SCOTT®

2008
Classic Specialized Catalogue

FOURTEENTH EDITION

STAMPS AND COVERS OF THE WORLD INCLUDING U.S. 1840–1940 (BRITISH COMMONWEALTH TO 1952)

EDITOR	James E. Kloetzel
ASSOCIATE EDITOR	William A. Jones
ASSISTANT EDITOR /NEW ISSUES & VALUING	Martin J. Frankevicz
ASSISTANT EDITOR	Charles Snee
VALUING ANALYST	Steven R. Myers
ADMINISTRATIVE ASSISTANT/IMAGE COORDINATOR	Beth L. Brown
DESIGN MANAGER	Teresa M. Wenrick
ADVERTISING	Phyllis Stegemoller
CIRCULATION/PRODUCT PROMOTION MANAGER	Tim Wagner
VICE PRESIDENT/EDITORIAL AND PRODUCTION	Steve Collins
PRESIDENT	William Fay
SPECIAL EDITORIAL CONSULTANT	**Sergio Sismondo**

Released November 2007

Scott Publishing Co.

911 Vandemark Road, Sidney, OH 45365-0828

A division of AMOS PRESS, INC., publishers of *Scott Stamp Monthly, Linn's Stamp News, Coin World* and *Coin World's Coin Values.*

Table of Contents

See Volumes 1 – 6 of the *Scott Standard Stamp Catalogue*
for stamps issued from 1941 to 2006
(British Commonwealth 1953-2006)

Scott Publishing Mission Statement

The Scott Publishing Team exists to serve the recreational, educational and commercial hobby needs of stamp collectors and dealers.

We strive to set the industry standard for philatelic information and products by developing and providing goods that help collectors identify, value, organize and present their collections.

Quality customer service is, and will continue to be, our highest priority. We aspire toward achieving total customer satisfaction.

Copyright Notice

Trademark Notice

ISBN 0-89487-414-7

Library of Congress Card No. 2-3301

Scott Publishing Co.

SCOTT 911 VANDEMARK ROAD, SIDNEY, OHIO 45365 937-498-0802

A short time ago, a friend and colleague, one of the world's top philatelic expertizers, relayed a conversation that he'd had recently with a German philatelic expert, who described the *Scott Classic Specialized Catalogue of Stamps & Covers* as the "best catalog of the world, in the world." This is high praise from an authority who is known not to bestow unearned compliments.

From the very beginning of the Classic catalogue in 1994 (for the 1995 first edition), the Scott editors have planned and worked to produce a specialized volume that could earn such accolades. We are gratified that some industry leaders have recognized that an important and very useful philatelic volume has emerged.

Users of the Classic catalogue realize that this volume has taken on a life of its own, with specialized listings in many areas for forerunners, cancels, pairs, blocks, shades and other varieties and, of course, covers.

We certainly are not done yet, as we already have several important enhancements planned for the next couple of years. This is an ongoing project, and we will continue working to ensure that the Scott Classic Specialized catalogue is the best and most essential one-volume worldwide catalogue for the classic period available.

The 2008 fourteenth edition of the Classic builds on its predecessors by including thoroughly revised values and added content in a wide range of collecting areas. Scott Associate Editor Bill Jones and Special Editorial Consultant Sergio Sismondo are the two individuals mainly responsible for pushing this project forward this year, and I thank Bill Jones for organizing much of the information for this Editor's Letter.

Tens of thousands of values have been carried into the Classic from the six-volume 2008 Scott Standard catalogues, and more than 12,000 additional value changes have been made for items listed only in the Classic. Additionally, more than 1,000 new numbered and valued items appear for the first time in this edition.

Value changes, nearly all increases, appear throughout the catalogue, but they are especially numerous in Belgian Congo; Ecuador; French, German and Italian colonies; Italian states and Italy proper; Jordan; Lithuania; Natal; Peru; Russia; Turkey; Uruguay and Venezuela. There are frequent and dramatic gains across the board in the Italian area.

Values for covers have been added for Alaouites, Albania (Italian occupation issues), Algeria (semipostals), Andorra (French), Annam & Tonkin, Austria (1925-40 issues), Benin, Fiume, French Congo, French Guiana, Inini, Italian Colonies, Italian East Africa, Italy (Scott 201-412 as well as airmails), Mauritania and Tripolitania. Values for covers have been updated in many areas, including French Polynesia, Italy and Italian area, Puerto Rico and Tahiti.

Major editorial enhancements appear throughout the catalog. Listings in several French areas countries have received significant additions, as have Hungary and the British area.

Forerunners — French stamps and covers used in overseas offices — appear for Algeria and St. Pierre & Miquelon. Some 270 different Algerian cancellations on three French letter-rate stamps used during 1849-76 are now listed. A total of 59 new Scott listings similarly have been added to St. Pierre & Miquelon for French Colonies general issues used in the colony during 1859-86.

In 1912, France surcharged existing Peace and Commerce keytype definitive stamps for many of its colonies, to create needed denominations from old, excess stocks. Two types of overprint, differing in the spacing between the two characters in the surcharged numerals, appeared on the overprint plates, with the second type appearing far less often than the first.

Although there are substantial differences in value between the two types, these were formerly briefly described in a footnote. With the 2008 edition, these types are now separately numbered and valued, with the expanded listings appearing for 15 French colonies.

An important addition has been made in French Guiana, where the T.A.G. (Transports Aériens Guyanais) airmails have been added this year. These crude, exotic stamps were produced by the pioneering airline La Sociéte des Transports Aériens Guyanais, which maintained service between Cayenne, Saint Laurent du Maroni and Inini, with less-regular flights to Paramaribo, Surinam, during 1920-22. These scarce and pricey airmail stamps have long been a favorite of air post collectors. They now appear as Scott CL1-CL15.

The first and second issues of Fiume have been reorganized and expanded to include both the typographed and handstamped versions of the first-issue overprints on Hungarian stamps and the three papers of the second issue, which represent three distinct printings. These more detailed listings are valued as unused hinged, never hinged, used, and in most cases, on cover.

Three new Hong Kong major numbers appear this year. Scott 36b and 44 were overprinted "S.O." (Stamp Office) and "S.D." (Stamp Duty) for use as revenue stamps. During 1891-93, they were also authorized for postal use. These postal fiscals appear for the first time in the 2008 Scott Classic Specialized catalogue as Scott 60A-60C.

Extensive editorial changes appear in Hungary. The 1874-81 St. Stephen's Crown monocolor sets have been extensively reorganized, and the various perforation varieties of both issues, as well as new color shade varieties, are now listed. The two watermark types of the 1898-99 set, differing in whether the crown appears within an oval or a circle, are now separately listed.

A significant addition to Hungarian listings comes with the addition of the stamps of Western Hungary. The 97 stamps were issued during September-December 1921 by local authorities, preceding the plebiscite that resulted in the district remaining a part of Hungary. They were sold at post offices within Western Hungary, and covers, though scarce, exist. They now appear at the end of the Hungarian section, under Western Hungary, as Scott 1-88 and J1-9.

A new Indian state appears with the listing of the Dungarpur issues of 1933-47. Dungarpur, a small state in northwestern India, issued 28 major varieties during this period, which were in use until they were replaced by Indian stamps in 1949. All are scarce.

In Morocco, the Cherifien issues of 1912-13 are listed for the first time. This postal service, operated by the Moroccan government, began handling the mails in 1892 in most major cities in the country. These stamps were used throughout the country until 1915, two years after the French authorities took control of the postal system. Formerly confined to a brief note within the French Offices in Morocco section, these stamps are now listed and valued under Morocco, since they were, indeed, the issues of that country's government before it came under French protection.

The expansion of the Czechoslovak Legion Post in Siberia that appeared in Volume 2 of the *2008 Scott Standard Postage Stamp Catalogue* appears in this edition of the Scott Classic Specialized catalogue for the first time. Be sure to read the footnotes carefully in order to be able to differentiate the valued original issues from remainders and later Prague reprints.

In addition to all these noteworthy changes, as usual hundreds of new varieties have been added throughout the volume, as well as many new listings for forerunners and multiples.

And, most importantly, remember that this hobby is a great gift. Enjoy.

James E. Kloetzel

James E. Kloetzel/Catalogue Editor

Acknowledgments

Our appreciation and gratitude go to the following individuals who have assisted us in preparing information included in this year's Scott Catalogues. Some helpers prefer anonymity. These individuals have generously shared their stamp knowledge with others through the medium of the Scott Catalogue.

Those who follow provided information that is in addition to the hundreds of dealer price lists and advertisements and scores of auction catalogues and realizations that were used in producing the catalogue values. It is from those noted here that we have been able to obtain information on items not normally seen in published lists and advertisements. Support from these people goes beyond data leading to catalogue values, for they also are key to editorial changes.

A special acknowledgment to Liane and Sergio Sismondo of The Classic Collector for their extraordinary assistance and knowledge sharing that has aided in the preparation of this year's Standard and Classic Specialized Catalogues.

Michael E. Aldrich (Michael E. Aldrich, Inc.)
A. R. Allison
AMEXFIL (Asociación Mexicana de Filatelia)
Robert Ausubel (Great Britain Collectors Club)
Dr. H.U. Bantz (S. W. Africa Stamp Study Group)
John Barone (Stamptracks)
Jack Hagop Barsoumian (International Stamp Co.)
William Batty-Smith (Sarawak Specialists' Society)
George G. Birdsall (Northland Auctions)
John Birkinbine II
Brian Bleckwenn
Chris Brainard
Roger S. Brody
Keith & Margie Brown
Bernard Bujnak
Lawrence A. Bustillo (Suburban Stamp Inc.)
A. Bryan Camarda (University Stamp Co.)
Alan C. Campbell
Tina & John Carlson (JET Stamps)
Joseph H. Chalhoub
Richard A. Champagne (Richard A. Champagne, Inc.)
Richard E. Clever (Asia Philatelics)
Leroy P. Collins III
Andrew Cronin (Canadian Society of Russian Philately)
Francis J. Crown, Jr.
Tony L. Crumbley (Carolina Coin and Stamp, Inc.)
Santiago Cruz
Tony Davis
Kenneth E. Diehl
Bob Dumaine
Esi Ebrani
Paul G. Eckman
Mehdi Esmaili (Iran Philatelic Study Circle)
Marty Farber
Jeffrey M. Forster
Robert S. Freeman
Ernest E. Fricks (France & Colonies Philatelic Society)
Richard Friedberg
Gregor Gätjens
Kay Gätjens
Bob Genisol (Sultan Stamp Center)
Michael A. Goldman (Regency Superior, Ltd.)
Richard B. Graham
Daniel E. Grau
Harry Hagendorf
Henry Hahn (Society for Czechoslovak Philately, Inc.)
Joe Hahn (Associated Collectors of El Salvador)
Bruce Hecht (Bruce L. Hecht Co.)
Robert R. Hegland
Stefan Heijtz
Clifford Herrick (Fidelity Trading Co.)
Steven Hines
Jack R. Hughes (Fellowship of Samoan Specialists)
Philip J. Hughes (Croatian Philatelic Society)
Wilson Hulme
Tom Jacks (Mountainside Stamps)
Eric Jackson
Michael Jaffe (Michael Jaffe Stamps, Inc.)
Peter C. Jeannopoulos
Stephen Joe (International Stamp Service)
Richard Juzwin (Richard Juzwin PTY LTD)
John Kardos
Allan Katz (Ventura Stamp Company)
Stanford M. Katz
Lewis Kaufman (The Philatelic Foundation)
Patricia A. Kaufmann
Dr. James W. Kerr
Matt Kewriga
William V. Kezbers
John L. Kimbrough
Eliot Landau
Lester C. Lanphear III
Steve Levine
Ulf Lindahl (Ethiopian Philatelic Society)
William A. Litle
Gary B. Little (Luxembourg Collectors Club)
Pedro Llach (Filatelia Llach S.L.)
Marcelo Loeb
George Luzitano
Dennis Lynch
Robert L. Markovits (Quality Investors, Ltd.)
William K. McDaniel
Gary N. McLean
Mark S. Miller (India Study Circle)
Allen Mintz (United Postal Stationery Society)
William E. Mooz
David Mordant
Gary M. Morris (Pacific Midwest Co.)
Peter Mosiondz, Jr.
Dr. Christian Mozek
Richard H. Muller (Richard's Stamps)
Albert Olejnik
John E. Pearson (Pittwater Philatelic Service)
John Pedneault
Donald J. Peterson (International Philippine Philatelic Society)
Stanley M. Piller (Stanley M. Piller & Associates)
Todor Drumev Popov
Peter W. W. Powell
Stephen Radin (Albany Stamp Co.)
Ghassan D. Riachi
Peter A. Robertson
Michael Rogers (Michael Rogers, Inc.)
Robert G. Rufe
Michael Ruggiero
Christopher Rupp
Mehrdad Sadri (Persiphila)
Richard H. Salz
Alex Schauss (Schauss Philatelics)
F. Burton Sellers
Guy Shaw
J. Randall Shoemaker (Professional Stamps Experts, Inc.)
Jeff Siddiqui (Pakistan Philatelic Study Circle)
Ray Simrak
Sergio & Liane Sismondo (The Classic Collector)
Jay Smith
Merle Spencer (The Stamp Gallery)
Frank J. Stanley, III
Richard Stark
Alfred E. Staubus
Philip & Henry Stevens (postalstationery.com)
Jerry Summers
James F. Taff
Jackson Taylor (Ferris Stamp Co.)
Scott R. Trepel (Robert A. Siegel Auction Galleries, Inc.)
Philip T. Wall
Jeffrey Ward
Daniel C. Warren
Richard A. Washburn
Giana Wayman (Asociacion Filatélica de Costa Rica)
Larry S. Weiss
William R. Weiss, Jr. (Weiss Auctions)
Ed Wener (Indigo)
Hans Westphal
Don White (Dunedin Stamp Centre)
Alan B. Whitman
Kirk Wolford (Kirk's Stamp Company)
Robert Wurdeman
Robert F. Yacano (K-Line Philippines)
Ralph Yorio
Val Zabijaka
Dr. Michal Zika (Album)
John P. Zuckerman (Robert A. Siegel Auction Galleries, Inc.)

Addresses, Telephone Numbers, Web Sites, E-Mail Addresses of General & Specialized Philatelic Societies

Collectors can contact the following groups for information about the philately of the areas within the scope of these societies, or inquire about membership in these groups. Aside from the general societies, we limit this list to groups that specialize in particular fields of philately, particular areas covered by the Scott Standard Postage Stamp Catalogue, and topical groups. Many more specialized philatelic societies exist than those listed below. These addresses were compiled in January 2001, and are, to the best of our knowledge, correct and current. Groups should inform the editors of address changes whenever they occur. The editors also want to hear from other such specialized groups not listed.

Unless otherwise noted all website addresses begin with http://

American Philatelic Society
100 Match Factory Place
Bellefonte PA 16823-1367
Ph: (814) 933-3803
www.stamps.org
E-mail: apsinfo@stamps.org

American Stamp Dealers Association
Jim Roselle
3 School St. Suite #205
Glen Cove NY 11542
Ph: (516) 759-7000
www.asdaonline.com
E-mail: asda@erols.com

International Society of Worldwide Stamp Collectors
Terry Myers, MD
9463 Benbrook Blvd. #114
Benbrook TX 76126
www.iswsc.org
E-mail: iswsc@hotmail.com

Royal Philatelic Society
41 Devonshire Place
London, United Kingdom W1G 6JY
www.rpsl.org.uk
E-mail: secretary@rpsl.org.uk

Royal Philatelic Society of Canada
PO Box 929, Station Q
Toronto, ON, Canada M4T 2P1
Ph: (888) 285-4143
www.rpsc.org
E-mail: info@rpsc.org

Young Stamp Collectors of America
Janet Houser
100 Match Factory Place
Bellefonte PA 16823-1367
Ph: (814) 933-3820
www.stamps.org/ysca/intro.htm
E-mail: ysca@stamps.org

Groups focusing on fields or aspects found in worldwide philately (some may cover U.S. area only)

American Air Mail Society
Stephen Reinhard
PO Box 110
Mineola NY 11501
www.americanairmailsociety.org
E-mail: sreinhard1@optonline.net

American First Day Cover Society
Douglas Kelsey
PO Box 16277
Tucson AZ 85732-6277
Ph: (520) 321-0880
www.afdcs.org
E-mail: afdcs@aol.com

American Revenue Association
Eric Jackson
PO Box 728
Leesport PA 19533-0728
Ph: (610) 926-6200
www.revenuer.org
E-mail: eric@revenuer.com

American Topical Association
Ray E. Cartier
PO Box 57
Arlington TX 76004-0057
Ph: (817) 274-1181
americantopicalassn.org
E-mail: americantopical@msn.com

Errors, Freaks and Oddities Collectors Club
Jim McDevitt
7643 Sequoia Dr., North
Mobile AL 36695-2809
Ph: (251) 607-9253
www.efoers.org
E-mail: cwouscg@aol.com

First Issues Collectors Club
Kurt Streepy
P.O. Box 288
Clear Creek IN 47426-0288
www.firstissues.org
E-mail: orders@firstissues.org

The Joint Stamp Issues Society
Pascal LeBlond
60-600 Rue Cormier
Gatineau, QC, Canada J9H 6B4
jointissues.ovh.org
E-mail: jointissues@yahoo.com

National Duck Stamp Collectors Society
Anthony J. Monico
PO Box 43
Harleysville PA 19438-0043
www.ndscs.org
E-mail: ndscs@hwcn.org

No Value Identified Club
Albert Sauvanet
Le Clos Royal B, Boulevard des Pas Enchantes
St. Sebastien-sur Loire, France 44230
E-mail: alain.vailly@irin.univ nantes.fr

The Perfins Club
Kurt Ottenheimer
462 West Walnut St.
Long Beach NY 11561
Ph: (516) 431-3412
E-mail: oak462@optonline.net

Postage Due Mail Study Group
John Rawlins
13, Longacre
Chelmsford
United Kingdom, CM1 3BJ
E-mail: john.rawlins2@ukonline.co.uk.

Post Mark Collectors Club
David Proulx
7629 Homestead Drive
Baldwinsville NY 13027
E-mail: stampdance@baldcom.net

Postal History Society
Kalman V. Illyefalvi
8207 Daren Court
Pikesville MD 21208-2211
Ph: (410) 653-0665
E-mail: kalphyl@juno.com

Precancel Stamp Society
Arthur Damm
176 Bent Pine Hill
North Wales PA 19454
Ph: (215) 368-6082
E-mail: shirldamm@comcast.net

United Postal Stationery Society
Stuart Leven
1445 Foxworthy Ave. #187
San Jose, CA 95118-1119
www.upss.org
E-mail: poststat@gmail.com

United States Possessions Philatelic Society
Geoffrey Brewster
6453 E. Stallion Rd.
Paradise Valley AZ 85253
Ph: (480) 607-7184

Groups focusing on U.S. area philately as covered in the Standard Catalogue

Canal Zone Study Group
Richard H. Salz
60 27th Ave.
San Francisco CA 94121-1026

Carriers and Locals Society
John D. Bowman
232 Leaf Lane
Alabaster AL 35007
Ph: (205) 621-8449
www.pennypost.org
E-mail: johndbowman@charter.net

Confederate Stamp Alliance
Patricia A. Kaufmann
10194 N. Old State Road
Lincoln DE 19960
www.csalliance.org
E-mail: trishkauf@comcast.net

Hawaiian Philatelic Society
Kay H. Hoke
PO Box 10115
Honolulu HI 96816-0115
Ph: (808) 521-5721

Plate Number Coil Collectors Club
Ronald E. Maifeld
PO Box 54622
Cincinnati OH 45254-0622
Ph: (513) 213-4208
www.pnc3.org
E-mail: president@pnc3.org

United Nations Philatelists
Blanton Clement, Jr.
P.O. Box 146
Morrisville PA 19067-0146
www.unpi.com
E-mail: bclemjr@yahoo.com

United States Stamp Society
Executive Secretary
PO Box 6634
Katy TX 77491-6631
www.usstamps.org
E-mail: webmaster@usstamps.org

U.S. Cancellation Club
Roger Rhoads
6160 Brownstone Ct.
Mentor OH 44060
www.geocities.com/athens/2088/uscchome.htm
E-mail: rrrhoads@aol.com

U.S. Philatelic Classics Society
Rob Lund
2913 Fulton
Everett WA 98201-3733
www.uspcs.org
E-mail: membershipchairman@uspcs.org

Groups focusing on philately of foreign countries or regions

Aden & Somaliland Study Group
Gary Brown
PO Box 106
Briar Hill, Victoria, Australia 3088
E-mail: garyjohn951@optushome.com.au

American Society of Polar Philatelists (Antarctic areas)
Alan Warren
PO Box 39
Exton PA 19341-0039
www.polarphilatelists.org
E-mail: alanwar@att.net

Andorran Philatelic Study Circle
D. Hope
17 Hawthorn Dr.
Stalybridge, Cheshire, United Kingdom SK15 1UE
www.chy-an-piran.demon.co.uk/
E-mail: apsc@chy-an-piran.demon.co.uk

Australian States Study Circle of The Royal Sydney Philatelic Club
Ben Palmer
GPO 1751
Sydney, N.S.W., Australia 2001

Austria Philatelic Society
Ralph Schneider
PO Box 23049
Belleville IL 62223
Ph: (618) 277-6152
www.austriaphilatelicsociety.com
E-mail: rschneider39@charter.net

American Belgian Philatelic Society
Walter D. Handlin
1303 Bullens Lane.
Woodlin, PA 19094
groups.hamptonroads.com/ABPS
E-mail: wdhandlin1@comcast.net

Bechuanalands and Botswana Society
Neville Midwood
69 Porlock Lane
Furzton, Milton Keynes, United Kingdom MK4 1JY
www.nevsoft.com
E-mail: bbsoc@nevsoft.com

Bermuda Collectors Society
Thomas J. McMahon
PO Box 1949
Stuart FL 34995
www.bermudacollectorssociety.org

Brazil Philatelic Association
William V. Kriebel
1923 ManningSt.
Philadelphia PA 19103-5728
Ph: (215) 735-3697
E-mail: kriebewv@drexel.edu

British Caribbean Philatelic Study Group
Dr. Reuben A. Ramkissoon
3011 White Oak Lane
Oak Brook IL 60523-2513
Ph: (630) 963-1439
www.bcpsg.com
E-mail: rramkissoon@juno.com

British North America Philatelic Society (Canada & Provinces)
H. P. Jacobi
6-2168 150A St.
Surrey, B.C., Canada V4A 9W4
www.bnaps.org
E-mail: pjacobi@shaw.ca

British West Indies Study Circle
W. Clary Holt
PO Drawer 59
Burlington NC 27216
Ph: (336) 227-7461

Burma Philatelic Study Circle
Michael Whittaker
1, Ecton Leys, Hillside
Rugby, Warwickshire, United Kingdom, CV22 5SL
E-mail: whittaker2004@ntlworld.com

Ceylon Study Group
R. W. P. Frost
42 Lonsdale Road, Cannington
Bridgewater, Somerset, United Kingdom TA5 2JS
E-mail: rodney.frost@tiscali.co.uk

Channel Islands Specialists Society
Miss S. Marshall
3, La Marette, Alderney,
Channel Islands, United Kingdom, GY9 3UQ
E-mail: am012e5360@blueyonder.co.uk

China Stamp Society
Paul H. Gault
PO Box 20711
Columbus OH 43220
www.chinastampsociety.org
E-mail: secretary@chinastampsociety.org

Colombia/Panama Philatelic Study Group (COPAPHIL)
c/o James A. Cross
PO Box 2245
El Cajon CA 92021
www.copaphil.org
E-mail: jimacross@cts.com

Association Filatelic de Costa Rica
Giana Wayman
c/o Interlink 102, PO Box 52-6770
Miami, FL 33152
E-mail: scotland@racsa.co.cr

Society for Costa Rica Collectors
Dr. Hector R. Mena
PO Box 14831
Baton Rouge LA 70808
www.socorico.org
E-mail: hrmena@aol.com

Croatian Philatelic Society (Croatia & other Balkan areas)
Ekrem Spahich
502 Romero, PO Box 696
Fritch TX 79036-0696
Ph: (806) 273-5609
www.croatianstamps.com
E-mail: eckSpahich@cableone.net

Cuban Philatelic Society of America
Ernesto Cuesta
PO Box 34434
Bethesda MD 20827
www.philat.com/cpsa
E-mail: ecuesta@philat.com

Cyprus Study Circle
Jim Wigmore
19 Riversmeet, Appledore
Bideford, N. Devon, United Kingdom EX39 1RE
www.cyprusstudycircle.org/index.htm
E-mail: jameswigmore@aol.com

Society for Czechoslovak Philately
Phil Rhoade
28168 Cedar Trail
Cleveland MN 56017
www.czechoslovakphilately.org
E-mail: philip.rhoade@mnsu.edu

Danish West Indies Study Unit of the Scandinavian Collectors Club
Arnold Sorensen
7666 Edgedale Drive
Newburgh IN 47630
Ph: (812) 853-2653
dwistudygroup.com
E-mail: valbydwi@hotmail.com

East Africa Study Circle
Jonathan Smalley
1 Lincoln Close
Tweeksbury, United Kingdom B91 1AE
easc.org.uk
E-mail: jpasmalley@tiscali.co.uk

Egypt Study Circle
Mike Murphy
109 Chadwick Road
London, United Kingdom SE15 4PY
egyptstudycircle.org.uk
E-mail: egyptstudycircle@hotmail.com

Estonian Philatelic Society
Juri Kirsimagi
29 Clifford Ave.
Pelham NY 10803
Ph: (914) 738-3713

Ethiopian Philatelic Society
Ulf Lindahl
21 Westview Place
Riverside CT 06878
Ph: (203) 866-3540
home.comcast.net/~fbheiser/ethiopia5.htm
E-mail: ulindahl@optonline.net

Falkland Islands Philatelic Study Group
Carl J. Faulkner
Williams Inn, On-the-Green
Williamstown MA 01267-2620
Ph: (413) 458-9371

Faroe Islands Study Circle
Norman Hudson
28 Enfield Road
Ellesmere Port, Cheshire, United Kingdom CH65 8BY
www.faroeislandssc.org.
E-mail: jntropics@hotmail.com

Former French Colonies Specialist Society
BP 628
75367 Paris Cedex 08, France
www.colfra.com
E-mail: clubcolfra@aol.com

France & Colonies Philatelic Society
Edward Grabowski
741 Marcellus Drive
Westfield NJ 07090-2012
www.drunkenboat.net/frandcol/
E-mail: edjjg@alum.mit.edu

Germany Philatelic Society
PO Box 6547
Chesterfield MO 63006
www.gps.nu

German Democratic Republic Study Group of the German Philatelic Society
Ken Lawrence
PO Box 98
Bellefonte PA 16823-0098
Ph: (814) 422-0625
E-mail: apsken@aol.com

Gibraltar Study Circle
David R. Stirrups
34 Glamis Drive
Dundee, United Kingdom DD2 1QP
E-mail: drstirrups@dundee.ac.uk

Great Britain Collectors Club
Timothy Bryan Burgess
3547 Windmill Way
Concord CA 94518
www.gbstamps.com/gbcc
E-mail: Pennyred@earthlink.net

Hellenic Philatelic Society of America (Greece and related areas)
Dr. Nicholas Asimakopulos
541 Cedar Hill Ave.
Wyckoff NJ 07481
Ph: (201) 447-6262
E-mail: nick1821@aol.com

Haiti Philatelic Society
Ubaldo Del Toro
5709 Marble Archway
Alexandria VA 22315
www.haitiphilately.org
E-mail: u007ubi@aol.com

Hong Kong Stamp Society
Dr. An-Min Chung
3300 Darby Rd. Cottage 503
Haverford PA 19041-1064

Society for Hungarian Philately
Robert Morgan
2201 Roscomare Rd.
Los Angeles CA 90077-2222
www.hungarianphilately.org
E-mail: h.alan.hoover@hungarianphilately.org

India Study Circle
John Warren
PO Box 7326
Washington DC 20044
Ph: (202) 564-6876
www.indiastudycircle.org
E-mail: warren.john@epa.gov

Indian Ocean Study Circle
Mrs. S. Hopson
Field Acre, Hoe Benham
Newbury, Berkshire, United Kingdom RG20 8PD
www.iosc.org.uk

Society of Indo-China Philatelists
Ron Bentley
2600 North 24th Street
Arlington VA 22207
www.sicp-online.org
E-mail: ron.bentley@verizon.net

Iran Philatelic Study Circle
Mehdi Esmaili
PO Box 750096
Forest Hills NY 11375
www.iranphilatelic.org
E-mail: m.esmaili@earthlink.net

Eire Philatelic Association (Ireland)
David J. Brennan
PO Box 704
Bernardsville NJ 07924
eirephilatelicassoc.org
E-mail: brennan704@aol.com

Society of Israel Philatelists
Paul S. Aufrichtig
300 East 42nd St.
New York NY 10017

Italy and Colonies Study Circle
Andrew D'Anneo
1085 Dunweal Lane
Calistoga CA 94515
www.icsc.pwp.blueyonder.co.uk
E-mail: audanneo@napanet.net

International Society for Japanese Philately
Kenneth Kamholz
PO Box 1283
Haddonfield NJ 08033
www.isjp.org
E-mail: isjp@isjp.org

Korea Stamp Society
John E. Talmage
PO Box 6889
Oak Ridge TN 37831
www.pennfamily.org/KSS-USA
E-mail: jtalmage@usit.net

Latin American Philatelic Society
Jules K. Beck
30 1/2 Street #209
St. Louis Park MN 55426-3551

Latvian Philatelic Society
Aris Birze
569 Rougemount Dr.
Pickering, ON, Canada L1W 2C1

Liberian Philatelic Society
William Thomas Lockard
PO Box 106
Wellston OH 45692
Ph: (740) 384-2020
E-mail: tlockard@zoomnet.net

Liechtenstudy USA (Liechtenstein)
Paul Tremaine
PO Box 601
Dundee OR 97115
Ph: (503) 538-4500
www.liechtenstudy.org
E-mail: editor@liechtenstudy.org

Lithuania Philatelic Society
John Variakojis
3715 W. 68th St.
Chicago IL 60629
Ph: (773) 585-8649
www.filatelija.lt/lps/and
www.withgusto.org/lps/index.htm
E-mail: variakojis@earthlink.net

Luxembourg Collectors Club
Gary B. Little
7319 Beau Road
Sechelt, BC, Canada VON 3A8
www.luxcentral.com/stamps/LCC
E-mail: lcc@luxcentral.com

Malaya Study Group
David Tett
16 Broadway, Gustard Wood,
Wheathampstead, Herts, United Kingdom AL4 8LN
www.m-s-g/org/uk
E-mail: davidtett@aol.com

Malta Study Circle
Alec Webster
50 Worcester Road
Sutton, Surrey, United Kingdom SM2 6QB
E-mail: alecwebster50@hotmail.com

Mexico-Elmhurst Philatelic Society International
David Pietsch
PO Box 50997
Irvine CA 92619-0997
E-mail: mepsi@msn.com

Society for Moroccan and Tunisian Philately
206, bld. Pereire
75017 Paris, France
members.aol.com/Jhaik5814
E-mail: splm206@aol.com

Natal and Zululand Study Circle
Dr. Guy Dillaway
PO Box 181
Weston MA 02493
www.nzsc.demon.co.uk

Nepal & Tibet Philatelic Study Group
Roger D. Skinner
1020 Covington Road
Los Altos CA 94024-5003
Ph: (650) 968-4163
fuchs-online.com/ntpsc/
E-mail: colinhepper@hotmail.co.uk

American Society of Netherlands Philately
Jan Enthoven
221 Coachlite Ct. S.
Onalaska WI 54650
Ph: (608) 781-8612
www.cs.cornell.edu/Info/People/aswin /NL/neth
E-mail: jenthoven@centurytel.net

New Zealand Society of Great Britain
Keith C. Collins
13 Briton Crescent
Sanderstead, Surrey, United Kingdom CR2 0JN
www.cs.stir.ac.uk/~rgc/nzsgb
E-mail: rgc@cs.stir.ac.uk

Nicaragua Study Group
Erick Rodriguez
11817 S.W. 11th St.
Miami FL 33184-2501
clubs.yahoo.com/clubs/nicaraguastudygroup
E-mail: nsgsec@yahoo.com

Society of Australasian Specialists/Oceania
Henry Bateman
PO Box 4862
Monroe LA 71211-4862
Ph: (800) 571-0293 members.aol.com/stampsho/saso.html
E-mail: hbateman@jam.rr.com

Orange Free State Study Circle
J. R. Stroud
28 Oxford St.
Burnham-on-sea, Somerset, United Kingdom TA8 1LQ
www.ofssc.org
E-mail: jrstroud@classicfm.net

Pacific Islands Study Circle
John Ray
24 Woodvale Avenue
London, United Kingdom SE25 4AE
www.pisc.org.uk
E-mail: info@pisc.org.uk

Pakistan Philatelic Study Circle
Jeff Siddiqui
PO Box 7002
Lynnwood WA 98046
E-mail: jeffsiddiqui@msn.com

Centro de Filatelistas Independientes de Panama
Vladimir Berrio-Lemm
Apartado 0823-02748
Plaza Concordia Panama, Panama
E-mail: panahistoria@yahoo.es

Papuan Philatelic Society
Steven Zirinsky
PO Box 49, Ansonia Station
New York NY 10023
Ph: (718) 706-0616
E-mail: szirinsky@cs.com

International Philippine Philatelic Society
Robert F. Yacano
PO Box 100
Toast NC 27049
Ph: (336) 783-0768
E-mail: ryacano@tria.d.rr.com

Pitcairn Islands Study Group
Dr. Everett L. Parker
719 Moosehead Lake Rd.
Greenville ME 04441-9727
Ph: (207) 695-3163
www.pisg.org
E-mail: eparker@midmaine.net

Plebiscite-Memel-Saar Study Group of the German Philatelic Society
Clay Wallace
100 Lark Court
Alamo CA 94507
E-mail: clayw1@sbcglobal.net

Polonus Philatelic Society (Poland)
Chris Kulpinski
9350 E. Palm Tree Dr.
Scottsdale AZ 85255
Ph: (480) 585-7114
www.polonus.org
E-mail: ctk@kulpinski.net

International Society for Portuguese Philately
Clyde Homen
1491 Bonnie View Rd.
Hollister CA 95023-5117
www.portugalstamps.com
E-mail: cjh1491@sbcglobal.net

Rhodesian Study Circle
William R. Wallace
PO Box 16381
San Francisco CA 94116
www.rhodesianstudycircle.org.uk
E-mail: bwall8rscr@earthlink.net

Canadian Society of Russian Philately
Andrew Cronin
PO Box 5722, Station A
Toronto, ON, Canada M5W 1P2
Ph: (905) 764-8968
www3.sympatico.ca/postrider/postrider
E-mail: postrider@sympatico.ca

Rossica Society of Russian Philately
Edward J. Laveroni
P.O. Box 320997
Los Gatos CA 95032-0116
www.rossica.org
E-mail: ed.laveroni@rossica.org

Ryukyu Philatelic Specialist Society
Carmine J. DiVincenzo
PO Box 381
Clayton CA 94517-0381

St. Helena, Ascension & Tristan Da Cunha Philatelic Society
Dr. Everett L. Parker
719 Moosehead Lake Rd.
Greenville ME 04441-9727
Ph: (207) 695-3163
ourworld.compuserve.com/homepages/ ST_HELENA_ASCEN_TDC
E-mail: eparker@midmaine.net

St. Pierre & Miquelon Philatelic Society
Jim Taylor
7704 Birch Bay Dr.
Blaine WA 98230
E-mail: jamestaylor@wavehome.com

Associated Collectors of El Salvador
Joseph D. Hahn
1015 Old Boalsburg Rd. Apt G-5
State College PA 16801-6149
www.elsalvadorphilately.org
E-mail: joehahn2@yahoo.com

Fellowship of Samoa Specialists
Jack R. Hughes
PO Box 1260
Boston MA 02117-1260
members.aol.com/tongaJan/foss.html

Sarawak Specialists' Society
Stu Leven
PO Box 24764
San Jose CA 95154-4764
Ph: (408) 978-0193
www.britborneostamps.org.uk
E-mail: stulev@ix.netcom.com

Scandinavian Collectors Club
Donald B. Brent
PO Box 13196
El Cajon CA 92020
www.scc-online.org
E-mail: dbrent47@sprynet.com

Slovakia Stamp Society
Jack Benchik
PO Box 555
Notre Dame IN 46556

Philatelic Society for Greater Southern Africa
Alan Hanks
34 Seaton Drive
Aurora, ON, L4G 2KI, Canada

Spanish Philatelic Society
Robert H. Penn
1108 Walnut Drive
Danielsville PA 18038
Ph: (610) 767-6793

Sudan Study Group
c/o North American Agent
Richard Wilson
53 Middle Patent Road
Bedford NY 10506
www.sudanphilately.co.uk
E-mail: dadu1@verizon.net

American Helvetia Philatelic Society (Switzerland, Liechtenstein)
Richard T. Hall
PO Box 15053
Asheville NC 28813-0053
www.swiss-stamps.org
E-mail: secretary@swiss-stamps.org

Tannu Tuva Collectors Society
Ken Simon
513 Sixth Ave. So.
Lake Worth FL 33460-4507
Ph: (561) 588-5954
www.seflin.org/tuva
E-mail: p003115b@pb.seflin.org

Society for Thai Philately
H. R. Blakeney
PO Box 25644
Oklahoma City OK 73125
E-mail: HRBlakeney@aol.com

Transvaal Study Circle
J. Woolgar
132 Dale Street
Chatham, Kent ME4 6QH, United Kingdom
www.transvaalsc.org

Ottoman and Near East Philatelic Society (Turkey and related areas)
Bob Stuchell
193 Valley Stream Lane
Wayne PA 19087
www.oneps.org
E-mail: rstuchell@msn.com

Ukrainian Philatelic & Numismatic Society
George Slusarczuk
PO Box 303
Southfields NY 10975-0303
www.upns.org
E-mail: Yurko@warwick.net

Vatican Philatelic Society
Sal Quinonez
1 Aldersgate, Apt. 1002
Riverhead NY 11901-1830
Ph: (516) 727-6426
www.vaticanphilately.org

British Virgin Islands Philatelic Society
Giorgio Migliavacca
PO Box 7007
St. Thomas VI 00801-0007
www.islandsun.com/FEATURES/bviphil9198.html
E-mail: issun@candwbvi.net

West Africa Study Circle
Dr. Peter Newroth
Suite 603
5332 Sayward Hill Crescent
Victoria, BC, Canada V8Y 3H8
www.wasc.org.uk/

Western Australia Study Group
Brian Pope
PO Box 423
Claremont, Western Australia, Australia 6910

Yugoslavia Study Group of the Croatian Philatelic Society
Michael Lenard
1514 North 3rd Ave.
Wausau WI 54401
Ph: (715) 675-2833
E-mail: mjlenard@aol.com

Topical Groups

Americana Unit
Dennis Dengel
17 Peckham Rd.
Poughkeepsie NY 12603-2018
www.americanaunit.org
E-mail: info@americanaunit.org

Astronomy Study Unit
George Young
PO Box 632
Tewksbury MA 01876-0632
Ph: (978) 851-8283
www.fandm.edu/departments/astronomy/miscell/astunit.html
E-mail: george-young@msn.com

Bicycle Stamp Club
Norman Batho
358 Iverson Place
East Windsor NJ 08520
Ph: (609) 448-9547
members.tripod.com/~bicyclestamps
E-mail: normbatho@worldnet.att.net

Biology Unit
Alan Hanks
34 Seaton Dr.
Aurora, ON, Canada L4G 2K1
Ph: (905) 727-6993

Bird Stamp Society
Mrs. Rosie Bradley
31 Park View,
Chepsow, Gwent, United Kingdom NP16 5NA
www.bird-stamps.org/bss
E-mail: bradley666@lycos.co.uk

Canadiana Study Unit
John Peebles
PO Box 3262, Station "A"
London, ON, Canada N6A 4K3
E-mail: john.peebles@sympatico.ca

Captain Cook Study Unit
Brian P. Sandford
173 Minuteman Dr.
Concord MA 01742-1923
www.captaincooksociety.com
E-mail: US@captaincooksociety.com/

Casey Jones Railroad Unit
Norman E. Wright
33 Northumberland Rd.
Rochester NY 14618-2405
Ph: (585) 461-9792
www.uqp.de/cjr/index.htm
E-mail: normaned@rochester.rr.com

Cats on Stamps Study Unit
Mary Ann Brown
3006 Wade Rd.
Durham NC 27705
E-mail: mabrown@nc.rr.com

Chemistry & Physics on Stamps Study Unit
Dr. Roland Hirsch
20458 Water Point Lane
Germantown MD 20874
www.cpossu.org
E-mail: rfhirsch@cpossu.org

Chess on Stamps Study Unit
Anne Kasonic
7625 County Road #153
Interlaken NY 14847
E-mail: akasonic@capital.net

Christmas Philatelic Club
Linda Lawrence
312 Northwood Drive
Lexington KY 40505
Ph: (859) 293-0151
www.hwcn.org/link/cpc
E-mail: stamplinda@aol.com

Christopher Columbus Philatelic Society
Donald R. Ager
PO Box 71
Hillsboro NH 03244-0071
Ph: (603) 464-5379
E-mail: meganddon@tds.net

Collectors of Religion on Stamps
Verna Shackleton
425 North Linwood Avenue #110
Appleton WI 54914
www://my.vbe.com/~cmfourl/coros1.htm
E-mail: corosec@sbcglobal.net

Dogs on Stamps Study Unit
Morris Raskin
202A Newport Rd.
Monroe Township NJ 08831
Ph: (609) 655-7411
www.dossu.org
E-mail: mraskin@cellurian.com

Earth's Physical Features Study Group
Fred Klein
515 Magdalena Ave.
Los Altos CA 94024
epfsu.jeffhayward.com

Ebony Society of Philatelic Events and Reflections (African-American topicals)
Manuel Gilyard
800 Riverside Drive, Ste 4H
New York NY 10032-7412
www.esperstamps.org
E-mail: gilyardmani@aol.com

Embroidery, Stitchery, Textile Unit
Helen N. Cushman
1001 Genter St., Apt. 9H
La Jolla CA 92037
Ph: (619) 459-1194

Europa Study Unit
Donald W. Smith
PO Box 576
Johnstown PA 15907-0576
www.europanews.emperors.net
E-mail: eunity@aol.com or donsmith65@msn.com

Fine & Performing Arts
Deborah L. Washington
6922 So. Jeffery Boulevard
#7 - North
Chicago IL 60649
E-mail: brasslady@comcast.net

Fire Service in Philately
Brian R. Engler, Sr.
726 1/2 W. Tilghman St.
Allentown PA 18102-2324
Ph: (610) 433-2782
www.firestamps.com

Gay & Lesbian History on Stamps Club
Joe Petronie
PO Box 190842
Dallas TX 75219-0842
www.glhsc.org
E-mail: glhsc@aol.com

Gems, Minerals & Jewelry Study Unit
George Young
PO Box 632
Tewksbury MA 01876-0632
Ph: (978) 851-8283
www.rockhounds.com/rockshop/gmjsuapp.txt
E-mail: george-young@msn.com

Graphics Philately Association
Mark H Winnegrad
PO Box 380
Bronx NY 10462-0380
www.graphics-stamps.org
E-mail: indybruce1@yahoo.com

Journalists, Authors & Poets on Stamps
Ms. Lee Straayer
P.O. Box 6808
Champaign IL 61826
E-mail: lstraayer@dcbnet.com

Lighthouse Stamp Society
Dalene Thomas
8612 West Warren Lane
Lakewood CO 80227-2352
Ph: (303) 986-6620
www.lighthousestampsociety.org
E-mail: dalene1@champmail.com

Lions International Stamp Club
John Bargus
304-2777 Barry Rd. RR 2
Mill Bay, BC, Canada V0R 2P0
Ph: (250) 743-5782

Mahatma Gandhi On Stamps Study Circle
Pramod Shivagunde
Pratik Clinic, Akluj
Solapur, Maharashtra, India 413101
E-mail: drnanda@bom6.vsnl.net.in

Mask Study Unit
Carolyn Weber
1220 Johnson Drive, Villa 104
Ventura CA 93003-0540
E-mail: cweber@venturalink.net

Masonic Study Unit
Stanley R. Longenecker
930 Wood St.
Mount Joy PA 17552-1926
Ph: (717) 653-1155
E-mail: natsco@usa.net

Mathematical Study Unit
Estelle Buccino
5615 Glenwood Rd.
Bethesda MD 20817-6727
Ph: (301) 718-8898
www.math.ttu.edu/msu/
E-mail: m.strauss@ttu.edu

Medical Subjects Unit
Dr. Frederick C. Skvara
PO Box 6228
Bridgewater NJ 08807
E-mail: fcskvara@verizon.net

Mourning Stamps and Covers Club
John Hotchner
PO Box 1125
Falls Church VA 22041-0125
E-mail: jmhstamp@ix.netcom.com

Napoleonic Age Philatelists
Ken Berry
7513 Clayton Dr.
Oklahoma City OK 73132-5636
Ph: (405) 721-0044
www.nap-stamps.org
E-mail: krb2@earthlink.net

Old World Archeological Study Unit
Caroline Scannel
11 Dawn Drive
Smithtown NY 11787-1761
www.owasu.org
E-mail: editor@owasu.org

Petroleum Philatelic Society International
Linda W. Corwin
5427 Pine Springs Court
Conroe TX 77304
Ph: (936) 441-0216
E-mail: corwin@pdq.net

Philatelic Computing Study Group
Robert de Violini
PO Box 5025
Oxnard CA 93031-5025
www.pcsg.org
E-mail: dviolini@adelphia.net

Philatelic Lepidopterists' Association
Alan Hanks
34 Seaton Dr.
Aurora, ON, Canada L4G 2K1
Ph: (905) 727-6933

Rotary on Stamps Unit
Gerald L. Fitzsimmons
105 Calla Ricardo
Victoria TX 77904
rotaryonstamps.org
E-mail: glfitz@suddenlink.net

Scouts on Stamps Society International
Lawrence Clay
PO Box 6228
Kennewick WA 99336
Ph: (509) 735-3731
www.sossi.org
E-mail: rfrank@sossi.org

Ships on Stamps Unit
Les Smith
302 Conklin Avenue
Penticton, BC, Canada, V2A 2T4
Ph: (250) 493-7486
www.shipsonstamps.org
E-mail: lessmith440@shaw.ca

Space Unit
Carmine Torrisi
PO Box 780241
Maspeth NY 11378
Ph: (718) 386-7882
stargate.1usa.com/stamps/
E-mail: ctorrisi1@nyc.rr.com

Sports Philatelists International
Margaret Jones
5310 Lindenwood Ave.
St. Louis MO 63109-1758
www.sportstamps.org

Stamps on Stamps Collectors Club
Alf Jordan
156 West Elm Street
Yarmouth ME 04096
Ph: (650) 234-1136
www.stampsonstamps.org
E-mail: ajordan1@maine.rr.com

Windmill Study Unit
Walter J. Hollien
PO Box 346
Long Valley NJ 07853-0346
Ph: (862) 812-0030
E-mail: whollien@earthlink.net

Women on Stamps Study Unit
Hugh Gottfried
2232 26th St.
Santa Monica CA 90405-1902
E-mail: hgottfried@adelphia.net

Zeppelin Collectors Club
Cheryl Ganz
PO Box 77196
Washington DC 20013

Expertizing Services

The following organizations will, for a fee, provide expert opinions about stamps submitted to them. Collectors should contact these organizations to find out about their fees and requirements before submitting philatelic material to them. The listing of these groups here is not intended as an endorsement by Scott Publishing Co.

General Expertizing Services

American Philatelic Expertizing Service (a service of the American Philatelic Society)
100 Match Factory Place
Bellefonte PA 16823-1367
Ph: (814) 237-3803
Fax: (814) 237-6128
www.stamps.org
E-mail: ambristo@stamps.org
Areas of Expertise: Worldwide

B. P. A. Expertising, Ltd.
PO Box 137
Leatherhead, Surrey, United Kingdom KT22 0RG
E-mail: sec.bpa@tcom.co.uk
Areas of Expertise: British Commonwealth, Great Britain, Classics of Europe, South America and the Far East

Philatelic Foundation
70 West 40th St., 15th Floor
New York NY 10018
Ph: (212) 221-6555
Fax: (212) 221-6208
www.philatelicfoundation.org
E-mail:philatelicfoundation@verizon.net
Areas of Expertise: U.S. & Worldwide

Professional Stamp Experts
PO Box 6170
Newport Beach CA 92658
Ph: (877) STAMP-88
Fax: (949) 833-7955
www.collectors.com/pse
E-mail: pseinfo@collectors.com
Areas of Expertise: Stamps and covers of U.S., U.S. Possessions, British Commonwealth

Royal Philatelic Society Expert Committee
41 Devonshire Place
London, United Kingdom W1N 1PE
www.rpsl.org.uk/experts.html
E-mail: experts@rpsl.org.uk
Areas of Expertise: All

Expertizing Services Covering Specific Fields Or Countries

Canadian Society of Russian Philately Expertizing Service
PO Box 5722, Station A
Toronto, ON, Canada M5W 1P2
Fax: (416) 932-0853
Areas of Expertise: Russian areas

China Stamp Society Expertizing Service
1050 West Blue Ridge Blvd
Kansas City MO 64145
Ph: (816) 942-6300
E-mail: hjmesq@aol.com
Areas of Expertise: China

Confederate Stamp Alliance Authentication Service
c/o Patricia A. Kaufmann
10194 N. Old State Road
Lincoln DE 19960-9797
Ph: (302) 422-2656
Fax: (302) 424-1990
www.csalliance.org
E-mail: trishkauf@comcast.net
Areas of Expertise: Confederate stamps and postal history

Croatian Philatelic Society Expertizing Service
PO Box 696
Fritch TX 79036-0696
Ph: (806) 857-0129
E-mail: ou812@arn.net
Areas of Expertise: Croatia and other Balkan areas

Errors, Freaks and Oddities Collectors Club Expertizing Service
138 East Lakemont Dr.
Kingsland GA 31548
Ph: (912) 729-1573
Areas of Expertise: U.S. errors, freaks and oddities

Estonian Philatelic Society Expertizing Service
39 Clafford Lane
Melville NY 11747
Ph: (516) 421-2078
E-mail: esto4@aol.com
Areas of Expertise: Estonia

Hawaiian Philatelic Society Expertizing Service
PO Box 10115
Honolulu HI 96816-0115
Areas of Expertise: Hawaii

Hong Kong Stamp Society Expertizing Service
PO Box 206
Glenside PA 19038
Fax: (215) 576-6850
Areas of Expertise: Hong Kong

International Association of Philatelic Experts
United States Associate members:

Paul Buchsbayew
119 W. 57th St.
New York NY 10019
Ph: (212) 977-7734
Fax: (212) 977-8653
Areas of Expertise: Russia, Soviet Union

William T. Crowe
(see Professional Stamp Experts)
Areas of Expertise: United States

John Lievsay
(see American Philatelic Expertizing Service and Philatelic Foundation)
Areas of Expertise: France

Robert W. Lyman
P.O. Box 348
Irvington on Hudson NY 10533
Ph and Fax: (914) 591-6937
Areas of Expertise: British North America, New Zealand

Robert Odenweller
P.O. Box 401
Bernardsville, NJ 07924-0401
Ph and Fax: (908) 766-5460
Areas of Expertise: New Zealand, Samoa to 1900

Alex Rendon
P.O. Box 323
Massapequa NY 11762
Ph and Fax: (516) 795-0464
Areas of Expertise: Bolivia, Colombia, Colombian States

Sergio Sismondo
10035 Carousel Center Dr.
Syracuse NY 13290-0001
Ph: (315) 422-2331
Fax: (315) 422-2956
Areas of Expertise: British East Africa, Camerouns, Cape of Good Hope, Canada, British North America

International Society for Japanese Philately Expertizing Committee
32 King James Court
Staten Island NY 10308-2910
Ph: (718) 227-5229
Areas of Expertise: Japan and related areas, except WWII Japanese Occupation issues

International Society for Portuguese Philately Expertizing Service
PO Box 43146
Philadelphia PA 19129-3146
Ph: (215) 843-2106
Fax: (215) 843-2106
E-mail: s.s.washburne@worldnet.att.net
Areas of Expertise: Portugal and colonies

Mexico-Elmhurst Philatelic Society International Expert Committee
PO Box 1133
West Covina CA 91793
Areas of Expertise: Mexico

Ukrainian Philatelic & Numismatic Society Expertizing Service
30552 Dell Lane
Warren MI 48092-1862
Ph: (810) 751-5754
Areas of Expertise: Ukraine, Western Ukraine

V. G. Greene Philatelic Research Foundation
P.O. Box 204, Station Q
Toronto, ON, Canada M4T 2M1
Ph: (416) 921-2073
Fax: (416) 921-1282
E-mail: vggfoundation@on.aibn.com
www.greenefoundation.ca
Areas of Expertise: British North America

Information on Catalogue Values, Grade and Condition

Catalogue Value

The Scott Catalogue value is a retail value; that is, an amount you could expect to pay for a stamp in the grade of Very Fine with no faults. Any exceptions to the grade valued will be noted in the text. The general introduction on the following pages and the individual section introductions further explain the type of material that is valued. The value listed for any given stamp is a reference that reflects recent actual dealer selling prices for that item.

Dealer retail price lists, public auction results, published prices in advertising and individual solicitation of retail prices from dealers, collectors and specialty organizations have been used in establishing the values found in this catalogue. Scott Publishing Co. values stamps, but Scott is not a company engaged in the business of buying and selling stamps as a dealer.

Use this catalogue as a guide for buying and selling. The actual price you pay for a stamp may be higher or lower than the catalogue value because of many different factors, including the amount of personal service a dealer offers, or increased or decreased interest in the country or topic represented by a stamp or set. An item may occasionally be offered at a lower price as a "loss leader," or as part of a special sale. You also may obtain an item inexpensively at public auction because of little interest at that time or as part of a large lot.

Stamps that are of a lesser grade than Very Fine, or those with condition problems, generally trade at lower prices than those given in this catalogue. Stamps of exceptional quality in both grade and condition often command higher prices than those listed.

Values for pre-1900 unused issues are for stamps with approximately half or more of their original gum. Stamps with most or all of their original gum may be expected to sell for somewhat more, and stamps with less than half of their original gum may be expected to sell for somewhat less than the values listed. On rarer stamps, it may be expected that the original gum will be somewhat more disturbed than it will be on more common issues. Unused stamps issued from 1900 to the present are assumed to have full original gum. From breakpoints in most countries' listings, stamps are valued as never hinged, due to the wide availability of stamps in that condition. These notations are prominently placed in the listings and in the country information preceding the listings. Some countries also feature listings with dual values for hinged and never-hinged stamps.

Values for early and valuable stamps are for examples with certificates of authenticity from acknowledged expert committees, or examples sold with the buyer having the right of certification. This applies to examples with orignial gum as well are examples without gum. Beware of stamps offered "as is," as the gum on some unused stamps offered with"original gum" may be fraudulent, and stamps offered as unused without gum may in some cases be altered used stamps.

Grade

A stamp's grade and condition are crucial to its value. The accompanying illustrations show examples of Very Fine stamps from different time periods, along with examples of stamps in Fine to Very Fine and Extremely Fine grades as points of reference. When a stamp seller offers a stamp in any grade from fine to superb without further qualifying statements, that stamp should not only have the centering grade as defined, but it also should be free of faults or other condition problems.

FINE-VERY FINE stamps may be somewhat off center on one side, or slightly off center on two sides. Imperforate stamps will have two full margins, and the design will not touch any edge. For perforated stamps, the perfs are well clear of the design, but are still noticeably off center. *However, early issues of a country may be printed in such a way that the design naturally is very close to the edges. In these cases, the perforations may cut into the design very slightly.* Used stamps will not have a cancellation that detracts from the design.

VERY FINE stamps may be slightly off center on one or two sides, but the design will be well clear of the edge. The stamp will present a nice, balanced appearance. Imperforate stamps will have four full margins. *However, early issues of many countries may be printed in such a way that the perforations may touch the design on one or more sides. Where this is the case, a boxed note will be found defining the centering and margins of the stamps being valued.* Used stamps will have light or otherwise neat cancellations. This is the grade used to establish Scott Catalogue values.

EXTREMELY FINE stamps are close to being perfectly centered. Imperforate stamps will have even margins that are larger than full margins. *Even the earliest perforated issues will have perforations clear of the design on all sides.*

Scott Publishing Co. recognizes that there is no formally enforced grading scheme for postage stamps, and that the final price you pay or obtain for a stamp will be determined by individual agreement at the time of transaction.

Full Margins

The spacing of the designs of classic stamps on their plates differ widely between countries and often between issues of a single country or sometimes even between stamps within a single issue. Because margin size is a significant determinant of grade and value, the *Scott Classic Specialized Catalogue* often includes the dimensions of "full margins" in millimeters in the listings. "Full margin" (a term coined by Edwin Mueller in his catalogue of imperforate European stamps) is defined as half the space between two stamps on the plate. It is the margin that would result from a stamp being cut from its neighbor exactly in the center of the margin space between the stamps. Since the spacing of many early classics is somewhat irregular, the average spacing is used. The horizontal and vertical margins may not be equal on the plate, and in such instances both measurements are given, vertical margins first followed by horizontal margins. In instances where different printings of a single issue were made from plates differing in spacing, the smallest existing spacing is given. Scott has adopted the Mueller convention of giving 1/4mm as the smallest "full margin" measurement even in those cases where there was almost no space between the designs on a plate.

Condition

Grade addresses only centering and (for used stamps) cancellation. *Condition* refers to factors other than grade that affect a stamp's desirability.

Factors that can increase the value of a stamp include exceptionally wide margins, particularly fresh color, the presence of selvage, and plate or die varieties. Unusual cancels on used stamps (particularly those of the 19th century) can greatly enhance their value as well.

Factors other than faults that decrease the value of a stamp include loss of original gum, regumming, a hinge remnant or foreign object adhering to the gum, natural inclusions, straight edges, and markings or notations applied by collectors or dealers.

Faults include missing pieces, tears, pin or other holes, surface scuffs, thin spots, creases, toning, short or pulled perforations, clipped perforations, oxidation or other forms of color changelings, soiling, stains, and such man-made changes as reperforations or the chemical removal or lightening of a cancellation.

Grading Illustrations

On the following seven pages are illustrations of various stamps from countries appearing in *The Classic Specialized Catalogue.* These stamps are arranged by country, and they represent early or important issues that are often found in widely different grades in the marketplace. The editors believe the illustrations will prove useful in showing the margin size and centering that will be seen on the various issues.

Use this Illustrated Grading Chart in conjunction with the Illustrated Gum Chart that follows it to better understand the grade and gum condition of stamps valued in the Scott Catalogues.

In addition to the matters of margin size, centering and original gum, collectors are reminded that the very fine stamps valued in the Scott catalogues also will possess fresh color and intact perforations, and they will be free from defects.

The three grades shown for each stamp are computer manipulated using single digitized master illustrations.

Fine-Very Fine

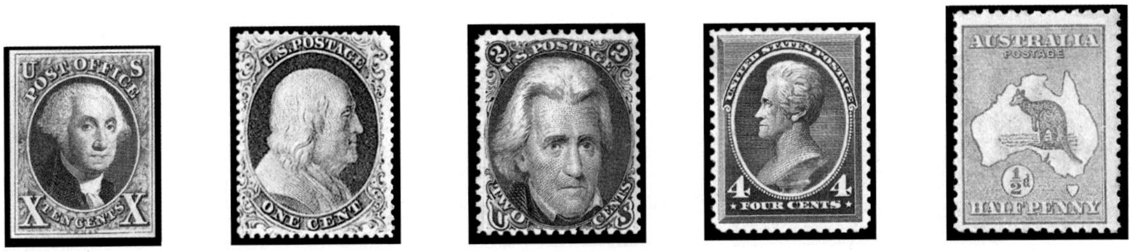

SCOTT CATALOGUES VALUE STAMPS IN THIS GRADE

Very Fine

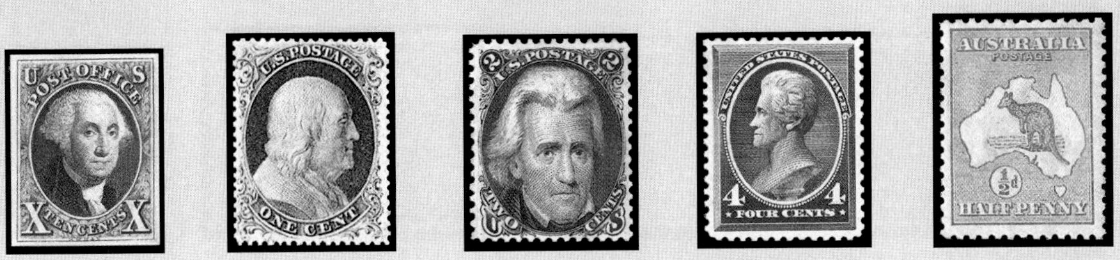

Extremely Fine

Fine-Very Fine

SCOTT CATALOGUES VALUE STAMPS IN THIS GRADE

Very Fine

Extremely Fine

Fine-Very Fine →

SCOTT CATALOGUES VALUE STAMPS IN THIS GRADE

Very Fine →

Extremely Fine →

Fine-Very Fine →

SCOTT CATALOGUES VALUE STAMPS IN THIS GRADE

Very Fine →

Extremely Fine →

Fine-Very Fine →

SCOTT CATALOGUES VALUE STAMPS IN THIS GRADE

Very Fine →

Extremely Fine →

Fine-Very Fine →

SCOTT CATALOGUES VALUE STAMPS IN THIS GRADE

Very Fine →

Extremely Fine →

Fine-Very Fine

SCOTT CATALOGUES VALUE STAMPS IN THIS GRADE

Very Fine

Extremely Fine

Fine-Very Fine

SCOTT CATALOGUES VALUE STAMPS IN THIS GRADE

Very Fine

Extremely Fine

Fine-Very Fine →

SCOTT CATALOGUES VALUE STAMPS IN THIS GRADE

Very Fine →

Extremely Fine →

Fine-Very Fine →

SCOTT CATALOGUES VALUE STAMPS IN THIS GRADE

Very Fine →

Extremely Fine →

Fine-Very Fine

SCOTT CATALOGUES VALUE STAMPS IN THIS GRADE

Very Fine

Extremely Fine

Fine-Very Fine

SCOTT CATALOGUES VALUE STAMPS IN THIS GRADE

Very Fine

Extremely Fine

Fine-Very Fine →

SCOTT CATALOGUES VALUE STAMPS IN THIS GRADE

Very Fine →

Extremely Fine →

Fine-Very Fine →

SCOTT CATALOGUES VALUE STAMPS IN THIS GRADE

Very Fine →

Extremely Fine →

For purposes of helping to determine the gum condition and value of an unused stamp, Scott Publishing Co. presents the following chart which details different gum conditions and indicates how the conditions correlate with the Scott values for unused stamps. Used together, the Illustrated Grading Chart on the previous pages and this Illustrated Gum Chart should allow catalogue users to better understand the grade and gum condition of stamps valued in the *Scott Classic Specialized Catalogue.*

Gum Categories:	MINT N.H.	ORIGINAL GUM (O.G.)				NO GUM

	Mint Never Hinged *Free from any disturbance*	**Lightly Hinged** *Faint impression of a removed hinge over a small area*	**Hinge Mark or Remnant** *Prominent hinged spot with part or all of the hinge remaining*	**Large part o.g.** *Approximately half or more of the gum intact*	**Small part o.g.** *Approximately less than half of the gum intact*	**No gum** *Only if issued with gum*
Commonly Used Symbol:	★★	★	★	★	★	(★)
Pre-1900 Issues (Pre-1879 for U.S.)	Very fine pre-1900 stamps in these categories trade at a premium over Scott value			Scott Value for "Unused"		Scott "No Gum" listings for selected unused classic stamps
From 1900 to breakpoints for listings of never-hinged stamps	Scott "Never Hinged" listings for selected unused stamps	Scott Value for "Unused" (Actual value will be affected by the degree of hinging of the full o.g.)				
From breakpoints noted for many countries	Scott Value for "Unused"					

Never Hinged (NH; ★★): A never-hinged stamp will have full original gum that will have no hinge mark or disturbance. The presence of an expertizer's mark does not disqualify a stamp from this designation.

Original Gum (OG; ★): Pre-1900 stamps should have approximately half or more of their original gum. On rarer stamps, it may be expected that the original gum will be somewhat more disturbed that it will be on more common issues. Stamps issued from 1900 to the present should have full original gum. Original gum will show some disturbance caused by a previous hinge(s) which may be present or entirely removed. The actual value of a stamp issued from 1900 to the present will be affected by the degree of hinging of the full original gum.

Disturbed Original Gum: Gum showing noticeable effects of humidity, climate or hinging over more than half of the gum. The significance of gum disturbance in valuing a stamp in any of the Original Gum categories depends on the degree of disturbance, the rarity and normal gum condition of the issue and other variables affecting quality.

Regummed (RG; (★)): A regummed stamp is a stamp without gum that has had some type of gum privately applied at a time after it was issued. This normally is done to deceive collectors and/or dealers into thinking that the stamp has original gum and therefore has a higher value. A regummed stamp is considered the same as a stamp with none of its original gum for purposes of grading.

Catalogue Values for Stamps on Covers

Definition of a Cover

Covers are philatelically defined as folded letters, folded covers or envelopes, with or without postage stamps, that have passed through the mail and bear postal or other markings of philatelic interest. Before the introduction of envelopes about 1840, people folded letters and wrote the address on the outside. Many people covered their letters with an extra sheet of paper on the outside for the address, producing the term "cover." Used stamped envelopes and wrappers and other items of postal stationery also are considered covers. Additionally, a newspaper stamp properly used on a newspaper or newspaper wrapper is considered to be an "on cover" usage, as is a postage stamp used on a post card. Occasionally, the term "newsprint" is used; this refers to either a newspaper or a one-page printed leaflet.

Catalogue Value

The Scott Catalogue value for a stamp on cover, as for a stamp off cover, is a retail value; that is, an amount you could expect to pay for that cover in a grade of Very Fine, as defined below. Folded letters, folded covers, envelopes, stationery entires and newspapers are valued as whole and complete, not as fronts of letter sheets or envelopes or as fragments of newspapers or circulars. Values given are for covers bearing stamps that are "tied on" by the cancellation. A stamp is said to be "tied" to a cover when the cancellation or postmark falls on both the stamp and the cover. Exceptions, such as some of the listings for newspaper stamps used on newspapers, always will be noted. Values for bisected, trisected, etc. stamps on cover are for items on which the cancellation ties the stamp across the cut. Values for U.S. patriotic covers of the Civil War period (bearing pictorial designs of a patriotic nature) are for the most common designs.

It should be noted that conventions observed for calculating the catalogue value of a cover with several different stamps vary somewhat between countries and types of covers. In a general way, however, the most common procedure may be summarized as follows: the stamp which has the highest "value on cover" is counted with its on-cover value, while the other stamps are added on to the total with their normal value as used stamps "off cover."

The value generally is given for the stamps as they are most commonly found on a cover. In some cases a stamp is most commonly found alone, paying a specified rate for the envelope, given its weight, destination and method of intended delivery. For instance, a one-half ounce letter sent internally in England by ordinary first class mail during the 19th century needed one penny of postage. Since such letters were very common, it follows that stamps with denominations of one penny are most often found on envelopes or folded letters paying that one-half ounce internal rate. One penny stamps also are found on letters together with other stamps making up different rates. A pair of one penny stamps may pay for a double weight envelope, four one penny stamps for an envelope addressed to France, six one penny stamps for an envelope addressed to Prussia, Italy or Spain, and so forth. Since letters addressed abroad are less common than letters addressed internally, the value of the one penny stamps given refers to the single usage. That is not true across the board, as there are many stamps issued during the 19th century that are more scarce used singly than in combination with other stamps. In all these other cases, the value given is intended to reflect the least scarce of the combinations.

If the value of a single stamp on a cover is of particular philatelic

Countries with listings for stamps on covers in the *Scott Classic Specialized Catalogue of Stamps & Covers*

United States
Confederate States
Guam
Hawaii
Aden
La Aguera
Aitutaki
Alaouites
Albania
Algeria
Allenstein
Spanish Andorra
French Andorra
Anjouan
Antigua
Argentina
- Buenos Aires
- Cordoba
- Corrientes

Ascension
Australia
Austria
- Lombardy-Venetia

Austrian
- Offices in Crete
- Offices in the Turkish Empire

Barbados
Basutoland
Batum
Bechuanaland Protectorate
Belgian Congo
Belgium
Benin
Bermuda
Bolivia
Bosnia and Herzegovina
Brazil
British Columbia and Vancouver Island
British Guiana
British Honduras
Bulgaria
Cameroun
Canada
Cape Juby
Caroline Islands
Castellorizo
Ceylon
Chile
Cochin-China
Corfu
Cuba
Cyrenaica
Danish West Indies
Danzig
Denmark
Ecuador
Eritrea
Fiji
Fiume
Finland
France
French Offices Abroad
- China
- Egypt-Alexandria
- Egypt-Port Said

French Colonies
French Congo
French Guiana
French Morocco
French Polynesia
French Sudan
Gabon
German East Africa
German New Guinea
German South West Africa
German States
- Baden
- Bavaria
- Bergedorf
- Bremen
- Brunswick
- Hamburg
- Hanover
- Lubeck
- Mecklenburg-Schwerin
- Mecklenburg-Strelitz
- Oldenburg
- Prussia
- Saxony
- Schleswig-Holstein
- Thurn and Taxis
- Wurttemberg
- North German Confederation

Germany
German Offices Abroad
- China
- Morocco
- Turkish Empire

Great Britain
Great Britain Offices Abroad
- Morocco
- Turkish Empire

Greece
Guadeloupe
Heligoland
Hong Kong
Iceland
India
Indo-China
Inini
Italian Colonies
Italian East Africa
Italian States
- Modena
- Parma
- Romagna
- Roman States
- Sardinia
- Tuscany
- Two Sicilies

Italy
Italian Offices Abroad
- China
- Africa
- Crete
- Turkish Empire
- Aegean Islands

Ivory Coast
Kiauchau
Labuan
Libya
Liechtenstein
Luxembourg
Madagascar (French Offices)
Madeira
Malta
Mariana Islands
Marienwerder
Marshall Islands
Martinique
Mauritania
Mauritius
Monaco
Netherlands
New Brunswick
New Caledonia
Newfoundland
New Hebrides, French
New Zealand
Nicaragua
Northern Rhodesia
Norway
Nossi Be
Nova Scotia
Nyasaland Protectorate
Obock
Paraguay
Peru
Philippines
Portugal
Prince Edward Island
Puerto Rico
Reunion
Russia
Saar
Ste.-Marie de Madagascar
St. Pierre & Miquelon
Samoa
San Marino
Senegal
Senegambia & Niger
Somalia
Somali Coast
South Africa
Southern Rhodesia
South West Africa
Spain
Straits Settlements
Swaziland
Sweden
Switzerland
Tahiti
Tannu Tuva
Togo
Transvaal
Tripolitania
Tunisia
Upper Silesia
Upper Volta (Burkina Faso)
Uruguay
Venezuela
Zanzibar

importance, as in the case of the stamps that pay for reduced rates for the delivery of newspapers or other printed matter, then their different value for this usage is indicated in footnotes or as a separate listing. It clearly is impossible to add to a catalogue of worldwide stamps the detailed information regarding the relative scarcity and value of all rates and combinations. We have limited ourselves to some of the more noteworthy and important cases.

In the majority of cases, the value of a cover assumes that the stamps on it have been used in the period contemporaneous with their issuance. Late usages are sometimes considered premium items, but in most cases late and very late usages are of no significance in postal history and detract from the value of the cover.

Condition

When evaluating a cover, care must be given to the factors that determine the overall condition of the item. It is generally more difficult to grade and evaluate a cover than a stamp. The condition of the stamps affixed to the cover must be taken into account — always in relation to the criteria for the particular issue. The Scott Catalogue does specify the grade and condition of the stamps for which a value is given, so it is important to consult this information. In addition, the condition of the cover must be taken into account. Values are for covers that are reasonably well preserved given the period of usage and the country of origin. A tiny nick or tear, or slight reduction from opening, are normal for 19th century covers. Folded letters may be expected to have tears on the reverse from opening, and often they will have file folds. Unless these factors affect the stamps or postal markings, they should not detract from the on-cover values given in the catalogue.

Just as with stamps, various factors can lower the value of a cover. Missing pieces, serious tears, holes, creases, toning, stains and alterations of postal mark- ings are examples of factors that lower the value of a cover. The necessity of considering these factors for the cover, as well as having to consider the condition of the stamps on the cover, helps to explain why it is more difficult to determine the value of a cover than a stamp off cover.

Factors Enhancing the Value of a Cover

A further difficulty in the valuation of covers is the necessity of considering factors other than the stamps used on a cover and the condition of the stamps and the cover. As stated previously, catalogue values listed herein generally reflect the most common usages of stamps on covers that are reasonably well preserved given the period of usage. Consideration of factors that may enhance the value of covers for the most part is beyond the scope of the Scott Catalogue. However, it is critical to understand that there are many such factors. Following is a list of many of the factors which often will increase the value of a cover.

- postal markings indicating origin, transit and arrival;
- postal markings indicating rates paid, which include postage, registration, acknowledgment of receipt, express charges, insurance, postage due, forwarding and many others;
- postal markings indicating carriers such as stagecoaches, trains, ships, aircraft, etc.;
- markings applied by censors, other civilian or military authorities, and others;
- scarce or rare destinations and routings;
- interruptions in the delivery system due to accidents, wars, natural calamities, etc.;
- unusual combinations of stamps;
- printed or hand-drawn pictorial, advertising or patriotic cover designs;
- unusual quality of stamps, postal markings or cover;
- and, outside of postal history, particularly noteworthy addressee, sender or contents.

Catalogue Listing Policy

It is the intent of Scott Publishing Co. to list all postage stamps of the world in the *Scott Standard Postage Stamp Catalogue*. The only strict criteria for listing is that stamps be decreed legal for postage by the issuing country and that the issuing country actually have an operating postal system. Whether the primary intent of issuing a given stamp or set was for sale to postal patrons or to stamp collectors is not part of our listing criteria. Scott's role is to provide basic comprehensive postage stamp information. It is up to each stamp collector to choose which items to include in a collection.

It is Scott's objective to seek reasons why a stamp should be listed, rather than why it should not. Nevertheless, there are certain types of items that will not be listed. These include the following:

1. Unissued items that are not officially distributed or released by the issuing postal authority. If such items are officially issued at a later date by the country, they will be listed. Unissued items consist of those that have been printed and then held from sale for reasons such as change in government, errors found on stamps or something deemed objectionable about a stamp subject or design.

2. Stamps "issued" by non-existent postal entities or fantasy countries, such as Nagaland, Occusi-Ambeno, Staffa, Sedang, Torres Straits and others. Also, stamps "issued" in the name of legitimate stamp-issuing countries that are not authorized by those countries.

3. Semi-official or unofficial items not required for postage. Examples include items issued by private agencies for their own express services. When such items are required for delivery, or are valid as prepayment of postage, they are listed.

4. Local stamps issued for local use only. Postage stamps issued by governments specifically for "domestic" use, such as Haiti Scott 219-228, or the United States non-denominated stamps, are not considered to be locals, since they are valid for postage throughout the country of origin.

5. Items not valid for postal use. For example, a few countries have issued souvenir sheets that are not valid for postage. This area also includes a number of worldwide charity labels (some denominated) that do not pay postage.

6. Intentional varieties, such as imperforate stamps that look like their perforated counterparts and are issued in very small quantities. Also, other egregiously exploitative issues such as stamps sold for far more than face value, stamps purposefully issued in artificially small quantities or only against advance orders, stamps awarded only to a selected audience such as a philatelic bureau's standing order customers, or stamps sold only in conjunction with other products. All of these kinds of items are usually controlled issues and/or are intended for speculation. These items normally will be included in a footnote.

7. Items distributed by the issuing government only to a limited group, such as a stamp club, philatelic exhibition or a single stamp dealer or other private company. These items normally will be included in a footnote.

The fact that a stamp has been used successfully as postage, even on international mail, is not in itself sufficient proof that it was legitimately issued. Numerous examples of so-called stamps from non-existent countries are known to have been used to post letters that have successfully passed through the international mail system.

There are certain items that are subject to interpretation. When a stamp falls outside our specifications, it may be listed along with a cautionary footnote.

A number of factors are considered in our approach to analyzing how a stamp is listed. The following list of factors is presented to share with you, the catalogue user, the complexity of the listing process.

Additional printings — "Additional printings" of a previously issued stamp may range from an item that is totally different to cases where it is impossible to differentiate from the original. At least a minor number (a small-letter suffix) is assigned if there is a distinct change in stamp shade, noticeably redrawn design, or a significantly different perforation measurement. A major number (numeral or numeral and capital-letter combination) is assigned if the editors feel the "additional printing" is sufficiently different from the original that it constitutes a different issue.

Commemoratives — Where practical, commemoratives with the same theme are placed in a set. Occasionally, however, stamp sets that were released over a period of years have been separated. Appropriately placed footnotes will guide you to each set's continuation.

Definitive sets — Blocks of numbers generally have been reserved for definitive sets, based on previous experience with any given country. If a few more stamps were issued in a set than originally expected, they often have been inserted into the original set with a capital-letter suffix, such as U.S. Scott 634A. If many more stamps than the originally allotted block were released before the set was completed, two or more blocks of numbers may have been needed to accomodate the entire set or series. Appropriately placed footnotes will guide you to each set's continuation.

Overprints — The color of an overprint is always noted if it is other than black. Where more than one color of ink has been used on overprints of a single set, the color used is noted. Early overprint and surcharge illustrations were altered to prevent their use by forgers.

album accessories

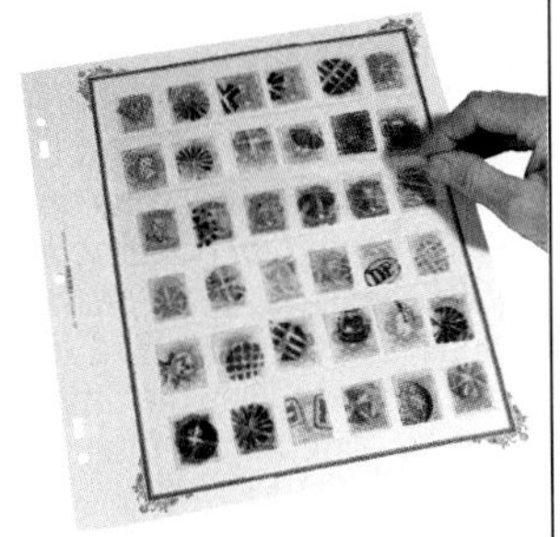

ADVANTAGE STOCK SHEETS

Advantage stock sheets fit directly in your 2-post or 3-ring National or Specialty album. Available with 1 to 8 pockets.

Sheets are sold in packages of 10.

- Stock sheets match album pages in every respect, including size, border, and color.
- Punched to fit perfectly in binder.
- Ideal for storing minor varieties and collateral material. A great place to keep new issues until the next supplement is available.
- Provides the protection of clear acetate pockets on heavyweight pages.

NATIONAL BORDER

Item			*Retail*	*AA**
AD11	1 Pocket	242mm	$15.99	$13.99
AD12	2 Pockets	119mm	$15.99	$13.99
AD13	3 Pockets	79mm	$15.99	$13.99
AD14	4 Pockets	58mm	$15.99	$13.99
AD15	5 Pockets	45mm	$15.99	$13.99
AD16	6 Pockets	37mm	$15.99	$13.99
AD17	7 Pockets	34mm	$15.99	$13.99
AD18	8 Pockets	31mm	$15.99	$13.99

SPECIALTY BORDER

Item			*Retail*	*AA**
AD21	1 Pocket	242mm	$15.99	$13.99
AD22	2 Pockets	119mm	$15.99	$13.99
AD23	3 Pockets	79mm	$15.99	$13.99
AD24	4 Pockets	58mm	$15.99	$13.99
AD25	5 Pockets	45mm	$15.99	$13.99
AD26	6 Pockets	37mm	$15.99	$13.99
AD27	7 Pockets	34mm	$15.99	$13.99
AD28	8 Pockets	31mm	$15.99	$13.99

BLANK PAGES

Ideal for developing your own album pages to be integrated with your album.

SPECIALTY SERIES PAGES (BORDER A)

(20 per pack)

Item		*Retail*	*AA**
ACC110		$7.74	$5.99
ACC111	Quadrille*	$7.74	$5.99

** Graph pattern printed on page.*

SPECIALTY/NATIONAL SERIES BINDERS

National series pages are punched for 3-ring and 2-post binders. The 3-ring binder is available in two sizes. The 2-post binder comes in one size. All Scott binders are covered with a tough green leatherette material that is washable and reinforced at stress points for long wear.

3-RING BINDERS & SLIPCASES

With the three ring binder, pages lay flat and the rings make turning the pages easy. The locking mechanism insure that the rings won't pop open even when the binder is full.

Item			*Retail*	*AA**
ACBR01	Small 3-Ring Binder	Holds up to 100 pages	$36.74	$29.99
ACBR03	Large 3-Ring Binder	Holds up to 250 pages	$36.74	$29.99
ACSR01	Small 3-Ring Slipcase.		$29.99	$24.99
ACSR03	Large 3-Ring Slipcase.		$29.99	$24.99

LARGE 2-POST BINDER & SLIPCASE

For the traditional Scott collector, we offer the standard hinge post binder. Scott album pages are punched with rectangular holes that fit on rectangular posts. The posts and pages are held by a rod that slides down from the top. With the post binder pages do not lie flat. However, filler strips are available for a minimal cost.

Item			*Retail*	*AA**
ACBS03	Large 2-Post Binder	Holds up to 250 pages	$52.99	$45.99
ACSS03	Large 2-Post Slipcase		$29.99	$24.99

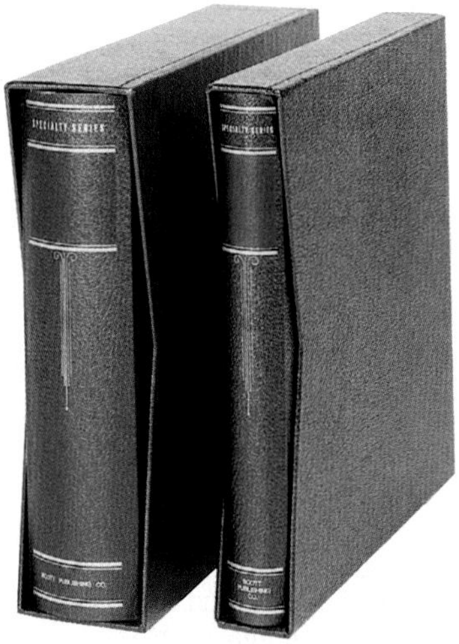

ALBUM PAGE DIVIDERS

Postage, air post, semi-postals; they're all right at your fingertips with National/Specialty Album Page Dividers. The dividers are a great way to keep your albums organized and save wear and tear on your pages.

Item		*Retail*	*AA**
ACC145	Package of 10	$4.49	$3.49

NATIONAL DIVIDER LABELS

35 clear, pressure sensitive labels for all categories of United States issues in the National Album.

Item	*Retail*	*AA**
ACC146	$4.49	$3.49

NATIONAL SERIES PAGES (BORDER B)

(20 per pack)

Item		*Retail*	*AA**
ACC120		$7.74	$5.99
ACC121	Quadrille*	$7.74	$5.99

PAGE PROTECTORS

Protect your stamps and album pages with a clear archival quality plastic sleeve. Sleeves fits over the entire page and protects pages from creases, fingerprints and tears. Scott Page protectors are pvc free and thin enough that they won't make your binder bulge. Page Protectors are available in two sizes. Sold in packages of 25.

2-Post Minuteman/International Pg Protectors

Item	*Retail*	*AA**
ACC165	$10.24	$7.99

National/Specialty Series Pg Protectors*

Item	*Retail*	*AA**
ACC166	$10.24	$7.99

*Punched to fit 2-post and 3-ring binder.

AMOS ADVANTAGE

To Order Call 1-800-572-6885

www.amosadvantage.com

1. AA* prices apply to paid subscribers of *Scott Stamp Monthly* and *Linn's*
2. Prices, terms and product availability subject to change.
3. **Shipping & Handling:**
United States: 10% of order total. Minimum charge $5.99 Maximum charge $30.00.
Canada: 15% of order total. Minimum charge $14.99 Maximum charge $45.00.
Foreign orders are shipped via DHL and billed actual freight. Credit cards only.

Understanding the Listings

On the opposite page is an enlarged "typical" listing from this catalogue. Below are detailed explanations of each of the highlighted parts of the listing.

1 Scott number — Scott catalogue numbers are used to identify specific items when buying, selling or trading stamps. Each listed postage stamp from every country has a unique Scott catalogue number. Therefore, Germany Scott 99, for example, can only refer to a single stamp. Although the Scott catalogue usually lists stamps in chronological order by date of issue, there are exceptions. When a country has issued a set of stamps over a period of time, those stamps within the set are kept together without regard to date of issue. This follows the normal collecting approach of keeping stamps in their natural sets.

When a country issues a set of stamps over a period of time, a group of consecutive catalogue numbers is reserved for the stamps in that set, as issued. If that group of numbers proves to be too few, capital-letter suffixes, such as "A" or "B," may be added to existing numbers to create enough catalogue numbers to cover all items in the set. A capital-letter suffix indicates a major Scott catalogue number listing. Scott uses a suffix letter only once. Therefore, a catalogue number listing with a capital-letter suffix will not also be found with the same letter (lower case) used as a minor-letter listing. If there is a Scott 16A in a set, for example, there will not also be a Scott 16a. However, a minor-letter "a" listing may be added to a major number containing an "A" suffix (Scott 16Aa, for example).

Suffix letters are cumulative. A minor "b" variety of Scott 16A would be Scott 16Ab, not Scott 16b.

There are times when a reserved block of Scott catalogue numbers is too large for a set, leaving some numbers unused. Such gaps in the numbering sequence also occur when the catalogue editors move an item's listing elsewhere or have removed it entirely from the catalogue. Scott does not attempt to account for every possible number, but rather attempts to assure that each stamp is assigned its own number.

Scott numbers designating regular postage normally are only numerals. Scott numbers for other types of stamps, such as air post, semi-postal, postal tax, postage due, occupation and others have a prefix consisting of one or more capital letters or a combination of numerals and capital letters.

2 Illustration number — Illustration or design-type numbers are used to identify each catalogue illustration. For most sets, the lowest face-value stamp is shown. It then serves as an example of the basic design approach for other stamps not illustrated. Where more than one stamp use the same illustration number, but have differences in design, the design paragraph or the description line clearly indicates the design on each stamp not illustrated. Where there are both vertical and horizontal designs in a set, a single illustration may be used, with the exceptions noted in the design paragraph or description line.

When an illustration is followed by a lower-case letter in parentheses, such as "A2(b)," the trailing letter indicates which overprint or surcharge illustration applies.

Illustrations normally are 70 percent of the original size of the stamp. An effort has been made to note all illustrations not illustrated at that percentage. Virtually all souvenir sheet illustrations are reduced even more. Overprints and surcharges are shown at 100 percent of their original size if shown alone, but are 70 percent of original size if shown on stamps. In some cases, the illustration will be placed above the set, between listings or omitted completely. Overprint and surcharge illustrations are not placed in this catalogue for purposes of expertizing stamps.

3 Paper color — The color of a stamp's paper is noted in italic type when the paper used is not white.

4 Listing styles — There are two principal types of catalogue listings: major and minor.

Major listings are in a larger type style than minor listings. The catalogue number is a numeral that can be found with or without a capital-letter suffix, and with or without a prefix.

Minor listings are in a smaller type style and have a small-letter suffix or (if the listing immediately follows that of the major number) may show only the letter. These listings identify a variety of the major item. Examples include perforation, color, watermark or printing method differences, multiples (some souvenir sheets, booklet panes and se-tenant combinations), and singles of multiples.

Examples of major number listings include 16, 28A, B97, C13A, 10N5, and 10N6A. Examples of minor numbers are 16a and C13Ab.

5 Basic information about a stamp or set — Introducing each stamp issue is a small section (usually a line listing) of basic information about a stamp or set. This section normally includes the date of issue, method of printing, perforation, watermark and, sometimes, some additional information of note. *Printing method, perforation and watermark apply to the following sets until a change is noted.* Stamps created by overprinting or surcharging previous issues are assumed to have the same perforation, watermark and printing method as the original. Dates of issue are as precise as Scott is able to confirm and often reflect the dates on first-day covers, rather than the actual date of release.

6 Denomination — This normally refers to the face value of the stamp; that is, the cost of the unused stamp at the post office at the time of issue. When a denomination is shown in parentheses, it does not appear on the stamp. This includes the non-denominated stamps of the United States, Brazil and Great Britain, for example.

7 Color or other description — This area provides information to solidify identification of a stamp. In many recent cases, a description of the stamp design appears in this space, rather than a listing of colors.

8 Year of issue — In stamp sets that have been released in a period that spans more than a year, the number shown in parentheses is the year that stamp first appeared. Stamps without a date appeared during the first year of the issue. Dates are not always given for minor varieties.

9 Value unused and Value used — The Scott catalogue values are based on stamps that are in a grade of Very Fine unless stated otherwise. Unused values refer to items that have not seen postal, revenue or any other duty for which they were intended. Pre-1900 unused stamps that were issued with gum must have at least most of their original gum. Later issues are assumed to have full original gum. From breakpoints specified in most countries' listings, stamps are valued as never hinged. Stamps issued without gum are noted. Modern issues with PVA or other synthetic adhesives may appear ungummed. Self-adhesive stamps are valued as appearing undisturbed on their original backing paper. For a more detailed explanation of these values, please see the "Catalogue Value," "Condition" and "Understanding Valuing Notations" sections elsewhere in this introduction.

In some cases, where used stamps are more valuable than unused stamps, the value is for an example with a contemporaneous cancel, rather than a modern cancel or a smudge or other unclear marking. For those stamps that were released for postal and fiscal purposes, the used value represents a postally used stamp. Stamps with revenue cancels generally sell for less. Scott values for used self-adhesive stamps are for examples either on piece or off piece.

Stamps separated from a complete se-tenant multiple usually will be worth less than a pro-rated portion of the se-tenant multiple, and stamps lacking the attached labels that are noted in the listings will be worth less than the values shown.

10 Changes in basic set information — Bold type is used to show any changes in the basic data given for a set of stamps. This includes perforation differences from one stamp to the next or a different paper, printing method or watermark.

11 Total value of a set — The total value of sets of three or more stamps issued after 1900 are shown. The set line also notes the range of Scott numbers and total number of stamps included in the grouping. The actual value of a set consisting predominantly of stamps having the minimum value of twenty cents may be less than the total value shown. Similary, the actual value or catalogue value of se-tenant pairs or of blocks consisting of stamps having the minimum value of twenty cents may be less than the catalogue values of the component parts.

A6

King George VI
A7

1938-44 Engr.

Perf. 12½

54	A6	½p	green	.20	*1.50*
54A	A6	½p	dk brown ('42)	.20	*2.00*
55	A6	1p	dark brown	1.75	.35
55A	A6	1p	green ('42)	.20	*.90*
56	A6	1½p	dark carmine	3.00	*4.50*
56A	A6	1½p	gray ('42)	.20	*5.75*
57	A6	2p	gray	4.00	1.25
57A	A6	2p	dark car ('42)	.20	*2.00*
58	A6	3p	blue	.50	.50
59	A6	4p	rose lilac	1.50	1.25
60	A6	6p	dark violet	2.00	1.25
61	A6	9p	olive bister	2.00	*3.25*
62	A6	1sh	orange & blk	1.75	*2.00*

Typo.
Perf. 14
Chalky Paper

63	A7	2sh	ultra & dl vio, *bl*	7.00	*11.00*
64	A7	2sh6p	red & blk, *bl*	8.00	*13.00*
65	A7	5sh	red & grn, *yel*	25.00	22.50
a.		5sh	dk red & dp grn, *yel* ('44)	55.00	*80.00*
66	A7	10sh	red & grn, *grn*	35.00	*45.00*

Wmk. 3

67	A7	£1	blk & vio, *red*	22.50	32.50
			Nos. 54-67 (18)	115.00	*150.50*
			Set, never hinged	200.00	

1 SCOTT NUMBER

2 ILLUS. NUMBER

3 PAPER COLOR

4 LISTING STYLES — MAJORS, MINORS

5 BASIC INFORMATION ON STAMP OR SET

6 DENOMINATION

7 COLOR OR OTHER DESCRIPTION

8 YEAR OF ISSUE

9 CATALOGUE VALUES — UNUSED, USED

10 CHANGES IN BASIC SET INFORMATION

11 TOTAL VALUE OF SET

Special Notices

Classification of stamps

The *Scott Standard Postage Stamp Catalogue* lists stamps by country of issue. The next level of organization is a listing by section on the basis of the function of the stamps. The principal sections cover regular postage, semi-postal, air post, special delivery, registration, postage due and other categories. Except for regular postage, catalogue numbers for all sections include a prefix letter (or number-letter combination) denoting the class to which a given stamp belongs.

The following is a listing of the most commonly used catalogue prefixes.

Prefix... Category
C..........Air Post
M..........Military
P...........Newspaper
N..........Occupation - Regular Issues
O..........Official
Q..........Parcel Post
J...........Postage Due
RA........Postal Tax
B..........Semi-Postal
E..........Special Delivery
MR........War Tax

Other prefixes used by more than one country include the following:
H..........Acknowledgment of Receipt
CO........Air Post Official
CQ........Air Post Parcel Post
RAC.......Air Post Postal Tax
CF.........Air Post Registration
CB.........Air Post Semi-Postal
CBO......Air Post Semi-Postal Official
CE.........Air Post Special Delivery
EY.........Authorized Delivery
S...........Franchise
G..........Insured Letter
GY.........Marine Insurance
MC........Military Air Post
MQ.......Military Parcel Post
NC........Occupation - Air Post
NL.........Occupation - Local Post
NO........Occupation - Official
NJ.........Occupation - Postage Due
NRA......Occupation - Postal Tax
NB.........Occupation - Semi-Postal
NE.........Occupation - Special Delivery
QY.........Parcel Post Authorized Delivery
AR.........Postal-fiscal
RAJ........Postal Tax Due
RAB.......Postal Tax Semi-Postal
F...........Registration
EB.........Semi-Postal Special Delivery
EO.........Special Delivery Official
QE.........Special Handling

Number changes

A listing of catalogue number additions, deletions and changes from the previous edition of the catalogue appears in each volume. Only number changes affecting the *Classic Specialized Catalogue* have been included in this volume. See *Classic Catalogue* Number Additions, Deletions & Changes in the table of contents for the location of this list.

Understanding valuing notations

The *minimum catalogue value* of an individual stamp or set is 20 cents. This represents a portion of the costs incurred to a dealer when he prepares an individual stamp for resale. As a point of philatelic-economic fact, the lower the value shown for an item in this catalogue, the greater the percentage of that value is attributed to dealer mark up and profit margin. In many cases, such as the 20-cent minimum value, that price does not cover the labor or other costs involved with stocking it as an individual stamp. The sum of minimum values in a set does not properly represent the value of a complete set primarily composed of a number of minimum-value stamps, nor does the sum represent the actual value of a packet made up of minimum-value stamps. Thus a packet of 1,000 different common stamps — each of which has a catalogue value of 20 cents — normally sells for considerably less than 200 dollars!

The *absence of a retail value* for a stamp does not necessarily suggest that a stamp is scarce or rare. In the U.S. listings, a dash in the value column means that the stamp is known in a stated form or variety, but information is either lacking or insufficient for purposes of establishing a usable catalogue value.

Stamp values in *italics* generally refer to items that are difficult to value accurately. For expensive items, such as those priced at $1,000 or higher, a value in italics indicates that the affected item trades very seldom. For inexpensive items, a value in italics represents a warning. One example is a "blocked" issue where the issuing postal administration may have controlled one stamp in a set in an attempt to make the whole set more valuable. Another example is an item that sold at an extreme multiple of face value in the marketplace at the time of its issue.

One type of warning to collectors that appears in the catalogue is illustrated by a stamp that is valued considerably higher in used condition than it is as unused. In this case, collectors are cautioned to be certain the used version has a genuine and contemporaneous cancellation. The type of cancellation on a stamp can be an important factor in determining its sale price. Catalogue values do not apply to fiscal or telegraph cancels, unless otherwise noted.

Some countries have released back issues of stamps in canceled-to-order form, sometimes covering as much as a 10-year period. The Scott Catalogue values for used stamps reflect canceled-to-order material when such stamps are found to predominate in the marketplace for the issue involved. Notes frequently appear in the stamp listings to specify which items are valued as canceled-to-order, or if there is a premium for postally used examples.

Many countries sell canceled-to-order stamps at a marked reduction of face value. Countries that sell or have sold canceled-to-order stamps at *full* face value include Australia, Netherlands, France and Switzerland. It may be almost impossible to identify such stamps if the gum has been removed, because official government canceling devices are used. Postally used copies of these items on cover, however, are usually worth more than the canceled-to-order stamps with original gum.

Abbreviations

Scott Publishing Co. uses a consistent set of abbreviations throughout this catalogue to conserve space, while still providing necessary information.

COLOR ABBREVIATIONS

amb	amber	crim	crimson	ol	olive
anil	aniline	cr	cream	olvn	olivine
ap	apple	dk	dark	org	orange
aqua	aquamarine	dl	dull	pck	peacock
az	azure	dp	deep	pnksh	pinkish
bis	bister	db	drab	Prus	Prussian
bl	blue	emer	emerald	pur	purple
bld	blood	gldn	golden	redsh	reddish
blk	black	grysh	grayish	res	reseda
bril	brilliant	grn	green	ros	rosine
brn	brown	grnsh	greenish	ryl	royal
brnsh	brownish	hel	heliotrope	sal	salmon
brnz	bronze	hn	henna	saph	sapphire
brt	bright	ind	indigo	scar	scarlet
brnt	burnt	int	intense	sep	sepia
car	carmine	lav	lavender	sien	sienna
cer	cerise	lem	lemon	sil	silver
chlky	chalky	lil	lilac	sl	slate
cham	chamois	lt	light	stl	steel
chnt	chestnut	mag	magenta	turq	turquoise
choc	chocolate	man	manila	ultra	ultramarine
chr	chrome	mar	maroon	Ven	Venetian
cit	citron	mv	mauve	ver	vermilion
cl	claret	multi	multicolored	vio	violet
cob	cobalt	mlky	milky	yel	yellow
cop	copper	myr	myrtle	yelsh	yellowish

When no color is given for an overprint or surcharge, black is the color used. Abbreviations for colors used for overprints and surcharges include: "(B)" or "(Blk)," black; "(Bl)," blue; "(R)," red; and "(G)," green.

Additional abbreviations in this catalogue are shown below:

Adm. .... Administration
AFL .... American Federation of Labor
Anniv. .... Anniversary
APS .... American Philatelic Society
Assoc. .... Association
ASSR. .... Autonomous Soviet Socialist Republic
b...................... Born
BEP .... Bureau of Engraving and Printing
Bicent. .... Bicentennial
Bklt. .... Booklet
Brit. .... British
btwn. .... Between
Bur. .... Bureau
c. or ca. .... Circa
Cat. .... Catalogue
Cent. .... Centennial, century, centenary
CIO .... Congress of Industrial Organizations
Conf. .... Conference
Cong. .... Congress
Cpl. .... Corporal
CTO .... Canceled to order
d...................... Died
Dbl. .... Double
EKU .... Earliest known use
Engr. .... Engraved
Exhib. .... Exhibition
Expo. .... Exposition
Fed. .... Federation
GB .... Great Britain
Gen. .... General
GPO .... General post office
Horiz. .... Horizontal
Imperf. .... Imperforate
Impt. .... Imprint
Intl. .... International
Invtd. .... Inverted
L...................... Left
Lieut., lt. .... Lieutenant
Litho. .... Lithographed
LL .... Lower left
LR .... Lower right
mm. .... Millimeter
Ms. .... Manuscript
Natl. .... National
No. .... Number
NY .... New York
NYC .... New York City
Ovpt. .... Overprint
Ovptd. .... Overprinted
P...................... Plate number
Perf. .... Perforated, perforation
Phil. .... Philatelic
Photo. .... Photogravure
PO .... Post office
Pr. .... Pair
P.R. .... Puerto Rico
Prec. .... Precancel, precanceled
Pres. .... President
PTT .... Post, Telephone and Telegraph
Rio .... Rio de Janeiro
Sgt. .... Sergeant
Soc. .... Society
Souv. .... Souvenir
SSR .... Soviet Socialist Republic, see ASSR
St. .... Saint, street
Surch. .... Surcharge
Typo. .... Typographed
UL .... Upper left
Unwmkd. .... Unwatermarked
UPU .... Universal Postal Union
UR .... Upper Right
US .... United States
USPOD .... United States Post Office Department
USSR .... Union of Soviet Socialist Republics
Vert. .... Vertical
VP .... Vice president
Wmk. .... Watermark
Wmkd. .... Watermarked
WWI .... World War I
WWII .... World War II

Examination

Scott Publishing Co. will not comment upon the genuineness, grade or condition of stamps, because of the time and responsibility involved. Rather, there are several expertizing groups that undertake this work for both collectors and dealers. Neither will Scott Publishing Co. appraise or identify philatelic material. The company cannot take responsibility for unsolicited stamps or covers sent by individuals.

How to order from your dealer

When ordering stamps from a dealer, it is not necessary to write the full description of a stamp as listed in this catalogue. All you need is the name of the country, the Scott catalogue number and whether the desired item is unused or used. For example, "Japan Scott 422 unused" is sufficient to identify the unused stamp of Japan listed as "422 A206 5y brown."

Basic Stamp Information

A stamp collector's knowledge of the combined elements that make a given stamp issue unique determines his or her ability to identify stamps. These elements include paper, watermark, method of separation, printing, design and gum. On the following pages each of these important areas is briefly described.

Paper

Paper is an organic material composed of a compacted weave of cellulose fibers and generally formed into sheets. Paper used to print stamps may be manufactured in sheets, or it may have been part of a large roll (called a web) before being cut to size. The fibers most often used to create paper on which stamps are printed include bark, wood, straw and certain grasses. In many cases, linen or cotton rags have been added for greater strength and durability. Grinding, bleaching, cooking and rinsing these raw fibers reduces them to a slushy pulp, referred to by paper makers as "stuff." Sizing and, sometimes, coloring matter is added to the pulp to make different types of finished paper.

After the stuff is prepared, it is poured onto sieve-like frames that allow the water to run off, while retaining the matted pulp. As fibers fall onto the screen and are held by gravity, they form a natural weave that will later hold the paper together. If the screen has metal bits that are formed into letters or images attached, it leaves slightly thinned areas on the paper. These are called watermarks.

When the stuff is almost dry, it is passed under pressure through smooth or engraved rollers - dandy rolls - or placed between cloth in a press to be flattened and dried.

Stamp paper falls broadly into two types: wove and laid. The nature of the surface of the frame onto which the pulp is first deposited causes the differences in appearance between the two. If the surface is smooth and even, the paper will be of fairly uniform texture throughout. This is known as *wove paper.* Early papermaking machines poured the pulp onto a continuously circulating web of felt, but modern machines feed the pulp onto a cloth-like screen made of closely interwoven fine wires. This paper, when held to a light, will show little dots or points very close together. The proper name for this is "wire wove," but the type is still considered wove. Any U.S. or British stamp printed after 1880 will serve as an example of wire wove paper.

Closely spaced parallel wires, with cross wires at wider intervals, make up the frames used for what is known as *laid paper.* A greater thickness of the pulp will settle between the wires. The paper, when held to a light, will show alternate light and dark lines. The spacing and the thickness of the lines may vary, but on any one sheet of paper they are all alike. See Russia Scott 31-38 for examples of laid paper.

Batonne, from the French word meaning "a staff," is a term used if the lines in the paper are spaced quite far apart, like the printed ruling on a writing tablet. Batonne paper may be either wove or laid. If laid, fine laid lines can be seen between the batons. The laid lines, which are a form of watermark, may be geometrical figures such as squares, diamonds, rectangles or wavy lines.

Quadrille is the term used when the lines in the paper form little squares. *Oblong quadrille* is the term used when rectangles, rather than squares, are formed. See Mexico-Guadalajara Scott 35-37 for examples of oblong quadrille paper.

Paper also is classified as thick or thin, hard or soft, and by color if dye is added during manufacture. Such colors may include yellowish, greenish, bluish and reddish.

Brief explanations of other types of paper used for printing stamps, as well as examples, follow.

Pelure — Pelure paper is a very thin, hard and often brittle paper that is sometimes bluish or grayish in appearance. See Serbia Scott 169-170.

Native — This is a term applied to handmade papers used to produce some of the early stamps of the Indian states. Stamps printed on native paper may be expected to display various natural inclusions that are normal and do not negatively affect value. Japanese paper, originally made of mulberry fibers and rice flour, is part of this group. See Japan Scott 1-18.

Manila — This type of paper is often used to make stamped envelopes and wrappers. It is a coarse-textured stock, usually smooth on one side and rough on the other. A variety of colors of manila paper exist, but the most common range is yellowish-brown.

Silk — Introduced by the British in 1847 as a safeguard against counterfeiting, silk paper contains bits of colored silk thread scattered throughout. The density of these fibers varies greatly and can include as few as one fiber per stamp or hundreds. U.S. revenue Scott R152 is a good example of an easy-to-identify silk paper stamp.

Silk-thread paper has uninterrupted threads of colored silk arranged so that one or more threads run through the stamp or postal stationery. See Great Britain Scott 5-6 and Switzerland Scott 14-19.

Granite — Filled with minute cloth or colored paper fibers of various colors and lengths, granite paper should not be confused with either type of silk paper. Austria Scott 172-175 and a number of Swiss stamps are examples of granite paper.

Chalky — A chalk-like substance coats the surface of chalky paper to discourage the cleaning and reuse of canceled stamps, as well as to provide a smoother, more acceptable printing surface. Because the designs of stamps printed on chalky paper are imprinted on what is often a water-soluble coating, any attempt to remove a cancellation will destroy the stamp. *Do not soak these stamps in any fluid.* To remove a stamp printed on chalky paper from an envelope, wet the paper from underneath the stamp until the gum dissolves enough to release the stamp from the paper. See St. Kitts-Nevis Scott 89-90 for examples of stamps printed on this type of chalky paper.

India — Another name for this paper, originally introduced from China about 1750, is "China Paper." It is a thin, opaque paper often used for plate and die proofs by many countries.

Double — In philately, the term double paper has two distinct meanings. The first is a two-ply paper, usually a combination of a thick and a thin sheet, joined during manufacture. This type was used experimentally as a means to discourage the reuse of stamps.

The design is printed on the thin paper. Any attempt to remove a cancellation would destroy the design. U.S. Scott 158 and other Banknote-era stamps exist on this form of double paper.

The second type of double paper occurs on a rotary press, when the end of one paper roll, or web, is affixed to the next roll to save time feeding the paper through the press. Stamp designs are printed over the joined paper and, if overlooked by inspectors, may get into post office stocks.

Goldbeater's Skin — This type of paper was used for the 1866 issue of Prussia, and was a tough, translucent paper. The design was printed in reverse on the back of the stamp, and the gum applied over the printing. It is impossible to remove stamps printed on this type of paper from the paper to which they are affixed without destroying the design.

Ribbed — Ribbed paper has an uneven, corrugated surface made by passing the paper through ridged rollers. This type exists on some copies of U.S. Scott 156-165.

Various other substances, or substrates, have been used for stamp manufacture, including wood, aluminum, copper, silver and gold foil, plastic, and silk and cotton fabrics.

Wove Laid Granite

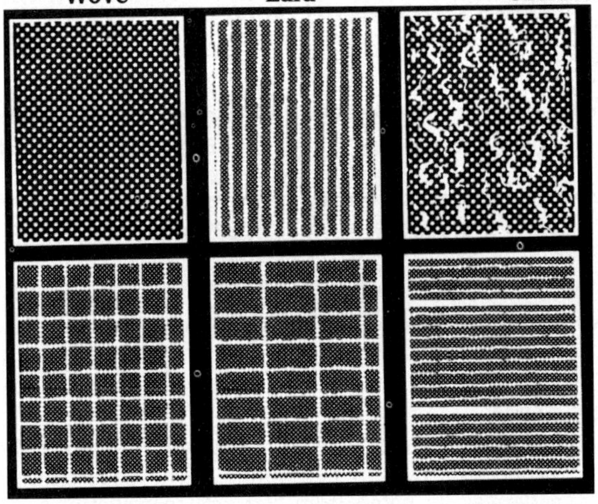

Quadrille Oblong Quadrille Laid Battone

Watermarks

Watermarks are an integral part of some papers. They are formed in the process of paper manufacture. Watermarks consist of small designs, formed of wire or cut from metal and soldered to the surface of the mold or, sometimes, on the dandy roll. The designs may be in the form of crowns, stars, anchors, letters or other characters or symbols. These pieces of metal - known in the paper-making industry as "bits" - impress a design into the paper. The design sometimes may be seen by holding the stamp to the light. Some are more easily seen with a watermark detector. This important tool is a small black tray into which a stamp is placed face down and dampened with a fast-evaporating watermark detection fluid that brings up the watermark image in the form of dark lines against a lighter background. These dark lines are the thinner areas of the paper known as the watermark. Some watermarks are extremely difficult to locate, due to either a faint impression, watermark location or the color of the stamp. There also are electric watermark detectors that come with plastic filter disks of various colors. The disks neutralize the color of the stamp, permitting the watermark to be seen more easily.

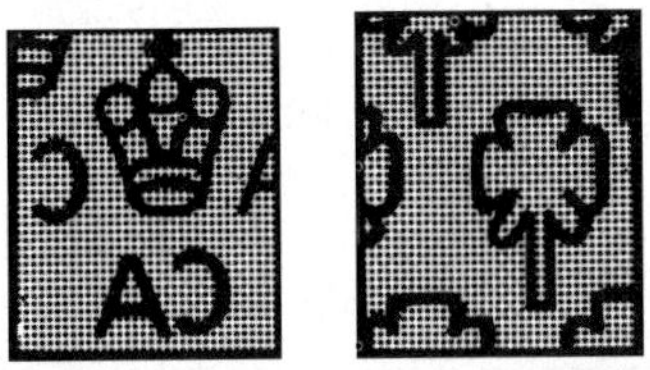

Multiple watermarks of Crown Agents and Burma

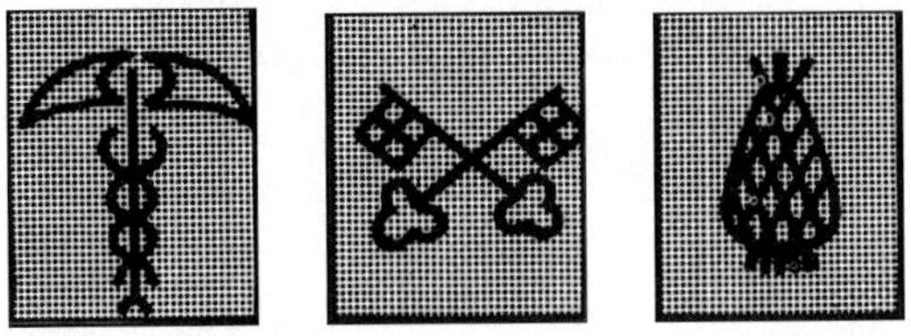

Watermarks of Uruguay, Vatican City and Jamaica

WARNING: Some inks used in the photogravure process dissolve in watermark fluids (Please see the section on Soluble Printing Inks). Also, see "chalky paper."

Watermarks may be found normal, reversed, inverted, reversed and inverted, sideways or diagonal, as seen from the back of the stamp. The relationship of watermark to stamp design depends on the position of the printing plates or how paper is fed through the press. On machine-made paper, watermarks normally are read from right to left. The design is repeated closely throughout the sheet in a "multiple-watermark design." In a "sheet watermark," the design appears only once on the sheet, but extends over many stamps. Individual stamps may carry only a small fraction or none of the watermark.

"Marginal watermarks" occur in the margins of sheets or panes of stamps. They occur on the outside border of paper (ostensibly outside the area where stamps are to be printed). A large row of letters may spell the name of the country or the manufacturer of the paper, or a border of lines may appear. Careless press feeding may cause parts of these letters and/or lines to show on stamps of the outer row of a pane.

Soluble Printing Inks

WARNING: Most stamp colors are permanent; that is, they are not seriously affected by short-term exposure to light or water. Some colors may fade from excessive exposure to light. There are stamps printed with inks that dissolve easily in water or in fluids used to detect watermarks. Use of these inks was intentional to prevent the removal of cancellations. Water affects all aniline inks, those on so-called safety paper and some photogravure printings - all such inks are known as *fugitive colors. Removal from paper of such stamps requires care and alternatives to traditional soaking.*

Separation

"Separation" is the general term used to describe methods used to separate stamps. The three standard forms currently in use are perforating, rouletting and die-cutting. These methods are done during the stamp production process, after printing. Sometimes these methods are done on-press or sometimes as a separate step. The earliest issues, such as the 1840 Penny Black of Great Britain (Scott 1), did not have any means provided for separation. It was expected the stamps would be cut apart with scissors or folded and torn. These are examples of imperforate stamps. Many stamps were first issued in imperforate formats and were later issued with perforations. Therefore, care must be observed in buying single imperforate stamps to be certain they were issued imperforate and are not perforated copies that have been altered by having the perforations trimmed away. Stamps issued imperforate usually are valued as singles. However, imperforate varieties of normally perforated stamps should be collected in pairs or larger pieces as indisputable evidence of their imperforate character.

PERFORATION

The chief style of separation of stamps, and the one that is in almost universal use today, is perforating. By this process, paper between the stamps is cut away in a line of holes, usually round, leaving little bridges of paper between the stamps to hold them together. Some types of perforation, such as hyphen-hole perfs, can be confused with roulettes, but a close visual inspection reveals that paper has been removed. The little perforation bridges, which project from the stamp when it is torn from the pane, are called the teeth of the perforation.

As the size of the perforation is sometimes the only way to differentiate between two otherwise identical stamps, it is necessary to be able to accurately measure and describe them. This is done with a perforation gauge, usually a ruler-like device that has dots or graduated lines to show how many perforations may be counted in the space of two centimeters. Two centimeters is the space universally adopted in which to measure perforations.

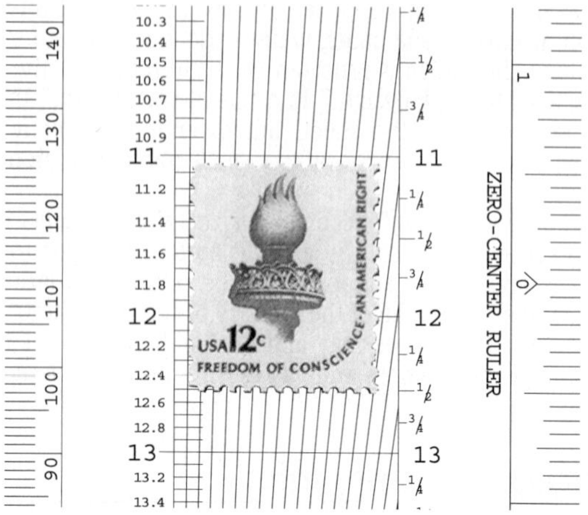

Perforation gauge

To measure a stamp, run it along the gauge until the dots on it fit exactly into the perforations of the stamp. If you are using a graduated-line perforation gauge, simply slide the stamp along the surface until the lines on the gauge perfectly project from the center of the bridges or holes. The number to the side of the line of dots or lines that fit the stamp's perforation is the measurement. For example, an "11" means that 11 perforations fit between two centimeters. The description of the stamp therefore is "perf. 11." If the gauge of the perforations on the top and bottom of a stamp differs from that on the sides, the result is what is known as *compound perforations.* In measuring compound perforations, the gauge at top and bottom is always given first, then the sides. Thus, a stamp that measures 11 at top and bottom and 10 1/2 at the sides is "perf. 11 x 10 1/2." See U.S. Scott 632-642 for examples of compound perforations.

Stamps also are known with perforations different on three or all four sides. Descriptions of such items are clockwise, beginning with the top of the stamp.

A perforation with small holes and teeth close together is a "fine perforation." One with large holes and teeth far apart is a "coarse perforation." Holes that are jagged, rather than clean-cut, are "rough perforations." *Blind perforations* are the slight impressions left by the perforating pins if they fail to puncture the paper. Multiples of stamps showing blind perforations may command a slight premium over normally perforated stamps.

The term *syncopated perfs* describes intentional irregularities in the perforations. The earliest form was used by the Netherlands from 1925-33, where holes were omitted to create distinctive patterns. Beginning in 1992, Great Britain has used an oval perforation to help prevent counterfeiting. Several other countries have started using the oval perfs.

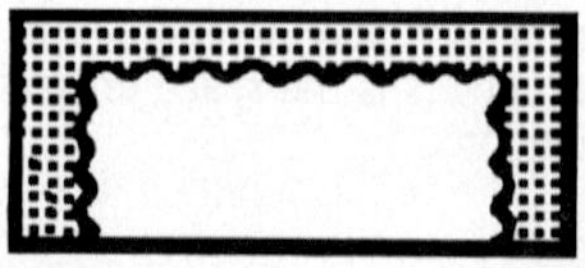

perce en arc

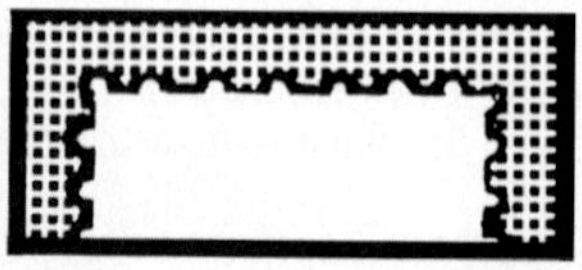

perce en lignes

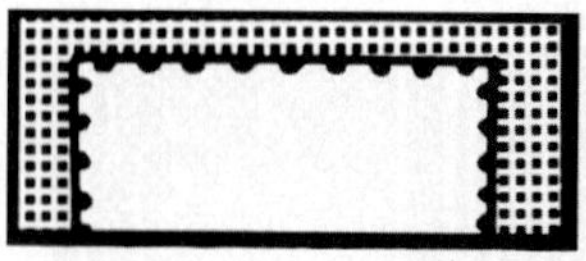

perce en points

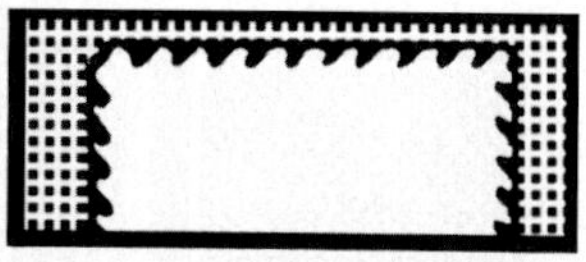

oblique roulette

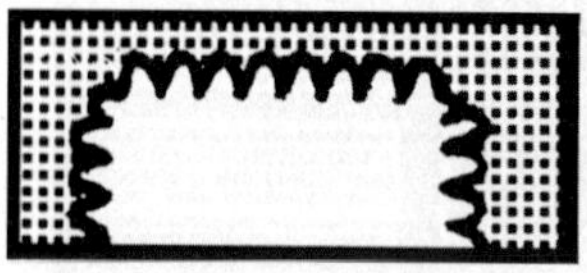

perce en scie

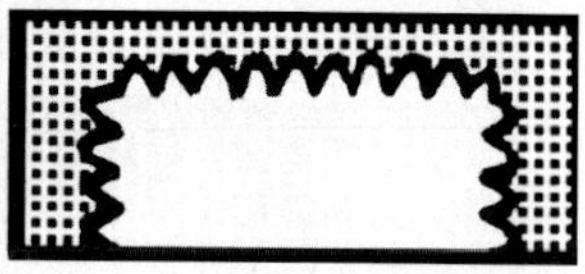

perce serpentin

ROULETTING

In rouletting, the stamp paper is cut partly or wholly through, with no paper removed. In perforating, some paper is removed. Rouletting derives its name from the French roulette, a spur-like wheel. As the wheel is rolled over the paper, each point makes a small cut. The number of cuts made in a two-centimeter space determines the gauge of the roulette, just as the number of perforations in two centimeters determines the gauge of the perforation.

The shape and arrangement of the teeth on the wheels varies. Various roulette types generally carry French names:

Perce en lignes - rouletted in lines. The paper receives short, straight cuts in lines. This is the most common type of rouletting. See Mexico Scott 500.

Perce en points - pin-rouletted. This differs from a small perforation because no paper is removed, although round, equidistant holes are pricked through the paper. See Mexico Scott 242-256.

Perce en arc and *perce en scie* - pierced in an arc or saw-toothed designs, forming half circles or small triangles. See Hanover (German States) Scott 25-29.

Perce en serpentin - serpentine roulettes. The cuts form a serpentine or wavy line. See Brunswick (German States) Scott 13-18.

Once again, no paper is removed by these processes, leaving the stamps easily separated, but closely attached.

DIE-CUTTING

The third and most recently developed major form of stamp separation is die-cutting. This is a method where a die in the pattern of separation is created that later cuts the stamp paper in a stroke motion. Although some standard stamps bear die-cut perforations, this process is primarily used for modern self-adhesive postage stamps.

Printing Processes

ENGRAVING (Intaglio, Line-engraving, Etching)

Master die - The initial operation in the process of line engraving is making the master die. The die is a small, flat block of softened steel upon which the stamp design is recess engraved in reverse.

Master die

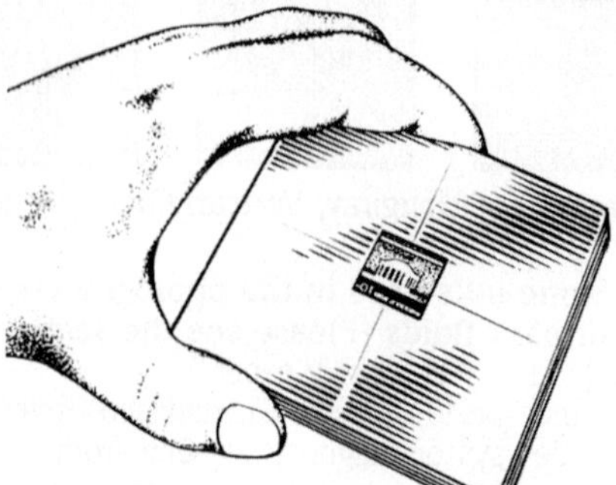

Photographic reduction of the original art is made to the appropriate size. It then serves as a tracing guide for the initial outline of the design. The engraver lightly traces the design on the steel with his graver, then slowly works the design until it is completed. At various points during the engraving process, the engraver hand-inks the die and makes an impression to check his progress. These are known as progressive die proofs. After completion of the engraving, the die is hardened to withstand the stress and pressures of later transfer operations.

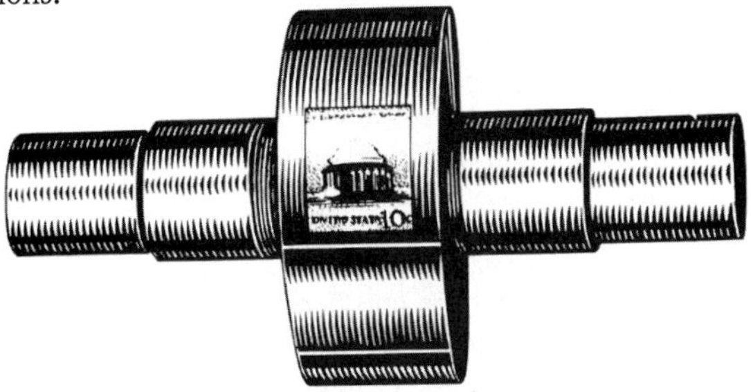

Transfer roll

Transfer roll — Next is production of the transfer roll that, as the name implies, is the medium used to transfer the subject from the master die to the printing plate. A blank roll of soft steel, mounted on a mandrel, is placed under the bearers of the transfer press to allow it to roll freely on its axis. The hardened die is placed on the bed of the press and the face of the transfer roll is applied to the die, under pressure. The bed or the roll is then rocked back and forth under increasing pressure, until the soft steel of the roll is forced into every engraved line of the die. The resulting impression on the roll is known as a "relief" or a "relief transfer." The engraved image is now positive in appearance and stands out from the steel. After the required number of reliefs are "rocked in," the soft steel transfer roll is hardened.

Different flaws may occur during the relief process. A defective relief may occur during the rocking in process because of a minute piece of foreign material lodging on the die, or some other cause. Imperfections in the steel of the transfer roll may result in a breaking away of parts of the design. This is known as a relief break, which will show up on finished stamps as small, unprinted areas. If a damaged relief remains in use, it will transfer a repeating defect to the plate. Deliberate alterations of reliefs sometimes occur. "Altered reliefs" designate these changed conditions.

Plate — The final step in pre-printing production is the making of the printing plate. A flat piece of soft steel replaces the die on the bed of the transfer press. One of the reliefs on the transfer roll is positioned over this soft steel. Position, or layout, dots determine the correct position on the plate. The dots have been lightly marked on the plate in advance. After the correct position of the relief is determined, the design is rocked in by following the same method used in making the transfer roll. The difference is that this time the image is being transferred from the transfer roll, rather than to it. Once the design is entered on the plate, it appears in reverse and is recessed. There are as many transfers entered on the plate as there are subjects printed on the sheet of stamps. It is during this process that double and shifted transfers occur, as well as re-entries. These are the result of improperly entered images that have not been properly burnished out prior to rocking in a new image.

Transferring the design to the plate

Following the entering of the required transfers on the plate, the position dots, layout dots and lines, scratches and other markings generally are burnished out. Added at this time by the siderographer are any required *guide lines, plate numbers* or other *marginal markings.* The plate is then hand-inked and a proof impression is taken. This is known as a plate proof. If the impression is approved, the plate is machined for fitting onto the press, is hardened and sent to the plate vault ready for use.

On press, the plate is inked and the surface is automatically wiped clean, leaving ink only in the recessed lines. Paper is then forced under pressure into the engraved recessed lines, thereby receiving the ink. Thus, the ink lines on engraved stamps are slightly raised, and slight depressions (debossing) occur on the back of the stamp. Prior to the advent of modern high-speed presses and more advanced ink formulations, paper had to be dampened before receiving the ink. This sometimes led to uneven shrinkage by the time the stamps were perforated, resulting in improperly perforated stamps, or misperfs. Newer presses use drier paper, thus both *wet* and *dry printings* exist on some stamps.

Rotary Press — Until 1914, only flat plates were used to print engraved stamps. Rotary press printing was introduced in 1914, and slowly spread. Some countries still use flat-plate printing.

After approval of the plate proof, older *rotary press plates* require additional machining. They are curved to fit the press cylinder. "Gripper slots" are cut into the back of each plate to receive the "grippers," which hold the plate securely on the press. The plate is then hardened. Stamps printed from these bent rotary press plates are longer or wider than the same stamps printed from flat-plate presses. The stretching of the plate during the curving process is what causes this distortion.

Re-entry — To execute a re-entry on a flat plate, the transfer roll is re-applied to the plate, often at some time after its first use on the press. Worn-out designs can be resharpened by carefully burnishing out the original image and re-entering it from the transfer roll. If the original impression has not been sufficiently removed and the transfer roll is not precisely in line with the remaining impression, the resulting double transfer will make the re-entry obvious. If the registration is true, a re-entry may be difficult or impossible to distinguish. Sometimes a stamp printed from a successful re-entry is identified by having a much sharper and clearer impression than its neighbors. With the advent of rotary presses, post-press re-entries were not possible. After a plate was curved for the rotary press, it was impossible to make a re-entry. This is because the plate had already been bent once (with the design distorted).

Double Transfer — This is a description of the condition of a transfer on a plate that shows evidence of a duplication of all, or a portion of the design. It usually is the result of the changing of the registration between the transfer roll and the plate during the rocking in of the original entry. Double transfers also occur when only a portion of the design has been rocked in and improper positioning is noted. If the worker elected not to burnish out the partial or completed design, a strong double transfer will occur for part or all of the design.

It sometimes is necessary to remove the original transfer from a plate and repeat the process a second time. If the finished re-worked image shows traces of the original impression, attributable to incomplete burnishing, the result is a partial double transfer.

Re-engraved — Alterations to a stamp design are sometimes necessary after some stamps have been printed. In some cases, either the original die or the actual printing plate may have its "temper" drawn (softened), and the design will be re-cut. The resulting impressions from such a re-engraved die or plate may differ slightly from the original issue, and are known as "re-engraved." If the alteration was made to the master die, all future printings will be consistently different from the original. If alterations were made to the printing plate, each altered stamp on the plate will be slightly different from each other, allowing specialists to reconstruct a complete printing plate.

Dropped Transfers — If an impression from the transfer roll has not been properly placed, a dropped transfer may occur. The final stamp image will appear obviously out of line with its neighbors.

Short Transfer — Sometimes a transfer roll is not rocked its entire length when entering a transfer onto a plate. As a result, the finished transfer on the plate fails to show the complete design, and the finished stamp will have an incomplete design printed. This is known as a "short transfer." U.S. Scott No. 8 is a good example of a short transfer.

TYPOGRAPHY (Letterpress, Surface Printing, Flexography, Dry Offset, High Etch)

Although the word "Typography" is obsolete as a term describing a printing method, it was the accepted term throughout the first century of postage stamps. Therefore, appropriate Scott listings in this catalogue refer to typographed stamps. The current term for this form of printing, however, is "letterpress."

As it relates to the production of postage stamps, letterpress printing is the reverse of engraving. Rather than having recessed areas trap the ink and deposit it on paper, only the raised areas of the design are inked. This is comparable to the type of printing seen by inking and using an ordinary rubber stamp. Letterpress includes all printing where the design is above the surface area, whether it is wood, metal or, in some instances, hardened rubber or polymer plastic.

For most letterpress-printed stamps, the engraved master is made in much the same manner as for engraved stamps. In this instance, however, an additional step is needed. The design is transferred to another surface before being transferred to the transfer roll. In this way, the transfer roll has a recessed stamp design, rather than one done in relief. This makes the printing areas on the final plate raised, or relief areas.

For less-detailed stamps of the 19th century, the area on the die not used as a printing surface was cut away, leaving the surface area raised. The original die was then reproduced by stereotyping or electrotyping. The resulting electrotypes were assembled in the required number and format of the desired sheet of stamps. The plate used in printing the stamps was an electroplate of these assembled electrotypes.

Once the final letterpress plates are created, ink is applied to the raised surface and the pressure of the press transfers the ink impression to the paper. In contrast to engraving, the fine lines of letterpress are impressed on the surface of the stamp, leaving a debossed surface. When viewed from the back (as on a typewritten page), the corresponding line work on the stamp will be raised slightly (embossed) above the surface.

PHOTOGRAVURE (Gravure, Rotogravure, Heliogravure)

In this process, the basic principles of photography are applied to a chemically sensitized metal plate, rather than photographic paper. The design is transferred photographically to the plate through a halftone, or dot-matrix screen, breaking the reproduction into tiny dots. The plate is treated chemically and the dots form depressions, called cells, of varying depths and diameters, depending on the degrees of shade in the design. Then, like engraving, ink is applied to the plate and the surface is wiped clean. This leaves ink in the tiny cells that is lifted out and deposited on the paper when it is pressed against the plate.

Gravure is most often used for multicolored stamps, generally using the three primary colors (red, yellow and blue) and black. By varying the dot matrix pattern and density of these colors, virtually any color can be reproduced. A typical full-color gravure stamp will be created from four printing cylinders (one for each color). The original multicolored image will have been photographically separated into its component colors.

For examples of the first photogravure stamps printed (1914), see Bavaria Scott 94-114.

LITHOGRAPHY (Offset Lithography, Stone Lithography, Dilitho, Planography, Collotype)

The principle that oil and water do not mix is the basis for lithography. The stamp design is drawn by hand or transferred from engraving to the surface of a lithographic stone or metal plate in a greasy (oily) substance. This oily substance holds the ink, which will later be transferred to the paper. The stone (or plate) is wet with an acid fluid, causing it to repel the printing ink in all areas not covered by the greasy substance.

Transfer paper is used to transfer the design from the original stone or plate. A series of duplicate transfers are grouped and, in turn, transferred to the final printing plate.

Photolithography — The application of photographic processes to lithography. This process allows greater flexibility of design, related to use of halftone screens combined with line work. Unlike photogravure or engraving, this process can allow large, solid areas to be printed.

Offset — A refinement of the lithographic process. A rubber-covered blanket cylinder takes the impression from the inked lithographic plate. From the "blanket" the impression is *offset* or transferred to the paper. Greater flexibility and speed are the principal reasons offset printing has largely displaced lithography. The term "lithography" covers both processes, and results are almost identical.

EMBOSSED (Relief) Printing

Embossing, not considered one of the four main printing types, is a method in which the design first is sunk into the metal of the die. Printing is done against a yielding platen, such as leather or linoleum. The platen is forced into the depression of the die, thus forming the design on the paper in relief. This process is often used for metallic inks.

Embossing may be done without color (see Sardinia Scott 4-6); with color printed around the embossed area (see Great Britain Scott 5 and most U.S. envelopes); and with color in exact registration with the embossed subject.

INK COLORS

Inks or colored papers used in stamp printing often are of mineral origin, although there are numerous examples of organic-based pigments. As a general rule, organic-based pigments are far more subject to varieties and change than those of mineral-based origin.

The appearance of any given color on a stamp may be affected by many aspects, including printing variations, light, color of paper, aging and chemical alterations.

Numerous printing variations may be observed. Heavier pressure or inking will cause a more intense color, while slight interruptions in the ink feed or lighter impressions will cause a lighter appearance. Stamps printed in the same color by water-based and solvent-based inks can differ significantly in appearance. Hand-mixed ink formulas (primarily from the 19th century) produced under different conditions (humidity and temperature) account for notable color variations in early printings of the same stamp (see U.S. Scott 248-250, 279B, for example). Different sources of pigment can also result in significant differences in color.

Light exposure and aging are closely related in the way they affect stamp color. Both eventually break down the ink and fade colors, so that a carefully kept stamp may differ significantly in color from an identical copy that has been exposed to light. If stamps are exposed to light either intentionally or accidentally, their colors can be faded or completely changed in some cases.

Papers of different quality and consistency used for the same stamp printing may affect color appearance. Most pelure papers, for example, show a richer color when compared with wove or laid papers. See Russia Scott 181a, for an example of this effect.

The very nature of the printing processes can cause a variety of differences in shades or hues of the same stamp. Some of these shades are scarcer than others, and are of particular interest to the advanced collector.

Gum

The Illustrated Gum Chart in the first part of this introduction shows and defines various types of gum condition. Because gum condition has an important impact on the value of unused stamps, we recommend studying this chart and the accompanying text carefully.

The gum on the back of a stamp may be shiny, dull, smooth, rough, dark, white, colored or tinted. Most stamp gumming adhesives use gum arabic or dextrine as a base. Certain polymers such as polyvinyl alcohol (PVA) have been used extensively since World War II.

The *Scott Standard Postage Stamp Catalogue* does not list items by types of gum. The *Scott Specialized Catalogue of United States Stamps* does differentiate among some types of gum for certain issues.

Reprints of stamps may have gum differing from the original issues. In addition, some countries have used different gum formulas for different seasons. These adhesives have different properties that may become more apparent over time.

Many stamps have been issued without gum, and the catalogue will note this fact. See, for example, United States Scott 40-47. Sometimes, gum may have been removed to preserve the stamp. Germany Scott B68, for example, has a highly acidic gum that eventually destroys the stamps. This item is valued in the catalogue with gum removed.

Reprints and Reissues

These are impressions of stamps (usually obsolete) made from the original plates or stones. If they are valid for postage and reproduce obsolete issues (such as U.S. Scott 102-111), the stamps are *reissues.* If they are from current issues, they are designated as *second, third,* etc., *printing.* If designated for a particular purpose, they are called *special printings.*

When special printings are not valid for postage, but are made from original dies and plates by authorized persons, they are *official reprints. Private reprints* are made from the original plates and dies by private hands. An example of a private reprint is that of the 1871-1932 reprints made from the original die of the 1845 New Haven, Conn., postmaster's provisional. *Official reproductions* or imitations are made from new dies and plates by government authorization. Scott will list those reissues that are valid for postage if they differ significantly from the original printing.

The U.S. government made special printings of its first postage stamps in 1875. Produced were official imitations of the first two stamps (listed as Scott 3-4), reprints of the demonetized pre-1861 issues (Scott 40-47) and reissues of the 1861 stamps, the 1869 stamps and the then-current 1875 denominations. Even though the official imitations and the reprints were not valid for postage, Scott lists all of these U.S. special printings.

Most reprints or reissues differ slightly from the original stamp in some characteristic, such as gum, paper, perforation, color or watermark. Sometimes the details are followed so meticulously that only a student of that specific stamp is able to distinguish the reprint or reissue from the original.

Remainders and Canceled to Order

Some countries sell their stock of old stamps when a new issue replaces them. To avoid postal use, the *remainders* usually are canceled with a punch hole, a heavy line or bar, or a more-or-less regular-looking cancellation. The most famous merchant of remainders was Nicholas F. Seebeck. In the 1880s and 1890s, he arranged printing contracts between the Hamilton Bank Note Co., of which he was a director, and several Central and South American countries. The contracts provided that the plates and all remainders of the yearly issues became the property of Hamilton. Seebeck saw to it that ample stock remained. The "Seebecks," both remainders and reprints, were standard packet fillers for decades.

Some countries also issue stamps *canceled-to-order (CTO),* either in sheets with original gum or stuck onto pieces of paper or envelopes and canceled. Such CTO items generally are worth less than postally used stamps. In cases where the CTO material is far more prevalent in the marketplace than postally used examples, the catalogue value relates to the CTO examples, with postally used examples noted as premium items. Most CTOs can be detected by the presence of gum. However, as the CTO practice goes back at least to 1885, the gum inevitably has been soaked off some stamps so they could pass as postally used. The normally applied postmarks usually differ slightly from standard postmarks, and specialists are able to tell the difference. When applied individually to envelopes by philatelically minded persons, CTO material is known as *favor canceled* and generally sells at large discounts.

Cinderellas and Facsimiles

Cinderella is a catch-all term used by stamp collectors to describe phantoms, fantasies, bogus items, municipal issues, exhibition seals, local revenues, transportation stamps, labels, poster stamps and many other types of items. Some cinderella collectors include in their collections local postage issues, telegraph stamps, essays and proofs, forgeries and counterfeits.

A *fantasy* is an adhesive created for a nonexistent stamp-issuing authority. Fantasy items range from imaginary countries (Occusi-Ambeno, Kingdom of Sedang, Principality of Trinidad or Torres Straits), to non-existent locals (Winans City Post), or nonexistent transportation lines (McRobish & Co.'s Acapulco-San Francisco Line).

On the other hand, if the entity exists and could have issued stamps (but did not) or was known to have issued other stamps, the items are considered *bogus* stamps. These would include the Mormon postage stamps of Utah, S. Allan Taylor's Guatemala and Paraguay inventions, the propaganda issues for the South Moluccas and the adhesives of the Page & Keyes local post of Boston.

Phantoms is another term for both fantasy and bogus issues.

Facsimiles are copies or imitations made to represent original stamps, but which do not pretend to be originals. A catalogue illustration is such a facsimile. Illustrations from the Moens catalogue of the last century were occasionally colored and passed off as stamps. Since the beginning of stamp collecting, facsimiles have been made for collectors as space fillers or for reference. They often carry the word "facsimile," "falsch" (German), "sanko" or "mozo" (Japanese), or "faux" (French) overprinted on the face or stamped on the back. Unfortunately, over the years a number of these items have had fake cancels applied over the facsimile notation and have been passed off as genuine.

Forgeries and Counterfeits

Forgeries and counterfeits have been with philately virtually from the beginning of stamp production. Over time, the terminology for the two has been used interchangeably. Although both forgeries and counterfeits are reproductions of stamps, the purposes behind their creation differ considerably.

Among specialists there is an increasing movement to more specifically define such items. Although there is no universally accepted terminology, we feel the following definitions most closely mirror the items and their purposes as they are currently defined.

Forgeries (also often referred to as *Counterfeits*) are reproductions of genuine stamps that have been created to defraud collectors. Such spurious items first appeared on the market around 1860, and most old-time collections contain one or more. Many are crude and easily spotted, but some can deceive experts.

An important supplier of these early philatelic forgeries was the Hamburg printer Gebruder Spiro. Many others with reputations in this craft included S. Allan Taylor, George Hussey, James Chute, George Forune, Benjamin & Sarpy, Julius Goldner, E. Oneglia and L.H. Mercier. Among the noted 20th-century forgers were Francois Fournier, Jean Sperati and the prolific Raoul DeThuin.

Forgeries may be complete replications, or they may be genuine stamps altered to resemble a scarcer (and more valuable) type. Most forgeries, particularly those of rare stamps, are worth only a small fraction of the value of a genuine example, but a few types, created by some of the most notable forgers, such as Sperati, can be worth as much or more than the genuine. Fraudulently produced copies are known of most classic rarities and many medium-priced stamps.

In addition to rare stamps, large numbers of common 19th- and early 20th-century stamps were forged to supply stamps to the early packet trade. Many can still be easily found. Few new philatelic forgeries have appeared in recent decades. Successful imitation of well-engraved work is virtually impossible. It has proven far easier to produce a fake by altering a genuine stamp than to duplicate a stamp completely.

Counterfeit (also often referred to as *Postal Counterfeit* or *Postal Forgery*) is the term generally applied to reproductions of stamps that have been created to defraud the government of revenue. Such items usually are created at the time a stamp is current and, in some cases, are hard to detect. Because most counterfeits are seized when the perpetrator is captured, postal counterfeits, particularly used on cover, are usually worth much more than a genuine example to specialists. The first postal counterfeit was of Spain's 4-cuarto carmine of 1854 (the real one is Scott 25). Apparently, the counterfeiters were not satisfied with their first version, which is now very scarce, and they soon created an engraved counterfeit, which is common. Postal counterfeits quickly followed in Austria, Naples, Sardinia and the Roman States. They have since been created in many other countries as well, including the United States.

An infamous counterfeit to defraud the government is the 1-shilling Great Britain "Stock Exchange" forgery of 1872, used on telegraph forms at the exchange that year. The stamp escaped detection until a stamp dealer noticed it in 1898.

Fakes

Fakes are genuine stamps altered in some way to make them more desirable. One student of this part of stamp collecting has estimated that by the 1950s more than 30,000 varieties of fakes were known. That number has grown greatly since then. The widespread existence of fakes makes it important for stamp collectors to study their philatelic holdings and use relevant literature. Likewise, collectors should buy from reputable dealers who guarantee their stamps and make full and prompt refunds should a purchased item be declared faked or altered by some mutually agreed-upon authority. Because fakes always have some genuine characteristics, it is not always possible to obtain unanimous agreement among experts regarding specific items. These students may change their opinions as philatelic knowledge increases. More than 80 percent of all fakes on the philatelic market today are regummed, reperforated (or perforated for the first time), or bear forged overprints, surcharges or cancellations.

Stamps can be chemically treated to alter or eliminate colors. For example, a pale rose stamp can be re-colored to resemble a blue shade of high market value. In other cases, treated stamps can be made to resemble missing color varieties. Designs may be changed by painting, or a stroke or a dot added or bleached out to turn an ordinary variety into a seemingly scarcer stamp. Part of a stamp can be bleached and reprinted in a different version, achieving an inverted center or frame. Margins can be added or repairs done so deceptively that the stamps move from the "repaired" into the "fake" category.

Fakers have not left the backs of the stamps untouched either. They may create false watermarks, add fake grills or press out genuine grills. A thin India paper proof may be glued onto a thicker backing to create the appearance an issued stamp, or a proof printed on cardboard may be shaved down and perforated to resemble a stamp. Silk threads are impressed into paper and stamps have been split so that a rare paper variety is added to an otherwise inexpensive stamp. The most common treatment to the back of a stamp, however, is regumming.

Some in the business of faking stamps have openly advertised foolproof application of "original gum" to stamps that lack it, although most publications now ban such ads from their pages. It is believed that very few early stamps have survived without being hinged. The large number of never-hinged examples of such earlier material offered for sale thus suggests the widespread extent of regumming activity. Regumming also may be used to hide repairs or thin spots. Dipping the stamp into watermark fluid, or examining it under longwave ultraviolet light often will reveal these flaws.

Fakers also tamper with separations. Ingenious ways to add margins are known. Perforated wide-margin stamps may be falsely represented as imperforate when trimmed. Reperforating is commonly done to create scarce coil or perforation varieties, and to eliminate the naturally occurring straight-edge stamps found in sheet margin positions of many earlier issues. Custom has made straight-edged stamps less desirable. Fakers have obliged by perforating straight-edged stamps so that many are now uncommon, if not rare.

Another fertile field for the faker is that of overprints, surcharges and cancellations. The forging of rare surcharges or overprints began in the 1880s or 1890s. These forgeries are sometimes difficult to detect, but experts have identified almost all. Occasionally, overprints or cancellations are removed to create non-overprinted stamps or seemingly unused items. This is most commonly done by removing a manuscript cancel to make a stamp resemble an unused example. "SPECIMEN" overprints may be removed by scraping and repainting to create non-overprinted varieties. Fakers use inexpensive revenues or pen-canceled stamps to generate unused stamps for further faking by adding other markings. The quartz lamp or UV lamp and a high-powered magnifying glass help to easily detect removed cancellations.

The bigger problem, however, is the addition of overprints, surcharges or cancellations - many with such precision that they are very difficult to ascertain. Plating of the stamps or the overprint can be an important method of detection.

Fake postmarks may range from many spurious fancy cancellations to a host of markings applied to transatlantic covers, to adding normally appearing postmarks to definitives of some countries with stamps that are valued far higher used than unused. With the increased popularity of cover collecting, and the widespread interest in postal history, a fertile new field for fakers has come about. Some have tried to create entire covers. Others specialize in adding stamps, tied by fake cancellations, to genuine stampless covers, or replacing less expensive or damaged stamps with more valuable ones. Detailed study of postal rates in effect at the time a cover in question was mailed, including the analysis of each handstamp used during the period, ink analysis and similar techniques, usually will unmask the fraud.

Restoration and Repairs

Scott Publishing Co. bases its catalogue values on stamps that are free of defects and otherwise meet the standards set forth earlier in this introduction. Most stamp collectors desire to have the finest copy of an item possible. Even within given grading categories there are variances. This leads to a controversial practice that is not defined in any universal manner: stamp *restoration.*

There are broad differences of opinion about what is permissible when it comes to restoration. Carefully applying a soft eraser to a stamp or cover to remove light soiling is one form of restoration, as is washing a stamp in mild soap and water to clean it. These are fairly accepted forms of restoration. More severe forms of restoration include pressing out creases or removing stains caused by tape. To what degree each of these is acceptable is dependent upon the individual situation. Further along the spectrum is the freshening of a stamp's color by removing oxide build-up or the effects of wax paper left next to stamps shipped to the tropics.

At some point in this spectrum the concept of *repair* replaces that of restoration. Repairs include filling thin spots, mending tears by reweaving or adding a missing perforation tooth. Regumming stamps may have been acceptable as a restoration or repair technique many decades ago, but today it is considered a form of fakery.

Restored stamps may or may not sell at a discount, and it is possible that the value of individual restored items may be enhanced over that of their pre-restoration state. Specific situations dictate the resultant value of such an item. Repaired stamps sell at substantial discounts from the value of sound stamps.

When the purchaser of an item has any reason to suspect that an item has been repaired, and the detection of such a repair is beyond his own ability, he should seek expert advice. There are services that specialize in giving such advice.

Terminology

Booklets — Many countries have issued stamps in small booklets for the convenience of users. This idea continues to become increasingly popular in many countries. Booklets have been issued in many sizes and forms, often with advertising on the covers, the panes of stamps or on the interleaving.

The panes used in booklets may be printed from special plates or made from regular sheets. All panes from booklets issued by the United States and many from those of other countries contain stamps that are straight edged on the sides, but perforated between. Others are distinguished by orientation of watermark or other identifying features. Any stamp-like unit in the pane, either printed or blank, that is not a postage stamp is considered to be a *label* in the catalogue listings.

Scott lists and values booklet panes only. Complete booklets are listed and valued in only a few cases, such as Grenada Scott 1055 and some forms of British prestige booklets. Individual booklet panes are listed only when they are not fashioned from existing sheet stamps and, therefore, are identifiable from their sheet stamp counterparts.

Panes usually do not have a used value assigned to them because there is little market activity for used booklet panes, even though many exist used and there is some demand for them.

Cancellations — The marks or obliterations put on stamps by postal authorities to show that they have performed service and to prevent their reuse are known as cancellations. If the marking is made with a pen, it is considered a "pen cancel." When the location of the post office appears in the marking, it is a "town cancellation." A "postmark" is technically any postal marking, but in practice the term generally is applied to a town cancellation with a date. When calling attention to a cause or celebration, the marking is known as a "slogan cancellation." Many other types and styles of cancellations exist, such as duplex, numerals, targets, fancy and others. See also "precancels," below.

Coil Stamps — These are stamps that are issued in rolls for use in dispensers, affixing and vending machines. Those coils of the United States, Canada, Sweden and some other countries are perforated horizontally or vertically only, with the outer edges imperforate. Coil stamps of some countries, such as Great Britain and Germany, are perforated on all four sides and may in some cases be distinguished from their sheet stamp counterparts by watermarks, counting numbers on the reverse or other means.

Errors — Stamps that have some major, consistent, unintentional deviation from the normal are considered errors. Errors include, but are not limited to, missing or wrong colors, wrong paper, wrong watermarks, inverted centers or frames on multicolor printing, inverted or missing surcharges or overprints, double impressions, missing perforations and others. Factually wrong or misspelled information, if it appears on all examples of a stamp, are not considered errors in the true sense of the word. They are errors of design. Inconsistent or randomly appearing items, such as misperfs or color shifts, are classified as freaks.

Overprints and Surcharges — Overprinting involves applying wording or design elements over an already existing stamp. Overprints can be used to alter the place of use (such as "Canal Zone" on U.S. stamps), to adapt them for a special purpose ("Porto" on Denmark's 1913-20 regular issues for use as postage due stamps, Scott J1-J7) or to commemorate a special occasion (United States Scott 647-648).

A *surcharge* is a form of overprint that changes or restates the face value of a stamp or piece of postal stationery.

Surcharges and overprints may be handstamped, typeset or, occasionally, lithographed or engraved. A few hand-written overprints and surcharges are known. The world's first surcharge was a handstamped "2" on the United States City Despatch Post stamps of 1846.

Precancels — Stamps that are canceled before they are placed in the mail are known as precancels. Precanceling usually is done to expedite the handling of large mailings and generally allow the affected mail pieces to skip certain phases of mail handling.

In the United States, precancellations generally identified the point of origin; that is, the city and state. This information appeared across the face of the stamp, usually centered between parallel lines. More recently, bureau precancels retained the parallel lines, but the city and state designations were dropped. Recent coils have a service inscription that is present on the original printing plate. These show the mail service paid for by the stamp. Since these stamps are not intended to receive further cancellations when used as intended, they are considered precancels. Such items often do not have parallel lines as part of the precancellation.

In France, the abbreviation *Affranchts* in a semicircle together with the word *Postes* is the general form of precancel in use. Belgian precancellations usually appear in a box in which the name of the city appears. Netherlands precancels have the name of the city enclosed between concentric circles, sometimes called a "lifesaver." Precancellations of other countries usually follow these patterns, but may be any arrangement of bars, boxes and city names.

Precancels are listed in the Scott catalogues only if the precancel changes the denomination (Belgium Scott 477-478); if the precanceled stamp is different from the non-precanceled version (such as untagged U.S. precancels); or if the stamp exists only precanceled (France Scott 1096-1099, U.S. Scott 2265).

Proofs and Essays — Proofs are impressions taken from an approved die, plate or stone in which the design and color are the same as the stamp issued to the public. Trial color proofs are impressions taken from approved dies, plates or stones in colors that vary from the final version. An essay is the impression of a design that differs in some way from the issued stamp. "Progressive die proofs" generally are considered to be essays.

Provisionals — These are stamps that are issued on short notice and intended for temporary use pending the arrival of regular issues. They usually are issued to meet such contingencies as changes in government or currency, shortage of necessary postage values or military occupation.

During the 1840s, postmasters in certain American cities issued stamps that were valid only at specific post offices. In 1861, postmasters of the Confederate States also issued stamps with limited validity. Both of these examples are known as "postmaster's provisionals."

Se-tenant — This term refers to an unsevered pair, strip or block of stamps that differ in design, denomination or overprint.

Unless the se-tenant item has a continuous design (see U.S. Scott 1451a, 1694a) the stamps do not have to be in the same order as shown in the catalogue (see U.S. Scott 2158a).

Specimens — The Universal Postal Union required member nations to send samples of all stamps they released into service to the International Bureau in Switzerland. Member nations of the UPU received these specimens as samples of what stamps were valid for postage. Many are overprinted, handstamped or initial-perforated "Specimen," "Canceled" or "Muestra." Some are marked with bars across the denominations (China-Taiwan), punched holes (Czechoslovakia) or back inscriptions (Mongolia).

Stamps distributed to government officials or for publicity purposes, and stamps submitted by private security printers for official approval, also may receive such defacements.

The previously described defacement markings prevent postal use, and all such items generally are known as "specimens."

Tete Beche — This term describes a pair of stamps in which one is upside down in relation to the other. Some of these are the result of intentional sheet arrangements, such as Morocco Scott B10-B11. Others occurred when one or more electrotypes accidentally were placed upside down on the plate, such as Colombia Scott 57a. Separation of the tete-beche stamps, of course, destroys the tete beche variety.

Dies of British Colonial Stamps

DIE A

DIE B

DIE A:
1. The lines in the groundwork vary in thickness and are not uniformly straight.
2. The seventh and eighth lines from the top, in the groundwork, converge where they meet the head.
3. There is a small dash in the upper part of the second jewel in the band of the crown.
4. The vertical color line in front of the throat stops at the sixth line of shading on the neck.

DIE B:
1. The lines in the groundwork are all thin and straight.
2. All the lines of the background are parallel.
3. There is no dash in the upper part of the second jewel in the band of the crown.
4. The vertical color line in front of the throat stops at the eighth line of shading on the neck.

DIE I

DIE II

DIE I:
1. The base of the crown is well below the level of the inner white line around the vignette.
2. The labels inscribed "POSTAGE" and "REVENUE" are cut square at the top.
3. There is a white "bud" on the outer side of the main stem of the curved ornaments in each lower corner.
4. The second (thick) line below the country name has the ends next to the crown cut diagonally.

DIE Ia.	DIE Ib.
1 as die II.	1 and 3 as die II.
2 and 3 as die I.	2 as die I.

DIE II:
1. The base of the crown is aligned with the underside of the white line around the vignette.
2. The labels curve inward at the top inner corners.
3. The "bud" has been removed from the outer curve of the ornaments in each corner.
4. The second line below the country name has the ends next to the crown cut vertically.

British Colonial and Crown Agents Watermarks

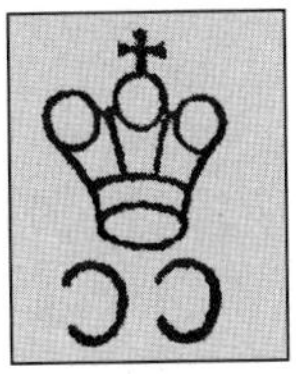

Wmk. 1
Crown and C C

Wmk. 2
Crown and C A

Wmk. 3
Multiple Crown and C A

Wmk. 4
Multiple Crown and Script C A

Wmk. 4a

Wmk. 314
St. Edward's Crown and C A Multiple

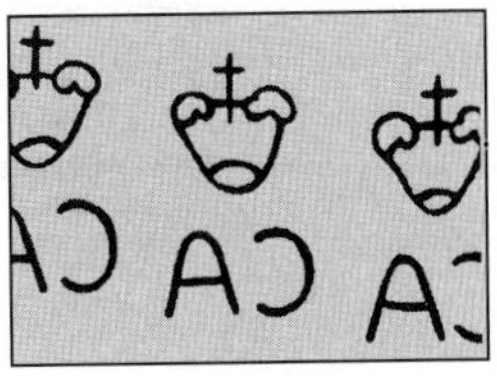

Wmk. 373

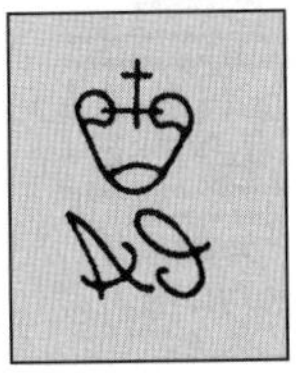

Wmk. 384

Watermarks 1 to 4, 314, 373, and 384, common to many British territories, are illustrated here to avoid duplication.

The letters "CC" of Wmk. 1 identify the paper as having been made for the use of the Crown Colonies, while the letters "CA" of the others stand for "Crown Agents." Both Wmks. 1 and 2 were used on stamps printed by De La Rue & Co.

Wmk. 3 was adopted in 1904; Wmk. 4 in 1921; Wmk. 314 in 1957; Wmk. 373 in 1974; and Wmk. 384 in 1985.

In Wmk. 4a, a non-matching crown of the general St. Edwards type (bulging on both sides at top) was substituted for one of the Wmk. 4 crowns which fell off the dandy roll. The non-matching crown occurs in 1950-52 printings in a horizontal row of crowns on certain regular stamps of Johore and Seychelles, and on various postage due stamps of Barbados, Basutoland, British Guiana, Gold Coast, Grenada, Northern Rhodesia, St. Lucia, Swaziland and Trinidad and Tobago. A variation of Wmk. 4a, with the non-matching crown in a horizontal row of crown-CA-crown, occurs on regular stamps of Bahamas, St. Kitts-Nevis and Singapore.

Wmk. 314 was intentionally used sideways, starting in 1966. When a stamp was issued with Wmk. 314 both upright and sideways, the sideways varieties usually are listed also – with minor numbers. In many of the later issues, Wmk. 314 is slightly visible.

Wmk. 373 is usually only faintly visible.

Crowned Circle Handstamps and Great Britain Stamps Used Abroad

Crowned Circle Handstamps

Prior to the introduction of postage stamps in a number of British colonies, British postal authorities furnished post offices in these colonies with crowned circle handstamps. Crowned circle handstamps also were issued to a number of British post offices in foreign countries. These handstamps were to be used on mail sent to foreign countries or on mail between two foreign ports. The postage paid by the sender was to be noted in manuscript on the cover.

Crowned circle handstamps from the colonies of British America are listed. Similar handstamps were also furnished to post offices in British possessions outside of British America, such as New Zealand, Lagos and the Ionian Islands; areas where Britain maintained consular offices, such as Cairo, Egypt; and British Postal Agency offices, such as Rio de Janeiro, Brazil and San Juan, Puerto Rico. These items are not listed at this time, but such expansion is planned for future editions.

Some of these handstamps were used for various purposes after the advent of postage stamps. Values are for covers with clearly legible handstamps, produced prior to the advent of the colony's stamps. The color of the handstamp is black unless otherwise noted.

Types of Crowned Circle Handstamps

Type I

Type II

Type III

Type IV

Type V

Type VI

Type VII

Type VIII

Type IX

Great Britain Stamps Used Abroad

In some British colonies, postage stamps of Great Britain were used prior to the introduction of the colony's own postage stamps. Special cancels, most of which show an alphanumeric code, were furnished to the postmasters in these colonies to be used on these Great Britain stamps. Cancels and Great Britain stamps were furnished to colonies outside of the British America area as well as to British consular offices and British Postal Agency offices, but only the obliterators of British colonies in British America are listed at this time.

Cancel numbers assigned and used by post offices in the British American colonies were numbered A01-A15, A18, A27-A37, A39-A49, A51-A62 and A64-A78. A typical example of these cancels is shown below. Similar cancels with different alphanumeric codes, not listed in this catalogue, were assigned to the other colonies, consular offices and Postal Agency offices, as were cancels that are not similar in appearance.

The values quoted are for very fine off cover examples of the Great Britain stamps specified in parentheses in the listing with a legible and clearly identifiable alphanumeric combination. Such examples on cover sell for more.

These listings generally are limited to off cover stamps only. Other stamps that may have been sent to these offices may exist on covers that bear these cancels, but the cancel may not be on the stamp. Such items would need to be collected as complete covers.

Any valid Great Britain stamp brought to these colonies prior to the introduction of the colony's own postage stamps would have received these cancels if properly posted, but in virtually all instances the Great Britain stamps specified in these listings are those that were sent to these colonies by British postal officals during the years noted in the listings.

These canceling devices were returned to Great Britain and put to use there, so some of these cancels may be found on other Great Britain stamps from later periods.

Type A

Type B

For a list of Crowned Circle handstamps and Great Britain stamps used abroad, see end of Index and Identifier.

British Commonwealth of Nations

Dominions, Colonies, Territories, Offices and Independent Members

Comprising stamps of the British Commonwealth and associated nations.

1. Great Britain

Great Britain: Including England, Scotland, Wales and Northern Ireland.

2. The Dominions, Present and Past

AUSTRALIA

The Commonwealth of Australia was proclaimed on January 1, 1901. It consists of six former colonies as follows:

New South Wales	South Australia	Tasmania
Queensland	Victoria	Western Australia

Territories belonging to, or administered by Australia: Nauru, New Guinea, Papua.

CANADA

The Dominion of Canada was created by the British North America Act in 1867. The following provinces were former separate colonies and issued postage stamps:

British Columbia and Vancouver Island	Newfoundland
New Brunswick	Nova Scotia
	Prince Edward Island

INDIA

The Republic of India was inaugurated on January 26, 1950. It succeeded the Dominion of India which was proclaimed August 15, 1947, when the former Empire of India was divided into Pakistan and the Union of India. The Republic is composed of about 40 predominantly Hindu states of three classes: governor's provinces, chief commissioner's provinces and princely states. India also has various territories, such as the Andaman and Nicobar Islands.

The old Empire of India was a federation of British India and the native states. The more important princely states were autonomous. Of the more than 700 Indian states, these 43 are familiar names to philatelists because of their postage stamps.

CONVENTION STATES

Chamba	Gwalior	Nabha
Faridkot	Jhind	Patiala

NATIVE FEUDATORY STATES

Alwar	Faridkot (1879-86)	Las Bela
Bamra	Hyderabad	Morvi
Barwani	Idar	Nandgaon
Bhopal	Indore	Nowanuggur
Bhor	Jaipur	Orchha
Bijawar	Jammu	Poonch
Bundi	Jammu and Kashmir	Rajpeepla
Bussahir	Jhalawar	Sirmoor
Charkhari	Jind (1875-76)	Soruth
Cochin	Kashmir	Travancore
Dhar	Kishangarh	Wadhwan
Duttia		

NEW ZEALAND

Became a dominion on September 26, 1907. The following islands and territories are, or have been, administered by New Zealand:

Aitutaki	Penrhyn
Cook Islands (Rarotonga)	Samoa (Western Samoa)
Niue	

SOUTH AFRICA

Under the terms of the South African Act (1909) the self-governing colonies of Cape of Good Hope, Natal, Orange River Colony and Transvaal united on May 31, 1910, to form the Union of South Africa. It became an independent republic May 3, 1961.

Under the terms of the Treaty of Versailles, South-West Africa, formerly German South-West Africa, was mandated to the Union of South Africa.

3. Colonies, Past and Present; ControlledTerritory and Independent Members of the Commonwealth

Aden
Antigua
Ascension
Bahamas
Bahrain
Barbados
Barbuda
Basutoland
Batum
Bechuanaland
Bechuanaland Prot.
Bermuda
British Central Africa
British East Africa
British Guiana
British Honduras
British New Guinea
British Solomon Islands
British Somaliland
Brunei
Bushire
Cameroons
Cape of Good Hope
Cayman Islands
Ceylon
Crete, British Administration
Cyprus
Dominica
East Africa & Uganda Protectorates
Egypt
Falkland Islands
Fiji
Gambia
German East Africa
Gibraltar
Gilbert & Ellice Islands
Gold Coast
Grenada
Griqualand West
Heligoland
Hong Kong
Ionian Islands
Jamaica
Kenya, Uganda & Tanzania
Kuwait
Labuan
Lagos
Leeward Islands
Madagascar
Malaya
- Federated Malay States
- Johore
- Kedah
- Kelantan
- Negri Sembilan
- Pahang
- Perak
- Selangor
- Sungei Ujong
- Trengganu

Maldive Islands
Malta
Mauritius
Mesopotamia
Montserrat
Natal
Nevis
New Britain
New Hebrides
Niger Coast Protectorate
Nigeria
North Borneo
Northern Nigeria
Northern Rhodesia
North West Pacific Islands
Nyasaland Protectorate
Orange River Colony
Palestine
Pitcairn Islands
Rhodesia
St. Christopher
St. Helena
St. Kitts-Nevis-Anguilla
St. Lucia
St. Vincent
Samoa
Sarawak
Seychelles
Sierra Leone
Solomon Islands
Somaliland Protectorate
Southern Nigeria
Southern Rhodesia
Straits Settlements
Sudan
Swaziland
Tanganyika
Tasmania
Tobago
Togo
Tonga
Transvaal
Trinidad
Trinidad and Tobago
Turks and Caicos
Turks Islands
Uganda
Virgin Islands
Zanzibar
Zululand

POST OFFICES IN FOREIGN COUNTRIES

Africa
- East Africa Forces
- Middle East Forces

Bangkok
China
Morocco
Turkish Empire

Colonies, Former Colonies, Offices, Territories Controlled by Parent States

Belgium
Belgian Congo
Ruanda-Urundi

Denmark
Danish West Indies
Faroe Islands
Greenland
Iceland

France
COLONIES PAST AND PRESENT, CONTROLLED TERRITORIES
Alaouites
Alexandretta
Algeria
Alsace & Lorraine
Anjouan
Annam & Tonkin
Benin
Cameroun
Castellorizo
Chad
Cilicia
Cochin China
Dahomey
Diego Suarez
Djibouti (Somali Coast)
French Congo
French Equatorial Africa
French Guiana
French Guinea
French India
French Morocco
French Sudan
Gabon
Grand Comoro
Guadeloupe
Indo-China
Inini
Ivory Coast
Latakia
Lebanon
Madagascar
Martinique
Mauritania
Mayotte
Memel
Middle Congo
Moheli
New Caledonia
New Hebrides
Niger Territory
Nossi-Be
Obock
Oceania (French Polynesia)
Reunion
Rouad, Ile
Ste.-Marie de Madagascar
St. Pierre & Miquelon
Senegal
Senegambia & Niger
Somali Coast
Syria
Tahiti
Togo
Tunisia
Ubangi-Shari
Upper Senegal & Niger
Upper Volta
Wallis & Futuna Islands

POST OFFICES IN FOREIGN COUNTRIES
China
Crete
Egypt
Turkish Empire
Zanzibar

Germany
EARLY STATES
Baden
Bavaria
Bergedorf
Bremen
Brunswick
Hamburg
Hanover
Lubeck
Mecklenburg-Schwerin
Mecklenburg-Strelitz
Oldenburg
Prussia
Saxony
Schleswig-Holstein
Wurttemberg

FORMER COLONIES
Cameroun (Kamerun)
Caroline Islands
German East Africa
German New Guinea
German South-West Africa
Kiauchau
Mariana Islands
Marshall Islands
Samoa
Togo

Italy
EARLY STATES
Modena
Parma
Romagna
Roman States
Sardinia
Tuscany
Two Sicilies
  Naples
  Neapolitan Provinces
  Sicily

FORMER COLONIES, CONTROLLED TERRITORIES, OCCUPATION AREAS
Aegean Islands
  Calimno (Calino)
  Caso
  Cos (Coo)
  Karki (Carchi)
  Leros (Lero)
  Lipso
  Nisiros (Nisiro)
  Patmos (Patmo)
  Piscopi
  Rodi (Rhodes)
  Scarpanto
  Simi
  Stampalia
Castellorizo
Corfu
Cyrenaica
Eritrea
Ethiopia (Abyssinia)
Fiume
Italian East Africa
Libya
Oltre Giuba
Saseno
Somalia (Italian Somaliland)
Tripolitania

POST OFFICES IN FOREIGN COUNTRIES
"ESTERO"*
Austria
Bengasi
China
  Peking
  Tientsin
Crete
Tripoli
Turkish Empire
  Constantinople
  Durazzo
  Janina
  Jerusalem
  Salonika
  Scutari
  Smyrna
  Valona

*Stamps overprinted "ESTERO" were used in various parts of the world.

Netherlands
Netherlands Antilles (Curacao)
Netherlands Indies
Netherlands New Guinea
Surinam (Dutch Guiana)

Portugal
COLONIES PAST AND PRESENT, CONTROLLED TERRITORIES
Angola
Angra
Azores
Cape Verde
Funchal
Horta
Inhambane
Kionga
Lourenco Marques
Macao
Madeira
Mozambique
Mozambique Co.
Nyassa
Ponta Delgada
Portuguese Africa
Portuguese Congo
Portuguese Guinea
Portuguese India
Quelimane
St. Thomas & Prince Islands
Tete
Timor
Zambezia

Russia
ALLIED TERRITORIES AND REPUBLICS, OCCUPATION AREAS
Armenia
Aunus (Olonets)
Azerbaijan
Batum
Estonia
Far Eastern Republic
Georgia
Karelia
Latvia
Lithuania
North Ingermanland
Ostland
Russian Turkestan
Siberia
South Russia
Tannu Tuva
Transcaucasian Fed. Republics
Ukraine
Wenden (Livonia)
Western Ukraine

Spain
COLONIES PAST AND PRESENT, CONTROLLED TERRITORIES
Aguera, La
Cape Juby
Cuba
Elobey, Annobon & Corisco
Fernando Po
Mariana Islands
Philippines
Puerto Rico
Rio de Oro
Spanish Guinea
Spanish Morocco
Spanish Sahara

POST OFFICES IN FOREIGN COUNTRIES
Morocco
Tangier
Tetuan

COMMON DESIGN TYPES

PORTUGAL & COLONIES

Pictured in this section are issues where one illustration has been used for a number of countries in the Catalogue. Not included in this section are overprinted stamps or those issues which are illustrated in each country.

Vasco da Gama

Fleet Departing CD20

Fleet Arriving at Calicut — CD21

Embarking at Rastello CD22

Muse of History CD23

San Gabriel, da Gama and Camoens CD24

Archangel Gabriel, the Patron Saint — CD25

Flagship San Gabriel — CD26

Vasco da Gama — CD27

Fourth centenary of Vasco da Gama's discovery of the route to India.

1898

Azores 93-100
Macao 67-74
Madeira 37-44
Portugal 147-154
Port. Africa 1-8
Port. Congo 75-98
Port. India 189-196
St. Thomas & Prince Islands...170-193
Timor 45-52

Pombal
POSTAL TAX
POSTAL TAX DUES

Marquis de Pombal — CD28

Planning Reconstruction of Lisbon, 1755 — CD29

Pombal Monument, Lisbon — CD30

Sebastiao Jose de Carvalho e Mello, Marquis de Pombal (1699-1782), statesman, rebuilt Lisbon after earthquake of 1755. Tax was for the erection of Pombal monument. Obligatory on all mail on certain days throughout the year.
Postal Tax Dues are inscribed 'Multa'

1925

Angola RA1-RA3, RAJ1-RAJ3
Azores RA9-RA11, RAJ2-RAJ4
Cape Verde RA1-RA3, RAJ1-RAJ3
Macao RA1-RA3, RAJ1-RAJ3
Madeira RA1-RA3, RAJ1-RAJ3
Mozambique RA1-RA3, RAJ1-RAJ3
Portugal RA11-RA13, RAJ2-RAJ4
Port. Guinea RA1-RA3, RAJ1-RAJ3
Port. India RA1-RA3, RAJ1-RAJ3
St. Thomas & Prince Islands RA1-RA3, RAJ1-RAJ3
Timor RA1-RA3, RAJ1-RAJ3

Vasco da Gama CD34

Mousinho de Albuquerque CD35

Dam CD36

Prince Henry the Navigator CD37

Affonso de Albuquerque CD38

Plane over Globe CD39

1938-39

Angola 274-291, C1-C9
Cape Verde 234-251, C1-C9
Macao 289-305, C7-C15
Mozambique 270-287, C1-C9
Port. Guinea 233-250, C1-C9
Port. India 439-453, C1-C8
St. Thomas & Prince Islands ... 302-319, 323-340, C1-C18
Timor 223-239, C1-C9

FRENCH COMMUNITY

Colonial Exposition

People of French Empire CD70

Women's Heads CD71

France Showing Way to Civilization CD72

"Colonial Commerce" CD73

International Colonial Exposition, Paris.

1931

Cameroun 213-216
Chad 60-63
Dahomey 97-100
Fr. Guiana 152-155
Fr. Guinea 116-119
Fr. India 100-103
Fr. Polynesia 76-79
Fr. Sudan 102-105
Gabon 120-123
Guadeloupe 138-141
Indo-China 140-142
Ivory Coast 92-95
Madagascar 169-172
Martinique 129-132
Mauritania 65-68
Middle Congo 61-64
New Caledonia 176-179
Niger 73-76
Reunion 122-125
St. Pierre & Miquelon 132-135
Senegal 138-141
Somali Coast 135-138
Togo 254-257
Ubangi-Shari 82-85
Upper Volta 66-69
Wallis & Futuna Isls. 85-88

Paris International Exposition
Colonial Arts Exposition

"Conoial Resources}
CD74 CD77

Overseas Commerce CD75

Exposition Building and Women CD76

"France and the Empire" CD78

Cultural Treasures of the Colonies CD79

Souvenir sheets contain one imperf. stamp.

1937

Cameroun 217-222A
Dahomey 101-107
Fr. Equatorial Africa 27-32, 73
Fr. Guiana 162-168
Fr. Guinea 120-126
Fr. India 104-110
Fr. Polynesia 117-123
Fr. Sudan 106-112
Guadeloupe 148-154
Indo-China 193-199
Inini 41
Ivory Coast 152-158
Kwangchowan 132
Madagascar 191-197
Martinique 179-185
Mauritania 69-75
New Caledonia 208-214
Niger 72-83
Reunion 167-173
St. Pierre & Miquelon 165-171
Senegal 172-178
Somali Coast 139-145
Togo 258-264
Wallis & Futuna Isls. 89

Curie

Pierre and Marie Curie CD80

40th anniversary of the discovery of radium. The surtax was for the benefit of the Intl. Union for the Control of Cancer.

1938

Cameroun B1
Cuba B1-B2
Dahomey B2
France B76
Fr. Equatorial Africa B1
Fr. Guiana B3
Fr. Guinea B2
Fr. India B6
Fr. Polynesia B5
Fr. Sudan B1
Guadeloupe B3
Indo-China B14
Ivory Coast B2
Madagascar B2
Martinique B2
Mauritania B3
New Caledonia B4
Niger B1
Reunion B4
St. Pierre & Miquelon B3
Senegal B3
Somali Coast B2
Togo B1

Caillie

Rene Calle and Map of Northwestern Africa — CD81

Death centenary of Rene Caillie (1799-1838), French explorer.
All three denominations exist with colony name omitted.

1939

Dahomey	108-110
Fr. Guinea	161-163
Fr. Sudan	113-115
Ivory Coast	160-162
Mauritania	109-111
Niger	84-86
Senegal	188-190
Togo	265-267

New York World's Fair

Natives and New York Skyline CD82

1939

Cameroun	223-224
Dahomey	111-112
Fr. Equatorial Africa	78-79
Fr. Guiana	169-170
Fr. Guinea	164-165
Fr. India	111-112
Fr. Polynesia	124-125
Fr. Sudan	116-117
Guadeloupe	155-156
Indo-China	203-204
Inini	42-43
Ivory Coast	163-164
Kwangchowan	121-122
Madagascar	209-210
Martinique	186-187
Mauritania	112-113
New Caledonia	215-216
Niger	87-88
Reunion	174-175
St. Pierre & Miquelon	205-206
Senegal	191-192
Somali Coast	179-180
Togo	268-269
Wallis & Futuna Isls.	90-91

French Revolution

Storming of the Bastille — CD83

French Revolution, 150th anniv. The surtax was for the defense of the colonies.

1939

Cameroun	B2-B6
Dahomey	B3-B7
Fr. Equatorial Africa	B4-B8, CB1
Fr. Guiana	B4-B8, CB1
Fr. Guinea	B3-B7
Fr. India	B7-B11
Fr. Polynesia	B6-B10, CB1
Fr. Sudan	B2-B6
Guadeloupe	B4-B8
Indo-China	B15-B19, CB1
Inini	B1-B5
Ivory Coast	B3-B7
Kwangchowan	B1-B5
Madagascar	B3-B7, CB1
Martinique	B3-B7
Mauritania	B4-B8
New Caledonia	B5-B9, CB1
Niger	B2-B6
Reunion	B5-B9, CB1
St. Pierre & Miquelon	B4-B8
Senegal	B4-B8, CB1
Somali Coast	B3-B7
Togo	B2-B6
Wallis & Futuna Isls.	B1-B5

Plane over Coastal Area CD85

All five denominations exist with colony name omitted.

1940

Dahomey	C1-C5
Fr. Guinea	C1-C5
Fr. Sudan	C1-C5
Ivory Coast	C1-C5
Mauritania	C1-C5
Niger	C1-C5
Senegal	C12-C16

BRITISH COMMONWEALTH OF NATIONS

The listings follow established trade practices when these issues are offered as units by dealers. The Peace issue, for example, includes only one stamp from the Indian state of Hyderabad. The U.P.U. issue includes the Egypt set. Pairs are included for those varieties issues with bilingual designs se-tenant.

Silver Jubilee

Windsor Castle and King George V CD301

Reign of King George V, 25th anniv.

1935

Antigua	77-80
Ascension	33-36
Bahamas	92-95
Barbados	186-189
Basutoland	11-14
Bechuanaland Protectorate	117-120
Bermuda	100-103
British Guiana	223-226
British Honduras	108-111
Cayman Islands	81-84
Ceylon	260-263
Cyprus	136-139
Dominica	90-93
Falkland Islands	77-80
Fiji	110-113
Gambia	125-128
Gibraltar	100-103
Gilbert & Ellice Islands	33-36
Gold Coast	108-111
Grenada	124-127
Hong Kong	147-150
Jamaica	109-112
Kenya, Uganda, Tanganyika	42-45
Leeward Islands	96-99
Malta	184-187
Mauritius	204-207
Montserrat	85-88
Newfoundland	226-229
Nigeria	34-37
Northern Rhodesia	18-21
Nyasaland Protectorate	47-50
St. Helena	111-114
St. Kitts-Nevis	72-75
St. Lucia	91-94
St. Vincent	134-137
Seychelles	118-121
Sierra Leone	166-169
Solomon Islands	60-63
Somaliland Protectorate	77-80
Straits Settlements	213-216
Swaziland	20-23
Trinidad & Tobago	43-46
Turks & Caicos Islands	71-74
Virgin Islands	69-72

The following have different designs but are included in the omnibus set:

Great Britain	226-229
Offices in Morocco	67-70, 226-229, 422-425, 508-510
Australia	152-154
Canada	211-216
Cook Islands	98-100
India	142-148
Nauru	31-34
New Guinea	46-47
New Zealand	199-201
Niue	67-69
Papua	114-117
Samoa	163-165
South Africa	68-71
Southern Rhodesia	33-36
South-West Africa	121-124

249 stamps

Coronation

Queen Elizabeth and King George VI CD302

1937

Aden	13-15
Antigua	81-83
Ascension	37-39
Bahamas	97-99
Barbados	190-192
Basutoland	15-17
Bechuanaland Protectorate	121-123
Bermuda	115-117
British Guiana	227-229
British Honduras	112-114
Cayman Islands	97-99
Ceylon	275-277
Cyprus	140-142
Dominica	94-96
Falkland Islands	81-83
Fiji	114-116
Gambia	129-131
Gibraltar	104-106
Gilbert & Ellice Islands	37-39
Gold Coast	112-114
Grenada	128-130
Hong Kong	151-153
Jamaica	113-115
Kenya, Uganda, Tanganyika	60-62
Leeward Islands	100-102
Malta	188-190
Mauritius	208-210
Montserrat	89-91
Newfoundland	230-232
Nigeria	50-52
Northern Rhodesia	22-24
Nyasaland Protectorate	51-53
St. Helena	115-117
St. Kitts-Nevis	76-78
St. Lucia	107-109
St. Vincent	138-140
Seychelles	122-124
Sierra Leone	170-172
Solomon Islands	64-66
Somaliland Protectorate	81-83
Straits Settlements	235-237
Swaziland	24-26
Trinidad & Tobago	47-49
Turks & Caicos Islands	75-77
Virgin Islands	73-75

The following have different designs but are included in the omnibus set:

Great Britain	234
Offices in Morocco	82, 439, 514
Canada	237
Cook Islands	109-111
Nauru	35-38
Newfoundland	233-243
New Guinea	48-51
New Zealand	223-225
Niue	70-72
Papua	118-121
South Africa	74-78
Southern Rhodesia	38-41
South-West Africa	125-132

202 stamps

Peace

King George VI and Parliament Buildings, London CD303

Return to peace at the close of World War II.

1945-46

Aden	28-29
Antigua	96-97
Ascension	50-51
Bahamas	130-131
Barbados	207-208
Bermuda	131-132
British Guiana	242-243
British Honduras	127-128
Cayman Islands	112-113
Ceylon	293-294
Cyprus	156-157
Dominica	112-113
Falkland Islands	97-98
Falkland Islands Dep.	1L9-1L10
Fiji	137-138
Gambia	144-145
Gibraltar	119-120
Gilbert & Ellice Island	52-53
Gold Coast	128-129
Grenada	143-144
Jamaica	136-137
Kenya, Uganda, Tanganyika	90-91
Leeward Islands	116-117
Malta	206-207
Mauritius	223-224
Montserrat	104-105
Nigeria	71-72
Northern Rhodesia	46-47
Nyasaland Protectorate	82-83
Pitcairn Island	9-10
St. Helena	128-129
St. Kitts-Nevis	91-92
St. Lucia	127-128
St. Vincent	152-153
Seychelles	149-150
Sierra Leone	186-187
Solomon Islands	80-81
Somaliland Protectorate	108-109
Trinidad & Tobago	62-63
Turks & Caicos Islands	90-91
Virgin Islands	88-89

The following have different designs but are included in the omnibus set:

Great Britain	264-265
Offices in Morocco	523-524
Aden	
Kathiri State of Seiyun	12-13
Qu'aiti State of Shihr and Mukalla	12-13
Australia	200-202
Basutoland	29-31
Bechuanaland Protectorate	137-139
Burma	66-69
Cook Islands	127-130
Hong Kong	174-175
India	195-198
Hyderabad	51
New Zealand	247-257
Niue	90-93
Pakistan-Bahawalpur	O16
Samoa	191-194
South Africa	100-102
Southern Rhodesia	67-70
South-West Africa	153-155
Swaziland	38-40
Zanzibar	222-223

164 stamps

Silver Wedding Issue

King George VI and Queen Elizabeth

CD304 CD305

1948-49

Aden 30-31
Kathiri State of Seiyun 14-15
Qu'aiti State of Shihr and
Mukalla 14-15
Antigua 98-99
Ascension 52-53
Bahamas 148-149
Barbados 210-211
Basutoland 39-40
Bechuanaland Protectorate 147-148
Bermuda 133-134
British Guiana 244-245
British Honduras 129-130
Cayman Islands 116-117
Cyprus 158-159
Dominica 114-115
Falkland Islands 99-100
Falkland Islands Dep. 1L11-1L12
Fiji 139-140
Gambia 146-147
Gibraltar 121-122
Gilbert & Ellice Islands 54-55
Gold Coast 142-143
Grenada 145-146
Hong Kong 178-179
Jamaica 138-139
Kenya, Uganda, Tanganyika 92-93
Leeward Islands 118-119
Malaya
Johore 128-129
Kedah 55-56
Kelantan 44-45
Malacca 1-2
Negri Sembilan 36-37
Pahang 44-45
Penang 1-2
Perak 99-100
Perlis 1-2
Selangor 74-75
Trengganu 47-48
Malta 223-224
Mauritius 229-230
Montserrat 106-107
Nigeria 73-74
North Borneo 238-239
Northern Rhodesia 48-49
Nyasaland Protectorate 85-86
Pitcairn Island 11-12
St. Helena 130-131
St. Kitts-Nevis 93-94
St. Lucia 129-130
St. Vincent 154-155
Sarawak 174-175
Seychelles 151-152
Sierra Leone 188-189
Singapore 21-22
Solomon Islands 82-83
Somaliland Protectorate 110-111
Swaziland 48-49
Trinidad & Tobago 64-65
Turks & Caicos Islands 92-93
Virgin Islands 90-91
Zanzibar 224-225

The following have different designs but are included in the omnibus set:

Great Britain 267-268
Offices in Morocco 93-94, 525-526
Bahrain 62-63
Kuwait 82-83
Oman 25-26
South Africa 106
South-West Africa 159

138 stamps

U.P.U. Issue

Mercury and Symbols of Communications — CD306

Plane, Ship and Hemispheres — CD307

Mercury Scattering Letters over Globe CD308

U.P.U. Monument, Bern CD309

Universal Postal Union, 75th anniversary.

1949

Aden 32-35
Kathiri State of Seiyun 16-19
Qu'aiti State of Shihr and
Mukalla 16-19
Antigua 100-103
Ascension 57-60
Bahamas 150-153
Barbados 212-215
Basutoland 41-44
Bechuanaland Protectorate 149-152
Bermuda 138-141
British Guiana 246-249
British Honduras 137-140
Brunei 79-82
Cayman Islands 118-121
Cyprus 160-163
Dominica 116-119
Falkland Islands 103-106
Falkland Islands Dep. 1L14-1L17
Fiji 141-144
Gambia 148-151
Gibraltar 123-126
Gilbert & Ellice Islands 56-59
Gold Coast 144-147
Grenada 147-150
Hong Kong 180-183
Jamaica 142-145
Kenya, Uganda, Tanganyika 94-97
Leeward Islands 126-129
Malaya
Johore 151-154
Kedah 57-60
Kelantan 46-49
Malacca 18-21
Negri Sembilan 59-62
Pahang 46-49
Penang 23-26
Perak 101-104
Perlis 3-6
Selangor 76-79
Trengganu 49-52
Malta 225-228
Mauritius 231-234
Montserrat 108-111
New Hebrides, British 62-65
New Hebrides, French 79-82
Nigeria 75-78
North Borneo 240-243
Northern Rhodesia 50-53
Nyasaland Protectorate 87-90
Pitcairn Islands 13-16
St. Helena 132-135
St. Kitts-Nevis 95-98
St. Lucia 131-134
St. Vincent 170-173
Sarawak 176-179
Seychelles 153-156
Sierra Leone 190-193
Singapore 23-26
Solomon Islands 84-87
Somaliland Protectorate 112-115
Southern Rhodesia 71-72
Swaziland 50-53
Tonga 87-90
Trinidad & Tobago 66-69
Turks & Caicos Islands 101-104
Virgin Islands 92-95
Zanzibar 226-229

The following have different designs but are included in the omnibus set:

Great Britain 276-279
Offices in Morocco 546-549
Australia 223
Bahrain 68-71
Burma 116-121
Ceylon 304-306
Egypt 281-283
India 223-226
Kuwait 89-92
Oman 31-34
Pakistan-Bahawalpur 26-29, O25-O28
South Africa 109-111
South-West Africa 160-162

319 stamps

University Issue

Arms of University College CD310

Alice, Princess of Athlone CD311

1948 opening of University College of the West Indies at Jamaica.

1951

Antigua 104-105
Barbados 228-229
British Guiana 250-251
British Honduras 141-142
Dominica 120-121
Grenada 164-165
Jamaica 146-147
Leeward Islands 130-131
Montserrat 112-113
St. Kitts-Nevis 105-106
St. Lucia 149-150
St. Vincent 174-175
Trinidad & Tobago 70-71
Virgin Islands 96-97

28 stamps

Classic Specialized Additions, Deletions & Number Changes

Number in 2007 Catalogue	Number in 2008 Catalogue
United States	
new	249a
new	279a
new	279e
279e	279j
new	279k
new	283a
new	530c
new	599b
new	681a
new	830a
new	C23a
new	E5a
new	U505b
new	R5e
R5e	R5f
new	R6f
new	R13f
new	R15f
new	R18e
R18e	R18f
new	R24e
new	R24f
new	R27e
new	R28e
new	R33c
new	R34g
new	R36e
new	R39e
new	R40e
new	R40f
new	R42e
new	R46e
new	R56e
new	R58e
new	R59e
new	R59f
new	R60e
new	R68e
new	R70e
new	R71e
new	R81e
new	R82e
new	R83e
new	R84e
new	R85f
new	R106a
new	R106b
new	R109b
new	R109c
Aden	
new	A134-A154
Alaouites	
new	3b
new	14b
Algeria	
new	A6G
new	A6S
new	A15S
new	A58L
new	3a
new	39a
new	49c
new	54b
new	58a
new	63b
new	66b
new	78b
Andorra (Fr.)	
new	P1a
Argentina — Buenos Aires	
new	10a
new	10b
new	10c
Argentina — Buenos Aires	
new	10d
new	10e
Australia	
new	25a
new	J10c
new	J11c
new	J11d
new	J40c
Bahrain	
new	15a
Barbados	
new	57f
Batum	
new	55a
new	56a
Bechuanaland	
new	6c
new	7c
new	8a
new	29a
new	29b
new	29c
new	29d
Benin	
new	2a
new	15b
new	15Ac
new	24a
Cape of Good Hope	
new	26a
Cilicia	
new	76A
Colombia	
C8a	deleted
Czechoslovakia — Czechoslovak Legion Post	
new	A1
1	1a
1a	1
2	2a
2a	2
3	3a
3a	3
new	4a
new	5a
new	6a-14a
Dahomey	
new	34b
new	32a-41b
new	47a
new	64a
Dominican Republic	
new	8a
new	17
new	22
Eritrea	
new	58a
new	64b
new	81a
new	84b
new	J23a
new	J27a
Fiume	
new	1a
new	3a-20a
Fiume	
new	21a-23a
new	24a
new	27a
new	28a
new	28b
new	29a
new	30a
new	30b
new	31a
new	31b
new	32a
new	33a
new	33b
new	34a
new	35a
new	36a
new	36b
new	36c
new	37a
new	38a
new	39a
new	40a
new	40b
new	40c
new	40d
new	41a
new	41b
new	41c
new	42a
new	42b
new	42c
new	43a
France	
new	37d
new	49a
new	S1a
French Congo	
new	14a
French Equatorial Africa	
100b	deleted
new	109a
new	124a
French Guiana	
new	12a
new	13a
new	17b
new	92a
new	87a-93b
French Guinea	
new	55a
new	56b
new	48a-62a
Gabon	
new	15c
new	72a-83c
Gambia	
new	12a
new	13b
new	13c
15	15a
new	15
new	16a
new	17a
new	18e
new	18f
new	18g
new	19a
new	45a
new	47a
new	70a
new	70b
new	71b
new	74a
Gambia	
new	75a
new	75b
new	76a
new	76b
new	76c
new	80a
new	102a
new	113a
Gibraltar	
new	32a
new	49Ab
new	50a
new	50b
new	52a
new	56b
new	57a
new	59a
new	66a
new	69a
new	78a
new	81a
Gilbert & Ellice Islands	
new	14a
new	44a
new	46a
new	46b
new	48a
48a	48b
Gold Coast	
new	11a
new	13b
new	18b
new	21a
new	23a
new	36a
new	50a
new	51a
new	53a
new	54a
new	56a
new	63a
Grand Comoro	
new	20b
new	20c-29a
Great Britain	
37c	deleted
40c	deleted
new	40c
Guadeloupe	
new	83a-85a
Haiti	
new	32b
Hong Kong	
new	60A-60C
Hungary	
13a	deleted
14b	deleted
14c	deleted
14d	deleted
15b	deleted
15c	deleted
15d	deleted
16a	deleted
17a	deleted
new	13a
new	13b
new	13c
new	13d
new	13e
new	14b
new	14c

Number in 2007 Catalogue	Number in 2008 Catalogue
Hungary	
new	14d
new	14e
new	15b
new	15c
new	15d
new	15e
new	15f
new	15g
new	15h
new	16a
new	16b
new	17a
new	17b
new	17c
new	17d
18-22	deleted
18a	deleted
18c-22b	deleted
new	18
new	18a
new	18b
new	18c
new	18d
new	18e
new	18f
new	18g
new	18h
new	18i
new	19
new	19a
new	19b
new	19c
new	19d
new	19e
new	19f
new	19g
new	19h
new	20
new	20a
new	20b
new	20c
new	20d
new	21
new	21a
new	21b
new	21c
new	21d
new	21e
new	22
new	22a
new	22b
new	22c
new	22d
new	22e
35A-46	deleted
35Ab-46a	deleted
new	35A-46
new	35Ab-46a
new	35Ac-46b
new	35Ad-46c
Western Hungary	
new	1-88
new	J1-J9
India	
Dungarpur	
new	1-28
Iran	
36	37
37	36
Italian States	
Roman States	
new	19c
new	19d
new	19e
new	21d
new	21e
new	22d
new	22e
new	22f
new	22g
Italian States	
Roman States	
new	22h
new	22i
new	22j
new	23l
new	23m
new	23n
new	23o
new	23p
new	24d
new	24e
new	25i
new	25j
new	25k
new	25l
new	25m
new	25n
new	25o
new	25p
Tuscany	
new	1a
new	13a
new	13b
Two Sicilies	
2e	deleted
new	2e
4c	deleted
7b	deleted
Italy	
new	114a
new	119b
119b	119c
new	121b
121b	121c
new	130a
new	B18a
Ivory Coast	
new	37a-41a
Jamaica	
new	51a
Liberia	
new	118b
new	118c
new	118d
Libya	
new	1b
new	3e
new	3f
new	3g
new	3h
new	4c
new	4d
new	4e
new	6c
new	8a
8a	8b
new	11a
new	13a
new	14a
new	15a
new	39c
new	39d
new	39e
new	40b
new	41b
new	42b
new	B1a
new	B3a
new	B4a
new	E1a
new	E2a
Madagascar	
new	115a
new	116b
new	116c
Madagascar	
new	117a
new	118b
new	118c
Malta	
new	A113
new	54a
Martinique	
new	101a-104a
Mayotte	
new	26b
new	22a-32a
Mexico	
O2a	O2b
New	O2a
Mohell	
new	17a-22a
Morocco	
new	A1-A14
New Brunswick	
new	2d
New Caledonia	
new	117b-121a
Nigeria	
new	3a
new	4a
Reunion	
new	14d
new	99a-106a
St. Helena	
new	22c
new	24a
new	33c
new	33d
new	33e
new	34a
new	57a
new	58a
St. Kitts-Nevis	
new	28a
St. Lucia	
new	40e
new	40f
new	40g
new	40h
new	40i
new	41h
new	42d
new	42e
St. Pierre and Miquelon	
new	A1-A59
new	1a
new	1b
new	2b
new	2c
new	3a
new	4a
new	5a
new	6a
new	6b
new	7a
new	7b
new	7c
new	8a
new	8b
new	9a
new	10a
new	10b
new	11a
new	11b
new	15b
St. Pierre and Miquelon	
new	117b
new	110a-120a
Senegal	
new	73a-78a
Somalia	
new	10a
new	18b
new	19a
new	19b
new	28a-31a
new	29b
new	31b
new	89a
new	J12c
new	J19b
new	Q45a
South Australia	
new	36a
new	91
new	91a
O36	deleted
O41	deleted
O41a	deleted
Spain	
new	59a
new	233a
Tasmania	
new	98d
Tunisia	
new	1a
new	2a
new	3a
new	5a
new	7a
new	8a
new	JA1-JA25a
Victoria	
new	35A

HAGNER STOCK SHEETS & ACCESSORIES

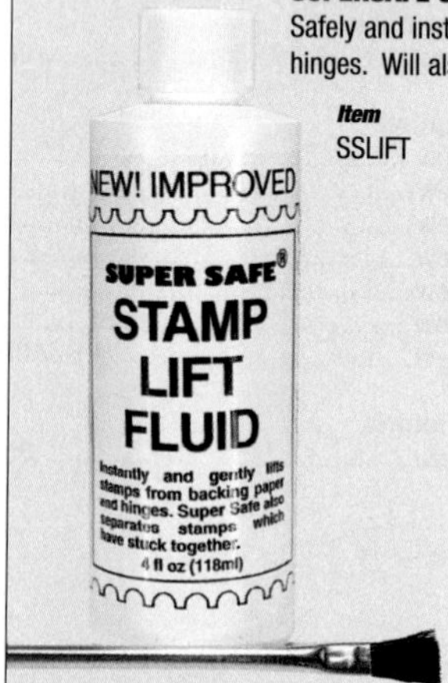

SUPERSAFE STAMP LIFT

Safely and instantly lifts stamps apart from backing paper and hinges. Will also work on stamps that are stuck together.

Item	*Retail*	*AA**
SSLIFT	$3.99	**$3.75**

APAK STAMP DRYING BOOK

Removing stamps from covers has never been easier. No more soggy newspapers or newsprint smudges on your stamps. With the specially coated paper, stamps pop right off. Stamps are flat, dry and ready for mounting. There are 10 glossy sheets sandwiched between 11 sheets of commercial grade blotting paper. Use this book over and over again for clean and easy stamp removal.

Item	*Retail*	*AA**
DB10	$14.95	**$12.99**

HAGNER STOCK SHEETS

The original Hagner Stock sheets are made from archival quality pH board and feature pure polyester film pockets that are glued to each page with special chemically inert glue. For more than 40 years, collectors all over the world have come to rely on Hagner stock sheets for their long-term stamp protection. Single-sided stock sheets are available in black or white.

Item			*Retail*	*AA**
HGB01	One Pocket 242 mm	Black (Single-sided)	$5.25	**$4.35**
HGB11	One Pocket 242 mm	Black (Double-sided)	$9.00	**$7.25**
HGW01	One Pocket 242 mm	White (Single-sided)	$5.25	**$4.35**
HGB02	Two Pocket 119 mm	Black (Single-sided)	$5.25	**$4.35**
HGB22	Two Pocket 119 mm	Black (Double-sided)	$8.25	**$7.25**
HGW02	Two Pocket 119 mm	White (Single-sided)	$5.25	**$4.35**
HGB03	Three Pocket 79 mm	Black (Single-sided)	$5.25	**$4.35**
HGB33	Three Pocket 79 mm	Black (Double-sided)	$9.00	**$7.25**
HGW03	Three Pocket 79 mm	White (Single-sided)	$5.25	**$4.35**
HGB04	Four Pocket 58 mm	Black (Single-sided)	$5.25	**$4.35**
HGB44	Four Pocket 58 mm	Black (Double-sided)	$9.00	**$7.25**
HGW04	Four Pocket 58 mm	White (Single-sided)	$5.25	**$4.35**
HGB05	Five Pocket 45 mm	Black (Single-sided)	$5.25	**$4.35**
HGB55	Five Pocket 45 mm	Black (Double-sided)	$9.00	**$7.25**
HGW05	Five Pocket 45 mm	White (Single-sided)	$5.25	**$4.35**
HGB06	Six Pocket 37 mm	Black (Single-sided)	$5.25	**$4.35**
HGB66	Six Pocket 37 mm	Black (Double-sided)	$9.00	**$7.25**
HGW06	Six Pocket 37 mm	White (Single-sided)	$5.25	**$4.35**
HGB07	Seven Pocket 31 mm	Black (Single-sided)	$5.25	**$4.35**
HGB77	Seven Pocket 31 mm	Black (Double-sided)	$9.00	**$7.25**
HGW07	Seven Pocket 31 mm	White (Single-sided)	$5.25	**$4.35**
HGB08	Eight Pocket 27 mm	Black (Single-sided)	$5.25	**$4.35**
HGB88	Eight Pocket 27 mm	Black (Double-sided)	$9.00	**$7.25**
HGW08	Eight Pocket 27 mm	White (Single-sided)	$5.25	**$4.35**
HGB09	Multi Pocket	Black (Single-sided)	$5.25	**$4.35**
HGB99	Multi Pocket	Black (Double-sided)	$9.00	**$7.25**
HGW09	Multi Pocket	White (Single-sided)	$5.25	**$4.35**

(Pocket sizes on Multi-pocket stock sheet are 36 mm, 67mm and 139mm).

AMOS ADVANTAGE

1. *AA prices apply to paid subscribers of *Scott Stamp Monthly* and *Linn's*
2. Prices, terms and product availability subject to change.
3. **Shipping & Handling:**
   United States: 10% of order total. Minimum charge $5.99 Maximum charge $30.00.
   Canada: 15% of order total. Minimum charge $14.99 Maximum charge $45.00.
   Foreign orders are shipped via DHL and billed actual freight. Credit cards only.

To Order Call 1-800-572-6885

www.amosadvantage.com

UNITED STATES

yu-ˌnī-təd ˈstāts

GOVT. — Republic
AREA — 3,615,211 sq. mi.
POP. — 226,545,805 (1980)
CAPITAL — Washington, DC

In addition to the 48 States and the District of Columbia, the Republic includes Alaska, Hawaii, Guam, the Commonwealth of Puerto Rico, the Virgin Islands, American Samoa, Wake, Midway, and a number of small islands in the Pacific Ocean, all of which use stamps of the United States.

100 Cents = 1 Dollar

Catalogue values for unused stamps in this country are for Never Hinged items, beginning with Scott 772 in the regular postage section, Scott C19 in the air post section, Scott RW1 in the hunting permit stamps section.

Watermarks

Wmk. 190 — "USPS" in Single-lined Capitals

Wmk. 191 — Double-lined "USPS" in Capitals

Wmk. 190PI — PIPS, used in the Philippines
Wmk. 191PI — PIPS, used in the Philippines
Wmk. 191C — US-C, used for Cuba
Wmk. 191R — USIR

POSTMASTERS' PROVISIONALS

Values for Envelopes are for entires.

Alexandria, Va.

A1

Type I — 40 asterisks in circle.
Type II — 39 asterisks in circle.

1846 **Typeset** ***Imperf.***
1X1 A1 5c black, *buff,* Type I —
a. 5c black, *buff,* Type II 100,000.
On cover (I or II) 200,000.
1X2 A1 5c black, *blue,* Type I, on cover —

All known copies of Nos. 1X1-1X2 are cut to shape.

Annapolis, Md.

ENVELOPE

E1

1846
2XU1 E1 5c carmine red *300,000.*

Handstamped impressions of the circular design with "2" in blue or red exist on envelopes and letter sheets. Values: blue $5,000, red $10,000.

A letter sheet exists with circular design and "5" handstamped in red. Values: blue $3,500, red $5,000.

A similar circular design in blue was used as a postmark.

Baltimore, Md.

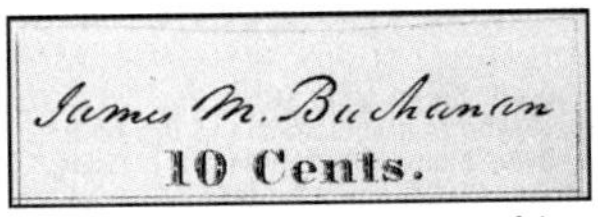

Signature of Postmaster — A1

1845 **Engr.** ***Imperf.***
3X1 A1 5c black *6,000.*
On cover *13,500.*
Vertical pair on cover *35,000.*
3X2 A1 10c black, on cover *70,000.*
3X3 A1 5c black, *bluish* *65,000.* *5,500.*
On cover *13,000.*
3X4 A1 10c black, *bluish* *60,000.*
On cover —

Nos. 3X1-3X4 were printed from a plate of 12 (2x6) containing nine 5c and three 10c.

ENVELOPES

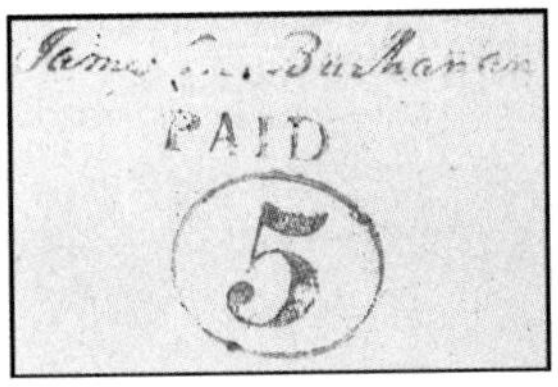

E1

The color given is that of the "PAID 5" and oval. "James M. Buchanan" is handstamped in black, blue or red. The paper is manila, buff, white, salmon or grayish.

1845 **Handstamped**
Various Papers
3XU1 E1 5c blue *6,500.*
3XU2 E1 5c red *9,000.*
3XU3 E1 10c blue *16,000.*
3XU4 E1 10c red *19,000.*

On the formerly listed "5+5" envelopes, the second "5" in oval is believed not to be part of the basic prepaid marking.

Boscawen, N. H.

A1

1846(?) **Typeset** ***Imperf.***
4X1 A1 5c dull blue, *yellowish,* on cover *300,000.*

Brattleboro, Vt.

Initials of Postmaster (FNP) — A1

Plate of 10 (5x2).

1846 **Engr.** ***Imperf.***
5X1 A1 5c black, *buff* *10,000.*
On cover *35,000.*
Two singles on cover *230,000.*

Lockport, N. Y.

A1

Handstamped, "5" in Black Ms
1846
6X1 A1 5c red, *buff,* on cover *300,000.*

Millbury, Mass.

George Washington—A1

Printed from a Woodcut
1846 ***Imperf.***
7X1 A1 5c blue, *bluish* *130,000.* *50,000.*
On cover *125,000.*

New Haven, Conn.

ENVELOPES

E1

1845 **Handstamped**
Signed in Blue, Black, Magenta or Red
8XU1 E1 5c red (Bl or M) *100,000.*
8XU2 E1 5c red, *light bluish* (Bk) *125,000.*
8XU3 E1 5c dull blue, *buff* (Bl) *125,000.*
8XU4 E1 5c dull blue (Bl) *125,000.*

Values of Nos. 8XU1-8XU4 are a guide to value. They are based on auction realizations and retail sales and take condition into consideration. All New Haven envelopes are of almost equal rarity. An entire of No. 8XU2 is the finest example known. The other envelopes are valued according to condition as much as rarity.

Reprints were made at various times between 1871 and 1932. They differ in shade and paper from the originals.

New York, N. Y.

George Washington — A1

Plate of 40 (5x8). Nos. 9X1d, 9X2, 9X2d and 9X3 unused are valued without gum.

1845-46 **Engr.** ***Imperf.***
Bluish Wove Paper
9X1 A1 5c blk, signed ACM, connected ('46) 1,500. 525.
On cover 650.
On cover to France or England *2,250.*
On cover to other European countries *5,500.*
Pair on cover *2,100.*
Pair on cover to England *4,500.*
Pair on cover to Canada *5,500.*
Strip of 3 on cover *9,000.*
Strip of 4 on cover *20,000.*
a. Signed ACM, AC connected 1,750. 575.
On cover 725.
On cover to France or England *2,250.*
On cover to other European countries *6,000.*
Pair on cover *2,100.*
b. Signed A.C.M. *3,750.* 700.
On cover 850.
On cover to France or England *2,750.*
On cover to other European countries *6,000.*
Pair on cover *3,250.*
c. Signed MMJr *10,000.*
On cover —
Pair on cover front *26,500.*
d. Signed RHM *13,000.* *3,500.*
On cover *5,500.*
On cover from New Hamburgh, N.Y. *12,500.*
e. Without signature 3,500. 750.
On cover 1,100.
On cover to France or England *2,250.*
On cover to other European countries *6,000.*
On cover, July 15, 1845 *30,000.*
Pair on cover *2,600.*

These stamps were usually initialed "ACM" in magenta ink, as a control, before being sold or passed through the mails.

A plate of 9 (3x3) was made from which proofs were printed in black on white and deep blue papers; also in blue, green, brown and red on white bond paper. Stamps from this plate were not issued, and it is possible that it is an essay, as the design differs slightly from the issued stamps from the sheet of 40.

1847 **Engr.** ***Imperf.***
Blue Wove Paper
9X2 A1 5c blk, signed ACM, connected *6,500.* 3,500.
On cover *5,750.*
Pair on cover —
a. Signed RHM —
b. Signed ACM, AC connected *5,000.*
d. Without signature *11,000.* *7,250.*

On the listing example of No. 9X2a the "R" is illegible and does not match those of the other "RHM" signatures.

1847 **Engr.** ***Imperf.***
Gray Wove Paper
9X3 A1 5c blk, signed ACM, connected 5,250. 2,250.
On cover *5,250.*
On cover to Europe *8,500.*
Pair on cover *8,750.*
a. Signed RHM *7,000.*
b. Without signature *12,000.*

Providence, R.I.

A1 & A2

1846 **Engr.** ***Imperf.***
10X1 A1 5c gray black 350. *1,750.*
On cover, tied by postmark *20,000.*
On cover, pen canceled *4,500.*
Two on cover —

10X2 A2 10c gray black 1,150. *15,000.*
On cover, pen canceled *35,000.*
a. Se-tenant with 5c 2,000.

Plate of 12 (3x4) contains 11-5c and 1-10c.

Reprints were made in 1898. Each stamp bears one of the following letters on the back: B. O. G. E. R. T. D. U. R. B. I. N. Value of 5c, $50; 10c, $125; sheet, $725.

Reprint singles or sheets without back print sell for more.

St. Louis, Mo.

A1

A2

A3

Nos. 11X1-11X8 unused are valued without gum.

1845-46 Engr. *Imperf.*

Greenish Wove Paper

11X1 A1 5c black *10,000.* *7,000.*
On cover *16,000.*
Two on cover *22,500.*
Strip of 3 on cover *42,500.*

11X2 A2 10c black *10,000.* *7,000.*
On cover *12,500.*
Pair on cover *20,000.*
Strip of 3 on cover *37,500.*

11X3 A3 20c black *140,000.*
On cover —
On cover, #11X5, two #11X3 *300,000.*

Three varieties of 5c, 3 of 10c, 2 of 20c.

1846

Gray Lilac Paper

11X4 A1 5c black — *45,000.*
On cover —

11X5 A2 10c black *10,000.* *7,000.*
On cover *10,500.*
Strip of 3 on cover *42,500.*

11X6 A3 20c black *82,500.* *45,000.*
On cover *35,000.*
Pair on cover *110,000.*
Pair, 20c + 10c, on cover *100,000.*

One variety of 5c, 3 of 10c, 2 of 20c.

No. 11X6 unused is unique. It is in the grade of fine and valued thus.

1847

Pelure Paper

11X7 A1 5c black, *bluish* — *10,000.*
On cover *15,000.*
Two on cover *35,000.*

11X8 A2 10c black, *bluish* *12,000.*
On cover *17,500.*
a. Impression of 5c on back —

Three varieties of 5c, 3 of 10c.

Used values are for pencanceled copies.

Manuscript Cancels on Used Stamps

Manuscript (pen) cancels reduce the value of used stamps by about 50%. See the Scott U.S. Specialized Catalogue for individual valuations.

GENERAL ISSUES

All Issues from 1847 to 1894 are Unwatermarked.

Benjamin Franklin
A1

George Washington
A2

1847, July 1 Engr. *Imperf.*

1 A1 5c red brn, *bluish* 6,750. 600.
No gum 2,600.
Pen cancel 300.
On cover 675.
a. 5c dark brown, *bluish* 8,750. 750.
No gum 3,400.
b. 5c orange brown, *bluish* 9,000. 900.
No gum 3,650.
c. 5c red orange, *bluish* *20,000.* *7,500.*
No gum 8,000.
d. 5c brown orange 1,500.
No gum *4,500.*
e. Double impression —

The only known double impression shows part of the design doubled.

2 A2 10c black, *bluish* *35,000.* 1,400.
No gum *16,000.*
Pen cancel 750.
On cover 1,700.
a. Diagonal half used as 5c on cover *13,000.*
b. Vertical half used as 5c on cover *35,000.*
c. Horizontal half used as 5c on cover —

REPRODUCTIONS

Actually, official imitations made from new plates by order of the Post Office Department.

A3

A4

1875 *Imperf.*

Bluish Paper Without Gum

3 A3 5c red brown 800.
4 A4 10c black 975.

Reproductions. The letters R. W. H. & E. at the bottom of each stamp are less distinct on the reproductions than on the originals.

5c. On the originals the left side of the white shirt frill touches the oval on a level with the top of the "F" of "Five." On the reproductions it touches the oval about on a level with the top of the figure "5." On the originals the bottom of the right leg of the "N" in "CENTS" is blunt. On the reproductions the "N" comes to a point at the bottom.

10c. On the reproductions, line of coat at left points to right tip of "X" and line of coat at right points to center of "S" of CENTS. On the originals, line of coat points to "T" of TEN and between "T" and "S" of CENTS. The bottom of the right leg of the "N" of "CENTS" shows the same difference as on the 5c originals and reproductions. On the reproductions the eyes have a sleepy look, the line of the mouth is straighter, and in the curl of hair near the left cheek is a strong black dot, while the originals have only a faint one.

Franklin — A5

ONE CENT

Type I. Has complete curved lines outside the labels with "U.S. Postage" and "One Cent." The scrolls below the lower label are turned under, forming little balls. The ornaments at top are substantially complete.

Values for type I are for stamps showing the marked characteristics plainly. Copies of type I showing the balls indistinctly sell for much lower prices.

Type Ib. Same as type I, but balls below the bottom label are not so clear. The plumelike scrolls at bottom are not complete.

A6

Type Ia. Same as type I at bottom, but top ornaments and outer line at top are partly cut away.

Type Ic. Same as type Ia, but bottom right plume and ball ornament incomplete. Bottom left plume complete or nearly complete.

A7

Type II. Same as type I at top, but the little balls of the bottom scrolls and the bottoms of the lower plume ornaments are missing. The side ornaments are substantially complete.

A8

Type III. The top and bottom curved lines outside the labels are broken in the middle. The side ornaments are substantially complete.

Type IIIa. Similar to type III with the outer line broken at top or bottom but not both.

A9

Type IV. Similar to type II, but with the curved lines outside the labels recut at top or bottom or both.

THREE CENTS

Washington — A10

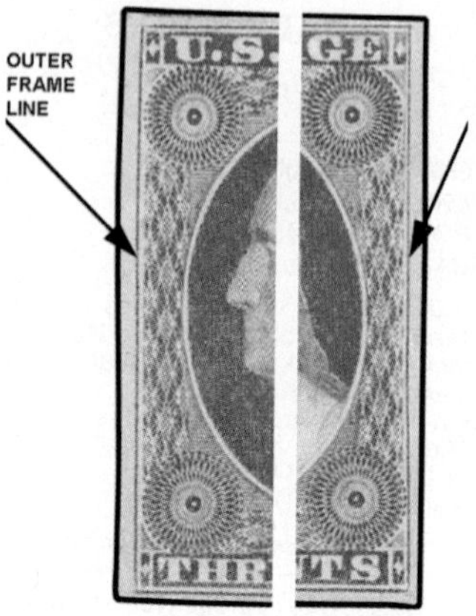

Type I

Type I. There is an outer frame line on all four sides. The outer frame lines at the sides are always recut, but the inner lines at the sides are not.

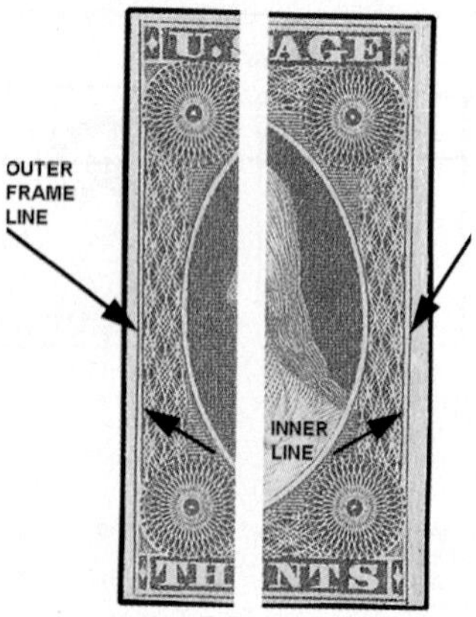

Type II

Type II. As Type I, but with the inner lines at the sides also recut.

FIVE CENTS

Type I. There are projections on all four sides.

Washington — A12

TEN CENTS

Type I. The "shells" at the lower corners are practically complete. The outer line below the label is very nearly complete. The outer lines are broken above the middle of the top label and the "X" in each upper corner.

A13

Type II. The design is complete at the top. The outer line at the bottom is broken in the middle. The shells are partly cut away.

A14

Type III. The outer lines are broken above the top label and the "X" numerals. The outer line at the bottom and the shells are partly cut away, similar to type II.

A15

Type IV. The outer lines have been recut at top or bottom or both.

Types I, II, III and IV have complete ornaments at the sides of the stamps and three pearls at each outer edge of the bottom panel.

Washington — A16

In Nos. 5-17, the 1c, 3c, and 12c have very small margins between the stamps. The 5c and 10c have moderate size margins. The values of these stamps take the margin size into consideration.

Values for No. 5A, 6b and 19b are for the less distinct positions. Best examples sell for more.

Values for No. 16 are for outer line recut at top. Other recuts sell for more.

1851-57 ***Imperf.***

5	A5	1c blue, I	*225,000.*	*80,000.*
		On cover		90,000.

Values for No. 5 are for copies with margins touching or slightly cutting into the design. Value unused is for an example with no gum.

5A	A5	1c blue, Ib	*17,500.*	*8,500.*
		No gum	*7,500.*	
		On cover		*8,500.*
6	A6	1c blue, Ia ('57)	*40,000.*	*12,500.*
		No gum	*20,000.*	
		On cover		17,000.
b.		Type Ic	*7,000.*	*2,750.*
		No gum	*3,250.*	
		On cover		4,250.
7	A7	1c blue, II	1,200.	170.
		No gum	500.	
		On cover		200.
8	A8	1c blue, III	*20,000.*	3,500.
		No gum	*7,500.*	
		On cover		3,750.

Values for type III are for at least a 2mm break in each outer line. Examples of type III with wider breaks in outer lines command higher prices; those with smaller breaks sell for much less.

8A	A8	1c blue, IIIa	*5,000.*	1,200.
		No gum	2,250.	
		On cover		1,300.

Stamps of type IIIa with bottom line broken command higher prices than those with top line broken. See note after No. 8 on width of break of outer lines.

9	A9	1c bl, IV ('52)	850.00	130.00
		No gum	325.00	
		On cover		150.00
a.		Printed on both sides, reverse inverted		—
10	A10	3c org brown, I	4,000.	150.00
		No gum	1,750.	
		On cover		210.00

Only one example of No. 10a is recorded.

10A	A10	3c org brown, II	4,000.	150.00
		No gum	1,750.	
b.		Printed on both sides		*12,000.*
11	A10	3c dull red, I	325.00	15.00
		No gum	105.00	
		On cover		600.00
11A	A10	3c dull red, II	325.00	15.00
		No gum	105.00	
c.		Vertical half used as 1c on cover		*5,000.*
d.		Diagonal half used as 1c on cover		*5,000.*
e.		Double impression		*5,000.*
12	A11	5c red brown, I ('56)	*30,000.*	950.
		No gum	*12,500.*	
		On cover		1,450.
13	A12	10c grn, I ('55)	*18,000.*	950.
		No gum	*7,750.*	
		On cover		1,050.
14	A13	10c grn, II ('55)	5,500.	200.
		No gum	2,200.	
		On cover		260.
15	A14	10c grn, III ('55)	5,500.	200.
		No gum	2,200.	
		On cover		260.
16	A15	10c grn, IV ('55)	*35,000.*	1,700.
		No gum	*16,000.*	
		On cover		2,000.
17	A16	12c black	6,500.	350.
		No gum	2,400.	
		On cover (single)		1,500.
a.		Diagonal half used as 6c on cover		*2,750.*
b.		Vertical half used as 6c on cover		*8,500.*
c.		Printed on both sides		*25,000.*

Same Designs as 1851-56 Issues

Franklin — A20

ONE CENT

Type V. Similar to type III of 1851-57 but with side ornaments partly cut away.

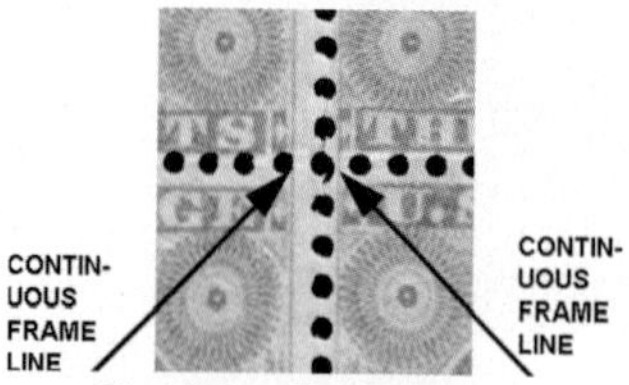

Washington Type III — A21

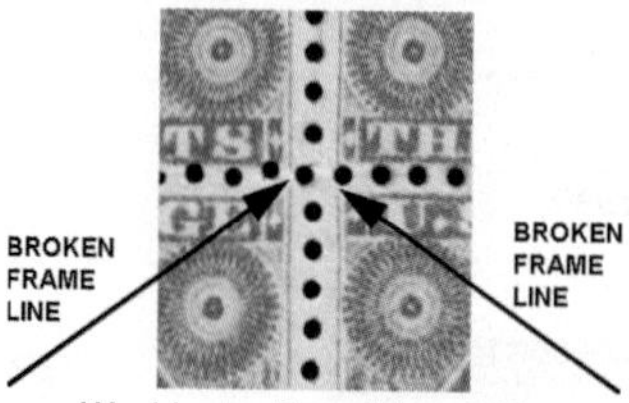

Washington Type IV — A21a

THREE CENTS

Type III. The outer frame line has been removed at top and bottom. The side frame lines were recut so as to be continuous from the top to the bottom of the plate. Stamps from the top or bottom rows show the ends of the side frame lines and may be mistaken for type IIa.

Type IV. The side frame lines extend only to the top and bottom of the stamp design.

Jefferson — A22

FIVE CENTS

Type II. The projections at top and bottom are partly cut away.

Washington (Two typical examples) A23

TEN CENTS

Type V. The side ornaments are slightly cut away. Usually only one pearl remains at each end of the lower label but some copies show two or three pearls at the right side.

At the bottom the outer line is complete and the shells nearly so. The outer lines at top are complete except over the right "X."

Washington A17

Franklin A18

Washington — A19

TWELVE CENTS

Plate I. Outer frame lines complete.

Plate III. Outer frame lines noticeably uneven or broken, sometimes partly missing.

Nos. 18-39 have small or very small margins. The values take into account the margin size.

1857-61 ***Perf. 15½***

18	A5	1c blue, I ('61)	2,500.	700.
		No gum	1,000.	
		On cover		850.
19	A6	1c blue, Ia	*40,000.*	*10,000.*
		No gum	*19,000.*	
		On cover		12,500.
b.		Type Ic	*4,500.*	*2,250.*
		No gum	2,100.	
		On cover		3,000.
20	A7	1c blue, II	1,250.	300.
		No gum	525.	
		On cover		350.
21	A8	1c blue, III	*17,500.*	2,750.
		No gum	*7,750.*	
		On cover		3,250.
a.		Horiz. pair, imperf. btwn.		*23,000.*
22	A8	1c blue, IIIa	2,750.	550.
		No gum	*1,100.*	
		On cover		600.
b.		Horiz. pair, imperf. btwn.		*5,000.*

One pair of No. 22b has been reported. Beware of pairs with blind perforations.

23	A9	1c blue, IV	9,000.	850.
		No gum	4,000.	
		On cover		1,050.
24	A20	1c blue, V	180.00	45.00
		No gum	75.00	
		On cover		52.50
b.		Laid paper		*1,750.*
25	A10	3c rose, I	3,000.	125.00
		No gum	1,250.	
		On cover		140.00
b.		Vert. pair, imperf. horiz.		*10,000.*
25A	A10	3c rose, II	4,750.	375.
26	A21	3c dull red, III	85.	9.00
		No gum	27.50	
		On cover		10.50
b.		Horiz. pair, imperf. vert., II	*4,000.*	—
c.		Vert. pair, imperf. horiz., II		*12,000.*
d.		Horiz. pair, imperf btwn., II		—
e.		Dbl. impression, II		*2,500.*
f.		As "a," horiz. strip of 3, imperf. vert., IIa, on cover		*14,500.*
26A	A21a	3c dull red, IV	450.	100.00
		No gum	150.	
		On cover		140.00
27	A11	5c brick red, I ('58)	*80,000.*	1,800.
		No gum	*20,000.*	
		On cover		2,200.
28	A11	5c red brn, I	6,500.	1,200.
		No gum	2,600.	
		On cover		1,400.
b.		5c bright red brown	8,500.	1,750.
		No gum	3,250.	
28A	A11	5c Indian red, I ('58)	*90,000.*	3,750.
		No gum	*25,000.*	
		On cover		5,250.
29	A11	5c brn, I ('59)	3,500.	450.
		No gum	1,500.	
		On cover		575.
30	A22	5c org brn, II ('61)	1,250.	1,300.
		No gum	550.	
		On cover		2,400.
30A	A22	5c brn, II ('60)	2,400.	325.
		No gum	1,000.	
		On cover		375.
b.		Printed on both sides		*40,000.*
31	A12	10c green, I	30,000.	1,300.
		No gum	*10,000.*	
		On cover		1,500.
32	A13	10c green, II	6,500.	300.
		No gum	2,750.	
		On cover		350.
33	A14	10c green, III	6,500.	300.
		No gum	2,750.	
		On cover		350.
34	A15	10c green, IV	*50,000.*	2,500.
		No gum	*22,500.*	
		On cover		2,900.
35	A23	10c grn, V ('59)	275.00	65.00
		No gum	110.	
		On cover		77.50
36	A16	12c black, plate I	2,000.	375.
		No gum	875.	
		On cover (single)		650.
a.		Diagonal half used as 6c on cover (I)		*17,500.*
b.		12c black, plate III ('59)	825.	225.
		No gum	360.	
		On cover (single)		650.
c.		Horizontal pair, imperf. between (I)		*12,500.*
37	A17	24c gray lil ('60)	1,700.	400.
a.		24c gray	1,700.	400.
		No gum	650.	
		On cover		1,050.
38	A18	30c orange ('60)	2,500.	500.
		No gum	1,050.	
39	A19	90c blue ('60)	3,500.	*9,500.*
		No gum	1,500.	
		On cover		225,000.
		Pen cancel		2,900.

See Die and Plate proofs in the Scott United States Specialized Catalogue for imperfs. of the 12c, 24c, 30c, 90c.

No. 28A unused is valued in the grade of fine. Only three examples are recorded with any amount of original gum.

Genuine cancellations on the 90c are rare.

REPRINTS OF 1857-60 ISSUE

White Paper

Without Gum

1875 ***Perf. 12***

40	A5	1c bright blue	*625.*	
41	A10	3c scarlet	*3,250.*	
42	A22	5c orange brown	*1,400.*	
43	A12	10c blue green	*3,000.*	—
44	A16	12c greenish blk	*3,250.*	
45	A17	24c black violet	*3,250.*	—
46	A18	30c yellow orange	*3,250.*	
47	A19	90c deep blue	*4,750.*	
		Nos. 40-47 (8)	*22,775.*	

Nos. 41-46 are valued in the grade of fine. Exist imperf., value, set of singles $25,000.

Washington — A27a

The paper of former Nos. 55-62 (Nos. 63E11e, 65-E15h, 67-E9e, 69-E6e, 72-E6h, Essay section, Nos. 70eTC, 71bTC, Trial Color Proof section, Scott U.S. Specialized) is thin and semitransparent. That of the postage issues is thicker and more opaque, except Nos. 62B, 70c and 70d.

1861

62B	A27a	10c dark green	*8,000.*	1,500.
		No gum	*3,750.*	
		On cover		2,000.
		On patriotic cover		3,000.

Franklin — A24

1c. A dash has been added under the tip of the ornament at right of the numeral in upper left corner.

Washington — A25

3c. Ornaments at corners have been enlarged and end in a small ball.

Jefferson — A26

5c. A leaflet has been added to the foliated ornaments at each corner.

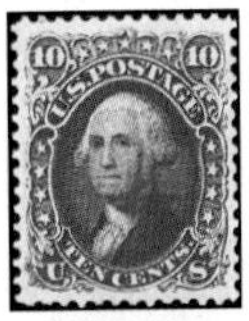
Washington — A27

A27

10c. A heavy curved line has been cut below the stars and an outer line added to the ornaments above them.

Washington — A28

12c. Ovals and scrolls have been added to the corners.

Washington A29

Franklin A30

Washington — A31

90c. Parallel lines form an angle above the ribbon with "U. S. Postage"; between these lines a row of dashes has been added and a point of color to the apex of the lower pair.

1861-62 ***Perf. 12***

No.	Design	Description	Unused	Used
63	A24	1c blue	375.00	50.00
		No gum	140.00	
		On cover (single)		57.50
		On patriotic cover		225.00
a.		1c ultramarine	*2,500.*	*600.00*
		No gum	1,000.	
b.		1c dark blue	750.00	350.00
		No gum	275.00	
c.		Laid paper	*11,000.*	*9,000.*
d.		Vert. pair, imperf. horiz.		—
e.		Printed on both sides	—	*4,000.*
64	A25	3c pink	*14,000.*	1,000.
		No gum	*5,500.*	
		On cover (pink)		1,100.
		On patriotic cover (pink)		1,300.
a.		3c pigeon blood pink	*45,000.*	*4,000.*
		No gum	*15,000.*	
		On cover		*4,750.*
		On patriotic cover		*7,000.*
b.		3c rose pink	600.00	160.00
		No gum	260.00	
		On cover		190.00
		On patriotic cover		250.00
65	A25	3c rose	150.00	3.00
		No gum	50.00	
		On cover		3.50
		On patriotic cover		40.00
b.		Laid paper	—	500.00
d.		Vert. pair, imperf. horiz.	*6,000.*	*750.00*
e.		Printed on both sides	*22,500.*	*5,000.*
f.		Double impression		*7,500.*

The 3c lake can be found under No. 66 in the Trial Color Proofs section of the Scott U.S. Specialized Catalogue. The imperf 3c lake under No. 66P in the same section. The imperf 3c rose can be found in the Die and Plate Proofs section of the Specialized.

No.	Design	Description	Unused	Used
67	A26	5c buff	*25,000.*	1,100.
		No gum	*11,000.*	
		On cover		1,350.
a.		5c brown yellow	*27,500.*	1,300.
		No gum	*12,000.*	
b.		5c olive yellow	—	3,000.
		On cover, #67, 67a or 67b		1,150.
		On patriotic cover		4,000.

Values for Nos. 67, 67a, 67b reflect the normal small margins.

No.	Design	Description	Unused	Used
68	A27	10c green	1,250.	60.00
		No gum	500.00	
		On cover		75.00
		On patriotic cover		375.00
		On cover to Canada		100.00
a.		10c dark green	1,500.	85.00
		No gum	600.00	
b.		Vert. pair, imperf. horiz.		*3,500.*
69	A28	12c black	2,100.	120.00
		No gum	875.00	
		On domestic cover		160.00
		On patriotic cover		900.00
		On cover to France or Germany with #65		180.00
70	A29	24c red lilac ('62)	3,000.	300.00
		No gum	1,200.	
		On cover		350.00
		On patriotic cover		*3,000.*
a.		24c brown lilac	3,250.	225.00
		No gum	1,300.	
b.		24c steel blue	16,500.	900.00
		No gum	*6,500.*	
		On cover		1,350.
c.		24c violet, thin paper	*35,000.*	2,000.
		No gum	*14,000.*	
d.		24c pale gray vio, thin paper	17,500.	2,500.
		No gum	6,000.	
71	A30	30c orange	2,500.	200.00
		No gum	1,000.	
		On cover to France or Germany		400.00
		On patriotic cover		*3,500.*
a.		Printed on both sides		—

Values for No. 71 are for copies with small margins, especially at sides. Large margined examples sell for much more.

No.	Design	Description	Unused	Used
72	A31	90c blue	3,500.	550.
		No gum	1,500.	
		On cover		*25,000.*
a.		90c pale blue	3,500.	550.
		No gum	1,500.	
b.		90c dark blue	4,250.	700.
		No gum	1,800.	

Nos. 70c, 70d are on a thinner, harder and more transparent paper than Nos. 70, 70a, 70b, or the later Nos. 78, 78a, 78b and 78c.

Designs as 1861 Issue

Andrew Jackson A32

Abraham Lincoln A33

1861-66 ***Perf. 12***

No.	Design	Description	Unused	Used
73	A32	2c black ('63)	400.00	70.00
		No gum	150.00	
		On cover		90.00
		On patriotic cover		*2,000.*
a.		Diag. half used as 1c as part of 3c rate on cover		1,750.
b.		Diagonal half used alone as 1c on cover		*3,000.*
c.		Horiz. half used as 1c as part of 3c rate on cover		*3,500.*
d.		Vert. half used as 1c as part of 3c rate on cover		2,000.
e.		Printed on both sides		*4,000.*
f.		Laid paper	—	*15,000.*

The 3c scarlet can be found under No. 74 in the Scott U.S. Specialized Catalogue Trial Color Proofs section.

No.	Design	Description	Unused	Used
75	A26	5c red brown ('62)	6,000.	600.
		No gum	2,250.	
		On cover		900.
		On patriotic cover		*2,500.*
76	A26	5c brown ('63)	1,700.	150.
		No gum	675.	
		On cover		200.
		On patriotic cover		850.
a.		5c black brown	2,000.	275.
		No gum	800.	
b.		Laid paper		—
77	A33	15c black ('66)	4,500.	225.
		No gum	1,750.	
		On cover to France or Germany		300.
78	A29	24c lilac ('62)	2,750.	250.
a.		24c grayish lilac	2,750.	300.
b.		24c gray	2,750.	300.
		No gum	875.	
		On cover, #78, 78a or 78b		325.
c.		24c blackish violet	*60,000.*	*15,000.*
		No gum	*25,000.*	
		On cover		20,000.
d.		Printed on both sides		*25,000.*

Values for Nos. 75, 76, 76a reflect the normal small margins.

Grill

Same as 1861-66 Issues
Embossed with grills of various sizes

Grill with Points Up

Grills A and C were made by a roller covered with ridges shaped like an inverted V. Pressing the ridges into the stamp paper forced the paper into the pyramidal pits between the ridges, causing irregular breaks in the paper.

Grill B was made by a roller with raised bosses.

A. Grill covering the entire stamp

1867 ***Perf. 12***

No.	Design	Description	Unused	Used
79	A25	3c rose	8,500.	1,750.
		No gum	2,750.	
		On cover		2,250.
b.		Printed on both sides		—
80	A26	5c brown	—	*130,000.*
a.		5c dark brown		*130,000.*
81	A30	30c orange		*100,000.*

An essay which is often mistaken for No. 79 (#79-E15) shows the points of the grill as small squares faintly impressed in the paper, but not cutting through it. On No. 79 the grill breaks through the paper. Copies free from defects are rare.

Eight copies of Nos. 80, 80a, and eight copies of No. 81 are known. All are more or less faulty and/or off-center. Values are for off-center examples with small perforation faults.

The imperf. of the 3c rose can be found in the Scott U.S. Specialized Catalogue Die and Plate Proofs section.

B. Grill about 18x15mm (22 by 18 points)

No.	Design	Description	Unused	Used
82	A25	3c rose		*200,000.*

The four known copies of No. 82 are valued in the grade of fine.

C. Grill about 13x16mm (16 to 17 by 18 to 21 points)

No.	Design	Description	Unused	Used
83	A25	3c rose	6,500.	1,100.
		No gum	2,500.	
		On cover		1,300.

The grilled area on each of four C grills in the sheet may total about 18x15mm when a normal C grill adjoins a fainter grill extending to the right or left edge of the stamp. This is caused by a partial erasure on the grill roller when it was changed to produce C grills instead of the all-over A grill.

The imperf. can be found in the Scott U.S. Specialized Catalogue Die and Plate Proofs section.

Grill with Points Down

The grills were produced by rollers with the surface covered by pyramidal bosses. On the Z grill the tips of the pyramids are very short horizontal ridges. On the D, E and F grills the ridges are vertical.

D. Grill about 12x14mm (15 by 17 to 18 points)

84 A32 2c black 16,000. 4,500.
No gum 8,000.
On cover 5,000.

No. 84 is valued in the grade of fine.

85 A25 3c rose 6,750. 1,200.
No gum 3,000.
On cover 1,250.

Z. Grill about 11x14mm (13 to 14 by 17 to 18 points)

85A A24 1c blue 3,000,000.
85B A32 2c black 15,000. 1,500.
No gum 6,500.
On cover 1,650.
85C A25 3c rose 25,000. 3,750.
No gum 9,500.
On cover 4,250.
85D A27 10c green 225,000.
85E A28 12c black 14,000. 2,500.
No gum 5,750.
On cover 3,000.
85F A33 15c black 750,000.

Two copies of No. 85A are known. One is contained in the New York Public Library collection.

Six copies of No. 85D are known. One is in the New York Public Library collection. Value is for a well-centered example with small faults.

Two copies of No. 85F are documented, one in the grade of very good, the other extremely fine. Value is for the extremely fine example.

E. Grill about 11x13mm (14 by 15 to 17 points)

86 A24 1c blue 4,000. 550.
No gum 1,750.
a. 1c dull blue 4,000. 525.
No gum 1,750.
On cover, #86 or 86a 650.
87 A32 2c black 1,900. 200.
No gum 800.
On cover 300.
a. Diagonal half used as 1c on cover 2,000.
b. Vertical half used as 1c on cover 2,000.
88 A25 3c rose 1,200. 27.50
No gum 450.
On cover 32.50
a. 3c lake red 1,350. 50.
No gum 525.
89 A27 10c green 5,500. 325.
No gum 2,400.
On cover 425.
90 A28 12c black 5,250. 400.
No gum 2,300.
On cover 550.
91 A33 15c black 12,000. 700.
No gum 5,000.
On cover 925.

F. Grill about 9x13mm (11 to 12 by 15 to 17 points)

92 A24 1c blue 3,500. 550.
No gum 1,200.
a. 1c pale blue 3,000. 475.
No gum 950.
On cover 600.
93 A32 2c black 550. 60.00
No gum 225.
On cover 75.
a. Vertical half used as 1c as part of 3c rate on cover 1,250.
b. Diagonal half used as 1c as part of 3c rate on cover 1,250.
c. Horizontal half used alone as 1c on cover 2,500.
d. Diagonal half used alone as 1c on cover 2,500.
94 A25 3c red 425. 10.
a. 3c rose 425. 10.
No gum 150.
On cover, #94 or 94a 11.
c. Vert. pair, imperf. horiz. 1,500.
d. Printed on both sides 7,500.

The imperf. 3c can be found in the Scott U.S. Specialized Catalogue Die and Plate Proofs section.

95 A26 5c brown 3,750. 875.
No gum 1,400.
On cover 925.
a. 5c black brown 4,500. 1,200.
No gum 1,700.

Values for Nos. 95, 95a reflect the normal small margins.

96 A27 10c yellow green 3,500. 250.
a. 10c dark green 3,500. 350.
No gum 1,150.
On cover, #96 or 96a 300.
97 A28 12c black 3,500. 300.
No gum 1,400.
On cover 350.
98 A33 15c black 4,500. 375.
No gum 1,750.
On cover 425.
99 A29 24c gray lilac 8,500. 1,300.
No gum 3,500.
On cover 2,250.
100 A30 30c orange 8,500. 900.
No gum 3,500.
On cover 2,000.

Values for No. 100 are for copies with small margins, especially at sides. Large-margined examples sell for much more.

101 A31 90c blue 14,500. 2,200.
No gum 5,850.
On cover 100,000.

Some authorities believe that more than one size of grill probably existed on one of the grill rolls.

Re-issue of 1861-66 Issues
Without Grill
Hard White Paper
White Crackly Gum

1875 *Perf. 12*

102 A24 1c blue 950. 1,250.
No gum 450.
On cover —
103 A32 2c black 4,500. 7,000.
No gum 2,500.
104 A25 3c brown red 5,000. 12,500.
No gum 2,600.
105 A26 5c brown 3,500. 6,000.
No gum 1,850.
106 A27 10c green 4,250. 20,000.
No gum 2,200.
107 A28 12c black 5,000. 9,500.
No gum 2,700.
108 A33 15c black 5,500. 16,000.
No gum 3,000.
109 A29 24c deep violet 7,000. 17,500.
No gum 3,750.
110 A30 30c brownish org 7,250. 17,500.
No gum 4,000.
111 A31 90c blue 7,500. 110,000.
No gum 4,150.

These stamps can be distinguished from the 1861-66 issues by the shades and the paper which is hard and very white instead of yellowish. The gum is white and crackly. The gum is almost always yellowed with age, and unused stamps with original gum are valued with such gum.

Used value for No. 111 is for a sound, centered example. Two of the five copies are known thus.

Franklin — A34

Post Horse and Rider — A35

Locomotive A36

Washington A37

Shield and Eagle — A38

S. S. Adriatic — A39

Landing of Columbus — A40

FIFTEEN CENTS
Type I. Picture unframed.

A40a

Type II. Picture framed.
Type III. Same as type I but without fringe of brown shading lines around central vignette.

"The Declaration of Independence" A41

Shield, Eagle and Flags A42

Lincoln — A43

G. Grill measuring 9½x9mm (12 by 11 to 11½ points)

1869 *Perf. 12*

112 A34 1c buff 850. 175.
No gum 360.
On cover, single 300.
b. Without grill 10,000.
113 A35 2c brown 800. 100.
No gum 325.
On cover, single 140.
b. Without grill 2,800.
c. Half used as 1c on cover, diagonal, vert. or horiz. 6,000.
d. Printed on both sides 9,000.
114 A36 3c ultramarine 350. 20.
No gum 140.
On cover 25.
a. Without grill 12,500.
b. Vertical one third used as 1c on cover —
c. Vertical two thirds used as 2c on cover 5,000.
d. Double impression 3,500.
e. Printed on both sides —
115 A37 6c ultramarine 3,250. 250.
No gum 1,350.
On cover 450.
b. Vertical half used as 3c on cover 50,000.

No. 115 is the most difficult value in this issue to find well-centered. Such examples sell for much more.

116 A38 10c yellow 2,750. 150.
No gum 1,100.
On cover 425.
117 A39 12c green 2,750. 160.
No gum 1,100.
On cover 500.
118 A40 15c brn & blue, Type I 10,000. 750.
No gum 4,250.
On cover 1,900.
a. Without grill 15,000.
119 A40a 15c brn & blue, Type II 4,000. 275.
No gum 1,750.
On cover 900.
b. Center inverted 1,000,000. 17,500.
No gum —
c. Center dbl., one invtd. 80,000.
120 A41 24c green & vio 9,500. 775.
No gum 4,250.
On cover 12,500.
a. Without grill 13,500.
b. Center inverted 325,000. 20,000.
On cover 105,000.
121 A42 30c blue & car 8,000. 550.
No gum 3,750.
On cover 32,500.
a. Without grill 12,000.
b. Flags inverted 350,000. 80,000.
No gum 210,000.
122 A43 90c car & black 13,000. 2,400.
No gum 5,500.
a. Without grill 20,000.

Values of varieties of Nos. 112-122 without grill are for copies with full original gum.

Most copies of Nos. 119b, 120b are faulty. Values are for fine centered copies with only minimal faults. No. 120b unused is valued without gum, as all of the three examples available to collectors are without gum.

Re-issues of the 1869 Issue
Without Grill
Hard White Paper
White crackly gum (somewhat yellowed with age)

1875 *Perf. 12*

123 A34 1c buff 675. 400.
No gum 325.
On cover 3,000.
124 A35 2c brown 800. 900.
No gum 375.
On cover 12,500.
125 A36 3c blue 5,500. 27,500.
No gum 3,250.
On cover —

Used value for No. 125 is for an attractive fine to very fine copy with minimal faults.

126 A37 6c blue 2,250. 2,750.
No gum 1,050.
On cover —
127 A38 10c yellow 2,250. 2,000.
No gum 1,150.
On cover 22,500.
128 A39 12c green 3,000. 3,250.
No gum 1,600.
On cover —
129 A40 15c brown & blue, type III 1,900. 1,300.
No gum 1,050.
On cover 22,500.
a. Imperf. horiz., single 6,250. 7,000.
No gum 4,250.

Type III is same as type I but without fringe of brown shading lines around central vignette.

130 A41 24c green & violet 2,750. 1,750.
No gum 1,200.
On cover 27,500.
131 A42 30c ultra & car 3,250. 3,000.
No gum 1,700.
132 A43 90c car & black 4,750. 6,500.
No gum 2,250.

1880-81

Soft Porous Paper

133 A34 1c buff 375. 350.
No gum 170.
On cover 1,900.
a. 1c brown orange ('81) 250. 300.

No. 133 was issued with gum, No. 133a without gum.

Printed by the National Bank Note Company

Franklin — A44

A44

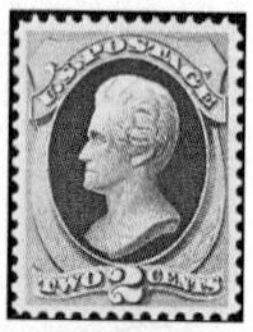

Jackson — A45

A45

Washington — A46

A46

Lincoln — A47

A47

Edwin M. Stanton — A48

A48

Jefferson — A49

A49

Henry Clay — A50

A50

Daniel Webster — A51

A51

Gen. Winfield Scott A52

Alexander Hamilton A53

Commodore O. H. Perry — A54

Two varieties of grill are known on this issue.

H. Grill about 10x12mm
(11 to 13 by 14 to 16 points)
On all values, 1c to 90c
I. Grill about 8½x10mm
(10 to 11 by 10 to 13 points)
On 1, 2, 3, 6, 7c

On the 1870-71 stamps the grill impressions are usually faint or incomplete. This is especially true of the H grill, which often shows only a few points.

Values for 1c — 7c are for stamps showing well defined grills.

White Wove Paper

1870-71 ***Perf. 12***

134	A44	1c ultramarine	2,750.	200.00
		No gum	1,100.	
		On cover		230.00
135	A45	2c red brown	1,300.	80.00
		No gum	550.00	
		On cover		105.00
a.		Diagonal half used as 1c on cover		—
b.		Vertical half used as 1c on cover		—
136	A46	3c green	800.00	27.50
		No gum	325.00	
		On cover		32.50
a.		Pair, one without grill, on cover		—

The imperf. 3c can be found in the Scott U.S. Specialized Catalogue Die and Plate Proofs section.

137	A47	6c carmine	5,750.	525.
		No gum	2,300.	
		On cover		750.
138	A48	7c vermilion ('71)	4,500.	525.
		No gum	1,800.	
		On cover		700.
139	A49	10c brown	7,000.	800.
		No gum	2,750.	
		On cover		1,000.
140	A50	12c dull violet	*27,500.*	3,250.
		No gum	*14,000.*	
		On cover		*6,500.*
141	A51	15c orange	8,500.	1,300.
		No gum	3,250.	
		On cover		2,000.
142	A52	24c purple	—	7,000.
		On cover		—
143	A53	30c black	19,000.	3,750.
		No gum	8,250.	
		On cover		4,750.
144	A54	90c carmine	20,000.	2,500.
		No gum	9,000.	
		On cover		—

Without Grill
White Wove Paper

1870-71 ***Perf. 12***

145	A44	1c ultramarine	700.	20.00
		No gum	260.	
		On cover		22.50
146	A45	2c red brown	400.	17.50
		No gum	160.	
		On cover		20.00
a.		Diagonal half used as 1c on cover		*700.00*
b.		Vertical half used as 1c on cover		*800.00*
c.		Double impression		800.00
147	A46	3c green	325.	1.75
		No gum	120.	
		On cover		2.25
a.		Printed on both sides		*12,500.*
b.		Double impression		*40,000.*

The imperf. 3c can be found in the Scott U.S. Specialized Catalogue Die and Plate Proofs section.

148	A47	6c carmine	1,200.	35.00
		No gum	475.	
		On cover		50.00
a.		Vert. half used as 3c on cover		*3,500.*
b.		Double impression		—
149	A48	7c vermilion ('71)	1,300.	95.00
		No gum	500.	
		On cover		160.00
150	A49	10c brown	1,750.	30.00
		No gum	675.	
		On cover		45.00
151	A50	12c dull violet	3,000.	200.00
		No gum	1,200.	
		On cover		450.00
152	A51	15c bright orange	3,250.	200.00
		No gum	1,300.	
		On cover		350.00
a.		Double impression		*6,000.*
153	A52	24c purple	2,300.	200.00
		No gum	925.	
		On cover		*1,500.*
154	A53	30c black	7,500.	275.00
		No gum	3,000.	
		On cover		825.00
155	A54	90c carmine	5,500.	350.00
		No gum	2,400.	
		On cover		—

Printed by the Continental Bank Note Co.

Designs of the 1870-71 Issue with secret marks on the values from 1c to 15c as described and illustrated below.

Franklin — A44a

1c. In pearl at left of numeral "1" is a small crescent.

Jackson — A45a

2c. Under the scroll at the left of "U. S." there is a small diagonal line. This mark seldom shows clearly. The stamp, No. 157, can be distinguished by its color.

Washington — A46a

3c. The under part of the upper tail of the left ribbon is heavily shaded.

Lincoln — A47a

6c. The first four vertical lines of the shading in the lower part of the left ribbon have been strengthened.

Stanton — A48a

7c. Two small semi-circles are drawn around the ends of the lines that outline the ball in the lower right hand corner.

Jefferson — A49a

10c. There is a small semi-circle in the scroll at the right end of the upper label.

Clay — A50a

12c. The balls of the figure "2" are crescent shaped.

Webster — A51a

15c. In the lower part of the triangle in the upper left corner two lines have been made heavier forming a "V." This mark can be found on some of the Continental and American (1879) printings, but not all stamps show it.

Secret marks were added to the dies of the 24c, 30c and 90c but new plates were not made from them. The various printings of these stamps can be distinguished only by the shades and paper.

White Wove Paper, thin to thick
Without Grill*

1873 ***Perf. 12***

156	A44a	1c ultramarine	300.	5.00
		No gum	100.	
		On cover		6.50
e.		With grill	*2,000.*	
f.		Imperf., pair	—	*1,500.*
157	A45a	2c brown	450.	22.50
		No gum	175.	
		On cover		27.50
c.		With grill	*1,850.*	*750.00*
d.		Double impression	—	*5,000*
e.		Vertical half used as 1c on cover		—
158	A46a	3c green	140.	1.00
		No gum	45.	
		On cover		1.20
e.		With grill	*500.*	
h.		Horiz. pair, imperf. vert.		—
i.		Horiz. pair, imperf. btwn.		*1,300.*
j.		Double impression		*10,000.*
k.		Printed on both sides		*12,000.*

The imperf. 3c, with and without grill, can be found in the Scott U.S. Specialized Catalogue Die and Plate Proofs section.

159	A47a	6c dull pink	475.	20.00
		No gum	180.	
		On cover		47.50
a.		Diagonal half used as 3c on cover		*4,000.*
b.		With grill	*1,800.*	
160	A48a	7c orange ver	1,500.	90.00
		No gum	600.	
		On cover		175.00
a.		With grill	*3,500.*	
161	A49a	10c brown	1,300.	25.00
		No gum	500.	
		On cover		40.00
c.		With grill	*3,750.*	
d.		Horiz. pair, imperf. btwn.		*2,750.*
162	A50a	12c blk vio	2,750.	125.00
		No gum	1,150.	
		On cover		325.00
a.		With grill	*5,500.*	
163	A51a	15c yell orange	3,000.	140.00
		No gum	1,250.	
		On cover		325.00
a.		With grill	*5,750.*	
164	A52	24c purple		*357,500.*
165	A53	30c gray blk	3,500.	130.00
		No gum	1,400.	
		On cover		*725.00*
c.		With grill	*22,500.*	
166	A54	90c rose carmine	2,750.	275.00
		No gum	1,250.	
		On cover		*7,500.*

The Philatelic Foundation has certified as genuine a 24c on vertically ribbed paper, and that is the stamp listed as No. 164. Specialists believe that only Continental used ribbed paper. It is not known for sure whether or not Continental also printed the 24c value on regular paper; if it did, specialists currently are not able to distinguish these from No. 153. The Catalogue value reflects a 2004 auction sale price realized.

* All values except 24c, 90c exist with experimental (J) grill, about 7x9½mm.

Special Printing of the 1873 Issue

Hard, White Wove Paper
Without Gum

1875 ***Perf. 12***

167	A44a	1c ultramarine	*18,000.*	
168	A45a	2c dark brown	*8,250.*	
169	A46a	3c blue green	*22,500.*	—
		On cover		—
170	A47a	6c dull rose	*22,500.*	
171	A48a	7c redish ver	*5,500.*	
172	A49a	10c pale brown	*21,000.*	
173	A50a	12c dark violet	*7,250.*	
174	A51a	15c bright orange	*21,000.*	
175	A52	24c dull purple	*5,000.*	*17,500.*
176	A53	30c greenish blk	*16,500.*	
177	A54	90c vio carmine	*21,000.*	

Although perforated, these stamps were usually cut apart with scissors. As a result, the perforations are often much mutilated and the design is frequently damaged.

These can be distinguished from the 1873 issue by the shades, also by the paper, which is very white instead of yellowish.

These and the subsequent issues listed under this heading are special printings of stamps then in current use which, together with the reprints and reissues, were made for sale to collectors. They were available for postage.

Zachary Taylor — A55

Yellowish Wove Paper

1875, June 21 ***Perf. 12***

178	A45a	2c vermilion	475.	12.50
		No gum	190.	
		On cover		15.00
b.		Half used as 1c on cover		*750.00*
c.		With grill	900.	*2,750.*

The imperf. 2c can be found in the Scott U.S. Specialized Catalogue Die and Plate Proofs section.

179	A55	5c blue	850.	25.00
		No gum	325.	
		On cover		37.50
c.		With grill	4,500.	

Almost all of the stamps of the Continental Bank Note Co. printing including the Department stamps and some of the Newspaper stamps may be found upon a paper which shows more or less of the characteristics of a ribbed paper.

Special Printing of the 1875 Issue

Hard, White Wove Paper
Without Gum

1875

180	A45a	2c carmine ver	*80,000.*
181	A55	5c bright blue	*450,000.*

Printed by the American Bank Note Company

Same as 1870-75 Issues
Soft Porous Paper
Varying from Thin to Thick

1879 ***Perf. 12***

182	A44a	1c dark ultra	350.00	4.50
		Never hinged	1,200.	
		No gum	125.00	
		On cover		4.75
183	A45a	2c vermilion	150.	3.25
		Never hinged	525.00	
		No gum	55.	
		On cover		3.75
a.		Double impression	—	*5,500.*
184	A46a	3c green	120.	.80
		Never hinged	425.00	
		No gum	40.	
		On cover		.90
b.		Double impression		—

The imperf. 3c can be found in the Scott U.S. Specialized Catalogue Die and Plate Proofs section.

185	A55	5c blue	550.00	15.00
		Never hinged	*1,900.*	
		No gum	220.	
		On cover		25.00
186	A47a	6c pink	1,100.	27.50
		Never hinged	*4,000.*	
		No gum	450.00	
		On cover		47.50
187	A49	10c brn (without secret mark)	3,500.	27.50
		Never hinged	*12,000.*	
		No gum	1,400.	
		On cover		50.00
188	A49a	10c brown (with secret mark)	2,500.	27.50
		Never hinged	*8,500.*	
		No gum	1,000.	
		On cover		42.50
189	A51a	15c red orange	350.00	25.00
		Never hinged	900.00	
		No gum	140.	
		On cover		87.50
190	A53	30c full black	1,100.	80.00
		Never hinged	*4,000.*	
		No gum	450.	
		On cover		425.00
191	A54	90c carmine	2,500.	325.00
		Never hinged	*8,500.*	
		No gum	1,000.	
		On cover		*5,000.*

The ABN Co. used many Continental plates to print the postage, Departmental and Newspaper stamps. Therefore, stamps bearing the Continental imprint were not always its product.

The ABN Co. also used the National 90c plate and possibly the 30c plate.

Early printings of No. 188 were from Continental plates 302 and 303 which contained the normal secret mark of 1873. After those plates were re-entered by the ABN Co. in 1880, pairs or multiple pieces contained combinations of normal, hairline or missing marks. The pairs or other multiples usually found contain at least one hairline mark which tended to disappear as the plate wore.

ABN Co. plates 377 and 378 were made in 1881 from the National transfer roll of 1870. No. 187 from those plates has no secret mark.

Perf 12 Trial/color Proofs on gummed stamp paper exist, as a 15c without speciman overprint.

The ABN Co. used many Continental plates to print the postage, Departmental and Newspaper stamps. Therefore, stamps bearing the Continental imprint were not always its product. The imperf. 90c can be found in the Scott U.S. Specialized Catalogue Die and Plate Proofs section.

Identification by Paper Type:

Collectors traditionally have identified American Banlk Note Co. issues by the soft, porous paper on which they were printed. However, the Continental Bank Note Co. occasionally used a soft paper from August 1878 through early 1879, before the consolidation of the companies. When the consolidation occurred on Feb. 4, 1879, American Bank Note Co. took over the presses, plates, paper, ink, and the employees of Continental. Undoubtedly they also acquired panes of finished stamps and sheets of printed stamps that had not yet been gummed and/or perforated. Since the soft paper that was in use at the time of the consolidation and after is approximately the same texture and thickness as the soft paper that American Bank Note Co. began using regularly in June or July of 1879, all undated soft paper stamps have traditionally been classified as American Bank Note Co. printings.

However, if a stamp bears a dated cancellation or is on a dated cover from Feb. 3, 1879 or earlier, collectors (especially specialist collectors) must consider the stamp to be a Continental Bank Note printing. Undated stamps off cover, and stamps and covers dated Feb. 4 or later, traditionally have been considered to be American Bank Note Co. printings since that company held the contract to print U.S. postage stamps beginning on that date. Only the most dedicated and serious specialist students attempt to determine the stamp printer of the issues on soft, portous paper in an absolute manner (by scientifically testing the paper and/or comparing printing records).

Special Printing of the 1879 Issue

Soft Porous Paper
Without Gum

1880 ***Perf. 12***

192	A44a	1c dark ultra	*50,000.*
193	A45a	2c black brown	*25,000.*
194	A46a	3c blue green	*75,000.*
195	A47a	6c dull rose	*65,000.*
196	A48a	7c scar vermilion	*8,000.*
197	A49a	10c deep brown	*45,000.*
198	A50a	12c black purple	*15,000.*
199	A51a	15c orange	*40,000.*
200	A52	24c dark violet	*12,500.*
201	A53	30c grnsh black	*24,000.*
202	A54	90c dull carmine	*40,000.*
203	A45a	2c scar vermilion	*125,000.*
204	A55	5c deep blue	*325,000.*

Nos. 192 and 194 are valued in the grade of fine.

No. 197 was printed from Continental plate 302 (or 303) after plate was re-entered, therefore stamp may show normal, hairline or missing secret mark.

IMPORTANT INFORMATION REGARDING VALUES FOR NEVER-HINGED STAMPS

Collectors should be aware that the values given for never-hinged stamps from No. 205 on are for stamps in the grade of very fine. The never-hinged premium as a percentage of value will be larger for stamps in extremely fine or superb grades, and the premium will be smaller for fine-very fine, fine or poor examples. This is particularly true of the issues of the late-19th and early-20th centuries. For example, in the grade of very fine, an unused stamp from this time period may be valued at $100 hinged and $160 never hinged. The never-hinged premium is thus 60%. But in a grade of extremely fine, this same stamp will not only sell for more hinged, but the never-hinged premium will increase, perhaps to 100%-300% or more over the higher extremely fine value. In a grade of superb, a hinged copy will sell for much more than a very fine copy, and additionally the never-hinged premium will be much larger, perhaps as large as 300%-400%. On the other hand, the same stamp in a grade of fine or fine-very fine not only will sell for less than a very fine stamp in hinged condition, but additionally the never-hinged premium will be smaller than the never-hinged premium on a very fine stamp, perhaps as small as 15%-30%.

Please note that the above statements and percentages are NOT a formula for arriving at the values of stamps in hinged or never-hinged condition in the grades of very good, fine, fine to very fine, extremely fine or superb. The percentages given apply only to the size of the premium for never-hinged condition that might be added to the stamp value for hinged condition. Further, the percentages given are only generalized estimates. Some stamps or grades may have percentages for never-hinged condition that are higher or lower than the ranges given.

For values of the most popular U.S. stamps in the grades of very good, fine, fine to very fine, extremely fine and superb, see the *Scott Valuing Supplement*, updated and issued twice each year in April and October.

James A. Garfield — A56

1882, Apr. 10 ***Perf. 12***

205	A56	5c yellow brown	325.	10.00
		Never hinged	1,000.	
		No gum	120.	
		On cover		18.50

Special Printing

Soft Porous Paper
Without Gum

1882

205C	A56	5c gray brown	*75,000.*

Designs of 1873 Re-engraved

Franklin — A44b

1c. The vertical lines in the upper part of the stamp have been so deepened that the background often appears to be solid. Lines of shading have been added to the upper arabesques.

Washington — A46b

3c. The shading at the sides of the central oval appears only about one-half the previous width. A short horizontal dash has been cut about 1mm below the "TS" of "CENTS."

Lincoln — A47b

6c. On the original stamps four vertical lines can be counted from the edge of the panel to the outside of the stamp. On the re-engraved stamps there are but three lines in the same place.

Jefferson — A49b

10c. On the original stamps there are five vertical lines between the left side of the oval and the edge of the shield. There are only four lines on the re-engraved stamps. In the lower part of the latter, also, the horizontal lines of the background have been strengthened.

1881-82 *Perf. 12*

206	A44b 1c gray blue	95.00	1.00
	Never hinged	300.00	
	No gum	27.50	
	On cover		1.50
207	A46b 3c blue green	100.00	.55
	Never hinged	325.00	
	No gum	30.00	
	On cover		.70
c.	Double impression		—
208	A47b 6c rose ('82)	900.00	100.00
	Never hinged	3,250.	
	No gum	300.00	
	On cover (rose)		180.00
a.	6c deep brown red	700.00	160.00
	Never hinged	2,150.	
	No gum	225.00	
	On cover		*425.00*
209	A49b 10c brown ('82)	200.00	6.00
	Never hinged	600.00	
	No gum	60.00	
	On cover		11.00
b.	10c black brown	2,500.	325.00
	Never hinged	5,000.	
	No gum	825.00	
	On cover		*525.00*
c.	Double impression		—
	Nos. 206-209 (4)	1,295.	107.55

Specimen stamps without overprint exist in a brown shade that differs from No. 209 and in green. The unoverprinted brown specimen is cheaper than No. 209.

Washington
A57

Jackson
A58

1883, Oct. 1 *Perf. 12*

210	A57 2c red brown	50.00	.60
	Never hinged	160.00	
	No gum	17.50	
	On cover		.70
211	A58 4c blue green	350.00	22.50
	Never hinged	1,100.	
	No gum	120.00	
	On cover		50.00

Imperfs. can be found in the Scott U.S. Specialized Catalogue Die and Plate Proofs section.

Special Printing

Soft Porous Paper

1883-85

211B	A57 2c pale red brown	450.	—
	Never hinged	950.	
	No gum	175.	
c.	Horiz. pair, imperf. btwn.	*2,000.*	
	Never hinged	*3,000.*	
211D	A58 4c deep blue green	*50,000.*	

No. 211D is without gum.

Franklin — A59

1887 *Perf. 12*

212	A59 1c ultramarine	120.00	2.25
	Never hinged	400.00	
	No gum	45.00	
	On cover		3.00
213	A57 2c green	50.00	.50
	Never hinged	150.00	
	No gum	17.50	
	On cover		.65
b.	Printed on both sides		—
214	A46b 3c vermilion	80.00	62.50
	Never hinged	240.00	
	No gum	27.50	
	On cover (single)		105.00
	Nos. 212-214 (3)	250.00	65.25

Imperf. 1c, 2c can be found in the Scott U.S. Specialized Catalogue Die and Plate Proofs section.

1888 *Perf. 12*

215	A58 4c carmine	250.00	22.50
	Never hinged	800.	
	No gum	90.00	
	On cover		45.00
216	A56 5c indigo	275.00	15.00
	Never hinged	900.	
	No gum	100.	
	On cover		27.50
217	A53 30c orange brn	475.	120.00
	Never hinged	1,500.	
	No gum	170.	
	On cover		*1,400.*
218	A54 90c purple	1,200.	260.
	Never hinged	4,000.	
	No gum	475.	
	On cover		*10,000.*
	Nos. 215-218 (4)	2,200.	417.50

Imperfs. can be found in the Scott U.S. Specialized Catalogue Die and Plate Proofs section.

Franklin
A60

Washington
A61

Jackson
A62

Lincoln
A63

Grant
A64

Garfield
A65

William T. Sherman
A66

Daniel Webster
A67

Henry Clay
A68

Jefferson
A69

Perry — A70

1890-93 *Perf. 12*

219	A60 1c dull blue	30.00	.60
	Never hinged	90.00	
	On cover		.65
219D	A61 2c lake	250.00	5.00
	Never hinged	800.00	
	On cover		7.00
220	A61 2c carmine	27.50	.55
	Never hinged	80.00	
	On cover		.60
a.	Cap on left "2"	150.00	10.00
	Never hinged	450.00	
c.	Cap on both "2's"	700.00	30.00
	Never hinged	2,000.	
221	A62 3c purple	90.00	7.50
	Never hinged	275.00	
	On cover		16.00
222	A63 4c dark brown	120.00	4.00
	Never hinged	360.00	
	On cover		15.00
223	A64 5c chocolate	100.00	4.00
	Never hinged	300.00	
	On cover		14.00
224	A65 6c brown red	90.00	20.00
	Never hinged	275.00	
	On cover		35.00
225	A66 8c lilac ('93)	70.00	14.00
	Never hinged	210.00	
	On cover		30.00
226	A67 10c green	225.00	3.75
	Never hinged	675.00	
	On cover		10.00
227	A68 15c indigo	300.00	25.00
	Never hinged	925.00	
	On cover		65.00
228	A69 30c black	450.00	35.00
	Never hinged	1,400.	
	On cover		*600.00*
229	A70 90c orange	700.00	140.00
	Never hinged	2,250.	
	On cover		—
	Nos. 219-229 (12)	2,452.	259.40

The "cap on right 2" variety is due to imperfect inking, not a plate defect.

Imperfs. can be found in the Scott U.S. Specialized Catalogue Die and Plate Proofs section.

Columbian Exposition Issue

Columbus in Sight of Land
A71

Landing of Columbus
A72

Flagship of Columbus
A73

Fleet of Columbus
A74

Columbus Soliciting Aid from Isabella
A75

Columbus Welcomed at Barcelona
A76

Columbus Restored to Favor
A77

Columbus Presenting Natives
A78

Columbus Announcing his Discovery
A79

Columbus at La Rábida
A80

Recall of Columbus A81

Isabella Pledging her Jewels A82

Columbus in Chains A83

Columbus Describing his Third Voyage A84

Isabella & Columbus A85

Columbus A86

1893 ***Perf. 12***

230	A71 1c deep blue	22.50	.40
	Never hinged	60.00	
	On cover		.90
231	A72 2c brown violet	21.00	.30
	Never hinged	57.50	
	On cover		.35
232	A73 3c green	60.00	15.00
	Never hinged	150.00	
	On cover		32.50
233	A74 4c ultra	90.00	7.50
	Never hinged	230.00	
	On cover		22.50
a.	4c blue (error)	19,000.	16,500.
	Never hinged	34,000.	
234	A75 5c chocolate	95.00	8.00
	Never hinged	260.00	
	On cover		22.50
235	A76 6c purple	90.00	22.50
	Never hinged	230.00	
a.	6c red violet	90.00	22.50
	Never hinged	230.00	
	On cover, #235 or 235a		50.00
236	A77 8c magenta	80.00	11.00
	Never hinged	200.00	
	On cover		22.50
237	A78 10c black brown	150.00	8.00
	Never hinged	350.00	
	On cover		32.50
238	A79 15c dark green	250.00	70.00
	Never hinged	750.00	
	On cover		225.00
239	A80 30c orange brown	300.00	90.00
	Never hinged	900.00	
	On cover		400.00
240	A81 50c slate blue	600.00	180.00
	Never hinged	1,800.	
	On cover		625.00
241	A82 $1 salmon	1,200.	650.
	Never hinged	4,000.	
	No gum	625.	
	On cover		2,000.
242	A83 $2 brown red	1,250.	600.
	Never hinged	4,100.	
	No gum	625.	
	On cover		2,100.
243	A84 $3 yellow green	1,900.	1,000.
	Never hinged	6,250.	
	No gum	1,000.	
a.	$3 olive green	1,900.	1,000.
	Never hinged	6,250.	
	No gum	1,000.	
	On cover, #243 or 243a		2,600.
244	A85 $4 crimson lake	2,600.	1,300.
	Never hinged	8,500.	
	No gum	1,300.	
a.	$4 rose carmine	2,600.	1,300.
	Never hinged	8,500.	
	No gum	1,300.	
	On cover		4,000.
245	A86 $5 black	3,000.	1,500.
	Never hinged	10,000.	
	No gum	1,500.	
	On cover		4,750.

World's Columbian Expo., Chicago, May 1-Oct. 30, 1893.

Nos. 230-245 are known imperf., but were not regularly issued. (See Scott U.S. Specialized Catalogue Die and Plate Proofs for the 2c.)

Never-Hinged Stamps

See note before No. 205 regarding premiums for never-hinged stamps.

Bureau Issues

Starting in 1894, the Bureau of Engraving and Printing at Washington has produced most U.S. postage stamps. Until 1965 Bureau-printed stamps were engraved except Nos. 525-536, which are offset. The combination of lithography and engraving (see No. 1253) was first used in 1964, and photogravure (see No. 1426) in 1971.

Franklin A87

Washington A88

Jackson A89

Lincoln A90

Grant A91

Garfield A92

Sherman A93

Webster A94

Clay A95

Jefferson A96

Perry A97

James Madison A98

John Marshall — A99

TWO CENTS

Triangle A (Type I)

Triangle B (Type II)

Type I. The horizontal lines of the ground work run across the triangle and are of the same thickness within it as without.

Type II. The horizontal lines cross the triangle but are thinner within it than without.

Triangle C (Types III and IV)

Type III. The horizontal lines do not cross the double frame lines of the triangle. The lines within the triangle are thin, as in type II. Otherwise, design as type II.

Type IV

Type IV. Same triangle C as type III, but other design differences including, (1) re-cutting and lengthening of hairline, (2) shaded toga button, (3) strengthening of lines on sleeve, (4) additional dots on ear, (5) "T" of "TWO" straight at right, (6) background lines extend into white oval opposite "U" of "UNITED." Many other differences exist.

ONE DOLLAR

Type I

Type I. The circles enclosing "$1" are broken where they meet the curved line below "One Dollar." The 15 left vert. rows of impressions from plate 76 are Type I, the balance Type II.

Type II

Type II. The circles are complete.

1894 **Unwmk.** ***Perf. 12***

246	A87 1c ultramarine	32.50	5.00
	Never hinged	95.00	
	On cover		20.00
247	A87 1c blue	75.00	3.00
	Never hinged	225.00	
	On cover		17.50
248	A88 2c pink, Type I	30.00	7.50
	Never hinged	87.50	
	On cover		15.00
249	A88 2c car lake, Type I	175.00	5.50
	Never hinged	550.00	
	On cover		11.50
a.	Double impression		—
250	A88 2c car, Type I	30.00	2.50
	Never hinged	85.00	
	On cover		3.50
a.	2c rose, type I	30.00	4.50
	Never hinged	85.00	
	On cover		5.50
b.	2c scarlet, type I ('95)	30.00	2.50
	Never hinged	85.00	
	On cover		3.50
c.	Vert. pair, imperf. horiz.	4,500.	
d.	Horiz. pair, imperf. btwn.	2,000.	
251	A88 2c car, Type II	350.00	11.00
	Never hinged	1,000.	
	On cover		20.00
a.	2c scarlet, type II	350.00	7.50
	Never hinged	1,000.	
	On cover		13.50
252	A88 2c car, Type III	130.00	11.00
	Never hinged	400.00	
	On cover		15.00
a.	2c scarlet, type III	130.00	11.00
	Never hinged	400.00	
	On cover		15.00
b.	Horiz. pair, imperf. vert.	5,000.	
c.	Horiz. pair, imperf. btwn.	5,500.	
253	A89 3c purple	125.00	10.00
	Never hinged	400.00	
	On cover		25.00
254	A90 4c dark brown	175.00	7.50
	Never hinged	525.00	
	On cover		21.00
255	A91 5c chocolate	125.00	7.00
	Never hinged	375.00	
	On cover		20.00
c.	Vert. pair, imperf. horiz.	4,000.	
256	A92 6c dull brown	175.00	25.00
	Never hinged	500.00	
	On cover		47.50
a.	Vert. pair, imperf. horiz.	2,000.	
257	A93 8c vio brn ('95)	175.00	18.50
	Never hinged	525.00	
	On cover		45.00
258	A94 10c drk grn	325.00	15.00
	Never hinged	1,000.	
	On cover		35.00
259	A95 15c drk blue	325.00	60.00
	Never hinged	1,000.	
	On cover		115.00
260	A96 50c orange	600.	135.00
	Never hinged	1,900.	
	On cover		1,000.
261	A97 $1 black, Type I	1,200.	350.
	Never hinged	3,750.	
	No gum	375.	
	On cover		2,750.
261A	A97 $1 black, Type II	2,400.	750.
	Never hinged	7,250.	
	No gum	750.	
	On cover		4,500.
262	A98 $2 bright blue	3,250.	1,250.
	Never hinged	9,750.	
	No gum	1,250.	
	On cover		5,000.
263	A99 $5 drk grn	5,000.	2,600.
	Never hinged	16,000.	
	No gum	2,500.	
	On cover		—

For imperfs. and the 2c pink, vert. pair, imperf. horiz., see Scott U.S. Specialized Catalogue Die and Plate Proofs.

Same as 1894 Issue

1895 **Wmk. 191** ***Perf. 12***

264	A87 1c blue	6.50	.50
	Never hinged	19.00	
	On cover		1.25
265	A88 2c car, Type I	30.00	3.00
	Never hinged	90.00	
	On cover		5.00
266	A88 2c car, Type II	35.00	5.00
	Never hinged	110.00	
	On cover		8.50
267	A88 2c car, Type III	5.50	.40
	Never hinged	16.00	
	On cover		.55
a.	2c pink, type III ('97	12.50	1.25
	Never hinged	40.00	
	On cover		1.50
b.	2c vermilion, type III ('99)	50.00	9.00
c.	2c rose carmine, type III ('99)	—	—

The three left vertical rows from plate 170 are Type II, the balance being Type III.

268	A89 3c purple	37.50	2.00
	Never hinged	115.00	
	On cover		8.00
269	A90 4c drk brn	50.00	3.00
	Never hinged	150.00	
	On cover		11.00
270	A91 5c choc.	37.50	3.00
	Never hinged	115.00	
	On cover		7.50
271	A92 6c dull brn	130.00	7.50
	Never hinged	390.00	
	On cover		27.50
a.	Wmkd. USIR	12,500.	10,000.
272	A93 8c vio brn	75.00	2.50
	Never hinged	225.00	
	On cover		14.00
a.	Wmkd. USIR	6,000.	1,000.
273	A94 10c drk grn	100.00	2.00
	Never hinged	300.00	
	On cover		15.00
274	A95 15c drk blue	250.00	15.00
	Never hinged	750.00	
	On cover		55.00
275	A96 50c orange	325.00	35.00
	Never hinged	1,000.	
	On cover		400.00
a.	50c red orange	375.00	42.50
	Never hinged	1,150.	
	On cover		400.00
276	A97 $1 blk, Type I	700.00	95.00
	Never hinged	2,100.	
	No gum	200.00	
	On cover		2,250.

276A A97 $1 blk, Type II — 1,500. — 225.00
Never hinged — 4,500.
No gum — 475.00
On cover — — *3,750.*
277 A98 $2 bright blue — 1,200. — 450.00
Never hinged — 3,600.
No gum — 400.00
a. $2 drk blue — 1,200. — 450.00
Never hinged — 3,600.
No gum — 400.00
On cover — — *3,500.*
278 A99 $5 drk grn — 2,400. — 650.00
Never hinged — 7,250.
No gum — 900.00
On cover — — *12,500.*

For imperfs. and the 1c horiz. pair, imperf. vert., see Scott U. S. Specialized Catalogue Die and Plate Proofs.
For "I.R." overprints see Nos. R155-R158.

TEN CENTS

Type I

Type I. Tips of foliate ornaments do not impinge on white curved line below "TEN CENTS."

Type II

Type II. Tips of ornaments break curved line below "E" of "TEN" and "T" of "CENTS."

1897-1903 Wmk. 191 ***Perf. 12***

279 A87 1c deep green, horiz. wmk. — 9.00 — .50
Never hinged — 25.00
On cover — — .60
a. Vertical watermark — *40.00* — *7.50*
Never hinged — *120.00*
279B A88 2c red, type IV ('99) — 9.00 — .40
Never hinged — 25.00
On cover — — .50
c. 2c rose carmine, type IV ('99) — 300.00 — 150.00
Never hinged — 750.00
d. 2c orange red, type IV, horiz. wmk. ('00) — 11.50 — .55
Never hinged — 32.50
On cover — — .70
e. 2c org red, IV, vert. wmk. — *35.00* — *5.00*
Never hinged — *110.00*
f. 2c carmine, type IV — 10.00 — .50
Never hinged — 27.50
On cover — — .65
g. 2c pink, type IV — 50.00 — 1.75
Never hinged — 150.00
On cover — — 2.00
h. 2c vermilion, type IV ('99) — 11.00 — .55
Never hinged — 30.00
On cover — — .75
i. 2c brown orange, type IV ('99) — *150.00* — *15.00*
Never hinged — *425.00*
j. Booklet pane of 6, IV, horiz. wmk. ('00) — *450.00* — *1,250.*
Never hinged — 900.00
k. Booklet pane of 6, IV, vert. wmk. ('02) — *450.00* — *1,250.*
Never hinged — 900.00
280 A90 4c rose brn ('98) — 30.00 — 3.00
Never hinged — 90.00
a. 4c lilac brown — 30.00 — 3.00
Never hinged — 90.00
b. 4c orange brown — 30.00 — 3.00
Never hinged — 90.00
On cover, #280, 280a or 280b — — 11.00
281 A91 5c dk bl ('98) — 35.00 — 2.00
Never hinged — 110.00
On cover — — 10.00
282 A92 6c lake ('98) — 50.00 — 6.00
Never hinged — 160.00
On cover — — 17.50
a. 6c purple lake — 75.00 — 12.50
Never hinged — 225.00
282C A94 10c brown, Type I ('98) — 210.00 — 6.00
Never hinged — 625.00
On cover — — 17.50
283 A94 10c org brn, II, horiz. wmk. — 160.00 — 5.00
Never hinged — 500.00
On cover — — 17.50
a. Vertical watermark ('00) — *225.00* — *10.00*
Never hinged — *700.00*
284 A95 15c ol grn ('98) — 175.00 — 10.00
Never hinged — 550.00
On cover — — 32.50
Nos. 279-284 (8) — 678.00 — 32.90

For "I.R." overprints see Nos. R153-R154.

Trans-Mississippi Exposition Issue

Marquette on the Mississippi A100

Farming in the West — A101

Indian Hunting Buffalo A102

Frémont on the Rocky Mountains A103

Troops Guarding Wagon Train — A104

Hardships of Emigration A105

Western Mining Prospector A106

Western Cattle in Storm A107

Mississippi River Bridge A108

1898, June 17 Wmk. 191 ***Perf. 12***

285 A100 1c dk yel grn — 30.00 — 6.50
Never hinged — 80.00
On cover — — 9.75
286 A101 2c copper red — 30.00 — 2.50
Never hinged — 80.00
On cover — — 3.50
287 A102 4c orange — 140.00 — 24.00
Never hinged — 400.00
On cover — — 57.50
288 A103 5c dull blue — 140.00 — 22.50
Never hinged — 400.00
On cover — — 50.00
289 A104 8c vio brn — 200.00 — 45.00
Never hinged — 600.00
On cover — — 115.00
a. Vert. pair, imperf. horiz. — *27,500.*
290 A105 10c gray violet — 180.00 — 32.50
Never hinged — 550.00
On cover — — 90.00
291 A106 50c sage grn — 700.00 — 190.00
Never hinged — 2,100.
On cover — — 1,750.
292 A107 $1 black — 1,250. — 650.00
Never hinged — 3,750.
No gum — 650.00
On cover — — *4,000.*
293 A108 $2 orange brn — 2,250. — 1,050.
Never hinged — 6,500.
No gum — 1,050.
On cover — — *12,500.*
Nos. 285-293 (9) — 4,920. — 2,023.

Trans-Mississippi Exposition, Omaha, Neb., June 1 to Nov. 1, 1898.
For "I.R." overprints see #R158A-R158B.

Never-Hinged Stamps
See note before No. 205 regarding premiums for never-hinged stamps.

Pan-American Exposition Issue

Fast Lake Navigation A109

"Empire State" Express — A110

Electric Automobile A111

Bridge at Niagara Falls — A112

Canal Locks at Sault Ste. Marie — A113

Fast Ocean Navigation A114

1901, May 1 Wmk. 191 ***Perf. 12***

294 A109 1c grn & black — 20.00 — 3.00
Never hinged — 45.00
On cover — — 4.50
a. Center inverted — *11,000.* — *13,000.*
Never hinged — *19,000.*
On cover — — —
295 A110 2c car & black — 17.50 — 1.00
Never hinged — 42.50
On cover — — 1.50
a. Center inverted — *45,000.* — *60,000.*
296 A111 4c dp red brn & black — 85.00 — 15.00
Never hinged — 200.00
On cover — — 37.50
a. Center inverted — *35,000.* — —
297 A112 5c ultra & black — 95.00 — 14.00
Never hinged — 225.00
On cover — — 40.00
298 A113 8c brn vio & black — 120.00 — 50.00
Never hinged — 280.00
On cover — — 110.00
299 A114 10c yel brn & black — 160.00 — 25.00
Never hinged — 375.00
On cover — — 125.00
Nos. 294-299 (6) — 497.50 — 108.00
Nos. 294-299, never hinged — 1,168.

Buffalo, NY, May 1-Nov. 1, 1901.
No. 296a was a special printing.
Almost all unused copies of Nos. 295a and 296a have partial or disturbed gum. Values are for examples with full original gum that is slightly disturbed.

Franklin A115

Washington A116

Jackson A117

Grant A118

Lincoln A119

Garfield A120

Martha Washington A121

Webster A122

Benjamin Harrison
A123

Clay
A124

Jefferson
A125

David G. Farragut
A126

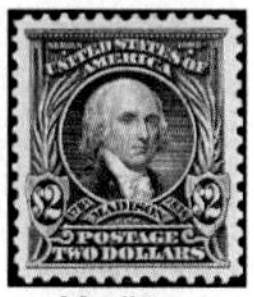
Madison
A127

Marshall
A128

1902-03 Wmk. 191 *Perf. 12*

300	A115 1c blue grn ('03)	12.00	.25
	Never hinged	30.00	
	On cover		.30
b.	Booklet pane of 6	600.00	*12,500.*
	Never hinged	1,150.	
301	A116 2c carmine ('03)	16.00	.40
	Never hinged	40.00	
	On cover		.45
c.	Booklet pane of 6	500.00	*2,250.*
	Never hinged	950.00	
302	A117 3c brt vio ('03)	55.00	3.50
	Never hinged	140.00	
	On cover		11.00
303	A118 4c brown ('03)	60.00	2.30
	Never hinged	150.00	
	On cover		12.50
304	A119 5c blue ('03)	60.00	2.00
	Never hinged	150.00	
	On cover		7.50
305	A120 6c claret ('03)	72.50	5.00
	Never hinged	180.00	
	On cover		15.00
306	A121 8c vio black	45.00	3.00
	Never hinged	110.00	
	On cover		8.00
307	A122 10c pale red brn ('03)	70.00	2.80
	Never hinged	175.00	
	On cover		9.00
308	A123 13c purple blk	50.00	9.00
	Never hinged	125.00	
	On cover		37.50
309	A124 15c ol grn ('03)	200.00	12.00
	Never hinged	500.00	
	On cover		80.00
310	A125 50c orange ('03)	475.00	27.50
	Never hinged	1,400.	
	On cover		700.00
311	A126 $1 black ('03)	750.00	80.00
	Never hinged	2,100.	
	No gum	180.00	
	On cover		1,500.
312	A127 $2 dk bl ('03)	1,200.	225.00
	Never hinged	3,250.	
	No gum	300.00	
	On cover		2,500.
313	A128 $5 dk grn ('03)	3,000.	750.00
	Never hinged	*8,000.*	
	No gum	850.00	
	On cover		*5,000.*
	Nos. 300-313 (14)	6,065.	1,122.

For listings of designs A127 and A128 with Perf. 10, see Nos. 479 and 480.

1906-08 *Imperf.*

314	A115 1c blue green	16.00	15.00
	Never hinged	35.00	
	On cover		22.50
314A	A118 4c brown ('08)	*75,000.*	*45,000.*
	Never hinged	*120,000.*	
	On cover		*130,000.*
315	A119 5c blue ('08)	240.	*1,250.*
	Never hinged	425.	
	On cover, pair		*45,000.*

No. 314A was issued imperforate but all copies were privately perforated with large oblong perforations at the sides (Schermack type III).

Beware of examples of No. 304 with perforations removed.

Used examples of Nos. 314 and 315 must have contemporaneous cancels.

Coil Stamps

Imperforate stamps are known fraudulently perforated to resemble coil stamps and part perforate varieties.

1908 *Perf. 12 Horizontally*

316	A115 1c bl grn	*55,000.*	
	Pair	150,000.	
317	A119 5c blue	*6,000.*	—
	Never hinged	*17,500.*	
	Pair	17,500.	
	Never hinged	*45,000.*	

Perf. 12 Vertically

318	A115 1c bl grn	*6,000.*	
	Never hinged	*11,500.*	
	Pair	16,500.	

Coil stamps for use in vending and affixing machines are perforated on two sides only, either horizontally or vertically. They were first issued in 1908, using perf. 12. This was changed to 8½ in 1910, and to 10 in 1914.

Imperforate sheets of certain denominations were sold to the vending machine companies which applied a variety of private perforations and separations.

Several values of the 1902 and later issues are found on an apparently coarse ribbed paper caused by worn blankets on the printing press and are not true paper varieties.

All examples of Nos. 316-318 must be accompanied by certificates of authenticity issued by recognized expertizing committees.

No. 318 is valued in the grade of fine.

Washington — A129

Type I

Type II

Type I. Leaf next to left "2" penetrates the border.

Type II. Strong line forming border left of leaf.

1903, Nov. 12 Wmk. 191 *Perf. 12*

319	A129 2c carmine (I)	6.00	.25
	Never hinged	15.00	
	On cover		.30
a.	2c lake (I)	—	—
b.	2c carmine rose (I)	10.00	.40
	Never hinged	25.00	
	On cover		.60
c.	2c scarlet (I)	10.00	.30
	Never hinged	25.00	
	On cover		.40
d.	Vert. pair, imperf. horiz. (#319)	*7,500.*	
	Never hinged	*15,000.*	
e.	Vert. pair, imperf. btwn. (#319)	*2,500.*	
f.	2c lake (II)	10.00	.30
	Never hinged	25.00	
	On cover		.35
g.	Booklet pane of 6, car (I)	125.00	*550.00*
	Never hinged	240.00	
h.	As "g" (II)	600.00	
	Never hinged	950.00	
i.	2c carmine (II)	75.00	*50.00*
	Never hinged	175.00	
	On cover		*150.00*
j.	2c carmine rose (II)	70.00	1.75
	Never hinged	160.00	
k.	2c scarlet (II)	70.00	.65
	Never hinged	160.00	
n.	As "g," car rose (I)	250.00	*650.00*
	Never hinged	450.00	
p.	As "g," scarlet (I)	185.00	*575.00*
	Never hinged	350.00	
q.	As "g," lake (II)	300.00	*750.00*
	Never hinged	575.00	

1906, Oct. 2 *Imperf.*

320	A129 2c carmine (I)	16.00	*17.50*
	Never hinged	35.00	
	On cover		22.50
a.	2c lake (II)	45.00	45.00
	Never hinged	100.00	
	On cover		—
b.	2c scarlet (I)	18.50	15.00
	Never hinged	40.00	
	On cover		22.50
c.	2c carmine rose (I)	60.00	42.50
	Never hinged	130.00	
d.	2c carmine (II)	*100.00*	*250.00*
	On cover		600.00

No. 320d was issued imperforate, but all copies were privately perforated with large oblong perforations at the sides (Schermack Type III).

Used examples of Nos. 320-320d must have contemporaneous cancels.

Coil Stamps

1908 *Perf. 12 Horizontally*

321	A129 2c car, pair (I)	*375,000.*	*200,000.*
	On cover, single		225,000.

Four authenticated unused pairs are known. Value of the unused pair represents 2002 auction sale price of a fresh, lightly hinged, fine-very fine pair.

The used value is for a single on cover, of which 2 authenticated examples are known, both used from Indianapolis in 1908. Numerous counterfeits exist.

Perf. 12 Vertically

322	A129 2c carmine	*7,000.*	
	Never hinged	*12,500.*	
	Pair	18,000.	

Louisiana Purchase Exposition Issue

Robert R. Livingston
A130

Thomas Jefferson
A131

James Monroe
A132

William McKinley
A133

Map of Louisiana Purchase
A134

1904, Apr. 30 Wmk. 191 *Perf. 12*

323	A130 1c green	30.00	5.00
	Never hinged	75.00	
	On cover		7.00
324	A131 2c carmine	27.50	2.00
	Never hinged	70.00	
	On cover		3.00
a.	Vert. pair, imperf. horiz.	*17,500.*	
325	A132 3c violet	90.00	30.00
	Never hinged	225.00	
	On cover		65.00
326	A133 5c dark blue	95.00	25.00
	Never hinged	240.00	
	On cover		50.00
327	A134 10c red brown	175.00	30.00
	Never hinged	440.00	
	On cover		125.00
	Nos. 323-327 (5)	417.50	92.00
	Nos. 323-327, never hinged	1,050.	

Louisiana Purchase Expo., St. Louis, Mo., Apr. 30 to Dec. 1, 1904.

Jamestown Exposition Issue

Captain John Smith — A135

Founding of Jamestown
A136

Pocahontas
A137

1907 Wmk. 191 *Perf. 12*

328	A135 1c green	30.00	5.00
	Never hinged	75.00	
	On cover		8.00
329	A136 2c carmine	35.00	4.50
	Never hinged	85.00	
	On cover		6.00
330	A137 5c blue	150.00	30.00
	Never hinged	350.00	
	On cover		82.50
	Nos. 328-330 (3)	215.00	39.50
	Nos. 328-330, never hinged	510.00	

Jamestown Expo., Hampton Roads, Va., Apr. 26 to Dec. 1.

Franklin
A138

Washington
A139

Washington — A140

There are several types of some of the 2c and 3c stamps of this and succeeding issues. These types are described under the dates when they first appeared.

Illustrations of Types I-VII of the 2c (A140) and Types I-IV of the 3c (A140) are reproduced by permission of H. L. Lindquist.

Type I

THREE CENTS

Type I. The top line of the toga rope is weak and the rope shading lines are thin. The fifth line from the left is missing.

The line between the lips is thin.

Used on both flat plate and rotary press printings.

1908-09 Wmk. 191 *Perf. 12*

331	A138 1c green	7.25	.40
	Never hinged	18.00	
	On cover		.55
a.	Booklet pane of 6	160.00	*450.00*
	Never hinged	285.00	
332	A139 2c carmine	6.75	.35
	Never hinged	16.00	
	On cover		.40
a.	Booklet pane of 6	135.00	*400.00*
	Never hinged	230.00	
333	A140 3c dp vio, Type I	35.00	3.00
	Never hinged	85.00	
	On cover		8.50
334	A140 4c orange brown	42.50	1.50
	Never hinged	100.00	
	On cover		7.00
335	A140 5c blue	55.00	2.50
	Never hinged	125.00	
	On cover		8.50
336	A140 6c red orange	70.00	6.50
	Never hinged	175.00	
	On cover		22.50
337	A140 8c olive green	50.00	3.00
	Never hinged	110.00	
	On cover		18.00
338	A140 10c yellow ('09)	75.00	2.00
	Never hinged	190.00	
	On cover		10.00
339	A140 13c bl grn ('09)	42.50	19.00
	Never hinged	100.00	
	On cover		110.00
340	A140 15c pale ultra ('09)	70.00	6.50
	Never hinged	175.00	
	On cover		125.00
341	A140 50c violet ('09)	350.00	20.00
	Never hinged	800.00	
	On cover		5,000.

342 A140 $1 vio brn ('09) 550.00 100.00
Never hinged 1,250.
On cover 6,000.
Nos. 331-342 (12) 1,354. 164.75

For listings of China Clay papers see the Scott U.S. Specialized Catalogue.

For listing of other perforated sheet stamps of designs A138, A139 and A140 see

#357-366	*Bluish Paper*	
#374-382, 405-407	*Single line wmk.*	*Perf. 12*
#423A-423C	*Single line wmk.*	*Perf. 12x10*
#423D-423E	*Single line wmk.*	*Perf. 10x12*
#424-430	*Single line wmk.*	*Perf. 10*
#461	*Single line wmk.*	*Perf. 11*
#462-469	*Unwmkd.*	*Perf. 10*
#498-507	*Unwmkd.*	*Perf. 11*
#519	*Double line wmk.*	*Perf. 11*
#525-530, 536	*Offset printing*	
#538-546	*Rotary press printing*	

Imperf

343 A138 1c green 4.50 4.50
Never hinged 9.50
On cover 10.00
344 A139 2c carmine 5.50 3.00
Never hinged 11.50
On cover 7.50
345 A140 3c dp violet, Type I 10.50 *20.00*
Never hinged 22.00
On cover 60.00
346 A140 4c org brown ('09) 17.50 22.50
Never hinged 37.50
On cover 90.00
347 A140 5c blue ('09) 32.50 35.00
Never hinged 70.00
On cover 125.00
Nos. 343-347 (5) 70.50 85.00

For listings of other imperforate stamps of designs A138, A139 and A140 see

#383 & 384, 408 & 409, 459	*Single line wmk.*
#481-485	*Unwmkd.*
#531-535	*Offset printing*

Coil Stamps

1908-10 ***Perf. 12 Horizontally***

348 A138 1c green 37.50 *50.00*
Never hinged 80.00
On cover 70.00
349 A139 2c carmine ('09) 80.00 80.00
Never hinged 175.00
On cover 37.50
350 A140 4c orange brown ('10) 160.00 *190.00*
Never hinged 350.00
On cover 250.00
351 A140 5c blue ('09) 175.00 *250.00*
Never hinged 375.00
On cover 625.00
Nos. 348-351 (4) 452.50 570.00

1909 ***Perf. 12 Vertically***

352 A138 1c green 95.00 *175.00*
Never hinged 210.00
On cover 100.00
353 A139 2c carmine 95.00 100.00
Never hinged 210.00
On cover 120.00
354 A140 4c orange brown 220.00 *250.00*
Never hinged 475.00
On cover 300.00
355 A140 5c blue 235.00 *275.00*
Never hinged 500.00
On cover 350.00
356 A140 10c yellow 3,250. *4,500.*
Never hinged 7,000.
On cover 10,000.

Beware of stamps offered as No. 356 which may be examples of No. 338 with perforations trimmed at top and/or bottom.

For listings of other coil stamps of designs A138, A139 and A140 see

#385-396, 410-413, 441-458	*Single line wmk.*
#486-496	*Unwmkd.*

Bluish Paper

This was made with 35 per cent rag stock instead of all wood pulp. The grayish blue color goes through the paper showing clearly on the back as well as on the face.

1909 ***Perf. 12***

357 A138 1c green 100.00 100.00
Never hinged 210.00
On cover 220.00
358 A139 2c carmine 90.00 100.00
Never hinged 190.00
On cover 190.00
359 A140 3c dp violet, Type I 2,000. *5,000.*
Never hinged 4,250.
On cover —
360 A140 4c orange brown *24,000.*
Never hinged *65,000.*
361 A140 5c blue 6,000. *15,000.*
Never hinged *15,000.*
On cover 27,500.
362 A140 6c red orange 1,500. *15,000.*
Never hinged 3,750.
On cover 22,500.
363 A140 8c olive green *27,500.*
Never hinged *40,000.*
364 A140 10c yellow 1,900. *6,250.*
Never hinged 4,500.
On cover —
365 A140 13c blue green 3,000. *2,250.*
Never hinged 6,500.
On cover —
366 A140 15c pale ultra 1,500. *11,000.*
Never hinged 3,250.
On cover —

Nos. 360, 363 not regularly issued.

Lincoln Centenary of Birth Issue

Lincoln — A141

1909, Feb. 12 Wmk. 191 ***Perf. 12***

367 A141 2c carmine 5.50 2.00
Never hinged 12.00
On cover 4.00

Imperf

368 A141 2c carmine 17.50 22.50
Never hinged 35.00
On cover 35.00

Bluish Paper

1909 ***Perf. 12***

369 A141 2c carmine 225.00 *275.00*
Never hinged 425.00
On cover 425.00

Alaska-Yukon Pacific Exposition Issue

William H. Seward — A142

1909, June 1 Wmk. 191 ***Perf. 12***

370 A142 2c carmine 8.75 2.25
Never hinged 17.50
On cover 5.00

1909 ***Imperf.***

371 A142 2c carmine 21.00 24.00
Never hinged 42.50
On cover 42.50

Seattle, Wash., June 1 to Oct. 16.

Hudson-Fulton Celebration Issue

"Half Moon" and Steamship A143

1909, Sept. 25 Wmk. 191 ***Perf. 12***

372 A143 2c carmine 12.00 4.75
Never hinged 25.00
On cover 8.50

Imperf

373 A143 2c carmine 25.00 27.50
Never hinged 50.00
On cover 40.00

Tercentenary of the discovery of the Hudson River and Centenary of Robert Fulton's steamship.

Designs of 1908-09 Issue

1910-11 Wmk. 190 ***Perf. 12***

374 A138 1c green 7.00 .25
Never hinged 16.00
On cover .30
a. Booklet pane of 6 225.00 *300.00*
Never hinged 375.00
375 A139 2c carmine 7.00 .25
Never hinged 16.00
On cover .30
a. Booklet pane of 6 125.00 *200.00*
Never hinged 200.00
b. 2c lake *900.00*
Never hinged *1,900.*
c. Double impression *600.00*
Never hinged *1,200.*
376 A140 3c dp vio, Type I ('11) 21.50 2.00
Never hinged 47.50
On cover 8.00
377 A140 4c brown ('11) 34.00 1.00
Never hinged 75.00
On cover 7.50
378 A140 5c blue ('11) 34.00 .75
Never hinged 75.00
On cover 5.25
379 A140 6c red orange ('11) 37.50 1.00
Never hinged 85.00
On cover 13.00
380 A140 8c ol grn ('11) 115.00 15.00
Never hinged 260.00
On cover 45.00
381 A140 10c yellow ('11) 110.00 6.00
Never hinged 250.00
On cover 22.50
382 A140 15c pale ultra ('11) 275.00 17.50
Never hinged 625.00
On cover 100.00
Nos. 374-382 (9) 641.00 43.75

1910 ***Imperf.***

383 A138 1c green 2.25 2.00
Never hinged 5.00
On cover 5.00
384 A139 2c carmine 3.75 2.50
Never hinged 8.00
On cover 3.50

Coil Stamps

1910 ***Perf. 12 Horizontally***

385 A138 1c green 45.00 30.00
Never hinged 100.00
On cover 55.00
386 A139 2c carmine 90.00 90.00
Never hinged 200.00
On cover 250.00

1910-11 ***Perf. 12 Vertically***

387 A138 1c green 200.00 125.00
Never hinged 425.00
On cover 160.00
388 A139 2c carmine 1,250. *1,600.*
Never hinged 2,750.
On cover 1,750.
389 A140 3c dp vio, Type I ('11) *65,000.* *11,000.*
Never hinged *150,000.*
On cover 27,500.

Stamps offered as No. 388 frequently are privately perforated examples of No. 384, or examples of No. 375, with top and/or bottom perfs trimmed.

No. 389 is valued in the grade of fine.

Stamps offered as No. 389 sometimes are examples of No. 376 with top and/or bottom perfs trimmed.

Beware also of plentiful fakes in the marketplace of Nos. 385-387.

Expertization by competent authorities is recommended.

1910 ***Perf. 8½ Horizontally***

390 A138 1c green 5.00 *12.50*
Never hinged 11.00
On cover 15.00
391 A139 2c carmine 42.50 45.00
Never hinged 90.00
On cover 60.00

1910-13 ***Perf. 8½ Vertically***

392 A138 1c green 30.00 50.00
Never hinged 65.00
On cover 70.00
393 A139 2c carmine 47.50 42.50
Never hinged 100.00
On cover 60.00
394 A140 3c dp vio, Type I ('11) 60.00 60.00
Never hinged 135.00
On cover 110.00
395 A140 4c brown ('12) 62.50 62.50
Never hinged 140.00
On cover 105.00
396 A140 5c blue ('13) 60.00 60.00
Never hinged 135.00
On cover 105.00
Nos. 392-396 (5) 260.00 275.00

Beware also of plentiful fakes in the marketplace of Nos. 390-393.

Panama-Pacific Exposition Issue

Vasco Nunez de Balboa — A144

Pedro Miguel Locks, Panama Canal — A145

Golden Gate — A146

Discovery of San Francisco Bay — A147

1913 Wmk. 190 ***Perf. 12***

397 A144 1c green 20.00 2.00
Never hinged 45.00
On cover 3.50
398 A145 2c carmine 20.00 1.00
Never hinged 45.00
On cover 1.75
a. 2c carmine lake *1,500.*
Never hinged *2,500.*
b. 2c lake *5,000.*
399 A146 5c blue 80.00 10.00
Never hinged 180.00
On cover 27.50
400 A147 10c orange yellow 135.00 22.50
Never hinged 300.00
On cover 57.50
400A A147 10c orange 225.00 19.00
Never hinged 500.00
On cover 75.00
Nos. 397-400A (5) 480.00 54.50
Nos. 397-400A, never hinged 1,070.

1914-15 ***Perf. 10***

401 A144 1c green 27.50 7.00
Never hinged 70.00
On cover 16.00
402 A145 2c carmine ('15) 75.00 2.75
Never hinged 190.00
On cover 6.50
403 A146 5c blue ('15) 175.00 19.00
Never hinged 425.00
On cover 55.00
404 A147 10c orange ('15) 900.00 70.00
Never hinged 2,100.
On cover 175.00
Nos. 401-404 (4) 1,177. 98.75
Nos. 401-404, never hinged 2,785.

San Francisco, Cal., Feb. 20 to Dec. 4.

TYPE I

Type I

TWO CENTS

Type I. There is one shading line in the first curve of the ribbon above the left "2" and one in the second curve of the ribbon above the right "2."

The button of the toga has a faint outline.

The top line of the toga rope, from the button to the front of the throat, is also very faint.

The shading lines at the face terminate in front of the ear with little or no joining, to form a lock of hair.

Used on both flat and rotary press printings.

1912-14 Wmk. 190 ***Perf. 12***

405 A140 1c green 7.00 .25
Never hinged 16.00
On cover .30
a. Vert. pair, imperf. horiz. 1,750 —
b. Booklet pane of 6 65.00 *75.00*
Never hinged 110.00
c. Double impression *1,250.*
406 A140 2c car, Type I 7.00 .25
Never hinged 16.00
On cover .30
a. Booklet pane of 6 65.00 *90.00*
Never hinged 110.00
b. Double impression 1,175.
c. 2c lake, type II *2,000.* *2,750.*
Never hinged *4,500.*
407 A140 7c black ('14) 80.00 14.00
Never hinged 180.00
On cover 75.00
Nos. 405-407 (3) 94.00 14.50

1912 ***Imperf.***

408 A140 1c green 1.00 .65
Never hinged 2.00
On cover 1.20
409 A140 2c carmine, Type I 1.20 .65
Never hinged 2.40
On cover 1.20

Coil Stamps

1912 ***Perf. 8½ Horizontally***

410 A140 1c green 6.00 *10.00*
Never hinged 13.00
On cover 14.00
411 A140 2c carmine, Type I 10.00 10.00
Never hinged 22.50
On cover 16.00

Perf. 8½ Vertically

412 A140 1c green 25.00 20.00
Never hinged 55.00
On cover 30.00
413 A140 2c carmine, Type I 55.00 20.00
Never hinged 120.00
On cover 27.50
Nos. 410-413 (4) 96.00 60.00

San Francisco, Cal., Feb. 20 to Dec. 4. Beware also of plentiful fakes in the marketplace of Nos. 410-413.

Franklin — A148

1912-14 Wmk. 190 ***Perf. 12***

414 A148 8c pale olive green 45.00 2.00
Never hinged 110.00
On cover 15.00
415 A148 9c sal red ('14) 55.00 13.50
Never hinged 130.00
On cover 50.00
416 A148 10c orange yellow 45.00 .75
Never hinged 110.00
On cover 2.70
a. 10c brown yellow *1,200.*
Never hinged *2,600.*
417 A148 12c cl brn ('14) 50.00 5.00
Never hinged 120.00
On cover 25.00
418 A148 15c gray 85.00 4.50
Never hinged 200.00
On cover 17.50
419 A148 20c ultra ('14) 200.00 18.50
Never hinged 450.00
On cover 150.00
420 A148 30c org red ('14) 125.00 17.50
Never hinged 280.00
On cover 250.00
421 A148 50c violet ('14) 450.00 30.00
Never hinged 1,000.
On cover 2,000.
Nos. 414-421 (8) 1,055. 91.75

No. 421 almost always has an offset of the frame lines on the back under the gum. No. 422 does not have this offset.

VALUES FOR VERY FINE STAMPS
Please note: Stamps are valued in the grade of Very Fine unless otherwise indicated.

1912, Feb. 12 Wmk. 191 ***Perf. 12***

422 A148 50c violet 260.00 22.50
Never hinged 600.00
On cover 2,000.
423 A148 $1 violet brown 550.00 75.00
Never hinged 1,200.
On cover 7,000.

Other stamps of type A148:

#431-440	*Single line wmk.*	*Perf. 10*
#460	*Double line wmk.*	*Perf. 10*
#470-478	*Unwmkd.*	*Perf. 10*
#508-518	*Unwmkd.*	*Perf. 11*

1914 Compound Perforations

As the Bureau of Engraving and Printing made the changeover to perf 10 from perf 12, in the normal course of their stamp production they perforated limited quantities of 1c, 2c and 5c stamps with the old 12-gauge perforations in one direction and the new 10-gauge perforations in the other direction. These were not production errors. These compound-perforation stamps previously were listed as Nos. 424a, 424b, 425c, 425d and 428a.

All examples of Nos. 423A-423E must be accompanied by certificates of authenticity issued by a recognized expertizing committee. Fakes made from perf 12, perf 10 and imperfs exist.

1914 Wmk. 190 ***Perf. 12x10***

423A A140 1c **green** *7,500.* *5,750.*
Never hinged —
On cover, pair 11,000.

Formerly No. 424a. Eight unused and 53 used examples are recorded. Value for unused is for a sound stamp with perfs touching or just cutting the design. Value for used is for a sound stamp in the grade of fine-very fine. Of the used examples, 20 are precanceled Quincy IL (very scarce) or Chicago (sometimes inverted). The block of four, single on postcard and pair on cover are each unique (top stamp of pair on cover with small piece missing).

423B A140 2c **rose red,** type I *175,000.* *18,500.*

Formerly No. 425d. One unused (a plate #7082 single) and 27 used examples are recorded. Value for used is for a sound stamp in the grade of fine-very fine. There are no precancels known on this issue.

423C A140 5c **blue** *20,000.*

Formerly No. 428a. 24 used examples are recorded. No unused examples are recorded. Three examples are precanceled: Tampa FL (2) and Rahway NJ (1). Value is for a sound stamp in the grade of fine-very fine. The pair is unique (one stamp creased, the other with a small tear).

1914 Wmk. 190 ***Perf. 10x12***

423D A140 1c **green** *16,000.*

Formerly No. 424b. 34 used examples are recorded. No unused examples are recorded. 32 examples are precanceled: Dayton OH (29), Buffalo NY (2) and Elkhart IN (1). Value is for a sound stamp in the grade of fine-very fine.

423E A140 2c **rose red,** type I —

Formerly No. 425c. Only one used example has been certified (by the Philatelic Foundation). It is well centered, has a machine cancel, and has small thinning and a crease.

1914-15 Wmk. 190 ***Perf. 10***

424 A140 1c green 2.50 .20
Never hinged 5.25
On cover .25
c. Vert. pair, imperf. horiz. *2,800.* *2,500.*
d. Booklet pane of 6 5.25 *7.50*
Never hinged 8.75
e. As "d," imperf. *2,000.*
f. Vert. pair, imperf. betw. and with straight edge at top *9,000.*

For former Nos. 424a and 424b, see Nos. 423A and 423D.

All known examples of No. 424e are without gum.

425 A140 2c rose red, Type I 2.30 .20
Never hinged 4.75
On cover .25
e. Booklet pane of 6 17.00 *25.00*
Never hinged 30.00
426 A140 3c dp vio, Type I 15.00 1.50
Never hinged 35.00
On cover 3.50
427 A140 4c brown 35.00 1.00
Never hinged 80.00
On cover 5.25
428 A140 5c blue 35.00 1.00
Never hinged 80.00
On cover 3.00
429 A140 6c red orange 50.00 2.00
Never hinged 115.00
On cover 9.00
430 A140 7c black 100.00 5.00
Never hinged 225.00
On cover 37.50
431 A148 8c pale olive green 37.50 3.00
Never hinged 87.50
On cover 8.00
432 A148 9c salmon red 50.00 9.00
Never hinged 115.00
On cover 27.50
433 A148 10c orange yellow 50.00 1.00
Never hinged 115.00
On cover 7.75
434 A148 11c dk grn ('15) 25.00 8.50
Never hinged 60.00
On cover 25.00
435 A148 12c claret brown 27.50 6.00
Never hinged 65.00
On cover 17.50
a. 12c copper red 32.50 7.00
Never hinged 75.00
On cover 20.00
437 A148 15c gray 135.00 7.25
Never hinged 300.00
On cover 52.50
438 A148 20c ultra 220.00 6.00
Never hinged 500.00
On cover 150.00
439 A148 30c orange red 260.00 16.00
Never hinged 600.00
On cover 250.00
440 A148 50c violet ('15) 575.00 16.00
Never hinged 1,300.
On cover 1,750.
Nos. 424-440 (16) 1,619. 83.65

For former Nos. 425c, 425d, and 428a, see Nos. 423E, 423B and 423C.

Coil Stamps

1914 ***Perf. 10 Horizontally***

441 A140 1c green 1.00 *1.50*
Never hinged 2.00
On cover 2.75
442 A140 2c carmine, Type I 10.00 *25.00*
Never hinged 22.50
On cover 35.00

1914 ***Perf. 10 Vertically***

443 A140 1c green 30.00 *40.00*
Never hinged 65.00
On cover 55.00
444 A140 2c carmine, Type I 50.00 25.00
Never hinged 125.00
On cover 35.00
445 A140 3c violet, Type I 250.00 225.00
Never hinged 575.00
On cover 300.00
446 A140 4c brown 140.00 140.00
Never hinged 325.00
On cover 190.00
447 A140 5c blue 50.00 100.00
Never hinged 110.00
On cover 125.00
Nos. 443-447 (5) 520.00 530.00

Beware also of plentiful fakes in the marketplace of Nos. 441-447.

TYPE II

Type II

TWO CENTS

Type II. Shading lines in ribbons as on type I.

The toga button, rope, and shading lines are heavy.

The shading lines of the face at the lock of hair end in a strong vertical curved line.

Used on rotary press printings only.

TYPE III

Type III

TWO CENTS

Type III. Two lines of shading in the curves of the ribbons.

Other characteristics similar to type II.

Used on rotary press printings only.

Fraudulently altered copies of Type III (Nos. 455, 488, 492 and 540) have had one line of shading scraped off to make them resemble Type II (Nos. 454, 487, 491 and 539).

ROTARY PRESS STAMPS

The Rotary Press stamps are printed from plates that are curved to fit around a cylinder. This curvature produces stamps that are slightly larger, either horizontally or vertically, than those printed from flat plates. Stamps from flat plates measure about 18½-19mm wide by 22mm high. When the impressions are placed sideways on the curved plates the stamps are 19½-20mm wide; when they are placed vertically the stamps are 23mm high.

Coil Stamps

Rotary Press Printing

1915-16 ***Perf. 10 Horizontally***

448 A140 1c green 7.50 *12.50*
Never hinged 16.00
On cover 20.00
449 A140 2c red, Type I 3,000. 600.00
Never hinged 6,500.
On cover 1,350.
450 A140 2c car, Type III ('16) 12.50 *20.00*
Never hinged 27.50
On cover 30.00

1914-16 ***Perf. 10 Vertically***

452 A140 1c green 10.00 *15.00*
Never hinged 21.00
On cover 20.00
453 A140 2c carmine rose, Type I 150.00 15.00
Never hinged 325.00
On cover 20.00
454 A140 2c red, Type II 82.50 20.00
Never hinged 175.00
On cover 40.00
455 A140 2c car, Type III 8.50 1.75
Never hinged 19.00
On cover 3.00
456 A140 3c violet, Type I ('16) 250.00 135.00
Never hinged 525.00
On cover 225.00
457 A140 4c brown ('16) 25.00 25.00
Never hinged 55.00
On cover 47.50
458 A140 5c blue ('16) 30.00 25.00
Never hinged 65.00
On cover 47.50
Nos. 452-458 (7) 556.00 236.75

1914, June 30 ***Imperf.***

459 A140 2c car, Type I 220.00 *1,300.*
Never hinged 350.00

No. 459 is a horizontal coil.

The used value is for a copy with a contemporaneous cancel.

Flat Plate Printings

1915, Feb. 8 Wmk. 191 ***Perf. 10***

460 A148 $1 violet black 850. 140.
Never hinged 1,900.
On cover 12,000.

1915, June 17 Wmk. 190 ***Perf. 11***

461	A140 2c pale carmine red, Type I	150.	*350.*
	Never hinged	325.	
	On cover		1,200.

Beware of fraudulently perforated examples of No. 409 being offered as No. 461.
The used value is for an example with a contemporaneous cancel.

Unwatermarked

From 1916 onward all postage stamps except Nos. 519 and 832b are on unwatermarked paper.

1916-17 Unwmk. ***Perf. 10***

462	A140 1c green	7.00	.35
	Never hinged	16.00	
	On cover		.50
a.	Booklet pane of 6	9.50	*12.50*
	Never hinged	16.00	
463	A140 2c car, Type I	4.50	.40
	Never hinged	10.00	
	On cover		.45
a.	Booklet pane of 6	110.00	*110.00*
	Never hinged	180.00	
464	A140 3c vio, Type I	75.00	17.50
	Never hinged	170.00	
	On cover		42.50
465	A140 4c org brn	45.00	2.50
	Never hinged	100.00	
	On cover		11.00
466	A140 5c blue	75.00	2.50
	Never hinged	170.00	
	On cover		13.00
467	A140 5c car (error in plate of 2c, '17)	*550.00*	850.00
	Never hinged	1,100.	
	On cover		5,000.
468	A140 6c red orange	95.00	9.00
	Never hinged	210.00	
	On cover		37.50
469	A140 7c black	130.00	15.00
	Never hinged	290.00	
	On cover		45.00
470	A148 8c olive green	60.00	8.00
	Never hinged	135.00	
	On cover		27.50
471	A148 9c salmon red	60.00	18.50
	Never hinged	135.00	
	On cover		42.50
472	A148 10c orange yel	110.00	2.50
	Never hinged	250.00	
	On cover		8.50
473	A148 11c dark green	45.00	18.50
	Never hinged	100.00	
	On cover		47.50
474	A148 12c claret brn	60.00	7.50
	Never hinged	135.00	
	On cover		22.50
475	A148 15c gray	200.00	16.00
	Never hinged	440.00	
	On cover		87.50
476	A148 20c lt ultra	250.00	17.50
	Never hinged	575.00	
	On cover		725.00
476A	A148 30c orange red	*4,000.*	
	Never hinged	*8,000.*	
477	A148 50c lt vio ('17)	1,100.	80.00
	Never hinged	2,400.	
	On cover		2,250.
478	A148 $1 violet black	800.00	25.00
	Never hinged	1,800.	
	On cover		3,000.
	Nos. 462-466,468-476,477-478 (16)	3,116.	240.75

No. 476A is valued in the grade of fine.

Types of 1903 Issue

1917, Mar. 22 ***Perf. 10***

479	A127 $2 dark blue	260.00	42.50
	Never hinged	575.00	
480	A128 $5 light green	220.00	40.00
	Never hinged	475.00	
	On cover		1,250.

Type Ia

TWO CENTS

Type Ia. Design characteristics similar to type I except that all lines of design are stronger.
The toga button, toga rope and rope shading lines are heavy. The latter characteristics are those of type II, which, however, occur only on impressions from rotary plates.
Used only on flat plates 10208 and 10209.

Type II

THREE CENTS

Type II. The top line of the toga rope is strong and the rope shading lines are heavy and complete.
The line between the lips is heavy.
Used on both flat plate and rotary press printings.

1916-17 ***Imperf.***

481	A140 1c green	.95	.65
	Never hinged	1.90	
	On cover		1.50
482	A140 2c car, Type I	1.30	1.25
	Never hinged	2.60	
	On cover		2.50
482A	A140 2c dp rose, Type Ia		*55,000.*
	On cover		60,000.

No. 482A was issued imperforate but all copies were privately perforated with large oblong perforations at the sides (Schermack type III).
No. 500 exists with imperforate top sheet margin. Copies have been altered by trimming perforations. Some also have faked Schermack perfs.

483	A140 3c vio, Type I ('17)	11.00	7.50
	Never hinged	24.00	
	On cover		20.00
484	A140 3c vio, Type II	8.50	5.00
	Never hinged	19.00	
	On cover		11.50
485	A140 5c car (error in plate of 2c) ('17)	*12,000.*	
	Never hinged	20,000.	
	Block of 9, #485 in middle	22,500.	
	Never hinged	32,500.	
	Block of 12, two middle stamps #485	42,500.	
	Never hinged	52,500.	

Although No. 485 is listed as a single stamp, such examples are not seen in the marketplace. The stamp is collected as the center stamp in a block of 9 with 8 No. 482 (the first value given being with No. 485 never hinged) or as two center stamps in a block of 12 (the first value given being with both examples of No. 485 never hinged). A second value is given for each block with all stamps in the block never hinged.

Coil Stamps

Rotary Press Printing

1916-19 ***Perf. 10 Horizontally***

486	A140 1c green ('18)	.85	.85
	Never hinged	1.75	
	On cover		1.15
487	A140 2c car, Type II	12.50	10.00
	Never hinged	26.00	
	On cover		15.00
488	A140 2c car, Type III ('19)	2.40	*3.25*
	Never hinged	5.00	
	On cover		5.00
489	A140 3c vio, Type I ('17)	4.50	2.25
	Never hinged	10.00	
	On cover		3.50
	Nos. 486-489 (4)	20.25	16.35

1916-22 ***Perf. 10 Vertically***

490	A140 1c green	.50	*.60*
	Never hinged	1.05	
	On cover		.80
491	A140 2c car, Type II	2,500.	750.00
	Never hinged	5,000.	
	On cover		1,100.
492	A140 2c car, Type III	9.00	1.00
	Never hinged	19.00	
	On cover		1.40
493	A140 3c vio, Type I ('17)	14.00	4.50
	Never hinged	30.00	
	On cover		8.00
494	A140 3c vio, Type II ('18)	10.00	2.00
	Never hinged	21.50	
495	A140 4c org brown ('17)	10.00	6.00
	Never hinged	21.50	
	On cover		10.00
496	A140 5c blue ('19)	3.25	2.50
	Never hinged	7.00	
	On cover		3.00
497	A148 10c org yel ('22)	19.00	15.00
	Never hinged	40.00	
	On cover		20.00
	Nos. 490,492-497 (7)	65.75	31.60

See note above #448 regarding #487, 491.

Blind Perfs.

Listings of imperforate-between varieties are for examples which show no trace of "blind perfs.," traces of impressions from the perforating pins which do not cut into the paper.

Types of 1912-14 Issue

Flat Plate Printings

1917-19 ***Perf. 11***

498	A140 1c green	.35	.25
	Never hinged	.75	
	On cover		.30
a.	Vert. pair, imperf. horiz.	900.00	
	Never hinged	*1,750.*	
b.	Horiz. pair, imperf. btwn.	*575.00*	
	Never hinged	*1,200.*	
c.	Vert. pair, imperf. btwn.	*700.00*	—
d.	Double impression	250.00	4,000.
e.	Booklet pane of 6	2.50	*2.00*
	Never hinged	4.25	
f.	Booklet pane of 30	*1,150.*	
	Never hinged	*1,800.*	
g.	Perf. 10 at top or bottom	*7,500.*	*30,000.*
	Never hinged	*11,500.*	
499	A140 2c rose, Type I	.35	.25
	Never hinged	.75	
	On cover		.30
a.	Vert. pair, imperf. horiz.	600.00	
	Never hinged	1,200.	
b.	Horiz. pair, imperf. vert.	*375.00*	*225.00*
	Never hinged	*750.00*	
c.	Vert. pair, imperf. btwn.	*1,000.*	*300.00*
e.	Booklet pane of 6	4.00	*2.50*
	Never hinged	6.75	
f.	Booklet pane of 30	*28,000.*	—
	Never hinged	*38,000.*	
g.	Double impression	200.00	—
	Never hinged	*400.00*	
	On cover		750.00
h.	2c lake, type I	500.00	350.00
	On cover		—
	Never hinged	1,000.	

No. 499b is valued in the grade of fine.

500	A140 2c dp rose, Type Ia	280.00	240.00
	Never hinged	600.00	
	On cover		650.00
501	A140 3c lt vio, Type I	11.00	.40
	Never hinged	25.00	
	On cover		.50
b.	Booklet pane of 6	75.00	*60.00*
	Never hinged	125.00	
c.	Vert. pair, imperf. horiz.	*2,500.*	
	Never hinged	*3,500.*	
d.	Double impression	*3,500.*	*2,750.*
502	A140 3c dk vio, Type II	14.00	.75
	Never hinged	32.50	
	On cover		1.00
b.	Booklet pane of 6	60.00	*55.00*
	Never hinged	100.00	
c.	Vert. pair, imperf. horiz.	*1,400.*	*750.00*

Never hinged 2,750.
On cover 1,500.
d. Double impression 750.00 750.00
e. Perf. 10 at top or bottom 15,000. 12,500.
Never hinged 21,500.

503 A140 4c brown 10.00 .40
Never hinged 22.50
On cover 2.10
b. Double impression —

504 A140 5c blue 9.00 .35
Never hinged 20.00
On cover .45
a. Horiz. pair, imperf. btwn. 3,250. —
b. Double impression 2,000. 900.00

505 A140 5c rose (error in plate of 2c) 350.00 550.00
Never hinged 700.00
On cover 2,250.

506 A140 6c red orange 12.00 .40
Never hinged 27.50
On cover 2.50
a. Perf. 10 at top or bottom 4,750. 6,500.

507 A140 7c black 27.50 1.25
Never hinged 65.00
On cover 7.75
a. Perf. 10 at top 20,000.

508 A148 8c olive bister 12.00 .65
Never hinged 27.50
On cover 2.75
b. Vert. pair, imperf. btwn. — —
c. Perf. 10 at top or bottom 15,000.

509 A148 9c salmon red 13.00 1.75
Never hinged 30.00
On cover 13.00
a. Perf. 10 at top or bottom 4,000. 6,500.

510 A148 10c orange yell 17.50 .25
Never hinged 40.00
On cover 2.00
a. 10c brown yellow 1,500. —
Never hinged 2,250.

511 A148 11c lt green 9.00 2.50
Never hinged 20.00
On cover 8.50
a. Perf. 10 at top or bottom 5,000. 4,500.
Never hinged 7,500.

512 A148 12c claret brown 9.00 .40
Never hinged 20.00
On cover 4.00
a. 12c brown carmine 10.50 .50
Never hinged 22.50
On cover 4.50
b. Perf. 10 at top or bottom 17,500. 6,000.

513 A148 13c apple grn ('19) 11.00 6.00
Never hinged 25.00
On cover 19.00

514 A148 15c gray 37.50 1.50
Never hinged 85.00
On cover 25.00
a. Perf. 10 at top or bottom 10,000.

515 A148 20c light ultra 45.00 .45
Never hinged 105.00
On cover 75.00
b. Vert. pair, imperf. btwn. 2,000. 1,750.
c. Double impression 1,250.
d. Perf. 10 at top or bottom — 15,000.

No. 515b is valued in the grade of fine.

Beware of pairs with blind perforations inside the design of the top stamp that are offered as No. 515b.

516 A148 30c orange red 37.50 1.50
Never hinged 85.00
On cover 150.00
a. Perf. 10 at top or bottom 20,000. 7,500.
Never hinged 40,000.
b. Double impression —

517 A148 50c red violet 65.00 [illegible]
Never hinged [illegible]
On cover [illegible]
b. Vert. [illegible] — 10,000.
[illegible] [illegible]op or bottom —

[illegible] A148 $1 violet brown 50.00 1.50
Never hinged 120.00
On cover 550.00
b. $1 deep brown 1,800. 1,250.
Never hinged 3,750.

Nos. 498-504,506-518 (20) 670.70 261.30

No. 518b is valued in the grade of fine to very fine.

Type of 1908-09 Issue

1917, Oct. 10 Wmk. 191 *Perf. 11*

519 A139 2c carmine 450.00 *1,400.*
Never hinged 900.00
On cover 2,750.

Fraudulently perforated copies of No. 344 are offered as No. 519. Obtaining a certificate from a recognized expertizing committee is strongly recommended.

The used value is for a stamp with a contemporaneous cancel.

Franklin — A149

1918, Aug. 19 Unwmk. *Perf. 11*

523 A149 $2 orange red & blk 625.00 250.00
Never hinged 1,300.
On cover 2,000.

524 A149 $5 dp grn & black 200.00 35.00
Never hinged 425.00
On cover 2,500.

See No. 547 for $2 carmine & black.

Types of 1912-14 Issue

Type IV

TWO CENTS

Type IV. Top line of toga rope is broken. Shading lines in toga button are so arranged that the curving of the first and last form a "D (reversed) ID."

Line of color in left "2" is very thin and usually broken.

Used on offset printings only.

Type V

TWO CENTS

Type V. Top line of toga is complete.

Five vertical shading lines in to[illegible]

Line of c[illegible] ally [illegible]

[illegible]ose and lip are as [illegible] the diagram.

Used on offset printings only.

Type Va

TWO CENTS

Type Va. Characteristics same as type V, except in shading dots of nose. Third row from bottom has 4 dots instead of 6. Overall height of type Va is ⅓mm less than type V.

Used on offset printings only.

Type VI

TWO CENTS

Type VI. General characteristics same as type V, except that line of color in left "2" is very heavy.

Used on offset printings only.

Type VII

TWO CENTS

Type VII. Line of color in left "2" is invariably continuous, clearly defined, and heavier than in type V or Va, but not as heavy as in type VI.

Additional vertical row of dots has been added to the upper lip.

Numerous additional dots have been added to hair on top of head.

Used on offset printings only.

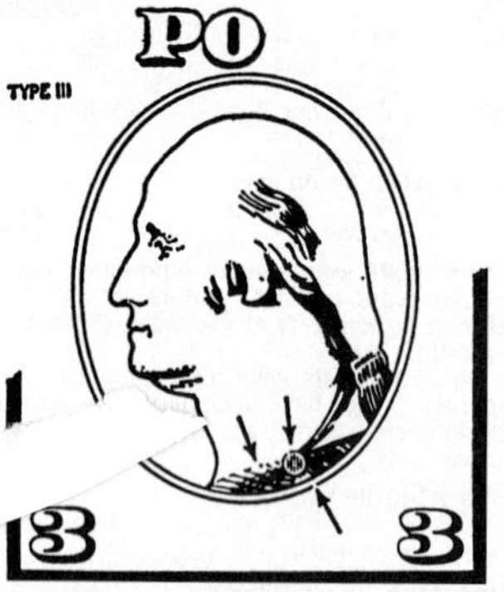

Type III

THREE CENTS

Type III. The top line of the toga rope is strong but the fifth shading line is missing as in type I.

Center shading line of the toga button consists of two dashes with a central dot.

The "P" and "O" of "POSTAGE" are separated by a line of color.

The frame line at the bottom of the vignette is complete.

Used on offset printings only.

Type IV

THREE CENTS

Type IV. Shading lines of toga rope are complete.

Second and fourth shading lines in toga button are broken in the middle and the third line is continuous with a dot in the center.

"P" and "O" of "POSTAGE" are joined.

Frame line at bottom of vignette is broken.

Used on offset printings only.

1918-20 Offset Printing *Perf. 11*

525 A140 1c gray green 2.50 .90
Never hinged 6.00
On cover 1.75
a. 1c dark green 7.00 1.75
Never hinged 17.50
c. Horiz. pair, imperf. btwn. 100.00 700.00
d. Double impression 40.00 —
Never hinged 90.00

526 A140 2c car, Type IV ('20) 27.50 4.00
Never hinged 62.50
On cover 11.00

527 A140 2c car, Type V ('20) 20.00 1.25
Never hinged 45.00
On cover 2.75
a. Double impression 75.00 —
Never hinged 160.00
b. Vert. pair, imperf. horiz. 850.00
c. Horiz. pair, imperf. vert. 1,000. —

528 A140 2c car, Type Va ('20) 9.50 .40
Never hinged 22.50
On cover .75
c. Double impression 55.00
Never hinged 125.00
g. Vert. pair, imperf. btwn. 2,500.

528A A140 2c car, Type VI ('20) 52.50 2.00
Never hinged 125.00
On cover 3.75
d. Double impression 180.00 —
Never hinged 400.00
f. Vert. pair, imperf. horiz. —
h. Vert. pair, imperf. btwn. 1,000.

528B A140 2c car, Type VII ('20) 22.50 .75
Never hinged 55.00
On cover 1.00
e. Double impression 80.00 400.00

529 A140 3c vio, Type III 3.60 .50
Never hinged 8.00
On cover .60
a. Double impression 45.00 —
Never hinged 100.00
b. Printed on both sides 2,500.

530 A140 3c pur, Type IV 1.80 .30
Never hinged 4.25
On cover .35
a. Double impression 35.00 —
b. Printed on both sides 350.00
Never hinged 650.00
c. Triple impression, Type IV 1,750.

Nos. 525-530 (8) 139.90 10.10

1918-20 *Imperf.*

531 A140 1c green ('19) 12.00 12.00
Never hinged 25.00
On cover 17.50

532 A140 2c car rose, Type IV ('20) 40.00 35.00
Never hinged 85.00
On cover 70.00

533 A140 2c car, Type V ('20) 110.00 95.00
Never hinged 230.00
On cover 210.00

534 A140 2c car, Type Va ('20) 14.00 9.00
Never hinged 30.00
On cover 16.00

534A A140 2c car, Type VI ('20) 47.50 32.50
Never hinged 100.00
On cover 45.00

534B A140 2c car, Type VII ('20) 2,100. 1,250.
Never hinged 3,600.
On cover 5,000.

535 A140 3c vio, Type IV 9.50 5.00
Never hinged 21.00
On cover 11.00
a. Double impression 95.00 —
Never hinged 200.00

Nos. 531-534A,535 (6) 233.00 188.50

1919, Aug. 15 *Perf. 12½*

536 A140 1c gray green 22.50 *27.50*
Never hinged 50.00
On cover 150.00
a. Horiz. pair, imperf. vert. *1,200.*

Victory Issue

"Victory" and Flags of the Allies — A150

Flat Plate Printing

1919, Mar. 3 **Engr.** ***Perf. 11***

537	A150	3c violet	10.00	3.25
		Never hinged	20.00	
		On cover		7.50
a.		3c deep red violet	*1,250.*	*2,250.*
		Never hinged	*2,100.*	
		On cover		—
b.		3c light reddish violet	125.00	35.00
		Never hinged	250.00	
		On cover		150.00
c.		3c red violet	150.00	40.00
		Never hinged	300.00	
		On cover		175.00

Victory of Allies in World War I.
No. 537a is valued in the grade of fine.

Rotary Press Printings

1919 ***Perf. 11x10***

Size: 19½ to 20mm wide by 22 to 22¼mm high

538	A140	1c green	11.00	8.50
		Never hinged	25.00	
		On cover		22.50
a.		Vert. pair, imperf. horiz.	50.00	*100.00*
		Never hinged	90.00	
539	A140	2c carmine rose, Type II	2,850.	*5,250.*
		Never hinged	4,250.	
		On cover		60,000.
540	A140	2c carmine rose, Type III	13.00	9.50
		Never hinged	30.00	
		On cover		25.00
a.		Vert. pair, imperf. horiz.	50.00	*100.00*
		Never hinged	100.00	
b.		Horiz. pair, imperf. vert.	*1,750.*	
541	A140	3c vio, Type II	45.00	30.00
		Never hinged	110.00	
		On cover		100.00

The part perforate varieties of Nos. 538a and 540a were issued in sheets and may be had in blocks; similar part perforate varieties, Nos. 490 and 492, are from coils and are found only in strips.

See note over No. 448 regarding No. 539.
No. 539 is valued in the grade of fine.

Size: 19x22½-22¾mm

1920, May 26 ***Perf. 10x11***

542	A140	1c green	14.00	1.50
		Never hinged	35.00	
		On cover		5.50

Size: 19x22½mm

1921 ***Perf. 10***

543	A140	1c green	.70	.40
		Never hinged	1.75	
		On cover		.45
a.		Horiz. pair, imperf. btwn.	*2,750.*	

Size: 19x22½mm

1922 ***Perf. 11***

544	A140	1c green	*22,500.*	*3,750.*
		Never hinged	*36,500.*	
		On cover		6,500.

No. 544 is valued in the grade of fine.

Size: 19½-20x22mm

1921 ***Perf. 11***

545	A140	1c green	200.00	210.00
		Never hinged	500.00	
		On cover		1,800.
546	A140	2c car rose, Type III	125.00	*175.00*
		Never hinged	300.00	
		On cover		775.00
a.		Perf. 10 on left side	*7,500.*	*10,000.*

Flat Plate Printing

1920, Nov. 1 ***Perf. 11***

547	A149	$2 carmine & black	160.00	40.00
		Never hinged	350.00	
		On cover		1,000.
a.		$2 lake & black	225.00	40.00
		Never hinged	500.00	

Pilgrim Tercentenary Issue

"Mayflower" A151

Landing of the Pilgrims — A152

Signing of the Compact — A153

1920, Dec. 21 ***Perf. 11***

548	A151	1c green	4.75	2.25
		Never hinged	12.00	
		On cover		3.50
549	A152	2c carmine rose	6.50	1.60
		Never hinged	17.50	
		On cover		2.50
550	A153	5c deep blue	45.00	14.00
		Never hinged	110.00	
		On cover		22.50
		Nos. 548-550 (3)	56.25	17.85
		Nos. 548-550, never hinged	139.50	

Tercentenary of the landing of the Pilgrims at Plymouth, Mass.

Nathan Hale A154

Franklin A155

Harding A156

Washington A157

Lincoln A158

Martha Washington A159

Theodore Roosevelt A160

Garfield A161

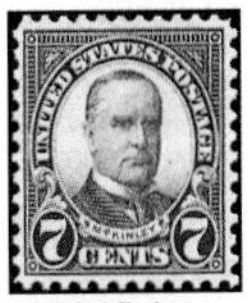

McKinley A162

Grant A163

Jefferson A164

Monroe A165

Rutherford B. Hayes A166

Grover Cleveland A167

American Indian A168

Statue of Liberty A169

Golden Gate — A170

Niagara Falls — A171

American Buffalo A172

Arlington Amphitheater A173

Lincoln Memorial A174

US Capitol A175

Head of Freedom Statue, Capitol Dome — A176

1922-25 ***Perf. 11***

551	A154	½c olive brn ('25)	.25	.20
		Never hinged	.50	
552	A155	1c dp grn ('23)	1.30	.20
		Never hinged	2.75	
a.		Booklet pane of 6	7.50	*4.00*
		Never hinged	12.50	
553	A156	1½c yel brn ('25)	2.30	.20
		Never hinged	4.75	
554	A157	2c car ('23)	1.20	.20
		Never hinged	2.50	
		On cover		.25
a.		Horiz. pair, imperf. vert.	*250.00*	
b.		Vert. pair, imperf. horiz.	*4,000.*	
c.		Booklet pane of 6	7.00	*3.00*
		Never hinged	12.00	
d.		Perf. 10 at top or bottom	*7,000.*	5,000.
		On cover		8,000.

No. 554d unused is unique. It is never hinged and has a natural straight edge at left. Value represents sale price at 2001 auction.

555	A158	3c violet ('23)	17.50	1.25
		Never hinged	37.50	
556	A159	4c yel brn ('23)	20.00	.50
		Never hinged	42.50	
		On cover		3.00
a.		Vert. pair, imperf. horiz.	*10,500.*	
b.		Perf. 10 at top or bottom	*3,000.*	*15,000.*
557	A160	5c dark blue	20.00	.30
		Never hinged	42.50	
a.		Imperf., pair	*2,000.*	
b.		Horiz. pair, imperf. vert.	—	
c.		Perf. 10 at top or bottom	—	*11,000.*
		On cover		17,500.
558	A161	6c red orange	37.50	1.00
		Never hinged	80.00	
559	A162	7c black ('23)	8.50	.75
		Never hinged	18.00	
560	A163	8c ol grn ('23)	50.00	1.00
		Never hinged	105.00	
561	A164	9c rose ('23)	14.00	1.25
		Never hinged	29.00	
562	A165	10c orange ('23)	17.50	.35
		Never hinged	37.50	
a.		Vert. pair, imperf. horiz.	*2,250.*	
		Never hinged	*3,250.*	
b.		Imperf., pair	*2,500.*	
c.		Perf. 10 at top or bottom	—	*8,500.*
563	A166	11c light blue	1.40	.60
		Never hinged	2.90	
a.		11c light bluish green	1.40	.60
		Never hinged	2.90	
d.		Imperf., pair		*20,000.*
564	A167	12c brn vio ('23)	6.00	.35
		Never hinged	13.00	
a.		Horiz. pair, imperf. vert.	*1,750.*	
565	A168	14c blue ('23)	4.00	.90
		Never hinged	8.50	
566	A169	15c gray	20.00	.30
		Never hinged	42.50	
567	A170	20c car rose ('23)	20.00	.30
		Never hinged	42.50	
a.		Horiz. pair, imperf. vert.	*2,000.*	
568	A171	25c yell grn	18.00	.75
		Never hinged	37.50	
b.		Vert. pair, imperf. horiz.	*2,500.*	
c.		Perf. 10 at one side	*5,000.*	*11,000.*
		Never hinged	*7,500.*	

No. 568b is valued in the grade of fine.

569	A172	30c ol brn ('23)	30.00	.60
		Never hinged	65.00	

570 A173 50c lilac 47.50 .40
Never hinged 100.00
571 A174 $1 vio brown ('23) 45.00 .65
Never hinged 95.00
572 A175 $2 dp blue ('23) 80.00 9.00
Never hinged 175.00
573 A176 $5 car & bl ('23) 110.00 15.00
Never hinged 240.00
a. $5 car lake & dark bl 200.00 20.00
Never hinged 375.00
Nos. 551-573 (23) 571.95 36.05
Nos. 551-573, never hinged 1,222.

No. 556a is unique. No. 562b is valued without gum and without blue pencil defacing lines. No. 568b is valued in the grade of fine.

For listings of other perforated stamps of designs A154 to A176 see

#578-579	*Perf. 11x10*
#581-591	*Perf. 10*
#594-595	*Perf. 11*
#632-642, 653, 692-696	*Perf. 11x10½*
#697-701	*Perf. 10½x11*

This series includes Nos. 622-623 (perf. 11).

1923-25 ***Imperf.***
575 A155 1c green 5.25 5.00
Never hinged 11.00
576 A156 1½c yel brn ('25) 1.30 1.50
Never hinged 2.70
577 A157 2c carmine 1.40 1.25
Never hinged 2.90
Nos. 575-577 (3) 7.95 7.75
Nos. 575-577, never hinged 16.60

The 1½c A156 rotary press imperforate is listed as No. 631.

Rotary Press Printings
Perf. 11x10

578 A155 1c green 85.00 *160.00*
Never hinged 190.00
On cover 700.00
579 A157 2c carmine 80.00 *140.00*
Never hinged 175.00
On cover 400.00

Nos. 578-579 were made from coil waste of Nos. 597, 599 and measure approximately 19¾x22¼mm.

1923-26 ***Perf. 10***
581 A155 1c green 11.00 .75
Never hinged 22.50
582 A156 1½c brown ('25) 5.50 .65
Never hinged 11.50
583 A157 2c car ('24) 2.75 .30
Never hinged 5.75
On cover 2.50
a. Booklet pane of 6 95.00 *150.00*
Never hinged 175.00
584 A158 3c violet ('25) 30.00 3.00
Never hinged 62.50
585 A159 4c yel brn ('25) 18.00 .65
Never hinged 37.50
On cover 15.00
586 A160 5c blue ('25) 18.00 .40
Never hinged 37.50
a. Horiz. pair, imperf. vert. 8,000.
587 A161 6c red org ('25) 9.25 .60
Never hinged 20.00
588 A162 7c black ('26) 12.50 6.25
Never hinged 26.00
589 A163 8c ol grn ('26) 27.50 4.50
Never hinged 57.50
590 A164 9c rose ('26) 6.00 2.50
Never hinged 13.00
591 A165 10c orange ('25) 60.00 .50
Never hinged 125.00
Nos. 581-591 (11) 200.50 20.10
Nos. 581-591, never hinged 433.75

No. 586a is unique, precanceled, with average centering and small faults, and it is valued as such.

Perf. 11

594 A155 1c green *16,000.* 15,000.
On cover 25,000.
595 A157 2c carmine 275.00 *375.00*
Never hinged 550.00
On cover 550.00

Nos. 594-595 were made from coil waste of Nos. 597 and 599, and measure approximately 19¾x22¼mm.

No. 594 unused is valued without gum; both unused and used are valued with perforations just touching frameline on one side.

Perf. 11

596 A155 1c green *130,000.*
Precanceled *110,000.*

No. 596 was made from rotary press sheet waste and measures approximately 19¼x22½mm. A majority of the copies carry the Bureau precancel "Kansas City, Mo." No. 596 is valued in the grade of fine.

ROTARY PRESS DOUBLE PAPER
The web of paper used on rotary presses must be continuous, therefore any break in the paper must be lapped and pasted, causing the "double paper" varieties. These are no longer listed since they may occur on any rotary press stamp.

Type I

Type II

Type I

Type II

Type I. No heavy hair lines at top center of head. Outline of left acanthus scroll generally faint at top and toward base at left side.

Type II. The heavy hair lines at top center of head; two being outstanding in the white area. Outline of left acanthus scroll very strong and clearly defined at top (under left edge of lettered panel) and at lower curve (above and to left of numeral oval). Type II is found only on Nos. 599A and 634A.

Coil Stamps
Rotary Press Printing

1923-29 ***Perf. 10 Vertically***
597 A155 1c green .25 .20
Never hinged .50
598 A156 1½c brown ('25) .90 .20
Never hinged 1.80
599 A157 2c car, Type I ('23) .35 .20
Never hinged .70
On cover 1.10
b. 2c carmine lake, I, never hinged *750.00*
599A A157 2c car, Type II ('29) 120.00 15.00
Never hinged 225.00
On cover 30.00
600 A158 3c violet ('24) 6.25 .20
Never hinged 12.50
On cover 6.00
601 A159 4c yellow brown 3.75 .35
Never hinged 7.50
On cover 14.00
602 A160 5c dk bl ('24) 1.50 .20
Never hinged 3.00
603 A165 10c orange ('24) 3.50 .20
Never hinged 7.00

Perf. 10 Horizontally

604 A155 1c green ('24) .30 .20
Never hinged .60
605 A156 1½c yel brn ('25) .30 .20
Never hinged .60
606 A157 2c carmine .30 .20
Never hinged .60
On cover 3.50
a. 2c carmine lake, never hinged *150.00*
Nos. 597-599,600-606 (10) 17.40 2.15
Nos. 597-599, 600-606, never hinged 34.80

Harding Memorial Issue

Warren G. Harding — A177

Flat Plate Printing
(19¼x22¼mm)

1923, Sept. 1 ***Perf. 11***
610 A177 2c black .55 .25
Never hinged 1.10
On cover .30
a. Horiz. pair, imperf. vert. *1,750.*

1923, Nov. 15 ***Imperf.***
611 A177 2c black 5.00 4.00
Never hinged 10.50

Rotary Press Printing
(19¼x22½mm)

1923, Sept. 12 ***Perf. 10***
612 A177 2c black 16.00 1.75
On cover 3.25
Never hinged 33.00

1923 ***Perf. 11***
613 A177 2c black *45,000.*

Tribute to President Warren G. Harding, who died August 2, 1923.
Nos. 610a, 613 valued in the grade of fine.

Huguenot-Walloon Tercentenary Issue

"New Netherland" A178

Landing at Fort Orange A179

Monument to Jan Ribault at Duvall County, Fla. — A180

Flat Plate Printings

1924, May 1 ***Perf. 11***
614 A178 1c dark green 2.25 3.25
Never hinged 4.25
On cover 4.50
615 A179 2c carmine rose 4.50 2.25
Never hinged 8.75
On cover 3.50
616 A180 5c dark blue 19.00 13.00
Never hinged 37.50
Nos. 614-616 (3) 25.75 18.50
Nos. 614-616, never hinged 50.50

Tercentenary of the settling of the Walloons and in honor of the Huguenots.

Lexington-Concord Issue

Washington at Cambridge A181

"Birth of Liberty," by Henry Sandham A182

The Minute Man, by Daniel Chester French A183

1925, Apr. 4 ***Perf. 11***
617 A181 1c deep green 2.00 2.50
Never hinged 4.00
On cover 3.75
618 A182 2c carmine rose 4.25 4.00
Never hinged 8.00
On cover 5.50
619 A183 5c dark blue 17.50 13.00
Never hinged 35.00
Nos. 617-619 (3) 23.75 19.50
Nos. 617-619, never hinged 47.00

150th anniv. of the Battle of Lexington-Concord.

Norse-American Issue

Sloop "Restaurationen" A184

Viking Ship A185

1925, May 18 ***Perf. 11***
620 A184 2c carmine & black 3.75 3.00
Never hinged 7.00
On cover 4.50
621 A185 5c dk blue & black 12.00 11.00
Never hinged 24.00

100th anniv. of the arrival in NY on Oct. 9, 1825, of the sloop "Restaurationen" with the first group of immigrants from Norway to the US.

Benjamin Harrison A186

Woodrow Wilson A187

1925-26 ***Perf. 11***
622 A186 13c green ('26) 12.00 .75
Never hinged 22.50
623 A187 17c black 13.00 .30
Never hinged 25.00

Sesquicentennial Exposition Issue

Liberty Bell — A188

1926, May 10 ***Perf. 11***
627 A188 2c carmine rose 2.75 .50
Never hinged 4.50
On cover 1.00

150th anniv. of the Declaration of Independence, Philadelphia, June 1-Dec. 1.

Statue of John Ericsson — A189

Alexander Hamilton's Battery — A190

Ericsson Memorial Issue

1926, May 29 ***Perf. 11***
628 A189 5c gray lilac 6.00 3.25
Never hinged 9.50

John Ericsson, builder of the "Monitor."

Battle of White Plains Issue

1926, Oct. 18 *Perf. 11*

629 A190 2c carmine rose 2.00 1.70
Never hinged 3.25
On cover 2.25

Battle of White Plains, NY, 150th anniv.

The existence of a genuine, no-spliced No. 629a has been questioned by specialists. The editors would like to see evidence of a non-spliced pair, imperf between.

International Philatelic Exhibition
Souvenir Sheet

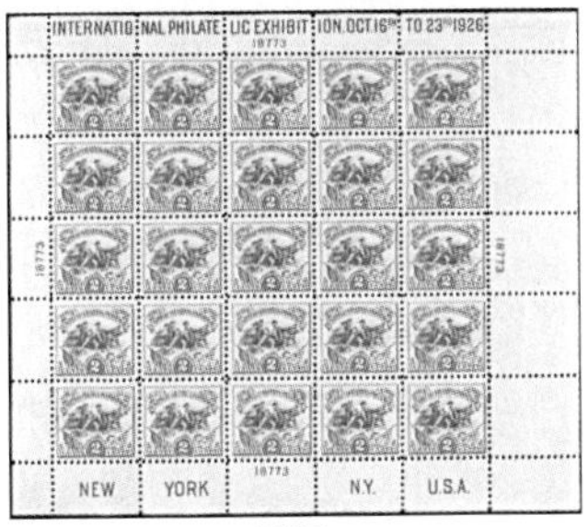

A190a

Illustration reduced.

1926, Oct. 18 *Perf. 11*

630 A190a 2c carmine rose, sheet of 25 375.00 450.00
Never hinged 600.00
On cover —

Intl. Phil. Exhib. in NYC, Oct. 16-23. Size: 158-160¼x136-146½mm.

Condition Valued:

Centering: Overall centering will average very fine, but individual stamps may be better or worse.

Perforations: No folds along rows of perforations.

Gum: There may be some light gum bends but no gum creases.

Hinging: There may be hinge marks in the selvage and on up to two or three stamps, but no heavy hingling or hinge remnants (except in the ungummed portion of the wide selvage).

Margins: Top panes should have about ½ inch bottom margin and 1 inch top margin.

Bottom panes should have about ½ inch top margin and just under ¾ inch bottom margin. Both will have one wide side (usually 1 inch plus) and one narrow (½ inch) side margin. The wide margin corner will have a small diagonal notch on top panes.

Types of 1922-26

Rotary Press Printings

1926, Aug. 27 *Imperf.*

631 A156 1½c yellow brown 1.90 1.70
Never hinged 2.75

1926-34 *Perf. 11x10½*

632 A155 1c green ('27) .20 .20
Never hinged .20
a. Booklet pane of 6 5.00 *4.00*
Never hinged 8.00
b. Vert. pair, imperf. btwn. *3,500.* *125.00*
Never hinged *5,500.*
c. Horiz. pair, imperf. btwn. *5,000.*

No. 632c is valued in the grade of fine and never hinged. It is possibly unique.

633 A156 1½c yel brown ('27) 1.70 .20
Never hinged 2.60
634 A157 2c car, Type I .20 .20
Never hinged .20
On cover .20
b. 2c carmine lake *500.00* —
Never hinged *900.00*
c. Horiz. pair, imperf. btwn. *7,000.*
d. Booklet pane of 6 1.50 *1.50*
Never hinged 2.50
e. As "d," carmine lake *2,000.*
Never hinged *4,000.*
634A A157 2c car, Type II ('28) 350.00 13.50
Never hinged 650.00
On cover 21.00
635 A158 3c violet ('27) .45 .20
Never hinged .60
On cover 2.00
a. 3c bright violet ('34) .20 .20
Never hinged .30
On cover .25
636 A159 4c yel brown ('27) 2.00 .20
Never hinged 3.00
On cover 8.00
637 A160 5c dk blue ('27) 2.00 .20
Never hinged 3.00
638 A161 6c red orange ('27) 2.00 .20
Never hinged 3.00
639 A162 7c black ('27) 2.00 .20
Never hinged 3.00
a. Vert. pair, imperf. btwn. 325.00 *250.00*
640 A163 8c ol grn ('27) 2.00 .20
Never hinged 3.00
641 A164 9c rose ('27) 2.00 .20
Never hinged 3.00
642 A165 10c orange ('27) 3.25 .20
Never hinged 5.00
Nos. 632-634,635-642 (11) 17.80 2.20
Nos. 632-634, 635-642 never hinged 26.60

The 1½c, 2c, 4c, 5c, 6c, 8c imperf. (dry print) are printer's waste.

For ½c, 11c-50c see Nos. 653, 692-701.

Vermont Sesquicentennial Issue

Green Mountain Boy — A191

Flat Plate Printing

1927, Aug. 3 *Perf. 11*

643 A191 2c carmine rose 1.20 .80
Never hinged 2.00
On cover 1.50

Battle of Bennington, Vt., and independence of the State of Vermont, 150th anniv.

"The Surrender of General Burgoyne at Saratoga," by John Trumbull
A192

Washington at Prayer — A193

Burgoyne Campaign Issue

1927, Aug. 3 *Perf. 11*

644 A192 2c carmine rose 3.25 2.10
Never hinged 5.50
On cover 3.00

Battles of Bennington, Oriskany, Fort Stanwix and Saratoga.

Valley Forge Issue

1928, May 26 *Perf. 11*

645 A193 2c carmine rose 1.00 .50
Never hinged 1.50
On cover .75
a. 2c lake —
Never hinged —

150th anniv. of Washington's encampment at Valley Forge, Pa.

Battle of Monmouth Issue

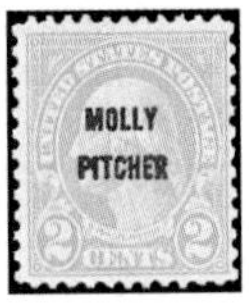

No. 634 Overprinted

Rotary Press Printing

1928, Oct. 20 *Perf. 11x10½*

646 A157 2c carmine 1.10 1.10
Never hinged 1.60
On cover 1.60
a. "Pitcher" only 500.00

The normal space between a vertical pair of the overprints is 18mm, but pairs are known with the space measuring 28mm.

150th anniv. of the Battle of Monmouth, NJ, and as a memorial to "Molly Pitcher" (Mary Ludwig Hays), the heroine of the battle.

Hawaii Sesquicentennial Issue

Nos. 634 and 637 Overprinted

Rotary Press Printing

1928, Aug. 13 *Perf. 11x10½*

647 A157 2c carmine 4.50 4.50
Never hinged 7.25
On cover 5.75
648 A160 5c dark blue 12.50 13.50
Never hinged 21.50
On cover 20.00

150th anniv. of the discovery of the Hawaiian Islands by Captain Cook.

These stamps were on sale at post offices in the Hawaiian Islands and at the Postal Agency in Washington, DC They were not on sale at post offices in the Continental US, though they were valid for postage there.

Normally the overprints were placed 18mm apart vertically, but pairs exist with a space of 28mm between the overprints.

Aeronautics Conference Issue

Wright Airplane A194

Globe and Airplane A195

Flat Plate Printing

1928, Dec. 12 *Perf. 11*

649 A194 2c carmine rose 1.10 .80
Never hinged 1.75
On cover 1.50
650 A195 5c blue 4.50 3.25
Never hinged 7.25

Intl. Civil Aeronautics Conf. at Washington, DC, Dec. 12-14, 1928, and of the 25th anniv. of the 1st airplane flight by the Wright brothers, Dec. 17, 1903.

George Rogers Clark Issue

Surrender of Fort Sackville A196

1929, Feb. 25 *Perf. 11*

651 A196 2c carmine & black .75 .50
Never hinged 1.10
On cover 1.00

150th anniv. of the surrender of Fort Sackville, the present site of Vincennes, Ind., to George Rogers Clark.

Type of 1925

Rotary Press Printing

1929, May 25 *Perf. 11x10½*

653 A154 ½c olive brown .20 .20
Never hinged .25

Edison's First Lamp
A197

Maj. Gen. John Sullivan
A198

Electric Light Jubilee Issue

1929 **Flat Plate Printing** *Perf. 11*

654 A197 2c carmine rose .65 .70
Never hinged 1.00
On cover 1.10

Rotary Press Printing
Perf. 11x10½

655 A197 2c carmine rose .60 .20
Never hinged .90
On cover .25

Coil Stamp (Rotary Press)
Perf. 10 Vertically

656 A197 2c carmine rose 13.00 1.75
Never hinged 21.00
On cover 2.75
Nos. 654-656 (3) 14.25 2.65

50th anniv. of invention of the incandescent lamp by Thomas Alva Edison, Oct. 21, 1879. Issued: #654, June 5; #655-656, June 11.

Sullivan Expedition Issue
Flat Plate Printing

1929, June 17 *Perf. 11*

657 A198 2c carmine rose .65 .60
Never hinged 1.00
On cover 1.00
a. 2c lake 360.00 300.00
Never hinged 575.00

150th anniv. of the Sullivan Expedition in NY State during the Revolutionary War.

Nos. 632-634, 635-642 Overprinted

Rotary Press Printing

1929 *Perf. 11x10½*

658 A155 1c green 2.25 2.00
Never hinged 4.00
a. Vert. pair, one without ovpt. *375.00*
659 A156 1½c brown 3.75 2.90
Never hinged 6.25
a. Vert. pair, one without ovpt. *425.00*
660 A157 2c carmine 4.25 1.00
Never hinged 7.00
661 A158 3c violet 20.00 15.00
Never hinged 37.50
a. Vert. pair, one without ovpt. *525.00*
Never hinged *675.00*
662 A159 4c yellow brown 20.00 9.00
Never hinged 37.50
a. Vert. pair, one without ovpt. *500.00*
663 A160 5c deep blue 12.50 9.75
Never hinged 24.00
664 A161 6c red orange 30.00 18.00
Never hinged 55.00
665 A162 7c black 30.00 27.50
Never hinged 55.00
666 A163 8c olive green 95.00 70.00
Never hinged 180.00
667 A164 9c light rose 14.00 11.25
Never hinged 26.00
668 A165 10c orange yel 25.00 12.00
Never hinged 45.00
Nos. 658-668 (11) 256.75 178.40
Nos. 658-668, never hinged 477.25

See note following No. 679.

Overprinted

669 A155 1c green 3.75 2.25
Never hinged 6.25
b. No period after "Nebr." (19338, 19339 UR 26, 36) 50.00
670 A156 1½c brown 3.50 2.50
Never hinged 5.75
671 A157 2c carmine 3.50 1.30
Never hinged 5.75
672 A158 3c violet 13.50 12.00
Never hinged 24.00
a. Vert. pair, one without ovpt. *500.00*
673 A159 4c yellow brown 20.00 15.00
Never hinged 35.00
674 A160 5c deep blue 18.00 15.00
Never hinged 32.50
675 A161 6c red orange 42.50 24.00
Never hinged 75.00
676 A162 7c black 22.50 18.00
Never hinged 42.50
677 A163 8c olive green 35.00 25.00
Never hinged 65.00
678 A164 9c light rose 40.00 27.50
Never hinged 70.00
a. Vert. pair, one without ovpt. *750.00*
679 A165 10c orange yel 120.00 22.50
Never hinged 230.00
Nos. 669-679 (11) 322.25 165.05
Nos. 669-679, never hinged 591.75

Nos. 658-660, 669-673, 677 and 678 are known with the overprints on vertical pairs spaced 32mm apart instead of the normal 22mm.

Important: Nos. 658-679 with original gum have either one horizontal gum breaker ridge per stamp or portions of two at the extreme top and bottom of the stamps, 21mm apart. Multiple complete gum breaker ridges indicate a fake overprint. Absence of the gum breaker ridges indicates either regumming or regumming and a fake overprint.

Gen. Anthony Wayne Memorial
A199

Lock No. 5, Monongahela River
A200

Battle of Fallen Timbers Issue
Flat Plate Printing

1929, Sept. 14 *Perf. 11*

680 A199 2c carmine rose .75 .75
Never hinged 1.10
On cover 1.10

General Anthony Wayne memorial and the 135th anniv. of the Battle of Fallen Timbers, Ohio.

Ohio River Canalization Issue

1929, Oct. 19 *Perf. 11*

681 A200 2c carmine rose .65 .65
Never hinged .95
On cover 1.10
a. 2c lake —

Completion of the Ohio River Canalization Project between Cairo, Ill. and Pittsburgh.

Massachusetts Bay Colony Issue

Mass. Bay Colony Seal — A201

1930, Apr. 8 *Perf. 11*

682 A201 2c carmine rose .55 .50
Never hinged .85
On cover 1.00

300th anniv. of the founding of the Massachusetts Bay Colony.

Carolina-Charleston Issue

Gov. Joseph West and Chief Shadoo, a Kiowa — A202

1930, Apr. 10 *Perf. 11*

683 A202 2c carmine rose 1.10 1.10
Never hinged 1.65
On cover 1.40

260th anniv. of the founding of the Province of Carolina, and the 250th anniv. of the City of Charleston, SC.

Warren G. Harding
A203

William H. Taft
A204

Type of 1922-26 Issue

Rotary Press Printing

1930 *Perf. 11x10½*

684 A203 1½c brown .35 .20
Never hinged .50
685 A204 4c brown .80 .25
Never hinged 1.25
On cover 5.00

Coil Stamps
Perf. 10 Vertically

686 A203 1½c brown 1.75 .20
Never hinged 2.50

687 A204 4c brown 3.25 .45
Never hinged 4.50
On cover 10.00

Braddock's Field Issue

Statue of Col. George Washington — A205

Flat Plate Printing

1930, July 9 *Perf. 11*

688 A205 2c carmine rose .90 .85
Never hinged 1.40
On cover 1.00

175th anniv. of the Battle of Braddock's Field, otherwise the Battle of Monongahela.

General von Steuben
A206

General Casimir Pulaski
A207

Von Steuben Issue

1930, Sept. 17 *Perf. 11*

689 A206 2c carmine rose .50 .50
Never hinged .75
On cover 1.05
a. Imperf., pair 2,750.
Never hinged 3,500.

Gen. Baron Friedrich Wilhelm von Steuben (1730-1794), German soldier who served with distinction in American Revolution.

Pulaski Issue

1931, Jan. 16 *Perf. 11*

690 A207 2c carmine rose .30 .25
Never hinged .40
On cover .50

150th anniv. (in 1929) of the death of Gen. Count Casimir Pulaski (1748-1779), Polish patriot and hero of American Revolution.

Types of 1922-26

Rotary Press Printing

1931 *Perf. 11x10½*

692 A166 11c light blue 2.50 .25
Never hinged 3.75
693 A167 12c brown violet 5.00 .20
Never hinged 8.00
694 A186 13c yellow green 1.90 .25
Never hinged 3.00
695 A168 14c dark blue 3.50 .45
Never hinged 5.50
696 A169 15c gray 7.75 .25
Never hinged 12.00

Perf. 10½x11

697 A187 17c black 4.25 .25
Never hinged 6.50
698 A170 20c carmine rose 7.75 .25
Never hinged 12.00
699 A171 25c blue green 8.00 .25
Never hinged 12.50
700 A172 30c brown 14.00 .25
Never hinged 22.50
701 A173 50c lilac 32.50 .25
Never hinged 52.50
Nos. 692-701 (10) 87.15 2.65
Nos. 692-701, never hinged 137.50

"The Greatest Mother" — A208

Count de Rochambeau, Washington, Count de Grasse — A209

Red Cross Issue
Flat Plate Printing

1931, May 21 *Perf. 11*

702 A208 2c black & red .20 .20
Never hinged .30
a. Red cross missing (foldover) *40,000.*

50th anniv. of the founding of the American Red Cross Society.

Yorktown Issue

1931, Oct. 19 *Perf. 11*

703 A209 2c car rose & blk .35 .25
Never hinged .50
a. 2c lake & black 4.50 .75
Never hinged 6.25
b. 2c dark lake & black *450.00*
Never hinged *800.00*
c. Horiz. pair, imperf. vert. *5,000.*
Never hinged *6,250.*

Surrender of Yorktown, sesquicentennial.

Washington Bicentennial Issue

Various Portraits of George Washington

A210

A211

A212

A213

A214

A215

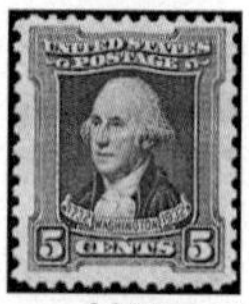

A216

A217

A218

A219

A220

A221

Rotary Press Printings

1932, Jan. 1 *Perf. 11x10½*

704 A210 ½c olive brown .20 .20
Never hinged .20
705 A211 1c green .20 .20
Never hinged .20
706 A212 1½c brown .40 .20
Never hinged .55
707 A213 2c carmine rose .20 .20
Never hinged .20
708 A214 3c deep violet .55 .20
Never hinged .80
709 A215 4c light brown .25 .20
Never hinged .35
710 A216 5c blue 1.50 .20
Never hinged 2.25
711 A217 6c red orange 3.00 .20
Never hinged 4.50
712 A218 7c black .25 .20
Never hinged .35
713 A219 8c olive bister 2.75 .50
Never hinged 4.00
714 A220 9c pale red 2.25 .20
Never hinged 3.25
715 A221 10c orange yellow 10.00 .20
Never hinged 15.00
Nos. 704-715 (12) 21.55 2.70
Nos. 704-715, never hinged 31.65

200th anniv. of the birth of Washington.

Skier — A222

Boy and Girl Planting Tree — A223

Olympic Winter Games Issue
Flat Plate Printing

1932, Jan. 25 *Perf. 11*

716 A222 2c carmine rose .40 .20
Never hinged .50
a. 2c lake —

Olympic Winter Games, Lake Placid, NY, Feb. 4-13.

Arbor Day Issue
Rotary Press Printing

1932, Apr. 22 *Perf. 11x10½*

717 A223 2c carmine rose .20 .20
Never hinged .20

60th anniv. of the 1st observance of Arbor Day in Nebr., April, 1872, and the birth centenary of Julius Sterling Morton, who conceived the plan and the name "Arbor Day," while a member of the Nebr. State Board of Agriculture.

10th Olympic Games Issue

Runner at Starting Mark
A224

Myron's Discobolus
A225

1932, June 15 *Perf. 11x10½*

718 A224 3c violet 1.40 .20
Never hinged 1.75
719 A225 5c blue 2.20 .20
Never hinged 2.75

Los Angeles, Cal., July 30-Aug. 14.

Washington — A226

1932, June 16 *Perf. 11x10½*

720 A226 3c deep violet .20 .20
Never hinged .20
b. Booklet pane of 6 35.00 *12.50*
Never hinged 60.00
c. Vert. pair, imperf. btwn. 700.00 *1,350.*
Never hinged 1,400.

Coil Stamps

Rotary Press Printing

1932, June 24 *Perf. 10 Vertically*

721 A226 3c deep violet 2.75 .20
Never hinged 3.50

1932, Oct. 12 *Perf. 10 Horizontally*

722 A226 3c deep violet 1.50 .35
Never hinged 2.00

Garfield Type of 1922-26 Issue

1932, Aug. 18 *Perf. 10 Vertically*

723 A161 6c deep orange 11.00 .30
Never hinged 15.00

William Penn
A227

Daniel Webster
A228

William Penn Issue
Flat Plate Printing

1932, Oct. 24 *Perf. 11*

724 A227 3c violet .35 .20
Never hinged .50
a. Vert. pair, imperf. horiz. —

250th anniv. of the arrival in America of William Penn (1644-1718), English Quaker and founder of Pennsylvania.

Daniel Webster Issue

1932, Oct. 24 *Perf. 11*

725 A228 3c violet .35 .25
Never hinged .50

Daniel Webster (1782-1852), statesman.

Georgia Bicentennial Issue

Gen. James Edward Oglethorpe — A229

1933, Feb. 12 *Perf. 11*

726 A229 3c violet .35 .20
Never hinged .50

200th anniv. of the Colony of Georgia founding and James Edward Oglethorpe, who landed from England, Feb. 12th, 1733, and personally supervised the establishing of the colony.

Peace of 1783 Issue

Washington's Headquarters, Newburgh, NY — A230

Rotary Press Printing

1933, Apr. 19 *Perf. 10½x11*

727 A230 3c violet .20 .20
Never hinged .20

150th anniv. of the Proclamation of Peace between the U.S. and Great Britain at the end of the Revolutionary War.
See No. 752.

Century of Progress Issue

Restoration of Fort Dearborn A231

Federal Building at Chicago, 1933 A232

1933, May 25 *Perf. 10½x11*

728 A231 1c yellow green .20 .20
Never hinged .25
729 A232 3c violet .25 .20
Never hinged .35

"Century of Progress" Intl. Phil. Exhib., Chicago, 1933 and 100th anniv. of the incorporation of Chicago as a city.

American Philatelic Society Issue
Souvenir Sheets
Without Gum
Flat Plate Printing

1933, Aug. 25 *Imperf.*

730 Sheet of 25 27.50 27.50
a. A231 1c deep yellow green .75 .50
731 Sheet of 25 25.00 25.00
a. A232 3c deep violet .65 .50

Sheet measures 134x120mm.
See Nos. 766-767.

National Recovery Act Issue

Group of Workers — A233

Rotary Press Printing

1933, Aug. 15 *Perf. 10½x11*

732 A233 3c violet .20 .20
Never hinged .20

Issued to direct attention to and arouse support of the nation for the NRA.

Byrd Antarctic Issue

World Map on van der Grinten's Projection — A234

Flat Plate Printing

1933, Oct. 9 *Perf. 11*

733 A234 3c dark blue .50 .50
Never hinged .60

Second Antarctic expedition of Rear Admiral Richard E. Byrd.
In addition to the 3 cents postage, letters sent by the ships of the expedition to be canceled in Little America were subject to a service charge of 50 cents each.
See Nos. 735, 753.

Kosciuszko Issue

Statue of Gen. Tadeusz Kosciuszko — A235

1933, Oct. 13 *Perf. 11*

734 A235 5c blue .55 .25
Never hinged .65
a. Horiz. pair, imperf. vert. 2,250.
Never hinged 2,800.

Gen. Tadeusz Kosciuszko (1746-1807), Polish soldier and statesman who served in American Revolution. 150th anniv. of grant of American citizenship.

National Stamp Exhibition Issue
Souvenir Sheet
Without Gum

1934, Feb. 10 *Imperf.*

735 Sheet of 6 12.00 10.00
a. A234 3c dark blue 1.90 1.65

Sheet measures 87x93mm. See #768.

a. Horizontal pair, imperf between 7,000.

Maryland Tercentenary Issue

"The Ark" and "The Dove" — A236

1934, Mar. 23 *Perf. 11*

736 A236 3c carmine rose .20 .20
Never hinged .20
a. Horiz. pair, imperf btwn. 7,000.

300th anniv. of the founding of Maryland.

Mothers of America Issue

Adaptation of Whistler's Portrait of his Mother A237

Rotary Press Printing

1934, May 2 *Perf. 11x10½*

737 A237 3c deep violet .20 .20
Never hinged .20

Flat Plate Printing
Perf. 11

738 A237 3c deep violet .20 .20
Never hinged .20

Mother's Day. See No. 754.

Wisconsin Tercentenary Issue

Nicolet's Landing A238

1934, July 7 *Perf. 11*

739 A238 3c deep violet .25 .20
Never hinged .40
a. Vert. pair, imperf. horiz. 350.00
Never hinged 600.00
b. Horiz. pair, imperf. vert. 500.00
Never hinged 850.00

Tercentenary of the arrival of French explorer Jean Nicolet at Green Bay, Wis.
See No. 755.

National Parks Issue

El Capitan, Yosemite (California) A239

Old Faithful, Yellowstone (Wyoming) A243

Grand Canyon (Arizona) A240

Mt. Rainier and Mirror Lake (Washington) — A241

Mesa Verde (Colorado) A242

Crater Lake (Oregon) A244

Great Head, Acadia Park (Maine) A245

Great White Throne, Zion Park (Utah) A246

Great Smoky Mts. (North Carolina) A248

Mt. Rockwell (Mt. Sinopah) and Two Medicine Lake, Glacier Natl. Park (Montana) A247

1934 **Flat Plate Printing** *Perf. 11*

740 A239 1c green .20 .20
Never hinged .25
a. Vert. pair, imperf. horiz., with gum 1,500.
Never hinged 2,100.
741 A240 2c red .20 .20
Never hinged .25
a. Vert. pair, imperf. horiz., with gum 575.00
Never hinged 975.00
b. Horiz. pair, imperf. vert., with gum 600.00
Never hinged 1,000.
742 A241 3c deep violet .20 .20
Never hinged .25
a. Vert. pair, imperf. horiz., with gum 700.00
Never hinged 1,200.
743 A242 4c brown .40 .40
Never hinged .60
a. Vert. pair, imperf. horiz., with gum 1,000.
Never hinged 1,700.
744 A243 5c blue .70 .65
Never hinged 1.00
a. Horiz. pair, imperf. vert., with gum 600.00
Never hinged 1,000.
745 A244 6c dark blue 1.10 .85
Never hinged 1.60
746 A245 7c black .60 .75
Never hinged .90
a. Horiz. pair, imperf. vert., with gum 600.00
Never hinged 1,000.
747 A246 8c sage green 1.60 1.50
Never hinged 2.40
748 A247 9c red orange 1.50 .65
Never hinged 2.25
749 A248 10c gray black 3.00 1.25
Never hinged 4.50
Nos. 740-749 (10) 9.50 6.65
Nos. 740-749, never hinged 14.00

National Parks Year.
Beware of fakes of the part-perforate errors of Nos. 740-749, including those with gum (see "without gum" note before No. 752).
See Nos. 750-751, 756-765, 769-770, 797.

American Philatelic Society Issue
Souvenir Sheet

1934, Aug. 28 *Imperf.*

750 Sheet of 6 30.00 27.50
Never hinged 37.50
a. A241 3c deep violet 3.50 3.25
Never hinged 4.50

Sheet measures approximately 98x93mm.
See #770.

Trans-Mississippi Philatelic Exposition Issue
Souvenir Sheet

1934, Oct. 10 *Imperf.*

751 Sheet of 6 12.50 12.50
Never hinged 16.00
a. A239 1c green 1.40 1.60
Never hinged 1.85

Sheet measures approximately 92x99mm.
See #769.

Special Printing (Nos. 752-771)

"Issued for a limited time in full sheets as printed, and in blocks thereof, to meet the requirements of collectors and others who may be interested" - From Postal Bulletin, No. 16614.

Issuance of the following 20 stamps in complete sheets resulted from the protest of collectors and others at the practice of presenting, to certain government officials, complete sheets of unsevered panes, imperforate (except Nos. 752 and 753) and generally ungummed.

Without Gum

Note: In 1940 the P.O. Department offered to and did gum full sheets of Nos. 756-765 and 769-770 sent in by owners. No other Special Printings were accepted for gumming.

Type of Peace Issue
Issued in sheets of 400
Rotary Press Printing

1935, Mar. 15 *Perf. 10½x11*

752 A230 3c violet .25 .20

Type of Byrd Issue
Issued in sheets of 200
Flat Plate Printing
Perf. 11

753 A234 3c dark blue .50 .45

No. 753 is similar to No. 733. Positive identification is by pairs or blocks showing a guide line between stamps. These lines are found only on No. 753.

Type of Mothers of America Issue
Issued in sheets of 200
Imperf

754 A237 3c deep violet .60 .60

Type of Wisconsin Issue
Issued in sheets of 200
Imperf

755 A238 3c deep violet .60 .60

Types of National Parks Issue
Issued in sheets of 200
Imperf

756	A239	1c green	.20	.20
757	A240	2c red	.25	.25
758	A241	3c deep violet	.50	.45
759	A242	4c brown	.95	.95
760	A243	5c blue	1.50	1.40
761	A244	6c dark blue	2.40	2.25
762	A245	7c black	1.50	1.40
763	A246	8c sage green	1.60	1.50
764	A247	9c red orange	1.90	1.75
765	A248	10c gray black	3.75	3.50
		Nos. 756-765 (10)	14.55	13.65

Souvenir Sheets
Type of Century of Progress Issue
Issued in sheets of 9 panes of 25 stamps each

Note: Single items from these sheets are identical with other varieties, 766 & 730, 766a & 730a, 767 & 731, 767a & 731a, 768 & 735, 768a & 735a, 769 & 756, 770 & 758.

Positive identification is by blocks or pairs showing wide gutters between stamps. These wide gutters occur only on Nos. 766-770 and measure, horiz., 13mm on Nos. 766-767; 16mm on No. 768, and 23mm on Nos. 769-770.

Imperf

766	Pane of 25	25.00	25.00
a.	A231 1c yellow green	.70	.50
767	Pane of 25	23.50	23.50
a.	A232 3c violet	.60	.50

National Exhibition Issue
Type of Byrd Issue
Issued in sheets of 25 panes of 6 stamps each, with vertical and horizontal gutters between panes
Imperf

768	Pane of 6	20.00	15.00
a.	A234 3c dark blue	2.80	2.40

Types of National Parks Issue
Issued in sheets of 20 panes of 6 stamps each, with vertical and horizontal gutters between panes
Imperf

769	Pane of 6	12.50	11.00
a.	A239 1c green	1.85	1.80
770	Pane of 6	30.00	24.00
a.	A241 3c deep violet	3.25	3.10

Type of Air Post Special Delivery
Issued in sheets of 200
Imperf

771 APSD1 16c dark blue 2.60 2.60

Catalogue values for unused stamps in this section, from this point to the end of the section, are for Never Hinged items.

VALUES FOR HINGED STAMPS AFTER NO. 771
This catalogue does not value unused stamps after No. 771 in hinged condition. Hinged unused stamps from No. 772 to the present are worth considerably less than the values given for unused stamps, which are for never-hinged examples.

Connecticut Tercentenary Issue

Charter Oak
A249

Rotary Press Printing
1935, Apr. 26 ***Perf. 11x10½***

772 A249 3c violet .30 .20

300th anniv. of the settlement of Conn.
See No. 778a.

California-Pacific Exposition Issue

View of San Diego Exposition
A250

1935, May 29 ***Perf. 11x10½***

773 A250 3c purple .30 .20

California-Pacific Expo., San Diego.
See No. 778b.

Boulder Dam Issue

Boulder Dam — A251

Flat Plate Printing
1935, Sept. 30 ***Perf. 11***

774 A251 3c purple .25 .20

Dedication of Boulder Dam.

Michigan Centenary Issue

Michigan State Seal
A252

Rotary Press Printing
1935, Nov. 1 ***Perf. 11x10½***

775 A252 3c purple .30 .20

Advance celebration of Michigan statehood centenary. Michigan was admitted to Union Jan. 26, 1837.
See No. 778c.

Texas Centennial Issue

Sam Houston, Stephen F. Austin and the Alamo
A253

1936, Mar. 2 ***Perf. 11x10½***

776 A253 3c purple .30 .20

Centennial of Texas independence.
See No. 778d.

Rhode Island Tercentenary Issue

Statue of Roger Williams — A254

1936, May 4 ***Perf. 10½x11***

777 A254 3c purple .35 .20

Settlement of Rhode Island, 1636.

Third International Philatelic Exhibition Issue
Souvenir Sheet

A254a

Illustration reduced.

Flat Plate Printing
1936, May 9 ***Imperf.***

778	A254a Sheet of 4	1.75	1.25
a.	A249 3c violet	.40	.30
b.	A250 3c violet	.40	.30
c.	A252 3c violet	.40	.30
d.	A253 3c violet	.40	.30

Sheet measures 98x66mm.

Arkansas Centennial Issue

Arkansas Post, Old and New State Houses
A255

Rotary Press Printing
1936, June 15 ***Perf. 11x10½***

782 A255 3c purple .30 .20

Centennial of Arkansas statehood.

Map of Oregon Territory
A256

Susan B. Anthony — A257

Oregon Territory Issue
1936, July 14 ***Perf. 11x10½***

783 A256 3c purple .25 .20

Centenary of Oregon Territory opening.

Susan B. Anthony Issue
1936, Aug. 26 ***Perf. 11x10½***

784 A257 3c dark violet .25 .20

Susan Brownell Anthony (1820-1906), woman suffrage advocate, honored on 16th anniv. of ratification of 19th Amendment granting American women the right to vote.

Army Issue

George Washington, Nathanael Greene and Mount Vernon — A258

Andrew Jackson, Winfield Scott and the Hermitage
A259

Generals Sherman, Grant and Sheridan
A260

Generals Robert E. Lee, "Stonewall" Jackson and Stratford Hall
A261

US Military Academy, West Point
A262

1936-37 ***Perf. 11x10½***

785	A258	1c green	.25	.20
786	A259	2c carmine ('37)	.25	.20
787	A260	3c purple ('37)	.35	.20
788	A261	4c gray ('37)	.55	.20
789	A262	5c ultra ('37)	.65	.25
		Nos. 785-789 (5)	2.05	1.05

Issued in honor of the United States Army.

Navy Issue

John Paul Jones and John Barry
A263

Stephen Decatur and Thomas MacDonough — A264

Admirals David G. Farragut and David D. Porter
A265

Admirals William T. Sampson, George Dewey and Winfield S. Schley
A266

Seal of US Naval Academy and Naval Cadets A267

1936-37 *Perf. 11x10½*

790	A263 1c green		.25	.20
791	A264 2c carmine ('37)		.25	.20
792	A265 3c purple ('37)		.35	.20
793	A266 4c gray ('37)		.55	.20
794	A267 5c ultra ('37)		.65	.25
	Nos. 790-794 (5)		2.05	1.05

Issued in honor of the United States Navy.

Northwest Ordinance Sesquicentennial Issue

Manasseh Cutler, Rufus Putnam and Map of Northwest Territory A268

1937, July 13 *Perf. 11x10½*
795 A268 3c red violet .30 .20

150th anniv. of the adoption of the Ordinance of 1787 and the creation of the Northwest Territory.

Virginia Dare Issue

Virginia Dare and Parents — A269

Flat Plate Printing

1937, Aug. 18 *Perf. 11*
796 A269 5c gray blue .30 .20

350th anniv. of the birth of Virginia Dare and the settlement at Roanoke Island. Virginia was the first child born in America of English parents (Aug. 18, 1587).

Society of Philatelic Americans
Souvenir Sheet

A269a

Illustration reduced.

1937, Aug. 26 *Imperf.*
797 A269a 10c blue green .60 .40

Sheet measures 67x78mm.

Constitution Sesquicentennial Issue

Signing of the Constitution A270

Rotary Press Printing

1937, Sept. 17 *Perf. 11x10½*
798 A270 3c bright red violet .35 .20

Sesquicentennial of the Signing of the Constitution, Sept. 17, 1787.

Territorial Issues
Hawaii

Statue of Kamehameha I, Honolulu — A271

1937, Oct. 18 *Perf. 10½x11*
799 A271 3c violet .30 .20

Alaska

Landscape with Mt. McKinley A272

1937, Nov. 12 *Perf. 11x10½*
800 A272 3c violet .30 .20

Puerto Rico

La Fortaleza, San Juan A273

1937, Nov. 25 *Perf. 11x10½*
801 A273 3c bright violet .30 .20

Virgin Islands

Charlotte Amalie A274

1937, Dec. 15 *Perf. 11x10½*
802 A274 3c light violet .30 .20

Presidential Issue

Benjamin Franklin A275

George Washington A276

Martha Washington A277

John Adams A278

Thomas Jefferson A279

James Madison A280

White House A281

James Monroe A282

John Q. Adams A283

Andrew Jackson A284

Martin Van Buren A285

William H. Harrison A286

John Tyler — A287

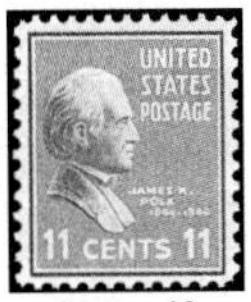

James K. Polk — A288

Zachary Taylor A289

Millard Fillmore A290

Franklin Pierce A291

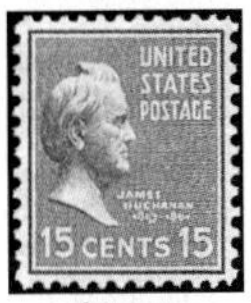

James Buchanan A292

Abraham Lincoln A293

Andrew Johnson A294

Ulysses S. Grant A295

Rutherford B. Hayes A296

James A. Garfield A297

Chester A. Arthur A298

Grover Cleveland A299

Benjamin Harrison A300

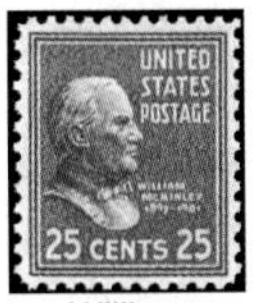

William McKinley A301

Theodore Roosevelt A302

William Howard Taft A303

Woodrow Wilson A304

Warren G. Harding A305

Calvin Coolidge A306

1938-54 *Perf. 11x10½*

803	A275	½c deep orange	.20	.20
804	A276	1c green	.20	.20
b.		Booklet pane of 6	2.00	*.50*
c.		Horiz. pair, imperf btwn. (from booklet pane)		—
805	A277	1½c bister brown	.20	.20
b.		Horiz. pair, imperf. btwn.	160.00	20.00
806	A278	2c rose carmine	.20	.20
b.		Booklet pane of 6	4.75	*.85*
807	A279	3c deep violet	.20	.20
a.		Booklet pane of 6	8.50	*2.00*
b.		Horiz. pair, imperf. btwn.	*1,500.*	—
c.		Imperf., pair	*2,750.*	
d.		As "a," imperf between vert.		—
808	A280	4c red violet	.75	.20
809	A281	4½c dark gray	.25	.20
810	A282	5c bright blue	.25	.20
811	A283	6c red orange	.25	.20
812	A284	7c sepia	.35	.20
813	A285	8c olive green	.35	.20
814	A286	9c rose pink	.35	.20
815	A287	10c brown red	.30	.20
816	A288	11c ultra	.65	.20
817	A289	12c bright violet	.90	.20
818	A290	13c blue green	1.25	.20
819	A291	14c blue	.90	.20
820	A292	15c blue gray	.50	.20
821	A293	16c black	1.10	.25
822	A294	17c rose red	1.00	.20
823	A295	18c brown car	2.00	.20
824	A296	19c bright violet	1.25	.35
825	A297	20c brt blue grn	.85	.20
826	A298	21c dull blue	1.25	.20
827	A299	22c vermilion	1.00	.40
828	A300	24c gray black	3.50	.20
829	A301	25c deep red lil	.80	.20
830	A302	30c deep ultra	3.75	.20
a.		30c blue	15.00	—
b.		30c deep blue	*250.00*	—
831	A303	50c lt red violet	5.00	.20

Flat Plate Printing

Perf. 11

832	A304	$1 pur & black	7.00	.20
a.		Vert. pair, imperf. horiz.	*1,500.*	
b.		Wmkd. USIR ('51)	175.00	65.00
1.		Hinged	110.00	
c.		$1 red violet & black ('54)	6.00	.20
d.		As "c," vert. pair, imperf. horiz.	*1,500.*	
e.		Vert. pair, imperf. btwn.	*2,750.*	
f.		As "c," vert. pair, imperf. btwn.	*8,500.*	
833	A305	$2 yel grn & blk	18.00	3.75
834	A306	$5 car & black	90.00	3.00
a.		$5 red brown & black	*3,000.*	*7,000.*
		Hinged	*2,000.*	
		Nos. 803-834 (32)	144.55	13.15

No. 805b used is always Bureau precanceled St. Louis Mo., and is generally with gum. Value is for gummed pair.

No. 832c is printed on thick white paper with smooth, colorless gum.

No. 834 can be chemically altered to resemble No. 834a. No. 834a should be purchased only with competent expert certification.

See Nos. 839-851.

Constitution Ratification Issue

Old Court House, Williamsburg, Va. — A307

Rotary Press Printing

1938, June 21 *Perf. 11x10½*

835 A307 3c deep violet .45 .20

150th anniv. of the ratification of the U.S. Constitution.

Landing of the Swedes and Finns — A308

Statue Symbolizing Colonization of the West — A309

Swedish-Finnish Tercentenary Issue

Flat Plate Printing

1938, June 27 *Perf. 11*

836 A308 3c red violet .35 .20

Tercentenary of the Swedish and Finnish settlement at Wilmington, Del.

Northwest Territory Issue

Rotary Press Printing

1938, July 15 *Perf. 11x10½*

837 A309 3c bright violet .30 .20

Sesquicentennial of the settlement of the Northwest Territory.

Iowa Territory Centennial Issue

Old Capitol, Iowa City A310

1938, Aug. 24 *Perf. 11x10½*

838 A310 3c violet .35 .20

Centenary of Iowa Territory.

Presidential Types of 1938
Coil Stamps

Rotary Press Printing

1939 *Perf. 10 Vertically*

839	A276	1c green	.30	.20
840	A277	1½c bister brown	.30	.20
841	A278	2c rose carmine	.40	.20
842	A279	3c deep violet	.50	.20
843	A280	4c red violet	7.50	.40
844	A281	4½c dark gray	.70	.40
845	A282	5c bright blue	5.00	.35
846	A283	6c red orange	1.10	.20
847	A287	10c brown red	11.00	1.00

Perf. 10 Horizontally

848	A276	1c green	.85	.20
849	A277	1½c bister brown	1.25	.30
850	A278	2c rose carmine	2.50	.40
851	A279	3c deep violet	2.50	.40
		Nos. 839-851 (13)	33.90	4.45

"Tower of the Sun" A311

Trylon and Perisphere A312

Golden Gate International Exposition Issue

Rotary Press Printing

1939, Feb. 18 *Perf. 10½x11*

852 A311 3c bright purple .30 .20

Golden Gate Intl. Expo., San Francisco.

New York World's Fair Issue

1939, Apr. 1 *Perf. 10½x11*

853 A312 3c deep purple .30 .20

Washington Inauguration Issue

George Washington Taking Oath of Office — A313

Flat Plate Printing

1939, Apr. 30 *Perf. 11*

854 A313 3c bright red violet .55 .20

Sesquicentennial of George Washington's inauguration as 1st president.

Baseball Centennial Issue

Sand-lot Baseball Game A314

Rotary Press Printing

1939, June 12 *Perf. 11x10½*

855 A314 3c violet 1.75 .20

Centennial of baseball.

Panama Canal Issue

Theodore Roosevelt, Gen. George W. Goethals and Gaillard Cut — A315

Flat Plate Printing

1939, Aug. 15 *Perf. 11*

856 A315 3c deep red violet .35 .20

25th anniv. of the Panama Canal opening.

Printing Tercentenary Issue

Stephen Daye Press — A316

Rotary Press Printing

1939, Sept. 25 *Perf. 10½x11*

857 A316 3c violet .25 .20

300th anniv. of printing in Colonial America.

50th Anniversary of Statehood Issue

Map of North and South Dakota, Montana and Washington A317

1939, Nov. 2 *Perf. 11x10½*

858 A317 3c rose violet .30 .20

50th anniv. of admission to Statehood of North Dakota, South Dakota, Montana and Washington.

Famous Americans Issues

Authors

Washington Irving — A318

James Fenimore Cooper — A319

Ralph Waldo Emerson A320

Louisa May Alcott A321

Samuel L. Clemens (Mark Twain) — A322

1940 *Perf. 10½x11*

859	A318	1c bright blue green	.20	.20
860	A319	2c rose carmine	.20	.20
861	A320	3c bright red violet	.25	.20
862	A321	5c ultra	.35	.20
863	A322	10c dark brown	1.75	1.20
		Nos. 859-863 (5)	2.75	2.00

Poets

Henry W. Longfellow A323

John Greenleaf Whittier A324

James Russell Lowell A325

Walt Whitman A326

James Whitcomb Riley — A327

1940 *Perf. 10½x11*

864	A323	1c bright blue green	.20	.20
865	A324	2c rose carmine	.20	.20
866	A325	3c bright red violet	.25	.20
867	A326	5c ultra	.40	.20
868	A327	10c dark brown	1.75	1.25
		Nos. 864-868 (5)	2.80	2.05

Educators

Horace Mann — A328

Mark Hopkins — A329

Charles W. Eliot — A330

Frances E. Willard — A331

Booker T. Washington — A332

1940 *Perf. 10½x11*

869	A328	1c bright blue green	.20	.20
870	A329	2c rose carmine	.20	.20
871	A330	3c bright red violet	.25	.20
872	A331	5c ultra	.40	.20
873	A332	10c dark brown	2.00	1.10
		Nos. 869-873 (5)	3.05	1.90

Scientists

John James Audubon A333

Dr. Crawford W. Long A334

Luther Burbank — A335

Dr. Walter Reed — A336

Jane Addams — A337

1940 *Perf. 10½x11*

874	A333	1c bright blue green	.20	.20
875	A334	2c rose carmine	.20	.20
876	A335	3c bright red violet	.25	.20
877	A336	5c ultra	.35	.20
878	A337	10c dark brown	1.50	.85
		Nos. 874-878 (5)	2.50	1.65

Composers

Stephen Collins Foster — A338

John Philip Sousa — A339

Victor Herbert
A340

Edward MacDowell
A341

Ethelbert Nevin — A342

1940 ***Perf. 10½x11***

879	A338	1c bright blue green	.20	.20
880	A339	2c rose carmine	.20	.20
881	A340	3c bright red violet	.25	.20
882	A341	5c ultra	.40	.20
883	A342	10c dark brown	3.75	1.20
		Nos. 879-883 (5)	4.80	2.00

Artists

Gilbert Charles Stuart — A343

James A. McNeill Whistler — A344

Augustus Saint-Gaudens
A345

Daniel Chester French
A346

Frederic Remington — A347

1940 ***Perf. 10½x11***

884	A343	1c bright blue green	.20	.20
885	A344	2c rose carmine	.20	.20
886	A345	3c bright red violet	.30	.20
887	A346	5c ultra	.50	.20
888	A347	10c dark brown	1.75	1.25
		Nos. 884-888 (5)	2.95	2.05

Inventors

Eli Whitney — A348

Samuel F. B. Morse — A349

Cyrus Hall McCormick
A350

Elias Howe
A351

Alexander Graham Bell — A352

1940 ***Perf. 10½x11***

889	A348	1c brt blue green	.25	.20
890	A349	2c rose carmine	.30	.20
891	A350	3c bright red violet	.30	.20
892	A351	5c ultra	1.10	.30
893	A352	10c dark brown	11.00	2.00
		Nos. 889-893 (5)	12.95	2.90
		Nos. 859-893 (35)	31.80	14.55

Pony Express Issue

Pony Express Rider
A353

1940, Apr. 3 ***Perf. 11x10½***

894	A353	3c henna brown	.40	.20

80th anniv. of the Pony Express.

Pan American Union Issue

The Three Graces from Botticelli's "Spring" — A354

1940, Apr. 14 ***Perf. 10½x11***

895	A354	3c light violet	.30	.20

Pan American Union founding, 50th anniv.

Idaho Statehood Issue

Idaho Capitol, Boise
A355

1940, July 3 ***Perf. 11x10½***

896	A355	3c bright violet	.25	.20

Idaho statehood, 50th anniv.

Wyoming Statehood Issue

Wyoming State Seal — A356

1940, July 10 ***Perf. 10½x11***

897	A356	3c brown violet	.30	.20

Wyoming statehood, 50th anniv.

Coronado Expedition Issue

"Coronado and His Captains," painted by Gerald Cassidy
A357

1940, Sept. 7 ***Perf. 11x10½***

898	A357	3c violet	.25	.20

400th anniv. of the Coronado Expedition.

National Defense Issue

Statue of Liberty — A358

90-millimeter Anti-aircraft Gun — A359

Torch of Enlightenment — A360

1940, Oct. 16 ***Perf. 11x10½***

899	A358	1c bright blue green	.20	.20
a.		Vert. pair, imperf. btwn.	*650.00*	—
b.		Horiz. pair, imperf. btwn.	35.00	—
900	A359	2c rose carmine	.20	.20
a.		Horiz. pair, imperf. btwn.	40.00	—
901	A360	3c bright violet	.20	.20
a.		Horiz. pair, imperf. btwn.	25.00	—
		Nos. 899-901 (3)	.60	.60

Thirteenth Amendment Issue

"Emancipation," Statue of Lincoln and Slave, by Thomas Ball — A361

1940, Oct. 20 ***Perf. 10½x11***

902	A361	3c deep violet	.25	.20

75th anniv. of the 13th Amendment to the Constitution.

AIR POST STAMPS

For prepayment of postage on all mailable matter sent by airmail.

Curtiss Jenny — AP1

Engraved (Flat Plate Printing)

1918 **Unwmk.** ***Perf. 11***

C1	AP1	6c orange	60.00	30.00
		Never hinged	125.00	
		On cover		50.00
C2	AP1	16c green	70.00	35.00
		Never hinged	150.00	
		On cover		55.00
C3	AP1	24c car rose & bl	70.00	35.00
		Never hinged	150.00	
		On cover		75.00
a.		Center inverted	*400,000.*	
		Never hinged	*850,000.*	
		Nos. C1-C3 (3)	200.00	100.00
		Nos. C1-C3, never hinged	425.00	

Wooden Propeller and Radiator
AP2

Emblem of Air Service
AP3

De Havilland Biplane — AP4

1923

C4	AP2	8c dark green	22.50	14.00
		Never hinged	45.00	
		On cover		22.50
C5	AP3	16c dark blue	70.00	30.00
		Never hinged	150.00	
		On cover		47.50
C6	AP4	24c carmine	80.00	30.00
		Never hinged	170.00	
		On cover		42.50
		Nos. C4-C6 (3)	172.50	74.00
		Nos. C4-C6, never hinged	365.00	

Map of US and Two Mail Planes — AP5

1926-27

C7	AP5	10c dark blue	2.50	.35
		Never hinged	4.50	
C8	AP5	15c olive brown	2.75	2.50
		Never hinged	5.25	
C9	AP5	20c yellow green ('27)	7.00	2.00
		Never hinged	13.50	
		Nos. C7-C9 (3)	12.25	4.85
		Nos. C7-C9, never hinged	23.25	

Lindbergh's Airplane "Spirit of St. Louis" — AP6

1927, June 18

C10	AP6	10c dark blue	7.00	2.50
		Never hinged	13.00	
a.		Booklet pane of 3	80.00	*65.00*
		Never hinged	130.00	

Singles from No. C10a are imperf. at sides or imperf. at sides and bottom.

Nos. C1-C10 were available for ordinary postage.

Beacon on Rocky Mountains
AP7

1928, July 25 ***Perf. 11***

C11	AP7	5c carmine & blue	5.00	.75
		Never hinged	9.50	
a.		Vertical pair, imperf. btwn.	*7,000.*	

Winged Globe — AP8

1930, Feb. 10 ***Perf. 11***

Size: 46½x19mm

C12	AP8	5c violet	9.00	.50
		Never hinged	17.50	
a.		Horiz. pair, imperf. btwn.	*4,500.*	

See Nos. C16-C17, C19.

Graf Zeppelin Issue

Zeppelin over Atlantic Ocean — AP9

Zeppelin between Continents — AP10

Zeppelin Passing Globe — AP11

1930, Apr. 19 ***Perf. 11***

C13 AP9 65c green	250.	160.
Never hinged	425.	
On cover		175.
C14 AP10 $1.30 brown	525.	375.
Never hinged	900.	
On cover		400.
C15 AP11 $2.60 blue	750.	575.
Never hinged	1,275.	
On cover		600.
Nos. C13-C15 (3)	1,525.	1,110.
Nos. C13-C15, never hinged	2,600.	

Issued for use on mail carried on first Europe-Pan-America round-trip flight of Graf Zeppelin, May, 1930.

Type of 1930 Issue

Rotary Press Printing

1931-32 ***Perf. 10½x11***

Size: 47½x19mm

C16 AP8 5c violet	5.00	.60
Never hinged	8.75	
C17 AP8 8c olive bister ('32)	2.25	.40
Never hinged	4.00	

Century of Progress Issue

Airship "Graf Zeppelin" — AP12

Flat Plate Printing

1933, Oct. 2 ***Perf. 11***

C18 AP12 50c green	55.00	55.00
Never hinged	100.00	
On cover		80.00

Flight of the "Graf Zeppelin" in Oct. 1933, to Miami, Akron and Chicago, and from the last city to Europe.

Catalogue values for unused stamps in this section, from this point to the end of the section, are for Never Hinged items.

Type of 1930 Issue

Rotary Press Printing

1934, June 30 ***Perf. 10½x11***

C19 AP8 6c dull orange	3.50	.25

Transpacific Issues

The "China Clipper" over the Pacific AP13

Flat Plate Printing

1935, Nov. 22 ***Perf. 11***

C20 AP13 25c blue	1.40	1.00

Issued to pay postage on mail carried on the Transpacific air post service inaugurated Nov. 22, 1935.

The "China Clipper" over the Pacific AP14

1937, Feb. 15 ***Perf. 11***

C21 AP14 20c green	11.00	1.75
C22 AP14 50c carmine	11.00	5.00

Eagle Holding Shield, Olive Branch and Arrows AP15

1938, May 14 ***Perf. 11***

C23 AP15 6c dk blue & carmine	.50	.20
a. Vert. pair, imperf. horiz.	325.00	—
b. Horiz. pair, imperf. vert.	*12,500.*	
c. ultra & carmine	150.00	*1,500.*

Transatlantic Issue

Winged Globe — AP16

1939, May 16 ***Perf. 11***

C24 AP16 30c dull blue	12.00	1.50

AIR POST SPECIAL DELIVERY STAMPS

To provide for the payment of both the postage and the special delivery fee in one stamp.

Great Seal of United States APSD1

Flat Plate Printing

1934 Unwmk. ***Perf. 11***

CE1 APSD1 16c dark blue	.60	.70
Never hinged	.80	

For imperforate variety see No. 771.

1936

CE2 APSD1 16c red & blue	.45	.25
Never hinged	.60	
a. Horiz. pair, imperf. vert.	*3,750.*	

SPECIAL DELIVERY STAMPS

When affixed to any letter or article of mailable matter, secured immediate delivery, between 7 A. M. and midnight, at any post office.

Messenger Running SD1

Flat Plate Printing

1885 Unwmk. ***Perf. 12***

E1 SD1 10c blue	500.00	70.00
Never hinged	1,100.	
On cover		130.00

Messenger Running SD2

1888

E2 SD2 10c blue	500.00	30.00
Never hinged	1,100.	
On cover		90.00

1893

E3 SD2 10c orange	260.00	40.00
Never hinged	600.00	
On cover		130.00

Messenger Running SD3

Line under "Ten Cents"

1894

E4 SD3 10c blue	850.00	55.00
Never hinged	2,100.	
On cover		210.00

1895 **Wmk. 191**

E5 SD3 10c blue	210.00	10.00
Never hinged	470.00	
On cover		20.00
a. Dots in curved frame above messenger (plate 882)	275.00	15.00
Never hinged	600.00	
b. Printed on both sides	—	

Messenger on Bicycle SD4

1902

E6 SD4 10c ultramarine	230.00	10.00
Never hinged	525.00	
a. 10c blue	230.00	10.00
Never hinged	525.00	
On cover		20.00

Helmet of Mercury and Olive Branch — SD5

1908

E7 SD5 10c green	70.00	45.00
Never hinged	150.00	
On cover		200.00

1911 Wmk. 190 ***Perf. 12***

E8 SD4 10c ultramarine	105.00	8.00
Never hinged	230.00	
b. 10c violet blue	120.00	12.00
Never hinged	270.00	
On cover		17.50

1914 ***Perf. 10***

E9 SD4 10c ultramarine	190.00	12.00
Never hinged	425.00	
On cover		45.00
a. 10c blue	240.00	15.00
Never hinged	525.00	
On cover		45.00

1916 Unwmk. ***Perf. 10***

E10 SD4 10c pale ultra	320.00	45.00
Never hinged	700.00	
On cover		100.00
a. 10c blue	350.00	50.00
Never hinged	750.00	
On cover		110.00

1917 ***Perf. 11***

E11 SD4 10c ultramarine	20.00	.75
Never hinged	45.00	
On cover		4.00
b. 10c gray violet	30.00	3.00
Never hinged	65.00	
c. 10c blue	65.00	4.00
Never hinged	140.00	
On cover		15.00
d. Perf. 10 at left		—

Postman and Motorcycle SD6

Post Office Truck SD7

1922-25

E12 SD6 10c gray violet	40.00	1.00
Never hinged	90.00	
On cover		2.00
a. 10c deep ultramarine	50.00	2.00
Never hinged	115.00	
On cover		3.50
E13 SD6 15c deep orange ('25)	27.50	1.75
Never hinged	55.00	
On cover		17.50
E14 SD7 20c black ('25)	2.00	1.00
Never hinged	4.25	
On cover		5.00
Nos. E12-E14 (3)	69.50	3.75

No. E13 measures 36½x21½mm
No. E16 measures 36¾x22¼mm
No. E14 measures 35½x21½mm
No. E19 measures 36¼x22mm

Rotary Press Printing

1927-31 ***Perf. 11x10½***

E15 SD6 10c gray violet	.65	.25
Never hinged	1.20	
a. 10c red lilac	.65	.25
Never hinged	1.20	
b. 10c gray lilac	.65	.25
Never hinged	1.20	
On cover		.30
c. Horiz. pair, imperf. btwn.	325.00	
Never hinged	*550.00*	

No. E15 measures 36½x21¾mm. Stamps from the flat plates measure 36x21½mm.

E16 SD6 15c orange ('31)	.70	.25
Never hinged	1.05	
On cover		1.50

REGISTRATION STAMP

Issued for the prepayment of registry fees; not usable for postage.

Eagle — RS1

Wmk. 190

1911, Dec. 1 Engr. ***Perf. 12***

F1 RS1 10c ultramarine	70.00	9.00
Never hinged	150.00	
On cover		50.00

POSTAGE DUE STAMPS

For affixing, by a postal clerk to any piece of mailable matter, to denote the amount to be collected from the addressee because of insufficient prepayment of postage.

Unused Values for Nos. J1-J14 are for stamps with full original gum.

D1

D2

Printed by the American Bank Note Company

1879 Unwmk. Engraved ***Perf. 12***

J1 D1 1c brown	90.00	14.00
Never hinged	250.00	
J2 D1 2c brown	425.00	18.00
Never hinged	1,100.	
J3 D1 3c brown	105.00	6.00
Never hinged	300.00	
J4 D1 5c brown	825.00	70.00
Never hinged	2,100.	
J5 D1 10c brown	950.00	70.00
Never hinged	2,500.	
a. Imperf., pair	*3,000.*	
J6 D1 30c brown	400.00	65.00
Never hinged	900.00	
J7 D1 50c brown	650.00	90.00
Never hinged	1,750.	
Nos. J1-J7 (7)	3,445.	333.00

Special Printing

1879

J8 D1 1c deep brown	*20,000.*
J9 D1 2c deep brown	*15,000.*
J10 D1 3c deep brown	*25,000.*
J11 D1 5c deep brown	*13,500.*
J12 D1 10c deep brown	*8,000.*
J13 D1 30c deep brown	*8,500.*
J14 D1 50c deep brown	*8,000.*

1884

J15 D1 1c red brown	75.00	7.00
Never hinged	200.00	

J16 D1 2c red brown 90.00 6.00
Never hinged 250.00
J17 D1 3c red brown 1,150. 300.00
Never hinged 2,500.
J18 D1 5c red brown 625.00 45.00
Never hinged 1,450.
J19 D1 10c red brown 625.00 35.00
Never hinged 1,450.
J20 D1 30c red brown 225.00 60.00
Never hinged 550.00
J21 D1 50c red brown 1,900. 225.00
Never hinged 4,250.
Nos. J15-J21 (7) 4,690. 678.00

1891
J22 D1 1c bright claret 35.00 2.00
Never hinged 95.00
J23 D1 2c bright claret 37.50 2.00
Never hinged 100.00
J24 D1 3c bright claret 75.00 16.00
Never hinged 200.00
J25 D1 5c bright claret 110.00 16.00
Never hinged 325.00
J26 D1 10c bright claret 180.00 30.00
Never hinged 550.00
J27 D1 30c bright claret 650.00 225.00
Never hinged 1,800.
J28 D1 50c bright claret 700.00 210.00
Never hinged 1,900.
Nos. J22-J28 (7) 1,787. 501.00

See Die and Plate Proofs in the Scott U.S. Specialized for imperfs. on stamp paper.

Printed by the Bureau of Engraving and Printing

1894
J29 D2 1c vermilion 2,750. 725.
Never hinged 5,500.
J30 D2 2c vermilion 850. 350.
Never hinged 2,100.

1894
J31 D2 1c deep claret 80.00 12.00
Never hinged 300.00
b. Vert. pair, imperf. horiz. —
J32 D2 2c deep claret 70.00 10.00
Never hinged 275.00
J33 D2 3c deep claret 220.00 50.00
Never hinged 600.00
J34 D2 5c deep claret 350.00 55.00
Never hinged 1,000.
J35 D2 10c deep claret 400.00 40.00
Never hinged 1,100.
J36 D2 30c deep claret 600.00 225.00
Never hinged 1,400.
a. 30c carmine 750.00 275.00
Never hinged 1,750.
b. 30c pale rose 500.00 200.00
Never hinged 1,250.
J37 D2 50c deep claret 2,000. 800.00
Never hinged 4,750.
a. 50c pale rose 1,800. 725.00
Never hinged 4,250.
Nos. J31-J37 (7) 3,720. 1,192.

Shades are numerous in the 1894 and later issues.
See Die and Plate Proofs in the Scott U.S. Specialized for 1c imperf. on stamp paper.

1895 **Wmk. 191**
J38 D2 1c deep claret 15.00 1.00
Never hinged 40.00
J39 D2 2c deep claret 15.00 1.00
Never hinged 40.00
J40 D2 3c deep claret 110.00 4.00
Never hinged 275.00
J41 D2 5c deep claret 115.00 4.00
Never hinged 290.00
J42 D2 10c deep claret 115.00 6.00
Never hinged 290.00
J43 D2 30c deep claret 700.00 70.00
Never hinged 1,800.
J44 D2 50c deep claret 450.00 50.00
Never hinged 1,200.
Nos. J38-J44 (7) 1,520. 136.00

1910-12 **Wmk. 190**
J45 D2 1c deep claret 45.00 5.00
Never hinged 130.00
a. 1c rose carmine 40.00 5.00
Never hinged 120.00
J46 D2 2c deep claret 45.00 2.00
Never hinged 130.00
a. 2c rose carmine 40.00 2.00
Never hinged 120.00
J47 D2 3c deep claret 675.00 50.00
Never hinged 1,750.
J48 D2 5c deep claret 130.00 12.00
Never hinged 300.00
a. 5c rose carmine 130.00 12.00
Never hinged 300.00
J49 D2 10c deep claret 140.00 20.00
Never hinged 360.00
a. 10c rose carmine 140.00 20.00
Never hinged 360.00
J50 D2 50c deep claret ('12) 1,150. 175.00
Never hinged 3,000.
Nos. J45-J50 (6) 2,185. 264.00

1914 ***Perf. 10***
J52 D2 1c carmine lake 90.00 15.00
Never hinged 260.00
a. 1c dull rose 95.00 15.00
Never hinged 270.00
J53 D2 2c carmine lake 70.00 1.00
Never hinged 200.00
a. 2c dull rose 75.00 2.00
Never hinged 210.00
b. 2c vermilion 75.00 2.00
Never hinged 210.00
J54 D2 3c carmine lake 1,150. 75.00
Never hinged 3,300.
a. 3c dull rose 1,100. 75.00
Never hinged 3,250.
J55 D2 5c carmine lake 55.00 6.00
Never hinged 160.00
a. 5c dull rose 45.00 4.00
Never hinged 150.00
J56 D2 10c carmine lake 80.00 4.00
Never hinged 220.00
a. 10c dull rose 85.00 5.00
Never hinged 240.00
J57 D2 30c carmine lake 250.00 25.00
Never hinged 575.00
J58 D2 50c carmine lake *17,500.* 1,400.
Never hinged *32,500.*
Nos. J52-J58 (7) 19,195. 1,526.

1916 **Unwmk.** ***Perf. 10***
J59 D2 1c rose 4,500. 675.00
Never hinged 10,000.
J60 D2 2c rose 275.00 75.00
Never hinged 750.00

1917 ***Perf. 11***
J61 D2 1c carmine rose 3.00 .25
Never hinged 10.00
a. 1c rose red 3.00 .25
Never hinged 10.00
b. 1c deep claret 3.00 .25
Never hinged 10.00
J62 D2 2c carmine rose 3.00 .25
Never hinged 10.00
a. 2c rose red 3.00 .25
Never hinged 10.00
b. 2c deep claret 3.00 .25
Never hinged 10.00
J63 D2 3c carmine rose 15.00 .80
Never hinged 40.00
a. 3c rose red 15.00 .80
Never hinged 40.00
b. 3c deep claret 15.00 .80
Never hinged 40.00
J64 D2 5c carmine 12.50 .80
Never hinged 37.50
a. 5c rose red 12.50 .80
Never hinged 37.50
b. 5c deep claret 12.50 .80
Never hinged 37.50
J65 D2 10c carmine rose 25.00 1.00
Never hinged 70.00
a. 10c rose red 25.00 1.00
Never hinged 70.00
b. 10c deep claret 25.00 1.00
Never hinged 70.00
J66 D2 30c carmine rose 90.00 2.00
Never hinged 260.00
a. 30c deep claret 90.00 2.00
Never hinged 260.00
J67 D2 50c carmine rose 150.00 1.00
Never hinged 370.00
a. 50c rose red 150.00 1.00
Never hinged 370.00
b. 50c deep claret 150.00 1.00
Never hinged 370.00
Nos. J61-J67 (7) 298.50 6.10

1925
J68 D2 ½c dull red 1.00 .25
Never hinged 1.75

D3

D4

1930 ***Perf. 11***
J69 D3 ½c carmine 4.50 1.90
Never hinged 10.00
J70 D3 1c carmine 3.00 .35
Never hinged 7.00
J71 D3 2c carmine 4.00 .35
Never hinged 9.00
J72 D3 3c carmine 21.00 2.75
Never hinged 50.00
J73 D3 5c carmine 19.00 5.00
Never hinged 45.00
J74 D3 10c carmine 45.00 2.00
Never hinged 100.00
J75 D3 30c carmine 150.00 4.00
Never hinged 325.00
J76 D3 50c carmine 200.00 2.00
Never hinged 450.00
J77 D4 $1 carmine 35.00 .35
Never hinged 70.00
a. $1 scarlet 30.00 .35
Never hinged 60.00
J78 D4 $5 carmine 40.00 .35
Never hinged 90.00
a. $5 scarlet 35.00 .35
Never hinged 75.00
Nos. J69-J78 (10) 521.50 19.05

Rotary Press Printing

1931-56 ***Perf. 11x10½***
J79 D3 ½c dull carmine .90 .20
Never hinged 1.30
J80 D3 1c dull carmine .20 .20
Never hinged .30
J81 D3 2c dull carmine .20 .20
Never hinged .30
J82 D3 3c dull carmine .25 .20
Never hinged .40
J83 D3 5c dull carmine .40 .20
Never hinged .60
J84 D3 10c dull carmine 1.10 .20
Never hinged 1.80
J85 D3 30c dull carmine 7.50 .25
Never hinged 11.50
J86 D3 50c dull carmine 9.00 .25
Never hinged 15.00

Perf. 10½x11
J87 D4 $1 scarlet ('56) 30.00 .25
Never hinged 47.50
Nos. J79-J87 (9) 49.55 1.95

J79a D3 ½c scarlet .90 .20
Never hinged 1.30
J80a D3 1c scarlet .20 .20
Never hinged .30
J81a D3 2c scarlet .20 .20
Never hinged .30
J82a D3 3c scarlet .25 .20
Never hinged .40
J83a D3 5c scarlet .40 .20
Never hinged .60
J84a D3 10c scarlet 1.10 .20
Never hinged 1.60
J85a D3 30c scarlet 7.50 .25
Never hinged 10.00
J86a D3 50c scarlet 10.00 .25
Never hinged 15.00
Nos. J79a-J86a (8) 20.55 1.70

UNITED STATES OFFICES IN CHINA

Issued for sale by the postal agency at Shanghai, at their surcharged value in local currency. Valid to the amount of their original values for the prepayment of postage on mail dispatched from the US postal agency at Shanghai to addresses in the US.

Nos. 498-499, 502-504, 506-510, 512, 514-518 Surcharged

1919 **Unwmk.** ***Perf. 11***
K1 A140 2c on 1c grn 25.00 *50.00*
Never hinged 70.00
K2 A140 4c on 2c rose, I 25.00 *50.00*
Never hinged 70.00
K3 A140 6c on 3c vio, II 57.50 *110.00*
Never hinged 140.00
K4 A140 8c on 4c brn 57.50 *110.00*
Never hinged 140.00
K5 A140 10c on 5c blue 65.00 *110.00*
Never hinged 170.00
K6 A140 12c on 6c red org 85.00 *160.00*
Never hinged 220.00
K7 A140 14c on 7c blk 87.50 *175.00*
Never hinged 225.00
K8 A148 16c on 8c ol bis 70.00 *120.00*
Never hinged 180.00
a. 16c on 8c olive green 60.00 *100.00*
Never hinged 150.00
K9 A148 18c on 9c sal red 65.00 *140.00*
Never hinged 170.00
K10 A148 20c on 10c org yel 60.00 *110.00*
Never hinged 160.00
K11 A148 24c on 12c brn car 80.00 *125.00*
Never hinged 200.00
a. 24c on 12c claret brown 105.00 *170.00*
Never hinged 270.00
K12 A148 30c on 15c gray 87.50 *190.00*
Never hinged 210.00
K13 A148 40c on 20c dp ultra 130.00 *275.00*
Never hinged 300.00
K14 A148 60c on 30c org red 120.00 *220.00*
Never hinged 280.00
K15 A148 $1 on 50c lt vio 575.00 *800.00*
Never hinged 1,300.
K16 A148 $2 on $1 vio brn 450.00 *700.00*
Never hinged 1,000.
a. Double surcharge *8,000.* *8,000.*
Never hinged *13,000.*
Nos. K1-K16 (16) 2,040. 3,445.

Nos. 498 and 528B Surcharged

1922, July 3
K17 A140 2c on 1c green 110.00 *160.00*
Never hinged 250.00
K18 A140 4c on 2c car, VII 100.00 *140.00*
Never hinged 230.00
a. "SHANGHAI" omitted *7,500.*
b. "CHINA" only *15,000.*

OFFICIAL STAMPS

The franking privilege having been abolished, as of July 1, 1873, these stamps were provided for each of the departments of Government for the prepayment of postage on official matter.

Penalty franks were first authorized in 1877, and their expanded use after 1879 reduced the need for official stamps, the use of which was finally abolished on July 5, 1884.

Designs, except Post Office, resemble those illustrated but are not identical. Each bears the name of Department. Portraits are as follows: 1c, Franklin; 2c, Jackson; 3c, Washington; 6c, Lincoln; 7c, Stanton; 10c, Jefferson; 12c, Clay; 15c, Webster; 24c, Scott; 30c, Hamilton; 90c, Perry.

Grade, condition and original gum are very important in valuing Nos. O1-O120 unused.

Printed by the Continental Bank Note Co.
Thin Hard Paper

O1

1873 **Unwmk.** **Engr.** ***Perf. 12***
Dept. of Agriculture
O1 O1 1c yellow 270.00 *180.00*
Never hinged 600.00
No gum 160.00
On wrapper *1,250.*
O2 O1 2c yellow 230.00 85.00
Never hinged 500.00
No gum 100.00
On cover *3,500.*
O3 O1 3c yellow 210.00 16.00
Never hinged 460.00
No gum 80.00
On cover *900.00*
O4 O1 6c yellow 240.00 60.00
Never hinged 525.00
No gum 95.00
On cover *7,500.*
O5 O1 10c yellow 500.00 200.00
Never hinged 1,150.
No gum 220.00
On cover —
O6 O1 12c yellow 425.00 260.00
Never hinged 950.00
No gum 250.00
On cover *11,000.*
O7 O1 15c yellow 425.00 230.00
Never hinged 950.00
No gum 225.00
O8 O1 24c yellow 425.00 220.00
Never hinged 950.00
No gum 225.00
O9 O1 30c yellow 500.00 270.00
Never hinged 1,200.
No gum 275.00
Nos. O1-O9 (9) 3,225. 1,521.

Special printings overprinted "SPECIMEN" follow No. O120.

Executive Dept.
O10 O1 1c carmine 850.00 475.00
Never hinged 2,250.
No gum 450.00
On cover *3,250.*
O11 O1 2c carmine 550.00 240.00
Never hinged 1,250.
No gum 240.00
On cover *3,750.*
O12 O1 3c carmine 700.00 210.00
Never hinged 1,600.
No gum 275.00
a. 3c violet rose 850.00 210.00
Never hinged 1,600.
No gum 325.00
On cover, #O12 or O12a *1,000.*
O13 O1 6c carmine 825.00 550.00
Never hinged 2,250.
No gum 325.00
On cover *3,500.*

O14 O1 10c carmine 1,100. 650.00
Never hinged 2,500.
No gum 600.00
On cover —
Nos. O10-O14 (5) 4,025. 2,125.

Special printings overprinted "SPECIMEN" follow No. O120.

Dept. of the Interior

O15 O1 1c vermilion 75.00 10.00
Never hinged 170.00
No gum 30.00
On cover 160.00
O16 O1 2c vermilion 70.00 12.00
Never hinged 160.00
No gum 30.00
On cover 65.00
O17 O1 3c vermilion 80.00 6.00
Never hinged 175.00
No gum 35.00
On cover 40.00
O18 O1 6c vermilion 70.00 10.00
Never hinged 160.00
No gum 27.50
On cover 95.00
O19 O1 10c vermilion 70.00 20.00
Never hinged 160.00
No gum 27.50
On cover 450.00
O20 O1 12c vermilion 90.00 12.00
Never hinged 200.00
No gum 35.00
On cover 450.00
O21 O1 15c vermilion 200.00 25.00
Never hinged 450.00
No gum 80.00
On cover 650.00
O22 O1 24c vermilion 180.00 20.00
Never hinged 400.00
No gum 60.00
On cover 2,500.
a. Double impression
O23 O1 30c vermilion 275.00 20.00
Never hinged 600.00
No gum 100.00
On cover —
O24 O1 90c vermilion 300.00 50.00
Never hinged 675.00
No gum 120.00
On cover 4,500.
Nos. O15-O24 (10) 1,410. 185.00

Special printings overprinted "SPECIMEN" follow No. O120.

Dept. of Justice

O25 O1 1c purple 250.00 100.00
Never hinged 550.00
No gum 100.00
On cover 1,750.
O26 O1 2c purple 310.00 110.00
Never hinged 700.00
No gum 120.00
On cover 1,500.
O27 O1 3c purple 320.00 35.00
Never hinged 725.00
No gum 110.00
On cover 575.00
O28 O1 6c purple 310.00 45.00
Never hinged 700.00
No gum 120.00
On cover 1,200.
O29 O1 10c purple 310.00 100.00
Never hinged 700.00
No gum 120.00
On cover 3,750.
O30 O1 12c purple 260.00 75.00
Never hinged 575.00
No gum 95.00
On cover 1,750.
O31 O1 15c purple 450.00 200.00
Never hinged 1,000.
No gum 210.00
On cover 1,250.
O32 O1 24c purple 1,250. 425.00
Never hinged 3,000.
No gum 550.00
On cover 8,000.
O33 O1 30c purple 1,250. 350.00
Never hinged 3,000.
No gum 550.00
On cover 22,000.
O34 O1 90c purple 1,900. 900.00
Never hinged 4,250.
No gum 800.00
On cover 26,000.
Nos. O25-O34 (10) 6,610. 2,340.

Special printings overprinted "SPECIMEN" follow No. O120.

Navy Dept.

O35 O1 1c ultramarine 160.00 50.00
Never hinged 350.00
No gum 65.00
On cover 750.00
a. 1c dull blue 160.00 50.00
Never hinged 350.00
No gum 65.00
O36 O1 2c ultramarine 160.00 25.00
Never hinged 350.00
No gum 65.00
On cover 350.00
a. 2c dull blue 160.00 25.00
Never hinged 350.00
No gum 65.00
O37 O1 3c ultramarine 170.00 15.00
Never hinged 375.00
No gum 60.00
On cover 160.00
a. 3c dull blue 170.00 15.00
Never hinged 375.00
No gum 60.00
O38 O1 6c ultramarine 150.00 25.00
Never hinged 325.00
No gum 55.00
On cover 750.00
a. 6c dull blue 150.00 25.00
Never hinged 325.00
No gum 55.00
O39 O1 7c ultramarine 650.00 230.00
Never hinged 1,500.
No gum 250.00
On cover 3,000.
a. 7c dull blue 650.00 230.00
Never hinged 1,500.
No gum 250.00
O40 O1 10c ultramarine 210.00 45.00
Never hinged 475.00
No gum 75.00
On cover 4,000.
a. 10c dull blue 210.00 45.00
Never hinged 475.00
No gum 75.00
O41 O1 12c ultramarine 220.00 45.00
Never hinged 500.00
No gum 80.00
On cover 3,000.
O42 O1 15c ultramarine 375.00 75.00
Never hinged 825.00
No gum 135.00
O43 O1 24c ultramarine 400.00 85.00
Never hinged 875.00
No gum 160.00
On cover 20,000.
a. 24c dull blue 375.00 80.00
Never hinged 825.00
No gum 150.00
O44 O1 30c ultramarine 325.00 50.00
Never hinged 725.00
No gum 125.00
O45 O1 90c ultramarine 1,050. 375.00
Never hinged 2,600.
No gum 450.00
a. Double impression 5,500.
Nos. O35-O45 (11) 3,870. 1,020.

Special printings overprinted "SPECIMEN" follow No. O120.

O6

Post Office Dept.

O47 O6 1c black 25.00 12.00
Never hinged 60.00
No gum 12.00
On cover 60.00
O48 O6 2c black 30.00 10.00
Never hinged 75.00
No gum 13.00
On cover 160.00
a. Double impression 600.00 400.00
O49 O6 3c black 10.00 2.00
Never hinged 25.00
No gum 3.00
On cover 20.00
a. Printed on both sides 7,500.
O50 O6 6c black 30.00 8.00
Never hinged 75.00
No gum 12.00
On cover 75.00
a. Diagonal half used as 3c on cover 5,750.
b. Double impression 3,000.
O51 O6 10c black 140.00 55.00
Never hinged 325.00
No gum 60.00
On cover 400.00
O52 O6 12c black 120.00 12.00
Never hinged 275.00
No gum 40.00
On cover 1,000.
O53 O6 15c black 140.00 20.00
Never hinged 325.00
No gum 50.00
On cover 5,000.
O54 O6 24c black 200.00 25.00
Never hinged 450.00
No gum 70.00
O55 O6 30c black 200.00 25.00
Never hinged 450.00
No gum 70.00
On cover —
O56 O6 90c black 220.00 25.00
Never hinged 500.00
No gum 80.00
Nos. O47-O56 (10) 1,115. 194.00

Stamps of the POD are often on paper with a gray surface. This is due to insufficient wiping of the plates during printing.

Special printings overprinted "SPECIMEN" follow No. O120.

Seward — O8

Dept. of State

O57 O1 1c dark green 260.00 75.00
Never hinged 575.00
No gum 110.00
On cover —
O58 O1 2c dark green 310.00 100.00
Never hinged 700.00
No gum 120.00
On cover 1,000.
O59 O1 3c bright green 220.00 25.00
Never hinged 500.00
No gum 85.00
On cover 450.00
O60 O1 6c bright green 220.00 30.00
Never hinged 500.00
No gum 85.00
On cover 650.00
O61 O1 7c dark green 290.00 65.00
Never hinged 650.00
No gum 95.00
On cover 1,000.
O62 O1 10c dark green 230.00 55.00
Never hinged 525.00
No gum 100.00
On cover 2,000.
O63 O1 12c dark green 310.00 125.00
Never hinged 700.00
No gum 140.00
On cover 1,500.
O64 O1 15c dark green 320.00 90.00
Never hinged 725.00
No gum 130.00
On cover 5,750.
O65 O1 24c dark green 525.00 230.00
Never hinged 1,200.
No gum 275.00
On cover 17,500.
O66 O1 30c dark green 500.00 180.00
Never hinged 1,150.
No gum 240.00
On cover —
O67 O1 90c dark green 1,050. 325.00
Never hinged 2,500.
No gum 525.00
On cover 62,500.
O68 O8 $2 green & black 1,500. 1,500.
Never hinged 3,000.
No gum 750.00
On cover 175,000.
O69 O8 $5 green & black 6,500. 12,000.
Never hinged 15,000.
No gum 3,250.
O70 O8 $10 green & black 4,750. 6,500.
Never hinged 11,500.
No gum 2,750.
O71 O8 $20 green & black 5,000. 4,000.
Never hinged 12,500.
No gum 2,500.

No. O71 used is valued with a blue or red favor cancel. Nos. O68-O71 with pen cancels sell for approximately 25-40% of the values shown.

Special printings overprinted "SPECIMEN" follow No. O120.

Treasury Dept.

O72 O1 1c brown 115.00 10.00
Never hinged 250.00
No gum 45.00
On cover 100.00
O73 O1 2c brown 120.00 8.00
Never hinged 275.00
No gum 40.00
On cover 75.00
O74 O1 3c brown 105.00 2.00
Never hinged 230.00
No gum 40.00
On cover 30.00
a. Double impression 5,000.
O75 O1 6c brown 115.00 4.00
Never hinged 250.00
No gum 40.00
On cover 75.00
O76 O1 7c brown 240.00 35.00
Never hinged 550.00
No gum 95.00
On cover 750.00
O77 O1 10c brown 230.00 12.00
Never hinged 525.00
No gum 90.00
On cover 450.00
O78 O1 12c brown 290.00 10.00
Never hinged 650.00
No gum 100.00
On cover 600.00
O79 O1 15c brown 290.00 12.00
Never hinged 650.00
No gum 100.00
On cover 850.00
O80 O1 24c brown 650.00 90.00
Never hinged 1,500.
No gum 270.00
O81 O1 30c brown 400.00 12.00
Never hinged 900.00
No gum 140.00
On cover 5,000.
O82 O1 90c brown 400.00 15.00
Never hinged 900.00
No gum 140.00
Nos. O72-O82 (11) 2,955. 210.00

Special printings overprinted "SPECIMEN" follow No. O120.

War Dept.

O83 O1 1c rose 230.00 15.00
Never hinged 525.00
No gum 90.00
On cover 140.00
O84 O1 2c rose 230.00 15.00
Never hinged 525.00
No gum 90.00
On cover 70.00
O85 O1 3c rose 230.00 5.00
Never hinged 525.00
No gum 90.00
On cover 40.00
O86 O1 6c rose 600.00 10.00
Never hinged 1,350.
No gum 250.00
On cover 60.00
O87 O1 7c rose 160.00 90.00
Never hinged 360.00
No gum 80.00
On cover —
O88 O1 10c rose 130.00 25.00
Never hinged 290.00
No gum 45.00
On cover 2,000.
O89 O1 12c rose 250.00 12.00
Never hinged 550.00
No gum 110.00
On cover 450.00
O90 O1 15c rose 80.00 15.00
Never hinged 175.00
No gum 30.00
On cover 3,000.
O91 O1 24c rose 80.00 12.00
Never hinged 175.00
No gum 30.00
On cover —
O92 O1 30c rose 125.00 12.00
Never hinged 275.00
No gum 45.00
On cover
O93 O1 90c rose 210.00 50.00
Never hinged 475.00
No gum 80.00
On cover
Nos. O83-O93 (11) 2,325. 261.00

Special printings overprinted "SPECIMEN" follow No. O120.

Printed by the American Bank Note Co.

1879 **Soft Porous Paper**

Dept. of Agriculture

O94 O1 1c yel, no gum 6,000.
O95 O1 3c yellow 550.00 100.00
Never hinged 1,250.
No gum 240.00
On cover —

Dept. of the Interior

O96 O1 1c vermilion 300.00 *275.00*
Never hinged 675.00
No gum 160.00
O97 O1 2c vermilion 10.00 3.00
Never hinged 22.50
No gum 3.00
On cover 150.00
O98 O1 3c vermilion 10.00 3.00
Never hinged 22.50
No gum 3.00
On cover 30.00
O99 O1 6c vermilion 10.00 *12.50*
Never hinged 22.50
No gum 3.00
On cover 200.00
O100 O1 10c vermilion 110.00 75.00
Never hinged 250.00
No gum 60.00
On cover 1,200.
O101 O1 12c vermilion 230.00 115.00
Never hinged 525.00
No gum 130.00
On cover —
O102 O1 15c vermilion 400.00 260.00
Never hinged 900.00
No gum 200.00
On cover —
O103 O1 24c vermilion 4,400. —
Never hinged 10,000.
No gum 2,100.

Dept. of Justice

O106 O1 3c bluish pur 175.00 100.00
Never hinged 400.00
No gum 80.00
On cover 700.00
O107 O1 6c bluish pur 450.00 250.00
Never hinged 1,000.
No gum 210.00
On cover —

Post Office Dept.

O108 O6 3c black 30.00 8.00
Never hinged 70.00
No gum 10.00
On cover —

Treasury Dept.

O109 O1 3c brown 80.00 10.00
Never hinged 175.00
No gum 35.00
On cover 110.00
O110 O1 6c brown 200.00 50.00
Never hinged 450.00
No gum 65.00
On cover 300.00
O111 O1 10c brown 260.00 80.00
Never hinged 575.00
No gum 90.00
On cover 750.00
O112 O1 30c brown 2,400. 425.00
Never hinged 5,500.
No gum 875.00
O113 O1 90c brown 4,500. 525.00
Never hinged 10,000.
No gum 1,650.
Nos. O109-O113 (5) 7,440. 1,090.

War Dept.

O114 O1 1c rose red 6.00 4.00
Never hinged 13.50
No gum 2.50
On cover 55.00
O115 O1 2c rose red 12.00 4.00
Never hinged 27.50
No gum 4.00
On cover 40.00
O116 O1 3c rose red 12.00 2.00
Never hinged 27.50
No gum 4.00
On cover 35.00
a. Imperf., pair 5,000.
b. Double impression 6,500.
O117 O1 6c rose red 11.00 3.00
Never hinged 25.00
No gum 4.00
On cover 50.00
O118 O1 10c rose red 65.00 50.00
Never hinged 150.00
No gum 26.00
On cover 1,800.

O119 O1 12c rose red 60.00 14.00
Never hinged 140.00
No gum 20.00
On cover —
O120 O1 30c rose red 220.00 100.00
Never hinged 500.00
No gum 90.00
Nos. O114-O120 (7) 386.00 177.00

SPECIAL PRINTINGS

Special printings of Official stamps were made in 1875 at the time the other Reprints, Re-issues and Special Printings were printed. They are ungummed.

Although perforated, these stamps were sometimes (but not always) cut apart with scissors. As a result the perforations may be mutilated and the design damaged.

All values exist imperforate.

Overprinted in Block Letters

1875 ***Perf. 12***

Thin, hard white paper
Type D

AGRICULTURE
Carmine Overprint

O1S D 1c yellow 30.00
a. "Sepcimen" error 2,500.
b. Small dotted "i" in "Specimen" 400.00
c. Horiz. ribbed paper 37.50
O2S D 2c yellow 55.00
a. "Sepcimen" error 3,000.
O3S D 3c yellow 300.00
a. "Sepcimen" error *11,000.*
O4S D 6c yellow 325.00
a. "Sepcimen" error *17,500.*
O5S D 10c yellow 325.00
a. "Sepcimen" error *15,000.*
O6S D 12c yellow 325.00
a. "Sepcimen" error *11,000.*
O7S D 15c yellow 325.00
a. "Sepcimen" error *11,000.*
O8S D 24c yellow 325.00
a. "Sepcimen" error *11,000.*
O9S D 30c yellow 325.00
a. "Sepcimen" error *13,500.*
Nos. O1S-O9S (9) 2,335.

EXECUTIVE
Blue Overprint

O10S D 1c carmine 30.00
a. Small dotted "i" in "Specimen" 500.00
b. Horiz. ribbed paper 35.00
c. As "b," small dotted "i" in "Specimen" 450.00
O11S D 2c carmine 55.00
O12S D 3c carmine 67.50
O13S D 6c carmine 67.50
O14S D 10c carmine 67.50
Nos. O10S-O14S (5) 287.50

INTERIOR
Blue Overprint

O15S D 1c vermilion 55.00
O16S D 2c vermilion 120.00
a. "Sepcimen" error *11,000.*
O17S D 3c vermilion 1,400.
O18S D 6c vermilion 1,400.
O19S D 10c vermilion 1,400.
O20S D 12c vermilion 1,400.
O21S D 15c vermilion 1,400.
O22S D 24c vermilion 1,400.
O23S D 30c vermilion 1,400.
O24S D 90c vermilion 1,400.
Nos. O15S-O24S (10) 11,375.

JUSTICE
Blue Overprint

O25S D 1c purple 30.00
a. "Sepcimen" error 1,900.
b. Small dotted "i" in "Specimen" 325.00
c. Horiz. ribbed paper 35.00
d. As "c," small dotted "i" in "Specimen" 450.00
O26S D 2c purple 55.00
a. "Sepcimen" error 2,500.
O27S D 3c purple 800.00
a. "Sepcimen" error *8,750.*
O28S D 6c purple 900.00
O29S D 10c purple 900.00
O30S D 12c purple 900.00
a. "Sepcimen" error *13,500.*
O31S D 15c purple 900.00
a. "Sepcimen" error *13,500.*
O32S D 24c purple 900.00
a. "Sepcimen" error *13,500.*
O33S D 30c purple 900.00
a. "Sepcimen" error *13,500.*
O34S D 90c purple 900.00
Nos. O25S-O34S (10) 7,185.

NAVY
Carmine Overprint

O35S D 1c ultramarine 32.50
a. "Sepcimen" error 2,500.
b. Double "Specimen" ovpt. *1,900.*
O36S D 2c ultramarine 60.00
a. "Sepcimen" error 3,250.
O37S D 3c ultramarine 1,000.
O38S D 6c ultramarine 1,100.
O39S D 7c ultramarine 450.00
a. "Sepcimen" error 8,250.
O40S D 10c ultramarine 1,100.
a. "Sepcimen" error *13,500.*
O41S D 12c ultramarine 1,000.
a. "Sepcimen" error *13,500.*
O42S D 15c ultramarine 1,000.
a. "Sepcimen" error *13,500.*
O43S D 24c ultramarine 1,000.
a. "Sepcimen" error *13,500.*
O44S D 30c ultramarine 1,000.
a. "Sepcimen" error *13,500.*
O45S D 90c ultramarine 1,000.
Nos. O35S-O45S (11) 8,742.

POST OFFICE
Carmine Overprint

O47S D 1c black 42.50
a. "Sepcimen" error 1,900.
b. Inverted overprint *2,750.*
O48S D 2c black 250.00
a. "Sepcimen" error 3,250.
O49S D 3c black 1,200.
a. "Sepcimen" error —
O50S D 6c black 1,100.
O51S D 10c black 900.00
a. "Sepcimen" error *11,000.*
O52S D 12c black 1,000.
O53S D 15c black 1,100.
a. "Sepcimen" error *13,500.*
O54S D 24c black 1,100.
a. "Sepcimen" error *11,000.*
O55S D 30c black 1,200.
O56S D 90c black 1,100.
a. "Sepcimen" error —
Nos. O47S-O56S (10) 8,992.

The existence of No. O49Sa has been questioned.

STATE
Carmine Overprint

O57S D 1c bluish green 30.00
a. "Sepcimen" error 1,900.
b. Small dotted "i" in "Specimen" 550.00
c. Horiz. ribbed paper 35.00
d. Double "Specimen" overprint *3,850.*
O58S D 2c bluish green 90.00
a. "Sepcimen" error *2,500.*
O59S D 3c bluish green 120.00
a. "Sepcimen" error 6,000.
O60S D 6c bluish green 275.00
a. "Sepcimen" error 8,250.
O61S D 7c bluish green 120.00
a. "Sepcimen" error 8,250.
O62S D 10c bluish green 500.00
a. "Sepcimen" error *13,500.*
O63S D 12c bluish green 550.00
a. "Sepcimen" error *11,000.*
O64S D 15c bluish green 550.00
O65S D 24c bluish green 550.00
a. "Sepcimen" error *11,000.*
O66S D 30c bluish green 550.00
a. "Sepcimen" error *15,000.*
O67S D 90c bluish green 550.00
a. "Sepcimen" error *11,000.*
O68S D $2 green & black *17,500.*
O69S D $5 green & black *25,000.*
O70S D $10 green & black *50,000.*
O71S D $20 green & black *85,000.*
Nos. O57S-O67S (11) 3,885.

TREASURY
Blue Overprint

O72S D 1c dark brown 75.00
O73S D 2c dark brown 350.00
O74S D 3c dark brown 1,400.
O75S D 6c dark brown 1,400.
O76S D 7c dark brown 850.00
O77S D 10c dark brown 1,350.
O78S D 12c dark brown 1,350.
O79S D 15c dark brown 1,350.
O80S D 24c dark brown 1,350.
O81S D 30c dark brown 1,350.
O82S D 90c dark brown 1,350.
Nos. O72S-O82S (11) 12,175.

WAR
Blue Overprint

O83S D 1c deep rose 30.00
a. "Sepcimen" error 1,400.
O84S D 2c deep rose 120.00
a. "Sepcimen" error 2,000.
O85S D 3c deep rose 1,000.
a. "Sepcimen" error *11,000.*
O86S D 6c deep rose 1,000.
a. "Sepcimen" error *15,000.*
O87S D 7c deep rose 325.00
a. "Sepcimen" error 10,000.
O88S D 10c deep rose 1,000.
a. "Sepcimen" error *13,500.*
O89S D 12c deep rose 1,000.
a. "Sepcimen" error *13,500.*
O90S D 15c deep rose 1,000.
a. "Sepcimen" error *13,500.*
O91S D 24c deep rose 1,000.
a. "Sepcimen" error *13,500.*
O92S D 30c deep rose 1,000.
a. "Sepcimen" error *13,500.*
O93S D 90c deep rose 1,000.
a. "Sepcimen" error *13,500.*
Nos. O83S-O93S (11) 8,475.

Printed by the American Banknote Company

SOFT POROUS PAPER

EXECUTIVE
Blue Overprint

O10xS D 1c violet rose 95.00

NAVY
Carmine Overprint

O35xS D 1c gray blue 100.00
a. Double overprint 1,200.

STATE

O57xS D 1c yellow green 180.00

Official Postal Savings Mail

These stamps were used to prepay postage on official correspondence of the Postal Savings Division of the POD. Discontinued Sept. 23, 1914.

O11

Printed by the Bureau of Engraving and Printing

1911 **Wmk. 191**

O121 O11 2c black 17.50 2.00
Never hinged 40.00
On cover 12.50
O122 O11 50c dark green 160.00 60.00
Never hinged 375.00
On cover 225.00
O123 O11 $1 ultra 200.00 15.00
Never hinged 450.00
On cover 110.00

Wmk. 190

O124 O11 1c dark violet 10.00 2.00
Never hinged 22.50
On cover 15.00
O125 O11 2c black 55.00 7.00
Never hinged 135.00
On cover 25.00
O126 O11 10c carmine 20.00 2.00
Never hinged 50.00
On cover 20.00
Nos. O121-O126 (6) 462.50 88.00

NEWSPAPER STAMPS

For the prepayment of postage on bulk shipments of newspapers and periodicals. From 1875 on, the stamps were affixed to pages of receipt books, sometimes canceled and retained by the post office. Discontinued on July 1, 1898.

Virtually all used stamps of Nos. PR1-PR4 are canceled by blue brush strokes. All are rare. Most used stamps of Nos. PR9-PR32, PR57-PR79 and PR81-PR89 are pen canceled (or uncanceled), with some of Nos. PR9-PR32 also known canceled by a thick blue brush stroke.

Handstamp cancellations on any of these issues are rare and sell for much more than catalogue values which are for pen-canceled examples.

Used values for Nos. PR90-PR125 are for stamps with handstamp cancellations.

Washington — N1

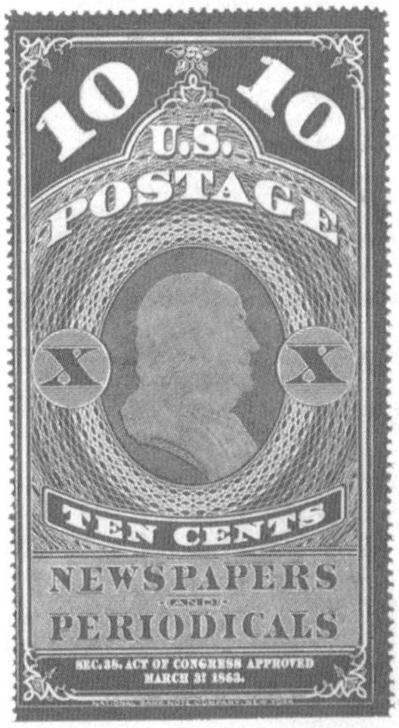

Franklin — N2

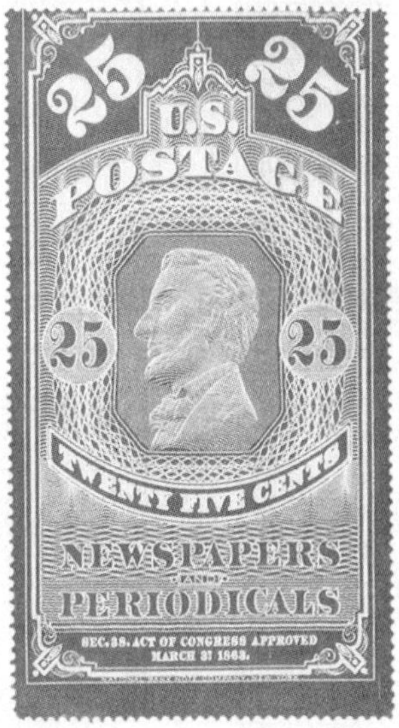

Lincoln — N3

Values for Nos. PR1-PR8 are for examples with perforations on all four sides. Examples with natural straight edges sell for somewhat less. Some panes were fully perforated, while others have natural straight edges either at top or bottom affecting five stamps in the pane of ten.

Printed by the National Bank Note Co.
Thin Hard Paper, No Gum

1865 Unwmk. Typo. *Perf. 12*
Size: 51x95mm

Colored Border

PR1	N1	5c dark blue	750.00	*2,000.*
a.		5c light blue	950.00	—
PR2	N2	10c blue green	300.00	*1,800.*
a.		10c green	300.00	*1,800.*
b.		Pelure paper	350.00	*1,800.*
PR3	N3	25c orange red	325.00	*2,400.*
a.		25c carmine red	350.00	2,400.
b.		Pelure paper	350.00	

Nos. PR1-PR3 used are valued with faults.

White Border
Yellowish Paper

PR4	N1	5c light blue	225.00	*2,400.*
a.		5c dark blue	250.00	—
b.		Pelure paper	275.00	—
		Nos. PR1-PR4 (4)	1,600.	

Reprints of 1865 Issue
Printed by the Continental Bank Note Co. using the original National Bank Note Co. plates

Hard White Paper, Without Gum

1875

PR5	N1	5c dull blue	200.00	
a.		Printed on both sides	*5,750.*	
PR6	N2	10c dk bluish grn	225.00	
a.		Printed on both sides	*4,250.*	
PR7	N3	25c dark carmine	250.00	
		Nos. PR5-PR7 (3)	675.00	

The 5c has white border, 10c and 25c have colored borders.

Printed by the American Bank Note Co.

1880 Soft Porous Paper
White Border

PR8	N1	5c dark blue	775.00

Statue of Freedom — N4

"Justice" — N5

Ceres — N6

"Victory" — N7

Clio — N8

Minerva — N9

Vesta — N10

"Peace" — N11

"Commerce"
N12

Hebe
N13

Indian Maiden — N14

> Values for used examples of Nos. PR9-PR113 are for fine-very fine examples for denominations to $3, and fine for denominations of $3 or higher. Some used Scott numbers may not exist without faults.

Printed by the Continental Bank Note Co.

Engraved Thin Hard Paper

1875 Size: 24x35mm

PR9	N4	2c black	280.00	30.00
		No gum	125.00	
PR10	N4	3c black	280.00	32.50
		No gum	125.00	
PR11	N4	4c black	280.00	30.00
		No gum	125.00	
PR12	N4	6c black	280.00	32.50
		No gum	125.00	
PR13	N4	8c black	325.00	47.50
		No gum	140.00	
PR14	N4	9c black	475.00	95.00
		No gum	200.00	
PR15	N4	10c black	350.00	37.50
		No gum	140.00	
PR16	N5	12c rose	800.00	90.00
		No gum	350.00	
PR17	N5	24c rose	875.00	115.00
		No gum	400.00	
PR18	N5	36c rose	875.00	125.00
		No gum	400.00	
PR19	N5	48c rose	1,250.	200.00
		No gum	500.00	
PR20	N5	60c rose	1,250.	115.00
		No gum	500.00	
PR21	N5	72c rose	1,250.	250.00
		No gum	500.00	
PR22	N5	84c rose	1,850.	375.00
		No gum	700.00	
PR23	N5	96c rose	1,350.	250.00
		No gum	550.00	
PR24	N6	$1.92 dark brn	1,650.	225.00
		No gum	725.00	
PR25	N7	$3 vermilion	1,800.	450.00
		No gum	725.00	
PR26	N8	$6 ultra	3,600.	550.00
		No gum	1,500.	
PR27	N9	$9 yellow	4,000.	600.00
		No gum	1,700.	
PR28	N10	$12 blue grn	4,500.	750.00
		No gum	1,750.	
PR29	N11	$24 dk gray vio	4,500.	800.00
		No gum	1,750.	
PR30	N12	$36 brn rose	5,000.	950.00
		No gum	2,000.	
PR31	N13	$48 red brn	6,250.	1,150.
		No gum	2,300.	
PR32	N14	$60 violet	6,500.	1,250.
		No gum	2,400.	

Special Printing of the 1875 Issue
Printed by the Continental Bank Note Co.

Hard White Paper, Without Gum

PR33	N4	2c gray blk	600.00	
a.		Horizontally ribbed paper	425.00	
PR34	N4	3c gray blk	600.00	
a.		Horizontally ribbed paper	425.00	
PR35	N4	4c gray blk	650.00	
a.		Horizontally ribbed paper	800.00	
PR36	N4	6c gray blk	850.00	
PR37	N4	8c gray blk	950.00	
PR38	N4	9c gray blk	1,050.	
PR39	N4	10c gray blk	1,300.	
PR40	N5	12c pale rose	1,500.	
PR41	N5	24c pale rose	2,100.	
PR42	N5	36c pale rose	2,800.	
PR43	N5	48c pale rose	3,750.	
PR44	N5	60c pale rose	3,750.	
PR45	N5	72c pale rose	4,400.	
PR46	N5	84c pale rose	4,800.	
PR47	N5	96c pale rose	*8,500.*	
PR48	N6	$1.92 dk brn	*22,500.*	
PR49	N7	$3 vermilion	*45,000.*	
PR50	N8	$6 ultra	*80,000.*	
PR51	N9	$9 yell	*160,000.*	
PR52	N10	$12 blue grn	*125,000.*	
PR53	N11	$24 dk gray vio	—	
PR54	N12	$36 brn rose	*250,000.*	
PR55	N13	$48 red brn	—	
PR56	N14	$60 violet	—	

Nos. PR33 to PR56 exist imperf. but were not regularly issued thus. Value, set $60,000.

Printed by the American Bank Note Co.

1879 Soft Porous Paper

PR57	N4	2c black	50.00	8.50
		No gum	20.00	
PR58	N4	3c black	60.00	10.50
		No gum	25.00	
PR59	N4	4c black	60.00	10.50
		No gum	25.00	
PR60	N4	6c black	105.00	21.00
		No gum	45.00	
PR61	N4	8c black	115.00	21.00
		No gum	47.50	
PR62	N4	10c black	115.00	21.00
		No gum	47.50	
PR63	N5	12c red	475.00	85.00
		No gum	200.00	
PR64	N5	24c red	475.00	85.00
		No gum	200.00	
PR65	N5	36c red	1,000.	240.00
		No gum	475.00	
PR66	N5	48c red	1,000.	180.00
		No gum	450.00	
PR67	N5	60c red	1,000.	160.00
		No gum	450.00	
a.		Imperf., pair	*4,000.*	
PR68	N5	72c red	1,250.	300.00
		No gum	575.00	
PR69	N5	84c red	1,250.	225.00
		No gum	575.00	
PR70	N5	96c red	1,200.	160.00
		No gum	525.00	
PR71	N6	$1.92 pale brn	550.00	135.00
		No gum	225.00	
PR72	N7	$3 red ver	625.00	150.00
		No gum	250.00	
PR73	N8	$6 blue	1,050.	230.00
		No gum	400.00	
PR74	N9	$9 orange	800.00	160.00
		No gum	325.00	
PR75	N10	$12 yellow grn	850.00	210.00
		No gum	325.00	
PR76	N11	$24 dk violet	800.00	260.00
		No gum	300.00	
PR77	N12	$36 Indian red	850.00	280.00
		No gum	350.00	
PR78	N13	$48 yel brn	900.00	390.00
		No gum	350.00	
PR79	N14	$60 purple	850.00	360.00
		No gum	350.00	
		Nos. PR57-PR70 (14)	8,155.	1,527.

See the Scott U.S. Specialized Catalogue Die and Plate Proof section for other imperforates.

Special Printing of the 1879 Issue
Printed by the American Bank Note Co.
Without Gum

1881

PR80	N4	2c intense black	1,350.

Regular Issue
With Gum

1885

PR81	N4	1c black	70.00	8.50
		No gum	35.00	
PR82	N5	12c carmine	180.00	20.00
		No gum	75.00	
PR83	N5	24c carmine	180.00	22.50
		No gum	75.00	
PR84	N5	36c carmine	280.00	37.50
		No gum	115.00	
PR85	N5	48c carmine	400.00	55.00
		No gum	175.00	
PR86	N5	60c carmine	525.00	80.00
		No gum	230.00	
PR87	N5	72c carmine	525.00	85.00
		No gum	230.00	
PR88	N5	84c carmine	800.00	200.00
		No gum	300.00	
PR89	N5	96c carmine	700.00	160.00
		No gum	275.00	
		Nos. PR81-PR89 (9)	3,660.	668.50

See the Scott U.S. Specialized Catalogue Die and Plate Proof section for imperforates.

Printed by the Bureau of Engraving and Printing
Soft Wove Paper with pale, whitish gum

1894

PR90	N4	1c intense black	425.00	*750.00*
		No gum	175.00	
PR91	N4	2c intense black	475.00	
		No gum	200.00	
PR92	N4	4c intense black	500.00	—
		No gum	225.00	
PR93	N4	6c intense black	3,750.	
		No gum	1,750.	
PR94	N4	10c intense black	1,150.	
		No gum	500.00	
PR95	N5	12c pink	2,600.	*1,500.*
		No gum	1,100.	
PR96	N5	24c pink	3,750.	*1,750.*
		No gum	1,850.	
PR97	N5	36c pink	*50,000.*	
PR98	N5	60c pink	*55,000.*	*7,500.*
PR99	N5	96c pink	*52,500.*	
PR100	N7	$3 scarlet	*60,000.*	
PR101	N8	$6 pale blue	*60,000.*	—
		No gum	*30,000.*	

Nos. PR90, PR95-PR98 used are valued with fine centering and small faults.

No. PR97 unused is valued in the grade of very good to fine. No. PR98 unused is valued in the grade of fine. Nos. PR99-PR100 unused are valued in the grade of fine-very fine.

Statue of Freedom
N15

"Justice"
N16

"Victory"
N17

Clio
N18

Vesta — N19

"Peace" — N20

"Commerce"
N21

Indian Maiden
N22

1895 Unwmk.
Sizes: 1c-50c, 21x34mm, $2-$100, 24x35mm

PR102	N15	1c black	230.	*100.*
		Never hinged	500.	
		No gum	90.	
PR103	N15	2c black	230.	*100.*
		Never hinged	500.	
		No gum	90.	
PR104	N15	5c black	300.	*150.*
		Never hinged	650.	
		No gum	125.	
PR105	N15	10c black	550.	*350.*
		Never hinged	1,150.	
		No gum	225.	
PR106	N16	25c carmine	750.	500.
		Never hinged	1,650.	
		No gum	300.	
PR107	N16	50c carmine	1,500.	*800.*
		Never hinged	3,250.	
		No gum	575.	
PR108	N17	$2 scarlet	1,500.	*600.*
		Never hinged	3,250.	
		No gum	575.	
PR109	N18	$5 ultra	2,100.	*1,100.*
		Never hinged	4,500.	
		No gum	800.	
PR110	N19	$10 green	3,750.	*1,300.*
		Never hinged	5,000.	
		No gum	900.	
PR111	N20	$20 slate	3,250.	*2,000.*
		Never hinged	6,500.	
		No gum	1,200.	
PR112	N21	$50 dull rose	2,900.	*750.*
		Never hinged	6,250.	
		No gum	1,100.	
PR113	N22	$100 purple	3,500.	*2,500.*
		Never hinged	7,000.	
		No gum	1,400.	
		Nos. PR102-PR113 (12)	20,560.	10,250.

1895-97 Wmk. 191

PR114	N15 1c black ('96)	8.00	25.00
	Never hinged	20.00	
	No gum	2.75	
PR115	N15 2c black	8.00	25.00
	Never hinged	20.00	
	No gum	2.75	
PR116	N15 5c black ('96)	13.00	40.00
	Never hinged	27.50	
	No gum	4.25	
PR117	N15 10c black	13.00	25.00
	Never hinged	27.50	
	No gum	4.25	
PR118	N16 25c carmine	20.00	65.00
	Never hinged	45.00	
	No gum	7.00	
PR119	N16 50c carmine	25.00	75.00
	Never hinged	55.00	
	No gum	8.50	
PR120	N17 $2 scar ('97)	30.00	110.00
	Never hinged	75.00	
	No gum	10.00	
PR121	N18 $5 dk bl ('96)	40.00	160.00
	Never hinged	100.00	
	No gum	13.50	
a.	$5 light blue	200.00	450.00
	Never hinged	450.00	
	No gum	67.50	
PR122	N19 $10 grn ('96)	42.50	160.00
	Never hinged	105.00	
	No gum	14.00	
PR123	N20 $20 slate ('96)	45.00	180.00
	Never hinged	110.00	
	No gum	15.00	
PR124	N21 $50 dl rose ('97)	75.00	225.00
	Never hinged	170.00	
	No gum	27.50	
PR125	N22 $100 pur ('96)	65.00	240.00
	Never hinged	150.00	
	No gum	22.50	
	Nos. PR114-PR125 (12)	384.50	1,330.
	Nos. PR114-PR125, never hinged	902.50	

In 1899 the Government sold 26,989 sets of these stamps, but, as the stock of the high values was not sufficient to make up the required number, the $5, $10, $20, $50 and $100 were reprinted. These are virtually indistinguishable from earlier printings.

For overprints see Nos. R159-R160.

PARCEL POST STAMPS

Issued for the prepayment of postage on parcel post packages only.

Post Office Clerk — PP1

City Carrier PP2

Railway Postal Clerk — PP3

Rural Carrier PP4

Mail Train — PP5

Steamship and Mail Tender PP6

Automobile Service PP7

Airplane Carrying Mail — PP8

Manufacturing — PP9

Dairying PP10

Harvesting PP11

Fruit Growing PP12

1913 Engr. Wmk. 190 *Perf. 12*

Q1	PP1 1c carmine rose	5.75	1.75
	Never hinged	14.00	
	On cover		6.00
Q2	PP2 2c carmine rose	6.75	1.40
	Never hinged	19.00	
	On cover		5.75
a.	Lake	*1,750.*	
Q3	PP3 3c carmine	13.50	6.50
	Never hinged	37.50	
	On cover		19.00
Q4	PP4 4c carmine rose	37.50	3.50
	Never hinged	110.00	
	On cover		65.00
Q5	PP5 5c carmine rose	32.50	2.50
	Never hinged	90.00	
	On cover		42.50
Q6	PP6 10c carmine rose	52.50	3.50
	Never hinged	120.00	
	On cover		55.00
Q7	PP7 15c carmine rose	67.50	15.00
	Never hinged	180.00	
	On cover		350.00
Q8	PP8 20c carmine rose	150.00	30.00
	Never hinged	325.00	
	On cover		750.00
Q9	PP9 25c carmine rose	67.50	8.50
	Never hinged	180.00	
	On cover		300.00
Q10	PP10 50c carmine rose	300.00	50.00
	Never hinged	700.00	
	On cover		—
Q11	PP11 75c carmine rose	110.00	40.00
	Never hinged	240.00	
	On cover		—
Q12	PP12 $1 carmine rose	375.00	45.00
	Never hinged	850.00	
	On cover		1,250.
	Nos. Q1-Q12 (12)	1,218.	207.65
	Nos. Q1-Q12, never hinged	2,865.	

No. Q2a is valued in the grade fine-very fine.

SPECIAL HANDLING STAMPS

For use on fourth-class mail to secure the same expeditious handling accorded to first-class mail matter.

PP13

1925-29 Unwmk. Engr. *Perf. 11*

QE1	PP13 10c yel grn ('28)	2.50	1.00
	Never hinged	4.25	
QE2	PP13 15c yel grn ('28)	2.75	.90
	Never hinged	4.50	
QE3	PP13 20c yel grn ('28)	4.50	1.50
	Never hinged	7.75	
QE4	PP13 25c yel grn ('29)	20.00	3.75
	Never hinged	37.50	
a.	25c deep green ('25)	25.00	12.00
	Never hinged	45.00	
	Nos. QE1-QE4 (4)	29.75	7.15
	Nos. QE1-QE4, never hinged	54.00	

PARCEL POST POSTAGE DUE STAMPS

For affixing by a postal clerk, to any parcel post package, to denote the amount to be collected from the addressee because of insufficient prepayment of postage.

PPD1

1913 Engr. Wmk. 190 *Perf. 12*

JQ1	PPD1 1c dark green	10.50	4.50
	Never hinged	26.00	
	On cover		150.00
JQ2	PPD1 2c dark green	85.00	17.50
	Never hinged	210.00	
	On cover		200.00
JQ3	PPD1 5c dark green	14.00	5.50
	Never hinged	35.00	
	On cover		185.00
JQ4	PPD1 10c dark green	175.00	45.00
	Never hinged	425.00	
	On cover		650.00
JQ5	PPD1 25c dark green	100.00	5.00
	Never hinged	260.00	
	On cover		—
	Nos. JQ1-JQ5 (5)	384.50	77.50
	Nos. JQ1-JQ5, never hinged	956.00	

CARRIERS' STAMPS

OFFICIAL ISSUES

Issued by the US Government to facilitate payment of fees for delivering and collecting letters.

Franklin OC1

Eagle OC2

1851 Unwmk. Engr. *Imperf.*

LO1	OC1 (1c) dull blue, *rose*	6,000.	6,500.
	On cover from Philadelphia		*17,500.*
	On cover from New York		*30,000.*
	On cover from New Orleans with 3c #10 (a 2nd #LO1 removed)		*30,000.*
LO2	OC2 1c blue	25.	60.
	On cover, used alone		500.
	On cover, precanceled		600.
	On cover, pair or 2 singles		*1,500.*
	On cover with block of 3, 1c #9		*4,500.*
	On cover with 3c #11		400.
	On cover with 3c #25		—
	On cover with 3c #26		*600.*
	On cover with strip of 3, 3c #26		—
	On 3c envelope #U1, #LO2 pen canceled		—
	On 3c envelope #U2, #LO2 pen canceled		—
	On cover with 3c #65 (Washington, D.C.)		*4,500.*
	Pair on cover (Cincinnati)		*1,000.*

1875

REPRINTS

Without Gum

LO3	OC1 (1c) blue, *rose*, imperf.	50.	
LO4	OC1 (1c) blue, perf. 12	*16,000.*	
LO5	OC2 1c blue, imperf.	25.	
LO6	OC2 1c blue, perf. 12	175.	

No. LO4 is valued in the grade of average to fine.

Reprints of the Franklin Carrier are printed in dark blue, instead of the dull blue or deep blue of the originals. The reprints of the Eagle carrier are on hard white paper, ungummed and sometimes perforated, and also on a coarse wove paper. Originals are on yellowish paper with brown gum.

SEMI-OFFICIAL ISSUES

Issued by officials or employees of the US Government for the purpose of securing or indicating payment of carriers' fees.

Baltimore, Md.

C1

1850-55 Typo. *Imperf.*

1LB1	C1 1c red, *bluish*	180.	160.
	On cover, tied by handstamp		*1,000.*
	On cover with 1c #9		—
	On cover (tied) with 3c #11		*500.*
1LB2	C1 1c blue, *bluish*	200.	150.
	On cover, tied		*1,000.*
a.	Bluish laid paper	—	—
1LB3	C1 1c blue	160.	100.
	On cover, tied by handstamp		*1,000.*
a.	Laid paper	190.	200.
	On cover, tied by handstamp		*1,000.*
b.	Block of 14 containing three tete-beche gutter pairs (unique)	*6,000.*	
1LB4	C1 1c green	—	1,000.
	On cover, tied by handstamp		*3,500.*
	On 3c envelope #U10		*3,500.*
1LB5	C1 1c red	2,250.	1,750.
	On cover, tied by handstamp		*4,500.*
	On cover (tied) with 3c #11		*5,000.*

Ten varieties.

C2

C3

1856 Typo.

1LB6	C2 1c blue	130.	90.
	On cover		400.
	On cover with 3c #11		*1,000.*
	On cover with 3c #26		*1,250.*
1LB7	C2 1c red	130.	90.
	On cover		300.
	On cover (tied) with 3c #26		350.
	On 3c envelope #U9, tied		*300.*

Shades exist of Nos. 1LB6-1LB7.

1857

1LB8	C3 1c black	65.	50.
	On cover, tied by handstamp		*125.*
	On cover (tied) with 3c #26		175.
	On 3c envelope #U9, tied		*225.*
	On 3c envelope #U10		*225.*
	On 3c envelope #U27, tied		*250.*
	Strip of 3 (not tied), on cover		*4,000.*
a.	"SENT"	100.	75.
	On cover, tied by handstamp		*175.*
	On cover with 3c #26		*250.*
	On 3c envelope #U9, tied		*250.*
	On 3c envelope #U10, tied		*250.*
b.	Short rays	100.	75.
	On cover (tied) with 3c #26		*600.*
1LB9	C3 1c red	100.	90.
	On cover		175.
	On cover with 3c #26		300.
	On 3c envelope #U9		325.
	On 3c envelope #U10		325.
a.	"SENT"	140.	110.
	On cover (tied) with 3c #26		*500.*
b.	Short rays	140.	110.
c.	As "b," double impression		*800.*

Ten varieties of C3.

BOSTON, MASS.

C6

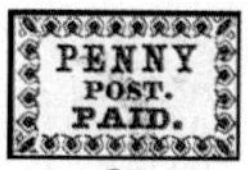

C7

1849-50 **Typeset**
3LB1 C6 1c blue 375.00 180.00
On cover, tied by handstamp 275.00
On cover with 5c #1 4,000.
On cover with two 5c #1 8,000.
On cover with 3c #10 450.00
a. Wrong ornament at left, on cover (not tied) 400.00
3LB2 C7 1c blue (shades), *slate* 190.00 100.00
On cover 220.00
On cover with 5c #1 12,500.
On cover with 3c #10 500.00
On cover with 3c #11 325.00
On 3c envelope #U2, #U5 or #U9 350.00

CHARLESTON, S. C.

C8

C10

1849 **Typo.**
4LB1 C8 2c black, *brn rose* 10,000.
On cover, not canceled, with certificate 17,000.
On cover (tied) with 10c #2 40,000.
4LB2 C8 2c black, *yellow,* cut to shape —
On cover, not tied, with certificate 12,500.
On cover with 10c #2 —

No. 4LB1 unused is a unique uncanceled stamp on piece. The used cut-to-shape stamp is also unique. Additionally, each of the listed covers bearing No. 4LB1 is unique.

No. 4LB2 unused (uncanceled) off cover is unique, as is the cover with #2. There are three recorded uses of No. 4LB2 alone on cover.

1854 **Typeset**
4LB3 C10 2c black 1,500.
On cover, tied by pen cancel 3,000.
On cover with 3c #11, tied 4,500.

C11

1849-50 **Typeset**
4LB5 C11 2c black, *bluish, pelure* 750. 500.
On cover with pair 5c #1b —
On cover with two 5c #1b —
On cover (tied) with 3c #11 4,000.
a. "Ceuts" 5,750.

No. 4LB5a is unique. It is without gum and is valued thus.

4LB7 C11 2c black, *yellow* 750. 1,000.
On cover, tied by handstamp 9,000.

Several varieties of C11.

C13

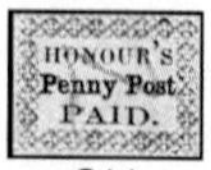

C14

C15

1851-58 **Typeset**
4LB8 C13 2c blk, *bluish* 350. 175.
On cover, tied by handstamp 700.
On cover (tied) with 3c #10 1,500.
On cover (tied) with 3c #11 1,500.
On cover (tied) with 3c #26 1,500.
a. Period after "Paid" 500. 250.
On cover 650.
b. "Cens" .700 900.
c. "Conours" and "Bents" —

4LB9 C13 2c blk, *bluish, pelure* 850. 950.
4LB11 C14 (2c) blk, *bluish* — 375.
On cover (handstamp tied) with 3c #11 15,000.
4LB12 C14 (2c) blk, *bluish, pelure* — —
4LB13 C15 (2c) blk, *bluish* ('58) 750. 400.
On cover with 3c #11, Aiken, S.C. postmark, tied by handstamp (unique0 6,000.
On cover with 3c #26, tied by pen cancel 4,000.
a. Comma after "PAID" 1,100.
b. No period after "Post" 1,400.

Several varieties of C13.

C16

C17

1851-58 **Typeset**
4LB14 C16 2c black, *bluish* 1,400. 900.
On cover with 3c #11 7,500.
On cover with 3c #26 6,000.
a. "Kingman's" erased 5,000.
4LB15 C17 2c black, *bluish* 800. 800.
On cover —
a. "Kingman's" erased, on cover with 3c #11, tied by pen cancel (unique) 4,500.

Several varieties of each.

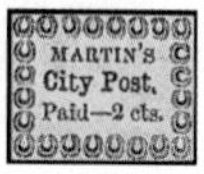

C18

1858 **Typeset**
4LB16 C18 2c black, *bluish* 8,000.

Several varieties.

Same as C19, but Inscribed "Beckmann's City Post"

1860
4LB17 C19 2c black —

One copy exists, on cover.

C19

C20

1859 **Typeset**
4LB18 C19 2c black, *bluish* 21,000.
On cover, uncanceled —
4LB19 C20 2c black, *bluish* 4,500. —
4LB20 C20 2c black, *pink* 200. —
4LB21 C20 2c black, *yellow* 200.

CINCINNATI, OHIO

C20a

1854 **Litho.** **Wove Paper**
9LB1 C20a 2c brown — 4,000.
On cover, tied by handstamp —
On cover, tied by pen cancel 4,500.
On cover with 1c #9 10,000.

CLEVELAND, OHIO

C20b

C20c

1854 **Wove Paper** **Litho.**
10LB1 C20b blue 5,000. 4,000.
On cover, tied by handstamp 15,000.
Pair on cover, canceled by pencil, with 3c #11, with certificate 17,000.

Vertically Laid Paper
10LB2 C20c 2c black, *bluish* 7,000. 7,000.
On cover —

LOUISVILLE, KY.

C21

C22

1857-58 **Litho.**
5LB1 C21 (2c) bluish green 125.
5LB2 C22 (2c) blue ('58) 250. 750.
On cover with 3c #26, tied by handstamp 6,250.
5LB3 C22 (2c) black ('58) 4,500. 15,000.

The value for No. 5LB3 used refers to the finer of the two known used (canceled) examples; it is on a piece with a 3c #26.

NEW YORK, N.Y.

C23

1842 **Engr.**
6LB1 C23 3c black, *grayish* 2,000.
On cover, tied by handstamp 11,500.

Used copies are Carriers' stamps only when canceled with the regular government cancellation "U.S." in octagonal frame (see illustration), "U.S.CITY DESPATCH POST," or New York circular postmark. When canceled "FREE" in frame they were used as local stamps (see No. 40L1 in the Scott Specialized Catalogue of United States Stamps).

C24

1842-45 **Engr.**
Unsurfaced Paper, Colored Through
6LB2 C24 3c black, *rosy buff* 2,500.
6LB3 C24 3c blk, *light blue* 550. 500.
On cover, tied by handstamp 1,750.
6LB4 C24 3c black, *green* 11,500.

Some authorities consider No. 6LB2 to be an essay, and No. 6LB4 to be a color changeling.

Glazed Paper, Surface Colored
6LB5 C24 3c black, *blue green (shades)* 200. 175.
On cover, tied by handstamp 600.
Five on cover 20,000.
a. Double impression 1,500.
b. 3c black, *blue* 650. 250.
On cover 750.
c. As "b," double impression 850.
d. 3c black, *green* 1,000. 900.
On cover —
e. As "d," double impression —
On cover —

6LB6 C24 3c **black,** *pink,* on cover front 14,500.

No. 6LB6 is unique.

No. 6LB5 Surcharged in Red — C25

1846
6LB7 C25 2c on 3c, on cover, not tied, with certificate 70,000.

The City Despatch 2c red is listed in the Scott United States Specialized Catalogue as a Local stamp.

C27

1849-50 **Typo.**
6LB9 C27 1c black, *rose* 100. 100.
On cover, tied by handstamp 250.
On cover with 5c #1 2,000.
6LB10 C27 1c black, *yellow* 100. 100.
On cover, tied by handstamp 250.
On cover with 5c #1 1,500.
6LB11 C27 1c black, *buff* 100. 100.
On cover 250.
On cover with 5c #1, not tied, with certificate 3,000.
a. Pair, one stamp sideways 2,850.

PHILADELPHIA, PA.

C28

C29

1849-50 **Typeset**
7LB1 C28 1c blk, *rose* (with letters L.P.) 450.
On cover, not canceled 2,000.
On cover with 5c #1 —
7LB2 C28 1c black, *rose* (with letter S) 3,000.
On cover, not canceled 4,500.
7LB3 C28 1c blk, *rose* (with letter H) 275.
On cover, tied by handstamp 3,750.
On cover, not canceled 1,000.
On cover with 5c #1 —
7LB4 C28 1c blk, *rose* (with letters L.S.) 400. 500.
On cover, not canceled 3,000.
7LB5 C28 1c black, *rose* (with letters J.J.) 7,500.
On cover with 5c #1, uncanceled 70,000.

The unique used No. 7LB5 is an uncanceled stamp on a cover front.

7LB6 C29 1c black, *rose* 300. 250.
On cover, tied by handstamp 2,500.
7LB7 C29 1c black, *blue, glazed* 1,000.
On cover, tied by handstamp 6,500.
On cover with 5c #1 —
7LB8 C29 1c blk, *ver,* glazed 700.
On cover, tied by handstamp 1,500.
On cover with 5c dark brown #1a, uncanceled 12,500.
On cover with 5c orange brown #1b, uncanceled 21,000.
7LB9 C29 1c blk, *yel,* glazed 2,750. 2,250.
On cover, not canceled 4,000.
On cover with 3c #10, uncanceled 2,000.

Several varieties of each.

Nos. 7LB1-7LB9 normally received no cancellation.

The 1c black on buff (unglazed), type C29, is believed to be a color changeling.

C30

C31

C32

1850-52 **Litho.**

No.	Description	Unused	Used
7LB11	C30 1c gold, *black*, glazed	175.	110.
	On cover, tied by handstamp		*600.*
	On cover with 5c #1		*3,500.*
	On cover (tied) with 3c #10		*800.*
7LB12	C30 1c blue	400.	275.
	On cover, tied by handstamp		*1,250.*
	On cover (tied) with 3c #10		*1,750.*
	On cover (tied) with 3c #11		*1,250.*
7LB13	C30 1c black	—	550.
	On cover, tied by handstamp		*2,500.*
	On cover (tied) with 3c #10		—
	On cover (not tied) with 3c #11		*3,250.*

25 varieties of C30.

Handstamped

No.	Description	Unused	Used
7LB14	C31 1c blue, *buff*	*3,250.*	
7LB16	C31 1c black		*5,000.*
	On cover with strip of 3, 1c #9		—
	On cover with 3c 1851 stamp removed, tied by handstamp		*7,000.*

1856(?)

No.	Description	Unused	Used
7LB18	C32 1c black	*1,250.*	*2,000.*
	On cover (cut diamond-shaped) with pair 1c #7 and single 1c #9		—
	On cover with strip of 3, 1c #7		17,000.
	On cover with 3c #11		*9,500.*
	On 3c envelope #U5		—
	On 3c envelope #U10, not canceled		*9,000.*

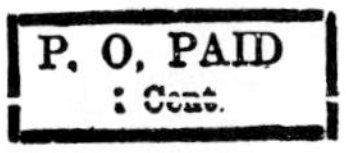

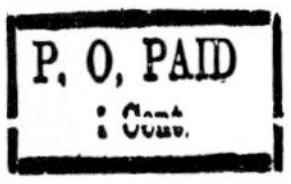

Labels of these designs are believed by most specialists not to be carrier stamps. Those seen are uncanceled, either off cover or affixed to stampless covers of the early 1850s. Some students believe they should be given carrier status.

ST. LOUIS, MO.

C36

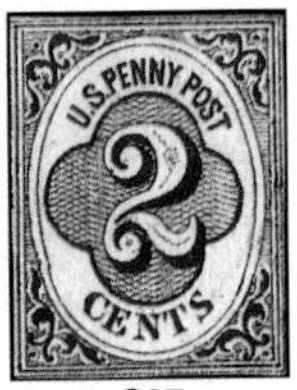
C37

Illustrations enlarged to show details of the two types (note upper corners especially).

1849 **Litho.**

No.	Description	Unused	Used
8LB1	C36 2c black	*7,000.*	*3,000.*
8LB2	C37 2c black	*6,000.*	—

C38

1857 **Litho.**

No.	Description	Unused	Used
8LB3	C38 2c blue	*22,500.*	
	On cover	*55,000.*	

Carrier stamps Nos. 9LB1, 10LB1-10LB2 are listed following No. 4LB21.

STAMPED ENVELOPES AND WRAPPERS

VALUES

Values are for cut squares in a grade of very fine. Very fine cut squares will have the design well centered within moderately large margins. Precanceled cut squares must include the entire precancellation. Values for unused entires are for those without printed or manuscript address. Values for letter sheets are for folded entires. Unfolded copies sell for more. A "full corner" includes back and side flaps and commands a premium. (Entire envelopes and wrappers are listed in the Scott U.S. Specialized Catalogue.)

Wrappers are listed with envelopes of corresponding designs, and indicated by prefix letter "W" instead of "U."

Envelopes with the stamp printed by error in colorless embossing from an uninked die, are "albinos." They are worth more than normal, inked impressions. Albinos of earlier issues, canceled while current, are scarce.

The papers of these issues vary greatly in texture, and in color from yellowish to bluish white and from amber to dark buff.

"+" Some authorities claim that Nos. U37, U48, U49, U110, U124, U125, U130, U133A, U137A, U137B, U137C, W138, U145, U162, U178A, U185, U220, U285, U286, U298, U299, UO3, UO32, UO38, UO45 and UO45A (each with "+" before number) were not regularly issued and are not known to have been used.

Washington

U1 U2

U1 — "THREE" in short label with curved ends; 13mm wide at top.

U2 — "THREE" in short label with straight ends; 15½mm wide at top.

U3

U4

U3 — "THREE" in short label with octagon ends.

U4 — "THREE" in wide label with straight ends; 20mm wide at top.

U5

U6

U5 — "THREE" in medium wide label with curved ends; 14½mm wide at top.

U7

U8

U7 — "TEN" in short label; 15⅓mm wide at top.

U8 — "TEN" in wide label 20mm wide at top.

On Diagonally Laid Paper

1853-55

No.	Description	Unused	Used
U1	U1 3c red	400.00	35.00
	Entire	2,250.	45.00
U2	U1 3c red, *buff*	100.00	25.00
	Entire	1,000.	30.00
U3	U2 3c red	1,300.	45.00
	Entire	6,000.	100.00
U4	U2 3c red, *buff*	350.00	40.00
	Entire	2,500.	75.00
U5	U3 3c red ('54)	6,250.	550.00
	Entire	*37,500.*	900.00
U6	U3 3c red, *buff* ('54)	4,750.	75.00
	Entire	—	150.00
U7	U4 3c red	5,500.	150.00
	Entire	—	300.00
U8	U4 3c red, *buff*	*8,750.*	175.00
	Entire	—	300.00
U9	U5 3c red ('54)	40.00	4.00
	Entire	150.00	9.00
U10	U5 3c red, *buff* ('54)	22.50	4.00
	Entire	72.50	6.00
U11	U6 6c red	325.00	90.00
	Entire	450.00	175.00
U12	U6 6c red, *buff*	175.00	90.00
	Entire	275.00	200.00
U13	U6 6c green	400.00	125.00
	Entire	750.00	225.00
U14	U6 6c green, *buff*	225.00	100.00
	Entire	450.00	225.00
U15	U7 10c green ('55)	500.00	100.00
	Entire	950.00	150.00
U16	U7 10c green, *buff* ('55)	190.00	75.00
	Entire	500.00	150.00
a.	10c pale green, *buff*	150.00	65.00
	Entire	425.00	125.00
U17	U8 10c green ('55)	550.00	140.00
	Entire	900.00	225.00
a.	10c pale green	400.00	125.00
	Entire	750.00	200.00
U18	U8 10c green, *buff* ('55)	400.00	90.00
	Entire	700.00	175.00
a.	10c pale green, *buff*	375.00	90.00
	Entire	750.00	175.00

Nos. U9, U10, U11, U12, U13, U14, U17 and U18 have been reprinted on white and buff papers, wove or vertically laid, and are not known entire. The originals are on diagonally laid paper. Value, set of 8 reprints on laid, $225. Reprints on wove sell for more.

U9

Franklin, Period after "POSTAGE." — U10

U10 — Bust touches inner frame-line at front and back.

No period after "POSTAGE" U11

Washington U12

Envelopes are on diagonally laid paper. Wrappers on vert. or horiz. laid paper, or on unwatermarked white paper (Nos. W22, or W25).

1860-61

No.	Description	Unused	Used
W18B	U9 1c blue ('61)	*5,750.*	
	Entire	—	
U19	U9 1c blue, *buff*	40.00	15.00
	Entire	90.00	32.50
W20	U9 1c blue, *buff* ('61)	70.00	50.00
	Entire	125.00	75.00
W21	U9 1c blue, *man* ('61)	60.00	45.00
	Entire	125.00	100.00
U21A	U9 1c blue, *org*, entire	*2,750.*	
W22	U9 1c blue, *org* ('61)	*4,250.*	
	Entire	*8,000.*	
U23	U10 1c blue, *org*	750.00	350.00
	Entire	1,000.	500.00
U24	U11 1c blue, *amber*	375.00	125.00
	Entire	725.00	225.00
W25	U11 1c blue, *man* ('61)	*7,500.*	*2,250.*
	Entire	*20,000.*	*5,750.*
U26	U12 3c red	35.00	20.00
	Entire	60.00	32.50
U27	U12 3c red, *buff*	26.00	13.00
	Entire	45.00	22.50
U28	U12+9 3c + 1c red & blue	375.00	275.00
	Entire	825.00	500.00
U29	U12+9 3c + 1c red & blue, *buff*	375.00	275.00
	Entire	825.00	500.00
U30	U12 6c red	3,500.	1,500.
	Entire	*6,500.*	
U31	U12 6c red, *buff*	4,000.	1,500.
	Entire	7,000.	*15,000.*
U32	U12 10c green	1,650.	450.00
	Entire	*14,000.*	650.00
U33	U12 10c green, *buff*	1,650.	375.00
	Entire	4,500.	550.00

Nos. U26-U27, U30-U33 have been reprinted on the same vertically laid papers as the reprints of the 1853-55 issue, and are not known entire. Value, Nos. U26-U27, $160; Nos. U30-U33, $100.

U13

U14

Washington

U15 U16

Envelopes are on diagonally laid paper.

1861

No.	Description	Unused	Used
U34	U13 3c pink	32.50	6.00
	Entire	62.50	13.00
U35	U13 3c pink, *buff*	32.50	6.00
	Entire	62.50	13.00
U36	U13 3c pink, *bl* (letter sheet)	82.50	60.00
	Entire	290.00	140.00
+U37	U13 3c pink, *org*	*5,500.*	
	Entire	*8,000.*	
U38	U14 6c pink	125.00	80.00
	Entire	210.00	190.00
U39	U14 6c pink, *buff*	82.50	62.50
	Entire	225.00	160.00
U40	U15 10c yell grn	47.50	30.00
	Entire	82.50	60.00
a.	10c blue green	47.50	30.00
	Entire	82.50	60.00
U41	U15 10c yel grn, *buff*	47.50	30.00
	Entire	82.50	52.50
a.	10c blue green, *buff*	47.50	30.00
	Entire	82.50	52.50
U42	U16 12c red & brn, *buff*	275.00	175.00
	Entire	550.00	*650.00*
a.	12c lake & brown, *buff*	*1,400.*	
U43	U16 20c red & bl, *buff*	325.00	200.00
	Entire	575.00	*1,250.*
U44	U16 24c red & grn, *buff*	300.00	200.00
	Entire	750.00	*1,500.*
a.	24c lake & green, *sal*	325.00	225.00
	Entire	850.00	*1,750.*
U45	U16 40c blk & red, *buff*	375.00	350.00
	Entire	850.00	*4,500.*

Nos. U38 and U39 have been reprinted on the same papers as the reprints of the 1853-55 issue and are not known entire. Value of two reprints, $60.

Jackson
U17

Jackson
U18

"U.S. POSTAGE" above

U17 — The downstroke and tail of the "2" unite near the point.

U18 — The downstroke and tail of the "2" touch but do not merge.

Jackson — U19

Jackson — U20

"U.S. POST" above

U19 — Stamp measures 24 to 25mm in width.

U20 — Stamp measures 25½ to 26¼mm in width.

Envelopes are on diagonally laid paper. Wrappers on vertically or horizontally laid paper.

1863-64

U46	U17 2c black, *buff*	55.00	21.00
	Entire	85.00	37.50
W47	U17 2c blk, *dk man*	85.00	50.00
	Entire	105.00	80.00
+U48	U18 2c black, *buff*	3,400.	
	Entire	6,250.	
+U49	U18 2c black, *org*	2,900.	
	Entire	5,750.	
U50	U19 2c blk, *buff* ('64)	19.00	9.50
	Entire	42.50	21.00
W51	U19 2c blk, *buff* ('64)	425.00	200.00
	Entire	650.00	350.00
U52	U19 2c blk, *org* ('64)	19.00	9.50
	Entire	37.50	18.00
W53	U19 2c blk, *dk man* ('64)	52.50	40.00
	Entire	175.00	140.00
U54	U20 2c blk, *buff* ('64)	19.00	9.50
	Entire	39.00	16.00
W55	U20 2c blk, *buff* ('64)	105.00	65.00
	Entire	160.00	120.00
U56	U20 2c blk, *org* ('64)	22.00	8.50
	Entire	34.00	16.00
W57	U20 2c blk, *lt man* ('64)	24.00	14.00
	Entire	37.50	24.00

Washington
U21

Washington
U22

1864-65

U58	U21 3c pink	12.00	1.60
	Entire	20.00	3.25
U59	U21 3c pink, *buff*	12.00	1.25
	Entire	20.00	3.00
U60	U21 3c brown ('65)	75.00	40.00
	Entire	140.00	125.00
U61	U21 3c brn, *buff* ('65)	60.00	30.00
	Entire	125.00	80.00
U62	U21 6c pink	110.00	29.00
	Entire	190.00	85.00
U63	U21 6c pink, *buff*	55.00	27.50
	Entire	110.00	50.00
U64	U21 6c purple ('65)	75.00	26.00
	Entire	100.00	55.00
U65	U21 6c pur, *buff* ('65)	60.00	20.00
	Entire	80.00	55.00
U66	U22 9c lem, *buff* ('65)	450.00	250.00
	Entire	625.00	1,000.
U67	U22 9c org, *buff* ('65)	160.00	90.00
	Entire	225.00	275.00
a.	9c orange yellow, *buff*	160.00	90.00
	Entire	225.00	275.00
U68	U22 12c brn, *buff* ('65)	325.00	275.00
	Entire	625.00	1,200.
U69	U22 12c red brn, *buff* ('65)	150.00	55.00
	Entire	200.00	360.00
U70	U22 18c red, *buff* ('65)	95.00	95.00
	Entire	200.00	800.00
U71	U22 24c bl, *buff* ('65)	100.00	95.00
	Entire	200.00	750.00
U72	U22 30c grn, *buff* ('65)	125.00	80.00
	Entire	200.00	1,500.
a.	30c yellow green, *buff*	125.00	80.00
	Entire	200.00	1,500.
U73	U22 40c rose, *buff* ('65)	125.00	250.00
	Entire	350.00	2,000.

Reay Issue

The engravings in this issue are finely executed.

Franklin — U23

Jackson — U24

U23 — Bust points to the end of the "N" of "ONE".

U24 — Bust narrow at back. Small, thick figures of value.

Washington
U25

Lincoln
U26

U25 — Queue projects below bust.

U26 — Neck very long at the back.

Stanton — U27

Jefferson — U28

U27 — Bust pointed at the back, figures "7" are normal.

U28 — Queue forms straight line with the bust.

Clay — U29

Webster — U30

U29 — Ear partly concealed by hair, mouth large, chin prominent.

U30 — Has side whiskers.

Scott — U31

Hamilton — U32

U31 — Straggling locks of hair at top of head; ornaments around the inner oval end in squares.

U32 — Back of bust very narrow, chin almost straight; labels containing figures of value are exactly parallel.

Perry — U33

U33 — Front of bust very narrow and pointed; inner lines of shields project very slightly beyond the oval.

1870-71

U74	U23 1c blue	45.00	30.00
	Entire	80.00	45.00
a.	1c ultramarine	72.50	35.00
	Entire	140.00	60.00
U75	U23 1c blue, *amber*	37.50	27.50
	Entire	60.00	40.00
a.	1c ultramarine, *amb*	70.00	30.00
	Entire	100.00	55.00
U76	U23 1c blue, *org*	22.50	10.00
	Entire	35.00	22.50
W77	U23 1c blue, *man*	45.00	37.50
	Entire	82.50	70.00
U78	U24 2c brown	40.00	16.00
	Entire	60.00	22.50
U79	U24 2c brown, *amb*	20.00	9.00
	Entire	40.00	17.50
U80	U24 2c brown, *org*	12.00	6.50
	Entire	17.50	11.00
W81	U24 2c brown, *man*	29.00	22.50
	Entire	62.50	57.50
U82	U25 3c green	8.50	1.00
	Entire	17.00	4.00
a.	3c brown (error), entire	13,000.	
U83	U25 3c green, *amb*	7.25	2.00
	Entire	18.00	5.00
U84	U25 3c green, *cream*	11.00	4.50
	Entire	17.00	10.00
U85	U26 6c dark red	32.50	16.00
	Entire	60.00	21.00
a.	6c vermilion	32.50	16.00
	Entire	75.00	20.00
U86	U26 6c dk red, *amb*	40.00	20.00
	Entire	75.00	30.00
a.	6c vermilion, *amber*	40.00	20.00
	Entire	75.00	30.00
U87	U26 6c dk red, *cr*	40.00	20.00
	Entire	80.00	30.00
a.	6c vermilion, *cream*	40.00	20.00
	Entire	80.00	30.00
U88	U27 7c ver, *amb* ('71)	55.00	190.00
	Entire	82.50	900.00
U89	U28 10c ol blk	975.00	900.00
	Entire	1,350.	1,250.
U90	U28 10c ol blk, *amb*	975.00	900.00
	Entire	1,350.	1,250.
U91	U28 10c brown	92.50	72.50
	Entire	140.00	125.00
U92	U28 10c brn, *amb*	110.00	75.00
	Entire	140.00	125.00
a.	10c dark brown, *amb*	110.00	52.50
	Entire	140.00	125.00
U93	U29 12c plum	125.00	82.50
	Entire	240.00	450.00
U94	U29 12c plum, *amb*	140.00	110.00
	Entire	240.00	650.00
U95	U29 12c plum, *cr*	275.00	250.00
	Entire	375.00	
U96	U30 15c red org	85.00	85.00
	Entire	175.00	
a.	15c orange	85.00	
	Entire	175.00	
U97	U30 15c red org, *amb*	210.00	300.00
	Entire	400.00	
a.	15c orange, *amber*	210.00	
	Entire	400.00	
U98	U30 15c red org, *cr*	325.00	350.00
	Entire	425.00	
a.	15c orange, *cream*	325.00	
	Entire	425.00	
U99	U31 24c purple	150.00	150.00
	Entire	200.00	
U100	U31 24c pur, *amb*	200.00	325.00
	Entire	375.00	
U101	U31 24c pur, *cream*	275.00	500.00
	Entire	475.00	
U102	U32 30c black	80.00	110.00
	Entire	300.00	750.00
U103	U32 30c blk, *amb*	250.00	500.00
	Entire	650.00	
U104	U32 30c blk, *cream*	250.00	500.00
	Entire	400.00	
U105	U33 90c carmine	175.00	350.00
	Entire	250.00	
U106	U33 90c car, *amb*	325.00	450.00
	Entire	800.00	4,500.
U107	U33 90c car, *cream*	300.00	2,500.
	Entire	800.00	5,000.

Plimpton Issue

The profiles in this issue are inferior to the fine engraving of the Reay issue.

U34

U35

U34 — Bust forms an angle at the back near the frame. Lettering poorly executed. Distinct circle in "O" of "POSTAGE."

U35 — Lower part of bust points to the end of the "E" in "ONE." Head inclined downward.

U36

U37

U36 — Bust narrow at back. Thin figures of value. The head of the "P" in "POSTAGE" is very narrow. The bust at front is broad and ends in sharp corners.

U37 — Bust broad. Figures of value in long ovals.

U38

U39

U38 — Similar to die 2 but the figure "2" at the left touches the oval.

U39 — Similar to die 2 but the "O" of "TWO" has the center netted instead of plain. The "G" of "POSTAGE" and the "C" of "CENTS" have diagonal crossline.

U40

U41

U40 — Bust broad; numerals in ovals short and thick.

U41 — Similar to die 5 but the ovals containing the numerals are much heavier. A diagonal line runs from the upper part of the "U" to the white frame-line.

U42

U43

U42 — Similar to die 5 but the middle stroke of "N" in "CENTS" is as thin as the vertical strokes.

U43 — Bottom of bust cut almost semi-circularly.

U44

U45

U44 — Thin lettering, long thin figures of value.

U45 — Thick lettering, well-formed figures of value, queue does not project below bust.

U46

U46 — Top of head egg-shaped; knot of queue well marked and projects triangularly.

Taylor — U47

Die 1

Die 2

Die 1 — Figures of value with thick curved tops.

Die 2 — Figures of value with long, thin tops.

U48

U49

U48 — Neck very short at the back.

U49 — Figures of value turned up at the ends.

U50

U51

U50 — Very large head.

U51 — Knot of queue stands out prominently.

U52

U53

U52 — Ear prominent, chin receding.

U53 — No side whiskers, forelock projects above head.

U54

U55

U54 — Hair does not project; ornaments around the inner oval end in points.

U55 — Back of bust rather broad, chin slopes considerably; labels containing figures of value are not exactly parallel.

U56

U56 — Front of bust sloping; inner lines of shields project considerably into the inner oval.

1874-86

Design U34

U108	1c dark blue	210.00	70.00
	Entire	275.00	110.00
a.	1c light blue	210.00	70.00
	Entire	275.00	125.00
U109	1c dk blue, *amb*	190.00	75.00
	Entire	210.00	140.00
+U110	1c dk blue, *cr*	1,750.	
U111	1c dk blue, *org*	25.00	17.50
	Entire	35.00	25.00
a.	1c light blue, *org*	25.00	17.50
	Entire	35.00	25.00
W112	1c dk blue, *man*	72.50	42.50
	Entire	110.00	75.00

Design U35

U113	1c light blue	1.90	1.00
	Entire	3.00	1.10
a.	1c dark blue	9.00	7.50
	Entire	29.00	20.00
U114	1c lt blue, *amb*	4.50	4.00
	Entire	8.25	6.00
a.	1c dark blue, *amb*	20.00	10.00
	Entire	30.00	20.00
U115	1c blue, *cr*	5.25	4.50
	Entire	10.50	6.50
a.	1c dark blue, *cr*	20.00	8.50
	Entire	32.50	20.00
U116	1c lt blue, *org*	.80	.40
	Entire	1.25	1.00
a.	1c dark blue, *org*	4.50	2.50
	Entire	16.00	8.00
U117	1c lt bl, *bl* ('80)	8.50	5.25
	Entire	13.50	9.00
U118	1c light blue, *fawn* ('79)	8.50	5.25
	Entire	15.00	10.00
U119	1c lt blue, *man* ('86)	9.00	3.25
	Entire	17.00	5.00
W120	1c lt blue, *man*	1.60	1.10
	Entire	2.75	1.75
a.	1c dark blue, *man*	9.00	8.00
	Entire	16.00	15.00
U121	1c lt blue, *amb man* ('86)	19.00	10.00
	Entire	29.00	20.00

Design U36

U122	2c brown	150.00	50.00
	Entire	175.00	85.00
U123	2c brown, *amb*	72.50	40.00
	Entire	125.00	70.00
+U124	2c brown, *cr*	1,250.	
+U125	2c brown, *org*	25,000.	
	Entire	45,000.	
W126	2c brown, *man*	175.00	85.00
	Entire	300.00	160.00
W127	2c ver, *man*	3,000.	250.00
	Entire	4,750.	5,000.

Design U37

U128	2c brown	60.00	35.00
	Entire	110.00	75.00
U129	2c brown, *amb*	85.00	45.00
	Entire	125.00	77.50
+U130	2c brown, *cr*	50,000.	
W131	2c brown, *man*	20.00	17.00
	Entire	29.00	26.00

Design U38

U132	2c brown	82.50	29.00
	Entire	125.00	80.00
U133	2c brown, *amb*	350.00	70.00
	Entire	575.00	140.00
+U133A	2c brown, *cr*	100,000.	

Design U39

U134	2c brown	1,500.	160.00
	Entire	2,250.	300.00
U135	2c brown, *amb*	525.00	125.00
	Entire	700.00	160.00
U136	2c brown, *org*	57.50	29.00
	Entire	87.50	37.50
W137	2c brown, *man*	85.00	40.00
	Entire	125.00	55.00
+U137A	2c vermilion	40,000.	
+U137B	2c ver, *amb*	40,000.	
	Entire	—	
+U137C	2c ver, *org*	100,000.	
+W138	2c ver, *man*	32,500.	

Design U40

U139	2c brown ('75)	62.50	37.50
	Entire	82.50	47.50
U140	2c brown, *amb* ('75)	97.50	62.50
	Entire	140.00	77.50
+U140A	2c reddish brown, *org* ('75)	25,000.	
	Entire	40,000.	
W141	2c brown, *man* ('75)	37.50	27.50
	Entire	45.00	32.50
U142	2c ver ('75)	10.00	5.00
	Entire	13.00	7.50
a.	2c pink	10.00	5.00
	Entire	13.00	7.50
U143	2c ver, *amber* ('75)	10.00	4.50
	Entire	13.00	5.75
U144	2c ver, *cr* ('75)	21.00	7.50
	Entire	26.00	12.50
+U145	2c ver, *org* ('75)	50,000.	
U146	2c ver, *bl* ('80)	140.00	40.00
	Entire	200.00	140.00
U147	2c ver, *fawn* ('75)	11.00	5.00
	Entire	17.00	7.00
W148	2c ver, *man* ('75)	4.75	3.75
	Entire	9.00	6.50

Design U41

U149	2c ver ('78)	62.50	32.50
	Entire	95.00	42.50
a.	2c pink	62.50	35.00
	Entire	95.00	45.00
U150	2c ver, *amber* ('78)	42.50	17.50
	Entire	62.50	22.50
U151	2c ver, *bl* ('80)	14.00	10.00
	Entire	21.00	15.00
a.	2c pink, *blue*	13.00	10.00
	Entire	17.50	12.50
U152	2c ver, *fawn* ('78)	15.00	4.75
	Entire	20.00	9.50

Design U42

U153	2c ver ('76)	77.50	27.50
	Entire	110.00	37.50
U154	2c ver, *amb* ('76)	400.00	90.00
	Entire	450.00	175.00
W155	2c ver, *man* ('76)	24.00	11.00
	Entire	47.50	20.00

Design U43

U156	2c ver ('81)	1,750.	175.00
	Entire	3,750.	500.00
U157	2c ver, *amb* ('81)	57,500.	35,000.
	Entire	110,000.	
W158	2c ver, *man* ('81)	110.00	62.50
	Entire	190.00	175.00

Design U44

U159	3c green	37.50	6.75
	Entire	62.50	17.50
U160	3c green, *amb*	40.00	11.50
	Entire	65.00	20.00
U161	3c green, *cr*	42.50	15.00
	Entire	70.00	30.00
+U162	3c green, *blue*	125,000.	

Design U45

U163	3c green	1.50	.30
	Entire	4.25	2.25
U164	3c green, *amb*	1.60	.70
	Entire	4.25	2.00
U165	3c green, *cr*	9.50	6.50
	Entire	19.00	9.00
U166	3c green, *blue*	8.50	6.25
	Entire	17.00	11.00
U167	3c green, *fawn* ('75)	5.25	3.50
	Entire	9.25	5.00

Design U46

U168	3c green ('81)	1,500.	80.00
	Entire	5,000.	275.00
U169	3c green, *amb* ('81)	325.00	110.00
	Entire	625.00	300.00
U170	3c grn, *bl* ('81)	12,500.	3,750.
	Entire	20,000.	4,750.
U171	3c green, *fawn* ('81)	45,000.	3,250.
	Entire		14,000.

Design U47

U172	5c blue, die 1 ('75)	15.00	9.00
	Entire	21.00	14.00
U173	5c blue, die 1, *amb* ('75)	15.00	10.00
	Entire	21.00	14.00
U174	5c blue, die 1, *cr* ('75)	125.00	42.50
	Entire	190.00	90.00
U175	5c blue, die 1, *bl* ('75)	40.00	16.00
	Entire	57.50	25.00
U176	5c blue, die 1, *fawn* ('75)	160.00	60.00
	Entire	300.00	
U177	5c blue, die 2 ('75)	14.00	8.00
	Entire	20.00	16.00
U178	5c blue, die 2, *amb* ('75)	12.00	8.00
	Entire	21.00	17.00
+U178A	5c blue, die 2, *cr* ('76)	14,000.	
	Entire	22,500.	
U179	5c blue, die 2, *blue* ('75)	32.50	11.00
	Entire	47.50	27.50
U180	5c blue, die 2, *fawn* ('75)	140.00	47.50
	Entire	240.00	140.00

Design U48

U181	6c red	10.00	6.75
	Entire	15.00	12.50
a.	6c vermilion	10.00	6.75
	Entire	15.00	12.50
U182	6c red, *amber*	15.00	6.75
	Entire	24.00	15.00
a.	6c vermilion, *amber*	15.00	6.75
	Entire	24.00	15.00
U183	6c red, *cream*	55.00	17.50
	Entire	87.50	40.00
a.	6c vermilion, *cream*	55.00	17.50
	Entire	87.50	40.00
U184	6c red, *fawn* ('75)	24.00	13.50
	Entire	35.00	29.00

Design U49

+U185	7c vermilion	1,800.	
U186	7c ver, *amber*	160.00	70.00
	Entire	200.00	

Design U50

U187	10c brown	45.00	22.50
	Entire	65.00	
U188	10c brown, *amb*	82.50	35.00
	Entire	160.00	

Design U51

U189	10c choc ('75)	8.00	4.25
	Entire	13.00	9.25
a.	10c bister brown	9.00	5.25
	Entire	13.00	10.50
b.	10c yellow ocher	4,500.	
	Entire	8,500.	
U190	10c choc, *amb* ('75)	9.00	7.25
	Entire	14.50	11.50
a.	10c bister brown, *amb*	9.00	7.75
	Entire	14.50	11.50
b.	10c yellow ocher, *amb*	3,500.	
	Entire	6,500.	
U191	10c brn, *oriental buff* ('86)	20.00	8.75
	Entire	22.50	11.50
U192	10c brn, *bl* ('86)	20.00	8.75
	Entire	22.50	15.00
a.	10c gray black, *blue*	18.00	8.25
	Entire	21.00	15.00
b.	10c red brown, *blue*	18.00	8.25
	Entire	21.00	15.00
U193	10c brown, *man* ('86)	19.00	10.00
	Entire	24.00	16.00
a.	10c red brown, *man*	19.00	10.00
	Entire	24.00	16.00
U194	10c brown, *amb man* ('86)	21.00	9.00
	Entire	27.50	17.50
a.	10c red brown, *amber manila*	21.00	9.00
	Entire	27.50	17.50

Design U52

U195	12c plum	475.00	100.00
	Entire	700.00	
U196	12c plum, *amb*	275.00	175.00
	Entire	350.00	
U197	12c plum, *cream*	225.00	150.00
	Entire	950.00	

Design U53

U198	15c orange	55.00	40.00
	Entire	92.50	55.00
U199	15c orange, *amb*	160.00	100.00
	Entire	300.00	
U200	15c org, *cream*	600.00	350.00
	Entire	1,100.	

Design U54

U201	24c purple	175.00	150.00
	Entire	250.00	
U202	24c purple, *amb*	200.00	125.00
	Entire	260.00	
U203	24c pur, *cream*	190.00	125.00
	Entire	750.00	

Design U55

U204	30c black	65.00	27.50
	Entire	90.00	65.00
U205	30c black, *amb*	75.00	60.00
	Entire	140.00	250.00
U206	30c black, *cream*	400.00	375.00
	Entire	800.00	
U207	30c blk, *oriental buff* ('86)	100.00	82.50
	Entire	160.00	
U208	30c blk, *bl* ('86)	110.00	82.50
	Entire	200.00	
U209	30c black, *man* ('86)	95.00	80.00
	Entire	160.00	
U210	30c black, *amb man* ('86)	175.00	85.00
	Entire	210.00	

Design U56

U211	90c carmine ('75)	110.00	85.00
	Entire	160.00	95.00
U212	90c car, *amb* ('75)	225.00	300.00
	Entire	275.00	
U213	90c car, *cr* ('75)	1,750.	
	Entire	3,250.	
U214	90c car, *oriental buff* ('86)	200.00	275.00
	Entire	300.00	300.00
U215	90c car, *bl* ('86)	200.00	250.00
	Entire	275.00	275.00
U216	90c car, *man* ('86)	175.00	250.00
	Entire	275.00	275.00
U217	90c car, *amb man* ('86)	150.00	200.00
	Entire	225.00	275.00

See Nos. U336-U347.

United States Centennial Issue

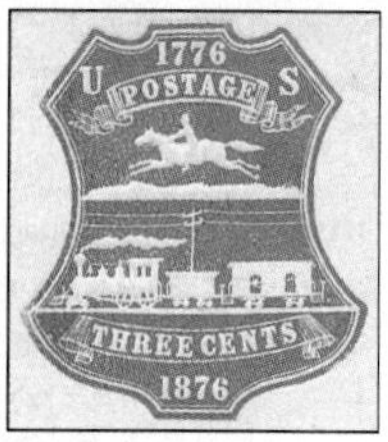

Single line under "POSTAGE" U57

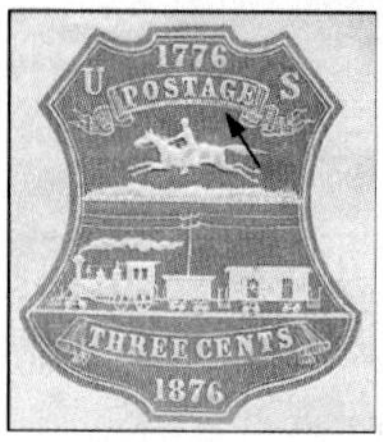

Double line under "POSTAGE" U58

1876

U218	U57 3c red	52.50	25.00
	Entire	77.50	50.00
U219	U57 3c green	45.00	17.50
	Entire	65.00	40.00
+U220	U58 3c red	*42,500.*	
	Entire	*60,000.*	
U221	U58 3c green	52.50	25.00
	Entire	85.00	50.00

Cent. of the US, and the World's Fair at Philadelphia.

See No. U582.

Garfield U59

Washington U60

1882-86

U222	U59 5c brown	5.75	3.00
	Entire	10.50	7.00
U223	U59 5c brown, *amb*	6.00	3.50
	Entire	11.00	8.50
U224	U59 5c brn, *oriental buff* ('86)	140.00	75.00
	Entire	200.00	
U225	U59 5c brown, *blue*	82.50	35.00
	Entire	125.00	75.00
U226	U59 5c brown, *fawn*	375.00	
	Entire	525.00	

1883, Oct.

U227	U60 2c red	4.50	2.25
	Entire	10.00	3.00
a.	2c brown (error), entire	*10,000.*	
U228	U60 2c red, *amber*	5.75	2.75
	Entire	10.50	6.00
U229	U60 2c red, *blue*	8.50	5.00
	Entire	13.00	8.00
U230	U60 2c red, *fawn*	9.25	5.25
	Entire	15.00	7.00

Wavy lines fine and clear — U61

Wavy lines thick and blurred — U62

Four Wavy Lines in Oval

1883, Nov.

U231	U61 2c red	5.50	2.50
	Entire	10.00	4.00
U232	U61 2c red, *amber*	6.50	3.75
	Entire	12.00	5.75
U233	U61 2c red, *blue*	11.00	7.50
	Entire	19.00	10.00
U234	U61 2c red, *fawn*	8.00	4.75
	Entire	12.00	6.00
W235	U61 2c red, *manila*	22.50	6.25
	Entire	32.50	12.50

1884, June

U236	U62 2c red	14.50	4.00
	Entire	22.50	7.75
U237	U62 2c red, *amber*	17.50	10.00
	Entire	27.50	11.00
U238	U62 2c red, *blue*	29.00	12.00
	Entire	40.00	15.00
U239	U62 2c red, *fawn*	25.00	11.00
	Entire	25.00	12.50

See Nos. U260-W269.

3½ links over left "2" — U63

2 links below right "2" — U64

Round "O" in "TWO." White lines above "WO" of "TWO" joined to form thick white dash. — U65

U240	U63 2c red	100.00	47.50
	Entire	160.00	72.50
U241	U63 2c red, *amber*	1,000.	325.00
	Entire	2,750.	750.00
U242	U63 2c red, *fawn*		*37,500.*
	Entire		*55,000.*
U243	U64 2c red	140.00	75.00
	Entire	175.00	100.00
U244	U64 2c red, *amber*	350.00	100.00
	Entire	500.00	125.00
U245	U64 2c red, *blue*	500.00	210.00
	Entire	650.00	225.00
U246	U64 2c red, *fawn*	450.00	170.00
	Entire	700.00	275.00
U247	U65 2c red	3,500.	750.00
	Entire	4,500.	*1,250.*
U248	U65 2c red, *amber*	5,250.	1,300.
	Entire	8,000.	*1,650.*
U249	U65 2c red, *fawn*	1,400.	500.00
	Entire	2,250.	*750.00*

See Nos. U270-U276.

Jackson — U66

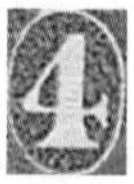

Die 1 — Numeral at left is 2¾mm wide

Die 2 — Numeral at left is 3¼mm wide

1883-86

U250	U66 4c grn, die 1	4.00	3.50
	Entire	6.50	6.00
U251	U66 4c grn, die 1, *amb*	5.00	3.50
	Entire	7.50	5.25
U252	U66 4c grn, die 1, *oriental buff* ('86)	13.00	9.00
	Entire	18.00	12.50
U253	U66 4c grn, die 1, *bl* ('86)	13.00	6.50
	Entire	18.00	8.00
U254	U66 4c grn, die 1, *man* ('86)	16.00	7.50
	Entire	21.00	15.00
U255	U66 4c grn, die 1, *amb man* ('86)	24.00	10.00
	Entire	32.50	15.00
U256	U66 4c grn, die 2	11.00	5.00
	Entire	19.00	6.75
U257	U66 4c grn, die 2, *amb*	15.00	7.00
	Entire	25.00	10.00
U258	U66 4c grn, die 2, *man* ('86)	15.00	7.50
	Entire	25.00	12.50
U259	U66 4c grn, die 2, *amb man* ('86)	15.00	7.50
	Entire	25.00	12.50

1884, May

U260	U61 2c brown	19.00	5.75
	Entire	21.00	9.00
U261	U61 2c brn, *amber*	19.00	6.50
	Entire	21.00	7.50
U262	U61 2c brn, *blue*	23.00	10.00
	Entire	29.00	14.00
U263	U61 2c brn, *fawn*	18.50	9.25
	Entire	20.00	12.50
W264	U61 2c brn, *manila*	19.00	11.50
	Entire	26.00	19.00

1884, June — **Retouched Die**

U265	U62 2c brown	20.00	6.50
	Entire	27.50	12.00
U266	U62 2c brn, *amber*	67.50	40.00
	Entire	75.00	50.00
U267	U62 2c brn, *blue*	25.00	9.00
	Entire	32.50	15.00
U268	U62 2c brn, *fawn*	18.00	11.00
	Entire	22.50	15.00
W269	U62 2c brn, *manila*	30.00	15.00
	Entire	35.00	24.00

2 Links Below Right "2"

U270	U64 2c brown	140.00	50.00
	Entire	175.00	110.00
U271	U64 2c brn, *amber*	500.00	110.00
	Entire	600.00	350.00
U272	U64 2c brn, *fawn*	*10,000.*	*3,000.*
	Entire	*12,000.*	*4,000.*

Round "O" in "Two"

U273	U65 2c brown	300.00	110.00
	Entire	400.00	200.00
U274	U65 2c brn, *amber*	300.00	110.00
	Entire	400.00	190.00
U275	U65 2c brn, *blue*		*20,000.*
	Entire		47,500.
U276	U65 2c brn, *fawn*	1,050.	700.00
	Entire	1,550.	*900.00*

Washington

U67 U68

U67 — Extremity of bust below the queue forms a point.

U68 — Extremity of bust is rounded.

Similar to U61

Two wavy lines in oval

1884-86

U277	U67 2c brown	.50	.20
	Entire	1.00	.40
a.	2c brown lake	22.50	21.00
	Entire	27.50	26.00
U278	U67 2c brn, *amber*	.65	.50
	Entire	1.75	.75
a.	2c brown lake, *amber*	35.00	25.00
	Entire	42.50	32.50
U279	U67 2c brn, *oriental buff* ('86)	5.00	2.10
	Entire	7.50	3.00
U280	U67 2c brn, *blue*	3.00	2.10
	Entire	4.50	3.50
U281	U67 2c brn, *fawn*	3.75	2.40
	Entire	5.75	4.00
U282	U67 2c brn, *man* ('86)	13.00	4.00
	Entire	17.50	6.50
W283	U67 2c brn, *man*	7.50	5.00
	Entire	11.00	6.50
U284	U67 2c brn, *amb man*('86)	9.00	5.75
	Entire	15.00	7.00
+U285	U67 2c red	775.00	
	Entire	1,650.	
+U286	U67 2c red, *blue*	325.00	
	Entire	375.00	
W287	U67 2c red, *man*	150.00	
	Entire	210.00	
U288	U68 2c brown	375.00	50.00
	Entire	850.00	150.00
U289	U68 2c brn, *amb*	18.00	13.00
	Entire	24.00	17.00
U290	U68 2c brn, *blue*	1,900.	300.00
	Entire	2,400.	*450.00*
U291	U68 2c brn, *fawn*	35.00	22.50
	Entire	45.00	27.50
W292	U68 2c brn, *man*	25.00	19.00
	Entire	35.00	22.50

Grant — US1

1886 — **Letter Sheet**

U293	US1 2c green, entire	30.00	20.00

See the Scott U.S. Specialized Catalogue for perforation and inscription varieties.

Franklin U69

Washington U70

U70 — Bust points between 3rd and 4th notches of inner oval; "G" of "POSTAGE" has no bar.

U71

U72

U71 — Bust points between second and third notches of inner oval; "G" of "POSTAGE" has a bar; ear is indicated by one heavy line; one vertical line at corner of mouth.

U72 — Frame same as die 2; upper part of head more rounded; ear indicated by two curved lines with two locks of hair in front; two vertical lines at corner of mouth.

Jackson — U73

Grant — U74

U75

U74 — There is a space between the beard and the collar of the coat. A button is on the collar.

U75 — The collar touches the beard and there is no button.

1887-94

U294	U69 1c blue	.55	.20
	Entire	1.00	.50
U295	U69 1c dk bl ('94)	7.50	2.50
	Entire	10.50	6.50
U296	U69 1c bl, *amb* ('94)	3.50	1.25
	Entire	6.00	3.50
U297	U69 1c dk blue, *amb* ('94)	47.50	22.50
	Entire	57.50	27.50
+U298	U69 1c bl, *oriental buff* ('94)	*15,000.*	
	Entire	*20,000.*	
+U299	U69 1c bl, *bl* ('94)	*20,000.*	
	Entire	*30,000.*	
U300	U69 1c bl, *man* ('94)	.65	.35
	Entire	1.25	.75
W301	U69 1c bl, *man* ('94)	.45	.30
	Entire	1.25	.60
U302	U69 1c dk blue, *man* ('94)	30.00	12.50
	Entire	37.50	20.00
U303	U69 1c dk blue, *man* ('94)	17.50	10.00
	Entire	25.00	15.00
U304	U69 1c bl, *amb man*	12.50	5.00
	Entire	17.50	7.50
U305	U70 2c green	19.00	10.50
	Entire	35.00	15.00
U306	U70 2c grn, *amb*	45.00	17.50
	Entire	55.00	22.50
U307	U70 2c grn, *oriental buff*	97.50	35.00
	Entire	125.00	50.00

U308 U70 2c grn, *blue* 20,000. 1,250.
Entire *22,000.*
U309 U70 2c grn, *man* 17,500. *750.00*
Entire *25,000.* 1,050.
U310 U70 2c grn, *amb man* 40,000. 1,250.
Entire — *3,500.*
U311 U71 2c green .35 .20
Entire .75 .25
a. 2c dark green ('94) .50 .30
Entire 1.10 .85
U312 U71 2c grn, *amb* .45 .20
Entire .80 .30
b. 2c dark green, *amber* ('94) .60 .35
U313 U71 2c grn, *oriental buff* .60 .25
Entire 1.20 .40
a. 2c dark green, *oriental buff* ('94) 2.00 1.00
Entire 4.00 4.00
U314 U71 2c grn, *blue* .65 .30
Entire 1.25 .40
a. 2c dark green, *blue* ('94) .85 .40
Entire 1.75 1.50
U315 U71 2c grn, *man* 1.75 .50
Entire 2.75 1.00
a. 2c dark green, *manila* ('94) 2.75 .75
Entire 4.00 1.50
W316 U71 2c grn, *man* 4.00 2.50
Entire 11.00 7.00
U317 U71 2c grn, *amb man* 2.75 1.90
Entire 6.00 3.00
a. 2c dark green, *amber manila* ('94) 4.00 3.00
Entire 7.50 4.00
U318 U72 2c green 150.00 12.50
Entire 200.00 45.00
U319 U72 2c grn, *amb* 190.00 25.00
Entire 275.00 50.00
U320 U72 2c grn, *oriental buff* 175.00 40.00
Entire 240.00 70.00
U321 U72 2c grn, *blue* 190.00 65.00
Entire 300.00 82.50
U322 U72 2c grn, *man* 275.00 65.00
Entire 325.00 110.00
U323 U72 2c grn, *amb man* 600.00 100.00
Entire 700.00 175.00
U324 U73 4c carmine 3.25 2.00
Entire 6.00 2.10
a. 4c lake 3.50 2.00
Entire 7.00 3.75
b. 4c scarlet ('94) 3.50 2.00
Entire 7.00 3.75
U325 U73 4c car, *amb* 3.75 3.50
Entire 7.50 4.00
a. 4c lake, *amber* 3.75 3.50
Entire 7.75 4.00
b. 4c scarlet, *amber* ('94) 4.00 3.75
Entire 8.00 4.25
U326 U73 4c car, *oriental buff* 8.00 3.50
Entire 16.00 6.25
a. 4c lake, *oriental buff* 8.00 3.50
Entire 16.00 6.25
U327 U73 4c car, *blue* 6.50 4.00
Entire 13.00 7.00
a. 4c lake, *blue* 6.50 4.00
Entire 13.00 6.00
U328 U73 4c car, *man* 9.00 7.00
Entire 13.00 7.50
a. 4c lake, *manila* 9.00 6.00
Entire 13.00 7.50
b. 4c pink, *manila* 15.00 10.00
Entire 21.00 12.50
U329 U73 4c car, *amb man* 7.50 3.25
Entire 13.50 5.00
a. 4c lake, *amb manila* 7.50 3.25
Entire 13.50 5.00
b. 4c pink, *amb manila* 16.00 10.00
Entire 22.50 12.50
U330 U74 5c blue 4.00 4.00
Entire 8.00 11.00
U331 U74 5c bl, *amber* 5.50 2.50
Entire 10.50 14.00
U332 U74 5c bl, *oriental buff* 6.00 4.00
Entire 17.00 18.00
U333 U74 5c bl, *blue* 10.50 6.00
Entire 17.00 15.00
U334 U75 5c blue ('94) 27.50 12.50
Entire 42.50 22.50
U335 U75 5c bl, *amb* ('94) 15.00 7.50
Entire 20.00 40.00
U336 U55 30c red brn 60.00 47.50
Entire 70.00 *475.00*
a. 30c yellow brown 60.00 47.50
Entire 70.00 *475.00*
b. 30c chocolate 60.00 47.50
Entire 70.00 *475.00*
U337 U55 30c red brn, *amb* 60.00 47.50
Entire 70.00 *475.00*
a. 30c yel brown, *amber* 60.00 47.50
Entire 70.00 *475.00*
b. 30c choc, *amber* 60.00 47.50
Entire 70.00 *475.00*
U338 U55 30c red brn, *oriental buff* 60.00 47.50
Entire 70.00 *475.00*
a. 30c yel brn, *oriental buff* 60.00 47.50
Entire 70.00 *475.00*
U339 U55 30c red brn, *bl* 60.00 47.50
Entire 70.00 *475.00*
a. 30c yellow brown, *blue* 60.00 47.50
Entire 70.00 *475.00*
U340 U55 30c red brn, *manila* 60.00 47.50
Entire 70.00 *475.00*
a. 30c brown, *manila* 60.00 47.50
Entire 70.00 *475.00*
U341 U55 30c red brn, *amb man* 60.00 47.50
Entire 70.00 *475.00*
a. 30c yel brn, *amb man* 60.00 47.50
Entire 70.00 *475.00*
U342 U56 90c purple 77.50 *90.00*
Entire 110.00 *1,050.*
U343 U56 90c pur, *amb* 92.50 90.00
Entire 140.00 *1,050.*
U344 U56 90c pur, *oriental buff* 92.50 90.00
Entire 150.00 *1,050.*
U345 U56 90c pur, *blue* 92.50 *90.00*
Entire 150.00 *1,050.*
U346 U56 90c pur, *man* 100.00 *92.50*
Entire 150.00 *1,050.*
U347 U56 90c pur, *amb man* 100.00 *92.50*
Entire 150.00 *1,050.*

Columbian Exposition Issue

Columbus and Liberty — U76

1893

U348 U76 1c deep blue 2.25 1.25
Entire 3.00 1.50
U349 U76 2c violet 1.75 .50
Entire 3.50 .60
a. 2c dark slate (error) *2,500.*
Entire *5,000.*
U350 U76 5c chocolate 8.50 7.50
Entire 13.00 10.00
a. 5c slate brown (error) 800.00 950.00
Entire *1,100.* *1,400.*
U351 U76 10c slate brown 35.00 30.00
Entire 70.00 60.00

Franklin U77

Washington U78

U78 — Bust points to first notch of inner oval and is only slightly concave below.

U79

U80

U79 — Bust points to middle of second notch of inner oval and is quite hollow below. Queue has ribbon around it.

U80 — Same as die 2 but hair flowing and no ribbon around queue.

Lincoln — U81

Pointed but not draped.

U82

U83

U82 — Bust broad and draped.

U83 — Head larger, inner oval has no notches.

Grant — U84

Similar to designs of 1887-95 but smaller

1899

U352 U77 1c green 1.10 .20
Entire 2.75 .50
U353 U77 1c grn, *amb* 5.50 1.50
Entire 8.75 2.75
U354 U77 1c grn, *oriental buff* 14.50 2.75
Entire 19.00 3.75
U355 U77 1c grn, *bl* 14.50 7.50
Entire 19.00 *12.50*
U356 U77 1c grn, *man* 2.40 .95
Entire 6.50 2.00
W357 U77 1c grn, *man* 2.50 1.10
Entire 9.00 4.00
U358 U78 2c carmine 3.00 1.75
Entire 8.00 3.25
U359 U78 2c car, *amb* 25.00 15.00
Entire 32.50 21.00
U360 U78 2c car, *oriental buff* 24.00 12.50
Entire 35.00 15.00
U361 U78 2c car, *blue* 65.00 35.00
Entire 77.50 50.00
U362 U79 2c carmine .35 .20
Entire .65 .30
a. 2c dark lake 30.00 30.00
Entire 37.50 35.00
U363 U79 2c car, *amb* 1.40 .20
Entire 3.00 .60
U364 U79 2c car, *oriental buff* 1.20 .20
Entire 3.00 .60
U365 U79 2c car, *blue* 1.50 .55
Entire 3.50 2.00
W366 U79 2c car, *man* 8.00 3.25
Entire 12.00 7.50
U367 U80 2c carmine 6.00 2.75
Entire 11.00 6.75
U368 U80 2c car, *amber* 9.00 6.75
Entire 15.00 12.00
U369 U80 2c car, *oriental buff* 25.00 12.50
Entire 32.50 20.00
U370 U80 2c car, *blue* 12.50 10.00
Entire 25.00 15.00
U371 U81 4c brown 20.00 13.00
Entire 30.00 18.00
U372 U81 4c brn, *amb* 20.00 13.00
Entire 32.50 24.00
U373 U82 4c brown *13,500.* 1,250.
Entire *20,000.*
U374 U83 4c brown 15.00 8.00
Entire 27.50 12.50
U375 U83 4c brn, *amb* 65.00 25.00
Entire 80.00 40.00
W376 U83 4c brn, *man* 20.00 10.00
Entire 35.00 25.00
U377 U84 5c blue 13.00 10.00
Entire 18.00 17.00
U378 U84 5c blue, *amb* 17.00 10.50
Entire 25.00 18.00

Franklin — U85

Washington — U86

U86 — "D" of "UNITED" contains vertical line at right that parallels the left vertical line. One short and two long vertical lines at right of "CENTS."

Grant — U87

Lincoln — U88

1903

U379 U85 1c green .80 .20
Entire 1.25 .35
U380 U85 1c green, *amb* 16.00 2.00
Entire 22.50 2.50
U381 U85 1c grn, *oriental buff* 19.00 2.50
Entire 26.00 3.50
U382 U85 1c green, *blue* 24.00 2.50
Entire 35.00 3.00
U383 U85 1c grn, *manila* 4.50 .90
Entire 6.00 1.25
W384 U85 1c grn, *manila* 3.00 .40
Entire 5.00 .80
U385 U86 2c carmine .50 .20
Entire .95 .35
a. 2c pink 2.00 1.50
Entire 3.00 2.00
b. 2c red 2.00 1.50
Entire 3.00 2.00
U386 U86 2c carmine, *amb* 2.50 .20
Entire 4.00 .80
a. 2c pink, *amber* 5.50 3.00
Entire 7.50 4.00
b. 2c red, *amber* 14.00 7.00
Entire 20.00 10.00
U387 U86 2c car, *oriental buff* 2.25 .30
Entire 3.50 .35
a. 2c pink, *oriental buff* 3.50 2.00
Entire 5.00 3.00
b. 2c red, *oriental buff* 4.00 2.25
Entire 5.50 3.25
U388 U86 2c carmine, *blue* 2.00 .50
Entire 3.00 .60
a. 2c pink, *blue* 22.50 14.00
Entire 30.00 18.00
b. 2c red, *blue* 22.50 14.00
Entire 30.00 18.00
W389 U86 2c car, *manila* 21.00 10.00
Entire 27.50 15.00
U390 U87 4c chocolate 22.50 12.50
Entire 32.50 15.00
U391 U87 4c choc, *amber* 24.00 12.50
Entire 35.00 15.00
W392 U87 4c choc, *manila* 25.00 12.50
Entire 50.00 40.00
U393 U88 5c blue 24.00 12.50
Entire 35.00 17.50
U394 U88 5c blue, *amber* 24.00 12.50
Entire 35.00 20.00

U89

"D" of "UNITED" is well rounded at right. The three lines at the right of "CENTS" and at the left of "TWO" are usually all short; the lettering is heavier and the ends of the ribbons slightly changed.

1904 **Re-cut Die**

U395 U89 2c carmine .75 .20
Entire 1.75 .45
a. 2c pink 5.50 2.50
U396 U89 2c car, *amber* 9.00 1.00
Entire 14.00 2.00
a. 2c pink, *amber* 11.00 3.00
U397 U89 2c car, *oriental buff* 6.00 1.10
Entire 8.50 1.50
a. 2c pink, *oriental buff* 7.50 2.75
U398 U89 2c carmine, *blue* 4.50 .90
Entire 6.00 1.40
a. 2c pink, *blue* 6.00 2.50
W399 U89 2c car, *manila* 16.00 10.00
Entire 35.00 25.00
a. 2c pink, *manila* 27.50 17.50
Entire 70.00 85.00

Franklin — U90

U90 Die 1

U90 Die 2

U90 Die 3

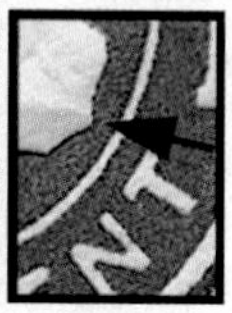

U90 Die 4

Die 1. Wide "D" in "UNITED."
Die 2. Narrow "D" in "UNITED."
Die 3. Wide "S-S" in "STATES" (1910).
Die 4. Sharp angle at back of bust, "N" and "E" of "ONE" are parallel (1912).

1907-16 **Die 1**

U400	U90 1c green	.35	.20
	Entire	.60	.30
a.	Die 2	.85	.25
	Entire	1.25	.45
b.	Die 3	.90	.35
	Entire	1.40	.65
c.	Die 4	.90	.30
	Entire	1.40	.45
U401	U90 1c green, *amber*	2.10	.40
	Entire	2.75	.60
a.	Die 2	2.60	.70
	Entire	3.50	.80
b.	Die 3	3.25	.75
	Entire	4.00	.80
c.	Die 4	2.10	.65
	Entire	3.00	.75
U402	U90 1c grn, *oriental buff*	10.50	1.00
	Entire	13.50	1.75
a.	Die 2	13.00	1.50
	Entire	18.50	1.75
b.	Die 3	15.50	1.50
	Entire	21.00	2.50
c.	Die 4	10.50	1.50
	Entire	13.50	2.25
U403	U90 1c green, *blue*	10.50	1.50
	Entire	13.50	2.25
a.	Die 2	13.00	3.00
	Entire	16.50	4.00
b.	Die 3	12.50	3.00
	Entire	16.00	3.25
c.	Die 4	9.50	1.25
	Entire	13.50	3.00
U404	U90 1c grn, *manila*	3.50	1.90
	Entire	6.00	2.75
a.	Die 3	4.50	3.00
	Entire	7.00	4.50
W405	U90 1c grn, *manila*	1.00	.25
	Entire	2.25	1.00
a.	Die 2	65.00	25.00
	Entire	90.00	30.00
b.	Die 3	12.00	4.00
	Entire	36.00	25.00
c.	Die 4	90.00	—
	Entire	—	—

Washington — U91

U91 Die 1

U91 Die 2

U91 Die 3

U91 Die 4

U91 Die 5

U91 Die 6

U91 Die 7

U91 Die 8

Die 1. Oval "O" in "TWO" and "C" in "CENTS," front of bust broad.
Die 2. Similar to 1 but hair in two distinct locks at top of head.
Die 3. Round "O" in "TWO" and "C" in "CENTS," coarse lettering.
Die 4. Similar to 3 but lettering fine and clear, hair lines clearly embossed. Inner oval thin and clear.
Die 5. All "S's" wide (1910).
Die 6. Similar to 1 but front of bust narrow (1913).
Die 7. Similar to 6 but upper corner of front of bust cut away (1916).
Die 8. Similar to 7 but lower stroke of "S" in "CENTS" is a straight line. Hair as in Die 2 (1916).

Die I

U406	U91 2c brown red	1.00	.20
	Entire	2.75	.30
a.	Die 2	45.00	7.00
	Entire	55.00	22.50
b.	Die 3	.90	.20
	Entire	2.75	1.00
U407	U91 2c brn red, *amb*	6.50	2.00
	Entire	9.00	5.00
a.	Die 2	375.00	65.00
	Entire	475.00	100.00
b.	Die 3	4.50	1.25
	Entire	7.00	1.90
U408	U91 2c brown red, *oriental buff*	8.75	1.50
	Entire	12.00	3.75
a.	Die 2	390.00	125.00
	Entire	475.00	150.00
b.	Die 3	7.50	2.50
	Entire	11.00	5.00
U409	U91 2c brn red, *blue*	5.75	2.00
	Entire	8.00	3.75
a.	Die 2	390.00	200.00
	Entire	500.00	475.00
b.	Die 3	5.75	1.75
	Entire	8.00	3.50
W410	U91 2c brn red, *man*	42.50	32.50
	Entire	55.00	42.50
U411	U91 2c carmine	.35	.20
	Entire	1.25	.35
a.	Die 2	.90	.20
	Entire	2.25	1.50
b.	Die 3	.80	.35
	Entire	1.50	.50
c.	Die 4	.65	.20
	Entire	1.25	.35
d.	Die 5	.65	.30
	Entire	1.75	.50
e.	Die 6	.60	.20
	Entire	1.50	.30
f.	Die 7	42.50	25.00
	Entire	55.00	30.00
g.	Die 8	42.50	25.00
	Entire	55.00	30.00
h.	Die 1, with added impression of 1c grn (#U400), entire	475.00	
i.	Die 1, with added impression of 4c blk (#U416a),entire	475.00	
U412	U91 2c carmine, *amb*	.30	.20
	Entire	1.10	.20
a.	Die 2	1.10	.25
	Entire	5.00	3.00
b.	Die 3	2.25	.45
	Entire	3.00	.75
c.	Die 4	.55	.25
	Entire	1.25	.40
d.	Die 5	.90	.35
	Entire	1.50	.55
e.	Die 6	.70	.35
	Entire	1.10	.50
f.	Die 7	37.50	25.00
	Entire	50.00	32.50
U413	U91 2c car, *oriental buff*	.55	.20
	Entire	.75	.25
a.	Die 2	2.25	.45
	Entire	5.00	3.75
b.	Die 3	9.00	3.00
	Entire	15.00	5.50
c.	Die 4	.55	.20
	Entire	1.25	.40
d.	Die 5	3.50	1.25
	Entire	5.00	3.25
e.	Die 6	.70	.35
	Entire	1.25	.55
f.	Die 7	105.00	45.00
	Entire	135.00	62.50
g.	Die 8	32.50	22.50
	Entire	50.00	27.50
U414	U91 2c carmine, *blue*	.60	.20
	Entire	1.40	.25
a.	Die 2	2.25	.35
	Entire	5.50	5.00
b.	Die 3	2.75	.60
	Entire	4.00	.70
c.	Die 4	.70	.25
	Entire	1.25	.45
d.	Die 5	2.25	.30
	Entire	3.00	.40
e.	Die 6	.65	.30
	Entire	1.10	.40
f.	Die 7	42.50	25.00
	Entire	50.00	35.00
g.	Die 8	42.50	25.00
	Entire	50.00	35.00
W415	U91 2c car, *manila*	5.00	2.00
	Entire	8.00	4.75
a.	Die 2	5.50	1.25
	Entire	8.00	4.50
b.	Die 5	5.50	2.50
	Entire	8.00	3.00
c.	Die 7	130.00	97.50
	Entire	175.00	125.00

U90 4c Die 1

U90 4c Die 2

U416	U90 4c black, die 2	6.00	3.00
	Entire	11.00	5.00
a.	Die 1	6.00	3.00
	Entire	11.00	5.00
U417	U90 4c black, *amb*, die 2	7.50	2.50
	Entire	12.00	4.00
a.	Die 1	7.50	2.50
	Entire	12.00	4.00

Die 1 — Tall "F" in "FIVE"

Die 2 — Short "F" in "FIVE"

U418	U91 5c blue, die 2	7.00	2.25
	Entire	13.50	6.50
a.	Die 1	7.00	2.25
	Entire	13.50	6.50
b.	5c blue, *buff*, die 2 (error)	*3,000.*	
c.	5c blue, *blue*, die 2 (error)	*3,000.*	
d.	5c blue, *blue*, die 1 (error), entire	*6,500.*	
U419	U91 5c blue, *amber*, die 2	16.50	11.00
	Entire	22.50	13.00
a.	Die 1	16.50	11.00
	Entire	22.50	13.00

Franklin — U92

Die 1

Die 2

Die 3

Die 4

Die 5

(The 1c and 4c dies are the same except for figures of value.)

Die 1. UNITED nearer inner circle than outer circle.
Die 2. Large U; large NT closely spaced.
Die 3. Knob of hair at back of neck. Large NT widely spaced.
Die 4. UNITED nearer outer circle than inner circle.
Die 5. Narrow oval C, (also O and G).

1915-32 **Die 1**

U420	U92 1c green ('17)	.25	.20
	Entire	.40	.20
a.	Die 2	150.00	55.00
	Entire	200.00	70.00
b.	Die 3	.35	.20
	Entire	.50	.25
c.	Die 4	.55	.40
	Entire	.80	.50
d.	Die 5	.45	.35
	Entire	.75	.45
U421	U92 1c grn, *amber* ('17)	.55	.30
	Entire	.80	.45
a.	Die 2	500.00	175.00
	Entire	700.00	200.00
b.	Die 3	1.40	.65
	Entire	2.00	.95
c.	Die 4	1.90	.85
	Entire	2.50	1.25
d.	Die 5	1.10	.55
	Entire	1.75	.80
U422	U92 1c grn, *oriental buff* ('17)	2.40	.90
	Entire	3.25	1.40
a.	Die 4	5.50	1.25
	Entire	8.00	2.75
U423	U92 1c grn, *bl* ('17)	.50	.35
	Entire	.90	.50
a.	Die 3	.80	.45
	Entire	1.25	.70
b.	Die 4	1.40	.65
	Entire	2.50	.35
c.	Die 5	.85	.35
	Entire	1.60	.65
U424	U92 1c grn, (unglazed), *manila* ('16)	7.00	4.00
	Entire	9.00	5.00
W425	U92 1c grn, (unglazed), *manila* ('16)	.25	.20
	Entire	.85	.20
a.	Die 3	190.00	125.00
	Entire	250.00	140.00
U426	U92 1c grn, (glazed) *brown* ('20)	45.00	15.00
	Entire	55.00	17.50
U427	U92 1c grn, (glazed) *brown* ('20)	65.00	30.00
	Entire	75.00	*40.00*
U428	U92 1c grn, (unglazed) *brown* ('20)	16.50	7.50
	Entire	24.00	9.00
W428A	U92 1c grn, (unglazed) *brown*, die 1 ('20, entire)		*3,000.*

Washington — U93

Die 1

Die 2

Die 3

Die 4

Die 5

Die 6

Die 7

Die 8

Die 9

(The 1½c, 2c, 3c, 5c, and 6c are the same except for figures of value.)

Die 1. Letters broad. Numerals vertical. Large head (9¼mm) from tip of nose to back of neck. E closer to inner circle than N of cents.

Die 2. Similar to 1; but U far from left circle.

Die 3. Similar to 2; but all inner circles very thin (Rejected Die).

Die 4. Large head as in Die 1. "C" of "CENTS" close to circle. Baseline of right numeral "2" slants downward to right. Left numeral "2" is larger.

Die 5. Small head (8¾mm) from tip of nose to back of neck. T and S of CENTS close at bottom.

Die 6. Similar to 5; but T and S of CENTS far apart at bottom. Left numeral slopes to right.

Die 7. Large head. Both numerals slope to right. Clean cut lettering. All letters T have short top strokes.

Die 8. Similar to 7; but all letters T have long top strokes.

Die 9. Narrow oval C (also O and G).

Die 1

U429 U93 2c car, *Dec. 20, 1915* .25 .20
Entire .40 .20
a. Die 2 16.00 7.00
Entire 25.00 10.00
b. Die 3 47.50 *50.00*
Entire 60.00 *200.00*
c. Die 4 32.50 15.00
Entire 45.00 20.00
d. Die 5 .55 .35
Entire 1.00 .45
e. Die 6 .65 .30
Entire 1.25 .60
f. Die 7 .70 .25
Entire 1.25 .75
g. Die 8 .50 .20
Entire 1.00 .50
h. Die 9 .50 .20
Entire 1.00 .45
i. 2c grn (error), die 1, entire *14,000.*
j. 2c car, die 1 with added impression of 1c grn (#U420), die 1 1,100.
Entire 1,500.
k. Die 1, with added impression of 4c blk (#U416a), entire 1,000.
l. Die 1, with added impression of 1c grn (#U400), die 1, entire 1,000.
m. As U429, with double impression, entire 1,750.

U430 U93 2c car, *amber* ('16) .30 .20
Entire .50 .20
a. Die 2 21.00 12.50
Entire 30.00 15.00
b. Die 4 52.50 25.00
Entire 70.00 30.00
c. Die 5 1.60 .35
Entire 2.25 .60
d. Die 6 1.25 .40
Entire 2.25 .75
e. Die 7 .75 .35
Entire 1.75 .95
f. Die 8 .70 .30
Entire 1.10 .45
g. Die 9 .65 .20
Entire 1.10 .35

U431 U93 2c car, *oriental buff* ('16) 2.25 .65
Entire 4.50 1.40
a. Die 2 210.00 *75.00*
Entire 275.00
b. Die 4 77.50 60.00
Entire 100.00 75.00
c. Die 5 3.50 2.00
Entire 6.00 2.75
d. Die 6 3.50 2.00
Entire 7.00 2.75
e. Die 7 3.50 2.00
Entire 6.00 3.25

U432 U93 2c carmine, *blue* ('16) .30 .20
Entire .60 .20
b. Die 2 42.50 25.00
Entire 60.00 35.00
c. Die 3 165.00 90.00
Entire 225.00 *110.00*
d. Die 4 67.50 50.00
Entire 100.00 55.00
e. Die 5 1.10 .30
Entire 2.00 .75
f. Die 6 1.10 .40
Entire 2.00 .60
g. Die 7 .85 .35
Entire 1.75 .65
h. Die 8 .65 .25
Entire 1.50 .50
i. Die 9 1.00 .30
Entire 2.75 .55
j. 2c purple (error), die 9 Entire —

U432A U93 2c car, *manila*, die 7, entire *55,000.*

W433 U93 2c car, *manila* ('16) .25 .20
Entire .50 .30

W434 U93 2c car, (glazed) *brn* ('20) 97.50 50.00
Entire 125.00 60.00

W435 U93 2c car, (unglazed) *brn* ('20) 97.50 50.00
Entire 125.00 60.00

U436 U93 3c purple ('32) .30 .20
Entire .60 .25
a. 3c dark violet, die 1 ('17) .60 .20
Entire 1.00 .25
b. 3c dark violet, die 5 ('17) 1.75 .75
Entire 3.25 .90
c. 3c dark violet, die 6 ('17) 2.10 1.40
Entire 3.25 1.50
d. 3c dark violet, die 7 ('17) 1.50 .95
Entire 3.00 1.00
e. 3c purple, die 7 ('32) .70 .30
Entire 1.75 .75
f. 3c purple, die 9 ('32) .45 .20
Entire .60 .30
g. 3c car (error), die 1 42.50 30.00
Entire 65.00 45.00
h. 3c car (error), die 5 37.50 30.00
Entire 60.00 45.00
i. 3c dk vio, die 1, with added impression of 1c grn (#U420), die 1, entire 900.00
j. 3c dk vio, die 1, with added impression of 2c car (#U429), die 1, entire 900.00 950.00

U437 U93 3c purple, *amb* ('32) .35 .20
Entire .60 .35
a. 3c dark violet, die 1 ('17) 5.50 1.25
Entire 9.00 2.25
b. 3c dark vio, die 5 ('17) 8.50 2.50
Entire 12.00 3.00
c. 3c dark vio, die 6 ('17) 8.50 2.50
Entire 12.00 3.00
d. 3c dark vio, die 7 ('17) 8.50 2.25
Entire 12.00 2.50
e. 3c purple, die 7 ('32) .75 .20
Entire 1.25 .30
f. 3c purple, die 9 ('32) .55 .20
Entire 1.00 .30
g. 3c car (error), die 5 500.00 350.00
Entire 525.00 *325.00*
h. 3c black (error), die 1 200.00 —
Entire 275.00

U438 U93 3c dk vio, *oriental buff* 27.50 1.65
Entire 35.00 2.00
a. Die 5 27.50 1.65
Entire 35.00 2.00
b. Die 6 37.50 3.50
Entire 50.00 4.50
c. Die 7 37.50 3.50
Entire 50.00 7.75

U439 U93 3c purple, *bl* ('32) .35 .20
Entire .75 .25
a. 3c dark violet, die 1 ('17) 8.50 2.00
Entire 15.00 6.00
b. 3c dark violet, die 5 ('17) 9.50 6.00
Entire 15.00 7.50
c. 3c dark violet, die 6 ('17) 9.50 6.00
Entire 15.00 7.50
d. 3c dark violet, die 7 ('17) 12.50 6.00
Entire 18.50 7.50
e. 3c purple, die 7 ('32) .75 .25
Entire 1.50 .50
f. 3c purple, die 9 ('32) .60 .20
Entire 1.50 .45
g. 3c car (error), die 5 375.00 300.00
Entire 475.00 *725.00*

U440 U92 4c black ('18) 1.75 .60
Entire 3.00 2.00
a. 4c black with added impression of 2c car (#U429), die 1, entire 450.00

U441 U92 4c black, *amb* ('18) 3.00 .85
Entire 5.00 2.00

U442 U92 4c blk, *bl* ('21) 3.50 .85
Entire 6.00 1.75

U443 U93 5c blue ('18) 3.50 2.75
Entire 6.00 3.25

U444 U93 5c blue, *amber* ('18) 4.00 1.60
Entire 7.00 3.50

U445 U93 5c bl, *blue* ('21) 4.25 3.25
Entire 8.50 4.25

See Nos. U481-U485, U529-U531.

Listings of double or triple surcharges of 1920-25 are for specimens with the surcharges directly or partly upon the stamp.

Surcharged

Type 1

1920-21

U446 U93 2c on 3c dk vio (U436, die 1) 16.00 10.00
Entire 25.00 12.50
a. Die 5 (U436b) 16.00 10.00
Entire 25.00 12.50

Surcharged

Type 2

Rose Surcharge

U447 U93 2c on 3c dk vio (U436, die 1) 10.00 6.50
Entire 17.50 8.50
b. Die 6 (U436c) 13.00 8.50
Entire 27.50 5.00

Black Surcharge

U447A U93 2c on 2c car (U429, die 1) *50,000.*

U447C U93 2c on 2c car, *amb* (U430, die 1) —

U448 U93 2c on 3c dk vio (U436, die 1) 2.75 2.00
Entire 4.00 2.50
a. Die 5 (U436b) 2.75 2.00
Entire 4.00 2.50
b. Die 6 (U436c) 3.50 2.00
Entire 5.00 2.50
c. Die 7 (U436d) 2.75 2.00
Entire 4.00 2.50

U449 U93 2c on 3c dk vio, *amb* (U437, die 1) 7.50 6.00
Entire 10.00 7.50
a. Die 5 (U437b) 13.00 7.50
Entire 17.50 10.00
b. Die 6 (U437c) 9.50 6.00
Entire 13.50 7.50
c. Die 7 (U437d) 8.50 6.50
Entire 12.00 8.00

U450 U93 2c on 3c dk vio, *oriental buff* (U438, die 1) 20.00 15.00
Entire 25.00 18.00
a. Die 5 (U438a) 20.00 15.00
Entire 25.00 18.00
b. Die 6 (U438b) 20.00 15.00
Entire 25.00 18.00
c. Die 7 (U438c) 135.00 90.00
Entire 175.00 125.00

U451 U93 2c on 3c dk vio, *blue* (U439, die 1) 16.00 10.50
Entire 22.50 11.50
b. Die 5 (U439b) 16.00 10.50
Entire 22.50 11.50
c. Die 6 (U439c) 16.00 10.50
Entire 22.50 11.50
d. Die 7 (U439d) 29.00 22.50
Entire 42.50 27.50

Surcharged

Type 3

Bars 2mm apart, 25 to 26 mm in length

U451A U90 2c on 1c grn (U400, die 1) *30,000.*
Entire —

U452 U92 2c on 1c grn (U420, die 1) 3,750.
Entire 4,250.
a. Die 3 (U420b) 3,750.
Entire 4,250.
b. As No. U452, dbl. surch. 4,500.
Entire 5,000.

U453 U91 2c on 2c car (U411b, die 3) 5,000.
Entire 8,000.
a. Die 1 (U411) 5,000.
Entire 8,000.

U453B U91 2c on 2c car, *bl* (U414e, die 6) 3,000.
Entire 3,750.

U453C U91 2c on 2c car, *oriental buff* (U413e, die 6) 2,500. *750.00*
Entire 3,250.
d. Die 1 (U413) 2,500.
Entire 3,250.

U454 U93 2c on 2c car (U429e, die 6) 150.00
Entire 200.00
a. Die 1 (U429) 350.00
Entire 400.00
b. Die 5 (U429d) 500.00
Entire 650.00
c. Die 7 (U429f) 150.00
Entire 200.00

U455 U93 2c on 2c car, *amb* (U430, die 1) 2,250.
Entire 4,250.
a. Die 6 (U430d) 2,250.
Entire 4,250.
b. Die 7 (U430e) 2,250.
Entire 4,250.

U456 U93 2c on 2c car, *oriental buff* (U431a, die 2) 300.00
Entire 375.00
a. Die 5 (U431c) 350.00
Entire 500.00
b. Die 7 (U431e) 800.00
Entire 850.00
c. As #U456, dbl. surch. 750.00

U457 U93 2c on 2c car, *bl* (U432f, die 6) 400.00
Entire 450.00
a. Die 5 (U432e) 400.00
Entire 500.00
b. Die 7 (U432g) 800.00
Entire 850.00

U458 U93 2c on 3c dk vio (U436, die 1) .55 .35
Entire .80 .45
a. Die 5 (U436b) .55 .40
Entire .80 .50
b. Die 6 (U436c) .55 .35
Entire .80 .45
c. Die 7 (U436d) .55 .35
Entire .80 .45
d. As #U458, dbl. surch. 25.00 7.50
Entire 35.00 10.00
e. As #U458, trip. surch. 110.00
Entire 160.00
f. As #U458, dbl. surch., one in magenta 110.00
Entire 150.00
g. As #U458, dbl. surch., types 2 & 3 140.00
Entire 190.00
h. As "a," dbl. surch. 27.50 15.00
Entire 37.50 20.00
i. As "a," triple surcharge 110.00
Entire 160.00
j. As "a," dbl. surch., both magenta 110.00
Entire 150.00
k. As "b," dbl. surch. 25.00 8.00
Entire 35.00 11.00
l. As "c," dbl. surch. 25.00 8.00
Entire 35.00 11.00
m. As "c," triple surcharge 110.00
Entire 150.00

U459 U93 2c on 3c dk vio, *amb* (U437c, die 6) 3.25 1.00
Entire 5.00 1.75
a. Die 1 (U437) 4.25 1.00
Entire 6.00 1.75
b. Die 5 (U437b) 4.25 1.00
Entire 6.00 1.75

c. Die 7 (U437d) 3.25 1.00
Entire 6.00 1.75
d. As #U459, dbl. surch. 35.00
Entire 50.00
e. As "a," dbl. surch. 35.00
Entire 50.00
f. As "b," dbl. surch. 35.00
Entire 50.00
g. As "b," dbl. surch., types 2 & 3 125.00
Entire 175.00
h. As "c," dbl. surch. 35.00
Entire 50.00
U460 U93 2c on 3c dk vio, *oriental buff* (U438a, die 5) 4.00 2.00
Entire 5.00 2.50
a. Die 1 (U438) 4.00 2.00
Entire 5.00 2.50
b. Die 6 (U438b) 4.25 2.00
Entire 6.00 2.50
c. As #U460, dbl. surch. 20.00
Entire 30.00
d. As "a," dbl. surch. 20.00
Entire 30.00
e. As "b," dbl. surch. 20.00
Entire 30.00
f. As "b," triple surcharge 150.00
Entire 250.00
U461 U93 2c on 3c dk vio, *bl* (U439, die 1) 6.50 1.00
Entire 9.00 1.50
a. Die 5 (U439b) 6.50 1.00
Entire 9.00 1.50
b. Die 6 (U439c) 6.50 1.00
Entire 9.00 1.50
c. Die 7 (U439d) 13.50 2.00
Entire 20.00 3.00
d. As #U461, dbl. surch. 20.00
Entire 30.00
e. As "a," dbl. surch. 20.00
Entire 30.00
f. As "b," dbl. surch. 20.00
Entire 30.00
g. As "c," dbl. surch. 20.00
Entire 30.00
U462 U87 2c on 4c choc (U390) 625.00 260.00
Entire 1,000. 500.00
U463 U87 2c on 4c choc, *amb* (U391) 1,250. 350.00
Entire 1,600. 500.00
U463A U90 2c on 4c blk (U416, die 2) 1,400. 400.00
Entire 2,000.
U464 U93 2c on 5c bl (U443) 1,400.
Entire 2,000.

Surcharged

Type 4

Bars 1mm apart, 21-23mm in length

U465 U92 2c on 1c grn (U420, die 1) 1,750.
Entire 2,900.
a. Die 3 (U420b) 2,000.
Entire 3,000.
U466 U91 2c on 2c car (U411e, die 6) *15,000.*
Entire *27,500.*
U466A U93 2c on 2c car (U429, die 1) 950.00
Entire 1,600.
c. Die 5 (U429d) 1,250.
Entire 1,750.
d. Die 6 (U429e) 1,250.
Entire 1,750.
e. Die 7 (U429f) 1,250.
Entire 1,750.
U466B U93 2c on 2c car, *amb* (U430) *15,000.*
Entire *27,500.*
U466C U93 2c on 2c car, *oriental buff (U431), entire* (U430) —
U466D U93 2c on 3c green, die 2 (U82) *7,500.*
U467 U45 2c on 3c grn (U163) 425.00
Entire 550.00
U468 U93 2c on 3c dk vio (U436, die 1) .70 .45
Entire 1.00 .75
a. Die 5 (U436b) .70 .50
Entire 1.00 .75
b. Die 6 (U436c) .70 .50
Entire 1.00 .75
c. Die 7 (U436d) .70 .50
Entire 1.00 .75
d. As #U468, dbl. surch. 20.00
Entire 30.00
e. As #U468, trip. surch. 100.00
Entire 150.00
f. As #U468, dbl. surch., types 2 & 4 125.00
Entire 175.00
g. As "a," double surcharge 20.00
Entire 30.00
h. As "b," double surcharge 20.00
Entire 30.00
i. As "c," double surcharge 20.00
Entire 30.00
j. As "c," triple surcharge 100.00
Entire 150.00
k. As "c," inverted surch. 75.00
Entire 125.00
l. 2c on 3c car (error) (U436h) 650.00
Entire 800.00
m. As #U468, triple surch., one inverted, entire *900.00*
U469 U93 2c on 3c dk vio, *amber* (U437, die 1) 3.75 2.25
Entire 5.00 2.75
a. Die 5 (U437b) 3.75 2.25
Entire 5.00 2.75
b. Die 6 (U437c) 3.75 2.25
Entire 5.00 2.75
c. Die 7 (U437d) 3.75 2.25
Entire 5.00 2.75
d. As No. U469, dbl. surch. 30.00
Entire 40.00
e. As "a," double surcharge 30.00
Entire 40.00
f. As "a," double surcharge, types 2 & 4 100.00
Entire 150.00
g. As "b," double surcharge 30.00
Entire 40.00
h. As "c," double surcharge 30.00
Entire 40.00
U470 U93 2c on 3c dk vio, *oriental buff* (U438, die 1) 6.00 2.50
Entire 10.00 4.00
a. Die 5 (U438a) 6.00 2.50
Entire 10.00 4.00
b. Die 6 (U438b) 6.00 2.50
Entire 10.00 4.00
c. Die 7 (U438c) 42.50 32.50
Entire 70.00 45.00
d. As No. U470, dbl. surch. 25.00
Entire 35.00
e. As No. U470, double surcharge, types 2 & 4 100.00
Entire 150.00
f. As "a," double surcharge 25.00
Entire 35.00
g. As "b," double surcharge 25.00
Entire 35.00
U471 U93 2c on 3c dk vio, *bl* (U439, die 1) 7.50 1.75
Entire 13.00 3.50
a. Die 5 (U439b) 7.50 1.75
Entire 13.00 3.50
b. Die 6 (U439c) 7.50 1.75
Entire 13.00 3.50
c. Die 7 (U439d) 10.50 6.00
Entire 22.50 10.00
d. As No. U471, dbl. surch. 30.00
Entire 40.00
e. As No. U471, double surcharge, types 2 & 4 175.00
Entire 250.00
f. As "a," double surcharge 30.00
Entire 40.00
g. As "b," double surcharge 30.00
Entire 40.00
U472 U87 2c on 4c choc (U390) 15.00 8.00
Entire 27.50 14.00
a. Double surcharge 150.00
U473 U87 2c on 4c choc, *amb* (U391) 16.50 10.00
Entire 27.50 13.50

Dbl. Surch., "1" and Type 4

U474 U93 2c on 1c on 3c dk vio (U436, die 1) 300.00
Entire 400.00
a. Die 5 (U436b) 400.00
Entire 575.00
b. Die 7 (U436d) 900.00
Entire 1,150.
U475 U93 2c on 1c on 3c dk vio, *amb* (U437, die 1) 300.00
Entire 475.00

Surcharged

Type 5

U476 U93 2c on 3c dk vio, *amb* (U437, die 1) 300.00
Entire 475.00
a. Die 6 (U437c) 750.00
Entire 1,000.
b. As #U476, double surch. —

Surcharged

Type 6

U477 U93 2c on 3c dk vio (U436, die 1) 140.00
Entire 190.00
a. Die 5 (U436b) 275.00
Entire 325.00
b. Die 6 (U436c) 275.00
Entire 325.00
c. Die 7 (U437d) 275.00
Entire 325.00
U478 U93 2c on 3c dk vio, *amb* (U437, die 1) 350.00
Entire 450.00

Handstamped Surcharge in Black or Violet — Type 7

U479 U93 2c on 3c dk vio (Bk) (U436, die 1) 450.00
Entire 550.00
a. Die 5 (U436) 900.00
Entire 1,100.
b. Die 7 (U436d) 450.00
Entire 550.00
U480 U93 2c on 3c dk vio (V) (U436d, die 7) *6,000.*
Entire *8,000.*
a. Double overprint —

Expertization by competent authorities is required for Nos. U476-U480.

Type of 1916-32 Issue

1925-34

Die 1

U481 U93 1½c brown .25 .20
Entire .60 .20
a. Die 8 .70 .25
Entire 1.00 .50
b. 1½c purple (error) ('34) 95.00
Entire 125.00
U482 U93 1½c brown, *amber* .95 .40
Entire 1.50 .60
a. Die 8 1.90 .75
Entire 2.50 .80
U483 U93 1½c brn, *bl* 1.60 .95
Entire 2.50 1.25
a. Die 8 2.40 1.25
Entire 3.25 1.40
U484 U93 1½c brown, *manila* 6.50 3.00
Entire 12.00 6.00
W485 U93 1½c brown, *manila* .85 .20
Entire 1.40 .45
a. With added impression of No. W433 120.00 —

Surcharged Type 8

1925

U486 U71 1½c on 2c grn (U311) 900.00
Entire 1,300.
U487 U71 1½c on 2c grn, *amb* (U312) 1,400.
Entire 1,850.
U488 U77 1½c on 1c grn (U352) 675.00
Entire 1,000.
U489 U77 1½c on 1c grn, *amb* (U353) 125.00 60.
Entire 200.00
U490 U90 1½c on 1c grn (U400, die 1) 6.75 3.50
Entire 11.00 5.50
a. Die 2 (U400a) 18.00 9.00
Entire 22.50 12.00
b. Die 3 (U400b) 42.50 17.50
Entire 55.00 22.50
c. Die 4 (U400c) 10.00 2.50
Entire 14.00 4.00
U491 U90 1½c on 1c grn, *amb* (U401c, die 4) 8.00 2.25
Entire 12.50 4.50
a. Die 1 (U401) 12.50 2.50
Entire 17.50 6.00
b. Die 2 (U401a) 120.00 65.00
Entire 140.00 95.00
c. Die 3 (U401b) 52.50 30.00
Entire 70.00 40.00
U492 U90 1½c on 1c grn, *oriental buff* (U402a, die 2) 600.00 150.00
Entire 700.00 175.00
a. Die 4 (U402c) 1,200. 250.00
Entire 1,500. 300.00
U493 U90 1½c on 1c grn, *bl* (U403c, die 4) 125.00 70.00
Entire 160.00 70.00
a. Die 2 (U403a) 125.00 70.00
Entire 160.00 90.00
U494 U90 1½c on 1c grn, *man* (U404, die 1) 400.00 100.00
Entire 550.00 150.00
a. Die 3 (U404a) 1,250.
Entire 1,500.
U495 U92 1½c on 1c grn (U420, die 1) .80 .25
Entire 1.10 .45
a. Die 2 (U420a) 85.00 52.50
Entire 125.00 90.00
b. Die 3 (U420b) 2.10 .70
Entire 3.00 .85
c. Die 4 (U420c) 2.10 .85
Entire 3.00 1.15
d. As No. U495, dbl. surch. 10.00 3.00
Entire 15.00 5.00
e. As "b," double surcharge 10.00 3.00
Entire 15.00 5.00
f. As "c," double surcharge 10.00 3.00
Entire 15.00 5.00
U496 U92 1½c on 1c grn, *amb* (U421, die 1) 21.00 12.50
Entire 30.00 15.00
a. Die 3 (U421b) 600.00
Entire 700.00
b. Die 4 (U421c) 21.00 12.50
Entire 30.00 15.00
U497 U92 1½c on 1c grn, *oriental buff* (U422, die 1) 4.50 1.90
Entire 7.00 2.25
a. Die 4 (U422b) 67.50
Entire 100.00
U498 U92 1½c on 1c grn, *bl* (U423c, die 4) 1.60 .75
Entire 2.50 1.00
a. Die 1 (U423) 2.75 1.50
Entire 4.50 2.00
b. Die 3 (U423b) 2.10 1.50
Entire 3.50 2.00
U499 U92 1½c on 1c grn, *man* (U424) 13.00 6.00
Entire 20.00 7.00
U500 U92 1½c on 1c grn, *brn (unglazed)* (U428) 85.00 30.00
Entire 100.00 35.00
U501 U93 1½c on 1c grn, *brn (glazed)* (U426) 85.00 25.00
Entire 100.00 35.00
U502 U93 1½c on 2c car (U429, die 1) 300.00 —
Entire 500.00
a. Die 5 (U429d) 400.00
Entire 575.00
b. Die 7 (U429f) 400.00
Entire 575.00
c. Die 6 (U429e) 425.00
Entire —
d. Die 8 (U429g) 500.00
U503 U93 1½c on 2c car, *oriental buff* (U431c, die 5) 400.00 —
Entire 525.00
a. Double surcharge —
b. Dbl. surch., one inverted *700.00*
U504 U93 1½c on 2c car, *bl* (U432, die 1) 450.00 —
Entire 525.00
a. Die 7 (U432g) 450.00
Entire 525.00

On Envelopes of 1925

U505 U93 1½c on 1½c brn (U481, die 1) 500.00
Entire 650.00
a. Die 8 (U481a) 500.00
Entire 650.00
b. As No. 505, double surcharge, entire —

U506 U93 1½c on 1½c brn, *bl* (U483a, die 8) 500.00
Entire 650.00

The paper of No. U500 is not glazed and appears to be the same as that used for wrappers of 1920.

Surcharged Type 9

Black Surcharge

U507 U69 1½c on 1c bl (U294) 3,250.
Entire 4,000.
U507A U69 1½c on 1c blue, *amb* (U296) —
U507B U69 1½c on 1c blue, *manila* (U300), entire 3,750.
U508 U77 1½c on 1c grn, *amb* (U353) 70.00
Entire 100.00
U508A U85 1½c on 1c grn (U379) 4,750.
Entire 6,750.
U509 U85 1½c on 1c grn, *amb* (U380) 16.00 10.00
Entire 30.00 15.00
a. Double surcharge 75.00
Entire 100.00
U509B U85 1½c on 1c grn, *oriental buff* (U381) 60.00 40.00
Entire 75.00 50.00
U510 U90 1½c on 1c grn (U400, die 1) 2.90 1.25
Entire 5.00 1.50
b. Die 2 (U400a) 9.50 4.00
Entire 13.50 6.00
c. Die 3 (U400b) 37.50 8.00
Entire 50.00 11.00
d. Die 4 (U400c) 4.25 1.25
Entire 8.00 2.00
e. As No. U510, double surcharge 25.00
Entire 50.00
U511 U90 1½c on 1c grn, *amb* (U401, die 1) 250.00 100.00
Entire 375.00 150.00
U512 U90 1½c on 1c grn, *oriental buff* (U402, die 1) 9.00 4.00
Entire 16.50 6.50
a. Die 4 (U402c) 21.00 14.00
Entire 30.00 17.00
U513 U90 1½c on 1c grn, *bl* (U403, die 1) 6.50 4.00
Entire 10.00 5.00
a. Die 4 (U403c) 6.50 4.00
Entire 10.00 5.00
U514 U90 1½c on 1c grn, *man* (U404, die 1) 34.00 9.00
Entire 45.00 22.50
a. Die 3 (U404a) 77.50 37.50
Entire 100.00 45.00
U515 U92 1½c on 1c grn (U420, die 1) .40 .20
Entire .75 .30
a. Die 2 (U420a) 21.00 15.00
Entire 30.00 20.00
b. Die 3 (U420b) .40 .20
Entire .75 .30
c. Die 4 (U420c) .40 .20
Entire .75 .30
d. As No. U515, dbl. surch. 10.00
Entire 15.00
e. As No. U515, inverted surch. 20.00
Entire 30.00
f. As No. U515, trip. surch. 20.00
Entire 30.00
g. As No. U515, dbl. surch., one invtd., entire —
h. As "b," double surcharge 10.00
Entire 15.00
i. As "b," inverted surcharge 20.00
Entire 30.00
j. As "b," triple surcharge 30.00
Entire 40.00
k. As "c," double surcharge 10.00
Entire 15.00
l. As "c," inverted surcharge 20.00
Entire 30.00

U516 U92 1½c on 1c grn, *amb* (U421c, die 4) 50.00 25.00
Entire 65.00 35.00
a. Die 1 (U421) 55.00 30.00
Entire 70.00 40.00
U517 U92 1½c on 1c grn, *oriental buff* (U422, die 1) 6.25 1.25
Entire 9.00 1.50
a. Die 4 (U422a) 7.25 1.50
Entire 10.00 2.00
U518 U92 1½c on 1c grn, *bl* (U423b, die 4) 6.00 1.25
Entire 8.00 1.50
a. Die 1 (U423) 7.75 2.50
Entire 11.00 3.00
b. Die 3 (U423a) 27.50 7.50
Entire 40.00 9.00
c. As "a," double surcharge 30.00
Entire 42.50
U519 U92 1½c on 1c grn, *man* (U424) 32.50 10.00
Entire 45.00 12.50
a. Double surcharge 100.00
U520 U93 1½c on 2c car (U429, die 1) 350.00 —
Entire 500.00
a. Die 5 (U429d) 350.00
Entire 500.00
b. Die 6 (U429e) 350.00
Entire 500.00
c. Die 7 (U429f) 400.00
Entire 550.00
U520D U93 1½c on 2c car, *amber* (U430c, die 5), entire —

Magenta Surcharge

U521 U92 1½c on 1c grn (U420b, die 3) 4.75 3.50
Entire 7.00 5.50
a. Double surcharge 75.00
Entire 125.00

Sesquicentennial Exposition Issue

Liberty Bell — U94

Die 1. The center bar of "E" of "POSTAGE" is shorter than top bar.
Die 2. The center bar of "E" of "POSTAGE" is of same length as top bar.

1926
U522 U94 2c carmine, die 1 1.10 .50
Entire 1.60 .95
a. Die 2 7.00 3.75
Entire 11.00 5.50

See note below No. 627.

Washington Bicentennial Issue

Mount Vernon — U95

2 cent:
Die 1. "S" of "POSTAGE" normal.
Die 2. "S" of "POSTAGE" raised.

1932
U523 U95 1c olive green 1.00 .80
Entire 1.50 1.75
U524 U95 1½c chocolate 2.00 1.50
Entire 2.75 2.50
U525 U95 2c car, die 1 .40 .20
Entire .50 .25
a. Die 2 70.00 20.00
Entire 85.00 27.50
b. Die 1, *blue*, entire (error) *40,000.*
U526 U95 3c violet 2.00 .35
Entire 2.50 .40
U527 U95 4c black 18.00 *20.00*
Entire 22.50 *35.00*
U528 U95 5c dark blue 4.00 3.50
Entire 4.75 4.75
Nos. U523-U528 (6) 27.40 26.35

Bicen. of the birth of Washington.

1932 **Die 7**
U529 U93 6c orange 7.00 4.00
Entire 10.00 7.50
U530 U93 6c orange, *amber* 13.00 10.00
Entire 18.00 12.50
U531 U93 6c orange, *blue* 13.00 10.00
Entire 18.00 12.50

AIR POST STAMPED ENVELOPES AND AIR LETTER SHEETS

UC1

UC2

UC1 — Vertical rudder is not semi-circular but slopes down to the left. The tail of the plane projects into the G of POSTAGE.

UC2 — Vertical rudder is semi-circular. The tail of the plane touches but does not project into the G of POSTAGE.

6c: Same as UC2 except 3 types of numeral.
Die 2a — Numeral "6" 6½mm wide.
Die 2b — Numeral "6" 6mm wide.
Die 2c — Numeral "6" 5½mm wide.
Die 3 — Vertical rudder leans forward. S closer to O than to T of POSTAGE. E of POSTAGE has short center bar.

1929-44 **Embossed**
UC1 UC1 5c blue 3.75 2.00
UC2 UC2 5c blue 11.50 5.00
UC3 UC2 6c org, die 2a ('34) 1.50 .40
a. No. UC3 with added impression of 3c pur (#U436a), entire without border *4,000.*
UC4 UC2 6c org, die 2b ('42) 3.00 2.00
UC5 UC2 6c org, die 2c ('44) .75 .30
UC6 UC2 6c org, die 3 ('42) 1.00 .35
a. 6c org, *blue* (error), entire *3,500.* *2,400.*
UC7 UC2 8c olive green ('32) 13.00 3.50

OFFICIAL STAMPED ENVELOPES

Post Office Department

"2" 9mm high — UO1

"3" 9mm high — UO2

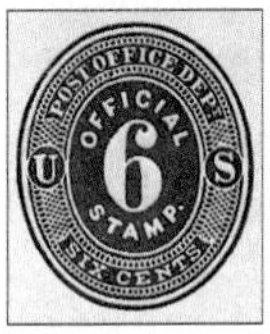
"6" 9½mm high — UO3

1873
UO1 UO1 2c black, *lemon* 24.00 10.00
Entire 35.00 15.00
UO2 UO2 3c black, *lemon* 16.00 6.50
Entire 29.00 11.00
+UO3 UO2 3c black *42,500.*
Entire *57,000.*
UO4 UO3 6c black, *lemon* 26.00 16.00
Entire 35.00 22.50

"2" 9¼mm high — UO4

"3" 9¼mm high — UO5

"6" 10½mm high — UO6

1874-79
UO5 UO4 2c black, *lemon* 10.50 4.25
Entire 15.00 7.00
UO6 UO4 2c black 140.00 35.00
Entire 190.00 55.00
UO7 UO5 3c black, *lemon* 3.00 .85
Entire 4.00 1.50
UO8 UO5 3c black 3,000. 2,250.
Entire 5,750.
UO9 UO5 3c black, *amber* 150.00 40.00
Entire 175.00 60.00
UO10 UO5 3c black, *blue* *45,000.*
Entire *50,000.*
UO11 UO5 3c blue, *blue* *45,000.*
Entire *50,000.*
UO12 UO6 6c black, *lemon* 16.00 6.50
Entire 26.00 12.50
UO13 UO6 6c black 3,250. 1,750.
Entire 4,000.

Postal Service

UO7

1877
UO14 UO7 black 7.00 4.50
Entire 11.50 6.00
UO15 UO7 black, *amber* 225.00 40.00
Entire 900.00 65.00
UO16 UO7 blue, *amber* 210.00 40.00
Entire 900.00 65.00
UO17 UO7 blue, *blue* 9.00 6.75
Entire 13.50 10.50

War Department

Franklin UO8

Jackson UO9

UO8 — Bust points to the end of "N" of "ONE."

UO9 — Bust narrow at the back.

Washington UO10

Lincoln UO11

UO10 — Queue projects below the bust.

UO11 — Neck very long at the back

Jefferson UO12

Clay UO13

UO12 — Queue forms straight line with bust.

UO13 — Ear partly concealed by hair, mouth large, chin prominent.

Webster
UO14

Scott
UO15

UO14 — Has side whiskers.

Hamilton — UO16

Back of bust very narrow, chin almost straight; the labels containing the letters "U S" are exactly parallel.

1873

Reay Issue

UO18	UO8 1c dark red	700.00	300.00
	Entire	1,100.	325.00
WO18A	UO8 1c dark red, *man*, entire		—
UO19	UO9 2c dark red	2,250.	400.00
	Entire	2,500.	
UO20	UO10 3c dark red	72.50	42.50
	Entire	100.00	70.00
UO21	UO10 3c dark red, *amb*	*40,000.*	
	Entire	*50,000.*	
UO22	UO10 3c dark red, *cr*	1,000.	300.00
	Entire	1,200.	350.00
UO23	UO11 6c dark red	325.00	100.00
	Entire	350.00	250.00
UO24	UO11 6c dark red, *cr*	8,250.	425.00
	Entire	10,000.	*2,000.*
UO25	UO12 10c dark red	*15,000.*	1,500.
	Entire	*22,500.*	4,000.
UO26	UO13 12c dark red	175.00	50.00
	Entire	200.00	—
UO27	UO14 15c dark red	160.00	55.00
	Entire	190.00	*375.00*
UO28	UO15 24c dark red	175.00	50.00
	Entire	200.00	*1,250.*
UO29	UO16 30c dark red	550.00	150.00
	Entire	675.00	500.00
UO30	UO8 1c vermilion	200.00	
	Entire	375.00	
WO31	UO8 1c ver, *man*	20.00	14.00
	Entire	35.00	25.00
+UO32	UO9 2c vermilion	500.00	
	Entire	—	
WO33	UO9 2c ver, *man*	210.00	
	Entire	350.00	
UO34	UO10 3c vermilion	100.00	40.00
	Entire	160.00	125.00
UO35	UO10 3c ver, *amb*	125.00	
	Entire	325.00	
UO36	UO10 3c ver, *cr*	17.00	12.50
	Entire	40.00	26.00
UO37	UO11 6c vermilion	87.50	
	Entire	150.00	
+UO38	UO11 6c ver, *cr*	575.00	
	Entire	*27,500.*	
UO39	UO12 10c vermilion	350.00	
	Entire	400.00	
UO40	UO13 12c vermilion	175.00	
	Entire	200.00	
UO41	UO14 15c vermilion	250.00	
	Entire	*3,000.*	
UO42	UO15 24c vermilion	450.00	
	Entire	600.00	
UO43	UO16 30c vermilion	500.00	
	Entire	600.00	

UO17

UO18

UO17 — Bottom serif on "S" is thick and short, bust at bottom below hair forms sharp point.

UO18 — Bottom serif on "S" is thick and short front part of bust is rounded.

UO19

UO20

UO19 — Bottom serif on "S" is short, queue does not project below bust.

UO20 — Neck very short at the back.

UO21

UO22

UO21 — Knot of queue stands out prominently.

UO22 — Ear prominent, chin receding.

UO23

UO24

UO23 — Has no side whiskers, forelock projects above head.

UO24 — Back of bust rather broad; chin slopes considerably; the labels containing letters "U S" are not exactly parallel.

1875

Plimpton Issue

UO44	UO17 1c red	190.00	85.00
	Entire	250.00	175.00
+UO45	UO17 1c red, *amb*	1,050.	
+UO45A	UO17 1c red, *org*	*37,500.*	
WO46	UO17 1c red, *man*	4.50	2.75
	Entire	9.00	6.50
UO47	UO18 2c red	140.00	—
	Entire	190.00	
UO48	UO18 2c red, *amb*	37.50	17.50
	Entire	45.00	27.50
UO49	UO18 2c red, *org*	70.00	17.50
	Entire	80.00	30.00
WO50	UO18 2c red, *man*	100.00	50.00
	Entire	225.00	—
UO51	UO19 3c red	17.50	10.00
	Entire	22.50	17.50
UO52	UO19 3c red, *amb*	22.50	10.00
	Entire	30.00	16.00
UO53	UO19 3c red, *cr*	7.25	3.75
	Entire	10.00	6.50
UO54	UO19 3c red, *bl*	4.00	2.75
	Entire	6.00	4.50
UO55	UO19 3c red, *fawn*	6.50	2.75
	Entire	11.50	4.00
UO56	UO20 6c red	65.00	30.00
	Entire	100.00	—
UO57	UO20 6c red, *amb*	95.00	40.00
	Entire	125.00	—
UO58	UO20 6c red, *cr*	225.00	85.00
	Entire	260.00	
UO59	UO21 10c red	250.00	80.00
	Entire	275.00	—
UO60	UO21 10c red, *amb*	1,250.	
	Entire	1,500.	
UO61	UO22 12c red	65.00	40.00
	Entire	190.00	*250.00*
UO62	UO22 12c red, *amb*	800.00	
	Entire	825.00	
UO63	UO22 12c red, *cr*	700.00	
	Entire	850.00	
UO64	UO23 15c red	250.00	140.00
	Entire	275.00	—
UO65	UO23 15c red, *amb*	950.00	
	Entire	1,200.	
UO66	UO23 15c red, *cr*	800.00	
	Entire	950.00	
UO67	UO24 30c red	170.00	140.00
	Entire	210.00	—
UO68	UO24 30c red, *amb*	950.00	
	Entire	2,400.	
UO69	UO24 30c red, *cr*	1,000.	
	Entire	1,350.	

Postal Savings Stamped Envelopes

UO25

1911

UO70	UO25 1c green	77.50	25.00
	Entire	110.00	42.50
UO71	UO25 1c grn, *oriental buff*	200.00	75.00
	Entire	250.00	90.00
UO72	UO25 2c carmine	13.50	4.00
	Entire	22.50	12.00
a.	2c car, *manila* (error)	*1,750.*	*1,000.*
	Entire	*2,500.*	*1,400.*

REVENUE STAMPS

Nos. R1-R102 were used to pay taxes on documents and proprietary articles including playing cards. Until Dec. 25, 1862, the law stated that a revenue stamp could be used only for payment of the tax upon the particular instrument or article specified on its face. After that date stamps, except the Proprietary, could be used indiscriminately.

Values quoted are for pen-canceled copies. Stamps with handstamped cancellations sell at higher prices. Stamps canceled with cuts, punches or holes sell for less. See the Scott U.S. Specialized Catalogue.

General Issue

First Issue. Head of Washington in Oval. Various Frames as Illustrated.

Nos. R1b to R42b, part perforate, occur perforated sometimes at sides only and sometimes at top and bottom only. The higher values, part perforate, are perforated at sides only. Imperforate and part perforate revenues often bring much more in pairs or blocks than as single copies.

The experimental silk paper is a variety of the old paper and has only a very few minute fragments of fiber.

Some of the stamps were in use eight years and were printed several times. Many color variations occurred, particularly when unstable pigments were used and the color was intended to be purple or violet, such as the 4c Proprietary, 30c and $2.50 stamps. Before 1868 dull colors predominate on these and the early red stamps. In later printings of the 4c Proprietary, 30c and $2.50 stamps, red predominates in the mixture, and on the dollar values the red is brighter. The early $1.90 stamp is dull purple, imperf. or perforated. In a later printing, perforated only, the purple is darker.

R1

R2

R3

R4

R5

1862-71 **Engr.** ***Perf. 12***

Old Paper

R1c	R1 1c Express, red	1.40
a.	Imperf.	70.00
b.	Part perf.	40.00
d.	Silk paper	120.00
e.	Vertical pair, imperf. between, old paper	*200.00*
R2c	R1 1c Playing Cards, red	160.00
a.	Imperf.	1,800.
b.	Part perf.	1,500.
R3c	R1 1c Proprietary, red	.50
a.	Imperf.	1,000.
b.	Part perf.	250.00
d.	Silk paper	45.00
R4c	R1 1c Telegraph, red	17.50
a.	Imperf.	600.00
R5c	R2 2c Bank Check, bl	.50
a.	Imperf.	1.25
b.	Part perf.	3.00
e.	Double impression	800.00
f.	As No. R5c, imperf btween	*400.00*
R6c	R2 2c Bank Check, org	.25
b.	Part perf.	55.00
d.	Silk paper	250.00
e.	Old paper, *green*	700.00
f.	As No. R6c, vert. half used as 1c on document	—
R7c	R2 2c Certificate, blue	30.00
a.	Imperf.	14.00
R8c	R2 2c Certificate, org	40.00
R9c	R2 2c Express, blue	.40
a.	Imperf.	14.00
b.	Part perf.	30.00
R10c	R2 2c Express, orange	12.50
b.	Part perf.	*750.00*
d.	Silk paper	120.00
R11c	R2 2c Playing Cards, bl	4.00
b.	Part perf.	250.00
R12c	R2 2c Playing Cards, org	50.00
R13c	R2 2c Proprietary, bl	.40
a.	Imperf.	*700.00*
b.	Part perf.	250.00
d.	Silk paper	100.00
e.	Ultramarine	300.00
f.	As No. R13c, horiz. half used as 1c on document	—
R14c	R2 2c Proprietary, org	60.00
R15c	R2 2c U.S. Int. Rev., org ('64)	.35
d.	Silk paper	.40
e.	Old paper, *green*	700.00
f.	As No. R15c, half used as 1c on document	—
R16c	R3 3c For. Exch., grn	4.50
b.	Part perf.	500.00
d.	Silk paper	100.00
R17c	R3 3c Playing Cards, grn ('63)	150.00
a.	Imperf.	*25,000.*
R18c	R3 3c Proprietary, grn	7.50
b.	Part perf.	500.00
d.	Silk paper	70.00
e.	As No. R18c, double impression	*1,000.*
f.	Printed on both sides, old paper	*3,500.*
R19c	R3 3c Telegraph, grn	2.75
a.	Imperf.	90.00
b.	Part perf.	27.50
R20c	R3 4c Inland Exch., brn ('63)	2.00
d.	Silk paper	110.00
R21c	R3 4c Playing Cards, slate ('63)	600.00
R22c	R3 4c Proprietary, purple	7.50
a.	Imperf.	—
b.	Part perf.	425.00
d.	Silk paper	150.00

Many shade and color variations of Nos. R21-R22. See foreword, "Revenue Stamps."

R23c	R3 5c Agreement, red	.50
d.	Silk paper	5.25
R24c	R3 5c Certificate, red	.50
a.	Imperf.	3.50
b.	Part perf.	13.00
d.	Silk paper	.55
e.	As No. R24c, half used as 2c on document	
f.	As No. R24c, impressions of R3 on back	*2,700.*
R25c	R3 5c Express, red	.40
a.	Imperf.	7.00
b.	Part perf.	7.00
R26c	R3 5c Foreign Exch., red	.50
b.	Part perf.	—
d.	Silk paper	375.00
R27c	R3 5c Inland Exch., red	.50
a.	Imperf.	8.25
b.	Part perf.	6.00
d.	Silk paper	17.50
e.	As No. R27b, double impression	—
R28c	R3 5c Playing Cards, red ('63)	35.00
e.	Double impression	*1,000.*

R29c	R3 5c Proprietary, red ('64)	27.50
d.	Silk paper	225.00
R30c	R3 6c Inland Exch., org ('63)	2.00
d.	Silk paper	150.00
R31c	R3 6c Proprietary, org ('71)	2,000.

Nearly all copies of No. R31 are faulty or repaired and poorly centered.

The Catalogue value is for a fine centered copy with minor faults which do not detract from its appearance.

R32c	R3 10c Bill of Lading, bl	1.50
a.	Imperf.	50.00
b.	Part perf.	425.00
R33c	R3 10c Certificate, blue	.35
a.	Imperf.	250.00
b.	Part perf.	700.00
d.	Silk paper	6.00
e.	As No. R33c, half used as 5c on document	200.00
R34c	R3 10c Contract, blue	.50
b.	Part perf.	450.00
d.	Silk paper	2.25
e.	Ultramarine, part perf.	650.00
f.	Ultramarine, old paper	1.00
g.	As No. R34c, half used as 5c on document	200.00
R35c	R3 10c For. Exch., bl	12.50
d.	Silk paper	—
e.	ultra, old paper	18.00
R36c	R3 10c Inland Exch., blue	.30
a.	Imperf.	350.00
b.	Part perf.	4.00
d.	Silk paper	70.00
e.	As No. R36c, half used as 5c on document	200.00
R37c	R3 10c Power of Attorney, blue	1.00
a.	Imperf.	850.00
b.	Part perf.	27.50
e.	As No. R37c, half used as 5c on document	200.00
R38c	R3 10c Proprietary, blue ('64)	17.50
R39c	R3 15c For. Exch., brn ('63)	15.00
e.	Double impression	1,000.
R40c	R3 15c Inland Exch., brn	1.75
a.	Imperf.	37.50
b.	Part perf.	12.50
e.	As No. R40b, double impression	1,200.
f.	As No. R40c, double impression	550.00
R41c	R3 20c For. Exch., red	60.00
a.	Imperf.	75.00
R42c	R3 20c Inland Exch., red	.45
a.	Imperf.	15.00
b.	Part perf.	20.00
d.	Silk paper	—
e.	As No. R42c, half used as 5c on document	200.00
R43c	R4 25c Bond, red	3.50
a.	Imperf.	250.00
b.	Part perf.	6.00
R44c	R4 25c Certificate, red	.50
a.	Imperf.	10.00
b.	Part perf.	6.00
d.	Silk paper	2.75
e.	Printed on both sides, old paper	4,500.
f.	Impression of No. R48 on back, old paper	—
R45c	R4 25c Entry of Goods, red	1.25
a.	Imperf.	20.00
b.	Part perf.	110.00
d.	Silk paper	60.00
R46c	R4 25c Insurance, red	.30
a.	Imperf.	11.00
b.	Part perf.	14.00
d.	Silk paper	5.50
e.	As No. R46c, double impression	500.00
R47c	R4 25c Life Insurance, red	9.50
a.	Imperf.	45.00
b.	Part perf.	475.00
R48c	R4 25c Power of Attorney, red	1.00
a.	Imperf.	8.00
b.	Part perf.	35.00
R49c	R4 25c Protest, red	7.50
a.	Imperf.	30.00
b.	Part perf.	700.00
R50c	R4 25c Warehouse Receipt, red	40.00
a.	Imperf.	47.50
b.	Part perf.	550.00
R51c	R4 30c For. Exch., lilac	55.00
a.	Imperf.	120.00
b.	Part perf.	2,000.
d.	Silk paper	—
R52c	R4 30c Inland Exch., lilac	8.00
a.	Imperf.	65.00
b.	Part perf.	75.00
d.	Silk paper	—

Many shade and color variations of Nos. R51-R52. See foreword, "Revenue Stamps."

R53c	R4 40c Inland Exch., brn	7.50
a.	Imperf.	1,200.
b.	Part perf.	8.00
f.	Double impression	—
R54c	R5 50c Conveyance, bl	.35
a.	Imperf.	17.00
b.	Part perf.	3.00
d.	Silk paper	3.00
e.	Ultramarine, old paper	.50
f.	Ultramarine, silk paper	—
R55c	R5 50c Entry of Goods, bl	.45
b.	Part perf.	15.00
d.	Silk paper	80.00
R56c	R5 50c For. Exch., blue	7.00
a.	Imperf.	60.00
b.	Part perf.	100.00
e.	As No. R56c, double impression	500.00
f.	As No. R56c, half used as 25c on document	200.00
R57c	R5 50c Lease, blue	9.00
a.	Imperf.	27.50
b.	Part perf.	140.00
R58c	R5 50c Life Insurance, bl	1.50
a.	Imperf.	40.00
b.	Part perf.	85.00
e.	As No. R58c, double impression	800.00
R59c	R5 50c Mortgage, blue	.65
a.	Imperf.	20.00
b.	Part perf.	4.50
d.	Silk paper	—
e.	As No. R59a, double impression	—
f.	As No. R59c, double impression	—
R60c	R5 50c Original Process, bl	1.00
a.	Imperf.	5.00
b.	Part perf.	600.00
d.	Silk paper	4.00
e.	As No. R60c, half used as 25c on document	—
R61c	R5 50c Passage Ticket, bl	2.00
a.	Imperf.	100.00
b.	Part perf.	275.00
R62c	R5 50c Probate of Will, bl	20.00
a.	Imperf.	50.00
b.	Part perf.	160.00
R63c	R5 50c Surety Bond, bl	.30
a.	Imperf.	275.00
b.	Part perf.	2.50
e.	Ultramarine, old paper	.75
R64c	R5 60c Inland Exch., org	8.00
a.	Imperf.	100.00
b.	Part perf.	75.00
d.	Silk paper	55.00
R65c	R5 70c For. Exch., green	12.00
a.	Imperf.	600.00
b.	Part perf.	175.00
d.	Silk paper	90.00

R6

R7

R8

R9

R10

(Illustration sideways) R11

Old Paper

R66c	R6 $1 Conveyance, red	25.00
a.	Imperf.	25.00
b.	Part perf.	700.00
d.	Silk paper	125.00
R67c	R6 $1 Entry of Goods, red	2.50
a.	Imperf.	42.50
d.	Silk paper	110.00
R68c	R6 $1 For. Exch., red	.75
a.	Imperf.	80.00
d.	Silk paper	100.00
e.	As No. R68c, diagonal half used as 50c on document	200.00
R69c	R6 $1 Inland Exch., red	.70
a.	Imperf.	15.00
b.	Part perf.	500.00
d.	Silk paper	3.75
R70c	R6 $1 Lease, red	4.00
a.	Imperf.	42.50
e.	As No. R70c, half used as 50c on document	—
R71c	R6 $1 Life Insurance, red	9.00
a.	Imperf.	200.00
e.	As No. R71c, half used as 50c on document	—
R72c	R6 $1 Manifest, red	35.00
a.	Imperf.	42.50
R73c	R6 $1 Mortgage, red	200.00
a.	Imperf.	25.00
R74c	R6 $1 Passage Ticket, red	275.00
a.	Imperf.	300.00
R75c	R6 $1 Power of Attorney, red	2.50
a.	Imperf.	90.00
R76c	R6 $1 Probate of Will, red	50.00
a.	Imperf.	90.00
R77c	R7 $1.30 For. Exch., org ('63)	75.00
a.	Imperf.	6,500.
R78c	R7 $1.50 Inland Exch., bl	6.00
a.	Imperf.	27.50
R79c	R7 $1.60 For. Exch., grn ('63)	120.00
a.	Imperf.	1,300.
R80c	R7 $1.90 For. Exch., pur ('63)	110.00
a.	Imperf.	10,000.
d.	Silk paper	—

Many shade and color variations of No. R80. See foreword, "Revenue Stamps."

R81c	R8 $2 Conveyance, red	3.50
a.	Imperf.	180.00
b.	Part perf.	2,000.
d.	Silk paper	40.00
e.	As No. R81c, half used as $1 on document	600.00
R82c	R8 $2 Mortgage, red	6.00
a.	Imperf.	135.00
d.	Silk paper	60.00
e.	As No. R82c, half used as $1 on document	—
R83c	R8 $2 Probate of Will, red ('63)	80.00
a.	Imperf.	5,500.
e.	As No. R83c, horiz. half used as $1 on document	750.00
R84c	R8 $2.50 Inland Exch., pur ('63)	20.00
a.	Imperf.	7,000.
d.	Silk paper	30.00
e.	As No. R84c, double impression	1,400.
R85c	R8 $3 Charter Party, grn	10.00
a.	Imperf.	175.00
d.	Silk paper	150.00
e.	As No. R85c, printed on both sides	2,300.
f.	As No. R85c, half used as $1.50 on document	—
g.	As No. R85c, impression of #RS208 on back	4,000.
R86c	R8 $3 Manifest, green	50.00
a.	Imperf.	175.00
R87c	R8 $3.50 Inland Exch., blue ('63)	65.00
a.	Imperf.	7,000.
e.	Printed on both sides	4,000.

Many shade and color variations of the $2.50. See foreword, "Revenue Stamps." The $3.50 has stars in upper corners.

R88c	R9 $5 Charter Party, red	9.00
a.	Imperf.	300.00
d.	Silk paper	80.00
R89c	R9 $5 Conveyance, red	10.00
a.	Imperf.	40.00
d.	Silk paper	125.00
R90c	R9 $5 Manifest, red	90.00
a.	Imperf.	185.00
R91c	R9 $5 Mortgage, red	22.50
a.	Imperf.	175.00
R92c	R9 $5 Probate of Will, red	25.00
a.	Imperf.	700.00
R93c	R9 $10 Charter Party, grn	32.50
a.	Imperf.	750.00
R94c	R9 $10 Conveyance, grn	70.00
a.	Imperf.	125.00
R95c	R9 $10 Mortgage, grn	35.00
a.	Imperf.	650.00
R96c	R9 $10 Probate of Will, green	40.00
a.	Imperf.	2,000.
R97c	R10 $15 Mortgage, blue	225.00
a.	Imperf.	2,700.
e.	Ultramarine, old paper	250.00
f.	Milky blue, old paper	275.00
R98c	R10 $20 Conveyance, org	110.00
a.	Imperf.	150.00
d.	Silk paper	175.00
R99c	R10 $20 Probate of Will, orange	2,000.
a.	Imperf.	2,000.
R100c	R10 $25 Mortgage, red ('63)	200.00
a.	Imperf.	1,400.
d.	Silk paper	250.00
e.	Horiz. pair, imperf. btwn., old paper	2,500.
R101c	R10 $50 U.S. Int. Rev., green ('63)	150.00
a.	Imperf.	250.00
R102c	R11 $200 U.S. Int. Rev., green & red ('64)	900.00
a.	Imperf.	2,500.

DOCUMENTARY STAMPS

Second Issue

After release of the First Issue revenue stamps, the Bureau of Internal Revenue received many reports of fraudulent cleaning and re-use. The Bureau ordered a Second Issue with new designs and colors, using a patented "chameleon" paper which is usually slightly violet or pinkish, with silk fibers.

R12

R12a

R13

R13a

R13b

Head of Washington in Black within Octagon. Various Frames and Numeral Arrangements.

1871 ***Perf. 12***

R103	R12 1c blue & black	60.00
	Cut cancel	22.50
a.	Inverted center	1,500.
R104	R12 2c blue & black	2.75
	Cut cancel	.20
a.	Inverted center	6,000.
R105	R12a 3c blue & black	35.00
	Cut cancel	12.50
R106	R12a 4c blue & black	100.00
	Cut cancel	35.00
a.	Horiz. half used as 2c on document	500.00

b. Vert. half used as 2c on document — *925.00*
R107 R12a 5c blue & black 2.00
Cut cancel .50
a. Inverted center *2,750.*
R108 R12a 6c blue & black 160.00
Cut cancel 55.00
R109 R12a 10c blue & black 1.50
Cut cancel .20
a. Inverted center *2,000.*
b. Double impression of center —
c. Half used as 5c on document *250.00*
R110 R12a 15c blue & black 55.00
Cut cancel 17.50
R111 R12a 20c blue & black 7.50
Cut cancel 2.75
a. Inverted center *11,500.*

Nos. R109a, R111a are valued in the grade of fine.

Head of Washington in Black within Circle

Various Frames

R112 R13 25c blue & black 1.25
Cut cancel .20
a. Inverted center *10,000.*
b. Sewing machine perf. 110.00
Cut cancel 65.00
c. Perf. 8 275.00
R113 R13 30c blue & black 110.00
Cut cancel 42.50
R114 R13 40c blue & black 90.00
Cut cancel 22.50
R115 R13a 50c blue & black 1.00
Cut cancel .20
a. Sewing machine perf. 75.00
b. Inverted center 1,000.
Punch cancellation 275.00
R116 R13a 60c blue & black 150.00
Cut cancel 50.00
R117 R13a 70c blue & black 70.00
Cut cancel 22.50
a. Inverted center *4,000.*
Cut cancel *2,000.*
R118 R13b $1 blue & black 8.00
Cut cancel 1.75
a. Inverted center *5,000.*
Punch cancel *900.00*
R119 R13b $1.30 blue & black 550.00
Cut cancel 150.00
R120 R13b $1.50 blue & black 19.00
Cut cancel 8.00
a. Sewing machine perf. 1,000.
R121 R13b $1.60 blue & black 575.00
Cut cancel 300.00
R122 R13b $1.90 blue & black 400.00
Cut cancel 120.00
R123 R13b $2 blue & black 20.00
Cut cancel 7.50
R124 R13b $2.50 blue & black 35.00
Cut cancel 16.00
R125 R13b $3 blue & black 45.00
Cut cancel 17.50
R126 R13b $3.50 blue & black 300.00
Cut cancel 100.00
R127 R13b $5 blue & black 27.50
Cut cancel 9.00
a. Inverted center *3,000.*
Punch cancel *950.00*
R128 R13b $10 blue & black 200.00
Cut cancel 70.00
R129 R13b $20 blue & black 650.00
Cut cancel 260.00
R130 R13b $25 blue & black 650.00
Cut cancel 275.00
R131 R13b $50 blue & black 650.00
Cut cancel 275.00
R132 R13b $200 red, bl & blk *6,500.*
Cut cancel *2,800.*
R133 R13b $500 red org, grn & blk *13,500.*

Fraudulently produced inverted centers exist, some excellently made.

Value for No. R133 is for a very fine appearing example with a light circular cut cancel or with minor flaws.

Third Issue

Violet "Chameleon" Paper with Silk Fibers. Various Frames and Numeral Arrangements.

1871-72 ***Perf. 12***

R134 R12 1c claret & blk ('72) 45.00
Cut cancel 20.00
R135 R12 2c orange & blk .40
Cut cancel .20
a. 2c vermilion & black (error) *650.00*
b. Inverted center 400.00
c. Imperf., pair —
R136 R12a 4c brown & blk ('72) 70.00
Cut cancel 21.00
R137 R12a 5c orange & black .35
Cut cancel .20
a. Inverted center *3,500.*

No. R137a is valued in the grade of fine.

R138 R12a 6c orange & blk ('72) 80.00
Cut cancel 25.00
R139 R12a 15c brown & blk ('72) 20.00
Cut cancel 5.00
a. Inverted center *15,000.*
R140 R13 30c orange & blk ('72) 30.00
Cut cancel 7.50
a. Inverted center *3,000.*
Cut cancel *1,750.*
R141 R13 40c brown & blk ('72) 65.00
Cut cancel 20.00
R142 R13a 60c orange & blk ('72) 95.00
Cut cancel 32.50
R143 R13a 70c green & blk ('72) 75.00
Cut cancel 22.50
R144 R13b $1 green & blk ('72) 2.00
Cut cancel .55
a. Inverted center *5,500.*
R145 R13b $2 ver & black ('72) 32.50
Cut cancel 14.00
R146 R13b $2.50 claret & blk ('72) 60.00
Cut cancel 22.00
a. Inverted center *25,000.*
R147 R13b $3 green & blk ('72) 60.00
Cut cancel 21.00
R148 R13b $5 ver & black ('72) 35.00
Cut cancel 12.50
R149 R13b $10 green & blk ('72) 200.00
Cut cancel 45.00
R150 R13b $20 org & blk ('72) 625.00
Cut cancel 260.00
a. $20 vermilion & black (error) 850.00

1874 ***Perf. 12***

R151 R12 2c org & blk, *grn* .20
Cut cancel .20
a. Inverted center 400.00

Liberty — R14

1875-78 ***Perf. 12***

R152a R14 2c bl, *blue*, silk paper .45
b. Wmk. 191R ('78) .35
c. Wmk. 191R, rouletted 32.50
d. Vert. pair, imperf. horiz. 525.00
e. As "b," imperf., pair *300.00*

The rouletted stamps probably were introduced in 1881.

Nos. 279, 267a, 267, 279Bg, 279B, 272-274 Overprinted in Red or Blue

I. R. — a I.R. — b

For Nos. R153-R160, values in the first column are for unused examples, values in the second column are for used.

1898 **Wmk. 191** ***Perf. 12***

R153 A87(a) 1c grn (R) 5.00 2.75
R154 A87(b) 1c grn (R) .35 .35
a. Overprint inverted 25.00 *18.00*
b. Ovpt. on back instead of face, invtd. —
c. Pair, one without ovpt. *10,000.*
R155 A88(b) 2c pink, III (Bl) .30 .25
b. 2c carmine, III .35 *.25*
c. As #R155, ovpt. invtd. 5.00 *4.00*
d. Vert. pair, one without ovpt. *1,500.*
e. Horiz. pair, one without ovpt. —
f. As #R155, ovpt. on back instead of face, invtd. —
R155A A88(b) 2c pink, IV (Bl) .25 .25
g. 2c carmine, IV .25 *.25*
h. As #R155A, ovpt. invtd. 2.75 *2.00*

Handstamped Type "b"

R156 A93 8c **vio brn** *5,250.*
R157 A94 10c **dark grn** *4,000.*
R158 A95 15c **dark blue** *6,500.*

Nos. R156-R158 were emergency provisionals, privately prepared, not officially issued.

Privately Prepared Provisionals

No. 285 Overprinted in Red

I. R.
L. H. C.

1898 **Wmk. 191** ***Perf. 12***

R158A A100 1c dk yel grn *12,500.* *10,000.*

Same Overprinted "I.R./P.I.D. & Son" in Red

R158B A100 1c dk yel grn *32,500.* *30,000.*

No. R158B is valued with small faults as each of the four recorded examples have faults.

Nos. R158A-R158B were overprinted with federal government permission by the Purvis Printing Co. upon order of Capt. L.H. Chapman of the Chapman Steamboat Line. Both the Chapman line and P.I. Daprix & Son operated freight-carrying steamboats on the Erie Canal. The Chapman Line touched at Syracuse, Utica, Little Falls and Fort Plain; the Daprix boat ran between Utica and Rome. 250 of each stamp were overprinted.

Dr. Kilmer & Co. provisional overprints are listed in the Scott Specialized Catalogue of United States Stamps under Private Die uMedicine Stamps, Nos. RS307-RS315.

Newspaper Stamp No. PR121 Surcharged Vertically in Red

1898 **Wmk. 191** ***Perf. 12***

Reading Down

R159 N18 $5 on $5 dk blue 500.00 200.00

Reading Up

R160 N18 $5 on $5 dk blue 140.00 110.00

Battleship — R15

Inscribed: "Series of 1898" and "Documentary."

There are 2 styles of rouletting for the 1898 proprietary and documentary stamps, an ordinary roulette 5½ and one where small rectangles of the paper are cut out, called hyphen hole perf. 7.

1898 **Wmk. 191R** ***Rouletted 5½***

R161 R15 ½c orange 4.00 *20.00*
R162 R15 ½c dark gray .30 .25
a. Vert. pair, imperf. horiz. 90.00
R163 R15 1c pale blue .20 .20
a. Vert. pair, imperf. horiz. 8.00
b. Imperf., pair *450.00*
R164 R15 2c car rose .30 .30
a. Vert. pair, imperf. horiz. 90.00
b. Imperf., pair 250.00
c. Horiz. pair, imperf. vert. —
R165 R15 3c dark blue 3.00 .35
R166 R15 4c pale rose 2.00 .35
a. Vert. pair, imperf. horiz. 155.00
R167 R15 5c lilac .55 .35
a. Pair, imperf. horiz. or vert. 250.00 160.00
b. Horiz. pair, imperf. btwn. *550.00*
R168 R15 10c dark brown 1.75 .25
a. Vert. pair, imperf. horiz. 35.00 30.00
b. Horiz. pair, imperf. vert. —
R169 R15 25c pur brown 5.00 .50
R170 R15 40c blue lilac 125.00 1.10
Cut cancellation .35
R171 R15 50c slate violet 25.00 .25
a. Imperf., pair *300.00*
R172 R15 80c bister 110.00 .50
Cut cancellation .20

No. R167b may not be genuine.

Hyphen Hole Perf. 7

R163p	1c	.30	.25
R164p	2c	.35	.25
R165p	3c	30.00	1.10
R166p	4c	11.00	1.60
R167p	5c	11.00	.25
R168p	10c	7.50	.25
R169p	25c	12.50	.30
R170p	40c	175.00	37.50
R171p	50c	55.00	.80
b.	Horiz. pair, imperf. btwn.	—	*250.00*
R172p	80c	210.00	50.00
	Cut cancellation		20.00

Commerce — R16

1898 ***Rouletted 5½***

R173 R16 $1 dark green 17.50 .25
a. Vert. pair, imperf. horiz. —
b. Horiz. pair, imperf. vert. — 325.00
p. Hyphen hole perf. 7 25.00 .65
Cut cancellation .30
R174 R16 $3 dark brown 37.50 1.00
Cut cancellation .25
a. Horiz. pair, imperf. vert. 500.00
p. Hyphen hole perf. 7 60.00 2.40
Cut cancellation .30
R175 R16 $5 orange red 60.00 1.90
Cut cancellation .25
R176 R16 $10 black 125.00 3.25
Cut cancellation .55
a. Horiz. pair, imperf. vert. —
R177 R16 $30 red 450.00 150.00
Cut cancellation 47.50
R178 R16 $50 gray brown 250.00 5.75
Cut cancellation 2.10

See Nos. R182-R183.

John Marshall — R17

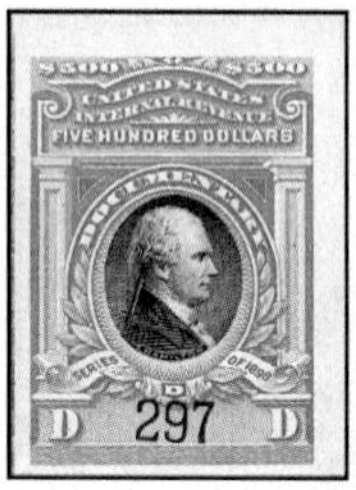
Alexander Hamilton — R18

James Madison — R19

Inscribed "Series of 1898"

1899 **Without Gum** ***Imperf.***

R179 R17 $100 yel brn & black 250.00 37.50
Cut cancellation 21.00
R180 R18 $500 car lake & black 1,400. 800.00
Cut cancellation 300.00
R181 R19 $1000 grn & blk 1,000. 375.00
Cut cancellation 150.00

See #R224-R227, R246-R252, R282-R286.

Type of 1898

1900 ***Hyphen-Hole Perf. 7***

R182 R16 $1 carmine 35.00 .55
Cut cancellation .30
R183 R16 $3 lake 225.00 52.50
Cut cancellation 9.00

Warning: The ink on No. R183 will run in water.

Surcharged in Black

a

b

Surcharged type "a"

1900

R184	R16	$1 gray	27.50	.40
		Cut cancellation		.25
a.		Horiz. pair, imperf. vert.		—
b.		Surcharge omitted	125.00	
		As "b", cut cancellation		82.50
R185	R16	$2 gray	27.50	.35
		Cut cancellation		.25
R186	R16	$3 gray	110.00	11.50
		Cut cancellation		4.25
R187	R16	$5 gray	72.50	9.00
		Cut cancellation		1.40
R188	R16	$10 gray	150.00	20.00
		Cut cancellation		3.25
R189	R16	$50 gray	1,200.	500.00
		Cut cancellation		125.00

Surcharged type "b"

1902

R190	R16	$1 green	40.00	3.50
		Cut cancellation		.30
a.		Inverted surcharge		*190.00*
R191	R16	$2 green	40.00	1.75
		Cut cancellation		.30
a.		Surcharged as #R185	110.00	75.00
b.		Surch. as #R185, in vio	*2,000.*	—
c.		As "a," double surcharge	*150.00*	
d.		As "a," triple surcharge	*850.00*	
R192	R16	$5 green	200.00	35.00
		Cut cancellation		4.25
a.		Surcharge omitted	250.00	
b.		Pair, one without surch.	*400.00*	
R193	R16	$10 green	425.00	125.00
		Cut cancellation		47.50
R194	R16	$50 green	2,000.	1,000.
		Cut cancellation		250.00

Warning: If Nos. R190-R194 are soaked, the center part of the surcharged numeral may wash off. Before surcharging, a square of soluble varnish was applied to the middle of some stamps.

R20

Liberty — R21

Inscribed "Series of 1914"

Offset Printing

1914 Wmk. 190 *Perf. 10*

R195	R20	½c rose	13.00	4.50
R196	R20	1c rose	2.50	.30
R197	R20	2c rose	3.50	.30
R198	R20	3c rose	75.00	30.00
R199	R20	4c rose	22.50	2.25
R200	R20	5c rose	9.00	.35
R201	R20	10c rose	7.00	.25
R202	R20	25c rose	47.50	.55
R203	R20	40c rose	30.00	2.50
R204	R20	50c rose	12.00	.35
R205	R20	80c rose	200.00	15.00
		Nos. R195-R205 (11)	422.00	56.35

Wmk. 191R

R206	R20	½c rose	1.60	.50
R207	R20	1c rose	.25	.20
R208	R20	2c rose	.30	.25
R209	R20	3c rose	1.50	.25
R210	R20	4c rose	4.00	.50
R211	R20	5c rose	1.75	.30
R212	R20	10c rose	.80	.20
R213	R20	25c rose	7.00	1.50
R214	R20	40c rose	110.00	14.00
		Cut cancellation		.45
R215	R20	50c rose	25.00	.25
		Cut cancellation		.20
R216	R20	80c rose	175.00	27.50
		Cut cancellation		1.00
		Nos. R206-R216 (11)	327.20	45.45

Engr.

R217	R21	$1 green	60.00	.55
		Cut cancellation		.25
a.		$1 yellow green	45.00	.25
R218	R21	$2 carmine	80.00	.75
		Cut cancellation		.20
R219	R21	$3 purple	100.00	3.75
		Cut cancellation		.50
R220	R21	$5 blue	90.00	4.00
		Cut cancellation		.55
R221	R21	$10 orange	200.00	5.25
		Cut cancellation		.80
R222	R21	$30 vermilion	600.00	19.00
		Cut cancellation		2.10
R223	R21	$50 violet	1,750.	1,000.
		Cut cancellation		350.00

See #R240-R245, R257-R259, R276-R281.

Portrait Types of 1899 Inscribed "Series of 1915" (#R224), or "Series of 1914"

1914-15 Without Gum *Perf. 12*

R224	R19	$60 brn *(Lincoln)*	200.00	140.00
		Cut cancellation		67.50
R225	R17	$100 grn *(Washington)*	67.50	45.00
		Cut cancellation		16.00
R226	R18	$500 blue	—	600.00
		Cut cancellation		250.00
R227	R19	$1000 orange	—	525.00
		Cut cancellation		275.00

The stamps of types R17, R18 and R19 in this and subsequent issues are issued in vert. strips of 4 which are imperf. at the top, bottom and right side; therefore, single copies are always imperf. on 1 or 2 sides.

R22

Offset Printing

1917 Wmk. 191R *Perf. 11*

R228	R22	1c carmine rose	.35	.20
R229	R22	2c carmine rose	.25	.20
R230	R22	3c carmine rose	1.75	.40
R231	R22	4c carmine rose	.75	.25
R232	R22	5c carmine rose	.30	.20
R233	R22	8c carmine rose	2.50	.35
R234	R22	10c carmine rose	.40	.20
R235	R22	20c carmine rose	.75	.25
R236	R22	25c carmine rose	1.50	.25
R237	R22	40c carmine rose	2.25	.50
R238	R22	50c carmine rose	2.50	.20
R239	R22	80c carmine rose	7.50	.25
		Nos. R228-R239 (12)	20.80	3.25

Type of 1914 without "Series 1914"

1917-33 Engr.

R240	R21	$1 yellow green	8.00	.25
a.		$1 green	6.75	.20
R241	R21	$2 rose	13.50	.25
R242	R21	$3 violet	50.00	1.10
		Cut cancellation		.25
R243	R21	$4 yel brn ('33)	35.00	1.90
		Cut cancellation		.25
R244	R21	$5 dark blue	22.50	.35
		Cut cancellation		.25
R245	R21	$10 orange	45.00	1.25
		Cut cancellation		.25

Portrait Types of 1899-1915 without "Series of" and Date

Portraits: $30, Grant. $100, Washington.

1917 Without Gum *Perf. 12*

R246	R17	$30 dp org, grn numerals	50.00	13.00
		Cut cancellation		2.25
a.		As "b," imperf., pair		*750.00*
b.		Numerals in blue	80.00	2.25
		As "b," cut cancellation		1.40
R247	R19	$60 brown	60.00	8.00
		Cut cancellation		.85
R248	R17	$100 green	37.50	1.25
		Cut cancellation		.40
R249	R18	$500 blue, red numerals	325.00	40.00
		Cut cancellation		12.50
a.		Numerals in orange	375.00	52.50
R250	R19	$1000 orange	150.00	12.50
		Cut cancellation		4.25
a.		Imperf., pair		*2,000.*

See note after No. R227.

1928-29 Offset Printing *Perf. 10*

R251	R22	1c carmine rose	2.10	1.60
R252	R22	2c carmine rose	.60	.30
R253	R22	4c carmine rose	7.00	4.00
R254	R22	5c carmine rose	1.60	.55
R255	R22	10c carmine rose	2.40	1.25
R256	R22	20c carmine rose	5.50	4.50
		Nos. R251-R256 (6)	19.20	12.20

Engr.

R257	R21	$1 green	175.00	45.00
		Cut cancellation		5.00
R258	R21	$2 rose	80.00	5.00
R259	R21	$10 orange	250.00	60.00
		Cut cancellation		26.00

1929 Offset Printing *Perf. 11x10*

R260	R22	2c carmine rose	3.00	2.75
R261	R22	5c carmine rose	2.00	1.90
R262	R22	10c carmine rose	9.25	6.75
R263	R22	20c carmine rose	15.00	8.25

Used values for Nos. R264-R734 are for copies which are neither cut nor perforated with initials. Copies with cut cancellations or perforated initials are valued in the Scott U. S. Specialized Catalogue.

Types of 1917-33 Overprinted in Black **SERIES 1940**

1940 Offset Printing *Perf. 11*

R264	R22	1c rose pink	3.50	2.40
R265	R22	2c rose pink	4.00	1.90
R266	R22	3c rose pink	10.00	4.25
R267	R22	4c rose pink	4.50	.60
R268	R22	5c rose pink	4.50	.95
R269	R22	8c rose pink	20.00	16.00
R270	R22	10c rose pink	2.25	.65
R271	R22	20c rose pink	3.00	.70
R272	R22	25c rose pink	7.50	1.40
R273	R22	40c rose pink	6.25	.90
R274	R22	50c rose pink	8.00	.55
R275	R22	80c rose pink	13.00	1.50
		Nos. R264-R275 (12)	86.50	31.80

Engr.

R276	R21	$1 green	60.00	1.00
R277	R21	$2 rose	60.00	1.75
R278	R21	$3 violet	80.00	30.00
R279	R21	$4 yellow brown	140.00	35.00
R280	R21	$5 dark blue	70.00	15.00
R281	R21	$10 orange	175.00	40.00

Types of 1917 Handstamped "Series 1940" like R264-R281 in Green (Nos. R282-R284, R286) or Violet (No. R285)

Perf. 12

Without Gum

R282	R17	$30 vermilion		1,000.
a.		With black 2-line handstamp in larger type		*12,500.*
R283	R19	$60 brown		1,500.
a.		As #R282a, cut cancel		—
R284	R17	$100 green		3,000.
R285	R18	$500 blue		2,000.
a.		As #R282a	*3,250.*	*3,850.*
b.		Blue handstamp, double transfer		—
R286	R19	$1000 orange		700.
a.		Double overprint (cut cancel)		—

Alexander Hamilton R23

Levi Woodbury R24

Thomas Corwin — R25

Portraits: 2c, Oliver Wolcott, Jr. 3c, Samuel Dexter. 4c, Albert Gallatin. 5c, George Washington Campbell. 8c, Alexander Dallas. 10c, William H. Crawford. 20c, Richard Rush. 25c, Samuel D. Ingham. 40c, Louis McLane. 50c, William J. Duane. 80c, Roger B. Taney. $2, Thomas Ewing. $3, Walter Forward. $4, John Canfield Spencer. $5, George M. Bibb. $10, Robert J. Walker. $20, William M. Meredith. $50, James Guthrie. $60, Howell Cobb. $100, P. F. Thomas. $500, John Adams Dix. $1,000, Salmon P. Chase.

Overprinted in Black Like Nos. R264-R281

1940 *Perf. 11*

Various Portraits

R288	R23	1c carmine	5.00	3.50
R289	R23	2c carmine	7.50	3.25
R290	R23	3c carmine	25.00	10.50
R291	R23	4c carmine	57.50	25.00
R292	R23	5c carmine	4.50	.70
R293	R23	8c carmine	80.00	60.00
R294	R23	10c carmine	4.00	.55
R295	R23	20c carmine	5.00	3.75
R296	R23	25c carmine	4.25	.60
R297	R23	40c carmine	60.00	25.00
R298	R23	50c carmine	6.25	.45
R299	R23	80c carmine	150.00	90.00
a.		Imperf, pair, without gum	*475.00*	
R300	R24	$1 carmine	37.50	.55
R301	R24	$2 carmine	70.00	.75
R302	R24	$3 carmine	160.00	87.50
a.		Imperf, pair, without gum	*1,400.*	
R303	R24	$4 carmine	95.00	32.50
R304	R24	$5 carmine	60.00	2.75
R305	R24	$10 carmine	100.00	6.25
R305A	R24	$20 carmine	*2,500.*	900.00
b.		Imperf, pair, without gum	*700.00*	

Various Frame Designs

Perf. 12

Without Gum

R306	R25	$30 carmine	160.00	42.50
R306A	R25	$50 carmine	—	*10,000.*
R307	R25	$60 carmine	300.00	62.50
a.		Vert. pair, imperf btwn.	*2,750.*	*1,450.*
R308	R25	$100 carmine	225.00	67.50
R309	R25	$500 carmine	—	*5,000.*
R310	R25	$1000 carmine	—	450.00

The $30 to $1,000 denominations in this and following similar issues, and the $2,500, $5,000 and $10,000 stamps of 1952-58 have straight edges on one or two sides. They were issued without gum through No. R723.

PROPRIETARY STAMPS

Stamps for use on proprietary articles were included in the first general issue of 1862-71. They are Nos. R3, R13-R14, R18, R22, R29, R31, R38.

Washington — RB1

Various Frames and Sizes

Violet or Green Paper with Silk Threads

1871-74 Engr. *Perf. 12*

a. left column = Violet Paper (1871)

b. right column = Green Paper (1874)

RB1	RB1	1c grn & blk	6.50	12.00
c.		Imperf.	80.00	
d.		Inverted center	*3,000.*	
RB2	RB1	2c grn & blk	7.50	27.50
c.		Invtd. center, *violet*	*40,000.*	*9,000.*
d.		Invtd. center, *green*		8,500.

No. RB2bc is valued with fine centering and small faults. RB2d is valued with small faults.

RB3	RB1	3c grn & blk	25.00	60.00
c.		Sewing machine perf.	500.00	
d.		Inverted center	*16,000.*	

No. RB3d is valued with small faults as 6 of the 7 recorded examples have faults.

RB4	RB1	4c grn & blk	14.00	22.50
c.		Inverted center	*19,000.*	

No. RB4c is valued with small faults as all recorded examples have faults.

RB5	RB1	5c grn & blk	150.00	160.00
c.		Inverted center	*130,000.*	

No. RB5c is unique. Value represents price realized in 2000 auction sale.

RB6	RB1	6c grn & blk	50.00	120.00
RB7	RB1	10c green & blk ('73)	225.00	60.00
RB8	RB1	50c green & blk ('73)	725.00	1,200.
RB9	RB1	$1 green & blk ('73)	*2,500.*	*12,000.*
RB10	RB1	$5 green & blk ('73)	*10,000.*	*40,000.*

No. RB10b is valued with small faults.

Washington — RB2

Various Frames and Sizes
Green Paper

Wmk. 191R, Unwmkd. (Silk Paper)

1875-81

b. left column = Perf.

c. right column = Rouletted 6

RB11	RB2	1c green	.50	125.00
a.		Silk paper	2.25	
d.		Vert. pair, imperf btwn.	300.00	
RB12	RB2	2c brown	2.00	140.00
a.		Silk paper	3.25	
RB13	RB2	3c orange	4.00	125.00
a.		Silk paper	14.00	
d.		Horiz. pair, imperf. btwn.		—
RB14	RB2	4c red brown	9.00	
a.		Silk paper	10.00	
RB15	RB2	4c red	6.00	250.00
RB16	RB2	5c black	125.00	*1,750.*
a.		Silk paper	175.00	
RB17	RB2	6c violet blue	25.00	400.00
a.		Silk paper	35.00	
RB18	RB2	6c violet	35.00	—
RB19	RB2	10c blue ('81)	350.00	

Many fraudulent roulettes exist.

Battleship — RB3

Rouletted 5½

1898 Wmk. 191R Engr.

RB20	RB3	⅛c yel grn	.25	.25
a.		Vert. pair, imperf. horiz.	—	
RB21	RB3	¼c brown	.20	.20
a.		¼c red brown	.20	.20
b.		¼c yellow brown	.20	.20
c.		¼c orange brown	.20	.20
d.		¼c bister	.20	.20
e.		Vert. pair, imperf. horiz.	—	
f.		Printed on both sides	—	
RB22	RB3	⅜c dp org	.30	.30
a.		Horiz. pair, imperf. vert.	10.50	
b.		Vert. pair, imperf. horiz.	—	
RB23	RB3	⅝c deep ultra	.25	.25
a.		Vert. pair, imperf. horiz.	77.50	—
b.		Horiz. pair, imperf. btwn.	*325.00*	
RB24	RB3	1c dark green	2.25	.40
a.		Vert. pair, imperf. horiz.	*325.00*	
RB25	RB3	1¼c violet	.35	.25
a.		1¼c brown violet	.35	.20
b.		Vert. pair, imperf. btwn.	—	
RB26	RB3	1⅞c dull blue	15.00	2.00
RB27	RB3	2c vio brown	1.40	.35
a.		Horiz. pair, imperf. vert.	52.50	
RB28	RB3	2½c lake	4.25	.35
a.		Vert. pair, imperf. horiz.	190.00	
RB29	RB3	3¾c olive gray	42.50	15.00
RB30	RB3	4c purple	16.00	1.50
RB31	RB3	5c brown org	15.00	1.50
a.		Vert. pair, imperf. horiz.	—	*325.00*
b.		Horiz. pair, imperf. vert.	—	*425.00*
		Nos. RB20-RB31 (12)	97.75	22.35

Hyphen Hole Perf. 7

RB20p	⅛c	.20	.20
RB21p	¼c	.20	.20
g.	¼c yellow brown	.20	.20
h.	¼c orange brown	.20	.20
RB22p	⅜c	.30	.25
RB23p	⅝c	.30	.25
RB24p	1c	26.00	13.00
RB25p	1¼c	.30	.25
c.	1¼c brown violet	.25	.20
RB26p	1⅞c	32.50	7.75
RB27p	2c	6.25	.80
RB28p	2½c	5.25	.30
RB29p	3¾c	72.50	21.00
RB30p	4c	62.50	18.00
RB31p	5c	67.50	21.00

See note before No. R161.

RB4

RB5

Offset Printing

1914 Wmk. 190 *Perf. 10*

RB32	RB4	⅛c black	.25	.35
RB33	RB4	¼c black	3.25	1.50
RB34	RB4	⅜c black	.35	.35
RB35	RB4	⅝c black	6.25	3.00
RB36	RB4	1¼c black	4.50	1.75
RB37	RB4	1⅞c black	57.50	20.00
RB38	RB4	2½c black	13.50	3.50
RB39	RB4	3⅛c black	125.00	62.50
RB40	RB4	3¾c black	50.00	25.00
RB41	RB4	4c black	75.00	40.00
RB42	RB4	4⅜c black	*3,000.*	—
RB43	RB4	5c black	150.00	100.00
		Nos. RB32-RB41,RB43 (11)	485.60	257.95

Wmk. 191R

RB44	RB4	⅛c black	.35	.30
RB45	RB4	¼c black	.25	.25
RB46	RB4	⅜c black	.75	.45
RB47	RB4	½c black	4.25	3.75
RB48	RB4	⅝c black	.30	.25
RB49	RB4	1c black	5.50	5.50
RB50	RB4	1¼c black	.65	.40
RB51	RB4	1½c black	4.25	3.00
RB52	RB4	1⅞c black	1.35	.90
RB53	RB4	2c black	6.50	9.50
RB54	RB4	2½c black	1.75	1.40
RB55	RB4	3c black	5.25	3.50
RB56	RB4	3⅛c black	7.00	4.50
RB57	RB4	3¾c black	14.00	10.00
RB58	RB4	4c black	.50	.30
RB59	RB4	4⅜c black	18.00	10.00
RB60	RB4	5c black	4.00	3.50
RB61	RB4	6c black	70.00	47.50
RB62	RB4	8c black	21.50	14.50
RB63	RB4	10c black	16.00	9.75
RB64	RB4	20c black	30.00	21.50
		Nos. RB44-RB64 (21)	212.15	150.75

1919 *Perf. 11*

RB65	RB5	1c dark blue	.25	.25
RB66	RB5	2c dark blue	.35	.25
RB67	RB5	3c dark blue	1.50	.75
RB68	RB5	4c dark blue	2.25	.75
RB69	RB5	5c dark blue	3.00	1.25
RB70	RB5	8c dark blue	20.00	13.50
RB71	RB5	10c dark blue	9.50	3.25
RB72	RB5	20c dark blue	14.00	5.00
RB73	RB5	40c dark blue	55.00	14.00
		Nos. RB65-RB73 (9)	105.85	39.00

FUTURE DELIVERY STAMPS

Issued to facilitate the collection of a tax upon each sale, agreement of sale or agreement to sell any products or merchandise at any exchange or board of trade, or other similar place for future delivery.

Documentary Stamps Nos. R228-R250 Overprinted in Black or Red

Offset Printing

1918-34 Wmk. 191R *Perf. 11*

Overprint Horizontal

(Lines 8mm apart)

RC1	R22	2c car rose	7.50	.25
RC2	R22	3c car rose ('34)	40.00	32.50
		Cut cancellation		18.00
RC3	R22	4c car rose	12.50	.25
RC3A	R22	5c car rose ('33)	85.00	7.50
RC4	R22	10c car rose	21.00	.35
a.		Double overprint	—	5.25
b.		"FUTURE" omitted	—	*210.00*
c.		"DELIVERY FUTURE"		37.50
RC5	R22	20c car rose	30.00	.25
a.		Double overprint		21.00
RC6	R22	25c car rose	65.00	.60
		Cut cancellation		.30
RC7	R22	40c car rose	75.00	1.25
		Cut cancellation		.35
RC8	R22	50c car rose	17.50	.35
a.		"DELIVERY" omitted	—	*110.00*
RC9	R22	80c car rose	135.00	13.50
		Cut cancellation		3.50
a.		Double overprint		37.50
		Cut cancellation		6.25
		Nos. RC1-RC9 (10)	488.50	56.80

Overprint Vertical, Reading Up

(Lines 2mm apart)

Engr.

RC10	R21	$1 green (R)	55.00	.35
		Cut cancellation		.20
a.		Overprint reading down		*300.00*
b.		Black overprint		—
		Cut cancellation		125.00
RC11	R21	$2 rose	65.00	.45
		Cut cancellation		.25
RC12	R21	$3 violet (R)	175.00	3.50
		Cut cancellation		.30
a.		Overprint reading down	—	52.50
RC13	R21	$5 dk bl (R)	100.00	.60
		Cut cancellation		.25
RC14	R21	$10 orange	125.00	1.35
		Cut cancellation		.30
a.		"DELIVERY FUTURE"		*110.00*
RC15	R21	$20 olive bis	250.00	7.50
		Cut cancellation		.65
		Nos. RC10-RC15 (6)	770.00	13.75

Perf. 12

Overprint Horizontal

(Lines 11½mm apart)

Without Gum

RC16	R17	$30 ver, green numerals	100.00	5.50
		Cut cancellation		1.75
a.		Numerals in blue	95.00	4.75
		Cut cancellation		2.00
b.		As "a," imperf.		*110.00*
RC17	R19	$50 olive grn	85.00	2.50
		Cut cancellation		.75
a.		$50 olive bister	85.00	2.75
		Cut cancellation		.25
RC18	R19	$60 brown	110.00	8.00
		Cut cancellation		1.00
a.		Vert. pair, imperf. horiz.		*425.00*
RC19	R17	$100 yel green ('34)	190.00	37.50
		Cut cancellation		9.00
RC20	R18	$500 blue, red numerals (R)	150.00	15.00
		Cut cancellation		6.50
a.		Numerals in orange	—	60.00
		Cut cancellation		12.50
RC21	R19	$1000 orange	175.00	7.50
		Cut cancellation		2.00
a.		Vert. pair, imperf. horiz.		*1,350.*
		Nos. RC16-RC21 (6)	810.00	76.00

See note after No. R227.

1923-24 Offset Printing *Perf. 11*

Overprint Horiz.

(Lines 2mm apart)

RC22	R22	1c carmine rose	1.10	.25
RC23	R22	80c carmine rose	150.00	3.00
		Cut cancellation		.55

Documentary Stamps of 1917 Overprinted in Red or Black

1925-34 Engr.

RC25	R21	$1 green (R)	70.00	1.25
		Cut cancellation		.25
RC26	R21	$10 orange (Bk) ('34)	175.00	25.00
		Cut cancellation		16.00

Overprinted like Nos. RC1-RC9

1928-29 Offset Printing *Perf. 10*

RC27	R22	10c carmine rose	*3,000.*	
RC28	R22	20c carmine rose	*3,000.*	

STOCK TRANSFER STAMPS

Issued to facilitate the collection of a tax on all sales or agreements to sell, or memoranda of sales or delivery of, or transfers of legal title to shares or certificates of stock.

Documentary Stamps Nos. R228 to R259 Overprinted in Black or Red

Offset Printing

1918-29 Wmk. 191R *Perf. 11*

Overprint Horiz. (Lines 8mm apart)

RD1	R22	1c car rose	1.00	.25
a.		Double overprint		—
RD2	R22	2c car rose	.25	.25
a.		Double overprint	—	5.00
		Cut cancellation		2.50
RD3	R22	4c car rose	.25	.25
a.		Double overprint	—	4.25
		Cut cancellation		2.10
b.		"STOCK" omitted		10.50
d.		Overprint lines 10mm apart	—	
RD4	R22	5c car rose	.30	.25
RD5	R22	10c car rose	.30	.25
a.		Double overprint	—	5.25
		Cut cancellation		2.75
b.		"STOCK" omitted		—
RD6	R22	20c car rose	.55	.25
a.		Double overprint		6.25
b.		"STOCK" double		—
RD7	R22	25c car rose	2.00	.25
		Cut cancellation		.20
RD8	R22	40c car rose ('22)	2.00	.25
RD9	R22	50c car rose	.70	.25
a.		Double overprint		
RD10	R22	80c car rose	8.00	.45
		Cut cancellation		.25
		Nos. RD1-RD10 (10)	15.35	2.70
		Set value		.90

Overprint Vertical, Reading Up

(Lines 2mm apart)

Engr.

RD11	R21	$1 green (R)	140.00	25.00
		Cut cancellation		7.00
a.		Ovpt. reading down	190.00	27.50
		Cut cancellation		9.00
RD12	R21	$1 green (Bk)	2.75	.30
a.		Pair, one without ovpt.	—	*160.00*
b.		Ovptd. on back instead of face, inverted	—	*110.00*
c.		Ovpt. reading down	—	6.00
d.		$1 yellow green	3.00	.25
RD13	R21	$2 rose	2.75	.25
a.		Ovpt. reading down		10.50
		Cut cancellation		1.50
b.		Vert. pair, imperf. horiz.	*500.00*	
RD14	R21	$3 violet (R)	25.00	6.00
		Cut cancellation		.30
RD15	R21	$4 yel brn	11.00	.25
		Cut cancellation		.20
RD16	R21	$5 dk blue (R)	7.00	.25
		Cut cancellation		.20
a.		Ovpt. reading down	32.50	1.35
		Cut cancellation		.25
RD17	R21	$10 orange	22.50	.45
		Cut cancellation		.20
RD18	R21	$20 ol bis ('21)	110.00	18.00
		Cut cancellation		5.00
		Nos. RD11-RD18 (8)	321.00	50.50

1918 Without Gum *Perf. 12*

Overprint Horizontal (Lines 11½mm apart)

RD19	R17	$30 ver, green numerals	37.50	5.75
		Cut cancellation		2.00
a.		Numerals in blue		60.00
RD20	R19	$50 olive green, *(Cleveland)*	125.00	62.50
		Cut cancellation		25.00
RD21	R19	$60 brown	225.00	25.00
		Cut cancellation		10.50
RD22	R17	$100 green	40.00	6.50
		Cut cancellation		3.00
RD23	R18	$500 blue (R)	400.00	150.00
		Cut cancellation		75.00
a.		Numerals in orange		150.00
RD24	R19	$1000 orange	250.00	95.00
		Cut cancellation		32.50

See note after No. R227.

1928-32 Offset Printing *Perf. 10*

Overprint Horiz. (Lines 8mm apart)

RD25	R22	2c carmine rose	4.75	.30
RD26	R22	4c carmine rose	4.75	.30
RD27	R22	10c carmine rose	4.75	.30
a.		Inverted overprint		*1,250.*
RD28	R22	20c carmine rose	5.00	.35
RD29	R22	50c carmine rose	9.00	.50

Overprint Vertical, Reading Up

(Lines 2mm apart)

Engr.

RD30	R21	$1 green	40.00	.35
a.		$1 yellow green	40.00	.50
RD31	R21	$2 car rose	3.75	.35
a.		Pair, one without overprint	*225.00*	*190.00*
RD32	R21	$10 orange	37.50	.50
		Cut cancellation		.25
		Nos. RD25-RD32 (8)	109.50	

Overprinted Horiz. in Black

1920-28 Offset Printing *Perf. 11*

RD33	R22	2c carmine rose	11.50	1.00
RD34	R22	10c carmine rose	2.75	.35
b.		Inverted overprint	*1,550.*	—
RD35	R22	20c carmine rose	5.25	.25
a.		Horiz. pair, one without overprint	*175.00*	
d.		Inverted overprint (perf. initials)		—
RD36	R22	50c carmine rose	4.50	.30

Engr.

RD37	R21	$1 green	60.00	12.50
		Cut cancellation		2.25
RD38	R21	$2 rose	65.00	12.50
		Cut cancellation		2.25
		Nos. RD33-RD38 (6)	149.00	26.90

Shifted overprints on the 10c, 20c and 50c result in "TRANSFER STOCK," "TRANSFER" omitted, "STOCK" omitted and other varieties.

Perf. 10

Offset Printing

RD39	R22	2c carmine rose	10.00	.95
RD40	R22	10c carmine rose	4.00	.55
RD41	R22	20c carmine rose	5.00	.25

Used values for Nos. RD42-RD372 are for copies which are neither cut nor perforated with initials. Copies with cut cancellations or perforated initials are valued in the Scott U.S. Specialized Catalogue.

Documentary Stamps of 1917-33 Overprinted in Black

1940 *Perf. 11*

RD42	R22	1c rose pink	4.00	.65
a.		"Series 1940" inverted	—	325.00

No. RD42a always comes with a natural straight edge at left.

RD43	R22	2c rose pink	4.00	.65
RD45	R22	4c rose pink	4.50	.35
RD46	R22	5c rose pink	5.00	.25
RD48	R22	10c rose pink	8.00	.35
RD49	R22	20c rose pink	10.50	.35
RD50	R22	25c rose pink	10.50	1.10
RD51	R22	40c rose pink	7.75	1.00
RD52	R22	50c rose pink	8.75	.35
RD53	R22	80c rose pink	100.00	70.00
		Nos. RD42-RD53 (10)	163.00	75.05

Engr.

RD54	R21	$1 green	37.50	.60
RD55	R21	$2 rose	42.50	1.00
RD56	R21	$3 violet	225.00	18.00
RD57	R21	$4 yel brown	90.00	1.60
RD58	R21	$5 dark blue	70.00	2.00
RD59	R21	$10 orange	200.00	10.00
RD60	R21	$20 olive bister	350.00	125.00
		Nos. RD54-RD60 (7)	1,015.	158.20

Stock Transfer Stamps of 1918 Handstamped in Blue "Series 1940"

1940 **Without Gum** *Perf. 12*

RD61	R17	$30 vermilion	*925.*	700.
RD62	R19	$50 olive green	*1,500.*	*2,000.*
a.		Dbl. ovpt. (perf. initials canc.)		*1,000.*
RD63	R19	$60 brown	*2,400.*	*2,200.*
RD64	R17	$100 green	*1,250.*	625.
RD65	R18	$500 blue		2,250.
RD66	R19	$1000 orange		*3,000.*

Levi Woodbury
ST2

Alexander Hamilton
ST1

Thomas Corwin — ST3

Portraits (see R23-R25): 2c, Wolcott. 4c, Gallatin. 5c, Campbell. 10c, Crawford. 20c, Rush. 25c, Ingham. 40c, McLane. 50c, Duane. 80c, Taney. $2, Ewing. $3, Forward. $4, Spencer. $5, Bibb. $10, Walker. $20, Meredith. $50, Guthrie. $60, Cobb. $100, Thomas. $500, Dix. $1,000, Chase.

Overprinted in Black **SERIES 1940**

1940 **Wmk. 191R** *Perf. 11*

Various Portraits

Size: 19x22mm

RD67	ST1	1c brt green	12.00	3.25
RD68	ST1	2c brt green	7.75	1.75
RD70	ST1	4c brt green	14.00	4.50
RD71	ST1	5c brt green	8.75	1.75
a.		Without overprint (cut canc.)		*275.00*
RD73	ST1	10c brt green	12.00	2.10
RD74	ST1	20c brt green	14.00	2.40
RD75	ST1	25c brt green	42.50	9.25
RD76	ST1	40c brt green	75.00	35.00
RD77	ST1	50c brt green	12.00	2.10
RD78	ST1	80c brt green	100.00	57.50
		Nos. RD67-RD78 (10)	298.00	119.60

Size: 21½x36¼mm

RD79	ST2	$1 brt green	47.50	4.25
a.		Without overprint (perf. initials canc.)		*240.00*
RD80	ST2	$2 brt green	50.00	10.50
RD81	ST2	$3 brt green	75.00	13.00
RD82	ST2	$4 brt green	300.00	210.00
RD83	ST2	$5 brt green	72.50	14.50
RD84	ST2	$10 brt green	175.00	42.50
RD85	ST2	$20 brt green	900.00	82.50

Perf. 12

Without Gum

Size: 28½x42mm

Various Frame Designs

RD86	ST3	$30 brt green	650.00	160.00
RD87	ST3	$50 brt green	725.00	475.00
RD88	ST3	$60 brt green	*3,000.*	1,100.
RD89	ST3	$100 brt green	—	325.00
RD90	ST3	$500 brt green	—	*2,000.*
RD91	ST3	$1000 brt green	—	*2,000.*

Nos. RD86-RD91 exist imperforate, without overprint.

HUNTING PERMIT STAMPS

The receipts of the sales of these "Migratory Bird Hunting" stamps help to maintain waterfowl life in the United States.

Unused values for all unused stamps in this section are for stamps with never-hinged original gum. Minor natural gum skips and bends are normal on Nos. RW1-RW20. No-gum stamps are without signature or other cancel.

Minor natural gum skips and bends are normal on Nos. RW1-RW20.

"No gum" stamps are without signature or other cancel.

Beginning with No. RW2, the used value is for stamps with manuscript signature.

Used Values

Used value for No. RW1 is for stamp with handstamp or manuscript cancel, though technically it was against postal regulations to deface the stamp or to apply a postal cancellation.

Beginning with No. RW2, the used values are for stamps with manuscript signatures.

Catalogue values for unused stamps in this section are for Never Hinged items.

Department of Agriculture

Various Designs Inscribed "U. S. Department of Agriculture"

HP1

Engraved; Flat Plate Printing

1934 **Unwmk.** *Perf. 11*

"Void after June 30, 1935"

RW1	HP1	$1 blue	800.00	140.00
		Hinged	400.00	
		No gum	160.00	
a.		Imperf., vertical pair		—
b.		Vert. pair, imperf. horiz.		—

1935 **"Void after June 30, 1936"**

RW2	$1 Canvasback Ducks Taking to Flight	700.00	160.00
	Hinged	350.00	
	No gum	200.00	

1936 **"Void after June 30, 1937"**

RW3	$1 Canada Geese in Flight	350.00	75.00
	Hinged	175.00	
	No gum	115.00	

1937 **"Void after June 30, 1938"**

RW4	$1 Scaup Ducks Taking to Flight	360.00	60.00
	Hinged	150.00	
	No gum	80.00	

1938 **"Void after June 30, 1939"**

RW5	$1 Pintail Drake and Duck Alighting	475.00	60.00
	Hinged	225.00	
	No gum	80.00	

Department of the Interior

Various Designs Inscribed "U. S. Department of the Interior"

Green-Winged Teal — HP6

1939 **"Void after June 30, 1940"**

RW6	HP6 $1 chocolate	275.00	45.00
	Hinged	125.00	
	No gum	60.00	

1940 **"Void after June 30, 1941"**

RW7	$1 Black Mallards	250.00	45.00
	Hinged	120.00	
	No gum	60.00	

CONFEDERATE STATES OF AMERICA

3¢ 1861 POSTMASTERS' PROVISIONALS

With the secession of South Carolina from the Union on Dec. 20, 1860, a new era began in U.S. history as well as its postal history. Other Southern states quickly followed South Carolina's lead, which in turn led to the formation of the provisional government of the Confederate States of America on Feb. 4, 1861.

President Jefferson Davis' cabinet was completed Mar. 6, 1861, with the acceptance of the position of Postmaster General by John H. Reagan of Texas. The provisional government had already passed regulations that required payment for postage in cash and that effectively carried over the U.S. 3c rate until the new Confederate Post Office Department took over control of the system.

Soon after entering on his duties, Reagan directed the postmasters in the Confederate States and in the newly seceded states to "continue the performance of their duties as such, and render all accounts and pay all moneys (sic) to the order of the Government of the U.S. as they have heretofore done, until the Government of the Confederate States shall be prepared to assume control of its postal affairs."

As coinage was becoming scarce, postal patrons began having problems buying individual stamps or paying for letters individually, especially as stamp stocks started to run short in certain areas. Even though the U.S. Post Office Department was technically in control of the postal system and southern postmasters were operating under Federal authority, the U.S.P.O. was hesitant in re-supplying seceded states with additional stamps and stamped envelopes.

The U.S. government had made the issuance of postmasters' provisionals illegal many years before, but the southern postmasters had to do what they felt was necessary to allow patrons to pay for postage and make the system work. Therefore, a few postmasters took it upon themselves to issue provisional stamps in the 3c rate then in effect. Interestingly, these were stamps and envelopes that the U.S. government did not recognize as legal, but they did do postal duty unchallenged in the Confederate States. Yet the proceeds were to be remitted to the U.S. government in Washington! Six authenticated postmasters' provisionals in the 3c rate have been recorded.

On May 13, 1861, Postmaster General Reagan issued his proclamation "assuming control and direction of postal service within the limits of the Confederate States of America on and after the first day of June," with new postage rates and regulations. The Federal government suspended operations in the Confederate States (except for western Virginia and the seceding state of Tennessee) by a proclamation issued by Postmaster General Montgomery Blair on May 27, 1861, effective from May 31, 1861, and June 10 for western and middle Tennessee. As Tennessee did not join the Confederacy until July 2, 1861, the unissued 3c Nashville provisional was produced in a state that was in the process of seceding, while the other provisionals were used in the Confederacy before the June 1 assumption of control of postal service by the Confederate States of America.

HILLSBORO, N.C.

A1

Handstamped Adhesive

1AX1	A1	3c **bluish black,** on cover	—

No. 1AX1 is unique. This is the same handstamp as used for No. 39X1. 3c usage is determined from the May 27, 1861 circular date stamp.

JACKSON, MISS.

E1

Handstamped Envelope

2AXU1	E1	3c **black**	*2,500.*

See Nos. 43XU1-43XU4.

MADISON COURT HOUSE, FLA.

A1

"CNETS"

Typeset Adhesive

3AX1	A1	3c **gold**	—	*10,000.*
		On cover		*65,000.*
a.		"CNETS"		*14,000.*

No. 3AX1 on cover and No. 3AX1a are each unique. See No. 137XU1.

NASHVILLE, TENN.

A1

Typeset Adhesive (5 varieties)

4AX1	A1	3c **carmine**	150.

No. 4AX1 was prepared by Postmaster McNish with the U.S. rate, but the stamp was never issued.

See Nos. 61X2-61XU2.

SELMA, ALA.

E1

Handstamped Envelope

5AXU1 E1 3c **black** 2,500.

See Nos. 77XU1-77XU3.

TUSCUMBIA, ALA.

E1

Handstamped Envelope

Impression at upper right

6AXU1 E1 3c **dull red,** *buff* 17,500.

See Nos. 84XU1-84XU3.

PROVISIONAL ISSUES

These stamps and envelopes were issued by individual postmasters generally during the interim between June 1, 1861, when the use of U.S. stamps stopped in the Confederacy, and Oct. 16, 1861, when the 1st Confederate Government stamps were issued. They were occasionally issued at later periods, especially in Texas, when regular issues of Government stamps were unavailable.

Canceling stamps of the post offices were often used to produce envelopes, some of which were supplied in advance by private citizens. These envelopes and other stationery therefore may be found in a wide variety of papers, colors, sizes and shapes, including patriotic and semi-official types. It is often difficult to determine whether the impression made by the canceling stamp indicates provisional usage or merely postage paid at the time the letter was deposited in the post office. Occasionally the same mark was used for both purposes.

The *press-printed* provisional envelopes are in a different category. They were produced in quantity, using envelopes procured in advance by the postmaster, such as those of Charleston, Lynchburg, Memphis, etc. *The press-printed envelopes are listed and valued on all known papers.*

The handstamped provisional envelopes are listed and valued according to type and variety of handstamp, but not according to paper. Many exist on such a variety of papers that they defy accurate, complete listing. The value of a handstamped provisional envelope is determined *primarily* by the clarity of the markings and its overall condition and attractiveness, rather than the type of paper. *All handstamped provisional envelopes, when used, should also show the postmark of the town of issue.*

Most handstamps are impressed at top right, although they exist from some towns in other positions.

Illustrations in this section are reduced in size.

XU numbers are envelope entires.

ABERDEEN, MISS.

E1

Handstamped Envelopes

1XU1 E1 5c black 6,000.
1XU2 E1 10c (ms.) on 5c black 12,500.

ABINGDON, VA.

E1a

Handstamped Envelopes

2XU1 E1a 2c black 11,000.
2XU2 E1a 5c black 1,250.
2XU3 E1a 10c black 2,200. 3,500.

No. 2XU1 is unique. The unused and used eamples ofNo. 2XU3 are each unique.

ALBANY, GA.

E1

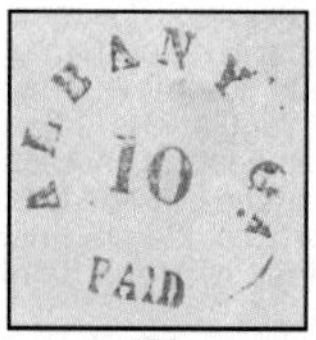

E2

E3

E4

Handstamped Envelopes

3XU1 E1 5c greenish blue 900.00
3XU2 E2 10c greenish blue 2,000.
3XU3 E2 10c on 5c grnsh blue 3,500.
3XU5 E3 5c greenish blue —
3XU6 E4 10c greenish blue 2,500.

The "10" in the No. 3XU2 marking is larger than the "10" in the No. 3XU3 marking.

Only one example each recorded of Nos. 3XU2, 3XU3 and 3XU6.

The existence of No. 3XU5 is in question. The editors would like to see an authenticated example of this marking.

ANDERSON COURT HOUSE, S.C.

E1

Handstamped Envelopes

4XU1 E1 5c black 500.00 2,250.
4XU2 E1 10c (ms.) black 3,000.

ATHENS, GA.

A1 — Type I

A1 — Type II

Typographed Adhesives

5X1 A1 5c purple (shades) 1,000. 1,500.
On cover 2,500.
Pair on cover 5,500.
Strip of 4 on cover (horiz.) 10,000.
a. Vertical tete beche pair 7,500.
Tete beche pair on cover 27,500.
5X2 A1 5c red — 4,750.
On cover 15,000.
Pair on cover —

The colorless ornaments in the four corners of No. 5X2 were recut, making them wider than those in No. 5X1.

Dangerous fakes exist of No. 5X1.

ATLANTA, GA.

E1

E2

E3

Handstamped Adhesives

6XU1 E1 5c red 3,500.
6XU2 E1 5c black 175.00 700.00
On patriotic cover 3,500.
6XU3 E1 10c on 5c black 1,500.
6XU4 E2 2c black 3,000.
6XU5 E2 5c black 1,500.
On patriotic cover 3,500.
6XU6 E2 10c black 950.00
6XU7 E2 10c on 5c black 2,500.
6XU8 E3 5c black 3,500.
6XU9 E3 10c black ("10" upright) 2,750.

Nos. 6XU1 and 6XU8 are each unique.

AUGUSTA, GA.

E1

Handstamped Envelope

7XU1 E1 5c black

Provisional status questioned. The only known example has a general C.S.A. issue used over the marking.

AUSTIN, MISS.

E1

Typographed Envelope

Typeset

8XU1 E1 5c red, *amber* 75,000.

No. 8XU1 is unique.

AUSTIN, TEX.

E1a

Handstamped Adhesive

9X1 E1a 10c **black** —
On cover, uncanceled 1,500.
On cover, tied —

Only one example of No. 9X1 tied on cover is recorded.

Handstamped Envelope

9XU1 E1a 10c black 1,750.

AUTAUGAVILLE, ALA.

E1

E2

Handstamped Envelopes

10XU1 E1 5c black 10,000.
10XU2 E2 5c black 12,500.

No. 10XU2 is unique.

BALCONY FALLS, VA.

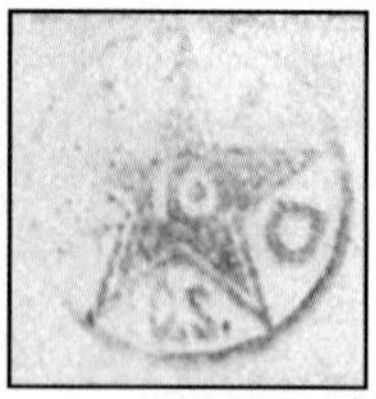

E1

Handstamped Envelope

122XU1 E1 10c blue 2,000.

BARNWELL COURT HOUSE, S.C.

E1

Handstamped Envelope

123XU1 E1 5c black 1,750.

These are two separate handstamps.

BATON ROUGE, LA.

A1

A2

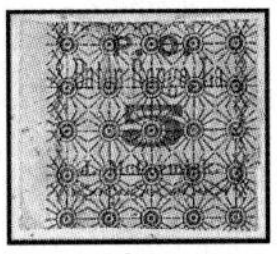
A3

A4

Ten varieties each of A1, A2 and A3

Typeset Adhesives

11X1	A1 2c green	*5,250.*	*5,000.*
	On cover		*20,000.*
a.	"McCcrmick"	*14,000.*	*8,500.*
	On cover		*22,500.*
11X2	A2 5c green & car	1,500.	1,400.
	On cover		2,750.
a.	"McCcrmick"	—	*2,000.*
	On cover		*6,500.*
11X3	A3 5c green & car	*4,500.*	*2,750.*
	On cover		*10,000.*
a.	"McCcrmick"		*3,500.*
11X4	A4 10c blue		*14,000.*
	On cover		*75,000.*

No. 11X4 on cover is unique.

BEAUMONT, TEX.

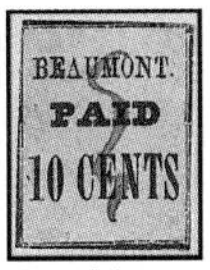

A1

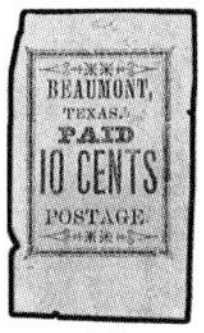

A2

Several varieties of A1

Typeset Adhesives

12X1	A1 10c black, *yellow,*		*12,500.*
12X2	A1 10c black, *pink*		*12,500.*
	On cover		*27,500.*
12X3	A2 10c black, *yellow,* on cover		*90,000.*

E1

A1

BLUFFTON, S.C.

Handstamped Envelope

124XU1	E1 5c black		*3,500.*

BRIDGEVILLE, ALA.

Handstamped Adhesive

13X1	A1 5c black & red		*20,000.*

CAMDEN, S.C.

E1

E2

Handstamped Envelopes

125XU1	E1 5c black		*4,500.*
125XU2	E2 10c black	*450.00*	

No. 125XU2 unused was privately carried and is addressed but has no postal markings. No. 125XU2 is indistinguishable from a handstamp paid cover when used.

CANTON, MISS.

E1

Handstamped Envelopes

14XU1	E1 5c black		2,750.
14XU2	E1 10c (ms.) on 5c black		5,000.

CAROLINA CITY, N.C.

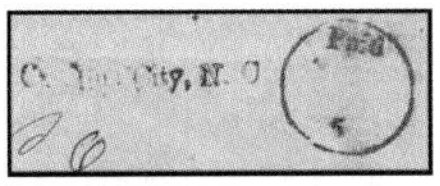
E1

Handstamped Envelope

118XU1	E1 5c black		*3,500.*

CARTERSVILLE, GA.

E1

Handstamped Envelope

126XU1	E1 (5c) red		*1,250.*

CHAPEL HILL, N.C.

E1

Handstamped Envelope

15XU1	E1 5c black		3,250.

CHARLESTON, S.C.

A1

E1

E2

Lithographed Adhesive

16X1	A1 5c blue	1,200.	850.00
	On cover		*2,250.*
	Pair, on cover		*5,000.*

Typographed from Woodcut Envelopes

16XU1	E1 5c blue	1,250.	*4,000.*
16XU2	E1 5c blue, *amber*	1,250.	*4,000.*
16XU3	E1 5c blue, *org*	1,250.	*4,000.*
16XU4	E1 5c blue, *buff*	1,250.	*4,000.*
16XU5	E1 5c blue, *blue*	1,250.	*4,000.*
16XU6	E2 10c blue, *org*		*77,500.*

Handstamped Envelope

16XU7	E2 10c black		*3,000.*

The No. 16XU6 entire is unique.

There is also only one copy known of No. 16XU7. It is a cut-out, not an entire. It may not have been mailed from Charleston and may not have paid postage.

CHARLOTTESVILLE, VA.

E1

Handstamped Envelopes

Manuscript Initials

127XU1	E1 5c blue		—
127XU2	E1 10c blue		—

CHATTANOOGA, TENN.

E1

Handstamped Envelopes

17XU2	E1 5c black		1,500.
17XU3	E1 5c on 2c black	*3,250.*	

CHRISTIANSBURG, VA.

E1

Handstamped Envelopes

Impressed at top right

99XU1	E1 5c black, *blue*		*2,250.*
99XU2	E1 5c blue		*2,000.*
99XU4	E1 5c green, on US envelope #U27		*4,500.*
99XU5	E1 10c blue		*3,500.*

COLAPARCHEE, GA.

E1

Control

Handstamped Envelope

119XU1	E1 5c black		*3,500.*

There are only two recorded examples of No. 119XU1, and both are used with general issue stamp from Savannah.

COLUMBIA, S.C.

E1

E2

Handstamped Envelopes

18XU1	E1 5c blue	550.00	*1,000.*
18XU2	E1 5c black	600.00	*1,250.*
18XU3	E1 10c on 5c blue		*3,500.*
18XU4	E2 5c blue (seal on front)		2,500.
a.	Seal on back		*1,250.*
18XU5	E2 10c blue (seal on back)		*2,750.*

Circular Seal similar to E2, 27mm diameter

18XU6	E2 5c blue (seal on back)		*4,000.*

E1

E1a

COLUMBIA, TENN.

Handstamped Envelope

113XU1	E1 5c red		*3,500.*

COLUMBUS, GA.

Handstamped Envelopes

19XU1	E1a 5c blue		800.
19XU2	E1a 10c red		*2,250.*

E1

E1a

COURTLAND, ALA.

Handstamped Envelopes from Woodcut

103XU1	E1 5c black		—
103XU2	E1 5c red		*10,000.*

Provisional status of No. 103XU1 questioned.

DALTON, GA.

Handstamped Envelopes

20XU1	E1a 5c black		600.00
a.	Denomination omitted (5c rate)		*725.00*
20XU2	E1a 10c black		800.00
20XU3	E1a 10c (ms.) on 5c black		1,500.

DANVILLE, VA.

A1

Design measures 60x37mm — E1

E2

E3

E4 

Typeset Adhesives
Wove Paper

21X1 A1 5c red		*5,500.*
On cover		—
Cut to shape		*4,000.*
On cover, cut to shape		*10,000.*

Only four rectangular-cut examples are recorded, one of which is reported to be on laid paper.

Two types: "SOUTHERN" in straight or curved line.

Typographed Envelopes

21XU1	E1 5c black	*5,500.*
21XU2	E1 5c black, *amber*	*5,500.*
21XU3	E1 5c black, *dark buff*	*5,250.*

An unissued 10c envelope (type E1, in red) is known. All recorded examples are envelopes on which added stamps paid the postage.

Handstamped Envelopes

21XU3A	E4 5c black (ms "WBP" initials)	*1,000.*
21XU4	E2 10c black	*2,500.*
21XU5	E2 10c blue	
21XU6	E3 10c black	*2,750.*
21XU7	E4 10c black (ms "WBP" initials)	—

The existence of No. 21XU5 has been questioned.

DEMOPOLIS, ALA.

E1

Handstamped Envelopes
Signature in ms.

22XU1	E1 5c black ("Jno. Y. Hall")	*3,500.*
22XU2	E1 5c black ("J. Y. Hall")	*3,500.*
22XU3	E1 5c (ms.) black ("J. Y. Hall")	*4,000.*

EATONTON, GA.

E1

E2

Handstamped Envelopes

23XU1	E1 5c black	*3,000.*
23XU2	E2 5c + 5c black	*5,000.*

EMORY, VA.

A1

E1

E2

Handstamped Adhesive
On sheet selvage of US 1857 1c stamps
Perf. 15 on Three Sides

24X1	A1 5c blue, on cover, ms. tied	*15,000.*

No. 24X1 exists with "5" above or below "PAID."

Handstamped Envelopes

24XU1	E1 5c blue	*2,000.*
24XU2	E2 10c blue	*10,000.*

Only one example recorded of No. 24XU2.

E1

E1a

FINCASTLE, VA.

Typeset Envelope

104XU1	E1 10c black	*20,000.*

No. 104XU1 is unique.

FORSYTH, GA.

Handstamped Envelope

120XU1	E1a 10c black	*1,750.*

Only one example recorded of No. 120XU1.

FRANKLIN, N.C.

E1

E1a

Typeset Envelope

25XU1	E1 5c blue, *buff*	*30,000.*

No. 25XU1 is unique.

FRAZIERSVILLE, S.C.

Handstamped Envelope
"5" manuscript

Only one example recorded of No. 128XU1.

128XU1	E1a 5c black	*2,250.*

FREDERICKSBURG, VA.

A1 

Typeset Adhesives
Ten varieties
Thin Bluish Paper

26X1	A1 5c blue, *bluish*	300.	850.
	On cover		*5,000.*
	Pair on cover		*12,000.*
26X2	A1 10c red (shades), *bluish*	1,250.	

GAINESVILLE, ALA.

E1

E2

Handstamped Envelopes

27XU1	E1 5c black	*5,000.*
27XU2	E2 10c black	*6,000.*

GALVESTON, TEX.

E1

E2

Handstamped Envelopes

98XU1	E1 5c black	500.00	*1,500.*
98XU2	E1 10c black		*2,000.*
98XU3	E2 10c black	550.00	*2,400.*
98XU4	E2 20c black		*3,500.*

GASTON, N.C.

E1

Handstamped Envelope

129XU1	E1 5c black	4,500.

Only one example recorded of No. 129XU1.

GEORGETOWN, S.C.

E1

Control

Handstamped Envelope

28XU1	E1 5c black	950.00

GOLIAD, TEX.

A1

A2

Typeset Adhesives
Several varieties of A1 and A2

29X1	A1 5c black	*12,000.*
29X2	A1 5c black, *gray*	*11,500.*
29X3	A1 5c black, *rose*	*12,000.*
29X4	A1 10c black	— *12,000.*
29X5	A1 10c black, *rose*	*12,000.*

Type A1 stamps bear ms. control: "Clarke P.M."

29X6	A2 5c black, *gray*	*10,000.*
a.	"Goilad"	*12,000.*
29X7	A2 10c black, *gray*	*12,000.*
	On cover	*25,000.*
a.	"Goilad"	*15,000.*
	On cover	*30,000.*
29X8	A2 5c black, *dark blue,* on cover	*7,000.*
29X9	A2 10c black, *dark blue*	*20,000.*

GONZALES, TEX.

A1

Illustration actual size.

Typographed Adhesives

30X1	A1 (5c) gold, *dark blue,* on cover	*15,000.*
30X2	A1 (10c) gold, *garnet,* on cover, *1864*	*12,500.*
30X3	A1 (10c) gold, *black,* on cover, *1865*	—

No. 30X1 must bear double-circle town cancel as validating control. The control was applied to the labels in the sheet before their sale as stamps. When used, the stamps bear an additional Gonzales double-circle postmark.

GREENSBORO, ALA.

E1

E2

Handstamped Envelopes

31XU1 E1 5c black *3,000.*
31XU2 E1 10c black *2,750.*
31XU3 E2 10c black *6,000.*

GREENSBORO, N.C.

E1

Handstamped Envelope

32XU1 E1 10c red 1,250.

GREENVILLE, ALA.

A1

A2

Typeset Adhesives

33X1 A1 5c blue & red *25,000.*
On cover *40,000.*
33X2 A2 10c red & blue —
On cover *40,000.*

GREENVILLE COURT HOUSE, S.C.

E1

E1a

Control

Handstamped Envelopes
Several types

34XU1 E1 5c black *2,000.*
34XU2 E1a10c black *2,250.*
34XU3 E1 20c (ms.) on 10c black *3,000.*

Envelopes must bear the black circle control on the back.

GREENWOOD DEPOT, VA.

A1

"PAID" Handstamped Adhesive
Value and signature ms.
Laid Paper

35X1 A1 10c black, *gray blue,* uncanceled, on cover *20,000.*

Six examples recorded of No. 35X1, all on covers. One of these is in the British Library collection. Of the remaining five, only one has the stamp tied to the cover.

GRIFFIN, GA.

E1

Handstamped Envelope

102XU1 E1 5c black 2,250.

A1

A1a

GROVE HILL, ALA.

Handstamped Adhesive

36X1 A1 5c black —
On cover *75,000.*

Two examples are recorded. One is on cover tied by the postmark. The other is canceled by magenta pen on a cover front.

HALLETTSVILLE, TEX.

Handstamped Adhesive
Ruled Letter Paper

37X1 A1a 10c black, *gray blue,* on cover *15,000.*

HAMBURGH, S.C.

E1

Handstamped Envelope

112XU1 E1 5c black *2,250.*

HARRISBURGH (Harrisburg), TEX.

E1

Handstamped Envelope

130XU1 E1 5c black —

No. 130XU1 is indistinguishable from a handstamp paid cover when used.

A1

A1a

HELENA, TEX.

Typeset Adhesives
Several varieties

38X1 A1 5c black, *buff* *7,500.* *6,000.*
38X2 A1 10c black, *gray* *5,000.*

On 10c "Helena" is in upper and lower case italics.

Used examples are valued with small faults or repairs, as all recorded have faults.

HILLSBORO, N.C.

Handstamped Adhesive

39X1 A1a 5c black, on cover *15,000.*

No. 39X1 is unique. See 3c 1861 Postmasters' Provisional No. 1AX1.

Manuscript Envelope

39XU1 10c "paid 10" —

No. 39XU1 has undated blue town cancel as control on face.

E1

E1a

HOLLANDALE, TEX.

Handstamped Envelope

132XU1 E1 5c black —

HOUSTON, TEX.

Handstamped Envelopes

40XU1 E1a 5c red — 750.00
40XU2 E1a 10c red — *1,500.*
40XU3 E1a 10c black *2,250.*
40XU4 E1a 5c + 10c red *2,500.*
40XU5 E1a 10c + 10c red *2,500.*
40XU6 E1a 10c (ms.) on 5c red *3,000.*

HUNTSVILLE, TEX.

E1

Control

Handstamped Envelope

92XU1 E1 5c black *5,000.*

No. 92XU1 exists with "5" outside or within control circle.

A1

E1

INDEPENDENCE, TEX.

Handstamped Adhesives

41X1 A1 10c black, *buff,* on cover, cut to shape, uncanceled *20,000.*
41X2 A1 10c black, *dull rose,* on cover

With small "10," "Pd" in manuscript

3 A1 10c black, *buff,* on cover, uncanceled, cut to shape 32,500.

No. 41X1 is unique. The existence of No. 41X2 has been questioned by specialists. The editors would like to see authenticated evidence of the existence of this item. All known examples of Nos. 41X1-41X3 are uncanceled on covers with black "INDEPENDANCE TEX." (sic) postmark.

No. 41X3 also exists cut square.

ISABELLA, GA.

Handstamped Envelope
"5" Manuscript

133XU1 E1 5c black *2,000.*

Only one example recorded of No. 133XU1.

E1

E1a

IUKA, MISS.

Handstamped Envelope

42XU1 E1 5c black *1,750.*

JACKSON, MISS.

Handstamped Envelopes

43XU1 E1a 5c black 575.00
43XU2 E1a 10c black *2,000.*
43XU3 E1a 10c on 5c black *2,750.*
43XU4 E1a 10c on 5c blue *2,750.*

The 5c also exists on a lettersheet. See No. 2AXU1.

E1

E1a

JACKSONVILLE, ALA.

Handstamped Envelope

110XU1 E1 5c black — *3,000.*

JACKSONVILLE, FLA.

Handstamped Envelope

134XU1 E1a 5c black —

Undated double circle postmark control on reverse.

A1

E1

JETERSVILLE, VA.

Handstamped "5"; ms. "AHA." Adhesive
Laid Paper

44X1 A1 5c black, vert. pair on cover, uncanceled *16,000.*

JONESBORO, TENN.

Handstamped Envelopes

45XU1 E1 5c black *3,750.*
45XU2 E1 5c dark blue *7,000.*

KINGSTON, GA.

E1

E2

E3

E4

Typeset Envelopes (design types E1-E2, E4 are handstamps; typeset design type E3 probably impressed by hand but possibly press printed)

46XU1 E1 5c black — 2,250.
46XU2 E2 5c black — 3,250.
46XU4 E3 5c black —
46XU5 E4 5c black *2,000.*

KNOXVILLE, TENN.

A1

Woodcut Adhesives

Grayish White Laid Paper

47X1 A1 5c brick red *1,400.* 1,400.
On cover, tied by handstamp *7,500.*
Pair on cover *7,500.*
47X2 A1 5c carmine *1,900.* *2,250.*
On cover, tied by handstamp *7,500.*
47X3 A1 10c green, on cover *57,750.*

The 5c has been reprinted in red, brown and chocolate on white and bluish wove and laid paper.

E1

E2

Typographed Envelopes

47XU1 E1 5c blue 750. 2,000.
47XU2 E1 5c blue, *orange* 750. 2,250.
47XU3 E1 10c red (cut to shape) *3,000.*
47XU4 E1 10c red, *orange* (cut to shape) *3,000.*

Only one example recorded of Nos. 47XU3 and 47XU4.

Handstamped Envelopes

47XU5 E2 5c black 750. *1,500.*
47XU6 E2 10c on 5c black *3,500.*

Type E2 exists with "5" above or below "PAID."

LA GRANGE, TEX.

E1

Handstamped Envelopes

48XU1 E1 5c black — 2,250.
48XU2 E1 10c black 3,000.

LAKE CITY, FLA.

E1

Control

Handstamped Envelope

96XU1 E1 10c black *2,000.*

Envelopes have black circle control mark, or printed name of E.R. Ives, postmaster, on face or back.

LAURENS COURT HOUSE, S.C.

E1

Handstamped Envelope

116XU1 E1 5c black *1,750.*

LENOIR, N.C.

A1

E1

Handstamped from Woodcut Adhesive

Paper has ruled lines in orange

49X1 A1 5c blue *7,250.* *6,750.*
On cover, pen-canceled *12,500.*
On cover, tied by handstamp *25,000.*

Handstamped Envelopes

49XU1 A1 5c black *3,500.*
49XU2 A1 10c (5c + 5c) blue *25,000.*
49XU3 E1 5c blue *4,500.*
49XU4 E1 5c black

No. 49XU2 is unique.
The existence of No. 49XU4 has been questioned.

LEXINGTON, MISS.

E1

Handstamped Envelopes

50XU1 E1 5c black *5,000.*
50XU2 E1 10c black *5,000.*

LEXINGTON, VA.

E1

Handstamped Envelopes

135XU1 E1 5c blue *500.00*
135XU2 E1 10c blue *750.00*

Nos. 135XU1-135XU2 by themselves are indistinguishable from a handstamp paid cover when used.

A1

A1a

LIBERTY, VA. (and SALEM, VA.)

Typeset Adhesive

Laid Paper

74X1 A1 5c blk, on cover, uncanceled, with Liberty postmark 35,000.
On cover, uncanceled, with Salem postmark *40,000.*

Three known on covers: two on covers with Liberty, Va. postmark, one on cover with Salem, Va., postmark.

LIMESTONE SPRINGS, S.C.

Handstamped Adhesive

121X1 A1a 5c black, on cover *10,000.*
Two on cover *15,000.*

Stamps are cut round or rectangular, on white or colored paper. Covers are not postmarked.

LIVINGSTON, ALA.

A1

Lithographed Adhesive

51X1 A1 5c blue *8,000.*
On cover *60,000.*
Pair on cover *120,000.*

The pair on cover is unique.

LYNCHBURG, VA.

A1

E1

Stereotyped Adhesive from Woodcut

52X1 A1 5c blue (shades) 1,800. *1,350.*
On cover *5,000.*
Pair on cover *20,000.*

Typographed Envelopes

52XU1 E1 5c black *3,000.*
52XU2 E1 5c black, *amber* 650. *3,000.*
52XU3 E1 5c black, *buff* *3,000.*
52XU4 E1 5c black, *brown* 900. *3,000.*
On patriotic cover —

MACON, GA.

A1

A2

A3

A4

E1

Typeset Adhesives

Several varieties of each. Ten of A2.

Wove Paper

53X1 A1 5c blk, *lt blue green* (shades) 900. 700.
On cover *4,000.*
Pair on cover *9,000.*
53X3 A2 5c black, *yellow* 2,500. 850.
On cover *4,750.*
Pair on cover *8,000.*
53X4 A3 5c blk, *yel* (shades) 2,750. 1,400.
On cover *6,000.*
Pair on cover *10,000.*
a. Vertical tete beche pair —
53X5 A4 2c black, *gray green* —
On cover *60,000.*

No. 53X4a is unique.
Dangerous fakes of No. 53X1 exist.

Laid Paper

53X6 A2 5c black, *yellow* *3,000.* *3,500.*
On cover *6,000.*
53X7 A3 5c black, *yellow* *6,000.*
On cover *9,000.*
53X8 A1 5c blk, *lt blue green* 1,750. *2,250.*
On cover *4,500.*

Handstamped Envelope

Two types of "PAID" and "5"

53XU1 E1 5c black 250. 575.

Values are for "PAID" over "5" variety. "5" over "PAID" is much scarcer.

MADISON, GA.

E1

E1a

Handstamped Envelope

136XU1 E1 5c red *500.*

No. 136XU1 is indistinguishable from a handstamp paid cover when used.

MADISON COURT HOUSE, FLA.

Typeset Envelope

137XU1 E1 5c black *23,000.*

No. 137XU1 is unique. See 3c 1861 Postmaster Provisional No. 3AX1.

MARIETTA, GA.

E1

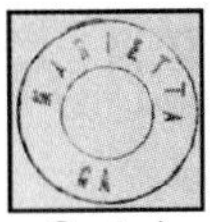

Control

E2

Handstamped Envelopes

54XU1 E1 5c black 400.
54XU2 E1 10c on 5c black *1,750.*
54XU3 E1 10c black
54XU4 E2 5c black *2,000.*

The existence of No. 54XU3 has been questioned by specialists. The editors would like to see authenticated evidence of this listing.

MARION, VA.

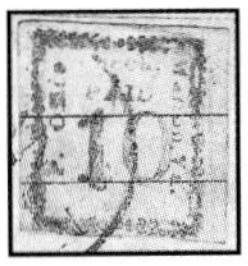

A1

Handstamped Numeral, Typeset Frame Adhesives

Wove Paper

55X1 A1 5c black *7,500.*
On cover *20,000.*
55X2 A1 10c black 16,500. *10,000.*
On cover *25,000.*

Bluish Laid Paper

55X3 A1 5c black — —

The 2c, 3c, 15c and 20c are believed to be bogus items printed later using the original typeset frame.

MEMPHIS, TENN.

A1

A2

Stereotyped Adhesives from Woodcut

56X1 A1 2c blue (shades) 100. *1,250.*
On cover *10,000.*
56X2 A2 5c red (shades) 150. 190.
On cover 1,750.
Pair on cover 3,500.
Strip of 4 on cover 7,000.
a. Tete beche pair 1,500.
On cover 10,000.
b. Pair, one sideways 750.
c. Pelure paper — —

Typographed Envelopes

56XU1 A2 5c red *2,500.*
56XU2 A2 5c red, *amber* *2,500.*
56XU3 A2 5c red, *orange* *2,500.*

MICANOPY, FLA.

E1

Handstamped Envelope

105XU1 E1 5c black *11,500.*

No. 105X1 is unique.

MILLEDGEVILLE, GA.

E1

E2

E3

Handstamped Envelopes

57XU1 E1 5c black 375.
a. Wide spacing between "I" and "D" of "PAID" 500.
57XU2 E1 5c blue 800.
57XU3 E1 10c on 5c black 1,000.
57XU4 E2 10c black 375. 1,000.
a. Wide spacing between "I" and "D" of "PAID" 400.
57XU5 E3 10c black 800.

On No. 57XU4, the "PAID/10" virtually always falls outside the Milledgeville control marking (as in illustration E1).

Two types of No. 57XU5; with tall, thin "1" of "10" and with short, fat "1." The latter is about twice as scarce.

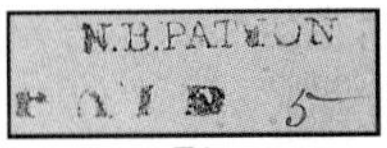

E1

E1a

MILTON, N.C.

Handstamped Envelope "5" Manuscript

138XU1 E1 5c black *2,000.*

MOBILE, ALA.

Lithographed Adhesives

58X1 A1 2c black 2,250. 1,100.
On cover *5,000.*
Pair on cover *20,000.*
Three singles on one cover *20,000.*
Five copies on one cover *20,000.*
58X2 A1 5c blue 350. 400.
On cover 1,800.
Pair on cover 2,400.
Strip of 3 on cover *6,000.*
Strip of 4 on cover *7,500.*
Strip of 5 on cover —

MONTGOMERY, ALA.

E1

E2

E3

Handstamped Envelopes

59XU1 E1 5c red 1,100.
59XU2 E1 5c blue 400. 900.
59XU3 E1 10c red 850.
59XU4 E1 10c blue 1,500.
59XU5 E1 10c black 850.
59XU6 E1 10c on 5c red *2,750.*

The 10c design is larger than the 5c.

59XU7 E2 2c red *2,500.*
59XU7A E2 2c blue *3,500.*
59XU8 E2 5c black *2,250.*
59XU9 E3 10c black *3,250.*
59XU10 E3 10c red *1,750.*

MT. LEBANON, LA.

A1

Woodcut Adhesive (mirror image of design)

60X1 A1 5c red brown, on cover *385,000.*

No. 60X1 is unique.

NASHVILLE, TENN.

A2

E1

Stereotyped Adhesives from Woodcut

Gray Blue Ribbed Paper

61X2 A2 5c carmine (shades) 850.00 600.00
On cover 2,500.
Pair on cover *6,000.*
a. Vertical tete beche pair *4,000.*
On cover *30,000.*
61X3 A2 5c brick red 850. 600.00
On cover 3,500.
Pair on cover *7,500.*
61X4 A2 5c gray (shades) 950.00 750.00
On cover *5,500.*
Pair on cover *7,250.*
61X5 A2 5c violet brown 1,000. 700.00
On cover 4,500.
Pair on cover *6,000.*
a. Vertical tete beche pair *5,000.* *4,000.*
On cover —
61X6 A2 10c green *4,500.*
On cover *20,000.*
On cover with No. 61X2 *25,000.*

Handstamped Envelopes

61XU1 E1 5c blue 900.
61XU2 E1 5c + 10c blue *2,750.*

NEW ORLEANS, LA.

A1

A2

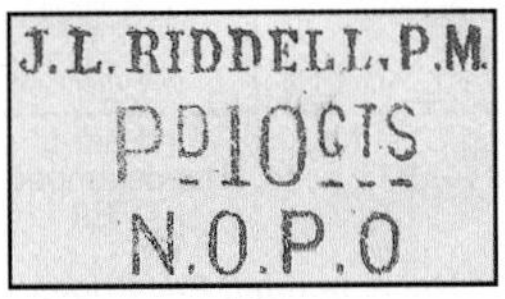

E1

Typographed Adhesives stereotyped from woodcut

62X1 A1 2c blue 175.00 600.
On cover *4,250.*
Pair on cover *10,000.*
Three singles on one cover *20,000.*
Strip of 5 on cover *30,000.*
a. Printed on both sides 1,750.
On cover *7,500.*
62X2 A1 2c red (shades) 150.00 *1,000.*
On cover *25,000.*
62X3 A2 5c brown, *white* 275.00 200.00
On cover 425.00
Pair on cover 850.00
Strip of 5 on cover *5,000.*
a. Printed on both sides *2,250.*
On cover *7,500.*
b. 5c ocher 700. 625.00
On cover 2,250.
Pair on cover 3,000.
62X4 A2 5c red brown, *bluish* 300. 200.
On cover 400.00
Pair on cover 675.00
Block of 4 on cover *5,000.*
a. Printed on both sides *2,750.*
62X5 A2 5c yel brn, *off-white* 140.00 240.00
On cover 850.00
Pair on cover 1,000.
Strip of 5 on cover —
62X6 A2 5c red — *7,500.*
62X7 A2 5c red, *bluish* *15,000.*

Handstamped Envelopes

62XU1 E1 5c black 4,500.
62XU2 E1 10c black *12,500.*
"J L. RIDDELL, P.M." omitted
62XU3 E1 2c black *9,500.*

A1

E1

NEW SMYRNA, FLA.

Handstamped Adhesive

63X1 A1 10c ("01") on 5c black *45,000.*

No. 63X1 is unique.

NORFOLK, VA.

Handstamped Envelopes

Ms Signature on Front or Back

139XU1 E1 5c blue — *1,250.*
139XU2 E1 10c blue *1,750.*

A1

E1

OAKWAY, S.C.

Handstamped Adhesive

115X1 A1 5c black, on cover *66,000.*

Two used examples of No. 115X1 are recorded, both on cover. Value represents 1997 auction realization for the cover on which the stamp is tied by manuscript "Paid."

PENSACOLA, FLA.

Handstamped Envelopes

106XU1 E1 5c black *3,750.*
106XU2 E1 10c (ms.) on 5c black *4,250.*

A1

A1a

PETERSBURG, VA.

Typeset Adhesive (10 varieties)

65X1 A1 5c red (shades) 2,250. 750.00
On cover 2,500.
Pair on cover *8,000.*
On cover with C.S.A. #1 *57,500.*

PITTSYLVANIA COURT HOUSE, VA.

Typeset Adhesives
Wove Paper

66X1 A1a 5c red 7,000. *6,000.*
On cover *55,000.*
Octagonally cut *5,000.*
On cover *20,000.*

Laid Paper

66X2 A1a 5c red *6,500.*
On cover *55,000.*
Octagonally cut *5,500.*
On cover *40,000.*

PLAINS OF DURA, GA.

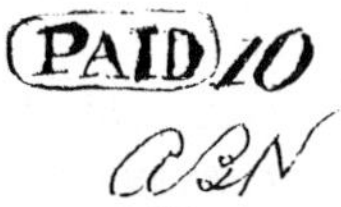

E1

Handstamped Envelopes
Ms. initials

140XU1 E1 5c black —
140XU2 E1 10c black —

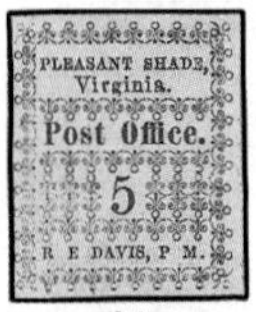
A1

E1

PLEASANT SHADE, VA.

Typeset Adhesive (5 varieties)

67X1 A1 5c blue 2,750. *20,000.*
On cover *27,500.*
Pair on cover *55,000.*

PLUM CREEK, TEX.

Manuscript Adhesive

141X1 E1 10c black, *blue,* on cover —

The ruled lines and "10" are done by hand. Size and shape of the stamp varies.

PORT GIBSON, MISS.

E1

Handstamped Envelope
Ms Signature

142XU1 E1 5c black —

A1

E1

PORT LAVACA, TEX.

Typeset Adhesive

107X1 A1 10c black, on cover *25,000.*

No. 107X1 is unique.

RALEIGH, N.C.

Handstamped Envelopes

68XU1 E1 5c red 600.00
68XU2 E1 5c blue *3,000.*

A1

E1

RHEATOWN, TENN.

Typeset Adhesive

Three varieties

69X1 A1 5c red 3,000. *3,750.*
On cover, ms. cancel *15,000.*
On cover, tied by handstamp *35,000.*

Stamps normally were canceled in manuscript.

RICHMOND, TEX.

Handstamped Envelopes

70XU1 E1 5c red 2,500.
70XU2 E1 10c red 2,000.
70XU3 E1 10c on 5c red *5,000.*
70XU4 E1 15c (ms.) on 10c red *5,000.*

E1

E1a

RINGGOLD, GA.

Handstamped Envelope

71XU1 E1 5c blue black *3,000.*

RUTHERFORDTON, N.C.

Handstamped Adhesive
"Paid 5cts" in ms.

72X1 E1a 5c black, cut round, on cover(uncanceled) *25,000.*

No. 72X1 is unique.

SALEM, N.C.

"Paid 5" in Ms. — E1

"Paid 5" Handstamped — E2

Handstamped Envelopes

73XU1 E1 5c black 1,750.
73XU2 E1 10c black *2,250.*
73XU3 E2 5c black *2,250.*
73XU4 E2 10c on 5c black *2,800.*

Reprints exist on various papers. They either lack the "Paid" and value or have them counterfeited.

SALISBURY, N.C.

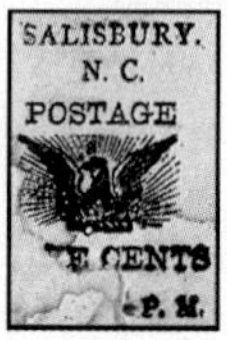
E1

Typeset Envelope
Impressed at top left

75XU1 E1 5c black, *greenish* *5,000.*

One example known with part of envelope torn away, leaving part of design missing. Illustration E1 partly suppositional.

SAN ANTONIO, TEX.

E1

E2

Control

Handstamped Envelopes

76XU1 E1 10c black 275.00 *2,000.*
76XU1A E2 5c black *1,500.*
76XU2 E2 10c black *2,500.*

Black circle control mark is on front or back.

SAVANNAH, GA.

E1

Control

E2

Handstamped Envelopes

101XU1 E1 5c black 400.00
101XU2 E2 5c black 600.00
101XU3 E1 10c black 750.00
101XU4 E2 10c black 750.00
101XU5 E1 10c on 5c black 1,500.
101XU6 E2 20c on 5c black *2,000.*

Envelope must bear octagonal control mark.
One example is known of No. 101XU6.

E1

E1a

SELMA, ALA.

Handstamped Envelopes
Signature in ms.

77XU1 E1 5c black *1,250.*
77XU2 E1 10c black *2,500.*
77XU3 E1 10c on 5c black *3,000.*

SPARTA, GA.

Handstamped Envelopes

93XU1 E1a 5c red — 1,750.
93XU2 E1a 10c red *2,500.*

Only one example recorded of No. 93XU2.

SPARTANBURG, S.C.

A1

A2

Handstamped Adhesives
on ruled or plain wove paper

78X1 A1 5c black *3,500.*
On cover *25,000.*
Pair on cover *30,000.*
a. "5" omitted —
78X2 A2 5c black, *bluish* *4,000.*
On cover *15,000.*
78X3 A2 5c black, *brown* *4,000.*
On cover *18,000.*

Most examples of Nos. 78X1-78X3 are cut round. Cut square examples in sound condition are worth much more.

STATESVILLE, N.C.

E1

Handstamped Envelopes

79XU1 E1 5c black 175.00 *675.00*
79XU2 E1 10c on 5c black *2,250.*

SUMTER, S.C.

E1

Handstamped Envelopes

80XU1 E1 5c black 400.
80XU2 E1 10c black 500.
80XU3 E1 10c on 5c black *800.*
80XU4 E1 2c (ms.) on 10c black *1,100.*

Used examples of Nos. 80XU1-80XU2 are indistinguishable from handstamped "Paid" covers.

TALBOTTOM, GA.

E1

Handstamped Envelopes

94XU1 E1 5c black 1,000.
94XU2 E1 10c black 1,000.
94XU3 E1 10c on 5c black *2,000.*

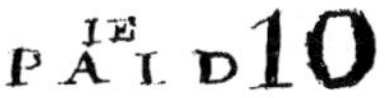
E1

A1

TALLADEGA, ALA.

Handstamped Envelopes

143XU1	E1	5c black	*1,200.*	—
143XU2	E1	10c black	*1,200.*	—

TELLICO PLAINS, TENN.

Typeset Adhesives
Laid Paper

81X1	A1	5c red	1,750.	—
		On cover		*50,000.*
81X2	A1	10c red	3,250.	

THOMASVILLE, GA.

E1

Control

E2

Handstamped Envelopes

82XU1	E1	5c black	575.00
82XU2	E2	5c black	900.00

TULLAHOMA, TENN.

E1

Control

Handstamped Envelope

111XU1 E1 10c black *3,000.*

E1

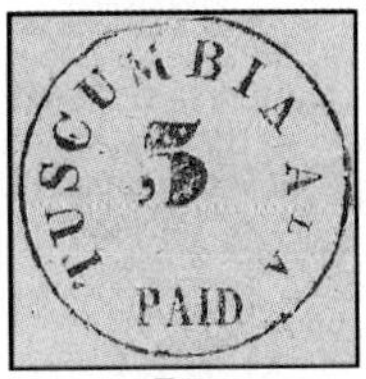
E1a

TUSCALOOSA, ALA.

Handstamped Envelopes

83XU1	E1	5c black	250.00
83XU2	E1	10c black	250.00

Used examples of Nos. 83XU1-83XU2 are indistinguishable from handstamped "Paid" covers.

TUSCUMBIA, ALA.

Handstamped Envelopes

84XU1	E1a	5c black	2,250.
84XU2	E1a	5c red	3,000.
84XU3	E1a	10c black	3,500.

See 3c 1861 Postmasters' Provisional No. 6AXU1.

A1

UNIONTOWN, ALA.

Typeset Adhesives in settings of 4 (2x2)

Four varieties of each value
Laid Paper

86X1	A1	2c dark blue, *gray blue,* on cover		—
86X2	A1	2c dark blue, sheet of 4	*57,500.*	
86X3	A1	5c green, *gray blue*	4,000.	3,250.
		On cover		*9,000.*
86X4	A1	5c green	4,000.	3,250.
		On cover		*7,500.*
		Pair on cover		*20,000.*
86X5	A1	10c red, *gray blue*		—
		On cover		*37,500.*

The item listed as No. 86X5 used is an uncanceled stamp on a large piece with part of addressee's name in manuscript.

UNIONVILLE, S.C.

A1

Handstamped Adhesive

Wove Paper with Blue Ruled Lines

87X1	A1	5c black, *grayish*	—
		On cover, uncanceled	*17,500.*
		On cover, tied	—
		Pair on patriotic cover	*32,500.*

The pair on patriotic cover is the only pair recorded.

VALDOSTA, GA.

E1

Control

Handstamped Envelopes

100XU1	E1	10c black	*2,000.*
100XU2	E1	5c +5c black	—

The black circle control must appear on front of the No. 100XU2 envelope or back of the No. 100XU1 envelope. There is one recorded cover each of Nos. 100XU1-100XU2.

VICTORIA, TEX.

Typeset Adhesives

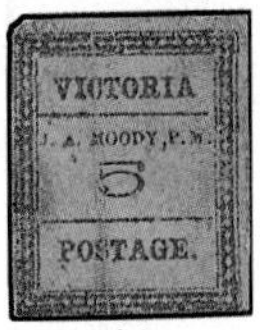

A1

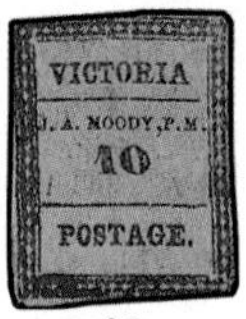

A2

88X1	A1	5c red brown, *green*	*9,000.*	
88X2	A1	10c red brown, *green*	*10,000.*	*5,500.*
		On cover		*115,000.*

Pelure Paper

88X3	A2	10c red brown, *green*	*10,000.*	*10,000.*

WALTERBOROUGH, S.C.

Handstamped Envelopes

E1

108XU1	E1	10c black, *buff*	*4,250.*
108XU2	E1	10c carmine	*4,250.*

WARRENTON, GA.

E1

Handstamped Envelopes

89XU1	E1	5c black	1,250.
89XU2	E1	10c (ms.) on 5c black	1,000.

E1

E1a

WASHINGTON, GA.

Handstamped Envelope

117XU1 E1 10c black *2,000.*

WEATHERFORD, TEX.

Handstamped Envelopes

Woodcut with "PAID" inserted in type

109XU1	E1a	5c black	*2,000.*
109XU2	E1a	5c + 5c black	*11,000.*

One example is known of No. 109XU2.

WINNSBOROUGH, S.C.

E1

Control

Handstamped Envelopes

97XU1	E1	5c black	*1,500.*
97XU2	E1	10c black	*3,500.*

Envelopes must bear black circle control on front or back.

WYTHEVILLE, VA.

E1

Control

Handstamped Envelope

114XU1 E1 5c black 900.00

For later additions, listed out of numerical sequence, see:

#74X1, Liberty, Va. (& Salem, Va.)
#92XU1, Huntsville, Tex.
#93XU1, Sparta, Ga.
#94XU1, Talbotton, Ga.
#96XU1, Lake City, Fla.
#97XU1, Winnsborough, S.C.
#98XU1, Galveston, Tex.
#99XU1, Christiansburg, Va.
#100XU1, Valdosta, Ga.
#101XU1, Savannah, Ga.
#102XU1, Griffin, Ga.
#103XU1, Courtland, Ala.
#104XU1, Fincastle, Va.
#105XU1, Micanopy, Fla.
#106XU1, Pensacola, Fla.
#107X1, Port Lavaca, Tex.
#108XU1, Walterborough, S.C.
#109XU1, Weatherford, Tex.
#110XU1, Jacksonville, Ala.
#111XU1, Tullahoma, Tenn.
#112XU1, Hamburgh, S.C.
#113XU1, Columbia, Tenn.
#114XU1, Wytheville, Va.
#115X1, Oakway, S.C.
#116XU1, Laurens Court House, S.C.
#117XU1, Washington, Ga.
#118XU1, Carolina City, N.C.
#119XU1, Colaparchee, Ga.
#120XU1, Forsyth, Ga.
#121XU1, Limestone Springs, S.C.
#122XU1, Balcony Falls, Va.
#123XU1, Barnwell Court House, S.C.
#124XU1, Bluffton, S.C.
#125XU1, Camden, S.C.
#126XU1, Cartersville, Ga.
#127XU1, Charlottesville, Va.
#128XU1, Fraziersville, S.C.
#129XU1, Gaston, N.C.
#130XU1, Harrisburgh, Tex.
#132XU1, Hollandale, Tex.
#133XU1, Isabella, Ga.
#134XU1, Jacksonville, Fla.
#135XU1, Lexington, Va.
#136XU1, Madison, Ga.
#137XU1, Madison Court House, Fla.
#138XU1, Milton, N.C.
#139XU1, Norfolk, Va.
#140XU1, Plains of Dura, Ga.
#141X1, Plum Creek, Tex.
#142XU1, Port Gibson, Miss.
#143XU1, Talladega, Ala.

GENERAL ISSUES

Jefferson Davis
A1

Thomas Jefferson
A2

1861 Unwmk. Litho. *Imperf.*

1	A1	5c green	275.00	175.00
		No gum	200.00	
		On cover		250.00
a.		5c light green	275.00	175.00
		No gum	175.00	
b.		5c dark green	350.00	200.00

	No gum	225.00	
c.	5c olive green	375.00	200.00
	No gum	250.00	
	On cover		300.00
2	A2 10c blue	300.00	200.00
	No gum	200.00	
	On cover		250.00
a.	10c light blue	300.00	190.00
	No gum	200.00	
b.	10c dark blue	600.00	275.00
	No gum	425.00	
	On cover		450.00
c.	10c indigo	*3,000.*	*2,500.*
	No gum	*2,000.*	
d.	Printed on both sides		—
e.	10c greenish blue	1,100.	350.00
	No gum	750.00	
	On cover		525.00

The earliest printings of No. 2 were made by Hoyer & Ludwig, the later ones by J. T. Paterson & Co. Stamps of the later printings usually have a small colored dash below the lowest point of the upper left spandrel.

See Nos. 4-5.

Andrew Jackson
A3

Jefferson Davis
A4

1862

3	A3 2c green	900.00	750.00
	No gum	575.00	
	On cover		*2,750.*
a.	2c bright yellow green	*2,000.*	—
	No gum	1,400.	
	On cover		*4,000.*
4	A1 5c blue	225.00	125.00
	No gum	140.00	
	On cover		250.00
a.	5c dark blue	250.00	175.00
	No gum	550.00	
b.	5c light milky blue	300.00	200.00
	No gum	190.00	
5	A2 10c rose	1,500.	500.00
	No gum	950.00	
	On cover		800.00
a.	10c carmine	*3,500.*	*1,900.*
	No gum	*2,250.*	
	On cover		*4,500.*

Typo.

6	A4 5c lt blue (London print)	15.00	*27.50*
	No gum	7.50	
	Pair on cover		100.00
7	A4 5c blue (local print)	18.00	*20.00*
	No gum	9.00	
	Pair on cover		95.00
a.	5c deep blue	20.00	*35.00*
	No gum	10.50	
	Pair on cover		95.00
b.	Printed on both sides	*2,500.*	*1,500.*
	Pair on cover		*4,000.*

No. 6 has fine, clear impression. No. 7 has coarser impression and the color is duller and often blurred.

Both 2c and 10c stamps, types A4 and A10, were privately printed in various colors.

Andrew Jackson — A5

1863 **Engr.**

8	A5 2c brown red	70.00	*350.00*
	No gum	40.00	
a.	2c pale red	90.00	*450.00*
	No gum	45.00	
	Single on cover, #8 or 8a		*1,500.*

A6

Jefferson Davis — A6a

Thick or Thin Paper

9	A6 10c blue	900.00	550.00
	No gum	650.00	
a.	10c milky blue	900.00	550.00
	No gum	650.00	
b.	10c gray blue	950.00	650.00
	No gum	675.00	
	On cover		1,600.
10	A6a 10c blue (with frame line)	5,000.	1,800.
	No gum	3,500.	
a.	10c milky blue	5,000.	1,800.
	No gum	3,500.	
b.	10c greenish blue	5,500.	1,900.
	No gum	4,000.	
c.	10c dark blue	5,500.	1,900.
	No gum	4,000.	
	On cover		*3,000.*

Values of Nos. 10, 10a, 10b and 10c are for copies showing parts of lines on at least three sides. Used stamps showing 4 complete lines sell for approximately 300% of the values given. Unused stamps showing 4 complete lines are exceedingly rare and will sell for many multiples of the values given.

A7

A8

There are many slight differences between A7 and A8, the most noticeable being the additional line outside the ornaments at the corners of A8.

11	A7 10c blue	15.00	*20.00*
	No gum	7.50	
	On cover		55.00
a.	10c milky blue	45.00	*47.50*
	No gum	32.50	
b.	10c dark blue	22.50	*25.00*
	No gum	14.00	
c.	10c greenish blue	20.00	18.00
	No gum	12.50	
d.	10c green	50.00	*45.00*
	No gum	35.00	
e.	Officially perforated 12½	300.00	275.00
	On cover		*750.00*

12	A8 10c blue	18.00	*20.00*
	No gum	9.00	
	On cover		75.00
	Pair on cover		200.00
a.	10c milky blue	45.00	*47.50*
	No gum	32.50	
b.	10c light blue	11.00	*20.00*
	No gum	7.50	
c.	10c greenish blue	20.00	*45.00*
	No gum	12.50	
d.	10c dark blue	18.00	*22.50*
	No gum	9.00	
e.	10c green	50.00	*45.00*
	No gum	35.00	
f.	Officially perforated 12½	325.00	400.00
	On cover		*750.00*

The paper of Nos. 11 and 12 varies from thin hard to thick soft. The so-called laid paper is probably due to thick streaky gum.

George Washington
A9

John C. Calhoun
A10

13	A9 20c green	40.00	*400.00*
	No gum	27.50	
a.	20c yellow green	70.00	*450.00*
	No gum	47.50	
b.	20c dark green	65.00	*500.00*
	No gum	45.00	
	On cover		*1,250.*
c.	Diagonal half used as 10c on cover		*2,000.*
d.	Horiz. half used as 10c on cover		*3,500.*

1862 **Typo.**

14	A10 1c orange	110.00	
	No gum	70.00	
a.	1c deep orange	130.00	
	No gum	90.00	

The 1c was never put in use.

CANAL ZONE

kə-ˈnal ˈzōn

LOCATION — A strip of land 10 miles wide, extending through the Republic of Panama, between the Atlantic and Pacific Oceans.

GOVT. — From 1904-79 a US Government Reservation.

AREA — 552.8 sq. mi.

POP. — 41,800 (est. 1976)

The Canal Zone, site of the Panama Canal, was leased in perpetuity to the US for a cash payment of $10,000,000 and a yearly rental.

100 Centavos = 1 Peso
100 Centesimos = 1 Balboa
100 Cents = 1 Dollar

Catalogue values for unused stamps in this country are for Never Hinged items, beginning with Scott 118 in the regular postage section and Scott C6 in the air post section.

Watermarks

Wmk. 190 — "USPS" in Single-lined Capitals

Wmk. 191 — Double-lined "USPS" in Capitals

Map of Panama — A1

Violet to Violet-blue Handstamp, "CANAL ZONE," on Panama Nos. 72-72c, 78 and 79

1904 **Unwmk.** **Engr.** ***Perf. 12***

1	A1 2c rose, both "PANAMA" up or down	600.	425.
a.	"CANAL ZONE" inverted	*1,000.*	850.
b.	"CANAL ZONE" double	*3,250.*	2,000.
c.	"CANAL ZONE" double, both inverted	*20,000.*	
d.	"PANAMA" reading down and up	750.	650.
e.	As "d," "CANAL ZONE" inverted	*9,000.*	*7,000.*
f.	Vert. pair, "PANAMA" reading up on top 2c, down on other	*2,100.*	*2,100.*
g.	As "f," "CANAL ZONE" inverted	*20,000.*	
2	A1 5c blue	300.	175.
a.	"CANAL ZONE" inverted	775.	600.
b.	"CANAL ZONE" double	2,250.	1,500.
c.	Pair, one without "CANAL ZONE"	*5,000.*	*5,000.*
d.	"CANAL ZONE" diagonal, running down to right	800.	700.
3	A1 10c yellow	400.	250.
a.	"CANAL ZONE" inverted	775.	600.
b.	"CANAL ZONE" double		*15,000.*
c.	Pair, one without "CANAL ZONE"	*6,000.*	*5,000.*
	Nos. 1-3 (3)	1,300.	850.00

On the 2c stamp "PANAMA" is normally about 13mm; on the 5c and 10c about 15mm.

Varieties of "PANAMA" overprint exist on the 2c with inverted "V" for "A," accent on "A," inverted "N," etc.

Counterfeit "CANAL ZONE" overprints exist.

U.S. Nos. 300, 319, 304, 306 and 307 Overprinted in Black

1904 **Wmk. 191**

4	A115 1c blue green	35.00	22.50
5	A129 2c carmine	30.00	25.00
a.	2c scarlet	35.00	30.00
6	A119 5c blue	110.00	65.00
7	A121 8c violet black	175.00	85.00
8	A122 10c pale red brown	150.00	90.00
	Nos. 4-8 (5)	500.00	287.50

Beware of fake overprints.

A2

A3

CANAL ZONE Regular Type

CANAL ZONE Antique Type

Black Overprint on Stamps of Panama

1904-06 **Unwmk.**

9	A2 1c green	2.75	2.25
a.	"CANAL" in antique type	100.00	100.00
b.	"ZONE" in antique type	70.00	70.00
c.	Inverted overprint	*5,500.*	*4,000.*
d.	Double overprint	*2,750.*	*2,000.*
10	A2 2c rose	4.50	3.00
a.	Inverted overprint	225.00	275.00
b.	"L" of "CANAL" sideways	2,500.	2,500.

Overprinted "CANAL ZONE" in Black, "PANAMA" and Bar in Red on Panama Nos. 77-79 "PANAMA" 15mm long

11	A3 2c rose	7.50	5.00
a.	"ZONE" in antique type	200.00	200.00
b.	"PANAMA" inverted, bar at bottom	675.00	675.00
12	A3 5c blue	8.00	3.75
a.	"CANAL" in antique type	75.00	65.00
b.	"ZONE" in antique type	75.00	65.00
c.	"CANAL ZONE" double	800.00	800.00
d.	"PANAMA" ovpt. dbl.	1,050.	1,000.
e.	"PANAMA" inverted, bar at bottom		2,000.
13	A3 10c yellow	22.50	12.50
a.	"CANAL" in antique type	200.00	200.00
b.	"ZONE" in antique type	175.00	160.00
c.	"PANAMA" ovpt. dbl.	650.00	650.00
d.	"PANAMA" overprint in red brown	27.50	27.50
	Nos. 11-13 (3)	38.00	21.25

With Added Surcharge in Red on Panama No. 81

14	A3 8c on 50c bis brn	32.50	22.50
a.	"ZONE" in antique type	1,150.	1,150.
b.	"CANAL ZONE" invtd.	450.00	425.00
c.	Rose brown overprint	40.00	40.00
d.	As "c," "CANAL" in antique type	2,000.	
e.	As "c," "ZONE" in antique type	2,000.	
f.	As "c," "8 cts" double	*1,100.*	
g.	As "c," "8" omitted	*4,250.*	

Panama No. 74 Overprinted "CANAL ZONE" in Regular Type in Black and Surch. Like No. 14 in Red. Both "PANAMA" Reading Up. "PANAMA" 13mm long.

1905

15	A3 8c on 50c bis brn	2,600.	*4,750.*
a.	"PANAMA" reading down & up	*7,500.*	—

On No. 15 with original gum the gum is almost always disturbed.

Map of Panama — A4

Panama Nos. 19 and 21 Surcharged in Black:

a
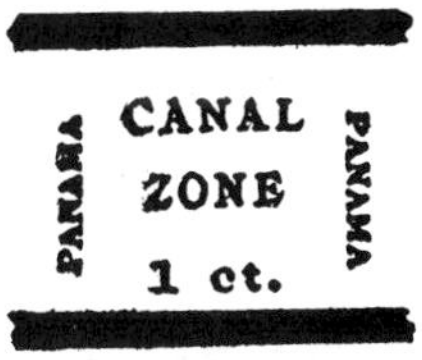

b
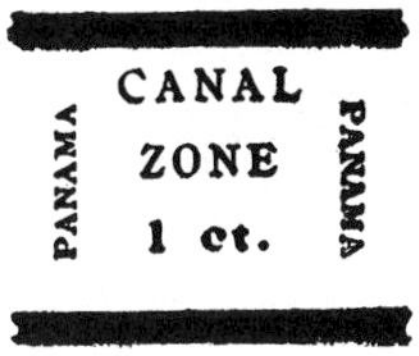

c
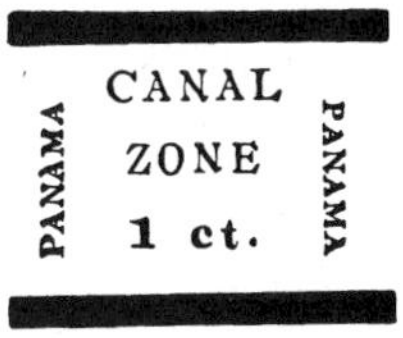

d
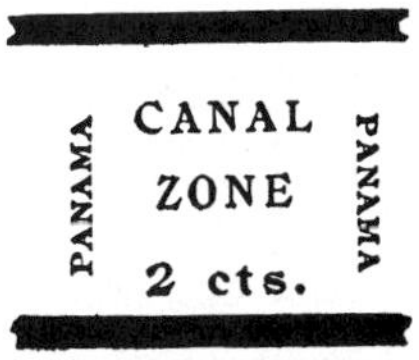

e
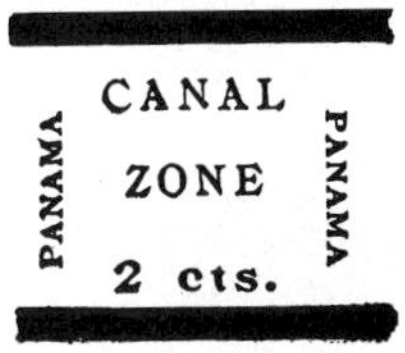

f
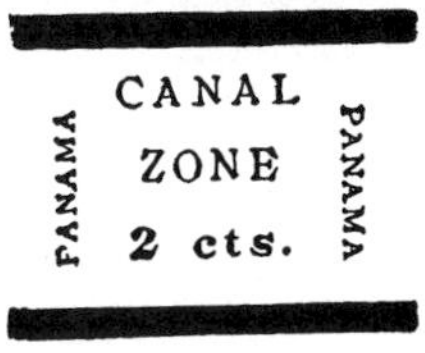

There were 3 printings of each denomination differing mainly in the relative position of the various parts of the surcharges. Varieties occur with invtd. "V" for the 3rd "A" in "PANAMA," "CA" spaced, "ZO" spaced, "2c" spaced, accents in various positions, and with bars shifted so that 2 bars appear on top or bottom of the stamp (either with or without the corresponding bar on top or bottom) and sometimes with only 1 bar at top or bottom.

1906

16	A4 1c on 20c vio, type a	2.00	1.60
a.	Surcharge type b	2.00	1.60
b.	Surcharge type c	2.00	1.60
c.	As #16, double surcharge		*2,000.*
17	A4 2c on 1p lake, type d	2.75	2.75
a.	Surcharge type e	2.75	2.75
b.	Surcharge type f	20.00	20.00

Panama No. 74 Overprinted "CANAL ZONE" in Regular Type in Black and Surcharged in Red

8 cts. (b) 8 cts (c)

Both "PANAMA" reading up

1905-06

18	A3 (b) 8c on 50c bis brn	55.00	50.00
a.	"ZONE" in antique type	200.00	180.00
b.	"PANAMA" down & up	175.00	160.00
19	A3 (c) 8c on 50c bis brn ('06)	55.00	45.00
a.	"CANAL" in antique type	210.00	180.00
b.	"ZONE" in antique type	210.00	180.00
c.	"8 cts." double	*1,100.*	*1,100.*
d.	"PANAMA" down & up	110.00	90.00

On Nos. 18-19 with original gum the gum is usually disturbed.

Panama No. 81 Overprinted "CANAL ZONE" in Regular Type in Black and Surcharged in Red Type "c" plus Period.

"PANAMA" reading up and down

20	A3 8c on 50c bis brn	45.00	40.00
a.	"CANAL" in antique type	200.00	180.00
b.	"ZONE" in antique type	200.00	180.00
c.	"8 cts" omitted	800.00	800.00
d.	"8 cts" double	*1,500.*	
e.	"cts. 8"		—

Numerous minor varieties of all these surcharges exist. Nos. 14, 18, 19 and 20 exist without CANAL ZONE overprint and are considered to be printer's waste.

Vasco Nunez de Balboa A5

Francisco Hernandez de Cordoba A6

Justo Arosemena A7

Manuel J. Hurtado A8

Jose de Obaldia — A9

Stamps of Panama Ovptd. in Black

1906-07

Overprint Reading Up

21	A6 2c red & black	25.00	25.00
a.	"CANAL" only	*4,000.*	

Overprint Reading Down

22	A5 1c green & black	2.25	1.25
a.	Horiz. pair, imperf. btwn.	1,300.	1,300.
b.	Vert. pair, imperf. btwn.	*2,000.*	*1,750.*
c.	Vert. pair, imperf. horiz.	*2,250.*	*1,750.*
d.	Invtd. ovpt., reading up	550.00	550.00
e.	Double overprint	275.00	275.00
f.	Dbl. ovpt., one reading up	1,750.	1,600.
g.	Inverted center and ovpt. reading up	*5,000.*	*5,000.*
23	A6 2c red & black	3.25	1.40
a.	Horiz. pair, imperf. btwn.	2,000.	1,750.
b.	Vertical pair, one without overprint	2,500.	2,500.
c.	Double overprint	650.00	650.00
d.	Dbl. ovpt., one diagonal	800.00	800.00
e.	Pair, Nos. 23, 23d	2,500.	
f.	2c carmine red & black	5.00	2.75
g.	As "f," inverted center and overprint reading up		*6,000.*
h.	As "d," one "ZONE CANAL"	*4,000.*	
i.	"CANAL" double	*4,000.*	
24	A7 5c ultra & black	6.50	2.25
c.	Double overprint	500.00	400.00
d.	"CANAL" only	*4,000.*	
e.	"ZONE CANAL"	*4,500.*	
25	A8 8c purple & black	22.50	8.00
a.	Horizontal pair, imperf. between and at left margin	2,000.	4,000.
26	A9 10c violet & black	20.00	8.00
a.	Dbl. ovpt., one reading up	*5,000.*	
b.	Overprint reading up	*5,500.*	
	Nos. 22-26 (5)	54.50	20.90

Nos. 22 to 25 occur with "CA" spaced.

Cordoba A11

Arosemena A12

Hurtado A13

Jose de Obaldia A14

Overprint Reading Down

1909

27	A11 2c ver & blk	12.50	5.50
a.	Horiz. pair, one without ovpt.	*2,600.*	
b.	Vert. pair, one without ovpt.	*3,500.*	
28	A12 5c dp bl & blk	45.00	12.50
29	A13 8c violet & black	40.00	14.00
30	A14 10c violet & black	40.00	15.00
a.	Horiz. pair, one without ovpt.	*2,400.*	
b.	Vert. pair, one without ovpt.	*3,000.*	
	Nos. 27-30 (4)	137.50	47.00

Nos. 27-30 occur with "CA" spaced.

Do not confuse #27 with #39d or 53a.

For designs A11-A14 with overprints reading up, see Nos. 32-35, 39-41, 47-48, 53-54, 56-57.

Vasco Nunez de Balboa — A15

Type I

Black Overprint, Reading Up

Type I Overprint: "C" with serifs both top and bottom. "L" "Z" and "E" with slanting serif.

Compare Type I overprint with Types II to V illustrated before Nos. 38, 46, 52 and 55. Illustrations of Types I to V are considerably enlarged and do not show actual spacing between lines of overprint.

1909-10

31	A15 1c dk green & blk	4.00	1.60
a.	Inverted center and overprint reading down		*22,500.*
c.	Bklt. pane of 6 handmade, perf. margins	575.00	
32	A11 2c vermilion & blk	4.50	1.60
a.	Vert. pair, imperf. horiz	1,000.	1,000.
c.	Bklt. pane of 6, handmade, perf. margins	750.00	
d.	Double overprint		—
33	A12 5c dp blue & blk	17.00	4.00
a.	Double overprint	375.00	375.00
34	A13 8c vio & blk ('10)	11.00	5.25
a.	Vert. pair, one without ovpt.	*1,750.*	
35	A14 10c violet & black	50.00	20.00
	Nos. 31-35 (5)	86.50	32.45

See Nos. 38, 46, 52, 55.

A16

A17

Black Surcharge

1911

36	A16 10c on 13c gray	6.00	2.25
a.	"10 cts." inverted	350.00	300.00
b.	"10 cts." omitted	350.00	

1914

37	A17 10c gray	55.00	12.50

Type II: "C" with serif at top only. "L" and "E" with vertical serifs. "O" tilts to left

Black Overprint, Reading Up

1912-16

38	A15 1c grn & blk ('13)	11.00	3.00
a.	Vert. pair, one without ovpt.	1,750.	1,750.
b.	Booklet pane of 6	625.00	
c.	As "b," handmade, perf. margins	1,000.	
39	A11 2c vermilion & blk	8.50	1.40
a.	Horiz. pair, right stamp without ovpt.	1,250.	
b.	Horiz. pair, left stamp without ovpt.	1,750.	
c.	Booklet pane of 6	550.00	
d.	Overprint reading down	200.00	
e.	As "d," inverted center	600.00	*750.00*
f.	As "e," booklet pane of 6 handmade, perf. margins	*80,000.*	
g.	As "c," handmade, perf. margins	1,000.	
h.	As #39, "CANAL" only		1,100.
40	A12 5c dp blue & blk	22.50	3.25
a.	With portrait of 2c		*10,000.*
41	A14 10c vio & blk ('16)	47.50	8.50
	Nos. 38-41 (4)	89.50	16.15

Map of Panama Canal A18

Balboa Takes Possession of the Pacific Ocean — A19

Gatun Locks — A20

Culebra Cut — A21

Blue Overprint, Type II

1915

42	A18 1c dark green & black	8.50	6.50
43	A19 2c carmine & black	10.00	4.25
44	A20 5c blue & black	11.00	5.75
45	A21 10c orange & black	22.50	11.00
	Nos. 42-45 (4)	52.00	27.50

Type III: Similar to Type I but letters appear thinner, particularly the lower bar of "L," "Z" and "E." Impressions are often light, rough and irregular, and not centered

Black Overprint, Reading Up

1915-20

46 A15 1c green & black 160.00 125.00
a. Overprint reading down 375.00
b. Double overprint 350.00
c. "ZONE" double *4,250.*
d. Dbl. ovpt,, one "ZONE CANAL" 2,000.
47 A11 2c orange ver & blk 3,250. 100.00
48 A12 5c dp blue & black 500.00 175.00
Nos. 46-48 (3) 3,910. 400.00

S.S. "Panama" in Culebra Cut — A22

S.S. "Panama" in Culebra Cut — A23

S.S. "Cristobal" in Gatun Locks — A24

Blue Overprint, Type II

1917

49 A22 12c purple & black 17.50 5.50
50 A23 15c brt blue & black 55.00 25.00
51 A24 24c yel brown & black 40.00 15.00
Nos. 49-51 (3) 112.50 45.50

Type IV: "C" thick at bottom, "E" with center bar same length as top and bottom bars

Black Overprint, Reading Up

1918-20

52 A15 1c green & black 32.50 11.00
a. Overprint reading down 175.00 —
b. Booklet pane of 6 650.00
c. Bklt. pane of 6, left vert. row of 3 without ovpt. *7,500.*
d. Bklt. pane of 6, right vert. row of 3 with dbl. ovpt. *7,500.*
e. Horiz. bklt. pair, left stamp without overprint *3,000.*
f. Horiz. bklt. pair, right stamp with dbl. overprint *3,000.*
g. Double overprint, bklt. single *3,000.*
53 A11 2c vermilion & blk 110.00 7.00
a. Overprint reading down 150.00 150.00
b. Horizontal pair, right stamp without overprint 2,000.
c. Booklet pane of 6 1,050.
d. Bklt. pane of 6, left vert. row of 3 without ovpt. *15,000.*
e. Horiz. bklt. pair, left stamp without overprint *3,000.* *4,500.*
54 A12 5c dp blue & black ('20) 150.00 35.00
Nos. 52-54 (3) 292.50 53.00

Normal spacing between words of overprint on Nos. 52 and 53 is 9¼mm. On No. 54 and the booklet printings of Nos. 52 and 53, the normal spacing is 9mm. Minor spacing varieties are known.

No. 53e used is unique and is on cover.

Type V: Smaller block type 1¾mm high. "A" with flat top

Black Overprint, Reading Up

1920-21

55 A15 1c lt green & black 22.50 3.50
a. Overprint reading down 300.00 225.00
b. Horiz. pair, right stamp without ovpt. 1,750.
c. Horiz. pair, left stamp without ovpt. 1,000.
d. "ZONE" only *4,250.* —
e. Booklet pane of 6 *2,250.*
f. "CANAL" double *1,750.*
56 A11 2c orange ver & blk 8.50 2.25
a. Double overprint 600.00
b. Double overprint, one reading down 650.00
c. Horiz. pair, right stamp without ovpt. 1,500.
d. Horiz. pair, left stamp without ovpt. 1,250.
e. Vert. pair, one without overprint 1,500.
f. "ZONE" double 1,250.
g. Booklet pane of 6 850.00
h. "CANAL" double 1,000.
57 A12 5c dp blue & black 300.00 55.00
a. Horiz. pair, right stamp without ovpt. *2,500.*
b. Horiz. pair, left stamp without ovpt. *2,500.*
Nos. 55-57 (3) 331.00 60.75

Drydock at Balboa A25

Ship in Pedro Miguel Locks — A26

Black Overprint, Type V

1920

58 A25 50c orange & black 275.00 160.00
59 A26 1b dk violet & black 175.00 65.00

Jose Vallarino A27

The "Land Gate" A28

Bolivar's Tribute — A29

Municipal Building in 1821 and 1921 — A30

Statue of Balboa — A31

Tomas Herrera — A32

Jose de Fabrega — A33

Black or Red Overprint, Type V

1921

60 A27 1c green 3.75 1.40
a. "CANAL" double *2,500.*
b. Booklet pane of 6 *1,000.*
61 A28 2c carmine 3.00 1.50
a. Overprint reading down 200.00 *225.00*
b. Double overprint 900.00
c. Vert. pair, one without overprint *3,500.*
d. "CANAL" double *1,900.*
f. Booklet pane of 6 *2,100.*
62 A29 5c blue (R) 11.00 4.50
a. Overprint reading down (R) 60.00
63 A30 10c violet 18.00 7.50
a. Overprint reading down 90.00
64 A31 15c light blue 47.50 17.50
65 A32 24c black brown 70.00 22.50
66 A33 50c black 150.00 100.00
Nos. 60-66 (7) 303.25 154.90

Experts question the status of the 5c blue with a small type V overprint in red or black.

Black Overprint, Type III

1924

67 A27 1c green 500. 200.
a. "ZONE CANAL" reading down 850.
b. "ZONE" reading down *1,900.*
c. Se-tenant pair, #67a and 67b *2,750.*

Coat of Arms — A34

Black Overprint

1924

68 A34 1c dark green 11.00 4.50
69 A34 2c carmine 8.25 2.75

The 5c to lb values were prepared but never issued. See listing in the Scott U.S. Specialized Catalogue.

US Nos. 551-554, 557, 562, 564-566, and 569-571 Overprinted in Red or Black

Type A

Letters "A" with Flat Tops

Flat Plate Printing

1924-25 ***Perf. 11***

70 A154 ½c olive brown (R) 1.25 .75
Never hinged 2.50
71 A155 1c deep green 1.40 1.00
Never hinged 2.25
a. Inverted overprint 500.00 500.00
b. "ZONE" inverted 350.00 325.00
c. "CANAL" only 1,750.
d. "ZONE CANAL" 500.00
e. Booklet pane of 6 80.00
72 A156 1½c yellow brown 1.90 1.70
Never hinged 3.00
73 A157 2c carmine 7.50 1.70
Never hinged 11.00
a. Booklet pane of 6 175.00
74 A160 5c dark blue 19.00 7.50
Never hinged 29.00
75 A165 10c orange 40.00 20.00
Never hinged 57.50
76 A167 12c brown violet 35.00 32.50
Never hinged 52.50
a. "ZONE" inverted *3,750.* *3,000.*
77 A168 14c dark blue 30.00 22.50
Never hinged 45.00
78 A169 15c gray 50.00 37.50
Never hinged 75.00
79 A172 30c olive brown 35.00 22.50
Never hinged 52.50
80 A173 50c lilac 77.50 45.00
Never hinged 115.00
81 A174 $1 violet brown 225.00 95.00
Never hinged 350.00
Nos. 70-81 (12) 523.55 287.65

The space between the two lines of the overprint, on both type A and B, varies on some settings.

US Nos. 554, 555, 557, 562, 564-567, 569-571 and 623 Overprinted in Black or Red

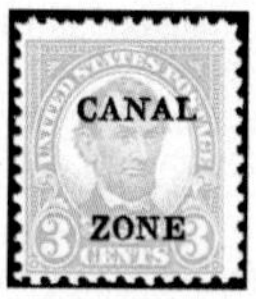

Type B

Letters "A" with Sharp Pointed Tops

1925-26

84 A157 2c carmine 30.00 8.00
Never hinged 45.00
a. "CANAL" ONLY *2,750.*
b. "ZONE CANAL" 500.00
c. Horiz. pair, one without overprint *3,500.*
d. Booklet pane of 6 175.00
e. Vertical pair, "a" and "b" se-tenant *2,750.*
85 A158 3c violet 4.00 3.25
Never hinged 6.00
a. "ZONE ZONE" 600.00 550.00
86 A160 5c dark blue 4.00 2.50
Never hinged 6.00
a. "ZONE ZONE" 1,250.
b. "CANAL" inverted 950.00
c. Inverted overprint 500.00
d. Pair, one without overprint *3,250.*
e. "ZONE CANAL" 350.00
f. "ZONE" only *2,000.*
g. Pair, one without ovpt., other ovpt. invtd. *2,500.*
h. "CANAL" only *2,250.*
87 A165 10c orange 35.00 13.00
Never hinged 52.50
a. "ZONE ZONE" *3,000.*
88 A167 12c brown violet 22.50 14.00
Never hinged 34.00
a. "ZONE ZONE" *5,250.*
89 A168 14c dark blue 27.50 16.00
Never hinged 42.50
90 A169 15c gray 7.50 4.50
Never hinged 10.50
a. "ZONE ZONE" *5,500.*
91 A187 17c black (R) 4.50 3.00
Never hinged 7.50
a. "ZONE" only 1,200.
b. "CANAL" only 1,700.
c. "ZONE CANAL" 300.00
92 A170 20c carmine rose 7.25 3.25
Never hinged 11.00
a. "CANAL" inverted *4,000.*
b. "ZONE" inverted *4,250.*
c. "ZONE CANAL" *3,600.*
93 A172 30c olive brown 5.75 4.00
Never hinged 8.00
94 A173 50c lilac 240.00 165.00
Never hinged 350.00
95 A174 $1 violet brown 150.00 60.00
Never hinged 225.00
Nos. 84-95 (12) 538.00 296.50

Overprint Type B on US Sesquicentennial Stamp No. 627

1926

96 A188 2c carmine rose 5.00 3.75
Never hinged 7.25

On this stamp there is a space of 5mm between the two words of the overprint.

Overprint Type B on US Nos. 583, 584 and 591

1927 ***Perf. 10***

97 A157 2c carmine 50.00 11.00
Never hinged 100.00
a. Pair, one without overprint *3,250.*
b. Booklet pane of 6 525.00
c. "CANAL" only *2,000.*
d. "ZONE" only *2,750.*
98 A158 3c violet 8.00 4.25
Never hinged 12.00
99 A165 10c orange 18.00 7.50
Never hinged 26.00
Nos. 97-99 (3) 76.00 22.75

Overprint Type B on US Nos. 632, 634, 635, 637 and 642

1927-31 ***Perf. 11x10½***

100 A155 1c green 2.25 1.40
Never hinged 3.50
a. Pair, one without overprint *5,500.*
101 A157 2c carmine 2.50 1.00
Never hinged 3.75
a. Booklet pane of 6 160.00
102 A158 3c violet 4.50 2.75
Never hinged 6.50
a. Booklet pane of 6, handmade, perf. margins *6,500.*
103 A160 5c dark blue 30.00 10.00
Never hinged 47.50
104 A165 10c orange 17.50 10.00
Never hinged 26.00
Nos. 100-104 (5) 56.75 25.15

Wet and Dry Printings

Canal Zone stamps printed by both the "wet" and "dry" process are Nos. 105, 108-109, 111-114, 117, 138-140, C21-C24, C26, J25, J27. Starting with Nos. 147 and C27, the Bureau of Engraving and Printing used the "dry" method exclusively. See note following US Scott 1029.

Maj. Gen. William Crawford Gorgas A35

Maj. Gen. George Washington Goethals A36

Gaillard Cut — A37

Maj. Gen. Harry Foote Hodges A38

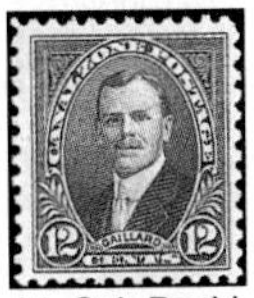

Lt. Col. David D. Gaillard A39

Maj. Gen. William L. Sibert — A40

Jackson Smith — A41

Rear Adm. Harry H. Rousseau A42

Col. Sydney B. Williamson A43

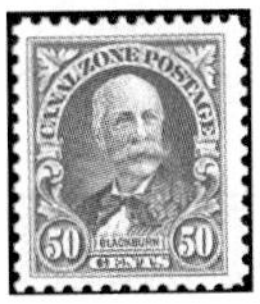

J.C.S. Blackburn — A44

1928-40			*Perf. 11*	
105	A35	1c green	.20	.20
		Never hinged	.25	
106	A36	2c carmine	.20	.20
		Never hinged	.25	
a.		Booklet pane of 6	15.00	*20.00*
		Never hinged	22.50	
107	A37	5c blue ('29)	1.00	.40
		Never hinged	1.30	
108	A38	10c orange ('32)	.20	.20
		Never hinged	.25	
109	A39	12c violet brown ('29)	.75	.60
		Never hinged	1.00	
110	A40	14c blue ('37)	.85	.85
		Never hinged	1.20	
111	A41	15c gray ('32)	.40	.35
		Never hinged	.55	
112	A42	20c olive brown ('32)	.60	.20
		Never hinged	.80	
113	A43	30c brown black ('40)	.80	.70
		Never hinged	1.10	
114	A44	50c lilac ('29)	1.50	.65
		Never hinged	2.00	
		Nos. 105-114 (10)	6.50	4.35

For surcharges & overprints see #J21-J24, O1-O8.

United States Nos. 720 and 695 Overprinted type B

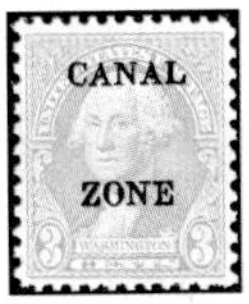

1933			*Perf. 11x10½*	
115	A226	3c deep violet	2.75	.25
		Never hinged	4.00	
b.		"CANAL" only	*2,600.*	
c.		Bklt. pane of 6, handmade, perf. margins	175.00	
116	A168	14c dark blue	4.50	3.50
		Never hinged	7.00	
a.		"ZONE CANAL"	*1,500.*	

Gen. George Washington Goethals — A45

1934, Aug. 15			*Perf. 11*	
117	A45	3c deep violet	.20	.20
		Never hinged	.25	
a.		Booklet pane of 6	45.00	*32.50*
		Never hinged	60.00	
b.		As "a," handmade, perf. margins	160.00	—

20th anniv. of the Panama Canal opening. See No. 153.

Catalogue values for unused stamps in this section, from this point to the end of the section, are for Never Hinged items.

US Nos. 803 and 805 Overprinted in Black

1939			*Perf. 11x10½*	
118	A275	½c deep orange	.20	.20
119	A277	1½c bister brown	.20	.20

Panama Canal Anniversary Issue

Balboa-Before — A46

Balboa-After — A47

Gaillard Cut-Before A48

Gaillard Cut-After A49

Bas Obispo-Before — A50

Bas Obispo-After A51

Gatun Locks-Before — A52

Gatun Locks-After A53

Canal Channel-Before A54

Canal Channel-After — A55

Gamboa-Before A56

Gamboa-After — A57

Pedro Miguel Locks-Before — A58

Pedro Miguel Locks-After A59

Gatun Spillway-Before A60

Gatun Spillway-After — A61

1939, Aug. 15			*Perf. 11*	
120	A46	1c yellow green	1.00	.30
121	A47	2c rose carmine	1.00	.35
122	A48	3c purple	1.00	.20
123	A49	5c dark blue	2.50	1.25
124	A50	6c red orange	5.00	3.00
125	A51	7c black	5.50	3.00
126	A52	8c green	7.00	3.50
127	A53	10c ultramarine	6.00	5.00
128	A54	11c blue green	11.00	8.00
129	A55	12c brown carmine	11.00	7.50
130	A56	14c dark violet	11.00	7.50
131	A57	15c olive green	15.00	6.00
132	A58	18c rose pink	16.00	8.50
133	A59	20c brown	17.50	7.50
134	A60	25c orange	25.00	17.50
135	A61	50c violet brown	30.00	6.00
		Nos. 120-135 (16)	165.50	85.10

25th anniv. of the Panama Canal.

AIR POST STAMPS

Nos. 105-106 Surcharged in Dark Blue

Type I — Flag of "5" pointing up **15**

Type II — Flag of "5" curved **15**

Flat Plat Printing

1929		Unwmk.	*Perf. 11*	
C1	A35	15c on 1c green, I	8.00	5.50
		Never hinged	12.00	
C2	A35	15c on 1c green, II	70.00	47.50
		Never hinged	115.00	
C3	A36	25c on 2c carmine	3.50	2.00
		Never hinged	5.25	
		Nos. C1-C3 (3)	81.50	55.00

Nos. 114 and 106 Surcharged

1929, Dec. 31				
C4	A44	10c on 50c lilac	7.50	6.50
		Never hinged	11.00	
C5	A36	20c on 2c carmine	5.00	1.75
		Never hinged	7.50	
a.		Dropped "2" in surcharge	80.00	60.00

Catalogue values for unused stamps in this section, from this point to the end of the section, are for Never Hinged items.

Gaillard Cut — AP1

1931-49			Engr.	
C6	AP1	4c red violet ('49)	.75	.70
C7	AP1	5c yellow green	.60	.45
C8	AP1	6c yellow brown ('46)	.75	.35
C9	AP1	10c orange	1.00	.35
C10	AP1	15c blue	1.25	.30
C11	AP1	20c red violet	2.00	.30
C12	AP1	30c rose lake ('41)	3.50	1.00
C13	AP1	40c yellow	3.50	1.10
C14	AP1	$1 black	8.50	1.90
		Nos. C6-C14 (9)	21.85	6.45

For overprints see Nos. CO1-CO14.

Douglas Plane over Sosa Hill — AP2

Planes and Map of Central America AP3

Pan American Clipper and Scene near Fort Amador AP4

Pan American Clipper at Cristobal Harbor AP5

Pan American Clipper over Gaillard Cut — AP6

Pan American Clipper Landing AP7

1939, July 15

C15 AP2	5c greenish black	3.75	2.25
C16 AP3	10c dull violet	3.25	3.00
C17 AP4	15c light brown	4.75	1.00
C18 AP5	25c blue	13.00	8.00
C19 AP6	30c rose carmine	13.00	7.75
C20 AP7	$1 green	35.00	27.50
	Nos. C15-C20 (6)	72.75	49.50

10th anniv. of Air Mail service and the 25th anniv. of the opening of the Panama Canal.

POSTAGE DUE STAMPS

Postage Due Stamps of the US Nos. J45a, J46a and J49a Overprinted in Black

1914, Mar. **Wmk. 190** ***Perf. 12***

J1 D2	1c rose carmine	85.00	15.00
J2 D2	2c rose carmine	250.00	42.50
J3 D2	10c rose carmine	1,000.	40.00

Castle Gate (See footnote) D1

Statue of Columbus D2

Pedro J. Sosa — D3

Blue Overprint, Type II, on Postage Due Stamps of Panama

1915 **Unwmk.**

J4 D1	1c olive brown	12.50	5.00
J5 D2	2c olive brown	225.00	17.50
J6 D3	10c olive brown	50.00	10.00

The 1c was intended to show a gate of San Lorenzo Castle, Chagres. By error the stamp actually shows the main gate of San Geronimo Castle, Portobelo.

Surcharged in Red

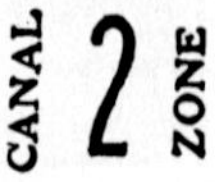

J7 D1	1c on 1c olive brn	110.00	15.00
J8 D2	2c on 2c olive brn	25.00	7.00
J9 D3	10c on 10c olive brn	22.50	5.00

Columbus Statue — D4

Capitol, Panama City — D5

Carmine Surcharge

1919

J10 D4	2c on 2c olive brown	30.00	12.50
J11 D5	4c on 4c olive brown	35.00	15.00
a.	"ZONE" omitted	*8,250.*	
b.	"4" omitted	*8,250.*	

Blue Overprint, Type V, on Postage Due Stamp of Panama

J11C D1	1c dark olive brown	—	10.00
a.	"CANAL ZONE" reading down	200.00	

US Postage Due Stamps Nos. J61, J62b and J65b Overprinted in Black

Letters "A" with Flat Tops

1924 ***Perf. 11***

J12 D2	1c carmine rose	100.00	27.50
J13 D2	2c deep claret	55.00	10.00
J14 D2	10c deep claret	225.00	50.00

US Postage Stamps Nos. 552, 554 and 562 Overprinted Type A and additional Overprint in Red or Blue

1925

J15 A155	1c deep green	90.00	13.00
J16 A157	2c carmine (Bl)	22.50	7.00
J17 A165	10c orange	50.00	11.00
a.	"POSTAGE DUE" double	450.00	
b.	"E" of "POSTAGE" missing	450.00	
c.	As "a" and "b"	*3,250.*	

"CANAL ZONE" Type B Overprinted on US Nos. J61, J62, J65, J65a

Letters "A" with Sharp Pointed Tops

1925

J18 D2	1c carmine rose	8.00	3.00
a.	"ZONE ZONE"	1,750.	
J19 D2	2c carmine rose	15.00	4.00
a.	"ZONE ZONE"	1,750.	
J20 D2	10c carmine rose	150.00	20.00
a.	Pair, one without overprint	*3,500.*	
b.	10c rose red	*250.00*	150.00
c.	As "b," double overprint	*450.00*	—

No. 107 Surcharged in Black

1929-30

J21 A37	1c on 5c blue	4.50	1.75
	Never hinged	9.00	
a.	"POSTAGE DUE" omitted	*5,500.*	
J22 A37	2c on 5c blue	7.50	2.50
	Never hinged	15.00	
J23 A37	5c on 5c blue	7.50	2.75
	Never hinged	15.00	
J24 A37	10c on 5c blue	7.50	2.75
	Never hinged	15.00	

On No. J23 the horizontal bars in the lower corners of the surcharge are omitted.

Canal Zone Seal — D6

1932-41

J25 D6	1c claret	.20	.20
	Never hinged	.25	
J26 D6	2c claret	.20	.20
	Never hinged	.25	
J27 D6	5c claret	.35	.20
	Never hinged	.40	
J28 D6	10c claret	1.40	1.50
	Never hinged	2.00	
J29 D6	15c claret ('41)	1.10	1.00
	Never hinged	1.50	
	Nos. J25-J29 (5)	3.25	3.10

The 1c and 5c are found in both "wet" and "dry" printings. (See note after US No. 1029.) The dry printings are in red violet.

GUAM

'gwäm

LOCATION — One of the Mariana Islands in the Pacific Ocean, about 1450 miles east of the Philippines
GOVT. — United States Possession
AREA — 206 sq. mi.
POP. — 9,000 (est. 1899)
CAPITAL — Agaña

Formerly a Spanish possession, Guam was ceded to the United States in 1898 following the Spanish-American War. Stamps overprinted "Guam" were superseded by the regular postage stamps of the United States in 1901.

100 Cents = 1 Dollar

US Nos. 279, 279B, 279Bc, 268, 280a, 281, 282, 272, 282C, 283, 284, 275, 275a, 276 and 276A Overprinted in Black (1c-50c) or Red ($1)

1899 **Wmk. 191** ***Perf. 12***

1 A87	1c deep green	20.00	*25.00*
	Never hinged	40.00	
	On cover		*200.00*
2 A88	2c red, type IV	17.50	*25.00*
	Never hinged	35.00	
	On cover		*200.00*
a.	2c rose carmine, IV	30.00	30.00
	Never hinged	60.00	
	On cover		*225.00*
3 A89	3c purple	140.00	*175.00*
	Never hinged	275.00	
	On cover		*400.00*
4 A90	4c lilac brown	135.00	*175.00*
	Never hinged	270.00	
	On cover		*450.00*
5 A91	5c blue	32.50	*45.00*
	Never hinged	65.00	
	On cover		*200.00*
6 A92	6c lake	125.00	*200.00*
	Never hinged	250.00	
	On cover		*450.00*
7 A93	8c violet brown	140.00	*200.00*
	Never hinged	275.00	
	On cover		*450.00*
8 A94	10c brown, type I	47.50	*55.00*
	Never hinged	95.00	
	On cover		*275.00*
9 A94	10c brown, type II	*3,750.*	—
	Never hinged	—	
10 A95	15c olive green	150.00	*175.00*
	Never hinged	300.00	
	On cover		*900.00*
11 A96	50c orange	350.00	*425.00*
	Never hinged	700.00	
	On cover		*1,250.*
a.	50c red orange	550.00	—
	Never hinged	1,100.	
12 A97	$1 black, type I	350.00	*400.00*
	Never hinged	700.00	
	On cover		*3,000.*
13 A97	$1 black, type II	*4,500.*	—
	Never hinged	—	
	Nos. 1-8,10-12 (11)	1,507.	*1,900.*

Counterfeit overprints exist.

SPECIAL DELIVERY STAMP

United States No. E5 Overprinted in Red

1899 **Wmk. 191** ***Perf. 12***

E1	SD3 10c blue	150.00	*200.00*
	Never hinged	275.00	
	On cover		*1,250.*

Guam Guard Mail stamps of 1930 are listed in the Scott Specialized United States Catalogue.

HAWAII

hə-'wä-yē

LOCATION — Group of 20 islands in the Pacific Ocean, about 2,000 miles southwest of San Francisco.
GOVT. — Former Kingdom and Republic
AREA — 6,435 sq. mi.
POP. — 150,000 (est. 1899)
CAPITAL — Honolulu

Until 1893 an independent kingdom, from 1893 to 1898 a republic, the Hawaiian Islands were annexed to the US in 1898.

100 Cents = 1 Dollar

> Values for Nos. 1-4 are for examples with minor damage that has been skillfully repaired.

A1

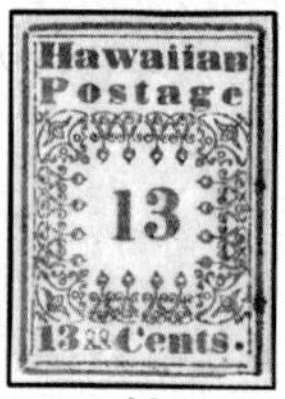

A2

A3

Pelure Paper

1851-52 **Unwmk.** **Typeset** ***Imperf.***

1 A1	2c blue	*660,000.*	*250,000.*
	On cover		*2,100,000.*
2 A1	5c blue	*55,000.*	*40,000.*
	On cover		*80,000.*
3 A2	13c blue	*37,000.*	*32,000.*
	On cover		*75,000.*
4 A3	13c blue	*52,500.*	*45,000.*
	On cover		*100,000.*

Two varieties of each.
No. 1 unused and on cover are unique.

King Kamehameha III
A4 A5

Thick White Wove Paper

1853 **Engr.**

5 A4	5c blue	2,250.	1,900.
	On cover		*4,000.*
	On cover with U.S. #17		*12,000.*
a.	Line through "Honolulu" (Pos. 2)	*3,250.*	*3,000.*

6 A5 13c dark red 600. *1,500.*
On cover *40,000.*
On cover with U.S. #11 (pair) *25,000.*
On cover with U.S. #17 *35,000.*
On cover with #5 and U.S. #17 *35,000.*
On cover with #5 and U.S. #36b *38,500.*

See #8-9. See Special Printings section, #10-11.

A6

1857

7 A6 5c on 13c dark red *7,000.* *17,000.*
On cover with pair U.S. #7, #15 *57,500.*
On cover with U.S. #14 *50,000.*
On cover with U.S. #11, 14 *55,000.*
On cover with U.S. #17 *60,000.*

1857

Thin White Wove Paper

8 A4 5c blue 650. *1,000.*
On cover *2,500.*
On cover with U.S. #11 —
On cover with U.S. #15 and #7 —
On cover with U.S. #17 *10,000.*
On cover with U.S. #26 —
On cover with U.S. #35 *11,000.*
On cover with U.S. #36 *10,000.*
On cover with U.S. #69 *12,500.*
On cover with U.S. #76 —
a. Line through "Honolulu" (Pos. 2) *1,250.* *1,250.*
On cover with U.S. #17 6,500.
b. Double impression *3,500.* *4,750.*

1861

Thin Bluish Wove Paper

9 A4 5c blue 350. 375.
On cover *5,000.*
On cover with U.S. #36b *3,250.*
On cover with U.S. #65 *3,000.*
On cover with U.S. #65 and #73 *6,500.*
On cover with U.S. #68 *4,250.*
On cover with U.S. #76 *7,000.*
a. Line through "Honolulu" (Pos. 2) *750.* *1,000.*

Re-issues

1868

Ordinary White Wove Paper

10 A4 5c blue 25.00
a. Line through "Honolulu" (Pos. 2) 55.00
11 A5 13c dull rose 300.00

Remainders of Nos. 10 and 11 were overprinted "SPECIMEN." Values, $60, $225 respectively.

Nos. 10 and 11 were never placed in use but copies (both with and without overprint) were sold at face value at the Honolulu post office.

REPRINTS (Official Imitations) 1889

5c Originals have two small dots near the left side of the square in the upper right corner. These dots are missing in the reprints.

13c The bottom of the 3 of 13 in the upper left corner is flattened in the originals and rounded in the reprints. The "t" of "Cts" on the left side is as tall as the "C" in the reprints, but shorter in the originals.

10R A4 5c **blue** 60.
Block of 4 275.
11R A5 13c **orange red** 300.
Block of 4 1,400.

On August 19, 1892, the remaining supply of reprints was overprinted in black "REPRINT." The reprints (both with and without overprint) were sold at face value.

Values for the Numeral stamps, Nos. 12-26, are for four-margin examples. Values for unused stamps are for examples without gum.

A7

A8

A9

1859-62 **Typeset**

12 A7 1c lt blue, *bluish white* *20,000.* *18,500.*
a. "1 Ce" omitted *22,500.*
b. "nt" omitted — —
13 A7 2c lt blue, *bluish white* *6,250.* *5,000.*
On cover *18,000.*
a. 2c dark blue, *grayish white* *6,750.* *5,000.*
b. Comma after "Cents" — *6,750.*
On cover *19,000.*
c. No period after "Leta" — —
14 A7 2c blk, *grnsh blue* ('62) *8,000.* *6,000.*
On cover *14,000.*
a. "2-Cents." — —

1863

15 A7 1c black, *grayish* 650. *3,000.*
On cover —
a. Tete beche pair *9,000.*
b. "NTER" —
c. Period omitted after "Postage" 850.
16 A7 2c black, *grayish* 1,000. 950.
On cover *5,000.*
a. "2" at top of rectangle *3,750.* *3,750.*
b. Printed on both sides — *21,000.*
c. "NTER" *3,250.* *6,500.*
d. 2c black, *grayish white* 1,000. 725.
e. Period omitted after "Cents" —
f. Overlapping impressions — —
g. "TAGE." — —
17 A7 2c dk blue, *bluish* *12,000.* *8,750.*
a. "ISL" — —
18 A7 2c black, *blue gray* *3,500.* *9,000.*
On cover *18,000.*

1864-65

19 A7 1c black 500. *10,000.*
20 A7 2c black 725. *1,500.*
On cover 19,000.
21 A8 5c blue, *blue* ('65) 850. 650.
On cover with U.S. #65 —
On cover with U.S. #68 —
On cover with U.S. #76 *8,250.*
a. Tete beche pair *10,500.*
b. 5c bluish black, *grayish white* *12,500.* *3,500.*
22 A9 5c blue, *blue* ('65) 550. *875.*
On cover *13,000.*
On cover with U.S. #76 *9,250.*
On cover with U.S. #63 and 76 —
a. Tete beche pair *20,000.*
b. 5c blue, *grayish white* —
c. Overlapping impressions —

1864 **Laid Paper**

23 A7 1c black 275. *2,500.*
On cover with U.S. #76 —
a. HA instead of HAWAIIAN *3,750.*
b. Tete beche pair *6,250.*
c. Tete beche pair, #23, 23a *18,000.*
24 A7 2c black 300. *1,050.*
a. "NTER" *3,750.*
b. "S" of "POSTAGE" omitted *1,500.*
c. Tete beche pair *5,500.*

A10

1865 **Wove Paper**

25 A10 1c dark blue 350.
a. Double impression —
b. With inverted impression of #21 *18,500.*
26 A10 2c dark blue 350.

Nos. 12-26 were typeset and were printed in settings of ten, each stamp differing from the others.

King Kamehameha IV
A11

1861-63 **Litho.**

Horizontally Laid Paper

27 A11 2c pale rose 325. 300.
On cover 1,000.
a. 2c carmine rose ('63) 3,000. 2,500.

Vertically Laid Paper

28 A11 2c pale rose 325. 300.
On cover *1,500.*
a. 2c carmine rose ('63) 300. *375.*
On cover *2,000.*

1869 **Engr.** **Thin Wove Paper**

29 A11 2c red 45.00 —

No. 29 was a re-issue sold only at the Honolulu post office, at first without overprint and later with overprint "CANCELLED."

See note following No. 51.

Princess Victoria Kamamalu — A12

King Kamehameha IV — A13

King Kamehameha V
A14 A15

Mataio Kekuanaoa — A16

1864-86 **Engr.** ***Perf. 12***

Wove Paper

30 A12 1c purple ('86) 11.00 8.00
On cover 150.00
a. 1c mauve ('71) 60.00 20.00
b. 1c violet ('78) 20.00 10.00
31 A13 2c vermilion ('86) 65.00 9.00
a. 2c rose vermilion 45.00 20.00
On cover 150.00
On cover with U.S. #76 *1,000.*
b. Half used as 1c on cover with #32 *8,500.*
32 A14 5c blue ('66) 175.00 30.00
On cover 250.00
On cover with any U.S. issues of 1861-67 *4,000.*
On cover with U.S. #116, 69 *25,000.*
33 A15 6c yellow green ('71) 45.00 9.00
On cover 300.00
a. 6c bluish green ('78) 35.00 9.00
On cover 300.00
On cover with U.S. #179 *1,500.*
On cover with U.S. #185 *800.00*
34 A16 18c dull rose ('71) 90.00 35.00
On cover 350.00
Nos. 30-34 (5) 386.00 91.00

No. 32 has traces of rectangular frame lines surrounding the design. Nos. 39 and 52C have no such frame lines.

For overprints see #53, 58-60, 65, 66C, 71.

King David Kalakaua
A17

Prince William Pitt Leleiohoku
A18

1875

35 A17 2c brown 8.50 3.00
On cover 200.00
36 A18 12c black 65.00 27.50
On cover 600.00

See Nos. 38, 43, 46. For overprints see Nos. 56, 62-63, 66, 69.

Princess Likelike
A19

King David Kalakaua
A20

Queen Kapiolani — A21

Statue of King Kamehameha I — A22

King William Lunalilo — A23

Queen Emma Kaleleonalani — A24

1882

37 A19 1c blue 11.00 6.00
On cover 40.00
38 A17 2c lilac rose 125.00 45.00
On cover 150.00
39 A14 5c ultramarine 15.00 3.25
On cover 27.50
a. Vert. pair, imperf. horiz. *5,000.* *4,250.*
40 A20 10c black 45.00 20.00
On cover 150.00
41 A21 15c red brown 60.00 25.00
On cover 200.00
Nos. 37-41 (5) 256.00 99.25

1883-86

42 A19 1c green 3.25 2.00
On cover 25.00
43 A17 2c rose ('86) 4.50 1.00
On cover 25.00
a. 2c dull red 62.50 21.00
44 A20 10c red brown ('84) 37.50 10.00
On cover 125.00
45 A20 10c vermilion 42.50 12.50
On cover 125.00
46 A18 12c red lilac 85.00 32.50
On cover 425.00
47 A22 25c dark violet 140.00 60.00
On cover 350.00
48 A23 50c red 175.00 85.00
On cover 500.00
49 A24 $1 rose red 275.00 250.00
On cover *8,000.*
Maltese cross cancellation 100.00
Nos. 42-49 (8) 762.75 453.00

Nos. 48-49 are valued used with postal cancels. Canceled-to-order cancels exist and are worth less.

Other fiscal cancellations exist on No. 49.

For overprints see Nos. 54-55, 57, 61-61B, 64, 67-68, 70, 72-73.

Reproduction and Reprint

Yellowish Wove Paper

1886-89 ***Imperf.***

50 A11 2c orange vermilion 160.00
51 A11 2c carmine ('89) 25.00

In 1885 the Postmaster General wished to have on sale complete sets of Hawaii's stamps as far back as type A11, but was unable to find either the stone from which Nos. 27 and 28, or the plate from which No. 29 was printed. He therefore sent a copy of No. 29 to the American Bank Note Co., with an order to engrave a new plate and print 10,000 stamps, of which 5000 were overprinted "Specimen" in blue.

The original No. 29 was printed in sheet of 15 (5x3), but the plate of these "Official Imitations" was made up of 50 stamps (10x5). Later, in 1887, the original die for No. 29 was discovered, and after retouching, a new plate was made and 37,500 stamps were printed. These, like the originals, were printed in sheets of 15. They were delivered during 1889 and 1890. In 1892 all remaining unsold in the Post Office were overprinted "Reprint."

No. 29 is red in color, and printed on very thin white wove paper. No. 50 is orange vermilion in color, on medium, white to buff paper. In No. 50 the vertical line on the left side of the portrait touches the horizontal line over the label "Elua Keneta", while in the other two varieties, Nos. 29 and 51, it does not touch the horizontal line by half a millimeter. In No. 51 there are three parallel lines on the left side of the King's nose, while in No. 29 and No. 50 there are no such lines. No. 51 is carmine in color and printed on thick, yellowish to buff wove paper.

It is claimed that both Nos. 50 and 51 were available for postage, although not made to fill a postal requirement.

Queen Liliuokalani — A25

1890-91 ***Perf. 12***

52 A25 2c dull violet ('91) 4.50 1.50
On cover 25.00
a. Vert. pair, imperf. horiz. *4,000.*
52C A14 5c deep indigo 120.00 150.00
On cover 500.00

Stamps of 1864-91 Overprinted in Red

Three categories of double overprints:
I. Both overprints heavy.
II. One overprint heavy, one of moderate strength.
III. One overprint heavy, one of light or weak strength.

1893

53 A12 1c purple 8.50 12.50
On cover 35.00
a. "189" instead of "1893" 575.00 —
b. No period after "GOVT" *265.00* *210.00*
f. Double overprint (III) *600.00*
54 A19 1c blue 8.50 *12.50*
On cover 40.00
b. No period after "GOVT" *140.00* *140.00*
e. Double overprint (II) *1,500.*
f. Double overprint (III) *400.00*
55 A19 1c green 1.75 *3.00*
On cover 25.00
d. Double overprint (I) *625.00* *450.00*
f. Double overprint (III) *200.00* *250.00*
g. Pair, one without ovpt. *10,000.*
56 A17 2c brown 12.00 *20.00*
On cover 60.00
b. No period after "GOVT" *300.00* —
57 A25 2c dull violet 1.50 1.25
On cover 25.00
a. "18 3" instead of "1893" *750.00* *500.00*
d. Double overprint (I) *1,300.* *650.00*
f. Double overprint (III) *175.00* *110.00*
g. Inverted overprint *4,000.* *4,500.*
58 A14 5c deep indigo 13.00 *25.00*
On cover 100.00
b. No period after "GOVT" *225.00* *250.00*
f. Double overprint (III) *1,250.*
59 A14 5c ultramarine 6.50 2.50
On cover 40.00
d. Double overprint (I) *6,500.*
e. Double overprint (II) *4,000.* *4,000.*
f. Double overprint (III) *600.00*
g. Inverted overprint *1,500.* *1,500.*
60 A15 6c green 17.50 *25.00*
On cover 135.00
e. Double overprint (II) *1,250.*
61 A20 10c black 12.00 *15.00*
On cover 125.00
e. Double overprint (II) *750.00* *650.00*
f. Double overprint (III) *200.00*
61B A20 10c red brown *14,000.* *29,000.*
62 A18 12c black 12.00 *17.50*
On cover 150.00
d. Double overprint (I) *2,000.*
e. Double overprint (II) *1,750.*
63 A18 12c red lilac 165.00 *250.00*
On cover 550.00
64 A22 25c dark violet 32.00 *40.00*
On cover 225.00
b. No period after "GOVT" *325.00* *325.00*
f. Double overprint (III) *1,000.*
Nos. 53-61,62-64 (12) 290.25 *424.25*

Overprinted in Black

65 A13 2c rose ver 80.00 *75.00*
On cover *450.00*
b. No period after "GOVT" *250.00* *250.00*
66 A17 2c rose 1.25 *2.25*
On cover 25.00
b. No period after "GOVT" 50.00 60.00
d. Double overprint (I) *4,000.*
e. Double overprint (II) *2,750.*
f. Double overprint (III) *300.00*
66C A15 6c green *14,000.* *29,000.*
On cover —
67 A20 10c vermilion 20.00 *30.00*
On cover 125.00
f. Double overprint (III) *1,250.*
68 A20 10c red brown 10.00 *13.00*
On cover 100.00
f. Double overprint (III) *4,000.*
69 A18 12c red lilac 325.00 *500.00*
On cover 950.00
70 A21 15c red brown 22.50 *30.00*
On cover 300.00
e. Double overprint (II) *2,000.*
71 A16 18c dull rose 35.00 *35.00*
On cover 225.00
a. "18 3" instead of "1893" *475.00* *475.00*
b. No period after "GOVT" *300.00* *300.00*
d. Double overprint (I) *600.00*
f. Double overprint (III) *250.00* —
g. Pair, one without ovpt. *3,500.*
h. As "b," double overprint (II) *1,750.*
72 A23 50c red 75.00 *90.00*
On cover 600.00
b. No period after "GOVT" *400.00* *400.00*
f. Double overprint (III) *1,000.*
73 A24 $1 rose red 135.00 *175.00*
On cover 750.00
b. No period after "GOVT" *450.00* 425.00
Nos. 65-66,67-73 (9) 703.75 *950.25*

Coat of Arms — A26

View of Honolulu — A27

Statue of Kamehameha I — A28

Stars and Palms — A29

S. S. "Arawa" — A30

Pres. Sanford Ballard Dole — A31

"CENTS" Added — A32

1894

74 A26 1c yellow 2.25 1.25
On cover 25.00
75 A27 2c brown 2.25 .60
On cover 25.00
76 A28 5c rose lake 5.00 2.00
On cover 25.00
77 A29 10c yellow green 7.50 5.00
On cover 45.00
78 A30 12c blue 15.00 *17.50*
On cover 150.00
79 A31 25c deep blue 20.00 13.50
On cover 100.00
Nos. 74-79 (6) 52.00 *39.85*

1899

80 A26 1c dark green 1.75 1.25
On cover 25.00
81 A27 2c rose 1.40 1.00
On cover 20.00
a. 2c salmon 1.50 1.25
b. Vert. pair, imperf. horiz. *4,500.*
82 A32 5c blue 7.50 3.25
On cover 25.00
Nos. 80-82 (3) 10.65 5.50

OFFICIAL STAMPS

Lorrin Andrews Thurston — O1

1896 **Unwmk.** **Engr.** ***Perf. 12***

O1 O1 2c green 40.00 17.50
On cover 400.00
O2 O1 5c black brown 40.00 17.50
On cover 450.00
O3 O1 6c deep ultra 40.00 17.50
On cover —
O4 O1 10c bright rose 40.00 17.50
On cover 500.00
O5 O1 12c orange 50.00 17.50
On cover —
O6 O1 25c gray violet 57.50 17.50
On cover —
Nos. O1-O6 (6) 267.50 105.00

Used values for #O1-O6 are for copies cto "FOREIGN OFFICE/HONOLULU H.I." in double circle without date.

The stamps of Hawaii were replaced by those of the United States.

ADEN

'ä-dᵊn

LOCATION — Southern Arabia
GOVT. — British colony and protectorate
AREA — 112,075 sq. mi.
POP. — 48,338
CAPITAL — Aden

Aden used India stamps before 1937.

12 Pies = 1 Anna
16 Annas = 1 Rupee

Catalogue values for unused stamps in this country are for Never Hinged items.

STAMPS OF INDIA USED IN ADEN

Type A

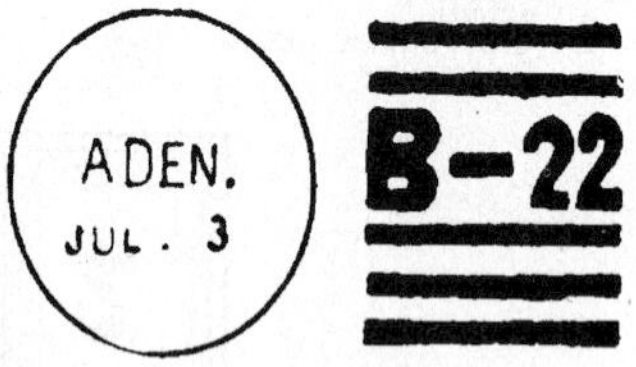

Type B

Stamps of India with Types A or B cancellations associated with circular datestamps of "ADEN," "ADEN CAMP," "ADEN STEAMER POINT" OR "ADEN CANTONMENT". Many other cancellations exist. Values shown are for the most common cancellation.

1854

A1 ½a blue, Die I (#2) *250.00*
Pair (#2) *900.00*
Strip or block of 4 (#2) *3,750.*
A4 1a red (#4) *350.00*
1a Pair (#4), #132 cancel *1,750.*
A7 2a green (#5) *500.00*
Pair (#5) *1,750.*
A11 4a bl & car (#6, 6a) *425.00*
Pair (#6, 6a) *1,100.*
Strip of 3 (#6, 6a) —

Values for #A11 are for stamps and covers bearing stamps that are cut to shape. Examples with complete margins sell for much more. Multiples will have a cancellation on each stamp.

Virtually all stamps of British India, including officials from 1854 to 1937, may be found used in Aden. The listings below include issues from 1855 to 1936. Values are for clear strikes of the more common postmarks.

1855-64 **Unwmk.**

Blue Glazed Paper

A13 4a black (#9) *90.00*
A14 8a rose (#10) *90.00*

1855-64 **Unwmk.** **White Paper**

A15 ½p blue (#11) *15.00*
A16 1a brown (#12) *17.50*
A17 2a dull rose (#13) *65.00*
A18 2a buff (#15) *65.00*
a. 2a orange (#15a) *75.00*
A19 4a black (#16) *25.00*
A20 4a green (#17) *25.00*
A21 8a rose (#18) *75.00*

1860-64 **Unwmk.**

A22 8p lilac (#19) *25.00*
A23 8p lilac, *bluish* (#19C) —

1865-67 **Wmk. 38**

A24 ½a blue (#20) *10.00*
A25 8p lilac (#21) *35.00*
A26 1a brown (#22) *10.00*
A27 2a orange (#23) *12.50*
a. 2a yellow (#23a) *17.50*
A28 4a green (#24) *75.00*
A29 8a rose (#25) —

1866-68 **Wmk. 38**

A30 4a green (#26) *15.00*
A31 4a blue green (#26B) *12.00*
A32 6a8p slate (#27) *75.00*
A33 8a rose ('68)(#28) *25.00*

1866 **Wmk. 36**

A34 6a violet (#29) —
A35 6a violet (#30) —

1873-76 **Wmk. 38**

A36 ½a blue (#31) *10.00*
A37 9p lilac (#32) —
A38 6a bister (#33) *12.00*
A39 12a red brown (#34) *50.00*
A40 1r slate (#35) *75.00*

1882-87 **Wmk. 39**

A41 ½a green (#36) *8.00*
A42 9p rose (#37) *12.00*
A43 1a maroon (#38) *7.00*
A44 1a6p bister brown (#39) *12.00*
A45 2a ultra (#40) *7.00*
A46 3a brown orange (#41) *10.00*
A47 4a olive green (#42) *10.00*
A48 4a6p green (#43) *20.00*
A49 8a red violet (#44) *14.00*
A50 12a violet, *red* (#45) *15.00*
A51 1r gray (#46) *25.00*

1891

A52 2½a on 4a6p green (#47) *12.50*

1892

A53 2a6p green (#48) *10.00*
A54 1r aniline car & grn (#49) *15.00*
A55 1r car rose & green (#49a) *25.00*

1895

A56 2r brown & rose (#50) —
A57 3r green & brown (#51) —
A58 5r vio & ultra (#52) —

1898

A59 ¼a on ½a green (#53) *10.00*

1899-1900

A60 3p car rose (#54) *7.00*
A61 3p gray (#55) *10.00*
A62 ½a light green (#56) *7.00*
A63 1a carmine rose (#57) *7.00*
A64 2a violet (#58) *8.00*
A65 2a6p ultramarine (#59) *10.00*

1902-09

A68 3p gray (#60) *7.00*
A69 ½a green (#61) *8.00*
A70 1a carmine rose (#62) *7.00*
A71 2a violet (#63) *7.00*
A72 2a6p ultramarine (#64) *9.00*
A73 3a brown orange (#65) *9.00*
A74 4a olive green (#66) *9.00*
A75 6a bister (#67) *25.00*
A76 8a red violet (#68) *10.00*
A77 12a red (#69) *20.00*
A78 1r car rose & grn (#70) *15.00*
A79 2r brown & rose (#71) *20.00*
A80 3r green & brown ('04) (#72) *75.00*
A81 5r vio & ultra ('04) (#73) *100.00*
A82 10r car rose & grn ('09) (#74) —

A83	15r ol gray & ultra ('09) (#75)	—
A84	25r ultra & org brn (#76)	—

1905

A85	¼p on ½a green (#77)	8.00

1906

A86	½a green (#78)	7.50
A87	1a carmine rose (#79)	7.50

1911-23

A88	3p gray (#80)	7.50
A89	½a green (#81)	7.50
A90	1a carmine rose (#82)	7.50
A91	1a dk brown (#83)	7.50
A92	2a dull violet (#84)	7.50
A93	2a6p ultramarine (#85)	17.50
A94	3a brown orange (#86)	7.50
A95	3a ultramarine (#87)	7.50
A96	4a olive green (#88)	7.50
A97	6a yel bister (#89)	7.50
A98	6a bister (#90)	7.50
A99	8a red violet (#91)	10.00
A100	12a claret (#92)	12.50
A101	1r grn & red brn (#93)	12.50
A102	2r brn & car rose (#94)	15.00
A103	5r vio & ultra (#95)	25.00
A104	10r car rose & grn (#96)	—
A105	15r ol grn & ultra (#97)	—
A106	25r ultra & brn org (#98)	—

1913-26

A107	2a6p ultramarine (#99)	7.50
A108	2a6p orange ('26) (#100)	17.50

1919

A109	1½a chocolate (#101)	8.00

1921-26

A110	1½a chocolate (#102)	20.00
A111	1½a rose ('26) (#103)	8.00

1921

A112	9p on 1a rose (#104)	7.50

1922

A113	¼p on ½a green (#105)	7.50

1926-36

A114	3p slate (#106)	7.50
A115	½a green (#107)	7.50
A116	1a dark brown (#108)	7.50
A117	1½a car rose ('29) (#109)	7.50
A118	2a dull violet (#110)	7.50
A119	2a vermilion ('34) (#111)	17.50
A120	2a6p buff (#112)	7.50
A121	3a ultramarine (#113)	7.50
A122	3a blue ('30) (#114)	7.50
A123	3a car rose ('32) (#115)	7.50
A124	4a olive green (#116)	7.50
A125	6a bister ('35) (#117)	10.00
A126	8a red violet (#118)	7.50
A127	12a claret (#119)	7.50
A128	1r grn & brn (#120)	7.50
A129	2r brn org & car rose (#121)	9.00
A130	5r dk vio & ultra (#122)	20.00
A131	10r carmine & green (#123)	—
A132	15r ol grn & ultra (#124)	—
A133	25r ultra & brn (#125)	—

1926-32

A134	2a dull violet (#126)	7.50
A135	2a vermilion ('32) (#127)	—
A136	4a olive green (#128)	7.50

1931, Feb. 9

A137	¼a brn & olive grn (#129)	12.50
A138	½a grn & vio (#130)	10.00
A139	1a choc & red vio (#131)	10.00
A140	2a blue green (#132)	30.00
A141	3a car & choc (#133)	40.00
A142	1r deep blue (#134)	75.00

1932

A143	9p dark green (#135)	7.50
A144	1a3p violet (#136)	7.50
A145	3a6p dark green (#137)	7.50

1934

A146	½a green (#138)	7.50
A147	1a dark brown (#139)	7.50

1935

A148	½a lt grn & blk (#142)	10.00
A149	9p dull grn & blk (#143)	10.00
A150	1a brn & blk (#144)	10.00
A151	1½a vio & blk (#145)	10.00
A152	2½a brn org & blk (#146)	10.00
A153	3½a blue & blk (#147)	15.00
A154	8a rose lil & blk (#148)	30.00

A cancellation reading "Support the Jubilee Fund / Aden" exists and is very scarce. Values on postcards or covers from $250.

OFFICIAL STAMPS OF INDIA USED IN ADEN

1866 **Unwmk.**

AO1	½a blue (#O1)	—
AO2	1a brown (#O3)	—
AO3	8a rose (#O4)	—

Wmk. 38

AO4	½a blue (#O5)	55.00
AO5	8p lilac (#O6)	—
AO6	1a brown (#O7)	55.00
AO7	2a yellow (#O8)	—
AO8	4a green (#O9)	—
AO9	4a green (#O10)	—

1866-73 **Wmk. 38**

AO10	½a blue (#O16)	10.00
AO11	½a blue, re-engraved (#O17)	—
AO12	1a brown (#O18)	10.00
AO13	2a orange (#O19)	17.50
AO14	4a green (#O20)	15.00
AO15	8a rose (#O21)	15.00

1874-82

AO16	½a blue, re-engraved (#O22)	10.00
AO17	1a brown (#O23)	8.00
AO18	2a orange (#O24)	50.00
AO19	4a green (#O25)	22.50
AO20	8a rose (#O26)	25.00

1883-87 **Wmk. 39**

AO21	½a green (#O27)	10.00
AO22	1a maroon (#O28)	10.00
AO23	2a ultra (#O29)	15.00
AO24	4a ol green (#O30)	10.00
AO25	8a red violet (#O31)	10.00
AO26	1r car rose & green (#O32)	10.00

1899-1900

AO28	3p car rose (#O33)	10.00
AO29	½a light green (#O34)	12.50
AO30	1a car rose (#O35)	10.00
AO31	2a violet (#O36)	12.50

1902-05

AO32	3p gray (#O37)	10.00
AO33	½a green (#O38)	10.00
AO34	1a carmine rose (#O39)	10.00
AO35	2a violet (#O40)	10.00
AO36	4a olive green (#O41)	10.00
AO37	6a bister (#O42)	10.00
AO38	8a red lilac (#O43)	12.50
AO39	1r car rose & grn ('05) (#O44)	15.00

1906-07

AO40	½a green (#O45)	10.00
AO41	1a carmine rose (#O46)	10.00

1909

AO42	2r brn & rose (#O47)	—
AO43	5r vio & ultra (#O48)	—
AO44	10r car rose & grn (#O49)	—
AO44a	10r red & grn (#O49a)	—
AO45	15r ol gray & ultra (#O50)	—
AO46	25r ultra & org brn (#O51)	—

1911-23

AO47	3p gray (#O52)	7.50
AO48	½a green (#O53)	7.50
AO49	1a carmine rose (#O54)	7.50
AO50	1a dk brown (#O55)	7.50
AO51	2a dull violet (#O56)	7.50
AO52	4a olive green (#O57)	7.50
AO53	6a bister (#O58)	10.00
AO54	8a red violet (#O59)	7.50
AO55	1r grn & brn (#O60)	12.50
AO56	2r brn & car rose (#O61)	25.00
AO57	5r vio & ultra (#O62)	—
AO58	10r car rose & grn (#O63)	—
AO59	15r ol grn & ultra (#O64)	—
AO60	25r ultra & brn org (#O65)	—

While only stamps of India were sold in Aden, stamps from other countries were canceled there. Aden was a major transfer point for mail from the Far East, Indian Ocean and East Africa and it was not uncommon for ships to arrive with uncanceled mail aboard. This included mail not canceled in the country of origin and letters posted at sea prior to the 1894 use of Paquebot markings. Such mail appropriately received Aden postmarks as it transited the country.

STAMPS OF CEYLON USED IN ADEN

Type A cancellation with associated circular datestamp.

1857-66

A168	1p blue (#3)	—
A169	2p deep green (#4)	300.00
a.	2p yellow green (#4a)	375.00
A170	5p org brn (#6)	—
A171	6p bis brn (#28)	—
A172	9p deep brn (#32)	—
A173	10p vermilion (#33)	—
A174	1sh violet (#34)	—
A175	1p blue (#46)	—
A176	6p chocolate brn (#53)	—
A177	9p brown (#55)	—

STAMPS OF GREAT BRITAIN USED IN ADEN

Type A cancellation with associated circular datestamp.

1856-62

A190	1p rose red (#20)	—
A191	4p rose (#26)	—
A192	6p lilac (#39)	—
A193	1sh green (#42)	—

STAMPS OF MAURITIUS USED IN ADEN

Type A cancellation with associated circular datestamp.

1848-63

A200	1p org red (#5b)	900.00
A201	9p magenta (#11)	—
A202	2p blue (#14c)	—
A203	2p blue (#15)	—
A204	6p blue (#18)	—
A205	1sh vermilion (#19)	—
A206	2p blue (#25)	—
A207	4p rose (#26)	—

Dhow — A1

Perf. 13x11½

1937, Apr. 1 **Engr.** **Wmk. 4**

1	A1 ½a lt green	4.00	2.40
	On cover		15.00
2	A1 9p dark green	4.00	3.00
	On cover		17.50
3	A1 1a black brown	4.00	1.00
	On cover		10.00
4	A1 2a red	4.00	2.75
	On cover		17.50
5	A1 2½a blue	4.50	1.25
	On cover		10.00
6	A1 3a carmine rose	10.50	8.00
	On cover		47.50
7	A1 3½a gray blue	8.00	3.75
	On cover		22.50
8	A1 8a rose lilac	25.00	7.50
	On cover		45.00
9	A1 1r brown	42.50	8.50
	On cover		50.00
10	A1 2r orange yellow	62.50	22.50
	On cover		140.00
11	A1 5r rose violet	115.00	80.00
	On cover		400.00
a.	5r reddish purple, aniline	375.00	95.00
	On cover		400.00
12	A1 10r olive green	375.00	400.00
	On cover		500.00
	Nos. 1-12 (12)	*659.00*	*540.65*
	Set, hinged	275.00	
	Set, perforated "SPECIMEN"	350.00	

Covers: Values for Nos. 10-12 are for over-franked covers, usually philatelic.

Common Design Types pictured following the introduction.

Coronation Issue

Common Design Type

1937, May 12 ***Perf. 13½x14***

13	CD302 1a black brown	.80	1.25
	On cover		4.00
14	CD302 2½a blue	.95	1.50
	On cover		6.00
15	CD302 3½a gray blue	1.25	3.00
	On cover		12.50
	Nos. 13-15 (3)	3.00	5.75
	Set, hinged	2.00	
	Set, perforated "SPECIMEN"	90.00	

Values are for covers with correct frankings. Philatelic covers sell for less.

Aidrus Mosque — A2

¾a, 5r, Camel Corpsman. 1a, 2r, Aden Harbor. 1½a, 1r, Adenese dhow. 2½a, 8a, Mukalla. 3a, 14a, 10r, Capture of Aden, 1839.

1939-48 **Engr.** **Wmk. 4** ***Perf. 12½***

16	A2 ½a green (7/42)	.45	.50
a.	½a yellow green	.55	.65
b.	½a blue green (9/48)	2.75	4.25
17	A2 ¾a red brn	1.75	1.25
a.	¾a brn vio	2.25	2.25
18	A2 1a brt lt blue	.25	.40
a.	1a light blue	1.75	.25
19	A2 1½a red	.75	.65
20	A2 2a dark brown	.25	.25
a.	2a sepia	3.75	2.25
21	A2 2½a brt ultra	.45	.30
22	A2 3a rose car & dk brn	.65	.25
23	A2 8a orange	.90	.40
b.	8a red orange	1.00	.45
23A	A2 14a lt bl & brn blk ('45)	2.50	1.00
24	A2 1r bright green	2.40	2.00
a.	1r emerald green	2.75	2.50
25	A2 2r dp mag & bl blk ('44)	5.00	2.40
a.	2r rose vio & indigo	7.00	3.00
26	A2 5r dp ol & lake brn (1/44)	16.00	9.50
a.	5r olive grn & red brn	12.50	8.75
27	A2 10r brt vio & brn	30.00	12.50
a.	10r dark pur & lake brn	30.00	12.50
	Nos. 16-27 (13)	61.35	31.40
	Set, cheapest shades, hinged	37.50	
	Set, perforated "SPECIMEN"	190.00	

Peace Issue

Common Design Type

Perf. 13½x14

1946, Oct. 15 **Engr.** **Wmk. 4**

28	CD303 1½a carmine	.20	1.50
29	CD303 2½a deep blue	.30	.65
a.	Wmk. inverted	*625.00*	
	Hinged	*475.00*	
	Set, perforated "SPECIMEN"	65.00	

Return to peace at end of World War II.

Silver Wedding Issue

Common Design Types

1949, Jan. 17 **Photo.** ***Perf. 14x14½***

30	CD304 1½a scarlet	.40	4.50

Engraved; Name Typographed

Perf. 11½x11

31	CD305 10r purple	30.00	37.50

25th anniv. of the marriage of King George VI and Queen Elizabeth.

UPU Issue

Common Design Types

Surcharged with New Values in Annas and Rupees

Engr.; Name typo. on Nos. 33-34

1949, Oct. 10 ***Perf. 13½, 11x11½***

32	CD306 2½a on 20c dp ultra	.60	1.60
33	CD307 3a on 30c dp car	1.90	1.60
34	CD308 8a on 50c org	1.25	1.60
35	CD309 1r on 1sh blue	1.75	3.00
	Nos. 32-35 (4)	5.50	7.80

75th anniv. of the formation of the UPU.

Nos. 18 and 20-27 Surcharged with New Values in Black or Carmine

1951, Oct. 1 **Wmk. 4** ***Perf. 12½***

36	A2 5c on 1a #18a	.20	.35
a.	On #18	.50	.50
37	A2 10c on 2a #20a	.20	.45
a.	On #20	.50	.50
b.	On 2a sepia brown	.50	.50

38 A2 15c on 2½a .20 *1.25*
a. Double surcharge *900.00*
Hinged *675.00*
39 A2 20c on 3a .30 *.40*
a. On 3a dp sepia & car rose 1.25 1.25
40 A2 30c on 8a #23b (C) .30 *.65*
41 A2 50c on 8a #23b .30 *.35*
a. Double surcharge, one albino *2,250.*
42 A2 70c on 14a 2.00 1.60
a. On 14a dk sepia & br lt blue 2.00 1.75
43 A2 1sh on 1r #24a .40 *.30*
44 A2 2sh on 2r #25 9.50 3.00
a. On #25a 7.50 6.50
b. On #25, albino surcharge *575.00*
45 A2 5sh on 5r #26 18.00 11.00
a. On 5r lake brown & sage green 16.50 12.50
46 A2 10sh on 10r #27 27.50 12.00
Nos. 36-46 (11) 58.90 31.35

Surcharge on No. 40 includes 2 bars.

Number 38a occured when one sheet was fed through the printing press twice, one time at a slight angle. Values for No. 38a are for examples with the surcharges clearly separated. Some positions have the 2nd overprint almost directly over the 1st, and, while rare, are in less demand and sell for less.

Nos. 37b, 39a, 42a and 45a are surcharged on stamps especially produced for this purpose and were not issued in these shades without surcharge.

KATHIRI

LOCATION — In Eastern Aden Protectorate
GOVT. — Sultanate
CAPITAL — Seiyun

The stamps of the Kathiri State of Seiyun were valid for use throughout Aden. Used copies generally bear Aden GPO or Aden Camp cancels. Examples with cancels from offices in the Eastern Protectorate command a premium.

Sultan Ja'far bin Mansur al Kathiri — A1

Seiyun — A2

Minaret at Tarim — A3

Designs: 2½a, Mosque at Seiyun. 3a, Palace at Tarim. 8a, Mosque at Seiyun, horiz. 1r, South Gate, Tarim. 2r, Kathiri House. 5r, Mosque at Tarim.

1942 Engr. Wmk. 4 *Perf. 13¾x14*
1 A1 ½a dark green .20 *.75*
a. Perf. 14 line .50 *1.00*
2 A1 ¾a copper brown .40 *1.60*
a. Perf. 14 line .55 *1.00*
3 A1 1a deep blue .75 .75
a. Perf. 14 line .75 *1.00*

Perf. 13x11½, 11½x13
4 A2 1½a dark car rose .75 *1.00*
a. 1½a dp car rose, analine 1.60 *2.00*
5 A3 2a sepia brown .40 *.95*
a. 2a sepia 1.25 *2.00*
6 A3 2½a deep blue 1.25 1.00
7 A2 3a dk car rose & dull brn 1.90 *2.75*
a. 3a car & sepia brn 2.00 *2.50*
8 A2 8a orange red 1.40 .90
9 A3 1r green 3.75 2.40
10 A2 2r rose vio & dk blue 7.50 *11.50*
a. 2r dp pur & dk bl 10.00 *12.50*
11 A3 5r gray green & fawn 24.00 19.00
Nos. 1-11 (11) 42.30 *42.60*
Set, perforated "SPECIMEN" 170.00

For surcharges see Nos. 20-27.

Nos. 4, 6 Ovptd. in Black or Red:

a

b

Perf. 13x11½, 11½x13
1946, Oct. 15 Wmk. 4
12 A2 (a) 1½a dark car rose .20 *.65*
13 A3 (b) 2½a deep blue (R) .25 .25
a. Inverted overprint 625.00
Hinged 425.00
b. Double overprint —
Set, perforated "SPECIMEN" 70.00

Victory of the Allied Nations in WWII.
All examples of No. 13b have the 2nd overprint almost directly over the 1st.

Silver Wedding Issue
Common Design Types

1949, Jan. 17 Photo. *Perf. 14x14½*
14 CD304 1½a scarlet .35 *2.50*

Engraved; Name Typo.
Perf. 11½x11
15 CD305 5r green 17.00 *10.00*

25th anniv. of the marriage of King George VI and Queen Elizabeth.

UPU Issue
Common Design Types
Surcharged with New Values in Annas and Rupees

Engr.; Name Typo. on Nos. 17-18
1949, Oct. 10 *Perf. 13½, 11x11½*
16 CD306 2½a on 20c dp ultra .25 *.50*
17 CD307 3a on 30c dp car 1.25 1.00
18 CD308 8a on 50c orange .55 *1.00*
19 CD309 1r on 1sh blue 1.00 *1.10*
Nos. 16-19 (4) 3.05 *3.60*

75th anniv. of the formation of the UPU.

Nos. 3 and 5-11 Surcharged with New Values in Carmine or Black
Perf. 14, 13x11½, 11½x13
1951, Oct. 1 Engr. Wmk. 4
20 A1 5c on 1a (C) .20 *1.00*
21 A3 10c on 2a #5a .30 *.65*
a. On #5 .40 *.75*
22 A3 15c on 2½a .50 *1.25*
23 A2 20c on 3a #7 .25 *2.10*
a. On #7a .50 *1.50*
24 A2 50c on 8a .30 *.75*
25 A3 1sh on 1r .95 *2.75*
26 A2 2sh on 2r #10 4.00 *29.00*
a. On #10a 12.50 *45.00*
27 A3 5sh on 5r 22.50 *40.00*
Nos. 20-27 (8) 29.00 77.50

QUAITI

LOCATION — In Eastern Aden Protectorate
GOVT. — Sultanate
CAPITAL — Mukalla

The stamps of the Quaiti State of Shihr and Mukalla were valid for use throughout Aden. Used copies generally bear Aden GPO or Aden Camp cancels. Examples with cancels from offices in the Eastern Protectorate command a premium.

Sultan Sir Saleh bin Ghalib al Qu'aiti — A1

Mukalla Harbor — A2

Buildings at Shibam — A3

Designs: 2a, Gateway of Shihr. 3a, Outpost of Mukalla. 8a, View of 'Einat. 1r, Governor's Castle, Du'an. 2r, Mosque in Hureidha. 5r, Meshhed.

1942 Engr. Wmk. 4 *Perf. 13¾x14*
1 A1 ½a blue green 1.00 .55
a. ½a olive green 27.50 *37.50*
b. Perf. 14 line .75 .50
2 A1 ¾a copper brown 1.90 .30
a. Perf. 14 line 1.25 1.00
3 A1 1a deep blue 1.00 1.00
a. Perf. 14 line 1.25 1.25
b. 1a blue 2.00 2.00

Perf. 13x11½, 11½x13
4 A2 1½a dk car rose 1.25 .55
a. 1½a car rose, analine 1.50 *1.25*
5 A2 2a black brown 1.50 *1.90*
a. 2a yellowish brown 25.00 *35.00*
b. 2a sepia 2.00 2.00
6 A3 2½a deep blue .50 .30
7 A2 3a dk car rose & dl brn .80 .80
a. 3a dp car & sepia 2.00 1.50
8 A3 8a orange red .50 .40
9 A2 1r green 3.50 3.75
a. Missing "A" in "CA" of watermark — *875.00*
10 A3 2r rose vio & dk blue 10.50 9.00
a. 2r dp pur & dp bl 15.00 12.50
11 A3 5r gray green & fawn 13.50 11.50
Nos. 1-11 (11) 35.95 30.05
Set, perforated "SPECIMEN" 160.00

For surcharges see Nos. 20-27.

Nos. 4, 6 Ovptd. in Black or Carmine like Kathiri Nos. 12-13
1946, Oct. 15 *Perf. 11½x13, 13x11½*
12 A2 (b) 1½a dk car rose .20 *.65*
13 A3 (a) 2½a deep blue (C) .25 .20
Set, perforated "SPECIMEN" 65.00

Victory of the Allied Nations in WWII.

Silver Wedding Issue
Common Design Types

1949, Jan. 17 Photo. *Perf. 14x14½*
14 CD304 1½a scarlet .55 *3.75*

Engraved; Name Typo.
Perf. 11½x11
15 CD305 5r green 17.00 10.50

25th anniv. of the marriage of King George VI and Queen Elizabeth.

UPU Issue
Common Design Types
Surcharged with New Values in Annas and Rupees

Engr.; Name Typo. on Nos. 17 and 18
1949, Oct. 10 *Perf. 13½, 11x11½*
16 CD306 2½a on 20c dp ultra .20 .20
17 CD307 3a on 30c dp car 1.10 .50
18 CD308 8a on 50c org .40 .80
19 CD309 1r on 1sh blue 1.00 1.00
a. Surcharge omitted *1,900.*
Hinged *1,400.*
Nos. 16-19 (4) 2.70 2.50

Nos. 3 and 5-11 and Types Surcharged with New Values in Carmine or Black
Perf. 14, 13x11½, 11½x13
1951, Oct. 1 Engr. Wmk. 4
20 A1 5c on 1a (C) .20 *.20*
21 A2 10c on 2a .20 *.20*
a. On #5a (12/18/46) 20.00 *30.00*
b. On #5b .50 *.75*
22 A3 15c on 2½a .20 *.20*
23 A2 20c on 3a #7 .30 *.65*
a. 20c on 3a #7a .40 .25
b. Double surcharge, one albino 250.00
24 A3 50c on 8a org red .55 *1.90*
a. 50c on 8a scarlet .20 *.40*
25 A2 1sh on 1r 2.10 .45
26 A3 2sh on 2r 9.50 *16.00*
27 A3 5sh on 5r 13.50 *25.00*
Nos. 20-27 (8) 26.55 *44.60*

AFGHANISTAN

af-'ga-nə-ˌstan

LOCATION — Central Asia, bounded by Iran, Russian Turkestan, India, Baluchistan and China
GOVT. — Constitutional Monarchy
AREA — 251,773 sq. mi.
POP. — 10,000,000
CAPITAL — Kabul

12 Shahi = 6 Sanar = 3 Abasi =
2 Krans = 1 Rupee Kabuli
60 Paisas = 1 Rupee (1921)
100 Pouls = 1 Rupee Afghani (1927)

CHARACTERS OF VALUE.

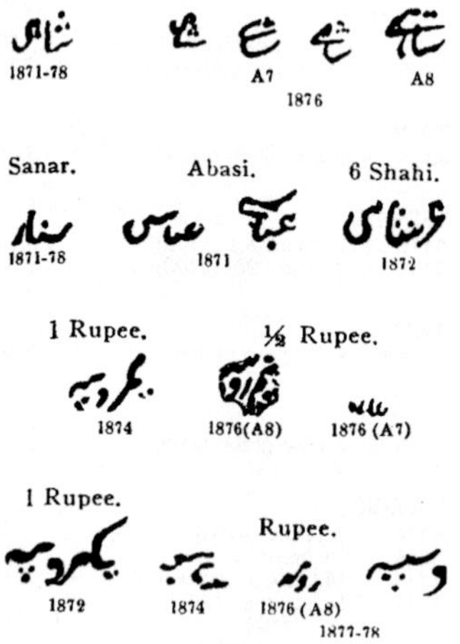

From 1871 to 1892 and 1898 the Moslem year date appears on the stamp. Numerals as follows:

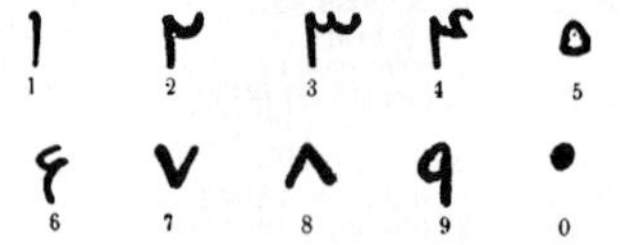

Until 1891 cancellation consisted of cutting or tearing a piece from the stamps. Such copies should not be considered as damaged.

Values are for cut square examples of good color. Cut to shape or faded copies sell for much less, particularly Nos. 2-10.

Nos. 2-108 are on laid paper of varying thickness except where wove is noted.

Until 1907 all stamps were issued ungummed.

The tiger's head on types A2 to A11 symbolizes the name of the contemporary amir, Sher (Tiger) Ali.

Kingdom of Kabul

Tiger's Head A2

(Both circles dotted)

1871 Unwmk. Litho. *Imperf.*

Dated "1288"

2	A2 1sh black		500.00	25.00
	On cover			800.00
3	A2 1sa black		600.00	32.50
	On cover			800.00
4	A2 1ab black		200.00	50.00
	On cover			900.00
	Nos. 2-4 (3)		1,300.	107.50

Thirty varieties of the shahi, 10 of the sanar and 5 of the abasi.

Similar designs without the tiger's head in the center are revenues.

A3

(Outer circle dotted)

Dated "1288"

5	A3 1sh black	300.00	35.00
6	A3 1sa black	175.00	27.50
7	A3 1ab black	175.00	22.50
	Nos. 5-7 (3)	650.00	85.00

Five varieties of each.

A4

1872

Toned Wove Paper

Dated "1289"

8	A4 6sh violet	*1,000.*	*650.*
	On cover		12,000.
9	A4 1rup violet	*1,500.*	*1,100.*

Two varieties of each. Date varies in location. Printed in sheets of 4 (2x2) containing two of each denomination.

Most used copies are smeared with a greasy ink cancel.

A4a

1873

White Laid Paper

Dated "1290"

10	A4a 1sh black	25.00	8.00
	On cover		300.00
a.	Corner ornament missing	*450.00*	*375.00*
b.	Corner ornament retouched	*60.00*	*30.00*

15 varieties. Nos. 10a, 10b are the sixth stamp on the sheet.

A5

1873

11	A5 1sh black	15.00	8.00
	On cover		300.00
11A	A5 1sh violet	*500.00*	

Sixty varieties of each.

1874

Dated "1291"

12	A5 1ab black	90.00	55.00
13	A5 ½rup black	45.00	22.50
14	A5 1rup black	37.50	20.00
	On cover		200.00
	Nos. 12-14 (3)	172.50	97.50

Five varieties of each.

Nos. 12-14 were printed on the same sheet. Se-tenant varieties exist.

A6

A7

1875

Dated "1292"

15	A6 1sa black	*325.00*	*250.00*
	On cover		1,000.
a.	Wide outer circle	*600.00*	
16	A6 1ab black	350.00	300.00
17	A6 1sa brown violet	75.00	40.00
a.	Wide outer circle	110.00	
18	A6 1ab brown violet	80.00	60.00

Ten varieties of the sanar, five of the abasi.

Nos. 15-16 and 17-18 were printed in the same sheets. Se-tenant pairs exist.

1876

Dated "1293"

19	A7 1sh black	300.00	175.00
	On cover		2,500.
20	A7 1sa black	375.00	200.00
	On cover		1,000.
21	A7 1ab black	600.00	300.00
22	A7 ½rup black	375.00	200.00
23	A7 1rup black	550.00	200.00
24	A7 1sh violet	375.00	200.00
25	A7 1sa violet	350.00	200.00
	On cover		2,000.
26	A7 1ab violet	425.00	200.00
27	A7 ½rup violet	200.00	150.00
28	A7 1rup violet	200.00	150.00

12 varieties of the shahi and 3 each of the other values.

A8

1876

Dated "1293"

29	A8 1sh gray	15.00	6.00
	On cover		300.00
30	A8 1sa gray	15.00	8.00
31	A8 1ab gray	42.50	20.00
32	A8 ½rup gray	50.00	25.00
33	A8 1rup gray	37.50	17.50
34	A8 1sh olive blk	125.00	
35	A8 1sa olive blk	175.00	
36	A8 1ab olive blk	350.00	
37	A8 ½rup olive blk	250.00	
38	A8 1rup olive blk	275.00	
39	A8 1sh green	30.00	7.00
40	A8 1sa green	35.00	15.00
41	A8 1ab green	60.00	37.50
42	A8 ½rup green	100.00	40.00
43	A8 1rup green	100.00	80.00
44	A8 1sh ocher	30.00	15.00
45	A8 1sa ocher	35.00	15.00
	On cover		400.00
46	A8 1ab ocher	60.00	27.50
47	A8 ½rup ocher	75.00	60.00
48	A8 1rup ocher	125.00	110.00
49	A8 1sh violet	37.50	15.00
50	A8 1sa violet	37.50	15.00
51	A8 1ab violet	50.00	15.00
52	A8 ½rup violet	70.00	22.50
53	A8 1rup violet	100.00	35.00

24 varieties of the shahi, 4 of which show denomination written:

12 varieties of the sanar, 6 of the abasi and 3 each of the ½ rupee and rupee.

A9

1877

Dated "1294"

54	A9 1sh gray	8.00	*15.00*
55	A9 1sa gray	6.00	10.00
56	A9 1ab gray	9.00	9.00
57	A9 ½rup gray	12.00	*20.00*
58	A9 1rup gray	12.00	*20.00*
59	A9 1sh black	18.00	
60	A9 1sa black	25.00	
61	A9 1ab black	42.50	
62	A9 ½rup black	45.00	
63	A9 1rup black	45.00	
64	A9 1sh green	32.50	32.50
	On cover		300.00
a.	Wove paper	35.00	
65	A9 1sa green	12.00	*12.00*
a.	Wove paper	16.00	15.00
66	A9 1ab green	14.00	*15.00*
a.	Wove paper	27.50	
67	A9 ½rup green	20.00	*20.00*
a.	Wove paper	30.00	*40.00*
68	A9 1rup green	20.00	*20.00*
a.	Wove paper	30.00	*40.00*
69	A9 1sh ocher	4.00	*6.00*
70	A9 1sa ocher	10.00	10.00
71	A9 1ab ocher	17.50	*25.00*
72	A9 ½rup ocher	30.00	*40.00*
73	A9 1rup ocher	30.00	*40.00*
74	A9 1sh violet	3.75	*10.00*
75	A9 1sa violet	9.50	*10.00*
76	A9 1ab violet	14.00	*14.00*
77	A9 ½rup violet	25.00	*25.00*
78	A9 1rup violet	25.00	25.00

25 varieties of the shahi, 8 of the sanar, 3 of the abasi and 2 each of the ½ rupee and rupee.

A10

A11

1878

Dated "1295"

79	A10 1sh gray	5.00	10.00
	On cover		300.00
80	A10 1sa gray	7.00	10.00
81	A10 1ab gray	7.00	10.00
82	A10 ½rup gray	10.00	15.00
83	A10 1rup gray	10.00	15.00
84	A10 1sh black	9.50	
85	A10 1sa black	9.50	
86	A10 1ab black	32.50	
87	A10 ½rup black	35.00	
88	A10 1rup black	35.00	
89	A10 1sh green	21.00	*55.00*
90	A10 1sa green	8.00	9.00
91	A10 1ab green	35.00	30.00
92	A10 ½rup green	30.00	*30.00*
93	A10 1rup green	60.00	40.00
	On cover		200.00
94	A10 1sh ocher	10.00	6.00
95	A10 1sa ocher	12.00	*15.00*
	On cover		50.00
96	A10 1ab ocher	45.00	35.00
97	A10 ½rup ocher	65.00	45.00
98	A10 1rup ocher	60.00	*40.00*
99	A10 1sh violet	8.00	*15.00*
100	A10 1sa violet	30.00	25.00
101	A10 1ab violet	16.00	15.00
102	A10 ½rup violet	55.00	35.00
103	A10 1rup violet	45.00	30.00
104	A11 1sh gray	5.00	6.00
105	A11 1sh black	*90.00*	50.00
106	A11 1sh green	8.00	7.50
107	A11 1sh ocher	8.00	8.00
	On cover		300.00
108	A11 1sh violet	6.00	6.00
	On cover		300.00

40 varieties of the shahi, 30 of the sanar, 6 of the abasi and 2 each of the ½ rupee and 1 rupee.

The 1876, 1877 and 1878 issues were printed in separate colors for each main post office on the Peshawar-Kabul-Khulm (Tashkurghan) postal route. Some specialists consider the black printings to be proofs or trial colors.

There are many shades of these colors.

1ab, Type I (26mm) — A12

1ab, Type II (28mm) — A13

A14

A15

Dated "1298", numerals scattered through design

Handstamped, in watercolor

1881-90

Thin White Laid Batonne Paper

109	A12 1ab violet	4.00	2.00
	On cover		100.00
109A	A13 1ab violet	8.00	3.00
	On cover		150.00
110	A12 1ab black brn	5.00	2.00
	On cover		100.00
111	A12 1ab rose	12.00	3.00
	On cover		50.00
b.	Se-tenant with No. 111A	16.00	
111A	A13 1ab rose	6.00	2.00
	On cover		100.00
112	A14 2ab violet	8.00	2.00
	On cover		50.00
113	A14 2ab black brn	10.00	6.00
	On cover		50.00
114	A14 2ab rose	20.00	10.00
	On cover		75.00
115	A15 1rup violet	10.00	2.00
116	A15 1rup black brn	12.00	8.00
117	A15 1rup rose	11.00	6.00

Thin White Wove Batonne Paper

118	A12 1ab violet	12.00	5.00
	On cover		200.00
119	A12 1ab vermilion	30.00	9.00
120	A12 1ab rose	30.00	25.00
121	A14 2ab violet	30.00	25.00
	On cover		600.00
122	A14 2ab vermilion	30.00	16.00
122A	A14 2ab black brn		
	On cover		200.00
123	A15 1rup violet	15.00	8.00
124	A15 1rup vermilion	14.00	7.50
125	A15 1rup black brn	19.00	8.00

Thin White Laid Batonne Paper

126	A12 1ab brown org	20.00	8.00
	On cover		300.00
126A	A13 1ab brn org (II)	20.00	8.00
	On cover		50.00
127	A12 1ab carmine lake	20.00	8.00
	On cover		100.00
a.	Laid paper	20.00	8.00
128	A14 2ab brown org	20.00	8.00
129	A14 2ab carmine lake	20.00	8.00
	On cover		70.00
130	A15 1rup brown org	35.00	15.00

131 A15 1rup car lake 35.00 15.00

Yellowish Laid Batonne Paper

132 A12 1ab purple 10.00 10.00
133 A12 1ab red 10.00 5.00

1884

Colored Wove Paper

133A A13 1ab purple, *yel* (II) 17.50 17.50
134 A12 1ab purple, *grn* 20.00
135 A12 1ab purple, *blue* 32.50 21.00
136 A12 1ab red, *grn* 37.50
137 A12 1ab red, *yel* 30.00
139 A12 1ab red, *rose* 50.00
140 A14 2ab red, *yel* 30.00
142 A14 2ab red, *rose* 30.00
143 A15 1rup red, *yel* 55.00 20.00
145 A15 1rup red, *rose* 65.00 25.00

Thin Colored Ribbed Paper

146 A14 2ab red, *yellow* 40.00
147 A15 1rup red, *yellow* 80.00
148 A12 1ab lake, *lilac* 40.00
149 A14 2ab lake, *lilac* 40.00
150 A15 1rup lake, *lilac* 40.00
151 A12 1ab lake, *green* 40.00
152 A14 2ab lake, *green* 40.00
153 A15 1rup lake, *green* 40.00

1886-88

Colored Wove Paper

155 A12 1ab black, *magenta* 60.00
156 A12 1ab claret brn, *org* 50.00
156A A12 1ab red, *org* 40.00
156B A14 2ab red, *org* 40.00
156C A15 1rup red, *org* 40.00

Laid Batonné Paper

157 A12 1ab black, *lavender* 40.00
158 A12 1ab cl brn, *grn* 40.00
159 A12 1ab black, *pink* 60.00
160 A14 2ab black, *pink* 100.00
161 A15 1rup black, *pink* 70.00

Laid Paper

162 A12 1ab black, *pink* 80.00
163 A14 2ab black, *pink* 80.00
164 A15 1rup black, *pink* 80.00
165 A12 1ab brown, *yel* 80.00
166 A14 2ab brown, *yel* 80.00
167 A15 1rup brown, *yel* 80.00
168 A12 1ab blue, *grn* 80.00
169 A14 2ab blue, *grn* 80.00
170 A15 1rup blue, *grn* 80.00

1891

Colored Wove Paper

175 A12 1ab green, *rose* 100.00
176 A15 1rup pur, *grn batonne* 100.00

Nos. 109-176 fall into three categories:

1. Those regularly issued and in normal postal use from 1881 on, handstamped on thin white laid or wove paper in strip sheets containing 12 or more impressions of the same denomination arranged in two irregular rows, with the impressions often touching or overlappng.

2. The 1884 postal issues provisionally printed on smooth or ribbed colored wove paper as needed to supplement low stocks of the normal white paper stamps.

3. The "special" printings made in a range of colors on several types of laid or wove colored papers, most of which were never used for normal printings. These were produced periodically from 1886 to 1891 to meet philatelic demands. Although nominally valid for postage, most of the special printings were exported directly to fill dealers' orders, and few were ever postally used. Many of the sheets contained all three denominations with impressions separated by ruled lines. Sometimes different colors were used, so se-tenant multiples of denomination or color exist. Many combinations of stamp and paper colors exist besides those listed.

Various shades of each color exist.

Type A12 is known dated "1297."

Counterfeits, lithographed or typographed, are plentiful.

Kingdom of Afghanistan

A16

A17

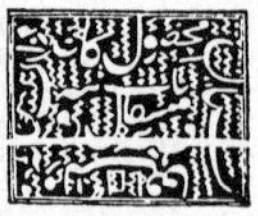

A18

Dated "1309"

1891 **Pelure Paper** **Litho.**

177 A16 1ab slate blue 1.00 1.00
a. Tete beche pair 17.00
178 A17 2ab slate blue 7.25 6.00
179 A18 1rup slate blue 15.00 12.00
Nos. 177-179 (3) 23.25 19.00

Revenue stamps of similar design exist in various colors.

Nos. 177-179 were printed in panes on the same sheet, so se-tenant gutter pairs exist. Examples in black or red are proofs.

A Mosque Gate and Crossed Cannons (National Seal) — A19

Dated "1310" in Upper Right Corner

1892

Flimsy Wove Paper

180 A19 1ab black, *green* 2.40 1.90
181 A19 1ab black, *orange* 3.00 3.00
182 A19 1ab black, *yellow* 2.40 1.90
183 A19 1ab black, *pink* 3.00 1.90
184 A19 1ab black, *lil rose* 3.00 3.00
185 A19 1ab black, *blue* 5.25 4.25
186 A19 1ab black, *salmon* 3.00 2.40
187 A19 1ab black, *magenta* 3.00 3.00
188 A19 1ab black, *violet* 3.00 3.00
188A A19 1ab black, *scarlet* 3.00 2.10

Many shades exist.

A20

A21

Undated

1894

Flimsy Wove Paper

189 A20 2ab black, *green* 7.75 7.75
190 A21 1rup black, *green* 12.00 12.00

24 varieties of the 2 abasi and 12 varieties of the rupee.

Nos. 189-190 and F3 were printed se-tenant in the same sheet. Pairs exist.

A21a

Dated "1316"

1898

Flimsy Wove Paper

191 A21a 2ab black, *pink* 3.00
192 A21a 2ab black, *magenta* 3.00
193 A21a 2ab black, *yellow* 1.40
193A A21a 2ab black, *salmon* 3.50
194 A21a 2ab black, *green* 1.75
195 A21a 2ab black, *purple* 2.10
195A A21a 2ab black, *blue* 21.00
Nos. 191-195A (7) 35.75

Nos. 191-195A were not regularly issued. Genuinely used copies are scarce. No. 195A was found in remainder stocks and probably was never released.

A22

A23

A24

1907 **Engr.** ***Imperf.***

Medium Wove Paper

196 A22 1ab blue green 25.00 10.00
a. 1ab emerald 20.00 6.00
b. Double impression 200.00
197 A22 1ab brt blue 21.00 13.00
198 A23 2ab deep blue 9.00 9.00
199 A24 1rup green 65.00 *15.00*
a. 1rup blue green 65.00 *15.00*

Zigzag Roulette 10

200 A22 1ab green 150.00 42.50
a. Double impression *500.00*
b. Printed on both sides *500.00*
201 A23 2ab blue 225.00 65.00
201A A24 1rup blue green *150.00 110.00*

1908 ***Perf. 12***

202 A22 1ab green 18.00 *24.00*
203 A23 2ab deep blue 6.00 6.00
a. Horiz. pair, imperf between *210.00*
204 A24 1rup blue green 42.50 21.00
Nos. 202-204 (3) 66.50 51.00

Twelve varieties of the 1 abasi, 6 of the 2 abasi, 4 of the 1 rupee.

Nos. 196-204 were issued in small sheets containing 3 or 4 panes. Gutter pairs, normal and tête bêche, exist.

A25

A26

A27

1909-19 **Typo.** ***Perf. 12***

205 A25 1ab ultra 3.50 1.25
a. Imperf., pair 24.00
206 A25 1ab red ('16) .75 .75
a. Imperf. 27.50
207 A25 1ab rose ('18) 1.00 .90
208 A26 2ab green .60 .30
a. Imperf., pair 24.00
b. Horiz. pair, imperf. btwn.
208C A26 2ab yellow ('16) 2.40 2.40
209 A26 2ab bis ('18-'19) 1.10 *1.50*
210 A27 1rup lilac brn 4.75 4.75
a. 1rup red brown 4.75 4.75
211 A27 1rup ol bis ('16) 7.25 7.25
Nos. 205-211 (8) 21.35 19.10

A28

1913

212 A28 2pa drab brown 12.00 3.00
a. 2pa red brown 12.00 3.00

No. 212 is inscribed "Tiket waraq dak" (Postal card stamps). It was usable only on postcards and not accepted for postage on letters.

Nos. 196-212 sometimes show letters of a papermaker's watermark, "Howard & Jones, London."

Royal Star — A29

1920, Aug. 24 ***Perf. 12***

Size: 39x47mm

214 A29 10pa rose 47.50 30.00
215 A29 20pa red brown 72.50 50.00
216 A29 30pa green 150.00 150.00
Nos. 214-216 (3) 270.00 230.00

Issued in sheets of two.

1921, Mar.

Size: 22½x28¼mm

217 A29 10pa rose 2.40 1.25
a. Perf. 11 ('27) 21.00 12.00
218 A29 20pa red brown 4.25 2.40
219 A29 30pa yel green 6.00 3.00
a. Tete beche pair 55.00 30.00
b. 30pa green 6.00 3.25
c. As "b," Tete beche pair 55.00 30.00
Nos. 217-219 (3) 12.65 6.65

Two types of the 10pa, three of the 20pa.

A30

Crest of King Amanullah A32

1924, Feb. 26 ***Perf. 12***

220 A30 10pa chocolate 50.00 30.00
a. Tete beche pair 150.00 80.00

6th Independence Day.

Printed in sheets of four consisting of two tete beche pairs, and in sheets of two. Two types exist.

Some authorities believe that Nos. Q15-Q16 were issued as regular postage stamps.

1925, Feb. 26 ***Perf. 12***

Size: 29x37mm

222 A32 10pa light brown 55.00 42.50

7th Independence Day.

Printed in sheets of 8 (two panes of 4).

1926, Feb. 28

Wove Paper

Size: 26x33mm

224 A32 10pa dark blue 6.00 6.00
- *a.* Imperf., pair 30.00
- *b.* Horiz. pair, imperf. btwn. 47.50
- *c.* Vert. pair, imperf. btwn.
- *d.* Laid paper 30.00 12.00

7th anniv. of Independence. Printed in sheets of 4, and in sheets of 8 (two panes of 4). Tete beche gutter pairs exist.

Tughra and Crest of Amanullah A33

1927, Feb.

225 A33 10pa magenta 10.00 9.00
- *a.* Vertical pair, imperf. between 60.00

Dotted Background

226 A33 10pa magenta 17.50 12.00
- *a.* Horiz. pair, imperf. between 77.50

The surface of No. 226 is covered by a net of fine dots.

8th anniv. of Independence. Printed in sheets of 8 (two panes of 4). Tete beche gutter pairs exist.

National Seal — A34

A35

A35a

A36

1927, Oct. ***Imperf.***

227 A34 15p pink 1.25 1.25
228 A35 30p Prus green 2.40 1.10
229 A36 60p light blue 3.50 3.00
- *a.* Tete beche pair 9.00
- *Nos. 227-229 (3)* 7.15 5.35

1927-30 ***Perf. 11, 12***

230 A34 15p pink 1.25 1.25
231 A34 15p ultra ('29) 1.25 1.25
232 A35 30p Prus green 2.40 1.25
233 A35a 30p dp green ('30) 1.25 1.10
234 A36 60p bright blue 2.40 1.25
- *a.* Tete beche pair 11.00 11.00

235 A36 60p black ('29) 3.00 2.10
- *Nos. 230-235 (6)* 11.55 8.20

Nos. 230, 232 and 234 are usually imperforate on one or two sides.

No. 233 has been redrawn. A narrow border of pearls has been added and "30," in European and Arabic numerals, inserted in the upper spandrels.

Tughra and Crest of Amanullah — A37

1928, Feb. 27

236 A37 15p pink 4.75 4.75
- *a.* Tete beche pair 11.00 9.00
- *b.* Horiz. pair, imperf. vert. 21.00 18.00
- *c.* As "a," imperf. vert., block of 4 30.00

9th anniv. of Independence. This stamp is always imperforate on one or two sides.

A 15p blue of somewhat similar design was prepared for the 10th anniv., but was not issued due to Amanullah's dethronement. Value, $15.

A38

A39

A40

A41

A42

1928-30 ***Perf. 11, 12***

237 A38 2p dull blue 2.50 1.60
- *a.* Vertical pair, imperf. between 17.50

238 A38 2p lt rose ('30) .25 .25
239 A39 10p gray green 1.00 .25
- *a.* Tete beche pair 12.00 5.00
- *b.* Vert. pair, imperf. horiz. 10.00 10.00
- *c.* Vertical pair, imperf. between

240 A39 10p choc ('30) 1.25 1.00
- *a.* 10p brown purple ('29) 8.00 4.00

241 A40 25p car rose 1.00 .25
242 A40 25p Prus green ('29) 1.50 1.00
243 A41 40p ultra 1.25 .55
- *a.* Tete beche pair 13.00 *15.00*

244 A41 40p rose ('29) 1.25 1.00
- *a.* Tete beche pair 12.50
- *b.* Vert. pair, imperf. horiz. 10.00

245 A42 50p red 1.00 .75
246 A42 50p dk blue ('29) 1.75 1.25
- *Nos. 237-246 (10)* 12.75 7.90

The sheets of these stamps are often imperforate at the outer margins.

Nos. 237-238 are newspaper stamps.

This handstamp was used for ten months by the Revolutionary Gov't in Kabul as a control mark on outgoing mail. It occasionally fell on the stamps but there is no evidence that it was officially used as an overprint. Unused copies were privately made.

Independence Monument A46

Wmk. Large Seal in the Sheet

1931, Aug. **Litho.** ***Perf. 12***

Laid Paper

Without Gum

262 A46 20p red 1.75 .85

13th Independence Day.

National Assembly Chamber A47

A48

A50

National Assembly Building A49

National Assembly Chamber A51

National Assembly Building A52

1932 **Unwmk.** **Typo.** ***Perf. 12***

Wove Paper

263 A47 40p olive .75 .35
264 A48 60p violet .85 .60
265 A49 80p dark red 1.10 .80
266 A50 1af black 10.00 5.75
267 A51 2af ultra 3.50 2.75
268 A52 3af gray green 4.25 2.50
- *Nos. 263-268 (6)* 20.45 12.75

Formation of the Natl. Council. Imperforate or perforated examples on ungummed chalky paper are proofs.

See Nos. 304-305.

Mosque at Balkh — A53

Kabul Fortress A54

Parliament House, Darul Funun — A55

Parliament House, Darul Funun — A56

Arch of Qalai Bist — A57

Memorial Pillar of Knowledge and Ignorance A58

Independence Monument A59

Minaret at Herat — A60

Arch of Paghman A61

Ruins at Balkh — A62

Minarets of Herat — A63

Great Buddha at Bamian — A64

1932 Typo. *Perf. 12*

269	A53	10p brown	.40	.20
270	A54	15p dk brown	.35	.25
271	A55	20p red	.45	.20
272	A56	25p dk green	.65	.20
273	A57	30p red	.65	.25
274	A58	40p orange	.75	.35
275	A59	50p blue	1.10	1.00
a.		Tete beche pair	5.50	
276	A60	60p blue	1.00	.75
277	A61	80p violet	1.90	1.40
278	A62	1af dark blue	3.50	.70
279	A63	2af dk red violet	3.75	2.00
280	A64	3af claret	4.25	2.50
		Nos. 269-280 (12)	18.75	9.80

Counterfeits of types A53-A65 exist.
See Nos. 290-295, 298-299, 302-303.

Entwined 2's — A65

Two types:
Type I — Numerals shaded. Size about 21x29mm.
Type II — Numerals unshaded. Size about 21¾x30mm.

1931-38 *Perf. 12, 11x12*

281	A65	2p red brn (I)	.25	.20
282	A65	2p olive blk (I) ('34)	.25	.50
283	A65	2p grnsh gray (I) ('34)	.35	.20
283A	A65	2p black (II) ('36)	.20	.40
284	A65	2p salmon (II) ('38)	.35	.40
284A	A65	2p rose (I) ('38)	.35	.50
b.		Imperf., pair	3.00	

Imperf

285	A65	2p black (II) ('37)	.75	.20
286	A65	2p salmon (II) ('38)	.25	.20
		Nos. 281-286 (8)	2.75	2.60

The newspaper rate was 2 pouls.

A66

A67

1932, Aug. *Perf. 12*

287 A66 1af Independence Monument 3.75 2.00

14th Independence Day.

1932, Oct. Typo.

1929 Liberation Monument, Kabul.

288 A67 80p red brown 1.60 1.10

Arch of Paghman — A68

1933, Aug.

289 A68 50p light ultra 3.00 1.10

15th Independence Day.

Types of 1932 and

Royal Palace, Kabul A69

Darrah- Shikari Pass, Hindu Kush — A70

1934-38 Typo. *Perf. 12*

290	A53	10p deep violet	.20	.20
291	A54	15p turq green	.30	.20
292	A55	20p magenta	.30	.20
293	A56	25p deep rose	.35	.20
294	A57	30p orange	.45	.25
295	A58	40p blue black	.60	.30
296	A69	45p dark blue	1.50	1.25
297	A69	45p red ('38)	.30	.20
298	A59	50p orange	.50	.20
299	A60	60p purple	.75	.30
300	A70	75p red	2.10	1.50
301	A70	75p dk blue ('38)	.60	.40
302	A61	80p brown vio	1.00	.60
303	A62	1af red violet	1.60	1.25
304	A51	2af gray black	3.00	2.10
305	A52	3af ultra	3.50	3.00
		Nos. 290-305 (16)	17.05	12.15

Nos. 290, 292, 300, 304, 305 exist imperf.

Independence Monument — A71

1934, Aug. Litho.

Without Gum

306	A71	50p pale green	2.50	2.00
a.		Tete beche pair	9.00	9.00

16th year of Independence. Each sheet of 40 (4x10) included 4 tete beche pairs as lower half of sheet was inverted.

Independence Monument — A74

Fireworks Display A75

1935, Aug. 15

Laid Paper

309 A74 50p dark blue 3.50 1.75

17th year of Independence.

1936, Aug. 15 *Perf. 12*

Wove Paper

310 A75 50p red violet 2.40 2.00

18th year of Independence.

Independence Monument and Nadir Shah — A76

1937

311	A76	50p vio & bis brn	1.90	1.60
a.		Imperf., pair	7.25	7.25

19th year of Independence.

Mohammed Nadir Shah
A77 A78

1938 *Perf. 11x12*

Without Gum

315	A77	50p brt blue & sepia	2.00	1.75
a.		Imperf. pair	17.00	17.00

20th year of Independence.

1939 *Perf. 11, 12x11*

317 A78 50p deep salmon 1.75 1.10

21st year of Independence.

National Arms A79

Parliament House, Darul Funun — A80

Royal Palace, Kabul A81

Independence Monument — A82

Independence Monument and Nadir Shah — A83

Mohammed Zahir Shah — A84

Mohammed Zahir Shah A85

Perf. 11, 11x12, 12x11, 12

1939-61 Typo.

318	A79	2p intense blk	.20	.40
318A	A79	2p brt pink ('61)	.20	.70
319	A80	10p brt purple	.20	.20
320	A80	15p brt green	.25	.20
321	A80	20p red lilac	.30	.20
322	A81	25p rose red	.35	.25
322A	A81	25p green ('41)	.25	.20
323	A81	30p orange	.30	.20
a.		Vert. pair, imperf between		—
324	A81	40p dk gray	.60	.30
325	A82	45p brt carmine	.60	.25
326	A82	50p dp orange	.45	.20
327	A82	60p violet	.60	.20
328	A83	75p ultra	1.75	.75
328A	A83	75p red vio ('41)	1.25	1.10
328C	A83	75p brt red ('44)	2.25	2.25
328D	A83	75p chnt brn ('49)	2.25	2.25
329	A83	80p chocolate	1.00	.75
a.		80p dull red violet (error)		
330	A84	1af brt red violet	1.25	.75
330A	A85	1af brt red vio ('44)	1.25	.60
331	A85	2af copper red	1.75	.75
a.		2af deep rose red	2.50	1.40
332	A84	3af deep blue	3.00	2.00
		Nos. 318-332 (21)	20.05	14.50

Many shades exist in this issue.
On No. 332 the King faces slightly left.
No. 318A issued with and without gum.
See #795A-795B. For similar design see #907A.

Mohammed Nadir Shah — A86

1940, Aug. 23 *Perf. 11*

333 A86 50p gray green 1.50 1.10

22nd year of Independence.

AIR POST STAMPS

Plane over Kabul AP1

Perf. 12, 12x11, 11

1939, Oct. 1 Typo. Unwmk.

C1	AP1	5af orange	5.00	2.25
a.		Imperf., pair ('47)	22.50	22.50
b.		Horiz. pair, imperf. vert.	20.00	
C2	AP1	10af blue	5.00	1.75
a.		10af lt bl	7.50	5.00
b.		Imperf., pair ('47)	22.50	
c.		Horiz. pair, imperf. vert.	20.00	

C3	AP1 20af emerald	10.00	5.00
a.	Imperf., pair ('47)	22.50	
b.	Horiz. pair, imperf. vert.	20.00	
c.	Vert. pair, imperf. horiz.	22.50	
	Nos. C1-C3 (3)	20.00	9.00

These stamps come with clean-cut or rough perforations. Counterfeits exist.

REGISTRATION STAMPS

R1

Dated "1309"

1891 Unwmk. Litho. *Imperf.*

Pelure Paper

F1	R1 1r slate blue	2.00	
a.	Tete beche pair	12.50	

Genuinely used copies of No. F1 are rare. Counterfeit cancellations exist.

R2

Dated "1311"

1893 Thin Wove Paper

F2	R2 1r black, *green*	1.60	

Genuinely used copies of No. F2 are rare. Counterfeit cancellations exist.

R3

Undated

1894

F3	R3 2ab black, *green*	7.50	*8.50*

12 varieties. See note below Nos. 189-190.

R4

Undated

1898-1900

F4	R4 2ab black, *deep rose*	3.50	3.50
F5	R4 2ab black, *lilac rose*	4.00	4.00
F6	R4 2ab black, *magenta*	5.00	4.00
F7	R4 2ab black, *salmon*	3.00	*3.50*
F8	R4 2ab black, *orange*	3.50	3.50
F9	R4 2ab black, *yellow*	3.50	*3.50*
F10	R4 2ab black, *green*	3.50	3.50
	Nos. F4-F10 (7)	26.00	25.50

Many shades of paper.

Nos. F4-F10 come in two sizes, measured between outer frame lines: 52x36mm, 1st printing; 46x33mm, 2nd printing. The outer frame line (not pictured) is 3-6mm from inner frame line.

Used on P.O. receipts.

OFFICIAL STAMPS

(Used only on interior mail.)

Coat of Arms O1

1909 Unwmk. Typo. *Perf. 12*

Wove Paper

O1	O1 red	1.00	1.00
a.	Carmine ('19?)	2.25	*6.00*

Later printings of No. O1 in scarlet, vermilion, claret, etc., on various types of paper, were issued until 1927.

Coat of Arms — O2

1939-68? Typo. *Perf. 11, 12*

O3	O2 15p emerald	.85	.65
O4	O2 30p ocher ('40)	1.10	1.10
O5	O2 45p dark carmine	1.00	1.00
O6	O2 50p brt car ('68)	.60	.60
a.	50p carmine rose ('55)	1.00	.60
O7	O2 1af brt red violet	1.50	1.40
	Nos. O3-O7 (5)	5.05	4.75

Size of 50p, 24x31mm, others 22½x28mm.

PARCEL POST STAMPS

Coat of Arms — PP1

PP2

PP3

PP4

1909 Unwmk. Typo. *Perf. 12*

Q1	PP1 3sh bister	1.00	*2.00*
a.	Imperf., pair	*1.00*	
Q2	PP2 1kr olive gray	1.60	*3.00*
a.	Imperf., pair		
Q3	PP3 1r orange	3.00	3.00
Q4	PP3 1r olive green	18.00	4.00
Q5	PP4 2r red	3.50	3.50
	Nos. Q1-Q5 (5)	27.10	15.50

1916-18

Q6	PP1 3sh green	1.60	*3.00*
Q7	PP2 1kr pale red	2.50	1.25
a.	1kr rose red ('18)	3.25	3.25
Q8	PP3 1r brown org	1.25	1.25
a.	1r deep brown ('18)	10.00	2.50
Q9	PP4 2r blue	4.50	*5.00*
	Nos. Q6-Q9 (4)	9.85	*10.50*

Nos. Q1-Q9 sometimes show letters of the papermaker's watermark "HOWARD & JONES LONDON."

Ungummed copies are remainders. They sell for one-third the price of mint examples.

Old Habibia College, Near Kabul — PP5

1921

Wove Paper

Q10	PP5 10pa chocolate	3.00	5.00
a.	Tete beche pair	15.00	15.00
Q11	PP5 15pa light brn	6.00	7.00
a.	Tete beche pair	20.00	
Q12	PP5 30pa red violet	9.00	7.00
a.	Tete beche pair	30.00	
b.	Laid paper	*15.00*	*10.00*
Q13	PP5 1r brt blue	10.00	9.00
a.	Tete beche pair	50.00	
	Nos. Q10-Q13 (4)	28.00	28.00

Stamps of this issue are usually perforated on one or two sides only.

The laid paper of No. Q12b has a papermaker's watermark in the sheet.

PP6

1924-26

Wove Paper

Q15	PP6 5kr ultra ('26)	35.00	35.00
Q16	PP6 5r lilac	15.00	15.00

A 15r rose exists, but is not known to have been placed in use.

PP7

PP8

1928-29 *Perf. 11, 11xImperf.*

Q17	PP7 2r yellow orange	10.00	3.00
Q18	PP7 2r green ('29)	3.00	3.00
Q19	PP8 3r deep green	7.50	4.00
Q20	PP8 3r brown ('29)	5.00	5.00
	Nos. Q17-Q20 (4)	25.50	15.00

POSTAL TAX STAMPS

Aliabad Hospital near Kabul PT1

Pierre and Marie Curie PT2

Perf. 12x11½, 12

1938, Dec. 22 Typo. Unwmk.

RA1	PT1 10p peacock grn	2.50	*4.00*
RA2	PT2 15p dull blue	2.50	*4.00*

Obligatory on all mail Dec. 22-28, 1938. The money was used for the Aliabad Hospital. See note with CD80.

AGUERA, LA

LOCATION — An administrative district in southern Rio de Oro on the northwest coast of Africa.

GOVT. — Spanish possession

AREA — Because of indefinite political boundaries, figures for area and population are not available.

100 Centimos = 1 Peseta

Type of 1920 Issue of Rio de Oro Overprinted

1920, June Typo. Unwmk. *Perf. 13*

1	A8	1c blue green	2.40	2.40
		Never hinged	3.25	
		On cover		65.00
2	A8	2c olive brown	2.40	2.40
		Never hinged	3.25	
		On cover		65.00
3	A8	5c deep green	2.40	2.40
		Never hinged	3.25	
		On cover		65.00
4	A8	10c light red	2.40	2.40
		Never hinged	3.25	
		On cover		65.00
5	A8	15c yellow	2.40	2.40
		Never hinged	3.25	
		On cover		65.00
6	A8	20c lilac	2.40	2.40
		Never hinged	3.25	
		On cover		65.00
7	A8	25c deep blue	2.40	2.40
		Never hinged	3.25	
		On cover		75.00
8	A8	30c dark brown	2.40	2.40
		Never hinged	3.25	
		On cover		75.00
9	A8	40c pink	2.40	2.40
		Never hinged	3.25	
		On cover		75.00
10	A8	50c bright blue	7.75	7.75
		Never hinged	10.00	
		On cover		125.00
11	A8	1p red brown	14.00	14.00
		Never hinged	17.50	
		On cover		250.00
12	A8	4p dark violet	45.00	45.00
		Never hinged	55.00	
		On cover		650.00
13	A8	10p orange	85.00	85.00
		Never hinged	110.00	
		On cover		1,300.
		Nos. 1-13 (13)	173.35	173.35
		Set, never hinged	275.00	

Values for Nos. 1-13 are for stamps with fine centering. Exceptional examples with very fine centering are scarce and command at least 50% premium.

Commercial covers are scarce. Philatelic covers sell for less.

Values for stamps in blocks of 4

1	A8	1c blue green	13.00	*14.00*
2	A8	2c olive brown	13.00	*14.00*
3	A8	5c deep green	13.00	*14.00*
4	A8	10c light red	13.00	*14.00*
5	A8	15c yellow	13.00	*14.00*
6	A8	20c lilac	13.00	*14.00*
7	A8	25c deep blue	13.00	*14.00*
8	A8	30c dark brown	13.00	*14.00*
9	A8	40c pink	13.00	*14.00*
10	A8	50c bright blue	30.00	*55.00*
11	A8	1p red brown	70.00	*75.00*
12	A8	4p dark violet	240.00	*250.00*
13	A8	10p orange	440.00	*475.00*

Values for Specimen Stamps (numbered A.000.000 on reverse)

1S	A8	1c blue green	7.50
2S	A8	2c olive brown	7.50
3S	A8	5c deep green	7.50
4S	A8	10c light red	7.50
5S	A8	15c yellow	7.50
6S	A8	20c lilac	7.50
7S	A8	25c deep blue	7.50
8S	A8	30c dark brown	7.50
9S	A8	40c pink	7.50
10S	A8	50c bright blue	19.00
11S	A8	1p red brown	19.00
12S	A8	4p dark violet	70.00
13S	A8	10p orange	140.00

King Alfonso XIII — A2

Two Types of 1c:

Type I: Two dots above "U" of "AGUERA," large letters.

Type II: No dots above "U" of "AGUERA," smaller letters.

1922, June

14	A2	1c turquoise bl (I)	1.10	1.10
		Never hinged	1.60	
		On cover		45.00
a.		Type II		95.00
15	A2	2c dark green	1.25	1.10
		Never hinged	1.60	
		On cover		45.00
16	A2	5c blue green	1.25	1.10
		Never hinged	1.60	
		On cover		45.00
17	A2	10c red	1.25	1.10
		Never hinged	1.60	
		On cover		45.00
18	A2	15c red brown	1.25	1.10
		Never hinged	1.60	
		On cover		45.00
19	A2	20c yellow	1.25	1.10
		Never hinged	1.60	
		On cover		45.00
20	A2	25c deep blue	1.25	1.10
		Never hinged	1.60	
		On cover		45.00
21	A2	30c dark brown	1.25	1.10
		Never hinged	1.60	
		On cover		52.50
22	A2	40c rose red	1.50	1.40
		Never hinged	2.10	
		On cover		57.50
23	A2	50c red violet	5.00	4.50
		Never hinged	7.50	
		On cover		77.50
24	A2	1p rose	10.00	9.25
		Never hinged	15.00	
		On cover		140.00
25	A2	4p violet	27.50	24.00
		Never hinged	35.00	
		On cover		350.00
26	A2	10p orange	40.00	37.50
		Never hinged	52.50	
		On cover		575.00
		Nos. 14-26 (13)	93.85	85.45
		Set, never hinged	140.00	

Values for stamps in blocks of 4

14	A2	1c turquoise bl (I)	7.25
15	A2	2c dark green	7.25
16	A2	5c blue green	7.25
17	A2	10c red	7.25
18	A2	15c red brown	7.25
19	A2	20c yellow	7.25
20	A2	25c deep blue	7.25
21	A2	30c dark brown	8.50
22	A2	40c rose red	8.50
23	A2	50c red violet	26.00
24	A2	1p rose	52.50
25	A2	4p violet	150.00
26	A2	10p orange	225.00

Values for Specimen Stamps (numbered A.000.000 on reverse)

14S	A2	1c turquoise bl (I)	5.75
15S	A2	2c dark green	5.75
16S	A2	5c blue green	5.75
17S	A2	10c red	5.75
18S	A2	15c red brown	5.75
19S	A2	20c yellow	5.75
20S	A2	25c deep blue	5.75
21S	A2	30c dark brown	8.50
22S	A2	40c rose red	8.50
23S	A2	50c red violet	11.00
24S	A2	1p rose	11.00
25S	A2	4p violet	35.00
26S	A2	10p orange	57.50

For later issues see Spanish Sahara.

AITUTAKI

ˌit-ə-ˈtäk-ē

LOCATION — One of the larger Cook Islands, in the South Pacific Ocean northeast of New Zealand

GOVT. — A dependency of the British dominion of New Zealand

AREA — 7 sq. mi.

POP. — 1,719

The Cook Islands were attached to New Zealand in 1901. Stamps of Cook Islands were used in 1932-72.

12 Pence = 1 Shilling

Watermark

Wmk. 61- Single-lined NZ and Star Close Together

Stamps of New Zealand Surcharged in Red or Blue:

a

b

1903 Engr. Wmk. 61 *Perf. 14*

1	A18(a)	½p green (R)	4.75	*7.00*
		On cover		125.00
2	A35(b)	1p rose (Bl)	5.00	*6.25*
		On cover		125.00

c

d

e

f

Perf. 11

3	A22(c)	2½p blue (R)	11.50	*15.00*
		On cover		125.00
4	A23(d)	3p yellow brn (Bl)	19.00	*16.00*
		On cover		140.00
5	A26(e)	6p red (Bl)	32.50	27.50
		On cover		175.00
6	A29(f)	1sh scarlet (Bl)	55.00	*90.00*
		On cover		350.00
a.		1sh orange red (Bl)	67.50	*100.00*
		On cover		375.00
b.		1sh orange brown (Bl)	125.00	*150.00*
		On cover		*750.00*
c.		As #6, no period after "Tiringi"	675.00	*850.00*
d.		As #6a, no period after "Tiringi"	800.00	*950.00*
e.		As #6b, no period after "Tiringi"	1,100.	*1,350.*

Values for covers are for commercially used and properly franked items. Philatelic usages also exist and sell for less.

1911, Sept. Typo. *Perf. 14x15*

7	A41(a)	½p yellow grn (R)	1.00	*4.25*
		Engr.		
		Perf. 14		
9	A22(c)	2½p deep blue (R)	8.50	*19.00*
a.		No period after "Ava"	175.00	*225.00*

g

h

1913-16 Typo.

10	A42(b)	1p rose (Bl)	3.25	*11.50*
		Engr.		
12	A41(g)	6p car rose (Bl) ('16)	47.50	*115.00*
13	A41(h)	1sh ver (Bl) ('14)	55.00	*150.00*

1916-17 *Perf. 14x14½*

17	A45(g)	6p car rose (Bl)	9.00	*29.00*
a.		Perf 14x13½	13.50	*57.50*
b.		Vert. pair, #17, 17a	57.50	*175.00*
18	A45(h)	1sh ver (Bl) ('17)	32.50	*95.00*
a.		Perf 14x13½	16.00	*100.00*
b.		Vert. pair, #17, 17a	140.00	*400.00*
		Nos. 1-18 (13)	284.50	*585.50*

New Zealand Stamps of 1909-19 Overprinted in Red or Dark Blue

1917-20 Typo. *Perf. 14x15*

19	A43	½p yellow grn ('20)	1.00	*6.25*
20	A42	1p car (Bl) ('20)	4.50	*30.00*
21	A47	1½p gray black	4.00	*32.50*
22	A47	1½p brown org ('19)	.85	*7.50*
23	A43	3p choc (Bl) ('19)	3.75	*18.00*

Engr. *Perf. 14x14½*

24	A44	2½p dull blue ('18)	1.90	*16.00*
a.		Perf 14x13½	2.25	*19.00*
b.		Vert. pair, #24, 24a	40.00	*140.00*
25	A45	3p vio brn (Bl) ('18)	1.75	*25.00*
a.		Perf 14x13½	2.00	*29.00*
b.		Vert. pair, #25, 25a	35.00	*160.00*
26	A45	6p car rose (Bl)	5.00	*22.50*
a.		Perf 14x13½	7.25	*24.00*
b.		Vert. pair, #26, 26a	47.50	*160.00*
27	A45	1sh vermilion (Bl)	12.50	*35.00*
a.		Perf 14x13½	16.00	*45.00*
b.		Vert. pair, #26, 26a	75.00	*200.00*
		Nos. 19-27 (9)	35.25	*192.75*

Landing of Capt. Cook A15

Avarua Waterfront A16

Capt. James Cook — A17

Palm — A18

Houses at Arorangi — A19

Avarua Harbor — A20

1920 Engr. Unwmk. *Perf. 14*

28	A15	½p green & black	3.75	26.00
29	A16	1p carmine & black	3.75	18.00
		Double derrick flaw	12.50	
30	A17	1½p brown & blk	6.25	*13.00*
31	A18	3p dp blue & blk	2.75	*15.00*
32	A19	6p slate & red brn	6.25	15.00
33	A20	1sh claret & blk	10.00	*22.50*
		Nos. 28-33 (6)	32.75	*109.50*

Inverted centers, double frames, etc. are from printers waste.

Rarotongan Chief (Te Po) — A21

1924-27 Wmk. 61 *Perf. 14*

34	A15	½p green & blk ('27)	2.10	*15.00*
35	A16	1p carmine & blk	6.25	*8.00*
		Double derrick flaw	17.00	
36	A21	2½p blue & blk ('27)	8.00	*62.50*
		Nos. 34-36 (3)	16.35	*85.50*

ALAOUITES

ˈal-au-ˌwītz

LOCATION — A division of Syria, in Western Asia.
GOVT. — Under French Mandate
AREA — 2,500 sq. mi.
POP. — 278,000 (approx. 1930)
CAPITAL — Latakia

This territory became an independent state in 1924, although still administered under the French Mandate. In 1930 it was renamed Latakia and Syrian stamps overprinted "Lattaquie" superseded the stamps of Alaouites. For these and subsequent issues see Latakia and Syria.

100 Centimes = 1 Piaster

Issued under French Mandate

Stamps of France Surcharged:

Nos. 1-6, 16-18

Nos. 7-15, 19-21

1925 Unwmk. *Perf. 14x13½*

1 A16 10c on 2c vio brn 2.25 *2.75*
On cover *30.00*
2 A22 25c on 5c orange 2.50 2.50
On cover *30.00*
3 A20 75c on 15c gray grn 4.00 4.00
On cover *50.00*
b. Wide spacing between "7" and "5" 21.00 21.00
4 A22 1p on 20c red brn 2.50 2.50
On cover *30.00*
5 A22 1.25p on 25c blue 2.50 *2.75*
On cover *30.00*
6 A22 1.50p on 30c red 10.00 10.00
On cover *65.00*
7 A22 2p on 35c violet 2.25 *3.00*
On cover *30.00*
On cover, single franking *40.00*
8 A18 2p on 40c red & pale bl 4.00 4.00
On cover *30.00*
On cover, single franking *40.00*
9 A18 2p on 45c grn & bl 10.50 10.50
On cover *85.00*
On cover, single franking *150.00*
10 A18 3p on 60c vio & ultra 4.25 *5.00*
On cover *45.00*
On cover, single franking *60.00*
11 A20 3p on 60c lt vio 12.50 12.50
On cover *60.00*
On cover, single franking *90.00*
b. Double surcharge 125.00 125.00
c. Small and raised figure "3" 80.00 80.00
12 A20 4p on 85c vermilion 2.00 2.00
On cover *35.00*
On cover, single franking *45.00*
13 A18 5p on 1fr cl & ol grn 5.00 5.00
On cover *50.00*
On cover, single franking *85.00*
14 A18 10p on 2fr org & pale bl 6.50 6.50
On cover *60.00*
On cover, single franking *100.00*
b. Wide spacing between "1" and "0" 35.00 35.00
15 A18 25p on 5fr bl & buff 10.00 10.00
On cover *65.00*
On cover, single franking *140.00*
Nos. 1-15 (15) 80.75 83.00

For overprints see Nos. C1-C4.

Same Surcharges on Pasteur Stamps of France

16 A23 50c on 10c green 2.25 *2.50*
On cover *30.00*
17 A23 75c on 15c green 2.00 2.00
On cover *30.00*
18 A23 1.50p on 30c red 2.00 *2.75*
On cover *25.00*
19 A23 2p on 45c red 3.00 *3.25*
On cover *30.00*
On cover, single franking *40.00*
20 A23 2.50p on 50c blue 4.00 4.00
On cover *30.00*
On cover, single franking *50.00*
21 A23 4p on 75c blue 3.75 *4.50*
On cover *40.00*
On cover, single franking *70.00*
Nos. 16-21 (6) 17.00 *19.00*

Inverted Surcharges

1a A16 10c on 2c vio brn 17.50
2a A22 25c on 5c orange 17.50
3a A20 75c on 15c gray grn 17.50
4a A22 1p on 20c red brn 17.50
5a A22 1.25p on 25c blue 17.50
6a A22 1.50p on 30c red 27.50
7a A22 2p on 35c violet 27.50
8a A18 2p on 40c red & pale bl 27.50
9a A18 2p on 45c grn & bl 27.50
10a A18 3p on 60c vio & ultra 15.00
11a A20 3p on 60c lt vio 15.00
12a A20 4p on 85c vermilion 15.00
13a A18 5p on 1fr cl & ol grn 15.00
14a A18 10p on 2fr org & pale bl 15.00
15a A18 25p on 5fr bl & buff 15.00
16a A23 50c on 10c green 12.50
17a A23 75c on 15c green 12.50
18a A23 1.50p on 30c red 12.50
19a A23 2p on 45c red 12.50
20a A23 2.50p on 50c blue 12.50
21a A23 4p on 75c blue 12.50

Stamps of Syria, 1925, Overprinted in Red, Black or Blue:

On A3, A5

On A4

1925, Mar. 1 *Perf. 12½, 13½*

25 A3 10c dk violet (R) 1.50 *1.75*
On cover *15.00*
a. Double overprint 24.00 24.00
b. Inverted overprint 20.00
26 A4 25c olive black (R) 1.75 *2.00*
On cover *13.50*
a. Inverted overprint 20.00
b. Blue overprint 28.00 28.00
27 A4 50c yellow green 1.25 *1.50*
On cover *12.00*
a. Inverted overprint 20.00 20.00
b. Blue overprint 30.00 30.00
c. Red overprint 28.00 28.00
d. "ALAOUITE," instead of "ALAOUITES" 17.50 17.50
28 A4 75c brown orange 1.50 *2.25*
On cover *12.00*
a. Inverted overprint 20.00
b. Double overprint 28.00 *28.00*
29 A5 1p magenta 2.00 2.00
On cover *15.00*
a. Inverted overprint 20.00
b. "ALACUITES," instead of "ALAOUITES" 14.00 14.00
c. "ALAOCITES," instead of "ALAOUITES" 17.50 15.00
d. "ALAO ITES," instead of "ALAOUITES" 14.00 14.00
e. "ALAOU ES," instead of "ALAOUITES" *20.00*
30 A4 1.25p deep green 2.25 2.25
On cover *12.50*
a. Red overprint 24.00 24.00
31 A4 1.50p rose red (Bl) 1.75 *2.00*
On cover *12.50*
a. Inverted overprint 20.00
b. Black overprint 24.00 24.00
32 A4 2p dk brown (R) 2.75 2.75
On cover *15.00*
On cover, single franking *20.00*
a. Blue overprint 38.00 38.00
b. Inverted overprint 20.00
33 A4 2.50p pck blue (R) 3.00 *3.00*
On cover *17.50*
On cover, single franking *25.00*
a. Black overprint 38.00 38.00
34 A4 3p orange brown 1.50 1.50
On cover *17.50*
On cover, single franking *30.00*
a. Inverted overprint 20.00
b. Blue overprint 38.00 38.00
35 A4 5p violet 2.75 2.75
On cover *20.00*
On cover, single franking *35.00*
a. Red overprint 38.00 38.00
36 A4 10p violet brown 3.00 *3.00*
On cover *25.00*
On cover, single franking *40.00*
37 A4 25p ultra (R) 5.00 *5.25*
On cover *27.50*
On cover, single franking *75.00*
Nos. 25-37 (13) 30.00 *32.00*

For overprints see Nos. C5-C19.

Stamps of Syria, 1925, Surcharged in Black or Red:

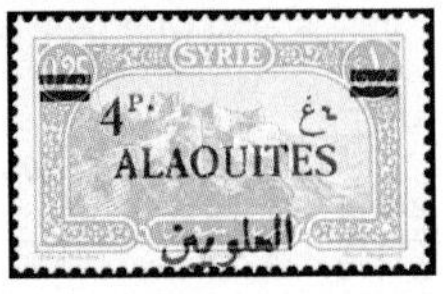
Nos. 38-42

Nos. 43-45

1926

38 A4 3.50p on 75c brn org 2.00 *2.75*
On cover *15.00*
a. Surcharged on face and back 12.00 12.00
39 A4 4p on 25c ol blk (R) 2.00 *2.25*
On cover *15.00*
40 A4 6p on 2.50p pck bl (R) 2.00 *2.25*
On cover *18.00*
41 A4 12p on 1.25p dp grn 2.50 *2.75*
On cover *25.00*
a. Inverted surcharge 27.50 27.50
42 A4 20p on 1.25p dp grn 3.50 3.50
On cover *45.00*
43 A4 4.50p on 75c brn org 4.00 2.75
On cover *18.00*
a. Inverted surcharge 27.50
44 A4 7.50p on 2.50p pck bl 4.00 2.75
On cover *18.00*
45 A4 15p on 25p ultra 9.00 5.00
On cover *35.00*
Nos. 38-45 (8) 29.00 *24.00*

For overprint see No. C21.

Syria #199 Ovptd. like #25 in Red

1928

46 A3 5c on 10c dk violet 1.50 1.50
On cover *12.50*
a. Double surcharge 24.00

Syria Nos. 178 and 174 Surcharged like Nos. 43-45 in Red

47 A4 2p on 1.25p dp green 12.50 7.00
On cover *45.00*
48 A4 4p on 25c olive black 9.00 5.00
On cover *30.00*

For overprint see No. C20.

49 A4 4p on 25c olive black 60.00 50.00
On cover *40.00*
a. Double impression
Nos. 46-49 (4) 83.00 63.50

AIR POST STAMPS

Nos. 8, 10, 13 & 14 with Additional Overprint in Black

1925, Jan. 1 Unwmk. *Perf. 14x13½*

C1 A18 2p on 40c 8.00 8.00
On cover *100.00*
On cover, single franking *110.00*
a. Overprint reversed 85.00
C2 A18 3p on 60c 9.00 *11.50*
On cover *55.00*
On cover, single franking *80.00*
a. Overprint reversed 75.00 75.00
C3 A18 5p on 1fr 8.00 8.00
On cover *60.00*
On cover, single franking *80.00*
C4 A18 10p on 2fr 8.50 8.50
On cover *55.00*
On cover, single franking *90.00*
Nos. C1-C4 (4) 33.50 *36.00*

Nos. 32, 34, 35 & 36 With Additional Overprint in Green

1925, Mar. 1 *Perf. 13½*

C5 A4 2p dark brown 2.75 2.75
On cover *25.00*
On cover, single franking *35.00*
C6 A4 3p orange brown 2.75 2.75
On cover *25.00*
On cover, single franking *40.00*
C7 A4 5p violet 2.75 2.75
On cover *30.00*
On cover, single franking *50.00*
C8 A4 10p violet brown 2.75 2.75
On cover *35.00*
On cover, single franking *65.00*
Nos. C5-C8 (4) 11.00 11.00

Nos. 32, 34, 35 & 36 With Additional Overprint in Red

1926, May 1

C9 A4 2p dark brown 4.00 4.00
On cover *25.00*
On cover, single franking *35.00*
C10 A4 3p orange brown 4.00 4.00
On cover *25.00*
On cover, single franking *40.00*
C11 A4 5p violet 4.00 4.00
On cover *35.00*
On cover, single franking *50.00*
C12 A4 10p violet brown 4.00 4.00
On cover *40.00*
On cover, single franking *70.00*
Nos. C9-C12 (4) 16.00 16.00

No. C9 has the original overprint in black.

Double or inverted overprints, original or plane, are known on most of Nos. C9-C12. Value, $75.

The red plane overprint was also applied to Nos. C5-C8. These are believed to have been essays, and were not regularly issued.

Nos. 27, 37 and Syria No. 177 with Type A4 overprint, With Additional Overprint of Airplane in Red or Black

1929, June-July

C17 A4 50c yel grn (R) 3.00 3.00
On cover *17.50*
a. Plane overprint double 150.00
b. Plane ovpt. on face and back 42.50
c. Pair with plane overprint tete beche 175.00
C18 A5 1p magenta (Bk) 6.00 6.00
On cover *40.00*
C19 A4 25p ultra (R) 30.00 30.00
On cover *125.00*
a. Plane overprint inverted 85.00 85.00
Nos. C17-C19 (3) 39.00 39.00

Nos. 47 and 45 With Additional Overprint of Airplane in Red

1929-30

C20 A4 2p on 1.25p ('30) 4.00 4.00
On cover *45.00*
a. Surcharge inverted 7.00
b. Double surcharge 6.00
C21 A4 15p on 25p (Bk + R) 35.00 35.00
On cover *110.00*
a. Plane overprint inverted 140.00 140.00

POSTAGE DUE STAMPS

Postage Due Stamps of France, 1893-1920, Surcharged Like No. 1 (Nos. J1-J2) or No. 7 (Nos. J3-J5)

1925 Unwmk. *Perf. 14x13½*

J1 D2 50c on 10c choc 3.75 *4.00*
On cover *50.00*
J2 D2 1p on 20c ol grn 3.75 *4.00*
On cover *50.00*
J3 D2 2p on 30c red 3.75 *4.00*
On cover *60.00*
J4 D2 3p on 50c vio brn 3.75 *4.00*
On cover *75.00*
J5 D2 5p on 1fr red brn, *straw* 4.50 4.50
On cover *80.00*
Nos. J1-J5 (5) 19.50 *20.50*

Postage Due Stamps of Syria, 1925, Overprinted Like No. 26 (Type D5) or No. 25 (Type D6) in Black, Blue or Red

1925 *Perf. 13½*

J6 D5 50c brown, *yel* 2.00 *2.25*
On cover *25.00*
J7 D6 1p vio, *rose* (Bl) 1.75 *2.25*
On cover *25.00*
a. Black overprint 50.00 50.00
b. Double overprint (Bk + Bl) 60.00 60.00
J8 D5 2p blk, *blue* (R) 3.00 3.00
On cover *25.00*
J9 D5 3p blk, *red org* 3.50 3.50
On cover *30.00*
J10 D5 5p blk, *bl grn* (R) 4.00 4.00
On cover *40.00*
Nos. J6-J10 (5) 14.25 15.00

The stamps of Alaouites were superseded in 1930 by those of Latakia.

ALBANIA

al-'bā-nē-ə

LOCATION — Southeastern Europe
GOVT. — Monarchy
AREA — 11,101 sq. mi.
POP. — 1,003,124
CAPITAL — Tirana

After the outbreak of World War I, the country fell into a state of anarchy when the Prince and all members of the International Commission left Albania. Subsequently General Ferrero in command of Italian troops declared Albania an independent country. A constitution was adopted and a republican form of government was instituted which continued until 1928 when, by constitutional amendment, Albania was declared to be a monarchy. The President of the republic, Ahmed Zogu, became king of the new state. Many unlisted varieties or surcharges and lithographed labels are said to have done postal duty in Albania and Epirus during this unsettled period.

On April 7, 1939, Italy invaded Albania. King Zog fled but did not abdicate. The King of Italy acquired the crown.

40 Paras = 1 Piaster = 1 Grossion
100 Centimes = 1 Franc (1917)
100 Qintar = 1 Franc

AUSTRIAN POST IN ALBANIA

The Austrian Empire maintained post offices in various coastal towns in Albania beginning in 1854, in conjunction with the operations of the Austrian Lloyd shipping line. The nine offices, with opening and closing dates, are listed in the table below. Since Italian was the official operational language, the names are shown in Italian with the modern equivalent in parentheses.

Post Office	Open	Close
Antivari (Bar)	1854	1878
Durazzo (Durres)	1854	1915
Janina (Ioannina)	1857	1914
Prevesa (Preveza)	1854	1914
Santi Quaranta (Sarande)	1870	1915
Sajada (Sayiadha)	1858	1912
San Giovanni Di Medua (Shengjin)	1879	1915
Scutari (Shkoder)	1901	1915
Valona (Vlore)	1854	1915

Values in the first column for Nos. 2A1-2A353 are for stamps without defects tied to piece with legible partial strikes of town cancellations; values in the second column are for stamps without defects tied to cover by complete strikes of town cancellations. Stamps with legible town cancellations off cover sell for 25-50% of the on-piece value.

Issue dates refer to dates of stamps' issue, not necessarily to their usage with specific Albanian postal markings.

ANTIVARI

Stamps of Lombardy-Venetia

Canceled in black with single circle date stamp with post office name, month and date, without year

1863 *Perf. 14*

2A1	2s yellow (#15)	575.00	2,000.
2A2	3s green (#16)	525.00	2,200.
2A3	5s rose (#17)	525.00	2,000.
2A4	10s blue (#18)	500.00	1,750.
2A5	15s yel brn (#19)	575.00	1,850.

1864-65 *Perf. 9½*

2A6	2s yellow (#20)	450.00	1,500.
2A7	3s green (#21)	200.00	850.00
2A8	5s rose (#22)	150.00	700.00
2A9	10s blue (#23)	125.00	500.00
2A10	15s yel brn (#24)	160.00	600.00

Stamps of Austrian Offices In the Turkish Empire

Canceled in black or red brown with single circle date stamp with post office name, month and date, without year

1867-83

Coarse Print

2A11	2s yellow (#1)	87.50	650.00
2A12	3s green (#2)	110.00	600.00
2A13	5s red (#3)	75.00	350.00
2A14	10s blue (#4)	70.00	300.00
2A15	15s brown (#5)	75.00	300.00
2A16	25s gray lilac (#6)	100.00	900.00
2A17	50s brown (#7)	110.00	*4,000.*

Fine Print

2A18	2s yellow (#7C)	1,200.	—
2A19	3s green (#7D)	85.00	475.00
2A20	5s red (#7E)	82.50	350.00
2A21	10s blue (#7F)	70.00	290.00
2A22	15s org brown (#7I)	175.00	975.00
2A23	25s gray lilac (#7J)	300.00	*5,250.*

Stamps of Lombardy-Venetia

Canceled in blue with single circle date stamp with post office name, month and date, without year

1863 *Perf. 14*

2A24	2s yellow (#15)	800.00	2,750.
2A25	3s green (#16)	750.00	2,850.
2A26	5s rose (#17)	750.00	1,650.
2A27	10s blue (#18)	700.00	2,400.
2A28	15s yel brn (#19)	800.00	2,500.

1864-65 *Perf. 9½*

2A29	2s yellow (#20)	525.00	1,650.
2A30	3s green (#21)	275.00	1,050.
2A31	5s rose (#22)	150.00	700.00
2A32	10s blue (#23)	190.00	675.00
2A33	15s yel brn (#24)	225.00	800.00

Stamps of Austrian Offices In the Turkish Empre

Canceled in blue with single circle date stamp with post office name, month and date, without year

1867-83

Coarse Print

2A34	2s yellow (#1)	125.00	825.00
2A35	3s green (#2)	150.00	750.00
2A36	5s red (#3)	120.00	500.00
2A37	10s blue (#4)	115.00	450.00
2A38	15s brown (#5)	120.00	475.00
2A39	25s gray lilac (#6)	145.00	1,100.
2A40	50s brown (#7)	150.00	*4,250.*

Fine Print

2A41	2s yellow (#7C)	1,250.	—
2A42	3s green (#7D)	125.00	625.00
2A43	5s red (#7E)	125.00	525.00
2A44	10s blue (#7F)	115.00	450.00
2A45	15s org brown (#7I)	225.00	1,125.
2A46	25s gray lilac (#7J)	350.00	*5,500.*

Stamps of Austria

Canceled in blue with single circle date stamp with post office name, month and date, without year

1863-64

2A47	2kr yellow (#22)	*1,150.*	—
2A48	3kr green (#23)	*1,150.*	—
2A49	5kr red (#24)	*1,150.*	—
2A50	10kr blue (#25)	*1,150.*	—
2A51	15kr yel brown (#26)	*1,150.*	—

DURAZZO

Stamps of Lombardy-Venetia

Canceled in black with single circle date stamp with post office name, month and date, without year

1863 *Perf. 14*

2A52	2s yellow (#15)	350.00	1,250.
2A53	3s green (#16)	300.00	1,350.
2A54	5s rose (#17)	300.00	1,100.
2A55	10s blue (#18)	250.00	850.00
2A56	15s yel brn (#19)	325.00	1,000.

1864-65 *Perf. 9½*

2A57	2s yellow (#20)	425.00	1,275.
2A58	3s green (#21)	160.00	675.00
2A59	5s rose (#22)	110.00	525.00
2A60	10s blue (#23)	85.00	325.00
2A61	15s yel brn (#24)	115.00	450.00

Stamps of Austrian Offices In the Turkish Empire

Canceled in black or red brown with single circle date stamp with post office name, month and date, without year

1867-83

Coarse Print

2A62	2s yellow (#1)	87.50	650.00
2A63	3s green (#2)	110.00	600.00
2A64	5s red (#3)	75.00	350.00
2A65	10s blue (#4)	70.00	300.00
2A66	15s brown (#5)	75.00	300.00
2A67	25s gray lilac (#6)	100.00	900.00
2A68	50s brown (#7)	110.00	*4,000.*

Fine Print

2A69	2s yellow (#7C)	1,200.	—
2A70	3s green (#7D)	85.00	475.00
2A71	5s red (#7E)	82.50	350.00
2A72	10s blue (#7F)	70.00	290.00
2A73	15s org brown (#7I)	175.00	975.00
2A74	25s gray lilac (#7J)	300.00	*5,250.*

Stamps of Lombardy-Venetia

Canceled in blue with single circle date stamp with post office name, month and date, without year

1863 *Perf. 14*

2A75	2s yellow (#15)	*1,300.*	*4,500.*
2A76	3s green (#16)	*1,250.*	*4,500.*
2A77	5s rose (#17)	*1,250.*	*4,250.*
2A78	10s blue (#18)	*1,200.*	*4,000.*
2A79	15s yel brn (#19)	*1,300.*	*4,100.*

1864-65 *Perf. 9½*

2A80	2s yellow (#20)	625.00	1,950.
2A81	3s green (#21)	375.00	1,350.
2A82	5s rose (#22)	325.00	1,200.
2A83	10s blue (#23)	300.00	1,000.
2A84	15s yel brn (#24)	325.00	1,100.

Stamps of Austrian Offices In the Turkish Empre

Canceled in blue with single circle date stamp with post office name, month and date, without year

1867-83

Coarse Print

2A85	2s yellow (#1)	125.00	825.00
2A86	3s green (#2)	150.00	750.00
2A87	5s red (#3)	120.00	500.00
2A88	10s blue (#4)	115.00	450.00
2A89	15s brown (#5)	120.00	475.00
2A90	25s gray lilac (#6)	145.00	1,100.
2A91	50s brown (#7)	150.00	*4,250.*

Fine Print

2A92	2s yellow (#7C)	1,250.	—
2A93	3s green (#7D)	125.00	625.00
2A94	5s red (#7E)	125.00	525.00
2A95	10s blue (#7F)	115.00	450.00
2A96	15s org brown (#7I)	225.00	1,125.
2A97	25s gray lilac (#7J)	350.00	*5,500.*

Stamps of Austrian Offices In the Turkish Empre

Canceled in black with "thimble" (diameter 20mm or less) circular date stamp with post office name and date

1867-83

Coarse Print

2A99	2s yellow (#1)	200.00	1,000.
2A100	3s green (#2)	215.00	950.00
2A101	5s red (#3)	185.00	700.00
2A102	10s blue (#4)	175.00	650.00
2A103	15s brown (#5)	175.00	650.00
2A104	25s gray lilac (#6)	200.00	1,250.
2A105	50s brown (#7)	215.00	*4,400.*

Fine Print

2A106	2s yellow (#7C)	1,300.	—
2A107	3s green (#7D)	200.00	825.00
2A108	5s red (#7E)	190.00	700.00
2A109	10s blue (#7F)	175.00	650.00
2A110	15s org brown (#7I)	290.00	1,325.
2A111	25s gray lilac (#7J)	400.00	*5,750.*

Use of this cancelation is known beginning in 1877.

Stamps of Austrian Offices In the Turkish Empre

Canceled in blue with "thimble" (diameter 20mm or less) circular date stamp with post office name and date

1867-83

Coarse Print

2A112	2s yellow (#1)	300.00	1,325.
2A113	3s green (#2)	325.00	1,250.
2A114	5s red (#3)	285.00	1,000.
2A115	10s blue (#4)	275.00	950.00
2A116	15s brown (#5)	280.00	975.00
2A117	25s gray lilac (#6)	300.00	1,575.
2A118	50s brown (#7)	325.00	*4,750.*

Fine Print

2A119	2s yellow (#7C)	1,400.	—
2A120	3s green (#7D)	300.00	1,125.
2A121	5s red (#7E)	285.00	1,000.
2A122	10s blue (#7F)	275.00	950.00
2A123	15s org brown (#7I)	385.00	1,625.
2A124	25s gray lilac (#7J)	500.00	*6,000.*

Use of this cancelation is known beginning in 1872.

Austrian Offices in Turkish Empire issues canceled in black with circular Durazzo date stamp with post office name, month, date and year date exist but are very rare.

JANINA

Stamps of Lombardy-Venetia

Canceled in black with single circle date stamp with post office name, month and date, without year

1863 *Perf. 14*

2A126	2s yellow (#15)	240.00	1,000.
2A127	3s green (#16)	200.00	1,200.
2A128	5s rose (#17)	200.00	900.00
2A129	10s blue (#18)	160.00	625.00
2A130	15s yel brn (#19)	225.00	725.00

1864-65 *Perf. 9½*

2A131	2s yellow (#20)	375.00	1,150.
2A132	3s green (#21)	125.00	550.00
2A133	5s rose (#22)	80.00	400.00
2A134	10s blue (#23)	50.00	200.00
2A135	15s yel brn (#24)	85.00	325.00

Stamps of Austrian Offices In the Turkish Empre

Canceled in black or red brown with single circle date stamp with post office name, month and date, without year

1867-83

Coarse Print

2A136	2s yellow (#1)	57.50	525.00
2A137	3s green (#2)	75.00	475.00
2A138	5s red (#3)	47.50	215.00
2A139	10s blue (#4)	40.00	165.00
2A140	15s brown (#5)	42.50	175.00
2A141	25s gray lilac (#6)	67.50	775.00
2A142	50s brown (#7)	75.00	*4,000.*

Fine Print

2A143	2s yellow (#7C)	1,175.	—
2A144	3s green (#7D)	55.00	350.00
2A145	5s red (#7E)	50.00	225.00
2A146	10s blue (#7F)	40.00	165.00
2A147	15s org brown (#7I)	150.00	850.00
2A148	25s gray lilac (#7J)	275.00	*5,250.*

Stamps of Austria

Canceled in black or red brown with single circle date stamp with post office name, month and date, without year

1867-83

Coarse Print

2A149	2kr yellow (#27)	625.00	—
2A150	3kr green (#28)	625.00	—
2A151	5kr red (#29)	625.00	—
2A152	10kr blue (#30)	625.00	*2,250.*
2A153	15kr brown (#31)	625.00	2,250.
2A154	25kr gray lilac (#32)	625.00	—
2A155	50kr brown (#33)	700.00	—

Fine Print

2A156	2kr yellow (#34)	625.00	—
2A157	3kr green (#35)	625.00	—
2A158	5kr red (#36)	625.00	—
2A159	10kr blue (#37)	625.00	*2,250.*
2A160	15kr org brown (#38)	625.00	2,250.
2A161	25kr gray (#39)	725.00	
2A162	50kr brown (#40)	750.00	—

Stamps of Austrian Offices In the Turkish Empre

Canceled in black with circular date stamp with post office name, month and date, with year date

1867-83

Coarse Print

2A163	2s yellow (#1)	57.50	525.00
2A164	3s green (#2)	75.00	475.00
2A165	5s red (#3)	47.50	215.00
2A166	10s blue (#4)	40.00	165.00
2A167	15s brown (#5)	42.50	175.00
2A168	25s gray lilac (#6)	67.50	775.00
2A169	50s brown (#7)	75.00	*4,000.*

Fine Print

2A170	2s yellow (#7C)	1,175.	—
2A171	3s green (#7D)	55.00	350.00
2A172	5s red (#7E)	50.00	225.00
2A173	10s blue (#7F)	40.00	165.00
2A174	15s org brown (#7I)	150.00	850.00
2A175	25s gray lilac (#7J)	275.00	*5,250.*

Use of this cancelation is known beginning in 1880.

PREVESA

Stamps of Lombardy-Venetia

Canceled in black with single circle date stamp with post office name, month and date, without year

1863 ***Perf. 14***

2A176	2s yellow (#15)	275.00	1,000.
2A177	3s green (#16)	225.00	1,150.
2A178	5s rose (#17)	225.00	900.00
2A179	10s blue (#18)	200.00	675.00
2A180	15s yel brn (#19)	275.00	800.00

1864-65 ***Perf. 9½***

2A181	2s yellow (#20)	375.00	1,150.
2A182	3s green (#21)	125.00	550.00
2A183	5s rose (#22)	80.00	400.00
2A184	10s blue (#23)	50.00	200.00
2A185	15s yel brn (#24)	85.00	325.00

Stamps of Austrian Offices In the Turkish Empre

Canceled in black with single circle date stamp with post office name, month and date, without year

1867-83

Coarse Print

2A186	2s yellow (#1)	37.50	450.00
2A187	3s green (#2)	57.50	400.00
2A188	5s red (#3)	27.50	140.00
2A189	10s blue (#4)	20.00	92.50
2A190	15s brown (#5)	24.00	100.00
2A191	25s gray lilac (#6)	50.00	700.00
2A192	50s brown (#7)	57.50	*3,850.*

Fine Print

2A193	2s yellow (#7C)	1,150.	—
2A194	3s green (#7D)	35.00	275.00
2A195	5s red (#7E)	32.50	150.00
2A196	10s blue (#7F)	20.00	87.50
2A197	15s org brown (#7I)	135.00	775.00
2A198	25s gray lilac (#7J)	250.00	*5,000.*

Stamps of Lombardy-Venetia

Canceled in blue with single circle date stamp with post office name, month and date, without year

1863 ***Perf. 14***

2A199	2s yellow (#15)	575.00	2,000.
2A200	3s green (#16)	525.00	2,200.
2A201	5s rose (#17)	525.00	2,000.
2A202	10s blue (#18)	500.00	1,750.
2A203	15s yel brn (#19)	575.00	1,850.

1864-65 ***Perf. 9½***

2A204	2s yellow (#20)	525.00	1,650.
2A205	3s green (#21)	275.00	1,050.
2A206	5s rose (#22)	220.00	875.00
2A207	10s blue (#23)	190.00	675.00
2A208	15s yel brn (#24)	225.00	800.00

Stamps of Austrian Offices In the Turkish Empre

Canceled in black with circular date stamp with post office name, month and date, with year date

1867-83

Coarse Print

2A209	2s yellow (#1)	57.50	525.00
2A210	3s green (#2)	75.00	475.00
2A211	5s red (#3)	47.50	215.00
2A212	10s blue (#4)	40.00	165.00
2A213	15s brown (#5)	42.50	175.00
2A214	25s gray lilac (#6)	67.50	775.00
2A215	50s brown (#7)	75.00	*4,000.*

Fine Print

2A216	2s yellow (#7C)	1,175.	—
2A217	3s green (#7D)	55.00	340.00
2A218	5s red (#7E)	50.00	225.00
2A219	10s blue (#7F)	40.00	165.00
2A220	15s org brown (#7I)	150.00	850.00
2A221	25s gray lilac (#7J)	275.00	*5,250.*

Use of this cancelation is known beginning in 1874.

DULCIGNO / S. GIOVANNI DI MEDUA

Stamps of Austrian Offices In the Turkish Empre

Canceled in black with circular date stamp with post office name, month and date, with year date

1867-83

Coarse Print

2A222	2s yellow (#1)	650.00	2,500.
2A223	3s green (#2)	675.00	2,450.
2A224	5s red (#3)	640.00	2,200.
2A225	10s blue (#4)	40.00	165.00
2A226	15s brown (#5)	625.00	2,150.
2A227	25s gray lilac (#6)	650.00	2,750.
2A228	50s brown (#7)	675.00	*5,750.*

Fine Print

2A229	2s yellow (#7C)	1,750.	—
2A230	3s green (#7D)	650.00	2,350.
2A231	5s red (#7E)	640.00	2,200.
2A232	10s blue (#7F)	625.00	2,150.
2A233	15s org brown (#7I)	725.00	2,800.
2A234	25s gray lilac (#7J)	850.00	*7,250.*

Stamps of Austrian Offices In the Turkish Empre

Canceled in blue with circular date stamp with post office name, month and date, with year date

1867-83

Coarse Print

2A235	2s yellow (#1)	1,150.	*4,250.*
2A236	3s green (#2)	1,150.	*4,000.*
2A237	5s red (#3)	1,150.	*3,900.*
2A238	10s blue (#4)	1,150.	*3,800.*
2A239	15s brown (#5)	1,150.	*3,750.*
2A240	25s gray lilac (#6)	1,150.	*4,375.*
2A241	50s brown (#7)	1,200.	*7,500.*

Fine Print

2A242	2s yellow (#7C)	*2,250.*	—
2A243	3s green (#7D)	1,100.	*4,000.*
2A244	5s red (#7E)	1,150.	*3,900.*
2A245	10s blue (#7F)	1,150.	*3,800.*
2A246	15s org brown (#7I)	1,250.	*4,400.*
2A247	25s gray lilac (#7J)	1,350.	*8,750.*

SAN GIOVANNI DI MEDUA

Stamps of Austrian Offices In the Turkish Empre

Canceled in black with circular date stamp with post office name, month and date, with year date

1867-83

Coarse Print

2A248	2s yellow (#1)	440.00	*1,825.*
2A249	3s green (#2)	450.00	1,750.
2A250	5s red (#3)	425.00	1,500.
2A251	10s blue (#4)	415.00	1,450.
2A252	15s brown (#5)	420.00	1,475.
2A253	25s gray lilac (#6)	450.00	2,100.
2A254	50s brown (#7)	450.00	*5,250.*

Fine Print

2A255	2s yellow (#7C)	1,400.	—
2A256	3s green (#7D)	300.00	1,625.
2A257	5s red (#7E)	285.00	1,500.
2A258	10s blue (#7F)	275.00	1,450.
2A259	15s org brown (#7I)	385.00	2,150.
2A260	25s gray lilac (#7J)	500.00	*6,500.*

Use of this cancelation is known beginning in March, 1881.

SANTI QUARANTA

Stamps of Austrian Offices In the Turkish Empre

Canceled in black with circular date stamp with post office name, month and date, with year date

1867-83

Coarse Print

2A261	2s yellow (#1)	200.00	1,000.
2A262	3s green (#2)	215.00	950.00
2A263	5s red (#3)	185.00	700.00
2A264	10s blue (#4)	175.00	650.00
2A265	15s brown (#5)	180.00	650.00
2A266	25s gray lilac (#6)	200.00	1,250.
2A267	50s brown (#7)	215.00	—

Fine Print

2A268	2s yellow (#7C)	1,300.	—
2A269	3s green (#7D)	200.00	825.00
2A270	5s red (#7E)	190.00	700.00
2A271	10s blue (#7F)	175.00	650.00
2A272	15s org brown (#7I)	290.00	1,325.
2A273	25s gray lilac (#7J)	400.00	*5,750.*

Use of this cancelation is known beginning in March 28, 1870.

Stamps of Austrian Offices In the Turkish Empre

Canceled in black with 23mm circular date stamp with post office name, month and date, with year date

1867-83

Coarse Print

2A274	2s yellow (#1)	300.00	1,325.
2A275	3s green (#2)	325.00	1,250.
2A276	5s red (#3)	285.00	1,000.
2A277	10s blue (#4)	275.00	950.00
2A278	15s brown (#5)	280.00	975.00
2A279	25s gray lilac (#6)	300.00	1,575.
2A280	50s brown (#7)	325.00	—

Fine Print

2A281	2s yellow (#7C)	1,400.	—
2A282	3s green (#7D)	300.00	1,125.
2A283	5s red (#7E)	285.00	1,000.
2A284	10s blue (#7F)	275.00	950.00
2A285	15s org brown (#7I)	385.00	1,625.
2A286	25s gray lilac (#7J)	500.00	*6,000.*

Use of this cancelation is known beginning in November, 1878.

SCUTARI D'ALBANIA

Stamps of Lombardy-Venetia

Canceled in black with "thimble" (diameter 20mm or less) circular date stamp with post office name and date

1864-65 ***Perf. 9½***

2A287	2s yellow (#20)	—	—
2A288	3s green (#21)	—	—
2A289	5s rose (#22)	*3,000.*	—
2A290	10s blue (#23)	*3,000.*	*11,500.*
2A291	15s yel brn (#24)	*3,000.*	—

Stamps of Austrian Offices In the Turkish Empre

Canceled in black with "thimble" circular date stamp with post office name and date

1867-83

Coarse Print

2A292	2s yellow (#1)	1,700.	—
2A293	3s green (#2)	1,750.	—
2A294	5s red (#3)	1,700.	—
2A295	10s blue (#4)	1,700.	*6,250.*
2A296	15s brown (#5)	1,700.	—
2A297	25s gray lilac (#6)	1,700.	—
2A298	50s brown (#7)	1,750.	—

Fine Print

2A299	2s yellow (#7C)	*2,800.*	—
2A300	3s green (#7D)	1,700.	—
2A301	5s red (#7E)	1,700.	—
2A302	10s blue (#7F)	1,700.	*6,250.*
2A303	15s org brown (#7I)	1,800.	—
2A304	25s gray lilac (#7J)	1,950.	—

Also known on Ottoman stamps, and on covers franked with Ottoman stamps.

VALONA

Stamps of Lombardy-Venetia

Canceled in black with single circle date stamp with post office name, month and date, without year

1863 ***Perf. 14***

2A305	2s yellow (#15)	800.00	2,750.
2A306	3s green (#16)	750.00	2,850.
2A307	5s rose (#17)	750.00	1,650.
2A308	10s blue (#18)	700.00	2,400.
2A309	15s yel brn (#19)	800.00	2,500.

1864-65 ***Perf. 9½***

2A310	2s yellow (#20)	625.00	1,950.
2A311	3s green (#21)	375.00	1,350.
2A312	5s rose (#22)	325.00	1,200.
2A313	10s blue (#23)	300.00	1,000.
2A314	15s yel brn (#24)	325.00	1,100.

Stamps of Austrian Offices In the Turkish Empre

Canceled in black or red brown with single circle date stamp with post office name, month and date, without year

1867-83

Coarse Print

2A315	2s yellow (#1)	87.50	650.00
2A316	3s green (#2)	110.00	600.00
2A317	5s red (#3)	77.50	340.00
2A318	10s blue (#4)	70.00	300.00
2A319	15s brown (#5)	75.00	300.00
2A320	25s gray lilac (#6)	100.00	900.00
2A321	50s brown (#7)	110.00	*4,000.*

Fine Print

2A322	2s yellow (#7C)	1,200.	—
2A323	3s green (#7D)	85.00	475.00
2A324	5s red (#7E)	82.50	350.00
2A325	10s blue (#7F)	70.00	290.00
2A326	15s org brown (#7I)	180.00	975.00
2A327	25s gray lilac (#7J)	300.00	*5,250.*

Stamps of Austrian Offices In the Turkish Empre

Canceled in blue with single circle date stamp with post office name, month and date, without year

1867-83

Coarse Print

2A328	2s yellow (#1)	125.00	825.00
2A329	3s green (#2)	150.00	750.00
2A330	5s red (#3)	120.00	500.00
2A331	10s blue (#4)	115.00	450.00
2A332	15s brown (#5)	120.00	475.00
2A333	25s gray lilac (#6)	145.00	1,100.
2A334	50s brown (#7)	150.00	*4,250.*

Fine Print

2A335	2s yellow (#7C)	1,250.	—
2A336	3s green (#7D)	125.00	625.00
2A337	5s red (#7E)	125.00	525.00
2A338	10s blue (#7F)	115.00	450.00
2A339	15s org brown (#7I)	225.00	1,125.
2A340	25s gray lilac (#7J)	350.00	*5,500.*

Stamps of Austrian Offices In the Turkish Empre

Canceled in black with circular date stamp with post office name, month and date, with year date

1867-83

Coarse Print

2A341	2s yellow (#1)	57.50	525.00
2A342	3s green (#2)	75.00	450.00
2A343	5s red (#3)	47.50	215.00
2A344	10s blue (#4)	40.00	165.00
2A345	15s brown (#5)	42.50	175.00
2A346	25s gray lilac (#6)	67.50	775.00
2A347	50s brown (#7)	75.00	*4,000.*

Fine Print

2A348	2s yellow (#7C)	1,175.	—
2A349	3s green (#7D)	55.00	340.00
2A350	5s red (#7E)	50.00	225.00
2A351	10s blue (#7F)	40.00	165.00
2A352	15s org brown (#7I)	150.00	850.00
2A353	25s gray lilac (#7J)	275.00	*5,250.*

GREEK CONSULAR POST IN EPIRUS

The Greek Postal Administration maintained facilities within the consular office at Ioannina, and in the postal agencies at Arta and Preveza.

Post Office	Open	Close
Arta (105)	1852	1881
Ioannina (99)	1852	1881
Preveza (104)	1853	1881

The post office of Arta became a regular Greek post office after annexation of that city on June 24, 1881.

Additional premiums for stamps of Greece with postmarks of the consular office in Epirus. The first column contains values for single stamps or for single stamps on piece; the second, for stamps on cover.

Rhombus of Dots with Numeral

Numeral 99	+25.	+150.
Numeral 104	+650.	*+2,000.*
Numeral 105	+275.	—

Circular Datestamps

Ioannina	+80.	*+375.*
Preveza	+800.	—
Arta (105) (until 6/23/81)	+80.	*+375.*
Arta (105) (after 6/24/81)	+20.	+150.

Greece annexed Arta on June 24, 1881. Greek stamps used from that date on are not "Used in Albania."

Watermarks

Wmk. 125 — Lozenges

Wmk. 220 — Double Headed Eagle

Stamps of Turkey Handstamped

Handstamped on Issue of 1908

Perf. 12, 13½ and Compound

1913, June **Unwmk.**

1	A19	2½pi violet brown	625.00	500.00

With Additional Overprint in Carmine 

2	A19	10pa blue green	600.00	550.00

Handstamped on Issue of 1909

4	A21	5pa ocher	350.00	350.00
5	A21	10pa blue green	250.00	175.00
6	A21	20pa car rose	250.00	175.00
7	A21	1pi ultra	210.00	175.00
		On newspaper or wrapper		*450.00*
8	A21	2pi blue black	350.00	325.00
10	A21	5pi dark violet	925.00	775.00
11	A21	10pi dull red	*3,250.*	*3,250.*

For surcharge see No. 19.

Additional values of 25pi dark green and 50pi red brown were overprinted and sold only to dealers. Values, 25pi $7,250, 50pi $14,000.

With Additional Overprint in Blue or Carmine

14	A21	20pa car rose (Bl)	650.00	675.00
15	A21	1pi brt blue (C)	1,300.	1,200.

Handstamped on Newspaper Stamp of 1911

17	A21	2pa olive green	350.00	350.00

Handstamped on Postage Due Stamp of 1908

18	A19	1pi black, *dp rose*	2,100.	1,850.

No. 18 was used for regular postage.

No. 6 Surcharged With New Value

19	A21	10pa on 20pa car rose	*850.00*	*850.00*

The overprint on #1-19 was handstamped and is found inverted, double, etc.

Nos. 6, 7 and 8 exist with the handstamp in red, blue or violet, but these varieties are not known to have been regularly issued.

A 2pa on 5pa newspaper stamp and a 2pi Postage due stamp exist with the handstamp, but these are not known to have been regularly issued. Values, $1,500 and 575.00, respectively.

Covers: Commercial covers of Nos. 1-19 are very scarce.

Excellent counterfeits exist of Nos. 1 to 19.

A1

Issued Without Gum

1913, July ***Imperf.***

Handstamped on White Laid Paper Without Eagle and Value

20	A1	(1pi) black	250.00	*350.00*
		Cut to shape	150.00	*225.00*
a.		Sewing machine perf.	450.00	*525.00*

Issued Without Gum

1913, Aug.

Value Typewritten in Violet With Eagle

21	A1	10pa violet	11.00	10.50
22	A1	20pa red & black	14.00	12.00
23	A1	1gr black	14.00	12.00
24	A1	2gr blue & violet	17.50	14.00
25	A1	5gr violet & blue	21.00	19.00
26	A1	10gr blue	21.00	19.00
		Nos. 21-26 (6)	98.50	88.50

Nos. 21-26 exist with the eagle inverted or omitted and with numerous errors in the figures of value and the spelling of the word "grosh."

A2

Skanderbeg (George Castriota) — A3

Issued Without Gum

1913, Nov. ***Perf. 11½***

Handstamped on White Laid Paper Eagle and Value in Black

27	A2	10pa green	3.50	3.00
b.		Eagle and value in green	1,500.	650.00
c.		10pa red (error)	20.00	20.00
d.		10pa violet (error)	20.00	20.00
29	A2	20pa red	5.25	4.25
b.		20pa green (error)	29.00	20.00
30	A2	30pa violet	5.25	4.25
a.		30pa ultramarine (error)	20.00	20.00
b.		30pa red (error)	20.00	20.00
31	A2	1gr ultramarine	7.00	6.25
a.		1gr green (error)	20.00	20.00
b.		1gr black (error)	20.00	20.00
c.		1gr violet (error)	20.00	20.00
33	A2	2gr black	10.50	7.00
a.		2gr violet (error)	25.00	25.00
b.		2gr blue (error)	25.00	25.00
		Nos. 27-33 (5)	31.50	24.75

The stamps of this issue are known with eagle or value inverted or omitted.

1st anniv. of Albanian independence.

1913, Dec. **Typo.** ***Perf. 14***

35	A3	2q orange brn & buff	3.50	1.75
36	A3	5q green & blue grn	3.50	1.75
37	A3	10q rose red	3.50	1.75
38	A3	25q dark blue	3.50	1.75
39	A3	50q violet & red	8.00	3.50
40	A3	1fr deep brown	20.00	10.00
		Nos. 35-40 (6)	42.00	*20.50*

For overprints and surcharges see Nos. 41-52, 105, J1-J9.

Nos. 35-40 Handstamped in Black or Violet

1914, Mar. 7

41	A3	2q orange brn & buff	37.50	37.50
42	A3	5q grn & bl grn (V)	37.50	37.50
43	A3	10q rose red	37.50	37.50
44	A3	25q dark blue (V)	37.50	37.50
45	A3	50q violet & red	37.50	37.50
46	A3	1fr deep brown	37.50	37.50
		Nos. 41-46 (6)	225.00	225.00

Issued to celebrate the arrival of Prince Wilhelm zu Wied on Mar. 7, 1914.

Nos. 35-40 Surcharged in Black:

a

b

1914, Apr. 2

47	A3	(a)	5pa on 2q	2.00	2.00
48	A3	(a)	10pa on 5q	2.00	2.00
49	A3	(a)	20pa on 10q	3.50	2.75
50	A3	(b)	1gr on 25q	3.50	3.50
51	A3	(b)	2gr on 50q	3.50	3.50
52	A3	(b)	5gr on 1fr	14.00	10.00
			Nos. 47-52 (6)	28.50	23.75

For overprints see Nos. 105, J6-J9.

Inverted Surcharge

47a	A3	(a)	5pa on 2q	15.00	15.00
48a	A3	(a)	10pa on 5q	14.00	14.00
49a	A3	(a)	20pa on 10q	15.00	15.00
50a	A3	(b)	1gr on 25q	15.00	15.00
51a	A3	(b)	2gr on 50q	18.00	18.00
52b	A3	(b)	5gr on 1fr	60.00	60.00
			Nos. 47a-52b (6)	137.00	137.00

Korce (Korytsa) Issues

A4

1914 **Handstamped** ***Imperf.***

52A	A4	10pa violet & red	140.00	140.00
c.		10pa black & red	200.00	200.00
53	A4	25pa violet & red	140.00	140.00
a.		25pa black & red	275.00	275.00

Nos. 52A-53a originally were handstamped directly on the cover, so the paper varies. Later they were also produced in sheets; these are rarely found. Nos. 52A-53a were issued by Albanian military authorities.

A5

A6

1917 **Typo. & Litho.** ***Perf. 11½***

54	A5	1c dk brown & grn	14.00	9.50
55	A5	2c red & green	14.00	9.50
56	A5	3c gray grn & grn	14.00	9.50
57	A5	5c green & black	12.50	6.25
58	A5	10c rose red & black	12.50	6.25
59	A5	25c blue & black	12.50	6.25
60	A5	50c violet & black	12.50	8.25
61	A5	1fr brown & black	12.50	8.25
		Nos. 54-61 (8)	104.50	63.75

1917-18

62	A6	1c dk brown & grn	2.25	1.90
63	A6	2c red brown & grn	2.25	1.90
a.		"CTM" for "CTS"	57.50	90.00
64	A6	3c black & green	2.25	1.90
a.		"CTM" for "CTS"	62.50	100.00
65	A6	5c green & black	3.25	3.25
66	A6	10c dull red & black	3.25	3.25
67	A6	50c violet & black	5.75	5.00
68	A6	1fr red brn & black	16.00	14.00
		Nos. 62-68 (7)	35.00	31.20

Counterfeits abound of Nos. 54-68, 80-81.

No. 65 Surcharged in Red

QARKU
I
KORÇËS
25 CTS

1918

80	A6	25c on 5c green & blk	140.00	200.00

A7

1918

81	A7	25c blue & black	60.00	85.00

General Issue

A8

A9

Handstamped in Rose or Blue

XV I MCMXIX

1919 ***Perf. 12½***

84	A8	(2)q on 2h brown	15.00	15.00
85	A8	5q on 16h green	15.00	15.00
86	A8	10q on 8h rose (Bl)	15.00	15.00
87	A8	25q on 64h blue	15.00	15.00
88	A9	25q on 64h blue	*300.00*	*300.00*
89	A8	50q on 32h violet	15.00	15.00
90	A8	1fr on 1.28k org, *bl*	15.00	15.00
		Nos. 84-90 (7)	*390.00*	*390.00*

See Nos. J10-J13. Compare with types A10-A14. For overprints see Nos 91-104.

Handstamped in Rose or Blue

1919, Jan. 16

91	A8	(2)q on 2h brown	14.00	14.00
92	A8	5q on 16h green	10.00	10.00
93	A8	10q on 8h rose (Bl)	10.00	10.00
94	A8	25q on 64h blue	14.00	14.00
95	A9	25q on 64h blue	45.00	45.00
96	A8	50q on 32h violet	14.00	14.00
97	A8	1fr on 1.28k org, *bl*	14.00	14.00
		Nos. 91-97 (7)	121.00	121.00

Handstamped in Violet

1919

98	A8	(2)q on 2h brown	15.00	15.00
99	A8	5q on 16h green	15.00	15.00
100	A8	10q on 8h rose	15.00	15.00
101	A8	25q on 64h blue	15.00	15.00
102	A9	25q on 64h blue	14.00	14.00
103	A8	50q on 32h violet	15.00	15.00
104	A8	1fr on 1.28k org, *bl*	15.00	15.00
		Nos. 98-104 (7)	104.00	104.00

No. 50 Overprinted in Violet

1919 ***Perf. 14***

105	A3	1gr on 25q blue	27.50	20.00

A10

A11

1919, June 5 ***Perf. 11½, 12½***

106	A10	10q on 2h brown	7.00	5.00
107	A11	15q on 8h rose	7.00	5.00
108	A11	20q on 16h green	7.00	5.00
109	A10	25q on 64h blue	7.00	5.00
110	A11	50q on 32h violet	7.00	5.00
111	A11	1fr on 96h orange	7.00	5.00
112	A10	2fr on 1.60k vio, buff	25.00	20.00
		Nos. 106-112 (7)	67.00	50.00

Nos. 106-108, 110 exist with inverted surcharge.

A12

A13

Black or Violet Surcharge

1919

113	A12	10q on 8h car	7.00	5.00
114	A12	15q on 8h car (V)	7.00	5.00
115	A13	20q on 16h green	7.00	5.00
116	A13	25q on 35h violet	7.00	5.00
117	A13	50q on 64h blue	20.00	14.00
118	A13	1fr on 96h orange	8.00	7.00
119	A12	2fr on 1.60k vio, buff	14.00	10.00
		Nos. 113-119 (7)	70.00	51.00

A14

A15

Overprinted in Blue or Black Without New Value

1920 ***Perf. 12½***

120	A14	1q gray (Bl)	100.00	70.00
121	A14	10q rose (Bk)	14.00	*18.00*
a.		Double overprint	125.00	*125.00*
122	A14	20q brown (Bl)	45.00	30.00
123	A14	25q blue (Bk)	525.00	*425.00*
124	A14	50q brown vio (Bk)	60.00	55.00
		Nos. 120-124 (5)	744.00	*598.00*

Counterfeit overprints exist of Nos. 120-128.

Surcharged with New Value

125	A14	2q on 10q rose (R)	14.00	*21.00*
126	A14	5q on 10q rose (G)	14.00	*18.00*
127	A14	25q on 10q rose (Bl)	14.00	14.00
128	A14	50q on 10q rose (Br)	14.00	*25.00*
		Nos. 125-128 (4)	56.00	78.00

Stamps of type A14 (Portrait of the Prince zu Wied) were not placed in use without overprint or surcharge.

Post Horn Overprinted in Black

1920 ***Perf. 14x13***

129	A15	2q orange	10.00	8.50
130	A15	5q deep green	17.50	15.00
131	A15	10q red	30.00	30.00
132	A15	25q light blue	57.50	30.00
133	A15	50q gray green	12.50	10.00
134	A15	1fr claret	12.50	10.00
		Nos. 129-134 (6)	140.00	103.50

Type A15 was never placed in use without post horn or "Besa" overprint.

Stamps of Type A15 (No Post Horn) Overprinted

1921

135	A15	2q orange	7.00	7.00
136	A15	5q deep green	7.00	7.00
137	A15	10q red	14.00	12.00
138	A15	25q light blue	25.00	21.00
139	A15	50q gray green	14.00	12.00
140	A15	1fr claret	14.00	12.00
		Nos. 135-140 (6)	81.00	71.00

For surcharge & overprints see #154, 156-157.

Stamps of these types, and with "TAKSE" overprint, were unauthorized and never placed in use. They are common.

Gjirokaster
A18

Korcha
A19

Designs: 5q, Kanina. 10q, Berati. 25q, Bridge at Vezirit. 50q, Rozafat. 2fr, Dursit.

1923 **Typo.** ***Perf. 12½, 11½***

147	A18	2q orange	1.10	1.40
148	A18	5q yellow green	.50	1.00
149	A18	10q carmine	.60	1.00
150	A18	25q dark blue	.60	1.00
151	A18	50q dark green	.60	1.00
152	A19	1fr dark violet	.60	1.40
153	A19	2fr olive green	3.00	5.50
		Nos. 147-153 (7)	7.00	*12.30*

For overprints & surcharges see #158-185, B1-B8.

No. 135 Surcharged

1922 ***Perf. 14x13***

154	A15	1q on 2q orange	3.00	3.50

Stamps of Type A15 (No Post Horn) Overprinted

1922

156	A15	5q deep green	3.50	*5.00*
157	A15	10q red	3.50	*5.00*

Nos. 147-151 Overprinted (top line in Black; diamond in Violet)

1924, Jan. ***Perf. 12½***

158	A18	2q red orange	8.50	*15.00*
159	A18	5q yellow green	8.50	*15.00*
160	A18	10q carmine	6.50	*11.00*
161	A18	25q dark blue	6.50	*11.00*
162	A18	50q dark green	10.00	*18.00*
		Nos. 158-162 (5)	40.00	70.00

The words "Mbledhje Kushtetuese" are in taller letters on the 25q than on the other values. Opening of the Constituent Assembly.

No. 147 Surcharged

1924

163	A18	1q on 2q red orange	2.75	*7.00*

Nos. 163, 147-152 Overprinted

1924

164	A18	1q on 2q orange	2.00	*6.75*
165	A18	2q orange	2.00	*6.75*
166	A18	5q yellow green	2.00	*6.75*
167	A18	10q carmine	2.00	*6.75*
168	A18	25q dark blue	2.00	*6.75*
169	A18	50q dark green	5.00	*12.50*
170	A19	1fr dark violet	5.00	*16.00*
		Nos. 164-170 (7)	20.00	*62.25*

Issued to celebrate the return of the Government to the Capital after a revolution.

Nos. 163, 147-152 Overprinted

1925

171	A18	1q on 2q orange	2.50	*5.00*
172	A18	2q orange	2.50	*5.00*
173	A18	5q yellow green	2.50	*5.00*
174	A18	10q carmine	2.50	*5.00*
175	A18	25q dark blue	2.50	*5.00*
176	A18	50q dark green	2.50	*6.00*
177	A19	1fr dark violet	5.00	*10.00*
		Nos. 171-177 (7)	20.00	*41.00*

Proclamation of the Republic, Jan. 21, 1925. The date "1921" instead of "1925" occurs once in each sheet of 50.

Nos. 163, 147-153 Overprinted

1925

178	A18	1q on 2q orange	1.00	*1.40*
a.		Inverted overprint	10.00	10.00
179	A18	2q orange	1.00	*1.40*
180	A18	5q yellow green	1.00	*1.40*
a.		Inverted overprint	10.00	10.00
181	A18	10q carmine	1.00	*1.40*
182	A18	25q dark blue	1.00	*1.40*
183	A18	50q dark green	1.00	*1.40*
184	A19	1fr dark violet	4.50	*3.50*
185	A19	2fr olive green	7.00	*3.50*
		Nos. 178-185 (8)	17.50	15.40

President Ahmed Zogu
A25 A26

1925 ***Perf. 13½, 13½x13***

186	A25	1q orange	.20	.20
187	A25	2q red brown	.20	.20
188	A25	5q green	.20	.20
189	A25	10q rose red	.20	.20
190	A25	15q gray brown	.75	*1.75*
191	A25	25q dark blue	.20	.20
192	A25	50q blue green	.75	*1.25*
193	A26	1fr red & ultra	1.50	1.75
194	A26	2fr green & orange	1.60	*1.75*
195	A26	3fr brown & violet	3.50	*4.00*
196	A26	5fr violet & black	4.00	5.00
		Nos. 186-196 (11)	13.10	16.50

No. 193 in ultramarine and brown, and No. 194 in green and brown were not regularly issued. Value, both $15.

For overprints & surcharges see #197-209, 238-248.

Nos. 186-196 Overprinted in Various Colors

1927

197	A25	1q orange (V)	.60	.85
198	A25	2q red brn (G)	.25	.30
199	A25	5q green (R)	1.00	.50
200	A25	10q rose red (Bl)	.25	.30
201	A25	15q gray brn (G)	6.00	*10.00*
202	A25	25q dk blue (R)	.50	.35
203	A25	50q blue grn (Bl)	.50	.35
204	A26	1fr red & ultra (Bk)	1.10	*.50*
205	A26	2fr green & org (Bk)	1.25	*.75*
206	A26	3fr brown & vio (Bk)	2.00	*1.40*
207	A26	5fr violet & blk (Bk)	3.50	*2.25*
		Nos. 197-207 (11)	16.95	17.55

No. 200 exists perf. 11.

For surcharges see Nos. 208-209, 238-240.

Nos. 200, 202 Surcharged in Black or Red

1928

208	A25	1q on 10q rose red	.45	.50
a.		Inverted surcharge	3.75	3.75
209	A25	5q on 25q dk blue (R)	.45	.50
a.		Inverted surcharge	3.75	3.75

A27

King Zog I — A28

Black Overprint

1928 ***Perf. 14x13½***

210	A27	1q orange brown	4.00	*7.25*
211	A27	2q slate	4.00	*7.25*
212	A27	5q blue green	4.00	*9.00*
213	A27	10q rose red	4.00	*9.00*
214	A27	15q bister	12.00	*35.00*
215	A27	25q deep blue	5.00	*9.00*
216	A27	50q lilac rose	8.00	*12.00*

Red Overprint

Perf. 13½x14

217	A28	1fr blue & slate	5.00	9.00
		Nos. 210-217 (8)	46.00	*97.50*

Compare with types A29-A32.

A29

A30

Black or Red Overprint

1928 ***Perf. 14x13½***

218	A29	1q orange brown	8.25	*20.00*
219	A29	2q slate (R)	8.25	*20.00*
220	A29	5q blue green	7.00	*8.25*
221	A29	10q rose red	7.00	*12.00*
222	A29	15q bister	9.00	*22.50*
223	A29	25q deep blue (R)	7.00	*12.00*
224	A29	50q lilac rose	7.00	*12.00*

Perf. 13½x14

225	A30	1fr blue & slate (R)	8.25	*20.00*
226	A30	2fr green & slate (R)	8.25	*20.00*
		Nos. 218-226 (9)	70.00	146.75

Proclamation of Ahmed Zogu as King of Albania.

A31

A32

Black Overprint

1928 *Perf. 14x13½*

227	A31	1q orange brown	.35	*1.10*
228	A31	2q slate	.35	*1.10*
229	A31	5q blue green	2.50	*3.00*
230	A31	10q rose red	.35	*1.10*
231	A31	15q bister	10.00	*20.00*
232	A31	25q deep blue	.35	*1.10*
233	A31	50q lilac rose	.65	*1.60*

Perf. 13½x14

234	A32	1fr blue & slate	1.25	*2.00*
235	A32	2fr green & slate	1.25	*3.00*
236	A32	3fr dk red & ol bis	5.00	*10.00*
237	A32	5fr dull vio & gray	5.00	*12.50*
		Nos. 227-237 (11)	27.05	56.50

The overprint reads "Kingdom of Albania."

Nos. 203, 202, 200 Surcharged in Black

1929 *Perf. 13½x13, 11½*

238	A25	1q on 50q blue green	.35	*.50*
239	A25	5q on 25q dark blue	.35	*.50*
240	A25	15q on 10q rose red	.55	*.75*
		Nos. 238-240 (3)	1.25	1.75

RROFT-MBRETI

Nos. 186-189, 191-194 Overprinted in Black or Red

8X1929.

1929 *Perf. 11½, 13½*

241	A25	1q orange	6.00	*17.50*
242	A25	2q red brown	6.00	*17.50*
243	A25	5q green	6.00	*17.50*
244	A25	10q rose red	6.00	*17.50*
245	A25	25q dark blue	6.00	*17.50*
246	A25	50q blue green (R)	8.00	*20.00*
247	A26	1fr red & ultra	12.00	*30.00*
248	A26	2fr green & orange	12.00	*30.00*
		Nos. 241-248 (8)	62.00	167.50

34th birthday of King Zog. The overprint reads "Long live the King."

Lake Butrinto — A33

King Zog I — A34

Zog Bridge — A35

Ruin at Zog Manor — A36

Perf. 14, 14½

1930, Sept. 1 **Photo.** **Wmk. 220**

250	A33	1q slate	.20	.20
251	A33	2q orange red	.20	.20
252	A34	5q yellow green	.20	.20
253	A34	10q carmine	.20	.20
254	A34	15q dark brown	.20	.20
255	A34	25q dark ultra	.20	.20
256	A33	50q slate green	.40	.30
257	A35	1fr violet	.85	.75
258	A35	2fr indigo	1.00	.85
259	A36	3fr gray green	3.25	1.90
260	A36	5fr orange brown	4.25	3.25
		Nos. 250-260 (11)	10.95	8.25

2nd anniversary of accession of King Zog I.

For overprints see Nos. 261-270, 299-309, J39. For surcharges see Nos. 354-360.

Nos. 250-259 Overprinted in Black

1934, Dec. 24

261	A33	1q slate	8.50	*10.00*
262	A33	2q orange red	8.50	*10.00*
263	A34	5q yellow green	8.50	8.50
264	A34	10q carmine	8.50	*10.00*
265	A34	15q dark brown	8.50	*10.00*
266	A34	25q dark ultra	8.50	*10.00*
267	A33	50q slate green	8.50	*14.00*
268	A35	1fr violet	8.50	*17.50*
269	A35	2fr indigo	9.00	*21.00*
270	A36	3fr gray green	12.50	*30.00*
		Nos. 261-270 (10)	89.50	141.00

Tenth anniversary of the Constitution.

Allegory of Death of Skanderbeg A37

Albanian Eagle in Turkish Shackles A38

5q, 25q, 40q, 2fr, Eagle with wings spread.

1937 **Unwmk.** *Perf. 14*

271	A37	1q brown violet	.20	.20
272	A38	2q brown	.40	.30
273	A38	5q lt green	.40	.40
274	A37	10q olive brown	.40	*.60*
275	A38	15q rose red	.60	*.80*
276	A38	25q blue	1.25	*1.50*
277	A37	50q deep green	3.00	2.50
278	A38	1fr violet	8.00	5.00
279	A38	2fr orange brown	10.00	7.50
		Nos. 271-279 (9)	24.25	18.80

Souvenir Sheet

280	Sheet of 3	15.00	*125.00*
a.	A37 20q red violet	3.00	*5.00*
b.	A38 30q olive brown	3.00	*5.00*
c.	A38 40q red	3.00	*5.00*

25th anniv. of independence from Turkey, proclaimed Nov. 26, 1912.

Queen Geraldine and King Zog — A40

1938 *Perf. 14*

281	A40	1q slate violet	.25	.30
282	A40	2q red brown	.25	.30
283	A40	5q green	.25	.30
284	A40	10q olive brown	1.00	.65
285	A40	15q rose red	1.00	.65
286	A40	25q blue	2.50	1.60
287	A40	50q Prus green	5.00	3.25
288	A40	1fr purple	10.00	6.50
		Nos. 281-288 (8)	20.25	13.55

Souvenir Sheet

289	Sheet of 4	30.00	*140.00*
a.	A40 20q dark red violet	6.00	*8.00*
b.	A40 30q brown olive	6.00	*8.00*

Wedding of King Zog and Countess Geraldine Apponyi, Apr. 27, 1938.

No. 289 contains 2 each of Nos. 289a, 289b.

Queen Geraldine — A42

National Emblems — A43

Designs: 10q, 25q, 30q, 1fr, King Zog.

1938

290	A42	1q dp red violet	.20	*.40*
291	A43	2q red orange	.20	*.40*
292	A42	5q deep green	.40	*.40*
293	A42	10q red brown	.40	*.70*
294	A42	15q deep rose	.80	*.90*
295	A42	25q deep blue	1.00	1.00
296	A43	50q gray black	7.00	4.50
297	A42	1fr slate green	10.00	6.50
		Nos. 290-297 (8)	20.00	14.80

Souvenir Sheet

298	Sheet of 3	18.00	*80.00*
b.	A43 20q Prussian green	4.50	*9.00*
c.	A42 30q deep violet	4.50	*9.00*

10th anniv. of royal rule. They were on sale for 3 days (Aug. 30-31, Sept. 1) only, during which their use was required on all mail.

No. 298 contains Nos. 294, 298b, 298c.

Issued under Italian Dominion

Nos. 250-260 Overprinted in Black

1939 **Wmk. 220** *Perf. 14*

299	A33	1q slate	1.25	*1.25*
		Never hinged	3.25	
300	A33	2q orange red	1.25	*1.25*
		Never hinged	3.25	
301	A34	5q yellow green	1.25	*1.25*
		Never hinged	3.25	
302	A34	10q carmine	1.25	*1.25*
		Never hinged	3.25	
303	A34	15q dark brown	2.00	*3.75*
		Never hinged	4.75	
304	A34	25q dark ultra	2.00	*3.75*
		Never hinged	4.75	
305	A33	50q slate green	2.50	*5.00*
		Never hinged	6.50	
306	A35	1fr violet	2.50	*5.00*
		Never hinged	6.50	
307	A35	2fr indigo	3.25	*9.50*
		Never hinged	8.00	
308	A36	3fr gray green	7.75	*22.50*
		Never hinged	19.00	
309	A36	5fr orange brown	10.00	*25.00*
		Never hinged	24.00	
		Nos. 299-309 (11)	35.00	79.50
		Set, on overfranked philatelic cover		160.00

Resolution adopted by the Natl. Assembly, Apr. 12, 1939, offering the Albanian Crown to Italy.

A46

A47

Native Costumes — A48

King Victor Emmanuel III A49 A50

Native Costume — A51

Monastery A52

Designs: 2fr, Bridge at Vezirit. 3fr, Ancient Columns. 5fr, Amphitheater.

1939 **Unwmk.** **Photo.** *Perf. 14*

310	A46	1q blue gray	1.25	.50
		Never hinged	3.25	
311	A47	2q olive green	1.25	.50
		Never hinged	3.25	
312	A48	3q golden brown	1.25	.50
		Never hinged	3.25	
313	A49	5q green	1.25	.20
		Never hinged	3.25	
314	A50	10q brown	1.25	.20
		Never hinged	3.25	
315	A50	15q crimson	1.25	.20
		Never hinged	3.25	
316	A50	25q sapphire	2.00	.80
		Never hinged	4.75	
317	A50	30q brt violet	2.50	1.40
		Never hinged	6.50	
318	A51	50q dull purple	3.25	3.25
		Never hinged	8.00	
319	A49	65q red brown	5.00	11.50
		Never hinged	13.00	
320	A52	1fr myrtle green	7.50	9.50
		Never hinged	19.00	
321	A52	2fr brown lake	11.50	19.00
		Never hinged	29.00	
322	A52	3fr brown black	19.00	35.00
		Never hinged	47.50	
323	A52	5fr gray violet	25.00	*50.00*
		Never hinged	65.00	
		Nos. 310-323 (14)	83.25	132.55
		Set, on overfranked philatelic cover		275.00

For overprints and surcharges see Nos. 331-353.

SEMI-POSTAL STAMPS

Nos. 148-151 Surcharged in Red and Black

1924, Nov. 1

B1	A18	5q + 5q yel grn	9.00	*25.00*
B2	A18	10q + 5q carmine	9.00	*25.00*
B3	A18	25q + 5q dark blue	9.00	*25.00*
B4	A18	50q + 5q dark grn	9.00	*25.00*
		Nos. B1-B4 (4)	36.00	100.00

Nos. B1 to B4 with Additional Surcharge in Red and Black

1924

B5	A18	5q + 5q + 5q yel grn	9.00	18.00
B6	A18	10q + 5q + 5q car	9.00	18.00
B7	A18	25q + 5q + 5q dk bl	9.00	18.00
B8	A18	50q + 5q + 5q dk grn	9.00	18.00
		Nos. B5-B8 (4)	36.00	72.00

AIR POST STAMPS

Airplane Crossing Mountains AP1

Wmk. 125

1925, May 30 **Typo.** *Perf. 14*

C1	AP1	5q green	1.50	*2.75*
C2	AP1	10q rose red	1.50	*2.75*
C3	AP1	25q deep blue	1.50	*2.75*
C4	AP1	50q dark green	2.50	*5.00*
C5	AP1	1fr dk vio & blk	4.25	*8.50*
C6	AP1	2fr ol grn & vio	7.00	*14.00*
C7	AP1	3fr brn org & dk grn	9.00	14.00
		Nos. C1-C7 (7)	27.25	49.75

Nos. C1-C7 exist imperf. Value $2,600.

For overprint see Nos. C8-C28.

Nos. C1-C7 Overprinted

1927, Jan. 18

C8	AP1	5q green	4.25	*8.50*
a.		Dbl. overprint, one invtd.	45.00	
C9	AP1	10q rose red	4.25	*8.50*
a.		Inverted overprint	40.00	
b.		Dbl. overprint, one invtd.	45.00	
C10	AP1	25q deep blue	3.50	*7.00*
C11	AP1	50q dark grn	2.50	*5.00*
a.		Inverted overprint	40.00	
C12	AP1	1fr dk vio & blk	2.50	*5.00*
a.		Inverted overprint	40.00	
b.		Double overprint	40.00	

C13 AP1 2fr ol grn & vio 5.50 *8.50*
C14 AP1 3fr brn org & dk grn 7.50 *12.00*
Nos. C8-C14 (7) 30.00 *54.50*

Nos. C1-C7 Overprinted

1928, Apr. 21

C15 AP1 5q green 4.25 *8.50*
a. Inverted overprint 60.00
C16 AP1 10q rose red 4.25 *8.50*
C17 AP1 25q deep blue 4.25 *8.50*
C18 AP1 50q dark green 9.00 *18.00*
C19 AP1 1fr dk vio & blk 45.00 *90.00*
C20 AP1 2fr ol grn & vio 45.00 *90.00*
C21 AP1 3fr brn org & dk grn 45.00 *90.00*
Nos. C15-C21 (7) 156.75 *313.50*

First flight across the Adriatic, Valona to Brindisi, Apr. 21, 1928.

The variety "SHQYRTARE" occurs once in the sheet for each value. Value 3 times normal.

Nos. C1-C7 Overprinted in Red Brown

1929, Dec. 1

C22 AP1 5q green 5.00 *7.00*
C23 AP1 10q rose red 5.00 *7.00*
C24 AP1 25q deep blue 5.00 *7.00*
C25 AP1 50q dk grn 100.00 *140.00*
C26 AP1 1fr dk vio & blk 175.00 *290.00*
C27 AP1 2fr ol grn 175.00 *290.00*
C28 AP1 3fr brn org & dk grn 175.00 *290.00*
Nos. C22-C28 (7) 640.00 *1,031.*

Excellent counterfeits exist.

King Zog and Airplane over Tirana AP2

AP3

1930, Oct. 8 Photo. Unwmk.

C29 AP2 5q yellow green .90 *1.40*
C30 AP2 15q rose red .90 *1.40*
C31 AP2 20q slate blue .90 *1.40*
C32 AP2 50q olive green 1.75 *2.00*
C33 AP3 1fr dark blue 2.75 *4.25*
C34 AP3 2fr olive brown 9.00 *14.00*
C35 AP3 3fr purple 21.00 14.00
Nos. C29-C35 (7) 37.20 *38.45*

For overprints and surcharges see Nos. C36-C45.

Nos. C29-C35 Overprinted

1931, July 6

C36 AP2 5q yellow grn 4.25 *8.50*
a. Double overprint *125.00*
C37 AP2 15q rose red 4.25 *8.50*
C38 AP2 20q slate blue 4.25 *8.50*
C39 AP2 50q olive grn 4.25 *8.50*
C40 AP3 1fr dark blue 25.00 *50.00*
C41 AP3 2fr olive brn 25.00 *50.00*
C42 AP3 3fr purple 21.00 *12.50*
a. Inverted overprint *250.00*
Nos. C36-C42 (7) 88.00 *146.50*

1st air post flight from Tirana to Rome.

Only a very small part of this issue was sold to the public. Most of the stamps were given to the Aviation Company to help provide funds for conducting the service.

Issued under Italian Dominion

Nos. C29-C30 Overprinted in Black

1939, Apr. 19 Unwmk. *Perf. 14*

C43 AP2 5q yel green 2.50 *7.00*
Never hinged 6.50
C44 AP2 15q rose red 2.50 *7.00*
Never hinged 6.50

No. C32 With Additional Surcharge

C45 AP2 20q on 50q ol grn 5.00 *11.50*
Never hinged 13.00
a. Inverted overprint — —
Nos. C43-C45 (3) 10.00 *25.50*
Set on flown cover 95.00

See note after No. 309.

King Victor Emmanuel III and Plane over Mountains AP4

1939, Aug. 4 Photo.

C46 AP4 20q brown 32.50 12.50
Never hinged 80.00
On commercial cover 40.00

Shepherds AP5

Map of Albania Showing Air Routes — AP6

Designs: 20q, Victor Emmanuel III and harbor view. 50q, Woman and river valley. 1fr, Bridge at Vezirit. 2fr, Ruins. 3fr, Women waving to plane.

1940, Mar. 20 Unwmk.

C47 AP5 5q green 1.25 *1.25*
Never hinged 3.25
C48 AP6 15q rose red 1.25 *1.90*
Never hinged 3.25
C49 AP5 20q deep blue 2.50 *3.25*
Never hinged 3.25
C50 AP6 50q brown 3.25 *9.50*
Never hinged 8.00
C51 AP5 1fr myrtle green 6.50 *12.50*
Never hinged 8.00
C52 AP6 2fr brown black 9.50 *19.00*
Never hinged 24.00
C53 AP6 3fr rose violet 16.00 *25.00*
Never hinged 40.00
Nos. C47-C53 (7) 40.25 *72.40*
Set on overfranked philatelic cover 175.00

SPECIAL DELIVERY STAMPS

Issued under Italian Dominion

King Victor Emmanuel III — SD1

1940 Unwmk. Photo. *Perf. 14*

E1 SD1 25q bright violet 4.50 *7.50*
Never hinged 11.00
E2 SD1 50q red orange 11.50 *18.00*
Never hinged 29.00
Set on overfranked philatelic cover 55.00

POSTAGE DUE STAMPS

Nos. 35-39 Handstamped in Various Colors

1914, Feb. 23 Unwmk. *Perf. 14*

J1 A3 2q org brn & buff (Bl) 9.00 3.50
J2 A3 5q green (R) 9.00 3.50
J3 A3 10q rose red (Bl) 12.50 3.50
J4 A3 25q dark blue (R) 15.00 3.50
J5 A3 50q vio & red (Bk) 22.50 11.50
Nos. J1-J5 (5) 68.00 25.50

The two parts of the overprint are handstamped separately. Stamps exist with one or both handstamps inverted, double, omitted or in wrong color.

Nos. 48-51 Overprinted in Black

1914, Apr. 16

J6 A3 (a) 10pa on 5q green 4.25 3.50
J7 A3 (a) 20pa on 10q rose red 4.25 3.50
J8 A3 (b) 1gr on 25q blue 4.25 3.50
J9 A3 (b) 2gr on 50q vio & red 4.25 3.50
Nos. J6-J9 (4) 17.00 14.00

Same Design as Regular Issue of 1919, Overprinted

1919, Feb. 10 *Perf. 11½, 12½*

J10 A8 (4)q on 4h rose 11.00 8.50
J11 A8 (10)q on 10k red, *grn* 11.00 8.50
J12 A8 20q on 2k org, *gray* 11.00 8.50
J13 A8 50q on 5k brn, *yel* 11.00 8.50
Nos. J10-J13 (4) 44.00 34.00

Fortress at Scutari — D3

D5

Post Horn Overprinted in Black

1920, Apr. 1 *Perf. 14x13*

J14 D3 4q olive green .70 *3.50*
J15 D3 10q rose red 1.40 *5.25*
J16 D3 20q bister brn 1.40 *5.25*
J17 D3 50q black 3.50 *14.00*
Nos. J14-J17 (4) 7.00 *28.00*

1922 *Perf. 12½, 11½*

Background of Red Wavy Lines

J23 D5 4q black, *red* 1.00 *3.50*
J24 D5 10q black, *red* 1.00 *3.50*
J25 D5 20q black, *red* 1.00 *3.50*
J26 D5 50q black, *red* 1.00 *3.50*
Nos. J23-J26 (4) 4.00 *14.00*

Same Overprinted in White

1925

J27 D5 4q black, *red* 1.75 *3.50*
J28 D5 10q black, *red* 1.75 *3.50*
J29 D5 20q black, *red* 1.75 *3.50*
J30 D5 50q black, *red* 1.75 *3.50*
Nos. J27-J30 (4) 7.00 *14.00*

The 10q with overprint in gold was a trial printing. It was not put in use.

D7

Coat of Arms — D8

Overprinted "QINDAR" in Red

1926, Dec. 24 *Perf. 13½x13*

J31 D7 10q dark blue .70 2.75
J32 D7 20q green .70 2.75
J33 D7 30q red brown 1.40 *5.75*
J34 D7 50q dark brown 2.50 *11.00*
Nos. J31-J34 (4) 5.30 *22.25*

Wmk. Double Headed Eagle (220)

1930, Sept. 1 Photo. *Perf. 14, 14½*

J35 D8 10q dark blue 6.50 *18.00*
J36 D8 20q rose red 1.25 *11.00*
J37 D8 30q violet 1.25 *11.00*
J38 D8 50q dark green 1.50 *11.00*
Nos. J35-J38 (4) 10.50 *51.00*

Nos. J36-J38 exist with overprint "14 Shtator 1943" (see Nos. 332-344) which is private and fraudulent on these stamps.

No. 253 Overprinted

1936 *Perf. 14*

J39 A34 10q carmine 9.00 *35.00*
a. Hyphens on each side of "Takse" ('39) 75.00 *175.00*

Issued under Italian Dominion

Coat of Arms — D9

1940 Unwmk. Photo. *Perf. 14*

J40 D9 4q red orange *37.50* *75.00*
Never hinged 95.00
J41 D9 10q bright violet *37.50* *75.00*
Never hinged 95.00
J42 D9 20q brown *37.50* *75.00*
Never hinged 95.00
J43 D9 30q dark blue *37.50* *75.00*
Never hinged 95.00
J44 D9 50q carmine rose *37.50* *75.00*
Never hinged 95.00
Nos. J40-J44 (5) *187.50* *375.00*

ALEXANDRETTA

ˌa-lig-ˌzan-ˈdre-tə

LOCATION — A political territory in northern Syria, bordering on Turkey
GOVT. — French mandate
AREA — 10,000 sq. mi. (approx.)
POP. — 220,000 (approx.)

Included in the Syrian territory mandated to France under the Versailles Treaty, the name was changed to Hatay in 1938. The following year France returned the territory to Turkey in exchange for certain concessions. See Hatay.

100 Centimes = 1 Piaster

Stamps of Syria, 1930-36, Overprinted or Surcharged in Black or Red:

a

b

c

d

e

1938 Unwmk. *Perf. 12x12½*

1	A6 (a)	10c vio brn	1.10	.90
2	A6 (a)	20c brn org	1.10	.90
		Perf. 13½		
3	A9 (b)	50c vio (R)	1.25	1.00
4	A10 (b)	1p bis brn	1.25	1.25
5	A9 (b)	2p dk vio (R)	2.00	2.00
6	A13 (b)	3p yel grn (R)	3.00	3.00
7	A10 (b)	4p yel org	3.50	3.50
8	A16 (b)	6p grnsh blk (R)	4.00	4.00
9	A18 (b)	25p vio brn	12.00	12.00
10	A15 (c)	75c org red	2.50	2.50
11	A10 (d)	2.50p on 4p yel org	4.00	3.00
12	AP2 (e)	12.50p on 15p org red	8.00	8.00
		Nos. 1-12 (12)	43.70	42.05

Issue dates: #1-9, Apr. 14, #10-12, Sept. 2.
Covers: Values for commercial covers begin at about $75.

Nos. 4, 7, 10-12 Overprinted in Black

1938, Nov. 10

13	A15	75c	37.50	37.50
14	A10	1p	25.00	25.00
15	A10	2.50p on 4p	16.00	16.00
16	A10	4p	19.00	19.00
17	AP2	12.50p on 15p	45.00	37.50
		Nos. 13-17 (5)	142.50	135.00

Death of Kemal Ataturk, pres. of Turkey.

AIR POST STAMPS

Air Post Stamps of Syria, 1937, Overprinted Type "b" in Red or Black

1938, Apr. 14 Unwmk. *Perf. 13*

C1	AP14	½p dark vio (R)	1.75	2.00
C2	AP15	1p black (R)	1.75	*2.00*
C3	AP14	2p blue grn (R)	2.50	*3.00*
C4	AP15	3p deep ultra	3.00	*4.00*
C5	AP14	5p rose lake	6.00	*10.00*
C6	AP15	10p red brown	6.75	*10.00*
C7	AP14	15p lake brown	8.00	*12.50*
C8	AP15	25p dk blue (R)	11.00	*16.00*
		Nos. C1-C8 (8)	40.75	*59.50*

POSTAGE DUE STAMPS

Postage Due Stamps of Syria, 1925-31, Ovptd. Type "b" in Black or Red

1938, Apr. 14 Unwmk. *Perf. 13½*

J1	D5	50c brown, *yel*	3.00	*3.00*
J2	D6	1p violet, *rose*	3.25	*3.25*
J3	D5	2p blk, *blue* (R)	4.00	4.00
J4	D5	3p blk, *red org*	6.00	*7.50*
J5	D5	5p blk, *bl grn* (R)	8.00	*8.50*
J6	D7	8p blk, *gray bl* (R)	11.00	*11.00*
		Nos. J1-J6 (6)	35.25	37.25

On No. J2, the overprint is vertical, reading up, other denominations, horizontal.
Stamps of Alexandretta were discontinued in 1938 and replaced by those of Hatay.

ALGERIA

al-ˈjir-ē-ə

LOCATION — North Africa
GOVT. — French Colony
AREA — 847,552 sq. mi.
POP. — 7,234,684
CAPITAL — Algiers

100 Centimes = 1 Franc

Catalogue values for unused stamps in this country are for Never Hinged items, beginning with Scott 109 in the regular postage section, and Scott B27 in the semi-postal section.

STAMPS OF FRANCE USED IN ALGERIA

Stamps of France used in Algeria

From 1849 to 1924, stamps of France were used at post offices in Algeria. From 1849 to 1862, stamps were canceled by a lozenge-shaped canceler with small numeral identifiers between 3710 and 4448, each of 83 post offices being identified by its number. From 1862 to 1876, similar cancelers, with larger numerals ranging from 5000 to 5177, were used by 156 post offices. After 1876, each post office used its own circular date stamp.

Grill and Town Cancels

Canceled with grill, on large piece with Algerian town name (first column) or on cover with town name on envelope (second column).

1849

On France No. 6

A6G A1 25c lt blue, *bluish*

Alger	60.00	250.00
Arzew	500.00	2,500.
Bouffarich	500.00	2,500.
Constantine	70.00	325.00
Cherchell	72.50	325.00
Dellys	72.50	325.00
Djidjeli	90.00	375.00
Douera	72.50	325.00
Douera + Coleah	500.00	2,500.
Mostaganem	65.00	300.00
Orleans-ville	200.00	1,000.
Philippeville	65.00	300.00
Tenez	65.00	300.00

The 25c value is the least expensive of the French stamps used in Algeria. Other values of the first issue exist used in Algeria and are worth more than the values shown.

Small Figures in Dotted Lozenge

Single (first column) or on cover (second column).

1849

On France No. 6

A6S A1 25c lt blue, *bluish*

3710 — Alger, *from*	45.00	125.00
3711 — L'Arba, *from*	325.00	3,000.
3712 — Arzew, *from*	225.00	1,750.
3713 — Aumale, *from*	110.00	725.00
3714 — Batna, *from*	90.00	650.00
3715 — Blidah, *from*	60.00	200.00
3716 — Bone, *from*	50.00	175.00
3717 — Bouffarich, *from*	200.00	1,600.
3718 — Bougie, *from*	90.00	675.00
3719 — Cherchell, *from*	100.00	675.00
3720 — Coleah, *from*	250.00	2,250.
3721 — Constantine, *from*	50.00	175.00
3722 — Dellys, *from*	180.00	1,350.
3723 — Dely-Ibrahim, *from*	350.00	3,250.
3724 — Djidjeli, *from*	180.00	1,400.
3725 — Douera, *from*	180.00	1,500.
3726 — Mascara, *from*	80.00	600.00
3727 — Medeah, *from*	80.00	300.00
3728 — Mers-el-Kebir, *from*	65.00	1,500.
3729 — Milianah, *from*	200.00	625.00
3730 — Mostaganem, *from*	80.00	225.00
3731 — Nemours, *from*	60.00	725.00
3732 — Oran, *from*	110.00	200.00
3733 — Orleansville, *from*	75.00	575.00
3734 — Philippeville, *from*	60.00	225.00
3735 — Setif, *from*	75.00	375.00
3736 — Sidi-Bel-Abbes, *from*	60.00	275.00
3737 — Stora, *from*	550.00	
3738 — Tenez, *from*	75.00	375.00
3739 — Tlemcen, *from*	70.00	300.00

All other values of the set exist used in Algeria. They are worth more than the values shown above, which are for cancellations on the 25c value.

1849

On France No. 15

A15S A3 25c blue, *bluish* (I)

3710 — Alger, *from*	1.50	7.50
3711 — L'Arba, *from*	50.00	425.00
3712 — Arzew, *from*	32.50	265.00
3713 — Aumale, *from*	17.50	115.00
3714 — Batna, *from*	15.00	80.00
3715 — Blidah, *from*	3.00	17.50
3716 — Bone, *from*	3.00	15.00
3717 — Bouffarik, *from*	32.50	225.00
3718 — Bougie, *from*	14.00	80.00
3719 — Cherchell, *from*	17.50	100.00
3720 — Coleah, *from*	40.00	300.00
3721 — Constantine, *from*	2.25	10.00
3722 — Dellys, *from*	30.00	200.00
3723 — Dely-Ibrahim, *from*	45.00	425.00
3724 — Djidjeli, *from*	32.50	225.00
3725 — Douera, *from*	32.50	225.00
3726 — Mascara, *from*	11.00	70.00
3727 — Medeah, *from*	11.00	70.00
3728 — Mers-el-Kebir, *from*	35.00	275.00
3729 — Milianah, *from*	12.00	70.00
3730 — Mostaganem, *from*	3.50	22.00
3731 — Nemours, *from*	17.50	115.00
3732 — Oran, *from*	2.25	11.00
3733 — Orleansville, *from*	12.00	87.50
3734 — Philippeville, *from*	3.50	17.50
3735 — Setif, *from*	10.00	52.50
3736 — Sidi-Bel-Abbes, *from*	3.50	21.00
3737 — Stora, *from*	140.00	2,500.
3738 — Tenez, *from*	12.00	175.00
3739 — Tlemcen, *from*	4.25	28.00
3751 — El Arrouch, *from*	60.00	650.00
3752 — Biskra, *from*	32.50	275.00
3753 — Boghar, *from*	45.00	550.00
3754 — La Calle, *from*	32.50	325.00
3755 — Gudiel, *from*	175.00	*4,250.*
3756 — Guelma, *from*	12.00	110.00
3757 — Lambese, *from*	115.00	1,225.
3758 — Milah, *from*	—	—
3759 — Saida, *from*	52.50	575.00
3760 — Smendou, *from*	62.50	625.00
3761 — St. Denis-du-Sig, *from*	14.00	115.00
3762 — Tebessa, *from*	42.50	400.00
3763 — Teniet-el-Haad, *from*	42.50	500.00
3764 — Tiaret, *from*	40.00	350.00
3774 — El Affroun, *from*	—	*3,500.*
3774 — Mouzaiaville, *from*	87.50	650.00
3775 — Ain Benian, *from*	—	—
3776 — Bou-Medfa, *from*	70.00	650.00
3777 — Marengo, *from*	30.00	275.00
3793 — Miserghin, *from*	52.50	625.00
3795 — Valmy d'Algerie, *from*	67.50	575.00
3846 — Penthievre, *from*	87.50	925.00
3912 — La Maison Carree, *from*	45.00	775.00
4005 — Soukaras, *from*	45.00	500.00
4007 — Laghouat, *from*	67.50	575.00
4104 — Jemmapes, *from*	32.50	325.00
4106 — La Reghaia, *from*	170.00	2,000.
4116 — Ain-Benida, *from*	27.50	300.00
4120 — Pont-l'Oued Djer, *from*	60.00	775.00
4122 — Staoueli, *from*	67.50	800.00
4187 — Gastonville, *from*	62.50	700.00
4189 — Lalla Maghrnia, *from*	62.50	500.00
4190 — Tizi-Ouzou, *from*	52.50	550.00
4361 — Bou Tkelis, *from*	67.50	750.00
4362 — Le tlelat, *from*	80.00	900.00
4363 — Ain-Temouchent *from*	45.00	475.00
4364 — Relizane *from*	62.50	625.00
4365 — Assi-Ameur, *from*	80.00	1,000.
4366 — Aboukir, *from*	250.00	3,150.
4367 — Ain Tedeles, *from*	62.50	625.00
4368 — La Stidia, *from*	180.00	*3,000.*
4369 — Fondouk, *from*	80.00	1,000.
4370 — Kouba, *from*	170.00	2,300.
4371 — Fort Napoleon, *from*	67.50	700.00
4372 — Dra-el-Mizan, *from*	95.00	1,150.
4373 — Rouiba, *from*	160.00	2,300.
4374 — Cheragas, *from*	160.00	*4,250.*
4446 — Geryville, *from*	225.00	*3,500.*
4447 — Oued-el-Hamman, *from*	200.00	*3,500.*
4448 — Sebdou, *from*	—	—

All other values of the set exist used in Algeria. They are worth more than the values shown above, which are for cancellations on the 25c value.

Large Figures in Dotted Lozenge

Single (first column) or on cover (second column).

1870-76

On France No. 58

A58L A13 25c blue, *bluish*

5000 — Aboukir, *from*	50.00	575.00
5001 — Ain Beida, *from*	62.50	700.00
5002 — Ain Beniam, *from*	—	—
5002 — Saint-Charles, *from*	67.50	775.00
5003 — Ain Tedeles, *from*	32.50	350.00
5004 — Ain Temouchena, *from*	14.00	110.00
5005 — Alger, *from*	1.40	3.50
5006 — L'Arba, *from*	14.00	125.00
5007 — El Arrouch *from*	17.50	125.00
5008 — Arzew, *from*	14.00	110.00
5009 — Assi-Ameur, *from*	62.50	550.00
5010 — Aumale, *from*	11.00	50.00
5011 — Batna, *from*	3.50	17.50
5012 — Biskra, *from*	10.00	42.50

5013 — Blidah, *from*	2.25	21.50
5014 — Boghar, *from*	28.50	225.00
5015 — Bone, *from*	3.50	11.00
5016 — Bou-Tletis, *from*	45.00	500.00
5017 — Bouffarik, *from*	9.25	42.50
5018 — Bougie, *from*	21.00	14.00
5019 — La Calle, *from*	52.50	175.00
5020 — Cheragas, *from*	52.50	1,000.
5020 — Palestro, *from*	52.50	550.00
5021 — Cherchell, *from*	12.00	60.00
5022 — Coleah, *from*	17.50	110.00
5023 — Constantine, *from*	2.25	8.50
5024 — Dellys, *from*	12.00	70.00
5025 — Dely-Ibrahim, *from*	32.50	265.00
5026 — Djidjeli, *from*	14.00	87.50
5027 — Douera, *from*	17.50	125.00
5028 — Dra-el-Mizan, *from*	45.00	550.00
5029 — Fondouk, *from*	35.00	465.00
5030 — Fort Napoleon, *from*	32.50	310.00
5030 — Fort National, *from*	32.50	225.00
5031 — Gastonville, *from*	40.00	475.00
5031 — Robertville, *from*	40.00	500.00
5032 — Geryville, *from*	52.50	625.00
5033 — Gudiel, *from*	—	—
5033 — Guyotville, *from*	52.50	750.00
5034 — Guelma, *from*	8.50	28.00
5035 — Jemmapes, *from*	9.50	55.00
5036 — Kouba, *from*	32.50	300.00
5037 — Laghouat *from*	28.00	225.00
5038 — Lalla Maghrnia, *from*	29.00	275.00
5039 — Lambese, *from*	32.50	300.00
5040 — La Maison Carree, *from*	30.00	240.00
5041 — Marengo, *from*	25.00	200.00
5042 — Mascara, *from*	3.50	14.00
5043 — Medeah, *from*	3.50	14.00
5044 — Mers-el-Kebir, *from*	28.00	225.00
5045 — Milah, *from*	—	—
5045 — Col des Beni Aicha, *from*	67.50	775.00
5046 — Milianah, *from*	5.00	17.50
5047 — Miserghin *from*	32.50	300.00
5048 — Mostaganem, *from*	3.50	14.00
5049 — Mouzaiaville, *from*	40.00	500.00
5050 — Nemours, *from*	8.50	42.50
5051 — Oran, *from*	1.50	5.00
5052 — Orleansville, *from*	3.50	14.00
5053 — Oued-el-Hammam, *from*	60.00	625.00
5054 — Penthievre, *from*	57.50	575.00
5055 — Philippeville, *from*	1.50	7.50
5056 — Pont de la Oued Djer, *from*	45.00	625.00
5056 — Bou Medfa, *from*	45.00	625.00
5057 — La Reghaia *from*	52.50	625.00
5057 — L'Alma, *from*	52.50	750.00
5058 — Relizane, *from*	11.00	70.00
5059 — Rouiba, *from*	35.00	675.00
5060 — Saida, *from*	12.00	110.00
5061 — Sebdou, *from*	52.50	550.00
5062 — Setif, *from*	3.50	14.00
5063 — Sidi-bel Abbes, *from*	3.00	11.00
5064 — Smendou, *from*	45.00	575.00
5065 — Soukaras, *from*	17.50	110.00
5066 — Staoueli, *from*	52.50	550.00
5067 — La Stidia, *from*	57.50	750.00
5068 — Stora, *from*	225.00	—
5069 — St-Cloud-d'Algerie, *from*	30.00	400.00
5070 — St. Denis-du-Sig, *from*	12.00	62.50
5071 — Tebessa, *from*	29.00	300.00
5072 — Tenez, *from*	12.00	60.00
5073 — Teniet-el-Haad, *from*	21.00	175.00
5074 — Le Tlelat, *from*	32.50	340.00
5075 — Tlemcen, *from*	3.50	14.00
5076 — Tiaret, *from*	8.50	55.00
5077 — Tizzi Ouzou, *from*	20.00	125.00
5078 — Valmy, *from*	52.50	500.00
5081 — Beni Mancour, *from*	62.50	800.00
5093 — Ain el Arba, *from*	62.50	775.00
5108 — Sidi-Moussa, *from*	80.00	825.00
5109 — Djelfa, *from*	14.00	200.00
5110 — Bou Kanifis, *from*	52.50	550.00
5111 — Collo, *from*	40.00	400.00
5112 — Duzerville, *from*	40.00	550.00
5113 — Mondovi, *from*	62.50	625.00
5114 — Barral, *from*	67.50	925.00
5115 — Hussein Dey, *from*	50.00	625.00
5116 — Birtouta, *from*	50.00	700.00
5117 — Berrouaghia, *from*	67.50	750.00
5117 — Gue de Constantine, *from*	67.50	2,100.
5120 — El Kantours, *from*	60.00	750.00
5120 — Bou Sfer, *from*	60.00	775.00
5122 — Les Trembles, *from*	60.00	650.00
5123 — Perregaux, *from*	60.00	700.00
5124 — Bizot, *from*	35.00	425.00
5125 — Bordj Bou-Arreridj, *from*	35.00	350.00
5126 — Ouled Mimoun, *from*	62.50	550.00
5126 — Lamoriciere, *from*	62.50	925.00
5127 — Gar Rouban, *from*	65.00	925.00
5128 — Daya, *from*	45.00	650.00
5130 — Oued-el-Halleg, *from*	45.00	550.00
5131 — Le Affroun, *from*	70.00	3,250.
5131 — Bou Saada, *from*	67.50	750.00
5133 — Kroubs, *from*	62.50	625.00
5134 — Bouguirat, *from*	62.50	625.00
5135 — L'Hilil *from*	45.00	550.00
5136 — Ammi-Moussa, *from*	62.50	625.00
5137 — Sidi-Ali-ben-Youd, *from*	60.00	750.00
5138 — Oued-Zenati, *from*	50.00	700.00
5140 — Affreville, *from*	52.50	650.00
5141 — Duperre, *from*	52.50	650.00
5142 — Boghari, *from*	62.50	700.00
5143 — Akbou, *from*	80.00	775.00
5144 — Khenchela, *from*	62.50	750.00
5145 — Zemmorah, *from*	67.50	775.00
5146 — Bordj Menaiel, *from*	62.50	700.00
5147 — La Chiffa, *from*	62.50	775.00
5148 — Rebeval, *from*	67.50	1,050.
5149 — La Senia, *from*	—	—
5150 — Oued-Athmenia, *from*	62.50	775.00
5151 — Birkadem, *from*	67.50	850.00
5152 — Ponteba, *from*	67.50	850.00
5157 — Oued-Slyt, *from*	80.00	1,000.
5158 — Oued-Fodda, *from*	80.00	1,000.
5159 — Akib-Zamoun, *from*	140.00	1,350.
5160 — Attatba, *from*	95.00	1,275.
5161 — Ain-Arnat, *from*	—	—
5162 — Sidi-Brahim, *from*	82.50	1,150.
5163 — Oued-Riou, *from*	90.00	1,750.
5164 — Henneya, *from*	225.00	3,500.
5165 — Ain Fekarin, *from*	140.00	2,750.
5166 — Bourkika, *from*	90.00	1,550.
5167 — Sidi-Ali, *from*	—	—
— Sidi-Ali straight-line cancellation, *from*		*3,600.*
5168 — Blad-el-Hadjadj, *from*	115.00	2,000.
5169 — Bordj-Bouira, *from*	260.00	*4,750.*
5171— Beni Saf, *from*	350.00	*5,000.*
5172 — Bir Rabalou, *from*	350.00	*5,000.*

ISSUES OF FRENCH ALGERIA

Stamps of France Overprinted in Red, Blue or Black:

a

b

c

d

1924-26 Unwmk. *Perf. 14x13½*

1	A16(a)	1c dk gray (R)	.20	.20
		Never hinged	.20	
		On cover		7.00
2	A16(a)	2c violet brn	.25	.20
		Never hinged	.40	
		On cover		7.00
3	A16(a)	3c orange	.25	.20
		Never hinged	.40	
		On cover		7.00
a.		Grayish paper	.35	.20
		Never hinged	.50	
		On cover		7.00
4	A16(a)	4c yel brn (Bl)	.25	.20
		Never hinged	.40	
		On cover		6.00
5	A22(a)	5c orange (Bl)	.25	.20
		Never hinged	.40	
		On cover		1.50
6	A16(a)	5c green ('25)	.50	.40
		Never hinged	.70	
		On cover		1.50
7	A23(a)	10c green	.40	.25
		Never hinged	.55	
		On cover		2.00
b.		Booklet pane of 10	6.00	
8	A22(a)	10c green ('25)	.65	.25
		Never hinged	.85	
		On cover		2.00
a.		Pair, one without overprint	1,200.	
		Never hinged	1,750.	
9	A20(a)	15c slate grn	.25	.20
		Never hinged	.40	
		On cover		1.00
10	A23(a)	15c green ('25)	1.00	.25
		Never hinged	.75	
		On cover		2.00
11	A22(a)	15c red brn (Bl) ('26)	.20	.20
		Never hinged	.20	
		On cover		—
12	A22(a)	20c red brn (Bl)	.40	.20
		Never hinged	.55	
		On cover		1.00
a.		Pair, one without overprint	1,200.	
		Never hinged	1,750.	
13	A22(a)	25c blue (R)	.40	.20
		Never hinged	.55	
		On cover		1.00
a.		Booklet pane of 10, *from*	140.00	
		Never hinged, *from*	190.00	
b.		Pair, one without overprint	1,400.	
		Never hinged	1,875.	
14	A23(a)	30c red (Bl)	1.40	.40
		Never hinged	2.00	
		On cover		2.00
15	A22(a)	30c cerise ('25)	.85	.65
		Never hinged	1.25	
a.		"ALGERIE" double	190.00	
		Never hinged	275.00	
16	A22(a)	30c lt bl (R) ('25)	.40	.25
		Never hinged	.55	
		On cover		3.50
a.		Booklet pane of 10	100.00	
		Never hinged	120.00	
17	A22(a)	35c violet	.40	.25
		Never hinged	.55	
		On cover		5.00
18	A18(b)	40c red & pale bl	.55	.25
		Never hinged	.75	
		On cover		2.50
19	A22(a)	40c ol brn (R) ('25)	.85	.65
		Never hinged	1.15	
		On cover		3.00
20	A18(b)	45c grn & bl (R)	.55	.40
		Never hinged	.75	
		On cover		7.00
a.		Double overprint	225.00	
		Never hinged	325.00	
21	A23(a)	45c red (Bl) ('25)	.75	.40
		Never hinged	1.00	
		On cover		5.00
22	A23(a)	50c blue (R)	.65	.50
		Never hinged	.85	
		On cover		5.00
23	A20(a)	60c lt violet	.75	.40
		Never hinged	1.00	
		On cover		7.00
a.		Inverted overprint		*2,500.*
24	A20(a)	65c rose (Bl)	.50	.40
		Never hinged	.65	
		On cover		3.50
25	A23(a)	75c blue (R)	.75	.50
		Never hinged	1.10	
		On cover		7.00
a.		Double overprint	275.00	
		Never hinged	375.00	
26	A20(a)	80c ver ('26)	1.20	.65
		Never hinged	1.75	
		On cover		14.00
27	A20(a)	85c ver (Bl)	.75	.55
		Never hinged	1.10	
		On cover		7.00
28	A18(b)	1fr cl & ol grn	1.25	.55
		Never hinged	1.85	
		On cover		3.50
a.		Background color omitted	200.00	
		Never hinged	350.00	
29	A22(a)	1.05fr ver ('26)	1.20	.55
		Never hinged	1.75	
		On cover		17.50
		On cover, single franking		60.00
30	A18(c)	2fr org & pale bl	1.50	.75
		Never hinged	2.10	
		On cover		11.00
		On cover, single franking		35.00
31	A18(b)	3fr vio & bl ('26)	3.75	1.25
		Never hinged	5.00	
		On cover		28.00
		On cover, single franking		82.50
a.		Background color omitted	200.00	
		Never hinged	350.00	
32	A18(d)	5fr bl & buff (R)	9.50	7.00
		Never hinged	14.00	
		On cover		35.00
		On cover, single franking		140.00
		Nos. 1-32 (32)	32.55	19.30

No. 15 was issued precanceled only. Values for precanceled stamps in first column are for those which have not been through the post and have original gum. Values in second column are for postally used, gumless stamps.

For surcharges see Nos. 75, P1.

Street in Kasbah, Algiers
A1

Mosque of Sidi Abd-er-Rahman
A2

La Pêcherie Mosque — A3

Marabout of Sidi Yacoub
A4

1926-39 Typo. *Perf. 14x13½*

33	A1	1c olive	.20	.20
		Never hinged	.20	
		On cover		5.00
a.		Imperforate	55.00	
		Never hinged	105.00	
34	A1	2c red brown	.20	.20
		Never hinged	.20	
		On cover		5.00
35	A1	3c orange	.20	.20
		Never hinged	.20	
		On cover		4.25
36	A1	5c blue green	.20	.20
		Never hinged	.20	
		On cover		1.50
37	A1	10c brt violet	.25	.20
		Never hinged	.40	
		On cover		1.50
a.		Booklet pane of 10	25.00	
		Never hinged	37.50	
38	A2	15c orange brn	.25	.20
		Never hinged	.40	
		On cover		1.50
a.		Imperforate	55.00	
		Never hinged	105.00	
39	A2	20c green	.25	.20
		Never hinged	.40	
		On cover		3.50
a.		yel grn, precanceled ('38)	1.40	.75
		Never hinged	1.80	
40	A2	20c deep rose	.20	.20
		Never hinged	.20	
		On cover		5.75
a.		Imperforate	55.00	
		Never hinged	110.00	
41	A2	25c blue grn	.25	.20
		Never hinged	.40	
		On cover		2.00
42	A2	25c blue ('27)	.50	.25
		Never hinged	.70	
		On cover		2.00
a.		Imperforate	55.00	
		Never hinged	115.00	
43	A2	25c vio bl ('39)	.20	.20
		Never hinged	.20	
		On cover		1.40
44	A2	30c blue	.40	.25
		Never hinged	.55	
		On cover		7.00
a.		Imperforate	55.00	
		Never hinged	110.00	
45	A2	30c bl grn ('27)	.90	.65
		Never hinged	1.40	
		On cover		3.50
46	A2	35c dp violet	1.25	1.00
		Never hinged	1.60	
		On cover		10.50
47	A2	40c olive green	.40	.20
		Never hinged	.55	
		On cover		2.50
a.		Booklet pane of 10	62.50	
		Never hinged	92.50	
b.		Imperforate	55.00	
		Never hinged	115.00	
48	A3	45c violet brn	.65	.25
		Never hinged	.90	
		On cover		2.75
49	A3	50c blue	.40	.25
		Never hinged	.55	
		On cover		1.50
a.		Booklet pane of 10	62.50	
		Never hinged	95.00	
b.		Imperforate	55.00	
		Never hinged	125.00	
c.		Vert. pair, #49 and 49b	175.00	
		Never hinged	250.00	
50	A3	50c dk red ('30)	.25	.20
		Never hinged	.40	
		On cover		1.50
a.		Booklet pane of 10	52.50	
		Never hinged	87.50	
b.		Imperforate	55.00	
		Never hinged	115.00	
51	A3	60c yellow grn	.40	.25
		Never hinged	.55	
		On cover		3.50
52	A3	65c blk brn ('27)	2.25	1.65
		Never hinged	3.00	
		On cover		7.00
53	A1	65c ultra ('38)	.40	.25
		Never hinged	.55	
		On cover		2.00
a.		Booklet pane of 10	28.00	
		Never hinged	42.50	
54	A3	75c carmine	.85	.50
		Never hinged	1.10	
		On cover		2.75
a.		Imperforate	55.00	

Never hinged 125.00
b. Vert. pair, #54 and 54a 175.00
Never hinged 250.00
55 A3 75c blue ('29) 3.50 .40
Never hinged 4.75
On cover 1.75
56 A3 80c orange red .75 .40
Never hinged 1.10
On cover 7.00
57 A3 90c red ('27) 6.00 2.75
Never hinged 8.00
On cover 6.00
On cover, single franking 12.50
a. Imperforate 55.00
Never hinged 110.00
58 A4 1fr gray grn & red brn .75 .40
Never hinged 1.10
On cover 7.00
On cover, single franking 14.00
a. Imperforate 125.00
Never hinged 175.00
59 A3 1.05fr lt brown .75 .50
Never hinged 1.10
On cover 7.00
On cover, single franking 14.00
60 A3 1.10fr mag ('27) 6.00 2.25
Never hinged 8.00
On cover 14.00
On cover, single franking 65.00
61 A4 1.25fr dk bl & ultra .90 .75
Never hinged 1.40
On cover 10.50
On cover, single franking 17.50
62 A4 1.50fr dk bl & ultra ('27) 4.00 .70
Never hinged 5.00
On cover 7.75
On cover, single franking 14.00
a. Imperforate 225.00
Never hinged 300.00
63 A4 2fr prus bl & blk brn 3.00 .70
Never hinged 4.25
On cover 6.50
On cover, single franking 8.50
a. Imperforate 85.00
Never hinged 125.00
b. 2fr Prus blue & black 6.00 2.50
Never hinged 9.00
64 A4 3fr violet & org 5.25 1.20
Never hinged 8.50
On cover 10.50
On cover, single franking 17.50
65 A4 5fr red & violet 8.75 3.50
Never hinged 14.00
On cover 21.00
On cover, single franking 35.00
a. "ALCERIE," instead of "ALGERIE" 37.50 22.50
Never hinged 80.00
66 A4 10fr ol brn & rose ('27) 52.50 32.50
Never hinged 80.00
On cover 70.00
On cover, single franking 125.00
a. Imperforate 110.00
Never hinged 625.00
b. 10fr sepia brn * dark red 55.00 35.00
Never hinged 80.00
On cover 77.50
On cover, single franking 140.00
67 A4 20fr vio & grn ('27) 5.50 4.00
Never hinged 7.50
On cover 13.00
On cover, single franking 25.00
Nos. 33-67 (35) 108.50 57.75

Type A4, 50c blue and rose red, inscribed "CENTENAIRE-ALGERIE" is France No. 255.

See design A24. For stamps and types surcharged see Nos. 68-74, 131, 136, 187, B1-B13, J27, P2.

Five Trees Instead of Four

58d A4 1fr gray grn & red brn 9.00 5.50
Never hinged 25.00
61d A4 1.25fr dk blue & ultra 11.00 6.50
Never hinged 32.00
62d A4 1.50fr dk blue & ultra ('27) 9.00 5.50
Never hinged 32.00
63d A4 2fr prus blue & blk brn 11.00 6.50
Never hinged 32.00
64d A4 3fr violet & orange 18.00 8.00
Never hinged 45.00
65d A4 5fr red & violet 70.00 55.00
Never hinged 140.00
66d A4 10fr olive brn & rose ('27) 475.00 375.00
Never hinged 675.00
67d A4 20fr violet & green ('27) 475.00 375.00
Never hinged 675.00

Stamps of 1926 Surcharged with New Values

1927

68 A2 10c on 35c dp violet .20 .20
69 A2 25c on 30c blue .20 .20
70 A2 30c on 25c blue grn .20 .20
71 A3 65c on 60c yel grn 1.10 .75
72 A3 90c on 80c org red .85 .60
73 A3 1.10fr on 1.05fr lt brn .55 .35
74 A4 1.50fr on 1.25fr dk bl & ultra 1.90 .75
Nos. 68-74 (7) 5.00 3.05

Bars cancel the old value on #68, 69, 73, 74.

No. 4 Surcharged

1927

75 A16 5c on 4c yellow brown .75 .25
a. Blue surcharge 975.00 *1,050.*
Never hinged 1,400.

Bay of Algiers A5

1930, May 4 **Engr.** ***Perf. 12½***

78 A5 10fr red brown 11.00 11.00
a. Imperf., pair 105.00
b. Perf 11 15.50 15.50
Never hinged 21.00
On cover 35.00

Cent. of Algeria and for Intl. Phil. Exhib. of North Africa, May, 1930.

One copy of No. 78 was sold with each 10fr admission.

Travel across the Sahara A6

Arch of Triumph, Lambese A7

Admiralty Building, Algiers A8

Kings' Tombs near Touggourt A9

El-Kebir Mosque, Algiers A10

Oued River at Colomb-Bechar A11

Sidi Bon Medine Cemetery at Tlemcen A13

View of Ghardaia A12

1936-41 **Engr.** ***Perf. 13***

79 A6 1c ultra .20 .20
80 A11 2c dk violet .20 .20
81 A7 3c dk blue grn .20 .20
82 A12 5c red violet .20 .20
83 A8 10c emerald .20 .20
84 A9 15c red .20 .20
85 A13 20c dk blue grn .20 .20
86 A10 25c rose vio .85 .35
87 A12 30c yellow grn .65 .20
88 A9 40c brown vio .20 .20
89 A13 45c deep ultra 1.25 .85
90 A8 50c red .65 .20
91 A6 65c red brn 4.00 2.50
92 A6 65c rose car ('37) .55 .20
93 A6 70c red brn ('39) .20 .20
94 A11 75c slate bl .55 .20
95 A7 90c henna brn 1.50 .85
96 A10 1fr brown .55 .20
97 A8 1.25fr lt violet .85 .45
98 A8 1.25fr car rose ('39) .45 .20
99 A11 1.50fr turq blue 1.50 .45
99A A11 1.50fr rose ('40) .60 .40
100 A12 1.75fr henna brn .35 .20
101 A7 2fr dk brown .55 .20
102 A6 2.25fr yellow grn 12.50 9.50
103 A12 2.50fr dk ultra ('41) .55 .40
104 A13 3fr magenta .65 .20
105 A10 3.50fr pck blue 3.75 2.75
106 A8 5fr slate blue .85 .20
107 A11 10fr henna brn .70 .35
108 A9 20fr turq blue 1.10 .70
Nos. 79-108 (31) 36.75 23.35

See Nos. 124-125, 162.

Nos. 82 and 100 with surcharge "E. F. M. 30frs" (Emergency Field Message) were used in 1943 to pay cable tolls for US and Canadian servicemen.

For other surcharges see Nos. 122, B27.

Catalogue values for unused stamps in this section, from this point to the end of the section, are for Never Hinged items.

Algerian Pavilion — A14

1937 ***Perf. 13***

109 A14 40c brt green .80 .60
110 A14 50c rose carmine .80 .20
111 A14 1.50fr blue 1.25 .60
112 A14 1.75fr brown black 1.25 .95
Nos. 109-112 (4) 4.10 2.35

Paris International Exposition.

Constantine in 1837 — A15

1937

113 A15 65c deep rose .55 .45
114 A15 1fr brown 5.00 .95
115 A15 1.75fr blue green .55 .45
116 A15 2.15fr red violet .75 .45
Nos. 113-116 (4) 6.85 2.30

Taking of Constantine by the French, cent.

Ruins of a Roman Villa — A16

1938

117 A16 30c green .75 .45
118 A16 65c ultra .35 .20
119 A16 75c rose violet .75 .55
120 A16 3fr carmine rose 2.50 2.25
121 A16 5fr yellow brown 4.00 3.50
Nos. 117-121 (5) 8.35 6.95

Centenary of Philippeville.

No. 90 Surcharged in Black

1938

122 A8 25c on 50c red .25 .25
Never hinged .40
On cover 3.00
a. Double surcharge 45.00 42.50
Never hinged 60.00
b. Inverted surcharge 39.00 35.00
Never hinged 50.00
c. Pair, one without surcharge 190.00
Never hinged 275.00

Types of 1936

1939

Numerals of Value on Colorless Background

124 A7 90c henna brown .20 .20
125 A10 2.25fr blue green .20 .20

For surcharge see No. B38.

American Export Liner Unloading Cargo A17

1939

126 A17 20c green 1.40 .80
127 A17 40c red violet 1.60 .90
128 A17 90c brown black .80 .40
129 A17 1.25fr rose 5.25 1.75
130 A17 2.25fr ultra 1.25 1.25
Nos. 126-130 (5) 10.30 5.10

New York World's Fair.

Type of 1926, Surcharged in Black

Two types of surcharge:
I — Bars 6mm
II — Bars 7mm

1939-40 ***Perf. 14x13½***

131 A1 1fr on 90c crimson (I) .25 .25
Never hinged .40
On cover 1.40
a. Booklet pane of 10 125.00
Never hinged 160.00
b. Double surcharge (I) 77.50
Never hinged 100.00
c. Inverted surcharge (I) 45.00
Never hinged 60.00
d. Pair, one without surch. (I) *1,250.*
Never hinged 1,650.
e. Type II ('40) 3.75 .60
Never hinged 5.00
On cover 2.90
f. Inverted surcharge (II) 62.50
Never hinged 62.50
g. Pair, one without surch. (II) *1,250.*
Never hinged 1,650.

SEMI-POSTAL STAMPS

Regular Issue of 1926 Surcharged in Black or Red

1927 **Unwmk.** ***Perf. 14x13½***

B1 A1 5c +5c bl grn .75 .75
On cover 32.50
B2 A1 10c +10c lilac .75 .75
On cover 32.50
B3 A2 15c +15c org brn .75 .75
On cover 30.00
B4 A2 20c +20c car rose .75 .75
On cover 40.00
B5 A2 25c +25c bl grn .75 .75
On cover 20.00
B6 A2 30c +30c lt bl .80 .80
On cover 40.00
B7 A2 35c +35c dp vio .80 .80
On cover 40.00

B8 A2 40c +40c ol grn .80 .80
On cover 17.50
B9 A3 50c +50c dp bl (R) .90 .90
On cover 17.50
a. Double surcharge 310.00 *325.00*
B10 A3 80c +80c red org .90 .90
On cover 40.00
B11 A4 1fr +1fr gray grn & red brn .90 .90
On cover 30.00
B12 A4 2fr +2fr Prus bl & blk brn 18.00 18.00
On cover 65.00
B13 A4 5fr +5fr red & vio 27.50 27.50
On cover 90.00
Nos. B1-B13 (13) 54.35 54.35

The surtax was for the benefit of wounded soldiers. Government officials speculated in this issue.

Railroad Terminal, Oran
SP1

Ruins at Djemila
SP2

Mosque of Sidi Abd-er-Rahman
SP3

Designs: 10c+10c, Rummel Gorge, Constantine. 15c+15c, Admiralty Buildings, Algiers. 25c+25c, View of Algiers. 30c+30c, Trajan's Arch, Timgad. 40c+40c, Temple of the North, Djemila. 75c+75c Mansourah Minaret, Tlemcen. 1f+1f, View of Ghardaia. 1.50f+1.50f, View of Tolga. 2f+2f, Tuareg warriors. 3f+3f, Kasbah, Algiers.

1930 Engr. *Perf. 12½*
B14 SP1 5c +5c orange 6.50 6.50
On cover 20.00
B15 SP1 10c +10c ol grn 6.50 6.50
On cover 20.00
B16 SP1 15c +15c dk brn 6.50 6.50
On cover 20.00
B17 SP1 25c +25c black 6.50 6.50
On cover 20.00
B18 SP1 30c +30c dk red 6.50 6.50
On cover 25.00
B19 SP1 40c +40c ap grn 6.50 6.50
On cover 17.50
B20 SP2 50c +50c ultra 6.75 6.75
On cover 17.50
B21 SP2 75c +75c red pur 6.75 6.75
On cover 17.50
B22 SP2 1fr +1fr org red 6.75 6.75
On cover 20.00
B23 SP2 1.50fr +1.50fr deep ultra 6.75 6.75
On cover 30.00
B24 SP2 2fr +2fr dk car 6.75 6.75
On cover 20.00
B25 SP2 3fr +3fr dk grn 6.75 6.75
On cover 40.00
B26 SP3 5fr +5fr grn & car 17.00 17.00
On cover 45.00
a. Center inverted 575.00
Never hinged 875.00
Nos. B14-B26 (13) 96.50 96.50

Centenary of the French occupation of Algeria. The surtax on the stamps was given to the funds for the celebration.

Nos. B14-B26 exist imperf. Value, set in pairs, $350.

Catalogue values for unused stamps in this section, from this point to the end of the section, are for Never Hinged items.

No. 102 Surcharged in Red

1938 *Perf. 13*
B27 A6 65c +35c on 2.25fr yel grn .75 .75
On cover 40.00
a. Inverted surcharge 190.00
b. Pair, one without surcharge 925.00

20th anniversary of Armistice.

René Caillié, Charles Lavigerie and Henri Duveyrier
SP14

1939 Engr.
B28 SP14 30c +20c dk bl grn 1.00 1.00
On cover 6.00
B29 SP14 90c +60c car rose 1.00 1.00
On cover 5.00
B30 SP14 2.25fr +75c ultra 11.00 11.00
On cover 30.00
B31 SP14 5fr +5fr brn blk 21.00 21.00
On cover 50.00
On cover, single franking 75.00
Nos. B28-B31 (4) 34.00 34.00

Pioneers of the Sahara.

French and Algerian Soldiers
SP15

1940 Photo. *Perf. 12*
B32 SP15 1fr +1fr bl & car .70 .70
On cover 5.00
a. Double surcharge 775.00
B33 SP15 1fr +2fr brn rose & blk .70 .70
On cover 5.00
B34 SP15 1fr +4fr dp grn & red 1.00 1.00
On cover 6.00
B35 SP15 1fr +9fr brn & car 1.40 1.40
On cover 9.00
Nos. B32-B35 (4) 3.80 3.80

The surtax was used to assist the families of mobilized men.

Nos. B32-B35 exist without surcharge. Value set, $140.

POSTAGE DUE STAMPS

D1

D2

Perf. 14x13½
1926-27 Typo. Unwmk.
J1 D1 5c light blue .20 .20
J2 D1 10c dk brn .20 .20
J3 D1 20c olive grn .45 .20
J4 D1 25c car rose .55 .45
J5 D1 30c rose red .70 .35
J6 D1 45c blue grn .90 .50
J7 D1 50c brn vio .20 .20
J8 D1 60c green ('27) 2.00 .70
J9 D1 1fr red brn, *straw* .20 .20
J10 D1 2fr lil rose ('27) .35 .20
J11 D1 3fr deep blue ('27) .35 .35
Nos. J1-J11 (11) 6.10 3.55

See Nos. J25-J26, J28-J32. For surcharges, see Nos. J18-J20.

1926-27
J12 D2 1c olive grn .20 .20
J13 D2 10c violet 1.10 .40
J14 D2 30c bister 1.10 .35
J15 D2 60c dull red .70 .35
J16 D2 1fr brt vio ('27) 14.50 3.00
J17 D2 2fr lt bl ('27) 11.50 1.10
Nos. J12-J17 (6) 29.10 5.40

See note below France No. J51. For surcharges, see Nos. J21-J24.

Stamps of 1926 Surcharged

1927
J18 D1 60c on 20c olive grn 1.40 .55
J19 D1 2fr on 45c blue grn 1.75 1.10
J20 D1 3fr on 25c car rose 1.10 .55
Nos. J18-J20 (3) 4.25 2.20

Recouvrement Stamps of 1926 Surcharged

1927-32
J21 D2 10c on 30c bis ('32) 3.50 2.50
J22 D2 1fr on 1c olive grn 2.00 1.10
J23 D2 1fr on 60c dl red ('32) 16.00 .55
J24 D2 2fr on 10c violet 11.00 9.50
Nos. J21-J24 (4) 32.50 13.65

NEWSPAPER STAMPS

Nos. 1 and 33 Surcharged in Red

1924-26 Unwmk. *Perf. 14x13½*
P1 A16 ½c on 1c dk gray .20 .20
On cover 40.00
a. Triple surcharge 190.00
P2 A1 ½c on 1c olive ('26) .20 .20

ALLENSTEIN

'a-lən-ˌshtin

LOCATION — In East Prussia
AREA — 4,457 sq. mi.
POP. — 540,000 (estimated 1920)
CAPITAL — Allenstein

Allenstein, a district of East Prussia, held a plebiscite in 1920 under the Versailles Treaty, voting to join Germany rather than Poland. Later that year, Allenstein became part of the German Republic.

100 Pfennig = 1 Mark

Stamps of Germany, 1906-20, Overprinted

Perf. 14, 14½, 14x14½, 14½x14
1920 Wmk. 125
1 A16 5pf green .35 *.70*
Never hinged .70
On cover 10.50
On cover, single franking 140.00
2 A16 10pf carmine .35 *.70*
Never hinged .70
On cover 10.50
On cover, single franking 20.00
3 A22 15pf dk vio .35 *.70*
Never hinged .70
On cover 10.50
On cover, single franking 14.00
4 A22 15pf vio brn 5.00 *8.50*
Never hinged 10.00
On cover 35.00
a. 15pf red brown 52.50 *275.00*
Never hinged 120.00
On cover 350.00
5 A16 20pf bl vio .35 *.90*
Never hinged .90
On cover 10.50
On cover, single franking 14.00
a. 20pf ultramarine 21.00 *85.00*
Never hinged 85.00
On cover 400.00
On cover, single franking 110.00
6 A16 30pf org & blk, *buff* .35 *.90*
Never hinged .90
On cover 10.50
7 A16 40pf lake & blk .35 *.70*
Never hinged .70
On cover 10.50
On cover, single franking 14.00
8 A16 50pf pur & blk, *buff* .35 *.70*
Never hinged .70
On cover 10.50
On cover, single franking 28.00
9 A16 75pf grn & blk .35 *.70*
Never hinged .70
On cover 14.00
On cover, single franking 70.00
10 A17 1m car rose 1.25 1.60
Never hinged 2.50
On cover —
On cover, single franking —
a. Double overprint — —
11 A17 1.25m green 1.25 2.10
Never hinged 2.50
On cover 5.00
On cover, single franking 57.50
a. Double overprint — —
b. 1.25m bluish green 10.00 28.00
Never hinged 20.00
On cover 70.00
On cover, single franking 175.00
12 A17 1.50m yel brn .85 *2.10*
Never hinged 2.10
On cover 35.00
On cover, single franking 70.00
a. 1.50m red brown 21.00 50.00
Never hinged 50.00
On cover 85.00
On cover, single franking 125.00
b. 1.50m dark brown 32.50 *90.00*
Never hinged 92.50
On cover 125.00
On cover, single franking 175.00
13 A21 2.50m lilac rose (shades) 2.10 *10.50*
Never hinged 4.00
On cover 27.50
On cover, single franking 105.00
14 A19 3m blk vio 2.10 *2.75*
Never hinged 4.00
On cover 42.50
a. Double overprint 260.00 *1,000.*
Never hinged 525.00
b. Inverted overprint — —
Nos. 1-14 (14) 15.35 *33.55*
Set, never hinged 31.00

The 5pf brown (Germany #118), 10pf orange (#119), 20pf green (#121), 30pf blue (#123) and 40pf (#124) exist with this overprint but were not regularly issued. Value, each: $75 hinged, $125 never hinged.

Overprinted

15 A16 5pf green .35 *.70*
Never hinged .70
On cover 11.00
16 A16 10pf carmine .35 *.70*
Never hinged .70
On cover 11.00
On cover, single franking 12.50
17 A22 15pf dark vio .35 *.70*
Never hinged .70
On cover 11.00
a. 15pf blackish violet 11.00 77.50
Never hinged 28.00
On cover 120.00
18 A22 15pf vio brn 19.00 *32.50*
Never hinged 42.50
On cover 70.00
a. 15pf red brown 55.00 *275.00*
Never hinged 110.00
19 A16 20pf blue vio .55 *1.10*
Never hinged 1.10
On cover 11.00
On cover, single franking 25.00
a. 20pf ultramarine 85.00 120.00
Never hinged 210.00
On cover 150.00
20 A16 30pf org & blk, *buff* .35 .70
Never hinged .70
On cover 11.00
On cover, single franking 17.50
21 A16 40pf lake & blk .35 .70
Never hinged .70
On cover 11.00
On cover, single franking 16.50
22 A16 50pf pur & blk, *buff* .35 .70
Never hinged .70
On cover 14.00
On cover, single franking 28.00
23 A16 75pf grn & blk .55 *1.10*
Never hinged 1.10
On cover 14.00
a. 75pf blue green & brownish black 10.50 *21.00*
Never hinged 21.00
On cover 70.00
24 A17 1m car rose 1.25 1.75
Never hinged 2.50
On cover 28.00
On cover, single franking 100.00
a. Inverted overprint 525.00 *700.00*
Never hinged 700.00
25 A17 1.25m green 1.25 *1.75*
Never hinged 2.50
On cover 28.00
On cover, single franking 42.50
a. 1.25m bluish green 8.50 *14.00*
Never hinged 17.50
On cover 52.50
On cover, single franking 85.00
26 A17 1.50m yel brn 1.10 *1.75*
Never hinged 1.75
On cover 28.00
On cover, single franking 62.50
a. 1.50m red brown 10.50 *50.00*
Never hinged 25.00
On cover 85.00
On cover, single franking 110.00
b. 1.50m dark brown 12.50 *62.50*

Never hinged 28.00
On cover 100.00
On cover, single franking 140.00
27 A21 2.50m lilac rose (shades) 2.10 *3.50*
Never hinged 4.25
On cover 28.00
On cover, single franking 100.00
28 A19 3m blk vio 1.40 1.75
Never hinged 2.50
On cover 35.00
On cover, single franking 140.00
a. Inverted overprint 350.00 *850.00*
Never hinged 625.00
b. Double overprint 175.00 *525.00*
Never hinged 525.00
Nos. 15-28 (14) 29.30 *49.40*
Set, never hinged 62.50

The 40pf carmine rose (Germany No. 124) exists with this oval overprint, but it is doubtful whether it was regularly issued. Value $90 hinged, $185 never hinged.

ANDORRA

an-'dor-ə

LOCATION — On the southern slope of the Pyrenees Mountains between France and Spain.
GOVT. — Co-principality
AREA — 179 sq. mi.
POP. — 5,231
CAPITAL — Andorre

Andorra is subject to the joint control of France and the Spanish Bishop of Urgel and pays annual tribute to both. The country has no monetary unit of its own, the peseta and franc both being in general use.

100 Centimos = 1 Peseta
100 Centimes = 1 Franc

SPANISH ADMINISTRATION

A majority of the Spanish Andorra stamps issued to about 1950 are poorly centered. The very fine examples that are valued will be somewhat off center. Very poorly centered examples (perfs cutting design) sell for less. Well centered stamps are scarce and sell for approximately twice the values shown (#1-24, E1-E3), or 50% more (#25-36, E4).

Stamps of Spain, 1922-26, Overprinted in Red or Black

Perf. 13½x12½, 12½x11½

1928 Unwmk.
1 A49 2c olive green .50 .50
Never hinged 1.20
On cover 25.00
a. 2c bronze green 2.50 2.50
Never hinged 6.00

Control Numbers on Back

2 A49 5c car rose (Bk) .75 .75
Never hinged 1.50
On cover 25.00
a. 5c rose 5.00 4.75
Never hinged 12.00
3 A49 10c green .75 .75
Never hinged 2.00
On cover 25.00
a. 10c bluish green 20.00 —
Never hinged 30.00
4 A49 15c slate blue 3.00 3.00
Never hinged 4.00
On cover 35.00
a. 15c dk slate green 9.00 9.00
Never hinged 15.00
5 A49 20c lilac 3.00 3.00
Never hinged 4.00
On cover 35.00
a. 20c violet 15.00 —
Never hinged 25.00
6 A49 25c rose red (Bk) 3.00 3.00
Never hinged 4.50
On cover 35.00
7 A49 30c brown 17.50 16.00
Never hinged 25.00
On cover 75.00
a. 30c grayish brown 19.00 19.00
Never hinged 30.00
b. As "a," inverted overprint 125.00 70.00
8 A49 40c deep blue 17.50 10.50
Never hinged 30.00
On cover 65.00
a. 40c grayish blue 35.00 30.00
Never hinged 57.50
9 A49 50c orange (Bk) 17.50 14.00
Never hinged 30.00
On cover 65.00
a. 50c yellow orange 35.00 30.00
Never hinged 57.50
10 A49a 1p blue blk 22.50 *22.50*
Never hinged 35.00
On cover 80.00
11 A49a 4p lake (Bk) 140.00 *170.00*
Never hinged 200.00
On cover 600.00
12 A49a 10p brown (Bk) 260.00 260.00
Never hinged 350.00
On cover —
a. Double overprint 550.00 *650.00*
Nos. 1-12 (12) 486.00 504.00
Set, never hinged 800.00

Counterfeit overprints exist.

Covers: Values for covers are for commercial items with proper frankings. Overfranked items and other philatelic covers sell for much less.

Values for stamps in blocks of 4

1	A49	2c olive green	2.75	2.75
a.		2c bronze green	13.00	*14.00*
2	A49	5c carmine rose (Bk)	3.25	3.25
a.		5c rose	29.00	29.00
3	A49	10c green	3.25	3.25
a.		10c bluish green	110.00	—
4	A49	15c slate blue	15.00	*16.00*
a.		15c dk slate green	50.00	*52.50*
5	A49	20c lilac	13.00	*17.50*
a.		20c violet	80.00	—
6	A49	25c rose red (Bk)	15.00	*17.50*
7	A49	30c brown	100.00	*110.00*
a.		30c grayish brown	95.00	—
8	A49	40c deep blue	100.00	70.00
a.		40c grayish blue	150.00	150.00
9	A49	50c orange (Bk)	95.00	90.00
a.		50c yellow orange	175.00	175.00
10	A49	1p blue black	250.00	130.00
11	A49	4p lake (Bk)	775.00	*900.00*
12	A49	10p brown (Bk)	1,600.	*1,750.*

Specimen Stamps, Numbered A.000.000 on Reverse

2S	A49	5c rose (Bk)	4.50
3S	A49	10c dark green	4.50
4S	A49	15c dk slate blue	25.00
5S	A49	20c grayish lilac (R)	27.50
6S	A49	25c rose red (Bk)	27.50
7S	A49	30c brown	140.00
8S	A49	40c dark blue	140.00
9S	A49	50c orange (Bk)	140.00
10S	A49	1p blue black	160.00
10aS	A49	1p blue black, perf 14	45.00
11S	A49	4p reddish violet (Bk)	1,000.
12S	A49	10p brown (Bk)	1,900.

1928 ***Perf. 14***

1b	A49	2c olive green	60.00	25.00
2b	A49	5c rose (Bk)	60.00	25.00
3b	A49	10c green	45.00	16.00
3c	A49	10c dark green	37.50	12.00
4b	A49	15c dk slate blue	60.00	25.00
5b	A49	20c grayish lilac (R)	60.00	25.00
5c	A49	20c lilac (C)	25.00	19.00
6a	A49	25c rose red (Bk)	45.00	19.00
b.		As "a," inverted overprint	110.00	65.00
7c	A49	30c brown	45.00	19.00
8b	A49	40c dark blue	45.00	9.50
8c	A49	40c dark blue	45.00	22.50
9b	A49	50c orange (Bk)	140.00	30.00
c.		As "b," inverted overprint	140.00	110.00
10a	A49	1p blue black	45.00	25.00
11a	A49	4p carmine lake (Bk)	140.00	80.00
11b	A49	4p reddish violet (Bk)	75.00	40.00
12b	A49	10p brown (Bk)	375.00	80.00

La Vall — A1

St. Juan de Caselles — A2

St. Julia de Loria — A3

St. Coloma — A4

General Council — A5

1929, Nov. 25 Engr. ***Perf. 14***
13 A1 2c olive green 1.10 .60
Never hinged 2.00

Control Numbers on Back

14 A2 5c carmine lake 4.00 1.25
Never hinged 7.00
15 A3 10c yellow green 4.00 *4.50*
Never hinged 7.25
16 A4 15c slate green 4.00 *4.50*
Never hinged 8.00
17 A3 20c violet 4.00 *4.50*
Never hinged 7.25
18 A4 25c carmine rose 8.50 6.25
Never hinged 14.00
19 A1 30c olive brown 160.00 175.00
Never hinged 250.00
20 A2 40c dark blue 6.75 3.00
Never hinged 14.00
21 A3 50c deep orange 6.75 4.50
Never hinged 13.50
22 A5 1p slate 14.50 14.50
Never hinged 35.00
23 A5 4p deep rose 110.00 110.00
Never hinged 160.00
24 A5 10p bister brown 125.00 *140.00*
Never hinged 170.00
Nos. 13-24 (12) 448.60 *468.60*
Set, never hinged 700.00

Nos. 13-24 exist imperforate. Value $1,000.

1931-38

Perf. 11½

13a	A1	2c	6.25	.80
		Never hinged	11.00	

Control Numbers on Back

14a	A2	5c	10.00	2.25
		Never hinged	17.50	
15a	A3	10c	10.00	2.00
		Never hinged	17.50	
16a	A4	15c	30.00	25.00
		Never hinged	41.00	
17a	A3	20c	10.00	6.00
		Never hinged	17.50	
18a	A4	25c	10.00	6.00
		Never hinged	17.50	
19a	A1	30c ('33)	175.00	65.00
		Never hinged	225.00	
20a	A2	40c ('35)	17.00	13.00
		Never hinged	25.00	
22a	A5	1p ('38)	40.00	25.00
		Never hinged	65.00	
		Nos. 13a-22a (9)	308.25	145.05
		Set, never hinged	425.00	

Without Control Numbers

1936-43 ***Perf. 11½x11***
25 A1 2c red brown ('37) 1.75 1.60
Never hinged 2.75
26 A2 5c dark brown 1.75 1.60
Never hinged 2.75
27 A3 10c blue green 10.00 3.25
Never hinged 25.00
a. 10c yellow green 110.00 62.50
Never hinged 150.00
28 A4 15c blue green ('37) 5.75 3.25
Never hinged 10.50
a. 15c yellow green 6.50 5.75
Never hinged 8.50
29 A3 20c violet 5.75 3.25
Never hinged 7.50
30 A4 25c deep rose ('37) 2.50 *3.25*
Never hinged 3.00
31 A1 30c carmine 4.50 3.25
Never hinged 6.25
31A A2 40c dark blue *725.00*
Never hinged *1,200.*
32 A1 45c rose red ('37) 1.90 1.60
Never hinged 2.90
33 A3 50c deep orange 8.50 5.75
Never hinged 10.00
34 A1 60c deep blue ('37) 5.75 3.25
Never hinged 7.50
34A A5 1p slate 2,150. —
Never hinged *4,000.*
35 A5 4p deep rose ('43) 25.00 *47.50*
Never hinged 72.50
36 A5 10p bister brn ('43) 47.50 *57.50*
Never hinged 85.00
Nos. 25-31,32-34,35-36 (12) 120.65 135.05
Set, never hinged 285.00

Nos. 26, 28, 32 exist imperforate. Value hinged, $275.

Beware of counterfeits of Nos. 31A and 34A. Purchase of copies with certificates is strongly advised.

SPANISH ADMINISTRATIONSPECIAL DELIVERY STAMPS

Special Delivery Stamp of Spain, 1905 Overprinted

1928 Unwmk. ***Perf. 14***

Without Control Number on Back

E1 SD1 20c red 100.00 95.00
Never hinged 150.00

With Control Number on Back

E2 SD1 20c pale red 60.00 37.50
Never hinged 80.00

Eagle over Mountain Pass — SD2

1929 ***Perf. 14***

With Control Number on Back

E3 SD2 20c scarlet 25.00 20.00
Never hinged 35.00

No. E3 perf 11½ is a specimen. Value, $300.

1937 ***Perf. 11½x11***

Without Control Number on Back

E4 SD2 20c red 7.75 *9.50*
Never hinged 10.00

FRENCH ADMINISTRATION

Stamps and Types of France, 1900-1929, Overprinted

Perf. 14x13½

1931, June 16 Unwmk.
1 A16 1c gray .70 *.70*
Never hinged 1.40
On cover 21.00
On cover, single franking 250.00
a. Double overprint *1,500.* *1,500.*
Never hinged *1,800.*
2 A16 2c red brown 1.00 *1.00*
Never hinged 1.75
On cover 21.00
On cover, single franking 160.00
3 A16 3c orange 1.00 *1.00*
Never hinged 1.75
On cover 21.00
On cover, single franking 160.00
4 A16 5c green 1.75 *1.75*
Never hinged 3.25
On cover 21.00
On cover, single franking 160.00
5 A16 10c lilac 3.00 *3.00*
Never hinged 6.00
On cover 21.00
On cover, single franking 160.00
6 A22 15c red brown 4.25 4.25
Never hinged 9.25
On cover 27.50
On cover, single franking 87.50
7 A22 20c red violet 7.00 7.00
Never hinged 14.00
On cover 37.50
On cover, single franking 160.00
8 A22 25c yellow brn 7.75 8.50
Never hinged 17.50
On cover 50.00
On cover, single franking 160.00
9 A22 30c green 7.00 7.00
Never hinged 16.00
On cover 50.00
On cover, single franking 160.00
10 A22 40c ultra 8.50 *10.00*
Never hinged 17.50
On cover 42.50
On cover, single franking 70.00
11 A20 45c lt violet 15.00 14.00
Never hinged 32.50
On cover 55.00
On cover, single franking 140.00
12 A20 50c vermilion 9.25 9.00
Never hinged 19.00
On cover 55.00
On cover, single franking 140.00
13 A20 65c gray green 21.00 21.00
Never hinged 42.50
On cover 100.00
On cover, single franking 250.00
14 A20 75c rose lilac 22.50 21.00
Never hinged 46.00
On cover 100.00
On cover, single franking 325.00
15 A22 90c red 27.50 *27.50*
Never hinged 56.00
On cover 125.00
On cover, single franking 350.00
16 A20 1fr dull blue 30.00 30.00
Never hinged 62.50
On cover 125.00
On cover, single franking 350.00
17 A22 1.50fr light blue 35.00 35.00
Never hinged 80.00
On cover 140.00
On cover, single franking 350.00

Overprinted 

18 A18 2fr org & pale bl 55.00 *60.00*
Never hinged 95.00
On cover 140.00
On cover, single franking 325.00
19 A18 3fr brt vio & rose 77.50 *85.00*
Never hinged 160.00
On cover 250.00
On cover, single franking 350.00
20 A18 5fr dk bl & buff 110.00 *110.00*
Never hinged 200.00
On cover 290.00
On cover, single franking 500.00
21 A18 10fr grn & red 225.00 *275.00*
Never hinged 450.00
On cover 1,050.
On cover, single franking —
22 A18 20fr mag & grn 290.00 *325.00*
Never hinged 600.00
On cover 1,250.
On cover, single franking —
Nos. 1-22 (22) 959.70 *1,056.*

See No. P1 for ½c on 1c gray.
Nos. 9, 15 and 17 were not issued in France without overprint.

Chapel of Meritxell
A50

Bridge of St. Anthony
A51

St. Miguel d'Engolasters
A52

Gorge of St. Julia
A53

Old Andorra
A54

1932-43 Engr. *Perf. 13*

23 A50 1c gray blk .35 *.35*
Never hinged .70
On cover 5.00
On cover, single franking 35.00
24 A50 2c violet .35 .35
Never hinged .70
On cover 5.00
On cover, single franking 35.00
25 A50 3c brown .35 .35
Never hinged .70
On cover 5.00
On cover, single franking 35.00
26 A50 5c blue green .55 .50
Never hinged 1.00
On cover 5.00
On cover, single franking 35.00
27 A51 10c dull lilac .75 .70
Never hinged 1.50
On cover 5.00
On cover, single franking 35.00
28 A50 15c deep red 1.50 1.50
Never hinged 3.00
On cover 8.50
On cover, single franking 35.00
29 A51 20c lt rose 10.50 8.50
Never hinged 21.00
On cover 50.00
On cover, single franking 100.00
30 A52 25c brown 4.25 4.25
Never hinged 7.75
On cover 60.00
On cover, single franking 175.00
31 A51 25c brn car ('37) 7.75 *11.00*
Never hinged 16.00
On cover 27.50
On cover, single franking 55.00
32 A51 30c emerald 3.25 3.25
Never hinged 5.75
On cover 30.00
On cover, single franking 77.50
33 A51 40c ultra 10.00 8.50
Never hinged 21.00
On cover 35.00
On cover, single franking 70.00
34 A51 40c brn blk ('39) .70 .70
Never hinged 1.75
On cover 7.00
On cover, single franking 55.00
35 A51 45c lt red 9.00 9.00
Never hinged 21.00
On cover 55.00
On cover, single franking 100.00
36 A51 45c bl grn ('39) 4.25 4.25
Never hinged 9.00
On cover 35.00
On cover, single franking 70.00
37 A52 50c lilac rose 10.00 10.00
Never hinged 21.00
On cover 42.50
On cover, single franking 85.00
38 A51 50c lt vio ('39) 4.25 4.25
Never hinged 8.75
On cover 35.00
On cover, single franking 70.00
38A A51 50c grn ('40) 1.50 1.75
Never hinged 3.00
On cover 37.50
On cover, single franking 100.00
39 A51 55c lt vio ('38) 18.00 14.00
Never hinged 37.50
On cover 70.00
On cover, single franking 110.00
40 A51 60c yel brn ('38) .70 .70
Never hinged 1.75
On cover 7.00
On cover, single franking 70.00
41 A52 65c yel grn 45.00 42.50
Never hinged 87.50
On cover 110.00
On cover, single franking 160.00
42 A51 65c blue ('38) 13.50 11.00
Never hinged 25.00
On cover 70.00
On cover, single franking 140.00
43 A51 70c red ('39) 1.75 1.75
Never hinged 3.50
On cover 14.00
On cover, single franking 70.00
44 A52 75c violet 8.50 7.00
Never hinged 17.50
On cover 42.50
On cover, single franking 140.00
45 A51 75c ultra ('39) 3.25 *3.50*
Never hinged 6.50
On cover 35.00
On cover, single franking 70.00
46 A51 80c green ('38) 22.50 18.00
Never hinged 45.00
On cover 110.00
On cover, single franking 210.00
46A A53 80c bl grn ('40) .30 .30
Never hinged .50
On cover 27.50
On cover, single franking 90.00
47 A53 90c deep rose 5.25 5.25
Never hinged 10.50
On cover 52.50
On cover, single franking 140.00
48 A53 90c dk grn ('39) 3.00 3.00
Never hinged 5.25
On cover 27.50
On cover, single franking 110.00
49 A53 1fr blue grn 15.00 10.50
Never hinged 32.50
On cover 55.00
On cover, single franking 90.00
50 A53 1fr scarlet ('38) 24.00 19.00
Never hinged 47.50
On cover 140.00
On cover, single franking 350.00
51 A53 1fr dp ultra ('39) .20 .20
Never hinged .40
On cover 7.00
On cover, single franking 70.00
51A A53 1.20fr brt vio ('42) .30 .30
Never hinged .50
On cover 5.00
On cover, single franking 42.50
52 A50 1.25fr rose car ('33) 42.50 32.50
Never hinged 87.50
On cover 55.00
On cover, single franking 110.00
52A A50 1.25fr rose ('38) 4.00 3.50
Never hinged 7.00
On cover 27.50
On cover, single franking 110.00
52B A53 1.30fr sepia ('40) .30 .30
Never hinged .50
On cover 60.00
On cover, single franking 160.00
53 A54 1.50fr ultra 17.50 14.00
Never hinged 35.00
On cover 60.00
On cover, single franking 110.00
53A A53 1.50fr crim ('40) .30 .30
Never hinged .50
On cover 55.00
On cover, single franking 140.00
54 A53 1.75fr violet ('33) 87.50 *100.00*
Never hinged 175.00
On cover 135.00
On cover, single franking 165.00
55 A53 1.75fr dk bl ('38) 37.50 32.50
Never hinged 70.00
On cover 150.00
On cover, single franking 350.00
56 A53 2fr red violet 8.50 8.50
Never hinged 17.50
On cover 27.50
On cover, single franking 90.00
56A A50 2fr rose red ('40) 1.25 .75
Never hinged 2.40
On cover 32.50
On cover, single franking 70.00
56B A50 2fr dk bl grn ('42) .30 .30
Never hinged .50
On cover 3.50
On cover, single franking 40.00
57 A50 2.15fr dk vio ('38) 50.00 40.00
Never hinged 100.00
On cover 175.00
On cover, single franking 375.00
58 A50 2.25fr ultra ('39) 7.00 7.00
Never hinged 14.00
On cover 35.00
On cover, single franking 110.00
58A A50 2.40fr red ('42) .45 .30
Never hinged .80
On cover 9.00
On cover, single franking 140.00
59 A50 2.50fr gray blk ('39) 7.00 7.00
Never hinged 14.00
On cover 42.50
On cover, single franking 115.00
59A A50 2.50fr dp ultra ('40) 2.00 2.00
Never hinged 4.00
On cover 35.00
On cover, single franking 70.00
60 A53 3fr orange brn 10.50 8.50
Never hinged 21.00
On cover 32.50
On cover, single franking 90.00
60A A50 3fr red brn ('40) .30 .30
Never hinged .50
On cover 35.00
On cover, single franking 70.00
60B A50 4fr sl bl ('42) .30 .30
Never hinged .50
On cover 10.00
On cover, single franking 70.00
60C A50 4.50fr dp vio ('42) 1.10 1.10
Never hinged 2.25
On cover 7.75
On cover, single franking 60.00
61 A54 5fr brown .50 .50
Never hinged 1.00
On cover 8.50
On cover, single franking 705.00
62 A54 10fr violet .70 .50
Never hinged 1.25
On cover 8.50
On cover, single franking 70.00
62B A54 15fr dp ultra ('42) .70 .70
Never hinged 1.40
On cover 12.00
On cover, single franking 70.00
63 A54 20fr rose lake .85 .55
Never hinged 1.40
On cover 8.50
On cover, single franking 62.50
63A A51 50fr turq bl ('43) 1.10 .90
Never hinged 2.25
On cover 13.00
On cover, single franking 70.00
Nos. 23-63A (56) 512.70 468.50

A 20c ultra exists. Value: unused, $21,250; never hinged $33,500.

No. 37 Surcharged with Bars and New Value in Black

1935, Sept. 25

64 A52 20c on 50c lil rose 14.00 12.50
a. Double surcharge *4,000.*

Coat of Arms
A55 A56

1936-42 *Perf. 14x13*

65	A55	1c black ('37)	.20	.20
66	A55	2c blue	.20	.20
67	A55	3c brown	.20	.20
68	A55	5c rose lilac	.20	.20
69	A55	10c ultra ('37)	.20	.20
70	A55	15c red violet	2.00	1.90
71	A55	20c emerald ('37)	.20	.20
72	A55	30c cop red ('38)	.45	*.55*
72A	A55	30c blk brn ('42)	.20	*.35*
73	A55	35c Prus grn ('38)	52.50	52.50
74	A55	40c cop red ('42)	.45	.45
75	A55	50c Prus grn ('42)	.45	.45
76	A55	60c turq bl ('42)	.45	.45
77	A55	70c vio ('42)	.45	.45
		Nos. 65-77 (14)	58.15	58.30

POSTAGE DUE STAMPS

Postage Due Stamps of France, 1893-1931, Overprinted

On Stamps of 1893-1926

1931-33 Unwmk. *Perf. 14x13½*

J1	D2	5c blue	1.75	1.75
J2	D2	10c brown	1.40	1.40
J3	D2	30c rose red	.70	.70
J4	D2	50c violet brn	1.40	1.40
J5	D2	60c green	22.50	22.50
J6	D2	1fr red brn, *straw*	1.00	1.00
J7	D2	2fr brt violet	10.00	10.00
J8	D2	3fr magenta	2.00	2.00
		Nos. J1-J8 (8)	40.75	40.75

On Stamps of 1927-31

J9	D4	1c olive grn	1.40	1.40
J10	D4	10c rose	3.50	3.50
J11	D4	60c red	19.00	19.00
J12	D4	1fr Prus grn ('32)	82.50	82.50
J13	D4	1.20fr on 2fr bl	57.50	57.50
J14	D4	2fr ol brn ('33)	160.00	160.00
J15	D4	5fr on 1fr vio	90.00	90.00
		Nos. J9-J15 (7)	413.90	413.90

D5

D6

1935-41 Typo.

J16	D5	1c gray grn	2.75	1.90
J17	D6	5c lt bl ('37)	6.75	*6.75*
J18	D6	10c brn ('41)	3.00	*4.25*
J19	D6	2fr vio ('41)	8.00	5.25
J20	D6	5fr red org ('41)	14.00	10.00
		Nos. J16-J20 (5)	34.50	*28.15*

NEWSPAPER STAMP

France No. P7 Overprinted

1931 Unwmk. *Perf. 14x13½*

P1 A16 ½c on lc gray .75 *.75*
Never hinged 1.40
a. Double overprint *2,000.*
Never hinged *3,000.*

ANGOLA

aŋ-'gō-lə

LOCATION — Southwestern Africa between Belgian Congo and South West Africa.
GOVT. — Portuguese colony
AREA — 481,351 sq. mi.
POP. — 3,484,300
CAPITAL — Luanda

1000 Reis = 1 Milreis
100 Centavos = 1 Escudo (1913)
100 Centavos = 1 Angolar (1932)

Watermark

Wmk. 232 — Maltese Cross

Portuguese Crown — A1

1870-77 Typo. Unwmk. *Perf. 12½*

Thin to Medium Paper

1	A1	5r gray black	2.25	1.40
b.		5r black	2.25	1.40
2	A1	10r yellow	20.00	16.00
a.		10r orange	22.50	16.00
3	A1	20r bister	2.25	2.00
b.		20r pale bister	2.25	2.00
4	A1	25r red	10.50	7.75
a.		25r rose	225.00	175.00
5	A1	40r blue ('77)	150.00	100.00
6	A1	50r green	50.00	14.00
a.		50r page green	50.00	14.00
7a	A1	100r lilac	9.75	4.75
b.		100r pale lilac	11.50	4.75
8a	A1	200r orange ('77)	6.00	4.00
9a	A1	300r choc ('77)	20.00	12.00

Perf. 13½

1a	A1	5r gray black	8.00	4.25
1c	A1	5r black	8.00	4.25
2b	A1	10r yellow	21.00	11.50
2c	A1	10r orange yellow	25.00	20.00
3a	A1	20r bister	450.00	375.00
4b	A1	25r red	21.00	20.00
4c	A1	25r rose	30.00	27.50
5a	A1	40r blue ('77)	225.00	160.00
6b	A1	50r green	1,050.	600.00
7	A1	100r lilac	4.75	3.25
7c	A1	100r lilac	4.75	3.25
8	A1	200r orange ('77)	4.00	2.00
9	A1	300r choc ('77)	4.75	3.25

Perf. 14

4d	A1	25r rose	500.00	350.00

Thick Paper

Perf. 12½

1d	A1	5r black	80.00	67.50
2d	A1	10r orange yellow	110.00	85.00
3c	A1	20r bister	110.00	85.00
4e	A1	25r red	55.00	50.00
6c	A1	50r green	80.00	67.50
7d	A1	100r lilac	110.00	65.00

1881-85 *Perf. 12½, 13½*

10	A1	10r green ('83)	7.50	4.25
a.		Perf. 12½	37.50	22.50
11	A1	20r carmine rose ('85)	18.00	13.50
12	A1	25r violet ('85)	12.00	4.75
a.		Perf. 13½	12.00	6.75
13	A1	40r buff ('82)	42.50	4.25
a.		Perf. 13½	10.50	4.75
15	A1	50r blue	40.00	9.00
a.		Perf. 13½	77.50	12.00
		Nos. 10-15 (5)	120.00	35.75

Two types of numerals are found on #2, 11, 13, 15.

The cliche of 40r in plate of 20r error, was discovered before the stamps were issued. All copies were defaced by a blue pencil mark. Value $1,600.

In perf. 12½, Nos. 1-4, 4a and 6, as well as 7a, were printed in 1870 on thicker paper and 1875 on normal paper. Stamps of the earlier printing sell for 2 to 5 times more than those of the 1875 printing.

Some reprints of the 1870-85 issues are on a smooth white chalky paper, ungummed and perf. 13½.

Other reprints of these issues are on thin ivory paper with shiny white gum and clear-cut perf. 13½.

Covers: covers bearing Nos. 1-15 are rare; values start at about $1,800.

King Luiz — A2

King Carlos — A3

1886 Embossed *Perf. 12½*

16	A2	5r black	15.00	6.25
a.		Perf. 13½	12.50	10.50
17	A2	10r green	15.00	6.25
a.		Perf. 13½	16.00	8.25
b.		10r deep green, perf 12½	7.75	4.25
18	A2	20r rose	22.50	12.50
a.		Perf. 13½	13.00	8.25
b.		20r carmine rose, Perf. 13½	13.00	8.25
c.		As "a," printed on reverse side	*55.00*	*65.00*
19	A2	25r red violet	15.00	4.00
a.		Double impression	*36.00*	*42.50*
b.		Triple impression	*85.00*	*100.00*
20	A2	40r chocolate	21.00	7.50
21	A2	50r blue	26.00	4.00
a.		Double impression	*37.50*	*42.50*
22	A2	100r yellow brn	35.00	10.00
23	A2	200r gray violet	50.00	13.00
24	A2	300r orange	50.00	14.00
		Nos. 16-24 (9)	249.50	77.50

For surcharges see #61-69, 172-174, 208-210.

Reprints of 5r, 20r & 100r have cleancut perf. 13½.

1893-94 Typo. *Perf. 11½, 12½, 13½*

Chalk-Surfaced Paper

Perf. 12½

26	A3	10r redsh violet	4.00	2.50
27	A3	15r chocolate	5.25	2.25
30	A3	50r light blue	5.25	2.25
31	A3	75r carmine	17.00	10.00
32	A3	80r lt green	13.00	7.00
33	A3	100r brown, *buff*	13.00	7.00
34	A3	150r car, *rose*	20.00	14.00
35	A3	200r dk blue, *lt bl*	22.50	14.00
36	A3	300r dk blue, *sal*	22.50	14.00

Perf. 11½

25	A3	5r yellow	3.00	1.25
27a	A3	15r chocolate	5.25	2.25
28	A3	20r lavender	5.25	2.25
29	A3	25r green	3.25	1.60
30a	A3	50r light blue	3.75	2.00
31a	A3	75r carmine	13.25	9.50
33a	A3	100r brown, *buff*	55.00	47.50
34a	A3	150r car, *rose*	16.00	10.00

Perf. 13½

35a	A3	200r dk blue, *lt bl*	14.00	12.00
36a	A3	300r dk blue, *sal*	14.00	12.00

Enamel Paper

Perf. 12½

29a	A3	25r green	3.00	1.50
30b	A3	50r light blue	5.50	3.25

Perf. 11½

25a	A3	5r yellow	2.25	1.60
26a	A3	10r redsh violet	2.50	1.80
29b	A3	25r green	3.25	3.00
31b	A3	75r carmine	9.25	7.75

Perf. 11½

25b	A3	5r yellow	1.80	1.50
29c	A3	25r green	3.00	2.00
30c	A3	50r light blue	7.75	6.25
31c	A3	75r carmine	7.75	6.25

For surcharges see Nos. 70-81, 175-179, 213-216, 234.

No. P1 Surcharged in Blue

1894, Aug.

37	N1	25r on 2½r brown	80.00	55.00

King Carlos — A5

1898-1903 *Perf. 11½*

Name and Value in Black except 500r

38	A5	2½r gray	.55	.40
39	A5	5r orange	.55	.40
40	A5	10r yellow grn	.55	.40
41	A5	15r violet brn	3.00	1.60
42	A5	15r gray green ('03)	1.50	1.40
43	A5	20r gray violet	.60	.50
44	A5	25r sea green	1.60	.65
45	A5	25r car ('03)	.75	.45
46	A5	50r blue	2.75	.90
47	A5	50r brown ('03)	7.50	3.75
48	A5	65r dull blue ('03)	7.75	5.75
49	A5	75r rose	10.00	6.00
50	A5	75r red violet ('03)	3.00	2.00
51	A5	80r violet	9.00	3.00
52	A5	100r dk blue, *blue*	1.90	1.25
53	A5	115r org brn, *pink* ('03)	12.00	7.50
54	A5	130r brn, *straw* ('03)	11.00	7.50
55	A5	150r brn, *straw*	10.00	5.75
56	A5	200r red vio, *pink*	5.50	1.75
57	A5	300r dk blue, *rose*	6.00	4.75
58	A5	400r dull bl, *straw* ('03)	5.50	3.50
59	A5	500r blk & red, *bl* ('01)	6.00	4.75
60	A5	700r vio, *yelsh* ('01)	30.00	15.00
		Nos. 38-60 (23)	137.00	78.95

For surcharges and overprints see Nos. 83-102, 113-117, 159-171, 181-183, 217-218, 221-225.

Stamps of 1886-94 Surcharged in Black or Red

Two types of surcharge:
I — 3mm between numeral and REIS.
II — 4½mm spacing.

1902 *Perf. 12½*

61	A2	65r on 40r choc	10.50	6.00
62	A2	65r on 300r org, I	10.50	6.00
a.		Type II	10.50	6.00
63	A2	115r on 10r green	8.75	4.75
a.		Inverted surcharge	60.00	40.00
b.		Perf. 13½	47.50	37.50
64	A2	115r on 200r gray vio	8.75	4.75
65	A2	130r on 50r blue	12.50	4.75
66	A2	130r on 100r brown	7.75	4.75
67	A2	400r on 20r rose	95.00	55.00
a.		Perf. 13½	150.00	95.00
68	A2	400r on 25r violet	21.00	11.00
69	A2	400r on 5r black (R)	17.50	13.00
a.		Double surcharge	60.00	40.00
		Nos. 61-69 (9)	192.25	110.00

For surcharges see Nos. 172-174, 208-210.

Perf. 11½, 12½, 13½

70	A3	65r on 5r yel, I	9.00	6.00
a.		Type II	10.00	10.00
71	A3	65r on 10r red vio, I	6.75	5.25
a.		Type II	6.75	5.25
b.		Perf. 11½, type I	10.50	6.25
c.		Perf. 11½, type II	10.50	6.25
72	A3	65r on 20r lav	10.50	6.25
a.		Type II	12.50	12.50
73		65r on 25r green	5.25	4.50
a.		Perf. 11½	12.50	12.50
74	A3	115r on 80r lt grn	13.50	8.25
75	A3	115r on 100r brn, *buff*	13.50	7.25
a.		Perf. 13½	50.00	40.00
76	A3	115r on 150r car, *rose*	16.00	12.50
a.		Perf. 13½	18.00	14.50
77	A3	130r on 15r choc	6.25	5.00
78	A3	130r on 75r carmine	8.00	7.50
a.		Perf. 13½	45.00	40.00
79	A3	130r on 300r dk bl, *sal*	18.00	15.00
80	A3	400r on 50r lt bl	8.00	5.25
81	A3	400r on 200r bl, *bl*	9.00	7.50
a.		Perf. 13½	225.00	150.00
82	N1	400r on 2½r brn	1.75	1.50
a.		Type II	1.75	1.50
		Nos. 70-82 (13)	125.50	91.75

For surcharges see #175-180, 211-216, 234-235.

Reprints of Nos. 65, 67, 68 and 69 have clean-cut perforation 13½.

Stamps of 1898 Overprinted — a

1902 *Perf. 11½*

83	A5	15r brown	2.10	1.40
84	A5	25r sea green	1.75	.80
85	A5	50r blue	3.75	1.75
86	A5	75r rose	6.25	5.00
		Nos. 83-86 (4)	13.85	8.95

For surcharge see No. 116.

No. 48 Surcharged in Black

1905

87	A5	50r on 65r dull blue	5.25	2.75

For surcharge see No. 183.

Stamps of 1898-1903 Overprinted in Carmine or Green—b

1911

88	A5	2½r gray	.45	.35
89	A5	5r orange yel	.45	.35
90	A5	10r light green	.45	.35
91	A5	15r gray green	.60	.50
92	A5	20r gray violet	.60	.50
93	A5	25r car (G)	.60	.50
94	A5	50r brown	2.50	1.50
95	A5	75r lilac	3.50	2.75
96	A5	100r dk blue, *bl*	5.25	3.00
97	A5	115r org brn, *pink*	3.00	1.50
98	A5	130r brn, *straw*	3.00	1.50
99	A5	200r red lil, *pnksh*	3.50	1.90
100	A5	400r dull bl, *straw*	3.50	1.50
101	A5	500r blk & red, *bl*	3.50	1.75
102	A5	700r violet, *yelsh*	3.50	2.00
		Nos. 88-102 (15)	34.40	19.95

Inverted and double overprints of Nos. 88-102 were made intentionally.

For surcharges see Nos. 217-218, 221-222, 224.

King Manuel II — A6

Ceres — A7

Overprinted in Carmine or Green

1912 *Perf. 11½x12*

103	A6	2½r violet	.50	*.30*
104	A6	5r black	.50	*.30*
105	A6	10r gray green	.50	.30
106	A6	20r carmine (G)	.50	.30
107	A6	25r violet brown	.50	.30
108	A6	50r dk blue	1.40	1.10
109	A6	75r bister brown	1.60	*1.40*
110	A6	100r brown, *lt green*	3.00	1.75
111	A6	200r dk green, *salmon*	3.00	1.75
112	A6	300r black, *azure*	3.00	1.75
		Nos. 103-112 (10)	14.50	9.25

For surcharges see Nos. 219-220, 226-227.

No. 91 Surcharged with New Values as

1912, June *Perf. 11½*
113 A5 2½r on 15r gray green 4.50 2.50
114 A5 5r on 15r gray green 4.75 2.50
115 A5 10r on 15r gray green 3.75 2.50
Nos. 113-115 (3) 13.00 7.50

Inverted and double surcharges of Nos. 113-115 were made intentionally.

Nos. 86 and 50 Surcharged "25" in Black and Overprinted in Violet — c

1912
116 A5 25r on 75r rose 70.00 50.00
117 A5 25r on 75r red violet 5.00 4.50
a. "REUPBLICA" 72.50 52.50
b. "25" omitted 72.50 52.50
c. "REPUBLICA" omitted 72.50 52.50

1914-26 Typo. *Perf. 12x11½, 15x14*
Name and Value in Black
118 A7 ¼c olive brown .25 .25
a. Inscriptions inverted 8.00
119 A7 ½c black .25 .25
120 A7 1c blue green .25 .25
121 A7 1c yel grn ('22) .20 .20
122 A7 1½c lilac brown .25 .25
123 A7 2c carmine .25 .25
124 A7 2c gray ('25) .45 .40
125 A7 2½c lt violet .25 .25
126 A7 3c orange ('21) .25 .25
127 A7 4c dull rose ('21) .25 .25
128 A7 4½c gray ('21) .25 .25
130 A7 5c blue .25 .25
131 A7 6c lilac ('21) .25 .25
132 A7 7c ultra ('21) .25 .25
133 A7 7½c yellow brn .30 .25
134 A7 8c slate .30 .25
135 A7 10c orange brn .30 .25
136 A7 12c olive brn ('21) .45 .35
137 A7 12c dp green ('25) .45 .40
138 A7 15c plum .25 .25
139 A7 15c brown rose ('21) .20 .20
140 A7 20c yel green 1.25 1.10
141 A7 24c ultra ('25) 1.25 .95
142 A7 25c choc ('25) 1.25 .95
143 A7 30c brown, *green* 2.25 2.00
144 A7 30c gray grn ('21) .45 .35
145 A7 40c brown, *pink* 2.25 2.00
146 A7 40c turq blue ('21) .95 .45
147 A7 50c orange, *sal* 7.50 6.25
148 A7 50c lt violet ('25) 1.10 .45
149 A7 60c dk blue ('22) 1.25 .70
150 A7 60c dp rose ('26) 65.00 45.00
151 A7 80c pink ('22) 1.40 .70
152 A7 1e green, *blue* 6.25 3.75
153 A7 1e rose ('22) 1.60 .70
154 A7 1e dp blue ('25) 2.75 1.60
155 A7 2e dk violet ('22) 1.75 .95
156 A7 5e buff ('25) 15.00 11.00
157 A7 10e pink ('25) 40.00 22.50
158 A7 20e pale turq ('25) 95.00 65.00
Nos. 118-158 (40) 254.15 171.95

Two kinds of paper, chalky-surfaced paper and ordinary, were used for Nos. 118-120, 122-123, 125, 130, 133-135, 138 and 140. Those on coated paper sell unused for 10 to 40 times the values listed; used for about 5 to 20 times.

All but #143, 145, 147 come perf 12x11½. All but #124, 137, 141-142, 146, 148, 151, 153-154, 156-158 come perf 15x14.

For surcharges see Nos. 228-229, 236-239.

Stamps of 1898-1903 Overprinted type "c" in Red or Green

On Stamps of 1898-1903

1914 *Perf. 11½, 12*
159 A5 10r yel green (R) 5.25 4.00
160 A5 15r gray green (R) 5.00 4.00
161 A5 20r gray violet (G) 2.00 1.50
163 A5 75r red violet (G) 2.00 1.00
164 A5 100r blue, *blue* (R) 3.00 2.75
165 A5 115r org brn, *pink* (R) 100.00
167 A5 200r red vio, *pnksh* (G) 2.00 1.25
169 A5 400r dl bl, *straw* (R) 37.50 37.50
170 A5 500r blk & red, *bl* (R) 5.00 4.50
171 A5 700r vio, *yelsh* (G) 24.00 20.00

Inverted and double overprints were made intentionally. No. 165 was not regularly issued. Red overprints on the 20r, 75r, 200r were not regularly issued. The 130r was not regularly issued without surcharge (No. 225).

On Nos. 63-65, 74-76, 78-79, 82
Perf. 11½, 12½, 13½
172 A2 115r on 10r (R) 16.00 16.00
a. Perf. 13½ 16.00 16.00
173 A2 115r on 200r (R) 22.50 22.50
174 A2 130r on 50r (R) 24.00 24.00
175 A3 115r on 80r (R) 175.00 175.00
176 A3 115r on 100r (R) 225.00 175.00
177 A3 115r on 150r (G) 190.00 160.00
178 A3 130r on 75r (G) 3.50 3.25
179 A3 130r on 300r (R) 7.50 6.25
a. Perf. 12½ 13.50 12.50
180 N1 400r on 2½r (R) .75 .55
a. Perf. 11½ 3.00 2.50
Nos. 172-180 (9) 664.25 582.55

Overprinted

On Stamps of 1902
Perf. 11½, 12
181 A5 50r blue (R) 2.00 1.60
182 A5 75r rose (G) 4.50 3.25

On No. 87
183 A5 50r on 65r dull blue (R) 4.25 2.75
Nos. 181-183 (3) 10.75 7.60

Inverted and double surcharges of Nos. 181-183 were made intentionally.

Common Design Types pictured following the introduction.

Vasco da Gama Issue of Various Portuguese Colonies

Common Design Types CD20-CD27 Surcharged

On Stamps of Macao

1913 *Perf. 12½ to 16*
184 ¼c on ½a blue grn 2.50 1.90
185 ½c on 1a red 2.50 1.90
186 1c on 2a red violet 2.50 1.90
187 2½c on 4a yel green 2.00 1.40
188 5c on 8a dk blue 2.00 1.40
189 7½c on 12a vio brn 8.50 5.75
190 10c on 16a bister brn 3.00 2.25
191 15c on 24a bister 3.50 2.25
Nos. 184-191 (8) 26.50 18.75

On Stamps of Portuguese Africa
Perf. 14 to 15
192 ¼c on 2½r blue grn 1.00 .75
193 ½c on 5r red 1.00 .75
194 1c on 10r red violet 1.00 .75
195 2½c on 25r yel grn 1.00 .75
196 5c on 50r dk blue 1.00 .75
197 7½c on 75r vio brn 5.75 5.00
198 10c on 100r bister brn 2.25 1.40
199 15c on 150r bister 2.50 1.75
Nos. 192-199 (8) 15.50 11.90

On Stamps of Timor
200 ¼c on ½a blue grn 2.50 2.00
201 ½c on 1a red 2.50 2.00
202 1c on 2a red vio 2.50 2.00
203 2½c on 4a yel grn 2.00 1.40
204 5c on 8a dk blue 2.00 1.40
205 7½c on 12a vio brn 8.50 5.75
206 10c on 16a bis brn 3.00 2.25
207 15c on 24a bister 3.50 2.25
Nos. 200-207 (8) 26.50 19.05
Nos. 184-207 (24) 68.50 49.70

Provisional Issue of 1902 Overprinted in Carmine

1915 *Perf. 11½, 12½, 13½*
208 A2 115r on 10r green 2.00 2.00
209 A2 115r on 200r gray vio 1.75 2.00
210 A2 130r on 100r brown 1.50 2.00
211 A3 115r on 80r lt green 1.40 1.25
212 A3 115r on 100r brn, *buff* 1.75 1.75
a. Perf. 11½ 77.50 72.50
213 A3 115r on 150r car, *rose* 1.50 1.50
214 A3 130r on 15r choc 1.40 1.25
a. Perf. 12½ 7.00 6.00
215 A3 130r on 75r carmine 2.40 2.00
216 A3 130r on 300r dk bl, *sal* 1.75 1.75
Nos. 208-216 (9) 15.45 15.50

Stamps of 1911-14 Surcharged in Black:

d

e

On Stamps of 1911

1919 *Perf. 11½*
217 A5 (d) ½c on 75r red lilac 2.50 2.00
218 A5 (d) 2½c on 100r blue, *grysh* 2.50 2.00

On Stamps of 1912
Perf. 11½x12
219 A6 (e) ½c on 75r bis brn 1.25 1.00
220 A6 (e) 2½c on 100r brn, *lt grn* 2.50 2.00

On Stamps of 1914
221 A5 (d) ½c on 75r red lil 1.50 1.25
222 A5 (d) 2½c on 100r bl, *grysh* 1.90 1.40
Nos. 217-222 (6) 12.15 9.65

Inverted and double surcharges were made for sale to collectors.

Nos. 163, 98 and Type of 1914 Surcharged with New Values and Bars in Black

1921
223 A5 (c) 00.5c on 75r 350.00 350.00
224 A5 (b) 4c on 130r (#98) 2.00 1.50
225 A5 (c) 4c on 130r brn, *straw* 5.75 5.25

Nos. 109 and 108 Surcharged with New Values and Bars in Black
226 A6 00.5c on 75c 1.50 1.25
227 A6 1c on 50r 1.60 1.50

Nos. 133 and 138 Surcharged with New Values and Bars in Black
228 A7 00.5c on 7½c 2.00 1.60
229 A7 04c on 15c 2.00 1.50
Nos. 224-229 (6) 14.85 12.60
Nos. 223-229 (7) 364.85 362.60

The 04c surcharge exists on the 15c brown rose, perf 12x11½, No. 139.

Nos. 81-82 Surcharged

1925 *Perf. 12½*
234 A3 40c on 400r on 200r bl, *bl* 1.00 .80
a. Perf. 13½ 5.25 4.00
235 N1 40c on 400c on 2½r brn .75 .75
a. Perf. 13½ .75 .75

Nos. 150-151, 154-155 Surcharged

1931 *Perf. 11½*
236 A7 50c on 60c deep rose 1.90 1.60
237 A7 70c on 80c pink 3.75 2.50
238 A7 70c on 1e deep blue 4.00 2.50
239 A7 1.40e on 2e dark violet 2.75 1.75
Nos. 236-239 (4) 12.40 8.35

Ceres — A14

Perf. 12x11½
1932-46 Typo. Wmk. 232
243 A14 1c bister brn .25 .20
244 A14 5c dk brown .30 .25
245 A14 10c dp violet .30 .25
246 A14 15c black .30 .25
247 A14 20c gray .30 .25
248 A14 30c myrtle grn .30 .25
249 A14 35c yel grn ('46) 7.50 3.50
250 A14 40c dp orange .40 .20
251 A14 45c lt blue 1.40 1.10
252 A14 50c lt brown .30 .20
253 A14 60c olive grn .90 .25
254 A14 70c orange brn .90 .25
255 A14 80c emerald .55 .20
256 A14 85c rose 4.50 2.00
257 A14 1a claret .95 .25
258 A14 1.40a dk blue 9.50 1.50
258A A14 1.75a dk blue ('46) 16.00 4.25
259 A14 2a dull vio 4.50 .45
260 A14 5a pale yel grn 9.50 1.50
261 A14 10a olive bis 18.00 4.50
262 A14 20a orange 47.50 4.50
Nos. 243-262 (21) 124.15 26.10
Set, never hinged 150.00

For surcharges see Nos. 263-267, 271-273, 294A-300, J31-J36.

Surcharged with New Value and Bars

5½mm between bars and new value.

1934
263 A14 10c on 45c lt bl 3.00 2.25
264 A14 20c on 85c rose 3.00 2.25
265 A14 30c on 1.40a dk bl 3.00 2.25
266 A14 70c on 2a dl vio 5.00 2.25
267 A14 80c on 5a pale yel grn 8.00 2.25
Nos. 263-267 (5) 22.00 11.25
Set, never hinged 29.00

See Nos. 294A-300.

Nos. J26, J30 Surcharged in Black

1935 Unwmk. *Perf. 11½*
268 D2 5c on 6c lt brown 2.00 1.25
269 D2 30c on 50c gray 2.00 1.25
270 D2 40c on 50c gray 2.00 1.25
Nos. 268-270 (3) 6.00 3.75
Set, never hinged 8.75

No. 255 Surcharged in Black

1938 Wmk. 232 *Perf. 12x11½*
271 A14 5c on 80c emerald .85 .50
272 A14 10c on 80c emerald 1.50 .75
273 A14 15c on 80c emerald 2.00 .75
Nos. 271-273 (3) 4.35 2.00
Set, never hinged 6.25

Vasco da Gama Issue
Common Design Types
Engr.; Name & Value Typo. in Black
Perf. 13½x13

1938, July 26 Unwmk.
274 CD34 1c gray green .25 .20
275 CD34 5c orange brn .30 .25
276 CD34 10c dk carmine .35 .25
277 CD34 15c dk violet brn .35 .25
278 CD34 20c slate .35 .25
279 CD35 30c rose violet .45 .30
280 CD35 35c brt green .95 .60
281 CD35 40c brown .30 .20
282 CD35 50c brt red vio .45 .20
283 CD36 60c gray black .95 .25
284 CD36 70c brown vio .95 .25
285 CD36 80c orange .95 .25
286 CD36 1a red .95 .25
287 CD37 1.75a blue 1.90 .80
288 CD37 2a brown car 2.75 .90
289 CD37 5a olive grn 12.50 .90
290 CD38 10a blue vio 25.00 1.00
291 CD38 20a red brown 35.00 3.25
Nos. 274-291 (18) 84.70 10.35
Set, never hinged 125.00

For surcharges see Nos. 301-304.

Marble Column and Portuguese Arms with Cross — A20

1938, July 29 *Perf. 12½*

292	A20	80c blue green	2.75	1.75
293	A20	1.75a deep blue	19.00	5.00
294	A20	20a dk red brown	55.00	24.00
		Nos. 292-294 (3)	76.75	30.75
		Set, never hinged	110.00	

Visit of the President of Portugal to this colony in 1938.

AIR POST STAMPS

Common Design Type

Perf. 13½x13

1938, July 26 Engr. Unwmk.

Name and Value in Black

C1	CD39	10c red orange	.35	.40
C2	CD39	20c purple	.35	.35
C3	CD39	50c orange	.35	.40
C4	CD39	1a ultra	.40	.40
C5	CD39	2a lilac brn	.85	.35
C6	CD39	3a dk green	1.60	.55
C7	CD39	5a red brown	3.75	.75
C8	CD39	9a rose carmine	6.00	1.60
C9	CD39	10a magenta	8.75	2.25
		Nos. C1-C9 (9)	22.40	7.05

No. C7 exists with overprint "Exposicao Internacional de Nova York, 1939-1940" and Trylon and Perisphere.

POSTAGE DUE STAMPS

D1

D2

1904 Unwmk. Typo. *Perf. 11½x12*

J1	D1	5r yellow grn	.30	.30
J2	D1	10r slate	.30	.30
J3	D1	20r yellow brn	.65	.40
J4	D1	30r orange	.65	.40
J5	D1	50r gray brown	.85	.65
J6	D1	60r red brown	7.25	4.50
J7	D1	100r lilac	3.00	2.25
J8	D1	130r dull blue	3.25	2.25
J9	D1	200r carmine	9.00	5.50
J10	D1	500r gray violet	7.50	4.75
		Nos. J1-J10 (10)	32.75	21.30

Postage Due Stamps of 1904 Overprinted in Carmine or Green

1911

J11	D1	5r yellow grn	.25	.25
J12	D1	10r slate	.25	.25
J13	D1	20r yellow brn	.25	.25
J14	D1	30r orange	.35	.25
J15	D1	50r gray brown	.35	.25
J16	D1	60r red brown	1.00	.75
J17	D1	100r lilac	1.00	.75
J18	D1	130r dull blue	1.10	.85
J19	D1	200r carmine (G)	1.40	.85
J20	D1	500r gray violet	1.50	1.40
		Nos. J11-J20 (10)	7.45	5.85

1921 *Perf. 11½*

J21	D2	½c yellow green	.25	.25
J22	D2	1c slate	.25	.25
J23	D2	2c orange brown	.25	.25
J24	D2	3c orange	.25	.25
J25	D2	5c gray brown	.25	.25
J26	D2	6c lt brown	.25	.25
J27	D2	10c red violet	.40	.30
J28	D2	13c dull blue	.70	.60
J29	D2	20c carmine	.70	.60
J30	D2	50c gray	.70	.60
		Nos. J21-J30 (10)	4.00	3.60

For surcharges see Nos. 268-270.

NEWSPAPER STAMP

N1

Perf. 11½, 12½, 13½

1893 Typo. Unwmk.

P1	N1	2½r brown	1.00	.70

No. P1 was also used for ordinary postage. For surcharges see Nos. 37, 82, 180, 235.

POSTAL TAX STAMPS

Pombal Issue

Common Design Types

1925, May 8 Unwmk. *Perf. 12½*

RA1	CD28	15c lilac & black	.75	.65
RA2	CD29	15c lilac & black	.75	.65
RA3	CD30	15c lilac & black	.75	.65
		Nos. RA1-RA3 (3)	2.25	1.95

"Charity"
PT1

Coat of Arms
PT2

1929 Litho. *Perf. 11*

Without Gum

RA4	PT1	50c dark blue	4.50	1.25

1939 Without Gum *Perf. 10½*

RA5	PT2	50c turq green	2.50	.25
RA6	PT2	1a red	8.00	1.60

A 1.50a, type PT2, was issued for fiscal use.

POSTAL TAX DUE STAMPS

Pombal Issue

Common Design Types

1925, May 8 Unwmk. *Perf. 12½*

RAJ1	CD28	30c lilac & black	.75	*.65*
RAJ2	CD29	30c lilac & black	.75	*.65*
RAJ3	CD30	30c lilac & black	.75	*.65*
		Nos. RAJ1-RAJ3 (3)	2.25	*1.95*

See note after Portugal No. RAJ4.

ANGRA

'aŋ-grə

LOCATION — An administrative district of the Azores, consisting of the islands of Terceira, Sao Jorge and Graciosa.

GOVT. — A district of Portugal

AREA — 275 sq. mi.

POP. — 70,000 (approx.)

CAPITAL — Angra do Heroismo

1000 Reis = 1 Milreis

STAMPS OF PORTUGAL USED IN ANGRA

Barred Numeral "48"

1853 Queen Maria II

A1	5r org brn (#1)	1,350.
A2	25r blue (#2)	75.00
A3	50r dp yel grn (#3)	1,400.
a.	50r blue grn (#3a)	2,000.
A4	100r lilac (#4)	3,750.

1855 King Pedro V (Straight Hair)

A5	5r red brn (#5)	1,450.
A6	25r blue, type II (#6)	67.50
a.	Type I (#6a)	75.00
A7	50r green (#7)	110.00
A8	100r lilac (#8)	140.00

1856-58

King Pedro V (Curled Hair)

A9	5r red brn (#9)	175.00
A10	25r blue, type II (#10)	120.00
a.	Type I (#10a)	85.00
A11	25r rose, type II (#11; '58)	27.50

1862-64 King Luiz

A12	5r brown (#12)	85.00
A13	10r orange (#13)	95.00
A14	25r rose (#14)	20.00
A15	50r yel green (#15)	125.00
A16	100r lilac (#16; '64)	140.00

1866-67 King Luiz

Imperf.

A17	5r black (#17)	120.00
A18	10r yellow (#18)	200.00
A19	20r bister (#19)	200.00
A20	25r rose (#20)	52.50
A21	50r green (#21)	160.00
A22	80r orange (#22)	160.00
A23	100r dk lilac (#23; '67)	210.00
A24	120r blue (#24)	150.00

Perf. 12½

A28	25r rose (#28)	120.00

King Carlos
A1 A2

Enamel surfaced paper

1892-93 Typo. Unwmk. *Perf. 12½*

1	A1	5r yellow	4.00	2.10
		Never hinged	4.75	
2	A1	10r redsh violet	4.00	2.00
		Never hinged	4.75	
3	A1	15r chocolate	6.00	3.50
		Never hinged	5.00	
4	A1	20r lavender	6.00	3.00
		Never hinged	7.50	
5	A1	25r green	5.00	.80
		Never hinged	5.75	
7	A1	50r blue	9.00	4.50
		Never hinged	11.00	
8	A1	75r carmine	10.00	6.00
		Never hinged	12.00	
9	A1	80r yellow green	12.00	11.50
		Never hinged	14.00	
10a	A1	100r brown, *yellow*	175.00	150.00
		Never hinged	210.00	
11	A1	150r car, *rose* ('93)	60.00	45.00
		Never hinged	72.50	
12	A1	200r dk blue, *bl* ('93)	60.00	45.00
		Never hinged	72.50	
13	A1	300r dk blue, *sal* ('93)	60.00	45.00
		Never hinged	72.50	

Enamel surfaced paper, Perf 13½

1b	A1	5r yellow	3.25	2.10
		Never hinged	3.75	
2a	A1	10r reddish violet	4.25	3.50
		Never hinged	5.00	
3a	A1	15r chocolate	4.25	3.75
		Never hinged	5.00	
4a	A1	20r lavender	4.25	3.25
		Never hinged	7.00	
7a	A1	50r blue	12.50	7.00
		Never hinged	15.00	
10	A1	100r brown, *yellow*	45.00	16.00
		Never hinged	52.50	
11a	A1	150r carmine, *rose*	70.00	60.00
		Never hinged	85.00	
12a	A1	200r dark blue, *blue* ('93)	70.00	60.00
		Never hinged	85.00	
13a	A1	300r dark blue, *salmon*	70.00	60.00
		Never hinged	85.00	

Enamel surfaced paper, perf 11½

1a	A1	5r yellow	14.00	7.00
		Never hinged	17.00	
5b	A1	25r green	6.00	1.25
		Never hinged	7.50	

Chalky surfaced paper with lozenges, Perf 12½

1c	A1	5r yellow	4.25	1.40
		Never hinged	5.25	

Chalky surfaced paper with lozenges, Perf 13½

1d	A1	5r yellow	4.50	1.60
		Never hinged	6.50	
5a	A1	25r green	10.00	6.00
		Never hinged	12.00	
7b	A1	50r blue	—	30.00
		Never hinged	—	

Reprints of 50r, 150r, 200r and 300r, made in 1900, are perf. 11½ and ungummed. Value, each $50. Reprints of all values, made in 1905, have shiny white gum and clean-cut perf. Value, each $22.50. 13½.

1897-1905 *Perf. 11½*

Name and Value in Black except Nos. 26 and 35

14	A2	2½r gray	.75	.50
		Never hinged	.90	
15	A2	5r orange	.75	.50
		Never hinged	.90	
a.		Diagonal half used as 2½r on newspaper or circular		*32.50*
16	A2	10r yellow grn	.75	.50
		Never hinged	.90	
17	A2	15r brown	10.00	7.00
		Never hinged	12.00	
18	A2	15r gray grn ('99)	1.00	.70
		Never hinged	1.90	
19	A2	20r gray violet	2.00	1.50
		Never hinged	2.40	
20	A2	25r sea green	3.25	1.40
		Never hinged	4.00	
21	A2	25r car rose ('99)	.75	.70
		Never hinged	1.00	
22	A2	50r dark blue	6.00	2.00
		Never hinged	7.25	
23	A2	50r ultra ('05)	15.00	12.50
		Never hinged	17.50	
24	A2	65r slate bl ('98)	1.40	.70
		Never hinged	1.60	
25	A2	75r rose	4.00	1.90
		Never hinged	4.75	
26	A2	75r gray brn & car, *straw*('05)	15.00	12.50
		Never hinged	17.50	
27	A2	80r violet	1.60	1.40
		Never hinged	2.00	
28	A2	100r dk blue, *bl*	3.00	2.00
		Never hinged	3.75	
29	A2	115r org brn, *pink*('98)	3.00	2.25
		Never hinged	3.50	
30	A2	130r gray brn, *straw*('98)	3.00	2.25
		Never hinged	3.50	
31	A2	150r lt brn, *straw*	3.00	2.00
		Never hinged	3.50	
32	A2	180r sl, *pnksh* ('98)	3.50	3.25
		Never hinged	4.00	
33	A2	200r red vio, *pnksh*	6.00	5.50
		Never hinged	7.25	
34	A2	300r blue, *rose*	9.00	7.00
		Never hinged	10.50	
35	A2	500r blk & red, *bl*	20.00	16.00
		Never hinged	24.00	
a.		Perf. 12½	30.00	20.00
		Never hinged	35.00	
		Nos. 14-35 (22)	112.75	84.05

Yellowish paper

15b	A2	5r orange	.65	.45
		Never hinged	.85	
21b	A2	25r carmine rose ('99)	1.00	.50
		Never hinged	1.20	
24b	A2	65r slate blue ('98)	1.10	.55
		Never hinged	1.50	
29a	A2	115r orange, *yellowish*	*6.75*	*3.75*
		Never hinged	*9.00*	

Azores stamps were used in Angra from 1906 to 1931, when they were superseded by those of Portugal.

ANJOUAN

'an-jü-wän

LOCATION — One of the Comoro Islands in the Mozambique Channel between Madagascar and Mozambique.

GOVT. — French Colony.

AREA — 89 sq. mi.

POP. — 20,000 (approx. 1912)

CAPITAL — Mossamondu

See Comoro Islands.

100 Centimes = 1 Franc

Navigation and Commerce — A1

Perf. 14x13½

1892-1907 Typo. Unwmk.

Name of Colony in Blue or Carmine

1	A1	1c black, *blue*	1.25	1.25
		Never hinged	1.90	
		On cover		140.00
2	A1	2c brown, *buff*	1.90	1.50
		Never hinged	3.00	
		On cover		140.00
3	A1	4c claret, *lav*	3.50	2.50
		Never hinged	5.50	
		On cover		160.00
4	A1	5c green, *grnsh*	6.25	4.00
		Never hinged	12.00	
		On cover		130.00

On newspaper or wrapper, single franking 425.00
5 A1 10c blk, *lavender* 8.00 5.00
Never hinged 14.00
On cover 125.00
6 A1 10c red ('00) 25.00 21.00
Never hinged 50.00
On cover 175.00
7 A1 15c blue, quadrille paper 10.50 7.00
Never hinged 20.00
On cover 125.00
8 A1 15c gray, *lt gray*('00) 17.50 14.00
Never hinged 35.00
On cover 140.00
9 A1 20c red, *green* 10.50 7.75
Never hinged 21.00
On cover 130.00
On cover, single franking 175.00
10 A1 25c black, *rose* 10.50 10.00
Never hinged 21.00
On cover 140.00
On cover, single franking 225.00
11 A1 25c blue ('00) 17.50 14.00
Never hinged 35.00
On cover 160.00
On cover, single franking 250.00
12 A1 30c brn, *bister* 25.00 14.00
Never hinged 50.00
On cover 110.00
On cover, single franking 240.00
13 A1 35c blk, *yel* ('06) 10.50 7.00
Never hinged 21.00
On cover 87.50
On cover, single franking 140.00
14 A1 40c red, *straw* 30.00 25.00
Never hinged 62.50
On cover 175.00
On cover, single franking 250.00
15 A1 45c blk, *gray grn* ('07) 105.00 100.00
Never hinged 225.00
On cover 525.00
On cover, single franking 625.00
16 A1 50c car, *rose* 35.00 25.00
Never hinged 70.00
On cover 225.00
On cover, single franking 325.00
17 A1 50c brn, *az* ('00) 25.00 25.00
Never hinged 50.00
On cover 225.00
On cover, single franking 300.00
18 A1 75c vio, *orange* 32.50 25.00
Never hinged 67.50
On cover 300.00
On cover, single franking 425.00
19 A1 1fr brnz grn, *straw* 70.00 62.50
Never hinged 160.00
On cover 475.00
On cover, single franking 575.00
Nos. 1-19 (19) 445.40 371.50

Perf. 13½x14 stamps are counterfeits.

Covers: Values are for commercial covers used at Anjouan.

Issues of 1892-1907 Surcharged in Black or Carmine

1912

Spacing between figures of surcharge 1.5mm (5c), 2mm (10c)

20 A1 5c on 2c brn, *buff* .90 .90
Never hinged 1.60
On cover 62.50
21 A1 5c on 4c cl, *lav* (C) 1.10 1.10
Never hinged 2.00
On cover 60.00
a. Pair, one without surcharge *775.00 775.00*
22 A1 5c on 15c blue (C) 1.10 1.10
Never hinged 1.75
On cover 62.50
a. Pair, one without surcharge *775.00 775.00*
23 A1 5c on 20c red, *green* 1.10 1.10
Never hinged 1.75
On cover 62.50
a. Pair, one without surcharge *775.00 775.00*
24 A1 5c on 25c blk, *rose* (C) 1.25 1.25
Never hinged 2.10
On cover 60.00
25 A1 5c on 30c brn, *bis* (C) 1.60 1.60
Never hinged 2.75
On cover 62.50
26 A1 10c on 40c red, *straw* 1.60 1.60
Never hinged 160.00
On cover 475.00
27 A1 10c on 45c black, *gray green* (C) 1.75 1.75
Never hinged 3.25
On cover 90.00
28 A1 10c on 50c car, *rose* 4.00 4.00
Never hinged 6.50
On cover 125.00
29 A1 10c on 75c vio, *org* 2.50 2.50
Never hinged 4.25
On cover 110.00
30 A1 10c on 1fr brnz grn, *straw* 3.25 3.25
Never hinged 5.25
On cover 125.00
a. Pair, one without surcharge *875.00 875.00*
Nos. 20-30 (11) 20.15 20.15

Spacing between figures of surcharge 2.25mm (5c), 2.75mm (10c)

20a A1 5c on 2c brn, *buff* 10.50 10.50
Never hinged 19.00
21b A1 5c on 4c cl, *lav* (C) 10.50 10.50
Never hinged 19.00
22b A1 5c on 15c blue (C) 12.00 12.00
Never hinged 21.00
23b A1 5c on 20c red, *green* 12.00 12.00
Never hinged 21.00
24a A1 5c on 25c blk, *rose* (C) 12.00 12.00
Never hinged 21.00
25a A1 5c on 30c brn, *bis* (C) 12.00 12.00
Never hinged 21.00
26a A1 10c on 40c red, *straw* 37.50 37.50
Never hinged 70.00
27a A1 10c on 45c black, *gray green* (C) 50.00 50.00
Never hinged 95.00
28a A1 10c on 50c car, *rose* 80.00 80.00
Never hinged —
29a A1 10c on 75c vio, *org* 75.00 75.00
Never hinged —
30b A1 10c on 1fr brnz grn, *straw* 80.00 80.00
Never hinged —
Nos. 20a-30b (11) 391.50 391.50

Nos. 20-30 were available for use in Madagascar and the Comoro archipelago.

The stamps of Anjouan were superseded by those of Madagascar, and in 1950 by those of Comoro Islands.

ANNAM AND TONKIN

a-'nam and 'tän-'kin

LOCATION — In French Indo-China bordering on the China Sea on the east and Siam on the west.
GOVT. — French Protectorate
AREA — 97,503 sq. mi.
POP. — 14,124,000 (approx. 1890)
CAPITAL — Annam: Hue; Tonkin: Hanoi

For administrative purposes, the Protectorates of Annam, Tonkin, Cambodia, Laos and the Colony of Cochin-China were grouped together and were known as French Indo-China.

100 Centimes = 1 Franc

Catalogue values for unused stamps are for examples without gum as most stamps were issued in that condition.

Stamps of French Colonies, 1881-86 Handstamped Surcharged in Black:

Perf. 14x13½

1888, Jan. 21 **Unwmk.**

1 A9 1c on 2c brn, *buff* 40.00 32.50
On cover *150.00*
a. Inverted surcharge 140.00 160.00
b. Sideways surcharge 140.00 150.00
2 A9 1c on 4c claret, *lav* 27.50 27.50
On cover *125.00*
a. Inverted surcharge 140.00 160.00
b. Double surcharge 160.00 175.00
c. Sideways surcharge 140.00 160.00
3 A9 5c on 10c blk, *lav* 37.50 27.50
On cover *125.00*
a. Inverted surcharge 140.00 140.00
b. Double surcharge 160.00 160.00

Hyphen between "A" and "T"

7 A9 1c on 2c brn, *buff* 260.00 300.00
On cover *1,000.*
a. Inverted surcharge 575.00 600.00
b. Sideways surcharge 375.00 410.00
c. Pair, Nos. 1, 7 160.00 160.00
8 A9 1c on 4c claret, *lav* 425.00 325.00
On cover *750.00*
9 A9 5c on 10c blk, *lav* 175.00 190.00
On cover *450.00*

A 5c on 2c was prepared but not issued. Value $6,750.

In these surcharges there are different types of numerals and letters.

There are numerous other errors in the placing of the surcharges, including double one inverted, double both inverted, double one sideways, and pair one without surcharge. Such varieties command substantial premiums.

These stamps were superseded in 1892 by those of Indo-China.

ANTIGUA

an-'tēg-ₑwₒə

LOCATION — In the West Indies, southeast of Puerto Rico
GOVT. — Presidency of the Leeward Islands Colony
AREA — 171 sq. mi.
POP. — 34,523
CAPITAL — St. John's

Antigua stamps were discontinued in 1890 and resumed in 1903. In the interim, stamps of Leeward Islands were used. Between 1903-1956, stamps of Antigua and Leeward Islands were used concurrently.

12 Pence = 1 Shilling
20 Shillings = 1 Pound

Catalogue values for unused stamps in this country are for Never Hinged items, beginning with Scott 96.

Watermark

Wmk. 5 — Star

PRE-STAMP POSTAL MARKINGS

Crowned Circle handstamp types I and IV are pictured in the Crowned Circle Handstamps and Great Britain Used Abroad section.

St. John's

1850

A1 I "Antigua" crowned circle handstamp in red, on cover 750.

Covers used from 1860-1869 are valued at $625.

English Harbor

1857

A2 IV "English Harbor" crowned circle handstamp, on cover 6,500.

STAMPS OF GREAT BRITAIN USED IN ANTIGUA

Numeral cancellation type A is pictured in the Crowned Circle Handstamps and Great Britain Used Abroad section.

1858-60

A02 (St. John's)

A3 A 1p rose red (#20) 625.
A4 A 2p blue (#17) 1,100.
A5 A 2p blue (#29, P8, 9) 950.
Plate 7 1,250.
A6 A 4p rose (#26) 650.
A7 A 6p lilac (#27) 200.
A8 A 1sh green (#28) 2,250.

A18 (English Harbor)

A9 A 2p blue (#29, P7) 11,500.
A10 A 4p rose (#26) 11,500.
A11 A 6p lilac (#27) 2,400.
A12 A 1sh green (#28) —

Forged cancellations exist.

Values for unused stamps are for examples with original gum as defined in the catalogue introduction. Any exceptions will be noted. Very fine examples of Nos. 1-8, 11, 18-20 will have perforations touching the design on at least one frameline due to the narrow spacing of the stamps on the plates. Stamps with perfs clear of the framelines on all four sides are extremely scarce and will command higher prices.

Queen Victoria
A1 A2

Rough Perf. 14-16

1862 Engr. Unwmk.

1 A1 6p blue green 900. 575.
On cover 5,000.
a. Perf. 11-13 6,000.
b. Perf. 11-13x14-16 3,250.
c. Perf. 11-13 compound with 14-16 3,500.

There is a question whether Nos. 1a-1c ever did postal duty.

Values for No. 1 are for stamps with perfs. cutting into the design. Values for No. 1b are for copies without gum.

1863-67 Wmk. 5

2 A1 1p dull rose 110.00 50.00
On cover 550.00
a. Vert. pair, imperf. btwn. 22,500.
b. Imperf., pair 2,750.
c. 1p lilac rose 150.00 65.00
On cover 625.00
3 A1 1p vermilion ('67) 275.00 30.00
On cover 450.00
a. Horiz. pair, imperf. btwn. 22,500.
4 A1 6p green 525.00 30.00
On cover 800.00
a. 6p yellow green 3,750. 95.00
On cover 1,650.
b. Pair, imperf. btwn. —
c. 6p dark green 625.00 27.50
On cover 900.00

1872 Wmk. 1 *Perf. 12½*

5 A1 1p lake 160.00 22.50
On cover 750.00
6 A1 1p vermilion 200.00 25.00
On cover 750.00
7 A1 6p blue green 550.00 12.00
On cover 550.00

1873-79 *Perf. 14*

8 A1 1p lake 160.00 11.00
On cover 350.00
a. Half used as ½p on cover 5,500.
b. 1p lake rose 160.00 13.50
On cover 375.00

Typo.

9 A2 2½p red brown ('79) 675.00 200.00
a. Large "2" with slanting bottom line 10,000. 3,000.
10 A2 4p blue ('79) 275.00 17.50

Engr.

11 A1 6p blue green ('76) 400.00 16.00
On cover 675.00

No. 9a is the result of damage to the plate.

1882-86 Typo. Wmk. 2

12 A2 ½p green 3.25 18.00
13 A2 2½p red brown 200.00 65.00
a. Large "2" with slanting bottom line 3,000. 1,250.
14 A2 2½p ultra ('86) 7.25 16.00
a. Large "2" with slanting bottom line 175.00 300.00
15 A2 4p blue 300.00 18.00
16 A2 4p brown org ('86) 2.50 3.25
17 A2 1sh violet ('86) 175.00 150.00

Engr.

18 A1 1p carmine ('84) 2.50 4.50
a. 1p rose 60.00 14.00
19 A1 6p deep green 65.00 140.00

No. 13a is the result of damage to the plate.

No. 18 was used for a time in St. Christopher and is identified by the "A12" cancellation.

1884 *Perf. 12*

20 A1 1p rose red 52.50 17.50
On cover 225.00

Seal of the Colony — A3

King Edward VII — A4

1903 Typo. Wmk. 1 *Perf. 14*

21 A3 ½p blue grn & blk 4.00 7.50
a. Bluish paper ('09) 100.00 100.00
22 A3 1p car & black 7.00 1.50
a. Bluish paper ('09) 92.50 92.50
23 A3 2p org brn & vio 8.00 27.50
24 A3 2½p ultra & black 9.50 17.50
25 A3 3p ocher & gray green 11.50 24.00
26 A3 6p black & red vio 35.00 60.00
27 A3 1sh violet & ultra 47.50 65.00
28 A3 2sh pur & gray green 80.00 110.00
29 A3 2sh6p red vio & blk 20.00 65.00
30 A4 5sh pur & gray green 75.00 115.00
Nos. 21-30 (10) 297.50 493.00
Set, overprinted "SPECIMEN" 165.00

1907 Chalky Paper

21b A3 ½p 3.50 5.00
24a A3 2½p 22.50 47.50
27a A3 1sh 47.50 92.50
30a A4 5sh 87.50 115.00

1908-20 Wmk. 3

31 A3 ½p green 3.50 5.25
a. ½p blue green ('17) 4.00 7.50
b. ½p dk grn, thick paper ('20) 3.00 5.00
32 A3 1p carmine 7.50 2.75
a. 1p scarlet ('15) 7.50 3.75
33 A3 2p org brn & dull vio ('12) 5.00 35.00
34 A3 2½p ultra 14.00 19.00
a. 2½p bright blue 19.00 24.00
35 A3 3p ocher & grn ('12) 7.00 22.50
a. 3p orange & dp grn ('18) 8.00 24.00
36 A3 6p blk & red vio ('11) 8.00 47.50
a. 6p grnsh black & magenta ('15) 8.00 50.00
37 A3 1sh vio & ultra 17.50 80.00
a. 1sh dk violet & dk blue ('15) 15.50 75.00
38 A3 2sh vio & green ('12) 85.00 105.00
Nos. 31-38 (8) 147.50 317.00

Nos. 33, 35 to 38 are on chalky paper.

For overprints see Nos. MR1-MR3.

George V — A6

St. John's Harbor — A7

1913

41 A6 5sh violet & green, chalky paper 85.00 140.00
a. 5sh bright green & dull violet, ordinary paper 75.00 125.00
Overprinted "SPECIMEN" 75.00

1921-29 Wmk. 4

42 A7 ½p green 2.75 .60
43 A7 1p rose red 3.25 .60
a. 1p bright scarlet ('29) 24.00 4.50
44 A7 1p dp violet ('23) 5.00 1.75
a. 1p mauve ('21) 14.00 8.00
45 A7 1½p orange ('22) 4.00 8.00
46 A7 1½p rose red ('26) 5.75 2.00
47 A7 1½p fawn ('29) 3.25 .75
48 A7 2p gray 3.50 .90
49 A7 2½p ultra 6.50 6.50
a. 2½ bright blue ('22) 7.00 20.00
50 A7 2½p orange ('23) 2.75 20.00

Chalky Paper

51 A7 3p violet, *yel* ('25) 5.75 10.00
52 A7 6p vio & red vio 4.75 7.50
53 A7 1sh black, *emer* ('29) 6.50 9.25
54 A7 2sh vio & ultra, *blue* ('27) 11.00 65.00
55 A7 2sh6p blk & red, *blue* ('27) 30.00 32.50
56 A7 3sh grn & vio ('22) 40.00 105.00
57 A7 4sh blk & red ('22) 50.00 75.00
Nos. 42-57 (16) 184.75 345.35

Wmk. 3

Chalky Paper

58 A7 3p violet, *yel* 4.75 14.00
59 A7 4p black & red, *yel* ('22) 2.40 6.50
60 A7 1sh black, *emerald* 4.50 10.50
61 A7 2sh vio & ultra, *bl* 14.00 22.50
62 A7 2sh6p blk & red, *bl* 18.00 57.50
63 A7 5sh grn & red, *yel* ('22) 9.00 60.00
64 A7 £1 vio & black, *red* ('22) 210.00 375.00
Nos. 58-64 (7) 262.65 546.00
Set, overprinted "SPECIMEN" 180.00

Old Dockyard, English Harbour — A8

Govt. House, St. John's — A9

Nelson's "Victory," 1805 — A10

Sir Thomas Warner's Ship, 1632 — A11

Perf. 12½

1932, Jan. 27 Engr. Wmk. 4

67 A8 ½p green 3.25 8.75
68 A8 1p scarlet 3.75 8.75
69 A8 1½p lt brown 3.50 5.50
70 A9 2p gray 4.50 22.50
71 A9 2½p ultra 4.50 8.75
72 A9 3p orange 4.50 14.00
73 A10 6p violet 16.00 14.00
74 A10 1sh olive green 20.00 32.50
75 A10 2sh6p claret 45.00 75.00
76 A11 5sh red brown & black 105.00 150.00
Nos. 67-76 (10) 210.00 340.75
Set, perforated "SPECIMEN" 210.00

Tercentenary of the colony.

Forged cancellations abound, especially dated "MY 18 1932."

Common Design Types pictured following the introduction.

Silver Jubilee Issue

Common Design Type

1935, May 6 *Perf. 13½x14*

77 CD301 1p car & blue 2.10 3.75
78 CD301 1½p gray blk & ultra 3.00 .80
79 CD301 2½p blue & brn 7.00 2.40
80 CD301 1sh brt vio & ind 9.50 15.00
Nos. 77-80 (4) 21.60 21.95
Set, never hinged 32.00
Set, perforated "SPECIMEN" 90.00

Coronation Issue

Common Design Type

1937, May 12 *Perf. 11x11½*

81 CD302 1p carmine .50 1.00
82 CD302 1½p brown .50 1.00
83 CD302 2½p deep ultra 1.00 1.75
Nos. 81-83 (3) 2.00 3.75
Set, never hinged 3.00
Set, perforated "SPECIMEN" 70.00

English Harbour — A14

Nelson's Dockyard — A15

Fort James — A16

St. John's Harbor — A17

1938-51 Engr. *Perf. 12½*

84 A14 ½p yel green .30 1.50
Never hinged .45
a. ½p green ('42) .30 1.50
Never hinged .45
85 A15 1p scarlet 2.00 3.25
Never hinged 3.25
a. 1p red ('42) 2.00 3.25
Never hinged 4.25
86 A15 1½p red brown ('43) 1.90 2.40
Never hinged 3.00
a. 1½p chocolate brown 4.25 1.50
Never hinged 6.75
b. 1½p lake browm ('49) 18.00 15.00
Never hinged 34.00
87 A14 2p gray .55 .70
Never hinged 1.10
a. 2p slate ('51) 4.50 5.75
Never hinged 9.00
88 A15 2½p ultra ('43) .70 .90
Never hinged 1.10
a. 2½p deep ultramarine .60 1.00
Never hinged 1.10
89 A16 3p pale orange ('44) .70 1.20
Never hinged 1.10
a. 3p orange .50 1.00
Never hinged 1.10
90 A17 6p purple 2.10 1.40
Never hinged 3.25
91 A17 1sh brown & blk 3.50 2.00
Never hinged 5.75
a. 1sh red brown & black ('49) 3.50 12.50
Never hinged 34.00
b. As "a," double frame, one albino 3,000.
Never hinged 4,000.
92 A16 2sh6p dp claret ('42) 17.00 15.00
Never hinged 26.00
a. 2sh6p brown purple 30.00 15.00
Never hinged 50.00
93 A17 5sh grayish olive green ('44) 10.00 8.75
Never hinged 15.00
a. 5sh olive green 15.00 12.50
Never hinged 25.00
94 A15 10sh red vio ('48) 11.50 32.50
Never hinged 17.00
95 A16 £1 Prussian blue ('48) 18.00 45.00
Never hinged 27.50
Nos. 84-95 (12) 68.25 114.60
Set, never hinged 105.00
Set, overprinted "SPECIMEN" 190.00

See Nos. 107-113, 115-116, 118-121, 136-142, 144-145.

For overprint see Nos. 125-126.

Catalogue values for unused stamps in this section, from this point to the end of the section, are for Never Hinged items.

Peace Issue

Common Design Type

1946, Nov. 1 Wmk. 4 *Perf. 13½x14*

96 CD303 1½p brown .25 .20
97 CD303 3p dp orange .25 .55
Set, overprinted "SPECIMEN" 65.00

Silver Wedding Issue

Common Design Types

1949, Jan. 3 Photo. *Perf. 14x14½*

98 CD304 2½p bright ultra .55 2.75

Engraved; Name Typographed

Perf. 11½x11

99 CD305 5sh dk brown olive 9.50 11.00

UPU Issue

Common Design Types

Perf. 13½, 11x11½

1949, Oct. 10 Wmk. 4

Engr.; Name Typo. on 3p and 6p

100 CD306 2½p deep ultra .45 .60
101 CD307 3p orange 1.90 2.75
102 CD308 6p purple .90 2.00
103 CD309 1sh red brown .90 1.50
Nos. 100-103 (4) 4.15 6.85

University Issue

Common Design Types

Perf. 14x14½

1951, Feb. 16 Engr. Wmk. 4

104	CD310	3c chocolate & blk	.45	*1.50*
105	CD311	12c purple & blk	.85	*1.75*

WAR TAX STAMPS

No. 31 and Type A3 Overprinted in Black or Red

1916-18 Wmk. 3 *Perf. 14*

MR1	A3	½p green	2.40	*2.90*
a.		Thick paper	4.00	
MR2	A3	½p green (R) ('17)	1.60	*2.90*
a.		Thick paper	7.50	
MR3	A3	1½p orange ('18)	1.10	*1.45*
a.		½p orange & yellow ('19)	1.10	*2.00*
b.		½p deep orange & yellow ('20)	1.10	*2.00*
		Nos. MR1-MR3 (3)	5.10	*7.25*
		Set, overprinted "SPECIMEN"	75.00	

ARGENTINA

ˌär-jən-ˈtē-nə

LOCATION — In South America
GOVT. — Republic
AREA — 1,084,120 sq. mi.
POP. — 12,760,880
CAPITAL — Buenos Aires

100 Centavos = 1 Peso

Watermarks

Wmk. 84 — Italic RA

Wmk. 85 — Small Sun, 4½mm

Wmk. 86 — Large Sun, 6mm

Wmk. 87 — Honeycomb

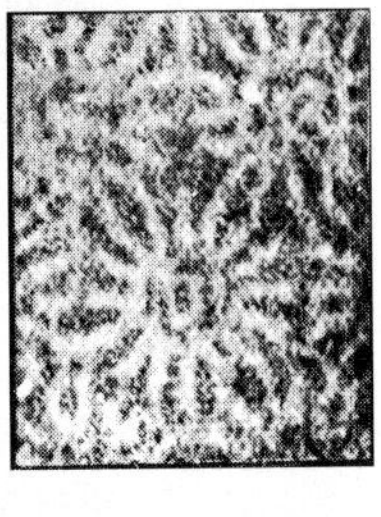

Wmk. 88 — Multiple Suns

Wmk. 89 — Large Sun

In this watermark the face of the sun is 7mm in diameter, the rays are heavier than in the large sun watermark of 1896-1911 and the watermarks are placed close together, so that parts of several frequently appear on one stamp. This paper was intended to be used for fiscal stamps and is usually referred to as "fiscal sun paper."

Wmk. 90 — RA in Sun

In 1928 watermark 90 was slightly modified, making the diameter of the Sun 9mm instead of 10mm. Several types of this watermark exist.

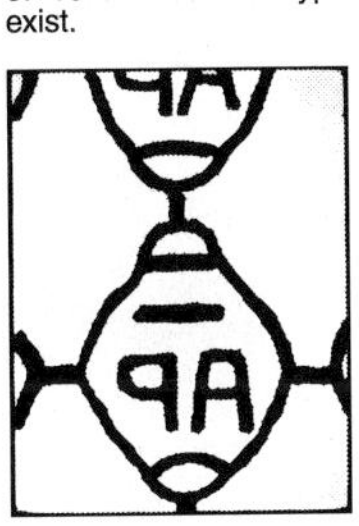

Wmk. 205 — AP in Oval

The letters "AP" are the initials of "AHORRO POSTAL." This paper was formerly used exclusively for Postal Savings stamps.

Wmk. 287 — Double Circle and Letters in Sheet

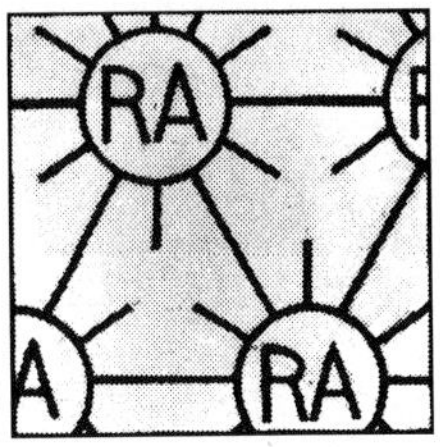

Wmk. 288 — RA in Sun with Straight Rays

PRE-STAMP POSTAL MARKINGS

Crowned Circle handstamp types I and VII are pictured in the Crowned Circle Handstamps and Great Britain Used Abroad section.

1851, Jan. 5

Crowned Circle Handstamps Types I or VII

Buenos Aires

A1	In red, on cover	900.00
A2	In black, on cover	900.00

Values are for clear cancellations on sound, fault-free stamps, with average to fine centering. In many cases, very fine copies are rare or non-existent.

STAMPS OF GREAT BRITAIN USED IN ARGENTINA

Numeral cancellation type A is pictured in the Crowned Circle Handstamps and Great Britain Used Abroad section.

1860-73

B32 (Buenos Aires)

A3	1p rose red (#20)	55.00
A4	1p rose red (#33, see footnote), *value from*	45.00

#A4 plate numbers P71-74, 76, 78-81, 85, 87, 89-97, 99, 101, 103-104, 107-108, 110, 112-114, 117-121, 123, 125, 127, 129-131, 135-136, 138-140, 142-143, 145, 147, 149-151, 155, 159, 163-164, 166, 169, 172.

A5	2p blue (#29, P8-9) *value from*	55.00
A6	2p blue, (#30, P12-14) *value from*	55.00
A7	3p rose (#37)	325.00
A8	3p rose (#44)	125.00
A9	3p rose (#49, P4-10) *value from*	55.00
A10	4p rose (#26)	125.00
A11	4p vermilion (#34, P3)	120.00
'a.	vermilion (#34a, P4)	125.00
A12	4p vermilion, plates 10-12 (#43), *value from*	60.00
a.	4p dull vermilion, plates 7-9, 13 (#43a), *value from*	60.00
A13	6p lilac (#27)	120.00
A14	6p lilac (#39, P3)	—
a.	6p lilac (#39b, P4)	—
A15	6p lilac (#45, P5)	95.00
	Plate 6	175.00
A16	6p dull violet (#50, P6)	105.00
A17	6p violet (#51, P8-9)	85.00
A18	6p brown, (#59, P11)	55.00
a.	6p pale buff, #59b, P11)	100.00
A19	9p straw (#40)	350.00
a.	9p bister (#40a)	400.00
A20	9p straw (#46)	575.00
A21	9p bister (#52)	350.00
A22	10p red brown (#53)	400.00
A23	1sh green (#28)	325.00
A24	1sh green (#42)	200.00
A25	1sh green (#48, P4)	190.00
A26	1sh green (#54, P4-6) *value from*	55.00
	Plate 7	90.00
A27	1sh green (#64, P8)	—
A28	2sh blue (#55)	250.00
A29	5sh rose (#57)	600.00

STAMPS OF ITALIAN OFFICES ABROAD USED IN ARGENTINA

Between 1874 and 1878, the Italian Consulate in Buenos Aires operated postal facilities for handling mail addressed to Italy. Stamps of the Italian Offices Abroad general issue were sold locally for franking this mail. These stamps were canceled on arrival at Genoa with a two-line italic postmark.

2A1	*"Da Buenos-Aires coi Postali Italiani"* on Italian stamps overprinted "ESTERO," from	300.00
	On cover, with stamps optd. "ESTERO", from	*9,000.*
2A2	*"Da Buenos-Aires coi Postali Italiani"* on cover, unpaid and with Italian Postage Due, from	1,500.

Mail could also be consigned to the Consular Agencies without prepayment of postage, in which case it was taxed upon arrival in Italy.

Mail could also be sent through the Consular Agencies to Europe by the English or French Paquet systems. Generally, these countries did not recognize the prepayment of postage by italian stamps, and such letters were assessed postage due charges and penalties upon arrival. Such covers are very rare.

Values for Unused

Unused values for Nos. 5-17 are for examples without gum. Examples with original gum command higher prices. Unused values of Nos. 1-4B and stamps after No. 17 are for examples with original gum as defined in the catalogue introduction.

Argentine Confederation

Symbolical of the Argentine Confederation

A1 A2

Unwmk.

1858, May 1 Litho. *Imperf.*

1	A1	5c red	1.50	*24.00*
		On cover		175.00
a.		Colon after "5"	1.75	*32.50*
		On cover		200.00
b.		Colon after "V"	1.75	*32.50*
		On cover		200.00
c.		Horiz. strip with all 9 types	20.00	
2	A1	10c green	2.50	*57.50*
		On cover		375.00
a.		With period after "10" (55R1)	20.00	*225.00*
		On cover		*750.00*
b.		10c dark green	3.25	*75.00*
		On cover		*475.00*
c.		As "a," dark green	30.00	*225.00*
		On cover		*750.00*
d.		10c pale green on thick paper	5.00	*110.00*
		On cover		*450.00*
e.		Horiz. strip with all 9 types	40.00	
f.		Diagonal half used as 5c on cover		*800.00*
g.		Horiz. half used as 5c on cover		*1,400.*
3	A1	15c blue	16.00	*160.00*
		On cover		1,750.
a.		15c dark blue	90.00	*240.00*
		On cover		*2,250.*
b.		Horiz. strip with all 9 types	150.00	
c.		Horiz. third used as 5c on cover		*6,500.*
d.		Vert. third used as 5c on cover		*8,000.*
e.		Diagonal third used as 5c on cover		*7,500.*
f.		Diagonal two-thirds used as 10c on cover		—
		Nos. 1-3 (3)	20.00	*241.50*

There are nine varieties of Nos. 1, 2 and 3. Counterfeits and forged cancellations of Nos. 1-3 are plentiful.

1860, Jan.

4	A2	5c red	3.25	*72.50*
		On cover		550.00
c.		Strip with all 8 types	30.00	
f.		5c blood red	240.00	
g.		As "f," strip with all 8 types	3,000.	
4A	A2	10c green	7.00	
d.		Strip with all 8 types	70.00	
h.		10c dark green	8.00	
4B	A2	15c blue	25.00	
e.		Strip with all 8 types	275.00	
i.		15c dark blue	27.50	
		Nos. 4-4B (3)	35.25	

Nos. 4A and 4B were never placed in use. Some compostitions of Nos. 4-4B contain 8 different types across the sheet. Other settings exist with minor variations. Counterfeits and forged cancellations of Nos. 4-4B are plentiful.

Argentine Republic

Seal of the Republic — A3

Broad "C" in "CENTAVOS," Accent on "U" of "REPUBLICA"

1862, Jan. 11

5	A3	5c rose	40.00	37.50
		On cover		150.00
a.		5c rose lilac	87.50	35.00
		On cover		160.00
6	A3	10c green	140.00	65.00
		On cover		375.00
b.		Diagonal half used as 5c on cover		*4,250.*
c.		5c dark green on ribbed paper	.00	225.00
7	A3	15c blue	275.00	225.00
		On cover		1,800.
a.		Without accent on "U"	*7,000.*	*3,000.*
b.		Tete beche pair	*55,000.*	—
i.		15c ultramarine	425.00	325.00

	On cover		2,000.
j.	Diagonal third used as 5c on cover		*5,000.*
k.	15c dark blue	450.00	350.00
	On cover		2,000.

Only one used example of No. 7b is known. It has faults. Two unused examples are known. One is sound with origional gum, the other is in a block, without gum, and has tiny faults.

Broad "C" in "CENTAVOS," No Accent on "U"

1863

7C	A3 5c rose	18.00	*21.00*
	On cover		110.00
d.	5c rose lilac	100.00	110.00
	On cover		300.00
e.	5c carmine rose	50.00	20.00
	On cover		140.00
m.	Worn plate (rose)	200.00	52.50
	On cover		175.00
n.	Worn plate (red)	225.00	60.00
	On cover		200.00
o.	Worn plate (lilac rose)	250.00	90.00
	On cover		250.00
p.	Accent between "P" and "U"	200.00	75.00
	On cover		*500.00*
7F	A3 10c yellow green	350.00	140.00
	On cover		650.00
g.	10c olive green	*500.00*	250.00
	On cover		1,000.
q.	10c green, ribbed paper	425.00	200.00
	On cover		*1,000.*
r.	Worn plate (green)	325.00	150.00
	On cover		750.00
s.	Worn plate (olive green)	425.00	160.00
	On cover		*1,100.*

Narrow "C" in "CENTAVOS," No Accent on "U"

1864

7H	A3 5c rose red	160.00	32.50
	On cover		165.00
t.	5c carmine rose	190.00	40.00
	On cover		220.00
u.	5c lilac rose	165.00	35.00
	On cover		200.00
v.	5c brick red		225.00
	On cover		—

The so-called reprints of 10c and 15c are counterfeits. They have narrow "C" and straight lines in shield. Nos. 7C and 7H have been extensively counterfeited.

Rivadavia Issue

Bernardino Rivadavia
A4 A5

Rivadavia — A6

1864-67 Engr. Wmk. 84 *Imperf.*

Clear Impressions

8	A4 5c brown rose	*1,300.*	*160.*
	On cover		1,500.
a.	5c orange red ('67)	*1,500.*	*160.*
	On cover		1,500.
9	A5 10c green	*2,000.*	*1,200.*
	On cover		*8,500.*
10	A6 15c blue	*7,500.*	*4,000.*
	On cover		*42,500.*

Perf. 11½

Dull to Worn Impressions

11	A4 5c brown rose ('65)	30.00	12.00
	On cover		60.00
11B	A4 5c lake	77.50	17.50
	On cover		75.00
12	A5 10c green	80.00	30.00
	On cover		180.00
a.	Diagonal half used as 5c on cover		*900.*
b.	Vert. half used as 5c on cover		*1,000.*
c.	Horiz. pair, imperf vert.		*1,750.*
13	A6 15c blue	275.00	110.00
	On cover		675.00

1867-72 Unwmk. *Imperf.*

14	A4 5c carmine ('72)	250.	65.
	On cover		425.00
15	A4 5c rose	200.	100.
	On cover		500.00
15A	A5 10c green	*4,000.*	*4,000.*
	On cover		—
16	A6 15c blue	*2,000.*	*1,750.*
	On cover		—

Nos. 15A-16 issued without gum.

1867 *Perf. 11½*

17	A4 5c carmine	350.00	150.00
	On cover		750.00

Nos. 14, 15 and 17 exist with part of papermaker's wmk. "LACROIX FRERES." Unused values, $600, $500 and $1,000, respectively.

Rivadavia
A7

Manuel Belgrano
A8

Jose de San Martin — A9

Groundwork of Horizontal Lines

1867-68 *Perf. 12*

18	A7 5c vermilion	200.00	15.00
	On cover		75.00
c.	Double impression		75.00
	On cover		—
18A	A8 10c green	60.00	18.00
	On cover		50.00
b.	Diag. half used as 5c on cover		*1,500.*
19	A9 15c blue	85.00	25.00
	On cover		250.00

Groundwork of Crossed Lines

20	A7 5c vermilion	15.00	1.00
	On cover		15.00
a.	Double impression		25.00
	On cover		—
21	A9 15c blue	100.00	25.00
	On cover		250.00

See Nos. 27, 33-34, 39 and types A19, A33, A34, A37. For surcharges and overprints see Nos. 30-32, 41-42, 47-51, O6-O7, O26.

Gen. Antonio G. Balcarce
A10

Mariano Moreno
A11

Carlos Maria de Alvear
A12

Gervasio Antonio Posadas
A13

Cornelio Saavedra — A14

1873

22	A10 1c purple	5.00	2.00
	On cover		20.00
	On cover, single franking		100.00
a.	1c gray violet	10.00	2.00
	On cover		20.00
	On cover, single franking		100.00
23	A11 4c brown	5.00	.40
	On cover		6.00
a.	4c red brown	100.00	2.00
	On cover		20.00
24	A12 30c orange	100.00	16.00
	On cover		400.00
a.	Vert. pair, imperf horiz.	*4,000.*	
25	A13 60c black	100.00	4.75
	On cover		1,000.
26	A14 90c blue	25.00	2.50
	On cover		2,500.
	Nos. 22-26 (5)	235.00	25.65

For overprints see Nos. O5, O12-O14, O19-O21, O25, O29.

1873

Laid Paper

27	A8 10c green	300.00	50.00
	On cover		250.00

Nos.18, 18A Surcharged in Black

Nos. 30-31

No. 32

1877, Feb.

Wove Paper

30	A7 1c on 5c vermilion	100.00	20.00
	On cover		*200.00*
a.	Inverted surcharge	500.00	250.00
31	A7 2c on 5c vermilion	150.00	60.00
	On cover		*350.00*
a.	Inverted surcharge	1,000.	500.00
32	A8 8c on 10c green	200.00	30.00
	On cover		*250.00*
b.	Inverted surcharge	1,800.	1,000.
	Nos. 30-32 (3)	450.00	110.00

Varieties also exist with double and triple surcharges, surcharge on reverse, 8c on No. 27, all made clandestinely from the original cliches of the surcharges.

Forgeries of these surcharges include the inverted and double varieties.

1876-77 *Rouletted*

33	A7 5c vermilion	175.00	75.00
	On cover		*500.00*
34	A7 8c lake ('77)	50.00	.50
	On cover		5.00

Belgrano
A17

Dalmacio Vélez Sarsfield
A18

San Martín — A19

1878 *Rouletted*

35	A17 16c green	10.00	1.10
	On cover		22.50
36	A18 20c blue	20.00	2.00
	On cover		150.00
37	A19 24c blue	100.00	2.00
	On cover		75.00
	Nos. 35-37 (3)	130.00	5.10

See No. 56. For overprints see Nos. O9-O10, O15-O17, O22, O28.

Vicente Lopez — A20

Alvear — A21

1877-80 *Perf. 12*

38	A20 2c yellow green	5.00	.75
	On cover		15.00
39	A7 8c lake ('80)	4.00	.50
	On cover		3.00
a.	8c brown lake	*50.00*	.50
	On cover		30.00
40	A21 25c lake ('78)	22.50	6.00
	On cover		1,500.
	Nos. 38-40 (3)	31.50	7.25

For overprints see Nos. O4, O11, O18, O24.

No. 18 Surcharged in Black

Large "P"

Small "P"

1882

Large "P" and Wide "V" in "PROVISORIO"

41	A7 ½c on 5c ver	2.00	2.00
	On cover		100.00
a.	Double surcharge	75.00	75.00
	On cover		*500.00*
b.	Inverted surcharge	35.00	35.00
	On cover		*500.00*
c.	"PROVISORIO" omitted	100.00	100.00
	On cover		*750.00*
d.	Fraction omitted	50.00	
e.	"PROVISOBIO"	32.50	32.50
	On cover		*500.00*
f.	Pair, one without surcharge	200.00	

Perforated across Middle of Stamp

42b	A7 ½c on 5c ver	30.00	22.50
	On cover		*500.00*

Small "P" and Narrow "V" in "PROVISORIO"

41g	A7 ½c on 5c ver	2.50	2.50
	On cover		100.00
41h	Double surcharge	32.50	32.50
	On cover		*500.00*
41i	Inverted surcharge	40.00	40.00
	On cover		*500.00*
41j	Fraction omitted	15.00	15.00
	On cover		*300.00*

Perforated across Middle of Stamp

42	A7 ½c on 5c ver	4.00	4.00
	On cover		400.00
a.	"PROVISORIQ"	40.00	40.00

A23

1882 Typo. *Perf. 12½, 14¼*

43	A23 ½c brown	1.50	1.00
	On cover		10.00
a.	Imperf., pair	100.00	80.00
44	A23 1c red, perf. 14	3.50	1.00
	On cover		5.00
a.	Perf. 12	9.00	4.25
	On cover		15.00
45	A23 12c ultra	100.00	10.00
	On cover		50.00
a.	Perf. 12	100.00	8.75
	On cover		50.00
46	A23 12c grnsh blue, perf. 14	250.00	12.00
	On cover		250.00
	Nos. 43-46 (4)	355.00	24.00

See type A29. For overprints see Nos. O2, O8, O23, O27.

No. 21 Surcharged in Red:

a

b

c

1884 Engr. *Perf. 12*

47	A9 (a) ½c on 15c blue	1.90	1.50
	On cover		50.00
a.	Groundwork of horiz. lines	150.00	80.00
	On cover		500.00
b.	Inverted surcharge	27.50	20.00
	On cover		*300.00*
48	A9 (b) 1c on 15c blue	16.00	13.00
	On cover		250.00
a.	Groundwork of horiz. lines	10.00	6.50
	On cover		*250.00*
b.	Inverted surcharge	80.00	57.50
c.	Double surcharge	40.00	32.50
	On cover		500.00

d. Triple surcharge 350.00

Nos. 20-21 Surcharged in Black

49 A7 (a) ½c on 5c ver 4.00 3.25
On cover 100.00
a. Inverted surcharge 160.00 110.00
On cover 1,000.
b. Date omitted 150.00 —
c. Pair, one without surcharge 375.00
d. Double surcharge 550.00
50 A9 (a) ½c on 15c blue 10.00 8.00
On cover 250.00
a. Groundwork of horiz. lines 32.50 26.00
On cover 500.00
b. Inverted surcharge 72.50 55.00
c. Pair, one without surcharge 325.00
51 A7 (c) 4c on 5c ver 10.00 6.50
On cover 100.00
a. Inverted surcharge 26.00 20.00
On cover 300.00
b. Double surcharge 325.00 200.00
On cover 1,250.
c. Pair, one without surcharge but with "4" in manuscript 550.00 350.00
d. Pair, one without surcharge 250.00
Nos. 47-51 (5) 41.90 32.25

A29

1884-85 Engr. *Perf. 12*

52 A29 ½c red brown 1.25 .50
On wrapper or newsprint 15.00
a. Horiz. pair, imperf vert. 300.00 250.00
53 A29 1c rose red 6.00 .50
On cover 5.00
a. Horiz. pair, imperf vert. 300.00 250.00
54 A29 12c 12c deep blue 50.00 1.25
On cover 10.00
a. grnsh blue ('85) 50.00 1.25
On cover 10.00
b. Horiz. pair, imperf vert. 300.00 250.00
Nos. 52-54 (3) 57.25 2.25

For overprints see Nos. O1, O3, O9.

San Martin Type of 1878

1887 Engr.

56 A19 24c blue 20.00 1.40
On cover 75.00

Justo Jose de Urquiza — A30

Lopez — A31

Miguel Juarez Celman A32

Rivadavia (Large head) A33

Rivadavia (Small head) A34

Domingo F. Sarmiento A35

Nicolas Avellaneda — A36

San Martin — A37

Julio A. Roca — A37a

Belgrano — A37b

Manuel Dorrego — A38

Moreno — A39

Bartolome Mitre — A40

CINCO CENTAVOS.
A33 — Shows collar on left side only.
A34 — Shows collar on both sides. Lozenges in background larger and clearer than in A33.

1888-90 Litho. *Perf. 11½*

57 A30 ½c blue 1.00 .50
On cover 75.00
b. Vert. pair, imperf. horiz. 125.00 65.00
c. Horiz. pair, imperf. vert. 125.00 65.00
58 A31 2c yel grn 25.00 7.00
On cover 150.00
b. Vert. pair, imperf. horiz. 80.00
c. Horiz. pair, imperf. vert. 200.00
59 A32 3c blue green 2.50 1.00
On cover 15.00
b. Horiz. pair, imperf. vert. 80.00
c. Horiz. pair, imperf. btwn. 100.00
d. Vert. pair, imperf. btwn. 25.00 25.00
60 A33 5c carmine 12.00 .60
On cover 30.00
b. Vert. pair, imperf. horiz. 100.00
61 A34 5c carmine 20.00 1.50
On cover 50.00
b. Vert. pair, imperf. btwn. 400.00
c. Vert. pair, imperf. horiz. 400.00
62 A35 6c red 50.00 18.00
On cover 250.00
b. Vert. pair, imperf. btwn. 150.00
c. Perf. 12 150.00 42.50
On cover 350.00
63 A36 10c brown 18.00 1.10
On cover 50.00
64 A37 15c orange 25.00 1.60
On cover 150.00
d. Vert. pair, imperf. btwn. 600.00
64A A37a 20c green 25.00 1.25
On cover 150.00
64B A37b 25c purple 40.00 2.50
On cover 500.00
65 A38 30c brown 50.00 3.00
On cover 500.00
b. 30c reddish chocolate brown 450.00 100.00
On cover 1,000.
c. Horiz. pair, imperf. btwn. 400.00 325.00
66 A39 40c slate, perf. 12 100.00 3.00
On cover 1,500.
a. Perf. 11½ 250.00 24.00
On cover 1,500.
b. Horiz. pair, imperf. btwn. (#66) 600.00
67 A40 50c blue 250.00 8.25
On cover 2,000.
Nos. 57-67 (13) 618.50 49.30

In this issue there are several varieties of each value, the difference between them being in the relative position of the head to the frame.

Imperf., Pairs

57a	A30	½c	75.00	60.00
58a	A31	2c	100.00	
59a	A32	3c	35.00	25.00
61a	A34	5c		100.00
62a	A35	6c	150.00	150.00
63a	A36	10c	55.00	
64c	A37	15c		200.00
65a	A38	30c	275.00	200.00

Values for Stamps with "MUESTRA" Overprint

59S	3c	blue green	30.00
63S	10c	brown	30.00
64S	15c	orange	30.00
64AS	20c	green	30.00
64BS	25c	purple	30.00
65S	30c	brown	30.00
66S	40c	slatee	30.00

Urquiza A41

Velez Sarsfield A42

Miguel Juarez Celman A43

Rivadavia (Large head) A44

Sarmiento A45

Juan Bautista Alberdi A46

1888-89 Engr. *Perf. 11½, 11½x12*

68 A41 ½c ultra .50 .30
On newspaper, single franking — 50.00
a. Vert. pair, imperf. horiz. — —
b. Imperf., pair 30.00 —
69 A42 1c brown 1.00 .50
On cover 3.00
a. Vert. pair, imperf. horiz. 65.00
b. Vert. pair, imperf. btwn. —
c. Imperf., pair 30.00
d. Horiz. pair, imperf. btwn. 100.00
70 A43 3c blue green 3.00 .80
On cover 6.00
71 A44 5c rose 3.00 .50
On cover 2.50
a. Imperf., pair 40.00 —
72 A45 6c blue black 2.00 .60
On cover 8.00
b. Perf. 11½x12 12.50 3.00
On cover 15.00
73 A46 12c blue 6.00 2.00
On cover 12.00
a. Imperf., pair 30.00
b. bluish paper 8.00 2.00
On cover 12.00
c. Perf. 11½ 10.00 3.00
On cover 15.00
Nos. 68-73 (6) 15.50 4.70

#69-70 exist with papermakers' watermarks.
See No. 77, types A50, A61. For surcharges see Nos. 83-84.

Jose Maria Paz — A48

Santiago Derqui — A49

Rivadavia (Small head) A50

Avellaneda A51

Moreno A53

Mitre A54

Posadas — A55

1890 Engr. *Perf. 11½*

75 A48 ¼c green .50 .30
On wrapper or newspaper, single franking 50.00
76 A49 2c violet 1.00 .50
On cover 2.00
a. 2c purple 1.00 .50
On cover 2.00
b. 2c slate 1.25 .30
On cover 2.50
c. Horiz. pair, imperf. btwn. 25.00 20.00
d. Imperf., pair 35.00
e. Perf. 11½x12 5.00 .50
On cover 3.00
77 A50 5c carmine 2.50 .30
On cover 2.50
a. Imperf., pair 50.00 25.00
b. Perf. 11½x12 5.00 .30
On cover 2.50
c. Vert. pair, imperf. btwn. 75.00 60.00
d. Horiz. pair, imperf. btwn. 75.00 60.00
78 A51 10c brown 3.00 .50
On cover 6.00
b. Imperf., pair 150.00
c. Vert. pair, imperf. btwn. 225.00
80 A53 40c olive green 6.00 1.00
On cover 450.00
a. Imperf., pair 40.00
b. Horiz. pair, imperf. btwn. 250.00
81 A54 50c orange 6.00 1.00
On cover 450.00
a. Imperf., pair 60.00
b. Perf. 11½x12 25.00 2.00
c. 50c lemon yellow 50.00
82 A55 60c black 15.00 3.00
a. Imperf., pair —
b. Vert. pair, imperf. btwn. 125.00 100.00
c. 60c blue black 25.00 2.50
Nos. 75-82 (7) 34.00 6.60

Type A50 differs from type A44 in having the head smaller, the letters of "Cinco Centavos" not as tall, and the curved ornaments at sides close to the first and last letters of "Republica Argentina."

Lithographed Surcharge on No. 73 in Black or Red

1890 *Perf. 11½x12*

83 A46 ¼c on 12c blue .50 .50
On wrapper, single franking 15.00
a. Perf. 11½ 40.00 35.00
b. Double surcharge 70.00 40.00
c. Inverted surcharge 80.00
84 A46 ¼c on 12c blue (R) .50 .50
On wrapper, single franking 15.00
a. Double surcharge 50.00 45.00
b. Perf. 11½ 8.00 6.00
On wrapper, single franking 45.00

Surcharge is different on #83 and 84.
Nos. 83-84 exist as pairs, one without surcharge. These were privately produced.

Rivadavia A57

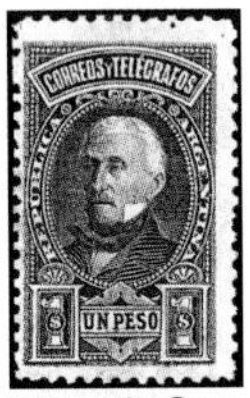
Jose de San Martin A58

Gregorio Araoz de Lamadrid A59

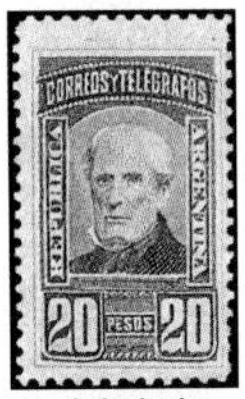
Admiral Guillermo Brown A60

1891 Engr. *Perf. 11½*

85 A57 8c carmine rose 1.25 .50
On cover 2.00
a. Imperf., pair 75.00
86 A58 1p deep blue 50.00 10.00
On cover —

87 A59 5p ultra 250.00 30.00
On cover —
88 A60 20p green 400.00 70.00
Nos. 85-88 (4) 701.25 110.50

Nos. 86-88 with violet oval or black boxed cancellations were used on parcels. Stamps so used are worth about 25% less than the values shown.

A 10p brown and a 50p red were prepared but not issued. Values: 10p $1,500 for fine, 50p $1,000 with rough or somewhat damaged perfs.

Velez Sarsfield A61

"Santa Maria," "Nina" and "Pinta" A62

1890 ***Perf. 11½***
89 A61 1c brown 1.00 .50
On cover 2.50
b. Horiz. pair, imperf. btwn. *550.00*

Type A61 is a re-engraving of A42. The figure "1" in each upper corner has a short horizontal serif instead of a long one pointing downward. In type A61 the first and last letters of "Correos y Telegrafos" are closer to the curved ornaments below than in type A42. Background is of horizontal lines (cross-hatching on No. 69).

1892, Oct. 12 Wmk. 85 ***Perf. 11½***
90 A62 2c light blue 7.50 2.50
On cover 30.00
a. Double impression 190.00
91 A62 5c dark blue 8.50 2.50
On cover, #90, 91 50.00

Discovery of America, 400th anniv. Counterfeits of Nos. 90-91 are litho.

Rivadavia A63

Belgrano A64

San Martin — A65

Perf. 11½, 12 and Compound
1892-95 Wmk. 85
92 A63 ½c dull blue .40 .20
On wrapper 10.00
a. ½c bright ultra 60.00 30.00
On wrapper *100.00*
93 A63 1c brown .60 .20
On cover 1.00
94 A63 2c green .75 .30
On cover 1.00
95 A63 3c orange ('95) 1.50 .30
On cover 1.50
96 A63 5c carmine 1.50 .30
On cover 1.00
b. 5c green (error) 1,.000. 1,000.
On cover *3,500.*
98 A64 10c carmine rose 12.00 .50
On cover 1.50
99 A64 12c deep blue ('93) 9.00 .50
On cover 1.50
100 A64 16c gray 15.00 .60
On cover 2.00
101 A64 24c gray brown 15.00 .60
On cover 3.00
b. Perf. 12 30.00 17.00
On cover 50.00
102 A64 50c blue green 22.50 .60
On cover 10.00
b. Perf. 12 30.00 6.00
On cover 25.00
103 A65 1p lake ('93) 11.00 .90
On cover 100.00
a. 1p red brown 18.00 5.00
On cover *175.00*
104 A65 2p dark green 22.50 2.50
On cover 150.00
a. Perf. 12 125.00 40.00
105 A65 5p dark blue 37.50 2.75
On cover 250.00
Nos. 92-105 (13) 149.25 10.25

Part-perforate varieties of Nos. 92-99 include vert. and/or horiz. pairs, imperf. between. Valued from $45.

The high values of this and succeeding issues are frequently punched with the word "INUTILIZADO," parts of the letters showing on each stamp. These punched stamps sell for only a small fraction of the catalogue values.

Examples of No. 95 in yellow shades are changelings.

Reprints of No. 96b have white gum. The original stamp has yellowish gum. Value $125.

Imperf., Pairs

92b	A63	½c	55.00
93a	A63	1c	55.00
94a	A63	2c	27.50
96a	A63	5c	27.50
98a	A64	10c	55.00
99a	A64	12c	55.00
100a	A64	16c	55.00
101a	A64	24c	55.00
102a	A64	50c	55.00
103b	A65	1p	60.00
105a	A65	5p	140.00

Nos. 102a, 103b and 105a exist only without gum; the other imperfs are found with or without gum, and values are the same for either condition.

Vertical Pairs, Imperf. Between

92c	A63	½c	125.00	
93b	A63	1c	100.00	
94b	A63	2c	50.00	
95a	A63	3c	250.00	
96c	A63	5c	45.00	—
98b	A64	10c	100.00	
99b	A64	12c	100.00	

Horizontal Pairs, Imperf. Between

93c	A63	1c	110.00	
94c	A63	2c	55.00	
96d	A63	5c	55.00	45.00
98c	A64	10c	110.00	

1896-97 Wmk. 86
106 A63 ½c slate .60 .30
On wrapper 10.00
a. ½c gray blue .60 .30
On wrapper 10.00
b. ½c indigo .60 .30
On wrapper 10.00
107 A63 1c brown .60 .30
On cover 1.00
108 A63 2c yellow green .60 .30
On cover 1.00
109 A63 3c orange .60 .30
On cover 1.50
110 A63 5c carmine .60 .30
On cover 1.00
a. Imperf., pair 100.00
111 A64 10c carmine rose 9.00 .30
On cover 1.50
112 A64 12c deep blue 4.50 .30
On cover 1.50
a. Imperf., pair —
113 A64 16c gray 12.00 .90
On cover 5.00
114 A64 24c gray brown 12.00 1.25
On cover 6.00
a. Imperf., pair 100.00 —
115 A64 30c orange ('97) 12.00 .70
On cover 5.00
116 A64 50c blue green 12.00 .70
On cover 10.00
117 A64 80c dull violet 17.50 .90
On cover 20.00
118 A65 1p lake 27.50 .90
On cover *40.00*
119 A65 1p20c black ('97) 12.00 3.25
On cover 125.00
120 A65 2p dark green 18.00 9.00
On cover 150.00
121 A65 5p dark blue 100.00 12.00
On cover 250.00
a. Perf. 12 350.00 100.00
Nos. 106-121 (16) 239.50 31.70

Vertical Pairs, Imperf. Between

106c	A63	½c	200.00	
107a	A63	1c	125.00	
108a	A63	2c	125.00	
109a	A63	3c	200.00	
110b	A63	5c	125.00	125.00
112b	A64	12c	125.00	100.00

Horizontal Pairs, Imperf. Between

107b	A63	1c	125.00	
108b	A63	2c	125.00	
110c	A63	5c	125.00	80.00
111a	A64	10c	125.00	
112c	A64	12c	125.00	

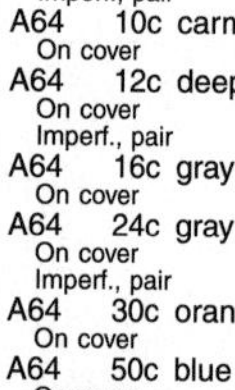
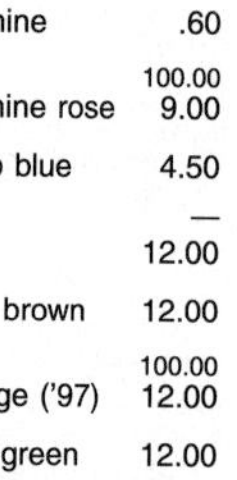
Allegory, Liberty Seated
A66 A67

Perf. 11½, 12 and Compound
1899-1903
122 A66 ½c yellow brown .40 .30
On cover, single franking 20.00
123 A66 1c green .60 .30
On cover 1.00
124 A66 2c slate .60 .30
On cover 1.00
125 A66 3c orange ('01) .80 .50
On cover 1.50
126 A66 4c yellow ('03) 1.40 .60
On cover 2.00
127 A66 5c carmine rose .60 .30
On cover 1.00
128 A66 6c black ('03) .90 .60
On cover 2.00
129 A66 10c dark green 1.40 .40
On cover 1.50
130 A66 12c dull blue .95 .60
On cover 2.00
131 A66 12c olive grn ('01) .95 .60
On cover 2.00
132 A66 15c sea green ('01) 2.50 .60
On cover 2.50
132B A66 15c dull blue ('01) 2.50 .60
On cover 2.50
133 A66 16c orange 8.00 6.00
On cover 25.00
134 A66 20c claret 1.90 .30
On cover 1.00
135 A66 24c violet 4.00 1.00
On cover 5.00
136 A66 30c rose 7.25 .60
On cover 5.00
137 A66 30c vermilion ('01) 4.00 .50
On cover 5.00
a. 30c scarlet 47.50 3.00
On cover 12.50
138 A66 50c brt blue 4.50 .50
On cover 10.00
139 A67 1p bl & blk, perf. 11½ 13.50 1.00
On cover *175.00*
a. Center inverted *1,500.* *525.00*
b. Perf. 12 300.00 150.00
140 A67 5p orange & blk 55.00 9.00
Punch cancellation 1.60
a. Center inverted *2,750.* —
141 A67 10p green & blk 60.00 15.00
Punch cancellation 1.75
a. Center inverted *3,600.*
Punch cancellation 675.00
142 A67 20p red & black 190.00 30.00
Punch cancellation 1.75
a. Center invtd.(punch cancel) *2,000.*
Nos. 122-142 (22) 361.75 69.60

Nos. 139-142 used are valued with violet oval or black boxed parcel cancels. Examples with letter cancels are worth ⅓rd more.

Part-perforate varieties of Nos. 122-129, 132, 138 include vert. and/or horiz. pairs, imperf. between. Valued from $3.

Imperf., Pairs

122a	A66	½c	30.00
123a	A66	1c	45.00
124a	A66	2c	15.00
125a	A66	3c	250.00
127a	A66	5c	15.00
128a	A66	6c	45.00
129a	A66	10c	45.00
132a	A66	15c	45.00

Vertical Pairs, Imperf. Between

122b	A66	½c	10.00	9.50
123b	A66	1c	10.00	9.50
124b	A66	2c	5.00	4.50
125b	A66	3c	210.00	150.00
126a	A66	4c	275.00	210.00
127b	A66	5c	4.50	2.50
128b	A66	6c	12.00	9.50
129b	A66	10c	75.00	
132c	A66	15c	12.00	9.50

Horizontal Pairs, Imperf. Between

122c	A66	½c	30.00	19.00
123c	A66	1c	47.50	27.50
124c	A66	2c	9.50	4.75
125c	A66	3c	210.00	150.00
126b	A66	4c	275.00	
127c	A66	5c	9.50	4.75
128c	A66	6c	17.00	9.50
129c	A66	10c	17.00	9.50
132d	A66	15c	35.00	21.00
138a	A66	50c	150.00	

River Port of Rosario A68

1902, Oct. 26 ***Perf. 11½, 11½x12***
143 A68 5c deep blue 3.50 1.75
On cover 20.00
a. Imperf., pair 95.00
b. Vert. pair, imperf. btwn. 60.00
c. Horiz. pair, imperf. btwn. 90.00

Completion of port facilities at Rosario.

San Martin
A69 A70

1908-09 Typo. ***Perf. 13½, 13½x12½***
144 A69 ½c violet .50 .30
145 A69 1c brnsh buff .50 .30
146 A69 2c chocolate .60 .30
147 A69 3c green .65 .40
148 A69 4c redsh violet 1.25 .40
149 A69 5c carmine .60 .30
150 A69 6c olive bister .75 .40
151 A69 10c gray green 1.75 .30
152 A69 12c yellow buff 1.00 .60
153 A69 12c dk blue ('09) 1.75 .30
154 A69 15c apple green 1.50 .75
155 A69 20c ultra 1.25 .30
156 A69 24c red brown 3.50 .60
157 A69 30c dull rose 6.00 .60
158 A69 50c black 6.00 .50
159 A70 1p sl bl & pink 17.50 2.50
Nos. 144-159 (16) 45.10 8.85

The 1c blue was not issued. Value $450.

Wmk. 86 appears on ½, 1, 6, 20, 24 and 50c. Other values have similar wmk. with wavy rays.

Stamps lacking wmk. are from outer rows printed on sheet margin.

Pyramid of May — A71

Nicolas Rodriguez Pena and Hipolito Vieytes — A72

Meeting at Pena's Home — A73

Designs: 3c, Miguel de Azcuenaga (1754-1833) and Father Manuel M. Alberti (1763-1811). 4c, Viceroy's house and Fort Buenos Aires. 5c, Cornelio Saavedra (1759-1829). 10c, Antonio Luis Beruti (1772-1842) and French distributing badges. 12c, Congress building. 20c, Juan Jose Castelli (1764-1812) and Domingo Matheu (1765-1831). 24c, First council. 30c, Manuel Belgrano (1770-1820) and Juan Larrea (1782-1847). 50c, First meeting of republican government, May 25, 1810. 1p, Mariano Moreno (1778-1811) and Juan Jose Paso (1758-1833). 5p, Oath of the Junta. 10p, Centenary Monument. 20p, Jose Francisco de San Martin (1778-1850).

Inscribed "1810 1910"
Various Frames

1910, May 1 Engr. ***Perf. 11½***
160 A71 ½c bl & gray bl .30 .20
161 A72 1c blue grn & blk .30 .30
b. Horiz. pair, imperf. btwn. *65.00*
162 A73 2c olive & gray .20 .30
163 A72 3c green .70 .40
164 A73 4c dk blue & grn .70 .40
165 A71 5c carmine .40 .25
166 A73 10c yel brn & blk 1.10 .50
167 A73 12c brt blue 1.10 .50
168 A72 20c gray brn & blk 3.25 .60
169 A73 24c org brn & bl 1.75 1.10
170 A72 30c lilac & blk 1.75 .90
171 A71 50c carmine & blk 4.50 1.10
172 A72 1p brt blue 9.50 3.25
173 A73 5p orange & vio 70.00 35.00
Punch cancel 2.50
174 A71 10p orange & blk 90.00 62.50
Punch cancel 3.00
175 A71 20p dp blue & ind 150.00 90.00
Punch cancel 4.50
Nos. 160-175 (16) 335.55 197.30

Centenary of the republic.

Center Inverted

160a	A71	½c	*800.00*
161a	A72	1c	*800.00*
162a	A73	2c	*800.00*
164a	A73	4c	*550.00*
167a	A73	12c	*700.00*
171a	A71	50c	*700.00*
173a	A73	5p	*700.00*

Domingo F. Sarmiento A87

Agriculture A88

1911, May 15 Typo. *Perf. 13½*

176	A87	5c gray brn & blk	.80	.40

Domingo Faustino Sarmiento (1811-88), pres. of Argentina, 1868-74.

Wmk. 86, without Face

1911 Engr. *Perf. 12*

Size: 19x25mm

177	A88	5c vermilion	.40	.20
178	A88	12c deep blue	5.00	.40
		Set value		.25

Wmk. 86, with Face

1911 Typo. *Perf. 13½x12½*

Size: 18x23mm

179	A88	½c violet	.25	.25
180	A88	1c brown ocher	.25	.25
181	A88	2c chocolate	.25	.25
a.		Perf. 13½	15.00	4.00
b.		Imperf., pair	40.00	
182	A88	3c green	.50	.40
183	A88	4c brown violet	.50	.25
184	A88	10c gray green	.50	.25
185	A88	20c ultra	4.00	.95
186	A88	24c red brown	6.00	3.50
187	A88	30c claret	3.00	.50
188	A88	50c black	6.00	.80
		Nos. 179-188 (10)	21.25	7.40

The 5c dull red is a proof. In this issue Wmk. 86 comes: straight rays (4c, 20c, 24c) and wavy rays (2c). All other values exist with both forms.

Wmk. 87 (Horiz. or Vert.)

1912-14 *Perf. 13½x12½*

189	A88	½c violet	.30	.25
190	A88	1c ocher	.30	.25
191	A88	2c chocolate	.50	.25
192	A88	3c green	.50	.40
193	A88	4c brown violet	.50	.40
194	A88	5c red	.40	.25
195	A88	10c deep green	1.75	.25
196	A88	12c deep blue	.60	.25
197	A88	20c ultra	3.00	.40
198	A88	24c red brown	6.00	2.00
199	A88	30c claret	5.00	7.00
200	A88	50c black	9.00	.90
		Nos. 189-200 (12)	27.85	12.60

See Nos. 208-212. For overprints see Nos. OD1-OD8, OD47-OD54, OD102-OD108, OD146-OD152, OD183-OD190, OD235-OD241, OD281-OD284, OD318-OD323.

Perf. 13½

189a	A88	½c	.80	.25
190a	A88	1c	.80	.25
191a	A88	2c	.80	.20
192a	A88	3c	35.00	16.00
193a	A88	4c	1.60	.70
194a	A88	5c	.30	.20
196a	A88	12c	3.25	.80
197a	A88	20c	5.00	.70
		Nos. 189a-197a (8)	47.55	19.10

A89

1912-13 *Perf. 13½*

201	A89	1p dull bl & rose	9.00	1.00
		Punch cancel		.30
202	A89	5p slate & ol grn	19.00	6.00
		Punch cancel		.60
203	A89	10p violet & blue	75.00	15.00
		Punch cancel		1.40
204	A89	20p blue & claret	210.00	75.00
		Punch cancel		2.00
		Nos. 201-204 (4)	313.00	97.00

1915 Unwmk. *Perf. 13½x12½*

208	A88	1c ocher	.50	.25
209	A88	2c chocolate	.90	.25
212	A88	5c red	.50	.25
		Nos. 208-212 (3)	1.90	.75

Only these denominations were printed on paper without watermark.

Other stamps of the series are known unwatermarked but they are from the outer rows of sheets the other parts of which are watermarked.

Francisco Narciso de Laprida A90

Declaration of Independence A91

Jose de San Martin — A92a A92

Perf. 13½, 13½x12½

1916, July 9 Litho. Wmk. 87

215	A90	½c violet	.60	.25
216	A90	1c buff	.50	.25

Perf. 13½x12½

217	A90	2c chocolate	.60	.25
218	A90	3c green	.60	.50
219	A90	4c red violet	.60	.50

Perf. 13½

220	A91	5c red	.50	.25
a.		Imperf., pair	40.00	
221	A91	10c gray green	1.50	.25
222	A92	12c blue	.90	.25
223	A92	20c ultra	2.40	1.10
224	A92	24c red brown	2.40	.60
225	A92	30c claret	3.50	.60
226	A92	50c gray black	3.25	5.00
227	A92a	1p slate bl & red	9.25	4.00
		Punch cancel		.50
a.		Imperf., pair	325.00	
228	A92a	5p black & gray grn	100.00	60.00
		Punch cancel		3.25
229	A92a	10p violet & blue	150.00	110.00
		Punch cancel		2.50
230	A92a	20p dull blue & cl	150.00	90.00
		Punch cancel		1.00
a.		Imperf., pair	650.00	
		Nos. 215-230 (16)	426.60	273.80

Cent. of Argentina's declaration of independence of Spain, July 9, 1816.

The watermark is either vert. or horiz. on Nos. 215-220, 222; only vert. on No. 221, and only horiz. on Nos. 223-230.

For overprints see #OD9, OD55-OD56, OD109, OD153, OD191-OD192, OD285, OD324.

A93

A94

A94a

Juan Gregorio Pujol — A95

1917 *Perf. 13½, 13½x12½*

231	A93	½c violet	.25	.25
232	A93	1c buff	.25	.25
233	A93	2c brown	.25	.25
234	A93	3c lt green	.70	.25
235	A93	4c red violet	.70	.25
236	A93	5c red	.25	.25
a.		Imperf., pair	15.00	
237	A93	10c gray green	.25	.25

Perf. 13½

238	A94	12c blue	.95	.25
239	A94	20c ultra	2.40	.30
240	A94	24c red brown	6.00	3.00
241	A94	30c claret	6.00	1.50
242	A94	50c gray black	6.00	.60
243	A94a	1p slate bl & red	6.00	.50
244	A94a	5p black & gray grn	19.00	3.00
		Punch cancel		1.50
245	A94a	10p violet & blue	47.50	12.00
		Punch cancel		1.00
246	A94a	20p dull blue & cl	90.00	50.00
		Punch cancel		.80
a.		Center inverted	1,200.	875.00
		Nos. 231-246 (16)	186.50	72.90

The watermark is either vert. or horiz. on Nos. 231-236, 238; only vert. on No. 237, and only horiz. on Nos. 239-246.

All known examples of No. 246a are off-center to the right.

1918, June 15 Litho. *Perf. 13½*

247	A95	5c bister & gray	.60	.25

Cent. of the birth of Juan G. Pujol (1817-61), lawyer and legislator.

Perf. 13½, 13½x12½

1918-19 Unwmk.

248	A93	½c violet	.25	.20
249	A93	1c buff	.25	.20
a.		Imperf., pair	14.00	
250	A93	2c brown	.25	.20
251	A93	3c lt green	.50	.20
252	A93	4c red violet	.50	.20
253	A93	5c red	.25	.20
254	A93	10c gray green	1.10	.20

Perf. 13½

255	A94	12c blue	1.25	.20
256	A94	20c ultra	1.40	.20
257	A94	24c red brown	2.40	.25
258	A94	30c claret	3.00	.30
259	A94	50c gray black	6.00	.40
		Nos. 248-259 (12)	17.15	2.75

The stamps of this issue sometimes show letters of papermakers' watermarks.

There were two printings, in 1918 and 1923, using different ink and paper.

1920 Wmk. 88 *Perf. 13½, 13½x12½*

264	A93	½c violet	.50	.20
265	A93	1c buff	.50	.20
266	A93	2c brown	.50	.20
267	A93	3c green	1.50	.90
268	A93	4c red violet	2.00	1.40
269	A93	5c red	.50	.20
270	A93	10c gray green	4.50	.20

Perf. 13½

271	A94	12c blue	2.50	.30
272	A94	20c ultra	4.00	.30
274	A94	30c claret	6.00	.70
275	A94	50c gray black	8.00	1.40
		Nos. 264-275 (11)	30.50	6.00

See #292-300, 304-307A, 310-314, 318, 322.

For overprints see Nos. OD10-OD20, OD57-OD71, OD74, OD110-OD121, OD154-OD159, OD161-OD162, OD193-OD207, OD209-OD211, OD242-OD252, OD254-OD255, OD286-OD290, OD325-OD328, OD330.

Belgrano's Mausoleum A96

Creation of Argentine Flag A97

Gen. Manuel Belgrano — A98

1920, June 18 *Perf. 13½*

280	A96	2c red	1.00	.25
a.		Perf. 13½x12½	2.00	.40
281	A97	5c rose & blue	1.00	.25
282	A98	12c green & blue	2.00	.90
		Nos. 280-282 (3)	4.00	1.40

Belgrano (1770-1820), Argentine general, patriot and diplomat.

Gen. Justo Jose de Urquiza — A99

Bartolome Mitre — A100

1920, Nov. 11

283	A99	5c gray blue	.60	.25

Gen. Justo Jose de Urquiza (1801-70), pres. of Argentina, 1854-60. See No. 303.

1921, June 26 Unwmk.

284	A100	2c violet brown	.50	.25
285	A100	5c light blue	.50	.25

Bartolome Mitre (1821-1906), pres. of Argentina, 1862-65.

Allegory, Pan-America — A101

1921, Aug. 25 *Perf. 13½*

286	A101	3c violet	.55	.30
287	A101	5c blue	.80	.20
288	A101	10c vio brown	1.40	.35
289	A101	12c rose	2.00	.75
		Nos. 286-289 (4)	4.75	1.60

Inscribed "Buenos Aires-Agosto de 1921" A102

Inscribed "Republica Argentina" A103

1921, Oct. *Perf. 13½x12½*

290	A102	5c rose	.30	.20
a.		Perf. 13½	1.25	.20
291	A103	5c rose	1.50	.20
a.		Perf. 13½	2.50	.20

1st Pan-American Postal Cong., Buenos Aires, Aug., 1921.

See Nos. 308-309, 319. For overprints see Nos. OD72, OD160, OD208, OD253, OD329.

1920 Wmk. 89 *Perf. 13½, 13½x12½*

292	A93	½c violet	1.60	.80
293	A93	1c buff	4.50	1.50
294	A93	2c brown	3.50	.50
297	A93	5c red	4.50	.35
298	A93	10c gray green	4.50	.35

Perf. 13½

299	A94	12c blue	3,000.	200.00
300	A94	20c ultra	12.00	1.00
		Nos. 292-298,300 (6)	30.60	4.50

1920

303	A99	5c gray blue	450.00	300.00

Perf. 13½, 13½x12½

1922-23 Wmk. 90

304	A93	½c violet	.50	.20
305	A93	1c buff	.50	.20
306	A93	2c brown	.50	.20
307	A93	3c green	.50	.40
307A	A93	4c red violet	1.50	1.00
308	A102	5c rose	2.50	.60
309	A103	5c red	.50	.25
310	A93	10c gray green	2.00	.20

Perf. 13½

311	A94	12c blue	1.00	.30
312	A94	20c ultra	1.50	.30
313	A94	24c red brown	15.00	6.00
314	A94	30c claret	6.00	.60
		Nos. 304-314 (12)	32.00	10.25

Paper with Gray Overprint RA in Sun

Perf. 13½, 13½x12½

1922-23 Unwmk.

318	A93	2c brown	3.00	1.00
319	A103	5c red	2.00	.30

Perf. 13½

322 A94 20c ultra 30.00 1.50
Nos. 318-322 (3) 35.00 2.80

San Martín
A104 A105
With Period after Value

1923, May Litho. Wmk. 90

323 A104 ½c red violet .50 .25
324 A104 1c buff .50 .25
325 A104 2c dark brown .50 .25
326 A104 3c lt green .50 .30
327 A104 4c red brown .50 .30
328 A104 5c red .50 .25
329 A104 10c dull green 3.50 .25
330 A104 12c deep blue .50 .25
331 A104 20c ultra 1.50 .25
332 A104 24c lt brown 3.50 3.00
333 A104 30c claret 15.00 .50
334 A104 50c black 7.50 .40

Without Period after Value

Wmk. 87 ***Perf. 13½***

335 A105 1p blue & red 6.00 .25
336 A105 5p gray lilac & grn 30.00 1.60
Punch cancel .60
337 A105 10p claret & blue 75.00 7.50
Punch cancel 1.00
338 A105 20p sl & brn lake 100.00 20.00
Punch cancel .60
a. Center inverted
Nos. 323-338 (16) 245.50 35.60

Nos. 335-338 and 353-356 canceled with round or oval killers in purple (revenue cancellations) sell for one-fifth to one-half as much as postally used copies.
For overprints see Nos. 399-404.

Design of 1923
Without Period after Value
Perf. 13½, 13½x12½

1923-24 Litho. Wmk. 90

340 A104 ½c red violet .50 .25
341 A104 1c buff .50 .25
342 A104 2c dk brown .50 .25
343 A104 3c green .60 .25
a. Imperf., pair 8.00
344 A104 4c red brown .60 .25
345 A104 5c red .50 .25
346 A104 10c dull green .50 .25
347 A104 12c deep blue .60 .25
348 A104 20c ultra .90 .25
349 A104 24c lt brown 2.50 1.10
350 A104 25c purple 1.10 .25
351 A104 30c claret 2.50 .25
352 A104 50c black 6.00 .25
353 A105 1p blue & red 2.00 .20
354 A105 5p dk vio & grn 15.00 .75
Punch cancel .20
355 A105 10p claret & blue 32.50 3.25
Punch cancel .20
356 A105 20p slate & lake 47.50 7.50
Punch cancel .20
Nos. 340-356 (17) 114.30 15.80

1931-33

Typographed

343b A104 3c 3.00 .40
345a A104 5c 4.50 .40
346a A104 10c 7.50 .40
347a A104 12c 15.00 3.00
348a A104 20c 50.00 2.50
350a A104 25c 37.50 1.75
351a A104 30c 21.00 1.10
Nos. 343b-351a (7) 138.50 9.55

The typographed stamps were issued only in coils and have a rough impression with heavy shading about the eyes and nose. Nos. 343 and 346 are known without watermark.
Nos. 341-345, 347-349, 351a may be found in pairs, one with period.
See note after No. 338. See Nos. 362-368.
For overprints see Nos. OD21-OD33, OD75-OD87, OD122-OD133, OD163-OD175, OD212-OD226, OD256-OD268, OD291-OD304, OD331-OD345.

Rivadavia — A106

1926, Feb. 8 ***Perf. 13½***

357 A106 5c rose .60 .25

Presidency of Bernardino Rivadavia, cent.

Rivadavia
A108

San Martin
A109

General Post Office, 1926 — A110

General Post Office, 1826 — A111

1926, July 1 ***Perf. 13½x12½***

358 A108 3c gray green .40 .25
359 A109 5c red .40 .25

Perf. 13½

360 A110 12c deep blue 1.25 .40
361 A111 25c chocolate 1.60 .20
a. "1326" for "1826" 15.00 5.00
Nos. 358-361 (4) 3.65 1.10

Centenary of the Post Office.
For overprints see #OD34, OD88, OD134, OD227-OD228, OD269, OD305, OD346.

Type of 1923-31 Issue
Without Period after Value

1927 Wmk. 205 ***Perf. 13½x12½***

362 A104 ½c red violet .50 .40
a. Pelure paper 2.50 2.50
363 A104 1c buff .50 .40
364 A104 2c dark brown .50 .25
a. Pelure paper .70 .70
365 A104 5c red .50 .30
a. Period after value 9.00 6.00
b. Pelure paper .70 .70
366 A104 10c dull green 5.00 3.00
367 A104 20c ultra 47.50 4.75

Perf. 13½

368 A105 1p blue & red 35.00 6.00
Nos. 362-368 (7) 89.50 15.10

Arms of Argentina and Brazil
A112

Wmk. RA in Sun (90)

1928, Aug. 27 ***Perf. 12½x13***

369 A112 5c rose red 1.50 .40
370 A112 12c deep blue 2.50 .70

Cent. of peace between the Empire of Brazil and the United Provinces of the Rio de la Plata.

Allegory, Discovery of the New World — A113

"Spain" and "Argentina" — A114

"America" Offering Laurels to Columbus
A115

1929, Oct. 12 Litho. ***Perf. 13½***

371 A113 2c lilac brown 2.00 .40
372 A114 5c light red 2.00 .40
373 A115 12c dull blue 6.00 1.00
Nos. 371-373 (3) 10.00 1.80

Discovery of America by Columbus, 437th anniv.

Spirit of Victory Attending Insurgents — A116

March of the Victorious Insurgents
A117

Perf. 13½x12½ (A116), 12½x13 (A117)

1930

374 A116 ½c violet gray 1.00 .40
375 A116 1c myrtle green 1.00 .40
376 A117 2c dull violet 1.00 .40
377 A116 3c green .50 .40
378 A116 4c violet .80 .70
379 A116 5c rose red .70 .25
380 A116 10c gray black 1.00 .60
381 A117 12c dull blue .50 .25
382 A117 20c ocher .50 .25
383 A117 24c red brown 2.25 1.50
384 A117 25c green 2.50 1.50
385 A117 30c deep violet 4.50 2.00
386 A117 50c black 6.25 2.50
387 A117 1p sl bl & red 11.00 10.00
388 A117 2p black & org 22.50 10.00
389 A117 5p dull grn & blk 92.50 35.00
390 A117 10p dp red brn & dull blue 110.00 40.00
391 A117 20p yel grn & dl bl 210.00 90.00
392 A117 50p dk grn & vio 750.00 550.00
Nos. 374-390 (17) 258.50 106.15

Revolution of 1930.
Nos. 387-392 with oval (parcel post) cancellation sell for less.
For overprint see No. 405.

1931 ***Perf. 12½x13***

393 A117 ½c red violet .50 .40
394 A117 1c gray black 1.10 .90
395 A117 3c green 1.00 .60
396 A117 4c red brown .80 .40
397 A117 5c red .70 .25
a. Plane omitted, top left corner 3.00 1.50
398 A117 10c dull green 1.50 .60
Nos. 393-398 (6) 5.60 3.15

Revolution of 1930.

Stamps of 1924-25 Overprinted in Red or Green

1931, Sept. 6 ***Perf. 13½, 13½x12½***

399 A104 3c green .40 .40
400 A104 10c dull green .60 .60
401 A104 30c claret (G) 4.50 2.50
402 A104 50c black 4.50 3.00

Overprinted in Blue

403 A105 1p blue & red 5.50 3.00
404 A105 5p dk violet & grn 60.00 20.00

No. 388 Overprinted in Blue

Perf. 12½x13

405 A117 2p black & orange 10.00 7.50
Nos. 399-405 (7) 85.50 37.00

1st anniv. of the Revolution of 1930.
See Nos. C30-C34.

Refrigeration Compressor — A118

Perf. 13½x12½

1932, Aug. 29 Litho.

406 A118 3c green 1.00 .50
407 A118 10c scarlet 2.00 .40
408 A118 12c gray blue 7.00 1.10
Nos. 406-408 (3) 10.00 2.00

6th Intl. Refrigeration Congress.

Port of La Plata
A119

Pres. Julio A. Roca — A120

Municipal Palace
A121

Cathedral of La Plata — A122

Dardo Rocha
A123

Perf. 13½x13, 13x13½ (10c)

1933, Jan.

409 A119 3c green & dk brn .40 .30
410 A120 10c orange & dk vio .60 .25
411 A121 15c dk bl & dp bl 2.50 1.50

412	A122	20c violet & yel brn	1.75	.90
413	A123	30c dk grn & vio brn	13.00	5.50
		Nos. 409-413 (5)	18.25	8.45

50th anniv. of the founding of the city of La Plata, Nov. 19th, 1882.

Christ of the Andes — A124

Buenos Aires Cathedral A125

1934, Oct. 1 ***Perf. 13x13½, 13½x13***

414	A124	10c rose & brown	.70	.20
415	A125	15c dark blue	1.40	.45

32nd Intl. Eucharistic Cong., Oct. 10-14.

"Liberty" with Arms of Brazil and Argentina A126

Symbolical of "Peace" and "Friendship" A127

1935, May 15 ***Perf. 13x13½***

416	A126	10c red	.85	.25
417	A127	15c blue	1.60	.50

Visit of Pres. Getulio Vargas of Brazil.

Belgrano A128

Sarmiento A129

Urquiza — A130

Louis Braille — A131

San Martin — A132

Brown — A133

Moreno A134

Alberdi A135

Nicolas Avellaneda A136

Rivadavia A137

Mitre A138

Bull (Cattle Breeding) A139

Martin Güemes A140

Agriculture A141

Merino Sheep (Wool) A142

Sugar Cane A143

Oil Well (Petroleum) — A144

Map of South America A145 A146

Fruit — A147

Iguacu Falls (Scenic Wonders) A148

Grapes (Vineyards) A149

Cotton — A150

Two types of A140:
Type I — Inscribed Juan Martin Guemes.
Type II — Inscribed Martin Güemes.

Perf. 13, 13½x13, 13x13½

1935-51 **Litho.** **Wmk. 90**

418	A128	½c red violet	.25	.20
419	A129	1c buff	.25	.20
a.		Typo.	.80	.20
420	A130	2c dark brown	.50	.20
421	A131	2½c black ('39)	.25	.20
422	A132	3c green	.50	.20
423	A132	3c lt gray ('39)	.50	.20
424	A134	3c lt gray ('46)	.50	.20
425	A133	4c lt gray	.50	.20
426	A133	4c sage green ('39)	.40	.20
427	A134	5c yel brn, typo.	.20	.20
a.		Tete beche pair, typo.	20.00	10.00
b.		Booklet pane of 8, typo.		
c.		Booklet pane of 4, typo.		
d.		Litho.	5.00	.50
428	A135	6c olive green	.40	.20
429	A136	8c orange ('39)	.40	.20
430	A137	10c car, typo.	.25	.20
431	A137	10c brown ('42)	.20	.20
a.		Typo.	2.00	.20
432	A138	12c brown	1.00	.20
433	A138	12c red ('39)	.25	.20
434	A139	15c slate bl ('36)	1.50	.20
435	A139	15c pale ultra ('39)	1.00	.20
436	A140	15c lt gray bl (II) ('42)	45.00	2.00
437	A140	20c lt ultra (I)	1.00	.20
438	A140	20c lt ultra (II) ('36)	1.00	.20
439	A140	20c bl gray (II) ('39)	.35	.20
439A	A139	20c dk bl & pale bl, ('42) 22x33mm	1.00	.20
440	A139	20c blue ('51)	.20	.20
a.		Typo.	.20	.20
441	A141	25c car ('36)	.50	.20
442	A142	30c org brn ('36)	.80	.20
443	A143	40c dk vio ('36)	.70	.20
444	A144	50c red & org ('36)	.70	.20
445	A145	1p brn blk & lt bl ('36)	25.00	1.00
446	A146	1p brn blk & lt bl ('37)	15.00	.30
a.		Chalky paper	100.00	2.00
447	A147	2p brn lake & dk ultra ('36)	1.00	.20
448	A148	5p ind & ol grn ('36)	3.00	.25
449	A149	10p brn lake & blk	15.00	1.00
450	A150	20p bl grn & brn ('36)	25.00	3.00
		Nos. 418-450 (34)	144.10	13.15

See Nos. 485-500, 523-540, 659, 668. For overprints see Nos. O37-O41, O43-O51, O53-O56, O58-O78, O108, O112, OD35-OD46, OD89-OD101, OD135-OD145, OD176-OD182C, OD229-OD234F, OD270-OD280, OD306-OD317, OD347-OD357.

No. 439A exists with attached label showing medallion. Value $42.50 unused, $22.50 used.

Souvenir Sheet

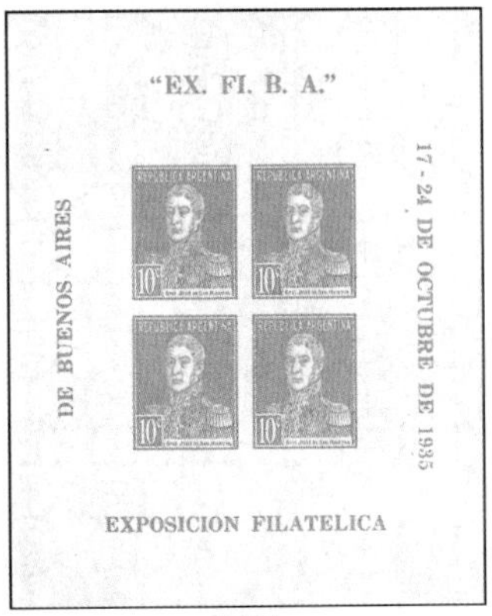

A151

Without Period after Value

1935, Oct. 17 **Litho.** ***Imperf.***

452	A151	Sheet of 4	75.00	35.00
a.		10c dull green	10.00	7.50

Phil. Exhib. at Buenos Aires, Oct. 17-24, 1935. The stamps were on sale during the 8 days of the exhibition only. Sheets measure 83x101mm.

Plaque — A152

1936, Dec. 1 ***Perf. 13x13½***

453	A152	10c rose	.80	.30

Inter-American Conference for Peace.

Domingo Faustino Sarmiento A153

"Presidente Sarmiento" A154

1938, Sept. 5

454	A153	3c sage green	.50	.50
455	A153	5c red	.50	.50
456	A153	15c deep blue	1.00	.50
457	A153	50c orange	3.00	1.00
		Nos. 454-457 (4)	5.00	2.50

50th anniv. of the death of Domingo Faustino Sarmiento, pres., educator and author.

1939, Mar. 16

458	A154	5c greenish blue	.50	.25

Final voyage of the training ship "Presidente Sarmiento."

Allegory of the UPU — A155

Coat of Arms — A157

Post Office, Buenos Aires — A156

Iguacu Falls — A158

Bonete Hill, Nahuel Huapi Park — A159

Allegory of Modern Communications A160

Argentina, Land of Promise A161

Lake Frias, Nahuel Huapi Park — A162

Perf. 13x13½, 13½x13

1939, Apr. 1 **Photo.**

459	A155	5c	rose carmine	.60	.25
460	A156	15c	grnsh black	.60	.40
461	A157	20c	brt blue	.60	.25
462	A158	25c	dp blue grn	1.10	.40
463	A159	50c	brown	1.60	.90
464	A160	1p	brown violet	2.50	2.40
465	A161	2p	magenta	15.00	15.00
466	A162	5p	purple	35.00	30.00
			Nos. 459-466 (8)	57.00	49.60

Universal Postal Union, 11th Congress.

Souvenir Sheets

A163

A164

1939, May 12 **Wmk. 90** ***Imperf.***

467	A163 Sheet of 4		6.00	4.25
a.	5c rose carmine (A155)		1.25	.75
b.	20c bright blue (A157)		1.25	.75
c.	25c deep blue green (A158)		1.25	.75
d.	50c brown (A159)		1.25	.75
468	A164 Sheet of 4		6.00	4.25

Issued in four forms:

a.	Unsevered horizontal pair of sheets, type A163 at left, A164 at right	25.00	15.00
b.	Unsevered vertical pair of sheets, type A163 at top, A164 at bottom	25.00	15.00
c.	Unsevered block of 4 sheets, type A163 at left, A164 at right	52.50	52.50
d.	Unsevered block of 4 sheets, type A163 at top, A164 at bottom	52.50	52.50

11th Cong. of the UPU and the Argentina Intl. Phil. Exposition (C.Y.T.R.A.).

No. 468 contains Nos. 467a-467d.

Family and New House A165

Perf. 13½x13

1939, Oct. 2 **Litho.** **Wmk. 90**

469	A165	5c bluish green	.50	.20

1st Pan-American Housing Congress.

Bird Carrying Record A166

Head of Liberty and Arms of Argentina A167

Record and Winged Letter A168

Perf. 13x13½, 13½x13 (#472)

1939, Dec. 11 **Photo.**

470	A166	1.18p indigo	15.00	10.00
471	A167	1.32p bright blue	15.00	10.00
472	A168	1.50p dark brown	50.00	30.00
		Nos. 470-472 (3)	80.00	50.00

These stamps were issued for the recording and mailing of flexible phonograph records.

Map of the Americas — A169

1940, Apr. 14 ***Perf. 13x13½***

473	A169	15c ultramarine	.50	.20

50th anniv. of the Pan American Union.

Souvenir Sheet

Reproductions of Early Argentine Stamps — A170

Wmk. RA in Sun (90)

1940, May 25 **Litho.** ***Imperf.***

474	A170 Sheet of 5	15.00	8.00
a.	5c dark blue (Corrientes A2)	2.00	1.50
b.	5c red (Argentina A1)	2.00	1.50
c.	5c dark blue (Cordoba #1)	2.00	1.50
d.	5c red (Argentina A3)	2.00	1.50
e.	10c dark blue (Buenos Aires A1)	2.00	1.50

100th anniv. of the first postage stamp.

AIR POST STAMPS

Airplane Circles the Globe — AP1

Eagle — AP2

Wings Cross the Sea — AP3

Condor on Mountain Crag — AP4

Perforations of Nos. C1-C37 vary from clean-cut to rough and uneven, with many skipped perfs.

Perf. 13x13½, 13½x13

1928, Mar. 1 **Litho.** **Wmk. 90**

C1	AP1	5c	lt red	1.25	.50
C2	AP1	10c	Prus blue	2.25	1.00
C3	AP2	15c	lt brown	2.25	.80
C4	AP1	18c	lilac gray	3.00	2.75
a.		18c brown lilac		3.25	2.75
b.		Double impression		*375.00*	
C5	AP2	20c	ultra	2.25	.80
C6	AP2	24c	deep blue	3.50	2.75
C7	AP3	25c	brt violet	3.50	1.50
C8	AP3	30c	rose red	5.25	1.00
C9	AP4	35c	rose	3.50	1.00
C10	AP1	36c	bister brn	2.50	1.50
C11	AP4	50c	gray black	4.00	.50
C12	AP2	54c	chocolate	3.50	2.00
C13	AP2	72c	yellow grn	4.75	2.00
a.		Double impression		*300.00*	
C14	AP3	90c	dk brown	9.00	1.75
C15	AP3	1p	slate bl & red	11.00	.65
C16	AP3	1.08p	rose & dk bl	16.00	4.50
C17	AP4	1.26p	dull vio & grn	20.00	8.00
C18	AP4	1.80p	blue & lil rose	20.00	8.00
C19	AP4	3.60p	gray & blue	42.50	19.00
			Nos. C1-C19 (19)	160.00	60.00

The watermark on No. C4a is larger than on the other stamps of this set, measuring 10mm across Sun.

Zeppelin First Flight

Air Post Stamps of 1928 Overprinted in Blue

1930, May

C20	AP2	20c	ultra	10.00	5.00
C21	AP4	50c	gray black	20.00	10.00
a.		Inverted overprint		*475.00*	
C22	AP3	1p	slate bl & red	21.00	10.00
a.		Inverted overprint		*650.00*	
C23	AP4	1.80p	blue & lil rose	55.00	25.00
C24	AP4	3.60p	gray & blue	150.00	70.00
			Nos. C20-C24 (5)	256.00	120.00

Overprinted in Green

C25	AP2	20c	ultra	10.00	6.00
C26	AP4	50c	gray black	12.50	9.00
C27	AP3	90c	dark brown	10.00	6.00
C28	AP3	1p	slate bl & red	20.00	12.50
C29	AP4	1.80p	blue & lil rose	600.00	400.00
a.		Thick paper		*850.00*	
			Nos. C25-C29 (5)	652.50	433.50

Air Post Stamps of 1928 Overprinted in Red or Blue

On AP1-AP2

On AP3-AP4

1931

C30	AP1	18c	lilac gray	2.00	1.50
C31	AP2	72c	yellow green	14.00	10.50
C32	AP3	90c	dark brown	14.00	10.50
C33	AP4	1.80p	bl & lil rose (Bl)	30.00	22.50
C34	AP4	3.60p	gray & blue	57.50	40.00
			Nos. C30-C34 (5)	117.50	85.00

1st anniv. of the Revolution of 1930.

Zeppelin Issue

Nos. C1, C4, C4a, C14 Overprinted in Blue or Red

On AP1

On AP3

1932, Aug. 4
C35 AP1 5c lt red (Bl) 3.00 2.00
C36 AP1 18c lilac gray (R) 12.50 9.00
a. 18c brown lilac (R) 100.00 60.00
C37 AP3 90c dark brown (R) 32.50 26.00
Nos. C35-C37 (3) 48.00 37.00

Plane and Letter — AP5

Mercury — AP6

Plane in Flight — AP7

Perf. 13½x13, 13x13½
1940, Oct. 23 Photo. Wmk. 90
C38 AP5 30c deep orange 5.00 .20
C39 AP6 50c dark brown 7.50 .20
C40 AP5 1p carmine 1.75 .20
C41 AP7 1.25p deep green .50 .20
C42 AP5 2.50p bright blue 1.25 .20
Nos. C38-C42 (5) 16.00 1.00

OFFICIAL STAMPS

Regular Issues Overprinted in Black

1884-87 Unwmk. *Perf. 12, 14*
O1 A29 ½c brown 12.00 10.00
O2 A23 1c red 8.00 6.00
b. Perf. 12 40.00 37.50
O3 A29 1c red .50 .35
On cover 25.00
b. Double overprint 75.00
O4 A20 2c green .50 .35
On cover 25.00
b. Double overprint 35.00 35.00
O5 A11 4c brown .50 .35
On cover 25.00
O6 A7 8c lake .50 .35
On cover 25.00
O7 A8 10c green 40.00 25.00
O8 A23 12c ultra (#45) 6.50 4.00
a. Perf. 14 325.00 125.00
O9 A29 12c grnsh blue .80 .65
On cover *35.00*
O10 A19 24c blue 1.25 1.00
On cover *50.00*
O11 A21 25c lake 16.00 12.50
O12 A12 30c orange 32.50 20.00
O13 A13 60c black 20.00 12.50
O14 A14 90c blue 20.00 16.00
b. Double overprint 50.00 45.00
Nos. O1-O14 (14) 159.05 109.05

Inverted Overprint

O1a A29 ½c 16.00 12.50
O2a A23 1c Perf. 14 50.00 40.00
c. Perf. 12 32.50 30.00
O3a A29 1c 1.60 1.00
O4a A20 2c 65.00 40.00
O5a A11 4c 40.00 32.50
O6a A7 8c 60.00 60.00
O8b A23 12c Perf. 12 12.50
O9a A29 12c 125.00 65.00
O10a A19 24c 2.75 1.60
O13a A13 60c 90.00 50.00
O14a A14 90c 50.00 40.00

1884 *Rouletted*
O15 A17 16c green 1.75 1.00
a. Double overprint 16.00 —
b. Inverted overprint 125.00
O16 A18 20c blue 8.00 7.00
a. Inverted overprint 60.00 40.00
O17 A19 24c blue 1.25 1.00
a. Inverted overprint 4.00 2.50
b. Double ovpt., one inverted 250.00 —
Nos. O15-O17 (3) 11.00 9.00

Overprinted Diagonally in Red

1885 *Perf. 12*
O18 A20 2c green 2.00 1.50
a. Inverted overprint 40.00 32.50
O19 A11 4c brown 2.00 1.40
a. Inverted overprint 40.00 32.50
b. Double overprint 50.00
O20 A13 60c black 20.00 16.00
O21 A14 90c blue 200.00 150.00

1885 *Rouletted*
O22 A19 24c blue 17.50 12.50

On all of these stamps, the overprint is found reading both upwards and downwards.

Counterfeits exist of No. O21 overprint and others.

Regular Issues Handstamped Horizontally in Black

1884 *Perf. 12, 14*
O23 A23 1c red 50.00 17.00
a. Perf. 12 150.00 100.00
O24 A20 2c green, diagonal overprint 25.00 15.00
a. Horizontal overprint 150.00 125.00
O25 A11 4c brown 10.00 8.00
O26 A7 8c lake 10.00 10.00
O27 A23 12c ultra 27.50 20.00

Overprinted Diagonally

O28 A19 24c bl, rouletted 20.00 15.00
O29 A13 60c black 15.00 10.00

Counterfeit overprints exist.

Liberty Head — O1

Perf. 11½, 12 and Compound
1901, Dec. 1 Engr.
O31 O1 1c gray .25 .20
On cover 20.00
b. Vert. pair, imperf. horiz. 50.00
c. Horiz. pair, imperf. vert. 50.00
O32 O1 2c orange brown .30 .20
On cover 25.00
O33 O1 5c red .40 .20
On cover 25.00
b. Vert. pair, imperf. horiz. 50.00
O34 O1 10c dark green .50 .20
On cover 35.00
O35 O1 30c dark blue 4.00 1.00
On cover 50.00
O36 O1 50c orange 2.00 1.00
On cover 75.00
Nos. O31-O36 (6) 7.45 2.80

Imperf, Pairs

O31a O1 1c 40.00
O32a O1 2c 40.00
O33a O1 5c 50.00
O34a O1 10c 40.00
O35a O1 30c 65.00
O36a O1 50c 50.00

Regular Stamps of 1935-51 Overprinted in Black

Perf. 13x13½, 13½x13, 13
1938-54 Wmk. RA in Sun (90)
O37 A129 1c buff ('40) .20 .20
O38 A130 2c dk brn ('40) .20 .20
O39 A132 3c grn ('39) .20 .20
O40 A132 3c lt gray ('39) .20 .20
O41 A134 5c yel brn .20 .20
O42 A195 5c car ('53) .20 .20
O43 A137 10c carmine .20 .20
O44 A137 10c brn ('39) .20 .20
O45 A140 15c lt gray bl, type II ('47) .20 .20
O46 A139 15c slate blue .50 .20
O47 A139 15c pale ultra ('39) .20 .20
O48 A139 20c blue ('53) .30 .20
O49 A141 25c carmine .20 .20
a. Overprint 11mm .20 .20
O49B A143 40c dk violet .90 .20
O50 A144 50c red & org .20 .20
a. Overprint 11mm .25 .20
O51 A146 1p brn blk & lt bl ('40) .20 .20
a. Overprint 11mm .25 .25
O52 A224 1p choc & lt bl ('51) .20 .20
a. Overprint 11mm .20 .20
O53 A147 2p brn lake & dk ultra (ovpt. 11mm) ('54) .70 .20
Nos. O37-O53 (18) 5.20 3.60

OFFICIAL DEPARTMENT STAMPS

Regular Issues of 1911-37 Overprinted in Black

Type I

Type II

Ministry of Agriculture (M. A.)
Type I

1913-37

On Stamp of 1911
OD1 A88 2c #181 .20 .20

On Stamps of 1912-14
OD2 A88 1c #190 .20 .20
OD3 A88 2c #191 .20 .20
OD4 A88 5c #194 .30 .20
OD5 A88 12c #196 .20 .20
Nos. OD2-OD5 (4) .90 .80

On Stamps of 1915-16
OD6 A88 1c #208 .20 .20
OD7 A88 2c #209 .20 .20
OD8 A88 5c #212 .20 .20
OD9 A91 5c #220 .20 .20
Nos. OD6-OD9 (4) .80 .80

On Stamp of 1917
OD10 A94 12c #238 .30 .20

On Stamps of 1918-19
OD11 A93 1c #249 .20 .20
OD12 A93 2c #250 .20 .20
OD13 A93 5c #253 .20 .20
OD14 A94 12c #255 .20 .20
OD15 A94 20c #256 .20 .20
Nos. OD10-OD15 (6) 1.30 1.20

On Stamps of 1920
OD16 A93 1c #265 .30 .25
OD17 A93 2c #266 .50 .25
OD18 A93 5c #269 .20 .20
Nos. OD16-OD18 (3) 1.00 .70

On Stamps of 1922-23
OD19 A94 12c #311 1.00 .40
OD20 A94 20c #312 25.00

On Stamps of 1923
OD21 A104 1c #324 .20 .20
OD22 A104 2c #325 .25 .20
OD23 A104 5c #328 .20 .20
OD24 A104 12c #330 .20 .20
OD25 A104 20c #331 .20 .20
Nos. OD21-OD25 (5) 1.05 1.00

On Stamps of 1923-31
OD26 A104 1c #341 .20 .20
OD27 A104 2c #342, I .20 .20
a. Type II 1.50 .75
OD28 A104 3c #343 .20 .20
OD29 A104 5c #345, II .20 .20
a. Type I .20 .20
OD30 A104 10c #346, II .20 .20
a. Type I .20 .20
OD31 A104 12c #347 .20 .20
OD32 A104 20c #348, I .20 .20
a. Type II .20 .20
OD33 A104 30c #351 .20 .20
Nos. OD26-OD33 (8) 1.60 1.60

On Stamp of 1926
OD34 A110 12c #360 .20 .20

Type II

On Stamps of 1935-37
OD35 A129 1c #419 .20 .20
OD36 A130 2c #420 .20 .20
OD37 A132 3c #422 .20 .20
OD38 A134 5c #427 .20 .20
OD39 A137 10c #430 .20 .20
OD40 A139 15c #434 .50 .20
OD41 A140 20c #437 .30 .20
OD42 A140 20c #438 .20 .20
OD43 A141 25c #441 .25 .20
OD44 A142 30c #442 .20 .20
OD45 A145 1p #445 2.50 1.50
OD46 A146 1p #446 .50 .25
Nos. OD35-OD46 (12) 5.45 3.75

Ministry of War (M. G.)
Type I

On Stamp of 1911
OD47 A88 2c #181 .20 .20

On Stamps of 1912-14
OD48 A88 1c #190 .20 .20
OD49 A88 2c #191 .75 .20
OD50 A88 5c #194 .20 .20
OD51 A88 12c #196 .20 .20
Nos. OD48-OD51 (4) 1.35 .80

On Stamps of 1915-16
OD52 A88 1c #208 6.00 .75
OD53 A88 2c #209 .60 .20
OD54 A88 5c #212 .75 .20
OD55 A91 5c #220 1.00 .25
OD56 A92 12c #222 1.00 .35
Nos. OD52-OD56 (5) 9.35 1.75

On Stamps of 1917
OD57 A93 1c #232 .30 .20
OD58 A93 2c #233 .40 .20
OD59 A93 5c #236 .30 .20
OD60 A94 12c #238 .60 .20
Nos. OD57-OD60 (4) 1.60 .80

On Stamps of 1918-19
OD61 A93 1c #249 .20 .20
OD62 A93 2c #250 .20 .20
OD63 A93 5c #253 .20 .20
OD64 A94 12c #255 .40 .20
OD65 A94 20c #256 1.25 .20
Nos. OD61-OD65 (5) 2.25 1.00

On Stamps of 1920
OD66 A93 2c #266 .40 .20
OD67 A93 5c #269 .40 .20
OD68 A94 12c #271 .35 .20
Nos. OD66-OD68 (3) 1.15 .60

On Stamp of 1920
OD69 A94 12c #299 2.00 .25

On Stamps of 1922-23
OD70 A93 1c #305 .75 .20
OD71 A93 2c #306 1.50 .45
OD72 A103 5c #309 .75 .20
OD73 A94 20c #312 .30 .20
Nos. OD70-OD73 (4) 3.30 1.05

On Stamp of 1922-23
OD74 A93 2c #318 5.00 .50

On Stamps of 1923
OD75 A104 1c #324 .20 .20
OD76 A104 2c #325 .20 .20
OD77 A104 5c #328 .20 .20
OD78 A104 12c #330 .20 .20
OD79 A104 20c #331 1.00 .20
Nos. OD75-OD79 (5) 1.80 1.00

On Stamps of 1923-31
OD80 A104 1c #341 1.25 .45
OD81 A104 2c #342 .20 .20
OD82 A104 3c #343, I .20 .20
a. Type II .40 .20
OD83 A104 5c #345, I .20 .20
a. Type II .20 .20
OD84 A104 10c #346, II .20 .20
a. Type I .60 .20
OD85 A104 20c #348, I .20 .20
a. Type II .40 .20
OD86 A104 30c #351, II .20 .20
a. Type I 1.00 .20
OD87 A105 1p #353 2.00 .30
Nos. OD80-OD87 (8) 4.45 1.95

On Stamp of 1926
OD88 A109 5c #359 .60 .20

Type II

On Stamps of 1935-37
OD89 A129 1c #419 .20 .20
OD90 A130 2c #420 .20 .20
OD91 A132 3c #422 .20 .20
OD92 A134 5c #427 .20 .20
OD93 A137 10c #430 .20 .20
OD94 A139 15c #434 .25 .20
OD95 A140 20c #437 1.00 .20
OD96 A140 20c #438 .25 .20
OD97 A141 25c #441 .20 .20
OD98 A142 30c #442 .20 .20
OD99 A144 50c #444 .25 .20
OD100 A145 1p #445 1.25 .50
OD101 A146 1p #446 .50 .25
Nos. OD89-OD101 (13) 4.90 2.95

Ministry of Finance (M. H.)
Type I

On Stamp of 1911
OD102 A88 2c #181 .20 .20

On Stamps of 1912-14
OD103 A88 1c #190 .20 .20
OD104 A88 2c #191 .20 .20
OD105 A88 5c #194 .20 .20
OD106 A88 12c #196 .20 .20
Nos. OD103-OD106 (4) .80 .80

On Stamps of 1915-16
OD107 A88 2c #209 .20 .20
OD108 A88 5c #212 .20 .20
OD109 A91 5c #220 .20 .20
Nos. OD107-OD109 (3) .60 .60

On Stamps of 1917

OD110 A93 2c #233 .20 .20
OD111 A93 5c #236 1.25 .20
OD112 A94 12c #238 .20 .20
Nos. OD110-OD112 (3) 1.65 .60

On Stamps of 1918-19

OD113 A93 2c #250 25.00
OD114 A93 5c #253 .20 .20
OD115 A94 12c #255 .45 .20
OD116 A94 20c #256 .45 .20

On Stamps of 1920

OD117 A93 1c #265 .75 .45
OD118 A93 2c #266 1.25 .45
OD119 A93 5c #269 .30 .20
OD120 A94 12c #271 .60 .20
Nos. OD117-OD120 (4) 2.90 1.30

On Stamp of 1922-23

OD121 A94 20c #312 12.50 2.50

On Stamps of 1923

OD122 A104 1c #324 .75 .40
OD123 A104 2c #325 .20 .20
OD124 A104 5c #328 .20 .20
OD125 A104 12c #330 .20 .20
OD126 A104 20c #331 .20 .20
Nos. OD122-OD126 (5) 1.55 1.20

On Stamps of 1923-31

OD127 A104 3c #343 7.00 1.50
OD128 A104 5c #345 .20 .20
OD129 A104 10c #346 .20 .20
OD130 A104 12c #347 7.00 3.75
OD131 A104 20c #348, I .20 .20
a. Type II .35 .20
OD132 A104 30c #351 .25 .20
OD133 A105 1p #353 .40 .20
Nos. OD127-OD133 (7) 15.25 6.25

On Stamp of 1926

OD134 A110 12c #360 12.50 12.50

Type II
On Stamps of 1935-37

OD135 A129 1c #419 .20 .20
OD136 A130 2c #420 .20 .20
OD137 A132 3c #422 .20 .20
OD138 A134 5c #427 .20 .20
OD139 A137 10c #430 .20 .20
OD140 A139 15c #434 .45 .20
OD141 A140 20c #437 .20 .20
OD142 A140 20c #438 .20 .20
OD143 A142 30c #442 .20 .20
OD144 A145 1p #445 2.00 1.00
OD145 A146 1p #446 .50 .20
Nos. OD135-OD145 (11) 4.55 3.00

Ministry of the Interior
(M. I.)
Type I
On Stamp of 1911

OD146 A88 2c #181 .25 .20

On Stamps of 1912-14

OD147 A88 1c #190 .20 .20
OD148 A88 2c #191 .20 .20
OD149 A88 5c #194 .20 .20
OD150 A88 12c #196 .20 .20
Nos. OD146-OD150 (5) 1.05 1.00

On Stamps of 1915-17

OD151 A88 2c #209 .80 .30
OD152 A88 5c #212 .75 .20
OD153 A91 5c #220 .60 .20
OD154 A93 5c #236 1.50 .20
Nos. OD151-OD154 (4) 3.65 .90

On Stamps of 1918-19

OD155 A93 2c #250 .20 .20
OD156 A93 5c #253 .20 .20

On Stamps of 1920

OD157 A93 1c #265 3.75 1.25
OD158 A93 5c #269 .75 .35

On Stamps of 1922-23

OD159 A93 2c #306 12.50 12.50
OD160 A103 5c #309 3.50 1.25
OD161 A94 12c #311 1.25 .40
OD162 A94 20c #312 1.25 .40
Nos. OD159-OD162 (4) 18.50 14.55

On Stamps of 1923

OD163 A104 1c #324 .20 .20
OD164 A104 2c #325 .20 .20
OD165 A104 5c #328 .20 .20
OD166 A104 12c #330 2.00 2.00
OD167 A104 20c #331 .75 .20
Nos. OD163-OD167 (5) 3.35 2.80

On Stamps of 1923-31

OD168 A104 1c #341 .20 .20
OD169 A104 2c #342 .20 .20
OD170 A104 3c #343, II .20 .20
a. Type I 1.25 .30
OD171 A104 5c #345, I .20 .20
a. Type II .20 .20
OD172 A104 10c #346, II .20 .20
OD173 A104 12c #347 .30 .20
OD174 A104 20c #348, II .20 .20
a. Type I .75 .20
OD175 A104 30c #351 .20 .20
Nos. OD168-OD175 (8) 1.70 1.60

Type II
On Stamps of 1935-37

OD176 A129 1c #419 .20 .20
OD177 A130 2c #420 .20 .20
OD178 A132 3c #422 .20 .20
OD178A A134 5c #427 .20 .20
OD179 A137 10c #430 .20 .20
OD180 A139 15c #434 .30 .20
OD181 A140 20c #437 .75 .20
OD182 A140 20c #438 .20 .20
OD182A A142 30c #442 .20 .20
OD182B A145 1p #445 2.00 1.00
OD182C A146 1p #446 .55 .20
Nos. OD176-OD182C (11) 5.00 3.00

Ministry of Justice and Instruction
(M. J. I.)
Type I
On Stamp of 1911

OD183 A88 2c #181 1.25 .20

On Stamps of 1912-14

OD184 A88 1c #190 1.50 .20
OD185 A88 2c #191 1.00 .20
OD186 A88 5c #194 .45 .20
OD187 A88 12c #196 .45 .20
Nos. OD184-OD187 (4) 3.40 .80

On Stamps of 1915-17

OD188 A88 1c #208 .30 .20
OD189 A88 2c #209 .30 .20
OD190 A88 5c #212 1.00 .20
OD191 A91 5c #220 .25 .20
OD192 A92 12c #222 .75 .20
Nos. OD188-OD192 (5) 2.60 1.00

On Stamps of 1917

OD193 A93 1c #232 .25 .20
OD194 A93 2c #233 .75 .20
OD195 A93 5c #236 .25 .20
OD196 A94 12c #238 17.50 5.00
Nos. OD193-OD196 (4) 18.75 5.60

On Stamps of 1918-19

OD197 A93 1c #249 .20 .20
OD198 A93 2c #250 .20 .20
OD199 A93 5c #253 .20 .20
OD200 A94 12c #255 .20 .20
OD201 A94 20c #256 .50 .20
Nos. OD197-OD201 (5) 1.30 1.00

On Stamps of 1920

OD202 A93 1c #265 .25 .20
OD203 A93 2c #266 .20 .20
OD204 A93 5c #269 .20 .20
OD205 A94 12c #271 .40 .20
Nos. OD202-OD205 (4) 1.05 .80

On Stamps of 1922-23

OD206 A93 1c #305 .25 .20
OD207 A93 2c #306 1.50 .50
OD208 A103 5c #309 .25 .20
OD209 A94 12c #311 10.00 1.75
OD210 A94 20c #312 1.50 .35
Nos. OD206-OD210 (5) 13.50 3.00

On Stamp of 1922-23

OD211 A93 2c #318 2.50 2.50

On Stamps of 1923

OD212 A104 1c #324 .20 .20
OD213 A104 2c #325 .20 .20
OD214 A104 5c #328 .20 .20
OD215 A104 12c #330 .20 .20
OD216 A104 20c #331 .50 .20
Nos. OD212-OD216 (5) 1.30 1.00

On Stamps of 1923-31

OD217 A104 ½c #340 2.00 .75
OD218 A104 1c #341, I .20 .20
a. Type II .20 .20
OD219 A104 2c #342 .20 .20
OD220 A104 3c #343, I .20 .20
a. Type II .20 .20
OD221 A104 5c #345, I .20 .20
a. Type II .20 .20
OD222 A104 10c #346, II .20 .20
a. Type I .30 .20
OD223 A104 12c #347, I .20 .20
a. Type II .30 .20
OD224 A104 20c #348, I .20 .20
a. Type II .20 .20
OD225 A104 30c #351 .20 .20
OD226 A105 1p #353 .40 .50
Nos. OD217-OD226 (10) 4.00 2.85

On Stamps of 1926

OD227 A109 5c #359 .20 .20
OD228 A110 12c #360 .20 .20

Type II
On Stamps of 1935-37

OD229 A129 1c #419 .20 .20
OD230 A130 2c #420 .20 .20
OD231 A132 3c #422 .20 .20
OD232 A134 5c #427 .20 .20
OD233 A137 10c #430 .20 .20
OD234 A139 15c #434 .45 .20
OD234A A140 20c #437 .20 .20
OD234B A140 20c #438 .20 .20
OD234C A141 25c #441 .20 .20
OD234D A142 30c #442 .20 .20
OD234E A145 1p #445 1.00 .60
OD234F A146 1p #446 .30 .20
Nos. OD229-OD234F (12) 3.55 2.80

Ministry of Marine
(M. M.)
Type I
On Stamp of 1911

OD235 A88 2c #181 .20 .20

On Stamps of 1912-14

OD236 A88 1c #190 .20 .20
OD237 A88 2c #191 .20 .20
OD238 A88 5c #194 2.00 .20
OD239 A88 12c #196 .20 .20
Nos. OD236-OD239 (4) 2.60 .80

On Stamps of 1915-16

OD240 A88 2c #209 .60 .20
OD241 A88 5c #212 .40 .20

On Stamps of 1917

OD242 A93 1c #232 .20 .20
OD243 A93 2c #233 .20 .20
OD244 A93 5c #236 .20 .20
Nos. OD242-OD244 (3) .60 .60

On Stamps of 1918-19

OD245 A93 1c #249 .20 .20
OD246 A93 2c #250 .20 .20
OD247 A93 5c #253 .25 .20
OD248 A94 12c #255 .25 .20
OD249 A94 20c #256 3.00 .35
Nos. OD245-OD249 (5) 3.90 1.15

On Stamps of 1920

OD250 A93 1c #265 .20 .20
OD251 A93 2c #266 .20 .20
OD252 A93 5c #269 .25 .20
Nos. OD250-OD252 (3) .65 .60

On Stamps of 1922-23

OD253 A103 5c #309 1.00 .20
OD254 A94 12c #311 7.00 7.00
OD255 A94 20c #312 7.00 1.50
Nos. OD253-OD254 (2) 8.00 7.20

On Stamps of 1923

OD256 A104 1c #324 .20 .20
OD257 A104 2c #325 .20 .20
OD258 A104 5c #328 .30 .20
OD259 A104 12c #330 .65 .20
OD260 A104 20c #331 .65 .20
Nos. OD256-OD260 (5) 2.00 1.00

On Stamps of 1923-31

OD261 A104 1c #341 .75 .25
OD262 A104 2c #342 .20 .20
OD263 A104 3c #343 .65 .20
OD264 A104 5c #345, I .20 .20
a. Type II .60 .20
OD265 A104 10c #346 .60 .20
OD266 A104 20c #348, II .60 .20
a. Type I .75 .20
OD267 A104 30c #351 1.00 .20
OD268 A105 1p #353 11.00 3.00
Nos. OD261-OD268 (8) 15.00 4.45

On Stamp of 1926

OD269 A109 5c #359 .50 .20

Type II
On Stamps of 1935-37

OD270 A129 1c #419 .20 .20
OD271 A130 2c #420 .20 .20
OD272 A132 3c #422 .20 .20
OD273 A134 5c #427 .20 .20
OD274 A137 10c #430 .25 .20
OD275 A139 15c #434 .30 .20
OD276 A140 20c #437 .40 .20
OD277 A140 20c #438 .30 .20
OD278 A142 30c #442 .25 .20
OD279 A145 1p #445 3.25 1.00
OD280 A146 1p #446 .75 .20
Nos. OD270-OD280 (11) 6.30 3.00

Ministry of Public Works
(M. O. P.)
Type I
On Stamp of 1911

OD281 A88 2c #181 .30 .20

On Stamps of 1912-14

OD282 A88 1c #190 .30 .20
OD283 A88 5c #194 .20 .20
OD284 A88 12c #196 1.50 .35
Nos. OD282-OD284 (3) 2.00 .75

On Stamps of 1916-19

OD285 A91 5c #220 10.00 1.00
OD286 A94 12c #238 25.00
OD287 A94 20c #256 25.00

On Stamps of 1920

OD288 A93 2c #266 6.00 2.50
OD289 A93 5c #269 2.00 .20
OD290 A94 12c #271 20.00 6.00
Nos. OD288-OD290 (3) 28.00 8.70

On Stamps of 1923

OD291 A104 1c #324 .40 .20
OD292 A104 2c #325 .30 .20
OD293 A104 5c #328 .40 .20
OD294 A104 12c #330 .60 .20
OD295 A104 20c #331 1.00 .20
Nos. OD291-OD295 (5) 2.70 1.00

On Stamps of 1923-31

OD296 A104 1c #341 .20 .20
OD297 A104 2c #342 .20 .20
OD298 A104 3c #343 .20 .20
OD299 A104 5c #345, I .20 .20
a. Type II .20 .20
OD300 A104 10c #346 .20 .20
OD301 A104 12c #347 9.00 1.25
OD302 A104 20c #348, I .20 .20
a. Type II 2.50 .50
OD303 A104 30c #351 .40 .20
OD304 A105 1p #353 20.00 6.00
Nos. OD296-OD304 (9) 30.60 8.65

On Stamp of 1926

OD305 A109 5c #359 .60 .20

Type II
On Stamps of 1935-37

OD306 A129 1c #419 .20 .20
OD307 A130 2c #420 .20 .20
OD308 A132 3c #422 .20 .20
OD309 A134 5c #427 .20 .20
OD310 A137 10c #430 .30 .20
OD311 A139 15c #434 .60 .20
OD312 A140 20c #437 .75 .20
OD313 A140 20c #438 .20 .20
OD314 A142 30c #442 .20 .20
OD315 A144 50c #444 .20 .20
OD316 A145 1p #445 2.00 1.00
OD317 A146 1p #446 .50 .25
Nos. OD306-OD317 (12) 5.55 3.25

Ministry of Foreign Affairs and Religion
(M. R. C.)
Type I
On Stamp of 1911

OD318 A88 2c #181 5.00 1.25

On Stamps of 1912-14

OD319 A88 1c #190 .20 .20
OD320 A88 2c #191 .20 .20
OD321 A88 5c #194 .40 .20
OD322 A88 12c #196 1.50 .25
Nos. OD319-OD322 (4) 2.30 .85

On Stamps of 1915-19

OD323 A88 5c #212 .40 .20
OD324 A91 5c #220 .20 .20
OD325 A94 20c #256 2.00 .75
Nos. OD323-OD325 (3) 2.60 1.15

On Stamps of 1920

OD326 A93 1c #265 .40 .20
OD327 A93 5c #269 .20 .20

On Stamps of 1922-23

OD328 A93 2c #306 9.00 3.50
OD329 A103 5c #309 27.50
OD330 A93 10c #311 22.50
Nos. OD328-OD330 (3) 59.00 3.50

On Stamps of 1923

OD331 A104 1c #324 .20 .20
OD332 A104 2c #325 .20 .20
OD333 A104 5c #328 .20 .20
OD334 A104 12c #330 .20 .20
OD335 A104 20c #331 .20 .20
Nos. OD331-OD335 (5) 1.00 1.00

On Stamps of 1923-31

OD336 A104 ½c #340 1.00 .50
OD337 A104 1c #341 .20 .20
OD338 A104 2c #342 .20 .20
OD339 A104 3c #343 .20 .20
OD340 A104 5c #345 .20 .20
OD341 A104 10c #346, II .20 .20
a. Type I 1.50 .20
OD342 A104 12c #347 .20 .20
OD343 A104 20c #348, I .20 .20
a. Type II .20 .20
OD344 A104 30c #351, I .20 .20
a. Type II .20 .20
OD345 A105 1p #353 .20 .20
Nos. OD336-OD346 (11) 3.20 2.50

On Stamp of 1926

OD346 A110 12c #360 .20 .20

Type II
On Stamps of 1935-37

OD347 A129 1c #419 .20 .20
OD348 A130 2c #420 .20 .20
OD349 A132 3c #422 .20 .20
OD350 A134 5c #427 .20 .20
OD351 A137 10c #430 .20 .20
OD352 A139 15c #434 .20 .20
OD353 A140 20c #437 .20 .20
OD354 A140 20c #438 .20 .20
OD355 A142 30c #442 .20 .20
OD356 A145 1p #445 2.50 1.25
OD357 A146 1p #446 1.00 .50
Nos. OD347-OD357 (11) 5.30 3.55

BUENOS AIRES

The central point of the Argentine struggle for independence. At intervals Buenos Aires maintained an independent government but after 1862 became a province of the Argentine Republic.

8 Reales = 1 Peso

Values of Buenos Aires Nos. 1-8 vary according to condition. Quotations are for fine copies. Very fine to superb specimens sell at much higher prices, and inferior or poor copies sell at reduced values, depending on the condition of the individual specimen.

Nos. 1-8 are normally found without gum, and the values below are for such items. Examples with original gum sell for higher prices.

Steamship — A1

1858 Unwmk. Typo. *Imperf.*

1 A1 1 (in) pesos lt brn *350.* *250.*
On cover *1,800.*
2 A1 2 (dos) pesos blue 175. 140.
On cover 800.
a. 2p indigo 200. *160.*
On cover *1,200.*
b. Diag. half used as 1p on cover *7,500.*
3 A1 3 (tres) pesos grn 1,500. *750.*
On cover 6,000.
a. 3p dark green 1,800. *825.*
On cover 7,500.
4 A1 4 (cuatro) pesos ver 4,750. *2,500.*
On cover *12,500.*
a. Half used as 2p on cover *15,000.*
5 A1 5 (cinco) pesos org 4,750. *2,500.*
On cover *10,000.*
a. 5p ocher 4,750. *2,500.*
On cover *10,000.*
b. 5p olive yellow 4,750. *2,500.*
On cover *10,000.*

Issued: #2-5, Apr. 29; #1, Oct. 26.

1858, Oct. 26

6 A1 4 (cuatro) reales brown 250. 200.
On cover 1,000.
a. 4r gray brown 250. 200.
On cover 1,000.
b. 4r yellow brown 250. 200.
On cover 1,000.

1859, Jan. 1

7 A1 1 (in) pesos blue 160. *225.*
On cover 1,000.
a. 1p indigo 200. *250.*
On cover 1,500.
b. Impression on reverse of stamp in blue *3,000.*
c. Double impression 250. *300.*
d. Vert. tete beche pair *65,000.*
e. Horiz. tete beche pair *45,000.*
f. Half used as 4r on cover *7,500.*
8 A1 1 (to) pesos blue 350. 225.
On cover 2,000.

No. 7e is valued with faults.

Nos. 1, 2, 3 and 7 have been reprinted on very thick, hand-made paper. The same four stamps and No. 8 have been reprinted on thin, hard, white wove paper.

Counterfeits of Nos. 1-8 are plentiful.

Liberty Head — A2

1859, Sept. 3

9 A2 4r green, *bluish* 250.00 160.00
On cover, pair 1,000.
On cover, single franking 2,000.
10 A2 1p blue, fine impression 35.00 17.50
On cover 100.00
a. 1p milky blue, blurred impression 150.00 50.00
On cover 400.00
b. 1p indigo 150.00 50.00
On cover 250.00
c. 1p greenish blue, blurred impression 200.00 75.00
On cover 500.00
d. Double impression 250.00 80.00
On cover 500.00
e. Partial double impression 100.00 40.00
On cover 250.00
11 A2 2p vermilion, fine impression 350.00 160.00
On cover 1,000.
a. 2p red, blurred impression 300.00 125.00
On cover 800.00
b. Vert. half used as 1p on cover *2,000.*

Both fine and blurred impressions of these stamps may be found. They have generally been called Paris and Local prints, respectively, but the opinion now obtains that the differences are due to the impression and that they do not represent separate issues. Values are for fine impressions. Rough or blurred impressions sell for less.

Many shades exist of Nos. 1-11.

1862, Oct. 4

12 A2 1p rose 200.00 100.00
On cover 500.00
13 A2 2p blue 350.00 75.00
On cover 360.00

All three values have been reprinted in black, brownish black, blue and red brown on thin hard white paper. The 4r has also been reprinted in green on bluish paper.

Values are for fine impressions. Rough or blurred impressions sell for less.

CORDOBA

A province in the central part of the Argentine Republic.

100 Centavos = 1 Peso

Arms of Cordoba — A1

Unwmk.

1858, Oct. 28 Litho. *Imperf.*

Laid Paper

1 A1 5c blue 125.
On cover, pen canceled *1,250.*
2 A1 10c black *2,500.*

Cordoba stamps were printed on laid paper, but stamps from edges of the sheets sometimes do not show any laid lines and appear to be on wove paper. Counterfeits are plentiful.

CORRIENTES

The northeast province of the Argentine Republic.

1 Real M(oneda) C(orriente) = 12½ Centavos M.C. = 50 Centavos

100 Centavos Fuertes = 1 Peso Fuerte

Nos. 1-2 were issued without gum. Nos. 3-8 were issued both with and without gum (values the same).

Ceres

A1 A2

Unwmk.

1856, Aug. 21 Typo. *Imperf.*

1 A1 1r black, *blue* 85.00 *175.00*
On cover *450.00*

No. 1 used is valued with pen cancellation.

Pen Stroke Through "Un Real"

1860, Feb. 8

2 A1 (3c) black, *blue* 350.00 *175.00*
On cover *1,250.*

No. 2 used is valued with pen cancellation.

1860-80

3 A2 (3c) black, *blue* 9.50 *30.00*
On cover 150.00
4 A2 (2c) blk, *yel grn*('64) 37.50 37.50
On cover 250.00
a. (2c) black, *blue green* 92.50 110.00
On cover 750.00
5 A2 (2c) blk, *yel*('67) 7.50 *19.00*
On cover 100.00
6 A2 (3c) blk, *dk bl*('71) 3.00 *19.00*
On cover 100.00
7 A2 (3c) blk, *rose red*('76) 100.00 50.00
On cover 275.00
a. (3c) black, *lil rose* ('75) 140.00 80.00
On cover 400.00
8 A2 (3c) blk, *dk rose*('79) 8.00 *32.50*
On cover 200.00
a. (3c) black, *red vio* ('77) 60.00 35.00
On cover 200.00
Nos. 3-8 (6) 165.50 188.00

Pen canceled examples of Nos. 3-8 sell for much less.

Printed from settings of 8 varieties, 3 or 4 impressions constituting a sheet. Some impressions were printed inverted and tete beche pairs may be cut from adjacent impressions.

From Jan. 1 to Feb. 24, 1864, No. 4 was used as a 5 centavos stamp but copies so used can only be distinguished when they bear dated cancellations.

The reprints show numerous spots and small defects which are not found on the originals. They are printed on gray blue, dull blue, gray green, dull orange and light magenta papers.

ARMENIA

är-ˈmē-nē-ə

LOCATION — South of Russia bounded by Georgia, Azerbaijan, Iran and Turkey
GOVT. — Republic
AREA — 11,306 sq. mi.
POP. — 1,109,200
CAPITAL — Yerevan

With Azerbaijan and Georgia, Armenia made up the Transcaucasian Federation of Soviet Republics.

Stamps of Armenia were replaced in 1923 by those of Transcaucasian Federated Republics.

100 Kopecks = 1 Ruble

Counterfeits abound of all overprinted and surcharged stamps.

Watermark

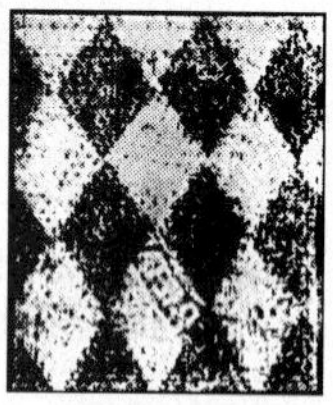

Diamonds — Wmk. 171

Perforations
Perforations are the same as the basic Russian stamps.

National Republic

Russian Stamps of 1902-19 Handstamped

At least thirteen types exist of both framed and unframed overprints ("a" and "c"). The device is the Armenian "H," initial of Hayasdan (Armenia). Inverted and double overprints are found.

Surcharged

Type I — Without periods (two types).
Type II — Periods after 1st "K" and "60."

Black Surcharge

1919 Unwmk. *Perf. 14x14½*

1 A14 60k on 1k orange (II) 2.50 2.50
a. Imperf. (I) 1.00 1.00
b. Imperf. (II) 1.00 1.00

Violet Surcharge

2 A14 60k on 1k orange (II) 1.00 1.00

Handstamped in Violet — a

Perf.

6 A15 4k carmine 3.00 3.00
7 A14 5k claret, imperf. 7.50 7.50
a. Perf. 5.00 5.00
9 A14 10k on 7k lt blue 5.00 5.00
10 A11 15k red brn & bl 3.00 3.00
11 A8 20k blue & car 2.00 2.00
13 A11 35k red brn & grn 4.00 4.00
14 A8 50k violet & green 3.50 3.50
15 A14 60k on 1k orange (II) 3.00 3.00
a. Imperf. (I) 5.00 5.00
b. Imperf. (II) 8.50 9.00
18 A13 5r dk bl, grn & pale bl 15.00 15.00
a. Imperf. 7.50 7.50
19 A12 7r dk green & pink 15.00 15.00
20 A13 10r scar, yel & gray 15.00 15.00

Handstamped in Black

31 A14 2k green, imperf. 1.00 1.00
a. Perf. 5.00 5.00
32 A14 3k red, imperf. 1.00 1.00
a. Perf. 5.00 5.00
33 A15 4k carmine .25 .25
34 A14 5k claret 1.00 1.00
a. Imperf. 5.00 5.00
36 A15 10k dark blue 2.00 .50
37 A14 10k on 7k lt blue .50 .50
38 A11 15k red brn & bl .50 .50
a. Imperf. 3.00 3.00
39 A8 20k blue & car 1.00 1.00
40 A11 25k green & gray vio 1.00 1.00
41 A11 35k red brn & grn 1.00 1.00
42 A8 50k violet & green 1.00 1.00
43 A14 60k on 1k orange (II) 2.50 2.50
43A A11 70k brown & org 1.00 1.00
b. Imperf. .50 .50
44 A9 1r pale brn, dk brn & org 1.50 1.50
a. Imperf. 1.00 1.00
45 A12 3½r mar & lt grn, imperf. 5.00 5.00
a. Perf. 5.00 5.00
46 A13 5r dk bl, grn & pale bl 4.00 4.00
a. Imperf. 6.00 6.00
47 A12 7r dk green & pink 6.00 6.00
48 A13 10r scar, yel & gray 50.00 50.00

Handstamped in Violet — c

Unwmk. *Perf.*
Wove Paper

62 A14 2k green, imperf. 10.00 10.00
a. Perf. 15.00 15.00
63 A14 3k red, imperf. 2.00 2.00
a. Perf. 10.00 10.00
64 A15 4k carmine 5.00 5.00
65 A14 5k claret 3.00 3.00
a. Imperf. 3.00 3.00
67 A15 10k dark blue 3.00 3.00
68 A14 10k on 7k lt bl 10.00 10.00
69 A11 15k red brn & bl 2.50 2.50
70 A8 20k blue & car 2.00 2.00
71 A11 25k grn & gray vio 2.00 2.00
72 A11 35k red brn & grn 2.00 2.00
73 A8 50k violet & grn 2.00 2.00
74 A14 60k on 1k org (II) 3.00 3.00
a. Imperf. (I) 3.00 3.00
b. Imperf. (II) 3.00 3.00
75 A9 1r pale brn, dk brn & org 2.00 2.00
a. Imperf. 2.00 2.00
76 A12 3½r mar & lt grn, imperf. 4.00 4.00
a. Perf. 5.00 5.00
77 A13 5r dk bl, grn & pale bl, imperf. 5.00 5.00
a. Perf. 4.00 4.00
78 A12 7r dk green & pink 10.00 10.00
79 A13 10r scar, yel & gray 10.00 10.00

Imperf

85 A11 70k brown & org 5.00 5.00

Handstamped in Black

Perf.

90 A14 1k orange 10.00 10.00
a. Imperf. 10.00 10.00
91 A14 2k green, imperf. 1.00 1.00
a. Perf. 7.50 7.50
92 A14 3k red, imperf. 1.00 1.00
a. Perf. 10.00 10.00
93 A15 4k carmine .50 .50
94 A14 5k claret 1.00 1.00
a. Imperf. 3.00 3.00
95 A14 7k light blue 15.00 15.00
96 A15 10k dark blue 12.00 12.00
97 A14 10k on 7k lt bl .50 .50
98 A11 15k red brn & bl .50 .50
99 A8 20k blue & car .50 .50
100 A11 25k grn & gray vio .50 .50
101 A11 35k red brn & grn .50 .50
102 A8 50k violet & grn .50 .50
102A A14 60k on 1k org, imperf. (I) .50 .50
b. Imperf. (II) .50 .50
c. Perf. (II) 2.50 2.50
103 A9 1r pale brn, dk brn & org 1.00 1.00
a. Imperf. 1.00 1.00
104 A12 3½r maroon & lt grn 4.00 4.00
a. Imperf. 5.00 5.00
105 A13 5r dk bl, grn & pale bl 10.00 10.00
a. Imperf. 5.00 5.00
106 A12 7r dk green & pink 3.00 3.00
107 A13 10r scar, yel & gray 25.00 25.00

Imperf

113 A11 70k brown & org 2.00 2.00

Handstamped in Violet or Black:

f

g

Violet Surcharge, Type f

1920 *Perf.*

120 A14 3r on 3k red, imperf. 5.00 5.00
a. Perf. 2.50 2.50
121 A14 5r on 3k red 4.00 4.00
122 A15 5r on 4k car 10.00 10.00
123 A14 5r on 5k claret, imperf. 10.00 10.00
a. Perf. 10.00 10.00
124 A15 5r on 10k dk blue 10.00 10.00
125 A14 5r on 10k on 7k lt bl 10.00 10.00
126 A8 5r on 20k bl & car

Imperf

127 A14 5r on 2k green 10.00 10.00
128 A11 5r on 35k red brn & grn 10.00 10.00

Black Surcharge, Type f or Type g (#130)

Perf.

130 A14 1r on 1k orange .50 .50
a. Imperf. .75 .75
131 A14 3r on 3k red .25 .25
a. Imperf. .25 .25
132 A15 3r on 4k carmine 10.00 10.00
133 A14 5r on 2k grn, imperf. 2.00 2.00
a. Perf. .25 .25
134 A14 5r on 3k red 10.00 10.00
a. Imperf. 2.50 2.50
135 A15 5r on 4k carmine 2.00 2.00
a. Imperf. .25 .25
136 A14 5r on 5k claret .50 .50
a. Imperf. .50 .50
137 A14 5r on 7k lt blue 2.00 2.00
138 A15 5r on 10k dk blue .50 .50
139 A14 5r on 10k on 7k lt bl .50 .50
140 A11 5r on 14k bl & rose 2.00 2.00
141 A11 5r on 15k red brn & blue .50 .50
a. Imperf. 2.00 2.00
142 A8 5r on 20k bl & car .50 .50
a. Imperf. 10.00 10.00
143 A11 5r on 20k on 14k bl & rose 12.00 12.00
144 A11 5r on 25k grn & gray vio 12.00 12.00

Black Surcharge, Type g or Type f (#148A, 151)

145 A14 10r on 1k org, imperf. .90 .90
a. Perf. *225.00 225.00*
146 A14 10r on 3k red *175.00 175.00*
147 A14 10r on 5k claret 15.00 15.00
a. Imperf. 6.00
148 A8 10r on 20k bl & car 15.00 15.00
148A A11 10r on 25k grn & gray vio 8.00 8.00
149 A11 10r on 25k grn & gray vio 5.00 5.00
a. Imperf. 8.00 8.00
150 A11 10r on 35k red brn & grn .50 .50
151 A8 10r on 50k brn vio & grn 10.00 10.00
152 A8 10r on 50k brn vio & grn 1.00 1.00
152A A11 10r on 70k brn & org, imperf. 3.00 3.00
b. Perf. *200.00 200.00*
152C A8 25r on 20k bl & car 4.00 4.00
153 A11 25r on 25k grn & gray vio 2.00 2.00
154 A11 25r on 35k red brn & grn 2.00 2.00
a. Imperf. 3.50 3.50
155 A8 25r on 50k vio & grn 4.00 4.00
a. Imperf. 5.00 5.00
156 A11 25r on 70k brn & org 8.00 8.00
a. Imperf. 5.00 5.00
157 A9 50r on 1r pale brn, dk brn & org, imperf. 1.00 1.00
a. Perf. 5.00 5.00
158 A13 50r on 5r dk bl, grn & lt bl 10.00 10.00
a. Imperf. 10.00 10.00
159 A12 100r on 3½r mar & lt grn 7.00 7.00
a. Imperf. 7.00 7.00
160 A13 100r on 5r dk bl, grn & pale bl 10.00 10.00
a. Imperf. 7.00 7.00
161 A12 100r on 7r dk grn & pink 10.00 10.00
a. Imperf. 35.00 35.00
162 A13 100r on 10r scar, yel & gray 10.00 10.00

Wmk. Wavy Lines (168)
Perf. 11½
Vertically Laid Paper

163 A12 100r on 3½r blk & gray *100.00 100.00*
164 A12 100r on 7r blk & yel *100.00 100.00*

1920 Unwmk. *Imperf.*
Wove Paper

166 A14 (g) 1r on 60k on 1k org (I) 12.00 12.00
168 A14 (f) 5r on 1k orange 10.00 10.00
173 A11 (f) 5r on 35k red brn & grn 5.00 5.00
177 A11 (g) 50r on 70k brn & org 5.00 5.00
179 A12 (g) 50r on 3½r mar & lt grn 2.00 2.00
181 A9 (g) 100r on 1r pale brn, dk brn & org 10.00 10.00

Romanov Issues Surcharged Type g or Type f (#185-187, 190)
On Stamps of 1913

1920 *Perf. 13½*

184 A16 1r on 1k brn org 20.00 20.00
185 A18 3r on 3k rose red 20.00 20.00
186 A19 5r on 4k dull red 10.00 10.00
187 A22 5r on 14k blue grn 60.00 60.00
187A A19 10r on 4k dull red 30.00
187B A26 10r on 35k gray vio & dk grn
187C A19 25r on 4k dull red 10.00 10.00
188 A26 25r on 35k gray vio & dk grn 2.75 2.75
189 A28 25r on 70k yel grn & brn 2.75 2.75
190 A31 50r on 3r dk vio 2.00 2.00
190A A16 100r on 1k brn org 100.00 100.00
190B A17 100r on 2k green 100.00 100.00
191 A30 100r on 2r brown 10.50 10.50
192 A31 100r on 3r dk vio 10.50 10.50

On Stamps of 1915, Type g
Thin Cardboard
Inscriptions on Back
Perf. 12

193 A21 100r on 10k blue 10.00
194 A23 100r on 15k brn 10.00
195 A24 100r on 20k ol grn 15.00

On Stamps of 1916, Type f
Perf. 13½

196 A20 5r on 10k on 7k brown 5.00 5.00
197 A22 5r on 20k on 14k bl grn 8.00 8.00

Surch. Type f or Type g (#204-205A, 207-207C, 210-211) over Type c
Type c in Violet
Perf.

200 A15 5r on 4k car 3.00 3.00
201 A15 5r on 10k dk bl 3.00 3.00
202 A11 5r on 15k red brn & bl 5.00 5.00
203 A8 5r on 20k blue & car 5.00 5.00
204 A11 10r on 25k grn & gray vio 10.00 10.00
205 A11 10r on 35k red brn & grn 3.00 3.00
205A A8 10r on 50k brn vio & grn 10.00 10.00
206 A8 25r on 50k brn vio & grn 150.00 150.00
207 A9 50r on 1r pale brn, dk brn & org, imperf. 3.50 3.50
a. Perf. 25.00 25.00
207B A12 100r on 3½r mar & lt grn 30.00
207C A12 100r on 7r dk grn & pink 9.00

Imperf

208 A14 5r on 2k green 25.00 25.00
209 A14 5r on 5k claret 25.00 25.00
210 A11 25r on 70k brn & org 25.00 25.00
211 A13 100r on 5r dk bl, grn & pale bl 2.00 2.00

Surcharged Type g or Type f (212-213, 215, 219-219A, 221-222) over Type c
Type c in Black
Perf.

212 A14 5r on 7k lt bl 150.00 150.00
213 A14 5r on 10k on 7k lt bl 5.00 5.00
214 A11 5r on 15k red brn & bl 1.00 1.00
215 A8 5r on 20k blue & car 3.00 3.00

215A	A11	10r on 5r on 25k grn & gray vio	5.00	5.00
216	A11	10r on 35k red brn & grn	2.00	2.00
217	A8	10r on 50k brn vio & grn	3.00	3.00
217A	A9	50r on 1r pale brn, dk brn & org	25.00	25.00
b.		Imperf.	2.00	2.00
217C	A12	100r on 3½r mar & lt grn	25.00	25.00
218	A13	100r on 5r dk bl, grn & pale bl	10.00	10.00
a.		Imperf.	2.00	2.00
219	A12	100r on 7r dk grn & pink	15.00	15.00
219A	A13	100r on 10r scar, yel & gray	10.00	10.00

Imperf

220	A14	1r on 60k on 1k org (I)	20.00	20.00
221	A14	5r on 2k green	5.00	5.00
222	A14	5r on 5k claret	5.00	5.00
223	A11	10r on 70k brn & org	10.00	10.00
224	A11	25r on 70k brn & org	3.00	3.00

Surcharged Type g or Type f (#233) over Type a

Type a in Violet

Imperf

231	A9	50r on 1r pale brn, dk brn & org	140.00	140.00
232	A13	100r on 5r dk bl, grn & pale bl	10.50	

Type a in Black

Perf.

233	A8	5r on 20k blue & car	5.00	5.00
233A	A11	10r on 25k grn & gray vio	55.00	55.00
234	A11	10r on 35k red brn & grn	200.00	200.00
235	A12	100r on 3½r mar & lt grn	5.00	5.00
a.		Imperf.	5.00	5.00

Imperf

237	A14	5r on 2k green	125.00	125.00
237A	A11	10r on 70k brn & org		

Surcharged Type a and New Value

Type a in Violet

Perf.

238	A11	10r on 15k red brn & blue	25.00	25.00

Type a in Black

239	A8	5r on 20k blue & car	3.00	3.00
239A	A8	10r on 20k blue & car	3.00	3.00
239B	A8	10r on 50k brn red & grn	20.00	

Imperf

240	A12	100r on 3½r mar & lt grn	15.00	15.00

Surcharged Type c and New Value

Type c in Black

1920 ***Perf.***

241	A15	5r on 4k red	5.00	5.00
242	A11	5r on 15k red brn & bl	3.00	3.00
243	A8	10r on 20k blue & car	5.00	5.00
243A	A11	10r on 25k grn & gray vio	3.00	3.00
244	A11	10r on 35k red brn & grn	3.00	3.00
a.		With additional surch. "5r"	5.00	5.00
245	A12	100r on 3½r mar & lt grn	5.00	5.00

Imperf

247	A14	3r on 3k red	7.00	7.00
248	A14	5r on 2k green	5.00	5.00
249	A9	50r on 1r pale brn, dk brn & org	5.00	5.00

Type c in Violet

249A	A14	5r on 2k green	6.50	

Postal Savings Stamps Surcharged

A1

A2

A3

Perf. 14½x15

Wmk. 171

250	A1	60k on 1k red & buff	50.00	50.00
251	A2	1r on 1k red & buff	50.00	50.00
252	A3	5r on 5k green & buff	50.00	50.00
253	A3	5r on 10k brn & buff	50.00	50.00

Russian Semi-Postal Stamps of 1914-18 Surcharged with Armenian Monogram and New Values like Regular Issues

On Stamps of 1914

Unwmk. ***Perf.***

255	SP5	25r on 1k red brn & dk grn, *straw*	60.00	60.00
256	SP5	25r on 3k mar & gray grn, *pink*	60.00	60.00
257	SP5	50r on 7 dk brn & dk grn, *buff*	75.00	75.00
258	SP5	100r on 1k red brn & dk grn, *straw*	75.00	75.00
259	SP5	100r on 3k mar & gray grn, *pink*	75.00	75.00
260	SP5	100r on 7k dk brn & dk grn, *buff*	75.00	75.00

On Stamps of 1915-19

261	SP5	25r on 1k org brn & gray	75.00	75.00
262	SP5	25r on 3k car & gray	75.00	75.00
263	SP5	50r on 10k dk bl & brn	25.00	25.00
264	SP5	100r on 1k org brn & gray	75.00	75.00
265	SP5	100r on 10k dk bl & brn	75.00	75.00

These surcharged semi-postal stamps were used for ordinary postage.

A set of 10 stamps in the above designs was prepared in 1920, but not issued for postal use, though some were used fiscally. Value of set, $10. Exist imperf with "SPECIMEN" overprint. Value of set, $15. Reprints exist.

Soviet Socialist Republic

Hammer and Sickle — A7

Mythological Monster — A8

Symbols of Soviet Republics on Designs from old Armenian Manuscripts A9

Ruined City of Ani — A10

Mythological Monster — A11

Armenian Soldier — A12

Soviet Symbols, Armenian Designs — A14

Mythological Monster A13

Mt. Alagöz and Plain of Shirak A15

Fisherman on River Aras — A16

Post Office in Erevan and Mt. Ararat A17

Ruin in City of Ani — A18

Street in Erevan — A19

Lake Sevan and Sevan Monastery — A20

Mythological Subject from old Armenian Monument — A21

Mt. Ararat — A22

1921 Unwmk. ***Perf. 11½, Imperf.***

278	A7	1r gray green	.50	
279	A8	2r slate gray	.50	
280	A9	3r carmine	.50	
281	A10	5r dark brown	.50	
282	A11	25r gray	.50	.50
283	A12	50r red	.30	
284	A13	100r orange	.30	
285	A14	250r dark blue	.30	
286	A15	500r brown vio	.30	
287	A16	1000r sea green	.40	
288	A17	2000r bister	1.75	
289	A18	5000r dark brown	1.00	
290	A19	10,000r dull red	1.00	
291	A20	15,000r slate blue	1.25	
292	A21	20,000r lake	1.50	
293	A22	25,000r gray blue	2.00	
294	A22	25,000r brown olive	8.00	
		Nos. 278-294 (17)	20.60	

Except the 25r, Nos. 278-294 were not regularly issued and used. Counterfeits exist.

For surcharges see Nos. 347-390.

Russian Stamps of 1909-17 Surcharged

Wove Paper

Lozenges of Varnish on Face

1921, Aug. ***Perf. 13½***

295	A9	5000r on 1r	*10.00*
296	A12	5000r on 3½r	*10.00*
297	A13	5000r on 5r	*10.00*
298	A12	5000r on 7r	*10.00*
299	A13	5000r on 10r	*10.00*
		Nos. 295-299 (5)	*50.00*

Nos. 295-299 were not officially issued. Counterfeits abound.

A23

Mt. Ararat & Soviet Star — A24

Soviet Symbols — A25

Crane — A26

Peasant — A27

Harpy — A28

Peasant Sowing — A29

Soviet Symbols — A30

Forging — A31

Plowing A32

1922 ***Perf. 11½***

300	A23	50r green & red	.85
301	A24	300r slate bl & buff	1.00
302	A25	400r blue & pink	1.00
303	A26	500r vio & pale lil	1.00
304	A27	1000r dull bl & pale bl	1.00
305	A28	2000r black & gray	1.25
306	A29	3000r black & grn	1.25
307	A30	4000r black & lt brn	1.25
308	A31	5000r blk & dull red	1.25
309	A32	10,000r black & pale rose	1.25
a.		Tête bêche pair	35.00
		Nos. 300-309 (10)	11.10

Nos. 300-309 were not issued without surcharge.

Stamps of types A23 to A32, printed in other colors than Nos. 300 to 309, are essays.

Nos. 300-309 with Handstamped Surcharge of New Values in Rose, Violet or Black

1922

310	10,000 on 50r (R)	*75.00*	*75.00*
311	10,000 on 50r (V)	*50.00*	*50.00*
312	10,000 on 50r	*25.00*	*25.00*
313	15,000 on 300r (R)	*100.00*	*100.00*
314	15,000 on 300r (V)	*75.00*	*75.00*
315	15,000 on 300r	*25.00*	*25.00*
316	25,000 on 400r (V)	*50.00*	*50.00*
317	25,000 on 400r	*25.00*	*25.00*
318	30,000 on 500r (R)	*100.00*	*100.00*
319	30,000 on 500r (V)	*50.00*	*50.00*
320	30,000 on 500r	*25.00*	*25.00*
321	50,000 on 1000r (R)	*100.00*	*100.00*
322	50,000 on 1000r (V)	*50.00*	*50.00*
323	50,000 on 1000r	*15.00*	*15.00*
324	75,000 on 3000r	*25.00*	*25.00*
325	100,000 on 2000r (R)	*100.00*	*100.00*
326	100,000 on 2000r (V)	*50.00*	*50.00*
327	100,000 on 2000r	*5.00*	*5.00*
328	200,000 on 4000r (V)	*10.00*	*10.00*
329	200,000 on 4000r	*10.00*	*10.00*
330	300,000 on 5000r (V)	*50.00*	*50.00*
331	300,000 on 5000r	*5.00*	*5.00*
332	500,000 on 10,000r (V)	*50.00*	*50.00*
333	500,000 on 10,000r	*10.00*	*10.00*
	Nos. 310-333 (24)	*1,080.*	*1,080.*

Forgeries exist.

Goose — A33

Armenian Woman at Well — A35

Armenian Village Scene A34

Mt. Ararat A36

Mt. Ararat A37

New Values in Gold Kopecks, Handstamped Surcharge in Black

1922 ***Imperf.***

334	A33	1(k) on 250r rose	15.00	15.00
335	A33	1(k) on 250r gray	20.00	20.00
336	A34	2(k) on 500r rose	8.00	8.00
337	A34	3(k) on 500r gray	8.00	8.00
338	A35	4(k) on 1000r rose	8.00	8.00
339	A35	4(k) on 1000r gray	15.00	15.00
340	A36	5(k) on 2000r gray	8.00	8.00
341	A36	10(k) on 2000r rose	8.00	8.00
342	A37	15(k) on 5000r rose	52.50	52.50
343	A37	20(k) on 5000r gray	8.00	8.00
		Nos. 334-343 (10)	150.50	150.50

Nos. 334-343 were issued for postal tax purposes.

Nos. 334-343 exist without surcharge but are not known to have been issued in that condition. Counterfeits exist of both sets.

Regular Issue of 1921 Handstamped with New Values in Black or Red

Short, Thick Numerals

1922 ***Imperf.***

347	A8	2(k) on 2r (R)	50.00	50.00
350	A11	4(k) on 25r (R)	30.00	30.00
353	A13	10(k) on 100r (R)	20.00	20.00
354	A14	15(k) on 250r	3.00	3.00
355	A15	20(k) on 500r	15.00	15.00
a.		With "k" written in red	10.00	10.00
357	A22	50(k) on 25,000r bl (R)	25.00	25.00
358	A22	50(k) on 25,000r brn ol (R)	125.00	125.00
359	A22	50(k) on 25,000r brn ol		
		Nos. 347-358 (7)	268.00	268.00

Perf. 11½

360	A7	1(k) on 1r, imperf.	*35.00*	*35.00*
a.		Perf.	*15.00*	*15.00*
361	A7	1(k) on 1r (R)	*35.00*	*35.00*
a.		Imperf.	*40.00*	*40.00*
362	A8	2(k) on 2r, imperf.	*40.00*	*40.00*
a.		Perf.	*40.00*	*40.00*
363	A15	2(k) on 500r	*50.00*	*50.00*
a.		Imperf.	*50.00*	*50.00*
364	A15	2(k) on 500r (R)	125.00	125.00
365	A11	4(k) on 25r, imperf.	*25.00*	*25.00*
a.		Perf.	*25.00*	*25.00*
366	A12	5(k) on 50r, imperf.	20.00	30.00
a.		Perf.	*25.00*	*25.00*
367	A13	10(k) on 100r	*20.00*	*20.00*
a.		Imperf.	*20.00*	*20.00*
368	A21	35(k) on 20,000r, imperf.	*75.00*	*75.00*
a.		With "k" written in violet	*75.00*	*75.00*
b.		Perf.	*75.00*	*75.00*
c.		As "a," perf.	*75.00*	*75.00*
d.		With "kop" written in violet, imperf.		
		Nos. 360-368 (9)	*425.00*	*435.00*

Manuscript Surcharge in Red

Perf. 11½

371	A14	1k on 250r dk bl	*40.00*	*40.00*

Handstamped in Black or Red

Tall, Thin Numerals

Imperf

377	A11	4(k) on 25r (R)	4.25	4.25
379	A13	10(k) on 100r	75.00	75.00
380	A15	20(k) on 500r	6.00	6.00
381	A22	50k on 25,000r bl	*75.00*	*75.00*
a.		Surcharged "50" only	50.00	50.00
382	A22	50k on 25,000r bl (R)	12.00	12.00
382A	A22	50k on 25,000r brn ol	24.00	24.00
		Nos. 377-382A (6)	*196.25*	*196.25*

On Nos. 381, 382 and 382A the letter "k" forms part of the surcharge.

Perf. 11½

383	A7	1(k) on 1r (R)	*40.00*	*40.00*
a.		Imperf.		
384	A14	1(k) on 250r	50.00	50.00
385	A15	2(k) on 500r	8.00	8.00
a.		Imperf.	20.00	20.00
386	A15	2(k) on 500r (R)	20.00	20.00
387	A9	3(k) on 3r	20.00	20.00
a.		Imperf.	20.00	20.00
388	A21	3(k) on 20,000r, imperf.	10.00	10.00
a.		Perf.	50.00	50.00
389	A11	4(k) on 25r	25.00	25.00
a.		Imperf.	100.00	100.00
390	A12	5(k) on 50r, imperf.	*10.00*	*10.00*
a.		Perf.	*15.00*	*15.00*
		Nos. 383-390 (8)	*183.00*	*183.00*

ASCENSION

ə-'sen,t,-shən

LOCATION — An island in the South Atlantic Ocean, 900 miles from Liberia

GOVT. — A part of the British Crown Colony of St. Helena

AREA — 34 sq. mi.

POP. — 188 (1931 census)

In 1922 Ascension was placed under the administration of the Colonial Office and annexed to the British Crown Colony of St. Helena. The only post office is at Georgetown.

12 Pence = 1 Shilling
20 Shillings = 1 Pound

STAMPS OF GREAT BRITAIN USED IN ASCENSION

Stamps of Great Britain with clearly legible circular or oval datestamps of Ascension.

1855-86

A1	1p red brown (#16), *from*	*5,000.*
A2	6p lilac, (#27)	—
A3	1p rose red (#33), *from*	*2,250.*
A4	6p lilac (#45, P5), *from*	*5,000.*
A5	1sh green (#48)	—
A6	1sh green (#54, P7)	—
A7	6p gray (#62, P15, 16), *from*	*4,250.*
A8	1p lilac (#89), *from*	55.00
A9	6p on 6p violet (#95)	—

Values for Nos. A1-A7 are for complete covers with the Great Britain stamps canceled on arrival in England and with an Ascension postmark struck elsewhere on the cover.

No. A3 exists with plate numbers 71, 74, 76, 78, 83, 85, 96, 100, 102-104, 122, 134, 154, 155, 157, 160, 168, 178. Value is for the most common plate numbers.

1887-92 **Victoria Jubilee**

A10	½p ver (#111)	82.50
A11	1½p vio & grn (#112)	390.00
A12	2p grn & car rose (#113)	180.00
A13	2½p vio, *blue* (#114)	85.00
A14	3p vio, *yel* (#115)	365.00
A15	4p brn & grn (#116)	275.00
A16	4½p car rose & grn (#117)	675.00
A17	5p lil & bl (#118)	275.00
A18	6p vio, *rose* (#119)	210.00
A19	9p bl & lil (#120)	550.00
A20	10p car rose & lil (#121)	725.00
A21	1sh green (#122)	625.00

1900

A22	½p blue grn (#125)	82.50
A23	1sh car rose & green (#126)	675.00

1902-11 **King Edward VII**

A24	½p gray grn (#127)	55.00
A25	1p carmine (#128)	25.00
	On cover	175.00
A26	1½p vio & grn (#129)	190.00
A27	2p grn & car (#130)	125.00
A28	2½p ultra (#131)	125.00
A29	3p vio, *yel* (#132)	190.00
A30	4p brn & grn (#133)	550.00
A31	4p orange (#144)	210.00
A32	5p lil & ultra (#134)	200.00
A33	6p dull vio (#135)	190.00
A34	7p gray (#145)	350.00
A35	9p ultra & vio (#136)	350.00
A36	10p car rose & vio (#137)	450.00
A37	1sh car rose & green (#138)	125.00
A38	2sh 6p dull vio (#139)	800.00
A39	5sh car rose (#140)	1,050.
A40	10sh ultra (#141)	*1,750.*
A41	£1 green (#142)	*4,500.*

Only one example is known of No. 41.

1911-12 **King George V**

A42	½p green (#151)	105.00
A43	½p yel grn (#153)	87.50
A44	1p scarlet (#154)	62.50

1912

A45		½p green (#157)	62.50	
A46		1p scarlet (#158)	62.50	

1912-22

A47		½p green (#159)	47.50	
A48		1p scarlet (#160)	27.50	
		On cover	175.00	
A49		1½p red brn (#161)	67.50	
A50		2p org, die 1 (#162)	55.00	
a.		Die II (#162a)	475.00	
A51		2½p ultra (#163)	77.50	
A52		3p bluish vio (#164)	100.00	
A53		4p slate grn (#165)	140.00	
A54		5p yel brn (#166)	140.00	
A55		6p rose lil (#167)	110.00	
A56		7p olive grn (#168)	450.00	
A57		8p black, *yel* (#169)	475.00	
A58		9p blk brn (#170)	425.00	
A59		9p olive grn (#183)	950.00	
A60		10p lt blue (#171)	425.00	
A61		1sh bister (#172)	150.00	
A62		2sh 6p gray brn (#179)	1,100.	
A63		5sh car rose (#180)	*1,800.*	

Catalogue values for unused stamps in this country are for Never Hinged items, beginning with Scott 50.

Stamps and Types of St. Helena, 1912-22 Overprinted in Black or Red

1922 Wmk. 4 *Perf. 14*

1	A9	½p green & blk	5.50	*22.50*
		On cover		*110.00*
2	A10	1p green	5.50	*20.00*
		On cover		*110.00*
3	A10	1½p rose red	19.00	*55.00*
		On cover		*325.00*
4	A9	2p gray & blk	19.00	15.00
		On cover		*110.00*
5	A9	3p ultra	14.50	*22.50*
		On cover		*110.00*
6	A10	8p dl vio & blk	30.00	*55.00*
		On cover		*190.00*
7	A10	2sh ultra & blk, *blue*	100.00	*140.00*
		On cover		*225.00*
8	A10	3sh vio & blk	150.00	*180.00*
		On cover		*265.00*

Wmk. 3

9	A9	1sh blk, *gray grn* (R)	32.50	*55.00*
		On cover		*275.00*
		Nos. 1-9 (9)	376.00	*565.00*
		Set, never hinged	600.00	
		Set, overprinted "SPECIMEN"	800.00	

Covers: Values for Nos. 7-8 on covers are for overfranked covers, usually philatelic.

All values are known with forged cancellations, many of them dated "MY 24 23."

Nos. 1, 4, 6 and 8 are from special printings, made expressly to be overprinted, and do not exist without overprint.

Seal of Colony — A3

1924-33 Typo. Wmk. 4 *Perf. 14*

Chalky Paper

10	A3	½p black & gray	4.00	*16.00*
11	A3	1p green & blk	6.25	*11.00*
a.		1p br bl grn & gray blk ('33)	110.00	*525.00*
12	A3	1½p rose red	8.50	*32.50*
13	A3	2p bluish gray & gray	18.00	10.00
14	A3	3p ultra	9.00	*17.00*
15	A3	4p blk & gray, *yel*	55.00	*90.00*
16	A3	5p ol & lil ('27)	11.00	*25.00*
17	A3	6p rose lil & gray	55.00	*110.00*
18	A3	8p violet & gray	17.50	*47.50*
19	A3	1sh brown & gray	22.50	*57.50*
20	A3	2sh ultra & gray, *blue*	62.50	*100.00*
21	A3	3sh blk & gray, *blue*	90.00	*100.00*
		Nos. 10-21 (12)	359.25	*616.50*

Set, never hinged	600.00
Set, overprinted "SPECIMEN"	725.00

View of Georgetown — A4

Map of Ascension — A5

Sooty Tern Breeding Colony A9

Designs: 1½p, Pier at Georgetown. 3p, Long Beach. 5p, Three Sisters. 5sh, Green Mountain.

1934, July 2 **Engr.**

23	A4	½p violet & blk	1.00	1.00
24	A5	1p lt grn & blk	2.00	1.40
25	A4	1½p red & black	2.00	*2.50*
26	A5	2p org & black	2.00	*2.75*
27	A4	3p ultra & blk	2.00	1.75
28	A4	5p blue & black	2.50	*3.75*
29	A5	8p dk brn & blk	5.00	*5.50*
30	A9	1sh carmine & blk	20.00	9.00
31	A5	2sh6p violet & blk	50.00	40.00
32	A4	5sh brown & blk	57.50	*65.00*
		Nos. 23-32 (10)	144.00	*132.65*
		Set, never hinged	200.00	
		Set, perforated "SPECIMEN"	425.00	

Common Design Types pictured following the introduction.

Silver Jubilee Issue

Common Design Type

1935, May 6 ***Perf. 11x12***

33	CD301	1½p car & dk blue	4.00	*9.00*
34	CD301	2p blk & ultra	12.50	*27.50*
35	CD301	5p ind & grn	19.00	*30.00*
36	CD301	1sh brn vio & indigo	27.50	*32.50*
		Nos. 33-36 (4)	63.00	*99.00*
		Set, never hinged	90.00	
		Set, perforated "SPECIMEN"	300.00	

25th anniv. of the reign of King George V.

Coronation Issue

Common Design Type

1937, May 19 ***Perf. 13½x14***

37	CD302	1p deep green	.75	1.50
38	CD302	2p deep orange	.60	.65
39	CD302	3p bright ultra	.60	.60
		Nos. 37-39 (3)	1.95	*2.75*
		Set, never hinged	3.50	
		Set, perforated "SPECIMEN"	275.00	

Georgetown — A11

Designs: No. 41, 41A, 2p, 4p, Green Mountain. No. 41D, 6p, 10sh, Three Sisters. 1½p, 2sh6p, Pier at Georgetown. 3p, 5sh, Long Beach.

Perf. 13, 13½ (#41, 44, 45), 14 (#43C)

1938-53

Center in Black

40	A11	½p violet ('44)	.35	*1.75*
		Never hinged	.65	
a.		Perf. 13½	1.75	1.25
		Never hinged	3.50	
41	A11	1p green	20.00	7.75
		Never hinged	37.50	
41A	A11	1p org yel, ('42)	.25	*.60*
		Never hinged	.45	
b.		Perf. 14 ('49)	.40	*15.00*
		Never hinged	.70	
c.		Perf. 13½	7.00	*8.75*
		Never hinged	13.50	
41D	A11	1p green ('49)	.45	*1.25*
		Never hinged	.75	
42	A11	1½p red, ('44)	.45	*.80*
		Never hinged	.85	
a.		Perf. 14 ('49)	1.30	*12.50*
		Never hinged	2.50	
b.		Perf. 13½	2.50	1.40
		Never hinged	4.50	
42C	A11	1½p lilac rose ('53)	.35	*8.25*
		Never hinged	.60	
d.		Perf. 14 ('49)	.40	*1.00*
		Never hinged	.70	
e.		1½p carmine, perf 14	5.25	6.50
		Never hinged	9.00	
43	A11	2p orange ('44)	.40	.40
		Never hinged	.80	
a.		Perf. 14 ('49)	1.50	*35.00*
		Never hinged	2.00	
b.		Perf. 13½	2.00	1.00
		Never hinged	3.75	
43C	A11	2p red ('49)	.75	2.00
		Never hinged	1.25	
44	A11	3p ultra	55.00	26.00
		Never hinged	95.00	
44A	A11	3p black, ('44)	.35	*.80*
		Never hinged	.70	
c.		Perf. 13½ ('40)	10.00	.90
		Never hinged	17.50	
44B	A11	4p ultra, ('44)	2.25	3.00
		Never hinged	4.50	
d.		Perf. 13½	8.00	3.25
		Never hinged	15.00	
45	A11	6p gray blue	4.50	1.50
		Never hinged	8.75	
a.		Perf. 13 ('44)	4.50	4.75
		Never hinged	8.75	
46	A11	1sh dk brn ('44)	3.25	2.00
		Never hinged	4.75	
a.		Perf. 13½	9.00	1.90
		Never hinged	16.00	
47	A11	2sh6p car ('44)	19.00	*35.00*
		Never hinged	30.00	
a.		Perf. 13½	29.00	10.50
		Never hinged	45.00	
b.		Frame printed doubly, one albino	*2,250.*	
		Never hinged	*3,250.*	
48	A11	5sh yel brn ('44)	25.00	26.00
		Never hinged	40.00	
a.		Perf. 13½	52.50	8.25
		Never hinged	100.00	
49	A11	10sh red vio ('44)	45.00	*52.50*
		Never hinged	62.50	
a.		Perf. 13½	55.00	45.00
		Never hinged	110.00	
b.		10sh brt analine red pur, perf 13	55.00	40.00
		Never hinged	110.00	
		Nos. 40-49 (16)	177.35	*169.60*
		Set, Never hinged	357.85	

Catalogue values for unused stamps in this section, from this point to the end of the section, are for Never Hinged items.

Peace Issue

Common Design Type

Perf. 13½x14

1946, Oct. 21 **Engr.** **Wmk. 4**

50	CD303	2p deep orange	.45	1.10
51	CD303	4p deep blue	.45	.65
		Set, perforated "SPECIMEN"	250.00	

Silver Wedding Issue

Common Design Types

1948, Oct. 20 Photo. ***Perf. 14x14½***

52	CD304	3p black	.55	.45

Engraved; Name Typographed

Perf. 11½x11

53	CD305	10sh red violet	50.00	*47.50*

The stamps formerly listed as Nos. 54-56 have been merged into the rest of the George VI definitive series as Nos. 41//43C.

UPU Issue

Common Design Types

Engr.; Name Typo. on Nos. 58, 59

1949, Oct. 10 ***Perf. 13½, 11x11½***

57	CD306	3p rose carmine	1.40	*1.25*
58	CD307	4p indigo	4.75	1.25
59	CD308	6p olive	1.75	2.75
60	CD309	1sh slate	4.50	3.00
		Nos. 57-60 (4)	12.40	8.25

AUSTRALIA

o-'strāl-yə

LOCATION — Oceania, south of Indonesia, bounded on the west by the Indian Ocean

GOVT. — Self-governing dominion of the British Commonwealth

AREA — 2,967,909 sq. mi.

POP. — 6,866,590

CAPITAL — Canberra

Australia includes the former British colonies of New South Wales, Victoria, Queensland, South Australia, Western Australia and Tasmania.

12 Pence = 1 Shilling
20 Shillings = 1 Pound

Catalogue values for unused stamps in this country are for Never Hinged items, beginning with Scott 197 in the regular postage section, Scott C6 in the air post section, and Scott J71 in the postage due section.

Watermarks

Wmk. 8 — Wide Crown and Wide A

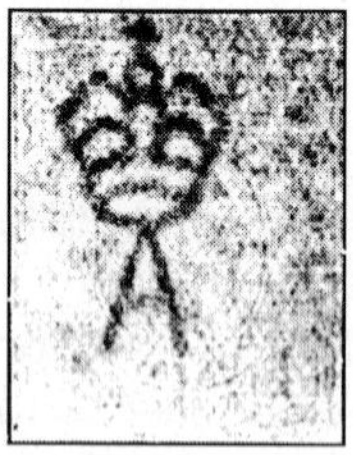

Wmk. 9 — Wide Crown and Narrow A

Wmk. 10 — Narrow Crown and Narrow A

Wmk. 11 — Multiple Crown and A

Wmk. 12 — Crown and Single-lined A

Wmk. 13 — Large Crown and Double-lined A

Wmk. 55 — Large Crown and NSW

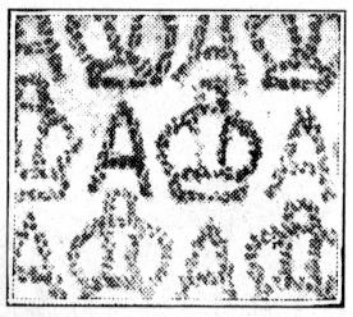

Wmk. 203 — Small Crown and A Multiple

Wmk. 228 — Small Crown and C of A Multiple

Kangaroo and Map — A1

Die I — The inside frameline has a break at left, even with the top of the letters of the denomination.

Die II — The frameline does not show a break (repaired die).

Die III — The left inside frameline shows a break opposite the face of the kangaroo.

Die IV — As Die III, with a break in the top outside frameline above the "ST" of "AUSTRALIA." The upper right inside frameline has an incomplete corner.

Dies are only indicated when there are more than one for any denomination.

1913 Typo. Wmk. 8 ***Perf. 11½, 12***

1	A1	½p green	8.00	4.00
		Never hinged	13.00	
		On cover		27.50
a.		½p yellow green	8.00	4.00
b.		½p deep green	8.00	4.00
c.		Wmk. sideways, crown pointing to left		*9,250.*
d.		Wmk. sideways, crown pointing to right		*11,500.*
e.		Wmk. inverted	40.00	11.50
f.		Printed on gummed side	*2,250.*	
2	A1	1p car (I)	10.00	1.00
		Never hinged	16.00	
		On cover		6.00
a.		1p red (I)	10.00	1.00
b.		1p pale red (I)	10.00	1.00
		Never hinged	16.00	
c.		1p rose red (I)	10.00	1.00
d.		1p carmine (II)	10.00	1.00
		Never hinged	16.00	
		On cover		6.00
e.		1p red (II)	11.00	1.00
f.		1p pale red (II)	11.00	1.00
g.		1p rose red (II)	11.00	1.00
h.		1p carmine (III)	12.50	1.25
		Never hinged	27.50	
		On cover		8.50
i.		1p red (III)	17.50	1.25
j.		1p pale red (III)	17.50	1.25
k.		1p rose red (III)	17.50	1.25
l.		As #2, wmk. sideways	*950.00*	*200.00*
m.		As "d," wmk. sideways	*1,000.*	*225.00*
n.		As #2, wmk. inverted	35.00	5.75
o.		As "d," wmk. inverted	35.00	5.75
p.		As "h," wmk. inverted	57.50	9.00
3	A1	2p gray	40.00	8.00
		Never hinged	120.00	
		On cover		30.00
a.		2p deep gray	35.00	7.00
b.		2p slate	35.00	7.00
c.		As #3, wmk. inverted	62.50	12.50
4	A1	2½p dark blue	45.00	17.00
		Never hinged	140.00	
		On cover		50.00
a.		2½p indigo	45.00	15.00
5	A1	3p ol bis, die I	87.50	12.00
		Never hinged	210.00	
		On cover		65.00
a.		Die II	275.00	100.00
		Never hinged	*600.00*	
		On cover		145.00
b.		Pair, #5-5a	575.00	290.00
c.		3p pale olive green (I)	87.50	10.00
		Never hinged	210.00	
d.		As "c," (II)	200.00	62.50
		Never hinged	*450.00*	
e.		Pair, #5c-5d	575.00	290.00
f.		3p green (I)	87.50	10.00
		Never hinged	210.00	
g.		As "f," (II)	200.00	62.50
		Never hinged	*450.00*	
h.		As #3, wmk. inverted	140.00	40.00
i.		As "a," wmk. inverted	450.00	160.00
j.		Pair, #5f-5g	575.00	290.00
6	A1	4p orange	90.00	27.50
		Never hinged	450.00	
		On cover		80.00
a.		4p deep orange	90.00	27.50
		Never hinged	450.00	
b.		4p yellow orange	350.00	50.00
		Never hinged	800.00	
		On cover		160.00

Many examples offered as #6b are either #6 or 6a with faded color.

7	A1	5p orange brown	100.00	42.50
		Never hinged	250.00	
		On cover		125.00
8	A1	6p ultra (II)	100.00	25.00
		Never hinged	325.00	
		On cover		140.00
a.		6p blue (II)	100.00	25.00
		Never hinged	275.00	
		On cover		160.00
b.		As #8, (III)	*3,250.*	*1,100.*
c.		As #8, wmk. inverted	130.00	57.50
d.		As "a," wmk. inverted	130.00	57.50
e.		As "b," wmk. inverted	*2,250.*	*750.00*
9	A1	9p purple	82.50	30.00
		Never hinged	350.00	
		On cover		145.00
a.		9p violet	82.50	22.50
b.		9p deep violet	82.50	22.50
10	A1	1sh blue green	100.00	20.00
		Never hinged	375.00	
		On cover		175.00
a.		1sh emerald	87.50	20.00
b.		As "a," analine ink	87.50	20.00
c.		As "a," wmk. inverted	400.00	75.00
11	A1	2sh brown	225.00	100.00
		Never hinged	900.00	
		On telegram form or parcel		285.00
a.		2sh dark brown	225.00	100.00
12	A1	5sh yellow & gray	400.00	200.00
		Never hinged	1,400.	
		On cover		—
a.		5sh chrome yel & gray	400.00	200.00
13	A1	10sh pink & gray	800.00	650.00
		Never hinged	3,250.	
		On cover		—
a.		10sh pink & slate	800.00	650.00
14	A1	£1 ultra & brown	2,000.	1,900.
		Never hinged	6,750.	
		On cover		—
a.		£1 ultra & red brn	2,100.	1,900.
15	A1	£2 dp rose & blk	5,000.	2,750.
		Never hinged	10,000.	
		On cover		—
a.		£2 rose & gray	4,500.	2,750.
		Never hinged	10,000.	
b.		£2 rose & jet black	4,500.	2,750.
		Never hinged	10,000.	
		Nos. 1-12 (12)	1,288.	487.00

On No. 4, "2½d" is colorless in solid blue background.

See Nos. 38-59, 96-102, 121-129, 206.

King George V
A2

Kookaburra (Kingfisher)
A3

1913-14 Unwmk. Engr. ***Perf. 11***

17	A2	1p carmine	4.25	5.75
		Never hinged	5.75	
a.		Vert. pair, imperf. between	*2,900.*	
18	A3	6p lake brown ('14)	90.00	55.00
		Never hinged	200.00	

See No. 95.

A4

ONE PENNY

Die I — Normal die, having outside the oval band with "AUSTRALIA" a white line and a heavy colored line.

Die Ia — As die I with a small white spur below the right serif at foot of the "1" in left tablet.

Die II — A heavy colored line between two white lines back of the emu's neck. A white scratch crossing the vertical shading lines at the lowest point of the bust.

TWO PENCE

Die I — The numeral "2" is thin. The upper curve is 1mm. across and a very thin line connects it with the foot of the figure.

Die II — The "2" is thicker than in die I. The top curve is 1½mm across and a strong white line connects it with the foot of the figure. There are thin vertical lines across the ends of the groups of short horizontal lines at each side of "TWO PENCE."

THREE PENCE

Die I — The ends of the thin horizontal lines in the background run into the solid color of the various parts of the design. The numerals are thin and the letters of "THREE PENCE" are thin and irregular.

Die II — The oval about the portrait, the shields with the numerals, etc., are outlined by thin white lines which separate them from the horizontal background lines. The numerals are thick and the letters of "THREE PENCE" are heavy and regular.

FIVE PENCE

Die I — The top of the flag of the "5" is slightly curved.

Die II — The top of the flag of the "5" is flat. There are thin white vertical lines across the ends of the short horizontal lines at each side of "FIVE PENCE."

1914-24 Typo. Wmk. 9 ***Perf. 14***

19	A4	½p emerald ('15)	2.75	1.00
		Never hinged	5.00	
a.		Thin "½" at right	*15,000.*	*4,500.*
20	A4	½p orange ('23)	2.50	2.50
		Never hinged	3.50	
21	A4	1p red (I)	4.25	1.00
		Never hinged	9.00	
a.		1p carmine rose (I)	8.25	1.00
		Never hinged	20.00	
b.		1p red (Ia)	425.00	6.00
		Never hinged	800.00	
c.		1p carmine (II) ('18)	60.00	30.00
		Never hinged	125.00	
d.		1p scar (I), rough paper	20.00	5.00

e. 1p rose red (Ia), rough paper 700.00 25.00
f. 1p brt rose (Ia), rough paper 500.00 100.00
22 A4 1p vio (I) ('22) 4.50 1.00
Never hinged 8.00
a. 1p red violet 6.50 2.00
Never hinged 10.00
23 A4 1p green (I) ('24) 3.50 1.50
Never hinged 6.25
24 A4 1½p choc ('18) 5.00 1.00
Never hinged 10.00
a. 1½p red brown 5.50 1.00
Never hinged 15.00
b. 1½p black brown 4.50 1.00
Never hinged 9.00
25 A4 1½p emerald ('23) 3.50 1.00
Never hinged 8.00
a. Rough paper 160.00 120.00
26 A4 1½p scarlet ('24) 3.00 .50
Never hinged 5.00
27 A4 2p brn org (I) ('20) 12.00 1.50
Never hinged 20.00
a. 2p orange (I) ('20) 12.00 2.00
Never hinged 25.00
b. Booklet pane of 6
28 A4 2p red (I) ('22) 10.00 2.00
Never hinged 20.00
29 A4 2p red brn (I) ('24) 20.00 10.00
Never hinged 30.00
30 A4 3p ultra (I) ('24) 25.00 5.00
Never hinged 55.00
31 A4 4p orange ('15) 40.00 2.50
Never hinged 75.00
a. 4p yellow 110.00 20.00
Never hinged 450.00
32 A4 4p violet ('21) 17.50 17.00
Never hinged 27.50
33 A4 4p lt ultra ('22) 55.00 10.00
Never hinged 110.00
34 A4 4p ol bis ('24) 27.50 10.00
Never hinged 55.00
35 A4 4½p violet ('24) 22.50 6.00
Never hinged 50.00
36 A4 5p org brn (I) ('15) 20.00 6.00
Never hinged 90.00
37 A4 1sh4p lt blue ('20) 110.00 25.00
Never hinged 400.00
Nos. 19-37 (19) 388.50 104.50

See Nos. 60-76, 113-120, 124.

1915 ***Perf. 11½, 12***
38 A1 2p gray 90.00 13.50
Never hinged 225.00
a. Wmk. inverted 1,250.
39 A1 2½p dark blue 75.00 32.50
Never hinged 150.00
40 A1 6p ultra (II) 225.00 25.00
Never hinged 700.00
a. Die III *3,200.* 1,100.
b. 6p bright blue (II) 200.00 50.00
c. As "b," Die III *1,800.* 600.00
d. As #40, wmk. inverted *2,500.*
41 A1 9p violet 225.00 50.00
Never hinged 1,000.
a. Wmk. inverted *1,250.* 650.00
42 A1 1sh blue green 200.00 27.50
Never hinged 850.00
43 A1 2sh brown 675.00 100.00
Never hinged 2,800.
44 A1 5sh yellow & gray 900.00 350.00
Never hinged 2,600.
a. Wmk. inverted 1,000. 350.00
b. Yellow double 14,000. 3,000.
Nos. 38-44 (7) 2,390. 598.50

1915-24 **Wmk. 10**
45 A1 2p gray (I) 27.50 8.00
Never hinged 42.50
a. Die II, shiny paper 37.50 14.00
Never hinged 55.00
46 A1 2½p dark blue 25.00 15.00
Never hinged 40.00
a. "1" of fraction omitted *39,000.* *11,000.*
47 A1 3p olive bister (I) 30.00 8.00
Never hinged 60.00
a. Die II 150.00 50.00
Never hinged 275.00
b. 3p lt olive (IV) 40.00 8.00
Never hinged 80.00
48 A1 6p ultra (II) 100.00 13.50
Never hinged 225.00
a. 6p chalky blue (III) 100.00 20.00
Never hinged 225.00
b. 6p ultra (III) 1,600. 500.00
c. As "c," (IV) 100.00 15.00
Never hinged 225.00
49 A1 6p yel brn (IV, '23) 25.00 6.00
Never hinged 50.00
50 A1 9p violet (IV) 70.00 16.00
Never hinged 160.00
a. 9p lilac (II) 70.00 16.00
Never hinged 160.00
51 A1 1sh blue grn (II, '16) 60.00 9.00
Never hinged 160.00
b. Die IV 60.00 9.00
52 A1 2sh brown ('16) 250.00 24.00
Never hinged 800.00
53 A1 2sh vio brn (II, '24) 110.00 30.00
Never hinged 250.00
54 A1 5sh yel & gray ('18) 250.00 100.00
Never hinged 700.00
55 A1 10sh brt pink & gray ('17) 650.00 325.00
Never hinged 1,500.
56 A1 £1 ultra & brn org ('16) 2,600. 1,750.
Never hinged 8,000.
a. £1 ultra & brn ('16) 2,400. 1,500.
Never hinged 7,500.
57 A1 £1 gray (IV, '24) 725.00 350.00
Never hinged 1,900.
58 A1 £2 dp rose & blk ('19) 4,500. 2,900.
Never hinged 10,000.
59 A1 £2 rose & vio brn ('24) 4,000. 2,650.
Never hinged 9,000.
Nos. 45-54 (10) 947.50 229.50

Perf. 14, 14½, 14½x14
1918-23 **Wmk. 11**
60 A4 ½p emerald 3.00 2.00
Never hinged 5.00
a. Thin "½" at right 110.00 90.00
61 A4 1p rose (I) 25.00 15.00
Never hinged 40.00
62 A4 1p dl grn (I) ('24) 8.00 8.00
Never hinged 12.00
63 A4 1½p choc ('19) 6.00 2.00
Never hinged 12.00
a. 1½p red brown ('19) 10.00 2.00
Never hinged 20.00
Nos. 60-63 (4) 42.00 27.00

1924 **Unwmk.** ***Perf. 14***
64 A4 1p green (I) 5.00 5.00
Never hinged 8.00
65 A4 1½p carmine 8.00 6.00
Never hinged 12.00

Perf. 14, 13½x12½
1926-30 **Wmk. 203**
66 A4 ½p orange 2.00 1.50
Never hinged 3.00
a. Perf. 14 ('27) 6.50 5.25
Never hinged 8.50
67 A4 1p green (I) 2.00 .75
Never hinged 3.00
a. 1p green (Ia) 47.50 *60.00*
Never hinged 65.00
b. Perf. 14 3.00 1.00
Never hinged 5.00
68 A4 1½p rose red ('27) 3.00 1.00
Never hinged 4.00
c. Perf. 14 ('26) 8.00 1.00
Never hinged 15.00
69 A4 1½p red brn ('30) 5.00 4.00
Never hinged 8.00
70 A4 2p red brn (II, '28) 7.00 4.00
Never hinged 10.50
a. Perf. 14 (I, '27) 40.00 25.00
Never hinged 75.00
71 A4 2p red (II) ('30) 10.00 .20
Never hinged 17.50
a. 2p red (I) ('30) 5.00 1.60
Never hinged 12.00
c. Unwmkd. (II) ('31) *1,600.* *2,000.*
72 A4 3p ultra (II) ('29) 25.00 5.00
Never hinged 40.00
a. 3p ultra (I) 50.00 20.00
Never hinged 125.00
b. Perf. 14 40.00 10.00
Never hinged 70.00
73 A4 4p ol bis ('29) 25.00 5.00
Never hinged 40.00
a. Perf. 14 ('28) 100.00 40.00
Never hinged 250.00
74 A4 4½p dk vio ('27) 20.00 7.00
Never hinged 30.00
a. Perf. 13½x12½ ('28) 75.00 25.00
Never hinged 125.00
75 A4 5p brn buff (II) ('30) 40.00 10.00
Never hinged 75.00
76 A4 1sh4p pale turq bl ('28) 175.00 25.00
Never hinged 425.00
a. Perf. 14 ('27) 200.00 125.00
Never hinged 650.00
Nos. 66-76 (11) 314.00 63.45

For surcharges & overprints see #106-107, O3-O4.

Parliament House, Canberra A5

Unwmk.
1927, May 9 **Engr.** ***Perf. 11***
94 A5 1½p brown red .90 .90
Never hinged 1.75
a. Vert. pair, imperf. btwn. *3,750.* *3,500.*
b. Horiz. pair, imperf. btwn. *4,750.* *4,750.*

Opening of Parliament House at Canberra.

Melbourne Exhibition Issue
Kookaburra Type of 1914
1928, Oct. 29
95 A3 3p deep blue 4.00 4.00
Never hinged 6.00
a. Pane of 4 150.00 *175.00*
Never hinged 225.00

No. 95a was issued at the Melbourne Intl. Phil. Exhib. No marginal inscription. Printed in sheets of 60 stamps (15 panes). No. 95 was printed in sheets of 120 and issued Nov. 2 throughout Australia.

Kangaroo-Map Type of 1913
Perf. 11½, 12
1929-30 **Wmk. 203** **Typo.**
96 A1 6p brown 24.00 20.00
Never hinged 45.00
97 A1 9p violet 55.00 20.00
Never hinged 120.00
98 A1 1sh blue green 60.00 11.00
Never hinged 140.00
99 A1 2sh red brown 110.00 25.00
Never hinged 325.00
100 A1 5sh yel & gray 325.00 120.00
Never hinged 800.00
101 A1 10sh pink & gray 550.00 625.00
Never hinged 1,400.
102 A1 £2 dl red & blk ('30) 4,000. 700.00
Never hinged 7,500.
Nos. 96-102 (7) 5,124. 1,521.

For overprint see No. O5.

Black Swan — A6

Capt. Charles Sturt — A7

Unwmk.
1929, Sept. 28 **Engr.** ***Perf. 11***
103 A6 1½p dull red 1.00 1.00
Never hinged 2.00

Centenary of Western Australia.

1930, June 2
104 A7 1½p dark red 1.00 1.00
Never hinged 2.00
105 A7 3p dark blue 3.50 3.00
Never hinged 6.00

Capt. Charles Sturt's exploration of the Murray River, cent.

Nos. 68 and 74a surcharged

1930 **Wmk. 203** ***Perf. 13½x12½***
106 A4 2p on 1½p rose red 1.00 1.00
Never hinged 2.00
107 A4 5p on 4½p dark violet 5.00 5.00
Never hinged 10.00

"Southern Cross" over Hemispheres A8

Perf. 11, 11½
1931, Mar. 19 **Unwmk.**
111 A8 2p dull red 1.00 1.00
Never hinged 2.00
112 A8 3p blue 4.75 2.00
Never hinged 8.00
Nos. 111-112,C2 (3) 12.75 10.00

Trans-oceanic flights (1928-1930) of Sir Charles Edward Kingsford-Smith (1897-1935).
See #C3 for similar design. For overprints see #CO1, O1-O2.

Types of 1913-23 Issues
Perf. 13½x12½
1931-36 **Typo.** **Wmk. 228**
113 A4 ½p orange ('32) 3.00 3.00
Never hinged 5.00
114 A4 1p green (I) 2.00 .25
Never hinged 3.00
115 A4 1½p red brn ('36) 6.00 6.00
Never hinged 8.00
116 A4 2p red (II) 2.00 .20
Never hinged 3.00
117 A4 3p ultra (II) ('32) 25.00 2.00
Never hinged 60.00
118 A4 4p ol bis ('33) 25.00 2.00
Never hinged 40.00
120 A4 5p brn buff (II) ('32) 20.00 2.00
Never hinged 30.00

Perf. 11½, 12; 13½x12½ (1sh4p)
121 A1 6p yel brn ('36) 22.50 22.50
Never hinged 37.50
122 A1 9p violet ('32) 30.00 5.00
Never hinged 85.00
124 A4 1sh4p lt blue ('32) 90.00 8.00
Never hinged 225.00
125 A1 2sh red brn ('35) 5.00 4.00
Never hinged 7.50
126 A1 5sh yel & gray ('32) 225.00 22.50
Never hinged 550.00
127 A1 10sh pink & gray ('32) 450.00 175.00
Never hinged 1,500.
128 A1 £1 gray ('35) 775.00 300.00
Never hinged 1,900.
129 A1 £2 dl rose & blk ('34) 3,250. 650.00
Never hinged 7,000.
Nos. 113-129 (15) 4,930. 1,202.

For redrawn 2sh see No. 206. For overprints see Nos. O6-O11.

Sydney Harbor Bridge — A9

Unwmk.
1932, Mar. 14 **Engr.** ***Perf. 11***
130 A9 2p red 2.00 2.00
Never hinged 3.00
131 A9 3p blue 4.00 4.00
Never hinged 6.75
132 A9 5sh gray green 475.00 300.00
Never hinged 1,100.

Wmk. 228
Perf. 10½
Typo.
133 A9 2p red 2.00 2.00
Never hinged 3.00

Opening of the Sydney Harbor Bridge on Mar. 19, 1932.
Value for 5sh, used, is for CTO copies.
For overprints see Nos. O12-O13.

Kookaburra A14

Male Lyrebird A16

1932, June 1 ***Perf. 13½x12½***
139 A14 6p light brown 15.00 1.00
Never hinged 25.00

1932, Feb. 15 **Unwmk.** ***Perf. 11***
Size: 21½x25mm
141 A16 1sh green 37.50 3.00
Never hinged 90.00

See #175, 300. For overprint see #O14.

Yarra Yarra Tribesman, Yarra River and View of Melbourne A17

Wmk. 228

1934, July 2 Engr. *Perf. 10½*

142 A17 2p vermilion 2.00 1.00
Never hinged 3.00
a. Perf. 11½ 5.00 4.00
Never hinged 8.00
143 A17 3p blue 3.00 3.00
Never hinged 6.00
a. Perf. 11½ 5.00 4.00
Never hinged 8.00
144 A17 1sh black 40.00 25.00
Never hinged 80.00
a. Perf. 11½ 50.00 35.00
Never hinged 95.00
Nos. 142-144 (3) 45.00 29.00

Centenary of Victoria.

Merino Sheep — A18

1934, Nov. 1 *Perf. 11½*

147 A18 2p copper red 3.00 1.00
Never hinged 4.00
a. Die II 25.00 5.00
148 A18 3p dark blue 10.00 8.00
Never hinged 15.00
149 A18 9p dark violet 35.00 30.00
Never hinged 75.00
Nos. 147-149 (3) 48.00 39.00

Capt. John Macarthur (1767-1834), "father of the New South Wales woolen industry."

Two dies of 2p: I, shading on hill in background uneven from light to dark. II, shading is uniformly dark.

Cenotaph in Whitehall, London — A19

George V on His Charger "Anzac" — A20

1935, Mar. 18 *Perf. 13½x12½*

150 A19 2p red 1.00 .35
Never hinged 2.00

Perf. 11

151 A19 1sh black 40.00 30.00
Never hinged 70.00

Anzacs' landing at Gallipoli, 20th anniv.

The 1sh perf 13½x12½ is a plate proof. Value, unused $2,000, mint never hinged $3,000.

1935, May 2 *Perf. 11½*

152 A20 2p red 1.00 .20
Never hinged 2.00
153 A20 3p blue 3.00 3.00
Never hinged 7.50
154 A20 2sh violet 40.00 35.00
Never hinged 75.00
Nos. 152-154 (3) 44.00 38.20

25th anniv. of the reign of King George V.

Amphitrite Joining Cables between Australia and Tasmania A21

1936, Apr. 1

157 A21 2p red 1.00 .65
Never hinged 2.00
158 A21 3p dark blue 3.25 3.00
Never hinged 5.25

Australia/Tasmania telephone link.

Proclamation Tree and View of Adelaide, 1936 — A22

1936, Aug. 3

159 A22 2p red 1.00 .50
Never hinged 2.00
160 A22 3p dark blue 3.25 3.25
Never hinged 5.00
161 A22 1sh green 12.00 10.00
Never hinged 25.00
Nos. 159-161 (3) 16.25 13.75

Centenary of South Australia.

Gov. Arthur Phillip at Sydney Cove — A23

1937, Oct. 1 *Perf. 13x13½*

163 A23 2p red 1.00 .25
Never hinged 3.00
164 A23 3p ultra 2.75 2.00
Never hinged 4.50
165 A23 9p violet 16.00 11.00
Never hinged 25.00
Nos. 163-165 (3) 19.75 13.25

150th anniversary of New South Wales.

Kangaroo A24

Queen Elizabeth A25

King George VI A26 A27

Koala — A28

Merino Sheep — A29

Kookaburra (Kingfisher) A30

Platypus A31

Queen Elizabeth and King George VI in Coronation Robes A32 A33

King George VI and Queen Elizabeth A34

Two Types of A25 and A26:

Type I — Highlighted background. Lines around letters of Australia Postage and numerals of value.

Type II — Background of heavy diagonal lines without the highlighted effect. No lines around letters and numerals.

Perf. 13½x14, 14x13½

1937-46 Engr. Wmk. 228

166 A24 ½p org, perf. 15x14 ('42) .50 .50
Never hinged 2.00
a. Perf. 13½x14 ('38) 1.00 .25
Never hinged 2.00
167 A25 1p emerald (I) 1.00 .90
Never hinged 2.00
168 A26 1½p dull red brn (II) 3.00 3.00
Never hinged 4.50
a. Perf. 15x14 ('41) 4.25 4.00
Never hinged 6.25
169 A26 2p scarlet (I) 1.00 .25
Never hinged 1.75
170 A27 3p ultramarine 30.00 10.00
Never hinged 50.00
a. 3p dp ultra, thin paper ('38) 30.00 3.00
Never hinged 50.00
171 A28 4p grn, perf. 15x14 ('42) 1.00 .25
Never hinged 2.00
a. Perf. 13½x14 ('38) 2.50 1.00
Never hinged 7.00
172 A29 5p pale rose vio, perf. 14x15 ('46) 1.25 1.00
Never hinged 2.00
a. Perf. 14x13½ ('38) 2.50 .80
Never hinged 4.00
173 A30 6p vio brn, perf. 15x14 ('42) .60 .25
Never hinged 1.50
a. Perf. 13½x14 10.00 2.00
Never hinged 20.00
b. 6p chocolate, perf. 15x14 1.00 .50
Never hinged 1.50
174 A31 9p sep, perf. 14x15 ('43) 1.75 .30
Never hinged 2.50
a. Perf. 14x13½ ('38) 4.00 1.25
Never hinged 8.00
175 A16 1sh gray grn, perf. 15x14 ('41) 1.00 .25
Never hinged 1.50
a. Perf. 13½x14 22.50 2.00
Never hinged 47.50
176 A27 1sh4p magenta ('38) 1.25 .80
Never hinged 2.00

Perf. 13½

177 A32 5sh dl red brn ('38) 8.00 4.00
Never hinged 15.00
a. Thin paper ('48) 3.50 3.00
Never hinged 4.50
178 A33 10sh dl gray vio ('38) 25.00 13.00
Never hinged 37.50
a. Thin paper ('48) 30.00 25.00
Never hinged 40.00
179 A34 £1 bl gray ('38) 60.00 27.50
Never hinged 90.00
a. Thin paper ('48) 60.00 55.00
Never hinged 90.00
Nos. 166-179 (14) 135.35 62.00

No. 175 measures 17½x21½mm.

Nos. 177-179 were issued on chalk-surfaced paper. Nos. 177a-179a were printed on a thin, rough ordinary paper. The watermark is more distinct on Nos. 177a-179a, while impressions are not as sharp as on Nos. 177-179.

See #223A, 293, 295, 298, 300. For surch. & overprints see #190, M1, M4-M5, M7.

1938-42 *Perf. 15x14*

180 A25 1p emerald (II) .75 .25
181 A25 1p dl red brn (II) ('41) .50 .25
181B A26 1½p bl grn (II) ('41) .50 .20
182 A26 2p scarlet (II) .60 .20
182B A26 2p red vio (II) ('41) .30 .20
183 A27 3p dk ultra ('40) 20.00 2.00
Never hinged 35.00
183A A27 3p dk vio brn ('42) .25 .20
Nos. 180-183A (7) 22.90 3.30
Set, never hinged 45.00

No. 183 differs from Nos. 170-170a in the shading lines on the king's left eyebrow which go downward, left to right, instead of the reverse. Also, more of the left epaulette shows.

For surcharges & ovpt. see #188-189, M3.

Coil Perforation

A special perforation was applied to stamps intended for use in coils to make separation easier. It consists of small and large holes (2 small, 10 large, 2 small) on the stamps' narrow side. Some of the stamps so perforated were sold in sheets.

This coil perforation may be found on Nos. 166, 181, 182, 182B, 193, 215, 223A, 231, 257, 315-316, 319, 319a and others.

Nurse, Sailor, Soldier and Aviator — A35

Perf. 13½x13

1940, July 15 Engr. Wmk. 228

184 A35 1p green 1.00 1.00
Never hinged 2.00
185 A35 2p red 1.00 1.00
Never hinged 2.00
186 A35 3p ultra 4.00 4.00
Never hinged 7.00
187 A35 6p chocolate 12.50 10.00
Never hinged 24.00
Nos. 184-187 (4) 18.50 16.00

Australia's participation in WWII.

No. 182 Surcharged in Blue

1941, Dec. 10 *Perf. 15x14*

188 A26 2½p on 2p red .50 .30
Never hinged 1.00

No. 183 Surcharged in Blue and Yellow

189 A27 3½p on 3p dk ultra .50 .35
Never hinged 1.00

No. 172a Surcharged in Purple

Perf. 14x13½

190 A29 5½p on 5p pale rose vio 4.00 4.00
Never hinged 4.75
Nos. 188-190 (3) 5.00 4.65

Queen Elizabeth A36 A37

King George VI A38 A39

George VI and Blue Wrens A40

Emu A41

1942-44 Engr. *Perf. 15x14*

191 A36 1p brown vio ('43) .25 .20
192 A37 1½p green .50 .20
193 A38 2p lt rose vio ('44) .50 .20
194 A39 2½p red .50 .20

195 A40 3½p ultramarine .75 .50
196 A41 5½p indigo 1.00 .20
Nos. 191-196 (6) 3.50 1.50
Set, never hinged 4.50

See #224-225. For overprint see #M2.

Catalogue values for unused stamps in this section, from this point to the end of the section, are for Never Hinged items.

Duke and Duchess of Gloucester A42

1945, Feb. 19 Engr. *Perf. 14½*

197 A42 2½p brown red .25 .20
198 A42 3½p bright ultra .35 .40
199 A42 5½p indigo .40 .40
Nos. 197-199 (3) 1.00 1.00

Inauguration of the Duke of Gloucester as Governor General.

Official Crest and Inscriptions A43

Dove and Australian Flag A44

Angel of Peace; "Motherhood" and "Industry" A45

1946, Feb. 18 Wmk. 228 *Perf. 14½*

200 A43 2½p carmine .20 .20
201 A44 3½p deep ultra .35 .45
202 A45 5½p deep yellow green .45 .35
Nos. 200-202 (3) 1.00 1.00

End of WWII. See #1456-1458.

Sir Thomas Mitchell and Map of Queensland A46

1946, Oct. 14

203 A46 2½p dark carmine .20 .20
204 A46 3½p deep ultra .60 .80
205 A46 1sh olive green .60 .40
Nos. 203-205 (3) 1.40 1.40

Sir Thomas Mitchell's exploration of central Queensland, cent.

Kangaroo-Map Type of 1913 Redrawn

1945, Dec. Typo. *Perf. 11½*

206 A1 2sh dk red brown 4.00 3.50

The R and A of AUSTRALIA are separated at the base and there is a single line between the value tablet and "Two Shillings." On No. 125 the tail of the R touches the A, while two lines appear between value tablet and "Two Shillings." There are many other minor differences in the design.

For overprint see No. M6.

John Shortland A47

Pouring Steel A48

Loading Coal — A49

1947, Sept. Engr. *Perf. 14½x14*

207 A47 2½p brown red .20 .20

Perf. 14½

208 A48 3½p deep blue .40 .50
209 A49 5½p deep green .40 .30
Nos. 207-209 (3) 1.00 1.00

150th anniv. of the discovery of the Hunter River estuary, site of Newcastle by Lieut. John Shortland. By error the 2½p shows his father, Capt. John Shortland.

Princess Elizabeth — A50

Perf. 14x14½

1947, Nov. 20 Wmk. 228

210 A50 1p brown violet .30 .40

See No. 215.

Hereford Bull A51

Crocodile A52

1948, Feb. 16 *Perf. 14½*

211 A51 1sh3p violet brown 2.00 1.00
212 A52 2sh chocolate 2.00 .30

See No. 302.

William J. Farrer — A53

Design: No. 214, Ferdinand von Mueller.

1948 *Perf. 14½x14*

213 A53 2½p red .20 .20
214 A53 2½p dark red .20 .20

William J. Farrer (1845-1906), wheat researcher, and Ferdinand von Mueller (1825-1896), German-born botanist.

Issue dates: #213, July 12. #214, Sept. 13.

Elizabeth Type of 1947

1948, Aug. Unwmk. *Perf. 14x14½*

215 A50 1p brown violet .20 .20

Scout in Uniform — A55

Arms of Australia — A56

1948, Nov. 15 Engr. Wmk. 228

216 A55 2½p brown red .20 .20

Pan-Pacific Scout Jamboree, Victoria, Dec. 29, 1948 to Jan. 9, 1949. See No. 249.

1949-50 Wmk. 228 *Perf. 14x13½*

218 A56 5sh dark red 4.00 .50
219 A56 10sh red violet 25.00 1.00
220 A56 £1 deep blue 37.50 7.00
221 A56 £2 green ('50) 150.00 21.00
Nos. 218-221 (4) 216.50 29.50

Henry Hertzberg Lawson (1867-1922), Author and Poet — A57

Perf. 14½x14

1949, June 17 Unwmk.

222 A57 2½p rose brown .25 .20

Outback Mail Carrier and Plane — A58

1949, Oct. 10

223 A58 3½p violet blue .40 .50

UPU, 75th anniv.

Types of 1938, 1942-44 & A59

Aborigine A59

John Forrest A60

1948-50 Unwmk. *Perf. 14½x14*

223A A24 ½p orange ('49) .20 .20
224 A37 1½p green ('49) .25 .20
225 A38 2p lt rose violet .30 .20

Wmk. 228

226 A59 8½p dark brown ('50) .50 .40
Nos. 223A-226 (4) 1.25 1.00

Issued: 2p, Dec.; ½p, Sept.; 1½p, 8/29; 8½p, 8/14.

See Nos. 248, 303.

1949, Nov. 28 Wmk. 228

227 A60 2½p brown red .20 .20

Forrest (1847-1918), explorer & statesman.

New South Wales
A61

Victoria
A62

First stamp designs.

Perf. 14½x14

1950, Sept. 27 **Unwmk.**
228 A61 2½p rose brown .25 .20
229 A62 2½p rose brown .25 .20
a. Pair, #228-229 1.00 1.00

Cent. of Australian adhesive postage stamps. Issued in sheets of 160 stamps containing alternate copies of Nos. 228 and 229.

Elizabeth
A63

George VI
A64

A65

A66

1950-51 **Engr.** **Unwmk.**
230 A63 1½p deep green .50 .40
231 A63 2p yellow grn ('51) .20 .20
232 A64 2½p violet brn ('51) .20 .20
233 A64 3p dull green ('51) .30 .20
Nos. 230-233 (4) 1.20 1.00

Issued: 1½p, 6/19; 2p, 3/28; 2½p, 5/23; 3p, 11/14.

1950-52 **Wmk. 228**
234 A64 2½p red .20 .20
235 A64 3p red ('51) .20 .20
236 A65 3½p red brown ('51) .30 .20
237 A65 4½p scarlet ('52) .40 .50
238 A65 6½p choc ('52) .30 .50
238A A65 6½p blue green ('52) .40 .20
239 A66 7½p deep blue ('51) .45 .50
Nos. 234-239 (7) 2.25 2.30

Issued: 2½p, 4/12; 3p, 2/28; 7½p, 10/31; 3½p, 11/28; 4½p, #238, 2/20; #238A, 4/9.

A67

Founding of the Commonwealth of Australia, 50th Anniv. — A68

Designs: No. 240, Sir Edmund Barton. No. 241, Sir Henry Parkes. 5½p, Duke of York opening first Federal Parliament. 1sh6p, Parliament House, Canberra.

Perf. 14½x14

1951, May 1 **Engr.** **Unwmk.**
240 3p carmine .40 .20
241 3p carmine .40 .20
a. A67 Pair, #240, 241 1.00 1.00
242 A68 5½p deep blue .80 *.70*
243 A68 1sh6p red brown 1.25 1.00
Nos. 240-243 (4) 2.85 2.10

Edward Hammond Hargraves
A69

King George VI
A70

Design: No. 245, Charles Joseph Latrobe (1801-1875), first governor of Victoria.

1951, July 2
244 A69 3p rose brown .25 .20
245 A69 3p rose brown .25 .20
a. Pair, #244, 245 1.00 1.00

Discovery of gold in Australia, cent. (No. 244); Establishment of representative government in Victoria, cent. (No. 245). Sheets contain alternate rows of Nos. 244 and 245.

1952, Mar. 19 **Wmk. 228** ***Perf. 14½***
247 A70 1sh½p slate blue 2.00 .75

Aborigine Type of 1950 Redrawn
Size: 20½x25mm
248 A59 2sh6p dark brown 4.00 1.00

Portrait as on A59; lettering altered and value repeated at lower left. See No. 303.

Scout Type of 1948
Dated "1952-53"
Perf. 14x14½

1952, Nov. 19 **Wmk. 228**
249 A55 3½p red brown .20 .20

Pan-Pacific Scout Jamboree, Greystanes, Dec. 30, 1952, to Jan. 9, 1953.

AIR POST STAMPS

Airplane over Bush Lands — AP1

Unwmk.
1929, May 20 **Engr.** ***Perf. 11***
C1 AP1 3p deep green 7.00 6.00
Never hinged 12.50
a. Booklet pane of 4 ('30) 400.00

Kingsford-Smith Type of 1931

1931, Mar. 19
C2 A8 6p gray violet 7.00 7.00
Never hinged 10.00

AP3

1931, Nov. 4
C3 AP3 6p olive brown 15.00 12.00
Never hinged 30.00

For overprint see No. CO1.

Mercury and Hemispheres
AP4

1934, Dec. 1 ***Perf. 11***
C4 AP4 1sh6p violet brown 32.50 6.00
Never hinged 75.00

Perf. 13x13½

1937, Oct. 22 **Wmk. 228**
C5 AP4 1sh6p violet brown 7.50 1.25
Never hinged 12.50

Catalogue values for unused stamps in this section, from this point to the end of the section, are for Never Hinged items.

Mercury and Globe — AP5

1949, Sept. 1 ***Perf. 14½***
C6 AP5 1sh6p sepia 2.00 .25

AIR POST OFFICIAL STAMP

No. C3 Overprinted

Perf. 11, 11½

1931, Nov. 17 **Unwmk.**
CO1 AP3 6p olive brown 22.50 *22.50*
Never hinged 35.00

Issued primarily for official use, but to prevent speculation, a quantity was issued for public distribution.

POSTAGE DUE STAMPS

Very fine examples of Nos. J1-J38 will have perforations touching the design on one or more sides due to the narrow spacing of the stamps on the plates. Stamps with perfs clear of the design on all four sides are scarce and will command higher prices.

D1

D2

1902 **Typo.** **Wmk. 55** ***Perf. 11½, 12***
J1 D1 ½p emerald 10.00 10.00
J2 D1 1p emerald 15.00 10.00
a. Perf. 11 *2,100.* *1,100.*
b. Perf. 11x11½ 400.00 200.00
J3 D1 2p emerald 27.50 10.00
a. Perf. 11x11½ 500.00 190.00
J4 D1 3p emerald 27.50 18.00
J5 D1 4p emerald 40.00 20.00
J6 D1 6p emerald 60.00 15.00
J7 D1 8p emerald 160.00 125.00
J8 D1 5sh emerald 300.00 100.00
Nos. J1-J8 (8) 640.00 308.00

Perf. 11½, 12, Compound with 11

1902-04
J9 D2 ½p emerald 15.00 *10.00*
a. Perf. 11 500.00 300.00
J10 D2 1p emerald, Perf 12x11 15.00 5.00
a. Perf. 11 175.00 35.00
b. Perf 11½ 350.00 175.00
c. Perf 11x11½ 32.50 10.00
J11 D2 2p emerald 20.00 5.00
a. Perf. 11 225.00 50.00
b. Perf 12 — 190.00
c. Perf 11x11½ 100.00 32.50
d. Perf 11x12 120.00 40.00
J12 D2 3p emerald 125.00 15.00
a. Perf. 11 150.00 55.00
b. Perf 12 400.00 150.00
J13 D2 4p emerald 100.00 20.00
a. Perf. 11 275.00 100.00
J14 D2 5p emerald 100.00 30.00
a. Perf. 11 375.00 75.00
b. Perf 12 75.00 20.00
J15 D2 6p emerald 125.00 25.00
a. Perf. 11 150.00 22.50
J16 D2 8p emerald 250.00 100.00
J17 D2 10p emerald 150.00 25.00
a. Perf 12x11½ 130.00 25.00
J18 D2 1sh emerald 110.00 25.00
a. Perf. 11 450.00 80.00
b. Perf 12x11½ 80.00 27.50
J19 D2 2sh emerald 175.00 25.00
a. Perf 11½, 12 175.00 35.00
J20 D2 5sh emerald 350.00 30.00
a. Perf. 11 1,000. 250.00

Perf. 11

J21 D2 10sh emerald *3,000.* *2,350.*
J22 D2 20sh emerald *6,500.* *4,000.*
Nos. J9-J20 (12) 1,535. 315.00

Perf. 11½, 12 Compound with 11

1906 **Wmk. 12**
J23 D2 ½p emerald 14.00 14.00
J24 D2 1p emerald 30.00 3.50
a. Perf. 11 *2,500.* *1,000.*
J25 D2 2p emerald 55.00 10.00
J26 D2 3p emerald 850.00 375.00
J27 D2 4p emerald 110.00 24.00
a. Perf. 11 *3,500.* *2,000.*
J28 D2 6p emerald 390.00 27.50
Nos. J23-J28 (6) 1,449. 454.00

1907 **Wmk. 13** ***Perf. 11½x11***
J29 D2 ½p emerald 37.50 *75.00*
J30 D2 1p emerald 225.00 100.00
J31 D2 2p emerald 325.00 250.00
J32 D2 4p emerald 425.00 200.00
J33 D2 6p emerald 475.00 250.00
Nos. J29-J33 (5) 1,487. 875.00

D3

D4

Perf. 11 (2sh, 10sh, 20sh), 11½x11 (1sh, 5sh)

1908-09 **Wmk. 12**
J34 D3 1sh emer ('09) 150.00 25.00
J35 D3 2sh emerald *1,500.* —
J36 D3 5sh emerald 375.00 57.50
J37 D3 10sh emerald *4,250.* —
J38 D3 20sh emerald *11,000.* —

1909-23 **Wmk. 13** ***Perf. 12x12½***
J39 D4 ½p green & car 27.50 *40.00*
a. Perf 11, green & rose ('14) 12.50 12.50
b. Perf 12½, green & scarlet ('13) 32.50 25.00
c. Perf 14 ('19) 12.50 12.50
J40 D4 1p green & car 20.00 7.50
a. Perf 11, yel grn & rose, thicker paper, thick yellowish gum 3,000. 1,200.
b. Perf 11, bright apple green & rose, thin paper, thin white gum ('14) 14.00 5.00
c. Perf 14 ('14) 60.00 15.00
J41 D4 2p green & car 27.50 5.00
a. Perf 11 — —
b. Perf 14 ('18) 25.00 6.50
J42 D4 3p green & car 30.00 12.50
a. Perf 14, green & rose ('16) 110.00 45.00
J43 D4 4p green & car 21.00 10.00
a. Perf 14 ('21) 150.00 60.00
J44 D4 6p green & car 30.00 12.00
a. Perf 11 — —
J45 D4 1sh green & car 29.00 8.00
a. Perf 14, yel grn & scarlet ('23) 40.00 20.00
J46 D4 2sh green & car 100.00 13.50
J47 D4 5sh green & car 150.00 15.00
J48 D4 10sh green & car 400.00 275.00
a. Perf 14, yel grn & scarlet ('21) 2,250.
J49 D4 £1 green & car 850.00 500.00
a. Perf 14, yel grn & scarlet ('21) 1,200.
Nos. J39-J49 (11) 1,685. 898.50

Nos. J39-J48 and J40a, J41a, J44a are from the 1909 printings and have thicker paper and thick yellowish gum. The other listings are from the 1912-23 printings on thinner paper with thin white gum.

1922-30 **Wmk. 10** ***Perf. 14, 11 (4p)***
J50 D4 ½p grn & car ('23) 8.00 5.00
J51 D4 1p green & car 6.50 2.00
J52 D4 1½p green & rose ('25) 3.75 3.25
J53 D4 2p green & car 8.00 3.75
J54 D4 3p green & car 15.00 2.75
J55 D4 4p green & car ('30) 15.00 7.00
a. Perf 14 45.00 20.00
J56 D4 6p green & car 32.50 16.00
Nos. J50-J56 (7) 88.75 39.75

1931-36 **Wmk. 228** ***Perf. 11***
J57 D4 ½p yel green & rose ('34) 20.00 20.00
J58 D4 1p yel grn & rose ('32) 7.75 2.00
a. Perf 14 12.00 10.00

J59	D4	2p yel grn & rose ('33)	9.00	2.00
a.		Perf 14	10.00	10.00
J60	D4	3p yel green & rose ('36)	125.00	100.00
J61	D4	4p yel green & rose ('34)	20.00	4.00
J62	D4	6p yel green & rose ('36)	475.00	425.00
J63	D4	1sh yel green & rose ('34)	60.00	26.00
		Nos. J57-J63 (7)	716.75	579.00

D5

Engraved; Value Typo.

1938 *Perf. 14½x14*

J64	D5	½p green & car	3.00	*3.00*
J65	D5	1p green & car	10.00	.75
J66	D5	2p green & car	10.00	.50
J67	D5	3p green & car	40.00	20.00
J68	D5	4p green & car	12.00	1.00
J69	D5	6p green & car	90.00	40.00
J70	D5	1sh green & car	50.00	17.50
		Nos. J64-J70 (7)	215.00	82.75

Catalogue values for unused stamps in this section, from this point to the end of the section, are for Never Hinged items.

Type of 1938
Value Tablet Redrawn

Original

Redrawn

Pence denominations: "D" has melon-shaped center in redrawn tablet. The redrawn 3p differs slightly, having semi-melon-shaped "D" center, with vertical white stroke half filling it.

1sh. 1938: Numeral "1" narrow, with six background lines above.

1sh. 1947: Numeral broader, showing more white space around dotted central ornament. Three lines above.

1946-57 **Wmk. 228**

J71	D5	½p grn & car ('56)	5.00	4.00
J72	D5	1p grn & car ('47)	3.25	.85
J73	D5	2p green & car	4.25	1.00
J74	D5	3p green & car	8.00	1.00
J75	D5	4p grn & car ('52)	8.00	1.25
J76	D5	5p grn & car ('48)	9.00	2.00
J77	D5	6p grn & car ('47)	10.00	2.50
J78	D5	7p grn & car ('53)	5.50	6.00
J79	D5	8p grn & car ('57)	20.00	17.50
J80	D5	1sh grn & car ('47)	17.00	2.25
		Nos. J71-J80 (10)	90.00	38.35

1953-54

White Tablet, Carmine Numeral

J81	D5	1sh grn & car ('54)	15.00	5.50
J82	D5	2sh green & car	20.00	12.50
J83	D5	5sh green & car	22.50	7.50
		Nos. J81-J83 (3)	57.50	25.50

Issued: 2sh, 5sh, Aug. 26; 1sh, Feb. 17.

MILITARY STAMPS

Nos. 166, 191, 183A, 173, 175, 206 and 177 Overprinted in Black:

a

b

c

1946

Wrong font "6"

AN AN

Normal & Narrow "N"

Perf. 14½x14, 15x14, 11½, 13½x13

1946-47 **Wmk. 228**

M1	A24(a)	½p orange	3.00	3.00
		Never hinged	5.00	
a.		Wrong font "6" in ovpt.	60.00	*125.00*
b.		Narrow "N"	60.00	*125.00*
M2	A36(b)	1p brown vio	3.00	3.00
		Never hinged	5.00	
a.		Blue overprint	100.00	67.50
		Never hinged	125.00	
M3	A27(b)	3p dk vio brn	3.00	*3.00*
		Never hinged	5.00	
a.		Double overprint	750.00	
M4	A30(a)	6p brn violet	10.50	10.00
		Never hinged	16.00	
a.		Wrong font "6" in ovpt.	140.00	*210.00*
b.		Narrow "N"	140.00	*210.00*
M5	A16(a)	1sh gray green	10.50	10.00
		Never hinged	16.00	
a.		Wrong font "6" in ovpt.	175.00	*225.00*
b.		Narrow "N"	175.00	*225.00*
M6	A1(c)	2sh dk red brn	30.00	40.00
		Never hinged	60.00	
M7	A32(c)	5sh dl red brn	125.00	*175.00*
		Never hinged	225.00	
a.		Thin paper (#177a) ('48)	100.00	*175.00*
		Never hinged	140.00	
		Nos. M1-M7 (7)	185.00	244.00

"B.C.O.F." stands for "British Commonwealth Occupation Force."

Issue dates: Nos. M1-M3, Oct. 11, 1946, Nos. M4-M7, May 8, 1947.

OFFICIAL STAMPS

OVERPRINTED AND PERFORATED OFFICIAL STAMPS

Overprinted and perforated Official stamps are comparatively more difficult to find well centered than the basic issues on which they are printed. This is because poorly centered sheets that had been discarded were purposely chosen to be overprinted to save money.

PERFORATED OFFICIAL STAMPS

In 1913-31, postage stamps were perforated "OS" for official Australian Federal and State government use. The first of such issues were punched with large initials 14mm high and containing 18 and 17 holes in the O and S, respectively. When stamps with this size initial fell apart, a smaller size was used. This was 8.5mm high and had 12 or 11 holes in the O and S. A third size OS, 9mm high was also used for a short time. Stamps exist with double or triple perforatioins. The system of perforated initials was replaced in 1931 by printed initials.

PERFORATED LARGE OS

OA Plus Scott Number

1913 **Wmk. 8**

OA1	A1	½p green	17.50	9.50
		Never hinged	30.00	
		On newspaper, postal card		65.00
e.		Wmk. inverted		80.00
OA2	A1	1p car (I)	16.00	3.50
		Never hinged	32.50	
		On circular, cover		30.00
d.		Die II	21.00	5.75
		Never hinged	35.00	
		On circular, cover		32.50
n.		As #OA2, wmk. inverted	80.00	8.00
o.		As "d," wmk. inverted	80.00	8.00
OA3	A1	2p gray	30.00	12.50
		Never hinged	47.50	
		On cover		85.00
OA4	A1	2½p dark blue	290.00	125.00
		Never hinged	525.00	
		On cover		350.00
OA5	A1	3p ol bis (I)	160.00	72.50
		Never hinged	275.00	
		On cover		175.00
a.		Die II	300.00	80.00
		Never hinged	*600.00*	
		On cover	250.00	
b.		Pair, #OA5-OA5a	*750.00*	
h.		As #OA5, wmk. inverted	110.00	50.00
i.		As "a," wmk. inverted	400.00	92.50
OA6	A1	4p orange	160.00	22.50
		Never hinged	300.00	
		On cover		85.00
b.		4p yellow orange	225.00	92.50
OA7	A1	5p org brn	140.00	32.50
		Never hinged	275.00	
		On cover		160.00
OA8	A1	6p ultra (I)	140.00	26.00
		Never hinged	325.00	
		On cover		160.00
c.		Wmk. inverted	225.00	80.00
OA9	A1	9p purple	125.00	47.50
		Never hinged	300.00	
		On cover		200.00
c.		Wmk. inverted		3,100.

All examples of the 9p purple with inverted watermark were released as #OA9c, of which 6 used specimens are known.

OA10	A1	1sh blue green	160.00	29.00
		Never hinged	310.00	
		On cover		250.00
c.		Wmk. inverted	600.00	190.00
OA11	A1	2sh brown	350.00	160.00
		Never hinged	1,200.	
		On cover		—
OA12	A1	5sh yel & gray	875.00	500.00
		Never hinged	1,510.	
		On cover		—
OA13	A1	10sh pink & gray	2,000.	1,250.
		Never hinged	3,250.	
		On cover		—
OA14	A1	£1 ultra & brn	3,100.	2,300.
		Never hinged	4,800.	
		On cover		—
OA15	A1	£2 dp rose & blk	5,750.	3,500.
		Never hinged	8,400.	
		On cover		—

PERFORATED SMALL OS

OB Plus Scott Number

1914 **Wmk. 8**

OB1	A1	½p green	14.00	10.00
		Never hinged	30.00	
		On newspaper, postcard		100.00
e.		Wmk. inverted		47.50
OB2	A1	1p car (I)	16.00	6.25
		Never hinged	30.00	
		On circular, cover		45.00
d.		Die II	25.00	3.50
		Never hinged	40.00	
		On circular, cover		25.00
h.		Die III	18.00	2.50
		Never hinged	35.00	
		On circular, cover		25.00
OB3	A1	2p gray	57.50	5.25
		Never hinged	92.50	
		On cover		65.00
c.		Wmk. inverted	92.50	14.00
OB4	A1	2½p dark blue	290.00	110.00
		Never hinged	600.00	
		On cover		300.00
OB5	A1	3p ol bis (I)	80.00	7.00
		Never hinged	160.00	
		On cover		100.00
a.		Die II	210.00	50.00
		Never hinged	*400.00*	
		On cover		150.00
b.		Pair, #OB5-OB5a	—	
h.		As # OB5, wmk. inverted		
i.		As "a," wmk. inverted	*310.00*	*80.00*
OB6	A1	4p orange	175.00	80.00
		Never hinged	350.00	
		On cover		240.00
b.		4p yellow orange	225.00	100.00
OB7	A1	5p org brn	140.00	47.50
		Never hinged	275.00	
		On cover		200.00
OB8	A1	6p ultra (II)	85.00	14.00
		Never hinged	200.00	
		On cover		125.00
c.		Wmk. inverted	210.00	75.00
OB9	A1	9p purple	85.00	26.00
		Never hinged	200.00	
		On cover		150.00
OB10	A1	1st blue green	100.00	26.00
		Never hinged	250.00	
		On cover		275.00
OB11	A1	2sh brown	225.00	110.00
		Never hinged	750.00	
		On cover		—
OB12	A1	5sh yel & gray	1,100.	575.00
		Never hinged	1,900.	
		On cover		—
OB13	A1	10sh pink & gray	2,300.	1,400.
		Never hinged	4,250.	
		On cover		—
OB14	A1	£1 ultra & brn	3,750.	2,300.
		Never hinged	5,250.	
		On cover		—
OB15	A1	£2 dp rose & black	6,250.	3,750.
		Never hinged	12,000.	
		On cover		—

1914-24 **Wmk. 9**

OB19	A4	½p emerald	11.50	3.00
OB20	A4	½p orange	18.00	11.50
OB21	A4	1p red (I)	12.50	.90
c.		1p carmine (II)	350.00	16.00
d.		1p scarlet (I), rough paper	24.00	7.00
e.		1p rose red (Ia), rough paper	250.00	16.00
f.		1p brt rose (Ia), rough paper	475.00	45.00
OB22	A4	1p violet (I)	26.00	15.00
OB23	A4	1p green (I)	8.50	2.50
OB24	A4	1½p choc	29.00	3.00
a.		1½p red brown	24.00	2.25
OB25	A4	1½p emerald	16.00	1.40
OB26	A4	1½p scarlet	7.50	.70
OB27	A4	2p brn org (I)	15.00	1.40
OB28	A4	2p red (I)	20.00	4.50
OB29	A4	2p red brn (I)	22.50	17.00
OB30	A4	3p ultra (I)	35.00	7.00
OB31	A4	4p orange	45.00	4.00
a.		4p yellow	250.00	55.00
OB32	A4	4p violet	47.50	15.00
OB33	A4	4p ultra	70.00	12.50
OB34	A4	4p ol bis	45.00	7.00
OB35	A4	4½p violet	120.00	14.00
OB36	A4	5p org brn (I)	57.50	10.00
a.		5p chestnut (I), rough paper	*1,500.*	140.00

All examples of the 5p chestnut on rough paper were released as #OB36a.

OB37	A4	1sh4p light blue	60.00	19.00

1915 **Wmk. 9**

OB38	A1	2p gray	92.50	12.50
OB40	A1	6p ultra (II)	150.00	17.50
a.		Die III	1,600.	450.00
OB41	A1	9p violet	210.00	75.00
OB42	A1	1sh blue green	210.00	45.00
OB43	A1	2sh brown	625.00	110.00
OB44	A1	5sh yellow & gray	800.00	150.00

1915-24 **Wmk. 10**

OB45	A1	2p gray (I)	22.50	5.75
a.		Die II	35.00	17.50
OB46	A1	2½p dark blue	55.00	14.00
OB47	A1	3p ol bis (I)	27.50	5.00
a.		Die II	100.00	47.50
b.		Die IV	27.50	16.00
OB48	A1	6p ultra (II)	40.00	7.00
b.		Die III	1,250.	400.00
c.		Die IV	55.00	16.00
OB49	A1	6p yel brn (IV)	25.00	3.00
OB50	A1	9p violet (II)	30.00	14.00
a.		9p lilac (III)	30.00	14.00
OB51	A1	1sh blue grn (I)	26.00	3.00
a.		Die IV	26.00	4.00
OB52	A1	2sh brown	125.00	17.00
OB53	A1	2sh vio brn (II)	62.50	14.00
OB54	A1	5sh yel & gray	200.00	52.50
OB55	A1	10sh brt pink & gray	450.00	70.00
OB56	A1	£1 ultra & brn	2,300.	1,400.
OB57	A1	£1 gray (IV)	800.00	400.00
OB58	A1	£2 rose & blk	2,300.	1,000.

1918-20 **Wmk. 11**

OB60	A4	½p emerald	17.50	7.00
OB61	A4	1p rose (I)	120.00	45.00
OB62	A4	1p green (I)	17.50	17.50
OB63	A4	1½p chocolate	21.00	2.90
a.		1½p red brown	25.00	2.60

1924 **Unwmk.**

OB64	A4	1p green	80.00	75.00
OB65	A4	1½p carmine	85.00	75.00

Perf. 14, 13½x12½

1926-30 **Wmk. 203**

OB66	A4	½p orange	4.50	1.40
a.		Perf. 14	200.00	85.00
OB67	A4	1p green (I)	4.50	1.40
a.		Die Ia	110.00	140.00
b.		Perf. 14	11.50	1.40
OB68	A4	1½p rose red	8.50	2.25
c.		Perf. 14	24.00	2.25
OB69	A4	1½p red brn	18.00	4.25
OB70	A4	2p red brn (II)	30.00	16.00
a.		Die I, perf. 14	140.00	45.00
OB71	A4	2p red (II)	18.00	4.25
OB72	A4	3p ultra (I)	32.50	5.75
a.		Die II	25.00	4.25
b.		Perf. 14	70.00	15.00
OB73	A4	4p ol bis	25.00	4.25
a.		Perf. 14	150.00	45.00
OB74	A4	4½p violet	150.00	40.00
a.		Perf. 13½x12½	110.00	110.00
OB75	A4	5p brown buff (II)	57.50	8.00
OB76	A4	1sh4p pale turq bl	260.00	27.50
a.		Perf. 14	350.00	140.00

1928

OB95	A3	3p deep blue	15.00	10.00

1928-30 **Wmk. 203**

OB96	A1	6p brown	26.00	4.50
OB97	A1	9p violet	50.00	6.25
OB98	A1	1sh blue green	26.00	4.50
OB99	A1	2sh red brown	75.00	10.00
OB100	A1	5sh yel & gray	225.00	85.00
OB101	A1	10sh pink & gray	2,000.	
OB102	A1	£2 dl red & blk	3,750.	

1930

OB104	A7	1½p dark red	11.50	8.00
OB105	A7	3p dark blue	16.00	9.25

PERFORATED MEDIUM OS

OC Plus Scott Number

1927

OC94	A5	1½p brown red	17.50	9.00

1929

OC103	A6	1½p dull red	17.50	11.50

1929

OCC1	AP1	3p deep green	26.00	14.00

OVERPRINTED OFFICIAL STAMPS

See note at beginning of section.

Overprinted

On Regular Issue of 1931

1931, May 4 Unwmk. *Perf. 11, 11½*

O1	A8	2p dull red	97.50	27.50
O2	A8	3p blue	325.00	60.00

These stamps were issued primarily for official use but to prevent speculation a quantity was issued for public distribution.

Used values are for cto copies.

Counterfeit overprints exist.

On Regular Issues of 1928-32

1932 Wmk. 203 *Perf. 13½x12½*

O3	A4	2p red (II)	20.00	10.00
O4	A4	4p olive bister	30.00	20.00

Perf. 11½, 12

O5	A1	6p brown	67.50	60.00

1932-33 Wmk. 228 *Perf. 13½x12½*

O6	A4	½p orange	6.00	2.75
a.		Inverted overprint	—	—
O7	A4	1p green (I)	3.50	1.00
O8	A4	2p red (II)	10.00	3.00
a.		Inverted overprint		—
O9	A4	3p ultra (II) ('33)	14.00	7.00
O10	A4	5p brown buff	42.50	40.00

Perf. 11½, 12

O11	A1	6p yellow brown	35.00	25.00
a.		Inverted overprint		—
		Nos. O6-O11 (6)	111.00	78.75

1932 Unwmk. *Perf. 11, 11½*

O12	A9	2p red	5.50	4.50
O13	A9	3p blue	18.00	18.00
O14	A16	1sh gray green	55.00	40.00
		Nos. O12-O14 (3)	78.50	62.50

AUSTRIA

'os-trē-ə

LOCATION — Central Europe
AREA — 32,378 sq. mi.
POP. — 6,760,233
CAPITAL — Vienna

Before 1867 Austria was an absolute monarchy, which included Hungary and Lombardy-Venetia. In 1867 the Austro-Hungarian Monarchy was established, with Austria and Hungary as equal partners. After World War I, in 1918, the different nationalities established their own states and only the German-speaking parts remained, forming a republic under the name "Deutschosterreich" (German Austria), which name was shortly again changed to "Austria." In 1938 German forces occupied Austria, which became part of the German Reich.

60 Kreuzer = 1 Gulden
100 Neu-Kreuzer = 1 Gulden (1858)
100 Heller = 1 Krone (1899)
100 Groschen = 1 Schilling (1925)

Unused stamps without gum sell for about one-third or less of the values quoted.

Watermarks

Wmk. 91 — "BRIEF-MARKEN" In Double-lined Capitals Across the Middle of the Sheet

Wmk. 140 — Crown

Issues of the Austrian Monarchy (including Hungary)

Coat of Arms — A1

NINE KREUZER

Type I. One heavy line around coat of arms center. On the 9kr the top of "9" is about on a level with "Kreuzer" and not near the top of the label. Each cliche has the "9" in a different position.

Type IA. As type I, but with 1¼mm between "9" and "K."

Type II. One heavy line around coat of arms center. On the 9kr the top of "9" is much higher than the top of the word "Kreuzer" and nearly touches the top of the label.

Type III. As type II, but with two, thinner, lines around the center.

Wmk. K.K.H.M. in Sheet or Unwmk.

1850 Typo. *Imperf.*

The stamps of this issue were at first printed on a rough hand-made paper, varying in thickness and having a watermark in script letters K.K.H.M., the initials of Kaiserlich Königliches Handels-Ministerium (Imperial and Royal Ministry of Commerce), vertically in the gutter between the panes. Parts of these letters show on margin stamps in the sheet. From 1854 a thick, smooth machine-made paper without watermark was used.

Thin to Thick Paper

1	A1 1kr yellow		1,550.	100.00
	No gum		350.00	
	On cover			340.00
a.	Printed on both sides		*1,900.*	125.00
b.	1kr orange		2,050.	125.00
	No gum		450.00	
	On cover			400.00
c.	1kr brown orange		3,100.	550.00
	No gum		700.00	
	On cover			1,950.
e.	1kr cadmium yellow		1,950.	110.00
	No gum		450.00	
	On cover			400.00
2	A1 2kr black		1,250.	72.50
	No gum		300.00	
	On cover			240.00
a.	Ribbed paper		—	*3,250.*
	On cover			*10,000.*
b.	2kr gray black		2,050.	110.00
	No gum		450.00	
	On cover			300.00
d.	Half used as 1kr on cover			*50,000.*

A cover bearing one example of the 2 kreuzer and a diagonally bisected example of the same stamp realized the equivalent of U.S. $50,950 at a Zurich auction in 2003.

d.	Half used as 1kr on cover, single franking		*42,500.*

A faulty cover bearing one example of the 2 kreuzer diagonally bisected, paying a 1 kreuzer rate, realized the equivalent of U.S. $41,520 at a Zurich auction in 2004.

e.	2kr silver gray ('50, 1st printing)	2,750.	575.00
	No gum	650.00	
	On cover		1,350.
3	A1 3kr red	725.00	3.50
	No gum	165.00	
	On cover		21.00
a.	Ribbed paper	*3,400.*	125.00
	No gum	775.00	
	On cover		400.00
b.	Laid paper	—	*13,000.*
	On cover		*19,000.*
c.	Printed on both sides		*8,600.*
d.	3kr dark carmine	1,500.	21.00
	No gum	350.00	
	On cover		82.50
4	A1 6kr brown	1,000.	7.25
	No gum	240.00	
	On cover		37.50
a.	Ribbed paper		*2,050.*
	On cover		*5,750.*
c.	Diagonal half used as 3kr on cover		*16,000.*
d.	6kr black brown	—	150.00
	On cover		350.00
e.	6kr pale reddish brown	1,250.	6.25
	No gum	300.00	
	On cover		35.00
5	A1 9kr blue, type II	2,050.	9.00
	No gum	475.00	
	On cover		40.00
a.	9kr blue, type I	*1,900.*	15.00
	No gum	450.00	
	On cover		90.00
b.	9kr blue, type IA	*13,500.*	*1,100.*
	On cover		*2,100.*
c.	Laid paper, type III		*11,500.*
d.	Printed on both sides, type II		*8,000.*
f.	9kr pale blue, type I	1,700.	11.00
	No gum	425.00	
	On cover		75.00
g.	9kr very dark blue, type III	2,050.	27.50
	No gum	500.00	
	On cover		60.00

1854

Machine-made Paper, Type III

1d	A1	1kr yellow	*1,250.*	90.00
		No gum	290.00	
		On cover		265.00
1f	A1	1kr cadmium yellow	*1,700.*	115.00
		No gum	400.00	
		On cover		315.00
1g	A1	1kr yellow ocher	*1,950.*	120.00
		No gum	475.00	
		On cover		340.00
1h	A1	1kr golden yellow	*3,100.*	200.00
		No gum	750.00	
		On cover		475.00
1i	A1	1kr mustard yellow		350.00
1j	A1	1kr lemon yellow	*1,250*	92.50
		No gum	310.00	
		On cover		275.00
2c	A1	2kr black	*1,550.*	67.50
		No gum	350.00	
		On cover		225.00
3e	A1	3kr red	*450.00*	2.50
		No gum	100.00	
		On cover		14.00
f.		3kr red, type I	*3,850.*	47.50
		No gum	900.00	
		On cover		175.00
4b	A1	6kr brown	*800.00*	6.00
		No gum	190.00	
		On cover		27.50
4f	A1	6kr reddish brown	*850.00*	5.50
		No gum	200.00	
		On cover		27.50
5e	A1	9kr blue	*900.00*	2.50
		No gum	200.00	
		On cover		15.00
5g	A1	9kr dark slate blue	*1,200.*	8.00
		No gum	300.00	
		On cover		35.00

Full margins = 1½mm.

In 1852-54, Nos. 1-5, rouletted 14, were used in Tokay and Homonna. A 12kr blue exists, but was not issued.

The reprints are type III in brighter colors, some on paper watermarked "Briefmarken" in the sheet.

For similar design see Lombardy-Venetia A1.

Values for used pairs

Hand-made Paper

1	A1	1kr yellow	310.00
		On cover	850.00
1b	A1	1kr orange	320.00
		On cover	900.00
1c	A1	1kr brown orange	1,100.
		On cover	2,400.
1e	A1	1kr cadmium yellow	340.00
		On cover	875.00
2	A1	2kr black	265.00
		On cover	2,600.
2b	A1	2kr gray black	260.00
		On cover	2,400.
2e	A1	2kr silver gray	1,500.
		On cover	—
3	A1	3kr red	17.50
		On cover	70.00
3d	A1	3kr dark carmine	47.50
		On cover	160.00
4	A1	6kr brown	75.00
		On cover	260.00
5	A1	9kr blue, type II	27.50
		On cover	425.00
5a	A1	9kr blue, type I	115.00
		On cover	325.00
5f	A1	9kr pale blue, type I	115.00
		On cover	325.00

Machine-made Paper, Type III

1d	A1	1kr yellow	250.00
		On cover	725.00
1f	A1	1kr cadmium yellow	440.00
		On cover	1,250.
1g	A1	1kr yellow ocher	360.00
		On cover	1,000.
1h	A1	1kr golden yellow	440.00
		On cover	1,250.
1j	A1	1kr lemon yellow	265.00
		On cover	725.00
2c	A1	2kr black	225.00
		On cover	2,200.
3e	A1	3kr red	12.00
		On cover	90.00
3f	A1	3kr red, type I	115.00
		On cover	250.00
4b	A1	6kr brown	62.50
		On cover	165.00
5e	A1	9kr blue	25.00
		On cover	90.00

Values for used strips of 3

Hand-made Paper

1	A1	1kr yellow	750.00
		On cover	1,550.
1b	A1	1kr orange	825.00
		On cover	1,700.
1c	A1	1kr brown orange	1,900.
		On cover	4,000.
1e	A1	1kr cadmium yellow	840.00
		On cover	1,725.
2	A1	2kr black	800.00
		On cover	1,750.

A used strip of eight of the 2 kreuzer black, hand-made paper, realized the equivalent of U.S. $24,535 at a Zurich auction in 2004.

2b	A1	2kr gray black	825.00
		On cover	1,575.
2e	A1	2kr silver gray	2,850.
3	A1	3kr red	57.50
		On cover	225.00
3d	A1	3kr dark carmine	165.00
		On cover	440.00
4	A1	6kr brown	360.00
		On cover	750.00

A used strip of eight of the 6 kreuzer brown, hand-made paper, realized the equivalent of U.S. $16,040 at a Zurich auction in 2004.

5	A1	9kr blue, type II	150.00
		On cover	675.00
5a	A1	9kr blue, type I	325.00
		On cover	775.00
5f	A1	9kr pale blue, type I	325.00

Machine-made Paper, Type III

1d	A1	1kr yellow	650.00
		On cover	1,400.
1f	A1	1kr cadmium yellow	1,100.
		On cover	*2,200.*
1g	A1	1kr yellow ocher	840.00
		On cover	1,675.
1h	A1	1kr golden yellow	1,100.
		On cover	2,150.
1j	A1	1kr lemon yellow	675.00
		On cover	1,400.
2c	A1	2kr black	725.00
		On cover	1,500.
3e	A1	3kr red	40.00
		On cover	325.00

3f	A1	3kr red, type I		300.00
		On cover		675.00
4b	A1	6kr brown		275.00
		On cover		640.00
5e	A1	9kr blue		120.00
		On cover		375.00

Values for used blocks of 4

Hand-made Paper

1	A1	1kr yellow		6,500.
1b	A1	1kr orange		7,250.
1c	A1	1kr brown orange		
1e	A1	1kr cadmium yellow		7,250.
2	A1	2kr black		11,000.
2b	A1	2kr gray black		12,000.
2e	A1	2kr silver gray		
3	A1	3kr red	12,000.	2,900.
3d	A1	3kr dark carmine	13,500.	4,750.
4	A1	6kr brown	13,500.	5,750.
4d	A1	6kr black brown		
5	A1	9kr blue, type II	37,500.	5,500.
5a	A1	9kr blue, type I	45,000.	5,750.
5f	A1	9kr pale blue, type I		5,750.

Machine-made Paper, Type III

1d	A1	1kr yellow		6,750.
1f	A1	1kr cadmium yellow		
1g	A1	1kr yellow ocher		7,500.
1h	A1	1kr golden yellow		
1j	A1	1kr lemon yellow		5,250.
2c	A1	2kr black	42,500.	11,000.
3e	A1	3kr red	8,250.	1,500.
3f	A1	3kr red, type I		5,000.
4b	A1	6kr brown	8,500.	5,000.
5e	A1	9kr blue	11,500.	2,250.

Values for stamps used in Lombardy-Venetia

Hand-made Paper

1	A1	1kr yellow, *from*	310.00
		On cover, *from*	4,500.
1b	A1	1kr orange, *from*	350.00
		On cover, *from*	4,750.
2	A1	2kr black, *from*	275.00
		On cover, *from*	3,100.
3	A1	3kr red, *from*	50.00
		On cover, *from*	350.00
3a	A1	3kr red (ribbed paper), *from*	210.00
		On cover, *from*	1,200.
4	A1	6kr brown, *from*	50.00
		On cover, *from*	400.00
5	A1	9kr blue (II)(from)	190.00
		On cover, *from*	1,700.
5a	A1	9kr blue (I)(from)	90.00
		On cover, *from*	900.00

Machine-made Paper, Type III

1d	A1	1kr yellow, *from*	550.00
		On cover, *from*	12,500.
2c	A1	2kr black, *from*	475.00
		On cover, *from*	8,500.
3e	A1	3kr red, *from*	275.00
		On cover, *from*	1,700.
4b	A1	6kr brown, *from*	310.00
		On cover, *from*	3,100.
5e	A1	9kr blue, *from*	410.00
		On cover, *from*	3,400.

Values for Stamps Cancelled First Day of Issue (June 1, 1850)

1	A1	1kr yellow	—
		On cover	—
2	A1	2kr black	—
		On cover	57,500.
3	A1	3kr red	1,150.
		On cover	21,500.

A 3 kreuzer stamp on small piece with first day cancellation, used in Fiume, realized the equivalent of U.S. $12,200 at a German auction in 2003.

A 3 kreuzer stamp on cover from Prague, with first day cancellation realized the equivalent of U.S. $16,985 at a Zurich auction in 2003.

4	A1	6kr brown	1,250.
		On cover	25,000.
5a	A1	9kr blue, type I	1,250.
		On cover	21,500.

Values for Stamps with Red Cancellations

Hand-Made Paper

1	A1	1kr yellow	3,000.
2	A1	2kr black	1,100.
3	A1	3kr red	550.00
4	A1	6kr brown	525.00
5	A1	9kr blue, type II	725.00

Machine-Made Paper

1a	A1	1kr yellow	1,050.
2c	A1	2kr black	400.00
3e	A1	3kr red	200.00
4b	A1	6kr brown	80.00
5e	A1	9kr blue	50.00

Values for Stamps with Blue Cancellations

Hand-Made Paper

1	A1	1kr yellow	900.00
2	A1	2kr black	850.00
3	A1	3kr red	210.00
4	A1	6kr brown	225.00
5	A1	9kr blue, type II	250.00

Machine-Made Paper

1a	A1	1kr yellow	650.00
2c	A1	2kr black	700.00
3e	A1	3kr red	110.00
4b	A1	6kr brown	105.00
5e	A1	9kr blue	140.00

Rouletted 14

1	A1	1kr yellow	—
		On cover, Tokay cancellation	—
2	A1	2kr black	—
		On cover, Tokay cancellation	—

A cover bearing one example of 1 kreuzer and one 2 kreuzer, both with Tokay roulettes realized the equivalent of U.S. $169,840 at a Zurich auction in 2003.

3	A1	3kr red	1,375.
		On cover, Tokay cancellation	11,500.

A cover bearing one example of the 3 kreuzer with Tokay roulettes realized U.S. $11,550 at a New York auction in 2003.

4	A1	6kr brown	1,875.
		On cover, Tokay cancellation	14,000.
5a	A1	9kr blue, type I	1,600.
		On cover, Tokay cancellation	12,500.

A cover bearing one example of the 3 kreuzer and one of the 6 kreuzer, both with Tokay roulettes, realized the equivalent of U.S. $20,045 at a Geneva auction in 2003.

This roulette was applied to stamps by the postmasters of the Tokay and Hommona post offices (now in Hungary) post offices during 1852-54.

A2

A3

Emperor Franz Josef — A4

A5

A6

1858-59 Embossed *Perf. 14½*

Two Types of Each Value.

Type I. Loops of the bow at the back of the head broken, except the 2kr. In the 2kr, the "2" has a flat foot, thinning to the right. The frame line in the UR corner is thicker than the line below. In the 5kr the top frame line is unbroken.

Type II. Loops complete. Wreath projects further at top of head. In the 2kr, the "2" has a more curved foot of uniform thickness, with a shading line in the upper and lower curves. The frame line UR is thicker than the line below. In the 5kr the top frame line is broken.

6	A2	2kr yellow, type II	1,050.	47.50
		No gum	210.00	
		On cover		110.00
a.		2kr yellow, type I	2,250.	400.00
		No gum	450.00	
		On cover		650.00
b.		2kr orange, type II	2,400.	240.00
		No gum	475.00	
		On cover		450.00
c.		Half used as 1kr on cover		36,000.
d.		2kr dark orange, type II	7,250.	650.00
		No gum	1,800.	
		On cover		1,450.

A cover bearing a 2 kreuzer dark orange and a 3 kreuzer pale green realized the equivalent of U.S. $18,870 at a Zurich auction in 2003.

7	A3	3kr black, type II	2,600.	210.00
		No gum	575.00	
		On cover		400.00
a.		3kr black, type I	1,575.	250.00
		No gum	325.00	
		On cover		450.00
b.		3kr gray black, type I	3,600.	525.00
		No gum	825.00	
		On cover		900.00
8	A3	3kr green, type II ('59)	1,350.	160.00
		No gum	290.00	
		On cover		300.00
a.		3k bluish green, type II ('59)	1,650.	190.00
		No gum	400.00	
		On cover		350.00
9	A4	5kr red, type II	400.00	1.10
		No gum	80.00	
		On cover		5.00
a.		5kr red, type I	825.00	22.50
		No gum	175.00	
		On cover		32.50
b.		5kr red, type II with type I frame	975.00	30.00
		No gum	225.00	
		On cover		55.00
10	A5	10kr brown, type II	825.00	2.75
		No gum	175.00	
		On cover		8.00
a.		10kr brown, type I	1,375.	42.50
		No gum	325.00	
		On cover		65.00
b.		Half used as 5kr on cover, single franking		16,000.

A cover bearing a diagonally bisected 10 kreuzer, paying a 5 kreuzer rate, realized the equivalent of U.S. $14,210 at a Zurich auction in 2004.

c.		Half used as 5kr on 15kr rate cover		22,000.
11	A6	15kr blue, type II	800.00	1.75
		No gum	160.00	
		On cover		5.00
a.		Type I	1,750.	18.00
		No gum	375.00	
		On cover		32.50
b.		Half used as 7kr on cover		—
c.		15k deep blue, Type I	1,800.	19.00
		No gum	450.00	
		On cover		37.50

The reprints are of type II and are perforated 10½, 11, 12, 12½ and 13. There are also imperforate reprints of Nos. 6 to 8.

For similar designs see Lombardy-Venetia A2-A6.

Values for used pairs

6	A2	2kr yellow, type II	110.00
		On cover	1,250.
6a	A2	2kr yellow, type I	875.00
		On cover	3,100.
6b	A2	2kr orange, type II	625.00
		On cover	—
7	A3	3kr black, type II	425.00
		On cover	2,000.
7a	A3	3kr black, type I	625.00
		On cover	2,250.
7b	A3	3kr gray black, type I	1,150.
		On cover	—
8	A3	3kr green, type II ('59)	375.00
		On cover	2,050.
9	A4	5kr red, type II	5.50
		On cover	18.00
9a	A4	5kr red, type I	42.50
		On cover	85.00
9b	A4	5kr red, type II with type I frame	65.00
		On cover	—
10	A5	10kr brown, type II	18.00
		On cover	45.00
10a	A5	10kr brown, type I	90.00
		On cover	160.00
11	A6	15kr blue, type II	17.00
		On cover	37.50
11a	A6	15kr blue, type I	4.00
		On cover	125.00

Values for used strips of 3

6	A2	2kr yellow, type II	200.00
		On cover	2,400.
6a	A2	2kr yellow, type I	1,450.
		On cover	4,400.
7	A3	3kr black, type II	850.00
		On cover	—
7a	A3	3kr black, type I	900.00
		On cover	—
7b	A3	3kr gray black, type I	2,600.
		On cover	—
8	A3	3kr green, type II ('59)	725.00
		On cover	—
9	A4	5kr red, type II	18.00
		On cover	110.00
9a	A4	5kr red, type I	75.00
		On cover	225.00
9b	A4	5kr red, type II with type 1 frame	110.00
		On cover	—
10	A5	10kr brown, type II	47.50
		On cover	250.00
10a	A5	10kr brown, type I	150.00
		On cover	325.00
11	A6	15kr blue, type II	29.00
		On cover	150.00
11a	A6	15kr blue, type I	110.00
		On cover	250.00

Values for used strips of 4

6	A2	2kr yellow, type II	475.00
6a	A2	2kr yellow, type I	2,050.
7	A3	3kr black, type II	1,150.
7a	A3	3kr black, type I	1,500.
7b	A3	3kr gray black, type II	2,800.
8	A3	3kr green, type II	1,100.
9	A4	5kr red, type II	60.00
9a	A4	5kr red, type II	190.00
9b	A4	5kr red, type II with type I frame	—
10	A5	10kr brown, type II	140.00
10a	A5	10kr brown, type I	300.00
11	A6	15kr blue, type II	87.50
11a	A6	15kr blue, type I	260.00

Values for used blocks of 4

6	A2	2kr yellow, type II		3,200.
6a	A2	2kr yellow, type I		7,750.
7	A3	3kr black, type II		4,250.
7a	A3	3kr black, type I	13,000.	5,250.
7b	A3	3kr gray black, type I		—

8 A3 3kr green, type II ('59) 4,750.
9 A4 5kr red, type II 3,500. 450.00
On cover 950.00
9a A4 5kr red, type I 900.00
On cover 1,550.
9b A4 5kr red, type II with type 1 frame —
10 A5 10kr brown, type II 725.00
On cover 1,600.
10a A5 10kr brown, type I 1,275.
On cover 2,900.
11 A6 15kr blue, type II 500.00
On cover 1,300.
11a A6 15kr blue, type I 1,100.
On cover 2,400.

Values for stamps, covers used in Lombardy-Venetia

6 A2 2kr yellow, type II, *from* 900.00
On cover, *from* 13,000.
6a A2 2kr yellow, type I, *from* 1,500.
On cover, *from* 15,000.
6b A2 2kr orange, type II, *from* 2,400.
On cover —
7 A3 3kr black, type II, *from* 350.00
On cover, *from* 3,650.
7a A3 3kr black, type I, *from* 400.00
On cover, *from* 4,000.
8 A3 3kr green, type II ('59)(from) 425.00
On cover, *from* 6,000.
9 A4 5kr red, type II, *from* 200.00
On cover, *from* 1,500.
9a A4 5kr red, type I, *from* 200.00
On cover, *from* 2,000.
10 A5 10kr brown, type II, *from* 190.00
On cover, *from* 2,400.
10a A5 10kr brown, type I, *from* 240.00
On cover, *from* 2,900.
11 A6 15kr blue, type II, *from* 240.00
On cover, *from* 4,250.
11a A6 15kr blue, type I, *from* 325.00
On cover, *from* 4,500.

Values for Stamps with Red Cancellations

6 A2 2kr yellow, type II 140.00
6a A2 2kr yellow, type I 650.00
6b A2 2kr orange, type II 4,150.
7 A3 3kr black, type II 210.00
7a A3 3kr black, type I 250.00
8 A3 3kr green, type II ('59) 225.00
9 A4 5kr red, type II 25.00
9a A4 5kr red, type I 150.00
10 A5 10kr brown, type II 20.00
10a A5 10kr brown, type I 80.00
11 A6 15kr blue, type II 11.00
11a A6 15kr blue, type I 75.00

Values for Stamps with Blue Cancellations

6 A2 2kr yellow, type II 1,100.
6a A2 2kr yellow, type I 1,600.
6b A2 2kr orange, type II 2,000.
7 A3 3kr black, type II 900.00
7a A3 3kr black, type I 1,000.
8 A3 3kr green, type II ('59) 575.00
9 A4 5kr red, type II 67.50
9a A4 5kr red, type I 82.50
10 A5 10kr brown, type II 75.00
10a A5 10kr brown, type I 150.00
11 A6 15kr blue, type II 82.50
11a A6 15kr blue, type I 140.00

Values for Stamps on Cover Cancelled First Day of Issue (Nov. 1, 1858)

6a A2 2kr yellow, type I 25,000.
7a A3 3kr black, type I 13,500.
9a A4 5kr red, type I 9,500.
10a A5 10kr brown, type I 11,500.
11a A6 15kr blue, type I 12,500.

Franz Josef — A7

Coat of Arms — A8

1860-61 Embossed *Perf. 14*

12 A7 2kr yellow 400.00 29.00
No gum 80.00
On cover 65.00
a. Half used as 1kr on cover 25,000.
13 A7 3kr green 325.00 25.00
No gum 72.50
On cover 62.50
a. 3kr yellow green 400.00 35.00
No gum 100.00
On cover 67.50
14 A7 5kr red 240.00 .50
No gum 50.00
On cover 4.00
a. 5kr deep red 325.00 2.75
No gum 80.00
On cover 10.00
15 A7 10kr brown 325.00 1.75
No gum 65.00
On cover 7.25
a. Half used as 5kr on cover 9,000.
b. 10kr deep brown 385.00 5.50
No gum 100.00
On cover 13.50
16 A7 15kr blue 425.00 1.10
No gum 87.50
On cover 5.00
a. 15k deep blue 550.00 4.00
No gum 140.00
On cover 10.00

Values for Pairs

12 A7 2kr yellow 1,300. 70.00
On cover 700.00
13 A7 3kr green 1,250. 72.50
On cover 975.00
14 A7 5kr red 800.00 4.00
On cover 17.50
15 A7 10kr brown 900.00 7.00
On cover 32.50
16 A7 15kr blue 1,050. 5.00
On cover 24.00

Values for Strips of 3

12 A7 2kr yellow 120.00
On cover 1,900.
13 A7 3kr green 110.00
On cover 1,800.
14 A7 5kr red 15.00
On cover 57.50
15 A7 10kr brown 29.00
On cover 160.00
16 A7 15kr blue 25.00
On cover 110.00

Values for Strips of 4

12 A7 2kr yellow 210.00
13 A7 3kr green 200.00
14 A7 5kr red 35.00
15 A7 10kr brown 87.50
16 A7 15kr blue 62.50

Values for Blocks of 4

12 A7 2kr yellow 4,400. 1,400.
On cover 4,000.
13 A7 3kr green 4,250. 1,400.
On cover 3,750.
14 A7 5kr red 2,400. 210.00
On cover 650.00
15 A7 10kr brown 3,250. 425.00
On cover 1,150.
16 A7 15kr blue 4,000. 310.00
On cover 900.00

Values for stamps, covers used in Lombardy-Venetia

12 A7 2kr yellow, *from* 550.00
On cover, *from* 13,750.
13 A7 3kr green, *from* 450.00
On cover, *from* 12,500.
14 A7 5kr red, *from* 165.00
On cover, *from* 1,900.
15 A7 10kr brown, *from* 225.00
On cover, *from* 2,100.
16 A7 15kr blue, *from* 375.00
On cover, *from* 5,750.

The reprints are perforated 9, 9½, 10, 10½, 11, 11½, 12, 12½, 13 and 13½.

There are also imperforate reprints of the 2 and 3kr.

For similar design see Lombardy-Venetia A7. For overprints see Poland Nos. J11-J12.

1863

17 A8 2kr yellow 550.00 95.00
No gum 110.00
On cover 190.00
a. Half used as 1kr on cover —
18 A8 3kr green 475.00 85.00
No gum 95.00
On cover 190.00
a. 3kr yellow green 700.00 100.00
No gum 175.00
On cover 250.00
19 A8 5kr rose 450.00 12.00
No gum 95.00
On cover 32.50
a. 5kr carmine rose 550.00 16.00
No gum 140.00
On cover 50.00
20 A8 10kr blue 1,250. 14.50
No gum 250.00
On cover 40.00
a. 10kr deep blue 1,350. 15.00
No gum 325.00
On cover 45.00
21 A8 15kr yellow brown 1,200. 15.00
No gum 240.00
On cover 45.00
a. 15kr deep brown 1,500. 20.00
No gum 375.00
On cover 60.00

Values for used pairs

17 A8 2kr yellow 240.00
18 A8 3kr green 210.00
19 A8 5kr rose 25.00
20 A8 10kr blue 32.50
21 A8 15kr yellow brown 40.00

Values for Stamps with Red Cancellations

17 A8 2kr yellow 1,650.
18 A8 3kr green 200.00
19 A8 5kr rose 45.00
20 A8 10kr blue 40.00
21 A8 15kr yellow brown 40.00

Values for Stamps with Blue Cancellations

17 A8 2kr yellow 475.00
18 A8 3kr green 275.00
19 A8 5kr rose 47.50
20 A8 10kr blue 95.00
21 A8 15kr yellow brown 87.50

For similar design see Lombardy-Venetia A1.

Wmk. 91, or, before July 1864, Unwmkd.

1863-64 *Perf. 9½*

22 A8 2kr yellow ('64) 175.00 11.50
No gum 35.00
On cover 37.50
a. Ribbed paper 450.00
On cover 1,250.
b. Half used as 1kr on cover 22,000.
c. 2kr deep yellow 200.00 15.50
No gum 50.00
On cover 50.00
23 A8 3kr green ('64) 175.00 12.00
No gum 35.00
On cover 45.00
a. 3kr deep green ('64) 210.00 17.00
No gum 55.00
On cover 60.00
24 A8 5kr rose 50.00 .40
No gum 10.00
On cover 4.50
a. Ribbed paper 650.00
On cover 2,100.
b. 5kr carmine rose 140.00 2.75
No gum 35.00
On cover 6.75
25 A8 10kr blue 225.00 3.00
No gum 42.50
On cover 10.00
a. Half used as 5kr on cover 18,000.
b. 10kr greenish blue 250.00 6.75
No gum 62.50
On cover 12.00
26 A8 15kr yellow brown 200.00 1.60
No gum 40.00
On cover 7.25
a. 15kr deep brown 240.00 2.25
No gum 60.00
On cover 10.00
Nos. 22-26 (5) 825.00 28.50

Values for Pairs

22 A8 2kr yellow ('64) 32.50
23 A8 3kr green ('64) 32.50
24 A8 5kr rose 1.50
25 A8 10kr blue 8.00
26 A8 15kr yellow brown 7.50

Values for Stamps with Red Cancellations

22 A8 2kr yellow ('64) 440.00
23 A8 3kr green ('64) 35.00
24 A8 5kr rose 17.50
25 A8 10kr blue 12.00
26 A8 15kr yellow brown 7.50

Values for Stamps with Blue Cancellations

22 A8 2kr yellow ('64) 110.00
23 A8 3kr green ('64) 30.00
24 A8 5kr rose 6.00
25 A8 10kr blue 13.00
26 A8 15kr yellow brown 9.50

Values for Stamps with Green Cancellations

22 A8 2kr yellow ('64) 750.00
23 A8 3kr green ('64) 750.00
24 A8 5kr rose 275.00

The reprints are perforated 10½, 11½, 13 and 13½. There are also imperforate reprints of the 2 and 3kr.

Issues of Austro-Hungarian Monarchy

From 1867 to 1871 the independent postal administrations of Austria and Hungary used the same stamps.

A9

A10

5 kr:

Type I. In arabesques in lower left corner, the small ornament at left of the curve nearest the figure "5" is short and has three points at bottom.

Type II. The ornament is prolonged within the curve and has two points at bottom. The corresponding ornament at top of the lower left corner does not touch the curve (1872).

Type III. Similar to type II but the top ornament is joined to the curve (1881). Two different printing methods were used for the 1867-74 issues. The first produced stamps on which the hair and whiskers were coarse and thick, from the second they were fine and clear.

1867-72 Wmk. 91 Typo. *Perf. 9½*

Coarse Print

27 A9 2kr yellow 110.00 2.50
Never hinged 200.00
On cover 11.00
a. Half used as 1kr on cover —
b. 2kr lemon yellow 175.00 5.00
Never hinged 290.00
On cover 17.50
c. 2kr ochre yellow 175.00 7.25
Never hinged 290.00
On cover 37.50
d. 2kr yellowish orange 110.00 2.25
Never hinged 190.00
On cover 12.50
e. 2kr deep orange 175.00 5.00
Never hinged 325.00
On cover 25.00
f. 2kr brown orange 260.00 14.50
Never hinged 475.00
On cover 65.00
28 A9 3kr green 125.00 2.40
Never hinged 200.00
On cover 14.00
a. 3kr pale yellow green 125.00 2.50
Never hinged 225.00
On cover 15.00
b. 3kr blue green 175.00 3.25
Never hinged 290.00
On cover 25.00
c. 3kr deep green 225.00 5.00
Never hinged 400.00
On cover 35.00
d. 3kr emerald green 275.00 12.50
Never hinged 500.00
On cover 75.00
29 A9 5kr rose, type II 80.00 .20
Never hinged 140.00
On cover 2.50
a. 5kr rose, type I 87.50 .20
Never hinged 150.00
On cover 2.50
b. Perf. 10½, type II 175.00
Never hinged 250.00
c. Cliché of 3kr in plate of 5kr 29,000.
d. 5kr lilac rose, type I 87.50 1.00
Never hinged 150.00
No gum 20.00
On cover 3.60
e. 5kr brick red, type II 135.00 1.60
Never hinged 225.00
No gum 22.00
On cover 6.75
f. 5kr violet red, type I 240.00 2.25
Never hinged 375.00
On cover 12.00
30 A9 10kr blue 260.00 2.00
Never hinged 425.00
On cover 35.00
On cover, single franking 45.00
a. Half used as 5kr on cover —
b. 10kr pale milky blue 300.00 5.00
Never hinged 500.00
On cover 35.00
c. 10kr deep blue 300.00 2.50
Never hinged 450.00
On cover 37.50
31 A9 15kr brown 260.00 5.50
Never hinged 460.00
On cover 17.00
a. 15kr deep brown 400.00 24.00
Never hinged 675.00
On cover 50.00
b. 15kr yellowish brown 290.00 6.50
Never hinged 500.00
On cover 24.00
c. 15kr gray brown 275.00 7.25
Never hinged 500.00
On cover 32.50
d. 15kr reddish brown 325.00 11.00
Never hinged 540.00
On cover 45.00
32 A9 25kr lilac 80.00 18.00
Never hinged 140.00
On cover 140.00
a. 25kr gray lilac 42.50 14.50
Never hinged 80.00
On cover 140.00
b. 25kr brown violet 310.00 55.00
Never hinged 540.00
On cover 300.00
c. 25kr violet 47.50 16.00
Never hinged 87.50
On cover 140.00
d. 25kr brownish lilac 80.00 32.50
Never hinged 140.00
On cover 200.00
e. 25kr dull gray 825.00 300.00
Never hinged 1,300.
On cover 1,000.

Perf. 12

33 A10 50kr light brown 37.50 110.00
Never hinged 57.50
On cover 2,400.
a. 50kr pale red brown 450.00 175.00
Never hinged 700.00
On cover 2,750.

A cover bearing a 50 kreuzer red brown, with 2 kreuzer yellow, 10 kreuzer blue and 15 kreuzer dark brown, addressed to Aden, realized the equivalent of U.S. $18,300 at a German auction in 2003.

b. 50kr brownish rose 450.00 275.00
Never hinged 700.00
On cover 3,000.
c. Pair, imperf. btwn., vert. or horizontal 650.00 1,350.

There are 3 known examples of No. 29c. Each has small defects.

Issues for Austria only

1874-80 *Perf. 9½*

Fine Print

34 A9 2kr yellow ('76) 13.00 .75
Never hinged 25.00
On cover 11.00
f. 2kr lemon yellow 17.00 10.00
Never hinged 37.50
On cover 17.50
35 A9 3kr green ('76) 60.00 .75
Never hinged 110.00
On cover 14.50
f. 3kr yellow green 80.00 .75
Never hinged 140.00
On cover 15.50
36 A9 5kr rose, type III 4.00 .20
Never hinged 8.00
On cover 3.00
f. 5kr carmine rose 4.00 .20
Never hinged 14.00
On cover 4.00
37 A9 10kr blue ('75) 150.00 .50
Never hinged 290.00
On cover 24.00
f. 10kr pale blue 190.00 .75
Never hinged 375.00
On cover 20.00
38 A9 15kr brown ('77) 8.00 6.50
Never hinged 18.00
On cover 50.00
f. 15kr deep chestnut brown 17.00 11.00
Never hinged 35.00
On cover 40.00
39 A9 25kr gray lil ('78) 1.00 160.00
Never hinged 2.50
On cover 8,000.
f. 25kr gray violet 20.00 190.00
Never hinged 37.50
On cover 8,000.
40 A10 50kr red brown 13.00 160.00
Never hinged 32.50
On cover 10,000.

Perf. 9

34a A9 2kr 225.00 55.00
On cover 500.00
35a A9 3kr 200.00 25.00
On cover 500.00
36a A9 5kr 80.00 3.00
On cover 125.00

37a A9 10kr 400.00 30.00
On cover 650.00
38a A9 15kr 575.00 110.00
On cover 900.00

Perf. 10½

34b A9 2kr 55.00 3.75
On cover 47.50
35b A9 3kr 95.00 2.25
On cover 47.50
36b A9 5kr 13.00 .75
On cover 25.00
37b A9 10kr 200.00 2.25
On cover 55.00
38b A9 15kr 225.00 22.50
On cover 175.00

Perf. 12

34c A9 2kr 250.00 140.00
On cover 440.00
35c A9 3kr 225.00 22.50
On cover 360.00
36c A9 5kr 55.00 4.25
On cover 110.00
37c A9 10kr 475.00 110.00
On cover 600.00
38c A9 15kr 750.00 160.00
On cover 925.00
40b A10 50kr brown ('80) 17.50 *160.00*
On cover *11,000.*
c. Perf. 10½x12 290.00 —

Perf. 13

34d A9 2kr 290.00 290.00
On cover 800.00
35d A9 3kr 200.00 30.00
On cover 360.00
36d A9 5kr 110.00 18.00
On cover 95.00
37d A9 10kr 250.00 85.00
On cover 500.00
38d A9 15kr 575.00 400.00
On cover —
40a A10 50kr 37.50 *210.00*
On cover —

Perf. 9x10½

34e A9 2kr 400.00 72.50
On cover —
35e A9 3kr 325.00 65.00
On cover —
36e A9 5kr 125.00 15.00
On cover —
37e A9 10kr 375.00 87.50
On cover —

Various compound perforations exist.

Values are for stamps that do not show the watermark. Stamps showing the watermark often sell for more.

For similar designs see Offices in the Turkish Empire A1-A2.

A11

Perf. 9, 9½, 10, 10½, 11½, 12, 12½

1883

Inscriptions in Black

41 A11 2kr brown 5.50 .40
Never hinged 13.50
On cover 10.00
42 A11 3kr green 5.50 .30
Never hinged 20.00
On cover 10.00
43 A11 5kr rose 67.50 .25
Never hinged 160.00
On cover 2.50
a. Vert. pair, imperf. btwn. 175.00 *350.00*
Never hinged 275.00
44 A11 10kr blue 4.00 .30
Never hinged 13.50
On cover 12.50
45 A11 20kr gray 50.00 3.50
Never hinged 140.00
On cover 200.00
c. Perf 9 *1,350.*
46 A11 50kr red lilac, perf 9½ 350.00 67.50
Never hinged 950.00
On cover *2,750.*
On parcel post receipt card 325.00
a. 50kr brown lilac & black, perf 10 325.00 100.00
On cover *3,250.*
On parcel post receipt card 350.00

The last printings of Nos. 41-46 are watermarked "ZEITUNGS-MARKEN" instead of "BRIEF-MARKEN." Values are for stamps that do not show watermark.

The 5kr has been reprinted in a dull red rose, perforated 10½.

For similar design see Offices in the Turkish Empire A3.

For surcharges see Offices in the Turkish Empire Nos. 15-19.

Values for stamps with "BRIEF-MARKEN" watermark

41a A11 2kr brown 8.00 .60
42a A11 3kr green 8.00 .60
43b A11 5kr rose 100.00 *.45*
44a A11 10kr blue 6.00 .50
45a A11 20kr gray 75.00 5.50
46b A11 50kr red lilac *425.00* *100.00*

Values for stamps with "ZEITUNGS-MARKEN" watermark

41b A11 2kr brown 27.50 11.00
42b A11 3kr green 27.50 11.00
43c A11 5kr rose *110.00* 8.75
44b A11 10kr blue 27.50 8.75
45b A11 20kr gray 85.00 32.50
46c A11 50kr red lilac *450.00* *160.00*

A12

A13

Perf. 9 to 13½, also Compound

1890-96 **Unwmk.**

Granite Paper

Numerals in black, Nos. 51-61

51 A12 1kr dark gray 1.40 .25
Never hinged 3.50
On cover 5.50
a. Pair, imperf. between 210.00 *450.00*
Never hinged 325.00
b. Half used as ½kr on cover *125.00*
As "b," on postcard 100.00
52 A12 2kr light brown .30 .25
Never hinged 2.40
On cover 2.00
53 A12 3kr gray green .40 .25
Never hinged 2.75
On cover 2.50
a. Pair, imperf. between 290.00 600.00
Never hinged 400.00
54 A12 5kr rose .40 .25
Never hinged 2.75
On cover 1.25
a. Pair, imperf. between 240.00 375.00
Never hinged 325.00
55 A12 10kr ultramarine 1.00 .25
Never hinged 5.00
On cover 5.50
a. Pair, imperf. between 325.00 550.00
Never hinged 475.00
56 A12 12kr claret 2.40 .35
Never hinged 10.00
On cover 40.00
On parcel post receipt card 9.00
a. Pair, imperf. between — 675.00
57 A12 15kr lilac 2.40 .35
Never hinged 10.00
On cover 12.50
On parcel post receipt card 11.00
a. Pair, imperf. between 425.00 750.00
Never hinged 575.00
58 A12 20kr olive green 35.00 2.00
Never hinged 95.00
On cover 300.00
On parcel post receipt card 13.50
59 A12 24kr gray blue 2.00 1.25
Never hinged 9.50
On cover 500.00
On parcel post receipt card 13.50
a. Pair, imperf. between 425.00 575.00
Never hinged 750.00
60 A12 30kr dark brown 2.50 .65
Never hinged 9.50
On cover 175.00
On parcel post receipt card 13.50
61 A12 50kr violet, perf 10 5.50 9.00
Never hinged 12.75
On cover *3,000.*
On parcel post receipt card 30.00
a. Perf 9½ 24.00 13.00
Never hinged 55.00
On cover *3,750.*
On parcel post receipt card 30.00

Engr.

62 A13 1gld dark blue 2.75 2.25
Never hinged 8.00
On cover *1,125.*
On parcel post receipt card 32.50
63 A13 1gld pale lilac ('96) 40.00 3.75
Never hinged 100.00
On cover *1,000.*
On parcel post receipt card 65.00
64 A13 2gld carmine 3.00 20.00
Never hinged 10.00
On cover *2,000.*
On parcel post receipt card 110.00
65 A13 2gld gray green ('96) 14.00 *40.00*
Never hinged 40.00
On cover *2,100.*
On parcel post receipt card 165.00
Nos. 51-65 (15) 113.05 80.85

Nearly all values of the 1890-1907 issues are found with numerals missing in one or more corners, some with numerals printed on the back.

For surcharges see Offices in the Turkish Empire Nos. 20-25, 28-31.

A14

Perf. 9 to 13½, also Compound

1891 **Typo.**

Numerals in black

66 A14 20kr olive green 1.75 .25
Never hinged 8.75
On cover 15.00
On parcel post receipt card 8.00
67 A14 24kr gray blue 3.00 .80
Never hinged 9.50
On cover 200.00
On parcel post receipt card 8.00
68 A14 30kr brown 1.75 .25
Never hinged 9.50
On cover 31.00
On parcel post receipt card 8.00
a. Pair, imperf. between 250.00 *575.00*
Never hinged 475.00
b. Perf. 9 100.00 45.00
Never hinged 200.00
On cover —
69 A14 50kr violet 1.75 .35
Never hinged 12.50
On cover *400.00*
On parcel post receipt card 10.00
Nos. 66-69 (4) 8.25 1.65

For surcharges see Offices in the Turkish Empire Nos. 26-27.

A15

A16

A17

A18

Perf. 10½ to 13½ and Compound

1899

Without Varnish Bars

Numerals in black, Nos. 70-82

70 A15 1h lilac .70 .20
Never hinged 2.00
On cover 4.00
On parcel post receipt card 8.00
b. Imperf. 55.00 *125.00*
Never hinged 110.00
Imperf, pair 140.00 *275.00*
Never hinged 240.00
c. Perf. 10½ 30.00 6.75
On cover 125.00
d. Numerals inverted *1,800.* *2,150.*
71 A15 2h dark gray 2.50 .55
Never hinged 16.00
On cover 5.00
On parcel post receipt card 8.00
72 A15 3h bister brown 6.00 .20
Never hinged 18.00
On cover 1.50
On parcel post receipt card 8.00
b. "3" in lower right corner sideways *2,400.*
73 A15 5h blue green 6.50 .20
Never hinged 17.50
On cover 1.00
On parcel post receipt card 8.00
c. Perf. 10½ 20.00 4.00
Never hinged 35.00
On cover 40.00
74 A15 6h orange .70 .20
Never hinged 2.00
On cover 2.75
On parcel post receipt card 8.00
75 A16 10h rose 15.00 .20
Never hinged 47.50
On cover 1.00
On parcel post receipt card 8.00
b. Perf. 10½ 800.00 175.00
Never hinged 1,200.
On cover —
76 A16 20h brown 4.75 .20
Never hinged 17.00
On cover 3.75
On parcel post receipt card 8.00
77 A16 25h ultramarine 55.00 .30
Never hinged 160.00
On cover 4.50
On parcel post receipt card 8.00
78 A16 30h red violet 17.50 2.25
Never hinged 60.00
On cover 18.75
On parcel post receipt card 12.50
b. Horiz. pair, imperf. btwn. 550.00 —
Never hinged 775.00
80 A17 40h green 29.00 3.00
Never hinged 85.00
On cover 25.00
On parcel post receipt card 12.50
81 A17 50h gray blue 16.00 3.50
Never hinged 50.00
On cover 37.50
On parcel post receipt card 12.50
b. All four "50's" parallel *2,500.*
82 A17 60h brown 45.00 1.10
Never hinged 125.00
On cover 30.00
On parcel post receipt card 12.50
b. Horiz. pair, imperf. btwn. 500.00 —
Never hinged 850.00
c. Perf. 10½ 95.00 4.00
Never hinged 150.00
On cover 27.50

Engr.

83 A18 1k carmine rose 5.50 .20
Never hinged 17.50
On cover 150.00
On parcel post receipt card 12.50
a. 1k carmine 5.50 .20
Never hinged 17.50
On cover 200.00
On parcel post receipt card 15.00
b. Vert. pair, imperf. btwn. 225.00 *300.00*
Never hinged 350.00
84 A18 2k gray lilac 47.50 .40
Never hinged 140.00
On cover *1,100.*
On parcel post receipt card 20.00
a. Vert. pair, imperf. btwn. 400.00 *600.00*
Never hinged 675.00
85 A18 4k gray green 9.50 15.00
Never hinged 34.00
On cover *900.00*
On parcel post receipt card 75.00
Nos. 70-85 (15) 261.15 27.50

For surcharges see Offices in Crete Nos. 1-7, Offices in the Turkish Empire Nos. 32-45.

1901 **With Varnish Bars**

70a A15 1h lilac 1.75 .40
Never hinged 4.00
On cover 4.00
71a A15 2h dark gray 2.00 .35
Never hinged 12.00
On cover 4.75
72a A15 3h bister brown .70 .20
Never hinged 2.00
On cover 2.00
73a A15 5h blue green .70 .20
Never hinged 2.00
On cover 1.00
74a A15 6h orange .70 .20
Never hinged 1.75
On cover 2.75
75a A16 10h rose .70 .20
Never hinged 2.75
On cover 1.00
76a A16 20h brown .70 .20
Never hinged 4.00
On cover 4.00
77a A16 25h ultra .85 .20
Never hinged 4.00
On cover 4.00
78a A16 30h red violet 1.75 .90
Never hinged 5.50
On cover 11.00
79 A17 35h green .85 .40
Never hinged 2.50
On cover 9.00
80a A17 40h green 1.60 3.50
Never hinged 5.50
On cover 19.00
81a A17 50h gray blue 4.00 8.00
Never hinged 9.50
On cover 37.50
82a A17 60h brown 2.00 .65
Never hinged 5.50
On cover 22.50
Nos. 70a-78a,79,80a-82a (13) 18.30 15.40

The diagonal yellow bars of varnish were printed across the face to prevent cleaning.

A19

A20

A21

Perf. 12½ to 13½ and Compound

1905-07 Typo.

Colored Numerals
Without Varnish Bars

86 A19 1h lilac .20 *.40*
Never hinged .35
On cover 3.25
87 A19 2h dark gray .20 .20
Never hinged .35
On cover 4.00
88 A19 3h bister brown .20 .20
Never hinged 1.40
On cover 1.65
89 A19 5h dk blue green 7.00 .20
Never hinged 22.00
On cover 1.00
90 A19 5h yellow grn ('06) .30 .20
Never hinged .65
On cover .60
91 A19 6h deep orange .30 .20
Never hinged 2.00
On cover 2.00
92 A20 10h carmine ('06) .45 .20
Never hinged 1.40
On cover .60
93 A20 12h violet ('07) 1.00 .75
Never hinged 3.50
On cover 110.00
On parcel post receipt card 8.00
94 A20 20h brown ('06) 3.25 .20
Never hinged 9.50
On cover 6.25
95 A20 25h ultra ('06) 3.50 .50
Never hinged 8.75
On cover 7.75
96 A20 30h red violet ('06) 8.00 .25
Never hinged 20.00
On cover 19.00

Black Numerals

97 A20 10h carmine 11.00 .20
Never hinged 67.50
On cover .75
98 A20 20h brown 29.00 2.00
Never hinged 110.00
On cover 7.50
99 A20 25h ultra 29.00 2.50
Never hinged 100.00
On cover 14.00
100 A20 30h red violet 55.00 4.50
Never hinged 160.00
On cover 25.00

White Numerals

101 A21 35h green 2.75 .25
Never hinged 13.50
On cover 8.00
102 A21 40h deep violet 2.75 .90
Never hinged 13.50
On cover 15.50
103 A21 50h dull blue 2.75 3.00
Never hinged 13.50
On cover 21.00
104 A21 60h yellow brown 2.75 .80
Never hinged 13.50
On cover 15.00
105 A21 72h rose 2.75 2.00
Never hinged 15.00
On cover 300.00
Nos. 86-105 (20) 162.15 19.45
Set, never hinged 415.00

For surcharges see Offices in Crete #8-14.

1904 ***Perf. 13x13½***

With Varnish Bars

86a A19 1h lilac .50 *1.00*
Never hinged 1.40
On cover 4.00
87a A19 2h dark gray 1.60 .90
Never hinged 5.50
On cover 11.00
88a A19 3h bister brown 2.00 .20
Never hinged 5.50
On cover 1.50
89a A19 5h dk blue green 3.50 .20
Never hinged 8.00
On cover 1.00
91a A19 6h deep orange 13.00 .35
Never hinged 27.50
On cover 2.25
97a A20 10h carmine 2.25 .20
Never hinged 12.00
On cover 1.00
98a A20 20h brown 30.00 1.25
Never hinged 90.00
On cover 6.75
99a A20 25h ultra 30.00 1.25
Never hinged 80.00
On cover 6.75
100a A20 30h red violet 45.00 2.25
Never hinged 125.00
On cover 13.50
101a A21 35h green 32.50 .80
Never hinged 85.00
On cover 67.50
102a A21 40h deep violet 30.00 3.50
Never hinged 85.00
On cover 67.50
103a A21 50h dull blue 30.00 8.75
Never hinged 85.00
On cover 67.50
104a A21 60h yellow brown 37.50 1.60
Never hinged 140.00
On cover 25.00
105a A21 72h rose 2.50 1.75
Never hinged 13.50
On cover 275.00
Nos. 86a-105a (14) 260.35 24.00
Set, never hinged 775.00

1904 ***Perf. 13x12½***

With Varnish Bars

86b A19 1h lilac .50 *1.10*
Never hinged 1.50
On cover 4.00
87b A19 2h dark gray 1.75 .75
Never hinged 5.50
On cover 11.00
88b A19 3h bister brown 2.25 .20
Never hinged 5.50
On cover 1.50
89b A19 5h dk blue green 7.50 .20
Never hinged 8.00
On cover 1.00
91b A19 6h deep orange 7.00 .35
Never hinged 27.50
On cover 2.50
97b A20 10h carmine 16.00 .20
Never hinged 12.00
On cover 1.00
98b A20 20h brown 26.00 1.90
Never hinged 90.00
On cover 6.75
99b A20 25h ultra 29.00 2.75
Never hinged 80.00
On cover 6.75
100b A20 30h red violet 55.00 4.25
Never hinged 125.00
On cover 13.50
101b A21 35h green 35.00 8.00
Never hinged 85.00
On cover 67.50
102b A21 40h deep violet 32.50 8.50
Never hinged 85.00
On cover 67.50
103b A21 50h dull blue 27.50 8.50
Never hinged 85.00
On cover 90.00
104b A21 60h yellow brown 42.50 1.75
Never hinged 140.00
On cover 25.00
Nos. 86b-104b (13) 282.50 38.45
Set, never hinged 495.00

Stamps of the 1901, 1904 and 1905 issues perf. 9 or 10½, also compound with 12½, were not sold at any post office, but were supplied only to some high-ranking officials. This applies also to the contemporaneous issues of Austrian Offices Abroad.

Karl VI — A22

Franz Josef — A23

Schönbrunn Castle — A24

Franz Josef — A25

Designs: 2h, Maria Theresa. 3h, Joseph II. 5h, 10h, 25h, Franz Josef. 6h, Leopold II. 12h, Franz I. 20h, Ferdinand I. 30h, Franz Josef as youth. 35h, Franz Josef in middle age. 60h, Franz Josef on horseback. 1k, Franz Josef in royal robes. 5k, Hofburg, Vienna.

1908-16 Typo. ***Perf. 12½***

Ordinary paper ('08-'13)

110 A22 1h gray black .30 *.80*
Never hinged .65
On cover 4.00
111 A22 2h blue violet .25 *.60*
Never hinged .65
On cover 4.00
112 A22 3h magenta .20 .20
Never hinged .65
On cover 3.75
113 A22 5h yellow green .20 .20
Never hinged .35
On cover .75
a. Booklet pane of 6 *25.00*
114 A22 6h orange brown 1.40 *1.75*
Never hinged 5.50
On cover 13.50
115 A22 10h rose .20 .20
Never hinged .35
On cover .75
a. Booklet pane of 6 *75.00*
116 A22 12h scarlet 1.40 *1.75*
Never hinged 6.75
On cover 16.50
117 A22 20h chocolate 1.75 .20
Never hinged 8.25
On cover 9.50
118 A22 25h ultramarine 2.50 .40
Never hinged 9.50
On cover 2.75
119 A22 30h olive green 10.00 .55
Never hinged 20.00
On cover 10.00
120 A22 35h slate 2.50 .20
Never hinged 21.50
On cover 8.00

Engr.

121 A23 50h dark green .65 .20
Never hinged 8.75
On cover 27.50
a. Vert. pair, imperf. btwn. 250.00 *400.00*
Never hinged 400.00
b. Horiz. pair, imperf. btwn. 250.00 *400.00*
Never hinged 400.00
122 A23 60h deep carmine .35 .20
Never hinged 1.40
On cover 17.00
a. Vert. pair, imperf. btwn. 275.00 *400.00*
Never hinged 400.00
b. Horiz. pair, imperf. btwn. 275.00 *400.00*
Never hinged 400.00
123 A23 72h dk brown 1.90 .35
Never hinged 12.00
On cover 85.00
124 A23 1k purple 12.00 .20
Never hinged 30.00
On cover 45.00
On cover, value declared 200.00
a. Vert. pair, imperf. btwn. 250.00 *375.00*
Never hinged 390.00
b. Horiz. pair, imperf. btwn. 250.00 *350.00*
Never hinged 340.00
125 A24 2k lake & olive grn 19.00 .35
Never hinged 65.00
On cover 80.00
On cover, value declared 400.00
126 A24 5k bister & dk vio 37.50 5.00
Never hinged 120.00
On cover (value declared) *750.00*
127 A25 10k blue, bis & dp brn 175.00 67.50
Never hinged 425.00
On cover (value declared) *1,250.*
Nos. 110-127 (18) 267.10 80.65
Set, never hinged 735.00

Chalky Paper ('08-'13)

110a A22 1h gray black .30 .20
Never hinged 2.00
On cover 3.50
111a A22 2h violet .25 .20
Never hinged 2.75
On cover 3.75
112a A22 3h magenta .45 .20
Never hinged 2.75
On cover 3.00
113b A22 5h yellow green .25 .25
Never hinged 1.40
On cover .75
c. Booklet pane of 6 *25.00*
114a A22 6h buff ('13) .75 .75
Never hinged 4.00
On cover 13.50
115b A22 10h rose .20 .20
Never hinged 1.40
On cover .75
c. Booklet pane of 6 *75.00*
116a A22 12h scarlet 1.40 1.00
Never hinged 6.75
On cover 15.50
117a A22 20h chocolate 6.75 .25
Never hinged 25.00
On cover 9.00
118a A22 25h deep blue 2.75 .25
Never hinged 15.50
On cover 2.50
119a A22 30h olive green 11.00 .30
Never hinged 37.50
On cover 27.50
120a A22 35h slate 2.50 .20
Never hinged 13.50
On cover 10.00

Wartime Printings on Grayish Paper ('16)

122c A23 60h deep carmine 1.25 *1.75*
On cover *67.50*
123a A23 72h dk brown 3.75 2.25
On cover —
124c A23 1k purple — 1.50
On cover —
125a A24 2k lake & olive grn — 3.75
On cover (value declared) —
126a A24 5k bister & dk vio — 9.00
On cover (value declared) —

Definitive set issued for the 60th year of the reign of Emperor Franz Josef.

Nos. 110a-120a, 121, and 123-127 were issued in 1908. Nos. 110-20 and 122 were issued in 1913.

All values exist imperforate. They were not sold at any post office, but presented to a number of high government officials. This applies also to all imperforate stamps of later issues, including semi-postals, etc., and those of the Austrian Offices Abroad.

Litho. forgeries of No. 127 exist.

For overprint and surcharge see #J47-J48. For similar designs see Offices in Crete A5-A6, Offices in the Turkish Empire A16-A17.

Birthday Jubilee Issue

Similar to 1908 Issue, but designs enlarged by labels at top and bottom bearing dates "1830" and "1910"

1910 Typo.

128 A22 1h gray black 4.00 *8.00*
Never hinged 11.50
On cover 34.00
129 A22 2h violet 7.75 *11.00*
Never hinged 17.50
On cover 55.00
130 A22 3h magenta 4.75 *8.75*
Never hinged 13.50
On cover 34.00
131 A22 5h yellow green .20 .30
Never hinged 2.00
On cover 7.50
132 A22 6h buff 3.50 *8.75*
Never hinged 11.50
On cover 50.00
133 A22 10h rose .20 .30
Never hinged 2.00
On cover 7.50
134 A22 12h scarlet 3.50 *8.75*
Never hinged 13.50
On cover 55.00
135 A22 20h chocolate 8.75 *11.00*
Never hinged 27.50
On cover 77.50
136 A22 25h deep blue 2.40 2.25
Never hinged 8.75
On cover 13.50
137 A22 30h olive green 3.50 *7.50*
Never hinged 16.00
On cover 77.50
138 A22 35h slate 3.50 *7.50*
Never hinged 16.00
On cover 100.00

Engr.

139 A23 50h dark green 4.75 *10.00*
Never hinged 16.00
On cover 150.00
140 A23 60h deep carmine 4.75 *10.00*
Never hinged 16.00
On cover 140.00
141 A23 1k purple 5.50 *12.00*
Never hinged 16.00
On cover 310.00
142 A24 2k lake & ol grn 150.00 *225.00*
Never hinged 250.00
On cover (value declared) *1,000.*
143 A24 5k bister & dk vio 110.00 *200.00*
Never hinged 175.00
On cover (value declared) *1,600.*
144 A25 10k blue, bis & dp brn 200.00 *325.00*
Never hinged 325.00
On cover (value declared) *2,200.*
Nos. 128-144 (17) 517.05 *856.10*
Set, never hinged 935.00

80th birthday of Emperor Franz Josef.
All values exist imperforate.
Litho. forgeries of Nos. 142-144 exist.

Austrian Crown — A37

Franz Josef — A38

Coat of Arms
A39 A40

Two sizes of Type A40:
Type I: 25x30mm
Type II: 26x29mm

1916-18 Typo.

145 A37 3h brt violet .20 .20
Never hinged .20
On cover 3.50
146 A37 5h lt green .20 .20
Never hinged .20
On cover 1.00
a. Booklet pane of 6 14.00
b. Booklet pane of 4 + 2 labels 27.50
147 A37 6h deep orange .25 *1.00*
Never hinged .70
On cover 20.00
148 A37 10h magenta .20 .20
Never hinged .20
On cover 1.00
a. Booklet pane of 6 27.50
149 A37 12h light blue .25 *1.75*
Never hinged 1.10
On cover 34.00
150 A38 15h rose red .40 .20
Never hinged 1.90
On cover 1.75
a. Booklet pane of 6 15.00

151 A38 20h chocolate 2.50 .20
Never hinged 12.00
On cover 10.00
152 A38 25h blue 4.75 .50
Never hinged 18.00
On cover 11.00
153 A38 30h slate 3.75 .80
Never hinged 18.00
On cover 13.50
154 A39 40h olive green .20 .20
Never hinged 1.40
On cover 5.00
155 A39 50h blue green .20 .20
Never hinged 1.40
On cover 15.50
156 A39 60h deep blue .20 .20
Never hinged 1.40
On cover 21.00
157 A39 80h orange brown .20 .20
Never hinged 1.40
On cover 27.50
158 A39 90h red violet .20 .20
Never hinged 1.40
On cover 67.50
159 A39 1k car, *yel* ('18) .25 .20
Never hinged 1.40
On cover 82.50

Engr.

160 A40 2k dark blue (I) 2.00 .20
Never hinged 5.50
On cover 110.00
a. Type II 10.00 1.00
Never hinged 27.50
161 A40 3k claret (I) 20.00 1.00
Never hinged 47.50
On cover 170.00
a. Type II 85.00 15.50
Never hinged 240.00
162 A40 4k deep green (I) 3.75 1.50
Never hinged 11.50
a. Type II 4.00 3.00
Never hinged 20.00
163 A40 10k deep violet (I) 24.00 *40.00*
Never hinged 72.50
a. Type II 110.00 *200.00*
On cover 340.00
Never hinged 225.00
Nos. 145-163 (19) 63.50 48.95
Set, never hinged 195.00

Stamps of type A38 have two varieties of the frame. Stamps of type A40 have various decorations about the shield.

Nos. 145-163 exist imperf. Value set, $475 hinged, $875 never hinged.

1917 Ordinary Paper

164 A40 2k light blue (I) 2.00 .25
Never hinged 4.00
On cover 115.00
a. Type II 2.40 .45
Never hinged 4.75
165 A40 3k carmine rose (I) 35.00 .75
Never hinged 85.00
On cover 175.00
a. Type II 225.00 140.00
Never hinged 1,700.
166 A40 4k yellow green (I) 2.00 1.10
Never hinged 6.00
a. Type II 20.00 19.00
Never hinged 67.50
167 A40 10k violet (I) 125.00 75.00
Never hinged 250.00
a. Type II 5,000. —
Never hinged *6,750.*
Nos. 164-167 (4) 164.00 77.10
Set, never hinged 345.00

Nos. 164-167 exist imperf. Value set, $400 hinged, $600 never hinged.

See Nos. 172-175 (granite paper). For overprints and surcharges see Nos. 181-199, C1-C3, J60-J63, N1-N5, N10-N19, N33-N37, N42-N51. Western Ukraine 2-7, 11-15, 19-28, 57-58, 85-89, 94-103, N3-N14, NJ13.

Emperor Karl I — A42

1917-18 Typo.

168 A42 15h dull red .20 .20
Never hinged .35
On cover 2.75
a. Booklet pane of 6 15.00
169 A42 20h dk green ('18) .20 .20
Never hinged 1.75
On cover 4.50
a. 20h green ('17) .50 .25
Never hinged 4.75
On cover 14.00
170 A42 25h blue .50 .20
Never hinged 5.00
On cover 12.00
171 A42 30h dull violet .30 .20
Never hinged 4.50
On cover 15.00
Nos. 168-171 (4) 1.20 .80
Set, never hinged 11.50

Nos. 168-171 exist imperf. Value set, $160 hinged, $275 never hinged.

For overprints and surcharges see Nos. N6-N9, N20, N38-N41, N52, N64. Western Ukraine 1, 8, 16-18, 90-93, N15-N18.

1918-19 Engr.

Granite Paper

172 A40 2k light blue .35 *.35*
Never hinged .65
On cover 125.00
a. Perf. 11½ 800.00 *1,000.*
Never hinged 1,350.
173 A40 3k carmine rose .35 *.75*
Never hinged .65
On cover 250.00
174 A40 4k yellow green ('19) 3.50 *20.00*
Never hinged 6.75
On cover 300.00
175 A40 10k lt violet ('19) 7.50 *24.00*
Never hinged 15.00
On cover 575.00
Nos. 172-175 (4) 11.70 *45.10*
Set, never hinged 23.00

Issues of the Republic

Austrian Stamps of 1916-18 Overprinted

1918-19 Unwmk. *Perf. 12½*

181 A37 3h bright violet .20 .20
Never hinged .30
On cover 3.50
182 A37 5h light green .20 .20
Never hinged .30
On cover 1.00
183 A37 6h deep orange .20 1.40
Never hinged 1.00
On cover 20.00
184 A37 10h magenta .20 .20
Never hinged .30
On cover .75
185 A37 12h light blue .35 *2.00*
Never hinged 1.40
On cover 34.00
a. 12h deep greenish blue 27.50
Never hinged 80.00
186 A42 15h dull red .30 *1.00*
Never hinged 1.50
On cover 3.00
187 A42 20h deep green .20 .20
Never hinged .45
On cover 1.00
188 A42 25h blue .20 .20
Never hinged .65
On cover 4.50
189 A42 30h dull violet .20 .20
Never hinged .65
On cover 2.00
190 A39 40h olive green .20 .20
Never hinged .65
On cover 6.75
191 A39 50h deep green .60 *1.10*
Never hinged 2.40
On cover 10.00
192 A39 60h deep blue .55 *1.00*
Never hinged 2.00
On cover 13.50
193 A39 80h orange brown .20 .20
Never hinged .65
On cover 13.50
a. Inverted overprint 225.00 275.00
Never hinged 375.00
194 A39 90h red violet .25 *.45*
Never hinged 1.00
On cover 20.00
195 A39 1k carmine, *yel* .20 *.35*
Never hinged 1.00
On cover 20.00

Granite Paper

196 A40 2k light blue .20 .20
Never hinged .20
On cover 34.00
a. Horiz. pair, imperf. between 275.00
Never hinged, #196a 400.00
b. Vert. pair, imperf. between 375.00
Never hinged, #196b 550.00
c. Perf. 11½ 80.00 95.00
Never hinged, #196c 140.00
On cover 300.00
197 A40 3k carmine rose .35 *.90*
Never hinged .80
On cover 140.00
198 A40 4k yellow green 1.00 *2.75*
Never hinged 2.40
On cover 240.00
a. Perf. 11½ 16.00 40.00
Never hinged 27.50
On cover —
199 A40 10k deep violet 6.75 *20.00*
Never hinged 12.50
On cover 475.00
Nos. 181-199 (19) 12.35 *32.75*
Set, never hinged 30.00

Nos. 181, 182, 184, 187-191, 194, 197 and 199 exist imperforate. Value: 181//194, each $18; 197, $150; 199, $225.

Post Horn — A43

Coat of Arms — A44

Allegory of New Republic — A45

1919-20 Typo. *Perf. 12½*

Ordinary Paper

200 A43 3h gray .20 .20
Never hinged .20
On cover 3.50
a. 3h deep gray 2.00 *4.00*
Never hinged 4.00
On cover 13.50
b. 3h gray black 140.00 *200.00*
Never hinged 275.00
On cover 340.00
201 A44 5h yellow green .20 .20
Never hinged .20
On cover 3.50
202 A44 5h gray ('20) .20 .20
Never hinged .20
On cover 3.50
a. 5h deep gray 7.50 *15.50*
Never hinged 15.50
On cover 34.00
b. 5h gray black 240.00 *340.00*
Never hinged 400.00
On cover —
203 A43 6h orange .20 *.55*
Never hinged .40
On cover 20.00
204 A44 10h deep rose .20 .20
Never hinged .20
On cover 1.00
205 A44 10h red ('20) .20 .20
Never hinged .20
On cover 1.00
a. Thick grayish paper ('20) .20 .20
Never hinged .20
On cover 1.50
206 A43 12h grnsh blue .20 *.80*
Never hinged .35
On cover 34.00
a. 12h deep greenish blue 47.50 *175.00*
Never hinged 175.00
On cover —
207 A43 15h bister ('20) .30 *.55*
Never hinged .55
On cover 3.50
a. Thick grayish paper ('20) .20 .20
Never hinged .20
On cover 1.40
208 A45 20h dark green .20 .20
Never hinged .20
On cover 1.00
a. 20h yellow green .20 .20
Never hinged .20
On cover 1.25
b. As "a," thick grysh paper ('20) .85 2.00
Never hinged 1.75
On cover 7.50
209 A44 25h blue .20 .20
Never hinged .20
On cover 4.00
a. 25h pale blue 15.00 *22.50*
Never hinged 32.50
On cover 37.50
b. 25h deep blue 190.00 *240.00*
Never hinged 325.00
On cover —
210 A43 25h violet ('20) .20 .20
Never hinged .20
On cover 2.00
211 A45 30h dark brown .20 .20
Never hinged .20
On cover 2.50
212 A45 40h violet .20 .20
Never hinged .20
On cover 3.75
213 A45 40h lake ('20) .20 .20
Never hinged .35
On cover 2.75
214 A44 45h olive green .20 *.75*
Never hinged .35
On cover 20.00
215 A45 50h dark blue .20 .20
Never hinged .20
On cover 2.00
a. Thick grayish paper ('20) .35 *.70*
Never hinged .70
On cover 2.75
216 A43 60h olive green ('20) .20 .20
Never hinged .20
On cover 4.75
217 A44 1k carmine, *yel* .20 .20
Never hinged .20
On cover 13.50
218 A44 1k light blue ('20) .20 .35
Never hinged .30
On cover 8.75
a. 1k deep blue 140.00 *240.00*
Never hinged 300.00
On cover —
Nos. 200-218 (19) 3.90 5.80
Set, never hinged 4.90

All values exist imperf. (For regularly issued imperfs, see Nos. 227-235.)

For overprints and surcharge see Nos. B11-B19, B30-B38, J102, N21, N27, N53, N58, N65, N71.

Parliament Building A46

1919-20 Engr. *Perf. 12½, 11½*

Granite Paper

219 A46 2k ver & blk .35 *.75*
Never hinged .70
On cover 67.50
a. Center inverted *3,250.*
Never hinged 4,250.
b. Perf. 11½ .75 *1.60*
Never hinged 1.50
On cover 40.00
220 A46 2½k olive bis ('20) .20 *.30*
Never hinged .35
On cover 6.75
221 A46 3k blue & blk brn .20 .35
Never hinged .35
On cover 10.00
a. Perf. 11½ 4.75 *7.50*
Never hinged 8.75
On cover 24.00
222 A46 4k carmine & blk .20 .20
Never hinged .35
On cover 13.50
a. Center inverted *1,750.* *1,750.*
Never hinged *2,250.*
b. Perf. 11½ 2.00 *3.75*
Never hinged 3.75
On cover 16.75
223 A46 5k black ('20) .20 .20
Never hinged .35
On cover 6.75
a. Perf. 11½x12½ 55.00 *82.50*
Never hinged 110.00
b. Perf. 11½ 3.00 *4.50*
Never hinged 5.00
On cover 17.50
224 A46 7½k plum .35 *.70*
Never hinged .70
On cover 6.75
a. Perf. 11½ 140.00 225.00
Never hinged 275.00
On cover —
b. Perf. 11½x12½ 65.00 125.00
Never hinged 130.00
225 A46 10k olive grn & blk brn .35 *.70*
Never hinged .70
On cover 13.50
a. Perf. 11½x12½ 175.00 300.00
Never hinged 325.00
b. Perf. 11½ 13.00 22.50
Never hinged 26.00
On cover 60.00
226 A46 20k lilac & red ('20) .20 *.35*
Never hinged .35
On cover 20.00
a. Center inverted *14,500.* *11,500.*
Never hinged 18,000.
b. Perf. 11½ 85.00 140.00
Never hinged 140.00
On cover 275.00
Nos. 219-226 (8) 2.05 *3.55*
Set, never hinged 3.85

A number of values exist imperforate between. Values, $300 to $400 a pair.

See No. 248. For overprints and surcharge see Nos. B23-B29, B43-B49.

1920 Typo. *Imperf.*

Ordinary Paper

227 A44 5h yellow green .30 *.75*
Never hinged .55
On cover 10.00
228 A44 5h gray .20 .20
Never hinged .20
On cover 3.50
229 A44 10h deep rose .20 .20
Never hinged .20
On cover 1.50
230 A44 10h red .20 .20
Never hinged .20
On cover 1.50
231 A43 15h bister .20 .20
Never hinged .20
On cover 4.00
232 A43 25h violet .20 .20
Never hinged .20
On cover 3.00
233 A45 30h dark brown .20 .20
Never hinged .20
On cover 3.50
234 A45 40h violet .20 .25
Never hinged .30
On cover 3.00
235 A43 60h olive green .20 .25
Never hinged .30
On cover 4.00
Nos. 227-235 (9) 1.90 2.45
Set, never hinged 2.35

Arms

A47 A48

1920-21 Typo. *Perf. 12½*

White Paper

238 A47 80h rose .20 .20
Never hinged .20
On cover .75
a. Thick grayish paper .20 .20
Never hinged .20
On cover .75
239 A47 1k black brown .20 .20
Never hinged .20
On cover .75
a. Thick grayish paper .20 .20

Never hinged .20
On cover .75
241 A47 1½k green ('21) .40 .20
Never hinged .80
On cover 1.75
a. Thick grayish paper .45 .20
Never hinged .20
On cover 1.25
242 A47 2k blue .20 .30
Never hinged .20
On cover 1.00
a. Thick grayish paper .20 .20
Never hinged .20
On cover 1.25
243 A48 3k yel grn & dk grn ('21) .20 *.30*
Never hinged .35
On cover 1.00
a. Thick grayish paper .20 .30
Never hinged .20
On cover 1.00
b. 3k pale green & blue green, white paper 8.00 *30.00*
Never hinged 17.50
On cover 57.50
c. 3k pale green & blue green, thick grayish paper 11.00 *28.00*
Never hinged 28.00
On cover 57.50
d. 3k dark green & blackish green, thick grayish paper 300.00 *475.00*
Never hinged 28.00
On cover 57.50
244 A48 4k red & claret ('21) .20 .20
Never hinged .35
On cover 2.00
a. Thick grayish paper .40 .30
Never hinged .55
On cover 2.00
245 A48 5k vio & claret ('21) .20 .20
Never hinged .35
On cover 1.75
a. Thick grayish paper .40 .30
Never hinged .70
On cover 1.75
246 A48 7½k yellow & brown ('21) .20 *.35*
Never hinged .35
On cover 2.25
247 A48 10k ultra & blue ('21) .20 *.20*
Never hinged .35
On cover 2.25
a. Thick grayish paper .40 .35
Never hinged .70
On cover 2.50
Nos. 238-247 (9) 2.00 2.15
Set, never hinged 3.25

For overprints and surcharges see Nos. B20-B22, B39-B42.

1921 **Engr.**

248 A46 50k dk violet, *yel* .85 *1.40*
Never hinged 1.40
On cover 67.50
a. Perf. 11½ 13.00 *65.00*
Never hinged 21.00
On cover 200.00

Symbols of Agriculture A49

Symbols of Labor and Industry A50

1922-24 **Typo.** ***Perf. 12½***

250 A49 ½k olive bister .20 *.60*
Never hinged .20
On cover 20.00
251 A50 1k brown .20 .20
Never hinged .20
On cover 6.75
252 A50 2k cobalt blue .20 .20
Never hinged .20
On cover 6.00
253 A49 2½k orange brown .20 .20
Never hinged .20
On cover 6.75
254 A50 4k dull violet .20 *1.00*
Never hinged .25
On cover 34.00
255 A50 5k gray green .20 .20
Never hinged .20
On cover 1.00
256 A49 7½k gray violet .20 .20
Never hinged .20
On cover 1.20
257 A50 10k claret .20 .20
Never hinged .20
On cover 1.00
258 A49 12½k gray green .20 .20
Never hinged .20
On cover 1.00
259 A49 15k bluish green .20 .20
Never hinged .20
On cover 8.00
260 A49 20k dark blue .20 .20
Never hinged .20
On cover 1.00
261 A49 25k claret .20 .20
Never hinged .20
On cover 1.00
262 A50 30k pale gray .20 .20
Never hinged .20
On cover 6.75
263 A50 45k pale red .20 .20
Never hinged .20
On cover 6.00
264 A50 50k orange brown .20 .20
Never hinged .20
On cover 1.50
265 A50 60k yellow green .20 .20
Never hinged .20
On cover 6.75
266 A50 75k ultramarine .20 .20
Never hinged .20
On cover 3.00
267 A50 80k yellow .20 .20
Never hinged .20
On cover 1.20
268 A49 100k gray .20 .20
Never hinged .20
On cover 1.00
269 A49 120k brown .20 .20
Never hinged .30
On cover 7.50
270 A49 150k orange .20 .20
Never hinged .20
On cover 3.50
271 A49 160k light green .20 .20
Never hinged .20
On cover 3.00
272 A49 180k red .20 .20
Never hinged .30
On cover 8.75
273 A49 200k pink .20 .20
Never hinged .20
On cover 1.00
274 A49 240k dark violet .20 .20
Never hinged .30
On cover 3.50
275 A49 300k light blue .20 .20
Never hinged .20
On cover 1.00
276 A49 400k deep green .85 .20
Never hinged 2.75
On cover 1.00
a. 400k gray green .85 .30
Never hinged 2.00
On cover 1.00
277 A49 500k yellow .20 .20
Never hinged .30
On cover 1.00
278 A49 600k slate .20 .20
Never hinged .35
On cover 2.00
279 A49 700k brown ('24) 2.10 .20
Never hinged 9.50
On cover 2.00
280 A49 800k violet ('24) 1.00 *1.50*
Never hinged 4.75
On cover 24.00
281 A50 1000k violet ('23) 1.75 .20
Never hinged 8.75
On cover 1.00
282 A50 1200k car rose ('23) 1.00 *.50*
Never hinged 6.00
On cover 8.00
283 A50 1500k orange ('24) 1.10 .20
Never hinged 6.00
On cover 1.50
284 A50 1600k slate ('23) 2.75 2.75
Never hinged 15.00
On cover 13.50
285 A50 2000k dp bl ('23) 4.00 1.50
Never hinged 17.50
On cover 3.50
286 A50 3000k lt blue ('23) 12.50 2.00
Never hinged 35.00
On cover 6.75
287 A50 4000k dk bl, *bl* ('24) 5.25 2.40
Never hinged 27.50
On cover 13.50
Nos. 250-287 (38) 37.90 18.25
Set, never hinged 140.00

Nos. 250-287 exist imperf. Value set, $500 hinged, $750 never hinged.

Symbols of Art and Science — A51

1922-24 **Engr.** ***Perf. 12½***

288 A51 20k dark brn .20 .20
Never hinged .20
On cover 6.75
a. Perf. 11½ 1.00 *1.25*
Never hinged 2.75
On cover 20.00
289 A51 25k blue .20 .20
Never hinged .20
On cover 3.00
a. Perf 11½ 1.00 *1.25*
Never hinged 2.75
On cover 25.00
b. 25k deep blue .40 .20
Never hinged .80
On cover 4.00
c. As "b," perf 11½ .70 *1.20*
Never hinged 2.75
On cover 27.50
290 A51 50k brown red .20 .20
Never hinged .20
On cover 3.50
a. Perf. 11½ 2.25 *2.50*
Never hinged 4.75
On cover 35.00
b. Vert. pair, imperf. btwn. 225.00 *300.00*
Never hinged 300.00
c. Perf 12½x11½ *1,150.*
d. 50k deep brownish red 4.00 3.75
Never hinged 8.00
On cover 27.50
291 A51 100k deep grn .20 .20
Never hinged .20
On cover 6.75
a. Perf. 11½ 5.50 *8.00*
Never hinged 10.75
On cover 45.00
b. Vert. pair, imperf. btwn. — *400.00*
Never hinged —
c. 100k pale olive green 1.10 *2.00*
Never hinged 2.25
On cover 10.00
292 A51 200k dark violet .20 .20
Never hinged .20
On cover 10.00
a. Perf. 11½ 8.00 *11.50*
Never hinged 16.00
On cover 67.50
b. Vert. pair, imperf. btwn. 375.00
Never hinged 475.00
293 A51 500k dp orange .50 *1.40*
Never hinged 1.00
On cover 30.00
294 A51 1000k blk vio, *yel* .20 .20
Never hinged .20
On cover 6.75
a. Perf. 11½ 175.00 *325.00*
Never hinged 400.00
On cover *1,000.*
b. Vert. pair, imperf. btwn. 325.00
Never hinged 425.00
c. Horiz. pair, imperf. btwn. 325.00
Never hinged 425.00
295 A51 2000k olive grn, *yel* .20 .20
Never hinged .35
On cover 10.00
a. 2000k yellow green, *yel* 6.75
Never hinged 13.50
b. Vert. pair, imperf. btwn. 325.00
Never hinged 400.00
296 A51 3000k claret brn ('23) 18.00 .75
Never hinged 36.00
On cover 17.00
297 A51 5000k gray black ('23) 5.00 1.60
Never hinged 10.00
On cover 55.00

Granite Paper

298 A51 10,000k red brown ('24) 6.00 *4.25*
Never hinged 12.00
On cover *475.00*
Nos. 288-298 (11) 30.90 9.40
Set, never hinged 60.00

On Nos. 281-287, 291-298 "kronen" is abbreviated to "k" and transposed with the numerals.

Nos. 288-298 exist imperf. Value set, $375 hinged, $625 never hinged.

Numeral A52

Fields Crossed by Telegraph Wires A53

White-Shouldered Eagle — A54

Church of Minorite Friars — A55

1925-32 **Typo.** ***Perf. 12***

303 A52 1g dark gray .20 .20
Never hinged 1.00
On cover 1.75
304 A52 2g claret .25 .20
Never hinged 1.40
On cover 1.50
a. 2g red lilac ('32) .55 .20
Never hinged 2.75
On cover 1.50
305 A52 3g scarlet .25 .20
Never hinged 1.40
On cover 1.25
306 A52 4g grnsh blue ('27) .50 .20
Never hinged 4.00
On cover 2.00
307 A52 5g brown orange .55 .20
Never hinged 4.75
On cover 1.75
308 A52 6g ultramarine .45 .20
Never hinged 5.50
On cover 2.75
a. 6g violet blue 1.75 .25
Never hinged 6.75
On cover 3.50
309 A52 7g chocolate .50 .20
Never hinged 6.00
On cover 1.75
310 A52 8g yellow green 2.40 .20
Never hinged 16.00
On cover 1.50
311 A53 10g orange .20 .20
Never hinged 1.00
On cover 1.50
313 A53 15g red lilac .20 .20
Never hinged 1.00
On cover 1.25
314 A53 16g dark blue .20 .20
Never hinged 1.00
On cover 1.50
315 A53 18g olive green .50 .55
Never hinged 3.50
On cover 2.00
316 A54 20g dark violet .50 .20
Never hinged 5.50
On cover 1.00
317 A54 24g carmine .50 .40
Never hinged 5.50
On cover 1.75
318 A54 30g dark brown .50 .20
Never hinged 5.50
On cover 2.50
319 A54 40g ultramarine .50 .20
Never hinged 5.50
On cover 2.50
320 A54 45g yellow brown .50 .20
Never hinged 6.00
On cover 4.25
321 A54 50g gray .70 .25
Never hinged 10.00
On cover 4.50
322 A54 80g turquoise blue 4.00 *4.50*
Never hinged 26.00
On cover 30.00

Perf. 12½
Engr.

323 A55 1s deep green 24.00 1.40
Never hinged 75.00
On cover 12.50
a. 1s light green 240.00 8.25
Never hinged 850.00
On cover 85.00
b. As "a," pair, imperf between 850.00
Never hinged 675.00
324 A55 2s brown rose 8.75 *11.00*
Never hinged 25.00
On cover 40.00
Nos. 303-324 (21) 46.15 *21.10*
Set, never hinged 210.00

#303-324 exist imperf. Value, set $400.
For type A52 surcharged see Nos. B118.

Güssing — A56

National Library, Vienna — A57

15g, Hochosterwitz. 16g, 20g, Durnstein. 18g, Traunsee. 24g, Salzburg. 30g, Seewiesen. 40g, Innsbruck. 50g, Worthersee. 60g, Hohenems. 2s, St. Stephen's Cathedral, Vienna.

1929-30 **Typo.** ***Perf. 12½***
Size: 25½x21½mm

326 A56 10g brown orange .75 .20
Never hinged 5.00
On cover 1.50
327 A56 10g bister ('30) .90 .20
Never hinged 6.75
On cover 1.50
328 A56 15g violet brown .70 *1.25*
Never hinged 3.00
On cover 9.25
329 A56 16g dark gray .20 .20
Never hinged .75
On cover 4.25
330 A56 18g blue green .55 *.45*
Never hinged 6.75
On cover 9.25
331 A56 20g dark gray ('30) 2.00 .20
Never hinged 18.00
On cover 6.00
332 A56 24g maroon 4.00 *6.00*
Never hinged 27.50
On cover 9.50
333 A56 24g lake ('30) 4.75 .45
Never hinged 34.00
On cover 2.50
334 A56 30g dark violet 6.75 .20
Never hinged 40.00
On cover 2.75
335 A56 40g dark blue 10.00 .25
Never hinged 60.00
On cover 2.50
336 A56 50g gray violet ('30) 27.50 .20
Never hinged 120.00
On cover 4.75
337 A56 60g olive green 27.50 .25
Never hinged 110.00
On cover 4.00

Engr.
Size: 21x26mm

338 A57 1s black brown 5.50 .25
Never hinged 34.00
On cover 12.50
a. Horiz. pair, imperf. btwn. 240.00
Never hinged 390.00
b. Vert. pair, imperf. btwn. 240.00
Never hinged 390.00
339 A57 2s dark green 11.50 8.75
Never hinged 50.00
On cover

a. Horiz. pair, imperf. btwn. 300.00
Never hinged 475.00
Nos. 326-339 (14) 102.60 18.85
Set, never hinged 485.00

#326, 328-330 and 332-339 exist imperf. Values, set of 12 unused hinged $1,300, never hinged $1,650.

Type of 1929-30 Issue

Designs: 12g, Traunsee. 64g, Hohenems.

1932 ***Perf. 12***

Size: 21x16½mm

340 A56 10g olive brown .75 .20
Never hinged 2.10
On cover 2.00
341 A56 12g blue green 1.40 .20
Never hinged 4.00
On cover 2.10
342 A56 18g blue green 1.40 *2.40*
Never hinged 3.50
On cover 5.00
343 A56 20g dark gray 1.40 .20
Never hinged 4.25
On cover 2.00
344 A56 24g carmine rose 5.00 .20
Never hinged 14.00
On cover 1.75
345 A56 24g dull violet 3.25 .20
Never hinged 8.50
On cover 1.75
346 A56 30g dark violet 17.00 .20
Never hinged 45.00
On cover 2.50
347 A56 30g carmine rose 5.50 .20
Never hinged 20.00
On cover 2.50
a. Vert. pair, imperf. btwn. 40.00
Never hinged, #347a 50.00
348 A56 40g dark blue 19.00 1.10
Never hinged 70.00
On cover 3.50
349 A56 40g dark violet 7.25 .30
Never hinged 29.00
On cover 3.50
350 A56 50g gray violet 24.00 .30
Never hinged 70.00
On cover 12.50
351 A56 50g dull blue 7.25 .30
Never hinged 25.00
On cover 4.00
352 A56 60g gray green 57.50 2.50
Never hinged 200.00
On cover 6.75
353 A56 64g gray green 24.00 .30
Never hinged 85.00
On cover 10.00
Nos. 340-353 (14) 174.70 8.60
Set, never hinged 575.00

For overprints and surcharges see Nos. B87-B92, B119-B121.
Nos. 340-353 exist imperf. Values, set unused hinged, $575, never hinged $725

Burgenland A67

Tyrol A68

Costumes of various districts: 3g, Burgenland. 4g, 5g, Carinthia. 6g, 8g, Lower Austria. 12g, 20g, Upper Austria. 24g, 25g, Salzburg. 30g, 35g, Styria. 45g, Tyrol. 60g, Vorarlberg bridal couple. 64g, Vorarlberg. 1s, Viennese family. 2s, Military.

1934-35 **Typo.** ***Perf. 12***

354 A67 1g dark violet .20 .20
Never hinged .20
On cover —
355 A67 3g scarlet .20 .20
Never hinged .20
On cover 1.25
356 A67 4g olive green .20 .20
Never hinged .20
On cover 3.50
357 A67 5g red violet .20 .20
Never hinged .20
On cover 2.00
358 A67 6g ultramarine .25 .25
Never hinged .50
On cover 2.50
359 A67 8g green .20 .20
Never hinged .25
On cover 2.00
360 A67 12g dark brown .20 .20
Never hinged .25
On cover 1.25
361 A67 20g yellow brown .20 .20
Never hinged .25
On cover 3.50
362 A67 24g grnsh blue .20 .20
Never hinged .25
On cover 1.25
363 A67 25g violet .25 .25
Never hinged .55
On cover 2.75
364 A67 30g maroon .25 .20
Never hinged .50
On cover 1.50
365 A67 35g rose carmine .35 .45
Never hinged 1.25
On cover 3.50

Perf. 12½

366 A68 40g slate gray .45 .25
Never hinged 1.75
On cover 1.50
367 A68 45g brown red .45 .25
Never hinged 1.75
On cover 3.50
368 A68 60g ultramarine .65 .65
Never hinged 2.75
On cover 2.75
369 A68 64g brown .65 .20
Never hinged 3.25
On cover 5.50
370 A68 1s deep violet 1.25 .55
Never hinged 7.00
On cover 7.75
371 A68 2s dull green 42.50 85.00
Never hinged 110.00
On cover 125.00

Designs Redrawn

Perf. 12 (6g), 12½ (2s)

372 A67 6g ultra ('35) .20 .20
Never hinged .35
On cover 2.00
373 A68 2s emerald ('35) 3.00 7.75
Never hinged 5.75
On cover 25.00
Nos. 354-373 (20) 51.85 97.60
Set, never hinged 140.00

The design of No. 358 looks as though the man's ears were on backwards, while No. 372 appears correctly.
On No. 373 there are seven feathers on each side of the eagle instead of five.
Nos. 354-373 exist imperf. Values, set unused hinged $375, never hinged $450.
For surcharges see Nos. B128-B131.

Dollfuss Mourning Issue

Engelbert Dollfuss — A85

1934-35 **Engr.** ***Perf. 12½***

374 A85 24g greenish black .45 .45
Never hinged 2.10
On overfranked cover 3.50
375 A85 24g indigo ('35) 1.10 1.10
Never hinged 3.75
On cover 5.00

Nos. 374-375 exist imperf. Value, each unused hinged $120, never hinged $150.

"Mother and Child," by Joseph Danhauser A86

"Madonna and Child," after Painting by Dürer — A87

1935, May 1

376 A86 24g dark blue .50 .30
Never hinged 2.10
On cover 2.75
a. Vert. pair, imperf. btwn. 275.00
Never hinged 350.00
b. Horiz. pair, imperf. btwn. 250.00
Never hinged 325.00

Mother's Day. No. 376 exists imperf. Value, unused hinged $150, never hinged $175.

1936, May 5 **Photo.**

377 A87 24g violet blue .30 *.45*
Never hinged 1.25
On cover 4.25

Mother's Day. No. 377 exists imperf. Value, unused hinged $150, never hinged $180.

Farm Workers — A88

Design: 5s, Factory workers.

1936, June **Engr.** ***Perf. 12½***

378 A88 3s red orange 13.00 17.00
Never hinged 29.00
On cover 40.00
379 A88 5s brown black 25.00 50.00
Never hinged 45.00
On cover 100.00

Nos. 378-379 exist imperf. Values, set unused hinged $210, never hinged $250.

Engelbert Dollfuss A90

Mother and Child — A91

1936, July 25

380 A90 10s dark blue 725.00 1,000.
Never hinged 1,100.
On cover 1,750.

Second anniv. of death of Engelbert Dollfuss, chancellor. Exists imperf. Value, $1,750.

1937, May 5 **Photo.** ***Perf. 12***

381 A91 24g henna brown .30 .45
On cover 4.50
Never hinged 1.25

Mother's Day. Exists imperf. Values, unused hinged $140, never hinged $165.

S.S. Maria Anna A92

Steamships: 24g, Uranus, 64g, Oesterreich.

1937, June 9

382 A92 12g red brown .60 .45
Never hinged 1.90
On cover 4.50
383 A92 24g deep blue .60 .45
Never hinged 1.90
On cover 3.50
384 A92 64g dark green .65 *1.10*
Never hinged 1.25
On cover 11.00
Nos. 382-384 (3) 1.85 *2.00*
Set, never hinged 7.75

Centenary of steamship service on Danube River. Exist imperf. Values, set unused hinged $350, never hinged $450.

First Locomotive, "Austria" A95

Designs: 25g, Modern steam locomotive. 35g, Modern electric train.

1937, Nov. 22

385 A95 12g black brown .20 .20
Never hinged .40
On cover 2.50
386 A95 25g dark violet .80 *1.25*
Never hinged 2.25
On cover 5.75
387 A95 35g brown red 2.00 *3.00*
Never hinged 4.25
On cover 9.25
Nos. 385-387 (3) 3.00 *4.45*
Set, never hinged 13.00

Centenary of Austrian railways. Exist imperf. Values, set unused hinged $90, never hinged $110.

Rose and Zodiac Signs — A98

1937 **Engr.** ***Perf. 13x12½***

388 A98 12g dark green .20 .25
Never hinged .20
On cover 1.75
389 A98 24g dark carmine .20 .25
Never hinged .45
On cover 1.75

Nos. 388-389 exist imperf. Values, set unused hinged $95, never hinged $120.

SEMI-POSTAL STAMPS

Issues of the Monarchy

Emperor Franz Josef — SP1

The Firing Step — SP2

Perf. 12½

1914, Oct. 4 **Typo.** **Unwmk.**

B1 SP1 5h green .20 *.35*
Never hinged .45
B2 SP1 10h rose .25 *.45*
Never hinged .70

Nos. B1-B2 were sold at an advance of 2h each over face value. Exist imperf.; value, set $50.

1915, May 1

Designs: 5h+2h, Cavalry. 10h+2h, Siege gun. 20h+3h, Battleship. 35h+3h, Airplane.

B3 SP2 3h + 1h violet brn .20 *.60*
Never hinged .30
B4 SP2 5h + 2h green .20 .20
Never hinged .20
B5 SP2 10h + 2h deep rose .20 .20
Never hinged .20
B6 SP2 20h + 3h Prus blue .70 *3.00*
Never hinged 1.75
B7 SP2 35h + 3h ultra 1.90 *6.50*
Never hinged 6.75
Nos. B3-B7 (5) 3.20 *10.50*
Set, never hinged 9.20

Exist imperf. Value, set $175 hinged and $325 never hinged.

Issues of the Republic

Types of Austria, 1919-20, Overprinted in Black

1920, Sept. 16 ***Perf. 12½***

B11 A44 5h gray, *yellow* .45 *1.25*
Never hinged 1.10
B12 A44 10h red, *pink* .35 *1.10*
Never hinged 1.10
B13 A43 15h bister, *yel* .30 *1.00*
Never hinged .85
B14 A45 20h dark grn, *bl* .30 *.85*
Never hinged .70

B15 A43 25h violet, *pink* .35 *.85*
Never hinged .70
B16 A45 30h brown, *buff* 1.40 *3.00*
Never hinged 2.75
B17 A45 40h carmine, *yel* .35 *.95*
Never hinged .85
B18 A45 50h dark bl, *blue* .35 *.70*
Never hinged .70
B19 A43 60h ol grn, *azure* 1.40 *3.25*
Never hinged 2.75
B20 A47 80h red .35 *.95*
Never hinged .70
B21 A47 1k orange brown .35 *.95*
Never hinged .70
B22 A47 2k pale blue .35 *1.10*
Never hinged .70

Granite Paper
Imperf

B23 A46 2½k brown red .35 *1.25*
Never hinged 1.10
B24 A46 3k dk blue & green .35 *1.40*
Never hinged 1.10
B25 A46 4k carmine & violet .55 *1.60*
Never hinged 1.40
B26 A46 5k blue .40 *1.40*
Never hinged 1.10
B27 A46 7½k yellow green .40 *1.40*
Never hinged 1.10
B28 A46 10k gray grn & red .40 *1.40*
Never hinged 1.40
B29 A46 20k lilac & orange .65 *2.00*
Never hinged 1.75
Nos. B11-B29 (19) 9.40 *26.40*
Set, never hinged 22.50

Carinthia Plebiscite. Sold at three times face value for the benefit of the Plebiscite Propaganda Fund.

Nos. B11-B19 exist imperf. Values, set unused hinged $120, never hinged $150.

Types of Regular Issues of 1919-21 Overprinted

1921, Mar. 1 ***Perf. 12½***

B30 A44 5h gray, *yellow* .25 *.65*
Never hinged .40
B31 A44 10h orange brown .25 *.65*
Never hinged .40
B32 A43 15h gray .25 *.65*
Never hinged .40
B33 A45 20h green, *yellow* .25 *.65*
Never hinged .40
B34 A43 25h blue, *yellow* .25 *.65*
Never hinged .40
B35 A45 30h violet, *bl* .45 *1.25*
Never hinged .80
B36 A45 40h org brn, *pink* .50 *1.60*
Never hinged 1.10
B37 A45 50h green, *blue* .90 *2.10*
Never hinged 2.10
B38 A43 60h lilac, *yellow* .35 *1.25*
Never hinged .80
B39 A47 80h pale blue .45 *1.10*
Never hinged .85
B40 A47 1k red org, *blue* .30 *1.00*
Never hinged .60
B41 A47 1½k green, *yellow* .20 *.65*
Never hinged .35
B42 A47 2k lilac brown .20 *.65*
Never hinged .35

Overprinted

B43 A46 2½k light blue .25 *.65*
Never hinged .45
B44 A46 3k ol grn & brn red .25 *.65*
Never hinged .45
B45 A46 4k lilac & orange .60 *1.90*
Never hinged 1.25
B46 A46 5k olive green .25 *.85*
Never hinged .45
B47 A46 7½k brown red .30 *.90*
Never hinged .55
B48 A46 10k blue & olive grn .25 *1.10*
Never hinged .45
B49 A46 20k car rose & vio .45 *1.40*
Never hinged .90
Nos. B30-B49 (20) 6.95 *20.30*
Set, never hinged 13.50

Nos. B30-B49 were sold at three times face value, the excess going to help flood victims. Exists imperf. Values, set unused hinged $250, never hinged $375.

Franz Joseph Haydn — SP9

View of Bregenz — SP16

Musicians: 5k, Mozart. 7½k, Beethoven. 10k, Schubert. 25k, Anton Bruckner. 50k, Johann Strauss (son). 100k, Hugo Wolf.

1922, Apr. 24 **Engr.** ***Perf. 12½***

B50 SP9 2½k brown, perf. 11½ 6.50 *10.50*
Never hinged 14.00
a. Perf. 12½ 9.25 *18.00*
Never hinged 25.00
B51 SP9 5k dark blue 1.10 *3.00*
Never hinged 2.10
B52 SP9 7½k black 1.75 *4.25*
Never hinged 3.50
a. Perf. 11½ 92.50 *175.00*
Never hinged 175.00
B53 SP9 10k dark violet 2.10 *5.00*
Never hinged 5.00
a. Perf. 11½ 3.50 *6.50*
Never hinged 8.50
B54 SP9 25k dark green 5.00 *9.25*
Never hinged 11.00
a. Perf. 11½ 4.25 *9.25*
Never hinged 9.25
B55 SP9 50k claret 2.10 *5.00*
Never hinged 5.00
B56 SP9 100k brown olive 5.75 *13.00*
Never hinged 14.00
a. Perf. 11½ 14.50 *42.50*
Never hinged 42.50
Nos. B50-B56 (7) 24.30 *50.00*
Set, never hinged 55.00

These stamps were sold at 10 times face value, the excess being given to needy musicians.

All values exist imperf. on both regular and handmade papers. Values, set unused hinged $350, never hinged $425.

A 1969 souvenir sheet without postal validity contains reprints of the 5k in black, 7½k in claret and 50k in dark blue, each overprinted "NEUDRUCK" in black at top. It was issued for the Vienna State Opera Centenary Exhibition.

1923, May 22 ***Perf. 12½***

Designs: 120k, Mirabelle Gardens, Salzburg. 160k, Church at Eisenstadt. 180k, Assembly House, Klagenfurt. 200k, "Golden Roof," Innsbruck. 240k, Main Square, Linz. 400k, Castle Hill, Graz. 600k, Abbey at Melk. 1000k, Upper Belvedere, Vienna.

Various Frames

B57 SP16 100k dk green 3.50 *8.50*
Never hinged 7.00
B58 SP16 120k deep blue 3.00 *7.75*
Never hinged 6.50
B59 SP16 160k dk violet 3.00 *7.75*
Never hinged 6.50
B60 SP16 180k red violet 3.00 *7.75*
Never hinged 6.50
B61 SP16 200k lake 3.00 *7.75*
Never hinged 5.75
B62 SP16 240k red brown 3.00 *7.75*
Never hinged 7.00
B63 SP16 400k dark brown 3.50 *8.50*
Never hinged 7.00
B64 SP16 600k olive brn 3.50 *10.00*
Never hinged 7.75
B65 SP16 1000k black 6.50 *12.00*
Never hinged 10.50
Nos. B57-B65 (9) 32.00 *77.75*
Set, never hinged 65.00

Nos. B57-B65 were sold at five times face value, the excess going to needy artists.

All values exist imperf. on both regular and handmade papers. Values, set hinged $350, never hinged $500.

Feebleness SP25

Siegfried Slays the Dragon SP30

Designs: 300k+900k, Aid to industry. 500k+1500k, Orphans and widow. 600k+1800k, Indigent old man. 1000k+3000k, Alleviation of hunger.

1924, Sept. 6 **Photo.**

B66 SP25 100k + 300k yel grn 3.50 *8.50*
Never hinged 6.25
B67 SP25 300k + 900k red brn 3.50 *9.25*
Never hinged 8.50
B68 SP25 500k + 1500k brn vio 3.50 *9.25*
Never hinged 10.50
B69 SP25 600k + 1800k pck bl 7.25 *16.00*
Never hinged 14.00
B70 SP25 1000k + 3000k brn org 9.25 *21.00*
Never hinged 16.00
Nos. B66-B70 (5) 27.00 *64.00*
Set, never hinged 55.00

The surtax was for child welfare and anti-tuberculosis work. Set exists imperf. Values, set unused hinged $350, never hinged $425.

1926, Mar. 8 **Engr.**

Designs: 8g+2g, Gunther's voyage to Iceland. 15g+5g, Brunhild accusing Kriemhild. 20g+5g, Nymphs telling Hagen the future. 24g+6g, Rudiger von Bechelaren welcomes the Nibelungen. 40g+10g, Dietrich von Bern vanquishes Hagen.

Design size 27½x28½mm

B71 SP30 3g + 2g olive blk 1.00 .70
Never hinged 1.75
On cover 4.00
B72 SP30 8g + 2g indigo .25 *.35*
Never hinged .35
On cover 4.00
B73 SP30 15g + 5g dk claret .25 *.35*
Never hinged .35
On cover 4.00
B74 SP30 20g + 5g olive grn .40 *.65*
Never hinged .70
On cover 7.50
B75 SP30 24g + 6g dk violet .40 *.65*
Never hinged .75
On cover 7.50
B76 SP30 40g + 10g red brn 3.50 *4.00*
Never hinged 9.50
On cover 11.00
Nos. B71-B76 (6) 5.80 *6.70*
Set, never hinged 13.50

Design size 28½x27½mm

B72a SP30 8g + 2g indigo .25 *.85*
Never hinged .85
On cover 5.00
B73a SP30 15g + 5g dk claret .45 *1.10*
Never hinged 1.10
On cover 5.75
B74a SP30 20g + 5g olive grn 17.50 *70.00*
Never hinged 60.00
On cover 100.00
B75a SP30 24g + 6g dk violet 2.50 *6.50*
Never hinged 5.75
On cover 18.00
B76a SP30 40g + 10g red brn 7.75 *8.50*
Never hinged 15.50
On cover 21.00
Nos. B72a-B76a (5) 28.45 *86.95*
Set, never hinged 80.00

Nibelungen issue.

The surtax was for child welfare. Nos. B71-B76 exist imperf. Values, set unused hinged $250, never hinged $325.

Pres. Michael Hainisch SP36

Pres. Wilhelm Miklas SP37

1928, Nov. 5

B77 SP36 10g dark brown 5.00 *10.50*
Never hinged 8.50
B78 SP36 15g red brown 5.00 *10.50*
Never hinged 8.50
B79 SP36 30g black 5.00 *10.50*
Never hinged 8.50
B80 SP36 40g indigo 5.00 *10.50*
Never hinged 8.50
Nos. B77-B80 (4) 20.00 *42.00*
Set, never hinged 34.00

Tenth anniversary of Austrian Republic. Sold at double face value, the premium aiding war orphans and children of war invalids.

Set exists imperf. Values, set unused hinged $250, never hinged $325.

1930, Oct. 4

B81 SP37 10g light brown 10.00 *21.00*
Never hinged 14.00
B82 SP37 20g red 10.00 *21.00*
Never hinged 14.00
B83 SP37 30g brown violet 10.00 *21.00*
Never hinged 14.00
B84 SP37 40g indigo 10.00 *21.00*
Never hinged 14.00
B85 SP37 50g dark green 10.00 *21.00*
Never hinged 14.00
B86 SP37 1s black brown 10.00 *21.00*
Never hinged 14.00
Nos. B81-B86 (6) 60.00 *126.00*
Set, never hinged 84.00

Nos. B81-B86 were sold at double face value. The excess aided the anti-tuberculosis campaign and the building of sanatoria in Carinthia.

Set exists imperf. Values, set unused hinged $450, never hinged $550.

Regular Issue of 1929-30 Overprinted in Various Colors

1931, June 20

B87 A56 10g bister (Bl) 35.00 *57.50*
Never hinged 77.50
B88 A56 20g dk gray (R) 35.00 *57.50*
Never hinged 77.50
B89 A56 30g dk violet (Gl) 35.00 *57.50*
Never hinged 77.50
B90 A56 40g dk blue (Gl) 35.00 *57.50*
Never hinged 77.50
B91 A56 50g gray vio (O) 35.00 *57.50*
Never hinged 77.50
B92 A57 1s black brn (Bk) 35.00 *57.50*
Never hinged 77.50
Nos. B87-B92 (6) 210.00 *345.00*
Set, never hinged 465.00

Rotary convention, Vienna.

Nos. B87 to B92 were sold at double their face values. The excess was added to the beneficent funds of Rotary International.

Exists imperf.

Ferdinand Raimund — SP38

Poets: 20g, Franz Grillparzer. 30g, Johann Nestroy. 40g, Adalbert Stifter. 50g, Ludwig Anzengruber. 1s, Peter Rosegger.

1931, Sept. 12

B93 SP38 10g dark violet 14.50 *29.00*
Never hinged 21.00
B94 SP38 20g gray black 14.50 *29.00*
Never hinged 21.00
B95 SP38 30g orange red 14.50 *29.00*
Never hinged 21.00
B96 SP38 40g dull blue 14.50 *29.00*
Never hinged 21.00
B97 SP38 50g gray green 14.50 *29.00*
Never hinged 21.00
B98 SP38 1s yellow brown 14.50 *29.00*
Never hinged 21.00
Nos. B93-B98 (6) 87.00 *174.00*
Set, never hinged 125.00

Nos. B93-B98 were sold at double face value. The surtax aided unemployed young people.

Set exists imperf. Values, set unused hinged $450, never hinged $550.

Chancellor Ignaz Seipel SP44

Ferdinand Georg Waldmüller SP45

1932, Oct. 12 ***Perf. 13***

B99 SP44 50g ultra 13.00 *25.00*
Never hinged 25.00

Msgr. Ignaz Seipel, Chancellor of Austria, 1922-29. Sold at double face value, the excess aiding wounded veterans of World War I.

Exists imperf. Values, unused hinged $250, never hinged $325.

1932, Nov. 21

Artists: 24g, Moritz von Schwind. 30g, Rudolf von Alt. 40g, Hans Makart. 64g, Gustav Klimt. 1s, Albin Egger-Lienz.

B100	SP45 12g slate green	21.00	*35.00*
	Never hinged	35.00	
B101	SP45 24g dp violet	18.00	*30.00*
	Never hinged	35.00	
B102	SP45 30g dark red	18.00	*30.00*
	Never hinged	35.00	
B103	SP45 40g dark gray	21.00	*32.50*
	Never hinged	35.00	
B104	SP45 64g dark brown	21.00	*32.50*
	Never hinged	35.00	
B105	SP45 1s claret	24.00	*50.00*
	Never hinged	35.00	
	Nos. B100-B105 (6)	123.00	*210.00*
	Set, never hinged	210.00	

Nos. B100 to B105 were sold at double their face values. The surtax was for the assistance of charitable institutions.

Set exists imperf. Values, set unused hinged $575, never hinged $725.

Mountain Climbing SP51

Designs: 24g, Ski gliding. 30g, Walking on skis. 50g, Ski jumping.

1933, Jan. 9 Photo. *Perf. 12½*

B106	SP51 12g dark green	7.25	*11.50*
	Never hinged	13.00	
B107	SP51 24g dark violet	100.00	*125.00*
	Never hinged	190.00	
B108	SP51 30g brown red	14.50	*21.00*
	Never hinged	21.00	
B109	SP51 50g dark blue	100.00	*125.00*
	Never hinged	190.00	
	Nos. B106-B109 (4)	221.75	*282.50*
	Set, never hinged	415.00	

Meeting of the Intl. Ski Federation, Innsbruck, Feb. 8-13.

These stamps were sold at double their face value. The surtax was for the benefit of "Youth in Distress."

#B106-B109 exist imperf. Values, set unused hinged $1,200, never hinged $1,500.

Stagecoach, after Painting by Moritz von Schwind — SP55

1933, June 23 Engr. *Perf. 12½*

Ordinary Paper

B110	SP55 50g deep ultra	150.00	*240.00*
	Never hinged	250.00	
	On cover		260.00
a.	Granite paper	325.00	*575.00*
	Never hinged	600.00	
	On cover		600.00

Sheets of 25.

Nos. B110 and B110a exist imperf. Values, unused hinged $675 and $1,500, never hinged $825 and $1,600.

Souvenir Sheet

Perf. 12

Granite Paper

B111	Sheet of 4	2,650.	*3,300.*
	Never hinged	3,150.	
	On cover (overfranked)		*4,000.*
a.	SP55 50g deep ultra	475.00	*750.00*
	Never hinged	650.00	
	On cover		*825.00*

Intl. Phil. Exhib., Vienna, 1933. In addition to the postal value of 50g the stamp was sold at a premium of 50g for charity and of 1.60s for the admission fee to the exhibition.

Size of No. B111: 126x103mm.

A 50g dark red in souvenir sheet, with dark blue overprint ("NEUDRUCK WIPA 1965"), had no postal validity.

Even though the margins No. B111 have no gum, the sheet sells for a premium when definitely never hinged.

No. B111 exists imperf. Value, unused $12,500.

St. Stephen's Cathedral in 1683 — SP56

Marco d'Aviano, Papal Legate — SP57

Designs: 30g, Count Ernst Rudiger von Starhemberg. 40g, John III Sobieski, King of Poland. 50g, Karl V, Duke of Lorraine. 64g, Burgomaster Johann Andreas von Liebenberg.

1933, Sept. 6 Photo. *Perf. 12½*

B112	SP56 12g dark green	22.50	*35.00*
	Never hinged	45.00	
B113	SP57 24g dark violet	21.00	*35.00*
	Never hinged	42.50	
B114	SP57 30g brown red	21.00	*35.00*
	Never hinged	42.50	
B115	SP57 40g blue black	30.00	*57.50*
	Never hinged	65.00	
B116	SP57 50g dark blue	21.00	*35.00*
	Never hinged	42.50	
B117	SP57 64g olive brown	25.00	*50.00*
	Never hinged	57.50	
	Nos. B112-B117 (6)	140.50	*247.50*
	Set, never hinged	295.00	

Deliverance of Vienna from the Turks, 250th anniv., and Pan-German Catholic Congress, Sept. 6, 1933.

The stamps were sold at double their face value, the excess being for the aid of Catholic works of charity.

Set exists imperf. Values, set unused hinged $850, never hinged $1,050.

Types of Regular Issue of 1925-30 Surcharged:

a

b

c

1933, Dec. 15

B118	A52(a) 5g + 2g ol grn	.20	*.85*
	Never hinged	.50	
B119	A56(b) 12g + 3g lt blue	.45	*1.10*
	Never hinged	.75	
B120	A56(b) 24g + 6g brn org	.20	*.85*
	Never hinged	.50	
B121	A57(c) 1s + 50g org red	37.50	*65.00*
	Never hinged	50.00	
	Nos. B118-B121 (4)	38.35	*67.80*
	Set, never hinged	52.50	

Winterhelp. Exists imperf. Values, set unused hinged $525, never hinged $650.

Anton Pilgram — SP62

Architects: 24g, J. B. Fischer von Erlach. 30g, Jakob Prandtauer. 40g, A. von Siccardsburg & E. van der Null. 60g, Heinrich von Ferstel. 64g, Otto Wagner.

1934, Dec. 2 Engr. *Perf. 12½*

Thick Yellowish Paper

B122	SP62 12g black	10.00	*21.00*
	Never hinged	15.00	
B123	SP62 24g dull violet	10.00	*21.00*
	Never hinged	15.00	
B124	SP62 30g carmine	10.00	*21.00*
	Never hinged	15.00	
B125	SP62 40g brown	10.00	*21.00*
	Never hinged	15.00	
B126	SP62 60g blue	10.00	*21.00*
	Never hinged	15.00	
B127	SP62 64g dull green	10.00	*21.00*
	Never hinged	15.00	
	Nos. B122-B127 (6)	60.00	*126.00*
	Set, never hinged	90.00	

Exist imperf. Values, set unused hinged $450, never hinged $550.

Nos. B124-B127 exist in horiz. pairs imperf. between. Value, each $160.

These stamps were sold at double their face value. The surtax on this and the following issues was devoted to general charity.

Types of Regular Issue of 1934 Surcharged in Black:

a

b

1935, Nov. 11 *Perf. 12, 12½*

B128	A67(a) 5g + 2g emerald	.40	*1.10*
	Never hinged	.70	
B129	A67(a) 12g + 3g blue	.75	*1.40*
	Never hinged	1.40	
B130	A67(a) 24g + 6g lt brown	.40	*1.10*
	Never hinged	.75	
B131	A68(b) 1s + 50g ver	35.00	*57.50*
	Never hinged	65.00	
	Nos. B128-B131 (4)	36.55	*61.10*
	Set, never hinged	67.50	

Winterhelp. Set exists imperf. Values, set unused hinged $125, never hinged $190.

Set without surcharge unused hinged $140, never hinged $190.

Prince Eugene of Savoy — SP68

Slalom Turn — SP74

Military Leaders: 24g, Field Marshal Laudon. 30g, Archduke Karl. 40g, Field Marshal Josef Radetzky. 60g, Admiral Wilhelm Tegetthoff. 64g, Field Marshal Franz Conrad Hotzendorff.

1935, Dec. 1 *Perf. 12½*

B132	SP68 12g brown	10.00	*21.00*
	Never hinged	17.00	
B133	SP68 24g dark green	10.00	*21.00*
	Never hinged	17.00	
B134	SP68 30g claret	10.00	*21.00*
	Never hinged	17.00	
B135	SP68 40g slate	10.00	*21.00*
	Never hinged	17.00	
B136	SP68 60g deep ultra	10.00	*21.00*
	Never hinged	17.00	
B137	SP68 64g dark violet	10.00	*21.00*
	Never hinged	17.00	
	Nos. B132-B137 (6)	60.00	*126.00*
	Set, never hinged	100.00	

These stamps were sold at double their face value. Set exists imperf. Values, set unused hinged $450, never hinged $550.

1936, Feb. 20 Photo.

Designs: 24g, Jumper taking off. 35g, Slalom turn. 60g, Innsbruck view.

B138	SP74 12g Prus green	2.40	*4.00*
	Never hinged	4.75	
B139	SP74 24g dp violet	4.25	*5.75*
	Never hinged	6.25	
B140	SP74 35g rose car	29.00	*55.00*
	Never hinged	50.00	
B141	SP74 60g sapphire	29.00	*52.50*
	Never hinged	50.00	
	Nos. B138-B141 (4)	64.65	*117.25*
	Set, never hinged	110.00	

Ski concourse issue. These stamps were sold at twice face value. Set exists imperf. Values, set unused hinged $450, never hinged $550.

St. Martin of Tours — SP78

Designs: 12g+3g, Medical clinic. 24g+6g, St. Elizabeth of Hungary. 1s+1s, "Flame of Charity."

1936, Nov. 2 Unwmk.

B142	SP78 5g + 2g dp green	.25	*.70*
	Never hinged	.35	
B143	SP78 12g + 3g dp violet	.25	*.70*
	Never hinged	.35	
B144	SP78 24g + 6g dp blue	.30	*.70*
	Never hinged	.35	
B145	SP78 1s + 1s dk car	6.50	*14.00*
	Never hinged	11.00	
	Nos. B142-B145 (4)	7.30	*16.10*
	Set, never hinged	12.00	

Winterhelp. Set exists imperf. Values, set unused hinged $175, never hinged $200.

Josef Ressel — SP82

Nurse and Infant — SP88

Inventors: 24g, Karl von Ghega. 30g, Josef Werndl. 40g, Carl Auer von Welsbach. 60g, Robert von Lieben. 64g, Viktor Kaplan.

1936, Dec. 6 Engr.

B146	SP82 12g dk brown	3.00	*7.25*
	Never hinged	6.00	
B147	SP82 24g dk violet	3.00	*7.25*
	Never hinged	6.00	
B148	SP82 30g dp claret	3.00	*7.25*
	Never hinged	6.00	
B149	SP82 40g gray violet	3.00	*7.25*
	Never hinged	6.00	
B150	SP82 60g vio blue	3.00	*7.25*
	Never hinged	6.00	
B151	SP82 64g dk slate green	3.00	*7.25*
	Never hinged	6.00	
	Nos. B146-B151 (6)	18.00	*43.50*
	Set, never hinged	36.00	

These stamps were sold at double their face value. Exists imperf. Values, set unused hinged $350, never hinged $450.

1937, Oct. 18 Photo.

12g+3g, Mother and child. 24g+6g, Nursing the aged. 1s+1s, Sister of Mercy with patient.

B152	SP88 5g + 2g dk green	.20	*.45*
	Never hinged	.25	
B153	SP88 12g + 3g dk brown	.20	*.45*
	Never hinged	.25	
B154	SP88 24g + 6g dk blue	.20	*.45*
	Never hinged	.25	
B155	SP88 1s + 1s dk carmine	4.00	*10.50*
	Never hinged	7.00	
	Nos. B152-B155 (4)	4.60	*11.85*
	Set, never hinged	7.75	

Winterhelp. Set exists imperf. Values, set unused hinged $90, never hinged $110.

Gerhard van Swieten — SP92

Physicians: 8g, Leopold Auenbrugger von Auenbrugg. 12g, Karl von Rokitansky. 20g, Joseph Skoda. 24g, Ferdinand von Hebra. 30g, Ferdinand von Arlt. 40g, Joseph Hyrtl. 60g, Theodor Billroth. 64g, Theodor Meynert.

1937, Dec. 5 Engr. *Perf. 12½*

B156 SP92 5g choc 2.10 5.00
Never hinged 3.50
B157 SP92 8g dk red 2.10 5.00
Never hinged 3.50
B158 SP92 12g brown blk 2.10 5.00
Never hinged 3.50
B159 SP92 20g dk green 2.10 5.00
Never hinged 3.50
B160 SP92 24g dk violet 2.10 5.00
Never hinged 3.50
B161 SP92 30g brown car 2.10 5.00
Never hinged 3.50
B162 SP92 40g dp olive grn 2.10 5.00
Never hinged 3.50
B163 SP92 60g indigo 2.10 5.00
Never hinged 3.50
B164 SP92 64g brown vio 2.10 5.00
Never hinged 3.50
Nos. B156-B164 (9) 18.90 *45.00*
Set, never hinged 30.00

These stamps were sold at double their face value. Set exists imperf. Values, set unused hinged $550, never hinged $725.

AIR POST STAMPS

Issues of the Monarchy

Types of Regular Issue of 1916 Surcharged

1918, Mar. 30 Unwmk. *Perf. 12½*

Grayish paper

C1 A40 1.50k on 2k lilac 1.40 5.00
Never hinged 3.75
On cover 90.00
C2 A40 2.50k on 3k ocher 7.25 22.50
Never hinged 25.00
On cover 110.00
a. Inverted surcharge *1,350.*
Never hinged 2,100.
b. Perf. 11½ 550.00 *650.00*
Never hinged 925.00
On cover 1,200.
c. Perf. 12½x11½ 50.00 *80.00*
Never hinged 95.00
On cover 90.00

Overprinted

C3 A40 4k gray 5.75 *15.00*
Never hinged 11.00
On cover —
Nos. C1-C3 (3) 14.40 *42.50*
Set, never hinged 40.00

White paper

C1a A40 1.50k on 2k lilac 3.00 *8.50*
Never hinged 5.75
On cover 140.00
C2d A40 2.50k on 3k ocher 7.25 *21.00*
Never hinged 12.00
On cover 175.00
C3a A40 4k gray 6.75 *20.00*
Never hinged 13.00
On cover —
On cover, overfranked 120.00
Nos. C1a-C3a (3) 17.00 *49.50*
Set, never hinged 26.00

Set exists imperf. Values, set unused hinged $325, never hinged $525.

Nos. C1-C3 also exist without surcharge or overprint. Values, set perf unused hinged $1,500, never hinged $2,500. Values, set imperf, unused hinged $1,500, never hinged $2,500.

Nos. C1-C3 were printed on grayish and on white paper.

A 7k on 10k red brown was prepared but not regularly issued. Value, perf. or imperf., $1,300 never hinged.

Issues of the Republic

Hawk — AP1

Wilhelm Kress — AP2

1922-24 Typo. *Perf. 12½*

C4 AP1 300k claret .30 *1.60*
Never hinged .65
On cover 77.50
C5 AP1 400k green ('24) 4.25 *14.50*
Never hinged 10.00
On cover 105.00
C6 AP1 600k bister .20 *1.10*
Never hinged .30
On cover 77.50
C7 AP1 900k brn orange .20 *1.10*
Never hinged .30
On cover 77.50

Engr.

C8 AP2 1200k brn violet .20 *1.10*
Never hinged .30
On cover 77.50
C9 AP2 2400k slate .20 *1.10*
Never hinged .30
On cover 77.50
C10 AP2 3000k dp brn ('23) 3.00 *8.25*
Never hinged 5.75
On cover 85.00
C11 AP2 4800k dark bl ('23) 3.00 *8.25*
Never hinged 5.75
On cover 95.00
Nos. C4-C11 (8) 11.35 *37.00*
Set, never hinged 22.50

Set exists imperf. Values, set unused hinged $250, never hinged $300.

Plane and Pilot's Head — AP3

Airplane Passing Crane — AP4

1925-30 Typo. *Perf. 12½*

C12 AP3 2g gray brown .35 *1.10*
Never hinged .80
On cover 2.25
C13 AP3 5g red .25 *.30*
Never hinged .45
On cover 1.50
a. Horiz. pair, imperf. btwn. 250.00
Never hinged 300.00
C14 AP3 6g dark blue 1.10 *1.75*
Never hinged 2.50
On cover 2.25
C15 AP3 8g yel green 1.10 *1.75*
Never hinged 2.50
On cover 2.50
C16 AP3 10g dp org ('26) 1.10 *1.75*
Never hinged 3.50
On cover 2.25
a. Horiz. pair, imperf. btwn. 300.00
Never hinged 350.00
C17 AP3 15g red vio ('26) .35 *.80*
Never hinged .65
On cover 1.75
a. Horiz. pair, imperf. btwn. 350.00
Never hinged 425.00
C18 AP3 20g org brn ('30) 13.00 7.75
Never hinged 25.00
On cover 13.50
C19 AP3 25g blk vio ('30) 5.00 *9.25*
Never hinged 8.50
On cover 17.50
C20 AP3 30g bister ('26) 10.00 *10.50*
Never hinged 21.00
On cover 19.00
C21 AP3 50g bl gray ('26) 18.00 16.00
Never hinged 35.00
On cover 27.50
C22 AP3 80g dk grn ('30) 3.00 *4.50*
Never hinged 4.25
On cover 10.50

Photo.

C23 AP4 10g orange red 1.10 *3.25*
Never hinged 1.75
On cover 5.50
a. Horiz. pair, imperf. btwn. 300.00
Never hinged 375.00
C24 AP4 15g claret .70 *1.75*
Never hinged 1.25
On cover 4.25
C25 AP4 30g brn violet .95 *2.50*
Never hinged 1.50
On cover 5.50
C26 AP4 50g gray black .95 *2.75*
Never hinged 1.50
On cover 4.25
C27 AP4 1s deep blue 8.50 *7.25*
Never hinged 35.00
On cover 10.50
C28 AP4 2s dark green 1.40 *3.50*
Never hinged 5.75
On cover 8.00
a. Vertical pair, imperf. btwn. 300.00
Never hinged 375.00
C29 AP4 3s red brn ('26) 55.00 *70.00*
Never hinged 92.50
On cover 90.00
C30 AP4 5s indigo ('26) 14.00 *29.00*
Never hinged 22.50
On cover 60.00

Size: 25½x32mm

C31 AP4 10s blk brown, *gray* ('26) 7.00 *20.00*
Never hinged 10.50
On cover 100.00
Nos. C12-C31 (20) 142.85 *195.45*
Set, never hinged 275.00

Exists imperf. Values, set unused hinged $800, never hinged $1,000.

Airplane over Güssing Castle — AP5

Airplane over the Danube — AP6

Designs (each includes plane): 10g, Maria-Worth. 15g, Durnstein. 20g, Hallstatt. 25g, Salzburg. 30g, Upper Dachstein and Schladminger Glacier. 40g, Lake Wetter. 50g, Arlberg. 60g, St. Stephen's Cathedral. 80g, Church of the Minorites. 2s, Railroad viaduct, Carinthia. 3s, Gross Glockner mountain. 5s, Aerial railway. 10s, Seaplane and yachts.

1935, Aug. 16 Engr. *Perf. 12½*

C32 AP5 5g rose violet .25 *.60*
Never hinged .35
On cover 1.75
C33 AP5 10g red orange .20 *.30*
Never hinged .20
On cover 1.75
C34 AP5 15g yel green .70 *1.75*
Never hinged 1.40
On cover 2.75
C35 AP5 20g gray blue .20 *.35*
Never hinged .25
On cover 2.25
C36 AP5 25g violet brn .20 *.35*
Never hinged .25
On cover 2.25
C37 AP5 30g brn orange .20 *.35*
Never hinged .25
On cover 2.25
C38 AP5 40g gray green .20 *.35*
Never hinged .25
On cover 2.50
C39 AP5 50g light sl bl .20 *.65*
Never hinged .35
On cover 2.50
C40 AP5 60g black brn .30 *.95*
Never hinged .60
On cover 4.25
C41 AP5 80g light brown .35 *1.25*
Never hinged .80
On cover 5.00
C42 AP6 1s rose red .30 *1.10*
Never hinged .60
On cover 4.25
C43 AP6 2s olive green 1.60 *5.75*
Never hinged 3.75
On cover 17.50
C44 AP6 3s yellow brn 7.00 *21.00*
Never hinged 17.50
On cover 35.00
C45 AP6 5s dark green 4.25 *15.00*
Never hinged 7.00
On cover 45.00
C46 AP6 10s slate blue 57.50 *110.00*
Never hinged 77.50
On cover 150.00
Nos. C32-C46 (15) 73.45 *159.75*
Set, never hinged 110.00

Set exists imperf. Values, set unused hinged $275, never hinged $325.

POSTAGE DUE STAMPS

Issues of the Monarchy

D1

D2

Perf. 10 to 13½

1894-95 Typo. Wmk. 91

J1 D1 1kr brown 1.90 1.00
Never hinged 6.25
On cover 17.00
Single franking on postcard 90.00
Single franking on printed matter 95.00
a. Perf. 13½ 45.00 37.50
Never hinged 67.50
On cover *75.00*
b. Half used as ½kr on cover *67.50*
J2 D1 2kr brown ('95) 2.50 1.90
Never hinged 7.50
On cover 14.00
a. Pair, imperf. btwn. 200.00 275.00
Never hinged 300.00
b. Half used as 1kr on cover *150.00*
J3 D1 3kr brown 3.00 1.00
Never hinged 8.00
On cover 9.25
On cover, single franking 11.50
a. Half used as 1½kr on cover *110.00*
J4 D1 5kr brown 3.00 .90
Never hinged 8.75
On cover 7.75
On cover, single franking 9.00
a. Perf. 13½ 25.00 15.00
Never hinged 37.50
On cover 45.00
b. Pair, imperf. btwn. 160.00 190.00
Never hinged 225.00
J5 D1 6kr brown ('95) 2.50 5.00
Never hinged 6.25
On cover 62.50
a. Half used as 3kr on cover *95.00*
J6 D1 7kr brown ('95) 1.25 4.50
Never hinged 3.00
On cover 100.00
a. Vert. pair, imperf. btwn. 275.00 —
Never hinged 425.00
b. Horiz. pair, imperf. btwn. 275.00 425.00
Never hinged 400.00
J7 D1 10kr brown 2.50 .50
Never hinged 13.50
On cover 16.00
a. Half used as 5kr on cover *110.00*
J8 D1 20kr brown 1.25 4.50
Never hinged 3.00
On cover 215.00
J9 D1 50kr brown 30.00 72.50
Never hinged 72.50
On cover *2,150.*
Nos. J1-J9 (9) 47.90 91.80

Values for Nos. J1-J9 are for stamps that do not show the watermark. Stamps showing the watermark often sell for more.

See Nos. J204-J231.

1899-1900 *Imperf.*

J10 D2 1h brown .25 .30
Never hinged 1.25
On cover 9.25
J11 D2 2h brown .25 .55
Never hinged 1.25
On cover 10.50
J12 D2 3h brown ('00) .25 .30
Never hinged 1.25
On cover 9.25
J13 D2 4h brown 1.75 1.50
Never hinged 5.50
On cover 12.50
J14 D2 5h brown ('00) 2.00 1.10
Never hinged 4.50
On cover 8.00
J15 D2 6h brown .30 .60
Never hinged 1.50
On cover 32.50
J16 D2 10h brown .25 .55
Never hinged 1.50
On cover 5.00
J17 D2 12h brown .50 1.75
Never hinged 2.10
On cover 62.50
J18 D2 15h brown .45 1.10
Never hinged 1.75
On cover 37.50
J19 D2 20h brown 16.00 3.50
Never hinged 50.00
On cover 16.00
J20 D2 40h brown 2.50 1.40
Never hinged 9.25
On cover *225.00*
J21 D2 100h brown 4.25 3.00
Never hinged 22.50
On cover *1,250.*
Nos. J10-J21 (12) 28.75 15.65

Perf. 10½, 12½, 13½ and Compound

J22 D2 1h brown .45 .20
Never hinged 1.50
On cover 5.00
J23 D2 2h brown .35 .20
Never hinged 1.50
On cover 4.25
J24 D2 3h brown ('00) .30 .20
Never hinged 1.50
On cover 10.00
J25 D2 4h brown .35 .20
Never hinged 1.75
On cover 11.50
J26 D2 5h brown ('00) .45 .20
Never hinged 2.10
On cover 4.25
J27 D2 6h brown .35 .20
Never hinged 1.75
On cover 6.25
J28 D2 10h brown .35 .20
Never hinged 2.50
On cover 3.00
J29 D2 12h brown .60 .65
Never hinged 3.00
On cover 40.00
J30 D2 15h brown .75 .80
Never hinged 3.75
On cover 21.50
J31 D2 20h brown 1.00 .25
Never hinged 5.00
On cover 10.50
J32 D2 40h brown 1.75 .45
Never hinged 7.50
On cover *210.00*

J33 D2 100h brown 18.00 1.75
Never hinged 82.50
On cover 950.00
Nos. J22-J33 (12) 24.70 5.30

Nos. J10-J33 exist on unwmkd. paper.
For surcharges see Offices in the Turkish Empire Nos. J1-J5.

D3

Ordinary Thin Paper

1910-13 Unwmk. *Perf. 12½*
J34b D3 1h carmine 2.25 1.40
Never hinged 9.25
On cover 14.00
J35 D3 2h carmine .25 .25
Never hinged .60
On cover 5.50
d. Half used as 1h on cover 77.50
J36 D3 4h carmine .20 .20
Never hinged .45
On cover 4.50
c. Half used as 2h on cover 77.50
d. Used as 5h with manuscript "5" on cover 175.00
J37 D3 6h carmine .20 .20
Never hinged .50
On cover 6.25
c. Used as 5h with manuscript "5" on cover 175.00
J38 D3 10h carmine .25 .20
Never hinged .60
On cover 1.25
c. Half used as 5h on cover 37.50
J39 D3 14h carmine ('13) 3.25 1.75
Never hinged 11.50
On cover 225.00
J40b D3 20h carmine 6.75 .20
Never hinged 21.00
On cover 6.75
c. Half used as 10h on cover 77.50
J41 D3 25h carmine ('10) 6.75 4.00
Never hinged 21.00
On cover *1,100.*
J42 D3 30h carmine 5.50 .25
Never hinged 19.00
On cover 45.00
J43 D3 50h carmine 7.50 .25
Never hinged 65.00
On cover 75.00
J44 D3 100h carmine 17.50 .45
Never hinged 52.50
On cover *1,100.*
Nos. J34b-J44 (11) 50.40 9.15

Chalky Paper

1908-13
J34a D3 1h carmine 1.35 *3.75*
Never hinged 2.75
On cover 17.50
J35a D3 2h carmine 2.10 *6.75*
Never hinged 9.25
On cover 32.50
J36a D3 4h carmine .65 *1.50*
Never hinged 2.50
On cover 7.50
J37a D3 6h carmine .80 *1.75*
Never hinged 2.50
On cover 10.50
J38a D3 10h carmine 3.75 .45
Never hinged 19.00
On cover 3.00
J40 D3 20h carmine 5.50 3.25
Never hinged 27.50
On cover 32.50
J42a D3 30h carmine 5.50 2.50
Never hinged 29.00
On cover 62.50
J43a D3 50h carmine 7.50 4.25
Never hinged 37.50
On cover 100.00
J44a D3 100h carmine 12.50 11.00
Never hinged 62.50
On cover 925.00

Thin Translucent Paper

1909
J34 D3 1h carmine .80 1.25
Never hinged 1.50
On cover 11.50
J35b D3 2h carmine 1.25 .90
Never hinged 5.50
On cover 8.75
J36b D3 4h carmine 9.25 .90
Never hinged 15.00
On cover 10.00
J37b D3 6h carmine .35 *.60*
Never hinged 1.00
On cover 11.50
J38b D3 10h carmine .30 .30
Never hinged 1.75
On cover 10.00
J40a D3 20h carmine 42.50 5.50
Never hinged 92.50
On cover 80.00
J44b D3 100h carmine 82.50 47.50
Never hinged 200.00
On cover *1,150.*

See Offices in the Turkish Empire type D3.

1911, July 16
J45 D3 5k violet 70.00 11.50
Never hinged 250.00
On cover —
J46 D3 10k violet 240.00 3.00
Never hinged 700.00
On cover —

Nos. J45-J46 exist imperf. Value, set unused hinged $900.

Regular Issue of 1908 Overprinted or Surcharged in Carmine or Black:

a

b

1916, Oct. 21
J47 A22 1h gray (C) .20 .20
Never hinged .25
On cover 12.50
a. Pair, one without overprint 125.00
Never hinged 200.00
J48 A22 15h on 2h vio (Bk) .20 *.60*
Never hinged .35
On cover 25.00
a. Inverted surcharge 325.00
Never hinged 625.00

D4

D5

Perf. 12½, 12½x13 (#J57-J59)
1916, Oct. 1
J49 D4 5h rose red .20 .20
Never hinged .20
On cover 4.00
J50 D4 10h rose red .20 .20
Never hinged .20
On cover 4.00
a. Half used as 5h on cover 52.50
J51 D4 15h rose red .20 .20
Never hinged .20
On cover 6.75
J52 D4 20h rose red .20 .20
Never hinged .20
On cover 4.00
J53 D4 25h rose red .20 *.65*
Never hinged .45
On cover 250.00
J54 D4 30h rose red .20 *.25*
Never hinged .20
On cover 16.00
a. Half used as 15h on cover 125.00
J55 D4 40h rose red .20 .30
Never hinged .35
On cover 12.50
a. Half used as 20h on cover 100.00
J56 D4 50h rose red .50 *1.60*
Never hinged 1.40
On cover 140.00
J57 D5 1k ultramarine .20 .20
Never hinged 1.25
On cover 475.00
a. Horiz. pair, imperf. btwn. 300.00 450.00
Never hinged 450.00
b. Perf 12½ 30.00 7.50
Never hinged 72.50
On cover *850.00*
J58 D5 5k ultramarine 1.90 2.40
Never hinged 6.75
a. Perf 12½ 67.50 40.00
Never hinged 140.00
J59 D5 10k ultramarine 2.00 1.25
Never hinged 7.75
a. Perf 12½ 125.00 70.00
Never hinged 275.00
Nos. J49-J59 (11) 6.00 *7.45*
Set, never hinged 19.00

Exists imperf. Value, set $225.
For overprints see J64-J74, Western Ukraine Nos. 54-55, NJ1-NJ6, Poland Nos. J1-J10.

Type of Regular Issue of 1916 Surcharged

1917
J60 A38 10h on 24h blue 1.10 .40
Never hinged 2.75
J61 A38 15h on 36h violet .30 .20
Never hinged .90
J62 A38 20h on 54h orange .20 *.30*
Never hinged .60
J63 A38 50h on 42h chocolate .20 .20
Never hinged .75
Nos. J60-J63 (4) 1.80 1.10
Set, never hinged 5.00

All values of this issue are known imperforate, also without surcharge, perforated and imperforate. Values, set imperf unused hinged $140, never hinged $200. Value of set without surcharge imperf unused hinged $110, never hinged $200. Same values for set without surcharge, perf 12½.
For overprints see Western Ukraine Nos. 57-58.

Issues of the Republic

Postage Due Stamps of 1916 Overprinted

1919
J64 D4 5h rose red .20 .20
Never hinged .25
a. Inverted overprint 225.00 300.00
Never hinged 300.00
J65 D4 10h rose red .20 .20
Never hinged .35
J66 D4 15h rose red .25 *.35*
Never hinged .65
J67 D4 20h rose red .25 *.35*
Never hinged .65
J68 D4 25h rose red 8.75 *13.50*
Never hinged 13.50
J69 D4 30h rose red .20 *.25*
Never hinged .30
J70 D4 40h rose red .25 *.60*
Never hinged .60
J71 D4 50h rose red .30 *1.25*
Never hinged .60
J72 D5 1k ultramarine 3.50 *8.00*
Never hinged 7.00
J73 D5 5k ultramarine 8.00 *10.50*
Never hinged 21.00
J74 D5 10k ultramarine 7.25 3.50
Never hinged 22.50
Nos. J64-J74 (11) 29.15 *38.70*
Set, never hinged 67.50

#J64, J65, J67, J70 exist imperf.

D6

D7

1920-21 *Perf. 12½*
J75 D6 5h bright red .20 *.30*
J76 D6 10h bright red .20 .20
J77 D6 15h bright red .20 *1.10*
J78 D6 20h bright red .20 .20
J79 D6 25h bright red .20 *.90*
J80 D6 30h bright red .20 *.25*
J81 D6 40h bright red .20 *.20*
J82 D6 50h bright red .20 *.20*
J83 D6 80h bright red .20 *.25*
J84 D7 1k ultramarine .20 *.20*
a. Thick grayish paper .20 .20
J85 D7 1½k ultra ('21) .20 .20
a. Thick grayish paper .20 .20
J86 D7 2k ultra ('21) .20 .20
a. Thick grayish paper .20 .20
J87 D7 3k ultra ('21) .20 *.50*
a. Thick grayish paper .20 .20
J88 D7 4k ultra ('21) .20 *.30*
a. Thick grayish paper .20 .30
J89 D7 5k ultramarine .20 *.20*
a. Thick grayish paper .50 2.00
J90 D7 8k ultra ('21) .20 *.50*
a. Thick grayish paper .20 .50
J91 D7 10k ultramarine .20 *.25*
a. Thick grayish paper .30 1.15
J92 D7 20k ultra ('21) .20 *.75*
a. Thick grayish paper .40 1.20
Nos. J75-J92 (18) *6.70*
Set, never hinged 3.50

Nos. J84 to J92 exist imperf. Values, set unused hinged $85, never hinged $115.

Imperf
J93 D6 5h bright red .20 *.35*
J94 D6 10h bright red .20 *.20*
J95 D6 15h bright red .20 *.90*
J96 D6 20h bright red .20 *.20*
J97 D6 25h bright red .20 *.90*
J98 D6 30h bright red .20 *.60*
J99 D6 40h bright red .20 *.35*
J100 D6 50h bright red .20 *.60*
J101 D6 80h bright red .20 *.35*
Nos. J93-J101 (9) *4.45*
Set, never hinged 1.40

No. 207a Surcharged in Dark Blue

1921, Dec. *Perf. 12½*
J102 A43 7½k on 15h bister .20 .20
Never hinged .20
On cover 6.00
a. Inverted surcharge 250.00 *425.00*
Never hinged 500.00

D8

D9

D10

1922
J103 D8 1k reddish buff .20 *.25*
J104 D8 2k reddish buff .20 *.25*
J105 D8 4k reddish buff .20 *.50*
J106 D8 5k reddish buff .20 *.25*
J107 D8 7½k reddish buff .20 *.65*
J108 D8 10k blue green .20 *.25*
J109 D8 15k blue green .20 *.50*
J110 D8 20k blue green .20 *.35*
J111 D8 25k blue green .20 *.80*
J112 D8 40k blue green .20 *.30*
J113 D8 50k blue green .20 *.90*
Nos. J103-J113 (11) *5.00*
Set, never hinged 1.75

Issue date: Nos. J108-J113, June 2.

1922-24
J114 D9 10k cobalt blue .20 *.30*
Never hinged .20
J115 D9 15k cobalt blue .20 *.35*
Never hinged .20
J116 D9 20k cobalt blue .20 *.45*
Never hinged .20
J117 D9 50k cobalt blue .20 *.35*
Never hinged .20
J118 D10 100k plum .20 .20
Never hinged .20
J119 D10 150k plum .20 *.20*
Never hinged .20
J120 D10 200k plum .20 .20
Never hinged .20
J121 D10 400k plum .20 .20
Never hinged .20
J122 D10 600k plum ('23) .20 *.35*
Never hinged .20
J123 D10 800k plum .20 .20
Never hinged .20
J124 D10 1,000k plum ('23) .20 .20
Never hinged .20
J125 D10 1,200k plum ('23) .20 *2.50*
Never hinged .25
J126 D10 1,500k plum ('24) .20 *.25*
Never hinged .30
J127 D10 1,800k plum ('24) 1.50 *5.25*
Never hinged 4.25
J128 D10 2,000k plum ('23) .30 *.85*
Never hinged 1.10
J129 D10 3,000k plum ('24) 5.75 *12.00*
Never hinged 12.00
J130 D10 4,000k plum ('24) 3.75 *9.75*
Never hinged 9.25
J131 D10 6,000k plum ('24) 6.75 *16.00*
Never hinged 22.50
Nos. J114-J131 (18) 20.65 *49.60*
Set, never hinged 50.00

J103-J131 sets exist imperf. Values, both sets unused hinged $240, never hinged $300.

D11

D12

1925-34 *Perf. 12½*
J132 D11 1g red .20 .20
Never hinged .20
J133 D11 2g red .20 .20
Never hinged .20
J134 D11 3g red .20 .20
Never hinged .20
J135 D11 4g red .20 .20
Never hinged .20
J136 D11 5g red ('27) .20 .20
Never hinged .20
J137 D11 6g red .20 *.45*
Never hinged .40
J138 D11 8g red .20 *.20*
Never hinged .40
J139 D11 10g dark blue .20 .20
Never hinged 1.40
J140 D11 12g dark blue .20 .20
Never hinged .20
J141 D11 14g dark blue ('27) .20 .20
Never hinged .30
J142 D11 15g dark blue .20 .20
Never hinged .20

J143 D11 16g dark blue ('29) .20 .20
Never hinged .70
J144 D11 18g dark blue ('34) 1.10 *3.50*
Never hinged 1.40
J145 D11 20g dark blue .20 .20
Never hinged .45
J146 D11 23g dark blue .25 .20
Never hinged 1.00
J147 D11 24g dark blue ('32) 1.10 .20
Never hinged 6.00
J148 D11 28g dark blue ('27) .90 .30
Never hinged 5.50
J149 D11 30g dark blue .20 .20
Never hinged 1.40
J150 D11 31g dark blue ('29) 1.10 .25
Never hinged 6.75
J151 D11 35g dark blue ('30) 1.10 .20
Never hinged 6.75
J152 D11 39g dark blue ('32) 1.40 .20
Never hinged 8.75
J153 D11 40g dark blue 1.25 *1.75*
Never hinged 4.25
J154 D11 60g dark blue .85 *1.10*
Never hinged 4.25
J155 D12 1s dark green 5.50 1.10
Never hinged 13.50
J156 D12 2s dark green 22.50 3.50
Never hinged 80.00
J157 D12 5s dark green 77.50 32.50
Never hinged 190.00
J158 D12 10s dark green 40.00 4.25
Never hinged 87.50
Nos. J132-J158 (27) 157.35 52.10
Set, never hinged 425.00

Issues of 1925-27 exist imperf. Values, set of 18 unused hinged $450, never hinged $550.
Issued: 3g, 2s-10s, Dec; 5g, 28g, 1/1; 14g, June; 31g, 2/1; 35g, Jan; 24g, 39g, Sept; 16g, May; 18g, 6/25; others, 6/1.

Coat of Arms
D13 D14

1935, June 1

J159 D13 1g red .20 .20
Never hinged .20
J160 D13 2g red .20 .20
Never hinged .20
J161 D13 3g red .20 .20
Never hinged .20
J162 D13 5g red .20 .20
Never hinged .20
J163 D13 10g blue .20 .20
Never hinged .20
J164 D13 12g blue .20 .20
Never hinged .20
J165 D13 15g blue .20 *.40*
Never hinged .30
J166 D13 20g blue .20 .20
Never hinged .40
J167 D13 24g blue .20 .20
Never hinged .75
J168 D13 30g blue .20 .20
Never hinged .75
J169 D13 39g blue .20 .20
Never hinged 1.25
J170 D13 60g blue .75 *.90*
Never hinged 1.55
J171 D14 1s green .75 .30
Never hinged 2.50
J172 D14 2s green 1.25 .70
Never hinged 6.25
J173 D14 5s green 2.75 2.50
Never hinged 13.50
J174 D14 10s green 3.75 .60
Never hinged 14.00
Nos. J159-J174 (16) 11.45 7.40
Set, never hinged 43.50

On #J163-J170, background lines are horiz.
Nos. J159-J174 exist imperf. Values, set unused hinged $200, never hinged $275.

MILITARY STAMPS

Issues of the Austro-Hungarian Military Authorities for the Occupied Territories in World War I

See Bosnia and Herzegovina for similar designs inscribed "MILITARPOST" instead of "FELDPOST."

Stamps of Bosnia of 1912-14 Overprinted

1915 Unwmk. *Perf. 12½*

M1 A23 1h olive green .20 *.45*
Never hinged .30
On cover 27.50
M2 A23 2h bright blue .20 *.35*
Never hinged .40
On cover 25.00
M3 A23 3h claret .20 *.35*
Never hinged .40
On cover 26.00
M4 A23 5h green .20 .20
Never hinged .25
On cover 16.00
M5 A23 6h dark gray .20 *.35*
Never hinged .45
On cover 37.50
M6 A23 10h rose carmine .20 .20
Never hinged .25
On cover 17.00
M7 A23 12h deep ol grn .20 *.45*
Never hinged .65
On cover 27.50
M8 A23 20h orange brn .20 *.60*
Never hinged .65
On cover 42.50
M9 A23 25h ultramarine .20 *.45*
Never hinged .65
On cover 42.50
M10 A23 30h orange red 1.90 *4.50*
Never hinged 5.00
On cover 50.00
M11 A24 35h myrtle grn 1.50 *3.75*
Never hinged 4.00
On cover 110.00
M12 A24 40h dark violet 1.50 *3.75*
Never hinged 4.00
On cover 140.00
M13 A24 45h olive brown 1.50 *3.75*
Never hinged 4.00
On cover 175.00
M14 A24 50h slate blue 1.50 *3.75*
Never hinged 4.00
On cover 175.00
M15 A24 60h brn violet .25 *1.00*
Never hinged .80
On cover 125.00
M16 A24 72h dark blue 1.50 *3.75*
Never hinged 4.00
On cover 137.50
M17 A25 1k brn vio, *straw* 1.60 *4.00*
Never hinged 4.00
On cover 240.00
M18 A25 2k dk gray, *blue* 1.60 *4.00*
Never hinged 4.00
On cover *340.00*
On postal money order or receipt 100.00
M19 A26 3k car, *green* 19.00 *37.50*
Never hinged 42.50
On cover —
On postal money order or receipt *100.00*
On overfranked philatelic cover 55.00
M20 A26 5k dk vio, *gray* 17.00 *27.50*
Never hinged 37.50
On cover —
On postal money order or receipt *100.00*
On overfranked philatelic cover 55.00
M21 A25 10k dk ultra, *gray* 125.00 210.00
Never hinged 225.00
On cover —
On postal money order or receipt *650.00*
On overfranked philatelic cover 375.00
Nos. M1-M21 (21) 175.65 *310.65*
Set, never hinged 350.00

Exists imperf. Values, set unused hinged $225, never hinged $450.
Nos. M1-M21 also exist with overprint double, inverted and in red. These varieties were made by order of an official but were not regularly issued.
Covers: On cover values are for stamps on postal money order receipts.

M1 M2
Emperor Franz Josef

Perf. 11½, 12½ and Compound

1915-17 Engr.

M22 M1 1h olive green .20 .20
Never hinged .25
On cover 7.50
M23 M1 2h dull blue .20 .25
Never hinged .30
On cover 7.50
Single franking on printed matter 20.00
M24 M1 3h claret .20 .20
Never hinged .25
On cover 7.50
M25 M1 5h green .20 .20
Never hinged .25
On cover 1.75
a. Perf. 11½ 62.50 *80.00*
Never hinged 115.00
b. Perf. 11½x12½ 92.50 *125.00*
Never hinged 175.00
c. Perf. 12½x11½ 110.00 *175.00*
Never hinged 210.00
M26 M1 6h dark gray .20 .25
Never hinged .25
On cover 11.50
M27 M1 10h rose carmine .20 .20
Never hinged .30
On cover 2.50
M28 M1 10h gray bl ('17) .20 .25
Never hinged .35
On cover 8.75
M29 M1 12h deep olive grn .20 .30
Never hinged .35
On cover 19.00
M30 M1 15h car rose ('17) .20 *.20*
Never hinged .20
On cover 4.25
a. Perf. 11½ 7.75 *17.00*
Never hinged 14.00
M31 M1 20h orange brn .25 *.35*
Never hinged 1.35
On cover 7.50
M32 M1 20h ol green ('17) .25 *.35*
Never hinged 1.35
On cover 11.50
M33 M1 25h ultramarine .20 *.25*
Never hinged .65
On cover 8.75
M34 M1 30h vermilion .20 *.35*
Never hinged .65
On cover 15.00
M35 M1 35h dark green .25 *.55*
Never hinged 1.25
On cover 26.00
M36 M1 40h dark violet .25 *.55*
Never hinged 1.25
On cover 26.00
M37 M1 45h olive brown .25 *.55*
Never hinged 1.25
On cover 37.50
M38 M1 50h myrtle green .25 *.55*
Never hinged 1.25
On cover 26.00
M39 M1 60h brown violet .25 *.55*
Never hinged 1.25
On cover 14.00
M40 M1 72h dark blue .25 *.55*
Never hinged 1.25
On cover 75.00
M41 M1 80h org brn ('17) .25 *.25*
Never hinged 1.35
On cover 37.50
M42 M1 90h magenta ('17) .70 *1.00*
Never hinged 3.00
On cover 87.50
M43 M2 1k brn vio, *straw* 1.25 *1.90*
Never hinged 6.25
On cover 60.00
M44 M2 2k dk gray, *blue* .75 1.00
Never hinged 3.75
On cover 75.00
M45 M2 3k car, *green* .70 *2.00*
Never hinged 3.25
On cover 190.00
M46 M2 4k dark violet, *gray* ('17) .60 *3.25*
Never hinged 2.50
On cover 375.00
M47 M2 5k dk vio, *gray* 16.00 *27.50*
Never hinged 35.00
On cover 500.00
M48 M2 10k dk ultra, *gray* 3.00 *7.50*
Never hinged 6.25
On cover 750.00
Nos. M22-M48 (27) 27.45 *51.05*
Set, never hinged 75.00

Nos. M22-M48 exist imperf. Values, set unused hinged $140, never hinged $275.

Emperor Karl I
M3 M4

1917-18 *Perf. 12½*

M49 M3 1h grnsh blue ('18) .20 .20
Never hinged .20
On cover 5.00
a. Perf. 11½ 4.75 *7.75*
Never hinged 8.75
M50 M3 2h red org ('18) .20 .20
Never hinged .20
On cover 5.00
M51 M3 3h olive gray .20 .20
Never hinged .20
On cover 5.00
a. Perf. 11½ 15.00 *27.50*
Never hinged 32.50
b. Perf. 11½x12½ 27.50 *52.50*
Never hinged 55.00
M52 M3 5h olive green .20 .20
Never hinged .20
On cover 3.00
M53 M3 6h violet .20 .20
Never hinged .25
On cover 7.50
M54 M3 10h orange brn .20 .20
Never hinged .20
On cover 1.90
M55 M3 12h blue .20 .20
Never hinged .25
On cover 12.50
a. Perf. 11½ 3.00 *5.50*
Never hinged 6.25
M56 M3 15h bright rose .20 .20
Never hinged .20
On cover 3.00
M57 M3 20h red brown .20 .20
Never hinged .20
On cover 5.00
M58 M3 25h ultramarine .20 .25
Never hinged .65
On cover 5.00
M59 M3 30h slate .20 .20
Never hinged .30
On cover 9.25
M60 M3 40h olive bister .20 .20
Never hinged .20
On cover 6.25
a. Perf. 11½ 1.90 *3.00*
Never hinged 3.75
M61 M3 50h deep green .20 .20
Never hinged .25
On cover 11.50
a. Perf. 11½ 7.75 *14.00*
Never hinged 15.00
M62 M3 60h car rose .20 .20
Never hinged .25
On cover 11.50
M63 M3 80h dull blue .20 .20
Never hinged .20
On cover 19.00
M64 M3 90h dk violet .25 *.45*
Never hinged .80
On cover 42.50
M65 M4 2k rose, *straw* .20 .25
Never hinged .35
On cover 32.50
a. Perf. 11½ 2.75 *5.00*
Never hinged 5.50
M66 M4 3k green, *blue* .85 *2.10*
Never hinged 2.50
On cover 150.00
M67 M4 4k rose, *green* 13.50 *17.00*
Never hinged 37.50
On cover 210.00
a. Perf. 11½ 26.00 *50.00*
Never hinged 52.50
M68 M4 10k dl vio, *gray* 1.00 *5.00*
Never hinged 2.75
On cover 625.00
a. Perf. 11½ 12.50 *25.00*
Never hinged 25.00
Nos. M49-M68 (20) 18.80 *27.85*
Set, never hinged 47.50

Nos. M49-M68 exist imperf. Values, set unused hinged $90, never hinged $175.
See No. M82. For surcharges and overprints see Italy Nos. N1-N19, Western Ukraine Nos. 34-53, 75-81.

Emperor Karl I — M5

1918 Typo. *Perf. 12½*

M69 M5 1h grnsh blue 16.00
Never hinged 45.00
M70 M5 2h orange 6.25
Never hinged 21.00
M71 M5 3h olive gray 6.25
Never hinged 21.00
M72 M5 5h yellow green .20
Never hinged .40
M73 M5 10h dark brown .20
Never hinged .40
M74 M5 20h red .55
Never hinged 2.25
M75 M5 25h blue .55
Never hinged 2.50
M76 M5 30h bister 75.00
Never hinged 165.00
M77 M5 45h dark slate 85.00
Never hinged 200.00
M78 M5 50h deep green 45.00
Never hinged 105.00
M79 M5 60h violet 90.00
Never hinged 200.00
M80 M5 80h rose 52.50
Never hinged 130.00
M81 M5 90h brown violet 1.75
Never hinged 3.50

Engr.

M82 M4 1k ol bister, *blue* .20
Never hinged .25
Nos. M69-M82 (14) 379.45
Set, never hinged 900.00

Nos. M69-M82 were on sale at the Vienna post office for a few days before the Armistice signing. They were never issued at the Army Post Offices. They exist imperf. Values, set unused hinged $675, never hinged $1,150.
For surcharges see Italy Nos. N20-N33.

MILITARY SEMI-POSTAL STAMPS

Emperor Karl I — MSP7

Empress Zita — MSP8

Perf. 12½x13

1918, July 20 Unwmk. Typo.

MB1 MSP7 10h gray green .25 .55
Never hinged .70
MB2 MSP8 20h magenta .25 .55
Never hinged .70

MB3 MSP7 45h blue .25 .55
Never hinged .70
Nos. MB1-MB3 (3) .75 1.65
Set, never hinged 2.10

These stamps were sold at a premium of 10h each over face value. The surtax was for "Karl's Fund."

For overprints see Western Ukraine Nos. 31-33.

Exist imperf. Values, set hinged unused $25, never hinged $55.

MILITARY NEWSPAPER STAMPS

Mercury — MN1

1916 Unwmk. Typo. *Perf. 12½*

MP1 MN1 2h blue .20 *.20*
Never hinged .20
On newspaper 12.50
a. Perf. 11½ 1.40 *1.60*
Never hinged 1.75
On newspaper —
b. Perf. 12½x11½ 150.00 *200.00*
Never hinged 250.00
On newspaper —
MP2 MN1 6h orange .50 *.80*
Never hinged 1.00
On newspaper 110.00
MP3 MN1 10h carmine .60 *.80*
Never hinged 1.20
On newspaper 110.00
MP4 MN1 20h brown .40 *.80*
Never hinged .90
On newspaper 150.00
a. Perf. 11½ 1.90 *5.00*
Never hinged 5.00
On newspaper —
Nos. MP1-MP4 (4) 1.70 *2.60*
Set, never hinged 3.25

Exist imperf. Values, Nos. MP2-MP3, unused hinged each $3.50, never hinged $4.50; Nos. MP1, MP4, unused hinged each $19, never hinged $45.

For surcharges see Italy Nos. NP1-NP4.

NEWSPAPER STAMPS

From 1851 to 1866, the Austrian Newspaper Stamps were also used in Lombardy-Venetia.

Values for unused stamps 1851-67 are for fine copies with original gum. Specimens without gum sell for about a third or less of the figures quoted.

Issues of the Monarchy

Mercury — N1

Three Types
Type I — The "G" has no crossbar.
Type II — The "G" has a crossbar.
Type IIa — as type II but the rosette is deformed. Two spots of color in the "G."

1851-56 Unwmk. Typo. *Imperf.*
Machine-made Paper

P1 N1 (0.6kr) bl, type IIa 175.00 110.00
No gum 30.00
On newspaper 250.00
On wrapper 240.00
a. Blue, type I 250.00 125.00
No gum 50.00
On newspaper 350.00
On wrapper 325.00
b. Ribbed paper 625.00 225.00
No gum 110.00
On newspaper 375.00
On wrapper 350.00
c. Blue, type II 600.00 250.00
No gum 125.00
On newspaper 750.00
On wrapper 750.00
P2 N1 (6kr) yel, type I *25,000.* *7,500.*
No gum *22,500.*
On newspaper
On newspaper *18,000.*
On wrapper *18,000.*
a. (6kr) brown orange, type I — *8,500.*
P3 N1 (30kr) rose, type I — *10,500.*
No gum *28,500.*
On newspaper *24,500.*
On wrapper *23,500.*
P4 N1 (6kr) scar, type II ('56) *67,500.* *50,000.*
No gum *32,500.*

Full margins = 1½mm at top and bottom, ½mm at sides.

Values for pairs

P1 N1 (0.6kr) blue, type IIa 375.00 220.00
On newspaper 500.00
P1a N1 (0.6kr) blue, type I 525.00 300.00
On newspaper 650.00
P1b N1 (0.6kr) blue, type I, ribbed paper 1,300. 475.00
On newspaper *800.00*
P1c N1 (0.6kr) blue, type II 1,250. 750.00
On newspaper —

Values for strips of 3

P1 N1 (0.6kr) blue, type IIa 600.00 375.00
On newspaper 900.00
P1a N1 (0.6kr) blue, type I 825.00 500.00
On newspaper 1,250.00
P1b N1 (0.6kr) blue, type I, ribbed paper *2,100.* 700.00
On newspaper 1,350.
P1c N1 (0.6kr) blue, type II — 1,450.
On newspaper —

Values for blocks of 4

P1 N1 (0.6kr) blue, type IIa *2,000.* *1,700.*
P1a N1 (0.6kr) blue, type I *2,250.* *3,000.*
P1b N1 (0.6kr) blue, type I, ribbed paper *4,500.* *3,250.*
P1c N1 (0.6kr) blue, type II — —

From 1852 No. P3 and from 1856 No. P2 were used as 0.6 kreuzer values.

Values for Nos. P2-P3 unused are for stamps without gum. Pale shades sell at considerably lower values.

Originals of Nos. P2 and P3 are usually in pale colors and poorly printed. Values are for stamps clearly printed and in bright colors. Numerous reprints of Nos. P1 to P4 were made between 1866 and 1904. Those of Nos. P2 and P3 are always well printed and in much deeper colors. All reprints are in type I, but occasionally show faint traces of a crossbar on "G" of "ZEITUNGS."

N2

N3

Two Types of the 1858-59 Issue
Type I — Loops of the bow at the back of the head broken.
Type II — Loops complete. Wreath projects further at top of head.

1858-59 Embossed

P5 N2 (1kr) blue, type I 650.00 625.00
No gum 75.00
On newspaper 1,150.
On wrapper 1,100.
a. (1kr) deep blue, type I 750.00 675.00
No gum 150.00
On newspaper 1,100.
On wrapper 875.00
P6 N2 (1kr) lilac, type II ('59) 875.00 300.00
No gum 100.00
On newspaper 600.00
On wrapper 575.00
a. (1kr) dark lilac, type II 1,450. 425.00
No gum 250.00
On newspaper 575.00
On wrapper 550.00
b. (1kr) dark slate lilac, type II — 650.00
On wrapper 1,300.
c. (1kr) gray, type II 2,100. 625.00
No gum 375.00
On newspaper 1,000.
On wrapper 950.00

Values for pairs

P5 N2 (1kr) blue, type I 1,400. *1,750.*
P6 N2 (1kr) lilac, type II 1,900. 750.00
P6a N2 (1kr) dark lilac, type II — 900.00

Values for strips of 3

P5 N2 (1kr) blue, type I *2,100.* *2,250.*
P6 N2 (1kr) lilac, type II *3,000.* *1,400.*
P6a N2 (1kr) dark lilac, type II —

Values for blocks of 4

P5 N2 (1kr) blue, type I *3,250.* *4,750.*
P6 N2 (1kr) lilac, type II *5,500.* *3,500.*
P6a N2 (1kr) dark lilac, type II — *5,500.*

1861

P7 N3 (1kr) gray 175.00 175.00
No gum 25.00
On newspaper 375.00
On wrapper 350.00
a. (1kr) gray lilac 625.00 240.00
No gum 120.00
On newspaper 525.00
On wrapper 475.00
b. (1kr) deep lilac 2,500. 750.00
No gum 475.00
On newspaper 1,500.
On wrapper 1,450.
c. (1kr) brownish lilac 500.00 260.00
No gum 100.00
On newspaper 600.00
On wrapper 575.00

Values for pairs

P7 N3 (1kr) gray 350.00 *425.00*
On newspaper 800.00
On wrapper 750.00
P7a N3 (1kr) gray lilac — 525.00
P7b N3 (1kr) deep lilac —

The embossing on the reprints of the 1858-59 and 1861 issues is not as sharp as on the originals.

N4

Wmk. 91, or, before July 1864, Unwmkd.

1863

P8 N4 (1.05kr) gray 45.00 15.00
No gum 8.00
On newspaper 85.00
On wrapper 75.00
a. Tete beche pair *125,000.*
b. (1.05kr) gray lilac 75.00 17.50
No gum 12.50
On newspaper 100.00
On wrapper 90.00
c. (1.05kr) brownish lilac 45.00 12.50
On newspaper 80.00
On wrapper 70.00

Values for pairs

P8 N4 (1.05kr) gray 90.00 35.00
P8b N4 (1.05kr) gray lilac 175.00 45.00

Values are for stamps that do not show the watermark. Stamps showing the watermark often sell for more.

The embossing of the reprints is not as sharp as on the originals.

Mercury
N5 N6

Three Types
Type I — Helmet not defined at back, more or less blurred. Two thick short lines in front of wing of helmet. Shadow on front of face not separated from hair.
Type II — Helmet distinctly defined. Four thin short lines in front of wing. Shadow on front of face clearly defined from hair.
Type III — Outer white circle around head is open at top (closed on types I and II). Greek border at top and bottom is wider than on types I and II.

1867-73 Typo. Wmk. 91
Coarse Print

P9 N5 (1kr) vio, type I 37.50 4.00
On newspaper 50.00
On wrapper 25.00
a. (1kr) violet, type II ('73) 125.00 18.00
On newspaper 165.00
On wrapper 95.00

1874-76
Fine Print

P9B N5 (1kr) violet, type III ('76) .55 .20
On newspaper 7.00
On wrapper 4.50
c. (1kr) gray lilac, type I ('76) 90.00 25.00
On newspaper 145.00
On wrapper 90.00
d. (1kr) violet, type II 27.50 5.00
On newspaper 80.00
On wrapper 50.00
e. Double impression, type III 175.00

Stamps of this issue, except No. P9Bc, exist in many shades, from gray to lilac brown and deep violet. Stamps in type III exist also privately perforated or rouletted.

1880

P10 N6 ½kr blue green 4.50 .85
On newspaper 30.00
On wrapper 16.00
a. ½kr yellow green 5.00 .95
On newspaper 32.50
On wrapper 17.50

Nos. P9B and P10 also exist on thicker paper without sheet watermark and No. P10 exists with unofficial perforation.

N7

1899 Unwmk. *Imperf.*
Without Varnish Bars

P11 N7 2h dark blue .20 .20
Never hinged .30
On newspaper 3.25
On wrapper 3.50
P12 N7 6h orange 2.00 1.75
Never hinged 4.00
On newspaper 47.50
On wrapper 45.00
P13 N7 10h brown .80 .75
Never hinged 2.00
On newspaper 27.50
On wrapper 25.00
P14 N7 20h rose 1.75 1.75
Never hinged 3.00
On newspaper 95.00
On wrapper 90.00
Nos. P11-P14 (4) 4.75 4.45

1901
With Varnish Bars

P11a N7 2h dark blue .60 .20
Never hinged 2.00
On newspaper 6.50
On wrapper 6.50
P12a N7 6h orange 8.50 11.50
Never hinged 17.50
On newspaper 150.00
On wrapper 150.00
P13a N7 10h brown 10.50 6.75
Never hinged 35.00
On newspaper 130.00
On wrapper 125.00
P14a N7 20h rose 19.00 26.00
Never hinged 35.00
On newspaper 260.00
On wrapper 250.00
Nos. P11a-P14a (4) 38.60 44.45

Nos. P11-P14 were re-issued in 1905.

Mercury
N8 N9

1908 *Imperf.*

P15 N8 2h dark blue 1.40 .20
Never hinged 1.50
On newspaper 4.50
On wrapper 4.25
a. Tete beche pair 250.00 300.00
Never hinged 300.00
P16 N8 6h orange 2.50 .30
Never hinged 5.50
On newspaper 40.00
On wrapper 35.00
P17 N8 10h carmine 2.50 .30
Never hinged 5.50
On newspaper 37.50
On wrapper 35.00
P18 N8 20h brown 2.75 .25
Never hinged 5.50
On newspaper 60.00
On wrapper 55.00
Nos. P15-P18 (4) 9.15 1.05

All values are found on chalky, regular and thin ordinary paper. They exist privately perforated.

1916 *Imperf.*

P19 N9 2h brown .20 .20
Never hinged .30
On newspaper 7.00
On wrapper 6.50
P20 N9 4h green .30 *.85*
Never hinged .60
On newspaper 60.00
On wrapper 55.00
P21 N9 6h dark blue .25 *.70*
Never hinged .55
On newspaper 60.00
On wrapper 55.00
P22 N9 10h orange .35 *.85*
Never hinged .80
On newspaper 60.00
On wrapper 55.00
P23 N9 30h claret .30 *.80*
Never hinged .55
On newspaper 80.00
On wrapper 75.00
Nos. P19-P23 (5) 1.40 3.40
Set, never hinged 2.75

Issues of the Republic

Newspaper Stamps of 1916 Overprinted

1919

P24 N9 2h brown .20 .20
Never hinged .20
On newspaper 2.00
On wrapper 1.50
P25 N9 4h green .25 *.70*
Never hinged .45
On newspaper 4.00
On wrapper 3.75
P26 N9 6h dark blue .20 *.70*
Never hinged .30
On newspaper 6.00
On wrapper 5.50
P27 N9 10h orange .25 *.90*
Never hinged .50
On newspaper 8.00
On wrapper 7.00
P28 N9 30h claret .20 *.50*
Never hinged .30
On newspaper 12.00
On wrapper 11.00
Nos. P24-P28 (5) 1.10 *3.00*
Set, never hinged 1.75

Mercury
N10 N11

1920-21 ***Imperf.***

P29 N10 2h violet .20 .20
Never hinged .20
P30 N10 4h brown .20 *.20*
Never hinged .20
P31 N10 5h slate .20 .20
Never hinged .20
P32 N10 6h turq blue .20 .20
Never hinged .20
P33 N10 8h green .20 *.30*
Never hinged .20
P34 N10 9h yellow ('21) .20 .20
Never hinged .20
P35 N10 10h red .20 .20
Never hinged .20
P36 N10 12h blue .20 *.30*
Never hinged .20
P37 N10 15h lilac ('21) .20 .20
Never hinged .20
a. Thick grayish paper .35 1.30
Never hinged .90
P38 N10 18h blue grn ('21) .20 *.25*
Never hinged .20
a. Thick grayish paper .20 *.35*
Never hinged .20
P39 N10 20h orange .20 *.25*
Never hinged .20
a. Thick grayish paper .20 *.45*
Never hinged .20
P40 N10 30h yellow brn ('21) .20 .20
Never hinged .20
a. Thick grayish paper .20 *.45*
Never hinged .20
P41 N10 45h green ('21) .20 *.35*
Never hinged .20
P42 N10 60h claret .20 .20
Never hinged .20
a. Thick grayish paper .20 *1.30*
Never hinged .25
P43 N10 72h chocolate ('21) .20 *.45*
Never hinged .20
P44 N10 90h violet ('21) .20 *.55*
Never hinged .25
a. Thick grayish paper .20 *1.00*
Never hinged .35
P45 N10 1.20k red ('21) .20 *.65*
Never hinged .25
P46 N10 2.40k yellow grn ('21) .20 *.55*
Never hinged .25
P47 N10 3k gray ('21) .20 *.40*
Never hinged .20
a. Thick grayish paper .20 *.80*
Never hinged .25
Nos. P29-P47 (19) 3.80 5.85
Set, never hinged 4.00

1921-22

P48 N11 45h gray .20 *.25*
P49 N11 75h brown org ('22) .20 *.35*
P50 N11 1.50k ol bister ('22) .20 *.50*
P51 N11 1.80k gray blue ('22) .20 *.55*
P52 N11 2.25k light brown .20 *.75*
P53 N11 3k dull green ('22) .20 *.55*
P54 N11 6k claret ('22) .20 *.65*
P55 N11 7.50k bister .20 *.85*
Nos. P48-P55 (8) 1.60 *4.45*
Set, never hinged 1.75

Nos. P24-P55 exist privately perforated.

NEWSPAPER TAX STAMPS

Values for unused stamps 1853-59 are for copies in fine condition with gum. Specimens without gum sell for about one-third or less of the figures quoted.

Issues of the Monarchy

NT1 NT2

Unwmk.

1853, Mar. 1 Typo. *Imperf.*

PR1 NT1 2kr green 1,650. 57.50
No gum 300.00
On newspaper 300.00
a. 2kr deep green 1,750. 72.50
No gum 300.00
On newspaper 325.00
b. 2kr yellow green 1,950. 100.00
No gum 350.00
On newspaper 350.00
c. 2kr blue green 1,900. 65.00
No gum 340.00
On newspaper 325.00

Full margins = 1¼mm at top and bottom, ¾mm at sides.

The reprints are in finer print than the more coarsely printed originals, and on a smooth toned paper.

Values for Nos. PR2-PR9 are for stamps that do not show the watermark. Stamps showing the watermark often sell for more.

Wmk. 91, or, before July 1864, Unwmkd.

1858-59

Two Types.
Type I — The banderol on the Crown of the left eagle touches the beak of the eagle.
Type II — The banderol does not touch the beak.

PR2 NT2 1kr blue, type II ('59) 42.50 5.50
No gum 6.00
On newspaper 17.50
a. 1kr blue, type I 1,100. 190.00
No gum 175.00
On newspaper 425.00
b. Printed on both sides, type II —
PR3 NT2 2kr brown, type II ('59) 40.00 6.75
No gum 7.00
On newspaper 16.00
a. 2kr red brown, type II 500.00 240.00
No gum 65.00
On newspaper 475.00
PR4 NT2 4kr brn, type I 425.00 *1,100.*
No gum 80.00
On newspaper 3,000.
a. 4kr deep brown, type I 575.00 1,250.
No gum 100.00
On newspaper 3,250.

Nos. PR2a, PR3a, and PR4 were printed only on unwatermarked paper. Nos. PR2 and PR3 exist on unwatermarked and watermarked paper.
Nos. PR2 and PR3 exist in coarse and (after 1874) in fine print, like the contemporary postage stamps.
The reprints of the 4kr brown are of type II and on a smooth toned paper.
Issue date: 4kr, Nov. 1.
See Lombardy-Venetia for the 1kr in black and the 2kr, 4fk in red.

NT3 NT4

1877 Redrawn

PR5 NT3 1kr blue 12.50 1.40
No gum 1.50
On newspaper 5.50
a. 1kr pale ultramarine *2,500.*
On newspaper *11,000.*
PR6 NT3 2kr brown 14.00 6.75
No gum 1.75
On newspaper 10.00

In the redrawn stamps the shield is larger and the vertical bar has eight lines above the white square and nine below, instead of five.
Nos. PR5 and PR6 exist also watermarked "WECHSEL" instead of "ZEITUNGS-MARKEN."

1890, June 1

PR7 NT4 1kr brown 9.00 1.00
No gum 1.35
On newspaper 6.00
PR8 NT4 2kr green 10.00 1.60
No gum 1.75
On newspaper 8.00

#PR5-PR8 exist with private perforation.

NT5

1890, June 1 Wmk. 91 *Perf. 12½*

PR9 NT5 25kr carmine 95.00 *200.00*
Never hinged 160.00
No gum 22.50
On newspaper *47.50*
Fiscal cancellation 425.00
a. Perf 13 100.00 *240.00*
Never hinged 175.00

Nos. PR1-PR9 did not pay postage, but were a fiscal tax, collected by the postal authorities on newspapers.

Values for stamps in pairs

PR1	NT1	2kr green	—	—
PR2	NT2	1kr blue, type II	65.00	35.00
PR2a	NT2	1kr blue, type I	2,700.	950.00
PR2b	NT2	1kr blue, printed on both sides		—
PR3	NT2	2kr brown, type II	87.50	—
PR3a	NT2	2kr red brown, type II	1,100.	—
PR4	NT2	4kr brown, type I	850.00	—
PR5	NT3	1kr blue	30.00	5.00
PR6	NT3	2kr brown	30.00	*50.00*
PR7	NT4	1kr brown	40.00	5.00
PR8	NT4	2kr green	40.00	6.00
PR9	NT5	25kr carmine	175.00	*425.00*

SPECIAL HANDLING STAMPS

(For Printed Matter Only) Issues of the Monarchy

Mercury
SH1

1916 Unwmk. *Perf. 12½*

QE1 SH1 2h claret, *yellow* .60 *1.60*
Never hinged 1.75
On cover 25.00
QE2 SH1 5h dp green, *yellow* .60 *1.60*
Never hinged 1.75
On cover 25.00

SH2

1917 *Perf. 12½*

QE3 SH2 2h claret, *yellow* .20 *.30*
Never hinged .30
On cover 25.00
a. Pair, imperf. between 175.00 *250.00*
Never hinged 200.00
b. Perf. 11½x12½ 55.00 *95.00*
Never hinged 110.00
On cover 175.00
c. Perf. 12½x11½ 80.00 *150.00*
Never hinged 165.00
On cover 225.00
d. Perf. 11½ 1.10 *2.50*
Never hinged 2.50
On cover 35.00
QE4 SH2 5h dp green, *yellow* .20 *.30*
Never hinged .30
On cover 21.00
a. Pair, imperf. between 160.00 *250.00*
Never hinged 175.00
b. Perf. 11½x12½ 45.00 *87.50*
Never hinged 95.00
On cover 175.00
c. Perf. 12½x11½ 70.00 *125.00*
Never hinged 140.00
On cover 250.00
d. Perf. 11½ 1.10 *2.50*
Never hinged 2.50
On cover 32.50

Nos. QE1-QE4 exist imperforate.

Issues of the Republic

Nos. QE3 and QE4 Overprinted

1919

QE5 SH2 2h claret, *yellow* .20 .20
Never hinged .20
On cover 9.00
a. Inverted overprint 325.00
Never hinged 375.00
b. Perf. 11½x12½ 5.25 *8.00*
Never hinged 10.50
On cover 85.00
c. Perf. 12½x11½ 65.00 *85.00*
Never hinged 125.00
On cover 175.00
d. Perf. 11½ .30 *.70*
Never hinged .65
On cover 17.50
QE6 SH2 5h deep green, *yellow* .20 .20
Never hinged .20
On cover 10.00
a. Perf. 11½x12½ 2.25 *3.75*
Never hinged 2.75
On cover 85.00
b. Perf. 12½x11½ 25.00 *35.00*
Never hinged 37.50
On cover 175.00
c. Perf. 11½ .20 *.45*
Never hinged .45
On cover 19.00

Nos. QE5 and QE6 exist imperforate. Value, set unused hinged $100.

SH3

Dark Blue Surcharge

1921

QE7 SH3 50h on 2h claret, *yellow* .20 *.20*
Never hinged .20
On cover 16.00

SH4

1922 *Perf. 12½*

QE8 SH4 50h lilac, *yellow* .20 *.40*
Never hinged .20
On cover 55.00

#QE5-QE8 exist in vertical pairs, imperf between. No. QE8 exists imperf. Value, unused hinged $110.

OCCUPATION STAMPS

Issued under Italian Occupation

Issued in Trieste

Austrian Stamps of 1916-18 Overprinted

1918 Unwmk. *Perf. 12½*

N1 A37 3h bright vio 1.25 1.25
Never hinged 2.75
a. Double overprint 40.00 40.00
b. Inverted overprint 40.00 40.00
N2 A37 5h light grn 1.40 1.25
Never hinged 2.75
a. Inverted overprint 40.00 40.00
c. Double overprint — 40.00
N3 A37 6h dp orange 2.00 2.00
Never hinged 4.00
N4 A37 10h magenta 13.00 3.25
Never hinged 25.00
a. Inverted overprint 40.00 40.00
N5 A37 12h light bl 2.75 2.50
Never hinged 5.50
a. Double overprint 40.00 40.00
N6 A42 15h dull red 1.40 1.25
Never hinged 2.75
a. Inverted overprint 40.00 40.00
b. Double overprint 40.00 40.00
N7 A42 20h dark green 1.40 1.25
Never hinged 2.75
a. Inverted overprint 40.00 40.00
c. Double overprint 95.00
N8 A42 25h deep blue 8.00 8.00
Never hinged 16.00
a. Inverted overprint 160.00 160.00
N9 A42 30h dl violet 2.75 2.50
Never hinged 5.50
N10 A39 40h olive grn 200.00 210.00
Never hinged 400.00
N11 A39 50h dark green 8.00 8.00
Never hinged 16.00
N12 A39 60h deep blue 20.00 20.00
Never hinged 40.00
N13 A39 80h orange brn 13.50 13.00
Never hinged 27.50
a. Inverted overprint —

N14 A39 1k car, *yel* 13.50 13.00
Never hinged 27.50
a. Double overprint 95.00
N15 A40 2k light bl 325.00 350.00
Never hinged 650.00
N16 A40 4k yellow grn 800.00 850.00
Never hinged 1,600.

Handstamped

N17 A40 10k dp violet *21,500.* *45,000.*
Never hinged *26,500.*

Granite Paper

N18 A40 2k light blue 450.00
Never hinged 900.00
N19 A40 3k car rose 400.00 400.00
Never hinged 800.00
Nos. N1-N14 (14) 288.95 287.25
Set, never hinged 575.00

Some authorities question the authenticity of No. N18. Counterfeits of Nos. N10, N15-N19 are plentiful.

Italian Stamps of 1901-18 Overprinted

Wmk. 140 Perf. 14

N20 A42 1c brown 2.00 4.50
Never hinged 5.00
a. Inverted overprint 22.50 22.50
N21 A43 2c orange brn 2.00 4.50
Never hinged 5.00
a. Inverted overprint 20.00 20.00
N22 A48 5c green 1.25 1.25
Never hinged 3.25
a. Inverted overprint 40.00 40.00
b. Double overprint 100.00
N23 A48 10c claret 1.25 1.25
Never hinged 3.25
a. Inverted overprint 60.00 60.00
b. Double overprint 100.00
N24 A50 20c brn orange 1.25 2.00
Never hinged 3.25
a. Inverted overprint 80.00 80.00
b. Double overprint 100.00 100.00
N25 A49 25c blue 1.25 2.50
Never hinged 3.25
a. Double overprint —
b. Inverted overprint 100.00 100.00
N26 A49 40c brown 10.00 20.00
Never hinged 25.00
a. Inverted overprint —
N27 A45 45c olive grn 3.25 6.75
Never hinged 8.00
a. Inverted overprint 125.00 125.00
N28 A49 50c violet 6.50 8.00
Never hinged 15.00
N29 A49 60c brown car 55.00 110.00
Never hinged 140.00
a. Inverted overprint —
b. Double overprint 250.00
N30 A46 1 l brn & green 25.00 40.00
Never hinged 67.50
a. Inverted overprint —
Nos. N20-N30 (11) 108.75 200.75
Set, never hinged 275.00

Italian Stamps of 1901-18 Surcharged

N31 A48 5h on 5c green 1.25 2.50
Never hinged 3.25
a. "5" omitted 90.00 90.00
b. Inverted surcharge 90.00 90.00
N32 A50 20h on 20c brn org 1.25 2.50
Never hinged 3.25
a. Double surcharge 90.00 90.00

Issued in the Trentino

Austrian Stamps of 1916-18 Overprinted

1918 Unwmk. Perf. 12½

N33 A37 3h bright vio 8.00 3.00
Never hinged 12.00
a. Double overprint 100.00 67.50
b. Inverted overprint 85.00 55.00
N34 A37 5h light grn 6.50 1.75
Never hinged 10.00
a. "8 nov. 1918" 2,100.
b. Inverted overprint 85.00 55.00
N35 A37 6h dp orange 85.00 40.00
Never hinged 125.00
N36 A37 10h magenta 6.50 2.00
Never hinged 10.00
a. "8 nov. 1918" 160.00 95.00
N37 A37 12h light blue 225.00 110.00
Never hinged 350.00
N38 A42 15h dull red 8.00 3.00
Never hinged 12.00
N39 A42 20h dark green 5.25 2.00
Never hinged 8.00
a. "8 nov. 1918" 200.00 110.00
b. Double overprint 100.00 67.50
c. Inverted overprint 40.00 22.50
d. 20h pale green 725.00
Never hinged 1,250.
N40 A42 25h deep blue 50.00 30.00
Never hinged 80.00
N41 A42 30h dl violet 20.00 10.00
Never hinged 30.00
N42 A39 40h olive grn 70.00 40.00
Never hinged 110.00
N43 A39 50h dark green 40.00 22.50
Never hinged 60.00
a. Inverted overprint 200.00 110.00
N44 A39 60h deep blue 67.50 35.00
Never hinged 100.00
a. Double overprint 200.00 110.00
N45 A39 80h orange brn 100.00 45.00
Never hinged 150.00
N46 A39 90h red violet 2,000. 1,000.
Never hinged 3,000.
N47 A39 1k car, *yel* 100.00 45.00
Never hinged 150.00
N48 A40 2k light blue 650.00 290.00
Never hinged 1,000.
N49 A40 4k yel green 3,000. 1,500.
Never hinged 4,500.
N50 A40 10k dp violet, black ovpt. 77,500.
Never hinged —
a. 10k dp violet, gray ovpt. 18,500. 25,000.
Never hinged 26,500.
b. 10k pale violet, gray ovpt. 12,500.
Never hinged 26,500.

A mint example of No. N50a sold for the equivalent of U.S. $20,750 at a Zurich auction in 1996.
A mint example of No. N50b sold for the equivalent of U.S. $26,290 at a Milan auction in 1998.

A cover with a complete set of Nos. N33-N50a sold for the equivalent of U.S. $14,380 at a New Jersey auction in 1998.

Granite Paper

N51 A40 2k light blue 1,000.
Never hinged 1,500.

Counterfeits of Nos. N33-N51 are plentiful.

Italian Stamps of 1901-18 Overprinted

Wmk. 140 Perf. 14

N52 A42 1c brown 2.00 6.50
Never hinged 5.00
a. Inverted overprint 87.50 87.50
b. Double overprint 87.50
N53 A43 2c orange brn 2.00 6.50
a. Inverted overprint 87.50 87.50
N54 A48 5c green 2.00 6.50
Never hinged 5.00
a. Inverted overprint 87.50 87.50
b. Double overprint 87.50 87.50
N55 A48 10c claret 2.00 6.50
Never hinged 5.00
a. Inverted overprint 125.00 125.00
b. Double overprint 87.50 87.50
N56 A50 20c brn orange 2.00 6.50
Never hinged 5.00
a. Inverted overprint 125.00 125.00
N57 A49 40c brown 80.00 55.00
Never hinged 200.00
N58 A45 45c olive grn 40.00 55.00
Never hinged 100.00
a. Double overprint 225.00 225.00
N59 A49 50c violet 40.00 55.00
Never hinged 100.00
N60 A46 1 l brn & green 40.00 55.00
Never hinged 100.00
a. Double overprint 225.00 225.00
Nos. N52-N60 (9) 210.00 252.50

Italian Stamps of 1906-18 Surcharged

N61 A48 5h on 5c green 2.00 3.25
Never hinged 5.00
N62 A48 10h on 10c claret 2.00 3.25
Never hinged 5.00
a. Inverted overprint 87.50 87.50
N63 A50 20h on 20c brn org 2.00 3.25
Never hinged 5.00
a. Double surcharge 87.50 87.50
Nos. N61-N63 (3) 6.00 9.75

General Issue

Italian Stamps of 1901-18 Surcharged

1919

N64 A42 1c on 1c brown 1.25 2.00
Never hinged 3.25
a. Inverted surcharge 20.00 20.00
N65 A43 2c on 2c org brn 1.25 2.00
Never hinged 3.25
a. Double surcharge 265.00
b. Inverted surcharge 16.00 16.00
c. Ovpted. "cerona" 67.50 67.50
N66 A48 5c on 5c green 1.25 1.25
Never hinged 3.25
a. Inverted surcharge 32.50 32.50
b. Double surcharge 100.00
N67 A48 10c on 10c claret 1.25 1.40
Never hinged 3.25
a. Inverted surcharge 52.50 52.50
b. Double surcharge 100.00 100.00
c. Ovpted. "oorona" 120.00
Never hinged 180.00
d. Ovpted. "corena" 120.00 120.00
N68 A50 20c on 20c brn org 1.25 1.25
Never hinged 3.25
a. Double surcharge 140.00 140.00
b. Half used as 10c on cover 275.00
N69 A49 25c on 25c blue 1.25 2.00
Never hinged 3.25
a. Double surcharge 140.00
N70 A49 40c on 40c brown 1.25 3.25
Never hinged 3.25
a. "ccrona" 125.00 125.00
N71 A45 45c on 45c ol grn 1.25 3.25
Never hinged 3.25
a. Inverted surcharge 110.00 140.00
N72 A49 50c on 50c violet .90 3.25
Never hinged 3.25
N73 A49 60c on 60c brn car .90 6.50
a. "00" for "60" 140.00 140.00
Never hinged 3.25

Surcharged

N74 A46 1cor on 1 l brn & grn 4.00 6.75
Never hinged 10.00
Nos. N64-N74 (11) 15.80 32.90

Surcharges similar to these but differing in style or arrangement of type were used in Dalmatia.

OCCUPATION SPECIAL DELIVERY STAMPS

Issued in Trieste

Special Delivery Stamp of Italy of 1903 Overprinted

1918 Wmk. 140 Perf. 14

NE1 SD1 25c rose red 30.00 37.50
Never hinged 60.00
a. Inverted overprint 125.00 125.00

General Issue

Special Delivery Stamps of Italy of 1903-09 Surcharged

1919

NE2 SD1 25c on 25c rose 2.00 2.50
Never hinged 5.00
a. Double surcharge 100.00 100.00
NE3 SD2 30c on 30c bl & rose 3.25 5.25
Never hinged 8.25
a. Pair, one stamp without surcharge 1,100.

OCCUPATION POSTAGE DUE STAMPS

Issued in Trieste

Postage Due Stamps of Italy, 1870-94, Overprinted

1918 Wmk. 140 Perf. 14

NJ1 D3 5c buff & mag 1.25 1.40
Never hinged 3.25
a. Inverted overprint 20.00 20.00
b. Double overprint 200.00
NJ2 D3 10c buff & mag 1.25 1.40
Never hinged 3.25
a. Inverted overprint 87.50 87.50
NJ3 D3 20c buff & mag 2.00 2.00
Never hinged 5.00
a. Double overprint 200.00
b. Inverted overprint 87.50 87.50
NJ4 D3 30c buff & mag 4.00 4.00
Never hinged 10.00
NJ5 D3 40c buff & mag 32.50 40.00
Never hinged 82.50
a. Inverted overprint 250.00 250.00
NJ6 D3 50c buff & mag 80.00 110.00
Never hinged 200.00
a. Inverted overprint 325.00 325.00
NJ7 D3 1 l bl & mag 290.00 325.00
Never hinged 450.00
Nos. NJ1-NJ7 (7) 411.00 483.80

General Issue

Postage Due Stamps of Italy, 1870-1903 Surcharged

1919

Buff & Magenta

NJ8 D3 5c on 5c 1.25 1.40
Never hinged 3.25
a. Inverted overprint 26.00 26.00
NJ9 D3 10c on 10c 1.25 1.40
Never hinged 3.25
a. Center and surcharge invtd. 200.00 200.00
NJ10 D3 20c on 20c 2.00 1.40
Never hinged 5.00
a. Double overprint 200.00 200.00
NJ11 D3 30c on 30c 2.00 2.50
Never hinged 5.00
NJ12 D3 40c on 40c 2.00 2.50
Never hinged 5.00
NJ13 D3 50c on 50c 3.25 5.00
Never hinged 8.25

Surcharged

NJ14 D3 1cor on 1 l bl & mag 3.25 6.75
Never hinged 8.25
NJ15 D3 2cor on 2 l bl & mag 47.50 110.00
Never hinged 72.50
NJ16 D3 5cor on 5 l bl & mag 47.50 110.00
Never hinged 72.50
Nos. NJ8-NJ16 (9) 110.00 240.95

AUSTRIAN OFFICES ABROAD

These stamps were on sale and usable at all Austrian post-offices in Crete and in the Turkish Empire.

100 Centimes = 1 Franc

OFFICES IN CRETE

Used values are italicized for stamps often found with false cancellations.

Stamps of Austria of 1899-1901 Issue, Surcharged in Black:

a

b

c

d

1903-04 Unwmk. *Perf. 12½, 13½*

On Nos. 73a, 75a, 77a, 81a

Granite Paper

With Varnish Bars

1 A15(a) 5c on 5h blue green 1.25 *4.25*
Never hinged 3.25
On cover *30.00*
a. Perf 13x12½ 45.00 *82.50*
Never hinged 110.00
On cover 160.00
2 A16(b) 10c on 10h rose .90 *4.50*
Never hinged 2.40
On cover *40.00*
3 A16(b) 25c on 25h ultra 40.00 25.00
Never hinged 80.00
On cover 240.00
a. Perf 13x12½ 67.50 *110.00*
Never hinged 140.00
On cover —
4 A17(c) 50c on 50h gray blue 10.00 *150.00*
Never hinged 26.50
On cover *1,000.*
a. Perf 13x12½ 20.00
Never hinged 52.50
On cover —

On Nos. 83, 83a, 84, 85

Without Varnish Bars

5 A18(d) 1fr on 1k car rose 2.00 *125.00*
Never hinged 3.00
On cover *1,500.*
a. 1fr on 1k carmine 8.00 —
Never hinged 26.50
b. Horiz. or vert. pair, imperf. between 200.00 —
Never hinged 325.00
6 A18(d) 2fr on 2k ('04) 9.00 *300.00*
Never hinged 26.50
7 A18(d) 4fr on 4k ('04) 11.00 *500.00*
Never hinged 30.00
On cover —
Nos. 1-7 (7) 74.15 1,108.

Surcharged on Austrian Stamps of 1904-05

1905

On Nos. 89, 97

Without Varnish Bars

8a A19(a) 5c on 5h blue green 65.00 50.00
Never hinged 150.00
On cover *110.00*
9 A20(b) 10c on 10h car .70 *13.50*
On cover *47.50*

On Nos. 89a, 97a, 99a, 103a

With Varnish Bars

8 A19(a) 5c on 5h bl grn 2.00 5.75
On cover *32.50*
b. Perf 13x12½ 13.50 *26.50*
Never hinged 32.50
On cover 67.50
9a A20(b) 10c on 10h carmine 30.00 42.50
On cover *140.00*
10 A20(b) 25c on 25h ultra 5.25 *125.00*
On cover *675.00*
b. Perf 13x12½ .35 *1.10*
Never hinged 1.00
On cover 675.00
11 A21(b) 50c on 50h dl bl .50 *425.00*
On cover —
b. Perf 13x12½ 6.75 *450.00*
Never hinged 16.75
On cover —

Surcharged on Austrian Stamps and Type of 1906-07

1907 *Perf. 12½, 13½*

Without Varnish Bars

12 A19(a) 5c on 5h yel green (#90) .60 *4.25*
Never hinged 1.50
On cover *26.50*
13 A20(b) 10c on 10h car (#92) .90 *37.50*
Never hinged 2.40
On cover *120.00*
14 A20(b) 15c on 15h vio .75 *32.50*
Never hinged 1.60
On cover *190.00*
Nos. 12-14 (3) 2.25 *74.25*

A5

A6

1908 Typo. *Perf. 12½*

15 A5 5c green, *yellow* .20 *.90*
Never hinged .45
On cover *10.00*
16 A5 10c scarlet, *rose* .35 *1.25*
Never hinged .75
On cover *13.50*
17 A5 15c brown, *buff* .40 *6.25*
Never hinged 1.20
On cover *75.00*
18 A5 25c dp blue, *blue* 12.00 5.50
Never hinged 32.50
On cover *75.00*
a. 25c deep blue, greenish blue paper 11.50 *23.00*
Never hinged 37.50
On cover *100.00*

Engr.

19 A6 50c lake, *yellow* 1.75 *35.00*
Never hinged 8.00
On cover *250.00*
20 A6 1fr brown, *gray* 2.50 *50.00*
Never hinged 9.25
On cover *450.00*
a. Vert pair, imperf. btwn. *160.00*
Never hinged *240.00*
Nos. 15-20 (6) 17.20 *98.90*

Nos. 15-18 are on paper colored on the surface only. All values exist imperforate.

60th year of the reign of Emperor Franz Josef, for permanent use.

Paper Colored Through

1914 Typo.

21 A5 10c rose, *rose* 1.00 *1,800.*
Never hinged 2.50
On cover *3,750.*
22 A5 25c ultra, *blue* .60 *225.00*
Never hinged 1.60
On cover *1,000.*
On parcel post receipt card *525.00*

Nos. 21 and 22 exist imperforate.

STAMPS OF LOMBARDY-VENETIA USED IN AUSTRIAN OFFICES IN THE TURKISH EMPIRE

From 1863 to 1867 the stamps of Lombardy-Venetia (Nos. 15 to 24) were used at the Austrian Offices in the Turkish Empire. Values for stamps are for examples with neat and legible town cancellations of the most common types from the larger post offices. Values for scarcer cancellation types and for cancellations from smaller post offices are much higher. Values for covers are also for the most common frankings. Covers bearing unusual frankings and unusual combinations of stamps are also worth much more.

Aegean Islands:	Leros, Meteline, Rhodes, Scio, Scio-Cesme
Albania:	Dulcigno San Giovanni di Medusa, Durazzo, Santi Quaranta, San Giovanni, Scutari, Valona
Bulgaria:	Burgas, Kustendje, Philippoli, Rustschuk, Sofia, Varna, Widdin
Crete:	Candia, La Canea, Rettimo
Cyprus:	Larnaca
Egypt:	Alexandria, Port Said
Greece:	Cavalla, Corfu, Janina, Lagos, Prevesa, Salonica, Sayada, Serres, Volo
Moldavia-Walachia:	Bakau, Berlad, Bottuschan, Bukarest, Czernawoda, Fokschan, Galatz, giurgevo, Ibralia, Jassy, Piatra, Ploeschti, Roman, Sulina, Tekutsch, Tultscha
Montenegro:	Antivari
Serbia:	Belgrade
Turkey (Ottoman Empire):	Adrianopoli, Alexandrette, Beyrut, Haifa (Caifa), Cesme, Constantinople, Dardanelles, Gallipoli, Ineboli, Jaffa, Jerusalem, Kerassunda, Latakia, Mersina, Rodosto, Samsun, Sinope, Smyrna, Tenedos, Trebizonde, Tripoli in Syria

1863 *Perf. 14*

A15 A8 2s yellow, *value from* 225.00
On cover, value from 875.00
Single franking, on cover, *value from* *5,200.*
A16 A8 3s green, *value from* 130.00
On cover, value from 1,000.
Single franking, on cover, *value from* *4,500.*
A17 A8 5s rose, *value from* 130.00
On cover, value from 675.00
Single franking, on cover, *value from* *2,750.*
A18 A8 10s blue, *value from* 82.50
On cover, value from 325.00
A19 A8 15s yellow brown, *value from* 175.00
On cover, value from 550.00

Nos. A15, A16 and A17 single frankings on covers or circulars are rare and worth much more than these values.

Values for Pairs, with legible cancellations

A15 A8 2s yellow, *value from* 450.00
On cover, value from 1,600.
A16 A8 3s green, *value from* 675.00
On cover, value from 2,900.
A17 A8 5s rose, *value from* 300.00
On cover, value from 1,250.
A18 A8 10s blue, *value from* 160.00
On cover, value from 675.00
A19 A8 15s yellow brown, *value from* 350.00
On cover, value from 1,250.

1864-65 Wmk. 91 *Perf. 9½*

A20 A8 2s yellow ('65), *value from* 400.00
On cover, value from 1,500.
Single franking, on cover —
A21 A8 3s green, *value from* 100.00
On cover, value from 600.00
Single franking, on cover, *value from* *2,750.*
A22 A8 5s rose, *value from* 47.50
On cover, value from 375.00
Single franking, on cover, *value from* *1,850.*
A23 A8 10s blue, *value from* 16.00
On cover, value from 67.50
A24 A8 15s yellow brown, *value from* 55.00
On cover, value from 240.00

Only one example is known of No. A20 on single franking cover.

Values for Pairs, with legible cancellations

A20 A8 2s yellow ('65), *value from* 800.00
On cover, value from 2,750.
A21 A8 3s green, *value from* 340.00
On cover, value from 2,750.
A22 A8 5s rose, *value from* 160.00
On cover, value from 825.00
A23 A8 10s blue, *value from* 50.00
On cover, value from 240.00
A24 A8 15s yellow brown, *value from* 110.00
On cover, value from 475.00

OFFICES IN THE TURKISH EMPIRE

100 Soldi = 1 Florin
40 Paras = 1 Piaster

Values for unused stamps are for copies with gum. Specimens without gum sell for about one-third or less of the figures quoted.

Used values are italicized for stamps often found with false cancellations.

For similar designs in Kreuzers, see early Austria.

A1

A2

Two different printing methods were used, as in the 1867-74 issues of Austria. They may be distinguished by the coarse or fine lines of the hair and whiskers and by the paper, which is more transparent on the later issue.

1867 Typo. Wmk. 91 *Perf. 9½*

Coarse Print

1 A1 2sld orange 1.60 *26.00*
Never hinged 3.25
On cover *2,400.*
a. 2sld yellow 60.00 35.00
Never hinged 95.00
On cover —
2 A1 3sld green 150.00 50.00
Never hinged 250.00
On cover *675.00*
a. 3sld dark green 240.00 90.00
Never hinged 350.00
On cover —
3 A1 5sld red 200.00 26.00
Never hinged 340.00
On cover —
a. 5sld carmine 175.00 14.50
Never hinged 275.00
On cover *800.00*
b. 5sld red lilac 190.00
Never hinged 290.00
On cover —
4 A1 10sld blue 150.00 2.00
Never hinged 240.00
On cover 24.00
a. 10sld light blue 200.00 2.75
Never hinged 300.00
On cover 27.50
b. 10sld dark blue 160.00 3.00
Never hinged 260.00
On cover 30.00
5 A1 15sld brown 24.00 6.50
Never hinged 40.00
On cover 40.00
a. 15sld dark brown 67.50 40.00
Never hinged 95.00
On cover 100.00
b. 15sld reddish brown 37.50 14.00
Never hinged 57.50
On cover 50.00
c. 15sld gray brown 87.50 14.00
Never hinged 140.00
On cover 47.50
6 A1 25sld violet 25.00 *35.00*
Never hinged 40.00
On cover *1,350.*
a. 25sld brown violet 37.50 *45.00*

Never hinged 57.50
On cover 1,350.
b. 25sld gray lilac 100.00 55.00
Never hinged 150.00
On cover 1,500.
7 A2 50sld brn, perf. 10½ 1.25 57.50
Never hinged 1.60
On cover 8,000.
a. Perf. 12 90.00 95.00
Never hinged 140.00
b. Perf. 13 300.00
Never hinged 500.00
k. Perf. 9 30.00 65.00
Never hinged 47.50
l. 50sld pale red brn, perf. 12 150.00 125.00
Never hinged 250.00
On cover 8,500.
m. Vert. pair, imperf. btwn. 325.00 650.00
Never hinged 475.00
n. Horiz. pair, imperf. btwn. 325.00 750.00
Never hinged 475.00
o. Perf. 10½x9 75.00 140.00
Never hinged 110.00

Perf. 9, 9½, 10½ and Compound

1876-83

Fine Print

7C A1 2sld yellow ('83) .20 2,200.
Never hinged .50
7D A1 3sld green ('78) 1.00 24.00
Never hinged 2.00
On cover, single franking 250.00
p. Perf. 10½x9 325.00
7E A1 5sld red ('78) .40 17.00
Never hinged .80
On cover —
q. Perf. 9 250.00
On cover —
7F A1 10sld blue 95.00 1.10
Never hinged 175.00
On cover, single franking 17.00
r. Perf. 10½ 150.00 7.25
Never hinged 300.00
On cover, single franking 67.50
s. Perf. 9 125.00 190.00
Never hinged 240.00
On cover, single franking 675.00
t. Perf. 10½x9 125.00
On cover, single franking 500.00
7I A1 15sld org brn ('81) 11.00 190.00
Never hinged 25.00
On cover, single franking 1,700.
u. Perf. 10½ 375.00
On cover —
7J A1 25sld gray lilac ('83) .60 350.00
Never hinged .80
On cover, single franking 13,500.
Nos. 7C-7J (6) 108.20

The 10 soldi has been reprinted in deep dull blue, perforated 10½.

A3

1883 ***Perf. 9½***

8 A3 2sld brown .20 150.00
Never hinged .30
On cover —
9 A3 3sld green 1.00 27.50
Never hinged 2.75
On cover, single franking 250.00
10 A3 5sld rose .20 17.50
Never hinged .50
On cover, single franking 200.00
a. Perf. 10 5.00 110.00
Never hinged 12.00
On cover —
11 A3 10sld blue .75 .50
Never hinged 1.50
On cover, single franking 20.00
a. Perf. 10½ 160.00
On cover —
12 A3 20sld gray, perf. 10 1.25 87.50
Never hinged 2.40
On cover —
a. Perf. 9½ 6.00 7.50
Never hinged 13.50
On cover, single franking 675.00
13 A3 50sld red lilac 1.00 17.50
Never hinged 2.25
On cover, single franking 2,000.
Nos. 8-13 (6) 4.40

No. 9 Surcharged

10 PARAS ON 3 SOLDI:

Type I — Surcharge 16½mm across. "PARA" about ½mm above bottom of "10." 2mm space between "10" and "P"; 1½mm between "A" and "10." Perf. 9½ only.

Type II — Surcharge 15¼ to 16mm across. "PARA" on same line with figures or slightly higher or lower. 1½mm space between "10" and "P"; 1mm between "A" and "10." Perf. 9½ and 10.

No. 9 Surcharged

1886 ***Perf. 9½***

14 A4 10pa on 3sld green, type II .65 16.00
Never hinged 1.00
On cover 140.00
a. 10pa on 3sld green, type I 200.00 375.00
Never hinged 340.00
b. Inverted surcharge, type I 2,000.
c. As #14, perf. 10 .30 5.50
Never hinged .50
On cover 45.00

Nos. 14 and 14c were overprinted in Vienna. Nos. 14a and 14b were overprinted in Constantinople.

Same surcharge on Austria Nos. 42-46

1888

15 A5 10pa on 3kr grn 3.25 10.00
Never hinged 8.00
On cover 55.00
a. "01 PARA 10" 650.00
16 A5 20pa on 5kr rose .50 7.75
Never hinged 1.40
On cover 65.00
a. Double surcharge 160.00
Never hinged 275.00
17 A5 1pi on 10kr blue 62.50 1.25
Never hinged 11.50
On cover 11.50
a. Perf. 13½ 300.00
b. Double surcharge 475.00
18 A5 2pi on 20kr gray 1.75 4.50
Never hinged 4.00
On cover 300.00
19 A5 5pi on 50kr vio 1.75 15.00
Never hinged 3.50
On cover 1,200.
Nos. 15-19 (5) 69.75 38.50

Austria Nos. 52-55, 58, 61 Surcharged

1890-92 Unwmk. ***Perf. 9 to 13½***

Granite Paper

20 A6 8pa on 2kr brn ('92) .20 .50
Never hinged .30
On cover 15.00
a. Perf. 9½ 15.00 15.00
Never hinged 75.00
On cover 75.00
21 A6 10pa on 3kr green .65 .50
Never hinged 1.00
On cover 12.00
a. Pair, imperf. between 475.00
22 A6 20pa on 5kr rose .25 .50
Never hinged .50
On cover 5.00
a. Perf 13½x11½ 85.00 67.50
Never hinged 140.00
23 A6 1pi on 10kr ultra .35 .20
Never hinged .75
On cover 6.00
a. Pair, imperf. between 475.00
24 A6 2pi on 20kr ol grn 5.00 25.00
Never hinged 13.50
On cover 600.00
a. Perf. 9½ 175.00
Never hinged 275.00
25 A6 5pi on 50kr violet 10.00 60.00
Never hinged 20.00
On cover 1,500.
a. Perf. 9½ 175.00
Never hinged 275.00
Nos. 20-25 (6) 16.45 86.70

Values on cover for Nos. 20-25 are for covers paying the correct rate. Overfranked covers are usually philatelic and have little value above that of the used stamps.

See note after Austria No. 65 on missing numerals, etc.

Austria Nos. 66, 69 Surcharged

1891 ***Perf. 10 to 13½***

26 A14 2pi on 20kr green 4.25 1.25
Never hinged 16.00
On cover 30.00
a. Perf. 9¼ 175.00 150.00
Never hinged 350.00
On cover 2,250.
27 A14 5pi on 50kr violet 2.75 2.75
Never hinged 6.75
On cover 375.00

Two types of the surcharge on No. 26 exist.

Austria Nos. 62-65 Surcharged

1892 ***Perf. 10½, 11½***

28 A8 10pi on 1gld blue 10.00 35.00
Never hinged 30.00
On cover —
29 A8 20pi on 2gld car 12.00 50.00
Never hinged 90.00
On cover —
a. Double surcharge

Values on cover for Nos. 28-29 are for overfranked complete covers, usually philatelic.

1896 ***Perf. 10½, 11½, 12½***

30 A8 10pi on 1gld pale lilac 13.50 20.00
Never hinged 17.00
On cover 1,500.
On overfranked cover 80.00
31 A8 20pi on 2gld gray grn 35.00 65.00
Never hinged 90.00
On overfranked cover 120.00

Austria Nos. 73, 75, 77, 81, 83-85 Surcharged

#32-35

#36-38

Perf. 12½, 13½ and Compound

1900

Without Varnish Bars

32 A9 10pa on 5h bl grn 4.00 .80
Never hinged 17.00
On cover 12.00
33 A10 20pa on 10h rose 5.00 .75
Never hinged 20.00
On cover 8.00
b. Perf. 12½x10½ 350.00 140.00
Never hinged 575.00
On cover —
34 A10 1pi on 25h ultra 3.00 .30
Never hinged 16.00
On cover 16.00
b. Perf. 10½ 17.00 9.50
Never hinged 57.50
On cover 20.00
35 A11 2pi on 50h gray bl 7.50 3.50
Never hinged 34.00
On cover 30.00
a. Perf. 10½ 20.00 20.00
Never hinged 70.00
On cover 30.00
36 A12 5pi on 1k car rose .50 .30
Never hinged 3.40
On cover 340.00
a. 5pi on 1k carmine 1.00 1.00
Never hinged 5.50
On cover 400.00
b. Horiz. or vert. pair, imperf. btwn. 140.00
Never hinged 210.00
37 A12 10pi on 2k gray lil 2.00 3.00
Never hinged 10.00
On cover 800.00
On parcel post receipt card 175.00
a. Horiz. pair, imperf. btwn.
38 A12 20pi on 4k gray grn 1.50 6.75
Never hinged 8.00
On cover 1,700.
On parcel post receipt card 450.00
Nos. 32-38 (7) 23.50 15.40

In the surcharge on Nos. 37 and 38 "piaster" is printed "PIAST."

1901

With Varnish Bars

32a A9 10pa on 5h blue green 1.50 2.50
Never hinged 8.75
On cover 15.00
33a A10 20pa on 10h rose 2.00 275.00
Never hinged 10.00
On cover 450.00
34a A10 1pi on 25h ultra 1.50 .50
Never hinged 6.75
On cover 6.75
35b A11 2pi on 50h gray blue 3.25 4.50
Never hinged 13.50
On cover 27.50
Nos. 32a-35b (4) 8.25 282.50

A4

A5

A6

1906 ***Perf. 12½ to 13½***

Without Varnish Bars

39 A4 10pa dark green 10.00 3.00
Never hinged 27.00
On cover 15.00
40 A5 20pa rose .80 .75
Never hinged 4.00
On cover 10.00
41 A5 1pi ultra .55 .30
Never hinged 3.50
On cover 8.75
42 A6 2pi gray blue .55 .75
Never hinged 3.50
On cover 27.00
Nos. 39-42 (4) 11.90 4.80

1903 With Varnish Bars

39a A4 10pa dark green 3.75 1.50
Never hinged 13.00
On cover 12.00
40a A5 20pa rose 2.00 .40
Never hinged 11.50
On cover 11.00
41a A5 1pi ultra 1.50 .30
Never hinged 8.00
On cover 8.75
42a A6 2pi gray blue 140.00 2.50
Never hinged 250.00
On cover 30.00

1907

Without Varnish Bars

43 A4 10pa yellow green .50 1.50
Never hinged 1.20
On cover 27.50
45 A5 30pa violet .50 3.25
Never hinged 1.50
On cover 87.50

A7

A8

1908 Typo. ***Perf. 12½***

46 A7 10pa green, *yellow* .20 .30
Never hinged .50
On cover 10.00
47 A7 20pa scarlet, *rose* .25 .30
Never hinged .50
On cover 10.00
48 A7 30pa brown, *buff* .30 .50
Never hinged .75
On cover 55.00
49 A7 1pi deep bl, *blue* 13.50 .20
Never hinged 37.50
On cover 8.00
a. 1pi greenish blue, *blue* 12.50 .65
Never hinged 42.50
On cover 12.00
50 A7 60pa vio, *bluish* .55 3.00
Never hinged 2.40
On cover 200.00

Engr.

51 A8 2pi lake, *yellow* .35 .20
Never hinged 2.00
On cover 85.00
52 A8 5pi brown, *gray* .60 .80
Never hinged 2.75
On cover 500.00
53 A8 10pi green, *yellow* 1.00 1.50
Never hinged 4.00
On cover 1,000.
54 A8 20pi blue, *gray* 2.00 3.50
Never hinged 6.75
On cover 1,750.
Nos. 46-54 (9) 18.75 10.30

Nos. 46-50 are on paper colored on the surface only. 60th year of the reign of Emperor Franz Josef I, for permanent use. All values exist imperforate.

1913-14 Typo.

Paper Colored Through

57 A7 20pa rose, *rose* ('14) .60 500.00
Never hinged 1.75
On cover 2,200.
58 A7 1pi ultra, *blue* .35 .50
Never hinged .75
On cover 6.75

Nos. 57 and 58 exist imperforate.

POSTAGE DUE STAMPS

Type of Austria D2 Surcharged

Black Surcharge

1902 Unwmk. *Perf. 12½, 13½*

J1	D2	10pa on 5h gray green	1.10	2.75
		Never hinged	6.00	
		On cover		5.00
a.		10pa on 5h yellow green	3.00	
		Never hinged	13.50	
J2	D2	20pa on 10h gray green	1.40	3.00
		Never hinged	8.75	
		On cover		340.00
a.		20pa on 10h yellow green	2.40	
		Never hinged	11.50	
J3	D2	1pi on 20h gray green	1.75	3.75
		Never hinged	8.00	
		On cover		340.00
a.		1pi on 20h yellow green	2.40	
		Never hinged	11.50	
J4	D2	2pi on 40h gray green	1.75	3.75
		Never hinged	9.50	
		On cover		575.00
a.		2pi on 40h yellow green	9.75	
		Never hinged	40.00	
J5	D2	5pi on 100h gray green	1.50	3.50
		Never hinged	8.00	
		On cover		1,000.
a.		5pi on 100h yellow green	3.00	
		Never hinged	20.00	
		Nos. J1-J5 (5)	7.50	16.75

D3

1908 Typo. *Perf. 12½*

Chalky Paper

J6	D3	¼pi pale green	3.00	9.50
		Never hinged	8.00	
		On cover		600.00
J7	D3	½pi pale green	1.75	*8.00*
		Never hinged	5.50	
		On cover		275.00
J8	D3	1pi pale green	2.00	*7.50*
		Never hinged	6.00	
		On cover		275.00
J9	D3	1½pi pale green	1.10	*19.00*
		Never hinged	3.40	
		On cover		375.00
J10	D3	2pi pale green	2.50	*16.00*
		Never hinged	6.00	
		On cover		550.00
J11	D3	5pi pale green	2.50	*12.00*
		Never hinged	8.00	
		On cover		*1,250.*
J12	D3	10pi pale green	16.00	*100.00*
		Never hinged	50.00	
		On cover		—
J13	D3	20pi pale green	11.00	*110.00*
		Never hinged	27.50	
		On cover		—
J14	D3	30pi pale green	16.00	11.50
		Never hinged	55.00	
		On cover		—
		Nos. J6-J14 (9)	55.85	*293.50*

Chalky paper

J6a	D3	¼pi dark green	2.00	*19.00*
		Never hinged	6.00	
		On cover		750.00
J7a	D3	½pi dark green	1.65	*19.00*
		Never hinged	6.00	
		On cover		750.00
J8a	D3	1pi dark green	1.75	*19.00*
		Never hinged	5.50	
		On cover		750.00
J9a	D3	1½pi dark green	1.40	*19.00*
		Never hinged	5.50	
		On cover		750.00
J10a	D3	2pi dark green	4.00	*24.00*
		Never hinged	11.00	
		On cover		—
J12a	D3	10pi dark green	55.00	*440.00*
		Never hinged	140.00	
		On cover		—
J13a	D3	20pi dark green	47.50	*500.00*
		Never hinged	110.00	
		On cover		—
J14a	D3	30pi dark green	85.00	34.00
		Never hinged	210.00	
		On cover		—
		Nos. J6a-J14a (8)	198.30	*1,074.*

Thin ordinary paper

J6b	D3	¼pi dark green	3.50	*34.00*
		Never hinged	9.50	
		On cover		850.00
J7b	D3	½pi dark green	1.50	*34.00*
		Never hinged	6.75	
		On cover		850.00
J8b	D3	1pi dark green	2.00	*27.50*
		Never hinged	6.75	
		On cover		850.00
J9b	D3	1½pi dark green	2.00	*75.00*
		Never hinged	6.75	
		On cover		—
J10b	D3	2pi dark green	3.00	*80.00*
		Never hinged	8.75	
		On cover		—
J11a	D3	5pi dark green	5.50	*40.00*
		Never hinged	13.50	
		On cover		—
J12b	D3	10pi dark green	50.00	*400.00*
		Never hinged	110.00	
		On cover		—
J13b	D3	20pi dark green	40.00	*475.00*
		Never hinged	100.00	
		On cover		—
J14b	D3	30pi dark green	26.00	*140.00*
		Never hinged	75.00	
		On cover		—
		Nos. J6b-J14b (9)	133.50	*1,305.*

Thick ordinary paper

J6c	D3	¼pi dark green	2.75	*34.00*
		Never hinged	10.00	
		On cover		675.00
J7c	D3	½pi dark green	1.35	*17.00*
		Never hinged	5.50	
		On cover		675.00
J8c	D3	1pi dark green	1.50	*17.00*
		Never hinged	5.50	
		On cover		675.00
J9c	D3	1½pi dark green	1.50	*67.50*
		Never hinged	6.00	
		On cover		850.00
J10c	D3	2pi dark green	2.00	*87.50*
		Never hinged	8.00	
		On cover		—
J11b	D3	5pi dark green	3.40	*24.00*
		Never hinged	12.00	
		On cover		—
J12c	D3	10pi dark green	40.00	*375.00*
		Never hinged	120.00	
		On cover		
J13c	D3	20pi dark green	42.50	*440.00*
		Never hinged	150.00	
		On cover		—
J14c	D3	30pi dark green	6.75	*24.00*
		Never hinged	20.00	
		On cover		—
		Nos. J6c-J14c (9)	101.75	*1,086.*

No. J6-J14 exist imperforate.
Forgeries exist.

LOMBARDY-VENETIA

Formerly a kingdom in the north of Italy forming part of the Austrian Empire. Milan and Venice were the two principal cities. Lombardy was annexed to Sardinia in 1859, and Venetia to the kingdom of Italy in 1866.

100 Centesimi = 1 Lira
100 Soldi = 1 Florin (1858)

Unused examples without gum of Nos. 1-24 are worth approximately 20% of the values given, which are for stamps with original gum as defined in the catalogue introduction.

For similar designs in Kreuzers, see early Austria.

Coat of Arms — A1

15 CENTESIMI:
Type I — "5" is on a level with the "1." One heavy line around coat of arms center.
Type II — As type I, but "5" is a trifle sideways and is higher than the "1."
Type III — As type II, but two, thinner, lines around center.
45 CENTESIMI:
Type I — Lower part of "45" is lower than "Centes." One heavy line around coat of arms center. "45" varies in height and distance from "Centes."
Type II — One heavy line around coat of arms center. Lower part of "45" is on a level with lower part of "Centes."
Type III — As type II, but two, thinner, lines around center.

Wmk. K.K.H.M. in Sheet or Unwmkd.

1850 Typo. *Imperf.*

Thick to Thin Paper

1	A1	5c buff	4,000.	175.00
		No gum	925.00	
		On cover		475.00
		On cover, single franking, printed matter		*1,425.*
a.		Printed on both sides	*13,750.*	400.00
		No gum	3,100.	
		On cover		1,100.
b.		5c yellow	*7,750.*	575.00
		No gum	1,650.	
		On cover		2,500.
		On cover, single franking		*3,750.*
c.		5c orange	4,750.	200.00
		No gum	1,200.	
		On cover		600.00
		On cover, single franking		*900.00*
d.		5c lemon yellow	—	*1,800.*
		On cover		*6,250.*
		On cover, single franking		7,000.
e.		5c greenish lemon yellow	—	*4,100.*
		On cover		*13,750.*
3	A1	10c black	4,000.	175.00
		No gum	1,050.	
		On cover		475.00
		On cover, single franking		725.00
a.		10c gray black	4,250.	175.00
		No gum	1,050.	
		On cover		475.00
		On cover, single franking		725.00
b.		10c silver gray	11,000.	1,100.
		No gum	2,500.	
		On cover		3,000.
		On cover, single franking		4,400.
e.		10c charcoal black	4,400.	200.00
		No gum	1,100.	
		On cover		750.00
		On cover, single franking		1,100.
4	A1	15c red, type III	1,600.	6.00
		No gum	400.00	
		On cover		21.00
a.		15c carmine, type III	1,750.	8.50
		No gum	450.00	
		On cover		30.00
b.		15c red, type I	*3,250.*	25.00
		No gum	825.00	
		On cover		92.50
c.		Ribbed paper, type II	—	825.00
		No gum	*27,500.*	
		On cover		1,300.
d.		Ribbed paper, type I	*19,000.*	275.00
		No gum	4,750.	
		On cover		525.00
f.		15c red, type II	*1,750.*	29.00
		No gum	400.00	
		On cover		150.00
h.		Laid paper, type III		*13,500.*
		On cover		*57,500.*
i.		15c carmine, type I	3,100.	40.00
		No gum	775.00	
		On cover		200.00
5	A1	30c brown	5,500.	20.00
		No gum	1,400.	
		On cover		65.00
a.		Ribbed paper	8,750.	150.00
		No gum	2,000.	
		On cover		325.00
c.		30c pale brown	4,600.	45.00
		No gum	1,150.	
		On cover		200.00
d.		30c reddish brown	5,400.	24.00
		No gum	1,350.	
		On cover		82.50
6	A1	45c blue, type III	*13,750.*	30.00
		No gum	3,100.	
		On cover		175.00
a.		45c blue, type I	*15,250.*	50.00
		No gum	3,750.	
		On cover		175.00
b.		Ribbed paper, type I	—	550.00
		No gum	27,500.	
		On cover		1,000.
c.		45c blue, type II	*110,000.*	60.00
		No gum	*27,500.*	
		On cover		225.00
e.		45c ultramarine, type III	*12,250.*	52.50
		No gum	3,100.	
		On cover		175.00
f.		45c pale grayish blue, type III	*21,000.*	190.00
		No gum	*5,250.*	
		On cover		750.00
g.		45c pale grayish ultramarine, type III	—	500.00
		On cover		2,000.
h.		45c sky blue, type I	*15,250.*	57.50
		No gum	4,000.	
		On cover		300.00

A cover bearing one example of the 15 centeimi, Type III, on laid paper (Scott 4h), sold for the equivalent of U.S. $40,500 at a Torino auction in 2003.

A mint example of the 45 centesimi blue, Type I, on hand-made paper (Scott No. 6a), was sold at a German auction for the equivalent of U.S. 16,755 in January, 2003.

1854

Machine-made Paper, Type III

3c	A1	10c black	*9,250.*	375.00
		No gum	2,300.	
		On cover		1,100.
3d	A1	10c gray black	*9,250.*	800.00
		No gum	2,300.	
		On cover		2,200.
4g	A1	15c pale red	*1,250.*	5.00
		No gum	325.00	
		On cover		13.50
4h	A1	15c salmon	1,250.	5.00
		No gum	325.00	
		On cover		13.50

5b A1 30c brown ('55) 5,250. 20.00
No gum 1,275.
On cover 60.00
5c A1 30c grayish brown, rough impression 10,000. 50.00
On cover 150.00
6d A1 45c blue 12,000. 62.50
No gum 2,750.
On cover 225.00
6h A1 45c cobalt 12,000. 62.50
No gum 2,750.
On cover 225.00

Full margins = 1½mm.

See note about the paper of the 1850 issue of Austria. *The reprints are type III, in brighter colors.*

Values for pairs
Thick to Thin Hand-made Paper

1 A1 5c buff 8,500. 360.00
On cover 1,200.
3 A1 10c black 8,500. 375.00
On cover 1,200.
4 A1 15c red, type III 3,500. 23.50
On cover 87.50
4b A1 15c red, type I 7,500. 87.50
On cover 310.00
4c A1 15c Ribbed paper, type II 5,500.
On cover —
4d A1 15c Ribbed paper, type I 575.00
On cover 1,350.
4f A1 15c red, type II 4,000. 72.50
On cover 225.00
4h A1 15c red, type III, laid paper —
5 A1 30c brown 12,500. 100.00
On cover 300.00
5a A1 30c Ribbed paper 525.00
On cover 1,500.
6 A1 45c blue, type III 175.00
On cover 650.00
6a A1 45c blue, type I 190.00
On cover 700.00
6b A1 45c Ribbed paper, type I 1,200.
On cover 3,100.
6c A1 45c blue, type II 240.00
On cover 875.00

Machine-made Paper

3c A1 10c black 775.00
On cover 6,750.
4g A1 15c pale red 2,750. 16.00
On cover 45.00
5b A1 30c brown 11,000. 62.50
On cover 225.00
6d A1 45c blue 26,000. 225.00
On cover 825.00

Values for strips of 3
Thick to Thin Hand-made Paper

1 A1 5c buff 13,500. 650.
On cover 2,200.
3 A1 10c black 13,500. 650.
On cover 2,200.
4 A1 15c red, type III 5,500. 160.
On cover 400.00
4b A1 15c red, type I 11,500. 400.00
On cover 1,050.
4d A1 15c Ribbed paper, type I 2,500.
On cover 6,100.
4f A1 15c red, type II 6,750. 325.00
On cover 1,000.
5 A1 30c brown 525.00
On cover 1,550.
5a A1 30c Ribbed paper 2,900.
On cover 8,500.
6 A1 45c blue, type III 900.00
On cover 2,250.
6a A1 45c blue, type I 950.00
On cover 2,400.
6b A1 45c Ribbed paper, type I 3,300.
On cover 10,000.
6c A1 45c blue, type II 1,100.
On cover 3,000.

Machine-made Paper

3c A1 10c black — 1,900.
On cover 4,750.
4g A1 15c pale red 4,250. 110.00
On cover 325.00
5b A1 30c brown 500.00
On cover 1,600.
6d A1 45c blue 1,000.
On cover 2,900.

Values for strips of 4

1 A1 5c buff 18,000. 3,100.
On cover 8,600.
3 A1 10c black 19,000. 3,600.
On cover 11,750.
4 A1 15c red, type III 7,500. 575.00
On cover 1,500.
4b A1 15c red, type I 15,000. 925.00
On cover 2,250.
4f A1 15c red, type II 9,500. 925.00
On cover 2,400.
5 A1 30c brown — 1,000.
On cover 2,500.
5a A1 30c ribbed paper 4,250.
On cover 10,000.
6 A1 45c blue, type III 1,500.
On cover 4,000.
6a A1 45c blue, type I 1,600.
On cover 4,400.
6b A1 45c blue, type I, ribbed paper 4,750.
On cover 11,750.
6c A1 45c blue, type II 2,000.
On cover 5,500.

Values for blocks of 4
Thick to Thin Hand-made Paper

1 A1 5c buff 46,000. 30,000.
On cover 70,000.
3 A1 10c black 29,000. 65,000.
4 A1 15c red, type III 12,500. 6,800.
On cover 21,000.
4b A1 15c red, type I 22,000.
On cover 72,500.
4f A1 15c red, type II 18,000. 17,500.
On cover 37,000.
5 A1 30c brown 47,500. 26,000.
On cover 68,000.
6 A1 45c blue, type III 22,000.
On cover 62,500.
6a A1 45c blue, type I 37,000.
On cover 117,500.
6c A1 45c blue, type II 70,000.

Machine-made Paper

3c A1 10c black —
On cover —
4g A1 15c pale red 6,000. 4,600.
On cover 10,750.
5b A1 30c brown 25,000. 13,750.
On cover 33,000.
6d A1 45c blue 60,000. 17,500.
On cover 50,000.

Values for stamps used in Austria
Thick to Thin Hand-made Paper

1 A1 5c buff (from) 475.
On cover (from) 8,000.
3 A1 10c black (from) 225.
On cover (from) 1,500.
4 A1 15c red, type III (from) 250.
On cover (from) 1,900.
4b A1 15c red, type I (from) 175.
On cover (from) 1,200.
4c A1 15c Ribbed paper, type II (from) 1,300.
On cover (from) 6,000.
4d A1 15c Ribbed paper, type I (from) 400.
On cover (from) 2,300.
4f A1 15c red, type II (from) 225.
On cover (from) 1,600.
5 A1 30c brown (from) 260.
On cover (from) 1,900.
5a A1 30c Ribbed paper (from) 325.
On cover (from) 2,000.
6 A1 45c blue, type III (from) 375.
On cover (from) 3,100.
6a A1 45c blue, type I (from) 325.
On cover (from) 2,200.
6b A1 45c Ribbed paper, type I (from) 1,100.
On cover (from)
6c A1 45c blue, type II (from) 350.
On cover (from) 2,600.

Machine-made Paper

3c A1 10c black (from) 625.
On cover (from) 3,100.
4g A1 15c pale red (from) 200.
On cover (from) 2,250.
5b A1 30c brown (from) 275.
On cover (from) 2,200.
6d A1 45c blue (from) 425.
On cover (from) 3,750.

A2

A3

A4

A5

A6

Two Types of Each Value.
Type I — Loops of the bow at the back of the head broken.
Type II — Loops complete. Wreath projects further at top of head.

1858-62 Embossed Perf. 14½

7 A2 2s yel, type II 1,100. 125.00
No gum 275.00
On cover 300.00
On cover, single franking 325.00
a. 2s yellow, type I 5,750. 575.00
No gum 1,450.
On cover 1,300.
On cover, single franking 1,400.
b. 2s bright yellow, type I 6,750. 625.00
No gum 1,750.
On cover 1,400.
8 A3 3s black, type II 9,000. 150.00
No gum 2,300.
On cover 375.00
On cover, single franking 425.00
a. 3s black, type I 4,100. 275.00
No gum 1,000.
On cover 625.00
On cover, single franking 700.00
b. Perf. 16, type I — 1,225.
On cover 3,200.
c. Perf. 15x16 or 16x15, type I 7,000. 400.00
No gum 1,750.
On cover 1,200.
d. 3s gray black, type I 5,500. 325.00
No gum 1,400.
On cover 850.00
9 A3 3s grn, type II ('62) 800.00 110.00
No gum 200.00
On cover 210.00
On cover, single franking 475.00
a. 3s bluish green 1,150. 150.00
No gum 350.00
On cover 275.00
10 A4 5s red, type II 425.00 7.50
No gum 110.00
On cover 20.00
a. 5s red, type I 1,375. 21.00
No gum 350.00
On cover 60.00
b. Printed on both sides, type II 5,000.
c. 5s bright red, type I 3,100. 80.00
No gum 775.00
On cover 240.00
11 A5 10s brown, type II 3,000. 15.00
No gum 775.00
On cover 45.00
a. 10s brown, type I 825.00 75.00
No gum 200.00
On cover 160.00
b. 10s dark brown, type I 1,250. 110.00
No gum 325.00
On cover 300.00
12 A6 15s blue, type II 3,500. 55.00
No gum 875.00
On cover 140.00
a. 15s blue, type I 6,100. 125.00
No gum 1,525.
On cover 325.00
b. Printed on both sides, type II 14,000.
c. 15s bright blue, type I 7,350. 140.00
No gum 2,000.
On cover 400.00
d. 15s bright blue, type II 4,000. 67.50
No gum 1,000.
On cover 200.00

The reprints are of type II and are perforated 10½, 11, 11½, 12, 12½ and 13. There are also imperforate reprints of Nos. 7-9.

Values for pairs

7 A2 2s yellow, type II 2,750. 275.00
On cover 775.00
On cover, pair only (4 soldi rate) 2,200.
7a A2 2s yellow, type I 12,000. 1,200.
On cover 2,750.
On cover, pair only (4 soldi rate) 5,250.
8 A3 3s black, type II 29,000. 325.00
On cover 850.00
On cover, pair only (6 soldi rate) 2,500.
8a A3 3s black, type I 5,500. 550.00
On cover 1,250.
8b A3 3s Perf. 16, type I 2,750.
On cover —
8c A3 3s Perf. 15x16 or 16x15, type I 1,050.
On cover 3,300.
9 A3 3s green, type II 2,600. 225.00
On cover 600.00
10 A4 5s red, type II 1,250. 17.50
On cover 55.00
10a A4 5s red, type I 3,000. 47.50
On cover 150.00
11 A5 10s brown, type II 9,000. 35.00
On cover 150.00
11a A5 10s brown, type I 1,800. 170.00
On cover 425.00
12 A6 15s blue, type II 10,000. 125.00
On cover 350.00
12a A6 15s blue, type I 13,750. 275.00
On cover 925.00

Values for used strips of 3

7 A2 2s yellow, type II 475.
On cover 1,700.
7a A2 2s yellow, type I 1,850.
On cover 5,500.
8 A3 3s black, type II 625.
On cover 2,300.
8a A3 3s black, type I 1,100.
On cover 3,100.
9 A3 3s green, type II 625.
On cover 2,500.
10 A4 5s red, type II 52.50
On cover 225.
10a A4 5s red, type I 240.
On cover 800.
11 A5 10s brown, type II 160.
On cover 675.
11a A5 10s brown, type I 550.
On cover 1,700.
12 A6 15s blue, type II 350.
On cover 1,500.
12a A6 15s blue, type I 850.
On cover 3,000.

A strip of three of the 3 soldi green (Scott No. 9), with another single example, and a 3 soldi black stamp (Scott No. 8) on a cover sent from Peschiera to Vienna sold for the equivalent of US $20,380 at a Zurich auction in 2004.

Values for strips of 4

7 A2 2s yellow, type II 1,250.
On cover 5,000.
7a A2 2s yellow, type I 3,500.
On cover 9,250.
8 A3 3s black, type II 1,400.
On cover 5,500.
8a A3 3s black, type I 2,300.
On cover 8,100.
9 A3 3s green, type II 1,550.
On cover 5,500.
10 A4 5s red, type II 250.
On cover 975.
10a A4 5s red, type I 800.
On cover 2,100.
11 A5 10s brown, type II 475.
On cover 1,500.
11a A5 10s brown, type I 1,100.
On cover 3,000.
12 A6 15s blue, type II 775.
On cover 3,000.
12a A6 15s blue, type I 1,700.
On cover 7,500.

Values for blocks of 4

7 A2 2s yellow, type II 6,000. 10,000.
On cover —
7a A2 2s yellow, type I —
8a A3 3s black, type I —
9 A3 3s green, type II 3,500. 17,500.
On cover —
10 A4 5s red, type II 2,300. 1,850.
On cover 8,500.
10a A4 5s red, type I 6,000. 7,250.
On cover 18,500.
11 A5 10s brown, type II 20,000. 6,750.
On cover —
11a A5 10s brown, type I 3,750. 14,500.
On cover 21,000.
12 A6 15s blue, type II 21,500. 6,750.
On cover 27,500.
12a A6 15s blue, type I 17,750.
On cover —

Values for stamps used in Austria

7 A2 2s yellow, type II (from) 775.
On cover (from) 13,750.
7a A2 2s yellow, type I (from) 1,500.
8 A3 3s black, type II (from) 310.
On cover (from) 1,850.
8a A3 3s black, type I (from) 425.
On cover (from) 1,750.
9 A3 3s green, type II (from) 375.
On cover (from) 2,000.
10 A4 5s red, type II (from) 190.
On cover (from) 1,550.
10a A4 5s red, type I (from) 210.
On cover (from) 1,850.
11 A5 10s brown, type II (from) 220.
On cover (from) 2,000.
11a A5 10s brown, type I (from) 300.
On cover (from) 2,500.
12 A6 15s blue, type II (from) 525.
On cover (from) 3,800.
12a A6 15s blue, type I (from) 525.
On cover (from) 5,500.

A7

A8

1861-62 Perf. 14

13 A7 5s red 4,250. 6.00
No gum 1,075.
On cover 18.50
14 A7 10s brown ('62) 6,750. 50.00
No gum 1,700.
On cover 140.00

The reprints are perforated 9, 9½, 10½, 11, 12, 12½ and 13. There are also imperforate reprints of the 2 and 3s.
The 2, 3 and 15s of this type exist only as reprints.

Values for pairs

13 A7 5s red 9,250. 13.50
On cover 45.00
14 A7 10s brown 14,500. 190.00
On cover 1,000.

Values for strips of 3

13 A7 5s red 47.50
On cover 210.00
14 A7 10s brown 840.00
On cover 2,750.

Values for strips of 4

13 A7 5s red 190.00
On cover 850.00
14 A7 10s brown 2,150.
On cover 6,750.

Values for blocks of 4

13 A7 5s red 18,500. 1,750.
On cover 5,500.
14 A7 10s brown 21,500.
On cover 70,000.

Values for stamps used in Austria

13 A7 5s red 210.00
On cover 1,850.
14 A7 10s brown 1,050.
On cover —

1863

15 A8 2s yellow 250.00 190.00
No gum 65.00
On cover 500.00
On cover, single franking 550.00
16 A8 3s green 3,350. 100.00
No gum 850.00
On cover 300.00
On cover, single franking 925.00
17 A8 5s rose 4,000. 27.50
No gum 1,000.
On cover 67.50
18 A8 10s blue 7,750. 125.00
No gum 1,900.
On cover 190.00
On cover, single franking 210.00
19 A8 15s yellow brown 6,150. 250.00
No gum 1,500.
On cover 725.00

Values for pairs

15 A8 2s yellow 575.00 375.00
On cover 1,700.
On cover, alone (4 soldi rate) 2,000.
16 A8 3s green 7,750. 325.00
On cover 1,300.
On cover, alone (6 soldi rate) 2,400.
17 A8 5s rose 9,000. 60.00
On cover 160.00
18 A8 10s blue 17,000. 260.00
On cover 575.00
19 A8 15s yellow brown 13,500. 525.00
On cover 1,800.

Values for strips of 3

15 A8 2s yellow 675.00
On cover 2,900.
16 A8 3s green 1,100.
On cover 4,600.

17 A8 5s rose 210.00
On cover 825.00
18 A8 10s blue 550.00
On cover 2,000.
19 A8 15s yellow brown 1,250.
On cover *4,500.*

Values for strips of 4

15 A8 2s yellow 1,525.
On cover *6,600.*
16 A8 3s green 2,250.
On cover *10,000.*
17 A8 5s rose 525.00
On cover 1,400.
18 A8 10s blue 2,000.
On cover 5,500.
19 A8 15s yellow brown 2,750.
On cover *7,500.*

Values for blocks of 4

15 A8 2s yellow *1,100.* *14,750.*
On cover *29,000.*
16 A8 3s green *20,000.*
On cover
17 A8 5s rose *3,250.*
On cover *7,750.*
18 A8 10s blue
19 A8 15s yellow brown *27,500.* *18,500.*
On cover *42,000.*

Values for stamps used in Austria

15 A8 2s yellow 700.00
On cover *14,000.*
16 A8 3s green 240.00
On cover 1,800.
17 A8 5s rose 240.00
On cover 2,000.
18 A8 10s blue 450.00
On cover 5,000.
19 A8 15s yellow brown 550.00
On cover *6,250.*

1864-65 Wmk. 91 *Perf. 9½*

20 A8 2s yellow ('65) 350.00 *550.00*
No gum 85.00
On cover 1,800.
On cover, single franking 2,000.
21 A8 3s green 45.00 37.50
No gum 11.00
On cover 85.00
On cover, single franking 275.00
22 A8 5s rose 6.00 6.25
No gum 1.50
On cover 17.00
23 A8 10s blue 55.00 17.50
No gum 14.00
On cover 35.00
On cover, single franking 40.00
24 A8 15s yellow brown 575.00 160.00
No gum 140.00
On cover 400.00

Nos. 15-24 reprints are perforated 10½ and 13. There are also imperforate reprints of the 2s and 3s.

Values for pairs

20 A8 2s yellow 775.00 *1,250.*
On cover *6,800.*
21 A8 3s green 100.00 77.50
On cover 190.00
On cover alone (6 soldi rate) *2,250.*
22 A8 5s rose 14.00 9.50
On cover 40.00
23 A8 10s blue 125.00 37.50
On cover 100.00
24 A8 15s yellow brown 1,300. 350.00
On cover 950.00

Values for strips of 3

20 A8 2s yellow 4,600.
On cover *9,000.*
21 A8 3s green 260.00
On cover *2,000.*
22 A8 5s rose 52.50
On cover 210.00
23 A8 10s blue 140.00
On cover 700.00
24 A8 15s yellow brown 625.00
On cover 2,000.

Values for strips of 4

20 A8 2s yellow 9,750.
21 A8 3s green 850.00
On cover *5,000.*
22 A8 5s rose 160.00
On cover 575.00
23 A8 10s blue *925.00*
On cover 3,000.
24 A8 15s yellow brown 2,000.
On cover 5,500.

Values for blocks of 4

20 A8 2s yellow 1,900. —
21 A8 3s green 190.00
22 A8 5s rose 30.00 *1,200.*
On cover *3,100.*
23 A8 10s blue 250.00 *9,250.*
On cover *26,000.*
24 A8 15s yellow brown 2,600. *7,750.*
On cover *20,500.*

Values for stamps used in Austria

20 A8 2s yellow 1,400.
21 A8 3s green 200.00
On cover 1,250.
22 A8 5s rose 140.00
On cover 1,800.
23 A8 10s blue 310.00
On cover *3,500.*
24 A8 15s yellow brown 450.00
On cover *4,500.*

NEWSPAPER TAX STAMPS

From 1853 to 1858 the Austrian Newspaper Tax Stamp 2kr green (No. PR1) was also used in Lombardy-Venetia, at the value of 10 centesimi.

NT1

Type I — The banderol of the left eagle touches the beak of the eagle.

Type II — The banderol does not touch the beak.

1858-59 Unwmk. Typo. *Imperf.*

PR1 NT1 1kr black, type I ('59) 1,850. *4,100.*
No gum 1,200.
On newspaper *15,250.*
PR2 NT1 2kr red, type II ('59) 400.00 92.50
No gum 175.00
On newspaper 375.00
a. Watermark 91 400.00 100.00
On newspaper —
PR3 NT1 4kr red, type I — *4,600.*
No gum *20,000.*
On newspaper *22,500.*

The reprints are on a smooth toned paper and are all of type II.

Values for blocks of 4

PR1 NT1 1kr black, type I 44,000.
PR2 NT1 2kr red, type II 3,300.

Values for stamps used in Austria

PR1 NT1 1kr black, type I *4,750.*
PR2 NT1 2kr red, type II *1,100.*

AZERBAIJAN

ˌa-zər-ˌbī-ˈjän

(Azerbaidjan)

LOCATION — Southernmost part of Russia in Eastern Europe, bounded by Georgia, Dagestan, Caspian Sea, Persia and Armenia
GOVT. — A Soviet Socialist Republic
AREA — 32,686 sq. mi.
POP. — 2,096,973 (1923)
CAPITAL — Baku

100 Kopecks = 1 Ruble

National Republic

Standard Bearer — A1

Farmer at Sunset — A2

Baku — A3

Temple of Eternal Fires — A4

1919 Unwmk. Litho. *Imperf.*

1 A1 10k multicolored .20 *.30*
2 A1 20k multicolored .20 *.30*
3 A2 40k green, yellow & blk .20 *.30*
4 A2 60k red, yellow & blk .25 *.35*
5 A2 1r blue, yellow & blk .35 *.50*
6 A3 2r red, bister & blk .35 *.50*
7 A3 5r blue, bister & blk .45 *.85*
8 A3 10r olive grn, bis & blk .65 *.95*
9 A4 25r blue, red & black 1.10 *20.00*
10 A4 50r ol grn, red & black 1.40 *1.75*
Nos. 1-10 (10) 5.15 *25.80*

The two printings of Nos. 1-10 are distinguished by the grayish or thin white paper. Both have yellowish gum. White paper copies are worth five times the above values.

For surcharges see Nos. 57-64, 75-80.

Soviet Socialist Republic

Symbols of Labor — A5

Oil Well — A6

Bibi Eibatt Oil Field — A7

Khan's Palace, Baku — A8

Globe and Workers — A9

Maiden's Tower, Baku — A10

Goukasoff House A11

Blacksmiths — A12

Hall of Judgment, Baku — A13

1922

15 A5 1r gray green .20 *.35*
16 A6 2r olive black .50 *.50*
17 A7 5r gray brown .20 *.35*
18 A8 10r gray .50 *.65*
19 A9 25r orange brown .20 *.40*
20 A10 50r violet .20 *.40*
21 A11 100r dull red .35 *.50*
22 A12 150r blue .35 *.50*
23 A9 250r violet & buff .35 *.50*
24 A13 400r dark blue .35 *.50*
25 A12 500r gray vio & blk .35 *.50*
26 A13 1000r dk blue & rose .35 *.60*
27 A8 2000r blue & black .35 *.50*
28 A7 3000r brown & blue .35 *.50*
a. Tete beche pair 15.00 15.00
29 A11 5000r black, *ol grn* .60 *.75*
Nos. 15-29 (15) 5.20 *7.50*

Counterfeits exist of Nos. 1-29. They generally sell for more than genuine copies.

For overprints and surcharges see Nos. 32-41, 43, 45-55, 65-72, 300-304, 307-333.

Nos. 15, 17, 23, 28, 27 Handstamped from Metal Dies in a Numbering Machine

1922

32 A5 10,000r on 1r 17.50 17.50
33 A7 15,000r on 5r 17.50 *27.50*
34 A9 33,000r on 250r 6.25 6.25
35 A7 50,000r on 3000r 29.00 9.00
36 A8 66,000r on 2000r 17.50 12.00
Nos. 32-36 (5) 87.75 72.25

Same Surcharges on Regular Issue and Semi-Postal Stamps of 1922

1922-23

36A A7 500r on 5r 150.00 *160.00*
37 A6 1000r on 2r 25.00 *30.00*
38 A8 2000r on 10r 15.00 8.00
39 A8 5000r on 2000r 7.50 3.00
40 A11 15,000r on 5000r 12.00 10.00
41 A5 20,000r on 1r 20.00 12.50
42 SP1 25,000r on 500r *50.00* —
43 A7 50,000r on 5r 50.00 50.00
44 SP2 50,000r on 1000r *50.00* —
45 A11 50,000r on 5000r 15.00 15.00
45A A8 60,000r on 2000r 100.00 *200.00*
46 A11 70,000r on 5000r 50.00 40.00
47 A6 100,000r on 2r 15.00 15.00
48 A8 200,000r on 10r 10.00 10.00
49 A9 200,000r on 25r 15.00 15.00
50 A7 300,000r on 3000r 35.00 35.00
51 A8 500,000r on 2000r 25.00 10.00

Revalued

52 A7 500r on #33 *500.00 500.00*
53 A11 15,000r on #46 *500.00 500.00*
54 A7 300,000r on #35 *500.00 500.00*
55 A8 500,000r on #36 *500.00 500.00*

The surcharged semi-postal stamps were used for regular postage.

Same Surcharges on Stamps of 1919

57 A1 25,000r on 10k .85 *1.25*
58 A1 50,000r on 20k .85 *1.25*
59 A2 75,000r on 40k 2.00 *3.00*
60 A2 100,000r on 60k .85 *1.25*
61 A2 200,000r on 1r .85 *1.25*
62 A3 300,000r on 2r 1.10 *1.25*
63 A3 500,000r on 5r 1.10 *1.25*
64 A2 750,000r on 40k 4.25 4.00
Nos. 57-64 (8) 11.85 *14.50*

Handstamped from Settings of Rubber Type in Black or Violet

100000
Nos. 65-66, 71-80

200.000
Nos. 67-70

On Stamps of 1922

65 A6 100,000r on 2r 25.00 25.00
66 A8 200,000r on 10r 75.00 *75.00*
67 A8 200,000r on 10r (V) 75.00 75.00
68 A9 200,000r on 25r (V) 75.00 75.00
a. Black surcharge 75.00 *75.00*
69 A7 300,000r on 3000r (V) 35.00 35.00
70 A8 500,000r on 2000r (V) 60.00 60.00
a. Black surcharge 75.00 *75.00*
72 A11 1,500,000r on 5000r (V) 125.00 125.00
a. Black surcharge 100.00 100.00

On Stamps of 1919

75 A1 50,000r on 20k 3.25
76 A2 75,000r on 40k 3.25
77 A2 100,000r on 60k 3.25

78	A2	200,000r on 1r	3.25
79	A3	300,000r on 2r	3.25
80	A3	500,000r on 5r	3.25

Inverted and double surcharges of Nos. 32-80 sell for twice the normal price.
Counterfeits exist of Nos. 32-80.

Baku Province

Regular and Semi-Postal Stamps of 1922 Handstamped in Violet or Black

БАКИНСКОЙ П. К.

The overprint reads "Bakinskoi P(ochtovoy) K(ontory)," meaning Baku Post Office.

1922		Unwmk.	Imperf.	
300	A5	1r gray green	*75.00*	
301	A7	5r gray brown	*75.00*	
302	A12	150r blue	*75.00*	
303	A9	250r violet & buff	*75.00*	
304	A13	400r dark blue	*65.00*	65.00
305	SP1	500r bl & pale bl	*75.00*	*100.00*
306	SP2	1000r brown & bis	*75.00*	
307	A8	2000r blue & black	*100.00*	*150.00*
308	A7	3000r brown & blue	*75.00*	
309	A11	5000r black, *ol grn*	*100.00*	
		Nos. 300-309 (10)	*790.00*	

Stamps of 1922 Handstamped in Violet

БАКИНСКАГО Г-П-Т-О.№1

Ovpt. reads: Baku Post, Telegraph Office No. 1.

1924

Overprint 24x2mm

312	A12	150r blue	*65.00*	
313	A9	250r violet & buff	*65.00*	
314	A13	400r dark blue	*65.00*	
317	A8	2000r blue & black	*65.00*	
318	A7	3000r brn & blue	*65.00*	
319	A11	5000r black, *ol grn*	*200.00*	

Overprint 30x3½mm

323	A12	150r blue	*75.00*	*100.00*
324	A9	250r violet & buff	*100.00*	
325	A13	400r dark blue	*100.00*	100.00
328	A8	2000r blue & black	*100.00*	100.00
329	A7	3000r brn & blue	*75.00*	
330	A11	5000r black, *ol grn*	*100.00*	

Overprinted on Nos. 32-33, 35

331	A5	10,000r on 1r	*500.00*
332	A7	15,000r on 5r	*500.00*
333	A7	50,000r on 3000r	*500.00*
		Nos. 312-333 (15)	*2,575.*

The overprinted semipostal stamps were used for regular postage.
A 24x2mm handstamp on #17, B1-B2, and 30x3½mm on #15, 17, B1-B2, was of private origin.

SEMI-POSTAL STAMPS

Carrying Food to Sufferers SP1

1922		Unwmk.	Imperf.	
B1	SP1	500r blue & pale blue	.40	*.75*

For overprint and surcharge see Nos. 42, 305.

Widow and Orphans — SP2

1922				
B2	SP2	1000r brown & bister	.75	*1.25*

Counterfeits exist.
For overprint and surcharge see #44, 306.

Russian stamps of 1909-18 were privately overprinted as above in red, blue or black by a group of Entente officers working with Russian soldiers returning from Persia. Azerbaijan was not occupied by the Allies. There is evidence that existing covers (some seemingly postmarked at Baku, dated Oct. 19, 1917, and at Tabriz, Russian Consulate, Apr. 25, 1917) are fakes.

AZORES

'ā-ˌzōrz

LOCATION — Group of islands in the North Atlantic Ocean, due west of Portugal
GOVT. — Integral part of Portugal, former colony
AREA — 922 sq. mi.
POP. — 253,935 (1930)
CAPITAL — Ponta Delgada

Azores stamps were supplanted by those of Portugal in 1931.

1000 Reis = 1 Milreis
100 Centavos = 1 Escudo (1912)

Stamps of Portugal Overprinted in Black or Carmine

A

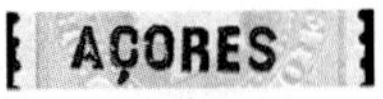

B

C

There are three types of surcharge. Type A: "C" and "O" rounded; "C" and "O" thinner; "C" and "O" raised. Type B: "C" and "O" rounded; "C" and "O" close together. Type C: "C" and "O" almost rectantgular.

Type A

1868		Unwmk.	Imperf.	
1	A14	5r black	*3,500.*	*2,250.*
2	A14	10r yellow	*13,750.*	*10,000.*
3	A14	20r bister	200.00	125.00
4	A14	50r green	200.00	125.00
5	A14	80r orange	200.00	125.00
6	A14	100r lilac	200.00	125.00

The reprints are on thick chalky white wove paper, ungummed, and on thin ivory paper with shiny white gum. Value $35-42.50 each.

1868-70			Perf. 12½	

5 REIS:
Type I — The "5" at the right is 1mm from end of label.
Type II — The "5" is 1½mm from end of label.

7	A14	5r black, type I (C)	60.00	30.00
a.		Type II	70.00	70.00
b.		As "a," double impression of stamp	125.00	110.00
8	A14	10r yellow	92.50	40.00
a.		Inverted overprint	*250.00*	*150.00*
b.		10r orange yellow	92.50	70.00
9	A14	20r bister	50.00	65.00
10	A14	25r rose	50.00	11.00
a.		Inverted overprint	—	—
b.		25r deep rose	70.00	11.00
11	A14	50r green	150.00	125.00
a.		50r pale green	200.00	190.00
12	A14	80r orange	150.00	125.00
13	A14	100r lilac ('69)	150.00	125.00
a.		100r pale mauve	200.00	200.00
14	A14	120r blue	150.00	125.00
a.		120r deep blue	175.00	125.00
15	A14	240r violet	600.00	400.00

The reprints are on thick chalky white paper ungummed, perf 13½, and on thin ivory paper with shiny white gum, perf 13½. Value $30 each.

Overprint Type B

1871-75			Perf. 12½	
21	A15	5r black (C)	13.50	8.75
a.		Inverted overprint	*47.50*	*42.50*
23	A15	10r yellow	29.00	25.00
a.		Inverted overprint	—	—
b.		Double overprint	60.00	47.50
24	A15	20r bister	30.00	26.00
a.		Ribbed paper	52.50	35.00
25	A15	25r rose	17.00	4.25
a.		Inverted overprint	—	—
d.		Dbl. impression of stamp	—	—
26	A15	50r green	85.00	42.50
e.		Ribbed paper	85.00	42.50
27	A15	80r orange	90.00	50.00
28	A15	100r lilac	90.00	60.00
a.		Perf. 14	195.00	150.00
29	A15	120r blue	175.00	125.00
a.		Inverted overprint	—	—
b.		Ribbed paper	325.00	260.00

Perf. 13½

21b	A15	5r black (C)	12.50	6.50
23c	A15	10r yellow	40.00	25.00
24b	A15	20r bister	60.00	30.00
25e	A15	25r rose	25.00	3.75
26a	A15	50r green	100.00	57.50
27a	A15	80r orange	125.00	62.50

Perf. 14

25c	A15	25r rose	165.00	57.50

Overprint Type A

Perf. 12½

21c	A15	5r black (C)	20.00	9.50
23d	A15	10r yellow	27.50	20.00
24c	A15	20r yellow	55.00	30.00
24d	A15	20r olive bister	32.50	21.00
24e	A15	20r yellow bister	32.50	21.00
24f	A15	20r bister, ribbed paper	37.50	24.00
25f	A15	25r rose	18.00	4.50
b.		Double overprint	37.50	27.50
25g	A15	25r rose, ribbed paper	30.00	7.75
26b	A15	50r green	100.00	27.50
27b	A15	80r orange	110.00	60.00
28b	A15	100r lilac	110.00	70.00
29c	A15	120r blue	150.00	95.00
30	A15	240r violet	850.00	675.00
30a	A15	240r violet, ribbed paper	1,000.	725.00

Overprint Type C

Perf. 12½

21d	A15	5r black (C)	13.00	6.75
23e	A15	10r yellow	27.50	12.50
24g	A15	20r bister	27.50	12.50
25h	A15	25r rose	16.00	3.25
26c	A15	50r green	80.00	25.00
27c	A15	80r orange	100.00	50.00
28c	A15	100r lilac	80.00	37.50
29d	A15	120r blue	160.00	80.00

Perf. 13½

21e	A15	5r black (C)	13.00	6.75
21f	A15	5r double impression of stamp	125.00	80.00
23f	A15	10r yellow	50.00	25.00
24h	A15	20r bister	50.00	25.00
25i	A15	25r rose	17.00	3.25
26d	A15	50r green	92.50	52.50
27d	A15	80r orange	140.00	62.50
28d	A15	100r lilac	110.00	45.00
29e	A15	120r blue	160.00	80.00

Perf. 14

28a	A15	100r lilac	175.00	100.00

The reprints are of type "b." All values exist are on thick chalky white paper ungummed, perf 13½ (value, each $29) and also on thin white paper with shiny white gum and perforated 13½ (value, each $30). The 5r, 10r, 15r, 50r and 120r also exist on thick chalky white paper ungummed, perf 12½. Value, each $80.

Overprint Type C in Black

1875-80			Perf. 13½	

15 REIS:
Type I — The figures of value, 1 and 5, at the right in upper label are close together.
Type II — The figures of value at the right in upper label are spaced.

32	A15	10r yellow green	150.00	125.00
33b	A15	15r lilac brown	70.00	47.50
a.		Inverted overprint	*150.00*	
34	A15	50r blue	140.00	60.00
a.		50r pale blue	175.00	95.00
35	A15	150r blue	200.00	175.00
36	A15	150r yellow	240.00	175.00
37	A15	300r violet	95.00	65.00

Perf. 12½

31	A15	10r blue green	150.00	125.00
32a	A15	10r yellow green	130.00	95.00
33b	A15	15r lilac brown	20.00	18.00
34b	A15	50r pale blue	175.00	95.00
35a	A15	150r blue	200.00	150.00

Overprint Type B

Perf. 13½

37a	A15	300r violet	100.00	67.50

Perf. 12½

33	A15	15r lilac brown	30.00	21.00
35b	A15	150r blue	210.00	150.00

The reprints have the same papers, gum and perforations as those of the preceding issue.

Overprint Type C in Black

1880			Perf. 12½	
38	A17	25r gray	150.00	95.00
a.		Perf 13½	150.00	42.50
39	A18	25r red lilac	60.00	9.50
a.		Perf 13½	60.00	9.50
b.		25r gray	—	—
c.		As "b," perf 13½	50.00	9.50
d.		As "c," double overprint		

Overprint Type C in Carmine or Black

Ordinary Paper

1881-82				
40	A16	5r black (C)	29.00	12.00
a.		perf 13½	27.50	12.00
41	A23	25r brown ('82)	55.00	8.00
b.		perf 13½	55.00	8.00
42	A19	50r blue	190.00	47.50
a.		perf 13½	190.00	47.50
		Nos. 40-42 (3)	274.00	67.50

Enamel Surfaced Paper

40b	A16	5r black (C)	160.00	95.00
41b	A16	25r brown ('82)	55.00	8.00
d.		perf 13½	55.00	8.00

Reprints of Nos. 38, 39, 39a, 40 and 42 have the same papers, gum and perforations as those of preceding issues.

Overprinted in Red or Black

d

1882-85			Perf. 12½	

Ordinary Paper

15, 20 REIS

Type I — The figures of value are some distance apart and close to the end of the label.
Type II — The figures are closer together and farther from the end of the label. On the 15 reis this is particularly apparent in the upper right figures.

43	A16	5r black (R)	20.00	10.00
45	A15	10r green	90.00	50.00
a.		Inverted overprint	—	—
47	A15	15r lilac brn	35.00	20.00
b.		Inverted overprint	—	—
48	A15	20r bister	70.00	40.00
a.		Inverted overprint	—	—
50	A23	25r brown	30.00	4.50
51	A15	50r blue	*1,800.*	*1,250.*
52	A24	50r blue	24.00	3.50
a.		Double overprint	—	—
53a	A15	80r orange	125.00	110.00
b.		Double overprint	—	—
54	A15	100r lilac	125.00	95.00
55	A15	150r blue	*1,500.*	*900.00*
56	A15	150r yellow	125.00	110.00
57	A15	300r violet	125.00	110.00
58	A21	5r slate (R)	25.00	6.00
60	A15	1000r black (R)	150.00	125.00

Perf. 13½

43a	A16	5r black (R)	29.00	14.00
45b	A15	10r green	97.50	62.50
47c	A15	15r lilac brown	75.00	85.00
48b	A15	20r bister	150.00	85.00
50a	A23	25r brown	26.00	4.50
51a	A15	50r blue	1,100.	925.00
52b	A24	50r blue	42.50	4.50

53c A15 80r orange 175.00 110.00
54a A15 100r lilac 150.00 110.00
55a A15 150r blue 900.00 800.00
56a A15 150r yellow 110.00 85.00
57a A15 300r violet 110.00 85.00
60a A15 1000r black ('85) (R) 140.00 125.00

Perf. 11½

50b A23 25r brown 26.00 4.50

Enamel Surfaced Paper

Perf. 12½

43b A16 5r black (R) 70.00 47.50
44 A21 5r slate 19.00 4.50
a. Double overprint —
c. Inverted overprint —
45d A15 10r green 125.00 110.00
46 A22 10r green ('84) 32.50 14.00
a. Double overprint —
47d A15 15r lilac brown 87.50 75.00
48c A15 20r bister 87.50 75.00
49 A15 20r carmine ('85) 150.00 125.00
a. Double overprint 190.00 —
50c A23 25r brown 27.50 4.50
52c A24 50r blue 27.50 4.50
53 A15 80r yellow 80.00 62.50
53b A15 80r orange 80.00 62.50
54b A15 100r lilac 62.50 55.00
56b A15 150r yellow 65.00 57.50
57b A15 300r violet 87.50 77.50
59 A24a 500r black (R) 195.00 175.00

Perf. 13½

44b A21 5r slate 32.50 11.00
45e A15 10r green 125.00 100.00
46b A22 10r green ('84) 32.50 14.00
47e A15 15r lilac brown 95.00 75.00
48e A15 20r bister 900.00 55.00
49b A15 20r carmine ('85) 150.00 125.00
50d A23 25r brown 30.00 4.50
52d A24 50r blue 37.50 14.00
53d A15 80r orange 95.00 75.00
56c A15 150r yellow 110.00 92.50
57c A15 300r violet 110.00 92.50

Perf. 11½

44d A21 5r slate 37.50 22.50
46c A22 10r green ('84) 32.50 14.00
50e A23 25r brown 27.50 4.50
52e A24 50r blue 27.50 4.50
58a A21 5r slate (R) 15.00 3.00

Reprints of the 1882-85 issues have the same papers, gum and perforations as those of preceding issues.

1887 Black Overprint

61 A25 20r pink 32.50 19.00
a. Inverted overprint — —
b. Double overprint — —
62 A26 25r lilac rose 35.00 3.00
a. Inverted overprint — —
b. Double ovpt., one invtd. — —
63 A26 25r red violet 35.00 3.00
a. Double overprint — —
64 A24a 500r red violet 150.00 110.00
a. Perf. 13½ 275.00 240.00
Nos. 61-64 (4) 252.50 135.00

Nos. 58-64 inclusive have been reprinted on thin white paper with shiny white gum and perforated 13½. Value: Nos. 58, 61-64, each $22.50; No. 59, $85; No. 60, $50.

Prince Henry the Navigator Issue

Portugal Nos. 97-109 Overprinted

1894, Mar. 4 ***Perf. 14***

65 A46 5r orange yel 3.50 3.00
Never hinged 7.00
a. Inverted overprint 60.00 60.00
66 A46 10r violet rose 3.50 3.00
Never hinged 7.00
a. Double overprint — —
b. Inverted overprint — —
67 A46 15r brown 4.25 4.00
Never hinged 8.25
68 A46 20r violet 4.50 4.25
Never hinged 8.50
a. Double overprint — —
69 A47 25r green 5.00 4.50
Never hinged 9.50
a. Double overprint 75.00 75.00
b. Inverted overprint 75.00 75.00
70 A47 50r blue 12.50 6.75
Never hinged 24.00
71 A47 75r dp carmine 22.50 9.50
Never hinged 47.50
72 A47 80r yellow grn 27.50 10.00
Never hinged 52.50
73 A47 100r lt brn, *pale buff* 27.50 8.00
Never hinged 52.50
a. Double overprint — —
74 A48 150r lt car, *pale rose* 35.00 19.00
Never hinged 77.50
75 A48 300r dk bl, *sal buff* 42.50 30.00
Never hinged 82.50
76 A48 500r brn vio, *pale lil* 75.00 45.00
Never hinged 150.00
77 A48 1000r gray blk, *yelsh* 150.00 70.00
Never hinged 300.00
a. Double overprint 700.00 500.00
Nos. 65-77 (13) 413.25 217.00

St. Anthony of Padua Issue

Portugal Nos. 132-146 Overprinted in Red or Black

1895, June 13 ***Perf. 12***

78 A50 2½r black (R) 3.00 1.25
79 A51 5r brown yel 9.50 3.00
80 A51 10r red lilac 9.50 4.50
81 A51 15r red brown 14.50 7.00
82 A51 20r gray lilac 16.00 9.50
83 A51 25r green & vio 10.00 3.00
84 A52 50r blue & brn 32.50 15.00
85 A52 75r rose & brn 47.50 40.00
86 A52 80r lt green & brn 55.00 47.50
87 A52 100r choc & blk 55.00 42.50
88 A53 150r vio rose & bis 110.00 100.00
89 A53 200r blue & bis 125.00 100.00
90 A53 300r slate & bis 150.00 110.00
91 A53 500r vio brn & grn 210.00 150.00
92 A53 1000r violet & grn 400.00 225.00
Nos. 78-92 (15) 1,247. 858.25

7th cent. of the birth of Saint Anthony of Padua.

Common Design Types pictured following the introduction.

Vasco da Gama Issue

Common Design Types

1898, Apr. 1 ***Perf. 14, 15***

93 CD20 2½r blue green 3.50 1.25
Never hinged 5.00
94 CD21 5r red 3.50 1.50
Never hinged 5.00
95 CD22 10r gray lilac 7.00 3.00
Never hinged 10.00
96 CD23 25r yellow green 7.00 3.00
Never hinged 10.00
97 CD24 50r dark blue 10.00 9.50
Never hinged 15.00
98 CD25 75r violet brown 21.00 14.00
Never hinged 32.50
99 CD26 100r bister brown 27.50 14.00
Never hinged 40.00
100 CD27 150r bister 42.50 30.00
Never hinged 62.50
Nos. 93-100 (8) 122.00 76.25

For overprints and surcharges see Nos. 141-148.

King Carlos — A28

King Manuel II — A29

1906 Typo. ***Perf. 11½x12***

101 A28 2½r gray .45 .40
Never hinged .50
a. Inverted overprint 35.00 35.00
102 A28 5r orange yel .45 .40
Never hinged .50
a. Inverted overprint 35.00 35.00
103 A28 10r yellow grn .45 .40
Never hinged .50
104 A28 20r gray vio .70 .50
Never hinged .80
105 A28 25r carmine .70 .40
Never hinged .80
106 A28 50r ultra 6.00 4.75
Never hinged 6.75
107 A28 75r brown, *straw* 2.10 *1.25*
Never hinged 2.40
108 A28 100r dk blue, *bl* 2.10 *1.40*
Never hinged 2.40
109 A28 200r red lilac, *pnksh* 2.25 *1.40*
Never hinged 2.60
110 A28 300r dk blue, *rose* 6.75 *5.75*
Never hinged 8.00
111 A28 500r black, *blue* 16.00 14.00
Never hinged 19.00
Nos. 101-111 (11) 37.95 30.65

"Acores" and letters and figures in the corners are in red on the 2½, 10, 20, 75 and 500r and in black on the other values.

1910, Apr. 1 ***Perf. 14x15***

112 A29 2½r violet .50 .40
113 A29 5r black .50 .40
114 A29 10r dk green .50 .40
115 A29 15r lilac brn .90 .65
116 A29 20r carmine 1.25 1.00
117 A29 25r violet brn .50 .50
a. Perf. 11½ 3.00 1.60
118 A29 50r blue 3.00 1.60
119 A29 75r bister brn 3.00 1.60
120 A29 80r slate 3.00 1.60
121 A29 100r brown, *lt grn* 5.00 3.75
122 A29 200r green, *sal* 5.00 3.75
123 A29 300r black, *blue* 3.00 2.75
124 A29 500r olive & brown 9.50 10.00
125 A29 1000r blue & black 21.00 19.00
Nos. 112-125 (14) 56.65 47.40

The errors of color 10r black, 15r dark green, 25r black and 50r carmine are considered to be proofs.

Stamps of 1910 Overprinted in Carmine or Green

1910

126 A29 2½r violet .40 .35
a. Inverted overprint 12.50 12.50
127 A29 5r black .40 .35
a. Inverted overprint 12.50 12.50
128 A29 10r dk green .40 .35
a. Inverted overprint 12.50 12.50
129 A29 15r lilac brn 1.90 1.40
a. Inverted overprint 12.50 12.50
130 A29 20r carmine (G) 1.90 1.40
a. Inverted overprint 22.50 22.50
b. Double overprint 22.50 22.50
131 A29 25r violet brn .40 .30
a. Perf. 11½ 65.00 57.50
132 A29 50r blue 1.40 1.25
133 A29 75r bister brn 1.40 .95
a. Double overprint 12.50 12.50
134 A29 80r slate 1.40 .95
135 A29 100r brown, *grn* 1.10 .90
136 A29 200r green, *sal* 1.10 *.95*
137 A29 300r black, *blue* 3.50 2.25
138 A29 500r olive & brn 4.50 *3.25*
139 A29 1000r blue & blk 11.00 *7.00*
Nos. 126-139 (14) 30.80 *21.65*

Vasco da Gama Issue Overprinted or Surcharged in Black:

d

e

f

1911 ***Perf. 14, 15***

141 CD20(d) 2½r blue green .65 .50
142 CD21(e) 15r on 5r red .65 .50
143 CD23(d) 25r yellow grn .65 .50
144 CD24(d) 50r dk blue 2.25 1.40
145 CD25(d) 75r violet brn 1.90 1.75
146 CD27(e) 80r on 150r bister 2.00 1.90
147 CD26(d) 100r yellow brn 2.10 1.90
a. Double surcharge 26.00 25.00
148 CD22(f) 1000r on 10r lilac 20.00 15.00
Nos. 141-148 (8) 30.20 23.45

Postage Due Stamps of Portugal Overprinted or Surcharged in Black "ACORES" and

1911 ***Perf. 12***

149 D1 5r black 1.25 1.10
150 D1 10r magenta 2.75 1.10
a. "Acores" double 20.00 15.00
151 D1 20r orange 5.25 3.75
152 D1 200r brn, *buff* 22.50 20.00
a. "Acores" inverted
153 D1 300r on 50r slate 22.50 19.00
154 D1 500r on 100r car, *pink* 22.50 18.00
Nos. 149-154 (6) 76.75 62.95

Ceres Issue of Portugal Overprinted in Black or Carmine

With Imprint

1912-31 ***Perf. 12x11½, 15x14***

155 A64 ¼c olive brown .55 .40
a. Inverted overprint 12.50 9.50
156 A64 ½c black (C) .55 .40
157 A64 1c deep green 1.10 .80
a. Inverted overprint 12.50
158 A64 1c dp brn ('18) .55 .40
a. Inverted overprint 17.50
159 A64 1½c choc ('13) 1.10 .80
a. Inverted overprint 12.50
160 A64 1½c dp grn ('18) .55 .50
a. Inverted overprint 17.50
161 A64 2c carmine .80 .65
a. Inverted overprint 20.00
162 A64 2c orange ('18) .55 .50
a. Inverted overprint 25.00
163 A64 2½c violet .80 .65
164 A64 3c rose ('18) .80 .65
165 A64 3c dull ultra ('25) .45 .35
166 A64 3½c lt grn ('18) .55 .50
167 A64 4c lt grn ('19) .55 .50
168 A64 4c orange ('30) .55 .50
169 A64 5c dp blue .80 .65
170 A64 5c yel brn ('18) .75 .65
171 A64 5c ol brn ('23) .55 .50
172 A64 5c blk brn ('30) 4.00 3.25
173 A64 6c dull rose ('20) .55 .50
174 A64 6c choc ('25) .55 .50
175 A64 6c red brn ('31) .40 *.30*
176 A64 7½c yel brn 6.75 3.75
177 A64 7½c dp bl ('18) 1.90 1.75
a. Perf 12x11½ 75.00 50.00
178 A64 8c slate ('13) .80 .70
179 A64 8c bl grn ('22) .80 .55
180 A64 8c orange ('25) 1.00 .95
181 A64 10c org brn .55 .45
182 A64 12c bl gray ('20) 2.75 1.75
183 A64 12c dp grn ('22) .90 .75
184 A64 13½c chlky bl ('20) 2.75 *1.90*
185 A64 14c dk bl, *yel* ('20) 2.25 *1.90*
186 A64 15c plum ('13) .85 .65
187 A64 15c blk (R) ('23) .55 .50
188 A64 16c brt ultra ('24) .95 .90
189 A64 16c dp bl ('30) 2.75 *1.90*
190 A64 20c vio brn, *grn* ('13) 12.50 7.00
191 A64 20c choc ('20) .90 .75
192 A64 20c dp grn ('23) 1.25 .95
a. Double overprint 22.50 22.50
193 A64 20c gray ('24) .80 .60
194 A64 24c grnsh bl ('21) .90 .55
195 A64 25c salmon ('23) .70 .50
196 A64 30c brn, *pink* ('13) 80.00 60.00
197 A64 30c brn, *yel* ('19) 2.25 1.90
198 A64 30c gray brn ('21) 1.90 1.60
199 A64 32c dp grn ('25) 2.75 2.40
200 A64 36c red ('21) .85 .65
201 A64 40c dp blue ('23) 1.00 .70
202 A64 40c blk brn ('24) 1.90 1.00
203 A64 40c brt grn ('30) 1.50 .75
204 A64 48c brt rose ('24) 5.00 3.00
205 A64 48c dull pink ('31) 3.50 3.00
206 A64 50c org, *sal* ('13) 6.50 2.75
207 A64 50c yellow ('23) 1.90 1.50
208 A64 50c bister ('30) 4.75 3.50
209 A64 50c red brn ('31) 4.75 3.50
210 A64 60c blue ('21) 1.90 1.50
211 A64 64c pale ultra ('24) 5.00 2.25
212 A64 64c brown rose ('31) 4.75 3.50
213 A64 75c dull rose ('23) 5.00 4.00

214	A64	75c car rose ('30)	4.75	3.50
215	A64	80c dull rose ('21)	2.50	2.10
216	A64	80c violet ('24)	2.50	1.90
217	A64	80c dk grn ('31)	4.75	3.00
218	A64	90c chlky bl ('21)	2.50	2.10
219	A64	96c dp rose ('26)	7.50	3.50
220	A64	1e dp grn, *bl*	7.00	6.00
221	A64	1e violet ('21)	2.50	2.10
222	A64	1e gray vio ('24)	3.75	3.25
223	A64	1e brn lake ('30)	40.00	27.50
224	A64	1.10e yel brn ('21)	2.75	2.10
225	A64	1.20e yel grn ('21)	3.25	2.10
226	A64	1.20e buff ('24)	8.25	6.00
227	A64	1.25e dk blue ('30)	2.75	2.25
228	A64	1.50e blk vio ('23)	9.75	6.75
229	A64	1.50e lilac ('25)	8.50	6.75
230	A64	1.60e dp bl ('25)	8.50	7.00
231	A64	2e slate grn ('21)	10.00	6.50
232	A64	2.40e apple grn ('26)	72.50	50.00
233	A64	3e lil pink ('26)	82.50	50.00
234	A64	3.20e gray grn ('25)	9.75	9.50
235	A64	5e emer ('24)	19.00	10.00
236	A64	10e pink ('24)	50.00	27.50
237	A64	20e pale turq ('25)	125.00	82.50
		Nos. 155-237 (83)	685.10	464.10

For same overprint on surcharged stamps see Nos. 300-306. For same design without imprint see Nos. 307-313.

Castello-Branco Issue

Stamps of Portugal, 1925, Overprinted in Black or Red

1925, Mar. 29 ***Perf. 12½***

238	A73	2c orange	.20	.20
239	A73	3c green	.20	.20
240	A73	4c ultra (R)	.20	.20
241	A73	5c scarlet	.20	.20
242	A74	10c pale blue	.20	.20
243	A74	16c red orange	.40	.30
244	A75	25c car rose	.40	.30
245	A74	32c green	.50	.50
246	A75	40c grn & blk (R)	.50	.50
247	A74	48c red brn	1.10	1.10
248	A76	50c blue green	1.10	1.00
249	A76	64c orange brn	1.10	1.00
250	A76	75c gray blk (R)	1.10	1.00
251	A75	80c brown	1.10	1.00
252	A76	96c car rose	1.40	1.10
253	A77	1.50e dk bl, *bl* (R)	1.40	1.10
254	A75	1.60e indigo (R)	1.50	1.40
255	A77	2e dk grn, *grn* (R)	2.50	2.10
256	A77	2.40e red, *org*	3.25	2.40
257	A77	3.20e blk, *grn* (R)	6.00	5.25
		Nos. 238-257 (20)	24.35	21.05

First Independence Issue

Stamps of Portugal, 1926, Overprinted in Red

1926, Aug. 13 ***Perf. 14, 14½***

Center in Black

258	A79	2c orange	.35	.35
259	A80	3c ultra	.35	.35
260	A79	4c yellow grn	.35	.35
261	A80	5c black brn	.35	.35
262	A79	6c ocher	.35	.35
263	A80	15c dk green	.75	.70
264	A81	20c dull violet	.75	.70
265	A82	25c scarlet	.75	.70
266	A81	32c deep green	.75	.70
267	A82	40c yellow brn	.75	.70
268	A82	50c olive bis	1.60	1.60
269	A82	75c red brown	1.75	1.75
270	A83	1e black violet	2.10	2.10
271	A84	4.50e olive green	8.75	8.75
		Nos. 258-271 (14)	19.70	19.45

The use of these stamps instead of those of the regular issue was obligatory on Aug. 13th and 14th, Nov. 30th and Dec. 1st, 1926.

Second Independence Issue

Same Overprint on Stamps of Portugal, 1927, in Red

1927, Nov. 29

Center in Black

272	A86	2c lt brown	.30	.30
273	A87	3c ultra	.30	.30
274	A86	4c orange	.30	.30
275	A88	5c dk brown	.30	.30
276	A89	6c orange brn	.30	.30
277	A87	15c black brn	.30	.30
278	A86	25c gray	1.25	1.25
279	A89	32c blue grn	1.25	1.25
280	A90	40c yellow grn	.75	.75
281	A90	96c red	3.25	3.25
282	A88	1.60e myrtle grn	3.25	3.25
283	A91	4.50e bister	9.00	8.75
		Nos. 272-283 (12)	20.55	20.30

Third Independence Issue

Same Overprint on Stamps of Portugal, 1928, in Red

1928, Nov. 27

Center in Black

284	A93	2c lt blue	.30	.30
285	A94	3c lt green	.30	.30
286	A95	4c lake	.30	.30
287	A96	5c olive grn	.30	.30
288	A97	6c orange brn	.30	.30
289	A94	15c slate	.65	.60
290	A95	16c dk violet	.75	.75
291	A93	25c ultra	.75	.75
292	A97	32c dk green	.80	.80
293	A96	40c olive brn	.80	.80
294	A95	50c red orange	1.75	1.75
295	A94	80c lt gray	1.75	1.75
296	A97	96c carmine	3.00	3.00
297	A96	1e claret	3.00	3.00
298	A93	1.60e dk blue	3.00	3.00
299	A98	4.50e yellow	8.75	8.50
		Nos. 284-299 (16)	26.50	26.20

A31

A32

1929-30 ***Perf. 12x11½, 15x14***

300	A31	4c on 25c pink ('30)	.75	.75
301	A31	4c on 60c dp blue	1.40	1.40
302	A31	10c on 25c pink	1.50	1.50
303	A31	12c on 25c pink	1.40	1.40
304	A31	15c on 25c pink	1.40	1.40
305	A31	20c on 25c pink	2.50	2.40
306	A31	40c on 1.10e yel brn	5.00	4.75
		Nos. 300-306 (7)	13.95	13.60

Black or Red Overprint

1930 ***Perf. 14***

Without Imprint at Foot

307	A32	4c orange	.90	.70
308	A32	5c dp brown	3.00	2.75
309	A32	10c vermilion	1.50	1.10
310	A32	15c black (R)	1.50	1.10
311	A32	40c brt green	1.40	.90
312	A32	80c violet	15.00	12.00
313	A32	1.60e dk blue	4.00	1.75
		Nos. 307-313 (7)	27.30	20.30

POSTAGE DUE STAMPS

D2

D3

Portugal Nos. J7-J13 Overprinted in Black

1904 **Unwmk.** ***Perf. 12***

J1	D2	5r brown	1.25	1.10
J2	D2	10r orange	1.40	1.10
J3	D2	20r lilac	2.25	1.10
J4	D2	30r gray green	2.25	1.75
a.		Double overprint		
J5	D2	40r gray violet	4.00	2.40
J6	D2	50r carmine	6.75	4.50
J7	D2	100r dull blue	8.50	8.25
		Nos. J1-J7 (7)	26.40	20.20

Same Overprinted in Carmine or Green (Portugal Nos. J14-J20)

1911

J8	D2	5r brown	.75	.65
J9	D2	10r orange	.75	.65
J10	D2	20r lilac	.95	.85
J11	D2	30r gray green	.95	.85
J12	D2	40r gray violet	1.50	1.10
J13	D2	50r carmine (G)	7.75	7.50
J14	D2	100r dull blue	2.75	2.75
		Nos. J8-J14 (7)	15.40	14.35

Portugal Nos. J21-J27 Overprinted in Black

1918

J15	D3	½c brown	.75	.75
a.		Inverted overprint	6.00	
b.		Double overprint	6.00	
J16	D3	1c orange	.75	.75
a.		Inverted overprint	6.00	
b.		Double overprint	6.00	
J17	D3	2c red lilac	.95	.85
a.		Inverted overprint	4.00	
b.		Double overprint	6.00	
J18	D3	3c green	.75	.75
a.		Inverted overprint	6.00	
b.		Double overprint	6.00	
J19	D3	4c gray	.75	.75
a.		Inverted overprint	6.00	
b.		Double overprint	6.00	
J20	D3	5c rose	.75	.75
b.		Double overprint	6.00	
J21	D3	10c dark blue	.75	.75
		Nos. J15-J21 (7)	5.45	5.35

Stamps and Type of Portugal Postage Dues, 1921-27, Overprinted in Black

1922-24 ***Perf. 11½x12***

J30	D3	½c gray green ('23)	.35	.35
J31	D3	1c gray green ('23)	.55	.45
J32	D3	2c gray green ('23)	.55	.45
J33	D3	3c gray green ('24)	.90	.45
J34	D3	8c gray green ('24)	.90	.45
J35	D3	10c gray green ('24)	.90	.45
J36	D3	12c gray green ('24)	.90	.45
J37	D3	16c gray green ('24)	.95	.45
J38	D3	20c gray green	.95	.45
J39	D3	24c gray green	.95	.45
J40	D3	32c gray green ('24)	.95	.45
J41	D3	36c gray green	.95	.60
J42	D3	40c gray green ('24)	.95	.60
J43	D3	48c gray green ('24)	.95	.60
J44	D3	50c gray green	.95	.60
J45	D3	60c gray green	1.00	.70
J46	D3	72c gray green	1.00	.70
J47	D3	80c gray green ('24)	5.00	4.25
J48	D3	1.20e gray green	5.75	4.75
		Nos. J30-J48 (19)	25.40	17.65

NEWSPAPER STAMPS

Newspaper Stamps of Portugal, Nos. P1, P1a, Overprinted Types c & d in Black or Red and:

N3

Perf. 12½, 13½ (#P4)

1876-88 **Unwmk.**

P1	N1	2½r (c) olive	13.00	5.50
a.		Inverted overprint		
b.		Perf 13½	8.00	3.50
P2	N1	2½r (d) olive ('82)	5.75	1.90
a.		Inverted overprint	—	—
b.		Double overprint	—	—
c.		Perf 13½	3.00	1.00
d.		2½r emerald green	3.00	1.00
e.		As "d," perf 13½	3.00	1.00
f.		As "d," perf 11½	20.00	3.00
g.		As "d," ribbed paper	3.00	1.00
P3	N3	2r black ('85)	6.00	3.00
a.		Inverted overprint	—	
b.		Double overprint, one inverted	—	
c.		Perf 13½	3.00	1.50
P4	N1	2½r (d) bister ('82)	5.75	1.90
a.		Double overprint	9.00	
b.		Perf 11½	20.00	3.00
c.		Perf 13½, ribbed paper	3.00	1.00
d.		Perf 11½, enamel paper	3.00	1.00
P5	N3	2r black (R) ('88)	19.00	16.00
a.		Perf 13½	10.00	6.00
		Nos. P1-P5 (5)	49.50	28.30

Reprints of the newspaper stamps have the same papers, gum and perforations as reprints of the regular issues. Value $2 each.

PARCEL POST STAMPS

Portugal Nos. Q1-Q17 Overprinted Like Nos. 155-237 in Black or Red

1921-22 **Unwmk.** ***Perf. 12***

Q1	PP1	1c lilac brown	.50	.45
a.		Inverted overprint	6.00	
Q2	PP1	2c orange	.50	.45
a.		Inverted overprint	6.00	
Q3	PP1	5c light brown	.50	.45
a.		Inverted overprint	6.00	
b.		Double overprint	6.00	
Q4	PP1	10c red brown	.75	.45
a.		Inverted overprint	6.00	
b.		Double overprint	6.00	
Q5	PP1	20c gray blue	.75	.45
a.		Inverted overprint	6.00	
b.		Double overprint	6.00	
Q6	PP1	40c carmine	.75	.45
a.		Double overprint	8.00	
Q7	PP1	50c black (R)	1.00	*1.90*
Q8	PP1	60c dark blue (R)	1.00	*1.90*
Q9	PP1	70c gray brown	2.50	1.25
a.		Double overprint	6.00	
Q10	PP1	80c ultra	2.50	1.25
Q11	PP1	90c light violet	2.50	1.25
Q12	PP1	1e light green	2.50	1.25
Q13	PP1	2e pale lilac	4.25	3.50
Q14	PP1	3e olive	7.75	3.75
Q15	PP1	4e ultra	9.00	3.75
Q16	PP1	5e gray	9.50	7.25
Q17	PP1	10e chocolate	40.00	21.00
		Nos. Q1-Q17 (17)	86.25	50.75

POSTAL TAX STAMPS

These stamps represent a special fee for the delivery of postal matter on certain days in the year. The money derived from their sale is applied to works of public charity.

Nos. 114 and 157 Overprinted in Carmine

1911-13 **Unwmk.** ***Perf. 14x15***

RA1	A29	10r dark green	1.50	1.10

The 20r of this type was for use on telegrams. Value $2.25 unused, $1.90 used.

Perf. 15x14

RA2	A30	1c deep green	5.00	3.75

The 2c of this type was for use on telegrams. Value $7.00 unused, $5.00 used.

Postal Tax Stamp of Portugal, No. RA4, Overprinted Like Nos. 155-237 in Black

1915 ***Perf. 12***

RA3	PT2	1c carmine	.65	.35

The 2c of this type was for use on telegrams. Value $1.10 unused, 85c used.

Postal Tax Stamp of 1915 Surcharged

1924

RA4	PT1	15c on 1c rose	1.10	*.90*

The 30c on 2c of this type was for use on telegrams. Value $3.00 unused, $1.90 used.

Comrades of the Great War Issue

Postal Tax Stamps of Portugal, 1925, Overprinted

1925, Apr. 8 *Perf. 11*

RA5	PT3	10c brown	1.10	1.10
RA6	PT3	10c green	1.10	1.10
RA7	PT3	10c rose	1.10	1.10
RA8	PT3	10c ultra	1.10	1.10
		Nos. RA5-RA8 (4)	4.40	4.40

The use of Nos. RA5-RA11 in addition to the regular postage was compulsory on certain days. If the tax represented by these stamps was not prepaid, it was collected by means of Postal Tax Due Stamps.

Pombal Issue

Common Design Types

1925 *Perf. 12½*

RA9	CD28	20c dp grn & blk	1.10	1.10
RA10	CD29	20c dp grn & blk	1.10	1.10
RA11	CD30	20c dp grn & blk	1.10	1.10
		Nos. RA9-RA11 (3)	3.30	3.30

POSTAL TAX DUE STAMPS

Postal Tax Due Stamp of Portugal Overprinted like Nos. RA5-RA8

1925, Apr. 8 Unwmk. *Perf. 11x11½*

RAJ1	PTD1	20c brown orange	1.10	.95

See note after No. RA8.

Pombal Issue

Common Design Types

1925, May 8 *Perf. 12½*

RAJ2	CD28	40c dp grn & blk	1.10	*1.10*
RAJ3	CD29	40c dp grn & blk	1.10	*1.10*
RAJ4	CD30	40c dp grn & blk	1.10	*1.10*
		Nos. RAJ2-RAJ4 (3)	3.30	*3.30*

See note after No. RA8.

BAHAMAS

bə-'hä-mə

LOCATION — A group of about 700 islands and 2,000 rocks in the West Indies, off the coast of Florida. Only 30 islands are inhabited.
GOVT. — British Colony
AREA — 5,353 sq. mi.
POP. — 209,505 (1980)
CAPITAL — Nassau

The principal island, on which the capital is located, is New Providence.

12 Pence = 1 Shilling
20 Shillings = 1 Pound

Catalogue values for unused stamps in this country are for Never Hinged items, beginning with Scott 130.

PRE-STAMP POSTAL MARKINGS

Crowned Circle handstamp type III is pictured in the Crowned Circle Handstamps and Great Britain Used Abroad section.

Nassau

1846-58

A1 III "Bahamas" crowned circle handstamp in red, on cover 2,600.

This handstamp, in black, was used from 1899-1935 denoting payment of postage for official mail.

STAMPS OF GREAT BRITAIN USED IN BAHAMAS

Numeral cancellation type A is pictured in the Crowned Circle Handstamps and Great Britain Used Abroad section.

1858-60

A05 (Nassau)

A2	A	1p rose red (#20)	2,600.
A3	A	2p blue (#29, P8)	1,500.
a.		Plate 7	1,500.
A4	A	4p rose (#26)	525.
A5	A	6p lilac (#27)	400.
A6	A	1sh green (#28)	2,600.

Values for unused stamps are for examples with original gum as defined in the catalogue introduction. Very fine examples of Nos. 2-26 will have perforations touching the design or frameline on at least one side due to the narrow spacing of the stamps on the plates. Stamps with perfs clear of the design or framelines on all four sides are extremely scarce and will command higher prices.

Pen cancellations usually indicate revenue use. Such stamps sell for much less than postally canceled copies. Beware of stamps with revenue or pen cancellations removed and forged postal cancellations added.

Queen Victoria
A1 A2

1859-60 Unwmk. Engr. *Imperf.*

1	A1	1p dull lake, thin paper ('60)	70.00	*1,700.*
a.		1p reddish lake, thick paper	*5,500.*	*2,600.*
b.		1p brownish lake, thick paper	*5,500.*	*2,600.*
		On cover		*17,500.*
c.		As "b," thin paper	*250.*	—

Most unused copies of #1 are remainders, and false cancellations are plentiful.

Stamps with pen cancellations may be postally used in inter-island mail. Certificates of authenticity are recommended.

A mint block of 12 stamps of the 1 penny reddish lake (Scott No. 1a) sold for the equivalent of U.S. $42,060 in a London auction in 1999.

A cover bearing one example of the 1 penny brownish lake (Scott No. 1b) sold for the equivalent of U.S. $16,460 in a London auction in 1999.

1861 *Rough Perf. 14 to 16*

2	A1	1p lake	925.	375.
a.		Clean-cut perf. ('60)	5,750.	800.
3	A2	4p dull rose	1,600.	475.
a.		Imperf. between, pair	*32,500.*	
4	A2	6p gray lilac	4,500.	700.
a.		Pale lilac	3,400.	575.

No. 2 exists perf 11 to 12½. This is a trial perforation by Perkins, Bacon and was not sent to the colony. Value, $2,600.

A mint block of 10 stamps of the 4 pence dull rose (Scott No. 3) sold for the equivalent of U.S. $34,750 in a London auction in 1999.

A mint block of 12 stamps of the 6 pence pale lilac (Scott No. 4a) sold for the equivalent of U.S. $40,230 in a London auction in 1999.

1862 *Perf. 11½, 12*

5	A1	1p lake	1,150.	200.
a.		Pair, imperf. between	*5,500.*	
b.		1p carmine lake	1,500.	225.
c.		Perf. 11½x11 or 12x11	2,600.	1,100.
d.		As "b," perf. 11½x11 or 12x11	2,300.	975.
6	A2	4p dull rose	3,750.	475.
a.		Perf. 11½x11 or 12x11	18,500.	2,050.
7	A2	6p gray violet	11,000.	575.
a.		Perf. 11½x11 or 12x11	19,500.	2,050.

No. 5a was not issued in the Bahamas. It is unique and faulty.

A mint example of the 6 pence gray violet (Scott No. 7) sold for the equivalent of U.S. $10,250 in a London auction in 1999.

Perf. 13

8	A1	1p brown lake	850.	150.
a.		1p carmine lake	1,050.	190.
9	A2	4p rose	3,150.	450.
10	A2	6p gray violet	3,750.	550.
a.		6p dull violet	3,150.	525.

Queen Victoria — A3

1863-65 Typo. Wmk. 1 *Perf. 12½*

11	A1	1p lake	115.00	75.00
a.		1p brown lake	105.00	70.00
b.		1p rose lake	140.00	80.00
c.		1p rose red	75.00	55.00
d.		1p red	70.00	55.00
12	A1	1p vermilion	75.00	50.00
13	A2	4p rose	375.00	70.00
a.		4p rose lake	525.00	92.50
b.		4p bright rose	350.00	70.00
14	A2	6p dk violet	190.00	80.00
a.		6p violet	300.00	105.00
b.		6p rose lilac	*7,500.*	*3,500.*
c.		6p lilac	450.00	80.00
15	A3	1sh green ('65)	2,850.	350.00

For surcharge see No. 26.

1863-81 *Perf. 14*

16	A1	1p vermilion	57.50	20.00
17	A1	1p car lake (anil.)	1,500.	
18	A2	4p rose	425.00	50.00
a.		4p deep rose ('76)	500.00	50.00
b.		4p dull rose	1,750.	50.00
19	A3	1sh green ('80)	9.25	8.75
a.		1shp dark green	300.00	45.00

Some copies of No. 16 show a light aniline appearance and care should be taken not to confuse these with No. 17. All known used copies of No. 17 bear fiscal cancels.

1882-98 **Wmk. 2**

20	A1	1p vermilion	500.00	70.00
21	A2	4p rose	925.00	70.00
22	A3	1sh green	45.00	17.50
23	A3	1sh blue grn ('98)	40.00	30.00

Perf. 12

24	A1	1p vermilion	55.00	22.50
25	A2	4p rose	625.00	60.00

No. 14a Surcharged in Black

1883 Wmk. 1 *Perf. 12½*

26	A2	4p on 6p violet	625.	475.
a.		Inverted surcharge	*16,000.*	*10,000.*

The surcharge, being handstamped, is found in various positions. Counterfeit overprints exist.

A mint example of the stamp with inverted surcharge (Scott No. 26a) sold for the equivalent of U.S. $13,980 in a London auction in 1999.

Queen Victoria — A5

Queen's Staircase — A6

1884-90 Typo. Wmk. 2 *Perf. 14*

27	A5	1p carmine rose	9.00	3.25
a.		1p pale rose	90.00	15.00
b.		1p car (aniline)	3.50	*8.50*
28	A5	2½p ultra	12.50	3.00
a.		2½p dull blue	90.00	22.50
b.		2½p bright blue	50.00	8.50
29	A5	4p yellow	12.50	5.00
30	A5	6p violet	7.50	*32.50*
31	A5	5sh olive green	75.00	*87.50*
32	A5	£1 brown	325.00	*275.00*
		Revenue cancellation		*55.00*
		Nos. 27-32 (6)	441.50	*406.25*

Cleaned fiscally used examples of No. 32 are often found with forged postmarks of small post offices added, especially dated "AU 29 94."

1901-03 Engr. Wmk. 1

33	A6	1p carmine & blk	11.50	*4.00*
34	A6	5p org & blk ('03)	10.00	*55.00*
35	A6	2sh ultra & blk ('03)	32.50	*57.50*
36	A6	3sh green & blk ('03)	45.00	*70.00*
		Nos. 33-36 (4)	99.00	*186.50*
		Set, overprinted "SPECIMEN"	150.00	

See Nos. 48, 58-62, 71, 78, 81-82.

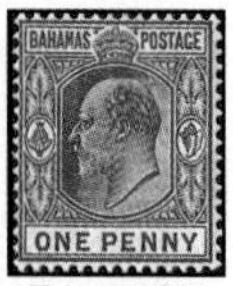

Edward VII
A7

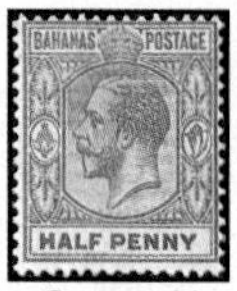

George V
A8

1902 Wmk. 2 Typo.

37	A7	1p carmine rose	2.00	3.25
38	A7	2½p ultra	8.50	1.75
39	A7	4p orange	20.00	*77.50*
a.		4p yellow ('10)	26.00	*80.00*
40	A7	6p bister brn	5.00	*25.00*
41	A7	1sh gray blk & car	26.00	*65.00*
a.		1sh brownish gray & carmine ('07)	26.00	*65.00*
42	A7	5sh violet & ultra	85.00	*100.00*
43	A7	£1 green & blk	300.00	*375.00*
		Nos. 38-43 (6)	444.50	*644.25*
		Set, overprinted "SPECIMEN"	325.00	

Beware of forged postmarks, especially dated "2 MAR 10."

1906-11 **Wmk. 3**

44	A7	½p green	5.75	4.00
		Overprinted "SPECIMEN"	62.50	
45	A7	1p car rose	32.50	1.75
46	A7	2½p ultra ('07)	32.50	32.50
47	A7	6p bister brn ('11)	30.00	*55.00*
		Nos. 44-47 (4)	100.75	*93.25*

1911-19 **Engr.**

48	A6	1p red & gray blk ('16)	6.00	3.00
a.		1p carmine & black ('11)	20.00	3.25
b.		1p carmine & gray black ('19)	8.50	6.75

For overprints see Nos. B1-B2.

1912-19 **Typo.**

49	A8	½p green	1.00	*11.00*
a.		½p yellow green	2.90	*17.00*
50	A8	1p car rose (aniline)	4.50	.45
b.		1p deep rose	9.25	2.50
c.		1p rose	12.50	3.50
d.		Inverted watermark	225.00	97.50
50A	A8	2p gray ('19)	3.00	*4.00*
51	A8	2½p ultra	6.00	*32.50*
a.		2½p deep blue	17.00	*42.50*
52	A8	4p orange	3.25	*17.00*
a.		4p orange yellow	6.25	*22.50*
53	A8	6p bister brown	2.25	*5.00*

Chalky Paper

54	A8	1sh black & car	2.25	*10.50*
a.		1sh jet black & carmine	16.00	*25.00*
55	A8	5sh violet & ultra	47.50	*80.00*
a.		5sh pale violet & deep blue	57.50	*85.00*
56	A8	£1 dull grn & blk	190.00	*350.00*
a.		£1 bright green & black	225.00	*375.00*
		Nos. 49-56 (9)	259.75	*510.45*
		Set, overprinted "SPECIMEN"	350.00	

1917-19 **Engr.**

58	A6	3p reddish pur, *buff*	6.00	4.00
a.		3p purple, *yellow*	6.25	*35.00*
59	A6	3p brown & blk ('19)	2.50	*3.00*
60	A6	5p violet & blk	3.25	*6.50*
61	A6	2sh ultra & black	35.00	*62.50*
62	A6	3sh green & black	75.00	62.50
		Nos. 58-62 (5)	121.75	*138.50*

Peace Commemorative Issue

King George V and Seal of Bahamas — A9

1920, Mar. 1 Engr. *Perf. 14*

65	A9	½p gray green	1.25	*6.25*
66	A9	1p deep red	3.25	1.10
67	A9	2p gray	3.25	*8.75*
68	A9	3p brown	3.25	*10.50*
69	A9	1sh dark green	20.00	*40.00*
		Nos. 65-69 (5)	31.00	*66.60*
		Set, overprinted "SPECIMEN"	190.00	

Types of 1901-12
Typo., Engr. (A6)

1921-34 **Wmk. 4**

70	A8	½p green ('24)	.60	.45
71	A6	1p car & black	1.10	*2.25*
72	A8	1p car rose	1.10	.20
73	A8	1½p fawn ('34)	8.00	1.25
74	A8	2p gray ('27)	1.75	*2.75*
75	A8	2½p ultra ('22)	1.10	*2.75*
76	A8	3p violet, *yel* ('31)	7.50	*19.00*
77	A8	4p yellow ('24)	1.75	*5.00*
78	A6	5p red vio & gray blk ('29)	5.00	*57.50*
79	A8	6p bister brn ('22)	.90	*1.75*
80	A8	1sh blk & red ('26)	3.25	*6.50*
81	A6	2sh ultra & blk ('22)	22.50	25.00
82	A6	3sh grn & blk ('24)	55.00	*75.00*
83	A8	5sh vio & ultra ('24)	40.00	*75.00*
84	A8	£1 grn & blk ('26)	200.00	*375.00*
		Nos. 70-84 (15)	349.55	*649.40*
		Set, ovptd/perf "SPECIMEN"	650.00	

The 3p, 1sh, 5sh and £1 are on chalky paper.

Seal of Bahamas — A10

1930, Jan. 2 **Engr.** ***Perf. 12***

85	A10	1p red & black	2.25	*3.25*
86	A10	3p dp brown & blk	4.50	*17.00*
87	A10	5p dk vio & blk	4.50	*17.00*
88	A10	2sh ultra & black	21.00	*57.50*
89	A10	3sh dp green & blk	47.50	*95.00*
		Nos. 85-89 (5)	79.75	*189.75*
		Set, perforated "SPECIMEN"	175.00	

The dates on the stamps commemorate important events in the history of the colony. The 1st British occupation was in 1629. The Bahamas were ceded to Great Britain in 1729 and a treaty of peace was signed by that country, France and Spain.

Type of 1930 Issue
Without Dates at Top

1931-46

90	A10	2sh ultra & black	11.50	5.00
a.		2sh ultra & slate purple	25.00	*32.50*
b.		2sh ind bl & slate purple	95.00	*45.00*
c.		2sh steel bl & slate pur	16.00	*2.50*
91	A10	3sh dp green & blk	9.00	5.25
a.		3sh deep grn & slate purple	32.50	30.00
b.		3sh deep grn & brownish blk	10.00	3.50
		Nos. 90a, 91a perf "SPECIMEN"	92.50	

Nos. 90a-91a are on thicker paper with yellowish gum, Later printings are on thinner white paper with colorless gum.

Issued: #90a, 91a, 7/14/31; #90b, 9/42; #90, 91b, 4/13/43; #90c 6/44; #91, 1946.

For overprints see Nos. 126-127.

Common Design Types
pictured following the introduction.

Silver Jubilee Issue
Common Design Type

1935, May 6 ***Perf. 13½x14***

92	CD301	1½p car & blue	1.25	*3.50*
93	CD301	2½p blue & brn	5.75	*10.50*
94	CD301	6p ol grn & lt bl	8.00	*15.00*
95	CD301	1sh brt vio & ind	8.00	*9.25*
		Nos. 92-95 (4)	23.00	*38.25*
		Set, never hinged	35.00	
		Set, perforated "SPECIMEN"	125.00	

Flamingos in Flight
A11

1935, May 22 ***Perf. 12½***

96	A11	8p car & ultra	7.00	3.75
		Never hinged	10.00	
		Perforated "SPECIMEN"	55.00	

Coronation Issue
Common Design Type

1937, May 12 ***Perf. 13½x14***

97	CD302	½p dp green	.20	.20
98	CD302	1½p brown	.25	1.25
99	CD302	2½p brt ultra	.40	1.25
		Nos. 97-99 (3)	.85	2.70
		Set, never hinged	1.10	
		Set, perforated "SPECIMEN"	70.00	

George VI — A12

Sea Gardens, Nassau
A13

Fort Charlotte
A14

Flamingos in Flight
A15

1938-46 **Typo.** **Wmk. 4** ***Perf. 14***

100	A12	½p green	.75	*1.60*
		Never hinged	1.10	
a.		½p bluish grn	1.10	*2.50*
		Never hinged	2.00	
b.		½p myrtle grn	4.00	*7.50*
		Never hinged	7.50	
101	A12	1p carmine	6.50	4.50
		Never hinged	9.75	
101A	A12	1p pale gray ('41)	.50	*.90*
		Never hinged	.70	
b.		1p olive gray	2.25	*3.75*
		Never hinged	3.75	
102	A12	1½p red brown	1.10	1.50
		Never hinged	1.75	
a.		1½p pale red brn	4.50	*2.90*
		Never hinged	7.50	
103	A12	2p gray	13.50	5.75
		Never hinged	21.00	
103B	A12	2p carmine ('41)	.75	.85
		Never hinged	1.10	
c.		"TWO PENCE" double		*8,500.*
d.		2p pale rose red	2.50	*3.75*
		Never hinged	3.75	
104	A12	2½p ultra	2.50	*1.90*
		Never hinged	3.75	
104A	A12	2½p lt violet ('43)	1.00	1.50
		Never hinged	1.40	
b.		"2½ PENNY" double	*2,750.*	—
		Never hinged	*3,750.*	
105	A12	3p lt violet	12.00	3.50
		Never hinged	18.00	
105A	A12	3p ultra ('43)	.45	*1.50*
		Never hinged	.70	
b.		3p bright ultra	3.00	*5.50*
		Never hinged	4.75	

Engr.
Perf. 12½

106	A13	4p red org & blue	.75	*1.25*
		Never hinged	1.10	
107	A14	6p blue & ol grn	.45	*1.25*
		Never hinged	.70	
108	A15	8p car & ultra	5.00	2.75
		Never hinged	7.75	

Typo.
Perf. 14

109	A12	10p yel org ('46)	2.00	.55
		Never hinged	2.90	

Ordinary Paper

110	A12	1sh black & bright red	9.00	1.00
		Never hinged	16.00	
a.		1sh gray blk & car, thick chalky paper	17.50	7.00
		Never hinged	26.00	
c.		1sh black & car	17.00	8.00
		Never hinged	25.00	
d.		1sh brownish gray & scar, thin chalky paper	250.00	75.00
		Never hinged	400.00	
e.		1sh pale brownish gray & crim	11.00	1.75
		Never hinged	16.00	
112	A12	5sh pur & ultra	18.00	14.00
		Never hinged	32.50	
a.		5sh lilac & blue	18.00	*17.00*
		Never hinged	27.50	
b.		5sh lilac & blue, thick chalky paper	140.00	110.00
		Never hinged	200.00	
c.		5sh reddish lil & bl, thin chalky paper	1,200.	575.00
		Never hinged	1,750.	
d.		5sh dull mauve & dp bl	65.00	62.50
		Never hinged	100.00	
e.		5sh brn pur & dp brt bl	27.50	12.50
		Never hinged	40.00	
113	A12	£1 bl grn & blk	45.00	*65.00*
		Never hinged	70.00	
a.		£1 dp gray grn & blk, thick chalky paper	200.00	160.00
		Never hinged	290.00	
b.		£1 gray grn & blk	100.00	*90.00*
		Never hinged	150.00	
		Nos. 100-113 (17)	119.25	*109.30*
		Set, never hinged	190.00	

See Nos. 154-156. For overprints see Nos. 116-125, 128-129.

No. 104 Surcharged in Black

1940, Nov. 28 ***Perf. 14***

115	A12	3p on 2½p ultra	1.10	*2.00*
		Never hinged	1.75	

Stamps of 1931-42 Overprinted in Black

1942, Oct. 12 ***Perf. 14, 12½, 12***

116	A12	½p green	.20	.60
		Never hinged	.35	
a.		Double overprint	800.00	
		Never hinged	1,250.	
117	A12	1p gray	.20	.60
		Never hinged	.35	
118	A12	1½p red brn	.30	.60
		Never hinged	.45	
119	A12	2p carmine	.35	.65
		Never hinged	.55	
120	A12	2½p ultra	.40	.65
		Never hinged	.55	
121	A12	3p ultra	.20	.65
		Never hinged	.35	
122	A13	4p red org & blue	.30	.85
		Never hinged	.45	
123	A14	6p blue & ol grn	.30	1.75
		Never hinged	.45	
124	A15	8p car & ultra	.75	.70
		Never hinged	1.75	
125	A12	1sh blk & car (#110c)	5.00	3.75
		Never hinged	8.00	
a.		On No. 110d	8.00	*7.50*
		Never hinged	12.50	
b.		On No. 110	4.50	*5.50*
		Never hinged	8.00	
126	A10	2sh dk ultra & blk	6.00	*10.50*
		Never hinged	9.25	
a.		On No. 90b	12.00	*21.00*
		Never hinged	17.50	
b.		On No. 90c	20.00	*30.00*
		Never hinged	30.00	
127	A10	3sh dp grn & sl pur(#91a)	5.00	*8.75*
		Never hinged	8.00	
a.		On No. 91b	30.00	*35.00*
		Never hinged	45.00	
128	A12	5sh lilac & ultra (#112a)	14.00	*14.00*
		Never hinged	23.00	
a.		On No. 112c	32.50	*19.00*
		Never hinged	47.50	
129	A12	£1 green & black	21.00	*27.50*
		Never hinged	35.00	
a.		On No. 113a	60.00	*80.00*
		Never hinged	92.50	
		Nos. 116-129 (14)	54.00	*71.55*
		Set, never hinged	87.50	
		Set, perforated "SPECIMEN"	525.00	

450th anniv. of the discovery of America by Columbus.

Nos. 125, 128-129 printed on chalky and ordinary paper.

Two printings of the basic stamps were overprinted, the first with dark gum, the second with white gum.

Catalogue values for unused stamps in this section, from this point to the end of the section, are for Never Hinged items.

Peace Issue
Common Design Type
Perf. 13½x14

1946, Nov. 11 **Engr.** **Wmk. 4**

130	CD303	1½p brown	.20	.35
131	CD303	3p deep blue	.20	.35
		Set, perforated "SPECIMEN"	70.00	

Infant Welfare Clinic
A16

Designs: 1p, Modern agriculture. 1½p, Sisal. 2p, Native straw work. 2½p, Modern dairying. 3p, Fishing fleet. 4p, Out island settlement. 6p, Tuna fishing. 8p, Paradise Beach. 10p, Modern hotel. 1sh, Yacht racing. 2sh, Water skiing. 3sh, Shipbuilding. 5sh, Modern transportation. 10sh, Modern salt production. £1, Parliament Building.

1948, Oct. 11 **Unwmk.** ***Perf. 12***

132	A16	½p orange	.35	.95
133	A16	1p olive green	.35	.35
134	A16	1½p olive bister	.40	.80
135	A16	2p vermilion	.35	.40
136	A16	2½p red brown	.70	.75
137	A16	3p brt ultra	.90	.90
138	A16	4p gray black	.65	.90
139	A16	6p emerald	1.90	.90
140	A16	8p violet	.75	.90
141	A16	10p rose car	.80	.75
142	A16	1sh olive brn	1.50	1.25
143	A16	2sh claret	6.25	*9.00*
144	A16	3sh brt blue	8.25	*9.00*
145	A16	5sh purple	9.00	6.50
146	A16	10sh dk gray	10.00	9.50
147	A16	£1 red orange	12.00	*13.50*
		Nos. 132-147 (16)	54.15	*56.35*

300th anniv., in 1947, of the settlement of the colony.

Silver Wedding Issue
Common Design Type
Perf. 14x14½

1948, Dec. 1 **Wmk. 4** **Photo.**

148	CD304	1½p red brown	.25	.25

Engr.; Name Typo.
Perf. 11½x11

149	CD305	£1 gray green	32.25	*45.00*

UPU Issue
Common Design Types
Engr.; Name Typo. on #151 & 152

1949, Oct. 10 ***Perf. 13½, 11x11½***

150	CD306	2½p violet	.30	*.35*
151	CD307	3p indigo	1.25	*1.50*
152	CD308	6p blue gray	.90	*1.25*
153	CD309	1sh rose car	1.50	1.50
		Nos. 150-153 (4)	3.95	4.60

George VI Type of 1938
Perf. 13½x14

1951-52 **Wmk. 4** **Typo.**

154	A12	½p claret ('52)	.80	*2.25*
a.		Wmk. 4a (error)	*3,750.*	
		Lightly hinged	2,500.	
155	A12	2p green	.90	.75
156	A12	3p rose red ('52)	.70	*2.75*
		Nos. 154-156 (3)	2.40	*5.75*

SEMI-POSTAL STAMPS

No. 48 Overprinted in Red

1917, May 18 **Wmk. 3** ***Perf. 14***

B1	A6	1p car & black	.40	*1.60*
		Overprinted "SPECIMEN"	75.00	

Type of 1911 Overprinted in Red

1919, Jan. 1

B2 A6 1p red & black .40 *2.25*
a. Double overprint *2,000.*
Overprinted "SPECIMEN" 62.50

This stamp was originally scheduled for release in 1918.

SPECIAL DELIVERY STAMPS

No. 34 Overprinted

1916 Wmk. 1 *Perf. 14*

E1 A6 5p orange & black 7.00 *45.00*
a. Double overprint *950.00 1,400.*
b. Inverted overprint *1,600. 1,600.*
c. Double ovpt., one invtd. *1,550. 1,500.*
d. Pair, one without overprint *25,000. 40,000.*

The No. E1 overprint exists in two types. Type I (illustrated) is much scarcer. Type II shows "SPECIAL" farther right, so that the letter "I" is slightly right of the vertical line of the "E" below it.

The first printing of 600 of no. E1 was sold in Canada from May 1, 1916, and under an agreement with the Canadian Post Office were used in combination with Canadian stamps and postmarked in Canada. Values for covers showing such use (canceled before December 13, 1916): from Toronto, $750; from Monrtreal, $800; from Ottawa, $1,200; from Winnipeg, $2,000.

Type of Regular Issue of 1903 Overprinted

1917, July 2 Wmk. 3

E2 A6 5p orange & black .80 *5.00*
Overprinted "SPECIMEN" 75.00

No. 60 Overprinted in Red

1918

E3 A6 5p violet & black .60 *1.75*
Overprinted "SPECIMEN" 75.00

WAR TAX STAMPS

Stamps of 1912-18 Overprinted

1918, Feb. 21 Wmk. 3 *Perf. 14*

MR1 A8 ½p green 9.00 *45.00*
a. Double overprint — —
b. Inverted overprint — —
MR2 A8 1p car rose 1.00 *1.00*
a. Double overprint — —
b. Inverted overprint — —
MR3 A6 3p brown, *yel* 3.75 *3.50*
a. Inverted overprint *1,250. 1,400.*
b. Double overprint *1,800. 2,000.*
MR4 A8 1sh black & red 110.00 *160.00*
a. Double overprint — —
Nos. MR1-MR4 (4) 123.75 *209.50*

Same Overprint on No. 48a

1918, July 10

MR5 A6 1p car & black 4.00 *5.50*
a. Double overprint *1,950. 2,050.*
b. Double ovpt., one invtd. *1,100.* —
c. Inverted overprint *1,750. 1,900.*

Nos. 49-50, 54 Overprinted in Black or Red

MR6 A8 ½p green 2.00 2.00
MR7 A8 1p car rose .65 .30
a. Watermarked sideways 675.00
MR8 A8 1sh black & red (R) 7.00 2.50
Nos. MR6-MR8 (3) 9.65 4.80
Set, overprinted "SPECIMEN" 115.00

Nos. 58-59 Overprinted

1918-19

MR9 A6 3p brown, *yel* .90 *3.25*
MR10 A6 3p brown & blk ('19) .90 *3.75*
Set, overprinted "SPECIMEN" 95.00

Nos. 49-50, 54 Overprinted in Red or Black

1919, July 14

MR11 A8 ½p green (R) .30 *1.25*
MR12 A8 1p car rose 1.10 *1.40*
MR13 A8 1sh black & red (R) 10.00 *24.00*
Nos. MR11-MR13 (3) 11.40 *26.65*

No. 59 Overprinted

MR14 A6 3p brown & black .80 *5.75*
Nos. MR11-MR14, overprinted "SPECIMEN" 115.00

BAHRAIN

bä-'rān

LOCATION — An archipelago in the Persian Gulf, including the islands of Bahrain, Muharraq, Sitra, Nebi Saleh, Kasasifeh and Arad.
GOVT. — British-protected territory
AREA — 255 sq. mi.
POP. — 350,798 (1981)
CAPITAL — Manama

12 Pies = 1 Anna
16 Annas = 1 Rupee

Catalogue values for unused stamps in this country are for Never Hinged items, beginning with Scott 62 in the regular postage section.

Indian Postal Administration

Stamps of India, 1926-32, Overprinted in Black

a

Wmk. Multiple Stars (196)

1933, Aug. 10 *Perf. 14*

1 A46 3p gray 4.00 .50
2 A47 ½a green 8.50 3.75
3 A68 9p dark green 4.25 3.25
4 A48 1a dark brown 8.00 2.75
5 A69 1a3p violet 9.00 2.50
6 A60 2a vermilion 11.50 19.00
7 A51 3a blue 21.00 *62.50*
8 A70 3a6p deep blue 4.25 .40
9 A61 4a olive green 20.00 *62.50*
10 A54 8a red violet 6.75 .40
11 A55 12a claret 8.50 1.50

Overprinted in Black

b

12 A56 1r green & brown 18.00 10.00
13 A56 2r brn org & car rose 32.50 *40.00*
14 A56 5r dk violet & ultra 150.00 *160.00*
Nos. 1-14 (14) 306.25 *369.05*

Stamps of India, 1926-32, Overprinted Type "a" in Black

1934

15 A72 1a dark brown 11.25 .45
a. Booklet, containing 16 #15 in four blocks of 4 *1,350.*
16 A51 3a carmine rose 5.50 .55
17 A52 4a olive green 5.75 .45
Nos. 15-17 (3) 22.50 1.45

The cover of No. 15a is red and black on tan, with Mysore Sandal Soup advertisement on front.

India Nos. 138, 111, 111a Overprinted Type "a" in Black

1935-37 *Perf. 13½x14, 14*

18 A71 ½a green 5.00 2.00
19 A49 2a vermilion 47.50 8.50
a. Small die ('37) 85.00 .30

India Stamps of 1937 Overprinted Type "a" in Black

1938-41 Wmk. 196 *Perf. 13½x14*

20 A80 3p slate 9.00 4.75
Never hinged 18.00
21 A80 ½a brown 4.00 .20
Never hinged 8.00
22 A80 9p green 5.25 2.75
Never hinged 10.25
23 A80 1a carmine 4.75 .20
Never hinged 9.50
24 A81 2a scarlet 3.75 2.75
Never hinged 5.75
26 A81 3a yel grn ('41) 9.00 7.50
Never hinged 13.50
27 A81 3a6p ultra 4.00 *4.50*
Never hinged 6.75
28 A81 4a dk brn ('41) 110.00 80.00
Never hinged 150.00
30 A81 8a bl vio ('40) 125.00 40.00
Never hinged 200.00
31 A81 12a car lake ('40) 95.00 50.00
Never hinged 140.00

Overprinted Type "b" in Black

32 A82 1r brn & slate 2.50 2.00
Never hinged 5.00
33 A82 2r dk brn & dk vio 9.00 9.00
Never hinged 15.00
34 A82 5r dp ultra & dk grn 12.50 15.00
Never hinged 17.00
35 A82 10r rose car & dk vio ('41) 50.00 42.50
Never hinged 75.00
36 A82 15r dk grn & dk brn ('41) 110.00 175.00
Never hinged 175.00
37 A82 25r dk vio & bl vio ('41) 80.00 *95.00*
Never hinged 120.00
Nos. 20-37 (16) 633.75 531.15
Set, never hinged 960.00

India Stamps of 1941-43 Overprinted Type "a" in Black

1942-44 Wmk. 196 *Perf. 13½x14*

38 A83 3p slate 1.40 2.25
Never hinged 2.75
39 A83 ½a rose vio ('44) 3.25 2.75
Never hinged 4.75
40 A83 9p lt green ('43) 10.00 20.00
Never hinged 15.00
41 A83 1a car rose ('44) 3.25 .85
Never hinged 6.25
42 A84 1a3p bister ('43) 6.50 21.00
Never hinged 9.50
43 A84 1½a dk pur ('43) 4.50 8.00
Never hinged 6.75
45 A84 2a scarlet ('43) 3.75 1.75
Never hinged 6.75
46 A84 3a violet ('43) 12.50 7.50
Never hinged 20.00
47 A84 3½a ultra 3.25 *90.00*
Never hinged 5.50
48 A85 4a chocolate 2.00 2.25
Never hinged 4.00
49 A85 6a peacock blue 10.00 *11.50*
Never hinged 17.00
50 A85 8a blue vio ('43) 3.50 4.00
Never hinged 6.25
51 A85 12a car lake 5.50 5.75
Never hinged 9.75
Nos. 38-51 (13) 69.40 *177.60*
Set, never hinged 115.00

British Postal Administration

See Oman (Muscat) for similar stamps with surcharge of new value only.

Great Britain Nos. 258 to 263, 243 and 248 Surcharged in Black

c

1948-49 Wmk. 251 *Perf. 14½x14*

52 A101 ½a on ½p green .35 *1.40*
Never hinged .55
53 A101 1a on 1p vermilion .35 *2.50*
Never hinged .55
54 A101 1½a on 1½p lt red brn .35 *3.50*
Never hinged .55
55 A101 2a on 2p lt orange .35 .20
Never hinged .55
56 A101 2½a on 2½p ultra .45 *4.25*
Never hinged .55
57 A101 3a on 3p violet .35 .20
Never hinged .55
58 A102 6a on 6p rose lilac .35 .20
Never hinged .55
59 A103 1r on 1sh brown 1.00 .20
Never hinged 1.40

Great Britain Nos. 249A, 250 and 251A Surcharged in Black

Wmk. 259 *Perf. 14*

60 A104 2r on 2sh6p yel grn 4.50 5.25
Never hinged 6.25
61 A104 5r on 5sh dull red 4.00 5.25
Never hinged 6.25
61A A105 10r on 10sh ultra 55.00 57.50
Never hinged 80.00
Nos. 52-61A (11) 67.05 80.45
Set, never hinged 100.00

Surcharge bars at bottom on No. 61A.
Issued: 10r, 7/4/49; others, 4/1/48.

Catalogue values for unused stamps in this section, from this point to the end of the section, are for Never Hinged items.

Silver Wedding Issue

Great Britain Nos. 267 and 268 Surcharged in Black

Perf. 14½x14, 14x14½

1948, Apr. 26 Wmk. 251

62 A109 2½a on 2½p 1.10 1.75
63 A110 15r on £1 37.50 *55.00*

Three bars obliterate the original denomination on No. 63.

Olympic Issue

Great Britain Nos. 271 to 274 Surcharged "BAHRAIN" and New Value in Black

1948, July 29 *Perf. 14½x14*

64 A113 2½a on 2½p brt ultra 1.10 *4.00*
a. Double surcharge *1,750. 2,500.*
65 A114 3a on 3p dp vio 1.10 *3.75*

66	A115	6a on 6p red vio	1.75	*3.75*
67	A116	1r on 1sh dk brn	2.75	*3.75*
		Nos. 64-67 (4)	6.70	*15.25*

A square of dots obliterates the original denomination on No. 67.

UPU Issue

Great Britain Nos. 276 to 279 Surcharged "BAHRAIN," New Value and Square of Dots in Black

1949, Oct. 10 Photo. *Perf. 14½x14*

68	A117	2½a on 2½p brt ultra	.65	*2.50*
69	A118	3a on 3p brt vio	.80	*4.00*
70	A119	6a on 6p red vio	.75	*3.25*
71	A120	1r on 1sh brown	1.50	2.50
		Nos. 68-71 (4)	3.70	*12.25*

Great Britain Nos. 280-285 Surcharged Type "c" in Black

1950-51 Wmk. 251

72	A101	½a on ½p lt org	2.75	2.75
73	A101	1a on 1p ultra	3.25	.30
74	A101	1½a on 1½p green	3.25	*14.50*
75	A101	2a on 2p lt red brn	1.75	.30
76	A101	2½a on 2½p ver	3.50	*14.50*
77	A102	4a on 4p ultra	3.75	1.75

Great Britain Nos. 286-288 Surcharged in Black

Three types of surcharge on No. 78: Type I, "2" level with "RUPEES;" Type II, "2" raised higher than "RUPEES," 15mm between "BAHRAIN" and "2 RUPEES;" Type III, as type II, but 16mm between "BAHRAIN" and "2 RUPEES."

Perf. 11x12

Wmk. 259

78	A121	2r on 2sh6p green, type I ('51)	30.00	11.50
a.		2r on 2sh6p, type II ('53)	90.00	45.00
b.		2r on 2sh6p, type III ('55)	925.00	105.00
79	A121	5r on 5sh dl red	16.00	6.00
80	A122	10r on 10sh ultra	35.00	9.50
		Nos. 72-80 (9)	99.25	*61.10*

Longer bars, at lower right, on No. 80.

Issued: 4a, Nov. 2, 1950; others, May 3, 1951.

Stamps of Great Britain, 1952-54, Surcharged "BAHRAIN" and New Value in Black or Dark Blue

1952-54 Wmk. 298 *Perf. 14½x14*

81	A126	½a on ½p red org ('53)	.25	.25
a.		"½" omitted	175.00	*200.00*
82	A126	1a on 1p ultra	.25	.20
83	A126	1½a on 1½p grn	.25	.25
84	A126	2a on 2p red brn	.25	.25
85	A127	2½a on 2½p scar	.55	*1.00*
86	A127	3a on 3p dk pur (Dk Bl)	1.00	.25
87	A128	4a on 4p ultra	5.00	.50
88	A129	6a on 6p lil rose	3.50	.45
89	A132	12a on 1sh3p dk grn	3.50	.75
90	A131	1r on 1sh6p dk bl	3.50	1.00
		Nos. 81-90 (10)	18.05	4.90

Issued: #83, 85, 12/5; #81-82, 84, 8/31/53; #87, 89-90, 11/2/53; #86, 88, 1/18/54.

BANGKOK

'baŋ‚käk

LOCATION — Capital of Siam (Thailand).

Stamps were issued by Great Britain under rights obtained in the treaty of 1855. These were in use until July 1, 1885, when the stamps of Siam were designated as the only official postage stamps to be used in the kingdom.

100 Cents = 1 Dollar

STAMPS OF STRAITS SETTLEMENTS USED IN BANGKOK

Oval postmark: "BRITISH CONSULATE BANGKOK" with Royal Arms in center

1877-82

A1	2c bister brown (#10)	450.00
A2	4c rose (#11)	450.00
A3	6c violet (#12)	500.00
A4	8c orange yellow (#13)	450.00
A5	10c on 30c claret (#22)	1,150.
A6	10c on 30c claret (#23)	1,150.
A8	12c blue (#14)	575.00

Excellent counterfeits of Nos. 1-22 are plentiful.

Stamps of Straits Settlements Overprinted in Black

1882 Wmk. 1 *Perf. 14*

1	A2	2c brown	*4,000.*	*1,750.*
2	A2	4c rose	*3,750.*	*1,500.*
b.		Double overprint		*8,750.*
3	A6	5c brown violet	*400.00*	*425.00*
4	A2	6c violet	*260.00*	*140.00*
5	A3	8c yel orange	*2,750.*	260.00
6	A7	10c slate	*450.00*	*140.00*
7	A3	12c blue	*1,100.*	*550.00*
8	A3	24c green	*800.00*	*175.00*
9	A4	30c claret	*50,000.*	*35,000.*
10	A5	96c olive gray	*8,500.*	*3,500.*

See note after No. 20.

1882-83 Wmk. 2

11	A2	2c brown	*550.00*	*400.00*
12	A2	2c rose ('83)	*62.50*	*52.50*
a.		Inverted overprint	*18,000.*	*12,500.*
b.		Double overprint	*3,200.*	*3,200.*
c.		Triple overprint	*11,500.*	
13	A2	4c rose	*675.00*	*375.00*
14	A2	4c brown ('83)	*90.00*	*80.00*
a.		Double overprint	4,000.	
15	A6	5c ultra ('83)	*290.00*	*200.00*
16	A2	6c violet ('83)	*210.00*	*125.00*
17	A3	8c yel orange	*190.00*	*75.00*
a.		Inverted overprint	*22,500.*	*12,500.*
18	A7	10c slate	*190.00*	*100.00*
19	A3	12c violet brn ('83)	*325.00*	*175.00*
20	A3	24c green	*6,750.*	*3,250.*

Double overprints must have two clear impressions. Partial double overprints exist on a number of values of these issues. They sell for a modest premium over catalogue value depending on how much of the impression is present.

1883 Wmk. 1

21	A5	2c on 32c pale red	*3,250.*	*3,000.*

On Straits Settlements No. 9

1885 Wmk. 38

22	A7	32c on 2a yel (B+B)	*40,000.*	—

BARBADOS

bär-'bā-‚dōs

LOCATION — A West Indies island east of the Windwards

GOVT. — British Colony

AREA — 166 sq. mi.

POP. — 270,500 (1981)

CAPITAL — Bridgetown

4 Farthings = 1 Penny

12 Pence = 1 Shilling

20 Shillings = 1 Pound

100 Cents = 1 Dollar (1950)

Catalogue values for unused stamps in this country are for Never Hinged items, beginning with Scott 207 in the regular postage section, and Scott J1 in the postage due section.

Watermarks

Wmk. 5 — Small Star

Wmk. 6 — Large Star

PRE-STAMP POSTAL MARKINGS

Crowned Circle handstamp type I is pictured in the Crowned Circle Handstamps and Great Britain Used Abroad section.

1849

A1	I	"Barbados" crowned circle handstamp in red, on cover	525.00
a.		Used with 1p stamp paying local postage, #A1 the overseas postage	*4,000.*

This handstamp was used 2/17/93 to 3/15/93 as a ½p stamp, 1/23/96 to 5/4/96 as a ¼p stamp. Value $100.

Values for unused stamps are for examples with original gum as defined in the catalogue introduction. Very fine examples of Nos. 10-42a, 44-59a will have perforations touching the design on at least one side due to the narrow spacing of the stamps on the plates and imperfect perforation methods. Stamps with perfs clear of the design on all four sides are extremely scarce and will command higher prices.

Britannia

A1 A2

1852-55 Unwmk. Engr. *Imperf.*

Blued Paper

1	A1	(½p) deep green	125.00	*375.00*
		On cover		—
a.		(½p) yellow green	*9,000.*	800.00
		On cover		—
2	A1	(1p) dark blue	35.00	*80.00*
		On cover		300.00
		On cover, pair		500.00
a.		(1p) blue	55.00	*225.00*
		On cover		400.00
3	A1	(2p) slate blue	29.00	
a.		(2p) grayish slate	275.00	*1,400.*
		On cover		—
b.		As "a," vert. half used as 1p on cover		*8,500.*
c.		(2p) deep slate	250.00	
4	A1	(4p) brown red ('55)	115.00	*325.00*
		On cover		—
		Nos. 1-4 (4)	304.00	

#3, 3c were not placed in use. No. 3c differs from No. 3a in the thickness and color of the gum which is yellowish and blotchy, as well as in shade. Beware of color changelings of Nos. 2-3 that may resemble No. 3a. Certificates of authenticity are required for Nos. 3a and 3b.

Use of #3b was authorized from 8/4-9/21/1854.

1855-58

White Paper

5	A1	(½p) deep green ('58)	175.00	*225.00*
a.		(½p) yellow green ('57)	600.00	125.00
6	A1	(1p) blue	45.00	*70.00*
a.		(1p) pale blue	110.00	*80.00*

It is believed that the (4p) brownish red on white paper exists only as No. 17b.

1859

8	A2	6p rose red	850.00	140.00
a.		6p deep rose red	850.00	210.00
9	A2	1sh black	260.00	85.00
a.		1sh brownish black	290.00	125.00

Pin-perf. 14

10	A1	(½p) pale yel grn	2,250.	500.00
11	A1	(1p) blue	2,250.	175.00
a.		1p deep blue	2,250.	175.00

Pin-perf. 12½

12	A1	(½p) pale yel grn	*8,500.*	800.00
12A	A1	(1p) blue	—	1,750.

Pin-perf. 14x12½

12B	A1	(½p) pale yel grn	—	*8,500.*

1861 *Clean-Cut Perf. 14 to 16*

13	A1	(½p) dark blue grn	140.00	13.50
14	A1	(1p) pale blue	925.00	80.00
a.		(1p) blue	800.00	75.00
b.		Half used as ½p on cover		—

Rough Perf. 14 to 16

15	A1	(½p) green	21.00	20.00
a.		(½p) blue green	62.50	*85.00*
b.		Imperf., pair	700.00	
c.		(½p) deep green	26.50	*30.00*
16	A1	(1p) blue	45.00	4.25
a.		Diagonal half used as ½p on cover		—
b.		Imperf., pair	850.00	*650.00*
c.		(1p) deep blue	45.00	4.25
17	A1	(4p) rose red	110.00	55.00
a.		(4p) brown red	160.00	62.50
b.		As "a," imperf., pair	1,350.	
c.		(4p) rose red, imperf., pair	900.00	
d.		(4p) lake rose	150.00	90.00
e.		As "d," imperf pair	1,500.	
18	A1	(4p) vermilion	290.00	95.00
a.		Imperf., pair	1,400.	
19	A2	6p rose red	375.00	17.00
a.		6p orange red ('64)	125.00	25.00

20 A2 6p orange ver 110.00 26.00
a. 6p vermilion 125.00 21.00
b. Imperf., pair 675.00 *1,000.*
c. 6p orange ('70) 150.00 40.00
21 A2 1sh brownish black 85.00 7.50
a. 1sh black 75.00 8.00
b. Horiz. pair, imperf. btwn. 7,500.
c. 1sh blue (error) *20,000.*

No. 21c was never placed in use. All copies are pen-marked (some have been removed) and have clipped perfs on one or more sides.

Use of #14b, 16a was authorized from 4/63-11/66.

Perf. 11 to 13

22 A1 (½p) deep green *11,000.*
23 A1 (1p) blue *2,500.*

Nos. 22 and 23 were never placed in use.

1870 Wmk. 6 *Rough Perf. 14 to 16*

24 A1 (½p) green 150.00 7.50
a. Imperf., pair (#24) 1,200.
b. (½p) yellow green 190.00 52.50
25 A1 (1p) blue 2,000. 62.50
a. Imperf., pair *3,000.*
b. 1p blue, *blue* *3,500.* 110.00
26 A1 (4p) dull red 1,100. 125.00
27 A2 6p vermilion 1,000. 80.00
28 A2 1sh black 450.00 21.00

1871 Wmk. 5

29 A1 (1p) blue 175.00 2.75
30 A1 (4p) rose red 1,150. 45.00
31 A2 6p vermilion 750.00 18.00
32 A2 1sh black 200.00 11.00

Clean-Cut Perf. 14½ to 16

33 A1 (1p) blue 325.00 2.75
a. Diagonal half used as ½p on cover —
34 A2 6p vermilion 975.00 95.00
35 A2 1sh black 175.00 11.00

Perf. 11 to 13x14½ to 16

36 A1 (½p) blue green 375.00 55.00
37 A1 (4p) vermilion 900.00 125.00

1873 *Perf. 14*

38 A2 3p claret 375.00 140.00

Wmk. 6

Clean-Cut Perf. 14½ to 16

39 A1 (½p) blue green 375.00 19.00
40 A1 (4p) rose red 1,250. 210.00
41 A2 6p vermilion 850.00 85.00
a. Imperf., pair 100.00 *1,750.*
b. Horiz. pair, imperf. btwn. 8,000.
42 A2 1sh black 175.00 16.00
a. Horiz. pair, imperf. btwn. 7,500.

No. 41 perf 11 to 12 was prepared, but not issued. Value, $8,000.

Britannia — A3

1873 Wmk. 5 *Perf. 15½x15*

43 A3 5sh dull rose 1,200. 375.00
Handstamped "SPECIMEN" 375.00

For surcharged bisects see Nos. 57-59.

1874 Wmk. 6 *Perf. 14*

44 A2 ½p blue green 40.00 8.00
45 A2 1p blue 100.00 3.25

Clean-Cut Perf. 14½ to 16

45A A2 1p blue *12,500.*

1875 Wmk. 1 *Perf. 12½*

46 A2 ½p yellow green 62.50 5.75
47 A2 4p scarlet 300.00 16.00
48 A2 6p orange 750.00 80.00
a. 6p bright yellow 1,150. 100.00
49 A2 1sh purple 575.00 4.00
Nos. 46-49 (4) 1,687. 105.75

1875-78 *Perf. 14*

50 A2 ½p yel green ('76) 15.00 1.00
51 A2 1p ultramarine 80.00 1.40
a. 1p gray blue 80.00 1.10
b. Half used as ½p on cover *1,300.*
c. Watermarked sideways *1,000.*
52 A2 3p violet ('78) 150.00 9.00
53 A2 4p rose red 150.00 10.50
a. 4p scarlet 210.00 4.50
b. As "a," perf. 14x12½ *9,000.*
54 A2 4p lake 575.00 4.50
55 A2 6p chrome yel 160.00 2.00
a. 6p yellow, wmkd. sideways 400.00 11.00

56 A2 1sh purple ('76) 175.00 5.00
a. 1sh violet *7,750.* 45.00
b. 1sh dull mauve 575.00 4.25
c. Half used as 6p on cover —

#48, 49, 55, 56 have the watermark sideways.

No. 53b was never placed in use.

A mint example of the one shilling aniline violet (Scott No. 56a) sold for the equivalent of U.S. $15,340 in a Singapore auction in 2003.

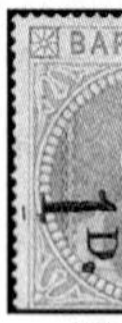

A4

A5

Large Surcharge, ("1" 7mm High, "D" 2¾mm High)

1878 Wmk. 5 *Perf. 15½x15*

Slanting Serif

57 A4 1p on half of 5sh *6,250.* 850.00
a. Unsevered pair *25,000.* *2,600.*
b. Unsevered horiz. pair, #57 + 58 *5,500.*
d. Unsevered horiz. pair, #57 + 58, imperf. between *35,000.*
e. Unsevered horiz. pair, #57 + 59 40,000. 8,500.
f. No period after "D" *18,750.* *2,250.*

Straight Serif

58 A4 1p on half of 5sh 7,250. 1,050.
a. Unsevered pair 4,000.

Small Surcharge, ("1" 6mm, "D" 2½mm High)

59 A5 1p on half of 5sh *9,500.* *1,200.*
a. Unsevered pair *32,500.* *5,250.*

On Nos. 57, 58 and 59 the surcharge is found reading upwards or downwards.

The perforation, which divides the stamp into halves, measures 11½ to 13.

The old denomination has been cut off the bottom of the stamps.

Queen Victoria — A6

1882-85 Typo. Wmk. 2 *Perf. 14*

60 A6 ½p green 21.00 1.75
a. ½p dull green 21.00 1.75
61 A6 1p carmine rose 26.00 1.10
a. 1p rose 75.00 2.50
b. Half used as ½p on cover 1,500.
62 A6 2½p dull blue 125.00 1.75
a. 2½p ultramarine 105.00 1.75
63 A6 3p magenta 5.00 *22.50*
a. 3p lilac 125.00 37.50
64 A6 4p slate 350.00 4.25
65 A6 4p brown ('85) 6.75 1.75
a. 4p pale brown ('85) 16.00 3.75
66 A6 6p olive gray 85.00 52.50
67 A6 1sh orange brown 32.50 24.00
68 A6 5sh bister 175.00 *225.00*
Nos. 60-68 (9) 826.25 *334.60*

No. 65 Surcharged in Black

1892

69 A6 ½p on 4p brown 2.75 *6.25*
a. Without hyphen 15.00 *27.50*
b. Double surcharge, one albino —
c. Double surch., red & black 850.00 *1,000.*
d. As "c," without hyphen 2,250. *3,000.*
e. Surcharged "PENNY HALF" 400.00 240.00

A8

Badge of Colony — A9

1892-1903 Wmk. 2

70 A8 1f sl & car ('96) 2.75 .20
71 A8 ½p green 2.75 .20
72 A8 1p carmine rose 5.50 .20
73 A8 2p sl & org ('99) 9.25 1.25
74 A8 2½p ultramarine 20.00 .25
75 A8 5p olive brn 8.00 5.25
76 A8 6p vio & car 19.00 3.00
77 A8 8p org & ultra 4.50 *26.00*
78 A8 10p bl grn & car 9.25 7.50
79 A8 2sh6p slate & org 55.00 57.50
80 A8 2sh6p pur & grn ('03) 115.00 *210.00*
Nos. 70-80 (11) 251.00 *311.35*
Set, ovptd. "SPECIMEN" 250.00

See Nos. 90-101. For surcharge see No B1.

Victoria Jubilee Issue

1897 Wmk. 1

81 A9 1f gray & car 5.75 .75
82 A9 ½p gray green 3.50 .75
83 A9 1p carmine rose 5.75 .75
84 A9 2½p ultra 8.50 1.00
85 A9 5p dk olive brn 22.50 20.00
86 A9 6p vio & car 30.00 27.50
87 A9 8p org & ultra 13.50 *29.00*
88 A9 10p bl grn & car 55.00 *62.50*
89 A9 2sh6p slate & org 85.00 62.50
Nos. 81-89 (9) 229.50 *204.75*
Set, ovptd. "SPECIMEN" 170.00

Bluish Paper

81a A9 1f gray & car 32.50 *35.00*
82a A9 ½p gray green 32.50 *35.00*
83a A9 1p carmine rose 45.00 *47.50*
84a A9 2½p ultra 45.00 *52.50*
85a A9 5p dk olive brn 260.00 *300.00*
86a A9 6p vio & car 150.00 160.00
87a A9 8p org & ultra 160.00 *175.00*
88a A9 10p bl grn & car 225.00 *275.00*
89a A9 2sh6p slate & org *140.00* *150.00*
Nos. 81a-89a (9) 1,090. *1,230.*

Badge Type of 1892-1903

1904-10 Wmk. 3

90 A8 1f gray & car 11.00 3.25
91 A8 1f brown ('09) 11.00 .35
92 A8 ½p green 21.00 .20
a. ½p blue green ('09) 26.00 1.40
93 A8 1p carmine rose 21.00 .20
94 A8 1p carmine ('09) 25.00 .20
95 A8 2p gray ('09) 8.50 *15.00*
96 A8 2½p ultramarine 24.00 .35
a. 2½p bright blue ('10) 57.50 10.75
97 A8 6p vio & car 20.00 *20.00*
98 A8 6p dl vio & vio ('10) 15.00 *20.00*
99 A8 8p org & ultra 57.50 *115.00*
100 A8 1sh blk, *grn* ('10) 12.50 *16.00*
101 A8 2sh6p pur & green 62.50 *140.00*
Nos. 90-101 (12) 289.00 *330.55*

Nelson Centenary Issue

Lord Nelson Monument — A10

1906 Engr. Wmk. 1

102 A10 1f gray & black 10.50 2.50
103 A10 ½p green & black 12.00 .40
104 A10 1p car & black 15.00 .25
105 A10 2p org & black 2.10 *5.50*
106 A10 2½p ultra & black 4.50 1.50
107 A10 6p lilac & black 22.50 *30.00*
108 A10 1sh rose & black 26.00 *62.50*
Nos. 102-108 (7) 92.60 *102.65*

See Nos. 110-112.

The "Olive Blossom" A11

1906, Aug. 15 Wmk. 3

109 A11 1p blk, green & blue 12.50 .30

Tercentenary of the 1st British landing.

Nelson Type of 1906

1907, July 6 Wmk. 3

110 A10 1f gray & black 6.25 6.25
111 A10 2p org & black 30.00 *32.50*
112 A10 2½p ultra & black 10.00 *30.00*
a. 2½p indigo & black 825.00 *1,000.*
Nos. 110-112 (3) 46.25 *68.75*

A12

A13

King George V — A14

1912 Typo.

116 A12 ¼p brown 1.90 1.90
117 A12 ½p green 4.75 .20
a. Booklet pane of 6
118 A12 1p carmine 11.00 .20
a. 1p scarlet 30.00 2.75
b. Booklet pane of 6
119 A12 2p gray 3.75 *17.50*
120 A12 2½p ultramarine 1.90 .60
121 A13 3p violet, *yel* 1.90 *17.50*
122 A13 4p blk & scar, *yel* 2.10 *22.50*
123 A13 6p vio & red vio 15.00 15.00
124 A14 1sh black, *green* 10.50 *17.50*
125 A14 2sh vio & ultra, *bl* 52.50 *60.00*
126 A14 3sh grn & violet 110.00 *125.00*
Nos. 116-126 (11) 215.30 *277.90*

Seal of the Colony — A15

1916-18 Engr.

127 A15 ¼p brown .90 .50
128 A15 ½p green 1.40 .20
129 A15 1p red 3.00 .20
130 A15 2p gray 6.00 *27.50*
131 A15 2½p ultramarine 4.25 3.00
132 A15 3p violet, *yel* 3.00 *8.75*
133 A15 4p red, *yel* 1.25 *17.50*
134 A15 4p red & black ('18) 1.00 *4.50*
135 A15 6p claret 5.00 *5.50*
136 A15 1sh black, *green* 8.75 *13.50*
137 A15 2sh violet, *blue* 20.00 9.25
138 A15 3sh dark violet 62.50 *160.00*
139 A15 3sh dk vio & grn ('18) 25.00 *87.50*
a. 3sh bright violet & green ('18) 300.00 *450.00*
Nos. 127-139 (13) 142.05 *337.90*

Nos. 134 and 139 are from a re-engraved die. The central medallion is not surrounded by a line and there are various other small alterations.

Victory Issue

Victory
A16 A17

1920, Sept. 9 **Wmk. 3**
140 A16 ¼p bister & black .35 .85
141 A16 ½p yel green & blk 1.25 .20
a. Booklet pane of 2
142 A16 1p org red & blk 5.00 .20
a. Booklet pane of 2
143 A16 2p gray & black 3.25 *10.00*
144 A16 2½p ultra & dk bl 3.50 *22.50*
145 A16 3p red lilac & blk 3.75 *8.00*
146 A16 4p gray grn & blk 4.00 *8.75*
147 A16 6p orange & blk 4.75 *19.00*
148 A17 1sh yel green & blk 12.50 *36.00*
149 A17 2sh brown & blk 35.00 *52.50*
150 A17 3sh orange & blk 40.00 *57.50*

1921, Aug. 22 **Wmk. 4**
151 A16 1p orange red & blk 21.00 .35
Nos. 140-151 (12) 134.35 *215.85*

A18 A19

1921-24 **Wmk. 4**
152 A18 ¼p brown .30 .20
153 A18 ½p green 1.90 .20
154 A18 1p carmine 1.00 .20
155 A18 2p gray 2.00 .25
156 A18 2½p ultramarine 1.90 *10.00*
158 A18 6p claret 4.25 *6.75*
159 A18 1sh blk, *emer* ('24) 60.00 *125.00*
160 A18 2sh dk vio, *blue* 12.50 *24.00*
161 A18 3sh dark violet 17.50 *75.00*

Wmk. 3
162 A18 3p violet, *yel* 2.50 *8.00*
163 A18 4p red, *yel* 2.25 *19.00*
164 A18 1sh black, *green* 7.00 *19.00*
Nos. 152-164 (12) 113.10 *287.60*

1925-35 **Wmk. 4** ***Perf. 14***
165 A19 ¼p brown .30 .20
166 A19 ½p green .60 .20
a. Perf. 13½x12½ ('32) 8.00 .20
b. Booklet pane of 10
167 A19 1p carmine .60 .20
a. Perf. 13½x12½ ('32) 7.50 .60
b. Booklet pane of 10
168 A19 1½p org, perf. 13½x12½ ('32) 2.50 1.25
a. Booklet pane of 6
b. Perf. 14 17.50 4.00
169 A19 2p gray .60 *4.00*
170 A19 2½p ultramarine .60 *1.00*
a. Perf. 13½x12½ ('32) 8.00 5.00
171 A19 3p vio brn, *yel* 1.25 .55
172 A19 3p red brn, *yel* ('35) 7.50 7.50
173 A19 4p red, *yel* .95 *1.25*
174 A19 6p claret 1.25 1.10
175 A19 1sh blk, *emerald* 2.50 *8.00*
a. Perf. 13½x12½ ('32) 62.50 37.50
176 A19 1sh brn blk, *yel grn* ('32) 5.50 *12.50*
177 A19 2sh violet, *bl* 8.75 8.00
178 A19 2sh6p car, *blue* ('32) 27.50 *35.00*
179 A19 3sh dark violet 14.00 *16.00*
Nos. 165-179 (15) 74.40 *96.75*

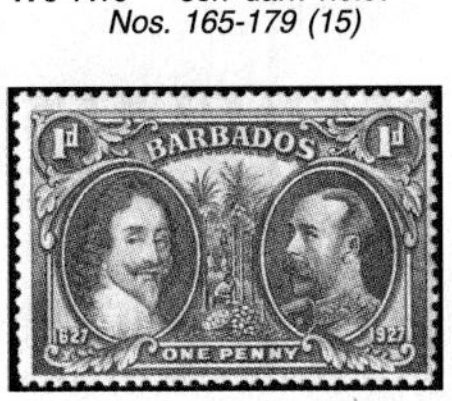

Charles I and George V — A20

1927, Feb. 17 ***Perf. 12½***
180 A20 1p carmine lake 1.25 .90

Tercentenary of the settlement of Barbados.

Common Design Types pictured following the introduction.

Silver Jubilee Issue
Common Design Type

1935, May 6 ***Perf. 11x12***
186 CD301 1p car & dk bl .60 .25
187 CD301 1½p blk & ultra 3.50 *6.50*
188 CD301 2½p ultra & brn 2.00 *4.00*
189 CD301 1sh brn vio & ind 10.00 *12.50*
Nos. 186-189 (4) 16.10 23.25
Set, never hinged 35.00

Coronation Issue
Common Design Type

1937, May 14 ***Perf. 13½x14***
190 CD302 1p carmine .20 .20
191 CD302 1½p brown .25 *.75*
192 CD302 2½p bright ultra .45 *.90*
Nos. 190-192 (3) .90 1.85
Set, never hinged 1.50

A21

1938-47 ***Perf. 13-14 & Compound***
193 A21 ½p green 4.50 .20
b. Perf. 14 52.50 1.50
c. Booklet pane of 10
193A A21 ½p bister ('42) .20 *.35*
194 A21 1p carmine 12.00 .20
b. Perf. 13½x13 200.00 5.00
c. Booklet pane of 10
194A A21 1p green ('42) .20 .20
d. Perf. 13½x13 3.25 1.00
195 A21 1½p red orange .20 *.50*
c. Perf. 14 3.50 .80
d. Booklet pane of 6
195A A21 2p rose lake ('41) .35 *3.00*
195B A21 2p bright rose red ('43) .20 *.80*
e. Perf. 14 .45 *2.10*
196 A21 2½p ultramarine .35 *.75*
197 A21 3p brown .20 *2.75*
b. Perf. 14 .25 .75
197A A21 3p deep bl ('47) .20 *2.10*
198 A21 4p black .20 .20
a. Perf. 14 .30 *5.50*
199 A21 6p violet .60 .50
199A A21 8p red vio ('46) .40 *2.50*
200 A21 1sh brn olive .75 .20
a. 1sh olive green 12.00 3.00
201 A21 2sh6p brown vio 5.25 1.75
201A A21 5sh indigo ('41) 2.40 *8.75*
Nos. 193-201A (16) 28.00 24.75
Set, never hinged 40.00

For surcharge see No. 209.

Kings Charles I, George VI Assembly Chamber and Mace A22

Perf. 13½x14
1939, June 27 **Engr.** **Wmk. 4**
202 A22 ½p deep green 1.40 1.25
203 A22 1p scarlet 1.40 .40
204 A22 1½p deep orange 1.40 .75
205 A22 2½p ultramarine 1.40 *5.50*
206 A22 3p yellow brown 1.40 *3.75*
Nos. 202-206 (5) 7.00 *11.65*
Set, never hinged 10.50

Tercentenary of the General Assembly.

Catalogue values for unused stamps in this section, from this point to the end of the section, are for Never Hinged items.

Peace Issue
Common Design Type

1946, Sept. 18
207 CD303 1½p deep orange .20 .20
208 CD303 3p brown .20 .20

Nos. 195e, 195B, Surcharged in Black

1947, Apr. 21 ***Perf. 14***
209 A21 1p on 2p brt rose red 1.00 1.00
a. Double surcharge —
b. Perf. 13½x13 3.75 *6.25*

Silver Wedding Issue
Common Design Types

Perf. 14x14½
1948, Nov. 24 **Photo.** **Wmk. 4**
210 CD304 1½p orange .20 .20

Engraved; Name Typographed
Perf. 11½x11
211 CD305 5sh dark blue 12.50 9.50

UPU Issue
Common Design Types

1949, Oct. 10 ***Perf. 13½, 11x11½***
212 CD306 1½p red orange .35 .35
213 CD307 3p indigo .55 .55
214 CD308 4p gray 1.00 1.00
215 CD309 1sh olive 1.40 1.40
Nos. 212-215 (4) 3.30 3.30

Dover Fort — A23

Admiral Nelson Statue — A24

Designs: 2c, Sugar cane breeding. 3c, Public buildings. 6c, Casting net. 8c, Intercolonial schooner. 12c, Flying Fish. 24c, Old Main Guard Garrison. 48c, Cathedral. 60c, Careenage. $1.20, Map. $2.40, Great Seal, 1660.

Perf. 11x11½ (A23), 13x13½ (A24)
1950, May 1 **Engr.** **Wmk. 4**
216 A23 1c slate .25 *1.90*
217 A23 2c emerald .20 *1.40*
218 A23 3c slate & brown 1.10 *2.00*
219 A24 4c carmine .30 .30
220 A23 6c blue .35 *1.50*
221 A23 8c choc & blue 1.10 *1.75*
222 A23 12c olive & aqua .90 .65
223 A23 24c gray & red .90 .35
224 A24 48c violet 7.75 4.50
225 A23 60c brn car & bl grn 8.50 6.00
226 A24 $1.20 olive & car 8.50 2.75
227 A23 $2.40 gray 15.00 12.50
Nos. 216-227 (12) 44.85 35.60

University Issue
Common Design Types

1951, Feb. 16 ***Perf. 14x14½***
228 CD310 3c turq bl & choc .75 .35
229 CD311 12c ol brn & turq bl 2.00 2.00

Stamp of 1852 A25

Perf. 13½
1952, Apr. 15 **Wmk. 4** **Engr.**
230 A25 3c slate bl & dp grn .20 .20
231 A25 4c rose pink & bl .25 *.60*
232 A25 12c emer & slate bl .30 *.60*
233 A25 24c gray blk & red brn .50 .50
Nos. 230-233 (4) 1.25 *1.90*

Centenary of Barbados postage stamps.

SEMI-POSTAL STAMP

No. 73 Surcharged in Red

Perf. 14
1907, Jan. 25 **Typo.** **Wmk. 2**
B1 A8 1p on 2p sl & org 3.25 *7.50*
a. No period after 1d 52.50 *87.50*
b. Inverted surcharge 2.00 *7.50*
c. Inverted surcharge, no period after 1d 47.50 *100.00*
d. Double surcharge 925.00 *1,000.*
e. Dbl. surch., both invtd. 925.00
f. Dbl. surch., one invtd. 1,200.
g. Vert. pair, one normal, one surcharge double 1,150.

POSTAGE DUE STAMPS

Catalogue values for unused stamps in this section are for Never Hinged items.

D1

1934-47 **Typo.** **Wmk. 4** ***Perf. 14***
J1 D1 ½p green ('35) 1.60 1.60
On cover *60.00*
J2 D1 1p black 1.60 1.60
On cover *60.00*
a. Half used as ½p on cover *2,500.*
J3 D1 3p dk car rose ('47) 26.00 26.00
On cover *175.00*
Nos. J1-J3 (3) 29.20 29.20

A 2nd die of the 1p was introduced in 1947.

Use of #J2a was authorized from Mar. 1934 through Feb. 1935. Some examples have "½d" written on the bisect in black or red ink.

On cover values are for properly franked commercial covers. Philatelic usages also exist and sell for less.

1950
J4 D1 1c green .35 *3.25*
On cover 60.00
J5 D1 2c black 1.25 *7.00*
On cover 60.00
J6 D1 6c carmine rose 1.25 *10.00*
On cover 125.00
Nos. J4-J6 (3) 2.85 *20.25*

Values are for 1953 chalky paper printing. Values on ordinary paper, unused $30, used $60.

Wmk. 4a (error)
J4a D1 1c green 300.00
J5a D1 2c black 500.00
J6a D1 6c carmine rose 200.00
Nos. J4a-J6a (3) 1,000.

WAR TAX STAMP

No. 118 Overprinted

1917 **Wmk. 3** ***Perf. 14***
MR1 A12 1p carmine .50 .20
a. Imperf., pair —

BARBUDA

bär-'büd-ə

LOCATION — Northernmost of the Leeward Islands, West Indies
GOVT. — Dependency of Antigua
AREA — 63 sq. mi.
POP. — 1,000 (estimated)
See Antigua.

12 Pence = 1 Shilling

Leeward Islands Stamps and Types of 1912-22 Overprinted in Black or Red

Die II

For description of dies I and II, see back of this section of the Catalogue.

1922, July 13 Wmk. 4 *Perf. 14*

1	A5	½p green	1.60	*11.00*
2	A5	1p rose red	1.60	*11.00*
3	A5	2p gray	1.60	*9.00*
4	A5	2½p ultramarine	1.60	*9.75*
5	A5	6p vio & red vio	2.25	*20.00*
6	A5	2sh vio & ultra, *bl*	14.50	*55.00*
7	A5	3sh green & violet	32.50	*87.50*
8	A5	4sh blk & scar (R)	40.00	*87.50*

Wmk. 3

9	A5	3p violet, *yel*	1.90	*15.00*
10	A5	1sh blk, *emer* (R)	1.75	*10.50*
11	A5	5sh grn & red, *yel*	80.00	*175.00*
		Nos. 1-11 (11)	179.30	*491.25*
		Set, never hinged	350.00	
		Set, overprinted "SPECIMEN"	260.00	

Beware of forgeries, especially used examples dated June 1, 1923.

Covers: Values for commercial covers with the 1p, 2p or 3p stamps begin at about $50. Other stamps are very scarce to rare on cover.

BASUTOLAND

bə-'sü-tə-ˌland

LOCATION — An enclave in the state of South Africa
GOVT. — British Crown Colony
AREA — 11,716 sq. mi.
POP. — 733,000 (est. 1964)
CAPITAL — Maseru

The Colony, a former independent native state, was annexed to the Cape Colony in 1871. In 1883 control was transferred directly to the British Crown. Stamps of the Cape of Good Hope were used from 1871 to 1910 and those of the Union of South Africa from 1910 to 1933.

12 Pence = 1 Shilling

Catalogue values for unused stamps in this country are for Never Hinged items, beginning with Scott 29 in the regular postage section and Scott J1 in the postage due section.

George V — A1

George VI — A2

Crocodile and River Scene

Perf. 12½

1933, Dec. 1 Engr. Wmk. 4

1	A1	½p emerald	1.25	*2.25*
		On cover		*8.00*
2	A1	1p carmine	1.00	*1.60*
		On cover		6.00
3	A1	2p red violet	1.25	*1.00*
		On cover		6.00
4	A1	3p ultra	1.10	*1.25*
		On cover		8.00
5	A1	4p slate	2.50	*9.00*
		On cover		30.00
6	A1	6p yellow	2.75	*2.25*
		On cover		9.00
7	A1	1sh red orange	2.75	*6.00*
		On cover		24.00
8	A1	2sh6p dk brown	24.00	*57.50*
		On cover		*200.00*
9	A1	5sh violet	57.50	*90.00*
		On cover		*275.00*
10	A1	10sh olive green	150.00	*175.00*
		On cover		*500.00*
		Nos. 1-10 (10)	244.10	*345.85*

Common Design Types pictured following the introduction.

Silver Jubilee Issue
Common Design Type

1935, May 4 *Perf. 13½x14*

11	CD301	1p car & blue	.70	*1.75*
12	CD301	2p gray blk & ultra	1.00	*1.50*
13	CD301	3p blue & brown	4.25	*5.75*
14	CD301	6p brt vio & indigo	4.25	*5.75*
		Nos. 11-14 (4)	10.20	*14.75*
		Set, never hinged	16.00	

Coronation Issue
Common Design Type

1937, May 12 *Perf. 13½x14*

15	CD302	1p carmine	.25	.30
16	CD302	2p rose violet	.40	.55
17	CD302	3p bright ultra	.50	.55
		Nos. 15-17 (3)	1.15	1.40
		Set, never hinged	1.60	

1938, Apr. 1 *Perf. 12½*

18	A2	½p emerald	.20	*1.75*
19	A2	1p rose car	.35	*1.00*
20	A2	1½p light blue	.30	*.65*
21	A2	2p rose lilac	.20	*.80*
22	A2	3p ultra	.20	*1.40*
23	A2	4p gray	1.10	*4.75*
24	A2	6p yel ocher	.45	*1.75*
25	A2	1sh red orange	.45	*1.40*
26	A2	2sh6p black brown	6.50	*11.00*
27	A2	5sh violet	17.50	*13.00*
28	A2	10sh olive green	17.50	*22.50*
		Nos. 18-28 (11)	44.75	*60.00*
		Set, never hinged	75.00	

Catalogue values for unused stamps in this section, from this point to the end of the section, are for Never Hinged items.

Peace Issue

South Africa Nos. 100-102 Overprinted

Basic stamps inscribed alternately in English and Afrikaans.

1945, Dec. 3 Wmk. 201 *Perf. 14*

29	A42	1p rose pink & choc, pair	.55	.70
	a.	Single, English	.20	.20
	b.	Single, Afrikaans	.20	.20
30	A43	2p vio & slate blue, pair	.55	.60
	a.	Single, English	.20	.20
	b.	Single, Afrikaans	.20	.20
31	A43	3p ultra & dp ultra, pair	.55	.85
	a.	Single, English	.20	.20
	b.	Single, Afrikaans	.20	.20
		Nos. 29-31 (3)	1.65	2.15

King George VI — A3

King George VI and Queen Elizabeth A4

Princess Margaret Rose and Princess Elizabeth A5

Royal British Family A6

Perf. 12½

1947, Feb. 17 Wmk. 4 Engr.

35	A3	1p red	.20	.20
36	A4	2p green	.20	.20
37	A5	3p ultra	.20	.20
38	A6	1sh dark violet	.20	.20
		Nos. 35-38 (4)	.80	.80

Visit of the British Royal Family, Mar. 11-12, 1947.

Silver Wedding Issue
Common Design Types

1948, Dec. 1 Photo. *Perf. 14x14½*

39	CD304	1½p brt ultra	.30	.20

Engr.; Name Typo.
Perf. 11½

40	CD305	10sh dk brown olive	35.00	*35.00*

UPU Issue
Common Design Types
Engr.; Name Typo. on 3p, 6p
Perf. 13½, 11x11½

1949, Oct. 10 Wmk. 4

41	CD306	1½p blue	.50	*1.25*
42	CD307	3p indigo	1.50	*2.50*
43	CD308	6p orange yel	1.50	*3.00*
44	CD309	1sh red brown	1.50	1.50
		Nos. 41-44 (4)	5.00	8.25

POSTAGE DUE STAMPS

Catalogue values for all unused stamps in this section are for Never Hinged items.

D1

1933-38 Wmk. 4 Typo. *Perf. 14*

J1	D1	1p dark red ('38)	1.60	*2.75*
		On cover		*80.00*
	a.	1p dark carmine	37.50	*45.00*
		On cover		*150.00*
	b.	Wmk. 4a (error)	92.50	
J2	D1	2p lt violet	.35	*15.00*
		On cover		*80.00*
	a.	Wmk. 4a (error)	100.00	

Nos. J1-J2 valued on chalky paper.
For surcharge see No. J7.
On cover values are for properly franked commercial covers. Philatelic usages also exist and sell for less.

OFFICIAL STAMPS

Nos. 1-3 and 6 Overprinted "OFFICIAL"

1934 Wmk. 4 Engr. *Perf. 12½*

O1	A1	½p emerald	*9,000.*	*5,500.*
O2	A1	1p carmine	*2,250.*	*2,100.*
O3	A1	2p red violet	*2,500.*	*800.*
O4	A1	6p yellow	*12,500.*	*5,500.*

Counterfeits exist.

BATUM

LOCATION — A seaport on the Black Sea.

Batum is the capital of Adzhar, a territory which, in 1921, became an autonomous republic of the Georgian Soviet Socialist Republic.

Stamps of Batum were issued under the administration of British forces which occupied Batum and environs between December, 1918, and July, 1920, following the Treaty of Versailles.

100 Kopecks = 1 Ruble

Counterfeits of Nos. 1-65 abound.

A1

1919 Unwmk. Litho. *Imperf.*

1	A1	5k green	7.50	*15.00*
		On cover		*500.00*
2	A1	10k ultramarine	7.50	*15.00*
		On cover		*500.00*
3	A1	50k yellow	3.50	*5.00*
		On cover		*350.00*
4	A1	1r red brown	5.25	*5.50*
		On cover		*375.00*
5	A1	3r violet	11.00	*17.50*
		On cover		*625.00*
6	A1	5r brown	11.50	*27.50*
		On cover		*675.00*
		Nos. 1-6 (6)	46.25	*85.50*

For overprints and surcharges see #13-20, 51-65.

Nos. 7-12, 21-50: numbers in parentheses are those of the basic Russian stamps.

Russian Stamps of 1909-17 Surcharged

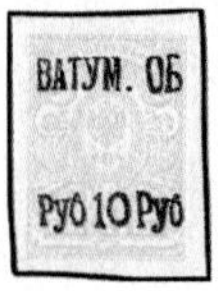

On Stamps of 1917

1919

7	10r on 1k orange (#119)	55.00	*70.00*
	On cover		*750.00*
8	10r on 3k red (#121)	25.00	*30.00*
	On cover		*700.00*

On Stamp of 1909-12
Perf. 14x14½

9	10r on 5k claret (#77)	425.00	450.00
	On cover		—

On Stamp of 1917

10	10r on 10k on 7k light blue (#117)	425.00	450.00
	On cover		—
	Nos. 7-10 (4)	930.00	1,000.

Russian Stamps of 1909-13 Surcharged

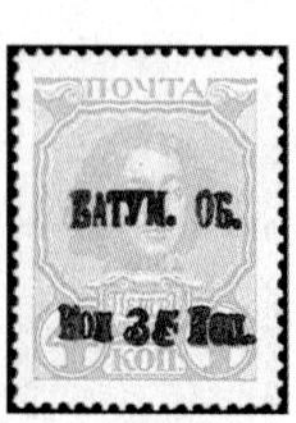

1919

11	35k on 4k carmine (#76)	*1,750.*	*5,500.*
	Unused on complete postcard	*5,000.*	
	On complete postcard		—
12	35k on 4k dull red (#91)	*6,500.*	*11,500.*
	Unused on complete postcard	*11,500.*	
	On complete postcard		—

This surcharge was intended for postal cards. A few cards which bore adhesive stamps were also surcharged.

Values are for stamps off card and without gum.

Type of 1919 Issue Overprinted

1919 Unwmk. *Imperf.*

13	A1	5k green	18.00	*14.50*
		On cover		*400.00*
14	A1	10k dark blue	16.00	*14.50*
		On cover		*400.00*
15	A1	25k orange	18.00	*14.50*
		On cover		*350.00*
16	A1	1r pale blue	5.00	*14.50*
		On cover		*325.00*
17	A1	2r salmon pink	1.25	*5.00*
		On cover		*325.00*
18	A1	3r violet	1.25	*5.00*
		On cover		*325.00*
19	A1	5r brown	1.50	*5.00*
		On cover		*325.00*
a.		"CCUPATION"	*450.00*	*450.00*
20	A1	7r dull red	5.00	*8.00*
		On cover		*350.00*
		Nos. 13-20 (8)	66.00	*81.00*

Russian Stamps of 1909-17 Surcharged in Various Colors:

10r & 50r

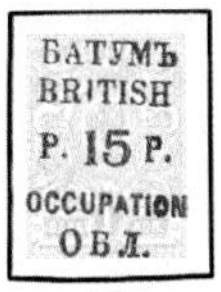

15r

On Stamps of 1917

1919-20 *Imperf.*

21	10r on 3k red (#121)	22.50	*25.00*
22	15r on 1k org (R) (#119)	50.00	*55.00*
23	15r on 1k org (Bk) (#119)	67.50	*72.50*
24	15r on 1k org (V) (#119)	67.50	*85.00*
25	50r on 1k org (#119)	475.00	*500.00*
26	50r on 2k green (#120)	625.00	*800.00*

On Stamps of 1909-17
Perf. 14x14½

27	50r on 2k green (#74)	625.00	675.00
28	50r on 3k red (#75)	1,250.	*1,350.*
29	50r on 4k car (#76)	850.00	*900.00*
30	50r on 5k claret (#77)	500.00	*575.00*
31	50r on 10k dk blue (R) (#79)	1,750.	*1,900.*
32	50r on 15k red brn & blue (#81)	550.00	*625.00*

Surcharged

On Stamps of 1909-17

33	25r on 5k cl (Bk) (#77)	47.50	55.00
34	25r on 5k cl (Bl) (#77)	47.50	55.00
35	25r on 10k on 7k lt blue (Bk) (#117)	140.00	*160.00*
36	25r on 10k on 7k lt blue (Bl) (#117)	80.00	*85.00*
37	25r on 20k on 14k bl & rose (Bk) (#118)	85.00	*100.00*
38	25r on 20k on 14k bl & rose (Bl) (#118)	85.00	*100.00*
39	25r on 25k grn & gray vio (Bk) (#83)	150.00	*160.00*
40	25r on 25k grn & gray vio (Bl) (#83)	110.00	125.00
41	25r on 50k vio & green (Bk) (#85a)	90.00	*100.00*
42	25r on 50k vio & green (Bl) (#85a)	85.00	*95.00*
43	50r on 2k green (#74)	115.00	140.00
44	50r on 3k red (#75)	115.00	140.00
45	50r on 4k car (#76)	110.00	115.00
46	50r on 5k claret (#77)	110.00	92.50

On Stamps of 1917
Imperf

47	50r on 2k green (#120)	400.00	*475.00*
48	50r on 3k red (#121)	475.00	*575.00*
49	50r on 5k claret (#123)	*1,350.*	*1,450.*

On Stamp of 1913
Perf. 13½

50	50r on 4k dull red (Bl) (#91)	72.50	*90.00*

Nos. 3, 13 and 15 Surcharged in Black or Blue:

1920 *Imperf.*

51	A1	25r on 5k green	37.50	*40.00*
52	A1	25r on 5k grn (Bl)	55.00	55.00
53	A1	25r on 25k orange	27.50	*30.00*
54	A1	25r on 25k org (Bl)	*125.00*	*125.00*
55	A1	50r on 50k yellow	22.50	*27.50*
a.		"50" cut in pieces	18.00	*19.00*
56	A1	50r on 50k yel (Bl)	110.00	110.00
a.		"50" cut in pieces	200.00	200.00
		Nos. 51-56 (6)	*377.50*	*387.50*

The figures of value in the surcharge on Nos. 55a and 56a were file-cut as a counter-forgery measure. Typically, the "5" is cut at bottom and on the right side of the loop. The zero is shorn at top and bottom, leaving the side bars intact. Nos. 55 and 56 are from early printings, before the handstamps were cut.

The surcharges on Nos. 21-56 inclusive are handstamped and are known double, inverted, etc.

Tree Type of 1919 Overprinted Like Nos. 13-20

1920

57	A1	1r orange brown	1.75	*10.00*
58	A1	2r gray blue	1.75	*10.00*
59	A1	3r rose	1.75	*10.00*
60	A1	5r black brown	1.75	*10.00*
61	A1	7r yellow	1.75	*10.00*
62	A1	10r dark green	1.75	*10.00*
63	A1	15r violet	2.25	*13.50*
64	A1	25r vermilion	2.00	*12.50*
65	A1	50r dark blue	2.25	*16.00*
		Nos. 57-65 (9)	17.00	*102.00*

The variety "BPITISH" occurs on #57-65. The "P" is actually a broken "R" and appears in Row 1, Pos. 19, in each sheet.

Nos. 57-65 exist without overprint.

BECHUANALAND

ˌbech-ˈwä-nə-ˌland

(British Bechuanaland)

LOCATION — Southern Africa
GOVT. — A British Crown Colony, which included the area of the former Stellaland, annexed in 1895 to the Cape of Good Hope Colony.
AREA — 51,424 sq. mi.
POP. — 72,700 (1891)
CAPITAL — Vryburg

British Bechuanaland stamps were also used in Bechuanaland Protectorate until 1897.

12 Pence = 1 Shilling
20 Shillings = 1 Pound

Watermarks

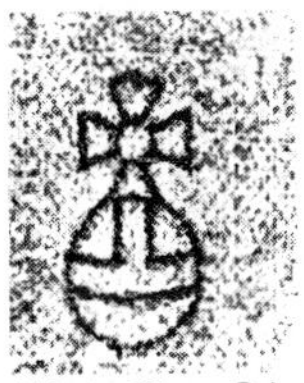

Wmk. 29 — Orb

Wmk. 14 — VR in Italics

Cape of Good Hope Stamps of 1871-85 Overprinted

1885-87 Wmk. 1 *Perf. 14*

Black Overprint

1	A6	4p blue ('86)	67.50	*80.00*

Wmk. 2

Black Overprint

3	A6	3p claret	40.00	*55.00*

Red Overprint

4	A6	½p black	18.00	27.50
a.		Overprint in lake	850.00	*1,000.*
b.		Double overprint in lake & blk	4,000.	*5,500.*

Wmk. Anchor (16)

Black Overprint

5	A6	½p black ('87)	8.50	*16.00*
a.		"ritish"	2,750.	*2,500.*
b.		Double overprint	3,750.	
6	A6	1p rose	13.50	10.50
a.		"ritish"	*7,500.*	*4,250.*
b.		Double overprint		*2,500.*
c.		Missing dot in first "i" of "British"	175.00	*175.00*
7	A6	2p bister	40.00	10.00
a.		"ritish"	6,750.	*4,250.*
b.		Double overprint		2,100.
c.		Missing dot in first "i" of "British"	425.00	175.00
8	A3	6p violet	125.00	45.00
a.		Missing dot in first "i" of "British"	1,250.	*575.00*
9	A3	1sh green ('86)	325.00	175.00
a.		"ritish"	*19,000.*	*14,000.*

There is no period after Bechuanaland in the genuine stamps.

Covers: Values for commercial covers begin at $400.

Black Ovpt. on Great Britain #111

1887 Wmk. 30

10	A54	½p vermilion	1.50	*1.50*
		Handstamped "SPECIMEN"	100.00	
a.		Double overprint	2,600.	

For overprints see Bechuanaland Protectorate Nos. 51-53.

A1

A2

A3

1887 Typo. Wmk. 29
Country Name in Black

11	A1	1p lilac	17.50	3.50
12	A1	2p lilac	85.00	10.00
a.		2p pale dull lilac	67.50	27.50
13	A1	3p lilac	4.25	*6.25*
a.		3p pale reddish lilac	72.50	22.50
14	A1	4p lilac	57.50	2.75
15	A1	6p lilac	67.50	9.00

Wmk. 14

16	A2	1sh green	35.00	6.75
17	A2	2sh green	57.50	45.00
18	A2	2sh6p green	67.50	67.50
19	A2	5sh green	105.00	*175.00*
		Pen cancellation		4.00
20	A2	10sh green	210.00	*400.00*
		Pen cancellation		27.50

Wmk. 29

21	A3	£1 lilac	1,000.	*1,300.*
		Pen cancellation		45.00
22	A3	£5 lilac	3,500.	*1,700.*
		Pen cancellation		190.00
		Nos. 11-22 handstamped "SPECIMEN"	1,050.	

The corner designs and central oval differs on No. 22.

For overprints see Bechuanaland Protectorate Nos. 54-58, 60-66. For surcharges see Nos. 23-28, 30, Cape of Good Hope No. 171.

Beware of cleaned pen (fiscal) cancellations and forged postmarks on Nos. 21-22.

Nos. 11-12, 14-16 Surcharged

1888

Country Name in Black

Black Surcharge

23	A1	1p on 1p lilac	8.50	7.50
a.		Double surcharge		
24	A1	6p on 6p lilac	125.00	20.00

Red Surcharge

25	A1	2p on 2p lilac	27.50	3.50
a.		"2" with curved tail	290.00	175.00
b.		On 1p pale dull lilac (#12a)	100.00	60.00
26	A1	4p on 4p lilac	350.00	*450.00*

Green Surcharge

27	A1	2p on 2p lilac		*4,000.*

Blue Surcharge

27A	A1	6p on 6p lilac		*13,500.*

Wmk. 14

Black Surcharge

28	A2	1sh on 1sh green	190.00	95.00

No. 29

No. 30

Green Ovpt. on Cape of Good Hope #41

1889 Wmk. 16

29	A4	½p black	4.75	*30.00*
a.		Double ovpt., one inverted	1,800.	
b.		Double ovpt., one vertical		—
c.		Pair, one stamp without ovpt.	5,750.	
d.		"British" omitted	*4,000.*	

1888 Wmk. 29
Black Surcharge on No. 13

30	A1	½p on 3p lilac & blk	190.00	*200.00*

Stamps with errors of spelling in the surcharge are fakes.

Cape of Good Hope Nos. 43-44 Overprinted in Black, Reading Up

1891 Wmk. 16

31	A4	1p rose	11.50	10.00
a.		Horiz. pair, one without overprint	—	
b.		"British" omitted	—	2,250.
c.		"Bechuanaland" omitted	2,400.	

32 A4 2p bister 3.75 3.00
a. Without period 325.00 *375.00*
Nos. 31-32 handstamped "SPECIMEN" 150.00

See Nos. 38-39.

Stamps of Great Britain Overprinted in Black

1891-94 Wmk. 30

33 A40 1p lilac 7.00 1.75
34 A56 2p green & car 14.00 4.75
35 A59 4p brown & green 3.00 .75
a. Half used as 2p on cover *2,750.*
36 A62 6p violet, *rose* 4.00 2.25
37 A65 1sh green ('94) 15.00 *19.00*
a. Half used as 6p on cover —
Nos. 33-37 (5) 43.00 *28.50*
Nos. 33-36 handstamped "SPECIMEN" 200.00

No. 35a was used at the Palapye Post Office in Nov. 1899. No. 37a was used at the Kanye Post Office in Dec. 1904.

For surcharges see Cape of Good Hope Nos. 172, 176-177.

Cape of Good Hope Nos. 43-44 Overprinted Like Nos. 31-32 but Reading Down

1893-95 Wmk. 16

38 A6 1p rose 2.75 2.75
a. No dots over the "i's" of "British" 140.00 *150.00*
b. "British" omitted 3,000.
c. As "a," reading up *3,000.*
d. Pair, one without overprint
e. Overprinted "Bechuanaland/British" 1,150. *1,300.*
39 A6 2p bister ('95) 5.50 2.75
a. Double overprint 1,500. 950.00
b. No dots over the "i's" of "British" 175.00 150.00
c. "British" omitted 725.00 625.00
d. As "b," reading up
e. Overprinted "Bechuanaland/British" 475.00 275.00

The missing dot-over-i variety exists only on this issue. Nos. 38c and 39d resulted from the sheets being fed into the press upside-down.

Cape of Good Hope No. 42 Overprinted

"BECHUANALAND" 16mm Long Overprint Lines 13mm Apart

1897

40 A6 ½p light green 3.00 *13.50*

"BECHUANALAND" 15mm Long Overprint Lines 10½mm Apart

41 A6 ½p light green 10.00 *55.00*

"BECHUANALAND" 15mm Long Overprint Lines 13½mm Apart

42 A6 ½p light green 24.00 *85.00*
Nos. 40-42 (3) 37.00 *153.50*

Nos. 40-42 actually are issues of Bechuanaland Protectorate.

BECHUANALAND PROTECTORATE

ˌbech-ˈwä-nə-ˌland prə-ˈtek-t(ə-)rət

LOCATION — In central South Africa, north of the Republic of South Africa, east of South West Africa and bounded on the north by the Caprivi Strip of Southwest Africa and on the east by Southern Rhodesia

GOVT. — British Protectorate

AREA — 222,000 sq. mi.

POP. — 540,400 (1964)

CAPITAL — Vryburg (to 1895), Mafeking

12 Pence = 1 Shilling
20 Shillings = 1 Pound

Catalogue values for unused stamps in this country are for Never Hinged items, beginning with Scott 137 in the regular postage section.

Additional Overprint in Black on Bechuanaland No. 10

a

b

c

1888-90 Wmk. 30 *Perf. 14*

51 A54(a) ½p vermilion ('90) 200.00 *375.00*
a. Double overprint 1,750.
b. "Protectorrte"
c. As "b," double overprint *14,000.*
52 A54(b) ½p vermilion ('88) 5.50 *35.00*
Handstamped "SPECIMEN" 100.00
a. Double overprint *375.00*
53 A54(c) ½p vermilion ('90) 190.00 *200.00*
a. Inverted overprint 87.50 *110.00*
b. Double overprint 125.00 *190.00*
c. As "a," double 700.00 700.00
d. "Portectorate" — —
e. As "a," "Portectorate" *7,500.* —

For surcharge see No. 68.

Bechuanaland Nos. 16-20 Overprinted Type "b" in Black

Wmk. 14

Country Name in Black

54 A2 1sh green 100.00 60.00
Handstamped "SPECIMEN" 125.00
a. First "o" omitted *5,750.* 3,500.
55 A2 2sh green 700.00 *1,000.*
a. First "o" omitted *17,000.* —
56 A2 2sh6p green 625.00 *925.00*
a. First "o" omitted *14,000.* —
57 A2 5sh green 1,400. *2,500.*
a. First "o" omitted *20,000.* —
58 A2 10sh green 4,750. *6,500.*
a. First "o" omitted *27,500.* —

Bechuanaland Nos. 11-15 Overprinted Type "b" and Surcharged in Black

1888 Wmk. 29

Country Name in Black

60 A1 1p on 1p lilac 9.25 *16.00*
a. Short "1" 475.00 *550.00*
61 A1 2p on 2p lilac 30.00 20.00
a. "2" with curved tail 800.00 550.00
63 A1 3p on 3p reddish lilac 150.00 *210.00*
64 A1 4p on 4p lilac 400.00 425.00
a. Small "4" *4,250.* *4,250.*
65 A1 6p on 6p lilac 80.00 47.50

In #60 the "1" is 2½mm high; in #60a, 2mm.

Value Surcharged in Red

66 A1 4p on 4p lilac 90.00 45.00

Cape of Good Hope Type of 1886 Overprinted in Green

1889 Wmk. 16

67 A6 ½p black 3.75 *50.00*
a. Double overprint 525.00 *750.00*
b. "Bechuanaland" omitted 1,750.
c. "Protectorate Bechuanaland" 1,300.
d. As "a," one reading as "c" 875.00 *1,000.*

Black Surcharge on Bechuanaland Protectorate No. 52

Wmk. 30

68 A54 4p on ½p ver 30.00 4.25
Handstamped "SPECIMEN" 150.00
a. Inverted surcharge *4,750.*
b. "rpence" omitted *7,000.*
c. "ourpence" omitted *11,750.*
d. As "c," inverted surcharge *16,000.*

Stamps of Great Britain 1881-87, Overprinted in Black

1897, Oct.

69 A54 ½p vermilion 1.25 *2.50*
70 A40 1p lilac 4.50 .85
71 A56 2p green & car 4.50 *4.00*
72 A58 3p violet, *yel* 6.25 *10.00*
73 A59 4p brown & green 17.00 16.00
74 A62 6p violet, *rose* 27.50 12.50
Nos. 69-74 (6) 61.00 45.85
Set, handstamped "SPECIMEN" 250.00

For surcharges see Cape of Good Hope Nos. 167-170, 173-175.

Same on Great Britain No. 125

1902, Feb. 25

75 A54 ½p blue green 1.75 *4.00*
Handstamped "SPECIMEN" 37.50

Stamps of Great Britain, 1902, Overprinted in Black

1904-12

76 A66 ½p gray green ('06) 2.25 2.25
77 A66 1p car ('05) 8.75 .65
78 A66 2½p ultra 8.75 5.75
a. Period after "P" of "Protectorate" 1,100. *1,400.*
79 A74 1sh scar & grn ('12) 45.00 *175.00*
a. 1sh carmine & green 47.50 *125.00*
Nos. 76-79 (4) 64.75 *183.65*

Same on Great Britain No. 143

1908

80 A66 ½p pale yel green 4.25 4.00

Transvaal No. 274 overprinted "Bechuanaland Protectorate," formerly listed as No. 81, now appears as No. AR1 in the Postal-Fiscal Stamps section.

Great Britain No. 154 Overprinted Like Nos. 76-79

1912, Sept. Wmk. 30 *Perf. 15x14*

82 A81 1p scarlet 2.25 .90
a. No cross on crown 175.00 87.50
b. 1p analine scarlet ('14) 160.00 92.50

Great Britain Stamps of 1912-13 Overprinted Like Nos. 76-79

Wmk. Crown and GvR (33)

1913-24

83 A82 ½p green 1.40 *2.00*
84 A83 1p scarlet ('15) 3.25 .85
a. 1p carmine ('22) 30.00 3.00
85 A84 1½p red brn ('20) 4.50 *3.50*
86 A85 2p reddish orange (I) 5.75 *5.25*
a. 2p orange (I) ('21) 22.50 4.50
b. 2p orange (II) ('24) 2.00 1.25
87 A86 2½p ultra 4.00 *25.00*
a. 2½p blue ('15) 12.50 *27.50*
88 A87 3p bluish violet 6.75 *13.50*
89 A88 4p slate green 7.25 *26.00*
90 A89 6p dull violet 8.00 *19.00*
a. Double overprint, one albino
91 A90 1sh bister 11.00 *25.00*
a. 1sh bister brown ('23) 30.00 *35.00*
Overprinted "SPECIMEN" 85.00
Nos. 83-91 (9) 51.90 *120.10*

The dies of No. 86 are the same as in Great Britain 1912-13 issue.

Overprinted

Wmk. 34 *Perf. 11x12*

92 A91 2sh6p dark brown ('15) 150.00 *300.00*
a. 2sh6p light brown ('16) 125.00 *300.00*
b. 2sh6p sepia brown ('17) 150.00 *260.00*
c. Double overprint, one albino, on #92 350.00
d. Triple overprint, one albino, on #92b —
93 A91 5sh rose carmine ('14) 190.00 *450.00*
a. 5sh carmine ('19) 350.00 *500.00*
b. Double overprint, one albino, on #93 450.00
c. Double overprint, one albino, on #93a 525.00

Nos. 92, 93 were printed by Waterlow Bros. & Layton; Nos. 92a, 93a were printed by Thomas De La Rue & Co.

Same Overprint On Retouched Stamps of 1919 (#179, 180)

1920-23

94 A91 2sh6p gray brown 100.00 *200.00*
95 A91 5sh car rose 140.00 *325.00*

Great Britain Stamps of 1924 Overprinted like Nos. 76-79

Wmk. Crown and Block GvR Multiple (35)

1925-27 *Perf. 15x14*

96 A82 ½p green ('27) 1.60 *2.00*
97 A83 1p scarlet 2.25 1.00
99 A85 2p deep org (II) 2.50 1.25
101 A87 3p violet ('26) 5.50 *22.50*
102 A88 4p slate green ('26) 5.50 *45.00*
103 A89 6p dull violet, chalky paper 45.00 *85.00*
a. 6p purple, ordinary paper 55.00 *57.50*
104 A90 1sh bister ('26) 11.00 *30.00*
Nos. 96-104 (7) 73.35 *186.75*

George V
A11

George VI, Cattle and Baobab Tree
A12

Perf. 12½

1932, Dec. 12 Engr. Wmk. 4

105 A11 ½p green 1.40 .35
a. Horiz. Pair, imperf between 20,500.
106 A11 1p carmine 1.25 .30
107 A11 2p red brown 1.25 .35
108 A11 3p ultra 1.40 3.00
109 A11 4p orange 1.40 *7.25*
110 A11 6p red violet 2.75 *5.00*
111 A11 1sh blk & ol grn 6.00 *8.00*
112 A11 2sh black & org 27.50 *55.00*
113 A11 2sh6p black & car 26.00 *35.00*
114 A11 3sh black & red vio 42.50 *50.00*
115 A11 5sh black & ultra 80.00 *85.00*
116 A11 10sh blk & red brown 160.00 *175.00*
Nos. 105-116 (12) 351.45 *424.25*

Common Design Types pictured following the introduction.

Silver Jubilee Issue
Common Design Type

1935, May 4 ***Perf. 11x12***

117 CD301 1p car & blue .25 *3.00*
118 CD301 2p black & ultra 1.00 3.00
119 CD301 3p ultra & brown 2.50 3.00
120 CD301 6p brown vio & ind 4.25 *3.00*
Nos. 117-120 (4) 8.00 12.00
Set, never hinged 20.00

Coronation Issue
Common Design Type

1937, May 12 ***Perf. 13½x14***

121 CD302 1p carmine .30 *.40*
122 CD302 2p brown .30 *1.10*
123 CD302 3p bright ultra .40 *1.50*
Nos. 121-123 (3) 1.00 3.00
Set, never hinged 1.50

1938, Apr. 1 ***Perf. 12½***

124 A12 ½p green 1.50 *2.50*
125 A12 1p rose car .50 .60
126 A12 1½p light blue 6.25 *2.25*
127 A12 2p brown .50 *.65*
128 A12 3p ultra .50 *2.50*
129 A12 4p orange 1.50 *3.75*
130 A12 6p rose violet 3.25 3.25
131 A12 1sh blk & ol grn 3.00 *4.50*
133 A12 2sh6p black & car 10.00 *14.00*
135 A12 5sh black & ultra 22.50 16.00
136 A12 10sh black & brn 10.50 *20.00*
Nos. 124-136 (11) 60.00 *70.00*
Set, never hinged 80.00

Catalogue values for unused stamps in this section, from this point to the end of the section, are for Never Hinged items.

Peace Issue

South Africa Nos. 100-102 Overprinted

Basic stamps inscribed alternately in English and Afrikaans.

1945, Dec. 3 Wmk. 201 ***Perf. 14***

137 A42 1p rose pink & choc, pair .30 .30
a. Single, English .20 .20
b. Single, Afrikaans .20 .20
138 A43 2p vio & slate blue, pair .40 .40
a. Single, English .20 .20
b. Single, Afrikaans .20 .20
139 A43 3p ultra & dp ultra, pair .50 .50
a. Single, English .25 .25
b. Single, Afrikaans .25 .25
Nos. 137-139 (3) 1.20 1.20

World War II victory of the Allies.

Royal Visit Issue
Types of Basutoland, 1947

Perf. 12½

1947, Feb. 17 Wmk. 4 Engr.

143 A3 1p red .20 .20
144 A4 2p green .20 .20
145 A5 3p ultra .20 .20
146 A6 1sh dark violet .20 .20
Nos. 143-146 (4) .80 .80

Visit of the British Royal Family, 4/17/47.

Silver Wedding Issue
Common Design Types

1948, Dec. 1 Photo. ***Perf. 14x14½***

147 CD304 1½p brt ultra .25 .20

Engr.; Name Typo.

Perf. 11½x11

148 CD305 10sh gray black 32.50 *40.00*

UPU Issue
Common Design Types

Engr.; Name Typo. on 3p and 6p

1949, Oct. 10 ***Perf. 13½, 11x11½***

149 CD306 1½p blue .25 .25
150 CD307 3p indigo .35 .35
151 CD308 6p red lilac .80 .80
152 CD309 1sh olive 1.50 1.50
Nos. 149-152 (4) 2.90 2.90

POSTAL-FISCAL STAMPS

Transvaal No. 274 Overprinted

1910, July Wmk. 3

AR1 A27 6p brn org & blk 190.00 *375.00*

This stamp was issued for fiscal use in January 1907, but the "POSTAGE" inscription was not obliterated, and examples were accepted for postal use during 1910-11.

Bechuanaland No. 16 surcharged "£5"

1918 Wmk. 29

AR2 A1 £5 on 1sh green *12,000.*

South Africa No. 3 overprinted "Bechuanaland Protectorate." in two lines

1922 Wmk. 177

AR3 A2 1p rose red 45.00 *140.00*
a. Double ovpt, one albino 160.00

POSTAGE DUE STAMPS

Postage Due Stamps of Great Britain Overprinted

On Stamp of 1914-22

1926 Wmk. 33 ***Perf. 14x14½***

J1 D1 1p carmine 6.75 *95.00*

On Stamps of 1924-30

Wmk. 35

J2 D1 ½p emerald 6.75 *57.50*

Overprinted

J3 D1 2p black brown 8.50 *100.00*
Nos. J1-J3 (3) 22.00 *252.50*
Set, never hinged 30.00

D2

1932 Wmk. 4 Typo. ***Perf. 14½***

J4 D2 ½p olive green 6.75 *55.00*
On cover *300.00*
J5 D2 1p carmine rose 8.00 *10.00*
On cover *275.00*
J6 D2 2p dull violet 10.00 *55.00*
On cover *300.00*
Nos. J4-J6 (3) 24.75 *120.00*
Set, never hinged 30.00
Set, perforated "SPECIMEN" 80.00

Chalky Paper

1958, Nov. 27

J5a D2 1p carmine 1.00 *12.00*
On cover *275.00*
J6a D2 2p violet 1.40 *16.00*
On cover *300.00*

On cover values are for properly franked commercial covers. Philatelic usages also exist and sell for less.

BELGIAN CONGO

'bel-jən 'käŋ-ˌgō

LOCATION — Central Africa
GOVT. — Belgian colony
AREA — 902,082 sq. mi. (estimated)
POP. — 12,660,000 (1956)
CAPITAL — Léopoldville

Congo was an independent state, founded by Leopold II of Belgium, until 1908 when it was annexed to Belgium as a colony.

100 Centimes = 1 Franc

Independent State

A1

A2

King Leopold II — A3

1886 Unwmk. Typo. ***Perf. 15***

1 A1 5c green 11.00 *22.50*
Never hinged 20.00
On cover —
2 A1 10c rose 5.25 *5.50*
Never hinged 6.50
On cover *550.00*
3 A2 25c blue 45.00 40.00
Never hinged 90.00
On cover *450.00*
a. 25c greenish blue 50.00 42.50
Never hinged 100.00
On cover *450.00*
b. 25c ultramarine 65.00 —
Never hinged 130.00
4 A3 50c olive green 8.50 8.50
Never hinged 11.00
On cover *750.00*
a. 50c dark olive 22.50 22.50
Never hinged 45.00
5 A1 5fr lilac 375.00 300.00
Never hinged 675.00
On cover —
a. Perf. 14 825.00 550.00
Never hinged —
b. 5fr deep lilac 725.00 475.00
Never hinged —
c. Imperforate —

Counterfeits exist.

Postal stationery with stamps added sell for considerably less.

For surcharge see No. Q1.

King Leopold II — A4

1887-94

6 A4 5c grn ('89) .75 *1.00*
Never hinged 1.00
On cover *125.00*
7 A4 10c rose ('89) 1.75 1.40
Never hinged 2.00
On cover *125.00*
8 A4 25c blue ('89) 1.75 1.40
Never hinged 2.00
On cover *300.00*
9 A4 50c reddish brown 52.50 25.00
Never hinged 90.00
On cover *500.00*
a. 50c deep brown 80.00 35.00
Never hinged 150.00
On cover *500.00*
10 A4 50c gray ('94) 3.75 *18.00*
Never hinged 4.50
On cover *2,000.*
11 A4 5fr violet 925.00 400.00
Never hinged —
On cover *6,750.*
12 A4 5fr gray ('92) 125.00 97.50
Never hinged 180.00
On cover, overfranked *1,000.*
On portion of parcel wrapper *1,250.*
13 A4 10fr buff ('91) 450.00 300.00
Never hinged 625.00
On cover, overfranked *2,000.*

The 25fr and 50fr in gray were not issued. Values, each $30., never hinged $40.

Counterfeits exist of Nos. 10-13, 25fr and 50fr, unused, used, genuine stamps with faked cancels and counterfeit stamps with genuine cancels.

Covers: Postal stationery with stamps added sell for considerably less. Values for Nos. 12-13 are for overfranked covers, usually philatelic.

For surcharges see Nos. Q3-Q6.

Port Matadi — A5

River Scene on the Congo, Stanley Falls — A6

Inkissi Falls — A7

Railroad Bridge on M'pozo River — A8

Hunting Elephants A9

Bangala Chief and Wife — A10

1894-1901 Engr. ***Perf. 12½ to 15***

14 A5 5c pale bl & blk 16.50 16.50
Never hinged 27.50
On cover *50.00*
15 A5 5c red brn & blk ('95) 3.75 1.50
Never hinged 5.25
On cover *25.00*
16 A5 5c grn & blk ('00) 2.00 .50
Never hinged 3.75
On cover *25.00*
a. Retouched 3.75 1.25
Never hinged 11.00
On cover 50.00
17 A6 10c red brn & blk 16.00 *18.00*
Never hinged 30.00
On cover *50.00*

18 A6 10c grnsh bl & blk ('95) 3.00 1.60
Never hinged 5.00
On cover 25.00
a. Center inverted 2,250. 2,500.
On cover 10,000.
19 A6 10c car & blk ('00) 4.00 .90
Never hinged 5.50
On cover 50.00
20 A7 25c yel org & blk 4.50 3.25
Never hinged 7.00
On cover 25.00
21 A7 25c lt bl & blk ('00) 4.75 2.25
Never hinged 7.00
On cover 9.00
a. Redrawn frame 1,100. 600.00
22 A8 50c grn & blk 1.75 1.75
Never hinged 2.75
On cover 60.00
23 A8 50c ol & blk ('00) 4.50 1.00
Never hinged 7.00
On cover 20.00
24 A9 1fr lilac & blk 25.00 16.50
Never hinged 40.00
On cover 275.00
a. 1fr rose lilac & black 350.00 27.50
Never hinged 575.00
On cover 275.00
25 A9 1fr car & blk ('01) 250.00 6.75
Never hinged 500.00
On cover 225.00
26 A10 5fr lake & blk 45.00 32.50
Never hinged 110.00
On cover 200.00
a. 5fr carmine rose & black 100.00 45.00
Never hinged 175.00
On cover 300.00
Nos. 14-26 (13) 380.75 103.00

No. 16a has a small circle touching the the frameline, about 2mm from the lower right corner

The frameline has been strenghtened at the top and bottom of No. 21a. It is thicker and more regular than on No. 21.

Covers: Postal stationery with stamps added sell for considerably less. Values for Nos. 26, 26a are for overfranked covers, usually philatelic.

For overprints see Nos. 31-32, 34, 36-37, 39.

Climbing Oil Palms — A11

Congo Canoe A12

1896

27 A11 15c ocher & blk 4.00 .90
Never hinged 6.50
On cover 25.00
28 A12 40c bluish grn & blk 4.00 3.50
Never hinged 6.50
On cover 30.00

For overprints see Nos. 33, 35.

Congo Village A13

River Steamer on the Congo A14

1898

29 A13 3.50fr red & blk 160.00 110.00
Never hinged 250.00
On cover 200.00
a. Perf. 14x12 450.00 275.00
Never hinged —
30 A14 10fr yel grn & blk 110.00 35.00
Never hinged 175.00
On cover —
a. Center inverted 25,000.
b. Perf. 12 650.00 37.50
Never hinged —
c. Perf. 12x14 400.00 —
Never hinged —
As "c," pen canceled 16.00

For overprints see Nos. 38, 40.

Belgian Congo

Overprinted

1908

31 A5 5c green & blk 7.25 7.25
Never hinged 20.00
On cover 45.00
a. Handstamped 3.50 2.00
Never hinged 6.00
As "a," on cover 25.00
32 A6 10c car & blk 12.00 12.00
Never hinged 30.00
On cover 45.00
a. Handstamped 3.50 2.00
Never hinged 6.00
As "a," on cover 25.00
33 A11 15c ocher & blk 7.25 7.25
Never hinged 20.00
On cover 35.00
a. Handstamped 7.00 3.50
Never hinged 12.00
As "a," on cover 35.00
34 A7 25c lt blue & blk 3.75 2.50
Never hinged 10.00
On cover 35.00
a. Handstamped 10.00 4.00
Never hinged 20.00
As "a," on cover 35.00
b. As "a," redrawn frame (#21a) 20.00 10.00
Never hinged 40.00
c. Double overprint (#34) 200.00
35 A12 40c bluish grn & blk 2.50 2.50
Never hinged 7.00
On cover 45.00
a. Handstamped 10.00 6.25
Never hinged 20.00
As "a," on cover 50.00
36 A8 50c olive & blk 4.25 2.50
Never hinged 8.50
On cover 25.00
a. Handstamped 4.75 3.50
Never hinged 12.00
As "a," on cover 25.00
b. As #36, inverted overprint 550.00
37 A9 1fr car & blk 20.00 2.50
Never hinged 50.00
On cover 100.00
a. Handstamped 50.00 10.00
Never hinged 75.00
As "a," on cover 85.00
38 A13 3.50fr red & blk 25.00 20.00
Never hinged 65.00
On cover 125.00
a. Handstamped 300.00 140.00
Never hinged 500.00
As "a," on cover 250.00
b. As #38, inverted overprint 600.00 —
39 A10 5fr car & blk 42.50 24.00
Never hinged 90.00
On cover 125.00
a. Handstamped 90.00 55.00
Never hinged 175.00
As "a," on cover 150.00
40 A14 10fr yel grn & blk 85.00 21.00
Never hinged 190.00
On cover 150.00
a. Perf. 14½ 250.00 —
Never hinged 500.00
b. Handstamped 175.00 55.00
Never hinged 350.00
As "a," on cover 150.00
c. Handstamped, perf. 14½ 400.00 225.00
Never hinged 700.00
d. As #40a, double overprint 400.00
Nos. 31-40 (10) 209.50 101.50

Most of the above handstamps are also found inverted and double.

There are two types of handstamped overprints, those applied in Brussels and those applied locally. There are eight types of each overprint. Values listed are the lowest for each stamp.

Covers: Values for Nos. 39, 39a, 40, 40b are for overfranked covers, usually philatelic.

Counterfeits of the handstamped overprints exist.

Port Matadi A15

River Scene on the Congo, Stanley Falls — A16

Climbing Oil Palms — A17

Railroad Bridge on M'pozo River — A18

1909 *Perf. 14*

41 A15 5c green & blk .75 1.00
Never hinged 2.50
On cover 15.00
42 A16 10c carmine & blk .75 .50
Never hinged 2.50
On cover 35.00
43 A17 15c ocher & blk 30.00 17.50
Never hinged 110.00
On cover 35.00
44 A18 50c olive & blk 3.50 2.50
Never hinged 10.00
On cover 25.00
Nos. 41-44 (4) 35.00 21.50

Port Matadi A19

River Scene on the Congo, Stanley Falls — A20

Climbing Oil Palms — A21

Inkissi Falls — A22

Congo Canoe A23

Railroad Bridge on M'pozo River — A24

Hunting Elephants A25

Congo Village A26

Bangala Chief and Wife — A27

River Steamer on the Congo A28

1910-15 **Engr.** *Perf. 14, 15*

45 A19 5c green & blk .75 .25
Never hinged 1.50
On cover 10.00
46 A20 10c carmine & blk .60 .25
Never hinged 1.50
On cover 10.00
a. 10c lake & black 30.00 30.00
Never hinged 50.00
On cover —
47 A21 15c ocher & blk .50 .25
Never hinged 1.10
On cover 20.00
48 A21 15c grn & blk ('15) .35 .25
Never hinged .85
On cover 10.00
a. Booklet pane of 10 14.00
49 A22 25c blue & blk 2.00 .35
Never hinged 3.50
On cover 10.00
50 A23 40c bluish grn & blk 2.50 2.25
Never hinged 3.50
On cover 20.00
51 A23 40c brn red & blk ('15) 4.50 2.40
Never hinged 14.00
On cover 20.00
52 A24 50c olive & blk 3.75 2.00
Never hinged 6.50
On cover 35.00
53 A24 50c brn lake & blk ('15) 7.00 2.40
Never hinged 20.00
On cover 25.00
54 A25 1fr carmine & blk 4.50 2.75
Never hinged 7.50
On cover 50.00
55 A25 1fr ol bis & blk ('15) 3.25 1.10
Never hinged 8.50
On cover 25.00
56 A26 3fr red & blk 16.00 13.00
Never hinged 35.00
On cover 100.00
57 A27 5fr carmine & blk 24.00 24.00
Never hinged 90.00
On cover 100.00
58 A27 5fr ocher & blk ('15) 2.25 1.10
Never hinged 4.50
On cover 75.00
59 A28 10fr green & blk 27.50 27.50
Never hinged 70.00
On cover 100.00
Nos. 45-59 (15) 99.45 79.85

Nos. 48, 51, 53, 55 and 58 exist imperforate.

Covers: Value for No. 59 is for overfranked cover, usually philatelic.

For overprints and surcharges see Nos. 64-76, 81-86, B5-B9.

Port Matadi A29

Stanley Falls, Congo River — A30

Inkissi Falls — A31

TEN CENTIMES.

Type I — Large white space at top of picture and two small white spots at lower edge. Vignette does not fill frame.

Type II — Vignette completely fills frame.

1915

60	A29	5c green & blk	.30	.20
a.		Booklet pane of 10	10.00	
61	A30	10c car & blk (II)	.30	.20
a.		10c carmine & black (I)	.30	.20
d.		Booklet pane of 10 (II)	15.00	
62	A31	25c blue & blk	1.50	.30
a.		Booklet pane of 10	90.00	
		Nos. 60-62 (3)	2.10	.70

Nos. 60 to 62 exist imperforate.
For surcharges see Nos. 77-80, 87, B1-B4.

Stamps of 1910 Issue Surcharged in Red or Black

1921

64	A23	5c on 40c bluish grn & blk (R)	.30	.25
65	A19	10c on 5c grn & blk (R)	.30	.25
66	A24	15c on 50c ol & blk (R)	.30	.25
67	A21	25c on 15c ocher & blk (R)	1.75	1.40
68	A20	30c on 10c car & blk	.40	*.60*
69	A22	50c on 25c bl & blk (R)	1.75	.90
		Nos. 64-69 (6)	4.80	3.65

The position of the new value and the bars varies on Nos. 64 to 69.

Overprinted

1921

70	A25	1fr carmine & blk	1.50	1.25
a.		Double overprint	20.00	
71	A26	3fr red & blk	3.00	3.00
72	A27	5fr carmine & blk	10.00	9.00
73	A28	10fr green & blk (R)	7.50	7.00
		Nos. 70-73 (4)	22.00	20.25

Belgian Surcharges

Nos. 51, 53, 60-62 Surcharged in Black or Red

1922

74	A24	5c on 50c	.40	.60
75	A29	10c on 5c (R)	.45	.25
76	A23	25c on 40c (R)	3.00	.55
77	A30	30c on 10c (II)	.40	.30
a.		30c on 10c (I)	.40	.30
b.		Double surcharge	4.75	4.75
78	A31	50c on 25c (R)	.50	.30
		Nos. 74-78 (5)	4.75	2.00

No. 74 has the surcharge at each side.

Congo Surcharges

Nos. 60, 51 Surcharged in Red or Black:

a

b

1922

80	A29	10c on 5c (R)	.65	.65
a.		Inverted surcharge	20.00	20.00
b.		Double surcharge	4.75	
c.		Double surch., one invtd.	40.00	
d.		Pair, one without surcharge	42.50	
e.		On No. 45	125.00	125.00
81	A23	25c on 40c	.85	.50
a.		Inverted surcharge	20.00	20.00
b.		Double surcharge	5.50	
c.		"25c" double		
d.		25c on 5c, No. 60	100.00	100.00

Nos. 55, 58 Surcharged with vertical bars over original values

1922

84	A25	10c on 1fr (R)	.90	.90
a.		Double surcharge	14.00	
b.		Inverted surcharge	20.00	20.00
85	A27	25c on 5fr	2.00	2.00

Nos. 68, 77 Handstamped

86	A20	25c on 30c on 10c	12.00	12.00
87	A30	25c on 30c on 10c (II)	10.00	10.00

Nos. 86-87 exist with handstamp surcharge inverted.
Counterfeit handstamped surcharges exist.

Ubangi Woman — A32

Watusi Cattle — A44

Designs: 10c, Baluba woman. 15c, Babuende woman. No. 90, 40c, 1.25fr, 1.50fr, 1.75fr, Ubangi man. 25c, Basketmaking. 30c, 35c, Nos. 101, 102, Carving wood. 50c, Archer. Nos. 92, 100, Weaving. 1fr, Making pottery. 3fr, Working rubber. 5fr, Making palm oil. 10fr, African elephant.

1923-27 Engr. *Perf. 12*

88	A32	5c yellow	.35	.20
89	A32	10c green	.20	.20
90	A32	15c olive brn	.20	.20
91	A32	20c olive grn ('24)	.20	.20
92	A44	20c green ('26)	.50	.20
93	A44	25c red brown	.25	.20
94	A44	30c rose red ('24)	.45	1.50
95	A44	30c olive grn ('25)	.20	.20
96	A44	35c green ('27)	1.00	.45
97	A32	40c violet ('25)	.20	.20
98	A44	50c gray blue	.25	.20
99	A44	50c buff ('25)	.60	.20
100	A44	75c red orange	.25	.20
101	A44	75c gray bl ('25)	1.00	.25
102	A44	75c salmon red ('26)	.80	.20
103	A44	1fr bister brn	.55	.25
104	A44	1fr dl blue ('25)	.40	.20
105	A44	1fr rose red ('27)	.85	.20
106	A32	1.25fr dl blue ('26)	.35	.20
107	A32	1.50fr dl blue ('26)	.35	.20
108	A32	1.75fr dl blue ('27)	3.75	3.50
109	A44	3fr gray brn ('24)	6.00	3.00
110	A44	5fr gray ('24)	10.00	6.50
111	A44	10fr gray blk ('24)	27.50	12.00

1925-26

112	A44	45c dk vio ('26)	.65	.35
113	A44	60c carmine rose	.60	.25
		Nos. 88-113 (26)	57.45	31.25

For surcharges see Nos. 114, 136-138, 157.

No. 107 Surcharged

1927, June 14

114	A32	1.75fr on 1.50fr dl bl	.80	.80

Sir Henry Morton Stanley — A45

1928, June 30 *Perf. 14*

115	A45	5c gray blk	.20	.20
116	A45	10c dp violet	.20	.20
117	A45	20c orange red	.50	.30
118	A45	35c green	1.25	.75
119	A45	40c red brown	.60	.20
120	A45	60c black brn	1.00	.50
121	A45	1fr carmine	.40	.20
122	A45	1.60fr dk gray	7.50	5.00
123	A45	1.75fr dp blue	1.25	.65
124	A45	2fr dk brown	.60	.30
125	A45	2.75fr red violet	5.00	.45
126	A45	3.50fr rose lake	1.00	.60
127	A45	5fr slate grn	.60	*.70*
128	A45	10fr violet blue	1.25	.75
129	A45	20fr claret	7.00	4.50
		Nos. 115-129 (15)	28.35	15.30

Sir Henry M. Stanley (1841-1904), explorer.

Nos. 118, 121-123, 125-126 Surcharged in Red, Blue or Black

1931, Jan. 15

130	A45	40c on 35c	1.50	1.50
131	A45	1.25fr on 1fr (Bl)	1.90	.30
132	A45	2fr on 1.60fr	.80	.40
133	A45	2fr on 1.75fr	.75	.30
134	A45	3.25fr on 2.75fr (Bk)	3.25	2.00
135	A45	3.25fr on 3.25fr (Bk)	6.00	6.00

Nos. 96, 108, 112 Surcharged in Red

Perf. 12½, 12

136	A44	40c on 35c grn	7.25	6.00
137	A44	50c on 45c dk vio	3.00	2.00

Surcharged

138	A32	2(fr) on 1.75fr dl bl	8.50	8.50
		Nos. 130-138 (9)	32.95	27.00

View of Sankuru River — A46

Flute Players — A50

Designs: 15c, Kivu Kraal. 20c, Sankuru River rapids. 25c, Uele hut. 50c, Musicians of Lake Leopold II. 60c, Batetelas drummers. 75c, Mangbetu woman. 1fr, Domesticated elephant of Api. 1.25fr, Mangbetu chief. 1.50fr, 2fr, Village of Mondimbi. 2.50fr, 3.25fr, Okapi. 4fr, Canoes at Stanleyville. 5fr, Woman preparing cassava. 10fr, Baluba chief. 20fr, Young woman of Irumu.

1931-37 Engr. *Perf. 11½*

139	A46	10c gray brn ('32)	.20	.20
140	A46	15c gray ('32)	.20	.20
141	A46	20c brn lil ('32)	.20	.20
142	A46	25c dp blue ('32)	.25	.25
143	A50	40c dp grn ('32)	.30	.30
144	A46	50c violet ('32)	.20	.20
b.		Booklet pane of 8	6.25	
145	A50	60c vio brn ('32)	.30	.30
146	A50	75c rose ('32)	.30	.30
b.		Booklet pane of 8	4.50	
147	A50	1fr rose red ('32)	.30	.30
148	A50	1.25fr red brown	.30	.30
b.		Booklet pane of 8	4.50	
149	A46	1.50fr dk ol gray ('37)	.30	.30
b.		Booklet pane of 8	6.00	
150	A46	2fr ultra ('32)	.35	.30
151	A46	2.50fr dp blue ('37)	.50	.30
b.		Booklet pane of 8	8.50	
152	A46	3.25fr gray blk ('32)	.80	.50
153	A46	4fr dl vio ('32)	.50	.30
154	A50	5fr dp vio ('32)	1.00	.40
155	A50	10fr red ('32)	1.25	1.00
156	A50	20fr blk brn ('32)	2.50	1.50
		Nos. 139-156 (18)	9.75	7.15

No. 109 Surcharged in Red

1932, Mar. 15 *Perf. 12*

157	A44	3.25fr on 3fr gray brn	7.50	5.00

King Albert Memorial Issue

King Albert — A62

1934, May 7 Photo. *Perf. 11½*

158	A62	1.50fr black	1.00	.80

No. 158 exists imperf. Value, $25.

Leopold I, Leopold II, Albert I, Leopold III A63

1935, Aug. 15 Engr. *Perf. 12½x12*

159	A63	50c green	2.00	2.00
160	A63	1.25fr dk carmine	1.50	.60
161	A63	1.50fr brown vio	1.40	.30
162	A63	2.40fr brown org	2.50	2.50
163	A63	2.50fr lt blue	2.50	2.00
164	A63	4fr brt violet	5.00	3.00
165	A63	5fr black brn	4.75	3.00
		Nos. 159-165 (7)	19.65	13.40

Founding of Congo Free State, 50th anniv.
Nos. 159-165 exist imperf. Value set, $1,750.
For surcharges see Nos. B21-B22.

Molindi River — A64

Bamboos — A65

Suza River — A66

Rutshuru River — A67

Karisimbi A68

Mitumba Forest A69

1937-38 Photo. *Perf. 11½*

166	A64	5c purple & blk	.30	.25
167	A65	90c car & brn	.70	.35
168	A66	1.50fr dp red brn & blk	.50	.40
169	A67	2.40fr ol blk & brn	.40	.30
170	A68	2.50fr dp ultra & blk	.65	.30
171	A69	4.50fr dk grn & brn	.85	.70
172	A69	4.50fr car & sep	.40	.30
		Nos. 166-172 (7)	3.80	2.60

National Parks.

Nos. 166-171 were issued Mar. 1, 1938. Exist imperf. Value, set $50.

No. 172 was issued in sheets of four measuring 140x111mm. It was sold by subscription, the subscription closing Oct. 20, 1937. Value, $3.00. Exists imperf. Value, $125.

See #B26. For surcharges see #184, 186.

SEMI-POSTAL STAMPS

Types of 1910-15 Issues Surcharged in Red

1918, May 15 Unwmk. *Perf. 14, 15*

B1	A29	5c + 10c grn & bl	.30	*.35*
B2	A30	10c + 15c car & bl (I)	.60	*.50*
B3	A21	15c + 20c bl grn & bl	.40	*.50*
B4	A31	25c + 25c dp bl & pale bl	1.50	*1.50*
B5	A23	40c + 40c brn red & bl	1.10	*1.00*
B6	A24	50c + 50c brn lake & bl	.40	*.45*
B7	A25	1fr + 1fr ol bis & bl	3.00	*3.00*
B8	A27	5fr + 5fr ocher & bl	15.00	*15.00*
B9	A28	10fr + 10fr grn & bl	140.00	*140.00*
		Nos. B1-B9 (9)	162.30	*162.30*
		Set, never hinged	400.00	

The position of the cross and the added value varies on the different stamps.

Nos. B1-B9 exist imperforate. Value, set never hinged, $425.

Perf 15 stamps are worth approximately twice the values shown.

SP1

Design: #B11 inscribed "Belgisch Congo."

1925, July 8 *Perf. 12½*

B10	SP1	25c + 25c carmine & blk	.40	*.40*
B11	SP1	25c + 25c carmine & blk	.40	*.40*
a.		Pair, Nos. B10-B11	.40	*.50*
		Never hinged	1.25	

Colonial campaigns in 1914-1918.

The surtax helped erect at Kinshasa a monument to those who died in World War I.

Nurse Weighing Child — SP3

First Aid Station SP5

20c+10c, Missionary & Child. 60c+30c, Congo hospital. 1fr+50c, Dispensary service. 1.75fr+75c, Convalescent area. 3.50fr+1.50fr, Instruction on bathing infant. 5fr+2.50fr, Operating room. 10fr+5fr, Students.

1930, Jan. 16 Engr. *Perf. 11½*

B12	SP3	10c + 5c ver	1.00	1.00
B13	SP3	20c + 10c dp brn	2.00	2.00
B14	SP5	35c + 15c dp grn	3.00	3.00
B15	SP5	60c + 30c dl vio	3.00	3.00
B16	SP3	1fr + 50c dk car	6.00	6.00
B17	SP5	1.75fr + 75c dp bl	5.50	5.50
B18	SP5	3.50fr + 1.50fr rose lake	8.00	8.00
B19	SP5	5fr + 2.50fr red brn	9.00	9.00
B20	SP5	10fr + 5fr gray blk	10.00	10.00
		Nos. B12-B20 (9)	47.50	47.50
		Set, never hinged	120.00	

The surtax was intended to aid welfare work among the natives, especially the children.

Nos. 161, 163 Surcharged "+50c" in Blue or Red

1936, May 15 *Perf. 12½x12*

B21	A63	1.50fr + 50c (Bl)	5.00	*6.00*
B22	A63	2.50fr + 50c (R)	4.50	3.00
		Set, never hinged	20.00	

Surtax was for the King Albert Memorial Fund.

Queen Astrid with Congolese Children — SP12

1936, Aug. 29 Photo. *Perf. 12½*

B23	SP12	1.25fr + 5c dark brown	.60	.45
B24	SP12	1.50fr + 10c dull rose	.65	.55
B25	SP12	2.50fr + 25c dark blue	1.00	.95
		Nos. B23-B25 (3)	2.25	1.95
		Set, never hinged	5.50	

Issued in memory of Queen Astrid. The surtax was for the aid of the National League for Protection of Native Children.

National Park Type of 1937-38 Souvenir Sheet

1938, Oct. 3 *Perf. 11½*

Star in Yellow

B26		Sheet of 6	40.00	40.00
		Never hinged	90.00	
a.		A64 5c ultra & light brown	6.50	6.50
b.		A65 90c ultra & light brown	6.50	6.50
c.		A66 1.50fr ultra & light brown	6.50	6.50
d.		A67 2.40fr ultra & light brown	6.50	6.50
e.		A68 2.50fr ultra & light brown	6.50	6.50
f.		A69 4.50fr ultra & light brown	6.50	6.50

Intl. Tourist Cong. A surtax of 3.15fr was for the benefit of the Congo Tourist Service. Exists imperf. Value $500.

Marabou Storks and Vultures — SP14

Buffon's Kob — SP15

Designs: 1.50fr+1.50fr, Pygmy chimpanzees. 4.50fr+4.50fr, Dwarf crocodiles. 5fr+5fr, Lioness.

1939, June 6 Photo. *Perf. 14*

B27	SP14	1fr + 1fr dp claret	6.50	6.50
B28	SP15	1.25fr + 1.25fr car	6.50	6.50
B29	SP15	1.50fr + 1.50fr brt pur	8.00	8.00
B30	SP14	4.50fr + 4.50fr sl grn	6.50	6.50
B31	SP15	5fr + 5fr brown	7.00	7.00
		Nos. B27-B31 (5)	34.50	34.50
		Set, never hinged	75.00	

Surtax for the Leopoldville Zoological Gardens. Exists imperf. Value $60.

Sold in full sets by subscription.

AIR POST STAMPS

Wharf on Congo River AP1

Congo "Country Store" AP2

View of Congo River AP3

Stronghold in the Interior — AP4

Unwmk.

1920, July 1 Engr. *Perf. 12*

C1	AP1	50c orange & blk	.40	.20
C2	AP2	1fr dull vio & blk	.65	.25
C3	AP3	2fr blue & blk	1.00	.50
C4	AP4	5fr green & blk	1.75	.90
		Nos. C1-C4 (4)	3.80	1.85
		Set, never hinged	8.50	

Kraal AP5

Porters on Safari AP6

1930, Apr. 2

C5	AP5	15fr dk brn & blk	3.50	1.25
C6	AP6	30fr brn vio & blk	3.75	1.50
		Set, never hinged	14.00	

Fokker F VII over Congo AP7

1934, Jan. 22 *Perf. 13½x14*

C7	AP7	50c gray black	.55	.20
C8	AP7	1fr dk carmine	.45	.20
a.		Booklet pane of 8	6.00	
C9	AP7	1.50fr green	.50	.20
C10	AP7	3fr brown	.35	.20
C11	AP7	4.50fr brt ultra	.75	.20
a.		Booklet pane of 8	10.00	
C12	AP7	5fr red brown	1.00	.35
C13	AP7	15fr brown vio	1.25	.50
C14	AP7	30fr red orange	2.00	1.00
C15	AP7	50fr violet	5.00	1.50
		Nos. C7-C15 (9)	11.85	4.35
		Set, never hinged	25.00	

The 1fr, 3fr, 4.50fr, 5fr, 15fr exist imperf.

No. C10 Surcharged in Blue with New Value and Bars

1936, Mar. 25

C16	AP7	3.50fr on 3fr brown	.40	.20

POSTAGE DUE STAMPS

In 1908-23 regular postage stamps handstamped "TAXES" or "TAXE," usually boxed, were used in lieu of postage due stamps.

D1

1923-29(?) Typo. Unwmk. *Perf. 14*

J1	D1	5c black brown	.20	.20
J2	D1	10c rose red	.25	.20
J3	D1	15c violet	.25	.20
J4	D1	30c green	.30	.25
J5	D1	50c ultramarine	.40	.35
J6	D1	50c blue ('29)	.45	.35
J7	D1	1fr gray	.55	.40
		Nos. J1-J7 (7)	2.40	1.95

PARCEL POST STAMPS

PP1

PP2

PP3

Handstamped Surcharges in Black or Blue on Nos. 5, 11-12

1887-93 Unwmk. *Perf. 15*

Q1 PP1 3.50fr on 5fr lilac 1,000. 750.00
Q3 PP2 3.50fr on 5fr vio 850.00 500.00
Q4 PP3 3.50fr on 5fr vio ('88) 675.00 325.00
Q6 PP3 3.50fr on 5fr gray ('93) 140.00 140.00
Never hinged 175.00

Nos. Q1, Q3-Q4, and Q6 are known with inverted surcharge and double surcharge, and No. Q6 in pair with unsurcharged stamp. These varieties sell for somewhat more than the normal surcharges.

Genuine stamps with counterfeit surcharges, counterfeit stamps with counterfeit surcharges, and both with counterfeit cancels exist.

BELGIUM

'bel-jəm

LOCATION — Western Europe, bordering the North Sea
GOVT. — Constitutional Monarchy
AREA — 11,778 sq. mi.
POP. — 9,853,000 (est. 1983)
CAPITAL — Brussels

100 Centimes = 1 Franc

Watermark

Wmk. 96 (With Frame)

Wmk. 96a (No Frame)

A1

A2

King Leopold I

Wmk. Two "L's" Framed (96)

1849 Engr. *Imperf.*

1 A1 10c brown *2,400.* 100.00
No gum 1,800.
On cover 175.00
a. 10c red brown *4,250.* 450.00
No gum 2,900.
On cover 750.00
b. 10c bister brown *2,900.* 140.00
No gum 2,100.
On cover 260.00
c. 10c dark brown *2,600.* 85.00
No gum 1,900.
On cover 210.00
2 A1 20c blue *2,650.* 57.50
No gum 2,000.
On cover 145.00
a. 20c milky blue *3,650.* 160.00
No gum 2,400.
On cover 400.00
b. 20c greenish blue *3,850.* 290.00
No gum 2,900.
On cover 500.00
c. 20c dark blue *3,100.* 62.50
No gum 2,100.
On cover 150.00

Full margins = ½mm.

The reprints are on thick and thin wove and thick laid paper unwatermarked.

A souvenir sheet containing reproductions of the 10c, 20c and 40c of 1849-51 with black burelage on back was issued Oct. 17, 1949, for the cent. of the 1st Belgian stamps. It was sold at BEPITEC 1949, an intl. stamp exhib. at Brussels, and was not valid. Value, $15.

Values for pairs

1 A1 10c brown 200.
On cover 450.
2 A1 20c blue 175.
On cover 425.

Values for strips of 3

1 A1 10c brown 900.
On cover 2,250.
2 A1 20c blue 675.
On cover 2,250.

Values for strips of 4

1 A1 10c brown 1,900.
On cover *10,000.*
2 A1 20c blue 1,600.
On cover *10,000.*

A cover sent from Herinnes to Charleroi bearing a strip of four of the 20 centimes blue (Scott No. 2) was sold for the equivalent of U.S. $10,000 in a Brussels auction in 2003.

Values for blocks of 4

1 A1 10c brown 3,500.
On cover —
2 A1 20c blue 3,750.
On cover —

1849-50 Thin Paper

3 A2 10c brown ('50) *2,500.* 100.00
No gum 2,100.
On cover 175.00
4 A2 20c blue ('50) *2,200.* 62.50
No gum 1,550.
On cover 140.00
5 A2 40c carmine rose *2,000.* 525.00
No gum 1,500.
On cover 1,000.

Full margins = ½mm.

Thick Paper

3a A2 10c brown ('50) *2,500.* 100.00
No gum 2,100.
On cover 175.00
4a A2 20c blue ('50) *2,200.* 62.50
No gum 1,550.
On cover 145.00
5a A2 40c carmine rose *2,000.* 525.00
No gum 1,550.
On cover 1,000.

Values for pairs

3 A2 10c brown ('50) 250.
On cover 400.
4 A2 20c blue ('50) 175.
On cover 290.
5 A2 40c carmine rose 1,150.
On cover 1,425.

Values for strips of 3

3 A2 10c brown ('50) 675.
On cover 1,000.
4 A2 20c blue ('50) 425.
On cover 675.
5 A2 40c carmine rose 1,775.
On cover 2,250.

Values for strips of 4

3 A2 10c brown ('50) 1,400.
On cover 2,250.
4 A2 20c blue ('50) 900.
On cover 1,350.
5 A2 40c carmine rose 2,250.
On cover 2,900.

Values for blocks of 4

3 A2 10c brown ('50) 2,500.
On cover 3,500.
4 A2 20c blue ('50) 1,600.
On cover 2,250.
5 A2 40c carmine rose 4,750.
On cover 5,500.

Wmk. Two "L's" Without Frame (96a)

1851-54

Thick Wove Paper

6 A2 10c brown 575.00 8.50
No gum 425.00
On cover 17.50
a. Ribbed paper ('54) 1,000. 62.50
7 A2 20c blue 750.00 8.00
No gum 525.00
On cover 17.50
a. Ribbed paper ('54) 1,000. 62.50
8 A2 40c car rose *3,900.* 110.00
No gum 2,300.
On cover 160.00
a. Ribbed paper ('54) *4,000.* 260.00

Full margins = ½mm.

Nos. 6a, 7a, 8a must have regular and parallel ribs covering the whole stamp.

Thin to Medium Wove Paper

6b A2 10c brown 650.00 9.00
No gum 425.00
On cover 17.50
7b A2 20c blue 800.00 8.50
No gum 525.00
On cover 17.50
8b A2 40c car rose *3,900.* 110.00
No gum 2,400.
On cover 175.00

Values for used pairs

6 A2 10c brown 22.50
On cover 65.00
7 A2 20c blue 22.50
On cover 67.50
8 A2 40c car rose 260.00
On cover 475.00

Values for strips of 3

6 A2 10c brown 80.00
On cover 140.00
7 A2 20c blue 85.00
On cover 145.00
8 A2 40c car rose 575.00
On cover 900.00

Values for strips of 4

6 A2 10c brown 140.00
On cover 275.00
7 A2 20c blue 140.00
On cover 275.00
8 A2 40c car rose 1,350.
On cover 2,000.

Values for blocks of 4

6 A2 10c brown 300.00
On cover 800.00
7 A2 20c blue 300.00
On cover 800.00
8 A2 40c car rose 2,750.
On cover 3,750.

Stamps 22mm high; Oval 17¼high

1861 Unwmk.

9 A2 1c green ('61) *225.00* 125.00
No gum 140.00
On wrapper 900.00
a. 1c pale green 225.00 140.00
No gum 150.00
On wrapper 925.00
b. 1c dark green 225.00 150.00
No gum 175.00
On wrapper 975.00
c. 1c deep bottle green 575.00 375.00
No gum 450.00
On wrapper 1,100.
10 A2 10c brown 450.00 9.00
No gum 325.00
On cover 15.00
a. 10c dark brown 475.00 11.00
No gum 325.00
On cover 15.00
11 A2 20c blue 475.00 9.00
No gum 325.00
On cover 15.00
a. 20c dark blue 490.00 10.50
No gum 340.00
On cover 15.00
12 A2 40c vermilion *3,650.* 80.00
No gum 2,100.
On cover 150.00
a. 40c carmine rose 3,650. 90.00
No gum 2,250.
On cover 160.00

Full margins = ½mm.

Nos. 9 and 13 were valid for postage on newspapers and printed matter only.

Reprints of Nos. 9-12 are on thin wove paper. The colors are brighter than those of the originals. They were made from the dies and show lines outside the stamps.

Values for pairs

9 A2 1c green 290.00
On cover 975.00
10 A2 10c brown 22.50
On cover 40.00
11 A2 20c blue 22.50
On cover 35.00
12 A2 40c vermilion 175.00
On cover 310.00

Values for strips of 3

9 A2 1c green 450.00
On cover 1,100.
10 A2 10c brown 57.50
On cover 90.00
11 A2 20c blue 57.50
On cover 90.00
12 A2 40c vermilion 575.00
On cover 1,000.

Values for strips of 4

9 A2 1c green 775.00
On cover 1,400.
10 A2 10c brown 110.00
On cover 180.00
11 A2 20c blue 125.00
On cover 190.00
12 A2 40c vermilion 1,500.
On cover 1,800.

Values for blocks of 4

9 A2 1c green 1,000.
On cover 2,250.
10 A2 10c brown 350.00
On cover 675.00
11 A2 20c blue 350.00
On cover 725.00
12 A2 40c vermilion 2,300.
On cover 3,600.

Stamps 21mm high; Oval 16½high

1858 Unwmk.

10b A2 10c brown 675.00 10.75
No gum 375.00
On cover 18.00
11b A2 20c blue 675.00 10.75
No gum 375.00
On cover 18.00
12b A2 40c vermilion 4,600. 110.00
No gum 3,000.
On cover 200.00

Values for pairs

10b A2 10c brown 35.00
On cover 150.00
11b A2 20c blue 35.00
On cover 150.00
12b A2 40c vermilion 260.00
On cover 775.00

Values for strips of 3

10 A2 10c brown 90.00
On cover 225.00
11 A2 20c blue 90.00
On cover 225.00
12 A2 40c vermilion 725.00
On cover 1,350.

Values for strips of 4

10 A2 10c brown 175.00
On cover 360.00
11 A2 20c blue 175.00
On cover 375.00
12 A2 40c vermilion 1,750.
On cover 2,500.

Values for blocks of 4

10 A2 10c brown 350.00
On cover 725.00
11 A2 20c blue 350.00
On cover 725.00
12 A2 40c vermilion *5,000.*
On cover *6,750.*

1865, Sept. *Perf. 14½*

13 A2 1c green 57.50 26.00
Never hinged 125.00
No gum 32.50
On wrapper 450.00
14 A2 10c brown 75.00 3.75
Never hinged 175.00
No gum 40.00
On cover 9.00
a. 10c reddish brown 100.00 4.50
Never hinged 225.00
No gum 52.50
On cover 9.50
15 A2 20c blue 75.00 3.50
Never hinged 175.00
No gum 40.00
On cover 9.00
a. 20c turquoise blue — 50.00
On cover 75.00
16 A2 40c carmine rose 425.00 25.00
Never hinged 950.00
No gum 240.00
On cover 60.00
a. 40c bright vermilion 500.00 67.50
Never hinged 1,100.
No gum 310.00
On cover 90.00
b. 40c pomegranate red 1,000. 110.00
Never hinged 2,250.
No gum 675.00
On cover 210.00

1863 *Perf. 12½*

13a A2 1c green 200.00 80.00
Never hinged 440.00
No gum 95.00
On wrapper 550.00
14b A2 10c brown 210.00 5.00
Never hinged 475.00
No gum 95.00
On cover 10.50
15b A2 20c blue 225.00 5.00
Never hinged 500.00
No gum 95.00
On cover 10.50
16c A2 40c carmine rose 1,150. 35.00
Never hinged 2,600.
No gum 625.00
On cover 75.00
16d A2 40c vermilion 1,300. 45.00
Never hinged 2,900.
No gum 675.00
On cover 90.00

1863, August *Perf. 12½x13½*

13b A2 1c green 75.00 45.00
Never hinged 175.00
No gum 37.50
On wrapper 475.00
13c A2 1c emerald green 85.00 42.50
Never hinged 190.00
No gum 40.00
On wrapper 525.00
14c A2 10c brown 110.00 4.00
Never hinged 250.00
No gum 52.50
On cover 10.00

15c	A2 20c blue	120.00	4.00
	Never hinged	275.00	
	No gum	40.00	
	On cover		10.00
16e	A2 40c carmine rose	650.00	35.00
	Never hinged	1,500.	
	No gum	350.00	
	On cover		75.00
16f	A2 40c bright vermilion	700.00	45.00
	Never hinged	1,600.	
	No gum	375.00	
	On cover		100.00

Values for Nos. 13-16f are for copies with perfs cutting into design.

King Leopold I — A3a

A3

A4

A4a

A5

London Print

1865 Typo. *Perf. 14*

17	A5 1fr pale violet	1,600.	110.00
	Never hinged	3,600.	
	No gum	1,000.	
	On cover		900.00

Brussels Print

Thick (Perf 15) or Thin (Perf 14½x14 Paper

1867 *Perf. 15*

18	A3 10c slate	160.00	2.25
	Never hinged	375.00	
	No gum	80.00	
	On cover		5.00
19	A3a 20c blue	275.00	2.00
	Never hinged	775.00	
	No gum	140.00	
	On cover		5.00
a.	20c lilac blue	425.00	2.75
	Never hinged	950.00	
	No gum	140.00	
	On cover		6.50
20	A4 30c brown	575.00	11.00
	Never hinged	1,300.	
	No gum	310.00	
	On cover		24.00
21	A4a 40c rose	725.00	20.00
	Never hinged	1,600.	
	No gum	350.00	
	On cover		110.00
22	A5 1fr violet	1,850.	97.50
	Never hinged	*4,150.*	
	No gum	900.00	
	On cover		775.00
a.	1fr lilac	1,900.	110.00
	Never hinged	*4,250.*	
	No gum	950.00	
	On cover		900.00

1865-66 *Perf. 14½x14*

18a	A3 10c slate	210.00	2.75
	Never hinged	475.00	
	No gum	100.00	
	On cover		5.00
b.	Pair, imperf. between		—
19b	A3a 20c blue	350.00	4.50
	Never hinged	775.00	
	No gum	175.00	
	On cover		5.00
19c	A3a 20c prussian blue	440.00	7.25
	Never hinged	1,000.	
	No gum	200.00	
	On cover		18.00
20a	A4 30c brown	675.00	11.50
	Never hinged	1,500.	
	No gum	350.00	
	On cover		24.00
b.	Pair, imperf. between	*2,000.*	
21a	A4a 40c rose	975.00	20.00
	Never hinged	2,200.	
	No gum	440.00	
	On cover		100.00
22b	A5 1f violet	1,800.	120.00
	Never hinged	*4,100.*	
	No gum	975.00	
	On cover		700.00
22c	A5 1f dark violet	2,300.	475.00
	Never hinged	*5,200.*	
	No gum	1,350.	
	On cover		1,600.

The reprints are on thin paper, imperforate and ungummed.

Coat of Arms — A6

1866-67 *Imperf.*

23	A6 1c gray	250.00	150.00
	Never hinged	600.00	
	On wrapper		750.00

Perf. 14½x14

24	A6 1c gray	57.50	16.00
	Never hinged	140.00	
	On wrapper		67.50
25	A6 2c blue ('67)	190.00	90.00
	Never hinged	475.00	
	On wrapper		775.00
a.	2c dark blue	200.00	100.00
	Never hinged	525.00	
	On wrapper		850.00
26	A6 5c brown	240.00	90.00
	Never hinged	550.00	
	On wrapper		525.00
a.	5c yellowish brown	250.00	92.50
	Never hinged	600.00	
	On wrapper		625.00

1867 *Perf. 15*

24a	A6 1c gray	45.00	16.00
	Never hinged	100.00	
	On wrapper		55.00
b.	1c bluish gray	300.00	100.00
	Never hinged	650.00	
	On wrapper		140.00
25b	A6 2c blue	140.00	90.00
	Never hinged	375.00	
	On wrapper		700.00
c.	2c ultramarine	150.00	110.00
	Never hinged	400.00	
	On wrapper		825.00
26b	A6 5c brown	175.00	90.00
	Never hinged	440.00	
	On wrapper		525.00
c.	5c yellowish brown	200.00	92.50
	Never hinged	500.00	
	On wrapper		625.00
d.	5c bister brown	190.00	95.00
	Never hinged	475.00	
	On wrapper		625.00

Nos. 23-26d were valid for postage on newspapers and printed matter only.

Counterfeits exist.

Reprints of Nos. 24-26 are on thin paper, imperforate and ungummed.

Imperf. varieties of 1869-1912 (between Nos. 28-105) are without gum.

A7

A8

A9

A10

A11

A12

A13

A14

King Leopold II — A15

1869-70 *Perf. 15*

28	A7 1c green	6.50	.30
	Never hinged	19.00	
	On cover, single franking		29.00
29	A7 2c ultra ('70)	20.00	1.50
	Never hinged	55.00	
	On cover, single franking		100.00
30	A7 5c buff ('70)	45.00	.75
	Never hinged	125.00	
	On cover, single franking		20.00
31	A7 8c lilac ('70)	80.00	50.00
	Never hinged	130.00	
	On cover, single franking		*725.00*
32	A8 10c green	20.00	.40
	Never hinged	50.00	
	On cover		3.75
33	A9 20c lt ultra ('70)	140.00	.90
	Never hinged	240.00	
	On cover		12.00
34	A10 30c buff ('70)	80.00	4.00
	Never hinged	135.00	
	On cover		10.00
a.	30c reddish ocher ('73)	75.00	4.00
	Never hinged	140.00	
	On cover		10.00
35	A11 40c brt rose ('70)	110.00	6.00
	Never hinged	240.00	
	On cover		120.00
a.	40c rose lilac	210.00	10.00
	Never hinged	400.00	
	On cover		135.00
36	A12 1fr dull lilac ('70)	350.00	17.00
	Never hinged	675.00	
	On cover		*725.00*
a.	1fr rose lilac	350.00	20.00
	Never hinged	700.00	
	On cover		*775.00*

The frames and inscriptions of Nos. 30, 31 and 42 differ slightly from the illustration.

Minor "broken letter" varieties exist on several values.

Nos. 28-30, 32-33, 35-38 also were printed in aniline colors. These are not valued separately.

See Nos. 40-43, 49-51, 55.

1875-78

37	A13 25c olive bister	150.00	1.50
	Never hinged	400.00	
	On cover		8.00
a.	25c ocher	160.00	1.60
	Never hinged	410.00	
	On cover		8.00
38	A14 50c gray	275.00	11.00
	Never hinged	625.00	
	On cover		150.00
	Roller cancel		12.50
a.	50c gray black	325.00	55.00
	Never hinged	650.00	
	On cover		200.00
b.	50c deep black	1,750.	275.00
	Never hinged	—	
	On cover		800.00
39	A15 5fr dp red brown	*1,700.*	1,450.
	Never hinged	3,100.	
	On cover		*11,000.*
	Roller cancel		700.00
a.	5fr pale brown ('78)	*3,750.*	1,450.
	Never hinged	—	
	On cover		*11,000.*
	Roller cancel		700.00

Dangerous counterfeits of No. 39 exist.

Printed in Aniline Colors

1881 *Perf. 14*

40	A7 1c gray green	20.00	.60
	Never hinged	30.00	
	On cover, single franking		32.50
41	A7 2c lt ultra	17.50	2.50
	Never hinged	50.00	
	On cover, single franking		90.00
42	A7 5c orange buff	57.50	1.10
	Never hinged	120.00	
	On cover		22.50
a.	5c red orange	57.50	1.10
	Never hinged	120.00	
	On cover		22.50
43	A8 10c gray green	30.00	.80
	Never hinged	50.00	
	On cover		5.00
44	A13 25c olive bister	75.00	2.50
	Never hinged	200.00	
	On cover		7.00
	Nos. 40-44 (5)	200.00	7.50

See note following No. 36.

A16

A17

A18

A19

1883

45	A16 10c carmine	27.50	2.50
	Never hinged	55.00	
	On cover		22.00
46	A17 20c gray	150.00	7.75
	Never hinged	425.00	
	On cover		60.00
47	A18 25c blue	260.00	35.00
	Never hinged	675.00	
	On cover		125.00
	Roller cancel		15.00
a.	25c dark blue	280.00	35.00
	Never hinged	700.00	
	On cover		175.00
48	A19 50c violet	260.00	35.00
	Never hinged	675.00	
	On cover		300.00
	Roller cancel		15.00
a.	50c deep violet	310.00	45.00
	Never hinged	825.00	
	On cover		310.00

A20

A21

A22

1884-85 *Perf. 14*

49	A7 1c olive green	13.50	.85
	Never hinged	35.00	
	On cover, single franking		60.00
50	A7 1c gray	4.00	.30
	Never hinged	11.00	
	On cover, single franking		15.00
51	A7 5c green	32.50	.40
	Never hinged	82.50	
	On cover		8.00
52	A20 10c rose, *bluish*	10.00	.40
	Never hinged	25.00	
	On cover		3.00
a.	Grayish paper	11.00	.50
	Never hinged	30.00	
	On cover		5.00
c.	Yellowish paper	*200.00*	35.00
	Never hinged	*400.00*	
	On cover		*100.00*
53	A21 25c blue, *pink* ('85)	11.00	.75
	Never hinged	27.50	
	On cover		7.25
a.	25c blue, *dark rose*	12.50	1.00
	Never hinged	32.50	
	On cover		7.00
54	A22 1fr brown, *grnsh*	*750.00*	17.50
	Never hinged	2,000.	
	On cover		*600.00*
a.	1fr deep green, *dk grn*	900.00	20.00
	Never hinged	2,400.	
	On cover		775.00

The frame and inscription of No. 51 differ slightly from the illustration.

See note after No. 36.

A23

A24

A25

A26

1886-91

55	A7 2c purple brn ('88)	12.50	1.50
	Never hinged	32.50	
	On cover, single franking		*70.00*
56	A23 20c olive, *grnsh*	140.00	1.25
	Never hinged	375.00	
	On cover		17.50
57	A24 35c vio brn, *brnsh* ('91)	18.00	3.00
	Never hinged	35.00	
	On cover		20.00
58	A25 50c bister, *yelsh*	9.50	2.25
	Never hinged	22.50	
	On cover		50.00
59	A26 2fr violet, *pale lil*	90.00	40.00
	Never hinged	100.00	
	On cover		*675.00*
	Roller cancel		6.00
a.	2fr vio, *brt lilac*	100.00	45.00
	Never hinged	135.00	
	On cover		*750.00*

Values quoted for Nos. 60-107 are for unused and used stamps with label attached. Stamps without label sell for much less.

Coat of Arms
A27

King Leopold
A28

1893-1900

60	A27 1c gray	1.10	.20
	Never hinged	1.35	
	On cover, single franking, without label		3.75
61	A27 2c yellow	1.25	1.10
	Never hinged	1.25	
	On cover, single franking, without label		200.00
a.	Wmkd. coat of arms in sheet ('95)	—	—
62	A27 2c violet brn ('94)	1.60	.30
	Never hinged	4.00	
	On cover, single franking, without label		23.00
63	A27 2c red brown ('98)	3.25	.50
	Never hinged	5.25	
	On cover, single franking, without label		30.00
64	A27 5c yellow grn	7.75	.30
	Never hinged	20.00	
	On cover, without label		2.50
65	A28 10c orange brn	5.00	.30
	Never hinged	5.50	
	On cover, without label		5.00
66	A28 10c brt rose ('00)	3.50	.40
	Never hinged	5.50	
	On cover, without label		6.00
67	A28 20c olive green	22.50	.60
	Never hinged	32.50	
	On cover, without label		18.00
68	A28 25c ultra	20.00	.50
	Never hinged	22.50	
	On cover, without label		5.00
a.	No ball to "5" in upper left corner	32.50	12.50
	Never hinged	62.50	
69	A28 35c violet brn	25.00	1.50
	Never hinged	50.00	
	On cover, without label		20.00
a.	35c red brown	42.50	2.40
	Never hinged	67.50	
	On cover, without label		22.50
70	A28 50c bister	62.50	20.00
	Never hinged	132.50	
	On cover, without label		85.00
71	A28 50c gray ('97)	57.50	2.50
	Never hinged	140.00	
	On cover, without label		72.50
72	A28 1fr car, *lt grn*	75.00	20.00
	Never hinged	175.00	
	On cover, without label		175.00
73	A28 1fr orange ('00)	90.00	5.00
	Never hinged	225.00	
	On cover, without label		185.00
a.	1fr yellow orange	105.00	6.00
	Never hinged	250.00	
	On cover, without label		200.00
74	A28 2fr lilac, *rose*	90.00	70.00
	Never hinged	150.00	
	On cover, without label		450.00
75	A28 2fr lilac ('00)	150.00	13.50
	Never hinged	300.00	
	On cover, without label		450.00

Covers: Values for covers are for commercial items with proper frankings and stamps without labels. Stamps on postcards and printed envelopes sell for less than the values quoted.

Values for covers bearing stamps with labels attached, and perforations clear of the design

60	A27	1c gray	7.00
61	A27	2c yellow	400.00
62	A27	2c violet brn	55.00
63	A27	2c red brown	70.00
64	A27	5c yellow grn	5.00
65	A28	10c orange brn	10.00
66	A28	10c brt rose	15.00
67	A28	20c olive green	40.00
68	A28	25c ultra	10.00
69	A28	35c violet brn	37.50
a.		35c red brown	47.50
70	A28	50c bister	190.00
71	A28	50c gray)	150.00
72	A28	1fr car, *lt grn*	425.00
73	A28	1fr orange	450.00
a.		1fr yellow orange	450.00
74	A28	2fr lilac, *rose*	950.00
75	A28	2fr lilac	1,000.

Very thin transparent paper (1904-05)

60a	A27 1c gray	3.75	2.50
	Never hinged	5.50	
62a	A27 2c violet brown	6.00	4.25
	Never hinged	12.00	
64a	A27 5c yellow green	11.00	10.00
	Never hinged	22.00	
66a	A28 10c bright rose	26.00	18.00
	Never hinged	52.50	
68b	A28 25c ultramarine	45.00	30.00
	Never hinged	80.00	
69b	A28 35c violet brown	50.00	32.50
	Never hinged	95.00	
71a	A28 50c gray	100.00	65.00
	Never hinged	200.00	
73b	A28 1fr orange	240.00	160.00
	Never hinged	440.00	

Antwerp Exhibition Issue

Arms of Antwerp — A29

1894

76	A29 5c green, *rose*	4.75	3.25
	Never hinged	12.50	
	On cover, with label		36.00
77	A29 10c carmine, *bluish*	3.75	2.50
	Never hinged	7.50	
	On cover, with label		32.50
78	A29 25c blue, *rose*	1.00	1.00
	Never hinged	1.00	
	On cover, with label		55.00
	Nos. 76-78 (3)	9.50	6.75

Brussels Exhibition Issue

St. Michael and Satan
A30 A31

1896-97 ***Perf. 14x14***

79	A30 5c dp violet	1.00	.60
	Never hinged	1.40	
	On cover, with label		27.50
	Sheet of 25	25.00	17.50
	Never hinged	40.00	
80	A31 10c orange brown	8.50	3.50
	Never hinged	20.00	
	On cover, with label		32.50
	Sheet of 25	425.00	300.00
	Never hinged	550.00	
81	A31 10c lilac brown	.50	.35
	Never hinged	.65	
	On cover, with label		22.50
	Sheet of 25	12.50	12.50
	Never hinged	16.00	
	Nos. 79-81 (3)	10.00	4.45

A32

A33

A34

A35

A36

A37

A38

A39

Two types of 1c:
I — Periods after "Dimanche" and "Zondag" in label.
II — No period after "Dimanche." Period often missing after "Zondag."

1905-11 ***Perf. 14***

82	A32 1c gray (I) ('07)	1.50	.20
	Never hinged	3.60	
	On cover, single franking, without label		3.00
a.	Type II ('08)	2.00	.60
	Never hinged	4.50	
	On cover, single franking, without label		5.00
83	A32 2c red brown ('07)	14.50	5.75
	Never hinged	45.00	
	On cover, single franking, without label		20.00
84	A32 5c green ('07)	11.50	.60
	Never hinged	32.50	
	On cover, without label		3.00
85	A33 10c dull rose	1.75	.60
	Never hinged	4.00	
	On cover, without label		5.00
86	A34 20c olive grn	26.00	1.00
	Never hinged	70.00	
	On cover, without label		20.00
87	A35 25c ultra	12.00	.85
	Never hinged	32.50	
	On cover, without label		5.00
a.	25c deep blue ('11)	13.50	2.00
	Never hinged	40.00	
	On cover, without label		7.25
88	A36 35c red brn	27.50	2.40
	Never hinged	75.00	
	On cover, without label		30.00
a.	35c purple brown ('05)	27.50	2.40
	Never hinged	72.50	
	On cover, without label		30.00
89	A37 50c bluish gray	95.00	4.00
	Never hinged	235.00	
	On cover, without label		85.00
90	A38 1fr yellow orange	110.00	8.00
	Never hinged	340.00	
	On cover, without label		175.00
a.	1fr orange ('09)	130.00	9.00
	Never hinged	360.00	
	On cover, without label		190.00
91	A39 2fr violet	75.00	22.50
	Never hinged	240.00	
	On cover, without label		—
	Bar cancellation		5.00
	Nos. 82-91 (10)	374.75	45.90

Values for covers bearing stamps with labels attached, and perforations clear of the design

82	A32	1c gray (I)	7.00
a.		Type II	12.00
83	A32	2c red brown	45.00
84	A32	5c green	7.00
85	A33	10c dull rose	12.00
86	A34	20c olive grn	40.00
87	A35	25c ultra	10.00
a.		25c deep blue	16.50
88	A36	35c red brn	65.00
a.		35c purple brown	70.00
89	A37	50c bluish gray	185.00
90	A38	1fr yellow orange	425.00
a.		1fr orange	450.00
91	A39	2fr violet	—

A40

A41

Lion of Belgium — A42

A43

King Albert I — A44

1912

92	A40 1c orange	.20	.20
	Never hinged	.20	
	On cover, single franking		2.00
93	A41 2c orange brn	.25	.45
	Never hinged	.40	
	On cover, single franking		20.00
94	A42 5c green	.20	.20
	Never hinged	.25	
	On cover		1.00
95	A43 10c red	.75	.40
	Never hinged	2.40	
	On cover		4.00
96	A43 20c olive grn	16.00	4.00
	Never hinged	35.00	
	On cover		22.50
a.	20c bronze green	90.00	27.50
	Never hinged	200.00	
	On cover		125.00
97	A43 35c bister brn	1.00	.70
	Never hinged	2.00	
	On cover		17.50
98	A43 40c green	16.00	14.50
	Never hinged	40.00	
	On cover		65.00
99	A43 50c gray	1.00	.80
	Never hinged	2.10	
	On cover		30.00
100	A43 1fr orange	4.00	3.00
	Never hinged	8.75	
	On cover		110.00
101	A43 2fr violet	17.50	17.50
	Never hinged	29.00	
	On cover		135.00
102	A44 5fr plum	80.00	25.00
	Never hinged	175.00	
	On cover		150.00
	Nos. 92-102 (11)	136.90	66.75

Counterfeits exist of Nos. 97-102. Those of No. 102 are common.

Covers: Values for stamps on cover are for stamps with labels attached. Covers bearing stamps without labels are worth about half of the values given.

For overprints see Nos. Q49-Q50, Q52, Q55-Q55A, Q57-Q60.

A45

Larger Head

1912-13

With Engraver's Name

103	A45 10c red	.40	.20
	Never hinged	1.25	
	On cover		3.00
104	A45 20c olive green ('13)	.40	.40
	Never hinged	.50	
	On cover		13.50
105	A45 25c ultramarine	4.25	*3.00*
	Never hinged	7.00	
	On cover		6.00
107	A45 40c green ('13)	.50	*.60*
	Never hinged	.70	
	On cover		42.50
	Nos. 103-107 (4)	5.55	4.20

Without Engraver's Name

1913-14

103a	A45 10c red	.20	.25
	Never hinged	.20	
	On cover		3.00
104a	A45 20c olive green ('14)	2.00	2.00
	Never hinged	2.40	
	On cover		32.50
105a	A45 25c ultramarine	.25	*.40*
	Never hinged	.30	
	On cover		7.00
	Nos. 103a-105a (3)	2.45	2.65

For overprints see #Q51, Q53-Q54, Q56.

Albert I
A46

Cloth Hall of Ypres
A47

Bridge of Dinant — A48

Library of Louvain — A49

Scheldt River at Antwerp
A50

Anti-slavery Campaign in the Congo A51

King Albert I at Furnes A52

Kings of Belgium Leopold I, Albert I, Leopold II A53

1915-20 Typo. *Perf. 14*

108 A46 1c orange .20 .20
Never hinged .20
On cover, single franking 4.00
109 A46 2c chocolate .20 .20
Never hinged .20
On cover, single franking 6.00
110 A46 3c gray blk ('20) .30 .20
Never hinged .80
On cover 2.00
111 A46 5c green 1.00 .20
Never hinged 3.25
On cover 1.00
112 A46 10c carmine .90 .20
Never hinged 3.00
On cover 1.00
a. 10c bright carmine 3.00 .30
Never hinged 6.75
On cover 2.00
113 A46 15c purple 1.50 .20
Never hinged 4.25
On cover 2.00
114 A46 20c red violet 3.00 .20
Never hinged 10.00
On cover 4.00
115 A46 25c blue .50 .40
Never hinged 1.10
On cover 6.75
a. 25c bright blue 1.10 .50
Never hinged 3.00
On cover 7.75

Engr.

116 A47 35c brown org & blk .50 .30
Never hinged 2.40
On cover 8.00
117 A48 40c green & black 1.00 .30
Never hinged 1.40
On cover 11.50
a. Vert. pair, imperf. btwn.
118 A49 50c car rose & blk 4.50 .30
Never hinged 12.50
On cover 11.00
119 A50 1fr violet 32.50 1.00
Never hinged 90.00
On cover 32.50
120 A51 2fr slate 21.00 2.00
Never hinged 57.50
On cover 55.00
a. 2fr gray black 25.00 2.40
Never hinged 67.50
On cover 57.50
b. 2fr pale gray 42.50 7.75
Never hinged 97.50
On cover 115.00
121 A52 5fr dp blue 275.00 125.00
Never hinged 775.00
On cover 325.00
Telegraph or railroad cancel 55.00
122 A53 10fr brown 20.00 20.00
Never hinged 35.00
On cover 175.00
Nos. 108-122 (15) 362.10 150.70

Perf 15

116a A47 35c brown orange & black 1.60 .80
Never hinged 5.00
On cover 8.00
117b A48 40c green & black 1.60 .80
Never hinged 5.00
On cover 11.50
118a A49 50c carmine rose & black 6.00 1.00
Never hinged 17.50
On cover 11.50
119a A50 1f violet 37.50 4.00
Never hinged 110.00
On cover 35.00
120c A51 2f slate 27.50 5.75
Never hinged 77.50
On cover 57.50
121a A52 5f deep blue 350.00 145.00
Never hinged 1,050.
On cover 500.00
122a A53 10f brown 25.00 25.00
Never hinged 50.00
On cover 175.00

Two types each of the 1c, 10c and 20c; three of the 2c and 15c; four of the 5c, differing in the top left corner.

See No. 138. For surcharges see Nos. B34-B47.

Perron of Liege (Fountain) A54

King Albert in Trench Helmet A55

Size: 18¼x28½mm

1919, July 25 *Perf. 11½*

123 A54 25c blue 2.40 .35
Never hinged 8.50
On cover 9.00
a. 25c deep blue 3.00 .45

Size: 18½x28mm

123b A54 25c blue 400.00 400.00
c. Sheet of 10 6,000. *6,000.*
Never hinged 7,000.

No. 123b is the first printing, which was issued in sheets of 10. Nos. 123 and 123a were later printings, issued in sheets of 100.

Perf. 11, 11½, 11½x11, 11x11½

1919

Size: 18½x22mm

124 A55 1c lilac brn .20 .20
Never hinged .20
125 A55 2c olive .20 .20
Never hinged .20
On cover, single franking 11.00

Size: 22x26

126 A55 5c green .20 .20
Never hinged .45
On cover 2.50
127 A55 10c carmine, 22x26¾mm .25 .25
Never hinged .50
On cover 2.00
a. Size: 22½x26mm 1.00 .60
Never hinged 2.00
On cover 6.00
128 A55 15c gray vio, 22x26¾mm .30 .30
Never hinged .60
On cover 3.50
a. Size: 22½x26mm 2.40 .60
Never hinged 5.50
On cover 6.75
129 A55 20c olive blk 1.10 1.10
Never hinged 2.00
On cover 23.50
130 A55 25c deep blue 1.60 1.60
Never hinged 2.75
On cover 14.00
131 A55 35c bister brn 3.00 3.00
Never hinged 3.50
132 A55 40c red 5.00 5.00
Never hinged 11.50
On cover 75.00
133 A55 50c red brn 9.50 10.00
Never hinged 19.00
On cover 135.00
134 A55 1fr lt orange 40.00 40.00
Never hinged 77.50
On cover 300.00
135 A55 2fr violet 375.00 375.00
Never hinged 575.00

Size: 28x33½mm

136 A55 5fr car lake 100.00 100.00
Never hinged 175.00
137 A55 10fr claret 110.00 110.00
Never hinged 275.00
Nos. 124-137 (14) 646.35 646.85
Set, never hinged 1,150.

Type of 1915 Inscribed: "FRANK" instead of "FRANKEN"

1919, Dec. *Perf. 14, 15*

138 A52 5fr deep blue 1.75 1.25
Never hinged 3.00
On cover 40.00

Town Hall at Termonde — A56

1920 *Perf. 11½*

139 A56 65c claret & black, 27x22mm .75 .20
Never hinged 1.50
On cover 12.00
a. Center inverted *67,500.*
b. Size: 26¼x22½mm 5.75 2.40
Never hinged 13.50
On cover 16.50

For surcharge see No. 143.

Nos. B48-B50 Surcharged in Red or Black

1921 *Perf. 12*

140 SP6 20c on 5c + 5c (R) .60 .25
Never hinged 1.90
On cover 10.00
a. Inverted surcharge 625.00 625.00
Never hinged 1,100.
On cover 2,200.
141 SP7 20c on 10c + 5c .40 .25
Never hinged 1.10
On cover 7.75
142 SP8 20c on 15c + 15c (R) .60 .25
Never hinged 1.90
On cover 10.00
a. Inverted surcharge 625.00 625.00
Never hinged 1,100.
On cover 2,200.

No. 139 Surcharged in Red

143 A56 55c on 65c claret & blk 1.50 .35
Never hinged 3.50
a. Pair, one without surcharge 2.25 .85
Never hinged 5.00
Nos. 140-143 (4) 3.10 1.10
Set, never hinged 8.50

A58

A59

1922-27 Typo. *Perf. 14*

144 A58 1c orange .20 .20
Never hinged .20
On cover, single franking 10.00
145 A58 2c olive ('26) .20 .20
Never hinged .25
On cover, single franking 13.50
146 A58 3c fawn .20 .20
Never hinged .20
On cover 2.50
147 A58 5c gray .20 .20
Never hinged .20
On cover 1.00
148 A58 10c blue grn .20 .20
Never hinged .30
On cover 1.00
149 A58 15c plum ('23) .20 .20
Never hinged .30
On cover 1.25
150 A58 20c black brn .20 .20
Never hinged .40
On cover 2.00
151 A58 25c magenta .20 .20
Never hinged .40
On cover 1.00
a. 25c dull violet ('23) .50 .20
Never hinged 1.10
On cover 1.25
152 A58 30c vermilion .50 .20
Never hinged .70
On cover 4.00
153 A58 30c rose ('25) .35 .20
Never hinged .70
On cover 5.00
154 A58 35c red brown .35 .30
Never hinged .50
On cover 11.50
155 A58 35c blue grn ('27) .80 .35
Never hinged 1.75
On cover 6.75
156 A58 40c rose .50 .20
Never hinged .70
On cover 6.75
157 A58 50c bister ('25) .50 .20
Never hinged .80
On cover 3.00
158 A58 60c olive brn ('27) 3.00 .20
Never hinged 9.50
On cover 1.00
159 A58 1.25fr dp blue ('26) 1.10 1.10
Never hinged 1.25
On cover 50.00
160 A58 1.50fr brt blue ('26) 1.60 .45
Never hinged 4.00
On cover 9.00
a. 1.50fr bright sky blue ('27) 7.75 2.00
Never hinged 19.50
On cover 10.00
b. 1.50fr intense bright blue ('30) 11.50 3.00
Never hinged 48.00
On cover 40.00
161 A58 1.75fr ultra ('27) 1.40 .20
Never hinged 5.00
On cover 1.25
a. Tete beche pair 5.00 5.00
Never hinged 10.00
c. Bklt. pane of 4 + 2 labels 40.00
Nos. 144-161 (18) 11.70 5.00
Set, never hinged 27.50

See Nos. 185-190. For overprints and surcharges see Nos. 191-195, 197, B56, O1-O6.

1921-25 Engr.
Perf. 11, 11x11½, 11½, 11½x11, 11½x12, 11½x12½, 12½

162 A59 50c dull blue .30 .20
Never hinged 1.60
On cover 3.00
163 A59 75c scarlet ('22) .25 .25
Never hinged .30
On cover 10.00
164 A59 75c ultra ('24) .45 .20
Never hinged .60
On cover 5.00
165 A59 1fr black brn ('22) .80 .20
Never hinged 2.00
On cover 6.50
166 A59 1fr dk blue ('25) .60 .20
Never hinged .80
On cover 7.00
167 A59 2fr dk green ('22) .90 .25
Never hinged 2.00
On cover 15.00
168 A59 5fr brown vio ('23) 13.50 *15.00*
Never hinged 18.00
On cover 40.00
169 A59 10fr magenta ('22) 9.00 6.50
Never hinged 25.00
On cover 165.00
Nos. 162-169 (8) 25.80 *22.80*
Set, never hinged 52.50

No. 162 measures 18x20¾mm and was printed in sheets of 100.

Philatelic Exhibition Issues

1921, May 26 *Perf. 11½*

170 A59 50c dark blue 3.50 3.50
Never hinged 4.75
a. Sheet of 25 200.00 175.00
Never hinged 225.00

No. 170 measures 17½x21¼mm, was printed in sheets of 25 and sold at the Philatelic Exhibition at Brussels.

The sheet normally has pin holes and a cancellation-like marking in the margin. These are considered unused and the condition valued here.

Souvenir Sheet

1924, May 24 *Perf. 11½*

171 Sheet of 4 140.00 140.00
Never hinged 260.00
a. A59 5fr red brown 10.00 10.00
Never hinged 12.00
On cover 35.00

Sold only at the Intl. Phil. Exhib., Brussels. Sheet size: 130x145mm.

The sheet normally has pin holes and a cancellation-like marking in the margin. These are considered unused and the condition valued here.

Kings Leopold I and Albert I — A60

1925 *Perf. 14*

172 A60 10c dp green 7.25 7.25
Never hinged 17.50
173 A60 15c dull vio 3.75 4.50
Never hinged 7.75
On cover 20.00
174 A60 20c red brown 3.75 4.50
Never hinged 7.75
175 A60 25c grnsh black 3.75 4.50
Never hinged 7.75
On cover 40.00
176 A60 30c vermilion 3.75 4.50
Never hinged 7.75
On cover 17.50
177 A60 35c lt blue 3.75 4.50
Never hinged 7.75
178 A60 40c brnsh blk 3.75 4.50
Never hinged 7.75
On cover 40.00
179 A60 50c yellow brn 3.75 4.50
Never hinged 7.75
On cover 30.00
180 A60 75c dk blue 3.75 4.50
Never hinged 7.75
181 A60 1fr dk violet 6.50 6.50
Never hinged 13.50
182 A60 2fr ultra 4.00 4.00
Never hinged 7.75
183 A60 5fr blue blk 3.75 4.50
Never hinged 7.75
184 A60 10fr dp rose 6.50 8.00
Never hinged 17.50
Nos. 172-184 (13) 58.00 66.25
Set, never hinged 126.00

75th anniv. of Belgian postage stamps.

Nos. 172-184 were sold only in sets and only by The Administration of Posts, not at post offices.

A61

1926-27 Typo.

185 A61 75c dk violet .75 .70
Never hinged 1.60
On cover 20.00
186 A61 1fr pale yellow .60 .35
Never hinged .75
On cover 15.00
187 A61 1fr rose red ('27) 1.00 .20
Never hinged 2.40
On cover 5.00
a. Tete beche pair 7.50 4.50
c. Bklt. pane 4 + 2 labels 25.00
188 A61 2fr Prus blue 2.50 .45
Never hinged 5.75
On cover 17.50
189 A61 5fr emerald ('27) 27.50 1.60
Never hinged 77.50
On cover 67.50
190 A61 10fr dk brown ('27) 60.00 7.75
Never hinged 160.00
On cover 175.00
Nos. 185-190 (6) 92.35 11.05
Set, never hinged 249.00

For overprints and surcharge see Nos. 196, Q174-Q175.

Stamps of 1921-27 Surcharged in Carmine, Red or Blue

1927

191 A58 3c on 2c olive (C) .20 .20
Never hinged .25
On cover, single franking 18.50
192 A58 10c on 15c plum (R) .20 .20
Never hinged .25
On cover 3.00
193 A58 35c on 40c rose (Bl) .45 .20
Never hinged .60
On cover 2.50
194 A58 1.75fr on 1.50fr brt bl (C) 2.25 .80
Never hinged 3.00
Nos. 191-194 (4) 3.10 1.40
Set, never hinged 3.75

Nos. 153, 185 and 159 Surcharged in Black

1929, Jan. 1

195 A58 5c on 30c rose .20 .20
Never hinged .20
On cover 4.50
196 A61 5c on 75c dk violet .20 .20
Never hinged .25
On cover 4.50
197 A58 5c on 1.25fr dp blue .20 .20
Never hinged .20
On cover 4.50
Nos. 195-197 (3) .60 .60
Set, never hinged .65

The surcharge on Nos. 195-197 is a precancelation which alters the value of the stamp to which it is applied.

Values for precanceled stamps in unused column are for those which have not been through the post and have original gum. Values in second column are for postally used, gumless stamps.

A63

A64

1929-32 Typo. *Perf. 14*

198 A63 1c orange .20 .20
Never hinged .20
199 A63 2c emerald ('31) .45 .45
Never hinged .50
200 A63 3c red brown .20 .20
Never hinged .20
201 A63 5c slate .20 .20
Never hinged .20
c. Bklt. pane of 4 + 2 labels 8.25
202 A63 10c olive grn .20 .20
Never hinged .20
On cover 1.00
c. Bklt. pane of 4 + 2 labels 4.50
203 A63 20c brt violet 1.00 .25
Never hinged 4.00
On cover 15.00
204 A63 25c rose red .45 .20
Never hinged 1.00
On cover 1.00
c. Bklt. pane of 4 + 2 labels 8.25
205 A63 35c green .60 .20
Never hinged 1.10
On cover 2.00
c. Bklt. pane of 4 + 2 labels 9.75
206 A63 40c red vio ('30) .30 .20
Never hinged 1.25
On cover 1.00
c. Bklt. pane of 4 + 2 labels 9.75
207 A63 50c dp blue .45 .20
Never hinged .80
On cover 1.00
c. Bklt. pane of 4 + 2 labels 8.25
208 A63 60c rose ('30) 2.00 .20
Never hinged 6.75
On cover 6.75
c. Bklt. pane of 4 + 2 labels 30.00
209 A63 70c org brn ('30) 1.10 .20
Never hinged 4.25
On cover 4.00
c. Bklt. pane of 4 + 2 labels 22.50
210 A63 75c dk blue ('30) 2.00 .20
Never hinged 7.75
On cover 2.40
b. 75c blue violet 2.40 .20
Never hinged 8.75
On cover 2.40
211 A63 75c dp brown ('32) 6.00 .20
Never hinged 26.00
On cover 2.00
b. Bklt. pane of 4 + 2 labels 100.00
Nos. 198-211 (14) 15.15 3.10
Set, never hinged 55.00

For overprints and surcharges see Nos. 225-226, 240-241, 254-256, 309, O7-O15.

Tete Beche Pairs

201a A63 5c .60 .60
Never hinged 1.10
202a A63 10c .30 .30
Never hinged .60
204a A63 25c 1.75 1.75
Never hinged 2.75
205a A63 35c 2.75 2.75
Never hinged 3.75
206a A63 40c 2.75 2.75
Never hinged 3.75
207a A63 50c 2.25 2.25
Never hinged 3.50
208a A63 60c 8.00 7.50
Never hinged 15.00
209a A63 70c 6.00 5.00
Never hinged 8.75
210a A63 75c 9.00 8.50
Never hinged 15.00
211a A63 75c 27.50 25.00
Never hinged 62.50
Nos. 201a-211a (10) 60.90 56.40
Set, never hinged 110.00

1929, Jan. 25 Engr. *Perf. 14½, 14*

212 A64 10fr dk brown 15.00 4.00
Never hinged 37.50
On cover 75.00
213 A64 20fr dk green 85.00 20.00
Never hinged 190.00
On cover 175.00
214 A64 50fr red violet 13.50 13.50
Never hinged 24.00
a. Perf. 14½ 37.50 40.00
Never hinged 87.50
215 A64 100fr brownish lake 13.50 13.50
Never hinged 25.00
a. Perf. 14½ 37.50 40.00
Never hinged 87.50
Nos. 212-215 (4) 127.00 51.00
Set, never hinged 276.50

Peter Paul Rubens — A65

Zenobe Gramme — A66

1930, Apr. 26 Photo. *Perf. 12½x12*

216 A65 35c blue green .40 .20
Never hinged 1.00
On cover 1.00
217 A66 35c blue green .40 .20
Never hinged 1.10
On cover 1.00

No. 216 issued for the Antwerp Exhibition, No. 217 the Liege Exhibition.

Leopold I, by Lievin de Winne — A67

Leopold II, by Joseph Leempoels — A68

Design: 1.75fr, Albert I.

1930, July 1 Engr. *Perf. 11½*

218 A67 60c brown violet .20 .20
Never hinged .35
On cover 1.25
219 A68 1fr carmine 1.10 1.10
Never hinged 2.50
On cover 3.50
220 A68 1.75fr dk blue 2.75 1.25
Never hinged 6.75
On cover 4.50
Nos. 218-220 (3) 4.05 2.55
Set, never hinged 9.90

Centenary of Belgian independence.
For overprints see Nos. 222-224.

Antwerp Exhibition Issue
Souvenir Sheet

Arms of Antwerp A70

1930, Aug. 9 *Perf. 11½*

221 A70 4fr Sheet of 1 100.00 87.50
Never hinged 275.00
On cover 140.00
a. Single stamp 70.00 40.00

Size: 142x141mm. Inscription in lower margin "ATELIER DU TIMBRE-1930-ZEGELFABRIEK." Each purchaser of a ticket to the Antwerp Phil. Exhib., Aug. 9-15, was allowed to purchase one stamps. The ticket cost 6 francs.

The sheet normally has pin holes and a cancellation-like marking in the margin. These are considered unused and the condition valued here.

Nos. 218-220 Overprinted in Blue or Red

1930, Oct.

222 A67 60c brown vio (Bl) 2.00 2.00
Never hinged 4.00
On cover 6.75
223 A68 1fr carmine (Bl) 8.25 7.75
Never hinged 15.00
On cover 24.00
224 A68 1.75fr dk blue (R) 14.50 14.50
Never hinged 35.00
On cover 42.50
Nos. 222-224 (3) 24.75 24.25
Set, never hinged 55.00

50th meeting of the administrative council of the Intl. Labor Bureau at Brussels.

The names of the painters and the initials of the engraver have been added at the foot of these stamps.

Stamps of 1929-30 Surcharged in Blue or Black:

1931, Feb. 20 *Perf. 14*

225 A63 2c on 3c red brown (Bl) .20 .20
Never hinged 2.00
226 A63 10c on 60c rose (Bk) .50 .20
Never hinged 1.75
On cover 8.50

The surcharge on No. 226 is a precancelation which alters the denomination. See note after No. 197.

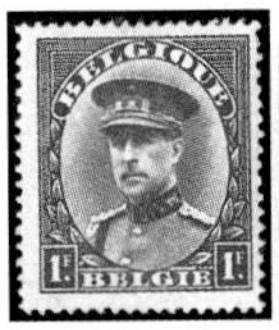

King Albert — A71a
A71

1931, June 15 Photo.

227 A71 1fr brown carmine .50 .20
Never hinged 1.00
On cover 3.00

1932, June 1

228 A71a 75c bister brown 1.25 .20
Never hinged 5.00
On cover 1.00
a. Tete beche pair 6.75 6.75
Never hinged 17.50
c. Bklt. pane 4 + 2 labels 27.50

See No. 257. For overprint see No. O18.

A72

1931-32 Engr.

229 A72 1.25fr gray black .75 .50
Never hinged 2.25
On cover 6.75
230 A72 1.50fr brown vio 1.25 .50
Never hinged 4.75
On cover 5.50
231 A72 1.75fr dp blue .80 .20
Never hinged 1.60
On cover 1.00
232 A72 2fr red brown 1.10 .20
Never hinged 2.40
On cover 5.50
233 A72 2.45fr dp violet 1.90 .40
Never hinged 8.00
On cover 11.50
234 A72 2.50fr black brn ('32) 10.00 .50
Never hinged 22.50
On cover 23.50
235 A72 5fr dp green 18.00 1.10
Never hinged 67.50
On cover 30.00
236 A72 10fr claret 45.00 12.50
Never hinged 140.00
On cover 77.50
Nos. 229-236 (8) 78.80 15.90
Set, never hinged 249.00

Nos. 206 and 209 Surcharged as No. 226, but dated "1932"

1932, Jan. 1

240 A63 10c on 40c red vio 2.50 .30
Never hinged 7.25
On cover 5.00
241 A63 10c on 70c org brn 2.00 .20
Never hinged 6.25
On cover 5.00

See note after No. 197.

Gleaner A73

Mercury A74

1932, June 1 Typo. *Perf. 13½x14*

245 A73 2c pale green .35 .35
Never hinged .50
246 A74 5c dp orange .20 .20
Never hinged .40
On cover, single franking 5.00
247 A73 10c olive grn .25 .20
Never hinged .40
On cover 1.00
a. Tete beche pair 4.00 4.00
Never hinged 5.75
c. Bklt. pane 4 + 2 labels 15.00
248 A74 20c brt violet 1.00 .20
Never hinged 3.25
On cover 37.50

249	A73 25c deep red	.60	.20
	Never hinged	2.00	
	On cover		1.60
a.	Tete beche pair	3.50	3.50
	Never hinged	5.00	
c.	Bklt. pane 4 + 2 labels	15.00	
250	A74 35c dp green	2.40	.20
	Never hinged	7.75	
	On cover		1.00
	Nos. 245-250 (6)	4.80	1.35
	Set, never hinged	14.50	

For overprints see Nos. O16-O17.

Auguste Piccard's Balloon — A75

1932, Nov. 26 Engr. *Perf. 11½*

251	A75 75c red brown	3.50	.30
	Never hinged	9.50	
	On cover		3.00
252	A75 1.75fr dk blue	13.50	2.10
	Never hinged	37.50	
	On cover		7.25
253	A75 2.50fr dk violet	17.00	11.50
	Never hinged	47.50	
	On cover		27.50
	Nos. 251-253 (3)	34.00	13.90
	Set, never hinged	97.50	

Issued in commemoration of Prof. Auguste Piccard's two ascents to the stratosphere.

Nos. 206 and 209 Surcharged as No. 226, but dated "1933"

1933, Nov. *Perf. 14*

254	A63 10c on 40c red vio	14.00	4.00
	Never hinged	32.50	
	On cover		55.00
255	A63 10c on 70c org brn	12.50	1.50
	Never hinged	32.50	
	On cover		7.00

No. 206 Surcharged as No. 226, but dated "1934"

1934, Feb.

256	A63 10c on 40c red vio	12.50	1.50
	Never hinged	35.00	
	On cover		8.00

For Nos. 254 to 256 see note after No. 197. Regummed copies of Nos. 254-256 abound.

King Albert Memorial Issue

Type of 1932 with Black Margins

1934, Mar. 10 Photo.

257	A71a 75c black	.30	.20
	Never hinged	.60	
	On cover		3.50

Congo Pavilion — A76

Designs: 1fr, Brussels pavilion. 1.50fr, "Old Brussels." 1.75fr, Belgian pavilion.

1934, July 1 *Perf. 14x13½*

258	A76 35c green	.75	.30
	Never hinged	2.50	
	On cover		3.00
259	A76 1fr dk carmine	1.25	.40
	Never hinged	4.25	
	On cover		2.00
260	A76 1.50fr brown	5.00	.80
	Never hinged	18.00	
	On cover		10.00
261	A76 1.75fr blue	5.00	.30
	Never hinged	19.00	
	On cover		5.00
	Nos. 258-261 (4)	12.00	1.80
	Set, never hinged	45.00	

Brussels Intl. Exhib. of 1935.

King Leopold III

A80 A81

1934-35 *Perf. 13½x14*

262	A80 70c olive blk ('35)	.35	.20
	Never hinged	1.00	
	On cover		1.00
a.	Tete beche pair	1.50	1.00
	Never hinged	2.25	
c.	Bklt. pane 4 + 2 labels	6.25	
263	A80 75c brown	.65	.25
	Never hinged	1.50	
	On cover		3.00

Perf. 14x13½

264	A81 1fr rose car ('35)	3.25	.35
	Never hinged	7.75	
	On cover		6.00
	Nos. 262-264 (3)	4.25	.80
	Set, never hinged	10.00	

For overprint see No. O19.

Coat of Arms — A82

1935-48 Typo. *Perf. 14*

265	A82 2c green ('37)	.20	.20
	Never hinged	.20	
a.	2c yellow green ('44)	.20	.20
	Never hinged	.30	
266	A82 5c orange	.20	.20
	Never hinged	.20	
	On cover		.75
267	A82 10c olive bister	.20	.20
	Never hinged	.20	
	On cover		.60
a.	Tete beche pair	.30	.25
	Never hinged	.50	
b.	Bklt. pane 4 + 2 labels	4.50	
268	A82 15c dk violet	.20	.20
	Never hinged	.20	
	On cover		4.00
269	A82 20c lilac	.20	.20
	Never hinged	.20	
	On cover		4.00
270	A82 25c carmine rose	.20	.20
	Never hinged	.20	
	On cover		1.25
a.	Tete beche pair	.30	.40
	Never hinged	.55	
c.	Bklt. pane 4 + 2 labels	4.50	
271	A82 25c yel org ('46)	.20	.20
	Never hinged	.20	
272	A82 30c brown	.20	.20
	Never hinged	.30	
	On cover		4.50
273	A82 35c green	.20	.20
	Never hinged	.20	
	On cover		1.00
a.	Tete beche pair	.30	.30
	Never hinged	.50	
c.	Bklt. pane 4 + 2 labels	3.00	
274	A82 40c red vio ('38)	.20	.20
	Never hinged	.90	
	On cover		1.25
275	A82 50c blue	.40	.20
	Never hinged	.80	
	On cover		1.00
276	A82 60c slate ('41)	.20	.20
	Never hinged	.20	
	On cover		1.00
277	A82 65c red lilac ('46)	.25	.20
	Never hinged	.75	
278	A82 70c lt blue grn ('45)	.25	.25
	Never hinged	.30	
	On cover		7.75
279	A82 75c lilac rose ('45)	.25	.20
	Never hinged	.70	
	On cover		3.00
280	A82 80c green ('48)	3.50	.40
	Never hinged	8.75	
	On cover		8.75
281	A82 90c dull vio ('46)	.20	.20
	Never hinged	.50	
	On cover		2.00
282	A82 1fr red brown ('45)	.20	.20
	Never hinged	.50	
	On cover		2.00
	Nos. 265-282 (18)	7.25	3.85
	Set, never hinged	17.00	

Several stamps of type A82 exist in various shades.

Nos. 265, 361 were privately overprinted and surcharged "+10FR." by the Association Belgo-Americaine for the dedication of the Bastogne Memorial, July 16, 1950. The overprint is in six types. Value $1.50 per set.

See design O1. For overprints and surcharges see Nos. 312-313, 361-364, 390-394, O20-O22, O24, O26-O28, O33.

A83 A83a

Perf. 14, 14x13½, 11½

1936-51 Photo.

Size: 17½x21¾mm

283	A83 70c brown	.30	.20
	Never hinged	.50	
	On cover		.75
a.	Tete beche pair	.80	.80
	Never hinged	1.40	
c.	Bklt. pane 4 + 2 labels	7.50	

Size: 20¾x24mm

284	A83a 1fr rose car	.30	.20
	Never hinged	1.00	
	On cover		1.50
285	A83a 1.20fr dk brown ('51)	.80	.20
	Never hinged	1.50	
	On cover		1.00
286	A83a 1.50fr brt red vio ('43)	.40	.30
	Never hinged	1.00	
	On cover		6.75
287	A83a 1.75fr dp ultra ('43)	.20	.20
	Never hinged	.40	
	On cover		16.00
288	A83a 1.75fr dk car ('50)	.20	.20
	Never hinged	.20	
	On cover		.75
289	A83a 2fr dk pur ('43)	1.00	1.00
	Never hinged	1.60	
	On cover		29.00
290	A83a 2.25fr grnsh blk ('43)	.25	.20
	Never hinged	.40	
	On cover		16.00
291	A83a 2.50fr org red ('51)	1.75	.30
	Never hinged	6.50	
	On cover		2.00
292	A83a 3.25fr chestnut ('43)	.20	.20
	Never hinged	.30	
	On cover		7.25
293	A83a 5fr dp green ('43)	1.00	.40
	Never hinged	3.25	
	On cover		24.00
	Nos. 283-293 (11)	6.40	3.40
	Set, never hinged	17.00	

Nos. 287-288, 290-291, 293 inscribed "Belgie-Belgique."

See designs A85, A91. For overprints and surcharges see #314, O23, O25, O29, O31, O34.

A84 A85

1936-51 Engr. *Perf. 14x13½*

294	A84 1.50fr rose lilac ('41)	.60	.35
	Never hinged	2.00	
	On cover		8.75
a.	1.50fr magenta ('36)	4.00	2.00
	Never hinged	9.75	
	On cover		14.00
b.	1.50fr rose ('39)	1.00	.40
	Never hinged	3.00	
	On cover		10.00
295	A84 1.75fr dull blue	.20	.20
	Never hinged	.70	
	On cover		5.00
a.	1.75fr ultramarine ('36)	2.00	.40
	Never hinged	4.75	
	On cover		5.00
b.	1.75fr blue black ('37)	2.75	.40
	Never hinged	6.75	
	On cover		5.75
296	A84 2fr dull vio	.40	.30
	Never hinged	1.50	
	On cover		6.75
a.	2fr lilac ('36)	1.50	.60
	Never hinged	4.75	
	On cover		9.00
b.	2fr red violet ('38)	1.00	.35
	Never hinged	6.75	
	On cover		7.75
297	A84 2.25fr gray vio ('41)	.25	.25
	Never hinged	.60	
	On cover		17.50
298	A84 2.45fr black	32.50	.70
	Never hinged	100.00	
	On cover		3.25
299	A84 2.50fr ol blk ('40)	2.00	.25
	Never hinged	8.75	
	On cover		13.50
300	A84 3.25fr org brn ('41)	.30	.20
	Never hinged	.50	
	On cover		5.75
301	A84 5fr dull green	2.40	.50
	Never hinged	7.00	
	On cover		16.50
a.	5fr yellow green ('37)	57.50	11.50
	Never hinged	165.00	
	On cover		16.50
b.	5fr olive green ('38)	2.40	.50
	Never hinged	7.25	
	On cover		1.75
302	A84 10fr vio brn	.60	.20
	Never hinged	.90	
	On cover		10.00
a.	10fr light brown	10.00	.20
	Never hinged	30.00	
	On cover		11.50
303	A84 20fr vermilion	1.00	.30
	Never hinged	2.40	
	On cover		30.00
a.	20fr rose orange ('36)	1.15	.40
	Never hinged	4.00	
	On cover		35.00

Perf. 11½

304	A84 3fr yel brn ('51)	.55	.20
	Never hinged	1.50	
	On cover		4.75
305	A84 4fr bl, *bluish* ('50)	4.75	.20
	Never hinged	5.00	
	On cover		2.00
a.	White paper	9.00	.20
	Never hinged	14.50	
306	A84 6fr brt rose car ('51)	2.75	.20
	Never hinged	10.00	
	On cover		9.00
307	A84 10fr brn vio ('51)	.55	.20
	Never hinged	1.25	
	On cover		3.00
308	A84 20fr red ('51)	1.10	.20
	Never hinged	2.50	
	On cover		6.75
	Nos. 294-308 (15)	49.95	4.25
	Set, never hinged	150.00	

See No. 1159. For overprint and surcharges see Nos. 316-317, O32.

No. 206 Surcharged as No. 226, but dated "1937"

1937 Unwmk. *Perf. 14*

309	A63 10c on 40c red vio	.20	.20
	Never hinged	.30	
	On cover		5.75

See note after No. 197.

1938-41 Photo. *Perf. 13½x14*

310	A85 75c olive gray	.25	.20
	Never hinged	.60	
	On cover		1.00
a.	Tete beche pair	.75	.80
	Never hinged	1.50	
c.	Bklt. pane 4 + 2 labels	6.75	
311	A85 1fr rose pink ('41)	.20	.20
	Never hinged	.20	
	On cover		1.00
a.	Tete beche pair	.25	.25
	Never hinged	.40	
b.	Booklet pane of 6	2.25	
c.	Bklt. pane 4 + 2 labels	2.25	
	Set, never hinged	.80	

For overprints and surcharges see Nos. 315, O25, O30, O35.

Nos. 272, 274, 283, 310, 299, 298 Surcharged in Blue, Black, Carmine or Red

a

b

c

1938-42

312	A82 (a) 10c on 30c (Bl)	.20	.20
	Never hinged	.20	
	On cover		3.50
313	A82 (a) 10c on 40c (Bl)	.20	.20
	Never hinged	.20	
	On cover		4.00
314	A83 (b) 10c on 70c (Bk)	.20	.20
	Never hinged	.20	
	On cover		3.50
315	A85 (b) 50c on 75c (C)	.20	.20
	Never hinged	.40	
	On cover		4.00
316	A84 (c) 2.25fr on 2.50fr (C)	.45	.45
	Never hinged	.70	
	On cover		57.50
317	A84 (c) 2.50fr on 2.45fr (R)	11.00	.20
	Never hinged	25.00	
	On cover		15.00
	Nos. 312-317 (6)	12.25	1.45
	Set, never hinged	26.00	

Issue date: No. 317, Oct. 31, 1938.

Basilica and Bell Tower — A86

Water Exhibition Buildings — A87

Designs: 1.50fr, Albert Canal and Park. 1.75fr, Eygenbilsen Cut in Albert Canal.

1938, Oct. 31 ***Perf. 14x13½, 13½x14***

318	A86	35c dk blue grn	.20	.20
		Never hinged	.30	
		On cover		3.00
319	A87	1fr rose red	.45	.30
		Never hinged	1.50	
		On cover		2.00
320	A87	1.50fr vio brn	1.10	.60
		Never hinged	4.75	
		On cover		5.50
321	A87	1.75fr ultra	1.25	.20
		Never hinged	4.25	
		On cover		4.00
		Nos. 318-321 (4)	3.00	1.30
		Set, never hinged	11.00	

Intl. Water Exhibition, Liège, 1939.

SEMI-POSTAL STAMPS

Values quoted for Nos. B1-B24 are for stamps with label attached. Copies without label sell for one-tenth or less.

St. Martin of Tours Dividing His Cloak with a Beggar
SP1 SP2

Unwmk.

1910, June 1 **Typo.** ***Perf. 14***

B1	SP1	1c gray	.75	.75
B2	SP1	2c purple brn	6.50	6.50
B3	SP1	5c peacock blue	1.90	1.90
B4	SP1	10c brown red	1.90	1.90
B5	SP2	1c gray green	1.90	1.90
B6	SP2	2c violet brn	5.00	5.00
B7	SP2	5c peacock blue	2.25	2.25
B8	SP2	10c carmine	2.25	2.25
		Nos. B1-B8 (8)	22.45	22.45
		Set, never hinged	65.00	

Overprinted "1911" in Black

1911, Apr. 1

B9	SP1	1c gray	20.00	16.00
a.		Inverted overprint		
B10	SP1	2c purple brn	57.50	42.50
B11	SP1	5c peacock blue	6.50	5.25
B12	SP1	10c brown red	6.50	5.25
B13	SP2	1c gray green	30.00	24.00
B14	SP2	2c violet brn	25.00	21.00
B15	SP2	5c peacock blue	6.50	5.25
B16	SP2	10c carmine	6.50	5.25
		Nos. B9-B16 (8)	158.50	124.50
		Set, never hinged	600.00	

Overprinted "CHARLEROI-1911"

1911, June

B17	SP1	1c gray	3.50	2.50
B18	SP1	2c purple brn	11.00	10.00
B19	SP1	5c peacock blue	6.50	6.50
B20	SP1	10c brown red	6.50	6.50
B21	SP2	1c gray green	3.50	2.50
B22	SP2	2c violet brn	11.00	9.00
B23	SP2	5c peacock blue	6.50	6.50
B24	SP2	10c carmine	6.50	6.50
		Nos. B17-B24 (8)	55.00	50.00
		Set, never hinged	175.00	

Nos. B1-B24 were sold at double face value, except the 10c denominations which were sold for 15c. The surtax benefited the national anti-tuberculosis organization.

King Albert I — SP3

1914, Oct. 3 **Litho.**

B25	SP3	5c green & red	*15.00*	*15.00*
B26	SP3	10c red	*1.50*	*1.50*
B27	SP3	20c violet & red	*45.00*	*45.00*
		Nos. B25-B27 (3)	61.50	61.50
		Set, never hinged	*125.00*	

Counterfeits of Nos. B25-B27 abound. Probably as many as 90% of the stamps on the market are counterfeits. Values are for genuine examples.

Merode Monument — SP4

1914, Oct. 3

B28	SP4	5c green & red	*4.50*	*3.00*
B29	SP4	10c red	*7.50*	*7.50*
B30	SP4	20c violet & red	*75.00*	*75.00*
		Nos. B28-B30 (3)	87.00	85.50
		Set, never hinged	*175.00*	

Counterfeits of Nos. B28-B30 abound. Probably as many as 90% of the stamps on the market are counterfeits. Values are for genuine examples.

King Albert I — SP5

1915, Jan. 1 ***Perf. 12, 14***

B31	SP5	5c green & red	5.00	3.00
a.		Perf. 12x14	16.00	12.00
B32	SP5	10c rose & red	20.00	6.00
B33	SP5	20c violet & red	25.00	14.00
a.		Perf. 14x12	500.00	250.00
b.		Perf. 12	50.00	32.50
		Nos. B31-B33 (3)	50.00	23.00
		Set, never hinged	150.00	

Nos. B25-B33 were sold at double face value. The surtax benefited the Red Cross.

Types of Regular Issue of 1915 Surcharged in Red:

Nos. B34-B40

Nos. B41-B43

Nos. B44-B47

1918, Jan. 15 **Typo.** ***Perf. 14***

B34	A46	1c + 1c dp orange	.50	.50
B35	A46	2c + 2c brown	.60	.60
B36	A46	5c + 5c blue grn	1.40	1.40
B37	A46	10c + 10c red	2.25	2.25
B38	A46	15c + 15c brt violet	3.25	3.25
B39	A46	20c + 20c plum	7.50	7.50
B40	A46	25c + 25c ultra	7.50	7.50
		Engr.		
B41	A47	35c + 35c lt vio & blk	10.00	10.00
B42	A48	40c + 40c dull red & blk	10.00	10.00
B43	A49	50c + 50c turq blue & blk	12.00	12.00
B44	A50	1fr + 1fr bluish slate	35.00	35.00
B45	A51	2fr + 2fr dp gray grn	100.00	100.00
B46	A52	5fr + 5fr brown	250.00	250.00
B47	A53	10fr + 10fr dp blue	500.00	500.00
		Nos. B34-B47 (14)	940.00	940.00
		Set, never hinged	2,000.	

Discus Thrower — SP6

Racing Chariot — SP7

Runner — SP8

1920, May 20 **Engr.** ***Perf. 12***

B48	SP6	5c + 5c dp green	1.40	1.40
B49	SP7	10c + 5c carmine	1.40	1.40
B50	SP8	15c + 15c dk brown	3.00	3.00
		Nos. B48-B50 (3)	5.80	5.80
		Set, never hinged	17.00	

7th Olympic Games, 1920. Surtax benefited wounded soldiers. Exists imperf.

For surcharges see Nos. 140-142.

Allegory: Asking Alms from the Crown SP9

Wounded Veteran SP10

1922, May 20

B51	SP9	20c + 20c brown	1.40	1.40

1923, July 5

B52	SP10	20c + 20c slate gray	1.75	1.75

Surtax on #B51-B52 was to aid wounded veterans.

SP11

SP12

St. Martin, by Van Dyck
SP13 SP14

1925, Dec. 15 **Typo.** ***Perf. 14***

B53	SP11	15c + 5c dull vio & red	.50	.20
B54	SP11	30c + 5c gray & red	.25	.20
B55	SP11	1fr + 10c chalky blue & red	1.25	1.40
		Nos. B53-B55 (3)	2.00	1.80

Surtax for the Natl. Anti-Tuberculosis League.

1926, Feb. 10

B56	SP12	30c + 30c bluish grn (red surch.)	.50	.50
B57	SP13	1fr + 1fr lt blue	7.25	7.25
B58	SP14	1fr + 1fr lt blue	1.10	1.25
		Nos. B56-B58 (3)	8.85	9.00

The surtax aided victims of the Meuse flood.

Lion and Cross of Lorraine — SP15

Queen Elisabeth and King Albert SP16

1926, Dec. 6 **Typo.** ***Perf. 14***

B59	SP15	5c + 5c dk brown	.25	.20
B60	SP15	20c + 5c red brown	.45	.40
B61	SP15	50c + 5c dull violet	.30	.20
		Engr. ***Perf. 11½***		
B62	SP16	1.50fr + 25c dk blue	.75	.70
B63	SP16	5fr + 1fr rose red	6.50	6.00
		Nos. B59-B63 (5)	8.25	7.50

Surtax was used to benefit tubercular war veterans.

Boat Adrift SP17

1927, Dec. 15 **Engr.** ***Perf. 11½, 14***

B64	SP17	25c + 10c dk brn	.70	.70
B65	SP17	35c + 10c yel grn	.70	.70
B66	SP17	60c + 10c dp violet	.60	.40
B67	SP17	1.75fr + 25c dk blue	1.50	*2.00*
B68	SP17	5fr + 1fr plum	4.50	*4.75*
		Nos. B64-B68 (5)	8.00	*8.55*

The surtax on these stamps was divided among several charitable associations.

Ogives of Orval Abbey — SP18

Monk Carving Capital of Column — SP19

Ruins of Orval Abbey SP20

Design: 60c+15c, 1.75fr+25c, 3fr+1fr, Countess Matilda recovering her ring.

1928, Sept. 15 **Photo.** ***Perf. 11½***

B69	SP18	5c + 5c red & gold	.20	.20
B70	SP18	25c + 5c dk vio & gold	.25	.25
		Engr.		
B71	SP19	35c + 10c dp grn	.70	.70
B72	SP19	60c + 15c red brn	.45	.20
B73	SP19	1.75fr + 25c dk blue	1.90	1.25
B74	SP19	2fr + 40c dp vio	15.00	12.50

B75 SP19 3fr + 1fr red 13.50 12.00

Perf. 14

B76 SP20 5fr + 5fr rose lake 9.00 9.00
B77 SP20 10fr + 10fr ol green 9.00 9.00
Nos. B69-B77 (9) 50.00 45.10

Surtax for the restoration of the ruined Orval Abbey.

St. Waudru, Mons — SP22

St. Rombaut, Malines — SP23

Designs: 25c + 15c, Cathedral of Tournai. 60c + 15c, St. Bavon, Ghent. 1.75fr + 25c, St. Gudule, Brussels. 5fr + 5fr, Louvain Library.

1928, Dec. 1 Photo. *Perf. 14, 11½*

B78 SP22 5c + 5c carmine .20 .20
B79 SP22 25c + 15c ol brn .25 .25

Engr.

B80 SP23 35c + 10c dp grn 1.00 1.00
B81 SP23 60c + 15c red brn .30 .30
B82 SP23 1.75fr + 25c vio bl 7.00 7.00
B83 SP23 5fr + 5fr red vio 14.00 14.00
Nos. B78-B83 (6) 22.75 22.75

The surtax was for anti-tuberculosis work.

Nos. B69-B77 with this overprint in blue or red were privately produced. They were for the laying of the 1st stone toward the restoration of the ruined Abbey of Orval. Value, set, $650.

Forgeries of the overprint exist.

Waterfall at Coo — SP28

Bayard Rock, Dinant — SP29

Designs: 35c+10c, Menin Gate, Ypres. 60c+15c, Promenade d'Orleans, Spa. 1.75fr+25c, Antwerp Harbor. 5fr+5fr, Quai Vert, Bruges.

1929, Dec. 2 Engr. *Perf. 11½*

B93 SP28 5c + 5c red brn .20 .25
B94 SP29 25c + 15c gray blk .65 .60
B95 SP28 35c + 10c green .80 .95
B96 SP28 60c + 15c rose lake .55 .50
B97 SP28 1.75fr + 25c dp blue 4.50 4.50

Perf. 14

B98 SP29 5fr + 5fr dl vio 27.50 27.50
Nos. B93-B98 (6) 34.20 34.30

Bornhem — SP34

Beloeil — SP35

Gaesbeek SP36

25c + 15c, Wynendaele. 70c + 15c, Oydonck. 1fr + 25c, Ghent. 1.75fr + 25c, Bouillon.

1930, Dec. 1 Photo. *Perf. 14*

B99 SP34 10c + 5c violet .25 *.30*
B100 SP34 25c + 15c olive brn .60 .60

Engr.

B101 SP35 40c + 10c brn vio .80 *1.00*
B102 SP35 70c + 15c gray blk .55 .55
B103 SP35 1fr + 25c rose lake 3.50 3.50
B104 SP35 1.75fr + 25c dp bl 4.50 2.75
B105 SP36 5fr + 5fr gray grn 27.50 *32.50*
Nos. B99-B105 (7) 37.70 *41.20*

Prince Leopold SP41

Queen Elisabeth SP42

Philatelic Exhibition Issue

Souvenir Sheet

1931, July 18 Photo. *Perf. 14*

B106 SP41 2.45fr + 55c car brn 140.00 140.00
Never hinged 350.00
a. Single stamp 70.00

Sold exclusively at the Brussels Phil. Exhib., July 18-21, 1931. Size: 122x159mm. Surtax for the Veterans' Relief Fund.

The sheet normally has pin holes and a cancellation-like marking in the margin. These are considered unused and the condition valued here.

1931, Dec. 1 Engr.

B107 SP42 10c + 5c red brn .30 *.50*
B108 SP42 25c + 15c dk vio 1.10 *1.25*
B109 SP42 50c + 10c dk grn .95 *1.10*
B110 SP42 75c + 15c blk brn .90 .70
B111 SP42 1fr + 25c rose lake 6.75 6.00
B112 SP42 1.75fr + 25c ultra 4.75 4.00
B113 SP42 5fr + 5fr brn vio 55.00 55.00
Nos. B107-B113 (7) 69.75 68.55

The surtax was for the National Anti-Tuberculosis League.

Désiré Cardinal Mercier — SP43

Mercier Protecting Children and Aged at Malines — SP44

Mercier as Professor at Louvain University — SP45

Mercier in Full Canonicals, Giving His Blessing SP46

1932, June 10 Photo. *Perf. 14½x14*

B114 SP43 10c + 10c dk violet .40 *.60*
B115 SP43 50c + 30c brt violet 2.25 *2.50*
B116 SP43 75c + 25c olive brn 2.25 2.25
B117 SP43 1fr + 2fr brown red 6.00 6.00

Engr. *Perf. 11½*

B118 SP44 1.75fr + 75c dp blue 70.00 *82.50*
B119 SP45 2.50fr + 2.50fr dk brn 70.00 70.00
B120 SP44 3fr + 4.50fr dull grn 70.00 70.00
B121 SP45 5fr + 20fr vio brn 80.00 *82.50*
B122 SP46 10fr + 40fr brn lake 175.00 *210.00*
Nos. B114-B122 (9) 475.90 *526.35*

Honoring Cardinal Mercier and to obtain funds to erect a monument to his memory.

Belgian Infantryman SP47

Sanatorium at Waterloo SP48

1932, Aug. 4 *Perf. 14½x14*

B123 SP47 75c + 3.25fr red brn 55.00 55.00
B124 SP47 1.75fr + 4.25fr dk blue 55.00 55.00

Honoring Belgian soldiers who fought in WWI and to obtain funds to erect a natl. monument to their glory.

1932, Dec. 1 Photo. *Perf. 13½x14*

B125 SP48 10c + 5c dk vio .30 *.90*
B126 SP48 25c + 15c red vio 1.00 *1.25*
B127 SP48 50c + 10c red brn 1.00 *1.25*
B128 SP48 75c + 15c ol brn 1.00 .80
B129 SP48 1fr + 25c dp red 13.00 10.50
B130 SP48 1.75fr + 25c dp blue 10.50 9.25
B131 SP48 5fr + 5fr gray grn 85.00 *90.00*
Nos. B125-B131 (7) 111.80 *113.95*

Surtax for the assistance of the Natl. Anti-Tuberculosis Society at Waterloo.

View of Old Abbey SP49

Ruins of Old Abbey — SP50

Count de Chiny Presenting First Abbey to Countess Matilda SP56

Restoration of Abbey in XVI and XVII Centuries SP57

Abbey in XVIII Century, Maria Theresa and Charles V — SP58

Madonna and Arms of Seven Abbeys SP60

Designs: 25c+15c, Guests, courtyard, 50c+25c, Transept. 75c+50c, Bell Tower. 1fr+1.25fr, Fountain. 1.25fr+1.75fr, Cloisters. 5fr+20fr, Duke of Brabant placing 1st stone of new abbey.

1933, Oct. 15 *Perf. 14*

B132 SP49 5c + 5c dull grn 35.00 *40.00*
B133 SP50 10c + 15c ol grn 32.50 *35.00*
B134 SP49 25c + 15c dk brn 32.50 *35.00*
B135 SP50 50c + 25c red brn 32.50 *35.00*
B136 SP50 75c + 50c dp grn 32.50 *35.00*
B137 SP50 1fr + 1.25fr cop red 32.50 *35.00*
B138 SP49 1.25fr + 1.75fr gray blk 32.50 *35.00*
B139 SP56 1.75fr + 2.75fr blue 37.50 *40.00*
B140 SP57 2fr + 3fr mag 37.50 *40.00*
B141 SP58 2.50fr + 5fr dull brn 37.50 *40.00*
B142 SP56 5fr + 20fr vio 40.00 *40.00*

Perf. 11½

B143 SP60 10fr + 40fr bl 225.00 *225.00*
Nos. B132-B143 (12) 607.50 *635.00*

The surtax was for a fund to aid in the restoration of Orval Abbey. Counterfeits exist.

"Tuberculosis Society" SP61

Peter Benoit SP62

1933, Dec. 1 Engr. *Perf. 14x13½*

B144	SP61	10c + 5c blk	.85	.85
B145	SP61	25c + 15c vio	3.00	3.00
B146	SP61	50c + 10c red brn	2.25	2.25
B147	SP61	75c + 15c blk brn	9.25	9.00
B148	SP61	1fr + 25c cl	10.50	10.50
B149	SP61	1.75fr + 25c vio bl	12.50	12.50
B150	SP61	5fr + 5fr lilac	115.00	115.00
		Nos. B144-B150 (7)	153.35	153.10

The surtax was for anti-tuberculosis work.

1934, June 1 Photo.

B151	SP62	75c + 25c olive brn	5.50	5.50

The surtax was to raise funds for the Peter Benoit Memorial.

SP63

King Leopold III — SP64

1934, Sept. 15

B152	SP63	75c + 25c ol blk	18.00	17.00
a.		Sheet of 20	750.00	750.00
B153	SP64	1fr + 25c red vio	17.00	16.00
a.		Sheet of 20	750.00	750.00

The surtax aided the National War Veterans' Fund. Sold for 4.50fr a set at the Exhibition of War Postmarks 1914-18, held at Brussels by the Royal Philatelic Club of Veterans. The price included an exhibition ticket. Sold at Brussels post office Sept. 18-22. No. B152 printed in sheets of 20 (4x5) and 100 (10x10). No. B153 printed in sheets of 20 (4x5) and 150 (10x15).

1934, Sept. 24

B154	SP63	75c + 25c violet	1.25	1.25
B155	SP64	1fr + 25c red brn	7.00	7.00

The surtax aided the National War Veterans' Fund. No. B154 printed in sheets of 100 (10x10); No. B155 in sheets of 150 (10x15). These stamps remained in use one year.

Crusader SP65

1934, Nov. 17 Engr. *Perf. 13½x14*

Cross in Red

B156	SP65	10c + 5c blk	1.25	1.25
B157	SP65	25c + 15c brn	1.75	1.75
B158	SP65	50c + 10c dull grn	1.75	1.75
B159	SP65	75c + 15c vio brn	.85	.85
B160	SP65	1fr + 25c rose	8.50	8.50
B161	SP65	1.75fr + 25c ultra	7.50	7.50
B162	SP65	5fr + 5fr brn vio	105.00	105.00
		Nos. B156-B162 (7)	126.60	126.60

The surtax was for anti-tuberculosis work.

Prince Baudouin, Princess Josephine and Prince Albert SP66

1935, Apr. 10 Photo.

B163	SP66	35c + 15c dk grn	.85	.75
B164	SP66	70c + 30c red brn	.85	.60
B165	SP66	1.75fr + 50c dk blue	3.00	*3.50*
		Nos. B163-B165 (3)	4.70	*4.85*

Surtax was for Child Welfare Society.

Stagecoach — SP67

Franz von Taxis — SP68

Queen Astrid — SP69

1935, Apr. 27

B166	SP67	10c + 10c ol blk	.60	.65
B167	SP67	25c + 25c bis brn	1.90	1.75
B168	SP67	35c + 25c dk green	2.50	2.25
		Nos. B166-B168 (3)	5.00	4.65

Printed in sheets of 10. Value, set of 3, $175.

Souvenir Sheet

1935, May 25 Engr. *Perf. 14*

B169	SP68	5fr + 5fr grnsh blk	125.00	125.00
a.		Single stamp	85.00	

Sheets measure 91½x117mm.

Nos. B166-B169 were issued for the Brussels Philatelic Exhibition (SITEB).

The sheet normally has pin holes and a cancellation-like marking in the margin. These are considered unused and the condition valued here.

1935 Photo. *Perf. 11½*

Borders in Black

B170	SP69	10c + 5c ol blk	.20	.20
B171	SP69	25c + 15c brown	.20	*.30*
B172	SP69	35c + 5c dk green	.20	*.25*
B173	SP69	50c + 10c rose lil	.65	.55
B174	SP69	70c + 5c gray blk	.20	.20
B175	SP69	1fr + 25c red	.90	.70
B176	SP69	1.75fr + 25c blue	2.00	1.50
B177	SP69	2.45fr + 55c dk vio	2.50	*2.75*
		Nos. B170-B177 (8)	6.85	6.45

Queen Astrid Memorial issue. The surtax was divided among several charitable organizations.

Issued: #B174, 10/31; others, 12/1.

Borgerhout Philatelic Exhibition Issue

Souvenir Sheet

Town Hall, Borgerhout SP70

1936, Oct. 3

B178	SP70	70c + 30c pur brn	50.00	35.00
a.		Single stamp	25.00	

Sheet measures 115x126mm.

The sheet normally has pin holes and a cancellation-like marking in the margin. These are considered unused and the condition valued here.

Town Hall and Belfry of Charleroi SP71

Prince Baudouin SP72

Charleroi Youth Exhibition

Souvenir Sheet

1936, Oct. 18 Engr.

B179	SP71	2.45fr + 55c gray blue	42.50	40.00
a.		Single stamp	25.00	

Sheet measures 95x120mm.

The sheet normally has pin holes and a cancellation-like marking in the margin. These are considered unused and the condition valued here.

1936, Dec. 1 Photo. *Perf. 14x13½*

B180	SP72	10c + 5c dk brown	.20	.20
B181	SP72	25c + 5c violet	.20	*.25*
B182	SP72	35c + 5c dk green	.20	*.25*
B183	SP72	50c + 5c vio brn	.30	*.35*
B184	SP72	70c + 5c ol grn	.20	.20
B185	SP72	1fr + 25c cerise	.65	.45
B186	SP72	1.75fr + 25c ultra	1.10	.65
B187	SP72	2.45fr + 2.55fr vio rose	3.00	*4.00*
		Nos. B180-B187 (8)	5.85	*6.35*

The surtax was for the assistance of the National Anti-Tuberculosis Society.

1937, Jan. 10

B188	SP72	2.45fr + 2.55fr slate	1.50	1.50

Intl. Stamp Day. Surtax for the benefit of the Brussels Postal Museum, the Royal Belgian Phil. Fed. and the Anti-Tuberculosis Soc.

Queen Astrid and Prince Baudouin SP73

Queen Mother Elisabeth SP74

1937, Apr. 15 *Perf. 11½*

B189	SP73	10c + 5c magenta	.20	.20
B190	SP73	25c + 5c ol blk	.20	*.25*
B191	SP73	35c + 5c dk grn	.20	*.25*
B192	SP73	50c + 5c violet	.50	*.55*
B193	SP73	70c + 5c slate	.20	*.30*
B194	SP73	1fr + 25c dk car	.65	.60
B195	SP73	1.75fr + 25c dp ultra	1.10	1.10
B196	SP73	2.45fr + 1.55fr dk brn	2.75	2.75
		Nos. B189-B196 (8)	5.80	6.00

The surtax was to raise funds for Public Utility Works.

1937, Sept. 15 *Perf. 14x13½*

B197	SP74	70c + 5c int black	.30	.30
B198	SP74	1.75fr + 25c brt ultra	.70	.70

Souvenir Sheet

Perf. 11½

B199	Sheet of 4	26.00	15.00
a.	SP74 1.50fr+2.50fr red brn	3.75	3.25
b.	SP74 2.45fr+3.55fr red vio	3.25	2.00

Issued for the benefit of the Queen Elisabeth Music Foundation in connection with the Eugene Ysaye intl. competition.

No. B199 contains two se-tenant pairs of Nos. B199a and B199b. Size: 111x145mm. On sale one day, Sept. 15, at Brussels.

The sheet normally has pin holes and a cancellation-like marking in the margin. These are considered unused and the condition valued here.

Princess Josephine-Charlotte SP75

1937, Dec. 1 *Perf. 14x13½*

B200	SP75	10c + 5c sl grn	.20	.20
B201	SP75	25c + 5c lt brn	.20	.20
B202	SP75	35c + 5c yel grn	.20	.20
B203	SP75	50c + 5c ol gray	.40	.35
B204	SP75	70c + 5c brn red	.20	.20
B205	SP75	1fr + 25c red	.70	.55
B206	SP75	1.75fr + 25c vio bl	.85	.70
B207	SP75	2.45fr + 2.55fr mag	3.25	*3.50*
		Nos. B200-B207 (8)	6.00	*5.90*

King Albert Memorial Issue

Souvenir Sheet

King Albert Memorial — SP76

1938, Feb. 17 *Perf. 11½*

B208	SP76	2.45fr + 7.55fr brn vio	13.00	11.00

Dedication of the monument to King Albert.

The sheet normally has pin holes and a cancellation-like marking in the margin. These are considered unused and the condition valued here.

King Leopold III in Military Plane SP77

1938, Mar. 15

B209	SP77	10c + 5c car brn	.20	*.30*
B210	SP77	35c + 5c dp grn	.35	*.90*
B211	SP77	70c + 5c gray blk	.65	.50
B212	SP77	1.75fr + 25c ultra	1.50	1.40
B213	SP77	2.45fr + 2.55fr pur	3.50	3.00
		Nos. B209-B213 (5)	6.20	6.10

The surtax was for the benefit of the National Fund for Aeronautical Propaganda.

Basilica of Koekelberg SP78

Interior View of the Basilica of Koekelberg
SP79

1938, June 1 **Photo.**

B214	SP78	10c + 5c lt brn	.20	.20
B215	SP78	35c + 5c grn	.20	.20
B216	SP78	70c + 5c gray grn	.20	.20
B217	SP78	1fr + 25c car	.65	.55
B218	SP78	1.75fr + 25c ultra	.65	.65
B219	SP78	2.45fr + 2.55fr brn vio	2.75	*3.50*

Engr.

B220	SP79	5fr + 5fr dl grn	11.00	10.50
		Nos. B214-B220 (7)	15.65	15.80

Souvenir Sheet

1938, July 21 **Engr.** ***Perf. 14***

B221	SP79	5fr + 5fr lt vio	14.00	14.00

The surtax was for a fund to aid in completing the National Basilica of the Sacred Heart at Koekelberg.

Nos. B214, B216 and B218 are different views of the exterior of the Basilica.

The sheet normally has pin holes and a cancellation-like marking in the margin. These are considered unused and the condition valued here.

Stamps of 1938 Surcharged in Black:

Nos. B222-B223

No. B224

1938, Nov. 10 ***Perf. 11½***

B222	SP78	40c on 35c+5c grn	.35	*.40*
B223	SP78	75c on 70c+5c gray grn	.50	*.60*
B224	SP78	2.50 +2.50fr on 2.45+2.55fr	4.50	*5.00*
		Nos. B222-B224 (3)	5.35	*6.00*

Prince Albert of Liege — SP81

1938, Dec. 10 **Photo.** ***Perf. 14x13½***

B225	SP81	10c + 5c brown	.20	.20
B226	SP81	30c + 5c mag	.20	*.30*
B227	SP81	40c + 5c olive gray	.20	*.30*
B228	SP81	75c + 5c slate grn	.20	.20
B229	SP81	1fr + 25c dk car	.55	*.75*
B230	SP81	1.75fr + 25c ultra	.55	*.75*
B231	SP81	2.50fr + 2.50fr dp grn	3.50	*5.50*
B232	SP81	5fr + 5fr brn lake	11.00	8.50
		Nos. B225-B232 (8)	16.40	16.50

Henri Dunant
SP82

Florence Nightingale
SP83

Queen Mother Elisabeth and Royal Children — SP84

Queen Astrid — SP86

King Leopold and Royal Children
SP85

Queen Mother Elisabeth and Wounded Soldier — SP87

1939, Apr. 1 **Photo.** ***Perf. 11½***
Cross in Carmine

B233	SP82	10c + 5c brn	.20	.20
B234	SP83	30c + 5c brn car	.30	.30
B235	SP84	40c + 5c ol gray	.20	*.30*
B236	SP85	75c + 5c slate blk	.40	.20
B237	SP84	1fr + 25c brt rose	1.90	1.10
B238	SP85	1.75fr + 25c brt ultra	.60	*.80*
B239	SP86	2.50fr + 2.50fr dl vio	1.25	*1.60*
B240	SP87	5fr + 5fr gray grn	4.25	*5.50*
		Nos. B233-B240 (8)	9.10	*10.00*

75th anniversary of the founding of the International Red Cross Society.

Rubens' House, Antwerp
SP88

"Albert and Nicolas Rubens" — SP89

Arcade, Rubens' House
SP90

"Helena Fourment and Her Children" — SP91

Rubens and Isabelle Brandt — SP92

Peter Paul Rubens — SP93

"The Velvet Hat" — SP94

"Descent from the Cross"
SP95

1939, July 1

B241	SP88	10c + 5c brn	.20	.20
B242	SP89	40c + 5c brn car	.20	.20
B243	SP90	75c + 5c ol blk	.35	.35
B244	SP91	1fr + 25c rose	1.40	1.40
B245	SP92	1.50fr + 25c sep	1.60	1.60
B246	SP93	1.75fr + 25c dp ultra	2.50	2.50
B247	SP94	2.50fr + 2.50fr brt red vio	8.25	*8.25*
B248	SP95	5fr + 5fr slate gray	10.50	10.50
		Nos. B241-B248 (8)	25.00	25.00

Issued to honor Peter Paul Rubens. The surtax was used to restore Rubens' home in Antwerp.

"Martin van Nieuwenhove" by Hans Memling (1430?-1495), Flemish Painter — SP96

1939, July 1

B249	SP96	75c + 75c olive blk	2.75	2.75

Twelfth Century Monks at Work — SP97

Reconstructed Tower Seen through Cloister — SP98

Monks Laboring in the Fields
SP99

Orval Abbey, Aerial View
SP100

Bishop Heylen of Namur, Madonna and Abbot General Smets of the Trappists — SP101

King Albert I and King Leopold III and Shrine — SP102

1939, July 20

B250	SP97	75c + 75c ol blk	2.50	2.75
B251	SP98	1fr + 1fr rose red	1.60	1.60
B252	SP99	1.50fr + 1.50fr dl brn	1.60	1.60
B253	SP100	1.75fr + 1.75fr saph	1.60	1.60
B254	SP101	2.50fr + 2.50fr brt red vio	7.25	6.50
B255	SP102	5fr + 5fr brn car	7.25	7.25
		Nos. B250-B255 (6)	21.80	21.30

The surtax was used for the restoration of the Abbey of Orval.

Bruges
SP103

Furnes
SP104

Belfries: 30c+5c, Thuin. 40c+5c, Lierre. 75c+5c, Mons. 1.75fr+25c, Namur. 2.50fr+2.50fr, Alost. 5fr+5fr, Tournai.

1939, Dec. 1 **Photo.** ***Perf. 14x13½***

B256	SP103	10c + 5c ol gray	.20	*.25*
B257	SP103	30c + 5c brn org	.25	*.35*
B258	SP103	40c + 5c brt red vio	.40	*.45*
B259	SP103	75c + 5c olive blk	.20	*.25*

Engr.

B260	SP104	1fr + 25c rose car	1.00	*1.25*
B261	SP104	1.75fr + 25c dk blue	1.00	*1.25*
B262	SP104	2.50fr + 2.50fr dp red brn	7.25	*8.00*
B263	SP104	5fr + 5fr pur	10.00	*11.00*
		Nos. B256-B263 (8)	20.30	*22.80*

Mons
SP111

Ghent
SP112

Coats of Arms: 40c+10c, Arel. 50c+10c, Bruges. 75c+15c, Namur. 1fr+25c, Hasselt. 1.75fr+50c, Brussels. 2.50fr+2.50fr, Antwerp. 5fr+5fr, Liege.

1940-41 Typo. *Perf. 14x13½*

B264 SP111 10c + 5c multi .20 .20
B265 SP112 30c + 5c multi .20 .20
B266 SP111 40c + 10c multi .20 .20
B267 SP112 50c + 10c multi .20 .20
B268 SP111 75c + 15c multi .20 .20
B269 SP112 1fr + 25c multi .30 .30
B270 SP111 1.75fr + 50c multi .45 .40
B271 SP112 2.50fr + 2.50fr multi 1.25 1.25
B272 SP111 5fr + 5fr multi 1.50 1.50
Nos. B264-B272 (9) 4.50 4.45

Nos. B264, B269-B272 issued in 1941. Surtax for winter relief. See No. B279.

Queen Elisabeth Music Chapel SP120

Bust of Prince Albert of Liege — SP121

1940, Nov. Photo. *Perf. 11½*

B273 SP120 75c + 75c slate 1.25 1.25
B274 SP120 1fr + 1fr rose red 1.25 1.25
B275 SP121 1.50fr + 1.50fr Prus grn 1.25 1.25
B276 SP121 1.75fr + 1.75fr ultra 1.25 1.25
B277 SP120 2.50fr + 2.50fr brn org 2.50 2.50
B278 SP121 5fr + 5fr red vio 3.00 3.00
Nos. B273-B278 (6) 10.50 10.50

The surtax was for the Queen Elisabeth Music Foundation. Nos. B273-B278 were not authorized for postal use, but were sold to advance subscribers either mint or canceled to order. See Nos. B317-B318.

AIR POST STAMPS

Fokker FVII/3m over Ostend AP1

Designs: 1.50fr, Plane over St. Hubert. 2fr, over Namur. 5fr, over Brussels.

Perf. 11½

1930, Apr. 30 Unwmk. Photo.

C1 AP1 50c blue .40 .40
C2 AP1 1.50fr black brn 2.25 2.50
C3 AP1 2fr deep green 2.00 .55
C4 AP1 5fr brown lake 1.75 .95
Nos. C1-C4 (4) 6.40 4.40
Set, never hinged 20.00

Exist imperf.

1930, Dec. 5

C5 AP1 5fr dark violet 30.00 30.00
Never hinged 45.00

Issued for use on a mail carrying flight from Brussels to Leopoldville, Belgian Congo, starting Dec. 7.
Exists imperf.

Nos. C2 and C4 Surcharged in Carmine or Blue

1935, May 23

C6 AP1 1fr on 1.50fr (C) .55 .40
C7 AP1 4fr on 5fr (Bl) 7.50 7.00
Set, never hinged 25.00

SPECIAL DELIVERY STAMPS

From 1874 to 1903 certain hexagonal telegraph stamps were used as special delivery stamps.

Town Hall, Brussels — SD1

Eupen — SD2

2.35fr, Street in Ghent. 3.50fr, Bishop's Palace, Liege. 5.25fr, Notre Dame Cathedral, Antwerp.

1929 Unwmk. Photo. *Perf. 11½*

E1 SD1 1.75fr dark blue .80 .30
E2 SD1 2.35fr carmine 1.50 .45
E3 SD1 3.50fr dark violet 10.00 9.00
E4 SD1 5.25fr olive green 5.50 5.25

1931

E5 SD2 2.45fr dark green 11.00 2.50
Nos. E1-E5 (5) 28.80 17.50
Set, never hinged 60.00

No. E5 Surcharged in Red

1932

E6 SD2 2.50fr on 2.45fr dk grn 9.00 1.25
Never hinged 25.00

POSTAGE DUE STAMPS

D1

D2

1870 Unwmk. Typo. *Perf. 15*

J1 D1 10c green 3.75 2.00
Never hinged 10.00
On cover 110.00
a. 10c deep green 4.50 3.00
Never hinged 12.50
On cover 120.00
J2 D1 20c ultra, thin paper 30.00 3.75
Never hinged 140.00
On cover 225.00

In 1909 many bisects of Nos. J1-J2 were created. The 10c bisect used as 5c on piece sells for $3.50.
No. J2 was also printed in aniline ink on thin paper. Value about the same.

1895-09 *Perf. 14*

J3 D2 5c yellow grn .20 .20
Never hinged .40
On cover 3.50
a. 5c green .85 .25
Never hinged 3.00
On cover 3.50
J4 D2 10c orange brn 17.50 1.75
Never hinged 57.50
On cover 15.00
J5 D2 10c carmine ('00) .20 .20
Never hinged .40
On cover 2.00
a. 10c rose 1.50 .40
Never hinged 3.00
On cover 2,000.
J6 D2 20c olive green .20 .20
Never hinged .40
On cover 3.50
J7 D2 30c pale blue ('09) .30 .25
Never hinged .80
On cover 17.50
J8 D2 50c yellow brn 17.50 5.00
Never hinged 57.50
On cover 85.00
J9 D2 50c gray ('00) .75 .45
Never hinged 1.60
On cover 30.00
a. 50c blackish gray 3.75 1.25
Never hinged 10.00
On cover 37.50
J10 D2 1fr carmine 20.00 11.50
Never hinged 50.00
On cover 850.00
J11 D2 1fr ocher ('00) 6.50 5.00
Never hinged 10.00
On cover 1,000.
Nos. J3-J11 (9) 63.15 24.55

1916 Redrawn

J12 D2 5c blue grn 25.00 7.00
Never hinged 72.50
On cover 22.50
J13 D2 10c carmine 42.50 11.00
Never hinged 140.00
On cover 15.00
J14 D2 20c dp gray grn 42.50 15.00
Never hinged 140.00
On cover 40.00
J15 D2 30c brt blue 6.00 5.00
Never hinged 14.00
On cover 50.00
J16 D2 50c gray 125.00 60.00
Never hinged 425.00
On cover 150.00
Nos. J12-J16 (5) 241.00 98.00

In the redrawn stamps the lions have a heavy, colored outline. There is a thick vertical line at the outer edge of the design on each side.

D3

D4

1919 *Perf. 14*

J17 D3 5c green .40 .50
J18 D3 10c carmine .95 .35
J19 D3 20c gray green 7.25 1.25
J20 D3 30c bright blue 1.40 .40
J21 D3 50c gray 2.75 .50
Nos. J17-J21 (5) 12.75 3.00

The 5c, 10c, 20c and 50c values also exist perf 14x15.

1922-32

J22 D4 5c dk gray .20 .20
J23 D4 10c green .20 .20
J24 D4 20c deep brown .20 .20
J25 D4 30c ver ('24) .65 .20
a. 30c rose red 1.00 .45
J26 D4 40c red brn ('25) .25 .20
J27 D4 50c ultra 1.90 .20
J28 D4 70c red brn ('29) .30 .20
J29 D4 1fr violet ('25) .45 .20
J30 D4 1fr rose lilac ('32) .55 .20
J31 D4 1.20fr ol grn ('29) .65 .45
J32 D4 1.50fr ol grn ('32) .65 .45
J33 D4 2fr violet ('29) .75 .20
J34 D4 3.50fr dp blue ('29) 1.00 .25
Nos. J22-J34 (13) 7.75 3.15

1934-46 *Perf. 14x13½*

J35 D4 35c green ('35) .40 .45
J36 D4 50c slate .20 .20
J37 D4 60c carmine ('38) .40 .30
J38 D4 80c slate ('38) .30 .20
J39 D4 1.40fr gray ('35) .65 .45
J39A D4 3fr org brn ('46) 1.50 .60
J39B D4 7fr brt red vio ('46) 2.25 3.25
Nos. J35-J39B (7) 5.70 5.45

See Nos. J54-J61.

MILITARY PARCEL POST STAMP

Type of Parcel Post Stamp of 1938 Surcharged with New Value and "M" in Blue.

1939 Unwmk. *Perf. 13½*

MQ1 PP19 3fr on 5.50fr copper red .30 .20
Never hinged .60

OFFICIAL STAMPS

For franking the official correspondence of the Administration of the Belgian National Railways.

Most examples of Nos. O1-O25 in the marketplace are counterfeits. Values are for genuine examples.

Regular Issue of 1921-27 Overprinted in Black

1929-30 Unwmk. *Perf. 14*

O1 A58 5c gray .20 .20
O2 A58 10c blue green .30 .40
O3 A58 35c blue green .40 .30
O4 A58 60c olive green .45 .30
O5 A58 1.50fr brt blue 8.00 6.25
O6 A58 1.75fr ultra ('30) 1.75 2.00
Nos. O1-O6 (6) 11.10 9.45

Same Overprint, in Red or Black, on Regular Issues of 1929-30

1929-31

O7 A63 5c slate (R) .25 .35
O8 A63 10c olive grn (R) .50 .40
O9 A63 25c rose red (Bk) 1.50 .85
O10 A63 35c dp green (R) 1.75 .50
O11 A63 40c red vio (Bk) 1.25 .45
O12 A63 50c dp blue (R) ('31) .80 .35
O13 A63 60c rose (Bk) 6.00 6.00
O14 A63 70c orange brn (Bk) 4.25 1.25
O15 A63 75c black vio (R) ('31) 4.00 .85
Nos. O7-O15 (9) 20.30 11.00

Overprinted on Regular Issue of 1932

1932

O16 A73 10c olive grn (R) .50 .60
O17 A74 35c dp green 9.00 .75
O18 A71a 75c bister brn (R) 1.50 .30
Nos. O16-O18 (3) 11.00 1.65

Overprinted on No. 262 in Red

1935 *Perf. 13½x14*

O19 A80 70c olive black 2.75 .25

Regular Stamps of 1935-36 Overprinted in Red

1936-38 *Perf. 13½, 13½x14, 14*

O20 A82 10c olive bister .20 .35
O21 A82 35c green .25 .40
O22 A82 50c dark blue .45 .35
O23 A83 70c brown 1.50 .65

Overprinted in Black or Red on Regular Issue of 1938

Perf. 13½x14

O24 A82 40c red violet (Bk) .30 .35
O25 A85 75c olive gray (R) .65 .30
Nos. O20-O25 (6) 3.35 2.40

NEWSPAPER STAMPS

Most examples of Nos. P1-P40 in the marketplace are counterfeits. Values are for genuine examples.

Parcel Post Stamps of 1923-27 Overprinted

Perf. 14½x14, 14x14½

1928 Unwmk.

P1 PP12 10c vermilion .25 .40
P2 PP12 20c turq blue .25 .40
P3 PP12 40c olive grn .25 .40
P4 PP12 60c orange .70 .90
P5 PP12 70c dk brown .45 .40
P6 PP12 80c violet .60 .70
P7 PP12 90c slate 2.25 2.00
P8 PP13 1fr brt blue .90 .60
a. 1fr ultramarine 12.00 5.00
P10 PP13 2fr olive grn 1.50 .60
P11 PP13 3fr orange red 1.60 .90

P12 PP13 4fr rose 2.25 1.10
P13 PP13 5fr violet 2.25 1.00
P14 PP13 6fr bister brn 4.50 1.75
P15 PP13 7fr orange 5.00 2.25
P16 PP13 8fr dk brown 6.00 2.75
P17 PP13 9fr red violet 10.00 3.00
P18 PP13 10fr blue green 9.00 2.75
P19 PP13 20fr magenta 15.00 7.00
Nos. P1-P8,P10-P19 (18) 62.75 28.90

Parcel Post Stamps of 1923-28 Overprinted

1929-31

P20 PP12 10c vermilion .25 .20
P21 PP12 20c turq blue .25 .20
P22 PP12 40c olive green .30 .20
a. Inverted overprint
P23 PP12 60c orange .55 .35
P24 PP12 70c dk brown .55 .20
P25 PP12 80c violet .60 .25
P26 PP12 90c gray 2.00 1.00
P27 PP13 1fr ultra .60 .25
a. 1fr bright blue 4.00 2.50
P28 PP13 1.10fr org brn ('31) 6.25 1.40
P29 PP13 1.50fr gray vio ('31) 6.25 1.90
P30 PP13 2fr olive green 2.00 .25
P31 PP13 2.10fr sl gray ('31) 17.00 12.00
P32 PP13 3fr orange red 2.25 .45
P33 PP13 4fr rose 2.25 .70
P34 PP13 5fr violet 3.00 .55
P35 PP13 6fr bister brn 3.75 1.00
P36 PP13 7fr orange 3.75 1.00
P37 PP13 8fr dk brown 3.75 1.00
P38 PP13 9fr red violet 5.25 1.50
P39 PP13 10fr blue green 3.75 1.10
P40 PP13 20fr magenta 13.00 4.50
Nos. P20-P40 (21) 77.35 30.00

PARCEL POST AND RAILWAY STAMPS

Values for used Railway Stamps (Chemins de Fer) stamps are for copies with railway cancellations. Railway Stamps with postal cancellations sell for twice as much.

Coat of Arms — PP1

1879-82 Unwmk. Typo. *Perf. 14*

Q1 PP1 10c violet brown 110.00 5.75
No gum 50.00
Q2 PP1 20c blue 275.00 17.50
No gum 140.00
Q3 PP1 25c green ('81) 375.00 10.00
No gum 175.00
Q4 PP1 50c carmine 1,750. 10.00
No gum 1,100.
Q5 PP1 80c yellow 2,000. 57.50
No gum 1,150.
Q6 PP1 1fr gray ('82) 275.00 16.00
No gum 140.00

Used copies of Nos. Q1-Q6 with pinholes, a normal state, sell for approximately 40-60 percent of the values given.

Most of the stamps of 1882-1902 (Nos. Q7 to Q28) are without watermark. Twice in each sheet of 100 stamps they have one of three watermarks: (1) A winged wheel and "Chemins de Fer de l'Etat Belge," (2) Coat of Arms of Belgium and "Royaume de Belgique," (3) Larger Coat of Arms, without inscription.

PP2

1882-94 *Perf. 15½x14¼*

Q7 PP2 10c brown ('86) 20.00 1.50
a. 10c rose brown 21.50 1.60
b. 10c chestnut brown 23.50 3.00
Q8 PP2 15c gray ('94) 8.75 7.25
Q9 PP2 20c blue ('86) 65.00 7.00
a. 20c ultramarine ('90) 75.00 4.00
b. 20c greenish blue ('90) 72.50 3.75
Q10 PP2 25c yel grn ('91) 72.50 4.25
a. 25c blue green ('87) 67.50 4.00
Q11 PP2 50c carmine 72.50 2.50
a. 50c rose ('82) 67.50 .75
b. 50c pomegranate 75.00 5.00
Q12 PP2 80c brnsh buff 72.50 .90
a. 80c bister ('83) 67.50 .80
Q13 PP2 80c lemon 75.00 1.60
Q14 PP2 1fr lavender 350.00 3.00
a. 1fr gray 385.00 3.50
b. 1fr bronze 425.00 4.50
Q15 PP2 2fr yel buff ('94) 210.00 67.50

Counterfeits exist.

PP3

Name of engraver below frame

1895-97

Numerals in Black, except 1fr, 2fr

Q16 PP3 10c red brown ('96) 11.00 .60
Never hinged 20.00
Q17 PP3 15c gray 11.00 7.00
Never hinged 18.00
Q18 PP3 20c blue 17.50 1.00
Never hinged 32.50
Q19 PP3 25c green 17.50 1.25
Never hinged 32.50
Q20 PP3 50c carmine 25.00 .80
Never hinged 50.00
Q21 PP3 60c violet ('96) 50.00 1.00
Never hinged 100.00
Q22 PP3 80c ol yel ('96) 50.00 1.40
Never hinged 100.00
Q23 PP3 1fr lilac brown 175.00 3.00
Never hinged 350.00
Q24 PP3 2fr yel buff ('97) 200.00 15.00
Never hinged 400.00

Counterfeits exist.

1901-02

Numerals in Black

Q25 PP3 30c orange 21.00 2.00
Never hinged 37.50
Q26 PP3 40c green 26.00 1.75
Never hinged 50.00
Q27 PP3 70c blue 50.00 1.40
Never hinged 100.00
a. Numerals omitted 750.00
b. Numerals printed on reverse 750.00
Q28 PP3 90c red 65.00 2.00
Never hinged 140.00
Nos. Q25-CQ28 (4) 162.00 7.15

Winged Wheel PP4

Without engraver's name

1902-14 *Perf. 15*

Q29 PP3 10c yel brn & slate .20 .20
Q30 PP3 15c slate & vio .20 .20
Q31 PP3 20c ultra & yel brn .20 .20
Q32 PP3 25c yel grn & red .20 .20
Q33 PP3 30c orange & bl grn .20 .20
Q34 PP3 35c bister & bl grn ('12) .35 .20
Q35 PP3 40c blue grn & vio .20 .20
Q36 PP3 50c pale rose & vio .20 .20
Q37 PP3 55c lilac brn & ultra ('14) .35 .20
Q38 PP3 60c violet & red .20 .20
Q39 PP3 70c blue & red .20 .20
Q40 PP3 80c lemon & vio brn .20 .20
Q41 PP3 90c red & yel grn .20 .20
Q42 PP4 1fr vio brn & org .20 .20
Q43 PP4 1.10fr rose & blk ('06) .20 .20
Q44 PP4 2fr ocher & bl grn .20 .20
Q45 PP4 3fr black & ultra .35 .20
Q46 PP4 4fr yel grn & red ('13) 1.25 .70
Q47 PP4 5fr org & bl grn ('13) .55 .55
Q48 PP4 10fr ol yel & brn vio ('13) .90 .55
Nos. Q29-Q48 (20) 6.55 5.20

Regular Issues of 1912-13 Handstamped in Violet

1915 *Perf. 14*

Q49 A42 5c green 160.00 160.00
Q50 A43 10c red 1,400. 1,400.
Q51 A45 10c red 200.00 200.00
a. With engraver's name 775.00 775.00
Q52 A43 20c olive grn *1,600. 1,600.*
Q53 A45 20c olive grn 225.00 225.00
a. With engraver's name 775.00 775.00
Q54 A45 25c ultra 225.00 225.00
a. With engraver's name 775.00 775.00
Q55 A43 35c bister brn 300.00 300.00
Q55A A43 40c green *2,500. 2,500.*
Q56 A45 40c green 275.00 275.00
Q57 A43 50c gray 275.00 275.00
Q58 A43 1fr orange 275.00 275.00
Q59 A43 2fr violet *1,650. 1,650.*
Q60 A44 5fr plum *3,500. 3,500.*

Excellent forgeries of this overprint exist.

PP5

PP6

1916 Litho. *Perf. 13½*

Q61 PP5 10c pale blue 1.10 .20
Q62 PP5 15c olive grn 1.40 .50
Q63 PP5 20c red 2.25 .50
Q64 PP5 25c lt brown 2.25 .50
Q65 PP5 30c lilac 1.40 .50
Q66 PP5 35c gray 1.40 .45
Q67 PP5 40c orange yel 3.00 1.50
Q68 PP5 50c bister 2.25 .45
Q69 PP5 55c brown 3.00 2.25
Q70 PP5 60c gray vio 2.25 .45
Q71 PP5 70c green 2.25 .45
Q72 PP5 80c red brown 2.25 .45
Q73 PP5 90c blue 2.25 .45
Q74 PP6 1fr gray 2.25 .45
Q75 PP6 1.10fr ultra *(Franken)* 27.50 21.00
Q76 PP6 2fr red 25.00 .45
Q77 PP6 3fr violet 25.00 .45
Q78 PP6 4fr emerald 45.00 1.50
Q79 PP6 5fr brown 45.00 3.00
Q80 PP6 10fr orange 45.00 1.50
Nos. Q61-Q80 (20) 241.80 37.00

Type of 1916 Inscribed "FRANK" instead of "FRANKEN"

1920

Q81 PP6 1.10fr ultra 2.00 .45

PP7

PP8

1920 *Perf. 14*

Q82 PP7 10c blue grn 1.75 .75
Q83 PP7 15c olive grn 1.75 1.10
Q84 PP7 20c red 1.75 .75
Q85 PP7 25c gray brn 2.50 .75
Q86 PP7 30c red vio 27.00 22.50
Q87 PP7 40c pale org 11.00 .75
Q88 PP7 50c bister 9.00 .75
Q89 PP7 55c pale brown 5.50 4.50
Q90 PP7 60c dk violet 10.00 .75
Q91 PP7 70c green 18.00 1.10
Q92 PP7 80c red brown 40.00 1.50
Q93 PP7 90c dull blue 10.00 .75
Q94 PP8 1fr gray 85.00 1.50
Q95 PP8 1.10fr ultra 26.00 2.00
Q96 PP8 1.20fr dk green 11.00 .75
Q97 PP8 1.40fr black brn 11.00 .75
Q98 PP8 2fr vermilion 110.00 1.25
Q99 PP8 3fr red vio 125.00 .85
Q100 PP8 4fr yel grn 125.00 .75
Q101 PP8 5fr bister brn 125.00 .75
Q102 PP8 10fr brown org 125.00 .75
Nos. Q82-Q102 (21) 881.25 45.30

PP9

PP10

Types PP7 and PP9 differ in the position of the wheel and the tablet above it.

Types PP8 and PP10 differ in the bars below "FR".

There are many other variations in the designs.

1920-21 Typo.

Q103 PP9 10c carmine .30 .20
Q104 PP9 15c yel grn .30 .20
Q105 PP9 20c blue grn .70 .20
Q106 PP9 25c ultra .65 .20
Q107 PP9 30c chocolate .85 .20
Q108 PP9 35c orange brn .90 .30
Q109 PP9 40c orange 1.10 .20
Q110 PP9 50c rose 1.10 .20
Q111 PP9 55c yel ('21) 4.50 3.25
Q112 PP9 60c dull rose 1.10 .20
Q113 PP9 70c emerald 3.00 .40
Q114 PP9 80c violet 2.25 .20
Q115 PP9 90c lemon 37.50 21.00
Q116 PP9 90c claret 4.50 .40
Q117 PP10 1fr buff 4.50 .35
Q118 PP10 1fr red brown 4.00 .30
Q119 PP10 1.10fr ultra 1.60 .45
Q120 PP10 1.20fr orange 6.25 .30
Q121 PP10 1.40fr yellow 10.00 1.75
Q122 PP10 1.60fr turq blue 18.00 .70
Q123 PP10 1.60fr emerald 40.00 .70
Q124 PP10 2fr pale rose 26.00 .30
Q125 PP10 3fr dp rose 24.00 .30
Q126 PP10 4fr emerald 24.00 .30
Q127 PP10 5fr lt violet 17.50 .30
Q128 PP10 10fr lemon 110.00 9.00
Q129 PP10 10fr dk brown 22.50 .30
Q130 PP10 15fr dp rose ('21) 22.50 .30
Q131 PP10 20fr dk blue ('21) 325.00 3.00
Nos. Q103-Q131 (29) 714.60 45.50

PP11

1922 Engr. *Perf. 11½*

Q132 PP11 2fr black 4.00 .20
Q133 PP11 3fr brown 37.50 .20
Q134 PP11 4fr green 9.00 .20
Q135 PP11 5r claret 9.00 .20
Q136 PP11 10fr yel brown 10.00 .20
Q137 PP11 15fr rose red 10.00 .25
Q138 PP11 20fr blue 67.50 .25
Nos. Q132-Q138 (7) 147.00 1.50

PP12

PP13

Perf. 14x13½, 13½x14

1923-40			Typo.	
Q139	PP12	5c red brn	.20	.25
Q140	PP12	10c vermilion	.20	.20
Q141	PP12	15c ultra	.20	.30
Q142	PP12	20c turq blue	.20	.20
Q143	PP12	30c brn vio ('27)	.20	.20
Q144	PP12	40c olive grn	.20	.20
Q145	PP12	50c mag ('27)	.20	.20
Q146	PP12	60c orange	.25	.20
Q147	PP12	70c dk brn ('24)	.20	.20
Q148	PP12	80c violet	.20	.20
Q149	PP12	90c sl ('27)	1.25	.20
Q150	PP13	1fr ultra	.35	.20
Q151	PP13	1fr brt blue ('28)	.55	.20
Q152	PP13	1.10fr orange	3.00	.30
Q153	PP13	1.50fr turq blue	3.25	.30
Q154	PP13	1.70fr dp brown ('31)	.75	.60
Q155	PP13	1.80fr claret	4.25	.60
Q156	PP13	2fr olive grn ('24)	.35	.20
Q157	PP13	2.10fr gray grn	7.50	.85
Q158	PP13	2.40fr dp violet	4.00	.85
Q159	PP13	2.70fr gray ('24)	12.00	.75
Q160	PP13	3fr org red	.45	.20
Q161	PP13	3.30fr brn ('24)	12.50	.75
Q162	PP13	4fr rose ('24)	.55	.20
Q163	PP13	5fr vio ('24)	.90	.20
Q163A	PP13	5fr brn vio ('40)	.45	.30
Q164	PP13	6fr bis brn ('27)	.50	.20
Q165	PP13	7fr org ('27)	.90	.20
Q166	PP13	8fr dp brown ('27)	.75	.20
Q167	PP13	9fr red vio ('27)	2.50	.20
Q168	PP13	10fr blue grn ('27)	1.10	.20
Q168A	PP13	10fr blk ('40)	4.00	3.75
Q169	PP13	20fr mag ('27)	1.90	.20
Q170	PP13	30fr turq grn ('31)	6.00	.40
Q171	PP13	40fr gray ('31)	55.00	.75
Q172	PP13	50fr bis ('27)	9.00	.30
		Nos. Q139-Q172 (36)	135.80	15.25

See Nos. Q239-Q262. For overprints see Nos. Q216-Q238. Stamps overprinted "Bagages Reisgoed" are revenues.

No. Q158 Surcharged

1924

Green Surcharge

Q173	PP13	2.30fr on 2.40fr violet	3.00	.50
		Never hinged	12.00	
a.		Inverted surcharge	57.50	

Type of Regular Issue of 1926-27 Overprinted

1928			Perf. 14	
Q174	A61	4fr buff	6.50	.90
Q175	A61	5fr bister	6.50	1.10
		Set, never hinged	40.00	

Central P.O., Brussels PP15

1929-30		Engr.	Perf. 11½	
Q176	PP15	3fr black brn	1.40	.20
Q177	PP15	4fr gray	1.40	.20
Q178	PP15	5fr carmine	1.40	.20
Q179	PP15	6fr vio brn ('30)	22.50	25.00
		Nos. Q176-Q179 (4)	26.70	25.60
		Set, never hinged	100.00	

No. Q179 Surcharged in Blue

1933

Q180	PP15	4(fr) on 6fr vio brn	25.00	.25
		Never hinged	90.00	

Modern Locomotive PP16

1934		Photo.	Perf. 13½x14	
Q181	PP16	3fr dk green	10.00	2.50
Q182	PP16	4fr red violet	3.00	.20
Q183	PP16	5fr dp rose	9.50	.20
		Nos. Q181-Q183 (3)	22.50	2.90
		Set, never hinged	120.00	

Modern Railroad Train — PP17

Old Railroad Train — PP18

1935		Engr.	Perf. 14x13½, 13½x14	
Q184	PP17	10c rose car	.30	.20
Q185	PP17	20c violet	.35	.20
Q186	PP17	30c black brn	.45	.30
Q187	PP17	40c dk blue	.55	.20
Q188	PP17	50c orange red	.55	.20
Q189	PP17	60c green	.65	.20
Q190	PP17	70c ultra	.70	.20
Q191	PP17	80c olive blk	.65	.20
Q192	PP17	90c rose lake	.85	.45
Q193	PP18	1fr brown vio	.85	.20
Q194	PP18	2fr gray blk	2.00	.20
Q195	PP18	3fr red org	2.50	.20
Q196	PP18	4fr violet brn	3.00	.20
Q197	PP18	5fr plum	3.25	.20
Q198	PP18	6fr dp green	3.50	.20
Q199	PP18	7fr dp violet	17.00	.20
Q200	PP18	8fr olive blk	17.00	.20
Q201	PP18	9fr dk blue	17.00	.20
Q202	PP18	10fr car lake	17.00	.20
Q203	PP18	20fr green	90.00	.20
Q204	PP18	30fr violet	90.00	2.00
Q205	PP18	40fr black brn	90.00	2.50
Q206	PP18	50fr rose car	100.00	2.00
Q207	PP18	100fr ultra	250.00	45.00
		Nos. Q184-Q207 (24)	708.15	55.85
		Set, never hinged	1,750.	

Centenary of Belgian State Railway.

Winged Wheel PP19

Surcharge in Red or Blue

1938		Photo.	Perf. 13½	
Q208	PP19	5fr on 3.50fr dk grn	6.50	.45
Q209	PP19	5fr on 4.50fr rose vio (Bl)	.20	.20
Q210	PP19	6fr on 5.50fr cop red (Bl)	.30	.20
a.		Half used as 3fr on piece		8.00
		Nos. Q208-Q210 (3)	7.00	.85
		Set, never hinged	50.00	

Nos. Q208-Q210 exist without surcharge. Value, set, $750.

See Nos. MQ1, Q297-Q299.

Symbolizing Unity Achieved Through Railroads PP20

1939		Engr.	Perf. 13½x14	
Q211	PP20	20c redsh brn	3.50	*3.75*
Q212	PP20	50c vio bl	3.50	*3.75*
Q213	PP20	2fr rose red	3.50	*3.75*
Q214	PP20	9fr slate grn	3.50	*3.75*
Q215	PP20	10fr dk vio	3.50	*3.75*
		Nos. Q211-Q215 (5)	17.50	*18.75*
		Set, never hinged	22.50	

Railroad Exposition and Cong. held at Brussels.

Parcel Post Stamps of 1925-27 Overprinted in Blue or Carmine

Perf. 14½x14, 14x14½

1940			Unwmk.	
Q216	PP12	10c vermilion	.20	.20
Q217	PP12	20c turq bl (C)	.20	.20
Q218	PP12	30c brn vio	.20	.20
Q219	PP12	40c ol grn (C)	.20	.20
Q220	PP12	50c magenta	.20	.20
Q221	PP12	60c orange	.20	*.25*
Q222	PP12	70c dk brn	.20	.20
Q223	PP12	80c vio (C)	.20	.20
Q224	PP12	90c slate (C)	.25	.25
Q225	PP13	1fr ultra (C)	.25	.20
Q226	PP13	2fr ol grn (C)	.25	.20
a.		Ovpt. inverted	100.00	75.00
Q227	PP13	3fr org red	.25	.20
Q228	PP13	4fr rose	.25	.20
Q229	PP13	5fr vio (C)	.25	.20
Q230	PP13	6fr bis brn	.35	.25
Q231	PP13	7fr orange	.35	.20
Q232	PP13	8fr dp brn	.35	.20
Q233	PP13	9fr red vio	.35	.20
Q234	PP13	10fr bl grn (C)	.35	.25
Q235	PP13	20fr magenta	.60	.25
Q236	PP13	30fr turq grn (C)	1.10	.75
Q237	PP13	40fr gray (C)	1.40	*2.00*
Q238	PP13	50fr bister	1.60	1.10
		Nos. Q216-Q238 (23)	9.55	8.10
		Set, never hinged	16.00	

ISSUED UNDER GERMAN OCCUPATION

German Stamps of 1906-11 Surcharged

Nos. N1-N6

Nos. N7-N9

Wmk. Lozenges (125)

1914-15			Perf. 14, 14½	
N1	A16	3c on 3pf brown	.45	.20
		On cover		5.50
N2	A16	5c on 5pf green	.40	.20
		On cover		2.75
N3	A16	10c on 10pf car	.50	.20
		On cover		2.75
N4	A16	25c on 20pf ultra	.50	.25
		On cover		2.75
		On cover, single franking		4.50
N5	A16	50c on 40pf lake & blk	2.50	1.25
		On cover		4.50
		On cover, single franking		8.50
N6	A16	75c on 60pf mag	.90	*1.25*
		On cover		8.50
		On cover, single franking		22.50
N7	A16	1fr on 80pf lake & blk, *rose*	2.50	1.75
		On cover		12.00
		On cover, single franking		27.50
N8	A17	1fr25c on 1m car	20.00	12.50
		On cover		42.50
		On cover, single franking		85.00
N9	A21	2fr50c on 2m gray bl	18.00	15.00
		On cover		125.00
		Nos. N1-N9 (9)	45.75	32.60
		Set, never hinged	160.00	

German Stamps of 1906-18 Surcharged

Nos. N10-N21

No. N22

Nos. N23-N25

1916-18				
N10	A22	2c on 2pf drab	.25	.25
		On cover		8.50
N11	A16	3c on 3pf brn	.35	.25
		On cover		3.00
N12	A16	5c on 5pf grn	.35	.25
		On cover		2.00
		On cover, single franking		3.00
N13	A22	8c on 7½pf org	.65	.35
		On cover		4.50
N14	A16	10c on 10pf car	.25	.25
		On cover		2.50
N15	A22	15c on 15pf yel brn	.65	.25
		On cover		3.00
N16	A22	15c on 15pf dk vio	.65	.45
		On cover		3.00
N17	A16	20c on 25pf org & blk, *yel*	.35	.35
		On cover		8.50
		On cover, single franking		27.50
N18	A16	25c on 20pf ultra	.35	.25
		On cover		5.50
		On cover, single franking		5.00
a.		25c on 20pf blue	.40	.25
		On cover		8.50
		On cover, single franking		17.50
N19	A16	40c on 30pf org & blk, *buff*	.40	.30
		On cover		5.50
		On cover, single franking		7.00
N20	A16	50c on 40pf lake & blk	.35	.30
		On cover		6.00
		On cover, single franking		9.00
N21	A16	75c on 60pf mag	1.00	*12.50*
		On cover		175.00
N22	A16	1fr on 80pf lake & blk, *rose*	2.00	*2.50*
		On cover		70.00
		On cover, single franking		115.00
N23	A17	1fr25c on 1m car	2.00	2.00
		On cover		85.00
		On cover, single franking		150.00
N24	A21	2fr50c on 2m gray bl	27.50	25.00
a.		2fr50c on 1m car (error)		*3,500.*
N25	A20	6fr25c on 5m sl & car	40.00	37.50
		On overfranked cover		450.00
		Nos. N10-N25 (16)	77.10	82.75
		Set, never hinged	145.00	

A similar series of stamps without "Belgien" was used in parts of Belgium and France while occupied by German forces. See France Nos. N15-N26.

BENIN

bə-'nin

LOCATION — West Coast of Africa
GOVT. — French Possession
AREA — 8,627 sq. mi.
POP. — 493,000 (approx.)
CAPITAL — Benin

In 1895 the French possessions known as Benin were incorporated into the colony of Dahomey.

100 Centimes = 1 Franc

Handstamped on Stamps of French Colonies

1892 Unwmk. *Perf. 14x13½*

Black Overprint

1 A9 1c blk, *bluish* 160.00 125.00
On cover 350.00
2 A9 2c brn, *buff* 140.00 115.00
On cover 350.00
3 A9 4c claret, *lav* 55.00 45.00
Never hinged 115.00
On cover 200.00
4 A9 5c grn, *grnsh* 21.00 15.00
Never hinged 42.50
On cover 100.00
On cover, single franking 350.00
a. Pair, one without overprint 325.00 350.00
5 A9 10c blk, *lavender* 70.00 55.00
On cover 130.00
On cover, single franking 350.00
6 A9 15c blue 27.50 12.50
Never hinged 60.00
On cover 100.00
On cover, single franking 350.00
a. Pair, one without overprint 325.00
7 A9 20c red, *grn* 200.00 175.00
On cover 525.00
8 A9 25c blk, *rose* 95.00 55.00
On cover 225.00
On cover, single franking 375.00
9 A9 30c brn, *yelsh* 160.00 140.00
On cover *450.00*
10 A9 35c blk, *orange* 160.00 140.00
On cover *550.00*
11 A9 40c red, *straw* 140.00 115.00
On cover *400.00*
12 A9 75c car, *rose* 350.00 300.00
On cover *650.00*
13 A9 1fr brnz grn, *straw* 375.00 325.00
On cover *700.00*

Red Overprint

14 A9 15c blue 90.00 60.00
On cover *150.00*

Blue Overprint

15 A9 5c grn, *grnsh* 2,100. 900.00
On cover *1,500.*
15A A9 15c blue 2,100. 900.00
On cover *1,500.*

The overprints of Nos. 1-15A are of four types, three without accent mark on "E." They exist diagonal.

Counterfeits exist of Nos. 1-19.

Inverted Overprint

2a	A9	2c brn, *buff*	160.00	160.00
4b	A9	5c grn, *grnsh*	95.00	70.00
5b	A9	10c blk, *lavender*	140.00	125.00
8b	A9	25c blk, *rose*	200.00	175.00
9b	A9	30c brn, *yelsh*	325.00	290.00
10b	A9	35c blk, *orange*	350.00	300.00
11b	A9	40c red, *straw*	300.00	240.00
12b	A9	75c car, *rose*	650.00	525.00
13b	A9	1fr brnz grn, *straw*	650.00	525.00
15b	A9	5c grn, *grnsh*	2,350.	1,100.
15Ac	A9	15c grn, *grnsh*	2,350.	1,100.

Red Overprint

14b	A9	15c blue	*110.00*	*95.00*

Double Overprint

4c	A9	5c grn, *grnsh*	125.00	95.00
5c	A9	10c blk, *lavender*	160.00	140.00
8c	A9	25c blk, *rose*	200.00	175.00
10c	A9	35c blk, *orange*	400.00	350.00
11c	A9	40c red, *straw*	350.00	325.00

Red Overprint

14c	A9	15c blue	*120.00*	*110.00*

Additional Surcharge in Red or Black

1892

16 A9 01c on 5c grn, *grnsh* 290.00 200.00
On cover *500.00*
a. Double surcharge 700.00 700.00
17 A9 40c on 15c blue 175.00 90.00
On cover 250.00
a. Double surcharge *3,000.*
18 A9 75c on 15c blue 775.00 475.00
On cover 1,100.
19 A9 75c on 15c bl (Bk) 2,800. 2,250.
On cover 5,250.

Counterfeits exist.

Navigation and Commerce
A3 A4

1893 Typo. *Perf. 14x13½*

Name of Colony in Blue or Carmine

20 A3 1c blk, *bluish* 3.50 2.25
Never hinged 5.75
On cover 110.00
21 A3 2c brn, *buff* 4.50 3.00
Never hinged 7.75
On cover 110.00
22 A3 4c claret, *lav* 4.25 3.00
Never hinged 7.00
On cover 11.00
23 A3 5c grn, *grnsh* 6.00 4.50
Never hinged 10.50
On cover 75.00
24 A3 10c blk, *lavender* 6.50 4.50
Never hinged 11.25
On cover 75.00
a. Name of country omitted *5,500.*
25 A3 15c blue, quadrille paper 30.00 21.00
Never hinged 60.00
On cover 70.00
26 A3 20c red, *grn* 17.00 12.00
Never hinged 32.50
On cover 100.00
On cover, single franking 150.00
27 A3 25c blk, *rose* 40.00 25.00
Never hinged 77.50
On cover 110.00
On cover, single franking 175.00
28 A3 30c brn, *bis* 19.00 14.00
Never hinged 39.00
On cover 140.00
On cover, single franking 200.00
29 A3 40c red, *straw* 4.25 4.25
Never hinged 7.00
On cover 100.00
On cover, single franking 200.00
30 A3 50c car, *rose* 4.50 4.25
Never hinged 8.50
On cover 140.00
On cover, single franking 225.00
31 A3 75c vio, *org* 9.50 7.75
Never hinged 16.00
On cover 225.00
On cover, single franking 375.00
32 A3 1fr brnz grn, *straw* 52.50 52.50
Never hinged 105.00
On cover 325.00
On cover, single franking *500.00*
Nos. 20-32 (13) 201.50 158.00

Perf. 13½x14 stamps are counterfeits.

1894 *Perf. 14x13½*

33 A4 1c blk, *bluish* 2.00 2.25
34 A4 2c brn, *buff* 2.75 2.25
Never hinged 2.75
On cover 75.00
35 A4 4c claret, *lav* 3.25 2.50
Never hinged 4.50
On cover 75.00
36 A4 5c grn, *grnsh* 4.25 2.75
Never hinged 5.25
On cover 75.00
37 A4 10c blk, *lavender* 4.50 4.00
Never hinged 7.75
On cover 35.00
38 A4 15c bl, quadrille paper 9.25 4.00
Never hinged 17.50
On cover 35.00
39 A4 20c red, *grn* 8.75 4.00
Never hinged 15.00
On cover 60.00
40 A4 25c blk, *rose* 10.50 5.00
Never hinged 18.50
On cover 60.00
On cover, single franking 100.00
41 A4 30c brn, *bis* 7.00 7.00
Never hinged 12.50
On cover 60.00
On cover, single franking 80.00
42 A4 40c red, *straw* 18.00 11.50
Never hinged 35.00
On cover 60.00
On cover, single franking 90.00
43 A4 50c car, *rose* 22.50 8.00
Never hinged 42.50
On cover 200.00
On cover, single franking 300.00
44 A4 75c vio, *org* 18.00 10.50
Never hinged 35.00
On cover 250.00
On cover, single franking 425.00
45 A4 1fr brnz grn, *straw* 5.00 4.25
Never hinged 8.50
On cover 300.00
On cover, single franking 400.00
Nos. 33-45 (13) 115.75 68.00

Perf. 13½x14 stamps are counterfeits.

POSTAGE DUE STAMPS

French Colony

Handstamped in Black on Postage Due Stamps of French Colonies

BENIN

1894 Unwmk. *Imperf.*

J1 D1 5c black 140.00 55.00
On cover 140.00
J2 D1 10c black 140.00 55.00
On cover 140.00
J3 D1 20c black 140.00 55.00
On cover 140.00
J4 D1 30c black 140.00 55.00
On cover 140.00
Nos. J1-J4 (4) 560.00 220.00

Nos. J1-J4 exist with overprint in various positions.

BERMUDA

ˌbər-'myü-də

LOCATION — A group of about 150 small islands of which only 20 are inhabited, lying in the Atlantic Ocean about 580 miles southeast of Cape Hatteras.
GOVT. — British Crown Colony
AREA — 20.5 sq. mi.
POP. — 54,893 (1980)
CAPITAL — Hamilton

4 Farthings = 1 Penny
12 Pence = 1 Shilling
20 Shillings = 1 Pound

Catalogue values for unused stamps in this country are for Never Hinged items, beginning with Scott 131.

PRE-STAMP POSTAL MARKINGS

Crowned Circle handstamp type I is pictured in the Crowned Circle Handstamps and Great Britain Used Abroad section.

1845

A1 I "Hamilton" crowned circle handstamp in red, on cover *4,250.*
A2 I "St. Georges" crowned circle handstamp in red, on cover *7,750.*
A3 I "Ireland Isle" crowned circle handstamp in red, on cover *7,750.*

Earliest known uses: #A1, 11/13/46. #A2, 8/1/45. #A3, 8/1/45.

See Nos. X4-X5 for use as adhesives.

POSTMASTER STAMPS

PM1

1848-56 Unwmk. *Imperf.*

X1 PM1 1p blk, *bluish* (1848) *125,000.*
On cover *160,000.*
a. Dated 1849 *135,000.*
X2 PM1 1p red, *bluish* (1856) *175,000.*
a. Dated 1854 *250,000.*
X3 PM1 1p red (1853) *160,000.*

PM2

1860

X4 PM2 (1p) red, *yellowish* *100,000.*

Same inscribed "HAMILTON"

1861

X5 PM2 (1p) red, *bluish* *130,000.*
X6 PM2 (1p) red *38,500.*

Nos. X1-X3 were produced and used by Postmaster William B. Perot of Hamilton. No. X4 is attributed to Postmaster James H. Thies of St. George's.

Only a few of each stamp exist. Values reflect actual sales figures for stamps in the condition in which they are found.

Values for unused stamps are for examples with original gum as defined in the catalogue introduction. Very fine examples of Nos. 1-1a, 2-15b will have perforations touching the design (or framelines where applicable) on at least one side due to the narrow spacing of the stamps on the plates. Stamps with perfs clear of the design on all four sides are scarce and will command higher prices.

Queen Victoria
A1 A2

A3

A4

A5

1865-74 Typo. Wmk. 1 *Perf. 14*

1 A1 1p rose red 110.00 1.75
a. 1p dull rose 140.00 8.00
b. Imperf. *30,000.* *17,000.*
2 A2 2p blue ('66) 450.00 30.00
a. 2p bright blue 450.00 19.00
3 A3 3p buff ('73) 600.00 80.00
On cover 400.00
a. 3p orange 2,050. 175.00
On cover 550.00
4 A4 6p brown lilac 1,100. 90.00
5 A4 6p lilac ('74) 30.00 17.00
On cover 600.00
6 A5 1sh green 450.00 67.50
On cover 600.00
Nos. 1-6 (6) 2,740. 286.25

See Nos. 7-9, 19-21, 23, 25. For surcharges see Nos. 10-15.

1882-1903 *Perf. 14x12½*

7 A3 3p buff 210.00 75.00
8 A4 6p violet ('03) 17.00 *27.50*
9 A5 1sh green ('94) 20.00 *150.00*
On cover 325.00
a. Vert. strip of 3, perf. all around & imperf. btwn. *13,750.*
Nos. 7-9 (3) 247.00 *252.50*

Handstamped Diagonally

1874 **Perf. 14**

10 A5 3p on 1sh green 1,700. 950.

Handstamped Diagonally

11 A1 3p on 1p rose 19,000. 20,000.
12 A5 3p on 1sh green 2,850. 975.00
a. "P" with top like "R" 2,300. 1,100.
On cover 5,500.

No. 11 is stated to be an essay, but a few copies are known used. Nos. 10-12 are found with double or partly double surcharges.

Surcharged in Black

1875

13 A2 1p on 2p blue 875.00 475.00
On cover 3,250.
a. Without period 16,000. 9,750.
b. Round "O" in "One" 1,650. 600.
14 A3 1p on 3p buff 550.00 425.00
a. Round "O" in "One" 800.00 500.00
15 A5 1p on 1sh green 625.00 310.00
On cover 1,750.
a. Inverted surcharge — 26,500.
b. Without period 18,500. 12,500.
c. Round "O" in "One" — 450.00

A6

A7

1880 **Wmk. 1**

16 A6 ½p brown 3.75 5.25
17 A7 4p orange 21.00 2.10
On cover 225.00

See Nos. 18, 24.

A8

A9

1883-1904 **Wmk. 2**

18 A6 ½p deep gray grn ('93) 3.50 1.00
a. ½p green ('92) 4.50 3.75
19 A1 1p aniline car ('89) 11.00 .30
a. 1p dull rose 200.00 5.25
b. 1p rose red 100.00 4.00
c. 1p carmine rose ('86) 75.00 .90
20 A2 2p blue ('86) 67.50 5.00
21 A2 2p brn pur ('98) 4.25 1.90
a. 2p aniline pur ('93) 17.50 4.50
22 A8 2½p ultra ('84) 6.75 .50
a. 2½p deep ultra 17.50 3.50
23 A3 3p gray ('86) 27.50 8.00
24 A7 4p brown org ('04) 37.50 62.50
25 A5 1sh ol bis ('93) 15.00 20.00
a. 1sh yellow brown 20.00 21.00
Nos. 18-25 (8) 173.00 99.20

Black Surcharge

1901

26 A9 1f on 1sh gray 3.00 1.25
Overprinted "SPECIMEN" 85.00
a. 1f on 1sh bluish gray 3.25 1.00
b. As "a," "F" in "FARTHING" doubled 6,750. 8,000.

The second "F" is inserted by hand.

Dry Dock — A10

1902-03

28 A10 ½p gray grn & blk ('03) 15.00 3.00
29 A10 1p car rose & brown 10.00 .20
30 A10 3p ol grn & violet 3.75 2.50
Nos. 28-30 (3) 28.75 5.70
Set, overprinted "SPECIMEN" 160.00

1906-10 **Wmk. 3**

31 A10 ¼p pur & brn ('08) 2.10 1.90
32 A10 ½p gray grn & blk 24.00 .80
33 A10 ½p green ('09) 17.50 3.50
34 A10 1p car rose & brn 32.50 .25
35 A10 1p carmine ('08) 12.50 .20
36 A10 2p orange & gray 9.25 13.50
37 A10 2½p blue & brown 20.00 8.75
38 A10 2½p ultra ('10) 15.00 8.00
39 A10 4p vio brn & blue ('09) 3.75 20.00
Nos. 31-39 (9) 136.60 56.90

Caravel A11

King George V A12

1910-24 **Engr.** **Perf. 14**

40 A11 ¼p brown ('12) 2.10 3.00
a. ¼p pale brown .70 1.75
41 A11 ½p yel green 1.90 .30
a. ½p dark green ('18) 9.25 1.50
42 A11 1p red (I) 19.00 .35
a. 1p carmine (I) ('19) 67.50 10.00
b. 1p rose red (I) ('16) 24.00 .35
43 A11 2p gray ('13) 3.75 12.50
44 A11 2½p ultra (I) ('12) 4.25 .75
45 A11 3p violet, *yel* ('13) 2.50 7.50
46 A11 4p red, *yellow* ('19) 7.50 15.00
47 A11 6p claret ('24) 12.50 9.00
a. 6p purple ('12) 18.00 23.00
48 A11 1sh blk, *green* ('12) 5.25 5.00
a. 1sh black, *olive* ('25) 6.00 19.00
Nos. 40-48, optd "SPECIMEN" 450.00

Typographed

Chalky Paper

49 A12 2sh ultra & dl vio, *bl* ('20) 22.50 62.50
50 A12 2sh6p red & blk, *bl* 35.00 100.00
51 A12 4sh car & black ('20) 75.00 200.00
52 A12 5sh red & grn, *yellow* 75.00 150.00
a. 5sh dp green & dp red, *yellow* 75.00 150.00
53 A12 10sh red & grn, *green* 225.00 425.00
a. 10sh red & green, *pale bluish green* ('22) 275.00 450.00
54 A12 £1 black & vio, *red* 400.00 700.00
Nos. 40-54 (16) 1,341. 1,690.
Nos. 49-54, optd "SPECIMEN" 900.00

Types I of 1p and 2½p are illustrated above Nos. 81-97.

The 1p was printed from two plates, the 2nd of which, #42a, exists only in carmine on opaque paper with a bluish tinge. Compare #MR1 (as #42) and MR2 (as #42a).

Revenue cancellations are found on Nos. 52-54.

See Nos. 81-97.

Seal of the Colony and King George V A13

1920-21 **Wmk. 3** **Ordinary Paper**

55 A13 ¼p brown 4.00 24.00
56 A13 ½p green 4.25 12.50
57 A13 2p gray 16.00 52.50

Chalky Paper

58 A13 3p vio & dl vio, *yel* 15.00 50.00
59 A13 4p red & blk, *yellow* 15.00 42.50
60 A13 1sh blk, *gray grn* 20.00 60.00

Ordinary Paper

Wmk. 4

67 A13 1p rose red 4.50 .35
68 A13 2½p ultra 18.00 16.00

Chalky Paper

69 A13 6p red vio & dl vio 32.50 92.50
Nos. 55-60,67-69 (9) 129.25 350.35

Issued: 6p, 1/19/21; others, 11/11/20.

King George V A14

1921, May 12 **Engr.**

71 A14 ¼p brown 1.90 4.50
72 A14 ½p green 3.50 7.50
73 A14 1p carmine 3.00 .45

Wmk. 3

74 A14 2p gray 7.50 35.00
75 A14 2½p ultra 11.00 3.75
76 A14 3p vio, *orange* 6.90 20.00
77 A14 4p scarlet, *org* 20.00 26.00
78 A14 6p claret 15.00 62.50
79 A14 1sh blk, *green* 29.00 62.50
Nos. 71-79 (9) 97.80 222.20

Tercentenary of "Local Representative Institutions" (Nos. 55-79).

Types of 1910-20 Issue

Types of 1p:

I II III

Types of 2½p:

I II

Three types of the 1d value: type I, figure "1" has pointed serifs, scroll at top left very weak; type II, thick "1" with square serifs, scroll weak; type III, thinner "1" with long square serifs, scroll complete with strong line. Two types of the 2½d value: type I, small "d," short, thick figures of value; type II, larger "d," taller, thinner figures of value.

1922-34 **Wmk. 4**

81 A11 ¼p brown ('28) 1.90 3.75
82 A11 ½p green 1.90 .20
83 A11 1p car, III ('28) 15.00 .35
a. 1p carmine, II ('26) 50.00 7.50
b. 1p carmine, I 21.00 .75
84 A11 1½p red brown ('34) 11.00 .45
85 A11 2p gray ('23) 1.90 1.90
86 A11 2½p ap grn ('23) 2.75 1.90
87 A11 2½p ultra, II ('32) 2.10 .90
a. 2½p ultra, I ('26) 3.00 .60
88 A11 3p ultra ('24) 20.00 32.50
89 A11 3p vio, *yellow* ('26) 5.00 1.25
90 A11 4p red, *yellow* ('24) 2.50 1.25
91 A11 6p claret ('24) 1.25 1.00
92 A11 1sh blk, *emer* ('27) 6.00 11.00
93 A11 1sh brn blk, *yel grn* ('34) 42.50 62.50

Chalky Paper

94 A12 2sh ultra & vio, *bl* ('27) 55.00 87.50
a. 2sh bl & dp vio, *dp bl* ('31) 67.50 100.00
95 A12 2sh 6p red & blk, *bl* ('27) 75.00 125.00
a. 2sh6p pale org ver & blk, *gray bl* ('30) 2,750. 2,250.
b. 2sh6p dp ver & blk, *deep blue* ('31) 100.00 150.00
96 A12 10sh red & grn, *emer* ('24) 160.00 300.00
a. 10sh dp red & pale grn, *dp emer* ('31) 175.00 350.00
97 A12 12sh 6p ocher & gray blk ('32) 300.00 425.00
On cover 3,000.
Nos. 81-97 (17) 703.80 1,056.

Revenue cancellations are found on Nos. 94-97.
For the 12sh6p with "Revenue" on both sides, see #AR1.

Common Design Types pictured following the introduction.

Silver Jubilee Issue
Common Design Type

1935, May 6 *Perf. 11x12*

100	CD301	1p car & dk bl	.40	.75
101	CD301	1½p blk & ultra	.60	*2.75*
102	CD301	2½p ultra & brn	1.00	1.50
103	CD301	1sh brn vio & ind	10.50	*20.00*
		Nos. 100-103 (4)	12.50	*25.00*
		Set, never hinged	17.50	

Hamilton Harbor — A15

Yacht "Lucie" — A17

South Shore — A16

Grape Bay — A18

Typical Cottage — A19

Scene at Par-la-Ville — A20

1936-40 *Perf. 12*

105	A15	½p blue green	.20	.20
106	A16	1p car & black	.55	.35
107	A16	1½p choc & black	1.25	.60
108	A17	2p lt bl & blk	6.00	2.00
109	A17	2p brn blk & turq bl ('38)	55.00	16.00
109A	A17	2p red & ultra ('40)	1.25	1.25
110	A18	2½p dk bl & lt bl	1.25	.30
111	A19	3p car & black	3.25	1.75
112	A20	6p vio & rose lake	1.00	.20
113	A18	1sh deep green	4.00	*11.50*
114	A15	1sh6p brown	.60	.25
		Nos. 105-114 (11)	74.35	34.40
		Set, never hinged	100.00	

No. 108, blue border and black center.
No. 109, black border, blue center.

Coronation Issue
Common Design Type

1937, May 14 *Perf. 13½x14*

115	CD302	1p carmine	.25	*.50*
116	CD302	1½p brown	.35	*1.00*
117	CD302	2½p bright ultra	.65	*1.00*
		Nos. 115-117 (3)	1.25	2.50
		Set, never hinged	1.75	

Hamilton Harbor — A21

Grape Bay — A22

St. David's Lighthouse A23

King George VI A25

Bermudian Water Scene and Yellow-billed Tropic Bird — A24

1938-51 **Wmk. 4** *Perf. 12*

118	A21	1p red & blk ('40)	.45	.40
a.		1p rose red & black	12.00	1.00
119	A21	1½p vio brn & blue	3.50	1.00
a.		1½p dl vio brn & bl ('43)	3.00	.20
120	A22	2½p blue & lt bl	6.50	.75
120A	A22	2½p ol brn & lt bl ('41)	1.90	.95
b.		2½p dk ol blk & pale blue ('43)	2.00	1.00
121	A23	3p car & blk	12.00	1.75
121A	A23	3p dp ultra & blk ('42)	1.00	.20
c.		3p brt ultra & blk ('41)	1.00	.20
121D	A24	7½p yel grn, bl & blk ('41)	3.75	1.50
122	A22	1sh green	1.25	.40

Typo.
Perf. 13

123	A25	2sh ultra & red vio, *bl* ('50)	10.00	9.00
a.		2sh ultra & vio, *bl,* perf. 14	7.00	2.50
b.		2sh ultra & dl vio, *bl* (mottled paper), perf. 14 ('42)	7.00	2.50
124	A25	2sh 6p red & blk, *bl*	11.00	6.50
a.		Perf. 14	20.00	6.50
125	A25	5sh red & grn, *yel*	12.50	11.50
a.		Perf. 14	45.00	15.00
126	A25	10sh red & grn, *grn* ('51)	30.00	*24.00*
a.		10sh brn lake & grn, *grn,* perf. 14	100.00	75.00
b.		10sh red & grn, *grn,* perf. 14 ('39)	175.00	150.00
127	A25	12sh 6p org & gray blk	65.00	55.00
a.		12sh 6p org & gray, perf. 14	85.00	45.00
b.		12sh 6p yel & gray, perf. 14 ('47)	550.00	450.00
c.		12sh 6p brn org & gray, perf. 14	200.00	80.00

Wmk. 3

128	A25	£1 blk & vio, *red* ('51)	40.00	*47.50*
a.		£1 blk & pur, *red,* perf. 14	225.00	100.00
b.		£1 blk & dk vio, *salmon,* perf. 14 ('42)	65.00	50.00
		Nos. 118-128 (14)	198.85	160.45
		Set, never hinged	325.00	

No. 127b is the so-called "lemon yellow" shade.
Revenue cancellations are found on Nos. 123-128. Copies with removed revenue cancellations and forged postmarks are abundant.

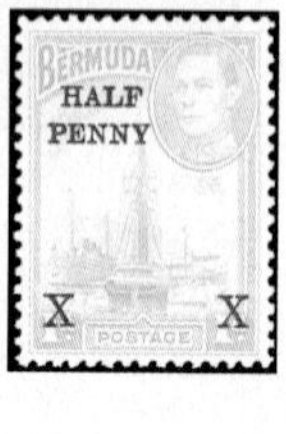

No. 118a Surcharged in Black

1940, Dec. 20 **Wmk. 4** *Perf. 12*

129	A21	½p on 1p rose red & blk	.30	1.25
		Never hinged	.50	

Catalogue values for unused stamps in this section, from this point to the end of the section, are for Never Hinged items.

Peace Issue
Common Design Type
Perf. 13½x14

1946, Nov. 6 **Engr.** **Wmk. 4**

131	CD303	1½p brown	.20	.20
132	CD303	3p deep blue	.30	.30

Silver Wedding Issue
Common Design Types

1948, Dec. 1 **Photo.** *Perf. 14x14½*

133	CD304	1½p red brown	.20	.20

Engr.; Name Typo.
Perf. 11½x11

134	CD305	£1 rose carmine	47.50	47.50

Postmaster Stamp of 1848 — A26

1949, Apr. 11 **Engr.** *Perf. 13x13½*

135	A26	2½p dk brown & dp bl	.20	.25
136	A26	3p dp blue & black	.25	.20
137	A26	6p green & rose vio	.45	.45
		Nos. 135-137 (3)	.90	.90

No. 137 shows a different floral arrangement.
Bermuda's first postage stamp, cent.

UPU Issue
Common Design Types
Engr.; Name Typo.

1949, Oct. 10 *Perf. 13½, 11x11½*

138	CD306	2½p slate	.50	*1.00*
139	CD307	3p indigo	1.25	1.00
140	CD308	6p rose violet	1.00	.80
141	CD309	1sh blue green	2.00	2.00
		Nos. 138-141 (4)	4.75	4.80

POSTAL-FISCAL STAMP

"Revenue Revenue" PF1

1936 **Typo.** **Wmk. 4** *Perf. 14*
Chalky Paper

AR1	PF1	2sh6p org & grayish blk	1,250.	*1,750.*
		Revenue cancel		75.00
		On cover		3,250.

#AR1 was authorized for postal use from Feb. 1 through May, 1937 and during Nov. and Dec. 1937. Used values are for examples with dated postal cancels indicating usage during the authorized periods. Beware of bogus and improperly dated favor cancels
Six covers are known properly used during those time periods.

WAR TAX STAMPS

No. 42 Overprinted

1918 **Wmk. 3** *Perf. 14*

MR1	A11	1p rose red	.90	*1.50*

No. 42a Overprinted

1920

MR2	A11	1p carmine	2.00	*2.50*

BOLIVIA

bə-'li-vē-ə

LOCATION — Central South America, separated from the Pacific Ocean by Chile and Peru.
GOVT. — Republic
AREA — 424,165 sq. mi.
POP. — 6,252,250 (est. 1984)
CAPITAL — Sucre (La Paz is the actual seat of government).

100 Centavos = 1 Boliviano

PRE-STAMP POSTAL MARKINGS

BRITISH CONSULAR OFFICES IN BOLIVIA

Crowned Circle handstamp type V is pictured in the Crowned Circle Handstamps and Great Britain Used Abroad section.

Cobija

1862, Mar. 29

A1	V	Crowned circle handstamp, in red, on cover	5,000.

STAMPS OF GREAT BRITAIN USED IN BOLIVIA

Numeral cancellation type A is pictured in the Crowned Circle Hanstamps and Great Britain Used Abroad section.

1865-78

C39 (Cobija)

A2	A	1p rose red (#33, P93, 95)	—
A3	A	2p blue (#30, P14)	—
A4	A	3p rose (#49, P6)	—
A5	A	3p rose (#61, P16, 19)	—
A6	A	4p pale ol grn (#70, P15)	550.00
A7	A	6p red violet (#51, P9)	525.00
A8	A	6p pale buff (#59b, P11)	—
A9	A	6p gray (#62, P13-16) (from)	400.00
A10	A	1sh green (#54, P4-5)	400.00
A11	A	1sh pale green (#64, P10-13)	400.00
A12	A	2sh blue (#55)	400.00
A13	A	5sh rose (#57, P2)	850.00

On Feb. 21, 1863, the Bolivian Government decreed contracts for carrying the mails should be let to the highest bidder, the service to commence on the day the bid was accepted, and stamps used for the payment of postage. On Mar. 18, the contract was awarded to Sr. Justiniano Garcia and was in effect until Apr. 29, 1863, when it was rescinded. Stamps in the form illustrated above were prepared in denominations of ½, 1, 2 and 4 reales. All values exist in black and in blue. The blue are twice as scarce as the black. Value, black, $75 each.

It is said that used copies exist on covers, but the authenticity of these covers remains to be established.

Condor — A1

A2

A3

72 varieties of each of the 5c, 78 varieties of the 10c, 30 varieties of each of the 50c and 100c.

The plate of the 5c stamps was entirely reengraved 4 times and retouched at least 6 times. Various states of the plate have distinguishing characteristics, each of which is typical of most, though not all the stamps in a sheet. These characteristics (usually termed types) are found in the shading lines at the right side of the globe. a, vertical and diagonal lines. b, diagonal lines only. c, diagonal and horizontal with traces of vertical lines. d, diagonal and horizontal lines. e, horizontal lines only. f, no lines except the curved ones forming the outlines of the globe.

1867-68 Unwmk. Engr. *Imperf.*

1	A1	5c yel grn, thin paper (a, b)	5.50	*10.00*
		Pair, on cover		3,250.
a.		5c blue green (a)	5.50	*14.00*
b.		5c deep green (a)	5.50	*14.00*
c.		5c ol grn, thick paper (a)	35.00	25.00
d.		5c yel grn, thick paper (a)	90.00	90.00
e.		5c yel grn, thick paper (b)	90.00	90.00
f.		5c blue green (b)	5.50	*14.00*
2	A1	5c green (d)	5.00	*10.00*
a.		5c green (c)	5.00	*10.00*
b.		5c green (e)	5.00	*10.00*
c.		5c green (f)	5.00	*10.00*
3	A1	5c vio ('68)	225.00	150.00
a.		5c rose lilac ('68)	175.00	140.00
		Revenue cancel		35.00
4	A3	10c brown	225.00	140.00
		On cover		10,000.
		Revenue cancel		55.00
5	A2	50c orange	27.50	
		Revenue cancel		14.00
6	A2	50c blue ('68)	*400.00*	
a.		50c dark blue ('68)	*400.00*	
		Revenue cancel		100.00
7	A3	100c blue	45.00	
		Revenue cancel		15.00
8	A3	100c green ('68)	175.00	
a.		100c pale blue grn ('68)	175.00	
		Revenue cancel		75.00

Used values are for postally canceled copies. Pen cancellations usually indicate that the stamps have been used fiscally and such stamps sell for about one-fifth as much as those with postal cancellations.

The 500c is an essay.

Reprints of Nos. 3,4, 6 and 8 are common. Value, $10 each. Reprints of Nos. 2 and 5 are scarcer. Value, $25 each.

Coat of Arms
A4 A5

1868-69 *Perf. 12*

Nine Stars

10	A4	5c green	22.50	12.50
11	A4	10c vermilion	40.00	15.00
12	A4	50c blue	45.00	25.00
13	A4	100c orange	55.00	27.50
14	A4	500c black	750.00	750.00

Eleven Stars

15	A5	5c green	15.00	7.50
16	A5	10c vermilion	25.00	12.50
a.		Half used as 5c on cover		400.00
17	A5	50c blue	40.00	22.50
18	A5	100c dp orange	42.50	22.50
19	A5	500c black	*2,250.*	*2,250.*

See Nos. 26-27, 31-34.

Arms and "The Law" — A6

1878 Various Frames *Perf. 12*

20	A6	5c ultra	10.00	2.00
21	A6	10c orange	10.00	2.00
a.		Half used as 5c on cover		50.00
22	A6	20c green	20.00	4.00
a.		Half used as 10c on cover		160.00
23	A6	50c dull carmine	110.00	20.00
		Nos. 20-23 (4)	150.00	28.00

A7 (11 Stars) A8 (9 Stars)

Numerals Upright

1887 *Rouletted*

24	A7	1c rose	2.25	1.80
25	A7	2c violet	2.25	1.90
26	A5	5c blue	7.25	3.00
27	A5	10c orange	7.25	5.00
		Nos. 24-27 (4)	19.00	11.70

See No. 37.

1890 *Perf. 12*

28	A8	1c rose	2.00	.80
29	A8	2c violet	3.00	2.00
30	A4	5c blue	4.50	.80
31	A4	10c orange	10.00	.95
32	A4	20c dk green	15.00	1.60
33	A4	50c red	6.25	1.60
34	A4	100c yellow	12.50	3.25
		Nos. 28-34 (7)	53.25	11.00

See Nos. 35-36, 38-39.

1893 Litho. *Perf. 11*

35	A8	1c rose	5.00	2.50
a.		Imperf. pair	100.00	
b.		Horiz. pair, imperf. vert.	20.00	
c.		Horiz. pair, imperf. btwn.	35.00	
36	A8	2c violet	5.00	2.50
a.		Block of 4 imperf. vert. and horiz. through center	50.00	
b.		Horiz. pair, imperf. btwn.	27.50	
c.		Vert. pair, imperf betwn.	27.50	
37	A7	5c blue	5.00	2.00
a.		Vert. pair, imperf. horiz.	27.50	
b.		Horiz. pair, imperf. btwn.	35.00	
38	A8	10c orange	17.00	6.00
a.		Horiz. pair, imperf. btwn.	50.00	
39	A8	20c dark green	75.00	30.00
a.		Imperf. pair, vert. or horiz.	250.00	
b.		Pair, imperf. btwn., vert. or horiz.	140.00	
		Nos. 35-39 (5)	107.00	43.00

Coat of Arms — A9

1894 Unwmk. Engr. *Perf. 14, 14½*

Thin Paper

40	A9	1c bister	1.50	1.25
41	A9	2c red orange	2.50	2.25
42	A9	5c green	1.50	1.25
43	A9	10c yellow brn	1.50	1.25
44	A9	20c dark blue	6.00	4.00
45	A9	50c claret	12.50	8.00
46	A9	100c brown rose	30.00	20.00
		Nos. 40-46 (7)	55.50	38.00

Stamps of type A9 on thick paper were surreptitiously printed in Paris on the order of an official and without government authorization. Some of these stamps were substituted for part of a shipment of stamps on thin paper, which had been printed in London on government order.

When the thick paper stamps reached Bolivia they were at first repudiated but afterwards were allowed to do postal duty. A large quantity of the thick paper stamps were fraudulently canceled in Paris with a cancellation of heavy bars forming an oval.

To be legitimate, copies of the thick paper stamps must have genuine cancellations of Bolivia. Value, on cover, each $125.

The 10c blue on thick paper is not known to have been issued.

Some copies of Nos. 40-46 show part of a papermakers' watermark "1011."

For overprints see Nos. 55-59.

President Tomas Frias — A10

President Jose M. Linares — A11

Pedro Domingo Murillo A12

Bernardo Monteagudo A13

Gen. Jose Ballivian — A14

Gen. Antonio Jose de Sucre — A15

Simon Bolivar — A16

Coat of Arms — A17

1897 Litho. *Perf. 12*

47	A10	1c pale yellow grn	1.50	1.00
a.		Vert. pair, imperf. horiz.	75.00	
b.		Vert. pair, imperf. btwn.	75.00	
48	A11	2c red	2.25	1.75
49	A12	5c dk green	1.50	.60
a.		Horiz. pair, imperf. btwn.	75.00	
50	A13	10c brown vio	1.75	1.00
a.		Vert. pair, imperf. btwn.	75.00	
51	A14	20c lake & blk	3.00	1.50
a.		Imperf., pair		150.00
52	A15	50c orange	4.75	2.50
53	A16	1b Prus blue	6.00	3.00
54	A17	2b red, yel, grn & blk	37.50	*50.00*
		Nos. 47-54 (8)	58.25	*61.35*

Excellent forgeries of No. 54, perf and imperf, exist, some postally used.

Reprint of No. 53 has dot in numeral. Same value.

Nos. 40-44 Handstamped in Violet or Blue

1899 *Perf. 14½*

55	A9	1c yellow bis	20.00	20.00
56	A9	2c red orange	35.00	30.00
57	A9	5c green	10.50	10.50
58	A9	10c yellow brn	13.00	10.50
59	A9	20c dark blue	45.00	35.00
		Nos. 55-59 (5)	123.50	106.00

The handstamp is found inverted, double, etc. Values twice the listed amounts. Forgeries of this handstamp are plentiful. "E.F." stands for Estado Federal.

The 50c and 100c (Nos. 45-46) were overprinted at a later date in Brazil.

Antonio José de Sucre — A18

Perf. 11½, 12

1899 Engr. Thin Paper

62	A18	1c gray blue	2.00	1.25
63	A18	2c brnsh red	2.00	1.25
64	A18	5c dk green	3.00	1.25
65	A18	10c yellow org	2.50	1.25
66	A18	20c rose pink	3.00	1.50
67	A18	50c bister brn	7.50	2.50
68	A18	1b gray violet	7.50	2.50
		Nos. 62-68 (7)	27.50	11.50

1901

69	A18	5c dark red	1.90	.60

Col. Adolfo Ballivian A19

Eliodoro Camacho A20

President Narciso Campero A21

Jose Ballivian A22

Gen. Andres Santa Cruz — A23

Coat of Arms — A24

1901-02 Engr.

70	A19	lc claret	.55	.20
71	A20	2c green	.55	.20
73	A21	5c scarlet	.55	.20
74	A22	10c blue	1.40	.20
75	A23	20c violet & blk	.80	.20
76	A24	2b brown	3.75	2.75
		Nos. 70-71,73-76 (6)	7.60	3.75

#73-74 exist imperf. Value, pairs, each $50.

For surcharges see #95-96, 193.

1904 Litho.

77	A19	1c claret	2.25	.55

In No. 70 the panel above "CENTAVO" is shaded with continuous lines. In No. 77 the shading is of dots.

See Nos. 103-105, 107, 110.

Coat of Arms of Dept. of La Paz — A25

Murillo — A26

Jose Miguel Lanza — A27

Ismael Montes — A28

1909 **Litho.** ***Perf. 11***

78	A25	5c blue & blk	10.50	7.75
79	A26	10c green & blk	10.50	7.75
80	A27	20c orange & blk	10.50	7.75
81	A28	2b red & black	10.50	7.75
		Nos. 78-81 (4)	42.00	31.00

Centenary of Revolution of July, 1809.
Nos. 78-81 exist imperf. and tête bêche.
Nos. 79-81 exist with center inverted.

Miguel Betanzos A29

Col. Ignacio Warnes A30

Murillo A31

Monteagudo A32

Esteban Arce — A33

Antonio Jose de Sucre — A34

Simon Bolivar — A35

Manuel Belgrano — A36

1909 **Dated 1809-1825** ***Perf. 11½***

82	A29	1c lt brown & blk	.55	.20
83	A30	2c green & blk	.55	.40
84	A31	5c red & blk	.55	.30
85	A32	10c dull bl & blk	.55	.25
86	A33	20c violet & blk	.65	.40
87	A34	50c olive bister & blk	1.00	.50
88	A35	1b gray brn & blk	1.00	.90
89	A36	2b chocolate & blk	1.60	1.00
		Nos. 82-89 (8)	6.45	3.95

War of Independence, 1809-1825.
Exist imperf. Value $200.
For surcharge see #97.

Warnes A37

Betanzos A38

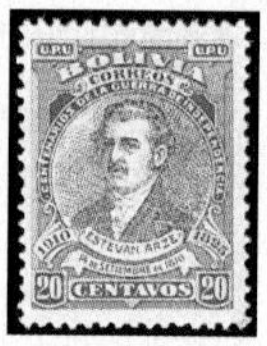

Arce — A39

Dated 1910-1825

1910 ***Perf. 13x13½***

92	A37	5c green & black	.40	.20
a.		Imperf., pair	5.00	
93	A38	10c claret & indigo	.40	.20
a.		Imperf., pair	10.00	
94	A39	20c dull blue & indigo	.70	.40
a.		Imperf., pair	5.00	
		Nos. 92-94 (3)	1.50	.80

War of Independence.
Nos. 92-94 may be found with parts of a papermaker's watermark: "A I & Co/EXTRA STRONG/9303."
Both perf and imperf exist with inverted centers.

Nos. 71 and 75 Surcharged in Black

1911 ***Perf. 11½, 12***

95	A20	5c on 2c green	.45	.20
a.		Inverted surcharge	7.50	7.50
b.		Double surcharge	7.50	
c.		Period after "1911"	3.00	1.00
d.		Blue surcharge	75.00	60.00
e.		Double dsurch., one invtd.	7.50	
96	A23	5c on 20c vio & blk	16.00	15.00
a.		Inverted surcharge	30.00	30.00
b.		Double surch., one invtd.	60.00	

No. 83 Handstamp Surcharged in Green

97	A30	20c on 2c grn & blk	*1,100.*	

This provisional was issued by local authorities at Villa Bella, a town on the Brazilian border. The 20c surcharge was applied after the stamp had been affixed to the cover. Excellent forgeries of No. 96-97 exist.

"Justice"
A40 A41

1912

Black or Dark Blue Overprint On Revenue Stamps

98	A40	2c green (Bk)	.35	.20
a.		Inverted overprint	7.50	
99	A41	10c ver (Bl)	1.10	.50
a.		Inverted overprint	7.50	

A42

A43

Red or Black Overprint

Engr.

100	A42	5c orange (R)	.45	.35
a.		Inverted overprint	7.50	
b.		Pair, one without overprint	7.50	
c.		Black overprint	40.00	

Red or Black Surcharge

101	A43	10c on 1c bl (R)	.55	.30
a.		Inverted surcharge	7.50	
b.		Double surcharge	7.50	
c.		Dbl. surcharge, one invtd.	7.50	
d.		Black surcharge	100.00	100.00
e.		As "d," inverted	125.00	
f.		As "d," double surcharge	110.00	
g.		Pair, one without black surch.	400.00	

Fakes of No. 101d are plentiful.

Revenue Stamp Surcharged

Type 1 —Serifed "1"s in date

Type 2 — Sans-serif "1"s in date

1917 **Litho.**

102	10c on 1c blue, Type 1	*1,750.*	*1,750.*
a.	10c on 1c, Type 2	—	—

Design similar to type A43.
1,000 copies of Nos. 102 and 102a were reportedly produced, with 90 percent of the issue being type 1 and the balance type 2.
Excellent forgeries exist.

Types of 1901 and

Frias — A45

Sucre — A46

Bolivar — A47

1913 **Engr.** ***Perf. 12***

103	A19	1c car rose	.25	.20
104	A20	2c vermilion	.25	.20
105	A21	5c green	.30	.20
106	A45	8c yellow	.85	.30
107	A22	10c gray	.50	.20
108	A46	50c dull violet	1.25	.35
109	A47	1b slate blue	2.25	.95
110	A24	2b black	5.50	3.25
		Nos. 103-110 (8)	11.15	5.65

No. 107, litho., was not regularly issued.

Nine values commemorating the Guiqui-La Paz railroad were printed in 1915 but never issued. Typographed forgeries exist.

Monolith of Tiahuanacu A48

Mt. Potosí A49

Lake Titicaca — A50

Mt. Illimani — A51

Legislature Building — A53

FIVE CENTAVOS.
Type I — Numerals have background of vertical lines. Clouds formed of dots.
Type II — Numerals on white background. Clouds near the mountain formed of wavy lines.

1916-17 **Litho.** ***Perf. 11½***

111	A48	½c brown	.20	.20
a.		Horiz. pair, imperf. vert.	15.00	
112	A49	1c gray green	.20	.20
a.		Imperf., pair	7.50	
113	A50	2c car & blk	.25	.20
a.		Imperf., pair	2.00	
b.		Vert. pair, imperf. horiz.		
c.		Center inverted	14.00	14.00
d.		Imperf., center inverted	17.50	
114	A51	5c dk blue (I)	.50	.20
a.		Imperf., pair	7.50	
b.		Vert. pair, imperf. horiz.	7.50	
c.		Horiz. pair, imperf. vert.	7.50	
115	A51	5c dk blue (II)	.50	.20
a.		Imperf., pair	7.50	
116	A53	10c org & bl	1.00	.20
a.		Imperf., pair	7.50	
b.		No period after "Legislativo"	1.00	.20
c.		Center inverted	47.50	47.50
d.		Vertical pair, imperf. between	5.00	
		Nos. 111-116 (6)	2.65	1.20

For surcharges see Nos. 194-196.

Coat of Arms
A54 A55

Printed by the American Bank Note Co.

1919-20 **Engr.** ***Perf. 12***

118	A54	1c carmine	.25	.20
119	A54	2c dk violet	4.75	3.00
120	A54	5c dk green	.50	.20
121	A54	10c vermilion	.50	.20
122	A54	20c dk blue	1.50	.30
123	A54	22c lt blue	.90	.75
124	A54	24c purple	.60	.50
125	A54	50c orange	4.75	.60
126	A55	1b red brown	6.00	1.75
127	A55	2b black brn	9.00	4.50
		Nos. 118-127 (10)	28.75	12.00

Printed by Perkins, Bacon & Co., Ltd.

1923-27 **Re-engraved** ***Perf. 13½***

128	A54	1c carmine ('27)	.20	.20
129	A54	2c dk violet	.30	.20
130	A54	5c dp green	.80	.20
131	A54	10c vermilion	14.00	10.00
132	A54	20c slate blue	1.75	.20
135	A54	50c orange	2.75	.60
136	A55	1b red brown	.70	.30
137	A55	2b black brown	.50	.30
		Nos. 128-137 (8)	21.00	12.00

There are many differences in the designs of the two issues but they are too minute to be illustrated or described.
Nos. 128-137 exist imperf.
See #144-146, 173-177. For surcharges see #138-143, 160, 162, 181-186, 236-237.

Stamps of 1919-20 Surcharged in Blue, Black or Red

1924 ***Perf. 12***

138	A54	5c on 1c car (Bl)	.40	.20
a.		Inverted surcharge	6.00	6.00
b.		Double surcharge	6.00	6.00
139	A54	15c on 10c ver (Bk)	.70	.50
a.		Inverted surcharge	6.00	6.00

140 A54 15c on 22c lt bl (Bk) .70 .30
a. Inverted surcharge 6.00 6.00
b. Double surcharge, one inverted *6.00 6.00*

No. 140 surcharged in red or blue probably are trial impressions. They appear jointly, and with black in blocks.

Same Surcharge on No. 131
Perf. 13½

142 A54 15c on 10c ver (Bk) .70 .25
a. Inverted surcharge 6.00 6.00

No. 121 Surcharged

Perf. 12

143 A54 15c on 10c ver (Bk) .90 .30
a. Inverted surcharge 6.00 6.00
b. Double surcharge 6.00 6.00
Noc. 138-143 (5) 3.40 1.55

Type of 1919-20 Issue
Printed by Waterlow & Sons
Second Re-engraving

1925 Unwmk. ***Perf. 12½***
144 A54 5c deep green .80 .20
145 A54 15c ultra .80 .20
146 A54 20c dark blue .65 .20
Nos. 144-146 (3) 2.25 .60

These stamps may be identified by the perforation.

Miner — A56

Condor Looking Toward the Sea A57

Designs: 2c, Sower. 5c, Torch of Eternal Freedom. 10c, National flower (kantuta). 15c, Pres. Bautista Saavedra. 50c, Liberty head. 1b, Archer on horse. 2b, Mercury. 5b, Gen. A. J. de Sucre.

1925 Engr. ***Perf. 14***
150 A56 1c dark green .90
151 A56 2c rose .90
152 A56 5c red, *grn* .65 .35
153 A56 10c car, *yel* .90 .75
154 A56 15c red brown .65 .25
155 A57 25c ultra 1.50 .50
156 A56 50c dp violet 1.50 .50
157 A56 1b red 3.00 1.25
158 A57 2b orange 3.50 1.75
159 A56 5b black brn 3.50 2.00
Nos. 150-159 (10) 17.00 7.35

Cent. of the Republic. The 1c and 2c were not released for general use.
Nos. 150-159 exist imperf. Value, $60 each pair.
For surcharges see Nos. C59-C62.

Stamps of 1919-27 Surcharged in Blue, Black or Red

1927
160 A54 5c on 1c car (Bl) 4.25 2.75
a. Inverted surcharge 22.50 22.50
b. Black surcharge 45.00 45.00

Perf. 12

162 A54 10c on 24c pur (Bk) 4.25 2.75
a. Inverted surcharge 60.00 60.00
b. Red surcharge 70.00 70.00

Coat of Arms — A66

Printed by Waterlow & Sons

1927 Litho. ***Perf. 13½***
165 A66 2c yellow .40 .20
166 A66 3c pink .50 .50
167 A66 4c red brown .40 .40
168 A66 20c lt ol grn .65 .20
169 A66 25c deep blue .65 .30
170 A66 30c violet .80 .80
171 A66 40c orange 1.50 1.25
172 A66 50c dp brown 1.50 .50
173 A55 1b red 1.75 1.25
174 A55 2b plum 2.50 2.50
175 A55 3b olive grn 2.90 2.50
176 A55 4b claret 4.00 3.50
177 A55 5b bister brn 4.75 4.00
Nos. 165-177 (13) 22.30 17.90

For overprints and surcharges see Nos. 178-180, 208, 211-212.

Type of 1927 Issue Overprinted

1927
178 A66 5c dark green .20 .20
179 A66 10c slate .45 .20
180 A66 15c carmine .65 .25
Nos. 178-180 (3) 1.30 .65

Exist with inverted overprint. Value $20 each.

Stamps of 1919-27 Surcharged

1928 ***Perf. 12, 12½, 13½***
Red Surcharge
181 A54 15c on 20c #122 9.00 9.00
182 A54 15c on 20c #132 9.00 9.00
a. Black surcharge 30.00
183 A54 15c on 20c #146 160.00 160.00

Black Surcharge
184 A54 15c on 24c #124 1.75 .90
a. Inverted surcharge 6.00 6.00
b. Blue surcharge 50.00
185 A54 15c on 50c #125 35.00 30.00
186 A54 15c on 50c #135 1.25 .65
Nos. 181-186 (6) 216.00 209.55

No. 183 exists with inverted surcharge.

Condor — A67

Hernando Siles — A68

Map of Bolivia — A69

Printed by Perkins, Bacon & Co., Ltd.

1928 Engr. ***Perf. 13½***
189 A67 5c green 1.50 .20
190 A68 10c slate .30 .20
191 A69 15c carmine lake .60 .20
Nos. 189-191 (3) 2.40 .60

Nos. 104, 111, 113, Surcharged in Various Colors

1930 ***Perf. 12, 11½***
193 A20 1c on 2c (Bl) 1.10 .90
a. "0.10" for "0.01" 20.00
194 A50 3c on 2c (Br) 1.10 .90
195 A48 25c on ½c (Bk) 1.40 .90
196 A50 25c on 2c (V) 1.40 .90
Nos. 193-196 (4) 5.00 3.60

The lines of the surcharges were spaced to fit the various shapes of the stamps. The surcharges exist inverted, double, etc.
Trial printings were made of the surcharges on #193 and 194 in black and on #196 in brown.

Mt. Potosi — A70

Mt. Illimani — A71

Eduardo Abaroa — A72

Map of Bolivia — A73

Sucre — A74

Bolivar — A75

1931 Engr. ***Perf. 14***
197 A70 2c green 1.40 .50
198 A71 5c light blue 1.40 .20
199 A72 10c red orange 1.40 .20
200 A73 15c violet 2.75 .20
201 A73 35c carmine 2.10 .85
202 A73 45c orange 2.10 .85
203 A74 50c gray 1.25 .55
204 A75 1b brown 1.75 .55
Nos. 197-204 (8) 14.15 3.90

No. 198 exists imperf.
See #207, 241. For surcharges see #209-210.

Symbols of 1930 Revolution — A76

1931 Litho. ***Perf. 11***
205 A76 15c scarlet 2.25 .40
a. Pair, imperf. between 15.00
206 A76 50c brt violet 1.10 .70
a. Pair, imperf. between 20.00

Revolution of June 25, 1930.
For surcharges see Nos. 239-240.

Map Type of 1931
Without Imprint

1932 Litho.
207 A73 15c violet 2.00 .35

Stamps of 1927-31 Surcharged

1933 ***Perf. 13½, 14***
208 A66 5c on 1b red .70 .35
a. Without period after "Cts" 1.40 1.40
209 A73 15c on 35c car .35 .35
a. Inverted surcharge 20.00
210 A73 15c on 45c orange .65 .30
a. Inverted surcharge 3.00 3.00
211 A66 15c on 50c dp brn 1.60 .30
212 A66 25c on 40c orange .35 .35
Nos. 208-212 (5) 3.65 1.65

The hyphens in "13-7-33" occur in three positions.

Coat of Arms — A77

1933 Engr. ***Perf. 12***
213 A77 2c blue green .30 .20
214 A77 5c blue .30 .20
215 A77 10c red .50 .30
216 A77 15c deep violet .35 .20
217 A77 25c dark blue .70 .55
Nos. 213-217 (5) 2.15 1.45

For surcharges see Nos. 233-235, 238.

Mariano Baptista — A78

Map of Bolivia — A79

1935
218 A78 15c dull violet .50 .35

1935
219 A79 2c dark blue .30 .20
220 A79 3c yellow .30 .20
221 A79 5c vermilion .30 .20
222 A79 5c blue grn .35 .20
223 A79 10c black brn .35 .20
224 A79 15c deep rose .35 .20
225 A79 15c ultra .35 .20
226 A79 20c yellow grn .40 .20
227 A79 25c lt blue .40 .20
228 A79 30c deep rose .80 .55
229 A79 40c orange .80 .55
230 A79 50c gray violet .80 .25
231 A79 1b yellow .80 .35
232 A79 2b olive brown .80 .70
Nos. 219-232 (14) 7.10 4.20

Regular Stamps of 1925-33 Surcharged in Black

1937 ***Perf. 11, 12, 13½***
233 A77 5c on 2c bl grn .25 .25
234 A77 15c on 25c dk bl .30 .30
235 A77 30c on 25c dk bl .50 .50
236 A55 45c on 1b red brn .60 .60
237 A55 1b on 2b plum .75 .75
a. "1" missing 7.50 7.50
238 A77 2b on 25c dk bl .75 .75

"Comunicaciones" on one line
239 A76 3b on 50c brt vio 1.25 1.25
a. "3" of value missing 7.00 7.00
240 A76 5b on 50c brt vio 1.25 1.25
Nos. 233-240 (8) 5.65 5.65

Exist inverted, double, etc.

President Siles — A80

1937 Unwmk. *Perf. 14*

241 A80 1c yellow brown	.30	.30

Native School — A81

Oil Wells — A82

Modern Factories A83

Torch of Knowledge A84

Map of the Sucre-Camiri R. R. — A85

Allegory of Free Education — A86

Allegorical Figure of Learning — A87

Symbols of Industry — A88

Modern Agriculture — A89

1938 Litho. *Perf. 10½, 11*

242 A81 2c dull red	.60	.45
243 A82 10c pink	.70	.30
244 A83 15c yellow grn	1.00	.30
245 A84 30c yellow	1.25	.35
246 A85 45c rose red	2.40	.85
247 A86 60c dk violet	1.90	.45
248 A87 75c dull blue	2.40	.35
249 A88 1b lt brown	3.50	.35
250 A89 2b bister	3.25	.80
Nos. 242-250 (9)	17.00	4.20

For surcharge see No. 314.

Llamas — A90

Vicuna — A91

Coat of Arms — A92

Cocoi Herons — A93

Chinchilla — A94

Toco Toucan — A95

Condor — A96

Jaguar — A97

1939, Jan. 21 *Perf. 10½, 11½x10½*

251 A90 2c green	.45	.30
252 A90 4c fawn	.45	.30
253 A90 5c red violet	.45	.30
254 A91 10c black	.65	.30
255 A91 15c emerald	.65	.35
256 A91 20c dk slate grn	.65	.30
257 A92 25c lemon	.70	.30
258 A92 30c dark blue	.65	.30
259 A93 40c vermilion	1.40	.30
260 A93 45c gray	1.40	.30
261 A94 60c rose red	1.40	.55
262 A94 75c slate blue	3.00	.55
263 A95 90c orange	2.25	.55
264 A95 1b blue	2.25	.55
265 A96 2b rose lake	3.00	.55
266 A96 3b dark violet	4.00	.85
267 A97 4b brown org	4.25	1.25
268 A97 5b gray brown	5.50	1.40
Nos. 251-268 (18)	33.10	9.30

All but 20c exist imperf.

Imperf. counterfeits with altered designs exist of some values.

For surcharges see Nos. 315-317.

Flags of 21 American Republics — A98

1940, Apr. Litho. *Perf. 10½*

269 A98 9b multicolored	2.25	1.10

Pan American Union, 50th anniversary.

AIR POST STAMPS

Aviation School AP1 AP2

1924, Dec. Unwmk. Engr. *Perf. 14*

C1 AP1 10c ver & blk	.25	.30
a. Inverted center	1,750.	
C2 AP1 15c carmine & blk	1.50	.50
C3 AP1 25c dk bl & blk	.60	.60
C4 AP1 50c orange & blk	1.50	1.25
C5 AP2 1b red brn & blk	.90	.95
C6 AP2 2b blk brn & blk	1.75	1.75
C7 AP2 5b dk vio & blk	5.50	5.50
Nos. C1-C7 (7)	12.00	10.85

Natl. Aviation School establishment.

These stamps were available for ordinary postage. Nos. C1, C3, C5 and C6 exist imperforate. Proofs of the 2b with inverted center exist imperforate and privately perforated.

For overprints and surcharges see Nos. C11-C23, C56-C58.

Emblem of Lloyd Aéreo Boliviano AP3

1928 Litho. *Perf. 11*

C8 AP3 15c green	2.10	1.40
a. Imperf., pair	50.00	
C9 AP3 20c dark blue	3.50	2.90
C10 AP3 35c red brown	2.90	2.10
Nos. C8-C10 (3)	8.50	6.40

No. C8 exists imperf. between.

For surcharges see #C24-C26, C53-C55.

Graf Zeppelin Issues

Nos. C1-C5 Surcharged or Overprinted in Various Colors:

Nos. C11, C19

Nos. C12-C18, C20-C23

1930, May 6 *Perf. 14*

C11 AP1 5c on 10c ver & blk (G)	9.50	9.50
C12 AP1 10c ver & blk (Bl)	9.50	9.50
C13 AP1 10c ver & blk (Br)	650.00	*925.00*
C14 AP1 15c car & blk (V)	9.50	9.50
C15 AP1 25c dk bl & blk (R)	9.50	9.50
C16 AP1 50c org & blk (Br)	9.50	9.50
C17 AP1 50c org & blk (R)	475.00	*600.00*
C18 AP2 1b red brn & blk (gold)	160.00	160.00

Experts consider the 50c with gold or silver overprint and 5c with black to be trial color proofs.

Nos. C11-C18 exist with the surcharges inverted, double, or double with one inverted, but the regularity of these varieties is questioned.

See notes following No. C23.

Surcharged or Overprinted in Bronze Inks of Various Colors

C19 AP1 5c on 10c ver & blk (G)	85.00	*85.00*
C20 AP1 10c ver & blk (Bl)	70.00	*70.00*
C21 AP1 15c car & blk (V)	85.00	*85.00*
C22 AP1 25c dk bl & blk (cop)	85.00	*85.00*
C23 AP2 1b red brn & blk (gold)	210.00	*210.00*
Nos. C19-C23 (5)	535.00	*535.00*

Flight of the airship Graf Zeppelin from Europe to Brazil and return via Lakehurst, NJ.

Nos. C19 to C23 were intended for use on postal matter forwarded by the Graf Zeppelin.

No. C18 was overprinted with light gold or gilt bronze ink. No. C23 was overprinted with deep gold bronze ink. Nos. C13 and C17 were overprinted with trial colors but were sold with the regular printings. The 5c on 10c is known surcharged in black and in blue.

No. C8-C10 Surcharged

1930, May 6 *Perf. 11*

C24 AP3 1.50b on 15c	70.00	70.00
a. Inverted surcharge	100.00	100.00
b. Comma instead of period after "1"	80.00	80.00
C25 AP3 3b on 20c	70.00	70.00
a. Inverted surcharge	100.00	100.00
b. Comma instead of period after "3"	80.00	80.00
C26 AP3 '6b on 35c	110.00	*110.00*
a. Inverted surcharge	125.00	125.00
b. Comma instead of period after "6"	110.00	110.00
Nos. C24-C26 (3)	250.00	250.00

Airplane and Bullock Cart — AP6

Airplane and River Boat — AP7

1930, July 24 Litho. *Perf. 14*

C27 AP6 5c dp violet	1.25	1.00
C28 AP7 15c red	1.25	1.00
C29 AP7 20c yellow	1.00	.90
C30 AP6 35c yellow grn	.80	.65
C31 AP7 50c deep blue	1.50	1.50
C32 AP6 1b lt brown	2.25	2.25
C33 AP7 2b deep rose	3.00	3.00
C34 AP6 3b slate	4.50	4.25
Nos. C27-C34 (8)	15.55	14.55

Nos. C27 to C34 exist imperforate.

For surcharge see No. C52.

Air Service Emblem AP8

1932, Sept. 16 *Perf. 11*

C35 AP8 5c ultra	2.75	2.00
C36 AP8 10c gray	1.75	1.40
C37 AP8 15c dark rose	1.75	1.40
C38 AP8 25c orange	1.75	1.40
C39 AP8 30c green	1.10	.70
C40 AP8 50c violet	2.75	2.00
C41 AP8 1b dk brown	2.75	2.00
Nos. C35-C41 (7)	14.60	10.90

Map of Bolivia — AP9

1935, Feb. 1 Engr. *Perf. 12*

C42 AP9 5c brown red	.20	.20
C43 AP9 10c dk green	.20	.20
C44 AP9 20c dk violet	.20	.20
C45 AP9 30c ultra	.25	.20
C46 AP9 50c orange	.30	.20
C47 AP9 1b bister brn	.30	.30
C48 AP9 1½b yellow	.70	.20
C49 AP9 2b carmine	.70	.30
C50 AP9 5b green	1.25	.40
C51 AP9 10b dk brown	2.50	.85
Nos. C42-C51 (10)	6.60	3.05

Nos. C1, C4, C10, C30 Surcharged in Red (#C52-C56) or Green (#C57-C58)

c

1937, Oct. 6 ***Perf. 11, 14***

C52 AP6 5c on 35c yel grn	.40	.30
a. "Carreo"	12.50	
b. Inverted surcharge		
C53 AP3 20c on 35c red brn	.50	.40
a. Inverted surcharge		
C54 AP3 50c on 35c red brn	.65	1.25
a. Inverted surcharge	17.50	
C55 AP3 1b on 35c red brn	1.25	.65
a. Inverted surcharge		
C56 AP1 2b on 50c org & blk	2.00	1.00
a. Inverted surcharge		
C57 AP1 12b on 10c ver & blk	6.50	4.75
a. Inverted surcharge	22.50	
C58 AP1 15b on 10c ver & blk	6.50	2.75
a. Inverted surcharge		

Regular Postage Stamps of 1925 Surcharged in Green or Red — d

Perf. 14

C59 A56 (d) 3b on 50c dp vio (G)	1.75	1.00
C60 A56 (d) 4b on 1b red (G)	2.25	1.40
C61 A57 (c) 5b on 2b org (G)	3.00	1.60
a. Double surcharge	90.00	
C62 A56 (d) 10b on 5b blk brn	5.00	3.25
a. Double surcharge	35.00	
Nos. C52-C62 (11)	29.80	18.35

No. C59-C62 exist with inverted surcharge, No. C62a with black and black and red surcharges.

Courtyard of Potosi Mint — AP10

Miner — AP11

Emancipated Woman AP12

Pincers, Torch and Good Will Principles AP15

Airplane over Field AP13

Airplanes and Liberty Monument AP14

Airplane over River AP16

Emblem of New Government AP17

Transport Planes over Map of Bolivia AP18

1938, May **Litho.** ***Perf. 10½***

C63 AP10 20c deep rose	.25	.25
C64 AP11 30c gray	.25	.25
C65 AP12 40c yellow	.25	.25
C66 AP13 50c yellow grn	.50	.25
C67 AP14 60c dull blue	.50	.25
C68 AP15 1b dull red	.75	.25
C69 AP16 2b bister	1.25	.25
C70 AP17 3b lt brown	1.25	.25
C71 AP18 5b dk violet	1.90	.25
Nos. C63-C71 (9)	6.90	2.25

40c, 1b, 2b exist imperf.

Chalice — AP19

Virgin of Copacabana AP20

Jesus Christ — AP21

Church of San Francisco, La Paz AP22

St. Anthony of Padua — AP23

1939, July 19 **Litho.** ***Perf. 13½, 10½***

C72 AP19 5c dull violet	.50	.25
a. Pair, imperf. between	40.00	
C73 AP20 30c lt bl grn	.70	.20
C74 AP21 45c violet bl	.70	.20
a. Vertical pair, imperf. between	45.00	
C75 AP22 60c carmine	.70	.35
C76 AP23 75c vermilion	.70	.60
C77 AP23 90c deep blue	.70	.25
C78 AP22 2b dull brown	1.10	.25
C79 AP21 4b deep plum	1.75	.40
C80 AP20 5b lt blue	4.25	.70
C81 AP19 10b yellow	5.50	1.10
Nos. C72-C81 (10)	16.60	4.30

2nd National Eucharistic Congress.
For surcharge see No. C112.

POSTAGE DUE STAMPS

D1

1931 **Unwmk.** **Engr.** ***Perf. 14, 14½***

J1 D1 5c ultra	1.25	*1.75*
J2 D1 10c red	1.40	*2.00*
J3 D1 15c yellow	2.00	*2.75*
J4 D1 30c deep green	2.00	*2.75*
J5 D1 40c deep violet	3.25	*4.25*
J6 D1 50c black brown	4.50	*5.75*
Nos. J1-J6 (6)	14.40	*19.25*

Symbol of Youth D2

Torch of Knowledge D3

Symbol of the Revolution of May 17, 1936 — D4

1938 **Litho.** ***Perf. 11***

J7 D2 5c deep rose	.50	.50
a. Pair, imperf. between		
J8 D3 10c green	.50	.50
J9 D4 30c gray blue	.50	.50
Nos. J7-J9 (3)	1.50	1.50

POSTAL TAX STAMPS

Worker — PT1

Imprint: "LITO. UNIDAS LA PAZ."

Perf. 13½x10½, 10½, 13½

1939 **Litho.** **Unwmk.**

RA1 PT1 5c dull violet	.80	.20
a. Double impression		

Redrawn

Imprint: "TALL. OFFSET LA PAZ."

1940 ***Perf. 12x11, 11***

RA2 PT1 5c violet	.65	.20
a. Horizontal pair, imperf. between	2.00	
b. Imperf. horiz., pair		

Tax of Nos. RA1-RA2 was for the Workers' Home Building Fund.

BOSNIA AND HERZEGOVINA

'bäz-nē-ə and ˌhert-sə-gō-'vē-nə

LOCATION — Dalmatia and Serbia

GOVT. — Provinces of Turkey under Austro-Hungarian occupation, 1879-1908; provinces of Austria-Hungary 1908-1918

AREA — 19,768 sq. mi.

POP. — 2,000,000 (approx. 1918)

CAPITAL — Sarajevo

Following World War I Bosnia and Herzegovina united with the kingdoms of Montenegro and Serbia, and Croatia, Dalmatia and Slovenia, to form the Kingdom of Yugoslavia (See Yugoslavia.)

100 Novcica (Neukreuzer) = 1 Florin (Gulden)

100 Heller = 1 Krone (1900)

Watermark

Wmk. 91 — BRIEF-MARKEN or (from 1890) ZEITUNGS-MARKEN in Double-lined Capitals, Across the Sheet

Coat of Arms — A1

Type I — The heraldic eaglets on the right side of the escutcheon are entirely blank. The eye of the lion is indicated by a very small dot, which sometimes fails to print.

Type II — There is a colored line across the lowest eaglet. A similar line sometimes appears on the middle eaglet. The eye of the lion is formed by a large dot which touches the outline of the head above it.

Type III — The eaglets and eye of the lion are similar to type I. Each tail feather of the large eagle has two lines of shading and the lowest feather does not touch the curved line below it. In types I and II there are several shading lines in these feathers, and the lowest feather touches the curved line.

Varieties of the Numerals

2 NOVCICA:
A — The "2" has curved tail. All are type I.
B — The "2" has straight tail. All are type II.

15 NOVCICA:
C — The serif of the "1" is short and forms a wide angle with the vertical stroke.
D — The serif of the "1" forms an acute angle with the vertical stroke.

The numerals of the 5n were retouched several times and show minor differences, especially in the flag.

Other Varieties

½ NOVCICA:
There is a black dot between the curved ends of the ornaments near the lower spandrels.
G — This dot touches the curve at its right. Stamps of this (1st) printing are litho.
H — This dot stands clear of the curved lines. Stamps of this (2nd) printing are typo.

10 NOVCICA:
Ten stamps in each sheet of type II show a small cross in the upper section of the right side of the escutcheon.

Perf. 9 to 13½ and Compound

1879-94 **Litho.** **Wmk. 91**

Type I

1 A1 ½n blk (type II) ('94)	22.00	*42.50*
Never hinged	34.00	
On wrapper or address label from printed matter		550.00
2 A1 1n gray	14.00	2.10
Never hinged	21.00	
On wrapper or address label from printed matter		275.00
c. 1n gray lilac		2.00
4 A1 2n yellow	21.00	1.40
Never hinged	30.00	
On postcard		19.00
On printed matter		210.00
5 A1 3n green	22.50	2.75
Never hinged	34.00	
Single franking on local cover		400.00
6 A1 5n rose red	40.00	.45
Never hinged	55.00	
On cover		16.00
7 A1 10n blue	140.00	1.00
Never hinged	210.00	
On cover		125.00

8 A1 15n brown (C) 135.00 8.50
Never hinged 200.00
On cover 375.00
a. 15n Brown (C) 300.00 42.50
Never hinged 500.00
On cover 1,100.
9 A1 20n gray green ('93) 575.00 11.50
Never hinged 950.00
On cover 1,600.
10 A1 25n violet 115.00 10.00
Never hinged 160.00
On cover *4,250.*
On other postal document 650.00
Nos. 1-10 (9) 1,084. 80.20

No. 2c was never issued. It is usually canceled by blue pencil marks and "mint" copies generally have been cleaned.

> *A fine cover sent from Sarajevo to Belgrade bearing a pair of 25n (Scott No. 10) sold for the equivalent of $10,425 at a Geneva auction in 2004.*

10½ to 13 and Compound

1894-98 **Typo.**

Type II

1a A1 ½n black 15.00 *21.00*
Never hinged 22.50
On wrapper or address label from printed matter 575.00
2a A1 1n gray 5.25 1.40
Never hinged 7.50
On wrapper or address label from printed matter 250.00
4a A1 2n yellow 3.00 .50
Never hinged 4.50
On postcard 7.25
5a A1 3n green 5.25 1.50
Never hinged 7.50
Single franking on local cover 300.00
6a A1 5n rose red 5.25 .75
Never hinged 7.50
On cover 7.25
7a A1 10n blue 6.00 1.10
Never hinged 10.50
On cover 87.50
b. Pair, imperf btw, perf 10½ all around *10,000.*
8b A1 15n brown 6.00 4.00
Never hinged 9.00
On cover 175.00
9a A1 20n gray green 6.75 5.00
Never hinged 9.75
On cover 1,450.
10a A1 25n violet 7.50 7.50
Never hinged 11.50
On cover —
On other postal document 275.00
Nos. 1a-10a (9) 60.00 42.75

Type III

6b A1 5n rose red ('98) 4.75 .45
Never hinged 7.25
c. Perf 10½ 13.00 1.50
Never hinged 19.00
d. Perf 11½ 72.50 2.50
Never hinged 110.00

All the preceding stamps exist in various shades.

Nos. 1a to 10a were reprinted in 1911 in lighter colors, on very white paper and perf. 12½. Value, set $25.

> *A very fine used pair imperforate between of the 10n blue (Scott No. 7b) sold for the equivalent of U.S. $10,425 at a Geneva auction in 2004.*

A2

A3

Perf. 10½, 12½ and Compound

1900 **Typo.**

11 A2 1h gray black .20 .20
Never hinged .60
On cover, postcard, newsprint or wrapper 36.00
12 A2 2h gray .20 .20
Never hinged .60
On cover, postcard, newsprint or wrapper 20.00
13 A2 3h yellow .20 .20
Never hinged .60
On cover 20.00
14 A2 5h green .20 .20
Never hinged .50
On cover 2.50
15 A2 6h brown .30 .20
Never hinged .75
On cover 27.50
16 A2 10h red .20 .20
Never hinged .50
On cover 2.50
17 A2 20h rose 150.00 10.00
Never hinged 310.00
On cover 210.00
18 A2 25h blue .75 .35
Never hinged 2.25
On cover 32.50
19 A2 30h bister brown 150.00 11.00
Never hinged 325.00
On cover 210.00
20 A2 40h orange 210.00 15.00
Never hinged 425.00
On cover 325.00
21 A2 50h red lilac .50 *.75*
Never hinged 1.60
On cover 575.00
22 A3 1k dark rose .75 .50
Never hinged 1.90
On cover —
23 A3 2k ultra 1.50 *1.75*
Never hinged 3.25
On cover —
24 A3 5k dull blue grn 3.00 *5.00*
Never hinged 6.25
On cover —
Nos. 11-24 (14) 517.80 45.55

All values of this issue except the 3h exist on ribbed paper.

Nos. 17, 19 and 20 were reprinted in 1911. The reprints are in lighter colors and on whiter paper than the originals. Reprints of Nos. 17 and 19 are perf. 10½ and those of No. 20 are perf. 12½. Value each $5.

Numerals in Black

1901-04 ***Perf. 12½***

25 A2 20h pink ('02) .70 .50
26 A2 30h bister brn ('03) .70 .50
27 A2 35h blue 1.25 .80
a. 35h ultramarine *250.00* 7.50
28 A2 40h orange ('03) .85 .85
29 A2 45h grnsh blue ('04) .90 .85
Nos. 25-29 (5) 4.40 3.50

Nos. 11-16, 18, 21-29 exist imperf. Most of Nos. 11-29 exist perf. 6½; compound with 12½; part perf.; in pairs imperf. between. These were supplied only to some high-ranking officials and never sold at any P.O.

View of Deboj A4

The Carsija at Sarajevo — A5

Designs: 2h, View of Mostar. 3h, Pliva Gate, Jajce. 5h, Narenta Pass and Prenj River. 6h, Rama Valley. 10h, Vrbas Valley. 20h, Old Bridge, Mostar. 25h, Bey's Mosque, Sarajevo. 30h, Donkey post. 35h, Jezero and tourists' pavilion. 40h, Mail wagon. 45h, Bazaar at Sarajevo. 50h, Postal car. 2k, St. Luke's Campanile, Jajce. 5k, Emperor Franz Josef.

Perf. 6½, 9½, 10½ and 12½, also Compounds

1906 **Engr.** **Unwmk.**

30 A4 1h black .20 .20
31 A4 2h violet .20 .20
32 A4 3h olive .20 .20
33 A4 5h dark green .30 .20
34 A4 6h brown .20 .20
a. Perf. 13½ 17.50 *25.00*
35 A4 10h carmine .45 .20
36 A4 20h dark brown .90 .20
a. Perf. 13½ 72.50 *92.50*
37 A4 25h deep blue 2.25 1.10
38 A4 30h green 2.25 .50
39 A4 35h myrtle green 2.25 .50
40 A4 40h orange red 2.25 .50
41 A4 45h brown red 2.25 1.40
42 A4 50h dull violet 2.25 1.10
43 A5 1k maroon 8.50 3.50
44 A5 2k gray green 6.75 *11.00*
45 A5 5k dull blue 6.00 *9.50*
Nos. 30-45 (16) 37.20 *30.50*

Nos. 30-45 exist imperf. Value, set $62.50 unused, $90 canceled.

For overprint and surcharges see #126, B1-B4.

Birthday Jubilee Issue

Designs of 1906 Issue, with "1830-1910" in Label at Bottom

1910 ***Perf. 12½***

46 A4 1h black .30 .30
47 A4 2h violet .30 .30
48 A4 3h olive .30 .30
49 A4 5h dark green .40 .20
50 A4 6h orange brn .40 .30
51 A4 10h carmine .45 .20
52 A4 20h dark brown 1.50 *2.10*
53 A4 25h deep blue 2.50 *3.50*
54 A4 30h green 2.10 *3.50*
55 A4 35h myrtle grn 2.10 *3.50*
56 A4 40h orange red 2.10 *4.25*
57 A4 45h brown red 3.50 *6.50*
58 A4 50h dull violet 3.75 *6.50*
59 A5 1k maroon 3.75 *7.50*
60 A5 2k gray green 22.50 *27.50*
61 A5 5k dull blue 1.50 *10.00*
Nos. 46-61 (16) 47.45 *76.45*

80th birthday of Emperor Franz Josef.

Scenic Type of 1906

Views: 12h, Jaice. 60h, Konjica. 72h, Vishegrad.

1912

62 A4 12h ultra 5.25 *6.00*
63 A4 60h dull blue 3.00 *5.25*
64 A4 72h carmine 14.50 *26.00*
Nos. 62-64 (3) 22.75 *37.25*

Value, imperf. set, $110.

See Austria for similar designs inscribed "FELDPOST" instead of "MILITARPOST."

Emperor Franz Josef
A23 A24

A25

A26

1912-14

Various Frames

65 A23 1h olive green .35 .20
66 A23 2h brt blue .35 .20
67 A23 3h claret .35 .20
68 A23 5h green .35 .20
69 A23 6h dark gray .35 .20
70 A23 10h rose car .35 .20
71 A23 12h dp olive grn .55 .30
72 A23 20h orange brn 3.00 .20
73 A23 25h ultra 1.50 .20
74 A23 30h orange red 1.50 .20
75 A24 35h myrtle grn 1.90 .20
76 A24 40h dk violet 5.25 .20
77 A24 45h olive brn 2.25 .30
78 A24 50h slate blue 2.75 .20
79 A24 60h brown vio 1.60 .20
80 A24 72h dark blue 3.00 *5.00*
81 A25 1k brn vio, *straw* 9.75 .50
82 A25 2k dk gray, *bl* 6.75 .85
83 A26 3k carmine, *grn* 10.00 *11.00*
84 A26 5k dk vio, *gray* 20.00 *27.50*
85 A25 10k dk ultra, *gray* ('14) 100.00 125.00
Nos. 65-85 (21) 171.90 173.05

Value, imperf. set, $375.

For overprints and surcharges see #127, B5-B8, Austria M1-M21.

A27

A28

1916-17 ***Perf. 12½***

86 A27 3h dark gray .20 *.30*
87 A27 5h olive green .20 *.60*
88 A27 6h violet .20 *.60*
89 A27 10h bister 1.50 *2.75*
90 A27 12h blue gray .30 *.75*
91 A27 15h car rose .20 .20
92 A27 20h brown .40 *.85*
93 A27 25h blue .40 *.85*
94 A27 30h dark green .40 *.85*
95 A27 40h vermilion .40 *.85*
96 A27 50h green .40 *.90*
97 A27 60h lake .40 *.90*
98 A27 80h orange brn 1.60 .50
a. Perf. 11½ 6.00 *9.00*
99 A27 90h dark violet 1.10 1.10
a. Perf. 11½ 875.00 —
101 A28 2k claret, *straw* .75 *2.25*
102 A28 3k green, *bl* 1.50 *4.00*
103 A28 4k carmine, *grn* 7.00 *16.00*
104 A28 10k dp vio, *gray* 16.00 *37.50*
Nos. 86-104 (18) 32.95 *71.75*

Value, imperf. set, $260.
For overprints see Nos. B11-B12.

Emperor Karl I
A29 A30

1917 ***Perf. 12½***

105 A29 3h olive gray .20 *.30*
a. Perf. 11½ 150.00 *275.00*
b. Perf. 12½x11½ 22.50 *60.00*
106 A29 5h olive green .20 .20
107 A29 6h violet .35 *.80*
108 A29 10h orange brn .20 .20
a. Perf. 11½x12½ 190.00 *275.00*
b. Perf. 11½ 350.00 —
109 A29 12h blue .50 *.80*
110 A29 15h brt rose .20 .20
111 A29 20h red brown .30 .20
112 A29 25h ultra .65 .65
113 A29 30h gray green .60 .30
114 A29 40h olive bis .35 .30
115 A29 50h dp green .75 .65
116 A29 60h car rose .65 .65
a. Perf. 11½ 22.50 *62.50*
117 A29 80h steel blue .30 *.35*
118 A29 90h dull violet 1.10 *1.60*
119 A30 2k carmine, *straw* 1.10 .70
120 A30 3k green, *bl* 21.00 *26.50*
121 A30 4k carmine, *grn* 7.50 *17.00*
122 A30 10k dp violet, *gray* 4.00 *17.50*
Nos. 105-122 (18) 39.95 *68.90*

Value, imperf. set, $85.

Nos. 47 and 66 Overprinted in Red

1918

126 A4 2h violet .60 *2.25*
b. Inverted overprint 30.00
d. Double overprint 18.50
f. Double overprint, one inverted —
127 A23 2h bright blue .60 *1.75*
a. Pair, one without overprint —
b. Inverted overprint 25.00
c. Double overprint 13.50
d. Double overprint, one inverted —

Emperor Karl I — A31

1918 **Typo.** ***Perf. 12½, Imperf.***

128 A31 2h orange 9.00
Never hinged 21.00

129	A31 3h dark green	9.00	
	Never hinged	21.00	
130	A31 5h lt green	9.00	
	Never hinged	21.00	
131	A31 6h blue green	9.00	
	Never hinged	21.00	
132	A31 10h brown	9.00	
	Never hinged	21.00	
133	A31 20h brick red	9.00	
	Never hinged	21.00	
134	A31 25h ultra	9.00	
	Never hinged	21.00	
135	A31 45h dk slate	9.00	
	Never hinged	21.00	
136	A31 50h lt bluish grn	9.00	
	Never hinged	21.00	
137	A31 60h blue violet	9.00	
	Never hinged	21.00	
138	A31 70h ocher	9.00	
	Never hinged	21.00	
139	A31 80h rose	9.00	
	Never hinged	21.00	
140	A31 90h violet brn	9.00	
	Never hinged	21.00	

Engr.

141	A30 1k ol grn, *grnsh*	*1,700.*	
	Never hinged	*2,750.*	
	Nos. 128-140 (13)	117.00	

Nos. 128-141 were prepared for use in Bosnia and Herzegovina, but were not issued there. They were sold after the Armistice at the Vienna post office for a few days.

SEMI-POSTAL STAMPS

Nos. 33 and 35 Surcharged in Red

1914 Unwmk. *Perf. 12½*

B1	A4 7h on 5h dk grn	.40	*.65*
B2	A4 12h on 10h car	.40	*.65*

Various minor varieties of the surcharge include "4" with open top, narrow "4" and wide "4."

Nos. B1-B2 exist with double and inverted surcharges. Value about $20 each.

#33, 35 Surcharged in Red or Blue

1915 *Perf. 12½*

B3	A4 7h on 5h (R)	10.50	*15.00*
a.	Perf. 9½	200.00	200.00
B4	A4 12h on 10h (Bl)	.30	*.50*

Nos. B3-B4 exist with double and inverted surcharges. Value about $28.50 each.

#68, 70 Surcharged in Red or Blue

1915

B5	A23 7h on 5h (R)	.85	*1.10*
a.	"1915" at top and bottom	40.00	*62.50*
B6	A23 12h on 10h (Bl)	1.40	*2.10*
a.	Surcharged "7 Heller."	45.00	*92.50*

Nos. B5-B6 are found in three types differing in length of surcharge lines:

I — date 18mm, denomination 14mm.
II — date 16mm, denomination 14mm.
III — date 18mm, denomination 16mm.

Nos. B5-B6 exist with double and inverted surcharges. Value $27 each.

Nos. B5a and B6a exist double and inverted.

#68, 70 Surcharged in Red or Blue

1916

B7	A23 7h on 5h (R)	.50	*.70*
B8	A23 12h on 10h (Bl)	.50	*.90*

Nos. B7-B8 exist with double and inverted surcharges. Value $20 each.

Wounded Soldier — SP1

Blind Soldier — SP2

1916 Engr.

B9	SP1 5h (+ 2h) green	1.10	*1.75*
B10	SP2 10h (+ 2h) magenta	1.75	*2.25*

Nos. B9-B10 exist imperf. Value, set $150.

Nos. 89, 91 Overprinted

1917

B11	A27 10h bister	.20	*.30*
B12	A27 15h carmine rose	.20	.20

Nos. B11-B12 exist imperf. Value set, $190.

Nos. B11-B12 exist with double and inverted overprint. Value $15 each.

Design for Memorial Church at Sarajevo SP3

Archduke Francis Ferdinand — SP4

Duchess Sophia and Archduke Francis Ferdinand SP5

1917 Typo. *Perf. 11½, 12½*

B13	SP3 10h violet black	.20	.30
B14	SP4 15h claret	.20	.30
B15	SP5 40h deep blue	.20	.30
	Nos. B13-B15 (3)	.60	.90

Assassination of Archduke Ferdinand and Archduchess Sophia. Sold at a premium of 2h each which helped build a memorial church at Sarajevo.

Exist imperf. Value, set $3.75.

Blind Soldier — SP6

Emperor Karl I — SP8

Design: 15h, Wounded soldier.

1918 Engr. *Perf. 12½*

B16	SP6 10h (+ 10h) grnsh bl	.60	*1.60*
B17	SP6 15h (+ 10h) red brn	.60	*1.60*

#B16-B17 exist imperf. Value, set $75.

1918 Typo. *Perf. 12½x13*

Design: 15h, Empress Zita.

B18	SP8 10h gray green	.35	*1.10*
B19	SP8 15h brown red	.35	*1.10*
B20	SP8 40h violet	.35	*1.10*
	Nos. B18-B20 (3)	1.05	*3.30*

Sold at a premium of 10h each which went to the "Karl's Fund."

#B18-B20 exist imperf. Value, set $135.

POSTAGE DUE STAMPS

D1

D2

Perf. 9½, 10½, 12½ and Compound

1904 Unwmk.

J1	D1	1h black, red & yel	.45	.20
J2	D1	2h black, red & yel	.45	.20
J3	D1	3h black, red & yel	.50	.20
J4	D1	4h black, red & yel	.50	.20
J5	D1	5h black, red & yel	2.00	.20
J6	D1	6h black, red & yel	.45	.20
J7	D1	7h black, red & yel	2.75	*3.25*
J8	D1	8h black, red & yel	2.75	1.60
J9	D1	10h black, red & yel	.65	.20
J10	D1	15h black, red & yel	.60	.20
J11	D1	20h black, red & yel	3.50	.30
J12	D1	50h black, red & yel	2.25	.30
J13	D1	200h black, red & grn	16.00	2.50
		Nos. J1-J13 (13)	32.85	9.55
		Set, never hinged	115.00	

Value, imperf. set, $150.

For overprints see Western Ukraine Nos. 61-72.

1916-18 *Perf. 12½*

J14	D2	2h red ('18)	.30	*.80*
J15	D2	4h red ('18)	.30	*.80*
J16	D2	5h red	.30	*.80*
J17	D2	6h red ('18)	.20	*1.10*
J18	D2	10h red	.30	*.80*
J19	D2	15h red	2.25	*8.75*
J20	D2	20h red	.30	*1.10*
J21	D2	25h red	.90	*3.00*
J22	D2	30h red	.75	*3.00*
J23	D2	40h red	9.00	*21.00*
J24	D2	50h red	22.50	*60.00*
J25	D2	1k dark blue	6.25	*11.50*
J26	D2	3k dark blue	22.50	*42.50*
		Nos. J14-J26 (13)	65.85	*155.15*
		Set, never hinged	200.00	

Nos. J25-J26 have colored numerals on a white tablet.

Value, imperf. set, $190.

For surcharges see Italy Nos. NJ1-NJ7.

NEWSPAPER STAMPS

Bosnian Girl — N1

1913 Unwmk. *Imperf.*

P1	N1 2h ultra	.50	1.00
P2	N1 6h violet	2.25	3.25
P3	N1 10h rose	2.50	3.00
P4	N1 20h green	2.75	3.50
	Nos. P1-P4 (4)	8.00	10.75

After Bosnia and Herzegovina became part of Yugoslavia stamps of type N1 perf., and imperf. copies surcharged with new values, were used as regular postage stamps. See Yugoslavia Nos. 1L21-1L22, 1L43-1L45.

SPECIAL HANDLING STAMPS

"Lightning" — SH1

1916 Unwmk. Engr. *Perf. 12½*

QE1	SH1 2h vermilion	.20	.20
a.	Perf. 11½x12½	350.00	250.00
QE2	SH1 5h deep green	.35	.35
a.	Perf. 11½	17.50	42.50

For surcharges see Italy Nos. NE1-NE2.

BRAZIL

brə-'zil

Brasil (after 1918)

LOCATION — On the north and east coasts of South America, bordering on the Atlantic Ocean.
GOVT. — Republic
AREA — 3,286,000 sq. mi.
POP. — 132,580,000 (est. 1984)
CAPITAL — Brasilia

Brazil was an independent empire from 1822 to 1889, when a constitution was adopted and the country became officially known as The United States of Brazil.

1000 Reis = 1 Milreis

> Values for unused stamps are for examples with original gum as defined in the catalogue introduction except for Nos. 1-38 and 42-52 which are valued without gum.

Watermarks

Wmk. 97 "CORREIO FEDERAL REPUBLICA DOS ESTADOS UNIDOS DO BRAZIL" in Sheet

Wmk. 98 "IMPOSTO DE CONSUMO REPUBLICA DOS ESTADOS UNIDOS DO BRAZIL" in Sheet

Wmk. 99 — "CORREIO"

Wmk. 100 — "CASA DA MOEDA" in Sheet

Because of the spacing of this watermark, a few stamps in each sheet may show no watermark.

Wmk. 101 — Stars and CASA DA MOEDA

Wmk. 193 — ESTADOS UNIDOS DO BRASIL

Wmk. 206 — Star-framed CM, Multiple

Wmk. 218 — E U BRASIL Multiple, Letters 8mm High

Wmk. 221 ESTADOS UNIDOS DO BRASIL, Multiple, Letters 6mm High

Wmk. 222 — CORREIO BRASIL and 5 Stars in Squared Circle

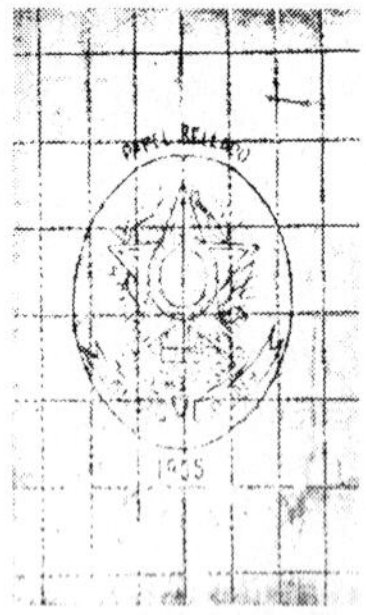

Wmk. 236 — Coat of Arms in Sheet

Watermark (reduced illustration) covers 22 stamps in sheet.

Wmk. 245 — Multiple "CASA DA MOEDA DO BRASIL" and Small Formee Cross

Wmk. 249 — "CORREIO BRASIL" multiple

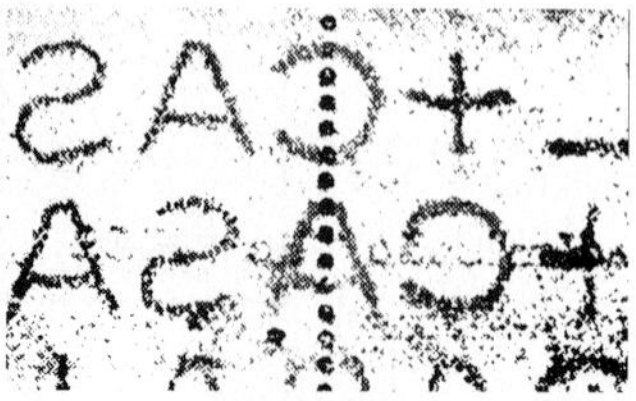

Wmk. 256 "CASA+DA+MOEDA+DO+BRAZIL" in 8mm Letters

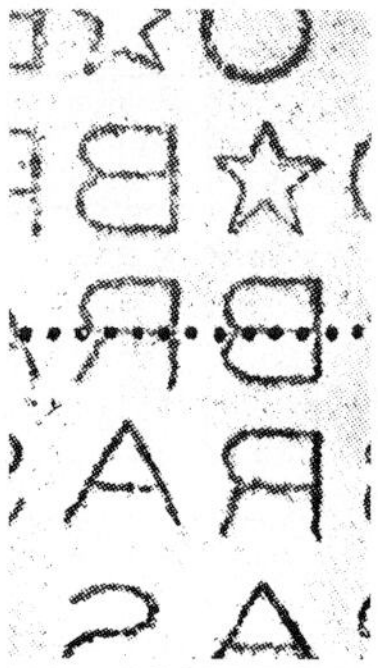

Wmk. 264 — "*CORREIO*BRASIL*" Multiple, Letters 7mm High

PRE-STAMP POSTAL MARKINGS

Crowned Circle handstamp type IX is pictured in the Crowned Circle Handstamps and Great Britain Used Abroad section.

Bahia

1851, Jan. 6

A1	IX	Crowned circle handstamp, on cover	*3,000.*
A2	IX	Crowned circle handstamp, in red, on cover	*5,500.*
A3	IX	Crowned circle handstamp, in green, on cover	—

Pernambuco

A4	IX	Crowned circle handstamp, on cover	*6,250.*
A5	IX	Crowned circle handstamp, in red, on cover	3,000.

Rio de Janeiro

A6	IX	Crowned circle handstamp, on cover	*2,900.*
A7	IX	Crowned circle handstamp, in red, on cover	800.00
A8	IX	Crowned circle handstamp, in green, on cover	—

> Values are for clear cancellations on sound, fault-free stamps, with average to fine centering. In many cases, very fine copies are rare or non-existent.

STAMPS OF GREAT BRITAIN USED IN BRAZIL

Type A

1860-73

Numeral Cancellation Type A, C81 (Bahia)

A9	A	1p rose red (#33, P90, 93, 96, 108, 113, 117, 135, 140, 147, 155) (from)	50.00
A10	A	1½p lake red (#32, P3)	125.00
A11	A	2p blue (#29, P9, 12)	85.00
A12	A	2p bl (#30, P13-14) (from)	75.00
A13	A	3p rose (#44)	—
A14	A	3p rose (#49, P4, 6, 8-10) (from)	60.00
A15	A	3p rose (#61, P11)	—
A16	A	4p ver (#43, P8-13) (from)	55.00
A17	A	6p lilac (#45, P5)	—
A18	A	6p dull violet (#50, P6)	160.00
A19	A	6p red vio (#51, P8-9) (from)	80.00
A20	A	6p pale buff (#59b, P11-12) (from)	110.00
a.		6p brown (#59, P11)	110.00
A21	A	6p gray (#60, P12)	—
A22	A	6p gray (#62, P13)	—
A23	A	9p straw (#46)	475.00
A24	A	9p bister (#52)	275.00
A25	A	1sh green (#48)	190.00
A26	A	1sh green (#54, P4-6) (from)	55.00
		Plate 7	55.00
A27	A	1sh deep green (#64a, P8-9) (from)	95.00
A28	A	2sh blue (#55)	300.00
A29	A	5sh rose (#57, P1)	550.00

Numeral Cancellation Type A, C82 (Pernambuco)

A30	A	1p rose red (#33, P85, 108, 111, 130-132, 149, 157, 159, 160, 187(from)	50.00
A31	A	2p blue (#29, P9, 12)	60.00
A32	A	2p blue (#30, P13-14) (from)	60.00
A33	A	3p rose (#44)	125.00
A34	A	3p rose (#49, P4-7, 10) (from)	60.00
A35	A	3p rose (#61, P11)	—
A36	A	4p vermilion (#43, P9-14) (from)	55.00
A37	A	6p lilac (#45, P5-6)	—
A38	A	6p dull violet (#50, P6)	90.00
A39	A	6p red violet (#51, P8-9) (from)	80.00
A40	A	6p brown (#59, P11)	90.00
a.		6p pale buff (#59b, P11-12)	60.00
A41	A	6p gray (#60, P12)	—
A42	A	9p straw (#46)	475.00
A43	A	9p bister (#52)	250.00
A44	A	10p red brown (#53)	325.00
A45	A	1sh green (#48)	190.00
A46	A	1sh green (#54, P4-6) (from)	55.00
		Plate 7	55.00
A47	A	2sh blue (#55)	275.00
A48	A	5sh rose (#57, P1)	550.00

Numeral Cancellation Type A, C83 (Rio de Janeiro)

A49	A	1p rose red (#20)	50.00
A50	A	1p rose red (#33, P71, 76, 80, 82, 86, 94, 103, 113, 117, 119, 123, 130, 132, 134-135, 146, 148, 159, 161, 166, 185, 200, 204 (from)	42.50
A51	A	2p blue (#29, P9, 12)	42.50
A52	A	2p blue (#30, P13-14) (from)	42.50
A53	A	3p rose (#49, P4-8) (from)	50.00
A54	A	3p rose (#61, P11)	—
A55	A	4p vermilion (#43, P8-13) (from)	55.00
A56	A	6p lilac (#45, P5)	110.00
A57	A	6p dull violet (#50, P6)	82.50
A58	A	6p red violet (#51, P8-9)	77.50
A59	A	6p brown (#59, P11)	82.50
a.		6p pale buff (#59b, P11)	50.00
A60	A	6p gray (#60, P12)	—
A61	A	9p straw (#46)	450.00
A62	A	9p bister (#52)	225.00
A63	A	10p red brown (#53)	300.00
A64	A	1sh green (#48)	150.00
A65	A	1sh green (#54, P4-6) (from)	50.00
		Plate 7	90.00
A66	A	1sh green (#64, P8-9) (from)	80.00
A67	A	2sh blue (#55)	150.00
A68	A	5sh rose (#57, P1)	550.00
		Plate 2	700.00

Issues of the Empire

A1

Grayish or Yellowish Paper

Unwmk.

1843, Aug. 1 Engr. *Imperf.*

Fine Impressions

1	A1 30r black	3,000.	550.
	On cover		*7,250.*
	On cover, single franking		*16,500.*
c.	Pair, #1-2		*300,000.*
d.	Strip of 3, 2 #1, 1 #2		*850,000.*

2	A1	60r black	600.	240.
		On cover		5,750.
3	A1	90r black	3,000.	1,200.
		On cover		13,000.

Nos. 1-3b were issued with gum, but very few unused examples retain even a trace of their original gum. Copies with original gum command substantial premiums.

Fine impressions are true black and have background lathework complete.

Most examples of Nos. 1-3b are printed on yellowish or grayish paper. They also exist on white paper, usually thin and somewhat translucent. Such examples are scarce and command premiums.

Nos. 1c and 1d are each unique.

Intermediate Impressions

1a	A1	30r	2,750.	450.
		On cover		7,250.
		On cover, single franking		16,500.
2a	A1	60r	550.	225.
		On cover		5,750.
3a	A1	90r	2,750.	1,100.
		On cover		13,000.

Intermediate impressions are grayish black and have weaker lathework in the background.

Worn Impressions

1b	A1	30r	2,750.	425.
		On cover		7,250.
		On cover, single franking		16,500.
2b	A1	60r	550.	225.
		On cover		5,750.
3b	A1	90r	2,500.	1,100.
		On cover		13,000.

Worn impressions have white areas in the background surrounding the numerals due to plate wear affecting especially the lathework.

A2

A3

Grayish or Yellowish Paper

1844-46

7	A2	10r black	100.00	20.00
		On cover		275.00
		On cover, single franking		—
8	A2	30r black	125.00	30.00
		On cover		300.00
9	A2	60r black	100.00	20.00
		On cover		250.00
10	A2	90r black	750.00	100.00
		On cover		675.00
11	A2	180r black	3,500.	1,350.
		On cover		10,000.
12	A2	300r black	5,250.	1,800.
		On cover		15,000.
13	A2	600r black	5,000.	2,000.
		On cover		—

Nos. 8, 9 and 10 exist on thick paper and are considerably scarcer.

Grayish or Yellowish Paper

1850, Jan. 1

21	A3	10r black	25.00	35.00
		On cover		300.00
		On cover, single franking		—
22	A3	20r black	75.00	100.00
		On cover		575.00
23	A3	30r black	10.00	3.00
		On cover		60.00
24	A3	60r black	10.00	2.50
		On cover		30.00
25	A3	90r black	80.00	12.00
		On cover		120.00
26	A3	180r black	80.00	55.00
		On cover		650.00
27	A3	300r black	325.00	60.00
		On cover		550.00
28	A3	600r black	375.00	90.00
		On cover		1,200.

No. 22 used is generally found precanceled with a single horizontal line in pen or blue crayon or with two diagonal pen lines. Value precanceled without gum, $75.

All values except the 90r were reprinted in 1910 on very thick paper.

1854

37	A3	10r blue	12.00	11.50
		On cover		400.00
		On cover, single franking		450.00
a.		10r pale blue	17.50	17.50
		On cover		450.00
b.		10r steel blue	85.00	50.00
		On cover		750.00
38	A3	30r blue	32.50	50.00
		On cover		500.00
a.		30r dark blue	70.00	50.00
		On cover		500.00
b.		30r steel blue	400.00	100.00
		On cover		750.00

A4

1861

39	A4	280r red	150.00	100.00
		No gum	100.00	
		On cover		1,200.
40	A4	430r yellow	225.00	140.00
		No gum	160.00	
		On cover		1,800.

Nos. 39-40 have been reprinted on thick white paper with white gum. They are printed in aniline inks and the colors are brighter than those of the originals.

1866 ***Perf. 13½***

42	A3	10r blue	125.00	150.00
		On cover		—
43	A3	20r black	900.00	400.00
		On cover		—
44	A3	30r black	300.00	150.00
		On cover		600.00
45	A3	30r blue	675.00	750.00
		On cover		—
46	A3	60r black	125.00	25.00
		On cover		600.00
47	A3	90r black	575.00	275.00
		On cover		675.00
48	A3	180r black	600.00	275.00
		On cover		—
49	A4	280r red	650.00	675.00
		On cover		2,500.
50	A3	300r black	750.00	400.00
		On cover		—
51	A4	430r yellow	600.00	350.00
		On cover		3,250.
52	A3	600r black	575.00	240.00
		On cover		3,250.

Fraudulent perforations abound. Purchases should be accompanied by certificates of authenticity.

A 10r black is questioned.

A5

A6

A7

A8

A8a

A9

Emperor Dom Pedro — A9a

100 reis

Type I — Left frameline weak and incomplete and composed of a single line which never touches the upper ornaments.

Type II — Left frameline incomplete and composed of a double outer line which does not touch the upper ornaments.

Type III — Left frameline complete and composed of two continuous outer lines which meet the upper ornaments.

Thick or Thin White Wove Paper

1866, July 1 ***Perf. 12***

53	A5	10r vermilion	12.00	5.00
		On cover		375.00
		On cover, single franking		500.00
b.		10r carmine vermilion	35.00	15.00
		On cover		375.00
		On cover, single franking		500.00
54	A6	20r red lilac	20.00	3.00
		On cover		325.00
		On cover, single franking		375.00
a.		20r dull violet	65.00	25.00
		On cover		400.00
		On cover, single franking		500.00
56	A7	50r blue	30.00	2.50
		On cover		60.00
		On cover, single franking		275.00
57	A8	80r slate violet	75.00	5.00
		On cover		160.00
		On cover, single franking		550.00
b.		80r rose lilac	100.00	10.00
		On cover		175.00
		On cover, single franking		600.00
58	A8a	100r blue green, type III	30.00	1.50
		On cover		25.00
a.		100r green (shades), type I	30.00	1.50
		On cover		35.00
c.		100r green (shades), type II	75.00	5.00
		On cover		67.50
59	A9	200r black	100.00	8.00
		On cover		80.00
a.		Half used as 100r on cover		1,500.
60	A9a	500r orange	200.00	35.00
		On cover		425.00
		Nos. 53-60 (7)	467.00	60.00

The 10r and 20r exist imperf. on both white and bluish paper. Some authorities consider them proofs.

Nos. 58 and 65 are found in three types.

Bluish Paper

53a	A5	10r	500.00	425.00
		On cover		—
54b	A6	20r	160.00	24.00
		On cover		—
56a	A7	50r	200.00	25.00
		On cover		350.00
57a	A8	80r	240.00	27.50
		On cover		—
58b	A8a	100r Type II	800.00	110.00
		On cover		275.00
d.		A8a 100r Type I	10,000.	—
		On cover		—

1876-77 ***Rouletted***

61	A5	10r vermilion ('77)	60.00	35.00
		On cover		275.00
		On cover, single franking		—
62	A6	20r red lilac ('77)	70.00	27.50
		On cover		250.00
		On cover, single franking		425.00
63	A7	50r blue ('77)	70.00	10.00
		On cover		275.00
		On cover, single franking		—
64	A8	80r violet ('77)	175.00	20.00
		On cover		375.00
65	A8a	100r green	40.00	1.25
		On cover		50.00
66	A9	200r black ('77)	80.00	7.50
		On cover		140.00
a.		Half used as 100r on cover		1,100.
67	A9a	500r orange	190.00	40.00
		On cover		700.00
		Nos. 61-67 (7)	685.00	141.25

A10

A11

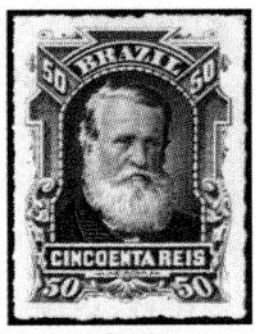
A12

A13

A14

A15

A16

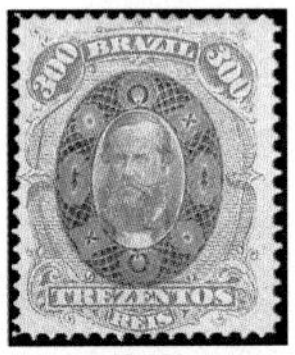
A17

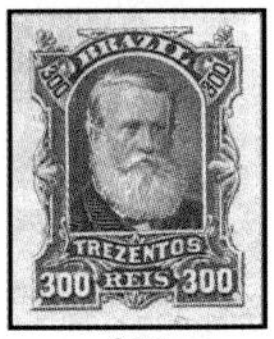
A18

A19

A20

1878-79 ***Rouletted***

68	A10	10r vermilion	12.00	3.00
		On cover		275.00
		On cover, single franking		500.00
69	A11	20r violet	15.00	2.50
		On cover		100.00
		On cover, single franking		500.00
a.		20r dark violet	24.00	6.00
		On cover		125.00
		On cover, single franking		600.00
b.		20r rose lilac	17.50	5.50
		On cover		125.00
		On cover, single franking		600.00
70	A12	50r blue	24.00	2.00
		On cover		100.00
		On cover, single franking		175.00
71	A13	80r lake	27.50	10.00
		On cover		375.00
		On cover, single franking		1,375.
72	A14	100r green	27.50	1.25
		On cover		35.00
73	A15	200r black	140.00	17.50
		On cover		200.00
a.		Half used as 100r on cover		1,200.
74	A16	260r dk brown	80.00	22.50
		On cover		550.00
75	A18	300r bister	80.00	6.00
		On cover		550.00
a.		One-third used as 100r on cover		10,000.
76	A19	700r red brown	160.00	85.00
		On cover		3,500.
77	A20	1000r gray lilac	190.00	37.50
		On cover		300.00
		On cover, single franking		2,000.
a.		Half used as 500r on cover		10,000.
		Nos. 68-77 (10)	756.00	187.25

1878, Aug. 21 ***Perf. 12***

78	A17	300r orange & grn	85.00	20.00
		On cover		600.00

Nos. 68-78 exist imperforate.

A21

A22

A23

Small Heads

Laid Paper

Perf. 13, 13½ and Compound

1881, July 15

79	A21	50r blue	125.00	18.00
		On cover		165.00
		On cover, single franking		375.00
80	A22	100r olive green	500.00	30.00
		On cover		165.00
81	A23	200r pale red brn	475.00	110.00
		On cover		250.00
a.		Half used as 100r on cover		1,750.

On Nos. 79 and 80 the hair above the ear curves forward. On Nos. 83 and 88 it is drawn backward. On the stamps of the 1881 issue the beard is smaller than in the 1882-85 issues and fills less of the space between the neck and the frame at the left.

See No. 88.

A24

A25

A26

A27

Two types each of the 100 and 200 reis.

100 REIS:

Type I — Groundwork formed of diagonal crossed lines and horizontal lines.

Type II — Groundwork formed of diagonal crossed lines and vertical lines.

200 REIS:

Type I — Groundwork formed of diagonal and horizontal lines.

Type II — Groundwork formed of diagonal crossed lines.

Larger Heads
Laid Paper

Perf. 12½ to 14 and Compound

1882-84

82 A24 10r black 10.00 *20.00*
On cover 275.00
83 A25 100r ol grn, type I 37.50 3.00
On cover 45.00
b. 100r dark green, type II 200.00 12.00
On cover 125.00
84 A26 200r pale red brn, type I 85.00 22.50
On cover 100.00
a. Half used as 100r on cover *1,100.*
85 A27 200r pale rose, type II 45.00 4.50
On cover 55.00
a. Diag. half used as 100r on cover 800.00
Nos. 82-85 (4) 177.50 50.00

See No. 86.

A28

A29

A30

Three types of A29

Type I — Groundwork of horizontal lines.

Type II — Groundwork of diagonal crossed lines.

Type III — Groundwork solid.

Perf. 13, 13½, 14 and Compound

1884-85

86 A24 10r orange 2.50 2.00
On cover 225.00
On cover, single franking 250.00
87 A28 20r slate green 30.00 3.00
On cover 275.00
a. 20r olive green 30.00 3.00
On cover 275.00
b. Half used as 10r on newspaper *3,000.*
88 A21 50r bl, head larger 30.00 3.00
On cover 60.00
On cover, single franking 115.00
90 A29 100r lilac, type I 125.00 2.50
On cover 65.00
a. 100r lilac, type II 450.00 75.00
On cover 275.00
b. 100r lilac, type III 325.00 55.00
On cover 250.00
91 A30 100r lilac 175.00 4.00
On cover 85.00

A31

A32

Southern Cross
A33

Crown
A34

Perf. 13, 13½, 14 and Compound

1885

92 A31 100r lilac 100.00 2.50
On cover 22.50

Compare design A31 with A35.

1887

93 A32 50r chalky blue 27.50 4.00
On cover 30.00
On cover, single franking 125.00
94 A33 300r gray blue 200.00 25.00
On cover 400.00
On cover, single franking 600.00
95 A34 500r olive 110.00 12.00
On cover 275.00
On cover, single franking 450.00

A35

A36

Entrance to Bay of Rio de Janeiro — A37

1888

96 A35 100r lilac 60.00 1.50
On cover 16.75
a. Imperf., pair 125.00 *160.00*
97 A36 700r violet 65.00 *100.00*
On cover *1,350.*
98 A37 1000r dull blue 250.00 100.00
On cover *1,400.*

Issues of the Republic

Southern Cross — A38

Wove Paper, Thin to Thick

Perf. 12½ to 14, 11 to 11½, and 12½ to 14x11 to 11½, Rough or Clean-Cut

Engraved; Typographed (#102)

1890-91

99 A38 20r gray green 2.00 1.50
On postcard 35.00
On cover, single franking 175.00
a. 20r blue green 2.00 1.50
On postcard 35.00
On cover, single franking 175.00
b. 20r emerald 16.00 6.00
On postcard 40.00
On cover, single franking 190.00
100 A38 50r gray green 5.00 1.50
On postcard 35.00
On cover, single franking 150.00
a. 50r olive green 12.00 6.00
On postcard 40.00
On cover, single franking 165.00
b. 50r yellow green 12.00 6.00
On postcard 40.00
On cover, single franking 165.00
c. 50r dark slate green 7.00 3.50
On postcard 40.00
On cover, single franking 165.00
d. Horiz. pair, imperf. btwn. —
101 A38 100r lilac rose 350.00 4.50
On cover *500.00*
102 A38 100r red lil, redrawn 25.00 1.50
On cover 20.00
a. Tete beche pair *15,000.* *16,500.*
On cover *35,000.*
103 A38 200r purple 8.00 1.50
On cover 30.00
a. 200r violet 10.00 2.00
On cover 32.50
b. 200r violet blue 22.50 3.00
On cover 35.00
104 A38 300r slate vio 150.00 25.00
On cover 175.00
a. 300r gray 75.00 8.50
On cover 150.00
b. 300r gray blue 85.00 8.50
On cover 150.00
c. 300r dark violet 75.00 5.00
On cover 150.00
105 A38 500r olive bister 17.50 8.00
On cover 150.00
a. 500r olive gray 17.50 10.00
On cover 165.00
106 A38 500r slate 17.50 12.00
On cover 175.00
107 A38 700r fawn 16.00 *16.00*
On cover 180.00
a. 700r chocolate 20.00 22.50
On cover 180.00
108 A38 1000r bister 15.00 3.00
On cover 225.00
a. 1000r yellow buff 30.00 7.50
On cover 240.00
Nos. 99-108 (10) 606.00 74.50

The redrawn 100r may be distinguished by the absence of the curved lines of shading in the left side of the central oval. The pearls in the oval are not well aligned and there is less shading at right and left of "CORREIO" and "100 REIS."

A 100 reis stamp of type A38 but inscribed "BRAZIL" instead of "E. U. DO BRAZIL" was not placed in issue but postmarked copies are known. A reprint on thick paper was made in 1910.

No. 101 exists imperf., not regularly issued.

For surcharges see Nos. 151-158.

Liberty Head
A39 A40

Perf. 12½ to 14, 11 to 11½ and 12½ to 14x11 to 11½

1891, May 1 **Typo.**

109 A39 100r blue & red 32.50 1.50
On cover 15.00
a. Frame inverted 100.00 90.00
On cover 500.00
b. Tete beche pair 675.00 *750.00*
On cover *2,500.*
c. 100r ultra & red 32.50 1.50
On cover 15.00

Perf. 11, 11½, 13, 13½, 14 and Compound

1893, Jan. 18 **Litho.**

111 A40 100r rose 75.00 1.75
On cover, single franking 37.50
a. 100r rose, perf 13 150.00 3.50
On cover, single franking 40.00

Sugarloaf Mountain — A41a
A41

Liberty Head — A42a
A42

Hermes — A43

Perf. 11 to 11½, 12½ to 14 and 12½ to 14x11 to 11½

1894-97 **Unwmk.**

112 A41 10r rose & blue 2.00 .80
On postcard, with other stamps 15.00
On cover, with other stamps 10.00
Single franking, on newspaper *150.00*
113 A41a 10r rose & blue 2.00 .80
On postcard, with other stamps 15.00
On cover, with other stamps 10.00
Single franking, on newspaper *150.00*
114 A41a 20r orange & bl ('97) 1.00 .30
On postcard, with other stamps 15.00
On cover, with other stamps 10.00
Single franking, on newspaper 50.00
a. 20r reddish orange & blue ('94) 1.75 .75
115 A41a 50r dk blue & blue 8.00 1.25
On postcard 3.00
Pair, on cover 10.00
a. 20r blue ('97) 6.00 4.00
116 A42 100r carmine & blk 4.00 .40
On cover 10.00
a. Vert. pair, imperf. btwn. *100.00*
b. 100r rose & black ('96) 9.00 .70
118 A42a 200r orange & blk 1.00 .40
a. Imperf. horiz., pair 80.00
b. Vert. pair, imperf. btwn. 80.00
c. 200r reddish orange & black ('94) 6.00 .60
119 A42a 300r green & blk 15.00 .60
On cover, single franking 25.00
a. 300r pale green & black ('94) 18.00 1.25
On cover, single franking 30.00
120 A42a 500r blue & blk 25.00 1.75
On cover 60.00
a. 500r indigo & black ('94) 190.00 6.00
121 A42a 700r lilac & blk 16.00 1.75
On cover 80.00
a. 700r lilac & black ('97) 18.00 1.75
On cover 80.00
122 A43 1000r green & vio 55.00 1.75
On cover 100.00
a. 1000r pale green & mauve ('94) 75.00 4.00
On cover 110.00
124 A43 2000r blk & gray lil 60.00 15.00
On cover 375.00
a. 2000r black & gray lilac, *chalky paper* ('94) 60.00 15.00
On cover 350.00
Nos. 112-124 (11) 189.00 24.80

Values for Nos. 112-124 are for the most common perforation variety of each stamp. Some perforations and combinations command premiums.

Values for this set are for stamps cut into the design on one or two sides due to the narrow spacing of the stamps in the setting of the plates and imperfect perforation methods. Between 1902 and 1905 these stamps were reissued with wider spacing between subjects and perforated 11½. These are listed as Nos. 113a-122b below.

The head of No. 116 exists in five types. See Nos. 140-150A, 159-161, 166-171d.

Wider Spacing Between Stamps

1902-05 ***Perf. 11½***

113a A41a 10r rose & bl 8.00 2.00
114b A41a 20r orange & bl 8.00 .50
119b A42a 300r green & blk 35.00 1.20
120b A42a 500r blue & blk 35.00 1.20
122b A43 1000r green & vio 275.00 10.00

Newspaper Stamps Surcharged:

a

b

c

Surcharged on 1889 Issue of type N1

1898 ***Rouletted***

Green Surcharge

125 (b) 700r on 500r yel 6.75 *10.00*
126 (c) 1000r on 700r yel 32.50 27.50
a. Surcharged "700r" 675.00 775.00
127 (c) 2000r on 1000r yel 27.50 15.00
128 (c) 2000r on 1000r brn 20.00 6.00

Violet Surcharge

129 (a) 100r on 50r brn yel 2.00 *45.00*
130 (c) 100r on 50r brn yel 65.00 50.00
131 (c) 300r on 200r blk 3.50 1.25
a. Double surcharge 160.00 275.00

The surcharge on No. 130 is handstamped. The impression is blurred and lighter in color than on No. 129. The two surcharges differ most in the shapes and serifs of the figures "1."

Counterfeits exist of No. 126a.

Black Surcharge

132 (b) 200r on 100r violet 3.50 1.25
a. Double surcharge 80.00 *175.00*
b. Inverted surcharge 80.00 *175.00*
132C (b) 500r on 300r car 5.50 3.00

133	(b)	700r on 500r green	8.00	2.00

Blue Surcharge

134	(b)	500r on 300r car	6.50	5.50

Red Surcharge

135	(c)	1000r on 700r ultra	22.50	15.00
a.		Inverted surcharge	200.00	—

Surcharged on 1890-94 Issues:

d

e

Perf. 11 to 14 and Compound

Black Surcharge

136	N3(e)	20r on 10r blue	3.00	6.00
137	N2(d)	200r on 100r red lilac	20.00	15.00
a.		Double surcharge	225.00	250.00
b.		200r on 100r pink	175.00	120.00

Surcharge on No. 137 comes blue to deep black.

Blue Surcharge

138	N3(e)	50r on 20r green	8.00	10.00

Red Surcharge

139	N3(e)	100r on 50r green	18.00	20.00
a.		Blue surcharge	12.50	

The surcharge on 139a exists inverted, and in pair, one without surcharge.

Types of 1894-97

1899

Perf. 5½-7 and 11-11½x5½-7

140	A41a	10r rose & bl	4.50	*12.00*
141	A41a	20r orange & bl	7.50	7.50
142	A41a	50r dk bl & lt bl	9.00	*30.00*
143	A42	100r carmine & blk	16.00	4.50
144	A42a	200r orange & blk	9.00	3.00
145	A42a	300r green & blk	60.00	7.50
		Nos. 140-145 (6)	106.00	64.50

Perf. 8½-9½, 8½-9½x11-11½

146	A41a	10r rose & bl	4.50	3.00
147	A41a	20r orange & bl	15.00	3.00
147A	A41a	50r dk bl & bl	125.00	30.00
148	A42	100r carmine & blk	30.00	1.50
149	A42a	200r orange & blk	15.00	1.00
150	A42a	300r green & blk	60.00	5.00
150A	A43	1000r green & vio	125.00	12.50
		Nos. 146-150A (7)	374.50	56.00

Nos. 140-150A are valued with perfs just cut into the design on one or two sides. Expect some irregularity of the perforations.

Issue of 1890-93 Surcharged in Violet or Magenta

Perf. 11 to 11½, 12½ to 14 and Compound

1899, June 25

151	A38	50r on 20r gray grn	2.00	*3.00*
a.		Double surcharge	125.00	125.00
152	A38	100r on 50r gray grn	2.00	*3.00*
b.		Double surcharge	100.00	100.00
153	A38	300r on 200r pur	7.50	*12.00*
a.		Double surcharge	250.00	—
b.		Pair, one without surcharge	425.00	—
154	A38	500r on 300r ultra, perf. 13	18.00	7.50
a.		500r on 300r gray lilac	30.00	9.00
b.		Pair, one without surcharge	425.00	*500.00*
c.		500r on 300r slate violet	37.50	15.00
155	A38	700r on 500r ol bis	24.00	6.00
a.		Pair, one without surcharge	425.00	—
156	A38	1000r on 700r choc	17.50	6.00
157	A38	1000r on 700r fawn	17.50	6.00
a.		Pair, one without surcharge	425.00	*500.00*
158	A38	2000r on 1000r yel buff	60.00	4.50
a.		2000r on 1000r bister	30.00	4.50
b.		Pair, one without surcharge	425.00	*500.00*
		Nos. 151-158 (8)	148.50	48.00

Types of 1894-97

Perf. 11, 11½, 13 and Compound

1900

159	A41a	50r green	10.00	.60
160	A42	100r rose	20.00	.30
a.		Frame around inner oval	100.00	4.00
161	A42a	200r blue	12.00	.35
		Nos. 159-161 (3)	42.00	1.25

Three types exist of No. 161, all of which have the frame around inner oval.

Cabral Arrives at Brazil — A44

Independence Proclaimed — A45

"Emancipation of Slaves" — A46

Allegory, Republic of Brazil — A47

1900, Jan. 1 Litho. *Perf. 12½*

162	A44	100r red	7.25	5.75
a.		Imperf., pair	400.00	500.00
163	A45	200r green & yel	7.25	5.75
164	A46	500r blue	7.25	5.75
165	A47	700r emerald	7.25	5.75
		Nos. 162-165 (4)	29.00	23.00

Discovery of Brazil, 400th anniversary.

Types of 1894-97

Wmk. (97? or 98?)

1905 *Perf. 11, 11½*

166	A41a	10r rose & bl	5.75	4.00
167	A41a	20r orange & bl	10.00	2.00
168	A41a	50r green	20.00	3.00
169	A42	100r rose	27.50	1.00
170	A42a	200r dark blue	16.00	1.00
171	A42a	300r green & blk	55.00	2.00
		Nos. 166-171 (6)	134.25	13.00

Positive identification of Wmk. 97 or 98 places stamp in specific watermark groups below.

Wmk. 97

166b	A41a	10r rose & blue	30.00	16.00
167b	A41a	20r orange & blue	30.00	8.00
168b	A41a	50r green	55.00	8.00
169b	A42	100r rose	200.00	30.00
170b	A42a	200r dark blue	125.00	4.00
171b	A42a	300r green & blk	375.00	30.00
171A	A43	1000r green & vio	290.00	30.00
		Nos. 166b-171A (7)	1,105.	126.00

Wmk. 98

166c	A41a	10r rose & blue	40.00	40.00
167c	A41a	20r orange & blue	80.00	20.00
168c	A41a	50r green	160.00	30.00
169c	A42	100r rose	80.00	4.00
170c	A42a	200r dark blue	125.00	4.00
171d	A42a	300r green & blk	290.00	30.00
		Nos. 166c-171d (6)	775.00	128.00

Allegory, Pan-American Congress — A48

1906, July 23 Litho. Unwmk.

172	A48	100r carmine rose	30.00	30.00
173	A48	200r blue	75.00	10.00

Third Pan-American Congress.

Aristides Lobo A48a

Benjamin Constant A49

Pedro Alvares Cabral A50

Eduardo Wandenkolk A51

Manuel Deodoro da Fonseca A52

Floriano Peixoto A53

Prudente de Moraes A54

Manuel Ferraz de Campos Salles A55

Francisco de Paula Rodrigues Alves — A56

Liberty Head — A57

A58

A59

1906-16 Engr. *Perf. 12*

174	A48a	10r bluish slate	.90	.20
175	A49	20r aniline vio	.90	.20
176	A50	50r green	.90	.20
a.		Booklet pane of 6 ('08)	40.00	*125.00*
177	A51	100r anil rose	2.00	.20
a.		Imperf. vert., coil ('16)	4.00	.35
b.		Booklet pane of 6 ('08)	80.00	*125.00*
178	A52	200r blue	2.00	.20
a.		Booklet pane of 6 ('08)	60.00	*125.00*
179	A52	200r ultra ('15)	2.00	.35
a.		Imperf. vert., coil ('16)	2.00	.35
180	A53	300r gray blk	3.50	.65
181	A54	400r olive grn	30.00	2.00
182	A55	500r dk violet	6.00	.65
183	A54	600r olive grn ('10)	3.00	1.00
184	A56	700r red brown	6.00	3.00
185	A57	1000r vermilion	32.50	1.00
186	A58	2000r yellow grn	20.00	.65
187	A58	2000r Prus blue ('15)	10.00	1.00
188	A59	5000r carmine rose	8.00	2.00
		Nos. 174-188 (15)	127.70	13.30

Allegorical Emblems: Liberty, Peace, Industry, etc. — A60

1908, July 14

189	A60	100r carmine	24.00	1.75

National Exhibition, Rio de Janeiro.

Emblems of Peace Between Brazil and Portugal A61

1908, July 14

190	A61	100r red	11.00	1.25

Opening of Brazilian ports to foreign commerce, cent. Medallions picture King Carlos I of Portugal and Pres. Affonso Penna of Brazil.

Bonifacio, Bolivar, Hidalgo, O'Higgins, San Martin, Washington — A62

1909

191	A62	200r deep blue	11.00	1.50

For surcharge see No. E1.

Nilo Peçanha A63

Baron of Rio Branco A64

1910, Nov. 15

192	A63	10,000r brown	11.00	3.00

1913-16

193	A64	1000r deep green	5.00	.50
194	A64	1000r slate ('16)	29.00	.65

Cabo Frio — A65

Perf. 11½

1915, Nov. 13 Litho. Wmk. 99

195	A65	100r dk grn, *yelsh*	5.00	4.00

Founding of the town of Cabo Frio, 300th anniversary.

Bay of Guajara A66

1916, Jan. 5

196	A66	100r carmine	11.00	6.00

City of Belem, 300th anniversary.

Revolutionary Flag — A67

1917, Mar. 6

197 A67 100r deep blue 18.00 8.50

Revolution of Pernambuco, Mar. 6, 1817.

Rodrigues Alves — A68

Unwmk.

1917, Aug. 31 Engr. *Perf. 12*

198 A68 5000r red brown 80.00 12.50

Liberty Head
A69 A70

Perf. 12½, 13, 13x13½.

1918-20 Typo. Unwmk.

200	A69	10r orange brn	.50	.25
201	A69	20r slate	.50	.25
202	A69	25r ol gray ('20)	.50	.25
203	A69	50r green	40.00	3.25
204	A70	100r rose	1.75	.25
a.		Imperf., pair	—	
205	A70	300r red orange	19.00	3.25
206	A70	500r dull violet	19.00	3.25
		Nos. 200-206 (7)	81.25	10.75

1918-20 Wmk. 100

207	A69	10r red brown	6.00	1.75
a.		Imperf., pair	—	
207B	A69	20r slate	1.50	1.50
c.		Imperf., pair	—	
208	A69	25r ol gray ('20)	.75	.50
209	A69	50r green	1.50	.50
210	A70	100r rose	50.00	.50
a.		Imperf., pair	—	
211	A70	200r dull blue	6.00	.50
212	A70	300r orange	47.50	5.00
213	A70	500r dull violet	47.50	9.00
214	A70	600r orange	2.50	*9.00*
		Nos. 207-214 (9)	163.25	28.25

Because of the spacing of this watermark, a few stamps in each sheet may show no watermark.

"Education" — A72

1918 Engr. *Perf. 11½*

215	A72	1000r blue	8.00	.30
216	A72	2000r red brown	35.00	10.00
217	A72	5000r dark violet	10.00	10.00
		Nos. 215-217 (3)	53.00	20.30

Watermark note below No. 257 also applies to Nos. 215-217.

See Nos. 233-234, 283-285, 404, 406, 458, 460. For surcharge see No. C30.

Railroad A73 "Industry" A74

"Aviation" A75 Mercury A76

"Navigation" — A77

Perf. 13½x13, 13x13½

1920-22 Typo. Unwmk.

218	A73	10r red violet	1.00	.40
219	A73	20r olive green	1.00	.40
220	A74	25r brown violet	.90	.40
221	A74	50r blue green	1.10	.40
222	A74	50r orange brn ('22)	1.90	.40
223	A75	100r rose red	3.75	.40
224	A75	100r orange ('22)	10.00	.40
225	A75	150r violet ('21)	1.90	.40
226	A75	200r blue	6.00	.40
227	A75	200r rose red ('22)	10.50	.40
228	A76	300r olive gray	17.00	.50
229	A76	400r dull blue ('22)	30.00	3.50
230	A76	500r red brown	24.00	.50
		Nos. 218-230 (13)	109.05	8.50

See Nos. 236-257, 265-266, 268-271, 273-274, 276-281, 302-311, 316-322, 326-340, 357-358, 431-434, 436-441, 461-463B, 467-470, 472-474, 488-490, 492-494. For surcharges see Nos. 356-358, 376-377.

Perf. 11, 11½

Engr. Wmk. 100

231	A77	600r red orange	2.75	.35
232	A77	1000r claret	7.00	.25
a.		Perf. 8½	50.00	7.50
233	A72	2000r dull violet	27.50	.75
234	A72	5000r brown	21.00	9.00
		Nos. 231-234 (4)	58.25	10.35

Nos. 233 and 234 are inscribed "BRASIL CORREIO." Watermark note below No. 257 also applies to Nos. 231-234.

See No. 282.

King Albert of Belgium and President Epitacio Pessoa A78

1920, Sept. 19 Engr. *Perf. 11½x11*

235 A78 100r dull red 1.00 1.00

Visit of the King and Queen of Belgium.

Types of 1920-22 Issue

Perf. 13x13½, 13x12½

1922-29 Typo. Wmk. 100

236	A73	10r red violet	.30	.20
237	A73	20r olive green	.30	.20
238	A75	20r gray violet ('29)	.30	.20
239	A74	25r brown violet	.35	.20
240	A74	50r blue grn	*3.25*	*35.00*
241	A74	50r org brn ('23)	.45	.35
242	A75	100r rose red	22.50	.40
243	A75	100r orange ('26)	.50	.20
244	A75	100r turq grn ('28)	.35	.20
245	A75	150r violet	2.50	.20
246	A75	200r blue	300.00	12.50
247	A75	200r rose red	.40	.20
248	A75	200r ol grn ('28)	2.50	3.00
249	A76	300r olive gray	1.90	.25
250	A76	300r rose red ('29)	.35	.25
251	A76	400r blue	1.90	.20
252	A76	400r orange ('29)	.75	.60
253	A76	500r red brown	7.50	.50
254	A76	500r ultra ('29)	8.50	.20
255	A76	600r brn org ('29)	7.50	3.00
256	A76	700r dull vio ('29)	7.50	1.75
257	A76	1000r turq bl ('29)	9.50	.70
		Nos. 236-257 (22)	379.10	*60.30*

Because of the spacing of the watermark, a few stamps in each sheet show no watermark.

A booklet exists with panes of 6 (2x3), created from the left margin blocks of sheet stamps of Nos. 241, 243, 247, 249 and 253. Once removed from the booklet, they cannot be separately identified.

"Agriculture" — A79

1922 Unwmk. *Perf. 13x13½*

258	A79	40r orange brown	.70	.35
259	A79	80r grnsh blue	.50	*3.25*

See Nos. 263, 267, 275.

Declaration of Ypiranga — A80

Dom Pedro I and Jose Bonifacio — A81

National Exposition and President Pessoa — A82

Unwmk.

1922, Sept. 7 Engr. *Perf. 14*

260	A80	100r ultra	5.00	.75
261	A81	200r red	7.00	.50
262	A82	300r green	7.00	.50
		Nos. 260-262 (3)	19.00	1.75

Cent. of independence and Natl. Exposition of 1922.

Agriculture Type of 1922

Perf. 13½x12

1923 Wmk. 100 Typo.

263 A79 40r orange brown .60 *.60*

Brazilian Army Entering Bahia — A83

Unwmk.

1923, July 12 Litho. *Perf. 13*

264 A83 200r rose 11.00 6.50

Centenary of the taking of Bahia from the Portuguese.

Types of 1920-22 Issues

Perf. 13x13½

1924 Typo. Wmk. 193

265	A73	10r red violet	9.00	6.00
266	A73	20r olive green	10.50	7.00
267	A79	40r orange brown	7.50	2.00
268	A74	50r orange brown	10.00	*30.00*
269	A75	100r orange	7.50	.75
270	A75	200r rose	10.50	.75
271	A76	400r blue	6.75	4.50
		Nos. 265-271 (7)	61.75	*51.00*

Arms of Equatorial Confederation, 1824 — A84

Unwmk.

1924, July 2 Litho. *Perf. 11*

272	A84	200r bl, blk, yel, & red	4.00	2.25
a.		Red omitted	275.00	275.00

Centenary of the Equatorial Confederation.

Chemically bleached fakes of No. 272a are more common than the genuine error. Expertization is advised.

Types of 1920-22 Issues

Perf. 9½ to 13½ and Compound

1924-28 Typo. Wmk. 101

273	A73	10r red violet	.75	.35
274	A73	20r olive gray	.75	.35
275	A79	40r orange brn	.75	.35
276	A74	50r orange brn	.75	.35
277	A75	100r red orange	2.25	.35
278	A75	200r rose	1.00	.35
279	A76	300r ol gray ('25)	10.00	.50
280	A76	400r blue	6.00	.35
281	A76	500r red brown	15.00	.45
		Engr.		
282	A77	600r red orange ('26)	2.50	.35
283	A72	2000r dull vio ('26)	7.50	.75
284	A72	5000r brown ('26)	22.50	.70
285	A72	10,000r rose ('28)	30.00	1.50
		Nos. 273-285 (13)	99.75	6.70

Nos. 283-285 are inscribed "BRASIL CORREIO."

Ruy Barbosa — A85

1925 Wmk. 100 *Perf. 11½*

286 A85 1000r claret 4.25 1.50

1926 Wmk. 101

287 A85 1000r claret 1.75 .35

"Justice" — A86

Scales of Justice and Map of Brazil — A87

Perf. 13½x13

1927, Aug. 11 Typo. Wmk. 206

288	A86	100r deep blue	1.10	.65
289	A87	200r rose	.90	.35

Founding of the law courses, cent.

Liberty Holding Coffee Leaves — A88

1928, Feb. 5

290	A88	100r blue green	1.75	.80
291	A88	200r carmine	1.10	.50
292	A88	300r olive black	9.00	.40
		Nos. 290-292 (3)	11.85	1.70

Introduction of the coffee tree in Brazil, bicent.

Official Stamps of 1919 Surcharged in Red or Black

Perf. 11, 11½

1928 Wmk. 100 Engr.

293	O3	700r on 500r org	6.25	6.00
a.		Inverted surcharge	175.00	175.00
294	O3	1000r on 100r rose red (Bk)	4.25	.60
295	O3	2000r on 200r dull bl	6.25	1.00
296	O3	5000r on 50r grn	6.25	1.25
297	O3	10,000r on 10r ol grn	30.00	2.50
		Nos. 293-297 (5)	53.00	11.35

#293-297 were used for ordinary postage.

Stamps in the outer rows of the sheets are often without watermark.

Ruy Barbosa — A89

Perf. 9, 9½x11, 11, and Compound

1929 **Wmk. 101**

300 A89 5000r blue violet		20.00	.75

See #405, 459. For surcharge see #C29.

Types of 1920-21 Issue

Perf. 13½x12½

1929	**Typo.**	**Wmk. 218**	
302 A75	20r gray violet	.35	.20
303 A75	50r red brown	.35	.20
304 A75	100r turq green	.55	.20
305 A75	200r olive green	22.50	5.00
306 A76	300r rose red	1.10	.20
307 A76	400r orange	1.25	*2.00*
308 A76	500r ultra	13.00	.45
309 A76	600r brown org	15.00	1.25
310 A76	700r dp violet	4.25	.20
311 A76	1000r turq blue	7.50	.20
	Nos. 302-311 (10)	65.85	9.90

Wmk. 218 exists both in vertical alignment and in echelon.

Wmk. in echelon

302a A75	20r	.50	.35
303a A75	50r	100.00	60.00
306a A76	300r	1.25	1.25
308a A76	500r	125.00	40.00
311a A76	1000r	10.00	10.00

Architectural Fantasies
A90 A91

Architectural Fantasy — A92

Perf. 13x13½

1930, June 20		**Wmk. 206**	
312 A90	100r turq blue	2.00	1.25
313 A91	200r olive gray	3.25	.80
314 A92	300r rose red	5.50	1.25
	Nos. 312-314 (3)	10.75	3.30

Fourth Pan-American Congress of Architects and Exposition of Architecture.

Types of 1920-21 Issues

1930	**Wmk. 221**	***Perf. 13x12½***	
316 A75	20r gray violet	.40	.35
317 A75	50r red brown	.40	.35
318 A75	100r turq blue	.80	.35
319 A75	200r olive green	4.75	1.25
320 A76	300r rose red	.95	.35
321 A76	500r ultra	2.40	.35
322 A76	1000r turq blue	40.00	1.50
	Nos. 316-322 (7)	49.70	4.50

Imperforates

From 1930 to 1947, imperforate or partly perforated sheets of nearly all commemorative and some definitive issues were obtainable.

Types of 1920-29 Issue

Perf. 11, 13½x13, 13x12½

1931-34	**Typo.**	**Wmk. 222**	
326 A75	10r deep brown	.25	.25
327 A75	20r gray violet	.25	.25
328 A74	25r brn vio ('34)	.25	1.25
330 A75	50r blue green	.25	.25
331 A75	50r red brown	.25	.25
332 A75	100r orange	.50	.25
334 A75	200r dp carmine	.75	.40
335 A76	300r olive green	1.00	.25
336 A76	400r ultra	1.40	.25
337 A76	500r red brown	6.00	.25
338 A76	600r brown org	6.00	.25
339 A76	700r deep violet	6.00	.25
340 A76	1000r turq blue	21.00	.25
	Nos. 326-340 (13)	43.90	4.40

Getulio Vargas and Joao Pessoa
A93

Vargas and Pessoa
A94

Oswaldo Aranha
A95 A96

Antonio Carlos
A97

Pessoa
A98

Vargas — A99

Unwmk.

1931, Apr. 29	**Litho.**	***Perf. 14***	
342 A93	10r + 10r lt bl	.20	*4.50*
343 A93	20r + 20r yel brn	.20	*3.25*
344 A95	50r + 50r bl grn, red & yel	.20	.20
a.	Red missing at left	.90	.90
345 A93	100r + 50r orange	.55	.45
346 A93	200r + 100r green	.55	.45
347 A94	300r + 150r multi	.55	.45
348 A93	400r + 200r dp rose	1.90	1.00
349 A93	500r + 250r dk bl	1.40	1.10
350 A93	600r + 300r brn vio	.95	*6.50*
351 A94	700r + 350r multi	1.75	.90
352 A96	1000r + 500r brt grn, red & yel	3.75	.55
353 A97	2000r + 1000r gray blk & red	7.50	.80
354 A98	5000r + 2500r blk & red	32.50	9.00
355 A99	10000r + 5000r brt grn & yel	80.00	17.50
	Nos. 342-355 (14)	132.00	46.65

Revolution of Oct. 3, 1930. Prepared as semi-postal stamps, Nos. 342-355 were sold as ordinary postage stamps with stated surtax ignored.

Nos. 306, 320 and 250 Surcharged

Wmk. E U BRASIL Multiple (218)

1931, July 20		***Perf. 13½x12½***	
356 A76	200r on 300r rose red	1.75	.90
a.	Wmk. in echelon	17.50	17.50
b.	Inverted surcharge	40.00	

Perf. 13x12½

Wmk. 221

357 A76	200r on 300r rose red	.30	.20
a.	Inverted surcharge	45.00	45.00

Perf. 13½x12½

Wmk. 100

358 A76	200r on 300r rose red	60.00	60.00

Map of South America Showing Meridian of Tordesillas — A100

Joao Ramalho and Tibiriça
A101

Martim Affonso de Souza
A102

King John III of Portugal
A103

Disembarkation of M. A. de Souza at Sao Vicente — A104

Wmk. 222

1932, June 3	**Typo.**	***Perf. 13***	
359 A100	20r dk violet	.40	.20
360 A101	100r black	.45	.35
361 A102	200r purple	1.25	.40
362 A103	600r red brown	2.10	2.25

Engr.

Wmk. 101

Perf. 9½, 11, 9½x11

363 A104	700r ultra	3.25	2.75
	Nos. 359-363 (5)	7.45	5.95

1st colonization of Brazil at Sao Vicente, in 1532, under the hereditary captaincy of Martim Affonso de Souza.

Revolutionary Issue

Map of Brazil — A105

Soldier and Flag — A106

Allegory: Freedom, Justice, Equality
A107

Soldier's Head
A108

"LEX" and Sword
A109

Symbolical of Law and Order — A110

Symbolical of Justice — A111

Perf. 11½

1932, Sept.	**Litho.**	**Unwmk.**	
364 A105	100r brown org	.55	2.40
365 A106	200r dk car	.45	.85
366 A107	300r gray green	2.40	4.25
367 A108	400r dark blue	8.75	8.75
368 A105	500r blk brn	8.75	8.75
369 A107	600r red	8.75	8.75
370 A106	700r violet	4.25	*8.75*
371 A108	1000r orange	2.10	*8.75*
372 A109	2000r dark brn	17.00	*24.00*
373 A110	5000r yellow grn	21.00	*40.00*
374 A111	10000r plum	24.00	*45.00*
	Nos. 364-374 (11)	98.00	160.25

Issued by the revolutionary forces in the state of Sao Paulo during the revolt of September, 1932. Subsequently the stamps were recognized by the Federal Government and placed in general use.

Excellent counterfeits of Nos. 373 and 374 exist. Favor cancels, applied at a later date, abound.

City of Vassouras and Illuminated Memorial — A112

Wmk. 222

1933, Jan. 15	**Typo.**	***Perf. 12***	
375 A112	200r rose red	1.40	.90

City of Vassouras founding, cent.

Nos. 306, 320 Surcharged

Perf. 13½x12½

1933, July 28		**Wmk. 218**	
376 A76	200r on 300r rose red	1.00	1.00
a.	Wmk. 218 in echelon (No. 306a)	15.00	15.00
b.	Wmk. 100 (No. 250)	125.00	125.00

Perf. 13x12½

Wmk. 221

377 A76	200r on 300r rose red	.45	.45
a.	Inverted surcharge	35.00	
b.	Double surcharge	35.00	

Religious Symbols and Inscriptions — A113

Wmk. 222

1933, Sept. 3	**Typo.**	***Perf. 13***	
378 A113	200r dark red	.90	.75

1st Natl. Eucharistic Congress in Brazil.

"Flag of the Race" A114

1933, Aug. 18
379 A114 200r deep red .90 .75

The raising of the "Flag of the Race" and the 441st anniv. of the sailing of Columbus from Palos, Spain, Aug. 3, 1492.

Republic Figure, Flags of Brazil and Argentina — A115

Wmk. 101
1933, Oct. 7 Engr. *Perf. 11½*
380 A115 200r blue .35 .25

Thick Laid Paper

1933, Dec. Wmk. 236 *Perf. 11, 11½*
381 A115 400r green 1.50 1.25
382 A115 600r brt rose 4.75 5.25
383 A115 1000r lt violet 7.25 4.75
Nos. 380-383 (4) 13.85 11.50

Visit of President Justo of the Argentina to Brazil, Oct. 2-7, 1933.

Allegory: "Faith and Energy" — A116

Allegory of Flight — A117

1933 Typo. Wmk. 222
384 A116 200r dark red .55 .20
385 A116 200r dark violet .70 .20

See Nos. 435, 471, 491.

Wmk. 236
1934, Apr. 15 Engr. *Perf. 12*
386 A117 200r blue .80 .50

1st Natl. Aviation Congress at Sao Paulo.

A118

Wmk. 222
1934, May 12 Typo. *Perf. 11*
387 A118 200r dark olive .40 .25
388 A118 400r carmine 2.25 2.25
389 A118 700r ultra 2.40 2.25
390 A118 1000r orange 5.75 1.00
Nos. 387-390 (4) 10.80 5.75

7th Intl. Fair at Rio de Janeiro.

Christ of Corcovado A119

1934, Oct. 20
392 A119 300r dark red 3.00 3.00
a. Tete beche pair 12.00 *12.00*
393 A119 700r ultra 11.00 11.00
a. Tete beche pair 32.50 32.50

Visit of Eugenio Cardinal Pacelli, later Pope Pius XII, to Brazil.

The three printings of Nos. 392-393, distinguishable by shades, sell for different prices.

José de Anchieta A120

Thick Laid Paper

1934, Nov. 8 Wmk. 236 *Perf. 11, 12*
394 A120 200r yellow brown .90 .60
395 A120 300r violet .75 .35
396 A120 700r blue 2.75 *3.00*
397 A120 1000r lt green 5.50 1.75
Nos. 394-397 (4) 9.90 5.70

Jose de Anchieta, S.J. (1534-1597), Portuguese missionary and "father of Brazilian literature."

A121

"Brazil" and "Uruguay" — A122

Wmk. 222
1935, Jan. 8 Typo. *Perf. 11*
398 A121 200r orange 1.10 .40
399 A122 300r yellow 1.40 1.25
400 A122 700r ultra 5.00 *8.00*
401 A121 1000r dk violet 12.50 8.00
Nos. 398-401 (4) 20.00 17.65

Visit of President Terra of Uruguay.

View of Town of Igarassu A123

1935, July 1
402 A123 200r maroon & brn 1.60 .55
403 A123 300r vio & olive brn 1.60 .45

Captaincy of Pernambuco founding, 400th anniv.

Types of 1918-29
Thick Laid Paper
Perf. 9½, 11, 12, 12x11

1934-36 Engr. Wmk. 236
404 A72 2000r violet 12.50 .60
405 A89 5000r blue vio ('36) 14.00 1.25
406 A72 10000r claret ('36) 15.00 1.75
Nos. 404-406 (3) 41.50 3.60

No. 404 is inscribed "BRASIL CORREIO."

Revolutionist A124

Bento Gonçalves da Silva — A125

Duke of Caxias A126

Perf. 11, 12
1935, Sept. 20-1936, Jan.
407 A124 200r black 1.10 .60
408 A124 300r rose lake 1.10 .60
409 A125 700r dull blue 4.50 4.50
410 A126 1000r light violet 5.00 1.60
Nos. 407-410 (4) 11.70 7.30

Centenary of the "Ragged" Revolution.

Federal District Coat of Arms A127

Wmk. 222
1935, Oct. 19 Typo. *Perf. 11*
411 A127 200r blue 4.00 4.00

8th Intl. Sample Fair held at Rio de Janeiro.

Coutinho's Ship — A128

Arms of Fernandes Coutinho — A129

1935, Oct. 25
412 A128 300r maroon 3.00 1.25
413 A129 700r turq blue 5.00 3.75

400th anniversary of the establishment of the first Portuguese colony at Espirito Santo by Vasco Fernandes Coutinho.

Gavea, Rock near Rio de Janeiro A130

1935, Oct. 12 Wmk. 245 *Perf. 11*
414 A130 300r brown & vio 2.75 1.50
415 A130 300r blk & turq bl 2.75 1.50
416 A130 300r Prus bl & ultra 2.75 1.50
417 A130 300r crimson & blk 2.75 1.50
Nos. 414-417 (4) 11.00 6.00

"Child's Day," Oct. 12.

Viscount of Cairu — A131

Perf. 11, 12x11
1936, Jan. 20 Engr. Wmk. 236
418 A131 1200r violet 10.00 3.50

Jose da Silva Lisboa, Viscount of Cairu (1756-1835).

View of Cametá A132

1936, Feb. 26 *Perf. 11, 12*
419 A132 200r brown orange 1.75 1.25
420 A132 300r green 1.75 1.00

300th anniversary of the founding of the city of Cameta, Dec. 24, 1635.

Coining Press A133

Thick Laid Paper

1936, Mar. 24 *Perf. 11*
421 A133 300r pur brn, *cr* 1.25 1.00

1st Numismatic Cong. at Sao Paulo, Mar., 1936.

Carlos Gomes — A134

"Il Guarany" — A135

Thick Laid Paper

1936, July 11 *Perf. 11, 11x12*
422 A134 300r dull rose 1.00 .35
423 A134 300r black brown 1.00 .35
424 A135 700r ocher 3.25 1.75
425 A135 700r blue 3.75 2.25
Nos. 422-425 (4) 9.00 4.70

Birth cent. of Antonio Carlos Gomes, who composed the opera "Il Guarany."

Scales of Justice — A136

Wmk. 222
1936, July 4 Typo. *Perf. 11*
426 A136 300r rose 2.00 .65

First National Judicial Congress.

Federal District Coat of Arms A137

1936, Nov. 13 Typo. Wmk. 249

427	A137	200r rose red	1.25	.55

Ninth International Sample Fair held at Rio de Janeiro.

Eucharistic Congress Seal — A138

1936, Dec. 17 Wmk. 245 *Perf. 11½*

428	A138	300r grn, yel, bl & blk	1.25	.50

2nd Natl. Eucharistic Congress in Brazil.

Botafogo Bay A139

Thick Laid Paper

Wmk. 236

1937, Jan. 2 Engr. *Perf. 11*

429	A139	700r blue	1.10	.45
430	A139	700r black	1.10	.45

Birth cent. of Francisco Pereira Passos, engineer who planned the modern city of Rio de Janeiro.

Types of 1920-21, 1933

Perf. 11, 11½ and Compound

1936-37 Typo. Wmk. 249

431	A75	10r deep brown	.20	.20
432	A75	20r dull violet	.20	.20
433	A75	50r blue green	.20	.20
434	A75	100r orange	.25	.20
435	A116	200r dk violet	1.10	.20
436	A76	300r olive green	.25	.20
437	A76	400r ultra	1.10	.20
438	A76	500r lt brown	1.75	.20
439	A76	600r brn org ('37)	4.00	.20
440	A76	700r deep violet	7.00	.20
441	A76	1000r turq blue	7.75	.20
		Nos. 431-441 (11)	23.80	2.20

Massed Flags and Star of Esperanto A140

1937, Jan. 19

442	A140	300r green	1.75	.50

Ninth Brazilian Esperanto Congress.

Bay of Rio de Janeiro A141

1937, June 9 Unwmk. *Perf. 12½*

443	A141	300r orange red & blk	1.00	.50
444	A141	700r blue & dk brn	2.50	.50

2nd South American Radio Communication Conf. held in Rio, June 7-19.

Globe — A142

Perf. 11, 12

1937, Sept. 4 Wmk. 249

445	A142	300r green	1.50	.50

50th anniversary of Esperanto.

Monroe Palace, Rio de Janeiro A143

Botanical Garden, Rio de Janeiro — A144

1937, Sept. 30 Unwmk. *Perf. 12½*

446	A143	200r lt brn & bl	.75	.35
447	A144	300r org & ol grn	.75	.35
448	A143	2000r grn & cerise	7.50	*12.50*
449	A144	10000r lake & indigo	70.00	60.00
		Nos. 446-449 (4)	79.00	73.20

Brig. Gen. Jose da Silva Paes — A145

Eagle and Shield — A146

1937, Oct. 11 Wmk. 249 *Perf. 11½*

450	A145	300r blue	.85	.35

Bicentenary of Rio Grande do Sul.

1937, Dec. 2 Typo. *Perf. 11*

451	A146	400r dark blue	.85	.35

150th anniversary of the US Constitution.

Bags of Brazilian Coffee A147

Frame Engraved, Center Typographed

1938, Jan. 17 Unwmk. *Perf. 12½*

452	A147	1200r multicolored	6.25	.45

Arms of Olinda A148

Perf. 11, 11x11½

1938, Jan. 24 Engr. Wmk. 249

453	A148	400r violet	.80	.35

4th cent. of the founding of the city of Olinda.

Independence Memorial, Ypiranga A149

1938, Jan. 24 Typo. *Perf. 11*

454	A149	400r brown olive	1.00	.35

Proclamation of Brazil's independence by Dom Pedro, Sept. 7, 1822.

Iguaçu Falls — A150

Perf. 12½

1938, Jan. 10 Unwmk. Engr.

455	A150	1000r sepia & yel brn	2.50	.85
456	A150	5000r ol blk & grn	27.50	20.00

Couto de Magalhaes A151

Perf. 11, 11x11½

1938, Mar. 17 Wmk. 249

457	A151	400r dull green	.80	.35

General Couto de Magalhaes (1837-1898), statesman, soldier, explorer, writer, developer.

Types of 1918-38

Perf. 11, 12x11, 12x11½, 12

1938 Engr. Wmk. 249

458	A72	2000r blue violet	12.00	.30
459	A89	5000r violet blue	45.00	.50
a.		5000r deep blue	37.50	.50
460	A72	10000r rose lake	50.00	1.50
		Nos. 458-460 (3)	107.00	2.30

No. 458 is inscribed "BRASIL CORREIO."

Types of 1920-22

1938 Wmk. 245 Typo. *Perf. 11*

461	A75	50r blue green	1.10	1.00
462	A75	100r orange	3.25	1.00
463	A76	300r olive green	1.10	3.00
463A	A76	400r ultra	225.00	150.00
463B	A76	500r red brown	1.10	*60.00*
		Nos. 461-463B (5)	231.55	215.00

National Archives Building A152

1938, May 20 Wmk. 249

464	A152	400r brown	.75	.35

Centenary of National Archives.

Souvenir Sheets

Sir Rowland Hill — A153

1938, Oct. 22 *Imperf.*

465	A153	Sheet of 10	20.00	20.00
a.		400r dull green, single stamp	1.25	1.25

Brazilian Intl. Philatelic Exposition (Brapex).

Issued in sheets measuring 106x118mm. A few perforated sheets exist.

President Vargas — A154

1938, Nov. 10 *Perf. 11*

Without Gum

466	A154	Sheet of 10	27.50	27.50
a.		400r slate blue, single stamp	1.75	1.75

Constitution of Brazil, set up by President Vargas, Nov. 10, 1937. Size: 113x135½mm.

Types of 1920-33

1939 Typo. Wmk. 256 *Perf. 11*

467	A75	10r red brown	.90	.90
468	A75	20r dull violet	.90	.30
469	A75	50r blue green	.90	.30
470	A75	100r yellow org	1.25	.30
471	A116	200r dk violet	1.60	.30
472	A76	400r ultra	3.00	.30
473	A76	600r dull orange	3.00	.30
474	A76	1000r turq blue	20.00	.30
		Nos. 467-474 (8)	31.55	3.00

View of Rio de Janeiro — A155

View of Santos — A156

1939, June 14 Engr. Wmk. 249

475	A155	1200r dull violet	2.25	.25

1939, Aug. 23

476	A156	400r dull blue	.50	.40

Centenary of founding of Santos.

Chalice Vine and Blossoms — A157

Eucharistic Congress Seal — A158

1939, Aug. 23

477	A157	400r green	1.50	.35

1st South American Botanical Congress held in January, 1938.

1939, Sept. 3

478	A158	400r rose red	.60	.35

Third National Eucharistic Congress.

Duke of Caxias, Army Patron — A159

1939, Sept. 12 Photo. *Rouletted*

479	A159	400r deep ultra	.60	.35

Issued for Soldiers' Day.

A159a

A159b

A159d

A159c

Designs: 400r, George Washington. 800r, Emperor Pedro II. 1200r, Grover Cleveland. 1600r, Statue of Friendship, given by US.

Unwmk.

1939, Oct. 7 Engr. *Perf. 12*

480	A159a	400r yellow orange	.70	.20
481	A159b	800r dark green	.35	.20
482	A159c	1200r rose car	.70	.20
483	A159d	1600r dark blue	.70	.20
		Nos. 480-483 (4)	2.45	.80

New York World's Fair.

Benjamin Constant A160

Fonseca on Horseback A161

Manuel Deodoro da Fonseca and President Vargas A162

Wmk. 249

1939, Nov. 15 Photo. *Rouletted*

484	A160	400r deep green	.45	.35
485	A162	1200r chocolate	1.10	.35

Engr. *Perf. 11*

486	A161	800r gray black	.65	.35
		Nos. 484-486 (3)	2.20	1.05

Proclamation of the Republic, 50th anniv.

President Roosevelt, President Vargas and Map of the Americas A163

1940, Apr. 14

487	A163	400r slate blue	1.00	.40

Pan American Union, 50th anniversary.

Types of 1920-33

1940-41 Typo. Wmk. 264 *Perf. 11*

488	A75	10r red brown	.80	.80
489	A75	20r dull violet	.80	.80
489A	A75	50r blue grn ('41)	1.50	*1.75*
490	A75	100r yellow org	2.50	.50
491	A116	200r violet	7.50	.50
492	A76	400r ultra	7.50	.25
493	A76	600r dull orange	10.00	.50
494	A76	1000r turq blue	22.50	.50
		Nos. 488-494 (8)	53.10	*5.60*

Map of Brazil — A164

1940, Sept. 7 Engr.

495	A164	400r carmine	.50	.30
a.		Unwmkd.	50.00	30.00

9th Brazilian Congress of Geography held at Florianopolis.

Victoria Regia Water Lily — A165

President Vargas — A166

Relief Map of Brazil — A167

1940, Oct. 30 Wmk. 249 *Perf. 11*

Without Gum

496	A165	1000r dull violet	1.40	1.75
a.		Sheet of 10	14.50	*27.50*
497	A166	5000r red	10.00	10.00
a.		Sheet of 10	125.00	*175.00*
498	A167	10,000r slate blue	15.00	7.50
a.		Sheet of 10	160.00	*175.00*
		Nos. 496-498 (3)	26.40	19.25

New York World's Fair.

All three sheets exist unwatermarked and also with papermaker's watermark of large globe and "AMERICA BANK" in sheet. A few imperforate sheets also exist.

Joaquim Machado de Assis — A168

Pioneers and Buildings of Porto Alegre — A169

1940, Nov. 1

499	A168	400r black	.60	.25

Birth centenary of Joaquim Maria Machado de Assis, poet and novelist.

1940, Nov. 2 Wmk. 264

500	A169	400r green	.40	.30

Colonization of Porto Alegre, bicent.

Proclamation of King John IV of Portugal — A173

1940, Dec. 1 Wmk. 249

501	A173	1200r blue black	1.75	.50

800th anniv. of Portuguese independence and 300th anniv. of the restoration of the monarchy.

No. 501 was also printed on paper with papermaker's watermark of large globe and "AMERICA BANK." Unwatermarked copies are from these sheets. Value of unwatermarked stamps, $125.

Brazilian Flags and Head of Liberty — A175

Wmk. 256

1940, Dec. 18 Engr. *Perf. 11*

502	A175	400r dull violet	.60	.20
b.		Unwmkd.	22.50	22.50

Wmk. 245

502A	A175	400r dull violet	75.00	50.00

10th anniv. of the inauguration of President Vargas.

SEMI-POSTAL STAMPS

In 1980 three stamps that were intended to be semi-postals were issued as postage stamps at the total combined face value. See Nos. 1681-1683.

National Philatelic Exhibition Issue

SP1

Wmk. Coat of Arms in Sheet (236)

1934, Sept. 16 Engr. *Imperf.*

Thick Paper

B1	SP1	200r + 100r dp claret	1.00	*2.50*
B2	SP1	300r + 100r ver	1.00	*2.50*
B3	SP1	700r + 100r brt bl	6.00	*22.50*
B4	SP1	1000r + 100r blk	7.50	*22.50*
		Nos. B1-B4 (4)	15.50	*50.00*

The surtax was to help defray the expenses of the exhibition. Issued in sheets of 60, inscribed "EXPOSICAO FILATELICA NACIONAL."

Red Cross Nurse and Soldier SP2

Wmk. 222

1935, Sept. 19 Typo. *Perf. 11*

B5	SP2	200r + 100r pur & red	1.75	1.25
B6	SP2	300r + 100r ol brn & red	2.00	.90
B7	SP2	700r + 100r turq bl & red	12.50	7.00
		Nos. B5-B7 (3)	16.25	9.15

3rd Pan-American Red Cross Conf. Exist imperf.

Three Wise Men and Star of Bethlehem — SP3

Angel and Child — SP4

Southern Cross and Child — SP5

Mother and Child — SP6

Wmk. 249

1939-40 Litho. *Perf. 10½*

B8	SP3	100r + 100r chlky bl & bl blk	.75	.75
a.		Horiz. or vert. pair, imperf. between	35.00	
B9	SP4	200r + 100r brt grnsh bl	1.10	1.00
a.		Horizontal pair, imperf. between	35.00	
B10	SP5	400r + 200r ol grn & ol	.80	.50
B11	SP6	1200r + 400r crim & brn red	3.25	1.50
a.		Vertical pair, imperf. between	35.00	
		Nos. B8-B11 (4)	5.90	3.75

Dates of issue: #B8, 12/20/39; #B9-B11, 2/26/40.

Surtax for charitable institutions.

For surcharges see Nos. C55-C59.

AIR POST STAMPS

Nos. O14-O29 Surcharged

1927, Dec. 28 Unwmk. *Perf. 12*

C1	O2	50r on 10r	.45	.35
a.		Inverted surcharge	325.00	
b.		Top ornaments missing	75.00	
C2	O2	200r on 1000r	2.25	*4.00*
a.		Double surcharge	325.00	
C3	O2	200r on 2000r	1.40	*7.50*
a.		Double surcharge	750.00	
b.		Double surcharge, one inverted	750.00	
C4	O2	200r on 5000r	1.50	1.00
a.		Double surcharge	325.00	—
b.		Double surcharge, one inverted	350.00	
c.		Triple surcharge	450.00	
C5	O2	300r on 500r	1.50	2.00
C6	O2	300r on 600r	.85	.90
b.		Pair, one without surch.	—	
C6A	O2	500r on 10r	375.00	425.00
C7	O2	500r on 50r	1.50	.65
a.		Double surcharge	300.00	
C8	O2	1000r on 20r	1.00	.45
a.		Double surcharge	300.00	—
C9	O2	2000r on 100r	2.25	1.40
a.		Pair, one without surcharge	—	
b.		Double surcharge	300.00	
C10	O2	2000r on 200r	3.50	1.50
C11	O2	2000r on 10,000r	2.25	.50
C12	O2	5000r on 20,000r	7.50	3.00
C13	O2	5000r on 50,000r	7.50	3.00
C14	O2	5000r on 100,000r	32.50	27.50
C15	O2	10,000r on 500,000r	35.00	20.00
C16	O2	10,000r on 1,000,000r	45.00	37.50
		Nos. C1-C6,C7-C16 (16)	145.95	111.25

Nos. C1, C1b, C7, C8 and C9 have small diamonds printed over the numerals in the upper corners.

Monument to de Gusmao — AP1

Santos-Dumont's Airship — AP2

Augusto Severo's Airship "Pax" — AP3

Santos-Dumont's Biplane "14 Bis" — AP4

Ribeiro de Barros's Seaplane "Jahu" — AP5

Perf. 11, 12½x13, 13x13½

1929 Typo. Wmk. 206

C17	AP1	50r blue grn	.35	.20
C18	AP2	200r red	1.40	.20
C19	AP3	300r brt blue	1.75	.20
C20	AP4	500r red violet	2.50	.20
C21	AP5	1000r orange brn	9.00	.40
		Nos. C17-C21 (5)	15.00	1.20

See #C32-C36. For surcharges see #C26-C27.

Bartholomeu de Gusmao AP6

Augusto Severo AP7

Alberto Santos-Dumont AP8

Perf. 9, 11 and Compound

1929-30 Engr. Wmk. 101

C22	AP6	2000r lt green ('30)	9.50	.50
C23	AP7	5000r carmine	9.50	1.25
C24	AP8	10,000r olive grn	9.50	1.75
		Nos. C22-C24 (3)	28.50	3.50

Nos. C23-C24 exist imperf.

See Nos. C37, C40.

Allegory: Airmail Service between Brazil and the US — AP9

1929 Typo. Wmk. 206

C25	AP9	3000r violet	10.00	1.75

Exists imperf. See Nos. C38, C41. For surcharge see No. C28.

Nos. C18-C19 Surcharged in Blue or Red

1931, Aug. 16 *Perf. 12½x13½*

C26	AP2	2500r on 200r (Bl)	30.00	25.00
C27	AP3	5000r on 300r (R)	35.00	30.00

No. C25 Surcharged

1931, Sept. 2 *Perf. 11*

C28	AP9	2500r on 3000r vio	27.50	*27.50*
a.		Inverted surcharge	160.00	—
b.		Surch. on front and back	160.00	

Regular Issues of 1928-29 Surcharged

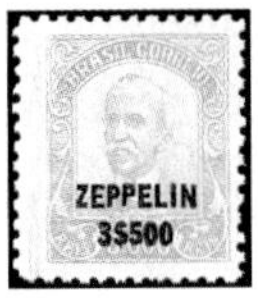

1932, May Wmk. 101 *Perf. 11, 11½*

C29	A89	3500r on 5000r gray lil	22.50	22.50
C30	A72	7000r on 10,000r rose	22.50	22.50
b.		Horiz. pair, imperf. between	*750.00*	

Imperforates

Since 1933, imperforate or partly perforated sheets of nearly all of the airmail issues have become available.

Flag and Airplane AP10

Wmk. 222

1933, June 7 Typo. *Perf. 11*

C31	AP10	3500r grn, yel & dk bl	6.00	2.00

See Nos. C39, C42.

1934 Wmk. 222

C32	AP1	50r blue grn	1.75	1.75
C33	AP2	200r red	2.25	.65
C34	AP3	300r brt blue	5.50	1.90
C35	AP4	500r red violet	2.25	.65
C36	AP5	1000r orange brn	7.50	.65
		Nos. C32-C36 (5)	19.25	5.60

1934 Wmk. 236 Engr. *Perf. 12x11*

Thick Laid Paper

C37	AP6	2000r lt green	4.50	1.50

Types of 1929, 1933

Perf. 11, 11½, 12

1937-40 Typo. Wmk. 249

C38	AP9	3000r violet	17.50	1.75
C39	AP10	3500r grn, yel & dk bl	3.00	1.50
		Engr.		
C40	AP7	5000r ver ('40)	4.00	.75
		Nos. C38-C40 (3)	24.50	4.00

Watermark note after #501 also applies to #C40.

Types of 1929-33

Perf. 11, 11½x12

1939-40 Typo. Wmk. 256

C41	AP9	3000r violet	1.50	.60
C42	AP10	3500r bl, dl grn & yel ('40)	1.50	.50

SPECIAL DELIVERY STAMPS

No. 191 Surcharged

1930 Unwmk. *Perf. 12*

E1	A62	1000r on 200r dp blue	6.00	1.75
a.		Inverted surcharge	500.00	

POSTAGE DUE STAMPS

D1

D2

1889 Unwmk. Typo. *Rouletted*

J1	D1	10r carmine	2.00	1.40
J2	D1	20r carmine	2.75	2.00
J3	D1	50r carmine	5.00	4.00
J4	D1	100r carmine	2.00	1.40
J5	D1	200r carmine	55.00	15.00
J6	D1	300r carmine	6.00	*8.00*
J7	D1	500r carmine	6.00	*8.00*
J8	D1	700r carmine	10.00	*14.00*
J9	D1	1000r carmine	10.00	10.00
		Nos. J1-J9 (9)	98.75	63.80

Counterfeits are common.

1890

J10	D1	10r orange	.60	.30
J11	D1	20r ultra	.60	.30
J12	D1	50r olive	1.25	.30
J13	D1	200r magenta	6.00	.60
J14	D1	300r blue green	3.00	1.50
J15	D1	500r slate	4.00	3.00
J16	D1	700r purple	4.50	*7.50*
J17	D1	1000r dk violet	5.50	5.00
		Nos. J10-J17 (8)	25.45	18.50

Counterfeits are common.

Perf. 11 to 11½, 12½ to 14 and Compound

1895-1901

J18	D2	10r dk blue ('01)	2.00	1.25
J19	D2	20r yellow grn	8.00	3.00
J20	D2	50r yellow grn ('01)	10.00	5.50
J21	D2	100r brick red	6.25	1.25
J22	D2	200r violet	6.00	.60
a.		200r gray lilac ('98)	12.00	2.00
J23	D2	300r dull blue	3.50	2.25
J24	D2	2000r brown	12.00	12.00
		Nos. J18-J24 (7)	47.75	25.85

1906 Wmk. 97

J25	D2	100r brick red	8.00	3.00

Wmk. (97? or 98?)

J26	D2	200r violet	7.50	1.25
a.		Wmk. 97	275.00	85.00
b.		Wmk. 98	12.50	50.00

D3

D4

1906-10 Unwmk. Engr. *Perf. 12*

J28	D3	10r slate	.20	.20
J29	D3	20r brt violet	.20	.20
J30	D3	50r dk green	.25	.20
J31	D3	100r carmine	1.75	.60
J32	D3	200r dp blue	1.00	.30
J33	D3	300r gray blk	.40	.60
J34	D3	400r olive grn	1.00	.90
J35	D3	500r dk violet	35.00	35.00
J36	D3	600r violet ('10)	1.25	*3.00*
J37	D3	700r red brown	35.00	30.00
J38	D3	1000r red	1.50	*3.00*
J39	D3	2000r green	4.75	5.50
J40	D3	5000r choc ('10)	1.50	*14.00*
		Nos. J28-J40 (13)	83.80	93.50

Perf. 12½, 11, 11x10½

1919-23 Typo.

J41	D4	5r red brown	.20	.25
J42	D4	10r violet	.25	.25
J43	D4	20r olive gray	.20	.20
J44	D4	50r green ('23)	.20	.20
J45	D4	100r red	1.10	1.00
J46	D4	200r blue	5.25	1.50
J47	D4	400r brown ('23)	1.40	1.25
		Nos. J41-J47 (7)	8.60	4.65

Perf. 12½, 12½x13½

1924-35 Wmk. 100

J48	D4	5r red brown	.25	.20
J49	D4	100r red	.75	.30
J50	D4	200r slate bl ('29)	1.00	.50
J51	D4	400r dp brn ('29)	1.50	1.00
J52	D4	600r dk vio ('29)	1.75	1.10
J53	D4	600r orange ('35)	.75	.50
		Nos. J48-J53 (6)	6.00	3.60

1924 Wmk. 193 *Perf. 11x10½*

J54	D4	100r red	45.00	45.00
J55	D4	200r slate blue	5.50	5.50

Perf. 11x10½, 13x13½

1925-27 Wmk. 101

J56	D4	20r olive gray	.20	.20
J57	D4	100r red	1.05	.30
J58	D4	200r slate blue	3.25	.35
J59	D4	400r brown	1.75	1.25
J60	D4	600r dk violet	4.25	2.50
		Nos. J56-J60 (5)	10.50	4.60

Wmk. E U BRASIL Multiple (218)

1929-30 *Perf. 12½x13½*

J61	D4	100r light red	.25	.20
J62	D4	200r blue black	.40	.25
J63	D4	400r brown	.40	.25
J64	D4	1000r myrtle green	.75	.50
		Nos. J61-J64 (4)	1.80	1.20

Perf. 11, 12½x13, 13

1931-36 Wmk. 222

J65	D4	10r lt violet ('35)	.20	.20
J66	D4	20r black ('33)	.20	.20
J67	D4	50r blue grn ('35)	.25	.20
J68	D4	100r rose red ('35)	.25	.20
J69	D4	200r sl blue ('35)	.40	.30
J70	D4	400r blk brn ('35)	2.00	2.00
J71	D4	600r dk violet	.35	.20
J72	D4	1000r myrtle grn	.50	.35
J73	D4	2000r brown ('36)	.80	.80
J74	D4	5000r indigo ('36)	1.25	1.00
		Nos. J65-J74 (10)	6.20	5.45

1938 Wmk. 249 *Perf. 11*

J75	D4	200r slate blue	2.00	.75

1940 Typo. Wmk. 256

J76	D4	10r light violet	.50	.50
J77	D4	20r black	.50	.50
J79	D4	100r rose red	.50	.50
J80	D4	200r myrtle green	1.25	.90
		Nos. J76-J80 (4)	2.75	2.40

OFFICIAL STAMPS

Pres. Affonso Penna
O1

Pres. Hermes da Fonseca
O2

Unwmk.

1906, Nov. 15 Engr. *Perf. 12*

O1	O1	10r org & grn	1.00	.30
O2	O1	20r org & grn	1.00	.30
O3	O1	50r org & grn	1.00	.30
O4	O1	100r org & grn	1.00	.30
O5	O1	200r org & grn	1.00	.30
O6	O1	300r org & grn	2.75	.60
O7	O1	400r org & grn	8.25	2.00
O8	O1	500r org & grn	4.00	1.25
O9	O1	700r org & grn	4.00	3.00
O10	O1	1000r org & grn	1.25	1.25
O11	O1	2000r org & grn	7.50	1.75
O12	O1	5000r org & grn	13.50	1.00
O13	O1	10,000r org & grn	13.50	1.25
		Nos. O1-O13 (13)	59.75	13.60

The portrait is the same but the frame differs for each denomination of this issue.

1913, Nov. 15

Center in Black

O14	O2	10r gray	.40	.50
O15	O2	20r ol grn	.40	.50
O16	O2	50r gray	.40	.50
O17	O2	100r ver	.40	.40
O18	O2	200r blue	.40	.40
O19	O2	500r orange	3.50	.65
O20	O2	600r violet	4.00	2.00
O21	O2	1000r blk brn	5.00	1.75
O22	O2	2000r red brn	7.50	1.75
O23	O2	5000r brown	8.75	3.50
O24	O2	10,000r black	15.00	7.50
O25	O2	20,000r blue	30.00	30.00
O26	O2	50,000r green	55.00	55.00
O27	O2	100,000r org red	200.00	200.00
O28	O2	500,000r brown	325.00	325.00
O29	O2	1,000,000r dk brn	350.00	350.00
		Nos. O14-O29 (16)	1,005.	979.45

The portrait is the same on all denominations of this series but there are eight types of the frame.

Pres. Wenceslau Braz — O3

Perf. 11, 11½

1919, Apr. 11 Wmk. 100

O30	O3	10r olive green	.50	*9.00*
O31	O3	50r green	1.25	1.25
O32	O3	100r rose red	2.00	.85
O33	O3	200r dull blue	3.50	.85
O34	O3	500r orange	9.25	*40.00*
		Nos. O30-O34 (5)	16.50	51.95

The official decree called for eleven stamps in this series but only five were issued.

For surcharges see Nos. 293-297.

NEWSPAPER STAMPS

N1

Rouletted

1889, Feb. 1 Unwmk. Litho.

P1	N1	10r yellow	3.00	3.00
a.		Pair, imperf. between	125.00	140.00
P2	N1	20r yellow	9.00	9.00
P3	N1	50r yellow	15.00	12.50
P4	N1	100r yellow	7.50	3.00
P5	N1	200r yellow	3.00	2.50
P6	N1	300r yellow	3.00	2.50
P7	N1	500r yellow	30.00	15.00
P8	N1	700r yellow	3.00	*20.00*
P9	N1	1000r yellow	3.00	*20.00*
		Nos. P1-P9 (9)	76.50	87.50

For surcharges see Nos. 125-127.

1889, May 1

P10	N1	10r olive	3.00	1.25
P11	N1	20r green	3.00	1.25
P12	N1	50r brn yel	3.00	1.25
P13	N1	100r violet	4.50	3.00
a.		100r deep violet	7.50	*20.00*
b.		100r lilac	14.00	3.00
P14	N1	200r black	4.50	3.00
P15	N1	300r carmine	17.50	17.50
P16	N1	500r green	75.00	*90.00*
P17	N1	700r pale blue	50.00	*55.00*
a.		700r ultramarine	90.00	*100.00*
b.		700r cobalt	425.00	*450.00*
P18	N1	1000r brown	17.50	*75.00*
		Nos. P10-P18 (9)	178.00	247.25

For surcharges see Nos. 128-135.

N2

N3

White Wove Paper Thin to Thick

Perf. 11 to 11½, 12½ to 14 and 12½ to 14x11 to 11½

1890 Typo.

P19	N2	10r blue	22.50	10.00
a.		10r ultramarine	22.50	10.00
P20	N2	20r emerald	70.00	20.00
P21	N2	100r violet	22.50	14.00
		Nos. P19-P21 (3)	115.00	44.00

For surcharge see No. 137.

1890-93

P22	N3	10r ultramarine	5.00	3.00
a.		10r blue	9.00	4.00
P23	N3	10r ultra, *buff*	3.00	3.00
P24	N3	20r green	10.00	3.00
a.		20r emerald	10.00	3.00
P25	N3	50r yel grn ('93)	25.00	15.00
		Nos. P22-P25 (4)	43.00	24.00

For surcharges see Nos. 136, 138-139.

POSTAL TAX STAMP

Icarus from the Santos-Dumont Monument at St. Cloud, France — PT1

Perf. 13½x12½, 11

1933, Oct. 1 Typo. Wmk. 222

RA1	PT1	100r deep brown	.70	.25

Honoring the Brazilian aviator, Santos-Dumont. Its use was obligatory as a tax on all correspondence sent to countries in South America, the US and Spain. Its use on correspondence to other countries was optional. The funds obtained were used for the construction of airports throughout Brazil.

BRITISH CENTRAL AFRICA

ˈbri-tish ˈsen-trəl ˈa-fri-kə

LOCATION — Central Africa, on the west shore of Lake Nyassa

GOVT. — British territory, under charter to the British South Africa Company

AREA — 37,800 sq. mi.

POP. — 1,639,329

CAPITAL — Zomba

In 1907 the name was changed to Nyasaland Protectorate, and stamps so inscribed replaced those of British Central Africa.

12 Pence = 1 Shilling
20 Shillings = 1 Pound

Rhodesia Nos. 2, 4-19 Overprinted in Black

1891-95 Unwmk. *Perf. 14*

1	A1	1p black	7.00	*6.00*
2	A2	2p gray green & ver	7.00	*5.00*
a.		Half used as 1p on cover ('95)		*3,000.*
3	A2	4p red brn & blk	7.50	*6.00*
4	A1	6p ultramarine	57.50	24.00
5	A1	6p dark blue	10.50	*9.50*
6	A2	8p rose & blue	17.50	*35.00*
a.		8p red & ultra	30.00	*52.50*
7	A1	1sh bis brown	19.00	13.00
8	A1	2sh vermilion	32.00	*60.00*
9	A1	2sh6p gray lilac	75.00	*100.00*
a.		2sh6p gray purple	75.00	*100.00*
10	A2	3sh brn & grn ('95)	75.00	*75.00*
11	A2	4sh gray & ver ('93)	70.00	*100.00*
12	A1	5sh yellow	82.50	*90.00*
13	A1	10sh green	165.00	*225.00*
14	A3	£1 blue	825.00	*650.00*
15	A3	£2 rose red	1,050.	—
16	A3	£5 yel green	1,800.	—
17	A3	£10 red brown	*3,850.*	*5,000.*
		Nos. 1-13 (13)	625.50	*748.50*

High values with fiscal cancellation are fairly common and can be purchased at a small fraction of the above values. This applies to subsequent issues also. The most common fiscal marking consists of an undated double-circle cancel with the words "BRITISH CENTRAL AFRICA" between the circles, and a town name in the center. This cancel exists in various sizes and is usually applied in black.

For surcharge see No. 20.

Rhodesia Nos. 13-14 Surcharged in Black

1892-93

18	A2	3sh on 4sh gray & ver ('93)	385.00	385.00
19	A1	4sh on 5sh yellow	90.00	*100.00*

No. 2 Surcharged in Black, with Bar

1895

20	A2	1p on 2p	11.50	*37.50*
a.		Double surcharge	*5,000.*	*3,500.*

A double surcharge, without period after "Penny," and measuring 16mm instead of 18mm, is from a trial printing made at Blantyre. Value, $650.

A4

Coat of Arms of the Protectorate — A5

1895 Unwmk. Typo. *Perf. 14*

21	A4	1p black	17.00	13.00
22	A4	2p green & black	30.00	14.00
23	A4	4p org & black	60.00	45.00
24	A4	6p ultra & black	75.00	8.75
25	A4	1sh rose & black	87.50	35.00
26	A5	2sh6p vio & black	235.00	350.00
27	A5	3sh yel & black	150.00	60.00
28	A5	5sh olive & blk	200.00	235.00
29	A5	£1 org & black	1,150.	450.00
30	A5	£10 ver & black	*6,500.*	*4,500.*
31	A5	£25 bl grn & blk	*11,500.*	—
		Nos. 21-28 (8)	854.50	760.75
		Nos. 21-29, overprinted "SPECIMEN"	425.00	

A mint example of the 25 pounds blue green and black (Scott No. 31) sold for U.S. $11,550 at a New York City auction in 2003.

1896 Wmk. 2

32	A4	1p black	4.00	6.00
33	A4	2p green & black	17.50	6.00
34	A4	4p org brown & blk	29.00	*20.00*
35	A4	6p ultra & black	32.50	15.00
36	A4	1sh rose & black	32.50	19.00

Wmk. 1 Sideways

37	A5	2sh6p vio rose & blk	160.00	*150.00*
38	A5	3sh yel & black	130.00	65.00
39	A5	5sh olive & blk	190.00	*225.00*
40	A5	£1 blue & blk	1,050.	600.00
41	A5	£10 ver & blk	*7,750.*	*4,500.*
		Overprinted "SPECIMEN"	210.00	
42	A5	£25 bl grn & blk	*15,000.*	—
		Overprinted "SPECIMEN"	375.00	
		Nos. 32-39 (8)	595.50	*506.00*
		Nos. 32-40, overprinted "SPECIMEN"	425.00	

A6

A7

1897-1901 Wmk. 2

43	A6	1p ultra & black	3.75	1.50
44	A6	1p rose & violet ('01)	3.00	.80
45	A6	2p yel & black	2.40	2.40

46 A6 4p car rose & blk 7.75 2.25
47 A6 4p ol green & violet ('01) 10.00 *13.00*
48 A6 6p green & black 52.50 5.00
49 A6 6p red brown & violet ('01) 4.50 3.50
50 A6 1sh gray lilac & blk 13.00 8.50

Wmk. 1

51 A7 2sh6p ultra & blk 62.50 *50.00*
52 A7 3sh gray grn & blk 225.00 *265.00*
53 A7 4sh car rose & blk 82.50 *92.50*
54 A7 10sh ol & black 175.00 *190.00*
55 A7 £1 dp vio & blk 325.00 190.00
56 A7 £10 org & black *5,600.* *2,150.*
Overprinted "SPECIMEN" 225.00
Nos. 43-54 (12) 641.90 *634.45*
Nos. 43-55, overprinted "SPECIMEN" 350.00

No. 52 Surcharged in Red

1897

57 A7 1p on 3sh 7.50 *11.50*
a. "PNNEY" 3,750. 3,250.
b. "PENN" 2,100. 1,750.
c. Double surcharge 675.00 975.00

A8

Type I — The vertical framelines are not continuous between stamps.
Type II — The vertical framelines are continuous between stamps.

1898, Mar. 11 Unwmk. *Imperf.*

Type I

Control on Reverse

58 A8 1p ver & ultra — 130.00
a. 1p ver & deep ultra 4,000. 130.00
b. No control on reverse 3,250. 185.00
c. Control double 500.00
d. Control on front *3,750.*
e. Pair, one without oval *16,250.*

Type II

Control on Reverse

f. 1p ver & ultra — 650.00

No Control on Reverse

g. 1p grayish blue & ver, initials on back 8,000. 925.00
h. No initials 4,250.
i. Oval inverted 15,000.
j. Oval double —
k. Pair, with 3 ovals —

Perf. 12

Type I

Control on Reverse

59 A8 1p ver & ultra 3,250. 26.00
a. 1p ver & deep ultra — 45.00
b. Two diff. controls on reverse — 700.00

No Control on Reverse

d. 1p ver & ultra 3,250. 100.00

There are 30 types of each setting of Nos. 58-59.
No. 58 issued without gum.
Control consists of figures or letters.
Initials are of Postmaster General (J.G. or J.T.G.).

A9

King Edward VII — A10

1903-04 Wmk. 2

60 A9 1p car & black 9.00 2.10
61 A9 2p vio & dull vio 4.25 2.25
62 A9 4p blk & gray green 3.00 *10.50*
63 A9 6p org brn & blk 3.75 *4.00*
64 A9 1sh pale blue & blk ('04) 4.50 *14.00*

Wmk. 1

65 A10 2sh6p gray green 57.50 *87.50*
66 A10 4sh vio & dl vio 82.50 *95.00*
67 A10 10sh blk & gray green 150.00 *265.00*
68 A10 £1 scar & blk 325.00 210.00
69 A10 £10 ultra & blk *5,600.* *3,750.*
Overprinted "SPECIMEN" 400.00
Nos. 60-68 (9) 639.50 *690.35*
Nos. 60-68, overprinted "SPECIMEN" 375.00

1907 Wmk. 3

70 A9 1p car & black 7.00 3.25
71 A9 2p vio & dull vio *12,500.*
72 A9 4p blk & gray grn *12,500.*
73 A9 6p org brn & blk 32.50 *52.50*

Nos. 71-72 were not issued.
British Central Africa stamps were replaced by those of Nyasaland Protectorate in 1908.

A mint example with sheet border at right of the 2 pence violet (Scott No. 71) sold for U.S. $19,250 at a New York City auction in 2003.
A mint example with sheet border at right of the 4 pence gray & green (Scott No. 72) sold for U.S. $19,250 at a New York City auction in 2003.

BRITISH COLUMBIA & VANCOUVER ISLAND

'bri-tish kə-'ləm-bē-ə

and van-'kü-vər 'ī-lənd

LOCATION — On the northwest coast of North America
GOVT. — British Colony
AREA — 355,900 sq. mi.
POP. — 694,300

In 1871 the colony became a part of the Canadian Confederation and the postage stamps of Canada have since been used.

12 Pence = 1 Shilling
20 Shillings = 1 Pound
100 Cents = 1 Dollar (1865)

Values for unused stamps are for examples with original gum as defined in the catalogue introduction. Very fine examples of Nos. 2 and 5-18 will have perforations touching the design on at least one side due to the narrow spacing of the stamps on the plates. Stamps with perfs clear of the design on all four sides are extremely scarce and will command much higher prices.

Queen Victoria — A1

1860 Unwmk. Typo. *Imperf.*

1 A1 2½p dull rose *9,000.*

No. 1 was not placed in use. It is ungummed and may be a proof or reprint.

Perf. 14

2 A1 2½p dull rose 400. 200.
Never hinged *600.*
On cover *1,100.*
a. 2½p pale dull rose *400.* *200.*
Never hinged *600.*
On cover *1,100.*

Two singles of the 2½ pence (Scott No. 2) on a very fine cover sent to Canada via San Francisco was sold for $10,000 at an American auction in 2003.
Two singles of the 2½ pence (Scott No. 2) on a very fine cover sent to Bergamo, Italy, via San Francisco was sold for $17,2500 at an American auction in 2004.

VANCOUVER ISLAND

A2

A3

1865 Wmk. 1 *Imperf.*

3 A2 5c rose *35,000.* *10,250.*
Never hinged *45,000.*
On cover *37,500.*
4 A3 10c blue 2,250. 975.00
Never hinged *3,500.*
On cover —

Perf. 14

5 A2 5c rose 310.00 185.00
Never hinged 450.00
On cover, *from* 650.00
6 A3 10c blue 250.00 180.00
Never hinged 450.00
On cover —

BRITISH COLUMBIA

Seal of British Columbia — A4

1865, Nov. 1

7 A4 3p blue 100.00 80.00
Never hinged 150.00
On cover, *from* 300.00
a. 3p pale blue 95.00 85.00
Never hinged 165.00
On cover, *from* 300.00

Type A4 of 1865 Surcharged in Various Colors

1867-69 *Perf. 14*

8 2c on 3p brown (Bk) 170.00 160.00
Never hinged 250.00
On cover, *from* 1,000.
9 5c on 3p brt red (Bk) ('69) 210.00 180.00
Never hinged 375.00
On cover, *from* 550.00
10 10c on 3p lilac rose (Bl) 1,300.
Never hinged 2,750.
11 25c on 3p orange (V) ('69) 220.00 180.00
Never hinged 325.00
On cover, *from* 800.00
12 50c on 3p violet (R) 750.00 *1,150.*
Never hinged 1,350.
13 $1 on 3p green (G) 1,250.
Never hinged 2,000.

Nos. 10 and 13 were not placed in use.

1869 *Perf. 12½*

14 5c on 3p brt red (Bk) 1,450. 1,100.
Never hinged *2,750.*
On cover —

15 10c on 3p lilac rose (Bl) 975.00 850.00
Never hinged *1,800.*
On cover —
16 25c on 3p orange (V) 625.00 625.00
Never hinged *1,200.*
On cover, *from* *1,400.*
17 50c on 3p violet (R) 850.00 725.00
Never hinged *1,700.*
On cover *2,000.*
18 $1 on 3p green (G) 1,400. 1,400.
Never hinged *2,500.*
On cover, *from* —

BRITISH EAST AFRICA

'bri-tish 'ēst 'a-fri-kə

LOCATION — Included all of the territory in East Africa under British control.

Postage stamps were issued by the British East Africa Company in 1896. Later the territory administered by this company was incorporated in the East Africa and Uganda Protectorate which, together with Kenya, became officially designated Kenya Colony.

16 Annas = 1 Rupee

STAMPS OF INDIA USED IN BRITISH EAST AFRICA

1890, July-Oct.

A1 ½a green (#36) *550.00*
A2 1a maroon (#38) *475.00*
A3 1a6p bister brown (#39) *800.00*
A4 2a ultramarine (#40) *925.00*
A5 3a brown orange (#41) *925.00*
A6 4a6p green (#43) *290.00*
A7 8a red violet (#44) *475.00*
A8 1r gray (#46) *925.00*

As Nos. 1-3 ran out, the Mombasa Post Office utilized unoverprinted Indian stamps for mail. Stamps so used were cancelled with the 21mm Mombasa circular datestamp with indicia C. Indian stamps were also used at Lamu during this period, and stamps with Lamu cancellations are worth much more than the values above.
Stamps of India with British East Africa cancellations at later dates originate on ship mail.

A1

A2

Queen Victoria

1890 Wmk. 30 *Perf. 14*

1 A1 ½a on 1p lilac 325.00 225.00
2 A2 1a on 2p grn & car rose 550.00 325.00
3 A3 4a on 5p lilac & bl 575.00 350.00

Covers: Commercial covers of this issue are rare. Values start at about $2,000.

Sun and Crown Symbolical of "Light and Liberty"
A4 A5

1890-94 Unwmk. Litho. *Perf. 14*

14 A4 ½a bister brown 1.10 *9.75*
b. ½a deep brown 1.00 *5.50*
c. As "b," horiz. pair, imperf. btwn. *1,850.* 750.00
d. As "b," vert. pair, imperf. btwn. 1,100. 575.00
f. ½a dull brown 4.25 *7.75*

15 A4 1a blue green 6.00 *7.50*
b. 1a deep blue green ('95) 1.00
16 A4 2a vermilion 3.25 *5.00*
17 A4 2½a black, *yel* ('91) 5.25 *6.00*
b. Vert. pair, imperf. btwn. 1,650. 700.00
c. Horiz. pair, imperf. btwn. 1,650. 525.00
d. 2½a black, *pale buff* ('92) 110.00 10.50
e. 2½a black, *yellow buff* ('91) 110.00 29.00
18 A4 3a black, *red* ('91) 5.50 *7.50*
b. Horiz. pair, imperf. btwn. 1,050 500.00
c. Vert. pair, imperf. btwn. 800.00 425.00
d. 3a black, *dull red* ('91) 15.00 *16.00*
19 A4 4a yellow brown 3.00 *8.25*
20 A4 4½a brown vio ('91) 3.00 *20.00*
b. 4½a gray violet ('91) 40.00 17.50
c. Horiz. pair, imperf. btwn. 1,650. 1,150.
d. Vert. pair, imperf. btwn. 1,150. 575.00
21 A4 5a black, *blue* ('94) 1.50 *13.00*
Handstamped "SPECIMEN" 52.50
22 A4 7½a black ('94) 1.50 *19.00*
Handstamped "SPECIMEN" 52.50
23 A4 8a blue 6.50 *11.00*
24 A4 8a gray 325.00 *325.00*
25 A4 1r rose 7.25 *10.50*
26 A4 1r gray 260.00 260.00
27 A5 2r brick red 17.00 *35.00*
28 A5 3r gray violet 11.00 *52.50*
29 A5 4r ultra 14.00 *52.50*
30 A5 5r gray green 35.00 *82.50*
Nos. 14-30 (17) 705.85 *925.00*

Some of the paper used for this issue had a papermaker's watermark and parts of it often can be seen on the stamps.

Values for Nos. 14c, 14d, 17b, 17c, 18b, 18c, 20c, 20d, unused, are for copies with little or no original gum. Stamps with natural straight edges are almost as common as fully perforated stamps from the early printings of Nos. 14-30, and for all printings of the rupee values. Values about the same.

For surcharges and overprints see Nos. 31-53.

1890-91 ***Imperf.***

Values for Pairs except No. 19b.

14a A4 ½a bister brown 1,200. 425.
14e A4 ½a deep brown 1,600. 625.
15a A4 1a blue green 2,900. 750.
16a A4 2a vermilion 2,100. 800.
17a A4 2½a black, *yellow* 1,150. 450.
18a A4 3a black, *red* 1,100. 450.
19a A4 4a yel brown 2,300. 1,100.
19b A4 4a gray 1,400. 1,650.
20a A4 4½a dull violet 1,750. 525.
23a A4 8a blue 4,000. 975.
25a A4 1r rose 9,250. 1,050.

A6

A7

Handstamped Surcharges

1891 ***Perf. 14***

31 A6 ½a on 2a ver ("A.D.") 5,750. 975.00
a. Double surcharge *7,250.*
32 A6 1a on 4a yel brn ("A.B.") 9,750. 2,200.

Nos. 31-32 are initialed in manuscript "A.D." or "A.B." See note below No. 35.

Manuscript Surcharges

1891-95

33 A6 ½a on 2a ver ("A.B.") 5,200. 975.00
a. "½ Annas" ("A.B.") 1,200.
b. Initialed "A.D." 2,900.
c. "½ Annas" ("A.D.") 2,500.
34 A6 ½a on 3a blk, *red*("T.E.C.R.") 500.00 57.50
b. Initialed "A.B." 8,000. 2,750.
34A A6 1a on 3a blk, *red*("V.H.M.") 8,250. 2,250.
c. Initialed "T.E.C.R." 6,350. 2,900.
35 A6 1a on 4a yel brn ("A.B.") 4,900. 1,750.

The manuscript initials on Nos. 31-35, given in parentheses, stand for Andrew Dick, Archibald Brown, Victor H. Mackenzie (1891) and T.E.C. Remington (1895).

Printed Surcharges

1894

36 A7 5a on 8a blue 77.50 *100.00*
37 A7 7½a on 1r rose 77.50 *100.00*
Set, handstamped "SPECIMEN" 100.00

Stamps of 1890-94 Handstamped in Black

1895

38 A4 ½a deep brown 87.50 29.00
39 A4 1a blue green 175.00 130.00
40 A4 2a vermilion 210.00 110.00
41 A4 2½a black, *yellow* 210.00 65.00
42 A4 3a black, *red* 92.50 57.50
43 A4 4a yel brown 60.00 42.50
44 A4 4½a gray violet 225.00 110.00
a. 4½a brown violet 1,300. 975.00
45 A4 5a black, *blue* 250.00 150.00
b. Inverted overprint *4,000.*
46 A4 7½a black 140.00 92.50
47 A4 8a blue 110.00 87.50
b. Inverted overprint *5,500.*
48 A4 1r rose 65.00 60.00
49 A5 2r brick red 525.00 300.00
50 A5 3r gray violet 260.00 140.00
b. Inverted overprint
51 A5 4r ultra 225.00 190.00
52 A5 5r gray green 500.00 *325.00*
Nos. 38-52 (15) 3,135. 1,889.

Double Overprints

38a A4 ½a 525. 500.
39a A4 1a 550. 525.
40a A4 2a 750. 550.
41a A4 2½a 750. 500.
43a A4 4a 550. 525.
44b A4 4½a gray violet 800. 650.
44c A4 4½a brown violet 3,200. 2,300.
45a A4 5a 1,050. 925.
46a A4 7½a 750. 650.
47a A4 8a 700. 700.
48a A4 1r 625. 650.
50a A5 3r 975. 975.
51a A5 4r 925. 925.
52a A5 5r 1,500. 1,500.

Surcharged in Red

1895

53 A4 2½a on 4½a gray vio 200.00 90.00
a. Double overprint (#44b) 1,050. 975.00

Stamps of India 1874-95 Overprinted or Surcharged

a

b

c

1895 **Wmk. Star (39)**

54 A17 ½a green 8.25 *6.50*
55 A19 1a maroon 7.00 *7.00*
56 A20 1a6p bister brn 5.00 *5.00*
57 A21 2a ultra 7.00 3.50
58 A28 2a6p green 9.00 3.00
59 A20(a) 2½a on 1a6p bis brn 110.00 47.50
a. "½" without fraction line 125.00
d. As "a," "1" of "½" invtd. 1,050. 700.00
62 A22 3a orange 13.00 *13.00*
63 A23 4a olive green 42.50 32.50
64 A25 8a red violet 32.50 *57.50*
a. 8a red lilac 97.50 80.00
65 A26 12a vio, *red* 25.00 *37.50*
66 A27 1r gray 110.00 75.00
67 A29 1r car & grn 52.50 *140.00*
a. Dbl. ovpt., one sideways 500.00 975.00
68 A30 2r bis & rose 110.00 *175.00*
69 A30 3r grn & brn 130.00 *175.00*
70 A30 5r vio & ultra 150.00 *190.00*
a. Double overprint 2,350.

Wmk. Elephant's Head (38)

71 A14 6a bister 45.00 *57.50*
Nos. 54-59,62-71 (16) 856.75 *1,025.*

"Brit1sh" for "British"

54a A17 ½a *6,500.* *5,750.*
55a A19 1a *7,750.* *4,000.*
57a A21 2a *7,750.* *7,750.*
58a A28 2a6p *4,400.*

"Br1tish" for "British"

54b A17 ½a 450.00
55b A19 1a 500.00
56a A19 1a6p 550.00
57b A21 2a 440.00 *300.00*
58b A28 2a6p 575.00 325.00
59b A20(a) 2½a on 1a6p *1,600.*
62a A22 3a 600.00 600.00
63a A23 4a 800.00 600.00
64b A25 8a red violet 875.00 750.00
64c A25 8a red lilac 1,600.
65a A26 12a 825.00 825.00
66a A27 1r gray 1,900.
67b A29 1r carmine & green 1,400.
71a A14 6a 1,450.

"Afr1ca" for "Africa"

54c A17 ½a 500.00
55c A19 1a 550.00
56b A19 1a6p 600.00
57c A21 2a 500.00 *350.00*
58c A28 2a6p 650.00 350.00
59c A20(a) 2½a on 1a6p 1,600.
62b A22 3a 725.00
63b A23 4a 825.00 650.00
64d A25 8a red violet 925.00 800.00
64e A25 8a red lilac 1,600.
65b A26 12a 875.00
66b A27 1r gray 1,900.
67c A29 1r carmine & green 1,450.
71b A14 6a 1,450.

Inverted "a" for "t"

64f A25 8a red lilac *15,000.*
67d A29 1r carmine & green *10,000.*

"Biitish" for "British"

58d A28 2a6p *8,750.*

"Bpitish" for "British"

58e A28 2a6p *8,750.*

"Eas" for "East"

58f A28 2a6p 1,200. *1,600.*

Letter "B" handstamped

68a A30 2r *6,500.* *6,500.*
69a A30 3r *6,500.* *6,500.*
70a A30 5r *6,000.* *6,000.*

No. 59 is surcharged in bright red; surcharges in brown red were prepared for the UPU, but not regularly issued as stamps. See note following No. 93.

Queen Victoria and British Lions — A8

1896-1903 Engr. Wmk. 2 ***Perf. 14***

72 A8 ½a yel green 3.00 1.00
73 A8 1a carmine 7.50 .50
a. 1a red 7.00 .50
74 A8 1a dp rose ('03) 27.50 4.75
75 A8 2a chocolate 6.00 *5.50*
76 A8 2½a dark blue 10.50 2.00
77 A8 3a gray 5.00 *9.50*
78 A8 4a deep green 7.00 4.00
79 A8 4½a orange 11.00 *19.00*
80 A8 5a dk ocher 9.00 5.00
81 A8 7½a lilac 6.50 *26.00*
82 A8 8a olive gray 6.50 *6.50*
83 A8 1r ultra 95.00 75.00
a. 1r pale blue 70.00 28.00
84 A8 2r red orange 77.50 30.00
85 A8 3r deep violet 77.50 37.50
86 A8 4r lake 70.00 82.50
87 A8 5r dark brown 65.00 47.50
Nos. 72-87 (16) 484.50 356.25
Set, ovptd. "SPECIMEN" 325.00

Zanzibar Nos. 38-40, 44-46 Overprinted in Black

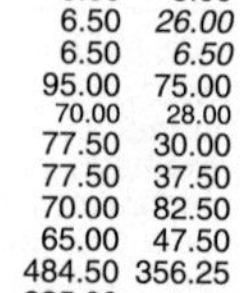

1897 **Wmk. Rosette (71)**

88 A2 ½a yel grn & red 62.50 52.50
89 A2 1a indigo & red 110.00 100.00
90 A2 2a red brn & red 42.50 24.00
91 A2 4½a org & red 57.50 35.00
a. Right serif of left-hand "4" omitted 900.00
b. Fraction bar at right omitted 900.00 550.00
92 A2 5a bister & red 62.50 40.00
a. "tish" omitted 1,750. 1,750.
93 A2 7½a lilac & red 57.50 40.00
a. Ovptd. on front and back —
b. "tish" omitted 1,900.
Nos. 88-93 (6) 392.50 291.50

Nos. 92a and 93b were apparently caused by the presence of foreign matter on the plate during overprinting.

The 1a with red overprint, which includes a period after "Africa", was sent to the UPU, but never placed in use. Nos. 88, 90-93 and 95-100 also exist with period (in black) in sets sent to the UPU. Some experts consider these essays.

Black Ovpt. on Zanzibar #39, 42 New Value Surcharged in Red

1897

95 A2(a) 2½a on 1a 125.00 75.00
a. Black overprint double *6,500.*
96 A2(b) 2½a on 1a 300.00 110.00
97 A2(c) 2½a on 1a 150.00 85.00
a. Black overprint double *7,000.*
98 A2(a) 2½a on 3a 125.00 62.50
99 A2(b) 2½a on 3a 300.00 110.00
100 A2(c) 2½a on 3a 150.00 70.00
Nos. 95-100 (6) 1,150. 512.50

A special printing of the 2½a surcharge on the 1a and 3a stamps was made for submission to the U.P.U. Stamps have a period after "Africa" in the overprint, and the surcharges included a "2" over "1" error in the fraction of the surcharge. These stamps were never placed in use. The fraction error appears on both the 1a and 3a stamps. Value, each, $1,500.

A10

1898 **Wmk. 1** **Engr.**

102 A10 1r gray blue 95.00 42.50
a. 1r dull blue ('01) 82.50 42.50
b. 1r ultramarine ('03) 400.00 275.00
103 A10 2r orange 110.00 110.00
104 A10 3r dk violet 130.00 *150.00*
105 A10 4r carmine 400.00 *475.00*
106 A10 5r black brown 325.00 *400.00*
107 A10 10r bister 375.00 *450.00*
Overprinted "SPECIMEN" 75.00
108 A10 20r yel green 875.00 *1,900.*
Overprinted "SPECIMEN" 150.00
109 A10 50r lilac 1,900. *7,000.*
Overprinted "SPECIMEN" 300.00
Nos. 102-107 (6) 1,435. *1,627.*
Nos. 102-106 ovptd. "SPECIMEN" 210.00

The stamps of this country were superseded in 1904 by the stamps of East Africa and Uganda Protectorate.

BRITISH GUIANA

'bri-tish gē-'a-nə, -'ä-nə

LOCATION — On the northeast coast of South America
GOVT. — British Crown Colony
AREA — 83,000 sq. mi.
POP. — 628,000 (estimated 1964)
CAPITAL — Georgetown

100 Cents = 1 Dollar

Catalogue values for unused stamps in this country are for Never Hinged items, beginning with Scott 242 in the regular postage section and Scott J1 in the postage due section.

STAMPS OF GREAT BRITAIN USED IN BRITISH GUIANA

Numeral cancellation type A is pictured in the Crowned Circle Handstamps and Great Britain Used Abroad section.

1858-60

A03 (Georgetown/Demerara)

A1 A 1p rose red (#20) 400.
A2 A 4p rose (#26) 190.
A3 A 6p lilac (#27) 140.
a. 6p lilac, blued paper (#27c) —
A4 A 1sh green (#28) 1,600.

A04 (New Amsterdam/Berbice)

A5 A 1p rose red (#20) 975.
A6 A 2p blue (#29, P8) 1,050.
Plate 7 1,050.
A7 A 4p rose (#26) 440.
A8 A 6p lilac (#27) 290.
A9 A 1sh green (#28) 1,950.

Values for unused stamps are for copies with original gum except for Nos. 6-12 and 35-53, which are valued without gum. Very fine examples of all stamps from No. 6 on will have four clear margins. Inferior copies sell at much reduced prices, depending on the condition of the individual specimen.

A1

1850-51 Typeset Unwmk. *Imperf.*

1 A1 2c blk, *pale rose,* cut to shape ('51) *250,000.*
2 A1 4c black, *orange* *50,000.*
Cut to shape *8,000.*
a. 4c black, *yellow* *60,000.*
Cut to shape *15,000.*
3 A1 4c blk, *yellow* (pelure) *80,000.*
Cut to shape *11,000.*
4 A1 8c black, *green* *32,500.*
Cut to shape *7,000.*
5 A1 12c black, *blue* *12,500.*
Cut to shape *4,500.*
a. 12c black, *pale blue* *18,000.*
Cut to shape *6,250.*
b. 12c black, *indigo* *18,000.*
Cut to shape *5,500.*
c. "1" of "12" omitted, cut to shape *90,000.*
d. "2" of "12" with straight bottom *5,500.*

These stamps were initialed before use by the Deputy Postmaster General or by one of the clerks of the Colonial Postoffice at Georgetown. The following initials are found:—E. T. E. D(alton); E. D. W(ight); G. B. S(mith); H. A. K(illikelley); W. H. L(ortimer). As these stamps are type-set there are several types of each value.

A used cut round example of the 4 cents on yellow paper (Scott No. 2a) sold for the equivalent of U.S. $14,645 in a Singapore auction in 2003.
A used cut square example of the 8 cents on green paper (Scott No. 4) sold for the equivalent of U.S. $24,400 in a German auction in 2003.
A used cut round example of the 4 cents on blue paper (Scott No. 5) on a cover addressed to Demerara sold for the equivalent of U.S. $15,140 in a London auction in 2003.
A used cut square example of the 12 cents on indigo paper (Scott No. 5b) sold for U.S. $10,450 in a New York City auction in 2003.

Ship and Motto of Colony — A2

Seal of the Colony — A3

1852 Litho.

6 A2 1c black, *magenta* 10,000. 5,250.
On cover *15,000.*
7 A2 4c black, *blue* 15,000. 9,500.
On cover *15,000.*

Both 1c and 4c are found in two types. Copies with paper cracked or rubbed sell for much less.
Some copies are initialed E. D. W(ight).
The reprints are on thicker paper and the colors are brighter. They are perforated 12½ and imperforate. Value $20 each.

A cover sent from Denerara to Cappuoy with the 4 cents on blue paper (Scott No. 7), and initialed "E.D.W.," sold for the equivalent of U.S. $14,710 in a London auction in 2003.

1853-59 *Imperf.*

Without Line above Value

8 A3 1c vermilion 4,500. 1,150.

A proof of #8 exists in reddish brown, value about $750.

Full or Partial White Line Above Value

Types of One Cent:
I: Larger "O" in "ONE," 1mm from end of value tablet.
II: Smaller "O" in "ONE," ¾mm from end of tablet.
III: "O" like Type II, "N" and "T" of "CENTS" widely spaced.
IV: Smaller "O" in "ONE," 1¼mm from end of tablet, letters in "ONE" are closely spaced.

9 A3 1c red (I) 3,500. 1,275.
a. Type II 4,000. 1,400.
b. Type III 5,250. 1,700.
c. Type IV *19,000.* 8,000.
d. 1c brownish red (I) *7,500.* 1,700.
e. 1c brownish red (II) *8,000.* 1,900.
f. 1c brownish red (III) — 2,250.
g. 1c brownish red (IV) — —
10 A3 4c blue 1,500. 525.00
a. 4c dark blue 2,600. 750.00
b. 4c pale blue 1,100. 450.00

On No. 9, "ONE CENT" varies from 11 to 13mm in width.

No. 10 Retouched; White Line above Value Removed

11 A3 4c blue 2,300. 700.00
a. 4c dark blue 3,750. 1,050.
b. 4c pale blue 1,725. 650.

Reprints of Nos. 8 and 10 are on thin paper, perf. 12½ or imperf. The 1c is orange red, the 4c sky blue.

1860

Numerals in Corners Framed

12 A3 4c blue 4,400. 575.00

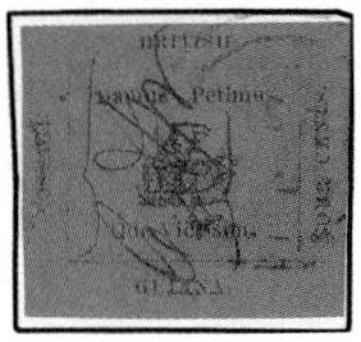
A4

1856 Typeset *Imperf.*

13 A4 1c black, *magenta* —
14 A4 4c black, *magenta* *7,750.*
With initials "C.A.W." (C.E. Watson) *14,000.*
a. 4c black, *rose carmine* *26,500.* *10,500.*
15 A4 4c black, *blue* *57,500.*
16 A4 4c black, *blue, paper colored through* *82,500.*

These stamps were initialed before being issued and the following initials are found: — E. T. E. D.; E. D. W.; W. H. L.; C. A. W. No. 13 is unique.

A very fine used example of the 4 cents on magenta (Scott No. 14), with the initials "C.A.W.," sold for the equivalent of U.S. $14,060 in a London auction in 2003.

A5

Wide space between value and "Cents"

1860-61 Litho. *Perf. 12*

Thick Paper

17 A5 1c brown red ('61) 375.00 110.00
18 A5 1c pink 1,625. 240.00
19 A5 2c orange 260.00 55.00
a. 2c deep orange 160.00 40.00
20 A5 8c rose 460.00 75.00
a. 8c brownish rose 600.00 110.00
21 A5 12c gray 460.00 47.50
a. 12c lilac 600.00 50.00
22 A5 24c green 1,150. 75.00
a. 24c deep green 1,600. 125.00

All denominations of type A5 above four cents are expressed in Roman numerals.
Bisects and trisects are found on covers. These were not officially authorized.
Nos. 21 and 21a are often found with a large red "5d" overprint about the same size as the stamp. This was an accounting marking to indicate postage payable by the Colonial Post Office to Great Britain for the overseas portion of postage collected.
The reprints of the 1c pink are perforated 12½; the other values have not been reprinted.

Thin Paper

1862-65

23 A5 1c brown 550.00 225.00
24 A5 1c black 110.00 57.50
25 A5 2c orange 110.00 52.50
26 A5 8c rose 160.00 70.00
27 A5 12c lilac 225.00 45.00
a. 12c purple 225.00 35.00
b. 12c grayish purple ('63) 250.00 47.50
28 A5 24c green 1,000. 110.00

Perf. 12½ and 13

29 A5 1c black 70.00 25.00
30 A5 2c orange 85.00 22.50
31 A5 8c rose 260.00 92.50
32 A5 12c lilac 675.00 125.00
33 A5 24c green 700.00 80.00

Medium Paper

33A A5 1c black 55.00 45.00
33B A5 2c deep orange ('64) 72.50 27.50
a. 2c orange ('62) 65.00 15.00
33C A5 8c pink 175.00 65.00
33D A5 12c lilac ('65) 575.00 110.00
33E A5 24c green 210.00 65.00
f. 24c deep green 325.00 85.00

Perf. 10

34 A5 12c gray lilac 575.00 92.50

Imperfs. are proofs. See Nos. 44-62.

A6

A7

A8

A9

A10

A11

1862 Typeset *Rouletted*

35 A6 1c black, *rose* *3,350.* *550.*
Unsigned 425.
36 A7 1c black, *rose* *4,250.* *750.*
Unsigned 475.
37 A8 1c black, *rose* *6,250.* *975.*
Unsigned 775.
38 A6 2c black, *yellow* *3,300.* *375.*
Unsigned 1,450.
39 A7 2c black, *yellow* *4,150.* *460.*
Unsigned 1,560.
40 A8 2c black, *yellow* *6,250.* *750.*
Unsigned 1,875.
41 A9 4c black, *blue* *4,750.* *925.*
Unsigned 875.
42 A10 4c black, *blue* *6,750.* *1,500.*
Unsigned
a. Without inner lines *4,750.* *925.*
As "a," unsigned 825.
43 A11 4c black, *blue* *3,600.* *700.*
Unsigned 775.

Nos. 35-43 were typeset, there being 24 types of each value. They were initialed before use "R. M. Ac. R. G.," being the initials of Robert Mather, Acting Receiver General.
The initials are in black on the 1c and in red on the 2c. An alkali was used on the 4c stamps, which, destroying the color of the paper, caused the initials to appear to be written in white.
Uninitialed stamps are remainders, few sheets having been found.
Specimens with roulette on all sides are valued higher.

Narrow space between value and "Cents"

1860 Thick Paper Litho. *Perf. 12*

44 A5 4c blue 350.00 62.50
c. 4c deep blue 525.00 92.50

Thin Paper

44A A5 4c pale blue 110.00 35.00
d. 4c blue 125.00 45.00

Perf. 12½ and 13

44B A5 4c blue 87.50 22.50

Medium Paper

1863-68 *Perf. 12½ and 13*

45 A5 1c black ('66) 55.00 29.00
46 A5 2c orange 60.00 7.50
a. 2c orange red ('65) 60.00 7.50
47 A5 4c gray blue ('64) 92.50 21.00
a. 4c blue 110.00 29.00
48 A5 8c rose ('68) 260.00 22.50
a. 8c carmine 300.00 25.00
49 A5 12c lilac ('67) 525.00 35.00
a. 12c brownish lilac 675.00 50.00
Nos. 45-49 (5) 992.50 115.00

1866 *Perf. 10*

50 A5 1c black 14.00 6.00
a. 1c gray black 17.50 14.00
51 A5 2c orange 32.50 4.25
a. 2c red orange 47.50 6.00
52 A5 4c blue 110.00 8.75
a. Half used as 2c on cover *6,400.*
b. 4c slate blue 110.00 15.00
c. 4c pale blue 95.00 11.00
53 A5 8c rose 160.00 29.00
a. Diagonal half used as 4c on cover *6,500.*
b. 8c brownish pink 200.00 32.50
c. 8c carmine 275.00 45.00
54 A5 12c lilac 210.00 20.00
a. Third used as 4c on cover —
b. 12c pale lilac ('67) 275.00 20.00
c. 12c gray lilac 225.00 19.00
d. 12c brownish gray 225.00 20.00
Nos. 50-54 (5) 526.50 68.00

1875 *Perf. 15*

58 A5 1c black 55.00 8.50
59 A5 2c orange 150.00 10.00
a. 2c red orange 150.00 10.00
60 A5 4c blue 260.00 110.00
61 A5 8c rose 260.00 87.50
62 A5 12c lilac 650.00 67.50
Nos. 58-62 (5) 1,375. 283.50

Seal of Colony
A12 A13

1863 ***Perf. 12***

63	A12 24c yellow green	190.00	12.50
a.	24c green	300.00	24.00

Perf. 12½ to 13

64	A12 6c blue	150.00	62.50
a.	6c milky blue	160.00	67.50
b.	6c greenish blue	165.00	72.50
c.	6c deep blue	250.00	85.00
65	A12 24c green	190.00	12.00
a.	24c yellow green	190.00	12.00
b.	24c blue green	250.00	24.00
66	A12 48c deep red	325.00	65.00
a.	48c rose	350.00	65.00
b.	48c pale red	290.00	65.00
	Nos. 63-66 (4)	855.00	152.00

1866 ***Perf. 10***

67	A12 6c blue	160.00	40.00
a.	6c ultramarine	175.00	65.00
b.	6c milky blue ('67)	150.00	37.50
68	A12 24c yellow green	210.00	8.75
a.	24c green	300.00	11.00
b.	24c blue green	260.00	9.25
69	A12 48c rose red	375.00	27.50
a.	48c crimson	375.00	32.50
	Perforated "SPECIMEN"	225.00	
	Handstamped "SPECIMEN"	290.00	
	Nos. 67-69 (3)	745.00	76.25

For surcharges see Nos. 83-92.

1875 ***Perf. 15***

70	A12 6c ultra	775.00	100.00
71	A12 24c yellow green	725.00	40.00
a.	24c deep green	1,100.	77.50

1876 Typo. Wmk. 1 ***Perf. 14***

72	A13 1c slate	3.00	1.50
a.	Perf. 14x12½		200.00
73	A13 2c orange	62.50	2.25
74	A13 4c ultra	140.00	15.00
a.	Perf. 12½	1,400.	225.00
75	A13 6c chocolate	82.50	8.00
76	A13 8c rose	125.00	1.00
77	A13 12c lilac	55.00	2.50
78	A13 24c green	65.00	4.00
79	A13 48c red brown	140.00	32.50
80	A13 96c bister	525.00	275.00
	Nos. 72-80 (9)	1,198.	341.75

See Nos. 107-111. For surcharges see Nos. 93-95, 98-101.

Stamps Surcharged by Brush-like Pen Lines

Surcharge Types:
Type a — Two horiz. lines.
Type b — Two lines, one horiz., one vert.
Type c — Three lines, two horiz., one vert.
Type d — One horiz. line.

On Nos. 75 and 67

1878 ***Perf. 10, 14***

82	A13(a) (1c) on 6c choc	42.50	*125.00*
83	A12(b) (1c) on 6c blue	190.00	82.50
84	A13(b) (1c) on 6c choc	325.00	125.00

On Nos. O3, O8-O10

85	A13(c) (1c) on 4c ultra	350.00	110.00
a.	Type b		*3,000.*
86	A13(c) (1c) on 6c choc	475.00	110.00
87	A5(c) (2c) on 8c rose	*2,750.*	325.00
88A	A13(b) (2c) on 8c rose	450.00	125.00

On Nos. O1, O3, O6-O7

89	A5(d) (1c) on 1c blk	250.00	82.50
89A	A5(d) (2c) on 8c rose	—	—
90	A13(d) (1c) on 1c sl	190.00	65.00
91	A13(d) (2c) on 2c org	375.00	72.50

The provisional values of Nos. 82 to 91 were established by various official decrees. The horizontal lines crossed out the old value, "OFFICIAL," or both.

Nos. 69 and 80 Surcharged with New Values in Black

No. 92

No. 93

No. 94

No. 95

1881

92	A12 1c on 48c red	50.00	5.50
a.	Without bar	—	700.00
93	A13 1c on 96c bister	4.50	*6.75*
a.	Without bar	—	
b.	Bar in red	—	
94	A13 2c on 96c bister	6.00	*12.00*
a.	Without bar	—	
b.	Bar in red	—	
95	A13 2c on 96c bister	55.00	*110.00*
a.	Bar in red	—	
	Nos. 92-95 (4)	115.50	*134.25*

Nos. O4, O5 and Unissued Official Stamps Surcharged with New Values

No. 96

No. 97

Nos. 98, 100

Nos. 99, 101

No. 102

1881

96	A5 1c on 12c lilac (#O4)	140.00	80.00
97	A13 1c on 48c red brn	175.00	110.00
98	A13 2c on 12c lilac	575.00	375.00
99	A13 2c on 12c lilac	87.50	32.50
a.	"2" inverted		
b.	"2" double	*925.00*	500.00
c.	Pair, #98-99	1,400.	1,500.
d.	As "c," "2" doubled	4,000.	
e.	"OFFICIAL" obliterated by bar		—
100	A13 2c on 24c green	725.00	725.00
101	A13 2c on 24c green	97.50	52.50
a.	"2" inverted		
d.	Double surcharge	1,275.	—
102	A12 2c on 24c green (#O5)	325.00	160.00

A27

Typeset

ONE AND TWO CENTS.
Type I — Ship with three masts.
Type II — Brig with two masts.

"SPECIMEN"
Perforated Diagonally across Stamp

1882 Unwmk. ***Perf. 12***

103	A27 1c black, *lil rose*, I	50.00	32.50
a.	Horiz. pair, imperf between		*6,000.*
b.	Without "Specimen"	725.00	425.00
104	A27 1c black, *lil rose*, II	50.00	32.50
a.	Without "Specimen"	725.00	425.00
105	A27 2c black, *yel*, I	82.50	55.00
a.	Without "Specimen"	600.00	500.00
b.	Diagonal half used as 1c on cover		—
106	A27 2c black, *yel*, II	90.00	55.00
a.	Without "Specimen"	625.00	500.00
	Nos. 103-106 (4)	272.50	175.00

Nos. 103-106 were typeset, 12 to a sheet, and, to prevent fraud on the government, the word *"Specimen"* was perforated across them before they were issued. There were 2 settings of the 1c and 3 settings of the 2c, so there are 24 types of the former and 36 of the latter.

Type of 1876

1882 Typo. Wmk. 2 ***Perf. 14***

107	A13 1c slate	9.50	.35
108	A13 2c orange	25.00	.35
a.	"2 CENTS" double		*6,500.*
109	A13 4c ultra	100.00	6.50
110	A13 6c brown	6.00	7.50
111	A13 8c rose	100.00	1.00
	Nos. 107-111 (5)	240.50	15.70

A very fine used pair of the 2 cents orange with value doubly printed (Scott 108a) sold for U.S. $11,550 at a New York City auction in 2003.

A28

A29

4 CENTS and $4
Type I — Figure "4" is 3mm high.
Type II — Figure "4" is 3½mm high.
6 CENTS
Type I — Top of "6" is flat.
Type II — Top of "6" turns downward.

"INLAND REVENUE" Overprint and Surcharged in Black

1889

112	A28 1c lilac	1.75	.55
113	A28 2c lilac	1.50	.50
114	A28 3c lilac	1.10	.40
115	A28 4c lilac, I	11.00	.40
116	A28 4c lilac, II	22.50	12.50
117	A28 6c lilac, I	22.50	4.75
118	A28 6c lilac, II	10.00	5.00
119	A28 8c lilac	1.75	.65
120	A28 10c lilac	6.75	2.75
121	A28 20c lilac	22.50	14.50
122	A28 40c lilac	24.00	25.00
123	A28 72c lilac	50.00	*65.00*
124	A28 $1 green	475.00	*600.00*
125	A28 $2 green	225.00	*275.00*
126	A28 $3 green	175.00	*225.00*
127	A28 $4 green, I	525.00	*725.00*
127A	A28 $4 green, II	1,650.	*2,000.*
128	A28 $5 green	325.00	*340.00*
	Nos. 112-128 (18)	3,550.	4,297.

For surcharges see Nos.129, 148-151B.

No. 113 Surcharged "2" in Red

1889

129	A29 2c on 2c lilac	2.25	.40

Inverted and double surcharges of "2" were privately made.

A30

A31

1889-1903 **Typo.**

130	A30 1c lilac & gray	4.50	2.00
131	A30 1c green ('90)	.85	.20
131A	A30 1c gray grn ('00)	2.00	*3.75*
132	A30 2c lilac & org	2.50	.20
133	A30 2c lil & rose ('00)	3.75	.30
134	A30 2c vio & blk, *red*('01)	1.40	.20
135	A30 4c lilac & ultra	5.00	2.25
a.	4c lilac & blue	24.00	2.50
136	A30 5c ultra ('91)	3.00	.25
137	A30 6c lilac & mar	8.00	*15.00*
a.	6c lilac & brown	40.00	19.00
138	A30 6c gray blk & ultra ('02)	7.50	*12.50*
139	A30 8c lilac & rose	14.00	1.75
140	A30 8c lil & blk ('90)	3.00	1.25
141	A30 12c lilac & vio	9.75	2.50
142	A30 24c lilac & grn	7.00	2.75
143	A30 48c lilac & ver	18.00	10.00
144	A30 48c dk gray & lil brn ('01)	35.00	32.50
a.	48c gray & purple brown	57.50	40.00
145	A30 60c gray grn & car ('03)	70.00	*210.00*
146	A30 72c lil & org brn	32.50	*42.50*
a.	72c lilac & yellow brown	75.00	*85.00*
147	A30 96c lilac & carmine	75.00	*80.00*
a.	96c lilac & rose	85.00	*92.50*
	Nos. 130-147 (19)	302.75	*419.90*

Stamps of the 1889-1903 issue with pen or revenue cancellation sell for a small fraction of the above quotations.
See Nos. 160-177.

Red Surcharge

1890

148	A31 1c on $1 grn & blk	1.40	.50
a.	Double surcharge	*190.00*	*125.00*
149	A31 1c on $2 grn & blk	2.25	.70
a.	Double surcharge	*90.00*	—
150	A31 1c on $3 grn & blk	2.25	1.40
a.	Double surcharge	*125.00*	—
151	A31 1c on $4 grn & blk, type I	2.25	*8.00*
a.	Double surcharge	*100.00*	
151B	A31 1c on $4 grn & blk, type II	14.00	*32.50*
c.	Double surcharge		
	Nos. 148-151B (5)	22.15	*43.10*

Mt. Roraima
A32

Kaieteur (Old Man's) Falls — A33

1898 Wmk. 1 **Engr.**

152	A32 1c car & gray blk	5.75	1.50
153	A33 2c indigo & brn	29.00	3.25
a.	Horiz. pair, imperf. between	*8,500.*	
b.	2c blue & brown	30.00	3.25
154	A32 5c brown & grn	55.00	4.50
155	A33 10c red & blue blk	29.00	22.50
156	A32 15c blue & red brn	35.00	18.00
	Nos. 152-156 (5)	153.75	49.75

60th anniv. of Queen Victoria's accession to the throne.

Nos. 154-156 Surcharged in Black

1899

157	A32 2c on 5c brn & grn	3.75	2.25
a.	Without period	125.00	85.00
158	A33 2c on 10c red & bl black	2.50	*2.50*
a.	"GENTS"	57.50	*80.00*
b.	Inverted surcharge	*550.00*	*625.00*
c.	Without period	25.00	*57.50*
159	A32 2c on 15c bl & red brown	1.50	1.50
a.	Without period	75.00	*75.00*
b.	Double surcharge	*800.00*	*975.00*
c.	Inverted surcharge	550.00	*750.00*
	Nos. 157-159 (3)	7.75	6.25

There are many slight errors in the setting of this surcharge, such as: small "E" in "CENTS"; no period and narrow "C"; comma between "T" and "S"; dash between "TWO" and "CENTS"; comma between "N" and "T."

Ship Type of 1889-1903

1905-10 **Wmk. 3**

Chalky Paper

160	A30 1c gray green	5.00	.35
a.	1c blue green, ordinary paper ('10)	17.50	3.00
b.	Booklet pane of 6		
161	A30 2c vio & blk, *red*	4.00	.20
162	A30 4c lilac & ultra	7.00	*14.00*
163	A30 5c lil & blue, *bl*	4.00	*7.50*
164	A30 6c gray black & ultra	17.50	*47.50*
165	A30 12c lilac & vio	25.00	*47.50*
166	A30 24c lil & grn ('06)	4.25	*5.00*
167	A30 48c gray & vio brn	16.00	*22.50*
168	A30 60c gray grn & car rose	16.00	*100.00*

169 A30 72c lil & org brn ('07)	37.50	*75.00*
170 A30 96c blk & red, *yel*('06)	40.00	*50.00*
Nos. 160-170 (11)	176.25	*369.55*

The 2c-60c exist on ordinary paper.

A34

George V — A35

Black Overprint

171 A34 $2.40 grn & vio	*190.00*	*300.00*

Ship Type of 1889-1903
Ordinary Paper

TWO CENTS
Type I — Only the upper right corner of the flag touches the mast.
Type II — The entire right side of the flag touches the mast.

1907

172 A30 2c red, type I	18.00	.20
b. 2c red, type II	9.75	.20
174 A30 4c brown & vio	2.60	.70
175 A30 5c blue	16.00	2.90
176 A30 6c gray & black	15.00	8.00
177 A30 12c orange & vio	4.75	4.75
Nos. 172-177 (5)	56.35	16.55

1913-16 *Perf. 14*

178 A35 1c green	1.75	.25
179 A35 2c scarlet	3.50	.20
a. 2c carmine	1.40	.20
180 A35 4c brn & red vio	4.25	.40
181 A35 5c ultra	2.00	1.10
182 A35 6c gray & black	3.00	1.40
183 A35 12c org & vio	1.50	1.10

Chalky Paper

184 A35 24c dl vio & grn	3.75	*4.50*
185 A35 48c blk & vio brn	25.00	20.00
186 A35 60c grn & car	17.50	*57.50*
187 A35 72c dl vio & org brn	47.50	*85.00*

Surface Colored Paper

188 A35 96c blk & red, *yel*	35.00	*70.00*

Paper Colored Through

189 A35 96c blk & red, *yel*('16)	22.50	*55.00*
Nos. 178-189 (12)	167.25	*296.45*

The 72c and late printings of the 2c and 5c are from redrawn dies. The ruled lines behind the value are thin and faint, making the tablet appear lighter than before. The shading lines in other parts of the stamps are also lighter.

1921-27 **Wmk. 4**

191 A35 1c green	5.50	.35
192 A35 2c rose red	4.90	.25
193 A35 2c dp vio ('23)	2.90	.20
194 A35 4c brn & vio	5.50	.20
195 A35 6c ultra	3.50	.35
196 A35 12c org & vio	3.00	1.75

Chalky Paper

197 A35 24c dl vio & grn	2.25	*5.25*
198 A35 48c blk & vio brn ('26)	11.00	4.00
199 A35 60c grn & car ('26)	11.50	*55.00*
200 A35 72c dl vio & brn org	26.00	*75.00*
201 A35 96c blk & red, *yel*('27)	22.50	*52.50*
Nos. 191-201 (11)	98.55	*194.85*

Plowing a Rice Field — A36

Indian Shooting Fish — A37

Kaieteur Falls — A38

Georgetown, Public Buildings A39

1931, July 21 **Engr.** ***Perf. 12½***

205 A36 1c blue green	2.75	1.40
206 A37 2c dk brown	2.25	.20
207 A38 4c car rose	2.00	.50
208 A39 6c ultra	2.50	*3.00*
209 A38 $1 violet	27.50	*55.00*
Nos. 205-209 (5)	37.00	*60.10*
Set, never hinged	75.00	

Cent. of the union of Berbice, Demerara and Essequibo to form the Colony of British Guiana.

A40

A41

Gold Mining — A42

Shooting Logs over Falls — A44

Kaieteur Falls — A43

Stabroek Market — A45

Sugar Cane in Punts — A46

Forest Road — A47

Victoria Regia Lilies — A48

Mt. Roraima — A49

Sir Walter Raleigh and Son — A50

Botanical Gardens A51

1934, Oct. 1 ***Perf. 12½***

210 A40 1c green	.70	*.90*
211 A41 2c brown	1.75	.80
212 A42 3c carmine	.35	.20
b. Perf. 12½x13½ ('43)	.70	*.90*
c. Perf. 13x13½ ('49)	.70	.20
213 A43 4c vio black	2.25	2.00
a. Vert. pair, imperf. horiz.	—	*18,500.*
214 A44 6c dp ultra	3.00	*4.25*
215 A45 12c orange	.20	.20
a. Perf. 13½x13 ('51)	.55	*1.10*
216 A46 24c rose violet	4.00	*8.00*
217 A47 48c black	8.00	*9.75*
218 A43 50c green	12.00	*20.00*
219 A48 60c brown	30.00	*31.00*
220 A49 72c rose violet	1.40	*2.50*
221 A50 96c black	22.50	*35.00*
222 A51 $1 violet	37.50	35.00
Nos. 210-222 (13)	123.65	*149.60*
Set, never hinged	225.00	

See Nos. 236, 238, 240.

Common Design Types pictured following the introduction.

Silver Jubilee Issue
Common Design Type

1935, May 6 ***Perf. 13½x14***

223 CD301 2c gray blk & ultra	.25	.20
224 CD301 6c blue & brown	1.25	*2.00*
225 CD301 12c indigo & grn	3.00	*6.00*
226 CD301 24c brt vio & ind	4.25	*7.50*
Nos. 223-226 (4)	8.75	15.70
Set, Never Hinged	17.50	

Coronation Issue
Common Design Type

1937, May 12 ***Perf. 13½x14***

227 CD302 2c brown	.20	.20
228 CD302 4c gray black	.40	.40
229 CD302 6c bright ultra	.45	.45
Nos. 227-229 (3)	1.05	1.05
Set, Never Hinged	1.40	

A52

A53

A54

A56

A55

A57

A58

Victoria Regia Lilies and Jacanas — A59

1938-52 **Engr.** **Wmk. 4** ***Perf. 12½***

230 A52 1c green	.30	.20
b. Perf. 14x13 ('49)	.30	*.90*
231 A53 2c violet blk, perf. 13x14 ('49)	.30	.20
b. Perf. 12½	.55	.20
232 A54 4c black & rose, perf. 13x14 ('52)	.35	.20
a. Perf. 12½	.60	.20
c. Vert. pair, imperf. between	*15,000.*	*8,000.*
233 A55 6c deep ultra, perf. 13x14 ('49)	.40	.35
a. Perf. 12½	.30	.20
234 A56 24c deep green	1.10	.20
a. Wmk. upright	22.50	11.00
235 A53 36c purple	1.60	.20
a. Perf. 13x14 ('51)	2.75	.35
236 A47 48c orange yel	.50	.60
a. Perf. 14x13 ('51)	1.25	1.25
237 A57 60c brown	9.50	7.00
238 A50 96c brown vio	2.25	*3.25*
a. Perf. 12½x13½ ('44)	4.00	*9.00*
239 A58 $1 deep violet	8.00	.50
a. Perf. 14x13 ('51)	250.00	*550.00*
240 A49 $2 rose vio ('45)	3.50	*20.00*
a. Perf. 14x13 ('50)	10.00	*20.00*
241 A59 $3 orange brn ('45)	19.00	*30.00*
a. Perf. 14x13 ('52)	20.00	*47.50*
Nos. 230-241 (12)	46.80	*62.70*
Set, Never Hinged	80.00	

The watermark on No. 234 is sideways.

Catalogue values for unused stamps in this section, from this point to the end of the section, are for Never Hinged items.

Peace Issue

Common Design Type

1946, Oct. 21 *Perf. 13½x14*

242 CD303 3c carmine .20 .20
243 CD303 6c deep blue .30 .20

Silver Wedding Issue

Common Design Types

1948, Dec. 20 Photo. *Perf. 14x14½*

244 CD304 3c scarlet .20 .20

Engr.

Perf. 11½x11

245 CD305 $3 orange brown 15.00 *19.00*

UPU Issue

Common Design Types

Engr.; Name Typo. on 6c and 12c

Perf. 13½, 11x11½

1949, Oct. 10 **Wmk. 4**

246 CD306 4c rose carmine .20 .20
247 CD307 6c indigo 1.40 .75
248 CD308 12c orange .20 *.75*
249 CD309 24c blue green .20 *.75*
Nos. 246-249 (4) 2.00 2.45

University Issue

Common Design Types

1951, Feb. 16 Engr. *Perf. 14x14½*

250 CD310 3c carmine & black .40 .20
251 CD311 6c dp ultra & black .45 .45

POSTAGE DUE STAMPS

Catalogue values for unused stamps in this section are for Never Hinged items.

D1

Perf. 13½x14

1940-52 **Typo.** **Wmk. 4**

J1 D1 1c green, *chalky paper* ('52) 1.75 *8.00*
On cover 100.00
a. Wmk. 4a (error) 140.00
Never hinged 75.00
b. 1c green, *ordinary paper* ('40) 7.00 8.00
Never hinged 3.25
J2 D1 2c black, *chalky paper* ('52) 2.00 *3.25*
On cover 100.00
a. Wmk. 4a (error) 125.00
b. 2c black, *ordinary paper* ('40) 25.00 2.25
J3 D1 4c ultra ('52) .35 *11.00*
On cover 200.00
a. Wmk. 4a (error) 125.00
J4 D1 12c carmine, *chalky paper* ('55) 18.00 *5.25*
a. 12c scarlet, *ordinary paper* ('40) 35.00 5.00
On cover 175.00
Nos. J1-J4 (4) 22.10 *27.50*

Cover values are for properly franked commercial items. Philatelic usages exist and sell for less.

WAR TAX STAMP

Regular Issue No. 179 Overprinted

1918, Jan. 4 **Wmk. 3** *Perf. 14*

MR1 A35 2c scarlet 1.40 .20

OFFICIAL STAMPS

Counterfeit overprints exist.

No. 50 Overprinted in Red **OFFICIAL**

1875 **Unwmk.** *Perf. 10*

O1 A5 1c black 65.00 17.50
a. Horiz. pair, imperf btwn. 4,250.

Nos. 51, 53-54, 68 Overprinted in Black

O2 A5 2c orange 210.00 17.50
O3 A5 8c rose 375.00 150.00
O4 A5 12c lilac 2,600. 575.00
O5 A12 24c green 1,300. 275.00

For surcharges see Nos. 87, 89, 89A, 96, 102.

Nos. 72-76 Overprinted "OFFICIAL" Similar to #O2-O5

1877 **Wmk. 1** *Perf. 14*

O6 A13 1c slate 300.00 95.00
a. Vert. pair, imperf btwn. *24,000.*
O7 A13 2c orange 140.00 17.50
O8 A13 4c ultramarine 100.00 35.00
O9 A13 6c chocolate 6,500. 700.00
O10 A13 8c rose 2,350. 525.00

The type A13 12c lilac, 24c green and 48c red brown overprinted "OFFICIAL" were never placed in use. A few copies of the 12c and 24c have been seen but the 48c is only known surcharged with new value for provisional use in 1881. See Nos. 97-101.

For surcharges see #85-86, 88A, 90-91.

A used vertical pair, imperforate between, of the 1 cent slate (Scott No. O6a) sold for the equivalent of U.S, $23,790 at a London auction in 2003.

BRITISH HONDURAS

'bri-tish hän-'dur-əs

LOCATION — Central America bordering on Caribbean on east, Mexico on north and Guatemala on west.
GOVT. — British Crown Colony
AREA — 8,867 sq. mi.
POP. — 130,000 (est. 1972)
CAPITAL — Belmopan

Before British Honduras became a colony (subordinate to Jamaica) in 1862, it was a settlement under British influence. In 1884 it became an independent colony.

12 Pence = 1 Shilling
100 Cents = 1 Dollar (1888)

Catalogue values for unused stamps in this country are for Never Hinged items, beginning with Scott 127 in the regular postage section, Scott J1 in the postage due section.

PRESTAMP POSTAL MARKINGS

Crowned Circle handstamp type II is pictured in the Crowned Circle Handstamps and Great Britain Used Abroad section.

1841

A1 II "Belize" crowned circle handstamp in red, on cover *4,750.*

STAMPS OF GREAT BRITAIN USED IN BRITISH HONDURAS

Numeral cancellation type A is pictured in the Crowned Circle Handstamps and Great Britain Used Abroad section.

1858-60

A06 (Belize)

A2 A 1p rose red (#20) 1,050.
A3 A 4p rose (#26) 440.
A4 A 6p lilac (#27) 440.
A5 A 1sh green (#28) 1,900.

Values for unused stamps are for examples with original gum as defined in the catalogue introduction. Very fine examples of Nos. 1-37 will have perforations touching the design on at least one side due to the narrow spacing of the stamps on the plates. Stamps with perfs clear of the design on all four sides are extremely scarce and will command higher prices.

Queen Victoria — A1

1866 **Unwmk.** **Typo.** *Perf. 14*

1 A1 1p pale blue 70.00 65.00
a. Horiz. pair, imperf. btwn.
b. 1p blue 90.00 80.00
2 A1 6p rose 350.00 175.00
3 A1 1sh green 375.00 140.00
a. Vert. pair, Nos. 1, 3 with gutter btwn. *55,000.*
b. Horiz. pair, Nos. 2, 3 with gutter btwn. *45,000.*

The 6p and 1sh were printed only in a sheet with the 1p. The 1p was later printed in sheets without the 6p and 1sh.

1872 **Wmk. 1** *Perf. 12½*

4 A1 1p pale blue 87.50 20.00
a. 1p deep blue ('74) 110.00 20.00
5 A1 3p reddish brn 150.00 87.50
a. 3p chocolate brn ('74) 190.00 110.00
6 A1 6p rose 325.00 47.50
a. 6p carmine rose ('74) 550.00 65.00
7 A1 1sh green 500.00 32.50
a. Horiz. pair, imperf. btwn. *16,250.*
b. 1sh deep green ('74) 450.00 25.00

For surcharges see Nos. 18-19.
No. 7a is unique and has faults.

1877-79 *Perf. 14*

8 A1 1p blue 75.00 11.50
a. Horiz. strip of 3, imperf. btwn. *7,500.*
b. 1p pale blue ('78) 90.00 19.00
9 A1 3p brown 150.00 20.00
10 A1 4p violet ('79) 200.00 10.00
11 A1 6p rose ('78) 450.00 200.00
12 A1 1sh green 275.00 13.00

For surcharges see Nos. 20-21, 29.

1882-87 **Wmk. 2**

13 A1 1p blue ('84) 52.50 18.00
14 A1 1p rose ('84) 26.00 15.00
a. Diagonal half used as ½p on cover
b. 1p carmine 57.50 21.00
15 A1 4p violet 87.50 5.50
16 A1 6p yellow ('85) 325.00 225.00
17 A1 1sh gray ('87) 300.00 190.00

For surcharges see Nos. 22-26, 28-35.

Stamps of 1872-87 Surcharged in Black

1888 **Wmk. 1** *Perf. 12½*

18 A1 2c on 6p rose 250.00 175.00
19 A1 3c on 3p brown *15,000.* *5,750.*

Perf. 14

20 A1 2c on 6p rose 160.00 140.00
a. Diagonal half used as 1c on cover *260.00*
b. Double surcharge 2,350. —
c. "2" with curved tail 1,600. —
21 A1 3c on 3p brown 100.00 100.00

Wmk. 2

22 A1 2c on 1p rose 9.75 *25.00*
a. Diagonal half used as 1c on cover 210.00
b. Double surcharge 1,050. 1,050.
c. Inverted surcharge 3,000. 2,650.
23 A1 10c on 4p violet 57.50 19.00
a. Inverted surcharge
24 A1 20c on 6p yellow 32.50 *40.00*
25 A1 50c on 1sh gray 450.00 *575.00*
a. "5" for "50" *11,750.*

No. 25 with Additional Surcharge in Red or Black

26 A1 2c (R) on 50c on 1sh gray 57.50 *110.00*
a. "TWO" in black *18,750.* *11,750.*
b. "TWO" double (Blk + R) *18,750.* *11,750.*
c. Diagonal half used as 1c on cover 250.00

A mint example of No. 26a with part of original gum realized the equivalent of U.S. $18,630 at a London auction in 2005.

A mint example of No. 26b with part of original gum realized the equivalent of U.S. $18,630 at a London auction in 2005.

Stamps of 1872-87 Surcharged in Black

c

1888-89

28 A1 2c on 1p rose .70 *2.50*
a. Diagonal half used as 1c on cover 100.00
29 A1 3c on 3p brown 3.75 1.60
30 A1 10c on 4p violet 14.00 1.00
a. Double surcharge *2,650.*
31 A1 20c on 6p yel ('89) 14.00 *16.00*
32 A1 50c on 1sh gray 32.50 *100.00*
Nos. 28-32 (5) 64.95 *121.10*

For other examples of this surcharge see Nos. 36, 47. For overprint see No. 51.

No. 30 with Additional Surcharge in Black or Red

1891

33 A1 6c (Blk) on 10c on 4p 1.50 *2.00*
a. "6" and bar inverted *3,500.* *925.00*
b. "6" only inverted *3,750.*
34 A1 6c (R) on 10c on 4p 1.75 *2.25*
a. "6" and bar inverted *525.00* *525.00*
b. "6" only inverted *3,750.*

Stamps similar to No. 33 but with "SIX" instead of "6," both with and without bar, were prepared but not regularly issued.

See No. 37.

No. 29 with Additional Surcharge in Black

35 A1 5c on 3c on 3p brown 1.50 *2.00*
a. Double surcharge of "Five" and bar 375.00 *400.00*
b. Wide space between "I" and "V" of "FIVE" 62.50 *80.00*

Black Surcharge, Type "c"

36 A1 6c on 3p blue 3.00 *18.00*

No. 36 with Additional Surcharge like Nos. 33-34 in Red

1891

37 A1 15c (R) on 6c on 3p blue 14.00 *30.00*
a. Double surcharge —

A8

A9

1891-98 Wmk. 2 *Perf. 14*

38 A8 1c green 2.75 1.25
39 A8 2c carmine rose 2.75 .25
40 A8 3c brown 7.00 4.25
41 A8 5c ultra ('95) 12.75 .80
42 A8 6c ultramarine 7.50 2.10
43 A8 10c vio & grn ('95) 10.50 9.50
a. 10c dull purple & green ('01) 12.50 8.50
44 A8 12c vio & green 3.00 2.50
a. 12c pale mauve & green 24.50 7.50
45 A8 24c yellow & blue 6.00 *15.00*
a. 24c orange & blue 32.50 *60.00*
46 A8 25c red brn & grn ('98) 85.00 *140.00*
Nos. 38-46 (9) 137.25 *175.65*

Numeral tablet on Nos. 43-46 has lined background with colorless value and "c."
For overprints see Nos. 48-50.

Type of 1866 Surcharged Type "c"

1892
47 A1 1c on 1p green .85 *1.60*

Regular Issue Overprinted in Black

1899

Overprint 12mm Long

48 A8 5c ultramarine 14.50 2.75
a. "BEVENUE" 100.00 *125.00*
49 A8 10c lilac & green 6.25 *17.00*
a. "BEVENUE" 210.00 *325.00*
c. "REVENU" 600.00
50 A8 25c red brn & grn 3.00 *37.50*
a. "BEVENUE" 125.00 *325.00*
c. "REVE UE" 2,250.
51 A1 50c on 1sh gray (No. 32) 400.00 350.00
a. "BEVENUE" 3,750. —
Nos. 48-51 (4) 423.75 *407.25*

Two lenghts of the overprint are found on the same pane: 12mm (43 to the pane) and 11mm (17 to the pane). The "U" is found in both a tall, narrow type and the more common small type.

Overprint 11mm Long

48b A8 5c 25.00 9.25
49b A8 10c 21.00 *50.00*
49d A8 10c "REVENU" 700.00 *825.00*
50b A8 25c 5.00 *60.00*
51b A1 50c 325.00 *500.00*

1899-1901
52 A9 5c gray blk & ultra, *bl* ('00) 17.00 2.75
53 A9 10c vio & grn ('01) 11.50 *8.00*
54 A9 50c grn & car rose 27.50 *62.50*
55 A9 $1 grn & car rose 80.00 *140.00*
56 A9 $2 green & ultra 110.00 *175.00*
57 A9 $5 green & black 325.00 *400.00*
Nos. 52-57 (6) 571.00 *788.25*

Numeral tablet on Nos. 53-54 has lined background with colorless value and "c."

King Edward VII — A10

1902-04 Typo. Wmk. 2
58 A10 1c gray grn & grn ('04) 3.00 *24.00*
59 A10 2c vio & blk, *red* 1.50 3.00
60 A10 5c gray blk & ultra, *blue* 8.00 .70
61 A10 20c dl vio & vio ('04) 6.50 *18.00*
Nos. 58-61 (4) 19.00 *45.70*
Set, overprinted "SPECIMEN" 57.50

1904-06 Chalky Paper Wmk. 3
62 A10 1c green 1.10 *2.40*
a. 1c green, ordinary paper 11.00 *14.50*
63 A10 2c vio & blk, *red* .80 *.20*
a. 2c vio & blk, *red*, ordinary paper 3.00 .35
64 A10 5c blk & ultra, *bl* ('05) 1.90 .20
65 A10 10c vio & grn ('06) 5.25 *11.50*
67 A10 25c vio & org ('06) 7.50 *50.00*
68 A10 50c grn & car rose ('06) 16.00 *75.00*
69 A10 $1 grn & car rose ('06) 57.50 *85.00*
70 A10 $2 grn & ultra ('06) 100.00 *175.00*
71 A10 $5 grn & blk ('06) 300.00 *325.00*
Nos. 62-71 (9) 490.05 *724.30*

The 1c and 2c exist also on ordinary paper.

1909

Ordinary Paper

72 A10 2c carmine 12.50 .20
73 A10 5c ultramarine 1.90 .20

1911
74 A10 25c black, *green* 5.00 *47.50*

Numeral tablet on #61, 65-68, 74 has lined background with colorless value and "c."

King George V
A11 A12

1913-17 Wmk. 3 *Perf. 14*
75 A11 1c green 4.00 1.60
a. 1c yellow green 8.00 2.75
76 A11 2c scarlet 3.25 1.60
a. 2c carmine 3.75 1.10
b. 2c bright scarlet ('15) 6.50 1.10
c. 2c red, *bluish* 13.50 9.00
77 A11 3c orange ('17) .85 .20
78 A11 5c ultra 2.25 1.10

Chalky Paper

79 A12 10c dl vio & ol grn 3.25 *7.00*
a. 10c purple & br green ('17) 17.50 *27.50*
80 A12 25c blk, *gray grn* 1.40 *12.50*
a. 25c black, *emerald* 2.00 *31.00*
b. 25c blk, *bl grn*, olive back 5.75 *12.50*
81 A12 50c vio & ultra, *bl* 13.50 *15.50*
82 A11 $1 black & scar 20.00 *52.50*
83 A11 $2 grn & dull vio 70.00 *85.00*
84 A11 $5 vio & blk, *red* 240.00 *275.00*
Nos. 75-84 (9) 357.65 *451.80*

See No. 91. For overprints see Nos. MR2-MR5.

With Moire Overprint in Violet

1915
85 A11 1c green 2.00 *12.50*
86 A11 2c carmine 2.25 .40
87 A11 5c ultramarine .25 *4.50*
Nos. 85-87 (3) 4.50 *17.40*

For overprint see No. MR1.

Peace Commemorative Issue

Seal of Colony and George V
A13

1921, Apr. 28 Engr.
89 A13 2c carmine 2.50 1.00

Similar to A13 but without "Peace Peace"

1922 Wmk. 4
90 A13 4c dark gray 4.50 .95

Type of 1913-17

1921 Typo. Wmk. 4
91 A11 1c green 3.50 *7.50*

A14

1922-33 Typo. Wmk. 4
92 A14 1c green ('29) .80 *1.10*
93 A14 2c dark brown .35 .20
94 A14 2c rose red ('27) .85 .70
95 A14 3c orange ('33) 3.50 1.00
96 A14 4c gray ('29) 1.25 .25
97 A14 5c ultramarine 1.00 .20

Chalky Paper

98 A14 10c olive grn & lil 1.25 .35
99 A14 25c black, *emerald* 1.50 *4.00*
100 A14 50c ultra & vio, *bl* 4.00 *9.00*
101 A14 $1 scarlet & blk 6.50 *12.50*
102 A14 $2 red vio & grn 34.00 *90.00*

Wmk. 3

103 A14 25c black, *emerald* 7.00 *45.00*
104 A14 $5 blk & vio, *red* 210.00 *240.00*
Nos. 92-104 (13) 272.00 *404.30*

For surcharges see Nos. B1-B5.

Common Design Types pictured following the introduction.

Silver Jubilee Issue

Common Design Type

Perf. 11x12

1935, May 6 Engr. Wmk. 4
108 CD301 3c black & ultra .65 .45
109 CD301 4c indigo & grn 1.10 *3.25*
110 CD301 5c ultra & brn 2.00 .75
111 CD301 25c brn vio & ind 4.00 3.75
Nos. 108-111 (4) 7.75 *8.20*
Set, never hinged 14.50

Coronation Issue

Common Design Type

1937, May 12 *Perf. 13½x14*
112 CD302 3c deep orange .20 .25
113 CD302 4c gray black .30 .25
114 CD302 5c bright ultra .50 *1.00*
Nos. 112-114 (3) 1.00 1.50
Set, never hinged 1.60

Mayan Figures
A15

Chicle Tapping — A16

Cohune Palm — A17

Local Products
A18

Grapefruit Industry
A19

Mahogany Logs in River — A20

Sergeant's Cay — A21

Dory — A22

Chicle Industry
A23

Court House, Belize — A24

Mahogany Cutting — A25

Seal of Colony — A26

1938 *Perf. 11x11½, 11½x11*
115 A15 1c green & violet .25 *1.10*
116 A16 2c car & black .25 *1.10*
a. Perf. 12 ('47) 1.10 .75
117 A17 3c brown & dk vio .25 *.80*
118 A18 4c green & black .25 *.80*
119 A19 5c slate bl & red vio .50 .50
120 A20 10c brown & yel grn .65 *.80*
121 A21 15c blue & brown .90 .80
122 A22 25c green & ultra 1.40 1.40
123 A23 50c dk vio & blk 9.00 4.00
124 A24 $1 ol green & car 16.00 8.50
125 A25 $2 rose lake & ind 18.00 *21.00*
126 A26 $5 brn & carmine 17.00 *30.00*
Nos. 115-126 (12) 64.45 *70.80*
Set, never hinged 105.00

Issued: 3c-5c, 1/10; 1c, 2c, 10c-50c, 2/14; $1-$5, 2/28.

Catalogue values for unused stamps in this section, from this point to the end of the section, are for Never Hinged items.

Peace Issue

Common Design Type

Perf. 13½x14

1946, Sept. 9 Engr. Wmk. 4
127 CD303 3c brown .20 .20
128 CD303 5c deep blue .20 .20

Silver Wedding Issue

Common Design Types

1948, Oct. 1 Photo. *Perf. 14x14½*
129 CD304 4c dark green .20 .20

Engraved; Name Typographed

Perf. 11½x11

130 CD305 $5 light brown 20.00 *30.00*

St. George's Cay — A27

H.M.S. Merlin — A28

1949, Jan. 10 Engr. *Perf. 12½*
131 A27 1c green & ultra .20 .20
132 A27 3c yel brn & dp blue .20 .20
133 A27 4c purple & brn ol .20 .30
134 A28 5c dk blue & brown 1.25 .45
135 A28 10c vio brn & blue grn 1.25 .45
136 A28 15c ultra & emerald 1.25 .45
Nos. 131-136 (6) 4.35 2.05

Battle of St. George's Cay, 150th anniv.

UPU Issue
Common Design Types
Perf. 13½, 11x11½

1949, Oct. 10 Engr. Wmk. 4

137 CD306	4c blue green	.35	.35
138 CD307	5c indigo	.55	.55
139 CD308	10c chocolate	.90	.90
140 CD309	25c blue	1.50	1.50
	Nos. 137-140 (4)	3.30	3.30

University Issue
Common Design Types

1951, Feb. 16 Engr. ***Perf. 14x14½***

141 CD310	3c choc & purple	.35	.35
142 CD311	10c choc & green	.65	.65

SEMI-POSTAL STAMPS

Regular Issue of 1921-29 Surcharged in Black or Red

1932 Wmk. 4 ***Perf. 14***

B1 A14	1c + 1c green	1.50	*5.00*
B2 A14	2c + 2c rose red	1.50	*4.75*
B3 A14	3c + 3c orange	2.50	*11.00*
B4 A14	4c + 4c gray (R)	3.25	*14.50*
B5 A14	5c + 5c ultra	5.00	*10.00*
	Nos. B1-B5 (5)	13.75	*45.25*

The surtax was for a fund to aid sufferers from the destruction of the city of Belize by a hurricane in Sept. 1931.

POSTAGE DUE STAMPS

Catalogue values for unused stamps in this section are for Never Hinged items.

D1

1923-64 Typo. Wmk. 4 ***Perf. 14***

J1 D1	1c black, *chalky paper* ('56)	.55	*24.00*
	Never hinged	.75	
	On cover		*165.00*
a.	1c black, *white ordinary paper* ('64)	25.00	*37.50*
	Never hinged	15.00	
b.	1c black, *yellowish thin paper* ('23)	2.50	*15.00*
J2 D1	2c black, *chalky paper* ('56)	.35	*20.00*
	Never hinged	.55	
	On cover		*165.00*
a.	2c black, *yellowish thin paper* ('23)	2.50	*8.50*
J3 D1	4c black, *chalky paper* ('56)	.60	*17.00*
	Never hinged	1.00	
	On cover		*275.00*
a.	4c black, *yellowish thin paper* ('23)	1.40	*6.50*
	Nos. J1-J3 (3)	1.50	*61.00*
	Nos. J1b, J2a, J3a, overprinted "SPECIMEN"	70.00	

On cover values are for properly franked commercial covers. Philatelic usages also exist and sell for less.

WAR TAX STAMPS

Nos. 85, 75 and 77 Overprinted

1916-17 Wmk. 3 ***Perf. 14***
With Moire Overprint

MR1 A11	1c green	.20	.75
a.	"WAR" inverted	200.00	*225.00*

Without Moire Overprint

MR2 A11	1c green ('17)	1.25	*3.00*
MR3 A11	3c orange ('17)	3.00	4.00
a.	Double overprint	350.00	*350.00*
	Nos. MR1-MR3 (3)	4.45	7.75

Nos. 75 and 77 Overprinted

1918

MR4 A11	1c green	.20	*.25*
MR5 A11	3c orange	.50	*1.50*

BRUNEI

'brü-ˌnī

LOCATION — On the northwest coast of Borneo
GOVT. — British Protectorate
AREA — 2,226 sq. mi.
POP. — 191,770 (1981)
CAPITAL — Bandar Seri Begawan

Although Brunei became a British protectorate in 1888, postage stamps were not issued until 1906, when the administration was transferred from the Sultan to the British Resident.

100 Cents (Sen) = 1 Dollar

Catalogue values for unused stamps in this country are for Never Hinged items, beginning with Scott 62.

Star and Local Scene — A1a

Perf. 13 to 13½

1895, July 22 Litho. Unwmk.

A1 A1a	½c brown (shades)	4.00	*22.50*
	Never hinged	5.50	
A2 A1a	1c brown lake (shades)	3.75	*17.50*
	Never hinged	5.25	
A3 A1a	2c black	4.50	*17.50*
	Never hinged	6.50	
A4 A1a	3c deep blue	4.50	*16.00*
	Never hinged	6.50	
A5 A1a	5c deep blue green	7.50	*19.00*
	Never hinged	10.50	
A6 A1a	8c plum	7.50	*35.00*
	Never hinged	10.50	
A7 A1a	10c orange red	9.25	*32.50*
	Never hinged	13.00	
a.	Imperf pair	*1,750.*	
A8 A1a	25c turquoise	82.50	*100.00*
	Never hinged	115.00	
A9 A1a	50c yellow green	22.50	*110.00*
	Never hinged	32.50	
A10 A1a	$1 yellow olive	24.00	*125.00*
	Never hinged	35.00	
	Nos. A1-A10 (10)	170.00	*495.00*

These stamps were valid within Brunei and to Labuan. Prior to Brunei's admission to the UPU in 1906, all overseas mail was sent through Labuan, where Labuan stamps were required for despatch abroad.

Covers bearing copies of A1-A10, mostly in combination with stamps of Labuan, are usually philatelic. Values start at about $425. Commercial uses of these stamps exist.

Labuan Stamps of 1902-03 Overprinted or Surcharged in Red:

1906 Unwmk. ***Perf. 12 to 16***

1 A38	1c violet & blk	37.50	*62.50*
a.	Black overprint	*2,400.*	*2,900.*
2 A38	2c on 3c brn & blk	4.00	*12.00*
a.	"BRUNEI." double	*4,400.*	*3,000.*
b.	"TWO CENTS." double	*6,500.*	
3 A38	2c on 8c org & blk	32.50	*92.50*
a.	"TWO CENTS." double	*12,000.*	
b.	"TWO CENTS." omitted, in pair with normal	*13,000.*	
4 A38	3c brown & blk	38.50	*100.00*
5 A38	4c on 12c yel & black	5.50	*6.00*
6 A38	5c on 16c org brn & green	52.50	*87.50*
7 A38	8c orange & blk	11.50	*35.00*
8 A38	10c on 16c org brn & green	7.50	*25.00*
9 A38	25c on 16c org brn & green	125.00	*140.00*
10 A38	30c on 16c org brn & green	125.00	*140.00*
11 A38	50c on 16c org brn & green	125.00	*140.00*
12 A38	$1 on 8c org & blk	125.00	*140.00*
	Nos. 1-12 (12)	689.50	*980.50*

The 25c surcharge reads: "25 CENTS."
Covers: Covers bearing this issue are rare.

Scene on Brunei River — A1

Two Types of 1908 1c, 3c:
Type I — Dots form bottom line of water shading. (Double plate.)
Type II — Dots removed. (Single plate.)

1907-21 Engr. Wmk. 3 ***Perf. 14***

13 A1	1c yel green & blk	2.75	*13.00*
14 A1	1c green (II) ('08)	.70	*2.50*
a.	Type I ('19)	1.00	*2.75*
c.	Type II, "A" missing from wmk.	250.00	
d.	Type II, "C" missing from wmk.	250.00	
15 A1	2c red & black	3.75	*5.25*
16 A1	2c brn & blk ('11)	4.50	*1.50*
17 A1	3c red brn & blk	12.50	*26.00*
18 A1	3c car (I) ('08)	6.00	1.75
a.	Type II ('17)	110.00	*45.00*
19 A1	4c lilac & blk	8.75	*11.50*
a.	4c reddish purple & gray black ('10)	80.00	70.00
20 A1	4c claret ('12)	5.50	.90
21 A1	5c ultra & blk	57.50	*110.00*
22 A1	5c org & blk ('08)	8.25	8.25
23 A1	5c orange ('16)	19.00	22.50
24 A1	8c orange & blk	8.75	*26.00*
25 A1	8c blue ('08)	7.25	*13.00*
26 A1	8c ultra ('16)	7.00	*30.00*
27 A1	10c dk green & blk	5.25	*9.00*
28 A1	10c violet, *yel* ('12)	2.40	2.00
b.	10c violet, *pale yellow* ('22)	1.60	*4.50*
29 A1	25c yel brn & blue	37.50	*57.50*
30 A1	25c violet ('12)	4.75	*20.00*
b.	25c deep dull purple ('20)	14.00	*20.00*
31 A1	30c black & pur	27.50	*26.00*
32 A1	30c org & red vio ('12)	10.50	*14.00*
33 A1	50c brown & grn	17.50	*27.50*
34 A1	50c blk, *grn* ('12)	32.50	*77.50*
35 A1	50c blk, *grnsh bl* ('21)	10.00	*42.50*
36 A1	$1 slate & red	70.00	*110.00*
37 A1	$1 red & blk, *bl* ('12)	25.00	*55.00*
38 A1	$5 lake, *grn* ('08)	175.00	*275.00*
39 A1	$25 blk, *red* ('08)	650.00	*1,200.*
	Nos. 13-38 (26)	570.10	*988.15*

Used value for No. 39 is for a CTO example dated before December 1941. CTOs dated later are worth about half the value given.

Stamps of 1908-21 Overprinted in Black: "MALAYA-BORNEO EXHIBITION, 1922" in Four Lines

1922

14b A1	1c green	2.25	*28.00*
16a A1	2c brown & black	5.00	*35.00*
18b A1	3c carmine	6.75	*40.00*
20a A1	4c claret	5.25	*50.00*
23a A1	5c orange	10.00	*60.00*
28a A1	10c violet, *yellow*	8.75	*60.00*
30a A1	25c violet	19.00	*90.00*
35a A1	50c greenish blue	60.00	*150.00*
37a A1	$1 red & black, *blue*	92.50	*225.00*
	Nos. 14b-37a (9)	209.50	*738.00*

Industrial fair, Singapore, Mar. 31-Apr. 15

Type of 1907 Issue

1924-37 Wmk. 4

43 A1	1c black ('26)	1.25	.90
44 A1	2c deep brown	1.25	*8.75*
45 A1	2c green ('33)	2.40	1.25
46 A1	3c green	1.00	*7.75*
47 A1	4c claret brown	1.75	1.50
48 A1	4c orange ('29)	2.40	1.25
49 A1	5c orange	6.50	*1.75*
50 A1	5c lt gray ('31)	21.00	14.00
51 A1	5c brown ('33)	19.50	.85
52 A1	8c ultra ('27)	7.00	6.00
53 A1	8c gray ('33)	18.50	.90
54 A1	10c violet, *yel* ('37)	18.50	*32.50*
55 A1	25c dk violet ('31)	11.00	*15.00*
56 A1	30c org & red vio ('31)	19.50	*19.00*
57 A1	50c black, *grn* ('31)	11.00	*17.50*
58 A1	$1 red & blk, *bl* ('31)	29.00	*87.50*
	Nos. 43-58 (16)	171.55	*216.40*

For overprints see Nos. N1-N20.

Dwellings in Town of Brunei A2

1924-31

59 A2	6c black	17.00	12.00
60 A2	6c red ('31)	5.50	*13.00*
61 A2	12c blue	5.50	*11.00*
	Nos. 59-61 (3)	28.00	*36.00*

See note after Nos. N1-N19.

Catalogue values for unused stamps in this section, from this point to the end of the section, are for Never Hinged items.

Types of 1907-24

1947-51 Engr. ***Perf. 14***

62 A1	1c brown	.65	*2.50*
63 A1	2c gray	.75	*5.25*
a.	Perf. 14½x13½ ('50)	2.40	*5.25*
64 A2	3c dark green	1.10	*6.50*
65 A1	5c deep orange	1.00	*1.60*
a.	Perf. 14½x13½ ('50)	4.25	*15.00*
66 A2	6c gray black	1.25	*6.00*
67 A1	8c scarlet	.50	*1.25*
a.	Perf. 13 ('51)	.65	*10.00*
68 A1	10c violet	.90	.40
a.	Perf. 14½x13½ ('50)	2.40	6.50
69 A1	15c brt ultra	1.90	*.90*
70 A1	25c red violet	3.00	1.25
a.	Perf. 14½x13½ ('51)	2.10	*9.50*
71 A1	30c dp org & gray blk	2.40	1.25
a.	Perf. 14½x13½ ('51)	2.10	*13.00*
72 A1	50c black	4.50	1.00
a.	Perf. 13 ('50)	2.10	*17.50*
73 A1	$1 scar & gray blk	12.00	.90
74 A1	$5 red org & grn ('48)	20.00	*21.00*
75 A1	$10 dp claret & gray blk ('48)	82.50	35.00
	Nos. 62-75 (14)	132.45	*84.80*

Sultan Ahmed and Pile Dwellings A3

1949, Sept. 22 Wmk. 4 ***Perf. 13***

76 A3	8c car & black	1.50	1.50
77 A3	25c red orange & pur	1.50	*1.90*
78 A3	50c blue & black	1.50	*1.90*
	Nos. 76-78 (3)	4.50	5.30

25th anniv. of the reign of Sultan Ahmed Tajudin Akhazul Khair Wad-din.

Common Design Types pictured following the introduction.

UPU Issue
Common Design Types
Engr.; Name Typo. on 15c and 25c

1949, Oct. 10 ***Perf. 13½, 11x11½***

79	CD306	8c rose car	1.50	1.50
80	CD307	15c indigo	5.00	2.40
81	CD308	25c red lilac	1.50	1.50
82	CD309	50c slate	1.50	1.50
		Nos. 79-82 (4)	9.50	6.90

Sultan Omar Ali Saifuddin — A4

River Kampong A5

Perf. 13½x13
1952, Mar. 1 **Engr.** **Wmk. 4**
Center in Black

83	A4	1c black	.25	.60
84	A4	2c red orange	.25	.60
85	A4	3c red brown	.25	.35
86	A4	4c green	.25	.20
87	A4	6c gray	.40	.20
88	A4	8c carmine	1.25	.20
89	A4	10c olive brown	.25	.20
90	A4	12c violet	1.75	.20
91	A4	15c blue	.75	.20
92	A4	25c purple	3.00	.25
93	A4	50c ultramarine	2.10	.35

Perf. 13

94	A5	$1 dull green	1.75	1.75
95	A5	$2 red	9.00	3.00
96	A5	$5 deep plum	19.00	8.25
		Nos. 83-96 (14)	40.25	16.35

See Nos. 101-114.

OCCUPATION STAMPS

Issued under Japanese Occupation
Stamps and Types of 1908-37 Handstamped in Violet, Red Violet, Blue or Red

Perf. 14, 14x11½ (#N7)
1942-44 **Wmk. 4**

N1	A1	1c black	8.25	*26.75*
N2	A1	2c green	70.00	*127.50*
N3	A1	2c dull orange	4.75	*10.50*
N4	A1	3c green	42.50	*87.50*
N5	A1	4c orange	5.50	*16.00*
N6	A1	5c brown	5.50	*16.00*
N7	A2	6c slate gray	85.00	*260.00*
N8	A2	6c red	775.00	775.00
N9	A1	8c gray (RV)	775.00	*975.00*
N10	A2	8c carmine	5.50	*14.00*
N11	A1	10c violet, *yel*	11.00	*30.00*
N12	A2	12c blue	30.00	*30.00*
N13	A2	15c ultra	21.00	*30.00*
N14	A1	25c dk violet	29.00	*70.00*
N15	A1	30c org & red vio	125.00	*290.00*
N16	A1	50c blk, *green*	45.00	*85.00*
N17	A1	$1 red & blk, *bl*	65.00	*110.00*

Wmk. 3

N18	A1	$5 lake, *green*	750.00	*2,000.*
N19	A1	$25 black, *red*	1,350.	*2,000.*

Overprints vary in shade. Nos. N3, N7, N10 and N13 without overprint are not believed to have been regularly issued.

No. N1 Surcharged in Red

1944 **Wmk. 4** ***Perf. 14***

N20	A1	$3 on 1c black	*6,000.*	*6,500.*
a.		On No. 43	*8,750.*	—

BULGARIA

ˌbəl-ˈgar-ē-ə

LOCATION — Southeastern Europe bordering on the Black Sea on the east and the Danube River on the north
GOVT. — Monarchy
AREA — 42,823 sq. mi.
POP. — 8,929,332 (1983)
CAPITAL — Sofia

In 1885 Bulgaria, then a principality under the suzerainty of the Sultan of Turkey, was joined by Eastern Rumelia. Independence from Turkey was obtained in 1908.

100 Centimes = 1 Franc
100 Stotinki = 1 Lev (1881)

Catalogue values for unused stamps in this country are for Never Hinged items, beginning with Scott 293 in the regular postage section, Scott B1 in the semi-postal section, Scott C15 in the airpost section, Scott E1 in the special delivery section.

Watermarks

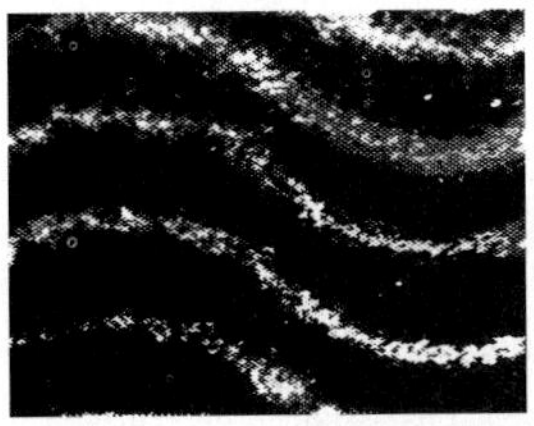
Wmk. 145 — Wavy Lines

Wmk. 168 — Wavy Lines and EZGV in Cyrillic

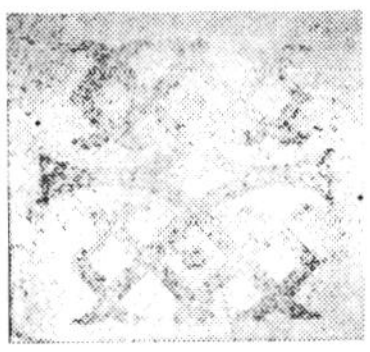
Wmk. 275 — Entwined Curved Lines

AUSTRIAN POST IN BULGARIA

The Austrian Empire maintained post offices in various cities in Bulgaria. The six offices established are listed below. The Austrian Lloyd Agency operated its own office. Filipopoli was open during two periods, the first while under Austrian occupation during the military campaign of 1854-57.
Burgas (Eastern Rumelia)
Filipopoli
Rustschuck
Sofia
Varna
Varna Lloyd Agency
Widdin

Values for Nos. 2A1-2A23 are for stamps without defects tied to cover by complete strikes of town cancellations. Stamps tied to piece with legible full strikes of town cancellations sell for 5-30% of the on-cover value. Stamps with partial strikes of town cancellations sell for 25-50% of the on-piece value.

Stamps of Lombardy-Venetia canceled with Austrian-Levant postmark of Rustschuck in black

2A1	2s yellow (#15)	1,250.
2A2	3s green (#16)	1,400.
2A3	5s rose (#17)	1,100.
2A4	10s blue (#18)	825.
2A5	15s yel brn (#19)	925.

Other Town Cancellations

Burgas (blk)	+2,100.
Burgas (bl)	+2,100.
Filipopoli	+625.
Rustschuck (bl)	+225.
Sofia	+1,250.

2A6	2s yellow (#20)	1,600.
2A7	3s green (#21)	825.
2A8	5s rose (#22)	650.
2A9	10s blue (#23)	400.
2A10	15s yel brn (#24)	525.

Other Town Cancellations

Burgas (blk)	+800.
Burgas (bl)	+825.
Filipopoli	+10.
Rustschuck (bl)	+800.
Sofia	+825.
Widdin (blk)	+1,450.
Widdin (bl)	+4,250.

Stamps of Austrian Levant canceled with Austrian-Levant blue circular date stamp of Varna
Course Print

2A11	2s yellow (#1a)	500.
2A12	3s green (#2)	425.
2A13	5s rose (#3)	100.
2A14	10s blue (#4)	45.
2A15	15s yel brn (#5)	55.
2A16	25s gray lilac (#6b)	800.
2A17	50s brown (#7	4,750.

Fine Print

2A18	2s yellow (#7C)	—
2A19	3s green (#7D)	250.
2A20	5s rose (#7E)	110.
2A21	10s blue (#7F)	40.
2A22	15s yel brn (#7I)	875.
2A23	25s gray lilac (#7J)	6,250.

Other Town Cancellations

Burgas	+525.
Filipopoli	+165.
Rustschuck	+70.
Sofia (blk)	+525.
Sofia (bl)	+2,500.
Varna, straight-line (blk)	+750.
Varna, straight-line (bl)	+1,150.
Varna, thimble (blk)	+325.
Varna, thimble (bl)	+525.
Varna, Bulgaria cancel	+750.
Varna Lloyd Agency	+525.
Widdin, thimble (blk)	+750.
Widdin, thimble (bl)	+1,150.

FRENCH IMPERIAL POST IN BULGARIA

Values for Nos. 3A1-3A8 are for stamps without defects tied to cover by complete strikes of the indicated cancels assigned to the French Post Office in Varna. Stamps off cover sell for 10-20% of the on-cover value.

Stamps of France canceled with small numerals "4018"

3A1	1c ol grn, *pale bl* (#12)	—
3A2	5c grn, *grnsh* (#13)	—
3A3	10c bister, *yelsh* (#14)	475.00
3A4	20c bl, *bluish* (#15)	500.00
3A5	40c org, *yelsh* (#18)	475.00
3A6	80c lake, *yelsh* (#19)	800.00
3A7	80c rose, *pnksh* (#20)	750.00

Stamp canceled with large numerals "5103"

3A8	40c pale org, *yelsh* (#35)	375.00

Lion of Bulgaria
A1 A2 A3

Perf. 14½x15
1879, May 1 **Wmk. 168** **Typo.**
Laid Paper

1	A1	5c black & orange	120.00	21.00
		On cover		2,500.
a.		5c black & yellow	90.00	20.00
		On cover		2,500.
2	A1	10c black & green	550.00	75.00
		On cover		800.00
b.		Vertical half used as 5c on cover		*3,750.*
3	A1	25c black & violet	325.00	18.00
		On cover		300.00
		On cover, single franking		600.00
a.		Imperf.		
b.		25c black & purple	225.00	17.00
		On cover		300.00
4	A1	50c black & blue	500.00	60.00
		On cover		1,250.
5	A2	1fr black & red	75.00	21.00
		On cover		1,500.

1881, Apr. 10

6	A3	3s red & silver	15.00	2.75
		On cover		200.00
a.		3s deep carmine & gray	15.00	2.75
		On cover		200.00
7	A3	5s black & orange	15.00	2.50
		On cover		200.00
a.		Background inverted		*1,750.*
b.		5s black & yellow	15.00	2.50
		On cover		200.00
8	A3	10s black & green	75.00	8.00
		On cover		500.00
a.		10s black & deep green	85.00	10.00
		On cover		500.00
9	A3	15s dp car red & green	75.00	8.00
		On cover		250.00
a.		15s car & pale green	85.00	10.00
		On cover		250.00
10	A3	25s black & violet	400.00	37.50
		On cover		250.00
a.		25s black & purple	350.00	35.00
		On cover		250.00
11	A3	30s blue & fawn	21.00	8.00
		On cover		300.00
a.		30s deep blue & brown	17.50	10.00
		On cover		300.00

1882, Dec. 4

12	A3	3s orange & yel	1.25	.50
		On cover		20.00
a.		Background inverted	*1,800.*	*1,000.*
13	A3	5s green & pale green	7.25	.60
		On cover		20.00
a.		5s rose & pale rose (error)	*1,900.*	*1,850.*
		On cover		*4,000.*
14	A3	10s rose & pale rose	9.50	.90
		On cover		20.00
15	A3	15s red vio & pale lil	7.25	.50
		On cover		25.00
16	A3	25s blue & pale blue	7.25	.60
		On cover		20.00
17	A3	30s violet & grn	7.25	.90
		On cover		30.00
18	A3	50s blue & pink	7.25	.90
		On cover		30.00
		Nos. 12-18 (7)	47.00	4.90

See Nos. 207-210, 286.

A4

A5

Surcharged in Black, Carmine or Vermilion

1884, May 1
Typo. Surcharge

19	A4	3s on 10s rose (Bk)	125.00	37.50
20	A4	5s on 30s blue & fawn (C)	125.00	37.50
20A	A4	5s on 30s bl & fawn (Bk)	*2,000.*	*2,000.*
21	A5	15s on 25s blue (C)	175.00	50.00

On some values the surcharge may be found inverted or double.

1885, Apr. 5

Litho. Surcharge

21B	A4 3s on 10s rose (Bk)	55.00	32.50
21C	A4 5s on 30s bl & fawn (V)	60.00	42.50
21D	A5 15s on 25s blue (V)	85.00	55.00
22	A5 50s on 1fr blk & red (Bk)	225.00	150.00
	On cover		800.00

Forgeries of Nos. 19-22 are plentiful.

Word below left star in oval has 5 letters
A6

Third letter below left star is "A"
A7

1885, May 25

23	A6 1s gray vio & pale gray	15.00	6.00
	On wrapper or newsprint		110.00
24	A7 2s sl grn & pale gray	14.00	5.00
	On cover		75.00

Word below left star has 4 letters
A8

Third letter below left star is "b" with cross-bar in upper half
A9

A10

1886-87

25	A8	1s gray vio & pale gray	1.00	.20
26	A9	2s sl grn & pale gray	1.00	.20
27	A10	1 l black & red ('87)	32.50	3.50
		Nos. 25-27 (3)	34.50	3.90

For surcharge see No. 40.

A11

Perf. 10½, 11, 11½, 13, 13½

1889 Wove Paper Unwmk.

28	A11	1s lilac	.65	.20
		On wrapper or newspaper		75.00
29	A11	2s gray	1.10	.20
30	A11	3s bister brown	.45	.20
31	A11	5s yellow green	4.50	.20
a.		Vert. pair, imperf. btwn.		
32	A11	10s rose	3.50	.20
33	A11	15s orange	10.50	.20
34	A11	25s blue	3.50	.20
35	A11	30s dk brown	6.00	.20
36	A11	50s green	.35	.30
37	A11	1 l orange red	.35	.40
		Nos. 28-37 (10)	30.90	2.30

The 10s orange is a proof.

Nos. 28-34 exist imperforate. Value, set $225.

See Nos. 39, 41-42. For overprints and surcharges see Nos. 38, 55-56, 77-81, 113.

No. 35 Surcharged in Black

1892, Jan. 26

38	A11 15s on 30s brn	12.00	1.00
a.	Inverted surcharge	*70.00*	*52.50*

1894 ***Perf. 10½, 11, 11½***

Pelure Paper

39	A11 10s red	7.00	.50
a.	Imperf.	*57.50*	

No. 26 Surcharged in Red

Wmk. Wavy Lines (168)

1895, Oct. 25 ***Perf. 14½x15***

Laid Paper

40	A9 1s on 2s	.90	.25
a.	Inverted surcharge	6.00	5.00
b.	Double surcharge	*62.50*	*62.50*
c.	Pair, one without surcharge	*125.00*	*125.00*

This surcharge on No. 24 is a proof.

Wmk. Coat of Arms in the Sheet

1896, Apr. 30 ***Perf. 11½, 13***

Wove Paper

41	A11	2 l rose & pale rose	2.75	1.75
42	A11	3 l black & buff	4.50	3.75

Coat of Arms
A14

Cherry Wood Cannon
A15

1896, Feb. 2 ***Perf. 13***

43	A14	1s blue green	.35	.20
		On wrapper or newspaper		75.00
44	A14	5s dark blue	.35	.20
45	A14	15s purple	.60	.30
46	A14	25s red	5.75	1.00
		Nos. 43-46 (4)	7.05	1.70

Baptism of Prince Boris.

Examples of Nos. 41-46 from sheet edges show no watermark.

Nos. 43, 45-46 were also printed on rough unwatermarked paper.

1901, Apr. 20 Litho. Unwmk.

53	A15	5s carmine	1.50	1.10
54	A15	15s yellow green	1.50	1.10

Insurrection of Independence in April, 1876, 25th anniversary.

Exist imperf. Forgeries exist.

Nos. 30 and 36 Surcharged in Black

1901, Mar. 24 Typo.

55	A11 5s on 3s bister brn	2.50	.90
a.	Inverted surcharge	42.50	42.50
b.	Pair, one without surcharge	*70.00*	*70.00*
56	A11 10s on 50s green	2.50	.90
a.	Inverted surcharge	50.00	50.00
b.	Pair, one without surcharge	*70.00*	*70.00*

Tsar Ferdinand
A17

Fighting at Shipka Pass
A18

ONE LEV:

Type I — The numerals in the upper corners have, at the top, a sloping serif on the left side and a short straight serif on the right.

Type II — The numerals in the upper corners are of ordinary shape without the serif at the right.

1901, Oct. 1-05 Typo. ***Perf. 12½***

57	A17	1s vio & gray blk	.20	.20
58	A17	2s brnz grn & ind	.25	.20
a.		Imperf.		
59	A17	3s orange & ind	.25	.20
60	A17	5s emerald & brn	2.25	.20
61	A17	10s rose & blk	1.50	.20
62	A17	15s claret & gray blk	.80	.20
63	A17	25s blue & blk	.80	.20
64	A17	30s bis & gray blk	18.00	.30
65	A17	50s dk blue & brn	1.00	.20
66	A17	1 l red org & brnz grn, type I	2.50	1.25
67	A17	1 l brn red & brnz grn, II ('05)	55.00	4.00
68	A17	2 l carmine & blk	5.00	.85
69	A17	3 l slate & red brn	6.00	2.25
		Nos. 57-69 (13)	93.55	10.25

For surcharges see Nos. 73, 83-85, 87-88.

1902, Aug. 29 Litho. ***Perf. 11½***

70	A18	5s lake	1.25	.45
71	A18	10s blue green	1.25	.45
72	A18	15s blue	6.25	2.00
		Nos. 70-72 (3)	8.75	2.90

Battle of Shipka Pass, 1877.

Imperf. copies are proofs.

Excellent forgeries of Nos. 70 to 72 exist.

No. 62 Surcharged in Black

1903, Oct. 1 ***Perf. 12½***

73	A17 10s on 15s	6.00	.40
a.	Inverted surcharge	*57.50*	*50.00*
b.	Double surcharge	*57.50*	*50.00*
c.	Pair, one without surcharge	*100.00*	*100.00*
d.	10s on 10s rose & black	*325.00*	*325.00*

Ferdinand in 1887 and 1907
A19

1907, Aug. 12 Litho. ***Perf. 11½***

74	A19	5s deep green	12.00	1.10
75	A19	10s red brown	18.00	1.10
76	A19	25s deep blue	42.50	2.10
		Nos. 74-76 (3)	72.50	4.30

Accession to the throne of Ferdinand I, 20th anniversary.

Nos. 74-76 imperf. are proofs. Nos. 74-76 exist in pairs imperforate between.

Stamps of 1889 Overprinted

1909

77	A11 1s lilac	1.25	.50
a.	Inverted overprint	21.00	17.50
b.	Double overprint, one inverted	24.00	24.00
78	A11 5s yellow green	1.25	.50
a.	Inverted overprint	25.00	25.00
b.	Double overprint	25.00	25.00

With Additional Surcharge

79	A11 5s on 30s brown (Bk)	2.00	.25
a.	"5" double		
b.	"1990" for "1909"	*700.00*	*550.00*
80	A11 10s on 15s org (Bk)	2.00	.50
a.	Inverted surcharge	17.50	17.50
b.	"1909" omitted	*27.50*	*27.50*
81	A11 10s on 50s dk grn (R)	2.00	.50
a.	"1990" for "1909"	100.00	100.00
b.	Black surcharge	52.50	52.50

Nos. 62 & 64

Surcharged with Value Only

83	A17 5s on 15s (Bl)	1.75	.60
a.	Inverted surcharge	21.00	21.00
84	A17 10s on 15s (Bl)	4.50	.40
a.	Inverted surcharge	21.00	21.00
85	A17 25s on 30s (R)	5.75	.90
a.	Double surcharge	70.00	70.00
b.	"2" of "25" omitted	87.50	87.50
c.	Blue surcharge	*300.00*	*175.00*

Nos. 59 and 62 Surcharged in Blue

1910, Oct.

87	A17 1s on 3s	4.25	.90
a.	"1910" omitted	21.00	
88	A17 5s on 15s	1.50	.60

Tsar Assen's Tower (Crown over lion)
A20

Tsar Ferdinand
A21

City of Trnovo
A22

Tsar Ferdinand
A23

Ferdinand
A24

Isker River
A25

Ferdinand
A26

Rila Monastery (Crown at UR)
A27

Tsar and Princes — A28

Ferdinand in Robes of Ancient Tsars — A29

Monastery of Holy Trinity — A30

View of Varna — A31

1911, Feb. 14 Engr. *Perf. 12*

89	A20	1s myrtle green	.25	.20
90	A21	2s car & blk	.25	.20
91	A22	3s lake & blk	.45	.20
92	A23	5s green & blk	1.25	.20
93	A24	10s dp red & blk	2.00	.20
94	A25	15s brown bister	4.50	.20
95	A26	25s ultra & blk	.55	.20
96	A27	30s blue & blk	4.50	.20
97	A28	50s ocher & blk	24.00	.25
a.		Center inverted		2,700.
98	A29	1 l chocolate	10.50	.20
99	A30	2 l dull pur & blk	2.50	.50
100	A31	3 l blue vio & blk	12.00	3.75
		Nos. 89-100 (12)	62.75	6.30

See Nos. 114-120, 161-162. For overprints and surcharges see Nos. 104-112, 188, B8, Greece N167-N178, N182-N187, Thrace 16-21, Romania 2N1-2N4.

Tsar Ferdinand — A32

1912, Aug. 2 Typo. *Perf. 12½*

101	A32	5s olive green	2.75	.85
a.		5s pale green	*325.00*	*150.00*
102	A32	10s claret	4.25	1.75
103	A32	25s slate	6.50	2.10
		Nos. 101-103 (3)	13.50	4.70

25th year of reign of Tsar Ferdinand.

Nos. 89-95 Overprinted in Various Colors

1913, Aug. 6 Engr.

104	A20	1s myrtle grn (C)	.20	.20
105	A21	2s car & blk (Bl)	.20	.20
107	A22	3s lake & blk (Bl Bk)	.20	.20
108	A23	5s grn & blk (R)	.20	.20
109	A24	10s dp red & blk (Bk)	.30	.20
110	A25	15s brown bis (G)	.55	.25
111	A26	25s ultra & blk (R)	2.75	.40
		Nos. 104-111 (7)	4.40	1.65

Victory over the Turks in Balkan War of 1912-1913.

No. 95 Surcharged in Red

1915, July 6

112	A26	10s on 25s	.50	.20

No. 28 Surcharged in Green

113	A11	3s on 1s lilac	3.50	4.50

Types of 1911 Re-engraved

1915, Nov. 7 *Perf. 11½, 14*

114	A20	1s dk bl grn	.20	.20
115	A23	5s grn & brn vio	1.40	.20
116	A24	10s red brn & brnsh blk	.25	.20
117	A25	15s olive green	.25	.20
118	A26	25s indigo & blk	.25	.20
119	A27	30s ol grn & red brn	.25	.20
120	A29	1 l dark brown	.30	.30
		Nos. 114-120 (7)	2.90	1.50

Widths: No. 114 is 19½mm; No. 89, 18½mm. No. 118 is 19¼mm; No. 95, 18¼mm. No. 120 is 20mm; No. 98, 19mm. The re-engraved stamps also differ from the 1911 issue in many details of design. Nos. 114-120 exist imperforate.

The 5s and 10s exist perf. 14x11½.

For Nos. 114-116 and 118 overprinted with Cyrillic characters and "1916-1917," see Romania Nos. 2N1-2N4.

Coat of Arms — A33

Peasant and Bullock — A34

Soldier and Mt. Sonichka — A35

View of Nish — A36

Town and Lake Okhrida — A37

Demir-Kapiya (Iron Gate) — A37a

View of Gevgeli — A38

Perf. 11½, 12½x13, 13x12½

1917-19 Typo.

122	A33	5s green	.30	.20
123	A34	15s slate	.20	.20
124	A35	25s blue	.20	.20
125	A36	30s orange	.20	.20
126	A37	50s violet	.50	.30
126A	A37a	2 l brn org ('19)	.50	.35
127	A38	3 l claret	1.75	1.75
		Nos. 122-127 (7)	3.65	3.20

Liberation of Macedonia. A 1 l dark green was prepared but not issued. Value $1.65.

For surcharges see Nos. B9-B10, B12.

View of Veles — A39

Monastery of St. Clement at Okhrida — A40

1918 *Perf. 13x14*

128	A39	1s gray	.20	.20
129	A40	5s green	.20	.20

Tsar Ferdinand A41

Plowing with Oxen A42

1918, July 1 *Perf. 12½x13*

130	A41	1s dark green	.20	.20
131	A41	2s dark brown	.20	.20
132	A41	3s indigo	.30	.20
133	A41	10s brown red	.30	.20
		Nos. 130-133 (4)	1.00	.80

Ferdinand's accession to the throne, 30th anniv.

1919 *Perf. 13½x13*

134	A42	1s gray	.20	.20

Sobranye Palace — A43

Tsar Boris III — A44

1919 *Perf. 11½x12, 12x11½*

135	A43	1s black	.20	.20
137	A43	2s olive green	.20	.20

For surcharges see Nos. 186, B1.

1919, Oct. 3

138	A44	3s orange brn	.20	.20
139	A44	5s green	.20	.20
140	A44	10s rose red	.20	.20
141	A44	15s violet	.20	.20
142	A44	25s deep blue	.20	.20
143	A44	30s chocolate	.20	.20
144	A44	50s yellow brn	.20	.20
		Nos. 138-144 (7)	1.40	1.40

1st anniv. of enthronement of Tsar Boris III.

Nos. 135-144 exist imperforate.

For surcharges see Nos. 187, B2-B7.

Birthplace of Vazov at Sopot and Cherrywood Cannon — A47

"The Bear Fighter"-a Character from "Under the Yoke" — A48

Ivan Vazov in 1870 and 1920 A49

Vazov — A50

The Monk Paisii — A52

Homes of Vazov at Plovdiv and Sofia A51

1920, Oct. 20 Photo. *Perf. 11½*

147	A47	30s brown red	.20	.20
148	A48	50s dark green	.20	.20
149	A49	1 l drab	.25	.30
150	A50	2 l light brown	.60	.55
151	A51	3 l black violet	.95	.65
152	A52	5 l deep blue	1.50	1.00
		Nos. 147-152 (6)	3.70	2.90

70th birthday of Ivan Vazov (1850-1921), Bulgarian poet and novelist.

Several values of this series exist imperforate and in pairs imperforate between.

Tsar Ferdinand
A53 A54

Mt. Shar — A55

Bridge over Vardar River — A56

View of Ohrid — A57

Perf. 13x14, 14x13

1921, June 11 Typo.

153	A53	10s claret	.20	.20
154	A54	10s claret	.20	.20
155	A55	10s claret	.20	.20
156	A56	10s rose lilac	.20	.20
157	A57	20s blue	.30	.20
		Nos. 153-157 (5)	1.10	1.00

Nos. 153-157 were intended to be issued in 1915 to commemorate the liberation of Macedonia. They were not put in use until 1921. A 50s violet was prepared but never placed in use. Value $1.75.

View of Sofia — A58

"The Liberator," Monument to Alexander II A59

Monastery at Shipka Pass — A62

Tsar Boris III — A63

Harvesting Grain — A64

Tsar Assen's Tower (No crown over lion) — A65

Rila Monastery (Rosette at upper right) — A66

1921-23 **Engr.** ***Perf. 12***

158	A58	10s blue gray	.20	.20
159	A59	20s deep green	.20	.20
160	A63	25s blue grn ('22)	.20	.20
161	A22	50s orange	.20	.20
162	A22	50s dk blue ('23)	2.50	2.50
163	A62	75s dull vio	.20	.20
164	A62	75s dp blue ('23)	.30	.20
165	A63	1 l carmine	.30	.20
166	A63	1 l dp blue ('22)	.30	.20
167	A64	2 l brown	.30	1.00
168	A65	3 l brown vio	1.40	1.10
169	A66	5 l lt blue	2.50	1.25
170	A63	10 l violet brn	6.75	2.10
		Nos. 158-170 (13)	15.35	9.55

For surcharge see No. 189.

Bourchier in Bulgarian Costume A67

James David Bourchier A68

View of Rila Monastery A69

1921, Dec. 31

171	A67	10s red orange	.20	.20
172	A67	20s orange	.20	.20
173	A68	30s dp gray	.20	.20
174	A68	50s bluish gray	.20	.20
175	A68	1 l dull vio	.20	.20
176	A69	1½ l olive grn	.20	.20
177	A69	2 l deep green	.20	.20
178	A69	3 l Prus blue	.45	.20
179	A69	5 l red brown	.85	.35
		Nos. 171-179 (9)	2.70	1.95

Death of James D. Bourchier, Balkan correspondent of the London Times.

For surcharges see Nos. B13-B16.

Postage Due Stamps of 1919-22 Surcharged as "a"

a

1924

182	D6	10s on 20s yellow	.20	.20
183	D6	20s on 5s gray grn	.20	.20
a.		20s on 5s emerald	7.00	7.00
184	D6	20s on 10s violet	.20	.20
185	D6	20s on 30s orange	.20	.20
		Nos. 182-185 (4)	.80	.80

Nos. 182 to 185 were used for ordinary postage.

Regular Issues of 1919-23 Surcharged in Blue or Red:

b

c

186	A43 (a)	10s on 1s black (R)	.20	.20
187	A44 (b)	1 l on 5s emer (Bl)	.20	.20
188	A22 (c)	3 l on 50s dk bl (R)	.20	.20
189	A63 (b)	6 l on 1 l car (Bl)	.60	.20
		Nos. 186-189 (4)	1.20	.80

The surcharge of No. 188 comes in three types: normal, thick and thin.

#182, 184-189 exist with inverted surcharge.

Lion of Bulgaria
A70 A71

Tsar Boris III — A72

New Sofia Cathedral — A73

Harvesting A74

1925 **Typo.** ***Perf. 13, 11½***

191	A70	10s red & bl, *pink*	.20	.20
192	A70	15s car & org, *blue*	.20	.20
193	A70	30s blk & buff	.20	.20
a.		Cliche of 15s in plate of 30s		
194	A71	50s choc, *green*	.20	.20
195	A72	1 l dull green	.50	.20
196	A73	2 l dk grn & buff	1.10	.20
197	A74	4 l lake & yellow	1.10	.20
		Nos. 191-197 (7)	3.50	1.40

Several values of this series exist imperforate and in pairs imperforate between.

See #199, 201. For overprint see #C2.

Cathedral of Sveta Nedelya, Sofia, Ruined by Bomb — A75

1926 ***Perf. 11½***

198	A75	50s gray black	.20	.20

A76

A77

Type A72 Re-engraved. (Shoulder at left does not touch frame)

1926

199	A76	1 l gray	.45	.20
a.		1 l green	.45	.20
201	A76	2 l olive brown	.50	.20

Center Embossed

202	A77	6 l dp bl & pale lemon	1.10	.20
203	A77	10 l brn blk & brn org	4.00	.75
		Nos. 199-203 (4)	6.05	1.35

For overprints see Nos. C1, C3-C4.

Christo Botev — A78

Tsar Boris III — A79

1926, June 2

204	A78	1 l olive green	.30	.20
205	A78	2 l slate violet	.90	.20
206	A78	4 l red brown	.90	.35
		Nos. 204-206 (3)	2.10	.75

Botev (1847-76), Bulgarian revolutionary, poet.

Lion Type of 1881

1927-29 ***Perf. 13***

207	A3	10s dk red & drab	.20	.20
208	A3	15s blk & org ('29)	.20	.20
209	A3	30s dk bl & bis brn ('28)	.20	.20
a.		30s indigo & buff	.20	.20
210	A3	50s blk & rose red ('28)	.20	.20
		Nos. 207-210 (4)	.80	.80

1928, Oct. 3 ***Perf. 11½***

211	A79	1 l olive green	.90	.20
212	A79	2 l deep brown	1.00	.20

St. Clement A80

Konstantin Miladinov A81

George S. Rakovski A82

Drenovo Monastery A83

Paisii — A84

Tsar Simeon — A85

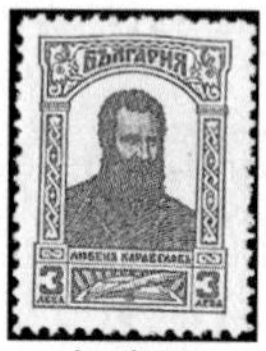
Lyuben Karavelov A86

Vassil Levski A87

Georgi Benkovski A88

Tsar Alexander II A89

1929, May 12

213	A80	10s dk violet	.20	.20
214	A81	15s violet brn	.40	.40
215	A82	30s red	.20	.20
216	A83	50s olive grn	.25	.20
217	A84	1 l orange brn	.60	.20
218	A85	2 l dk blue	.70	.20
219	A86	3 l dull green	1.50	.45
220	A87	4 l olive brown	2.50	.25
221	A88	5 l brown	1.50	.35
222	A89	6 l Prus green	2.25	.90
		Nos. 213-222 (10)	10.10	3.35

Millenary of Tsar Simeon and 50th anniv. of the liberation of Bulgaria from the Turks.

Royal Wedding Issue

Tsar Boris and Fiancee, Princess Giovanna A90

Queen Ioanna and Tsar Boris — A91

1930, Nov. 12 ***Perf. 11½***

223	A90	1 l green	.25	.25
224	A91	2 l dull violet	.25	.30
225	A90	4 l rose red	.25	.30
226	A91	6 l dark blue	.25	.40
		Nos. 223-226 (4)	1.00	1.25

Fifty-five copies of a miniature sheet incorporating one each of Nos. 223-226 were printed and given to royal, governmental and diplomatic personages.

Tsar Boris III
A92 A93

Perf. 11½, 12x11½, 13

1931-37 **Unwmk.**

227	A92	1 l blue green	.25	.20
228	A92	2 l carmine	.40	.20
229	A92	4 l red org ('34)	.75	.20
230	A92	4 l yel org ('37)	.20	.20
231	A92	6 l deep blue	.70	.20
232	A92	7 l dp bl ('37)	.20	.20
233	A92	10 l slate blk	8.75	.70
234	A92	12 l lt brown	.40	.20
235	A92	14 l lt brn ('37)	.30	.25
236	A93	20 l claret & org brn	1.00	.45
		Nos. 227-236 (10)	12.95	2.80

Nos. 230-233 and 235 have outer bars at top and bottom as shown on cut A92; Nos. 227-229 and 234 are without outer bars.

See Nos. 251, 279-280, 287. For surcharge see No. 252.

Balkan Games Issues

Gymnast A95

Soccer — A96

Riding — A97

Swimmer A100

"Victory" A101

Designs: 6 l, Fencing. 10 l, Bicycle race.

1931, Sept. 18 ***Perf. 11½***

237 A95	1 l lt green		1.25	.50
238 A96	2 l garnet		1.75	.50
239 A97	4 l carmine		3.25	.75
240 A95	6 l Prus blue		7.50	1.25
241 A95	10 l red org		20.00	3.75
242 A100	12 l dk blue		67.50	15.00
243 A101	50 l olive brn		62.50	35.00
	Nos. 237-243 (7)		163.75	56.75

1933, Jan. 5

244 A95	1 l blue grn	2.50	.95
245 A96	2 l blue	4.00	1.10
246 A97	4 l brn vio	6.00	1.10
247 A95	6 l brt rose	12.50	1.50
248 A95	10 l olive brn	90.00	20.00
249 A100	12 l orange	150.00	37.50
250 A101	50 l red brown	400.00	160.00
	Nos. 244-250 (7)	665.00	222.15

Nos. 244-250 were sold only at the philatelic agency.

Boris Type of 1931
Outer Bars at Top and Bottom Removed

1933 ***Perf. 13***

251 A92 6 l deep blue .80 .20

Type of 1931 Surcharged in Blue

1934

252 A92 2 (l) on 3 l ol brn 4.00 .25

Soldier Defending Shipka Pass A102

Shipka Battle Memorial A103

Color-Bearer A104

Veteran of the War of Liberation, 1878 — A105

Widow and Orphans — A106

Perf. 10½, 11½

1934, Aug. 26 **Wmk. 145**

253 A102	1 l green	.70	.40
254 A103	2 l pale red	.70	.25
255 A104	3 l bister brn	2.40	1.25
256 A105	4 l dk carmine	2.00	.60
257 A104	7 l dk blue	2.75	2.25
258 A106	14 l plum	17.00	8.00
	Nos. 253-258 (6)	25.55	12.75

Shipka Pass Battle memorial unveiling.

An unwatermarked miniature sheet incorporating one each of Nos. 253-258 was put on sale in 1938 in five cities at a price of 8,000 leva. Printing: 100 sheets.

1934, Sept. 21

259 A102	1 l bright green	.70	.40
260 A103	2 l dull orange	.70	.25
261 A104	3 l yellow	2.40	1.25
262 A105	4 l rose	2.00	.60
263 A104	7 l blue	2.75	2.25
264 A106	14 l olive bister	11.00	8.00
	Nos. 259-264 (6)	19.55	12.75

An unwatermarked miniature sheet incorporating one each of Nos. 259-263 was issued.

Velcho A. Djamjiyata A108

Capt. G. S. Mamarchev A109

1935, May 5 ***Perf. 11½***

265 A108	1 l deep blue	2.00	.40
266 A109	2 l maroon	2.00	.60

Bulgarian uprising against the Turks, cent.

Soccer Game — A110

Cathedral of Alexander Nevski — A111

Soccer Team — A112

Symbolical of Victory — A113

Player and Trophy — A114

The Trophy — A115

1935, June 14

267 A110	1 l green	12.00	.90
268 A111	2 l blue gray	12.00	1.40
269 A112	4 l crimson	12.00	2.25
270 A113	7 l brt blue	20.00	7.00
271 A114	14 l orange	20.00	9.00
272 A115	50 l lilac brn	250.00	110.00
	Nos. 267-272 (6)	326.00	130.55

5th Balkan Soccer Tournament.

Gymnast on Parallel Bars A116

Youth in "Yunak" Costume A117

Girl in "Yunak" Costume A118

Pole Vaulting A119

Stadium, Sofia — A120

Yunak Emblem — A121

1935, July 10

273 A116	1 l green	6.00	1.10
274 A117	2 l lt blue	6.00	1.10
275 A118	4 l carmine	8.00	2.25
276 A119	7 l dk blue	8.00	3.50
277 A120	14 l dk brown	10.00	4.00
278 A121	50 l red	170.00	80.00
	Nos. 273-278 (6)	208.00	91.95

8th tournament of the Yunak Gymnastic Organization at Sofia, July 12-14.

Boris Type of 1931

1935 **Wmk. 145** ***Perf. 12½, 13***

279 A92	1 l green	.30	.20
280 A92	2 l carmine	20.00	.20

Janos Hunyadi A122

King Ladislas Varnenchik A123

Varna Memorial A124

King Ladislas III — A125

Battle of Varna, 1444 — A126

1935, Aug. 4 ***Perf. 10½, 11½***

281 A122	1 l brown org	1.50	.60
282 A123	2 l maroon	2.75	.75
283 A124	4 l vermilion	15.00	4.00
284 A125	7 l dull blue	3.25	1.50
285 A126	14 l green	3.25	1.25
	Nos. 281-285 (5)	25.75	8.10

Battle of Varna, and the death of the Polish King, Ladislas Varnenchik (1424-44).

Lion Type of 1881

1935 **Wmk. 145** ***Perf. 13***

286 A3 10s dk red & drab .70 .20

Boris Type of 1933
Outer Bars at Top and Bottom Removed

1935

287 A92 6 l gray blue .60 .20

Dimitr Monument A127

Haji Dimitr — A128

Haji Dimitr and Stefan Karaja A129

Taking the Oath — A130

Birthplace of Dimitr A131

1935, Oct. 1 Unwmk. *Perf. 11½*

288	A127	1 l green	2.50	.45
289	A128	2 l brown	3.50	.90
290	A129	4 l car rose	10.00	2.75
291	A130	7 l blue	12.00	4.00
292	A131	14 l orange	15.00	3.50
		Nos. 288-292 (5)	43.00	11.60

67th anniv. of the death of the Bulgarian patriots, Haji Dimitr and Stefan Karaja.

Catalogue values for unused stamps in this section, from this point to the end of the section, are for Never Hinged items.

A132

A133

1936-39 *Perf. 13x12½, 13*

293	A132	10s red org ('37)	.20	.20
294	A132	15s emerald	.20	.20
295	A133	30s maroon	.20	.20
296	A133	30s yel brn ('37)	.20	.20
297	A133	30s Prus bl ('37)	.20	.20
298	A133	50s ultra	.20	.20
299	A133	50s dk car ('37)	.20	.20
300	A133	50s slate grn ('39)	.20	.20
		Nos. 293-300 (8)	1.60	1.60

Meteorological Station, Mt. Moussalla A134

Peasant Girl A135

Town of Nessebr A136

1936, Aug. 16 Photo. *Perf. 11½*

301	A134	1 l purple	2.50	.85
302	A135	2 l ultra	2.50	.75
303	A136	7 l dark blue	4.75	1.75
		Nos. 301-303 (3)	9.75	3.35

4th Geographical & Ethnographical Cong., Sofia, Aug. 1936.

Sts. Cyril and Methodius A137

Displaying the Bible to the People A138

1937, June 2

304	A137	1 l dk green	.25	.20
305	A137	2 l dk plum	.25	.20
306	A138	4 l vermilion	.45	.25
307	A137	7 l dk blue	1.75	1.10
308	A138	14 l rose red	1.75	1.10
		Nos. 304-308 (5)	4.45	2.85

Millennium of Cyrillic alphabet.

Princess Marie Louise A139

Tsar Boris III A140

1937, Oct. 3

310	A139	1 l yellow green	.35	.20
311	A139	2 l brown red	.25	.20
312	A139	4 l scarlet	.35	.20
		Nos. 310-312 (3)	.95	.60

Issued in honor of Princess Marie Louise.

1937, Oct. 3

313	A140	2 l brown red	.35	.20

19th anniv. of the accession of Tsar Boris III to the throne. See No. B11.

National Products Issue

Peasants Bundling Wheat A141

Sunflower A142

Wheat — A143

Chickens and Eggs — A144

Cluster of Grapes — A145

Rose and Perfume Flask — A146

Strawberries A147

Girl Carrying Grape Clusters A148

Rose — A149

Tobacco Leaves — A150

1938 *Perf. 13*

316	A141	10s orange	.20	.20
317	A141	10s red org	.20	.20
318	A142	15s brt rose	.30	.20
319	A142	15s deep plum	.30	.20
320	A143	30s golden brn	.20	.20
321	A143	30s copper brn	.20	.20
322	A144	50s black	.20	.20
323	A144	50s indigo	.20	.20
324	A145	1 l yel grn	.65	.20
325	A145	1 l green	.65	.20
326	A146	2 l rose pink	.60	.20
327	A146	2 l rose brn	.60	.20
328	A147	3 l dp red lil	1.25	.20
329	A147	3 l brn lake	1.25	.20
330	A148	4 l plum	.80	.20
331	A148	4 l golden brn	.80	.20
332	A149	7 l vio blue	1.50	1.50
333	A149	7 l dp blue	1.50	1.50
334	A150	14 l dk brown	2.25	1.90
335	A150	14 l red brn	2.25	1.90
		Nos. 316-335 (20)	15.90	10.00

Several values of this series exist imperforate.

Crown Prince Simeon A151 A153

Designs: 2 l, Same portrait as 1 l, value at lower left. 14 l, similar to 4 l, but no wreath.

1938, June 16

336	A151	1 l brt green	.20	.20
337	A151	2 l rose pink	.20	.20
338	A153	4 l dp orange	.20	.20
339	A151	7 l ultra	.80	.40
340	A153	14 l dp brown	.80	.40
		Nos. 336-340 (5)	2.20	1.40

First birthday of Prince Simeon.

Tsar Boris III A155 A156

Various Portraits of Tsar.

1938, Oct. 3

341	A155	1 l lt green	.20	.20
342	A156	2 l rose brown	.60	.20
343	A156	4 l golden brn	.20	.20
344	A156	7 l brt ultra	1.00	1.00
345	A156	14 l deep red lilac	.35	.25
		Nos. 341-345 (5)	2.35	1.85

Reign of Tsar Boris III, 20th anniv.

Early Locomotive A160

Designs: 2 l, Modern locomotive. 4 l, Train crossing bridge. 7 l, Tsar Boris in cab.

1939, Apr. 26

346	A160	1 l yel green	.25	.20
347	A160	2 l copper brn	.25	.20
348	A160	4 l red orange	1.50	.20
349	A160	7 l dark blue	3.50	.85
		Nos. 346-349 (4)	5.50	1.45

50th anniv. of Bulgarian State Railways.

Post Horns and Arrows — A164

Central Post Office, Sofia — A165

1939, May 14 Typo.

350	A164	1 l yellow grn	.25	.20
351	A165	2 l brt carmine	.30	.20

Establishment of the postal system, 60th anniv.

Gymnast on Bar — A166

Yunak Emblem — A167

Discus Thrower — A168

Athletic Dancer — A169

Weight Lifter — A170

1939, July 7 Photo.

352	A166	1 l yel grn & pale grn	.40	.20
353	A167	2 l brt rose	.45	.20
354	A168	4 l brn & gldn brn	.65	.35
355	A169	7 l dk bl & bl	1.50	.80
356	A170	14 l plum & rose vio	6.75	3.25
		Nos. 352-356 (5)	9.75	4.80

9th tournament of the Yunak Gymnastic Organization at Sofia, July 4-8.

Tsar Boris III — A171

Bulgaria's First Stamp — A172

1940-41 **Typo.**

356A	A171	1 l dl grn ('41)	.80	.20
357	A171	2 l brt crimson	.20	.20

1940, May 19 **Photo.** ***Perf. 13***

20 l, Similar design, scroll dated "1840-1940."

358	A172	10 l olive black	1.50	.90
359	A172	20 l indigo	1.50	.90

Cent. of 1st postage stamp. Exist imperf.

Peasant Couple and Tsar Boris — A174

Flags over Wheat Field and Tsar Boris — A175

Tsar Boris and Map of Dobrudja A176

1940, Sept. 20

360	A174	1 l slate green	.20	.20
361	A175	2 l rose red	.20	.20
362	A176	4 l dark brown	.20	.20
363	A176	7 l dark blue	1.60	1.25
		Nos. 360-363 (4)	2.20	1.85

Return of Dobrudja from Romania.

Fruit A177

Bees and Flowers A178

Plowing A179

Shepherd and Sheep A180

Tsar Boris III — A181

Perf. 10, 10½x11½, 11½, 13

1940-44 **Typo.** **Unwmk.**

364	A177	10s red orange	.20	.20
365	A178	15s blue	.20	.20
366	A179	30s olive brn ('41)	.20	.20
367	A180	50s violet	.20	.20
368	A181	1 l brt green	.20	.20
369	A181	2 l rose car	.20	.20
370	A181	4 l red orange	.20	.20
371	A181	6 l red vio ('44)	.30	.20
372	A181	7 l blue	.30	.20
373	A181	10 l blue grn ('41)	.30	.20
		Nos. 364-373 (10)	2.30	2.00

See Nos. 373A-377, 440. For overprints see Nos. 455-463, C31-C32.

1940-41 **Wmk. 145** ***Perf. 13***

373A	A180	50s violet ('41)	.20	.20
374	A181	1 l brt grn	.20	.20
375	A181	2 l rose car	.20	.20
376	A181	7 l dull blue	.45	.20
377	A181	10 l blue green	.65	.20
		Nos. 373A-377 (5)	1.70	1.00

Watermarked vertically or horizontally.

P. R. Slaveikov A182

Sofronii, Bishop of Vratza A183

Saint Ivan Rilski — A184

Martin S. Drinov — A185

Monk Khrabr — A186

Kolio Ficheto — A187

1940, Sept. 23 **Photo.** **Unwmk.**

378	A182	1 l brt bl grn	.20	.20
379	A183	2 l brt carmine	.20	.20
380	A184	3 l dp red brn	.20	.20
381	A185	4 l red orange	.20	.20
382	A186	7 l deep blue	1.00	.60
383	A187	10 l dp red brn	1.50	.85
		Nos. 378-383 (6)	3.30	2.25

Liberation of Bulgaria from the Turks in 1878.

Johannes Gutenberg A188

N. Karastoyanov, 1st Bulgarian Printer A189

1940, Dec. 16

384	A188	1 l slate green	.20	.20
385	A189	2 l orange brown	.20	.20

500th anniv. of the invention of the printing press and 100th anniv. of the 1st Bulgarian printing press.

SEMI-POSTAL STAMPS

Catalogue values for unused stamps in this section are for Never Hinged items.

Regular Issues of 1911-20 Surcharged:

a

b

c

Perf. 11½x12, 12x11½

1920, June 20 **Unwmk.**

B1	A43 (a)	2s + 1s ol grn	.20	.20
B2	A44 (b)	5s + 2½s grn	.20	.20
B3	A44 (b)	10s + 5s rose	.20	.20
B4	A44 (b)	15s + 7½s vio	.20	.20
B5	A44 (b)	25s + 12½s dp bl	.20	.20
B6	A44 (b)	30s + 15s choc	.20	.20
B7	A44 (b)	50s + 25s yel brn	.20	.20
B8	A29 (c)	1 l + 50s dk brn	.20	.20
B9	A37a (a)	2 l + 1 l brn org	.25	.25
B10	A38 (a)	3 l + 1½ l claret	.55	.45
		Nos. B1-B10 (10)	2.40	2.30

Surtax aided ex-prisoners of war. Value, Nos. B1-B7 imperf., $7.75.

Tsar Boris Type of 1937 Souvenir Sheet

1937, Nov. 22 **Photo.** ***Imperf.***

B11	A140	2 l + 18 l ultra	6.00	4.00

19th anniv. of the accession of Tsar Boris III to the throne.

Stamps of 1917-21 Surcharged in Black

1939, Oct. 22 ***Perf. 12½, 12***

B12	A34	1 l + 1 l on 15s slate	.20	.20
B13	A69	2 l + 1 l on 1½ l ol grn	.25	.25
B14	A69	4 l + 2 l on 2 l dp grn	.25	.25
B15	A69	7 l + 4 l on 3 l Prus bl	.75	.75
B16	A69	14 l + 7 l on 5 l red brn	1.00	1.00
		Nos. B12-B16 (5)	2.45	2.45

Surtax aided victims of the Sevlievo flood. The surcharge on #B13-B16 omits "leva."

AIR POST STAMPS

Regular Issues of 1925-26 Overprinted in Various Colors

1927-28 **Unwmk.** ***Perf. 11½***

C1	A76	2 l ol (R) ('28)	1.25	.70
C2	A74	4 l lake & yel (Bl)	1.75	.70
C3	A77	10 l brn blk & brn org (G) ('28)	30.00	13.00

Overprinted Vertically and Surcharged with New Value

C4	A77	1 l on 6 l dp bl & pale lem (C)	1.25	.70
a.		Inverted surcharge	*340.00*	*275.00*
b.		Pair, one without surcharge	*440.00*	
		Nos. C1-C4 (4)	34.25	15.10

Nos. C2-C4 overprinted in changed colors were not issued, value set $10.50.

Dove Delivering Message AP1

Junkers Plane, Rila Monastery AP2

1931, Oct. 28 **Typo.**

C5	AP1	1 l dk green	.20	.20
C6	AP1	2 l maroon	.20	.20
C7	AP1	6 l dp blue	.30	.20
C8	AP1	12 l carmine	.30	.30
C9	AP1	20 l dk violet	.65	.55
C10	AP1	30 l dp orange	1.00	1.25
C11	AP1	50 l orange brn	2.25	1.40
		Nos. C5-C11 (7)	4.90	4.10

Counterfeits exist. See Nos. C15-C18.

1932, May 9

C12	AP2	18 l blue grn	55.00	11.00
C13	AP2	24 l dp red	40.00	11.00
C14	AP2	28 l ultra	25.00	11.00
		Nos. C12-C14 (3)	120.00	33.00

Catalogue values for unused stamps in this section, from this point to the end of the section, are for Never Hinged items.

1938, Dec. 27

C15	AP1	1 l violet brown	.25	.20
C16	AP1	2 l green	.20	.20
C17	AP1	6 l deep rose	.70	.30
C18	AP1	12 l peacock blue	.85	.30
		Nos. C15-C18 (4)	2.00	1.00

Counterfeits exist.

Mail Plane — AP3

Plane over Tsar Assen's Tower — AP4

Designs: 4 l, Plane over Bachkovski Monastery. 6 l, Bojurishte Airport, Sofia. 10 l, Plane, train and motorcycle. 12 l, Planes over Sofia Palace. 16 l, Plane over Pirin Valley. 19 l, Plane over Rila Monastery. 30 l, Plane and Swallow. 45 l, Plane over Sofia Cathedral. 70 l, Plane over Shipka Monument. 100 l, Plane and Royal Cipher.

1940, Jan. 15 **Photo.** ***Perf. 13***

C19	AP3	1 l dk green	.20	.20
C20	AP4	2 l crimson	1.10	.20
C21	AP4	4 l red orange	.20	.20
C22	AP3	6 l dp blue	.20	.20
C23	AP4	10 l dk brown	.30	.20
C24	AP3	12 l dull brown	.50	.20
C25	AP3	16 l brt bl vio	.55	.25
C26	AP3	19 l sapphire	.75	.30
C27	AP4	30 l rose lake	1.10	.50
C28	AP4	45 l gray violet	2.75	.95
C29	AP4	70 l rose pink	2.75	1.25
C30	AP4	100 l dp slate bl	9.00	3.75
		Nos. C19-C30 (12)	19.40	8.20

SPECIAL DELIVERY STAMPS

Catalogue values for unused stamps in this section are for Never Hinged items.

Postman on Bicycle — SD1

Mail Car — SD2

Postman on Motorcycle — SD3

1939 Unwmk. Photo. *Perf. 13*

E1	SD1	5 l deep blue	.60	.20
E2	SD2	6 l copper brn	.25	.20
E3	SD3	7 l golden brn	.35	.20
E4	SD2	8 l red orange	.65	.20
E5	SD1	20 l bright rose	1.25	.40
		Nos. E1-E5 (5)	3.10	1.20

POSTAGE DUE STAMPS

D1

D2

Large Lozenge Perf. 5½ to 6½

1884 Typo. Unwmk.

J1	D1	5s orange	160.00	15.00
J2	D1	25s lake	77.50	10.00
J3	D1	50s blue	13.00	5.00
		Nos. J1-J3 (3)	250.50	30.00

1886 *Imperf.*

J4	D1	5s orange	75.00	2.50
J5	D1	25s lake	140.00	2.75
J6	D1	50s blue	5.00	2.75
		Nos. J4-J6 (3)	220.00	8.00

1887 *Perf. 11½*

J7	D1	5s orange	9.50	1.00
J8	D1	25s lake	9.50	1.00
J9	D1	50s blue	3.50	1.00
		Nos. J7-J9 (3)	22.50	3.00

Same, Redrawn

24 horizontal lines of shading in upper part instead of 30 lines

1892 *Perf. 10½, 11½*

J10	D1	5s orange	7.50	1.25
J11	D1	25s lake	7.50	1.25

1893

Pelure Paper

J12	D2	5s orange	10.00	3.50

D3

D4

1895 *Imperf.*

J13	D3	30s on 50s blue	7.00	2.00

Perf. 10½, 11½

J14	D3	30s on 50s blue	7.00	2.00

Wmk. Coat of Arms in the Sheet

1896 *Perf. 13*

J15	D4	5s orange	3.00	.75
J16	D4	10s purple	2.00	.75
J17	D4	30s green	1.40	.45
		Nos. J15-J17 (3)	6.40	1.95

Nos. J15-J17 are also known on unwatermarked paper from the edges of sheets.

In 1901 a cancellation, "T" in circle, was applied to Nos. 60-65 and used provisionally as postage dues.

D5

D6

1901-04 Unwmk. *Perf. 11½*

J19	D5	5s dl rose	.20	.20
J20	D5	10s yel grn	.40	.20
J21	D5	20s dl bl ('04)	3.25	.20
J22	D5	30s vio brn	.35	.20
J23	D5	50s org ('02)	5.50	4.00
		Nos. J19-J23 (5)	9.70	4.80

Nos. J19-J23 exist imperf. and in pairs imperf. between. Value, imperf., $250.

1915 Unwmk. *Perf. 11½*

Thin Semi-Transparent Paper

J24	D6	5s green	.20	.20
J25	D6	10s purple	.20	.20
J26	D6	20s dl rose	.20	.20
J27	D6	30s dp org	1.10	.20
J28	D6	50s dp bl	.35	.20
		Nos. J24-J28 (5)	2.05	1.00

1919-21 *Perf. 11½, 12x11½*

J29	D6	5s emerald	.20	.20
a.		5s gray green ('21)	.30	.20
J30	D6	10s violet	.20	.20
J31	D6	20s salmon	.20	.20
a.		20s yellow	.20	.20
J32	D6	30s orange	.20	.20
a.		30s red orange ('21)	.65	.65
J33	D6	50s blue	.20	.20
J34	D6	1 l emerald ('21)	.20	.20
J35	D6	2 l rose ('21)	.20	.20
J36	D6	3 l brown org ('21)	.35	.20
		Nos. J29-J36 (8)	1.75	1.60

Stotinki values of the above series surcharged 10s or 20s were used as ordinary postage stamps. See Nos. 182-185.

The 1919 printings are on thicker white paper with clean-cut perforations, the 1921 printings on thicker grayish paper with rough perforations.

Most of this series exist imperforate and in pairs imperforate between.

Heraldic Lion — D7

1932, Aug. 15

Thin Paper

J37	D7	1 l olive bister	.25	.20
J38	D7	2 l rose brown	.25	.20
J39	D7	6 l brown violet	.75	.35
		Nos. J37-J39 (3)	1.25	.75

Lion of Trnovo — D8

National Arms — D9

1933, Apr. 10

J40	D8	20s dk brn	.20	.20
J41	D8	40s dp bl	.20	.20
J42	D8	80s car rose	.20	.20
J43	D9	1 l org brn	.25	.20
J44	D9	2 l olive	.30	.25
J45	D9	6 l dl vio	.20	.20
J46	D9	14 l ultra	.25	.20
		Nos. J40-J46 (7)	1.60	1.45

POSTAL TAX STAMPS

The use of stamps Nos. RA1 to RA18 was compulsory on letters, etc., to be delivered on Sundays and holidays. The money received from their sale was used toward maintaining a sanatorium for employees of the post, telegraph and telephone services.

View of Sanatorium PT1

Sanatorium, Peshtera PT2

1925-29 Unwmk. Typo. *Perf. 11½*

RA1	PT1	1 l blk, *grnsh bl*	2.75	.20
RA2	PT1	1 l chocolate ('26)	2.75	.20
RA3	PT1	1 l orange ('27)	3.00	.30
RA4	PT1	1 l pink ('28)	4.50	.30
RA5	PT1	1 l vio, *pnksh* ('29)	4.75	.30
RA6	PT2	2 l blue green	.35	.20
RA7	PT2	2 l violet ('27)	.35	.20
RA8	PT2	5 l deep blue	3.00	.80
RA9	PT2	5 l rose ('27)	3.75	.40
		Nos. RA1-RA9 (9)	25.20	2.90

St. Constantine Sanatorium PT3

1930-33

RA10	PT3	1 l red brn & ol grn	4.00	.20
RA11	PT3	1 l ol grn & yel ('31)	.50	.20
RA12	PT3	1 l red vio & ol brn ('33)	.50	.20
		Nos. RA10-RA12 (3)	5.00	.60

Trojan Rest Home — PT4

Sanatorium PT5

1935 Wmk. 145 *Perf. 11, 11½*

RA13	PT4	1 l choc & red org	.30	.20
RA14	PT4	1 l emer & indigo	.30	.20
RA15	PT5	5 l red brn & indigo	1.40	.35
		Nos. RA13-RA15 (3)	2.00	.75

BURMA

'bər-mə

LOCATION — Bounded on the north by China; east by China, Laos and Thailand; south and west by the Bay of Bengal, and India.

GOVT. — Self-governing unit of the British Commonwealth

AREA — 261,789 sq. mi.

POP. — 35,313,905 (1983)

CAPITAL — Rangoon

Burma was part of India from 1826 until April 1, 1937, when it became a self-governing unit of the British Commonwealth and received a constitution.

12 Pies = 1 Anna

16 Annas = 1 Rupee

Catalogue values for unused stamps in this country are for Never Hinged items, beginning with Scott 35 in the regular postage section and Scott O28 in the official section.

Watermarks

Wmk. 254 — Elephant Heads

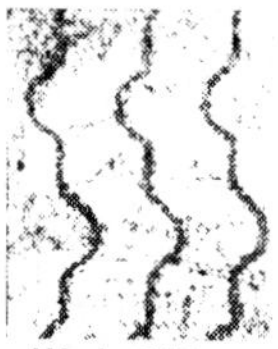
Wmk. 257 — Curved Wavy Lines

Stamps of India 1926-36 Overprinted

1937, Apr. 1 Wmk. 196 *Perf. 14*

1	A46	3p slate	.45	.20
		Never hinged	.75	
2	A71	½a green	.65	.20
		Never hinged	1.10	
3	A68	9p dark green	.70	.20
		Never hinged	1.25	
4	A72	1a dark brown	1.25	.20
		Never hinged	2.10	
5	A49	2a ver (small die)	.50	.20
		Never hinged	.85	
6	A57	2a6p buff	.40	.20
		Never hinged	.65	
7	A51	3a carmine rose	1.00	.50
		Never hinged	1.60	
8	A70	3a6p deep blue	1.75	.20
		Never hinged	3.00	
a.		3a6p dull blue	7.50	*8.00*
		Never hinged	11.00	
9	A52	4a olive green	.70	.20
		Never hinged	1.25	
10	A53	6a bister	.50	.60
		Never hinged	.85	
11	A54	8a red violet	1.25	.20
		Never hinged	2.10	
12	A55	12a claret	3.50	1.50
		Never hinged	6.00	

Overprinted

13	A56	1r green & brown	16.00	3.75
		Never hinged	27.50	
14	A56	2r brn org & car rose	16.50	15.00
		Never hinged	35.00	
15	A56	5r dk violet & ultra	22.50	*24.00*
		Never hinged	40.00	
16	A56	10r car & green	60.00	*75.00*
		Never hinged	110.00	
17	A56	15r ol green & ultra	225.00	135.00
		Never hinged	400.00	
18	A56	25r blue & ocher	450.00	425.00
		Never hinged	725.00	
		Nos. 1-18 (18)	682.65	

For overprints see #1N1-1N3, 1N25-1N26, 1N47.

King George VI

A1 A2

Royal Barge — A3

Elephant Moving Teak Log — A4

Farmer Plowing Rice Field — A5

Sailboat on Irrawaddy River — A6

Peacock — A7

George VI — A8

Perf. 13½x14

1938-40 Litho. Wmk. 254

18A	A1	1p red org ('40)	2.50	1.10
		Never hinged	3.50	
19	A1	3p violet	.20	*1.50*
		Never hinged	.25	
20	A1	6p ultramarine	.25	.20
		Never hinged	.25	
21	A1	9p yel green	.75	*1.25*
		Never hinged	1.25	
22	A2	1a brown violet	.25	.20
		Never hinged	.25	
23	A2	1½a turquoise green	.25	*1.75*
		Never hinged	.25	
24	A2	2a carmine	.50	.20
		Never hinged	.65	

Perf. 13

25	A3	2a6p rose lake	12.00	2.00
		Never hinged	17.50	
26	A4	3a dk violet	12.00	2.25
		Never hinged	17.50	
27	A5	3a6p dp blue & brt bl	1.25	*5.00*
		Never hinged	1.60	
28	A2	4a slate blue, perf. 13½x14	.75	.20
		Never hinged	.85	
29	A6	8a slate green	3.50	.40
		Never hinged	4.50	

Perf. 13½

30	A7	1r brt ultra & dk violet	3.50	.25
		Never hinged	4.50	
31	A7	2r dk vio & red brown	14.00	2.75
		Never hinged	20.00	
32	A8	5r car & dull vio	40.00	24.00
		Never hinged	60.00	
33	A8	10r gray grn & brn	50.00	50.00
		Never hinged	65.00	
		Nos. 18A-33 (16)	141.70	93.05
		Set, never hinged	250.00	

See Nos. 51-65. For overprints and surcharges see Nos. 34-50, O15-O27, 1N4-1N11, 1N28-1N30, 1N37-1N46, 1N48-1N49.

No. 25 Surcharged in Black

1940, May 6 ***Perf. 13***

34	A3	1a on 2a6p rose lake	3.00	1.50
		Never hinged	5.75	

Centenary of first postage stamp.

Catalogue values for unused stamps in this section, from this point to the end of the section, are for Never Hinged items.

Nos. 18A to 33 Overprinted in Black:

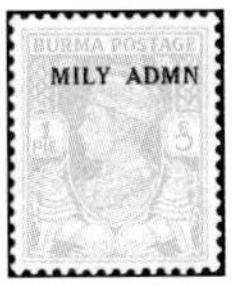

a

b

1945

35	A1(a)	1p red orange	.20	.20
36	A1(a)	3p violet	.20	*1.00*
37	A1(a)	6p ultramarine	.20	*.35*
38	A1(a)	9p yel green	.35	*1.10*
39	A2(a)	1a brown violet	.20	.20
40	A2(a)	1½a turq green	.20	.20
41	A2(a)	2a carmine	.20	.20
42	A3(b)	2a6p rose lake	2.25	*1.90*
43	A4(b)	3a dk violet	1.75	.20
44	A5(b)	3a6p dp bl & brt bl	.20	*.85*
45	A2(a)	4a slate blue	.20	*.75*
46	A6(b)	8a slate green	.20	*1.10*
47	A7(b)	1r brt ultra & dk vio	.45	*.60*
48	A7(b)	2r dk vio & red brown	.50	*1.40*
49	A8(b)	5r car & dull vio	.60	*1.40*
50	A8(b)	10r gray grn & brn	1.00	*1.40*
		Nos. 35-50 (16)	8.70	12.85

Types of 1938

Perf. 13½x14

1946, Jan. 1 Litho. Wmk. 254

51	A1	3p brown	.20	*2.50*
52	A1	6p violet	.20	*.40*
53	A1	9p dull green	.20	*3.50*
54	A2	1a deep blue	.20	.20
55	A2	1½a salmon	.20	.20
56	A2	2a rose lake	.20	*.50*

Perf. 13

57	A3	2a6p greenish blue	2.75	*4.50*
58	A4	3a blue violet	6.75	5.00
59	A5	3a6p ultra & gray blk	.75	*2.50*
60	A2	4a rose lil, perf. 13½x14	.50	.50
61	A6	8a deep magenta	2.25	4.75

Perf. 13½

62	A7	1r dp mag & dk vio	1.25	*1.90*
63	A7	2r salmon & red brn	7.50	*5.00*
64	A8	5r red brn & dk grn	7.50	*18.50*
65	A8	10r dk vio & car	11.00	*22.50*
		Nos. 51-65 (15)	41.45	72.45

For overprints see Nos. 70-84, O28-O42.

Burmese Man — A9

Burmese Woman — A10

Mythological Chinze — A11

Elephant Hauling Teak — A12

1946, May 2 ***Perf. 13***

66	A9	9p peacock green	.20	.20
67	A10	1½a brt violet	.20	.20
68	A11	2a carmine	.20	.20
69	A12	3a6p ultramarine	.40	.20
		Nos. 66-69 (4)	1.00	.80

Victory of the Allied Nations in WWII.

Nos. 51-65 Overprinted in Black

1947, Oct. 1 ***Perf. 13½x14, 13, 13½***

70	A1	3p brown	.85	.85
71	A1	6p violet	.20	*.40*
72	A1	9p dull green	.20	*.40*
a.		Inverted overprint	22.50	27.50
73	A2	1a deep blue	.20	*.40*
74	A2	1½a salmon	1.50	.20
75	A2	2a rose lake	.50	.25
76	A3	2a6p greenish bl	2.25	1.10
77	A4	3a blue violet	3.50	2.00
78	A5	3a6p ultra & gray blk	.90	*2.25*
79	A2	4a rose lilac	2.25	.50
80	A6	8a dp magenta	2.25	2.50
81	A7	1r dp mag & dk vio	5.50	1.40
82	A7	2r sal & red brn	5.50	4.75
83	A8	5r red brn & dk grn	5.50	*5.00*
84	A8	10r dk vio & car	3.75	*5.25*
		Nos. 70-84 (15)	34.85	*27.25*

The overprint is slightly larger on Nos. 76 to 78 and 80 to 84. The Burmese characters read "Interim Government."

Other denominations are known with the overprint inverted or double.

OFFICIAL STAMPS

Stamps of India, 1926-34, Overprinted in Black

1937 Wmk. 196 ***Perf. 14***

O1	A46	3p gray	2.00	.20
O2	A71	½a green	9.50	.20
O3	A68	9p dark green	4.50	.60
O4	A72	1a dark brown	4.75	.30
O5	A49	2a vermilion	11.00	.75
O6	A57	2a6p buff	5.75	3.25
O7	A52	4a olive grn	4.75	.40
O8	A53	6a bister	4.00	*12.00*
O9	A54	8a red violet	4.00	2.25
O10	A55	12a claret	4.00	*9.75*

Overprinted

O11	A56	1r green & brown	15.00	5.75
O12	A56	2r buff & car rose	35.00	*50.00*
O13	A56	5r dk vio & ultra	80.00	60.00
O14	A56	10r car & green	210.00	*175.00*
		Nos. O1-O14 (14)	394.25	*320.45*
		Set, never hinged	700.00	

For overprint see No. 1N27.

Regular Issue of 1938 Overprinted in Black

Perf. 13½x14, 13, 13½

1939 Wmk. 254

O15	A1	3p violet	.35	*.45*
O16	A1	6p ultramarine	.35	*.45*
O17	A1	9p yel green	4.50	4.50
O18	A2	1a brown violet	.40	*.50*
O19	A2	1½a turquoise green	4.25	2.25
O20	A2	2a carmine	1.50	.50
O21	A2	4a slate blue	5.50	.75

Overprinted

O22	A3	2a6p rose lake	19.00	17.00
O23	A6	8a slate green	17.00	5.00
O24	A7	1r brt ultra & dk vio	27.50	7.00
O25	A7	2r dk vio & red brn	30.00	*15.00*
O26	A8	5r car & dull vio	25.00	*16.00*
O27	A8	10r gray grn & brn	140.00	35.00
		Nos. O15-O27 (13)	275.35	104.40
		Set, never hinged	400.00	

For overprints see Nos. 1N12-1N16, 1N31-1N36, 1NO1.

Catalogue values for unused stamps in this section, from this point to the end of the section, are for Never Hinged items.

Nos. 51-56, 60 Overprinted Like Nos. O15-O21

1946 ***Perf. 13½x14***

O28	A1	3p brown	4.25	*4.50*
O29	A1	6p violet	2.25	*2.50*
O30	A1	9p dull green	.60	*3.75*
O31	A2	1a deep blue	.30	*2.25*
O32	A2	1½a salmon	.30	.40
O33	A2	2a rose lake	.35	*2.25*
O34	A2	4a rose lilac	.35	.90

Nos. 57, 61-65 Ovptd. Like Nos. O22-O27

Perf. 13, 13½

O35	A3	2a6p greenish blue	2.25	*8.00*
O38	A6	8a deep magenta	4.00	*4.25*
O39	A7	1r dp mag & dk vio	.75	*5.75*
O40	A7	2r salmon & red brn	8.25	*47.50*
O41	A8	5r red brn & dk grn	12.00	*52.50*
O42	A8	10r dk violet & car	20.00	*62.50*
		Nos. O28-O42 (13)	55.65	*197.05*

Nos. O28 to O42 Overprinted in Black

1947

O43	A1	3p brown	.50	*.55*
O44	A1	6p violet	3.25	*.25*
O45	A1	9p dull green	4.25	1.25

O46	A2	1a deep blue	4.25	1.10
O47	A2	1½a salmon	8.00	.60
O48	A2	2a rose lake	4.50	.30
O49	A3	2a6p greenish bl	30.00	15.00
O50	A2	4a rose lilac	17.50	.80
O51	A6	8a dp magenta	17.50	6.50
O52	A7	1r dp mag & dk vio	16.50	3.75
O53	A7	2r sal & red brn	16.50	22.50
O54	A8	5r red brn & dk grn	16.50	25.00
O55	A8	10r dk vio & car	16.50	35.00
		Nos. O43-O55 (13)	155.75	112.60

The overprint is slightly larger on Nos. O49 and O51 to O55. The Burmese characters read "Interim Government."

OCCUPATION STAMPS

Issued by Burma Independence Army (in conjunction with Japanese occupation officials)

Stamps of Burma, 1937-40, Overprinted in Blue, Black Blue, Black or Red

Henzada Issue

#1, 3, 5 Overprinted in Blue or Black

Henzada Type I

1942, May Wmk. 196 *Perf. 14*

1N1	A46	3p slate	5.00	15.00
1N2	A68	9p dark green	25.00	50.00
1N3	A49	2a vermilion	125.00	175.00

On 1938-40 George VI Issue

Perf. 13½x14

Wmk. 254

1N4	A1	1p red orange	200.00	250.00
1N5	A1	3p violet	30.00	45.00
1N6	A1	6p ultra	25.00	45.00
1N7	A1	9p yel green	400.00	
1N8	A2	1a brown violet	9.00	35.00
1N9	A2	1½a turq green	25.00	55.00
1N10	A2	2a carmine	25.00	55.00
1N11	A2	4a slate blue	50.00	85.00

On Official Stamps of 1939

1N12	A1	3p violet	75.00	200.00
1N13	A1	6p ultra	100.00	200.00
1N14	A2	1½a turq green	100.00	250.00
1N15	A2	2a carmine	275.00	400.00
1N16	A2	4a slate blue	1,350.	

Authorities believe this overprint was officially applied only to postal stationery and that the adhesive stamps existing with it were not regularly issued. It has been called "Henzada Type II."

Myaungmya Issue

1937 George V Issue Overprinted in Black

Myaungmya Type I

1942, May Wmk. 196 *Perf. 14*

1N25	A68	9p dk green	110.00
1N26	A70	3a6p deep blue	50.00

On Official Stamp of 1937, No. O8

1N27	A53	6a bister	75.00

On 1938-40 George VI Issue

Perf. 13½x14

Wmk. 254

1N28	A1	9p yel green	100.00
1N29	A2	1a brown vio	400.00
1N30	A2	4a sl blue (blk ovpt. over red)	175.00

On Official Stamps of 1939

1N31	A1	3p violet	27.50	50.00
1N32	A1	6p ultra	17.50	40.00
1N33	A2	1a brown vio	17.50	40.00
1N34	A2	1½a turq green	400.00	
1N35	A2	2a carmine	27.50	75.00
1N36	A2	4a slate blue	15.00	55.00

1938-40 George VI Issue Overprinted

Myaungmya Type II

1942, May

1N37	A1	3p violet	20.00	50.00
1N38	A1	6p ultra	60.00	85.00
1N39	A1	9p yel green	24.00	50.00
1N40	A2	1a brown vio	17.50	42.50
1N41	A2	2a carmine	24.00	60.00
1N42	A2	4a slate blue	40.00	80.00

Nos. 30-31 Overprinted

Myaungmya Type III

1N43	A7	1r brt ultra & dk vio	200.00
1N44	A7	2r dk vio & red brn	175.00

Pyapon Issue

No. 5 and 1938-40 George VI Issue Overprinted

1942, May

1N45	A1	6p ultra	75.00	
1N46	A2	1a brown vio	75.00	200.00
1N47	A49	2a vermilion	75.00	
1N48	A2	2a carmine	150.00	250.00
1N49	A2	4a slate blue	400.00	400.00
		Nos. 1N45-1N49 (5)	775.00	

Counterfeits of the peacock overprints exist.

OCCUPATION OFFICIAL STAMP

Myaungmya Issue

Burma No. O23 Overprinted in Black

1942, May Wmk. 254 *Perf. 13*

1NO1	A6	8a slate green	100.00

Overprint characters translate: "Office use." Two types of overprint differ mainly in base of peacock which is either 5mm or 8mm.

ISSUED UNDER JAPANESE OCCUPATION

Yano Seal — OS1

Wmk. ABSORBO DUPLICATOR and Outline of Elephant in Center of Sheet

Handstamped

1942, June 1 *Perf. 12x11*

Without Gum

2N1	OS1	1(a) vermilion	35.00	40.00

This stamp is the handstamped impression of the personal chop or seal of Shizuo Yano, chairman of the committee appointed to re-establish the Burmese postal system. It was prepared in Rangoon on paper captured from the Burma Government Offices. Not every stamp shows a portion of the watermark.

Farmer Plowing — OS2

Vertically Laid Paper

Without Gum

Wmk. ELEPHANT BRAND and Outline of Trumpeting Elephant Covering Several Stamps

1942, June 15 Litho. *Perf. 11x12*

2N2	OS2	1a scarlet	12.50	17.50

See illustration OS4.

Same, Surcharged with New Value

1942, Oct. 15

2N3	OS2	5c on 1a scarlet	11.50	17.00

Rice Harvest — A83

General Nogi — A84

Power Plant — A85

Admiral Togo — A86

Diamond Mountains, Korea — A89

Meiji Shrine, Tokyo — A90

Yomei Gate, Nikko — A91

Mount Fuji and Cherry Blossoms — A94

Torii of Miyajima Shrine — A96

Stamps of Japan, 1937-42, Handstamp Surcharged with New Value in Black

1942, Sept. Wmk. 257 *Perf. 13*

2N4	A83	¼a on 1s fawn	24.00	27.50
2N5	A84	½a on 2s crim	26.00	30.00
2N6	A85	¾a on 3s green	50.00	55.00
2N7	A86	1a on 5s brn lake	45.00	35.00
2N8	A89	3a on 7s dp green	90.00	95.00
2N9	A86	4a on 4s dk green	40.00	40.00
a.		4a on 4s + 2s dk green (#B5)	100.00	125.00
2N10	A90	8a on 8s dk pur & pale vio	150.00	150.00
a.		Red surcharge	225.00	250.00
2N11	A91	1r on 10s lake	18.00	22.50
2N12	A94	2r on 20s ultra	50.00	55.00
a.		Red surcharge	37.50	37.50
2N13	A96	5r on 30s pck bl	12.00	22.50
a.		Red surcharge	22.50	27.50
		Nos. 2N4-2N13 (10)	505.00	532.50

Numerous double, inverted, etc., surcharges exist.

Re-surcharged in Black

1942, Oct. 15

2N14	A83	1c on ¼a on 1s	40.00	40.00
2N15	A84	2c on ½a on 2s	45.00	45.00
2N16	A85	3c on ¾a on 3s	50.00	50.00
a.		"3C." in blue	175.00	
2N17	A86	5c on 1a on 5s	50.00	50.00
a.		"3C." in blue	125.00	
2N18	A89	10c on 3a on 7s	100.00	100.00
2N19	A86	15c on 4a on 4s	25.00	30.00
2N20	A90	20c on 8a on 8s (#2N10)	350.00	300.00
a.		On #2N10a	250.00	175.00
		Nos. 2N14-2N20 (7)	660.00	615.00

No. 2N16a was issued in the Shan States.

Done locally, numerous different handstamps of each denomination can exist.

Stamps of Japan, 1937-42, Handstamp Surcharged with New Value in Black

1942, Oct. 15

2N21	A83	1c on 1s fawn	17.50	17.50
2N22	A84	2c on 2s crim	37.50	30.00
2N23	A85	3c on 3s green	37.50	37.50
a.		"3C." in blue	85.00	100.00
2N24	A86	5c on 5s brn lake	40.00	42.50
a.		"5C." in violet	125.00	175.00
2N25	A89	10c on 7s dp grn	50.00	50.00
2N26	A86	15c on 4s dk grn	15.00	20.00
2N27	A90	20c on 8s dk pur & pale vio	100.00	75.00
		Nos. 2N21-2N27 (7)	297.50	272.50

Nos. 2N23a and 2N24a were issued in the Shan States.

Burma State Government Crest — OS3

Unwmk.

1943, Feb. 15 Litho. *Perf. 12*

Without Gum

2N29	OS3	5c carmine	10.00	12.50
a.		Imperf.	12.50	15.00

This stamp was intended to be used to cover the embossed George VI envelope stamp and generally was sold affixed to such envelopes. It is also known used on private envelopes.

Farmer Plowing — OS4

1943, Mar. Typo.

Without Gum

2N30	OS4	1c deep orange	1.00	1.00
2N31	OS4	2c yel green	1.00	1.50
2N32	OS4	3c blue	1.00	1.00
a.		Laid paper	10.00	10.00
2N33	OS4	5c carmine	.50	.65
a.		Small "5c"	3.00	4.00
b.		Imperf.		
2N34	OS4	10c violet brown	.75	.90
2N35	OS4	15c red violet	.25	.25
a.		Laid paper	10.00	
2N36	OS4	20c dull purple	.25	.75
2N37	OS4	30c blue green	.25	.75
		Nos. 2N30-2N37 (8)	5.00	6.80

Small "c" in Nos. 2N34 to 2N37.

Burmese Soldier Carving "Independence" OS5

Farmer Rejoicing OS6

Boy with Burmese Flag — OS7

Hyphen-hole Perf., Pin-Perf. x Hyphen-hole Perf.

1943, Aug. 1 **Typo.**

2N38	OS5	1c orange	1.00	*2.00*
a.		Perf. 11	3.50	*4.00*
2N39	OS6	3c blue	1.00	*2.00*
a.		Perf. 11	3.50	*4.00*
2N40	OS7	5c rose	1.00	*2.00*
a.		Perf. 11	3.50	*4.00*
		Nos. 2N38-2N40 (3)	3.00	*6.00*

Declaration of the independence of Burma by the Ba Maw government, Aug. 1, 1943.

Burmese Girl Carrying Water Jar — OS8

Elephant Carrying Teak Log — OS9

Watch Tower of Mandalay Palace — OS10

1943, Oct. 1 **Litho.** ***Perf. 12½***

2N41	OS8	1c dp salmon	17.00	*10.00*
2N42	OS8	2c yel green	.60	*1.25*
2N43	OS8	3c violet	.60	*1.00*
2N44	OS9	5c rose	.65	*1.00*
2N45	OS9	10c blue	.80	.60
2N46	OS9	15c vermilion	.80	*1.00*
2N47	OS9	20c yel green	.80	*1.25*
2N48	OS9	30c brown	.80	*1.25*
2N49	OS10	1r vermilion	.35	*3.00*
2N50	OS10	2r violet	.35	*5.00*
		Nos. 2N41-2N50 (10)	22.75	*25.35*

No. 2N49 exists imperforate. Canceled to order copies of Nos. 2N42-2N50 same values as unused.

Bullock Cart OS11

Shan Woman OS12

1943, Oct. 1 ***Perf. 12½***

2N51	OS11	1c brown	22.50	*35.00*
2N52	OS11	2c yel green	22.50	*35.00*
2N53	OS11	3c violet	20.00	*30.00*
2N54	OS11	5c ultra	4.50	*12.00*
2N55	OS12	10c blue	20.00	*35.00*
2N56	OS12	20c rose	22.50	*35.00*
2N57	OS12	30c brown	22.50	*35.00*
		Nos. 2N51-2N57 (7)	134.50	*217.00*

For use only in the Shan States. Perak No. N34 also used in Shan States. CTO's ½ used value.

Surcharged in Black

1944, Nov. 1

2N58	OS11	1c brown	4.00	*5.00*
2N59	OS11	2c yel green	.20	*1.25*
a.		Inverted surcharge	150.00	*200.00*
2N60	OS11	3c violet	2.50	*4.00*
2N61	OS11	5c ultra	1.25	1.50
2N62	OS12	10c blue	2.50	*3.50*
2N63	OS12	20c rose	.60	*1.50*
2N64	OS12	30c brown	.75	*1.50*
		Nos. 2N58-2N64 (7)	11.80	*18.25*

Top line of surcharge reads: "Bama naing ngan daw" (Burma State). Bottom line repeats denomination in Burmese. Surcharge applied when the Shan States came under Burmese government administration, Dec. 24, 1943. CTO's same value as unused.

BUSHIRE

bü-'shir

LOCATION — On Persian Gulf

Bushire is an Iranian port which British troops occupied Aug. 8, 1915.

20 Chahis (or Shahis) = 1 Kran
10 Krans = 1 Toman

Watermark

Wmk. 161 — Lion

ISSUED UNDER BRITISH OCCUPATION

Basic Iranian Designs

Ahmad Shah — A32

Imperial Crown — A33

King Darius, Farvahar overhead Overhead — A34

Ruins of Persepolis — A35

Iranian Stamps of 1911-13 Overprinted in Black

Perf. 11½, 11½x11

Typo. & Engr.

1915, Aug. 15 **Unwmk.**

N1	A32	1c green & org	65.00	*55.00*
N2	A32	2c red & sepia	65.00	45.00
N3	A32	3c gray brn & grn	67.50	*70.00*
N4	A32	5c brown & car	700.00	*700.00*
N5	A32	6c green & red brn	65.00	35.00
N6	A32	9c yel brn & vio	62.50	55.00
a.		Double overprint		
N7	A32	10c red & org brn	62.50	*55.00*
N8	A32	12c grn & ultra	75.00	*62.50*
N9	A32	1k ultra & car	110.00	45.00
a.		Double overprint	7,500.	
N10	A32	24c vio & grn	110.00	70.00
N11	A32	2k grn & red vio	260.00	200.00
N12	A32	3k vio & blk	400.00	*300.00*
N13	A32	5k red & ultra	300.00	175.00
N14	A32	10k ol bis & cl	300.00	175.00
		Nos. N1-N14 (14)	2,642.	2,042.

Forged overprints exist of Nos. N1-N29.

The Bushire overprint exists on Iran No. 537 but is considered a forgery.

Covers: Covers of this issue are scarce. Values start at $450.

No Period after "OCCUPATION"

N1b	A32	1c green & org	140.00	150.00
N2b	A32	2c red & sepia	140.00	140.00
N3b	A32	3c gray brn & grn	175.00	200.00
N5b	A32	6c green & red brn	140.00	110.00
N6b	A32	9c yel brn & vio	150.00	160.00
N7b	A32	10c red & org brn	160.00	175.00
N8b	A32	12c grn & ultra	190.00	200.00
N9b	A32	1k ultra & car	260.00	125.00
N10b	A32	24c vio & grn	290.00	200.00
N11b	A32	2k grn & red vio	850.00	525.00
N12b	A32	3k vio & blk	675.00	700.00
N13b	A32	5k red & ultra	525.00	460.00
N14b	A32	10k ol bis & cl	500.00	425.00

On Iranian Stamps of 1915

Perf. 11, 11½

1915, Sept. **Wmk. 161**

N15	A33	1c car & indigo	525.00	525.00
N16	A33	2c blue & car	8,500.	*8,500.*
N17	A33	3c dk grn	700.00	*700.00*
N18	A33	5c red	7,000.	*7,000.*
N19	A33	6c ol grn & car	6,250.	*6,250.*
N20	A33	9c yel brn & vio	1,100.	*1,000.*
N21	A33	10c bl grn & yel brn	1,750.	*1,500.*
N22	A33	12c ultra	1,750.	*1,750.*
N23	A34	1k sil, yel brn & gray	1,200.	900.00
N24	A33	24c yel brn & dk brn	1,000.	750.00
N25	A34	2k sil, bl & rose	1,000.	750.00
N26	A34	3k sil, vio & brn	1,000.	750.00
N27	A34	5k sil, brn & grn	1,500.	750.00
a.		Inverted overprint	—	—
N28	A35	1t gold, pur & blk	1,750.	*1,000.*
N29	A35	3t gold, cl & red brn	3,500.	*3,500.*

Persia resumed administration of Bushire post office Oct. 16, 1915.

Covers: Commercial covers of this issue are scarce. Values start at about $1,750.

CAMEROUN

ˌka-mə-ˈrün

(Kamerun)

LOCATION — On the west coast of Africa, north of the equator
AREA — 456,054 sq. mi.
POP. — 9,060,000 (est. 1983)
CAPITAL — Yaounde

Before World War I, Cameroun (Kamerun) was a German Protectorate. It was occupied during the war by Great Britain and France and in 1922 was mandated to these countries by the League of Nations.

100 Pfennig = 1 Mark
12 Pence = 1 Shilling
100 Centimes = 1 Franc

Watermark

Wmk. 125 — Lozenges

STAMPS OF GERMANY USED IN CAMEROUN

Type A

KAMERUN

Post Office opened 2/1/1887, was redesignated Duala 6/1/1901, and closed 9/27/1914.

1A1	A	3pf green (#37)	*1,750.*
1A2	A	5pf violet (#38)	225.00
1A3	A	10pf red (#39)	140.00
a.		10pf rose (#39b)	1,100.
1A4	A	20pf ultra (#40)	45.00
a.		20pf blue (#40b)	45.00
1A5	A	25pf red brn (#41a)	1,450.
1A6	A	50pf deep grayish ol grn (#42)	140.00
a.		50pf gray (#42a)	165.00
b.		50pf brt olive (#42b)	*1,100.*
c.		50pf dk ol grn (#42c)	225.00
1A7	A	2m dull vio pur (#36b)	725.00
a.		2m e lilac (#36d)	1,100.
1A8	A	3pf gray brn (#46)	47.50
a.		3pf brown (#46)	90.00
b.		3pf yel brn (#46a)	50.00
c.		3pf red brn (#46c)	50.00
d.		3pf brown ocher (#46f)	55.00
e.		3pf ol brn (#46e)	55.00
1A9	A	5pf blue green (#47)	25.00
a.		5pf yellow green (#47a)	47.50
b.		5pf deep green (#47b)	62.50
c.		5pf gray green (#47b)	62.50
1A10	A	10pf red (#48)	22.50
a.		10pf dark carmine (#48c)	250.00
b.		10pf brownish red (#48d)	*1,000.*
c.		10pf rose carmine (#48e)	37.50
1A11	A	20pf pale ultra (#49)	18.00
a.		20pf Prussian blue (#49a)	150.00
b.		20pf grayish ultra (#49b)	55.00
c.		20pf blue (#49c)	37.50
1A12	A	25pf red orange (#50)	150.00
a.		25pf org yel (#50b)	175.00
1A13	A	50pf lilac brn (#51)	50.00
a.		50pf brown red (#51c)	*3,250.*
b.		50pf red brown (#51d)	250.00
c.		50pf red lilac brn (#51d)	275.00
d.		50pf dull rose brn (#51e)	72.50
1A14	A	2m brown purple (#36)	62.50
a.		2m carmine lilac (#36e)	450.00

BIBUNDI

Post Office in operation 7/5/1891-1/8/1897, 5/22/1906-10/8/1914.

Type A Cancel with 2 Stars Below Year Date

2A1	A	3pf gray brn (#46)	240.00
a.		3pf brown (#46)	275.00
2A2	A	5pf blue grn (#47)	125.00
a.		5pf yel grn (#47a)	190.00
2A3	A	10pf red (#48)	110.00
a.		10pf brownish rose (#48e)	140.00
2A4	A	20pf blue (#49c)	140.00
a.		20pf pale ultra (#49)	—
2A5	A	25pf reddish org (#50)	575.00
a.		25pf org yel (#50b)	—
2A6	A	50pf lilac brn (#51)	250.00

Type B

BUEA
Post Office in operation 2/15/00-11/15/14.

3A1 B 3pf yel brn (#46a) 140.00
a. 3pf reddish brn (#46c) 140.00
b. 3pf brown ocher (#46f) 140.00
3A2 B 5pf blue green (#47) 165.00
3A3 B 10pf red (#48) 110.00
3A4 B 20pf pale ultra (#49) —
3A5 B 50pf lilac brn (#51) —
3A6 B 2m car lilac (#36e) 1,725.

DUALA/KAMERUN
Post Office in operation 6/1/01-9/27/14.

4A1 B 3pf yel brn (#46a) 50.00
a. 3pf red brn (#46c) 50.00
b. 3pf brn ocher (#46f) 55.00
4A2 B 5pf blue grn (#47) 25.00

GROS-BRATANGA
Post Office in operation 3/1/1893-12/31/1893.

5A1 A 3pf gray brn (#46) 240.00
5A2 A 5pf blue grn (#47) 190.00
a. 5pf yel grn (#47a) 240.00
5A3 A 10pf brownish rose (#48e) 210.00
a. 10pf car rose (#48d) —
5A4 A 20pf blue (#49c) 175.00
a. 20pf Prussian blue (#49e) 1,725.
5A5 A 25pf reddish org (#50) 575.00
a. 25pf org yel (#50b) 900.00
5A6 A 50pf lilac brn (#51) —

KRIBI
Post Office in operation 8/10/1894-10/13/1914.
Type A Cancel with 2 Stars Below Date

6A1 A 3pf yel brn (#46a) 70.00
a. 3pf red brn (#46c) 70.00
b. 3pf brn ocher (#46f) 70.00
c. 3pf gray brn (#46) 240.00
6A2 A 5pf blue grn (#47) 47.50
6A3 A 10pf red (#48) 85.00
a. 10pf brn rose (#48e) 110.00
b. 10pf brn red (#48f) 1,000.
6A4 A 20pf pale ultra (#49) 35.00
c. 20pf blue (#49c) 150.00
6A5 A 25pf red org (#50) 290.00
6A6 A 50pf lilac brn (#51) 87.50
a. 50pf dull rose brn (#51e) 210.00
6A7 A 2m brn purple (#36) 190.00
a. 2m car lilac (#36e) 450.00

RIO DEL REY
Post Office in operation 1/9/1897-8/1914.
Type A Cancel with 3 Stars Centered Below Date

7A1 A 3pf gray brown (#46) 240.00
a. 3pf yel brown (#46a) 190.00
b. 3pf red brown (#46c) 190.00
c. 3pf brown ocher (#46f) 190.00
7A2 A 5pf blue green (#47) 140.00
7A3 A 10pf red (#48) 85.00
7A4 A 20pf pale ultra (#49) 72.50
7A5 A 25pf red orange (#50) 575.00
7A6 A 50pf lilac brown (#51) 400.00

Several cancellation types exist. Values are for most common variety.

Type C

VIKTORIA
Post Office in operation 12/12/1888-9/1914, spelling changed to Victoria 12/1900.

8A1 C 3pf green (#37) —
8A2 C 5pf violet 1,250.
8A3 C 10pf red (#48) 375.00
8A4 C 20pf ultra (#40) 225.00
8A5 C 20pf blue (#49c) 225.00
8A6 C 50pf deep grayish ol grn (#42) 500.00
a. 50pf dk ol grn (#42c) 650.00
8A7 C 2m rose lilac (#36d) 2,750.

8A8 C 3pf yel brn (#46a) 50.00
a. 3pf red brn (#46c) 50.00
b. 3pf brn ocher (#46f) 55.00
c. 3pf ol brn (#46e) 55.00
d. 3pf brown (#46) 140.00
e. 3pf gray brn (#46) 140.00
8A9 C 5pf bl grn (#47) 42.50
a. 5pf yel grn (#47a) 70.00
b. 5pf deep grn (#47b) 250.00
c. 5pf gray grn (#47b) 250.00
8A10 C 10pf red (#48) 32.50
a. 10pf brnish red (#48c) 1,000.
b. 10pf car rose (#48d) 3,000.
c. 10pf brnish rose (#48e) 110.00
8A11 C 20pf pale ultra (#49) 27.50
a. 20pf grayish ultra (#49b) 425.00
b. 20pf blue (#49c) 110.00
8A12 C 25pf red org (#50) 290.00
a. 25pf org yel (#50b) 550.00
8A13 C 50pf lilac brn (#51) 50.00
a. 50pf dull rose brn (#51e) 210.00
8A14 C 2m brn pur (#36) 250.00

VICTORIA/KAMERUN

8A15 B 3pf yel brn (#46a) 140.00
a. 3pf red brn (#46c) 140.00
b. 3pf brn ocher (#46f) 140.00
8A16 B 2m brn pur (#36) 1,200.

Issued under German Dominion

Stamps of Germany Overprinted in Black

1897 Unwmk. ***Perf. 13½x14½***

1 A9 3pf yel brn 11.00 *16.00*
Never hinged 21.00
On cover 95.00
On cover, single franking 225.00
a. 3pf red brown 42.50 *125.00*
Never hinged 150.00
On cover 300.00
On cover, single franking 400.00
b. 3pf dark brown 16.00 *37.50*
Never hinged 50.00
On cover 140.00
On cover, single franking 275.00
c. 3pf olive brown 8.75 *37.50*
Never hinged 25.00
On cover 72.50
On cover, single franking 160.00
2 A9 5pf green 5.00 *8.00*
Never hinged 12.00
On cover 21.00
On cover, single franking 35.00
3 A10 10pf carmine 3.75 *4.00*
Never hinged 10.50
On cover 17.50
On cover, single franking 35.00
4 A10 20pf ultra 4.00 *8.00*
Never hinged 11.00
On cover 21.00
On cover, single franking 50.00
a. Diagonal half used as 10pf on cover 18,750.
5 A10 25pf orange 20.00 *35.00*
Never hinged 50.00
On cover 100.00
On cover, single franking 475.00
6 A10 50pf red brn 16.00 *29.00*
Never hinged 42.50
On cover 57.50
Nos. 1-6 (6) 59.75 *100.00*

Covers: Values for Nos. 1-5 are for covers paying the correct rates. No. 6 is for overfranked complete cover, usually philatelic.

A3

Kaiser's Yacht "Hohenzollern" — A4

1900 Unwmk. Typo. ***Perf. 14***

7 A3 3pf brown 1.25 *1.50*
Never hinged 2.75
On cover 50.00
On cover, single franking 35.00
8 A3 5pf green 13.50 1.10
Never hinged 35.00
On cover 17.50
On cover, single franking 14.50
9 A3 10pf carmine 40.00 1.25
Never hinged 80.00
On cover 17.50
10 A3 20pf ultra 25.00 2.25
Never hinged 52.50
On cover 21.00
a. Vertical half used as 10pf on cover (Longii, '11) 6,750.
11 A3 25pf org & blk, *yel* 1.40 *5.00*
Never hinged 3.50
On cover 42.50
12 A3 30pf org & blk, *sal* 1.75 *4.00*
Never hinged 3.75
On cover 42.50
13 A3 40pf lake & blk 1.75 *4.00*
Never hinged 3.75
On cover 42.50
14 A3 50pf pur & blk, *sal* 2.00 *6.00*
Never hinged 4.00
On cover 35.00
15 A3 80pf lake & blk, *rose* 2.75 *11.00*
Never hinged 12.00
On cover 35.00

Engr. ***Perf. 14½x14***

16 A4 1m carmine 67.50 *67.50*
Never hinged 140.00
On cover 110.00
17 A4 2m blue 5.00 *65.00*
Never hinged 14.00
On cover 110.00
18 A4 3m blk vio 5.00 *100.00*
Never hinged 17.50
On cover 175.00
19 A4 5m slate & car 125.00 *440.00*
Never hinged 325.00
On cover 875.00
Nos. 7-19 (13) 291.90 *708.60*

Covers: Values for Nos. 14-19 are for overfranked complete covers, usually philatelic.

1905-18 Wmk. 125 Typo.

20 A3 3pf brown ('18) .70
Never hinged 1.75
21 A3 5pf green .70 *1.60*
Never hinged 1.75
On cover 32.50
a. Bklt. pane of 6 15.00
b. Bklt. pane of 6, 2 #21 + 4 #22 62.50
c. Booklet pane of 5 + label 375.00
22 A3 10pf carmine ('06) 2.00 *1.40*
Never hinged 5.50
On cover 32.50
a. Bklt pane of 6 17.50
b. Booklet pane of 5 + label 500.00
23 A3 20pf ultra ('14) 2.75 *125.00*
Never hinged 7.00
On cover 425.00
On cover, single franking 850.00
a. 20pf dull blue ('17) 12.50
Never hinged 27.50
24 A4 1m carmine (26x17 perf holes) ('15) 8.50
Never hinged 21.00
a. 25x17 perf holes ('19) 10.00
Never hinged 35.00
25 A4 5m slate & carmine (26x17 perf holes) ('13) 37.50 *4,250.*
Never hinged 100.00
On cover *8,500.*
a. 5m slate & rose red (26x17 perf holes) 25.00
Never hinged 65.00
b. 5m slate & rose red (25x17 perf holes) ('19) 25.00
Never hinged 62.50
Nos. 20-25 (6) 52.15

The 3pf and 1m were not placed in use. Nos. 21a, 22a were made from sheet stamps.

The 3pf and 1m were not placed in use. **Covers:** Value for No. 25 is for overfranked complete cover, usually philatelic.

Issued under British Occupation

Stamps of German Cameroun Surcharged

#53

#62

Wmk. Lozenges (125) (#54-56, 65); Unwmk. (Other Values)

1915 ***Perf. 14, 14½***

Blue Surcharge

53 A3 ½p on 3pf brn 15.00 *40.00*
54 A3 ½p on 5pf grn 3.75 *11.00*
a. Double surcharge *1,000.*
55 A3 1p on 10pf car 1.50 *11.00*
a. "1" with thin serifs 15.00 *75.00*
b. Double surcharge 325.00
c. Black surcharge 18.00 *65.00*
d. As "c," "1" with thin serifs 240.00
e. "C.E.F." omitted 3,200.
f. "1d" double 2,100.

Black Surcharge

56 A3 2p on 20pf ultra 4.00 *24.00*
57 A3 2½p on 25pf org & blk, *yel* 13.50 *55.00*
a. Double surcharge *8,500.*
58 A3 3p on 30pf org & blk, *sal* 14.00 *45.00*
a. Large "3" in "3d" 900.00
b. Triple surcharge, two albino 290.00
59 A3 4p on 40pf lake & blk 13.50 *55.00*
a. Short "4" in "4d" 740.00 *1,050.*
60 A3 6p on 50pf pur & blk, *sal* 14.00 *55.00*
61 A3 8p on 80pf lake & blk, *rose* 13.50 *55.00*
62 A4 1sh on 1m car 190.00 *800.00*
a. "S" inverted 925.00 *3,000.*
63 A4 2sh on 2m bl 190.00 *800.00*
a. "S" inverted 925.00 *3,000.*
64 A4 3sh on 3m blk vio 190.00 *825.00*
a. "S" inverted 925.00 *3,000.*
b. Double surcharge *10,500.*
65 A4 5sh on 5m sl & car 240.00 *875.00*
a. "S" inverted 1,050. *3,250.*
Nos. 53-65 (13) 902.75 *3,651.*

The letters "C. E. F." are the initials of "Cameroons Expeditionary Force."

Numerous overprint varieties exist for #53-65.

Counterfeits exist of Nos. 54a, 54b.

Values for stamp with albino impressions of the surcharge

54c	½p on 5pf, double surcharge, one albino	240.00
55g	1p on 10pf, double surcharge, one albino	100.00
55h	1p on 10pf, triple surcharge, two albino	260.00
56a	2p on 20pf, double surcharge, one albino	225.00
57b	2½p on 25pf, double surcharge, one albino	—
58b	3p on 30pf, triple surcharge, two albino	290.00
59b	4p on 40pf, triple surcharge, two albino	260.00
59c	4p on 40pf, quadruple surcharge, three albino	1,900.
60a	6p on 50pf, double surcharge, one albino	210.00
61a	4p on 40pf, triple surcharge, two albino	1,250.
63b	8p on 80pf, double surcharge, one albino	1,700.
64c	3s on 3m, double surcharge, one albino	1,700.

See Cameroons for Nos. 66-77.

Issued under French Occupation

Gabon Nos. 37, 49-52, 54, 57-58, 60, 62-64, 66, 69-71 Overprinted

1915 Unwmk. ***Perf. 13½x14***

Inscribed "Congo Français"

101 A10 10c red & car 22.50 15.00
On cover 200.00

Inscribed "Afrique Equatoriale"

102 A10 1c choc & org 75.00 30.00
103 A10 2c blk & choc 125.00 100.00
104 A10 4c vio & dp bl 125.00 100.00
105 A10 5c ol gray & grn 26.00 15.00
105A A10 10c red & car *16,750.* *18,000.*
106 A10 20c ol brn & dk vio 150.00 150.00
107 A11 25c dp bl & choc 45.00 30.00
On cover 200.00
108 A11 30c gray blk & red 140.00 140.00
109 A11 35c dk vio & grn 47.50 30.00
a. Double overprint 1,400. —
110 A11 40c choc & ultra 140.00 140.00
111 A11 45c car & vio 160.00 140.00
112 A11 50c bl grn & gray 160.00 140.00
113 A11 75c org & choc 210.00 150.00
114 A12 1fr dk brn & bis 190.00 160.00
115 A12 2fr car & brn 210.00 190.00
Nos. 101-105,106-115 (15) 1,826. 1,530.

The overprint is vertical, reading up, on #101-106, 114-115, and horizontal on #107-113.

Stamps of Middle Congo, Issue of 1907, Overprinted

1916 Unwmk.

116 A1 1c ol gray & brn 75.00 75.00
117 A1 2c violet & brn 75.00 75.00
118 A1 4c blue & brown 80.00 75.00

119 A1 5c dk green & blue 22.50 22.50
120 A2 35c violet brn & bl 87.50 60.00
121 A2 45c violet & red 62.50 55.00

The overprint is vert., reading down, on #120-121.

Same Overprint On Stamps of French Congo, 1900

Wmk. Branch of Thistle (122)

Overprint Horizontal

122 A4 15c dull vio & ol grn 75.00 75.00
a. Inverted overprint 140.00 110.00

Wmk. Branch of Rose Tree (123)

Overprint Reading Up

123 A5 20c yellow grn & org 110.00 62.50
124 A5 30c car rose & org 75.00 60.00
125 A5 40c org brn & brt grn 52.50 47.50
126 A5 50c gray vio & lil 70.00 55.00
127 A5 75c red vio & org 62.50 55.00

Wmk. Branch of Olive (124)

128 A6 1fr gray lilac & ol 92.50 75.00
129 A6 2fr carmine & brn 92.50 75.00
Nos. 116-129 (14) 1,032. 867.50

Values are for copies centered in the grade of fine.

Counterfeits exist of Nos. 101-129.

Overprint Reading Down

123a A5 20c yellow grn & org 120.00 65.00
124a A5 30c car rose & org 85.00 70.00
125a A5 40c org brn & brt grn 65.00 60.00
126a A5 50c gray vio & lil 75.00 60.00
127a A5 75c red vio & org 70.00 55.00
128a A6 1fr gray lilac & ol 95.00 87.50
129a A6 2fr carmine & brn 110.00 92.50

Pairs, One Up, One Down

123b A5 20c yellow grn & org 2,100. 2,100.
124b A5 30c car rose & org 1,400. 1,400.
125b A5 40c org brn & brt grn 1,400. 1,400.
126b A5 50c gray vio & lil 1,400. 1,400.
127b A5 75c red vio & org 1,400. 1,400.
128b A6 1fr gray lilac & ol 1,600. 1,600.
129b A6 2fr carmine & brn 1,600. 1,600.

Stamps of Middle Congo, Issue of 1907 Overprinted

1916-17 **Unwmk.**

130 A1 1c ol gray & brn .30 .30
131 A1 2c violet & brn .35 .30
132 A1 4c blue & brn .60 .35
133 A1 5c dk green & bl .35 .30
134 A1 10c carmine & bl .70 .50
135 A1 15c brn vio & rose ('17) 1.40 .50
136 A1 20c brown & bl .60 .50
137 A2 25c blue & grn .60 .35
a. Triple overprint 425.00 *550.00*
138 A2 30c scarlet & grn .70 .50
a. Double overprint 325.00 *425.00*
139 A2 35c vio brn & bl .60 .50
140 A2 40c dull grn & brn 1.60 .85
141 A2 45c violet & red 1.60 .85
142 A2 50c blue grn & red 1.60 1.00
143 A2 75c brown & blue 1.60 1.00
144 A3 1fr dp grn & vio 1.10 .80
145 A3 2fr vio & gray grn 5.50 4.25
146 A3 5fr blue & rose 7.75 6.50
Nos. 130-146 (17) 26.95 19.35

No period after "Francaise"

130b A1 1c ol gray & brn 2.75 2.75
131b A1 2c violet & brn 2.75 2.75
137b A2 25c blue & grn 4.25 4.25
138 A2 30c scarlet & grn 4.25 4.25
139b A2 35c vio brn & bl 4.25 4.25
140b A2 40c dull grn & brn 4.75 4.75
141b A2 45c violet & red 5.25 5.25
142b A2 50c blue grn & red 5.25 5.25
144b A3 1fr dp grn & vio 9.00 9.00
Nos. 130b-144b (9) 42.50 42.50

Letter "s" of "Francaise" reversed

137c A2 25c blue & grn 3.75 3.75
138c A2 30c scarlet & grn 3.75 3.75
139c A2 35c vio brn & bl 3.75 3.75
140c A2 40c dull grn & brn 3.75 3.75
141c A2 45c violet & red 4.50 4.50
142c A2 50c blue grn & red 4.50 4.50
143c A2 75c brown & blue 4.50 4.50
144c A3 1fr dp grn & vio 4.50 4.50
145c A3 2fr vio & gray grn 17.50 17.50
146c A3 5fr blue & rose 24.00 24.00
Nos. 137c-146c (10) 74.50 74.50

Nos. 130-146 exist on ordinary paper and, with the exception of No. 135, on chalk surfaced paper.

On Nos. 137-146 there is 7mm between "Cameroun" and "Occupation."

Provisional French Mandate

Types of Middle Congo, 1907, Overprinted

1921

147 A1 1c ol grn & org .20 .20
148 A1 2c brown & rose .20 .20
149 A1 4c gray & lt grn .35 .30
150 A1 5c dl red & org .35 .30
a. Double overprint 850.00
151 A1 10c bl grn & lt grn .95 .45
152 A1 15c blue & org .35 .30
153 A1 20c red brn & ol .60 .50
154 A2 25c slate & org .80 .50
155 A2 30c rose & ver .95 .45
156 A2 35c gray & ultra .60 .45
157 A2 40c ol grn & org .80 .50
158 A2 45c brown & rose .60 .45
159 A2 50c blue & ultra .70 .45
160 A2 75c red brn & lt grn .80 .50
161 A3 1fr slate & org 1.60 1.10
162 A3 2fr ol grn & rose 4.75 3.25
163 A3 5fr dull red & gray 6.00 4.75
Nos. 147-163 (17) 20.60 14.65

Without Overprint

148b A1 2c brown & rose 160.00
149b A1 4c gray & lt grn 200.00
152b A1 15c blue & org 850.00 *450.00*
154b A2 25c slate & org 850.00
159b A2 50c blue & ultra 200.00

Nos. 152, 162, 163, 158, 160 Surcharged with New Value and Bars

1924-25

164 A1 25c on 15c bl & org ('25) .70 .70
165 A3 25c on 2fr ol grn & rose .95 .95
166 A3 25c on 5fr red & gray .95 .95
a. Pair, one without new value and bars
167 A2 65c on 45c brn & rose ('25) 1.10 1.10
168 A2 85c on 75c red brn & lt grn ('25) 1.60 1.60
Nos. 164-168 (5) 5.30 5.30

French Mandate

Herder and Cattle Crossing Sanaga River — A5

Tapping Rubber Tree — A6

Rope Suspension Bridge A7

1925-38 **Typo.** ***Perf. 14x13½***

170 A5 1c ol grn & brn vio, *lav* .20 .20
171 A5 2c rose & grn, *grnsh* .20 .20
172 A5 4c blue & blk .20 .20
173 A5 5c org & red vio, *lav* .20 .20
174 A5 10c red brn & org, *yel* .35 .30
175 A5 15c sl grn & grn .35 .30
176 A5 15c lilac & red ('27) .80 .50

Perf. 13½x14

177 A6 20c ol brn & red brn .50 .30
178 A6 20c green ('26) .35 .30
179 A6 20c brn red & ol brn ('27) .35 .35
180 A6 25c lt green & blk .60 .35
181 A6 30c bluish grn & ver .35 .20
182 A6 30c dk grn & grn ('27) .60 .35
183 A6 35c brown & black .75 .35
184 A6 35c dl grn & grn ('38) 1.50 1.00
185 A6 40c orange & vio 1.50 .85
186 A6 45c dp rose & cer .60 .35
187 A6 45c vio & org brn ('27) 1.75 1.25
188 A6 50c lt green & cer .60 .20
189 A6 55c ultra & car ('38) 1.25 1.10
190 A6 60c red vio & blk .60 .35
191 A6 60c brown red ('26) .60 .35
192 A6 65c indigo & brn .85 .70
193 A6 75c indigo & dp bl .60 .50
194 A6 75c org brn & red vio ('27) 1.00 .80
195 A6 80c carmine & brn ('38) 1.00 .80
196 A6 85c dp rose & bl 1.25 .85
197 A6 90c brn red & cer ('27) 2.00 .85

Perf. 14x13½

198 A7 1fr indigo & brn .85 .70
199 A7 1fr dull bl ('26) .40 .35
200 A7 1fr ol brn & red vio ('27) .85 .50
201 A7 1fr grn & dk brn ('29) 1.90 .80
202 A7 1.10fr rose red & dk brn ('28) 3.75 3.75
203 A7 1.25fr gray & dp bl ('33) 4.25 2.75
204 A7 1.50fr dull bl ('27) .65 .50
205 A7 1.75fr brn & org ('33) 1.25 1.00
206 A7 1.75fr dk bl & lt bl ('38) 1.90 1.00
207 A7 2fr dl grn & brn org 1.50 .75
208 A7 3fr ol brn & red vio ('27) 5.50 1.50
209 A7 5fr brn & blk, *bluish* 2.50 1.50
a. Cliché of 2fr in plate of 5fr *1,050.*
210 A7 10fr org & vio ('27) 11.00 5.00
211 A7 20fr rose & ol grn ('27) 14.50 8.50
Nos. 170-211 (42) 71.70 42.65

Shades exist for several values.

For overprints and surcharge see Nos. 212, 264, 276, 278, 279, B7-B9, B21.

No. 199 Surcharged with New Value and Bars in Red

1926

212 A7 1.25fr on 1fr dull blue .60 .50

Common Design Types pictured following the introduction.

Colonial Exposition Issue

Common Design Types

Name of Country in Black

1931 **Engr.** ***Perf. 12½***

213 CD70 40c deep green 4.00 2.50
214 CD71 50c violet 4.00 3.25
215 CD72 90c red orange 4.00 3.25
216 CD73 1.50fr dull blue 4.50 3.25
Nos. 213-216 (4) 16.50 12.25

Paris International Exposition Issue

Common Design Types

1937 ***Perf. 13***

217 CD74 20c deep violet 1.25 1.25
218 CD75 30c dark green 1.00 1.00
219 CD76 40c carmine rose 1.25 1.25
220 CD77 50c dark brown 1.25 1.25
221 CD78 90c red 1.25 1.25
222 CD79 1.50fr ultramarine 1.25 1.25
Nos. 217-222 (6) 7.25 7.25

French Colonial Art Exhibition

Common Design Type

Souvenir Sheet

1937 ***Imperf.***

222A CD77 3fr org red & blk 6.00 *6.50*

New York World's Fair Issue

Common Design Type

1939 ***Perf. 12½x12***

223 CD82 1.25fr carmine lake .95 .85
224 CD82 2.25fr ultra .95 .85

For overprints and surcharges see Nos. 280-281, B14-B17, B23, B25.

Mandara Woman — A19

Falls on M'bam River near Banyo — A20

Elephants A21

Man in Yaré — A22

1939-40 **Engr.** ***Perf. 13***

225 A19 2c black brn .20 .20
226 A19 3c magenta .20 .20
227 A19 4c deep ultra .20 .20
228 A19 5c red brown .20 .20
229 A19 10c dp bl grn .20 .20
230 A19 15c rose red .25 .20
231 A19 20c plum .25 .20
232 A20 25c black brn .50 .50
233 A20 30c dk red .60 .45
234 A20 40c ultra .60 .50
235 A20 45c slate green 2.00 1.60
236 A20 50c brown car .65 .40
237 A20 60c pck blue .60 .50
238 A20 70c plum 2.75 2.25
239 A21 80c Prus blue 2.00 1.75
240 A21 90c Prus blue .75 .50
241 A21 1fr car rose 1.50 .75
242 A21 1fr choc ('40) .95 .60
243 A21 1.25fr car rose 3.25 2.40
244 A21 1.40fr org red 1.00 .75
245 A21 1.50fr chocolate .80 .75
246 A21 1.60fr black brn 2.00 1.60
247 A21 1.75fr dk blue 1.10 .75
248 A21 2fr dk green .60 .60
249 A21 2.25fr dk blue 1.10 .75
250 A21 2.50fr brt red vio .95 .80
251 A21 3fr dk violet .95 .50
252 A22 5fr black brn .95 .65
253 A22 10fr brt red vio 1.50 1.25
254 A22 20fr dk green 3.00 2.10
Nos. 225-254 (30) 31.60 24.10

For overprints and surcharges see Nos. 255-263, 265-275, 277, 278A, 279A, B10-B13, B22, B24.

Stamps of 1925-40 Overprinted in Black or Orange "CAMEROUN FRANCAIS 27.8.40."

1940 ***Perf. 14x13½, 13½x14, 13***

255 A19 2c blk brn (O) .80 .80
256 A19 3c magenta .65 .65
257 A19 4c dp ultra (O) .65 .65
258 A19 5c red brn 3.25 2.75
259 A19 10c dp bl grn (O) .75 .75
260 A19 15c rose red .75 .75
260A A19 20c plum (O) 8.00 8.00
261 A20 25c blk brn .75 .75
b. Inverted overprint 175.00 175.00
261A A20 30c dk red 6.00 6.00
262 A20 40c ultra 4.00 4.00
263 A20 45c slate green 1.75 1.75
264 A6 50c lt grn & cer 1.25 1.00
a. Inverted overprint 160.00
265 A20 60c pck bl 4.00 4.00
266 A20 70c plum 1.10 1.10
267 A21 80c Prus bl (O) 4.00 3.25
268 A21 90c Prus bl (O) 1.00 1.00
269 A21 1.25fr car rose 1.00 1.00
270 A21 1.40fr org red 1.40 1.25
271 A21 1.50fr chocolate .75 .90
272 A21 1.60fr blk brn (O) 1.00 .90
273 A21 1.75fr dk bl (O) 1.50 1.25
274 A21 2.25fr dk bl (O) .75 .75
275 A21 2.50fr brt red vio .80 .80
276 A7 5fr brn & blk, *bluish* 15.00 12.50
277 A22 5fr black brn 12.00 11.00
278 A7 10fr org & vio 16.50 13.50
278A A22 10fr brt red vio 32.50 23.00
279 A7 20fr rose & ol grn 35.00 32.50
279A A22 20fr dk green 150.00 150.00

Same Overprint on Stamps of 1939

Perf. 12½x12

280 CD82 1.25fr car lake 4.00 4.00
281 CD82 2.25fr ultra 4.00 4.00
Nos. 255-281 (31) 314.90 294.55

Issued to note Cameroun's affiliation with General de Gaulle's "Free France" movement.

Numerous overprint varieties exist.

SEMI-POSTAL STAMPS

Curie Issue
Common Design Type

1938	**Unwmk.**	***Perf. 13***	
B1	CD80 1.75fr + 50c brt ultra	8.00	8.00

French Revolution Issue
Common Design Type

Photogravure; Name and Value Typographed in Black

1939

B2	CD83 45c + 25c green	9.00	9.00
B3	CD83 70c + 30c brown	9.00	9.00
B4	CD83 90c + 35c red org	9.00	9.00
B5	CD83 1.25fr + 1fr rose pink	9.00	9.00
B6	CD83 2.25fr + 2fr blue	11.00	11.00
	Nos. B2-B6 (5)	47.00	47.00

Stamps of 1925-33 Surcharged in Black

1940		***Perf. 14x13½***	
B7	A7 1.25fr + 2fr gray & dp bl	13.00	12.00
B8	A7 1.75fr + 3fr brn & org	13.00	12.00
B9	A7 2fr + 5fr dl grn & brn org	13.00	12.00
	Nos. B7-B9 (3)	39.00	36.00

The surtax was used for war relief work.

Regular Stamps of 1939 Surcharged in Black

1940		***Perf. 13***	
B10	A20 25c + 5fr blk brn	87.50	72.50
B11	A20 45c + 5fr slate grn	87.50	72.50
B12	A20 60c + 5fr peacock bl	95.00	75.00
B13	A20 70c + 5fr plum	95.00	75.00
	Nos. B10-B13 (4)	365.00	295.00

The surtax was used to purchase Spitfire planes for the Free French army.

POSTAGE DUE STAMPS

Man Felling Tree — D1

Perf. 14x13½

1925-27	**Unwmk.**	**Typo.**	
J1	D1 2c lt bl & blk	.25	.25
J2	D1 4c ol bis & red vio	.25	.25
J3	D1 5c vio & blk	.50	.50
J4	D1 10c red & blk	.50	.50
J5	D1 15c gray & blk	.60	.60
J6	D1 20c olive grn & blk	.60	.60
J7	D1 25c yel & blk	1.10	1.10
J8	D1 30c blue & org	1.10	1.10
J9	D1 50c brn & blk	1.60	1.60
J10	D1 60c bl grn & rose red	1.60	1.60
J11	D1 1fr dl red & grn, *grnsh*	1.60	1.60
J12	D1 2fr red & vio ('27)	3.25	3.25
J13	D1 3fr org brn & ultra ('27)	5.00	5.00
	Nos. J1-J13 (13)	17.95	17.95

Shades occur for several values.

Carved Figures — D2

1939	**Engr.**	***Perf. 14x13***	
J14	D2 5c brt red vio	.20	.20
J15	D2 10c Prus blue	.55	.55
J16	D2 15c car rose	.20	.20
J17	D2 20c blk brn	.20	.20
J18	D2 30c ultra	.35	.35
J19	D2 50c dk grn	.35	.35
J20	D2 60c brn vio	.65	.65
J21	D2 1fr dk vio	.80	.80
J22	D2 2fr org red	1.25	1.25
J23	D2 3fr dark blue	1.75	1.75
	Nos. J14-J23 (10)	6.30	6.30

CANADA

'ka-nə-də

LOCATION — Northern part of North American continent, except for Alaska
GOVT. — Self-governing dominion in the British Commonwealth of Nations
AREA — 3,851,809 sq. mi.
POP. — 24,907,100 (est. 1983)
CAPITAL — Ottawa

Included in the dominion are British Columbia, Vancouver Island, Prince Edward Island, Nova Scotia, New Brunswick and Newfoundland, all of which formerly issued stamps.

12 Pence = 1 Shilling
100 Cents = 1 Dollar (1859)

Catalogue values for unused stamps in this country are for Never Hinged items, beginning with Scott 268 in the regular postage section, Scott C9 in the air post section, Scott CE3 in the air post special delivery section, Scott CO1 in the air post official section, Scott E11 in the special delivery section, Scott EO1 in the special delivery official section, Scott J15 in the postage due section, and Scott O1 in the official section.

Values for unused stamps of #1-33 are for examples with partial original gum. Stamps without gum often trade at prices very close to those of stamps with partial gum. Examples with full original gum and lightly hinged are extremely scarce and generally sell for substantially more than the values listed.

Very fine examples of the perforated issues between Nos. 11-20 will have perforations touching the design or frameline on at least one side due to the narrow spacing of the stamps on the plates. Stamps with perfs clear of the designs on all four sides are extremely scarce and will command much higher prices.

PRE-STAMP POSTAL MARKINGS

Crown Circle Handstamp

Crowned Circle handstamp type II is pictured in the Crowned Circle Handstamps and Great Britain Used Abroad section.

1842-51

A1	II "Quebec" crowned circle handstamp in red, on cover	200.

Crown Circle handstamps exist also from Amherst, Nova Scotia, and St. Margaret's Bay, Nova Scotia, and St. John's, Newfoundland. These are listed under Nova Scotia and Newfoundland respectively.

POSTMASTER PROVISIONAL
New Carlisle, Gaspé

E1

ENVELOPE

1851, Apr.		**Typeset**
1X1	E1 3p black, entire	—

Only one example of No. 1X1 is recorded, an entire postmarked April 7, 1851, to Toronto.

Province of Canada

Beaver — A1

Prince Albert — A2

Queen Victoria — A3

1851	**Unwmk. Engr.**		***Imperf.***
	Laid Paper		
1	A1 3p red	*20,000.*	950.
	No gum	*15,000.*	
	On cover		*1,800.*
	Double transfer (pos. 47, pane A)		2,700.
a.	3p orange vermilion	—	950.
	No gum	—	
	On cover		*1,800.*
2	A2 6p slate violet	*20,000.*	1,500.
	No gum	*15,000.*	
	On cover		*3,100.*
a.	Diagonal half used as 3p on cover		*30,000.*
b.	6p grayish purple	*20,000.*	1,500.
	No gum	*15,000.*	
	On cover		*2,900.*
3	A3 12p black	*80,000.*	*60,000.*
	No gum	*55,000.*	
	On cover		*275,000.*

On some stamps the laid lines of Nos. 1-3 are practically invisible.

No. 1 double transfer position 47 shows extensive doubling of "EE PEN," above and below "POS," in and below "ANADA THR" and in all four numerals. Pane A is the upper pane.

1852-57

	Wove Paper		
4	A1 3p red	1,250.	200.
	No gum	1,150.	
	On cover		460.
	Double transfer (pos. 47, pane A)	*3,500.*	*650.*
	No gum	*2,250.*	
	On cover		*1,000.*
a.	3p brown red ('53)	1,300.	225.
	No gum	1,175.	
	On cover		500.
b.	Diagonal half used as 1½p on cover		*30,000.*
c.	Ribbed paper	3,250.	475.
	No gum	2,750.	
	On cover		575.
d.	Thin paper	1,250.	200.
	No gum	1,150.	
	On cover		460.
5	A2 6p slate gray ('55)	12,500.	1,250.
	No gum	10,000.	
	On cover		1,600.
a.	6p brownish gray	17,500.	2,500.
	No gum	13,000.	
	On cover		2,750.
b.	6p greenish gray	12,000.	1,250.
	No gum	9,500.	
	On cover		1,600.
c.	Diagonal half used as 3p on cover		*15,500.*
d.	Thick hard paper (gray vio) ('57)	14,000.	2,250.
	No gum	12,000.	
	On cover		2,600.

See note after No. 3 for characteristics of double transfer pos. 47 on No. 4. Pos. 47 is considered the most prominent double transfer, but many others exist. The double transfers exist on all shades and papers; values are for the most common shade and paper.

Most authorities believe the 12p black does not exist on wove paper.

Jacques Cartier — A4

1855

7	A4 10p blue	6,500.	1,500.
	No gum	5,000.	
	On cover		3,600.
a.	Thick paper	7,250.	1,850.
	No gum	6,400.	
	On cover		3,600.

Queen Victoria
A5 A6

1857

8	A5 ½p rose	750.	600.
	No gum	625.	
	On cover		850.
	On cover, single franking		1,100.
	On newspaper or circular		900.
a.	Horizontally ribbed paper	8,250.	2,250.
	No gum	7,500.	
	On cover		2,250.
b.	Vertically ribbed paper	8,500.	3,250.
	No gum	7,500.	
	On cover		3,250.
9	A6 7½p green	7,000.	2,750.
	No gum	5,000.	
	On cover		5,000.
a.	7½p deep green	6,750.	2,700.
	No gum	5,600.	
	On cover		5,500.

Very Thick Soft Wove Paper

10	A2 6p reddish pur	15,000.	4,750.
	No gum	12,500.	
	On cover		5,250.
a.	Half used as 3p on cover		*20,000.*

1858-59 Wove Paper *Perf. 12*

11	A5 ½p rose	2,400.	1,500.
	No gum	2,100.	
	On cover		1,350.
	On cover, single franking		2,000.
	On circular, single franking		1,700.
	On newspaper, single franking		2,000.
12	A1 3p red	6,000.	900.
	No gum	4,000.	
	On cover		1,000.
	Double transfer (pos. 47, pane A)		*1,100.*
	On cover		*2,000.*
13	A2 6p brown vio ('59)	11,000.	6,000.
	No gum	9,500.	
	On cover		8,000.
a.	6p gray violet	11,500.	6,500.
	No gum	10,000.	
	On cover		8,500.
b.	Diagonal half used as 3p on cover		*15,000.*

Nos. 11-13 values are for copies with perfs touching the design.

A7

A8

A9

A10

A11

A12

1859

14	A7 1c rose	350.00	75.00
	No gum	290.00	
	On cover		180.00
	On cover, single franking		190.00
	On circular		140.00
	On newspaper		240.00
a.	Imperf., pair	4,250.	
b.	1c deep rose	500.00	110.00
	No gum	325.00	
	On cover		350.00
	On cover, single franking		390.00
	On circular		225.00
	On newspaper		475.00
15	A8 5c vermilion	450.00	32.50
	No gum	375.00	
	On cover		47.50
	Major re-entry (pos. 28)	*1,800.*	*750.00*
	No gum	*1,500.*	
	On cover		*1,200.*
a.	Imperf., pair	11,500.	—
b.	Diagonal half used as 2½c on cover		*5,500.*
c.	5c brick red	550.00	35.00
	No gum	365.00	
	On cover		60.00
16	A9 10c black brn	9,000.	4,750.
	No gum	7,000.	
	On cover		*5,600.*
a.	Half used as 5c on cover		*7,500.*
17	A9 10c red lilac	900.00	130.00
	No gum	725.00	
	On cover		200.00
a.	10c violet	1,000.	135.00
	No gum	850.00	
	On cover		180.00
b.	10c brown	900.00	125.00
	No gum	700.00	
	On cover		200.00
c.	Imperf., pair	10,000.	
d.	Diagonal half used as 5c on cover		*3,500.*
e.	10c deep red purple	3,000.	700.00
	No gum	2,000.	
	On cover		1,050.
18	A10 12½c yel green	750.00	100.00
	No gum	625.00	
	On cover		300.00
a.	12½c blue green	900.00	120.00
	No gum	750.00	
	On cover		375.00
b.	Imperf., pair	3,500.	
19	A11 17c blue	900.00	175.00
	No gum	725.00	
	On cover		475.00
a.	17c slate blue	900.00	190.00
	No gum	725.00	
	On cover		475.00
b.	Imperf., pair	4,000.	

Nos. 14-19 values are for copies with perfs touching the design. Imperfs. are without gum.

Re-entries of the 5c are numerous. Many of them are slight and have only small premium value. The major re-entry has many lines of the design double, especially the outlines of the ovals and frame at left.

Nos. 14b, 15c, 16, 17b, 18a and 19 represent the 1st printings of the stamps. No. 17e is from a 2nd printing. All of these gauge closer to perf. 11¾, and this will aid in their proper identification.

No. 15b was used with a 10c for a 12½c rate.

1864

20	A12 2c rose	600.00	250.00
	No gum	350.00	
	On cover, single franking		1,350.
	On circular, single franking		1,200.
	On wrapper, single franking		2,250.
a.	2c deep claret rose	650.00	300.00
	No gum	450.00	
	On cover, single franking		1,500.
	On circular, single franking		1,350.
	On wrapper, single franking		2,350.
b.	Imperf., pair	3,000.	

Imperfs. are without gum.

Values are for copies with perfs touching the design.

On cover value is for a single franking on cover, circular or newspaper.

Dominion of Canada

Queen Victoria
A13 A14

A15

A16

A17

A18

A19

A20

1868-76 *Perf. 12, 11½x12 (5c)*

21	A13 ½c black	80.00	65.00
	No gum	57.50	
	On cover		1,000.
	On cover, single franking		2,000.
a.	Perf. 11½x12 ('73)	100.00	65.00
	No gum	62.50	
	On cover		1,000.
	On cover, single franking		2,000.
b.	Watermarked	*16,500.*	*7,250.*
	No gum	*15,000.*	
c.	Thin paper	100.00	60.00
	No gum	80.00	
	On cover		1,000.
	On cover, single franking		2,000.
22	A14 1c brown red	525.00	100.00
	No gum	400.00	
	On cover		175.00
a.	Watermarked	*2,500.*	400.00
	No gum	*1,600.*	
	On cover		—
b.	Thin paper	525.00	100.00
	No gum	425.00	
	On cover		210.00
23	A14 1c yellow org	1,200.	160.00
	No gum	925.00	
	On cover		225.00
a.	1c deep orange	1,500.	200.00
	No gum	1,100.	
	On cover		275.00
24	A15 2c green	525.00	80.00
	No gum	425.00	
	On cover		275.00
a.	Watermarked	2,500.	325.00
	No gum	1,900.	
	On cover		—
b.	Thin paper	650.00	85.00
	No gum	540.00	
	On cover		320.00
c.	Diagonal half used as 1c on cover		*3,500.*
25	A16 3c red	1,500.	32.50
	No gum	1,250.	
	On cover		40.00
a.	Watermarked	3,750.	325.00
	No gum	3,000.	
	On cover		—
b.	Thin paper	1,650.	35.00
	No gum	1,400.	
	On cover		45.00
26	A17 5c ol grn ('75)	1,200.	175.00
	No gum	950.00	
	On cover		400.00
a.	Perf. 12	*2,500.*	800.00
	No gum	2,000.	
	On cover		1,300.
b.	Imperf., pair	*11,000.*	
27	A18 6c dark brown	1,500.	100.00
	No gum	1,200.	
	On cover		190.00
a.	6c yellow brown	1,250.	100.00
	No gum	975.00	
	On cover		150.00
b.	Watermarked	*4,750.*	*1,500.*
	No gum	*3,100.*	
	On cover		—
c.	Thin paper	1,575.	140.00
	No gum	1,300.	
	On cover		225.00
d.	Diagonal half used as 3c on cover		*2,500.*
e.	Vert. half used as 3c on cover		—
f.	6c black brown, thin paper (Mar. '68, 1st printing)	2,000.	200.00
	No gum	1,600.	
	On cover		425.00
28	A19 12½c blue	925.00	100.00
	No gum	750.00	
	On cover		225.00
a.	Watermarked	*3,250.*	325.00
	No gum	*2,300.*	
	On cover		—
b.	Thin paper	875.00	120.00
	No gum	725.00	
	On cover		225.00
c.	Horiz. pair, imperf. vert.		—
d.	Vert. pair, imperf. horiz.		*12,500.*

29	A20	15c gray violet	75.00	40.00
		No gum	55.00	
		On cover		525.00
a.		Perf. 11½x12 ('74)	1,200.	250.00
		No gum	1,050.	
		On cover		850.00
b.		15c red lilac	800.00	100.00
		No gum	575.00	
		On cover		850.00
c.		Wmk. (Clutha Mills)	5,000.	1,000.
		No gum	3,600.	
		On cover		—
d.		Imperf., pair	1,150.	
		Never hinged	1,350.	
		No gum	800.00	
e.		Thin paper	600.00	120.00
		No gum	440.00	
		On cover		800.00
30	A20	15c gray	80.00	40.00
		No gum	60.00	
		On cover		525.00
a.		Perf. 11½x12 ('73)	1,000.	250.00
		No gum	800.00	
		On cover		1,500.
b.		15c blue gray ('75)	100.00	50.00
		No gum	70.00	
		On cover		525.00
c.		Very thick paper (dp vio)	*4,000.*	1,350.
		No gum	*3,000.*	
		On cover		1,900.
d.		Script wmk., Perf. 11½x12, ('76)	*15,000.*	*4,500.*
		No gum	*11,000.*	
		On cover		—
e.		15c deep blue	1,400.	250.00
		No gum	1,100.	
		On cover		725.00

The watermark on Nos. 21b, 22a, 24a, 25a, 27b, 28a and 29c consists of double-lined letters reading: "E. & G. BOTHWELL CLUTHA MILLS." The script watermark on No. 30d reads in full: "Alexr. Pirie & Sons." Values for all these watermarked stamps are for fine examples. Very fine examples are rare, seldom traded, and generally command premiums of about 100% over the values listed.

No. 26a unused is valued in the grade of fine. No. 26b is a unique pair.

The existence of No. 28c has been questioned.

Nos. 21-21c on cover values are for single frankings on cover or circular.

1868 **Laid Paper**

31	A14	1c brown red	18,500.	5,500.
		No gum	12,500.	
		On cover		6,500.
32	A15	2c green		*175,000.*
33	A16	3c bright red	14,000.	1,500.
		No gum	9,000.	
		On cover		2,250.

Only two examples of No. 32 are known, neither being very fine.

Montreal and Ottawa Printings

A21

A22

A23

A24

A25

A26

A27

1870-89 **Wove Paper** ***Perf. 12***

34	A21	½c black ('82)	12.50	8.00
		Never hinged	24.00	
		On cover		225.00
		On newspaper		250.00
		On unaddressed circular		300.00
		Pair with vertical gutter between	250.00	—
		Never hinged	460.00	
		On cover		*800.00*
a.		Imperf., pair	500.00	
		Never hinged	*750.00*	
b.		Horiz. pair, imperf. between	675.00	
		Never hinged	*1,000.*	
35	A22	1c yellow	40.00	1.10
		Never hinged	92.50	
		On cover		7.00
a.		1c orange ('70)	125.00	8.50
		Never hinged	240.00	
		On cover		11.00
b.		Imperf., pair	400.00	
		Never hinged	525.00	
c.		Diagonal half used as ½c on circular		3,500.
36	A23	2c green ('72)	60.00	2.00
		Never hinged	125.00	
		On cover		10.00
a.		Imperf., pair	600.00	
		Never hinged	*1,000.*	
b.		Diagonal half used as 1c on cover		1,600.
c.		Vertical half used as 1c on cover		1,600.
d.		2c blue green ('89)	80.00	4.00
		Never hinged	190.00	
		On cover		8.00
f.		Double impression	—	—
37	A24	3c orange red ('73)	90.00	2.00
		Never hinged	180.00	
		On cover		5.50
a.		3c rose ('71)	500.00	12.50
		Never hinged	*1,050.*	
		On cover		19.00
b.		3c copper red ('70)	1,100.	50.00
		Never hinged	*2,250.*	
		On cover		70.00
c.		3c dull red ('72)	100.00	2.50
		Never hinged	200.00	
		On cover		8.00
38	A25	5c sl green ('76)	725.00	20.00
		Never hinged	*1,400.*	
		On cover		62.50
39	A26	6c yel brn ('72)	550.00	20.00
		Never hinged	*1,050.*	
		On cover		37.50
a.		Diagonal half used as 3c on cover		500.00
c.		Imperf., pair	2,250.	
d.		6c brown ('75)	400.00	20.00
		Never hinged	*775.00*	
		On cover		35.00
40	A27	10c dull rose lilac ('77)	650.00	65.00
		Never hinged	*1,050.*	
		On cover		450.00
a.		10c magenta ('80)	675.00	70.00
		Never hinged	*925.00*	
		On cover		450.00
b.		10c deep lilac rose	650.00	65.00
		Never hinged	*800.00*	
		On cover		450.00

No. 34 on cover value is for single franking paying the circular rate.

No. 34a made with and without gum; values the same.

Copies of Nos. 36b and 36c postmarked "Halifax" are a private speculation.

1870 ***Perf. 12½***

37d	A24	3c copper red (Ottawa)	7,500.	1,150.
		Never hinged	*15,500.*	
		On cover		1,400.

1873-79 ***Perf. 11½x12***

35d	A22	1c orange	210.00	15.00
		Never hinged	420.00	
		On cover		50.00
36e	A23	2c green	350.00	20.00
		Never hinged	700.00	
		On cover		25.00
37e	A24	3c red	225.00	10.00
		Never hinged	500.00	
		On cover		13.00
38a	A25	5c slate green	600.00	40.00
		Never hinged	*1,350.*	
		On cover		60.00
39b	A26	6c yellow brown	650.00	50.00
		Never hinged	*1,350.*	
		On cover		60.00
40c	A27	10c dull rose lilac	1,000.	200.00
		Never hinged	*1,900.*	
		On cover		450.00
40d	A27	10c magenta	1,000.	200.00
		Never hinged	*1,900.*	
		On cover		450.00
40e	A27	10c pale milky rose lilac ('74)	1,300.	600.00
		Never hinged	*2,600.*	
		On cover		800.00

The gum on Nos. 35d-40c is always dull and usually blotchy or streaky. It is distinct from the earlier clear, smooth gum and from the bright shiny gums of the later periods.

Nos. 38 and 40 were printed at Montreal. Printings of Nos. 34 to 37, and 39 were made at Ottawa or Montreal and can be separated only by differences in paper and gum.

Ottawa Printing

A28

A29

1888-97 ***Perf. 12***

41	A24	3c brt vermilion	50.00	.80
		Never hinged	110.00	
		On cover		6.00
a.		3c rose carmine	400.00	10.00
		Never hinged	*875.00*	
		On cover		12.50
42	A25	5c gray	120.00	4.00
		Never hinged	300.00	
		On cover		32.50
43	A26	6c red brown	120.00	10.00
		Never hinged	300.00	
		On cover		32.50
a.		6c chocolate ('90)	200.00	27.50
		Never hinged	500.00	
		On cover		55.00
c.		5c on 6c re-entry	*3,600.*	*3,000.*
44	A28	8c violet black ('93)	140.00	4.50
		Never hinged	300.00	
		On cover		24.00
a.		8c blue gray	225.00	4.50
		Never hinged	475.00	
		On cover		24.00
b.		8c slate	180.00	4.50
		Never hinged	450.00	
		On cover		24.00
c.		8c gray	180.00	4.50
		Never hinged	450.00	
		On cover		24.00
45	A27	10c brown red ('97)	500.00	45.00
		Never hinged	975.00	
		On cover		225.00
a.		10c dull rose	475.00	40.00
		Never hinged	925.00	
		On cover		225.00
b.		10c pink	475.00	45.00
		Never hinged	925.00	
		On cover		240.00
46	A29	20c ver ('93)	375.00	100.00
		Never hinged	800.00	
		On cover		800.00
47	A29	50c dp blue ('93)	375.00	75.00
		Never hinged	800.00	
		On cover		700.00

Stamps of the 1870-93 issues are found on paper varying from very thin to thick, also occasionally on paper showing a distinctly ribbed surface.

The gum on Nos. 41-47 appears bright and shiny, often with a yellowish tint.

Values for Nos. 46-47 on cover are for single frankings paying the correct rate.

Imperf., Pairs

41b	A24	3c	325.
		Never hinged	500.
42a	A25	5c	600.
		Never hinged	1,000.
43b	A26	6c	500.
		Never hinged	700.
44d	A28	8c	650.
		Never hinged	825.
45c	A27	10c	500.
		Never hinged	600.
46a	A29	20c	1,100.
		Never hinged	*1,800.*
47a	A29	50c	1,100.
		Never hinged	*1,800.*

Nos. 41b-45c made with and without gum. Without gum sell for the same as the unused hinged price.

Imperforates and Part-Perforates

From 1859 through 1943 (Nos. 14a/262a), imperforate stamps were printed. The earliest imperforates through perhaps 1917 most likely were from imprimatur sheets (i.e. the first sheets from the approved plates, normally kept in government files) or proof sheets on stamp paper that once were in the post office archives. The imperforates from approximately 1927 to 1943 (often made both with and without gum) were specially created and traded for classic stamps needed for the post office museum, given as gifts to governmental or other dignitaries, or sold or given to favored persons.

The only imperforates from this entire period that were issued to the public were Nos. 90a and 136-138.

Similarly, almost all stamps that are known part-perforate (i.e., horizontal pairs imperforate vertically and vertical pairs imperforate horizontally) were specially made for trading purposes or as presentation items to be given to favored persons.

See the similar imperforates in the air post, Nos. CE1a and CE2a, special delivery, No. F2c (but not No. F1c which was an issued error), postage dues, and Nos. MR4b and MR4c.

Jubilee Issue

Queen Victoria, "1837" and "1897" — A30

1897, June 19 **Unwmk.** ***Perf. 12***

50	A30	½c black	100.00	100.00
		Never hinged	300.00	
		On cover		275.00
51	A30	1c orange	20.00	8.00
		Never hinged	50.00	
		On cover		15.00
52	A30	2c green	22.50	12.50
		Never hinged	55.00	
		On cover		17.50
53	A30	3c bright rose	15.00	2.25
		Never hinged	37.50	
		On cover		6.50
54	A30	5c deep blue	50.00	35.00
		Never hinged	125.00	
		On cover		85.00
55	A30	6c yellow brown	200.00	160.00
		Never hinged	500.00	
		On cover		275.00
56	A30	8c dark violet	65.00	50.00
		Never hinged	160.00	
		On cover		160.00
57	A30	10c brown violet	100.00	85.00
		Never hinged	250.00	
		On cover		250.00
58	A30	15c steel blue	200.00	160.00
		Never hinged	500.00	
		On cover		325.00
59	A30	20c vermilion	225.00	160.00
		Never hinged	550.00	
		On cover		325.00
60	A30	50c ultra	275.00	160.00
		Never hinged	725.00	
		On cover		350.00
61	A30	$1 lake	800.00	650.00
		Never hinged	2,150.	
		On cover		1,500.
62	A30	$2 dk purple	1,200.	500.00
		Never hinged	3,250.	
		On cover		1,000.
63	A30	$3 yel bister	1,250.	950.00
		Never hinged	3,400.	
		On cover		1,900.
64	A30	$4 purple	1,250.	950.00
		Never hinged	3,400.	
		On cover		1,900.
65	A30	$5 olive green	1,250.	950.00
		Never hinged	3,400.	
		On cover		1,500.
		Nos. 50-60 (11)	1,272.	932.75
		Nos. 50-60, never hinged	2,978.	

60th year of Queen Victoria's reign.

Roller and smudged cancels on Nos. 61-65 sell for less.

Covers: Value for No. 50 is for a single franking paying the correct rate. In combination with other postage it is worth much less. Values for Nos. 61-65 are for overfranked items, usually philatelic.

A31

A32

1897-98

66	A31	½c black	9.00	6.00
		Never hinged	21.50	
		On cover		200.00
67	A31	1c blue green	27.50	1.20
		Never hinged	70.00	
		On cover		2.50
68	A31	2c purple	27.50	2.00
		Never hinged	70.00	
		On cover		4.00
69	A31	3c carmine ('98)	40.00	.75
		Never hinged	100.00	
		On cover		2.00
70	A31	5c dk bl, *bluish*	120.00	7.50
		Never hinged	300.00	
		On cover		40.00
71	A31	6c brown	90.00	30.00
		Never hinged	225.00	
		On cover		450.00
72	A31	8c orange	190.00	11.00
		Never hinged	475.00	
		On cover		40.00
73	A31	10c brown vio ('98)	300.00	80.00
		Never hinged	750.00	
		On cover		650.00
		Nos. 66-73 (8)	804.00	138.45
		Nos. 66-73, never hinged	2,012.	

Values for Nos. 66, 71 and 73 on cover are for single frankings paying correct rates.

For surcharge see No. 87.

Imperf., Pairs

66a	A31	½c	325.
		Never hinged	600.
67a	A31	1c	325.
		Never hinged	600.
68a	A31	2c	325.
		Never hinged	600.
69a	A31	3c	650.
		Never hinged	1,200.
70a	A31	5c	325.
		Never hinged	600.
71a	A31	6c	650.
		Never hinged	1,200.
72a	A31	8c	500.
		Never hinged	925.
73a	A31	10c	500.
		Never hinged	925.

Nos. 66a, 67a, 68a and 70a made with and without gum. Specialists can distinguish printings made with and without gum by shade and paper quality. Without gum sell for about 95% of the unused hinged price.

1898-1902

TWO CENTS:

Type I — Frame of four very thin lines.
Type II — Frame of a thick line between two thin ones.

74 A32 ½c black 6.00 2.00
Never hinged 11.50
On cover 200.00
75 A32 1c gray green 27.50 .30
Never hinged 52.50
On cover 1.50
76 A32 2c purple (I) 27.50 .25
Never hinged 52.50
On cover 1.50
a. Thick paper ('99) 150.00 10.00
Never hinged 290.00
On cover 20.00
77 A32 2c car (I) ('99) 27.50 .25
Never hinged 52.50
On cover 1.50
a. 2c carmine (II) ('99) 35.00 .50
Never hinged 67.50
On cover 2.00
b. Booklet pane of 6 (II) ('00) 1,200. —
Never hinged 2,350.
78 A32 3c carmine 47.50 .90
Never hinged 90.00
On cover 1.50
79 A32 5c blue, *bluish* ('99) 200.00 2.00
Never hinged 400.00
On cover 40.00
b. Whiter paper ('99) 240.00 3.00
Never hinged 575.00
On cover 40.00
80 A32 6c brown 150.00 40.00
Never hinged 290.00
On cover 450.00
81 A32 7c ol yel ('02) 120.00 20.00
Never hinged 230.00
On cover 52.50
82 A32 8c orange 240.00 22.50
Never hinged 460.00
On cover 60.00
83 A32 10c brown vio 350.00 20.00
Never hinged 675.00
On cover 450.00
84 A32 20c ol grn ('00) 475.00 100.00
Never hinged 925.00
On cover 950.00
Nos. 74-84 (11) 1,671. 208.20
Nos. 74-84, never hinged 3,239.

Values for Nos. 74, 80, 83-84 on cover are for single frankings paying correct rates.

For surcharges see Nos. 88-88C.

Imperf., Pairs

74a A32 ½c 400.
Never hinged 650.
75a A32 1c 1,000.
Never hinged 1,600.
77c A32 2c (I) 400.
Never hinged 650.
77d A32 2c (II) *850.*
e. As No. 77b, imperf., 2 panes tete beche ('00) *12,000.*
79a A32 5c 900.
Never hinged 1,450.
80a A32 6c 900.
Never hinged 1,450.
81a A32 7c 500.
82a A32 8c 900.
Never hinged 1,450.
83a A32 10c 900.
Never hinged 1,250.
84a A32 20c 3,500.

Nos. 77e, 77e, 81a and 84a were made only without gum. No. 80a was made only with gum. Others either with or without gum and of these those without gum sell for about ⅔ of the values shown for unused hinged. Specialists can distinguish printings made with and without gum by shade and paper quality.

Imperial Penny Postage Issue

Map of British Empire on Mercator Projection A33

1898, Dec. 7 **Engr. & Typo.**

85 A33 2c black, lav & car 37.50 7.00
Never hinged 62.50
On cover 25.00
a. Imperf., pair 450.00
86 A33 2c black, bl & car 35.00 6.50
Never hinged 55.00
On cover 25.00
a. Imperf., pair 450.00
b. 2c black, deep bl & car 45.00 8.00
Never hinged 70.00
On cover 27.50

Imperfs. are without gum, and known in both the blue and deep blue shades of No. 86 and 86b; values the same.

Nos. 69 and 78 Surcharged in

1899, July

87 A31 2c on 3c carmine 15.00 6.50
Never hinged 40.00
On cover 11.00
88 A32 2c on 3c carmine 22.50 5.00
Never hinged 60.00
On cover 10.50

No. 78 Surcharged in Blue or Violet

A32a A32b

1899, Jan. 5

88B A32a 1(c) on ⅓ of 3c, on cover (Bl) *6,250.*
88C A32b 2(c) on ⅔ of 3c, on cover (V) *6,250.*

Nos. 88B-88C were prepared and used at Port Hood, Nova Scotia, without official authorization.

King Edward VII — A34

1903-08 **Engr.**

89 A34 1c green 27.50 .20
Never hinged 62.50
On cover 1.25
90 A34 2c carmine 32.50 .20
Never hinged 75.00
On cover 1.25
"Hairlines" plate cracks 60.00 6.00
Never hinged 120.00
On cover 10.00
b. Booklet pane of 6 1,100. *1,250.*
Never hinged *1,750.*
91 A34 5c blue, *blue* 200.00 4.00
Never hinged 450.00
On cover 30.00
b. Whiter paper 150.00 5.00
Never hinged 300.00
On cover 35.00
92 A34 7c olive bister 180.00 4.00
Never hinged 400.00
On cover 20.00
93 A34 10c brown lilac 375.00 8.50
Never hinged 850.00
On cover 300.00
94 A34 20c olive green ('04) 625.00 40.00
Never hinged 1,400.
On cover 400.00
95 A34 50c purple ('08) 750.00 140.00
Never hinged 1,700.
On cover 1,300.
Nos. 89-95 (7) 2,190. 196.90
Nos. 89-95, never hinged 4,938.

Values for Nos. 94 and 95 used are for examples with contemporaneous circular datestamps. Stamps with heavy cancellations or parcel cancellations sell for much less.

Hairlines: a pattern of fine lines across the face of the stamp caused by plate cracks. The values are for stamps with prominent and extensive lines. Values will be less for stamps with less prominent and less extensive cracks. See similar listings for Nos. 104, 104a, 106a, 106c.

Covers: values for Nos. 93-95 are for single frankings paying the correct rate.

Issued: 1c-10c, 7/1/03; 20c, 9/27/04; 50c, 11/19/08.

Imperf., Pairs

89a A34 1c 600.00
90a A34 2c 35.00 35.00
Never hinged 55.00
On cover 50.00
c. As No. 90b, imperf, 2 panes tete beche *12,000.*
91a A34 5c 1,000.
92a A34 7c 650.
93a A34 10c 1,000.

All imperfs except No. 90a made without gum.

No. 90a issued to the public with gum from plates 13 and 14. Also made without gum from plates 1 and 2, which are distinguishable by experts. Value, pair, plates 1 and 2 with certificate of authenticity, $350. Imperfs with black or red defacing lines are from experimental printings and are considered to be proofs.

Quebec Tercentenary Issue

Prince and Princess of Wales, 1908 — A35

Jacques Cartier and Samuel de Champlain A36

Queen Alexandra and King Edward A37

Champlain's Home in Quebec A38

Generals Montcalm and Wolfe — A39

View of Quebec in 1700 — A40

Champlain's Departure for the West — A41

Arrival of Cartier at Quebec A42

1908, July 16

96 A35 ½c black brown 4.75 4.00
Never hinged 12.00
On cover 200.00
Re-entry (line through "CANADA" - pos. 44) 45.00 45.00
Never hinged 110.00
On cover 350.00
97 A36 1c blue green 16.00 4.00
Never hinged 40.00
On cover 6.00
98 A37 2c carmine 27.50 1.25
Never hinged 70.00
On cover 5.00
99 A38 5c dark blue 60.00 42.50
Never hinged 150.00
On cover 150.00
100 A39 7c olive green 125.00 80.00
Never hinged 310.00
On cover 100.00
101 A40 10c dark violet 150.00 100.00
Never hinged 375.00
On cover 290.00
102 A41 15c red orange 180.00 100.00
Never hinged 450.00
On cover 325.00
103 A42 20c yellow brown 225.00 140.00
Never hinged 575.00
On cover 425.00
Nos. 96-103 (8) 788.25 471.75
Nos. 96-103, never hinged 1,982.

Covers: values for Nos. 96-103 are for properly franked items in the correct period of use.

Imperf., Pairs

96a A35 ½c 525.00
Never hinged 900.00
97a A36 1c 525.00
Never hinged 900.00
98a A37 2c 525.00
Never hinged 900.00
99a A38 5c 525.00
Never hinged 900.00
100a A39 7c 525.00
Never hinged 900.00
101a A40 10c 525.00
Never hinged 900.00
102a A41 15c 525.00
Never hinged 900.00
103a A42 20c 525.00
Never hinged 900.00

100 pairs of imperfs made, 50 with gum and 50 without. Due to demand, pairs without gum generally sell for 90-95% of the unused hinged price.

WET and DRY PRINTINGS

Before 1922, stamps were printed using dampened paper (wet printing). As the paper dried, it shrank slightly across the grain. In 1922, a new process was introduced that used much drier paper (dry printing) with little or no shrinkage. Additionally, on wet printings the gum does not extend to the edges of the pane and the design is more flat from the gummed side; on dry printings the gum extends to the edges of the pane and the designs shows some embossing effect when viewed from the gummed side.

The King George V Admiral issue, design A43, was printed from 1911 to 1925, and the earlier wet printings generally show a narrower design due to paper shrinkage

King George V — A43

Two dies of 1c.
Die I — The "N" of "ONE" is separated from the oval above it.
Die II — The "N" of "ONE" almost touches the oval above it.

Two dies of 3c carmine.
Die I — The "R" of "THREE" is separated from the oval above it. The bottom line of the vignette does not touch the heavy diagonal stroke at right.
Die II — The "R" of "THREE" almost touches the oval above it. The bottom horizontal line of the vignette touches the heavy diagonal stroke at right.

1911-25

104 A43 1c green 17.50 .20
Never hinged 45.00
On cover 1.25
"Hairlines" plate cracks (horiz.) 35.00 25.00
Never hinged 90.00
a. Booklet pane of 6 30.00 *32.50*
Never hinged 60.00
b. 1c blue green 22.50 .20
Never hinged 55.00
On cover 1.25
Major double transfer at lower right (35 LR 12) *2,500.* *1,250.*
On cover *2,500.*
c. 1c deep blue green 22.50 .20
Never hinged 55.00
On cover 1.25
As "c," "hairlines" plate cracks 50.00 6.50
Never hinged 100.00
On cover 7.50
105 A43 1c yellow, wet printing (I) ('22) 15.00 .20
Never hinged 40.00
On cover 1.25
a. Booklet pane of 4 + 2 labels 50.00 *55.00*
Never hinged 100.00
b. Booklet pane of 6 55.00 *55.00*
Never hinged 140.00
d. 1c orange yellow, dry printing (II) 15.00 .20
Never hinged 40.00
On cover 1.00
e. 1c lemon yellow, wet printing (I) 35.00 6.50
Never hinged 100.00
On cover 13.00
f. 1c yellow, dry printing (I) 29.00 .50
Never hinged 80.00
On cover —
106 A43 2c carmine 17.50 .20
Never hinged 45.00
On cover 1.25
a. Booklet pane of 6 35.00 35.00
Never hinged 70.00
As "a," "hairlines" plate cracks 52.50 52.50
Never hinged 90.00
b. 2c pink 125.00 16.00
Never hinged 325.00
On cover 25.00
c. 2c rose carmine 17.50 .20
Never hinged 45.00
On cover 1.25
As "c," "hairlines" plate cracks 45.00 4.50
Never hinged 75.00
On cover 7.50
d. As "c," booklet pane of 6 140.00 140.00
Never hinged 250.00
107 A43 2c yel green, wet printing ('22) 12.50 .20
Never hinged 32.50
On cover 2.00
a. Thin paper, wet printing ('24) 12.50 2.25
Never hinged 32.50
On cover 5.00
b. Booklet pane of 4 + 2 labels ('22) 60.00 *65.00*
Never hinged 120.00
c. Booklet pane of 6, wet printing ('22) 275.00 *300.00*
Never hinged 500.00
e. 2c green, dry printing ('23) 12.50 .20
Never hinged 32.50
On cover 2.00
f. As "c," dry printing 275.00 *300.00*
Never hinged 500.00
108 A43 3c brown, wet printing ('18) 15.00 .20
Never hinged 40.00
On cover 2.00
a. Booklet pane of 4 + 2 labels 80.00 *85.00*
Never hinged 160.00
b. 3c yellow brown, wet printing 27.50 .20
Never hinged 65.00
On cover 2.00
c. 3c brown, dry printing ('23) 15.00 .20
Never hinged 4.00
On cover 2.00
109 A43 3c car (I) ('23) 15.00 .20
Never hinged 40.00
On cover 2.00
a. Booklet pane of 4 + 2 labels 60.00 *65.00*
Never hinged 120.00
c. Die II ('24) 35.00 .20
Never hinged 90.00
On cover 3.50
d. 3c rose carmine (I) ('23) 35.00 3.50
Never hinged 90.00
On cover 10.00
110 A43 4c ol bis, wet printing ('22) 40.00 3.00
Never hinged 105.00
On cover, single franking 25.00
b. 4c olive yellow, wet printing 40.00 3.25
Never hinged 105.00
On cover, single franking 17.50
c. 4c golden yellow, wet printing 100.00 6.50
Never hinged 250.00
On cover, single franking 25.00
d. 4c yellow ocher, dry printing ('25) 40.00 3.50
Never hinged 105.00
On cover, single franking 17.50
111 A43 5c dark blue ('12) 120.00 .80
Never hinged 300.00
On cover 35.00
a. 5c indigo 200.00 2.00
Never hinged 450.00
On cover 35.00
b. 5c gray blue 160.00 1.00
Never hinged 400.00
On cover 35.00
112 A43 5c violet, wet printing ('22) 30.00 .65
Never hinged 77.50
On cover 27.50
a. Thin paper ('24) 25.00 6.50
Never hinged 65.00
On cover 35.00
c. Dry printing ('25) 45.00 1.40
Never hinged 100.00
On cover 35.00
113 A43 7c yel ocher ('12) 42.50 3.25
Never hinged 110.00
On cover 14.00
a. 7c olive bister ('15) 42.50 3.25
Never hinged 110.00
On cover 14.00
b. 7c straw 160.00 14.00
Never hinged 375.00
On cover 40.00
c. 7c sage green ('14) 325.00 27.50
Never hinged 775.00
On cover 50.00
114 A43 7c red brown, dry printing ('24) 20.00 10.00
Never hinged 52.50
On cover 15.00
On cover, single franking 35.00
b. 7c red brown, wet printing 24.00 14.00
Never hinged 65.00
On cover 15.00
On cover, single franking 35.00
115 A43 8c blue ('25) 30.00 10.00
Never hinged 77.50
On cover 20.00
On cover, single franking 45.00
116 A43 10c plum ('12) 250.00 2.50
Never hinged 650.00
On cover 25.00
On cover, single franking 45.00
a. 10c reddish purple 300.00 2.50
Never hinged 825.00
On cover 25.00
On cover, single franking 45.00
117 A43 10c blue, wet printing ('22) 42.50 2.00
Never hinged 110.00
On cover, single franking 27.50
a. Dry printing 42.50 2.00
Never hinged 110.00
On cover, single franking 27.50
118 A43 10c bis brn ('25) 37.50 2.00
Never hinged 100.00
On cover, single franking 27.50
b. 10c yellow brown 37.50 2.00
Never hinged 100.00
On cover, single franking 27.50
119 A43 20c ol grn, dry printing ('25) 100.00 1.75
Never hinged 260.00
On cover, single franking 150.00
b. 20c sage green, wet printing 175.00 6.00
Never hinged 425.00
On cover, single franking 150.00
c. 20c dk olive green, wet printing ('12) 110.00 2.00
Never hinged 240.00
On cover, single franking 150.00
d. 20c gray green, wet printing 110.00 5.00
Never hinged 275.00
On cover, single franking 150.00
120 A43 50c blk brn, dry printing ('25) 75.00 2.50
Never hinged 200.00
On cover, single franking 260.00
a. 50c black, wet printing ('12) 175.00 7.50
Never hinged 475.00
On cover, single franking 275.00
122 A43 $1 orange, dry printing ('23) 85.00 9.00
Never hinged 230.00
On cover, single franking 360.00
b. $1 deep orange, wet printing 170.00 14.00
Never hinged 375.00
On cover, single franking 360.00
Nos. 104-122 (18) 965.00 48.65
#104-122, never hinged 2,515.

For type A43 perforated 12x8 see No. 184.
For surcharges see Nos. 139-140.
Issued: #104, #106, 12/22/11; #105, 6/7/22; #108, 8/6/18; #109, 12/18/23; 4c, 7/7/22; #111, 1/17/12; #112, 2/2/22; #113, 116, 1/12/12; #114, 12/12/24; 8c, 9/1/25; #117, 2/20/22; #118, 8/1/25; 20c, 1/23/12; 50c, 1/26/12; $1, 7/22/23.

Imperf., Panes

105c As No. 105b, imperf, 2 panes tete beche *9,500.*
107d As No. 107c, imperf, 2 panes tete beche *9,500.*
109b As No. 109a, imperf, 2 panes tete beche *9,500.*

Imperf., Pairs

110a A43 4c 1,600.
Never hinged 2,900.
112b A43 5c 1,600.
Never hinged 2,900.
114a A43 7c 1,600.
Never hinged 2,900.
115a A43 8c 1,600.
Never hinged 2,900.
118a A43 10c 1,600.
Never hinged 2,900.
119a A43 20c 1,600.
Never hinged 2,900.
120b A43 50c 2,000.
Never hinged 3,600.
122a A43 $1 1,600.
Never hinged 2,900.

Nos. 105c and 109b made without gum, others with gum. About half of the No. 120b pairs have creases; value thus $500.

Two pairs of tete beche singles are known from No. 107d; value, unused, $1,750.

Coil Stamps

1913 ***Perf. 8 Horizontally***

123 A43 1c dark green 90.00 50.00
Never hinged 210.00
On cover 65.00
Pair 210.00 110.00
Never hinged 425.00
On cover 140.00
Paste-up pair 260.00 125.00
Never hinged 520.00
On cover 160.00
124 A43 2c carmine 90.00 50.00
Never hinged 210.00
On cover 75.00
Pair 210.00 110.00
Never hinged 425.00
On cover 275.00
Paste-up pair 260.00 190.00
Never hinged 520.00
On cover 225.00

1912-24 ***Perf. 8 Vertically***

125 A43 1c green 20.00 1.75
Never hinged 40.00
On cover 3.50
Pair 45.00 4.25
Never hinged 90.00

On cover 9.00
Paste-up pair 50.00 27.50
Never hinged 100.00
On cover 40.00
Major double transfer at lower right (35 LR 12) —

126 A43 1c orange yellow, dry printing (II) ('23) 10.00 6.50
Never hinged 20.00
On cover 8.50
Pair 21.00 17.00
Never hinged 42.00
On cover 22.50
Paste-up pair 32.50 27.50
Never hinged 55.00
On cover 32.50
a. As #126, block of 4 (II) 50.00 50.00
Never hinged 100.00
On cover, block of 4 62.50
On cover, vert. pair, commercial 27.50
On cover, vert. pair, 1st flight 16.00
b. 1c orange yellow, wet printing (I) 22.50 9.00
Never hinged 45.00
On cover 14.00
Pair 45.00 20.00
Never hinged 90.00
On cover 25.00
Paste-up pair 55.00 27.50
Never hinged 100.00
On cover 32.50
c. As "b," block of 4 (I) 400.00
Never hinged 675.00
d. 1c yellow, dry printing (I) 26.00 9.00
Never hinged 45.00
On cover 15.00
Pair 55.00 20.00
Never hinged 92.50
On cover 25.00
Paste-up pair 35.00 30.00
Never hinged 57.50
On cover 37.50

127 A43 2c carmine 30.00 1.75
Never hinged 60.00
On cover 3.50
Pair 60.00 6.50
Never hinged 120.00
On cover 9.00
Paste-up pair 75.00 35.00
Never hinged 140.00
On cover 42.50

128 A43 2c green ('22) 15.00 1.00
Never hinged 30.00
On cover 2.75
Pair 35.00 3.25
Never hinged 65.00
On cover 13.00
Paste-up pair 42.50 16.00
Never hinged 72.50
On cover 21.00
a. Block of 4 60.00 50.00
Never hinged 120.00
On cover, block of 4 60.00
On cover, vert. pair, commercial 20.00
On cover, vert. pair, 1st flight 12.50

129 A43 3c brown ('18) 22.50 1.25
Never hinged 45.00
On cover 3.50
Pair 50.00 4.00
Never hinged 100.00
On cover 13.50
Paste-up pair 60.00 20.00
Never hinged 120.00
On cover 25.00

130 A43 3c carmine, wet printing (I) ('24) 65.00 8.00
Never hinged 130.00
On cover 13.00
Pair 150.00 40.00
Never hinged 260.00
On cover, pair alone 65.00
Paste-up pair 190.00 80.00
Never hinged 300.00
On cover 95.00
a. Block of 4 (I) 800.00 550.00
Never hinged 1,300.
On cover, block of 4 —
On cover, vert. pair, commercial 325.00
On cover, vert. pair, 1st flight 250.00
b. Dry printing, die II 80.00 10.00
Never hinged 160.00
On cover 14.00
Pair 160.00 50.00
Never hinged 325.00
On cover, pair alone 60.00
Paste-up pair 190.00 90.00
Never hinged 375.00
On cover 110.00
Nos. 125-130 (6) 162.50 20.25
#125-130, never hinged 347.00

Nos. 126a and 128a were issued to the public. Nos. 126c and 130a were issued "by favor" as were the various other imperf and part-perfs of this era.

The used example of No. 125 with major double transfer is unique; it is defective.

Beware of fakes of No. 130a made from No. 138.

1915-24 ***Perf. 12 Horizontally***

131 A43 1c dark green 6.50 7.50
Never hinged 13.00
On cover 9.00
Pair 13.00 15.00
Never hinged 26.00
On cover, pair alone 20.00
Paste-up pair 16.00 16.00
Never hinged 32.00
On cover 25.00

132 A43 2c carmine 22.50 8.00
Never hinged 45.00
On cover 10.00
Pair 47.50 27.50
Never hinged 95.00
On cover, pair alone 50.00
Paste-up pair 55.00 35.00
Never hinged 110.00
On cover 55.00

133 A43 2c yellow grn ('24) 65.00 50.00
Never hinged 130.00
On cover 65.00
Pair 150.00 110.00
Never hinged 300.00
On cover, pair alone 160.00
Paste-up pair 160.00 125.00
Never hinged 320.00
On cover 190.00

134 A43 3c brown ('21) 9.00 5.00
Never hinged 18.00
On cover 9.00
Pair 18.00 12.50
Never hinged 36.00
On cover, pair alone 22.50
Paste-up pair 24.00 19.00
Never hinged 48.00
On cover 32.50
Nos. 131-134 (4) 103.00 70.50
#131-134, never hinged 206.00

"The Fathers of Confederation" — A44

1917, Sept. 15 ***Perf. 12***

135 A44 3c brown 40.00 1.25
Never hinged 100.00
On commercial cover 8.00
1st day cover 300.00
a. Imperf., pair 400.00

50th anniv. of the Canadian Confederation.
Imperfs. are without gum.
Value for No. 135 on commercial cover is for an example with stamp in grade of very fine. Value for grades below very fine are much less than the value shown.

1924 ***Imperf.***

136 A43 1c orange yellow 30.00 30.00
Never hinged 55.00
On cover, single franking 35.00
Pair 75.00 75.00
Never hinged 140.00
On cover 80.00

137 A43 2c green 30.00 30.00
Never hinged 55.00
On cover, single franking 35.00
Pair 75.00 75.00
Never hinged 140.00
On cover 80.00

138 A43 3c carmine (I) 15.00 15.00
Never hinged 24.00
On cover, single franking 17.00
Pair 40.00 40.00
Never hinged 75.00
On cover 45.00
Nos. 136-138 (3) 75.00 75.00
Nos. 136-138, never hinged 110.00

Plate Number Blocks

Before 1958, plate blocks consist of the printer's name and a plate number. As with single stamps, all plate blocks are valued in the grade of very fine, with listings for both hinged and never hinged through Nos. 262, C8, CE2, E10, and J14, and never hinged only from Nos. 268, B1, C9, CE3, C01, E11, EO1, J15, and O1. Some plate numbers and/or positions are worth more than others; only the most common are valued here.

No. 109 Surcharged:

a

b

1926 ***Perf. 12***

139 A43(a) 2c on 3c carmine (I) 52.50 52.50
Never hinged 85.00
On commercial cover 80.00
On 1st flight cover 55.00
Plate block of 8 500.00
Never hinged 775.00
a. Pair, one without surcharge 300.00
b. Double surcharge 200.00
c. Die II 500.00

140 A43(b) 2c on 3c carmine 26.00 22.50
Never hinged 42.50
On commercial cover 32.50
On 1st flight cover 29.00
Plate block of 8 300.00
Never hinged 475.00
a. Double surcharge 200.00
b. Triple surcharge 200.00
c. Double surch., one invtd. 300.00

First Day Covers

Values for first day covers are for addressed non-cacheted covers through No. 190, addressed cacheted covers from No. 191 to No. 277, and unaddressed covers with the most common cachets from No. 282 and later.

Sir John A. Macdonald A45

Sir Wilfrid Laurier A48

"The Fathers of Confederation" — A46

Parliament Building at Ottawa A47

Map of Canada A49

1927, June 29

141 A45 1c orange 3.25 1.20
Never hinged 6.00
1st day cover 100.00
Plate block of 8 35.00
Never hinged 52.50

142 A46 2c green 1.75 .20
Never hinged 3.25
1st day cover 100.00
Plate block of 4 42.50
Never hinged 60.00
Plate block of 6 21.00
Never hinged 31.00

143 A47 3c brown carmine 9.00 5.50
Never hinged 16.00
1st day cover 100.00
Plate block of 4 62.50
Never hinged 92.50
Plate block of 6 77.50
Never hinged 115.00

144 A48 5c violet 4.25 3.00
Never hinged 7.75
1st day cover 100.00
Plate block of 8 52.50
Never hinged 80.00

145 A49 12c dark blue 22.50 6.00
Never hinged 40.00
1st day cover 140.00
Plate block of 6 150.00
Never hinged 260.00
Nos. 141-145 (5) 40.75 15.90
#141-145, never hinged 73.00
Set of 5 stamps on one 1st day cover 350.00

60th year of the Canadian Confederation.

Imperf., Pairs

141a A45 1c 100.00
Never hinged 145.00
142a A46 2c 100.00
Never hinged 145.00
143a A47 3c 100.00
Never hinged 145.00
144a A48 5c 100.00
Never hinged 145.00
145a A49 12c 100.00
Never hinged 145.00

Horizontal Pairs, Imperf. Vertically

141b	A45	1c	100.00
		Never hinged	145.00
142b	A46	2c	100.00
		Never hinged	145.00
143b	A47	3c	100.00
		Never hinged	145.00
144b	A48	5c	100.00
		Never hinged	145.00
145b	A49	12c	100.00
		Never hinged	145.00

Vertical Pair, Imperf. Horizontally

141c	A45	1c	100.00
		Never hinged	145.00
142c	A46	2c	100.00
		Never hinged	145.00
143c	A47	3c	100.00
		Never hinged	145.00
144c	A48	5c	100.00
		Never hinged	145.00
145c	A49	12c	100.00
		Never hinged	145.00

Thomas d'Arcy McGee — A50

Laurier and Macdonald A51

Robert Baldwin and Sir Louis Hypolyte Lafontaine A52

1927, June 29

146 A50 5c violet		4.00	2.75
Never hinged		7.25	
1st day cover			100.00
Plate block of 8 (UR)		52.50	
Never hinged		80.00	
Plate block of 10 (UL)		62.50	
Never hinged		95.00	
147 A51 12c green		10.00	5.25
Never hinged		18.00	
1st day cover			125.00
Plate block of 6		95.00	
Never hinged		140.00	
148 A52 20c brown carmine		25.00	6.50
Never hinged		45.00	
1st day cover			125.00
Plate block of 4		125.00	
Never hinged		225.00	
Plate block of 6		180.00	
Never hinged		325.00	
Nos. 146-148 (3)		39.00	14.50
#146-148, never hinged		70.25	

Nos. 146-148 were to have been issued in July, 1926, as a commemorative series, but were withheld and issued June 29, 1927.

Imperf., Pairs

146a	A50	5c	100.00
		Never hinged	145.00
147a	A51	12c	100.00
		Never hinged	145.00
148a	A52	20c	100.00
		Never hinged	145.00

Horizontal Pairs, Imperf. Vertically

146b	A50	5c	100.00
		Never hinged	145.00
147b	A51	12c	100.00
		Never hinged	145.00
148b	A52	20c	100.00
		Never hinged	145.00

Vertical Pairs, Imperf. Horizontally

146c	A50	5c	100.00
		Never hinged	145.00
147c	A51	12c	100.00
		Never hinged	145.00
148c	A52	20c	100.00
		Never hinged	145.00

King George V — A53

Mt. Hurd from Bell-Smith's Painting "The Ice-crowned Monarch of the Rockies" A54

Quebec Bridge — A55

Harvesting Wheat A56

Schooner "Bluenose" A57

Parliament Building A58

1928-29

149 A53 1c orange	3.50	.35
Never hinged	6.50	
1st day cover (10/29/28)		140.00
Plate block of 8	29.00	
Never hinged	55.00	
a. Booklet pane of 6	22.50	16.00
Never hinged	32.50	
150 A53 2c green	1.75	.20
Never hinged	3.25	
1st day cover (10/17/28)		140.00
Plate block of 8	16.00	
Never hinged	30.00	
a. Booklet pane of 6	22.50	18.00
Never hinged	32.50	
151 A53 3c dk carmine	30.00	11.00
Never hinged	55.00	
1st day cover (12/12/28)		210.00
Plate block of 8	250.00	
Never hinged	475.00	
152 A53 4c bister ('29)	25.00	5.00
Never hinged	45.00	
1st day cover (8/16/29)		210.00
Plate block of 8	225.00	
Never hinged	400.00	
153 A53 5c dp violet	15.00	2.50
Never hinged	27.50	
1st day cover (12/12/28)		210.00
Plate block of 8	140.00	
Never hinged	260.00	
a. Booklet pane of 6	120.00	100.00
Never hinged	170.00	
154 A53 8c blue	17.50	6.50
Never hinged	32.50	
1st day cover (12/21/28)		210.00
Plate block of 8	160.00	
Never hinged	275.00	
155 A54 10c green	20.00	2.00
Never hinged	35.00	
1st day cover (12/5/28)		300.00
Plate block of 6	140.00	
Never hinged	250.00	
156 A55 12c gray ('29)	40.00	6.50
Never hinged	72.50	
1st day cover (1/8/29)		300.00
Plate block of 6	250.00	
Never hinged	450.00	
157 A56 20c dk car ('29)	55.00	11.00
Never hinged	100.00	
1st day cover (1/8/29)		300.00
Plate block of 6	350.00	
Never hinged	675.00	
158 A57 50c dk blue ('29)	200.00	60.00
Never hinged	400.00	
1st day cover (1/8/29)		3,500.
Plate block of 4	1,600.	
Never hinged	2,600.	
Plate block of 6	2,000.	
Never hinged	3,500.	
"Man on the Mast" plate flaw	1,400.	875.00
159 A58 $1 olive grn ('29)	275.00	75.00
Never hinged	550.00	
1st day cover (1/8/29)		2,000.
Plate block of 6	2,600.	
Never hinged	5,200.	
Nos. 149-159 (11)	682.75	180.05
#149-159, never hinged	1,328.	

Imperf., Panes

149c	As No. 149a, imperf, 2 panes tete beche	900.
	Never hinged	1,350.
150c	As No. 150a, imperf, 2 panes tete beche	900.
	Never hinged	1,350.
153c	As No. 153a, imperf, 2 panes tete beche	900.
	Never hinged	1,350.

Imperf., Pairs

149b	A53	1c	80.00
		Never hinged	110.00
150b	A53	2c	80.00
		Never hinged	110.00
151a	A53	3c	100.00
		Never hinged	140.00
152a	A53	4c	100.00
		Never hinged	140.00
153b	A53	5c	80.00
		Never hinged	110.00
154a	A53	8c	100.00
		Never hinged	140.00
155a	A54	10c	160.00
		Never hinged	225.00
156a	A55	12c	160.00
		Never hinged	225.00
157a	A56	20c	160.00
		Never hinged	225.00
158a	A57	50c	650.00
		Never hinged	950.00
159a	A58	$1	600.00
		Never hinged	875.00

Horizontal Pairs, Imperf. Vertically

149d	A53	1c	100.00
		Never hinged	140.00
150d	A53	2c	100.00
		Never hinged	140.00
151b	A53	3c	100.00
		Never hinged	140.00
152b	A53	4c	100.00
		Never hinged	140.00
153d	A53	5c	100.00
		Never hinged	140.00
154b	A53	8c	100.00
		Never hinged	140.00
155b	A54	10c	160.00
		Never hinged	230.00
156b	A55	12c	160.00
		Never hinged	230.00
157b	A56	20c	160.00
		Never hinged	230.00
158b	A57	50c	650.00
		Never hinged	950.00
159b	A58	$1	600.00
		Never hinged	875.00

Vertical Pairs, Imperf. Horizontally

149e	A53	1c	100.00
		Never hinged	140.00
150e	A53	2c	100.00
		Never hinged	140.00
151c	A53	3c	100.00
		Never hinged	140.00
152c	A53	4c	100.00
		Never hinged	140.00
153e	A53	5c	100.00
		Never hinged	140.00
154c	A53	8c	100.00
		Never hinged	140.00
155c	A54	10c	160.00
		Never hinged	230.00
156c	A55	12c	160.00
		Never hinged	230.00
157c	A56	20c	160.00
		Never hinged	230.00
158c	A57	50c	650.00
		Never hinged	950.00
159c	A58	$1	600.00
		Never hinged	875.00

Coil Stamps

1929 ***Perf. 8 Vertically***

160 A53 1c orange	35.00	20.00
Never hinged	62.50	
On commercial cover		20.00
Pair	70.00	50.00
Never hinged	140.00	
On commercial cover		45.00
Paste-up pair	90.00	65.00
Never hinged	150.00	
On commercial cover		50.00
Precanceled		10.00
161 A53 2c green	30.00	3.00
Never hinged	55.00	
On commercial cover		8.00
Pair	60.00	10.00
Never hinged	120.00	
On commercial cover		20.00
Paste-up pair	80.00	32.50
Never hinged	160.00	
On commercial cover		32.50

King George V A59

Library of Parliament A60

The Citadel at Quebec A61

Harvesting Wheat A62

Museum at Grand Pré and Monument to Evangeline A63

Mt. Edith Cavell A64

Two dies of 1c.

Die I — Three thick and one thin colored lines between "P" at right and ornament above it.

Die II — Four thick colored lines. Curved line in ball of ornament at right is longer than in die I.

Two dies of 2c.

Die I — The top of the letter "P" encloses a tiny dot of color.

Die II — The top of the "P" encloses a larger spot of color than in die I. The "P" appears almost like a "D."

1930-31 ***Perf. 11***

162 A59 1c orange	1.20	.50
Never hinged	2.50	
1st day cover (7/17/30)		70.00
Plate block of 4	8.00	
Never hinged	16.00	
163 A59 1c deep green (II)	2.00	.20
Never hinged	4.25	
On commercial cover		1.25
Plate block of 4	9.00	
Never hinged	19.00	
a. Booklet pane of 4 + 2 labels (II)	100.00	95.00
Never hinged	150.00	
b. Die I (12/6/30)	2.00	.20
Never hinged	4.25	
1st day cover (12/6/30)		40.00
c. Booklet pane of 6 (I)	20.00	20.00
Never hinged	30.00	
164 A59 2c dull green (I)	1.20	.20
Never hinged	2.50	
1st day cover (6/6/30)		70.00
Plate block of 4	7.00	
Never hinged	12.00	
a. Booklet pane of 6	30.00	30.00
Never hinged	45.00	
165 A59 2c deep red (I)	1.50	.20
Never hinged	3.25	
On commercial cover		2.00
Plate block of 4	7.00	
Never hinged	15.00	
a. Die II	2.00	.20
Never hinged	4.50	
1st day cover (11/17/30)		70.00
Plate block of 4	11.00	
Never hinged	22.50	
"Extended mustache" variety (65LR8)	70.00	52.50
Never hinged	120.00	
On commercial cover		70.00
b. Booklet pane of 6 (I)	22.50	22.50
Never hinged	35.00	
166 A59 2c dk brn (II) ('31)	2.00	.20
Never hinged	4.50	
On commercial cover		1.25
Plate block of 4	9.00	
Never hinged	19.00	
"Extended mustache" variety (65LR8)	70.00	52.50
Never hinged	120.00	
On commercial cover		70.00
a. Booklet pane of 4 + 2 labels (II)	120.00	120.00
Never hinged	180.00	
b. Die I	4.00	3.75
Never hinged	7.25	
1st day cover (7/4/31)		50.00
Plate block of 4	20.00	
Never hinged	32.50	
c. Booklet pane of 6 (I)	50.00	25.00
Never hinged	75.00	
167 A59 3c deep red ('31)	3.25	.20
Never hinged	7.25	
1st day cover (7/13/31)		100.00
Plate block of 4	14.00	
Never hinged	32.50	

a. Booklet pane of 4 + 2 labels 35.00 35.00
Never hinged 52.50
168 A59 4c yel bister 12.50 6.50
Never hinged 25.00
1st day cover (11/5/30) 100.00
Plate block of 4 60.00
Never hinged 120.00
169 A59 5c dl vio, rotary press 8.00 4.25
Never hinged 16.00
On commercial cover 14.00
Plate block of 4 35.00
Never hinged 7.00
a. Flat plate printing 6.00
Never hinged 13.00
1st day cover (6/18/30) 100.00
170 A59 5c dull blue 5.00 .30
Never hinged 10.00
1st day cover (11/13/30) 65.00
On commercial cover 10.00
Plate block of 4 22.50
Never hinged 45.00
171 A59 8c dark blue 25.00 12.00
Never hinged 50.00
1st day cover (8/13/30) 140.00
Plate block of 4 125.00
Never hinged 225.00
172 A59 8c red orange 6.00 5.00
Never hinged 12.00
1st day cover (11/5/30) 100.00
Plate block of 4 50.00
Never hinged 75.00
173 A60 10c olive green 12.50 1.20
Never hinged 25.00
1st day cover (9/15/30) 140.00
Plate block of 4 70.00
Never hinged 120.00
174 A61 12c gray black 25.00 5.25
Never hinged 50.00
1st day cover (12/4/30) 175.00
On commercial cover 11.00
1st flight cover 6.00
Plate block of 4 125.00
Never hinged 225.00
175 A62 20c brown red 40.00 1.20
Never hinged 80.00
1st day cover (12/4/30) 175.00
Plate block of 4 180.00
Never hinged 350.00
176 A63 50c dull blue 180.00 12.50
Never hinged 375.00
1st day cover (12/4/30) 350.00
Plate block of 4 1,400.
Never hinged 2,100.
177 A64 $1 dk ol green 180.00 25.00
Never hinged 375.00
1st day cover (12/4/30) 500.00
Plate block of 4 1,400.
Never hinged 2,000.
Nos. 162-177 (16) 505.15 74.70
#162-177, never hinged 1,042.

No. 169 rotary printing is distinguished unused from No. 169a flat plate printing by the former having gum ridges about 5mm apart.
See No. 201. For surcharge see No. 191. For overprint see No. 203.

Imperf., Pairs

163d A59 1c (II) 1,300.
Never hinged 2,000.
173a A60 10c 1,300.
Never hinged 2,000.
174a A61 12c 600.
Never hinged 900.
175a A62 20c 600.
Never hinged 900.
176a A63 50c 800.
Never hinged 1,200.
177a A64 $1 800.
Never hinged 1,200.

Coil Stamps

1930-31 ***Perf. 8½ Vertically***

178 A59 1c orange 12.50 8.50
Never hinged 25.00
On commercial cover 10.00
Pair 25.00 20.00
Never hinged 50.00
On cover 22.50
Joint line pair 35.00 22.50
Never hinged 70.00
On cover 25.00
179 A59 1c deep green 8.00 5.00
Never hinged 16.00
On commercial cover 6.00
Pair 16.00 13.00
Never hinged 32.00
On cover 15.00
Joint line pair 22.50 17.50
Never hinged 40.00
On cover 20.00
180 A59 2c dull green 5.25 2.75
Never hinged 10.50
On commercial cover 3.50
"Cockeyed King" variety 50.00
Never hinged 75.00
On cover 40.00
Pair 10.50 6.00
Never hinged 21.00
On cover 7.00
Joint line pair 17.50 12.50
Never hinged 30.00
On cover 15.00
"Cockeyed King" variety, left stamp in line pair 70.00 40.00
Never hinged 110.00
On cover 62.50
181 A59 2c deep red 22.50 2.25
Never hinged 45.00
On commercial cover 3.00
"Cockeyed King" variety 55.00 50.00
Never hinged 90.00
On cover 50.00
Pair 45.00 5.50
Never hinged 90.00
On cover 7.00
Joint line pair 65.00 14.00
Never hinged 125.00
On cover 15.00
"Cockeyed King" variety, left stamp in line pair 85.00 70.00
Never hinged 140.00
On cover 80.00
182 A59 2c dark brown ('31) 10.00 .65
Never hinged 20.00
On commercial cover 5.00
"Cockeyed King" variety 50.00 40.00
Never hinged 80.00
On cover 45.00
Pair 21.00 2.00
Never hinged 45.00
On cover 10.00
Joint line pair 30.00 5.50
Never hinged 60.00
On cover 13.00
"Cockeyed King" variety, left stamp in line pair 77.50 62.50
Never hinged 115.00
On cover 72.50
183 A59 3c deep red ('31) 16.00 .65
Never hinged 32.50
On commercial cover 2.00
Pair 32.50 1.60
Never hinged 67.50
On cover 4.00
Joint line pair 45.00 7.00
Never hinged 90.00
On cover 8.00
Nos. 178-183 (6) 74.25 19.80
#178-183, never hinged 149.00

A vertical "jump" in spacing invariably occurs at the line in line pairs of Nos. 178-183. Therefore, a very fine line pair will not contain perfectly centered stamps, but it should show attractive balanced centering. This also applies to the "cockeyed king" variety in a line pair, as this variety occurs on the stamp to the left of the joint line.

George V Type of 1912-25

1931, June 24 ***Perf. 12x8***

184 A43 3c carmine 5.25 4.00
Never hinged 14.00
1st day cover 550.00
Plate block of 8 85.00
Never hinged 140.00

Sir Georges Etienne Cartier — A65

1931, Sept. 30 ***Perf. 11***

190 A65 10c dark green 12.00 .20
Never hinged 27.50
1st day cover 550.00
Plate block of 4 70.00
Never hinged 140.00
a. Imperf., pair 425.00
Never hinged 650.00

First Day Covers

Values for first day covers are for addressed non-cacheted covers through No. 190, addressed cacheted covers from No. 191 to No. 277, and unaddressed covers with the most common cachets from No. 282 and later.

Nos. 165, 165a Surcharged

1932, June 21

191 A59 3c on 2c dp red (II) 1.25 .20
Never hinged 2.00
1st day cover 14.00
Plate block of 4 7.00
Never hinged 9.00
"Extended mustache" variety (65LR8) 70.00 55.00
Never hinged 100.00
On commercial cover 60.00
a. Die I 2.50 1.60
Never hinged 4.00
1st day cover 100.00
Plate block of 4 10.00
Never hinged 15.00

King George V — A66

Edward, Prince of Wales — A67

Allegory of British Empire A68

1932, July 12

192 A66 3c deep red 1.20 .20
Never hinged 2.40
1st day cover 8.50
Plate block of 4 5.50
Never hinged 11.00
193 A67 5c dull blue 6.50 2.00
Never hinged 13.00
1st day cover 11.00
Plate block of 4 52.50
Never hinged 105.00
194 A68 13c deep green 9.00 5.00
Never hinged 18.00
1st day cover 21.00
Plate block of 4 85.00
Never hinged 170.00
Nos. 192-194 (3) 16.70 7.20
#192-194, never hinged 32.40

Imperial Economic Conference, Ottawa.

Type of 1930 and

King George V — A69

Two dies of 3c.
Die I — Upper left tip of "3" level with horizontal line to its left.
Die II — Raised "3"; upper left tip of "3" is above horizontal line.

1932, Dec. 1

195 A69 1c dk grn, rotary press 1.20 .20
Never hinged 2.25
1st day cover 14.00
Plate block of 4 6.25
Never hinged 10.00
a. Booklet pane of 4 + 2 labels ('33) 67.50 67.50
Never hinged 105.00
b. Booklet pane of 6 ('33) 40.00 40.00
Never hinged 60.00
d. Flat plate printing 4.25
Never hinged 6.00
Plate block of 4 17.50
Never hinged 27.50
196 A69 2c black brown 1.25 .20
Never hinged 2.40
1st day cover 14.00
Plate block of 4 7.00
Never hinged 12.00
a. Booklet pane of 4 + 2 labels ('33) 90.00 90.00
Never hinged 135.00
b. Booklet pane of 6 ('33) 50.00 50.00
Never hinged 75.00
197 A69 3c deep red (I) 1.20 .20
Never hinged 2.25
1st day cover 14.00
Plate block of 4 14.00
Never hinged 19.00
a. Booklet pane of 4 + 2 labels ('33) 40.00 40.00
Never hinged 60.00
c. Die II 1.20 .20
Never hinged 2.25
On commercial cover 2.10
Plate block of 4 10.50
Never hinged 15.00
d. As "a," die II ('33) 32.50 32.50
Never hinged 50.00
198 A69 4c ocher 45.00 6.00
Never hinged 90.00
1st day cover 21.00
Plate block of 4 250.00
Never hinged 400.00
199 A69 5c dark blue 12.00 .20
Never hinged 24.00
1st day cover 21.00
Plate block of 4 52.50
Never hinged 105.00
a. Horiz. pair, imperf. vert. 1,250.
Never hinged 1,750.
200 A69 8c red orange 40.00 3.25
Never hinged 80.00
1st day cover 25.00
On commercial cover, single franking 42.50
Plate block of 4 175.00
Never hinged 350.00
201 A61 13c dull violet 40.00 3.25
Never hinged 80.00
1st day cover 30.00
Plate block of 4 200.00
Never hinged 350.00
Nos. 195-201 (7) 140.65 13.30
#195-201, never hinged 280.90
Set of 7, #195-201 on one 1st day cover 35.00

Type A66 has at the foot of the stamp "OTTAWA-CONFERENCE 1932". This inscription does not appear on the stamps of type A69.
Unused examples of No. 195 will show gum ridges about 5mm apart. The gum on No. 195d is flat.

Imperf., Pairs

195c A69 1c 200.00
Never hinged 300.00
196c A69 2c 200.00
Never hinged 300.00
197b A69 3c (I) 200.00
Never hinged 300.00
197e A69 3c (II) 1,650.
198a A69 4c 200.00
Never hinged 300.00
199b A69 5c 200.00
Never hinged 300.00
200a A69 8c 200.00
Never hinged 300.00
201a A69 13c 650.00
Never hinged 975.00

No. 197e exists as one unused block of 4.

Government Buildings, Ottawa — A70

1933, May 18 ***Perf. 11***

202 A70 5c dark blue 9.00 3.00
Never hinged 17.50
1st day cover 25.00
Plate block of 4 65.00
Never hinged 100.00
a. Imperf., pair 500.00
Never hinged 750.00

Meeting of the Executive Committee of the UPU at Ottawa, May and June, 1933.

No. 175 Overprinted in Blue

1933, July 24

203 A62 20c brown red 40.00 12.50
Never hinged 70.00
1st day cover 52.50
Plate block of 4 210.00
Never hinged 340.00
Broken "X" in "Exhibition" variety (pos. 19) 105.00 55.00
Never hinged 165.00
1st day cover 70.00
a. Imperf., pair 500.00

Never hinged 750.00
Imperf., pair with one broken "X" 3,500.
Never hinged 4,750.

World's Grain Exhibition and Conference at Regina.
Three examples are known of No. 203a with one stamp having the broken "X" variety. Two of these pairs are never hinged.

Steamship Royal William — A71

1933, Aug. 17

204 A71 5c dark blue 9.00 3.00
Never hinged 17.50
1st day cover 24.00
Plate block of 4 50.00
Never hinged 90.00
a. Imperf., pair 500.00
Never hinged 750.00

Centenary of the linking by steam of the Dominion, then a colony, with Great Britain, the mother country. The Royal William's 1833 voyage was the first Trans-Atlantic passage under steam all the way.

George V Type of 1932
Coil Stamps

1933 ***Perf. 8½ Vertically***

205 A69 1c dark green 12.50 2.50
Never hinged 22.50
On commercial cover 5.50
Pair 26.00 5.00
Never hinged 52.50
On cover 8.00
Joint line pair 35.00 7.00
Never hinged 65.00
On cover 17.00
206 A69 2c black brown 15.00 1.00
Never hinged 27.50
On commercial cover 5.00
Pair 35.00 2.10
Never hinged 60.00
On cover 7.00
Joint line pair 45.00 7.00
Never hinged 75.00
On cover 17.00
207 A69 3c deep red 12.50 .35
Never hinged 22.50
On commercial cover 5.00
Pair 26.00 1.00
Never hinged 47.50
On cover 8.75
Joint line pair 35.00 2.75
Never hinged 55.00
On cover 21.00
Nos. 205-207 (3) 40.00 3.85
Nos. 205-207, never hinged 72.50

Cartier's Arrival at Quebec — A72

1934, July 1 ***Perf. 11***

208 A72 3c blue 4.00 1.25
Never hinged 8.00
1st day cover 17.50
Plate block of 4 24.00
Never hinged 45.00
Horiz. strip of 4 with wide vert. gutter btwn. center stamps 275.00
Never hinged 400.00
a. Imperf., pair 525.00
Never hinged 800.00

Landing of Jacques Cartier, 400th anniv.

Group from Loyalists Monument, Hamilton, Ontario
A73

1934, July 1

209 A73 10c olive green 25.00 6.50
Never hinged 47.50
1st day cover 17.50
Plate block of 4 160.00
Never hinged 275.00
a. Imperf., pair 1,250.
Never hinged 1,900.

Emigration of the United Empire Loyalists from the US to Canada, 150th anniv.

Seal of New Brunswick — A74

1934, Aug. 16

210 A74 2c red brown 3.00 2.00
Never hinged 5.50
1st day cover 10.00
Plate block of 4 13.00
Never hinged 25.00
a. Imperf., pair 550.00
Never hinged 875.00

150th anniv. of the founding of the Province of New Brunswick.

Princess Elizabeth
A75

Duke of York
A76

King George V and Queen Mary — A77

Prince of Wales — A78

Windsor Castle
A79

Royal Yacht Britannia
A80

1935, May 4 ***Perf. 12***

211 A75 1c green .65 .30
Never hinged .95
1st day cover 5.50
Plate block of 6 9.50
Never hinged 14.00
"Weeping Princess" plate flaw (21UR1) 105.00 70.00
Never hinged 150.00
On cover 150.00
212 A76 2c brown 1.00 .20
Never hinged 1.50
1st day cover 5.50
Plate block of 6 8.00
Never hinged 12.00
213 A77 3c carmine 2.00 .20
Never hinged 3.25
1st day cover 5.50
Plate block of 6 19.00
Never hinged 29.00
214 A78 5c blue 5.25 2.50
Never hinged 8.50
1st day cover 14.00
Plate block of 6 62.50
Never hinged 95.00
215 A79 10c green 8.00 2.25
Never hinged 12.50
1st day cover 17.50
Plate block of 6 62.50
Never hinged 95.00
216 A80 13c dark blue 9.00 5.00
Never hinged 14.00
1st day cover 25.00
Plate block of 6 85.00
Never hinged 125.00
Plate block of 10 (LL position) 140.00
Never hinged 200.00
"Shilling mark" plate flaw between "1" and "3" of left "13" (78UR1) 425.00 350.00
Never hinged 600.00
On cover 300.00
Nos. 211-216 (6) 25.90 10.45
#211-216, never hinged 40.70
Set of 6, #211-216 on one 1st day cover 42.50

25th anniv. of the accession to the throne of George V.

Imperf., Pairs

211a A75 1c 200.00
Never hinged 300.00
212a A76 2c 200.00
Never hinged 300.00
213a A77 3c 200.00
Never hinged 300.00
214a A78 5c 200.00
Never hinged 300.00
215a A79 10c 200.00
Never hinged 300.00
216b A80 13c 200.00
Never hinged 300.00

King George V — A81

Royal Canadian Mounted Police — A82

Confederation Conference at Charlottetown, 1864 — A83

Niagara Falls — A84

Parliament Buildings, Victoria, B.C. — A85

Champlain Monument, Quebec
A86

1935, June 1 ***Perf. 12***

217 A81 1c green .30 .20
Never hinged .40
1st day cover 5.00
Plate block of 6 5.50
Never hinged 7.50
Plate block of 8 (pl. 3) 7.00
Never hinged 9.50
a. Bklt. pane of 4 + 2 labels 60.00 60.00
Never hinged 90.00
b. Booklet pane of 6 45.00 45.00
Never hinged 67.50
218 A81 2c brown .45 .20
Never hinged .65
1st day cover 5.00
Plate block of 6 5.50
Never hinged 7.50
Plate block of 8 7.00
Never hinged 9.50
a. Bklt. pane of 4 + 2 labels 60.00 60.00
Never hinged 90.00
b. Booklet pane of 6 40.00 40.00
Never hinged 60.00
219 A81 3c dk carmine .60 .20
Never hinged .90
1st day cover 5.00
Plate block of 6 10.50
Never hinged 15.00
Plate block of 8 14.00
Never hinged 20.00
a. Bklt. pane of 4 + 2 labels 30.00 30.00
Never hinged 45.00
c. Printed on gummed side 400.00
220 A81 4c yellowish orange 2.50 .50
Never hinged 3.75
1st day cover 7.00
Plate block of 6 50.00
Never hinged 75.00
221 A81 5c blue 3.25 .20
Never hinged 5.00
1st day cover 7.00
Plate block of 6 50.00
Never hinged 75.00
a. Horiz. pair, imperf. vert. 200.00
Never hinged 300.00
222 A81 8c dp orange 3.00 2.00
Never hinged 4.50
1st day cover 10.50
On commercial cover 26.00
On commercial cover, single franking 55.00
Plate block of 6 50.00
Never hinged 75.00
223 A82 10c car rose 7.00 .20
Never hinged 10.50
1st day cover 10.50
Plate block of 6 70.00
Never hinged 105.00
"Broken leg" on mountie variety 1,400. 1,050.
Never hinged 1,350.
224 A83 13c violet 8.00 .65
Never hinged 12.00
1st day cover 21.00
Plate block of 6 62.50
Never hinged 95.00
225 A84 20c olive green 20.00 .65
Never hinged 30.00
1st day cover 24.00
On commercial cover 15.00
Plate block of 6 175.00
Never hinged 250.00
226 A85 50c dull violet 30.00 5.00
Never hinged 45.00
1st day cover 50.00
Plate block of 6 250.00
Never hinged 325.00
227 A86 $1 deep blue 65.00 10.00
Never hinged 100.00
1st day cover 140.00
Plate block of 6 600.00
Never hinged 900.00
Nos. 217-227 (11) 140.10 19.80
#217-227, never hinged 212.70
Set of 11, #217-227 on one 1st day cover 160.00

No. 219c is valued in the grade of fine. Very fine examples are rare and sell for much more.

Imperf., Pairs

217c A81 1c 130.00
Never hinged 190.00
218c A81 2c 130.00
Never hinged 190.00
219b A81 3c 130.00
Never hinged 190.00
220a A81 4c 130.00
Never hinged 190.00
221b A81 5c 130.00
Never hinged 190.00
222a A81 8c 130.00
Never hinged 190.00
223a A82 10c 200.00
Never hinged 300.00
224a A83 13c 200.00
Never hinged 300.00
225a A84 20c 200.00
Never hinged 300.00
226a A85 50c 200.00
Never hinged 300.00
227a A86 $1 260.00
Never hinged 390.00

Coil Stamps

1935 ***Perf. 8 Vertically***

228 A81 1c green 12.50 2.50
Never hinged 19.00
On commercial cover 5.00
Pair 25.00 5.50
Never hinged 37.50
On cover 8.50
229 A81 2c brown 15.00 .80
Never hinged 22.50
On commercial cover 5.00
Pair 30.00 2.00
Never hinged 45.00
On cover 14.00
230 A81 3c dark carmine 12.50 .50
Never hinged 19.00
On commercial cover 5.00
Pair 25.00 2.00
Never hinged 37.50
On cover 14.00
Nos. 228-230 (3) 40.00 3.80
Nos. 228-230, never hinged 60.50

George VI — A87

George VI and Queen Elizabeth
A88

1937 ***Perf. 12***

231 A87 1c green .25 .20
Never hinged .40
1st day cover (4/1/37) 4.25
Plate block of 4 2.50
Never hinged 3.75
a. Booklet pane of 4 + 2 labels 15.00 *20.00*
Never hinged 22.50
b. Booklet pane of 6 5.00 *9.00*
Never hinged 7.50
232 A87 2c brown .60 .20
Never hinged .90
1st day cover (4/1/37) 4.25
Plate block of 4 3.00
Never hinged 4.50
a. Booklet pane of 4 + 2 labels 15.00 *17.50*
Never hinged 22.50

b.	Booklet pane of 6	9.00	*5.00*
	Never hinged	13.50	
233	A87 3c carmine	.60	.20
	Never hinged	.90	
	1st day cover (4/1/37)		4.25
	Plate block of 4	4.00	
	Never hinged	6.00	
a.	Booklet pane of 4 + 2 labels	5.00	*7.50*
	Never hinged	7.50	
234	A87 4c yellow	2.50	.20
	Never hinged	3.75	
	1st day cover (5/10/37)		6.25
	Plate block of 4	21.00	
	Never hinged	30.00	
235	A87 5c blue	3.00	.20
	Never hinged	4.50	
	1st day cover (5/10/37)		6.25
	Plate block of 4	21.00	
	Never hinged	30.00	
236	A87 8c orange	2.50	.45
	Never hinged	3.75	
	1st day cover (5/10/37)		6.25
	On commercial cover		7.50
	On commercial cover, single franking		55.00
	Plate block of 4	21.00	
	Never hinged	30.00	
	Nos. 231-236 (6)	9.45	1.45
	Nos. 231-236, never hinged	14.20	

Imperf., Pairs

231c	A87 1c	250.00	
	Never hinged	375.00	
232c	A87 2c	250.00	
	Never hinged	375.00	
233b	A87 3c	250.00	
	Never hinged	375.00	
234a	A87 4c	250.00	
	Never hinged	375.00	
235a	A87 5c	250.00	
	Never hinged	375.00	
236a	A87 8c	250.00	
	Never hinged	375.00	

1937, May 10

237	A88 3c carmine	.25	.20
	Never hinged	.35	
	1st day cover		2.75
	Plate block of 4	2.75	
	Never hinged	4.00	
a.	Imperf., pair	525.00	
	Never hinged	800.00	

Coronation of King George VI and Queen Elizabeth.

George VI Types of 1937
Coil Stamps

1937 ***Perf. 8 Vertically***

238	A87 1c green	2.00	1.00
	Never hinged	3.00	
	On commercial cover		5.00
	Pair	4.00	2.00
	Never hinged	6.00	
	On cover		7.00
239	A87 2c brown	3.00	.35
	Never hinged	4.50	
	On commercial cover		5.50
	Pair	6.00	1.40
	Never hinged	9.00	
	On cover		11.00
240	A87 3c carmine	6.00	.20
	Never hinged	9.00	
	On commercial cover		3.50
	Pair	12.00	.65
	Never hinged	18.00	
	On cover		11.00
	Nos. 238-240 (3)	11.00	1.55
	Nos. 238-240, never hinged	16.50	

Memorial Chamber, Parliament Building, Ottawa — A89

Entrance to Halifax Harbor A90

Fort Garry Gate, Winnipeg A91

Vancouver Harbor A92

Chateau de Ramezay, Montreal A93

1938 ***Perf. 12***

241	A89 10c dk carmine	9.00	.20
	Never hinged	13.50	
	1st day cover (7/28/38)		70.00
	Plate block of 4	50.00	
	Never hinged	75.00	
a.	10c carmine rose	9.00	.20
	Never hinged	13.50	
	1st day cover (6/15/38)		21.00
	Plate block of 4	35.00	
	Never hinged	52.50	
242	A90 13c deep blue	12.00	.50
	Never hinged	18.00	
	1st day cover (11/15/38)		21.00
	Plate block of 4	70.00	
	Never hinged	105.00	
243	A91 20c red brown	16.00	.40
	Never hinged	24.00	
	1st day cover (6/15/38)		24.00
	Plate block of 4	100.00	
	Never hinged	150.00	
244	A92 50c green	40.00	5.00
	Never hinged	60.00	
	1st day cover (6/15/38)		50.00
	Plate block of 4	180.00	
	Never hinged	275.00	
245	A93 $1 dull violet	75.00	6.50
	Never hinged	120.00	
	1st day cover (6/15/38)		95.00
	Plate block of 4	425.00	
	Never hinged	640.00	
a.	Vert. pair, imperf., horiz.	*3,000.*	
	Nos. 241-245 (5)	152.00	12.60
	#241-245, never hinged	235.00	

Imperf., Pairs

241b	A89 10c dark carmine	260.00	
	Never hinged	400.00	
241c	A89 10c carmine rose	260.00	
	Never hinged	400.00	
242a	A90 13c	260.00	
	Never hinged	400.00	
243a	A91 20c	260.00	
	Never hinged	400.00	
244a	A92 50c	260.00	
	Never hinged	400.00	
245b	A93 $1	450.00	
	Never hinged	675.00	

Princess Elizabeth and Princess Margaret Rose — A94

War Memorial, Ottawa — A95

King George VI and Queen Elizabeth A96

Unwmk.

1939, May 15 **Engr.** ***Perf. 12***

246	A94 1c green & black	.25	.20
	Never hinged	.30	
	1st day cover		2.10
	Plate block of 4	2.10	
	Never hinged	2.90	
247	A95 2c brown & black	.25	.20
	Never hinged	.30	
	1st day cover		2.10
	Plate block of 4	2.10	
	Never hinged	2.90	
248	A96 3c dk car & black	.25	.20
	Never hinged	.30	
	1st day cover		2.10
	Plate block of 4	2.10	
	Never hinged	2.90	
	Nos. 246-248 (3)	.75	.60
	Nos. 246-248, never hinged	.90	
	Set of 3, #246-248 on 1 1st day cover		3.50

Visit of George VI and Queen Elizabeth to Canada and the US.

This is the first issue of Canada that required the use of two separate plates, and each plate block shows two plate numbers (one for the frame and one for the vignette). 165 different plate number combinations are known, with a few being extremely scarce to rare. The scarcer plate combinations are worth large premiums.

Imperf., Pairs

246a A94 1c 325.00
Never hinged 475.00
247a A95 2c 325.00
Never hinged 475.00
248a A96 3c 325.00
Never hinged 475.00

A97

A98

King George VI — A99

Grain Elevators
A100

Farm Scene
A101

Parliament
Buildings — A102

"Ram"
Tank — A103

Corvette
A104

Munitions
Factory
A105

Destroyer
A106

1942-43 Engr. *Perf. 12*

249 A97 1c green .30 .20
Never hinged .40
1st day cover (7/1/42) 2.75
Plate block of 4 2.50
Never hinged 3.75
Vert. pair with full horiz. gutter betwn. (unique) *5,500.*
a. Booklet pane of 4 + 2 labels 3.00 *3.25*
Never hinged 4.50
b. Booklet pane of 6 4.00 *4.50*
Never hinged 6.00
c. Booklet pane of 3 ('43) 2.00 *4.00*
Never hinged 3.00
250 A98 2c brown .40 .20
Never hinged .60
1st day cover (7/1/42) 3.00
Plate block of 4 3.00
Never hinged 4.50
a. Booklet pane of 4 + 2 labels ('43) 6.00 *7.00*
Never hinged 9.00
b. Booklet pane of 6 8.00 *9.00*
Never hinged 12.00
d. Vert. strip of 3, imperf. horiz. *5,000.*

251 A99 3c dk carmine .60 .20
Never hinged .90
1st day cover (7/1/42) 3.00
Plate block of 4 3.50
Never hinged 5.25
a. Booklet pane of 4 + 2 labels 3.50 *4.50*
Never hinged 4.75
252 A99 3c rose violet ('43) .40 .20
Never hinged .60
1st day cover (6/30/43) 14.00
Plate block of 4 3.50
Never hinged 5.25
Horiz. pair with full vert. gutter btwn. *2,100.*
a. Booklet pane of 4 + 2 labels 3.00 4.25
Never hinged 4.50
b. Booklet pane of 3 2.75 *4.00*
Never hinged 4.00
c. Booklet pane of 6 ('47) 3.00 *4.00*
Never hinged 4.50
253 A100 4c greenish black 1.25 .60
Never hinged 1.90
1st day cover (7/1/42) 7.00
Plate block of 4 10.50
Never hinged 16.00
254 A98 4c dk car ('43) .60 .20
Never hinged .90
1st day cover (4/10/43) 16.00
Plate block of 4 3.10
Never hinged 6.25
a. Booklet pane of 6 4.50 *9.00*
Never hinged 6.75
b. Booklet pane of 3 2.75 *4.00*
Never hinged 4.25
255 A97 5c deep blue 1.20 .20
Never hinged 1.80
1st day cover (7/1/42) 7.75
Plate block of 4 9.50
Never hinged 14.00
256 A101 8c red brown 1.60 .50
Never hinged 2.40
1st day cover (7/1/42) 10.50
Plate block of 4 13.00
Never hinged 19.00
257 A102 10c brown 4.50 .20
Never hinged 6.75
1st day cover (7/1/42) 10.50
Plate block of 4 35.00
Never hinged 52.50
258 A103 13c dull green 5.00 3.50
Never hinged 7.50
1st day cover (7/1/42) 10.50
Plate block of 4 42.50
Never hinged 62.50
259 A103 14c dull grn ('43) 6.50 .35
Never hinged 9.75
1st day cover (4/17/43) 21.00
Plate block of 4 47.50
Never hinged 70.00
260 A104 20c chocolate 9.00 .20
Never hinged 13.50
1st day cover (7/1/42) 14.00
Plate block of 4 52.50
Never hinged 80.00
261 A105 50c violet 35.00 1.25
Never hinged 52.50
1st day cover (7/1/42) 22.50
Plate block of 4 160.00
Never hinged 240.00
262 A106 $1 deep blue 65.00 6.00
Never hinged 100.00
1st day cover (7/1/42) 70.00
Plate block of 4 425.00
Never hinged 625.00
Nos. 249-262 (14) 131.35 13.80
#249-262, never hinged 199.50

Canada's contribution to the war effort of the Allied Nations.

No. 250d totally imperf horiz. is unique. Beware of strips with blind perfs; these sell for much less.

For overprints see Nos. O1-O4.

Imperf., Pairs

249d A97 1c 200.00
Never hinged 300.00
250c A98 2c 200.00
Never hinged 300.00
251b A99 3c 200.00
Never hinged 300.00
252d A99 3c 200.00
Never hinged 300.00
253a A100 4c 200.00
Never hinged 300.00
254c A98 4c 200.00
Never hinged 300.00
255a A97 5c 200.00
Never hinged 300.00
256a A100 8c 200.00
Never hinged 300.00
257a A102 10c 325.00
Never hinged 500.00
258a A103 13c 325.00
Never hinged 500.00
259a A103 14c 325.00
Never hinged 500.00
260a A104 20c 325.00
Never hinged 500.00
261a A105 50c 325.00
Never hinged 500.00
262a A106 $1 325.00
Never hinged 500.00

Types of 1942
Coil Stamps

1942-43 *Perf. 8 Vertically*

263 A97 1c green ('43) 1.25 .50
Never hinged 1.80
On commercial cover 3.50
Pair 2.50 1.40
Never hinged 3.50
On cover 4.50
264 A98 2c brown 1.90 1.00
Never hinged 2.75
On commercial cover 3.50
Pair 3.75 2.50
Never hinged 5.25
On cover 5.00
265 A99 3c dark carmine 1.90 1.00
Never hinged 2.75
On commercial cover 3.50
Pair 3.75 2.50
Never hinged 5.25
On cover 12.50
266 A99 3c rose violet ('43) 3.00 .35
Never hinged 4.50
On commercial cover 2.75
Pair 6.00 1.75
Never hinged 9.00
On cover 12.00
267 A98 4c dk carmine ('43) 4.75 .25
Never hinged 7.25
On commercial cover 3.50
Pair 9.50 3.50
Never hinged 14.50
On cover 20.00
Nos. 263-267 (5) 12.80 3.10
Nos. 263-267, never hinged 19.05

See Nos. 278-281.

Catalogue values for unused stamps in this section, from this point to the end of the section, are for Never Hinged items.

Farm Scene, Ontario
A107

Great Bear Lake, Mackenzie
A108

Hydroelectric Station, Saint Maurice River
A109

Combine
A110

Logging, British Columbia
A111

Train Ferry, Prince Edward Island
A112

1946, Sept. 16 Engr. *Perf. 12*

268 A107 8c red brown 1.75 .60
1st day cover 4.50
Plate block of 4 9.00
269 A108 10c olive 2.25 .20
1st day cover 4.50
Plate block of 4 11.00
270 A109 14c black brown 3.75 .20
1st day cover 10.50
Plate block of 4 18.00
271 A110 20c slate black 5.00 .20
1st day cover 14.00
Plate block of 4 21.00
272 A111 50c dk blue green 22.50 1.50
1st day cover 24.00
Plate block of 4 100.00
273 A112 $1 red violet 45.00 3.00
1st day cover 37.50
Plate block of 4 225.00
Nos. 268-273 (6) 80.25 5.70
Set of 6, #268-273 on one 1st day cover 50.00

For overprints see Nos. O6-O10, O21-O23, O25.

Alexander Graham Bell — A113

Citizen of Canada — A114

1947, Mar. 3

274 A113 4c deep blue .25 .20
1st day cover 2.10
Plate block of 4 1.40

Birth centenary of Alexander Graham Bell.

1947, July 1

275 A114 4c deep blue .25 .20
1st day cover 2.10
Plate block of 4 1.40

Issued on the 80th anniv. of the Canadian Confederation, to mark the advent of Canadian Citizenship.

Princess Elizabeth — A115

Parliament Buildings Ottawa
A116

1948, Feb. 16

276 A115 4c deep blue .25 .20
1st day cover 2.10
Plate block of 4 1.40

Marriage of Princess Elizabeth to Lieut. Philip Mountbatten, R. N., on Nov. 20, 1947.

1948, Oct. 1

277 A116 4c gray .25 .20
1st day cover 2.10
Plate block of 4 1.00

Centenary of Responsible Government.

George VI Types of 1942
Coil Stamps

1948 *Perf. 9½ Vertically*

278 A97 1c green 6.00 1.80
On commercial cover 5.00
Pair 12.00 6.00
On cover 10.50
279 A98 2c brown 15.00 7.50
On commercial cover 7.00
Pair 30.00 19.00
On cover 20.00
280 A99 3c rose violet 9.00 2.00
On commercial cover 7.00
Pair 18.00 7.75
On cover 15.00
281 A98 4c dark carmine 13.50 2.25
On commercial cover 7.00
Pair 27.00 6.25
On cover 15.00
Nos. 278-281 (4) 43.50 13.55

First Day Covers

Values for first day covers are for addressed non-cacheted covers through No. 190, addressed cacheted covers from No. 191 to No. 277, and unaddressed covers with the most common cachets from No. 282 and later.

John Cabot's Ship "Matthew"
A117

1949, Apr. 1 Engr. *Perf. 12*

282 A117 4c deep green .20 .20
1st day cover 2.10
Plate block of 4 1.00

Entry of Newfoundland into confederation with Canada.

"Founding of Halifax, 1749"
A118

1949, June 21 **Unwmk.**

283 A118 4c purple .20 .20
1st day cover 2.10
Plate block of 4 1.00

200th anniv. of the founding of Halifax, Nova Scotia.

A119

A120

A121

A122

A123

1949, Nov. 15

284 A119 1c green .20 .20
1st day cover 5.50
Plate block of 4 .80
a. Booklet pane of 3 ('50) .60 *1.25*
285 A120 2c sepia .25 .20
1st day cover 5.50
Plate block of 4 1.30
286 A121 3c rose violet .35 .20
1st day cover 5.50
Plate block of 4 1.40
a. Booklet pane of 3 ('50) 2.00 *5.00*
b. Booklet pane of 4 + 2 labels ('50) 2.75 *3.50*
287 A122 4c dk carmine .55 .20
1st day cover 5.50
Plate block of 4 2.25
a. Booklet pane of 3 ('50) 10.00 10.00
b. Booklet pane of 6 ('50) 15.00 15.00
288 A123 5c deep blue 1.10 .20
1st day cover 5.50
Plate block of 4 6.00
Nos. 284-288 (5) 2.45 1.00
Set of 5, #284-288 on one 1st day cover 7.50

Stamps from booklet panes of 3 are imperf. on 2 or 3 sides.

"POSTES POSTAGE" Omitted

1950, Jan. 19

289 A119 1c green .20 .20
1st day cover 24.00
Plate block of 4 1.00
290 A120 2c sepia .30 .20
1st day cover 24.00
Plate block of 4 2.60
291 A121 3c rose violet .30 .20
1st day cover 24.00
Plate block of 4 1.75
292 A122 4c dark carmine .30 .20
1st day cover 24.00
Plate block of 4 1.75
293 A123 5c deep blue 1.25 .90
1st day cover 24.00
Plate block of 4 6.50
Nos. 289-293 (5) 2.35 1.70
Set of 5, #289-293 on one 1st day cover 42.50

See Nos. 295-300, 305-306, 309-310. For overprints see Nos. O12-O20.

Oil Wells, Alberta
A124

1950, Mar. 1 **Engr.** ***Perf. 12***

294 A124 50c dull green 10.00 1.00
1st day cover 27.50
Plate block of 4 52.50

Development of oil wells in Canada. For overprints see Nos. O11, O24.

Coil Stamps
Types of 1949
"POSTES POSTAGE" Omitted

1950 ***Perf. 9½ Vertically***

295 A119 1c green .65 .25
On commercial cover 3.50
Pair 1.30 .50
On cover 6.25
296 A121 3c rose violet 1.00 .50
On commercial cover 4.25
Pair 2.00 1.00
On cover 7.00

With "POSTES POSTAGE"
Perf. 9½ Vertically

297 A119 1c green .40 .20
On commercial cover 3.50
Pair .80 .50
On cover 6.25
298 A120 2c sepia 3.00 1.25
On commercial cover 4.25
Pair 6.00 2.75
On cover 9.50
299 A121 3c rose violet 1.80 .20
On commercial cover 3.50
Pair 3.75 .50
On cover 2.25
300 A122 4c dark carmine 15.00 .65
On commercial cover 10.50
Pair 30.00 2.25
On cover 27.50
Nos. 297-300 (4) 20.20 2.30

See note after No. 288.

Indians Drying Skins on Stretchers
A125

1950, Oct. 2 ***Perf. 12***

301 A125 10c black brown .80 .20
1st day cover 5.00
Plate block of 4 5.25

Canada's fur resources. For overprint see No. O26.

Fishing
A126

1951, Feb. 1 **Unwmk.**

302 A126 $1 bright ultra 47.50 9.00
1st day cover 62.50
Plate block of 4 210.00

Canada's fish resources. For overprint see No. O27.

Sir Robert Laird Borden
A127

William L. Mackenzie King
A128

1951, June 25 ***Perf. 12***

303 A127 3c turquoise green .20 .20
1st day cover 2.10
Plate block of 4 1.50
304 A128 4c rose pink .25 .20
1st day cover 2.10
Plate block of 4 1.50

George VI Types of 1949

1951 ***Perf. 12***

305 A120 2c olive green .20 .20
On commercial cover .75
Plate block of 4 .90
306 A122 4c orange vermilion .25 .20
On commercial cover .75
Plate block of 4 1.30
a. Booklet pane of 3 4.50 2.50
b. Booklet pane of 6 4.25 4.25

For overprints see Nos. O28-O29.

Coil Stamps
Perf. 9½ Vertically

309 A120 2c olive green 1.25 .50
On commercial cover 4.00
Pair 2.50 1.50
On cover 7.50
310 A122 4c orange vermilion 2.50 .60
On commercial cover 5.00
Pair 5.50 1.60
On cover 17.50

Trains of 1851 and 1951 — A129

"Threepenny Beaver" of 1851 — A130

Designs: 5c, Steamships City of Toronto and Prince George. 7c, Stagecoach and Plane.

1951, Sept. 24 **Unwmk.** ***Perf. 12***

311 A129 4c dark gray .50 .20
1st day cover 3.50
Plate block of 4 2.50
312 A129 5c purple 1.60 1.10
1st day cover 3.50
Plate block of 4 8.75
313 A129 7c deep blue 1.00 .25
1st day cover 3.50
Plate block of 4 5.25
314 A130 15c bright red 1.10 .25
1st day cover 3.50
Plate block of 4 6.00
Nos. 311-314 (4) 4.20 1.80
Set of 4, #311-314 on one 1st day cover 7.00

Centenary of British North American postal administration.

Princess Elizabeth and Duke of Edinburgh
A131

1951, Oct. 26 **Engr.**

315 A131 4c violet .20 .20
1st day cover 2.10
Plate block of 4 1.10

Visit of Princess Elizabeth, Duchess of Edinburgh and the Duke of Edinburgh to Canada and the US.

Symbols of Newsprint Paper Production
A132

1952, Apr. 1 **Unwmk.** ***Perf. 12***

316 A132 20c gray 1.25 .20
1st day cover 6.00
Plate block of 4 8.75

Canada's paper production. For overprint see No. O30.

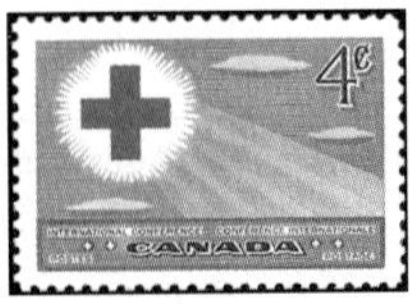

Red Cross on Sun — A133

1952, July 26 **Engr. and Litho.**

317 A133 4c blue & red .20 .20
1st day cover 2.10
Plate block of 4 1.25

18th Intl. Red Cross Conf., Toronto, July 1952.

Sir John J. C. Abbott
A134

Alexander Mackenzie
A135

1952, Nov. 3 **Engr.**

318 A134 3c rose lilac .20 .20
1st day cover 2.10
Plate block of 4 1.10
319 A135 4c orange vermilion .20 .20
1st day cover 2.10
Plate block of 4 1.10

Canada Goose
A136

1952, Nov. 3

320 A136 7c blue .35 .20
1st day cover 6.00
Plate block of 4 2.00

For overprint see No. O31.

Pacific Coast Indian House and Totem Pole — A137

1953, Feb. 2

321 A137 $1 gray 7.50 .75
1st day cover 30.00
Plate block of 4 35.00

For overprint see No. O32.

Natl. Wildlife Week — A138

1953, Apr. 1

322 A138 2c Polar bear .20 .20
1st day cover 2.10
Plate block of 4 1.10
323 A138 3c Moose .20 .20
1st day cover 2.10
Plate block of 4 1.20
324 A138 4c Bighorn sheep .25 .20
1st day cover 2.10
Plate block of 4 1.30
Nos. 322-324 (3) .65 .60
Set of 3, #322-324 on one 1st day cover 3.50

AIR POST STAMPS

Allegory of Flight — AP1

Unwmk.

1928, Sept. 21 **Engr.** ***Perf. 12***

C1 AP1 5c brown olive 12.50 3.50
Never hinged 22.50
1st day cover 87.50
Plate block of 6 105.00
Never hinged 160.00
"Swollen breast" variety (4UR2) 70.00 55.00
Never hinged 110.00
On commercial cover 70.00
Plate block of 6 (UR2) 175.00
Never hinged 275.00
a. Imperf., pair 225.00
Never hinged 310.00
b. Horiz. pair, imperf. vert. 175.00
Never hinged 250.00
c. Vert. pair, imperf. horiz. 175.00
Never hinged 250.00

For surcharge see No. C3.

For information on imperforate and part-perforate varieties, see note following No. 47a.

Allegory-Air Mail Circles Globe
AP2

1930, Dec. 4 *Perf. 11*

C2	AP2 5c olive brown	75.00	25.00
	Never hinged	125.00	
	1st day cover		140.00
	Plate block of 4	400.00	
	Never hinged	600.00	

For surcharge see No. C4.

No. C1 Surcharged

1932, Feb. 22 *Perf. 12*

C3	AP1 6c on 5c brown olive	10.00	3.25
	Never hinged	17.50	
	1st day cover		12.50
	Plate block of 6	105.00	
	Never hinged	160.00	
	"Swollen breast" variety (4UR2)	70.00	55.00
	Never hinged	110.00	
	On commercial cover		70.00
	Plate block of 6 (UR2)	175.00	
	Never hinged	275.00	
a.	Inverted surcharge	160.00	
	Never hinged	225.00	
b.	Double surcharge	550.00	
	Never hinged	775.00	
c.	Triple surcharge	325.00	
	Never hinged	450.00	
d.	Pair, one without surcharge	750.00	
	Never hinged	1,050.	

Counterfeit surcharges exist.
No. C3b is valued in the grade of fine.

No. C2 Surcharged in Dark Blue

1932, July 12 *Perf. 11*

C4	AP2 6c on 5c olive brown	30.00	10.00
	Never hinged	55.00	
	1st day cover		15.00
	Plate block of 4	210.00	
	Never hinged	325.00	

Daedalus
AP3

1935, June 1 **Engr.** *Perf. 12*

C5	AP3 6c red brown	3.00	1.00
	Never hinged	4.25	
	1st day cover		15.00
	Plate block of 6	21.00	
	Never hinged	32.50	
a.	Horiz. pair, imperf. vert.	*5,000.*	
b.	Imperf., pair	525.00	
	Never hinged	800.00	

No. C5a is believed to be unique and is the result of a pre-perforating paper foldover.

Mackenzie River Steamer and Seaplane
AP4

1938, June 15

C6	AP4 6c blue	3.00	.35
	Never hinged	4.25	
	1st day cover		14.00
	Plate block of 4	21.00	
	Never hinged	30.00	
a.	Imperf., pair	500.00	
	Never hinged	725.00	

Planes and Student Flyers
AP5

1942-43

C7	AP5 6c deep blue	4.75	.90
	Never hinged	7.00	
	1st day cover (7/1/42)		10.50
	Plate block of 4	24.00	
	Never hinged	35.00	
a.	Imperf., pair	500.00	
	Never hinged	725.00	
C8	AP5 7c deep blue ('43)	.90	.20
	Never hinged	1.30	
	1st day cover (4/16/43)		7.00
	Plate block of 4	5.50	
	Never hinged	8.50	
a.	Imperf., pair	500.00	
	Never hinged	725.00	

Canada's contribution to the war effort of the Allied Nations.

Catalogue values for unused stamps in this section, from this point to the end of the section, are for Never Hinged items.

Canada Geese in Flight — AP6

1946, Sept. 16

C9	AP6 7c deep blue	1.00	.20
	1st day cover		4.25
	Plate block of 4	4.50	
a.	Booklet pane of 4	3.00	3.00
	1st day cover		35.00

For overprints see Nos. CO1, CO2.

AIR POST SPECIAL DELIVERY STAMPS

Trans-Canada Airplane and Aerial View of a City — APSD1

1942-43 **Unwmk.** **Engr.** *Perf. 12*

CE1	APSD1 16c bright ultra	2.25	1.75
	Never hinged	3.25	
	1st day cover (7/1/42)		12.50
	Plate block of 4	12.50	
	Never hinged	19.00	
a.	Imperf., pair	500.00	
	Never hinged	725.00	
CE2	APSD1 17c brt ultra ('43)	2.75	2.50
	Never hinged	4.00	
	1st day cover (4/17/43)		32.50
	Plate block of 4	17.00	
	Never hinged	25.00	
a.	Imperf., pair	500.00	
	Never hinged	725.00	

Canada's contribution to the war effort of the Allied Nations.

Catalogue values for unused stamps in this section, from this point to the end of the section, are for Never Hinged items.

DC-4 Transatlantic Mail Plane Over Quebec — APSD2

1946, Sept. 16

CE3	APSD2 17c bright ultra	5.50	4.00
	1st day cover		12.50
	Plate block of 4	25.00	

Circumflex accent on second "E" of "EXPRES."

Corrected Die

1947, Dec. 3

CE4	APSD2 17c bright ultra	5.50	4.00
	1st day cover		120.00
	Plate block of 4	25.00	

Grave accent on the 2nd "E" of "EXPRES."

AIR POST OFFICIAL STAMPS

Catalogue values for unused stamps in this section are for Never Hinged items.

All cover values in this section are for uses on commercial covers.

No. C9 Overprinted in Black

1949 **Unwmk.** *Perf. 12*

CO1	AP6 7c deep blue	9.00	4.25
	On cover		21.00
	Plate block of 4	50.00	
a.	No period after "S"	80.00	50.00
	On cover		90.00
	Plate block of 4 (LL1, LL2)	120.00	

Same Overprinted

1950

CO2	AP6 7c deep blue	15.00	12.50
	On cover		27.50
	Plate block of 4	85.00	

SPECIAL DELIVERY STAMPS

All cover values in this section are for uses on commercial covers.

SD1

Unwmk.

1898, June 28 **Engr.** *Perf. 12*

E1	SD1 10c blue green	95.00	10.00
	Never hinged	250.00	
	On cover		140.00
	Plate block of 4 (pl. 2)	525.00	
	Never hinged	800.00	
	Plate block of 6 (pl. 1)	700.00	
	Never hinged	*1,600.*	
a.	10c green	95.00	10.00
	Never hinged	250.00	
	On cover		200.00
	Plate block of 4 (pl. 2)	525.00	
	Never hinged	800.00	
	Plate block of 6 (pl. 1)	700.00	
	Never hinged	*1,600.*	
b.	10c yellow green	140.00	17.50
	Never hinged	375.00	
	On cover		240.00
	Plate block of 4 (pl. 2)	725.00	
	Never hinged	1,250.	
	Plate block of 6 (pl. 1)	1,050.	
	Never hinged	*2,400.*	

Due to plate wear, the last examples of No. E1 printed show no shading in the value tablet areas. Such examples sell for only slightly more than normal stamps, either unused, used or on cover.

SD2

1922, Aug. 21

E2	SD2 20c carmine, dry printing (42½ wide)	80.00	8.00
	Never hinged	180.00	
	On cover		27.50
	Plate block of 4	1,050.	
	Never hinged	1,800.	
a.	20c scarlet, wet printing (41mm wide)	140.00	17.00
	Never hinged	250.00	
	On cover		30.00
	Plate block of 4	1,000.	
	Never hinged	1,500.	

Five Stages of Mail Transportation
SD3

1927, June 29

E3	SD3 20c orange	21.00	13.00
	Never hinged	42.50	
	On cover		45.00
	Plate block of 6	175.00	
	Never hinged	300.00	
a.	Imperf., pair	160.00	
	Never hinged	220.00	
b.	Horiz. pair, imperf. vert.	150.00	
	Never hinged	200.00	
c.	Vert. pair, imperf. horiz.	150.00	
	Never hinged	200.00	

No. E3 forms part of the Confederation Commemorative issue.

SD4

1930, Sept. 2 *Perf. 11*

E4	SD4 20c henna brown	57.50	14.00
	Never hinged	110.00	
	On cover		60.00
	Plate block of 4	275.00	
	Never hinged	500.00	

SD5

1933, Dec. 24

E5	SD5 20c henna brown	52.50	16.00
	Never hinged	95.00	
	On cover		52.50
	Plate block of 4	275.00	
	Never hinged	475.00	
a.	Imperf., pair	550.00	
	Never hinged	800.00	

Allegory of Progress — SD6

1935, June 1 *Perf. 12*

E6	SD6 20c dark carmine	9.00	6.50
	Never hinged	14.00	
	On cover		27.50
	Plate block of 4 (LL 1)	80.00	
	Never hinged	120.00	
	Plate block of 6	105.00	
	Never hinged	160.00	
a.	Imperf., pair	550.00	
	Never hinged	800.00	

Arms of Canada — SD7

1938-39

No.	Description	Unused	Used
E7	SD7 10c dk green (4/1/39)	5.25	3.25
	Never hinged	7.75	
	On cover		21.00
	Plate block of 4	42.50	
	Never hinged	60.00	
a.	Imperf., pair	550.00	
	Never hinged	800.00	
E8	SD7 20c dark carmine (6/15/38)	27.50	25.00
	Never hinged	42.50	
	On cover		50.00
	Plate block of 4 (LL 1)	190.00	
	Never hinged	250.00	
	Plate block of 6	250.00	
	Never hinged	*300.00*	
a.	Imperf., pair	550.00	
	Never hinged	800.00	

No. E8 Surcharged in Black

1939, Mar. 1

No.	Description	Unused	Used
E9	SD7 10c on 20c dk car	6.00	5.00
	Never hinged	8.25	
	On cover		24.00
	Plate block of 4 (LL 1)	32.50	
	Never hinged	45.00	
	Plate block of 6	47.50	
	Never hinged	65.00	

Coat of Arms and Flags SD8

1942, July 1 **Engr.**

No.	Description	Unused	Used
E10	SD8 10c green	2.50	1.80
	Never hinged	3.50	
	On cover		8.50
	Plate block of 4	18.00	
	Never hinged	24.00	
a.	Imperf., pair	550.00	
	Never hinged	800.00	

Canada's contribution to the war effort of the Allied Nations.

Catalogue values for unused stamps in this section, from this point to the end of the section, are for Never Hinged items.

Arms of Canada — SD9

1946, Sept. 16

No.	Description	Unused	Used
E11	SD9 10c green	2.75	1.10
	On cover		7.00
	Plate block of 4	12.50	

The laurel and olive branches symbolize Victory and Peace.

For overprints see Nos. EO1, EO2.

SPECIAL DELIVERY OFFICIAL STAMPS

Catalogue values for unused stamps in this section are for Never Hinged items.

All cover values in this section are for uses on commercial covers.

No. E11 Overprinted in Black

1950 **Unwmk.** ***Perf. 12***

No.	Description	Unused	Used
EO1	SD9 10c green	13.00	11.00
	On cover		60.00
	Plate block of 4	85.00	

Same Overprinted

No.	Description	Unused	Used
EO2	SD9 10c green	22.50	15.00
	On cover		70.00
	Plate block of 4	170.00	

REGISTRATION STAMPS

All cover values in this section are for uses on commercial covers.

R1

1875-88 **Unwmk.** **Engr.** ***Perf. 12***

No.	Description	Unused	Used
F1	R1 2c orange	90.00	4.50
	Never hinged	170.00	
	On cover		35.00
a.	2c vermilion	125.00	9.00
	Never hinged	210.00	
	On cover		35.00
b.	2c rose carmine	275.00	90.00
	Never hinged	500.00	
	On cover		120.00
c.	As "a," imperf., pair		—
d.	Perf. 12x11½	425.00	90.00
	Never hinged	775.00	
	On cover		150.00
F2	R1 5c dark green	125.00	5.00
	Never hinged	250.00	
	On cover		35.00
a.	5c blue green ('88)	130.00	5.00
	Never hinged	250.00	
	On cover		35.00
b.	5c yellow green	190.00	6.50
	Never hinged	375.00	
	On cover		35.00
c.	Imperf., pair	900.00	
	Never hinged	*1,300.*	
d.	Perf. 12x11½	1,300.	200.00
	Never hinged	*2,500.*	
	On cover		200.00
F3	R1 8c dull blue ('76)	375.00	275.00
	Never hinged	650.00	
	On cover		*7,250.*
a.	8c bright blue	450.00	350.00
	Never hinged	1,050.	
	On cover		*7,500.*
	Nos. F1-F3 (3)	590.00	284.50

Value for No. F3 on cover is for a correct usage in 1876-1877.

The used No. F1c is unique (fine centering).

POSTAGE DUE STAMPS

All cover values in this section are for uses on commercial covers.

On cover values are for stamps tied by postal cancellations such as datestamps or rollers. Covers with stamps uncanceled or tied by crayon marks sell for much less.

D1

D2

1906-28 **Unwmk.** **Engr.** ***Perf. 12***

No.	Description	Unused	Used
J1	D1 1c violet	14.00	4.25
	Never hinged	22.50	
	On cover		17.50
a.	Thin paper ('24)	32.50	7.00
	Never hinged	57.50	
b.	Imperf., pair	325.00	
c.	1c reddish violet ('28)	17.50	4.50
	Never hinged	32.50	
J2	D1 2c violet	14.00	.80
	Never hinged	22.50	
	On cover		10.50
a.	Thin paper ('24)	32.50	9.00
	Never hinged	57.50	
b.	Imperf., pair	325.00	
c.	2c reddish violet ('28)	17.50	.95
	Never hinged	30.00	
J3	D1 4c violet ('28)	60.00	20.00
	Never hinged	100.00	
	On cover		35.00
J4	D1 5c violet	14.00	1.50
	Never hinged	22.50	
	On cover		35.00
a.	As "c," thin paper	11.00	6.00
	Never hinged	20.00	
b.	Imperf., pair	325.00	
c.	5c reddish violet ('28)	17.50	1.75
	Never hinged	29.00	
J5	D1 10c violet ('28)	70.00	12.50
	Never hinged	130.00	
	On cover		*75.00*
	Nos. J1-J5 (5)	172.00	39.05
	#J1-J5, never hinged	247.50	

In 1924 there was a printing of Nos. J1, J2 and J4 on thin semi-transparent paper. Imperf pairs are without gum.

1930-32 ***Perf. 11***

No.	Description	Unused	Used
J6	D2 1c dark violet	11.00	3.75
	Never hinged	19.00	
	On cover, single franking		17.50
	Plate block of 4	210.00	
	Never hinged	325.00	
J7	D2 2c dark violet	6.00	.90
	Never hinged	11.00	
	On cover, single franking		14.00
	Plate block of 4	160.00	
	Never hinged	240.00	
J8	D2 4c dark violet	17.50	5.00
	Never hinged	32.50	
	On cover, single franking		17.50
	Plate block of 4	260.00	
	Never hinged	350.00	
J9	D2 5c dark violet	17.50	6.00
	Never hinged	32.50	
	On cover		*35.00*
	Plate block of 4	260.00	
	Never hinged	350.00	
J10	D2 10c dark violet ('32)	90.00	9.00
	Never hinged	170.00	
	On cover		*45.00*
	Plate block of 4	650.00	
	Never hinged	950.00	
a.	Vert. pair, imperf. horiz.	1,500.	—
	Never hinged	2,250.	
	Nos. J6-J10 (5)	142.00	24.65
	#J6-J10, never hinged	236.00	

No. J10a is valued in the grade of fine.

D3

D4

1933-34

No.	Description	Unused	Used
J11	D3 1c dark violet ('34)	12.00	6.00
	Never hinged	21.00	
	On cover, single franking		17.50
	Plate block of 4	62.50	
	Never hinged	95.00	
a.	Imperf., pair	325.00	
	Never hinged	475.00	
J12	D3 2c dark violet	6.00	1.10
	Never hinged	10.50	
	On cover, single franking		14.00
	Plate block of 4	52.50	
	Never hinged	80.00	
J13	D3 4c dark violet	12.00	6.50
	Never hinged	21.00	
	On cover, single franking		17.50
	Plate block of 4	62.50	
	Never hinged	95.00	
J14	D3 10c dark violet	25.00	5.00
	Never hinged	40.00	
	On cover		*45.00*
	Plate block of 4	140.00	
	Never hinged	200.00	
	Nos. J11-J14 (4)	55.00	18.60
	#J11-J14, never hinged	74.50	

Catalogue values for unused stamps in this section, from this point to the end of the section, are for Never Hinged items.

1935-65 ***Perf. 12***

No.	Description	Unused	Used
J15	D4 1c dark violet	.30	.20
	On cover, single franking		10.50
	Plate block of 4 (LL 1)	1.75	
	Plate block of 6	2.75	
	Plate block of 10	3.50	
a.	Imperf., pair	180.00	
b.	1c red violet ('40)	1.75	.50
	Plate block of 4 (LL 1)	8.50	
	Plate block of 6	14.00	
	Plate block of 10	19.00	
J16	D4 2c dark violet	.30	.20
	On cover, single franking		7.00
	Plate block of 4 (LL 1)	1.75	
	Plate block of 6	2.75	
	Plate block of 10	3.50	
a.	Imperf., pair	180.00	
c.	2c red violet	1.75	.50
	Plate block of 4 (LL 1, LL 2)	8.50	
	Plate block of 6	14.00	
	Plate block of 10	19.00	
J16B	D4 3c dark vio ('65)	2.00	1.25
	On cover, single franking		35.00
	Plate block of 4 (LL 1)	14.00	
	Plate block of 6	21.00	
	Plate block of 10	27.50	
J17	D4 4c dark violet	.35	.20
	On cover, single franking		10.50
	Plate block of 4 (LL 1)	2.10	
	Plate block of 6	3.50	
	Plate block of 10	4.25	
a.	Imperf., pair	180.00	
b.	4c red violet	1.40	.50
	Plate block of 4 (LL 1)	8.50	
	Plate block of 6	14.00	
	Plate block of 10	19.00	
J18	D4 5c dark vio ('48)	.40	.30
	On cover, single franking		17.50
	Plate block of 4 (LL 1)	2.75	
	Plate block of 6	4.50	
	Plate block of 10	5.50	
a.	5c red violet	2.75	1.00
	Plate block of 4 (LL 1)	14.00	
	Plate block of 6	21.00	
	Plate block of 10	27.50	
J19	D4 6c dark vio ('57)	2.25	1.25
	On cover, single franking		14.00
	Plate block of 4 (LL 1)	10.50	
	Plate block of 6	17.50	
	Plate block of 10	21.00	
J20	D4 10c dark violet	.40	.20
	On cover, single franking		10.50
	Plate block of 4 (LL 1)	2.50	
	Plate block of 6	3.75	
	Plate block of 10	5.00	
a.	Imperf., pair	180.00	
b.	10c red violet	1.40	.50
	Plate block of 4 (LL 1)	12.50	
	Plate block of 6	17.50	
	Plate block of 10	25.00	
	Nos. J15-J20 (7)	6.00	3.60

WAR TAX STAMPS

All cover values in this section are for uses on commercial covers.

WT1

WT2

Unwmk.

1915, Mar. 25 **Engr.** ***Perf. 12***

No.	Description	Unused	Used
MR1	WT1 1c green	21.00	.20
	Never hinged	47.50	
	On cover		1.40
MR2	WT1 2c carmine	21.00	.25
	Never hinged	47.50	
	On cover		3.50
a.	2c rose carmine	30.00	.40
	Never hinged	60.00	
	On cover		3.50

In 1915 postage stamps of 5, 20 and 50 cents were overprinted "WAR TAX" in two lines. These stamps were intended for fiscal use, the war tax on postal matter being 1 cent. A few of these stamps were used to pay postage.

1916

TWO DIES:

Die I — There is a colored line between two white lines below the large letter "T."

Die II — The right half of the colored line is replaced by two short diagonal lines and five small dots.

No.	Description	Unused	Used
MR3	WT2 2c + 1c car (I)	30.00	.20
	Never hinged	70.00	
	On cover		1.40

a.	2c + 1c carmine (II)	150.00	4.50
	Never hinged	350.00	
	On cover		7.50
b.	2c + 1c rose red (I)	42.50	.35
	Never hinged	85.00	
	On cover		1.25
MR4	WT2 2c + 1c brn (II)	17.50	.20
	Never hinged	40.00	
	On cover		1.00
a.	2c + 1c brown (I)	500.00	10.00
	Never hinged	900.00	
	On cover		15.00
b.	Imperf., pair (I)	160.00	
c.	Imperf., pair (II)	1,300.	

Nos. MR4b and MR4c were made without gum.

Perf. 12x8

MR5	WT2 2c + 1c car (I)	50.00	25.00
	Never hinged	120.00	
	On cover		30.00

Coil Stamps

Perf. 8 Vertically

MR6	WT2 2c + 1c car (I)	120.00	8.00
	Never hinged	260.00	
	On cover		10.00
	Pair	240.00	100.00
	Never hinged	400.00	
	On cover		*150.00*
	Paste-up pair	300.00	—
	Never hinged	500.00	
MR7	WT2 2c + 1c brn (II)	30.00	1.00
	Never hinged	65.00	
	On cover		6.25
	Pair	65.00	14.00
	Never hinged	120.00	
	On cover		15.00
	Paste-up pair	100.00	—
	Never hinged	175.00	
a.	2c + 1c brown (I)	150.00	7.50
	Never hinged	325.00	
	On cover		10.00
	Pair	300.00	75.00
	Never hinged	500.00	
	On cover		—
	Paste-up pair	325.00	—
	Never hinged	600.00	

OFFICIAL STAMPS

PERFORATED OFFICIAL STAMPS

Stamps perforated "O.H.M.S." (On His Majesty's Service) were introduced in May 1923 for use in the Receiver General's office of the Finance Department and by the Assistant Receiver Generals' offices in provincial cities. In 1935, the Post Office Department became responsible for perforating these stamps, and on March 28, 1939, the Treasury Board ruled that on and after June 30, 1939, all postage stamps used by government offices had to be perforated "O.H.M.S." These stamps continued to be produced until they were replaced by the overprinted "O.H.M.S." stamps in 1949.

The perforated initials can appear either upright, inverted, or sideways reading up or down on any given stamp, and further can be right-reading either from the front of the stamp or from the reverse. Thus, eight varieties are possible for each stamp, though not all stamps are known with all possible varieties. This catalogue values only the most common orientation.

The perfins come in two styles, as shown below. Stamps perforated with five holes in the vertical bars of the "H" are valued only used, because unused examples are rarely seen.

Values are for very fine examples with the stamp itself well centered and the perforations undamaged by encroaching perfin holes. Stamps in a grade below very fine and/or with damaged perforations will sell for less.

Beware of forgeries. On used stamps, be aware that ink from cancellations will tend to "bleed" into the perfin holes of genuine examples, whereas it will not on most forgeries, which almost always were made using already canceled stamps. As with all scarce issues that may be forged, dealing with reputable and knowledgable sources and using recognized expertizing authorities is recommened.

Stamps overprinted "O.H.M.S." or "G" follow No. OE11.

5-HOLE PERFINS

Large "O.H.M.S" 5 Holes in Vertical Bars of "H"

(OA plus Scott No.)

For die types of the 1c and 3c see postage.

1912-25 ***Perf. 12***

OA104	A43	1c green		47.50
OA105	A43	1c yellow (I) ('22)		42.50
d.		1c yellow (II)		42.50
OA106	A43	2c carmine		42.50
OA107	A43	2c yel green ('22)		32.50
a.		Thin paper ('24)		42.50
OA108	A43	3c brown ('18)		37.50
OA109	A43	3c car (I) ('23)		32.50
c.		Die II ('24)		37.50
OA110	A43	4c olive bister ('22)		42.50
OA111	A43	5c dark blue		47.50
OA112	A43	5c violet ('22)		42.50
a.		Thin paper ('24)		47.50
OA113	A43	7c yellow ocher		67.50
OA114	A43	7c red brn ('24)		57.50
OA115	A43	8c blue ('25)		67.50
OA116	A43	10c plum		67.50
OA117	A43	10c blue ('22)		47.50
OA118	A43	10c bis brn ('25)		32.50
OA119	A43	20c olive grn ('25)		47.50
OA120	A43	50c blk brn, dry printing ('25)		77.50
a.		50c black, wet printing		110.00
OA122	A43	$1 orange ('23)		115.00

Coil Stamp

1918 ***Perf. 8 Vertically***

OA129 A43 3c brown 360.00

50th Anniv. of the Canadian Confederation

1917 ***Perf. 12***

OA135 A44 3c brown 360.00

60th Year of the Canadian Confederation

1927

OA141	A45	1c orange	42.50
OA142	A46	2c green	57.50
OA143	A47	3c brown car	67.50
OA144	A48	5c violet	47.50
OA145	A49	12c dark blue	315.00

1927, June 29

OA146	A50	5c violet	42.50
OA147	A51	12c green	225.00
OA148	A52	20c brown car	140.00

Definitives

1928-29

OA149	A53	1c orange	52.50
OA150	A53	2c green	37.50
OA151	A53	3c dk car	77.50
OA152	A53	4c bister ('29)	105.00
OA153	A53	5c dp violet	37.50
OA154	A53	8c blue	100.00
OA155	A54	10c green	32.50
OA156	A55	12c gray ('29)	315.00
OA157	A56	20c dk car ('29)	95.00
OA158	A57	50c dk blue ('29)	420.00
OA159	A58	$1 olive grn ('29)	315.00

1930-31 ***Perf. 11***

For die types of the 1c and 2c see postage.

OA162	A59	1c orange	52.50
OA163	A59	1c deep green (II)	26.00
b.		Die I (12/6/30)	31.00
OA164	A59	2c dull green (I)	90.00
OA165	A59	2c deep red (I)	42.50
a.		Die II	37.50
OA166	A59	2c dk brn (II) ('31)	42.50
b.		Die I	47.50
OA167	A59	3c deep red ('31)	32.50
OA168	A59	4c yel bister	90.00
OA169	A59	5c dull violet	62.50
OA170	A59	5c dull blue	52.50
OA171	A59	8c dark blue	95.00
OA172	A59	8c red orange	80.00
OA173	A60	10c olive green	42.50
OA174	A61	12c gray black	175.00
OA175	A62	20c brown red	90.00
OA176	A63	50c dull blue	115.00
OA177	A64	$1 dk ol green	315.00

George V Type of 1912-25

1931 ***Perf. 12x8***

OA184 A43 3c carmine 95.00

Sir Georges Etienne Cartier

1931 ***Perf. 11***

OA190 A65 10c dark green 42.50

Nos. 165, 165a Surcharged

1932

OA191	A59	3c on 2c dp red (II)	52.50
a.		Die I	57.50

Imperial Economic Conference, Ottawa

1932

OA192	A66	3c deep red	37.50
OA193	A67	5c dull blue	57.50
OA194	A68	13c deep green	350.00

Type of 1930 and King George V

For die types of the 3c see postage.

1932

OA195	A69	1c dark green	32.50
OA196	A69	2c black brown	32.50
OA197	A69	3c deep red (I)	32.50
OA198	A69	4c ocher	95.00
OA199	A69	5c dark blue	47.50
OA200	A69	8c red orange	95.00
OA201	A61	13c dull violet	95.00

UPU Executive Meeting, Ottawa

1933

OA202 A70 5c dark blue 90.00

World's Grain Exhibition and Conference at Regina

1933

OA203 A62 20c brown red 100.00

Steamship Royal William

1933

OA204 A71 5c dark blue 90.00

Landing of Jacques Cartier, 400th Anniv.

1934

OA208 A72 3c blue 100.00

Emigration of the United Empire Loyalists from the US to Canada, 150th anniv.

1934

OA209 A73 10c olive green 105.00

150th anniv. of the Founding of the Province of New Brunswick

1934

OA210 A74 2c red brown 115.00

25th anniv. of the accession to the throne of George V

1935 ***Perf. 12***

OA211	A75	1c green	57.50
OA212	A76	2c brown	72.50
OA213	A77	3c carmine	95.00
OA214	A78	5c blue	90.00
OA215	A79	10c green	230.00
OA216	A80	13c dark blue	230.00

Definitives

1935

OA217	A81	1c green	37.50
OA218	A81	2c brown	62.50
OA219	A81	3c dk carmine	57.50
OA220	A81	4c yellow	100.00
OA221	A81	5c blue	57.50
OA222	A81	8c dp orange	100.00
OA223	A82	10c car rose	77.50
OA224	A83	13c violet	100.00
OA225	A84	20c olive green	105.00
OA226	A85	50c dull violet	72.50
OA227	A86	$1 deep blue	200.00

King George VI

1937

OA231	A87	1c green	4.75
OA232	A87	2c brown	5.75
OA233	A87	3c carmine	4.75
OA234	A87	4c yellow	13.50
OA235	A87	5c blue	11.50
OA236	A87	8c orange	23.00

Coronation of King George VI and Queen Elizabeth

1937

OA237 A88 3c carmine 90.00

George VI Types of 1937

Coil Stamp

1937 ***Perf. 8 Vertically***

OA240 A87 3c carmine 115.00

Pictorials

1938 ***Perf. 12***

OA241	A89	10c dk carmine	52.50
a.		10c carmine rose	42.50
OA242	A90	13c deep blue	52.50
OA243	A91	20c red brown	52.50
OA244	A92	50c green	115.00
OA245	A93	$1 dull violet	175.00

Visit of George VI and Queen Elizabeth to Canada and the U.S.

1939

OA246	A94	1c green & black	90.00
OA247	A95	2c brown & black	105.00
OA248	A96	3c dk car & black	90.00

Air Post Issues

1928

OAC1 AP1 5c brown olive 210.00

1930 ***Perf. 11***

OAC2 AP2 5c olive brown 315.00

No. C1 Surcharged

1932 ***Perf. 12***

OAC3 AP1 6c on 5c brn olive 210.00

No. C2 Surcharged in Dark Blue

1932 ***Perf. 11***

OAC4 AP2 6c on 5c olive brn 260.00

Daedalus

1935 ***Perf. 12***

OAC5 AP3 6c red brown 180.00

Mackenzie River Steamer and Seaplane

1938

OAC6 AP4 6c blue 52.50

Special Delivery Stamps

OAE1 SD1 10c blue green 210.00

1922

OAE2 SD2 20c carmine 210.00

1927

OAE3 SD3 20c orange 180.00

1930 ***Perf. 11***

OAE4 SD4 20c henna brown 180.00

1933

OAE5 SD5 20c henna brown 160.00

1935 ***Perf. 12***

OAE6 SD6 20c dark carmine 160.00

Arms of Canada

1938-39

OAE7	SD7	10c dk green ('39)	77.50
OAE8	SD7	20c dark carmine	115.00

No. E8 Surcharged in Black

1939

OAE9 SD7 10c on 20c dk car 115.00

4-HOLE PERFINS

Small "O.H.M.S" 4 Holes in Vertical Bars of "H"

(O plus Scott No.)

Definitives

1935 ***Perf. 12***

O223	A82	10c car rose	105.00	77.50
		Never hinged	140.00	
O224	A83	13c violet	130.00	77.50
		Never hinged	190.00	
O225	A84	20c olive green	160.00	95.00
		Never hinged	240.00	
O226	A85	50c dull violet	130.00	77.50
		Never hinged	190.00	
		Nos. O223-O226 (4)	525.00	327.50

George VI and Queen Elizabeth

1937

O231	A87	1c green	2.10	.20
		Never hinged	2.90	
O232	A87	2c brown	2.60	.20
		Never hinged	3.75	
O233	A87	3c carmine	2.60	.20
		Never hinged	3.75	
O234	A87	4c yellow	6.25	3.60
		Never hinged	9.00	

O235 A87 5c blue 4.25 .25
Never hinged 6.25
O236 A87 8c orange 21.00 8.50
Never hinged 30.00
Nos. O231-O236 (6) 38.80 12.95

Coronation of King George VI and Queen Elizabeth

1937
O237 A88 3c carmine 105.00 90.00
Never hinged 160.00

George VI Types of 1937
Coil Stamps

1937 ***Perf. 8 Vertically***
O239 A87 2c brown 105.00 77.50
Never hinged 160.00
O240 A87 3c carmine 105.00 77.50
Never hinged 160.00

Pictorials

1938 ***Perf. 12***
O241 A89 10c dk carmine 10.50 .45
Never hinged 16.00
a. 10c carmine rose 72.50 6.25
Never hinged 105.00
O242 A90 13c deep blue 16.00 2.60
Never hinged 25.00
O243 A91 20c red brown 47.50 3.10
Never hinged 70.00
O244 A92 50c green 77.50 16.00
Never hinged 120.00
O245 A93 $1 dull violet 165.00 62.50
Never hinged 250.00
Nos. O241-O245 (5) 316.50 84.65

Visit of George VI and Queen Elizabeth to Canada and the US.

1939
O246 A94 1c grn & blk 130.00 77.50
Never hinged 190.00
O247 A95 2c brn & blk 130.00 77.50
Never hinged 190.00
O248 A96 3c dk car & blk 130.00 77.50
Never hinged 190.00
Nos. O246-O248 (3) 390.00 232.50

Canada's Contribution to the War Effort of the Allied Nations

1942-43
O249 A97 1c green .50 .20
Never hinged .70
O250 A98 2c brown .75 .20
Never hinged 1.05
O251 A99 3c dk carmine 1.80 .60
Never hinged 2.60
O252 A99 3c rose violet ('43) 1.00 .20
Never hinged 1.50
O253 A100 4c greenish black 3.60 1.30
Never hinged 5.25
O254 A98 4c dk car ('43) .85 .20
Never hinged 1.20
O255 A97 5c deep blue 1.60 .20
Never hinged 2.25
O256 A101 8c red brown 10.50 3.50
Never hinged 15.00
O257 A102 10c brown 6.25 .30
Never hinged 9.00
O258 A103 13c dull green 7.25 6.25
Never hinged 11.00
O259 A103 14c dull grn ('43) 9.50 1.60
Never hinged 14.00
O260 A104 20c chocolate 13.00 1.30
Never hinged 19.00
O261 A105 50c violet 52.50 8.50
Never hinged 77.50
O262 A106 $1 deep blue 160.00 52.50
Never hinged 240.00
Nos. O249-O262 (14) 269.10 76.85

Peace Issue

1946
O268 A107 8c red brown 16.00 5.25
Never hinged 24.00
O269 A108 10c olive 4.25 .25
Never hinged 6.25
O270 A109 14c blk brn 5.25 1.00
Never hinged 8.00
O271 A110 20c slate black 6.25 1.00
Never hinged 9.50
O272 A111 50c dk bl grn 37.50 9.00
Never hinged 55.00
O273 A112 $1 red violet 90.00 32.50
Never hinged 140.00
Nos. O268-O273 (6) 159.25 49.00

"POSTES POSTAGE"

1949
O285 A120 2c sepia 1.00 1.00
Never hinged 1.50
O286 A121 3c rose violet 1.00 1.00
Never hinged 1.50

Air Post Issues

1928
OC1 AP1 5c brown olive 26.00 23.00
Never hinged 37.50

Daedalus

1935
OC5 AP3 6c red brown 95.00 85.00
Never hinged 140.00

Mackenzie River Steamer and Seaplane

1938
OC6 AP4 6c blue 4.25 1.60
Never hinged 6.25

Canada's Contribution to the War Effort of the Allied Nations

1942-43
OC7 AP5 6c deep blue 4.25 2.10
Never hinged 6.25
OC8 AP5 7c dp bl ('43) 4.25 .50
Never hinged 6.25

Canada Geese in Flight

1946
OC9 AP6 7c deep blue 3.10 .80
Never hinged 4.50

Air Post Special Delivery
Canada's Contribution to the War Effort of the Allied Nations

1942-43
OCE1 APSD1 16c brt ultra 32.50 26.00
Never hinged 50.00
OCE2 APSD1 17c brt ultra ('43) 21.00 21.00
Never hinged 31.00

DC-4 Transatlantic Mail Plane

1946-47
OCE3 APSD2 17c bright ultra 52.50 47.50
Never hinged 77.50

Circumflex accent on second "E" of "EXPRES."

Corrected Die

OCE4 APSD2 17c bright ultra ('47) 105.00 105.00
Never hinged 150.00

Grave accent on the 2nd "E" of "EXPRES."

Special Delivery Stamps

1933 ***Perf. 11***
OE5 SD5 20c henna brown 260.00 160.00
Never hinged 390.00

1935 ***Perf. 12***
OE6 SD6 20c dark carmine 130.00 77.50
Never hinged 195.00

Arms of Canada

1939
OE7 SD7 10c dk green ('39) 21.00 9.50
Never hinged 30.00

No. E8 Surcharged in Black

1939
OE9 SD7 10c on 20c dk car 160.00 95.00
Never hinged 240.00

Canada's Contribution to the War Effort of the Allied Nations

1942
OE10 SD8 10c green 21.00 12.50
Never hinged 30.00

Arms of Canada

1946
OE11 SD9 10c green 10.50 9.50
Never hinged 15.00

OVERPRINTED OFFICIAL STAMPS

Catalogue values for unused stamps in this section are for Never Hinged items.

All cover values in this section are for uses on commercial covers.

Nos. 249, 250, 252 and 254 Overprinted in Black

1949-50 **Unwmk.** ***Perf. 12***
O1 A97 1c green 2.00 1.75
On cover 7.00
Plate block of 4 13.00
a. No period after "S" 55.00 50.00
On cover 160.00
O2 A98 2c brown 9.00 7.25
On cover 21.00
Plate block of 4 160.00
a. No period after "S" 75.00 65.00
On cover 105.00
O3 A99 3c rose violet 2.00 1.10
On cover 7.00
Plate block of 4 13.00
O4 A98 4c dark carmine 2.50 .60
On cover 7.00
Plate block of 4 20.00

Nos. 269 to 273 Overprinted in Black

O6 A108 10c olive 3.50 .50
On cover 13.00
Plate block of 4 27.50
a. No period after "S" 60.00 55.00
Plate block of 4 (LL 1, LL 2) 200.00
O7 A109 14c black brown 4.00 2.00
On cover 13.00
Plate block of 4 42.50
a. No period after "S" 90.00 67.50
Plate block of 4 (LL 1) 125.00
O8 A110 20c slate black 12.50 2.75
On cover 12.00
Plate block of 4 100.00
a. No period after "S" 100.00 75.00
Plate block of 4 (LL 1, LL 2) 180.00
O9 A111 50c dk blue grn 200.00 100.00
On cover 175.00
Plate block of 4 1,400.
a. No period after "S" 550.00 450.00
Plate block of 4 (LL 1) 1,800.
O10 A112 $1 red violet 70.00 32.50
On cover 105.00
Plate block of 4 550.00
a. No period after "S" *2,000.*
Plate block of 4 (LL 1) *3,000.*
Nos. O1-O4,O6-O10 (9) 305.50 148.45

The "no period" varieties occur at 47LL1 & 47LL2 on some panes of #O6, O7, O8, on all panes of #O9, and on just a few panes of #O10.

Same Overprint on No. 294

1950
O11 A124 50c dull green 37.50 25.00
On cover 85.00
Plate block of 4 210.00

Nos. 284 to 288 Overprinted in Black

1950
O12 A119 1c green .40 .30
On cover 5.50
Plate block of 4 4.25
O13 A120 2c sepia 1.10 .75
On cover 5.50
Plate block of 4 5.25
O14 A121 3c rose violet 1.10 .50
On cover 5.50
Plate block of 4 6.75
O15 A122 4c dark carmine 1.10 .20
On cover 5.50
Plate block of 4 6.75
b. No period after "S" 60.00 50.00
O15A A123 5c deep blue 2.00 1.25
On cover 5.50
Plate block of 4 12.50
c. No period after "S" 60.00 50.00
On cover *90.00*
Nos. O12-O15A (5) 5.70 3.00

The "no period" varieties occur at 52LL1 on #O15 and at 52LL1, 78UL1 & 78UL2 on #O15A.

Stamps of 1946-50 Overprinted in Black

1950
O16 A119(a) 1c grn (#284) .50 .20
On cover 5.00
Plate block of 4 4.25
O17 A120(a) 2c sep (#285) 1.25 .80
On cover 5.00
Plate block of 4 8.50
O18 A121(a) 3c rose vio (#286) 1.25 .20
On cover 5.00
Plate block of 4 8.50
O19 A122(a) 4c dk car (#287) 1.25 .20
On cover 5.00
Plate block of 4 8.50
O20 A123(a) 5c dp bl (#288) 1.50 .85
On cover 5.00
Plate block of 4 16.00
O21 A108(b) 10c olive 2.25 .45
On cover 10.00
Plate block of 4 17.00
O22 A109(b) 14c black brn 6.50 2.00
On cover 10.50
Plate block of 4 40.00
O23 A110(b) 20c slate blk 14.00 1.00
On cover 10.50
Plate block of 4 105.00
O24 A124(b) 50c dull green 9.00 5.50
On cover 87.50
Plate block of 4 67.50
O25 A112(b) $1 red violet 100.00 65.00
On cover 105.00
Plate block of 4 525.00
Nos. O16-O25 (10) 137.50 76.20

Nos. 301-302 Overprinted Type "b"

1950-51
O26 A125 10c black brown 1.25 .20
On cover 8.50
Plate block of 4 9.50
a. Pair, one without "G" 725.00 500.00
O27 A126 $1 brt ultra ('51) 90.00 80.00
On cover 125.00
Plate block of 4 525.00

It is recommended that a certificate of authenticity be acquired for No. O26a.

Nos. 305-306 Overprinted Type "a"

1951-52 **Unwmk.** ***Perf. 12***
O28 A120 2c olive green .50 .20
On cover 4.25
Plate block of 4 3.00
O29 A122 4c orange ver ('52) .90 .20
On cover 4.25
Plate block of 4 5.25

No. 316 Overprinted Type "b"

1952
O30 A132 20c gray 2.00 .20
On cover 8.50
Plate block of 4 17.00

Nos. 320-321 Overprinted Type "b"

1952-53
O31 A136 7c blue 4.00 1.10
On cover 9.75
Plate block of 4 18.00
O32 A137 $1 gray ('53) 16.00 10.00
On cover 37.50
Plate block of 4 85.00

POST OFFICE SEALS

Values for Nos. OX1-OX4 used are for examples that are creased but not torn. Covers: All cover values in this section are for presentable covers with damage to the covers consistent with the application of the seal, which will be creasd but not torn.

POS1

1879 **Unwmk.** **Engr.** ***Perf. 12***
OX1 POS1 brown 225.00 140.00
Never hinged 600.00
On cover 1,050.

No. OX1 unused is very scarce with very fine centering, and rare very fine and never hinged; in fine condition values are 25-30% of those given for very fine.

POS2

1902-07

OX2 POS2 black, *bluish* 425.00 275.00
Never hinged 1,000.
On cover 1,200.
a. Imperf., pair 2,750.
OX3 POS2 black ('07) 105.00 52.50
Never hinged 240.00
On cover 550.00

No. OX2a is without gum.

POS3

1913

OX4 POS3 dark brown 55.00 35.00
Never hinged 120.00
On cover 550.00

CAPE JUBY

'kāp 'jü-bē

LOCATION — Northwest coast of Africa in Spanish Sahara
GOVT. — Spanish administration
AREA — 12,700 sq. mi.
POP. — 9,836
CAPITAL — Villa Bens (Cape Juby)

By agreement with France, Spain's Sahara possessions were extended to include Cape Juby and in 1916 Spanish troops occupied the territory. It is attached for administrative purposes to Spanish Sahara.

100 Centimos = 1 Peseta

STAMPS OF SPANISH MOROCCO USED IN CAPE JUBY

1915

Cancellations from "CABO JUBI" or "VILLA BENS"

A1 ¼c blue green (#39) 55.00
On cover 160.00
A2 2c dark brown (#40) 55.00
On cover 160.00
A3 5c green (#41) 55.00
On cover 160.00
A4 10c carmine (#42) 55.00
On cover 160.00
A5 15c violet (#43) 55.00
On cover 160.00
A6 20c olive green (#44) 55.00
On cover 160.00
A7 25c deep blue (#45) 55.00
On cover 160.00
A8 30c blue green (#46) 55.00
On cover 160.00
A9 40c rose (#47) 55.00
On cover 160.00
A10 50c slate blue (#48) 55.00
On cover 160.00
A11 1p lake (#49) 160.00
On cover 525.00
A12 4p deep violet (#50) 440.00
On cover 1,350.
A13 10p orange (#51) 440.00
On cover 1,350.
A14 20c red (#E2) 110.00
On cover 275.00

Values for stamps on cover are for philatelic covers, usually overfranked.

1917-19

A15 ¼c blue green (#52) 55.00
On cover 160.00
A16 2c dark brown (#53) 55.00
On cover 160.00
A17 5c green (#54) 55.00
On cover 160.00
A18 10c carmine (#55) 65.00
On cover 190.00
A19 25c deep blue (#58) 65.00
On cover 190.00
A20 30c blue green (#59) 65.00
On cover 225.00

Values for stamps on covers are for philatelic covers, usually overfranked.

Stamps of Rio de Oro, 1914 Surcharged in Violet, Red, Green or Blue

Two Types of Surcharge:
I: "CABO JUBI" in letters without serifs.
II: "CABO JUBI" in thin letters with serifs.

1916 **Unwmk.** ***Perf. 13***

Type I

1 A6 5c on 4p rose (V) 175.00 19.00
Never hinged 290.00
On cover 85.00
On registered cover 125.00
a. Inverted surcharge 250.00 30.00
d. Double surcharge 325.00 50.00
2 A6 10c on 10p dl vio (R) 40.00 19.00
Never hinged 57.50
On cover 85.00
On registered cover 125.00
a. Inverted surcharge 55.00 30.00
d. Double surcharge 75.00 50.00
2E A6 10c on 10p dl vio (V) 125.00 72.50
Never hinged 180.00
f. Double surcharge (R, V) 150.00 90.00
2G A6 10c on 10p dl vio (B) 125.00 72.50
Never hinged 180.00
3 A6 15c on 50c dk brn (G) 52.50 30.00
Never hinged 90.00
a. Inverted surcharge 57.50 30.00
4 A6 15c on 50c dk brn (R) 37.50 19.00
Never hinged 57.50
On cover 85.00
On registered cover 140.00
a. Inverted surcharge 55.00 30.00
5 A6 40c on 1p red vio (G) 77.50 35.00
Never hinged 130.00
a. Inverted surcharge 75.00 37.50
6 A6 40c on 1p red vio (R) 65.00 26.00
Never hinged 105.00
On cover 110.00
On registered cover 190.00
a. Inverted surcharge 75.00 42.50
Nos. 1-6 (8) 697.50 293.00
Set, never hinged 1,100.

Type II

1b A6 5c on 4p rose (V) 190.00 100.00
c. Inverted surcharge 425.00 200.00
2b A6 10c on 10p dl vio (R) 190.00 100.00
c. Inverted surcharge 425.00 190.00
3b A6 15c on 50c dk brn (G) 325.00 225.00
c. Inverted surcharge 425.00 200.00
4b A6 15c on 50c dk brn (R) 190.00 100.00
c. Inverted surcharge 425.00 200.00
5b A6 40c on 1p red vio (G) 425.00 —
c. Inverted surcharge 425.00 200.00
6b A6 40c on 1p red vio (R) 190.00 100.00
c. Inverted surcharge 425.00 200.00

Values for stamps in blocks of 4

Type I

1 A6 5c on 4p rose (V) 1,150. 140.00
2 A6 10c on 10p dl vio (R) 260.00 140.00
4 A6 15c on 50c dk brn (R) 260.00 140.00
6 A6 40c on 1p red viol (R) 425.00 200.00

Very fine examples of Nos. 1-6 will be somewhat off center. Well centered examples are uncommon and will sell for more.
Fakes of Nos. 1-6 are plentiful.

Stamps of Spain, 1876-1917, Overprinted in Red or Black

1919 ***Imperf.***

7 A21 ¼c bl grn (R) .30 .30
Never hinged .35
On cover 10.00

Perf. 13x12½, 14

8 A46 2c dk brn (Bk) .30 .30
Never hinged .35
On cover 10.00
a. Double overprint 19.00 16.00
b. Double overprint (Bk + R) 60.00 52.50
c. Imperf 30.00 22.50
9 A46 5c grn (R) .60 .60
Never hinged .90
On cover 12.50
a. Double overprint 19.00 16.00
b. Inverted overprint 30.00 *47.50*
c. Imperf (R) 30.00 22.50
d. Imperf (Bk) 60.00 60.00
10 A46 10c car (Bk) .70 .70
Never hinged 1.10
On cover 15.00
a. Double overprint (Bk + R) 60.00 52.50
b. Double overprint (Bk) 22.50 22.50
c. Imperf 30.00 22.50
11 A46 15c ocher (Bk) 3.00 3.00
Never hinged 4.25
On cover 25.00
b. Double overprint 19.00 16.00
c. Red control # 6.00 3.75
As "c," never hinged 8.75
d. As "c," inverted overprint 13.00
e. Imperf (Bk) 30.00 22.50
f. Imperf (R) 30.00 22.50
12 A46 20c ol grn (R) 16.00 16.00
Never hinged 25.00
On cover 130.00
a. Imperf 92.50 92.50
b. Imperf, control number omitted 190.00 190.00
13 A46 25c dp bl (R) 3.00 3.00
Never hinged 4.00
On cover 40.00
a. Double overprint 19.00 16.00
b. Imperf 30.00 22.50
14 A46 30c bl grn (R) 3.00 3.00
Never hinged 4.00
On cover 40.00
15 A46 40c rose (Bk) 3.25 3.25
Never hinged 4.25
On cover 40.00
a. Imperf 30.00 22.50
16 A46 50c sl bl (R) 3.50 3.50
Never hinged 5.00
On cover 55.00
17 A46 1p lake (Bk) 10.00 8.50
Never hinged 14.50
On cover 125.00
a. Imperf 35.00 35.00
18 A46 4p dp vio (R) 37.50 32.50
Never hinged 57.50
On cover 350.00
a. Imperf 40.00 40.00
19 A46 10p org (Bk) 52.50 42.50
Never hinged 75.00
On cover 725.00
a. Imperf 87.50 87.50
Nos. 7-19 (13) 133.65 117.15
Set, never hinged 225.00

Nos. 8-19 have blue control number on back.

Values for stamps in blocks of 4

7 A21 ¼c bl grn(R) 1.25 *1.50*
8 A46 2c dk brn (Bk) 1.25 *1.50*
9 A46 5c grn (R) 3.00 *4.00*
10 A46 10c car (Bk) 3.50 *4.50*
11 A46 15c ocher (Bk) 16.00 *24.50*
12 A46 20c ol grn (R) 90.00 *130.00*
13 A46 25c dp bl (R) 14.50 *19.00*
14 A46 30c bl grn (R) 14.50 *19.00*
15 A46 40c rose (Bk) 15.00 *19.50*
16 A46 50c sl bl (R) 19.00 *26.00*
17 A46 1p lake (Bk) 52.50 *64.00*
18 A46 4p dp vio (R) 190.00 *270.00*
19 A46 10p org (Bk) 275.00 *350.00*

Same on Stamps of Spain, 1920-21

1922 ***Imperf.***

20 A47 1c blue green (R) 25.00 14.00
Never hinged 42.50

Engr. ***Perf. 13x12½***

Blue Control Number on Back

23 A46 20c violet 140.00 40.00
Never hinged 200.00
On cover 225.00

A 2c and a 15c exist, values $400 and $10, respectively, for unused, hinged copies, $500 and $15 for never hinged.

Same on Stamps of Spain, 1922-23

1925 ***Perf. 13½x13***

25 A49 5c red vio 5.00 3.50
Never hinged 6.50
On cover 30.00
26 A49 10c bl grn 12.50 3.50
Never hinged 20.00
On cover 50.00
28 A49 20c violet 26.50 10.00
Never hinged 39.00
On cover 110.00
Nos. 25-28 (3) 44.00 17.00
Set, never hinged 65.00

Exists on Spain No. 331, 2c olive green. Value $300 unused hinged and $500 never hinged.

Seville-Barcelona Exposition Issue

CABO JUBY

Stamps of Spain, 1929, Overprinted in Red or Blue

1929 ***Perf. 11***

29 A52 5c rose lake (Bl) .45 .45
Never hinged .75
On cover 22.50
30 A53 10c green (R) .45 .45
Never hinged .75
On cover 22.50
31 A50 15c Prus bl (R) .45 .45
Never hinged .75
On cover 22.50
32 A51 20c pur (R) .45 .45
Never hinged .75
On cover 22.50
33 A50 25c brt rose (Bl) .45 .45
Never hinged .75
On cover 22.50
34 A52 30c blk brn (Bl) .45 .45
Never hinged .75
On cover 22.50
35 A53 40c dk bl (R) .45 .45
Never hinged .75
On cover 22.50
36 A51 50c dp org (Bl) .80 .80
Never hinged 1.75
On cover 32.50
37 A52 1p bl blk (R) 22.50 22.50
Never hinged 32.50
On cover —
38 A53 4p dp rose (Bl) 29.00 29.00
Never hinged 42.50
On cover —
39 A53 10p brn (Bl) 29.00 29.00
Never hinged 42.50
On cover —
Nos. 29-39 (11) 84.45 84.45
Set, never hinged 125.00

Stamps of Spanish Morocco, 1928-33, Overprinted in Black or Red

1934 ***Perf. 14***

40 A7 1c brt rose (Bk) .50 .50
Never hinged .65
On cover 18.00
41 A2 2c dk vio (R) 4.50 4.50
Never hinged 7.50
On cover 27.50
42 A2 5c dp bl (R) 5.00 5.00
Never hinged 7.50
On cover 27.50
43 A2 10c dk grn (Bk) 10.00 10.00
Never hinged 12.50
On cover 57.50
43A A10 10c dk grn (R) 3.00 3.00
Never hinged 4.00
On cover 27.50
44 A2 15c org brn (Bk) 25.00 25.00
Never hinged 47.50
On cover 150.00
45 A7 20c sl grn (R) 8.75 8.75
Never hinged 13.50
On cover 55.00
46 A3 25c cop red (Bk) 4.75 4.75
Never hinged 6.25
On cover 27.50
47 A10 30c red brn (Bk) 8.75 8.75
Never hinged 14.00
On cover 62.50
48 A13 40c dp bl (R) 32.50 32.50
Never hinged 50.00
On cover 175.00
49 A13 50c red org (Bk) 60.00 60.00
Never hinged 85.00
On cover 375.00
50 A4 1p yel grn (Bk) 45.00 45.00
Never hinged 70.00
On cover 250.00
51 A5 2.50p red vio (Bk) 90.00 90.00
Never hinged 140.00
On cover 600.00
52 A6 4p ultra (R) 115.00 115.00
Never hinged 210.00
On cover 725.00

No. 43A and 1c, 20c, 30c, 40c, 50c, with control numbers.

Same Overprint in Black on Stamp of Spanish Morocco, 1932

53 A2 1c car rose ("Ct") 2.10 2.10
Never hinged 3.25
On cover 27.50
Nos. 40-53 (15) 414.85 414.85
Set, never hinged 675.00

Stamps of Spanish Morocco, 1933-35, Overprinted in Black, Blue or Red

1935-36

54 A8 2c grn (R) .70 .70
55 A9 5c mag (Bk) 2.25 2.25
55A A10 10c dk grn (R) ('36) 11.00 11.00
56 A11 15c yel (Bl) 4.50 4.50
57 A12 25c crim (Bk) 50.00 50.00
58 A8 1p sl blk (R) 6.75 6.75
59 A9 2.50p brn (Bl) 30.00 30.00
60 A11 4p yel grn (R) 45.00 45.00
61 A12 5p blk (R) 37.50 37.50
Nos. 54-61 (9) 187.70 187.70
Set, never hinged 325.00

Same Overprint in Black or Red on Stamps of Spanish Morocco, 1935

1935 ***Perf. 13½***

62 A14 25c vio (R) 4.00 4.00
63 A15 30c crim (Bk) 4.00 4.00
64 A14 40c org (Bk) 5.25 5.25
65 A15 50c brt bl (R) 9.50 9.50
66 A14 60c dk bl grn (R) 11.50 11.50
67 A15 2p brn lake (Bk) 62.50 62.50

Same Overprint on Stamps of Spanish Morocco, 1933

Perf. 13½, 14

68 A7 1c brt rose (Bk) .30 .30

Perf. 14

69 A7 20c slate grn (R) 4.50 4.50
Nos. 62-69 (8) 101.55 101.55
Set, never hinged 160.00 160.00

Same Overprint on Stamps of Spanish Morocco, 1937

1937			*Perf. 13½*	
70	A21	1c dk bl (Bk)	.45	.45
71	A21	2c org brn (Bk)	.45	.45
72	A21	5c cer (Bk)	.45	.45
73	A21	10c emer (Bk)	.45	.45
74	A21	15c brt bl (Bk)	.45	.45
75	A21	20c red brn (Bk)	.45	.45
76	A21	25c mag (Bk)	.45	.45
77	A21	30c red org (Bk)	.45	.45
78	A21	40c org (Bk)	1.10	1.10
79	A21	50c ultra (R)	1.10	1.10
80	A21	60c yel grn (Bk)	1.10	1.10
81	A21	1p bl vio (Bk)	1.10	1.10
82	A21	2p Prus bl (Bk)	70.00	70.00
83	A21	2.50p gray blk (R)	70.00	70.00
84	A21	4p dk brn (Bk)	70.00	70.00
85	A22	10p vio blk (R)	70.00	70.00
		Nos. 70-85 (16)	288.00	288.00
		Set, never hinged	450.00	

1st Year of the Revolution.

Same Overprint in Black on Types of Spanish Morocco, 1939

Designs: 5c, Spanish quarter. 10c, Moroccan quarter. 15c, Street scene, Larache. 20c, Tetuan.

1939		Photo.	*Perf. 13½*	
86	A25	5c vermilion	.50	.50
87	A25	10c deep green	.50	.50
88	A25	15c brown lake	.50	.50
89	A25	20c bright blue	.50	.50
		Nos. 86-89 (4)	2.00	2.00
		Set, never hinged	2.75	

Same Overprint in Black or Red on Stamps of Spanish Morocco, 1940

1940			*Perf. 11½x11*	
90	A26	1c dk brn (Bk)	.25	.25
91	A27	2c ol grn (R)	.25	.25
92	A28	5c dk bl (R)	.25	.25
93	A29	10c dk red lil (Bk)	.25	.25
94	A30	15c dk grn (R)	.25	.25
95	A31	20c pur (R)	.25	.25
96	A32	25c blk brn (R)	.25	.25
97	A33	30c brt grn (Bk)	.30	.30
98	A34	40c slate grn (R)	.60	.60
99	A35	45c org ver (Bk)	.60	.60
100	A36	50c brn org (Bk)	.65	.65
101	A37	70c saph (R)	1.90	1.90
102	A38	1p ind & brn (Bk)	4.00	4.00
103	A39	2.50p choc & dk grn (Bk)	10.00	10.00
104	A40	5p dk cer & sep (Bk)	10.50	10.50
105	A41	10p dk ol grn & brn org (Bk)	26.00	26.00
		Nos. 90-105 (16)	56.30	56.30
		Set, never hinged	85.00	

Imperfs exist. Value, set $250.

SEMI-POSTAL STAMPS

Types of Semi-Postal Stamps of Spain, 1926, Overprinted

1926		Unwmk.	*Perf. 12½, 13*	
B1	SP1	1c orange	12.50	12.50
		Never hinged	19.00	
B2	SP2	2c rose	12.50	12.50
		Never hinged	19.00	
B3	SP3	5c blk brn	3.50	3.50
		Never hinged	4.50	
B4	SP4	10c dk grn	1.60	1.60
		Never hinged	2.25	
B5	SP1	15c dk vio	1.10	1.10
		Never hinged	1.40	
B6	SP4	20c vio brn	1.10	1.10
		Never hinged	1.40	
B7	SP5	25c dp car	1.10	1.10
		Never hinged	1.40	
B8	SP1	30c ol grn	1.10	1.10
		Never hinged	1.40	
B9	SP3	40c ultra	.45	.45
		Never hinged	1.40	
B10	SP2	50c red brn	.45	.45
		Never hinged	1.40	
B11	SP4	1p vermilion	.45	.45
		Never hinged	1.40	
B12	SP3	4p bister	1.60	1.60
		Never hinged	3.75	
B13	SP5	10p lt vio	3.50	3.50
		Never hinged	7.25	
		Nos. B1-B13 (13)	40.95	40.95
		Set, never hinged	65.00	

Nos. B12-B13 surcharged "Alfonso XIII" and new value are listed as Spain Nos. B68-B69. See Spain No. B6a.

AIR POST STAMPS

Spanish Morocco, Nos. C1 to C10 Overprinted "CABO JUBY" as on #54-61

1938, June 1		Unwmk.	*Perf. 13½*	
C1	AP1	5c brown	.25	.25
C2	AP1	10c brt grn	.25	.25
C3	AP1	25c crimson	.25	.25
C4	AP1	40c light blue	2.10	2.10
C5	AP2	50c brt mag	.25	.25
C6	AP2	75c dk bl	.25	.25
C7	AP1	1p sepia	.25	.25
C8	AP1	1.50p dp vio	1.90	1.90
C9	AP1	2p dp red brn	2.75	2.75
C10	AP1	3p brn blk	7.25	7.25
		Nos. C1-C10 (10)	15.50	15.50
		Set, never hinged	25.00	

SPECIAL DELIVERY STAMPS

Special Delivery Stamp of Spain Ovptd. "CABO JUBY" as on #7-28

1919		Unwmk.	*Perf. 14*	
E1	SD1	20c red (Bk)	3.25	3.25
b.		Double overprint	27.50	13.00

Spanish Morocco #E4 Overprinted "CABO JUBY" as on #40-52 in Red

1934				
E2	SD2	20c black	10.00	10.00

Spanish Morocco No. E5 Overprinted "CABO JUBY" as on Nos. 54-61

1935				
E3	SD3	20c vermilion	3.50	3.50

Same Ovpt. on Spanish Morocco #E6

1937			*Perf. 13½*	
E4	SD4	20c bright carmine	1.10	1.10

1st Year of the Revolution.

Same Ovpt. on Spanish Morocco #E8

1940			*Perf. 11½x11*	
E5	SD5	25c scarlet	.55	.55

SEMI-POSTAL SPECIAL DELIVERY STAMP

Type of Semi-Postal Special Delivery Stamp of Spain, 1926, Overprinted "CABO-JUBY" as on Nos. B1-B13

1926		Unwmk.	*Perf. 12½, 13*	
EB1	SPSD1	20c ultra & black	3.50	3.50

CAPE OF GOOD HOPE

'kāp əv 'gud 'hōp

LOCATION — In the extreme southern part of South Africa
GOVT. — British Colony
AREA — 276,995 sq mi. (1911)
POP. — 2,564,965 (1911)
CAPITAL — Cape Town

Cape of Good Hope joined with Natal, the Transvaal and the Orange River Colony in 1910, forming the Union of South Africa.

12 Pence = 1 Shilling

Watermarks

Wmk. 15 — Anchor

Wmk. 16 — Anchor

"Hope" Seated A1

Printed by Perkins, Bacon & Co.
Wmk. 15

1853, Sept. 1		Engr.	*Imperf.*	
1	A1	1p brick red, bluish paper	3,425.	225.00
a.		1p pale brick red, deeply blued paper	*4,500.*	350.00
b.		1p deep brick red, deeply blued paper	*5,750.*	375.00
f.		1p deep brick red, bluish paper	3,750.	260.00
2	A1	4p deep blue, lightly blued paper	1,500.	125.00
a.		4p deep blue, deeply blued paper	2,750.	180.00
b.		4p blue, bluish paper	1,600.	175.00

Watermark Sideways

1c	A1	1p As #1	—	375.00
1d	A1	1p As #1a	—	450.00
1e	A1	1p As #1b	—	450.00
1g	A1	1p As #1f	—	375.00
2c	A1	4p As #2	—	310.00
2d	A1	4p As #2a	*3,500.*	300.00
2e	A1	4p As #2b	—	310.00

Values for pairs

1	A1	1p	—	625.00
1a	A1	1p	—	975.00
1b	A1	1p	—	1,000.
1f	A1	1p	—	700.00
2	A1	4p	*4,100.*	350.00
2a	A1	4p	*7,500.*	500.00
2b	A1	4p	*4,400.*	475.00

Values for Blocks of 4

1	A1	1p	—	1,400.
1a	A1	1p	—	2,200.
1b	A1	1p	—	2,250.
1f	A1	1p	—	1,575.
2	A1	4p	*9,000.*	750.00
2a	A1	4p	*16,500.*	1,100.
2b	A1	4p	*9,600.*	1,000.

Counterfeits exist.

1855-58

White Paper

3	A1	1p rose ('57)	515.00	225.00
a.		1p dull red	750.00	290.00
b.		1p brick red	*5,750.*	1,000.
		As "b," Rouletted, unofficial		*3,500.*
4	A1	4p blue	550.00	57.50
		Rouletted, unofficial		*2,750.*
a.		Half used as 2p on cover		*40,000.*
b.		4p deep blue	750.00	57.50
e.		4p bright blue	700.00	57.50
5	A1	6p pale lilac ('58)	925.00	225.00
a.		6p rose lilac	*1,900.*	350.00
		As "a," Rouletted, unofficial		
b.		6p grayish lilac on bluish paper	*4,900.*	500.00
c.		6p slate purple on bluish paper	*4,000.*	1,150.
d.		Half used as 3p on cover		—
6	A1	1sh yellow grn ('58)	*3,150.*	210.00
		Rouletted, unofficial		*3,750.*
a.		1sh dark green	315.00	*575.00*
		As "a," Rouletted, unofficial		*4,000.*
b.		Half used as 6p on cover		—

Unofficially rouletted copies of 3b, 4, 5a, 6 and 6a require certificates of authenticity.

Watermark Sideways

3c	A1	1p As #3	—	500.00
3d	A1	1p As #3a	—	500.00
4c	A1	4p As#4	—	200.00
4d	A1	4p As #4b	—	200.00
5e	A1	6p As #5	—	1,050.
6c	A1	1sh As #6	—	1,050.

Values for Pairs

3	A1	1p	1,400.	625.00
3a	A1	1p	2,000.	800.00
3b	A1	1p	*16,000.*	2,800.
4	A1	4p	1,450.	160.00
4b	A1	4p	2,000.	160.00
4e	A1	4p	2,000.	160.00
5	A1	6p	3,000.	925.00
5a	A1	6p	*5,400.*	1,350.
5b	A1	6p	*13,250.*	2,000.
5c	A1	6p	*11,000.*	4,600.
6	A1	1sh	*8,750.*	*825.00*
6a	A1	1sh	825.	*2,300.*

Values for Blocks of 4

3	A1	1p	3,100.	1,850.
3a	A1	1p	4,500.	2,300.
3b	A1	1p		—
4	A1	4p	3,200.	450.00
4b	A1	4p	4,400.	450.00
4e	A1	4p	4,250.	450.00
5	A1	6p	5,250.	*1,850.*
5a	A1	6p	*12,000.*	*2,750.*
5b	A1	6p		*4,100.*
5c	A1	6p		*9,250.*
6	A1	1sh	*18,000.*	*1,650.*
6a	A1	1sh	1,800.	*4,600.*

Nos. 3-6 are known rouletted unofficially.
Counterfeits exist.
No. 4 was reproduced by the collotype process in an unwatermarked souvenir sheet distributed at the London Intl. Stamp Exhib. 1950.

A2

Printed by Saul Solomon & Co.

1861		Laid Paper	Unwmk.	Typo.
7	A2	1p vermilion	*16,000.*	2,550.
a.		1p carmine	*27,500.*	3,400.
b.		1p red	*40,000.*	4,900.
c.		1p milky blue (error)	*175,000.*	*32,500.*
d.		1p pale blue (error)		*35,000.*
9	A2	4p milky blue	*23,000.*	1,900.
a.		4p pale blue	*24,000.*	2,400.
b.		4p blue	*29,000.*	3,400.
c.		4p dark blue	*110,000.*	5,250.
d.		As #9, right corner retouched		7,000.
e.		As #9a, right corner retouched		6,250.
f.		4p vermilion (error)	*175,000.*	*65,000.*
g.		4p carmine (error)		*110,000.*
h.		Tête bêche pair, cliche error		*140,000.*

Values for Pairs

7	A2	1p	*45,000.*	*8,000.*
7a	A2	1p	*75,000.*	*10,500.*
7b	A2	1p	*110,000.*	*14,500.*
9	A2	4p	*67,500.*	*10,000.*
9a	A2	4p	*70,000.*	*11,500.*
9b	A2	4p	*87,500.*	*17,500.*
9c	A2	4p	*575,000.*	*27,500.*

Value for Used Blocks of 4

7	A2	1p	*26,000.*
7a	A2	1p	*35,000.*
7b	A2	1p	*50,000.*
9	A2	4p	*19,500.*
9a	A2	4p	*22,500.*
9b	A2	4p	*35,000.*
9c	A2	4p	*55,000.*

Nos. 7 and 9 are usually called Wood Blocks. The plates were made locally and composed of clichés mounted on wood. The errors were caused by a cliché of each value being mounted in the plate of the other value.

No. 9h is the unique pair with the two stamps positioned so that the inscription "POSTAGE" on one stamp is aligned next to the inscription "FOUR PENCE" on the adjoining stamp.

In 1883 plate proofs of both values on white paper, usually called "reprints," were made. The 1p is in dull orange red; the 4p in dark blue. These are known canceled, as a few were misused as stamps. The proofs do not include the errors.

Counterfeits exist.

Printed by De La Rue & Co.

1863-64 Wmk. 15 Engr.

12	A1	1p dark carmine	175.00	*260.00*
a.		1p reddish brown	450.00	290.00
b.		1p brownish red	450.00	260.00
13	A1	4p dark blue	190.00	62.50
a.		4p slate blue	2,400.	575.00
b.		4p steel blue	2,400.	325.00
c.		4p pale grayish blue	200.00	75.00
14	A1	6p purple	225.00	*525.00*
15	A1	1sh emerald	475.00	*525.00*
a.		1sh pale emerald	1,150.	—

Watermark Sideways

12c	A1	1p As #12	350.00	350.00
12d	A1	1p As #12a	575.00	350.00
12e	A1	1p As #12b	575.00	325.00
13d	A1	4p As #13	575.00	210.00
14a	A1	6p As #14		1,400.

Values for Pairs

12	A1	1p	475.00	*825.00*
12a	A1	1p	1,100.	925.00
12b	A1	1p	1,100.	850.00
13	A1	4p	475.00	210.00
13a	A1	4p	*6,000.*	1,850.
13b	A1	4p	*6,000.*	975.00
13c	A1	4p	500.00	250.00
14	A1	6p	575.00	*1,750.*
15	A1	1sh	1,150.	*2,100.*
15a	A1	1sh	*3,000.*	

Values for Blocks of 4

12	A1	1p	1,100.	*2,600.*
12a	A1	1p	3,000.	*2,850.*
12b	A1	1p	2,750.	*2,600.*
13	A1	4p	1,100.	*650.00*
13a	A1	4p	—	*5,750.*
13b	A1	4p	—	*3,000.*
13c	A1	4p	1,200.	*750.00*
14	A1	6p	1,400.	*5,250.*
15	A1	1sh	2,750.	*5,250.*
15a	A1	1sh	*7,000.*	

Nos. 12-15 can be distinguished from Nos. 3-6 not only by colors but because Nos. 12-15 often appear in a granular ink or with the background lightly printed in whole or part.

No. 12a, Wmk. 1, is believed to be a proof. Value, $17,000.

Counterfeits exist.

"Hope" and Symbols of Colony

A3 A6

Frame Line Around Stamp

1864-65 Typo. Wmk. 1 *Perf. 14*

16	A3	1p rose ('65)	95.00	27.50
a.		1p car red	100.00	29.00
17	A3	4p blue ('65)	115.00	3.75
a.		4p pale blue	115.00	3.75
b.		4p dull ultramarine	300.00	62.50
c.		4p deep blue ('72)	175.00	4.00
18	A3	6p bright violet	150.00	1.75
a.		6p dull violet	240.00	8.00
b.		6p pale lilac ('84)	125.00	25.00
19	A3	1sh yellow green	125.00	4.00
a.		1sh blue green	140.00	5.25
b.		1sh deep green	575.00	21.00
		Nos. 16-19 (4)	485.00	37.00

Watermark Inverted

16b	A3	1p rose	325.00	150.00
17d	A3	4p blue	475.00	175.00
18c	A3	6p bright violet	—	325.00
19d	A3	1sh yellow green	700.00	175.00

Watermark Reversed

19e	A3	1sh yellow green		—

Imperf. stamps are believed to be proofs.

For surcharges see Nos. 20-21, N3.

For types A3 and A6 with manuscript surcharge of 1d or overprints "G. W." or "G," see Griqualand West listings.

Stamps of 1864 Surcharged in Red or Black:

a

b

1868-74 Red Surcharge

20	A3(a)	4p on 6p	290.00	18.00
a.		"Peuce" for "Pence"	*2,100.*	900.00
b.		"Fonr" for "Four"		800.00
c.		Wmk inverted		*325.00*
21	A3(b)	1p on 6p ('74)	575.00	105.00
a.		"E" of PENNY omitted		1,150.

Space between words and bars varies from 12½-16mm on #20, and 16½-18mm on #21.

1876 Black Surcharge

22	A3 (b)	1p on 1sh green	95.00	57.50

Without Frame Line Around Stamp

1871-81 *Perf. 14*

23	A6	½p gray black ('75)	21.00	9.25
24	A6	1p rose ('72)	37.50	.70
25	A6	3p lilac rose ('80)	210.00	29.00
26	A6	3p claret ('81)	135.00	3.00
a.		3p pale claret	160.00	3.25
27	A6	4p blue ('76)	115.00	.85
a.		4p ultramarine	240.00	57.50
28	A6	5sh orange	400.00	18.00
		Nos. 23-28 (6)	918.50	60.80

Watermark Inverted

23a	A6	½p gray black	—	*115.00*
24a	A6	1p rose	*325.00*	*140.00*
25a	A6	3p lilac rose	—	*350.00*
26a	A6	3p claret	—	—
27b	A6	4p blue	*375.00*	*105.00*

For surcharges see Nos. 29-32, 39, 55.

No. 27 Surcharged in Red

1879

29	A6	3p on 4p blue	115.00	2.25
a.		"THE.EE"	2,250.	350.00
b.		"PENCB"	2,000.	275.00
c.		Double surcharge	*10,000.*	*3,750.*
d.		As "a," double surcharge	—	—

Type of 1871 Surcharged in Black

1880

30	A6	3p on 4p lilac rose	80.00	2.00
a.		Wmk. inverted		240.00

No. 25 Surcharged in Black

e

f

31	A6(e)	3p on 3p lilac rose	225.00	8.00
a.		Inverted surcharge	*9,500.*	1,100.
b.		Wmk inverted	—	*475.00*
32	A6(f)	3p on 3p lilac rose	87.50	1.75
a.		Inverted surcharge	925.00	45.00
b.		Vert. pair, #31-32	*1,100.*	*475.00*
c.		Wmk inverted	—	*175.00*

1882-83 Wmk. 2

33	A6	½p gray black	22.00	2.00
a.		½p black	26.00	2.00
b.		Wmk. inverted	—	*150.00*
34	A6	1p rose	55.00	1.10
a.		1p dp rose red	57.50	1.15
b.		Wmk inverted	—	*150.00*
35	A6	2p bister	92.50	.60
a.		2p dp bister	97.50	.60
b.		Wmk inverted	—	*150.00*
36	A6	3p claret	7.50	1.10
a.		3p dp claret	11.50	.90
b.		Wmk. inverted	—	*110.00*
37	A3	6p bright violet	105.00	.90
38	A6	5sh orange ('83)	925.00	275.00

For overprint see Rhodesia No. 49.

Nos. 26 and 36 Surcharged in Black

1882 Wmk. 1

39	A6	½p on 3p claret	*3,175.*	150.00
a.		Hyphen omitted		*3,750.*

Wmk. 2

40	A6	½p on 3p claret	29.00	3.75
a.		"ENNY"	2,300.	800.00
b.		"PENN"	1,150.	*700.00*
c.		Hyphen omitted	750.00	400.00
d.		Wmk. inverted		

1884-98 Wmk. 16

41	A6	½p gray black ('86)	4.50	.20
a.		Wmk. inverted	—	—
42	A6	½p yel green ('96)	1.75	.55
a.		½p green	3.25	.55
43	A6	1p rose ('85)	4.50	.20
a.		Wmk inverted	—	*92.50*
44	A6	2p bister	7.00	.20
a.		2p pale bister ('84)	26.00	1.00
b.		As "b," wmk inverted	—	*125.00*
45	A6	2p choc brown ('97)	2.35	.45
46	A6	3p red violet ('98)	8.00	1.00
47	A6	4p blue ('90)	11.00	.55
48	A6	4p pale ol grn ('97)	4.75	2.00
49	A3	6p violet	9.75	.25
a.		6p reddish purple	70.00	1.90
b.		6p bright mauve	11.50	.55
c.		As "a," wmk inverted	—	*225.00*
50	A3	1sh dull bluish grn ('89)	92.50	.45
a.		1sh green ('85)	160.00	5.50
b.		Wmk. inverted	—	*350.00*
51	A6	1sh blue grn ('94)	70.00	4.25
52	A6	1sh yel buff ('96)	9.25	1.10
53	A6	5sh orange ('87)	97.50	5.50
54	A6	5sh brown org ('96)	75.00	4.00
		Nos. 41-54 (14)	397.85	20.70

For surcharges see Nos. 58, 162, 165-166. For overprints see Rhodesia Nos. 43, 45-48.

Type of 1871 Surcharged in Black

1891, Mar.

55	A6	2½p on 3p deep magenta	3.75	.25
a.		"1" of "½" has straight serif	57.50	37.50
b.		2½p on 3p vio rose	4.75	1.10
c.		As "a," vio rose	60.00	42.50

Hope Seated — A13

1892-96

56	A13	2½p sage green	9.25	.20
a.		2½p olive green	11.50	.65
57	A13	2½p ultra ('96)	4.75	.20

For surcharge see No. N4. For overprint see Orange River Colony No. 55.

No. 44 Surcharged in Black

1893, Mar.

58	A6	1p on 2p bister	3.00	.55
a.		Double surcharge		450.00
b.		No period after "PENNY"	57.50	12.75
c.		1p on 2p pale bister (#44a)	4.50	1.10

Hope Standing A15

Table Mountain and Bay; Coat of Arms A16

1893-1902

59	A15	½p green ('98)	2.30	.20
60	A15	1p rose	1.45	.20
a.		1p carmine	3.50	1.10
61	A15	3p red violet ('02)	4.50	1.75
		Nos. 59-61 (3)	8.25	2.15

For surcharges see Nos. 163-164, N2. For overprints see Orange River Colony #54, 56, Rhodesia #44, Transvaal #236-236A.

1900, Jan.

62	A16	1p carmine rose	2.90	.25
a.		Wmk. inverted	—	110.00

King Edward VII — A17

Various frames.

1902-04 Wmk. 16

63	A17	½p emerald	2.60	.20
64	A17	1p car rose	2.35	.20
a.		Wmk. inverted	—	—
b.		Wmk. inverted and reversed	—	—
65	A17	2p brown ('04)	11.00	.95
a.		Wmk. inverted	—	—
66	A17	2½p ultra ('04)	3.25	*7.50*
67	A17	3p red violet ('03)	8.00	.90
68	A17	4p ol green ('03)	9.25	.75
69	A17	6p violet ('03)	17.50	.60
70	A17	1sh bister	14.00	.95
71	A17	5sh brown org ('03)	85.00	15.00
		Nos. 63-71 (9)	152.95	27.05

Imperf. stamps are proofs.

Cape of Good Hope stamps were replaced by those of Union of South Africa.

OFFICIAL STAMPS

PERFORATED OFFICIAL STAMPS

Stamps of Cape of Good Hope punched with an 11-hole double triangle device were used by the Stationery and Printed Forms Branch of the Cape of Good Hope Colonial Secretary's Department between 1904 and 1906. They are only known used.

1904-06

On Seated Hope Stamps of 1884/1897

OA1	A6	2p pale bister (#44a)	19.00
OA2	A6	2p choc brown (#45)	19.00
OA3	A6	3p red violet (#46)	25.00
OA4	A6	4p pale bister (#48)	25.00
OA5	A3	6p violet (#49)	23.00

On Standing Hope Stamps of 1898/1902

OA6	A15	½p green (#59)	25.00
OA7	A15	3p red violet (#61)	19.00

On Table Mountain Stamp of 1900

OA8	A16	1p carmine rose (#62)	19.00

On King Edward VII issue of 1902-04

OA9	A17	½p emerald (#63)	25.00
OA10	A17	1p car rose (#64)	15.00
OA11	A17	2p brown (#65)	23.00
OA12	A17	3p red violet (#67)	18.00
OA13	A17	4p ol green (#68)	19.00
OA14	A17	6p violet (#69)	21.00
OA15	A17	1sh bister (#70)	25.00
OA16	A17	5sh brown org (#71)	62.50

ISSUED IN MAFEKING

Excellent forgeries of Nos. 162-179 are known.

Stamps of Cape of Good Hope Surcharged

1900, Mar. 24

162 A6 1p on ½p grn *225.00 75.00*
163 A15 1p on ½p grn *275.00 85.00*
164 A15 3p on 1p rose *260.00 57.50*
165 A6 6p on 3p red vio *37,500. 290.00*
166 A6 1sh on 4p pale ol green *7,000. 400.00*

Stamps of Bechuanaland Protectorate Surcharged

1900 **Wmk. 30**

167 A54 1p on ½p ver 225.00 70.00
a. Inverted surcharge — *5,250.*
b. Vert. pair, surcharge tête bêche *32,500.*
168 A40 3p on 1p lilac 975.00 105.00
a. Double surcharge *25,000.*
169 A56 6p on 2p grn & car 2,200. 85.00
170 A58 6p on 3p vio, *yel* 5,750. 325.00
a. Inverted surcharge — *32,500.*
b. Double surcharge — —

The lettering of "Mafeking Besieged" shows varying breaks in various letters, and may have either a period or no punctuation after "Mafeking."

On Stamps of Bechuanaland
Wmk. 29

171 A1 6p on 3p violet & black *425.00 75.00*

Wmk. 30

172 A59 1sh on 4p brn & grn *1,500. 95.00*
a. Double surch., one inverted — *25,000.*
b. Triple surcharge — *25,000.*
c. Inverted surcharge — —
d. Double surcharge — *25,000.*

Stamps of Bechuanaland Protectorate Surcharged

173 A40 3p on 1p lilac 1,050. 85.00
a. Double surcharge — *8,000.*
174 A56 6p on 2p grn & car 1,200. 75.00
175 A62 1sh on 6p vio, *rose* 5,250. 95.00

On Stamps of Bechuanaland

176 A62 1sh on 6p vio, *rose* 20,000. 800.00
177 A65 2sh on 1sh green 10,000. 475.00

A fine mint example of the 1 shilling on 6 pence (Scott No. 176) sold for the equivalent of U.S. $13,077 at a London auction in 2003.

Sgt. Major Goodyear
M1

Gen. Robert S. S. Baden-Powell
M2

Wmk. OCEANA FINE Photographic Print

1900, Apr. *Perf. 12*

Laid Paper

178 M1 1p blue, *blue* 925.00 325.00
On cover *9,500.*
179 M2 3p blue, *blue*, 18½mm wide 1,400. 400.00
On cover 6,500.
a. Horiz. pair, imperf. between — *70,000.*
b. Double impression — *20,000.*
c. Reversed design *70,000. 42,500.*
180 M2 3p blue, *blue*, 21mm wide 8,750. 1,500.
On cover *12,500.*
a. 3p deep blue 9,250. 1,250.
On cover *13,500.*

The color of the paper varies from pale to deep blue.

OCEANA FINE is a sheet watermark and does not appear on every stamp.

Imperfs of No. 178 are proofs.

There is one used pair of No. 179a privately owned. There are 2 unused and 6 used examples of No. 179c privately owned.

Issued: #178, Apr. 6; #179-180, Apr. 10.

ISSUED IN VRYBURG

Under Boer Occupation

Cape of Good Hope Stamps of 1884-96 Surcharged

Two Types of Surcharge:
Type I — Surcharge 10mm high. Space between lines 5½mm.
Type II — Surcharge 12mm high. Space between lines 7½mm.

1899, Nov. **Wmk. 16** *Perf. 14*

N1 A6 ½p on ½p emer (I) 230. 92.50
a. Type II 2,000. 800.
N2 A15 1p on 1p rose (I) 260. 115.
a. Double surcharge —
b. Type II 2,200. 925.
N3 A3 2p on 6p vio (II) 2,500. 575.
N4 A13 2½p on 2½p ultra (I) 2,000. 500.
a. Type II *11,500. 5,000.*

Italic Z in "Z.A.R."

N1b A6 ½p on ½p *1,950. 800.00*
N2c A15 1p on 1p *2,200. 925.00*
N3a A3 2p on 6p *11,500. 4,900.*
N4b A13 2½p on 2½p *11,500. 5,000.*

"Z.A.R." stands for Zuid Afrikaansche Republiek (South African Republic).

Under British Occupation

Transvaal Stamps of 1895-96 Handstamped

1900 **Unwmk.** *Perf. 12½*

N5 A13 ½p green — *2,750.*
N6 A13 1p rose & grn *10,500. 5,000.*
N7 A13 2p brown & grn — —
N8 A13 2½p ultra & grn — —

CAPE VERDE

'kāp 'vərd

LOCATION — A group of 10 islands and five islets in the Atlantic Ocean, about 500 miles due west of Senegal.
GOVT. — Portuguese Territory
AREA — 1,557 sq. mi.
POP. — 296,093 (1980)
CAPITAL — Praia

1000 Reis = 1 Milreis
100 Centavos = 1 Escudo (1913)

BR. POSTAL AGENCY IN CAPE VERDE

FORERUNNERS — British Postal Agency

Crowned Circle handstamp type VII is pictured in the Crowned Circle Handstamps and Great Britain Used Abroad section.

St. Vincent (San Vicente)

1851

A1 VII Crowned circle handstamp on cover, Type VII, inscribed "PAID AT ST. VICENT C. DE V." *6,000.*

Crown of Portugal — A1

King Luiz — A2

1877 **Unwmk.** **Typo.** *Perf. 12½*

1 A1 5r black 2.75 1.25
2 A1 10r yellow 27.50 7.00
b. 10r orange yellow 30.00 11.00
3 A1 20r bister 2.50 1.00
a. 20r pale bister 2.00 1.00
4 A1 25r rose 1.40 .85
5 A1 40r blue 67.50 20.00
b. Cliche of Mozambique in Cape Verde plate, in pair with #5 1,100. 1,100.
d. 40r pale blue 75.00 40.00
6 A1 50r green 125.00 65.00
b. 50r yellow green 75.00 40.00
7 A1 100r lilac 5.50 1.90
b. 100r pale lilac 6.00 1.50
8 A1 200r orange 3.50 2.25
9 A1 300r brown 4.00 2.75
Nos. 1-9 (9) 239.65 102.00

Perf. 13½

1a A1 5r black 3.00 1.00
2a A1 10r yellow 30.00 11.00
3a A1 20r bister 2.00 1.00
4a A1 25r rose 7.50 4.00
5a A1 40r blue 75.00 40.00
c. Cliche of Mozambique in Cape Verde plate, in pair with #5a 1,500. 1,500.
6a A1 50r green 75.00 40.00
7a A1 100r lilac 6.00 1.50
8a A1 200r orange 7.50 4.75
Nos. 1a-8a (8) 206.00 103.25

1881-85 *Perf. 12½*

10 A1 10r green 1.75 1.25
11 A1 20r carmine ('85) 3.50 2.00
12 A1 25r violet ('85) 2.75 1.60
13 A1 40r yellow buff 1.75 1.00
a. Imperf. 1.00
b. Cliche of Mozambique in Cape Verde plate, in pair with #13 70.00 62.50
c. As "b," imperf. 35.00
14 A1 50r blue 4.50 2.50
Nos. 10-14 (5) 14.25 8.35

Reprints of the 1877-85 issues are on smooth white chalky paper, ungummed, and on thin white paper with shiny white gum. They are perf 13½.

Perf. 13½

10a A1 10r green 2.00 .90
11a A1 20r carmine ('85) 37.50 25.00
13d A1 40r yellow buff 3.50 2.50
e. Cliche of Mozambique in Cape Verde plate, in pair with #13d 100.00 75.00
14a A1 50r blue 5.50 3.00

1886 **Embossed** *Perf. 13½*
Chalk-Surfaced Paper

15 A2 5r black 2.50 1.75
a. Perf 12½ 3.75 1.65
16 A2 10r green 2.50 1.90
a. Perf 12½ 4.00 1.75

Perf. 12½

17 A2 20r carmine 5.00 2.75
a. Perf. 13½ 5.50 3.25
18 A2 25r violet 4.50 3.25
19 A2 40r chocolate 6.50 2.00
a. Perf. 13½ 7.25 3.75
20 A2 50r blue 5.50 2.00
21 A2 100r yel brown 5.50 2.75
22 A2 200r gray lilac 11.00 6.00
23 A2 300r orange 17.00 8.75
Nos. 15-23 (9) 60.00 31.15

The 25r, 50r and 100r have been reprinted in aniline colors with clean-cut Perf. 13½.

For surcharges see Nos. 59-67, 184-187.

King Carlos
A3 A4

1894-95 **Typo.** *Perf. 11½*

24 A3 5r orange .90 .75
25 A3 10r redsh violet .90 .75
26 A3 15r chocolate 2.25 1.50
27 A3 20r lavender 2.25 1.50
28 A3 25r dp green 1.90 1.40
29 A3 50r lt blue 1.90 1.40
31 A3 80r yel grn ('95) 7.00 4.50
32 A3 100r brn, *buff* ('95) 5.25 2.75
33b A3 150r car, *rose* 45.00 30.00
35 A3 300r dk blue, *sal* ('95) 20.00 9.50

Perf. 12½

26a A3 15r 90.00 67.50
28a A3 25r 3.50 2.75
30 A3 75r carmine ('95) 6.25 3.50
32a A3 100r 40.00 18.00
33a A3 150r 110.00 90.00
34a A3 200r 90.00 70.00

Perf. 13½

29a A3 50r 8.00 2.75
30a A3 75r 32.50 24.00
31a A3 80r 25.00 19.00
33 A3 150r car, *rose* ('95) 18.00 15.00
34 A3 200r dk blue, *lt blue* ('95) 18.00 15.00

For surcharges see Nos. 68-78, 137, 189-193, 201-205.

1898-1903 *Perf. 11½*
Name and Value in Black except 500r

36 A4 2½r gray .25 .20
37 A4 5r orange .30 .20
38 A4 10r lt green .40 .20
39 A4 15r brown 3.25 1.10
40 A4 15r gray green ('03) 1.00 .75
41 A4 20r gray violet 1.00 .50
42 A4 25r sea green 2.00 .70
a. Perf 12½ 35.00 20.00
43 A4 25r carmine ('03) .60 .30
44 A4 50r dark blue 2.25 .80
45 A4 50r brown ('03) 2.00 1.40
46 A4 65r slate blue ('03) 40.00 *40.00*
47 A4 75r rose 4.75 2.00
48 A4 75r lilac ('03) 1.75 1.25
49 A4 80r violet 4.75 2.25
50 A4 100r dk blue, *blue* 1.75 1.00
51 A4 115r org brn, *pink* ('03) 12.00 *13.50*
52 A4 130r brown, *straw* ('03) 12.00 *13.50*
53 A4 150r brown, *straw* 8.00 6.75
54 A4 200r red vio, *pnksh* 2.50 1.60
55 A4 300r dk blue, *rose* 8.00 3.00
56 A4 400r dull blue, *straw* ('03) 10.00 6.00
57 A4 500r blk & red, *blue* ('01) 8.00 3.00
58 A4 700r violet, *yelsh* ('01) 16.00 10.00
Nos. 36-58 (23) 142.55 110.00

For overprints and suecharges see Nos. 80-99, 139, 200.

Regular Issues Surcharged in Red or Black

Two spacing types of surcharge. See note above Angola No. 61.

On Issue of 1886

1902, Dec. 1 *Perf. 12½, 13½*

59 A2 65r on 5r black (R) 4.00 2.50
60 A2 65r on 200r gray lilac 4.00 2.50
61 A2 65r on 300r orange 4.00 2.50
62 A2 115r on 10r green 4.00 2.50
63 A2 115r on 20r rose 4.00 2.50
a. Perf 13½ 27.50 19.00
64 A2 130r on 50r blue 4.00 2.50
65 A2 130r on 100r brown 4.00 2.50
66 A2 400r on 25r violet 2.00 1.50
67 A2 400r on 40r choc 4.00 2.25
a. Perf 13½ 27.50 22.50

On Issue of 1894

Perf. 11½, 12½, 13½

68 A3 65r on 10r red violet 4.75 2.75
69 A3 65r on 20r lavender 4.50 2.50
70 A3 65r on 100r brown, *buff* 5.00 3.00
a. Perf 12½ 15.00 13.50

71 A3 115r on 5r orange 2.75 1.90
a. Inverted surcharge 45.00 45.00
72 A3 115r on 25r blue grn 2.75 1.75
a. Perf 11½ 45.00 25.00
73 A3 115r on 150r car, *rose* 4.75 3.75
a. Perf 13½ 20.00 12.00
74 A3 130r on 75r car 2.75 2.00
a. Perf 13½ 45.00 42.50
75 A3 130r on 80r yel grn 2.25 1.75
a. Perf 11½ 2.25 1.90
76 A3 130r on 200r dk blue, *blue* 3.00 1.75
77 A3 400r on 50r lt blue 3.25 2.25
a. Inverted surcharge 65.00 55.00
b. Perf 13½ 55.00 55.00
78 A3 400r on 300r dk blue, *sal* 1.75 1.10

On Newspaper Stamp of 1893

79 N1 400r on 2½r brown 1.25 1.10
a. Inverted surcharge 27.50
b. Perf 12½ 45.00 42.50
c. Perf 11½ 1.25 1.00
Nos. 59-79 (21) 72.75 46.85

Reprints of Nos. 59, 66, 67, and 77 have shiny white gum and clean-cut perforation 13½.

For overprint and surcharge see #137, 205-206.

Overprinted in Black On Nos. 39, 42, 44, 47

1902-03 ***Perf. 11½***

80 A4 15r brown 1.50 .80
81 A4 25r sea green 1.50 .80
82 A4 50r blue ('03) 1.75 1.00
83 A4 75r rose ('03) 2.25 1.40
a. Inverted overprint 42.50 42.50
Nos. 80-83 (4) 7.00 4.00

For overprint see No. 139.

No. 46 Surcharged in Black

1905, July 1

84 A4 50r on 65r slate blue 2.50 1.75

Stamps of 1898-1903 Overprinted in Carmine or Green

1911, Aug. 20

85 A4 2½r gray .20 .20
86 A4 5r orange .20 .20
87 A4 10r lt green .60 .50
88 A4 15r gray green .35 .20
89 A4 20r gray violet .65 .65
90 A4 25r carmine (G) .65 .30
91 A4 50r brown 4.00 2.75
92 A4 75r red lilac .85 .50
93 A4 100r dk blue, *blue* .85 .60
94 A4 115r org brn, *pink* .45 *1.25*
95 A4 130r brown, *straw* .45 *1.25*
96 A4 200r red vio, *pnksh* 3.25 3.25
97 A4 400r dull bl, *straw* 1.25 1.25
98 A4 500r blk & red, *bl* 1.50 1.00
99 A4 700r violet, *straw* 1.50 1.10
Nos. 85-99 (15) 16.75 15.00

King Manuel II — A5

Overprinted in Carmine or Green

1912 ***Perf. 11½x12***

100 A5 2½r violet .20 *1.25*
101 A5 5r black .20 .20
102 A5 10r gray grn .20 .20
103 A5 20r carmine (G) 1.25 .70
104 A5 25r vio brown .25 .20
105 A5 50r dk blue 2.00 1.60
106 A5 75r bister brn .45 .35
107 A5 100r brown, *lt grn* .45 .35
108 A5 200r dk green, *sal* .70 .60
109 A5 300r black, *azure* .70 .60

Perf. 14½x15

110 A5 400r black & blue 2.00 1.60
111 A5 500r ol grn & vio brn 2.00 1.60
Nos. 100-111 (12) 10.40 9.25

Common Design Types pictured following the introduction.

Vasco da Gama Issue of Various Portuguese Colonies

Common Design Types CD20-CD27 Surcharged

On Stamps of Macao

1913, Feb. 13 ***Perf. 12½ to 16***

112 ¼c on ½a blue grn 1.25 .75
113 ½c on 1a red .85 .75
114 1c on 2a red violet .85 .75
115 2½c on 4a yel grn .85 .75
116 5c on 8a dk blue 4.00 3.00
117 7½c on 12a vio brn 3.25 2.00
118 10c on 16a bister brn 1.40 1.25
119 15c on 24a bister 3.50 2.50
Nos. 112-119 (8) 15.95 11.75

On Stamps of Portuguese Africa
Perf. 14 to 15

120 ¼c on 2½r bl grn .65 .55
121 ½c on 5r red .65 .55
122 1c on 10r red vio .65 .55
123 2½c on 25r yel grn .65 .55
124 5c on 50r dk blue 1.25 .90
125 7½c on 75r vio brn 1.90 1.60
126 10c on 100r bis brn 1.25 1.10
127 15c on 150r bister 1.75 1.50
Nos. 120-127 (8) 8.75 7.30

On Stamps of Timor

128 ¼c on ½a bl grn .85 .75
129 ½c on 1a red .85 .75
130 1c on 2a red vio .85 .75
131 2½c on 4a yel grn .85 .75
132 5c on 8a dk blue 4.00 3.00
133 7½c On 12a vio brn 3.50 2.50
134 10c on 16a bis brn 1.40 1.25
135 15c on 24a bister 2.75 1.50
Nos. 128-135 (8) 15.05 11.25
Nos. 112-135 (24) 39.75 30.30

For surcharges see Nos. 197-198.

No. 75 Overprinted in Red

1913 ***Perf. 11½, 12½, 13½***

137 A3 130r on 80r yel grn 3.25 2.50

Nos. 73 and 76 overprinted but not issued. Values, $10, $12.

Same Overprint on No. 83 in Green

1914 ***Perf. 12***

139 A4 75r rose 3.25 2.50
a. "PROVISORIO" double (G and R) 45.00 40.00

Ceres — A6

Perf. 11½, 12x11½, 15x14

1914-26 **Typo.**

Name and Value in Black

144 A6 ¼c olive brn .20 .20
a. Imperf.
145 A6 ½c black .20 .20
146 A6 1c blue grn .85 .75
147 A6 1c yel grn ('22) .20 .20
148 A6 1½c lilac brown .20 .20
149 A6 2c carmine .20 .20
150 A6 2c gray ('26) .25 *5.00*
151 A6 2½c lt violet .20 .20
152 A6 3c org ('22) .30 .25
153 A6 4c rose ('22) .20 *1.60*
154 A6 4½c gray ('22) .20 *5.00*
155 A6 5c deep blue .75 .45
156 A6 5c brt blue ('22) .20 .20
157 A6 6c lilac ('22) .20 *2.75*
158 A6 7c ultra ('22) .20 *2.75*
159 A6 7½c yel brn .20 *1.00*
160 A6 8c slate .40 .30
161 A6 10c orange brn .20 .20
162 A6 12c blue grn ('22) .35 .25
163 A6 15c plum 4.00 3.00
164 A6 15c brn rose ('22) .25 .20
165 A6 20c yel grn .20 .20
166 A6 24c ultra ('26) 1.50 *1.40*
167 A6 25c choc ('26) 1.50 1.40
168 A6 30c brown, *grn* 3.00 3.00
169 A6 30c gray grn ('22) .75 .25
170 A6 40c brown, *pink* 3.00 3.00
171 A6 40c turq blue ('22) 1.75 .25
172 A6 50c orange, *sal* 3.00 3.00
173 A6 50c violet ('26) 1.75 .30
174 A6 60c dk blue ('22) 1.75 .45
175 A6 60c rose ('26) 1.75 .45
176 A6 80c brt rose ('22) 2.00 1.10
177 A6 1e green, *blue* 3.00 3.00
178 A6 1e rose ('22) 7.00 2.25
179 A6 1e dp blue ('26) 9.00 1.50
180 A6 2e dk violet ('22) 10.00 4.00
181 A6 5e buff ('26) 25.00 12.00
182 A6 10e pink ('26) 75.00 40.00
183 A6 20e pale turq ('26) 100.00 50.00
Nos. 144-183 (40) 260.70 152.45

For surcharge see No. 214.

Provisional Issue of 1902 Overprinted in Carmine

1915 ***Perf. 11½, 12½, 13½***

184 A2 115r on 10r green 2.50 2.00
a. Perf. 13½ 15.00 15.00
185 A2 115r on 20r rose 2.00 1.25
a. Perf. 13½ 15.00 15.00
186 A2 130r on 50r blue 2.00 1.10
187 A2 130r on 100r brown 1.50 .70
188 A3 115r on 5r orange 1.25 .40
a. Inverted overprint 30.00
189 A3 115r on 25r blue grn 1.50 .65
a. Perf. 11½ 15.00 15.00
190 A3 115r on 150r car, *rose* 1.00 .40
191 A3 130r on 75r carmine 2.00 .90
192 A3 130r on 80r yel grn 1.50 .70
a. Inverted overprint 30.00
193 A3 130r on 200r bl, *bl* 2.00 .90
a. Perf. 12½ 40.00 32.50
Nos. 184-193 (10) 17.25 9.00

War Tax Stamps of Portuguese Africa Surcharged

1921, Feb. 3 ***Perf. 15x14, 11½***

194 WT1 ¼c on 1c green .25 .25
195 WT1 ½c on 1c green .40 .30
a. "1/2" instead of "½" as shown 10.00 10.00
196 WT1 1c green .40 .30

Nos. 127 and 126 Surcharged

Perf. 14 to 15

197 CD27 2c on 15c on 150r 1.00 1.00
198 CD26 4c on 10c on 100r 1.25 1.00
a. On No. 118 (error) 150.00 150.00

The 4c surcharge also exists on No. 134. Value, $500.

No. 50 Surcharged

Perf. 12

200 A4 6c on 100r dk bl, *bl* 1.25 1.25
a. No accent on "U" of surcharge 12.50 8.00
Nos. 194-200 (6) 4.55 4.10

No. 200 has an accent on the "U" of the surcharge.

Stamps of 1913-15 Surcharged

1922, Apr. ***Perf. 11½, 12½, 13½***

On No. 137

201 A3 4c on 130r on 80r 1.25 1.25

On Nos. 191-193

202 A3 4c on 130r on 75r 1.60 1.60
203 A3 4c on 130r on 80r 1.25 1.25
204 A3 4c on 130r on 200r .90 .60
a. Perf. 12½ 15.00 15.00
Nos. 201-204 (4) 5.00 4.70

Surcharge of Nos. 201-204 with smaller $ occurs once in sheet of 28. Value eight times normal.

Nos. 78-79 Surcharged

1925 ***Perf. 13½, 11½***

205 A3 40c on 400r on 300r .60 .55
206 N1 40c on 400r on 2½r .40 .45

No. 176 Surcharged

1931, Nov. ***Perf. 12x11½***

214 A6 70c on 80c brt rose 2.75 1.40

Ceres — A7

1934, May 1 **Wmk. 232**

215 A7 1c bister .20 *.20*
216 A7 5c olive brown .20 .20
217 A7 10c violet .20 .20
218 A7 15c black .20 .20
219 A7 20c gray .20 .20
220 A7 30c dk green .20 .20
221 A7 40c red org .20 .20
222 A7 45c brt blue 1.40 .60
223 A7 50c brown .65 .45
224 A7 60c olive grn .65 .45
225 A7 70c brown org .65 .45
226 A7 80c emerald .65 .45
227 A7 85c deep rose 3.00 1.90
228 A7 1e maroon 2.10 .35
229 A7 1.40e dk blue 2.75 2.40
230 A7 2e dk violet 3.25 1.90
231 A7 5e apple green 14.50 3.75
232 A7 10e olive bister 24.00 14.00
233 A7 20e orange 45.00 18.00
Nos. 215-233 (19) 100.00 46.10

For surcharge see No. 256.

Vasco da Gama Issue
Common Design Types

1938 **Unwmk.** ***Perf. 13½x13***

Name and Value in Black

234 CD34 1c gray green .20 *.20*
235 CD34 5c orange brn .20 *.20*
236 CD34 10c dk carmine .20 .20
237 CD34 15c dk vio brn .70 .65
238 CD34 20c slate .35 .20
239 CD35 30c rose vio .35 .20
240 CD35 35c brt green .35 .20
241 CD35 40c brown .35 .20
242 CD35 50c brt red vio .35 .20
243 CD36 60c gray blk .35 .20
244 CD36 70c brown vio .35 .20
245 CD36 80c orange .30 .20
246 CD36 1e red .50 .20
247 CD37 1.75e blue 1.25 .55
248 CD37 2e dk blue grn 2.50 1.50
249 CD37 5e ol grn 5.75 1.50

250	CD38	10e blue vio	9.25	2.00
251	CD38	20e red brown	30.00	4.00
		Nos. 234-251 (18)	53.30	12.60

For surcharges see #255, 271-276, 288-292.

Outline Map of Africa — A8

1939, June 23 Litho. ***Perf. 11½x12***

252	A8	80c vio, *pale rose*	4.00	2.75
253	A8	1.75e blue, *pale bl*	32.50	25.00
254	A8	20e brown, *buff*	70.00	22.50
		Nos. 252-254 (3)	106.50	50.25

Visit of the President of Portugal in 1939.

AIR POST STAMPS

Common Design Type
Name and Value in Black

Perf. 13½x13

1938, July 26 **Unwmk.**

C1	CD39	10c red orange	.60	.50
C2	CD39	20c purple	.60	.50
C3	CD39	50c orange	.60	.50
C4	CD39	1e ultra	.60	.50
C5	CD39	2e lilac brown	1.40	.80
C6	CD39	3e dk green	1.75	1.40
C7	CD39	5e red brown	5.50	2.10
C8	CD39	9e rose carmine	9.00	3.75
C9	CD39	10e magenta	9.75	5.00
		Nos. C1-C9 (9)	29.80	15.05

No. C7 exists with overprint "Exposicao Internacional de Nova York, 1939-1940" and Trylon and Perisphere.

POSTAGE DUE STAMPS

D1

D2

1904 Unwmk. Typo. ***Perf. 12***

J1	D1	5r yellow grn	.40	*.25*
J2	D1	10r slate	.40	*.25*
J3	D1	20r yellow brn	.50	*.40*
J4	D1	30r red orange	1.25	*.40*
J5	D1	50r gray brown	.50	*.35*
J6	D1	60r red brown	9.25	4.25
J7	D1	100r lilac	1.75	1.25
J8	D1	130r dull blue	1.90	1.25
J9	D1	200r carmine	1.60	1.60
J10	D1	500r dull violet	5.00	*3.00*
		Nos. J1-J10 (10)	22.55	*13.00*

Overprinted in Carmine or Green

1911

J11	D1	5r yellow grn	.30	.20
J12	D1	10r slate	.30	.20
J13	D1	20r yellow brn	.35	.20
J14	D1	30r orange	.35	.20
J15	D1	50r gray brown	.65	.40
J16	D1	60r red brown	.65	.40
J17	D1	100r lilac	.65	.40
J18	D1	130r dull blue	.75	.65
J19	D1	200r carmine (G)	2.00	1.50
J20	D1	500r dull violet	2.50	1.75
		Nos. J11-J20 (10)	8.50	5.90

1921 ***Perf. 11½***

J21	D2	½c yellow grn	.30	.20
J22	D2	1c slate	.30	.20
J23	D2	2c red brown	.30	.20
J24	D2	3c orange	.30	.20
J25	D2	5c gray brown	.30	.20
J26	D2	6c lt brown	.30	.20
J27	D2	10c red violet	.30	.20
J28	D2	13c dull blue	.55	*.40*
J29	D2	20c carmine	.60	*.50*
J30	D2	50c gray	1.75	*1.10*
		Nos. J21-J30 (10)	5.00	*3.40*

NEWSPAPER STAMP

N1

1893 Typo. Unwmk. ***Perf. 11½***

P1	N1	2½r brown	1.50	.60
a.		Perf. 12½	3.00	1.50
b.		Perf. 13½	6.50	3.00

For surcharges see Nos. 79, 206.

POSTAL TAX STAMPS

Pombal Issue
Common Design Types

1925 Unwmk. Engr. ***Perf. 12½***

RA1	CD28	15c dull vio & blk	1.25	1.10
RA2	CD29	15c dull vio & blk	1.25	1.10
RA3	CD30	15c dull vio & blk	1.25	1.10
		Nos. RA1-RA3 (3)	3.75	3.30

POSTAL TAX DUE STAMPS

Pombal Issue
Common Design Types

1925 Unwmk. ***Perf. 12½***

RAJ1	CD28	30c dull vio & blk	.75	.70
RAJ2	CD29	30c dull vio & blk	.75	.70
RAJ3	CD30	30c dull vio & blk	.75	.70
		Nos. RAJ1-RAJ3 (3)	2.25	2.10

CAROLINE ISLANDS

'kar-ə-ˌlīn 'ī-ləndz

LOCATION — A group of about 549 small islands in the West Pacific Ocean, north of the Equator.
GOVT. — German colony
AREA — 550 sq. mi.
POP. — 40,000 (approx. 1915)

100 Pfennig = 1 Mark

Watermark

Wmk. 125 — Lozenges

Stamps of Germany 1889-90 Overprinted in Black

#1-6

#1a-6a

Overprinted at 56 degree Angle

1900 Unwmk. ***Perf. 13½x14½***

1	A9	3pf dk brown	12.00	*13.00*
		Never hinged	27.50	
		On cover		90.00
		On cover, single franking		100.00
2	A9	5pf green	17.00	*17.00*
		Never hinged	35.00	
		On cover		50.00
		On cover, single franking		60.00
3	A10	10pf carmine	18.00	*18.00*
		Never hinged	45.00	
		On cover		50.00
		On cover, single franking		60.00
4	A10	20pf ultra	22.50	*27.50*
		Never hinged	50.00	
		On cover		100.00
		On cover, single franking		125.00
5	A10	25pf orange	50.00	*65.00*
		Never hinged	130.00	
		On cover		160.00
		On cover, single franking		375.00
6	A10	50pf red brown	50.00	*65.00*
		Never hinged	125.00	
		On cover		100.00
		On cover, single franking		135.00
		Nos. 1-6 (6)	169.50	*205.50*

1899

Overprinted at 48 degree Angle

1a	A9	3pf light brown	450.00	*750.00*
		Never hinged	1,400.	
		On cover		1,450.
		On cover, single franking		1,700.
2a	A9	5pf green	500.00	550.00
		Never hinged	1,500.	
		On cover		1,750.
		On cover, single franking		1,750.
3a	A10	10pf carmine	60.00	*150.00*
		Never hinged	150.00	
		On cover		300.00
		On cover, single franking		325.00
4a	A10	20pf ultra	60.00	*150.00*
		Never hinged	150.00	
		On cover		300.00
		On cover, single franking		375.00
5a	A10	25pf orange	1,500.	*3,000.*
		Never hinged	3,400.	
		On cover		4,750.
		On cover, single franking		6,750.
6a	A10	50pf red brown	900.00	*1,500.*
		Never hinged	1,500.	
		On cover		2,750.
		On cover, single franking		3,500.

Covers: Values for Nos. 1-5, 1a-5a are for covers paying the correct rates. Nos. 6, 6a are for overfranked complete covers, usually philatelic.

A3

Kaiser's Yacht "Hohenzollern" — A4

1901, Jan. Typo. ***Perf. 14***

7	A3	3pf brown	1.00	*1.75*
		Never hinged	1.90	
		On cover		11.00
		On cover, single franking		18.00
8	A3	5pf green	1.00	*2.00*
		Never hinged	1.90	
		On cover		9.50
		On cover, single franking		11.00
9	A3	10pf carmine	1.00	*4.75*
		Never hinged	2.25	
		On cover		16.00
		On cover, single franking		22.50
a.		Half used as 5pf on cover, back-stamped in Jaluit ('05)		*110.00*
10	A3	20pf ultra	1.25	*8.50*
		Never hinged	3.50	
		On cover		30.00
		On cover, single franking		40.00
a.		Half used as 10pf on cover ('10)		*8,500.*
11	A3	25pf org & blk, *yel*	1.50	*14.00*
		Never hinged	3.75	
		On cover		65.00
		On cover, single franking		140.00
12	A3	30pf org & blk, *sal*	1.50	*14.00*
		Never hinged	3.75	
		On cover		70.00
		On cover, single franking		90.00
13	A3	40pf lake & blk	1.50	*16.00*
		Never hinged	3.75	
		On cover		75.00
		On cover, single franking		100.00
14	A3	50pf pur & blk, *sal*	2.00	*21.00*
		Never hinged	4.50	
		On cover		45.00
		On cover, single franking		50.00
15	A3	80pf lake & blk, *rose*	3.00	*25.00*
		Never hinged	6.00	
		On cover		55.00
		On cover, single franking		65.00

Engr. ***Perf. 14½x14***

16	A4	1m carmine	4.00	*60.00*
		Never hinged	10.00	
		On cover		110.00
		On cover, single franking		120.00
17	A4	2m blue	6.00	*75.00*
		Never hinged	17.00	
		On cover		120.00
		On cover, single franking		140.00
18	A4	3m black violet	9.00	*150.00*
		Never hinged	27.00	
		On cover		275.00
		On cover, single franking		300.00
19	A4	5m slate & carmine	150.00	550.00
		Never hinged	450.00	
		On cover		875.00
		On cover, single franking		1,100.
		Nos. 7-19 (13)	182.75	942.00

No. 9a is known as the "typhoon provisional" the stock of 5pf stamps having been destroyed during a typhoon. Covers (cards) without backstamp, value about $72.50.

Forged cancellations are found on #7-19.

Covers: Values for Nos. 14-19 are for overfranked complete envelopes, usually philatelic.

No. 7 Handstamp Surcharged **5 Pf**

1910, July 12

20	A3	5pf on 3pf brown		*5,500.*
a.		Inverted surcharge		*7,750.*
b.		Double surcharge		*11,000.*

Values are for stamps tied to cover. Stamps on piece sell for about 40% less.

1915-19 Wmk. 125 Typo.

21	A3	3pf brown ('19)	.85	
		Never hinged	1.90	
22	A3	5pf green	12.00	
		Never hinged	29.00	

Engr.

23	A4	5m slate & carmine (25x17 holes)	32.50	
		Never hinged	105.00	
a.		26x17 holes	32.50	
		Never hinged	170.00	
		Nos. 21-23 (3)	45.35	

Nos. 21-23 were not placed in use.

CASTELLORIZO

ˌkäs-tə-ˈlor-ə-ˌzō

(Castelrosso)

LOCATION — A Mediterranean island in the Dodecanese group lying close to the coast of Asia Minor and about 60 miles east of Rhodes.
GOVT. — Italian Colony
AREA — 4 sq. mi.
POP. — 2,238 (1936)

Formerly a Turkish possession, Castellorizo was occupied by the French in 1915 & ceded to Italy after World War I.

25 Centimes = 1 Piaster
100 Centimes = 1 Franc

Issued under French Occupation

Stamps of French Offices in Turkey Overprinted

1920 Unwmk. *Perf. 14x13½*

1 A2 1c gray 32.50 27.50
a. Inverted overprint 95.00 95.00
b. Double overprint 110.00 110.00
2 A2 2c vio brn 32.50 27.50
3 A2 3c red org 32.50 27.50
a. Inverted overprint 95.00 95.00
4 A2 5c green 37.50 32.50
a. Inverted overprint 95.00 95.00
5 A3 10c rose 40.00 40.00
On cover 675.00
6 A3 15c pale red 57.50 57.50
On cover 675.00
a. Inverted overprint 175.00 175.00
7 A3 20c brn vio 65.00 65.00
8 A5 1pi on 25c blue 65.00 65.00
On cover 675.00
a. Pair, one without overprint 240.00
9 A3 30c lilac 72.50 72.50

Overprint Reading Down

10 A4 40c red & pale bl (down) 125.00 125.00
a. Inverted ovpt (reading up) 500.00 500.00
11 A6 2pi on 50c bis brn & lav (down) 140.00 140.00
a. Inverted ovpt (reading up) 500.00 500.00
12 A6 4pi on 1fr cl & ol grn (down) 190.00 190.00
a. Double overprint 575.00 575.00
b. Inverted ovpt (reading up) 575.00 575.00
13 A6 20pi on 5fr dk bl & buff 525.00 500.00
a. Double overprint 1,050. *1,050.*
Nos. 1-13 (13) 1,415. 1,370.

No. 1-9 were overprinted in blocks of 25. Position 4 had "CASTELLÓRIZO" inverted and Positions 8 and 18 had "CASTELLORISO." The later variety also occurred in the setting of the form for Nos. 10-13.

"B. N. F." are the initials of "Base Navale Francaise".

Covers: Values for covers are for commercial items. Philatelic covers sell for less.

Overprinted in Black or Red

1920

On Stamps of French Offices in Turkey

14 A2 1c gray 18.00 18.00
15 A2 2c vio brn 18.00 18.00
16 A2 3c red org 19.00 19.00
17 A2 5c green (R) 19.00 19.00
19 A3 10c rose 20.00 20.00
On cover 675.00
20 A3 15c pale red 30.00 30.00
21 A3 20c brn vio 47.50 47.50
22 A5 1pi on 25c bl (R) 47.50 47.50
On cover 675.00
23 A3 30c lilac (R) 47.50 47.50
24 A4 40c red & pale bl 47.50 47.50
25 A6 2pi on 50c bis brn & lav 47.50 47.50
On cover 675.00
26 A6 4pi on 1fr claret & ol grn 55.00 55.00
28 A6 20pi on 5fr dk bl & buff 260.00 260.00
Nos. 14-28 (13) 676.50 676.50

On Nos. 25, 26 and 28 the two lines of the overprint are set wider apart than on the lower values.

"O.N.F." are the initials of "Occupation Navale Francaise."

"Casetllorizo" and "astellorizo" varieties are known on Nos. 14-23.

Overprint on 8pi on 2fr (#37), value $900 unused, $1,000 used.

Covers: Values for covers are for commercial items. Philatelic covers sell for less.

On Stamps of France

30 A22 10c red 30.00 17.50
a. Inverted overprint 150.00
31 A22 25c blue (R) 30.00 16.00
a. Inverted overprint 175.00

This overprint exists on 8 other 1900-1907 denominations of France (5c, 15c, 20c, 30c, 40c, 50c, 1fr, 5fr). These are believed not to have been issued or postally used.

Stamps of France, 1900-1907, Handstamped in Black or Violet

1920

33 A22 5c green 125.00 125.00
On cover *1,400.*
34 A22 10c red 125.00 125.00
On cover *1,400.*
35 A22 20c vio brn 125.00 125.00
36 A22 25c blue 125.00 125.00
On cover *1,400.*
37 A18 50c bis brn & lav 800.00 800.00
On cover *2,000.*
38 A18 1fr cl & ol grn (V) 800.00 800.00
Nos. 33-38 (6) 2,100. 2,100.

Nos. 1-38 are considered speculative.

Forgeries of overprints on Nos. 1-38 exist. They abound of Nos. 33-38.

Stamps of French Offices in Turkey handstamped "Occupation Francaise Castellorizo" were made privately.

Covers: Values for covers are for commercial items. Philatelic covers sell for less.

Issued under Italian Dominion

100 Centesimi = 1 Lira

Italian Stamps of 1906-20 Overprinted

1922 Wmk. 140 *Perf. 14*

51 A48 5c green 3.75 *19.00*
Never hinged 9.50
On cover 140.00
52 A48 10c claret 2.25 *19.00*
Never hinged 5.75
On cover 120.00
53 A48 15c slate 3.00 *19.00*
Never hinged 7.50
On cover 175.00
54 A50 20c brn org 2.25 *19.00*
Never hinged 5.75
On cover 120.00
a. Double overprint 275.00
55 A49 25c blue 2.25 *19.00*
Never hinged 5.75
On cover 140.00
56 A49 40c brown 37.50 22.50
Never hinged 95.00
On cover 190.00
57 A49 50c violet 37.50 22.50
Never hinged 95.00
On cover 200.00
58 A49 60c carmine 37.50 35.00
Never hinged 95.00
On cover 325.00
59 A49 85c chocolate 4.50 *40.00*
Never hinged 11.25
On cover 400.00
Nos. 51-59 (9) 130.50 *215.00*
Set, never hinged 325.00
Complete set, on over-franked cover 375.00

Map of Castellorizo; Flag of Italy — A1

1923

60 A1 5c gray green 3.00 *18.00*
Never hinged 7.50
On cover 340.00
61 A1 10c dull rose 3.00 *18.00*
Never hinged 7.50
On cover 340.00
62 A1 25c dull blue 3.00 *18.00*
Never hinged 7.50
On cover 300.00
63 A1 50c gray lilac 3.00 *18.00*
Never hinged 7.50
On cover 300.00
64 A1 1 l brown 3.00 *18.00*
Never hinged 7.50
On cover 450.00
Nos. 60-64 (5) 15.00 *90.00*
Set, never hinged 37.50
Complete set, on over-franked cover 425.00

Italian Stamps of 1901-20 Overprinted

1924

65 A48 5c green 1.50 *24.00*
Never hinged 3.75
On cover 225.00
66 A48 10c claret 1.50 *24.00*
Never hinged 3.75
On cover 120.00
67 A48 15c slate 1.50 *30.00*
Never hinged 3.75
On cover 190.00
68 A50 20c brn orange 1.50 *30.00*
Never hinged 3.75
On cover 190.00
a. Double overprint 100.00
69 A49 25c blue 1.50 *24.00*
Never hinged 3.75
On cover 175.00
70 A49 40c brown 1.50 *24.00*
Never hinged 3.75
On cover 190.00
71 A49 50c violet 1.50 *30.00*
Never hinged 3.75
On cover 175.00
72 A49 60c carmine 1.50 *37.50*
Never hinged 3.75
On cover 265.00
a. Double overprint 300.00
73 A49 85c red brown 1.50 *45.00*
Never hinged 3.75
On cover 450.00
74 A46 1 l brn & green 1.50 *45.00*
Never hinged 3.75
On cover 525.00
Nos. 65-74 (10) 15.00 *313.50*
Set, never hinged 37.50
Complete set, on over-franked cover 600.00

Ferrucci Issue

Types of Italian Stamps of 1930, Overprinted in Red or Blue

1930 Wmk. Crowns (140)

75 A102 20c violet 6.00 *6.00*
Never hinged 15.00
On cover 140.00
76 A103 25c dark green 6.00 *15.00*
Never hinged 15.00
On cover 175.00
77 A103 50c black 6.00 *6.00*
Never hinged 15.00
On cover 125.00
78 A103 1.25 l deep blue 6.00 *15.00*
Never hinged 15.00
On cover 265.00
79 A104 5 l + 2 l dp car (Bl) 22.50 *52.50*
Never hinged 55.00
On cover —
Nos. 75-79 (5) 46.50 *94.50*
Set, never hinged 115.00
Complete set, on over-franked cover 225.00

Garibaldi Issue

Types of Italian Stamps of 1932, Overprinted like Nos. 75-79 in Red or Blue

1932

80 A138 10c brown 22.50 *45.00*
Never hinged 55.00
On cover 190.00
81 A138 20c red brn (Bl) 22.50 *45.00*
Never hinged 55.00
On cover 140.00
82 A138 25c dp grn 22.50 *45.00*
Never hinged 55.00
On cover 175.00
83 A138 30c bluish slate 22.50 *45.00*
Never hinged 55.00
On cover 190.00
84 A138 50c red vio (Bl) 22.50 *45.00*
Never hinged 55.00
On cover 140.00
85 A141 75c cop red (Bl) 22.50 *45.00*
Never hinged 55.00
On cover 265.00
86 A141 1.25 l dull blue 22.50 *45.00*
Never hinged 55.00
On cover 375.00
87 A141 1.75 l + 25c brn 22.50 *45.00*
Never hinged 55.00
On cover —
88 A144 2.55 l + 50c org (Bl) 22.50 *45.00*
Never hinged 55.00
On cover —
89 A145 5 l + 1 l dl vio 22.50 *45.00*
Never hinged 55.00
On cover —
Nos. 80-89 (10) 225.00 *450.00*
Set, never hinged 550.00
Complete set, on over-franked cover 700.00

CAYMAN ISLANDS

ˌkā-ˈman ˈī-lənds

LOCATION — Three islands in the Caribbean Sea, about 200 miles northwest of Jamaica
GOVT. — Dependency of Jamaica
AREA — 100 sq. mi.
POP. — 18,285 (1982)
CAPITAL — George Town, located on Grand Cayman

12 Pence = 1 Shilling
20 Shilling = 1 Pound

STAMPS OF JAMAICA USED IN CAYMAN ISLANDS

Georgetown, Grand Cayman

Stamps of Jamaica canceled in purple with large double oval "GRAND CAYMAN * POST OFFICE" with date in center.

1889-94

A1 ½p gray green (#16a) 600.
A2 1p lilac & red vio (#24) 600.
A3 2p slate (#20) 5,500.
A4 2p green (#25) 1,050.
A5 2½p lilac & ultra (#26) 1,275.
A6 4p orange brown (#22a) 3,250.

Official Stamps

A7 ½p green, type II, OFFICIAL 17 to 17½mm (#O1) 1,400.
a. 1/2p green, type I, OFFICIAL 16mm (#O1a) 3,250.
A8 1p carmine rose (#O3) 1,400.
A9 2p slate (#O4) 4,250.

Stamps of Jamaica Canceled in purple or black with Single Circle Datestamp "GRAND CAYMAN/P.O." with date in center on two lines

1895-98

A10 ½p gray green (#16a) 700.
A11 1p lilac & red vio (#24) 550.
A12 2½p lilac & ultra (#26) 950.
A13 3p olive green (#21) 4,500.

Official Stamps

A14 ½p green, type I (#O1a) 2,750.
A15 1p carmine rose (#O3) 4,400.
A16 2p slate (#O4) 4,500.

Stamps of Jamaica Canceled with Double Circle Datestamp "GRAND CAYMAN * CAYMAN ISLANDS" with date in center on two lines

1898-1901

A17 ½p blue green (#16) 550.
a. 1/2p gray green (#16a) 550.
A18 1p lilac & red violet (#24) 550.
A19 1p red (#31) 600.
A20 2½p lilac & ultra (#26) 825.

Stake Bay, Cayman Brac

Stamps of Jamaica Canceled with Rectangular Postmark: "CAYMAN BRAC/CAYMAN ISLANDS"

1898-1900

A21 ½p gray green (#16a) 3,500.
A22 1p lilac & red vio (#24) 3,750.
A23 2p green (#25) 4,750.
A24 2½p lilac & ultra (#26) 3,750.

Stamps of Jamaica Canceled with Double Circle Datestamp "CAYMAN BRAC * CAYMAN ISLANDS" with date in center in two lines

1900-01

A25	½p gray green (#16a)	3,750.	
A26	1p lilac & red violet (#24)	3,500.	
A27	1p red (#31)	3,500.	
A28	2½p lilac & ultra (#26)	3,000.	

Catalogue values for unused stamps in this country are for Never Hinged items, beginning with Scott 112.

Victoria
A1

Edward VII
A2

1900 Typo. Wmk. 2 *Perf. 14*

1	A1	½p pale green	7.00	*17.00*
a.		½p green to deep green	14.00	*22.50*
2	A1	1p carmine rose	7.00	2.50
a.		1p carmine	15.00	14.00
		Set, Ovptd. "SPECIMEN"	150.00	

1901-03

3	A2	½p green ('02)	5.25	*29.00*
4	A2	1p car rose ('03)	11.50	*10.50*
5	A2	2½p ultramarine	11.50	*13.00*
6	A2	6p chocolate	32.50	*70.00*
7	A2	1sh brown orange	70.00	*125.00*
		Nos. 3-7 (5)	130.75	*247.50*
		Set, Ovptd. "SPECIMEN"	225.00	

1905 Wmk. 3

8	A2	½p green	8.00	*10.50*
9	A2	1p carmine rose	16.00	*20.00*
10	A2	2½p ultramarine	8.00	3.75
11	A2	6p chocolate	19.00	*45.00*
12	A2	1sh brown orange	37.50	*55.00*
		Nos. 8-12 (5)	88.50	*134.25*

For surcharge see No. 17.

1907, Mar. 13

13	A2	4p brown & blue	37.50	*70.00*
14	A2	6p ol green & rose	37.50	*80.00*
15	A2	1sh violet & green	65.00	*95.00*
16	A2	5sh ver & green	210.00	*350.00*
		Nos. 13-16 (4)	350.00	*595.00*
		Set, Ovptd. "SPECIMEN"	240.00	

Numerals of 4p, 1sh and 5sh of type A2 are in color on colorless tablet.

For surcharges see Nos. 18-20.

Nos. 9, 16, 13 Handstamped

No. 17

No. 18

No. 19

No. 20

1907-08

17	A2	½p on 1p	52.50	*87.50*
18	A2	½p on 5sh	300.00	*450.00*
a.		Inverted surcharge	*45,000.*	
b.		Double surcharge	*12,750.*	*12,750.*
c.		Double surcharge, one inverted		
d.		Pair, one without surcharge	*65,000.*	
19	A2	1p on 5sh	300.00	*400.00*
a.		Double surcharge	*21,000.*	*7,500.*
20	A2	2½p on 4p ('08)	1,800.	*3,250.*
a.		Double surcharge	*37,500.*	*24,000.*

The 1p on 4p is a revenue stamp not authorized for postal use, although postally used examples exist. Value for unused is about $300. Varieties exist: surcharge inverted $1,750, double $2,750, double, both inverted $2,750.

A3

A4

1907-09 *Perf. 14*

21	A3	½p green	2.75	*4.75*
22	A3	1p carmine rose	1.75	.85
23	A3	2½p ultramarine	4.00	4.00

Chalky Paper

24	A3	3p violet, *yellow*	3.75	*7.50*
25	A3	4p blk & red, *yel*	57.50	*80.00*
26	A3	6p purple & br pur	11.50	*40.00*
a.		6p purple & violet purple	37.50	*65.00*
27	A3	1sh black, *grn*	9.50	*25.00*
28	A3	5sh grn & red, *yel*	45.00	*70.00*
		Nos. 21-28 (8)	135.75	*232.10*

Issued: ½p, 1p, 12/27/07; 2½p, 3p, 4p, 5sh, 3/30/08; 6d, 10/2/08; 1sh, 4/5/09.

Forged cancellations are found on No. 28.

1908, Mar. 30 Wmk. 2

29	A3	1sh black, *green*	70.00	*100.00*
30	A3	10sh grn & red, *grn*	190.00	*260.00*
		Set of 9, #21-26, 28-30, Ovptd. "SPECIMEN"	375.00	

Numerals of 3p, 4p, 1sh and 5sh of type A3 are in color on plain tablet.

Forged cancellations are found on No. 30.

1908 Wmk. 3

Ordinary Paper

31	A4	¼p brown	2.10	.55
a.		¼p gray brown ('09)	4.00	1.10
		Ovpted "SPECIMEN"	100.00	

King George V
A5 A6

1912-20

32	A5	¼p brown ('13)	1.25	.50
33	A5	½p green	3.00	*6.00*
34	A5	1p carmine ('13)	3.50	2.75
35	A5	2p gray	1.10	*17.00*
36	A5	2½p ultra ('14)	8.50	*13.50*
a.		2½p deep bright blue ('17)	21.00	*29.00*

Chalky Paper

37	A5	3p vio, *yel* ('13)	2.75	*20.00*
a.		3p purple, *yellow* ('14)	17.50	*45.00*
b.		3p purple, *pale yellow* ('20)	4.00	*35.00*
c.		3p purple, *orange buff* ('20)	11.50	*35.00*
d.		3p purple, *buff* ('14)	—	—
38	A5	4p blk & red, *yel* ('13)	1.10	*11.00*
39	A5	6p vio & red vio ('13)	4.50	*9.00*
40	A5	1sh blk, *grn* ('13)	4.25	*27.50*
		Ovpted "SPECIMEN"	75.00	
41	A5	2sh vio & ultra, *bl*	14.50	*57.50*
42	A5	3sh green & vio	22.50	*77.50*
43	A5	5sh grn & red, *yel* ('14)	90.00	*190.00*
44	A5	10sh grn & red, *bl grn, olive back* ('18)	90.00	*160.00*
a.		10sh green & red, *grn* ('13)	125.00	*225.00*
		Ovpted "SPECIMEN"	110.00	
		Nos. 32-44 (13)	246.95	*592.25*

The first printings of the 3p, 1sh and 10sh have a white back.

For surcharges, see Nos. MR1-MR7.

1913, Nov. 19

Surface-colored Paper

45	A5	3p violet, *yel*	3.75	*9.50*
46	A5	1sh black, *green*	3.75	*4.00*
47	A5	10sh grn & red, *grn*	92.50	*160.00*
		Nos. 45-47 (3)	100.00	*173.50*
		Set, ovptd. "SPECIMEN"	100.00	

Numeral of ¼p, 2p, 3p, 4p, 1sh, 2sh, 3sh and 5sh of type A5 are in color on plain tablet.

1921-26 Wmk. 4 *Perf. 14*

50	A6	¼p yel brown ('22)	.55	*1.75*
51	A6	½p gray green ('22)	.55	.35
52	A6	1p rose red ('22)	1.50	*.90*
53	A6	1½p orange brn	1.90	.35
54	A6	2p gray ('22)	1.90	*4.75*
55	A6	2½p ultramarine ('22)	.60	*.60*
56	A6	3p violet, *yel* ('23)	1.25	*4.75*
57	A6	4½p olive grn ('23)	2.50	*3.25*
58	A6	6p claret ('22)	6.50	*37.50*
a.		6p deep claret	21.00	*45.00*
59	A6	1sh black, *grn* ('25)	11.50	*37.50*
60	A6	2sh violet, *blue* ('22)	17.00	*29.00*
61	A6	3sh violet ('22)	27.50	19.00
62	A6	5sh green, *yel* ('25)	29.00	*55.00*
63	A6	10sh car, *green* ('26)	72.50	*90.00*
		Nos. 50-63 (14)	174.75	*284.70*
		Set, ovptd. "SPECIMEN"	400.00	

Issued: 1½p, 4/4/21; ¼p, ½p, 1p, 2p, 2½p, 6p, 2sh, 3sh, 4/1/22; 3p, 4½p, 6/29/23; 5sh, 2/15/25; 1sh, 5/15/25; 10sh, 9/5/26.

1921-22 Wmk. 3

64	A6	3p violet, *org*	1.75	*9.50*
65	A6	4p red, *yel*	1.10	*4.75*
66	A6	1sh black, *green*	1.50	*11.50*
67	A6	5sh green, *yel*	19.00	*85.00*
68	A6	10sh car, *green*	72.50	*110.00*
		Nos. 64-68 (5)	95.85	*220.75*
		Set, ovptd. "SPECIMEN"	225.00	

Issued: 4p, 4/1/22; others, 4/4/21.

King William IV, King George V
A7

Perf. 12½

1932, Dec. 5 Wmk. 4 Engr.

69	A7	¼p brown	1.60	1.10
70	A7	½p green	3.00	*9.50*
71	A7	1p carmine	3.00	*9.50*
72	A7	1½p orange	3.00	3.00
73	A7	2p gray	3.00	*3.75*
74	A7	2½p ultramarine	3.00	1.75
75	A7	3p olive green	3.25	*6.00*
76	A7	6p red violet	11.50	*27.50*
77	A7	1sh brn & black	20.00	*37.50*
78	A7	2sh ultra & blk	55.00	*90.00*
79	A7	5sh green & blk	100.00	*140.00*
80	A7	10sh car & black	350.00	*375.00*
		Nos. 69-80 (12)	556.35	*704.60*
		Set, Perf "SPECIMEN"	575.00	

Centenary of the formation of the Cayman Islands Assembly.

Common Design Types pictured following the introduction.

Silver Jubilee Issue

Common Design Type

1935, May 6 *Perf. 13½x14*

81	CD301	½p green & black	.25	*1.25*
82	CD301	2½p blue & brown	1.25	*1.25*
83	CD301	6p ol grn & lt bl	1.25	*4.00*
84	CD301	1sh brt vio & ind	8.50	8.25
		Nos. 81-84 (4)	11.25	14.75
		Set, Perf "SPECIMEN"	150.00	

King George V
A8

Catboat
A9

Red-footed Boobies
A10

Conches and Coconut Palms — A11

Hawksbill Turtles
A12

1935-36 *Perf. 12½*

85	A8	¼p brown & blk	.55	*1.10*
86	A9	½p yel grn & ultra	1.10	*1.10*
87	A10	1p car & ultra	4.25	3.00
88	A11	1½p org & black	1.75	*2.40*
89	A9	2p brown vio & ultra	4.50	1.50
90	A12	2½p dp blue & blk	3.50	1.60
91	A8	3p ol grn & blk	2.75	*3.75*
92	A12	6p red vio & blk	9.25	6.00
93	A9	1sh org & ultra	7.25	*9.25*
94	A10	2sh black & ultra	50.00	50.00
95	A12	5sh green & blk	60.00	70.00
96	A11	10sh car & black	110.00	*125.00*
		Nos. 85-96 (12)	254.90	274.70
		Set, never hinged	450.00	
		Set, perf "SPECIMEN"	300.00	

Issued: #86, 2½p, 6p, 1sh, 1/1/36; others, 5/1/35.

Coronation Issue

Common Design Type

1937, May 13 *Perf. 11x11½*

97	CD302	½p deep green	.20	*1.50*
98	CD302	1p dark carmine	.25	.25
99	CD302	2½p deep ultra	.55	.55
		Nos. 97-99 (3)	1.00	2.30
		Set, never hinged	2.00	
		Set, Perf "SPECIMEN"	72.50	

Beach View, Grand Cayman
A13

Dolphin — A14

Hawksbill Turtles — A16

Map of the Islands
A15

Cayman Schooner
A17

Perf. 12½; 11½x13 or 13x11½ (A14, #111); 14 (#104, 107)

1938-43 Engr.

100	A13	¼p red orange	.35	*.60*
a.		Perf. 13½x12½ ('43)	.20	*.70*
101	A14	½p yel green	.50	*.60*
a.		Perf. 14 ('43)	.65	*1.50*

102 A15	1p carmine	.20	*.80*
103 A13	1½p black	.20	.20
104 A16	2p dp violet ('43)	.35	.30
a.	Perf. 11½x13	1.75	.45
105 A17	2½p ultra	.25	.20
106 A15	3p orange	.25	.20
107 A16	6p dk ol grn ('43)	1.40	1.40
a.	Perf. 11½x13	6.00	4.25
108 A14	1sh reddish brown	3.50	1.60
a.	Perf. 14 ('43)	2.50	2.10
109 A13	2sh green	26.00	15.00
110 A17	5sh deep rose	17.50	16.00
111 A16	10sh dark brown	12.50	9.75
a.	Perf. 14 ('43)	12.50	9.75
	Nos. 100-111 (12)	63.00	46.65
	Set, never hinged	135.00	
	Set of 14, #100-111, 114-115, Perf "SPECIMEN"	300.00	
	Set, Perf "SPECIMEN," Never hinged	400.00	

See Nos. 114-115.

Catalogue values for unused stamps in this section, from this point to the end of the section, are for Never Hinged items.

Peace Issue
Common Design Type

1946, Aug. 26 Wmk. 4 *Perf. 13½*

112 CD303 1½p black	.25	.20
113 CD303 3p orange	.25	.20
Set, ovptd. "SPECIMEN"	92.50	

Types of 1938

1947, Aug. 25 *Perf. 12½*

114 A17 2½p orange	3.50	.65
115 A15 3p ultramarine	3.50	.45

Silver Wedding Issue
Common Design Types

1948, Nov. 29 Photo. *Perf. 14x14½*

116 CD304 ½p dark green .20 .65

Perf. 11½x11

Engr.; Name Typo.

117 CD305 10sh blue violet 17.50 17.50

UPU Issue
Common Design Types

Engr.; Name Typo. on #119, 120

1949, Oct. 10 *Perf. 13½, 11x11½*

118 CD306 2½p orange	.30	*.70*
119 CD307 3p indigo	1.75	*2.00*
120 CD308 6p olive	.70	*2.00*
121 CD309 1sh red brown	.70	.40
Nos. 118-121 (4)	3.45	5.10

Catboat A18

Designs: ½p, Coconut grove. 1p, Green turtle. 1½p, Thatch rope industry. 2p, Caymanian seamen. 2½p, Map. 3p, Parrot fish. 6p, Bluff, Cayman Brac. 9p, George Town harbor. 1sh, Turtle "crawl". 2sh, Cayman schooner. 5sh, Boat-building. 10sh, Government offices.

Perf. 11½x11

1950, Oct. 2 Wmk. 4 Engr.

122 A18	¼p rose red & blue	.20	*.65*
123 A18	½p bl grn & red violet	.20	*1.50*
124 A18	1p dp blue & olive	.60	*.80*
125 A18	1½p choc & bl grn	.35	*.80*
126 A18	2p rose car & vio	1.40	*1.60*
127 A18	2½p sepia & aqua	1.40	.70
128 A18	3p bl & blue grn	1.75	1.60
129 A18	6p dp bl & org brn	2.10	1.50
130 A18	9p dk grn & rose red	8.50	2.10
131 A18	1sh red org & brn	3.75	3.00
132 A18	2sh red vio & vio	9.50	*12.00*
133 A18	5sh vio & olive	14.00	7.75
134 A18	10sh rose red & blk	19.00	16.00
	Nos. 122-134 (13)	62.75	50.00

WAR TAX STAMPS

No. 36 Surcharged:

a

b

1917, Feb. 26 Wmk. 3 *Perf. 14*

MR1 A5(a)	1½p on 2½p	11.00	*13.50*
a.	Fraction bar omitted	150.00	*210.00*
MR2 A5(b)	1½p on 2½p	2.10	*7.25*
a.	Fraction bar omitted	85.00	*150.00*

No. 1 exists with missing period. On No. 1 the distance between "WAR STAMP" and "1½" varies.

Surcharged

1917, Sept. 4

MR3 A5 1½p on 2½p ultra 900.00 *2,250.*

Surcharged

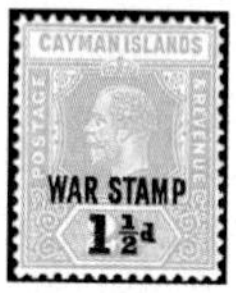

1917, Sept. 4

MR4 A5 1½p on 2½p ultra	.30	*.65*
a. Ovpted "SPECIMEN"	140.00	

No. 33 Overprinted

1919, Feb. 4

MR5 A5 ½p green .70 *3.00*

The "brownish paper" variety comes from the interleaving used for shipment from England.

Type of 1912-16 Surcharged

1919, Feb. 4

MR6 A5 1½p on 2½p orange .95 *1.50*

No. 35 Surcharged

1920, Mar. 10

MR7 A5 1½p on 2p gray 1.75 *8.50*

The "rose-tinted paper" variety comes from the interleaving used for shipment from England.

A surcharge in red was not issued.

CENTRAL LITHUANIA

ˈsen-trəl ˌli-thə-ˈwā-nē-ə

LOCATION — North of Poland and east of Lithuania

CAPITAL — Vilnius

At one time Central Lithuania was a grand duchy of Lithuania but at the end of the 18th Century it fell under Russian rule. After World War I, Lithuania regained her sovereignty but certain areas were occupied by Poland. During the Russo-Polish war this territory was seized by Lithuania whose claim was promptly recognized by the Soviet Government. Under the leadership of the Polish General Zeligowski the territory was recaptured and it was during this occupation the stamps of Central Lithuania came into being. Subsequently the territory became a part of Poland.

100 Fennigi = 1 Markka

Coat of Arms — A1

Perf. 11½, Imperf.

1920-21 Typo. Unwmk.

1	A1 25f red	.30	*.50*
2	A1 25f dark grn ('21)	.30	*.50*
3	A1 1m blue	.30	*.50*
4	A1 1m dark brn ('21)	.30	*.50*
5	A1 2m violet	.30	*.50*
6	A1 2m orange ('21)	.30	*.50*
	Nos. 1-6 (6)	1.80	*3.00*

For surcharges see Nos. B1-B5.

Lithuanian Stamps of 1919 Surcharged in Blue or Black

Perf. 11½x12, 12½x11½, 14

1920, Nov. 23 Wmk. 145

13 A5	2m on 15sk lil	12.50	*30.00*
a.	Inverted surcharge	*125.00*	
14 A5	4m on 10sk red	17.50	*25.00*
a.	Inverted surcharge	*125.00*	
15 A5	4m on 20sk dl bl (Bk)	17.50	*25.00*
a.	Inverted surcharge	*125.00*	
16 A5	4m on 30sk buff	12.00	*20.00*
a.	Inverted surcharge	*125.00*	
17 A6	6m on 50sk lt grn	12.00	*20.00*
a.	4m on 50sk (error)	*125.00*	
b.	10m on 50sk (error)	*125.00*	
c.	Surcharge inverted		—
18 A6	6m on 60sk vio & red	22.50	*40.00*
a.	4m on 60sk (error)	*125.00*	
b.	10m on 60sk (error)	*125.00*	
19 A6	6m on 75sk bis & red	22.50	*40.00*
a.	4m on 75sk (error)	*125.00*	
b.	10m on 75sk (error)	*125.00*	
20 A8	10m on 1auk gray & red	20.00	35.00
a.	Inverted surcharge	*190.00*	
21 A8	10m on 3auk lt brn & red	*475.00*	*800.00*
22 A8	10m on 5auk bl grn & red	*450.00*	*800.00*
	Nos. 13-20 (8)	136.50	*235.00*
	Nos. 13-22 (10)	*1,061.*	*1,835.*

The overprint on Nos. 17-19 is down-reading, i.e., the top of the overprint is at the right of the original design, the bottom at the left. The inverted overprint on No. 17c is up-reading.

Reprints of Nos. 17a, 17b, 18a, 18b, 19a, 19b. Value, each $45.

Counterfeits of Nos. 21-22 exist.

Lithuanian Girl — A2

Warrior — A3

Holy Gate of Vilnius — A4

Tower and Cathedral, Vilnius — A5

Rector's Insignia — A6

Gen. Lucien Zeligowski — A7

Perf. 11½, Imperf.

1920 Litho. Unwmk.

23	A2 25f gray	.20	*.75*
24	A3 1m orange	.20	*.75*
25	A4 2m claret	.30	*1.00*
26	A5 4m gray grn & buff	.70	*1.00*
27	A6 6m rose & gray	1.75	*1.00*
28	A7 10m brown & yellow	2.50	*3.25*
	Nos. 23-28 (6)	5.65	*7.75*

For surcharges see Nos. B13-B14, B17-B19.

St. Anne's Church, Vilnius — A8

St. Stanislas Cathedral, Vilnius — A9

White Eagle, White Knight Vytis — A10

Queen Hedwig and King Ladislas II Jagello — A11

Coat of Arms of Vilnius — A12

Poczobut Astronomical Observatory A13

Union of Lithuania and Poland — A14

Tadeusz Kosciuszko and Adam Mickiewicz A15

1921 *Perf. 14, Imperf.*

35	A8	1m dk gray & yel	.50	*1.00*
36	A9	2m rose & green	.50	*1.00*
37	A10	3m dark green	.60	*1.25*
38	A11	4m brown & buff	.60	*1.25*
39	A12	5m red brown	.60	*1.25*
40	A13	6m slate & buff	.60	*2.50*
41	A14	10m red vio & buff	1.50	*2.50*
42	A15	20m blk brn & buff	1.50	*2.50*
		Nos. 35-42 (8)	6.40	*13.25*

Set, perf. 13½, $150.

Peasant Girl Sowing — A16

White Eagle and Vytis — A17

Great Theater at Vilnius — A18

Allegory: Peace and Industry — A19

Gen. Zeligowski Entering Vilnius — A20

Gen. Zeligowski — A21

1921-22 *Perf. 11½, Imperf.*

53	A16	10m brown ('22)	6.00	*10.00*
54	A17	25m red & yel ('22)	7.50	*15.00*
55	A18	50m dk blue ('22)	6.00	*10.00*
56	A19	75m violet ('22)	6.00	*10.00*
57	A20	100m bl & bister	2.50	*5.75*
58	A21	150m ol grn & brn	2.50	*5.75*
		Nos. 53-58 (6)	30.50	*56.50*

Opening of the Natl. Parliament, Nos. 53-56; anniv. of the entry of General Zeligowski into Vilnius, Nos. 57-58.

SEMI-POSTAL STAMPS

Nos. 1-6 Surcharged in Black or Red

1921 **Unwmk.** *Perf. 11½, Imperf.*

B1	A1	25f + 2m red (Bk)	.50	*1.00*
B2	A1	25f + 2m dk green	.50	*1.00*
B3	A1	1m + 2m blue	1.50	*3.00*
B4	A1	1m + 2m dk brown	1.50	*3.00*
B5	A1	2m + 2m violet	1.00	*2.00*
B6	A1	2m + 2m orange	1.00	*2.50*
		Nos. B1-B6 (6)	6.00	*12.50*

The surcharge means "For Silesia 2 marks." The stamps were intended to provide a fund to assist the plebiscite in Upper Silesia.

Nos. 25, 26 Surcharged:

a

b

Perf. 11½, Imperf.

B13	A4 (a)	2m + 1(m) claret	2.75	10.00
B14	A5 (b)	4m + 1m gray green & buff	2.75	10.00

Nos. 25-26, 28 with inset

Perf. 11½, Imperf.

B17	A4	2m + 1m claret	.50	2.50
B18	A5	4m + 1m gray green & buff	.50	2.00
B19	A7	10m + 2m brn & yel	.90	3.75
		Nos. B13-B19 (5)	7.40	*28.25*

POSTAGE DUE STAMPS

University, Vilnius D1

Castle Hill, Vilnius D2

Castle Ruins, Troki — D3

Holy Gate, Vilnius — D4

St. Stanislas Cathedral D5

St. Anne's Church, Vilnius D6

1920-21 **Unwmk.** *Perf. 11½, Imperf.*

J1	D1	50f red violet	.35	*.60*
J2	D2	1m green	.35	*.60*
J3	D3	2m red violet	.45	*.60*
J4	D4	3m red violet	.65	*1.25*
J5	D5	5m red violet	.95	*2.50*
J6	D6	20m scarlet	2.25	*4.00*
		Nos. J1-J6 (6)	5.00	*9.55*

CEYLON

si-'län

LOCATION — An island in the Indian Ocean separated from India by the Gulf of Manaar

GOVT. — British Colony

AREA — 25,332 sq. mi.

POP. — 12,670,000 (est. 1971)

CAPITAL — Colombo

12 Pence = 1 Shilling
100 Cents = 1 Rupee (1872)

Values for unused stamps are for examples with original gum as defined in the catalogue introduction except for Nos. 2, 5, 8-9 which seldom have any remaining trace of their original gum. Many unused stamps of Ceylon, especially between Nos. 59 and 274, have toned gum or tropical stains. Values quoted are for stamps with fresh gum. Toned stamps have lower values, and common stamps with toned gum are worth very little.

Very fine examples of Nos. 1-15 will be cut square, will have small margins, but will show an intact design. Inferior examples with the design partly cut away will sell for much less, and examples with large margins will command higher prices. Very fine examples of Nos. 17-58b will have perforations just cutting into the design on one or more sides due to the narrow spacing of the stamps on the plates and to imperfect perforating methods. Stamps with perfs clear on all four sides are extremely scarce and will command substantially higher prices.

Catalogue values for unused stamps in this country are for Never Hinged items, beginning with Scott 290 in the regular postage section.

Watermarks

Wmk. 1a — 22½mm high, Oval Letters

Wmk. 1b — 21mm high, Round Letters

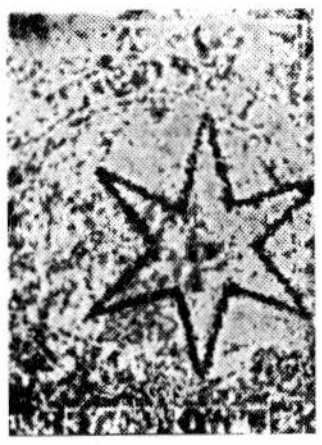
Wmk. 6 — Large Star

Queen Victoria
A1 A2

1857 **Engr.** **Wmk. 6** *Imperf.*
Blued Paper

1	A1	1p blue	—	225.
		On cover		1,600.
		On cover, single franking		1,900.
2	A1	6p plum	*10,000.*	525.
		On cover		4,700.
		On cover, single franking		5,800.

1857-59
White Paper

3	A1	1p dp turq	750.00	37.50
a.		1p blue	875.00	57.50
		On cover		325.00
		On cover, single franking		575.00
		Rouletted, unofficial	*9,000.*	
4	A1	2p deep grn	190.00	65.00
		On cover		525.00
		On cover, single franking		4,750.
		Rouletted, unofficial	*4,000.*	*1,750.*
a.		2p yellow green	575.00	105.00
		On cover		850.00
		On cover, single franking		—
5	A2	4p dl rose ('59)	*65,000.*	5,250.
		On cover		*26,500.*
		On cover, single franking		—
6	A1	5p org brown	1,750.	175.00
		On cover with other values		1,150.
		On cover, single franking		850.00
6A	A1	6p plum	2,250.	160.00
		On cover with other values		725.00
		On cover, single franking		575.00
7	A1	6p brown	7,500.	550.00
		On cover		3,750.
		On cover, single franking		—
a.		6p deep brown	9,250.	1,150.
		On cover		7,250.
		On cover, single franking		—
b.		6p pale brown	—	1,050.
		On cover		—
8	A2	8p brown ('59)	*27,500.*	1,750.
		On cover		*10,500.*
		On cover, single franking		—
9	A2	9p lil brn ('59)	*45,000.*	1,050.
		On cover		*8,750.*
		On cover, single franking		*11,500.*
10	A1	10p vermilion	925.00	350.00
		On cover with other values		7,500.
		On cover, single franking		3,750.
11	A1	1sh violet	5,500.	225.00
		On cover with other values		1,425.
		On cover, single franking		1,150.
12	A2	1sh9p green ('59)	950.00	925.00
		On cover, single franking		*21,500.*
		Rouletted, unofficial	*10,000.*	
a.		1sh9p yellow green	4,750.	3,500.
		On cover		—
13	A2	2sh blue ('59)	6,500.	1,400.
		On cover		—

Stamps of type A2 frequently have repaired corners.

Beware of Nos. 17-57 trimmed to resemble Nos. 3-13. Values are for stamps with clear margins on all sides.

No. 5 was reproduced by the collotype process in a souvenir sheet distributed at the London International Stamp Exhibition 1950. The paper is unwatermarked.

A3

1857-58 **Typo.** **Unwmk.**

14	A3	½p lilac ('58)	200.	*225.*
		On cover		2,500.
		Rouletted, unofficial	*9,000.*	
15	A3	½p lilac, *bluish*	4,000.	600.
		On cover		7,500.
		On cover, single franking		*11,500.*

Nos. 14-15, 38 are printed on surface-glazed paper. Values are for stamps without cracking of the surface, and examples showing cracking should be discounted.

Clean-Cut Perf. 14 to 15½

1861 **Wmk. 6** **Engr.**

17	A1	1p blue	175.00	18.00
		On cover		425.00
		On cover, single franking		425.00
a.		1p pale blue	1,275.	225.00
		On cover		—
18	A1	2p yel grn	220.00	27.50
		On cover		—
a.		2p green	210.00	32.50
		On cover with other stamps		750.00
b.		As "b," vert. pair, imperf between		—
19	A2	4p dull rose	2,300.	350.00
		On cover with other stamps		*8,000.*

20 A1 5p org brown 100.00 10.00
On cover 210.00
On cover, single franking 210.00
20A A1 6p brown 2,300. 140.00
On cover, single franking 1,275.
b. 6p bister brown 2,250. 215.00
On cover, single franking 2,750.
21 A2 8p brown 2,200. 575.00
On cover —
22 A2 9p lilac brown 7,500. 275.00
On cover with other stamps *6,500.*
23 A1 1sh violet 115.00 17.50
On cover 650.00
On cover, single franking 1,000.
24 A2 2sh blue 3,250. 750.00
On cover with other stamps *25,000.*

Rough Perf. 14 to 15½

25 A1 1p blue 150.00 9.00
On cover 210.00
On cover, single franking 210.00
b. Blued paper 625.00 24.00
On cover —
26 A1 2p yel green 500.00 92.50
On cover 900.00
On cover, single franking —
27 A2 4p rose red 500.00 105.00
On cover with other stamps *6,600.*
a. 4p dp rose red 550.00 115.00
28 A1 6p olive brown 975.00 105.00
On cover, single franking 875.00
On cover with other stamps
a. 6p deep brown 1,100. 115.00
On cover, single franking 1,100.
On cover with other stamps *1,550.*
b. 6p bister brown 1,750. 160.00
On cover, single franking 1,400.
On cover with other stamps *1,800.*
29 A2 8p brown 1,750. 650.00
On cover —
30 A2 8p yel brown 1,800. 400.00
On cover —
31 A2 9p olive brown 650.00 75.00
On cover 1,100.
On cover, single franking 1,550.
32 A2 9p deep brown 100.00 82.50
On cover, single franking 1,450.
a. 9p light brown 925.00 115.00
On cover, single franking —
33 A1 10p vermilion 300.00 25.00
On cover, single franking 1,000.
On cover with other stamps —
a. Imperf. vert., pair —
34 A1 1sh violet 300.00 17.50
On cover 425.00
35 A2 1sh9p green 825.00
36 A2 2sh blue 800.00 160.00
On cover —
a. 2sh deep blue 975.00 200.00
On cover —

The 1sh9p green was never placed in use.

1863 *Perf. 12½*

37 A1 10p vermilion 260.00 18.00
On cover 425.00
On cover, single franking 650.00

1864 Typo. Unwmk.

38 A3 ½p lilac 260.00 210.00
On cover, single franking *4,250.*

See note following No. 15.

1863 Engr. *Perf. 13*

39 A1 1p blue 160.00 7.00
On cover 225.00
On cover, single franking 350.00
40 A1 5p car brown 1,750. 175.00
On cover —
41 A1 6p deep brown 210.00 30.00
On cover with other stamps 725.00
On cover, single franking 650.00
a. 6p brown 210.00 30.00
On cover with other stamps 725.00
On cover, single franking 675.00
42 A2 9p brown 1,400 110.00
On cover, single franking *5,000.*
43 A1 1sh grayish violet 2,100. 92.50
On cover —

Parts of the papermaker's sheet watermark, "T. H. SAUNDERS 1862," may be found on some copies of Nos. 39-43.

Perf. 12

44 A1 1p blue 1,600. 150.00
On cover with other stamps 1,450.
On cover, single franking —
a. Horiz. pair, imperf. btwn. *14,000.*

Two Types of Watermark Crown and CC (1)

1863-67 Typo. Wmk. 1a *Perf. 12½*

45 A3 ½p lilac 55.00 40.00
On cover with other stamps 1,200.
On cover, single franking —
a. ½p reddish lilac 70.00 47.50
On cover with other stamps 1,750.
On cover, single franking 3,600.
b. ½p mauve 40.00 40.00
On cover —

Engr.

46 A1 1p blue 150.00 7.00
On cover 110.00
On cover, single franking 120.00
a. 1p dark blue 150.00 7.00
On cover 110.00
On cover, single franking 125.00
c. Perf. 11½ 3,000. 375.00
On cover 1,500.
On cover, single franking 1,800.
47 A1 2p gray green 87.50 14.00
On cover 200.00
On cover, single franking —
48 A1 2p emerald 175.00 115.00
On cover —
48A A1 2p yel green *10,000.* 475.00
On cover —
48B A1 2p bottle green *4,000.*
49 A1 2p olive 260.00 260.00
On cover —
50 A2 4p rose 440.00 105.00
On cover —
a. 4p carmine rose 750.00 175.00
On cover with other stamps *6,750.*
51 A1 5p car brown 210.00 80.00
On cover 1,200.
On cover, single franking 1,750.
52 A1 5p olive green 875.00 275.00
On cover *5,000.*
e. 5p deep sage green 2,100. 400.00
On cover *7,500.*
53 A1 6p choc brown 175.00 7.50
On cover 200.00
On cover, single franking 275.00
a. Perf. 13 1,850. 210.00
On cover, single franking —
b. 6p black brown 175.00 11.50
On cover 240.00
On cover, single franking 360.00
c. As "b," double impression *3,500.*
d. 6p reddish brown 220.00 14.00
54 A2 8p red brown 115.00 57.50
On cover 3,900.
On cover, single franking 8,000.
55 A2 9p brown 350.00 52.50
On cover 3,750.
On cover, single franking —
c. Perf. 13 5,000. 875.00
On cover —
56 A1 10p vermilion 2,100. 70.00
On cover with other stamps 900.00
On cover, single franking 700.00
a. 10p orange 4,600. 500.00
On cover —
58 A2 2sh blue 300.00 40.00
On cover with other stamps *14,500.*

The ½p, 1p blue, 2p olive, 4p and 5p green exist imperf.

Wmk. 1b

46d A1 1p blue 190.00 14.00
On cover 160.00
On cover, single franking 175.00
e. 1p dark blue 175.00 11.00
On cover 160.00
On cover, single franking 175.00
49d A1 2p orange yellow 110.00 6.50
On cover 725.00
On cover, single franking —
e. 2p olive yellow 150.00 14.00
On cover 850.00
On cover, single franking —
f. 2p olive green 175.00 30.00
On cover 2,150.
On cover, single franking —
50b A2 4p rose 225.00 65.00
On cover 1,750.
On cover, single franking *8,500.*
c. 4p carmine rose 125.00 40.00
On cover 1,750.
On cover, single franking —
52b A1 5p myrtle green 110.00 17.50
On cover 1,100.
On cover, single franking 1,100.
c. 5p olive green 125.00 17.50
On cover 2,300.
On cover, single franking 2,300.
d. 5p bronze green 45.00 *55.00*
On cover 2,150.
On cover, single franking 2,150.
53d A1 6p chocolate brown 45.00 *40.00*
On cover 575.00
On cover, single franking 575.00
e. 6p brown 100.00 11.50
On cover 250.00
On cover, single franking 900.00
54a A2 8p red brown 80.00 65.00
On cover 4,600.
On cover, single franking —
55a A2 9p dark brown 57.50 7.00
On cover 350.00
On cover, single franking 600.00
b. 9p bister brown 525.00 37.50
On cover 725.00
On cover, single franking 1,000.
56b A1 10p orange 105.00 12.50
On cover 675.00
On cover, single franking 625.00
c. 10p orange red 65.00 16.00
On cover 650.00
On cover, single franking 340.00
d. 10p vermilion *3,750.* 160.00
On cover —
On cover, single franking 2,000.
57 A1 1sh purple 110.00 9.25
On cover 440.00
On cover, single franking 450.00
a. 1sh reddish lilac 325.00 32.50
On cover 1,900.
On cover, single franking 1,900.
58a A2 2sh deep blue 150.00 14.00
On cover *13,500.*
On cover, single franking *17,250.*
b. 2sh indigo 260.00 22.50
On cover —

The 1p blue and 6p brown exist imperf. For overprints see Nos. O2, O4-O7.

A4

A5

1866 Typo. Wmk. 1 *Perf. 12½*

59 A5 3p rose 210.00 100.00
a. Imperf., pair *800.00*

For overprint see No. O3.

1868 *Perf. 14*

61 A4 1p blue 30.00 10.50
62 A5 3p rose 87.50 50.00

For overprint see No. O1.

A6

A7

A8

A9

A10

A11

A12

A13

A14

A15

A16

1872-80 *Perf. 14*

63 A6 2c brown 18.00 2.90
64 A7 4c gray 40.00 1.75
65 A7 4c lil rose ('80) 62.50 1.75
66 A8 8c orange 46.00 6.25
a. 8c orange yellow 32.50 7.00
67 A9 16c violet 100.00 3.00
68 A10 24c green 62.50 2.25
69 A11 32c slate bl ('77) 175.00 17.50
70 A12 36c blue 175.00 21.00
71 A13 48c rose 85.00 6.25
72 A14 64c red brn ('77) 300.00 75.00
73 A15 96c olive gray 225.00 30.00
Nos. 63-73 (11) 1,289. 167.65

For surcharges see #83-84, 94A-110, 112-114. For types surcharged see #124-129.

1872 *Perf. 12½*

74 A6 2c brown 2,900. 200.00
75 A7 4c gray 1,600. 300.00

1879 *Perf. 14x12½*

77 A6 2c brown 425.00 75.00
78 A7 4c gray 1,600. 40.00
79 A8 8c orange 450.00 55.00

Perf. 12½x14

82 A16 2r50c claret 550.00 350.00

The 32c and 64c are known perf. 14x12½, but were not regularly issued.

No. 82, perf. 12½, was not regularly issued.

See Nos. 142, 158. For surcharges see Nos. 111, 115, 130. For types surcharged see Nos. 160-161.

Nos. 68, 72 Surcharged

1882 *Perf. 14*

83 A10 16c on 24c green 27.50 7.50
84 A14 20c on 64c red brn 11.00 6.50
a. Double surcharge 1,300.

1883-99 Wmk. 2

85 A6 2c pale brown 65.00 2.00
86 A6 2c green ('84) 3.00 .20
a. Perf. 12 3,500.
87 A6 2c org brn ('99) 3.00 .40
88 A7 4c lilac rose 3.50 .35
89 A7 4c rose ('84) 4.50 *13.50*
a. Perf. 12 3,500.
90 A7 4c brt rose ('98) 8.75 *9.25*
91 A7 4c yellow ('99) 3.50 3.25
92 A8 8c orange 5.00 *9.25*
93 A9 16c violet 1,750. 175.00
94 A10 24c purple brown 1,250.
Overprinted "SPECIMEN" 525.00
b. Perf. 12 *3,750.*

Nos. 86a, 89a, 94 and 94b were never placed in use. A 48c brown, perf. 12, was prepared but not issued.

For surcharges and overprints see Nos.116-123, 143-151D, 155-156. O8-O9.

Issues of 1872-82 Surcharged:

a

b

c

d

1885 Wmk. 1 *Perf. 14*

94A A9 (a) 5c on 16c *3,250.*
95 A10 (a) 5c on 24c 3,250. 110.00
96 A11 (a) 5c on 32c 65.00 20.00
a. Inverted surcharge 1,500.
97 A12 (a) 5c on 36c 300.00 12.00
a. Inverted surcharge *2,250.*
98 A13 (a) 5c on 48c 1,250. 65.00
99 A14 (a) 5c on 64c 110.00 7.00
a. Double surcharge 1,150.
100 A15 (a) 5c on 96c 525.00 75.00
101 A9 (b) 10c on 16c *5,750.* 2,400.
102 A10 (b) 10c on 24c 500.00 125.00
103 A12 (b) 10c on 36c 450.00 200.00
104 A14 (b) 10c on 64c 475.00 175.00
105 A10 (b) 20c on 24c 65.00 21.00
106 A11 (c) 20c on 32c 75.00 65.00
107 A11 (c) 25c on 32c 18.00 5.25
108 A13 (c) 28c on 48c 45.00 7.00
a. Double surcharge 1,400.

109 A12 (b) 30c on 36c 16.50 10.50
a. Inverted surcharge 240.00 110.00
110 A15 (b) 56c on 96c 30.00 21.00

Perf. 12½

111 A16 (d) 1r12c on 2r50c 550.00 110.00

Perf. 14x12½

112 A11 (a) 5c on 32c 750.00 57.50
113 A14 (a) 5c on 64c 700.00 47.50
114 A14 (b) 10c on 64c 75.00 *110.00*
a. Vert. pair, imperf. btwn. 3,500.

Perf. 12½x14

115 A16 (d) 1r12c on 2r50c 110.00 50.00

Perf. 14

Wmk. 2

117 A7 (a) 5c on 4c rose 25.00 4.00
a. Inverted surcharge *350.00*
118 A8 (a) 5c on 8c org 82.50 8.00
a. Inverted surcharge *2,400.*
b. Double surcharge *1,750.*
119 A9 (a) 5c on 16c vio 110.00 12.50
a. Inverted surcharge *225.00*
120 A10 (a) 5c on 24c pur brn — 600.00
121 A9 (b) 10c on 16c vio *6,000.* 1,250.
122 A10 (b) 10c on 24c pur brn 15.00 7.00
123 A9 (b) 15c on 16c vio 12.50 8.75

A 5c on 4c lilac rose and a 5c on 24c green are known to exist and are considered to be a forgeries.

Types of 1872-80 Surcharged

e

f

g

1885-87

124 A 8 (e) 5c on 8c lilac 18.00 1.60
125 A10 (f) 10c on 24c pur brn 11.00 7.50
126 A 9 (f) 15c on 16c org 62.50 10.00
127 A11 (f) 28c on 32c sl bl 26.00 2.90
128 A12 (f) 30c on 36c ol grn 32.50 16.00
129 A15 (f) 56c on 96c ol gray 57.50 16.00

Wmk. 1 Sideways

130 A16 (g) 1r12c on 2r50c cl 42.50 *100.00*
Nos. 124-130 (7) *250.00* *154.00*

A23

A24

FIVE CENTS
Type I — Thin lines in background. Hair and curl clear.
Type II — Thicker lines in background. Heavier shading under chin.

1886 **Wmk. 2**

131 A23 5c lilac, type I 2.60 .20
a. Type II 2.60 .20

For overprint see No. O12.

1886-1900

132 A24 3c org brn & green ('93) 3.75 .50
133 A24 3c green ('00) 2.90 .60
134 A24 6c rose & blk ('99) 1.75 .50
135 A24 12c ol grn & car ('00) 4.50 *8.00*
136 A24 15c olive green 5.75 1.40
137 A24 15c ultra ('00) 6.25 1.50
138 A24 25c brown 4.25 1.10
a. 25c brown, value in ol yel 110.00 80.00
139 A24 28c slate 21.00 1.60
140 A24 30c vio & org brown ('93) 5.00 2.25
141 A24 75c blk & org brown ('00) 5.50 *7.00*
Nos. 132-141 (10) 60.65 *24.45*

Numeral tablet of 3c, 12c and 75c has lined background with colorless value and "c."
For surcharges & overprints see #152-154, 157, 159, O10-O11, O13-O17.

1887 **Wmk. 1**

142 A16 1r12c claret 25.00 22.50
Overprinted "SPECIMEN" 110.00

For overprint see No. O18.

Issue of 1883-84 Surcharged

1888-90 **Wmk. 2**

143 A7 2c on 4c lilac rose 1.60 .90
a. Inverted surcharge 22.50 20.00
b. Double surcharge, one invtd. 225.00
144 A7 2c on 4c rose 2.50 .35
a. Inverted surcharge 15.00 *16.00*
b. Double surcharge 250.00

Surcharged

145 A7 2c on 4c lilac rose .85 .35
a. Inverted surcharge 32.50 *35.00*
b. Double surcharge 75.00 75.00
c. Double surcharge, one invtd. 70.00 62.50
146 A7 2c on 4c rose 5.50 .20
a. Double surcharge, one invtd. 85.00 *92.50*
b. Double surcharge 80.00 *85.00*
c. Inverted surcharge 250.00

Surcharged

147 A7 2c on 4c lilac rose 75.00 32.50
a. Inverted surcharge 110.00 42.50
b. Double surcharge, one inverted 150.00
148 A7 2c on 4c rose 2.50 .85
a. Inverted surcharge 14.00 9.75
b. Double surcharge, one inverted 9.25 *11.50*
c. Double surcharge 150.00 125.00

Surcharged

149 A7 2c on 4c lilac rose 50.00 21.00
a. Inverted surcharge 150.00 35.00
150 A7 2c on 4c rose 3.00 1.25
a. Inverted surcharge 14.00 6.25
b. Double surcharge 110.00 110.00
c. Double surcharge, one inverted 14.00 7.00

Surcharged

151 A7 2c on 4c rose 11.50 1.10
a. Inverted surcharge 19.00 6.25
b. Double surcharge 100.00 100.00
c. Double surch., one invtd. 21.00 9.75
i. "S" of "Cents" inverted 210.00
151D A7 2c on 4c lilac rose 52.50 30.00
e. Inverted surcharge 80.00 45.00
f. Double surcharge 260.00
g. Double surch., one invtd. 100.00 100.00
h. "S" of "Cents" inverted 450.00

Counterfeit errors of surcharges of Nos. 143 to 151D are prevalent.

No. 136 Surcharged

1890

152 A24 5c on 15c ol green 2.90 2.25
a. "Flve" instead of "Five" 110.00 92.50
b. "REVENUE" omitted 190.00 160.00
c. Inverted surcharge 60.00 *55.00*
d. Double surcharge 110.00 *140.00*
e. As "a," inverted surcharge — 1,100.
f. Inverted "s" in "Cents" 70.00 *80.00*
g. As "f," inverted surcharge 1,250.
h. As "b," invtd. "s" in "Cents" 1,000.

Nos. 138-139 Surcharged

1891

153 A24 15c on 25c brown 12.50 *14.00*
154 A24 15c on 28c slate 16.00 9.75

Nos. 88, 89 and 139 Surcharged

1892

155 A7 3c on 4c lilac rose 1.10 *3.75*
156 A7 3c on 4c rose 4.25 *8.00*
a. Double surcharge, one invtd.
157 A24 3c on 28c slate 4.50 *4.00*
a. Double surcharge 140.00
Nos. 155-157 (3) 9.85 *15.75*

Type of 1879

1898

158 A16 2r50c violet, *red* 32.50 *62.50*

No. 136 Surcharged in Black

1899

159 A24 6c on 15c olive green .80 *.85*

Surcharged Type "g" in Black

1899 **Wmk. 1**

160 A16 1r50c on 2r50c gray 22.50 *52.50*
161 A16 2r25c on 2r50c yel 40.00 *92.50*

A35

1900 **Wmk. 1**

162 A35 1r50c car rose 22.50 *40.00*
163 A35 2r25c dull blue 35.00 *40.00*

King Edward VII

A36 A37

A38

A39

A40

1903-05 **Wmk. 2**

166 A36 2c org brown 2.25 .20
167 A37 3c green 2.25 1.10
168 A37 4c yel & blue 2.25 *4.00*
169 A38 5c dull lilac 1.75 .70
170 A39 6c car rose 11.00 1.75
171 A37 12c ol grn & car 5.75 *11.00*
172 A40 15c ultra 7.50 3.50
173 A40 25c bister 4.50 *9.25*
174 A40 30c vio & green 3.75 *4.50*
175 A37 75c bl & org ('05) 3.50 *21.00*
176 A40 1r50c gray ('04) 75.00 62.50
177 A40 2r25c brn & grn ('04) 75.00 57.50
Nos. 166-177 (12) 194.50 177.00

For overprints see Nos. O19-O24.

1904-10 **Wmk. 3**

178 A36 2c orange brown 1.75 .20
a. 2c orange 1.75 .55
179 A37 3c green 1.75 .20
180 A37 4c yel & blue 2.25 1.75
181 A38 5c dull lilac 2.50 1.40
a. Booklet pane of 12
182 A39 6c car rose 1.75 .20
183 A40 10c ol grn & vio ('10) 2.75 2.50
184 A37 12c ol grn & car 1.75 *2.00*
185 A40 15c ultra 2.25 .70
186 A40 25c bister ('05) 7.00 4.25
187 A40 25c slate ('10) 2.75 1.75
188 A40 30c vio & grn ('05) 2.75 *3.00*
189 A40 50c brown ('10) 4.50 *8.50*
190 A37 75c bl & org ('05) 6.00 *9.25*
191 A40 1r vio, *yel* ('10) 8.50 *11.50*
192 A40 1r50c gray ('05) 29.00 11.50
193 A40 2r scar, *yel* ('10) 17.50 *30.00*
194 A40 2r25c brn & grn 25.00 *32.50*
195 A40 5r blk, *grn* ('10) 42.50 *75.00*
196 A40 10r blk, *red* ('10) 100.00 *175.00*
Nos. 178-196 (19) 262.25 *371.20*

No. 181 exists on ordinary and chalky paper.

A41

A42

1908

197 A41 5c deep red violet 2.75 .20
a. Booklet pane of 12
198 A42 6c carmine rose 1.40 .20

1911, July 5

199 A40 3c green 1.10 .85

King George V

A44 A45

3 AND 6 CENTS
Type I — Small "c" after value, 2¼mm wide and 2mm high.
Type II — Large "c" after value, 2½mm wide and 2¼mm high.
1, 5 AND 9 CENTS are Type II, other denominations Type I.

Die I

For description of the dies, see front of this section of the Catalogue.

1912-25 **Wmk. 3**

200 A44 1c dp brn (Die Ib) ('20) 1.10 .20
201 A44 2c brown org .35 .20
202 A44 3c dp grn (Die Ia, type II) 2.90 .45
a. 3c deep green, die I, type I 5.00 1.25
203 A44 5c red violet 1.10 .70
204 A44 6c car (Die Ib, type II) 1.50 1.00
a. 6c carmine, die I, type I 1.75 .45
b. As "a," bklt. pane of 6
205 A44 10c olive green 3.50 2.00

206 A44 15c ultra 2.00 1.40

Chalky Paper

207 A44 25c yel & ultra 2.00 2.00
208 A44 30c green & vio 4.50 3.75
209 A44 50c black & scar 1.40 *2.00*
210 A44 1r violet, *yel* 3.75 *4.00*
211 A44 2r blk & red, *yel* 3.75 *12.50*
212 A44 5r blk, *green* 19.00 *32.50*
a. 5r black, *bl grn,* olive back 18.00 *40.00*
b. 5r blk, *emer* (Die II) ('20) 50.00 *110.00*
213 A44 10r vio & blk, *red* 70.00 *92.50*
a. Die II ('20) 85.00 *150.00*
214 A44 20r blk & red, *bl* 140.00 *150.00*
215 A45 50r dull violet 400.00
216 A45 100r gray black 1,600.
217 A45 500r gray green *5,250.*
218 A45 1000r vio, *red* ('25) *18,500.*
Nos. 200-214 (15) 256.85 *305.20*

Although Nos. 217 and 218 were theoretically available for postage it is not probable that they were ever used for other than fiscal purposes.

The 1r through 100r with revenue cancellations sell for minimal prices.

For surcharge & overprints see #223, MR1-MR3.

Die I
Surface-colored Paper

1913-14

220 A44 1r violet, *yellow* 3.50 *5.50*
221 A44 2r black & red, *yel* 3.00 *14.00*
222 A44 5r black, *green* 21.00 *37.50*
Nos. 220-222 (3) 27.50 *57.00*

No. 203 Surcharged

1918

223 A44 1c on 5c red violet .20 .25

For overprint see No. MR4.

Die I

1921-33 **Wmk. 4**

Ordinary Paper

225 A44 1c dp brn (Die Ib) ('27) .85 .40
226 A44 2c brn org (Die II) .70 .25
227 A44 3c green (Die Ia, type II) 3.00 .85
228 A44 3c slate (Die Ia, type II) ('22) .85 .20
229 A44 5c red vio (Die I) .55 .20
230 A44 6c carmine (Die Ib, type II) 2.25 .85
231 A44 6c vio (Die Ib, type II) ('22) 1.10 .20
232 A44 9c red, *yel* (Die II) ('26) .90 .35
233 A44 10c olive green 1.60 .45
a. Die II 2.00 .70
234 A44 12c scarlet, Die II 1.10 *2.50*
a. Die I ('25) 5.00 *6.25*
235 A44 15c ultramarine 3.75 *11.00*
236 A44 15c green, *yel,* Die II 1.75 1.10
a. Die I ('22) 1.75 1.40
237 A44 20c ultra, Die II ('24) 4.00 *.50*
a. Die I ('22) 4.00 *7.00*
238 A44 25c yel & blue 1.90 *2.10*
a. Die II 3.50 1.40

For surcharges see Nos. 248-249.

Chalky Paper

239 A44 30c green & violet 1.75 *3.00*
a. Die II 3.50 1.40
240 A44 50c blk & scar (Die II) 1.75 .90
a. Die I 62.50 *85.00*
241 A44 1r vio, *yel,* Die II 18.00 *27.50*
a. Die I 18.00 *30.00*
242 A44 2r blk & red, *yel* (Die II) 8.00 *8.50*
243 A44 5r blk, *emer,* (Die II) 32.50 *57.50*
244 A44 20r blk & red, *bl,* (Die II) 160.00 *210.00*
245 A45 50r dull vio 450.00 *800.00*
246 A45 100r gray black 1,750.
247 A45 100r ultra & dl vio ('27) 1,500.
Nos. 225-244 (20) 246.30 328.35

Nos. 228, 231 Surcharged

1926

248 A44 2c on 3c slate .90 *1.10*
a. Double surcharge 80.00
b. Bar omitted 85.00 *100.00*
249 A44 5c on 6c violet .55 .45
a. Double surcharge

A46

1927-29 **Chalky Paper** **Wmk. 4**

254 A46 1r red vio & dl vio ('28) 2.90 1.40
255 A46 2r car & green ('29) 4.25 3.00
256 A46 5r brn vio & grn ('28) 16.00 *22.50*
257 A46 10r org & green 40.00 *92.50*
258 A46 20r ultra & dl vio 110.00 *210.00*
Nos. 254-258 (5) 173.15 *329.40*

Common Design Types pictured following the introduction.

Silver Jubilee Issue
Common Design Type

1935, May 6 **Engr.** ***Perf. 13½x14***

260 CD301 6c gray blk & ultra .70 .30
261 CD301 9c indigo & green .80 1.00
262 CD301 20c blue & brown 4.50 2.50
263 CD301 50c brt vio & ind 5.25 6.50
Nos. 260-263 (4) 11.25 10.30

Tapping Rubber Tree — A47

Colombo Harbor — A49

Adam's Peak — A48

Picking Tea — A50

Coconut Palms — A53

Rice Terraces A51

River Scene A52

Temple of the Tooth, Kandy A54

Ancient Reservoir A55

Wild Elephants A56

View of Trincomalee A57

Perf. 11x11½, 11½x11; 11½x13, 13x11½ (A47, A48, A53); 14 (A56)

1935-36 **Wmk. 4**

264 A47 2c car rose & blk .35 *.45*
a. Perf. 14 10.00 .45
265 A48 3c olive & black .40 *.45*
a. Perf. 14 30.00 .40
266 A49 6c blue & black .35 .35
267 A50 9c org red & ol grn 1.10 .75
268 A51 10c dk vio & blk 1.40 *2.50*
269 A52 15c grn & org brn 1.10 .60
270 A53 20c ultra & black 2.00 *2.90*
271 A54 25c choc & dk ultra 1.60 1.40
272 A55 30c green & lake 2.50 *3.00*
273 A56 50c dk vio & blk 9.75 2.00
274 A57 1r brown & vio 21.00 18.00
Nos. 264-274 (11) 41.55 32.40

Issued: 2c, 15c, 25c, 5/1/35; 10c, 6/1/35; 1r, 7/1/35; 30c, 8/1/35; 3c, 10/1/35; 6c, 9c, 20c, 50c, 1/1/36.

Coronation Issue
Common Design Type

1937, May 12 ***Perf. 11x11½***

275 CD302 6c dark carmine .35 .20
a. Booklet pane of 10
276 CD302 9c deep green 1.25 *2.50*
a. Booklet pane of 10 150.00
277 CD302 20c deep ultra 1.75 *3.50*
Nos. 275-277 (3) 3.35 6.20
Set, never hinged 7.00

Types of 1935 with "Postage & Revenue Removed" and Picturing George VI and:

Ancient Guard Stone — A68

George VI — A69

Sigiriya (Lion Rock) — A61

Perf. 11x11½, 11½x11; 12 (#286)

1938-52 **Engr.** **Wmk. 4**

278 A47 2c car rose & blk ('44) .45 *.95*
a. Perf. 13½x13 ('38) 100.00 2.00
b. Perf. 13½ ('38) 2.00 .20
c. Perf. 12 ('49) 1.25 *4.00*
d. Perf. 11½x13 ('38) 9.00 2.00
279 A48 3c dk grn & blk ('42) .50 .20
a. Perf. 13x13½ ('38) 225.00 10.00
b. Perf. 14 ('41) 100.00 1.10
c. Perf. 13½ ('38) 3.50 .20
d. Perf. 12 ('46) .70 *.95*
e. Perf. 13x11½ 8.00 .50
280 A49 6c blue & black .20 .20
281 A61 10c blue & black 1.60 .20
282 A52 15c red brn & grn 1.25 .20
283 A50 20c dull bl & blk 2.25 .20
284 A54 25c choc & dk ultra 3.25 .25
285 A55 30c dk grn & rose car 8.00 2.25
286 A56 50c dk vio & blk ('46) 2.75 .20
a. Perf. 14 ('42) 90.00 29.00
b. Perf. 13x11½ ('38) 140.00 40.00
c. Perf. 13x13½ ('38) 300.00 3.00
d. Perf. 13½ ('38) 15.00 .35
e. Perf. 11½x11 ('42) 4.00 4.00
287 A57 1r dk brn & bl vio 10.50 1.40
288 A68 2r dark car & blk 9.25 2.90

Perf. *14* **Typo.**

289 A69 5r brn vio & grn 27.50 4.00
289A A69 10r yel org & dl grn ('52) 42.50 25.00
Nos. 278-289A (13) 110.00 37.95

No. 289A differs from type A69 in having "REVENUE" inscribed vertically at either side of the frame. This revenue 10r was valid for postage Dec. 1, 1952-Mar. 14, 1954.

See #292, 295. For surcharges see #290-291.

Catalogue values for unused stamps in this section, from this point to the end of the section, are for Never Hinged items.

No. 283 Surcharged in Black

1940, Nov. 5 ***Perf. 11x11½***

290 A50 3c on 20c dull bl & blk 3.00 .75

No. 280 Surcharged with New Value and Bars

1941, May 10

291 A49 3c on 6c blue & black .40 .20

Coconut Palms — A70

1943-47 **Wmk. 4** **Engr.** ***Perf. 12***

292 A70 5c red org & ol grn ('47) 2.00 .35
a. Perf. 13½ ('43) .35 .20

Peace Issue
Common Design Type

1946, Dec. 10 ***Perf. 13½x14***

293 CD303 6c deep blue .20 .20
294 CD303 15c brown .20 .20

Guard Stone Type of 1938

1947, Mar. 15 ***Perf. 11x11½***

295 A68 2r violet & black 2.40 1.75

Parliament Building, Colombo — A71

Adam's Peak A72

Dagoba at Anuradhapura A74

Temple of the Tooth, Kandy
A73

1947, Nov. 25 *Perf. 11x12, 12x11*

296 A71 6c deep ultra & black .20 .20
297 A72 10c car, orange & black .20 .20
298 A73 15c red vio & grnsh blk .20 .20
299 A74 25c brt green & bister .20 .20
Nos. 296-299 (4) .80 .80

New constitution of 1947.

National Flag
A75

D. S. Senanayake
A76

Engr., Flag Typo. (A75); Engr. (A76)
Perf. 12½x12, 12x12½, 13x12½

1949 **Wmk. 4**

300 A75 4c org brn, car & yel .20 .20
301 A76 5c dark green & brn .20 .20

Wmk. 290

302 A75 15c red org, car & yel .60 .20
303 A76 25c dp blue & brown .20 .50
Nos. 300-303 (4) 1.20 1.10

Size of No. 302: 28x22¼mm.
1st anniv. of Ceylon's independence.
Issued: #300-301, Feb. 4; #302-303, Apr. 5.

A77

A78

Design: 15c, Lion Rock and UPU symbols.

Wmk. 290

1949, Oct. 10 **Engr.** ***Perf. 12***

304 A77 5c dk green & brown .85 .20
305 A77 15c dark car & black 1.25 *2.50*
306 A78 25c ultra & black 1.25 1.25
Nos. 304-306 (3) 3.35 3.95

75th anniv. of the UPU.

Kandyan Dancer
A79

Kiri Vehera, Polonnaruwa
A80

Vesak Orchid — A81

Sigiriya — A82

Ratmalana, Plane — A83

Vatadage Ruins at Madirigiriya
A84

1950, Feb. 4 ***Perf. 12x12½***

307 A79 4c bright red & choc .20 .20
308 A80 5c green .20 .20
309 A81 15c pur & blue green 2.00 .35
310 A82 30c carmine & yel .35 *.50*

Perf. 11x11½, 11½x11

311 A83 75c red org & blue 5.50 .20
312 A84 1r red brn & dp blue 2.00 .35
Nos. 307-312 (6) 10.25 1.80

See Nos. 340-345.

Coconut Palms — A85

Star Orchid — A86

1951-52 Unwmk. Photo. ***Perf. 11½***

313 A85 10c gray & dark green 1.10 .75
314 A86 35c dk grn & rose brn ('52) 1.75 1.75
a. Corrected inscription ('54) 7.00 .70

On No. 314a a dot has been added above the third character in the second line of the Tamil inscription.
Issue dates: 10c, Aug. 1; 35c, Feb. 1.
See No. 351.

Mace and Symbols of Industry
A87

Perf. 12½x14

1952, Feb. 23 **Wmk. 290**

315 A87 5c green .20 .20
316 A87 15c brt ultramarine .40 .40

Colombo Plan Exhibition, February 1952.

WAR TAX STAMPS

Nos. 201, 202, 202a and 203 Overprinted

Die I

1918 **Wmk. 3** ***Perf. 14***

MR1 A44 2c brown orange .25 *.45*
a. Double overprint 30.00 35.00
b. Inverted overprint 40.00 *45.00*
MR2 A44 3c dp grn (Die Ia, type II) 2.00 .45
a. 3c dp green (Die I, type I) .20 *.55*
b. Double overprint (Die I) 70.00 *75.00*
MR3 A44 5c red violet .55 .35
a. Double overprint 37.50 *42.50*
b. Inverted overprint 92.50

Same Overprint on No. 223

MR4 A44 1c on 5c red violet .20 *.30*
a. Double overprint 160.00
Nos. MR1-MR4 (4) 3.00 1.55

OFFICIAL STAMPS

Regular Issues Overprinted

1869 **Wmk. 1** ***Perf. 12½, 14***

Black Overprint

O1 A4 1p blue 72.50
O2 A1 2p yellow 72.50
O3 A5 3p rose 125.00
O4 A2 8p red brown 72.50
O5 A1 1sh gray lilac 150.00

Red Overprint

O6 A1 6p brown 72.50
O7 A2 2sh blue 125.00
a. Imperf. *1,000.*
Nos. O1-O7 (7) 690.00

Nos. O1-O7 were never placed in use.
The overprint measures 15mm on #O1, O3.

Regular Issues Overprinted in Black or Red

1895-1900 **Wmk. 2** ***Perf. 14***

O8 A6 2c green 9.75 .50
O9 A6 2c org brn ('00) 8.00 .70
O10 A24 3c org brn & grn 11.50 .90
O11 A24 3c green ('00) 9.25 2.50
O12 A23 5c lilac 4.00 .35
O13 A24 15c olive green 14.00 .55
O14 A24 15c ultra ('00) 18.00 .70
O15 A24 25c brown 11.50 2.00
O16 A24 30c vio & org brn 15.00 .70
O17 A24 75c blk & org brn (R) ('99) 6.25 *7.50*

Wmk. 1

O18 A16 1r12c claret 85.00 62.50
a. Double ovpt., one albino 250.00
Nos. O8-O18 (11) 192.25 78.90

1903-04 **Wmk. 2**

O19 A36 2c orange brown 15.00 1.10
O20 A37 3c green 8.50 2.25
O21 A38 5c dull lilac 21.00 1.75
O22 A40 15c ultramarine 32.50 3.25
O23 A40 25c bister 25.00 21.00
O24 A40 30c violet & green 14.00 1.75
Nos. O19-O24 (6) 116.00 31.10

CHAD

'chad

(Tchad)

LOCATION — Central Africa, south of Libya
GOVT. — French Colony
AREA — 495,572 sq. mi.
POP. — 5,122,000 (est. 1984)
CAPITAL — N'djamena

A former dependency of Ubangi-Shari, Chad became a separate French colony in 1920. In 1934, the colonies of Chad, Gabon, Middle Congo and Ubangi-Shari were grouped in a single administrative unit known as French Equatorial Africa, with the capital at Brazzaville.

100 Centimes = 1 Franc

Types of Middle Congo, 1907-17, Overprinted

Perf. 14x13½, 13½x14

1922 **Unwmk.**

1 A1 1c red & violet .30 .30
a. Overprint omitted 160.00
2 A1 2c ol brn & salmon .40 .40
a. Overprint omitted 200.00
3 A1 4c ind & vio 1.00 1.00
4 A1 5c choc & grn 1.10 1.10
5 A1 10c dp grn & gray grn 2.00 2.00
6 A1 15c vio & red 2.10 2.10
7 A1 20c grn & vio 3.50 3.50
8 A2 25c ol brn & brn 8.00 8.00
9 A2 30c rose & pale rose 1.40 1.40
10 A2 35c dl bl & dl rose 2.50 2.50
11 A2 40c choc & grn 2.75 2.75
12 A2 45c vio & grn 2.00 2.00
13 A2 50c dk bl & pale bl 2.75 2.75
14 A2 60c on 75c vio, *pnksh* 3.25 3.25
a. "TCHAD" omitted 225.00
b. "60" omitted 225.00
15 A1 75c red & violet 2.75 2.75
16 A3 1fr indigo & salmon 10.00 10.00
17 A3 2fr indigo & violet 15.00 15.00
18 A3 5fr ind & olive brn 15.00 15.00
Nos. 1-18 (18) 75.80 75.80

See Nos. 26a, 32a, 38a, 55a.

Stamps of 1922 Overprinted in Various Colors:

Nos. 19-28

Nos. 29-50

1924-33

19 A1 1c red & vio .25 .25
a. "TCHAD" omitted 160.00
b. Double overprint 250.00
c. Violet omitted 210.00
20 A1 2c ol brn & sal .25 .25
a. "TCHAD" omitted 150.00
b. Double overprint 175.00
21 A1 4c ind & vio .25 .25
a. "TCHAD" omitted 675.00
22 A1 5c choc & grn (Bl) .90 .90
a. "TCHAD" omitted 150.00
23 A1 5c choc & grn .40 .40
a. "TCHAD" omitted 175.00
24 A1 10c dp grn & gray grn (Bl) .95 .65
25 A1 10c dp grn & gray grn .95 .65
26 A1 10c red org & blk ('25) .40 .40
a. "Afrique Equatoriale Française" omitted 160.00
b. "TCHAD" omitted 160.00
27 A1 15c vio & red .40 .40
28 A1 20c grn & vio .65 .65
a. "TCHAD" omitted 175.00
b. "Afrique Equatoriale Française" doubled 275.00
29 A2 25c ol brn & brn .40 .40
a. "Afrique Equatoriale Française" doubled 110.00
30 A2 30c rose & pale rose .55 .55
31 A2 30c gray & bl (R) ('25) .40 .40
32 A2 30c dk grn & grn ('27) 1.00 1.00
a. "Afrique Equatoriale Française" omitted 275.00
33 A2 35c indigo & dl rose .40 .40
34 A2 40c choc & grn 1.10 1.00
a. Double overprint (R + Bk) 210.00
35 A2 45c vio & grn .75 .75
a. Double overprint (R + Bk) 210.00
36 A2 50c dk bl & pale bl 1.25 1.10
a. Inverted overprint 125.00
37 A2 50c grn & vio ('25) 1.00 1.00
38 A2 65c org brn & bl ('28) 1.75 1.75
a. "Afrique Equatoriale Française" omitted 210.00
39 A2 75c red & vio 1.25 1.10
40 A2 75c dp bl & lt bl (R) ('25) .55 .55
a. "TCHAD" omitted 210.00
41 A2 75c rose & dk brn ('28) 2.25 2.25
42 A2 90c brn red & pink ('30) 6.00 6.00
43 A3 1fr ind & salmon 1.50 1.50
44 A3 1.10fr dl grn & bl ('28) 2.25 2.25
45 A3 1.25fr org brn & lt bl ('33) 6.50 6.50
46 A3 1.50fr ultra & bl ('30) 6.00 6.00
47 A3 1.75fr ol brn & vio ('33) 35.00 35.00
48 A3 2fr ind & vio 2.50 2.25
a. Double impression of frame 475.00

49 A3 3fr red vio ('30) 9.50 9.50
50 A3 5fr ind & ol brn 3.00 2.50
Nos. 19-50 (32) 90.30 88.55

See No. 58a.

Types of 1922 Overprinted like Nos. 29-50 and Surcharged with New Values

1924-27

51 A2 60c on 75c dk vio, *pnksh* .75 .75
a. "60" omitted 145.00
52 A3 65c on 1fr brn & ol grn ('25) 1.40 1.40
53 A3 85c on 1fr brn & ol grn ('25) 1.40 1.40
54 A2 90c on 75c brn red & rose red ('27) .95 .95
55 A3 1.25fr on 1fr dk bl & ultra (R) ('26) .35 .35
a. "Afrique Equatoriale Francaise" omitted 125.00
56 A3 1.50fr on 1fr ultra & bl ('27) 1.10 1.10
57 A3 3fr on 5fr org brn & dl red ('27) 3.25 3.25
58 A3 10fr on 5fr ol grn & cer ('27) 8.50 8.50
a. "10fr" omitted 325.00
59 A3 20fr on 5fr vio & ver ('27) 13.50 13.50
Nos. 51-59 (9) 31.20 31.20

Common Design Types pictured following the introduction.

Colonial Exposition Issue
Common Design Types

1931 Engr. *Perf. 12½*
Name of Country in Black

60 CD70 40c deep green 4.00 *4.00*
61 CD71 50c violet 4.00 *4.00*
62 CD72 90c red orange 4.00 *4.00*
63 CD73 1.50fr dull blue 4.00 *4.00*
Nos. 60-63 (4) 16.00 16.00

POSTAGE DUE STAMPS

Postage Due Stamps of France Overprinted

1928 Unwmk. *Perf. 14x13½*

J1 D2 5c light blue .20 .20
J2 D2 10c gray brown .20 .20
J3 D2 20c olive green .35 .35
J4 D2 25c bright rose .55 .55
J5 D2 30c light red .55 .55
J6 D2 45c blue green .95 .95
J7 D2 50c brown violet 1.25 1.25
J8 D2 60c yellow brown 1.25 1.25
J9 D2 1fr red brown 1.40 1.40
J10 D2 2fr orange red 3.25 3.25
J11 D2 3fr bright violet 2.75 2.75
Nos. J1-J11 (11) 12.70 12.70

Huts — D3

Canoe — D4

1930 Typo. *Perf. 14x13½, 13½x14*

J12 D3 5c dp bl & olive .40 .40
J13 D3 10c dk red & brn .40 .40
J14 D3 20c grn & brn .65 .65
J15 D3 25c lt bl & brn .90 .90
J16 D3 30c bis brn & Prus bl .90 .90
J17 D3 45c Prus bl & olive 1.25 1.25
J18 D3 50c red vio & brn 1.90 1.90
J19 D3 60c gray lil & bl blk 2.50 2.50
J20 D4 1fr bis brn & bl blk 2.50 2.50
J21 D4 2fr vio & brn 5.00 5.00
J22 D4 3fr dp red & brn 29.00 29.00
Nos. J12-J22 (11) 45.40 45.40

In 1934 stamps of Chad were superseded by those of French Equatorial Africa.

CHILE

'chi-lē

LOCATION — Southwest corner of South America
GOVT. — Republic
AREA — 292,135 sq. mi.
POP. — 11,682,260 (est. 1982)
CAPITAL — Santiago

100 Centavos = 1 Peso

STAMPS OF GREAT BRITAIN USED IN CHILE

Values are for clear cancellations on sound, fault-free stamps, with average to fine centering. In many cases, very fine copies are rare or non-existent.

Type A

Numeral Cancellation Type A, C37 (Caldera)

1865-81

A1 1p rose red, plates 71, 72, 88, 90, 95, 195 (#33), *value from* 62.50
A2 1½p lake red, plate 3 (#32a) —
A3 2p blue, plate 9 (#29) 67.50
A4 3p rose (#44) 100.00
A5 3p rose, plates 5, 7 (#49), *value from* *75.00*
A6 3p rose, plates 11, 12, 16-19 (#61), *value from* 62.50
A7 4p vermilion (#34a) —
A8 4p vermilion, plates 8, 11-14 (#43), *value from* 62.50
A9 4p pale olive green, plate 16 (#70) —
A10 6p lilac, plate 4 (#39b) 110.00
A11 6p lilac, plate 5 (#45) 150.00
Plate 6 150.00
A12 6p dull lilac, plate 6 (#50) 100.00
A13 6p violet, plates 8, 9 (#51), *value from* 100.00
A14 6p brown, plate 11 (#59) —
a. 6p pale buff, plate 11 (#59b) —
A15 6p gray, plate 12 (#60) —
A16 6p gray, plates 13-17 (#62), *value from* 62.50
A17 8p orange (#73) 400.00
A18 9p bister (#52) 275.00
A19 10p red brown (#53) 300.00
A20 1sh green, plate 4 (#48) —
A21 1sh green, plates 4-6 (#54), *value from* 62.50
A22 1sh green, plates 8, 10, 11 (#64), *value from* 95.00
Plates 12, 13, *value from, value from* 95.00
A23 2sh blue (#55) 250.00
a. 2sh cobalt blue (#55c) —
A24 2sh brown (#56) *2,250.*
A25 5sh rose, plate 2 (#57) 525.00

Numeral Cancellation Type A, C40 (Coquimbo)

1865-81

A26 ½p rose red, plate 14 (#58) —
A27 1p rose red (#20) —
A28 1p rose red, plates 85, 204 (#33) —
A29 2p blue, plate 9 (#29) —
A30 2p blue, plate 14 (#30) —
A31 3p rose (#44) —
A32 3p rose, plate 8 (#49) —
A33 3p rose, plate 9 (#61), *value from* 62.50
A34 4p vermilion, plate 4 (#34a)
A35 4p vermilion, plates 12, 14, *value from* (#43) 70.00
A36 4p pale olive green, plates 15, 16 (#70), *value from* 225.00
A37 6p lilac, plate 3 (#39) 95.00
a. Hair lines, plate 4 (#39b) —
A38 6p lilac, plate 5 (#45) —
A39 6p dull lilac, plate 6 (#50) 85.00
A40 6p violet, plates 6, 8, 9 (#51), *value from* 80.00
A41 6p brown, plate 11 (#59) —
a. 6p pale buff, plate 11 (#59b) 85.00
Plate 12 *240.00*
A42 6p gray, plate 12 (#60) 240.00
A43 6p gray, plates 13-16 (#62), *value from* 62.50
A44 8p orange (#73) —
A45 9p straw (#40) 350.00
A46 9p bister (#52) 250.00
A47 10p red brown (#53) —
A48 1sh green, plate 4 (#48) 190.00
A49 1sh green, plates 4-6 (#54), *value from* 62.50
A50 1sh green, plates 8-13 (#64), *value from* 90.00
A51 2sh blue (#55) 210.00
a. 2sh cobalt blue (#55c) —
A52 2sh brown (#56) *2,250.*
A53 5sh rose, plate 1 (#57) 550.00
Plate 2 700.00

VALPARAISO
Crowned Circle Handstamps

Crowned Circle handstamp types I and III are pictured in the Crowned Circle Handstamps and Great Britain Used Abroad section.

1846

A54 Crowned circle handstamp on cover, Type III, inscribed "PAID AT VALPARAISO" 450.00
A55 Crowned circle handstamp on cover, Type I, inscribed "PAID AT VALPARAISO" 525.00

Earliest known uses: A54, Oct. 31, 1846; A55, July 16, 1846.

Type B

Numeral Cancellation Type B, C30 (Type A)

1865-81

A56 ½p rose red, plates 6, 11-14 (#58), *value from* 75.00
A57 1p rose red, plates 80, 84, 85, 89, 91, 101, 106, 113, 122, 123, 138, 140, 141, 148, 149, 152, 157, 158, 162, 167, 175, 178, 181, 185-187, 189, 190, 195, 197-201, 207, 209-215, 217 (#33), *value from* 35.00
A58 1p red brown (#79) —
A59 1½p lake red, plate 1 (#32) *90.00*
Plate 3 60.00
A60 1½p red brown (#80) —
A61 2p blue, plate 9 (#29) 50.00
A62 2p blue, plates 13-15 (#30), *value from* 50.00
A63 2½p claret, plate 2 (#66) 225.00
A64 2½p claret, plates 4, 8 (#67), *value from* 190.00
A65 3p rose (#37) —
A66 3p rose (#44) —
A67 3p rose, plates 5-10 (#49), *value from* 57.50
A68 3p rose, plates 11, 12, 14, 16-19 (#61), *value from* 42.50
A69 4p vermilion, plate 4 (#34a) —
a. Hair lines (#34c) —
A70 4p vermilion, plates 9-14 (#43), *value from* 57.50
A71 4p vermilion, plate 15 (#69) 350.00
A72 4p pale olive green, plate 15 (#70), *value from* *225.00*
Plate 16 225.00
A73 4p gray brown, plate 17 (#71) —
A74 6p lilac, plate 3 (#39) 125.00
a. Hair lines, Plate 4 (#39b) *125.00*
A75 6p lilac, plate 5 (#45) —
Plate 6 —
A76 6p dull violet, plate 6 (#50) —
A77 6p violet, plates 6, 8, 9 (#51), *value from* 80.00
A78 6p brown, plates 11, 12 (#59), *value from* 50.00
a. 6p pale buff, plate 11 (#59b) 85.00
Plate 12 *240.00*
A79 6p gray, plate 12 (#60) 240.00
A80 6p gray, plates 13-17 (#62), *value from* 50.00
A81 6p gray, plate 17 (#86) —
A82 8p orange (#73) 350.00
A83 9p straw (#40) —
a. 9p bister (#40a) —
A84 9p straw (#46) —
A85 9p bister (#52) *225.00*
A86 10p red brown (#53) 300.00
A87 1sh green, plate 4 (#48) —
A88 1sh green, plates 4-6 (#54), *value from* 42.50
Plate 7 60.00
A89 1sh green, plates 8-11 (#64), *value from* 75.00
Plates 12, 13, *value from* 75.00
A90 1sh salmon, plate 13 (#87) 425.00
A91 2sh blue (#55) 150.00
a. 2sh cobalt blue (#55c) *1,700.*
A92 2sh brown (#56) *2,250.*
A93 5sh rose, plate 1 (#57) 550.00
Plate 2 700.00
A94 10sh gray green (#74) *3,100.*
A95 £1 brown lilac (#75) *4,250.*

Issues of the Republic

Values for Nos. 1-14 are for examples with four margins clear of the design. Because these stamps are printed closely together, large margins are not possible, without including portions of adjacent stamps or sheet margin. Values for stamps described as having three margins are for examples with margin touching the design on one side or one corner. Stamps with margins cutting into the design sell for much less than the values shown.

Unused stamps of the early issues are valued with a large portion of their original gum.

Pen cancellations are common on the 1862-67 issues. Such stamps sell for much less than the quoted values which are for those with handstamped postal cancellations.

Watermarks

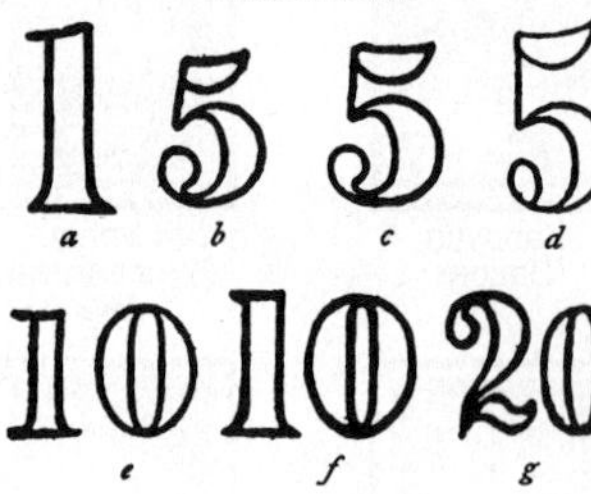

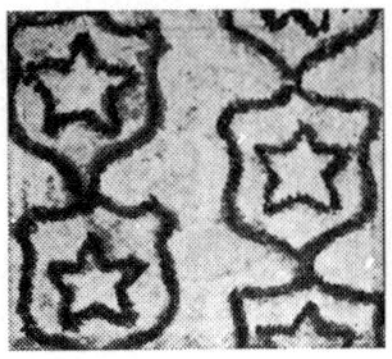

Wmk. 215 — Small Star in Shield, Multiple

Christopher Columbus — A1

London Prints

1853 Wmk. b Engr. *Imperf.*

Blued Paper

1 A1 5c brown red 375.00 85.00
On cover, stamp with three margins 150.00
a. White paper 110.00

Wmk. e

White Paper

2 A1 10c dp brt bl 400.00 100.00
On cover, stamp with three margins 350.00
a. Blued paper 150.00
b. Diag. half used as 5c on cover 350.00
c. Horiz. half used as 5c on cover 350.00
d. Vert. half used as 5c on cover 350.00

Used copies of Nos. 1-2 with three margins sell for 10-20 percent of the values shown.

Santiago Prints

Impressions Fine and Clear

1854 Wmk. b and e

White Paper

3 A1 5c pale red brn 325.00 55.00
On cover, stamp with three margins 140.00
a. 5c deep red brown *350.00* 55.00
b. 5c chestnut *575.00* 85.00
c. 5c chocolate *275.00*
d. Ribbed paper 95.00
e. Double impression 225.00
4 A1 5c burnt sienna 1,100. 175.00
On cover, stamp with three margins 475.00
a. 5c dull chocolate *2,000.* 850.00
5 A1 10c deep blue *875.00* 125.00
On cover, stamp with three margins 325.00
a. 10c slate blue 125.00
b. 10c greenish blue *375.00*
c. 10c sky blue 130.00
d. Diag. half used as 5c on cover 450.00
e. Horiz. half used as 5c on cover 450.00
f. Vert. half used as 5c on cover 450.00
6 A1 10c lt dl bl *875.00* 125.00
On cover, stamp with three margins 325.00
a. 10c pale blue 125.00
b. Diag. half used as 5c on cover 425.00
c. Horiz. half used as 5c on cover 425.00
d. Vert. half used as 5c on cover 425.00

Litho.

7 A1 5c pale brown *1,000.* 275.00
On cover, stamp with three margins 750.00
a. 5c red brown *1,450.* 275.00
On cover, stamp with three margins *750.00*
b. 5c deep brown *1,000.* 275.00
On cover, stamp with three margins *750.00*
c. 5c orange brown *1,000.* 275.00
On cover, stamp with three margins *750.00*
d. 5c chocolate brown *1,000.* 275.00
On cover, stamp with three margins *750.00*
e. 5c deep chocolate brown *1,000.* 275.00
On cover, stamp with three margins *750.00*
f. 5c deep red *1,400.* 275.00
On cover, stamp with three margins *750.00*

No. 5b is normally found on ribbed paper.

Used copies of Nos. 3, 5-7 with three margins sell for 15 percent of the values shown. Three-margin copies of No. 4 sell for about 20 percent.

London Print

1855 Blued Paper Wmk. c Engr.

8 A1 5c brown red 110.00 10.00
Fiscal cancellation 1.50
On cover, stamp with three margins 50.00
a. Thin paper 22.50
b. Ivory head 22.50
c. Cream paper without bluing 45.00

Santiago Prints

Impressions Worn and Blurred

1856-62 Wmk. b and e

White Paper

9 A1 5c rose red ('58) 37.50 7.00
Fiscal cancellation 1.00
On cover, stamp with three margins 27.50
On cover, stamp with four margins 55.00
a. 5c carmine red ('62) 90.00 18.00
b. 5c orange red ('61) *225.00* 100.00
c. 5c dull redsh brn ('57) *250.00* 22.50
d. 5c vermilion *125.00* 27.50
e. 5c salmon *125.00* 22.50
f. Printed on both sides *450.00* *250.00*
g. Double impression *450.00* 90.00
h. Very worn plate 18.00
i. Ribbed paper 60.00
10 A1 10c sky blue ('57) 125.00 18.50
Fiscal cancellation 1.75
On cover, stamp with three margins 55.00
On cover, stamp with four margins 110.00
a. 10c deep blue *125.00* 27.50
On cover, stamp with three margins 85.00
On cover, stamp with four margins 150.00
b. 10c light blue ('59) *150.00* 18.50
c. 10c indigo blue ('60) *175.00* 50.00
e. 10c deep slate blue ('57) 18.50
f. 10c greenish blue ('58) 27.50
g. 10c deep gray blue ('58) 18.50
h. 10c slate blue ('59) 18.50
i. 10c blue, *bluish* ('59) 27.50
j. 10c dark blue ('60) 27.50
k. Printed on both sides *250.00*
l. Very worn plate 37.50
m. 10c greenish blue, poor impression 27.50
n. As "j," half used as 5c on cover *125.00*
o. Any shade, horiz. half used as 5c on cover *140.00*
p. Any shade, vert. half used as 5c on cover *150.00*

London Prints

1862 Wmk. a, f and g

11 A1 1c lemon yellow 22.50 *27.50*
Fiscal cancellation 1.50
On cover, stamp with three margins 30.00
On cover, stamp with four margins 55.00
a. Double impression *350.00*
b. 1c greenish yellow 27.50
Fiscally used 3.00
12 A1 10c bright blue 32.50 15.00
Fiscally used 1.75
On cover, stamp with three margins 50.00
On cover, stamp with four margins 90.00
a. 10c deep blue 32.50 14.00
b. Blued paper — 17.50
c. Wmkd. "20" (error) *5,000.* *2,500.*
d. Diag. half used as 5c on cover 100.00
e. Horiz. half used as 5c on cover 110.00
f. Vert. half used as 5c on cover 125.00
13 A1 20c green 110.00 47.50
Fiscally used 5.50
On cover, stamp with three margins 150.00
On cover, stamp with four margins 300.00
a. 20c yellow green 110.00 47.50
b. 20c intense green — —
Nos. 11-13 (3) 165.00 90.00

No. 11a is only known fiscally used.

Santiago Print

1865 Wmk. d

14 A1 5c rose red 37.50 10.00
Fiscally used 1.50
On cover, stamp with three margins 30.00
On cover, stamp with four margins 55.00
a. 5c carmine red 37.50 9.25
b. Printed on both sides 300.00 *200.00*
c. Laid paper — *90.00*
d. Double impression, entire stamp *160.00*
e. 5c pale red 37.50 9.25
f. 5c vermilion 37.50 9.25
g. Vertically laid paper *100.00*
h. Very thin, silky paper 22.50
i. Thick paper (cardboard) 47.50
j. Partial double impression 100.00
k. Very worn plate 15.00

The 5c rose red (shades) on unwatermaked paper, either wove or ribbed, and on paper watermarked Chilean arms in the sheet are reprints made about 1870.

No. 13 has been reprinted in the color of issue and in fancy colors, both from the original engraved plate and from lithographic transfers. The reprints are on paper without watermark or with watermark CHILE and Star.

A2

A3

1867 Unwmk. *Perf. 12*

15 A2 1c orange 22.50 18.00
Never hinged 65.00
On cover, with other stamps 27.50
Pen cancellation .50
16 A2 2c black 27.50 *35.00*
Never hinged 75.00
On cover, with other stamps 45.00
Pen cancellation .65
17 A2 5c red 19.00 1.75
Never hinged 55.00
On cover 14.50
Pen cancellation .20
18 A2 10c blue 19.00 6.00
Never hinged 75.00
On cover 18.50
Pen cancellation .35
19 A2 20c green 27.50 3.00
Never hinged 75.00
On cover 55.00
Pen cancellation .45
Nos. 15-19 (5) 115.50 63.75

Unused values for Nos. 15-19 are for stamps with original gum.

Nos. 15-17 were used during stamp shortages between July 3 and August 28, 1881. So used, they are scarce,

1877 *Rouletted*

20 A3 1c gray 2.50 1.90
Never hinged 9.25
On cover 18.50
21 A3 2c orange 13.00 5.50
Never hinged 27.50
On cover 15.00
22 A3 5c dull lake 15.00 .55
Never hinged 22.50
On cover 4.50
23 A3 10c blue 12.50 2.50
Never hinged 27.50
On cover 14.00
a. Diagonal half used as 5c on cover —
24 A3 20c green 14.00 4.25
Never hinged 65.00
On cover 37.50
Nos. 20-24 (5) 57.00 14.70

The panel inscribed "CENTAVO" is straight on No. 22.

A4

A5

Columbus — A6

1878-99 *Rouletted*

25 A4 1c green ('81) 1.00 .20
Never hinged 2.50
On cover 3.75
26 A4 2c rose ('81) 1.00 .20
Never hinged 2.50
On cover 3.75
27 A5 5c dull lake ('78) 7.25 .90
Never hinged 18.00
On cover 9.00
28 A5 5c ultra ('83) 1.90 .50
Never hinged 5.50
On cover 3.75
29 A5 10c orange ('85) 2.75 .35
Never hinged 9.25
On cover 12.75
a. 10c yellow 9.00 1.90
Never hinged 27.50
On cover 18.50
30 A5 15c dk grn ('92) 3.00 .55
Never hinged 10.00
On cover 9.00
31 A5 20c gray ('86) 3.00 .55
Never hinged 10.00
On cover 14.00
32 A5 25c org brn ('92) 3.00 .55
Never hinged 10.00
On cover 9.00
33 A5 30c rose car ('99) 7.25 3.75
Never hinged 22.50
On cover 27.50
34 A5 50c lilac ('78) 45.00 27.50
Never hinged 100.00
On cover 135.00
35 A5 50c violet ('85) 3.00 2.00
Never hinged 10.00
On cover 14.50
36 A6 1p dk brn & blk ('92) 19.00 2.75
Never hinged 55.00
On cover 225.00
a. Imperf. horiz. or vert., pair 75.00
Never hinged 150.00
Nos. 25-36 (12) 97.15 39.80

For surcharge and overprint see Nos. 50, O16.

Columbus

A7 A8

1894 Re-engraved

37 A7 1c blue green .90 .25
Never hinged 2.25
On cover 3.75
38 A7 2c carmine lake .90 .25
Never hinged 2.25
On cover 3.75

In type A4 there is a small colorless ornament at each side of the base of the numeral, above the "E" and "V" of "CENTAVO." In type A7 these ornaments are missing, the figure "1" is broader than in type A4 and the head of the figure "2" is formed by a curved line instead of a ball.

1900-01

Type I — There is a heavy shading of short horizontal lines below "Chile" and the adjacent ornaments.

Type II — There is practically no shading below "Chile" and the ornaments.

Type I

39 A8 1c yel grn .80 .20
Never hinged 2.10
On cover 4.50
40 A8 2c brn rose 1.25 .20
Never hinged 2.50
On cover 4.50
41 A8 5c dp bl 6.50 .35
Never hinged 27.50
On cover 7.50
42 A8 10c violet 6.50 .70
Never hinged 18.50
On cover 9.25
43 A8 20c gray 6.50 2.50
Never hinged 16.50
On cover 12.75
44 A8 30c dp org ('01) 6.50 2.50
Never hinged 20.00
On cover 18.50
45 A8 50c red brn 7.50 2.50
Never hinged 24.00
On cover 27.50
Nos. 39-45 (7) 35.55 8.95

Type II

46 A8 1c yel grn ('01) .85 .20
Never hinged 2.25
On cover 4.50
47 A8 2c rose ('01) .85 .30
Never hinged 2.25
On cover 4.50
48 A8 5c dull blue ('01) 5.00 .25
Never hinged 19.00
On cover 6.50
a. Printed on both sides —
49 A8 10c vio ('01) 6.00 .85
Never hinged 20.00
On cover 13.00
Nos. 46-49 (4) 12.70 1.60

Nos. 40, 45 and 47 exist in vertical pairs, imperf horizontally, and horizontal pairs, imperf vertically. Nos. 42 and 48 exist in horizontal pairs, imperf between. No.43 exist in vertical pairs, imperf between. Value: unused $22.50, never hinged $45.

For surcharge see No. 57.

No. 33 Surcharged in Black

1900

Black Surcharge

50 A5 5c on 30c rose car 1.25 .35
Never hinged 2.50
On cover 6.50
a. Inverted surcharge 32.50 24.00
Never hinged 95.00
b. Double surcharge 90.00 60.00
Never hinged 95.00
c. Double surcharge, both invtd. 90.00 60.00
Never hinged 95.00
d. Double surcharge, one invtd. 90.00 60.00
Never hinged 95.00

Columbus — A10

1901-02 *Perf. 12*

51	A10	1c green	.50	.30
52	A10	2c carmine	.65	.20
53	A10	5c ultra	1.50	.20
54	A10	10c red & blk	2.25	.35
55	A10	30c vio & blk	6.75	.85
56	A10	50c red org & blk	7.25	2.25
		Nos. 51-56 (6)	18.90	4.15

No. 44 Surcharged in Dark Blue

1903 ***Rouletted***

57	A8	10c on 30c orange	1.90	.75
a.		Inverted surcharge	18.00	12.00
b.		Double surcharge	25.00	15.00
c.		Double surch., one inverted	25.00	15.00
d.		Double surch., both invtd.	25.00	15.00
e.		Stamp design printed on both sides		

Pedro de Valdivia — A11

Coat of Arms — A12

A13

Telegraph Stamps Surcharged or Overprinted in Black

Type I — Animal at left has neither mane nor tail.

Type II — Animal at left has mane and tail.

1904 *Perf. 12*

58	A11	1c on 20c ultra	.40	.30
a.		Imperf. horiz., pair	40.00	40.00
b.		Inverted surcharge	50.00	50.00
59	A13	2c yel brn, I	.35	.20
a.		Inverted overprint	20.00	20.00
b.		Pair, one without overprint	50.00	50.00
60	A13	5c red, I	.55	.20
a.		Inverted overprint	20.00	20.00
c.		Pair, one without overprint	50.00	50.00
61	A13	10c ol grn, I	1.50	.50
a.		Inverted overprint	50.00	50.00
		Nos. 58-61 (4)	2.80	1.20

Perf. 12½ to 16

62	A13	2c yel, brn, II	5.25	4.50
63	A11	3c on 5c brn red	37.50	32.50
a.		Inverted surcharge		
64	A12	3c on 1p brn, II	.45	.30
a.		Double surcharge	50.00	50.00
65	A13	5c red, II	6.25	5.50
a.		Inverted overprint		
66	A13	10c ol grn, II	14.50	10.00
67	A11	12c on 5c brn red	1.00	.45
a.		No star at left of "Centavos"	3.00	2.50
b.		Inverted surcharge	40.00	40.00
c.		Double surcharge	50.00	50.00
		Nos. 58-67 (10)	67.75	54.45

Counterfeits exist of the overprint and surcharge varieties of Nos. 57-67.

For overprint see No. O12.

A14

A15

Columbus — A16

1905-09 *Perf. 12*

68	A14	1c green	.25	.20
69	A14	2c carmine	.30	.20
70	A14	3c yel brn	.65	.30
71	A14	5c ultra	.70	.20
72	A15	10c gray & blk	1.10	.20
73	A15	12c lake & blk	5.50	2.25
74	A15	15c vio & blk	1.25	.20
75	A15	20c org brn & blk	2.25	.20
76	A15	30c bl grn & blk	3.50	.35
77	A15	50c ultra & blk	3.50	.40
78	A16	1p gold, grn & gray	16.00	11.00
		Nos. 68-78 (11)	35.00	15.50

A 20c dull red and black, type A15, was prepared but not issued. Value $125. "Specimen" copies of Nos. 74, 76-78 exist, punched to prevent postal use.

For surcharges and overprints see Nos. 79-82, O9, O11-O15.

Nos. 73, 78 Surcharged in Blue or Red

a

b

1910

79	A15 (a)	5c on 12c (Bl)	.50	.25
80	A16 (b)	10c on 1p (R)	1.10	.30
81	A16 (b)	20c on 1p (R)	1.60	.60
82	A16 (b)	1p (R)	3.00	1.10
		Nos. 79-82 (4)	6.20	2.25

The 1p is overprinted "ISLAS DE JUAN FERNANDEZ" only. The use of these stamps throughout Chile was authorized.

Independence Centenary Issue

Oath of Independence — A17

Monument to O'Higgins — A26

Gen. Manuel Blanco Encalada — A29

Designs: 2c, Battle of Chacabuco. 3c, Battle of Roble. 5c, Battle of Maipu. 10c, Naval Engagement of "Lautaro" and "Esmeralda." 12c, Capturing the "Maria Isabel." 15c, First Sortie of Liberating Forces. 20c, Abdication of O'Higgins. 25c, Chile's First Congress. 50c, Monument to José M. Carrera. 1p, Monument to San Martin. 5p, Gen. José Ignacio Zenteno. 10p, Adm. Lord Thomas Cochrane.

1910

Center in Black

83	A17	1c dk green	.20	.25
a.		Center inverted	*7,000.*	
84	A17	2c lake	1.10	.75
85	A17	3c red brown	.80	.45
86	A17	5c dp blue	.45	.20
87	A17	10c gray brn	1.20	.30
88	A17	12c vermilion	2.50	1.00
89	A17	15c slate	1.90	.55
90	A17	20c red orange	2.50	.85
91	A17	25c ultra	3.25	2.00
92	A26	30c violet	3.25	1.40
93	A26	50c olive grn	6.75	2.25
94	A26	1p yel org	14.00	5.25
95	A29	2p red	14.00	5.25
96	A29	5p yel grn	37.50	17.50
97	A29	10p dk violet	35.00	16.00
		Nos. 83-97 (15)	124.40	54.00

Columbus A32

De Valdivia A33

Mateo de Toro Zambrano A34

Bernardo O'Higgins A35

Ramón Freire — A36

F. A. Pinto — A37

Joaquín Prieto — A38

Manuel Bulnes — A39

Manuel Montt — A40

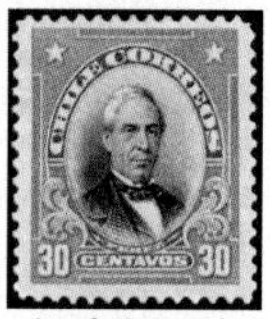

José Joaquín Pérez — A41

Federico Errázuriz Zanartu — A42

José de Balmaceda — A43

Designs: 1p, Anibal Pinto, 2p, Domingo Santa María. 10p, Federico Errázuriz Echaurren.

Outer backgrounds consist of horizontal and diagonal lines

1911 **Engr.** *Perf. 12*

98	A32	1c dp green	.25	.20
99	A33	2c scarlet	.25	.20
100	A34	3c sepia	.75	.25
101	A35	5c dk blue	.25	.20
102	A36	10c gray & blk	.75	.20
a.		Center inverted	800.00	600.00
103	A37	12c carmine & blk	1.00	.20
104	A38	15c violet & blk	.90	.20
a.		Center inverted	*1,000.*	
105	A39	20c org red & blk	1.75	.20
a.		Center inverted	50.00	50.00
106	A40	25c lt blue & blk	2.75	.60
107	A41	30c bis brn & blk	4.00	.30
108	A42	50c myr grn & blk	5.00	.30
109	A43	1p green & blk	9.00	.40
110	A43	2p ver & blk	17.50	1.75
111	A43	5p ol grn & blk	50.00	9.50
112	A43	10p org yel & blk	45.00	8.50
		Nos. 98-112 (15)	139.15	23.00

See Nos. 117, 121, 123, 127-128, 133-141, 143, 155A, 157-161, 165-169,171-172 and designs A47-A55, A57. For overprints see Nos. C6, C6B-C6D, C7-C8, C10-C11, C13-C21, O19-O22, O24-O27, O30-O34, O40.

Columbus A47

Toro Zambrano A48

Freire A49

O'Higgins A50

1912-13 **Engr.** *Perf. 12*

113	A47	2c scarlet	.20	.20
114	A48	4c black brn	.30	.20
115	A49	8c gray	1.00	.20
116	A50	10c blue & blk	1.00	.20
a.		Center inverted	500.00	400.00
b.		Imperf. horiz. or vert., pair	50.00	
117	A37	14c car & blk	1.50	.20
121	A38	40c violet & blk	5.75	.60
123	A40	60c lt blue & blk	14.00	1.75
		Nos. 113-123 (7)	23.75	3.35

See Nos. 125-126, 131, 164, 170, 173. For overprints see Nos. C6E, O18, O23, O28, O29.

Cochrane A52

Columbus A53

1915 **Engr.** *Perf. 13½x14*

124	A52	5c slate blue	.60	.35
a.		Imperf., pair	11.50	

See Nos. 155, 162-163. For overprints see Nos. O17, O37.

1918

125	A49	8c slate	17.50	.80

No. 125 is from a plate made in Chile to resemble No. 115. The top of the head is further from the oval, the spots of color enclosed in the figures "8" are oval instead of round, and there are many small differences in the design.

1921

Worn Plate

126	A49	8c gray	20.00	5.00

No. 126 differs from No. 125 in not having diagonal lines in the frame and only a few diagonal lines above the shoulders (due to wear), while No. 125 has diagonal lines in the oval up to the level of the forehead.

1915-25 **Typo.** *Perf. 13½ to 14½*

127	A32	1c gray green	.20	.20
128	A33	2c red	.20	.20
129	A53	4c brown ('18)	.25	.20

Frame Litho.; Head Engr.

131	A50	10c bl & blk	1.25	.20
a.		10c dark blue & black	1.25	.20
b.		Imperf., pair	110.00	
c.		Center inverted	325.00	
133	A38	15c vio & blk	.90	.20
134	A39	20c org red & blk	1.40	.20
a.		20c brown orange & blk	1.75	.20
135	A40	25c dl bl & blk	.55	.20
136	A41	30c bis brn & blk	1.75	.20
137	A42	50c dp grn & blk	1.75	.20

Perf. 14

138	A43	1p grn & blk	8.00	.20
139	A43	2p red & blk	9.75	.20
a.		2p vermilion & black	32.50	.60
140	A43	5p ol grn & blk ('20)	24.00	.60
141	A43	10p org & blk ('25)	25.00	1.75
		Nos. 127-141 (13)	75.00	4.55

The frames have crosshatching on the 15c, 20c, 30c, 2p, 5p and 10p. They have no crosshatching on the 10c, 25c, 50c and 1p.

Nos. 131a and 134a are printed from new head plates which give blacker and heavier impressions. No. 131a exists with; (a) frame litho., head engr.; (b) frame typo., head engr.; (c) frame typo., head litho. No. 134a is with frame typo., head engr.

A 4c stamp with portrait of Balmaceda and a 14c with portrait of Manuel de Salas were prepared but not placed in use. Both stamps were sent to the paper mill at Puente Alto for destruction. They were not all destroyed as some were privately preserved and sold.

Columbus
A54

Manuel Rengifo
A55

Types of 1915-20 Redrawn

1918-20 *Perf. 13½x14½*

143	A32	1c gray grn ('20)	.30	.20
144	A54	4c brown	.50	.20

No. 143 has all the lines much finer and clearer than No. 127. The white shirt front is also much less shaded.

1921

145	A55	40c dk vio & blk	2.00	.40

For overprints see Nos. C6A, C9.

Pan-American Congress Building — A56

Adm. Juan José Latorre — A57

1923, Apr. 25 **Typo.** *Perf. 14½x14*

146	A56	2c red	.20	.20
147	A56	4c brown	.20	.20

Typo.; Center Engr.

148	A56	10c blue & blk	.20	.20
149	A56	20c orange & blk	.75	.25
150	A56	40c dl vio & blk	1.00	.30
151	A56	1p green & blk	1.25	.50
152	A56	2p red & blk	5.00	.60
153	A56	5p dk grn & blk	17.00	4.50
		Nos. 146-153 (8)	25.60	6.75

Fifth Pan-American Congress.

Typographed; Head Engraved

1927 *Perf. 13½x14½*

154	A57	80c dk brn & blk	2.00	.60

Types of 1915-25 Issues
Inscribed: "Chile Correos"

Perf. 13½x14½

1928-31 **Engr.** **Wmk. 215**

155	A52	5c slate blue	.90	.20

Frame Typo.; Center Engr.

155A	A38	15c violet & blk	*350.00*	
156	A55	40c dk vio & blk	.40	.20
157	A42	50c dp grn & blk	1.75	.20

Perf. 14

158	A43	1p green & blk	.70	.20
159	A43	2p red & blk	3.25	.20
160	A43	5p ol grn & blk	6.50	.30
161	A43	10p orange & blk	6.50	1.25
		Nos. 155,156-161 (7)	20.00	2.55

Paper of #155-161 varies from thin to thick.

Types of 1915-25 Issues
Inscribed: "Correos de Chile"

1928 **Engr.** *Perf. 13½x14½*

162	A52	5c deep blue	.35	.20

1929 **Litho.**

163	A52	5c light green	.30	.20

Frame Litho.; Center Engr.

164	A50	10c blue & blk	1.25	.20
165	A38	15c violet & blk	1.50	.20
166	A39	20c org red & blk	3.50	.20
167	A40	25c blue & blk	.60	.20
168	A41	30c brown & blk	.45	.20
169	A42	50c dp grn & blk	.40	.20
		Nos. 163-169 (7)	8.00	1.40

Redrawn

1929 **Frame Typo.; Center Litho.**

170	A50	10c blue & blk	2.00	.20
171	A38	15c violet & blk	1.75	.20
172	A39	20c org red & blk	2.75	.20
		Nos. 170-172 (3)	6.50	.60

1931 **Unwmk.**

173	A50	10c blue & blk	.70	.20

In the redrawn stamps the lines behind the portraits are heavier and completely fill the ovals. There are strong diagonal lines above the shoulders. On #170 the head is larger than on #164, 173.

A58

Prosperity of Saltpeter Trade
A59 A60

Perf. 13½x14

1930, July 21 **Litho.** **Wmk. 215**

Size: 20x25mm

175	A58	5c yellow grn	.60	.40
176	A58	10c red brown	.60	.30
177	A58	15c violet	.60	.30
178	A59	25c deep gray	1.90	.60
179	A60	70c dark blue	4.50	1.50

Perf. 14

Size: 24½x30mm

180	A60	1p dk gray grn	3.75	.75
		Nos. 175-180 (6)	11.95	3.85

Cent. of the 1st shipment of saltpeter from Chile, July 21, 1830.

Manuel Bulnes
A61

Bernardo O'Higgins
A62

1931 *Perf. 13½, 14*

181	A61	20c dark brown	1.00	.30

For overprints see Nos. O35, O39.

1932

182	A62	10c deep blue	1.10	.35

For overprints see Nos. O36, O38.

Mariano Egana — A63

Joaquin Tocornal — A64

1934 *Perf. 13½x14*

183	A63	30c magenta	.60	.20

Perf. 14

184	A64	1.20p bright blue	1.00	.20

Centenary of the constitution.

José Joaquín Pérez — A65

1934 *Perf. 13½x14*

185	A65	30c bright pink	1.60	.35

Atacama Desert — A66

Designs: 10c, Fishing boats. 20c, Coquito palms. 25c, Sheep. 30c, Mining. 40c, Lonquimay forest. 50c, Colliery at Port Lota. 1p, Shipping at Valparaiso. 1.20p, Puntiagudo volcano. 2p, Diego de Almagro. 5p, Cattle. 10p, Mining saltpeter.

Wmk. 215

1936, Mar. 1 **Litho.** *Perf. 14*

186	A66	5c vermilion	.60	.30
187	A66	10c violet	.30	.25
188	A66	20c magenta	.40	.25
189	A66	25c grnsh blue	3.00	.80
190	A66	30c lt green	.30	.25
191	A66	40c blk, *cream*	3.00	.85
192	A66	50c bl, *bluish*	1.50	.30

Engr.

193	A66	1p dk green	1.60	.50
194	A66	1.20p dp blue	1.75	.70
195	A66	2p dk brown	2.00	.80
196	A66	5p copper red	5.00	2.25
197	A66	10p dk violet	12.00	8.00
		Nos. 186-197 (12)	31.45	15.25

400th anniv. of the discovery of Chile by Diego de Almagro.

Laja Waterfall — A78

Fishing in Chiloé — A84

Designs: 10c, Agriculture. 15c, Boldo tree. 20c, Nitrate Industry. 30c, Mineral spas. 40c, Copper mine. 50c, Mining. 1.80p, Osorno Volcano. 2p, Mercantile marine. 5p, Lake Villarrica. 10p, State railways.

Perf. 13½x14

1938-40 **Litho.** **Wmk. 215**

198	A78	5c brn car ('39)	.20	.20
199	A78	10c sal pink ('39)	.20	.20
200	A78	15c brn org ('40)	.20	.20
201	A78	20c light blue	.20	.20
202	A78	30c brt pink	.20	.20
203	A78	40c lt grn ('39)	.20	.20
204	A78	50c violet	.20	.20

Engr. *Perf. 14*

205	A84	1p orange brn	.20	.20
206	A84	1.80p deep blue	.45	.40
207	A84	2p car lake	.20	.20
208	A84	5p dk slate grn	.35	.20
209	A84	10p rose vio ('40)	.90	.20
		Nos. 198-209 (12)	3.50	2.60

See Nos. 217-227. For surcharge and overprints see Nos. 253, O41-O66, O70-O71.

Map of the Americas — A89

Unwmk.

1940, Sept. 11 **Litho.** *Perf. 14*

210	A89	40c dl grn & yel grn	.35	.20

Pan American Union, 50th anniversary.

SEMI-POSTAL STAMPS

S. S. Abtao and Captain Policarpo Toro
SP1

S. S. Abtao and Brother Eugenio Eyraud
SP2

Perf. 14½x15

1940, Mar. 1 **Engr.** **Unwmk.**

B1	SP1	80c + 2.20p dk grn & lake	1.50	1.40
B2	SP2	3.60p + 6.40p lake & dk grn	1.50	1.40
a.		Pair, #B1-B2	5.50	4.50

50th anniv. of Chilean ownership of Easter Is. Surtax used for charitable institutions.

Sheets containing 15 of each value, with 9 se-tenant pairs.

AIR POST STAMPS

Black Surcharge

Lithographed; Center Engraved

1927 **Unwmk.** *Perf. 13½x14*

Black Brown & Blue

C1	40c on 10c	275.00	36.00
C2	80c on 10c	275.00	40.00
C3	1.20p on 10c	275.00	50.00
C4	1.60p on 10c	275.00	50.00
C5	2p on 10c	275.00	50.00
	Nos. C1-C5 (5)	1,375.	226.00

Issued for air post service between Santiago and Valparaiso. The stamps picture Bernardo O'Higgins and are not known without surcharge.

Regular Issues of 1915-28 Overprinted or Surcharged in Black, Red or Blue

Inscribed: "Chile Correos"

1928-29 *Perf. 13½x14, 14*

C6	A39	20c brn org & blk (Bk)	.30	.25
C6A	A55	40c dk vio & blk (R)	.30	.20
C6B	A43	1p grn & blk (Bl)	1.50	.50
C6C	A43	2p red & blk (Bl)	2.00	.30
f.		2p ver & blk (Bl)	65.00	15.00
C6D	A43	5p ol grn & blk (Bl)	2.40	.75
C6E	A50	6p on 10c dp bl & blk (R)	40.00	22.50
C7	A43	10p org & blk (Bk) ('29)	9.50	3.00
C8	A43	10p org & blk (Bl)	35.00	22.50
		Nos. C6-C8 (8)	91.00	50.00

On Nos. C6B to C6D, C7 and C8 the overprint is larger than on the other stamps of the issue.

Same Overprint or Surcharge on Nos. 155, 156, 158-161
Inscribed: "Chile Correos"

1928-32 **Wmk. 215**

C9 A55 40c vio & blk (R) .55 .30
C10 A43 1p grn & blk (Bl) 1.50 .45
C11 A43 2p red & blk (Bl) 7.00 1.50
C12 A52 3p on 5c sl bl (R) 25.00 20.00
C13 A43 5p ol grn & blk (Bl) 6.00 1.50
C14 A43 10p org & blk (Bk) 27.50 7.25
Nos. C9-C14 (6) 67.55 31.00

Same Overprint on Nos. 166-169, 172 and 158 in Black or Red
Inscribed: "Correos de Chile"

1928-30

C15 A39 20c (#166) ('29) .75 .50
C16 A39 20c (#172) ('30) .35 .20
C17 A40 25c bl & blk (R) .45 .20
C18 A41 30c brn & blk .20 .20
a. Double ovpt., one inverted *250.00 250.00*
C19 A42 50c dp grn & blk (R) .25 .20
Nos. C15-C19 (5) 2.00 1.30

Inscribed: "Chile Correos"

1932 ***Perf. 13½x14, 14***

C21 A43 1p yel grn & blk (Bk) 2.75 1.50

Condor on Andes — AP1a

Airplane Crossing Andes — AP3

Los Cerrillos Airport — AP2

1931 **Litho.** ***Perf. 13½x14, 14½x14***

C22 AP1a 5c yellow grn .25 .20
C23 AP1a 10c yellow brn .25 .20
C24 AP1a 20c rose .25 .20
C25 AP2 50c dark blue 1.25 .40
C26 AP3 50c black brn .60 .20
C27 AP3 1p purple .50 .20
C28 AP3 2p blue blk .75 .25
a. 2p bluish slate .90 .40
C29 AP2 5p lt red 2.50 .25
Nos. C22-C29 (8) 6.35 1.90

For surcharges see Nos. C51-C53.

Airplane over City — AP4

Two Airplanes over Globe — AP9

Designs: 30c, 40c, 50c, Wings over Chile. 60c, Condor. 70c, Airplane and Star of Chile. 80c, Condor and Statue of Canpolican. 3p, 4p, 5p, Seaplane. 6p, 8p, 10p, Airplane. 20p, 30p, Airplane and Southern Cross. 40p, 50p, Airplane and symbols of space.

Perf. 13½x14

1934-39 **Engr.** **Wmk. 215**

C30 AP4 10c yel grn ('35) .25 .20
C31 AP4 15c dk grn ('35) .35 .20
C32 AP4 20c dp bl ('36) .20 .20
C33 AP4 30c blk brn ('35) .20 .20
C34 AP4 40c indigo ('38) .20 .20
C35 AP4 50c dk brn ('36) .20 .20
C36 AP4 60c vio blk ('35) .20 .20
C37 AP4 70c blue ('35) .35 .20
C38 AP4 80c ol blk ('35) .20 .20

Perf. 14

C39 AP9 1p slate blk .20 .20
C40 AP9 2p grnsh bl .20 .20
C41 AP9 3p org brn ('35) .25 .20
C42 AP9 4p brn ('35) .25 .20
C43 AP9 5p org red .25 .20
C44 AP9 6p yel brn ('35) .35 .20
a. 6p brown ('39) 2.50 1.75
C45 AP9 8p grn ('35) .30 .20
C46 AP9 10p brn lake .35 .20
C47 AP9 20p olive .35 .20
C48 AP9 30p gray blk .40 .20
C49 AP9 40p gray vio 1.00 .60
C50 AP9 50p brn vio 1.25 .60
Nos. C30-C50 (21) 7.30 5.00

Nos. C30-C50 have been re-issued in slightly different colors, with white gum. The first printings are considerably scarcer.
See Nos. C90-C107B, C148-C154.

Types of 1931 Surcharged in Black or Red

Perf. 13½x14, 14½x14

1940 **Wmk. 215**

C51 AP1a 80c on 20c lt rose .50 .20
C52 AP2 1.60p on 5p lt red 4.00 .70
C53 AP3 5.10p on 2p sl bl (R) 1.80 1.10
Nos. C51-C53 (3) 6.30 2.00

The surcharge on #C52 measures 21½mm.

ACKNOWLEDGMENT OF RECEIPT STAMPS

AR1

1894 **Unwmk.** ***Perf. 11½***

H1 AR1 5c brown .75 .50
a. Imperf., pair 3.00

The black stamp of design similar to AR1 inscribed "Avis de Paiement" was prepared for use on notices of payment of funds but was not regularly issued.

POSTAGE DUE STAMPS

D1

D2

Handstamped

1894 **Unwmk.** ***Perf. 13***

J1 D1 2c black, *straw* 11.00 5.00
J2 D1 4c black, *straw* 11.00 5.00
J3 D1 6c black, *straw* 11.00 5.00
J4 D1 8c black, *straw* 11.00 5.00
J5 D2 10c black, *straw* 11.00 5.00
J6 D1 16c black, *straw* 11.00 5.00
J7 D1 20c black, *straw* 11.00 5.00
J8 D1 30c black, *straw* 11.00 5.00
J9 D1 40c black, *straw* 11.00 5.00
Nos. J1-J9 (9) 99.00 45.00

J1a D1 2c black, *yellow* 45.00 42.50
J2a D1 4c black, *yellow* 37.50 30.00
J3a D1 6c black, *yellow* 27.50 25.00
J4a D1 8c black, *yellow* 11.00 9.00
J5a D2 10c black, *yellow* 11.00 9.00
J6a D1 16c black, *yellow* 11.00 9.00
J7a D1 20c black, *yellow* 11.00 9.00
J8a D1 30c black, *yellow* 11.00 9.00
J9a D1 40c black, *yellow* 11.00 9.00
Nos. J1a-J9a (9) 176.00 151.50

Counterfeits exist.

D3

1895 **Litho.** ***Perf. 11***

J19 D3 1c red, *yellow* 5.00 2.00
J20 D3 2c red, *yellow* 5.00 2.00
J21 D3 4c red, *yellow* 4.25 2.00
J22 D3 6c red, *yellow* 5.00 2.00
J23 D3 8c red, *yellow* 3.25 2.00
J24 D3 10c red, *yellow* 3.25 3.00
J25 D3 20c red, *yellow* 3.25 1.50
J26 D3 40c red, *yellow* 3.25 2.00
J27 D3 50c red, *yellow* 3.25 2.00
J28 D3 60c red, *yellow* 6.50 3.00
J29 D3 80c red, *yellow* 6.50 4.25
J30 D3 1p red, *yellow* 6.50 4.25
Nos. J19-J30 (12) 55.00 30.00

Nos. J19-J30 were printed in sheets of 100 (10x10) containing all 12 denominations.
Counterfeits of Nos. J19-J42 exist.

1896 ***Perf. 13½***

J31 D3 1c red, *straw* .75 .35
J32 D3 2c red, *straw* .75 .35
J33 D3 4c red, *straw* 1.00 .35
J34 D3 6c red, *straw* 2.00 .75
J35 D3 8c red, *straw* 1.00 .40
J36 D3 10c red, *straw* .75 .40
J37 D3 20c red, *straw* .75 .40
J38 D3 40c red, *straw* 12.00 10.00
J39 D3 50c red, *straw* 12.00 10.00
J40 D3 60c red, *straw* 12.00 10.00
J41 D3 80c red, *straw* 12.00 10.00
J42 D3 100c red, *straw* 25.00 21.00
Nos. J31-J42 (12) 80.00 64.00

D4

D5

1898 ***Perf. 13***

J43 D4 1c scarlet .35 .30
J44 D4 2c scarlet .90 .60
J45 D4 4c scarlet .35 .30
J46 D4 10c scarlet .35 .30
J47 D4 20c scarlet .35 .30
Nos. J43-J47 (5) 2.30 1.80

1924 ***Perf. 11½, 12½***

J48 D5 2c blue & red .75 .60
J49 D5 4c blue & red .75 .60
J50 D5 8c blue & red .75 .60
J51 D5 10c blue & red .75 .60
J52 D5 20c blue & red .75 .35
J53 D5 40c blue & red .75 .60
J54 D5 60c blue & red .75 .60
J55 D5 80c blue & red .75 .60
J56 D5 1p blue & red 1.00 .75
J57 D5 2p blue & red 1.75 1.25
J58 D5 5p blue & red 1.75 1.25
Nos. J48-J58 (11) 10.50 7.80

Nos. J48-J58 were printed in sheets of 150 containing all 11 denominations, and in sheets of 50 containing the five lower denominations, providing various se-tenants.
All values of this issue exist imperforate, also with center inverted, but are not believed to have been regularly issued. Those with inverted centers sell for about 10 times normal stamps.

OFFICIAL STAMPS

For Domestic Postage

O1

Single-lined frame
Control number in violet

1907 **Unwmk.** ***Imperf.***

O1 O1 dl bl, "CARTA" org 22.50 17.50
O2 O1 red, "OFICIO" bl 22.50 17.50
O3 O1 vio, "PAQUETE" red 22.50 17.50
O4 O1 org, *bl*, "EP" vio 22.50 17.50
Nos. O1-O4 (4) 90.00 70.00

The diagonal inscription in differing color indicates type of usage: CARTA for letters of ordinary weight; OFICIO, heavy letters to 100 grams; PAQUETE, parcels to 100 grams; E P (Encomienda Postal), heavier parcels; C (Certificado), as on No. O8, registration including postage.
Varieties include CARTA, PAQUETE and E P inverted, OFICIO omitted, etc.

Double-lined frame
Large control number in black
Perf. 11

O5 O1 bl, "CARTA" yel 8.00 7.00
O6 O1 red, "OFICIO" bl 8.00 5.25
O7 O1 brn, "PAQUETE" grn 8.00 5.25
O8 O1 grn, "C" red 110.00 82.50
Nos. O5-O8 (4) 134.00 100.00

Nos. O5-O8 exist in tête bêche pairs; with CARTA, OFICIO or PAQUETE double or inverted, and other varieties.
Counterfeits of Nos. O1-O8 exist.

For Foreign Postage

Regular Issues of 1892-1909 Overprinted in Red — a

On Stamps of 1904-09

1907 ***Perf. 12***

O9 A14 1c green 7.50 7.50
a. Inverted overprint 17.50
O10 A12 3c on lp brn 14.00 13.00
a. Inverted overprint 52.50
O11 A14 5c ultra 10.00 9.50
a. Inverted overprint 35.00
O12 A15 10c gray & blk 10.50 10.50
O13 A15 15c vio & blk 14.00 13.00
O14 A15 20c org brn & blk 14.00 14.00
O15 A15 50c ultra & blk 45.00 45.00

On Stamp of 1892
Rouletted

O16 A6 1p dk brn & blk 110.00 87.50
Nos. O9-O16 (8) 225.00 200.00

Counterfeits of Nos. O9-O16 exist.

Regular Issues of 1915-25 Overprinted in Red or Blue — b

1926 ***Perf. 13½x14, 14***

O17 A52 5c slate bl (R) 2.50 .50
O18 A50 10c bl & blk (R) 4.00 .75
O19 A39 20c org red & blk (Bl) 2.00 .40
O20 A42 50c dp grn & blk (Bl) 2.00 .40
O21 A43 1p grn & blk (R) 2.75 .70
O22 A43 2p ver & blk (Bl) 4.00 1.00
Nos. O17-O22 (6) 17.25 3.75

Nos. O21 and O22 are overprinted vertically at each side.
Nos. O17 to O22 were for the use of the Biblioteca Nacional.

Regular Issue of 1915-25 Overprinted in Red — c

1928 ***Perf. 13½x14, 14***

O23 A50 10c bl & blk 6.50 2.00
O24 A39 20c brn org & blk 3.00 1.00
O25 A40 25c dl bl & blk 7.50 1.00
O26 A42 50c dp grn & blk 4.00 1.00
O27 A43 1p grn & blk 5.00 1.50
Nos. O23-O27 (5) 26.00 6.50

The overprint on Nos. O23 to O26 is 16½mm high; on No. O27 it is 20mm.

Regular Issues of 1928-30 Overprinted in Red — d

On Stamp Inscribed: "Correos de Chile"

1930-31

O28 A50 10c bl & blk 3.00 1.50

Wmk. 215

On Stamps Inscribed: "Correos de Chile"

O29 A50 10c bl & blk 6.00 3.00
O30 A39 20c org red & blk .75 .50
O31 A40 25c bl & blk .75 .50
O32 A42 50c dp grn & blk 1.50 .75

On Stamps Inscribed: "Chile Correos"

O33 A42 50c dp grn & blk 1.50 .75
O34 A43 1p grn & blk 1.50 .75
Nos. O28-O34 (7) 15.00 7.75

Same Overprint on No. 181

1933 ***Perf. 13½x14***
O35 A61 20c dk brn .75 .25

Same Overprint in Red on No. 182

1935 **Wmk. 215**
O36 A62 10c deep blue .75 .50

No. 163 Ovptd. Type "b" in Red Inscribed: "Correos de Chile"

1934
O37 A52 5c lt grn .60 .50

Overprint "b" on No. 182

1935
O38 A62 10c dp bl .50 .50

Same Overprint in Black on No. 181

1936 **Wmk. 215** ***Perf. 13½x14***
O39 A61 20c dk brn 10.00 .50

Overprint "b" in Red on No. 158

1938 ***Perf. 14***
O40 A43 1p grn & blk 2.50 1.00

Nos. 204 and 205 Overprinted Type "d" in Black

1939 ***Perf. 13½x14, 14***
O41 A78 50c violet 4.00 2.50
O42 A84 1p org brn 5.00 4.00

Stamps of 1938-40 Overprinted Type "b" in Black, Red or Blue

1940-46 ***Perf. 13½x14, 14***
O43 A78 10c sal pink ('45) 2.00 1.75
O44 A78 15c brn org 1.00 .40
O45 A78 20c lt bl (R) ('42) 1.50 .60
O46 A78 30c brn pink (Bl) .75 .40
O47 A78 40c lt grn .75 .40
O48 A78 50c vio ('45) 4.00 .75
O49 A84 1p org brn ('42) 2.50 .75
O50 A84 1.80p dp bl (R) ('45) 10.00 6.00
O51 A84 2p car lake ('42) 2.00 1.25
Nos. O43-O51 (9) 24.50 12.30

Overprint "b" in Black on Nos. 223, 225

Unwmk.

O58 A84 1p brn org 2.50 1.50
O59 A84 2p car lake ('46) 5.00 2.00

CHINA

'chī-nə

LOCATION — Eastern Asia
GOVT. — Republic
AREA — 2,903,475 sq. mi.
POP. — 462,798,093 (1948)

10 Candareen = 1 Mace
10 Mace = 1 Tael
100 Cents = 1 Dollar (Yuan) (1897)

Watermarks

Wmk. 103 — Yin-Yang Symbol

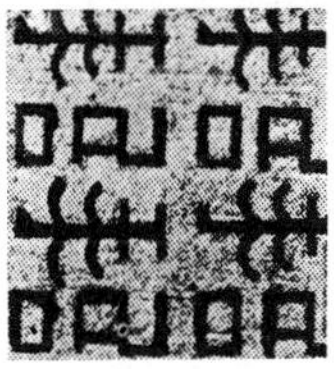

Wmk. 261 — Character Yu (Post) Multiple

Issues of the Imperial Maritime Customs Post

Imperial Dragon — A1

1878 **Unwmk.** **Typo.** ***Perf. 12½***

Thin Paper

Stamps printed 2½-3¼mm apart

1 A1 1c green 200.00 140.00
a. 1c dark green 350.00 175.00
2 A1 3c brown red 375.00 125.00
a. 3c vermilion 475.00 150.00
3 A1 5c orange 475.00 125.00
a. 5c bister orange 825.00 300.00

Imperforate essays of Nos. 1-3 have an extra circle near the dragon's lower left foot. Copies with the circle completely or mostly removed are proofs or unfinished stamps.

1882

Thin or Pelure Paper

Stamps printed 4½mm apart

4 A1 1c green 300.00 175.00
a. 1c dark green 325.00 185.00
5 A1 3c brown red 525.00 140.00
6 A1 5c orange yellow 9,500. 1,100.

1883 ***Rough to smooth Perf. 12½***

Medium to Thick Opaque Paper

Stamps printed 2½ to 3¼mm apart

7 A1 1c green 350.00 175.00
a. 1c dark green 425.00 210.00
b. 1c light green 400.00 225.00
c. Vert. pair, imperf. between 25,000.
8 A1 3c brown red 450.00 110.00
a. 3c vermilion 800.00 125.00
b. Vert. pair, imperf. between 25,000.
9 A1 5c yellow 775.00 150.00
a. 5c chrome yellow 950.00 160.00
b. Horiz. pair, imperf. btwn. 25,000.

Nos. 1-9 were printed from plates of 25, 20 or 15 individual copper dies, but only No. 5 exists in the 15-die setting. Many different printings and plate settings exist. All values occur in a wide variety of shades and papers. The effect of climate on certain papers has produced the varieties on so-called toned papers in Nos. 1-15.

Value for No. 8b is for a damaged copy.

Counterfeits, frequently with forged cancellations, occur in all early Chinese issues.

Imperial Dragon — A2

1885 **Wmk. 103** ***Perf. 12½***
10 A2 1c green 70.00 16.00
a. Vert. pair, imperf. btwn. 13,000. 13,000.
b. Horiz. pair, imperf. btwn. —
11 A2 3c lilac 130.00 20.00
a. Horiz. pair, imperf. btwn. 16,000. 16,000.
b. Vert. pair, imperf. btwn. 18,000.
12 A2 5c grnsh yellow 125.00 22.50
a. 5c bister brown 160.00 27.50
b. Vert. pair, imperf. btwn. 18,000. 18,000.
c. Horiz. pair, imperf. btwn. 18,000.
Nos. 10-12 (3) 325.00 58.50

1888 ***Perf. 11½-12***
13 A2 1c green 18.00 15.00
14 A2 3c lilac 60.00 10.50
b. Double impression 900.00
15 A2 5c grnsh yellow 95.00 27.50
b. Horiz. pair, imperf. vert. —
c. Double impression 600.00 600.00
Nos. 13-15 (3) 173.00 53.00

Nos. 10-15 were printed from plates made of 40 individual copper dies, arranged in two panes of 20 each. Several different settings exist of all values.

Imperforates of Nos. 13-15 are considered proofs by most authorities.

Stamps overprinted "Formosa" in English or Chinese are proofs.

For surcharges see Nos. 25-27, 75-77.

"Shou" and "Wu Fu" — A3

Dragon and Hydrangea Leaves — A4

"Pa Kua" Signs in Corners — A5

Dragon and Peony — A6

Carp, the Messenger Fish — A7

Dragon, "Pa Kua" and Immortelle A8

Dragons and "Shou" A9

Dragons and Giant Peony — A10

Junk on the Yangtse A11

1894 **Lithographed in Shanghai**
16 A3 1c orange red 10.00 *14.00*
a. Vert. pair, imperf. btwn. 1,750. 1,500.
b. Horiz. pair, imperf. btwn. 3,500. 3,500.
c. Vert. pair, imperf. horiz. 2,400. 2,400.
17 A4 2c green 16.00 8.00
a. Horiz. pair, imperf. btwn. 2,500. 2,500.
18 A5 3c orange 12.00 5.00
a. Vert. pair, imperf. btwn. 2,500. 2,500.
b. Horiz. pair, imperf. btwn. 3,000. 3,000.
19 A6 4c rose pink 57.50 60.00
a. Horiz. pair, imperf. btwn. 2,750.
20 A7 5c dull orange 90.00 100.00
a. Horiz. pair, imperf. btwn. 3,000. 3,000.
21 A8 6c dark brown 20.00 10.00
a. Vert. pair, imperf. btwn. 5,500.
b. Horiz. pair, imperf. btwn. 5,500.
22 A9 9c dark green 67.50 19.00
a. Imperf., pair 1,500.
b. Horiz. pair, imperf. vert. 3,000. 3,000.
c. Vert. pair, imperf. horiz. 3,000.
d. Vert. pair, imperf. btwn. 3,500. 3,500.
e. Tete beche pair, vert. 850.00 900.00
f. Tete beche pair, imperf. horiz. 4,000.
g. Tete beche pair, imperf. vert. 4,000. 4,000.
h. Vert. strip of 3, imperf. btwn. 4,000.
i. Tete beche pair, horiz. 1,000. 1,050.
23 A10 12c orange 150.00 92.50
24 A11 24c carmine 210.00 80.00
a. Vert. pair, imperf. btwn. 6,000.
Nos. 16-24 (9) 633.00 388.50

60th birthday of Tsz'e Hsi, the Empress Dowager. All values exist in several distinct shades.

On Mar. 20, 1896, the Customs Post was changed, by Imperial Edict, effective Jan. 1, 1897, to a National Post and the dollar was adopted as the unit of currency.

Time was required to work out details of the Imperial Post and design new stamps. As a provisional measure, stocks of Nos. 16-24 were ordered surcharged with new values in dollars and cents. It is believed that only the Shanghai office stock of Nos. 16-24 (plus any reserve stock at the printers) was surcharged with small figures of value. Other post offices throughout China were instructed to return all unoverprinted stocks on receipt of the new surcharges.

Early in the year it was apparent that all stamps would be exhausted before the new issues were ready (Nos. 86-97), and since the stones from which Nos. 16-24 had been printed no longer existed, new stones were made from the original transfers. A printing from the new stones was made early in 1897 and surcharged with large figures of value spaced 2½mm below the Chinese characters. During the surcharging, sheets from the 1894 (original) printing were received from outlying post offices and surcharged as they arrived. A small quantity of the 1897 printing reached the public without surcharge (Nos. 16n-24n).

Additional stamps were still required and another printing was made from the new stones and surcharged with large figures, but in a new setting with 1½mm between the Chinese characters and the value. Additional sheets of the 1894 printing were received from the most distant post offices and were also surcharged with the 1½mm setting. Thus there are four different sets of the large-figure surcharges. All these stamps were regularly issued but no attempt was made by the post office to separate printings. Some values are difficult to distinguish as to printing, particularly in used condition.

See No. 73. For surcharges see Nos. 28-72, 74.

1897 **Lithographed in Shanghai**
16n A3 1c pink *525.*
17n A4 2c olive green *750.*
18n A5 3c chrome yellow *500.*
p. 3c yellow buff *850.*
19n A6 4c pale rose *575.*
20n A7 5c yellow *575.*
21n A8 6c red brown *800.*

22n A9 9c yellowish green *2,750.*
p. 9c emerald green
23n A10 12c yellowish orange *2,800.*
24n A11 24c purplish red *1,350.*

The colors of the 1897 printings are pale or dull; the gum is thin and white. The 1894 printing has a thicker, yellowish gum.

The set of 9 values on thick unwatermarked paper is a special printing of 5,000 sets ordered by P. G. von Mollendorf, a Customs official, for presentation purposes. Value, set $1,500.

For surcharges see Nos. 47-55, 65-72.

Issues of the Chinese Government Post

Preceding Issues Surcharged in Black

Small Numerals 2½mm Below Chinese Characters
Surcharged on Nos. 13-15

1897, Jan. 2 *Perf. 11½-12*

25 A2 1c on 1c 18.00 *27.50*
26 A2 2c on 3c 125.00 60.00
27 A2 5c on 5c 50.00 19.00
Nos. 25-27 (3) 193.00 106.50

Surcharged on Nos. 16-24

28 A5 ½c on 3c 11.00 8.50
a. "1" instead of "½" 350.00 350.00
b. Horiz. pair, imperf. btwn. *3,000.*
c. Vert. pair, imperf. horiz. *3,000.* *2,250.*
d. Double surcharge *10,000.* *10,000.*
e. Vert. pair, imperf. btwn. *3,000.*
29 A3 1c on 1c 9.00 9.00
a. Inverted surcharge *9,000.* *3,500.*
30 A4 2c on 2c 11.00 6.50
a. Horiz. pair, imperf. vert. *2,000.*
b. Vert. pair, imperf. btwn. *2,000.*
c. Double surcharge *7,500.*
d. Inverted surcharge — *15,000.*
e. Horiz. pair, imperf. btwn. *2,000.*
31 A6 4c on 4c 11.00 7.00
a. Double surcharge *14,000.* *14,000.*
b. Vert. pair, imperf. btwn. *3,000.* *3,000.*
c. Horiz. pair, imperf. btwn. *3,000.* *3,000.*
32 A7 5c on 5c 12.00 6.00
a. Vert. pair, imperf. btwn. *3,000.* *3,000.*
33 A8 8c on 6c 14.00 7.50
a. Vert. pair, imperf. btwn. *2,100.* *2,100.*
b. Vert. strip of 3, imperf. btwn. *2,000.* *2,000.*
c. Horiz. pair, imperf. btwn. *2,250.* *2,250.*
34 A8 10c on 6c 45.00 50.00
b. Vert. pair, imperf. btwn. *2,100.* *2,100.*
c. Horiz. pair, imperf. vert. *2,400.* *2,400.*
35 A9 10c on 9c 240.00 85.00
a. Double surcharge *40,000.* *40,000.*
b. Inverted surcharge *15,000.* *15,000.*
36 A10 10c on 12c 200.00 125.00
a. Vert. pair, imperf. horiz. *1,500.*
b. Vert. pair, imperf. btwn. *1,500.* *1,800.*
37 A11 30c on 24c 250.00 140.00
a. Vert. pair, imperf. btwn. *7,500.*
Nos. 28-37 (10) 803.00 444.50

Small Numerals 4mm Below Chinese Characters

25a A2 1c on 1c green 50.00 50.00
28f A4 ½c on 3c orange 40.00 40.00
29b A3 1c on 1c vermilion 55.00 55.00
30f A4 2c on 2c dark green 35.00 35.00
31d A6 4c on 4c dark pink 35.00 35.00
32b A7 5c on 5c dull orange 35.00 35.00
33d A8 8c on 6c brown 25.00 25.00
35c A9 10c on 9c dark green 275.00 275.00
37b A11 30c on 24c dark red 400.00 250.00

Preceding Issues Surcharged in Black

Large Numerals
Numerals 2½mm below Chinese characters

1897, Mar.

Surcharged on Nos. 16-24

38 A5 ½c on 3c 2,000. 750.00
b. Inverted surcharge *4,500.*
39 A3 1c on 1c 550.00 160.00
40 A4 2c on 2c 290.00 240.00
41 A6 4c on 4c 350.00 300.00
b. Horiz. pair, imperf. btwn. *11,000.*
42 A7 5c on 5c 160.00 160.00
43 A8 8c on 6c 1,200. 1,200.
44 A9 10c on 9c 475.00 300.00
45 A10 10c on 12c *35,000.* 2,500.
46 A11 30c on 24c 950.00 1,000.
b. 2mm spacing between "30" and "cents." *15,000.*

Same Surcharge on Nos. 16n-24n

47 A5 ½c on 3c 11.00 *24.00*
a. "cen" for "cent" 850.00 850.00
b. Vert. pair, imperf. btwn. *1,500.* *1,500.*
c. Vert. pair, imperf. horiz. 1,100. 1,100.
d. As "a" and "c" *9,500.* *9,500.*
e. As "a" and "b" *7,500.* *7,500.*
f. Horiz. pair, imperf. btwn. *1,900.* *1,900.*
48 A3 1c on 1c 8.50 7.25
a. Horiz. pair, imperf. btwn. *2,500.*
49 A4 2c on 2c 7.00 5.25
50 A6 4c on 4c 11.00 9.00
a. Horiz. pair, imperf. btwn. *3,250.* *3,250.*
b. Vert. pair, imperf. btwn. *4,000.*
51 A7 5c on 5c 18.00 8.25
52 A8 8c on 6c 250.00 175.00
53 A9 10c on 9c 85.00 47.50
a. 10c on 9c emerald 90.00 52.50
b. Pair, one without surcharge 825.00
54 A10 10c on 12c 160.00 40.00
55 A11 30c on 24c 275.00 125.00
a. 2mm spacing btwn "30" and "cents" *1,000.* 400.00
b. Vert. pair, imperf. btwn. *6,250.*

All recorded unused copies of #45 are flawed.

Numerals 1½mm below Chinese characters

1897, May

Surcharged on Nos. 16-24

56 A5 ½c on 3c org yel 325.00 275.00
57 A3 1c on 1c 225.00 200.00
58 A4 2c on 2c — *1,250.*
59 A6 4c on 4c 175.00 160.00
60 A7 5c on 5c 125.00 100.00
61 A8 8c on 6c 900.00 675.00
62 A9 10c on 9c 225.00 160.00
63 A10 10c on 12c 850.00 650.00
64 A11 30c on 24c *27,500.* —

Same Surcharge on Nos. 16n-24n

65 A5 ½c on 3c 8.50 *9.00*
a. Inverted surcharge *3,000.* 3,000.
b. ½mm spacing *1,500.* *1,200.*
66 A3 1c on 1c 9.50 6.00
67 A4 2c on 2c 11.00 7.50
a. Inverted surcharge *8,750.* *8,750.*
b. Vert. pair, imperf. btwn. *8,500.*
68 A6 4c on 4c 175.00 110.00
a. Inverted surcharge 1,300. 1,300.
69 A7 5c on 5c 175.00 92.50
70 A9 10c on 9c 110.00 30.00
a. Inverted surcharge 1,000. 1,000.
71 A10 10c on 12c 225.00 60.00
72 A11 30c on 24c *13,000.* 2,600.

Same Surcharge (1½mm Spacing) on Type A12, and

A12

A12a

Redrawn Designs
Printed from New Stones

1897

73 A12 ½c on 3c yel 160.00 150.00
a. ½mm spacing *7,000.* *7,000.*
74 A12a 2c on 2c yel grn 42.50 16.50
a. Horiz. pair, imperf. btwn. *6,000.*

Nos. 73 and 74 were surcharged on stamps printed from new stones, which differ slightly from the originals. On No. 73 the numeral "3" and symbols in the four corner panels have been enlarged and strengthened. On No. 74, the numeral "2" has a thick, flat base.

Surcharged on Nos. 13-15

75 A2 1c on 1c green 325.00 *425.00*
76 A2 2c on 3c lilac 725.00 *700.00*
77 A2 5c on 5c grnsh yel 160.00 *300.00*

Revenue Stamps Surcharged in Black:

A13

a

b

c

d

e

f

g

1897 Unwmk. ***Perf. 12 to 15***

78 A13 (a) 1c on 3c red 190.00 110.00
a. No period after "cent" 210.00 160.00
b. Central character with large "box" 210.00 160.00
79 A13 (b) 2c on 3c red 525.00 160.00
a. Inverted surcharge *7,500.* *5,000.*
b. Inverted "S" in "CENTS" 650.00 400.00
c. No period after "CENTS" 650.00 400.00
d. Comma after "CENTS" 525.00 250.00
e. Double surcharge *25,000.* *25,000.*
f. Dbl. surch., both inverted *50,000*
g. Double surch. (blk & grn) *52,500.*
80 A13 (c) 2c on 3c red 175.00 175.00
81 A13 (d) 4c on 3c red *8,750.* *5,500.*
a. Double surcharge (blk & vio) *45,000.* *35,000.*
82 A13 (e) 4c on 3c red 275.00 125.00
83 A13 (f) $1 on 3c red *325,000.*
a. No period after "r" —
84 A13 (g) $1 on 3c red 1,300. 800.00
85 A13 (g) $5 on 3c red 7,500. 7,250.
a. Inverted surcharge *15,000.* *12,500.*

A few copies of the 3c red exist without surcharge; one canceled. No. 79 with green surcharge is a trial printing. Value for faulty upper left corner block, $190,000.

No. 79g is unique. The only canceled copy of #83 is in a museum.

Dragon — A14

Carp — A15

Wild Goose — A16

"Imperial Chinese Post"
Lithographed in Japan
Perf. 11, 11½, 12

1897, Aug. 16 **Wmk. 103**

86 A14 ½c purple brn 2.50 2.00
a. Horiz. pair, imperf. btwn. 475.00
87 A14 1c yellow 3.50 2.25
88 A14 2c orange 3.00 1.25
a. Vert. pair, imperf. horiz. 450.00
89 A14 4c brown 5.50 1.60
a. Horiz. pair, imperf. btwn. 750.00
90 A14 5c rose red 6.00 2.00
91 A14 10c dk green 17.50 1.60
92 A15 20c maroon 37.50 10.00
93 A15 30c red 65.00 20.00
94 A15 50c yellow grn 47.50 26.00
a. 50c black green 325.00
b. 50c blue green 675.00
95 A16 $1 car & rose 140.00 110.00
a. Horiz. pair, imperf. vert. —
96 A16 $2 orange & yel 950.00 850.00
a. Horiz. pair, imperf. vert. —
97 A16 $5 yel grn & pink 650.00 600.00

The inner circular frames and outer frames of Nos. 86-91 differ for each denomination.

No. 97 imperforate was not regularly issued. **Copies have been privately perforated and offered as No. 97**. Shades occur in most values of this issue.

A17

A18

A19

"Chinese Imperial Post"
Engraved in London

1898 Wmk. 103 ***Perf. 12 to 16***

98 A17 ½c chocolate 1.75 1.25
a. Vert. pair, imperf. btwn. 700.00 425.00
b. Vert. pair, imperf. horiz. 700.00 425.00
99 A17 1c ocher 2.50 1.00
a. Vert. pair, imperf. btwn. 200.00 200.00
b. Horiz. pair, imperf. btwn. 300.00 300.00
100 A17 2c scarlet 3.50 1.25
a. Vert. pair, imperf. btwn. 150.00 150.00
b. Horiz. pair, imperf. vert. 150.00 150.00
101 A17 4c orange brn 4.00 1.25
a. Vert. pair, imperf. btwn. 300.00
b. Horiz. pair, imperf. vert. 225.00 225.00
c. Horiz. pair, imperf. btwn. 525.00 525.00
d. Horiz. strip of 3, imperf. btwn. 700.00 700.00
102 A17 5c salmon 5.75 1.25
a. Vert. pair, imperf. btwn. 240.00 240.00
b. Horiz. pair, imperf. btwn. 275.00 275.00
c. Vert. pair, imperf. horiz. 275.00 275.00
d. 5c pale reddish orange 9.50 2.50
e. As "d," vert pair, imperf. btwn. 300.00 300.00
103 A17 10c dk blue grn 6.75 1.10
a. Vert. or horiz, pair, imperf. btwn — —
104 A18 20c claret 40.00 5.00
a. Horiz. pair, imperf. btwn. 600.00 600.00
b. Vert. pair, imperf. horiz. 600.00 600.00
c. Vert. pair, imperf. btwn. 675.00 675.00
105 A18 30c dull rose 25.00 8.00
a. Horiz. pair, imperf. btwn. 675.00
b. Vert. pair, imperf. horiz. 675.00
c. Vert. pair, imperf. btwn. 675.00
106 A18 50c lt green 40.00 8.50
a. Vert. pair, imperf. btwn. 600.00
107 A19 $1 red & pale rose 160.00 22.50
108 A19 $2 brn, red & yel 260.00 60.00
109 A19 $5 dp grn & sal 500.00 175.00
a. Horiz. pair, imperf. btwn. *7,500.*
b. Vert. pair, imperf. btwn. *7,750.*
Nos. 98-109 (12) 1,049. 286.10

No. 98 surcharged "B. R. A.-5-Five Cents" in three lines in black or green, was surcharged by British military authorities shortly after the Boxer riots for use from military posts in an occupied area along the Peking-Mukden railway. Usually canceled in violet.

See note following No. 122.

1900(?)-06 Unwmk. ***Perf. 12 to 16***

110 A17 ½c brown 1.50 1.25
a. Horiz. pair, imperf. btwn. 275.00 275.00
b. Vert. pair, imperf. btwn. 275.00 275.00
111 A17 1c ocher 1.50 1.25
a. Horiz. pair, imperf. btwn. 190.00 190.00
b. Vert. pair, imperf. btwn. 190.00 190.00
c. Vert. pair, imperf. horiz. 190.00 190.00
112 A17 2c scarlet 2.50 1.25
a. Horiz. pair, imperf. btwn. 160.00 160.00
b. Vert. pair, imperf. btwn. 160.00 160.00
c. Vert. pair, imperf. horiz. 160.00 160.00
d. Horiz. pair, imperf. vert. 160.00 160.00
e. Vert. strip of 3, imperf. btwn. 160.00 160.00
113 A17 4c orange brn 3.25 1.25
a. Horiz. pair, imperf. btwn. 275.00 275.00
b. Vert. pair, imperf. btwn. 275.00 275.00
114 A17 5c rose red 16.00 1.75
a. Vert. pair, imperf. btwn. 260.00 260.00
b. Vert. pair, imperf. horiz. 225.00 225.00
115 A17 5c orange 13.50 2.25
a. 5c yellow 175.00 25.00
b. Vert. pair, imperf. btwn. 300.00 300.00
c. Horiz. pair, imperf. btwn. 300.00 300.00
116 A17 10c green 10.50 1.25
a. Vert. pair, imperf. btwn. 225.00
b. Horiz. pair, imperf. btwn. 225.00
c. Vert. pair, imperf. horiz. 225.00
d. Vert. strip of 3, imperf. btwn. 400.00
117 A18 20c red brown 16.00 1.25
a. Horiz. pair, imperf. btwn. 375.00
b. Vert. pair, imperf. btwn. 325.00
c. Vert. pair, imperf. horiz. 325.00
118 A18 30c dull red 16.00 1.25
a. Vert. pair, imperf. btwn. 675.00
119 A18 50c yellow grn 27.50 1.75
a. Horiz. pair, imperf. btwn. 850.00
120 A19 $1 red & pale rose ('06) 85.00 12.00
121 A19 $2 brn red & yel ('06) 225.00 24.00
122 A19 $5 dp grn & sal 325.00 110.00
Nos. 110-122 (13) 743.25 160.50

See #124-130. For surcharges and overprints see #123, 134-177, J1-J6, Offices in Tibet 1-11.

Diagonal Half of No. 112 Surcharged on Stamp and Envelope

Postage
1 Cent
Paid

1903

No.	Design	Description	Unused	Used
123	A17	1c on half of 2c scarlet, on cover		*1,500.*

Used Oct. 22 to Oct. 24. Value is for cover mailed to post office other than sending office (Foochow) and bearing backstamp showing arrival date. Locally addressed or unaddressed covers without backstamps properly used are worth approximately $1,000. Others are worth less.

Forgeries are plentiful, particularly on pieces of cover. Certificates of authenticity are mandatory.

1905-10

No.	Design	Description	Unused	Used
124	A17	2c green ('08)	1.75	1.25
a.		Horiz. pair, imperf. btwn.	300.00	300.00
b.		Vert. pair, imperf. btwn.	300.00	300.00
c.		Horiz. pair, imperf. vert.	300.00	300.00
d.		Horiz. strip of 4, imperf. btwn.	675.00	675.00
125	A17	3c slate grn ('10)	2.75	1.25
a.		Horiz. pair, imperf. btwn.	225.00	
b.		Vert. pair, imperf. btwn.	225.00	
126	A17	4c vermilion ('09)	3.75	1.00
127	A17	5c violet	4.75	1.25
a.		5c lilac	5.50	1.25
b.		Horiz. pair, imperf. btwn.	325.00	
c.		Vert. pair, imperf. btwn.	325.00	
d.		Vert. pair, imperf. horiz.	275.00	
128	A17	7c maroon ('10)	8.75	4.50
129	A17	10c ultra ('08)	11.50	1.25
a.		Horiz. pair, imperf. btwn.	325.00	
b.		Vert. pair, imperf. btwn.	325.00	
c.		Vert. pair, imperf. horiz.	30.00	300.00
130	A18	16c olive grn ('07)	37.50	8.00
		Nos. 124-130 (7)	70.75	18.50

Temple of Heaven, Peking — A20

1909 *Perf. 14*

No.	Design	Description	Unused	Used
131	A20	2c orange & green	3.75	*4.50*
132	A20	3c orange & blue	5.00	*10.00*
133	A20	7c orange & brn vio	7.00	*5.25*
		Nos. 131-133 (3)	15.75	*19.75*

1st year of the reign of Hsuan T'ung, who later became Henry Pu-yi and then Emperor Kang Teh of Manchukuo.

Stamps of 1902-10 Overprinted with Chinese Characters

Foochow Issue

Overprinted in Red or Black

1912 *Perf. 12 to 16*

No.	Design	Description	Unused	Used
134	A17	3c slate grn (R)	175.	85.
135	A19	$1 red & pale rose	1,500.	1,400.
136	A19	$2 brn red & yel	2,250.	1,700.
137	A19	$5 dp grn & sal	3,750.	2,500.

The overprint "Ling Shih Chung Li" or "Provisional Neutrality," signified that the P.O. was conducted neutrally by agreement between the Manchu and opposing forces.

Nanking Issue

Overprinted in Red or Black

No.	Design	Description	Unused	Used
138	A17	1c ocher (R)	165.	100.
139	A17	3c slate grn (R)	150.	90.
140	A17	7c maroon	350.	250.
141	A18	16c olive grn (R)	1,500.	1,500.
142	A18	50c yellow grn (R)	1,500.	1,200.
143	A19	$1 red & pale rose	1,400.	1,100.
144	A19	$2 brn red & yel	2,750.	2,750.
145	A19	$5 dp green & sal	5,500.	5,500.

Vertical overprint reads: "Chung Hwa Min Kuo" (Republic of China).

Stamps of this issue were also used in Shanghai and Hankow.

Additional values were overprinted but not issued. Excellent forgeries of the overprints of Nos. 134-145 exist.

Issues of the Republic

Overprinted in Black or Red

Overprinted by the Maritime Customs Statistical Department, Shanghai

No.	Design	Description	Unused	Used
146	A17	½c brown	.70	.75
a.		Inverted overprint	37.50	37.50
b.		Double overprint	95.00	
147	A17	1c ocher (R)	1.10	.75
a.		Vert. pair, imperf. horiz.	190.00	190.00
b.		Inverted overprint	150.00	95.00
c.		Double overprint	190.00	150.00
d.		Horiz. pair, imperf. btwn.	275.00	240.00
e.		Horiz. pair, imperf. vert.	140.00	
f.		Pair, one without overprint	140.00	
148	A17	2c green (R)	.95	.75
a.		Vert. pair, imperf. btwn.	190.00	190.00
149	A17	3c slate grn (R)	1.40	.60
a.		Inverted overprint	100.00	60.00
b.		Horiz. or vert. pair, imperf. btwn	275.00	275.00
d.		Horiz. pair, imperf. vert.	110.00	
150	A17	4c vermilion	2.50	.60
a.		Vert. pair, imperf. btwn.	750.00	
151	A17	5c violet (R)	3.00	.40
a.		Horiz. pair, imperf. btwn.		
152	A17	7c maroon	4.50	1.25
153	A17	10c ultra (R)	4.75	.55
a.		Double overprint	190.00	
b.		Pair, one without overprint	700.00	
c.		Brownish red overprint	12.00	7.50
d.		Inverted overprint	240.00	240.00
154	A18	16c olive grn (R)	11.00	4.00
155	A18	20c red brown	9.00	2.75
156	A18	30c rose red	11.50	2.75
157	A18	50c yel grn (R)	20.00	2.75
158	A19	$1 red & pale rose	140.00	11.50
a.		Inverted overprint		*8,250.*
159	A19	$2 brn red & yel	100.00	32.50
a.		Inverted overprint	260.00	260.00
160	A19	$5 dp grn & sal	275.00	190.00
		Nos. 146-160 (15)	585.40	251.90

Stamps with blue overprint similar to the preceding were not an official issue but were privately made by a printer in Tientsin.

Overprinted in Red

Overprinted by the Commercial Press, Shanghai

This type differs in that the top character is shifted slightly to right and the bottom character is larger and has small "legs".

No.	Design	Description	Unused	Used
161	A17	1c ocher	3.25	.55
a.		Inverted overprint	375.00	375.00
b.		Vert. pair, imperf. btwn.	450.00	
c.		Double overprint	450.00	
162	A17	2c green	22.50	1.65
a.		Inverted overprint	1,100.	900.00
b.		Vert. pair, imperf. btwn.	260.00	
c.		Horiz. pair, imperf. btwn.	300.00	
d.		Horiz. strip of 3, imperf. btwn.	475.00	

Overprinted in Blue, Carmine or Black

Overprinted by Waterlow & Sons, London

No.	Design	Description	Unused	Used
163	A17	½c brown (Bl)	.75	.75
a.		Vert. pair, imperf. btwn.	1,050.	1,050.
164	A17	1c ocher (C)	.75	.75
a.		Horiz. pair, imperf. btwn.	190.00	
165	A17	2c green (C)	1.40	.60
166	A17	3c slate grn (C)	1.60	.65
a.		Inverted overprint		1,600.
167	A17	4c vermilion (Bk)	3.00	.90
168	A17	5c violet (C)	3.25	.85
169	A17	7c maroon (Bk)	20.00	14.00
170	A17	10c ultra (C)	8.00	1.40
a.		Vert. pair, imperf. btwn.	525.00	525.00
171	A18	16c olive grn (R)	26.00	7.75
172	A18	20c red brn (Bk)	17.50	2.10
173	A18	30c dull red (Bk)	57.50	4.00
174	A18	50c yellow grn (R)	77.50	8.00
175	A19	$1 red & pale rose (Bk)	125.00	10.50
176	A19	$2 brn red & yel (Bk)	250.00	125.00
177	A19	$5 dp grn & sal (C)	350.00	275.00
		Nos. 163-177 (15)	942.25	452.25

Due to instructions issued to postmasters throughout China at the time of the Revolution, a number of them prepared unauthorized overprints using the same characters as the overprints prepared by the government. While many were made in good faith, some, like the blue overprints from Tientsin, were bogus, and the status of certain others is extremely dubious.

Dr. Sun Yat-sen — A21

1912, Dec. 14 *Perf. 14½*

No.	Design	Description	Unused	Used
178	A21	1c orange	1.90	*2.60*
179	A21	2c yellow grn	1.90	*2.60*
180	A21	3c slate grn	1.90	*2.60*
181	A21	5c rose lilac	3.25	2.50
182	A21	8c dp brown	3.25	3.25
183	A21	10c dull blue	3.25	3.25
184	A21	16c olive grn	7.50	6.75
185	A21	20c maroon	15.00	7.50
186	A21	50c dk green	27.50	25.00
187	A21	$1 brown red	100.00	30.00
188	A21	$2 yellow brn	240.00	190.00
189	A21	$5 gray	85.00	*110.00*
		Nos. 178-189 (12)	490.45	386.05

Honoring the leader of the Revolution.

President Yuan Shih-kai — A22

1912, Dec. 14

No.	Design	Description	Unused	Used
190	A22	1c orange	1.00	1.00
191	A22	2c yellow green	1.00	1.00
192	A22	3c slate green	1.00	1.00
193	A22	5c rose lilac	1.00	1.10
194	A22	8c deep brown	3.50	2.25
195	A22	10c dull blue	2.75	1.40
196	A22	16c olive green	3.75	*4.25*
197	A22	20c maroon	3.00	*3.00*
198	A22	50c dark green	19.00	12.00
199	A22	$1 brown red	60.00	30.00
200	A22	$2 yellow brown	67.50	35.00
201	A22	$5 gray	225.00	225.00
		Nos. 190-201 (12)	388.50	317.00

Honoring the 1st pres. of the Republic.

Junk — A24

Reaping Rice — A25

Gateway, Hall of Classics, Peking — A26

DESIGN A24

London Printing: Vertical shading lines under top panel fine, junk with clear diagonal shading lines on sails, right pennant of junk usually long, lines in water weak except directly under junk.

Peking Printing: Vertical shading lines under top panel and inner vertical frame line much heavier, water and sails of junk more evenly and strongly colored, white wave over "H" of "CHINA" pointed upward, touching the junk.

DESIGN A25

London: Front hat brim thick and nearly straight, left foot touches shadow.

Peking: Front hat brim thin and strongly upturned, left foot and sickle clearly outlined in white, shadow of middle tree lighter than those of the right and left trees.

DESIGN A26

London: Light colored walk clearly defined almost to the doorway, figure in right doorway "T" shaped with strong horizontal cross-bar, white panel in base of central tower rectangular, vertical stroke in top left character uniformly thick at its base, tree to right of doorway ends in minute dots.

Peking: Walk more heavily shaded near doorway, especially at right; figure in right doorway more like a "Y", white panel at base of central tower is a long oval, right vertical stroke in top left character incurved near its base, tree at right has five prominent dots at top.

London Printing: By Waterlow & Sons, London, perf. 14 to 15.

Peking Printing: By the Chinese Bureau of Engraving and Printing, Peking, perf. 14.

London Printing

1913, May 5 *Perf. 14-15*

No.	Design	Description	Unused	Used
202	A24	½c black brn	.45	.20
a.		Horiz. or vert. pair, imperf. btwn.	190.00	
203	A24	1c orange	.45	.20
a.		Horiz. pair, imperf. btwn.	225.00	
b.		Vert. pair, imperf. btwn.	150.00	
c.		Horiz. strip of 5, imperf. btwn	600.00	
204	A24	2c yellow grn	1.50	.20
a.		Horiz. pair, imperf. btwn.	375.00	
205	A24	3c blue grn	3.75	.20
a.		Horiz. pair, imperf. btwn.	190.00	
b.		Vert. pair, imperf. btwn.		375.00
206	A24	4c scarlet	5.50	.40
207	A24	5c rose lilac	15.00	.40
208	A24	6c gray	2.50	.55
209	A24	7c violet	12.00	5.50
210	A24	8c brown org	22.50	1.40
211	A24	10c dk blue	19.00	.60
a.		Horiz. pair, imperf. btwn.	350.00	350.00
b.		Vert. pair, imperf. btwn.	375.00	275.00
212	A25	15c brown	17.50	4.00
213	A25	16c olive grn	9.00	1.10
214	A25	20c brown red	15.00	1.75
215	A25	30c brown vio	17.50	1.10
a.		Horiz. pair, imperf. btwn.	375.00	375.00
216	A25	50c green	32.50	2.50
217	A26	$1 ocher & blk	82.50	2.75
218	A26	$2 blue & blk	140.00	12.00
219	A26	$5 scarlet & blk	250.00	80.00
220	A26	$10 yel grn & blk	700.00	600.00
		Nos. 202-220 (19)	1,346.	714.85

First Peking Printing

1915 *Perf. 14*

221	A24	½c black brn	.45	.20
222	A24	1c orange	.45	.20
223	A24	2c yellow grn	.85	.20
224	A24	3c blue grn	.85	.20
225	A24	4c scarlet	9.25	.20
226	A24	5c rose lilac	3.75	.20
a.		Booklet pane of 4	110.00	
227	A24	6c gray	9.25	.25
228	A24	7c violet	11.00	3.75
229	A24	8c brown org	6.25	.25
230	A24	10c dk blue	7.25	.45
a.		Booklet pane of 4	110.00	
231	A25	15c brown	21.00	4.00
232	A25	16c olive grn	7.75	.45
233	A25	20c brown red	8.75	.45
234	A25	30c brown vio	7.75	.45
235	A25	50c green	19.00	.45
236	A26	$1 ocher & blk	62.50	.70
237	A26	$2 blue & blk	150.00	2.75
a.		Center inverted	*20,000.*	
238	A26	$5 scarlet & blk	375.00	25.00
239	A26	$10 yel grn & blk	550.00	160.00
		Nos. 221-239 (19)	1,251.	200.15

1919

240	A24	1½c violet	1.65	.40
241	A25	13c brown	4.00	.45
242	A26	$20 yellow & blk	2,250.	1,800.

Nos. 226 and 230 overprinted in red with five characters in vertical column were for postal savings use.

The higher values of the 1913-19 issues are often overprinted with Chinese characters, which are the names of various postal districts. Stamps were frequently stolen while in transit to post offices. The overprints served to protect them, since the stamps could only be used in the districts for which they were overprinted.

Compare designs A24-A26 with designs A29-A31. For surcharges and overprints see Nos. 247, 288, B1-B3, Sinkiang 1-38.

Yeh Kung-cho, Hsu Shi-chang and Chin Yun-peng
A27

1921, Oct. 10

243	A27	1c orange	5.00	1.50
244	A27	3c blue green	5.00	1.50
245	A27	6c gray	5.00	1.50
246	A27	10c blue	5.00	1.50
		Nos. 243-246 (4)	20.00	6.00

National Post Office, 25th anniversary.
For overprints see Sinkiang Nos. 39-42.

No. 224 Surcharged in Red

1922

247	A24	2c on 3c blue green	2.50	.50
a.		Inverted surcharge	*19,000.*	

Second Peking Printing

A29

A30

A31

Types of 1913-19 Issues Re-engraved

Type A29: Most of the whitecaps in front of the junk have been removed and the water made darker. The shading lines have been removed from the arabesques and pearls above the top inscription. The inner shadings at the top and sides of the picture have been cut away.

Type A30: The heads of rice in the side panels have a background of crossed lines instead of horizontal lines. The Temple of Heaven is strongly shaded and has a door. There are rows of pearls below the Chinese characters in the upper corners. The arabesques above the top inscription have been altered and are without shading lines.

Type A31: The curved line under the inscription at top is single instead of double. There are four vertical lines, instead of eight, at each side of the picture. The trees at the sides of the temple had foliage in the 1913-19 issues, but now the branches are bare. There are numerous other alterations in the design.

1923 *Perf. 14*

248	A29	½c black brown	.75	.20
a.		Horiz. pair, imperf. btwn.	165.00	165.00
b.		Horiz. pair, imperf. vert.	140.00	140.00
249	A29	1c orange	.45	.20
a.		Imperf., pair	110.00	
b.		Horiz. pair, imperf. vert.	110.00	
c.		Booklet pane of 6	90.00	
d.		Booklet pane of 4	45.00	
250	A29	1½c violet	1.40	.70
251	A29	2c yellow grn	.75	.20
252	A29	3c blue green	2.25	.20
a.		Booklet pane of 6	75.00	
253	A29	4c gray	10.00	.60
254	A29	5c claret	1.60	.35
a.		Booklet pane of 4	90.00	
255	A29	6c scarlet	3.25	.35
256	A29	7c violet	3.25	.35
257	A29	8c orange	6.50	.35
258	A29	10c blue	5.00	.25
a.		Booklet pane of 6	110.00	
b.		Booklet pane of 2	140.00	
259	A30	13c brown	11.50	.45
260	A30	15c dp blue	3.75	.45
261	A30	16c olive grn	4.50	.45
262	A30	20c brown red	3.75	.30
263	A30	30c purple	12.00	.30
264	A30	50c dp green	21.00	.45
265	A31	$1 org brn & sep	22.50	.55
266	A31	$2 blue & red brn	32.50	.80
267	A31	$5 red & slate	55.00	3.00
268	A31	$10 green & claret	300.00	32.50
269	A31	$20 plum & blue	500.00	110.00
		Nos. 248-269 (22)	1,001.	153.00

Nos. 249 and 275 exist with webbing watermark from experimental printing.

To prevent speculation and theft, the dollar denominations were overprinted with single characters in red for use in Kwangsi ($1-$20) and Kweichow ($1-$5).

See Nos. 275, 324. For surcharges and overprints see Nos. 274, 289, 311, 325, 330, 339-340, Szechwan 1-3, Yunnan 1-20, Manchuria 1-20, Sinkiang 47-69, 114, C1-C4.

Temple of Heaven, Peking — A32

1923, Oct. 17 *Perf. 14*

270	A32	1c orange	3.50	.95
271	A32	3c blue green	4.00	1.90
272	A32	4c red	7.50	1.90
273	A32	10c blue	11.00	2.50
		Nos. 270-273 (4)	26.00	7.25

Adoption of Constitution, October, 1923.
For overprints see Sinkiang Nos. 43-46.

No. 253 Surcharged in Red

1925

274	A29	3c on 4c gray	1.90	.20
a.		Inverted surcharge	*22,500.*	*10,000.*
b.		Vert. pair, imperf. btwn.		

Junk Type of 1923

1926

275	A29	4c olive green	1.25	.20
a.		Horiz. pair, imperf. vert.	175.00	
b.		Horiz. pair, imperf. btwn.	175.00	
c.		Horiz. strip of 3, imperf. btwn.	225.00	

Marshal Chang Tso-lin — A34

President Chiang Kai-shek — A35

1928, Mar. 1 *Perf. 14*

276	A34	1c brown orange	1.10	1.25
277	A34	4c olive green	2.75	3.00
278	A34	10c dull blue	6.75	4.00
279	A34	$1 red	40.00	*52.50*
		Nos. 276-279 (4)	50.60	60.75

Assumption of office by Marshal Chang Tso-lin. The stamps of this issue were only available for postage in the Provinces of Chihli and Shantung and at the Offices in Manchuria and Sinkiang.

For overprints see Manchuria Nos. 21-24, Sinkiang 70-73.

1929, May

280	A35	1c brown orange	.85	.35
281	A35	4c olive green	1.25	.65
282	A35	10c dark blue	10.00	1.00
283	A35	$1 dark red	60.00	45.00
		Nos. 280-283 (4)	72.10	47.00

Unification of China.
For overprints see Yunnan Nos. 21-24, Manchuria 25-28, Sinkiang 74-77.

Sun Yat-sen Mausoleum, Nanking — A36

1929, May 30 *Perf. 14*

284	A36	1c brown orange	1.00	.75
285	A36	4c olive green	.90	1.25
286	A36	10c dark blue	5.50	2.25
287	A36	$1 dark red	55.00	26.00
		Nos. 284-287 (4)	62.40	30.25

The transfer of Dr. Sun Yat-sen's remains from Peiping to the mausoleum at Nanking.

For overprints see Yunnan Nos. 25-28, Manchuria 29-32, Sinkiang 78-81.

Nos. 224 and 252 Surcharged in Red

1930

288	A24	1c on 3c blue green	1.10	2.00
289	A29	1c on 3c blue green	.85	.35
a.		No period after "Ct"	17.50	17.50

See Nos. 311, 325, 330.

Dr. Sun Yat-sen — A37

Type I — Double-lined circle in the sun.
Type II — Heavy, single-lined circle in the sun.

Printed by De la Rue & Co., Ltd., London

Perf. 11½x12½, 12½x13, 12½, 13½

1931, Nov. 12 **Engr.**

Type I

290	A37	1c orange	.45	.20
291	A37	2c olive green	.55	.30
292	A37	4c green	.85	.20
293	A37	20c ultra	1.10	.20
294	A37	$1 org brn & dk brn	8.25	.35
295	A37	$2 blue & org brn	22.50	2.25
296	A37	$5 dull red & blk	32.50	3.75
		Nos. 290-296 (7)	66.20	7.25

Stamps issued prior to 1933 were printed by a wet-paper process, and owing to shrinkage such stamps are 1-1½mm narrower than the later dry-printed stamps.

Early printings are perf. 12½x13. Nos. 304, 305 and 306 were later perf. 11½x12½.

1931-37

Type II

297	A37	2c olive grn	.35	.20
298	A37	4c green	.60	.20
299	A37	5c green ('33)	.35	.20
300	A37	15c dk green	3.75	1.25
301	A37	15c scarlet ('34)	.40	.20
302	A37	20c ultra ('37)	.75	.20
303	A37	25c ultra	.40	.60
304	A37	$1 org brn & dk brn	9.25	.50
305	A37	$2 blue & org brn	17.00	.90
306	A37	$5 dull red & blk	35.00	3.75
		Nos. 297-306 (10)	67.85	8.05

See #631-635. For surcharges and overprints see #341, 343, 678, 682, 684-685, 689-691, 768, 843, 1N1, 2N1-2N5, 2N57-2N59, 2N83-2N84, 2N101-2N106, 2N116, 2N124-2N126, 3N1-3N5, 4N1-4N5, 5N1-5N4, 6N1-6N5, 7N1-7N4, 7N54, 8N2-8N3, 8N43-8N44, 8N54, 8N57, 8N69-8N71, 8N85, 9N1-9N5, Taiwan 19, 21-22, Northeastern Provinces 44, Szechwan 4-11, Yunnan 29-44, Sinkiang 82-97.

"Nomads in the Desert" — A38

1932 **Unwmk.** *Perf. 14*

307	A38	1c deep orange	24.00	22.50
308	A38	4c olive green	24.00	22.50
309	A38	5c claret	24.00	22.50
310	A38	10c deep blue	24.00	22.50
		Nos. 307-310 (4)	96.00	90.00

Northwest Scientific Expedition of Sven Hedin. A small quantity of this issue was sold at face at Peking and several other cities. The bulk of the issue was furnished to Hedin and sold at $5 (Chinese) a set for funds to finance the expedition.

#252 Surcharged in Black Like #288

1932

311	A29	1c on 3c blue green	2.00	1.10

Martyrs Issue

Teng Keng
A39

Ch'en Ying-shih
A40

Chu Chih-hsin
A45

Sung Chiao-jen
A46

Huang Hsing
A47

Liao Chung-kai
A48

1932-34 *Perf. 14*

312	A39	½c black brown	.20	.20
313	A40	1c orange ('34)	.20	.20
314	A39	2½c rose lilac ('33)	.20	.20
315	A48	3c dp brown ('33)	.20	.20
316	A45	8c brown orange	.35	.20
317	A46	10c dull violet	.40	.20
318	A45	13c blue green	.50	.20
319	A46	17c brown olive	.40	.20
320	A47	20c brown red	.80	.20
321	A48	30c brown violet	1.25	.20
322	A47	40c orange	.95	.25
323	A40	50c green ('34)	3.50	.50
		Nos. 312-323 (12)	8.95	2.75

Perfs. 12 to 13 and compound and with secret marks are listed as Nos. 402-439. No. 316 re-drawn is No. 485.

For overprints and surcharge see Nos. 342, 472, 474, 478-479, 486-487, 490, 531-536, 539-541, 544-549, 616, 619, 622-624, 647-659, 662-663, 665, 669, 672, 698, 704, 711, 713-715, 720-721, 831, 846-847, 867, 870, 872, 881-882, J120-J121, 1N14-1N15, 1N59, 2N6-2N9, 2N32-2N56, 2N60, 2N76-2N82, 2N85-2N87-2N90, 2N107-2N115, 2N118, 2N121-2N123, 3N6-3N10, 3N34-3N55, 3N59, 4N6-4N9, 4N39-4N64, 4N69, 5N5-5N8, 5N34-5N60, 5N65, 6N6-6N8, 6N35-6N61, 6N66, 7N5-7N7, 7N30-7N53, 7N55, 7N59, 8N1, 8N4,

8N28-8N42, 8N45, 8N47-8N50, 8N60-8N61, 8N68, 8N73, 8N76-8N79, 8N89, 8N97, 8N99-8N100, 8N103-8N104, 9N72-9N77, Taiwan 14-17, 20, 28A, 74, Northeastern Provinces 6-8, 11, Szechwan 12-23, Yunnan 49-60, Sinkiang 102-113, 140-161, 197.

Junk Type of 1923 Issue

1933 *Perf. 14*

324 A29 6c brown 19.00 1.25

#275 Surcharged in Red Like #288

1933

325 A29 1c on 4c olive green 1.50 .30
a. No period after "Ct" 19.00 19.00

Tan Yuan-chang — A49

1933, Jan. 9

326 A49 2c olive green 2.25 .35
327 A49 5c green 2.25 .35
328 A49 25c ultra 7.00 1.50
329 A49 $1 red 62.50 19.00
Nos. 326-329 (4) 74.00 21.20

Tan Yuan-chang, more commonly known as Tan Yen-kai, a prominent statesman in China since the revolution of 1912 and Pres. of the Executive Dept. of the Natl. Government. Placed on sale Jan. 9, 1933, the date of the ceremony in celebration of the completion of the Tan Yuan-chang Memorial Hall and Tomb at Mukden.

For overprints see Yunnan Nos. 45-48, Sinkiang 98-101.

#251 Surcharged in Red Like #288

1935 *Perf. 14*

330 A29 1c on 2c yellow grn 2.25 .20

Emblem of New Life Movement A50

Four Virtues of New Life A51

Lighthouse — A52

1936, Jan. 1

331 A50 2c olive green .90 .75
332 A50 5c green 1.00 .25
333 A51 20c dark blue 5.00 .70
334 A52 $1 rose red 27.50 4.75
Nos. 331-334 (4) 34.40 6.45

"New Life" movement.

Methods of Mail Transportation A53

Maritime Scene — A54

Shanghai General Post Office — A55

Ministry of Communications, Nanking — A56

1936, Oct. 10

335 A53 2c orange .40 .40
336 A54 5c green .50 .20
337 A55 25c blue 4.00 .45
338 A56 $1 dk carmine 25.00 5.50
Nos. 335-338 (4) 29.90 6.55

Founding of the Chinese PO, 40th anniv.

Nos. 260 and 261 Surcharged in Red

1936, Oct. 11

339 A30 5c on 15c dp blue 1.00 .35
340 A30 5c on 16c olive grn 3.00 .85

No. 298 Surcharged in Red

1937

341 A37 1c on 4c green, type II 1.00 .40
a. Upper left character missing

Nos. 322 and 303 Surcharged in Black or Red

1938 *Perf. 12½, 14*

342 A47 8c on 40c orange (Bk) 1.50 .75
343 A37 10c on 25c ultra (R) 1.00 .20

Dr. Sun Yat-sen — A57

Type I — Coat button half circle. Six lines of shading above head. Top frame partially shaded with vertical lines.

Type II — Coat button complete circle. Nine lines of shading above head. Top frame partially shaded with vertical lines.

Type III — Coat button complete circle. Nine lines of shading above head. Top frame line fully shaded with vertical lines.

Printed by the Chung Hwa Book Co.

1938 Unwmk. Engr. *Perf. 12½*

Type I

344 A57 $1 henna & dk brn 70.00 9.75
345 A57 $2 dp blue & org brn 13.00 3.50
346 A57 $5 red & grnsh blk 100.00 14.00
Nos. 344-346 (3) 183.00 27.25

1939

Type II

347 A57 $1 henna & dk brn 13.00 .65
348 A57 $2 dp blue & org brn 16.00 3.00

1939-43

Type III

349 A57 2c olive green .20 .20
350 A57 3c dull claret .20 .20
351 A57 5c green .20 .20
352 A57 5c olive green .20 .20
353 A57 8c olive green .20 .20
354 A57 10c green .20 .20
355 A57 15c scarlet 1.10 2.00
356 A57 15c dk vio brn ('43) 15.00 30.00
357 A57 16c olive gray 1.50 .40
358 A57 25c dk blue .35 .70
359 A57 $1 henna & dk brn 1.75 .70
360 A57 $2 dp blue & org brn 3.50 .50
a. Imperf., pair 275.00
361 A57 $5 red & grnsh blk 2.25 .50
362 A57 $10 dk green & dull pur 13.50 2.00
363 A57 $20 rose lake & dk blue 47.50 45.00
Nos. 349-363 (15) 87.65 83.00

Several values exist imperforate, but these were not regularly issued. No. 361 imperforate is printer's waste.

See Nos. 368-401, 506-524. For surcharges and overprints see Nos. 440-448, 473, 475-477, 480-481, 482-484, 489, 537-538, 615, 618, 620, 660-661, 664, 666-668, 673-676, 680-681, 686, 688, 699-703, 707-709, 717, 719, 830, J67-J68, M2, M11-M12, 1N2-1N13, 1N23-1N42, 1N57-1N58, 2N10-2N31, 2N61-2N75, 2N86, 2N91-2N93, 2N117, 2N119-2N120, 3N11-3N33, 3N56-3N58, 3N60-3N61, 4N10-4N38, 4N65-4N68, 4N70-4N71, 5N9-5N33, 5N61-5N64, 5N66-5N68, 6N9-6N34, 6N62-6N65, 6N67-6N69, 7N8-7N29, 7N56-7N58, 7N60-7N61, 8N5-8N27, 8N46, 8N51-8N53, 8N55-8N56, 8N58-8N59, 8N62-8N67, 8N72, 8N74-8N75, 8N80-8N84, 8N86-8N88, 8N90, 8N95-8N96, 8N98, 8N101-8N102, 8N105-8N106, 9N6-9N71, 9N97, 9N99, Taiwan 78, 84, Northeastern Provinces 9-10, Sinkiang 115-139, 174-188, 196, 198.

Chinese and American Flags and Map of China — A58

Printed by American Bank Note Co.

Frame Engr., Center Litho.

1939, July 4 Unwmk. *Perf. 12*

Flag in Deep Rose and Ultramarine

364 A58 5c dark green 1.50 .50
365 A58 25c deep blue 1.75 .90
366 A58 50c brown 3.50 1.10
367 A58 $1 rose carmine 5.50 2.00
Nos. 364-367 (4) 12.25 4.50

150th anniv. of the US Constitution.

Type of 1939-41 Issue Re-engraved

2c, 1939-41

Re-engraved

8c, 1939-41

Re-engraved

1940 *Perf. 12½*

368 A57 2c olive green .20 .20
369 A57 8c olive green .20 .20

Type of 1938-41 Issue

1940 Unwmk. *Perf. 14*

Type III

370 A57 2c olive green 2.10 1.00
371 A57 5c green 4.25 2.10
372 A57 $1 henna & dk brn 75.00 15.00
373 A57 $2 dp blue & org brn 16.00 4.25
374 A57 $5 red & grnsh blk 21.00 15.00
375 A57 $10 dk grn & dull pur 62.50 12.00
Nos. 370-375 (6) 180.85 49.35

See surcharge note following No. 363.

Type of 1939-41

1940 Wmk. 261 *Perf. 12½*

Type III

376 A57 $1 henna & dk brn 6.00 8.00
377 A57 $2 dp blue & org brn 8.00 8.00
378 A57 $5 red & grnsh blk 8.00 17.50
379 A57 $10 dk green & dull pur 12.00 26.00
380 A57 $20 rose lake & dp blue 16.00 26.00
Nos. 376-380 (5) 50.00 85.50

See surcharge note following No. 363.

Printed by the Dah Tung Book Co.

Type III with Secret Marks

Five Cent

Type III — Characters joined

Secret Mark — Characters not joined

Eight Cent

Type III — Characters not joined

Secret Mark — Characters joined

Ten Cent

Type III — Characters sharp and well shaped

Secret Mark — Characters coarse and varying in thickness

Dollar Values

Type III

Secret Mark

1940 Unwmk. *Perf. 14*

381 A57 5c green .20 .20
382 A57 5c olive green .20 .20
383 A57 8c olive green .40 .20
a. Without "star" in uniform button 1.50 2.50
384 A57 10c green .20 .20
385 A57 30c scarlet .35 .20
386 A57 50c dk blue .45 .20
387 A57 $1 org brn & sepia 2.25 .20
388 A57 $2 dp blue & yel brn .90 .35
389 A57 $5 red & slate grn .90 .45
390 A57 $10 dk grn & dull pur 3.75 2.10
391 A57 $20 rose lake & dk blue 11.00 3.25
Nos. 381-391 (11) 20.60 7.55

Type III with Secret Marks

1940 Wmk. 261 *Perf. 14*

392 A57 5c green .20 .20
393 A57 5c olive green .20 .20
394 A57 10c green .35 .20
395 A57 30c scarlet .20 .20
396 A57 50c dk blue .55 .20
397 A57 $1 org brn & sepia 4.00 2.40
398 A57 $2 dp blue & yel brn 11.00 11.00
399 A57 $5 red & slate grn 10.00 10.00
400 A57 $10 dk grn & dull pur 14.00 15.00
401 A57 $20 rose lake & dk blue 22.50 18.00
Nos. 392-401 (10) 63.00 57.40

Nos. 383, 384, 385, 397, 400 and 401 exist perf. 12½, but were not issued with this perforation.

See surcharge note following No. 363.

Types of 1932-34
Martyrs Issue with Secret Mark

1932-34 Issue. In the left Chinese character in bottom row, the two parts are not joined.

Secret Mark, 1940-41 Issue. The two parts are joined.

Perf. 12½, 13 and Compound

1940-41 Wmk. 261

402	A39	½c	olive blk	.25	.20
403	A40	1c	orange	.25	.20
404	A46	2c	dp blue ('41)	.25	.20
405	A39	2½c	rose lilac	.25	.20
406	A48	3c	dp yellow brn	.25	.20
407	A39	4c	pale vio ('41)	.25	.20
408	A48	5c	dull red org ('41)	.25	.20
409	A45	8c	dp orange	.25	.20
410	A46	10c	dull violet	.25	.20
411	A45	13c	dp yellow grn	.25	.20
412	A48	15c	brown car	.25	.20
413	A46	17c	brown olive	.25	.20
414	A47	20c	lt blue	.25	.20
415	A45	21c	olive brn ('41)	1.00	*1.25*
416	A40	25c	red vio ('41)	.25	.20
417	A46	28c	olive ('41)	.25	.20
418	A48	30c	brown car	.25	.20
a.			Vert. pair, imperf. btwn.	125.00	
419	A47	40c	orange	.25	.20
420	A40	50c	green	.25	.20

Unwmk.

421	A39	½c	olive black	.20	.20
422	A40	1c	orange	.20	.20
a.			Without secret mark	2.25	2.25
b.			Horiz. pair, imperf. vert.	110.00	
423	A46	2c	dp blue	.20	.20
a.			Vert. pair, imperf. horiz.	100.00	
b.			Horiz. pair, imperf. between	160.00	
424	A39	2½c	rose lilac	.20	.20
425	A48	3c	dp yellow brn	.20	.20
426	A39	4c	pale violet	.20	.20
427	A48	5c	dull red org	.20	.20
428	A45	8c	dp orange	.20	.20
429	A46	10c	dull violet	3.00	.40
430	A45	13c	dp yel grn	.20	.20
431	A48	15c	brown car	.20	.20
432	A46	17c	brn olive	.20	.20
433	A47	20c	lt blue	.20	.20
a.			Vert. pair, imperf. horiz.	125.00	
b.			Horiz. pair, imperf. vert.	125.00	
434	A45	21c	olive brn	.20	.20
435	A40	25c	rose vio	.20	.20
436	A46	28c	olive	.20	.20
437	A48	30c	brown car	2.25	2.25
438	A47	40c	orange	.20	.20
439	A40	50c	green	3.00	.30
			Nos. 402-439 (38)	16.95	11.00

Several values exist imperforate, but they were not regularly issued.

Used values are for favor cancels. Postally used copies sell for more.

See surcharge note following No. 323.

Regional Surcharges.

The regional surcharges, Nos. 440-448, 482-484, 486-491, 525-549, have been listed according to the basic stamps, with black or red surcharges. The surcharges of the individual provinces, plus Hong Kong and Shanghai, are noted in small type. The numeral following each letter is the surcharge denomination. These surcharges are identified by the following letters:

a — Hong Kong
b — Shanghai
bx — Anhwei
c — Hunan
d — Kansu
e — Kiangsi
f — Eastern Szechwan
g — Chekiang
h — Fukien
i — Kwangsi
j — Kwangtung
k — Western Szechwan
l — Yunnan
m — Honan
n — Shensi
o — Kweichow
p — Hupeh

Regional Surcharges on Stamps of 1939-40:

Hong Kong — a4

Shanghai — b3

Hunan — c3

Kansu — d3

Kiangsi — e3

Eastern Szechwan — f3

Chekiang — g3

1940-41 Unwmk. *Perf. 12½, 14*

Carmine Surcharge

440	A57 4c on 5c ol grn (#382)	.55	.55
r.	Lower right character duplicated at left	30.00	32.50

Black Surcharge

441	A57 3c on 5c grn (#351) (b3)	1.10	1.25
442	A57 3c on 5c grn (#352) (c3, d3)	.60	1.60
443	A57 3c on 5c grn (#381) (b3)	.55	1.10
444	A57 3c on 5c ol grn (#382) (e3)	.65	.85
r.	Lower left character duplicated at right (Kiangsi)	42.50	42.50
	(b3) Shanghai	.65	1.40
	(f3) Eastern Szechwan	.65	1.60

The Kansu surcharges of #442 are of 6 types. Differences include formation of top part of fen character (at left of "3"), fen with low right hook, height of "3" (5-4mm), space between upper and lower characters (6-9mm), etc.

1940-41 Wmk. 261 *Perf. 14*

445	A57 3c on 5c grn (#392) (e3)	.55	1.25
r.	Lower left character duplicated at right (Kiangsi)	35.00	35.00
	(b3, c3) Shanghai, Hunan	.55	1.40
446	A57 3c on 5c ol grn (#393) (f3)	.65	1.60
	(b3) Shanghai	.85	1.60
r.	Lower left character duplicated at right (f3)	60.00	65.00

Red Surcharge

447	A57 3c on 5c grn (#392) (g3)	1.10	3.00
448	A57 3c on 5c ol grn (#393) (g3)	5.00	5.00

SEMI-POSTAL STAMPS

SP1

Red or Blue Surcharge

1920, Dec. 1 Unwmk. *Perf. 14, 15*

B1	SP1	1c on 2c green	4.50	1.50
B2	SP1	3c on 4c scar (B)	6.25	2.75
B3	SP1	5c on 6c gray	9.00	3.25
		Nos. B1-B3 (3)	19.75	7.50

The surcharge represents the actual franking value. The extra cent helped victims of the 1919 Yellow River flood.

AIR POST STAMPS

Curtiss "Jenny" over Great Wall (Bars of Republic flag on tail) — AP1

Unwmk.

1921, July 1 Engr. *Perf. 14*

C1	AP1	15c	bl grn & blk	29.00	27.50
C2	AP1	30c	scar & blk	29.00	27.50
C3	AP1	45c	dull vio & blk	29.00	27.50
C4	AP1	60c	dk blue & blk	35.00	32.50
C5	AP1	90c	ol grn & blk	47.50	45.00
			Nos. C1-C5 (5)	169.50	160.00

(Nationalist sun emblem on tail) — AP2

1929, July 5

C6	AP2	15c	blue grn & blk	3.75	.75
C7	AP2	30c	dk red & blk	7.50	2.50
C8	AP2	45c	dk vio & blk	14.50	6.75
C9	AP2	60c	dk blue & blk	17.50	8.50
C10	AP2	90c	ol grn & blk	14.50	14.50
			Nos. C6-C10 (5)	57.75	33.00

Junkers F-13 over Great Wall AP3

1932-37

C11	AP3	15c	gray grn	.45	.45
C12	AP3	25c	orange ('33)	.45	.45
C13	AP3	30c	red	7.00	.45
C14	AP3	45c	brown vio	.45	.45
C15	AP3	50c	dk brown ('33)	.45	.45
C16	AP3	60c	dk blue	.45	.45
C17	AP3	90c	olive grn	.45	.45
C18	AP3	$1	yellow grn ('33)	.45	.45
C19	AP3	$2	brown ('37)	1.25	.45
C20	AP3	$5	brown car ('37)	3.50	3.50
			Nos. C11-C20 (10)	14.90	7.55

See #C21-C40. For surcharges and overprints see #C41-C52, C54-C60, 9N111-9N114, 9NC1-9NC7, Szechwan C1, C3-C6, Sinkiang C5-C19.

Type of 1932-37, with secret mark

1932-37 Issue. Lower part of left character joined

Secret Mark, 1940-41 Issue. Separated.

Perf. 12, 12½, 12½x13, 13

1940-41 Wmk. 261

C21	AP3	15c	gray green	.50	.50
C22	AP3	25c	yellow org	.50	.50
C23	AP3	30c	red	.50	.50
a.			Vert. pair, imperf. between	200.00	
C24	AP3	45c	dull rose vio ('41)	.50	.50
C25	AP3	50c	brown	.50	.50
C26	AP3	60c	dp blue ('41)	.50	.50
C27	AP3	90c	olive ('41)	.50	.50
C28	AP3	$1	apple grn ('41)	.50	.50
C29	AP3	$2	lt brown ('41)	.50	.50
C30	AP3	$5	lake	1.25	1.25
			Nos. C21-C30 (10)	5.75	5.75

Unwmk.

Perf. 12½, 13, 13½

C31	AP3	15c	gray green ('41)	.45	.30
C32	AP3	25c	lt orange ('41)	.45	.30
C33	AP3	30c	lt red ('41)	.45	.30
C34	AP3	45c	dl rose vio ('41)	.45	.30
C35	AP3	50c	brown	.45	.30
C36	AP3	60c	blue ('41)	.45	.30
C37	AP3	90c	lt olive ('41)	.45	.30
C38	AP3	$1	apple grn ('41)	.65	.65
C39	AP3	$2	lt brown ('41)	1.50	1.50
C40	AP3	$5	lake ('41)	1.25	1.25
			Nos. C31-C40 (10)	6.55	5.50

For surcharges see note following No. C20.

SPECIAL DELIVERY STAMPS

Design: Dragon in irregular oval.

Stamp 8x2½ inches, divided into four parts by perforation or serrate rouletting.

Values of Nos. E1-E8 are for used mailer's receipts. Complete unused strips of four are exceptionally scarce because the first section (#1) was to remain in the P.O. booklet.

The mailer received the righthand section (#4), usually canceled, as a receipt. The middle two sections were canceled and attached to the letter. Upon arrival at the destination P.O. they were canceled again, usually on the back, with the righthand copy (#3) retained by that P.O. The lefthand copy (#2) was signed by the recipient and returned to the original P.O. as evidence of delivery. Sections 2 and 3 usually are thin or badly damaged.

Unused strips of three (#2-4) can be found of Nos. E3-E8.

"Chinese Imperial Post Office" in lines, repeated to form the background which is usually lighter in color than the rest of the design.

Dragon's head facing downward
Background with period after "POSTOFFICE."
No Date

1905 Unwmk. *Perf. 11*

E1	10c grass green	450.00

Serrate Roulette in Black

E2	10c deep green	325.00

Type, E3-E8

1907-10

Dragon's head facing forward

Background with no period after "POSTOFFICE"

No Date

E3	10c light bluish green	200.00	

1909-11

Background with date at bottom

E4	10c green (Feby 1909)	150.00	
E5	10c bl grn (Jan. 1911)	150.00	

1912

"IMPERIAL POST OFFICE" in serifed letters repeated to form the background.

No Date, No Border

Background of 30 or 28 lines

E6	10c green (30 lines)	70.00	
a.	28 lines	70.00	

Background of 35 lines of sans-serif letters

Colored Border

E8	10c green	140.00	

On No. E8 the medallion in the third section has Chinese characters in the background instead of the usual English inscriptions. E6 and E8 occur with many types of four-character overprints reading "Republic of China," applied locally but unofficially at various post offices.

Type, E9, E10

1913

Design: Wild Goose. Stamp 7½x2¾ inches, divided into five parts.

"CHINESE POST OFFICE" in sans-serif letters, repeated to form the background of 28 lines. With border.

Serrate Roulette in Black

E9	10c green	375.00	29.00

Unused values for Nos. E9-E10 are for complete strips of five parts. Used values are for single parts.

1914

"CHINESE POST OFFICE" in antique letters, forming a background of 29 or 30 lines. No border.

Serrate Roulette in Green

E10	10c green	90.00	3.00

On No. E9 the background is in sans-serif capitals, the Chinese and English inscriptions are on white tablets and the serial numbers are in black.

On No. E10 the background is in antique capitals and extends under the inscriptions. The serial numbers are in green.

NOTE:

In February, 1916, the Special Delivery Stamps were demonetized and became merely receipts without franking value. To mark this, four of the five sections of the stamp had the letters A, B, C, D either handstamped or printed on them.

POSTAGE DUE STAMPS

Regular Issue of 1902-03 Overprinted in Black

1904	**Unwmk.**	**Perf. 14 to 15**	
J1	A17 ½c chocolate	7.00	2.00
J2	A17 1c ocher	7.25	2.75
J3	A17 2c scarlet	8.00	3.75
J4	A17 4c red brn	8.50	4.25
J5	A17 5c salmon	17.00	7.50
J6	A17 10c dk blue grn	27.50	12.00
a.	Vert. pair, imperf. btwn.		475.00
	Nos. J1-J6 (6)	75.25	32.25

D1

1904		**Engr.**	
J7	D1 ½c blue	2.25	.50
a.	Horiz. pair, imperf. btwn.	350.00	325.00
J8	D1 1c blue	4.25	.50
J9	D1 2c blue	3.00	.50
a.	Horiz. pair, imperf. btwn.	400.00	350.00
J10	D1 4c blue	5.75	.60
J11	D1 5c blue	7.75	.60
J12	D1 10c blue	8.00	1.50
J13	D1 20c blue	22.50	4.00
J14	D1 30c blue	29.00	21.00
	Nos. J7-J14 (8)	82.50	29.20

Arabic numeral of value at left on #J12-J14.

1911			
J15	D1 1c brown	6.25	1.50
J16	D1 2c brown	13.00	13.00

The ½c, 4c, 5c and 20c in brown exist but were not issued as they arrived in China after the downfall of the Ching dynasty.

Issue of 1904 Overprinted in Red

1912			
J19	D1 ½c blue	425.	325.
J20	D1 4c blue	475.	400.
J21	D1 5c blue	550.	575.
J22	D1 10c blue	850.	650.
J23	D1 20c blue	1,800.	1,500.
J24	D1 30c blue	1,800.	1,500.

Nos. J15-J16 exist with this overprint, but were not regularly issued.

Nos. J25-J33

Nos. J34-J42

1912

Overprinted in Red

J25	D1 ½c blue	.20	.20
J26	D1 1c brown	.30	.30
a.	Horiz. pair, imperf. btwn.	550.00	
b.	Inverted overprint	225.00	
J27	D1 2c brown	.35	.30
J28	D1 4c blue	2.75	3.00
J29	D1 5c blue	95.00	90.00
J30	D1 5c brown	1.25	.80
a.	Inverted overprint	225.00	175.00
J31	D1 10c blue	5.00	1.10
J32	D1 20c blue	8.00	5.25
J33	D1 30c blue	11.50	10.00
	Nos. J25-J33 (9)	124.35	110.95

1912

Overprinted in Black

J34	D1 ½c blue	6.00	1.40
J35	D1 ½c brown	.70	.30
J36	D1 1c brown	.65	.55
a.	Inverted overprint	350.00	175.00
J37	D1 2c brown	3.00	4.25
J38	D1 4c blue	5.00	5.50
J39	D1 5c brown	9.50	7.00
a.	Horiz. pair, imperf. btwn.	700.00	
J40	D1 10c blue	11.50	16.00
J41	D1 20c brown	27.50	30.00
J42	D1 30c blue	57.50	35.00
	Nos. J34-J42 (9)	121.35	100.00

D4

D5 442srch

Printed by Waterlow & Sons

1913, May		**Perf. 14, 15**	
J43	D4 ½c blue	.60	.20
a.	Horiz. pair, imperf. btwn.	200.00	
J44	D4 1c blue	1.10	.20
J45	D4 2c blue	2.50	1.75
J46	D4 4c blue	2.00	.20
J47	D4 5c blue	3.00	.20
J48	D4 10c blue	6.00	4.25
J49	D4 20c blue	15.00	8.00
J50	D4 30c blue	19.00	4.00
	Nos. J43-J50 (8)	49.20	18.80

Printed by the Chinese Bureau of Engraving & Printing

1915	**Re-engraved**	**Perf. 14**	
J51	D4 ½c blue	.50	.55
J52	D4 1c blue	1.25	.20
J53	D4 2c blue	1.25	.20
J54	D4 4c blue	1.25	.20
J55	D4 5c blue	2.50	.50
J56	D4 10c blue	3.00	.70
J57	D4 20c blue	8.00	1.40
J58	D4 30c blue	32.50	3.25
	Nos. J51-J58 (8)	50.25	7.00

In the upper part of the stamps of type D4 there is an ornament of five marks like the letter "V". Below this is a curved label with an inscription in Chinese characters. On the 1913 stamps there are two complete background lines between the ornament and the label. The 1915 stamps show only one unbroken line at this place. There are other minute differences in the engraving of the stamps of the two issues.

1932		**Perf. 14**	
J59	D5 ½c orange	.20	.20
J60	D5 1c orange	.20	.20
J61	D5 2c orange	.20	.20
J62	D5 4c orange	.40	.20
J63	D5 5c orange	.40	.20
J64	D5 10c orange	.85	.45
J65	D5 20c orange	1.10	.55
J66	D5 30c orange	1.75	.55
	Nos. J59-J66 (8)	5.10	2.55

See Nos. J69-J79. For surcharges see Nos. 1NJ1, 9NJ1-9NJ4.

Regular Stamps of 1939 Overprinted in Black or Red

1940			
J67	A57 $1 henna & dk brn (Bk)	1.75	*5.00*
J68	A57 $2 dl bl & org brn (R)	1.75	*5.50*

Type of 1932

Printed by The Commercial Press, Ltd.

Perf. 12½, 12½x13, 13

1940-41		**Engr.**	
J69	D5 ½c yellow orange	.20	.30
J70	D5 1c yellow orange	.20	.30
J71	D5 2c yellow orange ('41)	.20	.30
J72	D5 4c yellow orange	.20	.30
J73	D5 5c yellow orange ('41)	.55	.30
J74	D5 10c yellow orange ('41)	.20	.30
J75	D5 20c yellow orange ('41)	.20	.30
J76	D5 30c yellow orange	.20	.30
J77	D5 50c yellow orange	.35	.35
J78	D5 $1 yellow orange	.35	.60
J79	D5 $2 yellow orange	.60	.60
	Nos. J69-J79 (11)	3.25	3.95

For surcharge see No. 1NJ1.

PROVINCES

Szechwan Province

Re-engraved Issue of China, 1923, Overprinted

1933	**Unwmk.**	***Perf. 14***	
1	A29 1c orange	6.25	.60
2	A29 5c claret	6.25	.85
3	A30 50c deep green	19.00	4.00
	Nos. 1-3 (3)	31.50	5.45

The overprint reads "For use in Szechwan Province exclusively".

Same on Sun Yat-sen Issue of 1931-37

Type II

1933-34		***Perf. 12½***	
4	A37 2c olive grn	.60	.60
5	A37 5c green	14.00	1.40
6	A37 15c dk green	4.50	1.75
7	A37 15c scar ('34)	4.00	7.00
8	A37 25c ultra	3.50	1.10
9	A37 $1 org brn & dk brn	12.00	2.40
10	A37 $2 bl & org brn	30.00	4.00
11	A37 $5 dl red & blk	77.50	22.50
	Nos. 4-11 (8)	146.10	40.75

Same on Martyrs Issue of 1932-34

1933		***Perf. 14***	
12	A39 ½c black brn	.50	.40
13	A40 1c orange	.45	.30
14	A39 2½c rose lilac	1.75	2.25
15	A48 3c deep brown	1.75	1.75
16	A45 8c brown org	1.10	.90
17	A46 10c dull violet	2.75	.30
18	A45 13c blue green	3.00	.60
19	A46 17c brown olive	3.25	.85
20	A47 20c brown red	4.00	.60
21	A48 30c brown violet	3.75	.60
22	A47 40c orange	8.25	.60
23	A40 50c green	22.50	.85
	Nos. 12-23 (12)	53.05	10.00

Yunnan Province

Stamps of China, 1923-26, Overprinted

The overprint reads "For exclusive use in the Province of Yunnan." It was applied to prevent stamps being purchased in the depreciated currency of Yunnan and used elsewhere.

1926 Unwmk. Perf. 14

1	A29	½c blk brn	1.10	.20
2	A29	1c orange	1.10	.20
3	A29	1½c violet	2.40	2.40
4	A29	2c yellow grn	1.75	.30
5	A29	3c blue green	1.75	.20
6	A29	4c olive grn	2.25	.30
7	A29	5c claret	2.25	.30
8	A29	6c red	3.25	.70
9	A29	7c violet	3.50	1.10
10	A29	8c brown org	3.00	.80
11	A29	10c dark blue	1.90	.20
12	A30	13c brown	1.10	1.10
13	A30	15c dark blue	1.10	1.10
14	A30	16c olive grn	2.25	1.10
15	A30	20c brown red	5.25	1.90
16	A30	30c brown vio	3.25	3.25
17	A30	50c deep green	3.50	3.25
18	A31	$1 org brn & sep	13.00	8.00
19	A31	$2 blue & red brn	22.50	8.00
20	A31	$5 red & slate	150.00	150.00
		Nos. 1-20 (20)	226.20	184.40

Unification Issue of China, 1929, Overprinted in Red

1929 Perf. 14

21	A35	1c brown org	1.10	1.10
22	A35	4c olive grn	2.25	*3.50*
23	A35	10c dark blue	4.00	*5.50*
24	A35	$1 dark red	70.00	55.00
		Nos. 21-24 (4)	77.35	65.10

Similar Overprint in Black on Sun Yat-sen Mausoleum Issue

Characters 15½-16mm apart

25	A36	1c brown orange	1.10	.85
26	A36	4c olive green	1.10	*2.25*
27	A36	10c dark blue	3.25	5.00
28	A36	$1 dark red	45.00	*40.00*
		Nos. 25-28 (4)	50.45	*48.10*

London Print Issue of China, 1931-37, Overprinted

1932-34 Unwmk. Perf. 12½

Type I (double circle)

29	A37	1c orange	1.75	1.75
30	A37	2c olive grn	2.00	*3.50*
31	A37	4c green	2.00	*3.50*
32	A37	20c ultra	1.75	*2.00*
33	A37	$1 org brn & dk brn	26.00	*35.00*
34	A37	$2 bl & org brn	50.00	*55.00*
35	A37	$5 dl red & blk	150.00	*190.00*
		Nos. 29-35 (7)	233.50	*290.75*

Type II (single circle)

36	A37	2c olive grn	17.00	14.00
37	A37	4c green	11.00	2.50
38	A37	5c green	10.00	6.75
39	A37	15c dk green	5.25	*5.75*
40	A37	15c scar ('34)	5.25	*6.50*
41	A37	25c ultra	7.00	5.50
42	A37	$1 org brn & dk brn	45.00	45.00
43	A37	$2 bl & org brn	77.50	77.50
44	A37	$5 dl red & blk	175.00	175.00
		Nos. 36-44 (9)	353.00	338.50

Nos. 36-39, 41-44 were overprinted in London as well as in Peking. The overprints differ in minor details. Value of London overprints (8), $350.

Tan Yuan-chang Issue of China, 1933, Overprinted

1933 Perf. 14

45	A49	2c olive green	1.10	1.10
46	A49	5c green	1.90	1.50
47	A49	25c ultra	3.25	*3.50*
48	A49	$1 red	50.00	40.00
		Nos. 45-48 (4)	56.25	46.10

Martyrs Issue of China, 1932-34, Overprinted

1933

49	A39	½c blk brown	1.00	.90
50	A40	1c orange	1.10	.80
51	A39	2½c rose lilac	2.25	2.50
52	A48	3c deep brown	3.50	1.25
53	A45	8c brown org	1.10	1.10
54	A46	10c dull vio	2.25	2.50
55	A45	13c blue grn	1.40	.60
56	A46	17c brn olive	7.00	7.00
57	A47	20c brown red	1.75	1.75
58	A48	30c brown vio	5.50	5.50
59	A47	40c orange	26.00	26.00
60	A40	50c green	26.00	26.00
		Nos. 49-60 (12)	78.85	75.90

China No. 324 was overprinted with characters arranged vertically, like Sinkiang No. 114, but was not issued.

Manchuria

Kirin and Heilungkiang Issue

Stamps of China, 1923-26, Overprinted

The overprint reads: "For use in Ki-Hei District" the two names being abbreviated.

The intention of the overprint was to prevent the purchase of stamps in Manchuria, where the currency was depreciated, and their resale elsewhere.

1927 Unwmk. Perf. 14

1	A29	½c black brn	1.10	.20
2	A29	1c orange	1.10	.20
3	A29	1½c violet	1.50	1.10
4	A29	2c yellow grn	1.50	.20
5	A29	3c blue grn	.85	.45
6	A29	4c olive grn	.30	.20
7	A29	5c claret	.85	.20
8	A29	6c red	1.50	1.10
9	A29	7c violet	3.00	1.10
10	A29	8c brown org	1.75	1.10
11	A29	10c dk blue	1.10	.30
12	A30	13c brown	2.25	1.75
13	A30	15c dk blue	2.25	1.75
14	A30	16c olive grn	2.25	1.60
15	A30	20c brown red	3.50	1.90
16	A30	30c brown vio	4.50	2.00
17	A30	50c dp green	7.00	2.40
18	A31	$1 org brn & sep	14.00	5.00
19	A31	$2 bl & red brn	37.50	11.00
20	A31	$5 red & slate	190.00	190.00
		Nos. 1-20 (20)	277.80	223.55

Several values of this issue exist with inverted overprint, double overprint and in pairs with one overprint omitted. These "errors" were not regularly issued. Forgeries also exist.

Chang Tso-lin Stamps of 1928 Overprinted in Red or Blue

1928 Perf. 14

21	A34	1c brown org (R)	1.75	1.10
22	A34	4c olive grn (R)	1.10	1.10
23	A34	10c dull blue (R)	3.00	2.25
24	A34	$1 red (Bl)	30.00	27.50
		Nos. 21-24 (4)	35.85	31.95

Unification Issue of China, 1929, Overprinted in Red as in 1928

1929

25	A35	1c brown orange	.80	.80
26	A35	4c olive green	2.25	2.00
27	A35	10c dark blue	8.00	7.50
28	A35	$1 dark red	65.00	*60.00*
		Nos. 25-28 (4)	76.05	*70.30*

Similar Overprint in Black on Sun Yat-sen Mausoleum Issue of China

Characters 15-16mm apart

1929 Perf. 14

29	A36	1c brown orange	1.40	*1.65*
30	A36	4c olive green	1.75	*1.90*
31	A36	10c dark blue	5.25	3.25
32	A36	$1 dark red	52.50	40.00
		Nos. 29-32 (4)	60.90	46.80

Sinkiang

Stamps of China, 1913-19, Overprinted in Black or Red

The first character of overprint is ½mm out of alignment, to the left, and the overprint measures 16mm.

1915 Unwmk. Perf. 14

1	A24	½c black brn	1.10	.60
2	A24	1c orange	1.10	.45
3	A24	2c yellow grn	1.50	.80
4	A24	3c slate grn	1.50	.40
5	A24	4c scarlet	3.00	.70
6	A24	5c rose lilac	2.25	.60
7	A24	6c gray	4.00	1.75
8	A24	7c violet	4.00	*5.25*
9	A24	8c brown orange	3.50	3.50
10	A24	10c dark blue	3.50	1.75
11	A25	15c brown	4.00	2.25
12	A25	16c olive grn	8.00	5.75
13	A25	20c brown red	8.00	4.50
14	A25	30c brown violet	9.00	7.00
15	A25	50c deep green	25.00	11.50
16	A26	$1 ocher & blk (R)	90.00	40.00
a.		Second & third characters of overprint transposed	*16,000.*	
		Nos. 1-16 (16)	169.45	86.80

Stamps of China, 1913-19, Overprinted in Black or Red

The five characters of overprint are correctly aligned and measure 15½mm.

1916-19

17	A24	½c black brn	1.25	1.50
18	A24	1c orange	2.00	1.10
19	A24	1½c violet	2.75	2.50
20	A24	2c yellow grn	2.00	1.10
21	A24	3c slate grn	3.50	.45
22	A24	4c scarlet	3.50	.75
23	A24	5c rose lilac	3.50	.55
24	A24	6c gray	5.00	.75
25	A24	7c violet	5.00	*7.00*
26	A24	8c brown org	5.50	5.25
27	A24	10c dark blue	5.50	.75
28	A25	13c brown	3.00	*5.00*
29	A25	15c brown	3.75	*5.25*
30	A25	16c olive grn	3.50	2.50
31	A25	20c brown red	2.75	1.90
32	A25	30c brown vio	4.25	3.75
33	A25	50c deep green	5.75	3.50
34	A26	$1 ocher & blk (R)	18.00	6.75
35	A26	$2 dk bl & blk (R)	17.50	7.50
36	A26	$5 scar & blk (R)	67.50	24.00
37	A26	$10 yel grn & blk (R)	175.00	110.00
38	A26	$20 yel & blk (R)	900.00	550.00
		Nos. 17-38 (22)	1,240.	741.85

For overprint see No. C4.

China Nos. 243-246 Overprinted

1921 Perf. 14

39	A27	1c orange	1.10	1.10
40	A27	3c blue green	2.25	2.25
41	A27	6c gray	8.50	6.00
42	A27	10c blue	50.00	50.00
		Nos. 39-42 (4)	61.85	59.35

Constitution Issue of China, 1923, Overprinted

1923

43	A32	1c orange	3.75	3.75
44	A32	3c blue green	4.25	4.25
45	A32	4c red	6.25	6.25
46	A32	10c blue	17.50	17.50
		Nos. 43-46 (4)	31.75	31.75

Stamps of China, 1923-26, Overprinted as in 1916-19, in Black or Red

1924

Re-engraved

47	A29	½c black brn	.90	*1.75*
48	A29	1c orange	.90	.70
49	A29	1½c violet	1.60	*3.00*
50	A29	2c yellow grn	2.50	.85
51	A29	3c blue grn	2.50	.75
52	A29	4c gray	2.50	*4.00*
53	A29	5c claret	.85	.60
54	A29	6c red	4.50	1.60
55	A29	7c violet	5.00	4.50
56	A29	8c org brn	*10.00*	*9.00*
57	A29	10c dark blue	4.00	1.10
58	A30	13c red brown	3.50	*5.00*
59	A30	15c deep blue	5.25	4.00
60	A30	16c olive grn	6.00	5.75
61	A30	20c brown red	5.00	3.75
62	A30	30c brown vio	5.75	4.00
63	A30	50c deep green	6.00	4.00
64	A31	$1 org brn & sep (R)	10.50	5.00
65	A31	$2 bl & red brn (R)	22.50	7.25
66	A31	$5 red & slate (R)	57.50	19.00
67	A31	$10 grn & claret (R)	175.00	100.00
68	A31	$20 plum & bl (R)	250.00	190.00
		Nos. 47-68 (22)	582.25	375.60

See #69, 114. For overprints see #C1-C3.

Same Overprint on China No. 275

1926

69	A29	4c olive green	2.50	2.50

Chang Tso-lin Stamps of China, 1928, Overprinted in Red or Blue

1928 Perf. 14

70	A34	1c brn org (R)	1.10	1.10
71	A34	4c ol grn (R)	1.75	1.75
72	A34	10c dull bl (R)	4.00	4.00
73	A34	$1 red (Bl)	30.00	30.00
		Nos. 70-73 (4)	36.85	36.85

Unification Issue of China, 1929, Overprinted in Red as in 1928

1929

74	A35	1c brown org	1.75	1.75
75	A35	4c olive grn	3.00	3.00
76	A35	10c dk blue	7.00	7.00
77	A35	$1 dk red	55.00	45.00
		Nos. 74-77 (4)	66.75	56.75

Similar Overprint in Black on Sun Yat-sen Mausoleum Issue of China

Characters 15mm apart

1929 Perf. 14

78	A36	1c brown org	1.10	1.10
79	A36	4c olive grn	1.60	*1.75*
80	A36	10c dark blue	3.75	*4.00*
81	A36	$1 dark red	47.50	37.50
		Nos. 78-81 (4)	53.95	44.35

Stamps of Sun Yat-sen Issue of 1931-37 Overprinted

1932 Type I Perf. 12½

82	A37	1c orange	1.00	*2.25*
83	A37	2c olive grn	1.75	*3.50*
84	A37	4c green	1.50	*3.75*

85 A37 20c ultra 2.25 *4.75*
86 A37 $1 org brn & dk brn 7.00 *11.50*
87 A37 $2 bl & org brn 14.00 *24.00*
88 A37 $5 dl red & blk 22.50 *35.00*
Nos. 82-88 (7) 50.00 *84.75*

No. 83 was overprinted in Shanghai in 1938. The overprint differs in minor details.

1932-38

Type II

89 A37 2c olive grn .25 *1.10*
90 A37 4c green .70 *2.25*
91 A37 5c green .45 *1.00*
92 A37 15c dk green .60 *2.25*
93 A37 15c scar ('34) .60 *2.25*
93A A37 20c ultra ('38) .45 *1.50*
94 A37 25c ultra .70 *2.25*
95 A37 $1 org brn & dk brn 5.25 *6.00*
96 A37 $2 bl & org brn 11.00 *17.50*
97 A37 $5 dl red & blk 22.50 *35.00*
Nos. 89-97 (10) 42.50 *71.10*

Nos. 89, 90 and 94 were overprinted in London, Peking and Shanghai. Nos. 92, 95-97 exist with London and Peking overprints. Nos. 91 and 93 exist with Peking and Shanghai overprints. No. 93A is a Shanghai overprint. The overprints differ in minor details.

Tan Yuan-chang Issue of China, 1933, Overprinted as in 1928

1933 ***Perf. 14***

98 A49 2c olive grn 2.40 2.40
99 A49 5c green 3.00 3.00
100 A49 25c ultra 9.50 9.50
101 A49 $1 red 47.50 40.00
Nos. 98-101 (4) 62.40 54.90

Stamps of China Martyrs Issue of 1932-34 Overprinted

1933-34

102 A39 ½c black brown .20 *1.25*
103 A40 1c orange 1.10 *1.50*
104 A39 2½c rose lilac .25 *1.10*
105 A48 3c deep brown .25 *1.10*
106 A45 8c brown orange .75 *1.25*
107 A46 10c dull violet .25 *1.10*
108 A45 13c blue green .25 *1.60*
109 A46 17c brown olive .25 *.85*
110 A47 20c brown red 1.10 *2.25*
111 A48 30c brown violet .40 *1.60*
112 A47 40c orange .60 *1.10*
113 A40 50c green .70 *2.25*
Nos. 102-113 (12) 6.10 *16.95*

Nos. 102-113 were originally overprinted in Peking. In 1938, Nos. 103-105, 108-112 were overprinted in Shanghai. The two overprints differ in minor details. No. 105, Shanghai overprint, is scarce. Value $35.

China No. 324 Overprinted as in 1916-19

1936 ***Perf. 14***

114 A29 6c brown 11.50 *12.00*

Stamps of China, 1939-40 Overprinted in Black

1940-45 Unwmk. *Perf. 12½*

Type III

115 A57 2c olive green .85 *1.00*
116 A57 3c dull claret ('41) .20 *1.50*
117 A57 5c green .20 *1.50*
118 A57 5c olive green .20 *1.50*
119 A57 8c olive green ('41) .20 *.75*
120 A57 10c green ('41) .20 *1.10*
121 A57 15c scarlet .55 *2.50*
122 A57 16c olive gray ('41) .40 *1.00*
123 A57 25c dark blue .55 *2.75*
124 A57 $1 hn & dk brn (type II) 6.25 *11.00*
125 A57 $2 dp bl & org brn (type I) 4.50 *11.00*
126 A57 $5 red & grnsh blk 26.00 *32.50*
Nos. 115-126 (12) 40.10 *68.10*

Perf. 14

With Secret Marks

127 A57 8c ol grn (#383a) 1.10 *1.65*
a. On #383 19.00 *22.50*
128 A57 10c green ('41) 9.50 *13.00*
129 A57 30c scarlet ('45) .30 *1.10*
130 A57 50c dk blue ('45) .55 *1.75*
131 A57 $1 org brn & sep .55 *2.25*
132 A57 $2 dp bl & org brn .55 *2.25*
133 A57 $5 red & sl grn .65 *3.75*
134 A57 $10 dk grn & dl pur 1.90 *2.75*
135 A57 $20 rose lake & dk bl 3.50 *5.50*
Nos. 127-135 (9) 18.60 *34.00*

Wmk. Character Yu (Post) (261)
Perf. 14

136 A57 5c olive green .20 *1.10*
137 A57 10c green .25 *1.75*
138 A57 30c scarlet .25 *2.25*
139 A57 50c dark blue .30 *1.10*
Nos. 136-139 (4) 1.00 *6.20*

AIR POST STAMPS

Sinkiang Nos. 53, 57, 59, 32 Overprinted in Red

1932-33 Unwmk. *Perf. 14*

C1 A29 5c claret ('33) 165. 90.
C2 A29 10c dk blue ('33) 165. 85.
C3 A30 15c deep blue 1,000. 275.
C4 A25 30c brown vio 400. 325.

Counterfeits exist of Nos. C1-C4.

Official Perforated Characters
For use on official mail, various Sinkiang stamps were perforated with an arrangement of four Chinese characters ("For Official Business Only"). These include Nos. 1-38, 47-69, 114.

OFFICES IN TIBET

12 Pies = 1 Anna
16 Annas = 1 Rupee

Stamps of China, Issues of 1902-10, Surcharged

1911 Unwmk. *Perf. 12 to 16*

1 A17 3p on 1c ocher 15.00 27.50
a. Inverted surcharge *3,500.*
2 A17 ½a on 2c grn 15.00 27.50
3 A17 1a on 4c ver 15.00 27.50
4 A17 2a on 7c mar 15.00 27.50
5 A17 2½a on 10c ultra 20.00 32.50
6 A18 3a on 16c ol grn 40.00 50.00
a. Large "S" in "Annas" *1,250.*
7 A18 4a on 20c red brn 40.00 50.00
8 A18 6a on 30c rose red 60.00 72.50
9 A18 12a on 50c yel grn 175.00 250.00
10 A19 1r on $1 red & pale rose 475.00 600.00
11 A19 2r on $2 red & yel 900.00 1,200.
Nos. 1-11 (11) 1,770. 2,365.

SHANGHAI

shaŋ-'hī

LOCATION — A city on the Whangpoo River, Kiangsu Province, China
POP. — 3,489,998

During 1842-1860, the Chinese government opened a number of ports for foreign trade, and European mercantile colonies were quickly established in these cities. The most active settlement was at Shanghai, where a British settlement was established in 1843, with French and American settlements soon following. The Shanghai Municipal Council was formed in 1854 to administer the foreign settlement. Virtually independent of Chinese control, the Council performed most government functions in Shanghai. Similar autonomous Western commercial settlements were later established in most of the treaty ports. Lack of confidence in existing Chinese postal services and dissatisfaction with the limited service provided by the British Hong Kong Postal Agency prompted the Shanghai Municipal Council to form the Shanghai Local Post in 1863. The first distinctive stamps for this service appeared in 1865, and Shanghai issues continued until 1897. Many of the other Chinese Treaty Ports joined the Shanghai Postal System, and the System handled more mail during its existence than the Imperial Customs Post, the Hong Kong Agencies, and all of the other foreign post offices. Ten of the ports within the system issued stamps during 1893-1897. On Nov. 1, 1897, the Shanghai Local Post was absorbed into the Imperial Chinese Post Office.

Cash Coin System

800-1600 Cash = 1 Tael

Dollar System

10 Cash = 1 Cent
10 Cents = 1 Chiao (Hao)
100 Cents = 1 Dollar (Yuan)
1 Dollar = .72 Tael

Tael System

10 Li = 1 Fen (Candereen)
10 Fen (Candereen) = 1 Ch'ien (Mace)
10 Ch'ien (Mace) = 1 Liang (Tael)

Covers: Although authenic used examples exist of many of Nos. 1-41a, covers are not known.

Margins: While unused stamps normally have wide margins and are valued in that condition, almost all known used examples have very narrow margins or are cut into the design, and are valued in that condition.

Watermarks

Wmk. 175 — Kung Pu (Municipal Council)

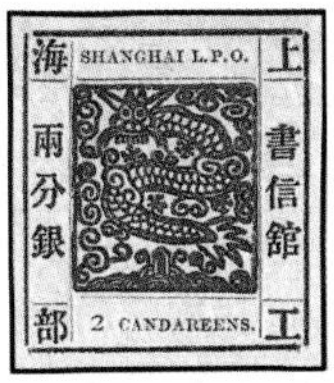

Dragon — A1

1865-66 Unwmk. Typo. *Imperf.*

Antique Numerals
Roman "I" in "I6"
"Candareens" Plural
Wove Paper

1 A1 2ca black 325.00 *2,250.*
a. Pelure paper 475.00
2 A1 4ca yellow 325.00 *3,250.*
a. Pelure paper 650.00 —
b. Double impression —
3 A1 8ca green 325.00 *3,750.*
a. 8ca yellow green 375.00
4 A1 16ca scarlet 750.00 *5,000.*
a. 16ca vermilion 675.00
b. Pelure paper 875.00
Nos. 1-4 (4) 1,725. 14,250.

No. 1: top character of three in left panel as illustrated. No. 5: top character is two horiz. lines.

Nos. 2, 3: center character of three in left panel as illustrated. Nos. 6, 7: center character much more complex.

Antique Numerals
"Candareens" Plural
Pelure Paper

5 A1 2ca black 325.00
a. Wove paper 275.00
6 A1 4ca yellow 550.00 —
7 A1 8ca deep green 550.00 —
Nos. 5-7 (3) 1,425.

Antique Numerals
"Candareen" Singular
Laid Paper

8 A1 1ca blue 325.00 *4,000.*
a. 1ca deep blue 175.00
9 A1 2ca black 3,250.
10 A1 4ca yellow 750.00
Nos. 8-10 (3) 4,325.

Wove Paper

11 A1 1ca blue 300.00 *5,000.*
12 A1 2ca black 625.00 *3,250.*
13 A1 4ca yellow 550.00 —
14 A1 8ca olive green 550.00 —
15 A1 16ca vermilion 300.00 —
a. "1" of "16" omitted —
Nos. 11-15 (5) 2,325.

Roman "I," Antique "2"
"Candareens" Plural Except on 1ca
Wove Paper

16 A1 1ca blue 650.00 *3,250.*
17 A1 12ca fawn 375.00
18 A1 12ca chocolate 375.00
Nos. 16-18 (3) 1,400.

Antique Numerals
"Candareens" Plural Except on 1ca
Wove Paper

19 A1 1ca indigo, pelure paper 275.00 *2,250.*
a. 1ca blue, wove paper 3,750.
b. 1ca indigo, wove paper 175.00
20 A1 3ca orange brown 250.00 *2,000.*
a. Pelure paper 325.00
21 A1 6ca red brown 150.00
22 A1 6ca fawn 450.00 —
23 A1 6ca vermilion 225.00
24 A1 12ca orange brown 125.00
25 A1 16ca vermilion 150.00 *775.00*
a. "1" of "16" omitted 500.00
Nos. 19-25 (7) 1,625.

Examples of No. 22 usually have the straight lines cutting through the paper.

Antique Numerals
Roman "I"
"Candareens" Plural Except on 1ca
Laid Paper

26 A1 1ca blue —
27 A1 2ca black 5,000.
28 A1 3ca red brown — —

Examples of No. 28 usually have the straight lines cutting through the paper.

Modern Numerals
"Candareen" Singular

29 A1 1ca slate blue 225.00 *2,250.*
a. 1ca dark blue 160.00 —
30 A1 3ca red brown 140.00

"Candareens" Plural Except the 1c

31 A1 2ca gray 190.00
a. 2ca black 125.00
32 A1 3ca red brown 160.00 *2,250.*

Coarse Porous Wove Paper

33a A1 1ca blue 160.00
34a A1 2ca black 210.00
b. Grayish paper 275.00
35a A1 3ca red brown 140.00
36a A1 4ca yellow 325.00
b. 4ca orange yellow 80.00
37a A1 6ca olive green 190.00
b. 6ca bronze green 95.00
38a A1 8ca emerald 225.00
b. 8ca green 95.00
39a A1 12ca orange vermilion 160.00
b. 12ca reddish orange 80.00
40a A1 16ca red 250.00 *875.00*
41a A1 16ca red brown 190.00 *875.00*
Nos. 33a-41a (9) 1,850.

Chinese characters change on same denomination stamps.

Nos. 1, 2, 11 and 32 exist on thicker paper, usually toned. Most authorities consider these four stamps and Nos. 33a-41a to be official reprints made to present sample sets to other post offices. The tone in this paper is an acquired characteristic, due to various causes. Many shades and minor varieties exist of Nos. 1-41a.

A2

A3

A4

A5

1866 Litho. *Perf. 12*
42 A2 2c rose 11.50 *14.00*
43 A3 4c lilac 25.00 *25.00*
44 A4 8c gray blue 27.50 *30.00*
45 A5 16c green 60.00 *70.00*
Nos. 42-45 (4) 124.00 139.00

Nos. 42-45 imperf. are proofs. See No. 50. For surcharges see Nos. 51-61, 67.

A6

A7

A8

A9

1866 *Perf. 15*
46 A6 1ca brown 6.00 5.50
a. "CANDS" 55.00 50.00
47 A7 3ca orange 25.00 *30.00*
48 A8 6ca slate 25.00 *30.00*
49 A9 12ca olive gray 60.00 *65.00*
Nos. 46-49 (4) 116.00 130.50

See Nos. 69-77. For surcharges see Nos. 62-66, 68, 78-83.

1872
50 A2 2c rose 85.00 *110.00*

Handstamp Surcharged in Blue, Red or Black

a 

1873 *Perf. 12*
51 A2 1ca on 2c rose 37.50 *50.00*
52 A3 1ca on 4c lilac 16.00 *18.00*
53 A3 1ca on 4c lilac (R) *1,750. 1,750.*
54 A3 1ca on 4c lilac (Bk) 20.00 *27.50*
55 A4 1ca on 8c gray bl 25.00 *27.50*
56 A4 1ca on 8c gray bl (R) *3,500. 3,500.*
57 A5 1ca on 16c green *2,750. 2,750.*
58 A5 1ca on 16c green (R) *4,000. 3,750.*

Perf. 15
59 A2 1ca on 2c rose 37.50 *42.50*

1875 *Perf. 12*
60 A2 3ca on 2c rose 70.00 70.00
61 A5 3ca on 16c green *1,100. 1,100.*

Perf. 15
62 A7 1ca on 3ca orange *4,000. 4,000.*
63 A8 1ca on 6ca slate 325.00 325.00
64 A8 1ca on 6ca slate (R) *2,500. 2,500.*
65 A9 1ca on 12ca ol gray 300.00 300.00
66 A9 1ca on 12ca ol gray (R) *2,500. 2,500.*
67 A2 3ca on 2c rose 250.00 250.00
68 A9 3ca on 12ca olive gray *6,000. 6,000.*

Counterfeits exist of Nos. 51-68.

Types of 1866

1875 *Perf. 15*
69 A6 1ca yel, *yel* 22.50 22.50
70 A7 3ca rose, *rose* 20.00 *22.50*

Perf. 11½
71 A6 1ca yel, *yel* 350.00 350.00

1876 *Perf. 15*
72 A6 1ca yellow 10.00 *12.50*
73 A7 3ca rose 50.00 *60.00*
74 A8 6ca green 65.00 *75.00*
75 A9 9ca blue 95.00 95.00
76 A9 12ca light brown 120.00 120.00
Nos. 72-76 (5) 340.00 362.50

1877 Engr. *Perf. 12½*
77 A6 1ca rose 1,000. *1,100.*

Stamps of 1875-76 Surcharged type "a" in Blue or Red

1877 Litho. *Perf. 15*
78 A7 1ca on 3ca rose, *rose* 250.00 250.00
79 A7 1ca on 3ca rose 42.50 42.50
80 A8 1ca on 6ca green 60.00 60.00
81 A9 1ca on 9ca blue 190.00 190.00
82 A9 1ca on 12ca lt brn 1,200. 1,000.
83 A9 1ca on 12ca lt brn (R) *3,250. 3,250.*

Counterfeits exist of Nos. 78-83.

A11

A12

A13

A14

1877 *Perf. 15*
84 A11 20 cash blue violet 12.00 *14.00*
a. 20 cash violet 10.00 10.00
85 A12 40 cash rose 14.50 13.00
86 A13 60 cash green 14.50 14.50
87 A14 80 cash blue 25.00 22.50
88 A14 100 cash brown 20.00 *27.50*
Nos. 84-88 (5) 86.00 91.50

Handstamp Surcharged in Blue

b 

1879 *Perf. 15*
89 A12 20 cash on 40c rose 19.00 19.00
90 A14 60 cash on 80c blue 25.00 *32.50*
91 A14 60 cash on 100c brn 25.00 *32.50*
Nos. 89-91 (3) 69.00 84.00

Types of 1877

1880 *Perf. 11½*
92 A11 20 cash violet 10.00 *11.00*
93 A12 40 cash rose 11.00 10.00
94 A13 60 cash green 9.50 *11.00*
95 A14 80 cash blue 12.00 *14.50*
96 A14 100 cash brown 13.50 *16.00*

Perf. 15x11½
97 A11 20 cash lilac 75.00 *95.00*
Nos. 92-97 (6) 131.00 157.50

Surcharged type "b" in Blue

1884 *Perf. 11½*
98 A12 20 cash on 40c rose 17.50 11.00
99 A14 60 cash on 80c blue 20.00 *22.50*
100 A14 60 cash on 100c brn 30.00 22.50
Nos. 98-100 (3) 67.50 56.00

Types of 1877

1884
101 A11 20 cash green 8.00 *9.00*

1885 *Perf. 15*
102 A11 20 cash green 5.00 3.50
103 A12 40 cash brown 6.50 *6.00*
104 A13 60 cash violet 11.00 *10.50*
a. 60 cash red violet 13.50 *20.00*
105 A14 80 cash buff 9.50 7.00
106 A14 100 cash yellow 11.50 *11.50*

Perf. 11½x15
107 A11 20 cash green 11.00 6.50
108 A13 60 cash red vio 12.00 9.00
Nos. 102-108 (7) 66.50 54.00

Surcharged type "b" in Blue

1886 *Perf. 15*
109 A14 40 cash on 80c buff 8.00 8.00
110 A14 60 cash on 100c yellow 11.00 10.00

Types of 1877

1888 *Perf. 15*
111 A11 20 cash gray 8.00 4.00
112 A12 40 cash black 8.00 *4.50*
113 A13 60 cash rose 11.50 9.00
a. Third character at left lacks dot at top 13.50 *15.00*
114 A14 80 cash green 11.00 7.50
115 A14 100 cash lt blue 14.00 *14.00*
Nos. 111-115 (5) 52.50 39.00

Handstamp Surcharged in Blue or Red Type "b" or:

c

d

1888 *Perf. 15*
116 A14(b) 40 cash on 100c yel 8.00 *9.00*
117 A14(b) 40 cash on 100c yel (R) 12.50 *14.00*
118 A12(c) 20 cash on 40c brn 17.50 17.50
119 A14(c) 20 cash on 80c buff 7.50 7.50
120 A12(d) 20 cash on 40c brn 15.00 *17.50*
Nos. 116-120 (5) 60.50 65.50

Inverted surcharges exist on Nos. 116-120; double on Nos. 116, 119, 120; omitted surcharges paired with normal stamp on Nos. 116, 119.

Handstamp Surcharged in Black and Red (100 cash) or Red (20 cash)

e 

1889 Unwmk.
121 A14(e) 100 cash on 20c on 100c yel 85.00 45.00
a. Without the surcharge "100 cash" 300.00
b. Blue & red surcharge —
122 A14(c) 20 cash on 80c grn 10.00 10.00
123 A14(c) 20 cash on 100c bl 10.00 10.00
Nos. 121-123 (3) 105.00 65.00

Counterfeits exist of Nos. 116-123.

1889 Wmk. 175 *Perf. 15*
124 A11 20 cash gray 4.75 3.50
125 A12 40 cash black 6.75 5.00
126 A13 60 cash rose 12.00 *13.00*
a. Third character at left lacks dot at top 17.00 *17.00*

Perf. 12
127 A14 80 cash green 9.00 *10.00*
128 A14 100 cash dk bl 11.50 8.50
Nos. 124-128 (5) 44.00 40.00

Nos. 124-126 are sometimes found without watermark. This is caused by the sheet being misplaced in the printing press, so that the stamps are printed on the unwatermarked margin of the sheet.

Shield with Dragon Supporters — A20

1890 Unwmk. Litho. *Perf. 15*
129 A20 2c brown 3.00 *3.75*
130 A20 5c rose 8.00 5.00
131 A20 15c blue 12.50 12.50

Nos. 129-131 imperforate are proofs.

Wmk. 175
132 A20 10c black 10.00 8.00
133 A20 15c blue 12.00 12.00
134 A20 20c violet 10.00 10.00
Nos. 129-134 (6) 55.50 51.25

See Nos. 135-141. For surcharges and overprints see Nos. 142-152, J1-J13.

1891 *Perf. 12*
135 A20 2c brown 2.00 2.00
136 A20 5c rose 6.00 6.00

1892
137 A20 2c green 3.50 2.25
138 A20 5c red 7.50 6.00
139 A20 10c orange 14.00 *15.00*
140 A20 15c violet 12.00 8.00
141 A20 20c brown 13.00 11.00
Nos. 137-141 (5) 50.00 42.25

No. 130 Handstamp Surcharged in Blue

f 

1892 Unwmk. *Perf. 15*
142 A20 2c on 5c rose 65.00 60.00

Counterfeits exist of Nos. 142-152.

Stamps of 1892 Handstamp Surcharged in Blue:

g

h

1893 Wmk. 175 *Perf. 12*
143 A20 ½c on 15c violet 10.00 8.00
144 A20 1c on 20c brown 10.00 8.00
a. ½c on 20c brown (error) *5,000.*

Surcharged in Blue or Red (#152) on Halves of #136 (#145-147), #138 (#148-150), #135 (#151), #137 (#152):

½Ct. *i* ½Ct. *j*

½Ct. *k* 1Ct. *m*

145 A20(i) ½c on half of 5c 7.50 6.50
146 A20(j) ½c on half of 5c 9.00 8.00
147 A20(k) ½c on half of 5c 80.00 70.00
148 A20(i) ½c on half of 5c 7.50 6.50
149 A20(j) ½c on half of 5c 8.50 6.50
150 A20(k) ½c on half of 5c 80.00 70.00
151 A20(m) 1c on half of 2c 3.00 2.50
c. Dbl. surch., one in green *350.00*
d. Dbl. surch., one in black *350.00*
152 A20(m) 1c on half of 2c 11.00 10.00
Nos. 145-152 (8) 206.50 180.00

The ½c surcharge setting of 20 (2x10) covers a vertical strip of 10 unsevered stamps, with horizontal gutter midway. This setting has 11 of type "i," 8 of type "j" and 1 of type "k." Nos. 145-152 are perforated vertically down the middle.

Inverted surcharges exist on Nos. 145-151. Double surcharges, one inverted, are also found in this issue.

Handstamped provisionals somewhat similar to Nos. 145-152 were issued in Foochow by the Shanghai Agency.

Coat of Arms — A24

Typo. (Dot)

Litho. (No Dot)

1893 Litho. *Perf. 13½x14*

Frame Inscriptions in Black

153 A24	½c orange, typo.	.40	.30
a.	½c orange, litho.	5.00	5.00
154 A24	1c brown, typo.	.40	.30
a.	1c brown, litho.	5.00	5.00
155 A24	2c vermilion	8.00	5.00
a.	Imperf, pair	100.00	
156 A24	5c blue	.75	.50
a.	Black inscriptions inverted	800.00	
157 A24	10c grn, typo. & litho.	2.50	*3.00*
a.	10c green, litho.	8.00	10.00
158 A24	15c yellow	.80	.75
159 A24	20c lil, typo. & litho.	2.75	*3.50*
a.	20c lilac, litho.	6.50	6.50
	Nos. 153-159 (7)	15.60	13.35

On Nos. 157 and 159, frame inscriptions are lithographed, rest of design typographed.

See Nos. 170-172. For overprints and surcharges see Nos. 160-166, 168-169.

Stamps of 1893 Overprinted in Black

1893, Dec. 14

160 A24	½c orange & blk	.40	.40
161 A24	1c brown & blk	.60	.60
a.	Double overprint	27.50	27.50
162 A24	2c vermilion & blk	.75	.75
a.	Inverted overprint	57.50	
163 A24	5c blue & black	3.00	*3.50*
a.	Inverted overprint	120.00	
164 A24	10c green & blk	7.00	*8.00*
165 A24	15c yellow & blk	4.00	4.00
166 A24	20c lilac & blk	6.00	*6.50*
	Nos. 160-166 (7)	21.75	23.75

50th anniv. of the first foreign settlement in Shanghai.

Mercury — A26

1893, Nov. 11 Litho. *Perf. 13½*

167 A26	2c vermilion & black	.80	.80

Nos. 158 and 159 Handstamp Surcharged in Black

1896 *Perf. 13½x14*

168 A24	4c on 15c yellow & blk	7.00	6.00
169 A24	6c on 20c lilac & blk (#159)	7.00	6.00
a.	On #159a	50.00	25.00

Surcharge occurs inverted or double on Nos. 168-169.

Arms Type of 1893

1896

170 A24	2c scarlet & blk	.30	*1.25*
a.	Black inscriptions inverted	150.00	
171 A24	4c orange & blk, *yel*	3.00	*3.25*
172 A24	6c car & blk, *rose*	2.50	*3.75*
	Nos. 170-172 (3)	5.80	*8.25*

POSTAGE DUE STAMPS

Postage Stamps of 1890-92 Handstamped in Black, Red or Blue

1892 Unwmk. *Perf. 15*

J1 A20	2c brown (Bk)	275.00	*300.00*
J2 A20	5c rose (Bk)	7.00	*7.50*
J3 A20	15c blue (Bk)	27.50	27.50

Wmk. 175

J4 A20	10c black (R)	17.50	*20.00*
J5 A20	15c blue (Bk)	15.00	*20.00*
J6 A20	20c violet (Bk)	12.50	*15.00*
	Nos. J1-J6 (6)	354.50	*390.00*

1892-93 *Perf. 12*

J7 A20	2c brown (Bk)	3.00	3.00
J8 A20	2c brown (Bl)	2.50	*3.00*
J9 A20	5c rose (Bl)	10.00	8.00
J10 A20	10c orange (Bk)	70.00	*75.00*
J11 A20	10c orange (Bl)	11.50	*9.00*
J12 A20	15c violet (R)	20.00	20.00
J13 A20	20c brown (R)	17.50	17.50
	Nos. J7-J13 (7)	134.50	*135.50*

D2

1893 Litho. *Perf. 13½*

J14 D2	½c orange & blk	.55	.55

Perf. 14x13½

J15 D2	1c brown & black	.60	.55
J16 D2	2c vermilion & black	.60	.55
J17 D2	5c blue & black	.90	.90
J18 D2	10c green & black	5.00	2.00
J19 D2	15c yellow & black	4.00	4.00
J20 D2	20c violet & black	1.50	1.50
	Nos. J14-J20 (7)	13.15	10.05

Stamps of Shanghai were discontinued in 1898.

CHINA TREATY PORTS

Wmk. 402 — Chinese Characters

AMOY

A seaport on an island located off the coast of Fukien Province, in south China. The Shanghai Local Post was handling mail from Amoy as early as 1863, but a formal branch office was not established until 1890. Shanghai stamps were used from 1890 until Mar. 31, 1895, when the post office was taken over by the Amoy Local Council. Amoy stamps were used from June 8, 1895, until Feb. 2, 1897, when mail services came under control of the Imperial Chinese Post Office.

All Amoy issues were printed by Schleicher and Schull, Duren, Germany.

Geese — A1

Type 1

Type 2

Perf. 11½

1895, June 8-1896 Unwmk. Litho.

1	A1	½c green	2.90	*3.50*
2	A1	1c rose red	2.90	27.50
a.		1c aniline rose red	2.90	*2.90*
3	A1	2c blue, Type 1	35.00	*42.50*
4	A1	2c blue, Type 2	10.00	*12.00*
5	A1	4c brown	10.00	*11.00*
6	A1	5c orange	11.00	*10.00*

Two lithographic stones were made for the ½ cent value, with the first used for the June 8, 1895, printing and the second used for a second printing on May 11, 1896, when Nos. 11-13 were printed. Plating details are needed to differentiate the two printings.

No. 1 also exists with papermaker's watermark "C S & S" in script letters.

Nos. 5 and 6 surcharged in two lines, wide "f"

1896, May 8

7	A1	Half Cent on 4c brown	42.50	*35.00*
8	A1	Half Cent on 5c orange	42.50	*35.00*

Nos. 5 and 6 surcharged "1/2"c, "2" with curved foot

1896, May 9

9	A1	½c on 4c brown	35.00	27.50
a.		"2" with straight foot	57.50	*47.50*
10	A1	½c on 5c orange	29.00	*25.00*
a.		"2" with straight foot	55.00	*42.50*
b.		Double surcharge	800.00	
c.		Double surcharge, one red	725.00	
d.		As "a." double surcharge	800.00	

1896, May 11 Wmk. 402

11	A1	15c gray black	12.00	*11.50*
12	A1	20c violet	14.00	*11.50*
13	A1	25c lilac rose	13.50	*11.50*

Nos. 5 and 6 surcharged in two lines, narrow "f"

1896, May 20

Unwmk.

Surcharged in Blue

14	A1	½c on 4c brown	42.50	*50.00*
a.		"G" instead of "C" in cent	500.00	*425.00*
15	A1	½c on 5c orange	45.00	*45.00*
a.		"G" instead of "C" in cent	500.00	*425.00*

Surcharged in Black

16	A1	½c on 4c brown	11.00	*11.50*
17	A1	½c on 5c orange	11.00	*11.50*

Nos. 11-13 surcharged, dropped "C"

1896, Oct. 1

Wmk. 402

18	A1	3c on 15c gray black	11.50	*17.50*
19	A1	6c on 20c violet	11.50	*17.50*
20	A1	10c on 25c lilac rose	11.50	*23.00*
a.		Blue surcharge with bar in black	*300.00*	
b.		Blue surcharge	—	
c.		Double surcharge, one blue, one black	—	

Nos. 11-13 surcharged in red (R) or black, "C" in line with other letters

1896, Oct. 9

21	A1	3c on 15c gray black (R)	14.00	*11.50*
a.		Brownish red surcharge	18.00	*13.50*
22	A1	6c on 20c violet (R)	14.00	*14.00*
23	A1	3c on 25c lilac rose	14.00	*14.00*
a.		Double surcharge	*300.00*	

POSTAGE DUE STAMPS

Nos. 1, 3-6 overprinted in red

Normal — "D" under "S"

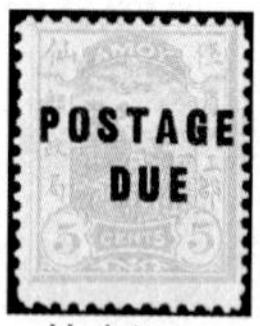

Variety — "DUE" shifted to right

Perf. 11½

1895, Oct. 14 Unwmk. Litho.

J1	A1	½c green	14.00	*16.00*
a.		Vertical pair, one without ovpt.	300.00	
b.		Vertical pair, one with red ovpt., one with black	—	
c.		"DUE" shifted to right	—	—
J2	A1	2c blue, type 1	*260.00*	*260.00*
a.		"DUE" shifted to right	*360.00*	
J3	A1	2c blue, type 2	14.00	*14.00*
a.		"DUE" shifted to right	275.00	*275.00*
J4	A1	4c brown	14.00	*14.00*
a.		"DUE" shifted to right	275.00	*275.00*
J5	A1	5c orange	14.00	*14.00*
a.		"DUE" shifted to right	275.00	*275.00*

Overprinted in Black

J6	A1	½c green	6.50	*6.25*
a.		Double overprint	*290.00*	*160.00*
b.		Inverted overprint	—	
c.		"DUE" shifted to right	275.00	*275.00*
J7	A1	1c rose red	*4.25*	5.00
a.		Double overprint	*425.00*	
b.		Inverted overprint	*450.00*	*450.00*
c.		"DUE" shifted to right	275.00	*275.00*
J8	A1	2c blue, type 1	*260.00*	—
J9	A1	2c blue, type 2	45.00	*37.50*
a.		"DUE" shifted to right	275.00	—
J10	A1	4c brown	26.00	*21.00*
a.		"DUE" shifted to right	275.00	*275.00*
J11	A1	5c orange	26.00	*21.00*
a.		"DUE" shifted to right	275.00	*275.00*

No. 2 overprinted in Roman (serifed) Type

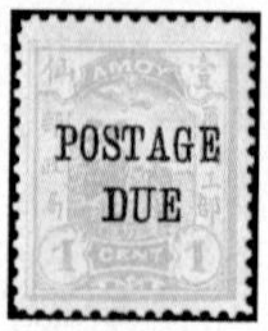

1896, June 1

J12	A1	1c rose red	*250.00*	*275.00*

CHEFOO

A seaport in Shantung Province, on the Straits of Pechile. It was opened to foreign trade by the Treaty of Peking in 1860 and by the 1890's had become a bustling city. Because of its pleasant climate, Chefoo became a favorite summer vacation area for foreigners in China. The Chefoo Local Post Committee was formed in mid-1893, and the first stamps for Chefoo were issued on Oct. 6, 1893. The Chefoo Local Post's operations were taken over by the Imperial Chinese Post Office on Feb. 2, 1897.

All Chefoo issues were printed by Schleicher and Schull, Duren, Germany. All were impressed with a faux watermark, the Chinese character for Yan, the first half of the Chinese name for Chefoo, Yan-Tai. Nos. 14-16 are impressed with two characters, for the full city name.

Smoke Tower and Semaphore — A1

Type 1: the right bottom of the "H" and the left bottom of the "E" of "CHEFOO" are clearly separated from each other; the ball of the semaphore is clear. Type 2: the "H" and the "E" of "CHEFOO" are nearly touching; the ball of the semaphore is not clear, and the rim is irregular; there is a hairline in the lower right of the outer frame.

Type 1

1893, Oct. 6 Litho. *Perf. 11½*

1	A1	½c green	14.50	11.00
2	A1	1c red	4.25	3.50
3	A1	2c ultramarine	14.50	*11.50*
a.		Vertical pair, imperf between	425.00	
b.		2c pale blue	14.50	*11.50*
4	A1	5c orange	14.50	*14.50*
a.		Imperforate	160.00	
5	A1	10c brown	14.50	*11.50*
a.		10c reddish brown	16.00	*12.50*

Type 2

1894, Jan.

6	A1	½c dark gray green	2.10	1.40
7	A1	5c red orange	4.25	4.25

Type 2; "Yan" Character Impressed on Front of Stamp

1894, March

8	A1	½c green	2.10	1.60
a.		"Yan" impression on back of stamp	5.75	5.75
9	A1	1c scarlet	1.10	1.00
a.		"Yan" impressed on back of stamp	5.75	5.75
10	A1	1c rose red	2.00	*3.50*
11	A1	2c blue	2.90	*3.25*
a.		Pair, imperf between	—	
12	A1	5c brown orange	4.50	4.50
a.		"Yan" impression inverted	11.00	
b.		"Yan" impression on back of stamp	6.75	6.75
13	A1	10c brown	5.00	5.00
a.		10c reddish brown	5.50	5.50

Harbor Scene — A2

"Yan Tai" Characters Impressed on Front of Stamp

1896, Jan.

14	A2	15c red brown & green	8.75	*11.00*
15	A2	20c red brown & violet	13.50	*11.50*
16	A2	25c violet & red	8.75	*11.00*

In Jan. 1896 a postal clerk overprinted 56 sets of Nos. 1-5 with a handstamped two-line "POSTAGE DUE" overprint, applied either horizontally or diagonally. These were sold from the post office but were never authorized and were later condemned by the Chefoo postmaster.

CHINKIANG

An ancient strategic city on the Yangtze River, 112 miles inland from Shanghai. Chinkiang became a Treaty Port in 1860, and in 1864 a British trading settlement was established in the city. By 1866, Chinkiang was a part of the Shanghai Postal System. On Aug. 6, 1894, postal operations were taken over by the Chinkiang Local Post Office. On Feb. 2, 1897, the Chinkiang mail service was absorbed into the Imperial Chinese Post.

All Chinkiang Local Post stamps were printed by Tokyo Tsukiji Foundry Co., Japan.

Golden Mountain — A1

Perf. 11½

1894, Aug. 6 Unwmk. Litho.

1	A1	½c rose	2.10	*2.90*
a.		Horiz. pair, imperf between	85.00	
b.		Vert. pair, imperf between	72.50	
c.		½c aniline rose	4.00	*4.00*
2	A1	1c blue	1.25	*1.25*
a.		Horiz. strip of 3, imperf vert.	160.00	160.00
b.		Perf 11½x11	7.50	7.50
3	A1	2c brown	4.00	*4.75*
a.		Perf 11½x11	7.50	7.50
4	A1	4c yellow	6.00	6.00
a.		Perf 11	6.25	6.25
5	A1	5c green	5.50	*5.75*
a.		Perf 11½x11	6.00	*6.00*
b.		Horiz. pair, imperf between	140.00	
c.		Vert. pair, imperf between	160.00	
6	A1	6c mauve	8.50	*6.50*
a.		Perf 11	7.25	*7.25*
b.		Perf 11½x11	6.00	*7.00*
c.		Perf 11x11½	8.00	8.00
d.		Horiz. pair, imperf between	110.00	
7	A1	10c orange	11.00	8.50
a.		Perf 11½x11	12.50	*12.50*
b.		Perf 11	9.50	9.50
c.		Perf 11x11½	10.00	10.00

Golden Mountain — A2

Type A2 is similar to A1, but clouds have been added to the sky, and shading added to the river.

1895, Apr. 9

8	A2	½c rose red	4.75	*4.25*
9	A2	1c blue	5.75	*5.75*
10	A2	2c brown	20.00	17.50
11	A2	4c yellow	13.50	*13.50*
12	A2	5c emerald green	13.50	*13.50*
13	A2	6c mauve	13.50	*14.00*
a.		Horiz. pair, imperf vert.	160.00	*95.00*
b.		Horiz. pair, imperf between	160.00	*140.00*
c.		Imperf, pair	—	
14	A2	10c orange	11.00	*11.00*
15	A2	15c carmine red	14.50	*16.00*

POSTAGE DUE STAMPS

Nos. 1-7 overprinted, narrow (1.5mm) spacing between "DUE" and Chinese characters

Perf. 11½

1894, Dec. 21 Unwmk. Litho.

J1 A1 ½c rose 7.25 *6.50*
a. Inverted overprint 47.50 *40.00*
b. Double overprint 80.00 47.50
J2 A1 1c blue 7.25 *5.00*
a. Inverted overprint 47.50 *42.50*
b. Double overprint, one inverted —
J3 A1 2c brown 7.25 *6.00*
a. Inverted overprint 47.50 *42.50*
b. Double overprint 110.00 110.00
J4 A1 4c yellow 7.50 *8.50*
a. Inverted overprint 65.00 50.00
b. Vert. pair, imperf between 110.00
c. Perf 11 9.50 9.50
J5 A1 5c green 7.25 *7.25*
a. Inverted overprint 57.50 55.00
J6 A1 6c mauve 9.00 8.50
a. Inverted overprint 65.00 57.50
b. Perf 11 8.00 8.00
c. As "b," inverted overprint 65.00 57.50
d. Perf 11x11½ 11.00 11.00
J7 A1 10c orange 7.00 7.00
a. Inverted overprint 65.00 60.00
b. Perf 11x11½ 9.00 7.25
c. Perf 11½x11 7.25 7.25
d. Vert. pair, imperf between 67.50

Nos. 1-7, 15 overprinted, wide (2.5mm) spacing between "DUE" and Chinese characters

Split "P" Variety

1895, Apr. 9

Overprinted in Red

J8 A1 ½c rose 110.00 *87.50*
a. Inverted overprint 140.00 125.00
b. Pair, one with inverted overprint *260.00 260.00*
c. Split "P" 175.00 175.00
d. Inverted overprint, Split "P" 200.00 200.00

Overprinted in Black over Red

J9 A1 ½c rose 160.00 *175.00*
a. Both overprints inverted 325.00 *325.00*
b. Pair, one with inverted overprint *325.00 325.00*
J10 A1 1c blue 160.00 *175.00*
a. Both overprints inverted 325.00 *325.00*
b. Pair, one with inverted overprint *325.00 325.00*
J11 A1 2c brown 160.00 *175.00*
a. Both overprints inverted 325.00 *325.00*
J12 A1 4c yellow 160.00 *175.00*
a. "DUE" omitted in red ovpt. 200.00
b. Both overprints inverted 325.00 *325.00*
J13 A1 5c green 160.00 *175.00*
a. Both overprints inverted 325.00 *325.00*
J14 A1 6c mauve 160.00 *175.00*
a. Both overprints inverted 325.00 *325.00*
J15 A1 10c orange 160.00 *175.00*
a. Both overprints inverted 325.00 *325.00*
b. Perf 11½x11 175.00 *175.00*
c. Perf 11x11½ 200.00 *200.00*
J16 A1 15c carmine 160.00 *175.00*
a. Both overprints inverted 325.00 *325.00*
b. Red overprint double

Overprinted in Black over Red, Split "P" Variety

J9c A1 ½c rose 200.00 *200.00*
d. Both overprints inverted *360.00 360.00*
J10c A1 1c blue 200.00 *200.00*
d. Both overprints inverted *360.00 360.00*
J11b A1 2c brown 200.00 *200.00*
c. Both overprints inverted *360.00 360.00*
J12c A1 4c yellow 200.00 *200.00*
d. Both overprints inverted *360.00 360.00*
J13b A1 5c green 200.00 *200.00*
c. Both overprints inverted *360.00 360.00*
J14b A1 6c mauve 200.00 *200.00*
c. Both overprints inverted *360.00 360.00*
J15d A1 10c orange 210.00 *210.00*
e. Both overprints inverted *360.00 360.00*
f. Perf 11x11½ 240.00 *240.00*
J12c A1 15c carmine 200.00 *200.00*
d. Both overprints inverted *360.00 360.00*

Overprinted in Black

J17 A1 ½c rose 5.00 4.25
a. Inverted overprint 160.00 45.00
b. Pair, one with inverted overprint *225.00*
c. "U" of "DUE" omitted *200.00* 200.00
d. "U" of "DUE" handstamped *200.00*
e. "DU" of "DUE" omitted *225.00*
f. "DU" handstamped *225.00*
J18 A1 1c blue 5.00 *4.25*
a. Inverted overprint 160.00
b. Double overprint, one inverted —
c. Pair, one with inverted overprint *225.00*
J19 A1 2c brown 15.00 15.00
a. Inverted overprint 160.00
b. Double overprint —
c. Horiz. pair, imperf between 110.00 *110.00*
d. Perf 11½x11 15.00 *16.00*
J20 A1 4c yellow 15.00 *16.00*
a. Inverted overprint 160.00 —
J21 A1 5c green 42.50 *45.00*
a. Inverted overprint 110.00
J22 A1 6c mauve 13.00 *14.00*
a. Inverted overprint 240.00
b. Double overprint, one inverted —
J23 A1 10c orange 8.50 *22.50*
a. Inverted overprint 160.00
b. Perf 11½x11 27.50 27.50
c. As "b," inverted overprint 160.00
d. Perf 11x11½ 22.00 22.00
J24 A1 15c carmine 11.00 *13.00*
a. Inverted overprint 160.00
b. Double overprint, one inverted 260.00

Overprinted in Black, Split "P" Variety

J17g A1 ½c rose 35.00 —
h. Inverted overprint 190.00
J18d A1 1c blue 35.00 —
e. Inverted overprint 190.00
J19e A1 2c brown 35.00 —
J20b A1 4c yellow 45.00 —
J21b A1 5c green 35.00 —
J22c A1 6c mauve 35.00 —
d. Inverted overprint 275.00
J23e A1 10c orange 35.00 —
f. Inverted overprint 160.00 160.00
g. Perf 11½x11 35.00 —
h. Perf 11x11½ 35.00
i. As "h," inverted overprint 190.00
J24c A1 15c carmine 35.00 —
d. Inverted overprint 190.00

Nos. 8-15 overprinted

1895

J25 A2 ½c rose 5.00 *9.00*
a. Inverted overprint 50.00 50.00
b. Double overprint —
J26 A2 1c blue 6.50 *10.00*
a. Inverted overprint 50.00 50.00
J27 A2 2c brown 22.50 *24.00*
a. Inverted overprint 75.00 75.00
b. Double overprint —
J28 A2 4c yellow 25.00 *27.50*
a. Inverted overprint 75.00 75.00
J29 A2 5c green 27.50 *30.00*
a. Inverted overprint 75.00 75.00
J30 A2 6c mauve 27.50 *32.50*
a. Inverted overprint 75.00 75.00
J31 A2 10c orange 25.00 *27.50*
a. Inverted overprint 75.00 75.00
J32 A2 15c carmine 25.00 *27.50*
a. Inverted overprint 75.00 75.00

Split "P" Variety

J25c A2 ½c rose 50.00 50.00
J26b A2 1c blue 50.00 50.00
J27c A2 2c brown 50.00 50.00
J28b A2 4c yellow 50.00 50.00
J29b A2 5c green 50.00 50.00
J30b A2 6c mauve 50.00 50.00
J31b A2 10c orange 50.00 50.00
J32b A2 15c carmine 50.00 50.00

D1

Perf. 11, 11½ (#J33, J36, J39)

1895, Apr. 9

J33 D1 ½c rose 5.00 5.00
a. Imperf 50.00
J34 D1 1c blue 5.00 5.00
a. Imperf 55.00
b. Vert. pair, imperf between 110.00 *110.00*
c. Perf 11½x11 5.75 5.75
J35 D1 2c brown 12.50 *15.00*
J36 D1 4c yellow 8.00 *11.00*
J37 D1 5c green 13.75 13.75
a. Perf 11½ 17.00 17.00
J38 D1 6c mauve 11.00 *12.50*
a. Imperf 15.00
b. Vert. pair, imperf between 52.50 *75.00*
J39 D1 10c orange 8.75 *10.00*
J40 D1 15c carmine 12.75 *15.00*
a. Perf 11½ 15.00 *17.50*

Nos. J37, J37a surcharged in red

1895, Sept. 11

J41 D1 FIVE CENTS on 5c green (#J37a) 20.00 *27.50*
a. Inverted surcharge 110.00 *90.00*
b. On #J37 22.50 *27.50*
c. Inverted surcharge 140.00 *140.00*

OFFICIAL STAMPS

Nos. 8-15 overprinted

1896

O1 A2 ½c rose 6.00 *8.00*
a. Inverted overprint *60.00*
O2 A2 1c blue 12.50 *16.00*
a. Inverted overprint *60.00*
O3 A2 2c brown 15.00 *16.50*
a. Inverted overprint *60.00*
O4 A2 4c yellow 20.00 20.00
a. Inverted overprint *100.00*
O5 A2 5c green 20.00 20.00
a. Inverted overprint *100.00*
O6 A2 6c mauve 20.00 20.00
a. Inverted overprint *100.00*
O7 A2 10c orange 22.50 *25.00*
a. Inverted overprint *100.00*
O8 A2 15c carmine 125.00 *135.00*
a. Inverted overprint *200.00*

Inverted overprint with period is probably from a trial printing.

CHUNGKING

An ancient port city on the Yangtze River, some 1,500 miles above Shanghai, which served as a main hub for trade between the interior provinces and the coast. Chungking was opened to foreign trade in 1890. Mail service to the outside world was slow and expensive, and on Nov. 1, 1893, the Chunking Local Post was established to provide improved services at lower rates. It opened offices in Ichang and Shanghai and issued its first stamps in Dec. 1893. It was replaced by the Imperial Chinese Post Office on Feb. 2, 1897, but, because of the lack of government service, the local post continued operations for a few months.

Nos. 1 and 2 were lithographed by Kelly and Walsh, Shanghai. Nos. 3-7 were lithographed by Tokyo Tsukiji Type Foundry Co., Tokyo, Japan, in sheets of 50 (10x5).

Forgeries exist of the rarer Chungking stamps and covers. These should be purchased with certificates of authenticity from knowledgeable authorities.

Pagoda and Junk — A1

Perf. 12½

1893, Dec. Unwmk. Litho.

1 A1 2c vermilion 47.50 47.50

1894, Mar. ***Imperfx12½***

2 A1 2c vermilion 16.50 *37.50*
a. Horiz. pair, imperf between —

No. 1 was printed in sheets of 40, with stamps perforated on all sides. No. 2 was printed in sheets of 10 stamps, arranged horizontally and perforated vertically only.

Pagoda and Junk, finer design — A2

Perf. 11½

1894, Dec. Unwmk. Litho.

3 A2 2c rose 2.00 *2.90*
a. Horiz. pair, imperf between 175.00
4 A2 4c blue 4.25 *5.25*
5 A2 8c orange 4.25 *7.50*
6 A2 16c mauve 4.25 *7.50*
a. Pair, imperf between —
b. Vert. strip of 3, imperf between 260.00
7 A2 24c green 5.75 *8.50*

POSTAGE DUE STAMPS

No. 2 handstamped "POSTAGE DUE" in English and Chinese

1895 Unwmk. Litho. ***Perf. 11½***

J1 A1 2c vermilion 200.00 200.00

Nos. 3-7 with this handstamp were made after Feb. 2, 1897, and do not appear to have been used. 2c-24c with black overprint, value $175 each. 2c, 16c and 24c, value $325 each.

Nos. 3-7 overprinted

Normal spacing between "POSTAGE" and "DUE" is 17.5mm. Narrow spacing is 16.5mm.

1895

J2 A2 2c rose 16.00 *12.50*
a. Narrow spacing 62.50
b. Double overprint —
c. Inverted overprint 90.00
J3 A2 4c blue 16.00 *13.50*
a. Narrow spacing 62.50
b. Inverted overprint —
J4 A2 8c orange 16.00 *13.50*
a. Narrow spacing 62.50
b. Inverted overprint —
J5 A2 16c mauve 16.00 *13.50*
a. Narrow spacing 62.50
b. Inverted overprint —
J6 A2 24c green 10.50 *19.00*
a. Narrow spacing 62.50
b. Inverted overprint —

FOOCHOW

A river port on the Min River, Foochow is the capital of Fukien province. It was one of the five original Treaty Ports, opened to foreign trade by the Treaty of Nanking in 1842. Foochow was soon the home of a large foreign community, with a considerable volume of commercial correspondence. By 1863, Shanghai was despatching mail to Foochow and at least as early of 1882 a Shanghai branch agency was operating in the port, using Shanghai stamps.

On Jan. 1, 1895, the Foochow Local Post Office was established, and Shanghai stamps were replaced with a "PAID" handstamp. Distinctive Foochow Local Post stamps were issued on Aug. 1. On Feb. 2, 1897, the Foochow Local Post was merged with the Imperial Chinese Postal Service.

All Foochow issues were lithographed by Waterlow and Sons, London, England, in sheets of 50 (5x10).

Cancellations

The more common cancellation is a circular date stamp inscribed "POSTAL SERVICE FOOCHOW CHINA." Used values are for stamps bearing this cancel. Covers are scarce. Value, $1,000.

Stamps cancelled with "POSTAL SERVICE PAGODA ANCHORAGE" command a $40 premium. Value on cover, $2,500.

Regatta Dragon Boat — A1

Perf. 13½-15

1895, Aug. 1 Unwmk. Litho.

1	A1 ½c blue	1.80	*2.50*
2	A1 1c green	1.80	*3.00*
a.	1c aniline green	13.50	*16.00*
3	A1 2c orange	6.50	*8.25*
a.	Imperf	45.00	
4	A1 5c ultramarine	8.50	*11.00*
a.	Imperf	45.00	
5	A1 6c carmine	9.00	*12.50*
a.	Imperf	45.00	
6	A1 10c yellow green	11.00	*12.50*
a.	Imperf	55.00	
7	A1 15c yellow brown	14.50	*20.00*
8	A1 20c violet	14.50	*20.00*
9	A1 40c red brown	16.00	*22.50*

New Colors

1896, July

10	A1 ½c yellow	2.25	*3.50*
11	A1 1c brown	2.25	*3.50*

Nos. 1-11 exist with a wide variety of perforations. The following perforations are known:

½c blue: 13½; 13½x14; 14; 14x13½; 14½; 14x14½; 14½x14; 13½x15; 13½x14x14x14.

1c green: 13½; 13½x14; 14; 14x13½; 14½; 14x14½; 15; 14x14½x15; 15x14½; 13½x14x14½14½.

2c orange: 14x14½; 15; 14x15; 15x14½.

5c ultramarine: 14; 14½; 14x14½; 14½; x14; 15; 14x14x14x14½.

6c carmine: 13½; 14; 14x13½; 14x14½.

10c yellow green: 14; 14½; 14½x14; 15; 14½x15; 15x14½; 15x14.

15c yellow brown: 14½; 15.

20c violet: 13½x14; 14; 14x13½; 14½; 14x14½.

40c red brown: 14½; 15.

½c yellow: 13½; 13½x14; 14; 14x13½; 14½; 14x14½; 14½x14; 15; 14½x13½; 14x14.

1c brown: 14; 14½; 15; 14½x15; 15x14½; 13½x14x14½14½.

HANKOW

A river port in Hupeh Province, situated at the junction of the Han and Yangtze Rivers, about 600 miles upriver from Shanghai. An important trading center for tea and other exports, Hankow was served by the Shanghai Local Post as early as 1863, and a Shanghai Agency post office was established in 1878.

The Hankow Municipal Council took over postal operations on Jan. 1, 1893, and the first stamps of the Hankow Local Post were released on May 20. This was the first of the Treaty Port issues. The postal service was absorbed by the Chinese Post Office on Feb. 2, 1897.

Worker Carrying Chests of Tea — A1

Rouletted Horiz. in Color

1893, May 20 Unwmk. Typo.

1	A1 2c violet, *lilac, surfaced paper*	85.00	60.00
2	A1 5c green, *salmon, surfaced paper*	225.00	110.00
a.	Printed on both sides	*450.00*	
3	A1 10c claret, *dull rose, unsurfaced paper*	225.00	110.00

Printed in vertical strips of 10 stamps, rouletted horizontally. Ten strips were sold in booklets of 100.

On the 2c and 5c values, the upper left Chinese character ("Hank'ow") is composed of two elements, the first being a four-sided box followed by an apostrophe. Only the second element ("Han") appears on the 10c value.

Worker Carrying Chests of Tea — A2

Yellow Stork Tower — A3

Municipal Building — A4

Rouletted Horiz. or Vert. (5c) in Color

1893, May 25-June

4	A2 2c violet, *lilac*	8.50	7.25
a.	Surface colored paper	*10.00*	10.00
5	A2 5c green, *salmon*	8.50	7.25
a.	5c green, *flesh*	*13.50*	13.50
b.	Printed on both sides	*18.00*	—
6	A2 10c carmine rose, *rose, surfaced paper*	11.50	*14.00*
a.	Vertically bisected to pay 5c registration		—
7	A3 20c blue, *buff*	17.50	*20.00*
8	A4 30c red, *yellow*	17.50	*24.00*

Nos. 4 and 6-8 were printed in vertical strips of 10, rouletted horizontally. No. 5 was printed in horizontal strips of 10, rouletted vertically.

Issue dates: 20c, 5/25; 30c, 5/26; 5c, 10c, early June; 2c, mid-June.

Faded copies of No. 6 are sometimes mistaken for No. 3. The unsurfaced paper of No. 3 is very rough and porous, while the surfaced paper of No. 6 is smoother and more uniform. Under shortwave ultraviolet light, No. 3 is a dark blue violet, No. 6 a bright red.

Rouletted Horiz. (2c) or Vert. (5c) in Color

1894, June

9	A2 2c violet, *buff*	11.50	8.50
a.	2c blue violet, *buff*	17.50	17.50
10	A2 5c green, *pale greenish buff*	13.50	8.50

Worker Carrying Chests of Tea — A5

City Gate & Pagoda — A6

Municipal Building — A7

Watermarked Chinese Characters

1894, Sept. *Perf. 15*

11	A5 2c green	7.25	*10.00*
12	A5 5c red brown	9.00	*10.00*
13	A5 10c blue	11.50	10.00
14	A6 20c orange red	14.50	13.50
15	A7 30c violet	16.00	15.00

Printed by Waterlow and Sons, London, in sheets of 100 (10x10).

Nos. 13-15 surcharged

1896, March-May

16	A5 ONE CENT on 10c blue	29.00	*29.00*
a.	Double surcharge, one inverted	*725.00*	
17	A6 TWO CENTS on 20c orange red	29.00	*29.00*
a.	Double surcharge	*500.00*	*500.00*
b.	"2" with curved foot	*75.00*	*75.00*
18	A7 FIVE CENTS on 30c violet	29.00	*29.00*
a.	Double surcharge	*350.00*	*350.00*

Worker Carrying Chests of Tea — A8

City Gate & Pagoda — A9

Municipal Building — A10

Perf. 11½-12

1894, Sept. Unwmk. Litho.

19	A8 2c green	4.25	*5.00*
20	A8 5c red brown	7.25	5.50
a.	Horizontal pair, imperf vertically	200.00	
21	A8 10c blue	13.50	*18.00*
a.	10c dark blue	15.00	*20.00*
b.	Vertical pair, imperf horizontally	210.00	
22	A9 20c orange brown	21.00	*18.00*
a.	20c yellow orange	22.50	22.00
b.	Aniline ink	*25.00*	*25.00*
23	A10 30c violet	11.00	*17.50*
a.	30c slate violet	11.00	*17.50*
b.	Short 2nd "L" in "LOCAL"	20.00	20.00
c.	Extra cross bar on "T" of "CENTS"	12.50	12.50
d.	Broken "S" in "CENTS"	13.50	13.50
e.	Horiz. pair, imperf between	210.00	*210.00*

Nos. 21 and 21a printed on both sides, No. 22 in black, No. 23 in black and No. 23 printed on both sides are proofs.

No. 23 Surcharged

1896, August

24	A10 ONE CENT on 30c violet, surcharged vertically	110.00	100.00
a.	Pair, one without surcharge	*850.00*	
b.	On #23b	140.00	
c.	Vertical pair, imperf horizontally	—	
d.	Inverted surcharge (reading down)	*350.00*	
e.	As "a," horiz. pair, imperf between	—	
25	A10 ONE CENT on 30c violet, surcharged horizontally	24.00	24.00
a.	On 30c slate violent (#23a)	24.00	24.00
b.	On #23b	*125.00*	125.00
c.	On #23c	160.00	
d.	Broken "O" in "ONE"	30.00	30.00
e.	Inverted surcharge	*95.00*	
f.	Horiz. pair, imperf between	*140.00*	
g.	Vertical pair, imperf horizontally	*100.00*	
h.	Double surcharge	*125.00*	

Nos. 19-23 overprinted "P.P.C."

1897, January

26	A8 2c green	*85.00*	—
27	A8 5c red brown	*85.00*	—
28	A8 10c blue	*85.00*	—
29	A9 20c orange brown	*85.00*	—
30	A10 30c violet	*85.00*	—

In January, 1897, after being ordered to close its offices on Feb. 2, 1897, the Hankow Local Post Office overprinted the stamps it had on hand with the letters "P.P.C." ("Pour Prendre Congee," French for "to take leave"). These stamps were used during the last few days that the post office was in operation. Covers exist and are very rare.

Dangerous forgeries of this overprint exist.

POSTAGE DUE STAMPS

Nos. 6-10 overprinted, Chinese in "Sung" type characters

1894

J1	A2 2c violet, *buff*	100.00	*125.00*
J2	A2 5c green, *pale green*	100.00	*120.00*
J3	A2 10c carmine, *rose*	100.00	*140.00*
J4	A3 20c blue, *buff*	100.00	*140.00*
J5	A4 30c red, *yellow*	100.00	*130.00*

Nos. 6-10 Overprinted, Chinese in ordinary characters, 2mm space between "POSTAGE" and "DUE"

Type 1 — small top character

Type 2 — large top character

Two types of overprint: Type 1, first vertical radical longer, top of left character 2½mm wide; Type 2, first vertical radical shorter, top of left character 3mm wide.

1894-96

J6	A2 2c violet, *buff*, type 1 ovpt.	11.50	*14.00*
a.	Inverted overprint	175.00	
b.	Double overprint	160.00	
c.	"E" of "POSTAGE" omitted	110.00	
d.	Type 2 ovpt.	150.00	*200.00*
J7	A2 5c green, *pale green*, type 1 ovpt.	15.00	15.00
a.	Inverted overprint	160.00	
b.	Double overprint	160.00	
c.	Double overprint, both inverted	275.00	
d.	Type 2 ovpt.	150.00	*200.00*
J8	A2 10c carmine, *rose* type 1 ovpt.	15.00	15.00
a.	Inverted overprint	200.00	
b.	Double overprint	200.00	
c.	Double overprint, both inverted	350.00	
d.	Type 2 ovpt.	110.00	*125.00*
J9	A3 20c blue, *buff*, type 1 ovpt.	65.00	57.50
a.	Inverted overprint	260.00	
b.	Double overprint	260.00	
c.	"E" of "POSTAGE" omitted	175.00	
d.	Type 2 ovpt.	150.00	—
J10	A4 30c red, *yellow*, type 1 ovpt.	35.00	29.00
a.	Inverted overprint	225.00	
b.	Double overprint	225.00	
c.	Triple overprint	—	
d.	"E" of "POSTAGE" omitted	140.00	*140.00*
e.	Wide space (4¼mm) between Chinese characters	—	
f.	Type 2 ovpt.	125.00	*135.00*

Nos. 6, 7, 9 overprinted, 3mm space between "POSTAGE" and "DUE"

1895

J11	A2 2c violet, *buff*, type 1 ovpt.	*290.00*	290.00
a.	Type 2 ovpt.	325.00	*325.00*
J12	A2 10c carmine, *rose* type 1 ovpt.	260.00	*260.00*
a.	Type 2 ovpt.	325.00	—
J13	A3 20c blue, *buff*, type 1 ovpt.	290.00	290.00
a.	Type 2 ovpt.	325.00	325.00

ICHANG

A river port on the north side of the Yangtze River, about 1,100 miles from Shanghai and 400 miles below Hankow. Ichang was the head of steam navigation on the Yangtze and so was the junction point of trade — most importantly, opium, tung oil and silk — between Szechuan and the rest of China.

Ichang was opened as a Treaty Port in 1876, and the first settlement of foreign traders soon followed, in 1878. The Ichang Local Post Office was established in Nov., 1894. Along with the other Treaty Port local posts, it was absorbed into the Chinese Post Office on Feb. 2, 1897.

All Ichang basic issues were lithographed by Tokyo Tsukiji Type Foundry Co., Tokyo, Japan.

Coin-like Design — A1

Brass Cash — A2

Ancient "Ichang" Character — A3

Stylized Pa Kua, "1894" — A4

Modern "Ichang" Character — A5

Pheasant — A6

Otter — A7

Map of the Foreign Settlement in Ichang — A8

Narrow Setting
Stamps Printed 3.5-4mm apart

Perf. 10¾-11½

1894, Dec. 1 Unwmk. Litho.

1	A1 ½ ca. brown	7.25	*9.00*
a.	Horiz. pair, imperf between	200.00	
2	A2 1 ca. olive brown	7.25	*11.50*
a.	Vert. pair, imperf between	290.00	175.00
3	A3 2 ca. red violet	12.00	*11.50*
4	A4 3 ca. gray	20.00	*14.50*
5	A5 5 ca. brown rose	10.00	*14.50*
a.	Horiz. pair, imperf between	400.00	
6	A6 1 m green	35.00	*57.50*
7	A7 15 ca. blue	40.00	*57.50*
8	A8 3 m carmine	40.00	*42.50*
a.	Vert. pair, imperf between	400.00	

Type A

Type B

Wide Setting
Stamps printed 5mm apart

Two types of 1 ca. value: Type A, 2 small triangles blank, open; Type B, 2 small triangles shaded closed.

1895

9	A1 ½ ca. red brown	8.50	4.50
10	A2 1 ca. bister brown (Type A)	21.00	17.50
11	A2 1 ca. bister brown (Type B)	11.50	*8.50*
12	A4 3 ca. gray lilac	17.50	*11.00*
a.	Horiz. pair, imperf vert.	—	
13	A3 2 ca. red violet	14.50	14.00
14	A8 3 m carmine	29.00	*30.00*

Handstamped with new value

1896

Surcharged in Violet

15	A8 2 ca. on 3m carmine (#8)	*600.00*	*550.00*
16	A8 2 ca. on 3m carmine (#14)	*110.00*	*72.50*

Surcharged in Black

17	A8 2 ca. on 3m carmine (#8)	65.00	*50.00*
18	A8 2 ca. on 3m carmine (#14)	110.00	*72.50*
a.	Pair, one without surcharge	725.00	
19	A8 2 ca. on 1 ca. bister brown (#10)	17.50	16.00
20	A8 2 ca. on 1 ca. bister brown (#11)	14.50	*11.50*
a.	Inverted surcharge	—	—
b.	Double surcharge	—	—

KEWKIANG

A river port in Kiangsi Province, on the Yangtze River, 458 miles upriver from Shanghai. Kewkiang was opened to foreign trade in 1858 and it appears that at least as early as 1865 an agent of the Shanghai Local Post was receiving and despatching mails. Shanghai Local Post stamps were used from Jan. 1, 1893, to June 1, 1894, when the Kewkiang Local Post took over postal operations. On Feb. 2, 1897, the Chinese Post Office took over postal services between cities, though the Kewkiang Local Post continued limited local delivery until late August.

All basic Kewkiang stamps were typographed by Central China Press, Kewkiang.

Pagoda — A1

Center Stroke Omitted

"Kiang" in Ancient Characters A2

"Kiang" in Modern Characters A3

"Kiang" in Modified Characters — A4

Unwmk.

1894, June 1 Typo. *Perf. 12*

On Native Paper

1	A1 ½c black, *rose*	3.00	3.00
a.	Stroke missing in "Kiang"	50.00	45.00
b.	As "a," corrected by hand	55.00	55.00
c.	Double impression	72.50	
2	A1 ½c red, *yellow*	3.00	3.00
a.	Stroke missing in "Kiang"	50.00	45.00
b.	As "a," corrected by hand	55.00	55.00
c.	Horiz. pair, imperf vert.	—	—
3	A2 1c gray black	3.00	3.00
4	A3 2c vermilion	4.00	4.25
a.	2c red, on European paper	5.75	5.50
5	A4 5c slate blue, *yellow*	5.00	*4.75*
6	A3 6c yellow	6.00	*5.75*
a.	6c ocher, on European paper	26.00	22.00
7	A2 10c black, *yellow buff*	8.50	8.50
a.	10c black, *yellow*	8.50	8.50
8	A4 15c red, *yellow*	8.50	*10.00*
a.	"1" of "15" omitted	110.00	*85.00*
9	A4 20c blue, *rose*	11.00	*11.00*
10	A3 40c black, *red*	12.00	*13.50*

Lu Shan Hills and Bridge Over Lung K'ai Ho Creek — A5

"Little Orphan Rock" — A6

1894, June 23

On Native Paper

11	A5 ½c black, *rose*	2.00	*4.25*
a.	Horiz. pair, imperf between	125.00	
12	A5 ½c red, *yellow*	2.00	*4.25*

1894, August On European Paper

13	A6 1c black	2.50	*4.25*
a.	Horiz. pair, imperf between	160.00	
b.	Double impression	175.00	

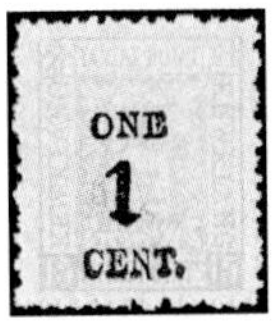

Nos. 6, 8, 9 surcharged in black or blue (#16)

1896, August

14	A4 HALF CENT on 20c	11.00	11.00
a.	Double surcharge	140.00	
b.	"1" of "½" inverted	16.00	16.00
c.	Inverted surcharge	140.00	
d.	Surcharge on reverse	200.00	
15	A4 ONE CENT on 15c	11.00	*11.00*
a.	Blue surcharge	140.00	110.00
b.	Surcharged on both sides	140.00	
c.	Pair, one without surcharge	375.00	
d.	On #8a	160.00	
e.	Wider space (3mm) between "1" and "CENT"	27.50	
16	A3 TWO CENTS on 6c (Bl)	12.50	12.50
a.	Black surcharge	175.00	140.00

POSTAGE DUE STAMPS

Nos. 4a//13 overprinted

Four types of overprint: type A, narrow setting, overprint slope 20 degrees, "D" larger (2½mm) and under "os" of "Postage;" type B, wide setting, overprint slope 20 degrees, "D" larger (2½mm) and under "st" of "Postage;" type C, wide setting, overprint slope 30-35 degrees, "D" smaller (2mm) and under "st" of "Postage;" type D, wide setting, overprint slope 40-45 degrees, "D" smaller (2mm) and under "ta" of "Postage."

Overprinted Type A

1895, Sept.

J1	½c black, *rose*	29.00	*40.00*
a.	"Postag"	160.00	*160.00*
J2	½c red, *yellow*	29.00	*40.00*
a.	"Postag"	160.00	*160.00*
b.	Inverted overprint	—	—
J3	1c black	26.00	*35.00*
a.	"Postag"	160.00	*160.00*
J4	2c red	75.00	*120.00*
a.	"Postag"	325.00	*325.00*
b.	Inverted overprint	—	—

Overprinted Type B

1896

J5	½c black, *rose*	14.50	9.00
a.	Inverted overprint	160.00	140.00
J6	½c red, *yellow*	11.00	9.00
a.	Inverted overprint	160.00	140.00
J7	1c black	10.00	*8.00*
J8	2c red	11.50	*11.00*
a.	Inverted overprint	160.00	140.00
J9	5c slate blue, *yellow*	14.50	*10.00*
a.	Inverted overprint	160.00	175.00
J10	6c yellow	16.00	*11.00*
J11	10c black, *yellow buff*	17.50	*14.00*
J12	15c red, *yellow*	20.00	*20.00*
a.	On #8a	*175.00*	175.00
J13	20c blue *rose*	29.00	29.00
J14	40c black, *red*	29.00	*29.00*

Overprinted in Red

J15	1c black	100.00	100.00
J16	10c black, *yellow buff*	425.00	*425.00*

Dangerous forgeries of Nos. J15-J16 exist.

Overprinted Type C

J17	½c black, *rose*	14.50	*8.50*
J18	½c red, *yellow*	10.50	*8.50*
J19	1c black	10.00	*8.00*
J20	2c red	11.50	11.00
J21	5c slate blue, *yellow*	14.50	10.00
J22	6c yellow	16.00	*11.00*
J23	10c black, *yellow buff*	17.50	14.00
J24	15c red, *yellow*	20.00	*20.00*
J25	20c blue *rose*	29.00	29.00
J26	40c black, *red*	29.00	*29.00*

Overprinted Type D

J27	½c black, *rose*	*14.50*	*13.50*
J28	½c red, *yellow*	*16.00*	*13.50*
J29	1c black	*17.50*	*11.50*
J30	2c red	*13.50*	*13.50*
J31	5c slate blue, *yellow*	*14.50*	*13.50*
J32	6c yellow	*14.50*	*13.50*
J33	10c black, *yellow buff*	*14.50*	*14.50*
J34	15c red, *yellow*	*16.00*	*16.00*
J35	20c blue *rose*	*21.00*	*26.00*
J36	40c black, *red*	*26.00*	*32.50*

NANKING

A river port on the Yangtze, about 200 miles upriver from Shanghai. An ancient and historical city, Nanking was opened to foreign settlement and trade by the Treaty of Peking in 1860. British and French settlement began in 1865, and a European community gradually developed. Nanking became a center of European missionary and educational work, and in 1885 an office of the Shanghai Agency was established. By 1896 the Nanking Local Post was operating in the city and on Sept. 20, 1896, the first Nanking local stamps were issued. Postal operations were taken over by the Chinese Post Office on Feb. 2, 1897.

All Nanking stamps were lithographed by Tokyo Tsukiji Type Foundry Co., Tokyo, Japan.

Stone Men at Approach to Ming Tomb — A1

The Drum Tower — A2

Stone Elephants at Approach to Ming Tomb — A3

Lotus Lake Scene — A4

Central Hall of the Confucian Temple — A5

The Great Bell — A6

"NANKING LOCAL POST" in double-lined Letters

Perf. 11½

1896, Sept. 20 Unwmk. Litho.

1	A1 ½c gray	6.50	*7.50*
a.	Horiz. pair, imperf between	290.00	
b.	Vert. pair, imperf between	290.00	
2	A2 1c rose	6.50	*7.50*
a.	Horiz. pair, imperf between	400.00	
3	A3 2c gray green	13.50	*15.00*
a.	Horiz. pair, imperf between	400.00	
4	A4 3c orange yellow	11.50	*9.00*
a.	3c yellow	11.50	*9.00*
5	A5 4c claret	13.50	*13.50*
6	A6 5c violet	14.00	12.50
7	A2 10c yellow green	17.50	12.50
a.	10c deep green	17.50	14.50
8	A2 20c brown	14.50	12.50

Nos. 1-8 were printed in sheets of 25 (5x5)

"NANKING LOCAL POST" in single-lined Letters

1896

9	A1 ½c salmon rose	5.75	*6.50*

No. 9 was printed in sheets of 25 (5x5).

"NANKING LOCAL POST" in single-lined Letters

1896 ***Perf. 12½***

10	A1 ½c lilac brown	7.25	*8.00*
11	A2 1c rose	12.50	*10.00*
12	A3 2c green	14.50	12.50
13	A4 3c yellow	16.00	15.00
a.	3c orange yellow	—	
14	A5 4c brown	17.50	16.00
15	A6 5c blue	17.50	*16.00*

1897 ***Imperf***

16	A2 1c rose	12.50	*15.00*

Nos. 10-16 were printed in sheets of 100 (10x10).

WEI HAI WEI

A port in Shantung province which, with adjoining territory, was leased to Great Britain in 1899. The Cornabe Co. operated a private courier post to Chefoo from Dec. 1898 until Mar. 1899, when a Chinese Imperial Post Office was opened. This was replaced by a British Post Office in Sept., 1899, which provided postal service, using Hong Kong stamps, until the territory was returned to China on Oct. 1, 1930.

Although not one of the Treaty Ports, Wei Hai Wei is generally collected with those issues.

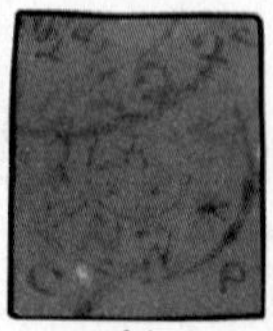

A1

A2

Before regular printed stamps were available, provisional stamps were made by impressing a Cornabe & Co. double circle chop on red native paper in black. The 2c stamp was handstamped once and "2c" was handwritten in the top right and left corners; the letters "C," standing for "Courier," and "P," standing for "Post," were written in the left and right lower corners respectively. The 5c stamps were produced by making two impressions of the Cornabe & Co. double circle chop on red native paper, one of which was inverted. "5c" was handwritten in each of the upper corners, and the words "Courier Post" were written below the stamped impressions. These stamps were signed in continuous horizontal rows on the back of the sheet by G.K. Fergusson, the Honorary Postmaster. 8 sheets of 98 stamps (14x7) or 784 stamps of the 2c denomination and 4 sheets of 98 stamps (14x7) or 392 stamps of the 5c denomination were produced.

1898, Dec. 8 Unwmk. ***Imperf***

1	A1 2c black, *red*	*225.00*	*260.00*
a.	Vertical signature of G.K. Fergusson	*625.00*	*625.00*
b.	"P.C." for "C.P."	*575.00*	*625.00*
c.	Chop inverted		—
d.	Chop double	*550.00*	
2	A2 5c black, *red*	*1,150.*	*1,100.*
a.	Vertical signature of G.K. Fergusson	*950.00*	*950.00*

A3

1899, Jan. 9 Litho. ***Perf. 11***

3	A3 2c red	125.00	*125.00*
4	A3 5c olive green	140.00	*160.00*
a.	Tete-beche pair		—
b.	Horiz. pair, imperf between	*1,350.*	1,350.
c.	5c emerald green	160.00	*175.00*
d.	5c green	160.00	*160.00*

Nos. 3-4 were lithographed by Kelly & Walsh, Shanghai, in sheets of 64 (8x8) stamps.

Reprints exist on thin paper.

WUHU

A port city on the Yangtze River, 282 miles from the sea. Wuhu was opened up as a Treaty Port in 1876, and a customs house was established in 1877. The Shanghai Local Post was operating in Wuhu by 1888. In June, 1894, the foreign community, composed mostly of Christian missionaries, established a local post, and stamps were issued in Nov. 1894. The Wuhu Local Post was replaced by the Chinese Post Office on Feb. 2, 1897, although it continued to provide service within the city for a short time after.

All basic Wuhu stamps were printed by the Lithographic Society of Shanghai.

Wild Fowl — A1

Rice Field — A2

Pheasants A3

Wuhu Pagoda A4

"Abundance" ("Fu") — A5

First Printing

11¾, 12¼ and compound

1894, Nov. 26 Unwmk. Litho.

1	A1 ½c black	8.50	6.50
a.	Imperf	13.50	9.00
b.	Perf 12	9.00	9.00
2	A2 ½c green	6.50	5.00
a.	Perf 11x11¾	22.50	18.00
3	A3 1c brown	8.50	5.75
a.	Perf 12	11.00	*11.00*
4	A2 2c yellow	7.25	*6.50*
a.	Perf 12	11.00	11.00
5	A4 5c carmine	7.25	*8.50*
a.	Imperf	12.50	*13.50*
6	A5 6c blue	10.00	10.00
7	A3 10c brown red	13.50	*13.50*
8	A4 15c olive green	13.50	*13.50*
9	A5 20c red	13.50	*13.00*
10	A1 40c brown	17.50	17.50

Second Printing

1894 ***Perf. 11***

11	A1 ½c grayish black	5.50	3.25
a.	Imperf	10.00	*12.00*
12	A2 ½c yellow green	4.25	2.90
a.	½c deep green	4.25	2.90
b.	Imperf	9.00	9.00
13	A3 1c grayish brown	7.25	4.00
a.	Imperf	*25.00*	
14	A2 2c orange yellow	6.00	5.75
a.	Imperf	*25.00*	
15	A4 5c red orange	8.00	*9.00*
a.	Imperf	13.50	10.00
16	A5 6c gray blue	8.00	*8.50*
a.	Imperf	13.50	10.00
17	A3 10c brown red	14.50	*11.50*
a.	Imperf	13.50	10.00
18	A4 15c olive green	13.50	*11.50*
a.	Imperf	*25.00*	
19	A5 20c orange red	12.50	11.00
a.	Imperf	*25.00*	
20	A1 40c yellow brown	15.00	15.00
a.	Imperf	*25.00*	

Nos. 1-10 surcharged with denomination in Chinese in black or red (R)

1895 ***11¾, 12¼ and compound***

21	A1 ½c black (R)	10.00	8.50
a.	Perf 12¼	13.50	—
22	A2 ½c green	8.00	7.25
23	A3 1c brown	6.25	5.00
a.	Perf 12	9.00	*7.25*
24	A2 2c yellow	7.25	*6.50*
25	A4 5c carmine	10.00	*10.00*
a.	Inverted surcharge	*110.00*	
26	A5 6c blue	14.50	*14.50*
27	A3 10c brown red	16.00	*14.50*
28	A4 15c olive green	17.50	14.50
29	A5 20c red	21.00	*22.50*
30	A1 40c brown	32.50	32.50

Nos. 11-20 surcharged with denomination in Chinese

31	A1 ½c grayish black (R)	10.00	8.50
a.	Inverted surcharge	110.00	
32	A1 ½c grayish black (Black)	72.50	
a.	Inverted surcharge	*210.00*	
33	A2 ½c green	8.00	7.25
a.	Inverted surcharge	110.00	
34	A3 1c brown	6.25	5.00
a.	Inverted surcharge	110.00	
b.	Horiz. pair, imperf between	200.00	
35	A2 2c orange yellow	7.25	6.50
a.	Inverted surcharge	110.00	
36	A4 5c red orange	10.00	*10.00*
a.	Inverted surcharge	110.00	
37	A5 6c gray blue	14.50	14.50
a.	Inverted surcharge	110.00	
38	A3 10c brown red	16.00	*14.50*
a.	Inverted surcharge	—	
39	A4 15c olive green	17.50	14.50
40	A5 20c red	21.00	
a.	Inverted surcharge	110.00	
41	A1 40c yellow brown	32.50	32.50
a.	Inverted surcharge	110.00	

Nos. 3//14 surcharged in black or red (R)

1895, Nov.

42	A3 ½c on 1c brown, perf 11¾ (R)	11.50	*9.00*
a.	"2" with straight foot	42.50	*29.00*
b.	Perf 11	13.50	*12.50*
c.	As "b," "2" with straight foot	65.00	*50.00*
d.	Perf 12¼	11.50	*9.00*
e.	As "d," "2" with straight foot	90.00	
f.	1c yellow brown, perf 11	125.00	125.00
43	A3 ½c on 1c brown, perf 12¼ (Black)	175.00	
a.	On 1c yellow brown, perf 11	175.00	
b.	Vert. pair, red and black surcharges setenant, perf 11	225.00	
c.	Vert. pair, red and black surcharges setenant, perf 12¼	225.00	
44	A2 5c on 2c yellow, perf 11	13.50	*14.50*
a.	Perf 12	13.50	*14.50*
b.	Double surcharge	325.00	

Other stamps with "5 Cent" surcharges, with and without a bar through the original value, exist but are of speculative nature and had no postal validity.

Cranes A6

Chinese Character ("Fortunate") A7

Chinese Characters ("Wuhu") — A8

Designs: 2c, 10c, owl; 6c, 40c stag.

1896, Feb. ***Perf. 10-10½***

45	A6 ½c lilac	11.50	8.50
46	A7 ½c yellow	8.50	*7.25*
47	A8 1c blue	7.25	6.75
48	A6 2c green	17.50	*14.50*
49	A7 5c yellow green	12.50	12.00
50	A6 6c yellow brown	16.00	18.00
51	A6 10c rose	21.00	19.00
52	A6 15c carmine	23.00	21.00
53	A8 20c rose	15.00	*20.00*
54	A6 40c carmine	21.00	*24.00*

Surcharged with values in Chinese characters

55	A6 ½c lilac	14.50	11.50
56	A7 ½c yellow	8.50	*8.50*
a.	Inverted surcharge	85.00	*57.50*
57	A8 1c blue	7.25	6.50
a.	Inverted surcharge	72.50	
b.	Vert. pair, one stamp with surcharge omitted	140.00	
58	A6 2c green	21.00	*17.50*
a.	Inverted surcharge	140.00	*100.00*
59	A7 5c yellow green	14.50	*11.50*
a.	Inverted surcharge	140.00	*140.00*
60	A6 6c yellow brown	14.00	*20.00*
a.	Inverted surcharge	85.00	*57.50*
61	A6 10c rose	35.00	*29.00*
a.	Inverted surcharge	140.00	100.00
62	A6 15c carmine	40.00	29.00
a.	Inverted surcharge	140.00	85.00
63	A8 20c rose	23.00	18.00
a.	Inverted surcharge	85.00	57.50
64	A6 40c carmine	26.00	*23.50*
a.	Inverted surcharge	85.00	57.50

In Jan. 1897, after being ordered to close its offices on Feb. 2, 1897, the Wuhu Local Post Office overprinted the stamps it had on hand with the letters "P.P.C." ("Pour Prendre Congee," French for "to take leave"). These stamps were used during the last few days that the post office was in operation. Covers exist and are very rare.

Nos. 45-54 overprinted

Nos. 45-54 Overprinted in Black

1897, Jan.

65	A6 ½c lilac	14.50	*17.50*
66	A7 ½c yellow	14.50	*17.50*
a.	Double overprint	—	—
67	A8 1c blue	14.50	17.50
68	A6 2c green	20.00	*35.00*
69	A7 5c yellow green	14.50	*17.50*
70	A6 6c yellow brown	16.00	*21.00*
71	A6 10c rose	29.00	*35.00*
72	A6 15c carmine	20.00	35.00
73	A8 20c rose	13.50	*23.00*
74	A6 40c carmine	17.00	*35.00*

Nos. 45-54 Overprinted in Red

75 A6 ½c lilac 17.50 17.50
76 A7 ½c yellow 16.00 20.00
77 A8 1c blue 14.50 29.00
78 A6 2c green 26.00 35.00
79 A7 5c yellow green 14.50 17.50
80 A6 6c yellow brown 17.50 21.00
81 A6 10c rose 35.00 35.00
82 A6 15c carmine 23.00 35.00
83 A8 20c rose 13.50 23.00
84 A6 40c carmine 35.00 35.00

Nos. 55-64 Overprinted in Black Above Chinese Characters

85 A6 ½c lilac 11.00 8.50
86 A7 ½c yellow 6.50 9.00
87 A8 1c blue 9.00 8.50
88 A6 2c green 17.50 20.00
89 A7 5c yellow green 8.50 9.00
90 A6 6c yellow brown 11.50 13.50
91 A6 10c rose 29.00 23.00
92 A6 15c carmine 26.00 23.00
93 A8 20c rose 23.00 26.00
94 A6 40c carmine 23.00 26.00

Nos. 55//62 Overprinted in Red Above Chinese Characters

95 A6 ½c lilac 11.50 10.00
96 A7 ½c yellow 8.50 8.50
97 A8 1c blue 8.50 8.50
98 A6 2c green 26.00 26.00
99 A7 5c yellow green 10.00 11.00
100 A6 6c yellow brown 13.50 14.50
101 A6 15c carmine 32.50 26.00

Nos. 55-64 Overprinted in Black Below Chinese Characters

102 A6 ½c lilac 8.50 11.00
103 A7 ½c yellow 7.75 10.00
104 A8 1c blue 7.25 11.50
105 A6 2c green 16.00 20.00
106 A7 5c yellow green 8.50 9.00
107 A6 6c yellow brown 11.00 13.50
108 A6 10c rose 29.00 23.00
109 A6 15c carmine 26.00 23.00
110 A8 20c rose 21.00 26.00
111 A6 40c carmine 24.00 26.00

Nos. 55//62 Overprinted in Red Below Chinese Characters

112 A6 ½c lilac 9.00 11.50
113 A7 ½c yellow 9.00 11.00
114 A8 1c blue 9.00 10.50
115 A6 2c green 16.00 20.00
116 A7 5c yellow green 11.00 11.00
117 A6 6c yellow brown 12.50 14.50
118 A6 15c carmine 32.50 26.00

POSTAGE DUE STAMPS

Regular postage stamps overprinted in black or red (R)

There are three types of overprint: type 1, "P" longer upright, extending to bottom; type 2, "P" short upright, "P" with loops at left; type 3, "P" short upright, "P" without loops at left. All three types exist on Nos. J1-J20, and types 1 and 2 exist on Nos. J28-J37.

Nos. 1-10 Overprinted

J1 A1 ½c black (R) 5.50 5.50
a. Inverted overprint 80.00
J2 A1 ½c black 90.00
J3 A2 ½c green 5.50 5.50
a. Inverted overprint 80.00
b. Perf 11x11¾ 27.50 27.50
J4 A3 1c brown 12.50 12.50
a. Inverted overprint 80.00
b. Perf 12¼ 12.50 12.50
J5 A2 2c yellow 10.00 7.25
a. Inverted overprint 80.00 80.00
J6 A4 5c carmine 10.00 10.00
J7 A5 6c blue 12.50 12.00
a. Inverted overprint 80.00 80.00
J8 A3 10c brown red 16.00 16.00
a. Inverted overprint 80.00 80.00
J9 A4 15c olive green 17.00 16.00
a. Inverted overprint 80.00 80.00
J10 A5 20c red 23.00 23.00
a. Inverted overprint 80.00 80.00
J11 A1 40c brown 29.00 25.00
a. Inverted overprint 80.00 80.00

Nos. 11-20 Overprinted

J12 A1 ½c black (R) 5.50 5.50
a. Inverted overprint 80.00
J13 A1 ½c black 85.00
J14 A2 ½c green 5.75 5.50
a. Inverted overprint 80.00
b. Perf 11x11¾ 27.50 27.50
J15 A3 1c brown 6.25 5.50
a. Inverted overprint 80.00
J16 A2 2c orange yellow 10.00 7.25
a. Inverted overprint 80.00
J17 A4 5c carmine 8.50 8.00
J18 A5 6c gray blue 12.50 12.00
a. Inverted overprint 80.00 80.00
J19 A3 10c brown red 17.00 16.00
a. Inverted overprint 80.00 80.00
J20 A4 15c olive green 17.00 16.00
a. Inverted overprint 80.00 80.00
b. "a" of "Postage" omitted 125.00

J21 A5 20c red 23.00 23.00
a. Inverted overprint 80.00 80.00
b. Vert. overprint, reading down 225.00 225.00
J22 A1 40c brown 29.00 25.00
a. Inverted overprint 80.00 80.00

Nos. 3//8 Overprinted Type 3

J23 A3 1c brown, perf 11¾ — —
a. Perf 12¼ — —
b. Imperf, "t" of "Postage" omitted —
J24 A2 2c orange yellow, imperf, "t" of "Postage" omitted — —
J25 A4 5c carmine, "t" of "Postage" omitted — —
J26 A3 10c brown red — —
J20 A4 15c olive green, imperf, overprint inverted — —

Nos. 45-54 Overprinted

J28 A6 ½c lilac 14.00 11.50
a. Inverted overprint 85.00 24.00
J29 A7 ½c yellow 7.25 7.25
a. Inverted overprint 57.50 42.50
J30 A8 1c blue 8.50 10.00
J31 A6 2c green 23.00 20.00
a. Inverted overprint 140.00 110.00
J32 A7 5c yellow green 13.50 12.00
J33 A6 6c yellow brown 17.50 16.00
J34 A6 10c rose 29.00 26.00
a. Inverted overprint 140.00 110.00
J35 A6 15c carmine 50.00 35.00
a. "a" of "Postage" omitted 160.00 50.00
J36 A8 20c rose 32.50 32.50
J37 A6 40c carmine 40.00 37.50

Nos. J28-J37 Overprinted

J38 A6 ½c lilac 11.00 10.00
a. Red overprint 32.50 35.00
b. Overprint reading down —
J39 A7 ½c yellow 8.50 8.50
a. Overprint reading down 65.00 57.50
J40 A8 1c blue 8.50 8.50
a. Red overprint, reading down 65.00 65.00
J41 A6 2c green 21.00 20.00
J42 A7 5c yellow green 10.00 8.50
J43 A6 6c yellow brown 13.50 11.50
J44 A6 10c rose 26.00 23.00
J45 A6 15c carmine 21.00 21.00
J46 A8 20c rose 21.00 21.00
J47 A6 40c carmine 23.00 23.00

CILICIA

sə-ˈli-sh̦ē-ˌə

LOCATION — A territory of Turkey, in Southeastern Asia Minor
AREA — 6,238 sq. mi.
POP. — 383,645
CAPITAL — Adana

British and French forces occupied Cilicia in 1918 and in 1919 its control was transferred to the French. Eventually part of Cilicia was assigned to the French Mandated Territory of Syria but by the Lausanne Treaty of 1923 which fixed the boundary between Syria and Turkey, Cilicia reverted to Turkey.

40 Paras = 1 Piaster

Issued under French Occupation

The overprint on Nos. 2-93 is often found inverted, double, etc.

Numbers in parentheses are those of basic Turkish stamps.

Turkish Stamps of 1913-19 Handstamped

Perf. 11½, 12, 12½, 13½

1919 Unwmk.

On Pictorial Issue of 1913

2 A24 2pa red lil (254) 1.60 1.40
3 A25 4pa dk brn (255) 1.50 1.25
4 A27 6pa dk bl (257) 17.50 10.00
5 A32 1¾pi sl & red brn (262) 2.50 1.75

On Issue of 1915

6 A17 1pi bl (300) 1.25 1.00
7 A21 20pa car rose (318) 1.25 1.00
9 A22 20pa car rose (330) 3.00 3.00

On Commemorative Issue of 1916

9A A41 5pa green (345) 110.00 70.00
10 A41 20pa ultra (347) 1.75 1.00
11 A41 1pi vio & blk (348) 2.00 1.25
12 A41 5pi yel brn & blk (349) 2.25 1.25

On Issue of 1916-18

13 A44 10pa grn (424) 1.50 1.10
14 A47 50pa ultra (428) 8.00 3.50
15 A51 25pi car, *straw* (434) 2.25 1.75
16 A52 50pi car (437) 1.75 1.25
17 A52 50pi ind (438) 16.00 13.00

On Issue of 1917

18 A53 5pi on 2pa Prus bl (547) 7.50 4.50

On Issue of 1919

19 A47 50pa ultra (555) 10.00 3.75
20 A48 2pi org brn & ind (556) 3.00 2.00
21 A49 5pi pale bl & blk (557) 15.00 4.00

On Newspaper Stamp of 1916

22 N3 5pa on 10pa gray grn (P137) 2.00 1.25

On Semi-Postal Stamps of 1915

22A A21 20pa car rose (B8) 72.50 55.00
22B A21 1pi ultra (B9) 1,500. 1,100.
22C A21 1pi ultra (B13) 1,100. 750.00

On Semi-Postal Stamps of 1916

23 A17 1pi bl (B19) 2.00 1.00
24 A21 20pa car rose (B28) 1.75 1.00
25 A21 1pi ultra (B29) 6.00 5.50

Turkish Stamps of 1913-18 Handstamped

1919

On Pictorial Issue of 1913

31 A24 2pa red lil (254) 1.50 1.00
32 A25 4pa dk brn (255) 2.00 1.75

On Issue of 1915

33 A17 1pi blue (300) 2.00 1.50
34 A22 20pa car rose (330) 2.00 1.50

On Commemorative Issue of 1916

35 A41 20pa ultra (347) 2.00 1.25
36 A41 1pi vio & blk (348) 1.25 1.00

On Issue of 1917

40 A53 5pi on 2pa Prus bl (547) 3.00 1.25

On Newspaper Stamp of 1916

41 N3 5pa on 10pa gray grn (P137) 3.00 1.75

On Semi-Postal Stamp of 1915

41A A21 20pa car rose (B8) 160.00 110.00

On Semi-Postal Stamps of 1916

42 A17 1pi blue (B19) 2.50 2.00
43 A21 20pa car rose (B28) 2.25 1.25
Nos. 31-43 (11) 181.50 124.25

Turkish Stamps of 1913-19 Handstamped

1919

On Pictorial Issue of 1913

51 A24 2pa red lil (254) 2.00 1.25
52 A25 4pa dk brn (255) 2.00 1.25

On Issue of 1915

53 A17 1pi blue (300) 2.00 1.00
55 A22 5pa ocher (328) 6.00 4.00
56 A22 20pa car rose (330) 2.00 1.50

On Commemorative Issue of 1916

57 A41 20pa ultra (347) 1.60 1.50
58 A41 1pi vio & blk (348) 1.60 1.50
59 A41 5pi yel brn & blk (349) 1.90 1.60

On Issue of 1916

59A A17 1pi blue (372) 70.00 55.00

On Issue of 1916-18

60 A43 5pa org (421) 7.00 5.00
61 A46 1pi dl vio (426) 3.50 2.00
63 A52 50pi grn, *straw* (439) 26.00 15.00

On Issue of 1917

64 A53 5pi on 2pa Prus bl (547) 8.00 4.00

On Newspaper Stamp of 1916

65 N3 5pa on 10pa gray grn (P137) 2.00 1.25

On Semi-Postal Stamp of 1915

65A A21 20pa car rose (B8) 850.00 675.00

On Semi-Postal Stamps of 1916

66 A17 1pi blue (B19) 8.00 2.50
67 A19 20pa car (B26) 9.00 4.00
68 A21 20pa car rose (B28) 125.00 67.50
69 A21 20pa car rose (B31) 6.00 2.50
Nos. 51-69 (19) 1,133. 847.35

Turkey No. 424 Handstamped

1919

71 A44 10pa green 2.75 2.50

"T.E.O." stands for "Territoires Ennemis Occupés."

Turkish Stamps of 1913-19 Overprinted in Black, Red or Blue

In this setting there are various broken and wrong font letters and the letter "i" is sometimes replaced by a "t."

1919 On Pictorial Issue of 1913

75 A30 1pi blue (R) (260) 2.25 .90

On Issue of 1915

76 A21 20pa car rose (318) 4.00 2.25

On Commemorative Issue of 1916

76A A41 5pa green (345) 150.00 75.00
77 A41 20pa ultra (347) 2.00 1.40
78 A41 1pi vio & blk (348) 2.50 1.00

On Issue of 1916-18

79 A43 5pa org (Bl) (421) 1.50 .60
80 A44 10pa green (424) 1.50 .60
81 A45 20pa dp rose (Bk) (425) 7.50 6.00

82 A45 20pa dp rose (Bl) (425) 1.25 .75
83 A48 2pi org brn & ind (429) 1.75 1.00
83C A49 5pi pale bl & blk (R) (430) 2.00 1.25
84 A51 25pi car, *straw* (434) 7.00 5.00
85 A52 50pi grn, *straw* (439) 105.00 65.00

On Issue of 1917

85A A53 5pi on 2pa Prus bl (547) —
86 A53 5pi on 2pa Prus bl (548) 6.50 5.50

On Newspaper Stamps of 1916-19

87 N3 5pa on 10p gray grn (P137) 2.50 2.00
88 N4 5pa on 2pa ol grn (P173) 1.00 .60

On Semi-Postal Stamps of 1915-17

90 A21 20pa car rose (B28) 2.75 1.75
91 A41 10pa car (B42) 1.50 .65
92 A11 10pa on 20pa vio brn (B38) 1.25 1.00
93 SP1 10pa red vio (B46) 2.00 1.25

It is understood that the newspaper and semi-postal stamps overprinted "Cilicie" were used as ordinary postage stamps.

A1

1920 Blue Surcharge ***Perf. 11½***

98 A1 70pa on 5pa red 2.50 .60
a. Double surcharge 30.00 30.00
b. Triple surcharge 200.00
99 A1 3½pi on 5pa red 3.50 2.00
a. Se-tenant with No. 98, horiz. pair 90.00
b. As "a," inverted surcharge 200.00
c. As "a," double surcharge 30.00 *32.50*

Nos. 98-99 exist with surcharge misspelled "PIATSRES," "OCCUPTTION," "OCCCPATION," "OCCUPITION". Value $9 each.

French Offices in Turkey No. 26 Surcharged

1920 ***Perf. 14x13½***

100 A3 20pa on 10c rose red 2.50 1.00
a. "PARAS" omitted 25.00 25.00
b. Surcharged on back 22.50 22.50

Three types of "20" exist on No. 100.

Stamps of France, 1900-17, Surcharged

1920

101 A16 5pa on 2c vio brn 1.00 .85
102 A22 10pa on 5c green 1.50 1.00
a. Inverted surcharge 17.50 *22.50*
103 A22 20pa on 10c red 2.00 1.75
104 A22 1pi on 25c blue 2.75 2.25
105 A20 2pi on 15c gray grn 6.00 5.00
106 A18 5pi on 40c red & gray bl 9.25 8.00
107 A18 10pi on 50c bis brn & lav 10.50 9.50
108 A18 50pi on 1fr cl & ol grn 125.00 125.00
109 A18 100pi on 5fr dk bl & buff 625.00 625.00
Nos. 101-109 (9) 783.00 778.35

Nos. 106 to 109 surcharged in four lines.
"O.M.F." stands for "Occupation Militaire Francaise."

Stamps of France, 1917, Surcharged

1920

110 A16 5pa on 2c vio brn 6.50
111 A22 10pa on 5c green 6.50
112 A22 20pa on 10c red 5.50
113 A22 1pi on 25c blue 5.50
114 A20 2pi on 15c gray grn 16.00
115 A18 5pi on 40c red & gray bl 55.00
116 A18 20pi on 1fr cl & ol grn 75.00
a. "O.M.F. Cilicie" omitted 300.00
b. Double surcharge 240.00
Nos. 110-116 (7) 170.00

On Nos. 115 and 116 "SAND. EST" is placed vertically. "Sand. Est" is an abbreviation of Sandjak de l'Est (Eastern County).
Nos. 110-116 were prepared for use, but never issued.

Stamps of France, 1900-17, Surcharged

1920

117 A16 5pa on 2c vio brn 1.25 .50
a. Inverted surcharge 12.50 12.50
b. Double surcharge 20.00 *21.00*
c. "Cililie" *10.00* *10.00*
d. Surcharge 5pi (error) 25.00 *26.00*
119 A22 10pa on 5c green 1.25 .50
a. Inverted surcharge 12.50 12.50
b. Surch. 5pa (error), invtd. 37.50 30.00
c. Surch. 5pa (error), upright 27.50 26.00
121 A22 20pa on 10c red 1.25 .50
a. Inverted surcharge 12.50 12.50
b. Surch. 10pa (error), invtd. 37.50 30.00
c. Surch. 10pa (error), upright 27.50 26.00
d. Double surcharge 22.50 21.00
122 A22 1pi on 25c blue 1.00 .50
a. Double surcharge 47.50 47.50
b. Inverted surcharge 12.50 12.50
123 A20 2pi on 15c gray grn 1.25 .75
a. Double surcharge 17.50 17.50
b. Inverted surcharge 12.50 12.50
124 A18 5pi on 40c red & gray bl 1.75 .90
a. Double surcharge 37.50 37.50
b. Inverted surcharge 12.50 12.50
c. "PIASRTES" 27.50 27.50
125 A18 10pi on 50c bis brn & lavender 2.75 1.60
a. "PIASRTES" 27.50 27.50
b. Double surcharge 37.50 37.50
c. Inverted surcharge 24.00 22.50
126 A18 50pi on 1fr claret & ol grn 7.50 3.50
a. "PIASRTES" 37.50 37.50
b. Inverted surcharge 32.50 26.00
127 A18 100pi on 5fr dk bl & buff 16.00 16.00
a. "PIASRTES" 72.50 72.50
b. Inverted surcharge 72.50 70.00
Nos. 117-127 (9) 34.00 24.75

This surcharge has "O.M.F." in thicker letters than the preceding issues.
There were two printings of this surcharge which may be distinguished by the space of 1 or 2mm between "Cilicie" and the numeral.
For overprints see Nos. C1-C2.

AIR POST STAMPS

Nos. 123 and 124 Handstamped

Perf. 14x13½

1920, July 15 **Unwmk.**

C1 A20 2pi on 15c gray grn *6,000.*
C2 A18 5pi on 40c red & gray bl *6,000.*
a. "PIASRTES"

A very limited number of Nos. C1 and C2 were used on two air mail flights between Adana and Aleppo. At a later date impressions from a new handstamp were struck "to oblige" on stamps of the regular issue of 1920 (Nos. 123, 124, 125 and 126) that were in stock at the Adana Post Office.

Counterfeits exist.

POSTAGE DUE STAMPS

Turkish Postage Due Stamps of 1914 Handstamped

Handstamped

1919 **Unwmk.** ***Perf. 12***

J1 D1 5pa claret 5.50 1.75
J2 D2 20pa red 5.50 1.75
J3 D3 1pi dark blue 8.00 3.50
J4 D4 2pi slate 8.00 3.50
Nos. J1-J4 (4) 27.00 10.50

Handstamped

J5 D1 5pa claret 5.50 1.75
J6 D2 20pa red 5.50 1.75
J7 D3 1pi dark blue 9.00 4.50
J8 D4 2pi slate 9.00 4.50
Nos. J5-J8 (4) 29.00 12.50

Handstamped

J9 D1 5pa claret 5.50 1.75
J10 D2 20pa red 5.50 1.75
J11 D3 1pi dark blue 8.00 3.50
J12 D4 2pi slate 10.00 4.50
Nos. J9-J12 (4) 29.00 11.50

Postage Due Stamps of France Surcharged

1921

J13 D2 1pi on 10c choc 7.25 4.00
J14 D2 2pi on 20c olive grn 7.25 4.00
J15 D2 3pi on 30c red 9.00 4.50
J16 D2 4pi on 50c vio brn 9.00 4.50
Nos. J13-J16 (4) 32.50 17.00

COCHIN CHINA

ˈkō-chən ˈchī-nə

LOCATION — The southernmost state of French Indo-China in the Cambodian Peninsula.
GOVT. — French Colony
AREA — 26,476 sq. mi.
POP. — 4,615,968
CAPITAL — Saigon

100 Centimes = 1 Franc

Values for unused stamps are for examples without gum, as most stamps were issued in that condition.

Surcharged in Black on Stamps of French Colonies:

a

b

c

1886-87 **Unwmk.** ***Perf. 14x13½***

1 A9(a) 5c on 25c yel, *straw* 160.00 110.00
On cover *2,000.*
2 A9(b) 5c on 2c brn, *buff* 18.00 *18.00*
On cover *1,500.*
3 A9(b) 5c on 25c yel, *straw* 22.00 22.00
On cover *1,200.*
a. Inverted surcharge 200.00 *200.00*
4 A9(c) 5c on 25c blk, *rose* ('87) 37.50 37.50
On cover *1,500.*
a. Double surch., one of type b *3,100.* *1,800.*
b. Triple surch., two of type b — —
c. Inverted surcharge — —
d. Double surch., both type "a" *2,250.* *2,500.*
e. Triple surch., types "a," "b" and "c" *6,750.*
Nos. 1-4 (4) 237.50 187.50

Covers: Values for covers are for commercial items with proper rates.

1888

5 A9 15c on half of 30c brn, *bis* 47.50

No. 5 was prepared but not issued.
The so-called Postage Due stamps were never issued.
Stamps of Cochin China were superseded by those of Indo-China in 1892.

COLOMBIA

kə-'ləm-bē-ə

LOCATION — On the northwest coast of South America, bordering on the Caribbean Sea and the Pacific Ocean
GOVT. — Republic
AREA — 456,535 sq. mi.
POP. — 28,240,000 (est. 1984)
CAPITAL — Bogota

In 1810 the Spanish Viceroyalty of New Granada gained its independence and with Venezuela and Ecuador formed the State of Greater Colombia. In 1832 this state split into three independent units as Venezuela, Ecuador and the Republic of New Granada. The name of the country has been, successively, Granadine Confederation (1858-61), United States of New Granada (1861), United States of Colombia (1861-65), and the Republic of Colombia (1885 to date).

100 Centavos = 1 Peso

In the earlier days many towns did not have handstamps for canceling and stamps were canceled with pen and ink. Pen cancellations, therefore, do not indicate fiscal use. (Postage stamps were not used for revenue purposes.) Used values for Nos. 1-128 are for stamps with illegible manuscript cancels or handstamp cancels of Bogota or Medellin. Stamps with legible manuscript or other handstamped town-name cancels sell for more.

Fractions of many Colombian stamps of both early and late issues are found canceled, their use to pay postage having been tolerated even though forbidden by the postal laws and regulations. Many are known to have been made for philatelic purposes.

Watermarks

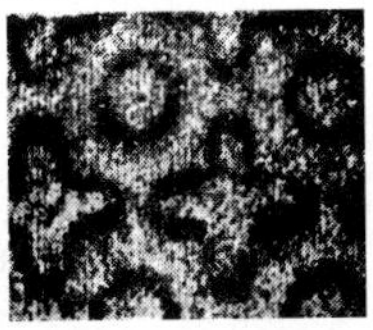

Wmk. 116 — Crosses and Circles

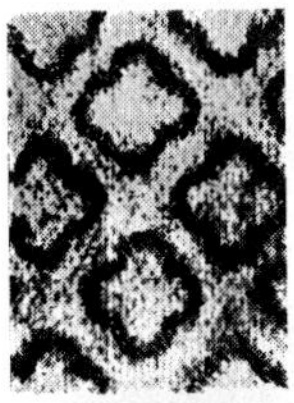

Wmk. 127 — Quatrefoils

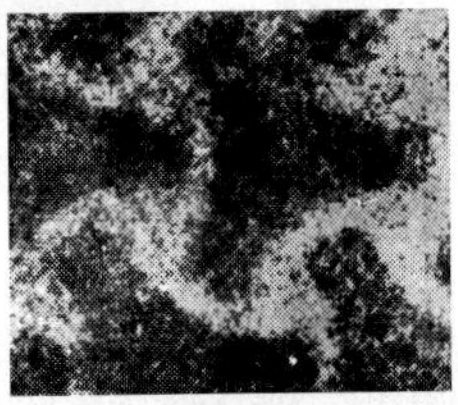

Wmk. 194 — Multiple Curvilinear Triangles

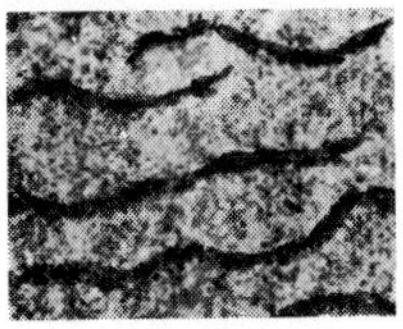

Wmk. 229 — Wavy Lines

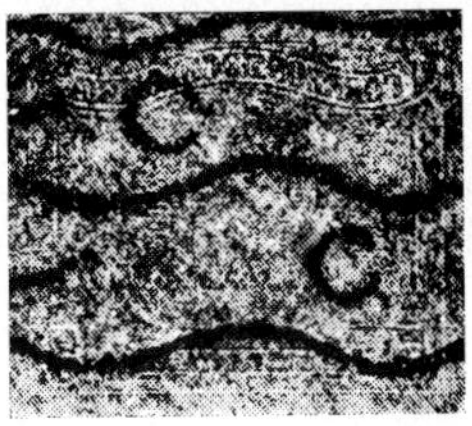

Wmk. 255 — Wavy Lines and C Multiple

STAMPS OF GREAT BRITAIN USED IN COLOMBIA

Crowned Circle handstamp types and numeral cancellation types A and B are pictured in the Crowned Circle Handstamps and Great Britain Used Abroad section.

Values are for clear cancellations on sound, fault-free stamps, with average to fine centering. In many cases, very fine copies are rare or non-existent.

CARTAGENA

Pre-Stamp Postal Markings

1841

A1 Crowned Circle handstamp Type II, on cover, inscribed "PAID AT CARTHAGENA" in red *1,500.*
A2 Crowned Circle handstamp Type I, on cover, inscribed "PAID AT CARTHAGENA" in black 1,100.

Earliest known uses: A1, 1/15/41; A2, 7/1/46.

Stamps of Great Britain, Canceled C56, Type A

1865-84

A3 ½p rose red (#58 P 10) —
A4 1p rose red (#33, P 78, 87, 100, 111, 113, 117, 119, 125, 172, 189, 217) *value from* 57.50
A5 2p blue (#29, P 9) 57.50
A6 2p blue (#30, P 14) 82.50
A7 3p rose (#44) —
A8 3p rose (#49, P 4, 5) —
A9 3p rose (#61, P 12, 17, 18) *value from* 57.50
A10 4p vermilion (#43, P 7-14) *value from* 57.50
A11 4p vermilion (#69, P 15) 350.00
A12 4p pale olive green (#70, P 15, 16) 225.00
A13 6p lilac (#45, P 5, 6) —
A14 6p dull violet (#50, P 6) 80.00
A15 6p violet (#51, P 8) 87.50
A16 6p gray (#60, P 12) 225.00
A17 6p gray (#62, P 13-16) *value from* 57.50
A18 8p orange (#73) 325.00
A19 9p straw (#46) —
A20 1sh green (#48, P 4) —
A21 1sh green (#54, P 4, 5, 7) *value from* 65.00
A22 1sh green (#64, P 12, 13) *value from* 75.00
Plates 8-11 *value from* 75.00
A23 1sh salmon (#87) —
A24 2sh blue (#55) 240.00
A25 5sh rose (#57, P 1) 600.00

Stamps of Great Britain, Canceled C65, Type B

A26 ½p rose red (#58, P 10) —
A27 1p rose red (#33, P 100, 106, 111, 123) *value from* 80.00
A28 1½p dull rose (#32) —
A29 2p blue (#29, P 9) 80.00
A30 2p lilac rose (#81) —
A31 2½p blue (#68) —
A32 3p rose (#49, P 9) —
A33 3p rose (#61, P 14, 17, 19, 20) —
A34 4p vermilion (#43, P 7-9, 11-14) *value from* 65.00
A35 4p vermilion (#69, P 15) 350.00
A36 4p pale olive green (#70, P 15, 16) 225.00
A37 6p dull violet (#50, P 6) 95.00
A38 6p violet (#51, P 8) 95.00
A39 6p pale buff (#51, P 8) —
A40 6p gray (#60, P 12) 225.00
A41 6p gray (#60, P 13, 15-17) *value from* 65.00
A42 8p orange (#73) 375.00
A43 9p straw (#46) 425.00
A44 1sh green (#48, P 4) 140.00
A45 1sh green (#54, P 4-7) *value from* 70.00
A46 1sh green (#64, P 12, 13) *value from* 80.00
Plates 8, 11 *value from* 80.00
A47 1sh salmon (#87) —
A48 2sh blue (#55) 425.00
A49 2sh brown (#56) *2,350.*
A50 5sh pale rose (#57a, P 1) 575.00
Plate 2 725.00
A51 5sh rose (#57, P 1) 600.00
Plate 2 725.00

The C65 canceler was supplied to the British post office in Cartagena in error. C56 was the obliterator assigned to Cartagena.

CHAGRES

Pre-Stamp Postal Markings

A52 Crowned Circle handstamp Type I, on cover, inscribed "PAID AT CHAGRES" in black —

Chagres is located in what is now the Republic of Panama. It was the chief Atlantic port of the isthmus from the 18th century and activity reached a zenith during the 1840s-1850s, when it was the Atlantic terminus for the trans-Isthmian route for miners en route to California.
Earliest known use: 9/16/46.

COLON

Pre-Stamp Postal Marking

A53 Crowned Circle handstamp Type VI, on cover, inscribed "PAID AT COLON" in red *5,000.*

Colon is located in what is now the Republic of Panama.
Earliest known use: 6/21/54.

Stamps of Great Britain, Canceled E88, Type B

1865-81

A54 1p rose red (#33, see footnote) *value from* 55.00

#A54 plate numbers 107, 121-123, 125, 127, 130, 131, 133, 136, 142, 150-153, 155-158, 160, 169-171, 174, 176, 178, 179, 184, 187, 188, 194, 195, 201, 209, 213, 214, 217.

A55 1p red brown (#79) 75.00
A56 1½p dull rose (#32, P 3) *110.00*
A57 2p blue (#30, P 14, 15) *value from* 55.00
A58 2p lilac rose (#81) —
A59 3p rose (#49, P 6, 9) —
A60 3p rose (#61, P 11, 12, 16, 18-20) *value from* 57.50
A61 4p vermilion (#43, P 10-14) *value from* 57.50
A62 4p vermilion (#69, P 15) —
A63 4p pale olive green (#70, P 15, 16) *value from* 225.00
A64 4p gray brown (#71, P 17) *350.00*
A65 4p gray brown (#84, P 17) *82.50*
A66 6p violet (#51, P 6, 8, 9) —
A67 6p pale buff (#59b, P 11) —
A68 6p brown (#59, P 11) 70.00
A69 6p gray (#60, P 12) —
A70 6p gray (#62, P 13-17) *value from* 57.50
A71 8p orange (#73) —
A72 9p bister (#52) 225.00
A73 10p red brown (#53) —
A74 1sh green (#54, P 4-7) *value from* 55.00
A75 1sh green (#64, P 8-13) *value from* 70.00
A76 1sh salmon (#65) *425.00*
A77 1sh salmon (#87, P 13) *150.00*
A78 2sh blue (#55) 160.00
A79 2sh brown (#56) *2,250.*
A80 5sh pale rose (#57a, P 1) 575.00
Plate 2 700.00
A81 5sh rose (#57, P 1) 575.00
Plate 2 700.00

PANAMA

Pre-Stamp Postal Marking

1846

A82 Crowned Circle handstamp Type I, on cover, inscribed "PAID AT PANAMA" in red *2,000.*

Panama is located in what is now the Republic of Panama.
Earliest known use: 8/24/46.

Stamps of Great Britain, Canceled C35, Type A or B

1865-81

A83 ½p rose red (#58 P 10-15, 19) *value from* 55.00
A84 1p rose red (#33, see footnote) *value from* 37.50

#A84 plate numbers 71, 72, 76, 81, 85, 87-89, 93, 95, 96, 101, 104, 114, 122, 124, 130, 138, 139, 142, 159, 168, 171, 172, 174, 179, 180, 184, 185, 187, 189, 191-193, 196, 197, 200, 203-205, 207-211, 213-215, 218, 224.

A85 1p red brown (#79) 47.50
A86 1½p lake red (#32a, P 3) 70.00
A87 1½p red brown (#80) —
A88 2p blue (#29, P 9) 42.50
Plate 12 80.00
A89 2p blue (#30, P 13-15) *value from* 42.50
A90 2p blue (#81) 110.00
A91 2½p claret (#66, P 1) 175.00
A92 2½p claret (#67, P 4, 12, 16) 130.00
A93 2½p blue (#68, P 19) —
A94 2½p blue (#82, P 22, 23) —
A95 3p rose (#37) 275.00
A96 3p rose (#44) —
A97 3p rose (#49, P 4-9) *value from* 52.50
A98 3p rose (#61, P 12, 14-20) *value from* 42.50
A99 3p rose (#83, P 20, 21) —
A100 4p vermilion (#34a, P4) 100.00
A101 4p vermilion, "hair-lines" (#34c, P 4) —
A102 4p vermilion (#43, P 7-14) *value from* 52.50
A103 4p vermilion (#69, P 15) 350.00
A104 4p pale olive green (#70, P 16) 225.00
Plate 15 *275.00*
A105 4p gray brown (#84, P 17, 18) *value from* 57.50
A106 5p deep indigo (#85) *160.00*
A107 6p lilac (#39, P 3) 87.50
A108 6p lilac (#39b, P 4) *150.00*
A109 6p lilac (#45, P 5) 80.00
Plate 6 *150.00*
A110 6p dull violet (#50, P 6) —
A111 6p violet (#51, P 6, 8, 9) *value from* 75.00
A112 6p pale buff (#59b, P 11) 80.00
Plate 12 *250.00*
A113 6p brown (#59, P 11) 52.50
A114 6p gray (#60, P 12) 225.00
A115 6p gray (#62, P 13-17) *value from* 52.50
A116 6p gray (#86, P 17) 75.00
A117 8p orange (#73) 275.00
A118 9p straw (#40) 300.00
A119 9p bister (#52) 275.00
A120 10p red brown (#53) 300.00
A121 1sh green (#48, P 4) 150.00
A122 1sh green (#54, P 4-6) *value from* 47.50
Plate 7 62.50
A123 1sh green (#64, P 12, 13) *value from* 57.50
Plates 8-11 *value from* 75.00
A124 1sh salmon (#65, P 13) 425.00
A125 1sh salmon (#87, P 13) *120.00*
A126 2sh blue (#55) 150.00
A127 2sh brown (#56) *2,250.*
A128 5sh pale rose (#57a, P 1) 550.00
Plate 2 700.00
A129 5sh rose (#57, P 1) 575.00
Plate 2 700.00

Later stamps of Great Britain are also known canceled "C35." These originate on mail posted aboard British civilian ships, and on other forms of ship mail which transited through Panama.

SANTA MARTHA

Pre-Stamp Postal Marking

1841

A130 Crowned Circle handstamp Type V, on cover, inscribed "PAID AT SANTA MARTHA" in red — *2,000.*

Earliest known use: 12/15/41.

Stamps of Great Britain, Canceled C62, Type A

1865-81

A131	½p rose red (#58 P 8)	*100.00*
A132	1p rose red (#33, P 33)	70.00
A133	2p blue (#29, P 9)	100.00
A134	2p blue (#30, P 14)	110.00
A135	4p vermilion (#43, P 7-9, 11-14) *value from*	65.00
A136	4p pale olive green (#70, P 15)	225.00
A137	4p gray brown (#71, P 17)	*350.00*
A138	4p gray brown (#84, P 17)	80.00
A139	6p lilac (#45, P 5)	95.00
A140	6p gray (#60, P 12)	—
A141	6p gray (#62, P 14)	—
A142	8p orange (#73)	325.00
A143	9p straw (#40)	—
A144	1sh green (#48, P 4)	175.00
A145	1sh green (#54, P 5, 7) *value from*	80.00
A146	1sh green (#64, P 8)	—
A147	2sh blue (#55)	325.00
A148	5sh rose (#57, P 2)	725.00

SAVANILLA (BARRANQUILLA)

Stamps of Great Britain, Canceled F69, Type B

1872-81

A149	½p rose red (#58 P 6)	95.00
A150	1p rose red (#33, P 122, 171) *value from*	70.00
A151	1½p lake red (#32a, P 3)	120.00
A152	3p rose (#49, P 7)	—
A153	3p rose (#61, P 20)	110.00
A154	3p rose (#83, P 20)	110.00
A155	4p ver (#43, P 12-14) *value from*	65.00
A156	4p ver (#69, P 15)	350.00
A157	4p pale ol grn (#70, P 16)	240.00
	Plate 15	*275.00*
A158	4p gray brn (#71, P 17)	*425.00*
A159	4p gray brn (#84, P 17)	82.50
A160	6p pale buff (#59b, P 11)	—
A161	6p gray (#86, P 16, 17) *value from*	87.50
A162	8p org (#73)	325.00
A163	1sh grn (#54, P 5, 7) *value from*	65.00
A164	1sh grn (#64, P 8, 11-13) *value from*	87.50
A165	1sh salmon (#65, P 13)	425.00
A166	2sh blue (#55)	240.00
A167	5sh rose (#57, P 2)	725.00

ISSUES OF COLOMBIA
Granadine Confederation

A1 A2 Coat of Arms

Type A1 — Asterisks in frame. Wavy lines in background.

Type A2 — Diamond-shaped ornaments in frame. Straight lines in background. Numerals larger.

1859 Unwmk. Litho. *Imperf.*

Wove Paper

1	A1	2½c green	95.00	95.00
a.		2½c yellow green	95.00	95.00
b.		2½c olive green	90.00	90.00
c.		2½c deep green	90.00	90.00
d.		2½c ochre	*125.00*	*125.00*
2	A1	5c blue	110.00	75.00
a.		Tête bêche pair	*3,500.*	*5,750.*
b.		"50" instead of "5"		*7,500.*
3	A1	5c violet	300.00	95.00
a.		Tête bêche pair	*5,000.*	*6,000.*
b.		"50" instead of "5"		*7,500.*
c.		50c blue violet	225.00	90.00
d.		50c lilac	225.00	90.00
e.		50c slate	250.00	100.00
4	A1	10c red brown	110.00	65.00
a.		10c buff	110.00	65.00
b.		10c bister brown	100.00	62.50
c.		10c yellow	100.00	62.50
d.		10c orange chestnut	100.00	62.50
e.		10c red orange	*125.00*	*90.00*
6	A1	20c blue	95.00	55.00
a.		20c gray blue	95.00	55.00
b.		Se-tenant with 5c		—
c.		Tête bêche pair	*25,000.*	*25,000.*
d.		20c pale ultramarine	*100.00*	*70.00*
7	A1	1p carmine	70.00	*100.00*
a.		1p rose	85.00	125.00
8	A1	1p rose, *bluish*	350.00	

The 2½c brown and 10c green are essays.

Reprints of No. 7 are in brown rose or brown red. Wavy lines of background are much broken; no dividing lines between stamps.

1860

Laid Paper

9	A2	5c lilac	250.00	175.00

Wove Paper

10	A2	5c gray lilac	65.00	50.00
a.		5c lilac	65.00	50.00
11	A2	10c yellow buff	65.00	45.00
a.		Tête bêche pair	*7,000.*	
12	A2	20c blue	160.00	110.00

United States of New Granada

Arms of New Granada — A3

1861

13	A3	2½c black	1,100.	300.00
14	A3	5c yellow	325.00	140.00
a.		5c buff	325.00	140.00
16	A3	10c blue	950.00	140.00
17	A3	20c red	400.00	190.00
18	A3	1p pink	950.00	300.00

There are 54 varieties of the 5c, 20c, and 1 peso.

Forgeries exist of Nos. 13-18.

United States of Colombia

Coat of Arms
A4 A5 A6

1862

19	A4	10c blue	200.	100.
20	A4	20c red	*3,600.*	600.
21	A4	50c green	200.	140.
22	A4	1p red lilac	475.	140.
23	A4	1p red lil, *bluish*	*4,250.*	*1,450.*

No. 23 is on a thinner, coarser wove paper than Nos. 19-22.

1863

24	A5	5c orange	80.00	52.50
a.		Star after "Cent"	90.00	60.00
25	A5	10c blue	180.00	25.00
a.		Period after "10"	175.00	22.50
26	A5	20c red	175.00	62.50
a.		Star after "Cent"	200.00	70.00
b.		Transfer of 50c in stone of 20c	*14,000.*	*4,500.*

Bluish Paper

28	A5	10c blue	140.00	27.50
a.		Period after "10"	150.00	30.00
29	A5	50c green	175.00	62.50
a.		Star after "Cent"	175.00	70.00

Ten varieties of each.

1864

Wove Paper

30	A6	5c orange	57.50	30.00
a.		Tête bêche pair	350.00	325.00
31	A6	10c blue	42.50	12.50
a.		Period after 10	42.50	12.50
32	A6	20c scarlet	80.00	45.00
33	A6	50c green	65.00	45.00
34	A6	1p red violet	275.00	140.00

Two varieties of each.

Arms of Colombia
A7 A9

A8

1865

35	A7	1c rose	8.00	8.00
a.		bluish pelure paper	22.50	17.50
36	A8	2½c black, *lilac*	16.00	11.00
37	A9	5c yellow	35.00	16.00
a.		5c orange	35.00	16.00
38	A9	10c violet	52.50	3.50
39	A9	20c blue	52.50	16.00
40	A9	50c green	92.50	42.50
41	A9	50c grn (small figures)	92.50	42.50
42	A9	1p vermilion	100.00	15.00
a.		1p rose red	100.00	15.00
b.		Period after "PESO"	120.00	17.50

Ten varieties of each of the 5c, 10c, 20c, and 50c, and six varieties of the 1 peso. No. 36 was used as a carrier stamp.

A10 A11 A12

A13 A14

A15 A16

1866

White Wove Paper

45	A10	5c orange	55.00	22.50
46	A11	10c lilac	13.00	4.25
a.		Pelure paper	17.50	10.00
47	A12	20c light blue	32.50	17.50
a.		Pelure paper	50.00	42.50
48	A13	50c green	13.00	10.00
49	A14	1p rose red, *bluish*	72.50	26.00
a.		1p vermilion	72.50	26.00
51	A15	5p blk, *green*	400.00	175.00
52	A16	10p blk, *vermilion*	275.00	160.00

There are several varieties of the 1 peso having the letters "U," "N," "S" and "O" smaller.

A17 A18

A19 A20

A21

TEN CENTAVOS:

Type I — "B" of "COLOMBIA" over "V" of "CENTAVOS".

Type II — "B" of "COLOMBIA" over "VO" of "CENTAVOS."

ONE PESO:

Type I — Long thin spear heads. Diagonal lines in lower part of shield.

Type II — Short thick spear heads. Horizontal and a few diagonal lines in lower part of shield.

Type III — Short thick spear heads. Crossed lines in lower part of shield. Ornaments at each side of circle are broken. (See No. 97.)

1868

53	A17	5c orange	55.00	42.50
54	A18	10c lilac (I)	3.25	.90
a.		10c red violet (I)	3.25	.90
b.		10c lilac (II)	3.25	.90
c.		10c red violet (II)	3.25	.90
d.		Printed on both sides	6.25	2.00
55	A19	20c blue	2.25	1.00
56	A20	50c yellow green	2.75	2.00
57	A21	1p ver (II)	3.25	1.75
a.		Tête bêche pair	110.00	85.00
b.		1p rose red (I)	45.00	22.50
c.		1p rose red (II)	3.00	1.75
		Nos. 53-57 (5)	66.50	48.15

See Nos. 83-84, 96-97.

Counterfeits or reprints.

10c — There is a large white dot at the upper left between the circle enclosing the "X" and the ornament below.

50c — There is a shading of dots instead of dashes below the ribbon with motto. There are crossed lines in the lowest section of the shield instead of diagonal or horizontal ones.

1p — The ornaments in the lettered circle are broken. There are crossed lines in the lowest section of the shield. These counterfeits, or reprints, are on white paper, wove and laid, on colored wove paper and in fancy colors.

A22

Two varieties

1869-70

Wove Paper

59	A22	2½c black, *violet*	3.50	2.10
a.		Laid paper ('70)	250.00	210.00
b.		Laid batonné paper ('70)	22.50	19.00

#59, 59a, 59b were used as carrier stamps.

Counterfeits, or reprints, are on magenta paper wove or ribbed.

A23 A24

1870

Wove Paper

62	A23	5c orange	1.60	1.10
a.		5c yellow	1.60	1.10
63	A24	25c black, *blue*	13.00	11.00

See No. 89.

In the counterfeits, or reprints, of No. 63, the top of the "2" of "25" does not touch the down stroke. The counterfeits are on paper of various colors.

A25 A26

5 pesos — The ornament at the left of the "C" of "Cinco" cuts into the "C," and the shading of the flag is formed of diagonal lines.

10 pesos — The stars have extra rays between the points, and the central part of the shield has some horizontal lines of shading at each end.

1870

Surface Colored, Chalky Paper

64	A25	5p blk, *green*	80.00	55.00
65	A26	10p blk, *vermilion*	92.50	55.00

See Nos. 77-79, 125-126.

A27

A28

A29

TEN CENTAVOS:
Type I — "S" of "CORREOS" 2½mm high. First "N" of "NACIONALES" small.
Type II — "S" of "CORREOS" 2mm high. First "N" of "NACIONALES" wide.

1871-74

Thin Porous Paper

66	A27	1c green ('72)	2.75	2.75
67	A27	1c rose ('73)	2.75	2.75
a.		1c carmine ('73)	2.75	2.75
68	A28	2c brown	1.25	1.25
a.		2c red brown	1.25	1.25
69	A29	10c vio (I) ('74)	2.00	1.60
a.		10c lilac (I) ('74)	2.00	1.60
b.		10c violet (II) ('74)	2.00	1.60
c.		10c lilac (II) ('74)	2.00	1.60
d.		Laid paper, as #69 ('72)	110.00	110.00
e.		Laid paper, as "b" ('72)	110.00	110.00
		Nos. 66-69 (4)	8.75	8.35

Counterfeits or reprints.

1c — The outer frame of the shield is broken near the upper left corner and the "A" of "Colombia" has no cross-bar.

2c — There are scratches across "DOS" and many white marks around the letters on the large "2." The counterfeits, or reprints, are on white wove and bluish white laid paper.

Condor — A30

Liberty Head
A31 A32

5 pesos, redrawn — The ornament at the left of the "C" only touches the "C," and the shading of the flag is formed of vertical and diagonal lines.

10 pesos, redrawn — The stars are distinctly five pointed, and there is no shading in the central part of the shield.

1877

Wove Paper

73	A30	5c purple	5.50	1.75
a.		5c lilac	5.50	1.75
74	A31	10c bister brown	2.75	.75
a.		10c red brown	2.75	.75
b.		10c violet brown	2.75	.75
75	A32	20c blue	3.25	1.10
a.		20c violet blue	6.50	2.75
77	A26	10p blk, *rose*	92.50	57.50
78	A25	5p blk, *lt grn,* redrawn	32.50	27.50
79	A26	10p blk, *rose,* redrawn	13.00	2.25
a.		10p blk, *dark rose,* redrawn	13.00	2.25
		Nos. 73-79 (6)	149.50	90.85

Stamps of the issues of 1871-77 are known with private perforations of various gauges, also with sewing machine perforation.

In the counterfeits, or reprints, of the 5 pesos the ornament at the left of the "C" of "Cinco" is separated from the "C" by a black line.

In the counterfeits, or reprints, of the 10 pesos the outer line of the double circle containing "10" is broken at the top, below "OS" of "Unidos," and the vertical lines of shading contained in the double circle are very indistinct. There is a colorless dash below the loop of the "P" of "Pesos."

1876-79

Laid Paper

80	A30	5c lilac	65.00	52.50
81	A31	10c brown	35.00	2.25
82	A32	20c blue	80.00	55.00
83	A20	50c green ('79)	77.50	52.50
84	A21	1p pale red (II) ('79)	50.00	12.50
		Nos. 80-84 (5)	307.50	174.75

1879

Wove Paper

89	A24	25c green	26.00	26.00

1881

Blue Wove Paper

93	A30	5c violet	16.00	10.50
a.		5c lilac	16.00	10.50
94	A31	10c brown	9.25	2.10
95	A32	20c blue	9.25	2.10
96	A20	50c yellow green	9.50	6.00
97	A21	1p ver (III)	13.00	6.00
		Nos. 93-97 (5)	57.00	26.70

For types of 1p, see note over No. 53.

Reprints of the 10c and 20c are much worn. On the 10c the letters "TAVOS" of "CENTAVOS" often touch. On the 20c the letters "NT" of "VEINTE" touch and the left arm of the "T" is too long. Reprints of the 25c, 50c and 1p have the characteristics previously described. The reprints are on white wove or laid paper, on colored papers, and in fancy colors. Stamps on green paper exist only as reprints.

A34

A35

A36

1 centavo — The period before "UNION" is round and there are rays between the stars and the condors.

2 centavos — The "2's" and "C's" in the corners are placed upright.

5 centavos — The last star at the right almost touches the frame.

10 centavos — The letters of the inscription are thin; there are rays between the stars and the condor.

1881 ***Imperf.***

White Wove Paper

103	A34	1c green	3.75	3.25
104	A35	2c vermilion	1.60	1.25
a.		2c rose	1.90	1.25
106	A34	5c blue	4.50	1.40
a.		Printed on both sides		
107	A36	10c violet	3.25	1.00
108	A34	20c black	3.50	1.60
		Nos. 103-108 (5)	16.60	8.50

The stamps of this issue are found with perforations of various gauges, also sewing machine perforation, all of which are unofficial.

See Nos. 112, 114-115.

Liberty Head — A37

A37a

1881 ***Imperf.***

109	A37	1c blk, *green*	2.50	*4.00*
110	A37	2c blk, *lilac rose*	2.50	*4.00*
111	A37	5c blk, *lilac*	6.50	1.50
		Nos. 109-111 (3)	11.50	*9.50*

Nos. 109 to 111 are found with regular or sewing machine perforation, unofficial.

Reprints:

1c — The top line of the stamp and the top frame extend to the left. 2c — There is a curved line over the scroll below the "AV" of "CENTAVOS."

5c — There are scratches across the "5" in the upper left corner. All three values were reprinted on the three colors of paper of the originals.

Redrawn

1 centavo — The period before "UNION" is square and the rays between the stars and the condor have been wholly or partly erased.

2 centavos — The "2's" and "C's" in the corners are placed diagonally.

5 centavos — The last star at the right touches the wing of the condor.

10 centavos — The letters of the inscription are thick; there are no rays under the stars; the last star at the right touches the wing of the condor and this wing touches the frame.

1883 ***Imperf.***

112	A34	1c green	4.75	4.25
113	A37a	2c rose	1.60	1.40
114	A34	5c blue	4.00	1.00
a.		5c ultramarine	4.00	1.00
b.		Printed on both sides, reverse ultra	25.00	20.00
115	A36	10c violet	5.00	1.40
		Nos. 112-115 (4)	15.35	8.05

The stamps of this issue are found with regular or sewing machine perforation, privately applied.

A38

A39

1883 ***Perf. 10½, 12, 13½***

116	A38	1c gray grn, *grn*	.80	.80
a.		Imperf., pair	4.00	4.00
117	A39	2c red, *rose*	.80	*1.10*
a.		2c org red, *rose*	.80	*1.10*
b.		2c red, *buff*	10.00	10.00
c.		Imperf., pair (#117 or 117a)	6.50	6.50
d.		"DE LOS" in very small caps	12.50	12.50
118	A38	5c blue, *bluish*	2.00	1.25
a.		5c dk bl, *bluish*	2.00	.90
b.		5c blue	2.75	2.00
c.		Imperf., pair (#118 or 118a)	6.50	6.50
d.		As "b," imperf., pair	10.00	10.00
119	A39	10c org, *yel*	1.00	*1.10*
a.		"DE LOS" in large caps	45.00	20.00
b.		Imperf., pair	13.00	13.00
120	A39	20c vio, *lilac*	1.10	1.10
a.		Imperf., pair	13.00	13.00
122	A38	50c brn, *buff*	2.25	2.50
a.		Perf. 12	2.25	2.50
123	A38	1p claret, *bluish*	4.25	1.60
a.		Imperf., pair	13.00	13.00
		Nos. 116-123 (7)	12.20	9.45

Redrawn Types of 1877

1883 (?) ***Perf. 10½, 12***

125	A25	5p orange brown	6.00	6.00
126	A26	10p black, *gray*	6.50	*7.25*

1886 ***Perf. 10½, 11½, 12***

127	A38	5p brown, *straw*	8.00	4.75
a.		Imperf., pair	26.00	26.00
128	A38	10p black, *rose*	8.00	4.75
a.		Imperf., pair	26.00	26.00

Republic of Colombia

A40

Simón Bolívar — A41

Pres. Rafael Núñez — A42

1886 ***Perf. 10½ and 13½***

129	A40	1c grn, *grn*	1.25	.60
a.		Imperf., pair	5.50	5.50
130	A41	5c blue, *bl*	1.25	.35
a.		5c ultra, *blue*	1.25	.35
b.		Imperf., pair (#130)	5.50	5.50
131	A42	10c orange	2.75	.60
a.		Imperf., pair	7.50	7.50
b.		Pelure paper	3.50	.85
		Nos. 129-131 (3)	5.25	1.55

Gen. Antonio Jose de Sucre y Alcala
A43

Gen. Antonio Nariño
A44

1887

133	A43	2c org red, *rose*	1.75	.85
a.		2c orange red, *yellowish*	4.50	4.50
b.		2c orange red	5.25	5.25
c.		Imperf., pair (#133)	8.00	8.00
134	A44	20c pur, *grysh*	2.25	.85
a.		Imperf., pair	6.50	6.50
b.		Pelure paper	2.75	1.75

Impressions of No. 134 on white, blue or greenish blue paper were not regularly issued.

Arms — A45

Nariño — A46

1888

135	A45	50c brn, *buff*	1.40	*1.50*
a.		Imperf., pair	4.75	4.75
136	A45	1p claret, *bluish*	6.00	1.75
137	A45	1p claret	2.50	1.25
138	A45	5p org brn	6.50	5.50
139	A45	5p black	11.00	8.00
140	A45	10p black, *rose*	16.00	5.50
		Nos. 135-140 (6)	43.40	23.50

See Nos. 154, 156-157.

1889

141	A46	20c pur, *grayish*	1.50	1.00
a.		Imperf., pair	7.50	7.50

Impressions on white, blue or greenish blue paper were not regularly issued.

A47

A48

A49

A50

A51

1890-91 ***Perf. 10½, 13½, 11***

142	A47	1c grn, *grn*	1.50	1.25
143	A48	2c org red, *rose*	.75	*.75*
144	A49	5c bl, *grnsh bl*	1.10	.35
a.		5c deep blue, *blue*	1.10	.35
b.		Imperf., pair	4.50	4.50
146	A50	10c brn, *yel*	.80	.35
a.		10c brown, *buff*	.80	.35
147	A51	20c vio, pelure paper	2.75	*3.50*
		Nos. 142-147 (5)	6.90	*6.20*

A52

A52a

A53

A53a

A54

Perf. 10½, 12, 13½, 14 to 15½

1892-99

Ordinary Paper

148	A47	1c red, *yel*	.65	.35
149	A52	2c red, *rose*	32.50	32.50
150	A52	2c green	.40	.25
a.		2c yellow green	.40	.25
151	A49	5c blk, *buff*	10.00	.30
152	A52a	5c org brn, *pale buff*	.85	.25
a.		5c red brown, *salmon* ('97)	.85	.25
153	A50	10c bis brn, *rose*	.60	.35
a.		10c brown, *brownish*	1.60	1.25
154	A53	20c brn, *bl*	.60	.35
a.		20c red brown, *blue*	.60	.35
b.		20c yel brn, *grnsh bl* ('97)	4.50	11.00
c.		20c brown, *buff* ('97)	15.00	11.00
155	A45	50c vio, *vio*	1.00	.60
156	A53a	50c red vio, *vio* ('99)	1.25	
157	A54	1p bl, *grnsh*	1.60	.75
a.		1p blue, *buff*	1.60	.75
158	A45	5p red, *pale rose*	6.00	2.75
159	A45	10p blue	12.50	2.75
a.		Thin, pale rose paper	22.50	6.00
		Nos. 148-159 (12)	67.95	
		Nos. 148-155,157-159 (11)		41.20

Type A53a is a redrawing of type A45. The letters of the inscriptions are slightly larger and the numerals "50" slightly smaller than in type A45.

The 20c brown on white paper is believed to be a chemical changeling.

Nos. 148, 150-152a, 153-155, 157, 159 exist imperf. Value per pair, $5-$7.50.

A56

1899

162	A56	1c red, *yellow*	.55	.30
163	A56	5c red brn, *sal*	.55	.30
164	A56	10c brn, *lil rose*	1.60	.80
165	A56	50c blue, *lilac*	1.10	1.00
		Nos. 162-165 (4)	3.80	2.40

Cartagena Issues

A57

1899 Blue Overprint *Imperf.*

167	A57	5c red, *buff*	24.00	24.00
a.		Sewing machine perf.	24.00	24.00
168	A57	10c ultra, *buff*	24.00	24.00
a.		Sewing machine perf.	24.00	24.00

Nos. 168 and 168a differ slightly from the illustration.

Bolivar No. 55 Overprinted with 7 Parallel Wavy Lines and:

A58

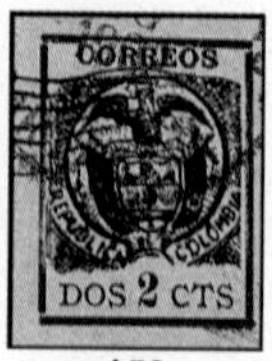
A59

A60

A61

Perf. 14 (#169), Sewing Machine Perf.

1899 Purple Overprint

169	A18	1c black	50.00	50.00
170	A58	1c brn, *buff*	17.00	17.00
a.		Altered from 10c	25.00	25.00
171	A59	2c blk, *buff*	17.00	17.00
a.		Altered from 10c	25.00	25.00
172	A60	5c mar, *grnsh bl*	15.00	15.00
a.		Perf. 12	15.00	15.00
b.		Without overprint	8.75	8.75
173	A61	10c red, *sal*	15.00	15.00
a.		Perf. 12	15.00	15.00
		Nos. 169-173 (5)	114.00	114.00

Types A58 and A59 illustrate Nos. 170a and 171a, which were made from altered plates of the 10c (No. 168). Nos. 170 and 171 were made from altered plate of the 5c denomination (No. 167), show part of the top flag of the "5" and differ slightly from the illustrations.

Nos. 170-173 exist imperf. Values about same as perf.

A62

1900 *Imperf.*

Purple Overprint

174	A62	5c red	20.00	20.00
a.		Perf. 12	27.50	27.50

A63

A64

"Gobierno Provisorio" at Top

1900 Litho. *Perf. 12 Vertically*

175	A63	1c (ctvo) blk, *bl grn*	35.00	6.50
a.		"cvo."	92.50	12.00
b.		"cvos."	35.00	6.50
c.		"centavo"	42.50	40.00
176	A63	2c black	25.00	4.00
177	A63	5c blk, *pink*	25.00	4.00
a.		Name at side (V)	50.00	7.50
178	A63	10c blk, *pink*	25.00	4.00
a.		Name at side (V)	50.00	7.50
179	A63	20c blk, *yellow*	35.00	6.50
a.		Name at side (G)	75.00	10.00
		Nos. 175-179 (5)	145.00	25.00

"Gobierno Provisional" at Top

Name at Side in Black or Green

180	A64	1c (ctvo.) blk, *bl grn*	35.00	5.00
a.		"centavo"	100.00	40.00
181	A64	2c blk, *bl grn*	20.00	5.00
182	A64	5c blk (G)	20.00	5.00
a.		"ctvos." smaller	40.00	7.50
183	A64	10c blk, *pink*	20.00	5.00
184	A64	20c blk, *yel* (G)	35.00	7.50
		Nos. 180-184 (5)	130.00	27.50

Issues of the rebel provisional government in Cucuta.

A65

A66

1901 *Sewing Machine Perf.*

Purple Overprint

185	A65	1c black	.85	.85
a.		Without overprint	1.90	1.90
b.		Double overprint	2.00	2.00
c.		Imperf., pair	2.00	2.00
d.		Inverted overprint	1.00	1.00
186	A66	2c blk, *rose*	.85	.85
a.		Imperf., pair	2.00	2.00
b.		Without overprint	1.90	1.90
c.		Double overprint	2.00	2.00

A67

A68

1901

Rose Overprint

187	A67	1c blue	.85	.85
a.		Imperf., pair	3.00	3.00
188	A68	2c brown	.85	.85
a.		Imperf., pair	3.00	3.00
b.		Without overprint	.85	.85

A69

A70

Sewing Machine or Regular Perf. 12, 12½

1902

Magenta Overprint

189	A69	5c violet	1.75	1.75
a.		Without overprint	1.75	1.75
b.		Double overprint	1.75	1.75
c.		Imperf., pair	3.75	3.75
190	A70	10c yel brn	1.75	1.75
a.		Double overprint	1.75	1.75
b.		Imperf., pair	3.75	3.75
c.		Without overprint	1.75	1.75
d.		Printed on both sides	2.50	2.50

A71

A72

1902

Magenta Overprint

191	A71	5c yel brn	1.75	1.75
a.		Without overprint	1.60	1.60
b.		Imperf., pair	5.00	5.00
192	A71	10c black	1.25	1.25
a.		Without overprint	1.00	1.00
b.		Imperf., pair	7.50	7.50
193	A72	20c maroon	4.00	2.50
b.		Imperf., pair	12.50	12.50
		Nos. 191-193 (3)	7.00	5.50

Nos. 191-193 exist tête bêche. Value of 10c and 20c, each $12.50.

Washed copies of Nos. 167-174, 185-193 are offered as "without overprint."

Barranquilla Issues

Magdalena River — A75

Iron Quay at Sabanilla — A76

La Popa Hill — A77

1902-03 *Imperf.*

194	A75	2c green	1.25	1.25
195	A75	2c dk bl	1.25	1.25
196	A75	2c rose	18.00	18.00
197	A76	10c scarlet	.85	.85
198	A76	10c orange	10.00	10.00
199	A76	10c rose	1.25	1.25
200	A76	10c maroon	1.40	1.40
201	A76	10c claret	1.40	1.40
202	A77	20c violet	2.75	2.75
a.		Laid paper		7.50
203	A77	20c dl bl	7.50	7.50
204	A77	20c dl bl, *pink*	110.00	110.00
205	A77	20c car rose	16.00	16.00
		Nos. 194-205 (12)	171.65	171.65

Sewing Machine Perf. and Perf. 12

194a	A75	2c green	7.50	7.50
195a	A75	2c dark blue	7.50	7.50
196a	A75	2c carmine	35.00	35.00
197a	A76	10c scarlet	3.50	3.50
198a	A76	10c orange	27.50	27.50
199a	A76	10c rose	5.50	5.50
200a	A76	10c maroon	5.50	5.50
201a	A76	10c claret	5.00	5.00
202b	A77	20c purple	.55	.55
c.		20c lilac	.55	.55
203a	A77	20c dull blue	7.50	7.50
204a	A77	20c dull blue, *rose*	140.00	140.00
205b	A77	20c carmine rose	55.00	55.00
		Nos. 194a-205b (12)	300.05	300.05

See Nos. 240-245.

Cruiser "Cartagena" — A78

Bolívar — A79

General Próspero Pinzón — A80

A81

A82

1903-04 *Imperf.*

209	A78	5c blue	2.10	2.10
210	A78	5c bister	3.50	3.50
211	A79	50c yellow	3.00	3.00
212	A79	50c green	3.50	3.50
213	A79	50c scarlet	3.50	3.50
214	A79	50c carmine	3.50	3.50
a.		50c rose	3.50	3.50
215	A79	50c pale brown	3.50	3.50
216	A80	1p yellow brn	1.25	1.25
217	A80	1p rose	2.00	2.00
218	A80	1p blue	2.00	2.00
219	A80	1p violet	20.00	20.00
220	A81	5p claret	4.25	4.25
221	A81	5p pale brown	6.50	6.50
222	A81	5p blue green	6.00	6.00
223	A82	10p pale green	6.25	6.25
224	A82	10p claret	20.00	20.00
		Nos. 209-224 (16)	90.85	90.85

Nos. 216 and 217 measure 20½x26½mm and No. 218, 18x24mm. Stamps of this issue exist with forged perforations.

Perf. 12

209a	A78	5c blue	7.50	7.50
210a	A78	5c bister	7.50	7.50
211a	A79	50c yellow	12.50	12.50
b.		50c orange	20.00	20.00
212a	A79	50c green	20.00	20.00
213a	A79	50c scarlet	9.00	9.00
214b	A79	50c rose	9.00	9.00
215a	A79	50c pale brown	9.00	9.00
216a	A80	1p yellow brown	4.00	4.00
217a	A80	1p rose	6.00	6.00
218a	A80	1p blue	7.50	6.00
219a	A80	1p violet	50.00	50.00
220a	A81	5p claret	16.00	16.00
221a	A81	5p pale brown	18.00	18.00
222a	A81	5p blue green	18.00	18.00
223a	A82	10p pale green	25.00	25.00
224a	A82	10p claret	60.00	60.00
		Nos. 209a-224a (16)	279.00	277.50

Laid Paper *Imperf.*

240	A76	10c dk bl, *lil*	5.00	5.00
241	A76	10c dk bl, *bluish*	3.00	3.00
242	A76	10c dk bl, *brn*	3.00	3.00
243	A76	10c dk bl, *sal*	7.50	7.50
244	A76	10c dk bl, *grnsh bl*	4.00	4.00
245	A76	10c dk bl, *dp rose*	3.00	3.00
		Nos. 240-245 (6)	25.50	25.50

Perf. 12

240a	A76	10c dk bl, *lilac*	10.50	10.50
241a	A76	10c dk bl, *bluish*	7.50	7.50
242a	A76	10c dk bl, *brn*	7.50	7.50
243a	A76	10c dk bl, *salmon*	55.00	55.00
244a	A76	10c dk bl, *grnsh bl*	16.00	16.00
245a	A76	10c dk bl, *deep rose*	7.50	7.50
		Nos. 240a-245a (6)	104.00	104.00

A82a

Imperf., Sewing Machine Perf.

1902			**Typeset**	
255	A82a	10c black, *rose*	3.50	3.50
256	A82a	20c blk, *orange*	2.50	2.50

This issue was printed in either Cali or Popayan.

Medellin Issue

A83

1902				
257	A83	1c grn, *straw*	.25	*.40*
258	A83	2c salmon, *rose*	.25	*.40*
259	A83	5c dp bl, *grnsh*	.25	*.40*
260	A83	10c pale brn, *straw*	.25	*.40*
261	A83	20c pur, *rose*	.35	*.40*
262	A83	50c dl rose, *grnsh*	1.75	*2.50*
263	A83	1p blk, *yellow*	3.50	*5.25*
264	A83	5p slate, *blue*	27.50	27.50
265	A83	10p dk brn, *rose*	17.50	17.50
		Nos. 257-265 (9)	51.60	54.75

For overprint see No. L8.

Imperf., Pairs

257a	A83	1c	8.50	8.50
258a	A83	2c	8.50	8.50
259a	A83	5c	8.50	8.50
260a	A83	10c	8.50	8.50
261a	A83	20c	8.50	8.50
262a	A83	50c	8.50	8.50
263a	A83	1p	22.50	22.50
264a	A83	5p	62.50	62.50
265a	A83	10p	50.00	50.00

Regular Issue

A84

A85

A86

A87

A88

A89

A90

A91

A92

1902			***Imperf.***	
266	A84	2c blk, *rose*	.20	.20
267	A85	4c red, *grn*	.20	.20
268	A86	5c grn, *bl*	.20	.20
269	A87	10c blk, *pink*	.20	.20
c.		10c blk, *rose*	.75	.75
270	A88	20c brn, *buff*	.20	.20
271	A89	50c dk grn, *rose*	1.10	1.10
272	A90	1p pur, *buff*	.45	.45
273	A91	5p grn, *bl*	3.25	3.25
274	A92	10p grn, *pale grn*	10.00	5.00
		Nos. 266-274 (9)	15.80	10.80

For overprint see No. H13.

Sewing Machine Perf.

266a	A84	2c blk, *rose*	1.50	1.50
267a	A85	4c red, *grn*	1.25	1.25
268a	A86	5c grn, *blue*	1.50	1.50
269a	A87	10c blk, *pink*	1.50	1.50
270a	A88	20c brn, *buff*	2.50	2.00
271a	A89	50c dk grn, *rose*	5.00	4.00
272a	A90	1p pur, *buff*	6.00	5.00
273a	A91	5p grn, *blue*	27.50	27.50
274a	A92	10p grn, *pale grn*	50.00	50.00
		Nos. 266a-274a (9)	96.75	94.25

1903			***Perf. 12***	
266b	A84	2c blk, *rose*	1.10	1.10
269b	A87	10c blk, *pink*	1.25	1.25
270b	A88	20c brn, *buff*	1.25	1.25
272b	A90	1p pur, *buff*	2.50	2.50
273b	A91	5p grn, *blue*	22.50	22.50
274b	A92	10p grn, *pale grn*	40.00	35.00
		Nos. 266b-274b (6)	68.60	63.60

1903			***Imperf.***	
284	A85	4c blue, *grn*	.25	.25
285	A86	5c blue, *blue*	.25	.25
286	A88	20c blue,*buff*	.25	.25
288	A89	50c blue, *rose*	1.40	1.40
		Nos. 284-288 (4)	2.15	2.15

Sewing Machine Perf.

284a	A85	4c blue, *grn*	1.75	1.40
285a	A86	5c blue, *blue*	1.75	1.40
286a	A88	20c blue, *buff*	2.50	2.00
288a	A89	50c blue, *rose*	5.00	4.50
		Nos. 284a-288a (4)	11.00	9.30

Perf. 12

284b	A85	4c blue, *grn*	2.00	2.00
285b	A86	5c blue, *blue*	2.00	2.00
286b	A88	20c blue, *buff*	2.75	2.75
288b	A89	50c blue, *rose*	7.50	7.50
		Nos. 284b-288b (4)	14.25	14.25

A93

1904		**Pelure Paper**	***Imperf.***	
303	A93	½c yellow brn	1.00	1.00
304	A90	1c blue green	1.00	1.00
a.		1c yellow green	1.00	1.00
306	A84	2c blue	.90	.60
307	A86	5c carmine	1.00	1.00
308	A87	10c violet	1.00	.90
		Nos. 303-308 (5)	4.90	4.50

For overprint see No. H13.

1904			***Perf. 13***	
303a	A93	½c yellow brown	3.00	3.00
304b	A90	1c blue green	4.00	3.50
c.		1c yellow green	5.00	4.50
306a	A84	2c blue	2.50	2.50

Perf. 12

307a	A86	5c carmine	2.25	2.25
308a	A87	10c violet	2.25	2.25
		Nos. 303a-308a (5)	14.00	13.50

A94

A95

Pres. José Manuel Marroquín — A96

Imprint: "Lit. J.L.Arango Medellin. Col."

1904		**Wove Paper**	***Perf. 12***	
314	A94	½c yellow	.65	.20
315	A94	1c green	.65	.20
316	A94	2c rose	.65	.20
317	A94	5c blue	1.00	.20
318	A94	10c violet	1.40	.20
319	A94	20c black	1.40	.25
320	A95	1p brown	15.00	2.50
321	A96	5p red & blk, *yel*	45.00	45.00
322	A96	10p bl & blk, *grnsh*	45.00	45.00
		Nos. 314-322 (9)	110.75	93.75

Redrawn

314a	A94	½c	.65	.20
315a	A94	1c	.65	.20
316a	A94	2c	.65	.20
317a	A94	5c	1.00	.20
319a	A94	20c	1.40	.20
		Nos. 314a-319a (5)	4.35	1.00

Imperf., Pairs

314b	A94	½c	2.50	2.50
315b	A94	1c	2.00	2.00
316b	A94	2c	2.50	2.50
317b	A94	5c	2.50	2.50
318a	A94	10c	3.25	3.25
319b	A94	20c	6.00	6.00
320a	A95	1p	50.00	50.00
		Nos. 314b-320a (7)	68.75	68.75

On the redrawn types, the imprint is close to the base of the design instead of being spaced from it. On the redrawn 2c and 5c, the lower end of the vertical white line below "OR" of "CORREOS" forms a hook which turns to the right instead of to the left as in the originals.

See Nos. 325-330. For surcharges see Nos. 351-354, L1-L7, L9-L13, L15-L25.

A97

100p has different frame.

1903			***Imperf.***	
323	A97	50p org yel, *pale pink*	75.00	75.00
324	A97	100p dk bl, *dk rose*	60.00	60.00

Imprint: "Lit. Nacional"

Perf. 10, 13, 13½ and Compound

1908				
325	A94	½c orange	.60	.20
a.		½c yellow	.60	.20
b.		Imperf., pair	2.00	1.50
c.		Without imprint	4.00	4.00
326	A94	1c yel grn	.60	.20
a.		Without imprint	.60	.20
d.		Imperf., pair	3.00	2.50
327	A94	2c red	.60	.20
a.		2c carmine	.60	.20
b.		Imperf., pair	3.00	2.50
328	A94	5c blue	.50	.20
a.		Imperf., pair	5.00	4.00
329	A94	10c violet	*40.00*	.70
330	A94	20c gray blk	*40.00*	.50
		Nos. 325-330 (6)	*82.30*	2.00

The above stamps may be easily distinguished from those of 1904 by the perforation, by the height of the design, 24mm instead of 23mm, and by the "Lit. Nacional" imprint.

Camilo Torres
A99

Policarpa Salavarrieta
A100

Bolívar Demanding Liberation of Slaves — A105

Designs: 2c, Nariño. 5c, Bolívar. 10c, Francisco José de Caldas. 20c, Francisco de Paula Santander. 10p, Bolívar Resigning.

1910, Aug.		**Engr.**	***Perf. 12***	
331	A99	½c violet & blk	.50	.25
a.		Center inverted	425.00	425.00
332	A100	1c deep green	.40	.25
333	A100	2c scarlet	.40	.25
334	A100	5c deep blue	1.25	.45
335	A100	10c plum	10.00	5.00
336	A100	20c black brn	15.00	5.50
337	A105	1p dk violet	65.00	20.00
338	A105	10p claret	250.00	200.00
		Nos. 331-338 (8)	342.55	231.70

Colombian independence centenary.

Caldas
A107

Monument to Battle of Boyacá
A113

View of Cartagena
A114

Coat of Arms
A118

Designs: 1c, Torres. 2c, Narino. 4c, Santander. 5c, Bolivar. 10c, Jose Maria Cordoba. 1p, Sucre. 2p, Rufino Cuervo. 5p, Antonio Ricaurte y Lozano.

1917		**Engr.**	***Perf. 14***	
339	A107	½c bister	.35	.20
340	A107	1c green	.30	.20
341	A107	2c car rose	.30	.20
342	A107	4c violet	.90	.30
343	A107	5c dull blue	2.25	.20
344	A107	10c gray	2.25	.20
345	A113	20c red	1.25	.20
346	A114	50c carmine	1.50	.20
347	A107	1p brt blue	11.00	.40
348	A107	2p orange	12.00	.45
349	A107	5p gray	30.00	8.50
350	A118	10p dk brown	35.00	10.00
		Nos. 339-350 (12)	97.10	21.05

The 1c, 5c, 10c, 50c, 2p, 5p and 10p also exist perf. 11½ and 11½ compounded with 14.

Litho. varieties of Nos. 343, 345 and 346 are counterfeits made to defraud the government.

Imperforate copies of Nos. 339-350 are not known to have been regularly issued.

See Nos. 373-374, 400-405. For overprints and surcharges see Nos. 369-370, 377, 409-410, 440, C1, O3, O5-O9.

Nos. 318-319, 329-330 Surcharged in Red

1918

On Issue of 1904

351	A94	½c on 20c black	1.00	.25
352	A94	3c on 10c violet	2.50	.50

On Issue of 1908

353	A94	½c on 20c gray blk	8.00	5.00
354	A94	3c on 10c violet	12.00	4.25
		Nos. 351-354 (4)	23.50	10.00

Nos. 351-354 inclusive exist with surcharge reading up or down. On one stamp in each sheet the letter "S" in "Especie" is omitted. All denominations exist with a small zero before the decimal in the surcharge.

A119

A120

1918 Litho. *Perf. 13½*

358 A119 3c red		.50	.20
a.	Imperf., pair	4.00	4.00

1920 Engr. *Perf. 14*

359 A120 3c red, *org*		.30	.20
a.	Imperf., pair	3.00	3.00

See #371-372. For surcharge see #453.

A121

A122

A123

Perf. 10, 13½ and Compound

1920-21 Litho.

360 A121	½c yellow	.50	.25
361 A121	1c green	.85	.20
362 A121	2c red	.65	.20
363 A122	3c green	.65	.20
a.	3c yellow green	.65	.20
364 A121	5c blue	.95	.25
365 A121	10c violet	3.00	1.50
366 A121	20c deep green	8.00	3.50
367 A123	50c dark red	8.00	3.50
	Nos. 360-367 (8)	22.60	9.60

The tablet with "PROVISIONAL" was added separately to each design on the various lithographic stones and its position varies slightly on different stamps in the sheet. For some values there were two or more stones, on which the tablet was placed at various angles.

Nos. 360-366 exist imperf.

See No. 375.

No. 342 Surcharged in Red

a

(15mm wide) — b

1921

369 A107 (a) 3c on 4c violet		.80	.25
a.	Double surcharge	13.00	
370 A107 (b) 3c on 4c violet		3.50	2.00

See No. 377.

Types of 1917-21

1923-24 Engr. *Perf. 13½*

371 A120	1½c chocolate	1.00	.50
372 A120	3c blue	.50	.20
373 A107	5c claret ('24)	2.00	.20
374 A107	10c blue	7.50	.40

Litho.

375 A121	10c dark blue	10.00	6.00
	Nos. 371-375 (5)	21.00	7.30

No. 342 Surcharged in Red

(18mm wide)

1924

377 A107 3c on 4c vio		3.00	1.25
a.	Double surcharge	12.00	
b.	Double surch., one invtd.	12.00	
c.	With added surch. "3cs." in red		

A124

1924-25 Litho. *Perf. 10, 10x13½*

379 A124	1c red	.70	.20
380 A124	3c dp blue ('25)	.70	.20

Exist imperf. Value, each pair $5.

A125

A126

Black, Red or Green Surch. & Ovpt.

Imprint of Waterlow & Sons

1925 *Perf. 14, 14½*

382 A125 1c on 3c bis brn		.30	.20
383 A126 4c violet (R)		.40	.20
a.	Inverted surcharge	7.00	7.00

Imprint of American Bank Note Co.

Perf. 12

384 A125 1c on 3c bis brn		6.00	5.00
a.	Inverted surcharge	15.00	15.00
385 A126 4c violet (G)		.40	.30
a.	Inverted overprint	7.50	7.50
	Nos. 382-385 (4)	7.10	5.70

Correos

Provisional

Revenue stamps of basic types A125 and A126 were handstamped as above in violet or blue by the Cali post office in 1925, but were not authorized by the government. Denominations so overprinted are 1c, 2c, 3c, 4c and 5c.

A127

A128

Perf. 10, 13½x10

1926 Litho. Wmk. 194

395 A127	1c gray green	.40	.20
396 A128	4c deep blue	.45	.20

Exist imperf. Value, each pair $4.

Types of 1917 and

Sabana Station — A129

1926-29 Unwmk. Engr. *Perf. 14*

400 A107	4c deep blue	.40	.20
401 A118	8c dark blue	.50	.20
402 A107	30c olive bister	4.75	.60
403 A129	40c brn & yel brn	7.50	1.00
404 A107	5p violet	7.50	.70
a.	Perf. 11 ('29)	12.00	1.00
405 A118	10p green	12.00	2.00
a.	Perf. 11 ('29)	25.00	4.00
	Nos. 400-405 (6)	32.65	4.70

For surcharges & overprint see #09-410, O4.

Death of Bolívar A130

1930, Dec. 17 *Perf. 12½*

408 A130	4c dk blue & blk	.45	.30

Cent. of the death of Simón Bolívar. See Nos. C80-C82.

Nos. 400 and 402 Surcharged in Red or Dark Blue

1932, Jan. 20 *Perf. 14*

409 A107 1c on 4c dp bl (R)		.30	.20
a.	Inverted surcharge	5.25	5.25
410 A107 20c on 30c ol bis		8.00	.70
a.	Inverted surcharge	17.50	
b.	Double surcharge	17.50	

Emerald Mine — A131

Oil Wells — A132

Coffee Cultivation A133

Platinum Mine — A134

Gold Mining — A135

Christopher Columbus — A136

Imprint: "Waterlow & Sons Ltd. Londres"

1932 Wmk. 229 *Perf. 12½*

411 A131	1c green	.50	.20
412 A132	2c red	.50	.20
413 A133	5c brown	.60	.20
414 A134	8c blue blk	3.75	.50
415 A135	10c yellow	2.75	.20
416 A136	20c dk blue	8.00	.35
	Nos. 411-416 (6)	16.10	1.65

See #441-442, 464-466a, 517. For surcharges see #455, 527, O1, O10-O11, O13, RA30.

Pedro de Heredia — A137

Coffee Picking — A138

Perf. 11½

1934, Jan. 10 Unwmk. Litho.

417 A137	1c dark green	2.25	.65
418 A137	5c chocolate	3.00	.55
419 A137	8c dark blue	2.25	.65
	Nos. 417-419 (3)	7.50	1.85

Cartagena, 400th anniv. See #C111-C114.

1934, Dec. Engr. *Perf. 12*

420 A138	5c brown	3.00	.20

Discus Thrower — A139

Post and Telegraph Building — A145

Allegory of Olympic Games at Barranquilla — A140

Foot Race A141

Tennis A142

Pier at Puerto Colombia A143

View of the Bay A144

Designs: 2c, Soccer. 10c, Hurdling. 15c, Athlete in stadium. 18c, Baseball. 24c, Swimming. 50c, View of Barranquilla. 2p, Monument to Flag. 5p, Coat of Arms. 10p, Condor.

1935, Jan. 26 Litho. *Perf. 11½*

421 A139	2c bluish grn & buff	1.25	.40
422 A139	4c deep green	1.25	.40
423 A140	5c dk brn & yel	1.25	.40
a.	Horiz. pair, imperf. btwn.	200.00	
424 A141	7c dk carmine	2.50	1.50
425 A142	8c blk & pink	2.00	2.00
426 A141	10c brown & bl	2.75	1.50
427 A143	12c indigo	3.25	2.50
428 A141	15c bl & red brn	5.50	4.25
429 A141	18c dk vio & buff	8.00	6.50
430 A144	20c purple & grn	6.50	5.50
431 A144	24c bluish grn & ultra	6.50	5.25
432 A144	50c ultra & buff	10.00	8.50
433 A145	1p drab & blue	92.50	50.00

434	A145	2p dull grn & gray	110.00	90.00
435	A145	5p pur blk & bl	350.00	275.00
436	A145	10p black & gray	425.00	400.00
		Nos. 421-436 (16)	1,028.	853.70

3rd Natl. Olympic Games, Barranquilla. Counterfeits of 10p exist.

Oil Wells — A155

Gold Mining — A157

Imprint: "American Bank Note Co."

1935, Mar. Unwmk. Engr. *Perf. 12*

437	A155	2c carmine rose	.35	.20
439	A157	10c deep orange	20.00	.20

See Nos. 468, 470, 498, 516. For surcharge and overprints see Nos. 496, 596, O2.

No. 347 Surcharged in Black

1935, Aug. *Perf. 14*

440	A107	12c on 1p brt bl	3.50	1.50

Types of 1932
Imprint: "Lit. Nacional Bogotá"

1935-36 Litho. *Perf. 11, 11½, 12½*

441	A131	1c lt green	.20	.20
a.		Imperf., pair	3.50	
442	A133	5c brown ('36)	.55	.20
a.		Imperf., pair	4.00	4.00

For surcharge see No. 527.

Bolívar A159

Tequendama Falls A160

Wmk. Wavy Lines. (229)

1937 Engr. *Perf. 12½*

443	A159	1c deep green	.20	.20
a.		Perf. 14		
444	A160	12c deep blue	3.25	1.10

See No. 570. For surcharges and overprints see Nos. 454, 456, C231, C326, O12.

Soccer Player — A161

Runner — A163

Discus Thrower — A162

1937, Jan. 4 Photo. Unwmk.

445	A161	3c lt green	1.40	.85
446	A162	10c carmine rose	3.00	1.75
447	A163	1p black	27.50	24.00
		Nos. 445-447 (3)	31.90	26.60

National Olympic Games, Manizales. For surcharge see No. 452.

Exposition Palace — A164

Stadium at Barranquilla A165

Monument to the Colors A166

1937, Jan. 4

448	A164	5c violet brown	2.00	.30
449	A165	15c blue	5.00	3.50
450	A166	50c orange brn	14.00	7.50
		Nos. 448-450 (3)	21.00	11.30

Barranquilla National Exposition.

Stamps of 1926-37 Surcharged in Black

1937-38 Unwmk. *Perf. 12½*

452	A161	1c on 3c lt grn	.75	.75
a.		Inverted surcharge	1.75	1.75
453	A118	5c on 8c dk bl	.40	.35
a.		Inverted surcharge	1.75	1.75

Wmk. 229

454	A160	2c on 12c dp bl	.40	.35
455	A134	5c on 8c bl blk	.45	.55
a.		Invtd. surcharge	1.50	1.50
456	A160	10c on 12c dp bl ('38)	4.25	.85
a.		Dbl. surcharge	8.50	8.50
		Nos. 452-456 (5)	6.25	2.85

Calle del Arco — A168

Entrance to Church of the Rosary — A169

Arms of Bogotá A170

Gonzálo Jiménez de Quesada A171

Bochica A172

Santo Domingo Convent A173

Mass of the Conquistadors — A174

1938, July 27 Unwmk. *Perf. 12½*

457	A168	1c yellow green	.20	.20
458	A169	2c scarlet	.20	.20
459	A170	5c brown blk	.25	.20
460	A171	10c brown	.60	.30
461	A172	15c brt blue	3.00	1.25
462	A173	20c brt red vio	3.00	1.25
463	A174	1p red brown	40.00	22.50
		Nos. 457-463 (7)	47.25	25.90

Bogotá, 400th anniversary.

Types of 1932
Imprint: "Litografia Nacional Bogotá"

1938, Dec. 5 Litho. *Perf. 10½, 11*

464	A132	2c rose	.80	.30
465	A135	10c yellow	2.00	.30
466	A136	20c dull blue	8.00	1.00
a.		20c dark blue, perf. 12½ ('44)	50.00	5.00
		Nos. 464-466 (3)	10.80	1.60

Types of 1935 and

Bolívar A175

Coffee Picking A176

Arms of Colombia A177

Christopher Columbus A178

Caldas A179

Sabana Station A180

Imprint: "American Bank Note Co."
Wmk. 255

1939, Mar. 3 Engr. *Perf. 12*

467	A175	1c green	.20	.20
468	A155	2c car rose	.20	.20
469	A176	5c dull brown	.20	.20
470	A157	10c deep orange	.40	.20
471	A177	15c dull blue	1.25	.20
472	A178	20c violet blk	14.00	.20
473	A179	30c olive bister	4.25	.30
474	A180	40c bister brn	13.00	2.75
		Nos. 467-474 (8)	33.50	4.25

See Nos. 497-499, 515, 518, 574. For surcharges and overprints see Nos. 506-507, 520-522, 596, RA26, RA47.

Gen. Santander A181

Allegory A182

Gen. Santander A183

Statue at Cúcuta A184

Birthplace of Santander A185

Church at Rosario A186

Paya — A187

Bridge at Boyacá — A188

Death of General Santander A189

Invasion of the Liberators A190

Perf. 13x13½, 13½x13

1940, May 6 Engr. Wmk. 229

475	A181	1c olive green	.20	.20
476	A182	2c dk carmine	.40	.25
477	A183	5c sepia	.20	.20
478	A184	8c carmine	1.50	1.50
479	A185	10c orange yel	.65	.50
480	A186	15c dark blue	1.75	1.10
481	A187	20c green	2.25	1.75
482	A188	50c violet	5.25	5.00
483	A189	1p deep rose	17.00	17.00
484	A190	2p orange	55.00	55.00
		Nos. 475-484 (10)	84.20	82.50

Death of General Francisco Santander, cent.

Tobacco Plant A194

Gen. Santander A195

Garcia Rovira — A196

R. Galan — A197

Antonio Sucre — A198

1940-43 Engr. Wmk. 255 *Perf. 12*

488	A194	8c rose car & grn	1.00	.55
489	A195	15c dp blue ('43)	1.10	.25
490	A196	20c gray blk ('41)	3.50	.40
491	A197	40c brown bis ('41)	2.10	.40
492	A198	1p black	6.75	.50
		Nos. 488-492 (5)	14.45	2.10

See #500, 554. For overprint see #RA28.

AIR POST STAMPS

No. 341 Overprinted

1919 Unwmk. *Perf. 14*

C1	A107	2c car rose		2,750.	1,300.
a.		Numerals "1" with serifs		*5,500.*	*3,250.*

Used for the first experimental flight from Barranquilla to Puerto Colombia, 6/18/19.
Values are for faulty copies.

Issued by Compania Colombiana de Navegacion Aerea

From 1920 to 1932 the internal airmail service of Colombia was handled by the Compania Colombiana de Navegacion Aerea (1920) and the Sociedad Colombo-Alemana de Transportes Aéreos, known familiarly as "SCADTA" (1920-1932).

These organizations, under government contracts, operated and maintained their own post offices and issued stamps which were the only legal franking for airmail service during this period, both in the internal and international mails. All letters had to bear government stamps as well.

Woman and Boy Watching Plane — AP1

Designs: No. C3, Clouds and small biplane at top. No. C4, Tilted plane viewed close-up from above. No. C5, Flier in plane watching biplane. No. C6, Lighthouse. No. C7, Fuselage and tail of biplane. No. C8, Condor on cliff. No. C9, Plane at rest; pilot foreground. No. C10, Ocean liner.

1920, Feb. Unwmk. Litho. *Imperf.*
Without Gum

C2	AP1	10c multicolored	2,500.	1,500.
C3	AP1	10c multicolored	3,000.	1,500.
C4	AP1	10c multicolored	3,500.	1,500.
C5	AP1	10c multicolored	2,750.	1,500.
C6	AP1	10c multicolored	2,400.	1,500.
C7	AP1	10c multicolored	8,500.	3,000.
C8	AP1	10c multicolored	4,500.	2,400.
C9	AP1	10c multicolored	2,750.	1,500.
C10	AP1	10c multicolored	3,500.	2,100.

Nos. C2-C10 were overprinted on the nine lighter-colored varieties of a set of 18 publicity labels produced by the Curtis Co. for inclusion with packs of cigarettes. These labels were printed setenant, in panes of 18 (3x6). Value for the set of 18 values without overprint: $4,000.

Flier in Plane Watching Biplane — AP2

1920, Mar.

C11	AP2	10c green	45.00	*70.00*

Four other 10c stamps, similar to No. C11, have two designs showing plane, mountains and water. They are printed in deep green or light brown red. Some authorities state that these four were not used regularly.

Issued by Sociedad Colombo-Alemana de Transportes Aereos (SCADTA)

Seaplane over Magdalena River — AP3

1920-21 Litho. *Perf. 12*

C12	AP3	10c yellow ('21)	35.00	30.00
C13	AP3	15c blue ('21)	40.00	32.50
C14	AP3	30c blk, *rose*	22.50	13.00
C15	AP3	30c rose ('21)	35.00	27.50
C16	AP3	50c pale green	35.00	30.00
		Nos. C12-C16 (5)	167.50	133.00

For surcharges see Nos. C17-C24, C36-C37.

No. C16 Handstamp Surcharged in Violet or Black:

(Illustrations of types "a" to "e" are reduced in size.)

VALOR 10 CENTAVOS
a

VALOR 10 CENTAVOS
b

Valor 10 Céntavos
c

VALOR 30 Ctvos
S.C.A.T.A
d

30¢ 30¢
e

$0 30
f

$0 30¢
g

1921

C17	AP3 (a)	10c on 50c	800.	750.
C18	AP3 (b)	10c on 50c	800.	750.
C19	AP3 (c)	10c on 50c	*800.*	*750.*
C20	AP3 (b)	30c on 50c	600.	525.
C21	AP3 (d)	30c on 50c	600.	525.
C22	AP3 (e)	30c on 50c	1,000.	1,000.
C23	AP3 (f)	30c on 50c	1,200.	1,000.
C24	AP3 (g)	30c on 50c	1,200.	1,000.

Plane over Magdalena River — AP4

Plane over Bogota Cathedral AP5

1921 *Perf. 11½*

C25	AP4	5c orange yellow	3.00	3.00
C26	AP4	10c slate green	1.25	1.00
C27	AP4	15c orange brown	1.25	1.10
C28	AP4	20c red brown	3.00	1.40
a.		Horiz. pair, imperf. vert.	*140.00*	
C29	AP4	30c green	1.40	.70
C30	AP4	50c blue	2.40	.75
C31	AP4	60c vermilion	50.00	22.50
C32	AP5	1p gray black	14.00	3.75
C33	AP5	2p rose	26.00	14.00
C34	AP5	3p violet	80.00	52.50
C35	AP5	5p olive green	225.00	210.00
		Nos. C25-C35 (11)	407.30	310.70

Exist imperf.
For surcharge see No. C52.

Nos. C16 and C12 Handstamp Surcharged

Illustration of type "h" is reduced in size.

VALOR 20 Ctvs.
h

30 cent.
i

1921-22 *Perf. 12*

C36	AP3 (h)	20c on 50c	2,250.	1,700.
C37	AP3 (i)	30c on 10c	500.	400.

Seaplane over Magdalena River — AP6

Plane over Bogota Cathedral AP7

1923-28 Wmk. 116 *Perf. 14x14½*

C38	AP6	5c orange yellow	1.00	.20
C39	AP6	10c green	1.00	.20
C40	AP6	15c carmine	1.00	.20
C41	AP6	20c gray	1.00	.20
C42	AP6	30c blue	1.00	.20
C43	AP6	40c purple ('28)	8.00	5.50
C44	AP6	50c green	1.25	.20
C45	AP6	60c brown	2.10	.20
C46	AP6	80c olive grn ('28)	21.00	20.00
C47	AP7	1p black	9.00	2.00
C48	AP7	2p red orange	13.00	4.00
C49	AP7	3p violet	27.50	17.50
C50	AP7	5p olive green	45.00	24.00
		Nos. C38-C50 (13)	131.85	74.40

For surcharges and overprints see Nos. C51, C53-C54, CF1.

Nos. C41 and C31 Surcharged in Carmine and Dark Blue:

No. C51

No. C52

1923

C51	AP6	30c on 20c gray (C)	60.00	40.00
C52	AP4	30c on 60c ver	52.50	27.50

Nos. C41-C42 Overprinted in Black

1928 Wmk. 116 *Perf. 14x14½*

C53	AP6	20c gray	42.50	40.00
C54	AP6	30c blue	42.50	40.00

Goodwill flight of Lt. Benjamin Mendez from New York to Bogota.

Magdalena River and Tolíma Volcano AP8

Columbus' Ship and Plane AP9

1929, June 1 Wmk. 127 *Perf. 14*

C55	AP8	5c yellow org	.65	.20
C56	AP8	10c red brown	.65	.20
C57	AP8	15c deep green	.65	.20
C58	AP8	20c carmine	.65	.20
C59	AP8	30c gray blue	.65	.20
C60	AP8	40c dull violet	.65	.25
C61	AP8	50c dk olive grn	1.25	.25
C62	AP8	60c orange brown	2.10	.25
C63	AP8	80c green	5.50	2.25
C64	AP9	1p blue	6.50	1.75
C65	AP9	2p brown orange	9.75	4.25
C66	AP9	3p pale rose vio	24.00	14.00
C67	AP9	5p olive green	60.00	26.00
		Nos. C55-C67 (13)	113.00	50.00

For surcharges and overprints see Nos. C80-C95, CF2, CF4.

For International Airmail

AP10

AP11

1929, June 1 Wmk. 127 *Perf. 14*

C68	AP10	5c yellow org	3.50	*4.25*
C69	AP10	10c red brown	.65	*1.75*
C70	AP10	15c deep green	.65	*1.75*
C71	AP10	20c carmine	.65	*2.10*
C72	AP10	25c violet blue	.65	.35
C73	AP10	30c gray blue	.65	.55
C74	AP10	50c dk olive grn	.65	*1.00*
C75	AP10	60c brown	1.50	*1.75*
C76	AP11	1p blue	3.00	*4.75*
C77	AP11	2p red orange	4.50	*5.75*
C78	AP11	3p violet	60.00	60.00
C79	AP11	5p olive green	80.00	*90.00*
		Nos. C68-79 (12)	156.40	*174.00*

This issue was sold abroad for use on correspondence to be flown from coastal to interior points of Colombia. Cancellations are those of the country of origin rather than Colombia.

For overprint see No. CF3.

Nos. C63, C66 and C64 Surcharged in Black:

m

n

1930, Dec. 15

C80	AP8(m)	10c on 80c	4.25	4.25
C81	AP9(n)	20c on 3p	8.25	*9.00*
C82	AP9(n)	30c on 1p	10.00	9.00
		Nos. C80-C82 (3)	22.50	*22.25*

Simon Bolivar (1783-1830).

Colombian Government Issues

Nos. C55-C67 Overprinted in Black:

o

p

Wmk. 127

1932, Jan. 1 Typo. ***Perf. 14***

C83	AP8(o)	5c yellow org	8.00	8.00
C84	AP8(o)	10c red brown	1.75	.50
C85	AP8(o)	15c deep green	3.00	3.00
C86	AP8(o)	20c carmine	1.50	.30
C87	AP8(o)	30c gray blue	1.50	.50
C88	AP8(o)	40c dull violet	2.00	1.00
C89	AP8(o)	50c dk ol grn	4.00	3.00
C90	AP8(o)	60c orange brn	3.25	3.00
C91	AP8(o)	80c green	14.00	14.00
C92	AP9(p)	1p blue	11.00	9.00
C93	AP9(p)	2p brown org	30.00	27.50
C94	AP9(p)	3p pale rose vio	60.00	52.50
C95	AP9(p)	5p olive green	100.00	*110.00*
		Nos. C83-C95 (13)	240.00	232.30

Coffee
AP12

Gold
AP16

Designs: 10c, 50c, Cattle. 15c, 60c, Petroleum. 20c, 40c, Bananas. 3p, 5p, Emerald.

1932-39 Wmk. 127 Photo. ***Perf. 14***

C96	AP12	5c org & blk brn	.90	.25
C97	AP12	10c lake & blk	1.00	.20
C98	AP12	15c bl grn & vio blk	.45	.20
C99	AP12	15c ver & vio blk ('39)	2.50	.20
C100	AP12	20c car & ol blk	.70	.20
C101	AP12	20c turq grn & ol blk ('39)	3.50	.30
C102	AP12	30c dk bl & blk brn	1.60	.20
C103	AP12	40c dk vio & ol bis	.85	.20
C104	AP12	50c dk grn & brnsh blk	3.50	1.25
C105	AP12	60c dk brn & blk vio	1.00	.25
C106	AP12	80c grn & blk brn	5.50	2.00
C107	AP16	1p dk bl & ol bis	9.00	1.25
C108	AP16	2p org brn & ol bis	10.00	2.25
C109	AP16	3p dk vio & emer	17.00	6.25
C110	AP16	5p gray blk & emer	47.50	20.00
		Nos. C96-C110 (15)	105.00	35.00

For overprint see No. CF5.

Nos. C104, C106-C108 Surcharged:

a

b

1934, Jan. 5

C111	AP12(a)	10c on 50c	3.50	3.50
C112	AP12(a)	15c on 80c	4.75	4.75
C113	AP16(b)	20c on 1p	5.25	5.25
C114	AP16(b)	30c on 2p	5.75	5.75
		Nos. C111-C114 (4)	19.25	19.25

400th anniversary of Cartagena.

Nos. C100 and C103 Surcharged in Black or Carmine:

1939, Jan. 15

C115	AP12	5c on 20c (Bk)	.35	.35
C116	AP12	5c on 40c (C)	.35	.25
C117	AP12	15c on 20c (Bk)	1.50	.50
	a.	Double surcharge	12.00	
	b.	Pair, one with dbl. surch.	14.00	
	c.	Inverted surcharge	12.00	12.00

No. CF5 Surcharged in Black

C118	AP12	5c on 20c	.70	.70
		Nos. C115-C118 (4)	2.90	1.80

Nos. C102-C103 Surcharged in Black or Red

1940, Oct. 20

C119	AP12	15c on 30c	1.25	.50
	a.	Inverted surcharge	12.00	
C120	AP12	15c on 40c (R)	2.00	.75
	a.	Double surcharge	12.00	

AIR POST REGISTRATION STAMPS

Issued by Sociedad Colombo-Alemana de Transportes Aereos (SCADTA)

No. C41 Overprinted in Red

1923 Wmk. 116 ***Perf. 14x14½***

CF1	AP6	20c gray	2.50	1.10

No. C58 Overprinted in Black

1929 Wmk. 127 ***Perf. 14***

CF2	AP8	20c carmine	4.50	1.10

Same Overprint on No. C71

CF3	AP10	20c carmine	6.50	6.00

Colombian Government Issues

Same Overprint on No. C86

1932

CF4	AP8	20c carmine	6.50	6.00

No. C100 Overprinted

CF5	AP12	20c car & ol blk	4.50	1.25

For surcharge see No. C118.

SCADTA — CONSULAR OVERPRINTS

The Sociedad Colombo-Alemana de Transportes Aéreos (SCADTA) was established in Colombia in December 1919 by a group of Colombian and German businessmen, with the aim of organizing efficient and reliable airline service within Colombia. In 1920 the Colombian government granted SCADTA the monopoly for carrying mail within the country and authorized it to establish and maintain its own post offices and to print its own stamps. These stamps represented the company's fees for air service, and all proceeds from their sale were retained by SCADTA. Airmail articles also required regular postage stamps, those of Colombia for domestic mail and, initially, for mail from abroad, or, later, stamps of the country of origin.

In order to encourage foreign airmail to Colombia, SCADTA made its stamps available at Colombian consular offices and trade missions, and through its own agents. For accounting purposes and to prevent speculation due to the frequent currency fluctuations of the period, one or two-letter control overprints were applied denoting the country of origin.

These stamps were superseded by Colombia Nos. C68-C79, which were sold abroad in the equivalent of U.S. gold dollars, thus eliminating the need to identify the various sales offices because of changes in rates of exchange.

NOTE: In order to maintain integrity of presentation, and for the convenience of the collector, the Scott editors have included SCADTA consular overprinted air post registration stamps within the air post sets with which they were issued.

UNITED STATES

Nos. C14, C16

Signed "G. Mejia" in red

1920, November

CLEU1	AP3	30c blk, *rose*	100.00	200.00
		On cover		2,000.
CLEU2	AP3	50c pale green	100.00	250.00
		On cover		5,000.
	a.	Black signature		—

Two examples of No. CLEU2 on cover are known. Nos. CLEU1 and CLEU2 exist together on a unique cover.

Nos. C25-C35 handstamped in black, letters 6½mm high

E. U.

1921-23

CLEU3	AP4	5c org yel	15.00	15.00
CLEU4	AP4	10c sl grn	15.00	15.00
CLEU5	AP4	15c org brn	15.00	15.00
CLEU6	AP4	20c red brown	15.00	15.00
CLEU7	AP4	30c green	10.00	10.00
CLEU8	AP4	50c blue	15.00	15.00
CLEU9	AP4	60c vermilion	22.50	25.00
CLEU10	AP5	1p gray black	30.00	30.00
CLEU11	AP5	2p rose	62.50	70.00
CLEU12	AP5	3p violet	87.50	100.00
CLEU13	AP5	5p ol grn	375.00	400.00

Nos. C25-C35 handstamped in violet, letters 6½mm high

CLEU14	AP4	5c org yel	15.00	17.50
CLEU15	AP4	10c sl grn	12.50	17.50
CLEU16	AP4	15c org brn	12.50	17.50
CLEU17	AP4	20c red brown	12.50	17.50
CLEU18	AP4	30c green	9.00	12.00
	a.	Double overprint	*750.00*	
CLEU19	AP4	50c blue	12.50	17.50
CLEU20	AP4	60c vermilion	30.00	25.00
CLEU21	AP5	1p gray black	27.50	37.50
CLEU22	AP5	2p rose	62.50	72.50
CLEU23	AP5	3p violet	110.00	125.00
CLEU24	AP5	5p ol grn	375.00	400.00

Nos. C38//51, CF1 handstamped in black, letters 6½mm high

1923

CLEU25	AP6	5c org yel	12.50	12.50
CLEU26	AP6	10c green	12.50	12.50
CLEU27	AP6	15c carmine	15.00	15.00
CLEU28	AP6	20c gray	15.00	15.00
CLEU29	AP6	30c blue	5.00	5.00
CLEU30	AP6	50c green	10.00	10.00
CLEU31	AP6	60c brown	10.00	10.00
CLEU32	AP7	1p black	20.00	20.00
CLEU33	AP7	2p red org	27.50	27.50
CLEU34	AP7	3p violet	50.00	50.00
CLEU35	AP7	5p ol grn	87.50	87.50
CLEU36	AP6	30c on 20c gray (C)	*1,250.*	*450.00*
	a.	"60" instead of "30" at left	—	—
CFLEU1	AP6	20c gray	37.50	37.50

Nos. C38//C51, CF1 handstamped in violet, letters 6½mm high

CLEU37	AP6	5c org yel	12.50	12.50
CLEU38	AP6	10c green	12.50	12.50
CLEU39	AP6	15c carmine	12.50	12.50
CLEU40	AP6	20c gray	12.50	12.50
CLEU41	AP6	30c blue	5.00	5.00
CLEU42	AP6	50c green	10.00	10.00
CLEU43	AP6	60c brown	10.00	10.00
CLEU44	AP7	1p black	20.00	20.00
CLEU45	AP7	2p red org	25.00	25.00
CLEU46	AP7	3p violet	50.00	50.00
CLEU47	AP7	5p ol grn	125.00	87.50
CLEU48	AP6	30c on 20c gray (C)	45.00	22.50
CFLEU2	AP6	20c gray	50.00	50.00

No. C41 handstamped in red, letters 6½mm high

CLEU49	AP6	20c gray	60.00	60.00

Nos. C38//50, CF1 overprinted in black, letters 10mm high

1923, June 4

CLEU50	AP6	5c org yel	4.50	4.50
CLEU51	AP6	10c green	2.00	2.00
CLEU52	AP6	15c carmine	3.00	3.00
CLEU53	AP6	20c gray	6.00	6.00
CLEU54	AP6	30c blue	2.00	2.00
CLEU55	AP6	50c green	5.00	5.00
CLEU56	AP6	60c brown	2.75	2.75
CLEU57	AP7	1p black	6.00	6.00
	a.	Double impression of basic stamp		*1,250.*
CLEU58	AP7	2p red org	17.50	17.50
CLEU59	AP7	3p violet	37.50	40.00
CLEU60	AP7	5p ol grn	55.00	55.00
CFLEU3	AP6	20c gray	12.50	12.50

Nos. CLEU50-CFLEU3 were lithograph overprinted by the Reichsdruckerei Berlin.

Nos. C40, C42 overprinted in black, letters 10mm high

EU

1928, Sept. 25

CLEU61	AP6	15c carmine	15.00	15.00
CLEU62	AP6	30c blue	5.00	5.00
	a.	Inverted overprint	*450.00*	*450.00*
	b.	Double overprint	*500.00*	*500.00*

Nos. CLEU61, CLEU62 were lithograph overprinted by Messrs. Fleming & Benedict for the New York agency. There were two printings of the 30c value, the first generally centered toward the top of the stamp, the second toward the bottom.

ARGENTINA & URUGUAY

Nos. C38//C50, CF1 handstamped in black, letters 5mm high

A-U.

1923

CLAU1	AP6	5c org yel	90.00	*90.00*
CLAU2	AP6	10c green	90.00	*90.00*
CLAU3	AP6	15c carmine	90.00	*90.00*
CLAU4	AP6	20c gray	90.00	*90.00*
CLAU5	AP6	30c blue	75.00	*75.00*
CLAU6	AP6	50c green	90.00	*90.00*
CLAU7	AP6	60c brown	90.00	*90.00*
CLAU8	AP7	1p black	125.00	*150.00*
CLAU9	AP7	2p red org	175.00	*200.00*
CLAU10	AP7	3p violet	400.00	*450.00*
CLAU11	AP7	5p ol grn	450.00	*500.00*

CFLAU1	AP6	20c gray	175.00	200.00

Nos. C38//C50, CF1 handstamped in black, letters 7½mm high

CLAU12	AP6	5c org yel	90.00	90.00
CLAU13	AP6	10c green	90.00	90.00
CLAU14	AP6	15c carmine	90.00	90.00
CLAU15	AP6	20c gray	90.00	90.00
CLAU16	AP6	30c blue	75.00	75.00
CLAU17	AP6	50c green	90.00	90.00
CLAU18	AP6	60c brown	90.00	90.00
CLAU19	AP7	1p black	125.00	150.00
CLAU20	AP7	2p red org	175.00	200.00
CLAU21	AP7	3p violet	400.00	450.00
CLAU22	AP7	5p ol grn	450.00	500.00
CFLAU2	AP6	20c gray	175.00	200.00

BARBADOS

No. C15 with manuscript overprint "G.M. Allayn" in black

1921, November

CLBA1	AP3	30c rose		
		On cover		—

BELGIUM

Nos. C38//50, CF1 overprinted in black, letters 10mm high

1923, Aug. 1

CLB1	AP6	5c org yel	6.00	6.00
CLB2	AP6	10c green	4.00	4.00
CLB3	AP6	15c carmine	6.00	6.00
CLB4	AP6	20c gray	3.50	3.50
CLB5	AP6	30c blue	3.50	3.50
CLB6	AP6	50c green	6.00	6.00
CLB7	AP6	60c brown	6.00	6.00
CLB8	AP7	1p black	15.00	16.00
CLB9	AP7	2p red org	20.00	22.50
CLB10	AP7	3p violet	75.00	80.00
CLB11	AP7	5p ol grn	87.50	90.00
CFLB1	AP6	20c gray, "R" 12mm high	100.00	100.00
a.		Overprint "R" 10mm high	37.50	37.50

Nos. CLB1-CFLB1 were lithograph overprinted by the Reichsdruckerei Berlin.

BOLIVIA

Nos. C38//50, CF1 handstamped in black, letters 6½mm high

1923

CLBO1	AP6	5c org yel	15.00	—
CLBO2	AP6	10c green	15.00	—
CLBO3	AP6	15c carmine	15.00	—
CLBO4	AP6	20c gray	15.00	—
CLBO5	AP6	30c blue	10.00	—
CLBO6	AP6	50c green	20.00	—
CLBO7	AP6	60c brown	30.00	—
CLBO8	AP7	1p black	37.50	—
CLBO9	AP7	2p red org	67.50	—
CLBO10	AP7	3p violet	87.50	—
CLBO11	AP7	5p ol grn	140.00	—
CFLBO1	AP6	20c gray	40.00	—

Nos. CLBO1-CFLBO1 were prepared but not issued. All used examples are either canceled by favor or are forgeries.

BRAZIL

Nos. C38//50, CF1 handstamped in black, letters 9½mm high

Br.

1923

CLBR1	AP6	5c org yel	20.00	20.00
CLBR2	AP6	10c green	20.00	20.00
CLBR3	AP6	15c carmine	20.00	20.00
CLBR4	AP6	20c gray	30.00	30.00
CLBR5	AP6	30c blue	20.00	20.00
CLBR6	AP6	50c green	40.00	40.00
CLBR7	AP6	60c brown	50.00	50.00
CLBR8	AP7	1p black	67.50	67.50
CLBR9	AP7	2p red org	100.00	110.00
CLBR10	AP7	3p violet	175.00	190.00
CLBR11	AP7	5p ol grn	375.00	400.00
CFLBR2	AP6	20c gray	67.50	67.50

Nos. C38//50, CF1 handstamped in black, letters 7mm high

1923

CLBR12	AP6	5c org yel	27.50	27.50
CLBR13	AP6	10c green	27.50	27.50
CLBR14	AP6	15c carmine	27.50	27.50
CLBR15	AP6	20c gray	37.50	37.50
CLBR16	AP6	30c blue	22.50	22.50
CLBR17	AP6	50c green	40.00	40.00
CLBR18	AP6	60c brown	40.00	40.00
CLBR19	AP7	1p black	50.00	55.00
CLBR20	AP7	2p red org	140.00	150.00
CLBR21	AP7	3p violet	225.00	250.00
CLBR22	AP7	5p ol grn	500.00	550.00
CFLBR3	AP6	20c gray	40.00	45.00

CANADA

Nos. C38//50, CF1 handstamped in black, letters 7mm high

1923

CLCA1	AP6	5c org yel	210.00	175.00
		Never hinged	275.00	
		On cover		1,750.
CLCA2	AP6	10c green	210.00	175.00
		Never hinged	275.00	
		On cover		1,750.
a.		Double overprint		750.00
CLCA3	AP6	15c carmine	210.00	150.00
		Never hinged	275.00	
		On cover		5,500.
CLCA4	AP6	20c gray	140.00	110.00
		Never hinged	175.00	
		On cover		—
CLCA5	AP6	30c blue	90.00	75.00
		Never hinged	115.00	
		On cover		1,400.
a.		Double overprint		—
CLCA6	AP6	50c green	210.00	210.00
		Never hinged	275.00	
		On cover		—
a.		Inverted overprint		—
CLCA7	AP6	60c brown	210.00	175.00
		Never hinged	275.00	
		On cover		2,250.
CLCA8	AP7	1p black	210.00	175.00
		Never hinged	275.00	
		On cover		—
CLCA9	AP7	2p red org	210.00	175.00
		Never hinged	275.00	
		On cover		—
CLCA10	AP7	3p violet	550.00	350.00
		Never hinged	700.00	
		On cover		—
CLCA11	AP7	5p ol grn	600.00	450.00
		Never hinged	750.00	
		On cover		—
CFLCA1	AP6	20c gray	700.00	550.00
		Never hinged	875.00	
		On cover		5,500.
a.		With manuscript red "R" overprint		—

On No. CFLCA1, the "R" is machine overprinted, while on No. CFLCA1a it is hand-written. The unique example of No. CFLCA1a is on cover.

CANAL ZONE

No. C42 overprinted "P", 10mm (#CLP60), and handstamped "C.Z." in violet, letters 6mm high

1923

CLCZ1	AP6	30c blue	5,000.	5,000.
		On cover		—

Five examples of No. CLCZ1 are known, three of them on cover. Forgeries exist.

CHILE

Nos. C38//50, CF1 handstamped in black, letters 7mm high

1923

CLCH1	AP6	5c org yel	20.00	20.00
CLCH2	AP6	10c green	20.00	20.00
CLCH3	AP6	15c carmine	20.00	17.50
CLCH4	AP6	20c gray	20.00	20.00
CLCH5	AP6	30c blue	15.00	12.50
CLCH6	AP6	50c green	20.00	20.00
CLCH7	AP6	60c brown	20.00	20.00
CLCH8	AP7	1p black	37.50	37.50
CLCH9	AP7	2p red org	45.00	45.00
CLCH10	AP7	3p violet	87.50	87.50
CLCH11	AP7	5p ol grn	175.00	175.00
CFLCH1	AP6	20c gray	50.00	50.00

COSTA RICA

Nos. C38//50, CF1 handstamped in black, letters 7½mm high

1923

CLCR1	AP6	5c org yel	15.00	15.00
CLCR2	AP6	10c green	15.00	15.00
CLCR3	AP6	15c carmine	20.00	20.00
CLCR4	AP6	20c gray	20.00	20.00
CLCR5	AP6	30c blue	10.00	5.00
CLCR6	AP6	50c green	40.00	40.00
CLCR7	AP6	60c brown	50.00	50.00
CLCR8	AP7	1p black	50.00	50.00
CLCR9	AP7	2p red org	75.00	75.00
CLCR10	AP7	3p violet	100.00	100.00
CLCR11	AP7	5p ol grn	175.00	175.00
CFLCR1	AP6	20c gray	50.00	50.00

CUBA

Nos. C38//50, CF1 handstamped in black, letters 7mm high without period, or 8mm high with period

1923

CLC1	AP6	5c org yel	20.00	20.00
CLC2	AP6	10c green	20.00	20.00
a.		Inverted overprint	—	—
CLC3	AP6	15c carmine	20.00	20.00
CLC4	AP6	20c gray	20.00	20.00
CLC5	AP6	30c blue	10.00	10.00
CLC6	AP6	50c green	30.00	30.00
CLC7	AP6	60c brown	30.00	30.00
CLC8	AP7	1p black	35.00	35.00
CLC9	AP7	2p red org	45.00	50.00
CLC10	AP7	3p violet	90.00	100.00
CLC11	AP7	5p ol grn	175.00	200.00
CFLC1	AP6	20c gray	40.00	45.00

No. C42 handstamped in violet, 8mm high

CLC12	AP6	30c blue	75.00	75.00

DENMARK, NORWAY & SWEDEN

Nos. C38//50, CF1 handstamped in violet, letters 10½mm high

D

1923

CLD1	AP6	5c org yel	62.50	62.50
CLD2	AP6	10c green	62.50	62.50
CLD3	AP6	15c carmine	100.00	100.00
CLD4	AP6	20c gray	62.50	62.50
CLD5	AP6	30c blue	30.00	30.00
CLD6	AP6	50c green	50.00	50.00
CLD7	AP6	60c brown	60.00	60.00
CLD8	AP7	1p black	100.00	100.00
CLD9	AP7	2p red org	120.00	120.00
CLD10	AP7	3p violet	275.00	275.00
CLD11	AP7	5p ol grn	375.00	375.00
CFLD1	AP6	20c gray	75.00	75.00

No. C42 handstamped in black, 10½mm high

CLD12	AP6	30c blue	125.00	125.00

Nos. CLD1-CLD12 were overprinted in Copenhagen.

Nos. C38//50, CF1 handstamped in violet, letters 7 or 8mm high

D

1923

CLD13	AP6	5c org yel	—	—
CLD14	AP6	10c green	—	—
CLD15	AP6	15c carmine	30.00	30.00
CLD16	AP6	20c gray	30.00	30.00
CLD17	AP6	30c blue	32.50	32.50
CLD18	AP6	50c green	62.50	62.50
CLD19	AP6	60c brown	75.00	75.00
CLD20	AP7	1p black	100.00	100.00
CLD21	AP7	2p red org	125.00	140.00
CLD22	AP7	3p violet	210.00	240.00
CLD23	AP7	5p ol grn	250.00	275.00
CFLD2	AP6	20c gray	—	—

Handstamped in Red

CLD24	AP6	5c org yel	30.00	30.00
CLD25	AP6	10c green	40.00	40.00
CLD26	AP6	15c carmine	30.00	30.00
CLD27	AP6	20c gray	40.00	40.00
CLD28	AP6	30c blue	32.50	32.50
CLD29	AP6	50c green	—	—
CLD30	AP6	60c brown	—	—
CLD31	AP7	1p black	—	—
CLD32	AP7	2p red org	—	—
CLD33	AP7	3p violet	—	—
CLD34	AP7	5p ol grn	—	—
CFLD3	AP6	20c gray	82.50	90.00

Nos. CLD13-CFLD3 were overprinted in Barranquilla.

Nos. C38//50, CF1 overprinted in black, letters 10mm high

1927, June 1

CLD35	AP6	5c	org yel	6.00	6.00
CLD36	AP6	10c	green	6.00	6.00
CLD37	AP6	15c	carmine	10.00	10.00
CLD38	AP6	20c	gray	10.00	10.00
CLD39	AP6	30c	blue	6.00	6.00
CLD40	AP6	50c	green	6.00	6.00
CLD41	AP6	60c	brown	10.00	10.00
CLD42	AP7	1p	black	10.00	10.00
CLD43	AP7	2p	red org	40.00	40.00
CLD44	AP7	3p	violet	50.00	50.00
CLD45	AP7	5p	ol grn	87.50	100.00
CFLD4	AP6	20c	gray	17.50	17.50

Nos. CLD35-CFLD4 were lithograph overprinted by the Reichsdruckerei Berlin.

FRANCE

Nos. C25-C35 handstamped in black, letters 8mm high

F

1921-23

CLF1	AP4	5c	org yel	20.00	25.00
CLF2	AP4	10c	sl grn	20.00	25.00
CLF3	AP4	15c	org brn	20.00	25.00
CLF4	AP4	20c	red brown	—	—
CLF5	AP4	30c	green	17.50	22.50
CLF6	AP4	50c	blue	12.50	17.50
CLF7	AP4	60c	vermilion	22.50	25.00
CLF8	AP5	1p	gray black	75.00	35.00
CLF9	AP5	2p	rose	67.50	75.00
CLF10	AP5	3p	violet	75.00	85.00
CLF11	AP5	5p	ol grn	*1,000.*	

Nos. C25-C35 handstamped in red, letters 8mm high
With or without period

1923

CLF12	AP4	5c	org yel	25.00	25.00
CLF13	AP4	10c	sl grn	15.00	15.00
CLF14	AP4	15c	org brn	12.50	12.50
CLF15	AP4	20c	red brown	25.00	25.00
CLF16	AP4	30c	green	30.00	30.00
CLF17	AP4	50c	blue	25.00	25.00
CLF18	AP4	60c	vermilion	40.00	40.00
CLF19	AP5	1p	gray black	20.00	20.00
CLF20	AP5	2p	rose	45.00	50.00
CLF21	AP5	3p	violet	80.00	90.00
CLF22	AP5	5p	ol grn	275.00	300.00

Nos. C25-C35 handstamped in violet, letters 8mm high
With or without period

CLF23	AP4	5c	org yel	300.00	300.00
CLF24	AP4	10c	sl grn	12.50	12.50
CLF25	AP4	15c	org brn	20.00	20.00
CLF26	AP4	20c	red brown	150.00	150.00
CLF27	AP4	30c	green	15.00	15.00
CLF28	AP4	50c	blue	12.50	12.50
CLF29	AP4	60c	vermilion	20.00	20.00
CLF30	AP5	1p	gray black	30.00	30.00
CLF31	AP5	2p	rose	67.50	75.00
CLF32	AP5	3p	violet	87.50	100.00
CLF33	AP5	5p	ol grn	800.00	*1,000.*

No. C29 handstamped in blue, letters 8mm high
With period

CLF34	AP4	30c	green	*100.00*	

Nos. C38//C50, CF1 handstamped in black, letters 6½ or 8mm high
Without period

CLF35	AP6	5c	org yel	15.00	15.00
CLF36	AP6	10c	green	12.50	12.50
CLF37	AP6	15c	carmine	30.00	30.00
CLF38	AP6	20c	gray	12.50	12.50
CLF39	AP6	30c	blue	10.00	10.00
CLF40	AP6	50c	green	12.50	12.50
CLF41	AP6	60c	brown	12.50	12.50
CLF42	AP7	1p	black	20.00	20.00
CLF43	AP7	2p	red org	20.00	25.00
CLF44	AP7	3p	violet	50.00	55.00
CLF45	AP7	5p	ol grn	75.00	85.00
CFLF1	AP6	20c	gray	25.00	27.50

Nos. C38//C50, CF1 handstamped in black, letters 6½ or 8mm high, with period

F.

1923

CLF46	AP6	5c	org yel	—	—
CLF47	AP6	10c	green	*12.50*	*12.50*
CLF48	AP6	15c	carmine	*30.00*	*30.00*
CLF49	AP6	20c	gray	*12.50*	*12.50*
CLF50	AP6	30c	blue	*10.00*	*10.00*
CLF51	AP6	50c	green	*12.50*	*12.50*
CLF52	AP6	60c	brown	*15.00*	*15.00*
CLF53	AP7	1p	black	—	—
CLF54	AP7	2p	red org	*30.00*	*35.00*
CLF55	AP7	3p	violet	*50.00*	*60.00*
CLF56	AP7	5p	ol grn	*90.00*	*100.00*
CFLF2	AP6	20c	gray	*25.00*	*27.50*

Nos. C38//C50, CF1 handstamped in violet, letters 6½ or 8mm high, without period

CLF57	AP6	5c	org yel	12.00	12.00
CLF58	AP6	10c	green	9.00	9.00
CLF59	AP6	15c	carmine	12.00	12.00
CLF60	AP6	20c	gray	9.00	9.00
CLF61	AP6	30c	blue	10.00	10.00
CLF62	AP6	50c	green	20.00	20.00
CLF63	AP6	60c	brown	20.00	20.00
CLF64	AP7	1p	black	20.00	20.00
CLF65	AP7	2p	red org	12.00	14.00
CLF66	AP7	3p	violet	100.00	*110.00*
CLF67	AP7	5p	ol grn	110.00	*120.00*
CFLF3	AP6	20c	gray	25.00	27.50

Nos. C38//C50, CF1 handstamped in violet, letters 6½ or 8mm high, with period

CLF68	AP6	5c	org yel	—	—
CLF69	AP6	10c	green	12.00	12.00
CLF70	AP6	15c	carmine	12.00	12.00
CLF71	AP6	20c	gray	12.00	12.00
CLF72	AP6	30c	blue	10.00	10.00
CLF73	AP6	50c	green	20.00	20.00
CLF74	AP6	60c	brown	20.00	20.00
CLF75	AP7	1p	black	—	—
CLF76	AP7	2p	red org	27.50	27.50
CLF77	AP7	3p	violet	100.00	*110.00*
CLF78	AP7	5p	ol grn	110.00	*120.00*
CFLF4	AP6	20c	gray	25.00	5.00

Nos. C42-C43 handstamped in red, letters 6½ or 8mm high

CLF79	AP6	30c	blue	30.00	30.00
CLF80	AP6	50c	green	37.50	37.50

Nos. C38//50, CF1 overprinted in black, letters 10mm high

1923, June 4

CLF81	AP6	5c	org yel	15.00	17.50
CLF82	AP6	10c	green	10.00	10.00
CLF83	AP6	15c	carmine	7.50	7.50
CLF84	AP6	20c	gray	10.00	10.00
a.			On 20c black	190.00	
CLF85	AP6	30c	blue	6.50	6.50
CLF86	AP6	50c	green	10.00	10.00
CLF87	AP6	60c	brown	10.00	10.00
CLF88	AP7	1p	black	15.00	15.00
CLF89	AP7	2p	red org	30.00	32.50
CLF90	AP7	3p	violet	67.50	75.00
CLF91	AP7	5p	ol grn	87.50	90.00
CFLF5	AP6	20c	gray	30.00	30.00

Nos. CLF81-CFLF5 were lithograph overprinted by the Reichsdruckerei Berlin.

GERMANY, AUSTRIA, CZECHOSLOVAKIA AND, LATER, HUNGARY & YUGOSLAVIA

Nos. C25-C35 handstamped in black or blue-black, letters 20mm high

1921-23

CLA1	AP4	5c	org yel	17.00	20.00
CLA2	AP4	10c	sl grn	10.00	17.50
a.			Overprint inverted	—	
CLA3	AP4	15c	org brn	17.00	15.00
CLA4	AP4	20c	red brown	12.50	17.50
a.			Horizontal pair, imperf vertically	*1,000.*	
b.			Vertical pair, imperf horizontally	—	
CLA5	AP4	30c	green	12.50	11.00
CLA6	AP4	50c	blue	15.00	22.50
CLA7	AP4	60c	vermilion	45.00	50.00
CLA8	AP5	1p	gray black	50.00	55.00
CLA9	AP5	2p	rose	55.00	65.00
CLA10	AP5	3p	violet	100.00	110.00
CLA11	AP5	5p	ol grn	500.00	*600.00*

No. CLA4 overprinted "R" in red

CFLA1	AP4	20c	red brown		*1,250.*

Nos. CLA1-CFLA1 were overprinted in Berlin prior to receipt of overprinted stamps from Barranquilla (Nos. CLA12-CLA22).

Three examples of No. CFLA1 are known. All are used.

Nos. C25-C35 handstamped in violet, letters 6½mm high

A

1921-23

CLA12	AP4	5c	org yel	12.50	—
CLA13	AP4	10c	sl grn	9.00	—
CLA14	AP4	15c	org brn	20.00	—
CLA15	AP4	20c	red brown	12.50	—
CLA16	AP4	30c	green	10.00	12.50
CLA17	AP4	50c	blue	12.50	17.50
CLA18	AP4	60c	vermilion	—	—
CLA19	AP5	1p	gray black	—	—
CLA20	AP5	2p	rose	70.00	75.00
CLA21	AP5	3p	violet	110.00	—
CLA22	AP5	5p	ol grn	500.00	—

Nos. C38//50, CF1 overprinted in black, letters 12mm high

1923, June 4

CLA23	AP6	5c	org yel	5.00	5.50
CLA24	AP6	10c	green	5.00	5.50
a.			Overprint inverted	300.00	
CLA25	AP6	15c	carmine	4.00	4.00
CLA26	AP6	20c	gray	4.00	4.00
CLA27	AP6	30c	blue	1.50	1.50
CLA28	AP6	50c	green	5.00	5.00
CLA29	AP6	60c	brown	5.00	5.00
CLA30	AP7	1p	black	6.00	6.00
CLA31	AP7	2p	red org	17.50	18.00
CLA32	AP7	3p	violet	37.50	37.50
CLA33	AP7	5p	ol grn	67.50	70.00
CFLA2	AP6	20c	gray	5.00	5.50

Nos. CLA23--CFLA2 were lithograph overprinted by the Reichsdruckerei Berlin.

Nos. C38 overprinted in black, letters 10mm high

A

1923 (?)

CLA34	AP6	5c	org yel	—	—

No. CLA34 was a proof, printed by the Reichsdruckerei Berlin, that was later put into service when supplies of No. CLA23 were depleted.

GREAT BRITAIN

Nos. C25-C35 handstamped in violet, letters 6½mm high

1921-23

CLGB1	AP4	5c	org yel	12.50	16.00
CLGB2	AP4	10c	sl grn	10.00	12.50
a.			Pair, one stamp without ovpt.	—	
CLGB3	AP4	15c	org brn	10.00	12.50
a.			Double overprint	—	
CLGB4	AP4	20c	red brown	12.50	16.00
CLGB5	AP4	30c	green	10.00	12.50
a.			Imperf	*200.00*	
CLGB6	AP4	50c	blue	25.00	30.00
CLGB7	AP4	60c	vermilion	—	
CLGB8	AP5	1p	gray black	50.00	55.00
CLGB9	AP5	2p	rose	110.00	125.00
CLGB10	AP5	3p	violet	150.00	175.00
a.			Double overprint		—
CLGB11	AP5	5p	ol grn	400.00	*450.00*

Handstamped in black

CLGB12	AP4	10c	sl grn	20.00	*20.00*
CLGB13	AP4	60c	vermilion	37.50	*37.50*
CLGB14	AP5	1p	gray black	30.00	*55.00*
CLGB15	AP5	2p	rose	175.00	*175.00*
CLGB16	AP5	3p	violet	175.00	*175.00*

Handstamped in red

CLGB17	AP4	50c	blue	*45.00*	*50.00*

Nos. C38//50, CF1 handstamped in black, letters 6mm high

1923

CLGB18	AP6	5c	org yel	15.00	15.00
CLGB19	AP6	10c	green	10.00	10.00
CLGB20	AP6	15c	carmine	10.00	10.00
CLGB21	AP6	20c	gray	10.00	10.00
CLGB22	AP6	30c	blue	5.00	5.00
CLGB23	AP6	50c	green	15.00	15.00
CLGB24	AP6	60c	brown	15.00	15.00
CLGB25	AP7	1p	black	20.00	20.00
CLGB26	AP7	2p	red org	50.00	50.00
CLGB27	AP7	3p	violet	75.00	75.00
CLGB28	AP7	5p	ol grn	125.00	125.00
CFLGB1	AP6	20c	gray	25.00	25.00

Handstamped in violet

CLGB29	AP6	5c	org yel	15.00	15.00
CLGB30	AP6	10c	green	10.00	10.00
CLGB31	AP6	15c	carmine	10.00	10.00
CLGB32	AP6	20c	gray	10.00	10.00
CLGB33	AP6	30c	blue	5.00	5.00
CLGB34	AP6	50c	green	15.00	15.00
CLGB35	AP6	60c	brown	15.00	15.00
CLGB36	AP7	1p	black	17.50	17.50
CLGB37	AP7	2p	red org	50.00	50.00
CLGB38	AP7	3p	violet	75.00	75.00
CLGB39	AP7	5p	ol grn	125.00	140.00
CFLGB2	AP6	20c	gray	17.50	20.00

Handstamped in red

CLGB40	AP6	5c	org yel	15.00	15.00
CLGB41	AP6	10c	green	10.00	10.00
CLGB42	AP6	15c	carmine	15.00	10.00
CLGB43	AP6	20c	gray	15.00	15.00
CLGB44	AP6	30c	blue	10.00	10.00
CLGB45	AP6	50c	green	15.00	11.50
CLGB46	AP6	60c	brown	20.00	20.00
CLGB47	AP7	1p	black	20.00	20.00
CLGB48	AP7	2p	red org	50.00	55.00
CLGB49	AP7	3p	violet	*175.00*	*190.00*
CLGB50	AP7	5p	ol grn	*250.00*	*275.00*
CFLGB3	AP6	20c	gray	25.00	25.00

Nos. C38//50, CF1 overprinted in black, letters 10mm high

1923, June 4

CLGB51	AP6	5c	org yel	20.00	22.50
CLGB52	AP6	10c	green	15.00	18.00
CLGB53	AP6	15c	carmine	15.00	18.00
CLGB54	AP6	20c	gray	15.00	18.00
CLGB55	AP6	30c	blue	8.00	8.00
CLGB56	AP6	50c	green	8.00	8.00
CLGB57	AP6	60c	brown	8.00	8.00
CLGB58	AP7	1p	black	20.00	22.50
a.			Double impression of basic stamp		*1,250.*
CLGB59	AP7	2p	red org	50.00	60.00
CLGB60	AP7	3p	violet	100.00	110.00
CLGB61	AP7	5p	ol grn	150.00	160.00
CFLGB4	AP6	20c	gray	60.00	60.00

Nos. CLGB51--CFLGB4 were lithograph overprinted by the Reichsdruckerei Berlin.

ITALY

Nos. C25-C35 handstamped in red, letter 7½mm high

I

1921-23

CLIT1	AP4	5c	org yel	20.00	20.00
CLIT2	AP4	10c	sl grn	15.00	15.00
CLIT3	AP4	15c	org brn	15.00	15.00
CLIT4	AP4	20c	red brown	20.00	20.00
CLIT5	AP4	30c	green	10.00	10.00
CLIT6	AP4	50c	blue	40.00	40.00
CLIT7	AP4	60c	vermilion	62.50	62.50
CLIT8	AP5	1p	gray black	75.00	75.00
CLIT9	AP5	2p	rose	110.00	125.00
CLIT10	AP5	3p	violet	160.00	175.00
CLIT11	AP5	5p	ol grn	750.00	900.00

Handstamped in violet

CLIT12	AP4	5c	org yel	17.50	17.50
CLIT13	AP4	10c	sl grn	15.00	15.00
CLIT14	AP4	15c	org brn	15.00	15.00
CLIT15	AP4	20c	red brown	25.00	25.00
CLIT16	AP4	30c	green	10.00	10.00
CLIT17	AP4	50c	blue	50.00	50.00
CLIT18	AP4	60c	vermilion	50.00	50.00
CLIT19	AP5	1p	gray black	100.00	100.00
CLIT20	AP5	2p	rose	150.00	175.00
CLIT21	AP5	3p	violet	300.00	350.00
CLIT22	AP5	5p	ol grn	750.00	900.00

Nos. C38//50, CF1 overprinted in black, letter 10mm high

1923, Dec. 11

CLIT23	AP6	5c	org yel	11.00	12.50
CLIT24	AP6	10c	green	5.00	5.50
CLIT25	AP6	15c	carmine	5.00	5.50
CLIT26	AP6	20c	gray	5.00	5.50
CLIT27	AP6	30c	blue	4.00	5.00
a.			Double ovpt., 10mm, 8mm		—
CLIT28	AP6	50c	green	7.50	7.50
CLIT29	AP6	60c	brown	7.50	7.50
CLIT30	AP7	1p	black	15.00	16.00
CLIT31	AP7	2p	red org	20.00	20.00
CLIT32	AP7	3p	violet	50.00	50.00
CLIT33	AP7	5p	ol grn	67.50	75.00
CFLIT1	AP6	20c	gray, "R" 12mm high	17.50	19.00
CFLIT2	AP6	20c	gray, "R" 10mm high	30.00	30.00

Nos. C47-C50 overprinted in black, letter 8mm high

CLIT34	AP7	1p	black	25.00	30.00
CLIT35	AP7	2p	red org	35.00	37.50
CLIT36	AP7	3p	violet	75.00	85.00
CLIT37	AP7	5p	ol grn	100.00	110.00

Nos. CLIT23--CFLIT37 were lithograph overprinted by the Reichsdruckerei Berlin.

MEXICO

The typewritten overprint "De Mexico" is known on postal stationery and reported on stamps of the 1923 issue.

NETHERLANDS & NETHERLANDS ANTILLES

Nos. C25-C35 handstamped in violet, letters 6mm high
With or without period

H.

1921-23

CLH1	AP4	5c	org yel	15.00	16.00
CLH2	AP4	10c	sl grn	15.00	16.00
CLH3	AP4	15c	org brn	15.00	16.00
CLH4	AP4	20c	red brown	20.00	22.50
CLH5	AP4	30c	green	10.00	11.00
CLH6	AP4	50c	blue	30.00	32.50
CLH7	AP4	60c	vermilion, ovpt. with period	37.50	40.00
a.			Overprint without period		—
CLH8	AP5	1p	gray black	110.00	125.00
CLH9	AP5	2p	rose	150.00	175.00
CLH10	AP5	3p	violet	210.00	240.00
CLH11	AP5	5p	ol grn	900.00	

Nos. C38//50, CF1 handstamped in black, letter 6mm high

1923

CLH12	AP6	5c	org yel	30.00	30.00
CLH13	AP6	10c	green	20.00	20.00
CLH14	AP6	15c	carmine	20.00	20.00
CLH15	AP6	20c	gray	32.50	32.50
CLH16	AP6	30c	blue	25.00	25.00
CLH17	AP6	50c	green	25.00	25.00
CLH18	AP6	60c	brown	40.00	40.00
CLH19	AP7	1p	black	50.00	50.00
CLH20	AP7	2p	red org	250.00	275.00
CLH21	AP7	3p	violet	150.00	175.00
CLH22	AP7	5p	ol grn	300.00	325.00
CFLH1	AP6	20c	gray	50.00	50.00

Nos. C38//50, CF1 handstamped in violet, letter 7mm high
Without period

1923

CLH23	AP6	5c	org yel	25.00	25.00
CLH24	AP6	10c	green	20.00	20.00
CLH25	AP6	15c	carmine	20.00	20.00
CLH26	AP6	20c	gray	17.50	17.50
CLH27	AP6	30c	blue	12.50	12.50
CLH28	AP6	50c	green	12.50	12.50
CLH29	AP6	60c	brown	20.00	20.00
CLH30	AP7	1p	black	30.00	30.00
CLH31	AP7	2p	red org	30.00	35.00
CLH32	AP7	3p	violet	50.00	55.00
CLH33	AP7	5p	ol grn	100.00	125.00
CFLH1	AP6	20c	gray	30.00	32.50

Nos. C42, C47 handstamped in red

CLH34	AP6	30c	blue	25.00	25.00
CLH35	AP7	3p	violet	100.00	125.00

Nos. C38//50, CF1 handstamped in black, letter 8mm high

1923

CLH36	AP6	5c	org yel	25.00	25.00
CLH37	AP6	10c	green	20.00	22.50
CLH38	AP6	15c	carmine	20.00	22.50
CLH39	AP6	20c	gray	20.00	22.00
CLH40	AP6	30c	blue	15.00	17.50
CLH41	AP6	50c	green	25.00	27.50
CLH42	AP6	60c	brown	25.00	27.50
CLH43	AP7	1p	black	40.00	45.00
CLH44	AP7	2p	red org	60.00	65.00
CLH45	AP7	3p	violet	90.00	100.00
CLH46	AP7	5p	ol grn	160.00	175.00
CFLH2	AP6	20c	gray	40.00	45.00

Nos. C38//50, CF1 overprinted in black, letter 10mm high

1923

CLH47	AP6	5c	org yel	15.00	17.50
CLH48	AP6	10c	green	6.00	7.00
CLH49	AP6	15c	carmine	6.00	7.00
CLH50	AP6	20c	gray	6.00	7.00
CLH51	AP6	30c	blue	5.00	6.00
CLH52	AP6	50c	green	6.00	7.00
CLH53	AP6	60c	brown	6.00	7.00
CLH54	AP7	1p	black	10.00	12.50
CLH55	AP7	2p	red org	20.00	22.50
CLH56	AP7	3p	violet	45.00	50.00
CLH57	AP7	5p	ol grn	75.00	85.00
CFLH3	AP6	20c	gray, "R" 12mm high	17.50	20.00
a.			"R" 10mm high	37.50	40.00

Nos. CLH47--CFLH3 were lithograph overprinted by the Reichsdruckerei Berlin.

PANAMA & CANAL ZONE

Nos. C25-C35 handstamped in violet, letters 7½mm high

P.

1921-23

CLP1	AP4	5c	org yel	15.00	17.50
CLP2	AP4	10c	sl grn	12.50	15.00
CLP3	AP4	15c	org brn	12.50	15.00
CLP4	AP4	20c	red brown	10.00	12.50
CLP5	AP4	30c	green	10.00	12.50
CLP6	AP4	50c	blue	17.50	20.00
CLP7	AP4	60c	vermilion	20.00	22.50
CLP8	AP5	1p	gray black	50.00	55.00
CLP9	AP5	2p	rose	110.00	125.00
CLP10	AP5	3p	violet	190.00	225.00
CLP11	AP5	5p	ol grn	375.00	400.00

Handstamped in black

CLP12	AP4	5c	org yel	25.00	27.50
CLP13	AP4	10c	sl grn	20.00	22.50
CLP14	AP4	15c	org brn	20.00	22.50
CLP15	AP4	20c	red brown	35.00	40.00
CLP16	AP4	30c	green	30.00	32.50
CLP17	AP4	50c	blue	40.00	45.00
CLP18	AP4	60c	vermilion	25.00	27.50
CLP19	AP5	1p	gray black	80.00	90.00
CLP20	AP5	2p	rose	225.00	250.00
CLP21	AP5	3p	violet	275.00	300.00
CLP22	AP5	5p	ol grn	350.00	400.00

Handstamped in red

CLP23	AP4	5c	org yel	15.00	17.50
CLP24	AP4	10c	sl grn	20.00	22.50
CLP25	AP4	15c	org brn	20.00	22.50
CLP26	AP4	20c	red brown	20.00	22.50
CLP27	AP4	30c	green	10.00	12.50
CLP28	AP4	50c	blue	15.00	17.50
CLP29	AP4	60c	vermilion	25.00	27.50
CLP30	AP5	1p	gray black	40.00	45.00
CLP31	AP5	2p	rose	175.00	190.00
CLP32	AP5	3p	violet	275.00	300.00
CLP33	AP5	5p	ol grn	575.00	650.00

Nos. C38//50, CF1 handstamped in violet, letter 6½mm high

1923

CLP34	AP6	5c	org yel	15.00	17.50
CLP35	AP6	10c	green	15.00	17.50
CLP36	AP6	15c	carmine	10.00	12.50
CLP37	AP6	20c	gray	20.00	20.00
CLP38	AP6	30c	blue	15.00	15.00
CLP39	AP6	50c	green	15.00	17.50
CLP40	AP6	60c	brown	20.00	22.50
CLP41	AP7	1p	black	20.00	22.50
CLP42	AP7	2p	red org	20.00	22.50
CLP43	AP7	3p	violet	50.00	55.00
CLP44	AP7	5p	ol grn	100.00	110.00
CFLP1	AP6	20c	gray	32.50	35.00

Handstamped in red

CLP45	AP6	5c	org yel	25.00	27.50
CLP46	AP6	10c	green	20.00	22.50
CLP47	AP6	15c	carmine	20.00	22.50
CLP48	AP6	20c	gray	20.00	22.50
CLP49	AP6	30c	blue	15.00	17.50
CLP50	AP6	50c	green	50.00	55.00
CLP51	AP6	60c	brown	50.00	55.00
CLP52	AP7	1p	black	70.00	80.00
CLP53	AP7	2p	red org	100.00	120.00
CLP54	AP7	3p	violet	150.00	175.00
CLP55	AP7	5p	ol grn	300.00	375.00
CFLP2	AP6	20c	gray	110.00	125.00

Nos. C38//50, CF1 overprinted in black, letter 10mm high

1923, June 4

CLP56	AP6	5c	org yel	7.50	7.50
CLP57	AP6	10c	green	7.50	7.50
CLP58	AP6	15c	carmine	7.50	7.50
CLP59	AP6	20c	gray	7.50	7.50
CLP60	AP6	30c	blue	2.50	2.50
CLP61	AP6	50c	green	12.50	12.50
CLP62	AP6	60c	brown	7.50	7.50
CLP63	AP7	1p	black	12.50	12.50
CLP64	AP7	2p	red org	17.50	19.00
CLP65	AP7	3p	violet	30.00	35.00
CLP66	AP7	5p	ol grn	55.00	65.00
CFLP3	AP6	20c	gray	10.00	12.50

Nos. CLP56--CFLP3 were lithograph overprinted by the Reichsdruckerei Berlin.

PERU

Nos. C38//50, CF1 handstamped in black, letter 7mm high

1923

CLPE1	AP6	5c	org yel	15.00	15.00
CLPE2	AP6	10c	green	15.00	15.00
CLPE3	AP6	15c	carmine	12.00	12.00
CLPE4	AP6	20c	gray	12.00	12.00
CLPE5	AP6	30c	blue	12.00	12.00
CLPE6	AP6	50c	green	20.00	20.00
CLPE7	AP6	60c	brown	20.00	20.00
CLPE8	AP7	1p	black	30.00	32.50
CLPE9	AP7	2p	red org	90.00	100.00
CLPE10	AP7	3p	violet	90.00	100.00
CLPE11	AP7	5p	ol grn	100.00	125.00
CFLPE1	AP6	20c	gray	22.50	25.00

Nos. C38//47 handstamped in red, letter 6½mm high

1923

CLPE12	AP6	5c	org yel	50.00	55.00
CLPE13	AP6	15c	carmine	40.00	45.00
CLPE14	AP6	20c	gray	45.00	50.00
CLPE15	AP6	50c	green	40.00	45.00
CLPE16	AP6	60c	brown	60.00	65.00
CLPE17	AP7	1p	black	87.50	95.00

SPAIN

Nos. C25-C35 handstamped in violet, letters 6½mm high
Without period, except for 30c

E

1921-23

CLE1	AP4	5c	org yel	14.00	17.50
a.			Pair, one with period, one without		—
CLE2	AP4	10c	sl grn	10.00	12.50
CLE3	AP4	15c	org brn	20.00	22.00
CLE4	AP4	20c	red brown	12.00	12.00
CLE5	AP4	30c	green	12.50	16.00
CLE6	AP4	50c	blue	18.00	22.00
CLE7	AP4	60c	vermilion	37.50	40.00
CLE8	AP5	1p	gray black	50.00	55.00
CLE9	AP5	2p	rose	62.50	70.00
CLE10	AP5	3p	violet	125.00	150.00
CLE11	AP5	5p	ol grn	500.00	600.00

No. CLE1 is unique.

Handstamped in red

CLE12	AP4	5c	org yel	25.00	30.00
CLE13	AP4	10c	sl grn	25.00	30.00
CLE14	AP4	15c	org brn	25.00	30.00
CLE15	AP4	20c	red brown	25.00	30.00
CLE16	AP4	30c	green	25.00	30.00
CLE17	AP4	50c	blue	37.50	45.00
CLE18	AP4	60c	vermilion	40.00	50.00
CLE19	AP5	1p	gray black	62.50	75.00
CLE20	AP5	2p	rose	75.00	85.00
CLE21	AP5	3p	violet	125.00	140.00
CLE22	AP5	5p	ol grn	625.00	750.00

Handstamped in black

CLE23	AP4	5c	org yel	22.50	25.00

Nos. C38//50, CF1 overprinted in black, letter 10mm high

1923, June 4

CLE24	AP6	5c	org yel	15.00	17.50
CLE25	AP6	10c	green	10.00	12.50
CLE26	AP6	15c	carmine	15.00	17.50
a.			Double overprint		—
CLE27	AP6	20c	gray	15.00	17.50
CLE28	AP6	30c	blue	10.00	10.00
CLE29	AP6	50c	green	12.50	14.00
CLE30	AP6	60c	brown	15.00	17.50
CLE31	AP7	1p	black	20.00	22.50
CLE32	AP7	2p	red org	45.00	55.00
CLE33	AP7	3p	violet	62.50	75.00

CLE34	AP7	5p ol grn	80.00	85.00
CFLE1	AP6	20c gray, "R" 12mm high	62.50	75.00
a.		"R" 10mm high	75.00	90.00

Nos. CLE24--CFLE1 were lithograph overprinted by the Reichsdruckerei Berlin.

SWEDEN & NORWAY

Nos. C38//50, CF1 overprinted in black, letter 10mm high

1927, March 10

CLSU1	AP6	5c org yel	10.00	12.00
CLSU2	AP6	10c green	7.50	7.50
CLSU3	AP6	15c carmine	7.50	7.50
CLSU4	AP6	20c gray	10.00	12.00
CLSU5	AP6	30c blue	6.00	6.00
CLSU6	AP6	50c green	7.50	7.50
CLSU7	AP6	60c brown	7.50	7.50
CLSU8	AP7	1p black	10.00	12.00
CLSU9	AP7	2p red org	27.50	30.00
CLSU10	AP7	3p violet	50.00	55.00
CLSU11	AP7	5p ol grn	65.00	70.00
CFLSU1	AP6	20c gray	17.50	17.50

Nos. CLSU1--CFLSU1 were lithograph overprinted by the Reichsdruckerei Berlin.

SWITZERLAND & LIECHTENSTEIN

Nos. C25-C35 handstamped in violet, letters 8mm high
Without period, except for 30c

S

1921-23

CLS1	AP4	5c org yel	15.00	17.50
CLS2	AP4	10c sl grn	15.00	17.50
CLS3	AP4	15c org brn	15.00	17.50
CLS4	AP4	20c red brown	—	—
CLS5	AP4	30c green, ovpt. with period	10.00	12.50
CLS6	AP4	50c blue	22.50	22.50
CLS7	AP4	60c vermilion	37.50	42.50
CLS8	AP5	1p gray black	62.50	70.00
CLS9	AP5	2p rose	62.50	70.00
CLS10	AP5	3p violet	325.00	*375.00*
CLS11	AP5	5p ol grn	450.00	*525.00*

Handstamped in black

CLS12	AP4	60c vermilion	—	—
CLS13	AP5	2p rose	325.00	*375.00*
CLS14	AP5	3p violet	650.00	*750.00*
CLS15	AP5	5p ol grn	—	—

Nos. C38//50, CF1 overprinted in black, letter 10mm high

1924, Jan. 1

CLS16	AP6	5c org yel	10.00	12.00
CLS17	AP6	10c green	6.00	7.50
CLS18	AP6	15c carmine	6.00	7.50
CLS19	AP6	20c gray	6.00	7.50
CLS20	AP6	30c blue	3.00	3.75
CLS21	AP6	50c green	7.50	9.00
CLS22	AP6	60c brown	6.00	7.50
CLS23	AP7	1p black	10.00	12.00
CLS24	AP7	2p red org	30.00	32.50
CLS25	AP7	3p violet	40.00	45.00
CLS26	AP7	5p ol grn	55.00	60.00
CFLS1	AP6	20c gray, "R" 12mm high	10.00	12.50
a.		"R" 10mm high	27.50	30.00

Nos. CLS16--CFLS1 were lithograph overprinted by the Reichsdruckerei Berlin.

VENEZUELA

Nos. C25-C35 handstamped in black, letters 8mm high

V

1921-23

CLV1	AP4	5c org yel	25.00	30.00
CLV2	AP4	10c sl grn	*20.00*	*25.00*
CLV3	AP4	15c org brn	20.00	25.00
CLV4	AP4	20c red brown	20.00	25.00
CLV5	AP4	30c green, ovpt. with period	17.50	20.00
CLV6	AP4	50c blue	*25.00*	*30.00*
CLV7	AP4	60c vermilion	25.00	30.00
CLV8	AP5	1p gray black	*90.00*	*100.00*
CLV9	AP5	2p rose	300.00	*350.00*
CLV10	AP5	3p violet	450.00	*500.00*
CLV11	AP5	5p ol grn	*1,250.*	*1,500.*

Handstamped in violet

CLV12	AP4	5c org yel	20.00	25.00
CLV13	AP4	10c sl grn	20.00	22.50
CLV14	AP4	15c org brn	20.00	22.50
CLV15	AP4	20c red brown	20.00	22.50
CLV16	AP4	30c green, ovpt. with period	22.50	25.00
CLV17	AP4	50c blue	*35.00*	*35.00*
CLV18	AP4	60c vermilion	50.00	50.00
CLV19	AP5	1p gray black	90.00	100.00
CLV20	AP5	2p rose	350.00	*400.00*
CLV21	AP5	3p violet	450.00	*500.00*
CLV22	AP5	5p ol grn	*800.00*	*1,000.*

Handstamped in red

CLV23	AP4	5c org yel	*17.50*	*25.00*
CLV24	AP4	10c sl grn	25.00	27.50
CLV25	AP4	15c org brn	*30.00*	*32.50*
CLV26	AP4	20c red brown	*30.00*	*32.50*
CLV27	AP4	30c green, ovpt. with period	*32.50*	*35.00*
CLV28	AP4	50c blue	35.00	40.00
CLV29	AP4	60c vermilion	*60.00*	*70.00*
CLV30	AP5	1p gray black	140.00	150.00
CLV31	AP5	2p rose	*400.00*	*450.00*
CLV32	AP5	3p violet	650.00	*750.00*
CLV33	AP5	5p ol grn	*1,000.*	*1,200.*

Nos. C38//50, CF1 handstamped in black, letter 8mm high

V

1923

CLV34	AP6	5c org yel	22.50	22.50
CLV35	AP6	10c green	17.50	17.50
CLV36	AP6	15c carmine	17.50	17.50
CLV37	AP6	20c gray	17.50	17.50
CLV38	AP6	30c blue	17.50	17.50
CLV39	AP6	50c green	40.00	40.00
CLV40	AP6	60c brown	40.00	40.00
CLV41	AP7	1p black	70.00	70.00
CLV42	AP7	2p red org	150.00	*175.00*
CLV43	AP7	3p violet	300.00	*350.00*
CLV44	AP7	5p ol grn	300.00	*350.00*
CFLV1	AP6	20c gray	30.00	35.00

Nos. C42//C50 handstamped in violet

CLV45	AP6	30c blue	*45.00*	*45.00*
CLV46	AP6	50c green	40.00	40.00
CLV47	AP7	1p black	50.00	50.00
CLV48	AP7	2p red org	90.00	*100.00*
CLV49	AP7	3p violet	100.00	*125.00*
CLV50	AP7	5p ol grn	125.00	*150.00*

Nos. C44//C48 handstamped in red

CLV51	AP6	50c green	40.00	45.00
CLV52	AP7	1p black	50.00	55.00
CLV53	AP7	2p red org	90.00	*100.00*

No. C42 with blue-black locally handstamp overprint, 12mm high

CLV54	AP6	30c blue		*200.00*

No. CLV54 was used mostly at Puerto Cabello.

Nos. C38//50, CF1 overprinted in black, letter 10mm high

1923, June 4

CLV55	AP6	5c org yel	22.50	22.50
CLV56	AP6	10c green	22.50	22.50
CLV57	AP6	15c carmine	15.00	15.00
CLV58	AP6	20c gray	15.00	15.00
CLV59	AP6	30c blue	15.00	15.00
CLV60	AP6	50c green	15.00	15.00
CLV61	AP6	60c brown	15.00	15.00
CLV62	AP7	1p black	22.50	22.50
CLV63	AP7	2p red org	45.00	52.50
CLV64	AP7	3p violet	85.00	*100.00*
CLV65	AP7	5p ol grn	180.00	*225.00*
CFLV2	AP6	20c gray	26.00	*30.00*

Nos. CLV55--CFLV2 were lithograph overprinted by the Reichsdruckerei Berlin.

SPECIAL DELIVERY STAMP

Special Delivery Messenger — SD1

1917 Unwmk. Engr. *Perf. 14*

E1	SD1	5c gray green	25.00	*75.00*

REGISTRATION STAMPS

R1

R2

1865 Unwmk. Litho. *Imperf.*

F1	R1	5c black	80.00	40.00
F2	R2	5c black	75.00	40.00

R3

R4

1870

White Paper

Vertical Lines in Background

F3	R3	5c black	2.25	1.90
F4	R4	5c black	2.25	1.90

Horizontal Lines in Background

F5	R3	5c black	7.50	6.50
F6	R4	5c black	2.25	1.90
		Nos. F3-F6 (4)	14.25	12.20

Reprints of Nos. F3 to F6 show either crossed lines or traces of lines in background.

R5

R6

1881 ***Imperf.***

F7	R5	10c violet	47.50	40.00
a.		Sewing machine perf.	55.00	47.50
b.		Perf. 11	60.00	50.00

1883 ***Perf. 12, 13½***

F8	R6	10c red, *orange*	1.50	*1.90*

R7

1889-95 ***Perf. 12, 13½***

F9	R7	10c red, *grysh*	5.25	2.50
F10	R7	10c red, *yelsh*	5.25	2.50
F11	R7	10c dp brn, *rose buff* ('95)	1.50	1.25
F12	R7	10c yel brn, *lt buff* ('92)	1.50	1.25
		Nos. F9-F12 (4)	13.50	7.50

Nos. F9-F12 exist imperf. Values same as for perf.

R9

1902 ***Imperf.***

F13	R9	20c red brown, *blue*	1.40	1.40
a.		Sewing machine perf.	3.75	3.75
b.		Perf. 12	3.75	3.75

Medellin Issue

R10

1902 ***Perf. 12***

Laid Paper

F16	R10	10c blk vio	12.50	12.50
a.		Wove paper	17.50	17.50

Regular Issue

1903 ***Imperf.***

F17	R9	20c blue, *blue*	1.40	1.40
a.		Sewing machine perf.	4.00	4.00
b.		Perf. 12	4.00	4.00

R11

1904 Pelure Paper *Imperf.*

F19	R11	10c purple	3.00	3.00
a.		Sewing machine perf.	4.00	3.00
b.		Perf. 12	5.00	4.00

R12

Imprint: "J. L. Arango"

1904 ***Perf. 12***

Wove Paper

F20	R12	10c purple	2.00	.50
a.		Imperf., pair	6.25	6.25

Imprint: "Lit. Nacional"

1909 ***Perf. 10, 14, 10x14, 14x10***

F21	R12	10c purple	2.25	.70
a.		Imperf., pair	5.00	5.00

For overprints see Nos. LF1-LF4.

Execution at Cartagena in 1816 — R13

1910, July 20 **Engr.** ***Perf. 12***

F22	R13	10c red & black	17.50	*75.00*

Centenary of National Independence.

Pier at Puerto Colombia — R14

Tequendama Falls — R15

Perf. 11, 11½, 14, 11½x14

1917, Aug. 25

F23	R14	4c green & ultra	.50	*2.50*
a.		Center inverted	575.00	575.00
F24	R15	10c deep blue	1.90	.60

R16

1925 **Litho.** ***Perf. 10x13½***

F25	R16	(10c) blue	3.50	1.50
a.		Imperf., pair	12.00	10.00
b.		Perf. 13½x10	6.00	4.00

ACKNOWLEDGMENT OF RECEIPT STAMPS

AR1

AR2

1893 **Unwmk.** **Litho.** ***Perf. 13½***

H1	AR1	5c ver, *blue*	4.25	4.25

1894 ***Perf. 12***

H2	AR1	5c vermilion	3.50	*4.00*

1902-03 ***Imperf.***

H3	AR2	10c blue, *blue*	2.75	4.00
a.		10c, blue, *greenish blue*	2.75	4.00
b.		Sewing machine perf.	2.75	4.00
c.		Perf. 12	2.75	4.00

The handstamp "AR" in circle is believed to be a postmark.

AR2a

Purple Handstamp

1903 ***Imperf.***

H4	AR2a	10c black, *pink*	20.00	20.00

AR3

AR4

1904 **Pelure Paper** ***Imperf.***

H12	AR3	5c pale blue	10.50	10.50
a.		Perf. 12	10.50	10.50

No. 307 Overprinted in Black, Green or Violet **A R**

H13	A86	5c carmine	17.50	17.50

1904 ***Perf. 12***

H16	AR4	5c blue	3.25	2.75
a.		Imperf., pair	8.75	8.75

For overprints see Nos. LH1-LH2.

General José Acevedo y Gómez — AR5

1910, July 20 **Engr.**

H17	AR5	5c orange & green	5.75	*16.00*

Centenary of National Independence.

Sabana Station AR6

Map of Colombia AR7

1917 ***Perf. 14***

H18	AR6	4c bister brown	1.75	*2.00*
H19	AR7	5c orange brown	1.50	*1.75*
a.		Imperf., pair	11.00	

LATE FEE STAMPS

LF1

LF2

1886 **Unwmk.** **Litho.** ***Perf. 10½***

I1	LF1	2½c blk, *lilac*	3.25	2.50
a.		Imperf., pair	12.00	12.00

1892 ***Perf. 12, 13½***

I2	LF2	2½c dk bl, *rose*	2.75	2.00
a.		Imperf., pair	12.00	
I3	LF2	2½c ultra, *pink*	2.75	2.00

LF3

LF4

1902 ***Imperf.***

I4	LF3	5c purple, *rose*	.85	.85
a.		Perf. 12	1.75	1.75

1914 ***Perf. 10, 13½***

I6	LF4	2c vio brown	4.00	4.00
I7	LF4	5c blue green	4.00	3.25

Retardo

Retardo
1921

Overprints illustrated above are unauthorized and of private origin.

POSTAGE DUE STAMPS

These are not, strictly speaking, postage due stamps but were issued to cover an additional fee, "Sobreporte," charged on mail to foreign countries with which Colombia had no postal conventions.

D1

D2

D3

1866 **Unwmk.** **Litho.** ***Imperf.***

J1	D1	25c black, *blue*	65.00	45.00
J2	D2	50c black, *yellow*	45.00	*65.00*
J3	D3	1p black, *rose*	140.00	*110.00*
		Nos. J1-J3 (3)	250.00	220.00

DEPARTMENT STAMPS

These stamps are said to be for interior postage, to supersede the separate issues for the various departments.

Regular Issues Handstamped in Black, Violet, Blue or Green — a

On Stamps of 1904

1909 **Unwmk.** ***Perf. 12***

L1	A94	½c yellow	2.00	2.00
a.		Imperf., pair	6.00	6.00
L2	A94	1c yel grn	3.00	2.00
L3	A94	2c red	4.50	3.00
a.		Imperf., pair	12.50	12.50
L4	A94	5c blue	5.00	3.25
L5	A94	10c violet	7.00	7.00
L6	A94	20c black	11.00	10.00
L7	A95	1p brown	18.00	17.00

On Stamp of 1902

L8	A83	10p dk brn, *rose*	20.00	20.00
		Nos. L1-L8 (8)	70.50	64.25

On Stamps of 1908

Perf. 10, 13, 13½ and Compound

L9	A94	½c orange	2.00	2.00
a.		Imperf., pair	6.00	6.00
L10	A94	1c green	4.00	3.25
a.		Without imprint	5.00	5.00
L11	A94	2c red	4.50	3.25
a.		Imperf., pair		
L12	A94	5c blue	4.50	3.25
a.		Imperf., pair	12.50	12.50
L13	A94	10c violet	6.00	6.00

On Tolima Stamp of 1888

Perf. 10½

L14	A23	1p red brn	12.50	12.50
		Nos. L9-L14 (6)	33.50	30.25

Regular Issues Handstamped — b

On Stamps of 1904

Perf. 12

L15	A94	½c yellow	2.00	2.00
L16	A94	1c yellow grn	3.50	3.00
L17	A94	2c red	6.00	5.00
L18	A94	5c blue	6.00	5.00
L19	A94	10c violet	8.00	6.00
L20	A94	20c black	11.00	11.00
L21	A94	1p brown	20.00	20.00
		Nos. L15-L21 (7)	56.50	52.00

On Stamps of 1908

Perf. 10, 13, 13½

L22	A94	½c orange	2.25	2.25
L23	A94	1c yellow grn	6.25	6.25
L24	A94	2c red	5.00	5.00
a.		Imperf., pair	12.50	12.50
L25	A94	5c light blue	6.00	5.00
		Nos. L22-L25 (4)	19.50	18.50

The handstamps on Nos. L1-L25 are, as usual, found inverted and double.

DEPARTMENT REGISTRATION STAMPS

Registration Stamps Handstamped like Nos. L1-L25

On Registration Stamp of 1904

1909 **Unwmk.** ***Perf. 12***

LF1	R12 (a)	10c purple	25.00	25.00
LF2	R12 (b)	10c purple	25.00	25.00

On Registration Stamp of 1909

Perf. 10, 13

LF3	R12 (a)	10c purple	25.00	25.00
LF4	R12 (b)	10c purple	25.00	25.00
		Nos. LF1-LF4 (4)	100.00	100.00

Nos. LF1-LF4 exist imperf. Value per pair, $100.

DEPARTMENT ACKNOWLEDGMENT OF RECEIPT STAMPS

Acknowledgment of Receipt Stamp of 1904 Handstamped like Nos. L1-L25

1909 **Unwmk.** ***Perf. 12***

LH1	AR4 (a)	5c blue	25.00	25.00
a.		Imperf., pair	100.00	
LH2	AR4 (b)	5c blue	25.00	25.00
a.		Imperf., pair	100.00	

LOCAL STAMPS FOR THE CITY OF BOGOTA

A1

Pelure Paper

1889 **Unwmk.** **Litho.** ***Perf. 12***

LX1	A1	½c black	.95	.95
a.		Imperf., pair	6.00	6.00

Impressions on bright blue and blue-gray paper were not regularly issued.

A2

A3

White Wove Paper

1896 ***Perf. 12, 13½***

LX2	A2	½c black	.95	.95

1903 ***Imperf.***

LX3	A3	10c black, *pink*	6.00	1.25
a.		Perf. 12	6.00	1.25

OFFICIAL STAMPS

Stamps of 1917-1937 Overprinted in Black or Red:

a

b

1937 Unwmk. ***Perf. 11, 12, 13½***

O1	A131 (a)	1c green	.20	.20
O2	A157 (a)	10c dp org	.20	.20
O3	A107 (b)	30c olive bis	1.75	1.00
O4	A129 (b)	40c brn & yel brn	1.50	.80
O5	A114 (b)	50c car	1.00	.50
O6	A107 (b)	1p lt bl	5.00	4.00
O7	A107 (b)	2p org	10.00	6.50
O8	A107 (b)	5p gray	37.50	27.50
O9	A118 (b)	10p dk brn	110.00	100.00

Wmk. 229
Perf. 12½

O10	A132 (a)	2c red	.20	.20
O11	A133 (a)	5c brn	.20	.20
O12	A160 (a)	12c dp bl (R)	1.00	.50
O13	A136 (b)	20c dk bl (R)	1.60	.60
		Nos. O1-O13 (13)	170.15	142.20

Tall, wrong font "I's" in OFICIAL exist on all stamps with "a" overprint.

POSTAL TAX STAMPS

"Greatest Mother" PT1

Perf. 11½
1935, May 27 Unwmk. Litho.

RA1	PT1	5c olive blk & scar	2.50	.75

Required on all mail during Red Cross Week in 1935 (May 27-June 3) and in 1936.

Mother and Child — PT2

Perf. 10½, 10½x11
1937, May 24 Unwmk.

RA2	PT2	5c red	1.50	.60

Required on all mail during Red Cross Week. The tax was for the Red Cross.

Ministry of Posts and Telegraphs Building
PT3 PT4

1939-45 Litho. ***Perf. 10½, 12½***

RA3	PT3	¼c dp bl	.20	.20
RA3A	PT3	¼c dk vio brn ('45)	.20	.20
RA4	PT3	½c pink	.20	.20
RA5	PT3	1c violet	.30	.20
RA5A	PT3	1c yel org ('45)	1.50	.60
RA6	PT3	2c pck grn	.40	.20
RA7	PT3	20c lt brn	3.50	1.25
		Nos. RA3-RA7 (7)	6.30	2.85

Obligatory on all mail. The tax was for the construction of the new Communications Building.

The 25c of type PT3 and PT4 were not usable on postal matter.

For overprint see No. 561.

Perf. 12½x13
1940, Jan. 20 Engr. Wmk. 229

RA8	PT4	¼c ultra	.20	.20
RA9	PT4	½c carmine	.20	.20
RA10	PT4	1c violet	.20	.20
RA11	PT4	2c bl grn	.25	.20
RA12	PT4	20c brown	1.00	.20
		Nos. RA8-RA12 (5)	1.85	1.00

See note after No. RA7. See No. RA18.

"Protection" — PT5

1940, Apr. 25 Wmk. 255 ***Perf. 12***

RA13	PT5	5c rose carmine	.25	.20

See No. RA17.

ANTIOQUIA

ˌant-ē-ˈō-kē-ə

Originally a State, now a Department of the Republic of Colombia. Until the revolution of 1885, the separate states making up the United States of Colombia were sovereign governments in their own right. On August 4, 1886, the National Council of Bogotá, composed of two delegates from each state, adopted a new constitution which abolished the sovereign rights of states, which then became departments with governors appointed by the President of the Republic. The nine original states represented at the Bogotá Convention retained some of their previous rights, as management of their own finances, and all issued postage stamps until as late as 1904. For Panama's issues, see Panama Nos. 1-30.

Coat of Arms
A1 A2

A3

A4

Wove Paper

1868 Unwmk. Litho. ***Imperf.***

1	A1	2½c blue	*1,000.*	*750.*
2	A2	5c green	*750.*	*575.*
3	A3	10c lilac	*3,000.*	*1,000.*
4	A4	1p red	*675.*	*750.*

Reprints of Nos. 1, 3 and 4 are on a bluish white paper and all but No. 3 have scratches across the design.

A5

A6

A7

A8

A9

A10

1869

5	A5	2½c blue	3.25	2.75
6	A6	5c green	5.00	4.50
7	A7	5c green	5.00	4.50
8	A8	10c lilac	6.25	3.25
9	A9	20c brown	6.25	3.25
10	A10	1p rose red	12.50	11.00
a.		1p vermilion	25.00	22.50
		Nos. 5-10 (6)	38.25	29.25

Reprints of Nos. 7, 8 and 10 are on a bluish white paper; reprints of Nos. 5 and 10a on white paper. The 10c blue is believed to be a reprint.

A11

A12

A13

A14

A15

A16

A17

A18

1873

12	A11	1c yellow grn	4.50	3.50
a.		1c green	4.50	3.50
13	A12	5c green	7.50	5.50
14	A13	10c lilac	22.50	19.00
15	A14	20c yellow brn	7.50	6.50
a.		20c dark brown	7.50	6.50
16	A15	50c blue	1.75	1.50
17	A16	1p vermilion	3.25	2.75
18	A17	2p black, *yellow*	7.75	7.00
19	A18	5p black, *rose*	55.00	47.50

A19

A20

Liberty Head
A21 A22

Pedro Justo Berrio — A23

1875-85

20	A19	1c blk, *grn*, unglazed ('76)	1.60	1.40
a.		Glazed paper	2.25	1.90
b.		1c blk, *lt grn*, laid paper ('85)	3.75	3.50
21	A19	1c black ('76)	1.10	1.00
a.		Laid paper	140.00	100.00
22	A19	1c bl grn ('85)	2.25	1.90
23	A19	1c red lil, laid paper ('85)	2.25	1.90
24	A20	2½c blue	2.25	1.90
a.		Pelure paper ('78)	*1,500.*	*1,100.*
25	A21	5c green	15.00	12.50
a.		Laid paper	140.00	80.00
26	A22	5c green	15.00	12.50
a.		Laid paper	140.00	80.00
27	A23	10c lilac	22.50	19.00
a.		Laid paper	140.00	110.00
28	A20	10c vio, pelure paper ('78)	*900.00*	675.00

Arms — A24

Liberty — A25

A26

A27

1878-85

29	A24	2½c blue, pelure paper	2.50	2.25
30	A24	2½c green ('83)	2.25	1.90
a.		Laid paper ('83)	70.00	47.50
31	A24	2½c blk, *buff* ('85)	6.25	5.50
32	A25	5c green ('83)	3.75	3.25
a.		Pelure paper	30.00	25.00
b.		Laid paper ('82)	37.50	11.00
33	A25	5c violet ('83)	8.75	6.50
a.		5c blue violet ('83)	8.75	6.50
34	A26	10c vio, laid paper ('82)	160.00	55.00
35	A26	10c scar ('83)	2.25	1.90
a.		Tete beche pair	50.00	45.00
36	A27	20c brown ('83)	3.75	3.25
a.		Laid paper ('82)	5.00	4.50

A28

A29

Liberty — A30

Coat of Arms — A31

1883-85

37	A28	5c brown	4.50	3.00
a.		Laid paper	190.00	75.00
38	A28	5c green ('85)	125.00	40.00
a.		Laid paper ('85)	140.00	65.00
39	A28	5c yel, laid paper ('85)	5.00	4.00
40	A29	10c bl grn, laid paper	5.00	4.50

41	A29	10c bl, *bl* ('85)	5.00	4.00
42	A29	10c lil, laid paper ('85)	9.50	6.50
a.		Wove paper ('85)	100.00	40.00
43	A30	20c bl, laid paper ('85)	4.50	4.00

1886

Wove Paper

55	A31	1c grn, *pink*	.55	.50
56	A31	2½c blk, *orange*	.55	.50
57	A31	5c ultra, *buff*	1.75	1.60
a.		5c blue, *buff*	3.25	2.75
58	A31	10c rose, *buff*	1.60	1.40
a.		Transfer of 50c in stone of 10c	75.00	65.00
59	A31	20c dk vio, *buff*	1.60	1.40
61	A31	50c yel brn, *buff*	2.75	2.50
62	A31	1p yel, *grn*	4.50	4.00
63	A31	2p green, *vio*	4.50	4.00
		Nos. 55-63 (8)	17.80	15.90

1887-88

64	A31	1c red, *vio*	.45	.40
65	A31	2½c lil, *pale lil*	.45	*.55*
66	A31	5c car, *buff*	.60	.55
67	A31	5c red, *grn*	3.25	1.60
68	A31	10c brn, *grn*	.65	*.80*
		Nos. 64-68 (5)	5.40	3.90

Medellin Issue

A32

A33

A34

A35

1888 **Typeset**

69	A32	2½c blk, *yellow*	14.00	12.50
70	A33	5c blk, *yellow*	7.50	6.75
71	A34	5c red, *yellow*	4.50	4.00
		Nos. 69-71 (3)	26.00	23.25

Two varieties of No. 69, six of No. 70 and ten of No. 71.

1889

72	A35	2½c red	7.00	6.00

Ten varieties including "eentavos."

Regular Issue

Coat of Arms
A36 A37

A38

A39

A40

A41

1889 **Litho.** ***Perf. 13½***

73	A36	1c blk, *rose*	.25	.25
74	A36	2½c blk, *blue*	.25	.25
75	A36	5c blk, *yellow*	.30	.30
76	A36	10c blk, *green*	.30	.30
		Nos. 73-76 (4)	1.10	1.10

1890

78	A37	20c blue	1.25	1.25
79	A38	50c vio brn	2.50	2.50
a.		Transfer of 20c in stone of 50c	82.50	82.50
80	A38	50c green	2.00	2.00
81	A39	1p red	1.75	1.75
82	A40	2p blk, *mag*	12.50	12.50
83	A41	5p blk, *org red*	20.00	20.00
		Nos. 78-83 (6)	40.00	40.00

Nos. 73-76, 82-83 exist imperf.

The so-called "errors" of Nos. 73 to 76, printed on paper of wrong colors, are essays or, possibly, reprints. They exist perforated and imperforate.

See No. 96.

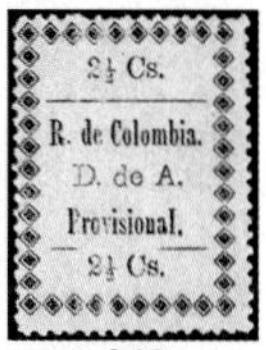
A42

A43

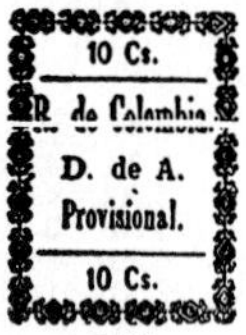
A44

A45

1890 **Typeset** ***Perf. 14***

84	A42	2½c blk, *buff*	2.00	2.00
85	A43	5c blk, *orange*	2.00	2.00
86	A44	10c blk, *buff*	6.00	6.00
87	A44	10c blk, *rose*	7.50	7.50
88	A45	20c blk, *orange*	7.50	7.50
		Nos. 84-88 (5)	25.00	25.00

20 varieties of the 5c, 10 each of the other values.

A46

A47

1892 **Litho.** ***Perf. 13½***

89	A46	1c brn, *brnsh*	.35	.35
90	A46	2½c pur, *lil*	.35	.35
92	A46	5c blk, *gray*	1.00	.50
a.		Transfer of 2½c in stone of 5c	150.00	
		Nos. 89-92 (3)	1.70	1.20

1893

93	A46	1c blue	.25	.25
94	A46	2½c green	.35	.35
95	A46	5c vermilion	.25	.25
96	A36	10c pale brown	.25	.25
		Nos. 93-96 (4)	1.10	1.10

1896 ***Perf. 14***

97	A47	2c gray	.25	.25
98	A47	2c lilac rose	.25	.25
99	A47	2½c brown	.25	.25
100	A47	2½c steel blue	.25	.25
101	A47	3c orange	.25	.25
102	A47	3c olive grn	.25	.25
103	A47	5c green	.25	.25
104	A47	5c yellow buff	.30	.30
105	A47	10c brown vio	.55	.55
106	A47	10c violet	.55	.55
107	A47	20c brown org	1.25	1.25
108	A47	20c blue	1.25	1.25
109	A47	50c gray brn	1.25	1.25
110	A47	50c rose	1.10	1.10
111	A47	1p blue & blk	16.00	16.00
112	A47	1p rose red & blk	16.00	16.00
113	A47	2p orange & blk	47.50	47.50
114	A47	2p dk grn & blk	47.50	47.50
115	A47	5p red vio & blk	82.50	82.50
116	A47	5p purple & blk	82.50	82.50
		Nos. 97-116 (20)	300.00	300.00

#115-116 with centers omitted are proofs.

General José María Córdoba — A48

1899 ***Perf. 11***

117	A48	½c grnsh bl	.20	.20
118	A48	1c slate blue	.20	.20
119	A48	2c slate brown	.20	.20
120	A48	3c red	.20	.20
121	A48	4c bister brown	.20	.20
122	A48	5c green	.20	.20
123	A48	10c scarlet	.20	.20
124	A48	20c gray violet	.20	.20
125	A48	50c olive bister	.20	.20
126	A48	1p greenish blk	.20	.20
127	A48	2p olive gray	.20	.20
		Nos. 117-127 (11)	2.20	2.20

Numerous part-perf. and imperf. varieties of Nos. 117-127 exist.

A49

A50

A50a

1901 **Typeset** ***Perf. 12***

128	A49	1c red	.20	.20
129	A50	1c ultra	.60	.60
130	A50	1c bister	.60	.60
130A	A50a	1c dull red	.60	.60
130B	A50a	1c ultra	4.00	4.00
		Nos. 128-130B (5)	6.00	6.00

Eight varieties of No. 128, four varieties of Nos. 129-130B.

A51

A52

Atanasio Girardot
A53

Dr. José Félix Restrepo
A54

1902 **Litho.** **Wove Paper**

131	A51	1c brt rose	.20	.20
a.		Laid paper	.60	.60
b.		Imperf., pair	2.50	
132	A51	2c blue	.20	.20
a.		Transfer of 3c in stone of 2c	5.00	5.00
133	A51	3c green	.20	.20
a.		Imperf., pair	4.00	
134	A51	4c dull violet	.20	.20
135	A52	5c rose red	.20	.20
136	A53	10c rose lilac	.20	.20
a.		Small head	5.00	5.00
b.		10c rose	.20	.20
137	A53	20c gray green	.20	.20
138	A53	30c brt rose	.20	.20
139	A53	40c blue	.20	.20
140	A53	50c brn, *yel*	.20	.20

Laid Paper

141	A54	1p purple & blk	.70	.70
142	A54	2p rose & blk	.70	.70
143	A54	5p sl bl & blk	1.25	1.25
		Nos. 131-143 (13)	4.65	4.65

1903

Wove Paper

143A	A51	1c blue	.20	.20
144	A51	2c violet	.20	.20
a.		Imperf.	2.50	

A55

A56

A57

Designs: 1p, Francisco Antonio Zea. 2p, Custodio Garcia Rovira. 3p, La Pola (Policarpa Salavarrieta). 4p, J. M. Restrepo. 5p, José Fernández Madrid. 10p, Juan del Corral.

1903-04

145	A55	4c yellow brn	.20	.20
146	A55	5c blue	.20	.20
147	A56	10c yellow	.20	.20
148	A56	20c purple	.20	.20
149	A56	30c brown	.60	.60
150	A56	40c green	.60	.60
151	A56	50c rose	.20	.20
152	A57	1p olive gray	.60	.60
153	A57	2p purple	.60	.60
154	A57	3p dark blue	.60	.60
155	A57	4p dull red	1.00	1.00
156	A57	5p red brown	3.00	1.50
157	A57	10p scarlet	6.50	3.50
		Nos. 145-157 (13)	14.50	10.00

Nos. 145-146, 151, 153-157 exist imperf. Value of pairs, $3 to $4.

Manizales Issue

Stamps of these designs are local private post issues.

OFFICIAL STAMPS Stamps of 1903-04 with overprint "OFICIAL" were never issued.

REGISTRATION STAMPS

R1

1896 **Unwmk.** **Litho.** ***Perf. 14***

F1	R1	2½c rose	1.10	1.10
F2	R1	2½c dull blue	1.10	1.10

Córdoba
R2

R3

R4

1899 *Perf. 11*
F3 R2 2½c dull blue .25 .25
F4 R3 10c red lilac .25 .25

1902 *Perf. 12*
F5 R4 10c purple, *blue* .30 .30
a. Imperf.

ACKNOWLEDGMENT OF RECEIPT STAMPS

AR1

1902-03 Unwmk. Litho. *Perf. 12*
H1 AR1 5c black, *rose* .90 .90
H2 AR1 5c slate ('03) .30 .30

LATE FEE STAMPS

Córdoba — LF1

1899 Unwmk. Litho. *Perf. 11*
I1 LF1 2½c dark green .25 .25
a. Imperf., pair 2.75

LF2

LF3

1901 Typeset *Perf. 12*
I2 LF2 2½c red violet .50 .50
a. 2½c purple .50 .50

1902 **Litho.**
I3 LF3 2½c violet .20 .20

City of Medellin

Stamps of the designs shown were not issued by any governmental agency but by the Sociedad de Mejoras Publicas.

BOLIVAR

bə-ˈlē-ˌvär

Originally a State, now a Department of the Republic of Colombia. (See Antioquia.)

A1

1863-66 Unwmk. Litho. *Imperf.*
1 A1 10c green *1,100.* *550.00*
a. Five stars below shield *2,400.* *2,200.*
2 A1 10c red ('66) 25.00 *27.50*
a. Diagonal half used as 5c on cover 55.00
b. Five stars below shield 75.00 67.50
3 A1 1p red 6.25 *7.25*

Fourteen varieties of each. Counterfeits of Nos. 1 and 1a exist.

Coat of Arms
A2 A3

A4

A5

1873
4 A2 5c blue 7.00 7.00
5 A3 10c violet 7.00 7.00
6 A4 20c yellow green 30.00 30.00
7 A5 80c vermilion 60.00 60.00
Nos. 4-7 (4) 104.00 104.00

A6

A7

A8

Bolívar — A9

1874-78
8 A6 5c blue 25.00 12.50
9 A7 5c blue ('78) 7.75 7.00
10 A8 10c violet ('77) 3.75 3.50
Nos. 8-10 (3) 36.50 23.00

Dated "1879"

1879 White Wove Paper *Perf. 12½*
11 A9 5c blue .25 .25
a. Imperf., pair .80
12 A9 10c violet .20 .20
13 A9 20c red .25 .25
a. 20c green (error) 10.00 10.00

Bluish Laid Paper

15 A9 5c blue .30 .30
a. Imperf., pair 2.00
16 A9 10c violet 1.60 1.60
a. Imperf., pair 4.00
17 A9 20c red .40 .40
a. Imperf., pair 1.75
Nos. 11-17 (6) 3.00 3.00

Stamps of 80c and 1p on white wove paper and 1p on bluish laid paper were prepared but not placed in use.

Dated "1880"

1880 White Wove Paper *Perf. 12½*
19 A9 5c blue .25 .25
a. Imperf., pair 1.60
20 A9 10c violet .35 .35
a. Imperf., pair 1.60
21 A9 20c red .35 .35
a. 20c green (error) 13.00 13.00
23 A9 80c green 2.25 2.25
24 A9 1p orange 2.50 2.50
a. Imperf., pair 5.50
Nos. 19-24 (5) 5.70 5.70

Bluish Laid Paper

25 A9 5c blue .25 .25
a. Imperf., pair 1.25
26 A9 10c violet 2.25 2.25
27 A9 20c red .35 .35
a. Imperf., pair 2.75
28 A9 1p orange 400.00
a. Imperf. *450.00*

A11

A12

A13

A15

A16

Dated "1882"
White Wove Paper

1882 *Perf. 12, 16x12*
29 A11 5c blue .35 .35
30 A12 10c lilac .25 .25
31 A13 20c red .35 .35
33 A15 80c green .65 .65
34 A16 1p orange .65 .65
Nos. 29-34 (5) 2.25 2.25

Nos. 29, 30 and 34 are known imperforate. They are printer's waste and were not issued through post offices.

A17

A18

1882 Engr. *Perf. 12*
35 A17 5p blue & rose red .60 .60
a. Imperf., pair 4.75
b. Perf. 16 7.50 6.25
c. Perf. 14 6.25 6.25
36 A17 10p brown & blue 1.60 1.60
a. Imperf., pair 8.00
b. Perf. 16 7.00 5.50
c. Rouletted 8.00 8.00

Dated "1883"

1883 Litho. *Perf. 12, 16x12*
37 A11 5c blue .20 .20
a. Imperf., pair .80
b. Perf. 12 3.00 1.00
38 A12 10c lilac .25 .25
39 A13 20c red .25 .25
41 A15 80c green .30 .30
42 A16 1p orange .60 .60
a. Perf. 16x12 2.00 2.00
Nos. 37-42 (5) 1.60 1.60

Dated "1884"

1884
43 A11 5c blue .30 .30
a. Perf. 12 10.00 9.25
44 A12 10c lilac .20 .20
45 A13 20c red .20 .20
a. Perf. 12 4.25 4.25
47 A15 80c green .25 .25
a. Perf. 12 2.00 2.00
48 A16 1p orange .30 .30
Nos. 43-48 (5) 1.25 1.25

Dated "1885"

1885
49 A11 5c blue .20 .20
50 A12 10c lilac .20 .20
51 A13 20c red .20 .20
53 A15 80c green .25 .25
54 A16 1p orange .30 .30
Nos. 49-54 (5) 1.15 1.15

The note after No. 34 will also apply to imperforate stamps of the 1884-85 issues.

1891 *Perf. 14*
55 A18 1c black .30 .30
56 A18 5c orange .30 .30
a. Imperf., pair .80
57 A18 10c carmine .30 .30
58 A18 20c blue .60 .60
59 A18 50c green .90 .90
60 A18 1p purple .90 .90
Nos. 55-60 (6) 3.30 3.30

For overprint see Colombia No. 169.

Bolívar
A19

José Fernández Madrid
A20

Manuel Rodriguez Torices
A21

José María García de Toledo
A22

1903 Laid Paper *Imperf.*
62 A19 50c dk bl, *pink* .60 .60
a. Bluish paper .60 .60
63 A19 50c sl grn, *pink* .60 .60
a. Rose paper 2.00 2.00
b. Greenish blue paper 3.00 3.00
c. Yellow paper 4.00 4.00
d. Brown paper 4.00 4.00
e. Salmon paper 7.50 7.50
64 A19 50c pur, *pink* 2.00 2.00
a. White paper 4.00 4.00
b. Brown paper 4.00 4.00
c. Greenish blue paper 4.00 4.00
d. Lilac paper 4.00 4.00
e. Rose paper 3.50 3.50
f. Yellow paper 4.00 4.00
g. Salmon paper 6.00 6.00
h. As "a," wove paper 9.00 9.00
65 A20 1p org, *sal* .60 .60
a. Yellow paper 4.50 4.50
b. Greenish blue paper 15.00 15.00
66 A20 1p gray grn, *lil* 1.40 1.40
a. Yellow paper 6.50 6.50
b. Salmon paper 7.50 7.50
c. Green paper 7.50 7.50
d. White wove paper 10.00
67 A21 5p car rose, *lil* .60 .60
a. Brown paper 1.10 1.10
b. Yellow paper 1.10 1.10
c. Greenish blue paper 4.50 4.50
d. Bluish paper 6.00 6.00
e. Salmon paper 7.50 7.50
f. Rose paper 9.00 9.00
68 A22 10p dk bl, *bluish* 1.25 1.25
a. Greenish blue paper 1.25 1.25
b. Rose paper 7.50 7.50
c. Salmon paper 7.50 7.50
d. Yellow paper 7.50 7.50
e. Brown paper 8.50 8.50
f. Lilac paper 10.00 10.00
g. White paper 9.00 9.00
69 A22 10p pur, *grnsh bl* 3.50 3.50
a. Bluish paper 7.50 7.50
b. Rose paper 6.75 6.75
c. Yellow paper 7.50 7.50
d. Brown paper 7.50 7.50
Nos. 62-69 (8) 10.55 10.55

Sewing Machine Perf.

Laid Paper

70 A19 50c dk bl, *pink* 1.00 1.00
a. Bluish paper 1.00 1.00
71 A19 50c sl grn, *pink* 2.00 2.00
72 A19 50c pur, *grnsh bl* 4.00 4.00
a. White paper 4.00 4.00
b. White wove paper 7.50
73 A20 1p org, *sal* 2.00 2.00
74 A20 1p gray grn, *lil* 9.00 9.00
a. Yellow paper 9.00 9.00
75 A21 5p car rose, *yel* 1.60 1.60
a. Lilac paper 4.00 4.00
b. Brown paper 4.00 4.00
c. Bluish paper 5.50 5.50
d. White wove paper 9.00

76 A22 10p dk bl, *grnsh bl* 4.50 4.50
a. Bluish paper 7.00 7.00
b. Yellow paper 9.00 9.00
c. As "b," wove paper 10.00
77 A22 10p pur, *grnsh bl* 7.00 7.00
a. Bluish paper 11.00 11.00
b. Rose paper 8.00 8.00
c. Yellow paper 11.00 11.00
Nos. 70-77 (8) 31.10 31.10

José María del Castillo y Rada — A23

Manuel Anguiano — A24

Pantaleón C. Ribón — A25

1904 ***Sewing Machine Perf.***
89 A23 5c black .25 .25
90 A24 10c brown .25 .25
91 A25 20c red .30 .30
92 A25 20c red brown .60 .60
Nos. 89-92 (4) 1.40 1.40

Imperf., pairs

89a A23 5c black 3.50 3.50
90a A24 10c brown 2.75 2.75
91a A25 20c red 6.50 6.50
92a A25 20c red brown 6.50 6.50

A26

A27

A28

1904 ***Imperf.***
93 A26 ½c black .65 .65
a. Tête bêche pair 3.50 3.50
94 A27 1c blue 1.10 1.10
95 A28 2c purple 1.25 1.25
Nos. 93-95 (3) 3.00 3.00

REGISTRATION STAMPS

Simón Bolívar
R1 R2

White Wove Paper
Perf. 12½, 16x12

1879 **Unwmk.** **Litho.**
F1 R1 40c brown .70 .70

Bluish Laid Paper

F2 R1 40c brown .70 .70
a. Imperf., pair 3.25

Dated "1880"

1880

White Wove Paper

F3 R1 40c brown .30 .30

Bluish Laid Paper

F4 R1 40c brown .65 .65
a. Imperf., pair 3.50

Dated "1882" to "1885"
White Wove Paper

1882-85 ***Perf. 16x12***
F5 R2 40c brown (1882) .30 .30
F6 R2 40c brown (1883) .25 .25
F7 R2 40c brown (1884) .25 .25
F8 R2 40c brown (1885) .30 .30
Nos. F5-F8 (4) 1.10 1.10

Perf. 12

F5a R2 40c 18.00
F6a R2 40c 9.25
F7a R2 40c 9.50
F8a R2 40c 2.50
Nos. F5a-F8a (4) 39.25

R3

Laid Paper

1903 ***Imperf.***
F9 R3 20c orange, *rose* .60 .60
a. Salmon paper 1.10 1.10
b. Greenish blue paper 6.00 6.00

Sewing Machine Perf.

F10 R3 20c orange, *rose* 2.50 2.50
a. Salmon paper 2.50 2.50
b. Greenish blue paper 6.00 6.00

R4

1904

Wove Paper

F11 R4 5c black 3.25 3.25

ACKNOWLEDGMENT OF RECEIPT STAMPS

AR1

AR2

1903 **Unwmk.** **Litho.** ***Imperf.***

Laid Paper

H1 AR1 20c org, *rose* 2.50 2.50
a. Yellow paper 1.25 1.25
b. Greenish blue paper 5.00 5.00
H2 AR1 20c dk bl, *yel* 2.00 2.00
a. Brown paper 3.50 3.50
b. Rose paper 2.50 2.50
c. Salmon paper 7.00 7.00
d. Greenish blue paper 7.00 7.00

Sewing Machine Perf.

H3 AR1 20c org, *grnsh bl* 6.25 6.25
a. Yellow paper 7.25 7.25
H4 AR1 20c dk bl, *yel* 7.25 7.25
a. Lilac paper 7.25 7.25
Nos. H1-H4 (4) 18.00 18.00

1904

Wove Paper

H5 AR2 2c red 1.10 1.10

LATE FEE STAMPS

LF1

1903 **Unwmk.** **Litho.** ***Imperf.***

Laid Paper

I1 LF1 20c car rose, *bluish* .60 .60
I2 LF1 20c pur, *bluish* .55 .55
a. Rose paper 2.00 2.00
b. Brown paper 2.00 2.00
c. Lilac paper 2.00 2.00
d. Yellow paper 6.25 6.25

Sewing Machine Perf.

I3 LF1 20c car rose, *bluish* 3.50 3.50
I4 LF1 20c pur, *bluish* 3.50 3.50
a. Rose paper 6.00 6.00
b. Lilac paper 6.00 6.00
c. Yellow paper 10.00 10.00
Nos. I1-I4 (4) 8.15 8.15

BOYACA

Originally a State, now a Department of the Republic of Colombia. (See Antioquia.)

Diego Mendoza Pérez — A1

1902 **Unwmk.** **Litho.** ***Perf. 13½***

Wove Paper

1 A1 5c blue green .70 .70
a. Bluish paper 90.00 90.00
b. Imperf., pair 12.50

Laid Paper
Perf. 12

2 A1 5c green 100.00 100.00

Coat of Arms
A2 A3

Gen. Próspero Pinzón — A4

A5

Monument of Battle of Boyacá — A6

President José Manuel Marroquin — A7

1903 **Litho.** ***Imperf.***
4 A2 10c dark gray .25 .25
5 A3 20c red brown .30 .30
6 A5 1p red 3.00 3.00
a. 1p claret 3.50 3.50
8 A6 5p black, *rose* 1.10 1.10
a. 5p black, *buff* 11.00 11.00
9 A7 10p black, *buff* 1.10 1.10
a. 10p black, *rose* 11.00 11.00
b. Tête bêche pair 15.00
Nos. 4-9 (5) 5.75 5.75

Perf. 12

10 A2 10c dark gray .30 .30
11 A3 20c red brown .35 .35
12 A4 50c green .30 .30
13 A4 50c dull blue 2.00 2.00
14 A5 1p red .30 .30
a. 1p claret 3.00 3.00
16 A6 5p black, *rose* 11.00 11.00
a. 5p black, *buff* 9.50 9.50
17 A7 10p black, *buff* 1.10 1.10
a. 10p black, *rose* 11.00 11.00
b. Tête bêche pair 12.00 12.00
Nos. 10-17 (7) 15.35 15.35

Statue of Bolívar — A8

1904
18 A8 10c orange .25 .25
a. Imperf., pair 3.50 3.50

CAUCA

Stamps of these designs were issued by a provincial post between 1879(?) and 1890.

Stamps of this design are believed to be of private origin and without official sanction.

Items inscribed "No hay estampillas" (No stamps available) and others inscribed "Manuel E. Jiménez" are considered by specialists to be receipt labels, not postage stamps.

CUNDINAMARCA

ˌkün-di-nə-ˈmär-kə

Originally a State, now a Department of the Republic of Colombia.
(See Antioquia.)

Coat of Arms
A1 A2

1870 Unwmk. Litho. *Imperf.*

1	A1	5c blue	4.75	4.75
2	A2	10c red	15.00	15.00

The counterfeits, or reprints, show traces of the cuts made to deface the dies.

A3

A4

A5

A6

1877-82

3	A3	10c red ('82)	3.25	3.25
a.		Laid paper ('77)	4.25	4.25
4	A4	20c green ('82)	7.00	7.00
a.		Laid paper ('77)	11.00	11.00
7	A5	50c purple ('82)	7.75	7.75
8	A6	1p brown ('82)	11.00	11.00
		Nos. 3-8 (4)	29.00	29.00

A7

1884

10	A7	5c blue	.75	.75
11	A7	5c blue (redrawn)	.75	.75
a.		Tête bêche pair	75.00	75.00

The redrawn stamp has no period after "COLOMBIA."

A8

A9

A10

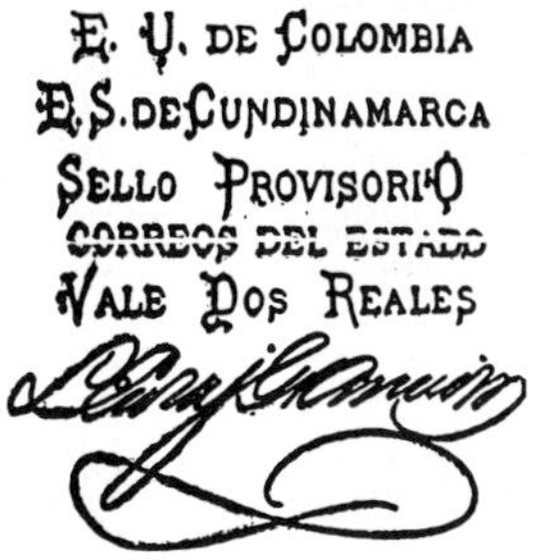

A11

1883 Typeset

13	A8	10c black, *yellow*	12.50	12.50
14	A9	50c black, *rose*	12.50	12.50
15	A10	1p black, *brown*	35.00	35.00
16	A11	2r black, *green*	*2,000.*	

Typeset varieties exist: 4 of the 10c, 2 each of 50c and 1p.

Some experts doubt that No. 16 was issued. The variety without signature and watermarked "flowers" is believed to be a proof. Forgeries exist.

A12

1886 Litho.

17	A12	5c blue	.75	.75
18	A12	10c red	4.50	4.50
19	A12	10c red, *lilac*	2.50	2.50
20	A12	20c green	3.75	3.75
a.		20c yellow green	4.50	4.50
21	A12	50c purple	5.00	5.00
22	A12	1p orange brown	5.25	5.25
		Nos. 17-22 (6)	21.75	21.75

Nos. 17 to 22 have been reprinted. The colors are aniline and differ from those of the original stamps. The impression is coarse and blurred.

A13

A14

A15

A16

A17

A18

A19

A20

A21

1904 *Perf. 10½, 12*

23	A13	1c orange	.25	.25
24	A14	2c gray blue	.25	.25
25	A15	3c rose	.35	.35
26	A15	5c olive grn	.35	.35
27	A16	10c pale brn	.35	.35
28	A17	15c pink	.35	.35
29	A18	20c blue, *grn*	.35	.35
30	A18	20c blue	.60	.60
31	A19	40c blue	.60	.60
32	A19	40c blue, *buff*	17.50	17.50
33	A20	50c red vio	.60	.60
34	A21	1p gray grn	.45	.45
		Nos. 23-34 (12)	22.00	22.00

Imperf

23a	A13	1c orange	.75	.75
24a	A14	2c blue	.75	.75
b.		2c slate	6.00	6.00
25a	A15	3c rose	.90	.90
26a	A15	5c olive green	1.50	1.50
27a	A16	10c pale brown	2.00	2.00
28a	A17	15c pink	.50	.50
29a	A18	20c blue, *green*	2.00	2.00
30a	A18	20c blue	2.00	2.00
31a	A19	40c blue	.70	.70
32a	A19	40c blue, *buff*	17.50	17.50
33a	A20	50c red violet	.70	.70
34a	A21	1p gray green	.70	.70
		Nos. 23a-34a (12)	30.00	30.00

REGISTRATION STAMPS

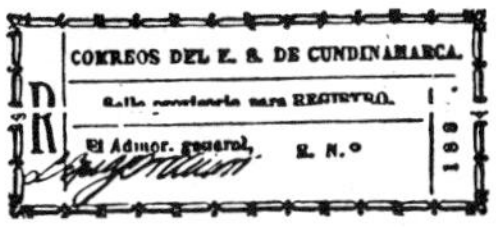

R1

1883 Unwmk. *Imperf.*

F1	R1	black, *orange*	15.00	16.00

R2

1904 *Perf. 12*

F2	R2	10c bister	.80	.80
a.		Imperf.	3.50	3.50

Magdalena

Items inscribed "No hay estampillas" (No stamps available) are considered by specialists to be not postage stamps but receipt labels.

Panama

Issues of Panama as a state and later Department of Colombia are listed with the Republic of Panama issues (Nos. 1-30).

SANTANDER

ˌsän-ˌtän-ˈdeˌəˌr

Originally a State, now a Department of the Republic of Colombia.

(See Antioquia.)

Coat of Arms
A1 A2

1884 Unwmk. Litho. *Imperf.*

1	A1	1c blue	.30	.30
a.		1c gray blue	.50	.50
2	A2	5c red	.50	.50
3	A2	10c bluish purple	1.75	1.75
a.		Tête bêche pair		
		Nos. 1-3 (3)	2.55	2.55

No. 2 exists unofficially perforated 14.

A3

A4

1886 *Imperf.*

4	A3	1c blue	.90	.90
5	A3	5c red	.30	.30
6	A3	10c red violet	.50	.50
a.		10c deep violet	.50	.50
b.		Inscribed "CINCO CENTAVOS"	25.00	25.00
		Nos. 4-6 (3)	1.70	1.70

The numerals in the upper corners are omitted on No. 5, while on No. 6 there are no numerals in the side panels. No. 6 exists unofficially perforated 12.

1887

7	A4	1c blue	.25	.25
a.		1c ultramarine	1.60	1.60
8	A4	5c red	1.60	1.60
9	A4	10c violet	5.00	5.00
		Nos. 7-9 (3)	6.85	6.85

A5

A6

A7

1889 *Perf. 11½ and 13½*

10	A5	1c blue	.30	.30
11	A6	5c red	1.25	1.25
12	A7	10c purple	.45	.45
a.		Imperf., pair	16.00	
		Nos. 10-12 (3)	2.00	2.00

A8

A9

1892 *Perf. 13½*

13	A8	5c red, *rose buff*	1.00	1.00

1895-96

14	A9	5c brown	.70	.70
15	A9	5c yel grn ('96)	.70	.70

A10

A11

A12

1899 *Perf. 10*

16	A10	1c black, *green*	.35	.35
17	A11	5c black, *pink*	.35	.35

Perf. 13½

18	A12	10c blue	.70	.70
a.		Perf. 12	1.00	1.00
		Nos. 16-18 (3)	1.40	1.40

A13

1903 ***Imperf.***

19	A13	50c red	.55	.55
a.		50c rose	.55	.55
b.		"SANTENDER"	2.50	2.50
c.		"Corrcos"	2.50	2.50
d.		"Corceos"	2.50	2.50
e.		Tête bêche pair	4.75	4.75
f.		Pair, one without overprint	2.75	2.75

The overprint "Correos de Departmento Bucaramanga" on the 50c red revenue stamp has been proved to be a cancellation.

A14

A15

Arms A16

Locomotive A17

A18

A19

A20

1904 ***Imperf.***

22	A14	5c dark green	.25	.25
a.		5c yellow green	.40	.40
24	A15	10c rose	.20	.20
25	A16	20c brown violet	.20	.20
26	A17	50c yellow	.20	.20
27	A18	1p black	.20	.20
28	A19	5p dark blue	.35	.35
29	A20	10p carmine	.40	.40
		Nos. 22-29 (7)	1.80	1.80

1905

30	A14	5c pale blue	.40	.40
31	A15	10c red brown	.40	.40
32	A16	20c yellow green	.40	.40
33	A17	50c red violet	.60	.60
34	A18	1p dark blue	.60	.60
35	A19	5p pink	.60	.60
36	A20	10p red	1.60	1.60
		Nos. 30-36 (7)	4.60	4.60

A21

1907 ***Imperf.***

37	A21	½c on 50c rose	.55	.55

City of Cucuta

Stamps of these and similar designs on white and yellow paper, with and without surcharges of ½c, 1c or 2c, are believed to have been produced without government authorization.

TOLIMA

tə-lē-mə

Originally a State, now a Department of the Republic of Colombia.
(See Antioquia.)

A1

1870 **Unwmk.** **Typeset** ***Imperf.***

White Wove Paper

1	A1	5c black	50.00	50.00
2	A1	10c black	75.00	75.00
a.		Vert. se-tenant pair	1,500.	1,500.

Printed from two settings. Setting I, ten types of 5c. Setting II, six types of 5c and four types of 10c.

Blue Laid Batonné Paper

3	A1	5c black	*950.00*	

Buff Laid Batonné Paper

4	A1	5c black	150.00	100.00

Blue Wove Paper

5	A1	5c black	70.00	45.00

Blue Vertically Laid Paper

6	A1	5c black	110.00	70.00
a.		Paper with ruled blue vertical lines		

Blue Horizontally Laid Paper

7	A1	5c black	100.00	75.00

Blue Quadrille Paper

8	A1	5c black	200.00	75.00

Ten varieties each of Nos. 3-5 and 7; 20 varieties each of Nos. 6 and 8.

Official imitations were made in 1886 from new settings of the type. There are only 2 varieties of each value. They are printed on blue and white paper, wove, batonné, laid, etc.

A2

A3

A4

A5

Yellowish White Wove Paper

1871 **Litho.** ***Imperf.***

9	A2	5c deep brown	2.25	2.25
a.		5c red brown	2.25	2.25
b.		Value reads "CINGO"	37.50	37.50
10	A3	10c blue	6.00	6.00
11	A4	50c green	7.75	7.75
12	A5	1p carmine	12.00	12.00
		Nos. 9-12 (4)	28.00	28.00

The 5p stamps, type A2, are bogus varieties made from an altered die of the 5c.

The 10c, 50c and 1 peso stamps have been reprinted on bluish white wove paper. They are from new plates and most copies show traces of fine lines with which the dies had been defaced. Reprints of the 5c have a large cross at the top. The 10c on laid batonné paper is known only as a reprint.

A6

A7

A8

A9

1879

Grayish or White Wove Paper

14	A6	5c yellow brown	.45	.45
a.		5c purple brown	.45	.45
15	A7	10c blue	.50	.50
16	A8	50c green, *bluish*	.50	.50
a.		White paper	1.60	1.60
17	A9	1p vermilion	2.25	2.25
a.		1p carmine rose	9.00	9.00
		Nos. 14-17 (4)	3.70	3.70

A10

Coat of Arms — A12

1883 ***Imperf.***

18	A6	5c orange	.45	.45
19	A7	10c vermilion	.90	.90
20	A10	20c violet	1.40	1.40
		Nos. 18-20 (3)	2.75	2.75

1884 ***Imperf.***

23	A12	1c gray	.20	.20
24	A12	2c rose lilac	.20	.20
a.		2c slate	.20	.20
25	A12	2½c dull orange	.20	.20
26	A12	5c brown	.20	.20
27	A12	10c blue	.35	.35
a.		10c slate	.25	.25
28	A12	20c lemon	.35	.35
a.		Laid paper	5.00	5.00
29	A12	25c black	.30	.30
30	A12	50c green	.30	.30
31	A12	1p vermilion	.40	.40
32	A12	2p violet	.60	.60
a.		Value omitted	27.50	27.50
33	A12	5p yellow	.40	.40
34	A12	10p lilac rose	1.10	1.10
a.		Laid paper	30.00	30.00
b.		10p gray	*160.00*	
		Nos. 23-34 (12)	4.60	4.60

A13

A14

Condor with Long Wings Touching Flagstaffs
A15 A16

1886 **Litho.** ***Perf. 10½, 11***

White Paper

36	A13	5c brown	1.25	1.25
a.		5c yellow brown	1.25	1.25
b.		Imperf., pair	16.00	
37	A14	10c blue	3.50	3.50
a.		Imperf., pair	16.00	
38	A15	50c green	3.00	3.00
a.		Imperf., pair	16.00	
39	A16	1p vermilion	2.50	2.50
a.		Imperf., pair	24.00	
		Nos. 36-39 (4)	10.25	10.25

No. 38 has been reprinted in pale gray green, perforated 10½, and No. 39 in bright vermilion, perforated 11½. The impressions show many signs of wear.

Lilac Tinted Paper

36c	A13	5c orange brown	12.00	12.00
37b	A14	10c blue	12.00	12.00
38b	A15	50c green	9.00	9.00
39b	A16	1p vermilion	8.00	8.00
		Nos. 36c-39b (4)	41.00	41.00

Items similar to A15 and A16 but with condor with long wings and upper flagstaffs omitted are forgeries.

A17

A18

Condor with Short Wings
A19 A20

1886 **White Paper** ***Perf. 12***

44	A19	1c gray	6.25	6.25
45	A17	2c rose lilac	6.50	6.50
46	A18	2½c dull org	19.00	19.00
47	A19	5c brown	8.50	8.00
48	A20	10c blue	8.00	8.00
49	A20	20c lemon	6.50	6.50
a.		Tête bêche pair	225.00	225.00
50	A20	25c black	6.25	6.25
51	A20	50c green	3.50	3.00
52	A20	1p vermilion	5.00	4.25
53	A20	2p violet	7.25	7.25
b.		Tête bêche pair	175.00	175.00
54	A20	5p orange	13.00	13.00
55	A20	10p lilac rose	7.25	7.25
		Nos. 44-55 (12)	97.00	95.25

Imperf., Pairs

44a	A19	1c	16.00	
47a	A19	5c	27.50	
48a	A20	10c	27.50	
52a	A20	1p	20.00	
53a	A20	2p	25.00	
54a	A20	5p	32.50	
55a	A20	10p	16.00	

A23

1888 ***Perf. 10½***

62	A23	5c red	.20	.20
63	A23	10c green	.30	.30
64	A23	50c blue	.75	.75
65	A23	1p red brown	1.75	1.75
		Nos. 62-65 (4)	3.00	3.00

For overprint see Colombia No. L14.

1895 ***Perf. 12, 13½***

66	A23	1c blue, *rose*	.25	.25
67	A23	2c grn, *lt grn*	.25	.25
68	A23	5c red	.20	.20
69	A23	10c green	.50	.50
70	A23	20c blue, *yellow*	.30	.30
71	A23	1p brown	2.00	2.00
		Nos. 66-71 (6)	3.50	3.50

Imperf., Pairs

62a	A23	5c	2.75	
63a	A23	10c	3.25	
64a	A23	50c	4.75	4.75
65a	A23	1p	7.25	
66a	A23	1c	7.25	
67a	A23	2c	7.25	
70a	A23	20c	8.00	

"No Hay Estampillas"

Items inscribed "No hay estampillas" (No stamps available) are considered by specialists to be not postage stamps but receipt labels.

"Honda Issue"

This item seems to be of private origin.

A24

A25

A26

A27

A28

A29

A30

A31

Sewing Machine or Regular Perf. 12

1903-04 **Litho.**

79	A24	4c black, *green*	.25	.25
80	A25	10c dull blue	.25	.25
81	A26	20c orange	.50	.50
82	A27	50c black, *rose*	.25	.25
a.		50c black, *buff*	.20	.20
84	A28	1p brown	.20	.20
85	A29	2p gray	.20	.20
86	A30	5p red	.20	.20
a.		Tête bêche pair	5.00	5.00
87	A31	10p black, *blue*	.25	.25
a.		10p black, *light green*	.25	.25
b.		10p black, *grn*, glazed	3.50	3.50
		Nos. 79-87 (8)	2.10	2.10

Imperf

79a	A24	4c black, *green*	.25	.25
80a	A25	10c dull blue	.20	.20
81a	A26	20c orange	1.10	1.10
82b	A27	50c black, *rose*	1.50	1.50
c.		50c black, *buff*	1.50	1.50
84a	A28	1p brown	.20	.20
85a	A29	2p gray	.25	.25
86b	A30	5p red	.25	.25
c.		Tête bêche pair	5.00	5.00
87c	A31	10p black, *blue*	2.25	2.25
d.		Tête bêche pair		
e.		10p black, *light green*	3.50	3.50
f.		10p black, *green*, glazed	18.00	18.00
		Nos. 79a-87c (8)	6.00	6.00

COOK ISLANDS

'kuk 'ī-lənds

(Rarotonga)

LOCATION — South Pacific Ocean, northeast of New Zealand
GOVT. — Dependency of New Zealand
AREA — 117 sq. mi.
POP. — 17,754 (1981)
CAPITAL — Rarotonga

Fifteen islands in Northern and Southern groups extend over 850,000 square miles of ocean.

Separate stamp issues used by Aitutaki (1903-32) and Penrhyn Islands (1902-32). Niue is included geographically, but administered separately. It issues separate stamps.

12 Pence = 1 Shilling
20 Shillings = 1 Pound

Catalogue values for unused stamps in this country are for Never Hinged items, beginning with Scott 127 in the regular postage section.

Watermarks

Wmk. 61 — Single-lined N Z and Star Close Together

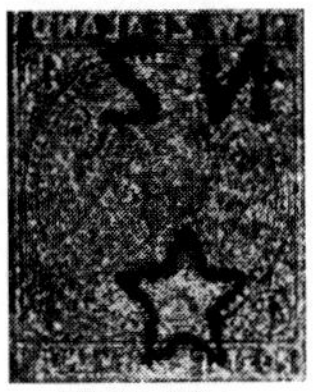
Wmk. 62 — Single-lined N Z and Star Wide Apart

A1

1892 Unwmk. Typo. *Perf. 12½*

Toned Paper

1	A1	1p black	32.50	30.00
2	A1	1½p violet	47.50	45.00
a.		1½p imperf, pair violet	*10,500.*	
3	A1	2½p blue	47.50	45.00
4	A1	10p carmine	160.00	150.00
		Nos. 1-4 (4)	287.50	270.00

White Paper

5	A1	1p black	32.50	30.00
a.		Vert. pair, imperf. between	*9,750.*	
6	A1	1½p violet	47.50	45.00
7	A1	2½p blue	47.50	45.00
8	A1	10p carmine	160.00	150.00
		Nos. 5-8 (4)	287.50	270.00

Nos. 1-8 were printed in sheets of 60 (6x10), from a setting of six slightly different cliches.

Queen Makea Takau — A2

Wrybill (Torea) — A3

1893-94 Wmk. 62 *Perf. 12x11½*

9	A2	1p brown	47.50	*52.50*
10	A2	1p blue ('94)	10.50	2.50
a.		Perf. 12½ with 12x11½	—	1,350.
11	A2	1½p brt violet	9.75	7.50
12	A2	2½p rose	45.00	*27.50*
a.		Perf. 12½ with 12x11½	2,100.	—
b.		2½p rose carmine	70.00	55.00
13	A2	5p olive gray	20.00	15.00
14	A2	10p green	80.00	*55.00*
		Nos. 9-14 (6)	212.75	*160.00*

1898-1900 *Perf. 11*

15	A3	½p blue ('00)	5.25	*7.00*
a.		"d" omitted at upper right	*1,750.*	
b.		½p steel blue (1st setting)	37.50	*52.50*
c.		½p steel blue (2nd setting)	23.00	*25.00*
16	A2	1p brown	19.00	*19.00*
a.		1p bistre brown ('00)	22.00	*24.00*
17	A2	1p blue	5.75	5.25
18	A2	1½p violet	10.50	7.50
a.		1½p deep mauve ('00)	10.50	7.50
19	A3	2p chocolate	8.00	7.50
a.		2p brown, thin toned paper	12.50	7.50
20	A2	2½p car rose	19.00	10.50
a.		2½p pale rose	55.00	45.00
21	A2	5p olive gray	27.50	20.00
22	A3	6p red violet	22.50	*27.50*
a.		6p purple, thin toned paper	29.00	*32.50*
23	A2	10p green	26.00	*45.00*
24	A3	1sh car rose	55.00	55.00
a.		1sh red, thin toned paper	70.00	*80.00*
		Nos. 15-24 (10)	198.50	*204.25*

The first setting of No. 15 is distinguished by the misplacement of the "½d" in each corner. In the second setting, these values are correctly positioned.

No. 17 Surcharged in Black

1899

25	A2	½p on 1p blue	40.00	*50.00*
a.		Double surcharge	1,000.	*1,050.*
b.		Inverted surcharge	1,200.	1,000.

No. 16 Overprinted in Black

1901

26	A2	1p brown	210.00	160.00
a.		Inverted overprint	2,100.	1,650.
c.		Double overprint	1,850.	*1,900.*

Some single stamps were overprinted by favor. Other varieties could exist.

Types of 1893-98

1902 Unwmk.

27	A3	½p green	5.00	*5.00*
a.		Vert. pair, imperf. horiz.	*1,400.*	
b.		½p blue green	7.50	*8.25*
28	A2	1p rose	14.00	*12.50*
a.		1p rose lake	12.50	7.50
29	A2	2½p dull blue	15.00	*24.00*
		Nos. 27-29 (3)	34.00	*41.50*

1902 Wmk. 61 *Perf. 11*

30	A3	½p green	3.25	*3.75*
a.		½p gray green	22.50	*55.00*
31	A2	1p rose	4.75	*3.50*
32	A2	1½p brt violet	4.75	*10.00*
33	A3	2p chocolate	5.75	*11.50*
a.		Figures of value omitted	*2,750.*	*3,250.*
b.		Perf. 11x14	*1,750.*	
34	A2	2½p dull blue	4.50	*8.00*
35	A2	5p olive gray	40.00	*55.00*
36	A3	6p purple	37.50	*32.50*
37	A2	10p blue green	55.00	*110.00*
38	A3	1sh car rose	55.00	*80.00*
a.		Perf. 11x14	*1,950.*	
		Nos. 30-38 (9)	210.50	*314.25*

1909-19 *Perf. 14, 14x14½, 14½x14*

39	A3	½p green, perf 14½x14 ('11)	7.00	*9.25*
a.		½p dp grn, perf 14 ('15)	5.50	*17.50*
b.		As "a," wmk upright	7.00	*12.50*
40	A2	1p red, wmk. sideways ('09)	10.00	9.00
a.		1p red, wmk. upright, perf 14	40.00	35.00
b.		1p red, chalky paper, perf 14	5.75	5.00
c.		1p red, chalky paper, perf 14x14½	6.50	*7.00*
41	A2	1½p purple, perf 14x15 ('16)	10.00	4.75
a.		1½p purple, perf 14 ('15)	87.50	47.50
42	A3	2p dp brown ('19)	5.75	*52.50*
43	A2	10p dp green ('18)	19.00	*100.00*
44	A3	1sh car rose ('19)	32.50	*100.00*
		Nos. 39-44 (6)	84.25	*275.50*

Nos. 39-40 are on both ordinary and chalky paper; Nos. 41-44 on chalky paper.

New Zealand Stamps of 1909-19 Surcharged in Dark Blue or Red

1919 Typo. *Perf. 14x15*

48	A43	½p yel green (R)	.45	*1.25*
a.		Pair, one without surcharge		
49	A42	1p carmine	1.25	*3.50*
50	A47	1½p brown org (R)	.60	*.90*
51	A43	2p yellow (R)	1.75	*2.00*
52	A43	3p chocolate	3.25	*15.00*

Engr. *Perf. 14x14½*

53	A44	2½p dull blue (R)	2.25	*2.75*
a.		Perf 14x13½	2.75	*7.50*
54	A45	3p violet brown	2.75	2.25
a.		Perf 14x13½	2.25	*9.50*
55	A45	4p purple	2.00	*5.00*
a.		Perf 14x13½	2.25	*6.50*
56	A44	4½p dark green	2.00	*9.50*
a.		Perf 14x13½	2.25	*8.00*
57	A45	6p car rose	2.00	*6.50*
a.		Perf 14x13½	3.50	*10.00*
58	A44	7½p red brown, perf 14x13½	1.75	*6.50*
59	A45	9p ol green (R)	2.25	*17.50*
a.		Perf 14x13½	3.75	*17.50*
60	A45	1sh vermilion	3.25	*21.00*
a.		Perf 14x13½	13.00	*35.00*
		Nos. 48-60 (13)	25.55	*93.65*

Vertical Pairs, Perf 14x14½ and 14x13½

53b	#53 + #53a	23.00	*52.50*
	Block of four, never hinged	65.00	
54b	#54 + #54a	25.00	*57.50*
	Block of four, never hinged	77.50	
55b	#55 + #55a	23.00	*65.00*
	Block of four, never hinged	67.50	
56b	#56 + #56a	23.00	*75.00*
	Block of four, never hinged	67.50	
57b	#57 + #57a	45.00	*100.00*
	Block of four, never hinged	140.00	
59b	#59 + #59a	45.00	*125.00*
	Block of four, never hinged	140.00	
60b	#60 + #60a	55.00	*140.00*
	Block of four, never hinged	175.00	

The Polynesian surcharge restates the denomination of the basic stamp.

Landing of Capt. Cook A4

Avarua Waterfront A5

Capt. James Cook — A6

Palm — A7

Houses at Arorangi — A8

Avarua Harbor — A9

1920 Unwmk. Engr. *Perf. 14*

61	A4	½p green & black	4.50	*21.00*
62	A5	1p car & black	5.50	*21.00*
a.		Center inverted	*550.00*	
63	A6	1½p blue & black	9.75	9.75
64	A7	3p red brn & blk	2.50	*6.25*
65	A8	6p org & red brn	3.50	*9.75*
66	A9	1sh vio & black	5.75	*20.00*
		Nos. 61-66 (6)	31.50	*87.75*

The stamps overprinted or inscribed "Rarotonga" were used throughout the Cook Islands.

For surcharges see Nos. 78, 79.

New Zealand Postal-Fiscal Stamps of 1906-13 Overprinted in Red or Dark Blue

a

Perf. 14, 14½, 14x14½

1921 Typo. Wmk. 61

67	PF1 2sh blue (R)	30.00	*62.50*
68	PF1 2sh6p brown	22.50	*60.00*
69	PF1 5sh green (R)	30.00	*75.00*
70	PF1 10sh claret	75.00	*110.00*
71	PF2 £1 rose	100.00	*210.00*
	Nos. 67-71 (5)	257.50	*517.50*

Types of 1920 Issue

1924-26 Engr. *Perf. 14*

72	A4 ½p yel grn & black	3.50	5.00
73	A5 1p carmine & black	7.00	2.50

Issued: ½p, May 13, 1926; 1p, Nov. 10, 1924.

New Zealand Stamps of 1926 Overprinted Type "a" in Red

1926-28 Typo. *Perf. 14, 14½x14*

74	A56 2sh blue ('27)	17.50	*45.00*
a.	2sh dark blue	11.50	*45.00*
75	A56 3sh violet ('28)	18.00	*47.50*

Rarotongan Chief (Te Po) — A10

Avarua Harbor — A11

1927, Oct. 15 Engr. *Perf. 14*

76	A10 2½p dk bl & red brn	5.75	*27.50*
77	A11 4p dull vio & bl grn	9.00	*20.00*

No. 63 Surcharged in Red

1931 Unwmk.

78	A6 2p on 1½p blue & blk	10.50	3.00

Same Surcharge on Type of 1920

Wmk. 61

79	A6 2p on 1½p blue & blk	5.25	*12.50*

No. 79 was not issued without surcharge.

New Zealand Postal-Fiscal Stamps of 1931-32 Overprinted Type "a" in Blue or Red

1931, Nov. 12 Typo.

80	PF5 2sh6p dp brown (Bl)	11.50	*25.00*
81	PF5 5sh green (R)	21.00	*62.50*
82	PF5 10sh dk car (Bl)	42.50	*110.00*
83	PF5 £1 pink (Bl) ('32)	100.00	*175.00*
	Nos. 80-83 (4)	175.00	*372.50*

See Nos. 103-108, 124A-126C.

Landing of Capt. Cook — A12

Capt. James Cook — A13

Double Canoe — A14

Islanders Unloading Ship — A15

View of Avarua Harbor — A16

R.M.S. Monowai — A17

King George V — A18

Unwmk.

1932, Mar. 16 Engr. *Perf. 13*

Center in Black

84	A12 ½p deep green	4.00	*18.00*
a.	Perf. 14	32.50	*100.00*
85	A13 1p brown lake	7.50	*5.00*
a.	Center inverted	8,500.	*8,500.*
b.	Perf. 14	17.50	*24.00*
86	A14 2p brown	3.50	*6.25*
b.	Perf. 14	10.00	*22.50*
87	A15 2½p dark ultra	12.50	*57.50*
b.	Perf. 14	16.00	*57.50*

Perf. 14

88	A16 4p ultra	17.50	*57.50*
a.	Perf. 13	22.50	*70.00*
b.	Perf. 14x13	35.00	*110.00*
89	A17 6p orange	5.00	*17.50*
a.	Perf. 13	27.50	*55.00*
90	A18 1sh deep violet	9.75	*25.00*
	Nos. 84-90 (7)	59.75	*186.75*

Nos. 84 to 90 were available for postage in Aitutaki, Penrhyn and Rarotonga and replaced the special issues for those islands.

Inverted centers of the 1p and 2p are from printers waste.

1933-36 Wmk. 61 *Perf. 14*

91	A12 ½p dp grn & blk	1.10	*5.00*
92	A13 1p dk car & black ('35)	1.40	*2.25*
93	A14 2p brn & blk ('36)	1.75	.60
94	A15 2½p dk ultra & blk	1.75	*2.50*
95	A16 4p blue & black	1.75	.60
96	A17 6p org & blk ('36)	2.00	*2.50*
97	A18 1sh dp vio & black ('36)	31.00	*42.50*
	Nos. 91-97 (7)	40.75	*55.95*

See Nos. 116-121.

Silver Jubilee Issue

Types of 1932 Overprinted in Black or Red

1935, May 7

98	A13 1p dk car & brn red	.30	*1.50*
99	A15 2½p dk ultra & bl (R)	.75	*2.50*
100	A17 6p dull org & green	3.00	*6.00*
	Nos. 98-100 (3)	4.05	*10.00*

The vertical spacing of the overprint is wider on No. 100.

New Zealand Stamps of 1926 Overprinted in Black

b

1936, July 15 Typo. *Perf. 14*

101	A56 2sh blue	15.00	*50.00*
102	A56 3sh violet	15.00	*80.00*

New Zealand Postal-Fiscal Stamps of 1931-35 Overprinted Type "b" in Black or Red

1932-36

103	PF5 2sh6p brown ('36)	21.00	*80.00*
104	PF5 5sh grn (R) ('36)	26.00	*100.00*
105	PF5 10sh dk car ('36)	55.00	*200.00*
106	PF5 £1 pink ('36)	85.00	*210.00*
107	PF5 £3 lt grn (R)	300.00	*550.00*
108	PF5 £5 dk blue (R)	210.00	*375.00*
	Nos. 103-108 (6)	697.00	*1,515.*

Issue dates: Mar. 1932, July 15, 1936.

New Zealand Stamps of 1937 Overprinted in Black

Perf. 14x13½

1937, June 1 Engr. Wmk. 253

109	A78 1p rose carmine	.20	.20
110	A78 2½p dark blue	.20	.20
111	A78 6p vermilion	.30	.30
	Nos. 109-111 (3)	.70	.70

King George VI A19

Village and Palms A20

Coastal Scene with Canoe — A21

1938, May 2 Wmk. 61 *Perf. 14*

112	A19 1sh dp violet & blk	5.00	*11.00*
113	A20 2sh dk red brn & blk	11.50	14.00
114	A21 3sh yel green & blue	26.00	*35.00*
	Nos. 112-114 (3)	42.50	60.00

See Nos. 122-124.

Mt. Ikurangi behind Avarua — A22

Perf. 13½x14

1940, Sept. 2 Engr. Wmk. 253

115	A22 3p on 1½p violet & blk	.70	.70

Issued only with surcharge. Stamps without surcharge are from the printer's archives.

Types of 1932-38

1944-46 Engr. *Perf. 14*

116	A12 ½p dk ol grn & blk ('45)	.80	*3.00*
117	A13 1p dk car & blk ('45)	1.10	1.00
118	A14 2p brn & blk ('46)	.70	*5.00*
119	A15 2½p dk bl & blk ('45)	.40	*1.75*
120	A16 4p blue & black	1.90	*10.00*
121	A17 6p org & black	.80	*1.75*
122	A19 1sh dp vio & blk	.80	*2.25*
123	A20 2sh dk red brn & blk	17.50	*40.00*
124	A21 3sh yel green & blue ('45)	16.00	*30.00*
	Nos. 116-124 (9)	40.00	94.75

New Zealand Nos. AR76, AR78, AR85 and Type of 1931 Postal-Fiscal Stamps Overprinted Type "b" in Black or Red

1943-50 Wmk. 253 Typo. *Perf. 14*

124A	PF5 2sh6p brn ('46)	9.00	*17.50*
125	PF5 5sh green (R)	6.00	*17.50*
126	PF5 10sh dp pink ('48)	27.50	*70.00*
126A	PF5 £1 pink ('47)	30.00	*75.00*
126B	PF5 £3 lt grn (R) ('46)	37.50	*150.00*
126C	PF5 £5 dk bl (R) ('50)	140.00	*325.00*
	Nos. 124A-126C (6)	250.00	*655.00*
	Set, never hinged	425.00	

For surcharges see Nos. 192-194.

Catalogue values for unused stamps in this section, from this point to the end of the section, are for Never Hinged items.

Peace Issue

New Zealand Nos. 248, 250, 254 and 255 Overprinted in Black or Blue:

c

d

Perf. 13x13½, 13½x13

1946, June 1 Engr.

127	A94 (c) 1p emerald	.50	.20
128	A96 (d) 2p rose vio (Bl)	.50	.50
129	A100(c) 6p org red & red brn	.80	.70
130	A101(c) 8p brn lake & blk (Bl)	.80	.70
	Nos. 127-130 (4)	2.60	2.10

Ngatangiia Channel, Rarotonga A23

Capt. James Cook Statue and Map of Cook Islands — A24

Designs: 1p, Cook and map of Hervey Isls. 2p, Rev. John Williams, his ship Messenger of Peace, and map of Rarotonga. 3p, Aitutaki map and palms. 5p, Mail plane landing at Rarotonga airport. 6p, Tongareva (Penrhyn) scene. 8p, Islander's house, Rarotonga. 2sh, Thatched house, mat weaver. 3sh, Steamer Matua offshore.

Perf. 13½x13, 13x13½

1949, Aug.1 Engr. Wmk. 253

131	A23 ½p brown & violet	.20	*1.00*
132	A23 1p green & orange	3.00	2.00
133	A23 2p carmine & brn	1.75	*2.00*
134	A23 3p ultra & green	1.50	*2.00*
135	A23 5p purple & grn	5.00	1.50
136	A23 6p car rose & blk	5.00	2.50
137	A23 8p orange & olive	.50	*3.75*
138	A24 1sh chocolate & bl	4.75	3.75
139	A24 2sh rose car & brn	3.50	*12.50*
140	A24 3sh bl grn & lt ultra	9.00	*22.50*
	Nos. 131-140 (10)	34.20	*53.50*

For surcharge see No. 147.

CORFU

kor-ˈfü

LOCATION — An island in the Ionian Sea opposite the Greek-Albanian border
GOVT. — A department of Greece
AREA — 245 sq. mi.
POP. — 114,620 (1938)
CAPITAL — Corfu

In 1923 Italy occupied Corfu (Kerkyra) during a controversy with Greece over the assassination of an Italian official in Epirus.

100 Centesimi = 1 Lira
100 Lepta = 1 Drachma

Watermark

Wmk. 140 — Crown

ISSUED UNDER ITALIAN OCCUPATION

Italian Stamps of 1901-23 Overprinted

1923, Sept. 20 Wmk. 140 *Perf. 14*

N1	A48	5c green	6.00	7.50
		Never hinged	8.00	
		On cover		70.00
N2	A48	10c claret	6.00	7.50
		Never hinged	8.00	
		On cover		70.00
N3	A48	15c slate	6.00	7.50
		Never hinged	8.00	
		On cover		80.00
N4	A50	20c brown orange	6.00	7.50
		Never hinged	8.00	
		On cover		80.00
N5	A49	30c orange brown	6.00	7.50
		Never hinged	8.00	
		On cover		115.00
N6	A49	50c violet	6.00	7.50
		Never hinged	8.00	
		On cover		70.00
N7	A49	60c blue	6.00	7.50
		Never hinged	8.00	
		On cover		90.00
a.		Vert. pair, one without overprint	*1,000.*	
N8	A46	1 l brown & green	6.00	7.50
		Never hinged	8.00	
		On cover		160.00
		Nos. N1-N8 (8)	48.00	60.00
		Set, never hinged	115.00	

Italian Stamps of 1901-23 Surcharged

1923, Sept. 24

N9	A48	25 l on 10c claret	60.00	30.00
		Never hinged	70.00	
		On cover		115.00
N10	A49	60 l on 25c blue	9.00	
		Never hinged	15.00	
N11	A49	70 l on 30c org brn	9.00	
		Never hinged	30.00	
N12	A49	1.20d on 50c violet	26.00	30.00
		Never hinged	45.00	
		On cover		115.00
N13	A46	2.40d on 1 l brn & grn	26.00	30.00
		Never hinged	45.00	
		On cover		160.00
N14	A46	4.75d on 2 l grn & org	13.50	
		Never hinged	20.00	
		Nos. N9-N14 (6)	143.50	
		Set, never hinged	360.00	
		#N9, N12-N13 on over-franked philatelic cover		550.00

Nos. N10, N11, N14 were not placed in use.

COSTA RICA

ˌkäs-tə-ˈrē-kə

LOCATION — Central America between Nicaragua and Panama
GOVT. — Republic
AREA — 19,344 sq. mi.
POP. — 2,450,226 (1984)
CAPITAL — San Jose

8 Reales= 100 Centavos= 1 Peso
100 Centimos= 1 Colon (1900)

Watermarks

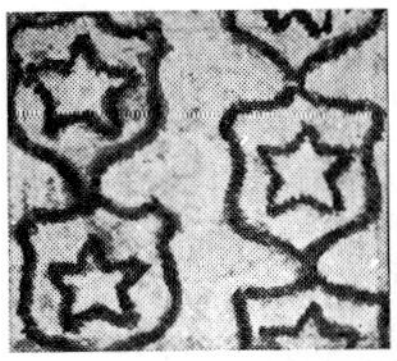

Wmk. 215 — Small Star in Shield, Multiple

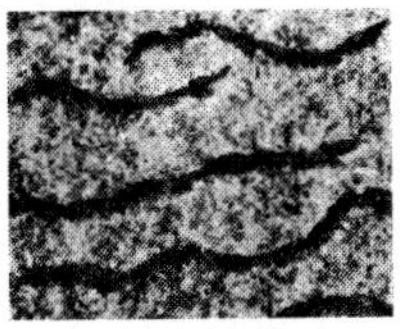

Wmk. 229 — Wavy Lines

Values for unused stamps are for examples with original gum as defined in the catalogue introduction. Very fine examples of Nos. 1-22 will have perforations just clear of the design on one or more sides due to the placement of the stamps on the plates and to imperfect perforating methods.

Coat of Arms — A1

1863 Unwmk. Engr. *Perf. 12*

1	A1	½r blue	.30	*1.00*
a.		½r light blue	.30	*1.00*
b.		Pair, imperf. horiz.	*1,500.*	
2	A1	2r scarlet	1.50	*2.00*
3	A1	4r green	15.00	*15.00*
4	A1	1p orange	40.00	*40.00*
		Nos. 1-4 (4)	56.80	58.00

The ½r was printed from two plates. The second is in light blue with little or no sky over the mountains.

Imperforate copies of Nos. 1-2 are corner copies from poorly perforated sheets.

Nos. 1-3 Surcharged in Red or Black:

a

b

c

d

e

1881-82

Red or Black Surcharge

7	A1(a)	1c on ½r ('82)	3.00	—
a.		On No. 1a	15.00	—
8	A1(b)	1c on ½r ('82)	18.00	—
9	A1(c)	2c on ½r, #1a	3.00	—
a.		On No. 1	8.00	—
12	A1(c)	5c on ½r	8.00	
13	A1(d)	5c on ½r ('82)	55.00	
14	A1(d)	10c on 2r (Bk) ('82)	70.00	—
15	A1(e)	20c on 4r ('82)	300.00	—

Overprints with different fonts and "OFICIAL" were never placed in use, and are said to have been surcharged to a dealer's order. The ½r surcharged "DOS CTS" is not a postage stamp. It probably is an essay.

Postally used copies of #7-15 are rare. #13-15 exist with a favor cancel having a hyphen between "San" and "Jose." Values same as unused. Fake cancellations exist.

Counterfeits exist of surcharges on #7-15.

Gen. Prospero Fernández A6

President Bernardo Soto Alfaro A7

1883, Jan. 1

16	A6	1c green	3.00	1.50
17	A6	2c carmine	3.00	1.50
18	A6	5c blue violet	30.00	2.00
19	A6	10c orange	140.00	12.00
20	A6	40c blue	2.00	*3.00*
		Nos. 16-20 (5)	178.00	20.00

Unused copies of 40c usually lack gum.

For overprints see Nos. O1-O20, O24, Guanacaste 1-38, 44.

1887

21	A7	5c blue violet	7.00	.50
22	A7	10c orange	4.00	3.00

Unused copies of 5c usually lack gum.

For overprints see Nos. O22-O23, Guanacaste 42-43, 45.

A8

A9

1889

Black Overprint

23	A8	1c rose	5.00	3.00
24	A9	5c brown	7.00	3.00

Vertical and inverted overprints are fakes.

For overprints see Guanacaste Nos. 47-54.

President Soto Alfaro
A10 A11

A12

A13

A14

A15

A16

A17

A18

A19

1889 *Perf. 14-16 & Compound*

25	A10	1c brown	.35	*.45*
a.		Horiz. pair, imperf. vert	*150.00*	
b.		Imperf. pair	*100.00*	
c.		Horiz. or vert. pair, imperf. btwn.	*150.00*	
26	A11	2c dark green	.35	*.45*
a.		Imperf., pair	50.00	
b.		Vert. pair, imperf. horiz.	125.00	
c.		Horiz. pair, imperf. btwn.	125.00	
27	A12	5c orange	.45	.35
a.		Imperf., pair		*250.00*
b.		Horiz. pair, imperf. btwn.	*150.00*	
28	A13	10c red brown	.40	.35
a.		Vert. or horiz. pair, imperf. btwn.	*150.00*	
29	A14	20c yellow green	.30	*.35*
a.		Vert. pair, imperf. horiz.	200.00	
b.		Horizontal pair, imperf. btwn.	*150.00*	
30	A15	50c rose red	1.00	
		Telegram cancel		.75
31	A16	1p blue	1.25	
		Telegram cancel		.75
32	A17	2p dull violet	6.00	
a.		2p slate	6.00	
		Telegram cancel		4.00
33	A18	5p olive green	25.00	
		Telegram cancel		10.00
34	A19	10p black	100.00	
		Telegram cancel		60.00
		Nos. 25-34 (10)	135.10	1.95

Nos. 30-34 normally were used on telegrams and most copies were removed from the forms and sold by the government.

For overprints see Nos. O25-O30, Guanacaste 55-67.

Arms of Costa Rica
A20 A21

A22

A23

A24

A25

A26

A27

A28

A29

1892 *Perf. 12-15 & Compound*

35	A20	1c grnsh blue	.30	*.40*
36	A21	2c yellow	.30	*.40*
37	A22	5c red lilac	.30	.25
a.		5c violet	60.00	.30
38	A23	10c lt green	.75	.35
a.		Horiz. pair, imperf. btwn.	—	*100.00*
39	A24	20c scarlet	12.00	.20
a.		Horiz. pair, imperf. btwn.	—	*100.00*
40	A25	50c gray blue	4.00	*4.25*
41	A26	1p green, *yel*	1.00	1.00
42	A27	2p brown red, *lilac*	3.00	1.00
a.		2p rose red, *pale lil*	12.00	1.00
43	A28	5p dk blue, *blue*	2.00	1.00
44	A29	10p brown, *pale buff*	35.00	5.00
a.		10p brown, *yellow*	8.00	
		Nos. 35-44 (10)	58.65	13.85

Imperfs. of Nos. 35-44 are proofs.
For overprints see Nos. O31-O36.

Statue of Juan Santamaría
A30

Juan Mora Fernández
A31

View of Port Limón — A32

Braulio Carillo ("Branlio" on stamp) — A33

National Theater — A34

José M. Castro — A35

Birris Bridge — A36

Juan Rafael Mora — A37

Jesús Jiménez
A38

Coat of Arms
A39

1901, Jan. *Perf. 12-15½*

45	A30	1c green & blk	3.25	.30
a.		Horiz. pair, imperf. btwn.	*150.00*	
46	A31	2c ver & blk	1.25	.30
47	A32	5c gray blue & blk	3.25	.30
a.		Vert. pair, imperf. btwn.	—	*150.00*
48	A33	10c ocher & blk	3.25	.35
49	A34	20c lake & blk	22.50	.25
a.		Vert. pair, imperf. btwn.	*150.00*	
50	A35	50c dull lil & dk bl	5.25	1.00
51	A36	1col ol bis & blk	110.00	3.50
52	A37	2col car rose & dk grn	16.00	3.00
53	A38	5col brown & blk	75.00	3.50
54	A39	10col yel grn & brn red	29.00	3.00
		Nos. 45-54 (10)	268.75	15.50

The 2c exists with center inverted.
Nos. 45-57 in other colors are private reprints made in 1948. They have little value.
For surcharge and overprints see Nos. 58, 78, O37-O44.

Remainders

In 1914 the government sold a large quantity of stamps at very much less than face value. The lot included most regular issues from 1901 to 1911 inclusive, postage due stamps of 1903 and official stamps of 1901-03. These stamps were canceled with groups of thin parallel bars. The higher valued used stamps, such as Nos. 64, 65-68a, sell for much less than the values quoted which are for stamps with regular postal cancellations. A few sell for much higher prices.

José M. Cañas — A40

Julián Volio — A41

Eusebio Figueroa Oreamuno — A42

1903 *Perf. 13½, 14, 15*

55	A40	4c red vio & blk	1.75	.70
56	A41	6c olive grn & blk	7.25	4.00
57	A42	25c gray lil & brn	16.00	.30
		Nos. 55-57 (3)	25.00	5.00

See note on private reprints following #54.
For overprints see Nos. 81, O45-O47.

No. 49 Surcharged in Black:

1905

58	A34	1c on 20c lake & blk	.50	.50
a.		Inverted surcharge	10.00	10.00
b.		Diagonal surcharge	.50	.50

Specimens surcharged in other colors are proofs.

Statue of Juan Santamaria
A43

Juan Mora Fernández
A44

José M. Cañas
A45

Mauro Fernández
A46

Braulio Carrillo — A47

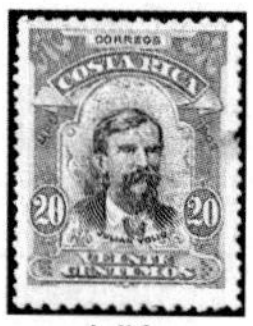
Julián Volio — A48

Eusebio Figueroa Oreamuno
A49

José M. Castro
A50

Jesús Jiménez — A51

Juan Rafael Mora — A52

Perf. 11x14, 14 (1c, 5c, 10c, 25c)

1907 **Unwmk.**

59	A43	1c red brn & ind	8.00	.40
a.		Perf. 11x14	60.00	3.00
b.		Imperf pair	15.00	—
60	A44	2c yel grn & blk	3.00	.30
a.		Perf. 14	3.00	.30
b.		Imperf pair	15.00	—
61	A45	4c car & indigo	12.00	2.50
a.		Perf. 14	500.00	40.00
b.		Imperf pair	15.00	—
62	A46	5c yel & dull bl	3.00	.30
a.		Perf. 11x14	60.00	1.00
b.		Imperf pair	15.00	—
63	A47	10c blue & blk	10.00	.50
a.		Perf. 11x14	20.00	1.00
b.		Imperf pair	30.00	—
64	A48	20c olive grn & blk	25.00	6.00
a.		Perf. 14	25.00	6.00
		Remainder cancel		2.00
b.		Imperf pair	—	
65	A49	25c gray lil & blk	3.00	3.00
		Remainder cancel		1.00
a.		Perf. 11x14	100.00	50.00
b.		Imperf pair	—	
66	A50	50c red lil & blue	55.00	25.00
		Remainder cancel		2.00
a.		Perf. 14	100.00	50.00
b.		Imperf pair	100.00	
67	A51	1col brown & blk	22.50	20.00
a.		Perf. 14	22.50	20.00
		Remainder cancel		2.00
b.		Imperf pair	—	
68	A52	2col claret & grn	160.00	100.00
		Remainder cancel		3.00
a.		Perf. 14	300.00	150.00
b.		Imperf pair	200.00	
		Nos. 59-68 (10)	301.50	158.00

The remainder cancel value applies to both perforations.

The imperforate varieties of the above set are valued without gum. Ungummed copies were probably placed on the market in London, while gummed copies appear to have been sent to Costa Rica and accepted for postal use. There is a small premium for gummed copies.

The 1c, 2c, 5c, 20c, 50c, 1 col and 2 col exist with center inverted.

Nos. 59-68 exist with papermaker's watermark.

No. 65b with brown vignette is a proof. Value, pair $40. The actual No. 65b (black vignette) is worth much more.

For overprints see Nos. 77, 79-80, 82-84, O48-O55, O60-O64.

Statue of Juan Santamaria
A53

Juan Mora Fernández
A54

José M. Cañas
A55

Mauro Fernández
A56

Braulio Carrillo
A57

Julián Volio
A58

Eusebio Figueroa Oreamuno
A59

Jesús Jiménez
A60

1910 *Perf. 12*

69	A53	1c brown	.20	.20
70	A54	2c dp green	.25	.20
71	A55	4c scarlet	.35	.35
72	A56	5c orange	1.00	.20
73	A57	10c deep blue	.25	.20
74	A58	20c olive grn	.50	.35
75	A59	25c dp violet	17.00	1.50
76	A60	1col dk brown	.50	.50
		Nos. 69-76 (8)	20.05	3.50

For overprints and surcharge see Nos. 111C-111J, B1, C2, O56-O59.

No. 60a Overprinted in Red

1911 *Perf. 14*

77	A44	2c yel grn & blk	1.50	1.00
a.		Inverted overprint	5.50	5.00
b.		Double overprint, both inverted	45.00	

Stamps of 1901-07 Overprinted in Red or Black

78	A30	1c grn & blk (R)	2.00	1.00
a.		Black overprint	32.50	18.00
b.		Inverted overprint		
79	A43	1c red brn & ind (Bk)	1.00	.40
a.		Inverted overprint	4.50	3.50
b.		Double overprint	5.50	5.00
80	A44	2c yel grn & blk (Bk)	1.00	.40
a.		Inverted overprint	3.75	3.50
b.		Dbl. ovpt., one as on No. 77	40.00	27.50
c.		Double overprint, one inverted	15.00	15.00
d.		Pair, one stamp No. 77	25.00	18.00
e.		Perf. 11x14	30.00	10.00

No. 55 Overprinted in Black

81 A40 4c red vio & blk 1.00 .65

Stamps of 1907 Overprinted in Blue, Black or Rose

Perf. 14, 11x14 (#83, 84)

82	A46 5c yel & bl (Bl)	1.50	.20
a.	"Habilitada"	3.25	2.50
b.	"2911"	5.50	3.25
c.	Roman "I" in "1911"	4.00	2.50
d.	Double overprint	5.50	5.00
e.	Inverted overprint	6.00	3.75
f.	Black overprint	—	2.00
g.	Triple overprint	6.00	
h.	Vert. pair, imperf. horiz.	*100.00*	
83	A47 10c blue & blk (Bk)	5.00	1.40
a.	As #83, Roman "I" in "1911"	7.00	5.00
c.	As #83, double overprint	20.00	11.50
d.	Perf. 14	45.00	5.00
84	A47 10c blue & blk (R)	15.00	12.50
a.	Roman "I" in "1911"	*100.00*	*100.00*
c.	Perf. 14	*100.00*	*100.00*
	Nos. 77-84 (8)	28.00	17.55

Many counterfeits of overprint exist.

A61

A62

A63

Telegraph Stamps Surcharged in Rose, Blue or Black

1911 ***Perf. 12***

86	A61 1c on 10c bl (R)	.30	.20
a.	"Coereos"	7.75	5.50
b.	Inverted surcharge		
87	A61 1c on 10c bl (Bk)	*200.00*	—
88	A61 1c on 25c vio (Bk)	.30	.20
a.	"Coereos"	8.00	5.50
b.	Pair, one without surcharge	20.00	
c.	Double surcharge	9.00	
e.	Double surch., one inverted	12.50	
89	A61 1c on 50c red brn (Bl)	.50	.40
a.	Inverted surcharge	5.50	5.00
b.	Double surcharge	4.50	
90	A61 1c on 1col brn (R)	.50	.40
91	A61 1c on 5col red (Bl)	.80	.55
92	A61 1c on 10col dk brn (R)	1.00	.70

Perf. 14

93	A62 2c on 5c brn org (Bk)	3.50	1.90
a.	Inverted surcharge	*9.00*	*3.75*
b.	"Corroes" inverted	*17.50*	
c.	Double surcharge	9.00	

Perf. 14x11

94	A62 2c on 10c bl (R)	100.00	
a.	Perf. 14	*300.00*	
b.	"Correos" inverted		
c.	As "b," perf. 14		
95	A62 2c on 50c cl (Bk)	.60	.50
a.	Inverted surcharge	4.50	3.25
b.	Double surcharge	12.50	
c.	Perf. 14	45.00	20.00
96	A62 2c on 1col brn (Bk)	1.00	.70
a.	Inverted surcharge	12.50	
b.	Double surcharge	16.00	
c.	Perf. 14	2.00	.80
97	A62 2c on 2col car (Bk)	.75	.60
a.	Inverted surcharge	8.00	5.00
b.	"Correos" inverted	10.00	5.50
c.	Double surcharge		
d.	Perf. 14	25.00	15.00
98	A62 2c on 5col grn (Bk)	.65	.65
a.	Inverted surcharge	10.00	7.00
b.	"Correos" inverted	*16.00*	*4.25*
c.	Perf. 14	6.00	3.00
99	A62 2c on 10col mar (Bk)	1.00	.65
a.	"Correos" inverted	*400.00*	

b.	Perf. 14	5.00	3.00

Perf. 12

100	A63 5c on 5c org (Bl)	.40	.25
a.	Double surcharge	25.00	15.00
b.	Inverted surcharge	25.00	8.50
c.	Pair, one without surcharge	16.00	

Counterfeits exist of Nos. 87, 94 and all minor varieties. Genuine "Coereos" errors do not exist on No. 87. Used copies of No. 94 with target cancels are counterfeits.

Nos. 93-99 exist with papermaker's watermark.

Coffee Plantation A64

1921, June 17 **Litho.** ***Perf. 11½***

103	A64 5c bl & blk	3.00	3.00
a.	Tête bêche pair	10.00	6.50
b.	Imperf., pair	*25.00*	
c.	As "a," imperf.	*125.00*	

Centenary of coffee raising in Costa Rica.

Liberty with Torch of Freedom — A65

1921 **Typo.** ***Perf. 11***

104	A65 5c violet	1.00	.40
a.	Imperf, pair	*100.00*	

Cent. of Central American independence.

Beware of trimmed singles that look like No. 104a.

For overprint see No. 111.

Juan Mora and Julio Acosta — A66

1921, Sept. 15 ***Perf. 11½***

105	A66 2c orange & blk	1.75	1.75
106	A66 3c green & blk	1.75	1.75
107	A66 6c scarlet & blk	3.00	3.00
108	A66 15c dk blue & blk	5.00	5.00
109	A66 30c orange brn & blk	6.50	6.50
	Nos. 105-109 (5)	18.00	18.00

Centenary of Central American independence. Issue requested by Costa Rican Philatelic Society. Authorized by decree calling for 2,000 of 30c and 5,000 each of other values. Many more were printed illegally including imperforates, color changes and inverted centers.

Each sheet of 20 (4x5) contains 5 tête-bêche pairs.

Simón Bolívar — A67

1921 **Engr.** ***Perf. 12***

110 A67 15c deep violet .75 .20

For overprint No. 110a see set following No. 111. For surcharge see No. 148

No. 104 Overprinted

1922 ***Perf. 11***

111	A65 5c violet	.75	.40
a.	Inverted overprint	10.00	
b.	Double overprint	15.00	

Stamps of 1910-1921 Overprinted in Blue, Red, Black or Gold

1922 ***Perf. 12***

111C	A53 1c brown (Bl)	.30	.20
111D	A54 2c deep green (R)	.40	.20
111E	A55 4c scarlet	.30	.20
111F	A56 5c orange	2.00	.35
111G	A57 10c deep blue (R)	.75	.35
111H	A67 15c deep violet (G)	3.50	2.00
	Nos. 111C-111H (6)	7.25	3.30

Inverted overprints occur on all values. Counterfeits exist.

No. 72 Overprinted

1923

111J	A56 5c orange	3.00	.75
k.	"VD." for "UD."	*75.00*	*75.00*

Jesús Jiménez — A68

1923, June 18 **Litho.** ***Perf. 11½***

112	A68 2c brown	.35	.35
113	A68 4c green	.35	.35
114	A68 5c blue	.50	.35
115	A68 20c carmine	.75	.45
116	A68 1col violet	1.00	1.10
	Nos. 112-116 (5)	2.95	2.60

Pres. Jesús Jiménez (1823-98).

Nos. 112-116, imperf, were not regularly issued. Value, set $5.

For overprints see Nos. O65-O69.

National Monument A70

Harvesting Coffee A71

Banana Growing A73

General Post Office — A74

Columbus Soliciting Aid of Isabella A75

Christopher Columbus A76

Columbus at Cariari — A77

Map of Costa Rica — A78

Manuel M. Gutiérrez — A79

1923-26 **Engr.** ***Perf. 12***

117	A70 1c violet	.25	.20
118	A71 2c yellow	.50	.20
119	A73 4c deep green	.75	.30
120	A74 5c light blue	1.50	.20
121	A74 5c yellow grn ('26)	.50	.20
122	A75 10c red brown	3.00	.20
123	A75 10c car rose ('26)	.50	.20
124	A76 12c carmine rose	10.00	3.00
125	A77 20c deep blue	10.00	.60
126	A78 40c orange	11.00	3.00
127	A79 1col olive green	2.00	.65
	Nos. 117-127 (11)	40.00	8.75

See #151-156. For surcharges & overprints see #136-140, 147, 189, 218, C2.

Rodrigo Arias Maldonado — A80

1924 ***Perf. 12½***

128	A80 2c dark green	.20	.20
a.	Perf. 14	.50	.25

See No. 162.

Map of Guanacaste A81

Mission at Nicoya — A82

1924 **Litho.** ***Perf. 12***

129	A81 1c carmine rose	.30	.20
130	A81 2c violet	.30	.20
131	A81 5c green	.30	.20
132	A81 10c orange	2.25	.50
133	A82 15c light blue	1.00	.45

134 A82 20c gray black 2.00 1.00
135 A82 25c light brown 3.00 1.50
Nos. 129-135 (7) 9.15 4.05

Centenary of annexation of Province of Guanacaste to Costa Rica.
Exist imperf. Value, set, $50.

Stamps of 1923 Surcharged:

a

b

1925

136 A74(a) 3c on 5c lt blue .30 .20
137 A75(a) 6c on 10c red brn .40 .25
138 A78(a) 30c on 40c orange 1.50 .40
139 A79(b) 45c on 1col ol grn 1.75 .50
a. Double surcharge 250.00
Nos. 136-139 (4) 3.95 1.35

No. 124 Surcharged

1926

140 A76 10c on 12c car rose 1.50 .30

College of San Luis, Cartago A83

Chapui Asylum, San José — A84

Normal School, Heredia A85

Ruins of Ujarrás A86

1926 **Unwmk.** **Engr.** ***Perf. 12½***

143 A83 3c ultra .50 .20
144 A84 6c dark brown .50 .20
145 A85 30c deep orange 2.00 .25
146 A86 45c black violet 4.00 1.00
Nos. 143-146 (4) 7.00 1.65

For surcharges see Nos. 190-190D, 217.

No. 124 Surcharged in Black:

1928, Jan. 7 ***Perf. 12***

147 A76 10c on 12c car rose 4.50 4.50

Issued in honor of Col. Charles A. Lindbergh during his Good Will Tour of Central America.
The surcharge has been privately reprinted using an original die. They can be distinguished by distinct dots under the "10s." All errors and inverted surcharges are reprints.

No. 110 Surcharged

1928

148 A67 5(c) on 15c dp violet .20 .20
a. Inverted surcharge 27.50

Type I — A88

Type II

Type III

Type IV

Type V

Surcharge Typo. (I-V) & Litho. (V)

1929 ***Perf. 12½***

149 A88 5c on 2col car (I) .50 .20
a.-d. Types II-V .60 .20

Telegraph Stamp Surcharged for Postage as in 1929, Surcharge Lithographed

1929

150 A88 13c on 40c deep grn .35 .25
a. Inverted surcharge 1.00 1.00

Excellent counterfeits exist of No. 150a.

Types of 1923-26 Issues Dated "1929"
Imprint of Waterlow & Sons

1930 **Size: 26x21½mm** ***Perf. 12½***

151 A70 1c dark violet .35 .20
155 A74 5c green .35 .20
156 A75 10c carmine rose .35 .20
Nos. 151-156 (3) 1.05 .60

Juan Rafael Mora — A89

1931

157 A89 13c carmine rose .60 .20

For surcharge see No. 209.

Seal of Costa Rica Philatelic Society ("Octubre 12 de 1932") A90

1932, Oct. 12 ***Perf. 12***

158 A90 3c orange .25 .20
159 A90 5c dark green .40 .25
160 A90 10c carmine rose .50 .25
161 A90 20c dark blue .85 .30
Nos. 158-161 (4) 2.00 1.00

Phil. Exhib., Oct. 12, 1932. See #179-183.

Maldonado Type of 1924

1934 ***Perf. 12½***

162 A80 3c dark green .20 .20

Red Cross Nurse — A91

1935, May 31 ***Perf. 12***

163 A91 10c rose carmine 7.50 .25

50th anniv. of the founding of the Costa Rican Red Cross Society.

Air View of Cartago A92

Miraculous Statuette and View of Cathedral A93

Vision of 1635 — A94

1935, Aug. ***Perf. 12½***

164 A92 5c green .20 .20
165 A93 10c carmine .30 .20
166 A92 30c orange .45 .20
167 A94 45c dark violet 1.10 .55
168 A93 50c blue black 1.75 1.00
Nos. 164-168 (5) 3.80 2.15

Tercentenary of the Patron Saint, Our Lady of the Angels, of Costa Rica.

Map of Cocos Island — A95

1936, Jan. 29 ***Perf. 14, 11½ (25c)***

169 A95 4c ocher .25 .20
170 A95 8c dark violet .35 .20
171 A95 25c orange .50 .20
172 A95 35c brown vio .75 .20
173 A95 40c brown 1.00 .20
174 A95 50c yellow 1.10 .60
175 A95 2col yellow grn 11.00 10.00
176 A95 5col green 30.00 25.00
Nos. 169-176 (8) 44.95 36.60

Exist imperf. Value, set, $50.
For surcharges see #196-200, C55-C56.

Map of Cocos Island and Ships of Columbus A96

1936, Dec. 5 ***Perf. 12***

177 A96 5c green .20 .20
178 A96 10c carmine rose .20 .20

For overprints see Nos. 247, O80-O81.

Seal of Costa Rica Philatelic Society ("Diciembre 1937") — A97

1937

179 A97 2c dark brown .35 .20
180 A97 3c black .35 .20
181 A97 5c green .35 .20
182 A97 10c orange red .35 .20
Nos. 179-182 (4) 1.40 .80

Souvenir Sheet

Imperf

183 Sheet of 4 1.50 1.50
a. A97 2c dark brown .20 .20
b. A97 3c black .20 .20
c. A97 5c green .20 .20
d. A97 10c orange red .20 .20

Phil. Exhib., Dec. 1937.

Purple Guaria Orchid, National Flower — A98

Tuna A99

Native with Donkey Carrying Bananas A101

3c, Cacao pod. 10c, Coffee harvesting.

1937-38 **Wmk. 229** ***Perf. 12½***

184 A98 1c green & vio ('38) .55 .20
185 A98 3c chocolate ('38) .35 .20

Unwmk. ***Perf. 12***

186 A99 2c olive gray .40 .20
187 A101 5c dark green .55 .20
188 A101 10c carmine rose .90 .20
Nos. 184-188 (5) 2.75 1.00

National Exposition.

No. 125 Overprinted in Black

1938 Unwmk. *Perf. 12*

189	A77 20c deep blue	1.50	.20

No. 146 Surcharged in Red:

a

b

c

d

e

1940 *Perf. 12½*

190	A86(a) 15c on 45c blk vio	.60	.30
190A	A86(b) 15c on 45c blk vio	.60	.30
190B	A86(c) 15c on 45c blk vio	.60	.30
190C	A86(d) 15c on 45c blk vio	.60	.30
190D	A86(e) 15c on 45c blk vio	.60	.30
	Nos. 190-190D (5)	3.00	1.50

#190D exists with inverted surcharge. Value, $5.

Allegory A103

Overprinted "Dia Panamericano de la Salud / 2 Diciembre 1940" and Arc

1940, Dec. 2 Engr. *Perf. 12*

191	A103 5c green	.20	.20
192	A103 10c rose carmine	.25	.20
193	A103 20c deep blue	.55	.25
194	A103 40c brown	1.50	1.25
195	A103 55c orange yellow	2.50	2.25
	Nos. 191-195 (5)	5.00	4.15

Pan-American Health Day. See #C46-C54. Exist without overprint.

POSTAL-FISCAL STAMPS

From April 1884 through September 1889 revenue stamps were permitted for postal use, when post offices exhausted supplies of regular postage stamps.

Used values are for stamps with postal cancels.

PF1

PF2

1884 Engr. *Perf. 12*

AR1	PF1 1c rose	.50	*5.00*
AR2	PF1 2c light blue	*20.00*	5.00

1888

AR3	PF2 5c brown	.50	*3.00*
AR4	PF2 10c blue	.25	*3.00*

SEMI-POSTAL STAMPS

No. 72 Surcharged in Red

1922 Unwmk. *Perf. 12*

B1	A56 5c + 5c orange	1.00	.40

Issued for the benefit of the Costa Rican Red Cross Society. In 1928, owing to a temporary shortage of the ordinary 5c stamp, No. B1 was placed on sale as a regular 5c stamp, the surtax being disregarded.

Discus Thrower SP1

Trophy SP2

Parthenon SP3

1924 Litho. *Imperf.*

B2	SP1 5c dark green	1.50	*2.00*
B3	SP2 10c carmine	1.50	*2.00*
B4	SP3 20c dark blue	20.00	*20.00*
a.	Tête bêche pair	60.00	*60.00*

Perf. 12

B5	SP1 5c dark green	1.50	*2.00*
B6	SP2 10c carmine	1.50	*2.00*
B7	SP3 20c dark blue	3.00	*3.50*
a.	Tête bêche pair	14.00	*16.00*
	Nos. B2-B7 (6)	29.00	*31.50*

These stamps were sold at a premium of 10c each, to help defray the expenses of athletic games held at San José in Dec. 1924.

AIR POST STAMPS

Airplane AP1

Perf. 12½

1926, June 4 Unwmk. Engr.

C1	AP1 20c ultramarine	3.00	.50

No. 123 Overprinted

1930, Mar. 14 *Perf. 12*

C2	A75 10c carmine rose	2.00	.25

Inverted or double overprints are fakes.

AP3

1930-32 *Perf. 12½*

C3	AP3 5c on 10c dk brn ('32)	.40	.25
C4	AP3 20c on 50c ultra	.50	.25
C5	AP3 40c on 50c ultra	.60	.25
	Nos. C3-C5 (3)	1.50	.75

The existence of genuine inverted or double surcharges of Nos. C3-C5 is in doubt.

Telegraph Stamp Overprinted

1930, Mar. 19

C6	AP3 1col orange	2.00	.50

No. O79 Surcharged in Red

1930, Mar. 11

C7	O7 8c on 1col lilac & blk	.60	.50
C8	O7 20c on 1col lilac & blk	.90	.50
C9	O7 40c on 1col lilac & blk	1.75	1.50
C10	O7 1col on 1col lilac & blk	2.75	1.50
	Nos. C7-C10 (4)	6.00	4.00

AP6

AP7

Red Surcharge on Revenue Stamps

1931-32 *Perf. 12*

C11	AP6 2col on 2col gray grn	35.00	35.00
C12	AP6 3col on 5col lil brn	35.00	35.00
C13	AP6 5col on 10col gray blk	35.00	35.00
	Nos. C11-C13 (3)	105.00	105.00

There were two printings of this issue which were practically identical in the colors of the stamps and the surcharges.

Nos. C11 and C13 have the date "1929" on the stamp, No. C12 has "1930."

Black Overprint on Telegraph Stamp

1932, Mar. 8 *Perf. 12½*

C14	AP7 40c green	3.00	.30
a.	Inverted overprint	30.00	

Unofficial "proofs," inverts and double overprints were made from a defaced plate.

Mail Plane about to Land — AP8

Allegory of Flight AP9

1934, Mar. 14 *Perf. 12*

C15	AP8 5c green	.20	.20
C16	AP8 10c carmine rose	.20	.20
C17	AP8 15c chocolate	.35	.20
C18	AP8 20c deep blue	.40	.20
C19	AP8 25c deep orange	.50	.20
C20	AP8 40c olive blk	1.75	.20
C21	AP8 50c gray blk	.85	.20
C22	AP8 60c orange yel	1.50	.20
C23	AP8 75c dull violet	2.75	.45
C24	AP9 1col deep rose	1.50	.20
C25	AP9 2col lt blue	6.00	.90
C26	AP9 5col black	5.00	4.75
C27	AP9 10col red brown	9.00	8.00
	Nos. C15-C27 (13)	30.00	15.90

Stamps Nos. C15 to C27 with holes punched through were for use of government officials.

See Nos. C216-C219. For overprints see Nos. C67-C73, C92-C93, C103-C116, CO1-CO13.

Airplane over Poás Volcano — AP10

1937, Feb. 10

C28	AP10 1c black	.45	.35
C29	AP10 2c brown	.45	.35
C30	AP10 3c dk violet	.45	.35
	Nos. C28-C30 (3)	1.35	1.05

First Fair of Costa Rica.

Puntarenas AP11

National Bank AP12

Perf. 12, 12½

1937, Dec. 15 Unwmk.

C31	AP11 2c black gray	.20	.20
C32	AP11 5c green	.20	.20
C33	AP11 20c deep blue	.30	.20
C34	AP11 1.40col olive brn	2.50	2.50
	Nos. C31-C34 (4)	3.20	3.10

1938, Jan. 11 Wmk. 229 *Perf. 12½*

C35	AP12 1c purple	.20	.20
C36	AP12 3c red orange	.20	.20
C37	AP12 10c carmine rose	.30	.20
C38	AP12 75c brown	2.50	2.00
	Nos. C35-C38 (4)	3.20	2.60

Nos. C31-C38 for the Natl. Products Exposition held at San José, Dec. 1937.

Airport Administration Building, La Sabana — AP13

1940, May 2 Engr. Unwmk.

C39	AP13 5c green	.20	.20
C40	AP13 10c rose pink	.20	.20
C41	AP13 25c lt blue	.20	.20
C42	AP13 35c red brown	.20	.20
C43	AP13 60c red org	.30	.30
C44	AP13 85c violet	1.40	.90
C45	AP13 2.35col turq grn	6.00	5.50
	Nos. C39-C45 (7)	8.50	7.50

Opening of the Intl. Airport at La Sabana.

Duran Sanatorium AP14

Overprinted "Dia Panamericano de la Salud / 2 Diciembre 1940" and Bar in Black

1940, Dec. 2 *Perf. 12*

C46	AP14	10c scarlet	.20	.20
C47	AP14	15c purple	.20	.20
C48	AP14	25c lt blue	.35	.35
C49	AP14	35c bister brn	.50	.50
C50	AP14	60c pck green	.75	.75
C51	AP14	75c olive	2.00	2.00
C52	AP14	1.35col red org	6.00	6.00
C53	AP14	5col sepia	45.00	40.00
C54	AP14	10col red lilac	125.00	100.00
		Nos. C46-C54 (9)	180.00	150.00

Pan-American Health Day. Exist without overprint. Few copies of C53-C54 were sold for postal purposes, nearly all having been obtained by philatelic speculators.

No. 174 Surcharged in Black or Blue

1940, Dec. 17 *Perf. 14*

C55	A95	15c on 50c yel (Bk)	1.00	1.00
C56	A95	30c on 50c yel (Bl)	1.00	1.00

Pan-American Aviation Day, proclaimed by President F. D. Roosevelt.

The 15c surcharge exists normal and inverted on #171, value, normal, $30.

AIR POST OFFICIAL STAMPS

Air Post Stamps of 1934 Overprinted in Red

1934 **Unwmk.** *Perf. 12*

CO1	AP8	5c green	.20	.20
CO2	AP8	10c car rose	.20	.20
CO3	AP8	15c chocolate	.35	.35
CO4	AP8	20c deep blue	.55	.55
CO5	AP8	25c deep org	.55	.55
CO6	AP8	40c olive blk	1.00	.60
CO7	AP8	50c gray blk	1.00	.60
CO8	AP8	60c org yel	1.25	.75
CO9	AP8	75c dull vio	1.25	.75
CO10	AP9	1col deep rose	5.00	1.10
CO11	AP9	2col light blue	8.00	3.50
CO12	AP9	5col black	9.00	6.50
CO13	AP9	10col red brown	8.00	8.00
		Nos. CO1-CO13 (13)	36.35	23.65

For overprints see Nos. C103-C116.

POSTAGE DUE STAMPS

D1

D2

1903 **Unwmk.** **Engr.** *Perf. 14*

Numerals in Black

J1	D1	5c slate blue	6.00	.90
J2	D1	10c brown orange	6.00	.65
J3	D1	15c yellow green	3.00	1.75
J4	D1	20c carmine	4.00	1.60
J5	D1	25c slate gray	4.00	1.75
J6	D1	30c brown	5.00	2.50
J7	D1	40c olive bister	6.00	2.50
J8	D1	50c red violet	6.00	2.00
		Nos. J1-J8 (8)	40.00	13.65

1915 **Litho.** *Perf. 12*

J9	D2	2c orange	1.00	.50
J10	D2	4c dark blue	1.00	.50
J11	D2	8c gray green	1.00	.50
J12	D2	10c violet	1.00	.50
J13	D2	20c brown	1.00	.50
		Nos. J9-J13 (5)	5.00	2.50

OFFICIAL STAMPS

Values for unused stamps are for examples with original gum as defined in the catalogue introduction. Very fine examples of Nos. O1-O24 will have perforations just clear of the design on one or more sides.

Official stamps, to about 1915, normally were not canceled when affixed to official mail. Occasionally they were canceled in a foreign country of destination. Used values are for favor-canceled specimens or for stamps without gum.

Regular Issues Overprinted

Overprinted in Red, Black, Blue or Green

1883-85 **Unwmk.** *Perf. 12*

O1	A6	1c green (R)	2.00	1.00
O2	A6	1c green (Bk)	4.00	1.00
O3	A6	2c carmine (Bk)	4.00	1.25
O4	A6	2c carmine (Bl)	2.00	1.40
O5	A6	5c blue vio (R)	7.00	2.75
O6	A6	10c orange (G)	10.00	3.50
O7	A6	40c blue (R)	10.00	3.50
		Nos. O1-O7 (7)	39.00	14.40

Overprinted

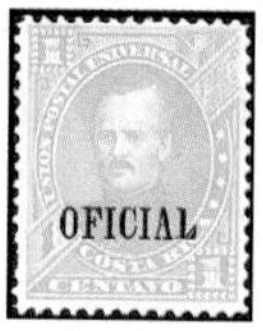

1886

O8	A6	1c green (Bk)	3.00	1.00
O9	A6	2c carmine (Bk)	3.00	1.50
O10	A6	5c blue vio (R)	20.00	10.00
O11	A6	10c orange (Bk)	20.00	10.00
		Nos. O8-O11 (4)	46.00	22.50

Overprinted

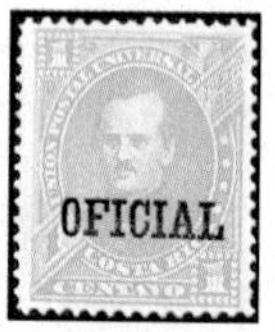

O12	A6	1c green (Bk)	3.00	.90
O13	A6	2c carmine (Bk)	3.00	1.25
O14	A6	5c blue vio (R)	20.00	10.00
O15	A6	10c orange (Bk)	20.00	10.00
		Nos. O12-O15 (4)	46.00	22.15

Nos. O8-O11 and O12-O15 exist se-tenant in vertical pairs.

Overprinted in Black

O16	A6	5c blue vio	50.00	30.00
O17	A6	10c orange	—	250.00

Overprinted

1887

O18	A6	1c green	1.00	.50
O19	A6	2c carmine	1.00	.45
O21	A6	10c orange	32.50	20.00
c.		Double overprint	37.50	
O22	A7	5c blue vio	10.00	3.00
O23	A7	10c orange	.75	.45
c.		Double overprint	25.00	
O24	A6	40c blue	1.00	.45
		Nos. O18-O24 (6)	46.25	24.85

Overprinted "OFICAL"

O18a	A6	1c green		
O19a	A6	2c carmine	*12.00*	*12.00*
O22a	A7	5c blue violet	*12.00*	
O23a	A7	10c orange	*12.00*	*2.75*
O24a	A6	40c blue	*15.00*	*15.00*
		Nos. O18a-O24a (4)	*51.00*	

Dangerous counterfeits exist of Nos. O18a-O24a.

Without Period

O18b	A6	1c green	12.00	8.00
O19b	A6	2c carmine	12.00	8.00
O22b	A7	5c blue violet	12.00	8.00
O23b	A7	10c orange	12.00	8.00
		Nos. O18b-O23b (4)	48.00	32.00

Nos. O18b-O23b are from a separate plate without periods. No. O23 exists without period (position 32). These must be collected in pairs.

Issues of 1889-1901 Overprinted

1889 *Perf. 14, 15*

O25	A10	1c brown	.20	.20
O26	A11	2c dk green	.20	.20
O27	A12	5c orange	.20	.20
O28	A13	10c red brown	.20	.20
O29	A14	20c yellow grn	.20	.20
O30	A15	50c rose red	1.00	1.00
		Nos. O25-O30 (6)	2.00	2.00

1892

O31	A20	1c grnsh blue	.25	.25
O32	A21	2c yellow	.25	.25
O33	A22	5c violet	.25	.25
O34	A23	10c lt green	5.00	1.00
O35	A24	20c scarlet	.20	.20
O36	A25	50c gray blue	.50	.50
		Nos. O31-O36 (6)	6.45	2.45

1901-02

O37	A30	1c green & blk	.35	.35
O38	A31	2c ver & blk	.35	.35
O39	A32	5c gray bl & blk	.35	.35
O40	A33	10c ocher & blk	.60	.60
O41	A34	20c lake & blk	.85	.85
O42	A35	50c lilac & dk bl	12.50	2.75
O43	A36	1col ol bis & blk	25.00	10.00
		Nos. O37-O43 (7)	40.00	15.25

No. 46 Overprinted in Green

1903

O44	A31	2c ver & blk	2.25	2.25
b.		"PROVISIORO"	8.00	8.00
d.		Inverted overprint	8.00	8.00
f.		As "b," inverted	10.00	8.00

Counterfeit overprints exist.

Regular Issue of 1903 Overprinted Like Nos. O25-O43

1903 *Perf. 14, 12½x14*

O45	A40	4c red vio & blk	1.10	1.10
O46	A41	6c ol grn & blk	1.25	1.25
O47	A42	25c gray lil & brn	8.00	4.50
		Nos. O45-O47 (3)	10.35	6.85

Counterfeit overprints exist.

Regular Issue of 1907 Overprinted

1908 *Perf. 14*

O48	A43	1c red brn & ind	.20	.20
O49	A44	2c yel grn & blk	.20	.20
O50	A45	4c car & ind	.20	.20
O51	A46	5c yel & dull bl	.20	.20
O52	A47	10c blue & blk	2.00	.90
O53	A49	25c gray lil & blk	.30	.20
O54	A50	50c red lil & bl	.50	.30
O55	A51	1col brown & blk	1.00	.70
		Nos. O48-O55 (8)	4.60	2.90

Various varieties of the overprint and basic stamps exist.

Imperf examples of Nos. O48, O49, O53 were found in 1970.

Regular Issue of 1910 Overprinted in Black

1917

O56	A56	5c orange	.25	.25
a.		Inverted overprint	5.00	3.00
O57	A57	10c deep blue	.20	.20
a.		Inverted overprint	3.00	3.00

No. 74 Surcharged

1920 **Red Surcharge** *Perf. 12*

O58	A58	15c on 20c olive grn	.50	.50

Nos. 72, 61, 59, 65-67 Surcharged or Overprinted

O59

O60

O61

O62

1921 **Black Surcharge** *Perf. 12*

O59	A56	10c on 5c orange	.30	.25
a.		"10 CTS." inverted	16.00	

Perf. 14

O60	A45	4c car & indigo	.30	.30
a.		"1291" for "1921"	11.00	
O61	A43	6c on 1c red brn & ind	.40	.40
O62	A49	20c on 25c gray lil & blk	.50	.40

Overprinted like No. O60

O63	A50	50c red lil & bl	2.50	1.50
O64	A51	1col brown & blk	5.00	2.75
		Nos. O59-O64 (6)	9.00	5.60

Nos. O60 to O64 exist with date and new values inverted. These may be printer's waste but probably were deliberately made.

Regular Issue of 1923 Overprinted

1923 *Perf. 11½*

O65	A68	2c brown	.20	.20
O66	A68	4c green	.20	.20
O67	A68	5c blue	.20	.20

O68 A68 20c carmine .20 .20
O69 A68 1col violet .30 .30
Nos. O65-O69 (5) 1.10 1.10

Nos. O65 to O69 exist imperforate but were not regularly issued in that condition.

O7

1926 Unwmk. Engr. *Perf. 12½*

O70 O7 2c ultra & blk .20 .20
O71 O7 3c mag & blk .20 .20
O72 O7 4c lt bl & blk .20 .20
O73 O7 5c grn & blk .20 .20
O74 O7 6c ocher & blk .20 .20
O75 O7 10c rose red & blk .20 .20
O76 O7 20c ol grn & blk .20 .20
O77 O7 30c red org & blk .20 .20
O78 O7 45c brown & blk .20 .20
O79 O7 1col lilac & blk .20 .20
Nos. O70-O79 (10) 2.00 2.00

See #O82-O94. For surcharges see #C7-C10.

Regular Issue of 1936 Overprinted in Black

1936 Unwmk. *Perf. 12*

O80 A96 5c green .20 .20
O81 A96 10c carmine rose .20 .20

Type of 1926

1937 *Perf. 12½*

O82 O7 2c vio & blk .20 .20
O83 O7 3c bis brn & blk .20 .20
O84 O7 4c rose car & blk .20 .20
O85 O7 5c ol grn & blk .20
O86 O7 8c blk brn & blk .20
O87 O7 10c rose lake & blk .20
O88 O7 20c ind & blk .20 .20
O89 O7 40c red org & blk .20 .20
O90 O7 55c dk vio & blk .30
O91 O7 1col brn vio & blk .25 .25
O92 O7 2col gray bl & blk .50 .50
O93 O7 5col dl yel & blk 2.50 2.50
O94 O7 10col blue & blk 20.00 20.00
Nos. O82-O94 (13) 25.15

Nine stamps of this series exist with perforated star (2c, 3c, 4c, 20c, 40c, 1col, 2col, 5col, 10col). These were issued to officials for postal purposes. Unpunched copies were sold to collectors but had no franking power. Values for unused are for unpunched.

GUANACASTE

ˌgwä-nə-ˈkästā

(A province of Costa Rica)

LOCATION — Northwestern coast of Central America
AREA — 4,000 sq. mi. (approx.)
POP. — 69,531 (estimated)
CAPITAL — Liberia

Residents of Guanacaste were allowed to buy Costa Rican stamps, overprinted "Guanacaste," at a discount from face value because of the province's isolation and climate, which makes it difficult to keep mint stamps. Use was restricted to the province.

Counterfeits of most Guanacaste overprints are plentiful.

For 1c and 2c stamps between Nos. 1-20, unused values are for examples with or without gum. For 5c stamps between Nos. 5-21, unused examples without gum sell for slightly more than the used value.

Very fine examples of Nos. 1-54 will have perforations just clear of the design on one or more sides.

Dangerous counterfeits exist of Nos. 1-54.

On Issue of 1883
Overprinted Horizontally in Black

16mm

1885 Unwmk. *Perf. 12*

1 A6 1c green 4.00 3.00
2 A6 2c carmine 4.00 3.00
a. "Gnanacaste" *250.00*
3 A6 10c orange 35.00 18.00
a. "Gnanacaste" *500.00*

Same Overprint in Red

4 A6 1c green 4.00 3.00
a. "Gnanacaste" *200.00*
b. Overprinted in black & red *300.00*
5 A6 5c blue violet 30.00 3.50
a. "Gnanacaste" *350.00*
6 A6 40c blue 25.00 18.00

Overprinted Horizontally in Black

17½mm

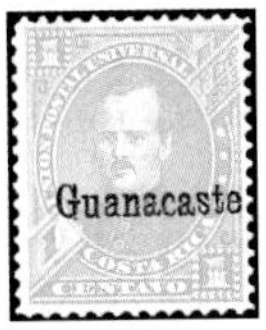

7 A6 1c green 10.00 7.00
8 A6 2c carmine 10.00 7.00
9 A6 5c blue violet 45.00 15.00
10 A6 10c orange 60.00 35.00
11 A6 40c blue 60.00 60.00

Same Overprint in Red

12 A6 5c blue violet 500.00 75.00
13 A6 40c blue *2,000.*

Overprinted Horizontally in Black

18½mm — c

14 A6 2c carmine 10.00 7.00
15 A6 10c orange 100.00 75.00

Same Overprint in Red

16 A6 1c green 7.00 7.00
a. Double ovpt., one in blk 250.00
17 A6 5c blue violet 45.00 15.00
18 A6 40c blue 75.00 75.00

Same Overprint, Vertically in Black

19 A6 1c green *5,000.*
20 A6 2c carmine *4,250.*
21 A6 5c blue violet 700.00 175.00
22 A6 10c orange 120.00 120.00

e f g h i

Overprinted Type e, Vertically

23 A6 1c green 3,000. 2,000.
24 A6 2c carmine 700.00 300.00
25 A6 5c blue violet 400.00 75.00
26 A6 10c orange 75.00 75.00

Overprinted Type f, Vertically

27 A6 1c green 2,000. 2,000.
28 A6 2c carmine 700.00 400.00
29 A6 5c blue violet 400.00 125.00
30 A6 10c orange 100.00 100.00

Overprinted Type g, Vertically

31 A6 1c green 2,500. 2,500.
32 A6 2c carmine 1,000. 1,000.
33 A6 5c blue violet 600.00 200.00
34 A6 10c orange 150.00 150.00

Overprinted Type h, Vertically

35 A6 1c green 2,000. 1,500.
36 A6 2c carmine 500.00 300.00
37 A6 5c blue violet 350.00 75.00
38 A6 10c orange 60.00 60.00

Overprinted Type i, Vertically

39 A6 1c green —
39A A6 2c carmine *275.00*
40 A6 5c blue violet 20.00
41 A6 10c orange *200.00*

On Issues of 1883-87

Overprinted Horizontally in Black

1888-89

42 A7 5c blue violet 15.00 3.00

Overprinted Horizontally in Black

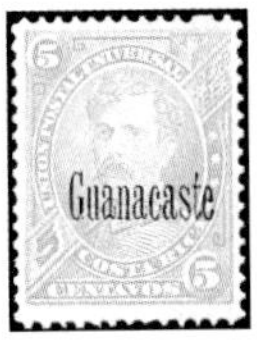

43 A7 5c blue violet 15.00 3.00

Overprinted Horizontally in Black

44 A6 2c carmine 3.00
45 A7 10c orange 3.00

Inverted overprints are fakes.

On Issue of 1889
Overprinted Like Nos. 7-13, Horizontally

1889

47 A8 2c blue 20.00

Vertically

48 A8 2c blue (c) 250.00
49 A8 2c blue (e) 75.00
51 A8 2c blue (f) 75.00
52 A8 2c blue (g) 250.00
54 A8 2c blue (h) 75.00

Nos. 47-54 are overprinted "Correos." Copies without "Correos" are known postally used. Unused examples are valued the same as Nos. 47-54, unused. The 1c without "Correos" is known postally used. The 1c with "Correos" is counterfeit.

On Nos. 25-33

Overprinted Horizontally in Black

1889 *Perf. 14 and 15*

55 A10 1c brown 5.00 3.00
56 A11 2c dark green 3.00 1.50
57 A12 5c orange 4.00 1.50
58 A13 10c red brown 4.00 1.50
59 A14 20c yellow green 1.00 1.50
60 A15 50c rose red 1.50 1.50
61 A16 1p blue 2.50 2.50
62 A17 2p violet 5.00 5.00
63 A18 5p olive green 35.00 30.00
Nos. 55-63 (9) 61.00 48.00

#61-63 with remainder cancels sell for about half the used values shown.

Overprinted "GUAGACASTE"

60a A15 50c rose red *300.00 300.00*
61a A16 1p blue *300.00 300.00*
62a A17 2p violet *350.00 350.00*
63a A18 5p olive green *500.00 500.00*

Values for #60a-63a used are for examples with remainder cancels.

Overprinted Horizontally in Black

64 A10 1c brown 2.00 1.50
a. Vert. pair, imperf. between
65 A11 2c dark green 2.00 1.50
66 A12 5c orange 2.00 1.50
67 A13 10c red brown 2.00 1.50
Nos. 64-67 (4) 8.00 6.00

CRETE

ˈkrēt

LOCATION — An island in the Mediterranean Sea south of Greece
GOVT. — A department of Greece
AREA — 3,235 sq. mi.
POP. — 336,150 (1913)
CAPITAL — Canea

Formerly Crete was a province of Turkey. After an extended period of civil wars, France, Great Britain, Italy and Russia intervened and declaring Crete an autonomy, placed it under the administration of Prince George of Greece as High Commissioner. In October, 1908, the Cretan Assembly voted for union with Greece and in 1913 the union was formally effected.

40 Paras = 1 Piaster
4 Metallik = 1 Grosion (1899)
100 Lepta = 1 Drachma (1900)

AUSTRIAN POST IN CRETE

The Austrian Empire maintained post offices in three cities in Crete.

Post Office	Open	Close
Candia	1858	1914
Canea	1845	1914
Rettimo	1858	1914

Values in the first column for Nos. 2A1-2A185 are for stamps without defects tied to piece with legible partial strikes of town cancellations; values in the second column are for stamps without defects tied to cover by complete strikes of town cancellations. Stamps with legible town cancellations off cover sell for 25-50% of the on-piece value.

Issue dates refer to dates of stamps' issue, not necessarily to their usage with specific Albanian postal markings.

CANDIA

Stamps of Lombardy-Venetia

Canceled in black or red brown with single circle date stamp with post office name, month and date, without year

1863 *Perf. 14*

2A1 2s yellow (#15) 450.00 1,500.
2A2 3s green (#16) 400.00 1,650.
2A3 5s rose (#17) 400.00 1,450.
2A4 10s blue (#18) 350.00 1,200.
2A5 15s yel brn (#19) 425.00 1,300.

1864-65 *Perf. 9½*

2A6 2s yellow (#20) 450.00 1,500.
2A7 3s green (#21) 200.00 850.00
2A8 5s rose (#22) 150.00 700.00
2A9 10s blue (#23) 125.00 500.00
2A10 15s yel brn (#24) 160.00 600.00

Stamps of Austrian Offices In the Turkish Empre

Canceled in black or red brown with single circle date stamp with post office name, month and date, without year

1867-83

Coarse Print

2A11 2s yellow (#1) 37.50 450.00
2A12 3s green (#2) 57.50 400.00
2A13 5s red (#3) 27.50 140.00

2A14	10s	blue (#4)	20.00	92.50
2A15	15s	brown (#5)	24.00	100.00
2A16	25s	gray lilac (#6)	50.00	700.00
2A17	50s	brown (#7)	57.50	*3,750.*

Fine Print

2A18	2s	yellow (#7C)	1,150.	—
2A19	3s	green (#7D)	35.00	275.00
2A20	5s	red (#7E)	32.50	150.00
2A21	10s	blue (#7F)	20.00	87.50
2A22	15s	org brown (#7I)	135.00	775.00
2A23	25s	gray lilac (#7J)	250.00	*5,000.*

Stamps of Austrian Offices In the Turkish Empire

Canceled in blue with single circle date stamp with post office name, month and date, without year

1867-83

Coarse Print

2A24	2s	yellow (#1)	125.00	825.00
2A25	3s	green (#2)	150.00	750.00
2A26	5s	red (#3)	120.00	500.00
2A27	10s	blue (#4)	115.00	450.00
2A28	15s	brown (#5)	120.00	475.00
2A29	25s	gray lilac (#6)	145.00	1,100.
2A30	50s	brown (#7)	150.00	*4,250.*

Fine Print

2A31	2s	yellow (#7C)	1,250.	—
2A32	3s	green (#7D)	125.00	625.00
2A33	5s	red (#7E)	125.00	525.00
2A34	10s	blue (#7F)	115.00	450.00
2A35	15s	org brown (#7I)	225.00	1,125.
2A36	25s	gray lilac (#7J)	350.00	*5,500.*

Stamps of Austrian Offices In the Turkish Empre

Canceled in black with circular date stamp with post office name, month and date, with year date

1867-83

Coarse Print

2A37	2s	yellow (#1)	37.50	450.00
2A38	3s	green (#2)	57.50	400.00
2A39	5s	red (#3)	27.50	140.00
2A40	10s	blue (#4)	20.00	92.50
2A41	15s	brown (#5)	24.00	100.00
2A42	25s	gray lilac (#6)	50.00	700.00
2A43	50s	brown (#7)	57.50	*3,750.*

Fine Print

2A44	2s	yellow (#7C)	1,150.	—
2A45	3s	green (#7D)	35.00	275.00
2A46	5s	red (#7E)	32.50	150.00
2A47	10s	blue (#7F)	20.00	87.50
2A48	15s	org brown (#7I)	135.00	775.00
2A49	25s	gray lilac (#7J)	250.00	*5,000.*

Stamps of Austrian Offices In the Turkish Empre

Canceled in blue with circular date stamp with post office name, month and date, with year date

1867-83

Coarse Print

2A50	2s	yellow (#1)	300.00	1,325.
2A51	3s	green (#2)	325.00	1,250.
2A52	5s	red (#3)	.28500	1,000.
2A53	10s	blue (#4)	275.00	950.00
2A54	15s	brown (#5)	280.00	975.00
2A55	25s	gray lilac (#6)	300.00	1,575.
2A56	50s	brown (#7)	325.00	*4,750.*

Fine Print

2A57	2s	yellow (#7C)	1,400.	—
2A58	3s	green (#7D)	300.00	1,125.
2A59	5s	red (#7E)	285.00	1,000.
2A60	10s	blue (#7F)	275.00	950.00
2A61	15s	org brown (#7I)	385.00	1,625.
2A62	25s	gray lilac (#7J)	500.00	*6,000.*

Candia Agencia del Lloyd Austriaco

Stamps of Lombardy-Venetia

Canceled with with oval postmark with ornaments in blue

1863 ***Perf. 14***

2A63	2s	yellow (#15)	—	—
2A64	3s	green (#16)	—	—
2A65	5s	rose (#17)	3,150.	12,000.
2A66	10s	blue (#18)	3,100.	11,050.
2A67	15s	yel brn (#19)	3,250.	12,000.

CANEA

Stamps of Lombardy-Venetia

Canceled in black or red brown with straight-line postmark with name of post office and date in italic letters

1863 ***Perf. 14***

2A68	2s	yellow (#15)	350.00	1,250.
2A69	3s	green (#16)	300.00	1,350.
2A70	5s	rose (#17)	300.00	1,100.
2A71	10s	blue (#18)	250.00	850.00
2A72	15s	yel brn (#19)	325.00	1,000.

1864-65 ***Perf. 9½***

2A73	2s	yellow (#20)	375.00	1,100.
2A74	3s	green (#21)	110.00	475.00
2A75	5s	rose (#22)	60.00	325.00
2A76	10s	blue (#23)	32.50	120.00
2A77	15s	yel brn (#24)	65.00	240.00

Stamps of Austrian Offices in the Turkish Empire

Canceled in black or red brown with straight-line postmark with name of post office and date in italic letters

1867-83

Coarse Print

2A78	2s	yellow (#1)	30.00	425.00
2A79	3s	green (#2)	47.50	350.00
2A80	5s	red (#3)	18.75	100.00
2A81	10s	blue (#4)	11.50	55.00
2A82	15s	brown (#5)	15.00	62.50
2A83	25s	gray lilac (#6)	40.00	675.00
2A84	50s	brown (#7)	47.50	*3,800.*

Fine Print

2A85	2s	yellow (#7C)	1,150.	—
2A86	3s	green (#7D)	27.50	225.00
2A87	5s	red (#7E)	22.50	115.00
2A88	10s	blue (#7F)	11.00	50.00
2A89	15s	org brown (#7I)	125.00	725.00
2A90	25s	gray lilac (#7J)	235.00	*5,000.*

Stamps of Lombardy-Venetia

Canceled in blue with straight-line postmark with name of post office and date in italic letters

1863 ***Perf. 14***

2A91	2s	yellow (#15)	450.00	1,500.
2A92	3s	green (#16)	400.00	1,650.
2A93	5s	rose (#17)	400.00	1,450.
2A94	10s	blue (#18)	350.00	1,200.
2A95	15s	yel brn (#19)	425.00	1,300.

1864-65 ***Perf. 9½***

2A96	2s	yellow (#20)	625.00	1,950.
2A97	3s	green (#21)	375.00	1,350.
2A98	5s	rose (#22)	325.00	1,200.
2A99	10s	blue (#23)	300.00	1,000.
2A100	15s	yel brn (#24)	325.00	1,100.

Stamps of Austrian Offices in the Turkish Empire

Canceled in blue with straight-line postmark with name of post office and date in italic letters

1867-83

Coarse Print

2A101	2s	yellow (#1)	130.00	825.00
2A102	3s	green (#2)	150.00	750.00
2A103	5s	red (#3)	120.00	500.00
2A104	10s	blue (#4)	115.00	450.00
2A105	15s	brown (#5)	120.00	475.00
2A106	25s	gray lilac (#6)	145.00	1,100.
2A107	50s	brown (#7)	150.00	*4,250.*

Fine Print

2A108	2s	yellow (#7C)	1,250.	—
2A109	3s	green (#7D)	130.00	625.00
2A110	5s	red (#7E)	125.00	525.00
2A111	10s	blue (#7F)	115.00	450.00
2A112	15s	org brown (#7I)	225.00	1,125.
2A113	25s	gray lilac (#7J)	340.00	*5,500.*

Stamps of Austrian Offices In the Turkish Empre

Canceled in black with circular date stamp with post office name, month and date, with year date

1867-83

Coarse Print

2A114	2s	yellow (#1)	30.00	425.00
2A115	3s	green (#2)	47.50	350.00
2A116	5s	red (#3)	18.75	100.00
2A117	10s	blue (#4)	1.50	55.000
2A118	15s	brown (#5)	15.00	62.50
2A119	25s	gray lilac (#6)	40.00	675.00
2A120	50s	brown (#7)	47.50	*3,800.*

Fine Print

2A121	2s	yellow (#7C)	1,150.	—
2A122	3s	green (#7D)	27.50	225.00
2A123	5s	red (#7E)	22.50	115.00
2A124	10s	blue (#7F)	11.00	55.00
2A125	15s	org brown (#7I)	125.00	725.00
2A126	25s	gray lilac (#7J)	235.00	*5,000.*

RETTIMO

Stamps of Lombardy-Venetia

Canceled in black with single circle date stamp with post office name, month and date, without year

1863 ***Perf. 14***

2A127	2s	yellow (#15)	450.00	1,500.
2A128	3s	green (#16)	400.00	1,650.
2A129	5s	rose (#17)	400.00	1,450.
2A130	10s	blue (#18)	350.00	1,200.
2A131	15s	yel brn (#19)	425.00	1,300.

1864-65 ***Perf. 9½***

2A132	2s	yellow (#20)	425.00	1,275.
2A133	3s	green (#21)	160.00	675.00
2A134	5s	rose (#22)	110.00	525.00
2A135	10s	blue (#23)	85.00	325.00
2A136	15s	yel brn (#24)	115.00	450.00

Stamps of Austrian Offices In the Turkish Empre

Canceled in black or red brown with single circle date stamp with post office name, month and date, without year

1867-83

Coarse Print

2A137	2s	yellow (#1)	37.50	450.00
2A138	3s	green (#2)	57.50	400.00
2A139	5s	red (#3)	27.50	140.00
2A140	10s	blue (#4)	20.00	92.50
2A141	15s	brown (#5)	24.00	100.00
2A142	25s	gray lilac (#6)	50.00	700.00
2A143	50s	brown (#7)	57.50	*3,850.*

Fine Print

2A144	2s	yellow (#7C)	1,150.	—
2A145	3s	green (#7D)	35.00	275.00
2A146	5s	red (#7E)	32.50	150.00
2A147	10s	blue (#7F)	20.00	87.50
2A148	15s	org brown (#7I)	135.00	775.00
2A149	25s	gray lilac (#7J)	250.00	*5,000.*

Stamps of Lombardy-Venetia

Canceled in blue with single circle date stamp with post office name, month and date, without year

1863 ***Perf. 14***

2A150	2s	yellow (#15)	575.00	2,000.
2A151	3s	green (#16)	525.00	2,200.
2A152	5s	rose (#17)	525.00	2,000.
2A153	10s	blue (#18)	500.00	1,750.
2A154	15s	yel brn (#19)	575.00	1,850.

1864-65 ***Perf. 9½***

2A155	2s	yellow (#20)	625.00	1,950.
2A156	3s	green (#21)	375.00	1,350.
2A157	5s	rose (#22)	325.00	1,200.
2A158	10s	blue (#23)	300.00	1,000.
2A159	15s	yel brn (#24)	325.00	1,100.

Stamps of Austrian Offices In the Turkish Empre

Canceled in blue with single circle date stamp with post office name, month and date, without year

1867-83

Coarse Print

2A160	2s	yellow (#1)	87.50	650.00
2A161	3s	green (#2)	110.00	600.00
2A162	5s	red (#3)	77.50	340.00
2A163	10s	blue (#4)	70.00	300.00
2A164	15s	brown (#5)	75.00	300.00
2A165	25s	gray lilac (#6)	100.00	900.00
2A166	50s	brown (#7)	110.00	*4,000.*

Fine Print

2A167	2s	yellow (#7C)	1,200.	—
2A168	3s	green (#7D)	85.00	475.00
2A169	5s	red (#7E)	82.50	350.00
2A170	10s	blue (#7F)	70.00	290.00
2A171	15s	org brown (#7I)	180.00	975.00
2A172	25s	gray lilac (#7J)	300.00	*5,250.*

Stamps of Austrian Offices In the Turkish Empre

Canceled in black with single circle date stamp with post office name, month and date, with year

1867-83

Coarse Print

2A173	2s	yellow (#1)	30.00	425.00
2A174	3s	green (#2)	47.50	350.00
2A175	5s	red (#3)	18.75	100.00
2A176	10s	blue (#4)	11.50	55.00
2A177	15s	brown (#5)	15.00	62.50
2A178	25s	gray lilac (#6)	40.00	675.00
2A179	50s	brown (#7)	45.00	*3,800.*

Fine Print

2A180	2s	yellow (#7C)	1,150.	—
2A181	3s	green (#7D)	27.50	225.00
2A182	5s	red (#7E)	22.50	115.00
2A183	10s	blue (#7F)	11.00	50.00
2A184	15s	org brown (#7I)	125.00	725.00
2A185	25s	gray lilac (#7J)	235.00	*5,000.*

Issued Under Joint Administration of France, Great Britain, Italy and Russia

British Sphere of Administration District of Heraklion (Candia)

A1

A2

Handstamped

1898 **Unwmk.** ***Imperf.***

1	A1	20pa violet	425.00	240.00

1898 **Litho.** ***Perf. 11½***

2	A2	10pa blue	8.50	3.00
		Never hinged	17.00	
a.		Horiz. pair, imperf. btwn.		
b.		Imperf., pair	260.00	
3	A2	20pa green	13.50	3.00
		Never hinged	20.00	
a.		Imperf., pair	260.00	

1899

4	A2	10pa brown	8.75	3.00
		Never hinged	17.50	
a.		Horiz. pair, imperf. btwn.		
b.		Imperf., pair	260.00	
5	A2	20pa rose	19.00	3.00
		Never hinged	24.00	
a.		Imperf., pair	260.00	

Used values for Nos. 2-5 are for stamps canceled by the straight-line "Heraklion" town postmark. Stamps canceled with any other postmark used for postal duty are scarce and worth much more.

Counterfeits exist of Nos. 1-5.

Russian Sphere of Administration District of Rethymnon

Coat of Arms

A3 A4

1899 **Handstamped** ***Imperf.***

10	A3	1m green	6.50	4.50
11	A3	2m black	6.50	4.50
12	A3	2m rose	250.00	200.00
13	A4	1m blue	80.00	25.00

Nos. 10-13 exist on both wove and laid papers. Counterfeits exist.

Poseidon's Trident — A5a

A5

1899 **Litho.** ***Perf. 11½***

With Control Mark Overprinted in Violet

Without Stars at Sides

14	A5	1m orange	80.	60.
15	A5	2m orange	80.	60.
16	A5	1gr orange	80.	60.
17	A5	1m green	80.	60.
18	A5	2m green	80.	60.
19	A5	1gr green	80.	60.
20	A5	1m yellow	80.	60.
21	A5	2m yellow	80.	60.
22	A5	1gr yellow	80.	60.
23	A5	1m rose	80.	60.
24	A5	2m rose	80.	60.
25	A5	1gr rose	80.	60.
26	A5	1m violet	80.	60.
27	A5	2m violet	80.	60.
28	A5	1gr violet	80.	60.
29	A5	1m blue	80.	60.
30	A5	2m blue	80.	60.
31	A5	1gr blue	80.	60.
32	A5	1m black	1,000.	900.
33	A5	2m black	1,000.	900.

34	A5	1gr black	1,000.	900.

With Stars at Sides

35	A5a	1m blue	25.00	15.00
36	A5a	2m blue	7.00	5.25
37	A5a	1gr blue	4.50	3.25
38	A5a	1m rose	50.00	40.00
39	A5a	2m rose	7.00	5.25
40	A5a	1gr rose	4.50	3.25
41	A5a	1m green	24.00	15.00
42	A5a	2m green	7.00	5.25
43	A5a	1gr green	7.00	5.25
44	A5a	1m violet	24.00	15.00
45	A5a	2m violet	7.00	5.25
46	A5a	1gr violet	4.50	4.25
		Nos. 35-46 (12)	171.50	122.00

Nearly all of Nos. 14 to 46 may be found without control mark, with double control marks and in various colors.

Counterfeits exist of Nos. 14-46.

Issued by the Cretan Government

Hermes — A6

Hera — A7

Prince George of Greece — A8

Talos — A9

Minos — A10

St. George and the Dragon — A11

1900, Mar. 1 Engr. *Perf. 14*

50	A6	1 l violet brown	.25	.25
51	A7	5 l green	1.25	.25
52	A8	10 l red	1.75	.25
53	A7	20 l carmine rose	6.25	1.25
		Nos. 50-53 (4)	9.50	2.00

See #64-71. For overprints and surcharges see #54-63, 72-73, 85, 88, 93, 97-99, 108, 111.

Overprinted

Red Overprint

54	A8	25 l blue	3.00	.85
55	A6	50 l lilac	3.00	1.25
56	A9	1d gray violet	13.00	11.00
57	A10	2d brown	25.00	25.00
58	A11	5d green & blk	120.00	120.00
		Nos. 54-58 (5)	164.00	158.10

Black Overprint

59	A8	25 l blue	3.00	.85
60	A6	50 l lilac	3.00	1.75
61	A9	1d gray violet	12.50	4.50
a.		Inverted overprint	*450.00*	*450.00*
62	A10	2d brown	22.50	22.50
63	A11	5d green & blk	60.00	60.00
		Nos. 59-63 (5)	101.00	89.60

1901

Without Overprint

64	A6	1 l bister		.90
65	A7	20 l orange	4.75	.90
66	A8	25 l blue	10.00	.60
67	A6	50 l lilac	30.00	22.50
68	A6	50 l ultra	13.50	13.00
69	A9	1d gray violet	30.00	25.00
70	A10	2d brown	10.00	8.50
71	A11	5d green & blk	12.00	10.00
		Nos. 64-71 (8)		81.40
		Nos. 65-71 (7)	110.25	

No. 64 is a revenue stamp that was used for postage for a short time. Unused, it can only be considered as a revenue.

Types A6 to A8 in olive yellow, and types A9 to A11 in olive yellow and black are revenue stamps.

See note following No. 53.

Surcharges with the year "1922" on designs A6, A8, A9, A11, A13, A15-A23 and D1 are listed under Greece.

No. 66 Overprinted in Black

1901

72	A8	25 l blue	32.50	.80
a.		First letter of ovpt. invtd.	300.00	200.00

No. 65 Surcharged in Black

1904, Dec.

73	A7	5 l on 20 l orange	4.50	.85
a.		Without "5" at right	100.00	50.00

Mycenaean Seal — A12

Britomartis (Cortyna Coin) — A13

Prince George — A14

Kydon and Dog (Cydonia Coin) — A15

Triton (Itanos Coin) — A16

Ariadne (Knossos Coin) — A17

Zeus as Bull Abducting Europa (Cortyna Coin) A18

Palace of Minos Ruins, Knossos A19

Arkadi Monastery and Mt. Ida — A20

1905, Feb. 15

74	A12	2 l dull violet	1.90	.45
75	A13	5 l yellow grn	5.00	.45
76	A14	10 l red	5.00	.45
77	A15	20 l blue grn	5.25	1.00
78	A16	25 l ultra	5.00	1.00
79	A17	50 l yellow brn	7.00	4.75
80	A18	1d rose car & dp brn	60.00	60.00
81	A19	3d orange & blk	50.00	40.00
82	A20	5d ol grn & blk	25.00	20.00
		Nos. 74-82 (9)	164.15	128.10

For overprints see Nos.86-87, 89, 91-92, 94-95, 104, 106, 109-110, 112-113, 115-120.

The so-called revolutionary stamps of 1905 were issued for sale to collectors and, so far as can be ascertained, were of no postal value whatever.

A. T. A. Zaimis A21

Prince George Landing at Suda A22

1907, Aug. 28

83	A21	25 l blue & blk	37.50	1.00
84	A22	1d green & blk	13.00	11.00

Administration under a High Commissioner.

For overprints see Nos. 90, 105, 107.

Stamps of 1900-1907 Overprinted in Black

1908, Sept. 21

85	A6	1 l violet brn	.60	.50
86	A12	2 l dull violet	.65	.50
87	A13	5 l yellow grn	.90	.50
88	A8	10 l red	1.75	.65
89	A15	20 l blue grn	4.50	.70
90	A21	25 l blue & blk	11.00	2.50
91	A17	50 l yellow brn	11.00	4.00
92	A18	1d rose car & dp brn	62.50	*65.00*
93	A10	2d brown	10.50	10.50
94	A19	3d orange & blk	37.50	32.50
95	A20	5d ol grn & blk	30.00	30.00
		Nos. 85-95 (11)	170.90	147.35

This overprint exists inverted and double, as well as with incorrect, reversed, misplaced and omitted letters. Similar errors are found on the Postage Due and Official stamps with this overprint.

Hermes by Praxiteles — A23

1908

96	A23	10 l brown red	3.00	.85
a.		Pair, one without overprint	25.00	
b.		Inverted overprint	25.00	
c.		Double overprint	35.00	

Nos. 96 and 114 were not regularly issued without overprint.

For overprints see Nos. 103, 114.

No. 53 Surcharged

1909

97	A7	5 l on 20 l car rose	110.00	*125.00*

Forgeries exist of No. 97.

On No. 65

98	A7	5 l on 20 l orange	1.75	1.00
a.		Inverted surcharge		

Overprinted on Nos. 64, J1

99	A6	1 l bister	1.75	1.75
100	D1	1 l red	1.75	1.75

No. J4 Surcharged

101	D1	2 l on 20 l red	1.75	1.75
b.		Inverted surcharge	75.00	
c.		Second letter of surcharge "D" instead of "P"	50.00	50.00

No. J4 Surcharged

102	D1	2 l on 20 l red	1.60	1.40

Overprinted in Black:

a

ϵΛΛΑΣ

b

c

103	A23(a)	10 l brown red	4.75	1.25
a.		Inverted overprint	85.00	
104	A15(a)	20 l blue grn	6.25	1.25
105	A21(c)	25 l blue & blk	12.50	4.00
106	A17(a)	50 l yellow brn	10.00	5.25
107	A22(b)	1d green & blk	12.50	11.00
108	A10(a)	2d brown	12.50	11.00
109	A19(b)	3d org & blk	90.00	75.00
110	A20(b)	5d ol grn & blk	27.50	27.50
		Nos. 103-110 (8)	176.00	136.25

Stamps of 1900-08 Overprinted in Red or Black

1909-10

111	A6	1 l violet brown	.45	.25
112	A12	2 l dull violet	.45	.25
113	A13	5 l yellow green	.45	.25
114	A23	10 l brown red (Bk)	.85	.25
115	A15	20 l blue green	3.00	.70

116	A16	25 l ultra	3.50	.75
117	A17	50 l yellow brn	9.00	6.75
118	A18	1d rose car & dp brn (Bk)	60.00	60.00
119	A19	3d orange & blk	50.00	50.00
120	A20	5d ol grn & blk	45.00	40.00
		Nos. 111-120 (10)	172.70	159.20

POSTAGE DUE STAMPS

D1

1901 Unwmk. Litho. *Perf. 14*

J1	D1	1 l red	.25	.25
J2	D1	5 l red	.95	.60
J3	D1	10 l red	1.50	.60
J4	D1	20 l red	1.90	1.50
J5	D1	40 l red	14.00	14.00
J6	D1	50 l red	14.00	14.00
J7	D1	1d red	20.00	18.00
J8	D1	2d red	14.00	14.00
		Nos. J1-J8 (8)	66.60	62.95

For overprints and surcharges see Nos. 100-102, J9-J26.

Surcharged in Black

Overprinted

1901

J9	D1	1d on 1d red	12.00	12.00

1908

J10	D1	1 l red	.60	.50
J11	D1	5 l red	1.10	.85
J12	D1	10 l red	1.25	.90
J13	D1	20 l red	3.00	2.25
J14	D1	40 l red	10.00	10.00
J15	D1	50 l red	10.00	10.00
J16	D1	1d red	125.00	125.00
J17	D1	1d on 1d red	10.00	10.00
J18	D1	2d red	17.50	17.50
		Nos. J10-J18 (9)	178.45	177.00

Nos. J10-J18 exist with inverted overprint. See note after No. 95.
Counterfeits of No. J16 exist.

Overprinted

1910

J19	D1	1 l red	.60	.25
J20	D1	5 l red	1.40	.25
J21	D1	10 l red	.85	.45
J22	D1	20 l red	4.25	1.75
J23	D1	40 l red	10.00	9.00
J24	D1	50 l red	12.50	11.00
J25	D1	1d red	27.50	27.50
J26	D1	2d red	27.50	27.50
		Nos. J19-J26 (8)	84.60	77.70

OFFICIAL STAMPS

O1

O2

Unwmk.
1908, Jan. 14 Litho. *Perf. 14*

O1	O1	10 l dull claret	18.50	2.50
O2	O2	30 l blue	42.50	2.50

Nos. O1-O2 exist imperf.

Overprinted

Overprinted

O3	O1	10 l dull claret	19.00	2.50
O4	O2	30 l blue	42.50	2.50

See note after No. 95.

1910

O5	O1	10 l dull claret	2.50	2.00
O6	O2	30 l blue	2.50	2.00

Nos. O5-O6 remained in use until 1922, nine years after union with Greece.

CUBA

ˈkyü-bə

LOCATION — The largest island of the West Indies; south of Florida
GOVT. — Republic
AREA — 44,206 sq. mi.
POP. — 6,743,000 (est. 1960)
CAPITAL — Havana

Formerly a Spanish possession, Cuba made several unsuccessful attempts to gain her freedom, which finally led to the intervention of the US in 1898. In that year under the Treaty of Paris, Spain relinquished the island to the US in trust for its inhabitants. In 1902 a republic was established and the Cuban Congress took over the government from the military authorities.

8 Reales Plata = 1 Peso
100 Centesimos = 1 Escudo or Peseta (1867)
1000 Milesimas = 100 Centavos = 1 Peso

Catalogue values for unused stamps in this country are for Never Hinged items, beginning with Scott RA1 in the postal tax section.

Pen cancellations are common on the earlier stamps of Cuba. Stamps so canceled sell for very much less than those with postmark cancellations.

Watermarks

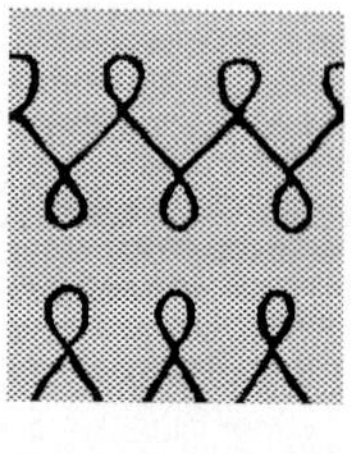
Wmk. 104 — Loops

Loops from different rows may or may not be directly opposite each other.

Wmk. 105 — Crossed Lines

Wmk. 106 — Star

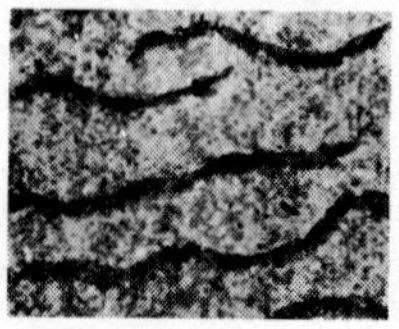
Wmk. 229 — Wavy Lines

FORERUNNERS

Crowned Circle handstamp types are pictured in the Crowned Circle Handstamps and Great Britain Used Abroad section.

BRITISH POST OFFICES IN CUBA

Havana

British P.O. opened 1762; stamps supplied 1865; closed May 30, 1877

Pre-Stamp Postal Markings

1841

A1	Crowned Circle handstamp Type II, on cover, inscribed "PAID AT HAVANA"	1,000.
A2	Crowned Circle handstamp Type IV, on cover, inscribed "PAID AT HAVANA" in black	1,000.
A3	Crowned Circle handstamp Type V, on cover, inscribed "PAID AT HAVANA"	850.00

Earliest known uses: A1, 11/13/41; A2, 1848; A3, 7/14/48

Stamps of Great Britain, Canceled C58, or with Circular Date Stamp

1865-77

A4	½p rose red (#58 P 6, 12), *value from*	80.00
A5	1p rose red (#33, P 86, 90, 93, 115, 120, 123, 144, 146, 171, 174, 208), *value from*	62.50
A6	2p blue (#29, P 9)	80.00
A7	2p blue (#30, P 14, 15), *value from*	80.00
A8	3p rose (#49, P 4)	140.00
A9	3p rose (#61, P 18, 19)	—
A10	4p vermilion (#43, P 7, 8, 10-14), *value from*	70.00
A11	4p vermilion (#69, P 15)	310.00
A12	6p lilac (#45, P 5)	—
A13	6p gray (#62, P 15)	—
A14	8p orange (#73)	—
A15	9p bister (#52)	290.00
A16	10p red brown (#53)	310.00
A17	1sh green (#48, P 4)	175.00
A18	1sh green (#54, P 4, 5), *value from*	70.00
	Plate 7	*100.00*
A19	1sh green (#64, P 10, 12, 13), *value from*	92.50
A20	2sh blue (#55)	225.00
A21	5sh rose (#57, P 1)	600.00
	Plate 2	600.00
a.	5sh pale rose (#57a, P 1)	475.00
	Plate 2	500.00

St. Jago de Cuba

British P.O. opened 1841; stamps supplied 1866; closed May 30, 1877

Pre-Stamp Postal Markings

1841

A22	Crowned Circle handstamp Type III, on cover, inscribed "PAID AT ST JAGO-DE-CUBA" in red	*6,250.*

Earliest known use: 12/15/41.

Stamps of Great Britain, Canceled C88

1866-77

A23	½p rose red (#58 P 4, 6, 14)	—
A24	1p rose red (#33, P 100, 105, 106, 109, 111, 120, 123, 138, 144, 146-148, 171, 208) *value from*	140.00
A25	1½p lake red (#32 P 3)	—
A26	2p blue (#29, P 13, 14)	—
A27	2p blue (#30, P 13, 14)	140.00
A28	3p rose (#49, P 5)	140.00
A29	4p vermilion (#43, P 9-14) *value from*	140.00
A30	4p vermilion (#69, P 15)	500.00
A31	6p violet (#51, P 6, 8, 9) *value from*	350.00
A32	6p pale buff (#59b, P 11)	—
A33	9p straw (#46)	—
A34	9p bister (#52)	—
A35	10p red brown (#53)	490.00
A36	1sh green (#54, P 4-6) *value from*	310.00
A37	1sh green (#64, P 9-13)	—
A38	2sh blue (#55)	—
A39	5sh rose (#57)	—

Issued under Spanish Dominion

Used also in Puerto Rico: Nos. 1-3, 9-14, 17-21, 32-34, 35A-37, 39-41, 43-45, 47-49, 51-53, 55-57.
Used also in the Philippines: Nos. 2-3.
Identifiable cancellations of those countries will increase the value of the stamps.

Queen Isabella II — A1

Blue Paper

1855 Typo. Wmk. 104 *Imperf.*

1	A1	½r p blue green	65.00	5.50
		On cover		27.50
a.		½r p blackish green	75.00	10.00
		On cover		32.50
2	A1	1r p gray green	55.00	3.75
		On cover		25.00
3	A1	2r p carmine	325.00	11.00
		On cover		100.00
4	A1	2r p orange red	825.00	17.50
		On cover		160.00
		Nos. 1-4 (4)	1,270.	37.75

See Nos. 9-14. For surcharges see Nos. 5-8, 15.

Counterfeit surcharges are plentiful.

Nos. 3-4 Surcharged

1855-56

5	A1	¼r p on 2r p car	750.00	200.00
		On cover		525.00
a.		Without fraction bar	*1,400.*	550.00
6	A1	¼r p on 2r p org red		550.00
		On cover		1,000.

Surcharged

7	A1	¼r p on 2r p car	650.00	190.00
		On cover		*800.00*
a.		Without fraction bar		725.00
8	A1	¼r p on 2r p org red	1,000.	450.00
		On cover		*1,200.*
a.		Without fraction bar		1,150.

The "Y ¼" surcharge met the "Ynterior" rate for delivery within the city of Havana.

Rough Yellowish Paper

1856 **Wmk. 105**
9 A1 ½r p yellow grn 6.50 .80
On cover 7.50
a. ½r p greenish blue 5.50 .80
On cover 9.00
10 A1 1r p green 775.00 17.50
On cover 29.00
a. 1r p emerald *1,100.* 20.00
On cover 45.00
11 A1 2r p orange red 375.00 15.00
On cover 175.00

White Smooth Paper

1857 **Unwmk.**
12 A1 ½r p blue 3.25 .65
On cover 5.00
a. ½r p milky blue (cleaned plate) 5.75 1.00
On cover 12.50
13 A1 1r p gray green 3.00 .65
On cover 8.00
a. 1r p pale yellow green 2.75 .65
On cover 10.00
c. 1r p pale green (cleaned plate) 5.00 1.00
On cover 15.00
14 A1 2r p dull rose 17.50 3.00
On cover 75.00
a. 2r p carmine 12.00 3.25
On cover 100.00
b. 2r p orange red 11.00 3.00
On cover 75.00
Nos. 12-14 (3) 23.75 4.30

Surcharged

1860
15 A1 ¼r p on 2r p dl rose 225.00 80.00
On cover 275.00
a. 1 of ¼ inverted 325.00 140.00
b. "1 ⅘" instead of "1 ¼" —

Queen Isabella II
A2 A3

1862-64 ***Imperf.***
16 A2 ¼r p black 19.00 15.00
On cover 110.00
17 A3 ¼r p blk, *buff* ('64) 19.00 14.00
On cover —
18 A3 ½r p green ('64) 4.75 .70
On cover 6.50
19 A3 ½r p grn, *pale rose* ('64) 11.00 2.00
On cover 15.00
a. ½r p grn,*rose lilac* 15.00 2.00
On cover 15.00
20 A3 1r p bl, *sal* ('64) 4.75 1.00
On cover 7.50
a. Diagonal half used as ½r p on cover 125.00
21 A3 2r p ver, *buff* ('64) 25.00 6.00
On cover 60.00
a. 2r p red, *buff* 30.00 6.75
On cover —
Nos. 16-21 (6) 83.50 38.70

No. 17 Overprinted in Black

1866
22 A3 ¼r p black, *buff* 70.00 *75.00*
On cover 325.00

Exists with handstamped "1866."

A5 A6

1866
23 A5 5c dull violet 40.00 26.00
On cover 47.50
24 A5 10c blue 2.50 1.00
On cover 7.50
25 A5 20c green 1.50 1.00
On cover 12.50
a. Diag. half used as 10c on cover 150.00
26 A5 40c rose 9.50 8.00
On cover 40.00
Nos. 23-26 (4) 53.50 36.00

Stamps Dated "1867"

1867 ***Perf. 14***
27 A5 5c dull violet 40.00 21.00
On cover 100.00
28 A5 10c blue 19.00 1.40
On cover 9.00
a. Imperf., pair 110.00 6.50
b. Diagonal half used as 5c on cover 140.00
29 A5 20c green 12.00 1.90
On cover 12.50
a. Imperf., pair 110.00 70.00
b. Diag. half used as 10c on cover 150.00
30 A5 40c rose 15.00 10.00
On cover —
Nos. 27-30 (4) 86.00 34.30

Stamps Dated "1868"

1868
31 A6 5c dull violet 18.00 8.25
On cover 25.00
32 A6 10c blue 3.75 1.75
On cover 7.50
a. Diagonal half used as 5c on cover 140.00
33 A6 20c green 5.50 3.00
On cover 15.00
a. Diag. half used as 10c on cover 140.00
34 A6 40c rose 14.00 8.00
On cover 60.00
a. Diag. half used as 20c on cover 175.00
Nos. 31-34 (4) 41.25 21.00

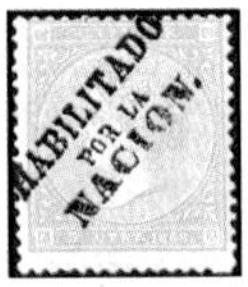

Nos. 31-34 Overprinted in Black

1868
35 A6 5c dull violet 62.50 29.00
On cover 175.00
35A A6 10c blue 62.50 29.00
On cover 150.00
b. Diag. half used as 5c on cover *275.00*
36 A6 20c green 62.50 29.00
On cover —
37 A6 40c rose 62.50 29.00
On cover —
Nos. 35-37 (4) 250.00 116.00

1869 **Stamps Dated "1869"**
38 A6 5c rose 37.50 12.00
On cover 175.00
39 A6 10c red brown 3.75 1.75
On cover 10.00
a. Diagonal half used as 5c on cover 125.00
40 A6 20c orange 6.50 2.25
On cover 15.00
41 A6 40c dull violet 30.00 9.50
On cover —
Nos. 38-41 (4) 77.75 25.50

Nos. 38-41 Ovptd. Like Nos. 35-37

42 A6 5c rose 150.00 42.50
On cover —
43 A6 10c red brown 45.00 32.50
On cover 200.00
a. Diagonal half used as 5c on cover —
44 A6 20c orange 37.50 32.50
On cover 200.00
a. Diag. half used as 10c on cover —
45 A6 40c dull violet 65.00 32.50
On cover —
Nos. 42-45 (4) 297.50 140.00

"Espana"
A8 A9

1870 ***Perf. 14***
46 A8 5c blue 150.00 55.00
On cover 275.00
47 A8 10c green 2.75 .85
On cover 10.00
a. Diagonal half used as 5c on cover 150.00
48 A8 20c red brown 2.75 .85
On cover 15.00
a. Diag. half used as 10c on cover 225.00
49 A8 40c rose 200.00 30.00
On cover 250.00

1871
50 A9 12c red lilac 20.00 10.00
On cover 50.00
a. Imperf., pair 85.00 —
51 A9 25c ultra 2.25 .85
On cover 10.00
a. Imperf., pair 40.00 —
b. Diagonal half used as 12c on cover 140.00
52 A9 50c gray green 2.25 .85
On cover 15.00
a. Imperf., pair 15.00 —
b. Diagonal half used as 25c on cover 140.00
53 A9 1p pale brown 27.50 9.00
On cover 90.00
a. Imperf., pair 125.00 —
Nos. 50-53 (4) 52.00 20.70

King Amadeo — A10

1873 ***Perf. 14***
54 A10 12½c dark green 22.50 14.00
On cover 80.00
55 A10 25c gray 2.25 .85
On cover 10.00
a. Diagonal half used as 12½c on cover 82.50
b. 25c lilac 6.00 1.10
On cover 15.00
c. As "b," half used as 12½c on cover 110.00
56 A10 50c brown 1.50 .80
On cover 15.00
a. Imperf., pair 55.00 —
b. Half used as 25c on cover 90.00
57 A10 1p red brown 300.00 40.00
On cover 150.00
a. Diagonal half used as 50c on cover 260.00

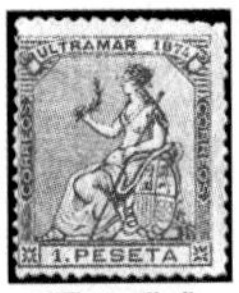

"España" Coat of Arms
A11 A12

1874
58 A11 12½c brown 18.00 8.25
On cover 50.00
a. Half used as 5c on cover 140.00
59 A11 25c ultra .90 .55
On cover 7.50
a. Diagonal half used as 12½c on cover 100.00
60 A11 50c dp violet 1.60 .80
On cover 12.50
a. Diagonal half used as 25c on cover 110.00
61 A11 50c gray 1.60 .80
On cover 12.50
a. Diagonal half used as 25c on cover 110.00
62 A11 1p carmine 210.00 60.00
On cover —
a. Imperf., pair 600.00 210.00
Nos. 58-62 (5) 232.10 70.40

Examples of Nos. 61, 63-65, 67-87 with fine impressions in slightly different colors are proofs.

1875
63 A12 12½c lt violet .80 .80
On cover 50.00
a. Imperf., pair 75.00
64 A12 25c ultra .40 .30
On cover 7.50
a. Imperf., pair 75.00
b. Diagonal half used as 12½c on cover 70.00
65 A12 50c blue green .45 .35
On cover 12.50
a. Imperf., pair 75.00
b. Diag. half used as 25c on cover 65.00
66 A12 1p brown 7.25 4.50
On cover —
b. Diag. half used as 50c on cover 125.00
Nos. 63-66 (4) 8.90 5.95

King Alfonso XII
A13 A14

1876
67 A13 12½c green 1.60 1.40
On cover 35.00
a. 12½c emerald green 1.75 1.75
On cover 45.00
68 A13 25c gray .70 .30
On cover 7.50
a. Diagonal half used as 12½c on cover 80.00
b. 25c pale violet 1.40 .25
On cover 7.50
d. 25c bluish gray 2.00 .30
On cover 10.00
69 A13 50c ultra .70 .35
On cover 7.50
a. Imperf., pair 14.00
b. Diag. half used as 25c on cover 65.00
70 A13 1p black 7.75 3.25
a. Imperf., pair 35.00
b. Diag. half used as 50c on cover 100.00
Nos. 67-70 (4) 10.75 5.30

1877
71 A14 10c lt green 22.50
72 A14 12½c gray 6.00 2.75
On cover 12.50
a. Imperf., pair 35.00
b. Diagonal half used on cover 65.00
73 A14 25c dk green .55 .45
On cover 7.50
a. Imperf., pair 35.00
b. Diagonal half used as 12½c on cover 65.00
74 A14 50c black .55 .45
On cover 7.50
a. Imperf., pair 35.00
b. Half used as 25c on cover 75.00
75 A14 1p brown 25.00 12.50
On cover —
Nos. 71-75 (5) 54.60

No. 71 was not placed in use.

Stamps Dated "1878"

1878
76 A14 5c blue .55 .45
On cover 15.00
77 A14 10c black 62.50
78 A14 12½c brown bis 3.25 1.75
On cover 12.50
a. 12½c gray bister 4.00 1.50
On cover 17.50
c. Diagonal half used on cover 65.00
79 A14 25c yel green .20 .20
On cover 7.50
b. No. 79 or 79c, diagonal half used as 12½c on cover 60.00
c. 25c deep green .20 .20
On cover 7.50
80 A14 50c dk blue grn .35 .20
On cover 7.50
b. Diagonal half used as 25c on cover 60.00
81 A14 1p carmine 10.00 4.50
b. 1p rose 6.75 3.50
Nos. 76-81 (6) 76.85 7.10

No. 77 was not placed in use.

Imperf., Pairs

76a	A14	5c blue	21.00
77a	A14	10c black	125.00
78b	A14	12½c brown bister	21.00
79a	A14	25c deep green	21.00
80a	A14	50c dk blue green	100.00
81a	A14	1p carmine	72.50

Stamps Dated "1879"

1879
82 A14 5c slate black .55 .25
On cover 15.00
83 A14 10c orange 140.00 75.00
84 A14 12½c rose .55 .25
On cover 12.50
85 A14 25c ultra .45 .25
On cover 7.50
a. Diagonal half used as 12½c on cover 65.00
b. Imperf., pair 40.00 —
86 A14 50c gray .45 .25
On cover 7.50
a. Diag. half used as 25c on cover 65.00
87 A14 1p olive bister 16.00 8.50
Nos. 82-87 (6) 158.00 84.50

A15 A16

A17

1880
88 A15 5c green .35 .20
On cover 12.50
89 A15 10c lake 80.00
90 A15 12½c gray .35 .20
On cover 7.50
91 A15 25c gray blue .35 .20
On cover 7.50
a. Diagonal half used as 12½c on cover 75.00
92 A15 50c brown .40 .20
On cover 7.50
a. Diagonal half used as 25c on cover 65.00

93 A15 1p yellow brn 5.50 2.50
a. Diagonal half used as 50c on cover 90.00
Nos. 88-93 (6) 86.95 3.30

No. 89 was not placed in use.

1881

94 A16 1c green .25 .20
On cover 7.50
95 A16 2c lake 40.00
96 A16 2½c olive bister .45 .30
On cover 7.50
97 A16 5c gray blue .25 .20
On cover 7.50
a. Diag. half used as 2½c on cover 55.00
98 A16 10c yellow brown .35 .20
On cover 7.50
a. Diagonal half used as 5c on cover 55.00
99 A16 20c dark brown 5.00 4.00
On cover 20.00
Nos. 94-99 (6) 46.30 4.90

No. 95 was not placed in use.

1882

100 A17 1c green .40 .35
On cover 7.50
a. Diag. half used as ½c on cover 50.00
101 A17 2c lake 2.40 .35
On cover 20.00
a. Diag. half used as 1c on cover 50.00
102 A17 2½c dk brown 5.25 1.75
On cover 7.50
103 A17 5c gray blue 2.40 .50
On cover 7.50
a. Diag. half used as 2½c on cover 65.00
104 A17 10c olive bister .60 .20
On cover 7.50
a. Diag. half used as 5c on cover 50.00
105 A17 20c red brown 80.00 27.50
On cover —
a. Diag. half used as 10c on cover 110.00
Nos. 100-105 (6) 91.05 30.65

See #121-131. For surcharges see #106-120.

Issue of 1882 Surcharged or Overprinted in Black, Blue or Red:

a

b

c

d

e

1883

Type "a"

106 A17 5 on 5c (R) 1.90 1.00
On cover 50.00
a. Triple surcharge
b. Double surcharge 19.00 19.00
c. Inverted surcharge 25.00 25.00
d. Without "5" in surcharge 14.00 14.00
e. Dbl. surch., types "a" & "d"
107 A17 10 on 10c (Bl) 1.90 1.10
On cover 60.00
a. Inverted surcharge
b. Double surcharge 22.50 22.50
108 A17 20 on 20c 25.00 21.00
On cover —
a. "10" instead of "20" 65.00 65.00
b. Double surcharge

Type "b"

109 A17 5 on 5c (R) 1.90 1.00
On cover 40.00
a. Inverted surcharge 22.50 22.50
b. Double surcharge 19.00 19.00
110 A17 10 on 10c (Bl) 5.50 2.25
On cover 60.00
a. Inverted surcharge 27.50 27.50
b. Double surcharge
111 A17 20 on 20c 55.00 27.50
On cover —
a. Double surcharge
b. Dbl. surch., types "b" & "c"

Type "c"

112 A17 5 on 5c (R) 1.60 1.00
On cover 50.00
a. Inverted surcharge 27.50 27.50
b. Dbl. surch., types "c" & "d" —
113 A17 10 on 10c (Bl) 5.50 2.50
On cover 75.00
a. Inverted surcharge 32.50 32.50
b. Double surcharge 32.50 32.50
114 A17 20 on 20c 37.50 20.00
On cover —
a. "10" instead of "20" 82.50 65.00
b. Double surcharge 82.50 82.50
c. Dbl. surch., types "a" & "c"

Type "d"

115 A17 5 on 5c (R) 1.50 .95
On cover 50.00
a. Inverted surcharge 27.50 27.50
b. Double surcharge 22.50 22.50
116 A17 10 on 10c (Bl) 2.25 1.60
On cover 70.00
a. Inverted surcharge 27.50 27.50
b. Double surcharge 25.00 25.00
117 A17 20 on 20c 55.00 22.50
On cover —
a. Dbl. surch., types "a" & "d"

Type "e"

118 A17 5c gray blue (R) 1.90 1.40
On cover 65.00
a. Double overprint 30.00 30.00
119 A17 10c olive bis (Bl) 4.50 4.50
On cover 100.00
a. Double overprint 32.50 32.50
120 A17 20c red brown 140.00 35.00
On cover —
a. Double overprint 110.00 110.00
Nos. 106-120 (15) 340.95 143.30

Handstamped overprints and surcharges are counterfeits.

Numerous other varieties exist.

Type of 1882

Original

1st retouch

2d retouch

The differences between the stamps of 1882 and the various retouches are as follows:

Original state: The medallion is surrounded by a heavy line of color of nearly even thickness, touching the horizontal line below the word "Cuba" (or "Filipinas," "Puerto Rico," as the case may be); the opening in the hair above the temple is narrow and pointed.

1st retouch: The line around the medallion is thin, except at the upper right, and does not touch the horizontal line above it; the opening in the hair is slightly wider and a trifle rounded; the lock of hair above the forehead is shaped like a broad "V" and ends in a point; there is a faint white line below it, which is not found on the stamps in the original state. Owing to wear of the plate the shape of the lock of hair and the width of the white line below it vary.

2nd retouch: The opening in the hair forms a semi-circle; the lock above the forehead is nearly straight, having only a slight wave, and the white line is much broader than before.

1883-86

121 A17 1c grn, 2nd retouch 110.00 45.00
On cover —
122 A17 2½c olive bister .40 .20
On cover 6.00
124 A17 2½c violet .40 .25
On cover 12.50
a. 2½c red lilac ('85) .85 .50
On cover 6.00
b. 2½c ultramarine 95.00 —
125 A17 5c gray bl, 1st retouch 2.25 .30
On cover 6.00
a. Diag. half used as 2½c on cover 45.00
126 A17 5c gray bl, 2nd retouch 22.50 2.50
On cover 12.00
a. Diag. half used as 2½c on cover 50.00
127 A17 10c brn, 1st retouch 2.75 .50
On cover 6.00
a. Diagonal half used as 5c on cover 40.00
128 A17 20c olive bister 13.00 2.75
On cover 15.00
Nos. 121-128 (7) 151.30 51.50

1888

129 A17 2½c red brown 1.60 .90
On cover 10.00
130 A17 10c blue 1.25 .80
On cover 10.00
a. Diagonal half used as 5c on cover 175.00
131 A17 20c brnsh gray 12.00 4.00
On cover 25.00
Nos. 129-131 (3) 14.85 5.70

King Alfonso XIII
A18 A19

1890-97

132 A18 1c gray brown 12.50 6.00
On cover 13.50
133 A18 1c ol gray ('91) 7.50 3.25
On cover 13.50
134 A18 1c ultra ('94) 3.25 .35
On cover 12.50
135 A18 1c dk vio ('96) .90 .25
On cover 5.00
136 A18 2c slate blue 7.00 2.00
On cover 12.50
137 A18 2c lilac brn ('91) 1.50 .45
On cover 13.50
138 A18 2c rose ('94) 30.00 5.00
On cover 13.50
139 A18 2c claret ('96) 7.75 .75
On cover 10.00
140 A18 2½c emerald 9.50 4.00
On cover 13.50
141 A18 2½c salmon ('91) 45.00 9.00
On cover —
142 A18 2½c lilac ('94) 3.00 .25
On cover 12.50
143 A18 2½c rose ('96) .65 .20
On cover 10.00
144 A18 5c olive gray .75 .60
On cover 12.50
145 A18 5c emerald ('91) .90 .40
On cover 12.50
146 A18 5c sl blue ('96) .50 .20
On cover 5.00
147 A18 10c brown violet 2.75 .75
On cover —
148 A18 10c claret ('91) 1.75 .40
On cover 12.50
149 A18 10c emerald ('96) 2.25 .20
On cover 12.50
150 A18 20c dk violet .75 .55
On cover —
151 A18 20c ultra ('91) 8.25 7.25
On cover —
152 A18 20c red brn ('94) 24.00 9.50
On cover 45.00
153 A18 20c violet ('96) 14.00 4.75
On cover —
154 A18 40c orange brn ('97) 29.00 11.00
On cover —
155 A18 80c lilac brn ('97) 52.50 17.00
On cover —
Nos. 132-155 (24) 265.95 84.10

Imperf., Pairs

134a	A18	1c	ultramarine	80.00
138a	A18	2c	rose	85.00
142a	A18	2½c	lilac	80.00
145a	A18	5c	emerald	85.00
148a	A18	10c	claret	75.00
152a	A18	20c	red brown	125.00

1898

156	A19	1m	orange brn	.20	.20
157	A19	2m	orange brn	.20	.20
158	A19	3m	orange brn	.20	.20
159	A19	4m	orange brn	4.25	1.40
160	A19	5m	orange brn	.20	.20
161	A19	1c	black vio	.20	.20
162	A19	2c	dk blue grn	.20	.20
163	A19	3c	dk brown	.20	.20
164	A19	4c	orange	12.50	3.50
165	A19	5c	car rose	.85	.20
166	A19	6c	dk blue	.25	.20
167	A19	8c	gray brown	.90	.35
168	A19	10c	vermilion	.90	.35
169	A19	15c	slate green	4.25	.35
170	A19	20c	maroon	.50	.20
171	A19	40c	dark lilac	2.00	.35
172	A19	60c	black	2.00	.35
173	A19	80c	red brown	13.00	6.75
174	A19	1p	yel green	13.00	6.75
175	A19	2p	slate blue	25.00	6.75
			Nos. 156-175 (20)	80.80	28.90

Nos. 156-160 were issued for use on newspapers.

Nos. 156-175 exist imperf. Value, unused pairs, $1,500.

For surcharges see Nos. 176-189C, 196-200.

Issued under Administration of the United States

Puerto Principe Issue

Issues of Cuba of 1898 and 1896 Surcharged:

HABILITADO 1 cent.
a

HABILITADO 1 cents.
b

HABILITADO 2 cents.
c

HABILITADO 2 cents.
d

HABILITADO 3 cents.
e

HABILITADO 3 cents.
f

HABILITADO 5 cents.
g

HABILITADO 5 cents.
h

HABILITADO 5 cents.
i

HABILITADO 5 cents.
j

HABILITADO 3 cents.
k

HABILITADO 3 cents.
l

m

HABILITADO 10 cents.

Types a, c, d, e, f, g and h are 17½mm high, the others are 19½mm high.

Black Surcharge On Nos. 156, 157, 158 and 160

1898-99

176 (a) 1c on 1m org brn 50.00 30.00
177 (b) 1c on 1m org brn 45.00 35.00
a. Broken figure "I" 75.00 65.00
b. Inverted surcharge 200.00
d. As "a," inverted *250.00*
178 (c) 2c on 2m org brn 24.00 18.00
a. Inverted surcharge 250.00 50.00
179 (d) 2c on 2m org brn 40.00 35.00
a. Inverted surcharge 350.00 100.00
179B (k) 3c on 1m org brn 300.00 175.00
c. Double surcharge 1,500. 750.00
179D (l) 3c on 1m org brn *1,500. 750.00*
e. Double surcharge — —
179F (e) 3c on 2m org brn *1,500.*

Value is for copy with minor faults.

179G (f) 3c on 2m org brn — *2,000.*

Value is for copy with minor faults.

180 (e) 3c on 3m org brn 30.00 30.00
a. Inverted surcharge 110.00
181 (f) 3c on 3m org brn 75.00 75.00
a. Inverted surcharge 200.00
182 (g) 5c on 1m org brn 700.00 200.00
a. Inverted surcharge 500.00
183 (h) 5c on 1m org brn 1,300. 500.00
a. Inverted surcharge 700.00
184 (g) 5c on 2m org brn 750.00 250.00
185 (h) 5c on 2m org brn 1,500. 500.00
186 (g) 5c on 3m org brn 650.00 175.00
a. Inverted surcharge 1,200. 700.00
187 (h) 5c on 3m org brn 400.00
a. Inverted surcharge 1,000.
188 (g) 5c on 5m org brn 80.00 60.00
a. Inverted surcharge 400.00 200.00
b. Double surcharge — —
189 (h) 5c on 5m org brn 350.00 250.00
a. Inverted surcharge 400.00
b. Double surcharge — —

The 2nd printing of Nos. 188-189 has shiny ink. Values are for the 1st printing.

189C (i) 5c on 5m org brn 7,500.

Black Surcharge on No. P25

190 (g) 5c on ½m bl grn 250.00 75.00
a. Inverted surcharge 500.00 150.00
b. Pair, right stamp without surcharge 500.00

Value for No. 190b is for pair with unsurcharged copy at right. Exists with unsurcharged stamp at left.

191 (h) 5c on ½m bl grn 300.00 90.00
a. Inverted surcharge 200.00
192 (i) 5c on ½m bl grn 550.00 200.00
a. Dbl. surch., one diagonal 11,500.
193 (j) 5c on ½m bl grn 800.00 300.00

Red Surcharge on No. 161

196 (k) 3c on 1c blk vio 65.00 35.00
a. Inverted surcharge 325.00
197 (l) 3c on 1c blk vio 125.00 55.00
a. Inverted surcharge 400.00
198 (i) 5c on 1c blk vio 25.00 30.00
a. Inverted surcharge 125.00
b. Surcharge vert. reading up 3,500.
c. Double surcharge 400.00 600.00
d. Double invtd. surch. —

No. 198b exists reading down.

199 (j) 5c on 1c blk vio 55.00 55.00
a. Inverted surcharge 250.00
b. Vertical surcharge 2,000.
c. Double surcharge 1,000. 600.00
200 (m) 10c on 1c blk vio 20.00 50.00
a. Broken figure "I" 40.00 100.00

Black Surcharge on Nos. P26-P30

201 (k) 3c on 1m bl grn 350. 350.
a. Inverted surcharge 450.
b. "EENTS" 550. 450.
c. As "b," inverted 850.
202 (l) 3c on 1m bl grn 550. 400.
a. Inverted surcharge 850.
203 (k) 3c on 2m bl grn 850. 400.
a. "EENTS" 1,250. 500.
b. Inverted surcharge 850.
c. As "a," inverted 950.
204 (l) 3c on 2m bl grn 1,250. 600.
a. Inverted surcharge 750.
205 (k) 3c on 3m bl grn 900. 400.
a. Inverted surcharge 500.
b. "EENTS" 1,250. 450.
c. As "b," inverted 700.
206 (l) 3c on 3m bl grn 1,200. 550.
a. Inverted surcharge 700.
211 (i) 5c on 1m bl grn — 1,800.
a. "EENTS" 2,500.
212 (j) 5c on 1m bl grn 2,500.
213 (i) 5c on 2m bl grn — 1,800.
a. "EENTS" 1,900.
214 (j) 5c on 2m bl grn 1,900.
215 (i) 5c on 3m bl grn 550.
a. "EENTS" 1,000.
216 (j) 5c on 3m bl grn — 1,000.
217 (i) 5c on 4m bl grn 2,500. 900.
a. "EENTS" 3,000. 1,500.
b. Inverted surcharge 2,000.
c. As "a," inverted 2,000.
218 (j) 5c on 4m bl grn 1,500.
a. Inverted surcharge 2,000.
219 (i) 5c on 8m bl grn 2,500. 1,250.
a. Inverted surcharge 1,500.
b. "EENTS" — 1,800.
c. As "b," inverted 2,500.
220 (j) 5c on 8m bl grn 2,000.
a. Inverted surcharge 2,500.

Beware of forgeries of the Puerto Principe issue. Obtaining expert opinions is recommended.

United States Nos. 279, 267, 267b, 279Bf, 279Bh, 268, 281, 282C and 283 Surcharged in Black

1899 Wmk. 191 *Perf. 12*

221 A87 1c on 1c yel grn 5.25 .40
On cover 15.00
222 A88 2c on 2c red-dish car, type III 10.00 .75
On cover 22.50
b. 2c on 2c vermilion, type III 10.00 .75
222A A88 2c on 2c red-dish car, type IV 6.00 .40
On cover 12.50
c. 2c on 2c vermilion, type IV 6.00 .40
d. As #222A, inverted surcharge *5,500.* *5,000.*
223 A88 2½c on 2c red-dish car, type III 5.00 .80
On cover 20.00
b. 2½c on 2c vermilion, type III 5.00 .80
223A A88 2½c on 2c red-dish car, type IV 3.50 .50
On cover 12.50
c. 2½c on 2c vermilion 3.50 .50
224 A89 3c on 3c pur 14.00 1.75
On cover 25.00
a. Period btwn. "B" and "A" 37.50 35.00
225 A91 5c on 5c bl 14.00 2.00
On cover 30.00
226 A94 10c on 10c brn, type I 25.00 6.50
On cover 115.00
b. "CUBA" omitted *5,500.* *4,000.*
226A A94 10c on 10c brn, type II *6,500.*
Nos. 221-226 (8) 82.75 13.10

The 2½c was sold and used as a 2c stamp.
Excellent counterfeits of this and the preceding issue exist, especially inverted and double surcharges.

Issues of the Republic under U.S. Military Rule

Statue of Columbus A20

Royal Palms A21

"Cuba" A22

Ocean Liner A23

Cane Field — A24

Wmk. US-C (191C)

1899 Engr. *Perf. 12*

227 A20 1c yel grn 3.75 .20
On cover 2.00
228 A21 2c carmine 3.75 .20
a. 2c scarlet 3.75 .20
On cover 2.00
b. Booklet pane of 6 ('02) *3,750.*
229 A22 3c purple 3.75 .20
On cover 4.00
230 A23 5c blue 5.00 .20
On cover 4.00
231 A24 10c brown 12.00 .50
On cover 6.50
Nos. 227-231 (5) 28.25 1.30

No. 228b was issued by the Republic.
See Nos. 233-237. For surcharge see No. 232.

Issues of the Republic

No. 229 Surcharged in Carmine

1902, Sept. 30

232 A22 1c on 3c purple 1.50 .50
a. Inverted surcharge 150.00 150.00
b. Surcharge sideways (numeral horizontal) 200.00 200.00
c. Double surcharge 200.00 200.00

Counterfeits of the errors are plentiful.

Re-engraved

The re-engraved stamps of 1905-07 may be distinguished from the issue of 1899 as follows:

ORIGINAL RE-ENGRAVED

1c — The ends of the label inscribed "Centavo" are rounded instead of square.
2c — The foliate ornaments, inside the oval disks bearing the numerals of value, have been removed.
5c — Two lines forming a right angle have been added in the upper corners of the label bearing the word "Cuba."
10c — A small ball has been added to each of the square ends of the label bearing the word "Cuba."

1905 Unwmk. *Perf. 12*

233 A20 1c green 1.60 .20
234 A21 2c rose 1.10 .20
a. Booklet pane of 6 150.00
236 A23 5c blue 37.50 1.00
237 A24 10c brown 3.00 .45
Nos. 233-237 (4) 43.20 1.85

Maj. Gen. Antonio Maceo — A26

1907

238 A26 50c gray bl & blk 1.10 .75

Bartolomé Masó A27

Máximo Gómez A28

Julio Sanguily A29

Ignacio Agramonte A30

Calixto García A31

José M. Rodriquez y Rodriquez (Mayia) A32

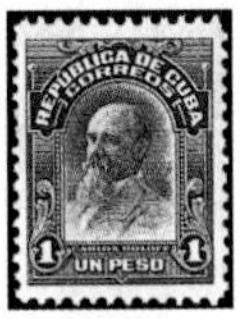

Carlos Roloff — A33

1910, Feb. 1

239 A27 1c grn & vio .85 .20
a. Center inverted 260.00 260.00
240 A28 2c car & grn 1.60 .20
a. Center inverted 575.00 575.00
241 A29 3c vio & bl 1.10 .20
242 A30 5c bl & grn 16.00 .80
243 A31 8c ol & vio 1.10 .30
244 A32 10c brn & bl 6.75 .65
a. Center inverted 850.00
245 A26 50c vio & blk 1.60 .50
246 A33 1p slate & blk 7.75 4.00
Nos. 239-246 (8) 36.75 6.85
Set, never hinged 50.00

1911-13

247 A27 1c green .55 .20
248 A28 2c car rose .70 .20
a. Booklet pane of 6 ('13) 82.50
250 A30 5c ultra 1.75 .20
251 A31 8c ol grn & blk 1.10 .60
252 A33 1p black 5.00 2.00
Nos. 247-252 (5) 9.10 3.20
Set, never hinged 16.00

Map of Cuba — A34

1914-15

253 A34 1c green .75 .20
a. Booklet pane of 6 87.50
254 A34 2c car rose .90 .20
a. Booklet pane of 6 87.50
255 A34 2c red ('15) 1.40 .20
a. Booklet pane of 6 87.50
256 A34 3c violet 4.50 .30
257 A34 5c blue 6.25 .20
258 A34 8c ol grn 5.00 .60
259 A34 10c brown 9.25 .30
260 A34 10c ol grn ('15) 11.00 .45
261 A34 50c orange 70.00 8.75
262 A34 1p gray 100.00 20.00
Nos. 253-262 (10) 209.05 31.20
Set, never hinged 300.00

Complete set of eight 1914 stamps, imperf. pairs, value $1,250.
Nos. 253, 254, 256 and E5 exist with "1917 GOB./CONSTITUCIONAL/CAMAGUEY" overprint. These were not authorized.

Gertrudis Gómez de Avellaneda, Cuban Poetess (1814-73) A34a

1914

263 A34a 5c blue 14.00 5.00
Never hinged 22.50

José Martí A35

Máximo Gómez A36

José de la Luz Caballero A37

Calixto García A38

Ignacio Agramonte A39

Tomás Estrada Palma A40

José A. Saco — A41

Antonio Maceo — A42

Carlos Manuel de Céspedes — A43

1917-18 Unwmk. *Perf. 12*

264	A35	1c bl grn	.75	.20
a.		Booklet pane of 6	40.00	
b.		Booklet pane of 30	250.00	
265	A36	2c rose	.75	.20
a.		Booklet pane of 6	50.00	
b.		Booklet pane of 30	210.00	
266	A36	2c lt red ('18)	.60	.20
a.		Booklet pane of 6	50.00	
267	A37	3c violet	.75	.20
a.		Imperf. pair	275.00	
b.		Booklet pane of 6	50.00	
268	A38	5c dp bl	.75	.20
269	A39	8c red brn	3.50	.20
270	A40	10c yel brn	2.25	.20
271	A41	20c gray grn	14.00	1.60
272	A42	50c dl rose	14.00	.70
273	A43	1p black	14.50	.70
		Nos. 264-273 (10)	51.85	4.40
		Set, never hinged	75.00	

1925-28 Wmk. 106 *Perf. 12*

274	A35	1c bl grn	1.10	.20
a.		Booklet pane of 6	350.00	
275	A36	2c brt rose	1.20	.20
a.		Booklet pane of 6	75.00	
b.		Booklet pane of 30	350.00	
276	A38	5c dp bl	2.50	.20
277	A39	8c red brn ('28)	5.75	.60
278	A40	10c yel brn ('27)	7.00	.70
279	A41	20c olive grn	11.00	1.10
		Nos. 274-279 (6)	28.55	3.00
		Set, never hinged	40.00	

1926 *Imperf.*

280	A35	1c blue green	1.40	1.00
281	A36	2c brt rose	1.40	1.00
282	A38	5c deep blue	1.75	1.40
		Nos. 280-282 (3)	4.55	3.40
		Set, never hinged	5.00	

See Nos. 304-310. For overprint and surcharge see Nos. 317-318, 644.

Arms of Republic A44

1927, May 20 Unwmk. *Perf. 12*

283	A44	25c violet	16.00	3.50
		Never hinged	24.00	

25th anniversary of the Republic.
For surcharges see Nos. 355, C3.

Tomás Estrada Palma A45

Designs: 2c, Gen. Gerardo Machado. 5c, Morro Castle. 8c, Havana Railway Station. 10c, Presidential Palace. 13c, Tobacco Plantation. 20c, Treasury Building. 30c, Sugar Mill. 50c, Havana Cathedral. 1p, Galician Clubhouse, Havana.

1928, Jan. 2 Wmk. 106

284	A45	1c deep green	.45	.20
285	A45	2c brt rose	.50	.20
286	A45	5c deep blue	.75	.30
287	A45	8c lt red brn	3.00	.90
288	A45	10c bister brn	.75	.55
289	A45	13c orange	1.50	.55
290	A45	20c olive grn	1.75	.65
291	A45	30c dk violet	4.25	.55
292	A45	50c carmine rose	6.50	2.10
293	A45	1p gray black	13.00	5.00
		Nos. 284-293 (10)	32.45	11.00
		Set, never hinged	50.00	

Sixth Pan-American Conference.

Capitol, Havana A55

1929, May 18

294	A55	1c green	.25	.25
295	A55	2c carmine rose	.30	.30
296	A55	5c blue	.45	.30
297	A55	10c bister brn	.75	.50
298	A55	20c violet	3.25	2.75
		Nos. 294-298 (5)	5.00	4.10
		Set, never hinged	9.00	

Opening of the Capitol, Havana.

Hurdler — A56

1930, Mar. 15 Engr.

299	A56	1c green	.50	.35
300	A56	2c carmine	.50	.40
301	A56	5c deep blue	.65	.40
302	A56	10c bister brn	1.00	.85
303	A56	20c violet	7.00	3.00
		Nos. 299-303 (5)	9.65	5.00
		Set, never hinged	17.50	

2nd Central American Athletic Games.

Types of 1917 Portrait Issue
Flat Plate Printing

1930-45 Wmk. 106 Engr. *Perf. 10*

304	A35	1c blue green	.75	.25
a.		Booklet pane of 6	50.00	
b.		Booklet pane of 30	—	
305	A36	2c brt rose	75.00	—
a.		Booklet pane of 6	1,200.	
305B	A37	3c dk rose vio ('42)	4.00	.75
c.		Booklet pane of 6	42.50	
306	A38	5c dk blue	2.75	.20
306A	A39	8c red brn ('45)	2.75	.25
307	A40	10c brown	2.75	.25
a.		10c yellow brown ('35)	3.50	.75
307B	A41	20c olive grn ('41)	4.75	.75
		Nos. 304-307B (7)	92.75	2.45

Nos. 305 and 305B were printed for booklet panes and all copies have straight edges.
For surcharge see No. 644.

Rotary Press Printing

308	A35	1c blue grn	1.10	.20
309	A36	2c brt rose	1.10	.20
a.		Booklet pane of 50		
310	A37	3c violet	1.50	.20
a.		3c dull violet ('38)	1.10	.20
b.		3c rose violet ('41)	1.10	.20
c.		Booklet pane of 50		
		Nos. 308-310 (3)	3.70	.60

Flat plate stamps measure 18½x21½mm; rotary press, 19x22mm.

The Mangos of Baragua — A57

War Memorial — A61

Battle of Mal Tiempo A58

Battle of Coliseo A59

Maceo, Gómez and Zayas A60

Wmk. 229

1933, Apr. 23 Photo. *Perf. 12½*

312	A57	3c dk brown	1.40	.30
313	A58	5c dk blue	1.25	.35
314	A59	10c emerald	2.25	.35
315	A60	13c red	2.75	.90
316	A61	20c black	5.50	2.10
		Nos. 312-316 (5)	13.15	4.00
		Set, never hinged	35.00	

War of Independence and dedication of the "Soldado Invasor" (the American Army that came to the aid of the revolution against Spain)monument.

Types of 1917 Issues with Carmine or Black Overprint Reading Up or Down

Rotary Press Printing

Wmk. 106

1933, Dec. 23 Engr. *Perf. 10*

317	A35	1c blue green (C)	1.75	.20

With Additional Surcharge of New Value and Bars

318	A37	2c on 3c vio (Bk)	1.75	.20

Establishment of a revolutionary junta.
Catalogue values for Nos. 317-318 unused are for examples with overprint reading up. Values for overprint reading down, $4.

Dr. Carlos J. Finlay — A62

1934, Dec. 3 Engr. *Perf. 10*

319	A62	2c dark carmine	1.00	.25
320	A62	5c dark blue	2.75	.65
		Set, never hinged	6.00	

Cent. of the birth of Dr. Carlos J. Finlay (1833-1915), physician-biologist who found that a mosquito transmitted yellow fever.

Pres. José Miguel Gómez — A63

Gómez Monument A64

1936, May *Perf. 10*

322	A63	1c green	1.50	.25
323	A64	2c carmine	2.25	.30
		Set, never hinged	7.00	

Unveiling of a monument to Gen. José Miguel Gómez, ex-president.

Matanzas Issue

Map of Cuba A65

2c, Map of Free Zone. 4c, S. S. "Rex" in Matanzas Bay. 5c, Ships in Matanzas Bay. 8c, Caves of Bellamar. 10c, Valley of Yumuri. 20c, Yumuri River. 50c, Ships Leaving Port.

Wmk. 229

1936, May 5 Photo. *Perf. 12½*

324	A65	1c blue green	.40	.20
325	A65	2c red	.60	.20
326	A65	4c claret	1.00	.20
327	A65	5c ultra	1.50	.20
328	A65	8c orange brn	2.50	.55
329	A65	10c emerald	2.75	.55
330	A65	20c brown	5.25	2.10
331	A65	50c slate	9.75	3.00
		Nos. 324-331,C18-C21,CE1,E8 (14)	43.15	16.05
		Set, never hinged	60.00	

Exist imperf. Value 20% more.

"Peace and Work" A73

Máximo Gómez Monument — A74

Torch — A75

"Independence" — A76

"Messenger of Peace" — A77

1936, Nov. 18 *Perf. 12½*

332	A73 1c emerald	.50	.20
333	A74 2c crimson	.60	.20
334	A75 4c maroon	.70	.20
335	A76 5c ultra	2.75	.45
336	A77 8c dk green	4.00	1.00
	Nos. 332-336,C22-C23,E9 (8)	17.80	3.75
	Set, never hinged	50.00	

Maj. Gen. Máximo Gómez, birth centenary.

Issued both perf and imperf. Values for imperfs are approx. 400% higher.

Sugar Cane — A78

Primitive Sugar Mill — A79

Modern Sugar Mill — A80

Wmk. 106

1937, Oct. 2 Engr. *Perf. 10*

337	A78 1c yellow green	.75	.40
338	A79 2c red	.40	.25
339	A80 5c bright blue	.85	.40
	Nos. 337-339 (3)	2.00	1.05
	Set, never hinged	4.00	

Cuban sugar cane industry, 400th anniv.

Argentine Emblem — A81

Mountain Scene (Bolivia) — A82

Arms of Brazil — A83

Canadian Scene — A84

Camilo Henriquez (Chile) A85

Gen, Francisco de Paula Santander (Colombia) A86

Natl. Monument (Costa Rica) — A87

Autograph of José Marti (Cuba) — A88

Columbus Lighthouse (Dominican Rep.) — A89

Juan Montalvo (Ecuador) — A90

Abraham Lincoln (US) A91

Quetzal and Scroll (Guatemala) A92

Arms of Haiti A93

Francisco Morazán (Honduras) A94

Fleet of Columbus — A95

Wmk. 106

1937, Oct. 13 Engr. *Perf. 10*

340	A81 1c deep green	.60	.60
341	A82 1c green	.60	.60
342	A83 2c carmine	.60	.60
343	A84 2c carmine	.60	.60
344	A85 3c violet	1.60	1.60
345	A86 3c violet	1.60	1.60
346	A87 4c bister brown	1.90	1.90
347	A88 4c bister brown	3.50	3.50
348	A89 5c blue	1.75	1.75
349	A90 5c blue	1.75	1.75
350	A91 8c citron	12.50	12.50
351	A92 8c citron	3.00	3.00
352	A93 10c maroon	3.00	3.00
353	A94 10c maroon	3.00	3.00
354	A95 25c rose lilac	30.00	30.00
	Nos. 340-354,C24-C29,E10-E11 (23)	125.50	125.50
	Set, never hinged	160.00	

Nos. 340-354 were sold by the Cuban PO for 3 days, Oct. 13-15, during which no other stamps were sold. They were postally valid for the full face value. Proceeds from their three-day sale above 30,000 pesos were paid by the Cuban POD to the Assoc. of American Writers and Artists. Remainders were overprinted "SVP" (Without Postal Value).

No. 283 Surcharged in Green

1937, Nov. 19 Unwmk. *Perf. 12*

355	A44 10c on 25c violet	12.50	2.00
	Never hinged	19.00	

Centenary of Cuban railroads.

Ciboney Indian and Cigar — A96

Cigar and Globe — A97

Tobacco Plant and Cigars — A98

1939, Aug. 28 Wmk. 106 *Perf. 10*

356	A96 1c yellow green	.35	.20
357	A97 2c red	.50	.20
358	A98 5c brt ultra	.90	.25
	Nos. 356-358 (3)	1.75	.65
	Set, never hinged	3.00	

General Calixto García A99 A100

1939, Nov. 6 *Perf. 10, Imperf.*

359	A99 2c dark red	.75	.20
360	A100 5c deep blue	1.00	.30
	Set, never hinged	3.00	

Birth centenary of General Garcia.

Values are for perf examples. Value of imperfs approx. 20% higher.

Gonzalo de Quesada — A101

1940, Apr. 30 Engr. *Perf. 10*

361	A101 2c rose red	.60	.25
	Never hinged	1.50	

Pan American Union, 50th anniversary.

Rotary Club Emblem, Cuban Flag and Tobacco Plant — A102

Lions Emblem, Cuban Flag and Royal Palms — A103

1940, May 18 Wmk. 106 *Perf. 10*

362	A102 2c rose red	1.00	.50
	Never hinged	1.60	

Rotary Intl. Convention held at Havana.

1940, July 23

363	A103 2c orange vermilion	1.00	.50
	Never hinged	1.60	

Lions International Convention, Havana.

Dr. Nicolás J. Gutiérrez A104

1940, Oct. 28

364	A104 2c orange ver	.50	.25
365	A104 5c blue	.75	.25
a.	Sheet of four, imperf., unwmkd.	4.50	3.00
	Never hinged	6.50	
b.	As "a," black overprint ('51)	5.00	4.00
	Never hinged	7.50	
	Set, never hinged	3.00	

100th anniv. of the publication of the 1st Cuban Medical Review, "El Repertorio Medico Habanero."

No. 365a contains 2 each of Nos. 364-365 imperf. and sold for 25c.

For overprint see No. C43A.

In 1951 No. 365a was overprinted in black: "50 Aniversario Descubrimiento Agente Transmisor de la Flebre Amarilla por el Dr. Carlos J. Finlay Honor a los Martires de la Ciencia 1901 1951." The overprint is illustrated over No. C43A, but does not include the plane and "Correo Aereo."

SEMI-POSTAL STAMPS

Common Design Types pictured following the introduction.

Curie Issue

Common Design Type

Wmk. 106

1938, Nov. 23 Engr. *Perf. 10*

B1	CD80 2c + 1c salmon	3.25	1.00
B2	CD80 5c + 1c deep ultra	3.25	1.25
	Set, never hinged	12.00	

40th anniv. of the discovery of radium by Pierre and Marie Curie. Surtax for the benefit of the Intl. Union for the Control of Cancer.

AIR POST STAMPS

Seaplane over Havana Harbor AP1

Wmk. 106

1927, Nov. 1 Engr. *Perf. 12*

C1	AP1 5c dark blue	3.00	.25
	Never hinged	4.00	

For overprint see No. C30.

Type of 1927 Issue Overprinted

1928, Feb. 8
C2 AP1 5c carmine rose 1.60 1.60
Never hinged 2.50

No. 283 Surcharged in Red

1930, Oct. 27 **Unwmk.**
C3 A44 10c on 25c violet 1.60 1.60
Never hinged 2.50

Airplane and Coast of Cuba — AP3

For Foreign Postage

1931, Feb. 26 Wmk. 106 *Perf. 10*
C4 AP3 5c green .45 .20
C5 AP3 10c dk blue .45 .20
C6 AP3 15c rose .90 .30
C7 AP3 20c brown .90 .20
C8 AP3 30c dk violet 1.25 .20
C9 AP3 40c dp orange 2.75 .35
C10 AP3 50c olive grn 3.25 .35
C11 AP3 1p black 5.25 .90
Nos. C4-C11 (8) 15.20 2.70
Set, never hinged 25.00

See No. C40. For surcharges see Nos. C16-C17, C203, C225.

Airplane AP4

For Domestic Postage

1931-46
C12 AP4 5c rose vio ('32) .35 .20
a. 5c brown violet ('36) .35 .20
C13 AP4 10c gray blk .35 .20
C14 AP4 20c car rose 2.50 .85
C14A AP4 20c rose pink ('46) 1.10 .20
C15 AP4 50c dark blue 4.25 .90
Nos. C12-C15 (5) 8.55 2.35
Set, never hinged 15.00

See #C130. For overprints see #C31, E29-E30.

Type of 1931 Surcharged in Black

1935, Apr. 24 ***Perf. 10***
C16 AP3 10c + 10c red 11.00 7.50
Never hinged 18.00
a. Double surcharge 110.00

Imperf
C17 AP3 10c + 10c red 25.00 *25.00*
Never hinged 30.00

Matanzas Issue

Air View of Matanzas AP5

10c, Airship "Macon." 20c, Airplane "The Four Winds." 50c, Air View of Fort San Severino.

Wmk. 229
1936, May 5 Photo. *Perf. 12½*
C18 AP5 5c violet .75 .25
C19 AP5 10c yellow orange .90 .40
C20 AP5 20c green 3.25 1.75
C21 AP5 50c greenish slate 8.00 3.00
Nos. C18-C21 (4) 12.90 5.40
Set, never hinged 20.00

Exist imperf. Value 20% more.

"Lightning" AP9

Allegory of Flight AP10

1936, Nov. 18
C22 AP9 5c violet 1.25 .25
C23 AP10 10c orange brown 2.00 .35
Set, never hinged 4.25

Major Gen. Maximo Gomez, birth cent.

Flat Arch (Panama) — AP11

Carlos Antonio López (Paraguay) — AP12

Inca Gate, Cuzco (Peru) — AP13

Atlacatl (Salvador) AP14

José Enrique Rodó (Uruguay) AP15

Simón Bolívar (Venezuela) AP16

Wmk. 106
1937, Oct. 13 Engr. *Perf. 10*
C24 AP11 5c red 7.00 7.00
C25 AP12 5c red 7.00 7.00
C26 AP13 10c blue 7.00 7.00
C27 AP14 10c blue 7.00 7.00
C28 AP15 20c green 9.50 9.50
C29 AP16 20c green 9.50 9.50
Nos. C24-C29 (6) 47.00 47.00
Set, never hinged 60.00

See note after No. 354.

Type of 1927 Overprinted in Black

1938, May Wmk. 106
C30 AP1 5c dark orange 2.75 1.50
Never hinged 4.00

1st airplane flight from Key West to Havana, made by Domingo Rosillo, 1913.

Type of 1931-32 Overprinted

1939, Oct. 15
C31 AP4 10c emerald 21.00 6.00
Never hinged 27.50

Issued in connection with an experimental postal rocket flight held at Havana.

Sir Rowland Hill, Map of Cuba and First Stamps of Britain, Spanish Cuba and Republic of Cuba — AP17

1940, Nov. 28 Engr. Wmk. 106
C32 AP17 10c brown 3.00 2.00
Never hinged 4.00

Souvenir Sheet
Unwmk. *Imperf.*
C33 Sheet of 4 11.00 11.00
Never hinged 22.50
a. AP17 10c light brown 2.75 1.25
Never hinged 3.50

Cent. of the 1st postage stamp.
Sheet sold for 60c.
No. C33 exists with each of the four stamps overprinted in black: "Exposicion de la ACNU/24 de Octubre de 1951/Dia de las Naciones" and "Historia de la Aviacion" in lower margin. Value, $60.
For overprints see Nos. C39, C211.

Poet José Heredia and Palms AP18

Heredia and Niagara Falls — AP19

1940, Dec. 30 Wmk. 106
C34 AP18 5c emerald 1.40 1.00
C35 AP19 10c greenish slate 2.40 1.50
Set, never hinged 5.00

Death cent. of José Maria Heredia y Campuzano (1803-39), poet and patriot.

AIR POST SPECIAL DELIVERY STAMPS

Matanzas Issue

Matanzas Harbor APSD1

Wmk. 229
1936, May 5 Photo. *Perf. 12½*
CE1 ASPD1 15c light blue 3.25 2.25

Exists imperf. Value $5 unused, $2.50 used.

SPECIAL DELIVERY STAMPS

Issued under US Administration

US No. E5 Surcharged in Red

1899 Wmk. 191 *Perf. 12*
E1 SD3 10c on 10c blue 160.00 100.00
a. No period after "CUBA" 575.00 400.00

Issues of the Republic under US Military Rule

Special Delivery Messenger SD2

Inscribed: "Immediata"

1899 Wmk. U S-C (191C) Engr.
E2 SD2 10c orange 55.00 15.00

Issues of the Republic
Inscribed: "Inmediata"

1902 ***Perf. 12***
E3 SD2 10c orange 1.00 .75

J. B. Zayas SD3

1910 Unwmk.
E4 SD3 10c orange & blue 14.00 3.25
Never hinged 20.00
a. Center inverted 1,250.

Airplane and Morro Castle SD4

1914, Feb. 24 ***Perf. 12***
E5 SD4 10c dark blue 15.00 1.25

Exists imperf. Value, pair $500.

1927 Wmk. Star (106)
E6 SD4 10c deep blue 12.00 .50
Never hinged 18.00

1935 ***Perf. 10***
E7 SD4 10c blue 12.00 .40
Never hinged 15.00

Matanzas Issue

Mercury SD5

Wmk. Wavy Lines (229)

1936, May 5 Photo. *Perf. 12½*

E8	SD5	10c deep claret	3.25	1.40

Exists imperf. Value $6 unused, $2.50 used.

"Triumph of the Revolution" — SD6

1936, Nov. 18

E9	SD6	10c red orange	6.00	1.10

Maj. Gen. Máximo Gómez (1836-1905).

Temple of Quetzalcoatl (Mexico) SD7

Ruben Dario (Nicaragua) SD8

Wmk. 106

1937, Oct. 13 Engr. *Perf. 10*

E10	SD7	10c deep orange	6.25	6.25
E11	SD8	10c deep orange	6.25	6.25

Issued for the benefit of the Association of American Writers and Artists. See note after No. 354.

POSTAGE DUE STAMPS

Issued under Administration of the United States

Postage Due Stamps of the US Nos. J38, J39, J41 and J42 Surcharged in Black like Nos. 221-226A

1899 Wmk. 191 *Perf. 12*

J1	D2	1c on 1c dp claret	45.00	5.25
J2	D2	2c on 2c dp claret	45.00	5.25
a.		Inverted surcharge		*4,000.*
J3	D2	5c on 5c dp claret	45.00	5.25
J4	D2	10c on 10c dp claret	27.50	2.50
		Nos. J1-J4 (4)	162.50	18.25

Issues of the Republic

D1

1914 Unwmk. Engr. *Perf. 12*

J5	D1	1c carmine rose	6.50	1.00
J6	D1	2c carmine rose	8.00	1.00
J7	D1	5c carmine rose	12.00	2.00
		Nos. J5-J7 (3)	26.50	4.00

1927-28

J8	D1	1c rose red	3.50	.70
J9	D1	2c rose red	5.50	.70
J10	D1	5c rose red	6.50	1.00
		Nos. J8-J10 (3)	15.50	2.40

NEWSPAPER STAMPS

Issued under Spanish Dominion

N1 N2

1888 Unwmk. Typo. *Perf. 14*

P1	N1	½m black	.20	*.25*
P2	N1	1m black	.20	*.30*
P3	N1	2m black	.20	*.30*
P4	N1	3m black	1.50	1.00
P5	N1	4m black	1.90	*2.00*
P6	N1	8m black	7.25	*8.50*
		Nos. P1-P6 (6)	11.25	*12.35*

1890

P7	N2	½m red brown	.50	*.65*
P8	N2	1m red brown	.50	*.65*
P9	N2	2m red brown	.80	*.95*
P10	N2	3m red brown	1.00	*1.10*
P11	N2	4m red brown	7.50	5.50
P12	N2	8m red brown	7.50	5.50
		Nos. P7-P12 (6)	17.80	14.35

1892

P13	N2	½m violet	.20	*.30*
P14	N2	1m violet	.20	*.30*
P15	N2	2m violet	.20	*.30*
P16	N2	3m violet	1.00	.35
P17	N2	4m violet	3.75	1.90
P18	N2	8m violet	8.00	3.00
		Nos. P13-P18 (6)	13.35	6.15

1894

P19	N2	½m rose	.20	*.30*
a.		Imperf. pair	22.50	
P20	N2	1m rose	.45	.35
P21	N2	2m rose	.50	.35
P22	N2	3m rose	1.90	1.40
P23	N2	4m rose	3.25	1.60
P24	N2	8m rose	5.50	4.00
		Nos. P19-P24 (6)	11.80	8.00

1896

P25	N2	½m blue green	.20	*.30*
P26	N2	1m blue green	.20	*.30*
P27	N2	2m blue green	.20	*.30*
P28	N2	3m blue green	2.50	1.50
P29	N2	4m blue green	5.25	*7.00*
P30	N2	8m blue green	9.50	*10.00*
		Nos. P25-P30 (6)	17.85	*19.40*

For surcharges see Nos. 190-193, 201-220.

POSTAL TAX STAMPS

Catalogue values for unused stamps in this section are for Never Hinged items.

Mother and Child — PT1

Nurse with Child — PT2

Wmk. Star. (106)

1938, Dec. 1 Engr. *Perf. 10*

RA1	PT1	1c bright green	1.25	.20

The tax benefited the National Council of Tuberculosis fund for children's hospitals. Obligatory on all mail during December and January. This note applies also to Nos. RA2-RA4, RA7-RA10, RA12-RA15, RA17-RA21.

1939, Dec. 1

RA2	PT2	1c orange vermilion	.75	.20

"Health" Protecting Children — PT3

1940, Dec. 1

RA3	PT3	1c deep blue	.75	.20

CYPRUS

ˈsī-prəs

LOCATION — An island in the Mediterranean Sea off the coast of Turkey
GOVT. — British Colony
AREA — 3,572 sq. mi.
POP. — 645,500 (1982)
CAPITAL — Nicosia

12 Pence = 1 Shilling
40 Paras = 1 Piaster
9 Piasters = 1 Shilling
20 Shillings = 1 Pound

Catalogue values for unused stamps in this country are for Never Hinged items, beginning with Scott 156 in the regular postage section.

STAMPS OF GREAT BRITAIN USED IN CYPRUS

Numeral cancellations on stamps of Great Britain.

When more than one plate number is shown, value is for the least expensive.

1878-81

982 (Famagusta)

A1	½p rose (#58, P11, 13), *value from*	800.
A2	1p rose red (#33, P145, 174, 181, 193, 202, 206, 215), *value from*	550.
A3	2p blue (#30, P13-15), *value from*	1,100.
A4	2½p claret (#67, P13, 16), *value from*	1,275.
A5	6p gray (#62, P15)	
A6	1sh green (#64, P12)	2,250.
A7	1sh salmon (#87, P14)	—

974 (Kyrenia)

A8	½p rose (#58, P13)	
A9	1p rose red (#33, P168, 171, 193, 196, 206, 207, 209, 220), *value from*	650.
A10	2p blue (#30, P13, 15), *value from*	1,000.
A11	2½p claret (#67, P12-15), *value from*	1,150.
A12	4p pale ol grn (#64, P16)	
A13	6p gray (#62, P16)	

942 (Larnaca)

A14	½p rose (#58, P11-15, 19-20), *value from*	300.
A15	1p rose red (#33), *value from*	195.

#A15 plate numbers: 129, 131, 146, 154, 170, 171, 174-179, 181-184, 187, 188, 190-210, 212-218, 220-222, 225.

A16	1½p lake red (#32, P3)	1,975.
A17	2p blue (#29, P9)	275.
A18	2p blue (#30, P13-15), *value from*	260.
A19	2½p claret (#67, P4-6, 8, 10, 12-17), *value from*	70.
A20	2½p ultra (#68, P17-20), *value from*	575.
A21	2½p ultra (#82, P21)	—
A22	4p pale ol grn (#64, P15-16), *value from*	640.
A23	6p gray (#62, P15-17), *value from*	575.
A24	6p pale buff (#59b, P11)	2,200.
A25	8p orange (#73)	*5,250.*
A26	1sh green (#64, P12-13), *value from*	1,050.
A27	1sh salmon (#87, P14)	—
A28	5sh rose (#87, P2)	*5,250.*

975 (Limassol)

A29	½p rose (#58, P11, 13, 15, 19), *value from*	525.
A30	1p rose red (#33), *value from*	325.

#A30 plate numbers: 160, 171, 173-175, 177, 179, 184, 187, 190, 191, 193, 195-198, 200, 202, 206-210, 213, 215, 216, 218, 220-222, 225.

A31	1½p lake red (#32, P3)	2,100.
A32	2p blue (#30, P14, 15), *value from*	475.
A33	2½p claret (#67, P11-16), *value from*	200.
A34	2½p ultra (#68, P17, 19, 20), *value from*	1,400.
A35	4p pale ol grn (#64, P16)	800.

969 (Nicosia)

A36	½p rose (#58, P12-15, 20), *value from*	525.
A37	1p rose red (#33), *value from*	325.

#A37 plate numbers: 170, 171, 174, 189, 190, 192, 193, 195, 196, 198, 200, 202, 203, 205-207, 210, 212, 214, 215, 218, 221, 222, 225.

A38	2p blue (#30, P14, 15), *value from*	525.
A39	2½p claret (#67, P10-16), *value from*	200.
A40	2½p ultra (#68, P20)	
A41	4p pale ol grn (#70, P16)	950.
A42	6p gray (#62, P16)	950.

981 (Paphos)

A43	½p rose (#58, P13, 15)	
A44	1p rose red (#33, P196, 201, 202, 204, 206, 213, 217), *value from*	575.
A45	2p blue (#30, P15), *value from*	1,000.
A46	2½p claret (#67, P13-16), *value from*	575.

AUSTRIAN OFFICES IN CYPRUS

Values in the first column for Nos. 2A1-2A78 are for stamps without defects tied to piece with legible partial strikes of town cancellations; values in the second column are for stamps without defects tied to cover by complete strikes of town cancellations. Stamps with legible town cancellations off cover sell for 25-50% of the on-piece value.

Issue dates refer to dates of stamps' issue, not necessarily to their usage with specific Cyprian postal markings.

Larnaca

Stamps of Lombardy-Venetia canceled in black with straight-line postmark with name of post office and date, italic lettering

1863 *Perf. 14*

2A1	2s yellow (#15)	*1,300.*	*4,500.*
2A2	3s green (#16)	*1,250.*	*4,500.*
2A3	5s rose (#17)	*1,250.*	*4,250.*
2A4	10s blue (#18)	*1,200.*	*4,000.*
2A5	15s yel brn (#19)	*1,300.*	*4,100.*

1864-65 *Perf. 9½*

2A6	2s yellow (#20)	975.00	*3,150.*
2A7	3s green (#21)	725.00	*2,550.*
2A8	5s rose (#22)	675.00	2,400.
2A9	10s blue (#23)	650.00	2,200.
2A10	15s yel brn (#24)	675.00	2,300.

Stamps of Lombardy-Venetia canceled in blue with straight-line postmark with name of post office and date, italic lettering

1863 *Perf. 14*

2A11	5s rose (#17)	*1,800.*	*6,750.*
2A12	10s blue (#18)	*1,800.*	*6,500.*
2A13	15s yel brn (#19)	*1,850.*	*6,600.*

1864-65 *Perf. 9½*

2A14	2s yellow (#20)	1,500.	*4,750.*
2A15	3s green (#21)	1,250.	*4,250.*
2A16	5s rose (#22)	1,175.	4,000.
2A17	10s blue (#23)	1,150.	3,800.
2A18	15s yel brn (#24)	1,175.	4,000.

Larnacca di Cipro

Stamps of Lombardy-Venetia canceled in black with single circle date stamp with post office name, month and date, without year

1863 *Perf. 14*

2A19	2s yellow (#15)	575.00	2,000.
2A20	3s green (#16)	525.00	2,200.
2A21	5s rose (#17)	525.00	2,000.
2A22	10s blue (#18)	500.00	1,750.
2A23	15s yel brn (#19)	575.00	1,850.

1864-65 *Perf. 9½*

2A24	2s yellow (#20)	625.00	1,950.
2A25	3s green (#21)	375.00	1,350.
2A26	5s rose (#22)	325.00	1,200.
2A27	10s blue (#23)	300.00	1,000.
2A28	15s yel brn (#24)	325.00	1,100.

Stamps of Austrian Offices In the Turkish Empire

Canceled in black or red brown with single circle date stamp with post office name, month and date, without year

1867-83

Coarse Print

2A29	2s yellow (#1)	300.00	1,325.
2A30	3s green (#2)	325.00	1,250.
2A31	5s red (#3)	285.00	1,000.

2A32	10s blue (#4)	275.00	950.00
2A33	15s brown (#5)	280.00	975.00
2A34	25s gray lilac (#6)	300.00	1,575.
2A35	50s brown (#7)	325.00	*4,750.*

Fine Print

2A36	2s yellow (#7C)	1,400.	—
2A37	3s green (#7D)	300.00	1,125.
2A38	5s red (#7E)	285.00	1,000.
2A39	10s blue (#7F)	275.00	950.
2A40	15s org brown (#7I)	385.00	1,625.
2A41	25s gray lilac (#7J)	500.00	*6,000.*

Stamps of Austria

Canceled in black or red brown with single circle date stamp with post office name, month and date, without year

1867-83

Coarse Print

2A42	2kr yellow (#27)	625.00	—
2A43	3kr green (#28)	625.00	—
2A44	5kr red (#29)	625.00	—
2A45	10kr blue (#30)	625.00	*2,250.*
2A46	15kr brown (#31)	625.00	*2,250.*
2A47	25kr gray lilac (#32)	625.00	—
2A48	50kr brown (#33)	700.00	—

Fine Print

2A49	2kr yellow (#34)	625.00	—
2A50	3kr green (#35)	625.00	—
2A51	5kr red (#36)	625.00	—
2A52	10kr blue (#37)	625.00	*2,250.*
2A53	15kr org brown (#38)	625.00	*2,250.*
2A54	25kr gray (#39)	725.00	
2A55	50kr brown (#40)	750.00	—

Stamps of Austrian Offices In the Turkish Empire

Canceled in blue with single circle date stamp with post office name, month and date, without year

1867-83

Coarse Print

2A56	2s yellow (#1)	300.00	1,325.
2A57	3s green (#2)	325.00	1,250.
2A58	5s red (#3)	285.00	1,000.
2A59	10s blue (#4)	275.00	950.
2A60	15s brown (#5)	280.00	975.
2A61	25s gray lilac (#6)	300.00	1,575.
2A62	50s brown (#7)	325.00	*4,750.*

Fine Print

2A63	2s yellow (#7C)	1,400.	—
2A64	3s green (#7D)	300.00	1,125.
2A65	5s red (#7E)	285.00	1,000.
2A66	10s blue (#7F)	275.00	950.
2A67	15s org brown (#7I)	385.00	1,625.
2A68	25s gray lilac (#7J)	500.00	*6,000.*

1863 ***Perf. 14***

2A69	2s yellow (#15)	—	—
2A70	3s green (#16)	—	—
2A71	5s rose (#17)	*1,800.*	*6,750.*
2A72	10s blue (#18)	*1,800.*	*6,500.*
2A73	15s yel brn (#19)	*1,850.*	*6,600.*

1864-65 ***Perf. 9½***

2A74	2s yellow (#20)	1,500.	4,750.
2A75	3s green (#21)	1,250.	4,250.
2A76	5s rose (#22)	1,175.	4,000.
2A77	10s blue (#23)	1,150.	3,800.
2A78	15s yel brn (#24)	1,175.	4,000.

BRITISH ADMINISTRATION

Values for unused stamps are for examples with original gum as defined in the catalogue introduction. Very fine examples of Nos. 1, 2 and 7-10 will have perforations touching the design on at least one or more sides due to the narrow spacing of the stamps on the plates and to imperfect perforation methods. Stamps with perfs clear on all four sides are scarce and will command higher prices.

Queen Victoria — A1

A2

A3

A4

A5

A6

A7

Various Watermarks as in Great Britain (#20, 23, 25, 27 & 29)

1880 **Typo.** ***Perf. 14***

1	A1	½p rose (P 15)	125.00	110.00
		Plate 12	210.00	*300.00*
		Plate 19	5,750.	950.00
b.		Double overprint (P 15)		*15,500.*
2	A2	1p red (P 216)	19.00	*45.00*
		Plate 217	13.00	*45.00*
		Plate 174	1,400.	1,400.
		Plate 181	400.00	200.00
		Plate 184	14,500.	2,750.
		Plate 193	800.00	
		Plate 196	700.00	
		Plate 201	14.00	*57.50*
		Plate 205	65.00	57.50
		Plate 208	110.00	65.00
		Plate 215	13.00	*57.50*
		Plate 218	21.00	*65.00*
		Plate 220	550.00	475.00
b.		Double overprint (P 218)	5,400.	
		Double overprint (P 208)	*17,500.*	
c.		Pair, one without ovpt. (P 208)	*22,000.*	
3	A3	2½p claret (P 14)	2.75	*9.25*
		Plate 15	4.00	*27.50*
4	A4	4p lt ol grn (P 16)	140.00	*240.00*
5	A5	6p ol gray (P 16)	575.00	*750.00*
6	A6	1sh green (P 13)	750.00	525.00

Black Surcharge

7	A7	30 paras on 1p red (P 216)	110.00	*95.00*
		Plate 201	140.00	100.00
		Plate 217	200.00	200.00
		Plate 220	175.00	*190.00*
b.		Dbl. surch., one invtd. (P 220)	1,500.	*1,350.*
		Dbl. surch., one invtd. (P 216)	4,250.	

No. 2 Surcharged

18mm Long

1881

8	A2	½p on 1p (205, 216)	80.00	*100.00*
		Plate 174	175.00	*350.00*
		Plate 181	175.00	*200.00*
		Plate 201	110.00	*140.00*
		Plate 205	80.00	*100.00*
		Plate 208	190.00	*325.00*
		Plate 215	750.00	*800.00*
		Plate 217	925.00	825.00
		Plate 218	525.00	*640.00*
		Plate 220	300.00	*375.00*
a.		"HALFPENN" (P216)	2,100.	2,100.

16mm Long

9	A2	½p on 1p (P 201)	140.00	*190.00*
		Plate 216	400.00	*450.00*
		Plate 218		*11,500.*
a.		Double surcharge (P 201, 216)	3,200.	2,900.

13mm Long

10	A2	½p on 1p red (P 215)	52.50	*75.00*
		Plate 205	290.00	
		Plate 217	150.00	92.50
		Plate 218	80.00	*110.00*
c.		Double surcharge (P 215)	550.00	*700.00*
		Double surcharge (P 205)	800.00	
e.		Triple surcharge (P 215)	800.00	
		Triple surcharge (P 205)	*4,000.*	
		Triple surcharge (P 217)	—	
		Triple surcharge (P 218)	*4,000.*	
h.		Quadruple surch. (P 205, 215)	*5,000.*	
j.		"CYPRUS" double (P 218)	*5,500.*	

A8

1881, July **Typo.** **Wmk. 1**

11	A8	½pi emerald green	210.00	52.50
12	A8	1pi rose	425.00	37.50
13	A8	2pi ultramarine	525.00	37.50
14	A8	4pi olive green	1,050.	325.00
15	A8	6pi olive gray	1,750.	500.00

Postage and revenue stamps of Cyprus with "J.A.B." (the initials of Postmaster J.A. Bulmer) in manuscript, or with "POSTAL SURCHARGE" (with or without "J. A. B."), were not Postage Due stamps but were employed for accounting purposes between the chief PO at Larnaca and the sub-offices.

See Nos. 19-25, 28-37. For surcharges see Nos. 16-18, 26-27.

A9

A10

Black Surcharge

1882 **Wmk. 1**

16	A9	½pi on ½pi grn	700.00	85.00
17	A10	30pa on 1pi rose	1,750.	125.00

1884 **Wmk. 2**

18	A9	½pi on ½pi green	160.00	10.00
a.		Double surcharge		*3,200.*

See Nos. 26, 27.

1882-94 **Die B**

For description of Dies A and B see "Dies of British Colonial Stamps" in Table of Contents.

19	A8	½pi green	5.75	.80
20	A8	30pa violet	5.75	5.75
21	A8	1pi rose	13.00	2.25
22	A8	2pi blue	16.00	2.00
23	A8	4pi pale ol grn	25.00	*27.50*
b.		4pi olive green	25.00	20.00
24a	A8	6pi	190.00	*650.00*
25a	A8	12pi	150.00	*375.00*
		Nos. 19-25a (7)	405.50	*1,063.*

Die A

19a	A8	½pi	18.00	1.75
b.		½pi emerald	*5,750.*	475.00
20a	A8	30pa lilac	70.00	22.50
21a	A8	1pi	100.00	2.25
22a	A8	2pi	140.00	2.25
23a	A8	4pi	400.00	27.50
c.		4pi deep olive green ('83)	575.00	35.00
24	A8	6pi olive gray	55.00	19.00
25	A8	12pi brown org	200.00	40.00
		Overprinted "SPECIMEN"	*925.00*	
		Nos. 19a-25 (7)	983.00	115.25

A11

Type I — Figures "½" 8mm apart.
Type II — Figures "½" 6mm apart.
The space between the fraction bars varies from 5½ to 8½mm but is usually 6 or 8mm.

Black Surcharge Type I

1886 **Wmk. 2**

26	A11	½pi on ½pi grn	400.00	15.00
a.		Type II	250.00	80.00
b.		Double surcharge, type II		

Wmk. 1

27	A11	½pi on ½pi grn	*8,750.*	500.00
a.		Type II	*19,500.*	

No. 27a probably is a proof.

1894-96 **Wmk. 2**

28	A8	½pi grn & car rose	4.75	1.50
29	A8	30pa violet & green	2.75	1.75
30	A8	1pi rose & ultra	7.25	1.50
31	A8	2pi ultra & mar	7.50	1.50
32	A8	4pi ol green & vio	19.00	5.25
33	A8	6pi ol gray & grn	14.50	*16.00*
34	A8	9pi brown & rose	18.00	20.00
35	A8	12pi brn org & blk	20.00	*60.00*
36	A8	18pi slate & brown	52.50	52.50
37	A8	45pi dk vio & ultra	110.00	*150.00*
		Nos. 28-37 (10)	256.25	*310.00*
		Set, optd. "SPECIMEN"	375.00	

King Edward VII
A12

King George V
A13

1903 **Typo.**

38	A12	½pi grn & car rose	4.50	1.40
39	A12	30pa violet & green	11.00	3.75
a.		30pa mauve & green	18.00	7.50
40	A12	1pi carmine rose & ultra	21.00	4.25
41	A12	2pi ultra & mar	62.50	12.50
42	A12	4pi ol green & vio	32.50	22.50
43	A12	6pi ol brown & grn	45.00	*140.00*
44	A12	9pi brn & car rose	110.00	*225.00*
45	A12	12pi org brn & blk	15.00	*62.50*
46	A12	18pi black & brown	92.50	*175.00*
47	A12	45pi dk vio & ultra	225.00	*575.00*
		Nos. 38-47 (10)	619.00	*1,221.*
		Set, optd. "SPECIMEN"	500.00	

1904-07 **Wmk. 3**

48	A12	5pa bis & blk ('07)	1.10	.80
49	A12	10pa org & grn ('07)	3.50	.55
a.		10pa yellow & green	42.50	6.25
50	A12	½pi grn & car rose	5.25	.20
51	A12	30pa reddish violet & green	16.00	1.75
a.		30pa violet & green ('10)	19.00	2.90
52	A12	1pi car rose & ultra	6.50	1.10
53	A12	2pi ultra & maroon	8.00	2.00
54	A12	4pi ol grn & red vio	13.00	9.25
55	A12	6pi ol brn & green	17.50	*17.00*
56	A12	9pi brn & car rose	35.00	9.75
a.		9pi yel brn & carmine rose	32.50	25.00
57	A12	12pi org brn & blk	29.00	*45.00*
58	A12	18pi black & brown	35.00	12.50
59	A12	45pi dk vio & ultra	85.00	*160.00*
		Nos. 48-59 (12)	254.85	*259.90*

1912

61	A13	10pa orange & green	3.75	2.90
a.		10pa org yel & br green ('15)	2.50	1.40
62	A13	½pi grn & car rose	2.00	.20
a.		½pi yel green & carmine	8.50	2.25
63	A13	30pa violet & green	2.90	.70
64	A13	1pi car & ultra	4.50	2.00
a.		1pi carmine & blue ('15)	15.00	4.75
65	A13	2pi ultra & maroon	7.50	2.25
66	A13	4pi ol grn & red vio	4.75	*5.50*
67	A13	6pi ol brn & green	4.00	*9.75*
68	A13	9pi brn & car rose	27.50	*30.00*
a.		9pi yellow brown & carmine	30.00	*32.50*
69	A13	12pi org brn & blk	18.00	*42.50*
70	A13	18pi black & brown	30.00	*35.00*
71	A13	45pi dl vio & ultra	92.50	*140.00*
		Nos. 61-71 (11)	197.40	*270.80*
		Set, optd. "SPECIMEN"	475.00	

1921-23 **Wmk. 4**

72	A13	10pa orange & grn	8.00	*9.50*
73	A13	10pa gray & yellow	14.00	8.50
74	A13	30pa violet & grn	2.90	.45
75	A13	30pa green	8.00	.45
76	A13	1pi rose & ultra	20.00	*30.00*
77	A13	1pi violet & car	3.50	*4.50*
78	A13	1½pi orange & blk	6.25	*5.50*
79	A13	2pi ultra & red vio	22.50	15.00
80	A13	2pi rose & ultra	11.00	*25.00*
81	A13	2¾pi ultra & red vio	8.00	*10.50*
82	A13	4pi ol grn & red vio	14.00	*20.00*
83	A13	6pi ol brn & green	19.00	*75.00*
84	A13	9pi brn & carmine	30.00	*80.00*
a.		9pi yellow brown & carmine	97.50	*140.00*

85 A13 18pi black & brn 70.00 *150.00*
86 A13 45pi dl vio & ultra 200.00 *290.00*
Nos. 72-86 (15) 437.15 *724.40*
Set, optd. "SPECIMEN" 625.00

Wmk. 3

87 A13 10sh grn & red, *yel* 425.00 *875.00*
88 A13 £1 vio & black, *red* 1,150. *2,100.*
Nos. 87-88, optd. "SPECIMEN" 575.00

Years of issue: Nos. 73, 75, 77-78, 80-81, 87-88, 1923; others, 1921.

Forged cancellations exist on Nos. 83-88, including a dangerous "LIMASSOL 14 MR 25" fake postmark.

A14

1924-28 Chalky Paper Wmk. 4

89 A14 ¼pi gray & brn org 1.10 .20
90 A14 ½pi gray blk & blk 3.00 *10.00*
91 A14 ½pi grn & dp grn ('25) 2.50 1.10
92 A14 ¾pi grn & dp grn 2.50 1.10
93 A14 ¾pi gray blk & blk ('25) 2.25 .20
94 A14 1pi brn vio & org brown 2.25 .80
95 A14 1½pi org & black 2.25 *8.50*
96 A14 1½pi carmine ('25) 2.90 .35
97 A14 2pi car & green 2.50 *15.00*
98 A14 2pi org & black ('25) 8.00 4.25
99 A14 2½pi ultra ('25) 3.50 .35
100 A14 2¾pi ultra & dull vio 3.75 3.50
101 A14 4pi ap grn & vio 3.75 3.75
102 A14 4½pi black & yel, *emer* 4.00 4.00
103 A14 6pi grn ol & grn 4.25 *6.25*
104 A14 9pi brn & dk vio 7.00 5.00
105 A14 12pi org brn & blk 10.50 *62.50*
106 A14 18pi blk & org 22.50 5.75
Revenue cancel 1.00
107 A14 45pi gray vio & ultra 42.50 *42.50*
Revenue cancel 1.50
108 A14 90pi grn & red, *yel* 100.00 *200.00*
Revenue cancel 3.00
109 A14 £5 blk, *yel* ('28) 3,200. *7,000.*
Overprinted "SPECIMEN" 1,000.
Revenue cancel 175.00

Wmk. 3

110 A14 £1 vio & black, *red* 350.00 *800.00*
Revenue cancel 10.00
Nos. 89-108 (20) 231.00 *375.10*

Nos. 96 and 99 are on ordinary paper.

Silver Coin of Amathus — A15

Philosopher Zeno — A16

Map of Cyprus — A17

Discovery of Body of St. Barnabas — A18

Cloisters of Bella Paise Monastery — A19

Badge of the Colony — A20

Hospice of Umm Haram at Larnaca — A21

Statue of Richard Coeur de Lion, London — A22

St. Nicholas Cathedral, Famagusta — A23

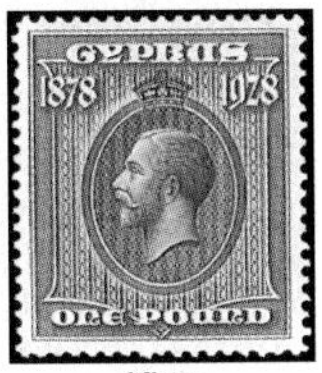

King George V — A24

Perf. 12

1928, Feb. 1 Engr. Wmk. 4

114 A15 ¾pi dark violet 3.00 1.10
115 A16 1pi Prus bl & blk 3.50 1.75
116 A17 1½pi red 5.00 2.25
117 A18 2½pi ultramarine 4.00 *2.50*
118 A19 4pi dp red brown 6.25 *7.00*
119 A20 6pi dark blue 8.50 *24.00*
120 A21 9pi violet brown 8.50 *12.50*
121 A22 18pi dk brn & blk 21.00 *21.00*
122 A23 45pi dp blue & vio 45.00 *55.00*
123 A24 £1 ol brn & deep blue 225.00 *350.00*
Nos. 114-123 (10) 329.75 *477.10*
Set, optd. "SPECIMEN" 625.00

50th year of Cyprus as a British colony.

Ruins of Vouni Palace — A25

Columns at Salamis — A26

Peristerona Church — A27

Soli Theater — A28

Kyrenia Castle and Harbor — A29

Kolossi Castle — A30

St. Sophia Cathedral — A31

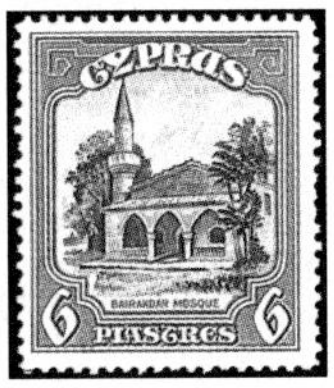

Bairakdar Mosque — A32

Queen's Window, St. Hilarion Castle — A33

Buyuk Khan, Nicosia — A34

Forest Scene — A35

1934, Dec. 1 Engr. *Perf. 12½*

125 A25 ¼pi yel brn & ultra 1.10 .55
Never hinged 1.50
a. Vert. pair, imperf. between *26,500.* *18,500.*
126 A26 ½pi green 1.60 1.10
Never hinged 1.75
a. Vert. pair, imperf. between *12,750.* *14,000.*
127 A27 ¾pi violet & blk 1.90 .20
Never hinged 2.50
a. Vert. pair, imperf. between *29,000.*
128 A28 1pi brown & blk 1.40 .90
Never hinged 2.50
a. Vert. pair, imperf. between *15,000.* *15,000.*
b. Horiz. pair, imperf. btwn. *11,750.*
129 A29 1½pi rose red 2.75 .60
Never hinged 3.50
130 A30 2½pi dark ultra 2.75 2.00
Never hinged 4.00
131 A31 4½pi dk car & blk 3.50 *4.25*
Never hinged 7.50
132 A32 6pi blue & black 10.00 *14.00*
Never hinged 20.00
133 A33 9pi dl vio & blk brown 9.00 *5.50*
Never hinged 17.50
134 A34 18pi ol grn & black 45.00 *32.50*
Never hinged 90.00
135 A35 45pi blk & emer 75.00 *57.50*
Never hinged 315.00
Nos. 125-135 (11) 154.00 *119.10*
Set, never hinged 300.00
Set, perf "SPECIMEN" 400.00

Common Design Types pictured following the introduction.

Silver Jubilee Issue
Common Design Type

1935, May 6 *Perf. 11x12*

136 CD301 ¾pi gray blk & ultra 1.90 .40
Never hinged 3.00
137 CD301 1½pi car & dk bl 4.25 2.75
Never hinged 5.50
138 CD301 2½pi ultra & brn 4.00 *1.60*
Never hinged 6.50
139 CD301 9pi brn vio & ind 16.00 *17.00*
Never hinged 22.50
Nos. 136-139 (4) 26.15 *21.75*
Set, never hinged 40.00
Set, perf "SPECIMEN" 175.00

Coronation Issue
Common Design Type

1937, May 12 *Perf. 11x11½*

140 CD302 ¾pi dark gray .35 .20
Never hinged .65
141 CD302 1½pi dark carmine .60 *.85*
Never hinged 1.00
142 CD302 2½pi deep ultra 1.25 *1.40*
Never hinged 2.10
Nos. 140-142 (3) 2.20 2.45
Set, never hinged 4.00
Set, perf "SPECIMEN" 100.00
Same, never hinged 150.00

Ruins of Vouni Palace — A36

Columns at Salamis — A37

Peristerona Church — A38

Soli Theater — A39

Kyrenia Castle and Harbor — A40

Kolossi Castle — A41

Map of Cyprus — A42

Bairakdar Mosque — A43

Citadel, Famagusta — A44

Buyuk Khan — A45

Forest Scene A46

King George VI A47

1938-44 Wmk. 4 *Perf. 12½*

143 A36 ¼pi yel brn & ultra .20 .20
Never hinged .20
144 A37 ½pi green .30 .20
Never hinged .55
145 A38 ¾pi violet & blk 7.00 .55
Never hinged 15.00
146 A39 1pi orange .40 .20
Never hinged .85
a. Perf. 13½x12½ ('44) 350.00 30.00
Never hinged 460.00
147 A40 1½pi rose car 2.50 1.60
Never hinged 6.00
147A A40 1½pi lt vio ('43) .25 .30
Never hinged .55
147B A38 2pi carmine & blk ('42) .35 .20
Never hinged .75
c. Perf. 12½x13½ ('44) 2.00 *7.50*
Never hinged 2.50
148 A41 2½pi ultramarine 10.00 3.50
Never hinged 26.00
148A A41 3pi dp ultra ('42) .80 .20
Never hinged 1.60
149 A42 4½pi gray .35 .20
Never hinged .75
150 A43 6pi blue & black .60 *1.10*
Never hinged 1.35
151 A44 9pi dk vio & blk 1.00 .20
Never hinged 2.45
152 A45 18pi ol grn & blk 2.00 .90
Never hinged 6.50
153 A46 45pi blk & emer 9.00 2.75
Never hinged 20.00
154 A47 90pi blk & brt vio 16.00 5.50
Never hinged 24.00
155 A47 £1 ind & dl red 35.00 26.00
Never hinged 52.50
Nos. 143-155 (16) 85.75 43.60
Set, never hinged 175.00
Set, perf "SPECIMEN" 400.00
Same, never hinged 475.00

See Nos. 164-166.

Catalogue values for unused stamps in this section, from this point to the end of the section, are for Never Hinged items.

Peace Issue
Common Design Type

1946, Oct. 21 Engr. *Perf. 13½x14*
156 CD303 1½pi purple .20 .20
157 CD303 3pi deep blue .20 .20

Silver Wedding Issue
Common Design Types

1948, Dec. 20 Photo. *Perf. 14x14½*
158 CD304 1½pi purple .55 .20

Engr.; Name Typo.
Perf. 11½x11
159 CD305 £1 dark blue 45.00 *55.00*

UPU Issue
Common Design Types
Perf. 13½, 11x11½

1949, Oct. 10 Engr. Wmk. 4
160 CD306 1½pi violet .45 *.75*
161 CD307 2pi deep carmine 1.75 1.75
162 CD308 3pi indigo .80 *1.10*
163 CD309 9pi rose violet 1.75 1.75
Nos. 160-163 (4) 4.75 5.35

Types of 1938-43

1951, July 2 Engr. *Perf. 12½*
164 A37 ½pi purple 2.40 .20
165 A40 1½pi deep green 3.00 .55
166 A41 4pi deep ultra 3.25 .30
Nos. 164-166 (3) 8.65 1.05

CYRENAICA

ˌsir-ə-ˈnā-ə-kə

LOCATION — In northern Africa bordering on the Mediterranean Sea
GOVT. — Italian colony
AREA — 75,340 sq. mi.
POP. — 225,000 (approx. 1934)
CAPITAL — Bengasi (Benghazi)

100 Centesimi = 1 Lira

Used values in italics are for postally used stamps. CTO's sell for about the same as unused, hinged stamps.

Watermark

Wmk. 140 — Crown

Propaganda of the Faith Issue

Italy Nos. 143-146 Overprinted

1923, Oct. 24 Wmk. 140 *Perf. 14*
1 A68 20c ol grn & brn org 7.25 *35.00*
Never hinged 11.00
On overfranked cover *225.00*
2 A68 30c claret & brn org 7.25 *35.00*
Never hinged 11.00
On overfranked cover *225.00*
a. Vert. pair, imperf between and at bottom *550.00*
b. Vert. strip of 3, imperf between and at bottom *625.00*
3 A68 50c violet & brn org 4.25 *42.50*
Never hinged 7.50
On overfranked cover *150.00*
4 A68 1 l blue & brown orange 4.25 *42.50*
Never hinged 7.50
On overfranked cover *300.00*
a. Vert. pair, imperf between *550.00*
b. Vert. strip of 3, imperf between and at bottom *625.00*
Nos. 1-4 (4) 23.00 *155.00*
Set, never hinged 57.50
Set on overfranked cover *500.00*

Fascisti Issue

Italy Nos. 159-164 Overprinted in Red or Black

1923, Oct. 29 Unwmk. *Perf. 14*
5 A69 10c dk grn (R) 7.25 *13.00*
Never hinged 12.50
On commercial cover *140.00*
6 A69 30c dk vio (R) 7.25 *13.00*
Never hinged 12.50
On commercial cover *140.00*
7 A69 50c brn car 7.25 *14.50*
Never hinged 12.50
On commercial cover *140.00*

Wmk. 140
8 A70 1 l blue 7.25 *35.00*
Never hinged 12.50
On commercial cover *250.00*
9 A70 2 l brown 7.25 *42.50*
Never hinged 12.50
On commercial cover *375.00*
10 A71 5 l blk & bl (R) 7.25 *47.50*
Never hinged 12.50
On commercial cover —
Nos. 5-10 (6) 43.50 *165.50*
Set, never hinged 110.00
Set on overfranked cover *375.00*

Manzoni Issue

Italy Nos. 165-170 Overprinted in Red

1924, Apr. 1 *Perf. 14*
11 A72 10c brn red & blk 11.50 *35.00*
Never hinged 18.00
12 A72 15c bl grn & blk 11.50 *35.00*
Never hinged 18.00
13 A72 30c blk & slate 11.50 *35.00*
Never hinged 18.00
14 A72 50c org brn & blk 11.50 *35.00*
Never hinged 18.00
15 A72 1 l bl & blk 72.50 *250.00*
Never hinged 150.00
a. Double overprint *875.00*
As "a," never hinged *1,100.*
16 A72 5 l vio & blk 475.00 *1,900.*
Never hinged 1,200.
Nos. 11-16 (6) 593.50 *2,290.*
Set, never hinged 1,450.
Set on overfranked cover *3,750.*

Vertical overprints on Nos. 11-14 are essays. On Nos. 15-16 the overprint is vertical at the left.

All examples of No. 15a are poorly centered.

Commercial covers of this issue are very rare.

Victor Emmanuel Issue

Italy Nos. 175-177 Overprinted

1925-26 Unwmk. *Perf. 11*
17 A78 60c brn car .75 *7.25*
Never hinged .90
On commercial cover *100.00*
18 A78 1 l dark blue .75 *7.25*
Never hinged 1.25
On commercial cover *150.00*
19 A78 1.25 l dk bl ('26) 2.75 *14.50*
Never hinged 6.75
On commercial cover *225.00*
a. Perf. 13½ 175.00 *475.00*
Never hinged 350.00
Nos. 17-19 (3) 4.25 *29.00*
Set, never hinged 11.00

Issue dates: Nov. 1925, July 1926.

Saint Francis of Assisi Issue

Italian Stamps of 1926 Overprinted

1926, Apr. 12 Wmk. 140 *Perf. 14*
20 A79 20c gray green 2.10 *10.00*
Never hinged 4.00
On commercial cover 80.00
21 A80 40c dark violet 2.10 *10.00*
Never hinged 4.00
On commercial cover 95.00
22 A81 60c red brown 2.10 *18.00*
Never hinged 4.00
On commercial cover *95.00*

Overprinted in Red

Unwmk.
23 A82 1.25 l dk bl, perf. 11 2.10 *25.00*
Never hinged 4.00
On commercial cover *160.00*
a. Pair, one with albino surcharge *725.00*
Never hinged *900.00*
24 A83 5 l + 2.50 l ol grn 4.50 *50.00*
Never hinged 11.50
On commercial cover —
a. Double surcharge, one black, one red *1,100.*
Never hinged *1,400.*
Nos. 20-24 (5) 12.90 *113.00*
Set, never hinged 32.50
Set on overfranked cover 275.00

Volta Issue

Type of Italy 1927, Overprinted

1927, Oct. 10 Wmk. 140 *Perf. 14*
25 A84 20c purple 5.75 *27.50*
Never hinged 14.00
On commercial cover 140.00
a. Overprint omitted *2,400.*
Never hinged 3,750.
26 A84 50c dp org 7.25 *18.00*
Never hinged 18.00
On commercial cover 140.00
a. Dot omitted after figures of value 42.50 *57.50*
b. Double overprint *150.00*
c. Overprinted "Cirenaica" and "Eritrea" (inverted) *325.00*
27 A84 1.25 l brt bl 11.50 *45.00*
Never hinged 27.50
On commercial cover 250.00
Nos. 25-27 (3) 24.50 *90.50*
Set, never hinged 62.50
Set on overfranked cover 250.00

#25 exists with overprint omitted. See Italy.

Monte Cassino Issue

Types of 1929 Issue of Italy, Overprinted in Red or Blue

1929, Oct. 14
28 A96 20c dk grn (R) 4.25 *16.00*
Never hinged 10.00
On commercial cover 125.00
29 A96 25c red org (Bl) 4.25 *16.00*
Never hinged 10.00
On commercial cover 110.00
30 A98 50c + 10c crim (Bl) 4.25 *18.00*
Never hinged 10.00
On commercial cover 80.00
31 A98 75c + 15c ol brn (R) 4.25 *18.00*
Never hinged 10.00
On commercial cover 125.00
32 A96 1.25 l + 25c dk vio (R) 10.00 *32.50*
Never hinged 20.00
On commercial cover 190.00
33 A98 5 l + 1 l saph (R) 10.00 *35.00*
Never hinged 20.00

Overprinted in Red

Unwmk.

34 A100 10 l + 2 l gray brn 10.00 *50.00*
Never hinged 20.00
Nos. 28-34 (7) 47.00 *185.50*
Set, never hinged 115.00
Set on overfranked cover 275.00

Royal Wedding Issue

Type of Italian Stamps of 1930 Overprinted

1930, Mar. 17 Wmk. 140

35 A101 20c yel grn 1.40 *4.25*
Never hinged 2.75
On commercial cover 80.00
a. Without overprint *18,500.*
Never hinged *27,500.*
36 A101 50c + 10c dp org 1.10 *7.25*
Never hinged 2.25
On commercial cover 100.00
37 A101 1.25 l + 25c rose red 1.10 *14.50*
Never hinged 2.25
On commercial cover 250.00
Nos. 35-37 (3) 3.60 *26.00*
Set, never hinged 8.75
Set on overfranked cover 150.00

Ferrucci Issue

Types of Italian Stamps of 1930, Overprinted in Red or Blue

1930, July 26

38 A102 20c violet (R) 2.75 *3.50*
Never hinged 4.50
On commercial cover 65.00
39 A103 25c dk grn (R) 2.75 *3.50*
Never hinged 4.50
On commercial cover 80.00
40 A103 50c black (R) 2.75 *7.25*
Never hinged 4.50
On commercial cover 65.00
41 A103 1.25 l dp bl (R) 2.75 *14.00*
Never hinged 4.50
On commercial cover 160.00
42 A104 5 l + 2 l dp car 7.25 *25.00*
Never hinged 16.50
Nos. 38-42 (5) 18.25 *53.25*
Set, never hinged 47.50
Set on overfranked cover 150.00

Virgil Issue

Types of Italian Stamps of 1930 Overprinted in Red or Blue

1930, Dec. 4

43 A106 15c vio blk 1.10 *7.25*
Never hinged 2.25
On commercial cover 80.00
44 A106 20c org brn (Bl) 1.10 *2.75*
Never hinged 2.25
On commercial cover 55.00
45 A106 25c dk grn 1.10 *2.75*
Never hinged 2.25
On commercial cover 47.50
46 A106 30c lt brn (Bl) 1.10 *2.75*
Never hinged 2.25
On commercial cover 55.00
47 A106 50c dl vio 1.10 *2.75*
Never hinged 2.25
On commercial cover 40.00
48 A106 75c rose red (Bl) 1.10 *7.75*
Never hinged 2.25
On commercial cover 110.00
49 A106 1.25 l gray bl 1.10 *7.25*
Never hinged 2.25
On commercial cover 160.00

Unwmk.

50 A106 5 l + 1.50 l dk vio 3.25 *30.00*
Never hinged 12.50
On commercial cover —
51 A106 10 l + 2.50 l ol brn (Bl) 3.25 *42.50*
Never hinged 12.50
Nos. 43-51 (9) 14.20 *105.75*
Set, never hinged 37.50
Set on overfranked cover 300.00

Saint Anthony of Padua Issue

Types of Italian Stamps of 1931 Overprinted in Blue or Red

1931, May 7 Wmk. 140

52 A116 20c brown (Bl) 1.50 *16.00*
Never hinged 3.50
On commercial cover 65.00
53 A116 25c green (R) 1.50 *5.75*
Never hinged 3.50
On commercial cover 65.00
54 A118 30c gray brn (Bl) 1.50 *5.75*
Never hinged 3.50
On commercial cover 95.00
55 A118 50c dl vio (Bl) 1.50 *5.75*
Never hinged 3.50
On commercial cover 65.00
56 A120 1.25 l slate bl (R) 1.50 *16.00*
Never hinged 3.50
On commercial cover 225.00

Overprinted like Nos. 23-24 in Red or Black

Unwmk.

57 A121 75c black, Opt. Type 1 (R) 1.50 *29.00*
Never hinged 3.50
On commercial cover 190.00
a. Overprint Type 2 *26.00* *72.50*
58 A122 5 l + 2.50 l dk brn, Opt. Type 1 4.25 *60.00*
Never hinged 5.00
a. Overprint Type 2 *57.50* *160.00*
Nos. 52-58 (7) 13.25 *138.25*
Set, never hinged 32.50
Set on overfranked cover 375.00

Overprint on Nos. 57-58: Type 1, 14½mm wide; Type 2, 13mm wide.

Carabineer A1

1934, Oct. 16 Photo. Wmk. 140

59 A1 5c dk ol grn & brn 3.50 *18.00*
Never hinged 7.75
On commercial cover 175.00
60 A1 10c brn & blk 3.50 *18.00*
Never hinged 7.75
On commercial cover 150.00
61 A1 20c scar & indigo 3.50 *14.50*
Never hinged 7.75
On commercial cover 150.00
62 A1 50c pur & brn 3.50 *14.50*
Never hinged 7.75
On commercial cover 125.00
63 A1 60c org brn & ind 3.50 *21.00*
Never hinged 7.75
On commercial cover 175.00
64 A1 1.25 l dk bl & grn 3.50 *35.00*
Never hinged 7.75
On commercial cover 225.00
Nos. 59-64 (6) 21.00 *121.00*
Set, never hinged 55.00
Set on overfranked cover 240.00

2nd Colonial Art Exhibition held at Naples. See Nos. C24-C29.

SEMI-POSTAL STAMPS

Many issues of Italy and Italian Colonies include one or more semipostal denominations. To avoid splitting sets, these issues are generally listed as regular postage unless all values carry a surtax.

Holy Year Issue

Italian Semi-Postal Stamps of 1924 Overprinted in Black or Red

1925, June 1 Wmk. 140 *Perf. 12*

B1 SP4 20c + 10c dk grn & brn 2.75 *18.00*
Never hinged 6.75
On commercial cover 140.00
B2 SP4 30c + 15c dk brn & brn 2.75 *20.00*
Never hinged 6.75
On commercial cover 125.00
B3 SP4 50c + 25c vio & brn 2.75 *18.00*
Never hinged 6.75
On commercial cover 125.00
B4 SP4 60c + 30c dp rose & brn 2.75 *22.50*
Never hinged 6.75
On commercial cover 190.00
B5 SP8 1 l + 50c dp bl & vio (R) 2.75 *27.50*
Never hinged 6.75
B6 SP8 5 l + 2.50 l org brn & vio (R) 2.75 *42.50*
Never hinged 6.75
Nos. B1-B6 (6) 16.50 *148.50*
Set, never hinged 42.50
Set on overfranked cover 325.00

Colonial Institute Issue

"Peace" Substituting Spade for Sword — SP1

1926, June 1 Typo. *Perf. 14*

B7 SP1 5c + 5c brown .85 *7.25*
Never hinged 2.25
On commercial cover 100.00
B8 SP1 10c + 5c olive grn .85 *7.25*
Never hinged 2.25
On commercial cover 87.50
B9 SP1 20c + 5c blue grn .85 *7.25*
Never hinged 2.25
On commercial cover 62.50
B10 SP1 40c + 5c brown red .85 *7.25*
Never hinged 2.25
On commercial cover 62.50
B11 SP1 60c + 5c orange .85 *7.25*
Never hinged 2.25
On commercial cover 100.00
B12 SP1 1 l + 5c blue .85 *16.00*
Never hinged 2.25
On commercial cover 175.00
Nos. B7-B12 (6) 5.10 *52.25*
Set, never hinged 7.50
Set on overfranked cover 160.00

Surtax for Italian Colonial Institute.

Types of Italian Semi-Postal Stamps of 1926 Overprinted like Nos. 17-19

1927, Apr. 21 Unwmk. *Perf. 11*

B13 SP10 40c + 20c dk brn & blk 2.10 *27.50*
Never hinged 5.00
On commercial cover 100.00
B14 SP10 60c + 30c brn red & ol brn 2.10 *27.50*
Never hinged 5.00
On commercial cover 110.00
B15 SP10 1.25 l + 60c dp bl & blk 2.10 *45.00*
Never hinged 5.00
On commercial cover 210.00
a. Double overprint *875.00*
As "a," never hinged *1,100.*
B16 SP10 5 l + 2.50 l dk grn & blk 3.50 *65.00*
Never hinged 8.00
Nos. B13-B16 (4) 9.80 *165.00*
Set, never hinged 25.00
Set on overfranked cover 325.00

The surtax on these stamps was for the charitable work of the Voluntary Militia for Italian National Defense.

Allegory of Fascism and Victory — SP2

1928, Oct. 15 Wmk. 140 *Perf. 14*

B17 SP2 20c + 5c bl grn 2.25 *10.50*
Never hinged 4.50
On commercial cover 95.00
B18 SP2 30c + 5c red 2.25 *10.50*
Never hinged 4.50
On commercial cover 95.00
B19 SP2 50c + 10c purple 2.25 *18.00*
Never hinged 4.50
On commercial cover 87.50
B20 SP2 1.25 l + 20c dk bl 2.75 *21.00*
Never hinged 5.00
On commercial cover 350.00
Nos. B17-B20 (4) 9.50 *60.00*
Set, never hinged 22.50
Set on overfranked cover 200.00

46th anniv. of the Societa Africana d'Italia. The surtax aided that society.

Types of Italian Semi-Postal Stamps of 1926 Overprinted in Red or Black like Nos. 52-56

1929, Mar. 4 Unwmk. *Perf. 11*

B21 SP10 30c + 10c red & blk 3.50 *18.00*
Never hinged 8.25
On commercial cover 100.00
B22 SP10 50c + 20c vio & blk 3.50 *21.00*
Never hinged 8.25
On commercial cover 100.00
B23 SP10 1.25 l + 50c brn & bl 4.25 *35.00*
Never hinged 10.00
On commercial cover 225.00
B24 SP10 5 l + 2 l ol grn & blk (Bk) 4.25 *65.00*
Never hinged 10.00
Nos. B21-B24 (4) 15.50 *139.00*
Set, never hinged 40.00
Set on overfranked cover 325.00

Surtax for the charitable work of the Voluntary Militia for Italian Natl. Defense.

Types of Italian Semi-Postal Stamps of 1926 Overprinted in Black or Red like Nos. 52-56

1930, Oct. 20 *Perf. 14*

B25 SP10 30c + 10c dk grn & bl grn (Bk) 14.50 *20.00*
Never hinged 35.00
On commercial cover 140.00
B26 SP10 50c + 10c dk grn & vio 14.50 *27.50*
Never hinged 35.00
On commercial cover 125.00
B27 SP10 1.25 l + 30c ol brn & red brn 14.50 *40.00*
Never hinged 35.00
On commercial cover 250.00
B28 SP10 5 l + 1.50 l ind & grn 47.50 *87.50*
Never hinged 120.00
On commercial cover 125.00
Nos. B25-B28 (4) 91.00 *175.00*
Set, never hinged 225.00
Set on overfranked cover 375.00

Surtax for the charitable work of the Voluntary Militia for Italian Natl. Defense.

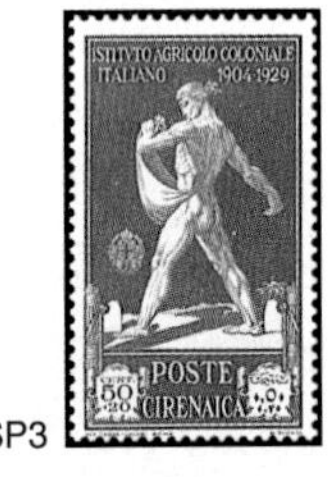

Sower — SP3

1930, Nov. 27 Photo. Wmk. 140

B29 SP3 50c + 20c ol brn 3.50 *18.00*
Never hinged 6.50
On commercial cover 110.00
B30 SP3 1.25 l + 20c dp bl 3.50 *18.00*
Never hinged 6.50
On commercial cover 150.00
B31 SP3 1.75 l + 20c green 3.00 *20.00*
Never hinged 6.50
On commercial cover 200.00
B32 SP3 2.55 l + 50c purple 5.75 *32.50*
Never hinged 13.00
On commercial cover 300.00

B33 SP3 5 l + 1 l dp car 6.75 *47.50*
Never hinged 13.00
Nos. B29-B33 (5) 22.50 *136.00*
Set, never hinged 55.00
Set on overfranked cover 250.00

25th anniv. of the Italian Colonial Agricultural Institute. The surtax was for the aid of that institution.

AIR POST STAMPS

Air Post Stamps of Tripolitania, 1931, Overprinted in Blue like Nos. 38-42

1932, Jan. 7 Wmk. 140 *Perf. 14*

C1 AP1 50c rose car 1.40 .35
Never hinged 1.75
On commercial cover 18.00
C2 AP1 60c dp org 4.50 *10.50*
Never hinged 11.00
On commercial cover 125.00
C3 AP1 80c dl vio 4.50 *18.00*
Never hinged 11.00
On commercial cover 210.00
Nos. C1-C3 (3) 10.40 *28.85*
Set, never hinged 26.00
Set on overfranked cover 150.00

Air Post Stamps of Tripolitania, 1931, Overprinted in Blue

1932, May 12

C4 AP1 50c rose car 1.40 1.75
Never hinged 2.75
On commercial cover 16.50
C5 AP1 80c dull violet 4.50 *20.00*
Never hinged 11.00
On commercial cover 210.00
Set, never hinged 14.50
Set on flight cover 125.00

This overprint was also applied to the 60c, Tripolitania No. C9. The overprinted stamp was never used in Cyrenaica, but was sold at Rome in 1943 by the Postmaster General for the Italian Colonies. Value $5.

Arab on Camel — AP2

Airplane in Flight AP3

1932, Aug. 8 Photo.

C6 AP2 50c purple 7.25 .20
Never hinged 9.00
On commercial cover 3.75
C7 AP2 75c brn rose 7.25 7.25
Never hinged 14.00
On commercial cover *95.00*
C8 AP2 80c deep blue 7.25 8.50
Never hinged 14.00
On commercial cover *125.00*
C9 AP3 1 l black 2.75 .20
Never hinged 4.50
On commercial cover 5.75
C10 AP3 2 l green 2.75 *8.50*
Never hinged 5.50
On commercial cover *250.00*
C11 AP3 5 l deep car 5.75 *18.00*
Never hinged 10.00
On commercial cover *440.00*
Nos. C6-C11 (6) 33.00 *42.65*
Set, never hinged 82.50
Set on flight cover *210.00*

For surcharges and overprint see #C20-C23.

Graf Zeppelin Issue

Zeppelin and Clouds forming Pegasus AP4

Zeppelin and Ancient Galley AP5

Zeppelin and Giant Bowman AP6

1933, Apr. 15

C12 AP4 3 l dk brn 7.25 *92.50*
Never hinged 16.00
On commercial cover *275.00*
C13 AP5 5 l purple 7.25 *92.50*
Never hinged 16.00
On commercial cover *325.00*
C14 AP6 10 l dp grn 7.25 *175.00*
Never hinged 16.00
On commercial cover *500.00*
C15 AP5 12 l deep blue 7.25 *200.00*
Never hinged 16.00
On commercial cover *725.00*
C16 AP4 15 l carmine 7.25 *200.00*
Never hinged 16.00
On commercial cover *725.00*
C17 AP6 20 l black 7.25 *250.00*
Never hinged 16.00
On commercial cover *725.00*
Nos. C12-C17 (6) 43.50 *1,010.*
Set, never hinged 105.00
Set on flight cover *2,750.*
Set on 6 flight covers *3,300.*

North Atlantic Crossing Issue

Airplane Squadron and Constellations — AP7

1933, June 1

C18 AP7 19.75 l grn & dp bl 14.00 *500.00*
Never hinged 32.50
On commercial cover *1,800.*
C19 AP7 44.75 l red & indigo 14.00 *500.00*
Never hinged 32.50
On commercial cover *1,800.*
Set, never hinged 65.00
Set on flight cover *3,500.*

Type of 1932 Overprinted and Surcharged

1934, Jan. 20

C20 AP3 2 l on 5 l org brn 2.75 *57.50*
Never hinged 5.50
On commercial cover 200.00
C21 AP3 3 l on 5 l yel grn 2.75 *57.50*
Never hinged 5.50
On commercial cover 200.00
C22 AP3 5 l ocher 2.75 *65.00*
Never hinged 5.50
On commercial cover 240.00
C23 AP3 10 l on 5 l rose 4.25 *65.00*
Never hinged 6.25
On commercial cover 325.00
Nos. C20-C23 (4) 12.50 *245.00*
Set, never hinged 26.00
Set on flight cover *900.00*

For use on mail to be carried on a special flight from Rome to Buenos Aires.

Transport Plane AP8

Venus of Cyrene AP9

1934, Oct. 9

C24 AP8 25c sl bl & org red 3.50 *20.00*
Never hinged 7.75
On commercial cover 125.00
C25 AP8 50c dk grn & ind 3.50 *16.00*
Never hinged 7.75
On commercial cover 110.00
C26 AP8 75c dk brn & org red 3.50 *14.50*
Never hinged 7.75
On commercial cover 150.00
a. Imperf. 1,700.
Never hinged 2,000.
C27 AP9 80c org brn & ol grn 3.50 *20.00*
Never hinged 7.75
On commercial cover 175.00
C28 AP9 1 l scar & ol grn 3.50 *22.50*
Never hinged 7.75
On commercial cover 210.00
C29 AP9 2 l dk bl & brn 3.50 *37.50*
Never hinged 7.75
On commercial cover 275.00
Nos. C24-C29 (6) 21.00 *130.50*
Set, never hinged 52.50
Set on flight cover 300.00

2nd Colonial Arts Exhib. held at Naples.

AIR POST SEMI-POSTAL STAMPS

King Victor Emmanuel III SPAP1

Wmk. 104

1934, Nov. 5 Photo. *Perf. 14*

CB1 SPAP1 25c + 10c gray grn 5.75 *12.50*
Never hinged 9.00
On cover 125.00
CB2 SPAP1 50c + 10c brn 5.75 *12.50*
Never hinged 9.00
On cover 125.00
CB3 SPAP1 75c + 15c rose red 5.75 *12.50*
Never hinged 9.00
On cover 150.00
CB4 SPAP1 80c + 15c brn blk 5.75 *12.50*
Never hinged 9.00
On cover 175.00
CB5 SPAP1 1 l + 20c red brn 5.75 *12.50*
Never hinged 9.00
On cover 200.00
CB6 SPAP1 2 l + 20c brt bl 5.75 *12.50*
Never hinged 9.00
CB7 SPAP1 3 l + 25c pur 20.00 *65.00*
Never hinged 42.50
CB8 SPAP1 5 l + 25c org 20.00 *65.00*
Never hinged 42.50
CB9 SPAP1 10 l + 30c dp vio 20.00 *65.00*
Never hinged 42.50
CB10 SPAP1 25 l + 2 l dp grn 20.00 *65.00*
Never hinged 42.50
Nos. CB1-CB10 (10) 114.50 *335.00*
Set, never hinged 275.00
Set on flown cover 875.00

65th birthday of King Victor Emmanuel III and the non-stop flight, Rome-Mogadiscio.

AIR POST SEMI-POSTAL OFFICIAL STAMP

Type of Air Post Semi-Postal Stamps, 1934, Overprinted Crown and "SERVIZIO DI STATO" in Black

1934, Nov. 5 Wmk. 140 *Perf. 14*

CBO1 SPAP1 25 l + 2 l cop red *2,400.*
Never hinged *3,000.*
On flight cover *1,475.*

CZECHOSLOVAKIA

ˌche-kə-slō-ˈvä-kē-ə

LOCATION — Central Europe
GOVT. — Republic
AREA — 49,355 sq. mi.
POP. — 15,395,970 (1983)
CAPITAL — Prague

The Czechoslovakian Republic consists of Bohemia, Moravia and Silesia, Slovakia and Ruthenia (Carpatho-Ukraine). In March 1939, a German protectorate was established over Bohemia and Moravia, as well as over Slovakia which had meanwhile declared its independence. Ruthenia was incorporated in the territory of Hungary. These territories were returned to the Czechoslovak Republic in 1945, except for Ruthenia, which was ceded to Russia.

100 Haleru = 1 Koruna

Catalogue values for unused stamps in this country are for Never Hinged items, beginning with Scott B144 in the semi-postal section, Scott EX1 in the personal delivery section, and Scott P14 in the newspaper section.

Watermarks

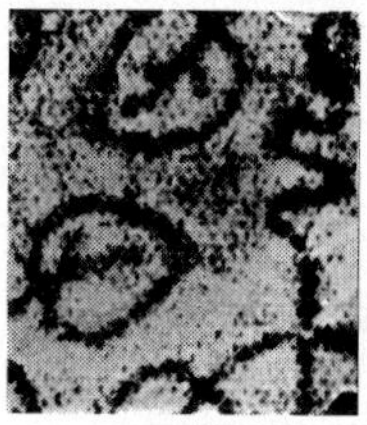

Wmk. 107 — Linden Leaves (Vertical)

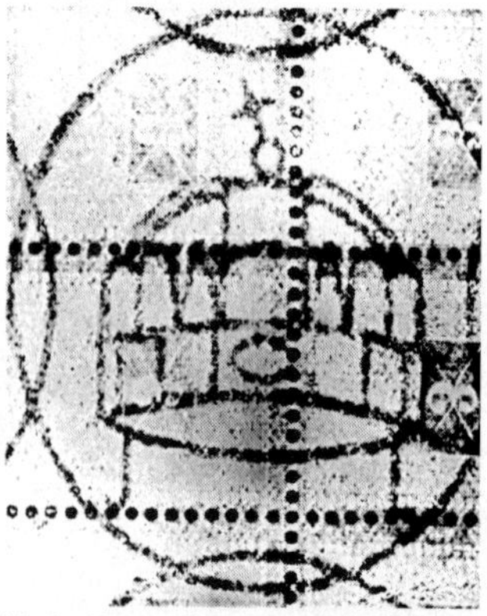

Wmk. 135 — Crown in Oval or Circle, Sideways

Wmk. 136

Wmk. 136a

Stamps of Austria overprinted "Ceskoslovenska Republika," lion and "Cesko Slovensky Stat," "Provisorni Ceskoslovenska Vlada" and Arms, and "Ceskoslovenska Statni Posta" and Arms were made privately. A few of them were passed through the post but all have been pronounced unofficial and unauthorized by the Postmaster General.

During the occupation of part of Northern Hungary by the Czechoslovak forces, stamps of Hungary were overprinted "Cesko Slovenska Posta," "Ceskoslovenska Statni Posta" and Arms, and "Slovenska Posta" and Arms. These stamps were never officially issued though copies have passed the post.

Hradcany at Prague — A1

1918-19 Unwmk. Typo. *Imperf.*

1	A1	3h red violet	.20	.20
2	A1	5h yellow green	.20	.20
3	A1	10h rose	.20	.20
4	A1	20h bluish green	.20	.20
5	A1	25h deep blue	.25	.20
6	A1	30h bister	.45	.20
7	A1	40h red orange	.45	.20
8	A1	100h brown	1.25	.20
9	A1	200h ultra	2.25	.20
10	A1	400h purple	3.50	.20

On the 3h-40h "Posta Ceskoslovenska" is in white on a colored background; on the higher values the words are in color on a white background.

The 25h in ultramarine was not valid for postage.

Nos. 1-6 exist as tete-beche gutter pairs.

See #368, 1554, 1600. For surcharges see #B130, C1, C4, J15, J19-J20, J22-J23, J30.

Perf. 11½, 13½

13	A1	5h yellow green	.65	.20
a.		Perf. 11½x10¾	1.90	.45
14	A1	10h rose	.30	.20
15	A1	20h bluish green	.30	.20
a.		Perf. 11½	.30	.20
16	A1	25h deep blue	.60	.20
a.		Perf. 11½	1.25	.65
20	A1	200h ultra	4.25	.20
		Nos. 1-10,13-16,20 (15)	15.05	3.00

All values of this issue exist with various private perforations and copies have been used on letters.

The 3, 30, 40, 100 and 400h formerly listed are now known to have been privately perforated.

For overprints see Eastern Silesia Nos. 2, 5, 7-8, 14, 16, 18, 30.

A2

Type II — Sun behind cathedral. Colorless foliage in foreground.

Type III — Without sun. Shaded foliage in foreground.

Type IV — No foliage in foreground. Positions of buildings changed. Letters redrawn.

1919 *Imperf.*

23	A2	1h dark brown (II)	.20	.20
25	A2	5h blue green (IV)	.40	.20
27	A2	15h red (IV)	.85	.20
29	A2	25h dull violet (IV)	.65	.20
30	A2	50h dull violet (II)	.40	.20
31	A2	50h dark blue (IV)	.40	.20
32	A2	60h orange (III)	1.25	.20
33	A2	75h slate (IV)	.85	.20
34	A2	80h olive grn (III)	.95	.20
36	A2	120h gray black (IV)	2.50	.30
38	A2	300h dark green (III)	6.50	.65
39	A2	500h red brown (IV)	8.50	.50
40	A2	1000h violet (III)	19.00	.75
a.		1000h bluish violet	42.50	1.60
		Nos. 23-40 (13)	42.45	4.00

For overprints see Eastern Silesia Nos. 1, 3-4, 6, 9-13, 15, 17, 20-21.

1919-20 *Perf. 11½, 13¾, 13¾x11½*

41	A2	1h dk brown (II)	.20	.20
42	A2	5h blue grn (IV), perf. 13½	.40	.20
a.		Perf. 11½	25.00	3.25
43	A2	10h yellow grn (IV)	.40	.20
a.		Imperf.	21.00	19.00
b.		Perf. 11¾	13.00	1.25
44	A2	15h red (IV)	.40	.20
a.		Perf. 11½x10¾	30.00	3.75
b.		Perf. 11½x13¾	85.00	19.00
c.		Perf. 13¾x10¾	125.00	26.00
45	A2	20h rose (IV)	.40	.20
a.		Imperf.	82.50	77.50
46	A2	25h dull vio (IV), perf. 11½	.65	.25
a.		Perf. 11½x10¾	5.00	.95
b.		Perf. 13¾x10¾	175.00	32.50
47	A2	30h red violet (IV)	.35	.20
a.		Imperf.	190.00	190.00
b.		Perf. 13¾x13½	550.00	160.00
c.		30h deep violet	.70	.20
d.		As "c," perf. 13¾x13½	625.00	190.00
e.		As "c," imperf.	190.00	140.00
50	A2	60h orange (III)	.30	.20
a.		Perf. 13¾x13½	12.50	6.25
53	A2	120h gray black (IV)	3.75	.95
		Nos. 41-53 (9)	6.85	2.60

Nos. 43a, 45a, 47a and 47e were imperforate by accident and not issued in quantities as were Nos. 23 to 40.

Rouletted stamps of the preceding issues are said to have been made by a postmaster in a branch post office at Prague, or by private firms, but without authority from the Post Office Department.

The 50, 75, 80, 300, 500 and 1000h have been privately perforated.

Unlisted color varieties of types A1 and A2 were not officially released, and some are printer's waste.

For surcharges and overprints see Nos. B131, C2-C3, C5-C6, J16-J18, J21, J24-J29, J31, J42-J43, Eastern Silesia 22-29.

Pres. Thomas Garrigue Masaryk — A4

1920 *Perf. 13½*

61	A4	125h gray blue	1.50	.20
a.		125h ultramarine	30.00	19.00
62	A4	500h slate, *grysh*	4.75	1.50
a.		Imperf.	20.00	7.00
63	A4	1000h blk brn, *brnsh*	8.00	2.40
		Nos. 61-63 (3)	14.25	4.10

#61, 61a, 63 imperf. were not regularly issued.

For surcharge and overprints see Nos. B131, Eastern Silesia 31-32.

Carrier Pigeon with Letter — A5

Czechoslovakia Breaking Chains to Freedom — A6

Hussite Priest — A7

Agriculture and Science — A8

Two types of 40h:

Type I: 9 leaves by woman's hip.

Type II: 10 leaves by woman's hip.

1920 *Perf. 14*

65	A5	5h dark blue	.20	.20
a.		Perf. 13¾	*325.00*	*150.00*
66	A5	10h blue green	.20	.20
a.		Perf. 13¾	*225.00*	110.00
67	A5	15h red brown	.20	.20
68	A6	20h rose	.20	.20
69	A6	25h lilac brown	.20	.20
70	A6	30h red violet	.20	.20
71	A6	40h red brown (I)	.60	.20
a.		As "b," tête bêche pair	6.75	2.00
b.		Perf. 13½	1.50	.20
c.		Type II	.25	.20
72	A6	50h carmine	.50	.20
73	A6	60h dark blue	.50	.20
a.		As "b," tête bêche pair	6.00	4.00
b.		Perf. 13½	2.00	.25

Photo.

74	A7	80h purple	.20	.20
75	A7	90h black brown	.30	.20

Typo.

76	A8	100h dark green	1.00	.20
77	A8	200h violet	1.50	.20
78	A8	300h vermilion	3.50	.20
a.		Perf. 13¾x13½	7.00	.35
79	A8	400h brown	6.00	.45
80	A8	500h deep green	7.00	.45
a.		Perf. 13¾x13½	100.00	5.50
81	A8	600h deep violet	9.00	.45
a.		Perf. 13¾x13½	275.00	7.00
		Nos. 65-81 (17)	31.30	4.15

No. 69 has background of horizontal lines.

Imperfs. were not regularly issued.

Nos. 71 and 73 exist as tete-beche gutter pairs.

For surcharges and overprint see Nos. C7-C9, J44-J56.

1920-25 *Perf. 14*

Two types of 20h:

Type I: Base of 2 is long, interior of 0 is angular.

Type II: Base of 2 is short, interior of 0 is an oval.

Two types of 25h:

Type I: Top of 2 curves up.

Type II: Top of 2 curves down.

82	A5	5h violet	.20	.20
a.		As "b," tête bêche pair	2.00	1.00
b.		Perf. 13½	1.00	.35
83	A5	10h olive bister	.20	.20
a.		As "b," tête bêche pair	2.25	1.50
b.		Perf. 13½	.80	.20
84	A5	20h deep orange (I)	1.00	.20
a.		As "b," tête bêche pair	30.00	14.00
b.		Perf. 13½	6.00	.90
c.		Type II	.20	.20
85	A5	25h blue green (I)	.20	.20
a.		Type II	.20	.20
86	A5	30h deep violet ('25)	3.00	.20
87	A6	50h yellow green	1.00	.20
a.		As "b," tête bêche pair	60.00	27.50
b.		Perf. 13½	12.00	2.00
88	A6	100h dark brown	1.00	.20
a.		Perf. 13½	15.00	.25
89	A6	150h rose	4.50	.50
a.		Perf. 13½	80.00	1.10
90	A6	185h orange	3.00	.20
91	A6	250h dark green	5.00	.25
		Nos. 82-91 (10)	19.10	2.35

Imperfs. were not regularly issued.

Nos. 82-84, 87 exist as tete-beche gutter pairs.

Type of 1920 Issue Redrawn

Type I — Rib of leaf below "O" of POSTA is straight and extends to tip. White triangle above book is entirely at left of twig. "P" has a stubby, abnormal appendage.

Type II — Rib is extremely bent; does not reach tip. Triangle extends at right of twig. "P" like Type I.

Type III — Rib of top left leaf is broken in two. Triangle like Type II. "P" has no appendage.

1923 *Perf. 13¾, 13¾x13½*

92	A8	100h red, *yellow*, III, perf. 14x13½	1.00	.20
a.		Type I, perf. 13¾	1.25	.20
b.		Type I, perf. 13¾x13½	1.25	.20
c.		Type II, perf. 13¾	1.50	.20
d.		Type II, perf. 13¾x13½	1.50	.20
e.		Type III, perf. 13¾	7.00	.20
93	A8	200h blue, *yellow*, II, perf. 14	5.00	.20
a.		Type II, perf. 13¾x13½	8.50	.25
b.		Type III, perf. 13¾	8.50	.25
c.		Type III, perf. 13¾x13½	52.50	.50
94	A8	300h violet, *yellow*, I, perf. 13¾	3.75	.20
a.		Type II, perf. 13¾	35.00	.25
b.		Type II, perf. 13¾x13½	50.00	.50
c.		Type III, perf. 13¾x13½	7.00	.20
d.		Type III, perf. 13¾	24.00	.35
		Nos. 92-94 (3)	9.75	.60

President Masaryk
A9 A10

Perf. 13¾x13½, 13¾

1925 Photo. Wmk. 107

Size: 19½x23mm

95	A9	40h brown orange	.75	.20
96	A9	50h olive green	1.50	.20
97	A9	60h red violet	1.75	.20
		Nos. 95-97 (3)	4.00	.60

Distinctive Marks of the Engravings.

I, II, III — Background of horizontal lines in top and bottom tablets. Inscriptions in Roman letters with serifs.

IV — Crossed horizontal and vertical lines in the tablets. Inscriptions in Antique letters without serifs.

I, II, IV — Shading of crossed diagonal lines on the shoulder at the right.

III — Shading of single lines only.

I — "T" of "Posta" over middle of "V" of "Ceskoslovenska." Three short horizontal lines in lower part of "A" of "Ceskoslovenska."

II — "T" over right arm of "V." One short line in "A."

III — "T" as in II. Blank space in lower part of "A."

IV — "T" over left arm of "V."

Wmk. Horizontally (107)

Engr.

I. First Engraving

Size: 19¾x22½mm

98	A10	1k carmine	.85	.20
99	A10	2k deep blue	2.00	.25
100	A10	3k brown	4.00	.65
101	A10	5k blue green	1.40	.45
		Nos. 98-101 (4)	8.25	1.55

Wmk. Vertically (107)

Size: 19¼x23mm

101A	A10	1k carmine	100.00	4.00
101B	A10	2k deep blue	100.00	12.50
101C	A10	3k brown	250.00	12.50
101D	A10	5k blue green	5.00	2.00

II. Second Engraving

Wmk. Horizontally (107)

Size: 19x21½mm

102	A10	1k carmine	42.50	.50
103	A10	2k deep blue	3.50	.25
104	A10	3k brown	3.50	.50
		Nos. 102-104 (3)	49.50	1.25

III. Third Engraving

Size: 19-19½x21½-22mm

Perf. 10

105	A10	1k carmine rose	1.00	.20
a.		Perf. 14	12.50	.20

IV. Fourth Engraving

Size: 19x22mm

1926 *Perf. 10*

106	A10	1k carmine rose	1.00	.20

Perf. 14

108	A10	3k brown	4.50	.20

There is a 2nd type of No. 106: with long mustache. Same values. See No. 130, design SP3.

Karlstein Castle — A11

1926, June 1 Engr. *Perf. 10*

109	A11	1.20k red violet	.50	.30
110	A11	1.50k car rose	.30	.20
111	A11	2.50k dark blue	3.00	.30
		Nos. 109-111 (3)	3.80	.80

See Nos. 133, 135.

Karlstein Castle — A12

Pernstein Castle — A13

Orava Castle
A14

Masaryk
A15

Strahov
Monastery — A16

Hradcany at
Prague
A17

Great
Tatra — A18

1926-27 Engr. Wmk. 107

114	A13	30h gray green	1.25	.20
115	A14	40h red brown	.50	.20
116	A15	50h deep green	.50	.20
117	A15	60h red vio, *lil*	.85	.20
118	A16	1.20k red violet	4.00	1.50

Perf. 13½

119	A17	2k blue	.75	.20
a.		2k ultramarine	5.50	.75
120	A17	3k deep red	1.50	.20
121	A18	4k brown vio ('27)	3.50	.40
122	A18	5k dk green ('27)	12.50	2.25
		Nos. 114-122 (9)	25.35	5.35

No. 116 exists in two types. The one with short, straight mustache at left sells for several times as much as that with longer wavy mustache.

See Nos. 137-140.

Coil Stamps

Perf. 10 Vertically

123	A12	20h brick red	.50	.40
a.		Vert. pair, imperf. horiz.	100.00	
124	A13	30h gray green	.35	.20
a.		Vert. pair, imperf. horiz.	100.00	
125	A15	50h deep green	.25	.20
		Nos. 123-125 (3)	1.10	.80

See No. 141.

1927-31 Unwmk. *Perf. 10*

126	A13	30h gray green	.25	.20
127	A14	40h deep brown	.70	.20
128	A15	50h deep green	.20	.20
129	A15	60h red violet	.70	.20
130	A10	1k carmine rose	1.10	.20
131	A15	1k deep red	.75	.20
132	A16	1.20k red violet	.40	.20
133	A11	1.50k carmine ('29)	.55	.20
134	A13	2k deep green ('29)	.50	.20
135	A11	2.50k dark blue	5.50	.30
136	A14	3k red brown ('31)	.60	.20
		Nos. 126-136 (11)	11.25	2.30

No. 130 exists in two types. The one with longer mustache at left sells for several times as much as that with the short mustache.

1927-28 *Perf. 13½*

137	A17	2k ultra	.85	.20
138	A17	3k deep red ('28)	1.90	.65
139	A18	4k brown violet ('28)	6.00	1.00
140	A18	5k dark green ('28)	6.25	.50
		Nos. 137-140 (4)	15.00	2.35

Coil Stamp

1927 *Perf. 10 Vertically*

141	A12	20h brick red	.50	.20

Catalogue values for unused stamps in this section, from this point to the end of the section, are for Never Hinged items.

Hradec Castle
A19

Brno Cathedral
A25

Masaryk — A27

10th anniv. of Czech. independence: 40h, Town Hall, Levoca. 50h, Telephone exchange, Prague. 60h, Town of Jasina. 1k, Hluboka Castle. 1.20k, Pilgrims' House, Velehrad. 2.50k, Great Tatra. 5k, Old City Square, Prague.

1928, Oct. 22 *Perf. 13½*

142	A19	30h black	.20	.20
143	A19	40h red brown	.20	.20
144	A19	50h dark green	.20	.20
145	A19	60h orange red	.20	.20
146	A19	1k carmine	.20	.20
147	A19	1.20k brown vio	.45	.40
148	A25	2k ultra	.55	.40
149	A19	2.50k dark blue	1.50	.75
150	A27	3k dark brown	1.00	.60
151	A25	5k deep violet	1.75	1.25
		Nos. 142-151 (10)	6.25	4.40

From one to three sheets each of Nos. 142-148, perf 12½, appeared on the market in the early 1950's.

Coat of Arms — A29

1929-37 *Perf. 10*

152	A29	5h dark ultra ('31)	.20	.20
153	A29	10h bister brn ('31)	.20	.20
154	A29	20h red	.20	.20
155	A29	25h green	.20	.20
156	A29	30h red violet	.20	.20
157	A29	40h dk brown ('37)	.40	.20
a.		40h red brown ('29)	1.00	.20
		Nos. 152-157 (6)	1.40	1.20

Coil Stamp

Perf. 10 Vertically

158	A29	20h red	.20	.20

For overprints see Bohemia and Moravia Nos. 1-5, Slovakia 2-6.

St. Wenceslas
A30

Founding St.
Vitus' Cathedral
A31

Design: 3k, 5k, St. Wenceslas martyred.

1929, May 14 *Perf. 13½*

159	A30	50h gray green	.40	.20
160	A30	60h slate violet	.60	.20
161	A31	2k dull blue	1.25	.40
162	A30	3k brown	1.50	.20
163	A30	5k brown violet	5.50	1.50
		Nos. 159-163 (5)	9.25	2.50

Millenary of the death of St. Wenceslas.

Statue of St.
Wenceslas and
National Museum,
Prague — A33

1929 *Perf. 10*

164	A33	2.50k deep blue	.65	.20

Brno Cathedral
A34

Tatra Mountain
Scene
A35

Design: 5k, Old City Square, Prague.

1929, Oct. 15 *Perf. 13½*

165	A34	3k red brown	1.75	.20
166	A35	4k indigo	4.50	.50
167	A35	5k gray green	5.00	.30
		Nos. 165-167 (3)	11.25	1.00

See No. 183.

A37

Type I 

Type II 

Two types of 50h:

I — A white space exists across the bottom of the vignette between the coat, shirt and tie and the "HALERU" frame panel.

II — An extra frame line has been added just above the "HALERU" panel which finishes off the coat and tie shading evenly.

1930, Jan. 2 *Perf. 10*

168	A37	50h myrtle green (II)	.20	.20
a.		Type I	.75	.20
169	A37	60h brown violet	.50	.20
170	A37	1k brown red	.20	.20
		Nos. 168-170 (3)	.90	.60

See No. 234.

Coil Stamp

1931 *Perf. 10 Vertically*

171	A37	1k brown red	.75	.40

President
Masaryk — A38

St. Nicholas'
Church,
Prague — A39

1930, Mar. 1 *Perf. 13½*

175	A38	2k gray green	1.00	.25
176	A38	3k red brown	1.50	.25
177	A38	5k slate blue	5.25	1.50
178	A38	10k gray black	13.00	3.00
		Nos. 175-178 (4)	20.75	5.00

Eightieth birthday of President Masaryk.

1931, May 15

183	A39	10k black violet	10.00	2.50

Krivoklat
Castle — A40

Krumlov
Castle — A42

Design: 4k, Orlik Castle.

1932, Jan. 2 *Perf. 10*

184	A40	3.50k violet	2.00	.80
185	A40	4k deep blue	2.25	.35
186	A42	5k gray green	2.50	.35
		Nos. 184-186 (3)	6.75	1.50

A43

A44

Miroslav Tyrs — A45

1932, Mar. 16

187	A43	50h yellow green	.35	.20
188	A43	1k brown carmine	.90	.20
189	A44	2k dark blue	6.25	.35
190	A44	3k red brown	12.50	.35
		Nos. 187-190 (4)	20.00	1.10

1933, Feb. 1

191	A45	60h dull violet	.25	.20

Miroslav Tyrs (1832-84), founder of the Sokol movement; and the 9th Sokol Congress (#187-190).

First Christian Church at Nitra
A46 A47

1933, June 20

192	A46	50h yellow green	.35	.20
193	A47	1k carmine rose	3.50	.20

Prince Pribina who introduced Christianity into Slovakia and founded there the 1st Christian church in A.D. 833.

All gutter pairs are vertical.

Bedrich Smetana,
Czech Composer and
Pianist, 50th Death
Anniv. — A48

1934, Mar. 26 Engr. *Perf. 10*

194	A48	50h yellow green	.30	.20

Consecration of Legion Colors at Kiev,
Sept. 21, 1914 — A49

Ensign Heyduk with Colors A51

Legionnaires A52

1k, Legion receiving battle flag at Bayonne.

1934, Aug. 15 ***Perf. 10***
195 A49 50h green .30 .20
196 A49 1k rose lake .45 .20
197 A51 2k deep blue 1.75 .20
198 A52 3k red brown 2.50 .20
Nos. 195-198 (4) 5.00 .80

20th anniv. of the Czechoslovakian Legion which fought in WWI.

Antonin Dvorák, (1841-1904), Composer — A53

1934, Nov. 22
199 A53 50h green .30 .20

Pastoral Scene — A54

1934, Dec. 17 ***Perf. 10***
200 A54 1k claret .40 .20
a. Souv. sheet of 15, perf. 13½ 150.00 *200.00*
b. As "a," single stamp 7.00 6.00
201 A54 2k blue 1.10 .35
a. Souv. sheet of 15, perf. 13½ 500.00 *750.00*
b. As "a," single stamp 30.00 17.50

Centenary of the National Anthem.
Nos. 200a & 201a have thick paper, darker shades, no gum. Forgeries exist.

President Masaryk
A55 A56

1935, Mar. 1
202 A55 50h green, *buff* .35 .20
203 A55 1k claret, *buff* .40 .20
204 A56 2k gray blue, *buff* 2.00 .25
205 A56 3k brown, *buff* 3.25 .25
Nos. 202-205 (4) 6.00 .90

85th birthday of President Masaryk. See No. 235.

Monument to Czech Heroes at Arras, France — A57

1935, May 4
206 A57 1k rose .75 .20
207 A57 2k dull blue 1.50 .35

20th anniversary of the Battle of Arras.

Gen. Milan Stefánik A58

Sts. Cyril and Methodius A59

1935, May 18
208 A58 50h green .20 .20

1935, June 22
209 A59 50h green .25 .20
210 A59 1k claret .35 .20
211 A59 2k deep blue 1.40 .25
Nos. 209-211 (3) 2.00 .65

Millenary of the arrival in Moravia of the Apostles Cyril and Methodius.

Masaryk — A60

Statue of Macha, Prague — A61

1935, Oct. 20 ***Perf. 12½***
212 A60 1k rose lake .20 .20

No. 212 exists imperforate. See No. 256. For overprints see Bohemia and Moravia Nos. 9-10, Slovakia 12.

1936, Apr. 30
213 A61 50h deep green .20 .20
214 A61 1k rose lake .30 .20

Karel Hynek Macha (1810-1836), Bohemian poet.

Jan Amos Komensky (Comenius) — A61a

Pres. Eduard Benes A62

Gen. Milan Stefánik A63

1936
215 A61a 40h dark blue .20 .20
216 A62 50h dull green .20 .20
217 A63 60h dull violet .20 .20
Nos. 215-217 (3) .60 .60

See #252, 255. For overprints see Bohemia and Moravia #6, 8, Slovakia 7, 9-11.

Castle Palanok near Mukacevo A64

Town of Banska Bystrica A65

Castle at Zvikov — A66

Ruins of Castle at Strecno — A67

Castle at Cesky Raj A68

Palace at Slavkov (Austerlitz) A69

Statue of King George of Podebrad A70

Town Square at Olomouc — A71

Castle Ruins at Bratislava A72

1936, Aug. 1
218 A64 1.20k rose lilac .20 .20
219 A65 1.50k carmine .20 .20
220 A66 2k dark blue green .20 .20
221 A67 2.50k dark blue .30 .20
222 A68 3k brown .30 .20
223 A69 3.50k dark violet 1.00 .30
224 A70 4k dark violet .50 .20
225 A71 5k green .45 .20
226 A72 10k blue 1.10 .30
Nos. 218-226 (9) 4.25 2.00

For overprints and surcharge see Nos. 237-238, 254A, Bohemia and Moravia 11-12, 14-19, Slovakia 13-14, 16-23.

President Benes — A73

Soldiers of the Czech Legion — A74

1937, Apr. 26 Unwmk. ***Perf. 12½***
227 A73 50h deep green .20 .20

For overprints see Nos. 236, Slovakia 8.

1937, June 15
228 A74 50h deep green .20 .20
229 A74 1k rose lake .25 .20

20th anniv. of the Battle of Zborov.

Cathedral at Prague — A75

Jan Evangelista Purkyne — A76

1937, July 1
230 A75 2k green .75 .20
231 A75 2.50k blue 1.00 .50

Founding of the "Little Entente," 16th anniv

1937, Sept. 2
232 A76 50h slate green .20 .20
233 A76 1k dull rose .20 .20

150th anniv. of the birth of Purkyne, Czech physiologist.

Masaryk Types of 1930-35

1937, Sept. ***Perf. 12½***
234 A37 50h black .20 .20

With date "14.IX. 1937" in design

235 A56 2k black .30 .20

Death of former President Thomas G. Masaryk on Sept. 14, 1937.

International Labor Bureau Issue

Stamps of 1936-37 Overprinted in Violet or Black

1937, Oct. 6 ***Perf. 12½***
236 A73 50h dp green (Bk) .25 .20
237 A65 1.50k carmine (V) .35 .20
238 A66 2k dp green (V) .50 .35
Nos. 236-238 (3) 1.10 .75

Bratislava Philatelic Exhibition Issue

Souvenir Sheet

A77

1937, Oct. 24 ***Perf. 12½***
239 A77 Sheet of 2 1.75 *2.00*
a. 50h dark blue .50 .50
b. 1k brown carmine .50 .50

The stamps show a view of Poprad Lake (50h) and the tomb of General Milan Stefanik (1k).

No. 239 overprinted with the Czechoslovak arms and "Czecho-Slovak Participation New York World's Fair 1939, Czecho-Slovak Pavilion" were privately produced to finance Czechoslovak participation in the exhibition. The overprint exists in black, green, red, blue, gold and silver.

No. 239 overprinted "Liberation de la Tchechoslovaquie, 28-X-1945" etc., was sold at a philatelic exhibition in Brussels, Belgium.

St. Barbara's Church, Kutna Hora — A79

Peregrine Falcon, Sokol Emblem — A80

1937, Dec. 4
240 A79 1.60k olive green .20 .20

For overprints see Bohemia and Moravia Nos. 13, Slovakia 15.

1938, Jan. 21

241	A80	50h deep green	.20	.20
242	A80	1k rose lake	.25	.20

10th Intl. Sokol Games. Imperf. copies of No. 242 are essays. Nos. 241-242 se-tentant with labels sell slightly higher.

Legionnaires

A81 A82

Legionnaire — A83

1938

243	A81 50h deep green	.20	.20
244	A82 50h deep green	.20	.20
245	A83 50h deep green	.20	.20
	Nos. 243-245 (3)	.60	.60

20th anniv. of the Battle of Bachmac, Vouziers and Doss Alto. #243-245 se-tentant with label sell slightly higher.

Jindrich Fügner, Co-Founder of Sokol Movement — A84

1938, June 18 ***Perf. 12½***

246	A84 50h deep green	.20	.20
247	A84 1k rose lake	.20	.20
248	A84 2k slate blue	.40	.20
	Nos. 246-248 (3)	.80	.60

10th Sokol Summer Games. Nos. 246-248 se-tenant with labels sell slightly higher.

View of Pilsen — A85

Cathedral of Kosice — A86

1938, June 24

249 A85 50h deep green .20 .20

Provincial Economic Council meeting, Pilsen. For overprint see Bohemia & Moravia #7.

1938, July 15 ***Perf. 12½***

250 A86 50h deep green .20 .20

Kosice Cultural Exhibition.

Prague Philatelic Exhibition Issue

Souvenir Sheet

Vysehrad Castle — Hradcany — A87

1938, June 26 ***Perf. 12½***

251 A87 Sheet of 2	4.00	3.00
a. 50h dark blue	1.25	1.25
b. 1k deep carmine	1.25	1.25

See No. 3036.

Stefánik Type of 1936

1938, Nov. 21

252 A63 50h deep green .20 .20

Allegory of the Republic — A89

1938, Dec. 19 **Unwmk.**

253 A89 2k lt ultra	.30	.20
254 A89 3k pale brown	.30	.20

20th anniv. of Independence. See No. B153.

"Wir sind frei!"

Stamps of Czechoslovakia, 1918-37, overprinted with a swastika in black or red and "Wir sind frei!" were issued locally and unofficially in 1938 as Czech authorities were evacuating and German authorities arriving. They appeared in the towns of Asch, Karlsbad, Reichenberg-Maffersdorf, Rumburg, etc.

The overprint, sometimes including a surcharge or the town name (as in Karlsbad), exists on many values of postage, air post, semi-postal, postage due and newspaper stamps.

No. 226 Surcharged in Orange Red

1939, Jan. 18 **Unwmk.** ***Perf. 12½***

254A A72 300h on 10k blue 1.00 *1.50*

Opening of the Slovakian Parliament.

View of Jasina — A89a

Perf. 12½

1939, Mar. 15 **Engr.** **Unwmk.**

254B A89a 3k ultra 11.00 *25.00*

Inauguration of the Carpatho-Ukraine Diet, Mar. 2, 1939.

Printed for use in the province of Carpatho-Ukraine but issued in Prague at the same time.

Used value is for red commemorative cancel.

Stefánik Type of 1936

1939 **Engr.** ***Perf. 12½***

255 A63 60h dark blue 40.00 20.00

Used exclusively in Slovakia.

Masaryk Type of 1935 with hyphen in Cesko-Slovensko

1939, Apr. 23

256 A60 1k rose lake .20 .20

SEMI-POSTAL STAMPS

Nos. B1-B123 were sold at 1½ times face value at the Philatelists' Window of the Prague P.O. for charity benefit. They were available for ordinary postage.

Almost all stamps between Nos. B1-B123 are known with misplaced or inverted overprints and/or in pairs with one stamp missing the overprint.

The overprints of Nos. B1-B123 have been well forged.

Austrian Stamps of 1916-18 Overprinted in Black or Blue

a

Two sizes of type A40:
Type I: 25x30mm.
Type II: 26x29mm.

1919 ***Perf. 12½***

B1	A37	3h brt violet	.20	*.25*
B2	A37	5h lt green	.20	*.25*
B3	A37	6h dp orange (Bl)	.60	.50
B4	A37	6h dp orange (Bk)	*2,000.*	*2,000.*
B5	A37	10h magenta	.60	*.75*
B6	A37	12h lt blue	.60	*.65*
B7	A42	15h dull red	.20	*.25*
B8	A42	20h dark green	.20	*.25*
a.		20h green	100.00	100.00
B9	A42	25h blue	.30	*.40*
B10	A42	30h dull violet	.30	*.40*
B11	A39	40h olive grn	.30	*.40*
B12	A39	50h dk green	.30	*.40*
B13	A39	60h dp blue	.30	*.40*
B14	A39	80h orange brn	.30	*.40*
B15	A39	90h red violet	.70	*.75*
B16	A39	1k car, *yel* (Bl)	.50	*.60*
B17	A39	1k car, *yel* (Bk)	125.00	100.00
B18	A40	2k light blue (I)	1.90	1.90
a.		2k dark blue (II)	2,750.	1,750.
b.		2k light blue (II)	1.90	1.90
c.		2k dark blue (I)	8,500.	4,000.
B19	A40	3k car rose (I)	50.00	27.50
a.		3k claret (I)	2,500.	900.00
b.		3k carmine rose (II)	2,000.	1,000.
c.		3k claret (II)	5,500.	4,000.
B20	A40	4k yellow grn (I)	20.00	15.00
a.		4k deep green (I)	55.00	45.00
b.		4k yellow grn (II)	45.00	40.00
B21	A40	10k violet	300.00	160.00
a.		10k deep violet	375.00	275.00
b.		10k black violet	450.00	300.00

The used value of No. B18a is for copies which have only a Czechoslovakian cancellation. Some of the copies of Austria No. 160 which were officially overprinted with type "a" and sold by the post office, had previously been used and lightly canceled with Austrian cancellations. These canceled-before-overprinting copies, which were postally valid, sell for about one-fourth as much.

Granite Paper

B22	A40	2k light blue	2.00	2.00
B23	A40	3k carmine rose	7.25	6.00

The 4k and 10k on granite paper with this overprint were not regularly issued.

Excellent counterfeits of Nos. B1-B23 exist.

Austrian Newspaper Stamps Overprinted

b

Imperf

On Stamp of 1908

B26 N8 10h carmine 2,250. 2,000.

On Stamps of 1916

B27	N9 2h brown	.20	.20
B28	N9 4h green	.25	.25
B29	N9 6h deep blue	.20	.20
B30	N9 10h orange	2.75	2.75
B31	N9 30h claret	1.10	1.10
	Nos. B27-B31 (5)	4.50	4.50

Austrian Special Handling Stamps Overprinted in Blue or Black Stamps of 1916 Overprinted

c

Perf. 12½

B32	SH1 2h claret, *yel* (Bl)	40.00	35.00
B33	SH1 5h dp grn, *yel* (Bk)	*1,200.*	*900.00*

Stamps of 1917 Overprinted

d

B34	SH2 2h cl, *yel* (Bl)	.25	*.35*
a.	Vert. pair, imperf. btwn.	*250.00*	
B35	SH2 2h cl, *yel* (Bk)	60.00	35.00
B36	SH2 5h grn, *yel* (Bk)	.25	.25

Austrian Air Post Stamps, #C1-C3, Overprinted Type "c" Diagonally

B37	A40 1.50k on 2k lil	200.00	200.00
B38	A40 2.50k on 3k ocher	200.00	200.00
B39	A40 4k gray	1,000.	900.00

1919

Austrian Postage Due Stamps of 1908-13 Overprinted Type "b"

B40	D3	2h carmine	*4,500.*	*2,750.*
B41	D3	4h carmine	25.00	15.00
B42	D3	6h carmine	12.50	8.00
B43	D3	14h carmine	90.00	35.00
B44	D3	25h carmine	45.00	20.00
B45	D3	30h carmine	375.00	300.00
B46	D3	50h carmine	875.00	825.00

Austria Nos. J49-J56 Overprinted Type "b"

B47	D4	5h rose red	.20	*.30*
B48	D4	10h rose red	.20	*.30*
B49	D4	15h rose red	.20	*.30*
B50	D4	20h rose red	2.00	1.50
B51	D4	25h rose red	1.25	1.00
B52	D4	30h rose red	.50	.50
B53	D4	40h rose red	2.00	1.75
B54	D4	50h rose red	400.00	250.00

Austria Nos. J57-J59 Overprinted Type "a"

B55	D5	1k ultra	12.50	10.00
B56	D5	5k ultra	55.00	35.00
B57	D5	10k ultra	375.00	200.00

Austria Nos. J47-J48, J60-J63 Overprinted Type "c" Diagonally

B58	A22	1h gray	32.50	30.00
B59	A23	15h on 2h vio	125.00	110.00
B60	A38	10h on 24h blue	90.00	85.00
B61	A38	15h on 36h vio	1.00	1.00
B62	A38	20h on 54h org	90.00	85.00
B63	A38	50h on 42h choc	1.00	1.00

Hungarian Stamps Ovptd. Type "b"

1919 **Wmk. 137** ***Perf. 15***

On Stamps of 1913-16

B64	A4	1f slate	2,400.	1,600.
B65	A4	2f yellow	3.50	2.50
B66	A4	3f orange	45.00	25.00
B67	A4	6f olive green	4.50	4.50
B68	A4	50f lake, *bl*	1.25	1.00
B69	A4	60f grn, *sal*	50.00	20.00
B70	A4	70f red brn, *grn*	2,400.	1,600.

On Stamps of 1916

B71	A8	10f rose	300.00	175.00
B72	A8	15f violet	160.00	100.00

On Stamps of 1916-18

B73	A9	2f brown orange	.20	.20
B74	A9	3f red lilac	.20	.20
B75	A9	5f green	.20	.20
B76	A9	6f grnsh blue	.60	.60
B77	A9	10f rose red	1.40	*2.25*
B78	A9	15f violet	.25	.25
B79	A9	20f gray brown	5.50	5.00
B80	A9	25f dull blue	.80	.75
B81	A9	35f brown	6.75	6.75
B82	A9	40f olive green	1.75	1.50

Overprinted Type "d"

B83	A10	50f red vio & lil	.80	.80
B84	A10	75f brt bl & pale bl	.75	.75
B85	A10	80f yel grn & pale grn	1.10	1.10
B86	A10	1k red brn & cl	1.40	1.40
B87	A10	2k ol brn & bis	5.50	5.50
B88	A10	3k dk vio & ind	37.50	37.50
B89	A10	5k dk brn & lt brn	140.00	90.00

B90 A10 10k vio brn & vio 1,250. 800.00

Overprinted Type "b"

On Stamps of 1918

B91 A11 10f scarlet .25 .25
B92 A11 20f dark brown .30 .30
B93 A11 25f deep blue 1.40 1.25
B94 A12 40f olive grn 1.50 1.25
B95 A12 50f lilac 67.50 25.00

On Stamps of 1919

B96 A13 10f red 7.00 6.00
B97 A13 20f dk brn *6,750.* —

Same Overprint On Hungarian Newspaper Stamp of 1914

Imperf

B98 N5 (2f) orange .20 *.30*

Same Overprint On Hungarian Special Delivery Stamp

Perf. 15

B99 SD1 2f gray grn & red .25 *.35*

Same Ovpt. On Hungarian Semi-Postal Stamps

B100 SP3 10f + 2f rose red .55 *.60*
B101 SP4 15f + 2f violet .90 .90
B102 SP5 40f + 2f brn car 7.00 3.50
Nos. B98-B102 (5) 8.90 5.65

Hungarian Postage Due Stamps of 1903-18 Overprinted Type "b"

1919 Wmk. 135 *Perf. 11½, 12*
B103 D1 50f green & black *525.00 525.00*

Wmk. Crown (136, 136a)

Perf. 11½x12, 15

B104 D1 1f green & black *1,200. 1,000.*
B105 D1 2f green & black *1,000. 750.*
B106 D1 12f green & black *4,250. 3,000.*
B107 D1 50f green & black 275. 150.

Wmk. Double Cross (137)

Perf. 15

On Stamps of 1914

B110 D1 1f green & black 1,250. 600.
B111 D1 2f green & black 700. 550.
B112 D1 5f green & black 1,325. 900.
B113 D1 12f green & black *5,250. 4,000.*
B114 D1 50f green & black 275. 150.

On Stamps of 1915-18

B115 D1 1f green & red 175.00 140.00
B116 D1 2f green & red 1.00 .80
B117 D1 5f green & red 12.50 10.00
B118 D1 6f green & red 1.50 1.50
B119 D1 10f green & red .60 .60
a. Pair, one without overprint
B120 D1 12f green & red 2.00 2.00
B121 D1 15f green & red 7.50 5.00
B122 D1 20f green & red 1.00 1.00
B123 D1 30f green & red 80.00 70.00
Nos. B115-B123 (9) 281.10 230.90

Excellent counterfeits of Nos. B1-B123 exist.

Bohemian Lion Breaking its Chains — SP1

Mother and Child — SP2

Perf. 11½, 13¾ and Compound

1919 Typo. Unwmk.

Pinkish Paper

B124 SP1 15h gray green .20 .20
B125 SP1 25h dark brown .20 .20
a. 25h light brown *5.00* 2.50
B126 SP1 50h dark blue .20 .20

Photo.

Yellowish Paper

B127 SP2 75h slate .20 .20
B128 SP2 100h brn vio .20 .20
B129 SP2 120h vio, *yel* .20 .20
Nos. B124-B129 (6) 1.20 1.20

Nos. B124-B126 commemorate the 1st anniv. of Czechoslovak independence. Nos. B127-B129 were sold for the benefit of Legionnaires' orphans. Imperforates exist.

See No. 1581.

Regular Issues of Czechoslovakia Surcharged in Red:

a

b

1920 *Perf. 13¾*
B130 A1(a) 40h + 20h bister .50 .50
B131 A2(a) 60h + 20h green .50 .50
B132 A4(b) 125h + 25h gray bl 1.00 1.00
Nos. B130-B132 (3) 2.00 *2.00*

President Masaryk — SP3

Wmk. Linden Leaves (107)

1923 Engr. *Perf. 13¾x14¾*
B133 SP3 50h gray green .75 .50
B134 SP3 100h carmine 1.00 .60
B135 SP3 200h blue 3.00 1.25
B136 SP3 300h dark brown 3.25 2.25
Nos. B133-B136 (4) 8.00 4.60

5th anniv. of the Republic.

The gum was applied through a screen and shows the monogram "CSP" (Ceskoslovenska Posta). These stamps were sold at double their face values, the excess being given to the Red Cross and other charitable organizations.

International Olympic Congress Issue

Semi-Postal Stamps of 1923 Overprinted in Blue or Red

1925
B137 SP3 50h gray green 10.00 8.50
B138 SP3 100h carmine 14.50 12.00
B139 SP3 200h blue (R) 72.50 55.00
Nos. B137-B139 (3) 97.00 75.50
Set, never hinged 150.00

These stamps were sold at double their face values, the excess being divided between a fund for post office clerks and the Olympic Games Committee.

Sokol Issue

Semi-Postal Stamps of 1923 Overprinted in Blue or Red

1926
B140 SP3 50h gray green 1.60 1.00
B141 SP3 100h carmine 3.25 1.50
B142 SP3 200h blue (R) 15.00 9.50
a. Double overprint
B143 SP3 300h dk brn (R) 20.00 16.00
Nos. B140-B143 (4) 39.85 28.00

These stamps were sold at double their face values, the excess being given to the Congress of Sokols, June, 1926.

Catalogue values for unused stamps in this section, from this point to the end of the section, are for Never Hinged items.

Midwife Presenting Newborn Child to its Father; after a Painting by Josef Manes
SP4 SP5

1936 Unwmk. Engr. *Perf. 12½*
B144 SP4 50h + 50h green .45 .20
B145 SP5 1k + 50h claret .45 .35
B146 SP4 2k + 50h blue 1.90 .95
Nos. B144-B146 (3) 2.80 1.50

SP6

"Lullaby" by Stanislav Sucharda SP7

1937 *Perf. 12½*
B147 SP6 50h + 50h dull green .50 .20
B148 SP6 1k + 50h rose lake .75 .50
B149 SP7 2k + 1k dull blue 1.75 1.00
Nos. B147-B149 (3) 3.00 1.70

President Masaryk and Little Girl in Native Costume — SP8

1938 *Perf. 12½*
B150 SP8 50h + 50h deep green .25 *.20*
B151 SP8 1k + 50h rose lake .35 *.25*

Souvenir Sheet

Imperf

B152 SP8 2k + 3k black 3.50 2.40

88th anniv. of the birth of Masaryk (1850-1937).

Allegory of the Republic Type Souvenir Sheet

1938 *Perf. 12½*
B153 A89 2k (+ 8k) dark blue 2.50 2.50

The surtax was devoted to national relief for refugees.

AIR POST STAMPS

Nos. 9, 39-40, 20, and Types of 1919 Surcharged in Red, Blue or Green:

1920 Unwmk. *Imperf.*
C1 A1 14k on 200h (R) 15.00 15.00
a. Inverted surcharge 125.00
C2 A2 24k on 500h (Bl) 40.00 30.00
a. Inverted surcharge 225.00
C3 A2 28k on 1000h (G) 30.00 30.00
a. Inverted surcharge 150.00
b. Double surcharge 200.00
Nos. C1-C3 (3) 85.00 75.00

Perf. 13¾

C4 A1 14k on 200h (R) 22.50 14.00
a. Perf. 13¾x13½ 90.00 52.50
C5 A2 24k on 500h (Bl) 45.00 32.50
a. Perf. 13¾x13½ 100.00 77.50

Perf. 13¾x13½

C6 A2 28k on 1000h (G) 20.00 22.50
a. Inverted surcharge 400.00 —
b. Perf. 13¾ 475.00 350.00
c. As "b," invtd. surcharge 350.00 —
Nos. C4-C6 (3) 87.50 69.00
Nos. C1-C6 (6) 172.50 144.00

Excellent counterfeits of the overprint are known.

Stamps of 1920 Surcharged in Black or Violet:

1922, June 15 *Perf. 13¾*
C7 A8 50h on 100h dl grn 1.50 1.50
a. Inverted surcharge 150.00
b. Double surcharge 160.00
C8 A8 100h on 200h vio 2.00 3.25
a. Inverted surcharge 150.00
C9 A8 250h on 400h brn (V) 5.00 7.50
a. Inverted surcharge 275.00
Nos. C7-C9 (3) 8.50 12.25

Fokker Monoplane AP3

Smolik S 19 AP4

Smolik S 19 — AP5

Fokker over Prague AP6

1930, Dec. 16 Engr. *Perf. 13½*
C10 AP3 50h deep green .20 .20
C11 AP3 1k deep red .25 .25
C12 AP4 2k dark green .60 .55
C13 AP4 3k red violet 1.25 1.00
C14 AP5 4k indigo 1.00 .80
C15 AP5 5k red brown 1.50 1.50
C16 AP6 10k vio blue 3.50 3.50
a. 10k ultra 6.25 6.50
C17 AP6 20k gray violet 4.50 3.00
Nos. C10-C17 (8) 12.80 10.80

Two types exist of the 50h, 1k and 2k, and three types of the 3k, differing chiefly in the size of the printed area. A "no hill at left" variety of the 3k exists.

Imperf. copies of Nos. C10-C17 are proofs.

Perf. 12

C10a AP3 50h deep green 1.90 1.90
C11a AP3 1k deep red 18.00 18.00
C12a AP4 2k dark green 14.00 14.00
C14a AP5 4k indigo 6.00 6.25
C17a AP6 20k gray violet 4.00 3.00

Perf. 12x13½, 13½x12

C11b AP3 1k deep red 2.75 2.75
C12b AP4 2k dark green 9.25 9.25

Perf. 13¾x12¼

C17b AP6 20k gray violet *1,100.*

Perf. 12½

C15a AP5 5k red brown *2,000.*

Type of 1930 with hyphen in Cesko-Slovensko

1939, Apr. 22 *Perf. 13½*
C18 AP3 30h rose lilac .20 .20

SPECIAL DELIVERY STAMPS

Doves — SD1

1919-20 Unwmk. Typo. *Imperf.*
E1 SD1 2h red vio, *yel* .20 .20
E2 SD1 5h yel grn, *yel* .20 .20
E3 SD1 10h red brn, *yel* ('20) .40 .40
Nos. E1-E3 (3) .80 .80

For overprints and surcharge see Nos. P11-P13, Eastern Silesia E1-E2.

1921 **White Paper**
E1a SD1 2h red violet 8.00
E2a SD1 5h yellow green 5.25
E3a SD1 10h red brown 100.00
Nos. E1a-E3a (3) 113.25

It is doubted that Nos. E1a-E3a were regularly issued.

PERSONAL DELIVERY STAMPS

Catalogue values for unused stamps in this section are for Never Hinged items.

PD1

Design: No. EX2, "D" in each corner.

1937 Unwmk. Photo. *Perf. 13½*
EX1 PD1 50h blue .20 .25
EX2 PD1 50h carmine .20 .25

POSTAGE DUE STAMPS

D1

1918-20 Unwmk. Typo. *Imperf.*
J1 D1 5h deep bister .20 .20
J2 D1 10h deep bister .20 .20
J3 D1 15h deep bister .20 .20
J4 D1 20h deep bister .20 .20
J5 D1 25h deep bister .20 .20
J6 D1 30h deep bister .30 .20
J7 D1 40h deep bister .30 .25
J8 D1 50h deep bister .30 .20
J9 D1 100h blk brn 1.25 .20
J10 D1 250h orange 4.75 1.40
J11 D1 400h scarlet 6.50 1.40
J12 D1 500h gray grn 2.50 .20
J13 D1 1000h purple 3.50 .25
J14 D1 2000h dark blue 15.00 .60
Nos. J1-J14 (14) 35.40 5.70

For surcharges and overprints see Nos. J32-J41, J57, Eastern Silesia J1-J11.

Nos. 1, 33-34, 10 Surcharged in Blue

1922
J15 A1 20h on 3h red vio .20 .20
J16 A2 50h on 75h slate .60 .20
J17 A2 60h on 80h olive grn .45 .20
J18 A2 100h on 80h olive grn 1.50 .20
J19 A1 200h on 400h purple 2.25 .20
Nos. J15-J19 (5) 5.00 1.00

Same Surcharge on Nos. 1, 10, 30-31, 33-34, 36, 40 in Violet

1923-26
J20 A1 10h on 3h red vio .20 .20
J21 A1 20h on 3h red vio .50 .20
J22 A1 30h on 3h red vio .20 .20
J23 A1 40h on 3h red vio .20 .20
J24 A2 50h on 75h slate 1.60 .20
J25 A2 60h on 50h dk vio ('26) 4.50 1.25
J26 A2 60h on 50h dk bl ('26) 4.50 1.50
J27 A2 60h on 75h slate .50 .20
J28 A2 100h on 80h ol grn 27.50 .20
J29 A2 100h on 120h gray blk 1.10 .20
J30 A1 100h on 400h pur ('26) 1.10 .20
J31 A2 100h on 1000h dp vio ('26) 1.60 .20
Nos. J20-J31 (12) 43.50 4.75

Postage Due Stamp of 1918-20 Surcharged in Violet

1924
J32 D1 50h on 400h scar .75 .20
J33 D1 60h on 400h scar 2.75 .50
J34 D1 100h on 400h scar 1.75 .20
Nos. J32-J34 (3) 5.25 .90

Postage Due Stamps of 1918-20 Surcharged with New Values in Violet as in 1924

1925
J35 D1 10h on 5h bister .20 .20
J36 D1 20h on 5h bister .20 .20
J37 D1 30h on 15h bister .20 .20
J38 D1 40h on 15h bister .20 .20
J39 D1 50h on 250h org .95 .20
J40 D1 60h on 250h org 1.25 .50
J41 D1 100h on 250h org 1.90 .20
Nos. J35-J41 (7) 4.90 1.70

Stamps of 1918-19 Surcharged with New Values in Violet as in 1922

1926 *Perf. 14, 11½*
J42 A2 30h on 15h red .50 .30
J43 A2 40h on 15h red .50 .30

On #J44-J49

On #J50-J56

1926 Violet Surcharge *Perf. 14*
J44 A8 30h on 100h dk grn .20 .20
J45 A8 40h on 200h violet .25 .20
J46 A8 40h on 300h ver .95 .25
a. Perf. 14x13½ 60.00
J47 A8 50h on 500h dp grn .50 .20
a. Perf. 14x13½ 2.75
J48 A8 60h on 400h brown 1.00 .20
J49 A8 100h on 600h dp vio 2.50 .35
a. Perf. 14x13½ 30.00 1.25
Nos. J44-J49 (6) 5.40 1.40

1927 **Violet Overprint**
J50 A6 100h dark brown .55 .20
a. Perf. 13½ *200.00* 10.00

Surcharged with New Value in Violet
J51 A6 40h on 185h org .20 .20
J52 A6 50h on 20h car .20 .20
a. 50h on 50h carmine (error) *35,000.*
J53 A6 50h on 150h rose .20 .20
a. Perf. 13½ 12.50 2.00
J54 A6 60h on 25h brown .25 .20
J55 A6 60h on 185h orange .55 .20
J56 A6 100h on 25h brown .55 .20
Nos. J50-J56 (7) 2.50 1.40

No. J52a is known only used.

No. J12 Surcharged in Violet

1927 *Imperf.*
J57 D1 200h on 500h gray grn 6.00 2.50

Catalogue values for unused stamps in this section, from this point to the end of the section, are for Never Hinged items.

D5

1928 *Perf. 14x13½*
J58 D5 5h dark red .20 .20
J59 D5 10h dark red .20 .20
J60 D5 20h dark red .20 .20
J61 D5 30h dark red .20 .20
J62 D5 40h dark red .20 .20
J63 D5 50h dark red .20 .20
J64 D5 60h dark red .20 .20
J65 D5 1k ultra .20 .20
J66 D5 2k ultra .50 .20
J67 D5 5k ultra .75 .20
J68 D5 10k ultra 1.90 .20
J69 D5 20k ultra 3.75 .30
Nos. J58-J69 (12) 8.50 2.50

LOCAL OFFICIAL STAMPS

Coat of Arms — L1

Typo. & Embossed

1918, Nov. 7 ***Die Cut Perf 12***
OL1 L1 10h blue 10.00 *15.00*
Never hinged 16.00
On cover 35.00
a. 10h pale blue 35.00 35.00
Never hinged 50.00
On cover 85.00
OL2 L1 20h bright carmine 7.00 7.00
Never hinged 10.00
On cover 35.00

In the first weeks of independence, the Czechoslovak National Council employed the Czech Scouts to maintain a local post in Prague, and Nos. OL1-OL2 were issued for this service. These stamps were in use Nov. 7-25, after which regular postal operations were resumed.

Nos. OL1 and OL2 were printed on grayish paper with yellow gum. A later printing on white paper with white gum was made for sale to collectors. These reprints sell for substantially less than the values above.

The scout delivery service was revived for one day, December 21, 1918, as part of the celebration of Thomas G. Masaryk's arrival in Czechoslovakia. 600 copies of No. OL1 and 1,000 copies of OL2 were overprinted "Prijezd presidenta Masaryka." ("Arrival of President Masaryk") in three lines.

NEWSPAPER STAMPS

Windhover — N1

1918-20 Unwmk. Typo. *Imperf.*
P1 N1 2h gray green .20 .20
P2 N1 5h green ('20) .20 .20
a. 5h dark green .40 .20
P3 N1 6h red .30 .25
P4 N1 10h dull violet .20 .20
P5 N1 20h blue .20 .20
P6 N1 30h gray brown .20 .20
P7 N1 50h orange ('20) .30 .20
P8 N1 100h red brown ('20) .40 .20
Nos. P1-P8 (8) 2.00 1.65

Nos. P1-P8 exist privately perforated.
For surcharges and overprints see Nos. P9-P10, P14-P16, Eastern Silesia P1-P5.

Stamps of 1918-20 Surcharged in Violet

1925-26
P9 N1 5h on 2h gray green .50 .40
P10 N1 5h on 6h red ('26) .25 *.40*

Special Delivery Stamps of 1918-20 Overprinted in Violet

1926
P11 SD1 5h apple grn, *yel* .20 .20
a. 5h dull green, *yellow* .50 .40
P12 SD1 10h red brn, *yel* .20 .20

With Additional Surcharge of New Value
P13 SD1 5h on 2h red vio, *yel* .35 .35
Nos. P11-P13 (3) .75 .75

Catalogue values for unused stamps in this section, from this point to the end of the section, are for Never Hinged items.

Newspaper Stamps of 1918-20 Overprinted in Violet

1934
P14 N1 10h dull violet .20 .20
P15 N1 20h blue .20 .20
P16 N1 30h gray brown .20 .20
Nos. P14-P16 (3) .60 .60

Overprinted for use by commercial firms only.

Carrier Pigeon — N2

1937 *Imperf.*
P17 N2 2h bister brown .20 .20
P18 N2 5h dull blue .20 .20
P19 N2 7h red orange .20 .20
P20 N2 9h emerald .20 .20
P21 N2 10h henna brown .20 .20
P22 N2 12h ultra .20 .20
P23 N2 20h dark green .20 .20
P24 N2 50h dark brown .20 .20
P25 N2 1k olive gray .20 .20
Nos. P17-P25 (9) 1.80 1.80

For overprint see Slovakia Nos. P1-P9.

Bratislava Philatelic Exhibition Issue
Souvenir Sheet

1937 *Imperf.*
P26 N2 10h henna brn, sheet of 25 4.00 4.00

CZECHOSLOVAK LEGION POST

The Czechoslovak Legion in Siberia issued these stamps for use on its mail and that of local residents. Forgeries exist.

Russia No. 79 Overprinted

1918	Typo.	Perf. 14x14½	
A1	A15 10k dark blue	1,750.	—

No. A1 was sold for a few days in Chelyabinsk. It was withdrawn because of a spelling error ("CZESZKJA," instead of "CZESZKAJA").

This overprint was also applied to Russia Nos. 73-78, 80-81, 83-85, 119-121, 123 and 130-131. These were trial printings, never sold to the public, although favor-cancelled covers exist.

Urn and Cathedral at Irkutsk — A1

Armored Railroad Car — A2

Sentinel — A3

1919-20	Litho.	Imperf.	
1	A1 25k carmine	10.50	—
	Never hinged	21.00	
a.	Perf 11½ ('20)	10.50	—
	Never hinged	21.00	
2	A2 50k yellow green	10.50	—
	Never hinged	21.00	
a.	Perf 11½ ('20)	10.50	—
	Never hinged	21.00	
3	A3 1r red brown	14.00	—
	Never hinged	28.00	
a.	Perf 11½ ('20)	14.00	—
	Never hinged	28.00	

Nos. 1-3 were printed by Makusin & Posochin in Irkutsk and were delivered to the Czech Field Post, imperforate and ungummed, in Dec. 1919. A crackled yellow gum was applied to stamps sold at Field Post offices. In Jan. 1920 a quantity of sheets was perforated 11½.

Nos. 1 and 2 exist in wide horizontal gutter pairs, containing one of each denomination. Value, $700 unused, $1,000 never hinged. No. 3 exists in wide vertical gutter pairs. Value, $1,700 unused, $3,000 never hinged.

Later, ungummed imperforate remainders were sent to Prague, where a smooth white gum was applied. Some of these remainder sheets were perforated 11½ and a large proportion were perforated 13¼. Value, set: $2.50 unused; $5 never hinged.

Nos. 1-3 and 1a-3a exist overprinted "Balicky do vlasti 50R" ("Packages to the homeland, 50 Rubles") and "Prvi Jugoslavenski puk u Sibiriji" ("First Jugoslav Regiment in Siberia"). Nos. 1-3 also exist overprinted "Vlak cs cerv.krize" ("Train of the Czechoslovak Red Cross"). All are rare.

Lion of Bohemia — A4

Type 1

Type 2

Two types: 1 — 6 points on star-like mace head at right of goblet; large saber handle; measures 20x25¼mm. 2 — 5 points on mace head; small saber handle; measures 19½x25mm.

Perce en Arc in Blue

1920		Embossed	
4	A4 (25k) blue & rose, ty 1	1.50	—
	Never hinged	2.50	
a.	Type 2	1.50	—
	Never hinged	2.50	

No. 4 was printed in Prague in 1919 and received in Siberia in 1920. It was overprinted "1920" (No. 5), which was in turn surcharged in various denominations (Nos. 6-14).

There were three printings of No. 4, all of which received the subsequent overprintings. The first printing has a steel blue frame and carmine center. The second printing has a gray-blue frame and red center. The first and second printings were sent to Siberia, apparently in similar quantities, and values for Nos. 4-14 are for examples from these printings.

A third printing was made in Prague in the 1920s to create copies for sale to collectors. Stamps of the third printing have a deep blue frame and carmine center, with heavy carmine inking at the top of the oval. Values for examples of Nos. 4-14 from this philatelic printing are much lower.

1st, 2nd

3rd

No. 4 Overprinted

1920			
5	A4 (25k) bl & rose, type 1	5.00	—
	Never hinged	10.00	
a.	Type 2	5.00	—
	Never hinged	10.00	

No. 5 (type 1) Surcharged with New Values in Green

6	A4 2k bl & rose	25.00
	Never hinged	50.00
7	A4 3k bl & rose	25.00
	Never hinged	50.00
8	A4 5k bl & rose	25.00
	Never hinged	50.00
9	A4 10k bl & rose	25.00
	Never hinged	50.00
10	A4 15k bl & rose	25.00
	Never hinged	50.00
11	A4 25k bl & rose	25.00
	Never hinged	50.00
12	A4 35k bl & rose	25.00
	Never hinged	50.00
13	A4 50k bl & rose	25.00
	Never hinged	50.00
14	A4 1r bl & rose	25.00
	Never hinged	50.00
	Nos. 6-14 (9)	225.00
	Set, never hinged	450.00

Surcharged on No. 5a (type 2)

6a	A4 2k bl & rose	25.00
	Never hinged	50.00
7a	A4 3k bl & rose	25.00
	Never hinged	50.00
8a	A4 5k bl & rose	25.00
	Never hinged	50.00
9a	A4 10k bl & rose	25.00
	Never hinged	50.00
10a	A4 15k bl & rose	25.00
	Never hinged	50.00
11a	A4 25k bl & rose	25.00
	Never hinged	50.00
12a	A4 35k bl & rose	25.00
	Never hinged	50.00
13a	A4 50k bl & rose	25.00
	Never hinged	50.00
14a	A4 1r bl & rose	25.00
	Never hinged	50.00
	Nos. 6a-14a (9)	225.00
	Set, never hinged	450.00

BOHEMIA AND MORAVIA

Catalogue values for unused stamps in this country are for never hinged items, beginning with Scott 20 in the regular postage section, Scott B1 in the semipostal section, Scott J1 in the postage due section, and Scott P1 in the newspaper section.

German Protectorate

Stamps of Czechoslovakia, 1928-39, Overprinted in Black

Perf. 10, 12½, 12x12½

1939, July 15				Unwmk.	
1	A29	5h	dk ultra	.20	.20
2	A29	10h	brown	.20	.20
3	A29	20h	red	.20	.20
4	A29	25h	green	.20	.20
5	A29	30h	red vio	.20	.20
6	A61a	40h	dk bl	2.50	4.75
7	A85	50h	dp grn	.20	.20
8	A63	60h	dl vio	2.50	4.75
9	A60	1k	rose lake (212)	.75	1.75
10	A60	1k	rose lake (256)	.30	.85
11	A64	1.20k	rose lilac	3.00	6.25
12	A65	1.50k	carmine	2.50	4.75
13	A79	1.60k	olive grn	2.50	4.75
a.			"Mähnen"	16.00	27.50
14	A66	2k	dk bl grn	1.10	1.75
15	A67	2.50k	dk bl	3.00	4.50
16	A68	3k	brown	3.00	4.75
17	A70	4k	dk vio	3.50	5.00
18	A71	5k	green	3.50	5.75
19	A72	10k	blue	4.75	9.50
			Nos. 1-19 (19)	34.10	60.30
			Set, never hinged	45.00	

The size of the overprint varies, Nos. 1-10 measure 17½x15½mm, Nos. 11-16 19x18mm, Nos. 17 and 19 28x17½mm and No. 18 23½x23mm.

Catalogue values for unused stamps in this section, from this point to the end of the section, are for never hinged items.

Linden Leaves and Closed Buds — A1

1939-41	Photo.		Perf. 14	
20	A1	5h dark blue	.20	.20
21	A1	10h blk brn	.20	.20
22	A1	20h crimson	.20	.20
23	A1	25h dk bl grn	.20	.20
24	A1	30h dp plum	.20	.20
24A	A1	30h golden brn ('41)	.20	.20
25	A1	40h orange ('40)	.20	.20
26	A1	50h slate grn ('40)	.20	.20
		Nos. 20-26 (8)	1.60	1.60

See Nos. 49-51.

Castle at Zvikov — A2

Karlstein Castle — A3

St. Barbara's Church, Kutna Hora — A4

Cathedral at Prague — A5

Brno Cathedral — A6

Town Square, Olomouc — A7

1939		Engr.	Perf. 12½	
27	A2	40h dark blue	.20	.20
28	A3	50h dk bl grn	.20	.20
29	A4	60h dl vio	.20	.20
30	A5	1k dp rose	.20	.20
31	A6	1.20k rose lilac	.40	.60
32	A6	1.50k rose car	.20	.20
33	A7	2k dk bl grn	.20	.20
34	A7	2.50k dark blue	.20	.20
		Nos. 27-34 (8)	1.80	2.00

No. 31 measures 23½x29½mm, No. 42 measures 18½x23mm.

See #52-53, 53B. For overprints see #60-61.

Zlin — A8

Iron Works at Moravská Ostrava — A9

Prague — A10

1939-40				
35	A8	3k dl rose vio	.20	.20
36	A9	4k slate ('40)	.20	.20
37	A10	5k green	.40	.40
38	A10	10k lt ultra	.30	.60
39	A10	20k yel brn	.90	1.25
		Nos. 35-39 (5)	2.00	2.65

Types of 1939 and

Neuhaus A11

Lainsitz Bridge near Bechyne A14

Pernstein Castle — A12

Samson Fountain, Budweis — A15

Pardubice Castle — A13

Kromeriz
A16

Wallenstein Palace, Prague — A17

1940 **Engr.** ***Perf. 12½***

40	A11	50h dk bl grn	.20	.20
41	A12	80h dp bl	.25	*.40*
42	A6	1.20k vio brn	.40	.25
43	A13	2k gray grn	.20	.20
44	A14	5k dk bl grn	.20	.20
45	A15	6k brn vio	.20	*.25*
46	A16	8k slate grn	.20	*.30*
47	A17	10k blue	.45	.30
48	A10	20k sepia	1.10	*1.50*
		Nos. 40-48 (9)	3.20	*3.60*

No. 42 measures 18½x23mm; No. 31, 23½x29½mm.

SEMI-POSTAL STAMPS

Catalogue values for unused stamps in this section are for never hinged items.

Nurse and Wounded Soldier — SP1

Perf. 13½

1940, June 29 **Photo.** **Unwmk.**

B1	SP1	60h + 40h indigo	.55	*.60*
B2	SP1	1.20k + 80h deep plum	.70	*.65*

Surtax for German Red Cross.

Labels alternate with stamps in sheets of #B1-B2.

PERSONAL DELIVERY STAMPS

PD1

1939-40 **Unwmk.** **Photo.** ***Perf. 13½***

EX1	PD1	50h indigo & blue ('40)	.45	*.80*
EX2	PD1	50h carmine & rose	.55	*1.10*

POSTAGE DUE STAMPS

Catalogue values for unused stamps in this section are for never hinged items.

D1

1939-40 **Unwmk.** **Typo.** ***Perf. 14***

J1	D1	5h dark carmine	.20	.20
J2	D1	10h dark carmine	.20	.20
J3	D1	20h dark carmine	.20	.20
J4	D1	30h dark carmine	.20	.20
J5	D1	40h dark carmine	.20	.20
J6	D1	50h dark carmine	.20	.20
J7	D1	60h dark carmine	.20	.20
J8	D1	80h dark carmine	.20	.20
J9	D1	1k bright ultra	.20	*.30*
J10	D1	1.20k brt ultra ('40)	.25	*.35*
J11	D1	2k bright ultra	.70	*.80*
J12	D1	5k bright ultra	.85	.85
J13	D1	10k bright ultra	1.25	1.25
J14	D1	20k bright ultra	2.40	2.40
		Nos. J1-J14 (14)	7.25	*7.55*

NEWSPAPER STAMPS

Catalogue values for unused stamps in this section are for never hinged items.

Carrier Pigeon — N1

1939 **Unwmk.** **Typo.** ***Imperf.***

P1	N1	2h ocher	.20	.20
P2	N1	5h ultra	.20	.20
P3	N1	7h red orange	.20	.20
P4	N1	9h emerald	.20	.20
P5	N1	10h henna brown	.20	.20
P6	N1	12h dark ultra	.20	.20
P7	N1	20h dark green	.20	*.25*
P8	N1	50h red brown	.20	*.35*
P9	N1	1k greenish gray	.20	*.35*
		Nos. P1-P9 (9)	1.80	2.15

No. P5 Overprinted in Black

1940

P10	N1	10h henna brown	.20	*.30*

Overprinted for use by commercial firms.

DAHOMEY

də-'hō-mē

LOCATION — West coast of Africa
AREA — 43,483 sq. mi.
POP. — 3,030,000 (est. 1974)
CAPITAL — Porto-Novo

Formerly a native kingdom including Benin, Dahomey was annexed by France in 1894. It became part of the colonial administrative unit of French West Africa in 1895.

100 Centimes = 1 Franc

See French West Africa No. 71 for stamp inscribed "Dahomey" and "Afrique Occidentale Francaise."

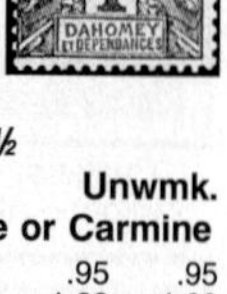

Navigation and Commerce — A1

Perf. 14x13½

1899-1905 **Typo.** **Unwmk.**

Name of Colony in Blue or Carmine

1	A1	1c black, *lil bl* ('01)	.95	.95
2	A1	2c brown, *buff* ('04)	1.60	1.00
3	A1	4c claret, *lav* ('04)	1.75	1.40
4	A1	5c yellow grn ('04)	4.25	2.40
5	A1	10c red ('01)	3.50	2.40
6	A1	15c gray ('01)	3.50	1.25
7	A1	20c red, *grn* ('04)	13.00	9.50
8	A1	25c black, *rose* ('99)	11.50	5.00
9	A1	25c blue ('01)	12.50	11.00
10	A1	30c brown, *bis* ('04)	17.00	8.75
11	A1	40c red, *straw* ('04)	18.00	11.00
12	A1	50c brn, *az* (name in red) ('01)	16.00	14.50
12A	A1	50c brn, *az* (name in bl) ('05)	25.00	16.00
13	A1	75c dp vio, *org* ('04)	65.00	42.50
14	A1	1fr brnz grn, *straw* ('04)	32.50	22.50
15	A1	2fr violet, *rose* ('04)	80.00	55.00
16	A1	5fr red lilac, *lav* ('04)	100.00	77.50
		Nos. 1-16 (17)	406.05	282.65

Perf. 13½x14 stamps are counterfeits.

For surcharges see Nos. 32-41.

Gen. Louis Faidherbe
A2

Oil Palm — A3

Dr. Noel Eugène Ballay
A4

1906-07 ***Perf. 13½x14***

Name of Colony in Red or Blue

17	A2	1c slate	.95	.80
18	A2	2c chocolate	1.25	.85
19	A2	4c choc, *gray bl*	2.25	1.75
20	A2	5c green	6.50	1.75
21	A2	10c carmine (B)	16.00	2.75
22	A3	20c black, *azure*	10.00	8.95
23	A3	25c blue, *pnksh*	10.00	9.00
24	A3	30c choc, *pnksh*	11.50	9.00
25	A3	35c black, *yellow*	65.00	9.00
26	A3	45c choc, *grnsh* ('07)	14.50	10.00
27	A3	50c deep violet	14.50	11.00
28	A3	75c blue, *orange*	17.50	13.50
29	A4	1fr black, *azure*	21.00	16.00
30	A4	2fr blue, *pink*	85.00	85.00
31	A4	5fr car, *straw* (B)	75.00	75.00
		Nos. 17-31 (15)	350.95	254.35

#2-3, 6-7, 9-13 Surcharged in Black or Carmine

1912 ***Perf. 14x13½***

Spacing between figures of surcharge 1.5mm (5c), 2mm (10c)

32	5c on 2c brn, *buff*	1.25	1.25
33	5c on 4c claret, *lav* (C)	1.10	1.10
a.	Double surcharge	200.00	
34	5c on 15c gray (C)	1.25	1.25
35	5c on 20c red, *grn*	1.10	1.10
36	5c on 25c blue (C)	1.25	1.25
a.	Inverted surcharge	160.00	
b.	Pair, one without surcharge	600.00	
37	5c on 30c brown, *bis* (C)	1.25	1.25
38	10c on 40c red, *straw*	1.25	1.25
a.	Inverted surcharge	250.00	
39	10c on 50c brn, *az*, name in bl (C)	1.60	1.60
40	10c on 50c brn, *az*, name in red (C)	850.00	900.00
41	10c on 75c violet, *org*	4.25	4.25
a.	Double surcharge	*4,500.*	
	Nos. 32-39,41 (9)	14.30	14.30

Spacing between figures of surcharge 2.25mm (5c), 2.75mm (10c)

32a	5c on 2c brn, *buff*	8.50	8.50
33b	5c on 4c claret, *lav* (C)	7.75	7.75
c.	Double surcharge, both wider spacing	1,400.	
d.	Double surcharge, one narrow and one wide spacing	4,000.	
34a	5c on 15c gray (C)	9.25	9.25
35a	5c on 20c red, *grn*	7.75	7.75
36b	5c on 25c blue (C)	9.25	9.25
c.	Inverted surcharge	1,400.	
37a	5c on 30c brown, *bis* (C)	8.50	8.50
38b	10c on 40c red, *straw*	60.00	60.00
c.	Inverted surcharge	2,250.	
39a	10c on 50c brn, *az*, name in bl (C)	125.00	125.00
40a	10c on 50c brn, *az*, name in red (C)	8,750.	
41b	10c on 75c violet, *org*	190.00	190.00
	Nos. 32a-39a,41b (9)	426.00	426.00

Man Climbing Oil Palm — A5

1913-39 ***Perf. 13½x14***

42	A5	1c violet & blk	.20	.20
43	A5	2c choc & rose	.20	.20
44	A5	4c black & brn	.20	.20
45	A5	5c yel grn & bl grn	.80	.35
46	A5	5c vio brn & vio ('22)	.35	.35
47	A5	10c org red & rose	.80	.45
a.		Half used as 5c on wrapper or printed matter		—
48	A5	10c yel grn & bl grn ('22)	.50	.50
49	A5	10c red & ol ('25)	.20	.20
50	A5	15c brn org & dk vio ('17)	.45	.35
51	A5	20c gray & choc	.35	.35
52	A5	20c bluish grn & grn ('26)	.20	.20
53	A5	20c mag & blk ('27)	.20	.20
54	A5	25c ultra & dp blue	1.40	.95
55	A5	25c vio brn & org ('22)	.70	.70
56	A5	30c choc & vio	2.00	1.60
57	A5	30c red org & rose ('22)	2.10	2.10
58	A5	30c yellow & vio ('25)	.20	.20
59	A5	30c dl grn & grn ('27)	.20	.20
60	A5	35c brown & blk	.60	.45
61	A5	35c bl grn & grn ('38)	.20	.20
62	A5	40c black & red org	.45	.45
63	A5	45c gray & ultra	.45	.45
64	A5	50c chocolate & brn	4.25	4.00
a.		Half used as 25c on cover		*500.00*
65	A5	50c ultra & bl ('22)	1.00	1.00
66	A5	50c brn red & bl ('26)	.85	.85
67	A5	55c gray grn & choc ('38)	.50	.35
68	A5	60c vio, *pnksh* ('25)	.20	.20
69	A5	65c yel brn & ol grn ('26)	.80	.80
70	A5	75c blue & violet	.80	.80
71	A5	80c henna brn & ultra ('38)	.20	.20
72	A5	85c dk bl & ver ('26)	1.00	1.00
73	A5	90c rose & brn red ('30)	.60	.50
74	A5	90c yel bis & red org ('39)	.75	.35
75	A5	1fr blue grn & blk	.80	.55
76	A5	1fr dk bl & ultra ('26)	1.00	1.00
77	A5	1fr yel brn & lt red ('28)	1.10	.80
78	A5	1fr dk red & red org ('38)	.75	.65
79	A5	1.10fr vio & bis ('28)	3.50	3.00
80	A5	1.25fr dp bl & dk brn ('33)	13.00	5.00
81	A5	1.50fr dk bl & lt bl ('30)	.95	.55
82	A5	1.75fr dk brn & dp buff ('33)	3.00	1.50
83	A5	1.75fr ind & ultra ('38)	1.00	.55
84	A5	2fr yel org & choc	.80	.80
85	A5	3fr red violet ('30)	2.00	.55
86	A5	5fr violet & dp bl	1.60	1.50
		Nos. 42-86 (45)	53.20	37.35

The 1c gray and yellow green and 5c dull red and black are Togo Nos. 193a, 196a.

Nos. 47a and 64a were authorized for use in Paouignan during the last part of November 1921. Other values exist as bisects but were not authorized.

For surcharges see #87-96, B1, B8-B11.

Type of 1913 Surcharged

1922-25

87	A5 60c on 75c vio, *pnksh*	.80	.80
a.	Double surcharge	140.00	
88	A5 65c on 15c brn org & dk vio ('25)	1.25	1.25
89	A5 85c on 15c brn org & dk vio ('25)	1.10	1.10
	Nos. 87-89 (3)	3.15	3.15

Stamps and Type of 1913-39 Surcharged with New Value and Bars

1924-27

90	A5 25c on 2fr org & choc	.80	.80
91	A5 90c on 75c cer & brn red ('27)	1.10	1.10
92	A5 1.25fr on 1fr dk bl & ultra (R) ('26)	.95	.95
93	A5 1.50fr on 1fr dk bl & grnsh bl ('27)	1.50	1.50
94	A5 3fr on 5fr olvn & dp org ('27)	7.25	7.25
95	A5 10fr on 5fr bl vio & red brn ('27)	5.75	5.75
96	A5 20fr on 5fr ver & dl grn ('27)	5.75	5.75
	Nos. 90-96 (7)	23.10	23.10

Common Design Types pictured following the introduction.

Colonial Exposition Issue

Common Design Types

1931 Engr. *Perf. 12½*

Name of Country in Black

97	CD70 40c deep green	4.25	4.25
98	CD71 50c violet	4.25	4.25
99	CD72 90c red orange	4.25	4.25
100	CD73 1.50fr dull blue	4.25	4.25
	Nos. 97-100 (4)	17.00	17.00

Paris International Exposition Issue

Common Design Types

1937 Engr. *Perf. 13*

101	CD74 20c deep violet	1.10	1.10
102	CD75 30c dark green	1.10	1.10
103	CD76 40c carmine rose	1.25	1.25
104	CD77 50c dark brown	1.25	1.25
105	CD78 90c red	1.25	1.25
106	CD79 1.50fr ultra	1.25	1.25
	Nos. 101-106 (6)	7.20	7.20

Souvenir Sheet

Imperf

107	CD77 3fr dp blue & blk	5.75	*7.25*

Caillié Issue

Common Design Type

1939, Apr. 5 Engr. *Perf. 12½x12*

108	CD81 90c org brn & org	.90	.90
109	CD81 2fr brt violet	.90	.90
110	CD81 2.25fr ultra & dk blue	1.10	1.10
	Nos. 108-110 (3)	2.90	2.90

New York World's Fair Issue

Common Design Type

1939 Engr.

111	CD82 1.25fr carmine lake	.80	.80
112	CD82 2.25fr ultra	.80	.80

SEMI-POSTAL STAMPS

Regular Issue of 1913 Surcharged in Red

1915 Unwmk. *Perf. 14x13½*

B1	A5 10c + 5c orange red & rose	.90	.90

Curie Issue

Common Design Type

1938 *Perf. 13*

B2	CD80 1.75fr + 50c brt ultra	7.25	7.25

French Revolution Issue

Common Design Type

1939 Photo.

Name and Value Typo. in Black

B3	CD83 45c + 25c green	6.50	6.50
B4	CD83 70c + 30c brown	6.50	6.50
B5	CD83 90c + 35c red org	6.50	6.50
B6	CD83 1.25fr + 1fr rose pink	6.50	6.50
B7	CD83 2.25fr + 2fr blue	6.50	6.50
	Nos. B3-B7 (5)	32.50	32.50

AIR POST STAMPS

Common Design Type

1940 Unwmk. Engr. *Perf. 12½*

C1	CD85 1.90fr ultra	.20	.30
C2	CD85 2.90fr dk red	.40	.40
C3	CD85 4.50fr dk gray grn	.65	.65
C4	CD85 4.90fr yel bister	.85	.85
C5	CD85 6.90fr deep org	1.10	1.10
	Nos. C1-C5 (5)	3.20	3.30

POSTAGE DUE STAMPS

Dahomey Natives — D1

D2

1906 Unwmk. Typo. *Perf. 14x13½*

J1	D1 5c grn, *grnsh*	1.75	1.75
J2	D1 10c red brn	3.00	3.00
J3	D1 15c dark blue	5.75	5.75
J4	D1 20c blk, *yellow*	4.25	4.25
J5	D1 30c red, *straw*	6.00	6.00
J6	D1 50c violet	17.50	17.50
J7	D1 60c blk, *buff*	10.00	10.00
J8	D1 1fr blk, *pinkish*	27.50	27.50
	Nos. J1-J8 (8)	75.75	75.75

1914

J9	D2 5c green	.20	.20
J10	D2 10c rose	.35	.35
J11	D2 15c gray	.35	.35
J12	D2 20c brown	.80	.80
J13	D2 30c blue	.95	.95
J14	D2 50c black	1.10	1.10
J15	D2 60c orange	1.40	1.40
J16	D2 1fr violet	1.40	1.40
	Nos. J9-J16 (8)	6.55	6.55

Type of 1914 Issue Surcharged

1927

J17	D2 2fr on 1fr lilac rose	4.00	4.00
J18	D2 3fr on 1fr org brn	4.00	4.00

DALMATIA

dal-ˈmā-shə̄-ə

LOCATION — A promontory in the northwestern part of the Balkan Peninsula, together with several small islands in the Adriatic Sea.

GOVT. — Part of the former Austro-Hungarian crownland of the same name.

AREA — 113 sq. mi.

POP. — 18,719 (1921)

CAPITAL — Zara.

Stamps were issued during Italian occupation. This territory was subsequently annexed by Italy.

100 Centesimi = 1 Corona = 1 Lira

Used values are for postally used copies.

Issued under Italian Occupation

Italy No. 87 Surcharged

1919, May 1 Wmk. 140 *Perf. 14*

1	A46 1cor on 1 l brn & grn	3.00	*10.00*

Italian Stamps of 1906-08 Surcharged — a

1921-22

2	A48 5c on 5c green	1.75	*2.00*
3	A48 10c on 10c claret	1.75	*2.00*
4	A49 25c on 25c blue ('22)	4.00	3.50
5	A49 50c on 50c vio ('22)	5.00	4.00

Italian Stamps of 1901-10 Surcharged — b

6	A46 1cor on 1 l brn & grn ('22)	7.75	9.00
7	A46 5cor on 5 l bl & rose ('22)	60.00	50.00
8	A51 10cor on 10 l gray grn & red ('22)	60.00	50.00
	Nos. 1-8 (8)	143.25	130.50

Surcharges similar to these but differing in style or arrangement of type were used in Austria under Italian occupation.

SPECIAL DELIVERY STAMPS

Italian Special Delivery Stamp No. E1 Surcharged type "a"

1921 Wmk. 140 *Perf. 14*

E1	SD1 25c on 25c rose red	3.25	*4.00*
a.	Double surcharge	110.00	150.00

Italian Special Delivery Stamp Surcharged **LIRE 1,20 DI CORONA**

1922

E2	SD2 1.20 l on 1.20 l	75.00	150.00

No. E2 was not placed in use.

POSTAGE DUE STAMPS

Italian Postage Due Stamps and Type Surcharged types "a" or "b"

1922 Wmk. 140 *Perf. 14*

J1	D3 (a) 50c on 50c buff & mag	2.25	*3.00*
J2	D3 (b) 1cor on 1 l bl & red	6.25	*6.00*
J3	D3 (b) 2cor on 2 l bl & red	42.50	*55.00*
J4	D3 (b) 5cor on 5 l bl & red	42.50	*55.00*
	Nos. J1-J4 (4)	93.50	*119.00*

DANISH WEST INDIES

ˈdā-nish ˈwest ˈin-dēs

LOCATION — A group of islands in the West Indies, lying east of Puerto Rico

GOVT. — Danish Colony

AREA — 132 sq. mi.

POP. — 27,086 (1911)

CAPITAL — Charlotte Amalie

The US bought these islands in 1917 and they became the US Virgin Islands, using US stamps and currency. However, for the first six months of U.S. ownership, until September 30, 1917, a postal transition period existed. During this period, either U.S., D.W.I. or mixed frankings could be used. The domestic printed matter or postcard rate was 5 bits or 1 cent, and the foreign printed matter or postcard rate was 10 bits, 2 cents, or 5 bits + 1 cent. The domestic minimum weight letter rate was 10 bits, 2 cents, or 5 bits + 1 cent, while the foreign minimum letter rate was 25 bits, 5 cents, or any combination of U.S. and D.W.I. stamps that together totalled 25 bits or 5 cents.

Letters posted to foreign destinations during the transition period are rare because of World War I. Values for covers listed here are for the period before the transition. Transition-period covers, including those with mixed franking, sell for much more.

100 Cents = 1 Dollar

100 Bit = 1 Franc (1905)

FORERUNNERS

Crowned Circle handstamp types are pictured in the Crowned Circle Handstamps and Great Britain Used Abroad section.

BRITISH POST OFFICES IN DANISH WEST INDIES

St. Thomas

British P.O. opened Jan., 1809; stamps supplied July 3, 1865; closed to the public Sept. 1, 1877; closed for receiving mail in transit 1879

Pre-Stamp Postal Markings

1849-55

A1	Crowned Circle handstamp Type I, on cover, inscribed "PAID AT ST. THOMAS"	575.
A2	Crowned Circle handstamp Type IX, on cover, inscribed "PAID AT ST. THOMAS" in black	1,900.

Earliest known uses: A1, 2/20/49; A2, 5/1/55.

Stamps of Great Britain, Canceled C51, or with Circular Date Stamp (Several types exist)

1865-79

A3	½p rose red (#58 P 5, 6, 8, 10-12), *value from*	42.50
A4	1p rose red (#20)	—
A5	1p rose red (#33, P 71, 72, 79, 81, 84-90, 93-102, 105-114, 116-125, 127, 129-131, 133, 134, 136-142, 144-152, 154-167, 169-182, 184-187, 189, 190, 197) *value from*	30.00
A6	1½p lake red (#32, P1, 3), *value from*	75.00
A7	2p blue (#29, P 9)	35.00
	Plate 12	*350.00*
A8	2p blue (#30, P 13-15), *value from*	35.00
A9	3p rose (#44, P 4)	100.00
A10	3p rose (#49, P 4-10)	50.00
A11	3p rose (#61, P 11-12, 14-19), *value from*	35.00
A12	4p vermilion (#34)	85.00
a.	Hair-lines (#34c)	100.00
A13	4p vermilion (#43, P 7-14), *value from*	57.50
A14	4p vermilion (#69, P 15)	350.00
A15	4p pale olive green (#70, P 15, 16)	225.00
A16	6p lilac (#39c, P 4)	175.00
A17	6p lilac (#45, P 5)	85.00
	Plate 6	160.00
A18	6p dull violet (#50, P 6)	85.00

A19 6p violet (#51, P 6, 8, 9), *value from* 80.00
A20 6p brown (#59, P 11) 50.00
a. 6p pale buff (#59b, P 11) 100.00
Plate 12 250.00
A21 6p gray (#60, P 12) 240.00
A22 6p gray (#62, P 13-16), *value from* 50.00
A23 8p orange (#73) 310.00
A24 9p straw (#40) 325.00
a. 9p bister (#40a) 350.00
A25 9p straw (#46) 425.00
A26 9p bister (#52) 225.00
A27 10p red brown (#53) 310.00
A28 1sh green (#48, P 4) 160.00
A29 1sh green (#54, P 4-7) *value from* 35.00
A30 1sh green (#64, P 8-13) *value from* 70.00
A31 2sh blue (#55) 150.00
A32 5sh rose (#57, P 1) 550.00
Plate 2 700.00

Issued under Danish Dominion Watermarks

Wmk. 111 — Small Crown

Wmk. 112 — Crown

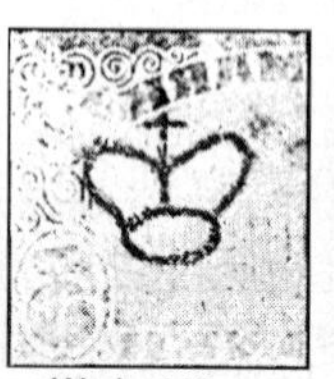
Wmk. 113 — Crown

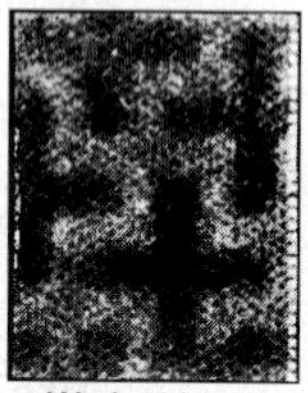
Wmk. 114 — Multiple Crosses

Coat of Arms — A1

Yellowish Paper
Yellow Wavy-line Burelage, UL to LR

1856 Wmk. 111 Typo. *Imperf.*
1 A1 3c dk car, brown gum 190. *250.*
On cover 3,000.
a. 3c dark carmine, yellow gum 200. *250.*
On cover 3,000.
b. 3c carmine, white gum *4,000.* —

Reprint: 1981, carmine, back-printed across two stamps ("Reprint by Dansk Post og Telegrafmuseum 1978"), value, pair, $10.

White Paper
Yellow Wavy-line Burelage, UR to LL

1866
2 A1 3c rose 40.00 *70.00*
On cover 3,000.

No. 2 reprints unwatermarked: 1930 carmine, value $75. 1942 rose carmine, back-printed across each row ("Nytryk 1942 G. A. Hagemann Danmark og Dansk Vestindiens Friemaerker Bind 2"), value $50.

1872 *Perf. 12½*
3 A1 3c rose 90.00 *275.00*
On cover *7,500.*

1873

Without Burelage
4 A1 4c dull blue 225.00 *425.00*
On cover —
a. Imperf., pair 750.00
b. Horiz. pair, imperf. vert. 550.00

#4 reprints, unwatermarked, imperf.: 1930, ultramarine, value $85. 1942, blue back-printed like 1942 reprint of #2, value $50.

A2

Normal Frame

Inverted Frame

The arabesques in the corners have a main stem and a branch. When the frame is in normal position, in the upper left corner the branch leaves the main stem half way between two little leaflets. In the lower right corner the branch starts at the foot of the second leaflet. When the frame is inverted the corner designs are, of course, transposed.

White Wove Paper, Varying from Thin to Thick

1874-79 Wmk. 112 *Perf. 14x13½*
5 A2 1c green & brn red 17.50 *27.50*
On cover 250.00
a. 1c grn & rose lilac, thin paper 75.00 *125.00*
b. 1c grn & red violet, medium paper 40.00 *65.00*
c. 1c green & violet, thick paper 17.50 *27.50*
e. Inverted frame 17.50 *27.50*
f. As "a," inverted frame *425.00*
6 A2 3c blue & carmine 22.50 20.00
On cover 225.00
a. 3c light blue & rose carmine, thin paper 65.00 50.00
b. 3c deep blue & dark carmine, medium paper 35.00 17.00
c. 3c greenish blue & lake, thick paper 22.50 17.00
d. Imperf., pair 325.00 —
e. Inverted frame 21.00 15.00
f. As "a," inverted frame *350.00*
7 A2 4c brn & dull blue 16.00 *19.00*
On cover 225.00
b. 4c brown & ultramarine 175.00 *225.00*
c. Diag. half used as 2c on cover 125.00
d. As "b," inverted frame *750.00* *1,250.*
8 A2 5c green & gray ('76) 27.50 22.50
a. 5c yellow green & dark gray, thin paper 47.50 32.50
b. Inverted frame 27.50 22.50
On cover 250.00
9 A2 7c lilac & orange 30.00 *85.00*
On cover 1,100.
a. 7c lilac & yellow 77.50 77.50
b. Inverted frame 52.50 *125.00*
10 A2 10c blue & brn ('76) 24.00 *27.50*
On cover 300.00
a. 10c dark blue & black brown, thin paper 70.00 45.00
b. "cent.s" 30.00 30.00
c. Inverted frame 24.00 27.50
11 A2 12c red lilac & yel green ('77) 42.50 *175.00*
On cover 1,750.
a. 12c lilac & deep green 130.00 *185.00*
12 A2 14c lilac & green 500.00 *850.00*
On cover —
a. Inverted frame *2,000.* *2,750.*
13 A2 50c violet, thin paper ('79) 175.00 *300.00*
On cover 2,500.
a. 50c gray violet, thick porous paper 225.00 *350.00*

The central element in the fan-shaped scrollwork at the outside of the lower left corner of Nos. 5a and 7b looks like an elongated diamond.

See Nos. 16-20. For surcharges see Nos. 14-15, 23-28, 40.

Nos. 9 and 13 Surcharged in Black

1887-95
14 A2 1c on 7c lilac & org 77.50 *200.00*
On cover 3,000.
a. 1c on 7c lilac & yellow 82.50 *210.00*
b. Double surcharge 225.00 *450.00*
c. Inverted frame 95.00 *300.00*
15 A2 10c on 50c violet ('95) 37.50 *62.50*
On cover 275.00

Type of 1874-79

1896-1901 *Perf. 13*
16 A2 1c green & red vio ('98) 12.00 *20.00*
On cover 150.00
a. Normal frame 260.00 375.00
17 A2 3c blue & lake ('98) 12.00 *16.00*
On cover 150.00
a. Normal frame 230.00 *375.00*
18 A2 4c bister & dull blue ('01) 16.00 14.00
On cover 150.00
a. Diagonal half used as 2c on cover 90.00
b. Inverted frame 50.00 *80.00*
On cover 250.00
c. As "b," diagonal half used as 2c on cover 300.00
19 A2 5c green & gray 35.00 32.50
On cover 325.00
a. Normal frame 675.00 *975.00*
20 A2 10c blue & brown ('01) 70.00 *140.00*
On cover 1,150.
a. Inverted frame 850.00 *1,450.*
b. "cent.s" 160.00 150.00
Nos. 16-20 (5) 145.00 *222.50*

Arms — A5

1900
21 A5 1c light green 2.75 2.75
On cover 80.00
On cover, single franking 300.00
22 A5 5c light blue 16.50 *22.50*
On cover 300.00

See Nos. 29-30. For surcharges see Nos. 41-42.

Nos. 6, 17, 20 Surcharged:

c

d

Surcharge "c" in Black

1902 *Perf. 14x13½*
23 A2 2c on 3c blue & car 450.00 *500.00*
On cover *4,000.*
a. "2" in date with straight tail 475.00 *525.00*
b. Normal frame *3,500.*

Perf. 13
24 A2 2c on 3c blue & lake 10.00 *27.50*
On cover 160.00
a. "2" in date with straight tail 12.00 *30.00*
b. Dated "1901" 450.00 *500.00*
c. Normal frame 150.00 *225.00*
d. Dark green surcharge 1,750. —
e. As "d" & "a" —
f. As "d" & "c" — —
25 A2 8c on 10c blue & brn 22.50 *37.50*
On cover 225.00
a. "2" with straight tail 27.50 *40.00*
b. On No. 20b 32.50 *45.00*
c. Inverted frame 230.00 *375.00*

Only one copy of No. 24f can exist.

Surcharge "d" in Black
27 A2 2c on 3c blue & lake 11.00 *35.00*
On cover 500.00
a. Normal frame 225.00 *375.00*
28 A2 8c on 10c blue & brn 12.00 12.00
On cover 175.00
a. On No. 20b 18.50 *25.00*
b. Inverted frame 200.00 *400.00*

1903 Wmk. 113
29 A5 2c carmine 7.00 *20.00*
On cover 125.00
30 A5 8c brown 24.00 *45.00*
On cover 250.00

King Christian IX — A8

St. Thomas Harbor — A9

1905 Typo. *Perf. 13*
31 A8 5b green 3.50 3.00
On cover 35.00
32 A8 10b red 3.50 3.00
On cover 35.00
33 A8 20b green & blue 8.00 7.50
On cover 150.00
34 A8 25b ultramarine 8.00 *9.50*
On cover 85.00
35 A8 40b red & gray 8.00 7.50
On cover 225.00
36 A8 50b yellow & gray 9.00 *11.00*
On cover 250.00

Frame Typo., Center Engr.
Wmk. Two Crowns (113)
Perf. 12
37 A9 1fr green & blue 17.50 *40.00*
On cover 625.00
38 A9 2fr org red & brown 30.00 *55.00*
On cover 1,100.
39 A9 5fr yellow & brown 70.00 *250.00*
On cover 1,750.
Nos. 31-39 (9) 157.50 *386.50*

Philatelic covers are valued at approximately 25% of these figures.

Nos. 18, 22, 30 Surcharged in Black

1905 Wmk. 112 *Perf. 13*
40 A2 5b on 4c bis & dull blue 15.00 *40.00*
On cover 250.00
a. Inverted frame 40.00 *75.00*
41 A5 5b on 5c light blue 12.50 *32.50*
On cover 250.00

Wmk. 113
42 A5 5b on 8c brown 12.50 *32.50*
On cover 250.00

Frederik VIII A10

Christian X A11

Frame Typo., Center Engr.
1907-08 Wmk. 113 *Perf. 13*
43 A10 5b green 1.75 1.75
On cover 22.50
44 A10 10b red 1.75 1.75
On cover 22.50
45 A10 15b violet & brown 3.50 *3.75*
On cover 125.00
46 A10 20b green & blue 30.00 27.50
On cover 110.00
47 A10 25b blue & dk blue 1.75 2.25
On cover 35.00
48 A10 30b claret & slate 47.50 47.50
On cover 350.00
49 A10 40b ver & gray 5.25 *8.50*
On cover 210.00
50 A10 50b yellow & brown 5.25 *13.50*
On cover 210.00
Nos. 43-50 (8) 96.75 106.50

1915 Wmk. 114 *Perf. 14x14½*
51 A11 5b yellow green 3.50 *3.50*
On cover 45.00
52 A11 10b red 3.50 *35.00*
On cover 100.00
53 A11 15b lilac & red brown 4.00 *40.00*
On cover 300.00
54 A11 20b green & blue 4.00 *40.00*
On cover 350.00
55 A11 25b blue & dark blue 4.00 *10.00*
On cover 100.00
56 A11 30b claret & black 4.00 *70.00*
On cover 900.00
57 A11 40b orange & black 4.00 *70.00*
On cover 550.00
58 A11 50b yellow & brown 4.00 *70.00*
On cover 650.00
Nos. 51-58 (8) 31.00 *338.50*

Forged and favor cancellations exist.

POSTAGE DUE STAMPS

Royal Cipher, "Christian 9 Rex" D1

1902 Unwmk. Litho. *Perf. 11½*
J1 D1 1c dark blue 4.00 *15.00*
On cover 400.00

J2 D1 4c dark blue 9.00 *20.00*
On cover *350.00*
J3 D1 6c dark blue 17.50 *55.00*
On cover *450.00*
J4 D1 10c dark blue 15.00 *60.00*
On cover *400.00*

There are five types of each value. On the 4c they may be distinguished by differences in the figures "4"; on the other values the differences are minute.

Used values of Nos. J1-J4 are for canceled copies. Uncanceled examples without gum have probably been used. Value 60% of unused.

On cover values are for copies tied by cancellation.

Counterfeits of Nos. J1-J4 exist.

D2

1905-13 ***Perf. 13***
J5 D2 5b red & gray 4.00 *6.25*
On cover *450.00*
J6 D2 20b red & gray 7.00 *12.50*
On cover *450.00*
J7 D2 30b red & gray 6.00 *12.50*
On cover *450.00*
J8 D2 50b red & gray 5.50 *32.50*
On cover *900.00*
a. Perf. 14x14½ ('13) 35.00 *125.00*
b. Perf. 11½ 300.00

All values of this issue are known imperforate, but were not regularly issued.

Used values of Nos. J5-J8 are for canceled copies. Uncanceled examples without gum have probably been used. Value 60% of unused.

On cover values are for copies tied by cancellation.

Counterfeits of Nos. J5-J8 exist.

Danish West Indies stamps were replaced by those of the US in 1917, after the US bought the islands.

DANZIG

ˈdanˌtˌ-sig

LOCATION — In northern Europe bordering on the Baltic Sea
AREA — 754 sq. mi.
POP. — 407,000 (approx. 1939)
CAPITAL — Danzig

Established as a "Free City and State" under the protection of the League of Nations in 1920, Danzig was seized by Germany in 1939.

100 Pfennig = 1 Gulden (1923)
100 Pfennig = 1 Mark

Watermarks

Wmk. 108 — Honeycomb

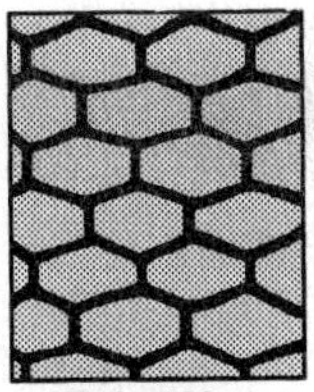
Wmk. 109 — Webbing

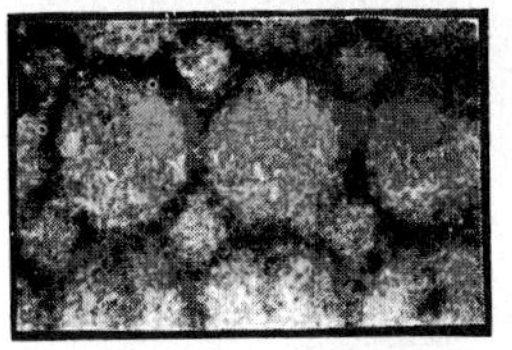
Wmk. 110 — Octagons

Wmk. 125 — Lozenges

Wmk. 237 — Swastikas

Used Values of 1920-23 are for favor-canceled stamps unless otherwise noted.

German Stamps of 1906-20 Overprinted in Black

Perf. 14, 14½, 15x14½
1920 **Wmk. 125**
1 A16 5pf green .25 .25
Never hinged 1.75
Postally used *2.00*
On cover *4.50*
a. Pair, one without overprint 75.00
Never hinged 225.00
b. Double overprint —
2 A16 10pf car rose .25 .25
Never hinged 1.25
Postally used *1.90*
On cover *4.50*
a. 10pf deep carmine 19.00 *22.50*
Never hinged 92.50
Postally used *130.00*
On cover *180.00*
3 A22 15pf violet brown .25 .25
Never hinged 1.75
Postally used *3.50*
On cover *5.75*
4 A16 20pf blue violet .25 *1.10*
Never hinged 1.25
Postally used *3.50*
On cover *7.50*
5 A16 30pf org & blk, *buff* .25 .25
Never hinged 1.25
Postally used *2.25*
On cover *7.50*
a. Pair, one without overprint — —
6 A16 40pf car rose .25 .25
Never hinged 1.25
Postally used *1.50*
On cover *7.50*
7 A16 50pf pur & blk, *buff* .50 .25
Never hinged 1.40
Postally used *3.50*
On cover *7.50*
a. Pair, one without overprint 140.00
Never hinged 375.00
8 A17 1m red .50 .60
Never hinged 2.50
Postally used *4.25*
On cover *9.25*
a. Pair, one without overprint 75.00
Never hinged 225.00
9 A17 1.25m green .50 .60
Never hinged 2.50
Postally used *4.25*
On cover *9.25*
a. 1.25m deep bluish green 22.50 *30.00*
Never hinged 125.00
Postally used *110.00*
On cover *150.00*
10 A17 1.50m yellow brn .90 .85
Never hinged 4.25
Postally used *5.25*
On cover *13.00*
11 A21 2m blue 3.00 *4.75*
Never hinged 12.00
Postally used *26.00*
On cover *45.00*
a. Double overprint *350.00*
Never hinged *750.00*
b. 2m blue black 100.00 *110.00*
Never hinged 300.00
Postally used *600.00*
On cover *725.00*
12 A21 2.50m lilac rose 1.75 *3.25*
Never hinged 8.50
Postally used *11.50*
On cover *23.00*
a. 2.50m deep lilac rose 2.75 *10.00*
Never hinged 10.00
Postally used *15.00*
On cover *35.00*
b. 2.50m lake rose 75.00 *100.00*
Never hinged 225.00
Postally used *525.00*
On cover *700.00*
13 A19 3m black violet 7.00 *10.00*
Never hinged 40.00
Postally used *100.00*
On cover *350.00*
a. 3m blackish slate-violet 60.00 *110.00*
Never hinged 200.00
Postally used *700.00*
On cover *850.00*
14 A16 4m black & rose 4.75 *6.00*
Never hinged 27.50
Postally used *35.00*
On cover *85.00*
15 A20 5m slate & car (25x17 holes) 1.75 *2.00*
Never hinged 10.00
Postally used *35.00*
On cover *75.00*
a. Center & "Danzig" invtd. *10,500.*
Never hinged —
b. Inverted overprint *17,500.*
c. 5m slate & car (26x17 holes) *2,300.*
Never hinged 6,500.
Nos. 1-15 (15) 22.15 30.65
Set, never hinged 100.00

The 5pf brown, 10pf orange and 40pf lake and black with this overprint were not regularly issued. Value for trio, $450.

For surcharges see Nos. 19-23, C1-C3.

Issued: 40pf, 9/13; 1.50m, 3m 7/20; 4m, 12/21; others 6/14.

Nos. 5, 4 Surcharged in Various Sizes

1920
19 A16 5pf on 30pf (V) .20 .20
Never hinged .75
Postally used *2.00*
On cover *3.75*
20 A16 10pf on 20pf (R) .20 .20
Never hinged .75
Postally used *1.75*
On cover *3.75*
a. Double surcharge 87.50 —
Never hinged 225.00
21 A16 25pf on 30pf (G) .20 .20
Never hinged .75
Postally used *1.75*
On cover *5.75*
a. Inverted surcharge 75.00 —
Never hinged 225.00
22 A16 60pf on 30pf (Br) .70 .85
Never hinged 3.50
Postally used *4.25*
On cover *9.00*
a. Double surcharge 75.00 240.00
Never hinged 225.00
23 A16 80pf on 30pf (V) .70 .85
Never hinged 3.50
Postally used *5.00*
On cover *9.00*

Issued: #21, 8/10. #20, 8/17. #19, 22-23, 11/1.

German Stamps Surcharged in Various Styles

Gray Burelage with Points Up
25 A16 1m on 30pf org & blk, *buff* (Bk) .70 *1.10*
Never hinged 3.75
Postally used *4.00*
On cover *15.00*
a. Pair, one without surcharge
e. Double burlage, both pointing up 55.00 *100.00*
Never hinged 175.00
Postally used *225.00*
26 A16 1¼m on 3pf brn (R) .70 *1.10*
Never hinged 4.25
Postally used *4.50*
On cover *17.00*
e. Double burelage, both pointing up 67.50 *140.00*
Never hinged 225.00
Postally used *275.00*
27 A22 2m on 35pf red brn (Bl) .85 *1.10*
Never hinged 6.00
Postally used *4.50*
On cover *15.00*
d. Surcharge omitted 70.00 —
Never hinged 260.00
e. Double burelage, both pointing up 70.00 *140.00*
Never hinged 225.00
Postally used *275.00*
28 A22 3m on 7½pf org (G) .85 *1.10*
Never hinged 4.25
Postally used *7.50*
On cover *19.00*
d. Double surcharge 150.00
Never hinged 375.00
e. Double burelage, both pointing up 62.50 *115.00*
Never hinged 180.00
Postally used *225.00*
29 A22 5m on 2pf gray (R) .85 *1.10*
Never hinged 4.25
Postally used *9.25*
On cover *22.50*
30 A22 10m on 7½pf org (Bk) 3.00 *7.00*
Never hinged 24.00
Postally used *20.00*
On cover *125.00*
d. Double surcharge 37.50
Never hinged 190.00
e. Double burelage, both pointing up 70.00 *115.00*
Never hinged 190.00
Postally used *225.00*
Nos. 19-30 (11) 8.95 *14.80*
Set, never hinged 47.50

Gray Burelage with Points Down
26a A16 1¼m on 3pf brown 36.00 *42.50*
Never hinged 92.50
Postally used *92.50*
On cover *140.00*
f. Double burelage, both pointing down 37.50 *150.00*
Never hinged 250.00
Postally used *300.00*
27a A22 2m on 35pf red brn 300.00 *325.00*
Never hinged *1,000.*
Postally used *700.00*
On cover *900.00*
28a A22 3m on 7½pf orange 11.00 *13.50*
Never hinged 35.00
Postally used *42.50*
On cover *75.00*
29a A22 5m on 2pf gray 11.50 *30.00*
Never hinged 37.50
Postally used *125.00*
On cover *190.00*
30a A22 10m on 7½pf orange 5.75 *11.00*
Never hinged 25.00
Postally used *42.50*
On cover *140.00*
Nos. 26a-30a (5) 364.25 *422.00*
Set, never hinged 1,440.

Violet Burelage with Points Up
25b A16 1m on 30pf org & blk, *buff* 57.50 37.50
Never hinged 225.00
Postally used *70.00*
On cover *150.00*
26b A16 1¼m on 3pf brown 4.50 *6.50*
Never hinged 17.50
Postally used *26.00*
On cover *45.00*
g. Double burelage, both pointing up 190.00 *225.00*
Never hinged 750.00
27b A22 2m on 35pf red brn 11.50 *37.50*
Never hinged 45.00
Postally used *125.00*
On cover *190.00*
f. Double burelage, both pointing up 190.00 *225.00*
Never hinged 750.00
28b A22 3m on 7½pf orange 2.25 *2.25*
Never hinged 10.50
Postally used *9.00*
On cover *37.50*
f. Double burelage, both pointing up 190.00 *225.00*
Never hinged 750.00
29b A22 5m on 2pf gray 1.10 *2.10*
Never hinged 3.50
Postally used *11.50*
On cover *35.00*
30b A22 10m on 7½pf orange 1.10 *2.10*
Never hinged 3.50
Postally used *11.50*
On cover *30.00*
g. Double burelage, both pointing up 175.00 *225.00*
Never hinged 700.00
Nos. 25b-30b (6) 77.95 *87.95*
Set, never hinged 275.00

Violet Burelage with Points Down
25c A16 1m on 30pf org & blk, *buff* 1.10 2.50
Never hinged 4.00
Postally used *9.25*
On cover *15.00*
d. Double burelage, both pointing down 190.00 *225.00*
Never hinged 750.00
26c A16 1¼m on 3pf brown 5.50 *11.00*
Never hinged 22.50
Postally used *32.50*
On cover *60.00*
d. Double burelage, both pointing down 190.00 *225.00*
Never hinged 750.00
27c A22 2m on 35pf red brn 21.00 *50.00*
Never hinged 97.50
Postally used *240.00*
On cover *300.00*
g. Double burelage, both pointing down 190.00 *225.00*
Never hinged 750.00
28c A22 3m on 7½pf orange 40.00 *85.00*
Never hinged 175.00
Postally used *300.00*
On cover *375.00*
g. Double burelage, both pointing down 190.00 *225.00*
Never hinged 750.00
29c A22 5m on 2pf gray 4.50 *8.50*
Never hinged 22.50
Postally used *35.00*
On cover *45.00*

e. Double burelage, both pointing down 190.00 *225.00*
Never hinged 750.00
30c A22 10m on 7½pf orange 13.50 *29.00*
Never hinged 57.50
Postally used *100.00*
On cover 140.00
h. Double burelage, both pointing down 190.00 *225.00*
Never hinged 750.00
i. Double burelage, one pointing up, one down 190.00 *225.00*
Never hinged 750.00
Nos. 25c-30c (6) 85.60 *186.00*
Set, never hinged 400.00

Burelage Omitted

25f A16 1m on 30pf org & blk, *buff* 3.00 *5.50*
Never hinged 11.50
Postally used *19.00*
On cover 45.00
26h A16 1¼m on 3pf brown 100.00 *150.00*
Never hinged 300.00
Postally used *550.00*
On cover 925.00
27h A22 2m on 35pf red brn 125.00 *150.00*
Never hinged 375.00
Postally used *600.00*
On cover 1,000.
28h A22 3m on 7½pf orange 210.00 *350.00*
Never hinged 750.00
Postally used *750.00*
On cover 1,200.
29f A22 5m on 2pf gray 210.00 *350.00*
Never hinged 750.00
Postally used *750.00*
On cover 1,200.
30j A22 10m on 7½pf orange 8.50 *19.00*
Never hinged 19.00
Postally used *92.50*
On cover 125.00

Excellent counterfeits of the surcharges are known.

German Stamps of 1906-20 Overprinted in Blue

1920

31 A22 2pf gray 110.00 *200.00*
Never hinged 350.00
Postally used *425.00*
On cover *1,900.*
32 A22 2½pf gray 150.00 *300.00*
Never hinged 500.00
Postally used *525.00*
On cover *3,100.*
33 A16 3pf brown 11.00 *40.00*
Never hinged 35.00
Postally used *45.00*
On cover 115.00
a. Double overprint 55.00 —
Never hinged 140.00
34 A16 5pf green .55 .60
Never hinged 1.90
Postally used *1.90*
On cover 7.50
a. Double overprint 72.50
Never hinged 190.00
35 A22 7½pf orange 40.00 *57.50*
Never hinged 145.00
Postally used *140.00*
On cover 275.00
36 A16 10pf carmine 3.75 *7.00*
Never hinged 14.50
Postally used *27.00*
On cover 60.00
a. 10pf dark rose red 12.50 25.00
Never hinged 62.50
Postally used *150.00*
On cover 225.00
b. Double overprint —
37 A22 15pf dk violet .55 *.75*
Never hinged 2.25
Postally used *4.25*
On cover 7.50
a. 15pf deep brownish violet 30.00 *52.50*
Never hinged 115.00
Postally used *190.00*
On cover 225.00
b. Double overprint 70.00
Never hinged 175.00
38 A16 20pf blue violet .55 *.75*
Never hinged 2.25
Postally used *4.50*
On cover 7.50

Overprinted in Carmine or Blue

39 A16 25pf org & blk, *yel* .55 *.75*
Never hinged 2.25
Postally used *2.60*
On cover 7.50
40 A16 30pf org & blk, *buff* 50.00 *85.00*
Never hinged 160.00
Postally used *170.00*
On cover 350.00
42 A16 40pf lake & blk 2.25 *2.50*
Never hinged 6.25
Postally used *17.50*
On cover 60.00
a. Inverted overprint —
b. Double overprint —
c. 40pf red & black 15.00 *22.50*
Never hinged 92.50
Postally used *100.00*
On cover 140.00
43 A16 50pf pur & blk, *buff* 175.00 *300.00*
Never hinged 500.00
Postally used *775.00*
On cover *2,700.*
44 A16 60pf mag (Bl) 1,250. *1,800.*
Never hinged 2,300.
Postally used *2,900.*
On cover —
45 A16 75pf green & blk .55 *.75*
Never hinged 2.25
Postally used *4.50*
On cover 10.00
46 A16 80pf lake & blk, *rose* 3.00 *4.25*
Never hinged 8.50
Postally used *35.00*
On cover 115.00
47 A17 1m carmine 1,200. *2,000.*
Never hinged 2,300.
Postally used *2,900.*
On cover —
a. Double overprint *3,750.*

Overprinted in Carmine

48 A21 2m gray blue 1,200. *2,000.*
Never hinged 2,300.
Postally used *2,900.*
On cover —

Counterfeit overprints of Nos. 31-48 exist.
Nos. 44, 47 and 48 were issued in small quantities and usually affixed directly to the mail by the postal clerk.
For surcharge see No. 62.
Issued: 5pf, 15pf, 20pf, 25pf, 75pf, 8/20. Others, 8/30.

A8

Hanseatic Trading Ship — A9

Serrate Roulette 13½

1921, Jan. 31 Typo. Wmk. 108

49 A8 5pf brown & violet .30 .20
Never hinged 1.10
Postally used *1.50*
On cover 3.00
50 A8 10pf orange & dk vio .30 .20
Never hinged 1.10
Postally used *1.50*
On cover 3.75
51 A8 25pf green & car rose .50 .65
Never hinged 1.90
Postally used *1.75*
On cover 3.75
52 A8 40pf carmine rose 3.50 3.25
Never hinged 14.00
Postally used *6.00*
On cover 11.50
53 A8 80pf ultra .50 .50
Never hinged 1.90
Postally used *7.00*
On cover 11.50
54 A9 1m car rose & blk 1.50 1.40
Never hinged 5.75
Postally used *4.25*
On cover 15.00
55 A9 2m dk blue & dk grn 6.00 4.75
Never hinged 20.00
Postally used *21.00*
On cover 35.00
56 A9 3m blk & grnsh bl 1.75 *1.60*
Never hinged 7.00
Postally used *7.00*
On cover 15.00
57 A9 5m indigo & rose red 1.75 *1.60*
Never hinged 7.00
Postally used *8.50*
On cover 19.00
58 A9 10m dk grn & brn org 3.50 *4.25*
Never hinged 14.00
Postally used *30.00*
On cover 45.00
Nos. 49-58 (10) 19.60 *18.40*
Set, never hinged 75.00

Issued in honor of the Constitution.
Nos. 49 and 50 with center in red instead of violet and Nos. 49-51, 54-58 with center inverted are probably proofs. All values of this issue exist imperforate but are not known to have been regularly issued in that condition.

1921, Mar. 11 *Perf. 14*

59 A8 25pf green & car rose .70 *1.10*
Never hinged 3.00
Postally used *1.75*
On cover 9.25
60 A8 40pf carmine rose 1.10 1.10
Never hinged 3.00
Postally used *2.60*
On cover 9.25
61 A8 80pf ultra 5.25 *10.50*
Never hinged 24.00
Postally used *23.00*
On cover 37.50
Nos. 59-61 (3) 7.05 *12.70*
Set, never hinged 30.00

No. 45 Surcharged in Black

1921, May 6 Wmk. 125

62 A16 60pf on 75pf .50 *.90*
Never hinged 3.25
Postally used *4.25*
On cover 9.25
a. Double surcharge 82.50 *100.00*
Never hinged 190.00
Postally used *575.00*
b. Pair, one stamp without "Danzig" overprint 37.50 *150.00*
Never hinged 115.00
Postally used —
c Double surcharge, one inverted 75.00 70.00
Never hinged 190.00
Postally used *260.00*
d. Surcharge "60" in center of design 15.00 *35.00*
Never hinged 52.50
Postally used *70.00*
On cover 115.00

Surcharge on #62 normally appears at top of design.

Arms — A11

Coat of Arms — A12

Wmk. 108 (Upright or Sideways)

1921-22 *Perf. 14*

63 A11 5(pf) orange .20 .20
Never hinged .90
Postally used *3.50*
On cover 4.50
64 A11 10(pf) dark brown .20 .20
Never hinged .70
Postally used *2.00*
On cover 4.50
65 A11 15(pf) green .20 .20
Never hinged .70
Postally used *1.60*
On cover 3.75
66 A11 20(pf) slate .20 .20
Never hinged .70
Postally used *1.60*
On cover 3.75
67 A11 25(pf) dark green .20 .20
Never hinged .70
Postally used *1.60*
On cover 3.75
68 A11 30(pf) blue & car .25 .20
Never hinged .85
Postally used *1.25*
On cover 3.75
a. Center inverted 45.00
Never hinged 115.00
69 A11 40pf green & car .20 .20
Never hinged .70
Postally used *1.60*
On cover 3.00
a. Center inverted 45.00
Never hinged 115.00
70 A11 50pf dk grn & car .20 .20
Never hinged .70
Postally used *1.60*
On cover 3.50
71 A11 60pf carmine .45 .35
Never hinged 1.50
Postally used *2.90*
On cover 5.25
72 A11 80pf black & car .35 *.45*
Never hinged .85
Postally used *2.60*
On cover 5.75

Paper With Faint Gray Network

73 A11 1m org & car .20 *.35*
Never hinged .70
Postally used *1.60*
On cover 3.25
a. Center inverted 45.00
Never hinged 115.00
b. Background omitted 5.75 *30.00*
Never hinged 15.00
On cover 75.00
74 A11 1.20m blue violet 1.25 1.00
Never hinged 5.00
Postally used *3.50*
On cover 11.50
a. Background omitted 7.50 *30.00*
Never hinged 23.00
On cover 110.00
75 A11 2m gray & car 3.25 *3.50*
Never hinged 10.50
Postally used *7.50*
On cover 15.00
a. Background omitted 15.00 *45.00*
Never hinged 45.00
On cover 125.00
76 A11 3m violet & car 9.00 8.75
Never hinged 30.00
Postally used *29.00*
On cover 45.00

Serrate Roulette 13½
Wmk. 108 Upright

77 A12 5m grn, red & blk 1.25 *2.50*
Never hinged 5.50
Postally used *15.00*
On cover 30.00
78 A12 9m rose, red & org ('22) 2.50 *7.75*
Never hinged 14.00
Postally used *140.00*
On cover 190.00
a. Background omitted 37.50
Never hinged 115.00
79 A12 10m ultra, red & blk 1.25 *2.50*
Never hinged 5.50
Postally used *23.00*
On cover 37.50
a. Background omitted 60.00
Never hinged 150.00
80 A12 20m red & black 1.25 *2.50*
Never hinged 11.00
Postally used *45.00*
On cover 75.00
a. Background omitted 60.00
Never hinged 150.00
Nos. 63-80 (18) 22.40 *31.25*
Set, never hinged 80.00

Wmk. 108 Sideways

77a A12 5m grn, red & blk 1.25 *2.60*
Never hinged 5.25
Postally used *60.00*
On cover 75.00
78a A12 9m rose, red & org 2.60 *7.75*
Never hinged 14.00
Postally used *170.00*
On cover 225.00
79a A12 10m ultra, red & blk 1.25 *2.60*
Never hinged 4.50
Postally used *70.00*
On cover 100.00
80a A12 20m red & blk 1.25 *2.60*
Never hinged 4.50
Postally used *130.00*
On cover 180.00

In this and succeeding issues the mark values usually have the face of the paper covered with a gray network. This network is often very faint and occasionally is omitted.
Nos. 64-76 exist imperf. Value, each $10-$37.50 unused, $30-$100 never hinged.
See Nos. 81-93, 99-105. For surcharges and overprints see Nos. 96-98, O1-O33.
Issued: #63-76, 6/3/21. #77, 79-80, 8/1/21. #78, 2/1/22. #77a-80a, 3/1922.

Type of 1921 and

A13

Coat of Arms — A13a

1922 Wmk. 108 Upright *Perf. 14*

81 A11 75(pf) deep vio .20 .20
Never hinged .50
Postally used *1.60*
On cover 3.75
82 A11 80(pf) green .20 .20
Never hinged .50
Postally used *30.00*
On cover 57.50
83 A11 1.25m vio & car .20 .20
Never hinged .50
Postally used *1.90*
On cover 3.75
84 A11 1.50m slate gray .20 .35
Never hinged .50
Postally used *1.90*
On cover 3.75
85 A11 2m car rose .20 .20
Never hinged .50
Postally used *1.60*
On cover 3.75
86 A11 2.40m dk brn & car .90 *1.40*
Never hinged 3.50
Postally used *25.00*
On cover 55.00

87 A11 3m car lake .20 .35
Never hinged .50
Postally used 1.90
On cover 3.75
a. dark carmine red 30.00 11.50
Never hinged 150.00
Postally used 275.00
On cover 300.00
88 A11 4m dark blue .70 1.40
Never hinged 3.50
Postally used 7.50
On cover 11.50
89 A11 5m deep grn .20 .35
Never hinged .50
Postally used 1.50
On cover 3.75
a. Wmk. sideways 15.00 52.50
Never hinged 60.00
Postally used 250.00
On cover 450.00
90 A11 6m car lake .20 .35
Never hinged .50
Postally used 1.50
On cover 3.75
a. 6m car rose, wmk. 109 sideways 1,800.
Never hinged 3,900.
91 A11 8m light blue .20 .70
Never hinged 1.25
Postally used 19.00
On cover 27.00
92 A11 10m orange .20 .35
Never hinged .50
Postally used 1.60
On cover 3.75
93 A11 20m org brn .20 .35
Never hinged .50
Postally used 1.60
On cover 3.75
94 A13 50m gold & car 2.00 4.00
Never hinged 7.00
Postally used 175.00
On cover 200.00
a. 50m gold & red 52.50 85.00
Never hinged 190.00
Postally used 500.00
On cover 690.00
95 A13a 100m metallic grn & red 3.25 10.00
Never hinged 14.00
Postally used 1,900.
On cover 2,300.
Nos. 81-95 (15) 9.05 20.40
Set, never hinged 35.00

Wmk. 108 Sideways

94b A13 50m gold & car 1.25 3.75
Never hinged 7.00
Postally used 175.00
On cover 225.00
c. As "a" 7.00 12.50
Never hinged 26.00
Postally used 175.00
On cover 200.00
95b A13a 100m metallic grn & red 3.00 5.00
Never hinged 10.50
Postally used 200.00
On cover 350.00

No. 95 has buff instead of gray network.
Nos. 81-83, 85-86, 88 exist imperf. Value, each $12.50.
Nos. 94-95 exist imperf. Value, each $50
Issued: 75pf, 80pf, 1.25m, 2m, 2.40m, 4m, 2/1. 50m, 100m, 3/10. 1.50m, 3m, 8m, 7/29. 6m, 20m, 10/30. 5m, 10m, 11/9.

Nos. 87, 88 and 91 Surcharged in Black or Carmine

1922

96 A11 6m on 3m car lake .20 .45
Never hinged .70
Postally used 2.50
On cover 3.75
a. Double surcharge
97 A11 8m on 4m dk blue .20 .80
Never hinged .70
Postally used 15.00
On cover 23.00
a. Double surcharge 50.00 62.50
Never hinged 115.00
b. Pair, one without surcharge 115.00
Never hinged 300.00
98 A11 20m on 8m lt bl (C) .20 .45
Never hinged .70
Postally used 9.25
On cover 13.00
Nos. 96-98 (3) .60 1.70
Set, never hinged 2.10

Issued: #97, 5/15. #96, 98, 10/2.

Wmk. 109 Sideways

1922-23 *Perf. 14*

99 A11 4m dark blue .20 .35
Never hinged .80
Postally used 2.25
On cover 7.50
100 A11 5m dark green .20 .35
Never hinged .80
Postally used 1.90
On cover 3.75
a. Wmk. 110 2,750.
Never hinged 3,850.
b. Wmk. 109 upright .45 .75
Never hinged 1.75
Postally used 4.50
On cover 7.50
102 A11 10m orange .20 .35
Never hinged .80
Postally used 1.60
On cover 3.75
b. Wmk. 109 upright .45 .75
Never hinged 1.75
Postally used 3.75
On cover 7.50
103 A11 20m orange brn .20 .35
Never hinged .80
Postally used 1.90
On cover 3.75
b. Wmk. 109 upright .45 .75
Never hinged 1.75
Postally used 3.50
On cover 8.50

Paper Without Network
Wmk. 109 Upright

104 A11 40m pale blue .20 .50
Never hinged .80
Postally used 9.25
On cover 19.00
105 A11 80m red .20 .50
Never hinged .80
Postally used 50.00
On cover 75.00
Nos. 99-105 (6) 1.20 2.40
Set, never hinged 5.00

Nos. 104-105 exist imperf. Value, each $17.50.
Issued: #99, 12/16/22. #104-105, 5/15/1923. Others, 1/1923.

A15

A15a

Coat of Arms
A16

1922-23 Wmk. 109 Upright *Perf. 14*

Paper With Gray Network

106 A15 50m pale bl & red .20 .35
Never hinged .70
Postally used 1.60
On cover 3.75
a. Wmk. sideways .45 .75
Never hinged 1.75
Postally used 3.75
On cover 7.50
107 A15a 100m dk grn & red .20 .35
Never hinged .70
Postally used 1.60
On cover 3.75
a. Wmk. sideways .45 .75
Never hinged 1.75
Postally used 4.50
On cover 10.00
108 A15a 150m violet & red .20 .35
Never hinged .70
Postally used 3.25
On cover 7.50
109 A16 250m violet & red .20 .35
Never hinged 1.60
Postally used 60.00
On cover 75.00
110 A16 500m gray blk & red .20 .35
Never hinged 1.60
Postally used 29.00
On cover 57.50
111 A16 1000m brn & red .20 .35
Never hinged 1.75
Postally used 20.00
On cover 37.50
112 A16 5000m silver & red 1.00 6.00
Never hinged 6.50
Postally used 60.00
On cover 100.00

Paper Without Network

113 A15 50m pale blue .40 .60
Never hinged .75
Postally used 140.00
On cover 180.00
114 A15a 100m deep green .40 .60
Never hinged .75
Postally used 4.50
On cover 9.25
115 A15 200m orange .40 .60
Never hinged .75
Postally used 2.25
On cover 5.75
Nos. 106-115 (10) 3.40 9.90
Set, never hinged 15.00

#108-112 exist imperf. Value, each $35 unused, $85 never hinged.
Nos. 113-115 exist imperf. Value, each $35 unused, $92.50 never hinged.
See Nos. 123-125. For surcharges and overprints see Nos. 126, 137-140, 143, 156-167, O35-O38.
Issued: #106, 11/21/22. #107, 12/14/22. 150m, 250m, 500m, 1000m, 1/24/23. 5000m, 2/27/23. #113, 200m, 7/20/23. #114, 4/27/23.

A17

1923 *Perf. 14*

Paper With Gray Network

117 A17 250m violet & red .20 .35
Never hinged .70
Postally used 8.50
On cover 15.00
118 A17 300m bl grn & red .20 .35
Never hinged .50
Postally used 2.75
On cover 5.75
119 A17 500m gray & red .20 .35
Never hinged .70
Postally used 2.10
On cover 5.75
120 A17 1000m brown & red .20 .40
Never hinged .70
Postally used 2.00
On cover 5.75
121 A17 3000m violet & red .20 .40
Never hinged .70
Postally used 14.00
On cover 15.00
123 A16 10,000m orange & red .35 .60
Never hinged 1.60
Postally used 13.00
On cover 19.00
124 A16 20,000m pale bl & red .35 1.10
Never hinged 1.75
Postally used 25.00
On cover 30.00
125 A16 50,000m green & red .35 1.25
Never hinged 1.75
Postally used 20.00
On cover 27.00
Nos. 117-125 (8) 2.05 4.80
Set, never hinged 10.00

#117, 119--121 exist imperf. Value, each $10.50 unused, $27.50 never hinged; #123-125 also exist imperf. Values each, $11.50 unused, $27.50 never hinged.
See #127-135. For surcharges & overprints see #141-142, 144-155, O39-O41.
Issued: 300m, 3/22. 250m, 5/15. 500m, 6/29. 1000m, 7/29. 3000m, 8/3. 10,000m, 8/8. 20,000m, 8/13. 50,000m, 8/20.

Network Omitted

117a A17 250m 11.50 11.50
Never hinged 37.50
Postally used 60.00
118a A17 300m 9.25 11.50
Never hinged 21.00
Postally used 57.50
119a A17 500m 6.00 11.50
Never hinged 27.00
Postally used 60.00
120a A17 1000m 6.00 11.50
Never hinged 27.00
Postally used 60.00
121a A17 3000m 11.50 13.00
Never hinged 37.50
Postally used 60.00
123a A16 10,000m 11.50 15.00
Never hinged 30.00
Postally used 70.00
124a A16 20,000m 15.00 15.00
Never hinged 45.00
Postally used 92.50
125a A16 50,000m 11.50 15.00
Never hinged 30.00
Postally used 92.50

#117a, 119a-121a exist imperf. Value each, $10.50 unused, $27.50 never hinged.

No. 124 Surcharged in Red

1923, Aug. 14

126 A16 100,000m on #124 1.10 7.00
Never hinged 3.75
Postally used 110.00
On cover 140.00
a. On #124a 5.75 15.00
Never hinged 15.00
Postally used 275.00
On cover —

No. 126 exists imperf. Value $37.50 unused, $92.50 never hinged.

1923 *Perf. 14*

Paper Without Network

127 A17 1000m brown .20 .35
Never hinged .50
Postally used 3.00
On cover 9.25
129 A17 5000m rose .20 .35
Never hinged .50
Postally used 1.60
On cover 5.75
131 A17 20,000m pale blue .20 .35
Never hinged .50
Postally used 1.60
On cover 5.75
132 A17 50,000m green .20 .35
Never hinged .50
Postally used 1.60
On cover 5.75
a. Wmk. 110 —
b. Wmk. two vert. interlaced ribbons 3,750.
Never hinged 7,500.

Paper With Gray Network

133 A17 100,000m deep blue .20 .35
Never hinged .50
Postally used 2.00
On cover 7.50
a. Network omitted 7.50 15.00
Never hinged 23.00
Postally used 55.00
134 A17 250,000m violet .20 .35
Never hinged .50
Postally used 2.00
On cover 10.00
a. Network omitted 7.50 15.00
Never hinged 23.00
Postally used 55.00
135 A17 500,000m slate .20 .35
Never hinged .50
Postally used 2.00
On cover 5.75
a. Network omitted 7.50 15.00
Never hinged 23.00
Postally used 55.00
Nos. 127-135 (7) 1.40 2.45
Set, never hinged 3.25

Nos. 127, 129, 131-135 exist imperf. Value each, $20 unused, $45 never hinged.

Issued: #127, 7/24. #129, 131, 8/25. #132, 9/1. #133, 9/11. #135, 9/16.

Abbreviations:
th=(tausend) thousand
mil=million

Nos. 115, 114, 132, and Type of 1923 Surcharged

1923 *Perf. 14*

Paper Without Network

137 A15 40th m on 200m .70 1.75
Never hinged 3.50
Postally used 140.00
On cover 190.00
a. Double surcharge 70.00
Never hinged 140.00
b. Pair, one without surch. —
138 A15 100th m on 200m .70 1.75
Never hinged 3.50
Postally used 26.00
On cover 45.00
139 A15 250th m on 200m 6.00 10.50
Never hinged 29.00
Postally used 250.00
On cover 350.00
140 A15a 400th m on 100m .35 .35
Never hinged 1.75
Postally used 6.00
On cover 15.00
a. Pair, one without surch. —
141 A17 500th m on #132 .30 .30
Never hinged 1.75
Postally used 4.50
On cover 12.50

On 10,000m

142 A17 1mil m org 2.75 6.00
Never hinged 14.50
Postally used 350.00
On cover 475.00

The surcharges on Nos. 140-142 differ in details from those on Nos. 137-139.

Type of 1923 Surcharged

Paper With Gray Network
On 1,000,000m

143 A16 10mil m org 1.40 1.40
Never hinged 2.00
Postally used 95.00
On cover 125.00
a. Network omitted 23.00 19.00

Never hinged 60.00
Postally used 450.00
Nos. 137-143 (7) 12.20 *22.05*
Set, never hinged 72.50

#142-143 exist imperf. Value: #142 unused $21, never hinged $50; #143 unused $19, never hinged $42.50.

Issued: #137-139, 9/1. #141, 9/8. #142, 9/13. #143, 10/1.

Type of 1923 Surcharged

Wmk. 109 Upright
Perf. 14

10,000m rose on paper without Network

144 A17 1mil m on 10,000m .20 *.35*
Never hinged .70
Postally used *1.90*
On cover 5.75
145 A17 2mil m on 10,000m .20 *.35*
Never hinged .70
Postally used *2.00*
On cover 5.75
146 A17 3mil m on 10,000m .20 *.35*
Never hinged .70
Postally used *2.00*
On cover 5.75
147 A17 5mil m on 10,000m .20 *.35*
Never hinged .70
Postally used *1.90*
On cover 5.75
b. Double surcharge 70.00
Never hinged 140.00

10,000m gray lilac on paper without Network

148 A17 10mil m on 10,000m .35 *.65*
Never hinged 1.40
Postally used *7.00*
On cover 15.00
149 A17 20mil m on 10,000m .35 *.65*
Never hinged 1.40
Postally used *8.50*
On cover 19.00
150 A17 25mil m on 10,000m .20 *.65*
Never hinged 1.00
Postally used *32.50*
On cover 47.50
151 A17 40mil m on 10,000m .20 *.65*
Never hinged 1.00
Postally used *32.50*
On cover 47.50
a. Double surcharge 52.50
Never hinged 140.00
152 A17 50mil m on 10,000m .20 *.75*
Never hinged 1.00
Postally used *11.00*
On cover 19.00

Type of 1923 Surcharged in Red

10,000m gray lilac on paper without Network

153 A17 100mil m on 10,000m .20 *.75*
Never hinged 1.00
Postally used *3.75*
On cover 7.50
154 A17 300mil m on 10,000m .20 *.75*
Never hinged 1.00
Postally used *11.00*
On cover 19.00
155 A17 500mil m on 10,000m .20 *.75*
Never hinged 1.00
Postally used *2.75*
On cover 7.50
Nos. 144-155 (12) 2.70 *7.00*
Set, never hinged 11.50

#144-147 exist imperf. Value, each $17 unused, $45 never hinged.. #148-155 exist imperf. Value, each $15 unused, $37.50 never hinged.

Issued: #148-150, 152, 10/15. #153, 10/22. #151, 154-155, 10/23.

Types of 1923 Surcharged

1923, Oct. 31 Wmk. 110 *Perf. 14*

156 A15 5pf on 50m .60 .35
Never hinged 2.25
Postally used *2.00*
On cover 3.75
157 A15 10pf on 50m .60 .35
Never hinged 2.25
Postally used *2.00*
On cover 3.75
158 A15a 20pf on 100m .60 .35
Never hinged 2.25
Postally used *2.00*
On cover 3.75
159 A15 25pf on 50m 5.75 *9.00*
Never hinged 15.00
Postally used *32.50*
On cover 50.00
160 A15 30pf on 50m 4.00 1.75
Never hinged 14.50
Postally used *5.00*
On cover 11.50
161 A15a 40pf on 100m 3.50 1.75
Never hinged 10.50
Postally used *8.50*
On cover 15.00
162 A15a 50pf on 100m 3.50 *2.50*
Never hinged 10.50
Postally used *11.50*
On cover 19.00
163 A15a 75pf on 100m 9.25 *14.50*
Never hinged 29.00
Postally used *50.00*
On cover 70.00

Type of 1923 Surcharged

1923, Nov. 5

164 A16 1g on 1mil m rose 6.25 5.25
Never hinged 21.00
Postally used *14.50*
On cover 45.00
165 A16 2g on 1mil m rose 14.50 *17.50*
Never hinged 35.00
Postally used *57.50*
On cover 150.00
166 A16 3g on 1mil m rose 32.50 *60.00*
Never hinged 100.00
Postally used *150.00*
On cover 350.00
167 A16 5g on 1mil m rose 30.00 *62.50*
Never hinged 100.00
Postally used *550.00*
On cover *750.00*
Nos. 156-167 (12) 111.05 *175.80*
Set, never hinged 375.00

Issued: #156-163, 10/31. #164-167, 11/5.

Coat of Arms — A19

1924-37 Wmk. 109 *Perf. 14*

168 A19 3pf brn, *yelsh* 1.25 1.25
Never hinged 4.00
On cover 5.75
a. 3pf dp brn, *white* 2.00 1.75
Never hinged 6.50
On cover 5.75
170 A19 5pf org, *yelsh* 3.25 .45
Never hinged 5.50
On cover 3.50
a. White paper 4.25 .50
Never hinged 14.50
On cover 3.50
c. Tête bêche pair 275.00
Never hinged 650.00
d. Syncopated perf., #170 10.50 9.00
Never hinged 29.00
On cover 26.00
e. Syncopated perf., #170a 20.00 10.50
Never hinged 60.00
On cover 26.00
171 A19 7pf yel grn 1.75 *2.40*
Never hinged 4.25
On cover 10.50
172 A19 8pf yel grn 3.25 *4.25*
Never hinged 6.25
On cover 15.00
173 A19 10pf grn, *yelsh* 7.75 .45
Never hinged 15.50
On cover 3.50
a. White paper 7.75 .45
Never hinged 20.00
On cover 3.50
c. 10pf blue grn, *yellowish* 4.50 .85
Never hinged 12.50
On cover 3.50
d. Tête bêche pair 275.00
Never hinged 650.00
e. Syncopated perf., #173 18.00 10.50
Never hinged 50.00
On cover 32.50
f. Syncopated perf., #173a 24.00 13.00
Never hinged 70.00
On cover 32.50
g. Syncopated perf., #173c 10.50 *14.50*
Never hinged 26.00
On cover —
175 A19 15pf gray 8.75 .45
Never hinged 21.00
On cover 3.50
a. 15pf dark greenish gray 6.00 .75
Never hinged 21.00
On cover 7.00
176 A19 15pf red, *yelsh* 2.75 1.00
Never hinged 7.00
On cover 3.50
a. White paper 2.75 .70
Never hinged 12.50
On cover 3.50
177 A19 20pf carmine & red 12.50 .65
Never hinged 34.50
On cover 5.75
a. 20pf dp lilac red & rose red 11.00 1.60
Never hinged 35.00
On cover 22.50
178 A19 20pf gray 2.00 1.75
Never hinged 5.25
On cover 7.00
179 A19 25pf slate & red 20.00 3.00
Never hinged 60.00
On cover 14.00
180 A19 25pf carmine 20.00 1.40
Never hinged 52.50
On cover 5.75
181 A19 30pf green & red 10.50 .75
Never hinged 35.00
On cover 7.00
a. 30pf dk grn & dk rose red 9.00 1.75
Never hinged 35.00
On cover 16.00
182 A19 30pf dk violet 2.00 *4.25*
Never hinged 5.25
On cover 10.50
183 A19 35pf ultra 2.25 1.10
Never hinged 8.50
On cover 8.50
a. 35pf greyish ultra 5.00 2.25
Never hinged 16.00
On cover 9.75
184 A19 40pf dk blue & blue 9.25 1.00
Never hinged 26.00
On cover 11.50
185 A19 40pf yel brn & red 7.00 *13.00*
Never hinged 29.00
On cover 32.50
186 A19 40pf dk blue 1.40 *3.50*
Never hinged 5.25
On cover 11.50
a. Imperf. 35.00
Never hinged 100.00
187 A19 50pf blue & red 12.50 7.00
Never hinged 40.00
On cover 22.50
a. Yellowish paper 12.50 7.00
Never hinged 37.50
On cover 27.50
b. 50pf dk ultra & dk rose red 14.50 10.50
Never hinged 52.50
On cover 32.50
188 A19 55pf plum & scar 7.25 *14.00*
Never hinged 17.50
On cover 57.50
189 A19 60pf dk grn & red 8.25 *16.00*
Never hinged 30.00
On cover 32.50
190 A19 70pf yel grn & red 3.25 *5.25*
Never hinged 10.50
On cover 40.00
191 A19 75pf violet & red, *yellowish* 5.75 *7.00*
Never hinged 15.50
On cover 32.50
a. White paper 12.50 *7.00*
Never hinged 40.00
On cover 32.50
b. 75pf dk pur & dk rose red 8.50 8.50
Never hinged 26.00
On cover 32.50
192 A19 80pf dk org brn & red 3.50 *7.00*
Never hinged 10.50
On cover 40.00
Nos. 168-192 (23) 156.15 *96.90*
Set, never hinged 450.00

The 5pf and 10pf with syncopated perforations (Netherlands type C) are coils.

See Nos. 225-232. For overprints and surcharges see Nos. 200-209, 211-215, 241-252, B9-B11, O42-O52.

Issued: #168, 10/1935. #168a, 2/19/27. #170, 2/1935. #170a, 173a, 175a, 1/19/24. #170d, 173e, 173g, 1937. #170e, 173f, 1932. #171, 4/27/33. #172, 8/14/37. #173, 3/1935. #173c, 6/24/37. #175, 3/1924. #176, 1936. #176a, 8/20/25. #177, 1/26/24. #178, 186, 6/20/35. #179, 181, 187, 191a, 3/12/24. #180, 6/5/25. #181a, 9/1930. #182, 8/21/35. #183, 1925. #183a, 1930. #184, 2/14/24. #185, 189, 4/15/35. #187a, 3/1938. #187b, 2/1930. #188, 4/17/37. #190, 192, 9/5/35. #191, 2/1937. #191b, 4/1932.

Oliva Castle and Cathedral
A20

St. Mary's Church
A23

Council Chamber on the Langenmarkt
A24

2g, Mottlau River & Krantor. 3g, View of Zoppot.

1924-32 Engr. Wmk. 125

193 A20 1g yel grn & blk 18.00 *37.50*
Never hinged 90.00
On cover 115.00
Parcel post cancel 18.00
194 A20 1g org & gray blk 14.00 3.25
Never hinged 65.00
On cover 11.50
Parcel post cancel 1.00
a. 1g red orange & blk 14.00 7.00
Never hinged 60.00
On cover 57.50
Parcel post cancel 1.00
195 A20 2g red vio & blk 37.50 *95.00*
Never hinged 160.00
On cover 225.00
Parcel post cancel 40.00
196 A20 2g rose & blk 3.50 *6.25*
Never hinged 12.00
On cover 19.00
Parcel post cancel 1.75
197 A20 3g dk blue & blk 3.50 *5.00*
Never hinged 18.00
On cover 37.50
Parcel post cancel 2.25
198 A23 5g brn red & blk 3.50 *6.25*
Never hinged 18.00
On cover 70.00
Parcel post cancel 1.90
199 A24 10g dk brn & blk 18.00 *75.00*
Never hinged 90.00
On cover 575.00
Parcel post cancel 18.00
Nos. 193-199 (7) 98.00 *228.25*
Set, never hinged 450.00

See No. 233. For overprints and surcharges see Nos. 210, 253-254, C31-C35.

Issued: #193, 195, 9/22/24. #194, 196, 11/28/24. #194a, 5/1932.

Stamps of 1924-25 Overprinted in Black, Violet or Red

1930, Nov. 15 Typo. Wmk. 109

200 A19 5pf orange 2.50 *3.50*
Never hinged 7.00
On cover 10.00
201 A19 10pf yellow grn (V) 4.50 4.25
Never hinged 9.25
On cover 10.00
202 A19 15pf red 6.00 *10.50*
Never hinged 12.50
On cover 23.00
203 A19 20pf carmine & red 3.00 *5.25*
Never hinged 7.75
On cover 10.00
204 A19 25pf slate & red 4.75 *10.50*
Never hinged 15.50
On cover 23.00
205 A19 30pf green & red 10.50 *24.00*
Never hinged 24.00
On cover 45.00
206 A19 35pf ultra (R) 40.00 *75.00*
Never hinged 110.00
On cover 215.00
207 A19 40pf dk bl & bl (R) 11.50 *35.00*
Never hinged 32.50
On cover 57.50
208 A19 50pf dp blue & red 40.00 *75.00*
Never hinged 100.00
On cover 150.00
209 A19 75pf violet & red 40.00 *75.00*
Never hinged 110.00
On cover 150.00

Engr. Wmk. (125)

210 A20 1g orange & blk (R) 40.00 *75.00*
Never hinged 110.00
On cover 150.00
Nos. 200-210 (11) 202.75 *393.00*
Set, never hinged 540.00

10th anniv. of the Free State. Counterfeits exist.

Nos. 171 and 183 Surcharged in Red Blue or Green:

Nos. 211-214

No. 215

1934-36

211 A19 6pf on 7pf (R) .80 *1.40*
Never hinged 3.75
On cover 5.75
212 A19 8pf on 7pf (Bl) 2.00 *2.00*
Never hinged 7.00
On cover 9.25
213 A19 8pf on 7pf (R) 1.10 1.70
Never hinged 5.50
On cover 9.25
214 A19 8pf on 7pf (G) .80 *1.70*
Never hinged 4.25
On cover 9.25
215 A19 30pf on 35pf (Bl) 12.00 *25.00*
Never hinged 37.50
On cover 37.50
a. on #183a 23.00 *70.00*
Never hinged 90.00
On cover 100.00
Nos. 211-215 (5) 16.70 *31.80*
Set, never hinged 55.00

Issued: #211, 215-216, 215a, 12/28/34. #212, 6/5/35. #213, 7/13/36. #214, 12/23/36.

Bathing Beach, Brösen
A25

View of Brösen Beach
A26

War Memorial at Brösen — A27

Skyline of Danzig — A28

1936, June 23 Typo. Wmk. 109

216 A25 10pf deep green	.70	.70
Never hinged	2.25	
On commercial cover		11.50
a. 10pf dark opal green	11.50	30.00
Never hinged	45.00	
On commercial cover		60.00
On first day cover		75.00
217 A26 25pf rose red	1.00	2.40
Never hinged	2.90	
On commercial cover		11.50
On first day cover		37.50
218 A27 40pf bright blue	1.75	4.50
Never hinged	6.00	
On commercial cover		19.00
On first day cover		37.50
Nos. 216-218 (3)	3.45	*7.60*
Set, never hinged	11.50	

Village of Brösen, 125th anniversary.
Exist imperf. Value each, $35 unused, $95 never hinged.

1937, Mar. 27

219 A28 10pf dark blue	.50	1.40
Never hinged	1.50	
On cover		4.50
220 A28 15pf violet brown	1.50	2.00
Never hinged	5.25	
On cover		7.50
Set, never hinged	6.75	
Set of 2, #219-220 on one 1st day cover		19.00

Air Defense League.

Danzig Philatelic Exhibition Issue
Souvenir Sheet

St. Mary's Church — A29

1937, June 6 Wmk. 109 *Perf. 14*

221 A29 50pf dark opal green	3.25	20.00
Never hinged	10.00	
On commercial cover		75.00
With Exhibition cancel		30.00
a. 10pf blackish green	15.00	42.50
Never hinged	37.50	
On commercial cover		87.50
With Exhibition cancel		57.50
On first day cover		100.00

Danzig Philatelic Exhib., June 6-8, 1937.
No. 221a is the first printing (June 6); No. 221 is the second printing (October).

Arthur Schopenhauer
A30 A31

Design: 40pf, Full-face portrait, white hair.

Unwmk.
1938, Feb. 22 Photo. *Perf. 14*

222 A30 15pf dull blue	1.60	3.00
Never hinged	3.75	
On commercial cover		7.50
223 A31 25pf sepia	3.25	7.25
Never hinged	10.50	
On commercial cover		15.00
224 A31 40pf orange ver	1.70	4.25
Never hinged	3.75	
On commercial cover		11.50
Nos. 222-224 (3)	6.55	*14.50*
Set, never hinged	18.00	
Set of 3, #222-224 on one 1st day cover		37.50

150th anniv. of the birth of Schopenhauer.

Type of 1924-35

1938-39 Typo. Wmk. 237 *Perf. 14*

225 A19 3pf brown	.90	4.00
Never hinged	1.75	
On cover		15.00
226 A19 5pf orange	.90	1.40
Never hinged	1.75	
On cover		15.00
b. Syncopated perf.	1.40	7.00
Never hinged	5.25	
On cover		13.00
227 A19 8pf yellow grn	4.00	16.00
Never hinged	12.00	
On cover		37.50
228 A19 10pf blue green	.90	1.25
Never hinged	1.75	
On cover		3.75
b. Syncopated perf.	3.00	8.75
Never hinged	10.50	
On cover		19.00
229 A19 15pf scarlet	2.50	6.25
Never hinged	5.25	
On cover		19.00
230 A19 25pf carmine	2.50	6.25
Never hinged	7.00	
On cover		23.00
231 A19 40pf dark blue	3.00	7.00
Never hinged	7.00	
On cover		55.00
232 A19 50pf brt bl & red	3.00	100.00
Never hinged	8.50	
On cover		115.00
Engr.		
233 A20 1g red org & blk	5.75	85.00
Never hinged	14.00	
On cover		115.00
Nos. 225-233 (9)	23.45	*227.15*
Set, never hinged	60.00	

Sizes: #233, 32½x21¼mm; #194, 31x21mm.
Nos. 226b and 228b are coils with Netherlands type C perforation.
Issued: 3pf, 7/1938. 5pf, 25pf, 7/23/38. 8pf, 9/1938. 10pf, 15pf, 1g, 10/1938. 40pf, 7/19/38. 50pf, 6/1939. #226b, 8/24/38. #228b, 7/18/38.

Knights in Tournament, 1500 — A33

French Leaving Danzig, 1814 — A35

Stamp Day: 10pf, Signing of Danzig-Sweden neutrality treaty, 1630. 25pf, Battle of Weichselmünde, 1577.

Unwmk.
1939, Jan. 7 Photo. *Perf. 14*

234 A33 5pf dark green	.80	2.25
Never hinged	2.00	
On commercial cover		7.50
235 A33 10pf copper brown	1.00	2.50
Never hinged	2.90	
On commercial cover		7.50
236 A35 15pf slate black	1.25	3.25
Never hinged	3.50	
On commercial cover		9.25
237 A35 25pf brown violet	1.40	3.50
Never hinged	4.25	
On commercial cover		17.00
Nos. 234-237 (4)	4.45	*11.50*
Set, never hinged	12.50	
Set of 4, #234-237 on one 1st day cover		30.00

Gregor Mendel — A37

15pf, Dr. Robert Koch. 25pf, Wilhelm Roentgen.

1939, Apr. 29 Photo. *Perf. 13x14*

238 A37 10pf copper brown	.40	1.10
Never hinged	1.40	
On commercial cover		5.75
239 A37 15pf indigo	.65	2.00
Never hinged	2.00	
On commercial cover		5.75
240 A37 25pf dark olive green	1.00	2.50
Never hinged	2.00	
On commercial cover		9.25
Nos. 238-240 (3)	2.05	*5.60*
Set, never hinged	5.50	
Set of 3, #238-240 on one 1st day cover		19.00

Issued in honor of the achievements of Mendel, Koch and Roentgen.

Issued under German Administration

Stamps of Danzig, 1925-39, Surcharged in Black:

a

b

c

1939 Wmk. 109 *Perf. 14*

241 A19(b) 4rpf on 35pf ultra	.75	2.00
Never hinged	1.75	
On cover		4.50
242 A19(b) 12rpf on 7pf yel grn	1.00	2.00
Never hinged	3.50	
On cover		4.50
243 A19(a) 20rpf gray	2.50	7.00
Never hinged	8.50	
On cover		11.50
Wmk. 237		
244 A19(a) 3rpf brown	1.00	2.00
Never hinged	2.00	
On cover		4.50
245 A19(a) 5rpf orange	1.00	2.00
Never hinged	2.00	
On cover		4.50
246 A19(a) 8rpf yellow grn	1.75	3.50
Never hinged	3.50	
On cover		7.50
247 A19(a) 10rpf blue grn	2.25	3.50
Never hinged	7.00	
On cover		7.50
248 A19(a) 15rpf scarlet	5.25	8.75
Never hinged	17.50	
On cover		17.00
249 A19(a) 25rpf carmine	5.75	10.50
Never hinged	14.00	
On cover		15.00
250 A19(a) 30rpf dk violet	2.25	3.75
Never hinged	5.25	
On cover		8.50
251 A19(a) 40rpf dk blue	3.00	5.25
Never hinged	7.00	
On cover		11.50
252 A19(a) 50rpf brt bl & red	4.50	7.00
Never hinged	10.50	
On cover		13.00
Thick Paper		
253 A20(c) 1rm on 1g red org & blk	12.50	40.00
Never hinged	40.00	
On cover		75.00
a. Thin white paper	21.00	115.00
Never hinged	70.00	
On cover		150.00
Wmk. 125		
Thin White Paper		
254 A20(c) 2rm on 2g rose & blk	15.00	37.50
Never hinged	52.50	
On cover		75.00
a. Thick paper	18.00	67.50
Never hinged	60.00	
On cover		90.00
b. As "a," "Deutsches Reich" omitted from surcharge	*1,000.*	—
Never hinged	*1,750.*	
c. As "a," "2 Reichmark" omitted from surcharge	*1,000.*	*1,750.*
Never hinged	*1,750.*	
Nos. 241-254 (14)	58.50	*134.75*
Set, never hinged	175.00	

#241-254 were valid throughout Germany.

SEMI-POSTAL STAMPS

St. George and Dragon — SP1

Wmk. 108
1921, Oct. 16 Typo. *Perf. 14*
Size: 19x22mm

B1 SP1 30pf + 30pf grn & org	.45	.70
Never hinged	.90	
Postally used		*110.00*
On cover		150.00
B2 SP1 60pf + 60pf rose & org	1.25	1.25
Never hinged	4.00	
Postally used		*110.00*
On cover		150.00
Size: 25x30mm		
Serrate Roulette 13½		
B3 SP1 1.20m + 1.20m dk bl & org	2.25	1.90
Never hinged	7.50	
Postally used		*110.00*
On cover		150.00
Nos. B1-B3 (3)	3.95	3.85
Set, never hinged	12.50	

Nos. B1-B3 exist imperf. Value each, $35 unused, $95 never hinged.

Aged Pensioner SP2

1923, Mar. Wmk. 109 *Perf. 14*
Paper With Gray Network

B4 SP2 50m + 20m lake	.20	.60
Never hinged	.65	
Postally used		*42.50*
On cover		100.00
B5 SP2 100m + 30m red vio	.20	.60
Never hinged	.65	
Postally used		*42.50*
On cover		100.00
Set, never hinged	1.25	

Nos. B4-B5 exist imperf. Value each, $19 unused, $100 never hinged.

Philatelic Exhibition Issue

Neptune Fountain — SP3

Various Frames.

1929, July 7 Engr. Unwmk.

B6 SP3 10pf yel grn & gray	2.00	2.25
Never hinged	7.00	
Exhibition cancellation		5.75
On cover		23.00
B7 SP3 15pf car & gray	2.00	2.25
Never hinged	7.00	
Exhibition cancellation		5.75
On cover		35.00
B8 SP3 25pf ultra & gray	7.50	7.00
Never hinged	26.00	
Exhibition cancellation		55.00
On cover		62.50
a. 25pf violet blue & black	32.50	62.50
Never hinged	100.00	
On cover		110.00
b. 25pf deep gray bl & blk	45.00	215.00

Never hinged 175.00
On cover 275.00
Nos. B6-B8 (3) 11.50 11.50
Set, never hinged 40.00
Set of 3, #B6-B8 on one 1st day cover 200.00

These stamps were sold exclusively at the Danzig Philatelic Exhibition, June 7-14, 1929, at double their face values, the excess being for the aid of the exhibition.

Regular Issue of 1924-25 Surcharged in Black

1934, Jan. 15 **Wmk. 109**

B9 A19 5pf + 5pf orange 11.50 *20.00*
Never hinged 32.50
On cover 57.50
B10 A19 10pf + 5pf yel grn 35.00 *45.00*
Never hinged 77.50
On cover 110.00
B11 A19 15pf + 5pf carmine 22.50 *37.50*
Never hinged 50.00
On cover 75.00
Nos. B9-B11 (3) 69.00 *102.50*
Set, never hinged 160.00

Surtax for winter welfare. Counterfeits exist.

Stock Tower — SP4

George Hall — SP6

City Gate, 16th Century SP5

1935, Dec. 16 **Typo.** ***Perf. 14***

B12 SP4 5pf + 5pf orange .65 *1.25*
Never hinged 1.60
On cover 5.50
B13 SP5 10pf + 5pf green 1.00 *2.00*
Never hinged 2.60
On cover 9.25
B14 SP6 15pf + 10pf scarlet 2.00 *3.25*
Never hinged 5.75
On cover 15.00
Nos. B12-B14 (3) 3.65 *6.50*
Set, never hinged 10.00
Set of 3, #B12-B14 on one 1st day cover 37.50

Surtax for winter welfare.

Milk Can Tower SP7

Frauentor SP8

Krantor — SP9

Langgarter Gate — SP10

High Gate SP11

1936, Nov. 25

B15 SP7 10pf + 5pf dk bl 1.60 *3.00*
Never hinged 5.00
On cover 15.00
a. Imperf. 52.50
Never hinged 140.00
B16 SP8 15pf + 5pf dull grn 1.60 *4.25*
Never hinged 5.00
On cover 15.00
B17 SP9 25pf + 10pf red brn 2.75 *5.75*
Never hinged 10.00
On cover 23.00
B18 SP10 40pf + 20pf brn & red brn 3.75 *9.50*
Never hinged 14.00
On cover 27.50
B19 SP11 50pf + 20pf bl & dk bl 6.25 *14.50*
Never hinged 17.00
On cover 37.50
Nos. B15-B19 (5) 15.95 *37.00*
Set, never hinged 50.00

Surtax for winter welfare.

SP12

SP13

1937, Oct. 30 **Wmk. 109 Sideways**

B20 SP12 25pf + 25pf dk car 2.50 *5.25*
Never hinged 10.50
On cover 45.00
a. Wmk. upright 10.50 *37.50*
Never hinged 35.00
On cover 92.50

Wmk. 109 Upright

B21 SP13 40pf + 40pf blue & red 2.50 *5.25*
Never hinged 10.50
On cover 45.00
a. Souvenir sheet of 2, #B20a-B21 50.00 *100.00*
Never hinged 100.00
Exposition cancellation 100.00
On cover 275.00

Founding of Danzig community at Magdeburg.

Madonna SP14

Mercury SP15

Weather Vane, Town Hall SP16

Neptune Fountain SP17

St. George and Dragon — SP18

1937, Dec. 13

B23 SP14 5pf + 5pf brt violet 3.50 *6.00*
Never hinged 7.00
On cover 11.50
B24 SP15 10pf + 10pf dk brn 3.50 *6.00*
Never hinged 7.00
On cover 11.50
B25 SP16 15pf + 5pf bl & yel brn 4.00 *6.00*
Never hinged 7.00
On cover 11.50
B26 SP17 25pf + 10pf bl grn & grn 4.00 *9.00*
Never hinged 10.50
On cover 19.00
B27 SP18 40pf + 25pf brt car & bl 7.50 *19.00*
Never hinged 21.00
On cover 37.50
Nos. B23-B27 (5) 22.50 *46.00*
Set, never hinged 52.50
Set of 5, #B23-B27 on one 1st day cover 100.00

Surtax for winter welfare. Designs are from frieze of the Artushof.

"Peter von Danzig" Yacht Race — SP19

Ships: 10pf+5pf, Dredger Fu Shing. 15pf+10pf, S. S. Columbus. 25pf+10pf, S. S. City of Danzig. 40pf+15pf, Peter von Danzig, 1472.

1938, Nov. 28 **Photo.** **Unwmk.**

B28 SP19 5pf + 5pf dk bl grn 1.25 *1.90*
Never hinged 4.25
On cover 15.00
B29 SP19 10pf + 5pf gldn brn 1.40 *3.00*
Never hinged 4.25
On cover 19.00
B30 SP19 15pf + 10pf ol grn 1.90 *3.00*
Never hinged 6.00
On cover 11.50
B31 SP19 25pf + 10pf indigo 2.50 *4.00*
Never hinged 8.50
On cover 13.00
B32 SP19 40pf + 15pf vio brn 3.25 *7.00*
Never hinged 11.50
On cover 20.00
Nos. B28-B32 (5) 10.30 *18.90*
Set, never hinged 35.00
Set of 5, #B28-B32 on one 1st day cover 57.50

Surtax for winter welfare.

AIR POST STAMPS

No. 6 Surcharged in Blue or Carmine

1920, Sept. 29 **Wmk. 125** ***Perf. 14***

C1 A16 40pf on 40pf 1.00 *2.75*
Never hinged 4.00
Postally used *10.50*
On flight cover 23.00
On commercial flown cover 45.00
a. Double surcharge 110.00 *200.00*
Never hinged 300.00
C2 A16 60pf on 40pf (C) 1.00 *2.75*
Never hinged 4.00
Postally used *11.00*
On flight cover 115.00
On commercial flown cover 225.00
a. Double surcharge 110.00 *200.00*
Never hinged 300.00
C3 A16 1m on 40pf 1.00 *2.75*
Never hinged 4.00
Postally used *14.50*
On flight cover 27.50
On commercial flown cover 55.00
Nos. C1-C3 (3) 3.00 *8.25*
Set, never hinged 12.00

Plane faces left on No. C2.

AP3

Plane over Danzig AP4

Wmk. (108) Upright

1921-22 **Typo.** ***Perf. 14***

C4 AP3 40(pf) blue green .25 *.45*
Never hinged 1.00
Postally used *5.00*
On commercial flown cover 27.50
C5 AP3 60(pf) dk violet .25 *.45*
Never hinged 1.00
Postally used *4.25*
On commercial flown cover 9.25
C6 AP3 1m carmine .25 *.45*
Never hinged 1.00
Postally used *4.50*
On commercial flown cover 11.50
C7 AP3 2m org brn .25 *.45*
Never hinged 1.00
Postally used *4.25*
On commercial flown cover 11.50

Serrate Roulette 13½

Size: 34½x23mm

C8 AP4 5m violet blue 1.00 *2.25*
Never hinged 4.00
Postally used *9.25*
On commercial flown cover 19.00
C9 AP4 10m dp grn 2.00 *4.25*
Never hinged 7.00
Postally used *37.50*
On commercial flown cover 60.00
Nos. C4-C9 (6) 4.00 *8.30*
Set, never hinged 15.00

Nos. C4-C9 exist imperf. Value, each $26 unused, $85 never hinged.

Issued: #C4-C5, C7-C8, 5/3/21. #C6, 4/3/21. #C9, 5/15/22.

Wmk. 108 Sideways

C4a AP3 40(pf) 19.00 *75.00*
Never hinged 55.00
C5a AP3 60(pf) 60.00 *35.00*
Never hinged 190.00
C6a AP3 1m — —
C7a AP3 2m 75.00 *140.00*
Never hinged 190.00
C8a AP4 5m 1,400. *2,300.*
Never hinged *2,700.*
b. imperf *1,900.* *3,000.*
Never hinged 3,750.
Postally used —
C9a AP4 10m 23.00 *57.50*
Never hinged 57.50

Issued: #C4a-C5a, C7a-C8a, 5/3/21. #C6a, 4/3/21. #C9a, 5/15/22.

1923 **Wmk. (109) Upright** ***Perf. 14***

C10 AP3 40(pf) blue green .35 *1.75*
Never hinged 1.50
Postally used *200.00*
On commercial flown cover 350.00
C11 AP3 60(pf) dk violet .35 *1.75*
Never hinged 1.50
Postally used *250.00*
On commercial flown cover 350.00
a. Double impression —
C12 AP3 1m carmine .35 *1.75*
Never hinged 1.50
Postally used *140.00*
On commercial flown cover 225.00
C13 AP3 2m org brown .35 *1.75*
Never hinged 1.50
Postally used *115.00*
On commercial flown cover 150.00
C14 AP3 25m pale blue .25 *.45*
Never hinged 1.25
Postally used *3.75*
On commercial flown cover 10.00

Serrate Roulette 13½

Size: 34½x23mm

C15 AP4 5m violet blue .35 *.80*
Never hinged 1.50
Postally used *115.00*
On commercial flown cover 190.00
C16 AP4 10m deep green .35 *.80*
Never hinged 1.50
Postally used *115.00*
On commercial flown cover 150.00

Paper With Gray Network

C17 AP4 20m org brn .35 *.80*
Never hinged 1.50
Postally used *27.50*

On commercial flown cover 57.50

Size: 40x23mm

C18 AP4 50m orange .25 .50
Never hinged 1.25
Postally used 23.00
On commercial flown cover 37.50
C19 AP4 100m red .25 .50
Never hinged 1.25
Postally used 3.00
On commercial flown cover 7.50
C20 AP4 250m dark brown .25 .50
Never hinged 1.25
Postally used 30.00
On commercial flown cover 57.50
C21 AP4 500m car rose .25 .50
Never hinged 1.25
Postally used 21.00
On commercial flown cover 30.00
Nos. C10-C21 (12) 3.70 *11.85*
Set, never hinged 17.00

#C11, C12, C14-C21 exist imperf. Value, #C11, C12, C15-C17, each $5.75 unused, $17.50 never hinged. Value, #C14, C18-C21, each $35 unused, $115 never hinged.

Issued: #C10, C13, C15-C16, 1/3/23. #C14, C18, C20-C21, 4/27/23. #C17, 1/10/23. #C19, 2/5/23.

Nos. C18, C19 and C21 exist with wmk. sideways, both perf and imperf. Value each, $57.50 unused, $150 never hinged.

Network Omitted

C18a AP4 50m 19.00 15.00
Never hinged 54.00
Postally used 100.00
C19a AP4 100m 8.50 23.00
Never hinged 23.00
Postally used 54.00
C20a AP4 250m 8.50 23.00
Never hinged 23.00
Postally used 100.00
C21a AP4 500m 14.00 15.00
Never hinged 37.50
Postally used 70.00

Issued: #C18a, C20a-C21a, 4/27/23. #C19a, 2/5/23.

Post Horn and Airplanes — AP5

1923, Oct. 18 ***Perf. 14***

Paper Without Network

C22 AP5 250,000m scarlet .25 1.00
Never hinged 1.00
Postally used 225.00
On commercial flown cover 300.00
C23 AP5 500,000m scarlet .25 1.00
Never hinged 1.00
Postally used 225.00
On commercial flown cover 300.00

Exist imperf. Value, each $42.50.

Surcharged

On 100,000m

C24 AP5 2mil m scarlet .25 1.00
Never hinged 1.00
Postally used 225.00
On commercial flown cover 300.00

On 50,000m

C25 AP5 5mil m scarlet .25 1.00
Never hinged 1.00
Postally used 225.00
On commercial flown cover 300.00
b. Cliché of 10,000m in sheet of 50,000m 30.00 70.00
Never hinged 90.00
Postally used 3,100.
c. As "b," surcharge omitted 6,250.
Never hinged 10,500.

Exist imperf. Value, each $100 unused, $260 never hinged.

Nos. C24 and C25 were not regularly issued without surcharge, although copies have been passed through the post. Values: C24 unused $7, never hinged $21; C25 unused $12, never hinged $21.

Plane over Danzig
AP6 AP7

1924

C26 AP6 10(pf) vermilion 22.50 4.75
Never hinged 75.00
On commercial flown cover 13.00
C27 AP6 20(pf) carmine rose 2.00 1.10
Never hinged 5.75
On commercial flown cover 9.25
C28 AP6 40(pf) olive brown 4.50 1.75
Never hinged 8.25
On commercial flown cover 11.50
C29 AP6 1g deep green 4.50 1.75
Never hinged 8.25
On commercial flown cover 15.00
C30 AP7 2½g violet brown 22.50 *32.50*
Never hinged 57.50
On commercial flown cover 92.50
Nos. C26-C30 (5) 56.00 *41.85*
Set, never hinged 150.00

Exist imperf. Value #C26, C30, $75 unused, $190 never hinged; others, each $35 unused, $100 never hinged.

Issued: #C26-C27, C29, 6/6. #C28, 6/4. #C30, 6/7.

Nos. 193, 195, 197-199 Surcharged in Various Colors

1932 **Wmk. 125**

C31 A20 10pf on 1g (G) 10.50 *20.00*
Never hinged 35.00
On commercial flown cover 57.50
C32 A20 15pf on 2g (V) 10.50 *20.00*
Never hinged 35.00
On commercial flown cover 57.50
C33 A20 20pf on 3g (Bl) 10.50 *20.00*
Never hinged 35.00
On commercial flown cover 57.50
C34 A23 25pf on 5g (R) 10.50 *20.00*
Never hinged 35.00
On commercial flown cover 57.50
C35 A24 30pf on 10g (Br) 10.50 *20.00*
Never hinged 35.00
On commercial flown cover 57.50
Nos. C31-C35 (5) 52.50 *100.00*
Set, never hinged 175.00

Intl. Air Post Exhib. of 1932. The surcharges were variously arranged to suit the shapes and designs of the stamps. The stamps were sold at double their surcharged values, the excess being donated to the exhibition funds.

No. C31 exists with inverted surcharge and with double surcharge. Value each, $75 unused, $190 never hinged.

Airplane
AP8 AP9

1935, Oct. 24 **Wmk. 109**

C36 AP8 10pf scarlet 2.00 .70
Never hinged 5.75
On commercial flown cover 2.90
C37 AP8 15pf yellow 2.00 1.00
Never hinged 5.75
On commercial flown cover 5.75
C38 AP8 25pf dark green 2.00 1.75
Never hinged 5.75
On commercial flown cover 9.25
C39 AP8 50pf gray blue 8.00 *9.25*
Never hinged 22.00
On commercial flown cover 30.00
C40 AP9 1g magenta 4.00 *9.25*
Never hinged 16.00
On commercial flown cover 30.00
Nos. C36-C40 (5) 18.00 *21.95*
Set, never hinged 55.00
Set of 5, #C36-C40 on one 1st day cover 57.50

Nos. C36 and C40 exist imperf. Values: C36 unused $19, never hinged $57.50; C40 unused $27.50, never hinged $75.

See Nos. C42-C45.

Souvenir Sheet

St. Mary's Church — AP10

1937, June 6 ***Perf. 14***

C41 AP10 50pf dark grayish blue 3.50 *20.00*
Never hinged 10.00
On commerical cover 75.00
Exhibition cancellation 26.00
a. 50pf dark ultramarine 15.00 *140.00*
Never hinged 37.50
On commerical cover 150.00
Exhibition cancellation 57.50
On first day cover 115.00

C41a is the first printing (June 6); C41 is the second printing (October).

Danzig Phil. Exhib., June 6-8, 1937.

Type of 1935

1938-39 **Wmk. 237**

C42 AP8 10pf scarlet 2.25 *5.75*
Never hinged 5.25
On commercial flown cover 11.50
C43 AP8 15pf yellow ('39) 2.25 *5.75*
Never hinged 5.25
On commercial flown cover 22.50
C44 AP8 25pf dark green 2.25 *7.00*
Never hinged 5.25
On commercial flown cover 30.00
C45 AP8 50pf gray blue ('39) 3.50 *17.50*
Never hinged 15.50
On commercial flown cover 92.50
Nos. C42-C45 (4) 10.25 *36.00*
Set, never hinged 32.50

Issued: #C42, C44, 7/1938. #C43, 7/8/38. #C44, 2/13/39.

POSTAGE DUE STAMPS

Danzig Coat of Arms
D1 D2

1921-22 Typo. Wmk. (108) ***Perf. 14***

Paper Without Network

J1 D1 10(pf) deep violet .25 .35
Never hinged .70
Postally used 9.25
On cover 45.00
J2 D1 20(pf) deep violet .25 .35
Never hinged .70
Postally used 9.25
On cover 45.00
J3 D1 40(pf) deep violet .25 .35
Never hinged .70
Postally used 11.50
On cover 45.00
J4 D1 60(pf) deep violet .25 .35
Never hinged .70
Postally used 12.50
On cover 45.00
J5 D1 75(pf) dp violet ('22) .25 .35
Never hinged .70
Postally used 23.00
On cover 92.50
J6 D1 80(pf) deep violet .25 .35
Never hinged .70
Postally used 11.50
On cover 45.00
J7 D1 120(pf) deep violet .25 .35
Never hinged .75
Postally used 14.00
On cover 45.00
J8 D1 200(pf) dp violet ('22) 1.00 1.25
Never hinged .70
Postally used 30.00
On cover 75.00
J9 D1 240(pf) deep violet .25 .35
Never hinged 1.40
Postally used 23.00
On cover 57.50
J10 D1 300(pf) dp violet ('22) 1.00 1.25
Never hinged 2.60
Postally used 17.00
On cover 70.00
J11 D1 400(pf) deep violet 1.00 1.25
Never hinged 2.60
Postally used 18.50
On cover 92.50
J12 D1 500(pf) deep violet 1.00 1.25
Never hinged 2.60
Postally used 18.50
On cover 40.00
J13 D1 800(pf) deep violet ('22) 1.00 *1.25*
Never hinged 2.60
Postally used 42.50
On cover 95.00
J14 D1 20m dp violet ('22) 1.00 *1.25*
Never hinged 2.60
Postally used 37.50
On cover 92.50
Nos. J1-J14 (14) 8.00 *10.30*
Set, never hinged 20.00

Nos. J1-J14 exist imperf. Value, each $20 unused, $55 never hinged.

1923 **Wmk. 109 Sideways**

J15 D1 100(pf) deep violet .60 .70
Never hinged 1.75
Postally used 575.00
On cover 750.00
J16 D1 200(pf) deep violet 2.10 3.50
Never hinged 5.75
Postally used 750.00
On cover 1,000.
J17 D1 300(pf) deep violet .60 .70
Never hinged 1.75
Postally used 750.00
On cover 1,000.
J18 D1 400(pf) deep violet .60 .70
Never hinged 1.60
Postally used 700.00
On cover 925.00
J19 D1 500(pf) deep violet .60 .70
Never hinged 1.60
Postally used 240.00
On cover 250.00
a. Wmk. Upright .50 .80
Never hinged 1.60
Postally used 170.00
On cover 250.00
J20 D1 800(pf) deep violet 1.40 3.50
Never hinged 4.50
Postally used 1,500.
On cover 1,850.
J21 D1 10m deep violet .60 .80
Never hinged 1.60
Postally used 23.00
On cover 57.50
a. Wmk. Upright .50 .80
Never hinged 1.60
Postally used 150.00
On cover 190.00
J22 D1 20m deep violet .60 .80
Never hinged 1.60
Postally used 60.00
On cover 140.00
J23 D1 50m deep violet .60 .90
Never hinged 1.60
Postally used 15.00
On cover 75.00

Paper With Gray Network

J24 D1 100m deep violet .60 .85
Never hinged 1.60
Postally used 23.00
On cover 75.00
J25 D1 500m deep violet .60 .85
Never hinged 1.60
Postally used 15.00
On cover 75.00
Nos. J15-J25 (11) 8.90 14.00
Set, never hinged 29.00

#J15, J17, J22-J25 exist imperf. Value each, $10 unused, $30 never hinged.

Issued: #J15, J21, J23, 1/10. #J16-J20, J22, 1/1923. #J19a, J21a, J24-J25, 4/3.

Nos. J22-J23 and Type of 1923 Surcharged

1923, Oct. 1

Paper without Network

J26 D1 5000m on 50m .35 .70
Never hinged 2.00
Postally used 1,100.
On cover —
J27 D1 10,000m on 20m .35 .70
Never hinged 2.00
Postally used 1,100.
On cover —
J28 D1 50,000m on 500m .35 .70
Never hinged 2.00
Postally used 1,100.
On cover —
J29 D1 100,000m on 20m .35 1.25
Never hinged 2.00
Postally used 1,300.
On cover —
Nos. J26-J29 (4) 1.40 3.35
Set, never hinged 8.00

On No. J26 the numerals of the surcharge are all of the larger size.

A 1000(m) on 100m deep violet was prepared but not issued. Value, $145, never hinged $350.

Nos. J26-J28 exist imperf. Value each, $14.50 unused, $35 never hinged.

1923-28 **Wmk. 110**

J30 D2 5(pf) blue & blk .90 .80
Never hinged 1.75
On cover 35.00
J31 D2 10(pf) blue & blk .60 .75
Never hinged 1.10
On cover 23.00

J32 D2 15(pf) blue & blk 1.40 1.10
Never hinged 3.50
On cover 57.50
J33 D2 20(pf) blue & blk 1.75 *2.25*
Never hinged 3.50
On cover 70.00
J34 D2 30(pf) blue & blk 7.25 2.25
Never hinged 17.50
On cover 70.00
J35 D2 40(pf) blue & blk 2.00 *3.00*
Never hinged 5.25
On cover 115.00
J36 D2 50(pf) blue & blk 2.00 *2.25*
Never hinged 5.25
On cover 60.00
J37 D2 60(pf) blue & blk 13.00 *17.50*
Never hinged 35.00
On cover 240.00
J38 D2 100(pf) blue & blk 14.00 7.00
Never hinged 40.00
On cover 140.00
J39 D2 3g blue & car 7.25 *45.00*
Never hinged 37.50
On cover 350.00
a. "Guldeu" instead of "Gulden" 300.00 *1,000.*
Never hinged 1,000.
Nos. J30-J39 (10) 50.15 *81.90*
Set, never hinged 150.00

Used values of Nos. J30-J39 are for postally used copies.
See Nos. J43-J47.

Postage Due Stamps of 1923 Issue Surcharged in Red

1932, Dec. 20
J40 D2 5pf on 40(pf) 2.00 *10.50*
Never hinged 7.00
On cover 170.00
J41 D2 10pf on 60(pf) 40.00 10.50
Never hinged 95.00
On cover 150.00
J42 D2 20pf on 100(pf) 2.00 *8.00*
Never hinged 7.00
On cover 170.00
Nos. J40-J42 (3) 44.00 *29.00*
Set, never hinged 110.00

Type of 1923

1938-39 Wmk. 237 *Perf. 14*
J43 D2 10(pf) bl & blk ('39) 1.10 *14.00*
Never hinged 4.25
On cover *300.00*
J44 D2 30(pf) bl & blk 1.90 *14.50*
Never hinged 7.00
On cover *300.00*
J45 D2 40(pf) bl & blk ('39) 5.50 *32.50*
Never hinged 21.00
On cover *575.00*
J46 D2 60(pf) bl & blk ('39) 6.75 *32.50*
Never hinged 26.00
On cover *575.00*
J47 D2 100(pf) bl & blk 10.50 *50.00*
Never hinged 30.00
On cover *700.00*
Nos. J43-J47 (5) 25.75 *143.50*
Set, never hinged 90.00

OFFICIAL STAMPS

Regular Issues of 1921-22 Overprinted

a

1921-22 Wmk. 108 *Perf. 14x14½*
O1 A11 5(pf) orange .25 .20
Never hinged .70
Postally used *27.50*
On cover 110.00
O2 A11 10(pf) dark brown .20 *.20*
Never hinged .50
Postally used *6.25*
On cover 70.00
a. Inverted overprint 35.00
Never hinged 100.00
O3 A11 15(pf) green .20 *.20*
Never hinged .50
Postally used *6.25*
On cover 70.00
O4 A11 20(pf) slate .20 *.20*
Never hinged .50
Postally used *6.25*
On cover 75.00
O5 A11 25(pf) dark green .20 *.20*
Never hinged .50
Postally used *5.75*
On cover 70.00
O6 A11 30(pf) blue & car .50 *.70*
Never hinged 1.40
Postally used *5.75*
On cover 70.00
O7 A11 40(pf) grn & car .25 *.25*
Never hinged .50
Postally used *11.50*
On cover 70.00
O8 A11 50(pf) dk grn & car .25 *.25*
Never hinged .50
Postally used *5.25*
On cover 54.00
O9 A11 60(pf) carmine .25 *.25*
Never hinged .50
Postally used *4.50*
On cover 50.00
O10 A11 75(pf) dp vio .20 *.35*
Never hinged .70
Postally used *2.75*
On cover 37.50
O11 A11 80(pf) black & car 1.00 *1.10*
Never hinged 2.90
Postally used *15.00*
On cover 70.00
O12 A11 80(pf) green .20 *1.75*
Never hinged .70
Postally used *200.00*
On cover *300.00*

Paper With Faint Gray Network

O14 A11 1m org & car .20 *.25*
Never hinged .50
Postally used *2.25*
On cover 37.50
O15 A11 1.20m blue violet 1.60 1.10
Never hinged 4.00
Postally used *23.00*
On cover 92.50
O16 A11 1.25m vio & car .20 *.35*
Never hinged .70
Postally used *62.50*
On cover —
O17 A11 1.50m slate gray .20 *.35*
Never hinged .50
Postally used *6.50*
On cover 37.50
O18 A11 2m gray & car 18.00 13.50
Never hinged 60.00
Postally used *57.50*
On cover 115.00
a. Inverted overprint 75.00
Never hinged 190.00
O19 A11 2m car rose .20 *.35*
Never hinged .70
Postally used *3.00*
On cover 45.00
O20 A11 2.40m dk brn & car 1.25 *2.50*
Never hinged 8.00
Postally used *60.00*
On cover 115.00
O21 A11 3m violet & car 12.50 *13.00*
Never hinged 40.00
Postally used *55.00*
On cover 110.00
O22 A11 3m car lake .20 *.35*
Never hinged .50
Postally used *10.00*
On cover 45.00
O23 A11 4m dk blue 1.00 .75
Never hinged 8.00
Postally used *75.00*
On cover 115.00
O24 A11 5m dp grn .20 *.35*
Never hinged .50
Postally used *30.00*
On cover 75.00
O25 A11 6m car lake .20 *.35*
Never hinged .50
Postally used *13.00*
On cover 70.00
O26 A11 10m orange .20 *.35*
Never hinged .50
Postally used *9.25*
On cover 57.50
O27 A11 20m org brn .20 *.35*
Never hinged .50
Postally used *19.00*
On cover 75.00
Nos. O1-O27 (26) 39.85 *39.55*
Set, never hinged 135.00

Double overprints exist on Nos. O1-O2, O5-O7, O10 and O12.
Issued: #O10, O12, O16-O17, O19-O20, O22-O27, 1922.

Same Overprint on No. 96

O28 A11 6m on 3m .20 *.75*
Never hinged .60
Postally used *13.00*
On cover 70.00
a. Inverted overprint 27.50
Never hinged 75.00

No. 77 Overprinted

Serrate Roulette 13½
1922 Wmk. 108 Sideways
O29 A12 5m grn, red & blk 4.00 *7.00*
Never hinged 15.00
Postally used *100.00*
On cover *150.00*
a. Wmk. upright 4.25 *8.50*
Never hinged 20.00
Postally used *92.50*
On cover *140.00*

Nos. 99-103, 106-107 Overprinted Type "a"

1922-23 Wmk. 109 *Perf. 14*
O30 A11 4m dark blue .20 *.50*
Never hinged .70
Postally used *35.00*
On cover 115.00
O31 A11 5m dark green .20 *.85*
Never hinged 1.00
Postally used *42.50*
On cover 100.00
O32 A11 10m orange .20 *.50*
Never hinged .70
Postally used *7.50*
On cover 57.50
O33 A11 20m orange brn .20 *.50*
Never hinged .70
Postally used *7.50*
On cover 85.00
O34 A15 50m pale blue & red .20 *.50*
Never hinged .70
Postally used *7.00*
On cover 30.80
O35 A15a 100m dk grn & red .20 *.50*
Never hinged .70
Postally used *12.50*
On cover 57.50

Nos. 113-115, 118-120 Overprinted Type "a"

O36 A15 50m pale blue .20 *.45*
Never hinged .70
Postally used *1,100.*
On cover *1,400.*
a. Inverted overprint 21.00
Never hinged 52.50
O37 A15a 100m dark green .20 *.45*
Never hinged .70
Postally used *300.00*
On cover 500.00
O38 A15 200m orange .20 *.45*
Never hinged .70
Postally used *30.00*
On cover 190.00
a. Inverted overprint 21.00
Never hinged 52.50

Paper With Gray Network

O39 A17 300m bl grn & red .20 *.50*
Never hinged .70
Postally used *275.00*
On cover 450.00
O40 A17 500m gray & red .20 *.45*
Never hinged .70
Postally used *425.00*
On cover *750.00*
a. Network omitted 14.00 *5.75*
Never hinged 37.50
O41 A17 1000m brn & red .20 *.45*
Never hinged .70
Postally used *92.50*
On cover 225.00
a. Network omitted 14.00 *5.75*
Never hinged 37.50
Nos. O30-O41 (12) 2.40 *6.10*
Set, never hinged 8.75

Issued: #O30, 12/16/22. #O31-O34, 1/10/23. #O36-O40, 7/20/23. #O41, 7/29/23.

Regular Issue of 1924-25 Overprinted

1924-25 *Perf. 14x14½*
O42 A19 5pf red orange 2.50 *3.00*
Never hinged 6.25
On cover 23.00
a. 5pf orange 11.50 *8.50*
Never hinged 37.50
On cover 37.50
O43 A19 10pf green 2.50 2.25
Never hinged 21.00
On cover 19.00
a. 10pf dark green 2.00 2.25
Never hinged 5.75
On cover 13.00
O44 A19 15pf gray 2.25 1.90
Never hinged 7.00
On cover 15.00
a. 15pf dk greenish gray 5.00 3.75
Never hinged 17.00
On cover 27.50
O45 A19 15pf red 22.50 8.75
Never hinged 54.00
On cover 19.00
O46 A19 20pf car & red 2.50 1.40
Never hinged 7.00
On cover 19.00
O47 A19 25pf slate & red 26.00 26.00
Never hinged 52.50
On cover 115.00
O48 A19 30pf green & red 3.75 2.50
Never hinged 8.50
On cover 23.00
a. 30pf dk grn & rose red 27.50 11.00
Never hinged 92.50
On cover 57.50
O49 A19 35pf ultra 52.50 50.00
Never hinged 140.00
On cover 100.00
O50 A19 40pf dk bl & dull bl 7.25 7.00
Never hinged 17.50
On cover 70.00
O51 A19 50pf dp blue & red 21.00 *32.50*
Never hinged 60.00
On cover 275.00
O52 A19 75pf violet & red 42.50 *100.00*
Never hinged 125.00
On cover 300.00
Nos. O42-O52 (11) 185.25 *235.30*
Set, never hinged 500.00

Double overprints exist on Nos. O42-O44, O47, O50-O52.

Issued: #O42-O43, O44a, O46, O50, 3/1/24. #O42a, O45, O49, 1925. #O48, O51-O52, 3/12/24.

DENMARK

'den-,märk

LOCATION — Northern part of a peninsula which separates the North and Baltic Seas, and includes the surrounding islands
GOVT. — Kingdom
AREA — 16,631 sq. mi.
POP. — 5,112,130 (1984)
CAPITAL — Copenhagen

96 Skilling = 1 Rigsbank Daler
100 Ore = 1 Krone (1875)

Values for unused stamps are for examples with original gum as defined in the catalogue introduction. Very fine examples of Nos. 9-37 and O1-O9 will have perforations clear of the framelines but with the design noticeably off center. Well centered stamps are quite scarce and will command substantial premiums.

Watermarks

Wmk. 111 — Small Crown

Wmk. 112 — Crown

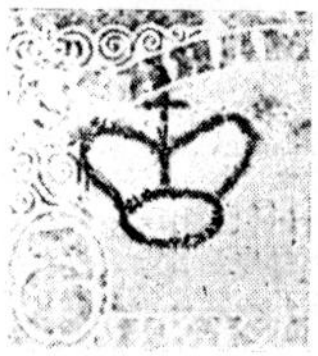

Wmk. 113 — Crown

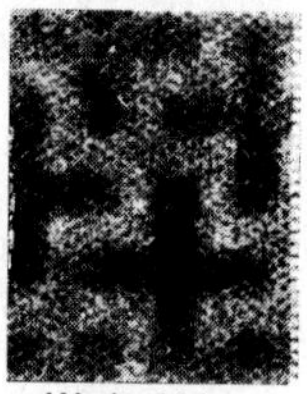

Wmk. 114 — Multiple Crosses

4:17 PM 6/5/20074:17 PM 6/5/2007

A1

Royal Emblems — A2

1851 Typo. Wmk. 111 *Imperf.*
With Yellow Brown Burelage
1 A1 2rs blue *2,250.* 975.00
On cover 2,000.
a. First printing *6,750.* *1,850.*
On cover 6,500.
2 A2 4rs brown 475.00 32.50
On cover 90.00
a. First printing 575.00 57.50
On cover 160.00
b. 4rs yellow brown 825.00 47.50
On cover 125.00

Full margins = 1mm.

The first printing of Nos. 1 and 2 had the burelage printed from a copper plate, giving a clear impression with the lines in slight relief. The subsequent impressions had the burelage typographed, with the lines fainter and not rising above the surface of the paper.

Nos. 1-2 were reprinted in 1885 and 1901 on heavy yellowish paper, unwatermarked and imperforate, with a brown burelage. No. 1 was also reprinted without burelage, on both yellowish and white paper. Value for least costly reprint of No. 1, $50.

No. 2 was reprinted in 1951 in 10 shades with "Colour Specimen 1951" printed on the *back. It was also reprinted in 1961 in 2 shades without burelage and with "Farve Nytryk 1961" printed on the back. Value for least costly reprint of No. 2, $8.50.*

Dotting in Spandrels
A3

Wavy Lines in Spandrels
A4

1854-57

3	A3 2s blue ('55)	55.00	50.00
	Never hinged	85.00	
	On cover		175.00
4	A3 4s brown	250.00	11.00
	Never hinged	500.00	
	On cover		26.00
a.	4s yellow brown	275.00	11.00
	Never hinged	550.00	
	On cover		27.50
5	A3 8s green ('57)	250.00	55.00
	Never hinged	425.00	
	On cover		275.00
	On cover, single franking		325.00
a.	8s yellow green	250.00	60.00
	Never hinged	450.00	
	On cover		275.00
	On cover, single franking		325.00
6	A3 16s gray lilac ('57)	475.00	150.00
	Never hinged	1,000.	
	On cover		750.00
	On cover, single franking		900.00
	Nos. 3-6 (4)	1,030.	266.00

Full margins = 1mm.

See No. 10. For denominations in cents see Danish West Indies Nos. 1-4.

1858-62

7	A4 4s yellow brown	57.50	8.00
	Never hinged	120.00	
	On cover		22.50
a.	4s brown	60.00	8.00
	Never hinged	140.00	
	On cover		22.50
b.	Wmk. 112 ('62)	55.00	9.00
	Never hinged	125.00	
	On cover		24.00
8	A4 8s green	725.00	82.50
	Never hinged	1,900.	
	On cover		375.00
	On cover, single franking		450.00

Full margins = 1mm.

Nos. 2 to 8 inclusive are known with unofficial perforation 12 or 13, and Nos. 4, 5, 7 and 8 with unofficial roulette 9½.

Nos. 3, 6-8 were reprinted in 1885 on heavy yellowish paper, unwatermarked, imperforate and without burelage. Nos. 4-5 were reprinted in 1924 on white paper, unwatermarked, imperforate, gummed and without burelage. Value for No. 3, $11; Nos. 4-5, each $100; No. 6, $15; Nos. 7-8, each $10.

1863 Wmk. 112 *Rouletted 11*

9	A4 4s brown	80.00	13.00
	Never hinged	140.00	
	On cover		32.50
a.	4s deep brown	80.00	13.00
	Never hinged	140.00	
	On cover		32.50
b.	4s red brown	77.50	18.00
	Never hinged	140.00	
	On cover		35.00
10	A3 16s violet	1,300.	450.00
	On cover		4,250.
	On cover, single franking		5,400.

Royal Emblems — A5

1864-68 *Perf. 13*

11	A5 2s blue ('65)	55.00	27.50
	Never hinged	140.00	
	On cover		62.50
12	A5 3s red vio ('65)	72.50	67.50
	Never hinged	190.00	
	On cover		325.00
	On cover, single franking		625.00
13	A5 4s red	35.00	7.00
	Never hinged	60.00	
	On cover		16.00
14	A5 8s bister ('68)	250.00	90.00
	Never hinged	450.00	
	On cover		325.00
15	A5 16s olive green	425.00	160.00
	Never hinged	825.00	
	On cover		325.00
	On cover, single franking		475.00
	Nos. 11-15 (5)	837.50	352.00

Nos. 11-15 were reprinted in 1886 on heavy yellowish paper, unwatermarked, imperforate and without gum. The reprints of all values except the 4s were printed in two vertical rows of six, inverted with respect to each other, so that horizontal pairs are always tête bêche. Value $10 each.

Nos. 13 and 15 were reprinted in 1942 with printing on the back across each horizontal row: "Nytryk 1942. G. A. Hagemann: Danmarks og Vestindiens Frimaerker, Bind 2." Value, $65 each.

Imperf, single

11a	A5 2s blue	90.00	90.00
	As "a," pair	225.00	225.00
12a	A5 3s red violet	125.00	
	As "a," pair	450.00	
13a	A5 4s red	72.50	85.00
	On cover		*2,000.*
	As "a," pair	225.00	—
14a	A5 8s bister	350.00	
	As "a," pair	775.00	
15a	A5 16s olive green	425.00	
	As "a," pair	900.00	

1870 *Perf. 12½*

11b	A5 2s blue	240.00	310.00
	Never hinged	525.00	
	On cover		500.00
12b	A5 3s red violet	400.00	575.00
	Never hinged	775.00	
	On cover		925.00
14b	A5 8s bister	400.00	400.00
	Never hinged	925.00	
	On cover		825.00
15b	A5 16s olive green	625.00	*1,250.*
	Never hinged	1,250.	
	On cover		2,600.
	Nos. 11b-15b (4)	1,665.	2,535.

A6

NORMAL FRAME

INVERTED FRAME

The arabesques in the corners have a main stem and a branch. When the frame is in normal position, in the upper left corner the branch leaves the main stem half way between two little leaflets. In the lower right corner the branch starts at the foot of the second leaflet. When the frame is inverted the corner designs are, of course, transposed.

1870-71 Wmk. 112 *Perf. 14x13½*

Paper Varying from Thin to Thick

16	A6 2s gray & ultra ('71)	70.00	25.00
	Never hinged	135.00	
	On cover		47.50
a.	2s gray & blue	70.00	25.00
	Never hinged	135.00	
	On cover		45.00
17	A6 3s gray & brt lil ('71)	72.50	85.00
	Never hinged	160.00	
	On cover		200.00
18	A6 4s gray & car	35.00	7.00
	Never hinged	100.00	
	On cover		18.00
19	A6 8s gray & brn ('71)	160.00	65.00
	Never hinged	400.00	
	On cover		190.00
20	A6 16s gray & grn ('71)	225.00	150.00
	Never hinged	575.00	
	On cover		525.00
	On cover, single franking		625.00

Perf. 12½

21	A6 2s gray & bl ('71)	1,750.	*2,900.*
	Never hinged	3,100.	
	On cover		5,650.
	On cover, single franking		6,250.
22	A6 4s gray & car	125.00	100.00
	Never hinged	260.00	
	On cover		125.00
24	A6 48s brn & lilac	400.00	250.00
	Never hinged	925.00	
	On cover		*1,600.*
	On cover, single franking		*2,250.*

Nos. 16-20, 24 were reprinted in 1886 on thin white paper, unwatermarked, imperforate and without gum. These were printed in sheets of 10 in which 1 stamp has the normal frame (value $32.50 each) and 9 the inverted (value $11 each).

Imperf, single

16b	A6 2s	*210.*	
17a	A6 3s	*190.*	
18a	A6 4s	*175.*	
19a	A6 8s	*200.*	
20a	A6 16s	*350.*	
24a	A6 48s	*350.*	—

Inverted Frame

16c	A6 2s	825.	625.
17b	A6 3s	1,900.	1,500.
18b	A6 4s	625.	77.50
	On cover		*225.*
19b	A6 8s	1,250.	725.
20b	A6 16s	1,700.	1,250.
24b	A6 48s	2,100.	1,450.

1875-79 *Perf. 14x13½*

25	A6 3o gray blue & gray	13.00	9.00
	Never hinged	22.50	
	On cover		35.00
	On cover, single franking		75.00
a.	1st "A" of "DANMARK" missing	45.00	125.00
	Never hinged	110.00	
b.	Imperf	*750.00*	
c.	Inverted frame	13.00	10.50
	Never hinged	22.50	
	On cover		40.00
26	A6 4o slate & blue	20.00	.40
	Never hinged	52.50	
	On cover		3.75
a.	4o gray & blue	20.00	.90
	Never hinged	52.50	
	On cover		3.75
b.	4o slate & ultra	70.00	12.00
	Never hinged	175.00	
	On cover		30.00
c.	4o gray & ultra	60.00	9.50
	Never hinged	155.00	
	On cover		30.00
d.	Imperf	60.00	—
	On cover		—
	Pair	—	
e.	As #26, inverted frame	20.00	.40
	Never hinged	52.50	
	On cover		3.50
f.	As "b," inverted frame	400.00	240.00
	On cover		—
27	A6 5o rose & blue ('79)	25.00	62.50
	Never hinged	42.50	
	On cover		625.00
	On cover, single franking		800.00
a.	Ball of lower curve of large "5" missing	87.50	225.00
	Never hinged	175.00	
b.	Inverted frame	825.00	*1,850.*
	Never hinged	1,550.	
28	A6 8o slate & car	17.50	.40
	Never hinged	45.00	
	On cover		2.75
a.	8o gray & carmine	35.00	4.00
	Never hinged	110.00	
	On cover		16.00
b.	Imperf	70.00	—
	On cover		—
	Pair	—	
c.	Inverted frame	17.50	.40
	Never hinged	45.00	
	On cover		2.75
d.	8o gray & analine red ('86)	35.00	4.00
	Never hinged	120.00	
	On cover		17.50
e.	As "d," imperf	150.00	—
	On cover		—
f.	As "d," inverted frame (pos. 69)	400.00	120.00
29	A6 12o sl & dull lake	8.50	3.50
	Never hinged	13.00	
	On cover		40.00
	On cover, single franking		60.00
a.	12o gray & bright lilac	35.00	6.75
	Never hinged	87.50	
	On cover		60.00
b.	12o gray & dull magenta	42.50	8.75
	Never hinged	87.50	
	On cover		65.00
c.	Inverted frame	8.00	3.00
	Never hinged	17.50	
	On cover		42.50
30	A6 16o slate & brn	32.50	3.00
	Never hinged	72.50	
	On cover		35.00
	On cover, single franking		67.50
a.	16o light gray & brown	40.00	4.00
	Never hinged	77.50	
	On cover		52.50
	On cover, single franking		85.00
b.	Inverted frame	26.00	3.25
	Never hinged	60.00	
	On cover		35.00
31	A6 20o rose & gray	70.00	26.00
	Never hinged	160.00	
	On cover		97.50
a.	20o carmine & gray	70.00	26.00
	Never hinged	175.00	
	On cover		95.00
b.	Inverted frame	70.00	26.00
	Never hinged	175.00	
	On cover		97.50
32	A6 25o gray & green	42.50	26.00
	Never hinged	87.50	
	On cover		240.00
	On parcel post receipt card		225.00
a.	Inverted frame	70.00	57.50
	Never hinged	175.00	
	On cover		310.00
33	A6 50o brown & vio	47.50	22.50
	Never hinged	125.00	
	On cover		200.00
	On parcel post receipt card		165.00
a.	50o brown & blue violet	325.00	110.00
	Never hinged	625.00	
	On cover		1,050.
b.	Inverted frame	47.50	25.00
	Never hinged	130.00	
	On cover		200.00
34	A6 100o gray & org ('77)	80.00	45.00
	Never hinged	175.00	
	On cover		210.00
	On parcel post receipt card		210.00
a.	Imperf, single	225.00	
b.	Inverted frame	87.50	45.00
	Never hinged	175.00	
	On cover		275.00
c.	100o greenish gray & orange yellow ('87)	80.00	45.00
	Never hinged	175.00	
	On cover		225.00
d.	100o bluish gray & orange yellow ('91)	82.50	37.50
	Never hinged	175.00	
	On cover		225.00
	Nos. 25-34 (10)	356.50	198.30
	Set, never hinged	800.00	

The stamps of this issue on thin semi-transparent paper are far scarcer than those on thicker paper.

See Nos. 41-42, 44, 46-47, 50-52. For surcharges see Nos. 55, 79-80, 136.

Arms — A7

Two types of numerals in corners:

1882

Small Corner Numerals

35	A7 5o green	210.00	82.50
	Never hinged	400.00	
	On cover		825.00
	On cover, single franking		950.00
37	A7 20o blue	160.00	35.00
	Never hinged	450.00	
	On cover		120.00

1884-88

Larger Corner Numerals

38	A7 5o green	11.00	1.40
	Never hinged	35.00	
	On cover		18.00
a.	Imperf	—	
39	A7 10o carmine ('85)	11.00	1.40
	Never hinged	35.00	
	On cover		18.00
a.	Small numerals in corners ('88)	400.00	*525.00*
	Never hinged	725.00	
	On cover		*7,500.*
b.	Imperf, single	140.00	
c.	Pair, Nos. 39, 39a	475.00	*775.00*
	Never hinged	825.00	
40	A7 20o blue	17.50	1.75
	Never hinged	45.00	
	On cover		22.50
a.	Pair, Nos. 37, 40	300.00	*675.00*
	Never hinged	575.00	
	On cover		2,500.
b.	Imperf	—	
	Nos. 38-40 (3)	39.50	4.55
	Set, never hinged	110.00	

Stamps with large corner numerals have white line around crown and lower oval touches frame.

The plate for No. 39, was damaged and 3 clichés in the bottom row were replaced by clichés for post cards, which had small numerals in the corners.

Two clichés with small numerals were inserted in the plate of No. 40.

See Nos. 43, 45, 48-49, 53-54. For surcharge see No. 56.

1895-1901 Wmk. 112 *Perf. 13*

41	A6 3o blue & gray	3.75	2.25
	Never hinged	4.50	
	On cover		13.50
42	A6 4o slate & bl ('96)	3.00	.30
	Never hinged	6.25	
	On cover		2.00
43	A7 5o green	5.00	.55
	Never hinged	17.50	
	On cover		2.50
44	A6 8o slate & car	3.00	.35
	Never hinged	9.00	
	On cover		2.00
45	A7 10o rose car	17.50	.55
	Never hinged	35.00	
	On cover		4.00
46	A6 12o sl & dull lake	3.50	3.00
	Never hinged	8.75	
	On cover		35.00
47	A6 16o slate & brown	12.50	3.00
	Never hinged	20.00	
	On cover		45.00
48	A7 20o blue	17.50	1.75
	Never hinged	45.00	
	On cover		10.00
49	A7 24o brown ('01)	5.00	2.75
	Never hinged	13.50	
	On cover		90.00
	On cover, single franking		225.00
50	A6 25o gray & grn ('98)	52.50	9.00
	Never hinged	100.00	
	On cover		110.00
51	A6 50o brown & vio ('97)	35.00	12.50
	Never hinged	70.00	
	On cover		105.00
	On cover, single franking		225.00
52	A6 100o slate & org	45.00	22.50
	Never hinged	87.50	
	On cover		100.00
	On cover, single franking		240.00
	Nos. 41-52 (12)	203.25	58.50
	Set, never hinged	425.00	

Inverted Frame

41b	A6 3o	7.25	4.25
	Never hinged	11.50	
	On cover		14.00
42a	A6 4o	3.00	.35
	Never hinged	5.50	
	On cover		2.00
44a	A6 8o	3.00	.40
	Never hinged	7.50	
	On cover		2.00
46a	A6 12o	8.00	3.00
	Never hinged	11.50	
	On cover		35.00
47a	A6 16o	15.00	3.00
	Never hinged	22.50	
	On cover		60.00
50a	A6 25o	30.00	13.50
	Never hinged	70.00	
	On cover		140.00

51a A6 50o 55.00 14.50
Never hinged 95.00
On cover 150.00
52a A6 100o 45.00 22.50
Never hinged 87.50
On cover 150.00
Nos. 41b-52a (8) 166.25 61.50
Set, never hinged 300.00

1902-04 **Wmk. 113**

41c A6 3o blue & gray 2.50 2.25
Never hinged 4.50
On cover 13.50
42b A6 4o slate & blue 11.00 13.50
Never hinged 17.50
On cover 40.00
43a A7 5o green 1.60 .20
Never hinged 4.50
On cover 2.75
44d A6 8o slate & carmine 275.00 210.00
Never hinged 575.00
On cover *1,900.*
45a A7 10o rose carmine 2.40 .20
Never hinged 6.25
On cover 3.00
48a A7 20o blue 13.00 2.50
Never hinged 30.00
On cover 13.00
50b A6 25o gray & green 5.75 3.00
Never hinged 12.50
On cover 85.00
51b A6 50o brown & violet 20.00 11.50
Never hinged 35.00
On cover 100.00
On cover, single franking 200.00
52b A6 100o slate & orange 18.00 9.00
Never hinged 35.00
On cover 120.00
On cover, single franking 265.00
Nos. 41c-52b (9) 349.25 252.15
Set, never hinged 625.00

Inverted Frame

41d A6 3o 45.00 32.50
Never hinged 105.00
On cover 70.00
42c A6 4o 95.00 62.50
Never hinged 225.00
On cover 170.00
50c A6 25o 125.00 40.00
Never hinged 260.00
On cover 105.00
51c A6 50o 160.00 97.50
Never hinged 300.00
On cover 175.00
52c A6 100o 125.00 100.00
Never hinged 300.00
On cover 225.00
Nos. 41d-52c (5) 550.00 332.50
Set, never hinged 1,200.

1902 **Wmk. 113**

53 A7 1o orange .60 .45
Never hinged .85
On cover 3.50
a. Imperf — —
54 A7 15o lilac 9.00 .55
Never hinged 17.50
On cover 20.00
a. Imperf, single *3,750.*

Nos. 44d, 44, 49 Surcharged:

a

b

1904-12 **Wmk. 113**

55 A6(a) 4o on 8o sl & car 2.50 3.50
Never hinged 4.50
On cover 17.50
a. Wmk. 112 ('12) 10.00 *35.00*
Never hinged 13.50
On cover 105.00
b. As "a," inverted frame — *3,250.*
Never hinged —

Wmk. 112

56 A7(b) 15o on 24o brown 3.00 5.00
Never hinged 4.50
On cover 30.00
a. Short "15" at right 15.00 *50.00*
Never hinged 32.50
Set, never hinged 9.00

A10

King Christian IX
A11

King Frederik VIII
A12

1905-17 **Wmk. 113** ***Perf. 13***

57 A10 1o orange ('06) 1.25 .40
Never hinged 4.50
On cover 1.75
58 A10 2o carmine 2.50 .25
Never hinged 8.75
On cover 3.50
a. Perf. 14x14½ ('17) 2.25 *11.00*
Never hinged 4.50
On cover 26.00
59 A10 3o gray 5.25 .45
Never hinged 13.00
On cover 1.50
60 A10 4o dull blue 4.50 .45
Never hinged 13.00
On cover 3.00
a. Perf. 14x14½ ('17) 6.50 *20.00*
Never hinged 13.00
On cover 45.00
61 A10 5o dp green ('12) 2.50 .20
Never hinged 6.00
On cover 1.00
62 A10 10o dp rose ('12) 3.50 .20
Never hinged 11.00
On cover 1.25
63 A10 15o lilac 13.00 1.25
Never hinged 35.00
On cover 8.75
64 A10 20o dk blue ('12) 22.50 .50
Never hinged 65.00
On cover 8.75
Nos. 57-64 (8) 55.00 3.70
Set, never hinged 160.00

The three wavy lines in design A10 are symbolical of the three waters which separate the principal Danish islands.

See Nos. 85-96. For surcharges and overprints see Nos. 163, 181, J1, J38, Q1-Q2.

1904-05 **Engr.**

65 A11 10o scarlet 1.60 .20
Never hinged 4.00
On cover 1.35
66 A11 20o blue 13.00 1.75
Never hinged 30.00
On cover 11.00
67 A11 25o brown ('05) 17.50 2.50
Never hinged 52.50
On cover 40.00
On cover, single franking 45.00
68 A11 50o dull vio ('05) 45.00 *52.50*
Never hinged 125.00
On cover 225.00
On cover, single franking 265.00
69 A11 100o ocher ('05) 8.75 *35.00*
Never hinged 13.00
On cover 130.00
On cover, single franking 225.00
Nos. 65-69 (5) 85.85 *91.95*
Set, never hinged 225.00

1905-06 **Re-engraved**

70 A11 5o green 2.25 .20
Never hinged 5.50
71 A11 10o scarlet ('06) 9.00 .20
Never hinged 22.50
Set, never hinged 28.00

The re-engraved stamps are much clearer than the originals, and the decoration on the king's left breast has been removed.

1907-12

72 A12 5o green 1.00 .20
Never hinged 1.75
a. Imperf.
73 A12 10o red 1.75 .20
Never hinged 3.50
a. Imperf.
74 A12 20o indigo 6.00 .20
Never hinged 20.00
a. 20o bright blue ('11) 8.00 .70
Never hinged 17.50
75 A12 25o olive brn 10.00 .40
Never hinged 35.00
76 A12 35o dp org ('12) 2.50 2.50
Never hinged 4.75
77 A12 50o claret 15.00 3.25
Never hinged 40.00
78 A12 100o bister brn 50.00 1.90
Never hinged 200.00
Nos. 72-78 (7) 86.25 8.65
Set, never hinged 305.00

Nos. 47, 31 and O9 Surcharged:

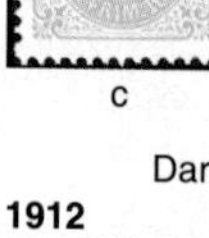
c

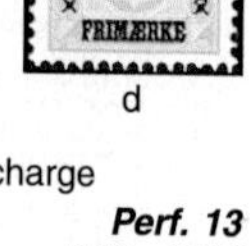
d

Dark Blue Surcharge

1912 **Wmk. 112** ***Perf. 13***

79 A6(c) 35o on 16o 8.00 *35.00*
Never hinged 16.00
a. Inverted frame 150.00 *375.00*
Never hinged 300.00

Perf. 14x13½

80 A6(c) 35o on 20o 16.00 *55.00*
Never hinged 27.50
a. Inverted frame 55.00 *125.00*

Never hinged 110.00

Black Surcharge

81 O1(d) 35o on 32o 15.00 *60.00*
Never hinged 27.50
Nos. 79-81 (3) 39.00 *150.00*
Set, never hinged 71.00

General Post Office, Copenhagen — A15

1912 **Engr.** **Wmk. 113** ***Perf. 13***

82 A15 5k dark red 300.00 100.00
Never hinged 525.00

See Nos. 135, 843.

Perf. 14x14½

1913-30 **Typo.** **Wmk. 114**

85 A10 1o dp orange ('14) .20 .20
Never hinged .35
a. Bklt. pane, 2 ea #85, 91 + 2 labels 18.00
86 A10 2o car ('13) 1.25 .20
Never hinged 3.75
a. Imperf 100.00 *200.00*
b. Booklet pane, 4 + 2 labels 24.00
87 A10 3o gray ('13) 2.25 .20
Never hinged 7.00
88 A10 4o blue ('13) 3.25 .20
Never hinged 10.50
a. Half used as 2o on cover 1,000.
89 A10 5o dk brown ('21) .55 .20
Never hinged .90
a. Imperf 150.00
b. Booklet pane, 4 + 2 labels 12.50
90 A10 5o lt green ('30) .90 .20
Never hinged 2.25
a. Booklet pane, 4 + 2 labels 12.50
b. Booklet pane of 50
91 A10 7o apple grn ('26) 2.25 .90
Never hinged 4.50
a. Booklet pane, 4 + 2 labels 15.00
92 A10 7o dk violet ('30) 7.50 2.25
Never hinged 22.50
93 A10 8o gray ('21) 3.00 1.25
Never hinged 6.00
94 A10 10o green ('21) .75 .20
Never hinged 1.50
a. Imperf 150.00
b. Booklet pane, 4 + 2 labels 32.50
95 A10 10o bister brn ('30) 1.25 .20
Never hinged 2.75
a. Booklet pane, 4 + 2 labels 14.00
b. Booklet pane of 50
96 A10 12o violet ('26) 12.50 4.00
Never hinged 35.00
Nos. 85-96 (12) 35.65 10.00
Set, never hinged 97.00

No. 88a was used with No. 97 in Faroe Islands, Jan. 3-23, 1919.

See surcharge and overprint note following #64.

King Christian X
A16 A17

1913-28 **Typo.** ***Perf. 14x14½***

97 A16 5o green .90 .20
Never hinged 2.50
a. Booklet pane of 4 10.00
98 A16 7o orange ('18) 1.75 .95
Never hinged 3.25
99 A16 8o dk gray ('20) 4.50 3.50
Never hinged 11.00
100 A16 10o red 1.25 .20
Never hinged 2.25
a. Imperf 175.00
b. Booklet pane of 4 10.00
101 A16 12o gray grn ('18) 5.00 6.00
Never hinged 7.00
102 A16 15o violet 1.25 .20
Never hinged 3.75
103 A16 20o dp blue 6.25 .20
Never hinged 22.50
104 A16 20o brown ('21) .60 .20
Never hinged 1.00
105 A16 20o red ('26) .90 .20
Never hinged 1.75
106 A16 25o dk brown 7.50 .35
Never hinged 25.00
107 A16 25o brn & blk ('20) 40.00 3.00
Never hinged 95.00
108 A16 25o red ('22) 2.25 .60
Never hinged 3.25
109 A16 25o yel grn ('25) 2.50 .35
Never hinged 3.75
110 A16 27o ver & blk ('18) 18.00 *32.50*
Never hinged 35.00
111 A16 30o green & blk ('18) 14.00 1.40
Never hinged 45.00
112 A16 30o orange ('21) 1.75 1.40
Never hinged 3.25
113 A16 30o dk blue ('25) 1.25 .35
Never hinged 2.00
114 A16 35o orange 11.00 1.75
Never hinged 37.50
115 A16 35o yel & blk ('19) 4.00 3.50
Never hinged 7.50
116 A16 40o vio & blk ('18) 8.00 2.25
Never hinged 35.00
117 A16 40o gray bl & blk ('20) 25.00 4.25
Never hinged 50.00
118 A16 40o dk blue ('22) 3.50 .75
Never hinged 5.75
119 A16 40o orange ('25) 1.25 .60
Never hinged 2.25
120 A16 50o claret 27.50 2.00
Never hinged 65.00
121 A16 50o claret & blk ('19) 40.00 .95
Never hinged 100.00
122 A16 50o lt gray ('22) 5.50 .20
Never hinged 17.50
a. 50o dark gray ('21) 35.00 3.00
Never hinged 100.00
123 A16 60o brn & bl ('19) 25.00 3.00
Never hinged 87.50
a. 60o brown & ultra ('19) 125.00 9.00
Never hinged 350.00
124 A16 60o grn bl ('21) 6.00 .60
Never hinged 16.00
125 A16 70o brn & grn ('20) 15.00 1.40
Never hinged 45.00
126 A16 80o bl grn ('15) 27.50 9.00
Never hinged 62.50
127 A16 90o brn & red ('20) 8.00 2.25
Never hinged 22.50
128 A16 1k brn & bl ('22) 30.00 1.40
Never hinged 87.50
129 A16 2k gray & cl ('25) 35.00 11.00
Never hinged 85.00
130 A16 5k vio & brn ('27) 4.50 4.25
Never hinged 6.00
131 A16 10k ver & yel grn ('28) 165.00 30.00
Never hinged 525.00
Nos. 97-131 (35) 551.40 130.75
Set, never hinged 1,475.

#97 surcharged "2 ORE" is Faroe Islands #1.

Nos. 87 and 98, 89 and 94, 89 and 104, 90 and 95, 97 and 103, 100 and 102 exist se-tenant in coils for use in vending machines.

For surcharges and overprints see Nos. 161-162, 176-177, 182-184, J2-J8, M1-M2, Q3-Q10.

1913-20 **Engr.**

132 A17 1k yellow brown 57.50 .60
Never hinged 150.00
133 A17 2k gray 65.00 3.00
Never hinged 250.00
134 A17 5k purple ('20) 8.00 7.00
Never hinged 20.00
Nos. 132-134 (3) 130.50 10.60
Set, never hinged 420.00

For overprint see No. Q11.

G.P.O. Type of 1912

Perf. 14x14½

1915 **Wmk. 114** **Engr.**

135 A15 5k dark red ('15) 250.00 90.00
Never hinged 875.00

Nos. 46 and O10 Surcharged in Black type "c" and:

e

1915 **Wmk. 112** **Typo.** ***Perf. 13***

136 A6 (c) 80o on 12o 18.00 *67.50*
Never hinged 32.50
a. Inverted frame 275.00 *500.00*
Never hinged 400.00
137 O1 (e) 80o on 8o 30.00 *80.00*
Never hinged 40.00
a. "POSTERIM" 40.00 *160.00*
Never hinged 52.50
Set, never hinged 70.00

Newspaper Stamps Surcharged

On Issue of 1907

1918 **Wmk. 113** ***Perf. 13***

138 N1 27o on 1o olive 60.00 *200.00*
Never hinged 110.00
139 N1 27o on 5o blue 60.00 *200.00*
Never hinged 110.00
140 N1 27o on 7o car 60.00 *200.00*
Never hinged 110.00
141 N1 27o on 10o dp lil 60.00 *200.00*
Never hinged 110.00
142 N1 27o on 68o yel brn 4.00 *22.50*
Never hinged 7.50
143 N1 27o on 5k rose & yel grn 3.50 *12.50*
Never hinged 6.50

144 N1 27o on 10k bis & bl 4.00 *20.00*
Never hinged 8.50
Nos. 138-144 (7) 251.50 *855.00*
Set, never hinged 462.50

On Issue of 1914-15
Wmk. Multiple Crosses (114)
Perf. 14x14½

145 N1 27o on 1o ol gray 2.50 *9.50*
Never hinged 4.00
146 N1 27o on 5o blue 4.75 *20.00*
Never hinged 7.50
147 N1 27o on 7o rose 2.50 *6.50*
Never hinged 4.00
148 N1 27o on 8o green 3.50 *9.50*
Never hinged 5.50
149 N1 27o on 10o dp lil 2.50 *7.75*
Never hinged 4.00
150 N1 27o on 20o green 3.50 *9.00*
Never hinged 5.00
151 N1 27o on 29o org yel 2.50 *6.50*
Never hinged 4.00
152 N1 27o on 38o orange 18.00 *65.00*
Never hinged 30.00
153 N1 27o on 41o yel brn 6.00 *32.50*
Never hinged 8.50
154 N1 27o on 1k bl grn & mar 2.50 *6.50*
Never hinged 4.00
Nos. 145-154 (10) 48.25 *172.75*
Set, never hinged 76.50

Kronborg Castle — A20

Sonderborg Castle — A21

Roskilde Cathedral — A22

Perf. 14½x14, 14x14½
1920, Oct. 5 **Typo.**

156 A20 10o red 2.25 .25
Never hinged 4.75
157 A21 20o slate 1.75 .25
Never hinged 4.00
158 A22 40o dark brown 7.00 3.00
Never hinged 15.00
Nos. 156-158 (3) 11.00 3.50
Set, never hinged 23.75

Reunion of Northern Schleswig with Denmark.
See #159-160. For surcharges see #B1-B2.

1921
159 A20 10o green 3.25 .35
Never hinged 9.00
160 A22 40o dark blue 25.00 4.25
Never hinged 65.00
Set, never hinged 70.00

Stamps of 1918 Surcharged in Blue

1921-22
161 A16 8o on 7o org ('22) 1.40 *2.50*
Never hinged 4.25
162 A16 8o on 12o gray grn 1.40 *6.00*
Never hinged 4.25
Set, never hinged 9.00

No. 87 Surcharged

1921
163 A10 8o on 3o gray 1.75 *2.25*
Never hinged 3.25

Christian X A23

Christian IV A24

A25

A26

1924, Dec. 1 ***Perf. 14x14½***
164 A23 10o green 4.00 3.50
Never hinged 7.25
165 A24 10o green 4.00 3.50
Never hinged 7.25
166 A25 10o green 4.00 3.50
Never hinged 7.25
167 A26 10o green 4.00 3.50
Never hinged 7.25
a. Block of 4, #164-167 20.00 *35.00*
Never hinged 40.00
168 A23 15o violet 4.00 3.50
Never hinged 7.25
169 A24 15o violet 4.00 3.50
Never hinged 7.25
170 A25 15o violet 4.00 3.50
Never hinged 7.25
171 A26 15o violet 4.00 3.50
Never hinged 7.25
a. Block of 4, #168-171 20.00 *35.00*
Never hinged 40.00
172 A23 20o dark brown 4.00 3.50
Never hinged 7.25
173 A24 20o dark brown 4.00 3.50
Never hinged 7.25
174 A25 20o dark brown 4.00 3.50
Never hinged 7.25
175 A26 20o dark brown 4.00 3.50
Never hinged 7.25
a. Block of 4, #172-175 20.00 *35.00*
Never hinged 40.00
Nos. 164-175 (12) 48.00 42.00
Set, never hinged 87.00
#167a, 171a, 175a, never hinged 120.00

300th anniv. of the Danish postal service.

Stamps of 1921-22 Surcharged:

k

l

1926
176 A16 (k) 20o on 30o org 3.50 *8.00*
Never hinged 5.25
177 A16 (l) 20o on 40o dk bl 4.00 *11.00*
Never hinged 7.25
Set, never hinged 12.50

A27

A28

1926, Mar. 11 ***Perf. 14x14½***
178 A27 10o dull green .60 .20
Never hinged 1.00
179 A28 20o dark red 1.00 .20
Never hinged 1.50
180 A28 30o dark blue 3.75 .45
Never hinged 6.25
Nos. 178-180 (3) 5.35 .85
Set, never hinged 8.75

75th anniv. of the introduction of postage stamps in Denmark.

Stamps of 1913-26 Surcharged in Blue or Black

No. 181

Nos. 182-184

1926-27 ***Perf. 14x14½***
181 A10 7o on 8o gray (Bl) .60 *2.00*
Never hinged 1.75
182 A16 7o on 27o ver & blk 3.00 *7.50*
Never hinged 4.75
183 A16 7o on 20o red ('27) .55 .40
Never hinged 1.00
184 A16 12o on 15o violet 2.00 *3.25*
Never hinged 4.00

Surcharged on Official Stamps of 1914-23

185 O1 (e) 7o on 1o org 3.00 *6.50*
Never hinged 8.50
186 O1 (e) 7o on 3o gray 4.50 *16.00*
Never hinged 8.75
187 O1 (e) 7o on 4o blue 2.50 *6.50*
Never hinged 3.00
188 O1 (e) 7o on 5o grn 35.00 *77.50*
Never hinged 50.00
189 O1 (e) 7o on 10o grn 2.50 *6.50*
Never hinged 3.00
190 O1 (e) 7o on 15o vio 2.25 *6.50*
Never hinged 3.50
191 O1 (e) 7o on 20o ind 10.00 *32.50*
Never hinged 17.50
a. Double surcharge *525.00* *675.00*
Never hinged *725.00*
Nos. 181-191 (11) 65.90 *165.15*
Set, never hinged 105.00

Caravel A30

Christian X A31

1927 **Typo.** ***Perf. 14x14½***
192 A30 15o red 2.50 .20
Never hinged 7.50
193 A30 20o gray 6.00 .65
Never hinged 18.00
194 A30 25o light blue .60 .20
Never hinged 1.00
195 A30 30o ocher .50 .20
Never hinged 1.50
196 A30 35o red brown 11.50 .65
Never hinged 35.00
197 A30 40o yel green 10.00 .20
Never hinged 27.50
Nos. 192-197 (6) 31.10 2.10
Set, never hinged 90.50

See #232-238J. For surcharges & overprints see #244-245, 269-272, Q12-Q14, Q19-Q25.

1930, Sept. 26
210 A31 5o apple grn 1.60 .20
Never hinged 2.50
a. Booklet pane, 4 + 2 labels 17.50
211 A31 7o violet 6.00 2.25
Never hinged 12.50
212 A31 8o dk gray 15.00 15.00
Never hinged 35.00
213 A31 10o yel brn 2.75 .20
Never hinged 4.50
a. Booklet pane, 4 + 2 labels 25.00
214 A31 15o red 5.50 .20
Never hinged 20.00
215 A31 20o lt gray 16.00 3.00
Never hinged 32.50
216 A31 25o lt blue 6.00 .60
Never hinged 12.50
217 A31 30o yel buff 6.00 1.50
Never hinged 12.50
218 A31 35o red brown 8.00 2.50
Never hinged 17.50
219 A31 40o dp green 7.50 .80
Never hinged 16.00
Nos. 210-219 (10) 74.35 26.25
Set, never hinged 165.50

60th birthday of King Christian X.

Wavy Lines and Numeral of Value — A32

Type A10 Redrawn

1933-40 **Unwmk.** **Engr.** ***Perf. 13***
220 A32 1o gray blk .20 .20
Never hinged .20
221 A32 2o scarlet .20 .20
Never hinged .20
222 A32 4o blue .25 .20
Never hinged .50
223 A32 5o yel grn .65 .20
Never hinged 1.25
a. 5o gray green 16.00 *20.00*
Never hinged 20.00
b. Tête bêche gutter pair 5.50 *10.00*
Never hinged 9.00
c. Booklet pane of 4 8.00
d. Bklt. pane, 1 #223a, 3 #B6 25.00
e. As "b," without gutter, never hinged 12.00
224 A32 5o rose lake ('38) .20 .20
Never hinged .20
a. Booklet pane of 4 .30
b. Booklet pane of 10 .65
224C A32 6o orange ('40) .20 .20
Never hinged .25
225 A32 7o violet .80 .20
Never hinged 1.50
226 A32 7o yel grn ('38) .70 .20
Never hinged 1.25
226A A32 7o lt brown ('40) .20 .20
Never hinged .30
227 A32 8o gray .50 .20
Never hinged 1.00
227A A32 8o yellow grn ('40) .20 .20
Never hinged .25
228 A32 10o yellow org 7.00 .20
Never hinged 13.00
a. Tête bêche gutter pair 20.00 20.00
Never hinged 35.00
b. Booklet pane of 4 57.50
c. As "a," without gutter, never hinged 45.00
229 A32 10o lt brown ('37) 4.50 .20
Never hinged 7.25
a. Booklet pane of 4 50.00
b. Booklet pane of 4, 1 #229, 3 #B7 22.50
230 A32 10o violet ('38) .50 .20
Never hinged .85
a. Booklet pane of 4 2.50
b. Bklt. pane, 2 #230, 2 #B10 4.00
Nos. 220-230 (14) 16.10 2.80
Set, never hinged 28.00

Design A10 was typographed. They had a solid background with groups of small hearts below the heraldic lions in the upper corners and below "DA" and "RK" of "DANMARK." The numerals of value were enclosed in single-lined ovals.

Design A32 is line-engraved and has a background of crossed lines. The hearts have been removed and the numerals of value are now in double-lined ovals. Two types exist of some values.

The 1ö, No. 220, was issued on fluorescent paper in 1969.

No. 230 with wide margins is from booklet pane No. 230b.

Surcharges of 20, 50 & 60öre on #220, 224 and 224C are listed as Faroe Islands #2-3, 5-6.

See Nos. 318, 333, 382, 416, 437-437A, 493-498, 629, 631, 688-695, 793-795, 883-886, 1114. For overprints and surcharges see Nos. 257, 263, 267-268, 355-356, Q15-Q17, Q31, Q43.

Certain Tête Bêche Pairs of 1938-55 issues which reached the market in 1971, and were not regularly issued, are not listed. This group comprises 24 different major-number vertical pairs of types A32, A47, A61 and SP3 (13 with gutters, 11 without), and pairs of some minor numbers and shades. They were removed from booklet pane sheets.

Type of 1927 Issue
Type I

Type I — Two columns of squares between sail and left frame line.

1933-34 **Engr.** ***Perf. 13***
232 A30 20o gray 8.50 .20
Never hinged 16.00
233 A30 25o blue 45.00 15.00
Never hinged 100.00
234 A30 25o brown ('34) 17.50 .20
Never hinged 42.50
235 A30 30o orange yel .60 .80
Never hinged 1.25
236 A30 30o blue ('34) .75 .20
Never hinged 1.50
237 A30 35o violet .30 .20
Never hinged .60
238 A30 40o yellow grn 3.00 .20
Never hinged 5.75
Nos. 232-238 (7) 75.65 16.80
Set, never hinged 167.50

Type II

Type II — One column of squares between sail and left frame line.

1933-40
238A A30 15o deep red 2.00 .20
Never hinged 3.00
k. Booklet pane of 4 22.50
l. Bklt. pane, 1 #238A, 3 #B8 35.00
238B A30 15o yel grn ('40) 5.00 .20
Never hinged 9.00
238C A30 20o gray blk ('39) 3.00 .20
Never hinged 6.00
238D A30 20o red ('40) .40 .20
Never hinged .75
238E A30 25o dp brown ('39) .40 .20
Never hinged .75
238F A30 30o blue ('39) 1.50 .25
Never hinged 2.50
238G A30 30o orange ('40) .40 .20
Never hinged .75
238H A30 35o violet ('40) .50 .30
Never hinged 1.00
238I A30 40o yel grn ('39) 8.00 .20
Never hinged 16.00
238J A30 40o blue ('40) .75 .20
Never hinged 1.25
Nos. 238A-238J (10) 21.95 2.15
Set, never hinged 41.00

Nos. 232-238J, engraved, have crosshatched background. Nos. 192-197, typographed, have solid background.

No. 238A surcharged 20 ore is listed as Faroe Islands No. 4.

See note on surcharges and overprints following No. 197.

King Christian X — A33

1934-41 *Perf. 13*

239	A33 50o gray	.75	.20
	Never hinged	1.75	
240	A33 60o blue grn	1.50	.20
	Never hinged	5.00	
240A	A33 75o dk blue ('41)	.30	.20
	Never hinged	.50	
241	A33 1k lt brown	2.50	.20
	Never hinged	8.00	
242	A33 2k dull red	3.75	.65
	Never hinged	9.50	
243	A33 5k violet	5.00	2.25
	Never hinged	17.00	
	Nos. 239-243 (6)	13.80	3.70
	Set, never hinged	42.00	

For overprints see Nos. Q26-Q27.

Nos. 233, 235 Surcharged in Black

1934, June 9

244	A30 4o on 25o blue	.40	.40
	Never hinged	.50	
245	A30 10o on 30o org yel	1.50	*1.75*
	Never hinged	2.75	
	Set, never hinged	3.25	

"The Ugly Duckling" A34

Andersen A35

"The Little Mermaid" — A36

1935, Oct. 4 *Perf. 13*

246	A34 5o lt green	1.75	.20
	Never hinged	5.00	
a.	Tête bêche gutter pair	8.50	*9.00*
	Never hinged	17.00	
b.	Booklet pane of 4	17.50	
c.	As "a," without gutter, never hinged	19.00	
247	A35 7o dull vio	1.50	*2.00*
	Never hinged	3.75	
248	A36 10o orange	3.00	.20
	Never hinged	8.50	
a.	Tête bêche gutter pair	11.50	*15.00*
	Never hinged	21.00	
b.	Booklet pane of 4	30.00	
c.	As "a," without gutter, never hinged	29.00	
249	A35 15o red	7.50	.20
	Never hinged	22.50	
a.	Tête bêche gutter pair	30.00	*24.00*
	Never hinged	57.50	
b.	Booklet pane of 4	75.00	
c.	As "a," without gutter, never hinged	62.50	
250	A35 20o gray	8.50	1.10
	Never hinged	22.50	
251	A35 30o dl bl	1.75	.30
	Never hinged	3.50	
	Nos. 246-251 (6)	24.00	*4.00*
	Set, never hinged	66.00	

Centenary of the publication of the earliest installment of Hans Christian Andersen's "Fairy Tales."

Nikolai Church A37

Hans Tausen A38

Ribe Cathedral — A39

1936 *Perf. 13*

252	A37 5o green	.90	.20
	Never hinged	2.50	
a.	Booklet pane of 4	17.50	
253	A37 7o violet	1.00	*1.75*
	Never hinged	2.00	
254	A38 10o lt brown	1.25	.20
	Never hinged	3.25	
a.	Booklet pane of 4	18.00	
255	A38 15o dull rose	2.00	.20
	Never hinged	4.50	
256	A39 30o blue	8.00	1.00
	Never hinged	21.50	
	Nos. 252-256 (5)	13.15	3.35
	Set, never hinged	33.75	

Church Reformation in Denmark, 400th anniv.

No. 229 Overprinted in Blue

1937, Sept. 17

257	A32 10o lt brown	.85	*1.50*
	Never hinged	2.00	

Jubilee Exhib. held by the Copenhagen Phil. Club on their 50th anniv. The stamps were on sale at the Exhib. only, each holder of a ticket of admission (1k) being entitled to purchase 20 stamps at face value; of a season ticket (5k), 100 stamps.

Yacht and Summer Palace, Marselisborg A40

Christian X in Streets of Copenhagen A41

Equestrian Statue of Frederik V and Amalienborg Palace — A42

1937, May 15 *Perf. 13*

258	A40 5o green	.65	.20
	Never hinged	1.75	
a.	Booklet pane of 4	10.50	
259	A41 10o brown	.65	.20
	Never hinged	1.75	
a.	Booklet pane of 4	10.50	
260	A42 15o scarlet	.65	.20
	Never hinged	1.75	
a.	Booklet pane of 4	12.00	
261	A41 30o blue	11.50	1.75
	Never hinged	22.50	
	Nos. 258-261 (4)	13.45	2.35
	Set, never hinged	27.75	

25th anniv. of the accession to the throne of King Christian X.

Emancipation Column, Copenhagen — A43

1938, June 20 *Perf. 13*

262	A43 15o scarlet	.40	.20
	Never hinged	1.00	

Abolition of serfdom in Denmark, 150th anniv.

No. 223 Overprinted in Red on Alternate Stamps

1938, Sept. 2

263	A32 5o yellow grn, pair	2.75	*5.25*
	Never hinged	7.50	

10th Danish Philatelic Exhibition.

Bertel Thorvaldsen A44

Statue of Jason A45

1938, Nov. 17 **Engr.** *Perf. 13*

264	A44 5o rose lake	.20	.20
	Never hinged	.50	
265	A45 10o purple	.45	.20
	Never hinged	.75	
266	A44 30o dark blue	1.10	.30
	Never hinged	2.25	
	Nos. 264-266 (3)	1.75	.70
	Set, never hinged	3.50	

The return to Denmark in 1838 of Bertel Thorvaldsen, Danish sculptor.

Stamps of 1933-39 Surcharged with New Values in Black:

a

b

c

1940

267	A32 (a) 6o on 7o yel grn	.20	.20
	Never hinged	.20	
268	A32 (a) 6o on 8o gray	.20	.20
	Never hinged	.20	
269	A30 (b) 15o on 40o #238	.60	*3.00*
	Never hinged	1.00	
270	A30 (b) 15o on 40o #238I	.60	.65
	Never hinged	.80	
271	A30 (c) 20o on 15o dp red	.80	.20
	Never hinged	1.25	
272	A30 (b) 40o on 30o #238F	.60	.20
	Never hinged	1.00	
	Nos. 267-272 (6)	3.00	*4.45*
	Set, never hinged	4.45	

SEMI-POSTAL STAMPS

Nos. 159, 157 Surcharged in Red

Wmk. Multiple Crosses (114)

1921, June 17 *Perf. 14½x14*

B1	A20 10o + 5o green	9.00	*32.50*
	Never hinged	22.50	
B2	A21 20o + 10o slate	11.00	*40.00*
	Never hinged	32.50	
	Set, never hinged	55.00	

Crown and Staff of Aesculapius SP1

Dybbol Mill SP2

1929, Aug. 1 **Engr.**

B3	SP1 10o yellow green	2.50	*3.50*
	Never hinged	4.50	
a.	Booklet pane of 2	21.00	
B4	SP1 15o brick red	4.00	*6.00*
	Never hinged	8.50	
a.	Booklet pane of 2	25.00	
B5	SP1 25o deep blue	17.50	*21.00*
	Never hinged	32.50	
a.	Booklet pane of 2	100.00	
	Nos. B3-B5 (3)	24.00	*30.50*
	Set, never hinged	45.00	

These stamps were sold at a premium of 5 öre each for benefit of the Danish Cancer Committee.

1937, Jan. 20 **Unwmk.** *Perf. 13*

B6	SP2 5o + 5o green	.40	*.75*
	Never hinged	.75	
B7	SP2 10o + 5o lt brown	1.75	*3.00*
	Never hinged	4.25	
B8	SP2 15o + 5o carmine	1.75	*3.00*
	Never hinged	4.25	
	Nos. B6-B8 (3)	3.90	*6.75*
	Set, never hinged	9.25	

The surtax was for a fund in memory of H. P. Hanssen, statesman.

Nos. 223a and B6, Nos. 229 and B7, Nos. 238A and B8 are found se-tenant in booklets. For booklet panes, see Nos. 223d, 229b and 238e.

Queen Alexandrine — SP3

1939-40 *Perf. 13*

B9	SP3 5o + 3o rose lake & red ('40)	.20	.20
	Never hinged	.40	
a.	Booklet pane of 4	2.00	2.00
B10	SP3 10o + 5o dk violet & red	.20	.20
	Never hinged	.50	
B11	SP3 15o + 5o scarlet & red	.30	*.50*
	Never hinged	.50	
	Nos. B9-B11 (3)	.70	.90
	Set, never hinged	1.40	

The surtax was for the Danish Red Cross.

Nos. 230 and B10 have been issued se-tenant in booklets. See No. 230b. In this pane No. 230 measures 23½x31mm from perf. to perf.

AIR POST STAMPS

Airplane and Plowman AP1

Towers of Copenhagen AP2

Wmk. Multiple Crosses (114)

1925-29 **Typo.** *Perf. 12x12½*

C1	AP1 10o yellow green	16.00	*25.00*
	Never hinged	32.50	
C2	AP1 15o violet ('26)	32.50	*42.50*
	Never hinged	82.50	
C3	AP1 25o scarlet	27.50	*37.50*
	Never hinged	47.50	
C4	AP1 50o lt gray ('29)	65.00	*125.00*
	Never hinged	160.00	

C5 AP1 1k choc ('29) 55.00 *125.00*
Never hinged 140.00
Nos. C1-C5 (5) 196.00 *355.00*
Set, never hinged 500.00

Unwmk.

1934, June 9 Engr. *Perf. 13*

C6 AP2 10o orange .50 *1.00*
Never hinged 1.00
C7 AP2 15o red 1.75 *3.50*
Never hinged 4.00
C8 AP2 20o Prus blue 2.00 *4.00*
Never hinged 4.50
C9 AP2 50o olive black 2.00 *4.00*
Never hinged 4.50
C10 AP2 1k brown 8.00 *15.00*
Never hinged 16.00
Nos. C6-C10 (5) 14.25 *27.50*
Set, never hinged 30.00

LATE FEE STAMPS

LF1

Coat of Arms — LF2

Perf. 14x14½

1923 Typo. Wmk. 114

I1 LF1 10o green 8.00 1.00
Never hinged 27.50
a. Double overprint —

No. I1 was, at first, not a postage stamp but represented a tax for the services of the post office clerks in filling out postal forms and writing addresses. In 1923 it was put into use as a Late Fee stamp.

1926-31

I2 LF2 10o green 3.75 .95
Never hinged 18.00
I3 LF2 10o brown ('31) 3.50 .35
Never hinged 12.00
Set, never hinged 30.00

1934 Unwmk. Engr. *Perf. 13*

I4 LF2 5o green .20 .20
Never hinged .25
I5 LF2 10o orange .20 .20
Never hinged .25
Set, never hinged 1.00

POSTAGE DUE STAMPS

Regular Issues of 1913-20 Overprinted

Perf. 14x14½

1921, May 1 Wmk. 114

J1 A10 1o deep orange 1.00 *1.50*
Never hinged 3.00
J2 A16 5o green 3.00 2.25
Never hinged 8.00
J3 A16 7o orange 2.50 1.75
Never hinged 5.00
J4 A16 10o red 13.50 7.50
Never hinged 35.00
J5 A16 20o deep blue 8.00 4.50
Never hinged 21.00
J6 A16 25o brown & blk 20.00 2.50
Never hinged 45.00
J7 A16 50o claret & blk 6.50 3.00
Never hinged 13.00
Nos. J1-J7 (7) 54.50 23.00
Set, never hinged 130.00

Same Overprint in Dark Blue On Military Stamp of 1917

1921, Nov. 23

J8 A16 10o red 8.50 6.00
Never hinged 20.00
a. "S" inverted 100.00 *150.00*
Never hinged 200.00

Numeral of Value — D1

Typographed (Solid Panel)

1921-30 *Perf. 14x14½*

J9 D1 1o orange ('22) .50 .40
Never hinged 1.10
J10 D1 4o blue ('25) 2.00 1.10
Never hinged 6.00
J11 D1 5o brown ('22) 2.00 .65
Never hinged 6.00
J12 D1 5o lt green ('30) .75 .60
Never hinged 2.40
J13 D1 7o apple grn ('27) 10.50 10.50
Never hinged 26.00
J14 D1 7o dk violet ('30) 22.50 22.50
Never hinged 60.00
J15 D1 10o yellow grn ('22) 2.00 .40
Never hinged 6.00
J16 D1 10o lt brown ('30) 1.00 .35
Never hinged 3.50
J17 D1 20o grnsh blue ('21) 1.25 .50
Never hinged 2.75
a. Double impression 2,100.
J18 D1 20o gray ('30) 1.25 .85
Never hinged 4.50
J19 D1 25o scarlet ('23) 2.00 .70
Never hinged 8.25
J20 D1 25o violet ('26) 1.75 .90
Never hinged 5.00
J21 D1 25o lt blue ('30) 3.75 2.25
Never hinged 8.25
J22 D1 1k dk blue ('21) 55.00 4.50
Never hinged 105.00
J23 D1 1k brn & dk bl ('25) 7.00 3.50
Never hinged 13.00
J24 D1 5k purple ('25) 15.00 7.00
Never hinged 32.50
Nos. J9-J24 (16) 128.25 56.70
Set, never hinged 290.00

Engraved (Lined Panel)

1934-55 Unwmk. *Perf. 13*

J25 D1 1o slate .20 .20
Never hinged .20
J26 D1 2o carmine .20 .20
Never hinged .20
J27 D1 5o yellow green .20 .20
Never hinged .20
J28 D1 6o dk olive ('41) .40 .20
Never hinged .45
J29 D1 8o magenta ('50) 1.25 *1.50*
Never hinged 2.25
J30 D1 10o orange .20 .20
Never hinged .25
J31 D1 12o dp ultra ('55) .30 .25
Never hinged .35
J32 D1 15o violet ('37) .40 .20
Never hinged .60
J33 D1 20o gray .35 .20
Never hinged .50
J34 D1 25o blue .40 .20
Never hinged .60
J35 D1 30o green ('53) .40 .20
Never hinged .60
J36 D1 40o claret ('49) .50 .20
Never hinged .70
J37 D1 1k brown .65 .25
Never hinged .75
Nos. J25-J37 (13) 5.45 *4.00*
Set, never hinged 8.00

No. 96 Surcharged in Black

1934 Wmk. 114 *Perf. 14x14½*

J38 A10 15o on 12o violet 1.50 .70
Never hinged 7.00

MILITARY STAMPS

Nos. 97 and 100 Overprinted in Blue

1917 Wmk. 114 *Perf. 14x14½*

M1 A16 5o green 7.50 *16.00*
Never hinged 22.50
a. "S" inverted 190.00 *275.00*
Never hinged 325.00
M2 A16 10o red 8.00 *13.00*
Never hinged 20.00
a. "S" inverted 150.00 *200.00*
Never hinged 250.00
Set, never hinged 42.50
#M1a, M2a, never hinged 600.00

The letters "S F" are the initials of "Soldater Frimaerke" (Soldier's Stamp).
For overprint see No. J8.

OFFICIAL STAMPS

Small State Seal — O1

Wmk. Crown (112)

1871 Typo. *Perf. 14x13½*

O1 O1 2s blue 130.00 80.00
Never hinged 350.00
On cover 120.00
a. 2s ultra 130.00 80.00
Never hinged 315.00
On cover 120.00
b. Imperf *250.00*
As "b," pair *900.00*
O2 O1 4s carmine 45.00 9.00
Never hinged 120.00
On cover 27.50
a. Imperf *200.00*
As "a," pair *900.00*
O3 O1 16s green 310.00 210.00
Never hinged 850.00
On cover 1,750.
a. Imperf *300.00*
As "a," pair *950.00*

Perf. 12½

O4 O1 4s carmine 4,100. 360.00
On cover 400.00
O5 O1 16s green 310.00 360.00
Never hinged 725.00
On cover 1,650.
#O1-O3, O5, never hinged 2,000.

Nos. O4-O5 values are for copies with defective perfs.

Nos. O1-O3 were reprinted in 1886 upon white wove paper, unwatermarked and imperforate. Value $10 each.

1875 *Perf. 14x13½*

O6 O1 3o violet 6.00 *10.00*
Never hinged 18.00
On cover 110.00
O7 O1 4o grnsh blue 6.00 2.50
Never hinged 22.00
On cover 16.00
O8 O1 8o carmine 6.00 1.25
Never hinged 22.00
On cover 8.00
a. Imperf —
O9 O1 32o green 20.00 20.00
Never hinged 47.50
On cover 160.00
Nos. O6-O9 (4) 38.00 *33.75*
Set, never hinged 110.00

For surcharge see No. 81.

1899-02 *Perf. 13*

O9A O1 3o red lilac ('02) 2.75 *3.75*
Never hinged 5.75
On cover 26.00
c. Imperf *210.00*
As "c," pair *575.00*
O9B O1 4o blue 1.75 1.60
Never hinged 3.50
On cover 14.00
O10 O1 8o carmine 11.00 11.00
Never hinged 40.00
On cover 62.50
Nos. O9A-O10 (3) 15.50 16.35
Set, never hinged 50.00

For surcharge see No. 137.

1902-06 Wmk. 113

O11 O1 1o orange 1.10 *1.60*
Never hinged 2.40
On cover 13.50
O12 O1 3o red lilac ('06) .70 .65
Never hinged 1.40
On cover 13.00
O13 O1 4o blue ('03) 1.50 1.25
Never hinged 3.50
On cover 21.00
O14 O1 5o green 1.25 .55
Never hinged 3.00
On cover 7.50
O15 O1 10o carmine 1.25 1.10
Never hinged 4.50
On cover 7.75
Nos. O11-O15 (5) 5.80 5.15
Set, never hinged 15.00

1914-23 Wmk. 114 *Perf. 14x14½*

O16 O1 1o orange 1.10 1.25
Never hinged 1.50
On cover 20.00
O17 O1 3o gray ('18) 3.00 3.00
Never hinged 5.00
On cover 65.00
O18 O1 4o blue ('16) 30.00 *50.00*
Never hinged 42.50
On cover 125.00
O19 O1 5o green ('15) .75 .35
Never hinged 1.60
On cover 10.00
O20 O1 5o choc ('23) 3.50 *5.00*
Never hinged 4.50
Postally used 17.00
On cover —
O21 O1 10o red ('17) 5.50 .75
Never hinged 10.00
On cover 25.00
O22 O1 10o green ('21) 1.00 *1.50*
Never hinged 2.00
On cover 25.00
O23 O1 15o violet ('19) 10.00 *27.50*
Never hinged 21.00
On cover 100.00
O24 O1 20o indigo ('20) 12.50 6.25
Never hinged 32.50
On cover 57.50
Nos. O16-O24 (9) 67.35 *95.60*
Set, never hinged 120.00

For surcharges see Nos. 185-191.
No. O20 is valued CTO.
Official stamps were discontinued Apr. 1, 1924.

NEWSPAPER STAMPS

Postal documents as listed below were official Post Office forms supplied to publishers. Newspaper stamps were affixed to the forms to pay postage for the delivery of bundles of papers.

Numeral of Value — N1

1907 Typo. Wmk. 113 *Perf. 13*

P1 N1 1o olive 10.00 2.75
Never hinged 40.00
On postal document 325.00
P2 N1 5o blue 21.00 14.00
Never hinged 95.00
On postal document 325.00
P3 N1 7o carmine 9.00 1.25
Never hinged 55.00
On postal document 250.00
P4 N1 10o deep lilac 30.00 3.00
Never hinged 140.00
On postal document 325.00
P5 N1 20o green 19.00 1.40
Never hinged 125.00
On postal document 325.00
P6 N1 38o orange 30.00 1.50
Never hinged 140.00
On postal document 400.00
P7 N1 68o yellow brown 80.00 25.00
Never hinged 400.00
On postal document 450.00
P8 N1 1k bl grn & claret 19.00 3.00
Never hinged 125.00
On postal document 325.00
P9 N1 5k rose & yel grn 160.00 37.50
Never hinged 550.00
On postal document 525.00
P10 N1 10k bister & blue 160.00 37.50
Never hinged 625.00
On postal document 525.00
Nos. P1-P10 (10) 538.00 126.90
Set, never hinged 2,300.

For surcharges see Nos. 138-144.

1914-15 Wmk. 114 *Perf. 14x14½*

P11 N1 1o olive gray 7.00 1.40
Never hinged 80.00
On postal document 325.00
P12 N1 5o blue 25.00 7.00
Never hinged 140.00
On postal document 325.00
P13 N1 7o rose 25.00 1.40
Never hinged 140.00
On postal document 275.00
P14 N1 8o green ('15) 20.00 1.40
Never hinged 125.00
On postal document 325.00
P15 N1 10o deep lilac 25.00 1.50
Never hinged 160.00
On postal document 325.00
P16 N1 20o green 225.00 2.75
Never hinged 625.00
On postal document 325.00
a. Imperf., pair *825.00*
P17 N1 29o orange yel ('15) 40.00 2.75
Never hinged 315.00
On postal document 325.00
P18 N1 38o orange 1,550. 125.00
Never hinged 2,250.
On postal document —
P19 N1 41o yellow brn ('15) 45.00 2.00
Never hinged 325.00
On postal document 325.00
P20 N1 1k blue grn & mar 77.50 2.50
Never hinged 475.00
On postal document 275.00
Nos. P11-P17,P19-P20 (9) 489.50 22.70
Set, never hinged 2,400.

For surcharges see Nos. 145-154.

PARCEL POST STAMPS

These stamps were for use on postal packets sent by the Esbjerg-Fano Ferry Service.

Regular Issues of 1913-30 Overprinted

1919-41 Wmk. 114 *Perf. 14x14½*

Q1	A10	10o green ('22)	8.00	*13.00*
		Never hinged	30.00	
Q2	A10	10o bister brn ('30)	9.00	6.50
		Never hinged	27.50	
Q3	A16	10o red	27.50	*55.00*
		Never hinged	75.00	
a.		"POSFFAERGE"	150.00	*350.00*
		Never hinged	250.00	
Q4	A16	15o violet	11.50	*27.50*
		Never hinged	27.50	
a.		"POSFFAERGE"	150.00	*350.00*
		Never hinged	250.00	
Q5	A16	30o orange ('22)	10.00	*21.00*
		Never hinged	24.00	
Q6	A16	30o dk blue ('26)	3.00	3.00
		Never hinged	5.25	
Q7	A16	50o cl & blk ('20)	180.00	*200.00*
		Never hinged	290.00	
Q8	A16	50o lt gray ('22)	18.00	11.00
		Never hinged	45.00	
a.		50o dark gray ('22)	125.00	*250.00*
		Never hinged	350.00	
Q9	A16	1k brn & bl ('24)	40.00	17.00
		Never hinged	105.00	
Q9A	A16	5k vio & brn ('41)	1.50	1.50
		Never hinged	2.10	
Q10	A16	10k ver & grn ('30)	55.00	*85.00*
		Never hinged	75.00	

Engr.

Q11	A17	1k yellow brn	75.00	*140.00*
		Never hinged	190.00	
a.		"POSFFAERGE"	1,400.	*2,250.*
		Nos. Q1-Q11 (12)	438.50	*580.50*
		Set, never hinged	900.00	

1927-30

Q12	A30	15o red ('27)	13.00	10.50
		Never hinged	22.50	
Q13	A30	30o ocher ('27)	11.00	11.00
		Never hinged	19.00	
Q14	A30	40o yel grn ('30)	12.50	10.50
		Never hinged	37.50	
		Set, never hinged	80.00	

Overprinted on Regular Issues of 1933-40

1936-42 Unwmk. *Perf. 13*

Q15	A32	5o rose lake ('42)	.20	.20
		Never hinged	.20	
Q16	A32	10o yellow org	15.00	*25.00*
		Never hinged	32.50	
Q17	A32	10o lt brown ('38)	1.00	*1.40*
		Never hinged	1.50	
Q18	A32	10o purple ('39)	.20	.20
		Never hinged	.25	
Q19	A30	15o deep red	.40	*1.00*
		Never hinged	.60	
Q20	A30	30o blue, I	3.25	*4.25*
		Never hinged	5.25	
Q21	A30	30o blue, II ('40)	6.00	*12.00*
		Never hinged	13.50	
Q22	A30	30o org, II ('42)	.35	*.60*
		Never hinged	.55	
Q23	A30	40o yel grn, I	3.25	*4.25*
		Never hinged	5.25	
Q24	A30	40o yel grn, II ('40)	6.00	*11.00*
		Never hinged	13.50	
Q25	A30	40o blue, II ('42)	.40	*1.00*
		Never hinged	.60	
Q26	A33	50o gray	1.00	*1.50*
		Never hinged	1.25	
Q27	A33	1k lt brown	.80	*1.25*
		Never hinged	1.10	
		Nos. Q15-Q27 (13)	37.85	*63.65*
		Set, never hinged	85.00	

DIEGO-SUAREZ

dē-ˌā-gō ˈswär-əs

LOCATION — A town at the northern end of Madagascar
GOVT. — French Colony
POP. — 12,237

From 1885 to 1896 Diego-Suarez, (Antsirane), a French naval base, was a separate colony and issued its own stamps. These were succeeded by stamps of Madagascar.

100 Centimes = 1 Franc

Values for unused stamps are for examples with original gum as defined in the catalogue introduction except for Nos. 6-10 and J1-J2 which are valued without gum.

Stamps of French Colonies Handstamp Surcharged in Violet

1890 Unwmk. *Perf. 14x13½*

1	A9	15c on 1c blk, *bl*	210.00	72.50
2	A9	15c on 5c grn, *grnsh*	550.00	72.50
3	A9	15c on 10c blk, *lav*	250.00	67.50
4	A9	15c on 20c red, *grn*	550.00	67.50
5	A9	15c on 25c blk, *rose*	90.00	40.00

Inverted Surcharge

1a	A9	15c on 1c blk, *bl*	425.00	190.00
2a	A9	15c on 5c grn, *grnsh*	1,000.	275.00
3a	A9	15c on 10c blk, *lav*	1,000.	400.00
4a	A9	15c on 20c red, *grn*	1,000.	275.00
5a	A9	15c on 25c blk, *rose*	425.00	210.00

Double Surcharge

1b	A9	15c on 1c blk, *bl*	650.00	300.00
2b	A9	15c on 5c grn, *grnsh*	2,600.	
3b	A9	15c on 10c blk, *lav*	1,150.	400.00
4b	A9	15c on 20c red, *grn*	1,150.	400.00
c.		Dble. surch., both inverted		750.00
5b	A9	15c on 25c blk, *rose*	475.00	210.00

Counterfeits exist.

Ship Flying French Flag — A2

France — A5

Symbolical of Union of France and Madagascar
A3 A4

1890 Litho. *Imperf.*

6	A2	1c black	850.00	190.00
7	A3	5c black	800.00	150.00
8	A4	15c black	175.00	72.50
9	A5	25c black	200.00	80.00

Counterfeits exist of Nos. 6-9.

A6

1891

10	A6	5c black	250.00	72.50

Excellent counterfeits exist of No. 10.

Stamps of French Colonies Surcharged in Red or Black:

No. 11

No. 12

1892 *Perf. 14x13½*

11	A9	5c on 10c blk, *lav* (R)	150.00	80.00
a.		Inverted surcharge	350.00	325.00
12	A9	5c on 20c red, *grn*	140.00	55.00
a.		Inverted surcharge	350.00	325.00

Stamps of French Colonies Overprinted in Black or Red

1892

13	A9	1c blue (R)	23.50	14.50
14	A9	2c brown, *buff*	23.50	14.50
15	A9	4c claret, *lav*	40.00	32.50
16	A9	5c green, *grnsh*	85.00	65.00
17	A9	10c black, *lavender*	29.00	23.50
b.		Double overprint	165.00	125.00
18	A9	15c blue, *pale blue*	23.50	14.00
19	A9	20c red, *grn*	25.00	23.50
20	A9	25c black, *rose*	23.50	12.50
21	A9	30c brown, *bis* (R)	925.00	675.00
22	A9	35c black, *yellow*	925.00	675.00
23	A9	75c carmine, *rose*	55.00	35.00
a.		Double overprint		325.00
24	A9	1fr brnz grn, *straw* (R)	62.50	42.50
a.		Double overprint	165.00	150.00

Inverted Overprint

13a	A9	1c	160.	140.
14a	A9	2c	160.	140.
15a	A9	4c		250.
16a	A9	5c	160.	140.
17a	A9	10c	160.	140.
20a	A9	25c	160.	140.
21a	A9	30c		1,250.
22a	A9	35c		1,250.

Navigation and Commerce
A10 A11

1892 Typo. *Perf. 14x13½*
Name of Colony in Blue or Carmine

25	A10	1c black, *blue*	1.75	1.75
26	A10	2c brown, *buff*	2.10	2.10
27	A10	4c claret, *lav*	2.25	2.25
28	A10	5c green, *grnsh*	4.75	4.75
29	A10	10c black, *lavender*	6.50	5.00
30	A10	15c bl, quadrille paper	12.50	8.00
31	A10	20c red, *green*	17.50	12.50
32	A10	25c black, *rose*	12.50	11.50
33	A10	30c brown, *bister*	16.50	12.50
34	A10	40c red, *straw*	21.00	16.00
35	A10	50c carmine, *rose*	36.00	22.00
36	A10	75c violet, *org*	40.00	29.00
37	A10	1fr brnz grn, *straw*	57.50	36.00
		Nos. 25-37 (13)	230.85	163.35

Perf. 13½x14 stamps are counterfeits.

1894 *Perf. 14x13½*

38	A11	1c black, *blue*	1.50	1.50
39	A11	2c brown, *buff*	2.10	1.75
40	A11	4c claret, *lav*	2.40	2.10
41	A11	5c green, *grnsh*	4.00	3.75
42	A11	10c black, *lavender*	5.75	5.00
43	A11	15c blue, quadrille paper	9.50	4.75
44	A11	20c red, *grn*	16.00	10.00
45	A11	25c black, *rose*	8.00	6.50
46	A11	30c brown, *bister*	9.50	4.50
47	A11	40c red, *straw*	9.50	4.75
48	A11	50c carmine, *rose*	14.50	10.00
49	A11	75c violet, *org*	9.50	6.50
50	A11	1fr brnz grn, *straw*	22.00	18.00
		Nos. 38-50 (13)	114.25	79.10

Bisected stamps of type A11 are mentioned in note after Madagascar No. 62.

For surcharges see Madagascar #56-57, 61-62.

Perf. 13½x14 stamps are counterfeits.

POSTAGE DUE STAMPS

D1

D2

1891 Unwmk. Litho. *Imperf.*

J1	D1	5c violet	175.00	57.50
J2	D2	50c black	185.00	72.50

Excellent counterfeits exist of Nos. J1-J2.

Postage Due Stamps of French Colonies Overprinted Like Nos. 13-24

1892

J3	D1	1c black	97.50	57.50
J4	D1	2c black	97.50	47.50
a.		Inverted overprint	325.00	210.00
J5	D1	3c black	97.50	50.00
J6	D1	4c black	97.50	47.50
J7	D1	5c black	97.50	57.50
J8	D1	10c black	25.00	22.50
a.		Inverted overprint	325.00	225.00
J9	D1	15c black	25.00	22.50
a.		Double overprint	475.00	400.00
J10	D1	20c black	160.00	92.50
a.		Double overprint	475.00	400.00
J11	D1	30c black	90.00	47.50
a.		Inverted overprint	325.00	225.00
J12	D1	60c black	875.00	650.00
J13	D1	1fr brown	2,200.	1,150.

DOMINICA

ˌdä-mə-ˈnē-kə

LOCATION — The largest island of the Windward group in the West Indies. Southeast of Puerto Rico.
AREA — 290 sq. mi.
POP. — 74,859 (1981)
CAPITAL — Roseau

Formerly a Presidency of the Leeward Islands, Dominica became a separate colony under the governor of the Windward Islands on January 1, 1940.

12 Pence = 1 Shilling
20 Shillings = 1 Pound
100 Cents = 1 Dollar (1949)

Catalogue values for unused stamps in this country are for Never Hinged items, beginning with Scott 112.

PRE-STAMP POSTAL MARKINGS

Crowned Circle handstamp type I is pictured in the Crowned Circle Handstamps and Great Britain Used Abroad section.

1845

A1	I	"Dominica" crowned circle handstamp in red, on cover	625.00

This marking was used in black as a cancel from 1874 to 1883.

STAMPS OF GREAT BRITAIN USED IN DOMINICA

Numeral cancellation type A is pictured in the Crowned Circle Handstamps and Great Britain Used Abroad section.

1858-60

A07 (Roseau)

A2	A	1p rose red (#20)	310.00
A3	A	2p blue (#29, P7)	850.00
A4	A	4p rose (#26)	375.00
A5	A	6p lilac (#27)	350.00
A6	A	1sh green (#28)	1,600.

Queen Victoria — A1

Perf. 12½

1874, May 4 Typo. Wmk. 1

1	A1	1p violet	170.00	55.00
2	A1	6p green	625.00	115.00
3	A1	1sh deep lilac rose	375.00	80.00
		Nos. 1-3 (3)	1,170.	250.00

During 1875-87 some issues were manuscript dated with village names. These are considered postally used. Stamps with entire village names sell for much more, starting at $100.

1877-79 ***Perf. 14***

4	A1	½p bister ('79)	14.50	*57.50*
5	A1	1p violet	7.00	2.30
a.		Diagonal or vertical half used as ½p on cover		2,100.
6	A1	2½p red brown ('79)	260.00	32.50
7	A1	4p blue ('79)	125.00	4.00
8	A1	6p green	170.00	22.50
9	A1	1sh dp lilac rose	140.00	57.50
		Nos. 4-9 (6)	716.50	176.30

For surcharges see Nos. 10-15.

No. 5 Bisected and Surcharged in Black or Red:

½
a

b

c

1882

10	A1(a)	½p on half of 1p	210.00	47.50
a.		Inverted surcharge	1,150.	900.00
b.		Surcharge tete beche pair	*1,900.*	*1,750.*
11	A1(b)	½p on half of 1p	72.50	27.50
a.		Surch. reading downward	72.50	27.50
b.		Double surcharge	900.00	
12	A1(c)	½p on half of 1p (R)	35.00	19.00
a.		Inverted surcharge	1,150.	550.00
b.		Double surcharge	1,850.	750.00
		Nos. 10-12 (3)	317.50	94.00

The existence of genuine copies of No. 10b has been questioned.

Nos. 8 and 9 Surcharged in Black

1886

13	A1	½p on 6p green	6.50	6.00
14	A1	1p on 6p green	*24,000.*	*12,500.*
15	A1	1p on 1sh	16.00	*19.00*
a.		Double surcharge	6,250.	3,500.

All copies of No. 14 may have small pin marks which may have been part of the surcharging process.

1883-89 Wmk. 2

16	A1	½p bister ('83)	3.75	*11.50*
17	A1	½p green ('86)	1.70	*6.25*
18	A1	1p violet ('86)	32.50	14.00
a.		Half used as ½p on cover		2,200.
19	A1	1p dp carmine ('89) ('87)	3.25	*7.50*
a.		1p rose ('87)	18.00	*20.00*
b.		Vert. half used as ½p on cover		2,100.
20	A1	2½p red brn ('84)	160.00	3.00
21	A1	2½p ultra ('88)	4.25	*5.75*
22	A1	4p gray ('86)	3.75	*5.75*
23	A1	6p orange ('88)	11.00	*55.00*
24	A1	1sh dp lil rose ('88)	180.00	*325.00*
		Nos. 16-24 (9)	400.20	*433.75*

Roseau, Capital of Dominica — A6

King Edward VII — A7

1903 Wmk. 1 ***Perf. 14***

Ordinary Paper

25	A6	½p gray green	4.75	2.90
26	A6	1p car & black	9.50	.90
27	A6	2p brn & gray grn	3.00	*5.25*
28	A6	2½p ultra & blk	6.00	4.75
29	A6	3p black & vio	9.50	4.00
30	A6	6p org brn & blk	5.25	21.00
31	A6	1sh gray grn & red vio	32.50	*47.50*
32	A6	2sh red vio & blk	30.00	*32.50*
33	A6	2sh6p ocher & gray grn	21.00	*85.00*
34	A7	5sh brown & blk	105.00	*160.00*
		Nos. 25-34 (10)	226.50	*363.80*
		Set, ovptd "SPECIMEN"	175.00	

1906-07

Chalky Paper

25a	A6	½p gray green	16.00	*21.00*
26a	A6	1p car & black	32.50	6.75
27a	A6	2p brn & gray grn	30.00	*42.50*
28a	A6	2½p ultra & blk ('07)	24.00	*57.50*
29a	A6	3p black & vio	42.50	*35.00*
31a	A6	1sh gray grn & red vio	85.00	*175.00*

1907-20 Wmk. 3

Chalky Paper

35	A6	½p gray green	4.00	3.75
36	A6	1p car & black	2.40	.50
37	A6	2p brn & gray grn	6.25	*19.00*
38	A6	2½p ultra & black	5.25	25.00
39	A6	3p black & vio	4.75	*16.00*
40	A6	3p vio, *yel*, chalky paper ('09)	3.50	*5.00*
a.		3p vio, *yel*, ordinary paper ('12)	3.50	5.00
b.		3p vio, *pale yel*, ordinary paper ('20)	9.75	18.00
41	A6	6p org brn & blk ('08)	60.00	*95.00*
42	A6	6p vio & dl vio, chalky paper ('09)	11.50	*17.50*
a.		6p vio & dl vio, ordinary paper ('15)	4.00	*20.00*
43	A6	1sh gray grn & red vio	4.50	*62.50*
44	A6	1sh blk, *green*, chalky paper ('10)	3.50	3.25
a.		1sh blk, *green*, ordinary paper ('15)	3.50	*4.50*
45	A6	2sh red vio & blk ('08)	27.50	*37.50*
46	A6	2sh ultra & vio, *bl* ('19)	30.00	*97.50*
47	A6	2sh6p ocher & gray grn ('08)	25.00	*70.00*
48	A6	2sh6p red & blk, *bl* ('20)	30.00	*100.00*
49	A7	5sh brn & blk ('08)	70.00	70.00
		Nos. 35-49 (15)	288.15	*622.50*

For type surcharged see No. 55.

1908-09 Ordinary Paper

50	A6	½p green	3.25	2.75
51	A6	1p scarlet	1.75	.55
a.		1p carmine	3.50	.35
52	A6	2p gray ('09)	4.00	*14.00*
53	A6	2½p ultramarine	9.50	*7.00*
		Nos. 50-53 (4)	18.50	*24.30*

King George V — A8

1914 Chalky Paper ***Perf. 14***

54	A8	5sh grn & scar, *yel*	70.00	*92.50*

Type of 1903 Surcharged

1920

55	A6	1½p on 2½p orange	3.00	*5.25*

1921 Wmk. 4

Ordinary Paper

56	A6	½p green	3.00	*17.50*
57	A6	1p rose red	2.25	*4.50*
58	A6	1½p orange	4.00	*12.50*
59	A6	2p gray	3.50	*4.00*
60	A6	2½p ultra	2.25	*10.00*
61	A6	6p vio & dl vio	3.00	*42.50*
62	A6	2sh ultra & vio, *bl*	37.50	*105.00*
63	A6	2sh6p red & blk, *bl*	37.50	*110.00*
		Nos. 56-63 (8)	93.00	*306.00*

No. 61 is on chalky paper.

Seal of Colony and George V — A9

1923-33 Chalky Paper Wmk. 4

65	A9	½p green & blk	2.00	.70
66	A9	1p violet & blk	2.30	1.90
67	A9	1p scar & black	10.50	1.15
68	A9	1½p car & black	3.25	.75
69	A9	1½p dp brn & blk	10.50	.80
70	A9	2p gray & black	2.00	.55
71	A9	2½p org & black	1.70	*10.50*
72	A9	2½p ultra & black	4.75	2.30
73	A9	3p ultra & black	1.75	*14.00*
74	A9	3p red & blk, *yel*	1.75	1.15
75	A9	4p brown & blk	2.75	*6.25*
76	A9	6p red vio & blk	4.00	*8.00*
77	A9	1sh blk, *emerald*	2.60	*3.25*
78	A9	2sh ultra & blk, *bl*	11.50	*22.50*
79	A9	2sh6p red & blk, *bl*	21.00	*22.50*
80	A9	3sh vio & blk, *yel*	3.75	*14.00*
81	A9	4sh red & blk, *emer*	12.50	*25.00*
82	A9	5sh grn & blk, *yel*	25.00	*55.00*
		Nos. 65-82 (18)	123.60	*190.30*

Issue years: Nos. 80, 82, 1927; Nos. 72, 74, 1928; Nos. 67, 69, 1933; others, 1923.

1923 Wmk. 3

83	A9	3sh vio & blk, *yel*	5.00	*72.50*
84	A9	5sh grn & blk, *yel*	11.00	*57.50*
85	A9	£1 vio & blk, *red*	275.00	*400.00*
		Nos. 83-85 (3)	291.00	*530.00*

Common Design Types pictured following the introduction.

Silver Jubilee Issue

Common Design Type

Perf. 13½x14

1935, May 6 Wmk. 4 Engr.

90	CD301	1p car & blue	.25	.30
91	CD301	1½p gray blk & ultra	.85	1.50
92	CD301	2½p blue & brn	3.00	*3.75*
93	CD301	1sh brt vio & ind	3.00	*5.25*
		Nos. 90-93 (4)	7.10	10.80
		Set, never hinged	15.00	

Coronation Issue

Common Design Type

1937, May 12 ***Perf. 11x11½***

94	CD302	1p dark carmine	.20	.20
95	CD302	1½p brown	.20	.20
96	CD302	2½p deep ultra	.35	*.60*
		Nos. 94-96 (3)	.75	1.00
		Set, never hinged	1.25	

Fresh-Water Lake — A10

Layou River — A11

Picking Limes — A12

Boiling Lake — A13

1938-47 Wmk. 4 ***Perf. 12½***

97	A10	½p grn & red brn	.20	.20
98	A11	1p car & gray	.20	.20
99	A12	1½p rose vio & grn	.20	*.95*
100	A13	2p brn blk & dp rose	.40	*1.25*
101	A12	2½p ultra & rose vio	3.25	2.50
102	A11	3p red brn & ol	.20	*.50*
103	A12	3½p red vio & brt ultra	1.00	*2.10*
104	A10	6p vio & yel grn	.50	*1.60*
105	A10	7p org brn & grn	.85	*1.75*
106	A13	1sh olive & vio	1.75	1.60
107	A11	2sh red vio & blk	4.00	*10.00*
108	A10	2sh6p scar ver & blk	8.75	6.50

109 A11 5sh dk brn & bl 4.75 *10.00*
110 A13 10sh dl org & blk 9.75 *19.00*
Nos. 97-110 (14) 35.80 *58.15*
Set, never hinged 60.00

Issued: 3½p, 7p, 2sh, 10sh, 10/15/47; others, 8/15/38.

King George VI — A14

1940, Apr. 15 Photo. *Perf. 14½x14*
111 A14 ¼p brown violet .20 .20

Catalogue values for unused stamps in this section, from this point to the end of the section, are for Never Hinged items.

Peace Issue
Common Design Type

1946, Oct. 14 Engr. *Perf. 13½x14*
112 CD303 1p carmine .20 .20
113 CD303 3½p deep blue .20 .20

Silver Wedding Issue
Common Design Types

1948, Dec. 1 Photo. *Perf. 14x14½*
114 CD304 1p scarlet .25 .25

Engraved; Name Typographed
Perf. 11½x11
115 CD305 10sh orange brn 14.50 *30.00*

UPU Issue
Common Design Types
Engr.: Name Typo. on 6c and 12c

1949, Oct. 10 *Perf. 13½, 11x11½*
116 CD306 5c blue .20 .20
117 CD307 6c chocolate 1.10 1.10
118 CD308 12c rose violet .55 .55
119 CD309 24c olive .30 .30
Nos. 116-119 (4) 2.15 2.15

University Issue
Common Design Types

1951, Feb. 16 Engr. *Perf. 14x14½*
120 CD310 3c purple & green .60 .40
121 CD311 12c dp car & dk bl grn .80 .60

George VI A15

Drying Cocoa A16

Picking Oranges — A17

Designs: 2c and 60c, Carib Baskets. 3c and 48c, Lime Plantation. 4c, Picking Oranges. 5c, Bananas. 6c, Botanical Gardens. 8c, Drying Vanilla Beans. 12c and $1.20, Fresh Water Lake. 14c, Layou River. 24c, Boiling Lake.

Perf. 14½x14
1951, July 1 Photo. Wmk. 4
122 A15 ½c brown .20 .20

Perf. 13x13½
Engr.
123 A16 1c red org & blk .20 .25
124 A16 2c dp grn & red brn .20 .20
125 A16 3c red vio & bl grn .20 .60
126 A16 4c dk brn & brn org .40 .70
127 A16 5c rose red & blk .95 .25
128 A16 6c org brn & ol grn 1.00 .25
129 A16 8c dp bl & dp grn .65 .60
130 A16 12c emer & gray .50 1.60
131 A16 14c pur & blue 1.10 1.60
132 A16 24c rose car & red vio .90 .25
133 A16 48c red org & bl grn 3.00 *7.25*
134 A16 60c gray & car 3.00 *6.00*
135 A16 $1.20 gray & emer 4.75 *6.00*

Perf. 13½x13
136 A17 $2.40 gray & org 26.00 *35.00*
Nos. 122-136 (15) 43.05 *60.75*

Nos. 125, 127, 129 and 131 Overprinted in Black or Carmine

1951, Oct. 15 *Perf. 13x13½*
137 A16 3c red vio & bl green .25 .25
138 A16 5c rose red & black .45 .45
139 A16 8c dp blue & dp grn (C) .55 .55
140 A16 14c purple & blue (C) .90 .90
Nos. 137-140 (4) 2.15 2.15

Adoption of a new constitution for the Windward Islands, 1951.

WAR TAX STAMPS

No. 50 Surcharged in Red

1916 Wmk. 3 *Perf. 14*
MR1 A6 ½p on ½p green .80 *.80*

No. 50 Overprinted in Black

1918
MR2 A6 ½p green 3.25 *6.75*

Nos. 50, 40 in Black or Red

1918
MR3 A6 ½p green .20 *.55*
MR4 A6 3p violet, *yel* (R) 1.60 *4.50*

Type of 1908-09 Surcharged in Red

1919
MR5 A6 1½p on 2½p orange .20 *.60*

DOMINICAN REPUBLIC

də-ˈmi-ni-kən ri-ˈpə-blik

LOCATION — Comprises about two-thirds of the island of Hispaniola in the West Indies.
GOVT. — Republic
AREA — 18,700 sq. mi.
POP. — 5,982,000 (est. 1983)
CAPITAL — Santo Domingo

8 Reales = 1 Peso
100 Centavos = 1 Peso (1880)
100 Centimos = 1 Franco (1883)
100 Centavos = 1 Peso (1885)

Watermarks

Wmk. 115 — Diamonds

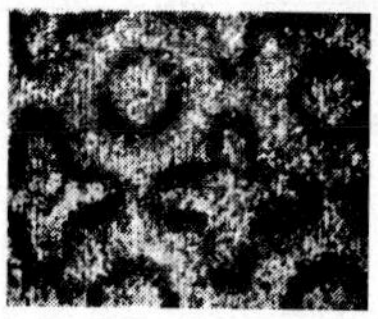
Wmk. 116 — Crosses and Circles

FORERUNNERS

BRITISH POST OFFICES IN DOMINICAN REPUBLIC

Puerto Plata

British P.O. opened by 1867; closed 1871; reopened 1876; closed 1881

Stamps of Great Britain, Canceled C86, or with Circular Date Stamp

1876-81
A1 ½p rose red (#58, P 10, 12, 14), *value from* 80.00
A2 1p rose red (#33, P 123, 130, 136, 146, 151, 178, 199, 200, 205, 217) *value from* 62.50
A3 1½p lake red (#32, P 3) 110.00
A4 2p blue (#30, P 13, 14), *value from* 80.00
A5 2½p claret (#67, P 13, 14), *value from* 160.00
A6 3p rose (#61, P 18) 92.50
A7 4p vermilion (#43, P 14) 92.50
A8 4p vermilion (#69, P 15) 350.00
A9 4p pale olive green (#70, P 15) 225.00
A10 6p violet (#51, P 8) —
A11 6p gray (#62, P 15) 80.00
A12 8p orange (#73) 350.00
A13 1sh green (#54, P 4, 7) *value from* 70.00
A14 1sh green (#64, P 11-13) *value from* 80.00
A15 2sh blue (#55) 250.00
A16 5sh rose (#57, P 2) —

Santo Domingo

British P.O. opened by 1867; closed 1871; reopened 1876; closed 1881

Stamps of Great Britain, Canceled C87, or with Circular Date Stamp

1876-81
A17 ½p rose red (#58, P 5, 6, 8, 10, 11, 13), *value from* 92.50
A18 1p rose red (#33, P 146, 154, 171, 173, 174, 176, 178, 186, 190, 197, 220) *value from* 70.00
A19 1½p lake red (#32, P 3) 115.00
A20 2p blue (#30, P 13, 14), *value from* 100.00
A21 3p rose (#61, P 18) —
A22 4p vermilion (#43, P 11, 12, 14) 100.00
A23 4p vermilion (#69, P 15) 375.00
A24 4p pale olive green (#70, P 15) 260.00
A25 6p gray (#62, P 15) —
A26 8p orange (#73) —
A27 9p bister (#52) —
A28 1sh green (#54, P 4) —
A29 1sh green (#64, P 10-13) *value from* 92.50
A30 2sh blue (#55) —

Dominican Republic

Coat of Arms
A1 A2

1865 Unwmk. Typo. *Imperf.*
Wove Paper
1 A1 ½r black, *rose* 600. 600.
2 A1 1r black, *dp green* 975. 950.

Twelve varieties of each.

Laid Paper
3 A2 ½r black, *pale green* 550. 475.
4 A2 1r black, *straw* 1,700. 1,100.

Twelve varieties of the ½r, ten of the 1r.

A3

A4

1866 Laid Paper Unwmk.
5 A3 ½r black, *straw* 200. 150.
6 A3 1r black, *pale green* 2,500. 2,000.
7 A4 1r black, *pale green* 175. 125.

Nos. 5-8 have 21 varieties (sheets of 21).

Wmk. 115
8 A3 1r black, *pale green* 13,000. 13,000.
a. "CORREOS" and "Un Real" doubled 21,000.

The unique example of No. 8a is centered in the grade of fine, has a shallow thin spot and pinhole.

1866-67 Wove Paper Unwmk.
9 A3 ½r black, *rose* ('67) 47.50 47.50
10 A3 1r blk, *pale green* 85.00 75.00
a. Inscription dbl., top & bottom *400.00* *400.00*
11 A3 1r black, *blue* ('67) 50.00 30.00
a. 1r black, *light blue* ('67) 50.00 30.00
b. No space btwn. "Un" and "real" *600.00* 500.00
c. Without inscription at top & bottom *1,500.* 1,000.
d. Inscription invtd., top & bottom —
Nos. 9-11 (3) 182.50 152.50

1867-71
Pelure Paper
13 A3 ½r black, *rose* 150.00 75.00
15 A3 ½r black, *lav* ('68) 250.00 210.00
a. Without inscription at top and bottom 525.00
b. Dbl. inscriptions, one invtd. *425.00*
16 A3 ½r black, *grnsh gray* ('68) 260.00 225.00
17 A3 ½r black, *yellow* ('68) 12,000.
18 A3 ½r black, *ol* ('69) 3,000. 5,500.
22 A3 1r black, *blue* 4,000.
23 A3 1r black, *lavender* 225.00 200.00
24 A4 1r black, *rose* ('68) 225.00 225.00
25 A4 1r black, *mag* ('69) 2,250. 1,300.
26 A4 1r black, *sal* ('71) 300.00 225.00

Value for No. 17 is for an example with very fine centering and small faults. Value for No. 22 is for a faulty example with very fine centering and appearance.

1870-73
Ordinary Paper
27 A3 ½r black, *magenta* 2,500. 4,750.
28 A3 ½r blue, *rose* (blk inscription) ('71) 50.00 42.50
a. Blue inscription 500.00 500.00
b. Without inscription at top and bottom
29 A3 ½r black, *yel* ('73) 30.00 21.00
a. Without inscription at top and bottom 700.00 700.00

30 A4 1r black, *vio* ('73) 30.00 21.00
a. Without inscription at top and bottom 700.00 700.00
31 A4 1r black, *dk grn* 60.00 50.00

Nos. 9-31 have 21 varieties (sheets of 21). Nos. 29 and 30 are known pin-perforated, unofficially.

Bisects are known of several of the early 1r stamps.

A5

A6

1879 ***Perf. 12½x13***
32 A5 ½r violet 2.50 1.50
a. Imperf., pair 9.00 9.00
b. Horiz. pair, imperf. vert. 17.00
33 A5 ½r violet, *bluish* 2.50 1.50
a. Imperf., pair 9.00 7.50
34 A5 1r carmine 3.50 1.50
a. Imperf., pair 11.50 9.00
b. Perf. 13 11.50 7.50
c. Perf. 13x12½ 11.50 7.50
35 A5 1r carmine, *sal* 2.50 1.50
a. Imperf., pair 8.25 8.25
Nos. 32-35 (4) 11.00 6.00

In 1891 15 stamps of 1879-83 were surcharged "U P U," new values and crossed diagonal lines.

1880 **Typo.** ***Rouletted in Color***
36 A6 1c green 1.25 .90
b. Laid paper 50.00 50.00
37 A6 2c red 1.00 .75
a. Pelure paper 40.00 40.00
b. Laid paper 40.00 40.00
38 A6 5c blue 1.25 .60
39 A6 10c rose 3.25 .90
40 A6 20c brown 2.00 .75
41 A6 25c violet 2.25 1.10
42 A6 50c orange 2.50 1.50
43 A6 75c ultra 5.00 2.50
a. Laid paper 40.00 40.00
44 A6 1p gold 6.50 4.00
a. Laid paper 50.00 50.00
b. Double impression 42.50 42.50
Nos. 36-44 (9) 25.00 13.00

1881

Network Covering Stamp

45 A6 1c green .90 .45
46 A6 2c red .90 .45
47 A6 5c blue 1.25 .45
48 A6 10c rose 1.50 .60
49 A6 20c brown 1.50 .80
50 A6 25c violet 1.75 .90
51 A6 50c orange 2.00 1.25
52 A6 75c ultra 6.00 4.00
53 A6 1p gold 8.00 6.50
Nos. 45-53 (9) 23.80 15.40

Preceding Issues (Type A6) Surch. with Value in New Currency:

a

b

5

céntimos.

c

d

1

Franco.

e

1

franco

f

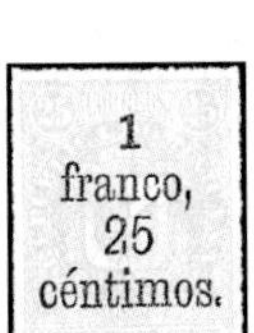

g

5

h francos.

5

francos i

1883

Without Network

54 (a) 5c on 1c green 1.40 1.50
b. Inverted surcharge 21.00 21.00
c. Surcharged "25 céntimos" 50.00 50.00
d. Surcharged "10 céntimos" 27.50 27.50
55 (b) 5c on 1c green 25.00 9.00
b. Double surcharge 100.00
c. Inverted surcharge 65.00 65.00
56 (c) 5c on 1c green 17.00 9.50
b. Surcharged "10 céntimos" 35.00 35.00
c. Surcharged "25 céntimos" 37.50 37.50
57 (a) 10c on 2c red 5.00 3.00
a. Inverted surcharge 27.50 27.50
d. Surcharged "5 céntimos" 52.50 52.50
e. Surcharged "25 céntimos" 75.00 75.00
58 (c) 10c on 2c red 4.50 3.50
a. "Céntimso"
b. Inverted surcharge 37.50 37.50
c. Surcharged "25 céntimos" 60.00 60.00
d. "10" omitted 60.00
59 (a) 25c on 5c blue 6.50 4.00
a. Surcharged "5 céntimos" 52.50
b. Surcharged "10 céntimos" 52.50 52.50
c. Surcharged "50 céntimos" 75.00 75.00
d. Inverted surcharge 50.00 50.00
60 (c) 25c on 5c blue 7.50 3.50
a. Inverted surcharge 45.00 37.50
b. Surcharged "10 céntimos" 45.00 37.50
e. "25" omitted 75.00
f. Surcharged on back 75.00
61 (a) 50c on 10c rose 25.00 11.50
a. Inverted surcharge 50.00 45.00
62 (c) 50c on 10c rose 35.00 17.50
a. Inverted surcharge 52.50 52.50
63 (d) 1fr on 20c brown 15.00 9.75
64 (e) 1fr on 20c brown 17.50 9.75
a. Comma after "Franco," 27.50 27.50
65 (f) 1fr on 20c brown 25.00 17.50
a. Inverted surcharge 75.00
66 (g) 1fr25c on 25c violet 21.00 15.00
a. Inverted surcharge 65.00 65.00
67 (g) 2fr50c on 50c orange 15.00 10.50
a. Inverted surcharge 35.00 27.50
68 (g) 3fr75c on 75c ultra 27.50 25.00
b. Inverted surcharge 60.00 60.00
c. Laid paper 75.00 75.00
70 (i) 5fr on 1p gold 550.00 500.00
a. "s" of "francos" inverted 700.00 700.00

With Network

71 (a) 5c on 1c green 3.00 2.50
b. Inverted surcharge 22.50 22.50
c. Double surcharge 22.50 22.50
d. Surcharged "25 céntimos" 42.50 42.50
e. "5" omitted 75.00 75.00
72 (b) 5c on 1c green 21.00 9.00
b. Inverted surcharge 60.00 60.00
73 (c) 5c on 1c green 27.50 11.50
b. Surcharged "10 céntimos" 50.00 42.50
c. Surcharged "25 céntimos" 60.00
74 (a) 10c on 2c red 3.75 2.25
a. Surcharged "5 céntimos" 52.50 45.00
b. Surcharged "25 céntimos" 67.50 67.50
c. "10" omitted 57.50
75 (c) 10c on 2c red 3.00 2.00
a. Inverted surcharge 30.00 17.00
76 (a) 25c on 5c blue 7.50 3.50
a. Surcharged "10 céntimos" 75.00
b. Surcharged "5 céntimos" 60.00
c. Surcharged "50 céntimos" 67.50
77 (c) 25c on 5c blue 60.00 30.00
a. Inverted surcharge
b. Surcharged on back
78 (a) 50c on 10c rose 25.00 7.50
a. Inverted surcharge 50.00 30.00
b. Surcharged "25 céntimos" 60.00
79 (c) 50c on 10c rose 30.00 9.50
a. Inverted surcharge 60.00
80 (d) 1fr on 20c brown 12.00 9.75
81 (e) 1fr on 20c brown 14.50 12.50
a. Comma after "Franco" 35.00 35.00
b. Inverted surcharge 75.00
82 (f) 1fr on 20c brown 25.00 20.00
83 (g) 1fr25c on 25c violet 45.00 30.00
a. Inverted surcharge 75.00
84 (g) 2fr50c on 50c orange 19.00 12.50
a. Inverted surcharge 35.00 27.50
85 (g) 3fr75c on 75c ultra 45.00 42.50
86 (h) 5fr on 1p gold 140.00 140.00
a. Inverted surcharge
87 (i) 5fr on 1p gold 190.00 190.00

Many minor varieties exist in Nos. 54-87: accent on "i" of "centimos"; "5" with straight top; "1" with straight serif.

A7

A7a

1885-91 **Engr.** ***Perf. 12***
88 A7 1c green .90 .45
89 A7 2c vermilion .90 .45
90 A7 5c blue 1.25 .45
91 A7a 10c orange 2.00 .60
92 A7a 20c dark brown 2.00 .75
93 A7a 50c violet ('91) 7.00 6.00
94 A7 1p carmine ('91) 18.00 12.00
95 A7 2p red brown ('91) 22.50 14.00
Nos. 88-95 (8) 54.55 34.70

Nos. 93, 94, 95 were issued without gum.
Imperf. varieties are proofs.
For surcharges see Nos. 166-168.

Coat of Arms — A8

1895 ***Perf. 12½x14***
96 A8 1c green 1.10 .45
97 A8 2c orange red 1.10 .45
98 A8 5c blue 1.10 .45
99 A8 10c orange 2.25 1.40
Nos. 96-99 (4) 5.55 2.75

Exist imperforate but were not issued.

1897 ***Perf. 14***
96a A8 1c green 1.40 .50
97a A8 2c orange red 8.00 .75
98a A8 5c blue 1.40 .75
99a A8 10c orange 2.75 1.50
Nos. 96a-99a (4) 13.55 3.50

Voyage of Diego Méndez from Jamaica — A9

Enriquillo's Revolt — A10

Sarcophagus of Columbus
A11

"Española" Guarding Remains of Columbus
A12

Toscanelli Replying to Columbus
A13

Bartolomé de las Casas Defending Indians — A14

Columbus at Salamanca
A15

Columbus' Mausoleum
A16

1899, Feb. 27 **Litho.** ***Perf. 11½***
100 A9 1c brown violet 5.00 4.00
102 A10 2c rose red 1.75 .70
103 A11 5c blue 2.00 .70
104 A12 10c orange 4.25 1.25
a. Tête bêche pair 42.50 42.50
105 A13 20c brown 6.50 5.00
106 A14 50c yellow green 8.00 6.00
a. Tête bêche pair 57.50 57.50
107 A15 1p black, *gray bl* 20.00 15.00
108 A16 2p bister brown 37.50 37.50

1900, Jan.
109 A11 ¼c black .70 *1.25*
110 A15 ½c black .70 *1.25*
110A A9 1c gray green .70 .50
Nos. 100-110A (11) 87.10 73.15

Nos. 100-110A were issued to raise funds for a Columbus mausoleum.

Imperf., Pairs

100a A9 1c brown violet 15.00
102a A10 2c rose red 5.00
103a A11 5c blue 5.75
104b A12 10c orange 8.75
105a A13 20c brown 15.00
106b A14 50c yellow green 17.50
c. As "b," tête bêche pair 125.00
107a A15 1p black, *gray blue* 42.50
108a A16 2p bister brown 70.00
109a A11 ¼c black 2.10 *2.50*
110b A15 ½c black 2.10 *2.50*
110c A9 1c gray green 3.50

Map of Hispaniola — A17

A18

1900, Oct. 21 **Unwmk.** ***Perf. 14***
111 A17 ¼c dark blue .65 .40
112 A17 ½c rose .65 .40
113 A17 1c olive green .65 .40
114 A17 2c deep green .65 .40
115 A17 5c red brown .65 .40
a. Vertical pair, imperf. between 17.50

Perf. 12
116 A17 10c orange .65 .40
117 A17 20c lilac 2.75 2.10
a. 20c rose (error) 5.75 5.75
118 A17 50c black 2.50 2.25
119 A17 1p brown 2.75 2.25
Nos. 111-119 (9) 11.90 9.00

Several varieties in design are known in this issue. They were deliberately made. Counterfeits of Nos. 111-119 abound.

1901-06 **Typo.** ***Perf. 14***
120 A18 ½c carmine & vio .65 .35
121 A18 ½c blk & org ('05) 1.50 .85
122 A18 ½c grn & blk ('06) .80 .30
123 A18 1c ol grn & vio .65 .20
124 A18 1c blk & ultra ('05) 1.50 .70
125 A18 1c car & blk ('06) 1.00 .45
126 A18 2c dp grn & vio .70 .20
127 A18 2c blk & vio ('05) 2.00 .60
128 A18 2c org brn & blk ('06) 1.00 .20
129 A18 5c org brn & vio .75 .25
130 A18 5c black & cl ('05) 2.25 1.00
131 A18 5c blue & blk ('06) 1.25 .30
132 A18 10c orange & vio 1.25 .35
133 A18 10c blk & grn ('05) 3.75 2.00
134 A18 10c red vio & blk ('06) 1.25 .35
135 A18 20c brn vio & vio 2.25 .70
136 A18 20c blk & ol ('05) 11.50 7.50
137 A18 20c ol grn & blk ('06) 6.50 2.50
138 A18 50c gray blk & vio 7.00 5.00
139 A18 50c blk & red brn ('05) 40.00 30.00
140 A18 50c brn & blk ('06) 7.50 7.00
141 A18 1p brn & vio 16.00 9.50
142 A18 1p blk & gray ('05) 175.00 *200.00*

143 A18 1p violet & blk ('06) 17.50 12.00
Nos. 120-143 (24) 303.55 282.30

Issued: 11/15/01; 5/11/05; 8/17/06.
See #172-176. For surcharges see #151-156.

Francisco Sánchez — A19

Juan Pablo Duarte — A20

Ramón Mella — A21

Ft. Santo Domingo — A22

1902, Feb. 25 Engr. *Perf. 12*
144 A19 1c dk green & blk .25 .25
145 A20 2c scarlet & blk .25 .25
146 A20 5c blue & blk .25 .25
147 A19 10c orange & blk .25 .25
148 A21 12c purple & blk .25 .25
149 A21 20c rose & blk .35 .35
150 A22 50c brown & blk .50 .50
Nos. 144-150 (7) 2.10 2.10

Center Inverted
144a A19 1c 5.00 3.50
145a A20 2c 5.00 3.50
146a A20 5c 5.00 3.50
148a A21 12c 5.00 3.50
149a A21 20c 5.00 3.50
150a A22 50c 5.00 3.50
Nos. 144a-150a (6) 30.00 21.00

400th anniversary of Santo Domingo.
Imperforate varieties of Nos. 144 to 150 were never sold to the public.

Nos. 138, 141 Surcharged in Black

1904, Aug.
151 A18 2c on 50c 7.00 6.00
152 A18 2c on 1p 10.50 7.00
b. "2" omitted 50.00 50.00
153 A18 5c on 50c 3.75 2.10
154 A18 5c on 1p 4.00 3.50
155 A18 10c on 50c 7.00 6.50
156 A18 10c on 1p 7.00 6.50
Nos. 151-156 (6) 39.25 31.60

Inverted Surcharge
151a A18 2c on 50c 14.00 14.00
152a A18 2c on 1p 14.00 14.00
c. As "a," "2" omitted 80.00 80.00
153a A18 5c on 50c 5.00 3.50
154a A18 5c on 1p 7.00 6.50
155a A18 10c on 50c 14.00 14.00
156a A18 10c on 1p 10.00 10.00
Nos. 151a-156a (6) 64.00 62.00

Official Stamps of 1902 Overprinted

Red Overprint
1904, Aug. 16
157 O1 5c dk blue & blk 5.00 2.75
a. Inverted overprint 6.50 5.50

Black Overprint
158 O1 2c scarlet & blk 12.50 4.00
a. Inverted overprint 15.00 5.00
159 O1 5c dk blue & blk 3,500. 3,500.
160 O1 10c yellow grn & blk 9.25 9.00
a. Inverted overprint 12.50 12.50

Surcharged

161 O1 1c on 20c yellow & blk 4.00 2.75
a. Inverted surcharge 6.50 5.00

Nos. J1-J2 Surcharged or Overprinted

Surcharged "CENTAVOS"
1904-05
Black Surcharge
162 D1 1c on 2c olive gray 250.00 200.00
a. "entavos" —
b. "Dominican" 350.00 300.00
c. "Centavo" 350.00 300.00

Carmine Surcharge or Overprint
163 D1 1c on 2c olive gray 2.25 1.00
a. Inverted surcharge 3.50 2.50
b. "Domihicana" 15.00 15.00
c. As "b," inverted 40.00 40.00
d. "Dominican" 10.50 10.50
e. "Centavos" omitted 30.00 30.00
g. "entavos" 30.00
163F D1 1c on 4c olive gray 35.00 7.00
164 D1 2c olive gray .80 .50
a. "Domihicana" 11.00 11.00
b. Inverted overprint 1.90 1.90
c. As "a," inverted 25.00 25.00
d. "Dominican" 5.75 5.75
e. "Centavo" omitted 12.50 10.00
f. "entavos" 12.50 12.50
g. As "f," inverted 40.00 40.00
h. As "d," inverted 40.00 40.00

Surcharged "CENTAVO"
165 D1 1c on 4c olive gray .80 .65
a. "Domihicana" 10.00 10.00
c. Inverted surcharge 1.75 1.75
d. "1" omitted 3.50 3.50
e. As "a," inverted 32.50 32.50
f. As "d," inverted 40.00 40.00
g. Double surcharge 30.00 30.00

No. 92 Surcharged in Red

1905, Apr. 4
166 A7a 2c on 20c dk brown 7.00 5.00
a. Inverted surcharge 15.00 15.00
167 A7a 5c on 20c dk brown 4.00 1.75
a. Inverted surcharge 16.00 16.00
b. Double surcharge 25.00 25.00
168 A7a 10c on 20c dk brown 7.00 5.00
Nos. 166-168 (3) 18.00 11.75

Nos. 166-168 exist with inverted "A" for "V" in "CENTAVOS" in surcharge.

Nos. J2, J4, J3 Surcharged:

1906, Jan. 16 *Perf. 14*
Red Surcharge
169 D1 1c on 4c olive gray .85 .50
a. Inverted surcharge 10.50 10.50
b. Double surcharge 25.00

1906, May 1
Black Surcharge
170 D1 1c on 10c olive gray 1.00 .40
a. Inverted surcharge 10.50 10.50
b. Double surcharge 14.00 14.00
c. "OMINICANA" 20.00 20.00
d. As "c," inverted 150.00
171 D1 2c on 5c olive gray 1.00 .40
a. Inverted surcharge 10.50 10.50
b. Double surcharge 35.00

The varieties small "C" or small "A" in "REPUBLICA" are found on #169, 170, 171.

Arms Type of 1901-06
1907-10 Wmk. 116
172 A18 ½c grn & blk ('08) .75 .20
173 A18 1c carmine & blk .75 .20
174 A18 2c orange brn & blk .75 .20
175 A18 5c blue & blk .75 .25
176 A18 10c red vio & blk ('10) 8.00 1.00
Nos. 172-176 (5) 11.00 1.85

No. O6 Overprinted in Red

1911, July 11 *Perf. 13½x14, 13½x13*
177 O2 2c scarlet & black 1.25 .50
a. "HABILITAOO" 8.75 6.00
b. Inverted overprint 21.00
c. Double overprint 21.00

A23

Juan Pablo Duarte — A24

1911-13 *Perf. 14*
Center in Black
178 A23 ½c orange ('13) .25 .20
179 A23 1c green .25 .20
180 A23 2c carmine .25 .20
181 A23 5c gray blue ('13) .75 .20
182 A23 10c red violet 1.25 .45
183 A23 20c olive green 8.00 7.00
184 A23 50c yellow brn ('12) 3.25 3.25
185 A23 1p violet ('12) 5.50 3.50
Nos. 178-185 (8) 19.50 15.00

See Nos. 230-232.

1914, Apr. 13 *Perf. 13x14*
Background Red, White and Blue
186 A24 ½c orange & blk .55 .30
187 A24 1c green & blk .55 .30
188 A24 2c rose & blk .55 .30
189 A24 5c slate & blk .55 .40
190 A24 10c magenta & blk 1.25 .70
191 A24 20c olive grn & blk 2.25 *1.90*
192 A24 50c brown & blk 3.00 *2.75*
193 A24 1p dull lilac & blk 5.00 4.00
Nos. 186-193 (8) 13.70 10.65

Cent. of the birth of Juan Pablo Duarte (1813-1876), patriot and revolutionary.

Official Stamps of 1909-12 Surcharged in Violet or Overprinted in Red:

a

b

1915, Feb. *Perf. 13½x13, 13½x14*
194 O2 (a) ½c on 20c orange & blk .50 .35
a. Inverted surcharge 6.00 6.00
b. Double surcharge 8.75 8.75
c. "Habilitado" omitted 5.25 5.25
195 O2 (b) 1c blue grn & blk .80 .25
a. Inverted overprint 6.00 6.00
b. Double overprint 7.00
c. Overprinted "1915" only 12.50
196 O2 (b) 2c scarlet & blk .80 .25
a. Inverted overprint 5.25 5.25
b. Double overprint 7.75 7.75
c. Overprinted "1915" only 8.75
d. "1915" double
197 O2 (b) 5c dk blue & blk 1.00 .25
a. Inverted overprint 7.00 7.00
b. Double overprint 8.75 8.75
c. Double ovpt., one invtd. 27.50
d. Overprinted "1915" only 8.50
198 O2 (b) 10c yel grn & blk 2.75 2.40
a. Inverted overprint 15.00
199 O2 (b) 20c orange & blk 9.00 6.50
a. "Habilitado" omitted
Nos. 194-199 (6) 14.85 10.00

#194, 196-198 are known with both perforations. #195, 199 are only perf. 13½x13.
The variety capital "I" for "1" in "Habilitado" occurs once in each sheet in all denominations.

A25

Type of 1911-13 Redrawn
Overprinted "1915" in Red

TWO CENTAVOS:
Type I — "DOS" in small letters.
Type II — "DOS" in larger letters with white dot at each end of the word.

1915 Unwmk. Litho. *Perf. 11½*
200 A25 ½c violet & blk .75 .20
a. Imperf., pair 5.75
201 A25 1c yel brn & blk .75 .20
a. Imperf., pair 6.50
b. Vert. pair, imperf. horiz. 10.50
c. Horiz. pair, imperf. vert. 10.50
202 A25 2c ol grn & blk (I) 3.75 .25
a. Imperf., pair 10.00
203 A25 2c ol grn & blk (II) 6.00 .20
a. Center omitted 87.50
b. Frame omitted 87.50
c. Imperf., pair 15.00
d. Horiz. pair, imperf. vert. 15.00
204 A25 5c magenta & blk 3.25 .25
a. Pair, one without overprint 65.00
b. Imperf., pair 6.50
205 A25 10c gray blue & blk 3.75 .50
a. Imperf., pair 7.75
b. Horiz. pair, imperf. vert. 35.00
206 A25 20c rose red & blk 6.50 1.40
a. Imperf., pair 12.50
207 A25 50c green & blk 8.50 4.00
a. Imperf., pair 25.00
208 A25 1p orange & blk 17.50 7.00
a. Imperf., pair 52.50
Nos. 200-208 (9) 50.75 14.00

Type of 1915 Overprinted "1916" in Red
1916
209 A25 ½c violet & blk 1.25 .20
a. Imperf., pair 21.00
210 A25 1c green & blk 2.00 .20
a. Imperf., pair 21.00

Type of 1915 Overprinted "1917" in Red
1917-19
213 A25 ½c red lilac & blk 2.25 .30
a. Horiz. pair, imperf. btwn. 47.50 47.50
214 A25 1c yellow grn & blk 1.50 .20
a. Vert. pair, imperf. btwn. 50.00
215 A25 2c olive grn & blk 1.40 .20
a. Imperf., pair 35.00
216 A25 5c magenta & blk 16.00 .70
Nos. 213-216 (4) 21.15 1.40

Type of 1915 Overprinted "1919" in Red
1919
219 A25 2c olive grn & blk 10.00 .20

Type of 1915 Overprinted "1920" in Red
1920-27
220 A25 ½c lilac rose & blk .50 .25
a. Horiz. pair, imperf. btwn. 25.00 25.00
b. Inverted overprint
c. Double overprint
d. Double overprint, one invtd.
221 A25 1c yellow grn & blk .75 .20
a. Overprint omitted 70.00
b. Horiz. pair, imperf. btwn. 40.00
222 A25 2c olive grn & blk .75 .20
a. Vertical pair, imperf. between 27.50
223 A25 5c dp rose & blk 9.00 .50
224 A25 10c blue & black 5.00 .25
225 A25 20c rose red & blk ('27) 7.00 .50
226 A25 50c green & blk ('27) 52.50 17.50
Nos. 220-226 (7) 75.50 19.40

Type of 1915 Overprinted "1921" in Red
1921
227 A25 1c yellow grn & blk 3.00 .30
a. Horiz. pair, imperf. btwn. 45.00 45.00
b. Imperf., pair 45.00 45.00
228 A25 2c olive grn & blk 5.00 .30
a. Vert. pair, imperf. btwn. 45.00

Redrawn Design of 1915 without Overprint

1922

230	A25 1c green		2.25	.20
231	A25 2c carmine (II)		2.50	.20
232	A25 5c blue		4.00	.25
	Nos. 230-232 (3)		8.75	.65

Exist imperf.

A26 A27

Second Redrawing

TEN CENTAVOS:

Type I — Numerals 2mm high. "DIEZ" in thick letters with large white dot at each end.

Type II — Numerals 3mm high. "DIEZ" in thin letters with white dot with colored center at each end.

1924-27

233	A26	1c green	.90	.20
a.		Vert. pair, imperf. btwn.	35.00	35.00
234	A26	2c red	.70	.20
235	A26	5c blue	1.10	.20
236	A26	10c pale bl & blk (I) ('26)	12.00	3.00
236A	A26	10c pale bl & blk (II)	22.50	1.10
236B	A26	50c gray grn & blk ('26)	45.00	27.50
237	A26	1p orange & blk ('27)	16.00	10.50
		Nos. 233-237 (7)	98.20	42.70

In the second redrawing the shield has a flat top and the design differs in many details from the stamps of 1911-13 and 1915-22.

1927

238	A27	½c lilac rose & blk	.30	.20

Exhibition Pavilion — A28

1927 **Unwmk.** ***Perf. 12***

239	A28	2c carmine	.80	.50
240	A28	5c ultra	1.75	.50

Natl. and West Indian Exhib. at Santiago de los Caballeros.

Ruins of Columbus' Fortress A29

1928

241	A29	½c lilac rose	.60	.35
242	A29	1c deep green	.50	.20
a.		Horiz. pair, imperf. btwn.	25.00	
243	A29	2c red	.50	.20
244	A29	5c dark blue	1.50	.35
245	A29	10c light blue	1.75	.30
246	A29	20c rose	3.00	.40
247	A29	50c yellow green	10.50	6.50
248	A29	1p orange yellow	27.50	20.00
		Nos. 241-248 (8)	45.85	28.30

Reprints exist of 1c, 2c and 10c.

Issued: 1c, 2c, 10c, Oct. 1; others, Dec.

Horacio Vasquez — A30

Convent of San Ignacio de Loyola — A31

1929, May-June

249	A30	½c dull rose	.50	.30
250	A30	1c gray green	.50	.20
251	A30	2c red	.60	.20
252	A30	5c dark ultra	1.25	.35
253	A30	10c pale blue	1.75	.50
		Nos. 249-253 (5)	4.60	1.55

Signing of the "Frontier" treaty with Haiti. Issue dates: 2c, May; others, June.

Imperf., Pairs

249a	A30	½c	12.50
250a	A30	1c	12.50
251a	A30	2c	12.50
252a	A30	5c	14.00

1930, May 1 ***Perf. 11½***

254	A31	½c red brown	.65	.45
a.		Imperf., pair	55.00	55.00
255	A31	1c deep green	.50	.20
256	A31	2c vermilion	.50	.20
a.		Imperf., pair	60.00	
257	A31	5c deep blue	1.25	.35
258	A31	10c light blue	3.00	1.00
		Nos. 254-258 (5)	5.90	2.20

Cathedral of Santo Domingo, First Church in America A32

1931 ***Perf. 12***

260	A32	1c deep green	.65	.20
a.		Imperf., pair	50.00	
261	A32	2c scarlet	.45	.20
a.		Imperf., pair	50.00	
262	A32	3c violet	.65	.20
263	A32	7c dark blue	2.00	.25
264	A32	8c bister	2.75	.85
265	A32	10c light blue	4.50	1.00
a.		Imperf., pair	35.00	
		Nos. 260-265 (6)	11.00	2.70

Issued: 3c-7c, Aug. 1; others, July 11.

For overprint see No. RAC8.

A33

Overprinted or Surcharged in Black

1932, Dec. 20 ***Perf. 12***

Cross in Red

265B	A33	1c yellow green	.50	.45
265C	A33	3c on 2c violet	.70	.55
265D	A33	5c blue	4.00	4.25
265E	A33	7c on 10c turq bl	5.50	5.75
		Nos. 265B-265E (4)	10.70	11.00

Proceeds of sale given to Red Cross. Valid Dec. 20 to Jan. 5, 1933.

Inverted and pairs, one without surcharge or overprint, exist on Nos. 265B-265D, as well as missing letters.

Fernando Arturo de Merino (1833-1906) as President — A35

Cathedral of Santo Domingo A36

Designs: ½c, 5c, 8c, Tomb of Merino. 1c, 3c, 10c, as Archbishop.

1933, Feb. 27 **Engr.** ***Perf. 14***

266	A35	½c lt violet	.45	.35
267	A35	1c yellow green	.60	.25
268	A35	2c lt red	1.00	.75
269	A35	3c deep violet	.70	.30
270	A35	5c dark blue	.80	.35
271	A35	7c ultra	1.40	.50
272	A35	8c dark green	1.75	.75
273	A35	10c orange yel	1.50	.50
274	A35	20c carmine rose	3.00	1.25
275	A36	50c lemon	11.25	6.00
276	A36	1p dark brown	24.75	14.00
		Nos. 266-276 (11)	47.20	25.00

For surcharges see Nos. G1-G7.

Tower of Homage, Ozama Fortress — A37

1932 **Litho.** ***Perf. 12***

278	A37	1c green	1.25	.20
279	A37	3c violet	.80	.20

Issue dates: 1c, July 2; 3c, June 22.

"CORREOS" added at left

1933, May 28

283	A37	1c dark green	.40	.20

President Rafael L. Trujillo
A38 A39

1933, Aug. 16 **Engr.** ***Perf. 14***

286	A38	1c yellow grn & blk	.75	.35
287	A39	3c dp violet & blk	.90	.35
288	A38	7c ultra & blk	2.00	.75
		Nos. 286-288 (3)	3.65	1.45

42nd birthday of President Rafael Leonidas Trujillo Molina.

San Rafael Bridge — A40

1934 **Litho.** ***Perf. 12***

289	A40	½c dull violet	.70	.35
290	A40	1c dark green	.90	.20
291	A40	3c violet	1.40	.20
		Nos. 289-291 (3)	3.00	.75

Opening of San Rafael Bridge.

Issue dates: ½c, 3c, Mar. 3; 1c, Feb. 17.

Trujillo Bridge A41

1934

292	A41	½c red brown	.50	.25
293	A41	1c green	.75	.20
294	A41	3c purple	1.10	.20
		Nos. 292-294 (3)	2.35	.65

Opening of the General Trujillo Bridge near Ciudad Trujillo.

Issue dates: 1c, Aug. 24. Others, Sept. 7.

Ramfis Bridge A42

1935, Apr. 6

295	A42	1c green	.45	.20
296	A42	3c yellow brown	.50	.20
297	A42	5c brown violet	1.60	1.00
298	A42	10c rose	3.25	1.40
		Nos. 295-298 (4)	5.80	2.80

Issued in commemoration of the opening of the Ramfis Bridge over the Higuamo River.

President Trujillo — A43

A44

A45

1935 ***Perf. 11***

299	A43	3c yellow & brown	.25	.20
300	A44	5c org red, bl, red & bis	.35	.20
301	A45	7c ultra, bl, red & brn	.50	.20
302	A44	10c red vio, bl, red & bis	.75	.20
		Nos. 299-302 (4)	1.85	.80

Ratification of a treaty setting the frontier between Dominican Republic and Haiti.

Issued: 3c, 10/29; 5c, 10c, 11/25; 7c, 11/8.

National Palace A46

1935, Apr. 1 ***Perf. 11½***

303	A46	25c yellow orange	2.75	.30

Obligatory for all mail addressed to the president and cabinet ministers.

Post Office, Santiago A47

1936

304	A47	½c bright violet	.30	.35
305	A47	1c green	.30	.20

Issue dates: ½c, Jan. 14; 1c, Jan. 4.

George Washington Ave., Ciudad Trujillo — A48

1936, Feb. 22

306	A48	½c brn & vio brn	.40	.45
a.		Imperf., pair	52.50	
307	A48	2c carmine & brn	.40	.30
308	A48	3c yellow org & red brn	.65	.20
309	A48	7c ultra, blue & brn	1.25	1.25
a.		Imperf., pair	52.50	
		Nos. 306-309 (4)	2.70	2.20

Dedication of George Washington Avenue, Ciudad Trujillo.

José Nuñez de Cáceres — A49

Felix M. del Monte — A55

Proposed National Library — A56

1c, Gen. Gregorio Luperon. 2c, Emiliano Tejera. 3c, Pres. Trujillo. 5c, Jose Reyes. 7c, Gen. Antonio Duverge. 25c, Francisco J. Peynado. 30c, Salome Urena. 50c, Gen. Jose M. Cabral. 1p, Manuel de Jesus Galvan. 2p, Gaston F. Deligne.

1936 Unwmk. Engr. *Perf. 13½, 14*

310	A49	½c dull violet	.30	.20
311	A49	1c dark green	.25	.20
312	A49	2c carmine	.30	.20
313	A49	3c violet	.30	.20
314	A49	5c deep ultra	.55	.30
315	A49	7c slate blue	1.00	.55
316	A55	10c orange	1.00	.30
317	A56	20c olive green	3.75	2.75
318	A55	25c gray violet	6.00	*8.00*
319	A55	30c scarlet	7.50	*10.00*
320	A55	50c black brown	8.00	5.50
321	A55	1p black	27.50	*32.50*
322	A55	2p yellow brown	65.00	*80.00*
		Nos. 310-322 (13)	121.45	*140.70*

The funds derived from the sale of these stamps were returned to the National Treasury Fund for the erection of a building for the National Library and Archives.

Issued: 3c, 7c, Mar. 18; others, May 22.

President Trujillo and Obelisk — A62

1937, Jan. 11 Litho. *Perf. 11½*

323	A62	1c green	.20	.20
324	A62	3c violet	.40	.20
325	A62	7c blue & turq blue	1.00	1.00
		Nos. 323-325 (3)	1.60	1.40

1st anniv. of naming Ciudad Trujillo.

Discus Thrower and Flag — A63

1937, Aug. 14

Flag in Red and Blue

326	A63	1c dark green	*8.00*	.75
327	A63	3c violet	*10.50*	.75
328	A63	7c dark blue	*19.00*	3.75
		Nos. 326-328 (3)	37.50	5.25

1st Natl. Olympic Games, Aug. 16, 1937.

Symbolical of Peace, Labor and Progress — A64

1937, Sept. 18 *Perf. 12*

329	A64	3c purple	.35	.20

"8th Year of the Benefactor."

Monument to Father Francisco Xavier Billini (1837-90) — A65

1937, Dec. 29

330	A65	½c deep orange	.20	.20
331	A65	5c purple	.45	.20

Globe and Torch of Liberty — A66

1938, Feb. 22 *Perf. 11½*

332	A66	1c green	.40	.20
333	A66	3c purple	.50	.20
334	A66	10c orange	1.00	.20
		Nos. 332-334 (3)	1.90	.60

150th anniv. of the Constitution of the US.

Pledge of Trinitarians, City Gate and National Flag — A67

1938, July 16 *Perf. 12*

335	A67	1c green, red & dk bl	.40	.20
336	A67	3c purple, red & bl	.45	.20
337	A67	10c orange, red & bl	.90	.40
		Nos. 335-337 (3)	1.75	.80

Trinitarians and patriots, Francisco Del Rosario Sanchez, Ramon Matias Mella and Juan Pablo Duarte, who helped free their country from foreign domination.

Seal of the University of Santo Domingo — A68

1938, Oct. 28

338	A68	½c orange	.30	.25
339	A68	1c dp green & lt green	.30	.20
340	A68	3c purple & pale vio	.40	.20
341	A68	7c dp blue & lt blue	.75	.35
		Nos. 338-341 (4)	1.75	1.00

Founding of the University of Santo Domingo, on Oct. 28, 1538.

Trylon and Perisphere, Flag and Proposed Columbus Lighthouse — A69

1939, Apr. 30 Litho. *Perf. 12*

Flag in Blue and Red

342	A69	½c red org & org	.35	.20
343	A69	1c green & lt green	.40	.20
344	A69	3c purple & pale vio	.40	.20
345	A69	10c orange & yellow	1.25	.65
		Nos. 342-345,C33 (5)	3.80	1.85

New York World's Fair.

A70

A71

1939, Sept. Typo.

346	A70	½c black & pale gray	.30	.20
347	A70	1c black & yel grn	.40	.20
348	A70	3c black & yel brn	.40	.20
349	A70	7c black & dp ultra	1.00	.90
350	A70	10c black & brt red vio	1.50	.40
		Nos. 346-350 (5)	3.60	1.90

José Trujillo Valdez (1863-1935), father of President Trujillo Molina.

1940, Apr. 14 Litho. *Perf. 11½*

Map of the Americas and flags of 21 American republics.

Flags in National Colors

351	A71	1c deep green	.35	.20
352	A71	2c carmine	.45	.20
353	A71	3c red violet	.60	.20
354	A71	10c orange	1.25	.20
355	A71	1p chestnut	15.00	9.50
		Nos. 351-355 (5)	17.65	10.30

Pan American Union, 50th anniv.

Sir Rowland Hill — A72

1940, May 6 *Perf. 12*

356	A72	3c brt red vio & rose lil	3.00	.40
357	A72	7c dk blue & lt blue	6.00	1.40

Centenary of first postage stamp.

Julia Molina Trujillo A73

1940, May 26

358	A73	1c grn, lt grn & dk grn	.35	.20
359	A73	2c brt red, buff & dp rose	.35	.25
360	A73	3c org, dl org & brn org	.50	.20
361	A73	7c bl, pale bl & dk bl	1.00	.35
		Nos. 358-361 (4)	2.20	1.00

Issued in commemoration of Mother's Day.

Map of Caribbean A74

1940, June 6 *Perf. 11½*

362	A74	3c brt car & pale rose	.40	.20
363	A74	7c dk blue & lt blue	.75	.20
364	A74	1p yel grn & pale grn	7.50	6.50
		Nos. 362-364 (3)	8.65	6.90

2nd Inter-American Caribbean Conf. held at Ciudad Trujillo, May 31 to June 6.

Marion Military Hospital — A75

1940, Dec. 24

365	A75	½c chestnut & fawn	.25	.20

AIR POST STAMPS

Map of Hispaniola — AP1

Perf. 11½

1928, May 31 Litho. Unwmk.

C1	AP1	10c deep ultra	4.50	2.00

1930

C2	AP1	10c ocher	3.00	2.00
a.		Vert. pair, imperf. btwn.	*600.00*	
C3	AP1	15c scarlet	6.00	3.00
C4	AP1	20c dull green	2.75	.50
C5	AP1	30c violet	6.00	3.25
		Nos. C2-C5 (4)	17.75	8.75

#C2-C5 have only "CENTAVOS" in lower panel. Issued: 10c, 20c, 1/24; 15c, 30c, 2/14.

1930

C6	AP1	10c light blue	1.50	.60
C7	AP1	15c blue green	3.00	.90
C8	AP1	20c yellow brown	3.25	.45
a.		Horiz. pair, imperf. vert.	450.00	450.00
C9	AP1	30c chocolate	5.50	1.50
		Nos. C6-C9 (4)	13.25	3.45

Issue dates: 10c, 15c, 20c, Sept.; 30c, Oct.

Batwing Sundial Erected in 1753 — AP2

1931-33 *Perf. 12*

C10	AP2	10c carmine	3.25	.50
C11	AP2	10c light blue	1.40	.50
C12	AP2	10c dark green	5.50	2.50
C13	AP2	15c rose lilac	2.50	.50
C14	AP2	20c dark blue	5.50	2.10
a.		Numerals reading up at left and down at right	5.00	2.50
b.		Imperf., pair	250.00	
C15	AP2	30c green	2.25	.25
C16	AP2	50c red brown	5.50	.50
C17	AP2	1p deep orange	7.50	2.50
		Nos. C10-C17 (8)	33.40	9.35

Issued: #C11, 7/2/32; #C12, 5/28/33; others 8/16.

Airplane and Ozama Fortress AP3

1933, Nov. 20

C18 AP3 10c dark blue 3.00 .50

Airplane and Trujillo Bridge AP4

1934, Sept. 20

C19 AP4 10c dark blue 3.00 .50

Symbolic of Flight AP5

1935, Apr. 29

C20 AP5 10c lt blue & dk blue 1.40 .40

AP6

1936, Feb. 11 ***Perf. 11½***

C21 AP6 10c dk bl & turq bl 2.25 .40

Allegory of Flight AP7

1936, Oct. 17

C22 AP7 10c dk bl, bl & turq bl 2.00 .30

Macoris Airport AP8

1937, Oct. 22

C23 AP8 10c green .90 .20

Fleet of Columbus AP9

Air Fleet AP10

Proposed Columbus Lighthouse — AP11

1937, Nov. 9 ***Perf. 12***

C24 AP9 10c rose red 1.50 1.25
C25 AP10 15c purple 1.25 .85
C26 AP11 20c dk bl & lt bl 1.25 .90
C27 AP10 25c red violet 1.75 1.00
C28 AP11 30c yellow green 1.50 1.00
C29 AP10 50c brown 3.25 1.25
C30 AP11 75c dk olive grn 9.00 9.00
C31 AP9 1p orange 5.50 1.75
Nos. C24-C31 (8) 25.00 17.00

Goodwill flight to all American countries by the planes "Colon," "Pinta," "Nina" and "Santa Maria."

#C30 was reproduced imperf. on #1019.

Pan American Clipper AP12

1938, July 30

C32 AP12 10c green 1.00 .20

Trylon and Perisphere, Plane and Proposed Columbus Lighthouse — AP13

1939, Apr. 30

C33 AP13 10c green & lt green 1.40 .60

New York World's Fair.

Airplane AP14

1939, Oct. 18

C34 AP14 10c green & dp green 1.40 .20
a. Pair, imperf. btwn. 450.00

Proposed Columbus Lighthouse, Plane and Caravels — AP15

Christopher Columbus and Proposed Lighthouse — AP16

Proposed Lighthouse — AP17

Christopher Columbus — AP18

Caravel — AP19

1940, Oct. 12

C35 AP15 10c sapphire & lt bl .85 .45
C36 AP16 15c org brn & brn 1.10 .75
C37 AP17 20c rose red & red 1.10 .75
C38 AP18 25c brt red lil & red vio 1.10 .35
C39 AP19 50c green & lt green 2.25 1.25
Nos. C35-C39 (5) 6.40 3.55

Discovery of America by Columbus and proposed Columbus memorial lighthouse in Dominican Republic.

AIR POST OFFICIAL STAMPS

Nos. O13-O14 Overprinted in Blue

Unwmk.

1930, Dec. 3 **Typo.** ***Perf. 12***

CO1 O3 10c light blue 10.50 *11.00*
a. Pair, one without ovpt. *900.00*
CO2 O3 20c orange 10.50 *11.00*

SPECIAL DELIVERY STAMPS

Biplane SD1

Perf. 11½

1920, Apr. **Unwmk.** **Litho.**

E1 SD1 10c deep ultra 5.50 1.25
a. Imperf., pair

Special Delivery Messenger — SD2

1925

E2 SD2 10c dark blue 16.00 4.50

SD3

1927

E3 SD3 10c red brown 5.00 1.25
a. "E EXPRESO" at top 55.00 55.00

INSURED LETTER STAMPS

Merino Issue of 1933 Surcharged in Red or Black

1935, Feb. 1 **Unwmk.** ***Perf. 14***

G1 A35 8c on 7c ultra .60 .20
a. Inverted surcharge 18.00
G2 A35 15c on 10c org yel .65 .20
a. Inverted surcharge 18.00
G3 A35 30c on 8c dk green 1.75 .90
G4 A35 45c on 20c car rose (Bk) 3.00 1.00
G5 A36 70c on 50c lemon 6.00 1.25
Nos. G1-G5 (5) 12.00 3.55

Merino Issue of 1933 Surcharged in Red

1940

G6 A35 8c on ½c lt vio 2.00 2.00
G7 A35 8c on 7c ultra 3.25 3.25

Coat of Arms — IL1

1940-45 **Litho.** ***Perf. 11½***

Arms in Black

G8 IL1 8c brown red .60 .25
a. 8c dk red, no shading on inner frame 1.00 .20
G9 IL1 15c dp orange ('45) 1.25 .20
G10 IL1 30c dk green ('41) 1.50 .20
a. 30c yellow green 1.50 .20
G11 IL1 45c ultra ('44) 1.50 .30
G12 IL1 70c olive brn ('44) 1.75 .30
Nos. G8-G12 (5) 6.60 1.25

See Nos. G13-G16, G24-G27.

POSTAGE DUE STAMPS

D1

1901 **Unwmk.** **Typo.** ***Perf. 14***

J1 D1 2c olive gray .70 .20
J2 D1 4c olive gray .90 .20
J3 D1 5c olive gray 1.50 .30
J4 D1 10c olive gray 2.75 .75
Nos. J1-J4 (4) 5.85 1.45

For surcharges and overprint see Nos. 162-165, 169-171.

1909 **Wmk. 116**

J5 D1 2c olive gray 1.50 .50
J6 D1 4c olive gray 1.50 .50
J7 D1 6c olive gray 2.00 .75
J8 D1 10c olive gray 4.00 2.50
Nos. J5-J8 (4) 9.00 4.25

1913

J9 D1 2c olive green .45 .20
J10 D1 4c olive green .50 .20
J11 D1 6c olive green .80 .35
J12 D1 10c olive green .90 .40
Nos. J9-J12 (4) 2.65 1.15

1922 **Unwmk.** **Litho.** ***Perf. 11½***

J13 D1 1c olive green .55 .55

OFFICIAL STAMPS

Bastion of February 27
O1

Unwmk.

1902, Feb. 25 Litho. *Perf. 12*

O1 O1 2c scarlet & blk .50 .30
O2 O1 5c dk blue & blk .65 .25
O3 O1 10c yel grn & blk .75 .45
O4 O1 20c yellow & blk 1.00 .40
a. Imperf., pair 10.00
Nos. O1-O4 (4) 2.90 1.40

For overprints and surcharge see #157-161.

Bastion of Feb. 27
O2

Columbus Lighthouse
O3

Perf. 13½x13, 13½x14

1909-12 Wmk. 116 Typo.

O5 O2 1c blue grn & blk .30 .20
O6 O2 2c scarlet & blk .35 .20
O7 O2 5c dk blue & blk .75 .30
O8 O2 10c yel grn & blk ('12) 1.10 .70
O9 O2 20c orange & blk ('12) 2.00 1.60
Nos. O5-O9 (5) 4.50 3.00

The 2c, 5c are found in both perforations; 1c, 20c perf. 13½x13; 10c perf. 13½x14.
For overprints and surcharge see #177, 194-199.

1928 Unwmk. *Perf. 12*

O10 O3 1c green .20 .20
O11 O3 2c red .20 .20
O12 O3 5c ultramarine .25 .25
O13 O3 10c light blue .30 .30
O14 O3 20c orange .45 .45
Nos. O10-O14 (5) 1.40 1.40

For overprints see Nos. CO1-CO2.

Proposed Columbus Lighthouse
O4

1937 Litho. *Perf. 11½*

O15 O4 3c dark purple .85 .20
O16 O4 7c indigo & blue .90 .30
O17 O4 10c orange yellow 1.00 .45
Nos. O15-O17 (3) 2.75 .95

Proposed Columbus Lighthouse
O5

1939-41

O18 O5 1c dp grn & lt grn .35 .20
O19 O5 2c crim & pale pink .35 .20
O20 O5 3c purple & lt vio .35 .20
O21 O5 5c dk bl & lt bl ('40) .60 .30
O21A O5 5c lt blue ('41) 1.50 1.00
O22 O5 7c brt bl & lt bl ('41) 1.10 .20
O23 O5 10c yel org & pale org ('41) 1.10 .35
O24 O5 20c brn org & buff ('41) 3.00 .50
O25 O5 50c brt red lil & pale lil ('41) 3.50 1.50
Nos. O18-O25 (9) 11.85 4.45

POSTAL TAX STAMPS

Santo Domingo after Hurricane
PT1

Hurricane's Effect on Capital
PT2

1930, Dec. Unwmk. Litho. *Perf. 12*

RA1 PT1 1c green & rose .20 .20
RA2 PT1 2c red rose .20 .20
RA3 PT2 5c ultra & rose .30 .20
RA4 PT2 10c yellow & rose .35 .30

Imperf

RA5 PT1 1c green & rose .40 .30
RA6 PT1 2c red & rose .50 .30
RA7 PT2 5c ultra & rose .60 .50
RA8 PT2 10c yellow & rose .90 .75
Nos. RA1-RA8 (8) 3.45 2.75

For surcharges see Nos. RAC1-RAC7.

Tête bêche Pairs

RA1a PT1 1c green & rose 1.75 1.75
RA2a PT1 2c red rose 1.75 1.50
RA3a PT1 5c ultra & rose 1.75 2.10
RA4a PT1 10c yellow & rose 2.10 2.10
RA5a PT1 1c green & rose 1.75 1.75
RA6a PT1 2c red & rose 1.75 1.75
RA7a PT1 5c ultra & rose 2.10 2.10
RA8a PT1 10c yellow & rose 2.10 2.10
Nos. RA1a-RA8a (8) 15.05 15.15

POSTAL TAX AIR POST STAMPS

Postal Tax Stamps Surcharged in Red or Gold

1930, Dec. 3 Unwmk. *Perf. 12*

RAC1 PT2 5c + 5c blk & rose (R) 25.00 25.00
a. Tête bêche pair 125.00
b. "Habilitado Para" missing 52.50
RAC2 PT2 10c + 10c blk & rose (R) 25.00 25.00
a. Tête bêche pair 125.00
b. "Habilitado Para" missing 52.50
c. Gold surcharge 95.00 95.00
d. As "c," tête bêche pair 450.00
e. As "c" and "b" 250.00

Nos. RAC1-RAC2 were on sale one day.

RAC4 PT2 5c + 5c ultra & rose (R) 6.00 6.00
a. Tête bêche pair 45.00
b. Inverted surcharge 42.50
c. Tête bêche pair, inverted surcharge 600.00
d. Pair, one without surcharge 190.00
e. "Habilitado Para" missing 15.00
RAC5 PT2 10c + 10c yel & rose (G) 4.50 4.50
a. Tête bêche pair 42.50
b. "Habilitado Para" missing 18.00

Imperf

RAC6 PT2 5c + 5c ultra & rose (R) 6.00 6.00
a. Tête bêche pair 52.50
b. "Habilitado Para" missing 18.00
RAC7 PT2 10c + 10c yel & rose (G) 6.00 6.00
a. Tête bêche pair 52.50
b. "Habilitado Para" missing 18.00
Nos. RAC1-RAC7 (6) 72.50 72.50

It was obligatory to use Nos. RA1-RA8 and RAC1-RAC7 on all postal matter, in amounts equal to the ordinary postage.
This surtax was for the aid of sufferers from the hurricane of Sept. 3, 1930.

No. 261 Overprinted in Green

1933, Oct. 11

RAC8 A32 2c scarlet .35 .30
a. Double overprint 9.00
b. Pair, one without overprint 375.00

By official decree a copy of this stamp, in addition to the regular postage, had to be used on every letter, etc., sent by the internal air post service.

EAST AFRICA AND UGANDA PROTECTORATES

ˈest ˈa-fri-kə and ü-ˈgan-də
prə-ˈtek-t̬ə-ˌrəts

LOCATION — Central East Africa, bordering on the Indian Ocean
GOVT. — Former British Protectorate
AREA — 350,000 sq. mi. (approx.)
POP. — 6,503,507 (approx.)
CAPITAL — Mombasa

This territory, formerly administered by the British East Africa Colony, was divided between Kenya Colony and the Uganda Protectorate. See Kenya, Uganda and Tanzania.

16 Annas = 1 Rupee
100 Cents = 1 Rupee (1907)

A1

A2

King Edward VII

1903 Typo. Wmk. 2 *Perf. 14*

1 A1 ½a gray green 5.00 *15.00*
2 A1 1a car & black 2.25 1.25
3 A1 2a vio & dull vio 10.50 3.00
4 A1 2½a ultramarine 14.50 *60.00*
5 A1 3a gray grn & brn 22.50 *67.50*
6 A1 4a blk & gray grn 13.50 *27.50*
7 A1 5a org brn & blk 22.50 *60.00*
8 A1 8a pale blue & blk 25.00 *50.00*

Wmk. 1

9 A2 1r gray green 20.00 *62.50*
a. On chalky paper 57.50 *100.00*
10 A2 2r vio & dull vio 85.00 *92.50*
11 A2 3r blk & gray grn 110.00 *190.00*
12 A2 4r lt green & blk 110.00 *190.00*
13 A2 5r car & black 125.00 *190.00*
14 A2 10r ultra & black 250.00 *425.00*
a. On chalky paper 350.00 *425.00*
15 A2 20r ol gray & blk 675.00 *1,400.*
16 A2 50r org brn & blk 1,700. *2,900.*
Nos. 1-14 (14) 815.75 *1,434.*
Set, ovptd "SPECIMEN" 350.00

1904-07 Wmk. 3 Chalky Paper

17 A1 ½a gray green 8.50 3.75
18 A1 1a car & black 9.25 2.00
19 A1 2a vio & dull vio 3.00 3.00
21 A1 3a gray grn & brn 4.25 *32.50*
22 A1 4a blk & gray grn 8.50 *21.00*
23 A1 5a org brn & blk 7.50 *32.50*
24 A1 8a pale blue & blk 8.00 21.00
25 A2 1r gray green 30.00 *70.00*
26 A2 2r vio & dl vio 42.50 *62.50*
27 A2 3r blk & gray grn 62.50 *110.00*
28 A2 4r lt green & blk 85.00 *160.00*
29 A2 5r car & black 95.00 *125.00*
29A A2 10r ultra & black 190.00 210.00
30 A2 20r ol gray & blk 625.00 *1,100.*
30A A2 50r org brn & blk 1,750. *3,100.*
Nos. 17-29 (12) 364.00 *643.25*

Ordinary Paper

17a A1 ½a gray green 9.75 3.50
18a A1 1a car & black 4.25 .90
19a A1 2a vio & dull vio 3.75 3.00
20 A1 2½a blue 9.25 *35.00*
a. 2½a blue & ultramarine 8.50 *19.00*
21a A1 3a gray grn & brn 4.25 *35.00*
22a A1 4a blk & gray grn 8.50 *20.00*
23a A1 5a org brn & blk 9.25 *17.50*
24a A1 8a pale blue & blk 8.00 *9.75*

1907-08

31 A1 1c brown ('08) 3.00 .20
32 A1 3c gray green 17.50 .80
a. 3c blue green 18.00 3.00
33 A1 6c carmine 3.25 .20
a. 6c carmine, single plate ('10) 16.00 .35
34 A1 10c citron & violet 11.00 10.00
35 A1 12c red vio & dl vio 12.00 3.50
36 A1 15c ultramarine 30.00 11.00
37 A1 25c blk & blue green 11.00 *8.50*
38 A1 50c org brn & green 14.50 14.50
39 A1 75c pale bl & gray blk ('08) 5.50 *40.00*
Nos. 31-39 (9) 107.75 *88.70*
Set, ovptd "SPECIMEN" 210.00

Nos. 31-33, 36 are on ordinary paper.
On No. 33a, there is a distinct white line separating the lower tablets from the rest of the design. This is not present on No. 33. The word "PROTECTORATE" is in taller letters on No. 33a.

A3

A4

King George V

1912-18 Ordinary Paper Wmk. 3

40 A3 1c black .40 *2.00*
41 A3 3c green 2.50 .70
a. Booklet pane of 6
b. 3c deep blue green ('17) 5.00 1.75
42 A3 6c carmine .80 .70
a. Booklet pane of 6
b. 6c scarlet ('17) 17.50 2.90
43 A3 10c yel orange 2.50 .55
a. 10c orange ('21) 11.50 3.50
44 A3 12c gray 3.25 .55
45 A3 15c ultramarine 3.25 .90

Chalky Paper

46 A3 25c scar & blk, *yel* .55 *1.50*
a. 25c scar & blk, *lemon* ('16) 12.50 12.50
Overprinted "SPECIMEN" 40.00
b. 25c scar & blk, *org buff* ('21) 50.00 19.00
c. 25c scar & blk, *pale yel* ('21) 11.50 5.75
47 A3 50c violet & black 1.90 1.50
48 A3 75c black, *green* 1.90 *21.00*
a. 75c black, *emerald* 13.50 *65.00*
b. 75c blk, *bl grn, olive back* 7.25 9.25
c. 75c blk, *emer, olive back* 50.00 *175.00*
49 A4 1r black, *green* 2.25 *5.25*
a. 1r black, *emerald* 6.00 *60.00*
50 A4 2r blk & red, *bl* 24.50 *45.00*
51 A4 3r gray grn & vio 24.50 *110.00*
52 A4 4r grn & red, *yel* 55.00 *125.00*
a. 4r grn & red, *pale yellow* 110.00 *190.00*
53 A4 5r dl vio & ultra 60.00 *175.00*
54 A4 10r grn & red, *grn* 150.00 *240.00*
55 A4 20r vio & blk, *red* 400.00 400.00
56 A4 20r bl & violet, *blue* ('18) 500.00 *550.00*
57 A4 50r gray grn & rose red 725.00 *975.00*
Overprinted "SPECIMEN" 175.00
a. 50r dull green & dull rose, ordinary paper 850.00 *925.00*

58 A4 100r blk & vio, *red* 6,000. 3,000.
Overprinted "SPECIMEN" 375.00
59 A4 500r red & grn, *grn* 22,000.
Overprinted "SPECIMEN" 750.00
Nos. 40-54 (15) 333.30 *729.65*
Nos. 40-54 (15), ovptd "SPECIMEN" 600.00

1914 Surface-colored Paper

60 A3 25c scarlet & blk, *yel* .60 *5.50*
61 A3 75c black, *green* 1.25 *19.50*
Nos. 60-61, ovptd "SPECIMEN" 75.00

Stamps of types A3 and A4 with watermark 4 are listed under Kenya, Uganda and Tanzania.

The 1r through 50r with revenue cancellations sell for minimal prices. The 100r and 500r were available for postage but were nearly always used fiscally.

For surcharge see No. 62.

No. 42 Surcharged 

1919

62 A3 4c on 6c carmine 1.50 .20
Handstamped "SPECIMEN" 70.00
a. Double surcharge 150.00 *240.00*
b. Without squares over old value 50.00 *85.00*
c. Pair, one without surcharge 1,900. *2,100.*
d. Inverted surcharge 325.00 *450.00*

For later issues see Kenya, Uganda and Tanzania.

For stamps of East Africa and Uganda overprinted "G. E. A." see German East Africa.

EASTERN RUMELIA

'ē-stərn rü-'mēl-yə

(South Bulgaria)

LOCATION — In southern Bulgaria
GOVT. — An autonomous unit of the Turkish Empire.
CAPITAL — Philippopolis (Plovdiv)

In 1885 the province of Eastern Rumelia revolted against Turkish rule and united with Bulgaria, adopting the new name of South Bulgaria. This union was assured by the Treaty of Bucharest in 1886, following the war between Serbia and Bulgaria.

40 Paras = 1 Piaster

Counterfeits of all overprints are plentiful.

No. 1 

A2

A3

Stamps of Turkey, 1876-84, Overprinted in Blue

1880 Unwmk. *Perf. 13½*

1 A5 ½pi on 20pa yel grn 42.50 34.00
a. Horiz. pair, one without overprint *400.00*
3 A2 10pa blk & rose *55.00*
4 A2 20pa vio & grn 55.00 42.50
6 A2 2pi blk & buff 72.50 62.50
7 A2 5pi red & bl 275.00 325.00
8 A3 10pa blk & red lil 37.50

Nos. 3 & 8 were not placed in use.

Inverted and double overprints of all values exist.

Same, with Extra Overprint "R. O."

9 A3 10pa blk & red lil 62.50 62.50

Crescent and Turkish Inscriptions of Value — A4

1881 Typo. *Perf. 13½*

10 A4 5pa blk & olive 7.00 .75
11 A4 10pa blk & green 11.50 .75
12 A4 20pa blk & rose 1.10 .75
b. Cliché of 10pa in plate of 20pa *400.00*
In pair with No. 12 *525.00*
13 A4 1pi blk & blue 3.75 3.00
14 A4 5pi rose & blue 35.00 *37.50*

Tête bêche pairs and imperforates were not placed in use, and were found only in the remainder stock. This is true also of No. 12b, and of a cliché of Turkey No. 63 in the 1pi plate.

Perf. 11½

10a A4 5pa blk & olive 11.00
11a A4 10pa blk & green 15.00
12a A4 20pa blk & rose 15.00
13a A4 1pi blk & blue 15.00
14a A4 5pi rose & blue 37.50

Nos. 10a-14a were not placed in use, and were found only in the remainder stock.

1884 *Perf. 11½*

15 A4 5pa lil & pale lil .40 .40
16 A4 10pa grn & pale grn .20 .40
17 A4 20pa car & pale rose .40
18 A4 1pi bl & pale bl .75
19 A4 5pi brn & pale brn *250.00*

Nos. 17-19 were not placed in use, and were found only in the remainder stock.

Nos. 15-19 imperf. are from remainders.

For overprints see Turkey Nos. 542-545.

Perf. 13½

15a A4 5pa lil & pale lil .75 *2.25*
16a A4 10pa grn & pale grn 11.00 11.00
17a A4 20pa car & pale rose 12.50
18a A4 1pi bl & pale bl 12.50
19a A4 5pi brn & pale brn *300.00*

Nos. 17a-19a were not placed in use, and were found only in the remainder stock.

South Bulgaria

Counterfeits of all overprints are plentiful.

Nos. 10-14 Overprinted in Two Types:

a

b

Type a — Four toes on each foot.
Type b — Three toes on each foot.

1885 Unwmk. *Perf. 13½*

Blue Overprint

20 A4 (a) 5pa blk & olive *225.00 250.00*
21 A4 (a) 10pa blk & grn *550.00 550.00*
22 A4 (a) 20pa blk & rose 225.00 —
a. Type "b" 225.00
b. Type "a," perf. 11½ 225.00 *250.00*
c. Type "b," perf. 11½ 190.00 —
23 A4 (a) 1pi blk & blue 37.50 *72.50*
a. Type "b" 50.00 *65.00*
24 A4 (b) 5pi rose & blue *375.00* —
a. Type "a" *725.00* —

Black Overprint

24B A4 (a) 20pa blk & rose 250.00 —
25 A4 (a) 1pi blk & bl 12.50 *25.00*
a. Type "b" 42.50 *55.00*
26 A4 (b) 5pi rose & bl *450.00* —

Same Overprint on Nos. 15-17

Perf. 11½

Blue Overprint

27 A4 (b) 5pa lil & pale lil, type "b" 15.00 *37.50*
a. Type "a" 22.50 *55.00*
b. Perf. 13½, type "b" 50.00 *65.00*
c. Perf. 13½, type "a" *225.00 250.00*
28 A4 (b) 10pa grn & pale grn 27.50 *50.00*
a. Type "a" 140.00 *225.00*
29 A4 (b) 20pa car & pale rose 175.00 *225.00*
a. Type "a" 175.00 *300.00*

Black Overprint

Perf. 13½

30 A4 (b) 5pa lil & pale lil 25.00 *45.00*
a. Type "a" 37.50 *57.50*
b. Type "b," perf. 11½ 37.50 *45.00*

Perf. 11½

31 A4 (a) 10pa grn & pale grn 37.50 *72.50*
a. Type "b" 45.00 —
b. Type "a," perf. 13½ 37.50 *57.50*
32 A4 (b) 20pa car & pale rose 37.50 *45.00*
a. Type "a" 37.50 *55.00*

Nos. 10-17 Handstamped in Black in Two Types:

a

b

Type a — First letter at top circular.
Type b — First letter at top oval.

1885 *Perf. 13½*

33 A4 (b) 5pa blk & olive *300.00* 250.00
a. Type "a" *250.00*
34 A4 (b) 10pa blk & grn *225.00* 250.00
a. Type "a" 300.00
35 A4 (b) 20pa blk & rose 60.00 *75.00*
a. Type "a" 100.00 *110.00*
36 A4 (a) 1pi blk & bl 55.00 *72.50*
a. Type "b" 90.00 *110.00*
37 A4 (a) 5pi rose & blue, type "a" *2,500.* —
a. Type "b" — —

Perf. 13½

38 A4 (a) 5pa lil & pale lil 15.00 18.00
a. Type "b" 15.00 *27.50*
b. Perf. 11½, type "a" 140.00 *180.00*
c. Perf. 11½, type "b" 140.00 *175.00*

Perf. 11½

39 A4 (a) 10pa grn & pale grn 17.50 *22.50*
a. Type "b" 37.50 37.50
40 A4 (a) 20pa car & pale rose 17.50 *32.50*
a. Type "b" 17.50 17.50

Nos. 20-40 exist with inverted and double handstamps. Overprints in unlisted colors are proofs.

The stamps of South Bulgaria were superseded in 1886 by those of Bulgaria.

EASTERN SILESIA

'ē-stərn sī-'lē-zhē-ə

LOCATION — In central Europe
GOVT. — Former Austrian crownland
AREA — 1,987 sq. mi.
POP. — 680,422 (estimated 1920)
CAPITAL — Troppau

After World War I, this territory was occupied by Czechoslovakia and eventually was divided between Poland and Czechoslovakia, the dividing line running through Teschen.

100 Heller = 1 Krone
100 Fennigi = 1 Marka

Plebiscite Issues

Stamps of Czechoslovakia 1918-20, Overprinted in Black, Blue, Violet or Red

1920 Unwmk. *Imperf.*

1 A2 1h dark brown .20 .30
2 A1 3h red violet .20 .20
3 A2 5h blue green 22.50 22.50
4 A2 15h red 11.00 11.00
5 A1 20h blue green .20 .20
6 A2 25h dull violet .75 .75
7 A1 30h bister (R) .20 .20
8 A1 40h red orange .30 .30
9 A2 50h dull violet .60 .45
10 A2 50h dark blue 2.50 1.50
11 A2 60h orange (Bl) .75 .75
12 A2 75h slate (R) .50 .75
13 A2 80h olive grn (R) .50 .75
14 A1 100h brown 1.10 1.10
15 A2 120h gray blk (R) 1.50 2.25
16 A1 200h ultra (R) 1.50 2.00
17 A2 300h green (R) 6.00 7.50
18 A1 400h purple (R) 2.00 3.00
20 A2 500h red brn (Bl) 5.00 6.00
a. Black overprint 6.00 9.00
21 A2 1000h violet (Bl) 12.50 13.50
a. Black overprint 60.00 75.00
Nos. 1-21 (20) 69.80 75.00

Perf. 11½, 13¾

22 A2 1h dark brown .20 .20
23 A2 5h blue green .30 .25
24 A2 10h yellow green .30 .25
a. Imperf. *250.00 200.00*
25 A2 15h red .50 .20
26 A2 20h rose .50 .35
a. Imperf. *300.00 250.00*
27 A2 25h dull violet .50 .35
28 A2 30h red violet (Bl) .35 .35
29 A2 60h orange (Bl) .50 .50
30 A1 200h ultra (R) 3.00 3.00
Nos. 22-30 (9) 6.15 5.45

The letters "S. O." are the initials of "Silésie Orientale."

Forged cancellations are found on #1-30.

Overprinted in Carmine or Violet 

31 A4 500h sl, *grysh* (C) 37.50
32 A4 1000h blk brn, *brnsh* 37.50

Excellent counterfeits of this overprint exist.

Stamps of Poland, 1919, Overprinted 

1920 *Perf. 11½*

41 A10 5f green .20 .20
42 A10 10f red brown .20 .20
43 A10 15f light red .20 .20
44 A11 25f olive green .20 .20
45 A11 50f blue green .20 .20

Overprinted 

46 A12 1k deep green .20 .20
47 A12 1.50k brown .20 .20
48 A12 2k dark blue .20 .20
49 A13 2.50k dull violet .20 .20
50 A14 5k slate blue .20 .20
Nos. 41-50 (10) 2.00 2.00

SPECIAL DELIVERY STAMPS

Czechoslovakia Special Delivery Stamps Overprinted in Blue

1920 Unwmk. *Imperf.*

E1 SD1 2h red violet, *yel* .20 .20
a. Black overprint 4.50 .80
E2 SD1 5h yellow green, *yel* .20 .20
a. Black overprint 7.00 5.00

Nos. E1-E2a exist on white paper.

POSTAGE DUE STAMPS

Czechoslovakia Postage Due Stamps Overprinted In Blue or Red

1920		Unwmk.	*Imperf.*	
J1	D1	5h deep bis (Bl)	.25	.20
a.		Black overprint	70.00	60.00
J2	D1	10h deep bister	.25	.20
J3	D1	15h deep bister	.25	.20
J4	D1	20h deep bister	.25	.20
J5	D1	25h deep bister	.25	.20
J6	D1	30h deep bister	.25	.20
J7	D1	40h deep bister	.50	.25
J8	D1	50h deep bister	2.50	3.00
J9	D1	100h blk brn (R)	2.50	3.00
J10	D1	500h gray grn (R)	5.50	4.50
J11	D1	1000h purple (R)	8.00	11.50
		Nos. J1-J11 (11)	20.50	23.45

Forged cancellations exist.

NEWSPAPER STAMPS

Czechoslovakia Newspaper Stamps Overprinted in Black like Nos. 1-30

1920		Unwmk.	*Imperf.*	
P1	N1	2h gray green	.30	.30
P2	N1	6h red	.20	.20
P3	N1	10h dull violet	.35	.20
P4	N1	20h blue	.55	.25
P5	N1	30h gray brown	.55	.25
		Nos. P1-P5 (5)	1.95	1.20

ECUADOR

'e-kwə-ˌdor

LOCATION — Northwest coast of South America, bordering on the Pacific Ocean
GOVT. — Republic
AREA — 116,270 sq. mi.
POP. — 8,420,000 (est. 1984)
CAPITAL — Quito

The Republic of Ecuador was so constituted on May 11, 1830, after the Civil War which separated the original members of the Republic of Colombia, founded by Simon Bolivar by uniting the Presidency of Quito with the Viceroyalty of New Grenada and the Captaincy of Venezuela. The Presidency of Quito became the Republic of Ecuador.

8 Reales = 1 Peso
100 Centavos = 1 Sucre (1881)

Watermarks

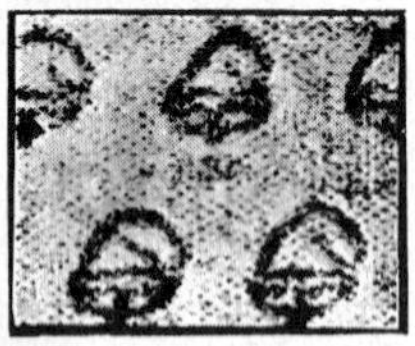

Wmk. 117 — Liberty Cap

Wmk. 127 — Quatrefoils

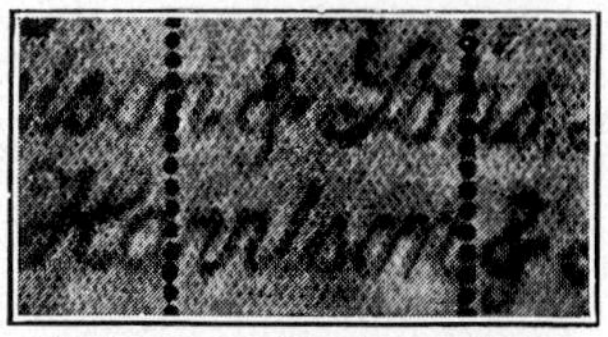

Wmk. 233 — "Harrison & Sons, London" in Script Letters

STAMPS OF GREAT BRITAIN USED IN ECUADOR

Guayaquil

Stamps of Great Britain cancelled Type A "C41"

1865-80		
A1	½p rose red, plates 5, 6 (#58), *value from*	70.00
A2	1p rose red ('57) (#20)	—
A3	1p rose red, plates 74, 78, 85, 92, 94, 105, 110, 115, 133, 140, 145, 166, 174, 180, 216 (#33), *value from*	50.00
A4	1½p lake red, plate 3 (#32)	100.00
A5	2p blue, plate 9 (#29)	55.00
A6	2p blue, plates 13, 14 (#30), *value from*	50.00
A7	3p rose ('62) (#37)	290.00
A8	3p rose ('65) (#44)	140.00
A9	3p rose ('67-'73), plates 6, 7, 9, 10 (#49), *value from*	57.50
A10	3p rose ('73-'80), plates 11, 12, 15-20 (#61), *value from*	57.50
A11	4p vermilion ('62), plate 4 (#34a)	140.00
A12	4p vermilion ('62), "hair lines" (#34c)	140.00
A13	4p vermilion ('65-'73), plates 7-14 (#43), *value from*	57.50
A14	4p vermilion ('76), plate 15 (#69)	350.00
A15	4p pale olive green, plate 15 (#70)	225.00
A16	4p pale olive green, plate 16 (#70)	225.00
A17	6p lilac, plate 4 (#39b)	175.00
A18	6p lilac ('65-'67), plate 5 (#45)	85.00
A19	6p lilac ('65-'67), plate 6 (#45)	85.00
A20	6p dull violet ('67), plate 6 (#50)	—
A21	6p violet ('67-'70), plates 6, 8, 9 (#51), *value from*	80.00
A22	6p pale buff ('72-'73), plate 11 (#59b)	92.50
A23	6p pale buff ('72-'73), plate 12 (#59b)	225.00
A24	6p brown ('72), plates 11, 12 (#59)	—
A25	6p gray ('73), plate 12 (#60)	—
A26	6p gray ('73), plates 13-16 (#60), *value from*	57.50
A27	8p orange ('76) (373)	375.00
A28	9p straw ('62) (#40)	310.00
A29	9p bister ('67) (#52)	225.00
A30	10p red brown ('67) (#53)	350.00
A31	1sh green ('65) (#48)	185.00
A32	1sh green ('67-'73), plates 4-6 (#54), *value from*	50.00
A33	1sh green ('67-'73), plate 7 (#54)	85.00
A34	1sh green ('73-'77), plates 8-11 (#64), *value from*	90.00
A35	1sh green ('73-'77), plates 12, 13 (#64), *value from*	85.00
A36	2sh blue ('67) (#55)	175.00
A37	2sh brown ('80) (#56)	*2,600.*
A38	5sh rose ('67-'74), plate 1 (#57)	550.00
A39	5sh rose ('67-'74), plate 2 (#57)	700.00

Issues of the Republic

Coat of Arms
A1 A2

1865-72 Unwmk. Typo. *Imperf.*

Quadrille Paper

1	A1	1r yellow ('72)	29.00	25.00
		On wrapper		150.00
		On cover		300.00

Wove Paper

2	A1	½r ultra	17.00	8.75
		On wrapper		125.00
		On cover		250.00
a.		½r gray blue ('67)	17.00	8.75
		On wrapper		100.00
		On cover		125.00
b.		Batonne paper ('70)	25.00	15.00
c.		Blue paper ('72)	125.00	82.50
d.		Embossed arms	—	400.00
e.		Watermarked	—	1,000.
3	A1	1r buff	22.50	11.00
		On wrapper		150.00
		On cover		300.00
a.		1r orange buff	27.50	13.00
		On wrapper		175.00
		On cover		325.00
4	A1	1r yellow	13.00	9.25
		On wrapper		125.00
		On cover		250.00
a.		1r olive yellow ('66)	19.00	15.00
		On wrapper		175.00
		On cover		400.00
b.		Laid paper	125.00	82.50
c.		Half used as ½r on cover		900.00
d.		Batonne paper	25.00	19.00
e.		Embossed arms	—	500.00
f.		Watermarked	—	1,000.
5	A1	1r green	190.00	22.50
		On wrapper		150.00
		On cover		300.00
a.		Half used as ½r on cover		*900.00*
b.		Embossed arms	—	*700.00*
c.		Watermarked	—	*1,000.*
6	A2	4r red ('66)	250.00	100.00
		On wrapper		*700.00*
		On cover		*1,000.*
a.		4r red brown ('66)	350.00	100.00
		On wrapper		*700.00*
		On cover		*1,100.*
b.		Arms in circle	250.00	150.00
c.		Printed on both sides	550.00	—
d.		Half used as 2r on cover		1,600.
e.		Embossed arms	—	*900.00*
f.		Watermarked	—	*2,000*
		Nos. 1-6 (6)	521.50	176.50

Letter paper embossed with arms of Ecuador was used in printing a number of sheets of Nos. 2, 4-6.

Papermakers' watermarks on No. 2e, 4f, 5c and 6f reads "Rolland Freres".

On the 4r the oval holding the coat of arms is usually 13½-14mm wide, but on about one-fifth of the stamps in the sheet it is 15-15½mm wide, almost a circle.

The 2r, 8r and 12r, type A1, are bogus.

Proofs of the ½r, type A1, are known in black and green.

An essay of type A2 shows the condor's head facing right.

1871-72

Blue-surface Paper

7	A1	½r ultra	22.50	14.00
		On wrapper		175.00
		On cover		350.00
8	A1	1r yellow	125.00	45.00
		On wrapper		*750.00*
		On cover		—

Unofficial reprints of types A1-A2 differ in color, have a different sheet makeup and lack gum. Type A1 reprints usually have a double frameline at left. All stamps on blue paper with horiz. blue lines are reprints.

A3

A4

1872 White Paper Litho. *Perf. 11*

9	A3	½r blue	13.00	3.00
10	A4	1r yellow	15.00	4.50
11	A3	1p rose	3.00	*10.00*
		Nos. 9-11 (3)	31.00	*17.50*

The 1r surcharged 4c is fraudulent.

A5

A6

A7

A8

A9

A10

1881, Nov. 1 Engr. *Perf. 12*

12	A5	1c yellow brn	.20	.20
13	A6	2c lake	.20	.20
14	A7	5c blue	2.60	.40
15	A8	10c orange	.20	.20
16	A9	20c gray violet	.20	.20
17	A10	50c blue green	.80	*2.00*
		Nos. 12-17 (6)	4.20	*3.20*

The 1c surcharged 3c, and 20c surcharged 5c are fraudulent.

For overprints see Nos. O1-O6.

No. 17 Surcharged in Black

DIEZ
CENTAVOS

1883, Apr.

18	A10	10c on 50c blue grn	19.00	15.00
a.		Double surcharge		

Dangerous forgeries exist.

A12

A13

A14

A15

1887

19	A12	1c blue green	.20	.20
20	A13	2c vermilion	.35	.20
21	A14	5c blue	1.10	.25
22	A15	80c olive green	2.00	*5.50*
		Nos. 19-22 (4)	3.65	*6.15*

For overprints see Nos. O7-O10.

President Juan Flores — A16

1892

23	A16	1c orange	.20	.20
24	A16	2c dk brown	.20	.20
25	A16	5c vermilion	.20	.20
26	A16	10c green	.20	.20
27	A16	20c red brown	.20	.20
28	A16	50c maroon	.20	*.30*
29	A16	1s blue	.20	*.70*
30	A16	5s purple	.50	*1.00*
		Nos. 23-30 (8)	1.90	*3.00*

The issues of 1892, 1894, 1895 and 1896 were printed by the Hamilton Bank Note Co., New York, to the order of N. F. Seebeck, who held a contract for stamps with the government of Ecuador.

No. 30 in green is said to be an essay or color trial.

For surcharges and overprints see Nos. 31-37, O11-O17.

Nos. 29 and 30 Surcharged in Black

1893

Surcharge Measures 25½x2½mm

31 A16 5c on 1s blue 2.00 2.00
32 A16 5c on 5s purple 4.75 3.50
  a. Double surcharge

Surcharge Measures 24x2¼mm

33 A16 5c on 1s blue 1.25 1.00
  a. Double surcharge, one inverted
34 A16 5c on 5s purple 5.00 4.00
  a. Double surcharge, one invtd.

Nos. 28-30 Surcharged in Black

35 A16 5c on 50c maroon .50 .45
  a. Inverted surcharge 1.75
36 A16 5c on 1s blue .85 .70
37 A16 5c on 5s purple 4.00 3.50
  Nos. 31-37 (7) 18.35 15.15

Pres. Juan Flores
A19

Pres. Vicente Rocafuerte
A20

38 A19 5c on 5s lake 1.00 1.00

It is stated that No. 38 was used exclusively as a postage stamp and not for telegrams.

1894 **Dated 1894** ***Perf. 12***

Various Frames

39 A20 1c blue .20 .20
40 A20 2c yellow brn .20 .20
41 A20 5c green .20 .20
  b. Perf. 14 2.90 1.00
42 A20 10c vermilion .35 .30
43 A20 20c black .55 .35
44 A20 50c orange 2.90 1.00
45 A20 1s carmine 4.75 2.00
46 A20 5s dark blue 6.00 3.00
  Nos. 39-46 (8) 15.15 7.25

1895

Same, Dated "1895"

47 A20 1c blue .45 .35
48 A20 2c yellow brn .45 .35
49 A20 5c green .35 .25
50 A20 10c vermilion .35 .20
51 A20 20c black .50 .50
52 A20 50c orange 1.75 1.10
53 A20 1s carmine 10.50 4.00
54 A20 5s dark blue 4.25 2.00
  Nos. 47-54 (8) 18.60 8.75

Reprints of the 2c, 10c, 50c, 1s and 5s of the 1894-95 issues are generally on thick paper. Original issues are on thin to medium thick paper. To distinguish reprints from originals, a comparison of paper thickness, paper color, gum, printing clarity and direction of paper weave is necessary. Value 20 cents each.

For overprints see #77-112, O20-O33, O50-O91.

A21

A22

A23

A24

A25

A26

A27

A28

1896 **Wmk. 117**

55 A21 1c dk green .35 .30
56 A22 2c red .35 .20
57 A23 5c blue .35 .20
58 A24 10c bister brn .30 *.45*
59 A25 20c orange .70 *1.00*
60 A26 50c dark blue 1.00 *1.50*
61 A27 1s yellow brn 2.00 *2.00*
62 A28 5s violet *7.00* *2.75*
  Nos. 55-62 (8) 12.05 *8.40*

Unwmk.

62A A21 1c dk green .50 .20
62B A22 2c red .55 .20
62C A23 5c blue .55 .35
62D A24 10c bister brn .35 *.70*
62E A25 20c orange 3.00 *2.75*
62F A26 50c dark blue 1.00 *1.40*
62G A27 1s yellow brn 3.00 *4.00*
62H A28 5s violet *7.50* *3.00*
  Nos. 62A-62H (8) *16.45* *12.60*

Reprints of Nos. 55-62H are on very thick paper, with paper weave direction vertical. Value 20 cents each.

For surcharges and overprints see Nos. 74, 76, 113-114, O34-O49.

Vicente Roca, Diego Noboa and José Olmedo — A28a

General Juan Francisco Elizalde — A28b

Perf. 11½

1896, Oct. 9 **Unwmk.** **Litho.**

63 A28a 1c rose .35 *.40*
64 A28b 2c blue .35 *.45*
65 A28a 5c green .50 *.50*
66 A28b 10c ocher .50 *.50*
67 A28a 20c red .70 *2.00*
68 A28b 50c violet 1.10 *3.25*
69 A28a 1s orange 2.00 *5.50*
  Nos. 63-69 (7) 5.50 *12.60*

Success of the Liberal Party in 1845 & 1895.

For overprints see Nos. 115-125.

A29

Black Surcharge

1896, Nov. ***Perf. 12***

70 A29 1c on 1c ver, "1893-1894" .50 .30
  a. Inverted surcharge 1.25 1.00
  b. Double surcharge 4.00 3.50
71 A29 2c on 2c bl, "1893-1894" 1.00 .85
  a. Inverted surcharge 2.00 1.75
72 A29 5c on 10c org, "1887-1888" 1.00 .30
  a. Inverted surcharge 2.00 .85
  b. Double surcharge 3.50 2.00
  c. Surcharged "2cts" .50 .40
  d. "1893-1894" 3.00 2.50
73 A29 10c on 4c brn, "1887-1888" 1.00 .55
  a. Inverted surcharge 2.00 .85
  b. Double surcharge 3.00 1.75
  c. Double surcharge, one inverted
  d. Surcharged "1 cto" 1.00 *1.40*
  e. "1891-1892" 8.50 6.75
  Nos. 70-73 (4) 3.50 2.00

Similar surcharges of type A29 include: Dated "1887-1888" — 1c on 1c blue green, 1c on 2c red, 1c on 4c brown, 1c on 10c yellow; 2c on 2c red, 2c on 10c yellow; 10c on 1c green.

Dated "1891-1892" — 1c on 1c blue green, 1c on 4c brown.

Dated "1893-1894" — 2c on 10c yellow; 10c on 1c vermilion, 10c on 10s black.

For overprints see Nos. O18-O19.

Nos. 59-60 Surcharged in Black or Red

1896, Oct. **Wmk. 117**

74 A25 5c on 20c orange 17.50 17.50
76 A26 10c on 50c dk bl (R) 17.50 17.50
  a. Double surcharge

The surcharge is diag., horiz. or vert.

Overprinted

On Issue of 1894

1897 **Unwmk.**

77 A20 1c blue 1.10 1.10
78 A20 2c yellow brn .95 .65
79 A20 5c green .45 .45
80 A20 10c vermilion 1.40 1.10
81 A20 20c black 1.50 1.40
82 A20 50c orange 3.25 1.60
83 A20 1s carmine 9.50 3.25
84 A20 5s dark blue 55.00 45.00
  Nos. 77-84 (8) 73.15 54.55

On Issue of 1895

85 A20 1c blue 3.00 2.75
86 A20 2c yellow brn 1.10 1.10
87 A20 5c green .95 .80
88 A20 10c vermilion 3.50 3.00
89 A20 20c black .95 .85
90 A20 50c orange 16.00 6.50
91 A20 1s carmine 7.25 3.75
92 A20 5s dark blue 7.25 7.25
  Nos. 85-92 (8) 40.00 26.00

Overprinted

On Issue of 1894

93 A20 1c blue .70 .45
94 A20 2c yellow brn .60 .35
95 A20 5c green .30 .25
96 A20 10c vermilion 1.75 .85
97 A20 20c black 1.90 1.25
98 A20 50c orange 3.50 1.40
99 A20 1s carmine 6.50 4.25
100 A20 5s dark blue 57.50 42.50
  Nos. 93-100 (8) 72.75 51.30

On Issue of 1895

101 A20 1c blue 1.60 .80
102 A20 2c yellow brn .80 .80
103 A20 5c green .85 .50
104 A20 10c vermilion 2.75 2.25
105 A20 20c black 2.50 .60
106 A20 50c orange .90 .90
107 A20 1s carmine 4.00 3.50
108 A20 5s dark blue 4.75 4.75
  Nos. 101-108 (8) 18.15 14.10

Overprints on Nos. 77-108 are to be found reading upward from left to right and downward from left to right, as well as inverted.

Overprinted **1897 Y 1898**

On Issue of 1894

1897

109 A20 10c vermilion 65.00 57.50

On Issue of 1895

110 A20 2c yellow brn *50.00* *45.00*
111 A20 1s carmine 65.00 57.50
112 A20 5s dark blue *65.00* *50.00*
  Nos. 109-112 (4) *245.00* *210.00*

Nos. 56, 59 Overprinted like Nos. 93-108

1897, June **Wmk. 117**

113 A22 2c red 50.00 40.00
114 A25 20c orange 55.00 47.50

Many forged overprints on Nos. 77-114 exist, made on original stamps and reprints.

Stamps or Types of 1896 Overprinted like Nos. 93-108

1897 **Unwmk.** ***Perf. 11½***

115 A28a 1c rose 1.25 1.25
116 A28b 2c blue 1.00 1.00
117 A28b 10c ocher 1.00 1.00
118 A28a 1s yellow 5.00 5.00
  Nos. 115-118 (4) 8.25 8.25

No. 63 Overprinted like Nos. 77-92

1897

119 A28a 1c rose .60 .50

Nos. 63-66 Overprinted in Black

1897

122 A28a 1c rose 2.25 2.00
123 A28b 2c blue 2.25 2.00
124 A28a 5c green 2.25 2.00
125 A28b 10c ocher 2.25 2.00
  a. Double overprint 5.25 4.75
  Nos. 122-125 (4) 9.00 8.00

The 20c, 50c and 1s with this overprint in black and all values of the issue overprinted in blue are reprints.

Overprint Inverted

122a A28a 1c 3.00 2.75
123a A28b 2c 3.00 2.75
124a A28a 5c 3.00 2.75
125b A28b 10c 2.75 2.75

Coat of Arms — A33

1897, June 23 **Engr.** ***Perf. 14-16***

127 A33 1c dk yellow grn .20 .20
128 A33 2c orange red .20 .20
129 A33 5c lake .20 .20
130 A33 10c dk brown .20 .20
131 A33 20c yellow .30 *.40*
132 A33 50c dull blue .30 *.65*
133 A33 1s gray .55 *.80*
134 A33 5s dark lilac .75 *1.10*
  Nos. 127-134 (8) 2.70 *3.75*

No. 135

No. 136

1899, May

135 A33 1c on 2c orange red 1.50 .80
136 A33 5c on 10c brown 1.25 .50
  a. Double surcharge

Luis Vargas Torres
A36

Abdón Calderón
A37

Juan Montalvo
A38

José Mejia
A39

Santa Cruz y Espejo — A40

Pedro Carbo — A41

José Joaquin Olmedo
A42

Pedro Moncayo
A43

1899 *Perf. 12½-16*

137	A36	1c gray blue & blk	.20	.20
a.		Horiz. pair, imperf. vert.		
138	A37	2c brown lil & blk	.20	.20
139	A38	5c lake & blk	.35	.20
140	A39	10c violet & blk	.35	.20
141	A40	20c green & blk	.35	.20
142	A41	50c lil rose & blk	.85	.55
143	A42	1s ocher & blk	4.00	1.75
144	A43	5s lilac & blk	7.25	5.00
		Nos. 137-144 (8)	13.55	8.30

1901

145	A36	1c scarlet & blk	.30	.20
146	A37	2c green & blk	.30	.20
147	A38	5c gray lil & blk	.30	.20
148	A39	10c dp blue & blk	.35	.25
149	A40	20c gray & blk	.35	.25
150	A41	50c lt blue & blk	1.10	.65
151	A42	1s brown & blk	4.00	1.75
152	A43	5s gray blk & blk	6.00	4.00
		Nos. 145-152 (8)	12.70	7.50

In July, 1902, following the theft of a quantity of stamps during a fire at Guayaquil, the Government authorized the governors of the provinces to handstamp their stocks. Many varieties of these handstamps exist.

Other control marks were used in 1907.

For overprints see Nos. O103-O106, O167.

A44

Surcharged on Revenue Stamp Dated 1901-1902

1903-06 *Perf. 14, 15*

153	A44	1c on 5c gray lil ('06)	.25	.20
154	A44	1c on 20c gray ('06)	3.25	2.25
155	A44	1c on 25c yellow	.50	.20
a.		Double surcharge		
156	A44	1c on 1s bl ('06)	26.00	25.00
157	A44	3c on 5c gray lil ('06)	3.25	2.00
158	A44	3c on 20c gray ('06)	8.50	7.50
159	A44	3c on 25c yel ('06)	8.00	7.50
159A	A44	3c on 1s blue ('06)	1.25	1.10
		Nos. 153-159A (8)	51.00	45.75

Counterfeits are plentiful.

See #191-197.

Capt. Abdón Calderón
A45 A46

1904, July 31 *Perf. 12*

160	A45	1c red & blk	.40	.30
161	A45	2c blue & blk	.50	.35
162	A46	5c yellow & blk	1.50	1.00
163	A45	10c red & blk	3.00	1.00
164	A45	20c blue & blk	8.00	2.50
165	A46	50c yellow & blk	65.00	35.00
		Nos. 160-165 (6)	78.40	40.15

Centenary of the birth of Calderón.

Presidents

Vicente Roca — A47

Diego Noboa — A48

Francisco Robles — A49

José M. Urvina — A50

García Moreno — A51

Jerónimo Carrión — A52

Javier Espinoza
A53

Antonio Borrero
A54

1907, July *Perf. 14, 15*

166	A47	1c red & blk	.35	.20
167	A48	2c pale blue & blk	.65	.20
168	A49	3c orange & blk	1.00	.20
169	A50	5c lilac rose & blk	1.25	.20
170	A51	10c dp blue & blk	2.50	.20
171	A52	20c yellow grn & blk	3.50	.35
172	A53	50c violet & blk	7.75	.70
173	A54	1s green & blk	10.00	2.00
		Nos. 166-173 (8)	27.00	4.05

The stamps of the 1907 issue frequently have control marks similar to those found on the 1899 and 1901 issues. These marks were applied to distinguish the stamps issued in the various provinces and to serve as a check on local officials.

Locomotive — A55

García Moreno — A56

Gen. Eloy Alfaro — A57

Abelardo Moncayo — A58

Archer Harman — A59

James Sivewright — A60

Mt. Chimborazo
A61

1908, June 25

174	A55	1c red brown	.75	*1.50*
175	A56	2c blue & blk	1.00	*1.60*
176	A57	5c claret & blk	1.90	*3.75*
177	A58	10c ocher & blk	1.40	*2.10*
178	A59	20c green & blk	1.40	*2.75*
179	A60	50c gray & blk	1.40	*2.75*
180	A61	1s black	2.75	*5.50*
		Nos. 174-180 (7)	10.60	19.95

Opening of the Guayaquil-Quito Railway.

José Mejía Vallejo — A62

Principal Exposition Building — A70

Designs: 2c, Francisco J. E. Santa Cruz y Espejo. 3c, Francisco Ascásubi. 5c, Juan Salinas. 10c, Juan Pio de Montúfar. 20c, Carlos de Montúfar. 50c, Juan de Dios Morales. 1s, Manuel R. de Quiroga.

1909, Aug. 10 *Perf. 12*

181	A62	1c green	.25	*.45*
182	A62	2c blue	.25	*.45*
183	A62	3c orange	.25	*.50*
184	A62	5c claret	.25	*.50*
185	A62	10c yellow brn	.30	*.50*
186	A62	20c gray	.30	*.70*
187	A62	50c vermilion	.30	*.70*
188	A62	1s olive grn	.35	*.95*
189	A70	5s violet	.75	*1.90*
		Nos. 181-189 (9)	3.00	*6.65*

National Exposition of 1909.

Surcharged

1909

190	A68	5c on 50c vermilion	.55	.50

Revenue Stamps Surcharged as in 1903

1910 *Perf. 14, 15*

Stamps Dated 1905-1906

191	A44	1c on 5c green	1.10	.85
192	A44	5c on 20c blue	4.75	1.00
193	A44	5c on 25c violet	9.00	1.75

Stamps Dated 1907-1908

194	A44	1c on 5c green	.20	.20
195	A44	5c on 20c blue	7.00	4.75
196	A44	5c on 25c violet	.60	.20

Stamp Dated 1909-1910

197	A44	5c on 20c blue	*40.00*	*30.00*
		Nos. 191-197 (7)	*62.65*	*38.75*

Presidents

Roca — A71

Noboa — A72

Robles — A73

Urvina — A74

Moreno — A75

Borrero — A76

1911-28 *Perf. 12*

198	A71	1c scarlet & blk	.40	.20
199	A71	1c orange ('16)	.40	.20
200	A71	1c lt blue ('25)	.20	.20
201	A72	2c blue & blk	.55	.20
202	A72	2c green ('16)	.55	.20
203	A72	2c dk violet ('25)	.55	.20
204	A73	3c orange & blk ('13)	1.10	.30
205	A73	3c black ('15)	.75	.20
206	A74	5c scarlet & blk	.95	.20
207	A74	5c violet ('15)	.95	.20
208	A74	5c rose ('25)	.35	.20
209	A74	5c dk brown ('28)	.35	.20
210	A75	10c dp blue & blk	1.10	.20
211	A75	10c dp blue ('15)	1.10	.20
212	A75	10c yellow grn ('25)	.35	.20
213	A75	10c black ('28)	.90	.20
214	A76	1s green & blk	6.00	1.10
215	A76	1s orange & blk ('27)	4.00	.20
		Nos. 198-215 (18)	20.55	4.60

For overprints see Nos. 260-262, 264-265, O107-O122, O124-O134, O156-O157, O160-O162, O164-O166, O168-O173, O175-O178, O183-O184, O189, RA1.

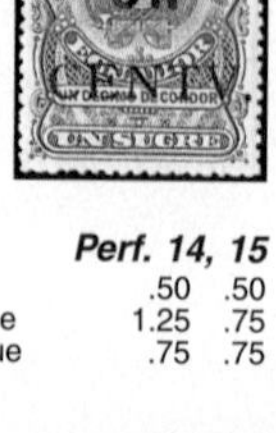

A77

1912 *Perf. 14, 15*

216	A77	1c on 1s green	.50	.50
217	A77	2c on 2s carmine	1.25	.75
218	A77	2c on 5s dull blue	.75	.75

219 A77 2c on 10s yellow	2.50	2.50
a. Inverted surcharge	8.00	6.00
Nos. 216-219 (4)	5.00	4.50

No. 216 exists with narrow "V" and small "U" in "UN" and Nos. 217, 218 and 219 with "D" with serifs or small "O" in "DOS."

Enrique Váldez — A78

Jerónimo Carrión — A79

Javier Espinoza — A80

1915-17 ***Perf. 12***

220 A78 4c red & blk	.20	.20
221 A79 20c green & blk ('17)	1.75	.20
222 A80 50c dp violet & blk	3.00	.45
Nos. 220-222 (3)	4.95	.85

For overprints see #O123, O135, O163, O174.

Olmedo — A86

Monument to "Fathers of the Country" — A95

Laurel Wreath and Star — A104

Designs: 2c, Rafael Ximena. 3c, Roca. 4c, Luis F. Vivero. 5c, Luis Febres Cordero. 6c, Francisco Lavayen. 7c, Jorge Antonio de Elizalde. 8c, Baltazar Garcia. 9c, Jose de Antepara. 15c, Luis Urdaneta. 20c, Jose M. Villamil. 30c, Miguel Letamendi. 40c, Gregorio Escobedo. 50c, Gen. Antonio Jose de Sucre. 60c, Juan Illingworth. 70c, Roca. 80c, Rocafuerte. 1s, Simon Bolivar.

1920

223 A86 1c yellow grn	.20	.20
224 A86 2c carmine	.20	.20
225 A86 3c yellow brn	.20	.20
226 A86 4c myrtle green	.30	.20
227 A86 5c pale blue	.30	.20
228 A86 6c red orange	.55	.30
229 A86 7c brown	1.50	.75
230 A86 8c apple green	.75	.35
231 A86 9c lake	2.75	1.25
232 A95 10c lt blue	1.00	.20
233 A86 15c dk gray	1.50	.35
234 A86 20c dk violet	1.50	.20
235 A86 30c brt violet	2.75	1.00
236 A86 40c dk brown	5.00	1.75
237 A86 50c dk green	3.50	.35
238 A86 60c dk blue	6.50	1.90
239 A86 70c gray	10.50	4.25
240 A86 80c orange yel	11.00	4.25
241 A104 90c green	11.50	4.25
242 A86 1s pale blue	16.00	7.00
Nos. 223-242 (20)	77.50	29.15

Cent. of the independence of Guayaquil.

For overprints and surcharges see Nos. 263, 274-292, O136-O155, O179-O182, O185-O188.

Postal Tax Stamp of 1924 Overprinted

1925

259 PT6 20c bister brown	1.50	1.50

Stamps of 1915-25 Overprinted in Black or Red Upright (1c, 3c, 5c) or Inverted (2c, 4c, 10c)

1926

260 A71 1c lt blue	5.50	4.75
261 A72 2c dk violet	5.50	4.75
262 A73 3c black (R)	5.50	4.75
263 A86 4c myrtle green	5.50	4.75
264 A74 5c rose	8.00	4.75
265 A75 10c yellow grn	8.00	4.75
Nos. 260-265 (6)	38.00	28.50

Quito-Esmeraldas railway opening.

Upright overprints on 2c, 4c, 10c and inverted overprints on 1c, 3c, 5c sell for more.

Postal Tax Stamps of 1920-24 Overprinted

1927

266 PT6 1c olive green	.20	.20
a. "POSTAI"	1.40	.85
b. Double overprint	2.00	.85
c. Inverted overprint	2.00	.85
267 PT6 2c deep green	.20	.20
a. "POSTAI"	1.40	.85
b. Double overprint	2.00	.85
268 PT6 20c bister brown	.70	.20
a. "POSTAI"	8.50	5.00
Nos. 266-268 (3)	1.10	.60

Quito Post Office — A109

1927, June

269 A109 5c orange	.25	.20
270 A109 10c dark green	.35	.20
271 A109 20c violet	.40	.20
Nos. 269-271 (3)	1.00	.60

Opening of new Quito P.O.

For overprint see No. O190.

Postal Tax Stamp of 1924 Overprinted in Dark Blue

POSTAL

1928

273 PT6 20c bister brown	.25	.20
a. Double overprint, one inverted	2.00	.70

See No. 339 for 10c with same overprint.

Nos. 235, 239-240 Overprinted in Red Brown and Surcharged in Dark Blue

1928, July 8

274 A86 10c on 30c violet	5.00	5.00
275 A86 50c on 70c gray	6.00	6.00
276 A86 1s on 80c org yel	7.00	7.00
Nos. 274-276 (3)	18.00	18.00

Quito-Cayambe railway opening.

Stamps of 1920 Surcharged

1928, Oct. 9

277 A86 1c on 1c yel grn	10.00	10.00
278 A86 1c on 2c car	.20	.20
279 A86 2c on 3c yel brn	1.50	1.50
a. Dbl. surch., one reading up	20.00	20.00
280 A86 2c on 4c myr grn	1.00	1.00
281 A86 2c on 5c lt blue	.40	.30
a. Dbl. surch., one reading up	20.00	20.00
282 A86 2c on 7c brown	50.00	50.00
283 A86 5c on 6c red org	.25	.20
a. "5 ctvos." omitted	25.00	25.00
284 A86 10c on 7c brown	.85	.85
285 A86 20c on 8c apple grn	.25	.20
a. Double surcharge		
286 A95 40c on 10c blue	2.75	2.75
287 A86 40c on 15c dk gray	.85	.85
288 A86 50c on 20c dk vio	9.50	9.50
289 A86 1s on 40c dk brown	3.00	3.00
290 A86 5s on 50c dk green	3.50	3.50
291 A86 10s on 60c dk blue	13.00	13.00

With Additional Surcharge in Red

292 A86 10c on 2c on 7c brn	.35	.35
a. Red surcharge double	20.00	20.00
Nos. 277-292 (16)	97.40	97.20

National Assembly of 1928.

Counterfeit overprints exist of #277-291.

A111

A112

Surcharged in Various Colors

1928, Oct. 31 ***Perf. 14***

293 A111 5c on 20c gray lil (Bk)	1.00	.85
294 A111 10c on 20c gray lil (R)	1.00	.85
295 A111 20c on 1s grn (O)	1.00	.85
296 A111 50c on 1s grn (Bl)	1.25	.70
297 A111 1s on 1s grn (V)	1.60	.90
298 A111 5s on 2s red (G)	5.00	4.50
299 A111 10s on 2s red (Br)	6.00	6.00
a. Black surcharge	5.00	5.00
Nos. 293-299 (7)	16.85	14.65

Quito-Otavalo railway opening.

See Nos. 586-587.

Postal Tax Stamp of 1924 Overprinted in Red

1929 ***Perf. 12***

302 PT6 2c deep green	.20	.20

There are two types of overprint on No. 302 differing slightly.

1929

Red Overprint

303 A112 1c dark blue	.20	.20
a. Overprint reading down	.20	.20

See Nos. 586-587.

Plowing — A113

Cultivating Cacao — A114

Cacao Pod — A115

Loading Sugar Cane — A119

Growing Tobacco — A116

Exportation of Fruits — A117

Landscape — A118

Scene in Quito A120

Scene in Quito A121

Olmedo — A122

Monument to Simón Bolívar — A125

Designs: 2s, Sucre. 5s, Bolivar.

1930, Aug. 1 ***Perf. 12½***

304 A113 1c yellow & car .20 .20
305 A114 2c yellow & grn .20 .20
306 A115 5c dp grn & vio brn .25 .20
307 A116 6c yellow & red .30 .20
308 A117 10c orange & ol grn .30 .20
309 A118 16c red & yel grn .35 .25
310 A119 20c ultra & yel .55 .20
311 A120 40c orange & sepia .75 .35
312 A121 50c orange & sepia .75 .40
313 A122 1s dp green & blk 2.75 .45
314 A122 2s dk blue & blk 4.25 .75
315 A122 5s dk violet & blk 7.75 1.50
316 A125 10s car rose & blk 26.50 5.00
Nos. 304-316 (13) 44.90 9.90

Centenary of founding of republic.
For surcharges and overprints see Nos. 319-320, 331-338, RA25, RA33, RA43.

A126

A127

Red Overprint

1933 ***Perf. 15***

317 A126 10c olive brown .50 .20

Blue Overprint

318 A127 10c olive brown .30 .20
a. Inverted overprint 5.00 5.00

For overprint see No. 339.

Nos. 307, 309 Surcharged in Black

1933 ***Perf. 12½***

319 A116 5c on 6c yellow & red .25 .20
320 A118 10c on 16c red & yel grn .40 .20
a. Inverted overprint 4.00 4.00

Landscape
A128

Mt. Chimborazo
A129

1934-45 ***Perf. 12***

321 A128 5c violet .90 .45
322 A128 5c blue .90 .45
323 A128 5c dark brown .90 .45
323A A128 5c slate blk ('45) .90 .45
324 A128 10c rose .90 .45
325 A128 10c dark green .90 .45
326 A128 10c brown .90 .45
327 A128 10c orange .90 .45
328 A128 10c olive green .90 .45
329 A128 10c gray blk ('35) .90 .45
329A A128 10c red lilac ('44) .90 .45

Perf. 14

330 A129 1s carmine rose 1.10 .50
Nos. 321-330 (12) 11.00 5.45

Stamps of 1930 Surcharged or Ovptd. in various colors similar to:

1935 ***Perf. 12½***

331 A116 5c on 6c (Bl) .45 .35
332 A116 10c on 6c (G) .65 .35
333 A119 20c (R) .90 .35
334 A120 40c (G) 1.25 .35
335 A121 50c (G) 1.50 .40
336 A122 1s on 5s (Gold) 3.50 1.00
337 A122 2s on 5s (Gold) 4.75 1.60
338 A125 5s on 10s (Bl) 8.00 4.25
Nos. 331-338,C35-C38 (12) 55.00 28.65

Unveiling of a monument to Bolivar at Quito, July 24, 1935.

The 5-stamp Sociedad Colombista Panamericana series of 1935 and 5 air-mail stamps of a similar design are not recognized by this Catalogue as having been issued primarily for postal purposes.

Telegraph Stamp Overprinted Diagonally in Red like No. 273

1935 ***Perf. 14½***

339 A126 10c olive brown .25 .25

Map of Galápagos Islands
A130

Galapagos Land Iguana
A131

Galápagos Tortoise — A132

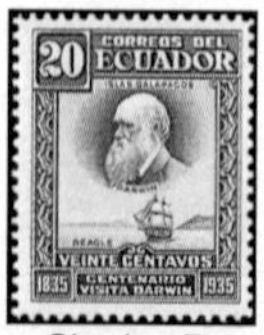

Charles R. Darwin — A133

Columbus
A134

Island Scene
A135

1936 ***Perf. 14***

340 A130 2c black 1.00 .25
341 A131 5c olive grn 1.25 .25
342 A132 10c brown 2.25 .30
343 A133 20c dk violet 2.50 .40
344 A134 1s dk carmine 4.00 .75
345 A135 2s dark blue 6.00 1.25
Nos. 340-345 (6) 17.00 3.20

Cent. of the visit of Charles Darwin to the Galápagos Islands, Sept. 17, 1835.
For overprints see Nos. O191-O195.

Tobacco Stamp Overprinted in Black

1936 ***Rouletted 7***

346 PT7 1c rose red .25 .25
a. Horiz. pair, imperf. vert.
b. Double surcharge

No. 346 is similar to type PT7 but does not include "CASA CORREOS."

Louis Godin, Charles M. de la Condamine and Pierre Bouguer
A136

Portraits: 5c, 20c, Antonio Ulloa, La Condamine and Jorge Juan.

1936 **Engr.** ***Perf. 12½***

347 A136 2c deep blue .35 .30
348 A136 5c dark green .35 .30
349 A136 10c deep orange .35 .30
350 A136 20c violet .55 .30
351 A136 50c dark red .85 .30
Nos. 347-351,C39-C42 (9) 4.50 2.45

Bicentenary of Geodesical Mission to Quito.

Independence Monument — A137

1936 ***Perf. 13½x14***

352 A137 2c green 2.00 1.10
353 A137 5c dark violet 2.00 1.10
354 A137 10c carmine rose 2.00 1.10
355 A137 20c black 2.00 1.10
356 A137 50c blue 2.75 1.75
357 A137 1s dark red 3.75 3.25
Nos. 352-357,C43-C50 (14) 42.50 37.40

1st Intl. Philatelic Exhibition at Quito.

Coat of Arms — A138

Overprint in Black or Red

1937 ***Perf. 12½***

359 A138 5c olive green 1.25 .30
360 A138 10c dark blue (R) 1.25 .25

For overprint see No. 562.

Andean Landscape
A139

Atahualpa, the Last Inca
A140

Hat Weavers — A141

Coast Landscape
A142

Gold Washing
A143

1937, Aug. 19 ***Perf. 11½***

361 A139 2c green .25 .25
362 A140 5c deep rose .25 .25
363 A141 10c blue .25 .25
364 A142 20c deep rose .75 .30
365 A143 1s olive green 1.00 .35
Nos. 361-365 (5) 2.50 1.40

For overprints see Nos. O196-O200.

"Liberty" Carrying Flag of Ecuador — A144

Engraved and Lithographed

1938, Feb. 22 ***Perf. 12***

Center Multicolored

366 A144 2c blue .25 .20
367 A144 5c violet .30 .20
368 A144 10c black .40 .20
369 A144 20c brown .55 .20
370 A144 50c black .85 .20
371 A144 1s olive blk 1.25 .30
372 A144 2s dk brn 2.50 .40
Nos. 366-372,C57-C63 (14) 13.35 3.80

US Constitution, 150th anniversary.
For overprints and surcharges see Nos. 413-415, 444-446, RA46, RA52.

A145

A146

A147

A148

Designs: 10c, Winged figure holding globe. 50c, Cactus, winged wheel. 1s, "Communications." 2s, "Construction."

Perf. 13, 13x13½

1938, Oct. 30 **Engr.**

373 A145 10c bright ultra .20 .20
374 A146 50c deep red violet .20 .20
375 A147 1s copper red .35 .20
376 A148 2s dark green .55 .20
Nos. 373-376 (4) 1.30 .80

Progress of Ecuador Exhibition.
For overprints see Nos. C105-C113.

Parade of Athletes — A149

Runner — A150

Basketball — A151

Wrestlers A152

Diver A153

1939, Mar. ***Perf. 12***

377	A149	5c carmine rose	2.25	.45
378	A150	10c deep blue	2.75	.55
379	A151	50c gray olive	4.25	.75
380	A152	1s dull violet	6.00	.75
381	A153	2s dull olive green	8.75	.95
		Nos. 377-381,C65-C69 (10)	45.00	5.60

First Bolivarian Games (1938), Bogota.

Dolores Mission A154

Trylon and Perisphere A155

1939, June 16 ***Perf. 12½x13***

382	A154	2c blue green	.25	.25
383	A154	5c rose red	.25	.25
384	A154	10c ultra	.25	.25
385	A154	50c yellow brown	.60	.25
386	A154	1s black	.95	.25
387	A154	2s purple	1.25	.40
		Nos. 382-387,C73-C79 (13)	6.25	3.05

Golden Gate International Exposition.
For surcharges see Nos. 429, 436.

1939, June 30

388	A155	2c lt olive green	.35	.35
389	A155	5c red orange	.35	.35
390	A155	10c ultra	.35	.35
391	A155	50c slate gray	.50	.35
392	A155	1s rose carmine	.90	.35
393	A155	2s black brown	1.00	.40
		Nos. 388-393,C80-C86 (13)	6.20	3.55

New York World's Fair.
For surcharge see No. 437.

Flags of the 21 American Republics — A156

1940 ***Perf. 12***

394	A156	5c dp rose & blk	.20	.20
395	A156	10c dk blue & blk	.20	.20
396	A156	50c Prus green & blk	.30	.20
397	A156	1s dp violet & blk	.50	.30
		Nos. 394-397,C87-C90 (8)	3.60	2.35

Pan American Union, 50th anniversary.

AIR POST STAMPS

In 1928-30, the internal airmail service of Ecuador was handled by the Sociedad Colombo-Alemana de Transportes Aereos ("SCADTA") under government sanction. During this period SCADTA issued stamps which were the only legal franking for airmail service except that handled under contract with Pan American-Grace Airways. SCADTA issues are Nos. C1-C6, C16-C25, CF1-CF2.

Colombia Air Post Stamps of 1923 Surcharged in Carmine

"Provisional" at 45 degree Angle

Perf. 14x14½

1928, Aug. 28 **Wmk. 116**

C1	AP6	50c on 10c green	110.00	70.00
C2	AP6	75c on 15c car	210.00	160.00
C3	AP6	1s on 20c gray	70.00	42.50
C4	AP6	1½s on 30c blue	45.00	35.00
C5	AP6	3s on 60c brown	85.00	52.50
		Nos. C1-C5 (5)	520.00	360.00

"Provisional" at 41 degree Angle

1929, Mar. 20

C1a	AP6	50c on 10c green	125.00	110.00
C2a	AP6	75c on 15c carmine	225.00	175.00
C3a	AP6	1s on 20c gray	225.00	175.00
		Nos. C1a-C3a (3)	575.00	460.00

Same with "Cts." Between Surcharged Numerals

C6	AP6	50c on 10c green	*700.00*	*1,700.*

A 75c on 15c carmine with "Cts." between the surcharged numerals exists. There is no evidence that it was regularly issued or used.
For overprints see Nos. CF1-CF1a.

Plane over River Guayas — AP1

Unwmk.

1929, May 5 **Engr.** ***Perf. 12***

C8	AP1	2c black	.20	.20
C9	AP1	5c carmine rose	.20	.20
C10	AP1	10c deep brown	.20	.20
C11	AP1	20c dark violet	.45	.20
C12	AP1	50c deep green	.80	.45
C13	AP1	1s dark blue	3.00	2.75
C14	AP1	5s orange yellow	12.50	11.00
C15	AP1	10s orange red	67.50	57.50
		Nos. C8-C15 (8)	84.85	72.50

Establishment of commercial air service in Ecuador. The stamps were available for all forms of postal service and were largely used for franking ordinary letters.
Nos. C13-C15 show numerals in color on white background. Counterfeits of No. C15 exist.
See #C26-C31. For overprints and surcharge see #C32-C38, C287, CO1-CO12.

Jesuit Church La Compania AP2

Mount Chimborazo AP3

Wmk. 127

1929, Apr. 1 **Litho.** ***Perf. 14***

C16	AP2	50c red brown	2.25	2.25
C17	AP2	75c green	2.25	2.25
C18	AP2	1s rose	3.50	2.25
C19	AP2	1½s gray blue	3.50	2.25
C20	AP2	2s violet	5.75	4.50
C21	AP2	3s brown	5.75	4.50
C22	AP3	5s lt blue	20.00	14.00
C23	AP3	10s lt red	42.50	30.00
C24	AP3	15s violet	70.00	60.00
C25	AP3	25s olive green	92.50	70.00
		Nos. C16-C25 (10)	248.00	192.00

For overprint see No. CF2.

Plane Type of 1929

1930-44 **Unwmk.** **Engr.** ***Perf. 12***

C26	AP1	1s carmine lake	3.25	.55
C27	AP1	1s green ('44)	.50	.20
C28	AP1	5s olive green	5.00	3.75
C29	AP1	5s purple ('44)	1.00	.20
C30	AP1	10s black	15.00	5.50
C31	AP1	10s brt ultra ('44)	2.25	.30
		Nos. C26-C31 (6)	27.00	10.50

Nos. C26-C31 show numerals in color on white background.
For surcharge see No. C287.

Type of 1929 Overprinted in Various Colors

AP4

1930, June 4

C32	AP4	1s car lake (Bk)	22.50	22.50
a.		Double ovpt. (R Br + Bk)	75.00	
C33	AP4	5s olive grn (Bl)	22.50	22.50
C34	AP4	10s black (R Br)	22.50	22.50
		Nos. C32-C34 (3)	67.50	67.50

Flight of Capt. Benjamin Mendez from Bogota to Quito, bearing a crown of flowers for the tomb of Grand Marshal Sucre.

Air Post Official Stamps of 1929-30 Overprinted in Various Colors or Surcharged Similarly in Upper & Lower Case

1935, July 24

C35	AP1	50c deep green (Bl)	8.50	5.00
C36	AP1	50c olive brn (R)	8.50	5.00
C37	AP1	1s on 5s ol grn (Bk)	8.50	5.00
a.		Double surcharge	95.00	
C38	AP1	2s on 10s black (R)	8.50	5.00
		Nos. C35-C38 (4)	34.00	20.00

Unveiling of a monument to Bolívar at Quito, July 24th, 1935.

Geodesical Mission Issue

Nos. 349-351 Overprinted in Blue or Black and Type of Regular issue

1936, July 3 ***Perf. 12½***

C39	A136	10c deep orange (Bl)	.40	.20
C40	A136	20c violet (Bk)	.40	.20
C41	A136	50c dark red (Bl)	.40	.20
C42	A136	70c black	.85	.35
		Nos. C39-C42 (4)	2.05	.95

For surcharge see No. RA42.

Philatelic Exhibition Issue

Type of Regular Issue Overprinted "AEREA"

1936, Oct. 20 ***Perf. 13½x14***

C43	A137	2c rose	4.50	4.50
C44	A137	5c brown orange	4.50	4.50
C45	A137	10c brown	4.50	4.50
C46	A137	20c ultra	4.50	4.50
C47	A137	50c red violet	4.50	4.50
C48	A137	1s green	4.50	4.50
		Nos. C43-C48 (6)	27.00	27.00

Condor and Plane — AP6

Perf. 13½

C49	AP6	70c orange brown	.50	.50
C50	AP6	1s dull violet	.50	.50

Nos. C43-C50 were issued for the 1st Intl. Phil. Exhib. at Quito.

Condor over "El Altar" — AP7

1937-46 ***Perf. 11½, 12***

C51	AP7	10c chestnut	2.50	.20
C52	AP7	20c olive black	3.25	.20
C53	AP7	40c rose car ('46)	3.25	.20
C54	AP7	70c black brown	4.50	.20
C55	AP7	1s gray black	7.00	.20
C56	AP7	2s dark violet	12.00	.65
		Nos. C51-C56 (6)	32.50	1.65

Issue dates: 40c, Oct. 7; others, Aug. 19.
For overprints see #463-464, CO13-CO17.

Portrait of Washington, American Eagle and Flags — AP8

Engraved and Lithographed

1938, Feb. 9 ***Perf. 12***

Center Multicolored

C57	AP8	2c brown	.20	.20
C58	AP8	5c black	.20	.20
C59	AP8	10c brown	.20	.20
C60	AP8	20c dark blue	.40	.20
C61	AP8	50c violet	.90	.20
C62	AP8	1s black	1.60	.20
C63	AP8	2s violet	3.75	.90
		Nos. C57-C63 (7)	7.25	2.10

150th anniv. of the US Constitution.
In 1947, Nos. C61-C63 were overprinted in dark blue: "Primero la Patria!" and plane. These revolutionary propaganda stamps were later renounced by decree.
For overprints see #C102-C104, C139-C141.

No. RA35 Surcharged in Red

1938, Nov. 16 ***Perf. 13½***

C64	PT12	65c on 3c ultra	.20	.20

A national airmail concession was given to the Sociedad Ecuatoriano de Transportes Aereos (SEDTA) in July, 1938. No. RA35 was surcharged for SEDTA postal requirements. SEDTA operated through 1940.

Army Horseman — AP9

Woman Runner — AP10

Tennis — AP11

Boxing — AP12

Olympic Fire — AP13

1939, Mar. Engr. *Perf. 12*

C65	AP9	5c lt green	.75	.20
C66	AP10	10c salmon	1.00	.20
C67	AP11	50c redsh brown	5.25	.20
C68	AP12	1s black brown	6.25	.45
C69	AP13	2s rose carmine	7.75	1.10
		Nos. C65-C69 (5)	21.00	2.15

First Bolivarian Games (1938).

Plane over Chimborazo AP14

1939, May 1 *Perf. 13x12½*

C70	AP14	1s yellow brown	.20	.20
C71	AP14	2s rose violet	.35	.20
C72	AP14	5s black	.95	.20
		Nos. C70-C72 (3)	1.50	.60

Golden Gate Bridge and Mountain Peak — AP15

Empire State Building and Mountain Peak — AP16

1939 *Perf. 12½x13*

C73	AP15	2c black	.20	.20
C74	AP15	5c rose red	.20	.20
C75	AP15	10c indigo	.20	.20
C76	AP15	50c rose violet	.20	.20
C77	AP15	1s chocolate	.40	.20
C78	AP15	2s yellow brown	.50	.20
C79	AP15	5s emerald	1.00	.20
		Nos. C73-C79 (7)	2.70	1.40

Golden Gate International Exposition.
For surcharge & overprint see #434, CO18.

1939

C80	AP16	2c brown orange	.20	.20
C81	AP16	5c dark carmine	.20	.20
C82	AP16	10c indigo	.20	.20
C83	AP16	50c slate green	.20	.20
C84	AP16	1s deep orange	.40	.20
C85	AP16	2s dk red violet	.45	.20
C86	AP16	5s dark gray	1.10	.20
		Nos. C80-C86 (7)	2.75	1.40

New York World's Fair.
For surcharge see No. 435.

Map of the Americas and Airplane — AP17

1940, July 9

C87	AP17	10c red org & blue	.20	.20
C88	AP17	70c sepia & blue	.20	.20
C89	AP17	1s copper brn & blue	.40	.20
C90	AP17	10s black & blue	1.60	.85
		Nos. C87-C90 (4)	2.40	1.45

Pan American Union, 50th anniversary.

AIR POST REGISTRATION STAMPS

Issued by Sociedad Colombo-Alemana de Transportes Aereos (SCADTA)

Nos. C3 and C3a Overprinted "R" in Carmine

1928-29 Wmk. 116 *Perf. 14x14½*

CF1	AP6	1s on 20c (#C3)	110.00	100.00
a.		1s on 20c (#C3a) ('29)	140.00	110.00

No. C18 Overprinted "R" in Black

1929, Apr. 1 Wmk. 127 *Perf. 14*

CF2	AP2	1s rose	75.00	55.00

AIR POST OFFICIAL STAMPS

Nos. C8-C15 Overprinted in Red or Black

1929, May Unwmk. *Perf. 12*

CO1	AP1	2c black (R)	.50	.50
CO2	AP1	5c carmine rose	.50	.50
CO3	AP1	10c deep brown	.50	.50
CO4	AP1	20c dark violet	.50	.50
CO5	AP1	50c deep green	2.00	2.00
CO6	AP1	1s dark blue	2.00	2.00
a.		Inverted overprint	240.00	
CO7	AP1	5s orange yellow	9.00	7.75
CO8	AP1	10s orange red	105.00	75.00
		Nos. CO1-CO8 (8)	120.00	88.75

Establishment of commercial air service in Ecuador.
Counterfeits of No. CO8 exist.
See Nos. CO9-CO12. For overprints and surcharges see Nos. C35-C38.

1930, Jan. 9

CO9	AP1	50c olive brown	1.75	1.75
CO10	AP1	1s carmine lake	2.25	2.25
CO11	AP1	5s olive green	5.50	5.50
CO12	AP1	10s black	10.50	10.50
		Nos. CO9-CO12 (4)	20.00	20.00

For surcharges and overprint see Nos. C36-C38.

Air Post Stamps of 1937 Overprinted in Black

1937, Aug. 19

CO13	AP7	10c chestnut	.20	.20
CO14	AP7	20c olive black	.20	.20
CO15	AP7	70c black brown	.20	.20
CO16	AP7	1s gray black	.30	.20
CO17	AP7	2s dark violet	.35	.30
		Nos. CO13-CO17 (5)	1.25	1.10

For overprints see Nos. 463-464.

No. C79 Overprinted in Black

1940, Aug. 1 *Perf. 12½x13*

CO18	AP15	5s emerald	.80	.60

SPECIAL DELIVERY STAMPS

SD1

1928 Unwmk. *Perf. 12*

E1	SD1	2c on 2c blue	4.00	*4.50*
E2	SD1	5c on 2c blue	3.50	*4.50*
E3	SD1	10c on 2c blue	3.50	*3.00*
a.		"10 CTVOS" inverted	10.50	*13.00*
E4	SD1	20c on 2c blue	5.00	*4.50*
E5	SD1	50c on 2c blue	6.00	*4.50*
		Nos. E1-E5 (5)	22.00	*21.00*

POSTAGE DUE STAMPS

Numeral — D1

Coat of Arms — D2

1896 Engr. Wmk. 117 *Perf. 12*

J1	D1	1c blue green	2.90	*3.25*
J2	D1	2c blue green	2.90	*3.25*
J3	D1	5c blue green	2.90	*3.25*
J4	D1	10c blue green	2.90	*3.25*
J5	D1	20c blue green	2.90	*4.25*
J6	D1	50c blue green	2.90	*6.50*
J7	D1	100c blue green	2.90	*8.50*
		Nos. J1-J7 (7)	20.30	*32.25*

Reprints are on very thick paper with distinct watermark and vertical paper-weave direction. Value 15c each.

Unwmk.

J8	D1	1c blue green	*2.50*	*3.00*
J9	D1	2c blue green	*2.50*	*3.00*
J10	D1	5c blue green	*2.50*	*3.00*
J11	D1	10c blue green	*2.50*	*3.00*
J12	D1	20c blue green	*2.50*	*3.75*
J13	D1	50c blue green	*2.50*	*5.25*
J14	D1	100c blue green	*2.50*	*7.50*
		Nos. J8-J14 (7)	17.50	*28.50*

1929

J15	D2	5c deep blue	.20	.20
J16	D2	10c orange yellow	.30	.30
J17	D2	20c red	.20	.20
		Nos. J15-J17 (3)	.70	.70

OFFICIAL STAMPS

Regular Issues of 1881 and 1887 Handstamped in Black

1886 Unwmk. *Perf. 12*

O1	A5	1c yellow brown	.85	.85
O2	A6	2c lake	1.00	1.00
O3	A7	5c blue	2.25	*2.90*
O4	A8	10c orange	1.75	1.10
O5	A9	20c gray violet	1.75	1.75
O6	A10	50c blue green	5.00	3.75
		Nos. O1-O6 (6)	12.60	11.35

1887

O7	A12	1c green	1.10	.85
O8	A13	2c vermilion	1.10	1.10
O9	A14	5c blue	1.75	.85
O10	A15	80c olive green	5.75	3.25
		Nos. O7-O10 (4)	9.70	6.05

Nos. O1-O10 are known with red handstamp but these are believed to be speculative.
The overprint on the 1886-87 issues is handstamped and is found in various positions.

Flores — O1

Arms — O1a

1892

Carmine Overprint

O11	O1	1c ultramarine	.20	.20
O12	O1	2c ultramarine	.20	.20
O13	O1	5c ultramarine	.20	.20
O14	O1	10c ultramarine	.20	.30
O15	O1	20c ultramarine	.20	.30
O16	O1	50c ultramarine	.20	*.35*
O17	O1	1s ultramarine	.35	*.50*
		Nos. O11-O17 (7)	1.55	2.05

1894

O18	O1a	1c slate green (R)	8.50
O19	O1a	2c lake (Bk)	8.50

Nos. O18 and O19 were not placed in use.

Rocafuerte O20ovpt

Dated 1894

1894

Carmine Overprint

O20	O2	1c gray black	.20	*.35*
O21	O2	2c gray black	.20	.20
O22	O2	5c gray black	.20	.20
O23	O2	10c gray black	.25	*.35*
O24	O2	20c gray black	.35	.35
O25	O2	50c gray black	1.25	1.25
O26	O2	1s gray black	2.00	1.90
		Nos. O20-O26 (7)	4.45	4.60

Dated 1895

1895

Carmine Overprint

O27	O2	1c gray black	1.75	1.75
O28	O2	2c gray black	2.50	2.50
O29	O2	5c gray black	.50	.50
O30	O2	10c gray black	2.50	2.50
O31	O2	20c gray black	3.75	3.50
O32	O2	50c gray black	*25.00*	*25.00*
O33	O2	1s gray black	1.25	1.25
		Nos. O27-O33 (7)	*37.25*	*37.00*

Reprints of 1894-95 issues are on very thick paper with paper weave found both horizontal and vertical for all denominations. Generally they are blacker than originals.
For overprints see Nos. O50-O91.

Types of 1896 Overprinted in Carmine

1896 Wmk. 117

O34	A21	1c olive bister	.35	.35
O35	A22	2c olive bister	.35	.35
O36	A23	5c olive bister	.35	.35
O37	A24	10c olive bister	.35	.35
O38	A25	20c olive bister	.35	.35
O39	A26	50c olive bister	.35	.35
O40	A27	1s olive bister	1.00	1.00
O41	A28	5s olive bister	2.00	2.00
		Nos. O34-O41 (8)	5.10	5.10

Reprints of Nos. O34-O41 are on thick paper with vertical paper weave direction.

Unwmk.

O42	A21	1c olive bister	1.00	1.00
O43	A22	2c olive bister	1.00	1.00
O44	A23	5c olive bister	1.00	1.00
O45	A24	10c olive bister	1.00	1.00
O46	A25	20c olive bister	1.00	1.00
O47	A26	50c olive bister	1.00	*1.00*
O48	A27	1s olive bister	2.50	2.50
O49	A28	5s olive bister	3.50	3.50
		Nos. O42-O49 (8)	12.00	12.00

Reprints of Nos. O42-O49 all have overprint in black. Value 20 cents each.

#O20-O26 Overprinted

1897-98

O50	O2	1c gray black	*4.00*	*4.00*
O51	O2	2c gray black	*5.00*	*5.00*
O52	O2	5c gray black	*45.00*	*45.00*
O53	O2	10c gray black	*4.25*	*4.25*
O54	O2	20c gray black	*2.00*	*1.25*
O55	O2	50c gray black	*10.00*	*10.00*
O56	O2	1s gray black	*16.00*	*16.00*
		Nos. O50-O56 (7)	*86.25*	*85.50*

#O20-O26 Overprinted 1897 1898

O57 O2 1c gray black 1.25 1.25
O58 O2 2c gray black 3.00 1.00
O59 O2 5c gray black 35.00 35.00
O60 O2 10c gray black 45.00 45.00
O61 O2 20c gray black 1.25 1.25
O62 O2 50c gray black 4.75 3.75
O63 O2 1s gray black 60.00 60.00
Nos. O57-O63 (7) 150.25 147.25

#O20-O26 Overprinted **1897 Y 1898**

O64 O2 1c gray black 8.50 8.50
O65 O2 2c gray black 8.50 8.50
O66 O2 5c gray black 8.50 8.50
O67 O2 10c gray black 8.50 8.50
O68 O2 20c gray black 8.50 8.50
O69 O2 50c gray black 8.50 8.50
O70 O2 1s gray black 8.50 8.50
Nos. O64-O70 (7) 59.50 59.50

#O27-O33 Overprinted in Black like Nos. O50-O56

O71 O2 1c gray black 2.00 2.00
O72 O2 2c gray black 1.50 1.50
O73 O2 5c gray black 2.00 2.00
O74 O2 10c gray black 2.00 2.00
O75 O2 20c gray black 4.00 4.00
O76 O2 50c gray black 140.00 140.00
O77 O2 1s gray black 40.00 40.00
Nos. O71-O77 (7) 191.50 191.50

#O27-O33 Overprinted like #O57-O63

O78 O2 1c gray black .90 .90
O79 O2 2c gray black .70 .70
O80 O2 5c gray black 1.75 1.75
O81 O2 10c gray black .70 .70
O82 O2 20c gray black .70 .45
O83 O2 50c gray black 1.40 .55
O84 O2 1s gray black 6.00 6.00
Nos. O78-O84 (7) 12.15 11.05

#O27-O33 Overprinted like #O64-O70

O85 O2 1c gray black 40.00 40.00
O86 O2 2c gray black 1.10 1.10
O87 O2 5c gray black .70 .70
O88 O2 10c gray black 35.00 35.00
O89 O2 20c gray black 60.00 60.00
O90 O2 50c gray black 13.00 13.00
O91 O2 1s gray black 80.00 80.00
Nos. O85-O91 (7) 229.80 229.80

Many forged overprints of Nos. O50-O91 exist, made on the original stamps and reprints.

O3

Black Surcharge

1898-99 ***Perf. 15, 16***

O92 O3 5c on 50c lilac .25 .25
a. Inverted surcharge 2.00 2.00
O93 O3 10c on 20s org .50 .50
a. Double surcharge 2.75 1.50
O94 O3 10c on 50c lilac 70.00 70.00
O95 O3 20c on 50c lilac 1.90 1.90
O96 O3 20c on 50s green 1.90 1.90
Nos. O92-O96 (5) 74.55 74.55

Green Surcharge

O97 O3 5c on 50c lilac 1.00 1.00
a. Double surcharge 2.50
b. Double surcharge, blk and grn 6.00
c. Same as "b," blk surch. invtd. 2.50

Red Surcharge

1899

O98 O3 5c on 50c lilac 1.10 1.10
a. Double surcharge 2.50
b. Dbl. surch., blk and red 3.00
O99 O3 20c on 50s green 1.90 1.90
a. Inverted surcharge 5.00
b. Dbl. surch., red and blk 8.00

Similar Surcharge in Black

Value in Words in Two Lines

O100 O3 1c on 5c blue *325.00*

Red Surcharge

O101 O3 2c on 5c blue *575.00*
O102 O3 4c on 20c blue *400.00*

Types of Regular Issue of 1899 Overprinted in Black

1899 ***Perf. 14, 15***

O103 A37 2c orange & blk .35 *.80*
O104 A39 10c orange & blk .35 *.80*
O105 A40 20c orange & blk .25 *1.25*
O106 A41 50c orange & blk .25 *1.60*
Nos. O103-O106 (4) 1.20 *4.45*

For overprint see No. O167.

The above overprint was applied to remainders of the postage stamps of 1904 with the idea of increasing their salability. They were never regularly in use as official stamps.

Regular Issue of 1911-13 Overprinted in Black

1913 ***Perf. 12***

O107 A71 1c scarlet & blk 1.75 1.75
O108 A72 2c blue & blk 1.75 1.75
O109 A73 3c orange & blk 1.10 1.10
O110 A74 5c scarlet & blk 2.25 2.25
O111 A75 10c blue & blk 2.25 2.25
Nos. O107-O111 (5) 9.10 9.10

Regular Issue of 1911-13 Overprinted

Overprint 22x3½mm

1916-17

O112 A72 2c blue & blk 12.50 9.00
O113 A74 5c scarlet & blk 12.50 9.00
O114 A75 10c blue & blk 7.50 6.00
Nos. O112-O114 (3) 32.50 24.00

Overprint 25x4mm

O115 A71 1c scarlet & blk .55 .55
O116 A72 2c blue & blk .80 .80
a. Inverted overprint 2.50 2.50
O117 A73 3c orange & blk .50 .50
O118 A74 5c scarlet & blk .80 .80
O119 A75 10c blue & blk .80 .80
Nos. O115-O119 (5) 3.45 3.45

Same Overprint On Regular Issue of 1915-17

O120 A71 1c orange .70 .70
O121 A72 2c green .70 .70
O122 A73 3c black 1.10 1.10
O123 A78 4c red & blk 1.10 1.10
a. Inverted overprint 7.50
O124 A74 5c violet .70 .70
O125 A75 10c blue 1.40 1.40
O126 A79 20c green & blk 7.50 7.50
Nos. O120-O126 (7) 13.20 13.20

Regular Issues of 1911-17 Overprinted in Black or Red

O127 A71 1c orange .45 .45
O128 A72 2c green .35 .35
O129 A73 3c black (Bk) .45 .35
O130 A73 3c black (R) .40 .35
a. Inverted overprint
O131 A78 4c red & blk .45 .45
O132 A74 5c violet .85 .35
O133 A75 10c blue & blk 2.25 .85
O134 A75 10c blue .45 .45
O135 A79 20c green & blk 2.25 .85
Nos. O127-O135 (9) 7.90 4.45

Regular Issue of 1920 Overprinted

1920

O136 A86 1c green .65 .65
a. Inverted overprint 8.50 —
O137 A86 2c carmine .50 .50
O138 A86 3c yellow brn .65 .65
O139 A86 4c dark green 1.00 1.00
a. Inverted overprint 8.50 —
O140 A86 5c blue 1.00 1.00
O141 A86 6c orange .65 .65
O142 A86 7c brown 1.00 1.00
O143 A86 8c yellow green 1.25 1.25
O144 A86 9c red 1.60 1.60
O145 A95 10c blue 1.00 1.00
O146 A86 15c gray 5.50 5.50
O147 A86 20c deep violet 7.25 7.25
O148 A86 30c violet 8.50 8.50
O149 A86 40c dark brown 10.50 10.50
O150 A86 50c dark green 7.25 7.25
O151 A86 60c dark blue 8.50 8.50
O152 A86 70c gray 8.50 8.50
O153 A86 80c yellow 10.50 10.50
O154 A104 90c green 10.50 10.50
O155 A86 1s blue 22.50 22.50
Nos. O136-O155 (20) 108.80 108.80

Cent. of the independence of Guayaquil.

Stamps of 1911 Overprinted

1922

O156 A71 1c scarlet & blk 4.50 4.50
O157 A72 2c blue & blk 2.25 2.25

Revenue Stamps of 1919-1920 Overprinted like Nos. O156 and O157

1924

O158 PT3 1c dark blue 1.00 1.00
O159 PT3 2c green 6.25 6.25

Regular Issues of 1911-17 Overprinted OFICIAL

1924

O160 A71 1c orange 3.50 3.50
a. Inverted overprint 7.50

Overprinted in Black or Red

O161 A72 2c green .30 .30
O162 A73 3c black (R) .40 .40
O163 A78 4c red & blk .65 .65
O164 A74 5c violet .65 .65
O165 A75 10c deep blue .65 .65
O166 A76 1s green & blk 3.50 3.50
Nos. O160-O166 (7) 9.65 9.65

No. O106 with Additional Overprint

1924 ***Perf. 14, 15***

O167 A41 50c orange & blk 1.10 1.10

Nos. O160-O167 exist with inverted overprint.

No. 199 Overprinted

1924 ***Perf. 12***

O168 A71 1c orange 2.75 2.75

Regular Issues of 1911-25 Overprinted

1925

O169 A71 1c scarlet & blk 5.00 2.10
a. Inverted overprint 7.50
O170 A71 1c orange .30 .30
a. Inverted overprint 2.00
O171 A72 2c green .30 .30
a. Inverted overprint 2.00
O172 A73 3c black (Bk) .30 .30
O173 A73 3c black (R) .55 .55
O174 A78 4c red & blk .30 .30
O175 A74 5c violet .40 .40
O176 A74 5c rose .40 .40
O177 A75 10c deep blue .30 .30
Nos. O169-O177 (9) 7.85 4.95

Regular Issues of 1916-25 Overprinted Vertically Up or Down

1927, Oct.

O178 A71 1c orange 1.00 1.00
O179 A86 2c carmine 1.00 1.00
O180 A86 3c yellow brown 1.00 1.00
O181 A86 4c myrtle green 1.00 1.00
O182 A86 5c pale blue 1.00 1.00
O183 A75 10c yellow green 1.00 1.00
Nos. O178-O183 (6) 6.00 6.00

Regular Issues of 1920-27 Overprinted

1928

O184 A71 1c lt blue .65 .65
O185 A86 2c carmine .65 .65
O186 A86 3c yellow brown .65 .65
a. Inverted overprint 2.50
O187 A86 4c myrtle green .65 .65
O188 A86 5c lt blue .65 .65
O189 A75 10c yellow green .65 .65
O190 A109 20c violet 5.50 1.25
a. Overprint reading up 1.75 1.10
Nos. O184-O190 (7) 9.40 5.15

The overprint is placed vertically reading down on No. O190.

Regular Issue of 1936 Overprinted in Black

1936 ***Perf. 14***

O191 A131 5c olive green .75 .25
O192 A132 10c brown .75 .25
O193 A133 20c dark violet .95 .35
O194 A134 1s dark carmine 1.10 .55
O195 A135 2s dark blue 1.25 .85
Nos. O191-O195 (5) 4.80 2.25

Regular Postage Stamps of 1937 Overprinted in Black

1937 ***Perf. 11½***

O196 A139 2c green .20 .20
O197 A140 5c deep rose .20 .20
O198 A141 10c blue .20 .20
O199 A142 20c deep rose .20 .20
O200 A143 1s olive green .20 .20
Nos. O196-O200 (5) 1.00 1.00

POSTAL TAX STAMPS

Roca — PT1

1920 **Unwmk.** ***Perf. 12***

RA1 PT1 1c orange .30 .30

PT2

PT3

RA2 PT2 1c red & blue .55 .20
a. "de" inverted 5.25 5.25
b. Double overprint 5.00 .60
c. Inverted overprint 5.00 .60
RA3 PT3 1c deep blue .65 .20
a. Inverted overprint 3.00 1.00
b. Double overprint 3.00 1.00

For overprints see Nos. O158-O159.

PT4

PT5

Red or Black Surcharge or Overprint

Stamp Dated 1911-1912

RA4 PT4 20c deep blue 27.50 15.00

Stamp Dated 1913-1914

RA5 PT4 20c deep blue (R) 1.10 .35

Stamp Dated 1917-1918

RA6 PT4 20c olive green (R) 3.25 .55
a. Dated 1919-20 *12.50*
RA7 PT5 1c on 2c green .45 .20

Stamp Dated 1911-1912

RA8 PT5 1c on 5c green .45 .20
a. Double surcharge

Stamp Dated 1913-1914

RA9 PT5 1c on 5c green 4.00 .55
a. Double surcharge 6.00 4.00

On Nos. RA7, RA8 and RA9 the surcharge is found reading upward or downward.
For surcharges see Nos. RA15-RA16.

Post Office — PT6

1920-24 **Engr.**

RA10 PT6 1c olive green .20 .20
RA11 PT6 2c deep green .20 .20
RA12 PT6 20c bister brn ('24) .85 .20
RA13 PT6 2s violet 5.75 3.25
RA14 PT6 5s blue 10.00 5.75
Nos. RA10-RA14 (5) 17.00 9.60

For overprints and surcharge see Nos. 259, 266-268, 273, 302, RA17.

Revenue Stamps of 1917-18 Surcharged Vertically in Red reading up or down

1921-22

RA15 PT5 20c on 1c dk blue 27.50 3.25
RA16 PT5 20c on 2c green 27.50 3.25

No. RA12 Surcharged in Green

1924

RA17 PT6 2c on 20c bis brn .30 .20
a. Inverted surcharge 6.00 5.00
b. Double surcharge 2.00 2.00

PT7

1924 ***Rouletted 7***

RA18 PT7 1c rose red .45 .20
a. Inverted overprint 1.75

Similar Design, Eagle at left

Perf. 12

RA19 PT7 2c blue .45 .20
a. Inverted overprint 1.75 1.75

For overprints and surcharges see Nos. 346, O201, RA32, RA34, RA37, RA44-RA45, RA47.

PT8

Inscribed "Timbre Fiscal"

1924

RA20 PT8 1c yellow 2.25 .85
RA21 PT8 2c dark blue .70 .35

Inscribed "Region Oriental"

RA22 PT8 1c yellow .35 .30
RA23 PT8 2c dark blue .70 .35
Nos. RA20-RA23 (4) 4.00 1.85

Overprint on No. RA22 reads down or up.

Revenue Stamp Overprinted in Blue

1934

RA24 2c green .20 .20
a. Blue overprint inverted 1.75 1.75
b. Blue ovpt. dbl., one invtd. 2.00 1.25

Postage Stamp of 1930 Overprinted in Red

Perf. 12½

RA25 A119 20c ultra & yel .25 .20

Telegraph Stamp Overprinted in Red, like No. RA24, and Surcharged diagonally in Black

1934 ***Perf. 14***

RA26 2c on 10c olive brn .35 .20
a. Double surcharge 2.75

Overprint Blue, Surcharge Red

RA27 2c on 10c olive brn .35 .20

PT9

PT10

Symbols of Post and Telegraph Service PT11

1934-36 ***Perf. 12***

RA28 PT9 2c green .30 .20
a. Both overprints in red ('36) .30 .20

Postal Tax stamp of 1920-24, overprinted in red "POSTAL" has been again overprinted "CASA de Correos y Teleg. de Guayaquil" in black.

Perf. 14½x14

1934 **Photo.** **Wmk. 233**

RA29 PT10 2c yellow green .20 .20

For the rebuilding of the GPO at Guayaquil.
For surcharge see No. RA31.

1935

RA30 PT11 20c claret .25 .20

For the rebuilding of the GPO at Guayaquil.

No. RA29 Surcharged in Red and Overprinted in Black

1935

RA31 PT10 3c on 2c yel grn .20 .20
a. Double surcharge

Social and Rural Workers' Insurance Fund.

Tobacco Stamp Surcharged in Black

1936 **Unwmk.** ***Rouletted 7***

RA32 PT7 3c on 1c rose red .30 .20
a. Lines of words reversed 1.00 .20
b. Horiz. pair, imperf. vert.

Issued for the Social and Rural Workers' Insurance Fund.

No. 310 Overprinted in Black

1936 ***Perf. 12½***

RA33 A119 20c ultra & yel .30 .20
a. Double overprint

Tobacco Stamp Surcharged in Black

1936 ***Rouletted 7***

RA34 PT7 3c on 1c rose red .30 .20

Social and Rural Workers' Insurance Fund.

Worker — PT12

1936 **Engr.** ***Perf. 13½***

RA35 PT12 3c ultra .20 .20

Social and Rural Workers' Insurance Fund.
For surcharges see Nos. C64, RA36, RA53-RA54.

Surcharged in Black

1936

RA36 PT13 5c on 3c ultra .30 .20

This combines the 2c for the rebuilding of the post office with the 3c for the Social and Rural Workers' Insurance Fund.

National Defense Issue

Tobacco Stamp, Surcharged in Black

1936 ***Rouletted 7***

RA37 PT7 10c on 1c rose .45 .20
a. Double surcharge

Symbolical of Defense — PT14

1937-42 ***Perf. 12½***

RA38 PT14 10c deep blue .45 .20

A 1s violet and 2s green exist in type PT14.
For surcharge see No. RA40.

PT15

Overprinted or Surcharged in Black

1937 Engr. & Typo. *Perf. 13½*

RA39 PT15 5c lt brn & red 1.00 .25
d. Inverted overprint 10.00

1942 *Perf. 12, 11½*

RA39A PT15 20c on 5c rose pink & red 32.50 7.00
RA39B PT15 20c on 1s yel brn & red 32.50 7.00
RA39C PT15 20c on 2s grn & red 32.50 7.00
Nos. RA39A-RA39C (3) 97.50 21.00

A 50c dark blue and red exists.

No. RA38 Surcharged in Red

1937 Engr. *Perf. 12½*

RA40 PT14 5c on 10c dp blue .55 .20

Map of Ecuador — PT16

1938 *Perf. 14x13½*

RA41 PT16 5c carmine rose .35 .20

Social and Rural Workers' Insurance Fund.

No. C42 Surcharged in Red

1938 *Perf. 12½*

RA42 AP5 20c on 70c black .55 .20

No. 307 Surcharged in Red

1938

RA43 A116 5c on 6c yel & red .20 .20

This stamp was obligatory on all mail from Nov. 23rd to 30th, 1938. The tax was for the Intl. Union for the Control of Cancer.

Tobacco Stamp, Surcharged in Black

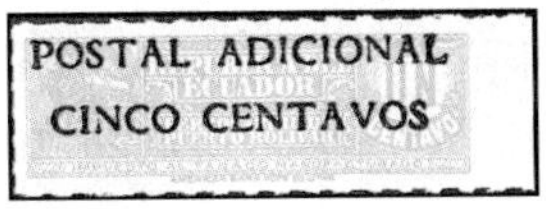

1939 *Rouletted*

RA44 PT7 5c on 1c rose .35 .20
a. Double surcharge
b. Triple surcharge

Tobacco Stamp, Surcharged in Blue

1940

RA45 PT7 5c on 1c rose red .50 .20
a. Double surcharge 3.50 3.50

No. 370 Surcharged in Carmine

1940 *Perf. 11½*

RA46 A144 20c on 50c blk & multi .25 .20
a. Double surcharge, one inverted

Tobacco Stamp, Surcharged in Black

TIMBRE PATRIOTICO
VEINTE CENTAVOS

1940 *Rouletted*

RA47 PT7 20c on 1c rose red 3.00 .50

Farmer Plowing PT17

Communication Symbols PT18

1940 *Perf. 13x13½*

RA48 PT17 5c carmine rose .35 .20

1940-43 *Perf. 12*

RA49 PT18 5c copper brown .35 .20
RA49A PT18 5c green ('43) .35 .20

For overprint and surcharges see #534, E6, I1.

EGYPT

'ē-jəpt

LOCATION — Northern Africa, bordering on the Mediterranean and the Red Sea
GOVT. — Monarchy
AREA — 386,900 sq. mi.
POP. — 46,000,000 (est. 1984)
CAPITAL — Cairo

Modern Egypt was a part of Turkey until 1914 when a British protectorate was declared over the country and the Khedive was deposed in favor of Hussein Kamil under the title of sultan. In 1922 the protectorate ended and the reigning sultan was declared king of the new monarchy.

40 Paras = 1 Piaster
1000 Milliemes = 100 Piasters = 1 Pound (1888)

Catalogue values for unused stamps in this country are for Never Hinged items, beginning with Scott B1 in the semi-postal section.

Watermarks

Wmk. 118 — Pyramid and Star

Wmk. 119 — Crescent and Star

Wmk. 120 — Triple Crescent and Star

Wmk. 195 — Multiple Crown and Arabic F

"F" in watermark stands for Fuad.

PRE-STAMP POSTAL MARKINGS

Crowned Circle handstamps types I, II and VII are pictured in the Crowned Circle Handstamps and Great Britain Used Abroad section.

Alexandria

1843, May 13

A1 II "Alexandria" crowned circle handstamp in red, on cover *3,150.*

Cairo

1859, Mar. 23

A2 VII "Cairo" crowned circle handstamp in red, on cover *4,250.*
A3 VII "Cairo" crowned circle handstamp in black, on cover *4,250.*

Suez

1847, July 16

A4 I "Suez" crowned circle handstamp in red, on cover *4,750.*
A5 I "Suez" crowned circle handstamp in black, on cover *4,750.*

STAMPS OF GREAT BRITAIN USED IN EGYPT

Numeral cancellation type A is pictured in the Crowned Circle Handstamps and Great Britain Used Abroad section.

1859-78

B01 (Alexandria, Cairo)

A6 ½p rose (#58, P5, 6, 8, 10, 13-15, 19-20), *from* 22.50
A7 1p rose red (#20) 8.00
a. 1p red brown (#20b) —
A8 1p rose red (#33, see footnote), *from* 11.00
A9 2p blue (#29, P7-9), *from* 11.00
A10 2p blue (#30, P13-15), *from* 11.00
A11 2½p claret (#66, P1-3) 40.00
a. Bluish paper (#66a, P1) 70.00
As "a," P2 *1,425.*
b. Lettered "LH-FL" (#66b) *1,500.*
A12 2½p claret (#67, P3-9), *from* 29.00
A13 3p rose (#37) 140.00
A14 3p rose (#44) 70.00
A15 3p rose (#49, P4-9), *from* 30.00
A16 3p rose (#61, P11-12, 14-16, 18, 19), *from* 30.00
A17 4p rose (#26) 47.50
A18 4p vermilion (#34) 47.50
a. Hairlines (#34b) 47.50
A19 4p vermilion (#43, P7-14), *from* 32.50
A20 4p vermilion (#69, P15) 190.00
A21 4p pale ol grn (#70, P15) 125.00
A22 6p lilac (#27) 55.00
A23 6p lilac (#39, P3) 47.50
a. Hairlines (#39b) 90.00
A24 6p lilac (#45, P5) 37.50
Plate 6 90.00
A25 6p dull violet (#50, P6) 47.50
A26 6p violet (#51, P8-9) 42.50
a. Imperf. (#51b, P8) *2,900.*
A27 6p brown (#59, P11) 32.00
a. 6p pale buff (#59b, P11) 80.00
As "a," plate 12 225.00
A28 6p gray (#60) 92.50
A29 6p gray (#62, P13-15), *from* 27.50
A30 9p straw (#40) 175.00
a. 9p bister (#40a) —
A31 9p straw (#46) —
A32 9p bister (#52) —
A33 10p red brown (#53) 150.00
A34 1sh green (#28) 140.00
A35 1sh green (#42) 85.00
A36 1sh green (#48) 40.00
A37 1sh green (#54, P4-6) 17.50
Plate 7 50.00
A38 1sh green (#64, P12-13) 32.00
Plates 8-11 45.00
A39 2sh blue (#55) 115.00
a. 2sh pale blue (#55a) 200.00
A40 5sh rose (#57, P1) 300.00
Plate 2 500.00

When more than one plate number is shown, value is for the least expensive.

A8 plate numbers: 71-74, 76, 78-99, 101-104, 106-115, 117-125, 127, 129-131, 133, 134, 136-140, 142-150, 152, 154, 156, 157, 159, 160, 162, 163, 165, 168-172, 174, 175, 177, 179-183, 185, 188, 190, 198, 200, 203, 206, 210, 220.

1859-78

B02 (Suez)

A41 ½p rose (#58, P6, 10-14), *from* 35.00
A42 1p rose red (#20) 11.50
A43 1p rose red (#33, see footnote) 13.50
A44 2p blue (#29, P9) 17.00
Plate 8 25.00
A45 2p blue (#30, P13) 17.00
Plates 14-15 25.00
A46 2½p claret (#66, P1-2) 40.00
Plate 3 50.00
a. Bluish paper (#66a, P1) 75.00
Plates 2-3 —
b. Lettered "LH-FL" (#66b) *1,700.*
A47 2½p claret (#67, P3-9), *from* 30.00
Plate 10 35.00
A48 3p rose (#37) 160.00
A49 3p rose (#44) 85.00
A50 3p rose (#49, P5-8, 10), *from* 30.00
A51 3p rose (#61, P12, 16) 30.00
A52 4p rose (#26) 62.50
A53 4p vermilion (#34) 55.00
a. Hairlines (#34b) 60.00
A54 4p vermilion (#43, P7-14), *from* 32.50
A55 4p vermilion (#69, P15) —
A56 4p pale ol grn (#70, P15) 150.00
A57 6p lilac (#27) 62.50
A58 6p lilac (#39, P3) 50.00
a. Hairlines (#39b) 90.00
A59 6p lilac (#45, P5) 42.50
Plate 6 100.00
A60 6p dull violet (#50, P6) 55.00
A61 6p violet (#51, P8-9) 42.50
A62 6p brown (#59, P11) 37.50
a. 6p pale buff (#59b, P11) 80.00
As "a," plate 12 2,750.
A63 6p gray (#60) 110.00
A64 6p gray (#62, P15-16) 32.50
Plates 13-14 32.50
A65 8p orange (#73) —
A66 9p straw (#40) 210.00
a. 9p bister (#40a) —
A67 9p bister (#52) —
A68 10p red brown (#53) 210.00
A69 1sh green (#28) 175.00
A70 1sh green (#42) 97.50
A71 1sh green (#48) 55.00
A72 1sh green (#54, P4-6) 22.50
Plate 7 45.00
A73 1sh green (#64, P12) 35.00
Plates 8-11 40.00
A74 2sh blue (#55) 180.00
a. 2sh pale blue (#55a) 225.00
A75 5sh rose (#57, P1) 350.00
Plate 2 600.00

When more than one plate number is shown, value is for the least expensive.

A8 plate numbers: 73-74, 78-81, 83-84, 86-87, 90-91, 93-94, 96-97, 100-101, 106-108, 110, 113, 118-125, 129-131, 134, 136-138, 140, 142-145, 147-154, 156, 158-168, 170, 174, 176-182, 184-187, 189-190, 198, 205.

Values for unused stamps are for examples with original gum as defined in the catalogue introduction. Very fine examples of Nos. 1-15 will have perforations that are clear of the framelines but with the design noticeably off center. Well centered stamps are extremely scarce and will command substantial premiums.

Turkish Numerals

Turkish Suzerainty

A1

A2

A3

A4

A5

A6

A7

Surcharged in Black

Wmk. 118

1866, Jan. 1 Litho. *Perf. 12½*

No.			Unused	Used
1	A1	5pa greenish gray	47.50	30.00
a.		Imperf., pair	225.00	
b.		Pair, imperf. between	350.00	
c.		Perf. 12½x13	57.50	55.00
d.		Perf. 13	300.00	350.00
e.		5pa gray	47.50	30.00
2	A2	10pa brown	65.00	32.50
a.		Imperf., pair	190.00	
b.		Pair, imperf. between	400.00	
c.		Perf. 13	200.00	*210.00*
d.		Perf. 12½x15	300.00	325.00
e.		Perf. 12½x13	92.50	55.00
3	A3	20pa blue	82.50	35.00
a.		Imperf., pair	275.00	
b.		Pair, imperf. between	450.00	
c.		Perf. 12½x13	110.00	95.00
d.		Perf. 13	475.00	275.00
e.		20pa greenish blue	82.50	35.00
4	A4	2pi yellow	110.00	47.50
a.		Imperf.	*125.00*	*125.00*
b.		Imperf. vert. or horiz., pair	400.00	400.00
c.		Perf. 12½x15	150.00	
d.		Diagonal half used as 1pi on cover		*2,600.*
e.		Perf. 12½x13, 13x12½	140.00	55.00
5	A5	5pi rose	300.00	250.00
a.		Imperf.	400.00	375.00
b.		Imperf. vert. or horiz., pair	*1,200.*	
d.		Inscription of 10pi, imperf.	950.00	850.00
e.		Perf. 12½x13, 13x12½	350.00	275.00
f.		As "d," perf. 12½x15	1,000.	850.00
6	A6	10pi slate bl	325.00	*325.00*
a.		Imperf.	*450.00*	450.00
b.		Pair, imperf. between	*2,250.*	
c.		Perf. 12½x13, 13x12½	550.00	550.00
d.		Perf. 13	*1,850.*	

Unwmk.

Typo.

No.			Unused	Used
7	A7	1pi rose lilac	67.50	5.50
a.		Imperf.	110.00	
b.		Horiz. pair, imperf. vert.	500.00	
c.		Perf. 12½x13, 13x12½	100.00	25.00
d.		Perf. 13	350.00	210.00
		Nos. 1-7 (7)	997.50	725.50

Single imperforates of types A1-A10 are sometimes simulated by trimming wide-margin copies of perforated stamps.

No. 4d must be dated between July 16 and July 31, 1867.

Proofs of #1-7 are on smooth white paper, unwatermarked and imperforate. Proofs of #7 are on thinner paper than No. 7a.

Sphinx and Pyramid — A8

Perf. 15x12½

1867 Litho. Wmk. 119

No.			Unused	Used
8	A8	5pa orange	25.00	11.00
a.		Imperf.	250.00	—
b.		Horiz. pair, imperf between	175.00	
c.		Vert. pair, imperf between	—	
9	A8	10pa lilac ('69)	62.50	11.00
a.		10pa violet	82.50	14.00
b.		Half used as 5pa on newspaper piece		850.00
11	A8	20pa yellow green ('69)	110.00	11.00
a.		20pa blue green	125.00	17.00
13	A8	1pi rose red	11.00	1.10
a.		Imperf, pair	150.00	
b.		Pair, imperf. between	300.00	
d.		Rouletted	70.00	
e.		1pi lake red	130.00	32.50
14	A8	2pi blue	125.00	17.00
a.		Imperf.	250.00	
b.		Horiz. pair, imperf. vert.	500.00	
d.		Perf. 12½	250.00	
15	A8	5pi brown	350.00	200.00
		Nos. 8-15 (6)	683.50	251.10

There are 4 types of each value, so placed that any block of 4 contains all types.

A9

A10

Clear Impressions
Thick Opaque Paper

Typographed by the Government at Boulac

Perf. 12½x13½ Clean-cut

1872 Wmk. 119

No.			Unused	Used
19	A9	5pa brown	9.25	5.00
20	A9	10pa lilac	9.00	3.75
21	A9	20pa blue	50.00	4.00
22	A9	1pi rose red	57.50	2.25
h.		Half used as 20pa on cover		700.00
23	A9	2pi dull yellow	97.50	15.00
j.		Half used as 1p on cover		1,200.
24	A9	2½pi dull violet	82.50	11.00
25	A9	5pi green	325.00	35.00
i.		Tête bêche pair		
		Nos. 19-25 (7)	630.75	76.00

Perf. 13½ Clean-cut

No.			Unused	Used
19a	A9	5pa brown	27.50	9.25
20a	A9	10pa dull lilac	9.00	4.25
21a	A9	20pa blue	90.00	20.00
22a	A9	1pi rose red	82.50	8.00
23a	A9	2pi dull yellow	55.00	8.00
24a	A9	2½pi dull violet	1,200.	225.00
25a	A9	5pi green	375.00	75.00

Litho.

No.			Unused	Used
21m	A9	20pa blue, perf. 12½x13½	150.00	80.00
21n	A9	20pa blue, perf. 13½	225.00	57.50
21p	A9	20pa blue, imperf.	250.00	
22m	A9	1pi rose red, perf. 12½x13½	550.00	20.00
22n	A9	1pi rose red, perf. 13½	875.00	50.00

Typographed
Blurred Impressions
Thinner Paper

Perf. 12½ Rough

1874-75 Wmk. 119

No.			Unused	Used
26	A10	5pa brown ('75)	7.25	3.50
e.		Imperf.	200.00	200.00
f.		Vert. pair, imperf. horiz.	1,000.	—
g.		Tête bêche pair	40.00	40.00
20b	A9	10pa gray lilac	10.00	3.50
g.		Tête bêche pair	225.00	225.00
21b	A9	20pa gray blue	90.00	4.00
k.		Half used as 10pa on cover		—
22b	A9	1pi vermilion	7.50	1.75
f.		Imperf.	—	150.00
g.		Tête bêche pair	150.00	125.00
23b	A9	2pi yellow	75.00	5.75
i.		Tête bêche pair	600.00	600.00
24b	A9	2½pi deep violet	9.25	3.50
e.		Imperf.	—	—
f.		Tête bêche pair	600.00	600.00
25b	A9	5pi yellow green	60.00	22.50
e.		Imperf.	400.00	—

No. 26f normally occurs tête-bêche.

Perf. 13½x12½ Rough

No.			Unused	Used
26c	A10	5pa brown	7.50	4.50
i.		Tête bêche pair	62.50	62.50
20c	A9	10pa gray lilac	12.00	3.25
i.		Tête bêche pair	225.00	*225.00*
21c	A9	20pa gray blue	8.50	3.75
h.		Pair, imperf. between	350.00	
22c	A9	1pi vermilion	55.00	3.25
i.		Tête bêche pair	500.00	500.00
23c	A9	2pi yellow	10.00	6.00
g.		Tête bêche pair	500.00	500.00
k.		Half used as 1pi on cover		*2,800.*

Perf. 12½x13½ Rough

No.			Unused	Used
23d	A9	2pi yellow ('75)	62.50	10.00
h.		Tête bêche pair	*1,000.*	
24d	A9	2½pi dp violet ('75)	45.00	12.50
i.		Tête bêche pair	*1,150.*	*1,000.*
25d	A9	5pi yel green ('75)	350.00	225.00

Nos. 24b, 24d Surcharged in Black

1879, Jan. 1 *Perf. 12½ Rough*

No.			Unused	Used
27	A9	5pa on 2½pi dull vio	8.75	8.75
a.		Imperf.	400.00	400.00
b.		Tête bêche pair	*7,500.*	
c.		Inverted surcharge	125.00	75.00
d.		Perf. 12½x13½ rough	11.00	*11.00*
e.		As "d," tête bêche pair	7,500.	
f.		As "d," inverted surcharge	140.00	95.00
28	A9	10pa on 2½pi dull vio	11.00	11.00
a.		Imperf.	400.00	400.00
b.		Tête bêche pair	*2,500.*	
c.		Inverted surcharge	125.00	82.50
d.		Perf. 12½x13½ rough	17.00	17.00
e.		As "d," tête bêche pair	3,000.	
f.		As "d," inverted surcharge	150.00	125.00

A11

A12

A13

A14

A15

A16

1879-1902 Typo. *Perf. 14x13½*

Ordinary Paper

No.			Unused	Used
29	A11	5pa brown	1.50	.60
30	A12	10pa violet	45.00	5.00
31	A12	10pa lilac rose ('81)	65.00	6.25
32	A12	10pa gray ('82)	13.25	1.60
33	A12	10pa green ('84)	.80	.65
34	A13	20pa ultra	62.50	2.25
35	A13	20pa rose ('84)	17.00	1.25
36	A14	1pi rose	25.00	.30
37	A14	1pi ultra ('84)	3.50	.20
38	A15	2pi orange yel	32.50	1.50
39	A15	2pi orange brn	25.00	1.50
40	A16	5pi green	70.00	8.75
41	A16	5pi gray ('84)	22.00	.50
a.		Chalky paper	16.00	.20
		Nos. 29-41 (13)	383.05	30.35

Chalky Paper

No.			Unused	Used
37a	A14	1pi ultra ('02)	3.00	.20
39a	A15	2pi orange brn ('02)	13.50	.20
41a	A16	5pi gray ('02)	18.00	.20

#29-31, 35-41 imperf are proofs.

For overprints see Nos. 42, O6-O7.

A17

1884, Feb. 1

No.			Unused	Used
42	A17	20pa on 5pi green	13.00	2.25
a.		Inverted surcharge	70.00	62.50

A18

A19

A20

A21

A22

A23

1888-1906

Ordinary Paper

No.			Unused	Used
43	A18	1m brown	.80	.20
44	A19	2m green	.65	.20
45	A20	3m maroon ('92)	6.00	1.10
46	A20	3m orange ('93)	2.25	.20
48	A22	5m carmine rose	1.75	.20
a.		5m rose, aniline ink	5.00	.20
49	A23	10p purple ('89)	30.00	.85
a.		10m purple, aniline ink	20.00	.85
		Nos. 43-49 (6)	41.45	2.75

Chalky Paper

No.			Unused	Used
43a	A18	1m pale brown ('02)	2.75	.20
44a	A19	2m green ('02)	1.10	.20
46a	A20	3m yel org ('02)	2.75	.20
47	A21	4m brown red ('06)	4.00	.20
a.		Half used as 2m on cover		—
48b	A22	5m rose ('02)	2.75	.20
49b	A23	10p mauve ('02)	25.00	.55

#43-44, 47-48 imperf are proofs.

For overprints see Nos. O2-O5, O8-O10, O14-O15.

Boats on Nile A24

Cleopatra A25

Ras-el-Tin Palace A26

Giza Pyramids A27

Sphinx A28

Colossi of Thebes A29

Pylon of Karnak and Temple of Khonsu — A30

Citadel at Cairo — A31

Rock Temple of Abu Simbel — A32

Aswan Dam — A33

Perf. 13½x14

1914, Jan. 8 Wmk. 119

Chalk-surfaced Paper

50	A24	1m olive brown	.45	*.60*
51	A25	2m dp green	.85	.20
52	A26	3m orange	1.00	.35
53	A27	4m red	1.50	.55
54	A28	5m lake	1.25	.20
a.		Booklet pane of 6	200.00	
55	A29	10m dk blue	3.00	.30

Perf. 14

56	A30	20m olive grn	5.00	.50
57	A31	50m red violet	10.00	.80
58	A32	100m black	22.50	1.00
59	A33	200m plum	29.00	2.75
		Nos. 50-59 (10)	74.55	7.25

All values of this issue exist imperforate on both watermarked and unwatermarked paper but are not known to have been issued in that condition.

See Nos. 61-69, 72-74. For overprints and surcharge see Nos. 60, 78-91, O11-O13, O16-O27, O30.

British Protectorate

No. 52 Surcharged

1915, Oct. 15

60	A26	2m on 3m orange	.90	.90
a.		Inverted surcharge	200.00	200.00

Scenic Types of 1914 and

Statue of Ramses II
A34 A35

1921-22 Wmk. 120 *Perf. 13½x14*

Chalk-surfaced Paper

61	A24	1m olive brown	.60	*.80*
62	A25	2m dp green	2.50	1.75
63	A25	2m red ('22)	2.00	.60
64	A26	3m orange	1.50	.70
65	A27	4m green ('22)	3.75	*4.00*
66	A28	5m lake	2.25	.20
67	A28	5m pink	2.50	.20
68	A29	10m dp blue	2.75	.20
69	A29	10m lake ('22)	2.25	.50
70	A34	15m indigo ('22)	3.00	.20
71	A35	15m indigo ('22)	16.00	2.50

Perf. 14

72	A30	20m olive green	10.00	.40
73	A31	50m maroon	12.00	.50
74	A32	100m black	55.00	6.75
		Nos. 61-74 (14)	116.10	19.30

For overprints see Nos. O28-O29.

Independent Kingdom

Stamps of 1921-22 Overprinted

1922, Oct. 10

78	A24	1m olive brown	.80	.60
a.		Inverted overprint	350.00	450.00
b.		Double overprint	200.00	—
79	A25	2m red	.60	.35
a.		Double overprint	200.00	—
80	A26	3m orange	1.25	.80
81	A27	4m green	.75	.50
b.		Inverted overprint	225.00	—
82	A28	5m pink	1.75	.20
83	A29	10m lake	1.75	.20
84	A34	15m indigo	4.00	.75
85	A35	15m indigo	3.25	.75

Perf. 14

86	A30	20m olive green	4.25	.50
a.		Inverted overprint	200.00	—
b.		Double overprint	300.00	—
87	A31	50m maroon	6.75	.50
a.		Inverted overprint	400.00	500.00
88	A32	100m black	17.00	1.00
a.		Inverted overprint	500.00	160.00
b.		Double overprint	400.00	150.00
		Nos. 78-88 (11)	42.15	6.15

Same Overprint on Nos. 58-59

Wmk. Crescent and Star (119)

90	A32	100m black	67.50	42.50
91	A33	200m plum	22.50	1.25

Proclamation of the Egyptian monarchy.

The overprint signifies "The Egyptian Kingdom, March 15, 1922." It exists in four types, one lithographed and three typographed on #78-87, but lithographed only on #88-91.

King Fuad
A36 A37

Wmk. 120

1923-24 Photo. *Perf. 13½*

Size 18x22½mm

92	A36	1m orange	.20	.20
93	A36	2m black	.50	.20
94	A36	3m brown	.75	.40
a.		Imperf., pair	200.00	
95	A36	4m yellow grn	.65	.50
96	A36	5m orange brn	.20	.20
a.		Imperf., pair	50.00	
97	A36	10m rose	1.10	.20
98	A36	15m ultra	2.25	.20

Perf. 14

Size: 22x28mm

99	A36	20m dk green	4.50	.20
100	A36	50m myrtle grn	6.75	.20
101	A36	100m red violet	19.00	.50
102	A36	200m violet ('24)	32.50	1.50
a.		Imperf., pair	300.00	
103	A37	£1 ultra & dk vio ('24)	150.00	22.50
a.		Imperf., pair	1,600.	
		Nos. 92-103 (12)	218.40	26.80

For overprints & surcharge see #167, O31-O38.

Thoth Carving Name of King Fuad — A38

1925, Apr. Litho. *Perf. 11*

105	A38	5m brown	6.25	4.00
106	A38	10m rose	9.25	6.75
107	A38	15m ultra	11.50	8.00
		Nos. 105-107 (3)	27.00	18.75

International Geographical Congress, Cairo.

Nos. 106-107 exist with both white and yellowish gum.

Oxen Plowing A39

1926 Wmk. 195 *Perf. 13x13½*

108	A39	5m lt brown	2.25	1.00
109	A39	10m brt rose	2.00	.90
110	A39	15m dp blue	2.25	.90
111	A39	50m Prus green	12.00	3.00
112	A39	100m brown vio	17.50	5.00
113	A39	200m brt violet	25.00	15.00
		Nos. 108-113 (6)	61.00	25.80

12th Agricultural and Industrial Exhibition at Gezira.

For surcharges see Nos. 115-117.

King Fuad — A40

Perf. 14x14½

1926, Apr. 2 Photo. Wmk. 120

114	A40	50p brn vio & red vio	90.00	16.50

58th birthday of King Fuad.

For overprint and surcharge see #124, 166.

Nos. 111-113 Surcharged

Perf. 13x13½

1926, Aug. 24 Wmk. 195

115	A39	5m on 50m Prus green	2.00	2.00
116	A39	10m on 100m brown vio	2.00	2.00
117	A39	15m on 200m brt violet	2.00	2.00
a.		Double surcharge	300.00	
		Nos. 115-117 (3)	6.00	6.00

Ship of Hatshepsut — A41

1926, Dec. 9 Litho. *Perf. 13x13½*

118	A41	5m brown & blk	2.25	1.40
119	A41	10m dp red & blk	3.25	1.50
120	A41	15m dp blue & blk	3.25	1.50
		Nos. 118-120 (3)	8.75	4.40

International Navigation Congress, Cairo.

For overprints see Nos. 121-123.

Nos. 118-120, 114 Overprinted

1926, Dec. 21

121	A41 (a)	5m	225.00	150.00
122	A41 (a)	10m	225.00	150.00
123	A41 (a)	15m	225.00	150.00

Perf. 14x14½

Wmk. 120

124	A40 (b)	50p	1,400.	875.00

Inauguration of Port Fuad opposite Port Said.

Nos. 121-123 have a block over "Le Caire" at lower left.

Forgeries of Nos. 121-124 exist.

Branch of Cotton A42

Perf. 13x13½

1927, Jan. 25 Wmk. 195

125	A42	5m dk brown & sl grn	1.25	.80
126	A42	10m dp red & slate grn	2.00	1.50
127	A42	15m dp blue & slate grn	2.00	1.50
		Nos. 125-127 (3)	5.25	3.80

International Cotton Congress, Cairo.

King Fuad
A43 A44

A45

A46

Perf. 13x13½

1927-37 Wmk. 195 Photo.

128	A43	1m orange	.35	.20
129	A43	2m black	.35	.20
130	A43	3m olive brn	.35	.20
131	A43	3m dp green ('30)	.65	.20
132	A43	4m yellow grn	.85	.40
133	A43	4m brown ('30)	1.00	.40
134	A43	4m dp green ('34)	.85	.40
135	A43	5m dk red brn ('29)	.95	.40
b.		5m chestnut	.95	.20
136	A43	10m dk red ('29)	1.25	.20
a.		10m orange red	1.25	.20
137	A43	10m purple ('34)	2.75	.20
138	A43	13m car rose ('32)	1.50	.40
139	A43	15m ultra	2.50	.20
140	A43	15m dk violet ('34)	5.25	.20
141	A43	20m ultra ('34)	9.25	.30

Early printings of Nos. 128, 129, 130, 132, 135, 136 and 139 were from plates with screen of vertical dots in the vignette; later printings show screen of diagonal dots.

Perf. 13½x14

142	A44	20m olive grn	3.25	.40
143	A44	20m ultra ('32)	4.00	.20
144	A44	40m olive brn ('32)	3.25	.20
145	A44	50m Prus green	3.50	.20
a.		50m greenish blue	5.50	.20
146	A44	100m brown vio	6.00	.20
a.		100m claret	9.00	.20
147	A44	200m deep violet	6.00	.50

Printings of Nos. 142, 145 and 146, made in 1929 and later, were from new plates with stronger impressions and darker colors.

Lithographed; Center Photogravure

Perf. 13x13½

148	A45	500m choc & Prus bl ('32)	110.00	10.00
a.		Entirely photogravure	110.00	22.50
149	A46	£1 dk grn & org brn ('37)	120.00	6.00
a.		Entirely photogravure	120.00	7.00
		Nos. 128-149 (22)	283.85	21.60

Statue of Amenhotep, Son of Hapu — A47

1927, Dec. 29 Photo. *Perf. 13½x13*

150	A47	5m orange brown	1.00	.40
151	A47	10m copper red	1.25	.45
152	A47	15m deep blue	2.50	.50
		Nos. 150-152 (3)	4.75	1.35

Statistical Congress, Cairo.

Imhotep — A48

Mohammed Ali Pasha — A49

1928, Dec. 15

153	A48	5m orange brown	1.00	.45
154	A49	10m copper red	1.10	.45

Intl. Congress of Medicine at Cairo and the cent. of the Faculty of Medicine at Cairo.

Prince Farouk — A50

1929, Feb. 11 Litho.

155	A50	5m choc & gray	1.60	1.10
156	A50	10m dull red & gray	1.90	1.25
157	A50	15m ultra & gray	1.90	1.25
158	A50	20m Prus blue & gray	1.90	1.25
		Nos. 155-158 (4)	7.30	4.85

Ninth birthday of Prince Farouk.

Nos. 155-158 with black or brown centers are trial color proofs. They were sent to the UPU, but were never placed on sale to the public, although some are known used.

Tomb Fresco at El-Bersheh — A51

1931, Feb. 15 *Perf. 13x13½*

163	A51	5m brown	.90	.55
164	A51	10m copper red	1.60	1.25
165	A51	15m dark blue	2.25	1.50
		Nos. 163-165 (3)	4.75	3.30

14th Agricultural & Industrial Exhib., Cairo.

Nos. 114 and 103 Surcharged with Bars and

1932 Wmk. 120 *Perf. 14x14½*

166	A40	50m on 50p	15.00	2.75

Perf. 14

167	A37	100m on £1	190.00	150.00

Locomotive of 1852 — A52

Perf. 13x13½

1933, Jan. 19 Litho. Wmk. 195

168	A52	5m shown	11.00	4.50
169	A52	13m 1859	17.00	8.00
170	A52	15m 1862	17.00	8.00
171	A52	20m 1932	17.00	8.00
		Nos. 168-171 (4)	62.00	28.50

International Railroad Congress, Heliopolis.

Commercial Passenger Airplane — A56

Dornier Do-X A57

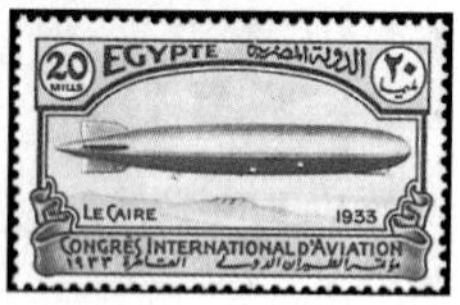

Graf Zeppelin A58

1933, Dec. 20 Photo.

172	A56	5m brown	5.00	1.75
173	A56	10m brt violet	12.00	7.25
174	A57	13m brown car	14.00	9.50
175	A57	15m violet	14.00	8.75
176	A58	20m blue	18.50	16.00
		Nos. 172-176 (5)	63.50	43.25

International Aviation Congress, Cairo.

A59

Khedive Ismail Pasha — A60

1934, Feb. 1 *Perf. 13½*

177	A59	1m dp orange	.50	*1.00*
178	A59	2m black	.55	*1.00*
179	A59	3m brown	.60	*1.25*
180	A59	4m blue green	.90	.40
181	A59	5m red brown	.95	.20
182	A59	10m violet	2.00	.20
183	A59	13m copper red	3.00	1.25
184	A59	15m dull violet	3.00	1.10
185	A59	20m ultra	2.00	.30
186	A59	50m Prus blue	7.00	.60
187	A59	100m olive grn	16.50	1.00
188	A59	200m dp violet	55.00	5.50

Perf. 13½x13

189	A60	50p brown	175.00	75.00
190	A60	£1 Prus blue	285.00	125.00
		Nos. 177-190 (14)	552.00	213.80

10th Congress of UPU, Cairo.

King Fuad — A61

1936-37 *Perf. 13½*

191	A61	1m dull orange	.40	*.60*
192	A61	2m black	1.25	.20
193	A61	4m dk green	1.40	.20
194	A61	5m chestnut	1.00	.20
195	A61	10m purple ('37)	1.75	.20
196	A61	15m brown violet	1.90	.40
197	A61	20m sapphire	2.25	.20
		Nos. 191-197 (7)	9.95	2.00

Entrance to Agricultural Building — A62

Agricultural Building — A63

Design: 15m, 20m, Industrial Building.

1936, Feb. 15 *Perf. 13½x13*

198	A62	5m brown	1.00	.85

Perf. 13x13½

199	A63	10m violet	1.25	.95
200	A63	13m copper red	1.50	2.00
201	A63	15m dark violet	1.10	1.00
202	A63	20m blue	2.25	2.00
		Nos. 198-202 (5)	7.10	6.80

15th Agricultural & Industrial Exhib., Cairo.

Signing of Treaty — A65

1936, Dec. 22 *Perf. 11*

203	A65	5m brown	.65	.55
204	A65	15m dk violet	.75	.70
205	A65	20m sapphire	2.00	.90
		Nos. 203-205 (3)	3.40	2.15

Signing of Anglo-Egyptian Treaty, Aug. 26, 1936.

King Farouk — A66

Medal for Montreux Conf. — A67

1937-44 Wmk. 195 *Perf. 13x13½*

206	A66	1m brown org	.30	.20
207	A66	2m vermilion	.30	.20
208	A66	3m brown	.30	.20
209	A66	4m green	.30	.20
210	A66	5m red brown	.50	.20
211	A66	6m lt yel grn ('40)	.60	.20
212	A66	10m purple	.30	.20
213	A66	13m rose car	.60	.35
214	A66	15m dk vio brn	.50	.20
215	A66	20m blue	.75	.35
216	A66	20m lil gray ('44)	.75	.20
		Nos. 206-216 (11)	5.20	2.50

For overprints see Nos. 301, 303, 345, 348, 360E, N3, N6, N8, N22, N25, N27.

1937, Oct. 15 *Perf. 13½x13*

217	A67	5m red brown	.50	.35
218	A67	15m dk violet	.75	.70
219	A67	20m sapphire	.80	.80
		Nos. 217-219 (3)	2.05	1.85

Intl. Treaty signed at Montreux, Switzerland, under which foreign privileges in Egypt were to end in 1949.

Eye of Ré — A68

1937, Dec. 8 *Perf. 13x13½*

220	A68	5m brown	.60	.70
221	A68	15m dk violet	.90	.70
222	A68	20m sapphire	1.10	.80
		Nos. 220-222 (3)	2.60	2.20

15th Ophthalmological Congress, Cairo, December, 1937.

King Farouk, Queen Farida — A69

1938, Jan. 20 *Perf. 11*

223	A69	5m red brown	6.50	4.00

Royal wedding of King Farouk and Farida Zulficar.

Inscribed: "11 Fevrier 1938"

1938, Feb. 11

224	A69	£1 green & sepia	150.00	110.00

King Farouk's 18th birthday.

Cotton Picker — A70

1938, Jan. 26 *Perf. 13½x13*

225	A70	5m red brown	.50	.50
226	A70	15m dk violet	2.00	.85
227	A70	20m sapphire	1.50	.75
		Nos. 225-227 (3)	4.00	2.10

18th International Cotton Congress at Cairo.

Pyramids of Giza and Colossus of Thebes
A71

1938, Feb. 1	*Perf. 13x13½*		
228 A71 5m red brown		1.00	.65
229 A71 15m dk violet		1.50	.80
230 A71 20m sapphire		1.75	.80
Nos. 228-230 (3)		4.25	2.25

Intl. Telecommunication Conf., Cairo.

Branch of Hydnocarpus — A72

1938, Mar. 21	*Perf. 13x13½*		
231 A72 5m red brown		1.00	.50
232 A72 15m dk violet		1.60	.60
233 A72 20m sapphire		1.60	.60
Nos. 231-233 (3)		4.20	1.70

International Leprosy Congress, Cairo.

King Farouk and Pyramids — A73

King Farouk
A74 A75

Backgrounds: 40m, Hussan Mosque. 50m, Cairo Citadel. 100m, Aswan Dam. 200m, Cairo University.

1939-46	**Photo.**	*Perf. 14x13½*	
234 A73 30m gray		.50	.20
a. 30m slate gray		.50	.20
234B A73 30m ol grn ('46)		.55	.20
235 A73 40m dk brown		.60	.20
236 A73 50m Prus green		.70	.20
237 A73 100m brown vio		1.00	.20
238 A73 200m dk violet		3.00	.20
	Perf. 13½x13		
239 A74 50p green & sep		6.75	2.00
240 A75 £1 dp bl & dk brn		14.50	4.00
Nos. 234-240 (8)		27.60	7.20

For £1 with A77 portrait, see No. 269D. See Nos. 267-269D. For overprints see Nos. 310-314, 316, 355-358, 360, 363-364, N13-N19, N32-N38.

SEMI-POSTAL STAMPS

Catalogue values for unused stamps in this section are for Never Hinged items.

Princess Ferial — SP1

	Perf. 13½x14		
1940, May 17	**Photo.**	**Wmk. 195**	
B1 SP1 5m + 5m copper brown		1.50	.50

AIR POST STAMPS

Mail Plane in Flight
AP1

	Perf. 13x13½		
1926, Mar. 10	**Wmk. 195**	**Photo.**	
C1 AP1 27m deep violet		17.00	15.00
1929, July 17			
C2 AP1 27m orange brown		4.50	2.25

Zeppelin Issue

No. C2 Surcharged in Blue or Violet

1931, Apr. 6			
C3 AP1 50m on 27m (Bl)		52.50	52.50
a. "1951" instead of "1931"		57.50	57.50
C4 AP1 100m on 27m (V)		52.50	*62.50*

Airplane over Giza Pyramids
AP2

1933-38	**Litho.**	*Perf. 13x13½*	
C5 AP2 1m orange & blk		.40	.25
C6 AP2 2m gray & blk		.80	.55
C7 AP2 2m org red & blk ('38)		2.00	.75
C8 AP2 3m ol brn & blk		.60	.20
C9 AP2 4m green & blk		.90	.45
C10 AP2 5m dp brown & blk		.40	.20
C11 AP2 6m dk green & blk		1.50	.65
C12 AP2 7m dk blue & blk		1.00	.55
C13 AP2 8m violet & blk		.60	.20
C14 AP2 9m dp red & blk		2.50	.75
C15 AP2 10m violet & brn		.75	.25
C16 AP2 20m dk green & brn		.60	.20
C17 AP2 30m dull blue & brn		.75	.20
C18 AP2 40m dp red & brn		15.00	.60
C19 AP2 50m orange & brn		12.00	.25
C20 AP2 60m gray & brn		3.75	.55
C21 AP2 70m dk blue & bl grn		3.50	.50
C22 AP2 80m ol brn & bl grn		3.50	.50
C23 AP2 90m org & bl grn		4.00	.50
C24 AP2 100m vio & bl grn		7.00	.50
C25 AP2 200m dp red & bl grn		10.00	1.00
Nos. C5-C25 (21)		71.55	9.60

See #C34-C37. For overprint see #C38.

SPECIAL DELIVERY STAMPS

Motorcycle Postman — SD1

	Perf. 13x13½		
1926, Nov. 28	**Photo.**	**Wmk. 195**	
E1 SD1 20m dark green		30.00	8.50
1929, Sept.			
E2 SD1 20m brown red & black		4.50	1.50

POSTAGE DUE STAMPS

D1 D2

Wmk. Crescent and Star (119)			
1884, Jan. 1	**Litho.**	*Perf. 10½*	
J1 D1 10pa red		40.00	9.00
a. Horiz. pair, imperf. vert.		150.00	
J2 D1 20pa red		175.00	50.00
J3 D1 1pi red		125.00	40.00
J4 D1 2pi red		225.00	11.00
J5 D1 5pi red		20.00	*60.00*
Nos. J1-J5 (5)		585.00	170.00
1886, Aug. 1		**Unwmk.**	
J6 D1 10pa red		52.50	7.00
a. Horiz. pair, imperf. vert.		135.00	
J7 D1 20pa red		225.00	30.00
J8 D1 1pi red		26.00	5.00
a. Pair, imperf. between		200.00	
J9 D1 2pi red		26.00	5.00
a. Pair, imperf. between		175.00	
Nos. J6-J9 (4)		329.50	47.00
1888, Jan. 1		*Perf. 11½*	
J10 D2 2m green		10.00	*15.00*
a. Horiz. pair, imperf. between		225.00	
J11 D2 5m rose red		35.00	14.00
J12 D2 1pi blue		140.00	40.00
a. Pair, imperf. between		300.00	
J13 D2 2pi yellow		150.00	20.00
J14 D2 5pi gray		210.00	190.00
a. Period after "PIASTRES"		275.00	250.00
Nos. J10-J14 (5)		545.00	279.00

Excellent counterfeits of #J1-J14 are plentiful.

There are 4 types of each of Nos. J1-J14, so placed that any block of 4 contains all types.

D3

	Perf. 14x13½		
1889	**Wmk. 119**	**Typo.**	
J15 D3 2m green		7.00	.55
a. Half used as 1m on cover			275.00
J16 D3 4m maroon		2.50	.55
J17 D3 1pi ultra		6.25	.55
J18 D3 2pi orange		6.00	.80
a. Half used as 1p on cover			—
Nos. J15-J18 (4)		21.75	2.45

Nos. J15-J18 exist on both ordinary and chalky paper. Imperf. examples of Nos. J15-J17 are proofs.

Black Surcharge

Type I Type II

Type I: the spacing between the last two Arabic characters at the right is 2mm. Type II: spacing is 3mm, and there is an added sign on top of the second character from the right.

1898			
J19 D4 3m on 2pi orange (I)		.65	*2.75*
a. Inverted surcharge		65.00	*82.50*
b. Pair, one without surcharge			—
c. Arabic "3" over "2"		125.00	
d. 3m on 2pi orange (II)		3.50	9.25
e. As "d," inverted surcharge		55.00	*65.00*
f. As "d," double surcharge		225.00	—

D5 D6

1921	**Wmk. 120**	*Perf. 14x13½*	
J20 D5 2m green		.25	.25
J21 D5 4m vermilion		1.10	.90
J22 D6 10m deep blue		1.25	1.00
Nos. J20-J22 (3)		2.60	2.15
1921-22			
J23 D5 2m vermilion		.25	.20
J24 D5 4m green		.25	.20
J25 D6 10m lake ('22)		.50	.40
Nos. J23-J25 (3)		1.00	.80

Nos. J18, J23-J25 Overprinted

1922, Oct. 10		**Wmk. 119**	
J26 D3 2pi orange		5.00	*5.00*
a. Overprint right side up		25.00	*25.00*
	Wmk. 120		
J27 D5 2m vermilion		.60	*.90*
J28 D5 4m green		.90	*.90*
J29 D6 10m lake		1.25	.90
Nos. J26-J29 (4)		7.75	7.70

Overprint on Nos. J26-J29 is inverted.

Arabic Numeral — D7

	Perf. 13x13½		
1927-56	**Litho.**	**Wmk. 195**	
	Size: 18x22½mm		
J30 D7 2m slate		.60	.40
J31 D7 2m orange ('38)		.80	.50
J32 D7 4m green		.60	.45
J33 D7 4m ol brn ('32)		6.25	4.25
J34 D7 5m brown		3.50	.80
J35 D7 6m gray grn ('41)		1.50	1.50
J36 D7 8m brn vio		1.00	.40
J37 D7 10m brick red ('29)		1.00	.30
a. 10m deep red		1.10	.35
J38 D7 12m rose lake ('41)		1.50	1.50
J38A D7 20m dk red ('56)		2.00	2.00
	Perf. 13½x14		
	Size: 22x28mm		
J39 D7 30m purple		4.25	2.25
Nos. J30-J39 (11)		23.00	14.35

See Nos. J47-J59. For overprints see Nos. J40-J46, NJ1-NJ7.

LOCAL STAMPS

SUEZ CANAL COMPANY

Steamship — L1

1868, July 8	**Litho.**	*Imperf.*	
L1 L1 1c black		275.00	*1,150.*
On cover			*22,500.*
L2 L1 5c green		100.00	*575.00*
On cover			*11,500.*
L3 L1 20c blue		35.00	*575.00*
On cover			*11,500.*
L4 L1 40c pink		150.00	*850.00*
On cover			*17,000.*

Nos. L1-L4 were issued by the Suez Canal Co. for use on letters and printed matter carried between canal ports. Items addressed to further destinations required additional French or Egyptian postage.

These issues were recognized officially by the French Consulate Offices at Port Said and Suez but not by the Egyptian Post Office, which suppressed their use at the end of August, 1868.

Nos. L1-L4 exist with portions of the papermaker's watermark, "LA + F" (La Croix Freres).

Many forgeries exist of the stamps of the Suez Canal Co., including excellent counterfeits created from the genuine plate of the 40c value, stolen from the company's archives.

MILITARY STAMPS

The "British Forces" and "Army post" stamps were special issues provided at a reduced rate for the purchase and use by the British military forces in Egypt and their families for ordinary letters sent to Great Britain and Ireland by concessionary arrangement made with the Egyptian government. From Nov. 1, 1932 to Feb. 29, 1936, in order to take advantage of the concessionary rate, it was mandatory to use #M1-M11 by affixing them to the backs of envelopes. An "Egypt Postage Prepaid" handstamp was applied to the face of the envelopes. Envelopes bearing these stamps were to be posted only at British military post boxes. Envelopes bearing the 1936-39 "Army Post" stamps (#M12-M15, issued by the Egyptian Postal Administration), also were sold at the concessionary rate and also were to be posted only at British military post boxes. The "Army Post" stamps were withdrawn in 1941, but the concession continued without the use of special stamps. The concession was finally canceled in 1951.

Imperf examples of Nos. M1-M4, M6, M9 (without overprint) and M10 are proofs.

M1

Unwmk.

1932, Nov. 1 Typo. *Perf. 11*
M1 M1 1pi red & deep blue 100.00 4.25
For similar design see #M3.

M2

1932, Nov. 26 Typo. *Perf. 11½*
M2 M2 3m blk, *sage grn* 55.00 *77.50*
See #M4, M6, M10.

M3

1933, Aug. Typo. *Perf. 11*
M3 M3 1pi red & deep blue 32.50 1.10

Camel Type of 1932

1933, Nov. 13 Typo. *Perf. 11½*
M4 M2 3m brown lake 8.75 *57.50*

M4

1934, June 1 Photo. *Perf. 14½x14*
M5 M4 1pi bright carmine 42.50 1.10
See #M7-M8. For overprint and surcharge see #M9, M11.

Camel Type of 1932

1934, Nov. 17 Typo. *Perf. 11½*
M6 M2 3m deep blue 8.25 *30.00*

Type of 1934

1934, Dec. 5 Photo. *Perf. 14½x14*
M7 M4 1pi green 4.50 4.50

Type of 1934

1935, Apr. 24 *Perf. 13½x14*
M8 M4 1pi bright carmine 2.90 *3.75*

Type of 1934 Overprinted in Red

1935, May 6 *Perf. 14*
M9 M4 1pi ultramarine 290.00 210.00

Camel Type of 1932

1935, Nov. 23 Typo. *Perf. 11½*
M10 M2 3m vermilion 2.25 *42.50*

No. M8 Surcharged

1935, Dec. 16 Photo. *Perf. 13½x14*
M11 M4 3m on 1pi brt car 19.00 *82.50*

Fuad Type of 1927
Inscribed "Army Post"

M5

1936, Mar. 1 Wmk. 195
M12 M5 3m green 1.10 1.10
M13 M5 10m carmine 2.50 .20

King Farouk — M6

1939, Dec. 16 *Perf. 13x13½*
M14 M6 3m green 1.90 *6.25*
M15 M6 10m carmine rose 2.50 .20

OFFICIAL STAMPS

O1

Wmk. Crescent and Star (119)

1893, Jan. 1 Typo. *Perf. 14x13½*
O1 O1 orange brown 1.25 .20
No. O1 exists on ordinary and chalky paper. Imperf. examples of No. O1 are proofs.

Regular Issues of 1884-93 Overprinted

1907
O2 A18 1m brown .80 .20
O3 A19 2m green .80 .20
O4 A20 3m orange .80 .20
O5 A22 5m car rose 1.10 .20
O6 A14 1pi ultra 1.60 .20
O7 A16 5pi gray 5.50 .20
Nos. O2-O7 (6) 10.60 1.20
Nos. O2-O3, O5-O7 imperf. are proofs.

Overprinted

1913
O8 A22 5m carmine rose 1.60 .20
a. Inverted overprint 27.50
b. No period after "S" 4.75 1.90

Regular Issues Overprinted

1914-15

On Issues of 1888-1906
O9 A19 2m green .25 .20
a. Inverted overprint 15.00 11.00
b. Double overprint 175.00
c. No period after "S" 4.50 3.25
O10 A21 4m brown red 1.10 .20
a. Inverted overprint 100.00 60.00

On Issue of 1914
O11 A24 1m olive brown .20 .20
a. No period after "S" 1.75 1.40
O12 A26 3m orange .20 .20
a. No period after "S" 3.75 2.75
O13 A28 5m lake .45 .20
a. No period after "S" 2.75 2.25
b. Two periods after "S" 2.75 2.25
Nos. O9-O13 (5) 2.20 1.00

Regular Issues Overprinted

1915, Oct.

On Issues of 1888-1906
O14 A19 2m green .55 .20
a. Inverted overprint 7.25 5.50
b. Double overprint 11.00
O15 A21 4m brown red .70 .20

On Issue of 1914
O16 A28 5m lake .45 .20
a. Pair, one without overprint 150.00
Nos. O14-O16 (3) 1.70 .60

1922 Wmk. 120

On Issue of 1921-22
O17 A24 1m olive brown 3.75 1.10
O18 A25 2m red 3.75 1.10
O19 A26 3m orange 65.00 65.00
O20 A28 5m pink 3.75 1.60
Nos. O17-O20 (4) 76.25 68.80

Regular Issues of 1921-22 Overprinted

1922
O21 A24 1m olive brn .25 .25
O22 A25 2m red .25 .20
O23 A26 3m orange 1.25 .90
O24 A27 4m green 1.75 1.25
a. Two periods after "H" none after "S" 72.50 72.50
O25 A28 5m pink .45 .20
a. Two periods after "H" none after "S" 37.50 37.50
O26 A29 10m deep blue 1.25 .70
O27 A29 10m lake ('23) 2.25 .70
a. Two periods after "H" none after "S" 55.00 42.50
O28 A34 15m indigo 1.50 .90
O29 A35 15m indigo 100.00 90.00
a. Two periods after "H" none after "S" 225.00 225.00
O30 A31 50m maroon 7.25 2.75

Regular Issue of 1923 Overprinted in Black or Red

1924 *Perf. 13½x14*
O31 A36 1m orange .45 .25
O32 A36 2m gray (R) .55 .35
O33 A36 3m brown 1.50 .60
O34 A36 4m yellow green 1.75 .70
O35 A36 5m orange brown .55 .20
O36 A36 10m rose 1.60 .25
O37 A36 15m ultra 1.75 .50

Perf. 14
O38 A36 50m myrtle green 4.50 1.40
Nos. O31-O38 (8) 12.65 4.25

O2

O3

Perf. 13x13½

1926-35 Litho. Wmk. 195

Size: 18½x22mm
O39 O2 1m lt orange .20 .20
O40 O2 2m black .20 .20
O41 O2 3m olive brn .20 .20
O42 O2 4m lt green .20 .20
O43 O2 5m brown .20 .20
O44 O2 10m dull red .45 .20
O45 O2 10m brt vio ('34) .20 .20
O46 O2 15m dp blue .65 .20
O47 O2 15m brown vio ('34) .25 .20
O48 O2 20m dp blue ('35) .35 .20

Perf. 13½

Size: 22½x27½mm
O49 O2 20m olive green 1.60 .20
O50 O2 50m myrtle green 1.25 .20
Nos. O39-O50 (12) 5.75 2.40

1938, Dec.

Size: 22½x19mm
O51 O3 1m orange .20 .20
O52 O3 2m red .20 .20
O53 O3 3m olive brown .20 .20
O54 O3 4m yel green .20 .20
O55 O3 5m brown .20 .20
O56 O3 10m brt violet .20 .20
O57 O3 15m rose violet .20 .20
O58 O3 20m blue .20 .20

Perf. 14x13½

Size: 26½x22mm
O59 O3 50m myrtle green .45 .20
Nos. O51-O59 (9) 2.05 1.80

ELOBEY, ANNOBON AND CORISCO

ˌel-ə-ˈbā, ˌan-ə-ˈbän and kə-ˈris-ˌₒkō

LOCATION — A group of islands near the Guinea Coast of western Africa.
GOVT. — Spanish colonial possessions administered as part of the Continental Guinea District. A second district under the same governor-general included Fernando Po.
AREA — 13¾ sq. mi.
POP. — 2,950 (estimated 1910)
CAPITAL — Santa Isabel

100 Centimos = 1 Peseta

King Alfonso XIII — A1

1903 Unwmk. Typo. *Perf. 14*

Control Numbers on Back

1	A1	¼c carmine	.65	.35
2	A1	½c dk violet	.65	.35
3	A1	1c black	.65	.35
4	A1	2c red	.65	.35
5	A1	3c dk green	.55	.35
6	A1	4c dk blue grn	.65	.35
7	A1	5c violet	.65	.35
8	A1	10c rose lake	1.40	1.40
9	A1	15c orange buff	4.00	1.50
10	A1	25c dark blue	6.25	5.00
11	A1	50c red brown	8.50	8.50
12	A1	75c black brn	8.50	*11.00*
13	A1	1p orange red	13.50	*16.50*
14	A1	2p chocolate	35.00	*50.00*
15	A1	3p dp olive grn	55.00	*60.00*
16	A1	4p claret	125.00	82.50
17	A1	5p blue green	140.00	85.00
18	A1	10p dull blue	275.00	140.00
		Nos. 1-18 (18)	676.60	463.85
		Set, never hinged	1,025.	

Dated "1905"

1905

Control Numbers on Back

19	A1	1c carmine	1.00	.55
20	A1	2c dp violet	4.50	.55
21	A1	3c black	1.00	.55
22	A1	4c dull red	1.00	.55
23	A1	5c dp green	1.00	.55
24	A1	10c blue grn	3.50	.75
25	A1	15c violet	4.00	3.50
26	A1	25c rose lake	4.00	3.50
27	A1	50c orange buff	7.75	5.00
28	A1	75c dark blue	7.75	5.00
29	A1	1p red brown	15.50	10.50
30	A1	2p black brn	17.00	16.00
31	A1	3p orange red	17.00	16.50
32	A1	4p dk brown	125.00	60.00
33	A1	5p bronze grn	140.00	62.50
34	A1	10p claret	325.00	190.00
		Nos. 19-34 (16)	675.00	376.00
		Set, never hinged	1,250.	

Nos. 19-22 Surcharged in Black or Red

1906

35 A1 10c on 1c rose (Bk)		10.00	6.00
a.	Inverted surcharge	10.00	6.00
b.	Value omitted	30.00	16.00
c.	Frame omitted	16.00	7.25
d.	Double surcharge	10.00	6.00
e.	Surcharged "15 cents"	30.00	16.00
f.	Surcharged "25 cents"	52.50	22.50
g.	Surcharged "50 cents"	37.50	22.50
h.	"1906" omitted	17.50	7.25
36 A1 15c on 2c dp vio (R)		10.00	6.00
a.	Frame omitted	12.00	5.50
b.	Surcharged "25 cents"	16.00	9.00
c.	Inverted surcharge	10.00	6.00
d.	Double surcharge	10.00	6.00
37 A1 25c on 3c blk (R)		10.00	6.00
a.	Inverted surcharge	10.00	6.00
b.	Double surcharge	10.00	6.00
c.	Surcharged "15 cents"	16.00	6.00
d.	Surcharged "50 cents"	25.00	11.00
38 A1 50c on 4c red (Bk)		10.00	6.00
a.	Inverted surcharge	10.00	6.00
b.	Value omitted	35.00	17.50
c.	Frame omitted	17.50	8.00
e.	Double surcharge	10.00	6.00
f.	"1906" omitted	17.50	8.00
g.	Surcharged "10 cents"	32.50	16.00
h.	Surcharged "25 cents"	32.50	16.00
	Nos. 35-38 (4)	40.00	24.00

Eight other surcharges were prepared but not issued: 10c on 50c, 75c, 1p, 2p and 3p; 15c on 50c and 5p; 50c on 5c.

Exist with surcharges in different colors; #35 in blue, red or violet, #36 in black or violet, #37 in black or violet, #38 in blue, violet or red. Value, set of 10, $135.

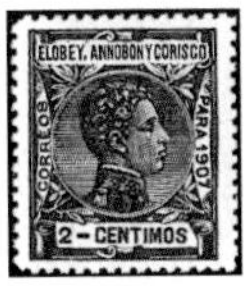

King Alfonso XIII — A2

1907

Control Numbers on Back

39	A2	1c dk violet	.45	.30
40	A2	2c black	.45	.30
41	A2	3c red orange	.45	.30
42	A2	4c dk green	.45	.30
43	A2	5c blue green	.45	.30
44	A2	10c violet	3.75	3.50
45	A2	15c carmine	1.25	1.25
46	A2	25c orange	1.25	1.25
47	A2	50c blue	1.25	1.25
48	A2	75c brown	3.75	1.60
49	A2	1p black brn	6.25	3.75
50	A2	2p orange red	9.50	4.25
51	A2	3p dk brown	8.75	4.25
52	A2	4p bronze grn	9.50	4.25
53	A2	5p claret	12.50	4.75
54	A2	10p rose	30.00	15.00
		Nos. 39-54 (16)	90.00	46.60
		Set, never hinged	160.00	

Stamps of 1907 Surcharged

1908-09

Black Surcharge

55	A2	5c on 3c red org ('09)	2.25	1.25
56	A2	5c on 4c dk grn ('09)	2.25	1.25
57	A2	5c on 10c violet	4.75	5.00
58	A2	25c on 10c violet	25.00	15.00
		Nos. 55-58 (4)	34.25	22.50

1910

Red Surcharge

59	A2	5c on 1c dark violet	1.75	.90
60	A2	5c on 2c black	1.75	.90

Nos. 55-60 exist with surcharge inverted (value set, $100 unused or used); with double surcharge, one black, one red (value set, $300 unused or used); with "PARA" omitted (value set, $150.00 unused or used)

The same 5c surcharge was also applied to Nos. 45-54, but these were not issued (value set, $250).

In 1909, stamps of Spanish Guinea replaced those of Elobey, Annobon and Corisco.

1909 CORREOS
10 cen de peseta

Revenue stamps surcharged as above were unauthorized although some were postally used.

EPIRUS

i-ˈpī-rəs

LOCATION — Southeastern Europe comprising parts of Greece and Albania.

This territory formerly belonged to Turkey but is now divided between Greece and Albania. The northern part of the Greek section, now a part of Albania, set up a provisional government during 1912-13 and issued postage stamps but it collapsed in 1916, following Greek occupation. The name "Epirus" is taken from the Greek word meaning "Mainland."

100 Lepta = 1 Drachma

Chimarra Issue

Double-headed Eagle, Skull and Crossbones — A1

Handstamped

1914 (Feb.) Unwmk. *Imperf.*

Control Mark in Blue

Without Gum

1	A1	1 l black & blue	190.00	150.00
2	A1	5 l blue & red	190.00	150.00
3	A1	10 l red & blk	190.00	150.00
4	A1	25 l blue & red	190.00	150.00
		Nos. 1-4 (4)	760.00	600.00

All values exist without control mark. This mark is a solid blue oval, about 12x8mm, containing the colorless Greek letters "SP," the first two letters of Spiromilios, the Chimarra commander.

All four exist with value inverted and the 1, 5 and 10 l with value double.

Some experts question the official character of this issue. Counterfeits are plentiful.

Provisional Government Issues

Infantryman with Rifle
A2 A3

Serrate Roulette 13½

1914 (Mar.) Litho.

5	A2	1 l orange	.40	.40
6	A2	5 l green	.40	.40
7	A3	10 l carmine	.40	.40
8	A3	25 l deep blue	.40	.40
9	A2	50 l brown	.85	.85
10	A2	1d violet	1.75	1.75
11	A2	2d blue	9.50	9.50
12	A2	5d gray green	12.00	12.00
		Nos. 5-12 (8)	25.70	25.70

15 values, 5 l to 5d, of Turkish stamps surcharged "Epirus Autonomous" and new values in Greek were on sale for a few days in Argyrokastron (Gjirokaster).

Flag of Epirus — A5

1914 (Aug.)

15	A5	1 l brown & blue	.55	*.65*
16	A5	5 l green & blue	.55	*.65*
17	A5	10 l rose red & blue	.60	*.70*
18	A5	25 l dk blue & blue	.70	*.75*
19	A5	50 l violet & blue	.90	*1.25*
20	A5	1d carmine & blue	4.50	*7.00*
21	A5	2d orange & blue	1.25	*1.75*
22	A5	5d dk green & blue	8.50	*9.00*
		Nos. 15-22 (8)	17.55	*21.75*

Koritsa Issue

A7

1914

26	A7	25 l dk blue & blue	4.50	4.50
27	A7	50 l violet & blue	7.50	7.50

Chimarra Issue

1911-23 Issues of Greece Overprinted

1914 (Aug.)

34	A24	1 l green	*22.50*	*22.50*
35	A25	2 l carmine	*21.00*	*21.00*
36	A24	3 l vermilion	*21.00*	*21.00*
37	A26	5 l green	*22.50*	*22.50*
38	A24	10 l carmine	*22.50*	*22.50*
39	A25	20 l slate	*42.50*	*42.50*
40	A25	25 l blue	*70.00*	*70.00*
41	A26	50 l violet brn	*95.00*	*95.00*
		Nos. 34-41 (8)	*317.00*	*317.00*

The 2 l and 3 l are engraved stamps of the 1911-21 issue, the others are lithographed stamps of the 1912-23 issue.

Overprint reads: "Greek Chimarra 1914."

Stamps of this issue are with or without a black monogram (S.S., for S. Spiromilios) in manuscript. Counterfeits are plentiful.

Stamps of the following designs were not regularly issued for postal purposes in the opinion of the editors.

From 1914: 1st design, 3 varieties. 2nd design, 6 varieties. 3rd design, 7 varieties. 4th and 5th designs, 15 varieties.

From 1920: 6th design, 4 varieties.

OCCUPATION STAMPS

Issued under Greek Occupation
Greek Occupation Stamps of 1913
Overprinted Horizontally

Serrate Roulette 13½

1914-15 Black Overprint Unwmk.

N1	O1	1 l brown	.65	.65
N2	O2	2 l red	.65	.65
b.		2 l rose	1.00	1.00
N4	O2	3 l orange	.75	.75
N5	O1	5 l green	2.25	2.00
N6	O1	10 l rose red	2.50	2.25
N7	O1	20 l violet	7.50	4.00
N8	O2	25 l pale blue	2.50	2.25
N9	O1	30 l gray green	11.00	10.00
N10	O2	40 l indigo	15.00	14.00
N11	O1	50 l dark blue	16.00	15.00
N12	O2	1d violet brown	65.00	65.00
		Nos. N1-N12 (11)	123.80	116.55

The overprint exists double on 6 denominations (1 l, 2 l both, 3 l, 5 l, 10 l and 1d); inverted on all but 25 l, 40 l; double, one inverted, 5 l. Values, $15 and up.

Red Overprint

N1a	O1	1 l brown	4.00
N2a	O2	2 l red	4.00
N4a	O2	3 l orange	4.00
N5a	O1	5 l green	4.00

Nos. N1a-N5a were not issued. Exist canceled.

Regular Issues of Greece, 1911-23, Overprinted

On Issue of 1911-21

1916 Engr.

N17	A24	3 l vermilion	7.25	7.25
N18	A26	30 l carmine rose	62.50	60.00
N19	A27	1d ultra	50.00	50.00
N20	A27	2d vermilion	62.50	60.00
N21	A27	3d carmine rose	75.00	75.00
N22	A27	5d ultra	350.00	350.00
a.		Double overprint	450.00	450.00
		Nos. N17-N22 (6)	607.25	602.25

Overprints on Nos. N18-N21 read up, on No. N22 reads down. Overprint on No. N17 exists reading down but most read up.

On Issue of 1912-23

1916 Litho.

N23	A24	1 l green	.85	.85
N24	A25	2 l carmine	.85	.85
N25	A24	3 l vermilion	1.25	1.25
N26	A26	5 l green	.85	.85
N27	A24	10 l carmine	1.10	1.10
N28	A25	20 l slate	1.25	1.25
N29	A25	25 l blue	2.25	2.25
N30	A26	30 l rose	7.00	7.00
N31	A25	40 l indigo	6.50	6.50
N32	A26	50 l violet brown	8.50	8.50
		Nos. N23-N32 (10)	30.40	30.40

Overprints on Nos. N28-N29, N31-N32 read up. Nos. N23-N27 N30 exist reading down but most read up.

In each sheet there are two varieties in the overprint: the "I" in "Epirus" omitted and an inverted "L" in place of the first letter of the word.

Counterfeits exist of Nos. N1-N32.

Postage stamps issued in 1940-41, during Greek occupation, are listed under Greece.

ERITREA

ˌer-ə-ˈtrē-ə

LOCATION — In northeast Africa, bordering on the Red Sea
GOVT. — Italian Colony
AREA — 15,754 sq. mi. (1936)
POP. — 600,573 (1931)
CAPITAL — Asmara

Eritrea was incorporated as a State of Italian East Africa in 1936.

100 Centesimi = 1 Lira

All used values to about 1916 are for postally used stamps. From 1916, used values in italics are for postally used stamps. CTO's, for stamps valued postally used, sell for about the same as unused, hinged stamps.

Watermark

Wmk. 140 — Crown

Stamps of Italy Overprinted

a

b

1892 Wmk. 140 *Perf. 14*

Overprinted Type "a" in Black

1	A6	1c bronze grn	7.50	6.00
		Never hinged	18.00	
		No gum	1.90	
		On cover		80.00
a.		Inverted overprint	440.00	400.00
		Never hinged	—	
b.		Double overprint	1,325.	
		Never hinged	1,650.	
c.		Vert. pair, one without overprint	2,500.	
		Never hinged	3,100.	
2	A7	2c org brn	3.75	3.00
		Never hinged	9.25	
		No gum	1.10	
		On cover		52.50
a.		Inverted overprint	400.00	375.00
		Never hinged	—	
b.		Double overprint	1,325.	
		Never hinged	1,650.	
3	A33	5c green	87.50	7.50
		Never hinged	225.00	
		No gum	18.00	
		On cover		50.00
a.		Inverted overprint	4,750.	2,750.
		Never hinged	5,900.	

Overprinted Type "b" in Black

4	A17	10c claret	110.00	7.50
		Never hinged	275.00	
		No gum	22.00	
		On cover		50.00
5	A17	20c orange	210.00	6.00
		Never hinged	550.00	
		No gum	45.00	
		On cover		37.50
6	A17	25c blue	800.00	30.00
		Never hinged	2,000.	
		No gum	160.00	
		On cover		240.00
7	A25	40c brown	8.75	*18.00*
		Never hinged	22.50	
		No gum	2.25	
		On cover		240.00
8	A26	45c slate grn	8.75	*21.00*
		Never hinged	22.50	
		No gum	2.25	
		On cover		260.00
9	A27	60c violet	8.75	42.50
		Never hinged	22.50	
		No gum	2.25	
		On cover		525.00
10	A28	1 l brn & yel	30.00	*42.50*
		Never hinged	75.00	
		No gum	6.00	
		On cover		600.00
11	A38	5 l bl & rose	440.00	325.00
		Never hinged	1,100.	
		No gum	87.50	
		On cover		*4,750.*
		Nos. 1-11 (11)	1,715.	*509.00*
		Set, never hinged	4,310.	

1895-99

Overprinted type "a" in Black

12	A39	1c brown ('99)	13.00	8.75
		Never hinged	32.50	
		No gum	2.75	
		On cover		65.00
13	A40	2c org brn ('99)	2.25	1.10
		Never hinged	5.50	
		No gum	.55	
		On cover		47.50
14	A41	5c green	2.25	1.10
		Never hinged	5.50	
		No gum	.55	
		On cover		30.00
a.		Inverted overprint	300.00	*2,600.*
		Never hinged	—	

Overprinted type "b" in Black

15	A34	10c claret ('98)	2.25	1.10
		Never hinged	5.50	
		No gum	.55	
		On cover		40.00
16	A35	20c orange	3.00	1.75
		Never hinged	7.50	
		No gum	.75	
		On cover		32.50
17	A36	25c blue	3.00	2.50
		Never hinged	7.50	
		No gum	.75	
		On cover		160.00
18	A37	45c olive grn	20.00	*18.00*
		Never hinged	50.00	
		No gum	5.25	
		On cover		375.00
		Nos. 12-18 (7)	45.75	*34.30*
		Set, never hinged	110.00	

1903-28

Overprinted type "a" in Black

19	A42	1c brown	.75	*1.10*
		Never hinged	1.90	
		On cover		15.00
a.		Inverted overprint	110.00	110.00
20	A43	2c orange brn	.75	*.55*
		Never hinged	1.90	
		On cover		15.00
21	A44	5c blue green	35.00	.55
		Never hinged	92.50	
		On cover		9.00
22	A45	10c claret	42.50	.55
		Never hinged	110.00	
		On cover		9.00
23	A45	20c orange	3.00	1.10
		Never hinged	7.50	
		On cover		13.50
24	A45	25c blue	300.00	14.50
		Never hinged	750.00	
		On cover		110.00
a.		Double overprint	550.00	—
		Never hinged	—	
25	A45	40c brown	375.00	21.00
		Never hinged	925.00	
		On cover		240.00
26	A45	45c olive grn	3.75	*7.50*
		Never hinged	9.25	
		On cover		150.00
27	A45	50c violet	100.00	25.00
		Never hinged	250.00	
		On cover		325.00
28	A46	75c dk red & rose ('28)	57.50	5.25
		Never hinged	160.00	
		On cover		160.00
29	A46	1 l brown & grn	3.75	.75
		Never hinged	9.25	
		On cover		87.50
30	A46	1.25 l bl & ultra ('28)	30.00	3.00
		Never hinged	75.00	
		On cover		130.00
31	A46	2 l dk grn & org ('25)	50.00	65.00
		Never hinged	120.00	
		On cover		275.00
32	A46	2.50 l dk grn & org ('28)	125.00	47.00
		Never hinged	325.00	
		On cover		400.00
33	A46	5 l blue & rose	25.00	37.00
		Never hinged	65.00	
		On cover		*2,750.*
		Nos. 19-33 (15)	1,152.	229.85
		Set, never hinged	2,900.	

Surcharged in Black

1905

34	A45	15c on 20c orange	35.00	9.25
		Never hinged	92.50	
		On cover		52.50

1908-28

Overprinted type "a" in Black

35	A48	5c green	.90	.85
		Never hinged	2.40	
		On cover		7.50
36	A48	10c claret ('09)	.90	.85
		Never hinged	2.40	
		On cover		11.00
37	A48	15c slate ('20)	14.50	8.75
		Never hinged	37.50	
		On cover		60.00
38	A49	20c green ('25)	13.00	10.50
		Never hinged	32.50	
		On cover		45.00
39	A49	20c lilac brn ('28)	4.25	3.00
		Never hinged	11.00	
		On cover		60.00
40	A49	25c blue ('09)	4.00	2.00
		Never hinged	10.00	
		On cover		26.00
41	A49	30c gray ('25)	13.50	13.00
		Never hinged	32.50	
		On cover		80.00
42	A49	40c brown ('16)	32.50	*30.00*
		Never hinged	82.50	
		On cover		110.00
43	A49	50c violet ('16)	11.00	1.75
		Never hinged	27.50	
		On cover		130.00
44	A49	60c brown car ('18)	18.00	20.00
		Never hinged	45.00	
		On cover		87.50
a.		Printed on both sides		*1,000.*
45	A49	60c brown org ('28)	75.00	*140.00*
		Never hinged	190.00	
		On cover		325.00
46	A51	10 l gray grn & red ('16)	250.00	*475.00*
		Never hinged	625.00	
		Nos. 35-46 (12)	437.55	*705.70*
		Set, never hinged	1,090.	

See No. 53.

A1

Government Building at Massaua — A2

1910-29 Unwmk. Engr. *Perf. 13½*

47	A1	15c slate	215.00	20.00
		Never hinged	850.00	
		On cover		110.00
a.		Perf. 11 ('29)	30.00	42.50
		Never hinged	75.00	
		On cover		375.00
48	A2	25c dark blue	4.25	*13.00*
		Never hinged	11.00	
		On cover		160.00
a.		Perf. 12	525.00	525.00

For surcharges see Nos. 51-52.

A3

Farmer Plowing — A4

1914-28

49	A3	5c green	.75	*2.25*
		Never hinged	1.90	
		On cover		45.00
a.		Perf. 11 ('28)	140.00	55.00
		Never hinged	375.00	
		On cover		300.00
50	A4	10c carmine	4.25	13.00
		Never hinged	11.00	
		On cover		160.00
a.		Perf. 11 ('28)	11.00	*37.50*
		Never hinged	27.50	
		On cover		260.00
b.		Perf. 13½x14	55.00	55.00
		Never hinged	140.00	
		On cover		*450.00*

No. 47 Surcharged in Red or Black

1916

51	A1	5c on 15c slate (R)	6.00	*13.00*
		Never hinged	14.50	
		On cover		175.00

52 A1 20c on 15c slate 2.25 3.75
Never hinged 5.50
On cover 87.50
a. "CEN" for "CENT" 30.00 30.00
Never hinged 75.00
b. "CENT" omitted 160.00 160.00
Never hinged 400.00
c. "ENT" 42.50 *42.50*
Never hinged 110.00
Set, never hinged 20.00

Italy No. 113 Overprinted in Black — f

1921 Wmk. 140 *Perf. 14*
53 A50 20c brown orange 3.75 *11.00*
Never hinged 9.25
On cover 45.00

Victory Issue

Italian Victory Stamps of 1921 Overprinted type "f" 13mm long

1922
54 A64 5c olive green 1.75 *6.50*
Never hinged 4.50
On cover 87.50
55 A64 10c red 1.75 *6.75*
Never hinged 4.50
On cover 140.00
56 A64 15c slate green 1.75 *10.00*
Never hinged 4.50
On cover 160.00
57 A64 25c ultra 1.75 *10.00*
Never hinged 4.50
On cover 200.00
Nos. 54-57 (4) 7.00 *33.25*
Set, never hinged 18.00
Set on overfranked, philatelic cover 160.00

Somalia Nos. 10-16 Overprinted In Black and Bars over Original Values

g

1922 Wmk. 140
58 A1 2c on 1b brn 4.50 *14.50*
Never hinged 11.00
On cover 87.50
a. Pair, one missing "ERITREA" 1,500.
Never hinged 1,850.
59 A1 5c on 2b bl grn 4.50 *10.00*
Never hinged 11.00
On cover 60.00
60 A2 10c on 1a claret 4.50 2.25
Never hinged 11.00
On cover 60.00
61 A2 15c on 2a brn org 4.50 2.25
Never hinged 11.00
On cover 60.00
62 A2 25c on 2½a blue 4.50 2.25
Never hinged 11.00
On cover 87.50
63 A2 50c on 5a yellow 14.50 10.00
Never hinged 37.50
On cover 160.00
a. "ERITREA" double *950.00*
64 A2 1 l on 10a lilac 14.50 18.00
Never hinged 37.50
On cover 275.00
a. "ERITREA" double 950.00 950.00
Never hinged 1,200.
b. Pair, one missing "ERITREA" *1,900.*
Never hinged *2,400.*
Nos. 58-64 (7) 51.50 *59.25*
Set, never hinged 125.00

See Nos. 81-87.

Propagation of the Faith Issue

Italy Nos. 143-146 Overprinted

1923
65 A68 20c ol grn & brn org 7.50 *35.00*
Never hinged 18.50
66 A68 30c claret & brn org 7.50 *35.00*
Never hinged 18.50
67 A68 50c vio & brn org 4.50 *42.50*
Never hinged 11.00
68 A68 1 l bl & brn org 4.50 *55.00*
Never hinged 11.00
Nos. 65-68 (4) 24.00 *167.50*
Set, never hinged 60.00

Fascisti Issue

Italy Nos. 159-164 Overprinted in Red or Black — j

1923 Unwmk. *Perf. 14*
69 A69 10c dk green (R) 7.50 *13.00*
Never hinged 18.50
On cover 190.00
70 A69 30c dk violet (R) 7.50 *13.00*
Never hinged 18.50
On cover 190.00
71 A69 50c brown carmine 7.50 *14.50*
Never hinged 18.50
On cover 190.00

Wmk. 140
72 A70 1 l blue 7.50 *35.00*
Never hinged 18.50
On cover 325.00
73 A70 2 l brown 7.50 *42.50*
Never hinged 18.50
On cover 475.00
74 A71 5 l black & blue (R) 7.50 *60.00*
Never hinged 18.50
Nos. 69-74 (6) 45.00 *178.00*
Set, never hinged 110.00
Set on overfranked, philatelic cover 475.00

Manzoni Issue

Italy Nos. 165-170 Overprinted in Red

1924 *Perf. 14*
75 A72 10c brown red & blk 11.50 *35.00*
Never hinged 30.00
76 A72 15c blue grn & blk 11.50 *35.00*
Never hinged 30.00
77 A72 30c black & slate 11.50 *35.00*
Never hinged 30.00
78 A72 50c org brn & blk 11.50 *35.00*
Never hinged 30.00
79 A72 1 l blue & blk 72.50 *250.00*
Never hinged 190.00
80 A72 5 l violet & blk 475.00 *2,000.*
Never hinged 1,200.
Nos. 75-79 (5) 118.50 *390.00*

On Nos. 79 and 80 the overprint is placed vertically at the left side.

Somalia Nos. 10-16 Overprinted type "g" in Blue or Red

1924
Bars over Original Values
81 A1 2c on 1b brn 11.50 *26.00*
a. Pair, one without "ERITREA" 1,475.
Never hinged 1,850.
On cover 130.00
82 A1 5c on 2b bl grn (R) 11.50 *16.00*
Never hinged 30.00
On cover 87.50
83 A2 10c on 1a rose red 7.50 *14.50*
Never hinged 18.50
On cover 65.00
84 A2 15c on 2a brn org 7.50 *14.50*
Never hinged 18.50
On cover 87.50
a. Pair, one without "ERITREA" 1,475.
Never hinged 1,850.
b. "ERITREA" inverted 950.00
Never hinged 1,200.
85 A2 25c on 2½a bl (R) 7.50 *10.50*
Never hinged 18.50
On cover 110.00
a. Double surcharge 750.00
Never hinged 950.00
86 A2 50c on 5a yellow 7.50 *18.00*
Never hinged 18.50
On cover 190.00
87 A2 1 l on 10a lil (R) 7.50 *26.00*
Never hinged 18.50
On cover 300.00
Nos. 81-87 (7) 60.50 *125.50*
Set, never hinged 150.00

Stamps of Italy, 1901-08 Overprinted type "j" in Black

1924
88 A42 1c brown 7.50 *8.75*
Never hinged 18.50
On cover 55.00
a. Inverted overprint 250.00
b. Vertical pair, one without ovpt. 950.00
Never hinged 1,200.
89 A43 2c orange brown 4.25 *7.50*
Never hinged 11.00
On cover 55.00
b. Vertical pair, one without ovpt. 950.00
Never hinged 1,200.
90 A48 5c green 7.50 *6.25*
Never hinged 18.50
On cover 32.50
Nos. 88-90 (3) 19.25 *22.50*
Set, never hinged 47.50

Victor Emmanuel Issue

Italy Nos. 175-177 Overprinted — k

1925-26 Unwmk. *Perf. 11*
91 A78 60c brown car 1.50 *6.00*
Never hinged 3.75
On cover 95.00
a. Perf. 13½ 22.00
Never hinged 22.00
On cover 275.00
92 A78 1 l dark blue 1.50 *8.75*
Never hinged 3.75
On cover 160.00
a. Perf. 13½ *17,750.* *4,400.*
Never hinged *22,000.*

Perf. 13½
93 A78 1.25 l dk blue ('26) 6.00 *26.00*
Never hinged 7.50
On cover 275.00
a. Perf. 11 1.10 *13.50*
Never hinged 15.00
On cover 375.00
Nos. 91-93 (3) 9.00 *40.75*
Set, never hinged 15.00

Saint Francis of Assisi Issue

Italian Stamps of 1926 Overprinted

1926 Wmk. 140 *Perf. 14*
94 A79 20c gray green 2.25 *10.00*
Never hinged 5.50
On cover 95.00
95 A80 40c dark violet 2.25 *10.00*
Never hinged 5.50
On cover 110.00
96 A81 60c red violet 2.25 *18.00*
Never hinged 5.50
On cover 110.00

Overprinted in Red

Unwmk. *Perf. 11*
97 A82 1.25 l dark blue 2.25 *26.00*
Never hinged 5.50
On cover 200.00

Perf. 14
98 A83 5 l + 2.50 l ol grn 5.75 *50.00*
Never hinged 15.00
Nos. 94-98 (5) 14.75 *114.00*
Set, never hinged 35.00
Set on overfranked philatelic cover 325.00

Italian Stamps of 1926 Overprinted type "f" in Black

1926 Wmk. 140 *Perf. 14*
99 A46 75c dk red & rose 52.50 14.50
Never hinged 125.00
On cover 80.00
a. Double overprint 300.00
100 A46 1.25 l blue & ultra 30.00 14.50
Never hinged 75.00
On cover 160.00
101 A46 2.50 l dk green & org 100.00 40.00
Never hinged 250.00
On cover 400.00
Nos. 99-101 (3) 182.50 69.00
Set, never hinged 450.00

Volta Issue

Type of Italy, 1927, Overprinted — o

1927
102 A84 20c purple 5.75 *30.00*
Never hinged 14.50
On cover 160.00
103 A84 50c deep orange 7.50 *18.00*
Never hinged 18.50
On cover 160.00
a. Double overprint 160.00
Never hinged 240.00
104 A84 1.25 l brt blue 11.50 *47.50*
Never hinged 30.00
On cover 300.00
Nos. 102-104 (3) 24.75 *95.50*
Set, never hinged 62.50

Italian Stamps of 1925-28 Overprinted type "a" in Black

1928-29
105 A86 7½c lt brown ('29) 14.50 *60.00*
Never hinged 37.50
On cover 225.00
106 A86 50c brt violet 52.50 52.50
Never hinged 130.00
On cover 100.00
Set, never hinged 160.00

Italian Stamps of 1927-28 Overprinted type "f"

1928-29
107 A86 50c brt violet 42.50 *42.50*
Never hinged 110.00
On cover 100.00

Unwmk. ***Perf. 11***

107A A85 1.75 l deep brown 65.00 30.00
Never hinged 160.00
On cover 120.00

Italy No. 192 Overprinted type "o"

1928 **Wmk. 140** ***Perf. 14***

108 A85 50c brown & slate 14.50 7.50
Never hinged 35.00
On cover 35.00

Monte Cassino Issue

Types of 1929 Issue of Italy Overprinted in Red or Blue

1929 ***Perf. 14***

109 A96 20c dk green (R) 4.50 *16.00*
Never hinged 11.00
On cover 190.00
110 A96 25c red orange (Bl) 4.50 *16.00*
Never hinged 11.00
On cover 130.00
111 A98 50c + 10c crim (Bl) 4.50 *18.00*
Never hinged 11.00
On cover 100.00
112 A98 75c + 15c ol brn (R) 4.50 *18.00*
Never hinged 11.00
On cover 190.00
113 A96 1.25 l + 25c dl vio (R) 10.00 *32.50*
Never hinged 26.00
On cover 240.00
114 A98 5 l + 1 l saph (R) 10.00 *35.00*
Never hinged 26.00

Overprinted in Red

Unwmk.

115 A100 10 l + 2 l gray brn 10.00 *52.50*
Never hinged 26.00
Nos. 109-115 (7) 48.00 *188.00*
Set, never hinged 125.00
Set on overfranked philatelic cover 375.00

Royal Wedding Issue

Type of Italian Stamps of 1930 Overprinted

1930 **Wmk. 140**

116 A101 20c yellow green 1.50 *4.25*
Never hinged 3.75
On cover 95.00
117 A101 50c + 10c dp orange 1.10 *7.50*
Never hinged 2.75
On cover 120.00
118 A101 1.25 l + 25c rose red 1.10 *14.50*
Never hinged 2.75
On cover 200.00
Nos. 116-118 (3) 3.70 *26.25*
Set, never hinged 9.25
Set on overfranked, philatelic cover 150.00

Lancer — A5

Scene in Massaua A6

2c, 35c, Lancer. 5c, 10c, Postman. 15c, Lineman. 25c, Askari (infantryman). 2 l, Railroad viaduct. 5 l, Asmara Deghe Selam. 10 l, Camels.

1930 **Wmk. 140** **Litho.** ***Perf. 14***

119 A5 2c brt bl & blk 2.25 *8.75*
Never hinged 5.50
On cover 95.00
120 A5 5c dk vio & blk 3.00 2.25
Never hinged 7.50
On cover 55.00
121 A5 10c yel brn & blk 3.00 1.10
Never hinged 7.50
On cover 30.00
122 A5 15c dk grn & blk 3.00 1.50
Never hinged 7.50
On cover 55.00
123 A5 25c gray grn & blk 3.00 1.10
Never hinged 7.50
On cover 35.00
124 A5 35c red brn & blk 7.50 *18.00*
Never hinged 18.50
On cover 100.00
125 A6 1 l dk bl & blk 3.00 1.10
Never hinged 7.50
On cover 37.50
126 A6 2 l choc & blk 7.50 *18.00*
Never hinged 18.50
On cover 240.00
127 A6 5 l ol grn & blk 10.00 *30.00*
Never hinged 26.00
On cover 625.00
128 A6 10 l dl bl & blk 16.00 *52.50*
Never hinged 40.00
Nos. 119-128 (10) 58.25 *134.30*
Set, never hinged 140.00
Set on overfranked philatelic cover 325.00

Ferrucci Issue

Types of Italian Stamps of 1930 Overprinted type "f" in Red or Blue

1930

129 A102 20c violet (R) 3.00 *3.75*
Never hinged 7.50
On cover 87.50
130 A103 25c dk green (R) 3.00 *3.75*
Never hinged 7.50
On cover 100.00
131 A103 50c black (R) 3.00 *7.50*
Never hinged 7.50
On cover 87.50
132 A103 1.25 l dp blue (R) 3.00 *14.50*
Never hinged 7.50
On cover 225.00
133 A104 5 l + 2 l dp car (Bl) 7.50 *26.00*
Never hinged 18.50
Nos. 129-133 (5) 19.50 *55.50*
Set, never hinged 47.50
Set on overfranked philatelic cover 200.00

Virgil Issue

Types of Italian Stamps of 1930 Overprinted in Red or Blue

1930 **Photo.**

134 A106 15c violet black 1.10 *7.50*
Never hinged 2.75
On cover 100.00
135 A106 20c orange brown 1.10 *3.00*
Never hinged 2.75
On cover 65.00
136 A106 25c dark green 1.10 *3.00*
Never hinged 2.75
On cover 60.00
137 A106 30c lt brown 1.10 *3.00*
Never hinged 2.75
On cover 65.00
138 A106 50c dull violet 1.10 *3.00*
Never hinged 2.75
On cover 50.00
139 A106 75c rose red 1.10 *6.00*
Never hinged 2.75
On cover 130.00
140 A106 1.25 l gray blue 1.10 *7.50*
Never hinged 2.75
On cover 200.00

Unwmk. **Engr.**

141 A106 5 l + 1.50 l dk vio 3.25 *35.00*
Never hinged 8.25
142 A106 10 l + 2.50 l ol brn 3.25 *55.00*
Never hinged 8.25
Nos. 134-142 (9) 14.20 *123.00*
Set, never hinged 35.00
Set on overfranked philatelic cover 375.00

Saint Anthony of Padua Issue

Types of Italian Stamps of 1931 Overprinted type "f" in Blue, Red or Black

1931 **Photo.** **Wmk. 140**

143 A116 20c brown (Bl) 1.50 *16.00*
Never hinged 3.75
On cover 80.00
144 A116 25c green (R) 1.50 *6.00*
Never hinged 3.75
On cover 80.00
145 A118 30c gray brn (Bl) 1.50 *6.00*
Never hinged 3.75
On cover 120.00
146 A118 50c dl violet (Bl) 1.50 *6.00*
Never hinged 3.75
On cover 80.00
147 A120 1.25 l slate bl (R) 1.50 *16.00*
Never hinged 3.75
On cover 225.00

Unwmk. **Engr.**

148 A121 75c black (R) 1.50 *30.00*
Never hinged 3.75
On cover 250.00
149 A122 5 l + 2.50 l dk brn (Bk) 6.00 *62.50*
Never hinged 15.00
Nos. 143-149 (7) 15.00 *142.50*
Set, never hinged 37.50
Set on overfranked philatelic cover 450.00

Victor Emmanuel III — A13

1931 **Photo.** **Wmk. 140**

150 A13 7½c olive brown 1.10 *3.75*
Never hinged 2.75
On cover 55.00
151 A13 20c slate bl & car 1.10 .20
Never hinged 2.75
On cover 2.50
152 A13 30c ol grn & brn vio 1.10 .20
Never hinged 2.75
On cover 2.50
153 A13 40c bl & yel grn 1.50 .20
Never hinged 3.75
On cover 13.50
154 A13 50c bis brn & ol .75 .20
Never hinged 1.90
On cover 2.50
155 A13 75c carmine rose 3.00 .20
Never hinged 7.50
On cover 13.50
156 A13 1.25 l violet & indigo 3.75 3.75
Never hinged 9.25
On cover 13.50
157 A13 2.50 l dull green 3.75 8.75
Never hinged 9.25
On cover 130.00
Nos. 150-157 (8) 16.05 17.25
Set, never hinged 40.00
Set on overfranked philatelic cover 110.00

Camel A14

Temple Ruins — A18

Designs: 2c, 10c, Camel. 5c, 15c, Shark fishery. 25c, Baobab tree. 35c, Pastoral scene. 2 l, African elephant. 5 l, Eritrean man. 10 l, Eritrean woman.

1934 **Photo.** **Wmk. 140**

158 A14 2c deep blue 1.50 *4.25*
Never hinged 3.75
On cover 30.00
159 A14 5c black 3.00 .35
Never hinged 7.50
On cover 3.00
160 A14 10c brown 3.00 .30
Never hinged 7.50
On cover 3.00
161 A14 15c orange brn 3.75 *1.50*
Never hinged 9.25
On cover 26.00
162 A14 25c gray green 3.00 .30
Never hinged 7.50
On cover 3.00
163 A14 35c purple 6.00 *8.75*
Never hinged 15.00
On cover 45.00
164 A18 1 l dk blue gray .75 .30
Never hinged 1.90
On cover 3.00
165 A14 2 l olive black 16.00 3.00
Never hinged 40.00
On cover 18.50
166 A18 5 l carmine rose 8.75 6.00
Never hinged 22.00
On cover 200.00
167 A18 10 l red orange 11.50 *20.00*
Never hinged 30.00
On cover 325.00
Nos. 158-167 (10) 57.25 *44.75*
Set, never hinged 140.00
Set on overfranked philatelic cover 260.00

Abruzzi Issue

Types of 1934 Issue Overprinted in Black or Red

1934

168 A14 10c dull blue (R) 11.50 *18.00*
Never hinged 30.00
On cover *225.00*
169 A14 15c blue 8.75 *18.00*
Never hinged 22.00
On cover *225.00*
170 A14 35c green (R) 5.25 *18.00*
Never hinged 13.00
On cover *240.00*
171 A18 1 l copper red 5.25 *18.00*
Never hinged 13.00
On cover *240.00*
172 A14 2 l rose red 16.00 *18.00*
Never hinged 40.00
173 A18 5 l purple (R) 8.75 *30.00*
Never hinged 22.00
174 A18 10 l olive grn (R) 8.75 *35.00*
Never hinged 22.00
Nos. 168-174 (7) 64.25 *155.00*
Set, never hinged 160.00
Set on overfranked philatelic cover 325.00

Grant's Gazelle A22

1934 **Photo.**

175 A22 5c ol grn & brn 3.75 *18.00*
Never hinged 9.25
On cover *225.00*
176 A22 10c yel brn & blk 3.75 *18.00*
Never hinged 9.25
On cover *190.00*
177 A22 20c scar & indigo 3.75 *14.50*
Never hinged 9.25
On cover *190.00*
178 A22 50c dk vio & brn 3.75 *14.50*
Never hinged 9.25
On cover *160.00*
179 A22 60c org brn & ind 3.75 *21.00*
Never hinged 9.25
On cover *225.00*
180 A22 1.25 l dk bl & grn 3.75 *35.00*
Never hinged 9.25
On cover *260.00*
Nos. 175-180 (6) 22.50 *121.00*
Set, never hinged 55.00
Set on overfranked philatelic cover 300.00

Second Colonial Arts Exhibition, Naples.
See Nos. C1-C6.

SEMI-POSTAL STAMPS

Many issues of Italy and Italian Colonies include one or more semipostal denominations. To avoid splitting sets, these issues are generally listed as regular postage, airmail, etc., unless all values carry a surtax.

Italy Nos. B1-B3 Overprinted type "f"

1915-16 **Wmk. 140** ***Perf. 14***

B1 SP1 10c + 5c rose 3.75 *14.50*
Never hinged 9.25
On cover 87.50
a. "EPITREA" 22.50 *32.50*
b. Inverted overprint 275.00 275.00
B2 SP2 15c + 5c slate 14.50 *26.00*
Never hinged 37.50
On cover 150.00
B3 SP2 20c + 5c orange 4.25 *30.00*
Never hinged 11.00
On cover 240.00
a. "EPITREA" 30.00 *47.50*
b. Inverted overprint 440.00 440.00
c. Pair, one without ovpt. — *2,400.*
Nos. B1-B3 (3) 22.50 *70.50*
Set, never hinged 55.00

No. B2 Surcharged

1916

B4 SP2 20c on 15c+5c slate 15.00 *30.00*
Never hinged 37.50
On cover 175.00
a. "EPITREA" 52.50 *87.50*
b. Pair, one without overprint 1,175.
Never hinged 1,475.
Nos. B1-B4 on overfranked philatelic cover *240.00*

Counterfeits exist of the minor varieties of Nos. B1, B3-B4.

Holy Year Issue

Italy Nos. B20-B25 Overprinted in Black or Red

1925 ***Perf. 12***

B5 SP4 20c + 10c dk grn & brn 3.00 *18.00*
Never hinged 7.50
On cover 150.00
B6 SP4 30c + 15c dk brn & brn 3.00 *20.00*
Never hinged 7.50
On cover 150.00
a. Double overprint
B7 SP4 50c + 25c vio & brn 3.00 *18.00*
Never hinged 7.50
On cover 150.00
B8 SP4 60c + 30c dp rose & brn 3.00 *24.00*
Never hinged 7.50
On cover 200.00
a. Inverted overprint
B9 SP8 1 l + 50c dp bl & vio (R) 3.00 *30.00*
Never hinged 7.50
B10 SP8 5 l + 2.50 l org brn & vio (R) 3.00 *42.50*
Never hinged 7.50
Nos. B5-B10 (6) 18.00 *152.50*
Set, never hinged 45.00
Set on overfranked philatelic cover 325.00

Colonial Institute Issue

"Peace" Substituting Spade for Sword — SP1

1926 **Typo.** ***Perf. 14***

B11 SP1 5c + 5c brown .90 *7.25*
Never hinged 2.25
On cover 130.00
B12 SP1 10c + 5c olive grn .90 *7.25*
Never hinged 2.25
On cover 100.00
B13 SP1 20c + 5c blue grn .90 *7.25*
Never hinged 2.25
On cover 80.00
B14 SP1 40c + 5c brown red .90 *7.25*
Never hinged 2.25
On cover 80.00
B15 SP1 60c + 5c orange .90 *7.25*
Never hinged 2.25
On cover 130.00
B16 SP1 1 l + 5c blue .90 *16.00*
Never hinged 2.25
On cover 225.00
Nos. B11-B16 (6) 5.40 *52.25*
Set, never hinged 13.50
Set on overfranked philatelic cover 225.00

The surtax of 5c on each stamp was for the Italian Colonial Institute.

Types of Italian Semi-Postal Stamps of 1926 Overprinted type "k"

1927 **Unwmk.** ***Perf. 11½***

B17 SP10 40c + 20c dk brn & blk 2.25 *30.00*
Never hinged 5.50
On cover 120.00
B18 SP10 60c + 30c brn red & ol brn 2.25 *30.00*
Never hinged 5.50
On cover 130.00
B19 SP10 1.25 l + 60c dp bl & blk 2.25 *47.50*
Never hinged 5.50
On cover 260.00
B20 SP10 5 l + 2.50 l dk grn & blk 3.75 *65.00*
Never hinged 9.25
Nos. B17-B20 (4) 10.50 *172.50*
Set, never hinged 25.00
Set on overfranked philatelic cover 400.00

The surtax on these stamps was for the charitable work of the Voluntary Militia for Italian National Defense.

Fascism and Victory SP2

Agriculture SP3

1928 **Wmk. 140** **Typo.** ***Perf. 14***

B21 SP2 20c + 5c blue grn 2.25 *11.00*
Never hinged 5.50
On cover 120.00
B22 SP2 30c + 5c red 2.25 *11.00*
Never hinged 5.50
On cover 120.00
B23 SP2 50c + 10c purple 2.25 *18.00*
Never hinged 5.50
On cover 110.00
B24 SP2 1.25 l + 20c dk blue 3.00 *22.50*
Never hinged 7.50
On cover 300.00
Nos. B21-B24 (4) 9.75 *62.50*
Set, never hinged 24.00
Set on overfranked philatelic cover 260.00

The surtax was for the Society Africana d'Italia, whose 46th anniv. was commemorated by the issue.

Types of Italian Semi-Postal Stamps of 1928 Overprinted type "f"

1929 **Unwmk.** ***Perf. 11***

B25 SP10 30c + 10c red & blk 3.75 *18.00*
Never hinged 9.25
On cover 130.00
B26 SP10 50c + 20c vio & blk 3.75 *22.50*
Never hinged 9.25
On cover 130.00
B27 SP10 1.25 l + 50c brn & bl 4.25 *37.50*
Never hinged 11.00
On cover 275.00
B28 SP10 5 l + 2 l olive grn & blk 4.25 *65.00*
Never hinged 11.00
Nos. B25-B28 (4) 16.00 *143.00*
Set, never hinged 40.00
Set on overfranked philatelic cover 400.00

Surtax for the charitable work of the Voluntary Militia for Italian Natl. Defense.

Types of Italian Semi-Postal Stamps of 1929 Overprinted type "f" in Black or Red

1930 ***Perf. 14***

B29 SP10 30c + 10c dk grn & bl grn (Bk) 19.00 *30.00*
Never hinged 47.50
On cover 190.00
B30 SP10 50c + 10c dk grn & vio 19.00 *40.00*
Never hinged 47.50
On cover 200.00
B31 SP10 1.25 l + 30c ol brn & red brn 19.00 *52.50*
Never hinged 47.50
On cover 310.00
B32 SP10 5 l + 1.50 l ind & grn 57.50 *140.00*
Never hinged 150.00
Nos. B29-B32 (4) 114.50 *262.50*
Set, never hinged 290.00
Set on overfranked philatelic cover 525.00

Surtax for the charitable work of the Voluntary Militia for Italian Natl. Defense.

1930 **Photo.** **Wmk. 140**

B33 SP3 50c + 20c ol brn 3.75 *18.00*
Never hinged 9.25
On cover 130.00
B34 SP3 1.25 l + 20c dp bl 3.75 *18.00*
Never hinged 9.25
On cover 190.00
B35 SP3 1.75 l + 20c green 3.75 *20.00*
Never hinged 9.25
On cover 240.00
B36 SP3 2.55 l + 50c purple 6.00 *32.50*
Never hinged 14.50
On cover 375.00
B37 SP3 5 l + 1 l dp car 6.00 *47.50*
Never hinged 14.50
Nos. B33-37 (5) 23.25 *136.00*
Set, never hinged 55.00
Set on overfranked philatelic cover 300.00

Italian Colonial Agricultural Institute, 25th anniv. The surtax aided that institution.

AIR POST STAMPS

Desert Scene AP1

Design: 80c, 1 l, 2 l, Plane and globe.

Wmk. Crowns (140)

1934 **Photo.** ***Perf. 14***

C1 AP1 25c sl bl & org red 3.75 *18.00*
Never hinged 9.25
On cover 160.00
C2 AP1 50c grn & indigo 3.75 *14.50*
Never hinged 9.25
On cover 130.00
C3 AP1 75c brn & org red 3.75 *14.50*
Never hinged 9.25
On cover 190.00
C4 AP1 80c org brn & ol grn 3.75 *18.00*
Never hinged 9.25
On cover 225.00
C5 AP1 1 l scar & ol grn 3.75 *22.50*
Never hinged 9.25
On cover 240.00
C6 AP1 2 l dk bl & brn 3.75 *35.00*
Never hinged 9.25
On cover 325.00
Nos. C1-C6 (6) 22.50 *122.50*
Set, never hinged 55.00
Set on overfranked philatelic cover 375.00

Second Colonial Arts Exhibition, Naples.

Plowing AP3

Plane and Cacti AP6

Designs: 25c, 1.50 l, Plowing. 50c, 2 l, Plane over mountain pass. 60c, 5 l, Plane and trees. 75c, 10 l, Plane and cacti. 1 l, 3 l, Bridge.

1936 **Photo.**

C7 AP3 25c deep green 2.25 *3.75*
Never hinged 5.50
On cover 55.00
C8 AP3 50c dark brown 1.50 .30
Never hinged 3.75
On cover 2.50
C9 AP3 60c brown orange 3.00 *8.75*
Never hinged 7.50
On cover 150.00
C10 AP6 75c orange brown 2.25 1.50
Never hinged 5.50
On cover 18.50
C11 AP3 1 l deep blue .75 .30
Never hinged 1.90
On cover 2.50
C12 AP3 1.50 l purple 3.00 .75
Never hinged 7.50
On cover 32.50
C13 AP3 2 l gray blue 3.00 *3.00*
Never hinged 7.50
On cover 80.00
C14 AP3 3 l copper red 16.00 17.50
Never hinged 40.00
On cover 160.00
C15 AP3 5 l green 10.00 6.00
Never hinged 25.00
On cover 325.00
C16 AP6 10 l rose red 21.00 8.00
Never hinged 55.00
On cover *600.00*
Nos. C7-C16 (10) 62.75 49.85
Set, never hinged 160.00
Set on overfranked philatelic cover 325.00

AIR POST SEMI-POSTAL STAMPS

King Victor Emmanuel III — SPAP1

1934 **Wmk. 140** **Photo.** ***Perf. 14***

CB1 SPAP1 25c + 10c 5.75 13.50
Never hinged 15.00
On cover 190.00
CB2 SPAP1 50c + 10c 5.75 13.50
Never hinged 15.00
On cover 190.00
CB3 SPAP1 75c + 15c 5.75 13.50
Never hinged 15.00
On cover 200.00
CB4 SPAP1 80c + 15c 5.75 13.50
Never hinged 15.00
On cover 240.00
CB5 SPAP1 1 l + 20c 5.75 13.50
Never hinged 15.00
On cover 260.00
CB6 SPAP1 2 l + 20c 5.75 13.50
Never hinged 15.00
CB7 SPAP1 3 l + 25c 20.00 65.00
Never hinged 52.50
CB8 SPAP1 5 l + 25c 20.00 65.00
Never hinged 52.50
CB9 SPAP1 10 l + 30c 20.00 65.00
Never hinged 52.50
CB10 SPAP1 25 l + 2 l 20.00 65.00
Never hinged 52.50
Nos. CB1-CB10 (10) 114.50 341.00
Set on overfranked philatelic flown cover 1,100.

65th birthday of King Victor Emmanuel III and the nonstop flight from Rome to Mogadiscio. Used values are for stamps canceled to order.

AIR POST SEMI-POSTAL OFFICIAL STAMP

Type of Air Post Semi-Postal Stamps, 1934, Overprinted Crown and "SERVIZIO DI STATO" in Black

1934 **Wmk. 140** ***Perf. 14***

CBO1 SPAP1 25 l + 2 l cop red *2,500.*
Never hinged *3,000.*
On flight cover 2,000.

SPECIAL DELIVERY STAMPS

Special Delivery Stamps of Italy, Overprinted type "a"

1907 **Wmk. 140** ***Perf. 14***

E1 SD1 25c rose red 18.00 18.00
Never hinged 45.00
On cover 120.00
a. Double overprint — —

1909

E2 SD2 30c blue & rose 85.00 *140.00*
Never hinged 210.00
On cover 440.00

1920

E3 SD1 50c dull red 2.25 *20.00*
Never hinged 5.50
On cover 190.00

"Italia" SD1

1924 Engr. Unwmk.

E4	SD1 60c dk red & brn	5.25	20.00
	Never hinged	13.00	
	On cover		100.00
a.	Perf. 13½	12.50	32.50
	Never hinged	32.50	
	On cover		225.00
E5	SD1 2 l dk blue & red	12.50	24.00
	Never hinged	32.50	
	On cover		325.00
	Set, never hinged	77.50	

For surcharges see Nos. E6-E8.

Nos. E4 and E5 Surcharged in Dark Blue or Red:

v

w

1926

E6	SD1 70c on 60c (Bl)	5.25	13.00
	Never hinged	13.00	
	On cover		120.00
E7	SD1 2.50 l on 2 l (R)	12.50	24.00
	Never hinged	32.50	
	On cover		400.00
	Set, never hinged	45.00	

Type of 1924 Surcharged in Blue or Black:

1927-35 Perf. 11

E8	SD1 1.25 l on 60c dk red & brn (Bl)	10.50	3.00
	Never hinged	26.00	
	On cover		9.25
a.	Perf. 14 (Bl) ('35)	75.00	15.00
	Never hinged	175.00	
	On cover		140.00
b.	Perf. 11 (Bk) ('35)	7,500.	600.00
	Never hinged	9,250.	
	On cover		2,250.
c.	Perf. 14 (Bk) ('35)	225.00	37.50
	Never hinged	440.00	
	On cover		275.00

AUTHORIZED DELIVERY STAMP

Authorized Delivery Stamp of Italy, No. EY2, Overprinted Type "f" in Black

1939-41 Wmk. 140 Perf. 14

EY1	AD2 10c dk brown ('41)	.60	
	Never hinged	1.50	
a.	10c reddish brown	16.00	30.00
	Never hinged	40.00	
	On cover		325.00

On No. EY1a, which was used in Italian East Africa, the overprint hits the figures "10." On No. EY1, which was sold in Rome, the overprint falls above the 10's.

POSTAGE DUE STAMPS

Postage Due Stamps of Italy Overprinted type "a" at Top

1903 Wmk. 140 Perf. 14

J1	D3 5c buff & mag	18.00	32.50
	Never hinged	27.50	
	On cover		375.00
a.	Double overprint	275.00	
J2	D3 10c buff & mag	14.50	32.50
	Never hinged	22.00	
	On cover		200.00
J3	D3 20c buff & mag	14.50	22.50
	Never hinged	22.00	
	On cover		200.00
J4	D3 30c buff & mag	20.00	26.00
	Never hinged	32.50	
	On cover		300.00
J5	D3 40c buff & mag	52.50	55.00
	Never hinged	77.50	
	On cover		310.00
J6	D3 50c buff & mag	75.00	55.00
	Never hinged	110.00	
	On cover		200.00
J7	D3 60c buff & mag	20.00	55.00
	Never hinged	32.50	
	On cover		475.00
J8	D3 1 l blue & mag	14.50	30.00
	Never hinged	22.00	
	On cover		325.00
J9	D3 2 l blue & mag	140.00	125.00
	Never hinged	225.00	
	On cover		800.00
J10	D3 5 l blue & mag	250.00	225.00
	Never hinged	375.00	
J11	D3 10 blue & mag l	2,350.	440.00
	Never hinged	3,500.	
	Set, #J1-J10, never hinged	950.00	

Same with Overprint at Bottom

1920-22

J1b	D3 5c buff & magenta	3.75	10.00
	Never hinged	5.50	
	On cover		375.00
c.	Numeral and ovpt. inverted	450.00	450.00
	Never hinged	—	
J2a	D3 10c buff & magenta	5.75	10.00
	Never hinged	8.75	
	On cover		160.00
J3a	D3 20c buff & magenta	750.00	300.00
	Never hinged	1,100.	
	On cover		1,850.
J4a	D3 30c buff & magenta	52.50	30.00
	Never hinged	77.50	
	On cover		300.00
J5a	D3 40c buff & magenta	42.50	32.50
	Never hinged	65.00	
	On cover		325.00
J6a	D3 50c buff & magenta	22.50	30.00
	Never hinged	35.00	
	On cover		160.00
J7a	D3 60c buff & magenta	22.50	30.00
	Never hinged	35.00	
	On cover		450.00
J8a	D3 1 l blue & magenta	40.00	30.00
	Never hinged	60.00	
	On cover		350.00
J9a	D3 2 l blue & magenta	1,350.	750.00
	Never hinged	2,000.	
	On cover		6,750.
J10a	D3 5 l blue & magenta	325.00	260.00
	Never hinged	500.00	
J11a	D3 10 l blue & magenta	50.00	67.50
	Never hinged	75.00	
	Set, never hinged	3,960.	

1903 Wmk. 140

J12	D4 50 l yellow	600.00	225.00
	Never hinged	875.00	
J13	D4 100 l blue	400.00	110.00
	Never hinged	600.00	

1927

J14	D3 60c buff & brown	100.00	115.00
	Never hinged	150.00	
	On cover		450.00

Postage Due Stamps of Italy, 1934, Overprinted type "j" in Black

1934

J15	D6 5c brown	.75	8.75
	Never hinged	1.90	
	On cover		375.00
J16	D6 10c blue	.75	1.10
	Never hinged	1.90	
	On cover		190.00
J17	D6 20c rose red	2.25	2.25
	Never hinged	5.50	
	On cover		160.00
a.	Inverted overprint	—	—
J18	D6 25c green	2.25	4.50
	Never hinged	5.50	
	On cover		160.00
J19	D6 30c red orange	2.25	8.75
	Never hinged	5.50	
	On cover		260.00
J20	D6 40c black brown	2.25	8.75
	Never hinged	5.50	
	On cover		300.00
J21	D6 50c violet	2.25	1.50
	Never hinged	5.50	
	On cover		130.00
J22	D6 60c black	4.50	16.00
	Never hinged	12.00	
	On cover		375.00
J23	D7 1 l red orange	2.25	2.25
	Never hinged	5.50	
	On cover		260.00
a.	Inverted overprint	450.00	—
	Never hinged	675.00	
J24	D7 2 l green	13.00	37.50
	Never hinged	32.50	
	On cover		375.00
J25	D7 5 l violet	22.50	42.50
	Never hinged	55.00	
J26	D7 10 l blue	26.00	47.50
	Never hinged	65.00	
J27	D7 20 l carmine rose	32.50	52.50
	Never hinged	82.50	
a.	Inverted overprint	450.00	—
	Never hinged	675.00	
	Nos. J15-J27 (13)	113.50	233.85
	Set, never hinged	275.00	

PARCEL POST STAMPS

These stamps were used by affixing them to the way bill so that one half remained on it following the parcel, the other half staying on the receipt given the sender. Most used halves are right halves. Complete stamps were obtainable canceled, probably to order. Both unused and used values are for complete stamps.

Parcel Post Stamps of Italy, 1914-17, Overprinted type "j" in Black on Each Half

1916 Wmk. 140 Perf. 13½

Q1	PP2 5c brown	95.00	125.00
	Never hinged	150.00	
Q2	PP2 10c deep blue	2,250.	2,750.
	Never hinged	3,400.	
Q3	PP2 25c red	215.00	225.00
	Never hinged	325.00	
Q4	PP2 50c orange	52.50	125.00
	Never hinged	77.50	
Q5	PP2 1 l violet	87.50	125.00
	Never hinged	140.00	
Q6	PP2 2 l green	67.50	125.00
	Never hinged	100.00	
Q7	PP2 3 l bister	675.00	400.00
	Never hinged	1,000.	
Q8	PP2 4 l slate	675.00	400.00
	Never hinged	1,000.	
	Set #Q1, Q3-Q8, never hinged	2,775.	

Halves Used

Q1, Q7-Q8	1.90
Q2	75.00
Q3	1.00
Q4	.20
Q5-Q6	.20

Overprinted type "f" on Each Half

1917-24

Q9	PP2 5c brown	3.00	6.00
	Never hinged	4.50	
	On parcel post receipt card		200.00
Q10	PP2 10c deep blue	3.00	6.00
	Never hinged	4.50	
Q11	PP2 20c black	3.00	6.00
	Never hinged	4.50	
Q12	PP2 25c red	3.00	6.00
	Never hinged	4.50	
	On parcel post receipt card		100.00
Q13	PP2 50c orange	6.00	9.00
	Never hinged	9.00	
	On parcel post receipt card		100.00
Q14	PP2 1 l violet	6.00	9.00
	Never hinged	9.00	
	On parcel post receipt card		150.00
Q15	PP2 2 l green	6.00	9.00
	Never hinged	9.00	
Q16	PP2 3 l bister	6.00	9.00
	Never hinged	9.00	
Q17	PP2 4 l slate	6.00	16.00
	Never hinged	9.00	
Q18	PP2 10 l rose lil ('24)	75.00	125.00
	Never hinged	110.00	
Q19	PP2 12 l red brn ('24)	175.00	260.00
	Never hinged	275.00	
Q20	PP2 15 l olive grn ('24)	175.00	160.00
	Never hinged	275.00	
Q21	PP2 20 l brn vio ('24)	225.00	300.00
	Never hinged	325.00	
	Nos. Q9-Q21 (13)	692.00	921.00
	Set, never hinged	1,050.	

Halves Used

Q9-Q16	.20
Q17	.20
Q18	.25
Q19	.75
Q20	.20
Q21	1.90

Parcel Post Stamps of Italy, 1927-39, Overprinted type "f" on Each Half

1927-37

Q21A	PP3 10c dp blue ('37)	3,875.	550.00
	Never hinged	5,250.	
Q22	PP3 25c red ('37)	375.00	37.50
	Never hinged	550.00	
Q23	PP3 30c ultra ('29)	3.00	13.00
	Never hinged	4.50	
	On parcel post receipt card		150.00
Q24	PP3 50c orange ('36)	450.00	26.00
	Never hinged	675.00	
Q25	PP3 60c red ('29)	3.00	13.50
	Never hinged	4.50	
	On parcel post receipt card		150.00
Q26	PP3 1 l brown vio ('36)	225.00	26.00
	Never hinged	350.00	
a.	1 l lilac	260.00	26.00
	Never hinged	400.00	
	On parcel post receipt card		100.00
Q27	PP3 2 l green ('36)	215.00	26.00
	Never hinged	325.00	
	On parcel post receipt card		125.00
Q28	PP3 3 l bister	7.50	21.00
	Never hinged	11.00	
Q29	PP3 4 l gray	7.50	21.00
	Never hinged	11.00	
Q30	PP3 10 l rose lilac ('36)	450.00	475.00
	Never hinged	675.00	
Q31	PP3 20 l lilac brn ('36)	450.00	475.00
	Never hinged	675.00	
	Nos. Q22-Q31 (10)	2,186.	
	Set, never hinged	3,675.	
	Nos. Q21A-Q31 (11)		1,684.

Halves Used

Q21A	15.00
Q22-Q25, Q27-Q28	.20
Q26, Q26a, Q29	.20
Q30	.75
Q31	1.50

ESTONIA

e-ˈstō-nē-ə

LOCATION — Northern Europe, bordering on the Baltic Sea and the Gulf of Finland
GOVT. — Republic
AREA — 18,353 sq. mi.
POP. — 1,542,000 (1986)
CAPITAL — Tallinn

Formerly a part of Russia, Estonia declared its independence in 1918. In 1940 it was incorporated in the Union of Soviet Socialist Republics.

100 Kopecks = 1 Ruble (1918)
100 Penni = 1 Mark (1919)
100 Sents = 1 Kroon (1928)

Watermark

Wmk. 207 — Arms of Finland in the Sheet

Illustration reduced. Watermark covers a large part of sheet.

A1

A2

1918-19 Unwmk. Litho. Imperf.

1	A1 5k pale red	.85	.85
2	A1 15k bright blue	.85	.85
3	A2 35p brown ('19)	1.00	.90
a.	Printed on both sides	100.00	
b.	35p olive	35.00	30.00
4	A2 70p olive grn ('19)	1.50	1.25
	Nos. 1-4 (4)	4.20	3.85

Nos. 1-4 exist privately perforated.

Russian Stamps of 1909-17 Handstamped in Violet or Black

1919, May 7 Perf. 14, 14½x15, 13½

8	A14 1k orange	1,750.	1,750.
9	A14 2k green	25.00	25.00
10	A14 3k red	30.00	26.00
11	A14 5k claret	25.00	22.50
12	A15 10k dk bl (Bk)	45.00	42.50
13	A15 10k dk bl	150.00	150.00
14	A14 10k on 7k lt bl	400.00	400.00

15	A11	15k red brn & bl	35.00	*35.00*
16	A11	25k grn & vio	40.00	*37.50*
17	A11	35k red brn & grn	*1,500.*	*1,500.*
18	A8	50k vio & grn	87.50	87.50
19	A9	1r pale brn, brn & org	150.00	150.00
20	A13	10r scar, yel & gray	*3,250.*	*3,250.*

Imperf

21	A14	1k orange	22.50	*22.50*
22	A14	2k green	*325.00*	*325.00*
23	A14	3k red	42.50	42.50
24	A9	1r pale brn, brn & red org	*210.00*	*210.00*
25	A12	3½r maroon & grn	*400.00*	*400.00*
26	A13	5r dk bl, grn & pale bl	*500.00*	*500.00*

Provisionally issued at Tallinn. This overprint has been extensively counterfeited. Values are for genuine examples competently expertized. No. 20 is always creased.

Gulls — A3

1919, May 13 ***Imperf.***

27	A3	5p yellow	2.25	*3.25*

A4

A5

A6

A7

Viking Ship — A8

1919-20 ***Perf. 11½***

28	A4	10p green	.25	.25

Imperf

29	A4	5p orange	.20	.20
30	A4	10p green	.20	.20
31	A5	15p rose	.20	.20
32	A6	35p blue	.25	.20
33	A7	70p dl vio ('20)	.25	.20
34	A8	1m bl & blk brn	1.25	.55
a.		Gray granite paper ('20)	.65	.40
35	A8	5m yel & blk	3.00	.95
a.		Gray granite paper ('20)	1.00	.50
36	A8	15m yel grn & vio ('20)	3.25	.65
37	A8	25m ultra & blk brn ('20)	4.75	2.50
		Nos. 28-37 (10)	13.60	5.90
		Set, never hinged	16.50	

The 5m exists with inverted center. Not a postal item.

See #76-77. For surcharges see #55, 57.

Skyline of Tallinn — A9

1920-24 ***Imperf.***

Pelure Paper

39	A9	25p green	.25	.25
40	A9	25p yellow ('24)	.25	*.30*
41	A9	35p rose	.25	.25
42	A9	50p green ('21)	.25	.25
43	A9	1m vermilion	.65	.25
44	A9	2m blue	.55	.25
45	A9	2m ultramarine	.45	.25
46	A9	2.50m blue	.65	.25
		Nos. 39-46 (8)	3.30	2.05
		Set, never hinged	9.00	

Nos. 39-46 with sewing machine perforation are unofficial.

For surcharge see No. 56.

Stamps of 1919-20 Surcharged

1920 ***Imperf.***

55	A5	1m on 15p rose	.50	.50
56	A9	1m on 35p rose	.60	.50
57	A7	2m on 70p dl vio	.85	.60
		Nos. 55-57 (3)	1.95	1.60
		Set, never hinged	4.00	

Weaver A10

Blacksmith A11

1922-23 **Typo.** ***Imperf.***

58	A10	½m orange ('23)	2.00	*3.00*
59	A10	1m brown ('23)	2.75	2.25
60	A10	2m yellow green	2.00	2.00
61	A10	2½m claret	5.00	3.00
62	A11	5m rose	5.00	3.00
63	A11	9m red ('23)	8.00	6.00
64	A11	10m deep blue	6.00	5.00
		Nos. 58-64 (7)	30.75	24.25
		Set, never hinged	60.00	

1922-25 ***Perf. 14***

65	A10	½m orange ('23)	.65	.20
66	A10	1m brown ('23)	.80	.20
67	A10	2m yellow green	1.40	.20
68	A10	2½m claret	1.40	.20
69	A10	3m blue green ('24)	1.50	.20
70	A11	5m rose	5.00	.20
71	A11	9m red ('23)	3.00	1.00
72	A11	10m deep blue	4.00	.20
73	A11	12m red ('25)	4.00	.90
74	A11	15m plum ('25)	4.00	.25
75	A11	20m ultra ('25)	15.00	.20
		Nos. 65-75 (11)	40.75	3.75
		Set, never hinged	75.00	

See No. 89. For surcharges see Nos. 84-88.

Viking Ship Type of 1920

1922, June 8 ***Perf. 14x13½***

76	A8	15m yel grn & vio	5.00	.60
77	A8	25m ultra & blk brn	9.00	2.00
		Set, never hinged	22.50	

Map of Estonia — A13

1923-24

Paper with Lilac Network

78	A13	100m ol grn & bl	20.00	2.75

Paper with Buff Network

79	A13	300m brn & bl ('24)	50.00	12.50
		Set, never hinged	110.00	

For surcharges see Nos. 106-107.

National Theater, Tallinn — A14

1924, Dec. 9 ***Perf. 14x13½***

Paper with Blue Network

81	A14	30m violet & blk	10.00	2.75

Paper with Rose Network

82	A14	70m car rose & blk	15.00	5.00
		Set, never hinged	25.00	

For surcharge see No. 105.

Vanemuine Theater, Tartu — A15

1927, Oct. 25

Paper with Lilac Network

83	A15	40m dp bl & ol brn	10.00	2.75
		Never hinged	15.00	

Stamps of 1922-25 Surcharged in New Currency in Red or Black

1928 ***Perf. 14***

84	A10	2s yellow green	1.50	.20
85	A11	5s rose red (B)	1.50	.20
86	A11	10s deep blue	2.00	.20
a.		Imperf., pair	*750.00*	—
87	A11	15s plum (B)	6.50	.25
88	A11	20s ultra	4.50	.30
		Nos. 84-88 (5)	16.00	1.15
		Set, never hinged	26.00	

10th anniversary of independence.

3rd Philatelic Exhibition Issue

Blacksmith Type of 1922-23

1928, July 6

89	A11	10m gray	5.00	*7.50*
		Never hinged	9.00	

Sold only at Tallinn Philatelic Exhibition. Exists imperf.

Arms — A16

Paper with Network in Parenthesis

1928-40 ***Perf. 14, 14½x14***

90	A16	1s dk gray (bl)	.30	.20
a.		Thick gray-toned laid paper ('40)	7.50	4.50
91	A16	2s yel grn (org)	.40	.20
92	A16	4s grn (brn) ('29)	.50	.20
93	A16	5s red (grn)	3.00	.20
a.		5 feet on lowest lion	35.00	25.00
94	A16	8s vio (buff) ('29)	1.60	.20
95	A16	10s lt bl (lilac)	2.00	.20
96	A16	12s crimson (grn)	1.50	.20
97	A16	15s yel (blue)	1.75	.20
98	A16	15s car (gray) ('35)	6.00	.45
99	A16	20s slate bl (red)	2.75	.20
100	A16	25s red vio (grn) ('29)	6.00	.20
101	A16	25s bl (brn) ('35)	6.00	.40
102	A16	40s red org (bl) ('29)	7.00	.30
103	A16	60s gray (brn) ('29)	10.00	.50
104	A16	80s brn (bl) ('29)	10.00	1.00
		Nos. 90-104 (15)	58.80	4.65
		Set, never hinged	85.00	

Types of 1924 Issues Surcharged:

1930, Sept. 1 ***Perf. 14x13½***

Paper with Green Network

105	A14	1k on 70m car & blk	7.00	3.00

Paper with Rose Network

106	A13	2k on 300m brn & bl	14.50	7.50

Paper with Blue Network

107	A13	3k on 300m brn & bl	35.00	18.00
		Nos. 105-107 (3)	56.50	28.50
		Set, never hinged	125.00	

University Observatory A17

University of Tartu A18

Paper with Network as in Parenthesis

1932, June 1 ***Perf. 14***

108	A17	5s red (yellow)	5.50	.60
109	A18	10s light bl (lilac)	1.50	.60
110	A17	12s car (blue)	8.00	2.75
111	A18	20s dk bl (green)	6.00	1.10
		Nos. 108-111 (4)	21.00	5.05
		Set, never hinged	55.00	

University of Tartu tercentenary.

Narva Falls — A19

Ancient Bard Playing Harp — A20

1933, Apr. 1 **Photo.** ***Perf. 14x13½***

112	A19	1k gray black	7.00	.65
		Never hinged	15.00	

See No. 149.

Paper with Network as in Parenthesis

1933, May 29 **Typo.** ***Perf. 14***

113	A20	2s green (orange)	1.50	.20
114	A20	5s red (green)	2.00	.20
115	A20	10s blue (lilac)	2.50	.20
		Nos. 113-115 (3)	6.00	.60
		Set, never hinged	12.50	

Tenth National Song Festival.

Nos. 113-115 exist imperf. Value $100.

Woman Harvester A21

Pres. Konstantin Päts A22

1935, Mar. 1 **Engr.** ***Perf. 13½***

116	A21	3k black brown	.50	*1.00*
		Never hinged	.65	

1936-40 **Typo.** ***Perf. 14***

117	A22	1s chocolate	.40	.25
118	A22	2s yellow green	.40	.25
119	A22	3s dp org ('40)	10.00	7.50
120	A22	4s rose vio	.75	.25
121	A22	5s lt blue grn	.75	.30
122	A22	6s rose lake	.90	.25
123	A22	6s dp green ('40)	25.00	25.00
124	A22	10s greenish blue	.80	.25
125	A22	15s crim rose ('37)	1.25	.25
126	A22	15s dp bl ('40)	4.00	2.25
127	A22	18s dp car ('39)	25.00	9.00
128	A22	20s brt vio	1.25	.35
129	A22	25s dk bl ('38)	6.00	.35
130	A22	30s bister ('38)	4.25	.35
131	A22	30s ultra ('39)	20.00	5.00
132	A22	50s org brn	7.00	.85
133	A22	60s brt pink	12.50	4.50
		Nos. 117-133 (17)	120.25	56.95
		Set, never hinged	175.00	

St. Brigitta Convent Entrance
A23

Ruins of Convent, Pirita River
A24

Front View of Convent — A25

Seal of Convent — A26

Paper with Network as in Parenthesis

1936, June 10 ***Perf. 13½***

134 A23 5s green (buff) .35 .20
135 A24 10s blue (lil) .55 .20
136 A25 15s red (org) .85 1.25
137 A26 25s ultra (brn) 1.25 *1.75*
Nos. 134-137 (4) 3.00 *3.40*
Set, never hinged 6.00

St. Brigitta Convent, 500th anniversary.

Harbor at Tallinn — A27

1938, Apr. 11 **Engr.** ***Perf. 14***

138 A27 2k blue .75 *1.25*
Never hinged .90

Friedrich R. Faehlmann
A28

Friedrich R. Kreutzwald
A29

1938, June 15 **Typo.** ***Perf. 13½***

139 A28 5s dark green .70 .50
140 A29 10s deep brown .70 .50
141 A29 15s dark carmine 1.00 .90
142 A28 25s ultra 1.60 1.40
a. Sheet of 4, #139-142 10.00 *12.00*
Nos. 139-142 (4) 4.00 3.30
Set, never hinged 9.00

Society of Estonian Scholars centenary.

Hospital at Pärnu — A30

Beach Hotel — A31

1939, June 20 **Typo.** ***Perf. 14x13½***

144 A30 5s dark green .70 .35
145 A31 10s deep red violet .50 .40
146 A30 18s dark carmine 1.50 1.50
147 A31 30s deep blue 1.75 1.75
a. Sheet of 4, #144-147 15.00 *25.00*
Nos. 144-147 (4) 4.45 4.00
Set, never hinged 10.00

Cent. of health resort and baths at Pärnu.

Narva Falls Type of 1933

1940, Apr. 15 **Engr.**

149 A19 1k slate green .70 *1.25*
Never hinged .85

The sky consists of heavy horizontal lines and the background consists of horizontal and vertical lines.

Carrier Pigeon and Plane — A32

1940, July 30 **Typo.**

150 A32 3s red orange .20 .20
151 A32 10s purple .20 .20
152 A32 15s rose brown .20 .20
153 A32 30s dark blue 1.00 .75
Nos. 150-153 (4) 1.60 1.35
Set, never hinged 2.50

Centenary of the first postage stamp. The 15s exists imperf. Value $5.

SEMI-POSTAL STAMPS

Assisting Wounded Soldier — SP1

Offering Aid to Wounded Hero — SP2

1920, June **Unwmk.** **Litho.** ***Imperf.***

B1 SP1 35p + 10p red & ol grn .25 *.35*
B2 SP2 70p + 15p dp bl & brn .25 *.35*

Surcharged

1920

B3 SP1 1m on No. B1 .30 .25
B4 SP2 2m on No. B2 .30 .25

Nurse and Wounded Soldier — SP3

1921, Aug. 1 ***Imperf.***

B5 SP3 2½ (3½)m org, brn & car .90 *1.00*
B6 SP3 5 (7)m ultra, brn & car .90 *1.00*

1922, Apr. 26 ***Perf. 13½x14***

B7 SP3 2½ (3½)m org, brn & car .90 *1.00*
a. Vert. pair, imperf. horiz. 30.00 30.00
B8 SP3 5 (7)m ultra, brn & car .90 *1.00*
a. Vert. pair, imperf. horiz. 30.00 30.00

Nos. B5-B8 Overprinted

1923, Oct. 8 ***Imperf.***

B9 SP3 2½ (3½)m 25.00 *25.00*
B10 SP3 5 (7)m 30.00 *30.00*

Perf. 13½x14

B11 SP3 2½ (3½)m 40.00 *40.00*
a. Vert. pair, imperf. horiz. 100.00 *160.00*
B12 SP3 5 (7)m 40.00 40.00
a. Vert. pair, imperf. horiz. 100.00 *160.00*
Nos. B9-B12 (4) 135.00 *135.00*

Excellent forgeries are plentiful.

Nos. B7 and B8 Surcharged

1926, June 15

B13 SP3 5 (6)m on #B7 3.50 3.50
a. Vert. pair, imperf. horiz. 20.00 20.00
B14 SP3 10 (12)m on #B8 4.00 4.00
a. Vert. pair, imperf. horiz. 20.00 20.00

Nos. B5-B14 had the franking value of the lower figure. They were sold for the higher figure, the excess going to the Red Cross Society.

Kuressaare Castle
SP4

Tartu Cathedral
SP5

Tallinn Castle
SP6

Narva Fortress
SP7

View of Tallinn — SP8

Laid Paper

Perf. 14½x14

1927, Nov. 19 **Typo.** **Wmk. 207**

B15 SP4 5m + 5m bl grn & ol, *grysh* .90 *1.00*
B16 SP5 10m + 10m dp bl & brn, *cream* .90 *1.00*
B17 SP6 12m + 12m rose red & ol grn, *bluish* .90 *2.00*

Perf. 14x13½

B18 SP7 20m + 20m bl & choc, *gray* 1.75 *2.00*
B19 SP8 40m + 40m org brn & slate, *buff* 1.75 *3.00*
Nos. B15-B19 (5) 6.20 *9.00*

The money derived from the surtax was donated to the Committee for the commemoration of War for Liberation.

Red Cross Issue

Symbolical of Succor to Injured — SP9

Symbolical of "Light of Hope" — SP10

1931, Aug. 1 **Unwmk.** ***Perf. 13½***

B20 SP9 2s + 3s grn & car 6.00 5.00
B21 SP10 5s + 3s red & car 6.00 5.00
B22 SP10 10s + 3s lt bl & car 6.00 5.00
B23 SP9 20s + 3s dk bl & car 7.50 7.50
Nos. B20-B23 (4) 25.50 *22.50*
Set, never hinged 35.00

Nurse and Child
SP11

Taagepera Sanatorium
SP12

Lorraine Cross and Flower — SP13

Paper with Network as in Parenthesis

1933, Oct. 1 ***Perf. 14, 14½***

B24 SP11 5s + 3s ver (grn) 5.00 4.25
B25 SP12 10s + 3s lt bl & red (vio) 5.00 4.25
B26 SP13 12s + 3s rose & red (grn) 5.00 4.75
B27 SP12 20s + 3s dk bl & red (org) 7.50 7.50
Nos. B24-B27 (4) 22.50 20.75
Set, never hinged 40.00

The surtax was for a fund to combat tuberculosis.

Coats of Arms

Narva — SP14

Pärnu — SP15

Tartu — SP16

Tallinn — SP17

Paper with Network as in Parenthesis

1936, Feb. 1 ***Perf. 13½***

B28 SP14 10s + 10s grn & ultra (gray) 3.50 *5.00*
B29 SP15 15s + 15s car & bl (gray) 3.50 *5.00*
B30 SP16 25s + 25s gray bl & red (brn) 4.50 *7.00*
B31 SP17 50s + 50s blk & dl org (ol) 10.00 *18.00*
Nos. B28-B31 (4) 21.50 *35.00*
Set, never hinged 35.00

Paide
SP18

Rakvere
SP19

Valga
SP20

Viljandi
SP21

Paper with Network as in Parenthesis

1937, Jan. 2 ***Perf. 13½x14***

B32 SP18 10s + 10s grn (gray) 3.00 *5.00*
B33 SP19 15s + 15s red brn (gray) 3.00 *5.00*
B34 SP20 25s + 25s dk bl (lil) 5.00 *6.00*
B35 SP21 50s + 50s dk vio (gray) 9.00 *10.00*
Nos. B32-B35 (4) 20.00 *26.00*
Set, never hinged 40.00

Baltiski — SP22

Võru — SP23

Haapsalu
SP24

Kuressaare
SP25

Designs are the armorial bearings of various cities

1938, Jan. 21
Paper with Gray Network

B36 SP22 10s + 10s dk brn 3.00 *3.25*
B37 SP23 15s + 15s car & grn 3.50 3.50
B38 SP24 25s + 25s dk bl & car 5.00 5.00
B39 SP25 50s + 50s blk & org yel 7.00 *8.75*
a. Sheet of 4, #B36-B39 35.00 30.00
Nos. B36-B39 (4) 18.50 *20.50*
Set, never hinged 40.00

Annual charity ball, Tallinn, Jan. 2, 1938.

Viljandimaa
SP27

Pärnumaa
SP28

Tartumaa
SP29

Harjumaa
SP30

Designs are the armorial bearings of various districts

1939, Jan. 10 *Perf. 13½*
Paper with Gray Network

B41 SP27 10s + 10s dk bl grn 3.50 *4.50*
B42 SP28 15s + 15s carmine 4.00 *5.00*
B43 SP29 25s + 25s dk blue 5.50 *7.25*
B44 SP30 50s + 50s brn lake 8.50 *15.00*
a. Sheet of 4, #B41-B44 30.00 *40.00*
Nos. B41-B44 (4) 21.50 *31.75*
Set, never hinged 40.00

Võrumaa
SP32

Järvamaa
SP33

Läänemaa
SP34

Saaremaa
SP35

Designs are the armorial bearings of various districts

1940, Jan. 2 **Typo.** *Perf. 13½*
Paper with Gray Network

B46 SP32 10s + 10s dp grn & ultra 2.50 *3.00*
B47 SP33 15s + 15s dk car & ultra 2.50 *3.00*
B48 SP34 25s + 25s dk bl & scar 3.00 *5.00*
B49 SP35 50s + 50s ocher & ultra 4.00 *8.00*
Nos. B46-B49 (4) 12.00 *19.00*
Set, never hinged 25.00

AIR POST STAMPS

Airplane
AP1

Unwmk.
1920, Mar. 13 **Typo.** *Imperf.*
C1 AP1 5m yel, blk & lt grn 3.00 *5.00*

No. C1 Overprinted "1923" in Red

1923, Oct. 1
C2 AP1 5m multicolored 7.00 *15.00*

No. C1 Surcharged in Red

1923, Oct. 1
C3 AP1 15m on 5m multi 10.00 *17.50*

Pairs of No. C1 Surcharged in Black or Red

1923, Oct.
C4 AP1 10m on 5m+5m (B) 7.50 *10.00*
C5 AP1 20m on 5m+5m 20.00 *22.50*
C6 AP1 45m on 5m+5m 80.00 *100.00*

Rough Perf. 11½

C7 AP1 10m on 5m+5m (B) *425.00 450.00*
C8 AP1 20m on 5m+5m *175.00 225.00*
Nos. C4-C8 (5) *707.50 807.50*

The pairs comprising Nos. C7 and C8 are imperforate between. Forged surcharges and perforations abound. Authentication is required.

Monoplane in Flight — AP2

Designs: Various views of planes in flight.

1924, Feb. 12 *Imperf.*
C9 AP2 5m yellow & blk 2.00 *4.00*
C10 AP2 10m blue & blk 2.00 *4.00*
C11 AP2 15m red & blk 2.00 *4.00*
C12 AP2 20m green & blk 2.00 *3.00*
C13 AP2 45m violet & blk 2.00 *6.00*
Nos. C9-C13 (5) 10.00 *21.00*

The paper is covered with a faint network in pale shades of the frame colors. There are four varieties of the frames and five of the pictures.

1925, July 15 *Perf. 13½*
C14 AP2 5m yellow & blk 1.50 *2.00*
C15 AP2 10m blue & blk 1.50 *2.00*
C16 AP2 15m red & blk 1.50 *3.00*
C17 AP2 20m green & blk 1.50 *2.50*
C18 AP2 45m violet & blk 1.50 *3.00*
Nos. C14-C18 (5) 7.50 *12.50*

Counterfeits of Nos. C1-C18 are plentiful.

OCCUPATION STAMPS

Issued under German Occupation
For Use in Tartu (Dorpat)

Russian Stamps of 1909-12 Surcharged

1918 **Unwmk.** *Perf. 14x14½*
N1 A15 20pf on 10k dk bl 35.00 *50.00*
N2 A8 40pf on 20k bl & car 35.00 *50.00*

Forged overprints exist.

ETHIOPIA

ˌē-thē-ˈō-pē-ə

(Abyssinia)

LOCATION — Northeastern Africa
GOVT. — Monarchy
AREA — 471,800 sq. mi.
POP. — 40,000,000 (est. 1984)
CAPITAL — Addis Ababa

During the Italian occupation (1936-1941) Nos. N1-N7 were used, also stamps of Italian East Africa, Eritrea and Somalia.

16 Guerche = 1 Menelik Dollar or 1 Maria Theresa Dollar
100 Centimes = 1 Franc (1905)
40 Paras = 1 Piaster (1908)
16 Mehalek = 1 Thaler or Talari (1928)
100 Centimes = 1 Thaler (1936)

Watermarks

Wmk. 140 — Crown

Wmk. 282 — Ethiopian Star and Amharic Characters, Multiple

Excellent forgeries of Nos. 1-86 exist.

Very Fine examples of Nos. 1-86 and J1-J42 will have perforations touching the design on one or more sides due to the narrow spacing of the stamps on the plates and imperfect perforating methods. Stamps with margins clear on all sides are scarce and command high premiums.

On March 9, 1894 Menelik II awarded Alfred Ilg a concession to develop a railway, including postal service. Ilg's stamps, Nos. 1-79, were valid locally and to Djibouti. Mail to other countries had to bear stamps of Obock, Somali Coast, etc.

Ethiopia joined the UPU Nov. 1, 1908.

Menelik II
A1

Lion of Judah
A2

Anharic numeral "8"

Perf. 14x13½

1895, Jan. Unwmk. Typo.

1	A1	¼g green	3.00	2.00
2	A1	½g red	3.00	2.00
3	A1	1g blue	3.00	2.00
4	A1	2g dark brown	3.00	2.00
5	A2	4g lilac brown	3.00	2.00
6	A2	8g violet	3.00	2.00
7	A2	16g black	3.00	2.00
		Nos. 1-7 (7)	21.00	14.00

For 4g, 8g and 16g stamps of type A1, see Nos. J3a, J4a and J7a.

Earliest reported use is Jan. 29, 1895.

Forged cancellations are plentiful.

For overprints see #8-86, J8-J28, J36-J42. For surcharges see #94-100, J29-J35.

Nos. 1-7 Handstamped in Violet or Blue

Overprint 9¼x2½mm, Serifs on "E"

1901, July 18

8	A1	¼g green	17.00	17.00
9	A1	½g red	17.00	17.00
10	A1	1g blue	17.00	17.00
11	A1	2g dark brown	17.00	17.00
12	A2	4g lilac brown	21.00	21.00
13	A2	8g violet	35.00	35.00
14	A2	16g black	42.50	42.50
		Nos. 8-14 (7)	166.50	166.50

Violet overprints were issued July 18, 1901, for postal use, while the blue overprints were issued in Jan. 1902 for philatelic purposes. The blue overprints were not used in the mails. Values for unused stamps are for examples with blue overprints. Unused stamps with violet overprints are worth much more.

Overprints 8¼mm wide are unofficial reproductions.

Nos. 1-7 Handstamped in Violet, Blue or Black

Overprint 11x3mm, Low Colons

1902, Apr. 1

15	A1	¼g green	6.00	6.00
16	A1	½g red	9.00	7.00
17	A1	1g blue	9.50	9.50
18	A1	2g dark brown	12.00	11.00
19	A2	4g lilac brown	19.00	15.00
20	A2	8g violet	26.00	26.00
21	A2	16g black	40.00	40.00
		Nos. 15-21 (7)	121.50	114.50

The handstamp reads "Bosta" (Post).

Overprints 10¾mm and 11mm wide with raised colons are unofficial reproductions.

Nos. 1-7 Handstamped in Black

Overprint 16x3¾mm

1903, Apr. 15

22	A1	¼g green	6.75	6.75
23	A1	½g red	10.00	10.00
24	A1	1g blue	12.00	12.00
25	A1	2g dark brown	14.00	14.00
26	A2	4g lilac brown	21.00	21.00
27	A2	8g violet	29.00	29.00
28	A2	16g black	42.50	42.50
		Nos. 22-28 (7)	135.25	135.25

The handstamp reads "Malekt." (Also "Melekt," message).

Original stamps have blurred colons. Unofficial reproductions have clean colons.

Nos. 22-28 have black overprints only. All other colors are fakes.

Nos. 1-7 Handstamped in Violet or Blue

Overprint 18¼mm Wide

1904, Dec.

36	A1	¼g green	12.00
37	A1	½g red	12.00
38	A1	1g blue	15.00
39	A1	2g dark brown	17.50
40	A2	4g lilac brown	22.50
41	A2	8g violet	45.00
42	A2	16g black	52.50
		Nos. 36-42 (7)	176.50

The handstamp reads "Malekathe" (message). This set was never issued.

Preceding Issues Surcharged with New Values in French Currency in Blue, Violet, Rose or Black:

a

b

Overprint 3mm High

1905, Jan. 1

On Nos. 1-7

43	A1 (a)	5c on ¼g	7.50	7.50
44	A1 (a)	10c on ½g	7.50	7.50
45	A1 (a)	20c on 1g	7.50	7.50
46	A1 (a)	40c on 2g	7.50	7.50
47	A2 (a)	80c on 4g	14.00	14.00
48	A2 (b)	1.60fr on 8g	17.50	21.00
49	A2 (b)	3.20fr on 16g	25.00	25.00
		Nos. 43-49 (7)	86.50	90.00

Nos. 48-49 exist with period or comma.

On No. 8, "Ethiopie" in Blue

50	A1 (a)	5c on ¼g	100.00	100.00

On No. 15, "Bosta" in Black

51	A1 (a)	5c on ¼g	30.00	30.00

On No. 22, "Malekt" in Black

52	A1 (a)	5c on ¼g	60.00	60.00

Unofficial reproductions exist of Nos. 50, 51, 52. The 5c on #36, 10c, 20c, 40c, 80c, and 1.60fr surcharges exist as unofficial reproductions only.

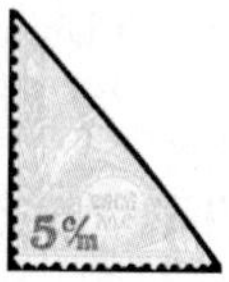

c

d

1905

On No. 2

54	A1 (c)	5c on half of ½g	5.00	5.00

On No. 21, "Bosta" in Black

55	A2 (d)	5c on 16g blk	200.00	100.00

On #55, "Bosta" is in black.

On No. 28, "Malekt" in Black

56	A2 (d)	5c on 16g blk	250.00	250.00
		Nos. 54-56 (3)	455.00	355.00

Nos. 55-56 issued Mar. 30.

The overprints and surcharges on Nos. 8 to 56 inclusive were handstamped, the work being very roughly done.

As is usual with handstamped overprints and surcharges there are many inverted and double, but most of them are fakes or unofficial reproductions.

Surcharged with New Values in Various Colors

and in Violet:

Overprint 14¾x3½mm

1906, Jan. 1

57	A1	5c on ¼g green	5.50	5.50
58	A1	10c on ½g red	8.50	8.50
59	A1	20c on 1g blue	8.50	8.50
60	A1	40c on 2g dk brn	8.50	8.50
61	A2	80c on 4g lilac brn	10.00	10.00
62	A2	1.60fr on 8g violet	15.00	15.00
63	A2	3.20fr on 16g black	32.50	32.50
		Nos. 57-63 (7)	88.50	88.50

Two types of the 4-character overprint ("Menelik"): 14x¾x3½mm and 16x4mm.

Surcharged with New Values

and in Violet Brown:

Overprint 16x4¼mm

1906, July 1

64	A1	5c on ¼g grn	7.25	7.25
a.		Surcharged "20"	50.00	50.00
65	A1	10c on ½g red	8.50	8.50
66	A1	20c on 1g blue	12.00	12.00
67	A1	40c on 2g dk brn	12.00	12.00
68	A2	80c on 4g lil brn	17.50	17.50
69	A2	1.60fr on 8g vio	17.50	17.50
70	A2	3.20fr on 16g blk	32.50	32.50
		Nos. 64-70 (7)	107.25	107.25

The control overprint reads "Menelik."

Surcharged in Violet:

e

f

1907, June 21

71	A1 (e)	¼ on ¼g grn	7.00	7.00
72	A1 (e)	½ on ½g red	7.00	7.00
73	A1 (f)	1 on 1g blue	8.25	8.25
74	A1 (f)	2 on 2g dk brn	9.00	9.00
a.		Surcharged "40"	50.00	
75	A2 (f)	4 on 4g lil brn	9.75	9.75
a.		Surcharged "80"	47.50	
76	A2 (f)	8 on 8g vio	21.00	21.00
77	A2 (f)	16 on 16g blk	27.50	27.50
		Nos. 71-77 (7)	89.50	89.50

Nos. 71-72 are also found with stars farther away from figures.

The control overprint reads "Dagmawi" ("Second"), meaning Emperor Menelik II.

Nos. 2, 23 Surcharged in Bluish Green

1908, Aug. 14

78	A1	1pi on ½g red (#2)	8.00	8.00
79	A1	1pi on ½g red (#23)	*850.00*	—

Official reproductions exist. Value, set $25.

Forgeries exist.

The surcharges on Nos. 57-78 are handstamped and are found double, inverted, etc.

Surcharged in Black

1908, Nov. 1

80	A1	¼p on ¼g grn	1.25	1.25
81	A1	½p on ½g red	1.25	1.25
82	A1	1p on 1g blue	1.75	1.75
83	A1	2p on 2g dk brn	3.00	3.00
84	A2	4p on 4g lil brn	4.25	4.25
85	A2	8p on 8g vio	10.00	10.00
86	A2	16p on 16g blk	15.00	15.00
		Nos. 80-86 (7)	36.50	36.50

Surcharges on Nos. 80-85 are found double, inverted, etc. Forgeries exist.

These are the 1st stamps valid for international mail.

King Solomon's Throne — A3

Menelik in Native Costume — A4

Menelik in Royal Dress — A5

1909, Jan. 29 ***Perf. 11½***

87	A3	¼g blue green	.60	.50
88	A3	½g rose	.65	.50
89	A3	1g green & org	3.50	1.25
90	A4	2g blue	2.50	1.50
91	A4	4g green & car	3.75	3.25
92	A5	8g ver & dp grn	9.00	5.75
93	A5	16g ver & car	12.50	9.00
		Nos. 87-93 (7)	32.50	21.75

For overprints see Nos. 101-115, J43-J49, J55-J56. For surcharges see Nos. 116-119.

Nos. 1-7 Handstamped and Surcharged in ms.

1911, Oct. 1 ***Perf. 14x13½***

94	A1	¼g on ¼g grn	40.00
95	A1	½g on ½g red	40.00
96	A1	1g on 1g blue	40.00
97	A1	2g on 2g dk brn	40.00
98	A2	4g on 4g lil brn	40.00
99	A2	8g on 8g violet	40.00
100	A2	16g on 16g black	40.00
		Nos. 94-100 (7)	280.00

Nos. 94-100 are provisionals used at Dire-Dawa for 5 days. The overprint is abbreviated from "Affranchissement Exceptionnel Faute Timbres" (Special Franking Lacking Stamps). The overprints and surcharges were applied to stamps on cover and then canceled.

Nos. 94-100 without surcharge are forgeries.

Stamps of 1909 Handstamped in Violet or Black:

Nos. 101-102

Nos. 104-107

1917, Mar. 30 *Perf. 11½*

101	A3	¼g blue grn (V)	4.00	4.00
102	A3	½g rose (V)	4.00	4.00
104	A4	2g blue (Bk)	5.00	5.00
105	A4	4g grn & car (Bk)	10.00	10.00
106	A5	8g ver & dp grn (Bk)	15.00	15.00
107	A5	16g ver & car (Bk)	30.00	30.00
		Nos. 101-107 (6)	68.00	68.00

Coronation of Empress Zauditu and appointment of Prince Tafari as Regent and Heir to the throne.

Exist with overprint inverted and double.

Stamps of 1909 Overprinted in Blue, Black or Red:

Nos. 108-111

Nos. 112-115

1917, Apr. 5-Oct. 1

108	A3	¼g blue grn (Bl)	1.00	1.00
109	A3	½g rose (Bl)	1.00	1.00
110	A3	1g grn & org (Bl)	2.00	2.00
111	A4	2g blue (R)	75.00	85.00
112	A4	2g blue (Bk)	1.00	1.00
113	A4	4g grn & car (Bl)	1.00	1.00
a.		Black overprint	10.00	10.00
114	A5	8g ver & dp grn (Bl)	1.00	1.00
115	A5	16g ver & car (Bl)	2.00	2.00
		Nos. 108-115 (8)	84.00	94.00

Coronation of Empress Zauditu.

Nos. 108-115 all exist with double overprint, inverted overprint, double overprint, one inverted, and various combinations.

Nos. 114-115 with Additional Surcharge

k

l

m

n

1917, May 28

116	A5 (k)	¼g on 8g	3.00	2.50
117	A5 (l)	½g on 8g	3.00	2.50
118	A5 (m)	1g on 16g	9.00	6.50
119	A5 (n)	2g on 16g	10.00	7.00
		Nos. 116-119 (4)	25.00	18.50

Nos. 116-119 all exist with the numerals double and inverted and No. 116 with the Amharic surcharge missing.

Sommering's Gazelle — A6

Prince Tafari — A9

Cathedral of St. George A12

Empress Waizeri Zauditu — A18

¼g, Giraffes. ½g, Leopard. 2g, Prince Tafari, diff. 4g, Prince Tafari, diff. 8g, White rhinoceros. 12g, Somali ostriches. 1t, African elephant. 2t, Water buffalo. 3t, Lions. 5t, 10t, Empress Zauditu.

1919, July 16 **Typo.** *Perf. 11½*

120	A6	⅛g violet & brn	.20	.20
121	A6	¼g bl grn & drab	.20	.20
122	A6	½g scar & ol grn	.20	.20
123	A9	1g rose lil & gray grn	.20	.20
124	A9	2g dp ultra & fawn	.20	.20
125	A9	4g turq bl & org	.20	*2.50*
126	A12	6g lt blue & org	.25	.20
127	A12	8g ol grn & blk brn	.35	.20
128	A12	12g red vio & gray	.50	.30
129	A12	1t rose & gray blk	.90	.40
130	A12	2t black & brown	2.50	
131	A12	3t grn & dp org	2.50	1.90
132	A18	4t brn & lil rose	3.00	2.50
133	A18	5t carmine & gray	4.00	4.00
134	A18	10t gray grn & bis	8.00	5.25
		Nos. 120-134 (15)	23.20	
		Nos. 120-129,131-134 (14)		18.25

No. 130 was not issued.

For overprints see Nos. J50-J54. For surcharges see Nos. 135-154.

Reprints have brownish gum that is cracked diagonally. Originals have smooth, white gum. Reprints exist imperf. and some values with inverted centers. Value for set, unused or canceled, $5.

No. 132 Surcharged in Blue

1919, Oct.

135	A18	4g on 4t brn & lil rose	3.00	3.00

Nos. 135-154

The Amharic surcharge indicates the new value and, therefore, varies on Nos. 135-154. There are numerous defective letters and figures, several types of the "2" of "½," the errors "guerhce," "gnerche," etc.

Many varieties of surcharge, such as double, inverted, lines transposed or omitted, and inverted "2" in "½," exist.

There are many irregularly produced settings in imitation of Nos. 136-154 which differ slightly from the originals. These may be essays or proofs.

Stamps of 1919 Surcharged

1921-22

136	A6	½g on ⅛g vio & brn ('22)	1.00	1.00
137	A6	1g on ¼g grn & db	2.50	1.00
138	A9	2g on 1g lil brn & gray grn ('22)	1.00	1.50
139	A18	2g on 4t brn & lil rose ('22)	35.00	15.00
140	A6	2½g on ½g scar & ol grn	1.00	*1.50*
141	A9	4g on 2g ultra & fawn ('22)	1.00	*1.25*
		Nos. 136-141 (6)	41.50	21.25

No. 139 has been forged.

Stamps and Type of 1919 Surcharged

1925-28

142	A12	½g on 1t rose & gray blk ('26)	1.00	1.00
a.		Without colon ('28)	12.50	12.50
143	A18	½g on 5t car & gray ('26)	2.00	1.00
144	A12	1g on 6g bl & org	1.00	1.00
145	A12	1g on 12g lil & gray	400.00	400.00
146	A12	1g on 3t grn & org ('26)	22.50	16.00
147	A18	1g on 10t gray grn & bis ('26)	1.00	*1.00*
		Nos. 142-147 (6)	427.50	420.00

On #142 the surcharge is at the left side of the stamp, reading upward. On #142a it is at the right, reading downward. The two surcharges are from different, though similar, settings. On #146 the surcharge is at the right, reading upward. See note following #154.

Type of 1919 Surcharged

1926

147A	A12	1g on 12g lil & gray	400.00

Forgeries exist.

Nos. 126-128 Surcharged

1926

148	A12	½g on 8g	3.00	1.25
149	A12	1g on 6g	80.00	50.00
150	A12	1g on 12g	350.00	
		Nos. 148-150 (3)	433.00	51.25

The Amharic line has 7 (½g) or 6 characters (1g).

Nos. 126-128, 131 Surcharged

1927

151	A12	½g on 8g	1.50	1.50
152	A12	1g on 6g	60.00	40.00
153	A12	1g on 12g	5.00	1.50
154	A12	1g on 3t	400.00	
		Nos. 151-154 (4)	466.50	43.00

The Amharic line has 7 (½g) or 4 characters (1g). No. 152 has the lines closer together than do the others.

Forgeries of No. 154 exist.

Prince Tafari — A22

Empress Zauditu — A23

1928, Sept. 5 **Typo.** *Perf. 13½x14*

155	A22	⅛m org & lt bl	.50	.45
156	A23	¼m ind & red org	.30	.45
157	A22	½m gray grn & blk	.50	.45
158	A23	1m dk car & blk	.30	.45
159	A22	2m dk bl & blk	.30	.45
160	A23	4m yel & olive	.30	.45
161	A22	8m vio & olive	.80	.45
162	A23	1t org brn & vio	.95	.65
163	A22	2t grn & bister	1.40	1.10
164	A23	3t choc & grn	2.25	1.25
		Nos. 155-164 (10)	7.60	6.15

For overprints and surcharges see Nos. 165-209, 217-230, C1-C10.

Preceding Issue Overprinted in Black, Violet or Red

1928, Sept. 1

165	A22	⅛m (Bk)	1.25	1.25
166	A23	¼m (V)	1.25	1.25
167	A22	½m (V)	1.25	1.25
168	A23	1m (V)	1.25	1.25
169	A22	2m (R)	1.25	1.25
170	A23	4m (Bk)	1.25	1.25
171	A22	8m (R)	1.25	1.25
172	A23	1t (Bk)	1.25	1.25
173	A22	2t (R)	1.90	1.90
174	A23	3t (R)	2.75	2.75
		Nos. 165-174 (10)	14.65	14.65

Opening of General Post Office, Addis Ababa.

Exist with overprint inverted, double, double, one inverted, etc.

Nos. 155, 157, 159, 161, 163 Handstamped in Violet, Red or Black

1928, Oct. 7

175	A22	⅛m (V)	1.40	1.40
176	A22	½m (R)	1.40	1.40
177	A22	2m (R)	1.40	1.40

178 A22 8m (Bk) 1.40 1.40
179 A22 2t (V) 1.40 1.40
Nos. 175-179 (5) 7.00 7.00

Crowning of Prince Tafari as king (Negus) on Oct. 7, 1928.
Nos. 175-177 exist with overprint vertical, inverted, double, etc.
Forgeries exist.

Nos. 155-164 Overprinted in Red or Green

1930, Apr. 3

180 A22 ⅛m org & lt bl (R) .25 .35
181 A23 ¼m ind & red org (G) .35 .35
182 A22 ½m gray grn & blk (R) .25 .35
183 A23 1m dk car & blk (G) .35 .35
184 A22 2m dk bl & blk (R) .35 .35
185 A23 4m yel & ol (R) .50 .50
186 A22 8m vio & ol (R) 1.00 1.00
187 A23 1t org brn & vio (R) 2.25 2.25
188 A22 2t grn & bis (R) 3.00 3.00
189 A23 3t choc & grn (R) 4.00 4.00
Nos. 180-189 (10) 12.30 12.50

Proclamation of King Tafari as King of Kings of Abyssinia under the name "Haile Selassie."
A similar overprint, set in four vertical lines, was printed on all denominations of the 1928 issue. It was not considered satisfactory and was rejected. The trial impressions were not placed on sale to the public, but some copies reached private hands and have been passed through the post.

Nos. 155-164 Overprinted in Red or Olive Brown

1930, Apr. 3

190 A22 ⅛m orange & lt bl .35 .35
191 A23 ¼m ind & red org (OB) .35 .35
192 A22 ½m gray grn & blk .75 .75
193 A23 1m dk car & blk (OB) .35 .35
194 A22 2m dk blue & blk .35 .35
195 A23 4m yellow & ol .60 .60
196 A22 8m violet & ol 1.00 1.00
197 A23 1t org brn & vio 2.25 2.25
198 A22 2t green & bister 3.00 3.00
199 A23 3t chocolate & grn 3.75 3.75
Nos. 190-199 (10) 12.75 12.75

Proclamation of King Tafari as Emperor Haile Selassie.
All stamps of this series exist with "H" of "HAILE" omitted and with many other varieties.

Nos. 155-164 Handstamped in Violet or Red

1930, Nov. 2

200 A22 ⅛m (V) .40 .40
201 A23 ¼m (V) .40 .40
202 A22 ½m (R) .40 .40
203 A23 1m (V) .40 .40
204 A22 2m (R) .40 .40
205 A23 4m (V) .40 .40
206 A22 8m (V or R) .90 .90
207 A23 1t (V) 1.25 1.25
208 A22 2t (V or R) 2.00 2.00
209 A23 3t (V or R) 3.00 3.00
Nos. 200-209 (10) 9.55 9.55

Coronation of Emperor Haile Selassie, Nov. 2, 1930.

Haile Selassie Coronation Monument, Symbols of Empire — A24

1930 Engr. *Perf. 12½*

210 A24 1g orange .40 .40
211 A24 2g ultra .40 .40
212 A24 4g violet .40 .40
213 A24 8g dull green .70 .65
214 A24 1t brown 1.00 1.00
215 A24 3t green 1.50 1.50
216 A24 5t red brown 1.50 1.50
Nos. 210-216 (7) 5.90 5.85

Coronation of Emperor Haile Selassie.
Issued: 4g, 11/2; others, 11/23.
Reprints of Nos. 210 to 216 exist. Colors are more yellow and the ink is thicker and slightly glossy. Ink on the originals is dull and granular. Value 35c each.

Nos. 158-160, 164 Surcharged in Green, Red or Blue

Type I

Type II

1931 *Perf. 13½x14*

217 A23 ⅛m on 1m .35 .35
218 A22 ⅛m on 2m (R) .35 .35
219 A23 ⅛m on 4m .35 .35
220 A23 ¼m on 1m (Bl) .35 .35
221 A22 ¼m on 2m (R) 1.00 1.00
222 A23 ¼m on 4m 1.00 1.00
225 A23 ½m on 1m (Bl) 1.00 1.00
226 A22 ½m on 2m (R) 1.00 1.00
227 A23 ½m on 4m, type II 1.00 1.00
a. ½m on 4m, type I 9.00 9.00
228 A23 ½m on 3t (R) 7.50 7.50
230 A22 1m on 2m (R) 1.25 1.25
Nos. 217-230 (11) 15.15 15.15

The ½m on ⅛m orange & light blue and ½m on ¼m indigo & red orange were clandestinely printed and never sold at the post office.
No. 230 with double surcharge in red and blue is a color trial.
Many varieties exist.
Issued: 1m, Apr.; others, 4/20.

Prince Makonnen A25

Empress Menen A27

View of Hawash River and Railroad Bridge A26

Designs: 2g, 8g, Haile Selassie (profile). 4g, 1t, Statue of Menelik II. 3t, Empress Menen (full face). 5t, Haile Selassie (full face).

Perf. 12½, 12x12½, 12½x12

1931, June 27 Engr.

232 A25 ⅛g red .40 .20
233 A26 ¼g olive green .40 .20
234 A25 ½g dark violet .40 .20
235 A27 1g red orange .50 .25
236 A27 2g ultra .50 .25
237 A25 4g violet .90 .40
238 A27 8g blue green 2.00 2.00
239 A25 1t chocolate 24.00 10.00
240 A27 3t yellow green 7.00 3.00
241 A27 5t red brown 12.00 5.50
Nos. 232-241 (10) 48.10 22.00

For overprints see Nos. B1-B5. For surcharges see Nos. 242-246.
Reprints of Nos. 232-236, 238-240 are on thinner and whiter paper than the originals. On originals the ink is dull and granular. On reprints, heavy, caked and shiny. Value 20c each.

Nos. 232-236 Surcharged in Blue or Carmine similar to cut

1936, Jan. 29 *Perf. 12x12½, 12½x12*

242 A25 1c on ⅛g red 2.00 1.00
243 A26 2c on ¼g ol grn (C) 2.00 1.00
244 A25 3c on ½g dk vio 2.00 1.10
245 A27 5c on 1g red org 2.50 1.50
246 A27 10c on 2g ultra (C) 3.25 1.90
Nos. 242-246 (5) 11.75 6.50

SEMI-POSTAL STAMPS

Types of 1931, Overprinted in Red at Upper Left

Perf. 12x12½, 12½x12

1936, Feb. 24 Unwmk.

B1 A27 1g light green .45 .45
B2 A27 2g rose .45 .45
B3 A25 4g blue .45 .45
B4 A27 8g brown .65 .65
B5 A25 1t purple .65 .65
Nos. B1-B5 (5) 2.65 2.65

Nos. B1-B5 were sold at twice face value, the surtax going to the Red Cross.

AIR POST STAMPS

Regular Issue of 1928 Handstamped in Violet, Red, Black or Green

Perf. 13½x14

1929, Aug. 17 Unwmk.

C1 A22 ⅛m orange & lt bl .90 *1.00*
C2 A23 ¼m ind & red org .90 *1.00*
C3 A22 ½m gray grn & blk .90 *1.00*
C4 A23 1m dk car & blk .90 *1.00*
C5 A22 2m dk blue & blk 1.00 *1.25*
C6 A23 4m yellow & olive 1.00 *1.25*
C7 A22 8m violet & olive 1.00 *1.25*
C8 A23 1t org brn & vio 1.25 *1.25*
C9 A22 2t green & bister 1.60 *2.00*
C10 A23 3t choc & grn 1.75 *2.00*
Nos. C1-C10 (10) 11.20 *13.00*

The overprint signifies "17 August 1929-Airplane of the Ethiopian Government." The stamps commemorate the arrival at Addis Ababa of the 1st airplane of the Ethiopian Government.
There are 3 types of the overprint: (I) 19½mm high; "colon" at right of bottom word. (II) 20mm high; same "colon." (III) 19½mm high; no "colon." Many errors exist.

Symbols of Empire, Airplane and Map — AP1

1931, June 17 Engr. *Perf. 12½*

C11 AP1 1g orange red .20 *.25*
C12 AP1 2g ultra .20 *.30*
C13 AP1 4g violet .20 *.40*
C14 AP1 8g blue green .50 *.80*
C15 AP1 1t olive brown 1.25 *1.00*
C16 AP1 2t carmine 2.25 *3.75*
C17 AP1 3t yellow green 3.25 *5.00*
Nos. C11-C17 (7) 7.85 *11.50*

Nos. C11 to C17 exist imperforate.
Reprints of C11 to C17 exist. Paper is thinner and gum whiter than the originals and the ink is heavy and shiny. Originals have ink that is dull and granular. Reprints usually sell at about one-tenth of above values.

POSTAGE DUE STAMPS

Very Fine examples of Nos. J1-J42 will have perforations touching the design on one or more sides.

Nos. 1-4 and unissued values Overprinted

Perf. 14x13½

1896, June 10 Unwmk.

Black Overprint

J1 A1 ¼g green 1.25
J2 A1 ½g red 1.25
J3 A1 4g lilac brown .90
a. Without overprint .90
J4 A1 8g violet .90
a. Without overprint .90

Red Overprint

J5 A1 1g blue 1.25
J6 A1 2g dark brown 1.25
J7 A1 16g black .90
a. Without overprint .90
Nos. J1-J7 (7) 7.70

Nos. J1-J7 were not issued.

Nos. 1-7 Handstamped in Various Colors:

a

b

1905, Jan. 1

J8 A1 (a) ¼g green 42.50 42.50
J9 A1 (a) ½g red 42.50 42.50
J10 A1 (a) 1g blue 42.50 42.50
J11 A1 (a) 2g dk brown 42.50 42.50
J12 A2 (a) 4g lilac brown 42.50 42.50
J13 A2 (a) 8g violet 42.50 42.50
J14 A2 (a) 16g black 42.50 42.50
Nos. J7-J14 (8) 298.40 297.50

1905, June 1

J15	A1 (b)	¼g green	42.50	42.50
J16	A1 (b)	½g red	42.50	42.50
J17	A1 (b)	1g blue	42.50	42.50
J18	A1 (b)	2g dark brown	42.50	42.50
J19	A2 (b)	4g lilac brown	42.50	42.50
J20	A2 (b)	8g violet	42.50	42.50
J21	A2 (b)	16g black	42.50	42.50
		Nos. J15-J21 (7)	297.50	297.50

Excellent forgeries of Nos. J8-J42 exist.

Nos. 1-7 Handstamped in Blue or Violet

1906, July 1

J22	A1	¼g green	10.00	10.00
J23	A1	½g red	10.00	10.00
J24	A1	1g blue	10.00	10.00
J25	A1	2g dark brown	10.00	10.00
J26	A2	4g lilac brown	10.00	10.00
J27	A2	8g violet	15.00	15.00
J28	A2	16g black	21.00	21.00
		Nos. J22-J28 (7)	86.00	86.00

Nos. J22-J27 exist with inverted overprint, also No. J22 with double overprint.

Forgeries exist.

With Additional Surcharge of Value Handstamped as on Nos. 71-77

1907, July 1

J29	A1 (e)	¼ on ¼g grn	14.00	14.00
J30	A1 (e)	½ on ½g red	14.00	14.00
J31	A1 (f)	1 on 1g blue	14.00	14.00
J32	A1 (f)	2 on 2g dk brown	14.00	14.00
J33	A2 (f)	4 on 4g lilac brn	14.00	14.00
J34	A2 (f)	8 on 8g violet	14.00	14.00
J35	A2 (f)	16 on 16g blk	22.50	22.50
		Nos. J29-J35 (7)	106.50	106.50

Nos. J30-J35 exist with inverted surcharge. Nos. J30, J33-J35 exist with double surcharge.

Nos. 1-7 Handstamped in Black

1908, Dec. 1

J36	A1	¼g green	1.00	.90
J37	A1	½g red	1.00	.90
J38	A1	1g blue	1.00	.90
J39	A1	2g dark brown	1.25	1.10
J40	A2	4g lilac brown	1.75	1.75
J41	A2	8g violet	4.00	4.50
J42	A2	16g black	12.50	14.00
		Nos. J36-J42 (7)	22.50	24.05

Nos. J36 to J42 exist with inverted overprint and Nos. J36, J37, J38 and J40 with double overprint.

Forgeries of Nos. J36-J56 exist.

Same Handstamp on Nos. 87-93

1912, Dec. 1 ***Perf. 11½***

J43	A3	¼g blue green	1.25	.85
J44	A3	½g rose	1.25	1.10

1913, July 1

J45	A3	1g green & org	4.25	3.00
J46	A4	2g blue	5.00	4.25
J47	A4	4g green & car	7.50	5.00
J48	A5	8g ver & dp grn	10.00	8.00
J49	A5	16g ver & car	25.00	19.00
		Nos. J43-J49 (7)	54.25	41.20

Nos. J43-J49, all exist with inverted, double and double, one inverted overprint.

Same Handstamp on Nos. 120-124 in Blue Black

1925-27 ***Perf. 11½***

J50	A6	⅛g violet & brn	*18.00*	*18.00*
J51	A6	¼g bl grn & db	*18.00*	*18.00*
J52	A6	½g scar & ol grn	*20.00*	*20.00*
J53	A9	1g rose lil & gray grn	*20.00*	*20.00*
J54	A9	2g dp ultra & fawn	*20.00*	*20.00*
		Nos. J50-J54 (5)	*96.00*	*96.00*

Same Handstamp on Nos. 110, 112

1930 (?)

J55	A3 (i)	1g green & org	*30.00*	*30.00*
J56	A4 (j)	2g blue	*30.00*	*30.00*

The status of Nos. J55-J56 is questioned.

OCCUPATION STAMPS

Issued under Italian Occupation

100 Centesimi = 1 Lira

OS1

Emperor Victor Emmanuel III — OS2

1936 **Wmk. 140** ***Perf. 14***

N1	OS1	10c orange brown	8.50	5.50
N2	OS1	20c purple	7.75	1.75
N3	OS2	25c dark green	3.75	.35
N4	OS2	30c dark brown	3.75	.85
N5	OS2	50c rose carmine	1.00	.20
N6	OS1	75c deep orange	15.00	4.00
N7	OS1	1.25 l deep blue	16.00	6.25
		Nos. N1-N7 (7)	55.75	18.90
		Set, never hinged	110.00	

Issued: #N3-N5, May 22; others Dec. 5.

For later issues see Italian East Africa.

FALKLAND ISLANDS

ˈfol-klənd ˈī-lənds

LOCATION — A group of islands about 300 miles east of the Straits of Magellan at the southern limit of South America

GOVT. — British Crown Colony

AREA — 4,700 sq. mi.

POP. — 1,813 (1980)

CAPITAL — Stanley

12 Pence = 1 Shilling

20 Shillings = 1 Pound

Catalogue values for unused stamps in this country are for Never Hinged items, beginning with Scott 97 in the regular postage section, Scott 1L1 in Falkland Island Dependencies regular issues, and Scott 2L1, 3L1, 4L1, 5L1 in the Issues for Separate Islands.

Values for unused stamps are for examples with original gum as defined in the catalogue introduction.

Nos. 1-4, 7-8, and some printings of Nos. 5-6, exist with straight edges on one or two sides, being the imperforate margins of the sheets. This occurs in 24 out of 60 stamps. Catalogue values are for stamps with perforations on all sides.

Queen Victoria — A1

1878-79 **Unwmk.** **Engr.** ***Perf. 14***

1	A1	1p claret	775.00	*500.00*
2	A1	4p dark gray ('79)	1,300.	200.00
3	A1	6p green	90.00	75.00
4	A1	1sh bister brown	72.50	75.00

No. 2 is known with paper maker's watermark "TURNER, CHAFFORD MILLS," in double-lined capital letters. Values, unused $2,500, used $475.

1883-95 **Wmk. 2**

5	A1	1p brt claret ('94)	120.00	95.00
	a.	1p claret	400.00	175.00
	b.	Horiz. pair, imperf. vert.	*52,500.*	
	c.	1p red brown ('91)	220.00	90.00
	d.	Diag. half of #5c used as ½p on cover		*3,000.*
6	A1	4p olive gray ('95)	12.00	27.50
	a.	4p gray black	425.00	95.00
	b.	4p olive gray black ('89)	150.00	57.50
	c.	4p brownish black ('94)	850.00	375.00

No. 6c has watermark reversed.

For surcharge see No. 19E.

1886 **Wmk. 2 Sideways**

7	A1	1p claret	75.00	57.50
	a.	1p brownish claret	110.00	55.00
	b.	Diagonal half of #7a used as ½p on cover		*2,600.*
8	A1	4p olive gray	450.00	50.00
	a.	4p pale gray black	725.00	72.50

For surcharge see No. 19.

1891-1902 **Wmk. 2**

9	A1	½p green ('92)	19.00	*18.00*
	a.	½p blue green	25.00	*30.00*
10	A1	½p yel green ('99)	2.25	*3.50*
11	A1	1p orange brown	80.00	67.50
	a.	Diagonal half used as ½p on cover		*2,250.*
11B	A1	1p pale red	6.50	5.00
12	A1	1p org red ('02)	13.00	4.75
	a.	1p Venetian red ('95)	23.00	20.00
13	A1	2p magenta ('96)	6.00	12.50
14	A1	2½p deep blue ('94)	275.00	160.00
15	A1	2½p ultra ('94)	30.00	12.50
	a.	2½p pale ultra ('98)	35.00	16.00
	b.	2½p dull blue	175.00	27.50
	c.	2½p deep ultra ('01)	40.00	40.00
	d.	2½p pale chalky ultra	160.00	50.00
16	A1	6p yellow ('96)	35.00	50.00
	a.	6p orange ('92)	65.00	50.00
17	A1	9p ver ('96)	42.50	*65.00*
	a.	9p salmon	50.00	*65.00*
18	A1	1sh gray brn ('95)	60.00	*65.00*
	a.	1sh bis brn ('96)	55.00	55.00
		Nos. 9-18 (11)	569.25	463.75

Nos. 7 and 5a Surcharged in Black

1891 **Wmk. 2 Sideways**

19	A1	½p on half of 1p, #7	650.	360.
	d.	Unsevered pair	3,000.	1,350.

Wmk. 2

19E	A1	½p on half of 1p, #5a	775.	325.
	f.	Unsevered pair	3,850.	1,700.

Genuine used bisects should be canceled with a segmented circular cork cancel. Any other cancel must be linked by date to known mail ship departures. This surcharge exists on "souvenir" bisects, including copies of No. 11, and can be found inverted, double and sideways.

A3

A4

1898 **Wmk. 1**

20	A3	2sh6p dark blue	275.00	300.00
21	A4	5sh brown red	225.00	275.00
		Set of two, ovptd. "SPECIMEN"	525.00	

A5

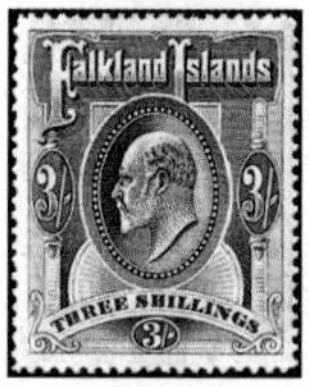

King Edward VII — A6

1904-07 Wmk. 3 *Perf. 14*

22	A5	½p	yellow green	5.25	1.80
23	A5	1p	red, wmk. sideways ('07)	1.20	*2.50*
a.			Wmk. upright ('04)	13.50	*1.80*
b.			Thick paper ('08)	19.00	2.00
24	A5	2p	dull vio ('05)	20.00	*32.50*
a.			2p reddish pur ('12)	260.00	310.00
25	A5	2½p	ultramarine	35.00	10.00
a.			2½p deep blue	300.00	200.00
26	A5	6p	orange ('05)	45.00	*57.50*
27	A5	1sh	bis brn ('05)	47.50	40.00
28	A6	3sh	gray green	160.00	150.00
a.			3sh green	150.00	120.00
29	A6	5sh	dull red ('05)	230.00	180.00
			Nos. 22-29 (8)	543.95	474.30
			Nos. 22-29 (8), ovptd. "SPECIMEN"	650.00	

King George V

A7 A8

1912-14

30	A7	½p	yellow green	3.00	3.25
31	A7	1p	red	4.50	2.50
32	A7	2p	brown violet	8.50	19.00
33	A7	2½p	deep ultra	9.50	*19.00*
34	A7	6p	orange	17.50	*22.50*
35	A7	1sh	bister brown	40.00	*37.50*
36	A8	3sh	dark green	100.00	*95.00*
37	A8	5sh	brown red	95.00	*120.00*
38	A8	5sh	plum ('14)	220.00	*220.00*
39	A8	10sh	red, *green*	200.00	*300.00*
40	A8	£1	black, *red*	525.00	*600.00*
			Nos. 30-40 (11)	1,223.	*1,438.*

For overprints see Nos. MR1-MR3.

1921-29 Wmk. 4

41	A7	½p	yellow green	3.50	*4.50*
42	A7	1p	red ('24)	6.00	1.50
43	A7	2p	brown vio ('23)	9.50	8.50
44	A7	2½p	dark blue	8.00	*20.00*
a.			2½p Prussian blue ('29)	375.00	*550.00*
45	A7	2½p	vio, *yel* ('23)	6.00	*42.50*
46	A7	6p	orange ('25)	9.50	*45.00*
47	A7	1sh	bister brown	20.00	*57.50*
48	A8	3sh	dk green ('23)	95.00	*190.00*
			Nos. 41-48 (8)	157.50	*369.50*

No. 43 Surcharged

1928

52	A7	2½p on 2p brn vio	*1,000.*	*1,000.*
a.		Double surcharge	*39,000.*	

Beware of forged surcharges.

King George V — A9

1929-31 *Perf. 14*

54	A9	½p	green	1.25	*3.00*
55	A9	1p	scarlet	4.00	.80
56	A9	2p	gray	3.25	3.00
57	A9	2½p	blue	3.25	*2.25*
58	A9	4p	deep orange	20.00	*14.00*
59	A9	6p	brown violet	20.00	*14.00*
60	A9	1sh	black, *green*	25.00	*35.00*
a.			1sh black, *emerald*	*26.00*	*30.00*
61	A9	2sh6p	red, *blue*	52.50	52.50
62	A9	5sh	green, *yel*	85.00	*100.00*
63	A9	10sh	red, *green*	160.00	*200.00*

Wmk. 3

64	A9	£1	black, *red*	350.00	425.00
			Nos. 54-64 (11)	724.25	849.55

Issue dates: 4p, 1931, others, Sept. 2.

Romney Marsh Ram — A10

Iceberg A11

Whaling Ship — A12

Port Louis A13

Map of the Islands A14

South Georgia A15

Blue Whale A16

Government House A17

Battle Memorial — A18

King Penguin — A19

Coat of Arms — A20

King George V — A21

1933, Jan. 2 Wmk. 4 *Perf. 12*

65	A10	½p	green & blk	2.00	6.00
66	A11	1p	dl red & blk	4.00	2.00
67	A12	1½p	lt bl & blk	16.00	*20.00*
68	A13	2p	ol brn & blk	12.50	*25.00*
69	A14	3p	dl vio & blk	17.50	*20.00*
70	A15	4p	orange & blk	20.00	*20.00*
71	A16	6p	gray & black	57.50	*65.00*
72	A17	1sh	ol grn & blk	50.00	*75.00*
73	A18	2sh6p	dp vio & blk	200.00	200.00
74	A19	5sh	yellow & blk	625.00	*850.00*
a.			5sh yellow orange & black	1,750.	*1,950.*
75	A20	10sh	lt brn & blk	700.00	*975.00*
76	A21	£1	rose & black	1,850.	*2,250.*
			Nos. 65-76 (12)	3,554.	*4,508.*

Cent. of the permanent occupation of the islands as a British colony.

Common Design Types pictured following the introduction.

Silver Jubilee Issue

Common Design Type

1935, May 7 *Perf. 11x12*

77	CD301	1p	carmine & blue	1.40	.50
78	CD301	2½p	ultra & brown	2.75	2.10
79	CD301	4p	indigo & grn	5.50	5.50
80	CD301	1sh	brn vio & ind	12.50	4.75
			Nos. 77-80 (4)	22.15	12.85
			Set, never hinged	37.50	

Coronation Issue

Common Design Type

1937, May 12 *Perf. 11x11½*

81	CD302	½p	deep green	.20	.20
82	CD302	1p	dark carmine	.35	*.50*
83	CD302	2½p	deep ultra	.60	*.80*
			Nos. 81-83 (3)	1.15	1.50
			Set, never hinged	2.00	

Whale Jawbones (Centennial Monument) — A22

#85, 86A, Black-necked swan. #85B, 86, Battle memorial. 2½p, 3p, Flock of sheep. 4p, Upland goose. 6p, R.R.S. "Discovery II." 9p, R.R.S. "William Scoresby." 1sh, Mt. Sugar Top. 1sh3p, Turkey vultures. 2sh6p, Gentoo penguins. 5sh, Sea lions. 10sh, Deception Island. £1, Arms of Colony.

1938-46 *Perf. 12*

84	A22	½p	green & blk	.20	.20
85	A22	1p	red & black	2.50	2.50
a.			1p rose carmine & black	16.00	1.75
85B	A22	1p	dk vio & blk	.20	.20
86	A22	2p	dk vio & blk	1.75	1.75
86A	A22	2p	rose car & black	.25	.25
87	A22	2½p	ultra & blk	1.50	1.25
87A	A22	3p	deep bl & black	.75	.75
88	A22	4p	rose vio & black	1.75	1.75
89	A22	6p	brown & blk	5.00	4.25
90	A22	9p	sl bl & blk	1.75	1.50
91	A22	1sh	dull blue	7.75	3.00
92	A22	1sh3p	carmine & blk	1.75	*3.00*
93	A22	2sh6p	gray black	37.50	21.00
94	A22	5sh	org brown & ultra	55.00	42.50
a.			5sh yel brown & indigo	625.00	300.00
95	A22	10sh	org & blk	60.00	42.50
96	A22	£1	dk vio & blk	125.00	85.00
			Nos. 84-96 (16)	302.65	211.40
			Set, never hinged	460.00	

Issued: #85B, 86A, 3p, 7/14/41; 1sh3p, 12/10/46; No. 94a, 1942; others, 1/3/38.

See Nos. 101-102. For overprints see Nos. 2L1-2L8, 3L1-3L8, 4L1-4L8.

Catalogue values for unused stamps in this section, from this point to the end of the section, are for Never Hinged items.

Peace Issue

Common Design Type

Perf. 13½x14

1946, Oct. 7 Engr. Wmk. 4

97	CD303	1p	purple	.35	.25
98	CD303	3p	deep blue	.55	.25

Silver Wedding Issue

Common Design Types

1948, Nov. 1 Photo. *Perf. 14x14½*

99	CD304	2½p	bright ultra	1.25	.60

Engr.; Name Typo.

Perf. 11½x11

100	CD305	£1	purple	110.00	75.00

Types of 1938-46

2½p, Upland goose. 6p, R.R.S. "Discovery II."

Perf. 12

1949, June 15 Engr. Wmk. 4

101	A22	2½p	dp blue & black	5.50	*7.25*
102	A22	6p	gray black	4.75	3.50

UPU Issue

Common Design Types

Engr.; Name Typo. on 3p, 1sh3p

1949, Oct. 10 *Perf. 13½, 11x11½*

103	CD306	1p	violet	.60	.60
104	CD307	3p	indigo	1.50	1.50
105	CD308	1sh3p	green	5.00	4.50
106	CD309	2sh	blue	11.00	9.50
			Nos. 103-106 (4)	18.10	16.10

Sheep A35

Arms of the Colony — A36

Designs: 1p, R.M.S. Fitzroy. 2p Upland goose. 2½p, Map. 4p, Auster plane. 6p, M.S.S. John Biscoe. 9p, "Two Sisters" peaks. 1sh, Gentoo penguins. 1sh 3p, Kelp goose and gander. 2sh 6p, Sheep shearing. 5sh, Battle memorial. 10sh, Sea lion and clapmatch. £1, Hulk of "Great Britain."

Perf. 13½x13, 13x13½

1952, Jan. 2 Engr. Wmk. 4

107	A35	½p	green	.70	*1.10*
108	A35	1p	red	1.50	.70
109	A35	2p	violet	3.50	*4.50*
110	A35	2½p	ultra & blk	.95	.95
111	A36	3p	deep ultra	1.00	*1.75*
112	A35	4p	claret	7.25	2.75
113	A35	6p	yellow brn	12.00	1.75
114	A35	9p	orange yel	9.00	3.50
115	A36	1sh	black	21.00	1.50
116	A35	1sh3p	red orange	13.00	*9.25*
117	A36	2sh6p	olive	16.00	*20.00*
118	A36	5sh	red violet	10.00	*15.00*
119	A35	10sh	gray	22.50	*25.00*
120	A35	£1	black	25.00	*32.50*
			Nos. 107-120 (14)	143.40	*120.25*

WAR TAX STAMPS

Regular Issue of 1912-14 Overprinted

1918, Oct. 7 Wmk. 3 *Perf. 14*
MR1 A7 ½p yellow green .55 *7.25*
MR2 A7 1p red .55 *4.00*
a. Double overprint *2,500.*
MR3 A7 1sh bister brown 6.50 *52.50*
a. Pair, one without overprint 8,000.
Nos. MR1-MR3 (3) 7.60 *63.75*

No. MR3a probably is caused by a foldover and is not constant.

FALKLAND ISLANDS DEPENDENCIES

Catalogue values for unused stamps in this section are for Never Hinged items.

Map of Falkland Islands — A1

Engr., Center Litho. in Black
1946, Feb. 1 Wmk. 4 *Perf. 12*
1L1 A1 ½p yellow green .95 *1.50*
1L2 A1 1p blue violet .95 *1.90*
1L3 A1 2p deep carmine .95 *1.90*
1L4 A1 3p ultramarine 1.90 *1.90*
1L5 A1 4p deep plum 1.90 *3.00*
1L6 A1 6p orange yellow 3.00 *3.50*
1L7 A1 9p brown 3.00 *3.50*
1L8 A1 1sh rose violet 5.75 *7.50*
Nos. 1L1-1L8 (8) 18.40 *24.70*

Nos. 1L1-1L8 were reissued in 1948, printed on more opaque paper with the lines of the map finer and clearer. Value for set, unused or used $120.
See No. 1L13.

Common Design Types pictured following the introduction.

Peace Issue
Common Design Type
1946, Oct. 4 *Perf. 13½x14*
1L9 CD303 1p purple .60 .20
1L10 CD303 3p deep blue 1.10 .20

Silver Wedding Issue
Common Design Types
1948, Dec. 6 Photo. *Perf. 14x14½*
1L11 CD304 2½p brt ultra 1.25 1.25
Perf. 11½x11
Engr.
1L12 CD305 1sh blue violet 5.75 5.75

Type of 1946
1949, Mar. 6 *Perf. 12*
Center Litho. in Black
1L13 A1 2½p deep blue 12.50 12.00

UPU Issue
Common Design Types
Engr.; Name Typo. on 2p, 3p
1949, Oct. 10 *Perf. 13½, 11x11½*
1L14 CD306 1p violet 1.60 1.90
1L15 CD307 2p deep carmine 4.25 1.90
1L16 CD308 3p indigo 6.50 4.25
1L17 CD309 6p red orange 11.00 8.50
Nos. 1L14-1L17 (4) 23.35 16.55

ISSUES FOR THE SEPARATE ISLANDS

Graham Land

Nos. 84, 85B, 86A, 87A, 88-91 Overprinted in Red

1944, Feb. 12 Wmk. 4 *Perf. 12*
2L1 A22 ½p green & black .55 .50
2L2 A22 1p dk vio & black .60 .60
2L3 A22 2p rose car & blk .90 .85
2L4 A22 3p deep bl & blk 1.25 1.10
2L5 A22 4p rose vio & blk 1.50 1.50
2L6 A22 6p brown & black 4.00 3.50
2L7 A22 9p slate bl & blk 3.00 3.00
2L8 A22 1sh dull blue 3.00 2.75
Nos. 2L1-2L8 (8) 14.80 13.80

South Georgia

1944, Apr. 3 Wmk. 4 *Perf. 12*
3L1 A22 ½p green & black .60 .50
3L2 A22 1p dark vio & blk .65 .60
3L3 A22 2p rose car & blk 1.00 .85
3L4 A22 3p deep bl & blk 1.40 1.10
3L5 A22 4p rose vio & blk 1.60 1.50
3L6 A22 6p brown & black 4.25 4.00
3L7 A22 9p slate bl & blk 3.25 3.00
3L8 A22 1sh dull blue 3.25 3.00
Nos. 3L1-3L8 (8) 16.00 14.55

South Orkneys

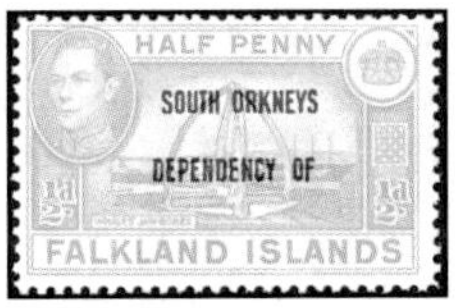

1944, Feb. 21 Wmk. 4 *Perf. 12*
4L1 A22 ½p green & black .55 .50
4L2 A22 1p dark vio & blk .60 .60
4L3 A22 2p rose car & blk .90 .85
4L4 A22 3p deep bl & blk 1.25 1.10
4L5 A22 4p rose vio & blk 1.50 1.50
4L6 A22 6p brown & black 4.00 3.50
4L7 A22 9p slate bl & blk 3.00 3.00
4L8 A22 1sh dull blue 3.00 2.75
Nos. 4L1-4L8 (8) 14.80 13.80

South Shetlands

1944 Wmk. 4 *Perf. 12*
5L1 A22 ½p green & black .50 .50
5L2 A22 1p dark vio & blk .60 .60
5L3 A22 2p rose car & blk .90 .85
5L4 A22 3p deep bl & blk 1.25 1.10
5L5 A22 4p rose vio & blk 1.50 1.50
5L6 A22 6p brown & black 4.00 3.50
5L7 A22 9p slate bl & blk 3.00 3.00
5L8 A22 1sh dull blue 3.00 2.75
Nos. 5L1-5L8 (8) 14.75 13.80

FAR EASTERN REPUBLIC

ˈfär ˈē-stərn ri-ˈpə-blik

LOCATION — In Siberia east of Lake Baikal
GOVT. — Republic
AREA — 900,745 sq. mi.
POP. — 1,560,000 (approx. 1920)
CAPITAL — Chita

A short-lived independent government was established here in 1920.

100 Kopecks = 1 Ruble

Watermark

Wmk. 171 — Diamonds

Vladivostok Issue
Russian Stamps Surcharged or Overprinted:

a

b

c

On Stamps of 1909-17
Perf. 14, 14½x15, 13½
1920 Unwmk.
2 A14(a) 2k green 8.00 *10.00*
3 A14(a) 3k red 8.00 *10.00*
4 A11(b) 3k on 35k red brn & grn 20.00 20.00
5 A15(a) 4k carmine 10.00 *12.00*
6 A11(b) 4k on 70k brn & org 6.00 *8.00*
8 A11(b) 7k on 15k red brn & bl 2.00 2.00
a. Inverted surcharge 50.00
b. Pair, one ovptd. "DBP" only
9 A15(a) 10k dark blue 50.00 *55.00*
a. Overprint on back 75.00
10 A12(c) 10k on 3½r mar & lt grn 15.00 *20.00*
11 A11(a) 14k blue & rose 30.00 30.00
12 A11(a) 15k red brn & bl 12.00 12.00
13 A8(a) 20k blue & car 65.00 65.00
14 A11(b) 20k on 14k bl & rose 6.00 *8.00*
a. Surcharge on back 30.00
15 A11(a) 25k green & vio 12.50 12.00
16 A11(a) 35k red brn & grn 30.00 30.00
17 A8(a) 50k brn vio & grn 10.00 *11.50*
18 A9(a) 1r pale brn, dk brn & org *500.00 500.00*

On Stamps of 1917
Imperf
21 A14(a) 1k orange 8.00 *8.50*
22 A14(a) 2k gray grn 3.00 2.50
23 A14(a) 3k red 8.00 *10.00*
25 A11(b) 7k on 15k red brn & dp bl 2.00 *5.00*
a. Pair, one without surcharge
b. Pair, one ovptd. "DBP" only
26 A12(c) 10k on 3½r mar & lt grn 10.00 *15.00*
27 A9(a) 1r pale brn, brn & red org 15.00 *20.00*

On Stamps of Siberia 1919
Perf. 14, 14½x15
30 A14(a) 35k on 2k green 5.00 *8.00*
a. "DBP" on back 25.00 *50.00*
Imperf
31 A14(a) 35k on 2k green 15.00 15.00
32 A14(a) 70k on 1k orange 7.00 *10.00*

Counterfeit surcharges and overprints abound, including digital forgeries.

Postal Savings Stamps Surcharged for Postal Use

A1

Perf. 14½x15
Wmk. 171
35 A1(b) 1k on 5k green, *buff* 15.00 15.00
36 A1(b) 2k on 10k brown, *buff* 35.00 35.00

The letters on these stamps resembling "DBP," are the Russian initials of "Dalne Vostochnaya Respublika" (Far Eastern Republic).

Chita Issue

A2

A2a

1921 Unwmk. Typo. *Imperf.*
38 A2 2k gray green 1.50 1.50
39 A2a 4k rose 3.00 3.00
40 A2 5k claret 3.00 3.00
41 A2a 10k blue 2.50 2.50
Nos. 38-41 (4) 10.00 10.00

For overprints see Nos. 62-65.

Blagoveshchensk Issue

A3

1921 Litho. *Imperf.*
42 A3 2r red 2.75 2.00
43 A3 3r dark green 2.75 2.00
44 A3 5r dark blue 2.75 2.00
a. Tête bêche pair 30.00 *50.00*
45 A3 15r dark brown 2.75 2.00
46 A3 30r dark violet 2.75 2.00
a. Tête bêche pair 30.00 *50.00*
Nos. 42-46 (5) 13.75 10.00

Remainders of Nos. 42-46 were canceled in colored crayon or by typographed bars. These sell for half of foregoing values.

Chita Issue

A4

A5

1922 Litho. *Imperf.*
49 A4 1k orange .55 *.85*
50 A4 3k dull red .30 *.45*
51 A5 4k dp rose & buff .30 *.45*
52 A4 5k orange brown .65 *.45*
53 A4 7k light blue .65 *1.25*
a. Perf. 11½ 1.00 2.00
b. Rouletted 9 2.00 2.00
c. Perf. 11½x roulетted 4.00 3.00
54 A5 10k dk blue & red .40 *.65*
55 A4 15k dull rose .55 *.85*
56 A5 20k blue & red .55 *.85*
57 A5 30k green & red org .65 *1.10*
58 A5 50k black & red org 1.25 *1.75*
Nos. 49-58 (10) 5.85 *8.65*

The 4k exists with "4" omitted. Value $100.

Vladivostok Issue

Stamps of 1921 Overprinted in Red

1922 *Imperf.*

62	A2 2k gray green	20.00	20.00
a.	Inverted overprint	100.00	
63	A2a 4k rose	20.00	20.00
a.	Inverted overprint	100.00	
b.	Double overprint	150.00	
64	A2 5k claret	15.00	15.00
a.	Inverted overprint	100.00	
b.	Double overprint	300.00	
65	A2a 10k blue	20.00	20.00
a.	Inverted overprint	100.00	
	Nos. 62-65 (4)	75.00	75.00

Russian revolution of Nov. 1917, 5th anniv.

Once in the setting the figures "22" of 1922 have the bottom stroke curved instead of straight. Value, each $40.

Vladivostok Issue

Russian Stamps of 1922-23 Surcharged in Black or Red

1923 *Imperf.*

66	A50 1k on 100r red	.40	*.75*
a.	Inverted surcharge	50.00	
67	A50 2k on 70r violet	.40	*.75*
68	A49 5k on 10r blue (R)	.40	*.75*
69	A50 10k on 50r brown	.90	*1.25*
a.	Inverted surcharge	50.00	
	Perf. 14½x15		
70	A50 1k on 100r red	.90	*1.25*
	Nos. 66-70 (5)	3.00	*4.75*

OCCUPATION STAMPS

Issued under Occupation of General Semenov

Chita Issue

Russian Stamps of 1909-12 Surcharged:

p. 1 p. a   **2p.50к.** b

c

1920 Unwmk. *Perf. 14, 14x15½*

N1	A15 (a) 1r on 4k car	50.00	*55.00*
N2	A8 (b) 2r50k on 20k bl & car	20.00	*40.00*
N3	A14 (c) 5r on 5k claret	20.00	*50.00*
a.	Double surcharge	60.00	
N4	A11 (a) 10r on 70k brn & org	20.00	*40.00*
	Nos. N1-N4 (4)	110.00	*185.00*

FAROE ISLANDS

'far-ˌō 'ī-lənds

(The Faroes)

LOCATION — North Atlantic Ocean
GOVT. — Part of the Kingdom of Denmark
AREA — 540 sq. mi.
POP. — 52,347 (1984)
CAPITAL — Thorshavn

100 Ore = 1 Krone

Denmark No. 97 Handstamp Surcharged

1919, Jan. Typo. *Perf. 14x14½*

1	A16 2o on 5o green	1,250.	350.00

Counterfeits of surcharge exist.

Denmark No. 88a, the bisect, was used with Denmark No. 97 in Faroe Islands Jan. 3-23, 1919.

Denmark Nos. 220, 224, 238A, 224C Surcharged in Blue or Black

Nos. 2, 5-6

No. 3

No. 4

1940-41 Engr. *Perf. 13*

2	A32 20o on 1o ('41)	45.00	85.00
3	A32 20o on 5o ('41)	40.00	30.00
4	A30 20o on 15o (Bk)	47.50	20.00
5	A32 50o on 5o (Bk)	250.00	75.00
6	A32 60o on 6o (Bk)	100.00	175.00
	Nos. 2-6 (5)	482.50	385.00
	Set, never hinged	675.00	

Issued during British administration.

FERNANDO PO

fər-'nan-ˌdō 'pō

LOCATION — An island in the Gulf of Guinea off west Africa.
GOVT. — Spanish Colony
AREA — 800 sq. mi.
POP. — 62,612 (1960)
CAPITAL — Santa Isabel

Together with the islands of Elobey, Annobon and Corisco, Fernando Po came under the administration of Spanish Guinea. Postage stamps of Spanish Guinea were used until 1960.

100 Centimos = 1 Escudo = 2.50 Pesetas
100 Centimos = 1 Peseta
1000 Milesimas = 100 Centavos = 1 Peso (1882)

FORERUNNERS

Crowned Circle handstamp type VII and Numeral Cancellation type B are pictured in the Crowned Circle Handstamps and Great Britain Used Abroad section.

P.O. at St. Thomas opened Apr. 1, 1858; canceller supplied 1874; closed in 1877

1859

A1	I Crowned circle handstamp Type VII inscribed "FERNANDO-P" in red, on cover,	5,750.

Earliest known use: 2/19/59.

STAMPS OF GREAT BRITAIN USED IN FERNANDO PO

Cancelled "247"

1874-77

A2	4p vermilion (#43, P 13, 14)	—
A3	4p vermilion (#69, P 15)	—
A4	6p gray (#62, P 13-16)	—

Issued under Spanish Dominion

Isabella II — A1

Alfonso XII — A2

1868 Unwmk. Typo. *Perf. 14*

1	A1 20c brown	450.00	125.00
a.	20c red brown	450.00	125.00

No. 1 is valued in the grade of fine, as illustrated. Examples with very fine centering are uncommon and sell for more.

Forgeries exist.

1879

Centimos de Peseta

2	A2 5c green	50.00	10.50
3	A2 10c rose	25.00	10.50
4	A2 50c blue	100.00	10.50
	Nos. 2-4 (3)	175.00	31.50

1882-89

Centavos de Peso

5	A2 1c green	10.50	4.00
6	A2 2c rose	16.00	6.75
7	A2 5c gray blue	52.50	9.50
8	A2 10c dk brown ('89)	72.50	4.75
	Nos. 5-8 (4)	151.50	25.00

Nos. 5-7 Handstamp Surcharged Type "a" in Blue, Black or Violet

a

1884-95

9	A2 50c on 1c green ('95)	95.00	19.00
11	A2 50c on 2c rose	29.00	6.00
12	A2 50c on 5c blue ('87)	105.00	25.00
	Nos. 9-12 (3)	229.00	50.00

Values above are for examples surcharged in blue or black. Stamps surcharged in violet are worth about 25% more.

Inverted and double surcharges exist. No. 12 exists overprinted in carmine. Value $80.

King Alfonso XIII — A4

1894-97 *Perf. 14*

13	A4 ⅛c slate ('96)	20.00	2.75
14	A4 2c rose ('96)	14.50	2.25
15	A4 5c blue grn ('97)	15.00	2.25
16	A4 6c dk violet ('96)	12.00	2.75
17	A4 10c blk vio ('94)	325.00	72.50
18	A4 10c lake ('95)	45.00	8.25
19	A4 10c org brn ('96)	9.50	2.25
20	A4 12½c dk brown ('96)	10.50	2.75
21	A4 20c slate bl ('96)	10.50	2.75
22	A4 25c claret ('96)	21.00	2.75
	Nos. 13-22 (10)	483.00	101.25

Stamps of 1894-97 Handstamped in Blue, Black or Red

b

c

Type "b" Surcharge

1896-98

23	A4 5c on 2c rose (Bl)	37.50	5.75
24	A4 5c on 10c brn vio (Bl)	110.00	16.00
25	A4 5c on 12½c brn (Bl)	25.00	4.75
a.	Black surcharge	25.00	4.75
	Nos. 23-25 (3)	172.50	26.50

Type "c" Surcharge

26	A4 5c on ⅛c slate (Bk)	22.00	6.25
27	A4 5c on 2c rose (Bl)	22.00	6.25
a.	Black surcharge	22.00	6.25
28	A4 5c on 5c green (R)	110.00	20.00
29	A4 5c on 6c dk vio (R)	17.50	12.50
a.	Violet surcharge	18.50	14.00
30	A4 5c on 10c org brn (Bk)	125.00	25.00
31	A4 5c on 12½c brn (R)	50.00	10.00
32	A4 5c on 20c sl bl (R)	27.50	9.50
33	A4 5c on 25c claret (Bk)	27.50	10.00
a.	Blue surcharge	27.50	12.00
	Nos. 26-33 (8)	401.50	99.50

Exist surcharged in other colors.

Type "a" Surch. in Blue or Black

1898-99

34	A4 50c on 2c rose	70.00	8.50
35	A4 50c on 10c brn vio	160.00	25.00
36	A4 50c on 10c lake	170.00	25.00
37	A4 50c on 10c org brn	160.00	25.00
38	A4 50c on 12½c brn (Bk)	140.00	16.50

The "a" surch. also exists on ⅛c, 5c & 25c. Values, $300, $200 and $190, respectively.

Arms

A5 A6

Revenue Stamps Handstamped in Blue

1897-98 *Imperf.*

39	A5 5c on 10c rose	32.50	15.00
40	A6 10c rose	27.50	13.00

A7

A8

A9

Arms — A9a

Revenue Stamps Handstamped in Black or Red

1899 *Imperf.*

41	A7	15c on 10c green	40.00	21.00
a.		Blue surcharge, vertical	35.00	19.00
42	A8	10c on 25c green	110.00	60.00
43	A9	15c on 25c green	175.00	110.00
43A	A9a	15c on 25c green (R)	*1,600.*	*1,000.*
b.		Black surcharge	*1,600.*	*1,000.*

Surcharge on No. 41 is either horizontal, inverted or vertical.
On No. 42 "CORREOS" is ovptd. in red.

King Alfonso XIII — A10

Double-lined shaded letters at sides.

1899 *Perf. 14*

44	A10	1m orange brn	1.90	.40
45	A10	2m orange brn	1.90	.40
46	A10	3m orange brn	1.90	.40
47	A10	4m orange brn	1.90	.40
48	A10	5m orange brn	1.90	.40
49	A10	1c black vio	1.90	.40
50	A10	2c dk blue grn	1.90	.40
51	A10	3c dk brown	1.90	.40
52	A10	4c orange	11.50	1.00
53	A10	5c carmine rose	1.90	.40
54	A10	6c dark blue	1.90	.40
55	A10	8c gray brn	7.00	.40
56	A10	10c vermilion	4.50	.40
57	A10	15c slate grn	4.50	.40
58	A10	20c maroon	12.00	1.00
59	A10	40c violet	82.50	17.50
60	A10	60c black	82.50	17.50
61	A10	80c red brown	82.50	17.50
62	A10	1p yellow grn	300.00	85.00
63	A10	2p slate blue	300.00	87.50
		Nos. 44-63 (20)	906.00	232.20

Nos. 44-63 exist imperf. Value for set, $1,275.
See Nos. 66-85. For surcharges see Nos. 64-65, 88-88B.

1900

Surcharged type "a"

64	A10	50c on 20c maroon	15.00	2.25
a.		Blue surcharge	30.00	4.50

Surcharged type "b"

64B	A10	5c on 20c maroon	200.00	10.00

Surcharged type "c"

65	A10	5c on 20c maroon	8.50	2.25
		Nos. 64-65 (3)	223.50	14.50

Dated "1900"

Solid letters at sides.

1900

66	A10	1m black	2.75	.50
67	A10	2m black	2.75	.50
68	A10	3m black	2.75	.50
69	A10	4m black	2.75	.50
70	A10	5m black	2.75	.50
71	A10	1c green	2.75	.50
72	A10	2c violet	2.75	.50
73	A10	3c rose	2.75	.50
74	A10	4c black brn	2.75	.50
75	A10	5c blue	2.75	.50
76	A10	6c orange	2.75	.50
77	A10	8c bronze grn	2.75	.50
78	A10	10c claret	2.75	.50
79	A10	15c dk violet	2.75	.50
80	A10	20c olive brn	2.75	.50
81	A10	40c brown	7.00	2.25
82	A10	60c green	15.00	2.50
83	A10	80c dark blue	16.00	3.75
84	A10	1p red brown	90.00	30.00
85	A10	2p orange	160.00	62.50
		Nos. 66-85 (20)	329.25	108.50
		Set, never hinged	475.00	

Nos. 66-85 exist imperf. Value, set *$1,600.*

A11

A12

Revenue Stamps Overprinted or Surcharged with Handstamp in Red or Black

1900 *Imperf.*

86	A11	10c blue (R)	35.00	16.00
87	A12	5c on 10c blue	90.00	37.50
		Set, never hinged	165.00	

Nos. 52 and 80 Surcharged type "a" in Violet or Black

1900

88	A10	50c on 4c orange (V)	14.00	4.00
a.		Green surcharge	22.50	12.00
88B	A10	50c on 20c ol brn	14.00	3.50
		Set, never hinged	37.50	

A13

A14

1901 *Perf. 14*

89	A13	1c black	2.25	.60
90	A13	2c orange brn	2.25	.60
91	A13	3c dk violet	2.25	.60
92	A13	4c lt violet	2.25	.60
93	A13	5c orange red	1.50	.60
94	A13	10c violet brn	1.50	.60
95	A13	25c dp blue	1.50	.60
96	A13	50c claret	2.25	.60
97	A13	75c dk brown	1.50	.60
98	A13	1p blue grn	50.00	5.00
99	A13	2p red brown	30.00	7.75
100	A13	3p olive grn	30.00	10.00
101	A13	4p dull red	32.50	10.00
102	A13	5p dk green	40.00	10.00
103	A13	10p buff	90.00	30.00
		Nos. 89-103 (15)	289.75	78.15
		Set, never hinged	500.00	

Dated "1902"

1902

Control Numbers on Back

104	A13	5c dk green	1.75	.35
105	A13	10c slate	2.00	.40
106	A13	25c claret	5.00	.65
107	A13	50c violet brn	11.50	2.25
108	A13	75c lt violet	11.50	2.25
109	A13	1p car rose	15.00	2.75
110	A13	2p olive grn	30.00	6.75
111	A13	5p orange red	42.50	15.00
		Nos. 104-111 (8)	119.25	30.40
		Set, never hinged	175.00	

Exist imperf. Value for set, *$850.*

1903 *Perf. 14*

Control Numbers on Back

112	A14	¼c dk violet	.35	.20
113	A14	½c black	.35	.20
114	A14	1c scarlet	.35	.20
115	A14	2c dk green	.35	.25
116	A14	3c blue grn	.35	.25
117	A14	4c violet	.35	.25
118	A14	5c rose lake	.40	.25
119	A14	10c orange buff	.45	.25
120	A14	15c blue green	1.75	.75
121	A14	25c red brown	2.25	1.00
122	A14	50c black brn	3.50	1.60
123	A14	75c carmine	12.00	3.00
124	A14	1p dk brown	17.50	5.00
125	A14	2p dk olive grn	24.00	6.25
126	A14	3p claret	24.00	6.25
127	A14	4p dark blue	30.00	10.00
128	A14	5p dp dull blue	45.00	13.50
129	A14	10p dull red	85.00	20.00
		Nos. 112-129 (18)	247.95	69.20
		Set, never hinged	400.00	

Dated "1905"

1905

Control Numbers on Back

136	A14	1c dp violet	.20	.20
137	A14	2c black	.20	.20
138	A14	3c vermilion	.20	.20
139	A14	4c dp green	.20	.20
140	A14	5c blue grn	.30	.25
141	A14	10c violet	1.25	.45
142	A14	15c car lake	1.25	.45
143	A14	25c orange buff	9.75	1.40
144	A14	50c green	6.00	2.10
145	A14	75c red brown	8.25	6.00
146	A14	1p dp gray brn	9.75	6.00
147	A14	2p carmine	17.50	9.00
148	A14	3p deep brown	27.50	10.50
149	A14	4p bronze grn	32.50	14.00
150	A14	5p claret	52.50	21.00
151	A14	10p deep blue	77.50	30.00
		Nos. 136-151 (16)	244.85	101.95
		Set, never hinged	450.00	

King Alfonso XIII — A15

1907

Control Numbers on Back

152	A15	1c blue black	.20	.20
153	A15	2c car rose	.20	.20
154	A15	3c dp violet	.20	.20
155	A15	4c black	.20	.20
156	A15	5c orange buff	.25	.20
157	A15	10c maroon	1.40	.35
158	A15	15c bronze grn	.45	.25
159	A15	25c dk brown	20.00	6.50
160	A15	50c blue green	.25	.25
161	A15	75c vermilion	.35	.25
162	A15	1p dull blue	2.00	.45
163	A15	2p brown	8.25	2.75
164	A15	3p lake	8.25	2.75
165	A15	4p violet	8.25	2.75
166	A15	5p black brn	8.25	2.75
167	A15	10p orange brn	8.25	2.75
		Nos. 152-167 (16)	66.75	22.80
		Set, never hinged	125.00	

No. 157 Handstamp Surcharged in Black or Blue

1908

168	A15	5c on 10c mar (Bk)	2.75	2.00
169	A15	5c on 10c mar (Bl)	9.00	5.50
		Set, never hinged	15.00	

The surcharge on Nos. 168-169 exist inverted, double, etc. The surcharge also exists on other stamps. A 25c on 10c also exists.

Seville-Barcelona Issue of Spain, 1929, Overprinted in Blue or Red

1929 *Perf. 11*

170	A52	5c rose lake	.20	.20
171	A53	10c green (R)	.20	.20
a.		Perf. 14	.65	.65
172	A50	15c Prus bl (R)	.25	.20
173	A51	20c purple (R)	.25	.20
174	A50	25c brt rose	.25	.20
175	A52	30c black brn	.25	.20
176	A53	40c dk blue (R)	.70	.70
177	A51	50c dp orange	1.50	1.50
178	A52	1p blue blk (R)	5.75	5.75
179	A53	4p deep rose	27.50	27.50
180	A53	10p brown	35.00	35.00
		Nos. 170-180 (11)	71.85	71.65
		Set, never hinged	120.00	

FIJI

'fē-ˌjē

LOCATION — Group of 332 islands (106 inhabited) in the South Pacific Ocean east of New Hebrides
GOVT. — British Colony
AREA — 7,078 sq. mi.
POP. — 646,561 (1981)
CAPITAL — Suva

12 Pence = 1 Shilling
20 Shillings = 1 Pound
100 Cents = 1 Dollar (1872-74)

Catalogue values for unused stamps in this country are for Never Hinged items, beginning with Scott 137 in the regular postage section and Scott B1 in the semi-postal section.

Values for unused stamps are for examples with original gum as defined in the catalogue introduction except for Nos. 1-10 which are valued without gum. Additionally, Nos. 1-10 are valued with roulettes showing on two or more sides, but expect small faults which do not detract from the appearance of the stamps. Very few examples of Nos. 1-10 will be found free of faults and these will command substantial premiums.

Watermark

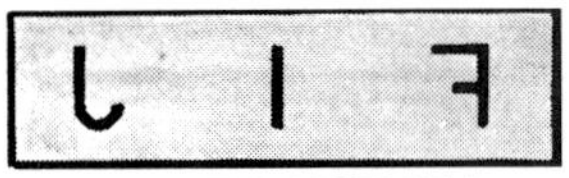

Wmk. 17 — FIJI POSTAGE Across Center Row of Sheet

A1

1870 **Unwmk.** **Typeset** *Rouletted*

Quadrille Paper

1	A1	1p black, *pink*	3,750.	4,000.
2	A1	3p black, *pink*	4,000.	4,000.
3	A1	6p black, *pink*	2,350.	2,750.
5	A1	1sh black, *pink*	1,750.	2,250.

1871 **Laid Batonne Paper**

6	A1	1p black, *pink*	1,000.	2,000.
7	A1	3p black, *pink*	1,750.	3,250.
8	A1	6p black, *pink*	1,300.	2,000.
9	A1	9p black, *pink*	2,200.	3,500.
a.		Comma after "EXPRESS"	*3,500.*	
10	A1	1sh black, *pink*	1,500.	1,600.

This service was established by the *Fiji Times*, a weekly newspaper, for the delivery of the newspaper. Since there was no postal service to the other islands, delivery of letters to agents of the newspaper on the islands was offered to the public.

Nos. 1-5 were printed in the same sheet, one horizontal row of 6 of each (6p, 1sh, 1p, 3p). Nos. 6-10 were printed from the same plate with three 9p replacing three 3p.

Most used examples have pen cancels.

Covers: Covers bearing Nos. 1-9 are very rare, values starting at about $22,000.

Up to three sets of imitations exist. One on pink laid paper, pin-perforated, measuring 22½x16mm. Originals measure 22½x18½mm. A later printing was made on pink wove paper.

Forgeries also exist plus fake cancellations.

Crown and "CR" (Cakobau Rex)

A2 A3

A4

1871 Typo. Wmk. 17 *Perf. 12½*

Wove Paper

15 A2 1p blue 62.50 140.00
16 A3 3p green 125.00 400.00
17 A4 6p rose 150.00 325.00
Nos. 15-17 (3) 337.50 865.00

Sheets of 50 (10x5).

For overprints and surcharges see Nos. 18-39.

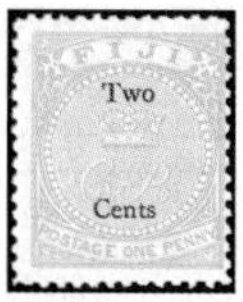

Stamps of 1871 Surcharged in Black

1872, Jan. 13

18 A2 2c on 1p blue 37.50 *57.50*
a. 2c on 1p pale blue 57.50 *75.00*
19 A3 6c on 3p green 75.00 75.00
20 A4 12c on 6p rose 100.00 85.00
Nos. 18-20 (3) 212.50 217.50

Nos. 18-20 with Additional Overprint in Black:

b

V.R.

c

1874, Oct. 10

21 A2(b) 2c on 1p blue 1,150. 325.00
22 A2(c) 2c on 1p blue 1,000. 300.00
a. Invtd. "A" instead of "V" 2,600. 1,500.
b. Period after "R" is a Maltese Cross 2,600. 1,500.
23 A3(b) 6c on 3p green 2,100. 1,000.
24 A3(c) 6c on 3p green 1,650. 775.00
a. Inverted "A" 4,250. 1,850.
b. Period after "R" is a Maltese Cross 4,250. 1,850.
25 A4(b) 12c on 6p rose 900.00 250.00
a. "V.R." inverted 5,750.
26 A4(c) 12c on 6p rose 725.00 225.00
a. Inverted "A" 2,250. 1,350.
b. Period after "R" is a Maltese Cross 2,250. 1,350.
c. "V.R." inverted — 5,000.

Types "b" and "c" were in the same sheet.

Nos. 23-26 with Additional Surcharge in Black or Red

2d.

1875

27 A3(b) 2p on 6c on 3p 1,950. 750.00
a. Period btwn. "2" and "d" 3,500. 1,400.
b. "V.R." double 4,000. 3,750.
28 A3(b) 2p on 6c on 3p (R) 750.00 325.00
a. Period btwn. "2" and "d" 1,750. 750.00
29 A3(c) 2p on 6c on 3p 1,650. 525.00
a. Inverted "A" 3,750. 1,400.
b. Period after "R" is a Maltese Cross 3,750. 1,400.
c. No period after "2d" 3,750. 1,400.
30 A3(c) 2p on 6c on 3p (R) 600.00 225.00
a. Inverted "A" 1,750. 750.00
b. Period after "R" is a Maltese Cross 1,750. 750.00
c. No period after "2d" 2,200. 925.00
31 A4(b) 2p on 12c on 6p 2,250. 950.00
a. Period btwn. "2" and "d"
b. No period after "2d"
c. "2d, VR" double 4,250.
32 A4(c) 2p on 12c on 6p 2,100. 900.00
a. Inverted "A" 2,750. 1,250.
b. No period after "2d"
c. "2d, VR" double 4,250.

Types of 1871 Overprinted or Surcharged in Black:

e

f

1876, Jan. 31 Unwmk.

Wove Paper

33 A2(e) 1p ultramarine 57.50 57.50
a. Inverted surcharge
b. Dbl. impression of stamp 1,000.
c. Horiz. pair, imperf vert. 1,000.
34 A3(e+f) 2p on 3p dk grn 52.50 60.00
a. Dbl. surch. "Two Pence"
b. 2p on 3p pale green 55.00 *62.50*
35 A4(e) 6p rose 70.00 65.00
a. 6p carmine rose 62.50 62.50
b. Surcharge inverted
c. Dbl. impression of stamp 2,850.
Nos. 33-35 (3) 180.00 182.50

1877 Laid Paper

36 A2(e) 1p ultramarine 20.00 *32.50*
a. Horiz. pair, imperf. vert. 1,100.
b. 1p deep blue 21.00 *32.50*
37 A3(e+f) 2p on 3p dk grn 65.00 *75.00*
a. 3p yellow green 65.00 *75.00*
b. Perf 10 400.00
c. Perf 11 350.00
d. Horiz. pair, imperf. vert. —
38 A3(e+f) 4p on 3p lilac 95.00 30.00
a. Horiz. pair, imperf. vert. 1,000.
39 A4(e) 6p rose 55.00 32.50
a. Horiz. pair, imperf. vert. 800.00
b. 6p carmine rose 55.00 40.00
Nos. 36-39 (4) 235.00 170.00

Many of the preceding stamps are known imperforate. They are printer's waste and were never issued.

A12

A13

Queen Victoria

A14 A15

Perf. 10-13½ & Compound

1878-90 Wove Paper Typo.

40 A12 1p ultra ('79) 10.00 7.50
a. 1p blue 60.00 3.75
41 A12 2p green 15.00 1.10
b. 2p ultramarine (error) *28,500.*
42 A12 4p brt vio ('90) 8.50 7.00
a. 4p mauve 11.50 8.50
43 A13 6p brt rose ('80) 7.50 4.25
a. Printed on both sides 1,150. 975.00
44 A14 1sh yel brn ('81) 40.00 10.00
a. 1sh deep brown 95.00 22.50

Litho.

45 A15 5sh blk & red brn ('82) 62.50 37.50
Nos. 40-45 (6) 143.50 67.35

No. 41b was not put on sale. All copies were supposed to be destroyed.

A quantity of No. 45 was sold as remainders, canceled-to-order with the following Suva dates: 15.DEC.00; 22.DE.1900; 28.DEC.1900; 12.DEC.01; 15.DEC.01; 16.DE.1901; 21.JUN.02; 15.DEC.02; 15. DE. 1902; and 21.DE.1902. Copies so cancelled are worth less than postally used examples.

No. 45 imperf was sold only as a remainder, canceled "Suva, 15.DEC.00."

A late printing of the 5sh, made from an electrotyped plate, exists in gray black and red orange, perf 12, differing from #45 in many details. It was also sold only as a remainder, canceled "Suva, 15.DEC.00." It is scarce.

For surcharges see Nos. 46-52.

Surcharged type "f" in Black

1878-90 Typo.

46 A12 2p on 3p green 6.50 *22.50*
47 A12 4p on 1p vio ('90) 47.50 30.00
48 A12 4p on 2p lilac ('83) 85.00 12.50
Nos. 46-48 (3) 139.00 65.00

Nos. 40-43 Surcharged in Black:

g

h

j

k

1891-92 *Perf. 10*

49 A12(g) ½p on 1p ('92) 50.00 75.00
50 A12(h) 2½p on 2p 50.00 57.50
a. Wider space (2mm) between "2" and "½" 150.00 *160.00*
51 A12(j) 5p on 4p ('92) 57.50 75.00
52 A13(k) 5p on 6p ('92) 62.50 80.00
a. "FIVE" and "PENCE" 3mm apart 75.00 80.00
Nos. 49-52 (4) 220.00 287.50

A18

Fijian Canoe — A19

A20

1891-96 *Perf. 10-12 & Compound*

53 A18 ½p grnsh blk ('92) 1.40 3.00
a. ½p gray 3.50 6.00
54 A19 1p black ('93) 5.00 5.50
55 A19 1p lilac rose ('96) 5.00 1.00
56 A19 2p green ('93) 6.50 1.10
a. Perf. 10x12 ('94) 700.00 425.00
57 A20 2½ red brown 5.75 5.75
58 A19 5p ultra ('93) 15.00 8.50
Nos. 53-58 (6) 38.65 24.85

Edward VII A22

George V A23

1903, Feb. 1 Wmk. 2 *Perf. 14*

59 A22 ½p gray grn & pale grn 2.60 2.25
60 A22 1p vio & blk, *red* 15.00 .65
61 A22 2p vio & orange 4.50 1.40
62 A22 2½p vio & ultra, *bl* 16.00 4.00
63 A22 3p vio & red vio 1.75 *4.50*
64 A22 4p violet & blk 1.75 *2.75*
65 A22 5p vio & green 1.75 *3.00*
66 A22 6p vio & car rose 1.75 *2.00*
67 A22 1sh grn & car rose 12.50 *70.00*
68 A22 5sh green & blk 62.50 *150.00*
69 A22 £1 gray & ultra 400.00 *550.00*
Revenue cancel 70.00
Nos. 59-68 (10) 120.10 *240.55*

Numerals of 2p, 4p, 6p and 5sh of type A22 are in color on plain tablet.

1904-12 Wmk. 3

Ordinary Paper

70 A22 ½p grn & pale grn ('04) 15.00 3.50
70A A22 ½p green ('08) 12.50 3.50
71 A22 1p vio & black, *red* ('04) 30.00 .20
72 A22 1p carmine ('06) 11.00 .20
73 A22 2½p ultra ('10) 7.50 *8.50*

Chalky Paper

74 A22 6p violet ('10) 15.00 *30.00*
75 A22 1sh grn & car rose ('09) 30.00 *45.00*
76 A22 1sh black, *green* ('11) 5.00 *11.00*
77 A22 5sh grn & scarlet, *yel* ('11) 65.00 *75.00*
78 A22 £1 vio & black, *red* ('12) 375.00 325.00
Nos. 70-77 (9) 191.00 *176.90*

Die I

For description of Dies I and II see "Dies of British Colonial Stamps" in Table of Contents.

1912-23

Ordinary Paper

79 A23 ¼p brown ('16) 1.50 .20
80 A23 ½p green 1.40 .55
81 A23 1p scarlet 2.25 .75
a. 1p carmine ('16) 2.25 .25
82 A23 2p gray ('14) 2.00 .20
83 A23 2½p ultra ('14) 3.50 4.00
84 A23 3p violet, *yel* 2.25 *4.00*
a. Die II ('21) 2.75 *25.00*
85 A23 4p black & red, *yel* ('14) 3.75 *15.00*
a. Die II ('23) 3.75 *27.50*

Chalky Paper

86 A23 5p dl vio & ol grn ('14) 5.50 *12.50*
87 A23 6p dl vio & red vio ('14) 2.40 *6.00*
88 A23 1sh black, *green* 1.10 *14.00*
a. 1sh black, *blue green*, ol back 4.50 *11.00*
b. 1sh black, *emerald* ('21) 6.25 *45.00*
c. Die II ('22) 3.25 *27.50*
89 A23 2sh 6p black & red, *blue* 37.50 *35.00*
90 A23 5sh grn & scar, *yellow* 37.50 *45.00*
91 A23 £1 vio & black, *red* 300.00 325.00
a. Die II ('21) 300.00 325.00
Revenue cancel 52.50

Surface-colored Paper

92 A23 1sh black, *green* 1.25 12.50
Nos. 79-90,92 (13) 101.90 *149.70*

Numerals of ¼p, 1½p, 2p, 4p, 6p, 2sh, 2sh6p and 5sh of type A23 are in color on plain tablet.

For overprints see Nos. MR1-MR2.

Die II

1922-27 Wmk. 4

Ordinary Paper

93 A23 ¼p dark brown 3.00 *27.50*
94 A23 ½p green .85 *2.40*
95 A23 1p rose red 2.75 1.25
96 A23 1p violet ('27) 1.40 .20
97 A23 1½p rose red ('27) 4.50 2.00
98 A23 2p gray 1.40 .20
99 A23 3p ultra ('23) 3.00 1.20
100 A23 4p blk & red, *yel* 5.75 7.50
101 A23 5p dl vio & ol green 1.75 *2.25*
102 A23 6p dl vio & red violet 2.40 1.50

Chalky Paper

103 A23 1sh blk, *emerald* 5.50 6.75
104 A23 2sh vio & ultra, *bl* ('27) 30.00 *67.50*
105 A23 2sh6p blk & red, *bl* 12.50 *35.00*
106 A23 5sh grn & scar, *yellow* 37.50 *75.00*
Nos. 93-106 (14) 112.30 *230.25*

Common Design Types pictured following the introduction.

Silver Jubilee Issue

Common Design Type

1935, May 6 *Perf. 13½x14*

110 CD301 1½p carmine & blue 1.10 *6.00*
111 CD301 2p gray blk & ultra 1.75 .40
112 CD301 3p blue & brown 3.00 3.00
113 CD301 1sh brt vio & indigo 6.00 6.00
Nos. 110-113 (4) 11.85 15.40
Set, never hinged 18.00

Coronation Issue

Common Design Type

1937, May 12 *Perf. 11x11½*

114	CD302	1p dark violet	.45	.25
115	CD302	2p gray black	.45	*.85*
116	CD302	3p indigo	.45	*.85*
		Nos. 114-116 (3)	1.35	1.95
		Set, never hinged	2.00	

Outrigger Canoe — A24

Fijian Village — A25

Outrigger Canoe A26

Map of Fiji Islands A27

Canoe and Arms of Fiji — A28

Sugar Cane — A29

Spear Fishing at Night — A30

Arms of Fiji — A31

Suva Harbor — A32

River Scene — A33

Fijian House — A34

Papaya Tree — A35

Bugler — A36

Designs: No. 121, Government buildings. 8p, 1sh5p, 1sh6p, Arms of Fiji.

Perf. 13½, 12½ (1p)

1938-55 **Engr.** **Wmk. 4**

117	A24	½p green	.25	1.00
c.		Perf. 14 ('41)	16.00	4.50
d.		Perf. 12 ('48)	.80	*4.00*
118	A25	1p blue & brn	.40	.25
119	A26	1½p rose car (empty canoe)	12.00	2.00
120	A27	2p grn & org brn (no "180 degree")	30.00	.50
121	A27	2p mag & grn	.45	.80
a.		Perf. 12 ('46)	.45	.90

Perf. 12½, 13x12 (6p), 14 (8p)

122	A28	3p dp ultra	.80	.40
123	A29	5p rose red & blue	32.50	13.00
124	A29	5p rose red & yel grn	.25	.40
125	A27	6p blk (no "180 degree")	50.00	16.00
126	A31	8p rose car	.80	3.00
a.		Perf. 13 ('50)	.55	*3.50*
127	A30	1sh black & yel	.60	.90

Perf. 14

128	A31	1sh5p car & black	.20	.20
128A	A31	1sh6p ultra	2.75	3.50
b.		Perf. 13 ('55)	1.10	*20.00*

Perf. 12½

129	A32	2sh vio & org	2.00	.55
130	A33	2sh6p brn & grn	2.25	2.00
131	A34	5sh dk vio & grn	2.25	2.25
131A	A35	10sh emer & brn org	27.50	*52.50*
131B	A36	£1 car & ultra	37.50	*65.00*
		Nos. 117-131B (18)	202.50	*164.25*

Issued: 1sh5p, 6/13/40; 5p, 10/1/40; #121, 5/19/42; 8p, 11/15/48; 10sh, £1, 3/13/50; 1sh6p, 8/1/50; others, 4/5/38.

Types of 1938-40 Redrawn

Perf. 13½ (1½p, 2p, 6p), 14 (2½p)

1940-49 **Wmk. 4**

132	A26	1½p rose car (man in canoe)	1.00	*1.00*
a.		Perf. 12 ('49)	.80	*1.60*
b.		Perf. 14 ('42)	14.50	*25.00*
133	A27	2p grn & org brn ("180 degree")	12.50	*21.00*
134	A27	2½p grn & org brn	.50	1.25
a.		Perf. 12 ('48)	.80	.60
b.		Perf. 13½ ('42)	.55	1.00
135	A27	6p blk ("180 degree")	2.50	3.00
a.		Perf. 12 ('47)	1.40	2.00
		Nos. 132-135 (4)	16.50	26.25

No. 132, type A26, has a man sitting in the canoe.

Nos. 133-135, type A27, have 180 degree added to the lower right hand corner of the design.

Issued: 2½p, Jan. 6, 1942; others Oct. 1, 1940.

No. 133 Surcharged in Black

1941, Feb. 10 *Perf. 13½*

136	A27	2½p on 2p grn & org brn	1.50	.40
		Never hinged	2.50	

Catalogue values for unused stamps in this section, from this point to the end of the section, are for Never Hinged items.

Peace Issue

Common Design Type

1946, Aug. 17 *Perf. 13½*

137	CD303	2½p bright green	.20	*.60*
138	CD303	3p deep blue	.20	.20

Silver Wedding Issue

Common Design Types

1948, Dec. 17 **Photo.** *Perf. 14x14½*

139	CD304	2½p dark green	.70	1.00

Engr.; Name Typo.

Perf. 11½x11

140	CD305	5sh blue violet	22.50	16.00

UPU Issue

Common Design Types

Engr.; Name Typo. on 3p, 8p

Perf. 13½, 11x11½

1949, Oct. 10 **Wmk. 4**

141	CD306	2p red violet	.65	.50
142	CD307	3p indigo	4.00	2.50
143	CD308	8p dp carmine	.65	*2.50*
144	CD309	1sh6p blue	.70	*1.10*
		Nos. 141-144 (4)	6.00	6.60

SEMI-POSTAL STAMPS

Catalogue values for unused stamps in this section are for Never Hinged items.

Children at Play — SP1

Rugby Player — SP2

Perf. 13x13½

1951, Sept. 17 **Engr.** **Wmk. 4**

B1	SP1	1p + 1p brown	.25	.25
B2	SP2	2p + 1p deep green	.30	.30

POSTAGE DUE STAMPS

D1

D2

D3

1917 **Unwmk.** **Typeset** *Perf. 11*

Laid Papers; Without Gum

J1	D1	½p black	850.00	425.00
J2	D2	½p black	550.00	300.00
J3	D3	1p black	375.00	92.50
J4	D3	2p black	325.00	75.00
J5	D3	3p black	400.00	92.50
J6	D3	4p black	850.00	425.00
		Nos. J1-J6 (6)	3,350.	1,410.

There were two printings of the 1/2p, 1p and 2p values. No. J1 is from the first printing of the 1/2p, and No. J2 is from the second. Examples of the 1/2p, 1p and 2p from the first printing are 25-27mm wide, while copies from the second printing are 23-24mm wide.

D4

D5

Perf. 14

1918, June 1 **Typo.** **Wmk. 3**

J7	D4	½p black	4.25	*20.00*
		On cover		*500.00*
J8	D4	1p black	4.25	*15.00*
		On cover		*150.00*
J9	D4	2p black	5.50	*22.50*
		On cover		*150.00*
J10	D4	3p black	7.00	*27.50*
		On cover		*2,000.*
J11	D4	4p black	8.25	*40.00*
		On cover		*750.00*
		Nos. J7-J11 (5)	29.25	*125.00*

Cover values for Nos. J7-J11 are for properly franked commercial items. Philatelic usages also exist and sell for less.

1940 **Wmk. 4** *Perf. 12½*

J12	D5	1p bright green	4.75	*62.50*
		On cover		*600.00*
J13	D5	2p bright green	8.50	*62.50*
		On cover		*600.00*
J14	D5	3p bright green	11.00	*77.50*
		On cover		*600.00*
J15	D5	4p bright green	12.00	*82.50*
		On cover		*650.00*
J16	D5	5p bright green	15.00	*82.50*
		On cover		*850.00*
J17	D5	6p bright green	8.00	*87.50*
		On cover		*750.00*
J18	D5	1sh dk carmine	20.00	*140.00*
		On cover		*750.00*
J19	D5	1sh6p dk carmine	20.00	*200.00*
		On cover		*750.00*
		Nos. J12-J19 (8)	99.25	*795.00*
		Set, never hinged	140.00	

Virtually all covers with Nos. J12-J19 are overfranked and of philatelic origin. The values above are for such covers.

WAR TAX STAMPS

Regular Issue of 1912-16 Overprinted

Die I

1916 **Wmk. 3** *Perf. 14*

MR1	A23	½p green	.85	*3.00*
a.		Inverted overprint	700.00	
b.		Double overprint		
MR2	A23	1p scarlet	2.00	.75
a.		1p carmine	30.00	26.00
b.		Pair, one without ovpt.	*9,000.*	
c.		Inverted overprint	800.00	

Most examples of #MR2b are within horiz. strips of 12.

FINLAND

'fin-lənd

(Suomi)

LOCATION — Northern Europe bordering on the Gulfs of Bothnia and Finland
GOVT. — Republic
AREA — 130,119 sq. mi.
POP. — 4,869,858 (1984)
CAPITAL — Helsinki

Finland was a Grand Duchy of the Russian Empire from 1809 until December 1917, when it declared its independence.

100 Kopecks = 1 Ruble
100 Pennia = 1 Markka (1866)

Catalogue values for unused stamps in this country are for Never Hinged items, beginning with Scott B39 in the semi-postal section.

Unused stamps are valued with original gum as defined in the catalogue introduction except for Nos. 1-3B which are valued without gum. Used values for Nos. 1-3B are for pen-canceled copies.

Very fine examples of the serpentine rouletted issues, Nos. 4-13c, will have roulettes cutting the design slightly on one or more sides and will have all "teeth" complete and intact. Stamps with roulettes clear of the design on all four sides are extremely scarce and sell for substantial premiums.

Watermarks

Wmk. 121 — Multiple Swastika

Wmk. 208 — Post Horn

Wmk. 168 — Wavy Lines and Letters

Issues under Russian Empire

Coat of Arms — A1

1856-58 Unwmk. Typo. *Imperf.*
Small Pearls in Post Horns
Wove Paper

1 A1 5k blue *6,000.* 1,400.
On cover, pen cancellation 5,250.
Pen and town cancellation 1,750.
On cover 7,250.
Town cancellation 2,750.
On cover 8,250.
a. Tête bêche pair *62,500.* *57,500.*
Pen and town cancellation *62,500.*
Town cancellation —
2 A1 10k rose 7,750. 360.
On cover, pen cancellation 875.
Pen and town cancellation 525.
On cover 1,650.
Town cancellation 850.
On cover 2,600.
a. Tête bêche pair *62,500.* *52,500.*
Pen and town cancellation *57,500.*
Town cancellation *62,500.*
e. 10k carmine 7,750. 400.
Pen and town cancellation 575.
Town cancellation 775.
f. 10k dark carmine 8,250. 450.
Pen and town cancellation 625.
Town cancellation 825.
g. 10k lilac red — 625.
Pen and town cancellation 1,050.
Town cancellation 1,600.

Cut to shape

1 A1 5k blue 125.
On cover, pen cancellation 1,050.
Pen and town cancellation 160.
On cover 1,575.
Town cancellation 200.
On cover 1,850.
2 A1 10k rose 42.50
On cover, pen cancellation 425.
Pen and town cancellation 67.50
On cover 525.
Town cancellation 77.50
On cover 625.

Wide Vertically Laid Paper

2C A1 10k rose ('58) — 1,250.
Pen and town cancellation 1,650.
Town cancellation 2,100.
d. Tête bêche pair —

Cut to shape

2C A1 10k rose 190.
Pen and town cancellation 250.
Town cancellation 325.

Full margins = 1 ½mm.

The wide vertically laid paper has 13-14 distinct lines per 2 centimeters. The 10k rose also exists on a narrow laid paper with lines sometimes indistinct. Value, 45 per cent of that for a wide laid paper example.

A 5k blue with small pearls exists on narrow vertically laid paper. It is rare.

Stamps on diagonally laid paper are envelope cut squares.

Large Pearls in Post Horns

1858 Wove Paper

3 A1 5k blue *7,750.* 1,250.
On cover, pen cancellation 3,600.
Pen and town cancellation 1,450.
On cover 6,750.
Town cancellation 2,250.
On cover 7,750.
a. Tête bêche pair *46,000.*
Pen and town cancellation *51,500.*

Cut to shape

3 A1 5k blue 95.00
On cover, pen cancellation 925.00
Pen and town cancellation 125.00
On cover 1,600.
Town cancellation 160.00
On cover 1,750.

Full margins = 1 ½mm.

1859 Wide Vertically Laid Paper

3B A1 5k blue — *15,500.*
Pen and town cancellation *21,000.*

Cut to shape

3B A1 5k blue 2,400.
Pen and town cancellation *3,200.*

Reprints of Nos. 2 and 3, made in 1862, are on brownish paper, on vertically laid paper, and in tête bêche pairs on normal and vertically laid paper. Reprints of 1871, 1881 and 1893 are on yellowish or white paper. Value for least costly of each, $85.

In 1956, Nos. 2 and 3 were reprinted for the Centenary with post horn watermark and gum. Value, $85 each.

Coat of Arms — A2

1860 *Serpentine Roulette 7½, 8*

Four types of indentation are noted:

I — Depth 1-1 ¼mm

II — Depth 1 ½-1 ¾mm

III — Depth 2-2 ¼mm

IV — Shovel-shaped teeth. Depth 1 ¼-1 ½mm

Wove Paper

4 A2 5k blue, *bluish*, I 625.00 160.00
On cover 1,050.
a. Roulette II 750.00 210.00
On cover 1,450.
b. Perf. vert.
5 A2 10k rose, *pale rose*, I 525.00 52.50
On cover 225.00
a. Roulette II 1,050. 150.00
On cover 775.00

A3

A4

1866-74 *Serpentine Roulette*

6 A3 5p pur brn, *lil*, I ('73) 350.00 160.00
On cover 1,250.
a. Roulette II 3,750.
On cover —
b. 5p red brn, *lil*, III ('71) 300.00 160.00
On cover 1,300.
7 A3 8p blk, *grn*, III ('67) 250.00 160.00
On cover *2,750.*
a. Ribbed paper, III ('72) 1,050. 825.00
On cover —
b. Roulette II ('74) 325.00 250.00
On cover *2,750.*
c. As "b," ribbed paper ('74) 310.00 210.00
On cover 2,100.
d. Roulette I ('73) 475.00 300.00
On cover *2,600.*
e. As "d," ribbed paper 1,050. 425.00
On cover —
f. Serpentine roulette 10 ½ ('67) *12,500.*
On cover —
8 A3 10p blk, *yel*, III ('70) 625.00 325.00
On cover 1,750.
a. 10p blk, *buff*, II 725.00 400.00
On cover 2,050.
b. 10p blk, *buff*, I ('73) 675.00 340.00
On cover 2,100.
9 A3 20p bl, *bl*, III 525.00 52.50
On cover 165.00
a. Roulette II 525.00 82.50
On cover 265.00
b. Roulette I ('73) 625.00 110.00
On cover 210.00
c. Roulette IV ('74) — *1,050.*
On cover —
d. Perf. horiz. —
e. Printed on both sides (40p blue on back) —
10 A3 40p rose, *lil rose*, III 460.00 62.50
On cover 250.00
a. Ribbed paper, III ('73) 625.00 190.00
On cover 525.00
b. Roulette II 475.00 77.50
On cover 240.00
c. As "b," ribbed paper ('73) 625.00 160.00
On cover 425.00
d. Roulette I 675.00 160.00
On cover 475.00
e. As "d," ribbed paper 625.00 110.00
On cover 375.00
f. Roulette IV — *2,100.*
g. As "f," ribbed paper — —
h. Serpentine roulette 10 ½ —
11 A4 1m yel brn, III ('67) 2,100. 800.00
On cover *13,500.*
a. Roulette II 2,600. 1,550.
On cover —

Nos. 7f and 10h are private roulettes and are also known in compound serpentine roulette 10 ½ and 7 ½.

Nos. 4-11 were reprinted in 1893 on thick wove paper. Colors differ from originals. Roulette type IV. Value for Nos. 4-5, each $40, Nos. 6-10, each $50. Value for No. 11, $55.

Thin or Thick Laid Paper

12 A3 5p red brn, *lil*, III 260.00 140.00
On cover 850.00
a. Roulette II 275.00 275.00
On cover *1,250.*
b. Roulette I 260.00 275.00
On cover 1,250.
d. 5p blk, *buff*, roul. III (error) *20,000.*
e. Tête bêche pair —
13 A3 10p black, *buff*, III 625.00 260.00
On cover 1,750.
a. 10p black, *yel*, II 775.00 260.00
On cover 1,750.
b. 10p black, *yel*, I 1,050. 675.00
On cover 2,600.
c. 10p red brown, *lil*, III (error) *7,250.* *6,500.*
On cover —

Forgeries of No. 13c exist.

Cover values for Nos. 6-13 are for covers bearing stamps with full teeth.

Nos. 6-13 with Short Teeth

Values below are for used stamps with one or two short roulettes. Stamps with teeth entirely missing or with several short roulettes are worth much less.

6	50.00
6a	*1,850.*
6b	40.00
7	40.00
7a	250.00
7b	75.00
7c	40.00
7d	80.00
7e	160.00
7f	*12,000.*
8	75.00
8a	100.00
8b	100.00
9	15.00
9a	27.50
9b	35.00
9c	450.00
10	17.50
10a	95.00
10b	17.50
10c	75.00
10d	40.00
10e	40.00
10f	*875.00*
10g	1,250.
11	200.00
11a	500.00
12	40.00
12a	60.00
12b	60.00
12d	*13,250.*
13	70.00
13a	75.00
13b	140.00
13c	*3,000.*

A5

A6

1875 *Perf. 14x13½*

16 A5 32p lake 2,050. 425.00
On cover 13,500.

1875-81 *Perf. 11*

17 A5 2p gray 45.00 52.50
Never hinged 92.50
On cover 725.00
On cover, single franking 525.00
On postal stationery 575.00
18 A5 5p orange 125.00 11.00
Never hinged 275.00
On cover 150.00
On cover, single franking 175.00
a. 5p yellow 125.00 11.00
Never hinged 275.00
On cover 150.00
On cover, single franking 175.00
19 A5 8p blue green 200.00 52.50
Never hinged 400.00
On cover 3,600.
On newsprint, single franking 6,250.
a. 8p yellow green 200.00 77.50
Never hinged 400.00
On cover 3,600.
On newsprint, single franking 6,250.
20 A5 10p brown ('81) 525.00 55.00
On cover 1,850.
On cover, single franking 3,250.

21 A5 20p ultra 140.00 3.00
Never hinged 260.00
On cover 37.50
a. 20p blue 150.00 5.25
Never hinged 260.00
On cover 42.50
b. 20p Prussian blue 310.00 35.00
On cover 310.00
c. Tête bêche pair 3,100.
22 A5 25p carmine ('79) 260.00 13.50
Never hinged 525.00
On cover 260.00
a. 25p rose 360.00 52.50
On cover 525.00
23 A5 32p carmine 410.00 57.50
On cover 525.00
a. 32p rose 500.00 160.00
Never hinged 675.00
On cover —
24 A5 1m violet ('77) 725.00 160.00
On cover *11,500.*
Nos. 17-24 (8) 2,430. 405.00

A souvenir card issued in 1974 for NORDIA 1975 reproduced a block of four of the unissued "1 MARKKAA" design.

Nos. 19, 23 were reprinted in 1893, perf. 12½. Value $17.50 each.

1881-83 ***Perf. 12½***

25 A5 2p gray 11.00 12.50
Never hinged 21.00
On cover 375.00
a. Imperf., pair 500.00
26 A5 5p orange 47.50 6.00
Never hinged 82.50
On cover 130.00
a. Tête bêche pair 6,250. 4,100.
b. Imperf. vert., pair —
c. Imperf. horiz., pair —
27 A5 10p brown 90.00 17.00
Never hinged 150.00
On cover *1,350.*
On cover, single franking 2,600.
28 A5 20p ultra 50.00 1.50
Never hinged 82.50
On cover 26.00
a. 20p blue 50.00 1.50
Never hinged 82.50
On cover 26.50
b. Tête bêche pair 2,600. 2,100.
c. Imperf., pair 65.00
29 A5 25p rose 40.00 9.25
Never hinged 70.00
On cover 260.00
a. 25p carmine 57.50 16.00
Never hinged 87.50
On cover 260.00
b. Tête bêche pair — —
30 A5 1m violet ('82) 360.00 40.00
Never hinged 525.00
On cover *9,500.*
Nos. 25-30 (6) 598.50 86.25

Nos. 27-29 were reprinted in 1893 in deeper shades, perf. 12½. Value $35 each.

Most copies of No. 28c are from printer's waste.

1881 ***Perf. 11x12½***

26d A5 5p orange 410.00 82.50
On cover *1,500.*
27a A5 10p brown 850.00 225.00
On cover *5,250.*
28d A5 20p ultra 525.00 40.00
On cover *1,500.*
28e A5 20p blue 525.00 40.00
On cover *1,500.*
29c A5 25p rose 625.00 160.00
On cover —
29d A5 25p carmine 525.00 110.00
On cover —
30a A5 1m violet 1,350.
On cover —

1881 ***Perf. 12½x11***

26e A5 5p orange 410.00 82.50
On cover *1,500.*
27b A5 10p brown — 300.00
On cover *5,250.*
28f A5 20p ultra 525.00 40.00
On cover *1,500.*
28g A5 20p blue 525.00 40.00
On cover *1,500.*
29e A5 25p rose — 260.00
On cover —
29f A5 25p carmine 525.00 100.00
On cover —

1885 ***Perf. 12½***

31 A5 5p emerald 16.00 .55
Never hinged 32.00
On cover 21.00
a. 5p yellow green 18.00 1.00
Never hinged 35.00
On cover 24.00
b. Tête bêche pair — *8,250.*
32 A5 10p carmine 24.00 2.50
Never hinged 40.00
On cover 67.50
a. 10p rose 24.00 2.50
Never hinged 40.00
On cover 67.50
33 A5 20p orange 30.00 .45
Never hinged 52.50
On cover 11.00
a. 20p yellow 35.00 1.60
Never hinged 52.50
On cover 16.00
b. Tête bêche pair — 3,250.
34 A5 25p ultra 57.50 3.25
Never hinged 77.50
On cover 77.50
a. 25p blue 52.50 2.75
Never hinged 77.50
On cover 77.50
35 A5 1m gray & rose 30.00 18.00
Never hinged 47.50
On cover *3,250.*
36 A5 5m green & rose 400.00 300.00
Never hinged 925.00
On cover —
37 A5 10m brown & rose 500.00 500.00
Never hinged 1,050.
On cover —

1889-92 ***Perf. 12½***

38 A6 2p slate ('90) .50 *.75*
Never hinged .85
On cover 55.00
39 A6 5p green ('90) 27.50 .20
Never hinged 57.50
On cover 7.50
40 A6 10p carmine ('90) 52.50 .50
Never hinged 100.00
On cover 8.50
a. 10p rose ('90) 67.50 .50
Never hinged 115.00
On cover 15.00
b. Imperf. 90.00 90.00
Never hinged 125.00
41 A6 20p orange ('92) 62.50 .30
Never hinged 100.00
On cover 9.25
a. 20p yellow ('90) 67.50 1.00
Never hinged 100.00
On cover 6.00
42 A6 25p ultra ('91) 62.50 .75
Never hinged 115.00
On cover 21.00
a. 25p blue 67.50 1.00
Never hinged 125.00
On cover 24.00
43 A6 1m slate & rose ('92) 4.00 3.25
Never hinged 6.50
On cover 110.00
a. 1m brnsh gray & rose ('90) 22.50 3.50
Never hinged 32.50
On cover 110.00
44 A6 5m green & rose ('90) 22.50 *62.50*
Never hinged 35.00
On cover *9,250.*
45 A6 10m brown & rose ('90) 32.50 *82.50*
Never hinged 52.50
On cover *5,250.*
Nos. 38-45 (8) 264.50 *150.75*

The 2p slate, perf. 14x13, is believed to be an essay.

See Nos. 60-63.

See Russia for types similar to A7-A18.

Finnish stamps have "dot in circle" devices or are inscribed "Markka," "Markkaa," "Pen." or "Pennia."

Imperial Arms of Russia

A7 A8 A9

A10 A11

Laid Paper

1891-92 **Wmk. 168** ***Perf. 14½x15***

46 A7 1k orange yel 4.50 *9.50*
Never hinged 5.25
On cover 140.00
47 A7 2k green 5.50 *8.00*
Never hinged 8.25
On cover 75.00
48 A7 3k carmine 10.50 *14.50*
Never hinged 13.00
On cover 75.00
49 A8 4k rose 12.50 12.50
Never hinged 17.00
On cover 55.00
50 A7 7k dark blue 5.50 2.25
Never hinged 11.25
On cover 26.50
51 A8 10k dark blue 12.50 *13.50*
Never hinged 26.00
On cover 105.00
52 A9 14k blue & rose 18.00 *24.00*
Never hinged 32.50
On cover 475.00
53 A8 20k blue & car 16.00 15.00
Never hinged 22.50
On cover 300.00
54 A9 35k violet & grn 22.50 *47.50*
Never hinged 32.50
On cover 1,500.
55 A8 50k violet & grn 27.50 30.00
Never hinged 52.50
On cover 1,300.

Perf. 13½

56 A10 1r brown & org 77.50 77.50
Never hinged 140.00
On cover 1,800.
57 A11 3½r black & gray 275.00 *400.00*
Never hinged 425.00
On cover 9,250.
a. 3½r black & yellow (error) *11,500.* *14,000.*
58 A11 7r black & yellow 200.00 *260.00*
Never hinged 340.00
On cover 9,500.
Nos. 46-58 (13) 687.50 *914.25*

Forgeries of Nos. 57, 57a, 58 exist.

Type of 1889-90

Wove Paper

1895-96 **Unwmk.** ***Perf. 14x13***

60 A6 5p green .50 .35
Never hinged 1.00
On cover 3.75
61 A6 10p rose .60 .45
Never hinged 1.25
On cover 3.75
62 A6 20p orange .50 .20
Never hinged 1.25
On cover 3.75
a. Imperf. 125.00 —
Never hinged 165.00
63 A6 25p ultra .80 .60
Never hinged 1.50
On cover 6.00
a. 25p blue 1.60 .65
Never hinged 3.00
On cover 6.50
b. Imperf. 100.00 —
Never hinged 125.00
Nos. 60-63 (4) 2.40 1.60

A12 A13

A14 A15

1901 **Litho.** ***Perf. 14½x15***

Chalky Paper

64 A12 2p yellow 4.00 4.00
Never hinged 6.25
On cover 12.50
65 A12 5p green 8.00 .65
Never hinged 15.00
On cover 3.75
66 A13 10p carmine 22.50 1.00
Never hinged 35.00
On cover 2.75
67 A12 20p dark blue 52.50 .55
Never hinged 1.00 82.50
On cover 2.75
68 A14 1m violet & grn 260.00 8.00
Never hinged 460.00
On cover 52.50

Perf. 13½

69 A15 10m black & gray 250.00 250.00
Never hinged 525.00
On cover 1,500.
Nos. 64-69 (6) 597.00 264.20

Imperf sheets of 10p and 20p, stolen during production, were privately perforated 11½ to defraud the P.O. Uncanceled imperfs. of Nos. 65-68 are believed to be proofs.

See Nos. 70-75, 82.

Types of 1901 Redrawn

No. 64 No. 70

2p. On No. 64, the "2" below "II" is shifted slightly leftward. On No. 70, the "2" is centered below "II."

No. 65 No. 71

5p. On No. 65, the frame lines are very close. On No. 71, a clear white space separates them.

Nos. 66, 67 Nos. 72, 73

10p, 20p. On Nos. 66-67, the horizontal central background lines are faint and broken. On Nos. 72-73, they are clear and solid, though still thin.

20p. On No. 67, "H" close to "2" with period midway. On No. 73 they are slightly separated with period close to "H."

No. 68 Nos. 74, 74a

1m. On No. 68, the "1" following "MARKKA" lacks serif at base. On Nos. 74-74a, this "1" has serif.

No. 69 No. 75

10m. On No. 69, the serifs of "M" and "A" in top and bottom panels do not touch. On No. 75, the serifs join.

Perf. 14¼x14¾, 14¼x14

1901-14 **Typo.**

Ordinary Paper

70 A12 2p orange .50 .70
Never hinged .60
On cover 6.00
71 A12 5p green 1.60 .20
Never hinged 3.00
On cover 2.00
a. Perf 14¼x14 ('06) 1.40 .40
Never hinged 2.50
On cover 3.00
72 A13 10p carmine 8.25 .20
Never hinged 18.00
On cover 2.00
a. Perf 14¼x14 ('07) 45.00 .20
Never hinged 92.50
On cover 2.00
b. Background inverted, perf 14¼x14¾ 13.50 2.00
Never hinged 26.00
c. Background inverted, perf 14¼x14 52.50 2.00
Never hinged 100.00
73 A12 20p dark blue 4.00 .20
Never hinged 10.00
On cover 2.00
a. Perf 14¼x14 ('06) 47.50 .65
Never hinged 80.00
On cover 3.00
74 A14 1m lil & grn, perf. 14¼x14 ('14) .75 .40
Never hinged 1.00
On cover 10.00
a. 1m violet & blue green, perf. 14¼x14¾ ('02) 8.00 .90
Never hinged 13.50
On cover 10.00
Nos. 70-74 (5) 15.10 1.70

Perf. 13½

75 A15 10m blk & drab ('03) 125.00 42.50
Never hinged 225.00
On cover 625.00

Imperf.

70a A12 2p 290.00 *410.00*
Never hinged 360.00
71b A12 5p 77.50 *160.00*
Never hinged 87.50
72a A13 10p 90.00 *160.00*
Never hinged 90.00
73a A12 20p 160.00 *160.00*
Never hinged 190.00
74b A14 1m 150.00 *160.00*
Never hinged 160.00

A16 A17 A18

1911-16 ***Perf. 14, 14¼x14¾***

77 A16 2p orange .20 .20
Never hinged .20
On cover 4.00
78 A16 5p green .25 .20
Never hinged .30
On cover 1.00
a. Imperf. 410.00
Never hinged 500.00
b. Perf. 14¼x14¾ 360.00 62.50
Never hinged 525.00
On cover *325.00*
79 A17 10p rose ('15) .20 .20
Never hinged .20
On cover 1.00
a. Imperf. 77.50 160.00
Never hinged 92.50

On cover 425.00
b. Perf. 14¼x14¾ ('16) 1.75 2.75
Never hinged 4.50
On cover 6.50
80 A16 20p deep blue .20 .20
Never hinged .30
On cover 2.00
a. Imperf. 150.00 1.10
Never hinged —
On cover 175.00
b. Perf. 14¼x14¾ 8.00 1.60
Never hinged 18.00
On cover 2.50
81 A18 40p violet & blue .20 .20
Never hinged .20
On cover 3.00
a. Perf. 14¼x14¾ 3,100. 3,100.
Nos. 77-81 (5) 1.05 1.00

There are three minor types of No. 79. Values are for the least expensive type.

Perf. 14½

82 A15 10m blk & grnsh gray ('16) 110.00 160.00
Never hinged 160.00
On cover 925.00
a. Horiz. pair, imperf. vert. 2,900.

Republic
Helsinki Issue

Arms of the Republic
A19 A20

Two types of the 40p.
Type I — Thin figures of value.
Type II — Thick figures of value.

Perf. 14, 14¼x14¾

1917-29 **Unwmk.**
83 A19 5p green .20 .20
84 A19 5p gray ('19) .20 .20
85 A19 10p rose .25 .20
a. Imperf., pair 200.00 250.00
86 A19 10p green ('19) 2.00 .40
a. Perf. 14¼x14¾ 1,800.
87 A19 10p lt blue ('21) .25 .20
88 A19 20p buff .25 .20
89 A19 20p rose ('20) .50 .20
90 A19 20p brown ('24) .50 .40
a. Perf. 14¼x14¾ .45 140.00
91 A19 25p blue .20 .20
92 A19 25p lt brown ('19) .20 .20
93 A19 30p green ('23) .25 .20
94 A19 40p violet (I) .20 .20
a. Perf. 14¼x14¾ 225.00 13.00
95 A19 40p bl grn (II) ('29) .20 .50
a. Type I ('24) 8.00 2.50
b. Perf. 14¼x14¾ .75 11.00
96 A19 50p orange brn .20 .20
97 A19 50p dp blue ('19) 2.50 .20
a. Perf. 14¼x14¾ 1,000.
98 A19 50p green ('21) 3.00 .20
a. Perf. 14¼x14¾ .30 2.50
99 A19 60p red vio ('21) .30 .20
a. Imperf., pair 75.00 100.00
100 A19 75p yellow ('21) .20 .30
101 A19 1m dull rose & blk 9.00 .20
102 A19 1m red org ('25) 4.50 12.50
103 A19 1½m bl grn & red vio ('29) .20 .20
a. Perf. 14¼x14¾ .20 .30
104 A19 2m green & blk ('21) 2.25 .50
105 A19 2m dk blue & ind ('22) 1.50 .20
a. Perf. 14¼x14¾ .50 1.00
106 A19 3m blue & blk ('21) 60.00 .20
107 A19 5m red vio & blk 14.00 .20
108 A19 10m brn & gray blk, perf. 14 .60 1.00
a. 10m light brown & black, perf. 14¼x14¾ ('29) 2.50 300.00
110 A19 25m dull red & yel ('21) .75 18.00
Nos. 83-108,110 (27) 104.20 37.40

Copies of a 2½p gray of this type exist. They are proofs from the original die which were distributed through the UPU. No plate was made for this denomination.

See Nos. 127-140, 143-152. For surcharge and overprints see Nos. 119-126, 153-154.

Vasa Issue

1918 **Litho.** ***Perf. 11½***
111 A20 5p green .20 .60
112 A20 10p red .20 .40
113 A20 30p slate .20 .95
114 A20 40p brown vio .20 .75
115 A20 50p orange brn .20 .95
116 A20 70p gray brown 1.50 10.00
117 A20 1m red & gray .30 .95
118 A20 5m red violet & gray 30.00 50.00
Nos. 111-118 (8) 32.80 64.60

Nos. 111-118 exist imperforate but were not regularly issued in that condition.

Sheet margin copies, perf. on 3 sides, imperf. on margin side, were sold by post office.

Stamps and Type of 1917-29 Surcharged

1919 ***Perf. 14***
119 A19 10p on 5p green .30 .35
120 A19 20p on 10p rose .30 .35
121 A19 50p on 25p blue .60 .35
122 A19 75p on 20p orange .30 .30
Nos. 119-122 (4) 1.50 1.35

Stamps and Type of 1917-29 Surcharged:

Nos. 123-125

No. 126

1921
123 A19 30p on 10p green .55 .35
124 A19 60p on 40p red violet 2.50 .75
125 A19 90p on 20p rose .35 .20
126 A19 1½m on 50p blue 1.25 .35
a. Thin "2" in "½" 9.00 4.75
b. Imperf., pair 225.00 300.00
Nos. 123-126 (4) 4.65 1.65

Arms Type of 1917-29
Perf. 14, 14¼x14¾

1925-29 **Wmk. 121**
127 A19 10p ultra ('27) .45 .75
128 A19 20p brown .45 .65
129 A19 25p brn org ('29) .65 40.00
130 A19 30p yel green .20 .20
a. Perf. 14¼x14¾ .20
131 A19 40p blue grn (I) ('26) 1.50 .35
a. Perf. 14¼x14¾ ('26) 2.75 .45
b. Type II ('28) 2.25 .35
c. As "b," perf. 14¼x14¾ ('28) 2.75 .45
132 A19 50p gray grn ('26) .35 .35
a. Perf. 14¼x14¾ ('26) .30 .35
133 A19 60p red violet .20 .20
134 A19 1m dp orange 3.25 .20
a. Perf. 14¼x14¾ 72.50 .45

Perf. 14¼x14¾

135 A19 1½m blue green & red violet, perf. 14¼x14¾ ('26) 3.50 .20
a. Perf. 14 ('26) 35.00 .20
136 A19 2m dk blue & indigo .30 .20
a. Perf. 14¼x14¾ .30 .30
137 A19 3m chlky blue & blk ('26) .90 .20
138 A19 5m red violet & blk .25 .20
139 A19 10m lt brn & blk ('27) 3.00 12.00
140 A19 25m dp org & yel ('27) 17.50 200.00
Nos. 127-140 (14) 32.50 255.50

No. 130a is not known cancelled during the period in which it was valid for postal use.

A21

Wmk. 208

1927, Dec. 6 **Typo.** ***Perf. 14***
141 A21 1½m deep violet .20 .30
142 A21 2m deep blue .25 1.00

10th anniv. of Finnish independence.

Arms Type of 1917-29
Perf. 14, 14¼x14¾

1927-29 **Wmk. 208**
143 A19 20p lt brown ('29) 1.00 8.50
144 A19 40p bl grn (II) ('28) .20 .20
145 A19 50p gray grn ('28) .20 .20
146 A19 1m dp orange .20 .20
a. Imperf., pair 125.00 140.00
b. Perf. 14 1.00 1.00
147 A19 1½m bl grn & red vio ('28) 1.50 .20
a. Perf. 14 700.00 9.00
148 A19 2m dk bl & ind ('28) .35 .30
149 A19 3m chlky bl & blk .35 .30
a. Perf. 14 1.50 1.50
150 A19 5m red vio & blk ('28) .60 .60
151 A19 10m lt brown & blk 1.00 29.00
152 A19 25m brown org & yel 1.10 110.00
Nos. 143-152 (10) 6.50 149.50

Nos. 146-147 Overprinted

1928, Nov. 10 **Litho.** **Wmk. 208**
153 A19 1m deep orange 6.50 12.50
154 A19 1½m bl grn & red vio 6.50 12.50

Nos. 153 and 154 were sold exclusively at the Helsinki Philatelic Exhibition, Nov. 10-18, 1928, and were valid only during that period.

S. S. "Bore" Leaving Turku — A23

Turku Cathedral — A24

Turku Castle — A25

Wmk. 208

1929, May 22 **Typo.** ***Perf. 14***
155 A23 1m olive green 1.40 2.75
156 A24 1½m chocolate 2.25 2.75
157 A25 2m dark gray .85 3.00
Nos. 155-157 (3) 4.50 8.50

Founding of the city of Turku (Abo), 700th anniv.

A26

1930-46 **Unwmk.** ***Perf. 14***
158 A26 5p chocolate .20 .20
159 A26 10p dull violet .20 .20
160 A26 20p yel grn .30 .35
161 A26 25p yel brn .20 .20
162 A26 40p blue grn 1.75 .35
163 A26 50p yellow .45 .35
164 A26 50p blue grn ('32) .20 .20
b. Imperf., pair 125.00 125.00
165 A26 60p dark gray .35 .45
165A A26 75p dp org ('42) .20 .20
166 A26 1m red org .45 .20
166B A26 1m yel grn ('42) .20 .20
167 A26 1.20m crimson .35 .50
168 A26 1.25m yel ('32) .20 .20
169 A26 1½m red vio 2.00 .20
170 A26 1½m car ('32) .20 .20
170A A26 1½m sl ('40) .20 .20
170B A26 1.75m org yel ('40) .55 .20
171 A26 2m indigo .30 .20
172 A26 2m dp vio ('32) 6.00 .20
173 A26 2m car ('36) .20 .20
Complete booklet, panes of 4 #161, 164, 166, 168, 173 5.00
173B A26 2m yel org ('42) .30 .20
173C A26 2m blue grn ('45) .20 .20
174 A26 2½m brt blue ('32) 2.00 .20
174A A26 2½m car ('42) .20 .20
174B A26 2.75m rose vio ('40) .20 .20
175 A26 3m olive blk 22.50 .20
175B A26 3m car ('45) .20 .20
175C A26 3m yel ('45) .35 .45
176 A26 3½m brt bl ('36) 5.50 .20
176A A26 3½m olive ('42) .20 .20
176B A26 4m olive ('45) .35 .20
176C A26 4½m saph ('42) .20 .20
176D A26 5m saph ('45) .35 .20
176E A26 5m pur ('45) .35 .20
j. Imperf., pair 125.00 125.00
176F A26 5m yel ('46) .70 .20
k. Imperf., pair 110.00 125.00
176G A26 6m car ('45) .35 .20
m. Imperf., pair 125.00 125.00
176H A26 8m pur ('46) .20 .20
176I A26 10m saph ('45) .70 .20
Nos. 158-176I (38) 49.35 8.85

See Nos. 257-262, 270-274, 291-296, 302-304. For surcharges and overprints see Nos. 195-196, 212, 221-222, 243, 250, 275, M2-M3.

Stamps of types A26-A29 overprinted "ITA KARJALA" are listed under Karelia, Nos. N1-N15.

Castle in Savonlinna A27

Lake Saima — A28

Woodchopper A29

1930 **Engr.**
177 A27 5m blue .20 .20
178 A28 10m gray lilac 50.00 2.50
179 A29 25m black brown .95 .20
Nos. 177-179 (3) 51.15 2.90

See #205, 305. For overprint see #C1.

Elias Lönnrot — A30

Seal of Finnish Literary Society — A31

1931, Jan. 1 **Typo.**
180 A30 1m olive brown 2.75 3.50
181 A31 1½m dull blue 14.00 3.50

Centenary of Finnish Literary Society.

A32

1931, Feb. 28

182	A32 1½m red	2.75	*6.00*
183	A32 2m blue	2.75	*7.00*

1st use of postage stamps in Finland, 75th anniv.

Nos. 162-163 Surcharged

1931, Dec.

195	A26 50p on 40p blue grn	1.40	.60
196	A26 1.25m on 50p yellow	4.00	1.50

Svinhufvud A33

Alexis Kivi A34

1931, Dec. 15

197	A33 2m gray blue & blk	1.50	*2.00*

Pres. Pehr Eyvind Svinhufvud, 70th birthday.

Lake Saima Type of 1930

1932-43 **Re-engraved**

205	A28 10m red violet ('43)	.35	.20
a.	10m dark violet	17.50	.50

On Nos. 205 and 205a the lines of the islands, the clouds and the foliage are much deeper and stronger than on No. 178.

1934, Oct. 10 **Typo.**

206	A34 2m red violet	2.25	2.25
	Never hinged	3.25	

Alexis Kivi, Finnish poet (1834-1872).

Bards Reciting the "Kalevala" A35

Goddess Louhi, As Eagle Seizing Magic Mill — A36

Kullervo — A37

1935, Feb. 28 **Engr.**

207	A35 1¼m brown lake	1.25	1.25
208	A36 2m black	3.00	.70
209	A37 2½m blue	3.00	1.75
	Nos. 207-209 (3)	7.25	3.70
	Set, never hinged	12.00	

Cent. of the publication of the "Kalevala" (Finnish National Epic).

No. 170 Surcharged in Black

1937, Feb.

212	A26 2m on 1½m car	3.25	.90
	Never hinged	7.00	

Gustaf Mannerheim — A38

Swede-Finn Co-operation in Colonization A39

1937, June 4 **Photo.** ***Perf. 14***

213	A38 2m ultra	.50	*.75*
	Never hinged	1.50	

70th birthday of Field Marshal Baron Carl Gustaf Mannerheim, June 4th, 1937.

1938, June 1

214	A39 3½m dark brown	1.25	*3.00*
	Never hinged	2.50	

Tercentenary of the colonization of Delaware by Swedes and Finns.

Early Post Office — A40

Designs: 1¼m, Mail delivery in 1700. 2m, Modern mail plane. 3½m, Helsinki post office.

1938, Sept. 6 **Photo.** ***Perf. 14***

215	A40 50p green	.35	.75
216	A40 1¼m dk blue	1.25	*2.25*
217	A40 2m scarlet	1.25	.90
218	A40 3½m slate black	3.50	*5.50*
	Nos. 215-218 (4)	6.35	9.40
	Set, never hinged	10.00	

300th anniv. of the Finnish Postal System.

Margin strips of each denomination (3 of #215, 2 each of #216, 217, 218) were pasted on to advertising sheets and stapled into a booklet. Value, $100.

Post Office, Helsinki — A44

1939-42 **Photo.**

219	A44 4m brown black	.20	.20

Engr.

219A	A44 7m black brn ('42)	.30	.20
219B	A44 9m rose lake ('42)	.30	.20
	Nos. 219-219B (3)	.80	.60
	Set, never hinged	2.25	

See No. 248.

University of Helsinki — A45

1940, May 1 **Photo.**

220	A45 2m dp blue & blue	.50	*.90*

300th anniv. of the founding of the University of Helsinki.

Nos. 168 and 173 Surcharged in Black

1940, June 16 **Typo.**

221	A26 1.75m on 1.25m yel	1.50	1.50
222	A26 2.75m on 2m carmine	4.50	.60

SEMI-POSTAL STAMPS

Arms — SP1

Unwmk.

1922, May 15 **Typo.** ***Perf. 14***

B1	SP1 1m + 50p gray & red	.75	*7.00*
	Never hinged	1.40	
a.	Perf. 13x13½	6.50	
	Never hinged	10.50	

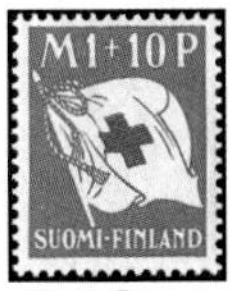

Red Cross Standard SP2

Symbolic SP3

Ship of Mercy — SP4

1930, Feb. 6

B2	SP2 1m + 10p red org & red	1.50	*7.50*
B3	SP3 1½m + 15p grysh grn & red	1.25	*7.50*
B4	SP4 2m + 20p dk bl & red	3.50	*35.00*
	Nos. B2-B4 (3)	6.25	*50.00*
	Set, never hinged	9.00	

The surtax on this and subsequent similar issues was for the benefit of the Red Cross Society of Finland.

Church in Hattula — SP5

SP8

Designs: 1½m+15p, Castle of Hameenlinna. 2m+20p, Fortress of Viipuri.

1931, Jan. 1 **Engr.**

Cross in Red

B5	SP5 1m + 10p gray grn	1.25	*9.00*
B6	SP5 1½m + 15p lil brn	6.50	11.00
B7	SP5 2m + 20p dull bl	1.10	*21.00*
	Nos. B5-B7 (3)	8.85	*41.00*
	Set, never hinged	22.50	

1931, Oct. 15 **Typo.** ***Rouletted 4, 5***

B8	SP8 1m + 4m black	15.00	*30.00*
	Never hinged	22.50	

The surtax was to assist the Postal Museum of Finland in purchasing the Richard Granberg collection of entire envelopes.

Helsinki University Library SP9

Nikolai Church at Helsinki SP10

2½m+25p, Parliament Building, Helsinki.

1932, Jan. 1 ***Perf. 14***

B9	SP9 1¼m + 10p ol bis & red	1.40	*9.25*
B10	SP10 2m + 20p dp vio & red	.70	*4.50*
B11	SP9 2½m + 25p lt blue & red	1.00	*15.00*
	Nos. B9-B11 (3)	3.10	*28.75*
	Set, never hinged	6.00	

Bishop Magnus Tawast SP12

Michael Agricola SP13

Design: 2½m+25p, Isacus Rothovius.

1933, Jan. 20 **Engr.**

B12	SP12 1¼m + 10p blk brn & red	2.50	*7.00*
B13	SP13 2m + 20p brn vio & red	.55	*3.00*
B14	SP13 2½m + 25p indigo & red	.75	*4.50*
	Nos. B12-B14 (3)	3.80	*14.50*
	Set, never hinged	7.50	

Evert Horn — SP15

Designs: 2m+20p, Torsten Stalhandske. 2½m+25p, Jakob (Lazy Jake) de la Gardie.

1934, Jan.

Cross in Red

B15	SP15 1¼m + 10p brown	.80	*2.25*
B16	SP15 2m + 20p gray lil	1.40	*4.00*
B17	SP15 2½m + 25p gray	.80	*2.75*
	Nos. B15-B17 (3)	3.00	*9.00*
	Set, never hinged	4.75	

Mathias Calonius SP18

Robert Henrik Rehbinder SP21

Designs: 2m+20p, Henrik C. Porthan. 2½m+25p, Anders Chydenius.

1935, Jan. 1

Cross in Red

B18	SP18 1¼m + 15p brown	.75	*2.25*
B19	SP18 2m + 20p gray lil	1.75	*4.00*
B20	SP18 2½m + 25p gray bl	.55	*2.25*
	Nos. B18-B20 (3)	3.05	*8.50*
	Set, never hinged	4.50	

1936, Jan. 1

2m+20p, Count Gustaf Mauritz Armfelt. 2½m+25p, Count Arvid Bernard Horn.

Cross in Red

B21 SP21 1¼m + 15p dk brn .50 *2.25*
B22 SP21 2m + 20p vio brn 2.75 *6.00*
B23 SP21 2½m + 25p blue .50 *2.25*
Nos. B21-B23 (3) 3.75 *10.50*
Set, never hinged 7.50

Type "Uusimaa" SP24

Type "Turunmaa" SP25

Design: 3½m+35p, Type "Hameenmaa."

1937, Jan. 1

Cross in Red

B24 SP24 1¼m + 15p brown .60 *2.25*
B25 SP25 2m + 20p brn lake 11.00 5.50
B26 SP24 3½m + 35p indigo .60 *2.50*
Nos. B24-B26 (3) 12.20 10.25
Set, never hinged 30.00

Aukuste Makipeska SP27

Skiing SP31

Designs: 1¼m+15p, Robert Isidor Orn. 2m+20p, Edward Bergenheim. 3½m+35p, Johan Mauritz Nordenstam.

1938, Jan. 5 **Engr.**

Cross in Red

B27 SP27 50p + 5p dk grn .45 *1.00*
B28 SP27 1¼m + 15p dk brn .90 *2.25*
B29 SP27 2m + 20p rose lake 4.50 4.50
B30 SP27 3½m + 35p dk blue .60 *2.25*
Nos. B27-B30 (4) 6.45 *10.00*
Set, never hinged 13.50

1938, Jan. 18

Designs: #B32, Skijumper. #B33, Skier.

B31 SP31 1.25m + 75p sl grn 2.50 *9.00*
B32 SP31 2m + 1m dk car 2.50 *9.00*
B33 SP31 3.50m + 1.50m dk blue 2.50 *9.00*
Nos. B31-B33 (3) 7.50 *27.00*
Set, never hinged 13.50

Ski championships held at Lahti.

Soldier SP34

Battlefield at Solferino SP35

1938, May 16

B34 SP34 2m + ½m blue 1.25 *3.00*
Never hinged 2.50

Victory of the White Army over the Red Guards. The surtax was for the benefit of the members of the Union of the Finnish Front.

1939, Jan. 2

Cross in Scarlet

B35 SP35 50p + 5p dk grn .60 *.90*
B36 SP35 1¼m + 15p dk brn .60 *1.50*
B37 SP35 2m + 20p lake 9.00 9.00
B38 SP35 3½m + 35p dk bl .50 *2.00*
Nos. B35-B38 (4) 10.70 13.40
Set, never hinged 22.50

Intl. Red Cross Soc., 75th anniv.

Catalogue values for unused stamps in this section, from this point to the end of the section, are for Never Hinged items.

Soldiers with Crossbows SP36

Arms of Finland SP40

1¼m+15p, Cavalryman. 2m+20p, Soldier of Charles XII of Sweden. 3½m+35p, Officer and soldier of War with Russia, 1808-1809.

1940, Jan. 3

Cross in Red

B39 SP36 50p + 5p dk grn .70 *1.00*
B40 SP36 1¼m + 15p dk brn 1.50 *1.60*
B41 SP36 2m + 20p lake 2.00 1.60
B42 SP36 3½m + 35p dp ultra 2.00 3.00
Nos. B39-B42 (4) 6.20 7.20

The surtax aided the Finnish Red Cross.

1940, Feb. 15 **Litho.**

B43 SP40 2m +2m indigo .40 *.80*

The surtax was given to a fund for the preservation of neutrality.

AIR POST STAMPS

No. 178 Overprinted in Red

1930, Sept. 24 **Unwmk.** ***Perf. 14***

C1 A28 10m gray lilac 125.00 *200.00*
Never hinged 200.00
a. 1830 for 1930 2,000. 3,250.

Overprinted expressly for use on mail carried in "Graf Zeppelin" on return flight from Finland to Germany on Sept. 24, 1930, after which trip the stamps ceased to be valid for postage. Forgeries are almost always on No. 205, rather than No. 178.

FIUME

ˈfyü-ˌmā

LOCATION — A city and surrounding territory on the Adriatic Sea
AREA — 8 sq. mi.
POP. — 44,956 (estimated 1924)

Formerly a port of Hungary, Fiume was claimed by Yugoslavia and Italy following World War I. During the discussion, the poet Gabriele d'Annunzio organized his legionnaires and seized Fiume, together with the islands of Arbe, Carnaro and Veglia, in the name of Italy. Yugoslavia recognized Italy's claim and the city was annexed in January, 1924.

100 Filler = 1 Korona
100 Centesimi = 1 Corona (1919)
100 Centesimi = 1 Lira

The overprints on Nos. 1-23a have been extensively forged. Even the inexpensive values are difficult to find with genuine overprints. Forgeries of many later issues also exist, most created for the packet trade in the 1920s. Values are for genuine stamps. Collectors should be aware that stamps sold "as is" are likely to be forgeries, and unexpertized collections should be assumed to consist of mostly forged stamps. Education plus working with knowledgeable dealers is mandatory in this collecting area. More valuable stamps should be expertized.

Hungarian Stamps of 1916-18 Typograph Overprinted

1918, Dec. 2 **Wmk. 137** ***Perf. 15***

On Stamps of 1916

White Numerals

1 A8 10f rose — —
a. Handstamped overprint 87.50 40.00
Never hinged 140.00
2 A8 15f violet 37.50 26.00
Never hinged 82.50
On cover 90.00

No. 1 with typographed overprint is unique.

Typographed Overprint
On Stamps of 1916-18
Colored Numerals

3 A9 2f brown orange 3.00 1.50
Never hinged 7.50
On cover 45.00
4 A9 3f red violet 3.00 1.50
Never hinged 7.50
On cover 45.00
5 A9 5f green 3.00 1.50
Never hinged 7.50
On cover 45.00
6 A9 6f grnsh blue 3.00 1.50
Never hinged 7.50
On cover 45.00
7 A9 10f rose red, inverted ovpt. *19,000.* *8,250.*
Never hinged *24,000.*
On cover —
8 A9 15f violet 3.00 1.50
Never hinged 7.50
On cover 45.00
9 A9 20f gray brown 3.00 1.50
Never hinged 7.50
On cover 45.00
10 A9 25f deep blue 11.00 1.75
Never hinged 27.50
On cover 75.00
11 A9 35f brown 6.00 3.00
Never hinged 15.00
On cover 100.00
12 A9 40f olive green 87.50 37.50
Never hinged 225.00
On cover 200.00

White Numerals

13 A10 50f red vio & lil 3.75 2.25
Never hinged 9.25
On cover 50.00
14 A10 75f brt bl & pale bl 8.75 3.00
Never hinged 22.50
On cover 50.00
15 A10 80f grn & pale grn 8.75 2.25
Never hinged 22.50
On cover 50.00
16 A10 1k red brn & claret 30.00 7.50
Never hinged 75.00
On cover 120.00
17 A10 2k ol brn & bis 3.75 2.25
Never hinged 9.25
On cover 200.00
18 A10 3k dk vio & ind 37.50 18.00
Never hinged 92.50
On cover *350.00*
19 A10 5k dk brn & lt brn 80.00 30.00
Never hinged 200.00
On cover *500.00*
20 A10 10k vio brn & vio 6,000. 2,750.
Never hinged *7,500.*
On cover —

Handstamped Overprint

3a A9 2f brown orange 15.00 11.00
Never hinged 22.50
4a A9 3f red violet 11.00 10.50
Never hinged 17.50
5a A9 5f green 9.00 10.50
Never hinged 13.50
6a A9 6f grnsh blue 30.00 15.00
Never hinged 45.00
7a A9 10f rose red *60.00* *22.50*
Never hinged *90.00*
8a A9 15f violet 37.50 15.00
Never hinged 55.00
9a A9 20f gray brown 260.00 95.00
Never hinged 390.00
10a A9 25f deep blue 75.00 15.00
Never hinged 110.00
11a A9 35f brown 60.00 15.00
Never hinged 90.00
12a A9 40f olive green 37.50 15.00
Never hinged 55.00

White Numerals

13a A10 50f red vio & lil 18.50 11.00
Never hinged 27.50
14a A10 75f brt bl & pale bl 87.50 18.50
Never hinged 140.00
15a A10 80f grn & pale grn 87.50 18.50
Never hinged 140.00
16a A10 1k red brn & claret 37.50 15.00
Never hinged 55.00
17a A10 2k ol brn & bis 67.50 18.50
Never hinged 100.00
18a A10 3k dk vio & ind 675.00 82.50
Never hinged 1,000.
19a A10 5k dk brn & lt brn 600.00 82.50
Never hinged 900.00
20a A10 10k vio brn & vio 250.00 130.00
Never hinged *375.00*

Inverted or double overprints exist on most of Nos. 4-15. No. 7 only exists with inverted overprint.

Typographed Overprint
On Stamps of 1918

21 A11 10f scarlet 3.00 3.00
Never hinged 7.50
On cover 30.00
22 A11 20f dark brown 2.25 1.50
Never hinged 5.50
On cover 35.00
23 A12 40f olive green 24.00 10.50
Never hinged 60.00
On cover 50.00

Handstamped Overprint
On Stamps of 1918

21a A11 10f scarlet 15.00 9.00
Never hinged 22.50
22a A11 20f dark brown 22.50 11.00
Never hinged 35.00
23a A12 40f olive green 15.00 9.00
Never hinged 22.50

The overprint on Nos. 3-23a was applied by 2 printing plates and 6 handstamps. Values are for the less costly. All genuine printed overprints on No. 7 are inverted and are extremely scarce.

Postage Due Stamps of Hungary, 1915-20 Ovptd. & Surcharged in Black

1919, Jan.

24 D1 45f on 6f green & red 10.50 11.00
Never hinged 26.00
On cover 75.00
a. Pair, one with inverted surcharge *900.00*
25 D1 45f on 20f green & red 26.50 11.00
Never hinged 60.00
On cover 80.00
Set, never hinged 85.00

Hungarian Savings Bank Stamp Surcharged in Black — A2

1919, Jan. 29

26 A2 15f on 10f dk violet 16.00 15.00
Never hinged 40.00
On cover 55.00

Overprints on Nos. 24-26 are typographed.

"Italy" — A3

Italian Flag on Clock-Tower in Fiume — A4

"Revolution" A5

Sailor Raising Italian Flag at Fiume (1918) A6

Nos. 30-43 exist on three types of paper: (A) grayish, porous paper, printed in sheets of 70 stamps (Jan, Feb. printings); (B) translucent or semi-translucent good quality white paper, printed in sheets of 70 stamps (March printing); and (C) good quality medium white paper, plain and opaque, sometimes grayish or yellowish, printed in sheets of 100 (April printing).

Perf. 11½

1919, April Unwmk. Litho.

Good Quality Medium White Paper (C)

27	A3	2c dull blue	1.50	1.50
		Never hinged	3.75	
		On cover		35.00
28	A3	3c gray brown	1.50	1.50
		Never hinged	3.75	
		On cover		40.00
a.		Perf 10½	1,100.	
		Never hinged	1,750.	
29	A3	5c yellow green	1.50	1.50
		Never hinged	3.75	
		On cover		35.00
30	A4	10c rose	37.50	26.00
		Never hinged	92.50	
		On cover		40.00
31	A4	15c violet	1.50	1.50
		Never hinged	3.75	
		On cover		35.00
32	A4	20c green	87.50	*140.00*
		Never hinged	225.00	
		On cover		*600.00*
33	A5	25c dark blue	2.25	1.50
		Never hinged	5.50	
		On cover		35.00
34	A6	30c deep violet	2.25	1.50
		Never hinged	5.50	
		On cover		35.00
a.		Perf 10½	1,100.	
		Never hinged	1,750.	
35	A5	40c brown	2.25	1.50
		Never hinged	5.50	
		On cover		35.00
36	A5	45c orange	2.25	2.25
		Never hinged	5.50	
		On cover		35.00
37	A6	50c yellow green	2.25	1.50
		Never hinged	5.50	
		On cover		35.00
a.		Perf 10½		—
38	A6	60c claret	2.25	1.50
		Never hinged	5.50	
		On cover		35.00
39	A6	1cor brown orange	3.75	2.25
		Never hinged	9.25	
		On cover		35.00
40	A6	2cor brt blue	3.75	2.25
		Never hinged	9.25	
		On cover		45.00
a.		Perf 10½	1,100.	
		Never hinged	1,750.	
41	A6	3cor orange red	4.50	2.25
		Never hinged	11.00	
		On cover		60.00
a.		Perf 10½		—
42	A6	5cor deep brown	22.50	22.50
		Never hinged	55.00	
		On cover		90.00
a.		Perf 10½	—	—
43	A6	10cor olive green	87.50	60.00
		Never hinged	225.00	
		On cover		*550.00*
		Nos. 27-43 (17)	266.50	271.00

1919, Jan.-Feb.

Poor Quality Grayish Paper (A)

30a	A4	10c rose	22.50	9.00
		Never hinged	55.00	
		On cover		45.00
31a	A4	15c violet	22.50	*26.00*
		Never hinged	55.00	
		On cover		50.00
32a	A4	20c emerald green	3.00	*3.00*
		Never hinged	7.50	
		On cover		*45.00*
33a	A5	25c light blue	11.00	1.50
		Never hinged	27.50	
		On cover		45.00
36a	A5	45c bister orange	3.00	3.00
		Never hinged	7.50	
		On cover		45.00
b.		Perf 10½	—	*1,250.*
38a	A6	60c claret	18.50	13.50
		Never hinged	47.50	
		On cover		45.00
39a	A6	1cor brown orange	6.00	3.00
		Never hinged	15.00	
		On cover		—
b.		Perf 10½	—	—
40b	A6	2cor cobalt blue	—	—
		Never hinged	—	
42b	A6	5cor deep brown	—	—
		Never hinged	—	
43a	A6	10cor olive green	24.00	*52.50*
		Never hinged	60.00	
		On cover		*150.00*

1919, Mar.

Good Quality Translucent White Paper (B)

27a	A3	2c dull blue	1.50	*3.00*
		Never hinged	3.75	
		On cover		25.00
28b	A3	3c gray brown	1.50	*3.00*
		Never hinged	3.75	
		On cover		25.00
29a	A3	5c yellow green	1.50	3.00
		Never hinged	3.75	
		On cover		25.00
30b	A4	10c ar rose	—	—
31b	A4	15c violet	2.25	*12.50*
		Never hinged	5.50	
		On cover		35.00
33b	A5	25c blue	2.25	*4.50*
		Never hinged	5.50	
		On cover		35.00
35a	A5	40c brown	2.25	3.00
		Never hinged	5.50	
		On cover		30.00
36c	A5	45c orange	150.00	*190.00*
		Never hinged	375.00	
		On cover		*500.00*
40c	A6	2cor cobalt blue	9.00	*11.00*
		Never hinged	22.50	
		On cover		*550.00*
d.		Perf 10½	*1,100.*	
		Never hinged	*1,750.*	
41b	A6	3cor org vermilion	9.00	*11.00*
		Never hinged	22.50	
		On cover		*550.00*
c.		Perf 10½		—
42c	A6	5cor choc brown	60.00	60.00
		Never hinged	150.00	
43b	A6	10cor olive green	87.50	*60.00*
		Never hinged	225.00	
		On cover		*550.00*

Part-perf. examples of most of this series are known.

For surcharges see Nos. 58, 60, 64, 66-69.

A7

A8

A9

A10

1919, July 28 *Perf. 11½*

46	A7	5c yellow green	1.50	.75
		Never hinged	3.75	
		On cover		*45.00*
47	A8	10c rose	1.50	.75
		Never hinged	3.75	
		On cover		*35.00*
48	A9	30c violet	6.00	2.25
		Never hinged	15.00	
		On cover		*45.00*
49	A10	40c yellow brown	1.50	*1.50*
		Never hinged	3.75	
		On cover		*40.00*
50	A10	45c orange	6.00	5.25
		Never hinged	15.00	
		On cover		*40.00*
51	A9	50c yellow green	6.00	5.25
		Never hinged	15.00	
		On cover		*40.00*
52	A9	60c claret	6.00	5.25
		Never hinged	15.00	
		On cover		*90.00*
a.		Perf. 13x12½	160.00	
		Never hinged	240.00	
b.		Perf. 10½	325.00	
		Never hinged	500.00	
53	A9	10cor olive green	6.00	*15.00*
		Never hinged	15.00	
		On cover		*450.00*
a.		Perf. 13x12½	52.50	*87.50*
		Never hinged	77.50	
		On cover		*600.00*
b.		Perf. 10½	325.00	325.00
		Never hinged	500.00	
		On cover		*750.00*
		Nos. 46-53 (8)	34.50	36.00
		Set, never hinged	85.00	

Five other denominations (25c, 1cor, 2cor, 3cor and 5cor) were not officially issued. Some copies of the 25c are known canceled, a few examples having been sold at post offices along with full sets of Nos. 46-53. Values: 25c blue, $800 unused, $1,200 never hinged, $1,750 used; 1cor brown orange, perf 11½, $110 unused, $275 never hinged; 1cor brown orange, perf 12½-13, unused $22.50, never hinged $55; 2cor blue, perf 11½, unused $67.50, never hinged $160; 2cor blue, perf 12½-13, unused $22.50, never hinged $55; 3cor vermilion, perf 11½, unused $52.50, never hinged, $130; 3cor vermilion, perf 12½-13, unused $87.50, never hinged $225; 5cor brown, perf 11½, unused $110, never hinged $275; 5cor brown, perf 12½-13, unused $110, never hinged $275.

For surcharges see Nos. 59, 61-63, 65, 70.

Stamps of 1919 Handstamp Surcharged

1919-20

58	A4	5c on 20c grn ('20)	.30	.30
59	A10	5c on 25c blue	.30	.30
60	A5	10c on 45c orange	.90	.30
61	A9	15c on 30c vio ('20)	.30	.30
62	A10	15c on 45c orange	.30	.30
63	A9	15c on 60c cl ('20)	.45	.50
64	A6	25c on 50c yel grn ('20)	8.75	*11.00*
65	A9	25c on 50c yel grn ('20)	.45	*.50*
66	A6	55c on 1cor brn org	18.00	9.00
67	A6	55c on 2cor brt bl	3.00	*3.50*
68	A6	55c on 3cor org red	3.00	3.00
69	A6	55c on 5cor dp brn	3.00	3.00
70	A9	55c on 10cor ol grn	13.00	8.75
		Nos. 58-70 (13)	51.75	*40.75*
		Set, never hinged	110.00	

Semi-Postal Stamps of 1919 Surcharged:

a

b

1919-20

73	SP6(a)	5c on 5c green	.30	.20
74	SP6(a)	10c on 10c rose	.30	.20
75	SP6(a)	15c on 15c gray	.30	.20
76	SP6(a)	20c on 20c org	.30	.20
77	SP9(a)	25c on 25c bl ('20)	.30	.20
78	SP7(b)	45c on 45c ol grn	.45	.35
79	SP7(b)	60c on 60c rose	.45	.35
80	SP7(b)	80c on 80c violet	.60	.50
81	SP7(b)	1cor on 1cor slate	.45	.35
82	SP8(a)	2cor on 2cor red brn	1.00	.80
83	SP8(a)	3cor on 3cor blk brn	2.40	1.90
84	SP8(a)	5cor on 5cor yel brn	3.00	2.50
85	SP8(a)	10cor on 10cor dk vio ('20)	1.00	.80
		Nos. 73-85 (13)	10.85	8.55
		Set, never hinged	21.00	

Double or inverted surcharges, or imperf. varieties, exist on most of Nos. 73-85.

There were three settings of the surcharges on Nos. 73-85 except No. 77 which is known only with one setting.

Gabriele d'Annunzio — A11

Severing the Gordian Knot — A12

1920, Sept. 12 Typo. ***Perf. 11½***

Pale Buff Background

86	A11	5c green	.55	.55
87	A11	10c carmine	.55	.55
88	A11	15c dark gray	.55	.55
89	A11	20c orange	.60	.60
90	A11	25c dark blue	.90	.90
91	A11	30c red brown	.95	.95
92	A11	45c olive gray	1.50	1.50
93	A11	50c lilac	1.50	1.50
94	A11	55c bister	1.50	1.50
95	A11	1 l black	7.75	*10.00*
96	A11	2 l red violet	7.75	*11.50*
97	A11	3 l dark green	7.75	*11.50*
98	A11	5 l brown	40.00	16.00
99	A11	10 l gray violet	7.75	*11.50*
		Nos. 86-99 (14)	79.60	*69.10*
		Set, never hinged	150.00	

Counterfeits of Nos. 86 to 99 are plentiful.

For overprints see Nos. 134-148.

1920, Sept. 12

Designs: 10c, Ancient emblem of Fiume. 20c, Head of "Fiume." 25c, Hands holding daggers.

100	A12	5c green	32.50	16.00
101	A12	10c deep rose	21.00	12.00
102	A12	20c brown orange	32.50	12.00
103	A12	25c indigo	21.00	*30.00*
a.		25c blue	60.00	60.00
		Nos. 100-103 (4)	107.00	70.00
		Set, never hinged	210.00	

Anniv. of the occupation of Fiume by d'Annunzio. They were available for franking the correspondence of the legionnaires on the day of issue only, Sept. 12, 1920.

Counterfeits of Nos. 100-103 are plentiful.

For overprints and surcharges see Nos. 104-133, E4-E9.

Nos. 100-103 Overprinted or Surcharged in Black or Red and New Values

1920, Nov. 20

104	A12	1c on 5c green	1.00	.40
105	A12	2c on 25c indigo (R)	.40	.40
a.		2c on 25c blue (R)	32.50	32.50
106	A12	5c green	14.00	1.00
107	A12	10c rose	14.00	1.00
108	A12	15c on 10c rose	1.00	.55
109	A12	15c on 20c brn org	.40	*.55*
110	A12	15c on 25c indigo (R)	.55	*.70*
a.		15c on 25c blue (R)	32.50	32.50
111	A12	20c brown orange	.70	.70
112	A12	25c indigo (R)	.70	.70
a.		25c blue (R)	3.50	3.50
113	A12	25c indigo (Bk)	70.00	70.00
a.		25c blue (Bk)	75.00	75.00
114	A12	25c on 10c rose	1.75	1.75
115	A12	50c on 20c brn org	4.00	1.25
116	A12	55c on 5c green	14.00	2.10
117	A12	1 l on 10c rose	24.00	10.00
118	A12	1 l on 25c indigo (R)	275.00	275.00
a.		1 l on 25c blue (R)	600.00	250.00
119	A12	2 l on 5c green	22.50	13.00
120	A12	5 l on 10c rose	92.50	50.00

121	A12	10 l on 20c brn org	325.00	190.00
		Nos. 104-121 (18)	861.50	619.10
		Set, never hinged	1,750.	

The Fiume Legionnaires of d'Annunzio occupied the islands of Arbe and Veglia in the Gulf of Carnaro Nov. 13, 1920-Jan. 5, 1921.

Varieties of overprint or surcharge exist for most of Nos. 104-121.

Nos. 113, 117-121, 125, 131 have a backprint.

Nos. 106-107, 111, 113, 115-116 Overprinted or Surcharged at top

1920, Nov. 18

122	A12	5c green	3.25	3.25
123	A12	10c rose	7.75	*8.50*
124	A12	20c brown org	17.50	12.00
125	A12	25c deep blue	9.50	*12.00*
126	A12	50c on 20c brn org	19.00	12.00
127	A12	55c on 5c green	19.00	12.00
		Nos. 122-127 (6)	76.00	59.75
		Set, never hinged	190.00	

The overprint on Nos. 122-125 comes in two widths: 11mm and 14mm. Values are for the 11mm width.

Nos. 106-107, 111, 113, 115-116 Overprinted or Surcharged at top

1920, Nov. 18

128	A12	5c green	3.25	3.25
129	A12	10c rose	7.75	*8.50*
130	A12	20c brown orange	17.50	12.00
131	A12	25c deep blue	9.50	*12.00*
132	A12	50c on 20c brn org	19.00	12.00
133	A12	55c on 5c green	19.00	12.00
		Nos. 128-133 (6)	76.00	59.75
		Set, never hinged	190.00	

The overprint on Nos. 128-131 comes in two widths: 17mm and 19mm. Values are for the 17mm width.

Nos. 122-133 exist with double and inverted overprints.

Counterfeits of these overprints exist.

Nos. 86-99 Overprinted

1921, Feb. 2

Pale Buff Background

134	A11	5c green	.35	.35
135	A11	10c carmine	.35	.35
136	A11	15c dark gray	.35	*.40*
137	A11	20c orange	1.25	.85
138	A11	25c dark blue	1.25	.85
139	A11	30c red brown	1.25	.85
140	A11	45c olive gray	.70	.70
141	A11	50c lilac	1.50	1.10
142	A11	55c bister	1.25	.80
143	A11	1 l black	75.00	72.50
144	A11	2 l red violet	15.00	11.50
145	A11	3 l dark green	15.00	11.50
146	A11	5 l brown	15.00	11.50
147	A11	10 l gray violet	15.00	11.50

With Additional Surcharge

148	A11	1 l on 30c red brown	.70	.70
		Nos. 134-148 (15)	143.95	125.45
		Set, never hinged	275.00	

Most of Nos. 134-143, 148 and E10-E11 exist with inverted or double overprint.

See Nos. E10-E11.

First Constituent Assembly

Nos. B4-B15 Overprinted

1921, Apr. 24

149	SP6	5c blue green	1.40	1.40
150	SP6	10c rose	1.40	1.40
151	SP6	15c gray	1.40	1.40
152	SP6	20c orange	1.40	1.40
153	SP7	45c olive green	4.25	4.00
154	SP7	60c car rose	4.25	4.00
155	SP7	80c brt violet	5.00	5.00

With Additional Overprint "L"

156	SP7	1 l on 1cor dk slate	7.00	7.00
157	SP8	2 l on 2cor red brn	32.50	1.00
158	SP8	3 l on 3cor black brn	32.50	32.50
159	SP8	5 l on 5cor yel brn	32.50	1.40
160	SP8	10 l on 10cor dk vio	35.00	35.00
		Nos. 149-160 (12)	158.60	95.50
		Set, never hinged	325.00	

The overprint exists inverted on several denominations.

Second Constituent Assembly

"Constitution" Issue of 1921 With Additional Overprint "1922"

1922

161	SP6	5c blue green	1.75	.85
162	SP6	10c rose	.20	*.35*
163	SP6	15c gray	7.75	2.75
164	SP6	20c orange	.85	.70
165	SP7	45c olive grn	6.00	3.00
166	SP7	60c car rose	.55	1.10
167	SP7	80c brt violet	.55	1.10
168	SP7	1 l on 1cor dk slate	.85	.70
169	SP8	2 l on 2cor red brn	7.75	4.25
170	SP8	3 l on 3cor blk brn	.75	*1.10*
171	SP8	5 l on 5cor yel brn	.55	*1.10*
		Nos. 161-171 (11)	27.55	17.00
		Set, never hinged	55.00	

Nos. 161-171 have the overprint in heavier type than Nos. 149-160 and "IV" in Roman instead of sans-serif numerals.

The overprint exists inverted or double on almost all values.

Venetian Ship — A16

Roman Arch — A17

St. Vitus — A18

Rostral Column — A19

1923, Mar. 23 ***Perf. 11½***

Pale Buff Background

172	A16	5c blue green	.35	.35
173	A16	10c violet	.35	.35
174	A16	15c brown	.35	.35
175	A17	20c orange red	.35	.35
176	A17	25c dark gray	.35	.35
177	A17	30c dark green	.35	.35
178	A18	50c dull blue	.35	.35
179	A18	60c rose	.55	*1.25*
180	A18	1 l dark blue	.55	*1.50*
181	A19	2 l violet brown	32.50	7.75
182	A19	3 l olive bister	24.00	14.50
183	A19	5 l yellow brown	24.00	19.00
		Nos. 172-183 (12)	84.05	46.45
		Set, never hinged	175.00	

Nos. 172-183 Overprinted

1924, Feb. 22

Pale Buff Background

184	A16	5c blue green	.35	*2.75*
185	A16	10c violet	.35	*2.75*
186	A16	15c brown	.60	*2.75*
187	A17	20c orange red	.60	*2.75*
188	A17	25c dk gray	.60	*2.75*
189	A17	30c dk green	.60	*2.75*
190	A18	50c dull blue	.60	*2.75*
191	A18	60c red	.60	*2.75*
192	A18	1 l dark blue	.60	*2.75*
193	A19	2 l violet brown	1.75	*6.00*
194	A19	3 l olive	2.75	*7.00*
195	A19	5 l yellow brown	2.75	*7.00*
		Nos. 184-195 (12)	12.15	*44.75*
		Set, never hinged	24.00	

The overprint exists inverted on almost all values.

Nos. 172-183 Overprinted

1924, Mar. 1

Pale Buff Background

196	A16	5c blue green	.35	*1.40*
197	A16	10c violet	.35	*1.40*
198	A16	15c brown	.35	*1.40*
199	A17	20c orange red	.35	*1.40*
200	A17	25c dark gray	.35	*1.40*
201	A17	30c dark green	.35	*1.40*
202	A18	50c dull blue	.35	*1.40*
203	A18	60c red	.35	*1.40*
204	A18	1 l dark blue	.35	*1.40*
205	A19	2 l violet brown	.70	*2.75*
206	A19	3 l olive	.70	*2.75*
207	A19	5 l yellow brown	.70	*2.75*
		Nos. 196-207 (12)	5.25	*20.85*
		Set, never hinged	10.00	

Postage stamps of Fiume were superseded by stamps of Italy.

SEMI-POSTAL STAMPS

Semi-Postal Stamps of Hungary, 1916-17 Overprinted

1918, Dec. 2 **Wmk. 137** ***Perf. 15***

B1	SP3	10f + 2f rose	2.40	1.25
a.		Inverted overprint	32.50	22.50
B2	SP4	15f + 2f dl vio	2.40	1.25
a.		Inverted overprint	62.50	22.50
B3	SP5	40f + 2f brn car	2.40	1.25
a.		Inverted overprint	35.00	17.50
		Nos. B1-B3 (3)	7.20	3.75
		Set, never hinged	17.50	

Examples of Nos. B1-B3 with overprint handstamped sell for higher prices.

Statue of Romulus and Remus Being Suckled by Wolf — SP6

Venetian Galley — SP7

Church of St. Mark's, Venice — SP8

Perf. 11½

1919, May 18 **Unwmk.** **Typo.**

B4	SP6	5c +5 l bl grn	7.50	4.25
B5	SP6	10c +5 l rose	7.50	4.25
B6	SP6	15c +5 l dk gray	7.50	4.25
B7	SP6	20c +5 l orange	7.50	4.25
B8	SP7	45c +5 l ol grn	7.50	4.25
B9	SP7	60c +5 l car rose	7.50	4.25
B10	SP7	80c +5 l lilac	7.50	4.25
B11	SP7	1cor +5 l dk slate	7.50	4.25
B12	SP8	2cor +5 l red brn	7.50	4.25
B13	SP8	3cor +5 l blk brn	7.50	4.25
B14	SP8	5cor +5 l yel brn	7.50	4.25
B15	SP8	10cor +5 l dk vio	7.50	4.25
		Nos. B4-B15 (12)	90.00	51.00
		Set, never hinged	175.00	

200th day of peace. The surtax aided Fiume students in Italy. "Posta di Fiume" is printed on the back of Nos. B4-B16.

The surtax is shown on the stamps as "LIRE 5" but actually was 5cor.

For surcharges and overprints see Nos. 73-85, 149-171, J15-J26.

Dr. Antonio Grossich — SP9

1919, Sept. 20

B16	SP9	25c + 2 l blue	1.40	1.40
		Never hinged	2.75	

Surtax for the Dr. Grossich Foundation.

SPECIAL DELIVERY STAMPS

Special Delivery Stamp of Hungary, 1916, Overprinted like Nos. 1-23

1918, Dec. 2 **Wmk. 137** ***Perf. 15***

E1	SD1	2f gray green & red	1.75	1.40
		Never hinged	3.25	

Handstamped overprints sell for more.

SD3

Perf. 11½

1920, Sept. 12 **Unwmk.** **Typo.**

E2	SD3	30c slate blue	16.00	12.00
E3	SD3	50c rose	16.00	12.00
		Set, never hinged	60.00	

For overprints see Nos. E10-E11.

Nos. 102 and 100 Surcharged

1920, Nov.

E4	A12 30c on 20c brn org	42.50	42.50
E5	A12 50c on 5c green	70.00	35.00

Nos. E4-E5 have a backprint.

Same Surcharge as on Nos. 124, 122

E6	A12 30c on 20c brn org	75.00	47.50
E7	A12 50c on 5c green	55.00	47.50

Overprint on Nos. E6-E7 is 11mm wide.

Same Surcharge as on Nos. 130, 128

E8	A12 30c on 20c brn org	75.00	47.50
E9	A12 50c on 5c green	55.00	47.50
	Nos. E4-E9 (6)	372.50	267.50
	Set, never hinged	900.00	

Overprint on Nos. E8-E9 is 17mm wide.

Nos. E2 and E3 Overprinted

1921, Feb. 2

E10	SD3 30c slate blue	7.00	8.75
E11	SD3 50c rose	10.50	8.75
	Set, never hinged	35.00	

Fiume in 16th Century SD4

1923, Mar. 23 *Perf. 11, 11½*

E12	SD4 60c rose & buff	10.50	6.00
E13	SD4 2 l dk bl & buff	10.50	7.75
	Set, never hinged	42.50	

Nos. E12-E13 Overprinted

1924, Feb. 22

E14	SD4 60c car & buff	.85	*4.25*
E15	SD4 2 l dk bl & buff	.85	*4.25*
	Set, never hinged	3.50	

Nos. E12-E13 Overprinted

1924, Mar. 1

E16	SD4 60c car & buff	.85	*3.50*
E17	SD4 2 l dk bl & buff	.85	*3.50*
	Set, never hinged	3.50	

POSTAGE DUE STAMPS

Postage Due Stamps of Hungary, 1915-1916, Overprinted

1918, Dec. Wmk. 137 *Perf. 15*

J1	D1 6f green & black	90.00	24.00
J2	D1 12f green & black	75.00	24.00
J3	D1 50f green & black	27.50	12.00
	Set, never hinged	290.00	
J4	D1 1f green & red	14.00	7.00
J5	D1 2f green & red	.55	.40
J6	D1 5f green & red	3.50	2.75
J7	D1 6f green & red	.55	.40
J8	D1 10f green & red	6.25	1.75
J9	D1 12f green & red	.70	.55
J10	D1 15f green & red	12.00	10.00
J11	D1 20f green & red	.70	.55
J12	D1 30f green & red	12.00	8.75
	Nos. J4-J12 (9)	50.25	32.15
	Set, never hinged	95.00	

The overprint on Nos. J1-J12 was applied both by press and handstamp. Values are for the less costly. Inverted and double overprints exist. Excellent forgeries exist.

Eagle — D2

Perf. 11½

1919, July 28 Unwmk. Typo.

J13	D2 2c brown	1.00	.80
J14	D2 5c brown	1.25	.80
	Set, never hinged	4.25	

Semi-Postal Stamps of 1919 with Overprint "Valore Globale" Surcharged:

1921, Mar. 21

J15	SP6 2c on 15c gray	.70	.70
J16	SP6 4c on 10c rose	.60	.55
J17	SP9 5c on 25c blue	.60	.55
J18	SP6 6c on 20c orange	.60	.55
J19	SP6 10c on 20c orange	.90	.90

Surcharged:

J20	SP7 20c on 45c olive grn	1.00	*1.40*
J21	SP7 30c on 1cor dk slate	1.25	*1.10*
J22	SP7 40c on 80c violet	.80	*.70*
J23	SP7 50c on 60c carmine	.80	*.70*
J24	SP7 60c on 45c olive grn	1.00	*1.40*
J25	SP7 80c on 45c olive grn	1.00	*1.40*

Surcharged like Nos. J15-J19

J26	SP8 1 l on 2cor red brown	1.75	*1.40*
	Nos. J15-J26 (12)	11.00	*11.35*
	Set, never hinged	21.00	

See note below No. 85 regarding settings of "Valore Globale" overprint.

NEWSPAPER STAMPS

Newspaper Stamp of Hungary, 1914, Overprinted like Nos. 1-23

1918, Dec. 2 Wmk. 137 *Imperf.*

P1	N5 (2f) orange	1.75	.70
	Never hinged	3.25	

Handstamped overprints sell for more.

Eagle N1

1919 Unwmk. *Perf. 11½*

P2	N1 2c deep buff	3.50	4.75

Re-engraved

P3	N1 2c deep buff	3.50	3.50
	Set, never hinged	14.00	

In the re-engraved stamp the top of the "2" is rounder and broader, the feet of the eagle show clearly and the diamond at bottom has six lines instead of five.

Steamer — N2

1920, Sept. 12

P4	N2 1c gray green	1.00	.70
	Never hinged	2.10	

No. P4 exists imperf.

FRANCE

ˈfranˌtˌs

LOCATION — Western Europe
GOVT. — Republic
AREA — 210,033 sq. mi.
POP. — 54,539,000 (est. 1984)
CAPITAL — Paris

100 Centimes = 1 Franc

Catalogue values for unused stamps in this country are for Never Hinged items, beginning with Scott 299 in the regular postage section, Scott B42 in the semi-postal section, Scott S1 for franchise stamps, and Scott N27 for occupation stamps.

Ceres — A1

FORTY CENTIMES

4
Type I

4
Type II

1849-50 Typo. Unwmk. *Imperf.*

1	A1 10c bis, *yelsh* ('50)	*1,500.*	300.00
	On cover, single franking		475.00
a.	10c dark bister, *yelsh*	1,700.	350.00
	On cover, single franking		575.00
b.	10c greenish bister	2,250.	375.00
	On cover, single franking		650.00
c.	10c deep greenish bister	4,000.	750.00
	On cover, single franking		1,350.
d.	Tête beche pair, bister, *yelsh*	*62,500.*	*14,000.*
	On cover		*25,000.*
e.	Tête beche pair, dark bister, *yelsh*	*66,000.*	*14,000.*
	On cover		*28,000.*
f.	Tête beche pair, greenish bister, *yelsh*	*72,500.*	*18,000.*
	On cover		*30,000.*
2	A1 15c green, *grnsh*	*18,500.*	800.00
	On cover, single franking		1,275.
a.	15c yellow green, *grnsh* ('50)	*18,500.*	900.00
	On cover, single franking		1,350.
b.	15c dark green	*19,500.*	900.00
	On cover, single franking		1,500.
c.	Tête bêche pair	—	
	On cover front		*240,000.*

A very fine example of 15 centimes yellow green, Scott No. 2a, realized the equivalent of U.S. $14,750 at a Weisbaden auction in 2005.

3	A1 20c blk, *yelsh*	300.00	40.00
	On cover, single franking		60.00
a.	20c black	400.00	45.00
	On cover, single franking		65.00
b.	20c black, *buff*	1,400.	225.00
	On cover, single franking		340.00
c.	Tête bêche pair	*9,000.*	*6,000.*
	On cover		*13,250.*
4	A1 20c dark blue	*2,350.*	
a.	20c blue, *bluish*	*2,200.*	
b.	20c blue, *yelsh*	*2,500.*	
c.	Tête bêche pair	*62,500.*	
e.	As "a," tête bêche pair	*55,000.*	
f.	As "b," tête bêche pair	*72,500.*	

6 A1 25c lt bl, bluish 5,500. 30.00
On cover, single franking 45.00
a. 25c blue, bluish ('50) 5,500. 32.50
On cover, single franking 45.00
b. 25c blue, yelsh 5,250. 40.00
On cover, single franking 60.00
c. Tête bêche pair 140,000. 11,000.
On cover 24,000.
7 A1 40c org, yelsh (I) ('50) 3,250. 475.00
With dark brownish gum 2,000.
On cover, single franking 550.00
a. 40c org ver, yelsh (I) 3,350. 475.00
On cover, single franking 650.00
b. 40c orange, yelsh (II) 22,000. 5,600.
On cover, single franking 11,000.
c. Pair, types I and II 35,000. 11,000.
On cover 15,000.
f. Pair, type II 92,500. 47,500.
On cover 57,500.
g. Vertical half used as 20c on cover 165,000.
8 A1 1fr vermilion, yelsh 65,000. 17,000.
On cover, single franking 40,000.
a. 1fr dull orange red 80,000. 18,500.
On cover, single franking 26,000.
b. Tête bêche pair 500,000. 125,000.
On cover 275,000.
c. 1fr pale ver ("Vervelle") 20,000.
d. As "c," tête bêche pair 365,000.

A cover bearing a single franking with 1fr vermilion, No. 8, realized the equivalent of U.S. $36,350 at a Geneva auction in 2004.

A tete-beche pair, No. 8b, in a used horizontal strip of three sold at a Paris auction in 2003 for the equivalent of U.S. $287,500.

9 A1 1fr light carmine 10,000. 700.00
On cover, single franking 2,000.
a. Tête bêche pair 165,000. 20,000.
On cover 50,000.
b. 1fr brown carmine 10,000. 900.00
On cover, single franking 1,300.
c. 1fr dark carmine, yelsh 10,000. 750.00
On cover, single franking 1,050.
e. 1fr red brown 16,000. 2,000.
On cover, single franking, from 2,500.

Full margins = ¾mm.

No. 4 was printed but not yet gummed when the rate change to 25c made them unnecessary. An essay with a red "25" surcharge on No. 4 was rejected.

An ungummed sheet of No. 8c was found in 1895 among the effects of Anatole A. Hulot, the printer. It was sold to Ernest Vervelle, a Parisian dealer, by whose name the stamps are known.

No. 9e exists used from the beginning of 1849. On-cover values: January to March dates, $6,000; April and May dates, $3,300; June and later dates, $2,500.

See Nos. 329-329e, 612-613, 624.

Values for stamps without gum

1 A1 10c bis, yelsh 550.
a. 10c dark bister, yelsh 500.
b. 10c greenish bister 775.
c. 10c deep greenish bister 1,750.
2 A1 15c green, grnsh 5,000.
a. 15c yellow green, grnsh 5,000.
b. 15c dark green 5,750.
3 A1 20c blk, yelsh 135.
a. 20c black 140.
b. 20c black, buff 475.
4 A1 20c dark blue 2,250.
a. 20c blue, bluish 2,300.
b. 20c blue, yellowish 2,750.
6 A1 25c lt bl, bluish 1,800.
a. 25c blue, bluish ('50) 1,850.
b. 25c blue, yelsh 1,850.
7 A1 40c org, yelsh (I) 1,000.
a. 40c org ver, yelsh (I) 1,000.
b. 40c orange, yelsh (II) 5,000.
c. Pair, types I and II 10,500.
f. Pair, type II 25,000.
8 A1 1fr vermilion, yelsh 33,000.
a. 1fr dull orange red 27,500
c. 1fr pale ver ("Vervelle") 20,000.
9 A1 1fr light carmine 2,500.
b. 1fr brown carmine 3,500.
c. 1fr dark carmine, yelsh 3,000.

e. 1fr red brown 6,000.

Values for blocks of 4

1 A1 10c bis, yelsh 8,400. 8,750.
On cover 13,500.
b. 10c greenish bister 13,250. 11,000.
On cover 14,000.
2 A1 15c green, grnsh 95,000. 55,000.
On cover 86,000.
b. 15c dark green 110,000. 66,000.
On cover 100,000.
3 A1 20c blk, yelsh 1,650. 3,700.
On cover 8,000.
a. 20c black 2,000. 4,250.
On cover 8,750.
4 A1 20c dark blue 10,000.
a. 20c blue, bluish 11,000.
b. 20c blue, yelsh 11,500.
6 A1 25c lt bl, bluish 23,000. —
a. 25c blue, bluish ('50) 29,500. 4,200.
On cover 6,000.
7 A1 40c org, yelsh (I) 20,000. 14,000.
On cover 20,000.
8 A1 1fr vermilion, yelsh 350,000. 110,000.
a. 1fr dull orange red 350,000. 120,000.
c. 1fr pale ver ("Vervelle") 140,000.
9b A1 1fr brown carmine 55,000. 12,500.
On cover 20,000.
c. 1fr dark carmine, yelsh 52,500. 11,500.
On cover 19,000.
d. 1fr red brown 280,000. —

Values for used pairs

1 A1 10c bis, yelsh 700.
a. 10c dark bister, yelsh 775.
b. 10c greenish bister 850.
c. 10c deep greenish bister 1,450.
2 A1 15c green, grnsh 1,900.
a. 15c yellow green, grnsh 2,000.
b. 15c dark green 2,000.
3 A1 20c blk, yelsh 90.
a. 20c black 100.
b. 20c black, buff 675.
6 A1 25c lt bl, bluish 67.50
a. 25c blue, bluish ('50) 80.
b. 25c blue, yelsh 90.
7 A1 40c org, yelsh (I) 900.
a. 40c org ver, yelsh (I) 1,250.
c. Pair, types I and II 11,750.
c. Pair, type II 45,000.
8 A1 1fr vermilion, yelsh 40,000.
a. 1fr dull orange red 42,500.
9 A1 1fr light carmine 1,600.
b. 1fr brown carmine 2,250.
c. 1fr dark carmine, yelsh 1,650.
e. 1fr red brown 4,500.

Values for pairs on cover

1 A1 10c bis, yelsh 1,100.
a. 10c dark bister, yelsh 1,200.
b. 10c greenish bister 1,275.
c. 10c deep greenish bister 2,200.
2 A1 15c green, grnsh 32,500.
a. 15c yellow green, grnsh 32,500.
b. 15c dark green 32,500.
3 A1 20c blk, yelsh 200.
a. 20c black 260.
b. 20c black, buff 800.
6 A1 25c lt bl, bluish 165.
a. 25c blue, bluish ('50) 165.
b. 25c blue, yelsh 185.
7 A1 40c org, yelsh (I) 1,250.
a. 40c org ver, yelsh (I) 1,350.
c. Pair, types I and II 16,500.
f. Pair, type II 62,500.
8 A1 1fr vermilion, yelsh 57,500.
a. 1fr dull orange red 60,000.
9 A1 1fr light carmine 2,400.
b. 1fr brown carmine 2,800.
c. 1fr dark carmine, yelsh 2,750.

Nos. 1, 4a, 6a, 7 and 13 are of similar designs and colors to French Colonies Nos. 9, 11, 12, 14, and 8. There are numerous shades of each. Identification by those who are not experts can be difficult, though cancellations can be used as a guide for used stamps.

Because of the date of issue the Colonies stamps are similar in shades and papers to the perforated French stamps, Nos. 23a, 54, 57-59, and are not as clearly printed. Except for No. 13, unused, the French Colonies stamps sell for much less than the values shown here for properly identified French versions.

Expertization of these stamps is recommended.

1862 **Re-issue**

1g A1 10c bister 375.
2d A1 15c yellow green 475.
3d A1 20c black, yellowish 325.
4d A1 20c blue 325.
6d A1 25c blue 350.
7d A1 40c orange (I) 475.
7e A1 40c orange (II) 10,000.
h. Pair, types I and II 15,000.
i. Pair, type II 28,500.
9d A1 1fr pale lake 475.

The re-issues are fine impressions in lighter colors and on whiter paper than the originals. An official imitation of the essay, 25c on 20c blue, also in a lighter shade and on whiter paper, was made at the same time as the re-issues.

Values for blocks of 4

1d A1 10c bister 1,600.
2d A1 15c yellow green 2,100.
3d A1 20c black, yellowish 1,450.
4d A1 20c blue 1,325.
6d A1 25c blue 1,600.
7d A1 40c orange (I) 2,000.
9d A1 1fr pale lake 2,200.

President Louis Napoleon — A2

Emperor Napoleon III — A3

1852

10 A2 10c pale bister, yelsh 28,500. 450.00
On cover, single franking 800.00
a. 10c dark bister, yelsh 32,000. 575.00
On cover, single franking 900.00
c. 10c dark brownish bister 36,500. 800.00
On cover, single franking 1,250.
11 A2 25c blue, bluish 2,300. 35.00
On cover, single franking 62.50
b. 25c dark blue, bluish 2,800. 52.50
On cover, single franking 80.00
c. 25c greenish blue 3,000. 90.00
On cover, single franking 140.00

Full margins = ¾mm.

Values for stamps without gum

10 A2 10c pale bister, yelsh 6,000.
a. 10c dark bister, yelsh 6,600.
c. 10c dark brownish bister 9,000.
11 A2 25c blue, bluish 800.
b. 25c dark blue, bluish 950.
c. 25c greenish blue 1,050.

Values for used pairs

10 A2 10c pale bister, yelsh 1,050.
11 A2 25c blue, bluish 80.

A sheet margin pair of 10 centimes, No. 10, realized the equivalent of U.S. $20,000 at a Geneva auction in 2004.

Values for pairs on cover

10 A2 10c pale bister, yelsh 1,850.
a. 10c dark bister, yelsh 2,400.
c. 10c dark brownish bister 2,800.
11 A2 25c blue, bluish 200.
b. 25c dark blue, bluish 250.
c. 25c greenish blue 360.

Values for used strips of 3

10 A2 10c pale bister, yelsh 2,350.
11 A2 25c blue, bluish 220.

Values for used strips of 4

10 A2 10c pale bister, yelsh 3,800.
11 A2 25c blue, bluish 500.

Values for used strips of 5

10 A2 10c pale bister, yelsh 7,500.
11 A2 25c blue, bluish 1,175.

Values for blocks of 4

10 A2 10c pale bister, yelsh 33,000.
On cover 60,000.
11 A2 25c blue, bluish 11,500. 1,750.
On cover 3,000.

1862 **Re-issue**

10b A2 10c bister 450.00
11a A2 25c blue 300.00

The re-issues are in lighter colors and on whiter paper than the originals.

Values for blocks of 4

10b A2 10c bister 2,100.
11a A2 25c blue 1,300.

1853-60 ***Imperf.***

Die I. The curl above the forehead directly below "R" of "EMPIRE" is made up of two lines very close together, often appearing to form a single thick line. There is no shading across the neck.

Die II. The curl is made of two distinct, more widely separated lines. There are lines of shading across the upper neck.

12 A3 1c ol grn, pale bl ('60) 150.00 65.00
On cover 145.00
On cover, single franking 300.00
a. 1c bronze grn, pale bluish 150.00 70.00
On cover 145.00
On cover, single franking 300.00
13 A3 5c grn, grnsh (I) ('54) 575.00 70.00
On cover 120.00
On cover, single franking 200.00
a. 5c dark green 1,050. 125.00
On cover 150.00
On cover, single franking 240.00
14 A3 10c bis, yelsh (I) 325.00 6.50
On cover, single franking 9.00
a. 10c yellow, yelsh (I) 1,400. 50.00
On cover, single franking 67.50
b. 10c bister brn, yelsh (I) 450.00 15.00
On cover, single franking 22.00
c. 10c bister, yelsh (II) ('60) 400.00 20.00
On cover, single franking 27.50
15 A3 20c bl, bluish (I) ('54) 140.00 1.00
On cover, single franking 1.50
a. 20c dark bl, bluish(I) 225.00 1.50
On cover, single franking 2.50
b. 20c milky blue (I) 225.00 11.00
On cover, single franking 14.50
c. 20c blue, lilac(I) 3,650. 62.50
On cover 85.00
d. 20c blue, bluish(II) ('60) 275.00 3.50
On cover 5.00
e. Half used as 10c on cover 16,500.
f. Tête-bêche pair 115,000.
16 A3 20c bl, grnsh(II) 3,800. 150.00
On cover, single franking 200.00
a. 20c blue, greenish(I) 4,650. 150.00
On cover 215.00
17 A3 25c bl, bluish(I) 1,900. 175.00
On cover, single franking 325.00
a. 25c milky blue (I) 2,000. 190.00
On cover, single franking 340.00
18 A3 40c org, yelsh(I) 1,900. 10.00
On cover, single franking 14.50
a. 40c org ver, yellowish 2,650. 14.00
On cover, single franking 22.50
b. Half used as 20c on cover 60,000.
19 A3 80c lake, yelsh (I) ('54) 2,500. 45.00
On cover, single franking 90.00
a. Tête bêche pair 350,000. 15,000.
On cover 57,500.
b. Half used as 40c on cover 35,000.
20 A3 80c rose, pnksh (I) ('60) 1,400. 35.00
On cover, single franking 55.00
a. Tete bêche pair 50,000. 9,500.
On cover, single franking 17,500.
b. 80c bright rose 1,650. 50.00
On cover, single franking 75.00
d. 80c pale rose 1,400. 37.50
On cover, single franking 67.50
e. 80c bright gooseberry red ("groseille") 3,300. 200.00
On cover, single franking 275.00
21 A3 1fr lake, yelsh (I) 6,500. 2,500.
On cover 5,000.
On cover, single franking 6,000.
a. Tête bêche pair 300,000. 100,000.
On cover 155,000.

Full margins = ¾mm.

Most values of the 1853-60 issue are known privately rouletted, pin-perf., perf. 7 and percé en scie.

A vertical mint pair of No. 19a was sold at a Paris auction in 2003 for the equivalent of $345,000.
A vertical pair of No. 19a on cover, addressed to Peru, was sold at a Paris auction in 2003 for the equivalent of $57,500.
A horizontal mint pair of No. 20a was sold at a Paris auction in 2003 for the equivalent of $46,000.
A horizontal pair of No. 20a on cover, addressed to Tuscany, was sold at a Paris auction in 2003 for the equivalent of $17,250.
An example of No. 21a, tête bêche pair within a mint block of 6, was sold at a Paris auction in 2003 for the equivalent of $431,250.

Values for bisected stamps on cover

14d A3 10c Nangis, *5/7/55* —
15e A3 20c Bordeaux, *Feb. '56* *12,000.*
15e A3 20c Marines, *Sep. '56)* *16,500.*
15e A3 20c Meru, *Sep. '56* *16,500.*
15e A3 20c Sainte-Sigolene, *Feb. '56* *18,000.*
15e A3 20c Vebron, *June '61-Jan '62* *16,500.*
15e A3 20c Villars-de-Lans, *Jan '58* *19,000.*
18b A3 40c Mosta-ganem, *May '60* *60,000.*
19b A3 80c Givors *35,000.*

Nos. 14d and 18b are unique.

Values for stamps without gum

12 A3 1c ol grn, *pale bl* 60.00
a. 1c bronze grn, *pale bluish* 65.00
13 A3 5c grn, *grnsh (I)* 200.00
a. 5c dark green 375.00
14 A3 10c bis, *yelsh* (I) 115.00
a. 10c yellow, *yelsh* (I) 540.00
b. 10c bister brn, *yelsh* (I) 165.00
c. 10c bister, *yelsh* (II) 150.00
15 A3 20c bl, *bluish* (I) 50.00
a. 20c dark bl, *bluish* (I) 82.50
b. 20c milky blue (I) 85.00
c. 20c blue, *lilac* (I) 1,150.
d. 20c blue, *bluish* (II) 105.00
16 A3 20c bl, *grnsh* (II) 1,125.
a. 20c blue, *greenish* (I) 1,450.
17 A3 25c bl, *bluish* (I) 725.00
a. 25c milky blue (I) 725.00
18 A3 40c org, *yelsh* (I) 625.00
a. 40c org ver, *yellowish* 775.00
19 A3 80c lake, *yelsh* (I) 775.00
20 A3 80c rose, *pnksh* (I) 475.00
20b A3 80c bright rose 525.00
20d A3 80c pale rose 475.00
20e A3 80c bright gooseberry red ("groseille") 1,500.
21 A3 1fr lake, *yelsh* (I) 1,600.

Values for pairs

12 A3 1c ol grn, *pale bl,* 150.00
a. 1c bronze grn, *pale bluish,* 165.00
13 A3 5c grn, *grnsh* (I) 150.00
a. 5c dark green 300.00
14 A3 10c bis, *yelsh* (I) 16.00
a. 10c yellow, *yelsh* (I) 125.00
b. 10c bister brn, *yelsh* (I) 52.50
c. 10c bister, *yelsh* (II) 47.50
15 A3 20c bl, *bluish* (I) 3.50
a. 20c dark bl, *bluish* (I) 3.50
b. 20c milky blue (I) 30.00
c. 20c blue, *lilac* (I) 165.00
d. 20c blue, *bluish* (II) 10.00
16 A3 20c bl, *grnsh* (II) 375.00
a. 20c blue, *greenish* (I) 375.00
17 A3 25c bl, *bluish* (I) 425.00
a. 25c milky blue (I) 450.00
18 A3 40c org, *yelsh* (I) 24.00
a. 40c org ver, *yellowish* 37.50
19 A3 80c lake, *yelsh* (I) 165.00
20 A3 80c rose, *pnksh* (I) 95.00
21 A3 1fr lake, *yelsh* (I) *4,750.*

Values for pairs on cover

12 A3 1c ol grn, *pale bl,* on cover, paying 2c rate 375.00
a. 1c bronze grn, *pale bluish,* on cover, paying 2c rate 385.00

13 A3 5c grn, *grnsh* (I) on cover, paying 10c rate 185.00
a. 5c dark green, on cover, paying 10c rate 350.00
14 A3 10c bis, *yelsh* (I) 18.50
a. 10c yellow, *yelsh* (I) 150.00
b. 10c bister brn, *yelsh* (I) 57.50
c. 10c bister, *yelsh* (II) 70.00
15 A3 20c bl, *bluish* (I) 4.00
a. 20c dark bl, *bluish* (I) 5.50
b. 20c milky blue (I) 37.50
c. 20c blue, *lilac* (I) 215.00
d. 20c blue, *bluish* (II) 11.00
16 A3 20c bl, *grnsh* (II) 500.00
a. 20c blue, *greenish* (I) 525.00
17 A3 25c bl, *bluish* (I) 875.00
a. 25c milky blue (I) 925.00
18 A3 40c org, *yelsh* (I) 37.50
a. 40c org ver, *yellowish* 55.00
19 A3 80c lake, *yelsh* (I) 225.00
20 A3 80c rose, *pnksh* (I) 150.00
Strip of 3 on cover 175.00
Strip of 4 on cover 275.00
Strip of 5 on cover 450.00
21 A3 1fr lake, *yelsh* (I) *11,750.*

Blocks of 4

12 A3 1c ol grn, *pale bl,* 725.00 875.00
On cover 1,750.
13 A3 5c grn, *grnsh* (I) 2,800. 925.00
On cover 1,750.
a. 5c dark green 4,800. 1,200.
On cover 2,200.
14 A3 10c bister, *yellowish* (I) 1,650. 225.00
On cover 400.00
c. 10c bister, *yellowish* (II) 2,150. 375.00
On cover 600.00
15 A3 20c blue, *bluish* (I) 675.00 72.50
On cover 135.00
a. 20c dark blue, *bluish* (I) 1,000. 100.00
On cover 175.00
d. 20c blue, *bluish* (II) 1,400. 375.00
On cover 525.00
16 A3 20c blue, *greenish* (II) *2,300.*
On cover *3,650.*
a. 20c blue, *greenish* (I) *1,350.*
On cover *2,200.*
17 A3 25c bl, *bluish* (I) 9,000. 2,000.
On cover 3,000.
18 A3 40c orange, *yellowish* (I) 9,250. 600.00
On cover 1,000.
19 A3 80c lake, *yellowish* (I) 14,000. 675.00
On cover 1,200.
20 A3 80c rose, *pinkish* (I) 7,250. 475.00
On cover 825.00
21 A3 1fr lake, *yellowish* (I) *22,500.* *20,000.*
On cover *35,000.*

1862 **Re-issue**

17c A3 25c blue (I) 350.
19c A3 80c lake (I) 1,350.
21c A3 1fr lake (I) 1,175.
d. Tête bêche pair *30,000.*

Blocks of 4

17c A3 25c blue (I) 1,525.
19c A3 80c lake (I) 6,350.
21c A3 1fr lake (I) 5,000.
d. Tête bêche pair in block *40,000.*

The re-issues are in lighter colors and on whiter paper than the originals.

No. 21d tête bêche pair in block of 6 was sold at a Paris auction in 2003 for the equivalent of $37,375.

1862-71 ***Perf. 14x13½***

22 A3 1c ol grn, *pale bl* (II) 140.00 30.00
On cover 70.00
On cover, single franking 110.00
a. 1c bronze grn, *pale bl* (II) 140.00 35.00
On cover 70.00
On cover, single franking 110.00
b. 1c bronze gold ("mordore") 325.00
23 A3 5c yel grn, *grnsh* (I) 150.00 8.00
On cover 22.00
On cover, single franking 50.00
a. 5c deep green, *grnsh* (I) 200.00 11.50
On cover 30.00
On cover, single franking 57.50
24 A3 5c grn, *pale bl* ('71) (I) 1,650. 90.00
On cover 110.00
On cover, single franking 240.00
25 A3 10c bis, *yelsh* (II) 1,100. 8.25
On cover, single franking 4.75
a. 10c yel brn, *yelsh* (II) 1,100. 4.00
On cover, single franking 5.00
26 A3 20c bl, *bluish* (II) 190.00 .90
On cover, single franking 1.00
a. Tête bêche pair (II) 3,300. 800.00
On cover 1,900.
b. 20c dark blue 250.00 .85
On cover, single franking 1.00
c. 20c pale blue 180.00 .65
On cover, single franking 1.00
d. 20c blue, *azure* 300.00 .85
On cover, single franking 1.00
27 A3 40c org, *yelsh* (I) 1,050. 6.75
On cover, single franking 8.75
a. 40c pale orange 1,050. 6.75
On cover, single franking 8.25
b. 40c yellow orange 1,150. 7.25
On cover, single franking 9.25
c. 40c bright orange 1,500. 8.75
On cover, single franking 12.00
28 A3 80c rose, *pnksh* (I) 1,000. 30.00
On cover 45.00
On cover, single franking 52.50
a. 80c bright rose, *pinkish* (I) 1,250. 35.00
On cover 55.00
On cover, single franking 67.50
b. 80c carmine rose (I) 1,600. 60.00
On cover 75.00
On cover, single franking 87.50
c. Tête bêche pair (I) *16,000.* *7,000.*
On cover *16,500.*

No. 26a imperf is from a trial printing.

A mint tete-beche pair of 80 centimes, No. 28c, realized the equivalent of U.S. $14,550 at a Geneva auction in 2004.

Values for stamps without gum

22 A3 1c ol grn, *pale bl* (II) 40.00
a. 1c bronze grn, *pale bl* (II) 40.00
b. 1c bronze gold ("mordore") 110.00
23 A3 5c yel grn, *grnsh* (I) 52.50
a. 5c deep green, *grnsh* (I) 67.50
24 A3 5c green, *pale bl* (I) 375.00
25 A3 10c bis, *yelsh* (II) 275.00
a. 10c yel brn, *yelsh* (II) 275.00
26 A3 20c bl, *bluish* (II) 57.50
b. 20c dark blue 85.00
c. 20c pale blue 60.00
d. 20c blue, *azure* 100.00
27 A3 40c org, *yelsh* (I) 300.00
a. 40c pale orange 300.00
b. 40c yellow orange 315.00
c. 40c bright orange 500.00
28 A3 80c rose, *pnksh* (I) 315.00
a. 80c bright rose, *pinkish* (I) 375.00
b. 80c carmine rose (I) 475.00

Values for used pairs

22 A3 1c ol grn, *pale bl* (II) 67.50
a. 1c bronze grn, *pale bl* (II) 70.00
23 A3 5c yel grn, *grnsh* (I) 18.50
a. 5c deep green, *grnsh* (I) 20.00
24 A3 5c green, *pale bl* (I) 225.00
25 A3 10c bis, *yelsh* (II) 8.00
a. 10c yel brn, *yelsh* (II) 8.50
26 A3 20c bl, *bluish* (II) 1.75
b. 20c dark blue 2.00
c. 20c pale blue 1.75
d. 20c blue, *azure* 2.00
27 A3 40c org, *yelsh* (I) 16.50
a. 40c pale orange 17.50
b. 40c yellow orange 18.00
c. 40c bright orange 18.00
28 A3 80c rose, *pnksh* (I) 77.50
a. 80c bright rose, *pinkish* (I) 110.00
b. 80c carmine rose (I) 140.00

Values for pairs on cover

22 A3 1c ol grn, *pale bl* (II) 340.00
a. 1c bronze grn, *pale bl* (II) 340.00
23 A3 5c yel grn, *grnsh* (I) 30.00
a. 5c deep green, *grnsh* (I) 37.50
24 A3 5c green, *pale bl* (I) 300.00
25 A3 10c bis, *yelsh* (II) 9.25
a. 10c yel brn, *yelsh* (II) 9.25
26 A3 20c bl, *bluish* (II) 2.00
b. 20c dark blue 2.75
c. 20c pale blue 2.00
d. 20c blue, *azure* 2.75
27 A3 40c org, *yelsh* (I) 23.50
a. 40c pale orange 23.50
b. 40c yellow orange 25.00
c. 40c bright orange 28.00
28 A3 80c rose, *pnksh* (I) 115.00
a. 80c bright rose, *pinkish* (I) 150.00
b. 80c carmine rose (I) 175.00

Values for strips of 3

22 A3 1c ol grn, *pale bl* (II) 110.00
On cover *400.00*
23 A3 5c yel grn, *grnsh* (I) 32.50
On cover *60.00*
24 A3 5c green, *pale bl* (I) 325.00
On cover *600.00*
25 A3 10c bis, *yelsh* (II) 22.00
On cover *35.00*
26 A3 20c bl, *bluish* (II) 4.00
On cover *12.50*
27 A3 40c org, *yelsh* (I) 30.00
On cover *75.00*
28 A3 80c rose, *pnksh* (I) 150.00
On cover *250.00*
Strip of 4 300.00
On cover *600.00*
Strip of 5 450.00
On cover *900.00*

Values for Blocks of 4

22 A3 1c ol grn, *pale bl* (II) 650.00 350.00
On cover 575.00
23 A3 5c yel grn, *grnsh* (I) 750.00 200.00
On cover 325.00
24 A3 5c green, *pale bl* (I) 11,000. 800.00
On cover 1,350.
25 A3 10c bis, *yelsh* (II) 5,750. 125.00
On cover 250.00
26 A3 20c bl, *bluish* (II) 825.00 67.50
On cover 125.00
27 A3 40c org, *yelsh* (I) 5,500. 250.00
On cover 450.00
28 A3 80c rose, *pnksh* (I) 4,750. 350.00
On cover 575.00

A4

A5

Napoleon III — A6

1863-70 ***Perf. 14x13½***

29 A4 1c brnz grn, *pale bl* ('70) 26.00 10.00
On cover 22.50
On cover, single franking 47.50
a. 1c olive green, *pale blue* 25.00 11.00
On cover 22.50
On cover, single franking 40.00
30 A4 2c red brn, *yelsh* 80.00 20.00
On cover 25.00
On cover, single franking 42.50
b. Half used as 1c on cover *30,000.*
31 A4 4c gray 210.00 42.50
On cover 70.00
On cover, single franking 290.00
a. Tete beche pair *17,500.* *10,750.*
On cover *32,500.*
d. Half used as 2c on cover *47,500.*
32 A5 10c bis, *yelsh* ('67) 400.00 6.75
On cover, single franking 8.00
c. Half used as 5c on cover with other stamps *3,250.*
d. Half used as 5c on cover, single franking *21,500.*
33 A5 20c bl, *bluish* ('67) 250.00 1.50
On cover, single franking 2.00
c. Half used as 10c on cover *44,000.*
34 A5 30c brn, *yelsh* ('67) 650.00 13.50
On cover 16.00
On cover, single franking 20.00
a. 30c dk brn, *yellowish* 1,000. 30.00
On cover 37.50
On cover, single franking 47.50
b. 30c pale brn, 625.00 13.50
On cover, single franking 20.00
35 A5 40c pale org, *yellowish* 650.00 8.75
On cover, single franking 10.00
a. 40c org, *yelsh* ('68) 675.00 11.00
On cover, single franking 14.00
c. Half used as 20c on cover *33,000.*
36 A5 80c rose, *pnksh* ('68) 850.00 20.00
On cover 25.00
On cover, single franking 30.00
a. 80c carmine, *yellowish* 1,150. 29.00
On cover 32.50
On cover, single franking 40.00
d. Half used as 40c on cover *42,500.*
e. Quarter used as 20c on cover *45,000.*
37 A6 5fr gray lil, *lav* ('69) *5,000.* 775.00
On cover 2,100.
On cover, single franking *16,000.*
a. "5" and "F" omitted *67,500.*
c. 5fr bluish gray, *lavender* *5,000.* 800.00
On cover 2,250.
On cover, single franking *16,000.*
d. As #37, "5" and "F" in light blue *5,250.* 875.00

No. 33 exists in two types, differing in the size of the dots at either side of POSTES.

On No. 37, the "5" and "F" vary in height from 3¾mm to 4½mm. These figures normally appear in gray but exist in blue or black.

All known copies of No. 37a are more or less damaged.

No. 29 was reprinted in 1887 by authority of Granet, Minister of Posts. The reprints show a *yellowish shade under the ultraviolet lamp. Value $850.*

For surcharge see No. 49.

Values for stamps without gum

29	A4	1c bronze green, *pale blue*	6.75
a.		1c olive green, *pale blue*	8.00
30	A4	2c red brown, *yellowish*	20.00
31	A4	4c gray	67.50
32	A5	10c bistre, *yellowish*	105.00
33	A5	20c blue, *bluish*	82.50
34	A5	30c brown, *yellowish*	200.00
a.		30c dark brown, *yellowish*	275.00
35	A5	40c orange, *yellowish*	200.00
a.		40c pale orange, *yellowish*	200.00
36	A5	80c rose, *pinkish*	240.00
a.		80c carmine, *yellowish*	375.00
37	A6	5fr gray lilac, *lavender*	1,425.
a.		5fr bluish gray, *lavender*	1,500.

Original Issue Imperfs

31c	A4	4c gray	250.	
32b	A5	10c bis, *yelsh*	375.	
33b	A5	20c bl, *bluish*	250.	
		On cover		13,250.
36c	A5	80c rose, *pnksh*	—	
		On cover		6,750.
37b	A6	5fr gray lil, *lav*	7,750.	
		Block of 4	37,500.	

Imperfs, "Rothschild" Re-issue
Paper Colors are the Same

29b	A4	1c olive green	850.
30a	A4	2c pale red brown	140.
31b	A4	4c pale gray	110.
32a	A5	10c pale bister	110.
33a	A5	20c pale blue	190.
34c	A5	30c pale brown	110.
35b	A5	40c pale orange	150.
36b	A5	80c rose	350.

The re-issues constitute the "Rothschild Issue." These stamps were authorized exclusively for the banker to use on his correspondence. Used copies exist.

Ceres

A7 A8

A9 A10

A11

Bordeaux Issue

On the lithographed stamps, except for type I of the 20c, the shading on the cheek and neck is in lines or dashes, not in dots. On the typographed stamps the shading is in dots. The 2c, 10c and 20c (types II and III) occur in two or more types. The most easily distinguishable are:

2c — Type A. To the left of and within the top of the left "2" are lines of shading composed of dots.

2c — Type B. These lines of dots are replaced by solid lines.

10c — Type A. The inner frame lines are of the same thickness as all other frame lines.

10c — Type B. The inner frame lines are much thicker than the others.

Three Types of the 20c.

A9 — The inscriptions in the upper and lower labels are small and there is quite a space between the upper label and the circle containing the head. There is also very little shading under the eye and in the neck.

A10 — The inscriptions in the labels are similar to those of the first type, the shading under the eye and in the neck is heavier and the upper label and circle almost touch.

A11 — The inscriptions in the labels are much larger than those of the two preceding types, and are similar to those of the other values of the same type in the set.

1870-71 Litho. *Imperf.*

38	A7	1c ol grn, *pale bl*	100.00	110.00
		On cover		300.00
		On cover, single franking		1,000.
a.		1c bronze green, *pale blue*	125.00	125.00
		On cover		325.00
		On cover, single franking		975.00
39	A7	2c red brn, *yelsh* (B)	190.00	190.00
		On cover		500.00
		On cover, single franking		1,825.
a.		2c brick red, *yelsh* (B)	625.00	525.00
		On cover		775.00
		On cover, single franking		2,000.
b.		2c chestnut, *yelsh* (B)	1,050.	575.00
		On cover		750.00
		On cover, single franking		2,000.
c.		2c chocolate, *yelsh* (A)	825.00	625.00
		On cover		900.00
		On cover, single franking		2,150.
40	A7	4c gray	200.00	175.00
		On cover		675.00
		On cover, single franking		*11,000.*
41	A8	5c yel green, *greenish*	190.00	125.00
		On cover		375.00
		On cover, single franking		3,150.
a.		5c grn, *grnsh*	275.00	175.00
		On cover		375.00
		On cover, single franking		3,150.
b.		5c emerald, *greenish*	3,000.	1,000.
		On cover		2,000.
		On cover, single franking		4,300.
42	A8	10c bis, *yelsh* (A)	675.00	50.00
		On cover		75.00
		On cover, single franking		100.00
a.		10c bister, *yellowish* (B)	700.00	75.00
		On cover, single franking		135.00
43	A9	20c bl, *bluish*	*16,000.*	450.00
		On cover		675.00
a.		20c dark blue, *bluish*	*19,000.*	600.00
		On cover, single franking		875.00
44	A10	20c bl, *bluish*	800.00	37.50
		On cover, single franking		50.00
a.		20c dark blue, *bluish*	1,000.	72.50
		On cover, single franking		95.00
b.		20c ultra, *bluish*	*16,500.*	*2,650.*
		On cover, single franking		*3,750.*
45	A11	20c bl, *bluish* ('71)	725.00	13.50
		On cover, single franking		17.50
a.		20c ultra, *bluish*	1,825.	500.00
		On cover, single franking		650.00
46	A8	30c brn, *yelsh*	250.00	160.00
		On cover		300.00
		On cover, single franking		300.00
a.		30c blk brn, *yelsh*	1,450.	575.00
		On cover		750.00
		On cover, single franking		825.00
47	A8	40c org, *yelsh*	325.00	90.00
		On cover, single franking		125.00
a.		40c yel orange, *yelsh*	1,000.	175.00
		On cover, single franking		300.00
b.		40c red orange, *yelsh*	500.00	150.00
		On cover, single franking		200.00
c.		40c scarlet, *yelsh*	*4,000.*	*1,350.*
		On cover, single franking		*1,900.*
d.		40c lemon yellow	*8,000.*	*1,600.*
		On cover, single franking		*2,000.*
e.		40c ochre	*5,750.*	*1,300.*
		On cover, single franking		*1,900.*
f.		40c orange vermilion	825.00	240.00
		On cover, single franking		300.00
g.		40c pale red	825.00	550.00
		On cover, single franking		775.00
48	A8	80c rose, *pinkish*	400.00	225.00
		On cover		450.00
		On cover, single franking		500.00
a.		80c dull rose, *pinkish*	400.00	210.00
		On cover		450.00
		On cover, single franking		500.00
b.		80c bright rose	575.00	240.00
		On cover		450.00
		On cover, single franking		500.00
c.		80c carmine rose	775.00	300.00
		On cover		500.00
		On cover, single franking		575.00
d.		80c deep carmine rose	975.00	525.00
		On cover		575.00
		On cover, single franking		925.00
e.		80c salmon	3,000.	1,350.
		On cover		1,700.
		On cover, single franking		2,000.
f.		80c reddish crimson	1,600.	800.00
		On cover		1,000.
		On cover, single franking		1,200.

All values of the 1870 issue are known privately rouletted, pin-perf and perf. 14.

See Nos. 50-53.

Values for stamps without gum

38	A7	1c olive green, *pale bl*	52.50
a.		1c bronze green, *pale blue*	52.50
39	A7	2c red brown, *yellowish* (B)	92.50
a.		2c brick red, *yellowish* (B)	250.00
b.		2c chestnut, *yellowish* (B)	425.00
c.		2c chocolate, *yellowish* (A)	300.00
40	A7	4c gray	92.50
41	A8	5c yellow green, *greenish*	97.50
a.		5c green, *grnsh*	125.00
b.		5c emerald, *greenish*	1,175.
42	A8	10c bister, *yellowish* (A)	240.00
a.		10c bister, *yellowish* (B)	240.00
43	A9	20c blue, *bluish*	*5,000.*
a.		20c dark blue, *bluish*	*5,750.*
44	A10	20c blue, *bluish*	240.00
a.		20c dark blue, *bluish*	275.00
b.		20c ultrmarine, *bluish*	5,000.
45	A11	20c blue, *bluish* ('71)	250.00
a.		20c ultramarine, *bluish*	675.00
46	A8	30c brown, *yellowish*	120.00
a.		30c black brown, *yellowish*	625.00
47	A8	40c orange, *yellowish*	150.00
a.		40c yellow orange, *yellowish*	525.00
b.		40c red orange, *yellowish*	200.00
c.		40c scarlet, *yellowish*	1,350.
d.		40c lemon yellow	*2,350.*
e.		40c ochre	*1,750.*
f.		40c orange vermilion	250.00
g.		40c pale red	300.00
48	A8	80c rose, *pinkish*	160.00
a.		80c dull rose, *pinkish*	190.00
b.		80c bright rose	260.00
c.		80c carmine rose	340.00
d.		80c deep carmine rose	475.00
e.		80c salmon	1,350.
f.		80c reddish crimson	675.00

A12

Blue Surcharge

1871 Typo. *Perf. 14x13½*

49	A12	10c on 10c bister	1,300.
		Without gum	600.00
		Block of 4, with gum	*6,000.*
a.		Pale blue surcharge	1,400.
		Without gum	650.00
		Block of 4, with gum	*6,500.*

#49 was never placed in use. Counterfeits exist.

A13 A14

Two types of the 40c as in the 1849-50 issue.

1870-73 Typo. *Perf. 14x13½*

50	A7	1c ol grn, *pale bl*	37.50	10.00
		On cover		22.50
		On cover, single franking		57.50
a.		1c bronze grn, *pale bl* ('72)	42.50	11.00
		On cover		21.00
		On cover, single franking		57.50
51	A7	2c red brn, *yelsh* ('70)	77.50	13.50
		On cover		22.50
		On cover, single franking		60.00
52	A7	4c gray ('70)	225.00	32.50
		On cover		85.00
		On cover, single franking		240.00
53	A7	5c yel grn, *pale bl* ('72)	140.00	6.75
		On cover		10.00
		On cover, single franking		16.50
a.		5c green	140.00	7.25
		On cover		11.00
		On cover, single franking		18.50
54	A13	10c bis, *yelsh*	500.00	50.00
		On cover		80.00
		On cover, single franking		145.00
a.		Tête beche pair	*4,750.*	*1,900.*
		On cover		*4,350.*
b.		Half used as 5c on cover		*3,750.*
55	A13	10c bis, *rose* ('73)	240.00	9.25
		On cover		11.00
		On cover, single franking		13.50
a.		Tête bêche pair	3,500.	1,500.
		On cover		2,900.
56	A13	15c bis, *yelsh* ('71)	300.00	3.25
		On cover		5.25
a.		Tête bêche pair	*37,500.*	*13,000.*
		On cover		*27,500.*
57	A13	20c dl bl, *bluish*	200.00	5.25
		On cover		8.00
a.		20c bright blue, *bluish*	325.00	6.75
		On cover		11.00
b.		Tête bêche pair	3,250.	1,300.
		On cover		3,000.
c.		Half used as 10c on cover		*55,000.*
d.		Quarter used as 5c on cover		*50,000.*
58	A13	25c bl, *bluish* ('71)	100.00	1.40
		On cover		2.00
a.		25c dk bl, *bluish*	150.00	1.40
		On cover		2.00
b.		Tête bêche pair	*6,500.*	*2,750.*
		On cover		*9,000.*
59	A13	40c org, *yelsh* (I)	425.00	5.25
		On cover		6.75
a.		40c orange yel, *yelsh* (I)	550.00	6.75
		On cover		9.25
b.		40c orange, *yelsh* (II)	2,750.	110.00
		On cover		210.00
c.		40c orange yel, *yelsh* (II)	2,750.	110.00
		On cover		220.00
d.		Pair, types I and II	*5,750.*	375.00
		On cover		775.00
e.		Pair, both type II	*17,500.*	2,150.
		On cover		2,500.
f.		Half used as 20c on circular		*22,000.*
g.		Half used as 20c on cover		*40,000.*

No. 58 exists in three main plate varieties, differing in one or another of the flower-like corner ornaments.

Margins on this issue are extremely small.

Nos. 54, 57 and 58 were reprinted imperf. in 1887. See note after No. 37.

Values for stamps without gum

50	A7	1c olive green, *pale bl*	10.00
a.		1c bronze green, *pale blue* ('72)	11.50
51	A7	2c red brown, *yellowish* ('70)	24.00
52	A7	4c gray	92.50
53	A7	5c yellow green, *pale blue*	42.50
a.		5c green	47.50
54	A13	10c bister, *yellowish*	160.00
55	A13	10c bister, *rose*	82.50
56	A13	15c bister, *yellowish*	92.50
57	A13	20c dull blue, *bluish*	67.50
a.		20c bright blue, *bluish*	100.00
58	A13	25c blue, *bluish*	37.50
a.		25c dark blue, *bluish*	42.50
59	A13	40c orange, *yellowish* (I)	140.00
a.		40c orange yellow, *yellowish* (I)	160.00
b.		40c orange, *yellowish* (II)	850.00
c.		40c orange yellow, *yellowish* (II)	850.00
d.		Pair, types I and II	*1,500.*
e.		Pair, both type II	*4,000.*

Imperf.

50b	A7	1c	250.00
51a	A7	2c	300.00
52a	A7	4c	575.00
53b	A7	5c yel grn, *pale bl*	250.00
55b	A13	10c	300.00
56b	A13	15c	300.00

"Ballons Montes" are letters which left Paris between Sept. 23, 1870, and Jan. 28, 1871, towards the end of the Franco-Prussian War. Placed under siege by the German army, the French capital was isolated from the rest of the world. With all other means of communication severed, Parisians took to the air, inaugurating what many consider to be the world's first air mail. Of the 67 balloons that were launched from Paris, 56 carried mail that passed through the Paris Post Office, including private letters, newspapers and official documents. While some balloons were unmanned, most carried at least a single person in addition to the 225-275 pounds of mail.

Ballons Montes can usually be identified by examination of the dates of posting, transit and arrival postmarks. Carried by capricious winds, each balloon landed in a different and unexpected location. Some crashed, some fell into the English Channel and many came down in German-controlled territory. When balloons landed in French territory or countries friendly to France, postal authorities enthusiastically aided the Parisians by sending the recovered mail by the most direct and efficient route to its destination. This use of a bewildering variety of postal routes is reflected in the unusual postal markings found on most Ballon Montes. While mail that fell into German hands was usually confiscated, on some occassions, German authorities actually helped deliver the mail to its intended destination. Mail confiscated by the Germans was posted following the conclusion of hostilities.

Ballon Montes are valued according to five criteria, three of which are reflected in the tables that follow. The base value is determined by the balloon that carried the cover. Values for the destination and the franking used to pay the postage are then added to the base value as premiums. Not reflected in the tables below are premiums for the nature and contents of the cover and any postmarks applied to the cover prior to its departure on the balloon. **Covers are valued in Very Fine condition.**

Base values for Ballons Montes

Scott #	Balloon Name	Date	Departure Time	Value From
BM1	*Neptune*	Sept. 23	08:00 a.m.	*6,750.*
BM2	*Ville de Florence*	Sept. 25	11:00 a.m.	500.
BM3	*Etats-Unis*	Sept. 29	10:30 a.m.	375.
a.	With transit postmark: *Gare de Mantes Sept. 29*			650.
BM4	*Celeste*	Sept. 30	09:30 a.m.	275.
BM5	Unnamed #1	Sept. 30	noon	190.
BM6	*Armand-Barbes*	Oct. 7	11:10 a.m.	160.
BM7	*George-Sand*	Oct. 7	11:10 a.m.	*4,000.*
BM8	Unnamed #2	Oct. 7	02:15 p.m.	225.
BM9	*Washington*	Oct. 12	08:00 a.m.	175.
a.	With transit postmark: *Douai Oct. 13*			325.
BM10	*Louis-Blanc*	Oct. 12	09:00 a.m.	160.
a.	With Travelling Post Office postmark: *Lille a Paris Oct. 12*			325.
BM11	*Godefroy-Cavaignac*	Oct. 14	10:00 a.m.	185.
a.	With transit postmark: *Chaumont Oct. 16*			425.
BM12	*Jean-Bart #1*	Oct. 14	01:15 p.m.	275.
BM13	*Jules-Favre #1*	Oct. 16	07:30 a.m.	160.
BM14	*Jean-Bart #2*	Oct. 16	09:50 a.m.	160.
BM15	*Victor Hugo*	Oct. 18	11:45 a.m.	200.
BM16	*Republique Universelle*	Oct. 19	09:15 a.m.	210.
a.	With transit postmark: *Renwez*			750.
b.	With transit postmark: *Rocroi*			750.
BM17	*Garibaldi*	Oct. 22	11:30 a.m.	200.
BM18	*Montgolfier*	Oct. 25	08:30 a.m.	425.
BM19	*Vauban*	Oct. 27	09:00 a.m.	200.
a.	With transit postmark: *Bar-le-Duc*			550.
BM20	*Bretagne*	Oct. 27	02:10 p.m.	*8,750.*
BM21	*Colonel Charras*	Oct. 29	noon	185.
BM22	*Fulton*	Nov. 2	08:45 a.m.	200.
BM23	*Ferdinand Flocon*	Nov. 4	09:30 a.m.	180.
a.	With transit postmark: *Nantes*			440.
BM24	*Galilee*	Nov. 4	02:00 p.m.	290.
BM25	*Ville de Chateaudun*	Nov. 6	09:45 a.m.	175.
BM26	Unnamed #3	Nov. 7	10:00 a.m.	*9,250.*
BM27	*Gironde*	Nov. 8	08:20 a.m.	220.
BM28	*Daguerre*	Nov. 12	09:00 a.m.	300.
BM29	*Niepce*	Nov. 12	09:15 a.m.	*6,250.*
BM30	*General Ulrich*	Nov. 18	11:15 p.m.	175.
a.	With transit postmark: *Luzarches*			325.
BM31	*Archimede*	Nov. 21	00:45 a.m.	200.
BM32	*Egalite*	Nov. 24	11:30 a.m.	*5,250.*
BM33	*Ville d'Orleans*	Nov. 24	11:30 p.m.	425.
a.	Re-posted from Norway			850.
b.	With transit postmark: *London Dec. 2/Dec. 4*			*1,350.*
BM34	*Jacquard*	Nov. 28	11:00 p.m.	*1,200.*
a.	With transit postmark: *Falmouth*			*4,000.*
b.	Re-posted from La Rochelle Dec. 21			*3,500.*
BM35	*Jules-Favre #2.*	Nov. 30	11:30 p.m.	185.
BM36	*Bataille de Paris*	Dec. 1	05:15 a.m.	*1,850.*
BM37	*Volta*	Dec. 2	08:00 a.m.	
BM38	*Franklin*	Dec. 5	01:00 p.m.	220.
a.	With transit postmark: *Nantes*			350.
BM39	*Armee de Bretagne*	Dec. 5	06:00 a.m.	*4,500.*
BM40	*Denis-Papin*	Dec. 7	01:00 a.m.	250.
BM41	*General Renault*	Dec. 11	02:15 a.m.	250.
a.	With transit postmark: *Foucarmont*			575.
BM42	*Ville de Paris*	Dec. 15	04:45 a.m.	285.
a.	Re-posted at Paris, July 1871			775.
BM43	*Parmentier*	Dec. 17	01:15 a.m.	210.
BM44	*Gutenberg*	Dec. 17	01:25 a.m.	*3,800.*
BM45	*Davy*	Dec. 18	05:00 a.m.	325.
a.	With transit postmark: *Beaune*			525.
BM46	*General Chanzy*	Dec. 20	02:00 a.m.	975.
BM47	*Lavoisier*	Dec. 22	02:30 a.m.	200.
BM48	*Delivrance*	Dec. 23	04:30 a.m.	225.
a.	With transit postmark: *Roche-sur-Yon*			425.
BM49	*Rouget-de-L'isle*	Dec. 24		*5,250.*
BM50	*Tourville*	Dec. 27	04:00 a.m.	200.
BM51	*Merlin de Douai*	Dec. 27	04:00 a.m.	*21,500.*
BM52	*Bayard*	Dec. 29	04:00 a.m.	210.
BM53	*Armee de la Loire*	Dec. 31	05:00 a.m.	210.
BM54	*Newton*	Jan. 4	01:00 a.m.	210.
BM55	*Duquesne*	Jan. 9	03:00 a.m.	200.
BM56	*Gambetta*	Jan. 10	04:15 a.m.	225.
BM57	*Kepler*	Jan. 11	03:00 a.m.	260.
a.	With transit postmark: *Paris a Brest*			400.
BM58	*Monge*	Jan. 13	00:30 a.m.	*8,500.*
BM59	*General Faidherbe*	Jan. 13	03:30 a.m.	215.
a.	With transit postmark: *Ste Foy*			550.
BM60	*Vaucanson*	Jan. 15	03:00 a.m.	210.

Base values for Ballons Montes

Scott #	Balloon Name	Date	Departure Time	Value From
BM61	*Steenackers*	Jan. 16	07:00 a.m.	*8,500.*
BM62	*Poste de Paris*	Jan. 18	03:00 a.m.	235.
BM63	*General Bourbaki*	Jan. 20	05:15 a.m.	220.
BM64	*General Daumesnil*	Jan. 22	04:00 a.m.	200.
BM65	*Torricelli*	Jan. 24	03:00 a.m.	300.
BM66	*Richard Wallace*	Jan. 27	03:30 a.m.	*1,700.*
BM67	*General Cambronne*	Jan. 28	05:45 a.m.	675.

Shortly after take-off, #BM8 crashed inside the French defensive lines and within sight of the encircling German forces. The mail carried by BM8 was salvaged and returned to Paris where it was re-posted on subsequent balloons.

#BM16 was also named *La Lafayette.* #BM20 was also named *le Normandie (A).*

#BM20, BM26, BM29, BM32, BM36, BM44, BM46, BM49, BM58 and BM61 only carried "Plis Confies," which did not pass through the Paris Post Office, but were delivered to either the balloon, the balloon company or the balloon's pilot directly. These covers normally carry postage and were canceled on transit or arrival. Covers passing through the Paris Post Office carry appropriate cancels.

No mail is known from #BM37.

Destinations of Mail Carried by Ballons Montes

Destination	Rate	Premium
French Area		
French Occupied Territory (without arrival pmk.)	20c	+175.
France Occupied Territory (French arrival pmk.)	20c	+850.
France Occupied Territory (German arrival pmk.)	20c	+2,350.
Island of Corsica	20c	+950.
Algeria	20c	+1,000.
Gabon	80c	+23,500.
Guadeloupe	50c	+5,000.
Martinique	50c	+5,000.
Monaco	20c	+8,500.
New Caledonia	70c	+17,000.
Reunion	50c	+12,750.
Senegal	50c	+12,750.
Tunisia	40c	+25,000.
Europe		
Austria	60c	+2,500.
Baden	30c	+1,950.
Bavaria	40c	+1,600.
Belgium	30c	+250.
Bremen	50c	+1,650.
Brunswick	50c	+1,700.
Bulgaria	50c	+7,750.
Canary Islands	40c	+4,000.
Canary Islands (Via England)	80c	+2,750.
Cyprus	40c	+7,000.
Denmark	50c	+4,000.
Denmark (Via Thurn & Taxis)	70c	+3,500.
Germany	40c, 50c	+2,100.
Gibraltar	40c	+4,750.
Great Britain	30c	+250.
Greece (Sea post)	60c	+7,750.
Isle of Wight	30c	+900.
Ireland	30c	+1,450.
Italy	40c	+1,700.
Jersey	30c	+550.
Liechtenstein	60c	+10,000.
Luxembourg	25c	+7,250.
Madeira	80c	+5,000.
Malta	40c	+7,000.
Montenegro	60c	+10,000.
Netherlands	40c	+850.
Norway	70c	+6,000.
Norway (Via Denmark)	1 Franc	+7,750.
Poland	80c	+11,500.
Portugal	40c	+2,600.
Prussia	40c	+1,600.
Rhodes	40c	+6,750.
Roman States	50c	+1,600.
Romania	40c	+12,000.
Russia (with arrival postmark)	80c	+10,000.
Russia (without arrival postmark)	80c	+2,250.
South Russia (with arrival postmark)	1 Franc	+11,500.
South Russia (without arrival postmark)	1 Franc	+2,600.
Saxony	50c	+1,750.
Scotland	30c	+1,300.
Spain	40c	+1,750.
Sweden (Via Denmark)	60c	+4,250.
Sweden (Via Thurn & Taxis)	70c	+6,000.
Switzerland	30c	+275.

Destinations of Mail Carried by Ballons Montes

Destination	Rate	Premium
Turkey (sea post)	40c	*+2,300.*
Turkey (land post)	80c	*+3,000.*
Walachia	50c	*+7,750.*
Other Areas		
Argentina	80c	*+12,750.*
Australia	80c	*+9,000.*
Bolivia	1 Fr	*+8,750.*
Brazil	80c	*+7,750.*
Canada	80c	*+30,000.*
Cape of Good Hope	80c	*+34,000.*
Ceylon	80c	*+7,000.*
Chile	80c	*+10,000.*
China	80c	*+25,000.*
Cuba	80c	*+8,000.*
Egypt	40c	*+4,250.*
Haiti	80c	*+10,000.*
Hong Kong	80c	
India	80c	*+13,000.*
Jamaica	80c	*+7,500.*
Japan	80c	*+26,000.*
Malaysia	80c	*+17,250.*
Mauritius	80c	*+15,000.*
Mexico	80c	*+10,000.*
Mexico (Via Panama)	1 Fr	*+10,000.*
Newfoundland	80c	*+10,000.*
Panama	80c	*+15,000.*
Paraguay	80c	*+8,750.*
Peru	1 Fr	*+10,000.*
Philippine Islands	80c	*+17,000.*
Puerto Rico	80c	*+17,000.*
Tangier	40c	*+6,750.*
United States	70c, 80c	*+3,000.*
United States (Interior)	1 Fr	*+3,500.*
Uruguay	80c	*+8,750.*
Venezuela	80c	*+8,750.*
West Indies	70c	*+6,000.*

Franking used on Mail Carried by Ballons Montes

France Scott #	Description	Premium
1853-1860		
15	20c blue, *bluish*	*+3,500.*
18	40c orange, *yellowish*	*+3,500.*
1862-1871		
22	1c olive green, *pale blue*	*+2,000.*
23	5c yellow green, *greenish*	+700.
25	10c bister, *yellowish*	+500.
26	20c blue, *bluish*	+235.
27	40c orange, *yellowish*	+900.
28	80c rose, *pinkish*	*+2,250.*
1863-1870		
29	1c bronze green, *pale blue*	*+1,600.*
30	2c red brown, *yellowish*	*+1,750.*
31	4c grey	*+1,750.*
32	10c bister, *yellowish*	no premium
33	20c blue, *bluish*	no premium
34	30c brown, *yellowish*	no premium
35	40c orange, *yellowish*	no premium
36	80c rose, *pinkish*	no premium
1870		
54	10c bister, *yellowish*	no premium
54a	10c bister, *yellowish*, tete beche pair	*+6,000.*
57	20c blue, *bluish*	no premium
57b	20c blue, *bluish*, tete beche pair	*+6,750.*

1872-75 ***Perf. 14x13½***

Larger Numerals

60	A14	10c bis, *rose* ('75)	300.00	10.00
		On cover		10.00
		On cover, single franking		13.50
a.		Cliché of 15c in plate of 10c	*3,750.*	*4,250.*
		On cover		*25,000.*
b.		Pair, #60, 60a	*7,500.*	*9,500.*
		On cover		—
61	A14	15c bister ('73)	310.00	3.50
		On cover		4.75
62	A14	30c brn, *yelsh*	550.00	5.50
		On cover		6.75
		On cover, single franking		8.00
63	A14	80c rose, *pnksh*	600.00	10.00
		On cover		17.00
		On cover, single franking		27.50
b.		80c carmine rose	725.00	13.50
		On cover		19.00
		On cover, single franking		30.00
c.		80c bright carmine	825.00	20.00
		On cover		22.50
		On cover, single franking		30.00

Values for stamps without gum

60	A14	10c bister, *rose* ('75)	100.00
61	A14	15c bister	120.00
62	A14	30c brown, *yellowish*	160.00
63	A14	80c rose, *pinkish*	200.00
b.		80c carmine rose	220.00
c.		80c bright carmine	250.00

Imperf.

62a	A14	30c	450.00
63a	A14	80c	650.00

Values for Nos. 64-240 are for stamps with all perforations clear of the framelines. Stamps with perforations touching the framelines on one or two sides are worth about 35% less than the values quoted. Values for stamps on cover are for average stamps on very fine, clean, complete covers.

Peace and Commerce ("Type Sage") — A15

Type I. The "N" of "INV" is under the "B" of "REPUBLIQUE."

Type II. The "N" of "INV" is under the "U" of "REPUBLIQUE."

1876-78 ***Perf. 14x13½***

Type I

64	A15	1c grn, *grnsh*	140.00	60.00
		Never hinged	175.00	
		On cover		200.00
		On cover, single franking		575.00
65	A15	2c grn, *grnsh*	1,325.	190.00
		Never hinged	1,750.	
		On cover		300.00
		On cover, single franking		500.00
66	A15	4c grn, *grnsh*	140.00	45.00
		Never hinged	175.00	
		On cover		180.00
		On cover, single franking		575.00
67	A15	5c grn, *grnsh*	600.00	37.50
		Never hinged	825.00	
		On cover		47.50
		On cover, single franking		67.50
68	A15	10c grn, *grnsh*	800.00	18.00
		Never hinged	1,000.	
		On cover		19.00
		On cover, single franking		40.00
69	A15	15c gray lil, *grysh*	800.00	14.50
		Never hinged	1,000.	
		On cover		19.00
		On cover, single franking		40.00
70	A15	20c red brn, *straw*	500.00	14.50
		Never hinged	675.00	
		On cover		27.50
		On cover, single franking		67.50
71	A15	20c bl, *bluish*	*37,500.*	
		Ovptd. "SPECIMEN," no gum	*12,500.*	
72	A15	25c ultra, *bluish*	*7,250.*	45.00
		Never hinged	*9,000.*	
		On cover		62.50
		On cover, single franking		67.50
73	A15	30c brn, *yelsh*	375.00	6.75
		Never hinged	480.00	
		On cover		9.00
		On cover, single franking		11.50
74	A15	40c red, *straw* ('78)	500.00	27.50
		Never hinged	675.00	
		On cover		40.00
		On cover, single franking		47.50
75	A15	75c car, *rose*	875.00	10.00
		Never hinged	1,075.	
		On cover		14.50
		On cover, single franking		26.50
76	A15	1fr brnz grn, *straw*	850.00	8.00
		Never hinged	1,000.	
		On cover		26.50
		On cover, single franking		75.00

No. 71 was never put into use.

The reprints of No. 71 are type II. They are imperforate or with forged perforation.

For overprints and surcharges see Offices in China Nos. 1-17, J7-J10, J20-J22, Offices in Egypt, Alexandria 1-15, Port Said 1-17, Offices in Turkish Empire 1-7, Cavalle 1-8, Dedeagh 1-8, Port Lagos 1-5, Vathy 1-9, Offices in Zanzibar 1-33, 50-54, Offices in Morocco 1-8, and Madagascar 14-27.

Values for stamps without gum

64	A15	1c green, *greenish*	42.50
65	A15	2c green, *greenish*	325.00
66	A15	4c green, *greenish*	40.00
67	A15	5c green, *greenish*	175.00
68	A15	10c green, *greenish*	215.00
69	A15	15c gray lilac, *grayish*	200.00
70	A15	20c red brown, *straw*	150.00
71	A15	20c blue, *bluish*	*17,500.*
72	A15	25c ultramarine, *bluish*	*1,650.*
73	A15	30c brown, *yellowish*	125.00
74	A15	40c red, *straw*	145.00
75	A15	75c carmine, *rose*	240.00
76	A15	1fr bronze green, *straw*	215.00

Values for Blocks of 4

64	A15	1c grn, *grnsh*	660.00	300.00
		Never hinged	800.00	
		On cover		675.00
65	A15	2c grn, *grnsh*	6,600.	1,850.
		Never hinged	8,250.	
		On cover		2,400.
66	A15	4c grn, *grnsh*	625.00	350.00
		Never hinged	800.00	
		On cover		1,150.
67	A15	5c grn, *grnsh*	3,300.	300.00
		Never hinged	3,650.	
		On cover		450.00
68	A15	10c grn, *grnsh*	3,850.	275.00
		Never hinged	4,500.	
		On cover		400.00
69	A15	15c gray lil, *grysh*	4,000.	275.00
		Never hinged	4,500.	
		On cover		425.00
70	A15	20c red brn, *straw*	2,500.	275.00
		Never hinged	3,200.	
		On cover		500.00
72	A15	25c ultra, *bluish*	*45,000.*	2,000.
		Never hinged	*52,000.*	
		On cover		2,250.
73	A15	30c brn, *yelsh*	1,850.	110.00
		Never hinged	2,200.	
		On cover		150.00
74	A15	40c red, *straw* ('78)	2,750.	210.00
		Never hinged	3,200.	
		On cover		300.00
75	A15	75c car, *rose*	4,250.	140.00
		Never hinged	5,250.	
		On cover		200.00
76	A15	1fr brnz grn, *straw*	4,000.	115.00
		Never hinged	5,000.	
		On cover		275.00

Imperf.

64a	A15	1c	95.00
		Never hinged	140.00
65a	A15	2c	500.00
		Never hinged	775.00
66a	A15	4c	95.00
		Never hinged	140.00
67a	A15	5c	325.00
		Never hinged	475.00
68a	A15	10c	350.00
		Never hinged	500.00
69a	A15	15c	350.00
		Never hinged	500.00
70a	A15	20c	250.00
		Never hinged	375.00
73a	A15	30c	175.00
		Never hinged	240.00
74a	A15	40c	175.00
		Never hinged	240.00
75a	A15	75c	350.00
		Never hinged	500.00
76a	A15	1fr	275.00
		Never hinged	400.00

1876-77 ***Perf. 14x13½***

Type II

77	A15	2c grn, *grnsh*	100.00	15.00
		Never hinged	125.00	
		On cover		26.50
		On cover, single franking		60.00
78	A15	5c grn, *grnsh*	24.00	.35
		Never hinged	27.50	
		On cover		.65
a.		Imperf.	140.00	
		Never hinged	200.00	
79	A15	10c grn, *grnsh*	925.00	190.00
		Never hinged	1,200.	
		On cover		210.00
		On cover, single franking		280.00
80	A15	15c gray lil, *grysh*	525.00	1.40
		Never hinged	750.00	
		On cover		2.00
		On cover, single franking		2.75
81	A15	25c ultra, *bluish*	400.00	1.00
		Never hinged	500.00	
		On cover		1.35
		On cover, single franking		1.65
a.		25c blue, *bluish*	400.00	1.40
		Never hinged	540.00	
		On cover		1.65
		On cover, single franking		2.00
b.		Pair, types I & II	*65,000.*	*15,500.*
		No gum	*15,250.*	
		On cover		*52,500.*
c.		Imperf.	250.00	
		Never hinged	375.00	
d.		25c ultramarine, *pale greenish*		*515.00*
		On cover		*900.00*

On cover, single franking — 1,250.
82 A15 30c yel brn, *yelsh* — 72.50 — 1.00
Never hinged — 100.00
On cover — 1.35
On cover, single franking — 3.75
a. 30c brown, *yellowish* — 80.00 — 1.40
Never hinged — 110.00
On cover — 1.75
On cover, single franking — 3.75
b. Imperf. — 400.00
Never hinged — 600.00
83 A15 75c car, *rose* ('77) — 1,725. — 82.50
Never hinged — 2,000.
On cover — 190.00
On cover, single franking — 400.00
84 A15 1fr brnz grn, *straw* ('77) — 125.00 — 5.25
Never hinged — 175.00
On cover — 24.00
On cover, single franking — 77.50
a. Imperf. — 925.00
Never hinged — 1,225.
b. 1fr deep olive green, *straw* — 125.00 — 6.75
Never hinged — 190.00
On cover — 28.00
On cover, single franking — 87.50

1877-80

86 A15 1c blk, *lil bl* — 2.75 — 1.00
Never hinged — 4.00
On cover — 1.60
On cover, single franking — 2.75
a. 1c black, *gray blue* — 2.75 — 1.00
Never hinged — 3.25
On cover, single franking — 1.60
On cover — 2.75
b. Imperf. — 75.00
Never hinged — 115.00
87 A15 1c blk, *Prus bl* ('80) — *9,000.* — *3,500.*
Never hinged — *14,000.*
No gum — 3,400.
On cover — *12,250.*
On cover, single franking — *15,000.*

Values for No. 87 are for copies with the perfs touching the design on at least one side.

88 A15 2c brn, *straw* — 3.25 — 1.40
Never hinged — 5.25
On cover — 2.00
On cover, single franking — 4.75
a. 2c brown, *yellow* — 4.75 — 1.50
Never hinged — 6.75
On cover — 2.25
On cover, single franking — 4.75
b. Imperf. — 37.50
Never hinged — 52.50
89 A15 3c yel, *straw* ('78) — 160.00 — 32.50
Never hinged — 240.00
On cover — 360.00
On cover, single franking — 725.00
a. Imperf. — 100.00
Never hinged — 140.00
90 A15 4c claret, *lav* — 4.00 — 1.50
Never hinged — 6.00
On cover — 8.00
On cover, single franking — 85.00
a. 4c vio brown, *lavender* — 5.50 — 3.75
Never hinged — 8.75
On cover — 10.00
On cover, single franking — 110.00
b. Imperf. — 50.00
Never hinged — 75.50
91 A15 10c blk, *lavender* — 26.00 — .75
Never hinged — 40.00
On cover — 1.60
On cover, single franking — 1.60
a. 10c black, *rose lilac* — 27.50 — 1.40
Never hinged — 30.00
On cover — 1.60
On cover, single franking — 1.60
b. 10c black, *lilac* — 30.00 — 1.40
Never hinged — 42.50
On cover — 1.60
On cover, single franking — 1.60
c. Imperf. — 55.00
Never hinged — 85.00
92 A15 15c blue ('78) — 20.00 — .40
Never hinged — 25.00
On cover — .65
On cover, single franking — 1.00
a. Imperf. — 75.00
Never hinged — 115.00
b. 15c blue, *bluish* — 300.00 — 3.50
Never hinged — 425.00
On cover — 4.75
On cover, single franking — 10.00
93 A15 25c blk, *red* ('78) — 800.00 — 20.00
Never hinged — 1,200.
No gum — 250.00
On cover — 36.00
On cover, single franking — 40.00
a. Imperf. — 500.00
Never hinged — 775.00
94 A15 35c blk, *yel* ('78) — 500.00 — 26.00
Never hinged — 700.00
On cover — 52.50
On cover, single franking — 95.00
a. 35c blk, *yel org* — 525.00 — 30.00
Never hinged — 800.00
On cover — 57.50
On cover, single franking — 120.00
b. Imperf. — 225.00
Never hinged — 325.00
95 A15 40c red, *straw* ('80) — 72.50 — 1.40
Never hinged — 110.00
On cover — 5.25
On cover, single franking — 6.75
a. 40c pale orange red, *straw* — 82.50 — 2.10
Never hinged — 125.00
On cover — 5.75
On cover, single franking — 6.75
b. Imperf. — 190.00
Never hinged — 280.00
96 A15 5fr vio, *lav* — 450.00 — 60.00
Never hinged — 700.00
On cover — 350.00
On cover, single franking — 2,650.
a. 5fr red lilac, *lavender* — 525.00 — 80.00
Never hinged — 725.00
On cover — 380.00
On cover, single franking — 3,000.
b. Imperf. — 625.00
Never hinged — 950.00

1879-90

97 A15 3c gray, *grysh* ('80) — 4.50 — 1.40
Never hinged — 5.25
On cover — 8.00
On cover, single franking — 55.00
a. Imperf. — 52.50
Never hinged — 80.00
98 A15 20c red, *yel grn* — 35.00 — 3.50
Never hinged — 45.00
On cover — 24.00
On cover, single franking — 100.00
a. 20c red, *deep green* ('84) — 45.00 — 5.00
Never hinged — 70.00
On cover — 27.50
On cover, single franking — 110.00
b. Imperf. — 80.00
Never hinged — 115.00
99 A15 25c yel, *straw* — 300.00 — 4.50
Never hinged — 390.00
On cover — 10.00
On cover, single franking — 12.00
a. Imperf. — 210.00
Never hinged — 300.00
100 A15 25c blk, *pale rose* ('86) — 62.50 — .65
Never hinged — 85.00
On cover — 2.60
On cover, single franking — 3.60
a. Imperf. — 110.00
101 A15 50c rose, *rose* ('90) — 160.00 — 2.00
Never hinged — 250.00
On cover — 7.25
On cover, single franking — 20.00
a. 50c carmine, *rose* — 160.00 — 2.75
Never hinged — 265.00
On cover — 9.25
On cover, single franking — 24.00
102 A15 75c dp vio, *org* ('90) — 200.00 — 27.50
Never hinged — 275.00
On cover — 90.00
On cover, single franking — 225.00
a. 75c deep violet, *yellow* — 225.00 — 35.00
Never hinged — 315.00
On cover — 100.00
On cover, single franking — 230.00

1892

Quadrille Paper

103 A15 15c blue — 12.50 — .30
Never hinged — 13.50
On cover — 1.40
On cover, single franking — 4.50
a. Imperf. — 160.00
Never hinged — 200.00

1898-1900

Ordinary Paper

104 A15 5c yel grn — 25.00 — 1.25
Never hinged — 30.00
On cover — 2.00
On cover, single franking — 4.75
a. Imperf. — 72.50
Never hinged — 110.00

Type I

105 A15 5c yel grn — 17.50 — 1.25
Never hinged — 21.00
On cover — 2.00
On cover, single franking — 2.25
a. Imperf. — 500.00
Never hinged — 725.00
No gum — 150.00
106 A15 10c blk, *lavender* — 27.50 — 2.00
Never hinged — 30.00
On cover — 3.25
On cover, single franking — 3.50
a. Imperf. — 210.00
Never hinged — 310.00
No gum — 67.50
107 A15 50c car, *rose* — 210.00 — 25.00
Never hinged — 260.00
On cover — 50.00
On cover, single franking — 80.00
108 A15 2fr brn, *azure* ('00) — 125.00 — 30.00
Never hinged — 150.00
On cover — 375.00
On cover, single franking — 3,600.
b. Imperf. — *2,150.*
Never hinged — *2,850.*
No gum — 675.00

See No. 226.

Reprints of A15, type II, were made in 1887 and left imperf. See note after No. 37. Value for set of 27, $3,300.

Liberty, Equality, Fraternity
A16

"The Rights of Man"
A17

Liberty and Peace
A18

1900-29 — *Perf. 14x13½*

109 A16 1c gray — .55 — .35
Never hinged — .85
On cover — .70
On cover, single franking — 1.60
110 A16 2c violet brn — .70 — .25
Never hinged — 1.00
On cover — .80
On cover, single franking — 3.25
111 A16 3c orange — .45 — .45
Never hinged — .70
On cover — 2.00
On cover, single franking — 6.00
a. 3c red — 15.00 — 5.50
Never hinged — 23.00
On cover — 16.50
112 A16 4c yellow brn — 3.25 — 1.40
Never hinged — 5.25
On cover — 3.00
On cover, single franking — 42.50
113 A16 5c green — 1.60 — .20
Never hinged — 3.00
On cover — .70
On cover, single franking — 1.40
b. Booklet pane of 10 — 325.00
114 A16 7½c lilac ('26) — .35 — .35
Never hinged — .70
115 A16 10c lilac ('29) — 3.00 — .35
Never hinged — 5.00
On cover — 5.00
On cover, single franking — 45.00
116 A17 10c carmine — 21.00 — 1.40
Never hinged — 65.00
On cover — 7.50
On cover, single franking — 10.50
a. Numerals printed separately — 24.00 — 7.50
Never hinged — 47.50
On cover — 10.00
On cover, single franking — 14.00
117 A17 15c orange — 6.00 — .35
Never hinged — 18.00
On cover — .70
On cover, single franking — .70
118 A17 20c brown vio — 50.00 — 6.25
Never hinged — 120.00
On cover — 13.50
On cover, single franking — 32.50
119 A17 25c blue — 92.50 — 1.40
Never hinged — 290.00
On cover — 4.00
On cover, single franking — 6.50
a. Numerals printed separately — 90.00 — 6.50
Never hinged — 225.00
On cover — 9.25
On cover, single franking — 16.00
120 A17 30c violet — 67.50 — 4.25
Never hinged — 175.00
On cover — 14.00
On cover, single franking — 32.50
121 A18 40c red & pale bl — 13.00 — .60
Never hinged — 37.50
On cover — 1.30
On cover, single franking — 1.50
122 A18 45c green & bl ('06) — 22.50 — 1.60
Never hinged — 50.00
On cover — 5.25
123 A18 50c bis brn & lav — 85.00 — 1.00
Never hinged — 200.00
On cover — 2.60

124 A18 60c vio & ultra ('20) 1.00 .75
Never hinged 1.20
On cover 3.50
125 A18 1fr claret & ol grn 24.00 .50
Never hinged 60.00
On cover 2.00
On cover, single franking 3.25
126 A18 2fr gray vio & yel 625.00 60.00
Never hinged 1,400.
On cover 210.00
On cover, single franking 1,500.
127 A18 2fr org & pale bl ('20) 37.50 .40
Never hinged 90.00
On cover 6.50
On cover, single franking 23.00
128 A18 3fr vio & bl ('25) 20.00 6.00
Never hinged 37.50
On cover 16.50
On cover, single franking 45.00
129 A18 3fr brt vio & rose ('27) 40.00 2.10
Never hinged 100.00
On cover 20.00
On cover, single franking 40.00
130 A18 5fr dk bl & buff 67.50 3.25
Never hinged 190.00
On cover 26.00
On cover, single franking 105.00
131 A18 10fr grn & red ('26) 95.00 13.50
Never hinged 200.00
On cover 30.00
On cover, single franking 60.00
132 A18 20fr mag & grn ('26) 150.00 30.00
Never hinged 325.00
On cover 100.00
On cover, single franking 300.00
Nos. 109-132 (24) 1,427. 136.70

In the 10c and 25c values, the first printings show the numerals to have been impressed by a second operation, whereas, in later printings, the numerals were inserted in the plates. Two operations were used for all 20c and 30c, and one operation for the 15c.

No. 114 was issued precanceled only. Values for precanceled stamps in first column are for those which have not been through the post and have original gum. Values in the second column are for postally used, gumless stamps.

See Offices in China Nos. 34, 40-44, Offices in Crete 1-5, 10-15, Offices in Egypt, Alexandria 16-20, 26-30, 77, 84-86, Port Said 18-22, 28-32, 83, 90-92, Offices in Turkish Empire 21-26, 31-33, Cavalle 9, Dedeagh 9.

For overprints and surcharge see Nos. 197, 246, C1-C2, M1, P7. Offices in China 57, 62-65, 71, 73, 75, 83-85, J14, J27, Offices in Crete 17-20, Offices in Egypt, Alexandria 31-32, 34-35, 40-48, 57-64, 66, 71-73, Port Said 33, 35-40, 43, 46-57, 59, 65-71, 73, 78-80, Offices in Turkish Empire 35-38, 47-49, Cavalle 13-15, Dedeagh 16-18, Offices in Zanzibar 39, 45-49, 55, Offices in Morocco 11-15, 20-22, 26-29, 35-41, 49-54, 72-76, 84-85, 87-89, B6.

Imperf.

109a A16 1c 50.00
Never hinged 72.50
110a A16 2c 60.00 55.00
Never hinged 90.00
Without gum 47.50
111b A16 3c 47.50
Never hinged 72.50
112a A16 4c Without gum 125.00
113a A16 5c 62.50
Never hinged 92.50
Without gum 57.50
116b A17 10c #116 or 116a 200.00 *125.00*
Never hinged 300.00
Without gum 125.00
117a A17 15c 160.00 *150.00*
Never hinged 240.00
Without gum 100.00
119b A17 25c #119 or 119a 400.00
Never hinged 600.00
Without gum 250.00
121a A18 40c 175.00 140.00
Never hinged 260.00
Without gum 100.00
122a A18 45c 200.00
Never hinged 300.00
Without gum 90.00
123a A18 50c 350.00 350.00
Never hinged 525.00
Without gum 250.00
124a A18 60c 450.00
Never hinged 725.00
Without gum 310.00
125a A18 1fr 210.00 210.00
Never hinged 300.00
Without gum 150.00
126a A18 2fr Without gum *1,150.*
127a A18 2fr 425.00
Never hinged 725.00
Without gum 300.00
128a A18 3fr *600.00* 450.00
Never hinged *925.00*
129a A18 3fr 375.00
Never hinged 525.00
130a A18 5fr 775.00
Never hinged 1,150.
Without gum 350.00

Nos. 112a and 126a are valued without gum.

Flat Plate & Rotary Press

The following stamps were printed by both flat plate and rotary press: Nos. 109-113, 144-146, 163, 166, 168, 170, 177-178, 185, 192 and P7.

"Rights of Man" A19

Sower A20

1902

133 A19 10c rose red 22.50 .85
Never hinged 85.00
On cover 3.00
134 A19 15c pale red 8.00 .35
Never hinged 24.00
On cover .65
135 A19 20c brown violet 62.50 10.50
Never hinged 180.00
On cover 17.00
On cover, single franking 45.00
136 A19 25c blue 72.50 1.50
Never hinged 225.00
On cover 4.00
On cover, single franking 8.00
137 A19 30c lilac 190.00 11.50
Never hinged 475.00
On cover 17.00
On cover, single franking 35.00
Nos. 133-137 (5) 355.50 24.70

Imperf.

133a A19 10c rose red 325.00 *225.00*
Never hinged 500.00
Without gum 180.00
134a A19 15c pale red 350.00 *225.00*
Never hinged 525.00
Without gum 230.00
135a A19 20c brown violet 600.00 *350.00*
Never hinged 925.00
Without gum 325.00
136a A19 25c blue 725.00 *475.00*
Never hinged 1,050.
137a A19 30c lilac *500.00*
Never hinged 1,475.

See Offices in China Nos. 35-39, Offices in Crete 6-10, Offices in Egypt, Alexandria 21-25, 81-82, Port Said 23-27, 87-88, Offices in Turkish Empire 26-30, Cavalle 10-11, Dedeagh 10-11.

For overprints and surcharges see Nos. M2, Offices in China 45, 58-61, 66-70, 76-82, J15-J16, J28-J30, Offices in Crete 16, Offices in Egypt, Alexandria 33, 36-39, 49-50, 52-56, 65, 67-70, B1-B4, Port Said 34, 41-42, 44-45, 57, 60-64, 77, 74-77, B1-B4, Offices in Turkish Empire 34, 39, Cavalle 12, Dedeagh 15, Offices in Zanzibar 40-44, 56-59, Offices in Morocco 16-19, 30-34, 42-48, 77-83, 86, B1-B5, B7, B9.

1903-38

138 A20 10c rose 6.00 .20
Never hinged 14.50
On cover .75
139 A20 15c slate grn 4.00 .20
Never hinged 6.75
On cover .75
b. Booklet pane of 10 450.00
140 A20 20c violet brn 50.00 1.40
Never hinged 110.00
On cover 7.00
On cover, single franking 32.50
141 A20 25c dull blue 55.00 1.00
Never hinged 130.00
On cover 3.50
On cover, single franking 5.00
142 A20 30c violet 140.00 4.25
Never hinged 325.00
On cover 10.00
On cover, single franking 20.00
143 A20 45c lt violet ('26) 4.50 1.40
Never hinged 8.50
On cover 5.50
On cover, single franking 35.00
144 A20 50c dull blue ('21) 20.00 .85
Never hinged 50.00
On cover 5.25
On cover, single franking 6.75
145 A20 50c gray grn ('26) 5.00 .85
Never hinged 8.50
On cover 2.00
On cover, single franking 16.50
146 A20 50c vermilion ('26) 1.00 .20
Never hinged 1.50
On cover .50
On cover, single franking .50
a. Booklet pane of 10 40.00
147 A20 50c grnsh bl ('38) 1.00 .35
Never hinged 1.75
On cover 1.40
On cover, single franking 4.00
148 A20 60c lt vio ('24) 4.25 1.25
Never hinged 9.00
On cover 4.00
On cover, single franking 5.25
149 A20 65c rose ('24) 2.00 1.00
Never hinged 4.00
On cover 4.00
On cover, single franking 30.00
150 A20 65c gray grn ('27) 5.25 1.50
Never hinged 10.50
On cover 6.75
On cover, single franking 40.00
151 A20 75c rose lil ('26) 4.00 .45
Never hinged 7.75
On cover 1.60
On cover, single franking 3.25
152 A20 80c ver ('25) 20.00 6.00
Never hinged 40.00
On cover 7.50
On cover, single franking 37.50
153 A20 85c ver ('24) 10.00 1.75
Never hinged 18.00
On cover 3.25
On cover, single franking 5.00
154 A20 1fr dull blue ('26) 4.75 .50
Never hinged 9.50
On cover 2.75
On cover, single franking 20.00
Nos. 138-154 (17) 336.75 23.15
Set, never hinged 725.00

See Nos. 941, 942A. For surcharges and overprints see Nos. 229-230, 232-233, 236, 256, B25, B29, B32, B36, B40, M3-M4, M6, Offices in Turkish Empire 46, 54.

Imperf.

138a A20 10c 150.00
Never hinged 225.00
Without gum 90.00
139a A20 15c 72.50 50.00
Never hinged 110.00
Without gum 40.00
140a A20 20c 275.00 140.00
Never hinged 460.00
Without gum 60.00
141a A20 25c 275.00
Never hinged 380.00
Without gum 72.50
142a A20 30c 475.00
Never hinged 675.00
Without gum 160.00
144a A20 50c 82.50
Never hinged 115.00
145a A20 50c 80.00
Never hinged 120.00
146b A20 50c Without gum 60.00
147a A20 50c 35.00
Never hinged 52.50
149a A20 65c 150.00
Never hinged 250.00
151a A20 75c 325.00
Never hinged 500.00
154a A20 1fr *750.00*
Never hinged 1,000.

Ground A21

No Ground A22

1906, Apr. 13
With Ground Under Feet of Figure

155 A21 10c red 2.00 1.40
Never hinged 3.25
On cover 4.00
On cover, single franking 4.75
a. Imperf., pair 400.00 200.00
Never hinged 550.00
No gum 250.00

1906-37

TEN AND THIRTY-FIVE CENTIMES

Type I — Numerals and letters of the inscriptions thin.

Type II — Numerals and letters thicker.

No Ground Under the Feet

156 A22 1c olive bis ('33) .20 .25
Never hinged .30
On cover 2.60
On cover, single franking 36.00
a. 1c bistre brown ('36) .20 .25
Never hinged .30
On cover 2.60
On cover, single franking 36.00
157 A22 2c dk green ('33) .20 .25
Never hinged .30
On cover 2.00
On cover, single franking 36.00
158 A22 3c ver ('33) .20 .25
Never hinged .30
On cover 14.00
On cover, single franking 60.00
159 A22 5c green ('07) 1.25 .20
Never hinged 2.25
On cover .70
a. Imperf., pair 40.00 30.00
Never hinged 57.50
Without gum 15.00
b. Booklet pane of 10 100.00
160 A22 5c orange ('21) .90 .20
Never hinged 1.75
On cover 1.00
a. Booklet pane of 10 72.50
161 A22 5c cerise ('34) .20 .20
Never hinged .30
On cover 3.00
On cover, single franking 100.00
162 A22 10c red (II) ('07) 1.25 .20
Never hinged 2.25
No gum 15.00
a. Imperf., pair 26.00 72.50
Never hinged 40.00
On cover 15.00
b. 10c red (I) ('06) 6.50 .75
Never hinged 20.00
On cover 2.25
On cover, single franking 3.50
c. Booklet pane of 10 (I) 125.00
d. Booklet pane of 10 (II) 75.00
e. Booklet pane of 6 (II) 240.00
163 A22 10c grn (II) ('21) .50 .25
Never hinged 1.00
On cover .70
a. 10c green (I) ('27) 29.00 30.00
Never hinged 36.00
On cover 55.00
On cover, single franking 140.00
b. Booklet pane of 10 (II) 150.00
c. Booklet pane of 10 (I) 3,200.
164 A22 10c ultra ('32) 1.25 .20
Never hinged 2.00
On cover 1.40
On cover, single franking 14.00
165 A22 15c red brn ('26) .20 .20
Never hinged .30
On cover .40
On cover, single franking .40
a. Booklet pane of 10 27.50
166 A22 20c brown 2.50 .25
Never hinged 6.50
On cover 1.60
On cover, single franking 3.50
a. Imperf., pair 60.00 65.00
Never hinged 80.00
Without gum 27.50
167 A22 20c red vio ('26) .20 .20
Never hinged .35
On cover .45
On cover, single franking .65
a. Booklet pane of 10 7.50
168 A22 25c blue 2.00 .20
Never hinged 4.00
On cover .40
a. Booklet pane of 10 37.50
b. Imperf, pair (dark blue) 26.00 40.00
Never hinged 40.00
c. Imperf, pair (pale blue) 150.00
Never hinged 240.00
169 A22 25c lt brown ('27) .20 .20
Never hinged .30
On cover .65
On cover, single franking 1.00
170 A22 30c orange 10.00 1.00
Never hinged 23.00
On cover 1.60
On cover, single franking 4.50
a. Imperf, pair 140.00 100.00
Never hinged 210.00
Without gum 80.00
171 A22 30c red ('21) 5.25 1.60
Never hinged 11.00
On cover 5.25
On cover, single franking 8.00
172 A22 30c cerise ('25) .70 .50
Never hinged 1.60
On cover 3.00
On cover, single franking 7.25
a. Booklet pane of 10 13.50
173 A22 30c lt blue ('25) 3.00 .35
Never hinged 4.75
On cover 1.75
On cover, single franking 7.25
a. Booklet pane of 10 35.00
174 A22 30c cop red ('37) .20 .25
Never hinged .40
On cover .70
On cover, single franking 2.00
a. Booklet pane of 10 9.00
175 A22 35c vio (II) ('26) 6.00 .65
Never hinged 10.50
On cover 1.60
a. Imperf, pair 125.00 125.00
Never hinged 175.00
Without gum 72.50
b. 35c violet (I) ('06) 110.00 5.25
Never hinged 240.00
On cover 16.50
On cover, single franking 14.00
c. As "b," Imperf, pair, without gum *650.00*
176 A22 35c grn ('37) .50 .45
Never hinged .90
On cover 2.00
On cover, single franking 4.50
177 A22 40c olive ('25) 1.25 .45
Never hinged 2.50
On cover 1.60
On cover, single franking 4.00
b. Booklet pane of 10 30.00
178 A22 40c ver ('26) 2.00 .60
Never hinged 4.00
On cover 1.60
On cover, single franking 3.50
a. Booklet pane of 10 25.00
179 A22 40c violet ('27) 1.50 .65
Never hinged 2.75
On cover 1.20
On cover, single franking 1.40
180 A22 40c lt ultra ('28) 1.00 .25
Never hinged 1.75
On cover .50
On cover, single franking 1.00
181 A22 1.05fr ver ('25) 7.50 6.50
Never hinged 15.00
On cover 10.40
On cover, single franking 40.00
182 A22 1.10fr cerise ('27) 9.00 2.00
Never hinged 17.00
On cover 6.50
On cover, single franking 23.00
a. 1.10fr bright rose 13.00 3.25
Never hinged 23.00
On cover 8.50
183 A22 1.40fr cerise ('26) 16.00 18.00
Never hinged 30.00
On cover 95.00
On cover, single franking 750.00
a. 1.40fr bright rose 20.00 20.00
Never hinged 36.00
184 A22 2fr Prus grn ('31) 11.00 1.25
Never hinged 18.00
On cover 12.00
On cover, single franking 45.00
a. 2fr blackish green 18.00 3.00
Never hinged 24.00
On cover 14.50
Nos. 156-184 (29) 85.95 37.55
Set, never hinged 170.00

The 10c and 35c, type I, were slightly retouched by adding thin white outlines to the sack of grain, the underside of the right arm and the back of the skirt. It is difficult to distinguish the retouches except on clearly-printed copies. The white outlines were made stronger on the stamps of type II.

Stamps of types A16, A18, A20 and A22 were printed in 1916-20 on paper of poor quality, usually grayish and containing bits of fiber. This is called G. C. (Grande Consommation) paper.

Nos. 160, 162b, 163, 175b and 176 also exist imperf.

See Nos. 241-241b. For surcharges and overprint see Nos. 227-228, 234, 238, 240, 400, B1, B24, B28, B31, B35, B37, B39, B41, M5, P8, Offices in Turkish Empire 40-45, 52, 55.

Louis Pasteur — A23

1923-26

185	A23	10c green	.50	.20
		Never hinged	.80	
		On cover		.65
		On cover, single franking		1.40
a.		Booklet pane of 10	15.00	
186	A23	15c green ('24)	1.10	.20
		Never hinged	2.25	
		On cover		1.10
		On cover, single franking		3.00
187	A23	20c green ('26)	2.25	.65
		Never hinged	3.50	
		On cover		4.25
		On cover, single franking		4.50
188	A23	30c red	.65	*1.10*
		Never hinged	1.25	
		On cover		3.00
		On cover, single franking		5.00
189	A23	30c green ('26)	.50	.35
		Never hinged	.85	
		On cover		3.00
		On cover, single franking		5.00
190	A23	45c red ('24)	1.50	1.50
		Never hinged	2.60	
		On cover		3.50
		On cover, single franking		7.25
191	A23	50c blue	3.50	.30
		Never hinged	6.00	
		On cover		3.50
		On cover, single franking		11.25
192	A23	75c blue ('24)	3.00	.80
		Never hinged	4.25	
		On cover		3.00
		On cover, single franking		5.00
a.		Imperf., pair	200.00	
		Never hinged	310.00	
		Without gum	175.00	
193	A23	90c red ('26)	7.75	2.50
		Never hinged	14.50	
		On cover		4.00
		On cover, single franking		7.50
194	A23	1fr blue ('25)	16.00	.25
		Never hinged	29.00	
		On cover		3.50
		On cover, single franking		24.00
195	A23	1.25fr blue ('26)	17.50	6.75
		Never hinged	32.50	
		On cover		17.00
		On cover, single franking		40.00
196	A23	1.50fr blue ('26)	4.00	.20
		Never hinged	9.25	
		On cover		1.60
		On cover, single franking		3.50
		Nos. 185-196 (12)	58.25	14.80
		Set, never hinged	120.00	

Nos. 185, 188 and 191 were issued to commemorate the cent. of the birth of Pasteur.

For surcharges and overprint see Nos. 231, 235, 257, B26, B30, B33, C4.

No. 125 Overprinted in Blue

1923, June 15

197	A18	1fr claret & ol grn	300.00	325.00
		Never hinged	500.00	
		On cover		475.00
		On cover, single franking		475.00

Allegory of Olympic Games at Paris A24

The Trophy A25

Milo of Crotona — A26

Victorious Athlete — A27

1924, Apr. 1 ***Perf. 14x13½, 13½x14***

198	A24	10c gray grn & yel grn	1.60	1.00
		Never hinged	4.50	
		On cover		2.10
		On cover, single franking		4.75
199	A25	25c rose & dk rose	2.25	.65
		Never hinged	5.25	
		On cover		2.10
		On cover, single franking		4.75
200	A26	30c brn red & blk	8.00	9.00
		Never hinged	16.50	
		On cover		22.00
		On cover, single franking		50.00
201	A27	50c ultra & dk bl	21.00	4.50
		Never hinged	65.00	
		On cover		27.50
		On cover, single franking		82.50
		Nos. 198-201 (4)	32.85	15.15
		Set, never hinged	100.00	

8th Olympic Games, Paris. Exist imperf.

Pierre de Ronsard (1524-85), Poet — A28

1924, Oct. 6 ***Perf. 14x13½***

219	A28	75c blue, *bluish*	1.50	1.10
		Never hinged	2.25	
		On cover		8.50
		On cover, single franking		16.50

"Light and Liberty" Allegory A29

Majolica Vase — A30

Potter Decorating Vase — A31

Terrace of Château A32

1924-25 ***Perf. 14x13½, 13½x14***

220	A29	10c dk grn & yel ('25)	.45	.60
		Never hinged	.80	
		On cover		1.40
		On cover, single franking		4.00
221	A30	15c ind & grn ('25)	.45	.60
		Never hinged	1.00	
		On cover		1.90
		On cover, single franking		*4.00*
a.		Imperf.	300.00	
		Never hinged	*475.00*	
b.		As "a," setenant with normal	375.00	
		Never hinged	*675.00*	
222	A31	25c vio brn & garnet	.70	.30
		Never hinged	1.40	
		On cover		1.90
		On cover, single franking		5.00
223	A32	25c gray bl & vio ('25)	1.10	.45
		Never hinged	1.75	
		On cover		1.90
		On cover, single franking		5.00
a.		Imperf.	*350.00*	
		Never hinged	*500.00*	
b.		As "a," setenant with normal	*475.00*	
		Never hinged	*700.00*	
224	A31	75c indigo & ultra	2.50	1.75
		Never hinged	5.00	
		On cover		5.25
		On cover, single franking		13.50
225	A29	75c dk bl & lt bl ('25)	13.00	5.25
		Never hinged	26.00	
		On cover		15.00
		On cover, single franking		27.50
a.		Imperf.	*300.00*	
		Never hinged	*425.00*	
b.		As "a," setenant with normal	*425.00*	
		Never hinged	*625.00*	
		Nos. 220-225 (6)	18.20	8.95
		Set, never hinged	35.00	

Intl. Exhibition of Decorative Modern Arts at Paris, 1925.

Philatelic Exhibition Issue

Souvenir Sheet

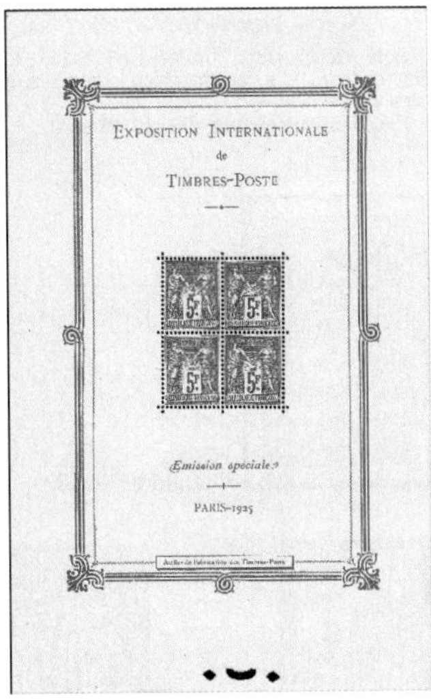

A32a

1925, May 2 ***Perf. 14x13½***

226	A32a	Sheet of 4, A15 II	700.00	700.00
		Never hinged	2,000.	
		On cover		*2,000.*
a.		Imperf. sheet	3,750.	1,400.
		Never hinged	6,000.	
b.		5fr carmine, perf.	75.00	85.00
		Never hinged	130.00	
		On cover		175.00
c.		5fr carmine, imperf.	675.00	
		Never hinged	1,000.	

These were on sale only at the Intl. Phil. Exhib., Paris, May, 1925. Size: 140x220mm.

Nos. 148-149, 152-153, 173, 175, 181, 183, 192, 195 Surcharged

1926-27

227	A22	25c on 30c lt bl	.20	.25
		Never hinged	.30	
		On cover		2.50
		On cover, single franking		4.25
228	A22	25c on 35c violet	.20	.25
		Never hinged	.30	
		On cover		2.75
		On cover, single franking		5.00
a.		Double surcharge	425.00	275.00
		Never hinged	575.00	
229	A20	50c on 60c lt vio ('27)	1.10	.85
		Never hinged	2.00	
		On cover		3.00
		On cover, single franking		6.00
230	A20	50c on 65c rose ('27)	.60	.45
		Never hinged	1.10	
		On cover		2.75
		On cover, single franking		6.00
a.		Inverted surcharge	*900.00*	*1,000.*
		Never hinged	*1,325.*	
231	A23	50c on 75c blue	2.75	1.00
		Never hinged	4.00	
		On cover		3.00
		On cover, single franking		6.75
232	A20	50c on 80c ver ('27)	1.00	.85
		Never hinged	1.75	
		On cover		4.00
		On cover, single franking		21.00
233	A20	50c on 85c ver ('27)	1.60	.65
		Never hinged	3.25	
		On cover		3.00
		On cover, single franking		8.00
234	A22	50c on 1.05fr ver	1.00	.60
		Never hinged	1.90	
		On cover		3.00
		On cover, single franking		6.75
235	A23	50c on 1.25fr blue	2.10	1.75
		Never hinged	4.00	
		On cover		3.75
		On cover, single franking		10.00
236	A20	55c on 60c lt vio	92.50	35.00
		Never hinged	175.00	
		On cover		110.00
		On cover, single franking		110.00
238	A22	90c on 1.05fr ver ('27)	1.75	2.00
		Never hinged	3.00	
		On cover		3.75
		On cover, single franking		8.50
240	A22	1.10fr on 1.40fr cer	.75	.85
		Never hinged	1.40	
		On cover		5.75
		On cover, single franking		35.00
		Nos. 227-240 (12)	105.55	44.50
		Set, never hinged	240.00	

Issue dates: Nos. 229-230, 232-234, 1927.

No. 236 is known only precanceled. See second note after No. 132.

Nos. 229, 230, 234, 238 and 240 have three bars instead of two. The 55c surcharge has thinner, larger numerals and a rounded "c." Width, including bars, is 17mm, instead of 13mm.

The 55c was used only precanceled at the Magasins du Louvre department store in Paris, August 1926.

Strasbourg Exhibition Issue

Souvenir Sheet

A32b

1927, June 4

241	A32b Sheet of 2	675.00	700.00
	Never hinged	1,600.	
	On cover		*1,400.*
a.	5fr light ultra (A22)	140.00	175.00
	Never hinged	275.00	225.00
	On cover		*300.00*
b.	10fr carmine rose (A22)	140.00	175.00
	Never hinged	275.00	225.00
	On cover		*300.00*
	In pair with #241a and label	360.00	425.00
	Never hinged	600.00	550.00

Sold at the Strasbourg Philatelic Exhibition as souvenirs. Size: 111x140mm.

Marcelin Berthelot (1827-1907), Chemist and Statesman — A33

1927, Sept. 7

242	A33 90c dull rose	1.40	.45
	Never hinged	2.25	
	On cover		2.00
	On cover, single franking		3.00

For surcharge see No. C3.

Lafayette, Washington, S. S. Paris and Airplane "Spirit of St. Louis" — A34

1927, Sept. 15

243	A34 90c dull red	1.00	1.25
	Never hinged	2.00	
	On cover		4.25
	On cover, single franking		6.50
a.	Value omitted	1,550.	1,350.
	Never hinged	*2,000.*	
	On cover		1,750.
244	A34 1.50fr deep blue	3.25	2.00
	Never hinged	5.50	
	On cover		4.25
	On cover, single franking		6.50
a.	Value omitted	1,150.	
	Never hinged	*1,450.*	
	Set, never hinged	6.50	

Visit of American Legionnaires to France, September, 1927. Exist imperf.

Joan of Arc — A35

1929, Mar.

245	A35 50c dull blue	1.25	.20
	Never hinged	2.10	
	On cover		.85
	On cover, single franking		2.00
a.	Booklet pane of 10	125.00	
	Never hinged	160.00	
b.	Imperf.	100.00	
	Never hinged	150.00	

500th anniv. of the relief of Orleans by the French forces led by Joan of Arc.

No. 127 Overprinted in Blue

1929, May 18

246	A18 2fr org & pale bl	375.00	400.00
	Never hinged	650.00	
	On cover		550.00
	On cover, single franking		550.00

Sold exclusively at the Intl. Phil. Exhib., Le Havre, May, 1929, for 7fr, which included a 5fr admission ticket.

Excellent counterfeits of No. 246 exist.

Reims Cathedral — A37

Die I, II, III

Die IV

Die I Die II Die III

Die I — The window of the 1st turret on the left is made of 2 lines. The horizontal line of the frame surrounding 3F is not continuous.

Die II — Same as Die I but the line under 3F is continuous.

Die III — Same as Die II but there is a deeply cut line separating 3 and F.

Die IV — Same as Die III but the window of the first turret on the left is made of three lines.

Mont-Saint-Michel — A38

Die I

Die II

Die I — The line at the top of the spire is broken.

Die II — The line is unbroken.

Port of La Rochelle A39

Dies I & II

Die III

Die I — The top of the "E" of "POSTES" has a serif. The oval of shading inside the "0" of "10 fr" and the outer oval are broken at their bases.

Die II — The same top has no serif. Interior and exterior of "0" broken as in Die I.

Die III — Top of "E" has no serif. Interior and exterior of "0" complete.

Pont du Gard, Nimes A40

Dies I & II

Die III

Die I — Shading of the first complete arch in the left middle tier is made of horizontal lines. Size 36x20¾mm. Perf. 13½.

Die II — Same, size 35½x21mm. Perf. 11.

Die III — Shading of same arch is made of three diagonal lines. Thin paper. Perf. 13.

1929-33 Engr. *Perf. 11, 13, 13½*

247	A37 3fr dk gray ('30) (I)	50.00	1.75
	Never hinged	85.00	
	On cover		5.00
	On cover, single franking		20.00
247A	A37 3fr dk gray ('30) (II)	100.00	2.75
	Never hinged	150.00	
	On cover		7.50
	On cover, single franking		30.00
247B	A37 3fr dk gray ('30) (III)	300.00	19.00
	Never hinged	450.00	
	On cover		*33.00*
	On cover, single franking		*60.00*
248	A37 3fr bluish sl ('31) (IV)	55.00	1.75
	Never hinged	90.00	
	On cover		5.00
	On cover, single franking		20.00
249	A38 5fr brn ('30) (I)	18.00	3.50
	Never hinged	30.00	
	On cover		5.00
	On cover, single franking		18.00
250	A38 5fr brn ('31) (II)	17.00	.50
	Never hinged	25.00	
	On cover		4.50
	On cover, single franking		15.50
251	A39 10fr lt ultra (I)	75.00	12.00
	Never hinged	125.00	
	On cover		20.00
	On cover, single franking		35.00
251A	A39 10fr ultra (II)	110.00	20.00
	Never hinged	160.00	
	On cover		30.00
	On cover, single franking		47.50
252	A39 10fr dk ultra ('31) (III)	55.00	5.00
	Never hinged	100.00	
	On cover		14.50
	On cover, single franking		30.00
253	A40 20fr red brown (I)	210.00	30.00
	Never hinged	325.00	
	On cover		75.00
	On cover, single franking		225.00
a.	20fr pale red brown (I)	925.00	275.00
	Never hinged	1,500.	
254	A40 20fr brt red brn ('30) (II)	675.00	275.00
	Never hinged	1,175.	
	On cover		540.00
	On cover, single franking		1,000.
254A	A40 20fr org brn ('31) (III)	200.00	27.50
	Never hinged	300.00	
	On cover		60.00
	On cover, single franking		210.00
b.	20fr pale orange brown (III)	240.00	30.00
	Never hinged	375.00	
	Nos. 247-254A (12)	1,865.	398.75

View of Algiers A41

1929, Jan. 1 Typo.

255	A41 50c blue & rose red	1.60	.25
	Never hinged	3.25	
	On cover		1.00
	On cover, single franking		3.50

Cent. of the 1st French settlement in Algeria.

Nos. 146 and 196 Overprinted

1930, Apr. 23 *Perf. 14x13½*

256	A20 50c vermilion	2.25	2.40
	Never hinged	4.50	
	On cover		6.50
	On cover, single franking		15.00
257	A23 1.50fr blue	15.00	11.00
	Never hinged	32.50	
	On cover		23.00
	On cover, single franking		30.00
	Set, never hinged	37.00	

Intl. Labor Bureau, 48th Congress, Paris.

Colonial Exposition Issue

Fachi Woman — A42

French Colonials A43

1930-31 Typo. *Perf. 14x13½*

258	A42 15c gray black	.90	.25
	Never hinged	1.90	
	On cover		.50
	On cover, single franking		2.40
259	A42 40c dark brown	1.90	.25
	Never hinged	3.50	
	On cover		.50
	On cover, single franking		1.00
260	A42 50c dark red	.55	.20
	Never hinged	.80	
	On cover		.70
	On cover, single franking		.70
a.	Booklet pane of 10	12.50	
261	A42 1.50fr deep blue	7.25	.50
	Never hinged	17.00	
	On cover		2.00
	On cover, single franking		3.00

Perf. 13½

Photo.

262	A43 1.50fr dp blue ('31)	32.50	2.10
	Never hinged	67.50	
	On cover		3.00
	On cover, single franking		5.25
	Nos. 258-262 (5)	43.10	3.30
	Set, never hinged	90.00	

No. 260 has two types: type 1 shows four short downward hairlines near top of head, type 2 has no lines. Booklet stamps are type 2.

Arc de Triomphe A44

1931 Engr. *Perf. 13*

263	A44 2fr red brown	32.50	.70
	Never hinged	45.00	
	On cover		3.50
	On cover, single franking		8.50

Peace with Olive Branch — A45

1932-39 Typo. *Perf. 14x13½*

264 A45 30c dp green		.80	.40
	Never hinged	1.40	
	On cover		1.40
	On cover, single franking		4.25
265 A45 40c brt violet		.25	.25
	Never hinged	.45	
	On cover		1.10
	On cover, single franking		3.50
266 A45 45c yellow brown		1.50	.80
	Never hinged	2.90	
	On cover		6.75
	On cover, single franking		32.50
267 A45 50c rose red		.20	.20
	Never hinged	.20	
	On cover		.35
	On cover, single franking		.75
a.	Imperf., pair	55.00	
	Never hinged	90.00	
b.	Booklet pane of 10	5.50	
	Never hinged	10.00	
268 A45 55c dull vio ('37)		.50	.20
	Never hinged	.80	
	On cover		.75
	On cover, single franking		2.10
269 A45 60c ocher ('37)		.25	.20
	Never hinged	.35	
	On cover		3.50
	On cover, single franking		21.00
270 A45 65c violet brown		.40	.40
	Never hinged	.65	
	On cover		.65
	On cover, single franking		4.25
271 A45 65c brt ultra ('37)		.25	.20
	Never hinged	.35	
	On cover		.65
	On cover, single franking		1.00
a.	Booklet pane of 10	7.00	
	Never hinged	10.00	
272 A45 75c olive green		.20	.25
	Never hinged	.25	
	On cover		.75
	On cover, single franking		3.00
273 A45 80c orange ('38)		.20	.20
	Never hinged	.20	
	On cover		.75
	On cover, single franking		3.50
274 A45 90c dk red		26.00	1.60
	Never hinged	47.50	
	On cover		4.00
	On cover, single franking		7.00
275 A45 90c brt green ('38)		.20	.20
	Never hinged	.20	
	On cover		.75
	On cover, single franking		4.00
276 A45 90c ultra ('38)		.60	.20
	Never hinged	1.00	
	On cover		.40
	On cover, single franking		1.00
a.	Booklet pane of 10	8.50	
	Never hinged	12.00	
277 A45 1fr orange		2.50	.20
	Never hinged	4.50	
	On cover		1.40
	On cover, single franking		5.00
278 A45 1fr rose pink ('38)		2.40	.35
	Never hinged	4.50	
	On cover		1.00
	On cover, single franking		3.50
279 A45 1.25fr brown ol		60.00	3.75
	Never hinged	120.00	
	On cover		5.00
	On cover, single franking		25.00
280 A45 1.25fr rose car ('39)		1.50	1.75
	Never hinged	2.75	
	On cover		2.75
	On cover, single franking		8.00
281 A45 1.40fr brt red vio ('39)		4.75	4.00
	Never hinged	8.25	
	On cover		10.00
	On cover, single franking		47.50
282 A45 1.50fr deep blue		.25	.25
	Never hinged	.45	
	On cover		.75
	On cover, single franking		4.00
283 A45 1.75fr magenta		3.50	.40
	Never hinged	6.25	
	On cover		1.00
	On cover, single franking		4.00
	Nos. 264-283 (20)	106.25	15.80
	Set, never hinged	205.00	

The 50c is found in 4 types, differing in the lines below belt and size of "c."

For surcharges and overprints see Nos. 298, 333, 401-403, 405-409, M7-M9, S1.

Le Puy-en-Velay — A46

1933 Engr. *Perf. 13*

290 A46 90c rose		2.75	.85
	Never hinged	4.25	
	On cover		1.50
	On cover, single franking		3.00

Aristide Briand A47

Paul Doumer A48

Victor Hugo — A49

1933, Dec. 11 Typo. *Perf. 14x13½*

291 A47 30c blue green		13.00	6.50
	Never hinged	24.00	
	On cover		8.50
	On cover, single franking		13.50
292 A48 75c red violet		22.50	1.40
	Never hinged	42.50	
	On cover		2.25
	On cover, single franking		6.75
293 A49 1.25fr claret		4.75	1.90
	Never hinged	8.25	
	On cover		4.25
	On cover, single franking		21.00
	Nos. 291-293 (3)	40.25	9.80
	Set, never hinged	75.00	

Dove and Olive Branch A50

Joseph Marie Jacquard A51

1934, Feb. 20

294 A50 1.50fr ultra		50.00	11.00
	Never hinged	72.50	
	On cover		21.00
	On cover, single franking		37.50

1934, Mar. 14 Engr. *Perf. 14x13*

295 A51 40c blue		2.25	.70
	Never hinged	3.75	
	On cover		1.10
	On cover, single franking		2.25

Jacquard (1752-1834), inventor of an improved loom for figured weaving.

Jacques Cartier A52

1934, July 18 *Perf. 13*

296 A52 75c rose lilac		22.50	1.75
	Never hinged	55.00	
	On cover		3.50
	On cover, single franking		13.00
297 A52 1.50fr blue		40.00	3.50
	Never hinged	95.00	
	On cover		5.25
	On cover, single franking		13.00
	Set, never hinged	150.00	

Cartier's discovery of Canada, 400th anniv.

No. 279 Surcharged

1934, Nov. *Perf. 14x13½*

298 A45 50c on 1.25fr brn ol		3.00	.40
	Never hinged	5.75	
	On cover		2.25
	On cover, single franking		11.00

Catalogue values for unused stamps in this section, from this point to the end of the section, are for Never Hinged items.

Breton River Scene A53

1935, Feb. Engr. *Perf. 13*

299 A53 2fr blue green		52.50	.80
	On cover		3.50
	On cover, single franking		13.00

S. S. Normandie A54

1935, Apr.

300 A54 1.50fr dark blue		21.00	1.60
	On cover		3.50
	On cover, single franking		6.75
a.	1.50fr pale blue ('36)	100.00	14.00
	On cover		32.50
	On cover, single franking		52.50
b.	1.50fr blue green ('36)	*17,500.*	*12,500.*
	Hinged	13,250.	
c.	1.50fr turquoise ('36)	325.00	32.50
	Hinged	210.00	
	On cover		72.50
	On cover, single franking		110.00

Maiden voyage of the transatlantic steamship, the "Normandie."

Benjamin Delessert A55

1935, May 20

301 A55 75c blue green		32.50	1.25
	On cover		3.25
	On cover, single franking		10.00

Opening of the International Savings Bank Congress, May 20, 1935.

View of St. Trophime at Arles A56

Victor Hugo (1802-85) A57

1935, May 3

302 A56 3.50fr dark brown		50.00	3.50
	On cover		7.25
	On cover, single franking		20.00

1935, May 30 *Perf. 14x13*

303 A57 1.25fr magenta		6.00	1.40
	On cover		4.25
	On cover, single franking		23.00

Cardinal Richelieu — A58

Jacques Callot — A59

1935, June 12 *Perf. 13*

304 A58 1.50fr deep rose		40.00	1.40
	On cover		2.50
	On cover, single franking		5.25

Tercentenary of the founding of the French Academy by Cardinal Richelieu.

1935, Nov. *Perf. 14x13*

305 A59 75c red		14.50	.60
	On cover		1.60
	On cover, single franking		5.00

300th anniv. of the death of Jacques Callot, engraver.

André Marie Ampère (1775-1836), Scientist, by Louis Boilly — A60

1936, Feb. 27 *Perf. 13*

306 A60 75c brown		25.00	1.60
	On cover		2.25
	On cover, single franking		6.75

Windmill at Fontvielle, Immortalized by Daudet — A61

1936, Apr. 27

307 A61 2fr ultra		4.25	.35
	On cover		2.25
	On cover, single franking		7.25

Publication, in 1866, of Alphonse Daudet's "Lettres de mon Moulin," 75th anniv.

Pilâtre de Rozier and his Balloon A62

1936, June 4

308 A62 75c Prus blue		25.00	2.00
	On cover		4.00
	On cover, single franking		11.00

150th anniversary of the death of Jean Francois Pilâtre de Rozier, balloonist.

Rouget de Lisle — A63

"La Marseillaise" — A64

1936, June 27

309 A63 20c Prus green		4.75	1.60
	On cover		2.60
	On cover, single franking		4.00
310 A64 40c dark brown		8.50	2.75
	On cover		4.00
	On cover, single franking		5.00

Cent. of the death of Claude Joseph Rouget de Lisle, composer of "La Marseillaise."

Canadian War Memorial at Vimy Ridge A65

1936, July 26

311 A65 75c henna brown 16.00 1.60
On cover 4.75
On cover, single franking 26.00
312 A65 1.50fr dull blue 24.00 7.00
On cover 13.00
On cover, single franking 24.00

Unveiling of the Canadian War Memorial at Vimy Ridge, July 26, 1936.

A66

Jean Léon Jaurès A67

1936, July 30

313 A66 40c red brown 4.25 1.10
On cover 1.40
On cover, single franking 3.75
314 A67 1.50fr ultra 20.00 2.10
On cover 4.00
On cover, single franking 8.00

Assassination of Jean Léon Jaurès (1859-1914), socialist and politician.

Herald — A68

Allegory of Exposition A69

1936, Sept. 15 Typo. ***Perf. 14x13½***

315 A68 20c brt violet .80 .40
On cover 1.40
On cover, single franking 6.00
316 A68 30c Prus green 3.25 1.25
On cover 2.00
On cover, single franking 21.00
317 A68 40c ultra 1.75 .40
On cover 1.00
On cover, single franking 3.50
318 A68 50c red orange 1.60 .20
On cover .70
On cover, single franking 1.10
319 A69 90c carmine 18.00 6.00
On cover 11.25
On cover, single franking 23.00
320 A69 1.50fr ultra 50.00 3.25
On cover 5.75
On cover, single franking 20.00
Nos. 315-320 (6) 75.40 11.50

Publicity for the 1937 Paris Exposition.

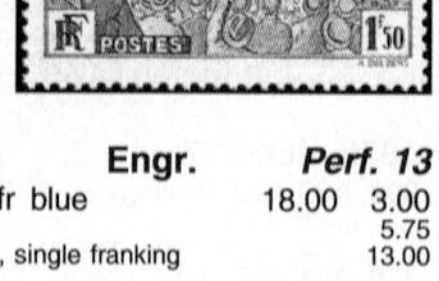

"Peace" A70

1936, Oct. 1 Engr. ***Perf. 13***

321 A70 1.50fr blue 18.00 3.00
On cover 5.75
On cover, single franking 13.00

Skiing A71

1937, Jan. 18

322 A71 1.50fr dark blue 9.00 1.40
On cover 2.75
On cover, single franking 4.50

Intl. Ski Meet at Chamonix-Mont Blanc.

Pierre Corneille, Portrait by Charles Le Brun — A72

1937, Feb. 15

323 A72 75c brown carmine 2.75 1.00
On cover 2.00
On cover, single franking 5.25

300th anniv. of the publication of "Le Cid."

Paris Exposition Issue

Exposition Allegory A73

1937, Mar. 15

324 A73 1.50fr turq blue 3.00 1.00
On cover 2.00
On cover, single franking 5.25

Jean Mermoz (1901-36), Aviator A74

Memorial to Mermoz — A75

1937, Apr. 22

325 A74 30c dk slate green .65 .40
On cover 2.25
On cover, single franking 6.75
326 A75 3fr dark violet 9.25 3.00
On cover 10.00
On cover, single franking 26.00
a. 3fr violet 10.50 3.75
On cover 10.50
b. 3fr gray violet (non-Fluorescent) 250.00 72.50
Hinged 150.00

Electric Train A76

Streamlined Locomotive A77

1937, May 31

327 A76 30c dk green 1.50 1.40
On cover 2.25
On cover, single franking 4.75
328 A77 1.50fr dk ultra 10.50 6.50
On cover 10.00
On cover, single franking 30.00

13th International Railroad Congress.

Intl. Philatelic Exhibition Issue

Souvenir Sheet

Ceres Type A1 of 1849-50 — A77a

1937, June 18 Typo. ***Perf. 14x13½***

329 A77a Sheet of 4 425.00 225.00
Lightly hinged in margins 200.00
On cover *450.00*
a. 5c ultra & dark brown 50.00 35.00
Lightly hinged 30.00
On cover *125.00*
b. 15c red & rose red 50.00 35.00
Lightly hinged 30.00
On cover *125.00*
c. 30c ultra & rose red 50.00 35.00
Lightly hinged 30.00
On cover *125.00*
d. 50c red & dark brown 50.00 35.00
Lightly hinged 30.00
On cover *125.00*
e. Sheet of 4, imperf 2,250.
Lightly hinged in margins 1,825.

Issued in sheets measuring 150x220mm.

The sheets were sold only at the exhibition in Paris, a ticket of admission being required for each sheet purchased.

René Descartes, by Frans Hals — A78

1937, June Engr. ***Perf. 13***

Inscribed "Discours sur la Méthode"

330 A78 90c copper red 2.75 1.10
On cover 2.25
On cover, single franking 8.00

Inscribed "Discours de la Méthode"

331 A78 90c copper red 9.00 1.40
On cover 2.25
On cover, single franking 10.00

3rd centenary of the publication of "Discours de la Méthode" by René Descartes.

France Congratulating USA — A79

1937, Sept. 17

332 A79 1.75fr ultra 3.25 1.50
On cover 2.25
On cover, single franking 3.75

150th anniv. of the US Constitution.

No. 277 Surcharged in Red

1937, Oct. ***Perf. 14x13½***

333 A45 80c on 1fr orange 1.40 .20
On cover 10.50
On cover, single franking 52.50
a. Inverted surcharge *1,000.*
Hinged *725.00*

Mountain Road at Iseran A80

1937, Oct. 4 Engr. ***Perf. 13***

334 A80 90c dark green 2.75 .25
On cover .65
On cover, single franking 3.50

Issued in commemoration of the opening of the mountain road at Iseran, Savoy.

Ceres — A81

1938-40 Typo. ***Perf. 14x13½***

335 A81 1.75fr dk ultra .85 .45
On cover .75
On cover, single franking 4.25
336 A81 2fr car rose ('39) .30 .20
On cover .75
On cover, single franking 11.00
337 A81 2.25fr ultra ('39) 11.00 .75
On cover .75
On cover, single franking 4.25
338 A81 2.50fr green ('39) 2.25 .40
On cover 1.00
On cover, single franking 4.25
339 A81 2.50fr vio blue ('40) .85 .45
On cover .85
On cover, single franking 5.00
340 A81 3fr rose lilac ('39) .80 .40
On cover 1.00
On cover, single franking 3.50
Nos. 335-340 (6) 16.05 2.65

For surcharges see Nos. 397-399.

Léon Gambetta (1838-82), Lawyer and Statesman — A82

1938, Apr. 2 Engr. ***Perf. 13***

341 A82 55c dark violet .45 .40
On cover 1.00
On cover, single franking 3.50

Arc de Triomphe of Orange A82a

Miners A83

Keep and Gate of Vincennes A86

Palace of the Popes, Avignon
A84

Medieval Walls of Carcassonne — A85

Port of St. Malo — A87

1938

342 A82a 2fr brown black 1.00 1.00
On cover 5.50
On cover, single franking 10.50
343 A83 2.15fr violet brn 6.75 .80
On cover 1.40
On cover, single franking 4.00
344 A84 3fr car brown 18.00 4.00
On cover 8.25
On cover, single franking 32.50
345 A85 5fr deep ultra 1.00 .35
On cover 2.40
On cover, single franking 14.50
346 A86 10fr brown, *blue* 2.00 1.50
On cover 3.25
On cover, single franking 37.50
347 A87 20fr dk blue green 57.50 15.00
On cover 23.00
On cover, single franking 42.50
Nos. 342-347 (6) 86.25 22.65

For surcharges see Nos. 410-414.

Clément Ader, Air Pioneer
A88

1938, June 16
348 A88 50fr ultra (thin paper) 110.00 50.00
Hinged 70.00
On cover 160.00
On cover, single franking 375.00
a. 50fr dark ultra (thick paper) 110.00 62.50
Hinged 72.50
On cover 160.00
On cover, single franking 375.00

Soccer Players
A89

1938, June 1
349 A89 1.75fr dark ultra 21.00 10.50
On cover 21.00
On cover, single franking 50.00

World Cup Soccer Championship.

Costume of Champagne Region — A90

Jean de La Fontaine — A91

1938, June 13
350 A90 1.75fr dark ultra 5.50 3.50
On cover 5.25
On cover, single franking 10.00

Tercentenary of the birth of Dom Pierre Pérignon, discoverer of the champagne process.

1938, July 8
351 A91 55c dk blue green .85 .80
On cover 1.00
On cover, single franking 2.00

Jean de La Fontaine (1621-1695) the fabulist.

Seal of Friendship and Peace, Victoria Tower and Arc de Triomphe
A92

1938, July 19
352 A92 1.75fr ultra .95 .65
On cover 2.00
On cover, single franking 4.00

Visit of King George VI and Queen Elizabeth of Great Britain to France.

Mercury
A93

Self-portrait
A95

1938-42 Typo. *Perf. 14x13½*
353 A93 1c dark brown ('39) .20 .20
On cover 8.50
On cover, single franking 67.50
354 A93 2c slate grn ('39) .20 .20
On cover 20.00
On cover, single franking 100.00
355 A93 5c rose .20 .20
On cover 8.50
On cover, single franking 50.00
356 A93 10c ultra .20 .20
On cover 2.00
On cover, single franking 25.00
357 A93 15c red orange .20 .20
On cover 2.75
On cover, single franking 47.50
358 A93 15c orange brn ('39) .80 .40
On cover 2.75
On cover, single franking 47.50
359 A93 20c red violet .20 .20
On cover 3.00
On cover, single franking 21.00
360 A93 25c blue green .20 .20
On cover 7.00
On cover, single franking 22.00
361 A93 30c rose red ('39) .20 .20
On cover 1.10
On cover, single franking 2.75
362 A93 40c dk violet ('39) .20 .20
On cover 1.00
On cover, single franking 2.00
363 A93 45c lt green ('39) .60 .40
On cover 6.50
On cover, single franking 10.50
364 A93 50c deep blue ('39) 3.00 .35
On cover 2.75
On cover, single franking 16.50
365 A93 50c dk green ('41) .45 .25
On cover 2.75
On cover, single franking 20.00
366 A93 50c grnsh blue ('42) .20 .20
On cover 1.00
On cover, single franking 4.00
367 A93 60c red orange ('39) .20 .20
On cover 2.75
On cover, single franking 12.00
368 A93 70c magenta ('39) .20 .20
On cover 1.00
On cover, single franking 2.00
369 A93 75c dk org brn ('39) 6.00 2.00
On cover 25.00
On cover, single franking 100.00
Nos. 353-369 (17) 13.25 5.80

No. 366 exists imperforate. See Nos. 455-458. For overprints and surcharge see #404, 499-502.

1939, Mar. 15 Engr. *Perf. 13*
370 A95 2.25fr Prussian blue 6.00 2.75
On cover 4.00
On cover, single franking 7.25

Paul Cézanne (1839-1906), painter.

Georges Clemenceau and Battleship Clemenceau — A96

1939, Apr. 18
371 A96 90c ultra .65 .45
On cover 1.75
On cover, single franking 3.25

Laying of the keel of the warship "Clemenceau," Jan. 17, 1939.

Statue of Liberty, French Pavilion, Trylon and Perisphere
A97

1939-40
372 A97 2.25fr ultra 12.00 5.25
On cover 7.25
On cover, single franking 13.00
373 A97 2.50fr ultra ('40) 13.00 7.50
On cover 11.50
On cover, single franking 16.50

New York World's Fair.

Joseph Nicéphore Niepce and Louis Jacques Mandé Daguerre
A98

1939, Apr. 24
374 A98 2.25fr dark blue 11.00 5.25
On cover 7.25
On cover, single franking 13.00

Centenary of photography.

Iris — A99

Pumping Station at Marly
A100

1939-44 Typo. *Perf. 14x13½*
375 A99 80c red brown ('40) .20 .20
On cover .65
On cover, single franking 6.75
376 A99 80c yellow grn ('44) .20 .20
On cover 3.00
On cover, single franking 10.00
377 A99 1fr green .80 .20
On cover .65
On cover, single franking 1.00
378 A99 1fr crimson ('40) .40 .35
On cover .65
On cover, single franking 1.00
a. Booklet pane of 10 7.50
379 A99 1fr grnsh blue ('44) .20 .20
On cover 1.40
On cover, single franking 5.25
380 A99 1.20fr violet ('44) .20 .20
On cover 1.00
On cover, single franking 2.00
381 A99 1.30fr ultra ('40) .20 .20
On cover 3.00
On cover, single franking 13.00
382 A99 1.50fr red org ('41) .20 .20
On cover 1.00
On cover, single franking 10.00
383 A99 1.50fr henna brn ('44) .20 .20
On cover 1.00
On cover, single franking 4.75
384 A99 2fr violet brn ('44) .20 .20
On cover 1.00
On cover, single franking 4.25
385 A99 2.40fr car rose ('44) .20 .20
On cover 2.00
On cover, single franking 110.00
386 A99 3fr orange ('44) .20 .20
On cover 2.00
On cover, single franking 8.00
387 A99 4fr ultra ('44) .20 .20
On cover 3.00
On cover, single franking 12.00
Nos. 375-387 (13) 3.40 2.75

1939 Engr. *Perf. 13*
388 A100 2.25fr brt ultra 18.00 4.00
On cover 5.75
On cover, single franking 13.00

France's participation in the International Water Exposition at Liège.

St. Gregory of Tours — A101

1939, June 10
389 A101 90c red .65 .40
On cover 1.00
On cover, single franking 3.00

14th centenary of the birth of St. Gregory of Tours, historian and bishop.

"The Oath of the Tennis Court" by Jacques David
A102

1939, June 20
390 A102 90c deep slate green 2.75 1.50
On cover 2.00
On cover, single franking 3.25

150th anniversary of French Revolution.

Cathedral of Strasbourg — A103

1939, June 23
391 A103 70c brown carmine 1.10 .80
On cover 1.40
On cover, single franking 3.25

500th anniv. of the completion of Strasbourg Cathedral.

Porte Chaussée, Verdun
A104

1939, June 23
392 A104 90c black brown .80 .70

23rd anniv. of the Battle of Verdun.

View of Pau
A105

1939, Aug. 25
393 A105 90c brt rose, *gray bl* .90 .40

Maid of Languedoc A106

Bridge at Lyons A107

1939

394 A106 70c black, *blue* .35 .35
On cover 3.00
On cover, single franking 20.00
395 A107 90c dull brown vio .80 .65
On cover 3.25
On cover, single franking 20.00

Imperforates

Nearly all French stamps issued from 1940 onward exist imperforate. Officially 20 sheets, ranging from 25 to 100 subjects, were left imperforate.

Georges Guynemer (1894-1917), World War I Ace — A108

1940, Nov. 7

396 A108 50fr ultra 12.50 7.25
On cover 60.00
On cover, single franking 180.00

Stamps of 1938-39 Surcharged in Carmine

1940-41 ***Perf. 14x13½***

397 A81 1fr on 1.75fr dk ultra .20 .20
On cover .65
On cover, single franking 3.00
398 A81 1fr on 2.25fr ultra ('41) .20 .20
On cover 1.00
On cover, single franking 3.00
399 A81 1fr on 2.50fr grn ('41) .85 .85
On cover 1.40
On cover, single franking 3.25
Nos. 397-399 (3) 1.25 1.25

Stamps of 1932-39 Surcharged in Carmine, Red (#408) or Black (#407)

1940-41 ***Perf. 13, 14x13½***

400 A22 30c on 35c grn ('41) .20 .20
On cover 1.75
On cover, single franking 10.00
401 A45 50c on 55c dl vio ('41) .20 .20
On cover 1.00
On cover, single franking 15.00
a. Inverted surcharge *725.00*
Lightly hinged *575.00*
402 A45 50c on 65c brt ultra ('41) .20 .20
On cover .65
On cover, single franking 15.00
403 A45 50c on 75c ol grn ('41) .25 .20
On cover 1.00
On cover, single franking 15.00
404 A93 50c on 75c dk org brn ('41) .20 .20
On cover 1.00
On cover, single franking 30.00
405 A45 50c on 80c org ('41) .25 .20
On cover 1.00
On cover, single franking 16.50
406 A45 50c on 90c ultra ('41) .20 .20
On cover 1.00
On cover, single franking 15.00
a. Inverted surcharge *425.00*
Lightly hinged *300.00*
b. "05" instead of "50" *6,750.*
Lightly hinged *5,000.*
407 A45 1fr on 1.25fr rose car (Bk) ('41) .20 .20
On cover 1.00
On cover, single franking 3.00
408 A45 1fr on 1.40fr brt red vio (R) ('41) .20 .20
On cover 1.00
On cover, single franking 4.00
a. Double surcharge *1,250.*
Lightly hinged *800.00*
409 A45 1fr on 1.50fr dk bl ('41) .75 .65
On cover 1.00
On cover, single franking 3.00
410 A83 1fr on 2.15fr vio brn .35 .20
On cover .65
On cover, single franking 3.00
a. Inverted surcharge *12,000.* *5,250.*
On cover *7,500.*
411 A85 2.50fr on 5fr dp ultra ('41) .35 .20
On cover 4.25
On cover, single franking 20.00
a. Double surcharge *275.00* 150.00
Lightly hinged *190.00*
412 A86 5fr on 10fr brn, *bl* ('41) 1.40 1.25
On cover 5.00
On cover, single franking 40.00
413 A87 10fr on 20fr dk bl grn ('41) 1.40 1.25
On cover 52.50
On cover, single franking 140.00
414 A88 20fr on 50fr dk ultra (#348a) ('41) 42.50 30.00
On cover 82.50
On cover, single franking 240.00
a. 20fr on 50fr ultra, thin paper (#348) 52.50 42.50
On cover 100.00
On cover, single franking 275.00
Nos. 400-414 (15) 48.65 35.35

SEMI-POSTAL STAMPS

No. 162 Surcharged in Red and:

No. B1

SP2

1914 Unwmk. Typo. ***Perf. 14x13½***

B1 A22 10c + 5c red 5.00 4.25
Never hinged 6.00
On cover 8.00
On cover, single franking 10.00
B2 SP2 10c + 5c red 27.50 3.00
Never hinged 55.00
On cover 8.75
On cover, single franking 11.00
a. Booklet pane of 10 525.00
Never hinged 700.00

Issue dates: #B1, Aug. 11; #B2, Sept. 10.
For overprint see Offices in Morocco #B8.

Widow at Grave SP3

War Orphans SP4

Woman Plowing — SP5

"Trench of Bayonets" SP6

Lion of Belfort SP7

"La Marseillaise" — SP8

1917-19

B3 SP3 2c + 3c vio brn 3.50 3.00
Never hinged 6.00
On cover 10.00
B4 SP4 5c + 5c grn ('19) 18.00 6.50
Never hinged 30.00
On cover 11.00
B5 SP5 15c + 10c gray green 25.00 16.00
Never hinged 50.00
On cover 27.50
B6 SP5 25c + 15c dp bl 75.00 40.00
Never hinged 125.00
On cover 55.00
B7 SP6 35c + 25c slate & vio 125.00 85.00
Never hinged 225.00
On cover 140.00
B8 SP7 50c + 50c pale brn & dk brn 225.00 125.00
Never hinged 450.00
On cover 225.00
B9 SP8 1fr + 1fr cl & mar 325.00 275.00
Never hinged 675.00
On cover 475.00
B10 SP8 5fr + 5fr dp bl & blk 1,300. 1,000.
Never hinged 2,700.
On cover *1,875.*
Nos. B3-B10 (8) 2,096. 1,550.

See #B20-B23. For surcharges see #B12-B19.

Hospital Ship and Field Hospital SP9

1918, Aug.

B11 SP9 15c + 5c sl & red 95.00 47.50
Never hinged 190.00
On cover 72.50

Semi-Postal Stamps of 1917-19 Surcharged

1922, Sept. 1

B12 SP3 2c + 1c violet brn .35 *.50*
Never hinged .70
On cover 2.75
B13 SP4 5c + 2½c green .50 *.70*
Never hinged 1.00
On cover 2.75
B14 SP5 15c + 5c gray grn 1.10 1.10
Never hinged 1.50
On cover 4.00
B15 SP5 25c + 5c deep bl 1.75 1.75
Never hinged 3.00
On cover 5.50
B16 SP6 35c + 5c slate & vio 10.00 10.00
Never hinged 16.00
On cover 27.50
B17 SP7 50c + 10c pale brn & dk brn 14.00 13.00
Never hinged 24.00
On cover 40.00
a. Pair, one without surcharge
B18 SP8 1fr + 25c cl & mar 22.50 22.50
Never hinged 40.00
On cover *110.00*
B19 SP8 5fr + 1fr bl & blk 110.00 125.00
Never hinged 210.00
On cover *300.00*
Nos. B12-B19 (8) 160.20 174.55
Set, never hinged 296.20

Style and arrangement of surcharge differs for each denomination.

Types of 1917-19

1926-27

B20 SP3 2c + 1c violet brn 1.00 1.00
Never hinged 1.50
On cover 2.75
B21 SP7 50c + 10c ol brn & dk brn 17.50 10.00
Never hinged 35.00
On cover 27.50
B22 SP8 1fr + 25c dp rose & red brn 40.00 30.00
Never hinged 80.00
On cover *87.50*
B23 SP8 5fr + 1fr sl bl & blk 87.50 75.00
Never hinged 160.00
On cover *300.00*
Nos. B20-B23 (4) 146.00 116.00

Sinking Fund Issues

Types of Regular Issues of 1903-07 Surcharged in Red or Blue

1927, Sept. 26

B24 A22 40c + 10c lt blue (R) 4.00 4.00
Never hinged 6.50
On cover 20.00
a. Missing first "e" in "Amortissement" 70.00 65.00
Never hinged 110.00
B25 A20 50c + 25c green (Bl) 6.00 6.00
Never hinged 8.50
On cover 27.50
a. Missing dot on "i" of "Caisse" 42.50 32.50
Never hinged 65.00

Surcharge on #B25 differs from illustration.

Type of Regular Issue of 1923 Surcharged in Black

B26 A23 1.50fr + 50c orange 9.50 9.50
Never hinged 16.00
On cover *40.00*
a. Pair, one without surcharge *2,000.*
Never hinged 2,700.
Nos. B24-B26 (3) 19.50 19.50

See Nos. B28-B33, B35-B37, B39-B41.

Industry and Agriculture SP10

1928, May Engr. ***Perf. 13½***

B27 SP10 1.50fr + 8.50fr dull blue 100.00 100.00
Never hinged 140.00
On cover 200.00
a. Blue green 425.00 425.00
Never hinged 600.00

Types of 1903-23 Issues Surcharged like Nos. B24-B26

1928, Oct. 1 ***Perf. 14x13½***

B28 A22 40c + 10c gray lilac (R) 8.75 8.00
Never hinged 16.00
On cover 25.00
a. Missing first "e" in "Amortissement" 62.50 *67.50*
Never hinged 110.00
B29 A20 50c + 25c orange brn (Bl) 22.50 20.00
Never hinged 40.00
On cover 40.00
a. Missing dot on "i" of "Caisse" 60.00 57.50
Never hinged 80.00

B30 A23 1.50fr + 50c rose lilac (Bk) 35.00 27.50
Never hinged 65.00
On cover 60.00
Nos. B28-B30 (3) 66.25 55.50

Types of 1903-23 Issues Surcharged like Nos. B24-B26

1929, Oct. 1

B31 A22 40c + 10c green 15.00 12.50
Never hinged 20.00
On cover 27.50
a. Missing first "e" in "Amortissement" 65.00 62.50
Never hinged 95.00
b. Missing dot on "i" of "Caisse" 45.00 45.00
Never hinged 62.50
B32 A20 50c + 25c lilac rose 22.50 22.50
Never hinged 40.00
On cover 45.00
a. Missing dot on "i" of "Caisse" 70.00 65.00
Never hinged 100.00
B33 A23 1.50fr + 50c chestnut 45.00 40.00
Never hinged 80.00
On cover 80.00
Nos. B31-B33 (3) 82.50 75.00

"The Smile of Reims" SP11

1930, Mar. 15 **Engr.** ***Perf. 13***

B34 SP11 1.50fr + 3.50fr red vio 65.00 65.00
Never hinged 90.00
On cover 100.00
On cover, single franking 160.00
a. Booklet pane of 4 250.00
Never hinged 400.00
b. Booklet pane of 8 550.00
Never hinged 800.00

Booklets containing No. B34 have two panes of 4 (#B34a) connected by a gutter, the complete piece constituting #B34b, which is stapled into the booklet through the gutter.

Types of 1903-07 Issues Surcharged like Nos. B24-B25

1930 Oct. 1 ***Perf. 14x13½***

B35 A22 40c + 10c cerise 18.00 13.00
Never hinged 32.50
On cover 27.50
a. Missing dot on "i" of "Caisse" 35.00 35.00
Never hinged 50.00
B36 A20 50c + 25c gray brown 30.00 24.00
Never hinged 55.00
On cover 50.00
a. Missing dot on "i" of "Caisse" 67.50 62.50
Never hinged 100.00
B37 A22 1.50fr + 50c violet 60.00 50.00
Never hinged 100.00
On cover 100.00
a. "C" below "t" of "Amortissement" 100.00 100.00
Never hinged 140.00
Nos. B35-B37 (3) 108.00 87.00

Allegory, French Provinces SP12

1931, Mar. 1 ***Perf. 13***

B38 SP12 1.50fr + 3.50fr green 110.00 110.00
Never hinged 190.00
On cover 175.00
On cover, single franking 215.00

Types of 1903-07 Issues Surcharged like Nos. B24-B25

1931, Oct. 1 ***Perf. 14x13½***

B39 A22 40c + 10c ol grn 35.00 30.00
Never hinged 62.50
On cover 60.00
a. Missing dot on "i" of "Caisse" 52.50 50.00
Never hinged 80.00
B40 A20 50c + 25c gray vio 80.00 75.00
Never hinged 150.00
On cover 135.00
a. Missing first "e" in "Amortissement" 125.00 125.00
Never hinged 175.00
B41 A22 1.50fr + 50c deep red 75.00 75.00
Never hinged 125.00
On cover 145.00
a. "C" below "t" of "Amortissement" 140.00 140.00
Never hinged 210.00
Nos. B39-B41 (3) 190.00 180.00

Catalogue values for unused stamps in this section, from this point to the end of the section, are for Never Hinged items.

"France" Giving Aid to an Intellectual SP13

Symbolic of Music SP14

1935, Dec. 9 **Engr.** ***Perf. 13***

B42 SP13 50c + 10c ultra 3.00 2.00
On cover 3.25
On cover, single franking 5.50
B43 SP14 50c + 2fr dull red 75.00 35.00
On cover 45.00
On cover, single franking 75.00

The surtax was for the aid of distressed and exiled intellectuals.
For surcharge see No. B47.

Statue of Liberty SP15

Children of the Unemployed SP16

1936-37

B44 SP15 50c + 25c dk blue ('37) 4.00 3.00
On cover 4.50
On cover, single franking 9.00
B45 SP15 75c + 50c violet 13.00 7.50
On cover 11.00
On cover, single franking 20.00

Surtax for the aid of political refugees.
For surcharge see No. B47.

1936, May

B46 SP16 50c + 10c copper red 4.50 3.00
On cover 5.50
On cover, single franking 8.00

The surtax was for the aid of children of the unemployed.

No. B43 Surcharged in Black

1936, Nov.

B47 SP14 20c on 50c + 2fr dull red 3.00 1.75
On cover 4.00
On cover, single franking 7.00

Jacques Callot SP17

Anatole France (Jacques Anatole Thibault) — SP18

Hector Berlioz SP19

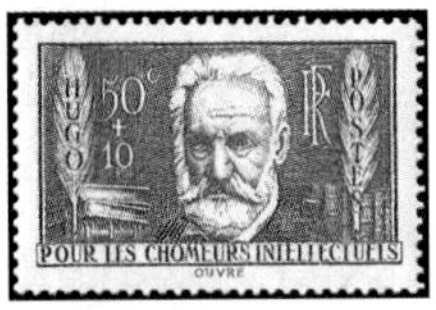
Victor Hugo SP20

Auguste Rodin SP21

Louis Pasteur SP22

1936-37 **Engr.**

B48 SP17 20c + 10c brown car 3.00 1.50
On cover 3.50
On cover, single franking 6.50
B49 SP18 30c + 10c emer ('37) 2.50 1.50
On cover 3.50
On cover, single franking 5.50
B50 SP19 40c + 10c emer 3.00 1.75
On cover 4.00
On cover, single franking 6.50
B51 SP20 50c + 10c copper red 4.50 2.50
On cover 3.75
On cover, single franking 5.00
B52 SP21 90c + 10c rose red ('37) 8.75 5.00
On cover 5.00
On cover, single franking 6.00
B53 SP22 1.50fr + 50c deep ultra 30.00 15.00
On cover 18.50
On cover, single franking 25.00
Nos. B48-B53 (6) 51.75 27.25

The surtax was used for relief of unemployed intellectuals.

1938

B54 SP18 30c + 10c brown car 2.50 1.75
On cover 3.50
On cover, single franking 5.50
B55 SP17 35c + 10c dull green 2.50 2.25
On cover 3.75
On cover, single franking 6.00
B56 SP19 55c + 10c dull vio 7.50 3.00
On cover 4.25
On cover, single franking 5.50
B57 SP20 65c + 10c ultra 8.00 3.00
On cover 4.25
On cover, single franking 5.50
B58 SP21 1fr + 10c car lake 6.50 3.00
On cover 4.25
On cover, single franking 6.00
B59 SP22 1.75fr + 25c dp blue 26.00 12.50
On cover 17.50
On cover, single franking 21.00
Nos. B54-B59 (6) 53.00 25.50

Tug of War SP23

Foot Race SP24

Hiking — SP25

1937, June 16

B60 SP23 20c + 10c brown 2.00 1.50
On cover 2.50
On cover, single franking 3.50
B61 SP24 40c + 10c red brown 2.00 1.50
On cover 2.50
On cover, single franking 3.50
B62 SP25 50c + 10c black brn 2.00 1.50
On cover 2.50
On cover, single franking 3.50
Nos. B60-B62 (3) 6.00 4.50

The surtax was for the Recreation Fund of the employees of the Post, Telephone and Telegraph.

Pierre Loti (Louis Marie Julien Viaud) SP26

1937, Aug.

B63 SP26 50c + 20c rose car 4.50 2.75
On cover 5.50
On cover, single franking 16.50

The surtax was for the Pierre Loti Monument Fund.

"France" and Infant SP27

1937-39

B64 SP27 65c + 25c brown vio 3.50 1.50
On cover 4.00
On cover, single franking 4.50
B65 SP27 90c + 30c pck bl ('39) 2.50 1.75
On cover 5.00
On cover, single franking 11.00

The surtax was used for public health work.

Winged Victory of Samothrace SP28

Jean Baptiste Charcot SP29

1937, Aug.

B66 SP28 30c blue green 100.00 35.00
On cover 42.50
On cover, single franking 77.50
B67 SP28 55c red 100.00 35.00
On cover 42.50
On cover, single franking 77.50
Set, hinged 110.00

On sale at the Louvre for 2.50fr. The surtax of 1.65fr was for the benefit of the Louvre Museum.

1938-39

B68 SP29 65c + 35c dk bl grn 1.50 1.50
On cover 2.00
On cover, single franking 4.50

B69 SP29 90c + 35c brt red vio ('39) 16.00 8.75
On cover 12.00
On cover, single franking 27.50

Surtax for the benefit of French seamen.

Palace of Versailles SP30

1938, May 9

B70 SP30 1.75fr + 75c dp bl 26.00 15.00
On cover 17.50
On cover, single franking 25.00

Natl. Exposition of Painting and Sculpture at Versailles.
The surtax was for the benefit of the Versailles Concert Society.

French Soldier SP31

Monument SP32

1938, May 16

B71 SP31 55c + 70c brown vio 5.25 3.50
On cover 5.50
On cover, single franking 16.00
B72 SP31 65c + 1.10fr pck bl 5.25 3.50
On cover 5.50
On cover, single franking 16.00

The surtax was for a fund to erect a monument to the glory of the French Infantrymen.

1938, May 25

B73 SP32 55c + 45c vermilion 15.00 8.00
On cover 13.00
On cover, single franking 25.00

The surtax was for a fund to erect a monument in honor of the Army Medical Corps.

Reims Cathedral SP33

"France" Welcoming Her Sons SP34

1938, July 10

B74 SP33 65c + 35c ultra 10.00 8.75
On cover 12.00
On cover, single franking 16.00

Completion of the reconstruction of Reims Cathedral, July 10, 1938.

1938, Aug. 8

B75 SP34 65c + 60c rose car 6.00 4.00
On cover 5.50
On cover, single franking 11.00

The surtax was for the benefit of French volunteers repatriated from Spain.

Curie Issue
Common Design Type

1938, Sept. 1

B76 CD80 1.75fr + 50c dp ultra 13.00 8.75
On cover 11.00
On cover, single franking 16.00

Victory Parade Passing Arc de Triomphe SP36

1938, Oct. 8

B77 SP36 65c + 35c brown car 4.50 3.00
On cover 5.00
On cover, single franking 6.00

20th anniversary of the Armistice.

Student and Nurse — SP37

1938, Dec. 1

B78 SP37 65c + 60c pck blue 11.00 6.00
On cover 8.00
On cover, single franking 13.00

The surtax was for Student Relief.

Blind Man and Radio SP38

1938, Dec.

B79 SP38 90c + 25c brown vio 11.00 6.00
On cover 8.00
On cover, single franking 13.00

The surtax was used to help provide radios for the blind.

Civilian Facing Firing Squad — SP39

Red Cross Nurse — SP40

1939, Feb. 1

B80 SP39 90c + 35c black brn 11.00 6.00
On cover 10.00
On cover, single franking 13.00

The surtax was used to erect a monument to civilian victims of World War I.

1939, Mar. 24

B81 SP40 90c + 35c dk sl grn, turq bl & red 9.50 6.00
On cover 7.00
On cover, single franking 10.00

75th anniv. of the Intl. Red Cross Soc.

Army Engineer SP41

1939, Apr. 3

B82 SP41 70c + 50c vermilion 7.50 5.00

Army Engineering Corps. The surtax was used to erect a monument to those members who died in World War I.

Ministry of Post, Telegraph and Telephone SP42

1939, Apr. 8

B83 SP42 90c + 35c turq blue 22.50 15.00
On cover 18.00
On cover, single franking 27.50

The surtax was used to aid orphans of employees of the postal system. Opening of the new building for the Ministry of Post, Telegraph and Telephones.

Mother and Child — SP43

Eiffel Tower — SP44

1939, Apr. 24

B84 SP43 90c + 35c red 2.50 1.75
On cover 3.25
On cover, single franking 6.50

The surtax was used to aid children of the unemployed.

1939, May 5

B85 SP44 90c + 50c red violet 10.00 6.00
On cover 8.00
On cover, single franking 16.00

50th anniv. of the Eiffel Tower. The surtax was used for celebration festivities.

Puvis de Chavannes — SP45

Claude Debussy SP46

Honoré de Balzac SP47

Claude Bernard SP48

1939-40

B86 SP45 40c + 10c ver 1.10 .70
On cover 2.25
On cover, single franking 4.25
B87 SP46 70c + 10c brn vio 5.50 1.90
On cover 3.25
On cover, single franking 6.50
B87A SP46 80c + 10c brn vio ('40) 6.00 5.00
On cover 7.00
On cover, single franking 8.75
B88 SP47 90c + 10c brt red vio 5.50 1.90
On cover 3.25
On cover, single franking 5.50
B88A SP47 1fr + 10c brt red vio ('40) 6.00 5.00
On cover 7.00
On cover, single franking 8.75
B89 SP48 2.25fr + 25c brt ultra 20.00 8.00
On cover 11.00
On cover, single franking 14.00
B89A SP48 2.50fr + 25c brt ultra ('40) 6.00 5.00
On cover 7.00
On cover, single franking 8.75
Nos. B86-B89A (7) 50.10 27.50

The surtax was used to aid unemployed intellectuals.

Mothers and Children
SP49 SP50

1939, June 15

B90 SP49 70c + 80c bl, grn & vio 3.50 3.25
On cover 4.50
On cover, single franking 11.00
B91 SP50 90c + 60c dk brn, dl vio & brn 5.75 4.25
On cover 4.50
On cover, single franking 10.00

The surtax was used to aid France's repopulation campaign.

"The Letter" by Jean Honoré Fragonard SP51

Statue of Widow and Children SP52

1939, July 6

B92 SP51 40c + 60c multi 3.50 2.75
On cover 4.00
On cover, single franking 6.00

The surtax was used for the Postal Museum.

1939, July 20

B93 SP52 70c + 30c brown vio 17.50 8.50
On cover 11.00
On cover, single franking 17.50

Surtax for the benefit of French seamen.

French Soldier SP53

Colonial Trooper SP54

1940, Feb. 15

B94 SP53 40c + 60c sepia 2.50 1.75
On cover 4.00
On cover, single franking 9.00
B95 SP54 1fr + 50c turq blue 2.50 1.75
On cover 4.00
On cover, single franking 9.00

The surtax was used to assist the families of mobilized men.

World Map Showing French Possessions — SP55

1940, Apr. 15

B96 SP55 1fr + 25c scarlet	2.50	1.60
On cover		3.50
On cover, single franking		4.50

Marshal Joseph J. C. Joffre SP56

Marshal Ferdinand Foch — SP57

Gen. Joseph S. Gallieni SP58

Woman Plowing SP59

1940, May 1

B97 SP56 80c + 45c choc	6.00	4.25
On cover		6.50
On cover, single franking		11.00
B98 SP57 1fr + 50c dk vio	5.50	3.50
On cover		6.50
On cover, single franking		11.00
B99 SP58 1.50fr + 50c brown red	5.50	3.50
On cover		6.50
On cover, single franking		11.00
B100 SP59 2.50fr + 50c indigo & dl bl	10.00	8.50
On cover		11.00
On cover, single franking		32.50
Nos. B97-B100 (4)	27.00	19.75

The surtax was used for war charities.

Doctor, Nurse, Soldier and Family SP60

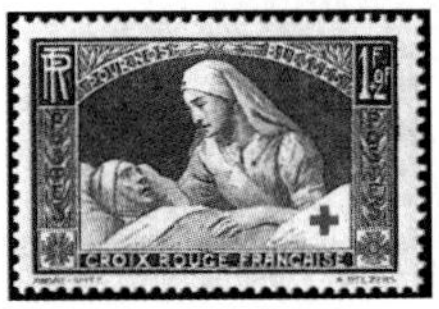

Nurse and Wounded Soldier SP61

1940, May 12

B101 SP60 80c + 1fr dk grn & red	6.50	4.25
On cover		8.75
On cover, single franking		55.00
B102 SP61 1fr + 2fr sep & red	8.00	4.25
On cover		7.75
On cover, single franking		12.50

The surtax was used for the Red Cross.

Nurse with Injured Children — SP62

1940, Nov. 12

B103 SP62 1fr + 2fr sepia	.85	.75
On cover		2.50
On cover, single franking		6.50

The surtax was used for victims of the war.

Wheat Harvest SP63

Sowing SP64

Picking Grapes SP65

Grazing Cattle SP66

1940, Dec. 2

B104 SP63 80c + 2fr brn blk	2.25	1.40
On cover		3.50
On cover, single franking		55.00
B105 SP64 1fr + 2fr chestnut	2.25	1.40
On cover		3.50
On cover, single franking		16.50
B106 SP65 1.50fr + 2fr brt vio	2.25	1.40
On cover		3.50
On cover, single franking		27.50
B107 SP66 2.50fr + 2fr dp grn	3.00	1.40
On cover		3.50
On cover, single franking		32.50
Nos. B104-B107 (4)	9.75	5.60

The surtax was for national relief.

AIR POST STAMPS

Nos. 127, 130 Overprinted in Dark Blue or Black

Perf. 14x13½

1927, June 25 **Unwmk.**

C1 A18 2fr org & bl (DB)	200.00	225.00
Never hinged	375.00	
On cover, stamp very fine		525.00
C2 A18 5fr dk bl & buff	200.00	225.00
Never hinged	375.00	
On cover, stamp very fine		525.00

On sale only at the Intl. Aviation Exhib. at Marseilles, June, 1927. One set could be purchased by each holder of an admission ticket. Excellent counterfeits exist.

Stamps centered in the grade of fine sell for about 30 percent less.

Nos. 242, 196 Surcharged

1928, Aug. 23

C3 A33 10fr on 90c	1,500.	1,500.
Never hinged	2,100.	
On cover		1,800.
a. Inverted surcharge	*14,500.*	*15,500.*
Never hinged	*19,000.*	
On cover		*18,500.*
b. Space between "10" and bars 6½mm	*2,600.*	*3,100.*
Never hinged	*3,600.*	
On cover		3,900.
C4 A23 10fr on 1.50fr	*7,500.*	*7,500.*
Never hinged	*11,000.*	
On cover		*9,000.*
a. Space between "10" and bars 6½mm	*9,500.*	*9,500.*
Never hinged	*14,000.*	
On cover		*11,500.*

Nos. C3-C4 received their surcharge in New York by order of the French consul general. They were for use in paying the 10fr fee for letters leaving the liner Ile de France on a catapulted hydroplane when the ship was one day off the coast of France on its eastward voyage.

The normal space between "10" and bars is 4½mm, but on 10 stamps in each pane of 50 the space is 6½mm. Counterfeits exist.

View of Marseille, Church of Notre Dame at Left — AP1

1930-31 **Engr.** ***Perf. 13***

C5 AP1 1.50fr dp carmine	16.00	3.00
Never hinged	26.00	
On cover		5.00
On cover, single franking		14.00
a. With perf. initials "E.I.P.A.30"	2,750.	3,750.
Never hinged	3,600.	
b. Pair, C5, C5a	3,400.	
Never hinged		
C6 AP1 1.50fr dk bl ('31)	14.00	1.40
Never hinged	25.00	
On cover		4.50
On cover, single franking		6.00
a. 1.50fr ultramarine	30.00	18.00
Never hinged	55.00	
On cover		27.50
On cover, single franking		42.50
b. As "a," with perf. initials "E.I.P.A.30"	325.00	300.00
Never hinged	500.00	
On cover		350.00
c. Pair, C6a, C6b	600.00	
Never hinged	1,100.	
d. 1.50fr bright ultra	290.00	175.00
Never hinged	450.00	

Nos. C5a, C6a were sold at the Intl. Air Post Exhib., Paris, Nov. 6-20, 1930, at face value plus 5fr, the price of admission.

Forgeries abound of Nos. C5a and C6b. Certificates from recognized authorities are recommended.

Blériot's Monoplane AP2

1934, Sept. 1 ***Perf. 13***

C7 AP2 2.25fr violet	15.00	4.50
Never hinged	26.00	
On cover		11.00
On cover, single franking		17.50

1st flight across the English Channel, by Louis Blériot.

Plane over Paris AP3

1936

C8 AP3 85c deep green	1.75	1.50
Never hinged	3.00	
On cover		4.50
On cover, single franking		12.50
a. 85c green	14.00	3.25
Never hinged	19.00	
C9 AP3 1.50fr blue	7.50	3.50
Never hinged	13.00	
On cover		6.50
On cover, single franking		11.00
C10 AP3 2.25fr violet	14.50	5.75
Never hinged	25.00	
On cover		10.00
On cover, single franking		17.50
C11 AP3 2.50fr rose	22.50	6.50
Never hinged	32.50	
On cover		11.00
On cover, single franking		16.50
C12 AP3 3fr ultra	15.00	1.10
Never hinged	25.00	
On cover		4.50
On cover, single franking		16.00
C13 AP3 3.50fr orange brn	50.00	18.00
Never hinged	85.00	
On cover		24.00
On cover, single franking		42.50
C14 AP3 50fr emerald	600.00	250.00
Never hinged	900.00	
On cover		425.00
On cover, single franking		900.00
a. 50fr deep green	800.00	475.00
Never hinged	1,250.	
b. 50fr green	650.00	275.00
Never hinged	1,000.	
Nos. C8-C14 (7)	711.25	286.35

Monoplane over Paris — AP4

Paper with Red Network Overprint

1936, July 10 ***Perf. 12½***

C15 AP4 50fr ultra	450.00	250.00
Never hinged	775.00	
On cover		425.00
On cover, single franking		875.00
a. Red network inverted	675.00	290.00
Never hinged	950.00	

Airplane and Galleon — AP5

Airplane and Globe AP6

1936, Aug. 17 ***Perf. 13***

C16 AP5 1.50fr dk ultra	11.50	3.50
Never hinged	22.50	
On cover		5.00
On cover, single franking		21.00
C17 AP6 10fr Prus green	250.00	100.00
Never hinged	450.00	
On cover		125.00
On cover, single franking		175.00

100th air mail flight across the South Atlantic.

POSTAGE DUE STAMPS

D1

D2

1859-70 **Unwmk.** **Litho.** ***Imperf.***

J1 D1 10c black	*22,500.*	175.00
No gum	4,500.	
On cover		500.00
J2 D1 15c black ('70)	100.00	175.00
No gum	35.00	
On cover		875.00

Full margins = 1mm.

In the lithographed stamps the central bar of the "E" of "CENTIMES" is very short, and the accent on "a" slants at an angle of 30 degree, for the 10c and 17 degree for the 15c, while on the typographed the central bar of the "E" is almost as wide as the top and bottom bars and the accent on the "a" slants at an angle of 47 degree.

No. J2 is known rouletted unofficially.

1859-78 Typo.

J3 D1 10c black 21.00 14.00
No gum 7.00
On cover 22.50
J4 D1 15c black ('63) 25.00 12.00
No gum 8.50
On cover 22.50
J5 D1 20c black ('77) *2,875.*
No gum 1,575.
J6 D1 25c black ('71) 110.00 42.50
No gum 40.00
On cover 77.50
J7 D1 30c black ('78) 175.00 100.00
No gum 60.00
On cover 225.00
J8 D1 40c blue ('71) 250.00 325.00
No gum 90.00
On cover 2,350.
a. 40c ultramarine *5,250.* *5,000.*
No gum 1,925.
On cover *17,500.*
b. 40c Prussian blue *1,900.*
No gum —
J9 D1 60c yellow ('71) 400.00 *850.00*
No gum 175.00
On cover *6,650.*
J10 D1 60c blue ('78) 50.00 *110.00*
No gum 16.00
On cover 1,125.
a. 60c dark blue 450.00 550.00
No gum 180.00
On cover *2,250.*
J10B D1 60c black *2,100.*
No gum 1,375.

Full margins = 1 ¼mm.

The 20c & 60c black were not put into use.

Nos. J3, J4, J6, J8 and J9 are known rouletted unofficially and Nos. J4, J6, J7 and J10 pin-perf. unofficially.

1882-92 ***Perf. 14x13½***

J11 D2 1c black 1.50 1.50
On cover 17.50
J12 D2 2c black 18.00 21.00
On cover 315.00
J13 D2 3c black 18.00 22.50
On cover 390.00
J14 D2 4c black 35.00 35.00
On cover 350.00
J15 D2 5c black 77.50 25.00
On cover 42.50
J16 D2 10c black 70.00 1.50
On cover 18.00
J17 D2 15c black 47.50 9.75
On cover 21.00
J18 D2 20c black 250.00 110.00
On cover 260.00
J19 D2 30c black 150.00 1.40
On cover 17.50
J20 D2 40c black 95.00 52.50
On cover 125.00
J21 D2 50c blk ('92) 425.00 150.00
On cover 300.00
J22 D2 60c blk ('84) 425.00 45.00
On cover 225.00
J23 D2 1fr black 525.00 325.00
On cover *3,400.*
J24 D2 2fr blk ('84) 1,000. 700.00
On cover *8,000.*
J25 D2 5fr blk ('84) 2,250. 1,400.
On cover —

Excellent counterfeits exist of Nos. J23-J25.

See Nos. J26-J45A. For overprints and surcharges see Offices in China Nos. J1-J6, J33-J40, Offices in Egypt, Alexandria J1-J5, Port Said J1-J8, Offices in Zanzibar 60-62, J1-J5, Offices in Morocco 9-10, 24-25, J1-J5, J10-J12, J17-J22, J35-J41.

1884

J26 D2 1fr brown 290.00 77.50
On cover 1,700.
J27 D2 2fr brown 150.00 110.00
On cover *7,000.*
J28 D2 5fr brown 325.00 300.00
On cover —

1893-1941

J29 D2 5c blue ('94) .25 .25
Never hinged .35
On cover .75
J30 D2 10c brown .25 .25
Never hinged .35
On cover .75
J31 D2 15c lt grn ('94) 21.00 1.00
Never hinged 35.00
On cover 2.75
J32 D2 20c ol grn ('06) 5.00 .45
Never hinged 8.50
On cover 1.50
J33 D2 25c rose ('23) 5.00 3.25
Never hinged 8.50
On cover 5.50
J34 D2 30c red ('94) .25 .20
Never hinged .35
On cover .75
J35 D2 30c org red ('94) 450.00 60.00
Never hinged 675.00
J36 D2 40c rose ('25) 10.50 3.50
Never hinged 17.00
On cover 5.50
J37 D2 45c grn ('24) 9.00 3.50
Never hinged 15.00
On cover 7.00
J38 D2 50c brn vio ('95) .35 .20
Never hinged .60
On cover .75
a. 50c lilac .35 .20
Never hinged .60
On cover .75
J39 D2 60c bl grn ('25) .75 .45
Never hinged 1.10
On cover 1.50
J40 D2 1fr rose, *straw* ('96) 475.00 275.00
Never hinged 675.00
On cover 350.00
J41 D2 1fr red brn, *straw* ('20) 8.50 .20
Never hinged 12.50
On cover .75
J42 D2 1fr red brn ('35) .80 .25
Never hinged 1.50
On cover .75
J43 D2 2fr red org ('10) 210.00 42.50
Never hinged 340.00
On cover 110.00
J44 D2 2fr brt vio ('26) .45 *.60*
Never hinged .70
On cover 2.50
J45 D2 3fr magenta ('26) .45 *.70*
Never hinged .70
On cover 2.50
J45A D2 5fr red org ('41) 1.40 1.60
Never hinged 2.25
On cover 7.00

D3

D4

1908-25

J46 D3 1c olive grn .75 *.85*
Never hinged 1.45
On cover 5.50
J47 D3 10c violet 1.10 .30
Never hinged 1.75
On cover 1.75
a. Imperf., pair 140.00
Never hinged 275.00
J48 D3 20c bister ('19) 35.00 .85
Never hinged 55.00
On cover 5.50
J49 D3 30c bister ('09) 14.00 .35
Never hinged 21.00
On cover 1.75
J50 D3 50c red ('09) 260.00 42.50
Never hinged 425.00
On cover 141.00
J51 D3 60c red ('25) 2.75 2.50
Never hinged 4.25
On cover 11.00
Nos. J46-J51 (6) 313.60 47.35

"Recouvrements" stamps were used to recover charges due on undelivered or refused mail which was returned to the sender.

For surcharges see Offices in Morocco Nos. J6-J9, J13-J16, J23-J26, J42-J45.

Nos. J49-J50 Surcharged

1917

J52 D3 20c on 30c bister 15.50 2.75
Never hinged 25.00
On cover 7.50
J53 D3 40c on 50c red 11.00 2.75
Never hinged 17.50
On cover 7.50
a. Double surcharge 335.00
Never hinged 460.00

In Jan. 1917 several values of the current issue of postage stamps were handstamped "T" in a triangle and used as postage due stamps.

Recouvrements Stamps of 1908-25 Surcharged

1926

J54 D3 50c on 10c lilac 3.50 2.75
Never hinged 5.75
On cover 7.50
J55 D3 60c on 1c ol grn 7.00 3.00
Never hinged 11.00
On cover 10.50
J56 D3 1fr on 60c red 14.00 7.75
Never hinged 25.00
On cover 17.50
J57 D3 2fr on 60c red 14.00 7.75
Never hinged 25.00
On cover 17.50
Nos. J54-J57 (4) 38.50 21.25

1927-31

J58 D4 1c olive grn ('28) .90 .90
Never hinged 1.40
On cover 4.25
J59 D4 10c rose ('31) 1.50 1.25
Never hinged 2.75
On cover 5.75
J60 D4 30c bister 4.25 .35
Never hinged 7.00
On cover 2.25
J61 D4 60c red 4.25 .35
Never hinged 7.95
On cover 1.50
J62 D4 1fr violet 12.00 2.75
Never hinged 21.00
On cover 11.50
J63 D4 1fr Prus grn ('31) 12.50 .50
Never hinged 22.50
On cover 3.50
J64 D4 2fr blue 70.00 32.50
Never hinged 125.00
On cover 70.00
J65 D4 2fr olive brn ('31) 110.00 20.00
Never hinged 200.00
On cover 60.00
Nos. J58-J65 (8) 215.40 58.60

Nos. J62 to J65 have the numerals of value double-lined.

Nos. J64, J62 Surcharged in Red or Black

1929

J66 D4 1.20fr on 2fr blue 35.00 8.50
Never hinged 67.50
On cover 25.00
J67 D4 5fr on 1fr vio (Bk) 55.00 10.00
Never hinged 100.00
On cover 30.00

No. J61 Surcharged

1931

J68 D4 1fr on 60c red 25.00 2.75
Never hinged 42.50
On cover 7.50

MILITARY STAMPS

Regular Issue Overprinted in Black or Red

1901-39 Unwmk. ***Perf. 14x13½***

M1 A17 15c orange ('01) 55.00 5.00
Never hinged 110.00
On cover 15.50
a. Inverted overprint 200.00 90.00
b. Imperf., pair 300.00
M2 A19 15c pale red ('03) 60.00 4.25
Never hinged 125.00
On cover 12.50
M3 A20 15c slate grn ('04) 45.00 4.00
Never hinged 87.50
On cover 13.00
a. No period after "M" 90.00 35.00
Never hinged 125.00
b. Imperf., pair 175.00
Never hinged 210.00
M4 A20 10c rose ('06) 27.50 5.00
Never hinged 52.50
On cover 14.00
a. No period after "M" 75.00 30.00
Never hinged 90.00
b. Imperf., pair 200.00
Never hinged 250.00
M5 A22 10c red ('07) .90 .60
Never hinged 1.75
On cover 4.00
a. Inverted overprint 72.50 42.50
Never hinged 100.00
b. Imperf., pair 140.00
Never hinged 175.00
M6 A20 50c vermilion ('29) 3.50 .60
Never hinged 5.75
On cover 4.25
a. No period after "M" 27.50 10.00
Never hinged 42.50
b. Period in front of F 27.50 10.00
Never hinged 42.50
M7 A45 50c rose red ('34) 2.25 .45
Never hinged 4.00
On cover 3.25
a. No period after "M" *20.00* *12.50*
b. Inverted overprint 100.00 77.50
Never hinged 140.00
M8 A45 65c brt ultra (R) ('38) .30 .30
Never hinged .45
On cover 2.75
a. No period after "M" 18.00 16.00
Never hinged 27.50
M9 A45 90c ultra (R) ('39) .40 .35
Never hinged .60
On cover 2.75
Nos. M1-M9 (9) 194.85 20.55

"F. M." are initials of Franchise Militaire (Military Frank). See No. S1.

NEWSPAPER STAMPS

Coat of Arms — N1

1868 Unwmk. Typo. ***Imperf.***

P1 N1 2c lilac 225.00 52.50
No gum 70.00
On newspaper 210.00
P2 N1 2c (+ 2c) blue 475.00 225.00
No gum 160.00
On newspaper *850.00*

Perf. 12½

P3 N1 2c lilac 35.00 16.00
No gum 12.00
On newspaper 55.00
P4 N1 2c (+ 4c) rose 200.00 77.50
No gum 52.50
On newspaper 375.00
P5 N1 2c (+ 2c) blue 57.50 25.00
No gum 22.50
On newspaper 85.00
P6 N1 5c lilac 950.00 500.00
No gum 325.00
On newspaper *3,500.*

Nos. P2, P4, and P5 were sold for face plus an added fiscal charge indicated in parenthesis. Nos. P1, P3 and P6 were used simply as fiscals.

The 2c rose and 5c lilac imperforate and the 5c rose and 5c blue, both imperforate and perforated, were never put into use.

Nos. P1-P6 were reprinted for the 1913 Ghent Exhibition and the 1937 Paris Exhibition (PEXIP).

No. 109 Surcharged in Red

1919 ***Perf. 14x13½***

P7 A16 ½c on 1c gray .20 .20
Never hinged .40
On cover 22.50
On printed matter, single franking 450.00
a. Inverted surcharge 950.00 875.00
Never hinged 1,500.
b. Double surcharge *5,750.*

No. 156 Surcharged

1933

P8 A22 ½c on 1c olive bister .20 *.30*
Never hinged .35
a. ½c on 1c brown bister .55 *.80*
Never hinged 1.00

FRANCHISE STAMPS

No. 276 Overprinted "F"

1939 Unwmk. ***Perf. 14x13½***

S1 A45 90c ultramarine 1.75 2.25
Never hinged 2.50
On cover 16.00
a. Period following "F" 17.50 17.50
Never hinged 25.00

No. S1 was for the use of Spanish refugees in France. "F" stands for "Franchise."

OCCUPATION STAMPS

FRANCO-PRUSSIAN WAR

Issued under German Occupation (Alsace and Lorraine)

OS1

1870 Typo. Unwmk. *Perf. 13½x14*

Network with Points Up

N1	OS1	1c bronze green	70.00	70.00
		On cover		160.00
		On cover, single franking		—
a.		1c olive grn	70.00	70.00
		On cover		160.00
		On cover, single franking		—
N2	OS1	2c dark brown	140.00	125.00
		On cover		250.00
		On cover, single franking		700.00
a.		2c red brown	140.00	125.00
		On cover		250.00
		On cover, single franking		700.00
N3	OS1	4c gray	150.00	85.00
		On cover		175.00
		On cover, single franking		550.00
N4	OS1	5c yel grn	150.00	12.00
		On cover		70.00
		On cover, single franking		125.00
a.		5c deep green	150.00	12.50
		On cover		70.00
		On cover, single franking		125.00
N5	OS1	10c bistre brn	125.00	5.00
		On cover		35.00
		On cover, single franking		40.00
a.		10c yellow brown	125.00	5.75
		On cover		35.00
		On cover, single franking		40.00
b.		Network lemon yellow	160.00	7.50
		On cover		70.00
		On cover, single franking		77.50
N6	OS1	20c ultra	140.00	12.00
		On cover		55.00
		On cover, single franking		67.50
a.		20c milky blue	125.00	12.00
		On cover		55.00
		On cover, single franking		67.50
N7	OS1	25c brown	175.00	85.00
		On cover		260.00
		On cover, single franking		300.00
a.		25c black brown	160.00	80.00
		On cover		240.00
		On cover, single franking		275.00

There are three varieties of the 4c and two of the 10c, differing in the position of the figures of value, and several other setting varieties.

Network with Points Down

N8	OS1	1c olive grn	425.00	*575.00*
		On cover		1,450.
N9	OS1	2c red brn	210.00	*500.00*
		On cover		1,100.
		On cover, single franking		1,575.
N10	OS1	4c gray	210.00	175.00
		On cover		300.00
		On cover, single franking		700.00
N11	OS1	5c yel grn	4,750.	500.00
		On cover		1,400.
		On cover, single franking		2,100.
N12	OS1	10c bister	210.00	17.00
		On cover		82.50
		On cover, single franking		95.00
a.		Network lemon yellow	225.00	50.00
		On cover		175.00
		On cover, single franking		210.00
N13	OS1	20c ultra	275.00	65.00
		On cover		275.00
		On cover, single franking		300.00
N14	OS1	25c brown	625.00	275.00
		On cover		600.00
		On cover, single franking		675.00

Official imitations have the network with points downward. The "P" of "Postes" is 2½mm from the border in the imitations and 3mm in the originals.

The word "Postes" measures 12¾ to 13mm on the imitations, and from 11 to 12½mm on the originals.

The imitations are perf. 13½x14½; originals, perf. 13½x14¼.

The stamps for Alsace and Lorraine were replaced by stamps of the German Empire on Jan. 1, 1872.

WORLD WAR I

German Stamps of 1905-16 Surcharged:

1916 Wmk. 125 *Perf. 14, 14½*

N15	A16	3c on 3pf brown	.70	.70
		Never hinged	2.10	
		On cover		85.00
N16	A16	5c on 5pf green	.70	*.70*
		Never hinged	2.10	
		On cover		85.00
N17	A22	8c on 7½pf org	1.40	1.40
		Never hinged	2.75	
		On cover		90.00
N18	A16	10c on 10pf car	1.40	1.40
		Never hinged	2.75	
		On cover		85.00
N19	A22	15c on 15pf yel brn	.70	.70
		Never hinged	2.10	
		On cover		90.00
N20	A16	25c on 20pf blue	.70	.70
		Never hinged	2.10	
		On cover		90.00
a.		25c on 20pf ultramarine	1.40	*1.40*
		Never hinged	4.25	
		On cover		140.00
N21	A16	40c on 30pf org & blk, *buff*	2.10	*2.10*
		Never hinged	5.00	
		On cover		150.00
N22	A16	50c on 40pf lake & blk	2.10	*2.10*
		Never hinged	5.50	
		On cover		210.00
N23	A16	75c on 60pf mag	9.75	*9.75*
		Never hinged	18.00	
		On cover		525.00
N24	A16	1fr on 80pf lake & blk, *rose*	9.75	*9.75*
		Never hinged	27.50	
		On cover		525.00

N25	A17	1fr25c on 1m car	37.50	*37.50*
		Never hinged	110.00	
a.		Double surcharge	—	
N26	A21	2fr50c on 2m gray bl	37.50	37.50
		Never hinged	110.00	
a.		Double surcharge	—	
		Nos. N15-N26 (12)	104.30	*104.30*

These stamps were also used in parts of Belgium occupied by the German forces.

Catalogue values for unused stamps in this section, from this point to the end of the section, are for Never Hinged items.

WORLD WAR II

Alsace

Issued under German Occupation

Values for unused copies of N27-N58 are for never hinged stamps.

Stamps of Germany 1933-36 Overprinted in Black

1940 Wmk. 237 *Perf. 14*

N27	A64	3pf olive bister	.70	*.50*
		On cover		1.75
N28	A64	4pf dull blue	.70	*.50*
		On cover		1.75
N29	A64	5pf brt green	.70	*.50*
		On cover		1.75
N30	A64	6pf dark green	.70	*.50*
		On cover		1.75
N31	A64	8pf vermilion	.70	*.50*
		On cover		1.75
N32	A64	10pf chocolate	.70	*.50*
		On cover		2.10
N33	A64	12pf dp carmine	.85	*.50*
		On cover		3.25
N34	A64	15pf maroon	.90	*.50*
		On cover		4.25
N35	A64	20pf brt blue	1.40	*.65*
		On cover		5.75
N36	A64	25pf ultra	1.40	*.65*
		On cover		2.75
N37	A64	30pf olive grn	1.40	*.65*
		On cover		6.25
N38	A64	40pf red violet	2.50	*.85*
		On cover		10.00
N39	A64	50pf dk grn & blk	6.00	*2.75*
		On cover		21.00
N40	A64	60pf claret & blk	6.00	*2.75*
		On cover		21.00
N41	A64	80pf dk blue & blk	14.00	*6.00*
		On cover		45.00
N42	A64	100pf orange & blk	14.00	5.75
		On cover		42.50
		Nos. N27-N42 (16)	52.65	24.05

Lorraine

Issued under German Occupation

Stamps of Germany 1933-36 Overprinted in Black

1940 Wmk. 237 *Perf. 14*

N43	A64	3pf olive bister	.95	*1.00*
		On cover		2.50
N44	A64	4pf dull blue	.95	*1.00*
		On cover		2.50
N45	A64	5pf brt green	.95	*1.00*
		On cover		2.50
N46	A64	6pf dark green	.95	.55
		On cover		2.50
N47	A64	8pf vermilion	.95	*1.00*
		On cover		2.50
N48	A64	10pf chocolate	1.25	.85
		On cover		3.25
N49	A64	12pf deep carmine	1.25	.85
		On cover		3.25
N50	A64	15pf maroon	1.25	1.00
		On cover		3.25
a.		Inverted surcharge	—	
N51	A64	20pf brt blue	1.40	1.00
		On cover		5.75
N52	A64	25pf ultra	1.40	1.00
		On cover		5.75
N53	A64	30pf olive grn	1.90	1.00
		On cover		7.75
N54	A64	40pf red violet	2.10	1.10
		On cover		10.50
N55	A64	50pf dk grn & blk	5.25	3.00
		On cover		17.50
N56	A64	60pf claret & blk	5.25	3.00
		On cover		19.00
N57	A64	80pf dk blue & blk	15.00	6.25
		On cover		52.50
N58	A64	100pf orange & blk	15.00	6.75
		On cover		42.50
		Nos. N43-N58 (16)	55.80	*30.35*

Besetztes Gebiet Nordfrankreich

These three words, in a rectangular frame covering two stamps, were handstamped in black on Nos. 267, 367 and 369 and used in the Dunkerque region in July-August, 1940. The German commander of Dunkerque authorized the overprint.

OFFICES IN CHINA

Prior to 1923 several of the world powers maintained their own post offices in China for the purpose of sending and receiving overseas mail. French offices were maintained in Canton, Hoi Hao (Hoihow), Kwangchowan (Kouang-tchéou-wan), Mongtseu (Mong-tseu), Packhoi (Paknoi), Tong King (Tchongk-ing), Yunnan Fou (Yunnanfu).

100 Centimes = 1 Franc

100 Cents = 1 Piaster

100 Cents = 1 Dollar

Peace and Commerce Stamps of France Overprinted in Red, Carmine or Black

1894-1900 Unwmk. *Perf. 14x13½*

1	A1	5c green, *greenish* (R)	2.25	2.00
		On cover		50.00
a.		5c green, *greenish* (C)	1.25	1.10
		On cover		50.00
2	A1	5c yel grn, I (R) ('00)	2.25	2.00
		On cover		50.00
a.		Type II	40.00	25.00
		On cover		350.00
3	A1	10c blk, *lav*, I (R)	6.00	1.75
		On cover		45.00
a.		Type II	20.00	8.50
b.		Type II (C)	17.50	11.00
4	A1	15c bl (R)	8.50	2.75
		On cover		65.00
5	A1	20c red, *grn*	5.00	3.25
		On cover		100.00
6	A1	25c blk, *rose* (C)	6.00	1.75
		On cover		50.00
a.		Double overprint	70.00	35.00
b.		Pair, one without overprint	225.00	
c.		Red overprint	10.50	1.75
7	A1	30c brn, *bis*	6.50	4.25
		On cover		100.00
8	A1	40c red, *straw*	6.75	5.50
		On cover		190.00
9	A1	50c car, *rose*, I	20.00	11.50
		On cover		100.00
a.		Carmine overprint	50.00	
b.		Type II (Bk)	13.00	6.50
		On cover		100.00
10	A1	75c dp vio, *org* (R)	62.50	45.00
		On cover		190.00
11	A1	1fr brnz grn, *straw*	12.50	4.50
		On cover		190.00
a.		Double overprint	275.00	*300.00*
12	A1	2fr brn, *az* ('00)	27.50	20.00
		On cover		350.00
12A	A1	5fr red lil, *lav*	60.00	42.50
		On cover		—
b.		Red overprint	450.00	
		Nos. 1-12A (13)	225.75	146.75

For surcharges and overprints see Nos. 13-17, J7-J10, J20-J23.

No. 11 Surcharged in Black **25**

13	A1	25c on 1fr brnz grn, *straw*	72.50	45.00
		On cover		275.00

No. 6 Surcharged in Red

1901

14	A1	2c on 25c blk, *rose*	825.00	250.00
		On cover		*1,250.*
15	A1	4c on 25c blk, *rose*	725.00	250.00
		On cover		*950.00*
16	A1	6c on 25c blk, *rose*	825.00	300.00
		On cover		*1,250.*
17	A1	16c on 25c blk, *rose*	250.00	150.00
		On cover		*1,250.*
a.		Black surcharge		*5,500.*
		Nos. 14-17 (4)	2,625.	950.00

Stamps of Indo-China Surcharged in Black

1902-04

18	A3	1c blk, *lil bl*	1.75	1.40
		On cover		85.00
19	A3	2c brn, *buff*	6.00	6.00
		On cover		85.00
20	A3	4c claret, *lav*	2.50	1.75
		On cover		85.00
21	A3	5c yellow grn	3.25	2.25
		On cover		60.00
22	A3	10c red	6.00	4.00
		On cover		60.00
23	A3	15c gray	5.50	5.00
		On cover		85.00
24	A3	20c red, *grn*	9.00	6.00
		On cover		125.00
25	A3	25c blk, *rose*	10.00	10.00
		On cover		95.00
26	A3	25c blue ('04)	6.50	5.25
		On cover		85.00
27	A3	30c brn, *bis*	8.00	6.00
		On cover		150.00
28	A3	40c red, *straw*	40.00	20.00
		On cover		150.00
29	A3	50c car, *rose*	55.00	55.00
		On cover		150.00
30	A3	50c brn, *az* ('04)	8.00	7.00
		On cover		110.00
31	A3	75c vio, *org*	30.00	25.00
		On cover		175.00
32	A3	1fr brnz grn, *straw*	35.00	35.00
		On cover		725.00
33	A3	5fr red lil, *lavender*	85.00	65.00
		On cover		—
		Nos. 18-33 (16)	311.50	254.65

The Chinese characters surcharged on Nos. 18-33 are the Chinese equivalents of the French values and therefore differ on each denomination. Another printing of these stamps was made in 1904 which differs from the first one principally in the size and shape of the letters in "CHINE," particularly the "H" which is much thinner in the second printing. Values are for the less expensive variety. Many varieties of surcharge exist.

Liberty, Equality and Fraternity
A3

"Rights of Man"
A4

A5

1902-03 **Typo.**

34	A3	5c green	1.75	1.40
		On cover		12.50
35	A4	10c rose red ('03)	1.75	1.40
		On cover		19.00
36	A4	15c pale red	1.75	1.40
		On cover		35.00
37	A4	20c brn vio ('03)	5.75	5.00
		On cover		100.00
38	A4	25c blue ('03)	4.25	2.10
		On cover		35.00
39	A4	30c lilac ('03)	6.00	5.75
		On cover		100.00
40	A5	40c red & pale bl	12.50	11.00
		On cover		90.00
41	A5	50c bis brn & lav	16.00	12.50
		On cover		75.00
42	A5	1fr claret & ol grn	21.00	12.00
		On cover		100.00
43	A5	2fr gray vio & yel	42.50	30.00
		On cover		—
44	A5	5fr dk bl & buff	60.00	47.50
		On cover		—
		Nos. 34-44 (11)	173.25	130.05

For surcharges and overprints see Nos. 45, 57-85, J14-J16, J27-J30.

Surcharged in Black

1903

45	A4	5c on 15c pale red	12.50	14.00
		On cover		65.00
a.		Inverted surcharge	77.50	47.50

Stamps of Indo-China, 1904-06, Surcharged as Nos. 18-33 in Black

1904-05

46	A4	1c olive grn	1.25	1.25
		On cover		90.00
47	A4	2c vio brn, *buff*	1.25	1.25
		On cover		90.00
47A	A4	4c cl, *bluish*	700.00	575.00
		On cover		*1,500.*
48	A4	5c deep grn	1.25	1.25
		On cover		50.00
49	A4	10c carmine	1.90	1.90
		On cover		50.00
50	A4	15c org brn, *bl*	2.25	1.75
		On cover		62.50
51	A4	20c red, *grn*	9.00	9.00
		On cover		100.00
52	A4	25c deep blue	7.25	4.00
		On cover		65.00
53	A4	40c blk, *bluish*	5.75	4.00
		On cover		100.00
54	A4	1fr pale grn	300.00	250.00
		On cover		500.00
55	A4	2fr brn, *org*	30.00	25.00
		On cover		—
56	A4	10fr org brn, *grn*	110.00	100.00
		On cover		—
		Nos. 46-56 (12)	1,169.	974.40

Many varieties of the surcharge exist.

Stamps of 1902-03 Surcharged in Black

1907

57	A3	2c on 5c green	1.25	1.10
		On cover		25.00
58	A4	4c on 10c rose red	1.25	1.10
		On cover		25.00
a.		Pair, one without surcharge		—
59	A4	6c on 15c pale red	2.00	1.60
		On cover		50.00
60	A4	8c on 20c brn vio	3.50	3.50
		On cover		100.00
a.		"8" inverted	42.50	42.50
61	A4	10c on 25c blue	1.10	.85
		On cover		37.50
62	A5	20c on 50c bis brn & lav	3.50	2.50
		On cover		65.00
a.		Double surcharge		
b.		Triple surcharge	300.00	300.00
63	A5	40c on 1fr claret & ol grn	14.00	9.00
		On cover		100.00
64	A5	2pi on 5fr dk bl & buff	16.00	9.00
		On cover		—
a.		Double surcharge	*1,750.*	*1,550.*
		Nos. 57-64 (8)	42.60	28.65

Stamps of 1902-03 Surcharged in Black

1911-22

65	A3	2c on 5c green	1.25	1.00
		On cover		25.00
66	A4	4c on 10c rose red	2.00	1.00
		On cover		25.00
67	A4	6c on 15c org	3.25	1.25
		On cover		50.00
68	A4	8c on 20c brn vio	1.75	1.25
		On cover		90.00
69	A4	10c on 25c bl ('21)	2.75	1.10
		On cover		75.00
70	A4	20c on 50c bl ('22)	45.00	32.50
		On cover		140.00
71	A5	40c on 1fr cl & ol grn	4.25	2.75
		On cover		100.00

No. 44 Surcharged

73	A5	$2 on 5fr bl & buff ('22)	125.00	92.50
		On cover		—
		Nos. 65-73 (8)	185.25	133.35

Types of 1902-03 Surcharged like Nos. 65-71

1922

75	A3	1c on 5c org	3.50	3.25
		On cover		250.00
76	A4	2c on 10c grn	4.25	4.00
		On cover		250.00
77	A4	3c on 15c org	5.75	4.50
		On cover		250.00
78	A4	4c on 20c red brn	7.25	6.00
		On cover		250.00
79	A4	5c on 25c dk vio	4.00	3.25
		On cover		250.00
80	A4	6c on 30c red	7.75	6.50
		On cover		250.00
82	A4	10c on 50c blue	9.00	6.75
		On cover		250.00
83	A5	20c on 1fr claret & ol grn	25.00	22.50
		On cover		—
84	A5	40c on 2fr org & pale bl	30.00	25.00
		On cover		300.00
85	A5	$1 on 5fr dk bl & buff	110.00	110.00
		On cover		—
		Nos. 75-85 (10)	206.50	191.75

POSTAGE DUE STAMPS

Postage Due Stamps of France Handstamped in Red or Black

1901-07 **Unwmk.** ***Perf. 14x13½***

J1	D2	5c lt bl (R)	4.25	2.50
J2	D2	10c choc (R)	7.25	4.25
		On cover		650.00
J3	D2	15c lt grn (R)	7.25	4.50
J4	D2	20c ol grn (R) ('07)	7.25	6.50
		On cover		650.00
J5	D2	30c carmine	10.00	7.75
		On cover		650.00
J6	D2	50c lilac	12.50	7.75
		On cover		650.00
		Nos. J1-J6 (6)	48.50	33.25

Stamps of 1894-1900 Handstamped in Carmine

A PERCEVOIR

1903

J7	A1	5c yel grn	*2,000.*	725.00
a.		Purple handstamp	*2,000.*	675.00
b.		5c green, *greenish*	*6,600.*	
J8	A1	10c blk, *lavender*	*6,500.*	*5,250.*
a.		Purple handstamp	*6,500.*	*5,250.*
J9	A1	15c blue	*2,000.*	675.00
a.		Purple handstamp	*2,000.*	675.00
J10	A1	30c brn, *bister*	*1,100.*	77.50
		On cover		*2,750.*
a.		Purple handstamp	*1,100.*	77.50

Same Handstamp on Stamps of 1902-03 in Carmine

1903

J14	A3	5c green	*1,250.*	625.
a.		Purple handstamp	*1,300.*	625.
J15	A4	10c rose red	525.	125.
		On cover		*3,000.*
a.		Purple handstamp	525.	125.
J16	A4	15c pale red	550.	125.
a.		Purple handstamp	550.	125.

Stamps of 1894-1900 Handstamped in Carmine

1903

J20	A1	5c yellow green	*1,700.*	250.
		On cover		*3,000.*
a.		Purple handstamp	*1,600.*	250.
b.		5c green, *greenish*	*6,600.*	
J21	A1	10c blk, *lavender*	*6,750.*	*7,000.*
a.		Purple handstamp	*6,750.*	*7,000.*
J22	A1	15c blue	825.	80.
a.		Purple handstamp	825.	80.
J23	A1	30c brn, *bister*	400.	65.
		On cover		*2,750.*
a.		Purple handstamp	400.	65.

Same Handstamp on Stamps of 1902-03 in Carmine or Purple

1903

J27	A3	5c green (C)	1,100.	550.00
a.		Purple handstamp	1,100.	550.00
J28	A4	10c rose red (C)	250.00	42.50
		On cover		*3,000.*
a.		Purple handstamp	250.00	42.50
J29	A4	15c pale red (C)	550.00	42.50
a.		Purple handstamp	550.00	42.50
J30	A4	30c lilac (P)	*9,000.*	*7,500.*

The handstamps on Nos. J7-J30 are found inverted, double, etc.

The cancellations on these stamps should have dates between Sept. 1, and Nov. 30, 1903, to be genuine.

Postage Due Stamps of France, 1893-1910 Surcharged like Nos. 65-71

1911

J33	D2	2c on 5c blue	1.40	1.10
a.		Double surcharge	90.00	—
J34	D2	4c on 10c choc	1.40	1.10
		On cover		625.00
a.		Double surcharge	90.00	—
J35	D2	8c on 20c ol grn	1.75	1.40
		On cover		625.00
a.		Double surcharge	90.00	—
J36	D2	20c on 50c lilac	1.75	1.40
		On cover		625.00
		Nos. J33-J36 (4)	6.30	5.00

1922

J37	D2	1c on 5c blue	60.00	55.00
J38	D2	2c on 10c brn	82.50	72.50
J39	D2	4c on 20c ol grn	100.00	72.50
J40	D2	10c on 50c brn vio	100.00	72.50
		Nos. J37-J40 (4)	342.50	272.50

CANTON

Stamps of Indo-China, 1892-1900, Overprinted in Red

1901 **Unwmk.** ***Perf. 14x13½***

1	A3	1c blk, *lil bl*	1.40	1.40
1A	A3	2c brn, *buff*	1.75	1.75
2	A3	4c claret, *lav*	3.25	3.25
2A	A3	5c grn, *grnsh*	500.00	500.00
3	A3	5c yel grn	2.25	2.25
4	A3	10c blk, *lavender*	5.00	5.00
5	A3	15c blue, quadrille paper	4.50	4.50
6	A3	15c gray	5.00	5.00
a.		Double overprint	16.00	
7	A3	20c red, *grn*	10.00	10.00
8	A3	25c blk, *rose*	8.50	8.50
9	A3	30c brn, *bister*	20.00	20.00
10	A3	40c red, *straw*	20.00	20.00
11	A3	50c car, *rose*	22.50	22.50
12	A3	75c dp vio, *org*	30.00	30.00
13	A3	1fr brnz grn, *straw*	30.00	30.00
14	A3	5fr red lil, *lav*	190.00	190.00
		Nos. 1-14 (16)	854.15	854.15

The Chinese characters in the overprint on Nos. 1-14 read "Canton." On Nos. 15-64, they restate the denomination of the basic stamp.

Surcharged in Black

1903-04

15	A3	1c blk, *lil bl*	2.75	2.50
16	A3	2c brn, *buff*	2.75	2.50
17	A3	4c claret, *lav*	2.75	2.50
18	A3	5c yellow green	2.75	2.50
19	A3	10c rose red	2.75	2.75
20	A3	15c gray	2.75	2.75
21	A3	20c red, *grn*	14.00	11.00
22	A3	25c blue	6.50	4.25
23	A3	25c blk, *rose* ('04)	5.00	4.25
24	A3	30c brn, *bister*	18.00	12.00
25	A3	40c red, *straw*	47.50	40.00
26	A3	50c car, *rose*	300.00	250.00
27	A3	50c brn, *az* ('04)	52.50	47.50
28	A3	75c dp vio, *org*	47.50	42.50
a.		"INDO-CHINE" inverted	*36,000.*	
29	A3	1fr brnz grn, *straw*	50.00	42.50
30	A3	5fr red lil, *lav*	55.00	47.50
		Nos. 15-30 (16)	612.50	517.00

Many varieties of the surcharge exist on #15-30.

Stamps of Indo-China, 1892-1906, Surcharged in Red or Black

A second printing of the 1906 surcharges of Canton, Hoi Hao, Kwangchowan, Mongtseu, Packhoi, Tong King and Yunnan Fou was made in 1908. The inks are grayish instead of full black and vermilion instead of carmine. Values are for the cheaper variety which usually is the second printing.

The 4c and 50c of the 1892 issue of Indo-China are known with this surcharge and similarly surcharged for other cities in China. The surcharges on these two stamps are always inverted. It is stated that they were irregularly produced and never issued.

1906

31	A4	1c ol grn (R)	1.40	1.40
32	A4	2c vio brn, *buff*	1.40	1.40
33	A4	4c cl, *bluish* (R)	1.40	1.40
34	A4	5c dp grn (R)	2.25	2.25
35	A4	10c carmine	2.50	2.50
36	A4	15c org brn, *bl*	7.25	7.25
37	A4	20c red, *grn*	3.50	3.50
38	A4	25c deep blue	3.50	3.50
39	A4	30c pale brn	4.50	4.50
40	A4	35c blk, *yel* (R)	3.25	3.25
41	A4	40c blk, *bluish* (R)	5.25	5.25
42	A4	50c bister brn	5.25	5.25
43	A3	75c dp vio, *org* (R)	45.00	45.00
44	A4	1fr pale grn	11.00	11.00
45	A4	2fr brn, *org* (R)	27.50	27.50
46	A3	5fr red lil, *lav*	62.50	62.50
47	A4	10fr org brn, *grn*	62.50	62.50
		Nos. 31-47 (17)	249.95	249.95

Surcharge exists inverted on 1c, 25c & 1fr.

Stamps of Indo-China, 1907, Surcharged "CANTON", and Chinese Characters, in Red or Blue

1908

48	A5	1c ol brn & blk	.70	.70
49	A5	2c brn & blk	.70	.70
50	A5	4c bl & blk	1.40	.95
51	A5	5c grn & blk	1.40	1.25
52	A5	10c red & blk (Bl)	1.75	1.40
53	A5	15c vio & blk	2.75	2.25
54	A6	20c vio & blk	3.25	2.75
55	A6	25c bl & blk	3.25	2.75
56	A6	30c brn & blk	5.75	5.25
57	A6	35c ol grn & blk	5.75	5.25
58	A6	40c brn & blk	7.25	5.75
59	A6	50c car & blk (Bl)	7.25	5.75
60	A7	75c ver & blk (Bl)	7.25	6.50
61	A8	1fr car & blk (Bl)	12.00	9.25
62	A9	2fr grn & blk	32.50	27.50
63	A10	5fr bl & blk	45.00	35.00
64	A11	10fr pur & blk	75.00	65.00
		Nos. 48-64 (17)	212.95	178.00

Nos. 48-64 Surcharged with New Values in Cents or Piasters in Black, Red or Blue

1919

65	A5	⅖c on 1c	.85	.80
66	A5	⅘c on 2c	.85	.80
67	A5	1⅗c on 4c (R)	.85	.80
68	A5	2c on 5c	1.10	*1.10*
69	A5	4c on 10c (Bl)	1.25	1.00
a.		Chinese "2" instead of "4"	25.00	25.00
70	A5	6c on 15c	1.75	1.75
71	A6	8c on 20c	3.50	1.75
72	A6	10c on 25c	3.50	1.25
73	A6	12c on 30c	1.40	1.40
a.		Double surcharge	92.50	92.50
74	A6	14c on 35c	1.40	1.25
a.		Closed "4"	6.75	6.75
75	A6	16c on 40c	1.40	1.25
76	A6	20c on 50c (Bl)	1.75	1.25
77	A7	30c on 75c (Bl)	1.75	1.25
78	A8	40c on 1fr (Bl)	8.00	5.00
79	A9	80c on 2fr (R)	12.00	6.75
80	A10	2pi on 5fr (R)	10.00	10.00
81	A11	4pi on 10fr (R)	11.50	11.50
		Nos. 65-81 (17)	62.85	48.90

HOI HAO

Stamps of Indo-China Overprinted in Red

1901 Unwmk. *Perf. 14x13½*

1	A3	1c blk, *lil bl*	2.50	2.50
2	A3	2c brn, *buff*	3.00	3.00
3	A3	4c claret, *lav*	3.00	3.00
4	A3	5c yel grn	3.25	3.25
5	A3	10c blk, *lavender*	5.75	5.25
6	A3	15c blue	1,450.	650.00
7	A3	15c gray	4.50	3.00
8	A3	20c red, *grn*	15.00	13.50
9	A3	25c blk, *rose*	12.50	6.75
10	A3	30c brn, *bister*	29.00	22.50
11	A3	40c red, *straw*	29.00	22.50
12	A3	50c car, *rose*	32.50	29.00
13	A3	75c dp vio, *org*	190.00	160.00
14	A3	1fr brnz grn, *straw*	650.00	550.00
15	A3	5fr red lil, *lav*	650.00	500.00
		Nos. 1-15 (15)	3,080.	1,974.

The Chinese characters in the overprint on Nos. 1-15 read "Hoi Hao." On Nos. 16-66, they restate the denomination of the basic stamp.

Surcharged in Black

1903-04

16	A3	1c blk, *lil bl*	1.25	1.25
17	A3	2c brn, *buff*	1.25	1.25
18	A3	4c claret, *lav*	2.50	2.50
19	A3	5c yel grn	2.50	2.50
20	A3	10c red	3.00	3.00
21	A3	15c gray	3.00	3.00
22	A3	20c red, *grn*	6.00	6.00
23	A3	25c blue	5.50	5.50
24	A3	25c blk, *rose* ('04)	3.50	3.50
25	A3	30c brn, *bister*	4.25	4.25
26	A3	40c red, *straw*	30.00	30.00
27	A3	50c car, *rose*	25.00	25.00
28	A3	50c brn, *az* ('04)	110.00	110.00
29	A3	75c dp vio, *org*	35.00	35.00
a.		"INDO-CHINE" inverted	*36,000.*	
30	A3	1fr brnz grn, *straw*	47.50	47.50
31	A3	5fr red lil, *lav*	150.00	160.00
		Nos. 16-31 (16)	430.25	440.25

Many varieties of the surcharge exist on #1-31.

Stamps of Indo-China, 1892-1906, Surcharged in Red or Black

1906

32	A4	1c ol grn (R)	2.00	2.00
33	A4	2c vio brn, *buff*	1.75	1.75
34	A4	4c cl, *bluish* (R)	3.00	3.00
35	A4	5c dp grn (R)	3.00	3.00
36	A4	10c carmine	3.25	3.25
37	A4	15c org brn, *bl*	6.00	6.00
38	A4	20c red, *grn*	5.50	5.50
39	A4	25c deep blue	6.50	6.50
40	A4	30c pale brn	6.50	6.50
41	A4	35c blk, *yel* (R)	11.00	11.00
42	A4	40c blk, *bluish* (R)	11.00	11.00
43	A4	50c gray brn	11.00	*11.00*
44	A3	75c dp vio, *org* (R)	27.50	27.50
45	A4	1fr pale grn	27.50	27.50
46	A4	2fr brn, *org* (R)	27.50	27.50
47	A3	5fr red lil, *lav*	90.00	90.00
48	A4	10fr org brn, *grn*	130.00	130.00
		Nos. 32-48 (17)	373.00	373.00

Stamps of Indo-China, 1907, Surcharged "HOI HAO" and Chinese Characters, in Red or Blue

1908

49	A5	1c ol brn & blk	.95	.95
50	A5	2c brn & blk	.95	.95
51	A5	4c bl & blk	1.10	1.10
52	A5	5c grn & blk	1.90	1.90
53	A5	10c red & blk (Bl)	1.90	1.90
54	A5	15c vio & blk	4.00	4.00
55	A6	20c vio & blk	5.25	5.25
56	A6	25c bl & blk	5.25	5.25
57	A6	30c brn & blk	5.25	5.25
58	A6	35c ol grn & blk	5.25	5.25
59	A6	40c brn & blk	5.50	5.50
61	A6	50c car & blk (Bl)	6.50	6.50
62	A7	75c ver & blk (Bl)	7.00	7.00
63	A8	1fr car & blk (Bl)	18.00	18.00
64	A9	2fr grn & blk	32.50	32.50
65	A10	5fr bl & blk	65.00	65.00
66	A11	10fr pur & blk	85.00	*85.00*
		Nos. 49-66 (17)	251.30	251.30

Nos. 49-66 Surcharged with New Values in Cents or Piasters in Black, Red or Blue

1919

67	A5	⅖c on 1c	.70	.70
68	A5	⅘c on 2c	.70	.70
69	A5	1⅗c on 4c (R)	1.10	1.10
70	A5	2c on 5c	1.40	1.40
71	A5	4c on 10c (Bl)	1.75	1.75
a.		Chinese "2" instead of "4"	7.25	7.25
72	A5	6c on 15c	1.50	1.50
73	A6	8c on 20c	2.75	2.75
a.		"S" of "CENTS" omitted	85.00	85.00
74	A6	10c on 25c	4.25	4.25
75	A6	12c on 30c	1.40	1.40
76	A6	14c on 35c	1.40	1.40
a.		Closed "4"	11.00	11.00
77	A6	16c on 40c	1.40	1.40
79	A6	20c on 50c (Bl)	1.75	1.75
80	A7	30c on 75c (Bl)	3.50	3.50
81	A8	40c on 1fr (Bl)	7.25	7.25
82	A9	80c on 2fr (R)	17.00	17.00
83	A10	2pi on 5fr (R)	47.50	47.50
a.		Triple surch. of new value	500.00	*500.00*
84	A11	4pi on 10fr (R)	140.00	*140.00*
		Nos. 67-84 (17)	235.35	235.35

KWANGCHOWAN

A Chinese Territory leased to France, 1898 to 1945.

Stamps of Indo-China, 1892-1906, Surcharged in Red or Black

1906 Unwmk. *Perf. 14x13½*

1	A4	1c ol grn (R)	2.00	2.00
2	A4	2c vio brn, *buff*	2.25	2.25
3	A4	4c cl, *bluish* (R)	3.25	3.25
4	A4	5c dp grn (R)	3.25	3.25
5	A4	10c carmine	3.50	3.50
6	A4	15c org brn, *bl*	9.50	9.50
7	A4	20c red, *grn*	4.00	4.00
8	A4	25c deep blue	3.50	3.50
9	A4	30c pale brn	3.50	3.50
10	A4	35c blk, *yel* (R)	5.75	5.75
11	A4	40c blk, *bluish* (R)	4.50	4.50
12	A4	50c bister brn	18.00	18.00
13	A3	75c dp vio, *org* (R)	25.00	25.00
14	A4	1fr pale grn	27.50	27.50
15	A4	2fr brn, *org* (R)	25.00	25.00
16	A3	5fr red lil, *lav*	175.00	175.00
17	A4	10fr org brn, *grn*	225.00	225.00
		Nos. 1-17 (17)	540.50	540.50

Various varieties of the surcharge exist on Nos. 2-10.

Stamps of Indo-China, 1907, Surcharged "KOUANG-TCHEOU" and Value in Chinese in Red or Blue

1908

18	A5	1c ol brn & blk	.95	.95
19	A5	2c brn & blk	.95	.95
20	A5	4c bl & blk	.95	.95
21	A5	5c grn & blk	1.00	1.00
22	A5	10c red & blk (Bl)	1.10	1.10
23	A5	15c vio & blk	2.50	2.50
24	A6	20c vio & blk	4.50	4.50
25	A6	25c bl & blk	4.75	4.75
26	A6	30c brn & blk	7.00	7.00
27	A6	35c ol grn & blk	10.00	10.00
28	A6	40c brn & blk	10.00	10.00
30	A6	50c car & blk (Bl)	10.00	10.00
31	A7	75c ver & blk (Bl)	11.00	11.00
32	A8	1fr car & blk (Bl)	15.00	15.00
33	A9	2fr grn & blk	25.00	25.00
34	A10	5fr bl & blk	55.00	55.00
35	A11	10fr pur & blk	80.00	80.00
a.		Double surcharge	650.00	650.00
b.		Triple surcharge	650.00	650.00
		Nos. 18-35 (17)	239.70	239.70

The Chinese characters overprinted on Nos. 1 to 35 repeat the denomination of the basic stamp.

Nos. 18-35 Surcharged with New Values in Cents or Piasters in Black, Red or Blue

1919

36	A5	⅖c on 1c	.60	.50
37	A5	⅘c on 2c	.60	.50
38	A5	1⅗c on 4c (R)	.70	.60
39	A5	2c on 5c	1.00	.60
a.		"2 CENTS" inverted	60.00	
40	A5	4c on 10c (Bl)	3.00	2.25
41	A5	6c on 15c	1.25	1.25
42	A6	8c on 20c	3.25	3.00
43	A6	10c on 25c	9.75	8.50
44	A6	12c on 30c	1.75	1.50
45	A6	14c on 35c	2.50	2.25
a.		Closed "4"	30.00	25.00
46	A6	16c on 40c	1.25	1.25
48	A6	20c on 50c (Bl)	1.40	1.40
49	A7	30c on 75c (Bl)	7.00	7.00
50	A8	40c on 1fr (Bl)	8.00	8.00
a.		"40 CENTS" inverted		
51	A9	80c on 2fr (R)	9.00	8.00
52	A10	2pi on 5fr (R)	140.00	125.00
53	A11	4pi on 10fr (R)	22.50	22.50
		Nos. 36-53 (17)	213.55	194.10

Stamps of Indo-China, 1922-23, Overprinted in Black, Red or Blue

1923

54	A12	⅒c blk & sal (Bl)	.20	.20
55	A12	⅕c dp bl & blk (R)	.20	.20
a.		Black overprint	85.00	
56	A12	⅖c ol brn & blk (R)	.20	.20
57	A12	⅘c brt rose & blk	.35	.35
58	A12	1c yel brn & blk (Bl)	.35	.35
59	A12	2c gray grn & blk (R)	.60	.60
60	A12	3c vio & blk (R)	.60	.60
61	A12	4c org & blk	.70	.70
62	A12	5c car & blk	.70	.70
63	A13	6c dl red & blk	.70	.70
64	A13	7c ol grn & blk	1.25	1.25
65	A13	8c black (R)	1.75	1.75
66	A13	9c yel & blk	1.75	1.75
67	A13	10c bl & blk	1.50	1.50
68	A13	11c vio & blk	1.50	1.50
69	A13	12c brn & blk	1.50	1.50
70	A13	15c org & blk	1.90	1.90
71	A13	20c bl & blk, *straw* (R)	1.90	1.90
72	A13	40c ver & blk, *bluish* (Bl)	2.25	2.25
73	A13	1pi bl grn & blk, *grnsh*	6.50	6.50
74	A13	2pi vio brn & blk, *pnksh* (Bl)	12.00	12.00
		Nos. 54-74 (21)	38.40	38.40

Indo-China Stamps of 1927 Overprinted in Black or Red

1927

75	A14	⅒c lt ol grn (R)	.20	.20
76	A14	⅕c yellow	.20	.20
77	A14	⅖c lt blue (R)	.35	.35
78	A14	⅘c dp brown	.35	.35
79	A14	1c orange	.50	.50
80	A14	2c blue grn (R)	.75	.75
81	A14	3c indigo (R)	.75	.75
82	A14	4c lilac rose	.75	.75
83	A14	5c deep violet	.75	.75
84	A15	6c deep red	.75	.75
85	A15	7c lt brown	.75	.75
86	A15	8c gray grn (R)	.85	.85
87	A15	9c red violet	1.00	1.00
88	A15	10c lt bl (R)	1.00	1.00
89	A15	11c orange	1.00	1.00
90	A15	12c myr grn (R)	1.00	1.00
91	A16	15c dl rose & ol brn	2.00	2.00
92	A16	20c vio & sl (R)	1.75	1.75
93	A17	25c org brn & lil rose	1.75	1.75
94	A17	30c dp bl & ol gray (R)	1.25	1.25
95	A18	40c ver & lt bl	1.25	1.25
96	A18	50c lt grn & sl (R)	1.60	1.60
97	A19	1pi dk bl, blk & yel (R)	3.25	3.25
98	A19	2pi red, dp bl & org (R)	4.00	4.00
a.		Double overprint	100.00	
		Nos. 75-98 (24)	27.80	27.80

Stamps of Indo-China, 1931-41, Overprinted in Black or Red

1937-41 *Perf. 13, 13½*

99	A20	⅒c Prus blue	.20	.20
100	A20	⅕c lake	.20	.20
101	A20	⅖c orange red	.20	.20
102	A20	½c red brown	.20	.20
103	A20	⅘c dk violet	.20	.20
104	A20	1c black brown	.20	.20
105	A20	2c dk green	.20	.20
a.		Inverted overprint	100.00	
106	A21	3c dk green	.60	.60
107	A21	3c yel brn ('41)	.20	.20
108	A21	4c dk blue (R)	.70	.70
109	A21	4c dk green ('41)	.20	.20
110	A21	4c yel org ('41)	1.60	1.60
111	A21	5c dp violet	.70	.70
112	A21	5c dp green ('41)	.35	.35
113	A21	6c orange red	.50	.50
114	A21	7c black (R) ('41)	.50	.50
115	A21	8c rose lake ('41)	.50	.50
116	A21	9c blk, *yel* (R) ('41)	.60	.60
d.		Black overprint	7.25	7.25
117	A22	10c dk blue (R)	.80	.80
118	A22	10c ultra, *pink* (R) ('41)	.60	.60
119	A22	15c dk bl (R)	.60	.60
120	A22	18c bl (R) ('41)	.35	.35
121	A22	20c rose	.60	.60
122	A22	21c olive grn	.60	.60
123	A22	22c green ('41)	.35	.35
124	A22	25c dp violet	2.40	2.40
125	A22	25c dk bl (R) ('41)	.60	.60
126	A22	30c orange brn	.60	.60
127	A23	50c dk brown	.80	.80
128	A23	60c dl violet	.80	.80
129	A23	70c lt bl (R) ('41)	.60	.60
130	A23	1pi yel green	1.40	1.40
131	A23	2pi red	1.40	1.40
		Nos. 99-131 (33)	20.35	20.35

Common Design Types pictured following the introduction.

Colonial Arts Exhibition Issue

Common Design Type

Souvenir Sheet

1937 Engr. *Imperf.*

132	CD79	30c grn & sepia	6.50	6.50

New York World's Fair Issue

Common Design Type

1939 Unwmk. *Perf. 12½x12*

133	CD82	13c car lake	.80	.80
134	CD82	23c ultra	.80	.80

SEMI-POSTAL STAMPS

French Revolution Issue

Common Design Type

1939 Unwmk. Photo. *Perf. 13*

Name and Value typo. in Black

B1	CD83	6c + 2c green	5.75	5.75
B2	CD83	7c + 3c brown	5.75	5.75
B3	CD83	9c + 4c red org	5.75	5.75
B4	CD83	13c + 10c rose pink	5.75	5.75
B5	CD83	23c + 20c blue	5.75	5.75
		Nos. B1-B5 (5)	28.75	28.75

MONGTSEU (MENGTSZ)

Stamps of Indo-China Surcharged in Black

1903-04 Unwmk. *Perf. 14x13½*

1	A3	1c blk, *lil bl*	6.50	6.50
2	A3	2c brn, *buff*	4.75	4.75
3	A3	4c claret, *lav*	5.75	5.75
4	A3	5c yel grn	4.25	4.25
5	A3	10c red	5.75	5.75
6	A3	15c gray	7.00	7.00
7	A3	20c red, *grn*	8.00	8.00

7C	A3	25c blk, *rose*	550.00	550.00
8	A3	25c blue	8.50	8.50
9	A3	30c brn, *bister*	9.00	9.00
10	A3	40c red, *straw*	50.00	50.00
11	A3	50c car, *rose*	325.00	325.00
12	A3	50c brn, *az* ('04)	82.50	82.50
13	A3	75c dp vio, *org*	75.00	75.00
a.		"INDO-CHINE" inverted	*50,000.*	
14	A3	1fr brnz grn, *straw*	80.00	80.00
15	A3	5fr red lil, *lav*	80.00	80.00
		Nos. 1-15 (16)	1,302.	1,302.

Many Surcharge varieties exist on #1-15.

Stamps of Indo-China, 1892-1906, Surcharged in Red or Black

1906

16	A4	1c ol grn (R)	1.25	1.25
17	A4	2c vio brn, *buff*	1.25	1.25
18	A4	4c cl, *bluish* (R)	1.25	1.25
19	A4	5c dp grn (R)	1.60	1.60
20	A4	10c carmine	1.50	1.50
21	A4	15c org brn, *bl*	3.50	3.50
22	A4	20c red, *grn*	3.00	3.00
23	A4	25c deep blue	3.50	3.50
24	A4	30c pale brn	4.50	4.50
25	A4	35c blk, *yel* (R)	4.00	4.00
26	A4	40c blk, *bluish* (R)	4.00	4.00
27	A4	50c bister brn	13.00	13.00
28	A3	75c dp vio, *org* (R)	40.00	40.00
a.		"INDO-CHINE" inverted	*50,000.*	
29	A4	1fr pale grn	16.00	16.00
30	A4	2fr brn, *org* (R)	42.50	42.50
31	A3	5fr red lil, *lav*	90.00	90.00
32	A4	10fr org brn, *grn*	125.00	125.00
a.		Chinese characters inverted	*1,350.*	*1,500.*
		Nos. 16-32 (17)	355.85	355.85

Inverted varieties of the surcharge exist on Nos. 19, 22 and 32.

Stamps of Indo-China, 1907, Surcharged "MONGTSEU" and Value in Chinese in Red or Blue

1908

33	A5	1c ol brn & blk	.70	.70
34	A5	2c brn & blk	.80	.80
35	A5	4c bl & blk	.80	.80
36	A5	5c grn & blk	.80	.80
37	A5	10c red & blk (Bl)	1.75	1.75
38	A5	15c vio & blk	1.75	1.75
39	A6	20c vio & blk	3.50	3.50
40	A6	25c bl & blk	10.00	10.00
41	A6	30c brn & blk	4.00	4.00
42	A6	35c ol grn & blk	4.75	4.75
43	A6	40c brn & blk	3.25	3.25
45	A6	50c car & blk (Bl)	4.50	4.50
46	A7	75c ver & blk (Bl)	8.50	8.50
47	A8	1fr car & blk (Bl)	8.50	8.50
48	A9	2fr grn & blk	11.50	11.50
49	A10	5fr bl & blk	67.50	67.50
50	A11	10fr pur & blk	95.00	95.00
		Nos. 33-50 (17)	227.60	227.60

The Chinese characters overprinted on Nos. 1 to 50 repeat the denomination of the basic stamp.

Nos. 33-50 Surcharged with New Values in Cents or Piasters in Black, Red or Blue

1919

51	A5	⅖c on 1c	.95	.95
52	A5	⅘c on 2c	.95	.95
53	A5	1⅗c on 4c	1.10	1.10
54	A5	2c on 5c	.95	.95
55	A5	4c on 10c (Bl)	1.75	1.75
56	A5	6c on 15c	2.00	2.00
57	A6	8c on 20c	4.25	4.25
58	A6	10c on 25c	3.50	3.50
59	A6	12c on 30c	2.50	2.50
60	A6	14c on 35c	2.25	2.25
a.		Closed "4"	9.50	9.50
61	A6	16c on 40c	3.25	3.25
63	A6	20c on 50c (Bl)	3.25	3.25
64	A7	30c on 75c (Bl)	3.50	3.50
65	A8	40c on 1fr (Bl)	6.00	6.00
66	A9	80c on 2fr (R)	6.00	6.00
a.		Triple surch., one inverted	400.00	400.00
67	A10	2pi on 5fr (R)	110.00	110.00
a.		Triple surch., one inverted	325.00	325.00
b.		Double surcharge	525.00	525.00
68	A11	4pi on 10fr (R)	22.50	22.50
		Nos. 51-68 (17)	174.70	174.70

PAKHOI

Stamps of Indo-China Surcharged in Black

1903-04 Unwmk. *Perf. 14x13½*

1	A3	1c blk, *lil bl*	4.75	4.75
2	A3	2c brn, *buff*	3.50	3.50
3	A3	4c claret, *lav*	3.50	3.50
4	A3	5c yel grn	3.50	3.50
5	A3	10c red	3.50	3.50
6	A3	15c gray	3.50	3.50
7	A3	20c red, *grn*	6.75	6.75
8	A3	25c blue	5.75	5.75
9	A3	25c blk, *rose*('04)	6.00	6.00
10	A3	30c brn, *bister*	6.50	6.50
11	A3	40c red, *straw*	40.00	40.00
12	A3	50c car, *rose*	275.00	275.00
13	A3	50c brn, *az* ('04)	37.50	37.50
14	A3	75c dp vio, *org*	47.50	47.50
a.		"INDO-CHINE" inverted	*36,000.*	
15	A3	1fr brnz grn, *straw*	47.50	47.50
16	A3	5fr red lil, *lav*	90.00	90.00
		Nos. 1-16 (16)	584.75	584.75

Many varieties of the surcharge exist.

Stamps of Indo-China 1892-1906, Surcharged in Red or Black

1906

17	A4	1c ol grn (R)	1.25	1.25
18	A4	2c vio brn, *buff*	1.25	1.25
19	A4	4c cl, *bluish* (R)	1.25	1.25
20	A4	5c dp grn (R)	1.25	1.25
21	A4	10c carmine	1.25	1.25
22	A4	15c org brn,*bl*	5.75	5.75
23	A4	20c red, *grn*	3.00	3.00
24	A4	25c deep blue	3.00	3.00
25	A4	30c pale brn	3.00	3.00
26	A4	35c blk, *yel* (R)	3.00	3.00
27	A4	40c blk, *bluish*(R)	3.00	3.00
28	A4	50c bister brn	5.75	5.75
29	A3	75c dp vio, *org* (R)	40.00	40.00
30	A4	1fr pale grn	17.50	17.50
31	A4	2fr brn, *org*(R)	29.00	29.00
32	A3	5fr red lil, *lav*	85.00	85.00
33	A4	10fr org brn, *grn*	87.50	87.50
		Nos. 17-33 (17)	291.75	291.75

Various surcharge varieties exist on #17-24.

Stamps of Indo-China, 1907, Surcharged "PAKHOI" and Value in Chinese in Red or Blue

1908

34	A5	1c ol brn & blk	.50	.50
35	A5	2c brn & blk	.50	.50
36	A5	4c bl & blk	.50	.50
37	A5	5c grn & blk	1.25	1.25
38	A5	10c red & blk (Bl)	1.25	1.25
39	A5	15c vio & blk	1.40	1.40
40	A6	20c vio & blk	1.40	1.40
41	A6	25c bl & blk	2.25	2.25
42	A6	30c brn & blk	2.25	2.25
43	A6	35c ol grn & blk	2.25	2.25
44	A6	40c brn & blk	2.25	2.25
46	A6	50c car & blk (Bl)	2.25	2.25
47	A7	75c ver & blk (Bl)	4.50	4.50
48	A8	1fr car & blk (Bl)	6.00	6.00
49	A9	2fr grn & blk	12.00	12.00
50	A10	5fr bl & blk	65.00	65.00
51	A11	10fr pur & blk	110.00	110.00
		Nos. 34-51 (17)	215.55	215.55

The Chinese characters overprinted on Nos. 1 to 51 repeat the denomination of the basic stamps.

Nos. 34-51 Surcharged with New Values in Cents or Piasters in Black, Red or Blue

1919

52	A5	⅖c on 1c	.60	.60
a.		"PAK-HOI" and Chinese double	150.00	150.00
53	A5	⅘c on 2c	.60	.60
54	A5	1⅗c on 4c (R)	.60	.60
55	A5	2c on 5c	1.40	1.40
56	A5	4c on 10c (Bl)	2.40	2.40
57	A5	6c on 15c	.95	.95
58	A6	8c on 20c	2.40	2.40
59	A6	10c on 25c	3.50	3.50
60	A6	12c on 30c	1.00	1.00
a.		"12 CENTS" double	140.00	140.00
61	A6	14c on 35c	.65	.65
a.		Closed "4"	7.25	7.25
62	A6	16c on 40c	1.75	1.75
64	A6	20c on 50c (Bl)	1.40	1.40
65	A7	30c on 75c (Bl)	3.00	3.00
66	A8	40c on 1fr (Bl)	7.25	7.25
67	A9	80c on 2fr (R)	6.00	6.00
68	A10	2pi on 5fr (R)	8.25	8.25
69	A11	4pi on 10fr (R)	20.00	20.00
		Nos. 52-69 (17)	61.75	61.75

TCHONGKING (CHUNGKING)

Stamps of Indo-China Surcharged in Black

1903-04 Unwmk. *Perf. 14x13½*

1	A3	1c blk, *lil bl*	3.00	3.00
2	A3	2c brn, *buff*	3.00	3.00
3	A3	4c claret, *lav*	3.50	3.50
4	A3	5c yel grn	3.50	3.50
5	A3	10c red	4.00	4.00
6	A3	15c gray	3.75	3.75
7	A3	20c red, *grn*	6.00	6.00
8	A3	25c blue	35.00	35.00
9	A3	25c blk, *rose* ('04)	7.50	7.50
10	A3	30c brn, *bister*	9.00	9.00
11	A3	40c red, *straw*	35.00	35.00
12	A3	50c car, *rose*	160.00	160.00
13	A3	50c brn, *az* ('04)	85.00	85.00
14	A3	75c vio, *org*	32.50	32.50
15	A3	1fr brnz grn, *straw*	40.00	40.00
16	A3	5fr red lil, *lav*	67.50	67.50
		Nos. 1-16 (16)	498.25	498.25

Many surcharge varieties exist on #1-14.

Stamps of Indo-China and French China, issued in 1902 with similar overprint, but without Chinese characters, were not officially authorized.

Stamps of Indo-China, 1892-1906, Surcharged in Red or Black

1906

17	A4	1c ol grn (R)	1.40	1.40
18	A4	2c vio brn, *buff*	1.40	1.40
19	A4	4c cl, *bluish* (R)	1.75	1.75
20	A4	5c dp grn (R)	2.00	2.00
21	A4	10c carmine	2.25	2.25
22	A4	15c org brn, *bl*	10.00	10.00
23	A4	20c red, *grn*	2.50	2.50
24	A4	25c deep blue	3.25	3.25
25	A4	30c pale brn	2.10	2.10
26	A4	35c blk, *yellow* (R)	3.25	3.25
27	A4	40c blk, *bluish* (R)	5.00	5.00
28	A4	50c bis brn	6.00	6.00
29	A3	75c dp vio, *org* (R)	35.00	35.00
30	A4	1fr pale grn	21.00	21.00
31	A4	2fr brn, *org* (R)	21.00	21.00
32	A3	5fr red lil, *lav*	75.00	75.00
33	A4	10fr org brn, *grn*	90.00	90.00
		Nos. 17-33 (17)	282.90	282.90

Variety "T" omitted in surcharge occurs once in each sheet of Nos. 17-33. Other surcharge varieties exist, such as inverted surcharge on 1c and 2c.

Stamps of Indo-China, 1907, Surcharged "TCHONGKING" and Value in Chinese in Red or Blue

1908

34	A5	1c ol brn & blk	.35	.35
35	A5	2c brn & blk	.50	.50
36	A5	4c bl & blk	.70	.70
37	A5	5c grn & blk	1.25	1.25
38	A5	10c red & blk (Bl)	1.25	1.25
39	A5	15c vio & blk	1.75	1.75
40	A6	20c vio & blk	2.75	2.75
41	A6	25c bl & blk	3.50	3.50
42	A6	30c brn & blk	2.25	2.25
43	A6	35c ol grn & blk	5.00	5.00
44	A6	40c brn & blk	10.00	10.00
45	A6	50c car & blk (Bl)	7.25	7.25
46	A7	75c ver & blk (Bl)	6.50	6.50
47	A8	1fr car & blk (Bl)	9.00	9.00
48	A9	2fr grn & blk	65.00	65.00
49	A10	5fr bl & blk	26.00	26.00
50	A11	10fr pur & blk	175.00	175.00
		Nos. 34-50 (17)	318.05	318.05

The Chinese characters overprinted on Nos. 1 to 50 repeat the denomination of the basic stamp.

Nos. 34-50 Surcharged with New Values in Cents or Piasters in Black, Red or Blue

1919

51	A5	⅖c on 1c	.80	.70
52	A5	⅘c on 2c	.80	.70
53	A5	1⅗c on 4c (R)	.80	.70
54	A5	2c on 5c	.95	.70
55	A5	4c on 10c (Bl)	.80	.70
56	A5	6c on 15c	.95	.85
57	A6	8c on 20c	2.00	.70
58	A6	10c on 25c	5.75	5.50
59	A6	12c on 30c	1.75	1.10
60	A6	14c on 35c	1.10	1.10
a.		Closed "4"	11.00	11.00
61	A6	16c on 40c	1.60	1.25
a.		"16 CENTS" double	80.00	80.00
62	A6	20c on 50c (Bl)	6.75	3.75
63	A7	30c on 75c (Bl)	1.75	1.75
64	A8	40c on 1fr (Bl)	3.50	2.10
65	A9	80c on 2fr (R)	3.25	3.00
66	A10	2pi on 5fr (R)	4.75	4.75
67	A11	4pi on 10fr (R)	11.00	11.00
		Nos. 51-67 (17)	48.30	40.35

YUNNAN FOU

(Formerly Yunnan Sen, later known as Kunming)

Stamps of Indo-China Surcharged in Black

1903-04 Unwmk. *Perf. 14x13½*

1	A3	1c blk, *lil bl*	5.50	5.50
2	A3	2c brn, *buff*	5.50	5.50
3	A3	4c claret, *lav*	5.50	5.50
4	A3	5c yel green	5.50	5.50
5	A3	10c red	5.50	5.50
6	A3	15c gray	5.50	5.50
7	A3	20c red, *grn*	7.50	7.50
8	A3	25c blue	5.50	5.50
9	A3	30c brn, *bister*	8.50	8.50
10	A3	40c red, *straw*	70.00	45.00
11	A3	50c car, *rose*	300.00	300.00
12	A3	50c brn, *az* ('04)	160.00	160.00
13	A3	75c dp vio, *org*	50.00	45.00
a.		"INDO-CHINE" inverted	*27,500.*	
14	A3	1fr brnz grn, *straw*	50.00	50.00
15	A3	5fr red lil, *lav*	95.00	95.00
		Nos. 1-15 (15)	779.50	749.50

The Chinese characters overprinted on Nos. 1 to 15 repeat the denomination of the basic stamp.

Many varieties of the surcharge exist.

Stamps of Indo-China, 1892-1906, Surcharged in Red or Black

1906 Unwmk. *Perf. 14x13½*

17	A4	1c ol grn (R)	2.25	2.25
18	A4	2c vio brn, *buff*	2.25	2.25
19	A4	4c cl, *bluish* (R)	2.25	2.25
20	A4	5c dp grn (R)	2.75	2.75
21	A4	10c carmine	4.00	4.00
22	A4	15c org brn, *bl*	9.00	9.00
23	A4	20c red, *grn*	3.75	3.75
24	A4	25c deep blue	4.00	4.00
25	A4	30c pale brn	3.75	3.75
26	A4	35c blk, *yel* (R)	6.00	6.00
27	A4	40c blk, *bluish* (R)	5.00	5.00
28	A4	50c bister brn	6.50	6.50
29	A3	75c dp vio, *org* (R)	42.50	42.50
30	A4	1fr pale grn	19.00	19.00
31	A4	2fr brn, *org* (R)	19.00	19.00
32	A3	5fr red lil, *lav*	60.00	60.00
33	A4	10fr org brn, *grn*	85.00	85.00
		Nos. 17-33 (17)	277.00	277.00

Various varieties of the surcharge exist on Nos. 18, 20, 21 and 27.

Stamps of Indo-China, 1907, Surcharged "YUNNANFOU," and Value in Chinese in Red or Blue

1908

34	A5	1c ol brn & blk	.80	.80
35	A5	2c brn & blk	.95	.95
36	A5	4c bl & blk	1.10	1.10
37	A5	5c grn & blk	1.75	1.75
38	A5	10c red & blk (Bl)	1.75	1.75
39	A5	15c vio & blk	4.25	4.25
40	A6	20c vio & blk	4.25	4.25
41	A6	25c bl & blk	5.75	5.75
42	A6	30c brn & blk	5.50	5.50
43	A6	35c ol grn & blk	5.00	5.00
44	A6	40c brn & blk	6.00	6.00
45	A6	50c car & blk (Bl)	7.00	7.00

46 A7 75c ver & blk (Bl) 6.75 6.75
47 A8 1fr car & blk (Bl) 11.00 11.00
48 A9 2fr grn & blk 19.00 19.00
a. "YUNANNFOU" *1,750. 1,750.*
49 A10 5fr bl & blk 42.50 42.50
a. "YUNANNFOU" *1,750. 1,750.*
50 A11 10fr pur & blk 82.50 82.50
a. "YUNANNFOU" *1,750. 1,750.*
Nos. 34-50 (17) 205.85 205.85

The Chinese characters overprinted on Nos. 17-50 repeat the denomination of the basic stamp.

Nos. 34-50 Surcharged with New Values in Cents or Piasters in Black, Red or Blue

1919
51 A5 ⅖c on 1c .60 .60
a. New value double 95.00
52 A5 ⅘c on 2c .85 .85
53 A5 1⅗c on 4c (R) .95 .95
54 A5 2c on 5c 1.25 1.25
a. Triple surcharge 150.00
55 A5 4c on 10c (Bl) .95 .95
56 A5 6c on 15c 1.75 1.75
57 A6 8c on 20c 2.50 2.50
58 A6 10c on 25c 2.50 2.50
59 A6 12c on 30c 1.75 1.75
60 A6 14c on 35c 6.25 3.50
a. Closed "4" 65.00 65.00
61 A6 16c on 40c 3.50 3.50
62 A6 20c on 50c (Bl) 2.00 2.00
63 A7 30c on 75c (Bl) 3.00 3.00
64 A8 40c on 1fr (Bl) 3.50 3.50
65 A9 80c on 2fr (R) 5.75 5.75
a. Triple surch., one inverted 175.00
66 A10 2pi on 5fr (R) 29.00 29.00
67 A11 4pi on 10fr (R) 15.00 15.00
Nos. 51-67 (17) 81.10 78.35

OFFICES IN CRETE

Austria, France, Italy and Great Britain maintained their own post offices in Crete during the period when that country was an autonomous state.

100 Centimes = 1 Franc

Liberty, Equality and Fraternity A1

"Rights of Man" A2

Liberty and Peace (Symbolized by Olive Branch) — A3

Perf. 14x13½
1902-03 Unwmk. Typo.
1 A1 1c gray 1.40 1.25
2 A1 2c violet brown 1.40 1.25
3 A1 3c red orange 1.40 1.25
4 A1 4c yellow brown 1.40 1.25
5 A1 5c green 1.40 1.25
6 A2 10c rose red 1.75 1.60
7 A2 15c pale red ('03) 2.40 1.75
8 A2 20c brown vio ('03) 3.25 2.50
9 A2 25c blue ('03) 4.25 2.50
10 A2 30c lilac ('03) 5.50 4.25
11 A3 40c red & pale bl 8.50 7.50
12 A3 50c bis brn & lav 12.00 8.50
13 A3 1fr claret & ol grn 16.00 14.00
14 A3 2fr gray vio & yel 25.00 22.50
15 A3 5fr dk blue & buff 45.00 40.00
Nos. 1-15 (15) 130.65 111.35

A4

A5

Black Surcharge

1903
16 A4 1pi on 25c blue 35.00 29.00
17 A5 2pi on 50c bis brn & lav 57.50 42.50
18 A5 4pi on 1fr claret & ol grn 85.00 77.50
19 A5 8pi on 2fr gray vio & yel 92.50 92.50
20 A5 20pi on 5fr dk bl & buff 160.00 140.00
Nos. 16-20 (5) 430.00 381.50

OFFICES IN EGYPT

French post offices formerly maintained in Alexandria and Port Said.

100 Centimes = 1 Franc

ALEXANDRIA

Stamps of France Overprinted in Red, Blue or Black

1899-1900 Unwmk. *Perf. 14x13½*
1 A15 1c blk, *lil bl* (R) 1.40 1.40
a. Double overprint 110.00
b. Triple overprint 125.00
2 A15 2c brn, *buff* (Bl) 2.10 1.75
3 A15 3c gray, *grysh* (Bl) 2.10 1.75
4 A15 4c cl, *lav* (Bl) 2.50 2.10
5 A15 5c yel grn, (I) (R) 4.00 2.10
On cover 65.00
a. Type II (R) 110.00 72.50
6 A15 10c blk, *lav,* (I) (R) 5.75 5.00
On cover 75.00
a. Type II (R) 42.50 25.00
7 A15 15c blue (R) 6.00 3.25
On cover 75.00
8 A15 20c red, *grn* 10.00 5.50
a. Double overprint
9 A15 25c blk, *rose* (R) 5.00 2.75
On cover 75.00
a. Inverted overprint 57.50
b. Double ovpt., one invtd. 110.00
10 A15 30c brn, *bis* 11.00 8.50
11 A15 40c red, *straw* 9.75 9.75
12 A15 50c car, *rose* (II) 24.00 12.50
a. Type I 125.00 18.00
13 A15 1fr brnz grn, *straw* 22.50 16.00
On cover 750.00
14 A15 2fr brn, *az* ('00) 65.00 62.50
15 A15 5fr red lil, *lav* 92.50 80.00
Nos. 1-15 (15) 263.60 214.85

Covers: Values are for commercial covers with correct postage rates. Postcards sell for somewhat less than covers. Philatelic covers sell for much less.

A2

A3

A4

1902-03
16 A2 1c gray .50 .20
a. 1c gray black .65 .40
17 A2 2c violet brn .50 .35
18 A2 3c red orange .50 .35
19 A2 4c yellow brn .75 .55
20 A2 5c green 1.10 .45
On cover 40.00
21 A3 10c rose red .95 .45
On cover 40.00
22 A3 15c orange 1.10 .75
On cover 35.00
a. 15c pale red ('03) 3.00 .90
On cover 37.50
23 A3 20c brn vio ('03) 2.00 1.00
On cover 52.50
24 A3 25c blue ('03) 1.00 .35
On cover 35.00
a. 25c dark blue 1.50 .50
On cover 52.50
25 A3 30c violet ('03) 5.00 2.75
26 A4 40c red & pale bl 3.50 1.40
27 A4 50c bis brn & lav 6.75 2.00
28 A4 1fr cl & ol grn 6.25 2.75
29 A4 2fr gray vio & yel 16.00 7.75
a. 2fr deep violet & yellow — —
30 A4 5fr dk bl & buff 19.00 11.00
Nos. 16-30 (15) 64.90 32.10

The 2c, 5c, 10c, 20c and 25c exist imperf. Value, each $32.50

See #77-86. For surcharges see #31-73, B1-B4.

Covers: Values are for commercial covers with correct postage rates. Postcards sell for somewhat less than covers. Philatelic covers sell for much less.

Stamps of 1902-03 Surcharged Locally in Black

1921
31 A2 2m on 5c green 5.00 2.75
32 A2 3m on 3c red org 5.00 3.75
a. Larger numeral 80.00 57.50
33 A3 4m on 10c rose 4.00 3.25
34 A2 5m on 1c dk gray 5.50 4.25
35 A2 5m on 4c yel brn 5.75 4.75
36 A3 6m on 15c orange 3.75 3.00
a. Larger numeral 65.00 65.00
37 A3 8m on 20c brn vio 5.00 3.25
a. Larger numeral 47.50 35.00
38 A3 10m on 25c blue 2.50 2.50
a. Inverted surcharge 30.00 30.00
b. Double surcharge 30.00 30.00
39 A3 12m on 30c vio 9.25 9.25
40 A2 15m on 2c vio brn 4.25 4.25

Nos. 26-30 Surcharged

41 A4 15m on 40c 12.50 11.00
42 A4 15m on 50c 7.50 7.50
43 A4 30m on 1fr 110.00 110.00
44 A4 60m on 2fr 160.00 160.00
a. Larger numeral 500.00 500.00
45 A4 150m on 5fr 250.00 250.00

Port Said Nos. 20 and 19 Surcharged like Nos. 32 and 40

45A A2 3m on 3c red org 100.00 100.00
46 A2 15m on 2c vio brn 92.50 92.50
Nos. 31-46 (17) 782.50 772.00

Alexandria No. 28 Surcharged with Two New Values

1921
46A A4 30m on 15m on 1fr 825.00 *875.00*

The surcharge "15 Mill." was made in error and is canceled by a bar.

The surcharges were lithographed on Nos. 31, 33, 38, 39 and 42 and typographed on the other stamps of the 1921 issue. Nos. 34, 36 and 37 were surcharged by both methods.

Alexandria Stamps of 1902-03 Surcharged in Paris

1921-23
47 A2 1m on 1c gray 2.25 1.60
48 A2 2m on 5c green 1.75 1.40
49 A3 4m on 10c rose 2.00 1.60
50 A3 4m on 10c green ('23) 1.40 1.40
51 A2 5m on 3c red org ('23) 4.75 3.50
52 A3 6m on 15c orange 1.40 1.10
53 A3 8m on 20c brn vio 1.40 .70
54 A3 10m on 25c blue .95 .90
55 A3 10m on 30c vio 2.75 2.25
56 A3 15m on 50c bl ('23) 3.50 2.25

Nos. 27-30 and Type of 1902 Surcharged

57 A4 15m on 50c 2.25 2.25
58 A4 30m on 1fr 2.50 1.60
59 A4 60m on 2fr *1,650. 1,650.*
60 A4 60m on 2fr org & pale bl ('23) 7.50 7.50
61 A4 150m on 5fr 9.25 5.50
Nos. 47-58,60-61 (14) 43.65 33.55

Stamps and Types of 1902-03 Surcharged with New Values and Bars in Black

1925
62 A2 1m on 1c gray .80 .80
63 A2 2m on 5c orange .80 .80
64 A2 2m on 5c green 1.00 1.00
65 A3 4m on 10c green .80 .80
66 A2 5m on 3c red org 1.00 .80
67 A3 6m on 15c orange .95 .80
68 A3 8m on 20c brn vio 1.25 .85
69 A3 10m on 25c blue .75 .60
70 A3 15m on 50c blue 1.40 .95
71 A4 30m on 1fr cl & ol grn 2.25 1.75
72 A4 60m on 2fr org & pale bl 3.00 2.75
73 A4 150m on 5fr dk bl & buff 3.75 3.00
Nos. 62-73 (12) 17.75 14.90

Types of 1902-03 Issue

1927-28
77 A2 3m orange ('28) 1.40 1.10
81 A3 15m slate blue 1.40 1.10
82 A3 20m rose lil ('28) 4.25 3.00
84 A4 50m org & blue 7.50 5.75
85 A4 100m sl bl & buff 10.00 7.50
86 A4 250m gray grn & red 16.00 10.00
Nos. 77-86 (6) 40.55 28.45

SEMI-POSTAL STAMPS

Regular Issue of 1902-03 Surcharged in Carmine

1915 Unwmk. *Perf. 14x13½*
B1 A3 10c + 5c rose .80 .80

Sinking Fund Issue

Type of 1902-03 Issue Surcharged in Blue or Black

1927-30
B2 A3 15m + 5m deep org 3.25 3.25
B3 A3 15m + 5m red vio ('28) 3.25 3.25
a. 15m + 5m violet ('30) 7.00 7.00

Type of 1902-03 Issue Surcharged as in 1927-28

1929
B4 A3 15m + 5m fawn 5.50 5.50

POSTAGE DUE STAMPS

Postage Due Stamps of France, 1893-1920, Surcharged in Paris in Black

1922 Unwmk. *Perf. 14x13½*
J1 D2 2m on 5c blue 1.60 1.60
J2 D2 4m on 10c brown 1.60 1.60
J3 D2 10m on 30c rose red 1.90 1.90
J4 D2 15m on 50c brn vio 2.25 2.25
J5 D2 30m on 1fr red brn, *straw* 3.00 3.00
Nos. J1-J5 (5) 10.35 10.35

D3

1928 Typo.
J6 D3 1m slate 1.25 1.25
J7 D3 2m light blue .85 .85
J8 D3 4m lilac rose 1.25 1.25
J9 D3 5m gray green 1.40 1.40
J10 D3 10m light red 1.60 1.60
J11 D3 20m violet brn 1.50 1.50

J12 D3 30m green 3.25 3.25
J13 D3 40m lt violet 3.75 3.75
Nos. J6-J13 (8) 14.85 14.85

#J6-J13 were also available for use in Port Said.

PORT SAID

Stamps of France Overprinted in Red, Blue or Black

1899-1900 Unwmk. *Perf. 14x13½*

1 A15 1c blk, *lil bl* (R) 1.25 .85
2 A15 2c brn, *buff* (bl) 1.25 .95
3 A15 3c gray, *grysh* (Bl) 1.25 1.25
4 A15 4c claret, *lav* (Bl) 1.25 1.25
5 A15 5c yel grn (I) (R) 6.25 4.50
On cover 110.00
a. Type II (R) 32.50 11.00
6 A15 10c blk, *lav* (I) (R) 9.00 9.00
On cover 110.00
a. Type II (R) 472.50 35.00
7 A15 15c blue (R) 9.00 5.50
On cover 110.00
8 A15 20c red, *grn* 10.00 7.50
9 A15 25c blk, *rose* (R) 8.50 3.00
On cover 110.00
a. Double overprint 160.00
b. Inverted overprint 160.00
10 A15 30c brn, *bister* 10.00 8.50
a. Inverted overprint 175.00
11 A15 40c red, *straw* 10.00 8.50
12 A15 50c car, *rose* (II) 13.00 10.00
a. Type I 250.00 80.00
b. Double overprint (II) 275.00
13 A15 1fr brnz grn, *straw* 20.00 11.00
On cover 725.00
14 A15 2fr brn, *az* ('00) 55.00 50.00
15 A15 5fr red lil, *lav* 82.50 67.50
Nos. 1-15 (15) 238.25 189.30

Covers: Values are for commercial covers with correct postage rates. Postcards sell for somewhat less than covers. Philatelic covers sell for much less.

Regular Issue Surcharged in Red

PORT SAID
VINGT
CINQ

1899

16 A15 25c on 10c blk, *lav* 92.50 24.00
On cover 150.00
a. Inverted surcharge 200.00

With Additional Surcharge "25" in Red

17 A15 25c on 10c blk, *lav* 350.00 125.00
a. "25" inverted 1,100. 925.00
b. "25" in black 2,150.
c. As "b," "VINGT CINQ" inverted 2,550.
d. As "b," "25" vertical 2,550.
e. As "c" and "d" 2,550.

A2

A3

A4

1902-03 Typo.

18 A2 1c gray .65 .45
a. 1c gray black .50 .50
19 A2 2c violet brn .75 .50
20 A2 3c red orange .60 .50
21 A2 4c yellow brown .75 .60
22 A2 5c blue green .80 .60
On cover 50.00
a. 5c yellow green 3.00 2.25
23 A3 10c rose red 1.25 .75
On cover 50.00
24 A3 15c pale red ('03) 2.25 1.50
On cover 40.00
a. 15c orange 3.00 1.75
On cover 40.00
25 A3 20c brn vio ('03) 2.25 1.50
On cover 50.00
26 A3 25c blue ('03) 2.00 1.25
On cover 45.00
a. 25c dark blue 4.25 3.50
27 A3 30c violet ('03) 4.25 3.50
28 A4 40c red & pale bl 4.00 3.00
29 A4 50c bis brn & lav 5.75 4.75
30 A4 1fr claret & ol grn 7.00 5.75
31 A4 2fr gray vio & yel 9.75 9.75
a. 2fr dark violet & yellow 9.75
32 A4 5fr dk bl & buff 24.00 21.00
Nos. 18-32 (15) 66.05 55.40

See #83-92. For surcharges see #33-80, B1-B4.

Stamps of 1902-03 Surcharged Locally

1921

33 A2 2m on 5c green 5.50 5.50
a. Inverted surcharge 30.00 30.00
34 A3 4m on 10c rose 4.75 4.75
a. Inverted surcharge 30.00 30.00
35 A2 5m on 1c 7.50 7.50
a. Inverted surcharge 55.00 55.00
c. Surcharged "2 Milliemes" 37.50 37.50
36 A2 5m on 2c 10.00 10.00
a. Surcharged "2 Milliemes" 45.00 45.00
b. As "a," inverted 75.00 75.00
37 A2 5m on 3c 6.50 6.50
a. Inverted surcharge 37.50 37.50
b. On Alexandria #18 275.00 275.00
38 A2 5m on 4c 6.75 6.75
a. Inverted surcharge 57.50 57.50
39 A2 10m on 2c 10.00 10.00
40 A2 10m on 4c 13.00 13.00
a. Inverted surcharge 60.00 60.00
41 A3 10m on 25c 4.75 4.75
a. Inverted surcharge 57.50 57.50
42 A3 12m on 30c 18.00 18.00
43 A2 15m on 4c 5.75 5.75
a. Inverted surcharge 57.50 57.50
44 A3 15m on 15c pale red 37.50 37.50
a. Inverted surcharge 75.00 75.00
45 A3 15m on 20c 37.50 37.50
a. Inverted surcharge 75.00 75.00
46 A4 30m on 50c 200.00 200.00
47 A4 60m on 50c 225.00 225.00
48 A4 150m on 50c 275.00 275.00

Nos. 46, 47 and 48 have a bar between the numerals and "Millièmes," which is in capital letters.

Same Surcharge on Stamps of French Offices in Turkey, 1902-03

49 A2 2m on 2c vio brn 75.00 75.00
50 A2 5m on 1c gray 57.50 57.50
a. "5" inverted — —
Nos. 33-50 (18) 1,000. 1,000.

Nos. 28-32 Surcharged

51 A4 15m on 40c 37.50 37.500
52 A4 15m on 50c 42.50 42.50
b. Bar below 15 35.00 35.00
53 A4 30m on 1fr 175.00 175.00
54 A4 60m on 2fr 60.00 60.00
55 A4 150m on 5fr 190.00 190.00
Nos. 51-55 (5) 505.00 509.50

Overprinted "MILLtEMES"

51a A4 15m on 40c 100.00 100.00
52a A4 15m on 50c 200.00 200.00
53a A4 30m on 1fr 500.00 525.00
54a A4 60m on 2fr 200.00 225.00
55a A4 150m on 5fr 550.00 575.00
Nos. 51a-55a (5) 1,550. 1,625.

Stamps of 1902-03 Surcharged in Paris

1921-23

56 A2 1m on 1c gray .85 .85
57 A2 2m on 5c green .85 .85
58 A3 4m on 10c rose 1.75 1.75
59 A2 5m on 3c red org 5.75 5.75
60 A3 6m on 15c orange 1.75 1.75
a. 6m on 15c pale red 8.50 8.50
61 A3 8m on 20c brn vio 1.75 1.75
62 A3 10m on 25c blue 2.00 2.00
63 A3 10m on 30c violet 4.75 4.75
64 A3 15m on 50c blue 4.25 4.25

Nos. 29-32 and Type of 1902 Surcharged

65 A4 15m on 50c 4.00 4.00
66 A4 30m on 1fr 5.50 5.50
67 A4 60m on 2fr 85.00 85.00
68 A4 60m on 2fr org & pale blue 7.50 7.50
69 A4 150m on 5fr 7.50 7.50
Nos. 56-69 (14) 133.20 133.20

Stamps and Types of 1902-03 Surcharged with New Values and Bars

1925

70 A2 1m on 1c gray .60 .60
71 A2 2m on 5c green .75 .75
72 A3 4m on 10c rose red .75 .75
73 A2 5m on 3c red org .80 .80
74 A3 6m on 15c orange .80 .80
75 A3 8m on 20c brn vio .75 .75
76 A3 10m on 25c blue 1.25 1.25
77 A3 15m on 50c blue 1.25 1.25
78 A4 30m on 1fr cl & ol grn 1.75 1.75
79 A4 60m on 2fr org & pale blue 1.75 1.75
80 A4 150m on 5fr dk bl & buff 2.25 2.25
Nos. 70-80 (11) 12.70 12.70

Types of 1902-03 Issue

1927-28

83 A2 3m orange ('28) 1.25 1.25
87 A3 15m slate bl 1.50 1.50
88 A3 20m rose lil ('28) 1.60 1.60
90 A4 50m org & blue 3.00 3.00
91 A4 100m slate bl & buff 3.50 3.50
92 A4 250m gray grn & red 5.75 5.75
Nos. 83-92 (6) 16.60 16.60

SEMI-POSTAL STAMPS

Regular Issue of 1902-03 Surcharged in Carmine

1915 Unwmk. *Perf. 14x13½*

B1 A3 10c + 5c rose .95 .95

Sinking Fund Issue

Type of 1902-03 Issue Surcharged like Alexandria Nos. B2-B3 in Blue or Black

1927-30

B2 A3 15m + 5m dp org (Bl) 1.75 1.75
B3 A3 15m + 5m red vio ('28) 1.75 1.75
a. 15m + 5m violet ('30) 3.50 3.50
B4 A3 15m + 5m fawn ('29) 2.25 2.25
Nos. B2-B4 (3) 5.75 5.75

POSTAGE DUE STAMPS

Postage Due Stamps of France, 1893-1906, Surcharged Locally in Black

15
Millièmes

1921 Unwmk. *Perf. 14x13½*

J1 D2 12m on 10c brown 37.50 37.50
J2 D2 15m on 5c blue 40.00 42.50
J3 D2 30m on 20c ol grn 42.50 42.00
a. Inverted surcharge 575.00 575.00
J4 D2 30m on 50c red vio *2,500. 2,900.*

Same Surcharged in Red or Blue

1921

J5 D2 2m on 5c bl (R) 32.50 32.50
a. Blue surcharge 240.00 240.00
J6 D2 4m on 10c brn (Bl) 32.50 32.50
a. Surcharged "15 Milliemes" 475.00 475.00
J7 D2 10m on 30c red (Bl) 32.50 32.50
a. Inverted surcharge 100.00 100.00
J8 D2 15m on 50c brn vio (Bl) 42.50 427.50
a. Inverted surcharge 100.00 100.00
Nos. J5-J8 (4) 140.00 525.00

Nos. J5-J8 exist with second "M" in "Milliemes" inverted, also with final "S" omitted.

Alexandria Nos. J6-J13 were also available for use in Port Said.

OFFICES IN TURKEY (LEVANT)

Various powers maintained post offices in the Turkish Empire before World War I by authority of treaties which ended with the signing of the Treaty of Lausanne in 1923. The foreign post offices were closed Oct. 27, 1923.

100 Centimes = 1 Franc
25 Centimes = 40 Paras = 1 Piaster

2ovpt

Stamps of France Surcharged in Black or Red

1885-1901 Unwmk. *Perf. 14x13½*

1 A1 1pi on 25c yel, *straw* 400.00 10.00
a. Inverted surcharge *1,950. 1,850.*
2 A1 1pi on 25c blk, *rose* (R) ('86) 3.50 .70
a. Inverted surcharge 300.00 275.00
3 A1 2pi on 50c car, *rose* (II) ('90) 12.50 1.75
a. Type I ('01) 260.00 35.00
4 A1 3pi on 75c car, *rose* 18.00 9.00
5 A1 4pi on 1fr brnz grn, *straw* 18.00 9.00
6 A1 8pi on 2fr brn, *az* ('00) 32.50 16.00
7 A1 20pi on 5fr red lil, *lav* ('90) 70.00 35.00
Nos. 1-7 (7) 554.50 81.45

A2

A3

A4

A5

A6

1902-07 Typo. *Perf. 14x13½*

21 A2 1c gray .35 .35
22 A2 2c vio brn .50 .35
23 A2 3c red org .50 .35
24 A2 4c yel brn 1.75 .75
a. Imperf., pair 57.50
25 A2 5c grn ('06) .75 .35
26 A3 10c rose red .75 .35
27 A3 15c pale red ('03) 1.75 .95
28 A3 20c brn vio ('03) 2.40 1.50
29 A3 25c blue ('07) 32.50 25.00
a. Imperf., pair 300.00
30 A3 30c lilac ('03) 3.50 1.75
31 A4 40c red & pale bl 3.50 2.00
32 A4 50c bis brn & lav ('07) 160.00 140.00
a. Imperf., pair 650.00

33 A4 1fr claret & ol grn ('07) 300.00 300.00
a. Imperf., pair 800.00

Black Surcharge

34 A5 1pi on 25c bl ('03) .80 .35
a. Second "I" omitted 7.50 6.25
b. Double surcharge 55.00 40.00
35 A6 2pi on 50c bis brn & lavender 2.50 .85
36 A6 4pi on 1fr cl & ol grn 3.00 1.00
a. Imperf., pair 550.00
37 A6 8pi on 2fr gray vio & yel 13.00 8.25
38 A6 20pi on 5fr dk bl & buff 5.75 3.00
Nos. 21-38 (18) 533.30 487.15

Nos. 29, 32-33 were used during the early part of 1907 in the French Offices at Harar and Diredawa, Ethiopia. Djibouti and Port Said stamps were also used.

No. 27 Surcharged in Green

1 Piastre

Beyrouth

1905

39 A3 1pi on 15c pale red 1,600. 250.
a. "Piastte" *4,750.* 950.

Stamps of France 1900-21 Surcharged:

On A22

On A20

On A18

1921-22

40 A22 30pa on 5c grn .60 .50
41 A22 30pa on 5c org .50 .50
42 A22 1pi20pa on 10c red .50 .50
43 A22 1pi20pa on 10c grn .75 .50
44 A22 3pi30pa on 25c bl .95 .50
45 A22 4pi20pa on 30c org 1.00 .65
a. "4" omitted 725.00
46 A20 7pi20pa on 50c bl 1.00 .65
47 A18 15pi on 1fr car & ol grn 1.60 1.25
48 A18 30pi on 2fr org & pale bl 8.25 5.75
49 A18 75pi on 5fr dk bl & buff 7.50 4.75
Nos. 40-49 (10) 22.65 15.55

Stamps of France, 1903-07, Handstamped

1923

52 A22 1pi20pa on 10c red 50.00 50.00
54 A20 3pi30pa on 15c gray grn 17.50 17.50
55 A22 7pi20pa on 35c vio 20.00 20.00
a. 1pi20pa on 35c violet 625.00 625.00
Nos. 52-55 (3) 87.50 87.50

CAVALLE (CAVALLA)

Stamps of France Overprinted or Surcharged in Red, Blue or Black

1893-1900 Unwmk. *Perf. 14x13½*

1 A15 5c grn, *grnsh* (R) 16.00 12.50
2 A15 5c yel grn (I) ('00) (R) 16.00 12.50
3 A15 10c blk, *lav* (II) 18.00 15.00
a. 10c black, *lavender* (I) 150.00 100.00
4 A15 15c blue (R) 32.50 18.00
5 A15 1pi on 25c blk, *rose* 22.50 16.00
6 A15 2pi on 50c car, *rose* 65.00 47.50
7 A15 4pi on 1fr brnz grn, *straw* (R) 70.00 60.00
8 A15 8pi on 2fr brn, *az* ('00) (Bk) 100.00 90.00
Nos. 1-8 (8) 340.00 271.50

A3

A4

A5

A6

1902-03

9 A3 5c green 1.50 1.25
10 A4 10c rose red ('03) 1.50 1.25
11 A4 15c orange 1.75 1.25
a. 15c pale red ('03) 7.50 7.50

Surcharged in Black

12 A5 1pi on 25c bl 3.00 1.75
13 A6 2pi on 50c bis brn & lav 7.50 4.75
14 A6 4pi on 1fr cl & ol grn 9.50 7.00
15 A6 8pi on 2fr gray vio & yel 12.00 12.00
Nos. 9-15 (7) 36.75 29.25

DEDEAGH (DEDEAGATCH)

Stamps of France Overprinted or Surcharged in Red, Blue or Black

1893-1900 Unwmk. *Perf. 14x13½*

1 A15 5c grn, *grnsh* (II) (R) 10.00 9.00
2 A15 5c yel grn (I) ('00) (R) 9.50 9.00
3 A15 10c blk, *lav* (II) 16.00 13.00
a. Type I 29.00 20.00
4 A15 15c blue (R) 22.50 18.00
5 A15 1pi on 25c blk, *rose* 24.00 22.50
6 A15 2pi on 50c car, *rose* 42.50 32.50
7 A15 4pi on 1fr brnz grn, *straw* (R) 55.00 45.00
8 A15 8pi on 2fr brn, *az* ('00) (Bk) 80.00 60.00
Nos. 1-8 (8) 259.50 209.00

A3

A4

A5

A6

1902-03

9 A3 5c green 1.40 1.25
10 A4 10c rose red ('03) 1.75 1.50
11 A4 15c orange 2.25 1.40

Black Surcharge

15 A5 1pi on 25c bl ('03) 2.25 1.75
16 A6 2pi on 50c bis brn & lav 7.00 6.00
a. Double surcharge 190.00
17 A6 4pi on 1fr cl & ol grn 12.50 10.00
18 A6 8pi on 2fr gray vio & yel 18.00 16.00
Nos. 9-18 (7) 45.15 37.90

PORT LAGOS

Stamps of France Overprinted or Surcharged in Red or Blue

1893 Unwmk. *Perf. 14x13½*

1 A15 5c grn, *grnsh* (R) 18.00 18.00
2 A15 10c blk, *lav* 37.50 30.00
3 A15 15c blue (R) 57.50 47.50
4 A15 1pi on 25c blk, *rose* 472.50 42.50
5 A15 2pi on 50c car, *rose* 125.00 70.00
6 A15 4pi on 1fr brnz grn, *straw* (R) 77.50 62.50
Nos. 1-6 (6) 788.00 270.50

VATHY (SAMOS)

Stamps of France Overprinted or Surcharged in Red, Blue or Black

1894-1900 Unwmk. *Perf. 14x13½*

1 A15 5c grn, *grnsh* (R) 5.50 4.75
2 A15 5c yel grn (I) ('00) (R) 5.50 4.75
a. Type II 55.00 55.00
3 A15 10c blk, *lav* (I) 11.00 9.50
a. Type II 35.00 25.00
4 A15 15c blue (R) 9.50 9.50
5 A15 1pi on 25c blk, *rose* 12.00 6.50
6 A15 2pi on 50c car, *rose* 20.00 16.00
7 A15 4pi on 1fr brnz grn, *straw* (R) 24.00 24.00
8 A15 8pi on 2fr brn, *az* ('00) (Bk) 50.00 50.00
9 A15 20pi on 5fr lil, *lav* ('00) (Bk) 75.00 75.00
Nos. 1-9 (9) 212.50 200.00

OFFICES IN ZANZIBAR

Until 1906 France maintained post offices in the Sultanate of Zanzibar, but in that year Great Britain assumed direct control over this protectorate and the French withdrew their postal system.

16 Annas = 1 Rupee

A1

A2

Stamps of France Surcharged in Red, Carmine, Blue or Black

1894-96 Unwmk. *Perf. 14x13½*

1 A1 ½a on 5c grn, *grnsh* 5.75 3.50
2 A1 1a on 10c blk, *lav* (Bl) 10.00 8.00
3 A1 1½a on 15c bl ('96) 15.00 13.00
a. "ANNAS" 75.00 65.00
b. Carmine surcharge 22.50 17.50
4 A1 2a on 20c red, *grn* ('96) (Bk) 12.10 10.00
a. "ANNA" 1,600. 1,600.
5 A1 2½a on 25c blk, *rose* (Bl) 7.50 5.75
a. Double surcharge 175.00
6 A1 3a on 30c brn, *bis* ('96) (Bk) 15.00 12.00
7 A1 4a on 40c red, *straw* ('96) (Bk) 17.50 17.00
8 A1 5a on 50c car, *rose* (Bl) 25.00 21.00
9 A1 7½a on 75c vio, *org* ('96) 375.00 300.00
10 A1 10a on 1fr brnz grn, *straw* 42.50 32.50
a. Carmine surcharge 50.00 40.00
11 A1 50a on 5fr red lil, *lav* ('96) (Bk) 240.00 200.00
Nos. 1-11 (11) 765.35 622.75

1894

12 A2 ½a & 5c on 1c blk, *lil bl* (R) 150.00 *175.00*
13 A2 1a & 10c on 3c gray, *grysh* (R) 140.00 *150.00*
14 A2 2½a & 25c on 4c cl, *lav* (Bk) 180.00 *200.00*
15 A2 5a & 50c on 20c red, *grn* (Bk) 180.00 *200.00*
16 A2 10a & 1fr on 40c red, *straw* (Bk) 350.00 *375.00*
Nos. 12-16 (5) 1,000. 1,100.

There are two distinct types of the figures 5c, four of the 25c and three of each of the others of this series.

Stamps of France Surcharged in Red, Carmine, Blue or Black

1896-1900

17 A15 ½a on 5c grn, *grnsh* (R) 6.75 5.50
a. Carmine surcharge 4.50 3.00
18 A15 ½a on 5c yel grn (I) (R) 5.75 5.00
a. Type II 6.50 5.00
19 A15 1a on 10c blk, *lav* (II) (Bl) 6.50 5.00
a. Type I 15.00 12.50
20 A15 1½a on 15c bl (R) 7.50 5.75
21 A15 2a on 20c red, *grn* 5.75 5.75
a. "ZANZIBAR" double 110.00
b. "ZANZIBAR" triple 140.00
22 A15 2½a on 25c blk, *rose* (Bl) 7.50 5.75
a. Inverted surcharge 175.00
23 A15 3a on 30c brn, *bis* 7.50 5.75
24 A15 4a on 40c red, *straw* 7.50 6.50
25 A15 5a on 50c rose, *rose* (II) (Bl) 30.00 20.00
a. Type I 90.00 75.00

26 A15 10a on 1fr brnz grn, *straw* (R) 18.00 13.00
a. Carmine surcharge 12.50 11.50
27 A15 20a on 2fr brn, *az* 22.50 13.00
a. "ZANZIBAS" 500.00 550.00
b. "ZANZIBAR" triple *1,200.*
28 A15 50a on 5fr lil, *lav* 55.00 47.50
a. "ZANZIBAS" *3,250.*
Nos. 17-28 (12) 348.50 217.65

For surcharges see Nos. 50-54.

A4

A5

1897

29 A4 2½a & 25c on ½a on 5c grn, *grnsh* 1,000. 140.
30 A4 2½a & 25c on 1a on 10c *lav* *3,250.* 750.
31 A4 2½a & 25c on 1½a on 15c blue *3,250.* 625.
32 A5 5a & 50c on 3a on 30c brn, *bis* *3,250.* 550.
33 A5 5a & 50c on 4a on 40c red, *straw* *3,250.* 700.

A6

A7

Printed on the Margins of Sheets of French Stamps

Perf. 14x13½ on one or more sides

1897

34 A6 2½a & 25c grn, *grnsh* 850.
35 A6 2½a & 25c blk, *lav* *2,900.*
36 A6 2½a & 25c blue *2,250.*
37 A7 5a & 50c brn, *bis* *2,250.*
38 A7 5a & 50c red, *straw* *2,100.*

There are 5 varieties of figures in the above surcharges.

A8

A9

A10

Surcharged in Red or Black

1902-03 ***Perf. 14x13½***

39 A8 ½a on 5c grn (R) 5.00 4.25
40 A9 1a on 10c rose red ('03) 5.00 5.00
41 A9 1½a on 15c pale red ('03) 11.00 9.50
42 A9 2a on 20c brn vio ('03) 12.00 10.00
43 A9 2½a on 25c bl ('03) 13.00 12.00
44 A9 3a on 30c lil ('03) 9.50 9.50
a. 5a on 30c (error) 240.00 *275.00*
45 A10 4a on 40c red & pale bl 20.00 18.00
46 A10 5a on 50c bis brn & lav 18.00 15.00
47 A10 10a on 1fr cl & ol grn 24.00 19.00
48 A10 20a on 2fr gray vio & yel 55.00 50.00
49 A10 50a on 5fr dk bl & buff 75.00 65.00
Nos. 39-49 (12) 876.15 713.40

For see Reunion Nos. 55-59.

Nos. 23-24 Surcharged in Black:

25 ▪ 2½ — a
50 ▪ 5 — b
1 fr ▪ 10 — c

1904

50 A15 25c & 2½a on 4a on 40c 750.
51 A15 50c & 5a on 3a on 30c 850.
52 A15 50c & 5a on 4a on 40c 850.
53 A15 1fr & 10a on 3a on 30c 1,500.
54 A15 1fr & 10a on 4a on 40c 1,500.

Nos. 39-40, 44 Surcharged in Red or Black:

2 / 25 — d
25c / 2½ — e
50c / cinq — f
1 fr / dix — g

55 A8 25c & 2a on ½a on 5c (R) *2,500.* 87.50
56 A9 25c & 2½a on 1a on 10c *4,500.* 90.00
a. Inverted surcharge 950.00
57 A9 25c & 2½a on 3a on 30c *1,750.*
a. Inverted surcharge *2,000.*
b. Double surch., both invtd. *2,500.*
58 A9 50c & 5a on 3a on 30c 900.00
59 A9 1fr & 10a on 3a on 30c 1,250.

No. J1-J3 With Various Surcharges Overprinted:

"Timbre" in Red

60 D1 ½a on 5c blue 350.00

Overprinted "Affrancht" in Black

61 D1 1a on 10c brown 350.00

With Red Bars Across "CHIFFRE" and "TAXE"

62 D1 1½a on 15c green 750.00

The illustrations are not exact reproductions of the new surcharges but are merely intended to show their relative positions and general styles.

POSTAGE DUE STAMPS

Postage Due Stamps of France Surcharged in Red, Blue or Black Like Nos. 17-28

1897 **Unwmk.** ***Perf. 14x13½***

J1 D2 ½a on 5c blue (R) 16.00 8.50
J2 D2 1a on 10c brn (Bl) 16.00 8.50
a. Inverted surcharge 110.00 *125.00*
J3 D2 1½a on 15c grn (R) 21.00 10.00
J4 D2 3a on 30c car (Bk) 21.00 16.00
J5 D2 5a on 50c lil (Bl) 21.00 17.00
a. 2½a on 50c lilac (Bl) 1,000. 875.00
Nos. J1-J5 (5) 36.00 25.50

For overprints see Nos. 60-62.

FRENCH COLONIES

'french 'kä-lə-nēz

From 1859 to 1906 and in 1944 and 1945 special stamps were issued for use in all French Colonies which did not have stamps of their own.

100 Centimes = 1 Franc

Perforations: Nos. 1-45 are known variously perforated privately.

Gum: Many of Nos. 1-45 were issued without gum. Some were gummed locally.

Reprints: Nos. 1-7, 9-12, 24, 26-42, 44 and 45 were reprinted officially in 1887. These reprints are ungummed and the colors of both design and paper are deeper or brighter than the originals. Value for Nos. 1-6, $20 each.

Eagle and Crown — A1

1859-65 **Unwmk.** **Typo.** ***Imperf.***

1 A1 1c ol grn, *pale bl* ('62) 16.50 *19.00*
On cover 275.00
2 A1 5c yel grn, *grnsh* ('62) 19.00 12.00
On cover 85.00
3 A1 10c bister, *yel* 25.00 6.50
On cover 26.00
a. Pair, one sideways 800.00 400.00
On cover *1,600.*
4 A1 20c bl, *bluish* ('65) 29.00 11.00
On cover 42.50
5 A1 40c org, *yelsh* 22.00 11.00
On cover 50.00
6 A1 80c car rose, *pnksh* ('65) 90.00 50.00
On cover 250.00
Nos. 1-6 (6) 201.50 109.50

Values for stamps on cover are for covers paying ordinary rates and emanating from the most populated colonies such as Martinique and Guadeloupe. Covers originating from more remote areas command premiums.

Values for stamps blocks of 4

1	A1	1c	ol grn, *pale bl*	87.50	*190.00*
2	A1	5c	yel grn, *grnsh*	90.00	*165.00*
3	A1	10c	bister, *yel*	120.00	55.00
a.	Block, one sideways			—	—
4	A1	20c	bl, *bluish*	130.00	*150.00*
5	A1	40c	org, *yelsh*	100.00	100.00
6	A1	80c	car rose, *pnksh*	450.00	*475.00*

Napoleon III
A2 A3

Ceres
A4

Napoleon III
A5

1871-72 ***Imperf.***

7 A2 1c ol grn, *pale bl* ('72) 57.50 50.00
On cover 290.00
8 A3 5c yel grn, *grnsh* ('72) 825.00 350.00
On cover 1,650.
9 A4 10c bis, *yelsh* 300.00 110.00
On cover 350.00
a. Tête bêche pair *35,000.* *16,500.*
On cover *47,500.*
10 A4 15c bis, *yelsh* ('72) 275.00 11.00
On cover 57.50
11 A4 20c blue, *bluish* 425.00 100.00
On cover 450.00
a. Tête bêche pair *12,000.* —
On cover *30,000.*
12 A4 25c bl, *bluish* ('72) 140.00 11.00
On cover 80.00
13 A5 30c brn, *yelsh* 125.00 40.00
On cover 140.00
14 A4 40c org, *yelsh* (I) 210.00 11.00
On cover 47.50
a. Type II *2,750.* *500.00*
On cover *1,100.*
b. Pair, types I & II *5,750.* *1,400.*
On cover *3,250.*
c. Type II, pair *13,500.* *5,000.*
On cover *22,000.*
15 A5 80c rose, *pnksh* 850.00 92.50
On cover 450.00
Nos. 7-15 (9) 3,207. 775.50

For 40c types I-II see illustrations over France #1.

See note after France No. 9 for additional information on Nos. 8-9, 11-12, 14.

Values for stamps blocks of 4

7	A2	1c	ol grn, *pale bl*	260.00	450.00
8	A3	5c	yel grn, *grnsh*	6,250.	*6,750.*
9	A4	10c	bis, *yelsh*	1,500.	1,400.
a.	Tête bêche pair			—	—
10	A4	15c	bis, *yelsh*	1,400.	120.00
11	A4	20c	blue, *bluish*	2,100.	1,100.
a.	Tête bêche pair			—	—
12	A4	25c	bl, *bluish*	675.00	95.00
13	A5	30c	brn, *yelsh*	575.00	275.00
14	A4	40c	org, *yelsh* (I)	1,300.	425.00
a.	Type II			—	—
b.	Block, 1 type II			—	—
c.	Block, 2 type II			—	—
15	A5	80c	rose, *pnksh*	4,300.	2,250.

Ceres
A6 A7

1872-77 ***Imperf.***

16 A6 1c ol grn, *pale bl* ('73) 11.00 *12.00*
On cover 175.00
17 A6 2c red brn, *yelsh* ('76) 400.00 650.00
On cover *8,500.*
18 A6 4c gray ('76) *8,900.* 475.00
On cover *12,000.*
19 A6 5c grn, *pale bl* 12.00 8.00
On cover 29.00
20 A7 10c bis, *rose* ('76) 190.00 11.00
On cover 57.50
21 A7 15c bister ('77) 425.00 82.50
On cover 460.00
22 A7 30c brn, *yelsh* 90.00 17.50
On cover 57.50
23 A7 80c rose, *pnksh* ('73) 500.00 125.00
On cover 650.00

No. 17 was used only in Cochin China, 1876-77. Excellent forgeries of Nos. 17 and 18 exist.

With reference to the stamps of France and French Colonies in the same designs and colors see the note after France No. 9.

Values for stamps blocks of 4

16	A6	1c	ol grn, *pale bl*	50.00	77.50
17	A6	2c	red brn, *yelsh*	2,000.	
18	A6	4c	gray	—	
19	A6	5c	grn, *pale bl*	50.00	70.00
20	A7	10c	bis, *rose*	875.00	175.00
21	A7	15c	bister	2,250.	1,050.
22	A7	30c	brn, *yelsh*	400.00	150.00
23	A7	80c	rose, *pnksh*	2,400.	775.00

Peace and Commerce
A8

Commerce
A9

1877-78 **Type I** ***Imperf.***

24 A8 1c grn, *grnsh* 22.00 *32.50*
On cover 200.00
25 A8 4c grn, *grnsh* 14.50 14.50
On cover 75.00
26 A8 30c brn, *yelsh* ('78) 32.50 *42.50*
On cover 125.00
27 A8 40c ver, *straw* 21.00 18.00
On cover 80.00
28 A8 75c rose, *rose* ('78) 62.50 *72.50*
On cover 290.00
a. 75c carmine, *rose* 110.00 95.00
On cover 525.00
29 A8 1fr brnz grn, *straw* 37.50 16.00
On cover 100.00
Nos. 24-29 (6) 190.00 196.00

Type II

30 A8 2c grn, *grnsh* 11.00 8.50
On cover 62.50
31 A8 5c grn, *grnsh* 14.50 4.25
On cover 26.00
32 A8 10c grn, *grnsh* 72.50 10.50
On cover 62.50
33 A8 15c gray, *grnsh* 225.00 62.50
On cover 290.00
34 A8 20c red brn, *straw* 45.00 7.25
On cover 35.00
35 A8 25c ultra *bluish* 32.50 7.50
On cover 40.00
a. 25c blue, *bluish* ('78) *3,750.* 140.00
On cover *625.00*
36 A8 35c vio blk, *org* ('78) 40.00 22.50
On cover 150.00
Nos. 30-36 (7) 440.50 123.00
Nos. 24-36 (13) 630.50 319.00

Values for stamps blocks of 4

24	A8	1c	grn, *grnsh*	125.00	200.00
25	A8	4c	grn, *grnsh*	65.00	100.00
26	A8	30c	brn, *yelsh*	150.00	210.00
27	A8	40c	ver, *straw*	90.00	175.00
28	A8	75c	rose, *rose*	290.00	375.00
a.	75c carmine, *rose*			625.00	600.00
29	A8	1fr	brnz grn, *straw*	175.00	190.00

Type II

30	A8	2c	grn, *grnsh*	47.50	55.00
31	A8	5c	grn, *grnsh*	70.00	70.00
32	A8	10c	grn, *grnsh*	300.00	110.00
33	A8	15c	gray, *grnsh*	1,000.	1,000.
34	A8	20c	red brn, *straw*	240.00	110.00
35	A8	25c	ultra, *bluish*	150.00	70.00
a.	25c blue, *bluish*			—	2,750.
36	A8	35c	vio blk, *org*	200.00	210.00

1878-80

Type II

38	A8	1c blk, *lil bl*	14.00	14.00
		On cover		110.00
39	A8	2c brn, *buff*	14.00	*19.00*
		On cover		80.00
40	A8	4c claret, *lav*	21.00	21.00
		On cover		100.00
41	A8	10c blk, *lav* ('79)	90.00	19.00
		On cover		92.50
42	A8	15c blue ('79)	22.50	11.00
		On cover		57.50
43	A8	20c red, *grn* ('79)	62.50	11.00
		On cover		57.50
44	A8	25c blk, *red* ('79)	500.00	225.00
		On cover		1,100.
45	A8	25c yel, *straw* ('80)	600.00	25.00
		On cover		80.00
		Nos. 38-45 (8)	1,324.	345.00

No. 44 was used only in Mayotte, Nossi-Be and New Caledonia. Forgeries exist.

The 3c yellow, 3c gray, 15c yellow, 20c blue, 25c rose and 5fr lilac were printed together with the reprints, and were never issued.

Values for stamps blocks of 4

38	A8	1c	blk, *lil bl*	62.50	125.00
39	A8	2c	brn, *buff*	62.50	125.00
40	A8	4c	claret, *lav*	95.00	160.00
41	A8	10c	blk, *lav*	400.00	190.00
42	A8	15c	blue	110.00	150.00
43	A8	20c	red, *grn*	310.00	150.00
44	A8	25c	blk, *red*	*2,750.*	—
45	A8	25c	yel, *straw*	*3,250.*	350.00

1881-86 ***Perf. 14x13½***

46	A9	1c blk, *lil bl*	4.25	3.50
		On cover		20.00
47	A9	2c brn, *buff*	4.25	3.75
		On cover		19.00
48	A9	4c claret, *lav*	4.25	4.25
		On cover		19.00
49	A9	5c grn, *grnsh*	5.00	2.25
		On cover		12.50
50	A9	10c blk, *lavender*	8.50	3.75
		On cover		12.50
51	A9	15c blue	12.50	2.25
		On cover		11.50
52	A9	20c red, *yel grn*	42.50	15.00
		On cover		47.50
53	A9	25c yel, *straw*	11.00	4.25
		On cover		14.50
54	A9	25c blk, *rose* ('86)	14.50	2.25
		On cover		14.50
55	A9	30c brn, *bis*	32.50	18.00
		On cover		70.00
56	A9	35c vio blk, *yel org*	32.50	25.00
		On cover		110.00
a.		35c violet black, *yellow*	82.50	42.50
		On cover		125.00
57	A9	40c ver, *straw*	35.00	24.00
		On cover		110.00
58	A9	75c car, *rose*	100.00	50.00
		On cover		200.00
59	A9	1fr brnz grn, *straw*	62.50	37.50
		On cover		110.00
		Nos. 46-59 (14)	369.25	195.75

Nos. 46-59 exist imperforate. They are proofs and were not used for postage, except the 10c.

For stamps of type A9 surcharged with numerals see: Cochin China, Diego Suarez, Gabon, Malagasy (Madagascar), Nossi-Be, New Caledonia, Reunion, Senegal, Tahiti.

Values for stamps blocks of 4

46	A9	1c	blk, *lil bl*	20.00	65.00
47	A9	2c	brn, *buff*	20.00	65.00
48	A9	4c	claret, *lav*	20.00	70.00
49	A9	5c	grn, *grnsh*	24.00	35.00
50	A9	10c	blk, *lavender*	42.50	62.50
51	A9	15c	blue	57.50	62.50
52	A9	20c	red, *yel grn*	200.00	190.00
53	A9	25c	yel, *straw*	55.00	65.00
54	A9	25c	blk, *rose*	55.00	65.00
55	A9	30c	brn, *bis*	140.00	150.00
56	A9	35c	vio blk, *yel org*	150.00	190.00
a.		35c	violet black, *yellow*	375.00	375.00
57	A9	40c	ver, *straw*	160.00	200.00
58	A9	75c	car, *rose*	460.00	690.00
59	A9	1fr	brnz grn, *straw*	290.00	400.00

POSTAGE DUE STAMPS

D1

1884-85 **Unwmk.** **Typo.** ***Imperf.***

J1	D1	1c black	2.75	2.75
J2	D1	2c black	2.75	2.75
J3	D1	3c black	2.75	2.75
J4	D1	4c black	3.25	2.75
J5	D1	5c black	4.25	2.10
J6	D1	10c black	6.50	4.25
J7	D1	15c black	10.50	8.25
J8	D1	20c black	10.50	8.75
J9	D1	30c black	12.00	6.50
J10	D1	40c black	16.00	6.50
J11	D1	60c black	25.00	13.50
J12	D1	1fr brown	25.00	16.00
a.		1fr black	250.00	
J13	D1	2fr brown	22.00	16.00
a.		2fr black	250.00	
J14	D1	5fr brown	75.00	50.00
a.		5fr black	325.00	

Nos. J12a, J13a and J14a were not regularly issued.

1894-1906

J15	D1	5c pale blue	.80	.80
J16	D1	10c gray brown	.80	.80
J17	D1	15c pale green	.90	.90
J18	D1	20c olive grn ('06)	.90	.90
J19	D1	30c carmine	1.75	1.10
J20	D1	50c lilac	1.75	1.10
J21	D1	60c brown, *buff*	3.00	1.75
a.		60c dark violet, *buff*	4.00	2.10
J22	D1	1fr red, *buff*	4.25	3.25
a.		1fr rose, *buff*	18.00	15.00
		Nos. J15-J22 (8)	14.15	10.60

For overprints see New Caledonia Nos. J1-J8.

FRENCH CONGO

ˈfrench ˈkäŋ‚gō

LOCATION — Central Africa
GOVT. — French possession

French Congo was originally a separate colony, but was joined in 1888 to Gabon and placed under one commissioner-general with a lieutenant-governor presiding in Gabon and another in French Congo. In 1894 the military holdings in Ubangi were attached to French Congo, and in 1900 the Chad military protectorate was added. Postal service was not established in Ubangi or Chad, however, at that time. In 1906 Gabon and Middle Congo were separated and French Congo ceased to exist as such. Chad and Ubangi remained attached to Middle Congo as the joint dependency of "Ubangi-Chari-Chad," and Middle Congo stamps were used there.

100 Centimes = 1 Franc

Watermarks

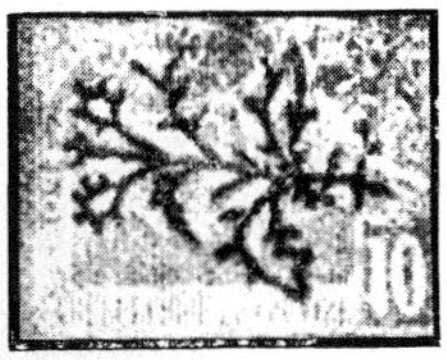

Wmk. 122 Thistle Branch

Wmk. 123 — Rose Branch

Wmk. 124 Olive Branch

Stamps of French Colonies Surcharged Horizontally in Red or Black

1891 **Unwmk.** ***Perf. 14x13½***

1	A9	5c on 1c blk, *lil bl* (R)	*5,100.*	*3,500.*
		On cover		*8,000.*
2	A9	5c on 1c blk, *lil bl*	140.00	72.50
		On cover		450.00
a.		Double surcharge	475.00	325.00
3	A9	5c on 15c blue	225.00	110.00
		On cover		450.00
a.		Double surcharge	525.00	250.00
5	A9	5c on 25c blk, *rose*	80.00	32.50
		On cover		450.00
a.		Inverted surcharge		

First "O" of "Congo" is a Capital, "Francais" with Capital "F"

1891-92

6	A9	5c on 20c red, *grn*	900.00	350.00
		On cover		600.00
7	A9	5c on 25c blk, *rose*	140.00	65.00
		On cover		450.00
a.		Surcharge vertical	190.00	60.00
8	A9	10c on 25c blk, *rose*	175.00	50.00
		On cover		450.00
a.		Inverted surcharge	325.00	110.00
b.		Surcharge vertical	150.00	72.50
c.		First "o" of "Congo" small		
d.		Double surcharge	300.00	140.00
9	A9	10c on 40c red, *straw*	1,900.	300.00
		On cover		600.00
10	A9	15c on 25c blk, *rose*	160.00	35.00
		On cover		450.00
a.		Surcharge vertical	190.00	57.50
b.		Inverted surcharge		
c.		Double surcharge	275.00	140.00

First "O" of Congo small
Surcharge Vert., Down or Up
No period

11	A9	5c on 25c blk, *rose*	200.00	85.00
		On cover		450.00
12	A9	10c on 25c blk, *rose*		—
13	A9	15c on 25c blk, *rose*	275.00	110.00
		On cover		500.00

Postage Due Stamps of French Colonies Surcharged in Red or Black Reading Down or Up

1892 ***Imperf.***

14	D1	5c on 5c blk (R)	125.00	100.00
		On cover		600.00
a.		Double surcharge	1,100.	
		On cover		675.00
15	D1	5c on 20c blk (R)	125.00	95.00
		On cover		675.00
16	D1	5c on 30c blk (R)	160.00	125.00
17	D1	10c on 1fr brown	125.00	95.00
a.		Double surcharge	3,250.	3,300.
b.		Surcharge horiz.		*1,800.*
c.		"Congo" omitted		*375.00*
		Nos. 14-17 (4)	535.00	415.00

Excellent counterfeits of Nos. 1-17 exist.

Navigation and Commerce — A3

1892-1900 **Typo.** ***Perf. 14x13½***

Colony Name in Blue or Carmine

18	A3	1c blk, *lil bl*	1.25	1.10
		On cover		75.00
19	A3	2c brn, *buff*	2.25	1.75
		On cover		75.00
a.		Name double	125.00	125.00
20	A3	4c claret, *lav*	2.25	2.10
		On cover		75.00
a.		Name in blk and in blue	125.00	125.00
21	A3	5c grn, *grnsh*	4.25	4.25
		On cover		60.00
22	A3	10c blk, *lavender*	16.50	14.00
		On cover		60.00
a.		Name double	625.00	450.00
23	A3	10c red ('00)	2.10	1.40
		On cover		45.00
24	A3	15c blue, quadrille paper	42.50	14.00
		On cover		60.00
25	A3	15c gray ('00)	7.50	5.00
		On cover		60.00
26	A3	20c red, *grn*	17.50	13.00
		On cover		125.00
27	A3	25c blk, *rose*	19.50	13.00
		On cover		90.00
28	A3	25c blue ('00)	8.50	8.00
		On cover		100.00
29	A3	30c brn, *bis*	22.50	15.00
		On cover		200.00
30	A3	40c red, *straw*	42.50	24.00
		On cover		200.00
31	A3	50c car, *rose*	37.50	23.00
		On cover		200.00
32	A3	50c brn, *az* ('00)	10.00	8.50
		On cover		275.00
a.		Name double	600.00	600.00
33	A3	75c dp vio, *org*	30.00	23.00
		On cover		300.00
34	A3	1fr brnz grn, *straw*	42.50	22.50
		On cover		450.00
		Nos. 18-34 (17)	309.10	193.60

Perf. 13½x14 stamps are counterfeits.
For surcharges see Nos. 50-51.

Leopard — A4

Bakalois Woman — A5

Coconut Grove — A6

1900 **Wmk. 122** ***Perf. 11***

35	A4	1c brn vio & gray lilac	.55	.55
		On cover		75.00
a.		Background inverted	62.50	62.50
36	A4	2c brn & org	.55	.55
		On cover		75.00
a.		2c dark red & red	140.00	*190.00*
b.		Imperf., pair	50.00	50.00
37	A4	4c scar & gray bl	1.10	.85
		On cover		75.00
a.		4c dark red & red	550.00	
b.		Background inverted	60.00	60.00
38	A4	5c grn & gray grn	2.00	.85
		On cover		60.00
a.		Imperf., pair	110.00	110.00
39	A4	10c dk red & red	5.50	2.25
		On cover		60.00
a.		Imperf., pair	110.00	110.00
40	A4	15c dl vio & ol grn	2.00	1.00
		On cover		60.00
a.		Imperf. pair	75.00	75.00

Wmk. 123

41	A5	20c yel grn & org	1.75	1.50
		On cover		75.00
42	A5	25c bl & pale bl	2.40	1.50
		On cover		75.00
43	A5	30c car rose & org	3.50	1.60
		On cover		100.00
44	A5	40c org brn & brt grn	4.25	2.00
		On cover		100.00
a.		Imperf., pair	75.00	75.00
b.		Center inverted	125.00	125.00
45	A5	50c gray vio & lil	5.50	5.00
		On cover		145.00
46	A5	75c red vio & org	11.00	6.50
		On cover		145.00
a.		Imperf., pair	75.00	75.00

Wmk. 124

47	A6	1fr gray lil & ol	17.50	12.00
		On cover		145.00
a.		Center inverted	225.00	225.00
b.		Imperf., pair	100.00	100.00
48	A6	2fr car & brn	30.00	20.00
		On cover		450.00
a.		Imperf., pair	200.00	200.00
49	A6	5fr brn org & gray	65.00	57.50
		On cover		*1,000.*
a.		5fr ocher & gray	650.00	*700.00*
b.		Center inverted	325.00	325.00
c.		Wmk. 123	325.00	225.00
d.		Imperf., pair	350.00	350.00
		Nos. 35-49 (15)	152.60	113.65

For surcharges see Nos. 52-53.

Nos. 26 and 29 Surcharged in Black

Valeur
15

1900 **Unwmk.** ***Perf. 14x13½***

50	A3	5c on 20c red, *grn*	*20,000.*	*5,000.*
a.		Double surcharge		*13,750.*
51	A3	15c on 30c brn, *bis*	*13,750.*	*2,000.*
a.		Double surcharge		*5,000.*

Nos. 43 and 48 Surcharged in Black:

a

0,40

b

1903		**Wmk. 123**		***Perf. 11***
52	A5	5c on 30c	225.00	110.00
		On cover		350.00
a.		Inverted surcharge	*2,150.*	

Wmk. 124

53	A6	10c on 2fr	275.00	90.00
		On cover		300.00
a.		Inverted surcharge	*2,200.*	
b.		Double surcharge	*2,400.*	

Counterfeits of the preceding surcharges are known.

FRENCH EQUATORIAL AFRICA

'french ,ē-kwə-'tōr-ē-əl 'a-fri-kə

LOCATION — North of Belgian Congo and south of Libya.
GOVT. — French Colony
AREA — 959,256 square miles
POP. — 4,491,785
CAPITAL — Brazzaville

In 1910 Gabon and Middle Congo, with its military dependencies, were politically united as French Equatorial Africa. The component colonies were granted administrative autonomy. In 1915 Ubangi-Chari-Chad was made an autonomous civilian colony and in 1920 Chad was made a civil colony. In 1934 the four colonies were administratively united as one colony, but this federation was not completed until 1936. Each colony had its own postal administration until 1936. The postal issues of the former colonial subdivisions are listed under the names of those colonies.

100 Centimes = 1 Franc

Stamps of Gabon, 1932, Overprinted "Afrique Equatoriale Francaise" and Bars Similar to "a" and "b" in Black

Perf. 13x13½, 13½x13

1936			**Unwmk.**	
1	A16	1c brown violet	.20	.20
2	A16	2c black, *rose*	.35	.35
3	A16	4c green	.85	.85
4	A16	5c grnsh blue	.95	.95
5	A16	10c red, *yel*	.85	.85
6	A17	40c brown violet	2.50	2.00
7	A17	50c red brown	1.90	1.50
8	A17	1fr yel grn, *bl*	22.50	10.00
9	A18	1.50fr dull blue	6.25	2.25
10	A18	2fr brown red	13.00	9.00
		Nos. 1-10 (10)	49.35	27.95

Stamps of Middle Congo, 1933 Overprinted in Black:

a

b

c

1936				
11	A4 (b)	1c lt brown	.20	.20
12	A4 (b)	2c dull blue	.20	.20
13	A4 (b)	4c olive green	1.10	1.10
14	A4 (b)	5c red violet	.65	.65
15	A4 (b)	10c slate	1.10	.70
16	A4 (b)	15c dk violet	1.50	1.10
17	A4 (b)	20c red, *pink*	1.50	1.00
18	A4 (b)	25c orange	2.40	1.60
19	A5 (a)	40c orange brn	3.25	1.75
20	A5 (c)	50c black violet	3.25	2.25
21	A5 (c)	75c black, *pink*	4.00	3.25
22	A5 (a)	90c carmine	4.00	2.50
23	A5 (c)	1.50fr dark blue	2.50	1.50
24	A6 (a)	5fr slate blue	42.50	22.50
25	A6 (a)	10fr black	25.00	16.00
26	A6 (a)	20fr dark brown	22.50	20.00
		Nos. 11-26 (16)	115.65	76.30

Common Design Types pictured following the introduction.

Paris International Exposition Issue
Common Design Types

1937, Apr. 15		**Engr.**		***Perf. 13***
27	CD74	20c dark violet	1.75	1.75
28	CD75	30c dark green	1.75	1.75
29	CD76	40c carmine rose	1.75	1.75
30	CD77	50c dk brn & bl	1.40	1.40
31	CD78	90c red	2.00	2.00
32	CD79	1.50fr ultra	2.00	2.00
		Nos. 27-32 (6)	10.65	10.65

Logging on Loéme River — A1

People of Chad — A2

Pierre Savorgnan de Brazza A3

Emile Gentil — A4

Paul Crampel A5

Governor Victor Liotard A6

Two types of 25c:
Type I — Wide numerals (4mm).
Type II — Narrow numerals (3½mm).

1937-40		**Photo.**		***Perf. 13½x13***
33	A1	1c brown & yel	.20	.20
34	A1	2c violet & grn	.20	.20
35	A1	3c blue & yel ('40)	.20	.20
36	A1	4c magenta & bl	.20	.20
37	A1	5c dk & lt green	.40	.20
38	A2	10c magenta & blue	.25	.20
39	A2	15c blue & buff	.25	.20
40	A2	20c brown & yellow	.40	*.55*
41	A2	25c cop red & bl (I)	.65	.20
a.		Type II	2.25	1.60
42	A3	30c gray grn & grn	.65	.45
43	A3	30c chlky bl, ind & buff ('40)	.30	.30
44	A2	35c dp grn & yel ('38)	.80	.55
45	A3	40c cop red & bl	.30	.25
46	A3	45c dk bl & lt grn	3.75	3.00
47	A3	45c dp grn & yel grn ('40)	.45	.45
48	A3	50c brown & yellow	.30	.20
49	A3	55c pur & bl ('38)	.65	.55
50	A3	60c mar & gray bl ('40)	.50	.50
51	A4	65c dk bl & lt grn	.65	.30
52	A4	70c dp vio & buff ('40)	.55	.55
53	A4	75c ol blk & dl yel	4.50	3.75
54	A4	80c brn & yel ('38)	.45	.45
55	A4	90c copper red & buff	.45	.30
56	A4	1fr dk vio & lt grn	1.75	.85
57	A3	1fr cer & dl org ('38)	2.50	.95
58	A4	1fr bl grn & sl grn ('40)	.45	*.45*
59	A5	1.25fr cop red & buff	1.00	.65
60	A5	1.40fr dk brn & pale grn ('40)	.90	.90
61	A5	1.50fr dk & lt blue	1.25	.50
62	A5	1.60fr dp vio & buff ('40)	.80	.80
63	A5	1.75fr brn & yel	1.50	.65
64	A4	1.75fr bl & lt bl ('38)	.55	.45
65	A5	2fr dk & lt green	.85	.55
66	A6	2.15fr brn, vio & yel ('38)	.65	.50
67	A6	2.25fr bl & lt bl ('39)	1.25	1.25
68	A6	2.50fr rose lake & buff ('40)	.90	.90
69	A6	3fr dk blue & buff	.60	.25
70	A6	5fr dk & lt green	1.25	.75
71	A6	10fr dk violet & bl	2.75	2.00
72	A6	20fr ol blk & dl yel	3.00	2.50
		Nos. 33-72 (40)	39.00	28.65

For overprints and surcharges see Nos. 80-127, 129-141, B2-B3, B10-B13, B22-B23.

Colonial Arts Exhibition Issue
Souvenir Sheet
Common Design Type

1937				***Imperf.***
73	CD79	3fr red brown	11.00	*12.00*
		Never hinged	15.00	

Count Louis Edouard Bouet-Willaumez and His Ship "La Malouine" — A7

1938, Dec. 5				***Perf. 13½***
74	A7	65c gray brown	.90	.90
75	A7	1fr deep rose	1.10	1.10
76	A7	1.75fr blue	1.25	1.25
77	A7	2fr dull violet	1.50	1.50
		Nos. 74-77 (4)	4.75	4.75
		Set, never hinged	8.50	

Centenary of Gabon.

New York World's Fair Issue
Common Design Type

1939, May 10		**Engr.**		***Perf. 12½x12***
78	CD82	1.25fr carmine lake	1.25	1.25
79	CD82	2.25fr ultra	1.25	1.25
		Set, never hinged	5.00	

Stamps of 1936-40, Overprinted in Carmine or Black:

Nos. 80-82, 84-88, 93

Nos. 83, 89-92, 94-125

1940-41				***Perf. 13½x13***
80	A1	1c brn & yel (C)	1.25	1.25
81	A1	2c vio & grn (C)	1.25	1.25
82	A1	3c blue & yel (C)	1.25	1.25
83	A4	4c ol grn (No. 13)	10.00	8.50
84	A1	5c dk grn & lt grn (C)	1.25	1.25
85	A2	10c magenta & bl	1.75	1.75
86	A2	15c blue & buff (C)	1.50	1.50
87	A2	20c brn & yel (C)	1.50	1.50
88	A2	25c cop red & bl	7.00	7.00
89	A3	30c gray grn & grn (C)	14.50	9.25
90	A3	30c gray grn & grn ('41)	2.25	2.25
91	A3	30c chlky bl, ind & buff (C) ('41)	7.25	6.00
92	A3	30c chlky bl, ind & buff ('41)	9.50	8.50
93	A2	35c dp grn & yel (C)	1.60	1.60
94	A3	40c cop red & bl	1.10	1.10
95	A3	45c dp grn & yel grn (C)	.85	.65
96	A3	45c dp grn & yel grn ('41)	1.10	1.10
97	A3	50c brn & yel (C)	5.75	4.75
98	A3	50c brn & yel ('41)	4.75	4.75
99	A3	55c pur & bl (C)	.85	.80
100	A3	55c pur & bl ('41)	1.10	1.10
101	A3	60c mar & gray bl	.80	.80
102	A4	65c dk bl & lt grn	.80	.80
103	A4	70c dp vio & buff	.80	.80
104	A4	75c ol blk & dl yel	45.00	45.00
105	A4	80c brown & yellow	.80	.80
106	A4	90c cop red & buff	1.00	1.00
107	A4	1fr bl grn & sl grn	7.25	7.25
108	A4	1fr bl grn & sl grn (C) ('41)	4.50	4.00
109	A3	1fr cer & dl org	2.00	2.00
110	A5	1.40fr dk brn & pale grn	.80	.80
111	A5	1.50fr dk bl & lt bl	.80	.80
112	A5	1.60fr dp vio & buff	.80	.80
113	A5	1.75fr brown & yel	1.40	1.40
114	A6	2.15fr brn, vio & yel	1.25	1.25
115	A6	2.25fr bl & lt bl (C)	.85	.85
116	A6	2.25fr bl & lt bl ('41)	2.50	2.50
117	A6	2.50fr rose lake & buff	.85	.85
118	A6	3fr dk bl & buff (C)	1.25	1.25
119	A6	3fr dk bl & buff ('41)	2.75	2.75
120	A6	5fr dk grn & lt grn (C)	3.00	3.00
121	A6	5fr dk grn & lt grn ('41)	90.00	50.00
122	A6	10fr dk vio & bl (C)	2.00	2.00
123	A6	10fr dk vio & bl ('41)	72.50	50.00
124	A6	20fr ol blk & dl yel (C)	1.75	1.75
125	A6	20fr ol blk & dl yel ('41)	11.50	10.00
		Nos. 80-125 (46)	334.30	259.55

For overprints and surcharges see Nos. 129-132, B12-B13, B22-B23.

Double Overprint

94a	A3	40c	21.00
96a	A3	45c	25.00
98a	A3	50c	25.00
100a	A3	55c	25.00
102a	A4	65c	21.00
103a	A4	70c	25.00
105a	A4	80c	25.00
106a	A4	90c	21.00
b.		one inverted	85.00
109a	A4	1fr One inverted	85.00
110a	A5	1.40fr	25.00
111a	A5	1.50fr	25.00
114a	A6	2.15fr	18.00
115a	A6	2.25fr	25.00
116a	A6	2.25fr	25.00
117a	A6	2.50fr	25.00
119a	A6	3fr	25.00
123a	A6	10fr	25.00
124a	A6	20fr	25.00
		Nos. 96a-124a (17)	470.00

Nos. 48, 51 Surcharged in Black or Carmine

1940				
126	A3	75c on 50c	.55	.55
a.		Double surcharge	25.00	
127	A4	1fr on 65c (C)	.55	.55
a.		Double surcharge	18.00	
		Set, never hinged	4.50	

Middle Congo No. 67 Overprinted in Carmine like No. 80

Perf. 13½

128	A4	4c olive green	45.00	37.50

Stamps of 1940 With Additional Overprint in Black

1940 *Perf. 13½x13*

129	A4	80c brown & yel	12.50	10.00
a.		Overprint without "2"	110.00	
130	A4	1fr bl grn & sl grn	12.50	10.00
131	A3	1fr cer & dull org	12.50	10.00
132	A5	1.50fr dk bl & lt bl	12.50	10.00
		Nos. 129-132 (4)	50.00	40.00
		Set, never hinged	80.00	

Arrival of General de Gaulle in Brazzaville, capital of Free France, Oct. 24, 1940.

These stamps were sold affixed to post cards and at a slight increase over face value to cover the cost of the cards.

For surcharges see Nos. B12-B13, B22-B23.

SEMI-POSTAL STAMPS

Common Design Type

1938, Oct. 24 **Engr.**

B1	CD80	1.75fr + 50c brt ultra	18.00	18.00
		Never hinged	27.50	

Nos. 51, 64 Surcharged in Black or Red

1938, Nov. 7 *Perf. 13x13½*

B2	A4	65c + 35c dk bl & lt grn (R)	1.60	1.60
B3	A4	1.75fr + 50c bl & lt bl	1.60	1.60
		Set, never hinged	6.00	

The surtax was for welfare.

French Revolution Issue

Common Design Type

Name and Value Typo. in Black

1939, July 5 **Photo.**

B4	CD83	45c + 25c green	12.00	12.00
B5	CD83	70c + 30c brown	12.00	12.00
B6	CD83	90c + 35c red org	12.00	12.00
B7	CD83	1.25fr + 1fr rose pink	12.00	12.00
B8	CD83	2.25fr + 2fr blue	12.00	12.00
		Nos. B4-B8 (5)	60.00	60.00
		Set, never hinged	85.00	

Surtax used for the defense of the colonies.

AIR POST STAMPS

Hydroplane over Pointe-Noire — AP1

Trimotor over Stanley Pool — AP2

1937 **Unwmk.** **Photo.** *Perf. 13½*

C1	AP1	1.50fr ol blk & yel	.20	.20
C2	AP1	2fr mag & blue	.35	.35
C3	AP1	2.50fr grn & buff	.35	.35
C4	AP1	3.75fr brn & lt grn	.55	.55
C5	AP2	4.50fr cop red & bl	.55	.55
C6	AP2	6.50fr bl & lt grn	1.10	1.10
C7	AP2	8.50fr red brn & yel	1.25	1.25
C8	AP2	10.75fr vio & lt grn	1.25	1.25
		Nos. C1-C8 (8)	5.60	5.60

For overprints and surcharges see #C9-C16, CB2.

Nos. C1, C3-C7 Overprinted in Black like Nos. 133-141

1940-41

C9	AP1	1.50fr ('41)	175.00	175.00
C10	AP1	2.50fr	1.40	1.40
C11	AP1	3.75fr ('41)	175.00	175.00
C12	AP2	4.50fr	1.75	1.75
C13	AP2	6.50fr	2.50	2.50
C14	AP2	8.50fr	1.40	1.40

No. C8 Surcharged in Carmine

C15	AP2	50fr on 10.75fr	7.50	7.50

No. C3 Surcharged in Black

C16	AP1	10fr on 2.50fr ('41)	65.00	65.00
		Nos. C9-C16 (8)	429.55	429.55

Counterfeits of Nos. C9 and C11 exist. See note following No. 141.

POSTAGE DUE STAMPS

Numeral of Value on Equatorial Butterfly — D1

1937 **Unwmk.** **Photo.** *Perf. 13*

J1	D1	5c redsh pur & lt bl	.20	.20
J2	D1	10c cop red & buff	.20	.20
J3	D1	20c dk grn & grn	.25	.20
J4	D1	25c red brn & buff	.25	.20
J5	D1	30c cop red & lt bl	.35	.35
J6	D1	45c mag & yel grn	.50	.50
J7	D1	50c dk ol grn & buff	.50	.50
J8	D1	60c redsh pur & yel	.65	.65
J9	D1	1fr brown & yel	.80	.80
J10	D1	2fr dk bl & buff	1.40	1.00
J11	D1	3fr red brn & lt grn	1.50	1.10
		Nos. J1-J11 (11)	6.60	5.70
		Set, never hinged	10.00	

FRENCH GUIANA

ˈfrench gē-ˈa-nə

LOCATION — On the northeast coast of South America bordering on the Atlantic Ocean.
GOVT. — French colony
AREA — 34,740 sq. mi.
POP. — 28,537 (1946)
CAPITAL — Cayenne

100 Centimes = 1 Franc

Stamps of French Colonies Surcharged in Black

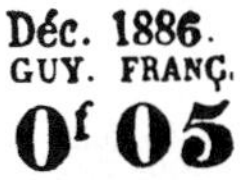

1886, Dec. **Unwmk.** *Imperf.*

1	A8	5c on 2c grn, *grnsh*	575.00	500.00
b.		No "f" after "O"	725.00	675.00

Perf. 14x13½

2	A9	5c on 2c brn, *buff*	450.00	450.00
b.		No "f" after "O"	400.00	350.00

Two types of No. 1: Surcharge 12mm high, and surcharge 10½mm high.

"Av" of Date Line Inverted-Reversed

1887, Apr. *Imperf.*

4	A8	20c on 35c blk, *org*	50.00	40.00

Date Line Reads "Avril 1887"

5	A8	5c on 2c grn, *grnsh*	110.00	95.00
6	A8	20c on 35c blk, *org*	250.00	210.00
7	A7	25c on 30c brn, *yelsh*	35.00	29.00
		On cover		*2,500.*

Variety "small f omitted" occurs on #5-7.

French Colonies Nos. 22 and 26 Surcharged

8	A7	5c on 30c brn, *yelsh*	115.00	110.00
a.		Double surcharge	575.00	575.00
b.		Inverted surcharge	850.00	850.00
c.		Pair, one without surcharge	1,150.	
9	A8	5c on 30c brn, *yelsh*	1,100.	1,100.

French Colonies Nos. 22 and 28 Surcharged:

1888

10	A7	5c on 30c brn, *yelsh*	110.00	90.00
		On cover		*3,000.*
b.		Double surcharge	575.00	575.00
c.		Inverted surcharge	425.00	400.00
11	A8	10c on 75c car, *rose*	250.00	250.00

Stamps of French Colonies Overprinted in Black

1892, Feb. 20 *Imperf.*

12	A8	2c grn, *grnsh*	650.00	725.00
		On cover		*4,000.*
a.		Inverted overprint	2,600.	
13	A7	30c brn, *yelsh*	115.00	115.00
a.		Inverted overprint	450.00	425.00
14	A8	35c blk, *orange*	*2,100.*	*2,100.*
15	A8	40c red, *straw*	110.00	110.00
16	A8	75c car, *rose*	115.00	110.00
a.		Inverted overprint	350.00	350.00
17	A8	1fr brnz grn, *straw*	130.00	125.00
a.		Inverted overprint	600.00	525.00
b.		Double overprint	600.00	525.00

1892 *Perf. 14x13½*

18	A9	1c blk, *lil bl*	35.00	27.50
		On cover		900.00
19	A9	2c brn, *buff*	32.50	30.00
		On cover		900.00
20	A9	4c claret, *lav*	30.00	30.00
		On cover		900.00
21	A9	5c grn, *grnsh*	32.50	27.50
		On cover		600.00
a.		Inverted overprint	92.50	
b.		Double overprint	92.50	
22	A9	10c blk, *lavender*	55.00	35.00
		On cover		500.00
a.		Inverted overprint	125.00	125.00
23	A9	15c blue	45.00	32.50
		On cover		400.00
24	A9	20c red, *grn*	40.00	32.50
		On cover		900.00
25	A9	25c blk, *rose*	65.00	30.00
		On cover		400.00
26	A9	30c brn, *bis*	32.50	29.00
		On cover		800.00
27	A9	35c blk, *orange*	175.00	175.00
		On cover		900.00
28	A9	40c red, *straw*	100.00	100.00
		On cover		900.00
a.		Inverted overprint	175.00	175.00
29	A9	75c car, *rose*	110.00	77.50
		On cover		900.00
30	A9	1fr brnz grn, *straw*	180.00	160.00
		On cover		—
		Nos. 18-30 (13)	932.50	786.50

French Colonies No. 51 Surcharged

1892, Dec.

31	A9	5c on 15c blue	42.50	29.00

Navigation and Commerce — A12

1892-1904 **Typo.** *Perf. 14x13½*

Name of Colony in Blue or Carmine

32	A12	1c blk, *lil bl*	1.50	1.00
		On cover		60.00
33	A12	2c brn, *buff*	1.00	.90
		On cover		60.00
34	A12	4c claret, *lav*	1.50	1.10
		On cover		60.00
a.		"GUYANE" double	175.00	
35	A12	5c grn, *grnsh*	8.50	7.50
		On cover		40.00
36	A12	5c yel grn ('04)	1.50	.70
		On cover		30.00
37	A12	10c blk, *lavender*	9.75	5.75
		On cover		40.00
38	A12	10c red ('00)	3.25	1.00
		On cover		40.00
39	A12	15c blue, quadrille paper	27.50	2.50
		On cover		40.00
40	A12	15c gray, *lt gray* ('00)	100.00	67.50
		On cover		180.00
41	A12	20c red, *grn*	18.00	11.00
		On cover		130.00
42	A12	25c blk, *rose*	16.00	3.25
		On cover		60.00
43	A12	25c blue ('00)	13.00	13.00
		On cover		75.00
44	A12	30c brn, *bis*	17.00	11.00
		On cover		275.00
45	A12	40c red, *straw*	17.00	12.00
		On cover		300.00
46	A12	50c car, *rose*	25.00	13.00
		On cover		300.00
47	A12	50c brn, *az* ('00)	20.00	16.00
		On cover		400.00
48	A12	75c dp vio, *org*	30.00	16.00
		On cover		550.00
49	A12	1fr brn grn, *straw*	12.50	10.50
		On cover		900.00
50	A12	2fr vio, *rose* ('02)	140.00	7.50
		On cover		2,000.
		Nos. 32-50 (19)	463.00	201.20

Perf. 13½x14 stamps are counterfeits.
For surcharges see Nos. 87-93.

Great Anteater — A13

Washing Gold — A14

Palm Grove at Cayenne A15

1905-28

51	A13	1c black	.30	.30
52	A13	2c blue	.30	.30
53	A13	4c red brn	.30	.30
54	A13	5c green	.90	.65
55	A13	5c org ('22)	.25	.25
56	A13	10c rose	1.00	.65
57	A13	10c grn ('22)	.50	.35
58	A13	10c red, *bluish* ('25)	.35	.35
59	A13	15c violet	1.10	.90
60	A14	20c red brn	.45	.35
61	A14	25c blue	2.00	1.25
62	A14	25c vio ('22)	.55	.50
63	A14	30c black	1.40	.60
64	A14	30c rose ('22)	.40	.40
65	A14	30c red org ('25)	.25	.25
66	A14	30c dk grn, *grnsh* ('28)	1.00	1.00
67	A14	35c blk, *yel* ('06)	.35	.30
68	A14	40c rose	.65	.60
69	A14	40c black ('22)	.25	.25
70	A14	45c olive ('07)	.70	.60
71	A14	50c violet	3.00	2.25
72	A14	50c blue ('22)	.45	.40
73	A14	50c gray ('25)	.65	.40
74	A14	60c lil, *rose* ('25)	.55	.50
75	A14	65c myr grn ('26)	.75	.60
76	A14	75c green	1.25	.80

77 A14 85c magenta ('26) .60 .60
78 A15 1fr rose .75 .75
79 A15 1fr bl, *bluish* ('25) .80 .70
80 A15 1fr bl, *yel grn* ('28) 2.25 2.25
81 A15 1.10fr lt red ('28) 1.25 1.25
82 A15 2fr blue 1.00 1.00
83 A15 2fr org red, *yel* ('26) 2.25 1.50
84 A15 5fr black 5.50 4.00
85 A15 10fr grn, *yel* ('24) 11.00 10.00
a. Printed on both sides 42.50 42.50
86 A15 20fr brn lake ('24) 14.00 13.00
Nos. 51-86 (36) 59.05 50.15

For surcharges see Nos. 94-108, B1-B2.

Issue of 1892 Surcharged in Black or Carmine

1912

Spacing between figures of surcharge 1.5mm (5c), 2mm (10c)

87 A12 5c on 2c brn, *buff* .75 .75
On cover 90.00
88 A12 5c on 4c cl, *lav* (C) .75 .75
On cover 90.00
89 A12 5c on 20c red, *grn* 1.00 1.00
On cover 90.00
90 A12 5c on 25c blk, *rose* (C) 3.00 3.00
On cover 120.00
91 A12 5c on 30c brn, *bis* (C) .95 .95
On cover 90.00
92 A12 10c on 40c red, *straw* .75 .75
On cover 90.00
a. Pair, one stamp without urcharge 875.00
93 A12 10c on 50c car, *rose* 3.00 3.00
On cover 120.00
a. Double surcharge 400.00
Nos. 87-93 (7) 10.20 10.20

Spacing between figures of surcharge 2.25mm (5c), 2.75mm (10c)

87a A12 5c on 2c brn, *buff* 17.00 17.00
88a A12 5c on 4c cl, *lav* (C) 10.00 10.00
89a A12 5c on 20c red, *grn* 17.00 17.00
90a A12 5c on 25c blk, *rose* (C) 25.00 25.00
91a A12 5c on 30c brn, *bis* (C) 17.00 17.00
92b A12 10c on 40c red, *straw* 110.00 110.00
93b A12 10c on 50c car, *rose* 225.00 225.00
Nos. 87a-93b (7) 421.00 421.00

No. 59 Surcharged in Various Colors

1922

94 A13 1c on 15c vio (Bk) .45 .45
95 A13 2c on 15c vio (Bl) .45 .45
a. Inverted surcharge 65.00
96 A13 4c on 15c vio (G) .45 .45
a. Double surcharge 57.50
97 A13 5c on 15c vio (R) .45 .45
Nos. 94-97 (4) 1.80 1.80

Type of 1905-28 Surcharged in Blue

1923

98 A15 10fr on 1fr grn, *yel* 16.00 16.00
99 A15 20fr on 5fr lilac, *rose* 16.00 16.00

Stamps and Types of 1905-28 Surcharged with New Value and Bars in Black or Red

1924-27

100 A13 25c on 15c vio ('25) .50 .50
101 A15 25c on 2fr bl ('24) .60 .60
a. Double surcharge 100.00
b. Triple surcharge 110.00
102 A14 65c on 45c ol (R) ('25) 1.10 1.10
103 A14 85c on 45c ol (R) ('25) 1.10 1.10
104 A14 90c on 75c red ('27) .95 .95
105 A15 1.05fr on 2fr lt yel brn ('27) .95 .95
106 A15 1.25fr on 1fr ultra (R) ('26) 1.10 1.10
107 A15 1.50fr on 1fr lt bl ('27) 1.10 1.10
108 A15 3fr on 5fr vio ('27) 1.25 1.25
a. No period after "F" 8.50 8.50
Nos. 100-108 (9) 8.65 8.65

Carib Archer — A16

Shooting Rapids, Maroni River A17

Government Building, Cayenne — A18

1929-40 ***Perf. 13½x14***

109 A16 1c gray lil & grnsh bl .20 .20
110 A16 2c dk red & bl grn .20 .20
111 A16 3c gray lil & grnsh bl ('40) .20 .20
112 A16 4c ol brn & red vio .20 .20
113 A16 5c Prus bl & red org .20 .20
114 A16 10c mag & brn .25 .25
115 A16 15c yel brn & red org .25 .25
116 A16 20c dk bl & ol grn .25 .25
117 A16 25c dk red & dk brn .40 .40

Perf. 14x13½

118 A17 30c dl & lt grn .50 .50
119 A17 30c grn & brn ('40) .30 .30
120 A17 35c Prus grn & ol grn ('38) .75 .75
121 A17 40c org brn & ol gray .25 .25
122 A17 45c grn & dk brn .75 .75
123 A17 45c ol grn & lt grn ('40) .55 .55
124 A17 50c dk bl & ol gray .30 .30
125 A17 55c vio bl & car ('38) 1.25 1.25
126 A17 60c sal & grn ('40) .50 .50
127 A17 65c sal & grn .75 .75
128 A17 70c ind & sl bl ('40) .90 .90
129 A17 75c ind & sl bl .90 .90
130 A17 80c blk & vio bl ('38) .70 .70
131 A17 90c dk red & ver .75 .75
132 A17 90c red vio & brn ('39) .80 .80
133 A17 1fr lt vio & brn .50 .50
134 A17 1fr car & lt red ('38) 1.75 1.75
135 A17 1fr blk & vio bl ('40) .55 .55

136 A18 1.05fr ver & olivine 4.75 4.50
137 A18 1.10fr ol brn & red vio 5.25 4.00
138 A18 1.25fr blk brn & bl grn ('33) .65 .65
139 A18 1.25fr rose & lt red ('39) .70 .70
140 A18 1.40fr ol brn & red vio ('40) .90 .90
141 A18 1.50fr dk bl & lt bl .35 .35
142 A18 1.60fr ol brn & bl grn ('40) .90 .90
143 A18 1.75fr brn red & blk brn ('33) 1.90 1.75
144 A18 1.75fr vio bl ('38) 1.40 .75
145 A18 2fr dk grn & rose red .50 .50
146 A18 2.25fr vio bl ('39) .90 .90
147 A18 2.50fr cop red & brn ('40) 1.00 1.00
148 A18 3fr brn red & red vio .70 .70
149 A18 5fr dl vio & yel grn 1.00 1.00
150 A18 10fr ol gray & dp ultra 1.25 1.25
151 A18 20fr indigo & ver 1.75 1.75
Nos. 109-151 (43) 38.80 36.50

Common Design Types pictured following the introduction.

Colonial Exposition Issue

Common Design Types

1931 **Engr.** ***Perf. 12½***

Name of Country in Black

152 CD70 40c dp green 4.50 4.50
153 CD71 50c violet 4.50 4.50
154 CD72 90c red orange 4.50 4.50
155 CD73 1.50fr dull blue 4.50 4.50
Nos. 152-155 (4) 18.00 18.00

Recapture of Cayenne by d'Estrées, 1676 — A19

Products of French Guiana A20

1935, Oct. 21 ***Perf. 13***

156 A19 40c gray brn 3.50 3.50
157 A19 50c dull red 7.25 5.75
158 A19 1.50fr ultra 3.50 3.50
159 A20 1.75fr lilac rose 9.50 8.50
160 A20 5fr brown 7.25 7.25
161 A20 10fr blue green 7.25 7.25
Nos. 156-161 (6) 38.25 35.75

Tercentenary of the founding of French possessions in the West Indies.

Paris International Exposition Issue

Common Design Types

1937, Apr. 15

162 CD74 20c deep violet 1.15 1.15
163 CD75 30c dark green 1.15 1.15
164 CD76 40c carmine rose 1.15 1.15
165 CD77 50c dark brown 1.25 1.25
166 CD78 90c red 1.25 1.25
167 CD79 1.50fr ultra 1.40 1.40
Nos. 162-167 (6) 7.35 7.35

Colonial Arts Exhibition Issue

Souvenir Sheet

Common Design Type

1937 ***Imperf.***

168 CD75 3fr violet 8.00 *10.00*

New York World's Fair Issue

Common Design Type

1939, May 10 **Engr.** ***Perf. 12½x12***

169 CD82 1.25fr car lake .95 .95
170 CD82 2.25fr ultra .95 .95

SEMI-POSTAL STAMPS

Regular Issue of 1905-28 Surcharged in Red

1915 **Unwmk.** ***Perf. 13½x14***

B1 A13 10c + 5c rose 12.00 12.00
On cover 90.00
a. Inverted surcharge 190.00 190.00
b. Double surcharge 190.00 190.00

Regular Issue of 1905-28 Surcharged in Rose

B2 A13 10c + 5c rose .95 .95
On cover 90.00

Curie Issue

Common Design Type

1938 ***Perf. 13***

B3 CD80 1.75fr + 50c brt ultra 10.00 10.00

French Revolution Issue

Common Design Type

1939 **Photo.**

Name and Value in Black

B4 CD83 45c + 25c green 9.25 9.25
B5 CD83 70c + 30c brown 9.25 9.25
B6 CD83 90c + 35c red org 9.25 9.25
B7 CD83 1.25fr + 1fr rose pink 9.25 9.25
B8 CD83 2.25fr + 2fr blue 9.25 9.25
Nos. B4-B8 (5) 46.25 46.25

AIR POST STAMPS

Cayenne AP1

Perf. 13½

1933, Nov. 20 **Unwmk.** **Photo.**

C1 AP1 50c orange brn .20 .20
C2 AP1 1fr yellow grn .35 .35
C3 AP1 1.50fr dk blue .50 .50
C4 AP1 2fr orange .50 .50
C5 AP1 3fr black .65 .65
C6 AP1 5fr violet .65 .65
C7 AP1 10fr olive grn .65 .65
C8 AP1 20fr scarlet .80 .80
Nos. C1-C8 (8) 4.30 4.30

AIR POST SEMI-POSTAL STAMP

French Revolution Issue

Common Design Type

Unwmk.

1939, July 5 **Photo.** ***Perf. 13***

Name & Value Typo. in Orange

CB1 CD83 5fr + 4fr brn blk 16.00 16.00

SOCIETE DE TRANSPORTS AERIENS GUYANAIS

During 1920-22, a pioneering airline, *La Société des Transports Aériens Guyanais* maintained service between Cayenne, Saint Laurent du Maroni and Inini, with less regular flights to Paramaribo, Surinam. During July-Oct. 1921, T.A.G. produced stamps to prepay the 75c internal airmail fee, under contract with the postal authorities. After October, these stamps were replaced by regular French Guiana issues.

Nos CL1-CL15 were issued without gum.

APSO1

1921, July 8 ***Imperf.***

CL1 APSO1 75c red violet, *bluish* 1,250. 1,100.
On cover *2,750.*
Block of 4 *5,500.* *5,500.*

1921, July 9 ***Pin-Perf***

CL2 APSO1 75c red violet, *orange brown* 2,600. 1,650.
On cover 2,500.
Block of 4 6,750. 6,750.

Nos CL1-CL2 were for use on the St. Laurent du Maroni-Cayenne Route. Used examples were usually cancelled by a manuscript signature in red ink.

All stamps were overprinted in red violet with a large oval inscribed "Societe Des Transports Aeriens Guyanais" on the front, and by a similar overprint, inscribed "St. Laurent du Maroni" on the reverse. Because the overprint covers four stamps, each individual stamp shows approximately one-fourth of the oval.

An unused single of No. CL1 realized the equivalent of U.S. $1,070 in a June, 2005, Paris auction. A used example of No. CL1 realized the equivalent of U.S. $1,090 in a May, 2006, Paris auction. A single example on cover realized the equivalent of U.S. $2,410 in a June, 2005, Paris auction.

An unused example of No. CL2 realized the equivalent of U.S. $2,295 in a May, 2006, Paris auction.

APSO2

1921, July 8 ***Imperf.***

CL3	APSO2 75c black, *grayish*	1,000.	500.00
	On cover		1,000.
	Tête-bche pair	*11,000.*	*6,250.*
CL4	APSO2 75c black, *bluish*	1,000.	550.00
	On cover		1,000.
	Tête-bche pair	*11,000.*	*7,250.*
CL5	APSO2 75c black, *salmon*	850.00	550.00
	On cover		1,100.

For flights from Cayene, St. Laurent du Maroni and return. Flown letters bearing Nos. CL3-CL15 were cancelled "Avion"

Because the letters "T.A.G." and the denomination "0.75" were printed separately from the rest of the design, their position on the stamp varies.

APSO3

1921, Sept.

Two dies: type I, lower part of right frame line straight; type II, lower part of right frame line curved outward. There are many minor differences between the two dies, but the angle of the frame line is sufficient for identification.

CL6	APSO3 75c black, *gray* (I)	950.00	675.00
	On cover		1,100.
	Tête-bche pair	*11,000.*	*11,000.*
CL7	APSO3 75c black, *bluish* (I)	1,100.	850.00
	On cover		1,350.
	Tête-bche pair	*11,000.*	*11,000.*
CL8	APSO3 75c black, *salmon* (I)	*11,000.*	
CL9	APSO3 75c black, *rose* (II)	800.00	800.00
	On cover		1,450.

For flights from Cayenne to St. Laurent du Maroni and return and from St. Laurent du Maroni to Inini and return.

APSO4

1921, Sept.

CL10	APSO4 75c black, *gray*	2,750.	2,750.
	On cover		*3,500.*
CL11	APSO4 75c black, *bluish*	2,750.	
CL12	APSO4 75c black, *salmon*	1,100.	900.00
	On cover		*1,250.*
CL13	APSO4 75c black, *rose*	900.00	900.00
	On cover		*1,250.*
CL14	APSO4 75c black, *yellow*	1,650.	1,400.
	On cover		*3,500.*
CL15	APSO4 75c black, *straw*	1,650.	900.00
	On cover		*3,500.*

Nos. CL10-CL15 were for use on all T.A.G. flights.

POSTAGE DUE STAMPS

Postage Due Stamps of France, 1893-1926, Overprinted

1925-27 **Unwmk.** ***Perf. 14x13½***

J1	D2 5c light blue	.45	.45
	On cover. *from*		200.00
J2	D2 10c brown	.55	.55
	On cover. *from*		200.00
J3	D2 20c olive green	.75	.75
	On cover. *from*		200.00
J4	D2 50c violet brown	.95	.95
	On cover. *from*		200.00
J5	D2 3fr magenta ('27)	7.75	7.75
	On cover. *from*		200.00

Surcharged in Black

J6	D2 15c on 20c ol grn	.50	.50
	On cover. *from*		200.00
a.	Blue surcharge	32.50	
J7	D2 25c on 5c lt bl	.80	.80
	On cover. *from*		200.00
J8	D2 30c on 20c ol grn	1.00	1.00
	On cover. *from*		200.00
J9	D2 45c on 10c brn	.95	.95
	On cover. *from*		200.00
J10	D2 60c on 5c lt bl	.95	.95
	On cover. *from*		200.00
J11	D2 1fr on 20c ol grn	1.40	1.40
	On cover. *from*		250.00
J12	D2 2fr on 50c vio brn	1.50	1.50
	On cover. *from*		250.00
	Nos. J1-J12 (12)	17.55	17.55

Royal Palms — D3

Guiana Girl — D4

1929, Oct. 14 **Typo.** ***Perf. 13½x14***

J13	D3 5c indigo & Prus bl	.30	.30
	On cover. *from*		300.00
J14	D3 10c bis brn & Prus grn	.30	.30
	On cover. *from*		300.00
J15	D3 20c grn & rose red	.30	.30
	On cover. *from*		300.00
J16	D3 30c ol brn & rose red	.30	.30
	On cover. *from*		300.00
J17	D3 50c vio & ol brn	.65	.65
	On cover. *from*		300.00
J18	D3 60c brn red & ol brn	.95	.95
	On cover. *from*		300.00
J19	D4 1fr dp bl & org brn	1.25	1.25
	On cover. *from*		300.00
J20	D4 2fr brn red & bluish grn	1.40	1.40
	On cover. *from*		300.00
J21	D4 3fr violet & blk	3.25	3.25
	On cover. *from*		300.00
	Nos. J13-J21 (9)	8.70	8.70

FRENCH GUINEA

'french 'gi-nē

LOCATION — On the coast of West Africa, between Portuguese Guinea and Sierra Leone.
GOVT. — Former French colony
AREA — 89,436 sq. mi.
POP. — 2,058,442 (est. 1941)
CAPITAL — Conakry

French Guinea stamps were replaced by those of French West Africa around 1944-45. French Guinea became the Republic of Guinea Oct. 2, 1958.

100 Centimes = 1 Franc

Navigation and Commerce
A1

Fulah Shepherd
A2

Perf. 14x13½

1892-1900 **Typo.** **Unwmk.**

Name of Colony in Blue or Carmine

1	A1 1c black, *lilac bl*	1.10	1.10
2	A1 2c brown, *buff*	1.60	1.60
3	A1 4c claret, *lav*	2.00	2.00
4	A1 5c green, *grnsh*	6.50	3.50
5	A1 10c blk, *lavender*	5.75	3.50
6	A1 10c red ('00)	32.50	29.00
7	A1 15c blue, quadrille paper	11.00	5.50
8	A1 15c gray, *lt gray* ('00)	80.00	75.00
9	A1 20c red, *grn*	16.00	10.00
10	A1 25c black, *rose*	10.00	6.00
11	A1 25c blue ('00)	19.00	17.50
12	A1 30c brown, *bis*	30.00	25.00
13	A1 40c red, *straw*	30.00	25.00
a.	"GUINEE FRANCAISE" double	350.00	350.00
14	A1 50c car, *rose*	32.50	26.00
15	A1 50c brown, *az* ('00)	29.00	25.00
16	A1 75c dp vio, *org*	45.00	37.50
17	A1 1fr brnz grn, *straw*	37.50	30.00
	Nos. 1-17 (17)	389.45	323.20

Perf. 13½x14 stamps are counterfeits.
For surcharges see Nos. 48-54.

1904

18	A2 1c black, *yel grn*	.70	.55
19	A2 2c vio brn, *buff*	.75	.75
20	A2 4c carmine, *bl*	1.10	.95
21	A2 5c green, *grnsh*	1.25	.95
22	A2 10c carmine	2.75	1.50
23	A2 15c violet, *rose*	7.50	3.50
24	A2 20c carmine, *grn*	10.00	9.50
25	A2 25c blue	12.50	7.50
26	A2 30c brown	17.50	16.00
27	A2 40c red, *straw*	24.00	18.00
28	A2 50c brown, *az*	24.00	18.00
29	A2 75c green, *org*	27.50	21.00
30	A2 1fr brnz grn, *straw*	37.50	32.50
31	A2 2fr red, *org*	72.50	72.50
32	A2 5fr green, *yel grn*	87.50	87.50
	Nos. 18-32 (15)	327.05	290.70

For surcharges see Nos. 55-62.

Gen. Louis Faidherbé
A3

Oil Palm — A4

Dr. Noel Eugène Ballay
A5

1906-07

Name of Colony in Red or Blue

33	A3 1c gray	.60	.60
34	A3 2c brown	.85	.75
35	A3 4c brown, *bl*	1.10	1.10
36	A3 5c green	2.50	1.60
37	A3 10c carmine (B)	20.00	2.00
38	A4 20c black, *blue*	5.00	3.00
39	A4 25c blue, *pnksh*	5.00	5.00
40	A4 30c brown, *pnksh*	6.25	3.00
41	A4 35c black, *yellow*	3.75	2.00
42	A4 45c choc, *grnsh gray*	5.00	3.25
43	A4 50c dp violet	10.00	8.00
44	A4 75c blue, *org*	6.25	3.00
45	A5 1fr black, *az*	16.00	16.00
46	A5 2fr blue, *pink*	32.50	32.50
47	A5 5fr car, *straw* (B)	50.00	45.00
	Nos. 33-47 (15)	164.80	126.80

Regular Issues Surcharged in Black or Carmine

1912

Spacing between figures of surcharge 1.5mm (5c), 2mm (10c)

On Issue of 1892-1900

48	A1 5c on 2c brown, *buff*	.80	.80
49	A1 5c on 4c cl, *lav* (C)	.80	.80
50	A1 5c on 15c blue (C)	.80	.80
51	A1 5c on 20c red, *grn*	3.00	3.00
52	A1 5c on 30c brn, *bis* (C)	3.50	3.50
53	A1 10c on 40c red, *straw*	1.75	1.75
54	A1 10c on 75c dp vio, *org*	6.25	6.25
a.	Double surcharge, inverted	210.00	

On Issue of 1904

55	A2 5c on 2c vio brn, *buff*	.80	.80
a.	Pair, one without surcharge	450.00	
b.	Inverted surcharge	140.00	
56	A2 5c on 4c car, *blue*	.80	.80
57	A2 5c on 15c violet, *rose*	.80	.80
58	A2 5c on 20c car, *grn*	.80	.80
59	A2 5c on 25c blue (C)	1.10	1.10
60	A2 5c on 30c brown (C)	1.50	1.50
61	A2 10c on 40c red, *straw*	1.25	1.25
62	A2 10c on 50c brn, *az* (C)	3.50	3.50
	Nos. 48-62 (15)	27.45	27.45

Spacing between figures of surcharge 2.25mm (5c), 2.75mm (10c)

48a	A1 5c on 2c brown, *buff*	75.00	75.00
49a	A1 5c on 4c cl, *lav* (C)	35.00	35.00
50a	A1 5c on 15c blue (C)	37.50	37.50
51a	A1 5c on 20c red, *grn*	175.00	175.00
52a	A1 5c on 30c brn, *bis* (C)	525.00	525.00
53a	A1 10c on 40c red, *straw*	37.50	37.50
54b	A1 10c on 75c dp vio, *org*	18.50	18.50
c.	Double surcharge, inverted		3,000.

On Issue of 1904

55c	A2 5c on 2c vio brn, *buff*	27.50	27.50
56a	A2 5c on 4c car, *blue*	27.50	27.50
57a	A2 5c on 15c violet, *rose*	27.50	27.50
58a	A2 5c on 20c car, *grn*	37.50	37.50
59a	A2 5c on 25c blue (C)	92.50	92.50
60a	A2 5c on 30c brown (C)	125.00	125.00
61a	A2 10c on 40c red, *straw*	35.00	35.00
62a	A2 10c on 50c brn, *az* (C)	52.50	52.50
	Nos. 48a-62a (15)	27.45	27.45

Ford at Kitim — A6

1913-33 *Perf. 13½x14*

63	A6	1c violet & bl	.20	.20
64	A6	2c brn & vio brn	.20	.20
65	A6	4c gray & black	.20	.20
66	A6	5c yel grn & bl grn	.80	.25
67	A6	5c brn vio & grn ('22)	.20	.20
68	A6	10c red org & rose	.75	.25
69	A6	10c yel grn & bl grn ('22)	.25	.25
70	A6	10c vio & ver ('25)	.45	.25
71	A6	15c vio brn & rose ('16)	.30	.25
72	A6	15c gray grn & yel grn ('25)	.25	.25
73	A6	15c red brn & rose lil ('27)	.25	.25
74	A6	20c brown & violet	.30	.25
75	A6	20c grn & bl grn ('26)	.65	.50
76	A6	20c brn red & brn ('27)	.65	.30
77	A6	25c ultra & blue	2.00	1.00
78	A6	25c black & vio ('22)	.50	.50
79	A6	30c vio brn & grn	1.10	.75
80	A6	30c red org & rose ('22)	.80	.75
81	A6	30c rose red & grn ('25)	.25	.25
82	A6	30c dl grn & bl grn ('28)	1.25	.90
83	A6	35c blue & rose	.40	.20
84	A6	40c green & gray	.80	.65
85	A6	45c brown & red	.85	.75
86	A6	50c ultra & black	5.75	3.25
87	A6	50c ultra & bl ('22)	.85	.50
88	A6	50c yel brn & ol ('25)	.45	.35
89	A6	60c vio, *pnksh* ('25)	.45	.35
90	A6	65c yel brn & sl bl ('26)	1.40	1.00
91	A6	75c red & ultra	1.25	1.00
92	A6	75c indigo & dl bl ('25)	.90	.80
93	A6	75c mag & yel grn ('27)	1.40	1.00
94	A6	85c ol grn & red brn ('26)	1.00	1.00
95	A6	90c brn red & rose ('30)	5.25	4.25
96	A6	1fr violet & black	1.25	.90
97	A6	1.10fr vio & ol brn ('28)	5.50	4.25
98	A6	1.25fr vio & yel brn ('33)	1.90	1.00
99	A6	1.50fr dk bl & lt bl ('30)	5.00	1.90
100	A6	1.75fr ol brn & vio ('33)	1.50	1.25
101	A6	2fr orange & vio brn	3.00	1.25
102	A6	3fr red violet ('30)	7.50	5.00
103	A6	5fr black & vio	11.00	11.00
104	A6	5fr dl bl & blk ('22)	5.00	2.25
		Nos. 63-104 (42)	73.75	51.65

Nos. 66 and 68 exist on both ordinary and chalky paper, No. 71 on chalky paper only.

For surcharges see Nos. 105-115, B1.

Nos. 66, 68 and 77 pasted on colored cardboard and overprinted "VALEUR D'ECHANGE" were used as emergency currency in 1920.

Type of 1913-33 Surcharged

1922

105	A6	60c on 75c violet, *pnksh*	.50	.50

Stamps and Type of 1913-33 Surcharged with New Value and Bars

1924-27

106	A6	25c on 2fr org & brn (R)	.35	.35
107	A6	25c on 5fr dull bl & blk	.35	.35
108	A6	65c on 75c rose & ultra ('25)	1.00	1.00
109	A6	85c on 75c rose & ultra ('25)	1.25	1.25
110	A6	90c on 75c brn red & cer ('27)	1.75	1.75
111	A6	1.25fr on 1fr dk bl & ultra ('26)	.85	.85
112	A6	1.50fr on 1fr dp bl & lt bl ('27)	1.40	1.40
113	A6	3fr on 5fr mag & sl ('27)	3.25	3.25
114	A6	10fr on 5fr bl & bl grn, *bluish* ('27)	6.50	6.50
115	A6	20fr on 5fr rose lil & brn ol, *pnksh* ('27)	14.50	14.50
		Nos. 106-115 (10)	31.20	31.20

Common Design Types pictured following the introduction.

Colonial Exposition Issue
Common Design Types

1931 **Engr.** *Perf. 12½*

Name of Country in Black

116	CD70	40c deep green	3.75	3.75
117	CD71	50c violet	3.75	3.75
118	CD72	90c red orange	3.75	3.75
119	CD73	1.50fr dull blue	3.75	3.75
		Nos. 116-119 (4)	15.00	15.00

Paris International Exposition Issue
Common Design Types

1937 *Perf. 13*

120	CD74	20c deep violet	1.25	1.25
121	CD75	30c dark green	1.25	1.25
122	CD76	40c carmine rose	1.40	1.40
123	CD77	50c dark brown	1.40	1.40
124	CD78	90c red	1.50	1.50
125	CD79	1.50fr ultra	1.50	1.50
		Nos. 120-125 (6)	8.30	8.30

Colonial Arts Exhibition Issue
Souvenir Sheet

Common Design Type

1937 *Imperf.*

126	CD76	3fr Prussian green	5.75	*7.00*

Guinea Village A7

Hausa Basket Workers A8

Forest Waterfall A9

Guinea Women — A10

1938-40 *Perf. 13*

128	A7	2c vermilion	.20	.20
129	A7	3c ultra	.20	.20
130	A7	4c green	.20	.20
131	A7	5c rose car	.20	.20
132	A7	10c peacock blue	.20	.20
133	A7	15c violet brown	.20	.20
134	A8	20c dk carmine	.20	.20
135	A8	25c pck blue	.20	.20
136	A8	30c ultra	.20	.20
137	A8	35c green	.45	.40
138	A8	40c blk brn ('40)	.20	.20
139	A8	45c dk green ('40)	.20	.20
140	A8	50c red brown	.40	.40
141	A9	55c dk ultra	.85	.75
142	A9	60c dk ultra ('40)	.65	.65
143	A9	65c green	.90	.65
144	A9	70c green ('40)	1.25	1.00
145	A9	80c rose violet	.50	.45
146	A9	90c rose vio ('39)	1.00	.95
147	A9	1fr orange red	2.50	1.40
148	A9	1fr brn blk ('40)	.40	.40
149	A9	1.25fr org red ('39)	1.10	1.00
150	A9	1.40fr brown ('40)	1.10	1.00
151	A9	1.50fr violet	2.25	1.40
152	A10	1.60fr org red ('40)	1.25	1.00
153	A10	1.75fr ultra	.60	.55
154	A10	2fr magenta	.85	.50
155	A10	2.25fr brt ultra ('39)	1.75	1.25
156	A10	2.50fr brn blk ('40)	1.25	1.00
157	A10	3fr peacock blue	.70	.30
158	A10	5fr rose violet	.70	.55
159	A10	10fr slate green	1.00	.80
160	A10	20fr chocolate	2.50	1.40
		Nos. 128-160 (33)	26.15	20.00

For surcharges see Nos. B8-B11.

Caillié Issue
Common Design Type

1939 **Engr.** *Perf. 12½x12*

161	CD81	90c org brn & org	.75	.75
162	CD81	2fr brt violet	.85	.85
163	CD81	2.25fr ultra & dk bl	.85	.85
		Nos. 161-163 (3)	2.45	2.45

René Caillié, French explorer, death cent.

New York World's Fair Issue
Common Design Type

1939

164	CD82	1.25fr carmine lake	.95	.95
165	CD82	2.25fr ultra	.95	.95

SEMI-POSTAL STAMPS

Regular Issue of 1913 Surcharged in Red

1915 **Unwmk.** *Perf. 13½x14*

B1	A6	10c + 5c org & rose	1.10	1.00

Exists on both ordinary and chalky paper.

Curie Issue
Common Design Type

1938 **Engr.** *Perf. 13*

B2	CD80	1.75fr + 50c brt ultra	7.50	7.50

French Revolution Issue
Common Design Type

1939 **Photo.**

Name and Value Typo. in Black

B3	CD83	45c + 25c green	7.50	7.50
B4	CD83	70c + 30c brown	7.50	7.50
B5	CD83	90c + 35c red org	7.50	7.50
B6	CD83	1.25fr + 1fr rose pink	7.50	7.50
B7	CD83	2.25fr + 2fr blue	7.50	7.50
		Nos. B3-B7 (5)	37.50	37.50

AIR POST STAMPS

Common Design Type

1940 **Unwmk.** **Engr.** *Perf. 12½x12*

C1	CD85	1.90fr ultra	.45	.45
C2	CD85	2.90fr dark red	.50	.50
C3	CD85	4.50fr dk gray grn	.65	.65
C4	CD85	4.90fr yellow bis	.65	.65
C5	CD85	6.90fr dp orange	1.00	1.00
		Nos. C1-C5 (5)	3.25	3.25

POSTAGE DUE STAMPS

Fulah Woman D1

Heads and Coast D2

1905 **Unwmk.** **Typo.** *Perf. 14x13½*

J1	D1	5c blue	1.40	1.40
J2	D1	10c brown	1.40	1.40
J3	D1	15c green	4.25	2.75
J4	D1	30c rose	4.25	2.75
J5	D1	50c black	7.25	7.25
J6	D1	60c dull orange	10.00	8.00
J7	D1	1fr violet	32.50	29.00
		Nos. J1-J7 (7)	61.05	52.55

1906-08

J8	D2	5c grn, *grnsh* ('08)	16.00	10.50
J9	D2	10c violet brn ('08)	4.25	4.25
J10	D2	15c dk blue ('08)	4.25	4.25
J11	D2	20c blk, *yellow*	4.25	3.25
J12	D2	30c red, *straw* ('08)	22.50	20.00
J13	D2	50c violet ('08)	18.00	18.00
J14	D2	60c blk, *buff* ('08)	18.00	16.00
J15	D2	1fr blk, *pnksh* ('08)	11.00	9.00
		Nos. J8-J15 (8)	98.25	85.25

D3

D4

1914

J16	D3	5c green	.20	.20
J17	D3	10c rose	.20	.20
J18	D3	15c gray	.35	.35
J19	D3	20c brown	.50	.50
J20	D3	30c blue	.50	.50
J21	D3	50c black	.90	.70
J22	D3	60c orange	1.40	1.40
J23	D3	1fr violet	1.40	1.40
		Nos. J16-J23 (8)	5.45	5.25

Type of 1914 Issue Surcharged

1927

J24	D3	2fr on 1fr lil rose	5.75	5.75
J25	D3	3fr on 1fr org brn	5.75	5.75

1938 **Engr.**

J26	D4	5c dk violet	.20	.20
J27	D4	10c carmine	.20	.20
J28	D4	15c green	.20	.20
J29	D4	20c red brown	.20	.20
J30	D4	30c rose violet	.20	.20
J31	D4	50c chocolate	.50	.50
J32	D4	60c peacock blue	.80	.80
J33	D4	1fr vermilion	.80	.80
J34	D4	2fr ultra	.80	.80
J35	D4	3fr black	1.25	1.25
		Nos. J26-J35 (10)	5.15	5.15

A 10c of type D4 without "RF" was issued in 1944 by the Vichy Government, but was not placed on sale in the colony.

FRENCH INDIA

ˈfrench ˈin-dē-ə

LOCATION — East coast of India bordering on Bay of Bengal.
GOVT. — French Territory
AREA — 196 sq. mi.
POP. — 323,295 (1941)
CAPITAL — Pondichéry

French India was an administrative unit comprising the five settlements of Chandernagor, Karikal, Mahé, Pondichéry and Yanaon.

100 Centimes = 1 Franc
24 Caches = 1 Fanon (1923)
8 Fanons = 1 Rupie

Navigation and Commerce — A1

A2

Perf. 14x13½

1892-1907 **Typo.** **Unwmk.**

Colony Name in Blue or Carmine

1	A1	1c blk, *lil bl*	.95	.70
2	A1	2c brn, *buff*	1.40	1.10
3	A1	4c claret, *lav*	1.75	1.60
4	A1	5c grn, *grnsh*	4.00	2.75
5	A1	10c blk, *lavender*	9.50	2.50
6	A1	10c red ('00)	3.25	1.75
7	A1	15c blue, quadrille paper	10.50	4.25
8	A1	15c gray, *lt gray* ('00)	25.00	22.50
9	A1	20c red, *grn*	5.25	4.00

ur
by
on.
ure
ow.
21st

...d red br...
color for this issue.

The auctioneer reports that only one block of 10 stamps has been found of this 68-year-old error, and of those, seven are held by the Smithsonian National Postal Museum in Washington, D.C.

As a result, only three examples are available to the collecting community.

The postal museum refers to the error as one of the most spec-

two mi... dish brown," the museu... "but somehow a few printed... rose red escaped detection. Whi... sunlight and exposure to chemicals can change a stamp's color, experts agree that neither could have caused this dramatic variant. Hence, it is a true error."

The error is listed in the Spink catalog with the Scott *Special-*

866
scal 4a
37
R

...port: U.S. stamp to honor Janis Joplin

American rock and blues singer and musician Janis Joplin (1943-70) is expected to be the subject of a United States stamp in 2014, according to an article published Jan. 9 by *The Wall Street Journal*.

Stefanie Cohen reports, "The [Joplin] estate has worked with the U.S. Postal Service to create a commemorative stamp, out later this year."

If issued, it is likely a Janis Joplin stamp would be part of the Music Icons series. A USPS spokesman contacted by *Linn's* would not confirm the report. ■

10	A1	25c blk, *rose*	3.50	1.75
11	A1	25c blue ('00)	13.50	11.00
12	A1	30c brn, *bis*	47.50	40.00
13	A1	35c blk, *yel* ('06)	13.50	7.00
14	A1	40c red, *straw*	5.25	5.00
15	A1	45c blk, *gray grn* ('07)	4.00	3.50
16	A1	50c car, *rose*	5.25	5.00
17	A1	50c brn, *az* ('00)	12.00	12.00
18	A1	75c dp vio, *org*	7.00	7.00
19	A1	1fr brnz grn, *straw*	9.50	9.50
		Nos. 1-19 (19)	182.60	142.90

Perf. 13½x14 stamps are counterfeits.

Nos. 10 and 16 Surcharged in Carmine or Black

1903

20	A1	5c on 25c blk, *rose*	260.00	165.00
21	A1	10c on 25c blk, *rose*	275.00	180.00
22	A1	15c on 25c blk, *rose*	90.00	90.00
23	A1	40c on 50c car, *rose* (Bk)	425.00	325.00
		Nos. 20-23 (4)	1,050.	760.00

Counterfeits of Nos. 20-23 abound.

1903

Revenue Stamp Surcharged in Black

24	A2	5c gray blue	22.50	22.50

The bottom of the revenue stamps were cut off.

Brahma — A5

Kali Temple near Pondichéry A6

1914-22 ***Perf. 13½x14, 14x13½***

25	A5	1c gray & blk	.25	.20
26	A5	2c brn vio & blk	.25	.20
27	A5	2c grn & brn vio ('22)	.25	.20
28	A5	3c brown & blk	.30	.25
29	A5	4c orange & blk	.30	.25
30	A5	5c bl grn & blk	.45	.45
31	A5	5c vio brn & blk ('22)	.25	.25
32	A5	10c dp rose & blk	.95	.95
33	A5	10c grn & blk ('22)	.60	.60
34	A5	15c vio & blk	.75	.75
35	A5	20c org red & blk	1.25	1.25
36	A5	25c blue & blk	1.25	1.25
37	A5	25c ultra & fawn ('22)	.80	.80
38	A5	30c ultra & blk	2.40	2.40
39	A5	30c rose & blk ('22)	.90	.90
40	A6	35c choc & blk	1.40	1.40
41	A6	40c org red & blk	1.40	1.40
42	A6	45c bl grn & blk	1.40	1.40
43	A6	50c dp rose & blk	1.25	1.25
44	A6	50c ultra & bl ('22)	1.50	1.50
45	A6	75c blue & blk	2.75	2.75
46	A6	1fr yellow & blk	2.75	2.75
47	A6	2fr violet & blk	4.25	4.25
48	A6	5fr ultra & blk	1.90	1.90
49	A6	5fr rose & blk ('22)	3.50	3.50
		Nos. 25-49 (25)	33.05	32.80

For surcharges see Nos. 50-79, 113-116, 156A, B1-B5.

No. 34 Surcharged in Various Colors

1922

50	A5	1c on 15c (Bk)	.60	.60
51	A5	2c on 15c (Bl)	.60	.60
53	A5	5c on 15c (R)	.60	.60
		Nos. 50-53 (3)	1.80	1.80

Stamps and Types of 1914-22 Surcharged with New Values in Caches, Fanons and Rupies in Black, Red or Blue:

1923-28

54	A5	1ca on 1c gray & blk (R)	.20	.20
55	A5	2ca on 5c vio brn & blk	.30	.30
a.		Horizontal pair, imperf. between	—	
56	A5	3ca on 3c brn & blk	.40	.40
57	A5	4ca on 4c org & blk	.60	.60
58	A5	6ca on 10c grn & blk	.65	.65
59	A6	6ca on 45c bl grn & blk (R)	.65	.65
60	A5	10ca on 20c dp red & bl grn ('28)	2.00	2.00
61	A5	12ca on 15c vio & blk	.65	.65
62	A5	15ca on 20c org & blk	1.00	1.00
63	A6	16ca on 35c lt bl & yel brn ('28)	2.00	2.00
64	A5	18ca on 30c rose & blk	1.75	1.75
65	A6	20ca on 45c grn & dl red ('28)	1.50	1.10
66	A5	1fa on 25c dp grn & rose red ('28)	2.75	2.75
67	A6	1fa3ca on 35c choc & blk (Bl)	.80	.80
68	A6	1fa6ca on 40c org & blk (R)	1.00	.90
69	A6	1fa12ca on 50c ultra & bl (Bl)	1.25	.90
70	A6	1fa12ca on 75c bl & blk (Bl)	1.00	.90
a.		Double surcharge	95.00	
71	A6	1fa16ca on 75c brn red & grn ('28)	2.50	2.25
72	A5	2fa9ca on 25c ultra & fawn (Bl)	1.00	.80
73	A6	2fa12ca on 1fr vio & dk brn ('28)	2.25	2.25
74	A6	3fa3ca on 1fr yel & blk (R)	1.10	1.00
a.		Double surcharge	125.00	
75	A6	6fa6ca on 2fr vio & blk (Bl)	3.50	3.50
76	A6	1r on 1fr grn & dp bl (R) ('26)	7.00	5.50
77	A6	2r on 5fr rose & blk (R)	5.50	5.00
a.		Double surcharge	100.00	
78	A6	3r on 2fr gray & bl vio (R) ('26)	15.00	12.50
79	A6	5r on 5fr rose & blk, *grnsh* ('26)	19.00	19.00
		Nos. 54-79 (26)	75.35	69.35

Nos. 60, 63, 66 and 73 have the original value obliterated by bars.

A7

A8

1929

80	A7	1ca dk gray & blk	.20	.20
81	A7	2ca vio brn & blk	.20	.20
82	A7	3ca brn & blk	.20	.20
83	A7	4ca org & blk	.25	.25
84	A7	6ca gray grn & grn	.25	.25
85	A7	10ca brn, red & grn	.25	.25
86	A8	12ca grn & lt grn	.60	.60
87	A7	16ca brt bl & blk	.75	.75
88	A7	18ca brn red & ver	.75	.75
89	A7	20ca dk bl & grn, *bluish*	.60	.60
90	A8	1fa gray grn & rose red	.60	.55
91	A8	1fa6ca red org & blk	.60	.55
92	A8	1fa12ca dp bl & ultra	.60	.55
93	A8	1fa16ca rose red & grn	.75	.75
94	A8	2fa12ca brt vio & brn	1.00	.80
95	A8	6fa6ca dl vio & blk	1.00	.80
96	A8	1r gray grn & dp bl	.95	.80
97	A8	2r rose & blk	1.40	.95
98	A8	3r lt gray & gray lil	2.50	1.60
99	A8	5r rose & blk, *grnsh*	2.50	1.75
		Nos. 80-99 (20)	15.95	13.15

For overprints and surcharges see Nos. 117-134, 157-176, 184-209G.

Common Design Types pictured following the introduction.

Colonial Exposition Issue

Common Design Types

1931 **Engr.** ***Perf. 12½***

100	CD70	10ca deep green	3.00	3.00
101	CD71	12ca violet	3.00	3.00
102	CD72	18ca red orange	3.00	3.00
103	CD73	1fa12ca dull blue	3.00	3.00
		Nos. 100-103 (4)	12.00	12.00

Paris International Exposition Issue

Common Design Types

1937 ***Perf. 13***

104	CD74	8ca dp violet	1.10	1.10
105	CD75	12ca dk green	1.10	1.10
106	CD76	16ca car rose	1.25	1.25
107	CD77	20ca dk brown	1.25	1.25
108	CD78	1fa12ca red	1.25	1.25
109	CD79	2fa12ca ultra	1.25	1.25
		Nos. 104-109 (6)	7.20	7.20

For overprints see Nos. 135-139, 177-181.

Colonial Arts Exhibition Issue

Souvenir Sheet

Common Design Type

1937 ***Imperf.***

110	CD79	5fa red violet	6.50	*8.75*

For overprint see No. 140.

New York World's Fair Issue

Common Design Type

1939 **Engr.** ***Perf. 12½x12***

111	CD82	1fa12ca car lake	.95	.95
112	CD82	2fa12ca ultra	1.25	1.25

For overprints see Nos. 141-142, 182-183.

SEMI-POSTAL STAMPS

Regular Issue of 1914 Surcharged in Red

1915 **Unwmk.** ***Perf. 14x13½***

B1	A5	10c + 5c rose & blk	1.25	1.25
a.		Inverted surcharge	140.00	140.00

There were two printings of this surcharge; in the first it was placed at the bottom of the stamp, in the second it was near the top.

Regular Issue of 1914 Surcharged in Red

1916

B2	A5	10c + 5c rose & blk	13.00	13.00
a.		Inverted surcharge	140.00	140.00
b.		Double surcharge	140.00	140.00

Surcharged

B3	A5	10c + 5c rose & blk	2.50	2.50

Surcharged

B4	A5	10c + 5c rose & blk	1.10	1.10

Surcharged

B5	A5	10c + 5c rose & blk	1.50	1.50

Curie Issue

Common Design Type

1938 **Engr.** ***Perf. 13***

B6	CD80	2fa12ca + 20ca brt ultra	7.25	7.25

French Revolution Issue

Common Design Type

1939 **Photo.**

Name and Value Typo. in Black

B7	CD83	18ca + 10ca grn	6.50	6.50
B8	CD83	1fa6ca + 12ca brn	6.50	6.50
B9	CD83	1fa12ca + 16ca red org	6.50	6.50

B10 CD83 1fa16ca + 1fa16ca rose pink 6.50 6.50
B11 CD83 2fa12ca + 3fa blue 6.50 6.50
Nos. B7-B11 (5) 32.50 32.50

POSTAGE DUE STAMPS

Postage Due Stamps of France Surcharged like Nos. 54-75 in Black, Blue or Red

1923 Unwmk. *Perf. 14x13½*

J1 D2 6ca on 10c brn .80 .80
J2 D2 12ca on 25c rose (Bk) .85 .85
J3 D2 15ca on 20c ol grn (R) 1.10 1.10
J4 D2 1fa6ca on 30c red 1.10 1.10
J5 D2 1fa12a on 50c brn vio 1.90 1.90
J6 D2 1fa15ca on 5c bl (Bk) 2.00 2.00
J7 D2 3fa3ca on 1fr red brn, *straw* 2.10 2.10
Nos. J1-J7 (7) 9.85 9.85

Types of Postage Due Stamps of French Colonies, 1884-85, Surcharged with New Values as in 1923 in Red or Black

Bars over Original Values

1928

J8 D1 4ca on 20c gray lil 1.10 1.10
J9 D1 1fa on 30c orange 2.10 2.10
J10 D1 1fa16ca on 5c bl blk (R) 2.10 2.10
J11 D1 3fa on 1fr lt grn 2.50 2.50
Nos. J8-J11 (4) 7.80 7.80

D3

1929 Typo.

J12 D3 4ca deep red .35 .35
J13 D3 6ca blue .50 .50
J14 D3 12ca green .50 .50
J15 D3 1fa brown .95 .95
J16 D3 1fa12ca lilac gray .95 .95
J17 D3 1fa16ca buff 1.25 1.25
J18 D3 3fa lilac 1.60 1.60
Nos. J12-J18 (7) 6.10 6.10

FRENCH MOROCCO

'french mə-'rä-ₗₒkō

LOCATION — Northwest coast of Africa
GOVT. — French Protectorate
AREA — 153,870 sq. mi.
POP. — 8,340,000 (estimated 1954)
CAPITAL — Rabat

100 Centimos = 1 Peseta
100 Centimes = 1 franc (1917)

French Offices in Morocco

A1

A2

Stamps of France Surcharged in Red or Black

1891-1900 Unwmk. *Perf. 14x13½*

1 A1 5c on 5c grn, *grnsh* (R) 8.50 3.50
On cover 20.00
a. Imperf., pair 110.00
2 A1 5c on 5c yel grn (II) (R) ('99) 24.00 21.00
On cover 70.00
a. Type I 24.00 17.50
3 A1 10c on 10c blk, *lav* (II) (R) 24.00 2.10
On cover 10.00
a. Type I 29.00 16.00
b. 10c on 25c black, *rose* 775.00
4 A1 20c on 20c red, *grn* 27.50 20.00
On cover *90.00*
5 A1 25c on 25c blk, *rose* (R) 21.00 2.50
On cover 11.00
a. Double surcharge 160.00
b. Imperf., pair 125.00

6 A1 50c on 50c car, *rose* (II) 70.00 29.00
On cover 55.00
a. Type I 300.00 210.00
7 A1 1p on 1fr brnz grn, *straw* 82.50 52.50
On cover 150.00
8 A1 2p on 2fr brn, *az* (Bk) ('00) 190.00 175.00
On cover 625.00
Nos. 1-8 (8) 447.50 305.60

No. 3b was never sent to Morocco.

France Nos. J15-J16 Overprinted in Carmine

1893

9 A2 5c black 1,900. 800.
On cover *1,400.*
10 A2 10c black 1,650. 575.
On cover *950.*

Counterfeits exist.

A3

18srch

A5

Surcharged in Red or Black

1902-10

11 A3 1c on 1c gray (R) ('08) 1.40 .80
a. Surcharge omitted
12 A3 2c on 2c vio brn ('08) 1.40 .95
13 A3 3c on 3c red org ('08) 1.50 .95
14 A3 4c on 4c yel brn ('08) 7.75 5.25
15 A3 5c on 5c grn (R) 6.00 2.50
a. Double surcharge 175.00
16 A4 10c on 10c rose red ('03) 4.50 1.50
a. Surcharge omitted
17 A4 20c on 20c brn vio ('03) 21.00 14.00
18 A4 25c on 25c bl ('03) 21.00 1.75
19 A4 35c on 35c vio ('10) 29.00 16.00
20 A5 50c on 50c bis brn & lav ('03) 40.00 9.25
21 A5 1p on 1fr cl & ol grn ('03) 82.50 55.00
22 A5 2p on 2fr gray vio & yel ('03) 110.00 67.50
Nos. 11-22 (12) 326.05 175.45

Nos. 11-14 exist spelled CFNTIMOS or GENTIMOS.

The 25c on 25c with surcharge omitted is listed as No. 81a.

For overprints and surcharges see Nos. 26-37, 72-79, B1, B3.

Postage Due Stamps Nos. J1-J2 Handstamped

1903

24 D2 5c on 5c light blue 1,100. 925.
On cover *1,100.*
25 D2 10c on 10c chocolate 2,100. 1,600.
On cover *2,000.*

Nos. 24 and 25 were used only on Oct. 10, 1903. Used copies were not canceled, the overprint serving as a cancellation.

Counterfeits exist.

Types of 1902-10 Issue Surcharged in Red or Blue

1911-17

26 A3 1c on 1c gray (R) .55 .50
27 A3 2c on 2c vio brn .55 .50
28 A3 3c on 3c orange .55 .50
29 A3 5c on 5c green (R) .80 .35
30 A4 10c on 10c rose .65 .35
a. Imperf., pair 200.00

31 A4 15c on 15c org ('17) 2.25 1.60
32 A4 20c on 20c brn vio 3.50 2.50
33 A4 25c on 25c blue (R) 1.75 1.25
34 A4 35c on 35c violet (R) 6.75 2.75
35 A5 40c on 40c red & pale bl ('17) 6.00 4.00
36 A5 50c on 50c bis brn & lav (R) 17.50 9.25
37 A5 1p on 1fr cl & ol grn 13.00 5.00
Nos. 26-37 (12) 53.85 28.55

For surcharges see Nos. B1, B3.

The Administration Cherifinne des Postes, Telegraphes et Telephones was formed in 1911 under French guidance, and stamps of this design were issued by the Cherifien posts in 1912-13. See listings under "Morocco."

French Protectorate

A6

A7

A8

Issue of 1911-17 Overprinted "Protectorat Francais"

1914-21

38 A6 1c on 1c gray .45 .30
39 A6 2c on 2c vio brn .45 .30
40 A6 3c on 3c orange .80 .35
41 A6 5c on 5c green .55 .35
a. New value omitted 210.00 210.00
42 A7 10c on 10c rose .45 .20
a. New value omitted 450.00 450.00
43 A7 15c on 15c org ('17) .65 .55
a. New value omitted 82.50 82.50
44 A7 20c on 20c brn vio 3.50 2.10
a. "Protectorat Francais" double 210.00 210.00
45 A7 25c on 25c blue 1.60 .35
a. New value omitted 250.00 250.00
46 A7 25c on 25c violet ('21) 1.00 .20
a. "Protectorat Francais" omitted 60.00 60.00
b. "Protectorat Francais" double 125.00 125.00
c. "Protectorat Francais" dbl. (R + Bk) 125.00 125.00
47 A7 30c on 30c vio ('21) 12.00 6.75
48 A7 35c on 35c violet 4.00 1.25
49 A8 40c on 40c red & pale bl 12.00 6.50
a. New value omitted 240.00 240.00
50 A8 45c on 45c grn & bl ('21) 32.50 29.00
51 A8 50c on 50c bis brn & lav 1.10 .35
a. "Protectorat Francais" invtd. 110.00 110.00
b. "Protectorat Francais" double *175.00 175.00*
52 A8 1p on 1fr cl & ol grn 2.40 .50
a. "Protectorat Francais" invtd. 240.00 240.00
b. New value double 140.00 140.00
c. New value dbl., one invtd. 140.00 140.00
53 A8 2p on 2fr gray vio & yel 4.00 1.10
a. New value omitted 125.00 125.00
b. "Protectorat Francais" omitted 85.00 85.00
c. New value double *125.00 125.00*
d. New value dbl., one invtd.
54 A8 5p on 5fr dk bl & buff 10.50 3.25
Nos. 38-54 (17) 87.95 53.40

For surcharges see Nos. B2, B4-B5.

Tower of Hassan, Rabat — A9

Mosque of the Andalusians, Fez — A10

City Gate Chella A11

Koutoubiah, Marrakesh A12

Bab Mansour, Meknes A13

Roman Ruins, Volubilis A14

1917 Engr. *Perf. 13½x14, 14x13½*

55 A9 1c grnsh gray .35 .35
56 A9 2c brown lilac .50 .35
57 A9 3c orange brn .50 .35
a. Imperf., pair 65.00 65.00
58 A10 5c yellow grn .50 .20
59 A10 10c rose red .65 .20
60 A10 15c dark gray .65 .20
a. Imperf., pair 47.50 47.50
61 A11 20c red brown 2.50 1.75
62 A11 25c dull blue 2.90 .70
63 A11 30c gray violet 3.25 2.10
64 A12 35c orange 3.25 2.10
65 A12 40c ultra 1.25 .70
66 A12 45c gray green 21.00 8.50
67 A13 50c dk brown 4.00 2.10
a. Imperf., pair 47.50 47.50
68 A13 1fr slate 8.50 2.75
a. Imperf., pair 47.50 47.50
69 A14 2fr black brown 125.00 70.00
70 A14 5fr dk gray grn 32.50 29.00
71 A14 10fr black 32.50 29.00
Nos. 55-71 (17) 239.80 150.35

See note following #115. See #93-105. For surcharges see #120-121.

Types of the 1902-10 Issue Overprinted

1918-24 *Perf. 14x13½*

72 A3 1c gray .30 .30
73 A3 2c violet brn .35 .35
74 A3 3c red orange .55 .55
75 A3 5c green .55 .35
76 A3 5c orange ('23) 1.25 1.25
77 A4 10c rose 1.25 .95
78 A4 10c green ('24) 1.10 .95
79 A4 15c orange 1.10 .70
80 A4 20c violet brn 1.90 1.40
81 A4 25c blue 1.60 1.40
a. "TANGER" omitted 325.00 300.00
82 A4 30c red org ('24) 1.90 1.90
83 A4 35c violet 2.25 1.75
84 A5 40c red & pale bl 2.50 1.60
85 A5 50c bis brn & lav 17.50 10.50
86 A4 50c blue 12.00 8.25
87 A5 1fr claret & ol grn 9.50 4.50

88	A5	2fr org & pale bl ('24)	57.50	55.00
89	A5	5fr dk bl & buff ('24)	47.50	47.50
		Nos. 72-89 (18)	160.60	139.20

Types of 1917 and

Tower of Hassan, Rabat — A15

Bab Mansour, Meknes A16

Roman Ruins, Volubilis A17

1923-27 **Photo.** ***Perf. 13½***

90	A15	1c olive green	.20	.20
91	A15	2c brown vio	.20	.20
92	A15	3c yellow brn	.20	.20
93	A10	5c orange	.20	.20
94	A10	10c yellow brn	.20	.20
95	A10	15c dk gray	.20	.20
96	A11	20c red brown	.20	.20
97	A11	20c red vio ('27)	.45	.45
98	A11	25c ultra	.20	.20
99	A11	30c deep red	.20	.20
100	A11	30c turq bl ('27)	.85	.50
101	A12	35c violet	.80	.50
102	A12	40c orange red	.20	.20
103	A12	45c deep green	.20	.20
104	A16	50c dull turq	.35	.20
105	A12	50c olive grn ('27)	.65	.20
106	A16	60c lilac	.70	.20
107	A16	75c red vio ('27)	.70	.35
108	A16	1fr deep brown	.50	.35
109	A16	1.05fr red brn ('27)	1.40	.60
110	A16	1.40fr dull rose ('27)	.65	.50
111	A16	1.50fr turq bl ('27)	1.10	.25
112	A17	2fr olive brn	1.25	.75
113	A17	3fr dp red ('27)	1.50	.75
114	A17	5fr dk gray grn	3.00	1.75
115	A17	10fr black	8.50	3.75
		Nos. 90-115 (26)	24.60	13.30

Nos. 90-110, 112-115 exist imperf. The stamps of 1917 were line engraved. Those of 1923-27 were printed by photogravure and have in the margin at lower right the imprint "Helio Vaugirard."

See #B36. For surcharges see #122-123.

No. 102 Surcharged in Black

1930

120	A12	15c on 40c orange red	1.25	1.25

Nos. 100, 106 and 110 Surcharged in Blue Similarly to No. 176

1931

121	A11	25c on 30c turq blue	2.00	1.60
a.		Inverted surcharge	85.00	85.00
122	A16	50c on 60c lilac	.80	.25
a.		Inverted surcharge	95.00	95.00
123	A16	1fr on 1.40fr rose	2.50	1.25
a.		Inverted surcharge	95.00	95.00
		Nos. 121-123 (3)	5.30	3.10

Old Treasure House and Tribunal, Tangier A18

Roadstead at Agadir A19

Post Office at Casablanca A20

Moulay Idriss of the Zehroun A21

Kasbah of the Oudayas, Rabat A22

Court of the Medersa el Attarine at Fez A23

Saadiens' Tombs at Marrakesh A25

Kasbah of Si Madani el Glaoui at Ouarzazat A24

1933-34 **Engr.** ***Perf. 13***

124	A18	1c olive blk	.20	.20
125	A18	2c red violet	.20	.20
126	A19	3c dark brown	.20	.20
127	A19	5c brown red	.20	.20
128	A20	10c blue green	.20	.20
129	A20	15c black	.20	.20
130	A20	20c red brown	.20	.20
131	A21	25c dark blue	.20	.20
132	A21	30c emerald	.35	.20
133	A21	40c black brn	.35	.20
134	A22	45c brown vio	.55	.50
135	A22	50c dk blue grn	.55	.20
a.		Booklet pane of 10	12.00	
b.		Booklet pane of 20	25.00	
136	A22	65c brown red	.20	.20
a.		Booklet pane of 10	12.00	
b.		Booklet pane of 20	25.00	
137	A23	75c red violet	.55	.20
138	A23	90c orange red	.35	.20
139	A23	1fr deep brown	.80	.35
140	A23	1.25fr black ('34)	1.10	.80
141	A24	1.50fr ultra	.35	.20
142	A24	1.75fr myr grn ('34)	.55	.20
143	A24	2fr yellow brn	3.25	.55
144	A24	3fr car rose	42.50	5.00
145	A25	5fr red brown	8.50	1.50
146	A25	10fr black	6.75	5.25
147	A25	20fr bluish gray	6.50	5.25
		Nos. 124-147 (24)	74.80	22.40

Booklets containing Nos. 135 and 136 each have two panes of 10 (#135a, 136a) connected by a gutter, the complete piece constituting No. 135b or 136b, which is stapled into the booklet through the gutter.

For surcharges see Nos. 148, 176, B13-B20.

No. 135 Surcharged in Red

1939

148	A22	40c on 50c dk bl grn	.55	.20

Mosque of Salé — A26

Sefrou — A27

Cedars — A28

Goatherd A29

Ramparts of Salé — A30

Scimitar-horned Oryxes — A31

Fez — A33

Valley of Draa A32

1939-42

149	A26	1c rose violet	.20	.20
150	A27	2c emerald	.20	.20
151	A27	3c ultra	.20	.20
152	A26	5c dk bl grn	.20	.20
153	A27	10c brt red vio	.20	.20
154	A28	15c dk green	.20	.20
155	A28	20c black grn	.20	.20
156	A29	30c deep blue	.20	.20
157	A29	40c chocolate	.20	.20
158	A29	45c Prus green	.55	.20
159	A30	50c rose red	1.50	.70
159A	A30	50c Prus grn ('40)	.20	.20
160	A30	60c turq blue	1.50	.55
160A	A30	60c choc ('40)	.20	.20
161	A31	70c dk violet	.20	.20
162	A32	75c grnsh blk	.35	.20
163	A32	80c pck bl ('40)	.20	.20
163A	A32	80c dk grn ('42)	.20	.20
164	A30	90c ultra	.20	.20
165	A28	1fr chocolate	.20	.20
165A	A32	1.20fr rose vio ('42)	.50	.20
166	A32	1.25fr henna brn	1.00	.50
167	A32	1.40fr rose violet	.35	.20
168	A30	1.50fr cop red ('40)	.20	.20
168A	A30	1.50fr rose ('42)	.20	.20
169	A33	2fr Prus green	.20	.20
170	A33	2.25fr dark blue	.50	.20
170A	A26	2.40fr red ('42)	.20	.20
171	A26	2.50fr scarlet	1.00	.50
171A	A26	2.50fr dp blue ('40)	.90	.35
172	A33	3fr black brown	.35	.20
172A	A26	4fr dp ultra ('42)	.20	.20
172B	A32	4.50fr grnsh blk ('42)	.55	.20
173	A31	5fr dark blue	.55	.35
174	A31	10fr red	.90	.55
174A	A31	15fr Prus grn ('42)	4.25	3.00
175	A31	20fr dk vio brn	1.60	1.40
		Nos. 149-175 (37)	20.55	13.50
		Set, never hinged	30.00	

See Nos. 197-219. For surcharges see Nos. 244, 261-262, B21-B24, B26, B28, B32.

No. 136 Surcharged in Black

1940

176	A22	35c on 65c brown red	1.40	.60
a.		Pair, one without surcharge	2.50	2.50

The surcharge was applied on alternate rows in the sheet, making No. 176a. This was done to make a pair equal 1fr, the new rate.

SEMI-POSTAL STAMPS

French Protectorate

No. 30 Surcharged in Red ✚ 5c

1914 **Unwmk.** ***Perf. 14x13½***

B1	A4	10c + 5c on 10c	*18,500.*	*22,000.*

Known only with inverted red surcharge.

Same Surcharge on No. 42 with "Protectorat Francais"

B2	A7	10c + 5c on 10c rose	4.25	4.25
a.		Double surcharge	125.00	125.00
b.		Inverted surcharge	140.00	140.00
c.		"c" omitted	67.50	67.50

On Nos. B1 and B2 the cross is set up from pieces of metal (quads), the horizontal bar being made from two long pieces, the vertical bar from two short pieces. Each cross in the setting of twenty-five differs from the others.

No. 30 Handstamp Surcharged in Red ✚ 5c

B3	A4	10c + 5c on 10c rose	*1,250.*	*975.*
		On cover		*2,250.*

No. B3 was issued at Oujda. The surcharge ink is water-soluble.

No. 42 Surcharged in Vermilion or Carmine

B4	A7	10c + 5c on 10c (V)	16.00	16.00
a.		Double surcharge	160.00	160.00
b.		Inverted surcharge	160.00	160.00
c.		Double surch., one invtd.	140.00	140.00
B5	A7	10c +5c on 10c (C)	350.00	400.00

On Nos. B4-B5 the horizontal bar of the cross is single and not as thick as on Nos. B1-B2.

No. B5 was sold largely at Casablanca.

SP1

SP2

Carmine Surcharge

1915

B6	SP1	5c + 5c green	2.25	1.75
a.		Inverted surcharge	225.00	225.00
B7	SP2	10c + 5c rose	3.00	3.00

No. B6 was not issued without the Red Cross surcharge. No. B7 was used in Tangier.

SP3

SP4

France No. B2 Overprinted in Black

B8	SP3	10c + 5c red	5.25	5.25

Carmine Surcharge

1917

B9	SP4	10c + 5c on 10c rose	2.10	2.10

On No. B9 the horizontal bar of the cross is made from a single, thick piece of metal.

Marshal Hubert Lyautey — SP5

1935, May 15 Photo. *Perf. 13x13½*

B10	SP5	50c + 50c red	8.25	8.25
B11	SP5	1fr + 1fr dk grn	8.25	8.25
B12	SP5	5fr + 5fr blk brn	32.50	32.50
		Nos. B10-B12 (3)	49.00	49.00
		Set, never hinged	110.00	

Stamps of 1933-34 Surcharged in Blue or Red

1938 ***Perf. 13***

B13	A18	2c + 2c red vio	4.00	4.00
B14	A19	3c + 3c dk brn	4.00	4.00
B15	A20	20c + 20c red brn	4.00	4.00
B16	A21	40c + 40c blk brn (R)	4.00	4.00
B17	A22	65c + 65c brn red	4.00	4.00
B18	A23	1.25fr + 1.25fr blk (R)	4.00	4.00
B19	A24	2fr + 2fr yel brn	4.00	4.00
B20	A25	5fr + 5fr red brn	4.00	4.00
		Nos. B13-B20 (8)	32.00	32.00
		Set, never hinged	45.00	

AIR POST STAMPS

French Protectorate

Biplane over Casablanca AP1

1922-27 Photo. Unwmk. *Perf. 13½*

C1	AP1	5c dp orange ('27)	.35	.35
C2	AP1	25c dp ultra	.85	.50
C3	AP1	50c grnsh blue	.35	.35
C4	AP1	75c dp blue	62.50	9.25
C5	AP1	75c dp green	.50	.20
C6	AP1	80c vio brn ('27)	1.40	.35
C7	AP1	1fr vermilion	.80	.35
C8	AP1	1.40fr brn lake ('27)	2.00	.95
C9	AP1	1.90fr dp blue ('27)	2.00	1.40
C10	AP1	2fr black vio	1.90	.80
a.		2fr deep violet	1.90	1.10
C11	AP1	3fr gray blk	2.00	1.35
		Nos. C1-C11 (11)	74.65	15.85

The 25c, 50c, 75c deep green and 1fr each were printed in two of three types, differing in frameline thickness, or hyphen in "Helio-Vaugirard" imprint.

Imperf., Pairs

C1a	AP1	5c	42.50
C2a	AP1	25c	55.00
C3a	AP1	50c	42.50
C4a	AP1	75c	475.00
C5a	AP1	75c	60.00
C6a	AP1	80c	47.50
C7a	AP1	1fr	55.00
C10b	AP1	2fr	175.00

Nos. C8-C9 Surcharged in Blue or Black

1931, Apr. 10

C12	AP1	1fr on 1.40fr (B)	1.40	1.40
a.		Inverted surcharge	240.00	240.00
C13	AP1	1.50fr on 1.90fr (Bk)	1.40	1.40

Rabat and Tower of Hassan AP2

Casablanca AP3

1933, Jan. Engr.

C14	AP2	50c dark blue	.60	.50
C15	AP2	80c orange brn	.60	.45
C16	AP2	1.50fr brown red	.60	.50
C17	AP3	2.50fr carmine rose	4.25	.85
C18	AP3	5fr violet	2.10	1.25
C19	AP3	10fr blue green	.80	.80
		Nos. C14-C19 (6)	8.95	4.35

For surcharges see Nos. CB22-CB23.

Storks and Minaret, Chella — AP4

Plane and Map of Morocco AP5

1939-40 ***Perf. 13***

C20	AP4	80c Prus green	.20	.20
C21	AP4	1fr dk red	.20	.20
C22	AP5	1.90fr ultra	.30	.20
C23	AP5	2fr red vio ('40)	.30	.20
C24	AP5	3fr chocolate	.30	.20
C25	AP4	5fr violet	1.10	.60
C26	AP5	10fr turq blue	1.00	.35
		Nos. C20-C26 (7)	3.40	1.95

AIR POST SEMI-POSTAL STAMPS

French Protectorate

Moorish Tribesmen SPAP1

Designs: 25c, Moor plowing with camel and burro. 50c, Caravan nearing Saffi. 75c, Walls, Marrakesh. 80c, Sheep grazing at Azrou. 1fr, Gate at Fez. 1.50fr, Aerial view of Tangier. 2fr, Aerial view of Casablanca. 3fr, Storks on old wall, Rabat. 5fr, Moorish fete.

Perf. 13½

1928, July 26 Photo. Unwmk.

CB1	SPAP1	5c dp blue	4.00	4.00
CB2	SPAP1	25c brn org	4.00	4.00
CB3	SPAP1	50c red	4.00	4.00
CB4	SPAP1	75c org brn	4.00	4.00
CB5	SPAP1	80c olive grn	4.00	4.00
CB6	SPAP1	1fr orange	4.00	4.00
CB7	SPAP1	1.50fr Prus bl	4.00	4.00
CB8	SPAP1	2fr dp brown	4.00	4.00
CB9	SPAP1	3fr dp violet	4.00	4.00
CB10	SPAP1	5fr brown blk	4.00	4.00
		Nos. CB1-CB10 (10)	40.00	40.00

These stamps were sold in sets only and at double their face value. The money received for the surtax was divided among charitable and social organizations. The stamps were not sold at post offices but solely by subscription to the Moroccan Postal Administration.

Overprinted in Red or Blue (25c, 50c, 75c, 1fr)

1929, Feb. 1

CB11	SPAP1	5c dp blue	4.00	4.00
CB12	SPAP1	25c brown org	4.00	4.00
CB13	SPAP1	50c red	4.00	4.00
CB14	SPAP1	75c org brn	4.00	4.00
CB15	SPAP1	80c olive grn	4.00	4.00
CB16	SPAP1	1fr orange	4.00	4.00
CB17	SPAP1	1.50fr Prus bl	4.00	4.00
CB18	SPAP1	2fr dp brown	4.00	4.00
CB19	SPAP1	3fr dp violet	4.00	4.00
CB20	SPAP1	5fr brown blk	4.00	4.00
		Nos. CB11-CB20 (10)	40.00	40.00

These stamps were sold at double their face values and only in Tangier. The surtax benefited various charities.

Marshal Hubert Lyautey SPAP10

1935, May 15 ***Perf. 13½***

CB21	SPAP10	1.50fr + 1.50fr blue	17.00	17.00

Nos. C14, C19 Surcharged in Red

1938 ***Perf. 13***

CB22	AP2	50c + 50c dk bl	4.50	4.50
CB23	AP3	10fr + 10fr bl grn	4.50	4.50

POSTAGE DUE STAMPS

French Offices in Morocco

Postage Due Stamps and Types of France Surcharged in Red or Black

1896 Unwmk. *Perf. 14x13½*

On Stamps of 1891-93

J1	D2	5c on 5c lt bl (R)	5.75	3.50
		On cover		125.00
J2	D2	10c on 10c choc (R)	8.50	3.50
		On cover		125.00
J3	D2	30c on 30c car	21.00	16.00
		On cover		125.00
a.		Pair, one without surcharge		
J4	D2	50c on 50c lilac	21.00	16.00
a.		"S" of "CENTIMOS" omitted	240.00	175.00
J5	D2	1p on 1fr lil brn	275.00	250.00

1909-10 On Stamps of 1908-10

J6	D3	1c on 1c ol grn (R)	1.75	1.75
J7	D3	10c on 10c violet	26.00	22.50
J8	D3	30c on 30c bister	32.50	29.00
J9	D3	50c on 50c red	45.00	45.00
		Nos. J6-J9 (4)	105.25	98.25

Postage Due Stamps of France Surcharged in Red or Blue

1911 On Stamps of 1893-96

J10	D2	5c on 5c blue (R)	2.90	2.90
J11	D2	10c on 10c choc (R)	11.00	11.00
a.		Double surcharge	110.00	110.00
J12	D2	50c on 50c lil (Bl)	13.00	13.00

On Stamps of 1908-10

J13	D3	1c on 1c ol grn (R)	1.75	1.75
J14	D3	10c on 10c vio (R)	5.25	5.25
J15	D3	30c on 30c bis (R)	5.75	5.75
J16	D3	50c on 50c red (Bl)	11.00	11.00
		Nos. J10-J16 (7)	50.65	50.65

For surcharges see Nos. JN23-J26.

French Protectorate

D4

D5

Type of 1911 Issue Overprinted "Protectorat Francais"

1915-17

J17	D4	1c on 1c black	.35	.35
a.		New value double	125.00	
J18	D4	5c on 5c blue	1.40	1.10
J19	D4	10c on 10c choc	1.75	1.25
J20	D4	20c on 20c ol grn	1.75	1.25
J21	D4	30c on 30c rose red	4.50	4.00
J22	D4	50c on 50c vio brn	6.50	4.50
		Nos. J17-J22 (6)	16.25	12.45

Nos. J13 to J16 With Additional Overprint "Protectorat Francais"

1915

J23	D3	1c on 1c ol grn	.95	.95
J24	D3	10c on 10c violet	1.90	1.60
J25	D3	30c on 30c bister	2.10	1.90
J26	D3	50c on 50c red	2.10	2.00
		Nos. J23-J26 (4)	7.05	6.45

1917-26 Typo.

J27	D5	1c black	.20	.20
J28	D5	5c deep blue	.20	.20
J29	D5	10c brown	.45	.20
J30	D5	20c olive green	2.00	1.10
J31	D5	30c rose	.20	.20
J32	D5	50c lilac brown	.45	.20
J33	D5	1fr red brn, *straw* ('26)	.90	.60
J34	D5	2fr violet ('26)	1.50	.90
		Nos. J27-J34 (8)	5.90	3.60

See #J49-J56, Morocco #J1-J4. For surcharges see #J46-J48.

Postage Due Stamps of France, 1882-1906 Overprinted

1918

J35	D2	1c black	.60	.60
J36	D2	5c blue	1.25	1.25
J37	D2	10c chocolate	1.25	1.25
J38	D2	15c green	3.00	3.00
J39	D2	20c olive green	4.25	4.00
J40	D2	30c rose red	8.75	8.50
J41	D2	50c violet brown	14.00	13.50
		Nos. J35-J41 (7)	33.10	32.10

Postage Due Stamps of France, 1908-19 Overprinted

1918

J42	D3	1c olive green	.60	.60
J43	D3	10c violet	1.75	1.75
J44	D3	20c bister	5.50	5.50
J45	D3	40c red	13.00	13.00
		Nos. J42-J45 (4)	20.85	20.85

PARCEL POST STAMPS

French Protectorate

PP1

1917 Unwmk. *Perf. 13½x14*

Q1	PP1	5c green	.70	.35
Q2	PP1	10c carmine	.70	.35
Q3	PP1	20c lilac brown	.70	.50
Q4	PP1	25c blue	1.25	.50
Q5	PP1	40c dark brown	1.90	.80
Q6	PP1	50c red orange	2.40	.60
Q7	PP1	75c pale slate	3.00	1.90
Q8	PP1	1fr ultra	4.00	.55
Q9	PP1	2fr gray	5.75	1.00
Q10	PP1	5fr violet	9.00	1.00
Q11	PP1	10fr black	13.00	1.00
		Nos. Q1-Q11 (11)	42.40	8.55

FRENCH OCEANIA

ˈfrench ˌpä-lə-ˈnē-zhə

(French Polynesia)

LOCATION — South Pacific Ocean
GOVT. — French Overseas Territory
AREA — 1,522 sq. mi.
POP. — 172,000 (est. 1984)
CAPITAL — Papeete

In 1903 various French Establishments in the South Pacific were united to form a single colony. Most important of the island groups are the Society Islands, Marquesas Islands, the Tuamotu group and the Gambier, Austral, and Rapa Islands. Tahiti, largest of the Society group, ranks first in importance.

100 Centimes = 1 Franc

Catalogue values for unused stamps in this country are for Never Hinged items, beginning with Scott 124 in the regular postage section, Scott B6 in the semi-postal section, and Scott CB1 in the airpost semi-postal section.

Navigation and Commerce — A1

Perf. 14x13½

1892-1907 Typo. Unwmk.

Name of Colony in Blue or Carmine

1	A1	1c black, *lil bl*	1.50	1.50
		On cover or postcard, in combination		115.00
2	A1	2c brown, *buff*	2.50	2.00
		On cover or postcard, in combination		115.00
3	A1	4c claret, *lav*	4.00	3.00
		On cover or postcard, in combination		115.00
4	A1	5c green, *grnsh*	10.50	7.75
		On cover		150.00
5	A1	5c yellow grn ('06)	2.50	1.75
		On cover		135.00
6	A1	10c blk, *lavender*	30.00	12.50
		On cover		200.00
7	A1	10c red ('00)	2.50	1.75
		On cover		175.00
8	A1	15c blue, quadrille paper	25.00	10.50
		On cover		200.00
9	A1	15c gray, *lt gray* ('00)	5.00	4.00
		On cover		300.00
10	A1	20c red, *grn*	20.00	8.00
		On cover		400.00
11	A1	25c black, *rose*	60.00	27.50
		On cover		135.00
12	A1	25c blue ('00)	20.00	13.50
		On cover		290.00
13	A1	30c brown, *bis*	19.00	13.50
		On cover		600.00
14	A1	35c black, *yel* ('06)	8.00	8.00
		On cover		600.00
15	A1	40c red, *straw*	150.00	87.50
		On cover		800.00
16	A1	45c blk, *gray grn* ('07)	7.00	*7.50*
		On cover		900.00
17	A1	50c car, *rose*	11.50	9.50
		On cover		210.00
18	A1	50c brown, *az* ('00)	300.00	240.00
		On cover		*2,250.*
19	A1	75c dp vio, *org*	13.50	10.50
		On cover		625.00
20	A1	1fr brnz grn, *straw*	15.50	12.50
		On cover		225.00
		Nos. 1-20 (20)	528.05	354.10

Perf. 13½x14 stamps are counterfeits.

For overprint and surcharge see #55, B1.

Covers: Values are for commercial covers with correct frankings. Philatelic covers sell for less.

Tahitian Girl — A2

Kanakas — A3

Fautaua Valley — A4

1913-30

21	A2	1c violet & brn	.20	.20
		On cover		50.00
22	A2	2c brown & blk	.20	.20
		On cover		50.00
23	A2	4c orange & bl	.20	.20
		On cover		60.00
24	A2	5c grn & yel grn	.95	.55
		On cover		52.50
25	A2	5c bl & blk ('22)	.20	.20
		On cover		55.00
26	A2	10c rose & org	1.75	.95
		On cover		55.00
27	A2	10c bl grn & yel grn ('22)	.95	.95
		On cover		55.00
28	A2	10c org red & brn red, *bluish* ('26)	1.50	1.50
		On cover		60.00
29	A2	15c org & blk ('15)	.65	.45
		On cover		60.00
a.		Imperf., pair	125.00	
30	A2	20c black & vio	1.10	.90
		On cover		60.00
a.		Imperf., pair	125.00	
31	A2	20c grn & bl grn ('26)	.95	.95
		On cover		62.50
32	A2	20c brn red & dk brn ('27)	1.50	1.50
		On cover		65.00
33	A3	25c ultra & blue	1.50	1.10
		On cover		62.50
34	A3	25c vio & rose ('22)	.50	.50
		On cover		55.00
35	A3	30c gray & brown	4.00	3.00
		On cover		75.00
a.		Imperf., pair	225.00	
36	A3	30c rose & red org ('22)	2.40	2.40
		On cover		75.00
37	A3	30c blk & red org ('26)	.65	.65
		On cover		60.00
38	A3	30c slate bl & bl grn ('27)	1.75	1.75
		On cover		65.00
39	A3	35c green & rose	1.10	1.10
		On cover		75.00
40	A3	40c black & green	1.10	1.10
		On cover		60.00
41	A3	45c orange & red	1.10	1.10
		On cover		60.00
42	A3	50c dk brown & blk	15.00	12.00
		On cover		*190.00*
43	A3	50c ultra & bl ('22)	.95	.95
		On cover		60.00
44	A3	50c gray & bl vio ('26)	.45	.45
		On cover		60.00
45	A3	60c green & blk ('26)	.65	.65
		On cover		65.00
46	A3	65c ol brn & red vio ('27)	3.00	3.00
		On cover		75.00
47	A3	75c vio brn & vio	2.10	2.10
		On cover		75.00
48	A3	90c brn red & rose ('30)	16.00	16.00
		On cover		*190.00*
49	A4	1fr rose & black	4.00	3.00
		On cover		82.50
50	A4	1.10fr vio & dk brn ('28)	1.50	1.50
		On cover		82.50
51	A4	1.40fr bis brn & vio ('29)	4.00	4.00
		On cover		82.50
52	A4	1.50fr ind & bl ('30)	16.00	16.00
		On cover		210.00
53	A4	2fr dk brown & grn	4.00	3.00
		On cover		150.00
54	A4	5fr violet & bl	9.50	9.50
		On cover		190.00
		Nos. 21-54 (34)	80.30	69.45

For surcharges see Nos. 56-71, B2-B4.

No. 7 Overprinted

1915

55	A1	10c red	3.50	3.50
a.		Inverted overprint	125.00	125.00

For surcharge see No. B1.

No. 29 Surcharged

1916

56	A2	10c on 15c org & blk	2.00	1.75

Nos. 22, 41 and 29 Surcharged

1921

57	A2	5c on 2c brn & blk	25.00	25.00
58	A3	10c on 45c org & red	25.00	25.00
59	A2	25c on 15c org & blk	5.75	5.75
		Nos. 57-59 (3)	55.75	55.75

On No. 58 the new value and date are set wide apart and without bar.

Types of 1913-30 Issue Surcharged in Black or Red

1923-27

60	A3	60c on 75c bl & brn	.40	.40
61	A4	65c on 1fr dk bl & ol (R) ('25)	1.25	1.25
62	A4	85c on 1fr dk bl & ol (R) ('25)	1.25	1.25
63	A3	90c on 75c brn red & cer ('27)	1.90	1.90
		Nos. 60-63 (4)	4.80	4.80

No. 26 Surcharged

1924

64	A2	45c on 10c rose & org	2.40	2.40
a.		Inverted surcharge	*2,500.*	*2,500.*

Stamps and Type of 1913-30 Surcharged with New Value and Bars in Black or Red

1924-27

65	A4	25c on 2fr dk brn & grn	.80	.80
66	A4	25c on 5fr vio & bl	.85	.85
67	A4	1.25fr on 1fr dk bl & ultra (R) ('26)	.85	.85
68	A4	1.50fr on 1fr dk bl & lt bl ('27)	2.10	2.10
69	A4	20fr on 5fr org & brt vio ('27)	24.00	18.00
		Nos. 65-69 (5)	28.60	22.60

Surcharged in Black or Red

1926

70	A4	3fr on 5fr gray & blue	2.10	1.75
71	A4	10fr on 5fr grn & blk (R)	4.75	4.25

Papetoai Bay, Moorea A5

1929, Mar. 25

72	A5	3fr green & dk brn	5.75	5.75
73	A5	5fr lt blue & dk brn	11.00	11.00
74	A5	10fr lt red & dk brn	32.50	32.50
75	A5	20fr lilac & dk brn	40.00	40.00
		Nos. 72-75 (4)	89.25	89.25

For overprints see Nos. 128, 130, 132, 134.

Common Design Types pictured following the introduction.

Colonial Exposition Issue

Common Design Types

1931, Apr. 13 Engr. *Perf. 12½*

Name of Country Printed in Black

76	CD70	40c deep green	5.75	5.75
77	CD71	50c violet	5.75	5.75
78	CD72	90c red orange	5.75	5.75
79	CD73	1.50fr dull blue	5.75	5.75
		Nos. 76-79 (4)	23.00	23.00

Spear Fishing A12

Tahitian Girl — A13

Idols A14

1934-39 Photo. *Perf. 13½, 13½x13*

80	A12	1c gray black	.20	.20
81	A12	2c claret	.20	.20
82	A12	3c lt blue ('39)	.20	.20
83	A12	4c orange	.35	.35
84	A12	5c violet	.55	.55
85	A12	10c dark brown	.20	.20
86	A12	15c green	.35	.35
87	A12	20c red	.35	.35
88	A13	25c gray blue	.55	.55
89	A13	30c yellow green	.95	.95
90	A13	30c orange brn ('39)	.50	.50
91	A14	35c dp green ('38)	2.75	2.75
92	A13	40c red violet	.35	.35
93	A13	45c brown orange	6.25	6.25
94	A13	45c dk green ('39)	.95	.95
95	A13	50c violet	.35	.35
96	A13	55c blue ('38)	5.00	5.00
97	A13	60c black ('39)	.50	.50
98	A13	65c brown	2.25	2.25
99	A13	70c brt pink ('39)	.80	.80
100	A13	75c olive green	6.25	6.25
101	A13	80c violet brn ('38)	1.10	1.10
102	A13	90c rose red	.55	.55
103	A14	1fr red brown	.55	.55
104	A14	1.25fr brown violet	5.75	5.75
105	A14	1.25fr rose red ('39)	.70	.70
106	A14	1.40fr orange yel ('39)	.70	.70
107	A14	1.50fr blue	.55	.55
108	A14	1.60fr dull vio ('39)	.95	.95
109	A14	1.75fr olive	5.00	5.00
110	A14	2fr red	.55	.55
111	A14	2.25fr deep blue ('39)	.70	.70
112	A14	2.50fr black ('39)	.80	.80
113	A14	3fr brown org ('39)	1.25	1.25
114	A14	5fr red violet ('39)	.75	.75
115	A14	10fr dark green ('39)	2.25	2.25
116	A14	20fr dark brown ('39)	2.25	2.25
		Nos. 80-116 (37)	54.25	54.25

For overprints see #126-127, 129, 131, 133, 135.

Paris International Exposition Issue

Common Design Types

1937 Engr. *Perf. 13*

117	CD74	20c deep violet	2.25	2.25
118	CD75	30c dark green	2.25	2.25
119	CD76	40c carmine rose	2.25	2.25
120	CD77	50c dk brown & blue	3.00	3.00
121	CD78	90c red	3.00	3.00
122	CD79	1.50fr ultra	3.75	3.75
		Nos. 117-122 (6)	16.50	16.50

Colonial Arts Exhibition Issue

Souvenir Sheet

Common Design Type

1937 *Imperf.*

123	CD78	3fr emerald	30.00	*42.50*

New York World's Fair Issue

Common Design Type

1939, May 10 Engr. *Perf. 12½x12*

124	CD82	1.25fr carmine lake	1.00	1.00
125	CD82	2.25fr ultra	1.00	1.00
		Set, never hinged	3.50	

SEMI-POSTAL STAMPS

Nos. 55 and 26 Surcharged in Red

1915 Unwmk. *Perf. 14x13½*

B1	A1	10c + 5c red	22.50	22.50
a.		"e" instead of "c"	57.50	57.50
b.		Inverted surcharge	160.00	160.00
B2	A2	10c + 5c rose & org	7.50	7.50
a.		"e" instead of "c"	40.00	40.00
b.		"c" inverted	47.50	47.50
c.		Inverted surcharge	225.00	225.00

Surcharged in Carmine

B3	A2	10c + 5c rose & org	3.25	3.25
a.		"e" instead of "c"	25.00	25.00
b.		Inverted surcharge	150.00	150.00

Surcharged in Carmine

1916

B4	A2	10c + 5c rose & org	3.25	3.25

Curie Issue

Common Design Type

1938 Engr. *Perf. 13*

B5	CD80	1.75fr + 50c brt ultra	14.00	14.00

French Revolution Issue

Common Design Type

1939 Photo.

Name and Value Typo. in Black

B6	CD83	45c + 25c grn	14.00	14.00
B7	CD83	70c + 30c brn	14.00	14.00
B8	CD83	90c + 35c red org	14.00	14.00
B9	CD83	1.25fr + 1fr rose pink	14.00	14.00
B10	CD83	2.25fr + 2fr blue	14.00	14.00
		Nos. B6-B10 (5)	70.00	70.00
		Set, never hinged	120.00	

AIR POST STAMP

Seaplane in Flight AP1

Perf. 13½

1934, Nov. 5 Unwmk. Photo.

C1	AP1	5fr green	.75	.75

For overprint see No. C2.

AIR POST SEMI-POSTAL STAMP

Catalogue values for unused stamps in this section are for Never Hinged items.

French Revolution Issue

Common Design Type

Unwmk.

1939, July 5 Photo. *Perf. 13*

Name and Value Typo. in Orange

CB1	CD83	5fr + 4fr brn blk	52.50	29.00

POSTAGE DUE STAMPS

Postage Due Stamps of French Colonies, 1894-1906, Overprinted

1926-27 Unwmk. *Perf. 14x13½*

J1	D1	5c light blue	.60	.60
J2	D1	10c brown	.60	.60
J3	D1	20c olive green	.95	.95
J4	D1	30c dull red	1.00	1.00
J5	D1	40c rose	2.25	2.25
J6	D1	60c blue green	2.25	2.25
J7	D1	1fr red brown, *straw*	2.25	2.25
J8	D1	3fr magenta ('27)	9.50	9.50

With Additional Surcharge of New Value

J9	D1	2fr on 1fr orange red	2.75	2.75
		Nos. J1-J9 (9)	22.15	22.15

Fautaua Falls, Tahiti — D2

Tahitian Youth — D3

1929 Typo. *Perf. 13½x14*

J10	D2	5c lt blue & dk brn	.50	.50
J11	D2	10c vermilion & grn	.60	.60
J12	D2	30c dk brn & dk red	1.25	1.25
J13	D2	50c yel grn & dk brn	1.00	1.00
J14	D2	60c dl vio & yel grn	2.75	2.75
J15	D3	1fr Prus bl & red vio	2.25	2.25
J16	D3	2fr brn red & dk brn	1.50	1.50
J17	D3	3fr bl vio & bl grn	1.50	1.50
		Nos. J10-J17 (8)	11.35	11.35

FRENCH SUDAN

'french sü-'dan

LOCATION — In northwest Africa, north of French Guinea and Ivory Coast

GOVT. — French Colony

AREA — 590,966 sq. mi.

POP. — 3,794,270 (1941)

CAPITAL — Bamako

In 1899 French Sudan was abolished as a separate colony and was divided among Dahomey, French Guinea, Ivory Coast, Senegal and Senegambia and Niger. Issues for French Sudan were resumed in 1921.

From 1906 to 1921 a part of this territory was known as Upper Senegal and Niger. A part of Upper Volta was added in 1933.

100 Centimes = 1 Franc

Navigation and Commerce

A1 A2

Stamps of French Colonies, Surcharged in Black

Perf. 14x13½

1894, Apr. 12 Unwmk.

1	A1	15c on 75c car, *rose*	3,200.	*1,600.*
		On cover		4,000.
2	A1	25c on 1fr brnz grn, *straw*	3,500.	*1,250.*
		On cover		3,500.

The imperforate stamp like No. 1 was made privately in Paris from a fragment of the lithographic stone which had been used in the Colony for surcharging No. 1.

Counterfeit surcharges exist.

1894-1900 Typo. *Perf. 14x13½*

Name of colony in Blue or Carmine

3	A2	1c blk, *lil bl*	1.25	1.25
		On cover		—
4	A2	2c brn, *buff*	1.75	1.75
		On cover		—
5	A2	4c claret, *lav*	4.25	4.25
		On cover		—
6	A2	5c grn, *grnsh*	7.25	7.25
		On cover		42.50
7	A2	10c blk, *lav*	16.00	16.00
		On cover		42.50
8	A2	10c red ('00)	5.50	5.50
		On cover		42.50
9	A2	15c blue, quadrille paper	5.00	5.00
		On cover		62.50
10	A2	15c gray, *lt gray* ('00)	5.75	5.75
		On cover		75.00
11	A2	20c red, *grn*	22.00	22.00
		On cover		*110.00*
12	A2	25c blk, *rose*	19.50	19.50
		On cover		67.50
13	A2	25c blue ('00)	5.75	5.75
		On cover		55.00
14	A2	30c brn, *bister*	32.50	32.50
		On cover		—
15	A2	40c red, *straw*	26.00	26.00
		On cover		125.00
16	A2	50c car, *rose*	40.00	40.00
		On cover		140.00
17	A2	50c brn, *az* ('00)	9.75	9.75
		On cover		*125.00*
18	A2	75c dp vio, *org*	37.50	37.50
		On cover		250.00
19	A2	1fr brnz grn, *straw*	7.00	7.00
		On cover		—
		Nos. 3-19 (17)	246.75	246.75

Perf. 13½x14 stamps are counterfeits.

Nos. 8, 10, 13, 17 were issued in error. They were accepted for use in the other colonies.

Covers: Values are for commercial with correct frankings. Philatelic covers sell for less.

Camel and Rider — A3

Stamps of Upper Senegal and Niger Overprinted in Black

1921-30 *Perf. 13½x14*

21	A3	1c brn vio & vio	.20	.20
22	A3	2c dk gray & dl vio	.20	.20
23	A3	4c blk & blue	.20	.20
24	A3	5c ol brn & dk brn	.20	.20
25	A3	10c yel grn & bl grn	.65	.20
26	A3	10c red vio & bl ('25)	.25	.20
27	A3	15c red brn & org	.25	.20
28	A3	15c yel grn & dp grn ('25)	.25	.20
29	A3	15c org brn & vio ('27)	1.25	1.25
30	A3	20c brn vio & blk	.25	.20
31	A3	25c blk & bl grn	.75	.60
a.		Booklet pane of 4	—	
32	A3	30c red org & rose	1.10	.75
33	A3	30c bl grn & blk ('26)	.45	.45
34	A3	30c dl grn & bl grn ('28)	1.40	1.40
35	A3	35c rose & vio	.30	.25
36	A3	40c gray & rose	.90	.65
37	A3	45c bl & ol brn	.75	.60
38	A3	50c ultra & bl	1.25	.95
39	A3	50c red org & bl ('26)	.90	.80
40	A3	60c vio, *pnksh* ('26)	.80	.50
41	A3	65c bis & pale bl ('28)	1.40	1.25
42	A3	75c org & ol brn	1.00	.80
43	A3	90c brn red & pink ('30)	4.25	4.25
44	A3	1fr dk brn & dl vio	1.10	.95
45	A3	1.10fr gray lil & red vio ('28)	2.25	2.25
46	A3	1.50fr dp bl & bl ('30)	4.75	4.75
47	A3	2fr grn & bl	1.60	1.40
48	A3	3fr red vio ('30)	9.50	9.50
a.		Double overprint	125.00	
49	A3	5fr vio & blk	5.00	4.25
		Nos. 21-49 (29)	43.15	39.40

Type of 1921 Surcharged

1922, Sept. 28

50	A3	60c on 75c vio, *pnksh*	.50	.50

Stamps and Type of 1921-30 Surcharged with New Values and Bars

1925-27

51	A3	25c on 45c	.50	.50
52	A3	65c on 75c	1.40	1.10
53	A3	85c on 2fr	1.40	1.40
54	A3	85c on 5fr	1.40	1.40
55	A3	90c on 75c brn red & sal pink ('27)	1.60	1.40
56	A3	1.25fr on 1fr dp bl & lt bl (R) ('26)	.95	.95
57	A3	1.50fr on 1fr dp bl & ultra ('27)	.95	.95
58	A3	3fr on 5fr dl red & brn org ('27)	4.25	3.75
59	A3	10fr on 5fr brn red & bl grn ('27)	17.00	14.00
60	A3	20fr on 5fr vio & ver ('27)	22.00	19.50
		Nos. 51-60 (10)	51.45	44.95

Sudanese Woman — A4

Entrance to the Residency at Djenné — A5

Sudanese Boatman — A6

1931-40 Typo. *Perf. 13x14*

61	A4	1c dk red & blk	.20	.20
62	A4	2c dp blue & org	.20	.20
63	A4	3c dk red & blk ('40)	.20	.20
64	A4	4c gray lil & rose	.20	.20
65	A4	5c indigo & grn	.20	.20
66	A4	10c ol grn & rose	.20	.20
67	A4	15c blk & brt vio	.25	.25
68	A4	20c hn brn & lt bl	.25	.25
69	A4	25c red vio & lt red	.25	.25
70	A5	30c grn & lt grn	.60	.35
71	A5	30c dk bl & red org ('40)	.25	.25
72	A5	35c ol grn & grn ('38)	.35	.35
73	A5	40c ol grn & pink	.25	.25
74	A5	45c dk bl & red org	.80	.35
75	A5	45c ol grn & grn ('40)	.35	.35
76	A5	50c red & black	.25	.25
77	A5	55c ultra & car ('38)	.35	.35
78	A5	60c brt bl & brn ('40)	.80	.80
79	A5	65c brt vio & blk	.50	.35
80	A5	70c vio bl & car rose ('40)	.50	.50
81	A5	75c brt bl & ol brn	2.25	1.50
82	A5	80c car & brn ('38)	.35	.35
83	A5	90c dp red & red org	1.50	.75
84	A5	90c brt vio & sl blk ('39)	.60	.60
85	A5	1fr indigo & grn	6.75	1.50
86	A5	1fr rose red ('38)	4.00	1.50
87	A5	1fr car & brn ('40)	.60	.60
88	A6	1.25fr vio & dl vio ('33)	.50	.50
89	A6	1.25fr red ('39)	.60	.60
90	A6	1.40fr brt vio & blk ('40)	.65	.65
91	A6	1.50fr dk bl & ultra	.50	.35
92	A6	1.60fr brn & dp bl ('40)	.60	.60
93	A6	1.75fr dk brn & dp bl ('33)	.65	.55
94	A6	1.75fr vio bl ('38)	.65	.55
95	A6	2fr org brn & grn	.70	.40
96	A6	2.25fr vio bl & ultra ('39)	.75	.75
97	A6	2.50fr lt brown ('40)	1.25	1.25
98	A6	3fr Prus grn & brn	.65	.25
99	A6	5fr red & blk	1.75	1.00
100	A6	10fr dull bl & grn	2.00	1.60
101	A6	20fr red vio & brn	2.75	2.25
		Nos. 61-101 (41)	37.00	24.20

For surcharges see Nos. B7-B10.

Common Design Types pictured following the introduction.

Colonial Exposition Issue
Common Design Types

1931, Apr. 13 Engr. *Perf. 12½*
Name of Country Printed in Black

102	CD70	40c deep green	3.00	3.00
103	CD71	50c violet	3.00	3.00
104	CD72	90c red orange	3.00	3.00
105	CD73	1.50fr dull blue	3.00	3.00

Paris International Exposition Issue
Common Design Types

1937, Apr. 15 *Perf. 13*

106	CD74	20c deep violet	1.00	1.00
107	CD75	30c dark green	1.25	1.25
108	CD76	40c carmine rose	1.25	1.25
109	CD77	50c dark brown	1.25	1.25
110	CD78	90c red	1.25	1.25
111	CD79	1.50fr ultra	1.25	1.25
		Nos. 106-111 (6)	7.25	7.25

Colonial Arts Exhibition Issue
Souvenir Sheet
Common Design Type

1937 Engr. *Imperf.*

112	CD77	3fr magenta & blk	7.50	*8.00*

Caillie Issue
Common Design Type

1939, Apr. 5 *Perf. 12½x12*

113	CD81	90c org brn & org	.75	.75
114	CD81	2fr brt violet	.75	.75
115	CD81	2.25fr ultra & dk bl	.75	.75

New York World's Fair Issue
Common Design Type

1939, May 10

116	CD82	1.25fr car lake	.90	.90
117	CD82	2.25fr ultra	.90	.90

SEMI-POSTAL STAMPS

Curie Issue
Common Design Type
Unwmk.

1938, Oct. 24 Engr. *Perf. 13*

B1	CD80	1.75fr + 50c brt ultra	10.00	10.00

French Revolution Issue
Common Design Type

1939, July 5 Photo.
Name and Value Typo. in Black

B2	CD83	45c + 25c green	8.50	8.50
B3	CD83	70c + 30c brown	8.50	8.50
B4	CD83	90c + 35c red orange	8.50	8.50
B5	CD83	1.25fr + 1fr rose pink	8.50	8.50
B6	CD83	2.25fr + 2fr blue	8.50	8.50
		Nos. B2-B6 (5)	42.50	42.50

AIR POST STAMPS

Common Design Type
Perf. 12½x12

1940, Feb. 8 Unwmk. Engr.

C1	CD85	1.90fr ultra	.25	.25
C2	CD85	2.90fr dark red	.35	.35
C3	CD85	4.50fr dk gray green	.75	.75
C4	CD85	4.90fr yellow bister	.75	.75
C5	CD85	6.90fr deep orange	.90	.90
		Nos. C1-C5 (5)	3.00	3.00

POSTAGE DUE STAMPS

D1

D2

Postage Due Stamps of Upper Senegal and Niger Overprinted

Perf. 14x13½

1921, Dec. Unwmk. Typo.

J1	D1	5c green	.35	.35
J2	D1	10c rose	.50	.50
J3	D1	15c gray	.65	.65
J4	D1	20c brown	.85	.85
J5	D1	30c blue	.85	.85
J6	D1	50c black	1.25	1.25
J7	D1	60c orange	1.50	1.50
J8	D1	1fr violet	1.90	1.90
		Nos. J1-J8 (8)	7.85	7.85

Type of 1921 Issue Surcharged

1927, Oct. 10

J9	D1	2fr on 1fr lilac rose	4.50	4.50
J10	D1	3fr on 1fr org brown	4.50	4.50

1931, Mar. 9

J11	D2	5c green	.20	.20
J12	D2	10c rose	.20	.20
J13	D2	15c gray	.20	.20
J14	D2	20c dark brown	.20	.20
J15	D2	30c dark blue	.35	.35
J16	D2	50c black	.35	.35
J17	D2	60c deep orange	.50	.50
J18	D2	1fr violet	.80	.80
J19	D2	2fr lilac rose	.95	.95
J20	D2	3fr red brown	1.00	1.00
		Nos. J11-J20 (10)	4.75	4.75

FUNCHAL

fün-'shäl

LOCATION — A city and administrative district in the Madeira island group in the Atlantic Ocean northwest of Africa

GOVT. — A part of the Republic of Portugal

POP. — 150,574 (1900)

Postage stamps of Funchal were superseded by those of Madeira. These, in turn, were displaced by the stamps of Portugal.

1000 Reis = 1 Milreis

STAMPS OF PORTUGAL USED IN FUNCHAL

Barred Numeral "51"

Queen Maria II

1853

A1	5r orange brown (#1)	1,425.
A2	25r blue (#2)	92.50
A3	50r deep yellow green (#3)	1,400.
a.	50r blue green (#3a)	—
A4	100r lilac (#4)	3,000.

1855 King Pedro V (Straight Hair)

A5	5r red brown (#5)	1,425.
A6	25r blue, type II (#6)	72.50
a.	Type I (#6a)	67.50
A7	50r green (#7)	110.00
A8	100r lilac (#8)	115.00

1856-58

King Pedro V (Curled Hair)

A9	5r brown (#9)	175.00
A10	25r blue, type II (#10)	110.00
a.	Type I (#10a)	110.00
A11	25r rose, type II (#11) ('58)	36.00

1862-64 King Luiz

A12	5r brown (#12)	110.00
A13	10r orange (#13)	115.00
A14	25r rose (#14)	40.00
A15	50r yellow green (#15)	110.00
A16	100r lilac (#16) ('64)	100.00

1866-67 King Luiz

Imperf.

A17	5r black (#17)	115.00
A18	10r yellow (#18)	175.00
A19	20r bister (#19)	175.00
A20	25r rose (#20) ('67)	132.50
A21	50r green (#21)	175.00
A22	80r orange (#22)	175.00
A23	100r dark lilac (#23) ('67)	225.00
A24	120r blue (#24)	115.00

Perf. 12½

A28	25r rose (#28)	95.00

King Carlos
A1 A2

1892-93 Typo. Unwmk.

Enamel Surfaced Paper, *Perf. 12½*

1	A1	5r yellow	3.00	1.50
		Never hinged	4.25	
a.		Half used as 2½r on entire newspaper		16.00
2	A1	10r red violet	2.50	1.50
		Never hinged	3.50	
3	A1	15r chocolate	3.25	2.50
		Never hinged	4.75	
4	A1	20r lavender	3.75	2.10
		Never hinged	5.00	
a.		Perf. 13½	8.75	6.25
5	A1	25r dark green	6.00	1.35
		Never hinged	8.00	
6	A1	50r ultramarine	7.00	5.50
		Never hinged	10.00	
7	A1	75r carmine	7.00	5.50
		Never hinged	10.00	
8	A1	80r yellow green	14.00	9.50
		Never hinged	20.00	
9	A1	100r brn, *yel* ('93)	9.00	4.00
		Never hinged	12.50	
a.		Diagonal half used as 50r on cover		32.50
11	A1	200r dk bl, *bl* ('93)	60.00	37.50
		Never hinged	82.50	
12	A1	300r dk bl, *sal* ('93)	60.00	47.50
		Never hinged	95.00	

Enamel Surfaced Paper, *Perf. 13½*

1c	A1	5r yellow	3.00	1.50
		Never hinged	4.00	
2a	A1	10r red violet	3.25	2.10
		Never hinged	4.75	
3a	A1	15r chocolate	4.50	2.10
		Never hinged	6.25	
4a	A1	20r lavender	8.75	6.25
		Never hinged	12.50	
6a	A1	50r ultramarine	8.75	5.50
		Never hinged	12.50	
7a	A1	75r carmine	8.75	5.50
		Never hinged	12.50	
8a	A1	80r yellow green	17.50	12.00
		Never hinged	20.00	
10	A1	150r car, *rose* ('93)	52.50	26.00
		Never hinged	72.50	

Enamel Surfaced Paper, *Perf. 11½*

1b	A1	5r yellow	4.00	2.75
5a	A1	25r dark green	4.75	1.00
6b	A1	50r ultramarine	4.75	2.10

Chalky Paper, *Perf. 12½*

3b	A1	15r chocolate	14.00	10.00
		Never hinged	20.00	
8b	A1	80r yellow green	16.00	11.00
		Never hinged	22.50	

Chalky Paper, *Perf. 13½*

6c	A1	50r ultramarine	12.50	7.25
		Never hinged	19.00	

Nos. 1-12 were issued on two types of paper: enamel surfaced, which is white, with a uniform low gloss; and chalky, which bears a low-gloss application in a pattern of tiny lozenges, producing a somewhat duller appearance.

The reprints of this issue have shiny white gum and clean-cut perforation 13½. The shades differ from those of the originals and the uncolored paper is thin.

1897-1905 *Perf. 11¾*

Name and Value in Black except Nos. 25 and 34

13	A2	2½r gray	.50	.35
		Never hinged	.60	
14	A2	5r orange	.50	.35
		Never hinged	.60	
15	A2	10r light green	.50	.35
		Never hinged	.60	
16	A2	15r brown	5.00	3.00
		Never hinged	7.25	
17	A2	15r gray grn ('99)	3.25	2.25
		Never hinged	4.50	
18	A2	20r gray vio	1.40	.75
		Never hinged	1.75	
19	A2	25r sea green	2.75	.75
		Never hinged	3.75	
20	A2	25r car rose ('99)	1.40	.55
		Never hinged	1.75	
a.		Booklet pane of 6	—	
21	A2	50r dark blue	6.00	4.00
		Never hinged	7.25	
a.		Perf. 12½	16.00	7.25
		Never hinged	18.00	
22	A2	50r ultra ('05)	1.50	.90
		Never hinged	1.75	
23	A2	65r slate blue ('98)	1.25	.90
		Never hinged	1.50	
24	A2	75r rose	1.40	.95
		Never hinged	2.00	
25	A2	75r brn & red, *yel* ('05)	2.00	1.40
		Never hinged	2.40	
26	A2	80r violet	1.40	1.10
		Never hinged	2.00	
27	A2	100r dark blue, *blue*	1.40	1.10
		Never hinged	2.00	
a.		Diagonal half used as 50r on cover		—
28	A2	115r org brn, *pink* ('98)	2.25	1.40
		Never hinged	3.00	
29	A2	130r gray brown, *buff* ('98)	2.25	1.40
		Never hinged	3.00	
30	A2	150r lt brn, *buff*	2.75	1.25
		Never hinged	3.75	
31	A2	180r sl, *pnksh* ('98)	2.25	1.40
		Never hinged	3.00	
32	A2	200r red vio, *pale lil*	3.00	2.10
		Never hinged	3.75	
33	A2	300r blue, *rose*	3.00	2.10
		Never hinged	3.75	
34	A2	500r blk & red, *bl*	3.50	2.40
		Never hinged	3.75	
a.		Perf. 12½	13.00	7.75
		Never hinged	15.00	
		Nos. 13-34 (22)	49.25	30.75

Yellowish Paper

13a	A2	2½r gray	.50	.35
		Never hinged	.60	
14a	A2	5r orange	.50	.35
		Never hinged	.60	
15a	A2	10r light green	.50	.35
		Never hinged	.60	

17a A2 15r gray grn ('99) 3.25 2.25
Never hinged 4.75
18a A2 20r gray vio 1.40 .75
Never hinged 1.75
20b A2 25r car rose ('99) 1.40 .55
Never hinged 1.75
23a A2 65r slate blue ('98) 1.25 .90
Never hinged 1.50
24a A2 75r rose 1.40 .95
Never hinged 2.00

GABON

ga-'bōⁿ

LOCATION — West coast of Africa, at the equator
GOVT. — French colony
AREA — 102,089 sq. mi.
POP. — 1,367,000 (est. 1984)
CAPITAL — Libreville

Gabon originally was under the control of French West Africa. In 1886, it was united with French Congo. In 1904, Gabon was granted a certain degree of colonial autonomy which prevailed until 1934, when it merged with French Equatorial Africa.

100 Centimes = 1 Franc

Stamps of French Colonies of 1881-86 Handstamp Surcharged in Black:

a

b

1886 Unwmk. *Perf. 14x13½*

1 A9 (a) 5c on 20c red, *grn* 425.00 400.00
a. "5" double 3,000.
2 A9 (b) 10c on 20c red, *grn* 425.00 400.00
a. "0" double 1,100. 1,000.
b. "10" double 1,100. 1,000.
3 A9 (b) 25c on 20c red, *grn* 70.00 62.50
On cover 1,200.
a. "25" double 550.00 425.00
b. "25" omitted 925.00 925.00
c. "GAB" inverted 700.00 600.00
e. 56 dots around "GAB" 5,250. 1,400.
On cover 4,500.
4 A9 (b) 50c on 15c bl 1,200. 1,400.
a. "GAB" omitted 2,700.
5 A9 (b) 75c on 15c bl 1,350. 1,700.
a. "75" double 4,250.

On Nos. 3 and 5 the surcharge slants down; on No. 4 it slants up. The number of dots varies.

Counterfeits of Nos. 1-15 exist.

Covers: Values are for commercial covers with correct frankings.

Handstamp Surcharged in Black — c

1888-89

6 A9 15c on 10c blk, *lav* 4,500. 1,050.
7 A9 15c on 1fr brnz grn, *straw* 1,800. 850.00
8 A9 25c on 5c grn, *grnsh* 1,200. 225.00
On cover 1,200.
a. Double surcharge 3,250. 3,250.
9 A9 25c on 10c blk, *lav* 5,000. 1,500.
10 A9 25c on 75c car, *rose* 2,800. 1,400.
On cover 5,000.

Official reprints exist.

Postage Due Stamps of French Colonies Handstamp Surcharged in Black — d

1889 *Imperf.*

11 D1 15c on 5c black 250.00 200.00
a. "TIMBRE" omitted 750.00 500.00
b. "15" omitted 750.00 525.00
12 D1 15c on 30c black 4,250. 3,000.
a. "GABON" omitted 5,400.
b. "15" omitted 5,400.
13 D1 25c on 20c black 92.50 77.50
On cover 675.00

Nos. 11 and 13 exist with "GABON," "TIMBRE" or "25" double.

A8

1889 Typeset

14 A8 15c blk, *rose* 1,400. 925.
a. "GAB" omitted 7,000.
15 A8 25c blk, *green* 925. 700.
On cover 2,750.
a. "GAB" omitted 2,400.
b. "GAB" inverted 2,300.
c. "GAB" double 4,500.

Ten varieties of each. Nos. 14-15 exist with small "f" in "Francaise."

Navigation and Commerce — A9

1904-07 Typo. *Perf. 14x13½*
Name of Colony in Blue or Carmine

16 A9 1c blk, *lil bl* .85 .70
On cover 55.00
a. "GABON" double 210.00
17 A9 2c brn, *buff* .95 .80
On cover 55.00
18 A9 4c claret, *lav* 1.75 1.25
On cover 55.00
19 A9 5c yellow green 2.10 1.75
On cover 30.00
20 A9 10c rose 7.00 5.50
On cover 30.00
21 A9 15c gray 7.75 5.50
On cover 30.00
22 A9 20c red, *grn* 11.00 8.25
On cover 75.00
23 A9 25c blue 9.25 5.50
On cover 40.00
24 A9 30c yel brn 11.00 11.00
On cover 75.00
25 A9 35c blk, *yel* ('06) 16.00 16.00
On cover 90.00
26 A9 40c red, *straw* 19.00 14.00
On cover 90.00
27 A9 45c blk, *gray grn* ('07) 32.50 32.50
On cover 140.00
28 A9 50c brn, *az* 15.00 15.00
On cover 100.00
29 A9 75c dp vio, *org* 20.00 20.00
On cover 140.00
30 A9 1fr brnz grn, *straw* 30.00 27.50
31 A9 2fr vio, *rose* 70.00 60.00
32 A9 5fr lil, *lav* 110.00 95.00
Nos. 16-32 (17) 364.15 320.25

Perf. 13½x14 stamps are counterfeits.
For surcharges see Nos. 72-84.

Covers: Values are for commercial covers with correct frankings. Philatelic covers sell for less.

Fang Warrior — A10

Fang Woman — A12

Libreville A11

Inscribed: "Congo Français"

1910 *Perf. 13½x14*

33 A10 1c choc & org 1.40 1.40
34 A10 2c black & choc 1.90 1.90
35 A10 4c vio & dp bl 1.90 1.90
36 A10 5c ol gray & grn 3.00 3.00
37 A10 10c red & car 4.25 4.25
38 A10 20c choc & dk vio 4.00 4.00
39 A11 25c dp bl & choc 4.00 4.00
40 A11 30c gray blk & red 26.00 26.00
41 A11 35c dk vio & grn 16.00 16.00
42 A11 40c choc & ultra 18.00 18.00
43 A11 45c carmine & vio 32.50 32.50
44 A11 50c bl grn & gray 50.00 50.00
45 A11 75c org & choc 80.00 77.50
46 A12 1fr dk brn & bis 80.00 77.50
47 A12 2fr carmine & brn 225.00 210.00
48 A12 5fr blue & choc 225.00 210.00
Nos. 33-48 (16) 772.95 737.95

Inscribed: "Afrique Equatoriale"

1910-22

49 A10 1c choc & org .20 .20
50 A10 2c black & choc .20 .20
a. 2c gray black & deep olive .30 .20
51 A10 4c vio & dp bl .35 .35
52 A10 5c ol gray & grn .50 .35
53 A10 5c gray blk & ocher ('22) .80 .80
54 A10 10c red & car .85 .70
55 A10 10c yel grn & bl grn ('22) .80 .80
56 A10 15c brn vio & rose ('18) .55 .50
57 A10 20c ol brn & dk vio 13.50 9.50
58 A11 25c dp bl & choc .70 .55
59 A11 25c Prus bl & blk ('22) .95 .95
60 A11 30c gray blk & red 1.10 .95
61 A11 30c rose & red ('22) 1.40 1.40
62 A11 35c dk vio & grn .55 .70
63 A11 40c choc & ultra 1.10 .80
64 A11 45c carmine & vio .95 .80
65 A11 45c blk & red ('22) 1.60 1.60
66 A11 50c bl grn & gray 1.10 .95
67 A11 50c dk bl & bl ('22) 1.00 1.00
68 A11 75c org & choc 5.00 4.75
69 A12 1fr dk brn & bis 2.75 2.50
70 A12 2fr car & brn 5.00 4.00
71 A12 5fr blue & choc 8.25 7.00
Nos. 49-71 (23) 49.20 41.35

For overprints & surcharges see #85-119, B1-B3.

Stamps of 1904-07 Surcharged in Black or Carmine

1912

Spacing between figures of surcharge 1.5mm (5c), 2mm (10c)

72 A9 5c on 2c brn, *buff* .95 .95
73 A9 5c on 4c cl, *lav* (C) .85 .85
74 A9 5c on 15c gray (C) .85 .85
75 A9 5c on 20c red, *grn* .80 .80
76 A9 5c on 25c bl (C) .85 .85
77 A9 5c on 30c pale brn (C) .55 .55
78 A9 10c on 40c red, *straw* .95 .95
79 A9 10c on 45c blk, *gray grn* (C) .95 .95
80 A9 10c on 50c brn, *az* (C) .85 .85
81 A9 10c on 75c dp vio, *org* .85 .85
82 A9 10c on 1fr brnz grn, *straw* .85 .85
83 A9 10c on 2fr vio, *rose* .95 .95
a. Inverted surcharge 250.00 250.00
84 A9 10c on 5fr lil, *lav* 3.00 3.00
Nos. 72-84 (13) 13.25 13.25

Spacing between figures of surcharge 2.25mm (5c), 2.75mm (10c)

72a A9 5c on 2c brn, *buff* 6.00 6.00
73a A9 5c on 4c cl, *lav* (C) 6.00 6.00
74a A9 5c on 15c gray (C) 6.00 6.00
75a A9 5c on 20c red, *grn* 6.00 6.00
76a A9 5c on 25c bl (C) 6.00 6.00
77a A9 5c on 30c pale brn (C) 8.50 8.50
78a A9 10c on 40c red, *straw* 21.00 21.00
79a A9 10c on 45c blk, *gray grn* (C) 27.50 27.50
80a A9 10c on 50c brn, *az* (C) 35.00 35.00
81a A9 10c on 75c dp vio, *org* 50.00 50.00
82a A9 10c on 1fr brnz grn, *straw* 57.50 57.50
83b A9 10c on 2fr vio, *rose* 57.50 57.50
c. Inverted surcharge 3,250. 3,250.
84 A9 10c on 5fr lil, *lav* 125.00 125.00
Nos. 72a-84 (13) 412.00 412.00

Stamps of 1910-22 Overprinted in Black, Blue or Carmine

On A10, A12

On A11

1924-31

85 A10 1c brown & org .20 .20
86 A10 2c blk & choc (Bl) .35 .35
87 A10 4c violet & ind .20 .20
88 A10 5c gray blk & ocher .35 .35
89 A10 10c yel grn & bl grn .70 .70
a. Double overprint (Bk & Bl) 110.00
90 A10 10c dk bl & brn ('26) (C) .20 .20
91 A10 15c brn vio & rose (Bl) .70 .70
92 A10 15c rose & brn vio ('31) (Bl) .90 .90
93 A10 20c ol brn & dk vio (C) .70 .70
a. Inverted overprint 125.00 125.00
94 A11 25c Prus bl & blk (C) .55 .55
95 A11 30c rose & red (Bl) .55 .55
96 A11 30c blk & org ('26) .55 .55
97 A11 30c dk grn & bl grn ('28) .70 .70
98 A11 35c dk vio & grn (Bl) .50 .50
99 A11 40c choc & ultra (C) .45 .45
100 A11 45c blk & red (Bl) 1.10 1.10
101 A11 50c dk bl & bl (C) .65 .65
102 A11 50c car & grn ('26) .65 .65
103 A11 65c dp bl & red org ('28) 3.25 2.90
104 A11 75c org & brn (Bl) 1.40 1.40
105 A11 90c brn red & rose ('30) 2.10 1.75
106 A12 1fr dk brn & bis 1.25 1.25
107 A12 1.10fr dl grn & rose red ('28) 5.00 4.25
108 A12 1.50fr pale bl & dk bl ('30) .90 .90
109 A12 2fr rose & brn 1.40 1.40
110 A12 3fr red vio ('30) 7.75 6.00
111 A12 5fr dp bl & choc 5.75 4.75
Nos. 85-111 (27) 38.80 34.60

Types of 1924-31 Issues Surcharged with New Values in Black or Carmine

1925-28

112 A12 65c on 1fr ol grn & brn .80 .80
113 A12 85c on 1fr ol grn & brn .95 .95
114 A11 90c on 75c brn red & cer ('27) 1.10 1.10
115 A12 1.25fr on 1fr dk bl & ultra (C) .55 .55
116 A12 1.50fr on 1fr lt bl & dk bl ('27) 1.10 1.10
117 A12 3fr on 5fr mag & ol brn 6.75 5.50
118 A12 10fr on 5fr org brn & grn ('27) 11.00 9.50
119 A12 20fr on 5fr red vio & org red ('27) 12.00 10.50
Nos. 112-119 (8) 34.25 30.00

Bars cover the old denominations on #114-119.

Common Design Types pictured following the introduction.

Colonial Exposition Issue
Common Design Types

1931 *Perf. 12½*
Name of Country in Black

120 CD70 40c dp green 2.50 2.50
121 CD71 50c violet 2.50 2.50
122 CD72 90c red orange 2.50 2.50
123 CD73 1.50fr dull blue 4.00 4.00
Nos. 120-123 (4) 11.50 11.50

Timber Raft on Ogowe River
A16

Count Savorgnan de Brazza — A17

Village of Setta Kemma
A18

1932-33 Photo. *Perf. 13x13½*

124	A16	1c brown violet	.20	.20
125	A16	2c blk, *rose*	.20	.20
126	A16	4c green	.20	.20
127	A16	5c grnsh blue	.20	.20
128	A16	10c red, *yel*	.20	.20
129	A16	15c red, *grn*	.55	.50
130	A16	20c deep red	.55	.50
131	A16	25c brown red	.55	.35
132	A17	30c yellow grn	1.25	1.00
133	A17	40c brown vio	1.75	.80
134	A17	45c blk, *dl grn*	1.50	1.00
135	A17	50c red brown	1.40	.80
136	A17	65c Prus blue	4.50	4.00
137	A17	75c blk, *red org*	3.00	2.10
138	A17	90c rose red	2.75	2.10
139	A17	1fr yel grn, *bl*	22.50	14.00
140	A18	1.25fr dp vio ('33)	1.50	1.10
141	A18	1.50fr dull blue	3.75	1.60
142	A18	1.75fr dp green ('33)	1.75	1.10
143	A18	2fr brn red	30.00	17.00
144	A18	3fr yel grn, *bl*	3.75	3.00
145	A18	5fr red brown	6.50	4.75
146	A18	10fr blk, *red org*	25.00	19.00
147	A18	20fr dk violet	40.00	29.00
		Nos. 124-147 (24)	153.55	104.70

SEMI-POSTAL STAMPS

No. 37 Surcharged in Red

1916 Unwmk. *Perf. 13½x14*

B1	A10	10c + 5c red & car	17.50	17.50
a.		Double surcharge	125.00	*140.00*

Same Surcharge on No. 54 in Red

B2	A10	10c + 5c red & car	22.50	22.50
a.		Double surcharge	125.00	*140.00*

No. 54 Surcharged in Red

1917

B3	A10	10c + 5c red & car	1.10	1.10

POSTAGE DUE STAMPS

Postage Due Stamps of France Overprinted

1928 Unwmk. *Perf. 14x13½*

J1	D2	5c light blue	.20	.20
J2	D2	10c gray brown	.20	.20
J3	D2	20c olive green	.70	.70
J4	D2	25c bright rose	.75	.75
J5	D2	30c light red	1.10	1.10
J6	D2	45c blue green	1.25	1.25
J7	D2	50c brown violet	2.00	2.00
J8	D2	60c yellow brown	2.00	2.00
J9	D2	1fr red brown	2.00	2.00
J10	D2	2fr orange red	3.25	3.25
J11	D2	3fr bright violet	3.75	3.75
		Nos. J1-J11 (11)	17.20	17.20

Chief Makoko, de Brazza's Aide — D3

Count Savorgnan de Brazza — D4

1930 Typo. *Perf. 13½x14*

J12	D3	5c dk bl & olive	.75	.75
J13	D3	10c dk red & brn	.80	.80
J14	D3	20c green & brn	1.10	1.10
J15	D3	25c lt bl & brn	1.10	1.10
J16	D3	30c bis brn & Prus bl	1.60	1.60
J17	D3	45c Prus bl & ol	2.50	2.50
J18	D3	50c red vio & brn	2.75	2.75
J19	D3	60c gray lil & bl blk	5.00	5.00
J20	D4	1fr bis brn & bl blk	7.00	7.00
J21	D4	2fr violet & brn	9.25	9.25
J22	D4	3fr dp red & brn	10.50	10.50
		Nos. J12-J22 (11)	42.35	42.35

Fang Woman — D5

1932 Photo. *Perf. 13x13½*

J23	D5	5c dk bl, *bl*	.95	.95
J24	D5	10c red brown	1.10	1.10
J25	D5	20c chocolate	1.60	1.60
J26	D5	25c yel grn, *bl*	1.60	1.60
J27	D5	30c car rose	1.75	1.75
J28	D5	45c red org, *yel*	6.50	6.50
J29	D5	50c dk violet	2.25	2.25
J30	D5	60c dull blue	3.25	3.25
J31	D5	1fr blk, *red org*	7.50	7.50
J32	D5	2fr dark green	8.50	8.50
J33	D5	3fr rose lake	7.75	7.75
		Nos. J23-J33 (11)	42.75	42.75

GAMBIA

'gam-bē-ə

LOCATION — Extending inland from the mouth of the Gambia River on the west coast of Africa
GOVT. — Republic in British Commonwealth
AREA — 4,068 sq. mi.
POP. — 695,886 (1983)
CAPITAL — Banjul

The British Crown Colony and Protectorate of Gambia became independent in 1965 and a republic in 1970.

12 Pence = 1 Shilling

Catalogue values for unused stamps in this country are for Never Hinged items, beginning with Scott 144.

Queen Victoria
A1 A2

Typographed and Embossed

1869, Jan. Unwmk. *Imperf.*

1	A1	4p pale brown	525.	225.
a.		4p brown	575.	200.
2	A1	6p deep blue	550.	225.
a.		6p blue	*625.*	*210.*
b.		6p pale blue	*2,500.*	*1,250.*

1874, Aug. Wmk. 1

3	A1	4p brown	450.	225.
a.		4p pale brown	425.	210.
4	A1	6p blue	375.	210.
a.		6p deep blue	375.	225.
b.		Panel sloping down from left to right	700.	400.

The name panel sloping down variety is from a top right corner position. A top left corner position exists with a less noticeable sloping of the panel down from right to left; it is worth less.

1880, June *Perf. 14*

5	A1	½p orange	10.00	*17.00*
6	A1	1p maroon	5.25	*7.00*
7	A1	2p rose	29.00	12.50
8	A1	3p ultra	75.00	37.50
9	A1	4p pale brown	225.00	17.00
a.		4p brown	225.00	16.00
10	A1	6p blue	100.00	52.50
a.		Panel sloping down from left to right	250.00	175.00
11	A1	1sh green	275.00	150.00
a.		1sh deep green	275.00	150.00
		Nos. 5-11 (7)	719.25	293.50

The watermark on Nos. 5-11 exists both upright and sideways.
See footnote following No. 4.

1886-93 Wmk. 2 Sideways

12	A1	½p gray grn	3.75	*2.50*
a.		½p deep green ('87)	4.00	2.50
13	A1	1p rose car ('87)	6.50	*9.00*
a.		1p maroon		*17,250.*
b.		1p aniline rose car	6.50	*11.00*
c.		1p pale carmine	6.50	*11.00*
14		2p deep orange	2.25	*9.25*
b.		2p orange	11.50	5.75
15	A1	2½p dp br blue	4.50	1.40
a.		2½ ultramarine ('87)	5.25	2.25
16	A1	3p gray	7.00	*17.00*
a.		3p slate gray ('86)	8.50	*16.00*
17	A1	4p dp brown	8.50	2.25
a.		4p brown ('87)	8.50	2.25
18	A1	6p slate green ('93)	12.50	*52.50*
a.		6p pale olive green ('86)	82.50	62.50
b.		6p bronze green ('89)	30.00	*62.50*
c.		As "a," panel sloping down from left to right	200.00	160.00
d.		As "b," panel sloping down from left to right	70.00	*110.00*
e.		6p olive green ('87)	70.00	62.50
f.		As "e," panel sloping down from left to right	190.00	160.00
g.		6p dp bronze grn ('89)	35.00	*62.50*
19	A1	1sh violet	6.25	*18.00*
a.		1sh purple	6.25	*22.50*
b.		1sh aniline violet	1,250.	
		Nos. 12-19 (8)	51.25	*111.90*

See footnote following No. 4.

1898, Jan. Typo. Wmk. 2

20	A2	½p gray green	3.25	2.00
21	A2	1p carmine rose	2.50	.85
22	A2	2p brn org & pur	7.00	4.00
23	A2	2½p ultramarine	2.25	*2.75*
24	A2	3p red vio & ultra	26.00	14.00
25	A2	4p brown & ultra	10.50	*35.00*
26	A2	6p ol grn & car rose	11.50	*30.00*
27	A2	1sh vio & green	32.50	*75.00*
		Nos. 20-27 (8)	95.50	*163.60*
		Set, ovptd. "SPECIMEN"	180.00	

King Edward VII — A3

1902-05 *Perf. 14*

28	A3	½p green	3.50	*2.75*
29	A3	1p car rose	4.50	1.10
30	A3	2p org & pur	3.75	2.25
31	A3	2½p ultramarine	32.50	20.00
32	A3	3p red vio & ultra	14.00	4.00
33	A3	4p brn & ultra	3.75	*27.50*
34	A3	6p ol grn & rose	6.25	*14.00*
35	A3	1sh bluish vio & green	47.50	*92.50*
36	A3	1sh6p grn & red, *yel*	8.00	*21.00*
37	A3	2sh black & org	55.00	*70.00*
38	A3	2sh6p pur & brn, *yel*	17.50	*70.00*
39	A3	3sh red & grn, *yel*	22.50	*70.00*
		Nos. 28-39 (12)	218.75	*395.10*
		Set, ovptd. "SPECIMEN"	210.00	

Numerals of 5p, 7½p, 10p, 1sh6p, 2sh, 2sh6p and 3sh of type A3 are in color on plain tablet.

Issue dates: 1p, Mar. 13. ½p, 3p, Apr. 19. 2p, 2½p, 4p, 6p, 1sh, 2sh, June 14. 1sh6p, 2sh6p, 3sh, Apr. 6, 1905.

For surcharges, see Nos. 65-66.

1904-09 Wmk. 3

41	A3	½p green	5.25	.35
42	A3	1p car rose	5.25	.20
a.		1p carmine ('09)	8.00	.20
43	A3	2p org & pur ('06)	14.00	2.50
44	A3	2p gray ('09)	1.90	12.50
45	A3	2½p br blue ('05)	7.00	5.50
a.		2½ ultra & br blue	17.50	*29.00*
46	A3	3p red vio & ultra	8.50	2.25
47	A3	3p vio, *yel* ('09)	4.00	1.10
a.		3p violet, *lemon yellow*	6.25	2.00
48	A3	4p brn & ultra ('06)	20.00	*45.00*
49	A3	4p blk & red, *yel* ('09)	1.40	.75
50	A3	5p gray & black	16.00	*22.50*
51	A3	5p org & vio ('09)	1.75	1.40
52	A3	6p ol grn & rose ('06)	20.00	*62.50*
53	A3	6p dull vio ('09)	2.50	2.50
54	A3	7½p blue grn & red	12.50	*42.50*
55	A3	7½p brn & ultra ('09)	2.75	2.75
56	A3	10p ol bis & red	24.00	*35.00*
57	A3	10p ol grn & car rose ('09)	2.75	*8.00*
58	A3	1sh violet & grn	25.00	*55.00*
59	A3	1sh blk, *grn* ('09)	3.75	*20.00*
60	A3	1sh 6p vio & grn ('09)	16.00	*70.00*
61	A3	2sh black & org	80.00	*100.00*
62	A3	2sh vio & bl, *bl* ('09)	16.00	*22.50*
63	A3	2sh 6p blk & red, *bl* ('09)	24.00	22.50
64	A3	3sh yel & grn ('09)	26.00	*55.00*
		Nos. 41-64 (24)	340.30	*592.30*

Nos. 38-39 Surcharged in Black:

a

b

Type a (I) — The word "PENNY" is 5mm from the horizontal bars.

Type a (II) — "PENNY" is 4mm from the bars.

1906, Apr. Wmk. 2

65	A3	½p on 2sh6p, type I	57.50	*70.00*
a.		Type II	62.50	*75.00*
66	A3	1p on 3sh	62.50	35.00
a.		Double surcharge	*2,150.*	*5,750.*

King George V — A4

1912-22 Wmk. 3

70	A4	½p dp green	2.00	*1.75*
a.		½p green	2.75	1.75
b.		½p pale green ('16)	4.00	3.75
71	A4	1p carmine	2.75	2.00
a.		1p scarlet ('16)	4.25	1.00
b.		1p rose red	2.75	2.00
72	A4	1½p ol brn & grn	.60	.35
73	A4	2p gray	.60	*3.25*
74	A4	2½p dp br blue	4.50	3.50
a.		2½p bright blue	5.00	2.75
75	A4	3p violet, *yel*	.60	.35
a.		3p violet, *lemon* ('17)	16.00	*20.00*
b.		3p violet, *org buff* ('20)	11.50	*9.50*
c.		3p violet, *pale yellow*	1.40	*1.10*

76	A4	4p	blk & red, *yel*	1.10	*11.50*
a.			4p blk & red, *lemon* ('17)	2.75	*8.50*
b.			4p blk & red, *org buff* ('20)	9.00	*12.50*
c.			4p blk & red, *pale yellow*	1.75	*9.50*
77	A4	5p	orange & vio	1.10	*2.25*
78	A4	6p	dl vio & red violet	1.10	*2.75*
79	A4	7½p	brn & ultra	1.40	*7.50*
80	A4	10p	ol grn & car rose	2.25	*20.00*
a.			10p dp ol grn & car rose	2.75	*17.50*
81	A4	1sh	blk, *green*	2.25	1.10
a.			1sh black, *emerald*	1.10	*22.50*
82	A4	1sh6p	vio & green	12.50	11.50
83	A4	2sh	vio & bl, *bl*	4.00	*7.00*
84	A4	2sh6p	blk & red, *bl*	3.75	*16.00*
85	A4	3sh	yel & green	9.75	*30.00*
86	A4	5sh	grn & red, *yel* ('22)	*92.50*	*150.00*
			Nos. 70-86 (17)	*142.75*	*270.80*
			Set, ovptd. "SPECIMEN"	400.00	

Numerals of 1½p, 5p, 7½p, 10p, 1sh6p, 2sh, 2sh6p, 3sh, 4sh and 5sh of type A3 are in color on colorless tablet. No. 86 is on chalky paper.

1921-22 **Wmk. 4**

87	A4	½p	green	.35	*20.00*
88	A4	1p	carmine	1.10	*5.75*
89	A4	1½p	ol grn & bl grn	1.40	*15.00*
90	A4	2p	gray	1.10	*2.50*
91	A4	2½p	ultramarine	.60	*7.00*
92	A4	5p	org & violet	2.00	*18.00*
93	A4	6p	dl vio & red vio	2.00	*20.00*
94	A4	7½p	brn & ultra	2.25	*35.00*
95	A4	10p	yel grn & car rose	8.00	*17.00*
96	A4	4sh	blk & red ('22)	*85.00*	*150.00*
			Nos. 87-96 (10)	*103.80*	*290.25*
			Set, ovptd. "SPECIMEN"	225.00	

No. 96 is on chalky paper.

George V and Elephant — A5

George V — A6

1922-27 **Engr.** **Wmk. 4**

Head and Shield in Black

102	A5	½p	green	.65	.65
a.			½p deep green ('25)	5.25	1.75
103	A5	1p	brown	.90	.20
104	A5	1½p	carmine	.95	.20
105	A5	2p	gray	1.10	3.75
106	A5	2½p	orange	1.10	*12.50*
107	A5	3p	ultramarine	1.10	.20
108	A5	4p	car, *org* ('27)	6.25	*22.50*
109	A5	5p	yellow green	2.40	*11.50*
110	A5	6p	claret	1.50	.35
111	A5	7½p	vio, *yel* ('27)	8.00	*62.50*
112	A5	10p	blue	5.50	*20.00*
113	A6	1sh	vio, *org* ('24)	2.75	1.40
a.			1sh dk violet, *yel buff* ('29)	50.00	50.00
114	A6	1sh6p	blue	12.50	*16.00*
115	A6	2sh	vio, *blue*	4.50	*4.75*
116	A6	2sh6p	dark green	5.00	*11.00*
117	A6	3sh	aniline vio	13.50	*55.00*
a.			3sh black purple	240.00	*475.00*
118	A6	4sh	brown	6.25	*18.00*
119	A6	5sh	dk grn, *yel* ('26)	13.50	*42.50*
120	A6	10sh	yellow green	80.00	*110.00*
			Nos. 102-120 (19)	167.45	*393.00*
			Set, ovptd. "SPECIMEN"	450.00	

1922, Sept. 1 **Wmk. 3**

Head & Shield in Black

121	A5	4p	carmine, *yel*	3.00	*3.50*
122	A5	7½p	violet, *yel*	3.75	*7.50*
123	A6	1sh	violet, *orange*	10.50	*26.00*
124	A6	5sh	dk green, *yel*	45.00	*140.00*
			Nos. 121-124 (4)	62.25	*177.00*
			Set, ovptd. "SPECIMEN"	160.00	

The Specimen overprint on No. 124 is handstamped.

Common Design Types pictured following the introduction.

Silver Jubilee Issue

Common Design Type

1935, May 6 **Wmk. 4** ***Perf. 11x12***

125	CD301	1½p	carmine & bl	.60	*.70*
126	CD301	3p	ultra & brn	.75	*1.25*
127	CD301	6p	ol grn & lt bl	1.40	*4.00*
128	CD301	1sh	brn vio & ind	4.50	*8.50*
			Nos. 125-128 (4)	7.25	*14.45*
			Set, never hinged	16.00	
			Set, perf "SPECIMEN"	110.00	

Coronation Issue

Common Design Type

1937, May 12 ***Perf. 11x11½***

129	CD302	1p	brown	.20	*.80*
130	CD302	1½p	dark carmine	.20	*.40*
131	CD302	3p	deep ultra	.50	*1.10*
			Nos. 129-131 (3)	.90	2.30
			Set, never hinged	1.60	
			Set, perf "SPECIMEN"	900.00	

King George VI and Elephant Badge of Gambia — A7

1938-46 ***Perf. 12***

132	A7	½p	bl grn & blk	.20	*.80*
133	A7	1p	brn & red vio	.20	*.55*
134	A7	1½p	rose red & brn lake	.25	2.25
a.			1½ scarlet & brn lake	4.00	2.75
b.			1½ br car & brn lake	175.00	13.50
134A	A7	1½p	gray black & ultra ('44)	.20	1.75
135	A7	2p	gray black & ultra	3.00	3.75
135A	A7	2p	rose red & brn lake ('43)	.65	2.50
136	A7	3p	blue & brt bl	.40	.20
136A	A7	5p	dk vio brn & olive ('41)	.45	.60
137	A7	6p	plum & ol grn	1.25	.40
138	A7	1sh	vio & sl blk	1.60	.20
138A	A7	1sh3p	bl & choc ('46)	2.00	2.75
139	A7	2sh	bl & dp rose	3.50	3.75
140	A7	2sh6p	sl grn & sep	10.00	2.75
141	A7	4sh	dk vio & red orange	17.00	2.75
142	A7	5sh	org red & dk blue	17.00	4.50
143	A7	10sh	blk & yel org	17.00	8.00
			Nos. 132-143 (16)	74.70	37.50
			Set, never hinged	110.00	
			Set, perf "SPECIMEN"	400.00	

Issued: 5p, Mar. 13; #135A, Oct. 1; #134A, Jan. 2; 1sh3p, Nov. 28; others, Apr. 1.

Catalogue values for unused stamps in this section, from this point to the end of the section, are for Never Hinged items.

Peace Issue

Common Design Type

1946, Aug. 6 **Engr.** ***Perf. 13½***

144	CD303	1½p	black	.20	.20
145	CD303	3p	deep blue	.20	.20
			Set, perf "SPECIMEN"	80.00	

Silver Wedding Issue

Common Design Types

1948, Dec. 24 **Photo.** ***Perf. 14x14½***

146	CD304	1½p	black	.25	.20

Perf. 11½x11

Engr.; Name Typo.

147	CD305	£1	purple	18.00	*19.00*

UPU Issue

Common Design Types

Engr.; Name Typo. on 3p, 6p

Perf. 13½, 11x11½

1949, Oct. 10 **Wmk. 4**

148	CD306	1½p	slate	.40	*1.40*
149	CD307	3p	indigo	1.90	2.00
150	CD308	6p	red lilac	.55	1.10
151	CD309	1sh	violet	.55	.45
			Nos. 148-151 (4)	3.40	4.95

GEORGIA

'jor-jə

LOCATION — In the southern part of Russia, bordering on the Black Sea and occupying the entire western part of Trans-Caucasia
GOVT. — A Soviet Socialist Republic
AREA — 25,760 sq. mi. (1920)
POP. — 2,372,403 (1920)
CAPITAL — Tbilisi (Tiflis)

Georgia was formerly a province of the Russian Empire and later a part of the Transcaucasian Federation of Soviet Republics. Stamps of Georgia were replaced in 1923 by those of Transcaucasian Federated Republics.

100 Kopecks = 1 Ruble

Tiflis

A 6k local stamp, imperforate and embossed without color on white paper, was issued in November, 1857, at Tiflis by authority of the viceroy. The square design shows a coat of arms.

National Republic

St. George
A1 A2

Perf. 11½, Imperf.

1919		**Litho.**	**Unwmk.**	
12	A1	10k blue	.20	.20
13	A1	40k red orange	.20	.20
a.		Tête bêche pair	25.00	25.00
14	A1	50k emerald	.20	.20
15	A1	60k red	.20	.20
16	A1	70k claret	.20	*.25*
17	A2	1r orange brown	.20	*.25*
		Nos. 12-17 (6)	1.20	1.30

Queen Thamar — A3

1920		***Perf. 11½, Imperf.***		
18	A3	2r red brown	.30	.30
19	A3	3r gray blue	.20	*.30*
20	A3	5r orange	.30	*.60*
		Nos. 18-20 (3)	.80	*1.20*

Nos. 12-20 with parts of design inverted, sideways or omitted are fraudulent varieties.
Overprints meaning "Day of the National Guard, 12, 12, 1920" (5 lines) and "Recognition of Independence, 27, 1, 1921" (4 lines) were applied, probably in Italy, to remainders taken by government officials who fled when Russian forces occupied Georgia.
"Constantinople" and new values were unofficially surcharged on stamps of 1919-20 by a consul in Turkey.

Soviet Socialist Republic

Soldier with Flag — A5 Peasant Sowing Grain — A6

Industry and Agriculture — A7

1922		**Unwmk.**	***Perf. 11½***	
26	A5	500r rose	3.50	3.25
27	A6	1000r bister brown	3.50	3.25
28	A7	2000r slate	6.50	6.00
29	A7	3000r brown	6.50	6.00
30	A7	5000r green	6.50	6.00
		Nos. 26-30 (5)	26.50	24.50

Forgeries exist of Nos. 26-30.
Nos. 26 to 30 exist imperforate but were not so issued. Value for set, $100.

Nos. 26-30 Handstamped with New Values in Violet

1923				
36	A6	10,000r on 1000r	5.00	5.00
a.		Black surcharge	15.00	*20.00*
b.		20,000r on 1000r	200.00	
37	A7	15,000r on 2000r, blk surch.	4.75	*6.50*
a.		Violet surcharge	20.00	20.00
38	A5	20,000r on 500r	4.50	*6.50*
a.		Black surcharge	10.00	5.00
39	A7	40,000r on 5000r	4.00	4.00
a.		Black surcharge	10.00	*10.00*
40	A7	80,000r on 3000r	4.50	*6.50*
a.		Black surcharge	10.00	*12.00*
		Nos. 36-40 (5)	22.75	*28.50*

There were two types of the handstamped surcharges, with the numerals 5½mm and 6½mm high. The impressions are often too indistinct to measure or even to distinguish the numerals.
Double and inverted surcharges exist, as is usual with handstamps.

Printed Surcharge in Black

43	A6	10,000r on 1000r	6.00	6.25
44	A7	15,000r on 2000r	4.00	4.00
45	A5	20,000r on 500r	2.00	2.00
46	A7	40,000r on 5000r	4.00	3.75
47	A7	80,000r on 3000r	4.00	4.00
		Nos. 43-47 (5)	20.00	*20.00*

Nos. 43, 45, 46 and 47 exist imperforate but were not so issued. Value $25 each.

Russian Stamps of 1909-18 Handstamp Surcharged

Type I. Surcharge 20x5½mm.
Type II. Surcharge 22x7¼mm.

1923			***Perf. 14½x15***	
48	A14	10,000r on 7k lt bl	200.00	200.00
49	A11	15,000r on 15k red brn & bl (I)	10.00	10.00
a.		Type II	10.00	10.00

Type I Surcharge Handstamped on Armenia No. 141

50	A11	15,000r on 5r on 15k red brn & bl	200.00	*300.00*
a.		Type II		
		Nos. 48-50 (3)	410.00	*510.00*

Russian Stamps and Types of 1909-18 Surcharged in Dark Blue or Black

1923			***Perf. 11½, 14½x15***	
51	A14	75,000r on 1k org	3.00	*4.25*
a.		Imperf.	50.00	*75.00*
52	A14	200,000r on 5k cl	4.00	*5.00*
53	A8	300,000r on 20k bl & car (Bk)	4.00	*5.00*
a.		Dark blue surcharge	50.00	*75.00*
54	A14	350,000r on 3k red	7.00	*8.00*
a.		Imperf.	6.00	*7.25*

Imperf

55	A14	700,000r on 2k grn	7.00	*10.00*
a.		Perf. 14½x15	27.50	*32.50*
		Nos. 51-55 (5)	25.00	*32.25*

SEMI-POSTAL STAMPS

SP1 SP2

SP3 SP4

Surcharge in Red or Black

1922		**Unwmk.**	***Perf. 11½***	
B1	SP1	1000r on 50r vio (R)	.50	*3.00*
B2	SP2	3000r on 100r brn red	.50	*3.00*
B3	SP3	5000r on 250r gray grn	.50	*3.00*
B4	SP4	10,000r on 25r blue (R)	.50	*3.00*
		Nos. B1-B4 (4)	2.00	*12.00*

Nos. B1-B4 exist imperf but were not so issued. Value slightly more than perforated examples.

GERMAN EAST AFRICA

'jər-mən 'ēst 'a-fri-kə

LOCATION — In East Africa, bordering on the Indian Ocean
GOVT. — German Colony
AREA — 384,180 sq. mi.
POP. — 7,680,132 (1913)
CAPITAL — Dar-es Salaam

Following World War I, the greater part of this German Colonial possession was mandated to Great Britain. The British ceded to the Belgians the provinces of Ruanda and Urundi. The Kionga triangle was awarded to the Portuguese and became part of the Mozambique Colony. The remaining area became the British Mandated Territory of Tanganyika.

64 Pesa = 1 Rupee
100 Heller = 1 Rupee (1905)
100 Centimes = 1 Franc (1916)

Stamps of Germany Surcharged in Black

Nos. 1-5 Nos. 6-10

1893		**Unwmk.**	***Perf. 13½x14½***	
		Surcharge 15¼mm long		
1	A9	2pes on 3pf brown	35.00	*47.50*
		Never hinged	125.00	
		On cover		275.00
a.		Surcharge 16¾mm long	*3,250.*	
		Never hinged	*4,500.*	
2	A9	3pes on 5pf green	42.50	*47.50*
		Never hinged	175.00	
		On cover		275.00
a.		Surcharge 14¼mm long	*700.00*	
		Never hinged	*1,700.*	
b.		Surcharge 16¼mm long	*900.00*	
		Never hinged	*1,750.*	
3	A10	5pes on 10pf car	30.00	24.00
		Never hinged	150.00	
		On cover		140.00
a.		Surcharge 14¼mm long	*2,400.*	
		Never hinged	*5,000.*	
b.		Surcharge 16¼mm long	*2,400.*	
		Never hinged	*5,000.*	
		Surcharge 16¼mm long		
4	A10	10pes on 20pf ultra	19.00	12.50
		Never hinged	100.00	
		On cover		67.50
		Surcharge 16¾mm long		
5	A10	25pes on 50pf red brn	35.00	27.50
		Never hinged	100.00	
		On cover		120.00
a.		Surcharge 17½mm long	*80.00*	*225.00*
		Never hinged	*250.00*	
		On cover		125.00
		Nos. 1-5 (5)	161.50	159.00

Covers: Value for No. 5 are for overfranked complete covers, usually philatelic.

1896				
6	A9	2pes on 3pf dk brn	1.60	*30.00*
		Never hinged	4.50	
		On cover		140.00
a.		2pes on 3pf light brown	24.00	*37.50*
		Never hinged	80.00	
		On cover		175.00
b.		2pes on 3pf grayish brown	9.50	9.00
		Never hinged	27.50	
		On cover		55.00
c.		2pes on 3pf reddish brown	35.00	*82.50*
		Never hinged	100.00	
		On cover		260.00
7	A9	3pes on 5pf green	2.10	4.00
		Never hinged	5.00	
		On cover		27.50
8	A10	5pes on 10pf car	2.25	3.75
		Never hinged	5.00	
		On cover		27.50
9	A10	10pes on 20pf ultra	4.50	4.50
		Never hinged	12.50	
		On cover		35.00
10	A10	25pes on 50pf red brn	19.00	*24.00*
		Never hinged	55.00	
		On cover		70.00
		Nos. 6-10 (5)	29.45	*66.25*

Covers: Value for No. 10 is for overfranked complete covers, usually philatelic.

A5

Kaiser's Yacht "Hohenzollern" — A6

1900		**Typo.**	***Perf. 14***	
11	A5	2p brown	2.40	1.40
		Never hinged	6.25	
		On cover		55.00
12	A5	3p green	2.40	1.60
		Never hinged	6.25	
		On cover		25.00
13	A5	5p carmine	2.75	2.00
		Never hinged	9.00	
		On cover		27.50
14	A5	10p ultra	4.50	4.00
		Never hinged	14.00	
		On cover		50.00
15	A5	15p org & blk, *sal*	4.50	*5.75*
		Never hinged	15.00	
		On cover		70.00
16	A5	20p lake & blk	6.25	*12.50*
		Never hinged	22.50	
		On cover		70.00
17	A5	25p pur & blk, *sal*	6.25	*12.50*
		Never hinged	20.00	
		On cover		35.00
18	A5	40p lake & blk, *rose*	7.50	*19.00*
		Never hinged	22.50	
		On cover		60.00
		Engr.		
		Perf. 14½x14		
19	A6	1r claret	17.00	*47.50*
		Never hinged	50.00	
		On cover		100.00
20	A6	2r yel green	8.25	*75.00*
		Never hinged	22.50	
		On cover		200.00
21	A6	3r car & slate	85.00	*175.00*
		Never hinged	375.00	
		On cover		425.00
a.		3r red & slate	100.00	175.00
		Never hinged	250.00	
		On cover		350.00
		Nos. 11-21 (11)	146.80	*356.25*

Covers: Values for Nos. 17-21 are for overfranked complete covers, usually philatelic.

Value in Heller

1905		**Typo.**	***Perf. 14***	
22	A5	2½h brown	2.25	1.50
		Never hinged	11.00	
		On cover		17.50
23	A5	4h dk olive green	10.00	5.00
		Never hinged	37.50	
		On cover		17.50
a.		4h green	11.50	*10.00*
		Never hinged	32.50	
		On cover		45.00
b.		4h dark yellowish green	9.75	*11.00*

Never hinged 20.00
On cover 42.50
24 A5 7½h carmine 9.00 1.40
Never hinged 27.50
On cover 14.00
25 A5 15h ultra 20.00 5.00
Never hinged 50.00
On cover 21.00
a. 15h violet blue 45.00 *16.00*
Never hinged 125.00
On cover 37.50
26 A5 20h org & blk, *yel* 9.75 *14.00*
Never hinged 27.50
On cover 30.00
27 A5 30h lake & blk 10.00 5.00
Never hinged 27.50
On cover 15.00
28 A5 45h pur & blk 22.50 *30.00*
Never hinged 50.00
On cover 70.00
29 A5 60h lake & blk, *rose* 22.50 *77.50*
Never hinged 100.00
On cover 225.00
Nos. 22-29 (7) 96.25 *125.40*

Covers: Values for Nos. 27-29 are for overfranked complete covers, usually philatelic.

1905-16 Wmk. Lozenges (125)

31 A5 2½h brn ('06) .85 .80
Never hinged 2.50
On cover 21.00
32 A5 4h grn ('06) .85 .55
Never hinged 2.75
On cover 14.00
b. Booklet pane of 4 + 2 labels 45.00
Never hinged 67.50
c. Booklet pane of 5 + label *195.00*
Never hinged 300.00
33 A5 7½h car ('06) 1.00 *1.40*
Never hinged 3.75
On cover 14.00
b. Booklet pane of 4 + 2 labels 45.00
Never hinged 65.00
c. Booklet pane of 5 + label *200.00*
Never hinged 300.00
34 A5 15h dk blue ('08) 1.90 1.25
Never hinged 7.75
On cover 17.50
a. 15h ultramarine ('06) 8.50 8.50
Never hinged 21.00
On cover 35.00
35 A5 20h org & blk, *yel* ('11) 2.00 *16.00*
Never hinged 7.00
On cover 55.00
36 A5 30h lake & blk ('09) 2.25 *6.50*
Never hinged 7.00
On cover 42.50
37 A5 45h pur & blk ('06) 4.50 *45.00*
Never hinged 15.00
On cover 250.00
38 A5 60h lake & blk, *rose* 26.00 *160.00*
Never hinged 62.50
On cover 350.00

Engr.

Perf. 14½x14

39 A6 1r red ('16) 9.75 *20,000.*
Never hinged 62.50
On cover *45,000.*
40 A6 2r yel grn 40.00
Never hinged 85.00
41 A6 3r car & sl ('08) 40.00 *190.00*
Never hinged 110.00
On cover 425.00
a. 3r red & blackish green ('08) 90.00 *250.00*
Never hinged 375.00
On cover 550.00
Nos. 31-41 (11) 129.10

No. 40 was never placed in use.

The frame of No. 41a fluoresces bright orange under ultra-violet light.

Booklet panes of 6 made from sheet stamps exist of the 4h and 7½h.

Forged cancellations are found on #35-39, 41.

Covers: Values for Nos. 37-38, 41 are for overfranked complete covers, usually philatelic.

In early 1916, German East African authorities ordered supplies of provisional stamps, printed by the press of the Evangelical Mission in Wuga. Three values in denominations most urgently needed were produced in March, but before they could be issued, new stocks of regular stamps were received from Germany. To prevent their capture by the British, the provisionals were buried until 1922, when they were retrieved by the German government and sold at auction. Because of their long storage in the tropical climate, 90-95% of the stamps were destroyed and those surviving are usually brittle and somewhat faded.

Values: 2½h violet brown, $50; 7½h, carmine, $20; 1r pink, $1,200.

OCCUPATION STAMPS

Issued Under Belgian Occupation

Stamps of Belgian Congo, 1915, Handstamped "RUANDA" in Black or Blue

1916 Unwmk. *Perf. 13½ to 15*

N1 A29 5c green & blk 21.00
N2 A30 10c carmine & blk 21.00
N3 A21 15c blue grn & blk 42.50
N4 A31 25c blue & blk 21.00
N5 A23 40c brown red & blk 21.00
N6 A24 50c brown lake & blk 30.00
N7 A25 1fr olive bis & blk 150.00
N8 A27 5fr ocher & blk *2,150.*
Nos. N1-N7 (7) 306.50

Stamps of Belgian Congo, 1915, Handstamped "URUNDI" in Black or Blue

N9 A29 5c green & blk 21.00
N10 A30 10c carmine & blk 21.00
N11 A21 15c bl grn & blk 42.50
N12 A31 25c blue & blk 21.00
N13 A23 40c brn red & blk 21.00
N14 A24 50c brn lake & blk 30.00
N15 A25 1fr ol bis & blk 150.00
N16 A27 5fr ocher & blk *2,150.*
Nos. N9-N15 (7) 306.50

Stamps of Belgian Congo overprinted "Karema," "Kigoma" and "Tabora" were not officially authorized.

Nos. N1-N16 exist with forged overprint.

Stamps of Belgian Congo, 1915, Overprinted in Dark Blue

1916 *Perf. 12½ to 15*

N17 A29 5c green & blk .70 .25
On cover —
b. Inverted overprint 135.00 —
N18 A30 10c carmine & blk 1.00 .40
On cover 32.50
N19 A21 15c bl grn & blk .75 .25
On cover 27.50
N20 A31 25c blue & blk 6.50 1.50
On cover 35.00
N21 A23 40c brn red & blk 12.50 5.50
On cover 65.00
N22 A24 50c brn lake & blk 15.00 5.50
On cover 45.00
N23 A25 1fr olive bis & blk 3.00 .65
On cover —
N24 A27 5fr ocher & blk 3.00 1.40
On cover —
Nos. N17-N24 (8) 42.45 15.45

Nos. N17-N18, N20-N22 Surcharged in Black or Red

1922

N25 A24 5c on 50c brn lake & blk .30 .30
Never hinged .65
On cover —
N26 A29 10c on 5c grn & blk (R) .30 .30
Never hinged .65
On cover 22.50
N27 A23 25c on 40c brn red & blk (R) 2.00 1.25
Never hinged 5.50
On cover 27.50
N28 A30 30c on 10c car & blk .30 .20
Never hinged .65
On cover 27.50
N29 A31 50c on 25c bl & blk (R) .30 .20
Never hinged .65
On cover 27.50
Nos. N25-N29 (5) 3.20 2.25

No. N25 has the surcharge at each side.

SEMI-POSTAL STAMPS

Issued under Belgian Occupation

Semi-Postal Stamps of Belgian Congo, 1918, Overprinted

1918 Unwmk. *Perf. 14, 15*

NB1 A29 5c + 10c grn & bl .40 .40
Never hinged .85
NB2 A30 10c + 15c car & bl .40 .40
Never hinged .85
NB3 A21 15c + 20c bl grn & bl .40 .40
Never hinged .85
NB4 A31 25c + 25c dp & pale bl .40 .40
Never hinged .85
NB5 A23 40c + 40c brn red & bl .65 .65
Never hinged 1.75
NB6 A24 50c + 50c brn lake & bl .85 .85
Never hinged 2.10
NB7 A25 1fr + 1fr ol bis & bl 2.40 2.40
Never hinged 3.00
NB8 A27 5fr + 5fr ocher & bl 7.25 7.25
Never hinged 11.00
NB9 A28 10fr + 10fr grn & bl 60.00 60.00
Never hinged 60.00
Nos. NB1-NB9 (9) 72.75 72.75

The letters "A.O." are the initials of "Afrique Orientale" (East Africa).

ISSUED UNDER BRITISH OCCUPATION

Issued Under British Occupation

Stamps of Nyasaland Protectorate, 1913-15 Overprinted

1916 Wmk. 3 *Perf. 14*

N101 A3 ½p green 1.60 *8.75*
a. Double overprint (R & Bk)
N102 A3 1p carmine 1.60 *3.50*
N103 A3 3p violet, *yel* 10.00 *19.00*
a. Double overprint *10,000.*
N104 A3 4p scar & blk, *yel* 32.50 *45.00*
N105 A3 1sh black, *green* 35.00 *47.50*
Nos. N101-N105 (5) 80.70 *123.75*
Set, ovptd. "SPECIMEN" 190.00

"N.F." stands for "Nyasaland Force."

Stamps of East Africa and Uganda, 1912-14, Overprinted in Black or Red

1917

N106 A3 1c black (R) .20 *.90*
N107 A3 3c blue green .20 .20
N108 A3 6c carmine .20 .20
N109 A3 10c brown orange .55 *.65*
a. Inverted overprint
N110 A3 12c gray .55 *2.50*
N111 A3 15c ultramarine .90 *2.50*
N112 A3 25c scar & blk, *yel* .90 *4.00*
N113 A3 50c violet & blk .90 *3.75*
N114 A3 75c blk, *bl grn,* olive back (R) 1.10 *5.00*
a. 75c black, *emerald* (R) 3.75 *50.00*

Overprinted

N115 A4 1r blk, *green*(R) 3.50 *8.00*
a. 1r black, *emerald* (R) 7.50 *62.50*
N116 A4 2r blk & red, *bl* 11.00 *50.00*
N117 A4 3r gray grn & vio 15.00 *92.50*
N118 A4 4r grn & red, *yel* 19.00 *100.00*
N119 A4 5r dl vio & ultra 42.50 *100.00*
N120 A4 10r grn & red, *grn* 85.00 *375.00*
a. 10r grn & red, *emerald* 100.00 *400.00*
N121 A3 20r vio & blk, *red* 210.00 *450.00*
N122 A3 50r gray grn & red 450.00 *925.00*
Nos. N106-N120 (15) 181.50 *745.20*

See Tanganyika for "G.E.A." overprints on stamps inscribed "East Africa and Uganda Protectorates" with watermark 4.

MAFIA ISLAND

Mafia is a small island on the Indian Ocean coast of German East Africa, near the mouth of the Rufiji River. It was captured by the British in December, 1914, and in January, 1915, the military authorities began to overprint stamps for the use of civilian personnel on the island. Overprinted stamps were used, until the island's transfer to Tanganyikan administration in 1918.

Stamps of German East Africa with Manuscript Overprint "G R Mafia J D M."

1915

NL1 A5 2½h brown *2,500.*
NL2 A5 4h green *2,500.*
a. Mss. "JDM GR Mafia" *3,000.*
NL3 A5 7½h carmine *2,500.*
a. Mss. "JDM GR Mafia"
NL4 A5 15h ultra *2,500.*
NL5 A5 20h org & blk, *yel* —
NL6 A5 30h lake & blk —
NL7 A5 45h pur & blk —
NL8 A6 2r yel grn —

Initials are those of Lt. Col. J.D. Mackay, Military Governor.

German East Africa #31//41, Zanzibar #141//146 Handstamped

Black Overprint

1915, Jan.

NL9 A5 2½h brown 650.00
NL10 A5 4h green 750.00
a. Double ovpt. —
NL11 A5 7½h carmine 550.00
a. Pair, one without ovpt. *4,750.*
NL12 A5 15h ultramarine 675.00
NL13 A5 20h org & blk, *yel* 750.00
NL14 A5 30h lake & blk 900.00
a. Pair, one without ovpt. *5,250.*
NL15 A5 45h pur & blk 950.00
a. Pair, one without ovpt. *5,250.*
NL16 A6 1r red *7,500.*
NL17 A6 2r yellow green *8,250.*
NL18 A6 3r car & slate *7,500.*

Deep Purple Overprint

NL19 A5 4h green 950.00
NL20 A5 7½h carmine 650.00
NL21 A5 15h ultramarine 750.00
NL22 A5 20h org & blk, *yel* 900.00
a. Pair, one without ovpt. *4,750.*
b. Double ovpt. —
NL23 A5 30h lake & blk 1,250.
a. Double ovpt. —
NL24 A5 45h pur & blk 1,175.

Reddish Violet Overprint

NL25 A5 2½h brown 275.00
a. Pair, one without ovpt. *2,750.*
b. Initialled "JDM" *1,750.*
NL26 A5 4h green 350.00
a. Pair, one without ovpt. *2,600.*
b. Initialled "JDM" *1,750.*
NL27 A5 7½h carmine 150.00
a. Pair, one without ovpt. *2,200.*
b. Initialled "JDM" *1,750.*
NL28 A5 15h ultramarine 225.00
a. Pair, one without ovpt. *2,350.*
b. Initialled "JDM" *1,750.*
NL29 A5 20h org & blk, *yel* 450.00
a. Pair, one without ovpt. *2,750.*
b. Initialled "JDM" *1,750.*
NL30 A5 30h lake & blk 475.00
a. Pair, one without ovpt. *2,750.*
b. Initialled "JDM" *1,750.*
NL31 A5 45h pur & blk 550.00
a. Pair, one without ovpt. *3,500.*
b. Initialled "JDM" *1,750.*

NL32	A6	1r red	*5,500.*	
NL33	A6	2r yellow green	*6,250.*	
NL34	A6	3r car & slate	*7,000.*	

The reddish violet overprint is often under-inked and may be faint.

On Zanzibar 1915 Issue
Surcharge in Black

NL35	1c gray (#141)	—	
NL36	3c yellow green (#142)	—	
NL37	6c carmine (#143)	*1,000.*	*1,000.*
NL38	15c ultramarine (#146)	—	

German East Africa #13//41, Zanzibar #141, 143 with same handstamped overprint and surcharged with new values

#NL44

#NL49

1915, May

On 1900 Issue

NL39	A5	6c on 5p carmine	—
NL40	A5	6c on 20p lake & black	—
NL41	A5	6c on 40p carmine	—

On 1905-16 Issues
Surcharge in Green, Violet or Black

NL42	A5	6c on 2½h brown	1,300.	*1,500.*
a.		Pair, one without surcharge		5,250.
b.		Inverted surcharge		
c.		Double surcharge		
NL43	A5	6c on 4h green	1,300.	*1,500.*
a.		Pair, one without surcharge		5,250.
b.		Inverted surcharge		
c.		Double surcharge		
NL44	A5	6c on 7½h carmine	1,350.	*1,650.*
a.		Pair, one without surcharge		
b.		Inverted surcharge		
c.		Double surcharge		
NL45	A5	6c on 15h ultramarine	1,350.	*1,650.*
a.		Double surcharge		
b.		Triple surcharge		
c.		Inverted surcharge		
NL46	A5	6c on 20h org & blk, *yel*	1,650.	*1,900.*
a.		Inverted surcharge		
NL47	A5	6c on 30h lake & blk	2,350.	*2,500.*
a.		Inverted surcharge		
NL48	A5	6c on 45h purple & black	2,350.	*2,500.*
a.		Pair, one without surcharge		
b.		Inverted surcharge		
NL49	A6	6c on 1r red	12,250.	
a.		Double surcharge		
NL50	A6	6c on 2r yellow green	13,750.	
a.		Double surcharge		
NL51	A6	6c on 3r carmine & slate	15,000.	

On Zanzibar 1914 Issue
Surcharge in Black

NL52	6c on 1c gray (#141)	—
NL53	6c on 6c carmine (#143)	—

German East Africa Fiscal Stamps Handstamped in Bluish Green or Violet

#NL56

1915, Sept.

Inscribed "Statistik Des Waaren-Verkhers"

NL54	24p vermilion, *buff*	875.00	*1,100.*
NL55	12½p brown	875.00	*1,150.*
a.	Pair, one without overprint		*4,000.*
NL56	25h dull green	875.00	*1,150.*
NL57	50h slate	875.00	*1,150.*
a.	Pair, one without overprint		*4,000.*
NL58	1r lilac	875.00	*1,150.*

#NL59

Inscribed "Ubersetzungs Gebuhren"

NL59	25h gray	875.00	*1,150.*

Handstamped in three lines, serifed type

1915, Sept.

On Nos. NL55-60

NL60	24p vermilion, *buff*, (#55)	1,150.
NL61	12½p brown (#56)	1,150.
a.	"G.R. POST MAFIA" inverted	
NL62	25h dull green (#57)	1,150.
NL63	50h slate (#58)	1,150.
NL64	1r lilac (#59)	1,150.
NL65	25h gray (#60)	1,150.
a.	Pair, one without overprint	*4,000.*

#NL67

On unoverprinted Fiscal Stamps

NL66	24p vermilion, *buff*	—
NL67	12½p brown	—
NL68	25h dull green	—
NL69	50h slate	—
NL70	1r lilac	—
NL71	25h gray	—
a.	Inverted ovpt.	

On German East African Stamps in Green, Violet or Black

NL72	A5	7½h carmine	—
NL73	A5	20h org & blk, *yel*	—
NL74	A5	30h lake & blk	—

On Zanzibar Stamps in Green, Violet or Black

NL75	1c gray (#141)	—
NL76	3c yellow green (#142)	—
NL77	6c carmine (#143)	—
NL78	15c ultramarine (#146)	—

On Indian Expeditionary Force Stamps (India #M34-M43) in Green, Greenish Black or Blue

NL79	3p gray (#M34)	40.00	*95.00*
a.	Pair, one without overprint		*1,150.*
NL80	½a green (#M35)	65.00	*100.00*
a.	Pair, one without overprint		*1,250.*
NL81	1a carmine rose (#M36)	70.00	*100.00*
NL82	2a violet (#M37)	110.00	*160.00*
NL83	2½a ultramarine (#M38)	140.00	*200.00*
NL84	3a orange brown (#M39)	140.00	*225.00*
a.	Pair, one without overprint		1,500.
NL85	4a olive green (#M40)	175.00	*250.00*
NL86	8a purple (#M41)	300.00	*400.00*
a.	Pair, one without overprint		*1,900.*
NL87	12a dull claret (#M42)	375.00	*550.00*
NL88	1r green & red brown (#M43)	450.00	*575.00*
a.	Double overprint, one inverted		*2,750.*

Handstamp exists inverted, double and sideways.

Handstamped in three lines, sans-serif italic type, in green, greenish black or blue

On Indian Expeditionary Force Stamps (India #M34-M43)

1916, Oct.

NL89	3p gray (#M34)	150.00	*175.00*
NL90	½a green (#M35)	160.00	*160.00*
NL91	1a carmine rose (#M36)	120.00	*140.00*
NL92	2a violet (#M37)	200.00	200.00
NL93	2½a ultramarine (#M38)	210.00	*225.00*
NL94	3a orange brown (#M39)	210.00	*225.00*
NL95	4a olive green (#M40)	350.00	*350.00*
NL96	8a purple (#M41)	450.00	*500.00*
NL97	12a dull claret (#M42)	475.00	*600.00*
NL98	1r green & red brown (#M43)	550.00	*575.00*

Some values exist with handstamp inverted.

GERMAN NEW GUINEA

ˈjər-mən ˈnü ˈgi-nē

LOCATION — A group of islands in the west Pacific Ocean, including a part of New Guinea and adjacent islands of the Bismarck Archipelago.
GOVT. — German Protectorate
AREA — 93,000 sq. mi.
POP. — 601,427 (1913)
CAPITAL — Herbertshohe (later Kokopo)

The islands were occupied by Australian troops during World War I and renamed "New Britain." By covenant of the League of Nations they were made a mandated territory of Australia in 1920. The old name of "New Guinea" has since been restored. Postage stamps were issued under all regimes. For other listings see New Britain (1914-15), North West Pacific Islands (1915-22) and New Guinea.

100 Pfennig = 1 Mark

Stamps of Germany Overprinted in Black

1897-99 Unwmk. *Perf. 13½x14½*

1	A9	3pf brown	7.75	*9.25*
		Never hinged	18.50	
		On cover		75.00
a.		3pf reddish brown ('99)	105.00	*190.00*
		Never hinged	325.00	
		On cover		450.00
b.		3pf yellow brown ('99)	29.00	*52.50*
		Never hinged	85.00	
		On cover		110.00
2	A9	5pf green	3.75	*5.25*
		Never hinged	6.75	
		On cover		67.50
3	A10	10pf carmine	6.00	*8.50*
		Never hinged	12.00	
		On cover		92.50
4	A10	20pf ultra	8.50	*13.00*
		Never hinged	20.00	
		On cover		150.00
5	A10	25pf orange ('98)	26.00	*50.00*
		Never hinged	60.00	
		On cover		150.00
a.		Inverted overprint	*2,750.*	
		Never hinged	*4,600.*	
6	A10	50pf red brown	30.00	*45.00*
		Never hinged	75.00	
		On cover		92.50
		Nos. 1-6 (6)	82.00	*131.00*

Covers: Value for No. 6 is for overfranked complete cover, usually philatelic.

Kaiser's Yacht "Hohenzollern"
A3 A4

1901 Typo. *Perf. 14*

7	A3	3pf brown	1.10	1.10
		Never hinged	2.25	
		On cover		92.50
8	A3	5pf green	7.00	1.10
		Never hinged	15.00	
		On cover		37.50
9	A3	10pf carmine	22.50	2.50
		Never hinged	60.00	
		On cover		45.00
10	A3	20pf ultra	1.40	*2.50*
		Never hinged	3.75	
		On cover		75.00
11	A3	25pf org & blk, *yel*	1.75	*15.00*
		Never hinged	3.75	
		On cover		150.00
12	A3	30pf org & blk, *sal*	1.75	*19.00*
		Never hinged	3.75	
		On cover		150.00
13	A3	40pf lake & blk	1.75	*21.00*
		Never hinged	3.75	
		On cover		150.00
14	A3	50pf pur & blk, *sal*	1.90	*18.00*
		Never hinged	3.75	
		On cover		52.50
15	A3	80pf lake & blk, *rose*	3.50	*26.00*
		Never hinged	6.00	
		On cover		75.00

Engr.
Perf. 14½x14

16	A4	1m carmine	3.75	*50.00*
		Never hinged	23.00	
		On cover		92.50
17	A4	2m blue	5.00	*62.50*
		Never hinged	23.00	
		On cover		130.00
18	A4	3m blk vio	6.75	*140.00*
		Never hinged	30.00	
		On cover		260.00
19	A4	5m slate & car	150.00	*450.00*
		Never hinged	375.00	
		On cover		800.00
		Nos. 7-19 (13)	208.15	*808.70*

Fake cancellations exist on Nos. 10-19.
Covers: Values for Nos. 14-19 are for overfranked complete cover, usually philatelic.

A5

A6

Wmk. Lozenges (125)

1914-19 Typo. *Perf. 14*

20	A3	3pf brown ('19)	.75	
		Never hinged	1.50	
21	A5	5pf green	1.50	
		Never hinged	3.00	
22	A5	10pf carmine	1.50	
		Never hinged	3.00	

Engr.

Perf. 14½x14

23	A6	5m slate & carmine	30.00	
		Never hinged	92.50	

Nos. 20-23 were never placed in use.
Nos. 21-23 have "NEUGUINEA" as one word without a hyphen.

GERMAN SOUTH WEST AFRICA

'jər-mən 'sauth 'west 'a-fri-kə

LOCATION — In southwest Africa, bordering on the South Atlantic.
GOVT. — German Colony
AREA — 322,450 sq. mi. (1913)
POP. — 94,372 (1913)
CAPITAL — Windhoek

The Colony was occupied by South African troops during World War I and in 1920 was mandated to the Union of South Africa by the League of Nations. See South-West Africa.

100 Pfennig = 1 Mark

Stamps of Germany Overprinted

1897 Unwmk. *Perf. 13½x14½*

1	A9	3pf dark brown	6.75	*9.50*
		Never hinged	26.00	
		On cover		67.50
a.		3pf yellow brown	40.00	*2,000.*
		Never hinged	140.00	
		On cover		—
b.		3pf olive brown	45.00	
		Never hinged	160.00	
c.		3pf reddish brown	—	*2,250.*
		Never hinged	—	
2	A9	5pf green	3.50	3.25
		Never hinged	11.00	
		On cover		26.00
3	A10	10pf carmine	17.00	13.00
		Never hinged	57.50	
		On cover		75.00
4	A10	20pf ultra	4.50	*4.25*
		Never hinged	22.50	
		On cover		30.00
5	A10	25pf orange	190.00	*20,000.*
		Never hinged	575.00	
6	A10	50pf red brown	190.00	
		Never hinged	575.00	
		Nos. 1-4 (4)	31.75	30.00

Nos. 5 and 6 were prepared for issue but were not sent to the Colony.

Overprinted "Deutsch-Südwestafrika"

1899

7	A9	3pf dark brown	3.25	*17.00*
		Never hinged	15.00	
		On cover		100.00
a.		3pf reddish brown	13.00	*72.50*
		Never hinged	50.00	
		On cover		500.00
b.		3pf yellow brown	5.50	*10.00*
		Never hinged	20.00	
		On cover		50.00
8	A9	5pf green	2.50	2.10
		Never hinged	10.00	
		On cover		19.00
9	A10	10pf carmine	2.50	2.50
		Never hinged	10.00	
		On cover		19.00
10	A10	20pf ultra	9.00	*11.50*
		Never hinged	42.50	
		On cover		45.00
11	A10	25pf orange	250.00	325.00
		Never hinged	925.00	
		On cover		750.00
12	A10	50pf red brown	9.00	8.50
		Never hinged	45.00	
		On cover		45.00

Covers: Value for No. 12 is for overfranked complete covers, usually philatelic.

Kaiser's Yacht "Hohenzollern"
A3 A4

1900 Typo. *Perf. 14*

13	A3	3pf brown	1.25	1.25
		Never hinged	9.25	
		On cover		60.00
14	A3	5pf green	16.00	.65
		Never hinged	45.00	
		On cover		15.00
15	A3	10pf carmine	11.50	.65
		Never hinged	45.00	
		On cover		15.00
16	A3	20pf ultra	24.00	1.25
		Never hinged	72.50	
		On cover		15.00
17	A3	25pf org & blk, *yel*	1.25	*4.25*
		Never hinged	5.25	
		On cover		22.50
18	A3	30pf org & blk, *sal*	18.00	2.25
		Never hinged	190.00	
		On cover		15.00
19	A3	40pf lake & blk	1.50	*2.75*
		Never hinged	5.25	
		On cover		15.00
20	A3	50pf pur & blk, *sal*	1.75	1.75
		Never hinged	6.25	
		On cover		15.00
21	A3	80pf lake & blk, *rose*	1.75	*7.50*
		Never hinged	6.25	
		On cover		35.00

Engr.

Perf. 14½x14

22	A4	1m carmine	90.00	*25.00*
		Never hinged	350.00	
		On cover		60.00
23	A4	2m blue	22.50	*30.00*
		Never hinged	92.50	
		On cover		70.00
24	A4	3m blk vio	26.00	*35.00*
		Never hinged	110.00	
		On cover		85.00
25	A4	5m slate & car	150.00	125.00
		Never hinged	375.00	
		On cover		350.00
		Nos. 13-25 (13)	365.50	*237.30*

Covers: Values for Nos. 20-25 are for overfranked complete covers, usually philatelic.

Wmk. Lozenges (125)

1906-19 Typo. *Perf. 14*

26	A3	3pf dk brn ('07)	.65	*13.00*
		Never hinged	1.90	
		On cover		50.00
a.		3pf yellow brown ('13)	.80	*2.90*
		Never hinged	2.00	
		On cover		32.50
27	A3	5pf green	.65	*1.10*
		Never hinged	1.90	
		On cover		19.00
b.		Bklt. pane of 6 (2 #27, 4 #28)	40.00	
		Never hinged	75.00	
c.		Booklet pane of 5 + label	*150.00*	
		Never hinged	*375.00*	
28	A3	10pf lt rose	.80	*1.10*
		Never hinged	3.75	
		On cover		15.00
a.		10pf red ('13)	3.00	*15.00*
		Never hinged	11.00	
		On cover		92.50
b.		Booklet pane of 5 + label	*225.00*	
		Never hinged	*450.00*	
29	A3	20pf ultra ('11)	.80	*3.00*
		Never hinged	3.75	
		On cover		22.50
30	A3	30pf org & blk, *pale yellow* ('11)	11.00	*42.50*
		Never hinged	52.50	
		On cover		925.00
a.		30pf orange & black, *pale orange* ('13)	5.75	—
		Never hinged	15.00	
		On cover		—

Engr.

Perf. 14½x14

31	A4	1m carmine ('12)	9.75	*55.00*
		Never hinged	50.00	
		On cover		275.00
32	A4	2m blue ('11)	9.75	*26.00*
		Never hinged	50.00	
		On cover		275.00
33	A4	3m blk vio ('19)	11.00	
		Never hinged	42.50	
a.		3m gray violet	22.50	
		Never hinged	140.00	
34	A4	5m slate & car	21.00	*225.00*
		Never hinged	75.00	
		On cover		850.00
a.		5m slate & rose red	42.50	
		Never hinged	275.00	
		Nos. 26-34 (9)	65.40	366.70

Nos. 33, 33a, 34a were never placed in use.
Booklet panes of 6 made from sheet stamps exist of the 5pf and 10pf.
Forged cancellations are found on #30-32, 34.
Covers: Values for Nos. 31-34 are for overfranked complete covers, usually philatelic.

GERMAN STATES

'jər-mən 'stāts

Watermarks

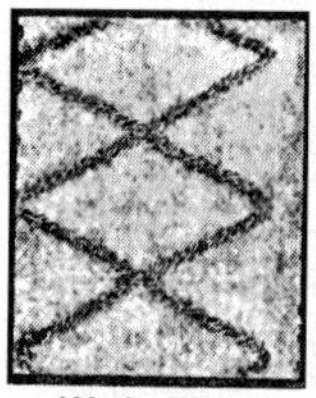
Wmk. 92 — 17mm wide

Wmk. 93 — 14mm wide

Wmk. 94 — Horiz. WavyLines Wide Apart

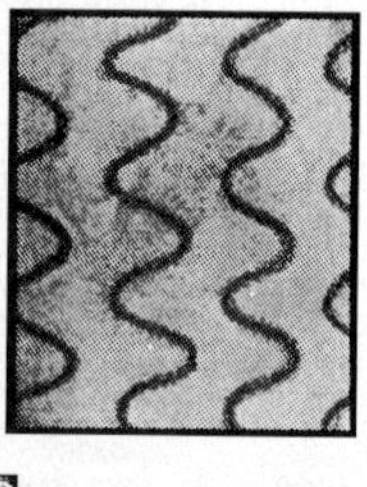
Wmk. 95v — Vert. Wavy Lines Close Together

Wmk. 95h — Horiz. Wavy Lines Close Together

Wmk. 102 — Post Horn

Wmk. 116 — Crosses and Circles

Wmk. 128 — Wavy Lines

Wmk. 130 — Wreath of Oak Leaves

Wmk. 148 — Small Flowers

Wmk. 162 — Laurel Wreath

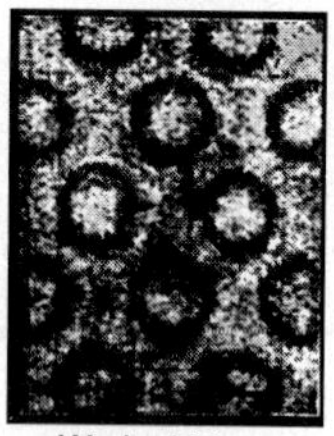
Wmk. 192 — Circles

BADEN

LOCATION — In southwestern Germany
GOVT. — Former Grand Duchy
AREA — 5,817 sq. mi.
POP. — 1,432,000 (1864)
CAPITAL — Karlsruhe (Principal city)

Baden was a member of the German Confederation. In 1870 it became part of the German Empire.

60 Kreuzer = 1 Gulden

Values for unused stamps are for examples with original gum as defined in the catalogue introduction except for Nos. 1-9 which are valued without gum. Very fine examples of Nos. 1-9 will have one or two margins touching the framelines due to the very narrow spacing of the stamps on the plates. Stamps with margins clear of the framelines on all four sides are scarce and sell for considerably more.

A1

1851-52 Unwmk. Typo. *Imperf.*

1	A1	1kr blk, *dk buff*	250.00	210.00
		With gum	440.00	
		On cover		500.00
2	A1	3kr blk, *yellow*	125.00	12.50
		With gum	225.00	
		On cover		35.00
3	A1	6kr blk, *yel grn*	400.00	40.00
		With gum	725.00	
		On cover		100.00
4	A1	9kr blk, *lil rose*	80.00	24.00
		With gum	175.00	
		On cover		82.50

Thin Paper (First Printing, 1851)

1a	A1	1kr black, *buff*	1,825.	675.00
		With gum	9,000.	
		On cover		1,500.
2a	A1	3kr black, *orange*	625.00	30.00
		With gum	1,450.	
		On cover		82.50
3a	A1	6kr black, *blue green*	2,000.	75.00
		With gum	3,250.	
		On cover		225.00

4a A1 9kr black, *deep rose* 2,550. 140.00
With gum 4,000.
On cover 400.00
4b A1 9kr black, *bl grn* (error) 1,300,000.
On cover *2,000,000.*

Values for pairs

1 A1 1kr blk, *dk buff* 1,450. 550.00
With gum 2,900.
On cover 1,500.
2 A1 3kr blk, *yellow* 325.00 47.50
With gum 800.00
On cover 87.50
Gutter pair (10) *8,000.*
On cover *40,000.*
3 A1 6kr blk, *yel grn* 825.00 150.00
With gum 1,550.
On cover 225.00
Gutter pair (2) *30,000.*
4 A1 9kr blk, *lil rose* 225.00 125.00
With gum 550.00
On cover 650.00

Thin Paper

1a A1 1kr black, *buff* — 1,800.
On cover 2,550.
Gutter pair (1) *115,000.*
2a A1 3kr black, *orange* 2,200. 150.00
With gum *4,400.*
On cover 175.00
3a A1 6kr black, *blue green* — 290.00
With gum *8,000.*
On cover 800.00
4a A1 9kr black, *deep rose* — 1,450.
With gum *8,750.*

Values for strips of 3

1 A1 1kr blk, *dk buff* 875.00
On cover 1,450.
2 A1 3kr blk, *yellow* 875.00 175.00
With gum 1,600.
On cover *4,000.*
3 A1 6kr blk, *yel grn* 550.00
On cover *1,300.*
4 A1 9kr blk, *lil rose* 360.00 375.00
With gum 875.00
On cover 800.00

Thin Paper

1a A1 1kr black, *buff* 2,600.
On cover *4,000.*
2a A1 3kr black, *orange* 2,900. 500.00
With gum *6,250.*
On cover 725.00
3a A1 6kr black, *blue green* 1,300.
On cover *2,600.*
4a A1 9kr black, *deep rose* 4,400.

Values for blocks of 4

1 A1 1kr blk, *dk buff* — *3,750.*
2 A1 3kr blk, *yellow* — *1,300.*
With gum *5,000.*
3 A1 6kr blk, *yel grn* — *3,750.*
With gum *7,500.*
4 A1 9kr blk, *lil rose* 550.00 *2,750.*
With gum *1,800.*

Thin Paper

1a A1 1kr black, *buff* — —
2a A1 3kr black, *orange* *4,000.* *2,400.*
With gum *8,000.*
3a A1 6kr black, *blue green* — —
With gum *22,000.*
4a A1 9kr black, *deep rose* — —
With gum *22,000.*

1853-58

6 A1 1kr black 150.00 22.50
With gum 375.00
On cover 100.00
a. Tête bêche gutter pair *45,000.*
7 A1 3kr black, *green* 150.00 16.00
With gum 300.00
On cover 22.50
8 A1 3kr black, *bl* ('58) 625.00 30.00
With gum 1,300.
On cover 100.00
a. Printed on both sides
9 A1 6kr black, *yellow* 240.00 24.00
With gum 500.00
On cover 62.50

Values for pairs

6 A1 1kr black 440.00 110.00
With gum 1,600.
On cover 225.00
7 A1 3kr blk, *green* 30.00
With gum 1,300.
On cover 45.00
8 A1 3kr blk, *blue,* (58) 1,450. 125.00
With gum 3,000.
On cover 175.00
9 A1 6kr blk, *yellow* 225.00
With gum 1,600.

Values for used strips of 3

6 A1 1kr black 160.00
On cover 260.00
7 A1 3kr blk, *green* 87.50
On cover 110.00
8 A1 3kr blk, *blue,* (58) 325.00
On cover 550.00
9 A1 6kr blk, *yellow* 725.00

Values for blocks of 4

6 A1 1kr black — *1,300.*
With gum 4,500.
7 A1 3kr blk, *green* *2,000.*
With gum 4,500.
On cover *3,000.*
8 A1 3kr blk, *blue,* (58) *2,200.*
With gum 7,250.
9 A1 6kr blk, *yellow* *8,000.*
With gum 6,600.

Full margins of Nos. 1-4, 6-9 = ½mm.

Reissues (1865) of Nos. 1, 2, 3, 6, 7 and 8 exist on thick paper and No. 9 on thin paper; the color of the last is brighter than that of the original.

Covers: Values for Nos. 1-9 on cover are for covers bearing stamps with one or more margins touching, but not into the design. Covers bearing stamps with full clear margins are rare and command substantial premiums.

Coat of Arms
A2 A3

1860-62 *Perf. 13½*

10 A2 1kr black 72.50 22.50
No gum 30.00
Never hinged 300.00
On cover 72.50
On cover, single franking 110.00
12 A2 3kr ultra ('61) 80.00 16.00
No gum 30.00
Never hinged 250.00
On cover 55.00
a. 3kr Prussian blue 275.00 50.00
No gum 100.00
Never hinged 800.00
On cover 87.50
b. 3kr violet ultramarine 375.00 160.00
No gum 150.00
On cover 440.00
13 A2 6kr red org ('61) 95.00 60.00
No gum 37.50
Never hinged 500.00
On cover 175.00
a. 6kr yellow orange ('62) 175.00 72.50
No gum 72.50
Never hinged 750.00
On cover 200.00
14 A2 9kr rose ('61) 240.00 160.00
No gum 87.50
Never hinged 1,000.
On cover 440.00

Copies of Nos. 10-14 and 18 with all perforations intact sell for considerably more.

Values for pairs

10 A2 1kr black 150.00 55.00
No gum 65.00
On cover 110.00
12 A2 3kr ultra 300.00 55.00
No gum 110.00
On cover 72.50
a. 3kr Prussian blue 1,100. 225.00
No gum 300.00
On cover 375.00
b. 3kr violet ultramarine 1,100. 550.00
No gum 325.00
On cover 875.00
13 A2 6kr red org 300.00 160.00
No gum 110.00
On cover 375.00
a. 6kr yellow orange 475.00 225.00
No gum 175.00
On cover 400.00
14 A2 9kr rose 550.00 375.00
No gum 225.00
On cover 800.00

Values for strips of 3

10 A2 1kr black 240.00 100.00
No gum 100.00
On cover 150.00
12 A2 3kr ultra 440.00 110.00
No gum 160.00
On cover 160.00
a. 3kr Prussian blue 1,800. 440.00
No gum 725.00
On cover 500.00
b. 3kr violet ultramarine 1,100.
On cover 1,600.
13 A2 6kr red org 525.00 375.00
No gum 175.00
On cover 650.00
a. 6kr yellow orange 650.00 400.00
No gum 250.00
On cover 650.00
14 A2 9kr rose 875.00 *1,000.*
No gum 375.00
On cover 1,450.

Values for blocks of 4

10 A2 1kr black 375.00 *875.00*
No gum 150.00
12 A2 3kr ultra 550.00 *725.00*
No gum 225.00
a. 3kr Prussian blue 3,250. 1,800.
No gum 875.00
b. 3kr violet ultramarine —
13 A2 6kr red org 725.00 *1,600.*
No gum 300.00
a. 6kr yellow orange 875.00 *2,000.*
No gum 375.00
14 A2 9kr rose 1,800. *2,600.*
No gum 725.00

1862 *Perf. 10*

15 A2 1kr black 57.50 72.50
Never hinged 200.00
On cover 140.00
On cover, single franking 360.00
a. 1kr silver gray *6,600.*
On cover *17,000.*
b. 1kr gray black 725.00 *825.00*
On cover *1,900.*
16 A2 6kr Prus bl ('62) 110.00 62.50
Never hinged 500.00
On cover 140.00
a. 6kr blue ('63) 140.00 95.00
Never hinged 600.00
On cover 150.00
17 A2 9kr brown 82.50 67.50
Never hinged 500.00
On cover 140.00
a. 9kr dark brown 350.00 275.00
Never hinged 1,200.
On cover 550.00
b. 9kr bister 140.00 *225.00*
Never hinged 700.00
On cover 310.00

Perf. 13½

18 A3 3kr rose 2,500. 310.00
No gum 700.00
On cover 675.00

Values for pairs

15 A2 1kr black 140.00 *175.00*
No gum 42.50
On cover 275.00
a. 1kr silver gray *19,000.*
b. 1kr gray black 1,800.
On cover *2,300.*
16 A2 6kr Prus bl 275.00 250.00
No gum 100.00
On cover 325.00
a. 6kr blue 340.00 250.00
No gum 140.00
On cover 350.00
17 A2 9kr brown 275.00 190.00
No gum 100.00
On cover 300.00
a. 9kr dark brown 925.00 650.00
No gum 350.00
On cover 875.00
b. 9kr bister 375.00 *500.00*
No gum 150.00
On cover 600.00
18 A3 3kr rose *5,500.* 700.00
No gum 1,800.
On cover 1,100.

Values for strips of 3

15 A2 1kr black 200.00 *350.00*
No gum 72.50
On cover 500.00
a. 1kr silver gray
b. 1kr gray black 4,000.
On cover 5,000.
16 A2 6kr Prus bl 400.00 375.00
No gum 140.00
On cover 625.00
a. 6kr blue 440.00 440.00
No gum 190.00
On cover 700.00
17 A2 9kr brown 400.00 400.00
No gum 140.00
On cover 700.00
a. 9kr dark brown 1,350. 1,100.
No gum 500.00
On cover 1,700.
b. 9kr bister 1,050.
No gum 250.00
On cover 1,700.
18 A3 3kr rose 1,350.
On cover 2,100.

Values for blocks of 4

15 A2 1kr black 275.00 *1,300.*
No gum 110.00
a. 1kr silver gray — —
b. 1kr gray black — —
16 A2 6kr Prus bl 1,300. 1,300.
No gum 225.00
a. 6kr blue 1,400. 1,400.
No gum 275.00
17 A2 9kr brown 1,600. *2,200.*
No gum 200.00
a. 9kr dark brown 2,900. *3,000.*
No gum 700.00
b. 9kr bister 2,300. *2,750.*
No gum 310.00
18 A3 3kr rose — 2,200.
strip of 4 — —

1862-65 *Perf. 10*

19 A3 1kr black ('64) 45.00 12.00
No gum 14.00
Never hinged 120.00
On cover 28.00
On cover, single franking 140.00
a. 1kr silver gray *2,100.*
On cover *3,600.*
b. 1kr gray black 375.00 260.00
On cover 500.00
20 A3 3kr rose 45.00 1.60
No gum 14.00
Never hinged 120.00
On cover 7.00
a. Imperf. *100,000.* *40,000.*
On cover *100,000.*
22 A3 6kr ultra ('65) 7.50 *22.50*
No gum 2.25
Never hinged 25.00
On cover 55.00
a. 6kr Prussian blue ('64) *575.00* 65.00
No gum 160.00
Never hinged 2,000.
On cover 160.00
23 A3 9kr brn ('64) 14.00 25.00
No gum 5.00
Never hinged 35.00
On cover 65.00
a. 9kr bister 375.00 90.00
No gum 100.00
Never hinged 700.00
On cover 160.00
b. Printed on both sides *6,500.*
c. 9kr dark brown 500.00 *440.00*
No gum 160.00
Never hinged 1,500.
On cover *1,300.*
24 A3 18kr green 375.00 575.00
No gum 110.00
Never hinged 1,200.
On cover 1,800.
On cover, single franking 2,900.
a. 18kr dark green 1,300. 1,300.
No gum 340.00
Never hinged 4,000.
On cover *8,250.*
On cover, single franking *8,250.*

25	A3 30kr deep orange	27.50	*1,300.*
	No gum	8.75	
	Never hinged	65.00	
	On cover		*4,400.*
	On cover, single franking		*19,000.*
a.	30kr yellow orange	140.00	*2,200.*
	No gum	45.00	
	Never hinged	600.00	
	On cover		*8,250.*
	On cover, single franking		*9,000.*

Forged cancellations are known on #25.

Values for pairs

19	A3 1kr black	140.00	37.50
	On cover		50.00
a.	1kr silver gray		*4,750.*
	On cover		*5,750.*
b.	1kr gray black		*725.00*
	On cover		1,100.
20	A3 3kr rose	110.00	4.25
	On cover		13.00
22	A3 6kr ultra	16.00	*55.00*
	On cover		87.50
a.	6kr Prussian blue	1,600.	160.00
	On cover		325.00
23	A3 9kr brown	37.50	*70.00*
	On cover		140.00
a.	9kr bister	875.00	225.00
	On cover		440.00
c.	9kr dark brown	1,300.	1,000.
	On cover		1,800.
24	A3 18kr green	1,400.	1,400.
	On cover		4,400.
a.	18kr dark green	3,600.	3,100.
	On cover		*5,800.*
25	A3 30kr deep orange	65.00	*3,250.*
	On cover		*14,500.*
a.	30kr yellow orange	375.00	*5,500.*
	On cover		*18,000.*

Values for strips of 3

19	A3 1kr black	190.00	65.00
	On cover		80.00
a.	1kr silver gray		*7,250.*
	On cover		*8,750.*
b.	1kr gray black		1,300.
	On cover		1,800.
20	A3 3kr rose	160.00	20.00
	On cover		37.50
22	A3 6kr ultra	27.50	*210.00*
	On cover		325.00
a.	6kr Prussian blue	2,300.	*625.00*
	On cover		1,100.
23	A3 9kr brown	57.50	*210.00*
	On cover		375.00
a.	9kr bister		375.00
	On cover		575.00
c.	9kr dark brown	2,000.	1,600.
	On cover		2,750.
24	A3 18kr green	4,400.	—
a.	18kr dark green		—
25	A3 30kr deep orange	110.00	*5,750.*
a.	30kr yellow orange	550.00	—

Values for blocks of 4

19	A3 1kr black	275.00	*725.00*
	Never hinged	600.00	
20	A3 3kr rose	225.00	*725.00*
	Never hinged	550.00	
22	A3 6kr ultra	37.50	*1,400.*
	Never hinged	70.00	
a.	6kr Prussian blue	3,250.	1,800.
23	A3 9kr brown	70.00	*1,300.*
	Never hinged	140.00	
c.	9kr dark brown	3,000.	—
	Never hinged	5,750.	
24	A3 18kr green	3,000.	—
25	A3 30kr deep orange	140.00	—
	Never hinged	300.00	
a.	30kr yellow orange	875.00	—
	Never hinged	2,500.	

A4

1868

26	A4 1kr green	4.00	*4.50*
	Never hinged	7.00	
	On cover		14.00
	On wrapper, single franking		70.00
27	A4 3kr rose	2.25	1.50
	Never hinged	4.25	
	On cover		7.00
28	A4 7kr dull blue	19.00	*32.50*
	Never hinged	37.50	
	On cover		87.50
a.	7kr sky blue	42.50	*92.50*
	Never hinged	70.00	
	On cover		275.00
	On cover, single franking		*700.00*

Forged cancellations are known on #28a.

Values for pairs

26	A4 1kr green	8.75	*11.50*
	On cover		30.00
27	A4 3kr rose	4.25	*8.75*
	On cover		19.00
28	A4 7kr dull blue	40.00	*92.50*
	On cover		190.00
a.	7kr sky blue	92.50	350.00
	On cover		825.00

Values for strips of 3

26	A4 1kr green	13.00	*19.00*
	On cover		37.50
27	A4 3kr rose	7.75	*37.50*
	On cover		57.50
28	A4 7kr dull blue	60.00	*300.00*
	On cover		440.00
a.	7kr sky blue	140.00	*1,100.*
	On cover		2,100.

Values for blocks of 4

26	A4 1kr green	16.00	*375.00*
	Never hinged	32.50	
27	A4 3kr rose	8.75	*1,600.*
	Never hinged	19.00	
28	A4 7kr dull blue	82.50	*2,750.*
	Never hinged	160.00	
a.	7kr sky blue	210.00	—
	Never hinged	350.00	

The postage stamps of Baden were superseded by those of the German Empire on Jan. 1, 1872, but Official stamps were used during the year 1905.

RURAL POSTAGE DUE STAMPS

RU1

1862 **Unwmk.** ***Perf. 10***

Thin Paper

LJ1	RU1 1kr blk, *yellow*	4.00	*275.00*
	Never hinged	6.50	
	On cover		575.00
a.	Thick paper	140.00	*575.00*
	Never hinged	250.00	
	On cover		1,300.
LJ2	RU1 3kr blk, *yellow*	2.25	*110.00*
	Never hinged	3.75	
	On cover		225.00
a.	Thick paper	110.00	*375.00*
	Never hinged	225.00	
	On cover		875.00
LJ3	RU1 12kr blk, *yellow*	26.00	*20,000.*
	Never hinged	65.00	
	On cover		*32,500.*
a.	Half used as 6kr on cover		*25,000.*
b.	Quarter used as 3kr on cover		—

On #LJ3, "LAND-POST" is a straight line.
Paper of #LJ1a, LJ2a is darker yellow.
Forged cancellations abound on #LJ1-LJ3.

Values for pairs

LJ1	RU1 1kr blk, *yellow*	8.75	*725.00*
	On cover		875.00
a.	Thick paper	250.00	*1,300.*
	On cover		1,800.
LJ2	RU1 3kr blk, *yellow*	5.00	*250.00*
	On cover		400.00
a.	Thick paper	225.00	*875.00*
	On cover		1,300.
LJ3	RU1 12kr blk, *yellow*	100.00	*29,000.*
	On cover		*47,500.*

Values for strips of 3

LJ1	RU1 1kr blk, *yellow*	14.50	*1,100.*
	On cover		1,400.
a.	Thick paper	400.00	*2,000.*
	On cover		2,750.
LJ2	RU1 3kr blk, *yellow*	725.00	*440.00*
	On cover		450.00
a.	Thick paper	375.00	*1,400.*
	On cover		1,800.
LJ3	RU1 12kr blk, *yellow*	140.00	—

Values for blocks of 4

LJ1	RU1 1kr blk, *yellow*	22.50	*1,800.*
	Never hinged	35.00	
a.	Thick paper	550.00	*2,900.*
	Never hinged	1,150.	
LJ2	RU1 3kr blk, *yellow*	10.00	*1,250.*
	Never hinged	20.00	
a.	Thick paper	400.00	*2,200.*
	Never hinged	1,000.	
LJ3	RU1 12kr blk, *yellow*	125.00	—
	Never hinged	375.00	

A used single of the 12kr stamp (Scott No. LJ3) tied to a small piece by a neat c.d.s., sold for the equivalent of U.S. $24,400 at a German auction in 2003.

OFFICIAL STAMPS

See Germany Nos. OL16-OL21.

BAVARIA

LOCATION — In southern Germany
GOVT. — Kingdom
AREA — 30,562 sq. mi. (1920)
POP. — 7,150,146 (1919)
CAPITAL — Munich

Bavaria was a member of the German Confederation and became part of the German Empire in 1870. After World War I, it declared itself a republic. It lost its postal autonomy on Mar. 31, 1920.

60 Kreuzer = 1 Gulden
100 Pfennig = 1 Mark (1874)

Values for unused stamps are for examples with original gum as defined in the catalogue introduction. Unused examples of the 1849-7 issues without gum sell for about 50-60% of the figures quoted.

A1

Broken Circle — A1a

Two plates used for No. 1:
Plate I: Rough impression, framelines around figure "1" broken or incomplete.
Plate II: Fine impression, framelines around "1" complete.

1849 **Unwmk.** **Typo.** ***Imperf.***

1	A1 1kr black (I)	725.00	*1,825.*
	Pen & postmark cancels		1,300.
	Pen cancel		1,300.
	On cover, postmark cancel		4,750.
	On cover, pen cancel		5,500.
	On cover, pen & postmark cancels		3,750.
	On printed matter, single franking		7,250.
	On printed matter, pair		*13,000.*
	Pair with gutter between	*19,000.*	*90,000.*
a.	1kr deep black (I)	2,175.	*2,900.*
	Pen cancel		1,750.
	Pen & postmark cancels		1,825.
	On cover, pen & postmark cancels		5,800.
b.	Tête bêche pair	*125,000.*	
c.	1kr black (II)	2,200.	2,000.
	Pen cancel		1,900.
	Pen & postmark cancels		1,450.
	On cover, pen & postmark cancels		4,400.
	On cover, pen cancel		6,500.
	On cover, postmark cancel		6,600.
	On printed matter, single franking		*8,000.*
d.	1kr deep black (II)	4,400.	3,250.
	On cover, pen & postmark cancels		7,250.

Full margins = 1mm. There are dividing lines between stamps.

With Silk Thread

2	A1a 3kr blue	45.00	2.25
	On cover		11.00
	On printed matter, single franking		225.00
	Pair with gutter between	*2,750.*	*12,000.*
	On cover		*26,000.*
a.	3kr greenish blue	45.00	2.25
	On cover		11.00
b.	3kr deep blue	45.00	2.25
	On cover		11.00
3	A1a 6kr brown	*6,500.*	190.00
	Pen cancel		225.00
	Pen & postmark cancels		125.00
	On cover		440.00
	Pair with gutter between	—	*30,000.*

Full margins = 1mm. There are dividing lines between stamps.

No. 1 exists with silk thread, from a single proof sheet, value about $4,000.

Values for pairs

1	A1 1kr black (I)	1,600.	*4,400.*
	Pen & postmark cancels		3,650.
	On cover		13,000.
a.	1kr deep black (I)	5,800.	*7,250.*
	Pen & postmark cancels		5,800.
	On cover		14,500.
c.	1kr black (II)		4,750.
d.	1kr deep black (II)		8,000.
2	A1a 3kr blue	110.00	14.50
	On cover		36.00
a.	3kr greenish blue	110.00	14.50
	On cover		36.00
b.	3kr deep blue	110.00	14.50
	On cover		36.00
3	A1a 6kr brown	*20,000.*	1,100.
	On cover		2,200.

Values for strips of 3

1	A1 1kr black (I)	2,900.	*8,000.*
	Pen & postmark cancels		6,500.
	On cover		*19,000.*
a.	1kr deep black (I)	8,000.	*12,500.*
	Pen & postmark cancels		9,500.
	On cover		20,000.
c.	1kr black (II)		9,500.
	On cover		19,000.
d.	1kr deep black (II)		13,000.
2	A1a 3kr blue	175.00	65.00
	On cover		130.00
a.	3kr greenish blue	175.00	65.00
	On cover		130.00

b. 3kr deep blue 200.00 72.50
On cover 140.00
3 A1a 6kr brown — —

Values for blocks of 4

1 A1 1kr black (I) 3,750. *58,000.*
a. 1kr deep black — —
2 A1a 3kr blue 290.00 *1,450.*
a. 3kr greenish blue 290.00 *1,450.*
b. 3kr deep blue 290.00 *1,450.*
3 A1a 6kr brown — —

Complete circle — A2

Coat of Arms — A3

1850-58 With Silk Thread

4 A2 1kr pink 90.00 19.00
Never hinged 150.00
On cover 65.00
On wrapper, single franking 140.00
On cover, single franking, local delivery 300.00
Pair with gutter between *2,200.* *25,000.*
On cover *50,000.*
a. 1kr lilac rose 375.00 40.00
Never hinged 575.00
On cover 87.50
5 A2 6kr brown 40.00 5.50
Never hinged 90.00
On cover 22.00
Pair with gutter between *3,650.* *14,500.*
On cover *32,500.*
a. Half used as 3kr on cover *15,750.*
6 A2 9kr yellow green 60.00 13.00
Never hinged 120.00
On cover 40.00
Pair with gutter between *2,200.* *14,500.*
On cover *44,000.*
a. 9kr blue green ('53) *11,000.* 150.00
On cover 500.00
Pair with gutter between — —
b. 9kr pale blue green *6,500.* 45.00
On cover 140.00
Pair with gutter between — *21,750.*
On cover *47,500.*
7 A2 12kr red ('58) 125.00 *125.00*
Never hinged 225.00
On cover 550.00
On cover, single franking 650.00
Pair with gutter between *3,650.* *26,000.*
8 A2 18kr yel ('54) 110.00 *190.00*
Never hinged 175.00
On cover 875.00
On cover, single franking 1,200.
Pair with gutter between *2,200.* *26,000.*

Full margins = 1mm. There are dividing lines between stamps.

Values for pairs

4 A2 1kr pink 225.00 110.00
On cover 300.00
a. 1kr lilac rose — 160.00
On cover 375.00
5 A2 6kr brown 100.00 45.00
On cover 65.00
6 A2 9kr yel grn 140.00 140.00
On cover 275.00
a. 9kr blue green — 575.00
On cover 1,100.
b. 9kr pale blue green — 260.00
On cover 475.00
7 A2 12kr red 275.00 *800.00*
On cover 1,300.
8 A2 18kr yellow 275.00 *875.00*
On cover 1,450.

Values for strips of 3

4 A2 1kr pink 350.00 140.00
On cover 375.00
a. 1kr lilac rose — 240.00
On cover 475.00
5 A2 6kr brown 160.00 *450.00*
On cover 625.00
6 A2 9kr yel grn 275.00 *325.00*
On cover 575.00
a. 9kr blue green 1,300.
On cover 2,200.
b. 9kr pale blue green 500.00
On cover 875.00
7 A2 12kr red 440.00 *2,000.*
On cover 3,000.
8 A2 18kr yellow 450.00 *2,000.*
On cover 2,200.

Values for blocks or strips of 4

4 A2 1kr pink 500.00 *2,400.*
a. 1kr lilac rose 3,000.
5 A2 6kr brown 260.00 *2,400.*
6 A2 9kr yel grn 375.00 *3,000.*
a. 9kr blue green 6,600.
b. 9kr pale blue green 6,000.
7 A2 12kr red 725.00 *7,250.*
8 A2 18kr yellow 800.00 *5,500.*

1862

9 A2 1kr yellow 60.00 17.50
Never hinged 92.50
On cover 87.50
On wrapper, single franking 175.00
On cover, single franking, local delivery 375.00
Pair with gutter between *2,200.* *25,000.*
10 A1a 3kr rose 140.00 2.25
Never hinged 225.00
On cover 11.00
On printed matter, single franking 225.00
On wrapper, single franking 300.00
a. 3kr carmine 45.00 4.75
Never hinged 65.00
On cover 13.50
Pair with gutter between *1,450.* *13,000.*
On cover *27,500.*
11 A2 6kr blue 65.00 8.75
Never hinged 92.50
On cover 32.50
Pair with gutter between 2,200. *14,500.*
On cover *44,000.*
a. 6kr ultra *1,750.* *9,000.*
b. Half used as 3kr on cover *10,000.*
12 A2 9kr bister 100.00 13.00
Never hinged 140.00
On cover 50.00
Pair with gutter between *2,750.* *19,000.*
13 A2 12kr yel grn 82.50 60.00
Never hinged 130.00
On cover 225.00
On cover, single franking 350.00
Pair with gutter between 2,750.
a. Half used as 6kr on cover *32,000.*
14 A2 18kr ver red 875.00 140.00
Never hinged 1,400.
On cover 1,100.
On cover, single franking 2,200.
a. 18kr pale red 140.00 *450.00*
Never hinged 210.00
On cover 1,800.
On cover, single franking *3,850.*
Pair with gutter between 2,500.

Full margins = 1mm. There are dividing lines between stamps.

No. 11a was not put in use.

Values for pairs

9 A2 1kr yellow 175.00 100.00
On cover 300.00
10 A1a 3kr rose 575.00 14.50
On cover 32.50
a. 3kr carmine 110.00 22.00
On cover 35.00
11 A2 6kr blue 140.00 110.00
On cover 175.00
12 A2 9kr bister 225.00 140.00
On cover 325.00
13 A2 12kr yel grn 175.00 350.00
On cover 825.00
14 A2 18kr ver red 2,500. 550.00
On cover 1,600.
a. 18kr pale red 440.00 *1,300.*
On cover 2,800.

Values for strips of 3

9 A2 1kr yellow 275.00 160.00
On cover 325.00
10 A1a 3kr rose 875.00 45.00
On cover 70.00
a. 3kr carmine 160.00 50.00
On cover 82.50
11 A2 6kr blue 550.00 350.00
On cover 625.00
12 A2 9kr bister 350.00 *725.00*
On cover 1,300.
13 A2 12kr yel grn 290.00 *875.00*
On cover 1,600.
14 A2 18kr ver red 2,200.
On cover 3,600.
a. 18kr pale red 650.00 —

Values for blocks or strips of 4

9 A2 1kr yellow 350.00 *2,200.*
10 A1a 3kr rose 1,100. 875.00
a. 3kr carmine 225.00 *1,300.*
11 A2 6kr blue 375.00 *1,800.*
12 A2 9kr bister 450.00 *7,100.*
13 A2 12kr yel grn 440.00 —
14 A2 18kr ver red — *5,500.*
a. 18kr pale red 825.00 —

1867-68 Embossed

15 A3 1kr yel grn 60.00 8.75
Never hinged 87.50
On cover 35.00
On wrapper, single franking 110.00
On cover, single franking, local delivery 190.00
Pair with gutter between 2,300. *11,500.*
a. 1kr dark blue green 300.00 44.00
Never hinged 450.00
On cover 125.00
Pair with gutter between *13,000.*
16 A3 3kr rose 60.00 1.40
Never hinged 100.00
On cover 7.00
Pair with gutter between 2,750. *11,000.*
a. Printed on both sides *5,000.*
17 A3 6kr ultra 42.50 17.00
Never hinged 62.50
On cover 110.00
Pair with gutter between 1,400.
a. Half used as 3kr on cover *75,000.*
18 A3 6kr bis ('68) 72.50 45.00
Never hinged 110.00
On cover 275.00
On cover, single franking 4,000.
Pair with gutter between 3,100.
a. Half used as 3kr on cover *32,000.*
19 A3 7kr ultra ('68) 375.00 11.50
Never hinged 725.00
On cover 55.00
Pair with gutter between 7,250.
a. 7kr Prus bl ('69) 3,300. 575.00
On cover 2,200.
b. 7kr royal bl ('69) 2,000. 375.00
Never hinged 2,200.
On cover 1,300.
20 A3 9kr bister 42.50 30.00
Never hinged 62.50
On cover 150.00
Pair with gutter between 1,500.
21 A3 12kr lilac 325.00 90.00
Never hinged 875.00
On cover 400.00
Pair with gutter between 6,600.
22 A3 18kr red 125.00 150.00
Never hinged 225.00
On cover 2,300.
On cover, single franking 3,200.
Pair with gutter between 2,200.

Full margins = 1¼mm.

The paper of the 1867-68 issues often shows ribbed or laid lines.

Values for pairs

15 A3 1kr yellow green 115.00 26.00
On cover 130.00
a. 1kr dk blue green 460.00 130.00
On cover 230.00
16 A3 3kr rose 125.00 13.00
On cover 42.50
17 A3 6kr ultra 87.50 *140.00*
On cover 325.00
18 A3 6kr bister 150.00 *275.00*
On cover *575.00*
19 A3 7kr ultra 1,100. 210.00
On cover 325.00
a. 7kr Prussian blue 2,500.
b. 7kr royal blue 1,600.
On cover 2,000.
20 A3 9kr bister 87.50 *250.00*
On cover 575.00
21 A3 12kr lilac 725.00 450.00
On cover 875.00
22 A3 18kr red 260.00 *875.00*
On cover 3,600.

Values for strips of 3

15 A3 1kr yellow green 200.00 50.00
On cover 110.00
a. 1kr dk blue green 825.00 225.00
On cover 375.00
16 A3 3kr rose 210.00 35.00
On cover 70.00
17 A3 6kr ultra 160.00 *650.00*
On cover *1,100.*
18 A3 6kr bister 250.00 *875.00*
On cover *1,400.*
19 A3 7kr ultra 1,800. 725.00
On cover 1,300.
20 A3 9kr bister 150.00 *1,100.*
On cover *1,800.*
21 A3 12kr lilac 1,300. *1,600.*
On cover *2,800.*
22 A3 18kr red 400.00 *2,200.*
On cover *5,400.*

Values for blocks of 4

15 A3 1kr yellow green 350.00 *1,400.*
16 A3 3kr rose 550.00 *725.00*
On cover *1,800.*
17 A3 6kr ultra 225.00 *3,250.*
18 A3 6kr bister 350.00 *4,000.*
19 A3 7kr ultra 3,200. 2,200.
20 A3 9kr bister 225.00
21 A3 12kr lilac 4,400. *5,000.*
22 A3 18kr red 575.00

1870-72 Wmk. 92 *Perf. 11½*
Without Silk Thread

23 A3 1kr green 11.00 1.25
Never hinged 17.50
On cover 7.00
Pair with gutter between 275.00
Never hinged 440.00
b. Unwmk. 225.00 92.50
Never hinged 400.00
c. 1kr deep yellow green 27.50 3.75
Never hinged 44.00
On cover 14.00
Pair with gutter between 350.00
Never hinged 575.00
24 A3 3kr rose 22.50 .70
Never hinged 35.00
On cover 5.75
Pair with gutter between 275.00
Never hinged 400.00
b. Unwmk. 150.00 62.50
Never hinged 175.00
25 A3 6kr bister 30.00 27.50
Never hinged 57.50
On cover 110.00
On cover, single franking 1,350.
Pair with gutter between 525.00
Never hinged 875.00
b. Unwmk. 150.00 125.00
Never hinged 250.00
26 A3 7kr ultra 2.75 *3.25*
Never hinged 5.00
On cover 22.00
Pair with gutter between 310.00
Never hinged 500.00
a. 7kr Prussian blue 19.00 11.00
Never hinged 29.00
On cover 50.00
c. 7kr dk ultra 575.00 150.00
On cover 650.00
d. 7kr ultra, unwmk. 150.00 110.00
Never hinged 250.00
27 A3 9kr pale brn ('72) 4.25 3.50
Never hinged 6.50
On cover 150.00
On parcel post receipt card, single franking 350.00
Pair with gutter between 525.00
Never hinged 875.00
28 A3 10kr yellow 4.50 *12.50*
Never hinged 8.00
On cover 150.00
On parcel post receipt card, single franking 325.00
On parcel post receipt card, two singles 325.00
On cover, two singles 440.00
Pair with gutter between 440.00
Never hinged 575.00
b. 10kr yellowish orange 15.00 *42.50*
Never hinged 30.00
On cover 250.00
On parcel post receipt card, single franking 350.00
On parcel post receipt card, two singles 400.00
On cover, two singles 625.00
Pair with gutter between 500.00
Never hinged 725.00
29 A3 12kr lilac 1,100. *4,125.*
Never hinged 1,800.
Pair with gutter between 6,500.
Never hinged 8,100.
30 A3 18kr dull brick red 8.75 *12.50*
Never hinged 18.00
On cover —
On parcel post receipt card 875.00
Pair with gutter between 500.00
Never hinged 725.00
b. 18kr dark brick red 225.00 62.50
Never hinged 400.00
On cover —
On parcel post receipt card 1,100.

The paper of the 1870-75 issues frequently appears to be laid with the lines either close or wide apart.

See Nos. 33-37.
Reprints exist.

Values for blocks of 4

23 A3 1kr green 57.50 *250.00*
Never hinged 110.00
b. 1kr deep yellow green 175.00 *350.00*
Never hinged 325.00
24 A3 3kr rose 125.00 *190.00*
Never hinged 225.00
25 A3 6kr bister 175.00 *875.00*
Never hinged 300.00
26 A3 7kr ultra 18.00 *575.00*
Never hinged 32.50
a. 7kr Prussian blue 110.00 *7,000.*
Never hinged 225.00
27 A3 9kr pale brown 42.50 *550.00*
Never hinged 70.00
28 A3 10kr yellow 25.00 *725.00*
Never hinged 35.00
b. 10kr yellowish orange 100.00
Never hinged 175.00
29 A3 12kr 5,500. *25,000.*
Never hinged 450.00
30 A3 18kr dull brick red 55.00 *425.00*
Never hinged 110.00
b. 18kr dark brick red 625.00

Imperf

23d A3 1kr *1,400.*
24c A3 3kr *1,400.* *1,400.*
25c A3 6kr *2,200.*
26e A3 7kr *2,200.*
30d A3 18kr *2,200.*

Wmk. 93

23a A3 1kr green 92.50 8.75
Never hinged 175.00
On cover 25.00
e. 1kr deep yellow green 140.00 32.50
Never hinged 250.00
On cover 70.00
24a A3 3kr rose 90.00 2.25
Never hinged 140.00
On cover 11.00
25a A3 6kr bister 150.00 65.00
Never hinged 275.00
On cover 225.00
On cover, single franking 1,750.
26b A3 7kr ultra 125.00 32.50
Never hinged 200.00
On cover 110.00
g. 7kr dk ultra 550.00
On cover —
27a A3 9kr pale brown 250.00 *450.00*
Never hinged 425.00
On parcel post receipt card 1,100.
On cover, single franking *2,200.*
28a A3 10kr yellow 225.00 *325.00*
Never hinged 350.00
On parcel post receipt card 875.00
On cover, single franking 1,400.
On parcel post receipt card, two singles 1,400.
On cover, two singles 2,000.
c. 10kr yellowish orange 230.00 230.00
Never hinged 425.00
On parcel post receipt card 700.00
On cover, single franking 1,300.
On parcel post receipt card, two singles 1,600.
29a A3 12kr lilac 325.00 *1,000.*
Never hinged 625.00
On cover 3,600.
On cover, single franking 4,400.
Pair with gutter between
30a A3 18kr dull brick red 375.00 150.00
Never hinged 625.00
On cover —
On parcel post receipt card 1,250.
c. 18kr dark brick red 250.00 225.00
Never hinged 450.00
On cover —
On parcel post receipt card 1,400.

Values for blocks of 4

23a A3 1kr green 575.00 425.00
e. 1kr deep yellow green 700.00
24a A3 3kr rose 500.00 400.00
25a A3 6kr bister 875.00
26b A3 7kr ultra 700.00
27a A3 9kr pale brown 2,000.
28a A3 10kr yellow 1,300.
c. 10kr yelsh org 1,600.
29a A3 12kr lilac, wmk. 92 1,600. *23,000.*
30c A3 18kr dull brick red 1,750.

Imperf

23f A3 1kr *1,600.*
24d A3 3kr *1,600.*
26f A3 7kr *2,200.*
30e A3 18kr *2,500.*

A4

A5

1874-75 Wmk. 92 *Imperf.*

31 A4 1m violet 575.00 72.50
Never hinged 875.00
On cover, single franking *7,250.*
On parcel post receipt card *1,400.*
a. 1m deep violet 925.00 150.00
Never hinged 1,600.
On cover *8,750.*
On parcel post receipt card *1,750.*

Perf. 11½

32 A4 1m violet ('75) 190.00 45.00
Never hinged 275.00
On cover, single franking *2,850.*

On parcel post receipt card 950.00
a. 1m deep violet 425.00 100.00
Never hinged 625.00
On cover, single franking *3,200.*
On parcel post receipt card 1,400.

Values for blocks of 4

31 A4 1m violet 7,250. 1,300.
31a A4 1m deep violet 8,750. 1,800.
32 A4 1m violet 1,400. 925.00
32a A4 1m deep violet 2,500.

See Nos. 46-47, 54-57, 73-76.

1875 Wmk. 94

33 A3 1kr green .65 *22.50*
Never hinged 1.25
On cover 110.00
Pair with gutter between 11.00
Never hinged 20.00
34 A3 3kr rose .65 *4.00*
Never hinged .95
On cover 37.50
Pair with gutter between 8.75
Never hinged 16.00
35 A3 7kr ultra 3.25 *250.00*
Never hinged 6.50
On cover 1,250.
Pair with gutter between 87.50
Never hinged 150.00
36 A3 10kr yellow 27.50 *250.00*
Never hinged 55.00
On cover *1,400.*
Two singles on cover 3,250.
Pair with gutter between 425.00
Never hinged 700.00
37 A3 18kr red 22.50 *57.50*
Never hinged 42.50
On cover *27,500.*
On parcel post receipt card *22,000.*
Pair with gutter between 275.00
Never hinged 575.00

Values for blocks of 4

33 A3 1kr green 2.75 *1,150.*
Never hinged 6.00
34 A3 3kr rose 3.75 *375.00*
Never hinged 6.50
35 A3 7kr ultra 18.00 *4,400.*
Never hinged 32.50
36 A3 10kr yel 175.00 *4,400.*
Never hinged 350.00
37 A3 18kr red 140.00 *2,300.*
Never hinged 275.00

False cancellations exist on #29, 29a, 33-37.

1876-78 Embossed *Perf. 11½*

38 A5 3pf lt grn 27.50 1.40
Never hinged 65.00
On cover 14.00
a. 3pf lt yel grn 65.00 10.00
Never hinged 140.00
On cover 55.00
39 A5 5pf dk grn 72.50 10.00
Never hinged 175.00
On cover 35.00
On cover, single franking 87.50
a. 5pf dk bluish grn 225.00 18.00
Never hinged 700.00
On cover 50.00
40 A5 5pf lilac ('78) 140.00 18.00
Never hinged 325.00
On cover 87.50
a. 5pf lt reddish vio 250.00 35.00
Never hinged 500.00
On cover 110.00
41 A5 10pf rose 140.00 .55
Never hinged 500.00
On cover 8.75
a. 10pf dk magenta 275.00 18.00
Never hinged 700.00
On cover 35.00
42 A5 20pf ultra 150.00 2.75
Never hinged 500.00
On cover 22.50
On postcard, single franking 140.00
a. 20pf gray blue 375.00 18.00
Never hinged 825.00
On cover 44.00
43 A5 25pf yel brn 140.00 5.00
Never hinged 350.00
On cover 650.00
On postcard, single franking 650.00
On cover, single franking 700.00
44 A5 50pf scarlet 47.50 4.75
Never hinged 87.50
On cover 1,500.
On parcel post receipt card 1,100.
45 A5 50pf brn ('78) 725.00 25.00
Never hinged 1,800.
On cover 1,500.
On parcel post receipt card 700.00
46 A4 1m violet 1,750. 82.50
Never hinged 3,250.
On cover 3,500.
On parcel post receipt card 625.00
47 A4 2m orange 19.00 7.25
Never hinged 44.00
On cover 2,200.
On parcel post receipt card 250.00

The paper of the 1876-78 issue often shows ribbed lines.

See Nos. 48-53, 58-72. For overprints and surcharge see Nos. 237, O1-O5.

Values for blocks of 4

38 A5 3pf green 140.00 110.00
Never hinged 275.00
On cover 275.00
a. 3pf lt yel grn 325.00 —
Never hinged 700.00
39 A5 5pf dk green 325.00 140.00
Never hinged 875.00
On cover 1,100.
a. 5pf dk bluish green 1,100. 175.00
On cover 1,100.
40 A5 5pf lilac 700.00 550.00
Never hinged 1,600.
On cover 1,750.
a. 5pf lt reddish violet 1,250. 700.00
Never hinged 2,500.
On cover 2,500.

41 A5 10pf rose 650.00 190.00
On cover 1,100.
42 A5 20pf ultramarine 140.00
a. 20pf gray blue 225.00
43 A5 25pf yel brn 300.00
44 A5 50pf scarlet 225.00 *460.00*
Never hinged 400.00
45 A5 50pf brown *5,750.*
46 A4 1m violet 8,750. *5,750.*
47 A4 2m orange 110.00 57.50
Never hinged 44.00

1881-1911 Wmk. 95v *Perf. 11½*

48 A5 3pf green 11.50 .45
Never hinged 28.00
On cover 11.50
49 A5 5pf lilac 17.00 1.25
Never hinged 32.50
On cover 14.00
50 A5 10pf carmine 11.00 .40
Never hinged 25.00
On cover 3.75
b. 10pf magenta 22.00 3.25
Never hinged 55.00
On cover 25.00
51 A5 20pf ultramarine 13.00 .65
Never hinged 25.00
On cover 8.75
52 A5 25pf yellow brown 110.00 3.25
Never hinged 225.00
On cover 350.00
On postal card, single franking 450.00
On cover, single franking, local delivery 650.00
On parcel post receipt card 250.00
53 A5 50pf deep brown 140.00 3.25
Never hinged 250.00
On cover 275.00
Two singles on cover 700.00
On parcel post receipt card 250.00
On cover, single franking 450.00
54 A4 1m rose lil ('00) 225.00 1.40
Never hinged 500.00
On cover 350.00
On parcel post receipt card 70.00
Two singles on parcel post receipt card 425.00
a. 1m brownish lilac, toned paper 62.50 3.00
Never hinged 140.00
On cover 350.00
On cover, single franking 1,100.
On parcel post receipt card 140.00
b. 1m brownish pur, toned paper 1,100. 110.00
Never hinged 2,500.
On cover 1,400.
On cover, single franking 2,500.
On parcel post receipt card 875.00
c. 1m brownish lilac, white paper 45.00 *50.00*
Never hinged 87.50
On cover 600.00
On parcel post receipt card 175.00
55 A4 2m orange ('01) 3.25 *4.50*
Never hinged 7.00
On cover 875.00
On cover, single franking 1,400.
Two singles on cover 2,300.
On parcel post receipt card 175.00
a. Toned paper ('90) 72.50 10.00
Never hinged 150.00
On cover 1,300.
On cover, single franking 1,800.
Two singles on cover 2,900.
On parcel post receipt card 275.00
56 A4 3m olive gray ('00) 18.00 *22.50*
Never hinged 32.50
On cover 2,200.
On cover, single franking 2,200.
On parcel post receipt card 550.00
a. White paper ('06) 140.00 *500.00*
Never hinged 250.00
On cover 2,900.
On cover, single franking 3,600.
On parcel post receipt card 1,300.
b. Yellowish translucent paper ('11) 100.00 *340.00*
Never hinged 150.00
On cover 2,200.
On cover, single franking *2,500.*
On parcel post receipt card *875.00*
57 A4 5m yellow green ('00) 18.00 *22.50*
Never hinged 32.50
On cover 2,200.
On cover, single franking 2,200.
On parcel post receipt card 700.00
a. White paper ('06) 140.00 *375.00*
Never hinged 225.00
On cover 2,900.
On cover, single franking 3,600.
On parcel post receipt card 1,300.
b. Yellowish translucent paper ('11) 70.00 *150.00*
Never hinged 110.00
On cover *2,200.*
On cover, single franking 2,500.
On parcel post receipt card 875.00

Nos. 54-55 are on white paper. Nos. 56-57 are on toned paper. A 2m lilac was not regularly issued.

Values for blocks of 4

48 A5 3pf green 65.00 55.00
Never hinged 140.00
On cover 110.00
49 A5 5pf lilac 82.50 37.50
Never hinged 32.50
On cover 110.00
50 A5 10pf carmine 55.00 37.50
Never hinged 125.00
On cover 55.00
b. 10pf magenta 140.00 55.00
Never hinged 375.00
51 A5 20pf ultramarine 62.50 50.00
Never hinged 125.00
52 A5 25pf yellow brown 550.00 87.50
Never hinged 1,100.
53 A5 50pf deep brown 575.00 110.00
Never hinged 1,150.
54 A4 1m rose 13.00 *37.50*
Never hinged 28.00
a. 1m brownish lilac, toned paper 275.00 70.00
Never hinged 650.00

e. 1m brownish lilac, white paper 250.00 —
Never hinged 550.00
55 A4 2m orange 18.00 *37.50*
Never hinged 35.00
a. Toned paper 440.00 70.00
Never hinged 925.00

Imperf

48a A5 3pf 400.00 *2,000.*
Never hinged 700.00
49a A5 5pf 1,800.
Never hinged 2,800.
50a A5 10pf 400.00 *2,000.*
Never hinged 700.00
On cover *2,500.*
51a A5 20pf 1,400.
Never hinged 3,250.
52a A5 25pf 1,400.
Never hinged 3,250.
53a A5 50pf 1,400.
Never hinged 3,250.
54d A4 1m rose 130.00
Never hinged 250.00
e. As "a." 3,600.
Never hinged 5,800.
55b A4 2m org 70.00
Never hinged 140.00
56c A4 3m As "a." 2,800.
Never hinged 550.00
57c A4 5m As "a." 275.00
Never hinged 550.00

1888-1900 Wmk. 95h *Perf. 14½*

White Paper

58 A5 2pf gray ('00) 1.50 .45
Never hinged 4.50
On cover 6.50
60 A5 3pf brown ('00) .20 *.40*
Never hinged .65
On cover 1.90
b. 3pf black brown 8.75 7.00
Never hinged 22.00
On cover 22.00
62 A5 5pf dk grn ('00) .20 *.40*
Never hinged .55
On cover 1.90
63 A5 10pf carmine .30 *.40*
Never hinged .55
On cover 1.90
64 A5 20pf ultra .30 *.40*
Never hinged .55
On cover 3.00
On postal card, single franking *28.00*
b. 20pf grayish blue .55 *1.10*
Never hinged 1.10
On cover 7.00
66 A5 25pf orange ('00) .35 *.55*
Never hinged .80
On cover 18.00
On cover, single franking 57.50
67 A5 30pf ol grn ('00) .40 *.70*
Never hinged 1.10
On cover 22.00
On postal card, single franking 70.00
68 A5 40pf yellow ('00) .40 *.95*
Never hinged 1.40
On cover 32.50
70 A5 50pf maroon ('00) .35 *1.40*
Never hinged .90
On cover 30.00
On cover, single franking 42.50
On parcel post receipt card 18.00
71 A5 80pf lilac ('00) 2.25 *4.00*
Never hinged 6.00
On cover 175.00
On cover, single franking 275.00
On parcel post receipt card 50.00

Values for blocks of 4

58 A5 2pf gray 60.00 *70.00*
Never hinged 150.00
On cover *110.00*
63 A5 10pf carmine 1.40 *2.75*
Never hinged 2.75
On cover *8.75*
64 A5 20pf ultra 1.40 *6.00*
Never hinged 2.75
On cover *8.75*
b. 20pf grayish blue 3.25 *14.00*
Never hinged 7.00
On cover 28.00

Imperf

58b A5 2pf 65.00
Never hinged 150.00
60c A5 3pf 65.00
Never hinged 140.00
62b A5 5pf 65.00
Never hinged 140.00
63c A5 10pf 62.50
Never hinged 140.00
64c A5 20pf 65.00
Never hinged 140.00
66b A5 25pf 65.00
Never hinged 175.00
70b A5 50pf 110.00
Never hinged 225.00

1888-99

Toned Paper

58a A5 2pf gray ('99) 11.00 3.50
Never hinged 32.50
On cover 14.00
59 A5 3pf green 9.25 2.10
Never hinged 32.50
On cover 11.00
60a A5 3pf dk ocher brn ('90) 9.25 .40
Never hinged 23.00
On cover 2.75
d. 3pf yel brn 26.00 5.25
Never hinged 62.50
On cover 13.50
61 A5 5pf lilac 22.50 3.25
Never hinged 62.50
On cover 18.00
a. 5pf brownish violet 18.00 7.00
Never hinged 55.00
On cover 28.00
62a A5 5pf dk green ('90) 9.25 .40
Never hinged 23.00
On cover 2.75
d. Imperf 550.00 *1,050.*
On cover *2,750.*

63a A5 10pf car red 6.00 .40
Never hinged 16.00
On cover 2.75
b. Imperf. 72.50 *175.00*
Never hinged 225.00
On cover 525.00
d. 10pf lilac red 18.00 7.00
Never hinged 55.00
On cover 17.50
64a A5 20pf ultra 8.75 1.25
Never hinged 26.00
On cover 5.00
d. 20pf grayish blue 13.00 3.25
Never hinged 35.00
On cover 10.50
65 A5 25pf yel brn 27.50 6.00
Never hinged 82.50
On cover 190.00
On cover, single franking 250.00
On parcel post receipt card 82.50
66a A5 25pf org ('90) 15.00 1.50
Never hinged 50.00
On cover 20.00
69 A5 50pf dp brn 57.50 3.25
Never hinged 150.00
On cover 150.00
On cover, single franking 175.00
On parcel post receipt card 77.50
70a A5 50pf mar ('90) 45.00 2.10
Never hinged 87.50
On cover 55.00
On parcel post receipt card 20.00
71a A5 80pf lilac ('99) 27.50 8.25
Never hinged 87.50
On cover 275.00
On cover, single franking 375.00
On parcel post receipt card 70.00

Values for blocks of 4

58a A5 2pf gray 55.00 *70.00*
On cover 110.00
59 A5 3pf green 50.00 35.00
Never hinged 150.00
60a A5 3pf dk ocher brn ('90) 70.00 7.00
Never hinged 150.00
On cover 21.00
d. 3pf yel brn 160.00 62.50
Never hinged 375.00
61 A5 5pf lilac 110.00 35.00
Never hinged 300.00
On cover 110.00
a. 5pf brownish violet 110.00 87.50
Never hinged 300.00
On cover 175.00
62a A5 5pf dk green 70.00 3.25
Never hinged 150.00
On cover 11.00
63a A5 10pf car red 28.00 7.00
Never hinged 82.50
On cover 14.00
d. 10pf lilac red 110.00 87.50
Never hinged 300.00
On cover 175.00
64a A5 20pf ultra 50.00 17.50
Never hinged 140.00
On cover 55.00
d. 20pf grayish blue 70.00 42.50
Never hinged 225.00
On cover 85.00
65 A5 25pf yel brn 140.00 42.50
Never hinged 400.00
66a A5 25pf org ('90) 87.50 14.00
Never hinged 275.00
On cover 70.00
69 A5 50pf dp brn 250.00 55.00
Never hinged 725.00
70a A5 50pf mar ('90) 225.00 28.00
Never hinged 450.00
On parcel post receipt card 110.00
71a A5 80pf lilac 150.00 100.00
Never hinged 425.00

1911, Jan. 23 Wmk. 95v

72 A5 5pf dark green .60 *8.50*
Never hinged 1.40
On cover *19.00*
On registered cover *55.00*
On first day cover *35.00*

1911, Jan. Wmk. 95h *Perf. 11½*

73 A4 1m rose lilac 4.00 *27.50*
Never hinged 7.00
On cover *350.00*
On parcel post receipt card *425.00*
74 A4 2m orange 17.00 *37.50*
Never hinged 20.00
On cover *1,400.*
On parcel post receipt card *875.00*
75 A4 3m olive gray 17.00 *57.50*
Never hinged 22.00
On cover *2,900.*
On parcel post receipt card *1,300.*
76 A4 5m pale yel grn 17.00 *57.50*
Never hinged 22.00
On cover *2,900.*
On parcel post receipt card *1,300.*
Nos. 73-76 (4) 55.00 180.00

Values for canceled to order and on philatelic covers

73 A4 1m rose lilac 92.50
On overfranked cover 65.00
74 A4 2m orange 14.00
On overfranked cover 82.50
75 A4 3m olive gray 22.00
On overfranked cover 140.00
76 A4 5m pale yellow green 22.00
On overfranked cover 210.00

See note after No. 91 concerning used values.

A6

A7

Prince Regent Luitpold A8

Perf. 14x14½

1911 Wmk. 95h Litho.

77 A6 3pf brn, *gray brn* .20 .20
Never hinged .75
On cover 1.25
a. "911" for "1911" 275.00 275.00
Never hinged 450.00
78 A6 5pf dk grn, *grn* .20 .20
Never hinged .75
On cover 1.25
a. Tête bêche pair 4.50 10.50
b. Booklet pane of 4 + 2 labels 100.00 150.00
c. Bklt. pane of 5 + label 225.00 375.00
d. Bklt. pane of 6 35.00
79 A6 10pf scar, *buff* .20 .20
Never hinged .75
On cover 1.25
a. Tête bêche pair 5.75 62.50
b. "911" for "1911" 15.00 15.00
Never hinged 25.00
d. Booklet pane of 5 + label 65.00 30.00
80 A6 20pf dp bl, *bl* 1.90 .75
Never hinged 7.00
On cover 3.75
81 A6 25pf vio brn, *buff* 2.90 1.10
Never hinged 11.00
On cover 13.50

Perf. 11½

Wmk. 95v

82 A7 30pf org buff, *buff* 1.50 .90
Never hinged 6.00
On cover 13.50
83 A7 40pf ol grn, *buff* 3.00 .90
Never hinged 9.25
On cover 13.50
84 A7 50pf cl, *gray brn* 2.50 1.40
Never hinged 10.50
On cover 25.00
84A A7 60pf dk grn, *buff* 2.50 1.40
Never hinged 10.50
On cover 25.00
85 A7 80pf vio, *gray brn* 8.75 4.75
Never hinged 20.00
On cover 70.00
86 A8 1m brn, *gray brn* 2.50 1.25
Never hinged 10.50
On parcel post receipt card 25.00
87 A8 2m dk grn, *grn* 2.50 6.25
Never hinged 10.50
On parcel post receipt card 35.00
88 A8 3m lake, *buff* 12.50 35.00
Never hinged 28.00
On parcel post receipt card 125.00
89 A8 5m dk bl, *buff* 11.00 25.00
Never hinged 28.00
On parcel post receipt card 175.00
90 A8 10m org, *yel* 22.50 42.50
Never hinged 37.50
On parcel post receipt card 310.00
91 A8 20m blk brn, *yel* 19.00 20.00
Never hinged 37.50
On parcel post receipt card 375.00
Nos. 77-91 (16) 93.65 141.80

90th birthday of Prince Regent Luitpold.
All values exist in 2 types except #84A.

Used values: Nos. 73-76 and 77-91 often were canceled en masse for accounting purposes. These cancels are perfectly clear, and used values are for stamps canceled thus. Postally used examples are worth about twice as much.

Imperf

77b A6 3pf 28.00
Never hinged 50.00
78e A6 5pf 12.50
Never hinged 23.00
79e A6 10pf 25.00
Never hinged 42.50
80a A6 20pf 25.00
Never hinged 42.50
81a A6 25pf 28.00
Never hinged 47.50
82a A7 30pf 28.00
Never hinged 47.50
83a A7 40pf 47.50
Never hinged 70.00
84b A7 50pf 28.00 87.50
Never hinged 47.50
85a A7 80pf 35.00 110.00
Never hinged 60.00
86a A8 1m 250.00
Never hinged 440.00
87a A8 2m 875.00
Never hinged 1,300.
88a A8 3m 550.00
89a A8 5m 350.00
Never hinged 550.00
90a A8 10m 350.00
Never hinged 550.00
91a A8 20m 350.00
Never hinged 550.00

Prince Regent Luitpold — A9

1911, June 10 Unwmk.

92 A9 5pf grn, yel & blk .45 .90
Never hinged .85
On cover 3.75
b. Horiz. pair, imperf. btwn. 140.00 225.00
93 A9 10pf rose, yel & blk .70 1.40
Never hinged 1.40
On cover 6.00
b. Pair, imperf. between 140.00 225.00

Silver Jubilee of Prince Regent Luitpold.

Used Values

given for Nos. 94-275, B1-B3 are for postally used. Canceled-to-order stamps, which abound, sell for same prices as unused.

A10

A11

King Ludwig III
A12 A13

Perf. 14x14½

1914-20 Wmk. 95h Photo.

Wartime & Later Printings ('16-'20)

Coarse Impressions, Dull Colors

94 A10 2pf gray ('18) .20 1.25
Never hinged .25
On cover 1.90
95 A10 3pf brown .20 1.25
Never hinged .30
On cover 1.90
96 A10 5pf yellow grn 1.10 1.40
Never hinged 2.75
On cover 1.90
a. 5pf dark green 1.10 1.40
Never hinged 2.75
On cover 1.90
b. Tête bêche pair 3.00 10.00
c. Booklet pane of 5 + 1 label 13.00 50.00
97 A10 7½pf dp green ('16) .20 1.40
On cover 1.90
a. Tête bêche pair 1.90 6.00
b. Booklet pane of 6 12.50
98 A10 10pf vermilion 1.40 1.40
Never hinged 2.75
On cover 1.90
a. Tête bêche pair 3.00 10.00
b. Booklet pane of 5 + 1 label 13.00 50.00
99 A10 10pf car rose ('16) .20 1.25
Never hinged .25
On cover 1.90
100 A10 15pf ver ('16) .20 1.25
Never hinged .25
On cover 1.90
a. Tête bêche pair 1.90 6.00
b. Booklet pane of 5 + 1 label 5.50 19.00
101 A10 15pf car ('20) 1.50 27.50
Never hinged 3.10
On cover 44.00
102 A10 20pf blue .20 1.25
Never hinged .30
On cover 1.90
103 A10 25pf gray .20 1.25
Never hinged .30
On cover 2.50
104 A10 30pf orange .80 1.25
Never hinged 2.25
On cover 1.90
105 A10 40pf olive grn .20 1.40
Never hinged .30
On cover 1.90
106 A10 50pf red brn .20 1.40
Never hinged .30
On cover 1.90
107 A10 60pf blue grn .80 1.40
Never hinged 2.25
On cover 3.25
108 A10 80pf violet .20 1.40
Never hinged .30
On cover 5.00

Perf. 11½

Wmk. 95v

109 A11 1m brown .20 1.40
Never hinged .35
On cover 8.75
110 A11 2m violet .20 2.50
Never hinged .45
On cover 13.50
111 A11 3m scarlet .30 5.00
Never hinged .65
On cover 25.00

Wmk. 95h

112 A12 5m deep blue .40 10.00
Never hinged .85
On cover 32.50
113 A12 10m yellow grn 1.40 50.00
Never hinged 2.75
On cover 110.00
114 A12 20m brown 2.50 72.50
Never hinged 5.75
On cover 175.00
Nos. 94-114 (21) 12.60 187.45

Pre-war Printings ('14-'15)

Clear Impressions, Bright Colors

Values for used stamps, covers and parcel post receipt cards with dated cancellations between Mar. 30, 1914, and Dec. 31, 1915.

95c A10 3pf brown 1.25
On cover 1.90
96d A10 5pf yellow grn 1.40
On cover 1.90
96e A10 5pf dark green 1.40
On cover 1.75
98c A10 10pf vermilion 1.40
On cover 1.90
102a A10 20pf blue 2.10
On cover 5.00
103a A10 25pf gray 7.00
On cover 22.00
104a A10 30pf orange 4.50
On cover 19.00
105a A10 40pf olive grn 7.00
On cover 19.00
106a A10 50pf red brn 7.00
On cover 19.00
107a A10 60pf blue grn 10.00
On cover 19.00
108a A10 80pf violet 10.00
On cover 30.00
109a A11 1m brown 6.50
On cover 25.00
110a A11 2m violet 12.50
On parcel post receipt card 57.50
111a A11 3m scarlet 5.00
On parcel post receipt card 25.00
112a A12 5m deep blue 70.00
On parcel post receipt card 250.00
113a A12 10m yellow grn 250.00
On parcel post receipt card 575.00
114a A12 20m brown 225.00
On parcel post receipt card 575.00
Nos. 95c-114a (17) 622.05

See #117-135. For overprints and surcharges see #115, 136-175, 193-236, B1-B3.

No. 94 Surcharged

1916 Wmk. 95h *Perf. 14x14½*

115 A13 2½pf on 2pf gray .20 .85
a. Double surcharge

Ludwig III Types of 1914-20

1916-20 *Imperf.*

117 A10 2pf gray .20 10.00
118 A10 3pf brown .20 12.00
119 A10 5pf pale yel grn .20 10.00
120 A10 7½pf dp green .20 10.00
a. Tête bêche pair 3.25 6.00
121 A10 10pf car rose .20 10.00
122 A10 15pf vermilion .20 10.00
a. Tête bêche pair 3.25 6.00
123 A10 20pf blue .20 12.00
124 A10 25pf gray .20 12.00
125 A10 30pf orange .20 12.00
126 A10 40pf olive grn .20 12.00
127 A10 50pf red brown .20 12.00
128 A10 60pf dark green .20 13.00
129 A10 80pf violet .20 13.00
130 A11 1m brown .35 13.00
131 A11 2m violet .35 13.00
132 A11 3m scarlet .45 22.50
133 A12 5m deep blue .75 30.00
134 A12 10m yellow green 1.25 57.50
135 A12 20m brown 1.75 90.00
Nos. 117-135 (19) 7.50 374.00

Stamps and Type of 1914-20 Overprinted:

a

b

Wmk. 95h or 95v

1919 *Perf. 14x14½*

Overprint "a"

136 A10 3pf brown .20 1.00
137 A10 5pf yellow grn .20 1.00
138 A10 7½pf deep green .20 1.00
139 A10 10pf car rose .20 1.00
140 A10 15pf vermilion .20 1.00
141 A10 20pf blue .20 1.00
142 A10 25pf gray .20 1.00
143 A10 30pf orange .20 1.00
144 A10 35pf orange .20 1.90
a. Without overprint 100.00
145 A10 40pf olive grn .20 1.10
146 A10 50pf red brown .20 1.10
147 A10 60pf dark green .20 1.10
148 A10 75pf red brown .20 .95
a. Without overprint 22.50 225.00
149 A10 80pf violet .20 1.25

Perf. 11½

Overprint "a"

150 A11 1m brown .20 1.10
151 A11 2m violet .20 1.25
152 A11 3m scarlet .40 3.50

Overprint "b"

153 A12 5m deep blue .90 10.00
154 A12 10m yellow green .95 37.50
155 A12 20m dk brown 1.50 37.50
Nos. 136-155 (20) 6.95 106.25

Inverted overprints exist on Nos. 137-143, 145-147, 149. Value, each $15.
Double overprints exist on Nos. 137, 139, 143, 145, 150. Values, $30-$75.

Imperf

Overprint "a"

156 A10 3pf brown .20 13.00
157 A10 5pf pale yel grn .20 13.00
158 A10 7½pf dp green .20 13.00
159 A10 10pf car rose .20 13.00
160 A10 15pf vermilion .20 13.00
161 A10 20pf blue .20 13.00
162 A10 25pf gray .20 13.00
163 A10 30pf orange .20 13.00
164 A10 35pf orange .20 17.00
a. Without overprint 13.00
165 A10 40pf olive grn .20 13.00
166 A10 50pf red brown .20 13.00
167 A10 60pf dk green .20 13.00
168 A10 75pf red brown .20 17.00
a. Without overprint 190.00
169 A10 80pf violet .20 17.00
170 A11 1m brown .20 20.00
171 A11 2m violet .40 22.50
172 A11 3m scarlet .55 35.00

Overprint "b"

173 A12 5m deep blue .75 42.50
174 A12 10m yellow grn .95 60.00
175 A12 20m brown 1.90 60.00
Nos. 156-175 (20) 7.55 434.00

Stamps of Germany 1906-19 Overprinted

1919 Wmk. 125 *Perf. 14, 14½*

176 A22 2½pf gray .20 .90
177 A16 3pf brown .20 .90
178 A16 5pf green .20 .90
179 A22 7½pf orange .20 .95
180 A16 10pf carmine .20 1.25
181 A22 15pf dk violet .20 1.00
a. Double overprint 375.00 1,050.
182 A16 20pf ultra .20 .90
183 A16 25pf org & blk, *yel* .20 1.25
184 A22 35pf red brown .20 1.40
185 A16 40pf lake & blk .20 1.40
186 A16 75pf green & blk .35 1.90
187 A16 80pf lake & blk, *rose* .35 2.50
188 A17 1m car rose .75 4.00
189 A21 2m dull blue 1.10 8.00
190 A19 3m gray violet 1.10 10.50
191 A20 5m slate & car 1.10 10.50
a. Inverted overprint 3,575.
Nos. 176-191 (16) 6.75 48.25

Bavarian Stamps of 1914-16 Overprinted:

c

d

Wmk. 95h or 95v

1919-20 *Perf. 14x14½*

Overprint "c"

193 A10 3pf brown .20 1.25
194 A10 5pf yellow grn .20 .95
195 A10 7½pf dp green .20 13.00
196 A10 10pf car rose .20 .95

197 A10 15pf vermilion .20 .95
198 A10 20pf blue .20 .95
199 A10 25pf gray .20 1.25
200 A10 30pf orange .20 1.25
201 A10 40pf olive grn .20 11.50
202 A10 50pf red brown .20 1.50
203 A10 60pf dk green .20 11.50
204 A10 75pf olive bister .35 11.50
205 A10 80pf violet .20 3.00

Perf. 11½

Overprint "c"

206 A11 1m brown .20 2.25
207 A11 2m violet .20 4.25
208 A11 3m scarlet .35 6.00

Overprint "d"

209 A12 5m deep blue .60 14.50
210 A12 10m yellow grn 1.25 30.00
211 A12 20m dk brown 1.90 50.00
Nos. 193-211 (19) 7.25 166.55

Imperf

Overprint "c"

212 A10 3pf brown .20 10.00
213 A10 5pf pale yel grn .20 10.00
214 A10 7½pf deep green .20 22.50
215 A10 10pf car rose .20 10.00
216 A10 15pf vermilion .20 10.00
217 A10 20pf blue .20 10.00
a. Double overprint 50.00
218 A10 25pf gray .20 10.00
219 A10 30pf orange .20 11.50
220 A10 40pf olive grn .20 11.50
221 A10 50pf red brn .20 11.50
222 A10 60pf dk green .20 11.50
223 A10 75pf olive bis .20 30.00
a. Without overprint 5.00
224 A10 80pf violet .20 11.50
225 A11 1m brown .20 18.00
226 A11 2m violet .20 18.00
227 A11 3m scarlet .45 22.50

Overprint "d"

228 A12 5m deep blue .60 32.50
229 A12 10m yellow grn 1.25 57.50
230 A12 20m brown 1.75 90.00
Nos. 212-230 (19) 7.05 408.50

Ludwig Type of 1914, Printed in Various Colors and Surcharged

1919 ***Perf. 11½***

231 A11 1.25m on 1m yel grn .20 1.25
232 A11 1.50m on 1m orange .20 2.75
233 A11 2.50m on 1m gray .35 5.25
Nos. 231-233 (3) .75 9.25

1920 ***Imperf.***

234 A11 1.25m on 1m yel grn .20 30.00
a. Without surcharge 325.00
235 A11 1.50m on 1m org .20 30.00
a. Without surcharge 6.50
236 A11 2.50m on 1m gray .35 30.00
a. Without surcharge 6.50
Nos. 234-236 (3) .75 90.00

No. 60 Surcharged in Dark Blue

1920 ***Perf. 14½***

237 A5 20pf on 3pf brown .20 1.25
a. Inverted surcharge 6.50 26.00
b. Double surcharge 80.00 190.00

Plowman A14

"Electricity" Harnessing Light to a Water Wheel A15

Sower — A16

Madonna and Child — A17

von Kaulbach's "Genius" — A18

TWENTY PFENNIG
Type I — Foot of "2" turns downward.
Type II — Foot of "2" turns upward.

Perf. 14x14½

1920 **Wmk. 95h** **Typo.**

238 A14 5pf yellow grn .20 1.00
239 A14 10pf orange .20 1.00
240 A14 15pf carmine .20 1.00
241 A15 20pf violet (I) .20 1.00
a. 20pf violet (II) 8.00 1,150.
242 A15 30pf dp blue .20 1.10
243 A15 40pf brown .20 1.10
244 A16 50pf vermilion .20 1.25
245 A16 60pf blue green .20 1.90
246 A16 75pf lilac rose .20 1.90

Perf. 12x11½

Wmk. 95v

247 A17 1m car & gray .35 1.90
248 A17 1¼m ultra & ol bis .20 1.90
249 A17 1½m dk grn & gray .20 2.75
250 A17 2½m blk & gray .20 12.00

Perf. 11½x12

Wmk. 95h

251 A18 3m pale blue .450 11.50
252 A18 5m orange .45 11.50
253 A18 10m deep green .75 22.50
254 A18 20m black 1.25 30.00
Nos. 238-254 (17) 9.70 105.30

Imperf. Pairs

238a A14 5pf yellow grn 55.00 350.00
239a A14 10pf orange 125.00
241b A15 20pf violet (I) 55.00
243a A15 40pf brown 110.00
244a A16 50pf vermilion 32.50
245a A16 60pf blue green 37.50
246a A16 75pf lilac rose 37.50
247a A17 1m car & gray 6.50 26.00
248a A17 1¼m ultra & ol bis 6.50 26.00
249a A17 1½m dk grn & gray 6.50 26.00
250a A17 2½m blk & gray 11.50 65.00
251a A18 3m pale blue 11.50 65.00
252a A18 5m orange 11.50 65.00
253a A18 10m deep green 11.50 65.00
254a A18 20m black 11.50 65.00

Perf. 12x11½

1920 **Litho.** **Wmk. 95v**

255 A17 2½m black & gray .40 30.00

On No. 255 the background dots are small, hazy and irregularly spaced. On No. 250 they are large, clear, round, white and regularly spaced in rows. The backs of the typo. stamps usually show a raised impression of parts of the design.

Stamps and Types of Preceding Issue Overprinted

1920

256 A14 5pf yellow green .20 1.10
a. Inverted overprint 26.00
b. Imperf., pair 37.50 375.00
257 A14 10pf orange .20 1.10
a. Imperf., pair 37.50 375.00
258 A14 15pf carmine .20 1.10
259 A15 20pf violet .20 1.10
a. Inverted overprint 26.00 650.00
b. Double overprint 13.00
c. Imperf., pair 50.00
260 A15 30pf deep blue .20 1.10
a. Inverted overprint 26.00
b. Imperf., pair 50.00 375.00
261 A15 40pf brown .20 1.10
a. Inverted overprint 26.00 450.00
b. Imperf., pair 50.00
262 A16 50pf vermilion .20 1.90
263 A16 60pf blue green .20 1.00
264 A16 75pf lilac rose .35 4.00
265 A16 80pf dark blue .35 2.25
a. Without overprint 100.00
b. Imperf., pair 50.00

Overprinted in Black or Red

266 A17 1m car & gray .35 1.75
a. Imperf., pair 50.00 375.00
b. Inverted overprint 47.50
267 A17 1¼m ultra & ol bis .35 1.75
a. Imperf., pair 47.50
268 A17 1½m dk grn & gray .40 2.75
a. Imperf., pair 47.50
269 A17 2m vio & ol bis .60 3.25
a. Without overprint 32.50
b. Imperf., pair 50.00
270 A17 2½m (#250) (R) .20 2.25
c. Imperf., pair 50.00
270A A17 2½m (#255) (R) .45 80.00
b. Imperf., pair 50.00

Overprinted

271 A18 3m pale blue 2.25 7.25
272 A18 4m dull red 2.75 8.50
a. Without overprint 47.50
273 A18 5m orange 2.25 8.00
274 A18 10m dp green 2.75 10.00
275 A18 20m black 5.00 10.50
Nos. 256-275 (21) 19.65 151.75

Nos. 256-275 were available for postage through all Germany, but were used almost exclusively in Bavaria.

SEMI-POSTAL STAMPS

Regular Issue of 1914-20 Surcharged in Black

1919 **Wmk. 95h** ***Perf. 14x14½***

B1 A10 10pf + 5pf car rose .35 1.50
a. Inverted surcharge 26.00 65.00
b. Surcharge on back 50.00
c. Imperf., pair 325.00
B2 A10 15pf + 5pf ver .35 1.50
a. Inverted surcharge 26.00 65.00
b. Imperf., pair 190.00
B3 A10 20pf + 5pf blue .35 1.90
a. Inverted surcharge 26.00 65.00
b. Imperf., pair 375.00
Nos. B1-B3 (3) 1.05 4.90

Surtax was for wounded war veterans.

POSTAGE DUE STAMPS

D1

D2

With Silk Thread

1862 **Typeset** **Unwmk.** ***Imperf.***

J1 D1 3kr black 125.00 325.00
Never hinged 175.00
No gum 57.50
Pen cancel 87.50
On cover 875.00
On cover, pen cancel 275.00
Pair with gutter between 1,300.
Never hinged 2,000.
No gum 700.00
a. "Empfange" 375.00 1,000.
Never hinged 600.00
On cover 2,200.

Values for Multiples

J1 D1 3kr Pair 250.00 1,100.
Never hinged 440.00
On cover 150.00
J1 D1 3kr Strip of 3 400.00 2,200.
Never hinged 650.00
On cover 1,700.
J1 D1 3kr Block or strip of 4 650.00 4,400.
Never hinged 1,000.

Full margins = 1¼mm at sides, ¾mm at top and bottom. There are vertical dividing lines between stamps.

Without Silk Thread

1870 **Typo.** **Wmk. 93** ***Perf. 11½***

J2 D1 1kr black 10.00 725.00
Never hinged 14.00
On cover 1,400.
Pair with gutter between 87.50
Never hinged 175.00
a. Wmk. 92 45.00 1,650.
Never hinged 87.50
On cover 2,500.
Pair with gutter between 200.00
Never hinged 350.00
J3 D1 3kr black 10.00 450.00
Never hinged 14.00
On cover 875.00
Pair with gutter between 110.00
Never hinged 210.00
a. Wmk. 92 50.00 950.00
Never hinged 87.50
On cover 1,750.
Pair with gutter between 225.00
Never hinged 425.00

Type of 1876 Regular Issue Overprinted in Red "Vom Empfänger zahlbar"

1876 **Wmk. 94**

J4 D2 3pf gray 14.00 350.00
Never hinged 40.00
On cover 87.50
Pair with gutter between 175.00
J5 D2 5pf gray 10.00 17.00
Never hinged 35.00
On cover 65.00
Pair with gutter between 150.00
J6 D2 10pf gray 3.25 1.25
Never hinged 13.00
On cover 14.00
Pair with gutter between 87.50
a. Vert. half used as 5pf on cover 2,800.
Nos. J4-J6 (3) 27.25 368.25

1883 **Wmk. 95v**

J7 D2 3pf gray 82.50 92.50
Never hinged 175.00
On cover 350.00
Pair with gutter between 550.00
J8 D2 5pf gray 55.00 60.00
Never hinged 110.00
On cover 175.00
Pair with gutter between 350.00
J9 D2 10pf gray 2.25 .55
Never hinged 7.00
On cover 7.00
Pair with gutter between 140.00
a. "Empfanger" 140.00 140.00
Never hinged 275.00
On cover 250.00
b. "zahlhar" 72.50 72.50
Never hinged 175.00
On cover 140.00
c. Imperf. 87.50
Never hinged 140.00
Nos. J7-J9 (3) 139.75 153.05

1895-1903 **Wmk. 95h** ***Perf. 14½***

J10 D2 2pf gray .60 1.40
Never hinged 1.25
On cover 10.50
Pair with gutter between 7.00 37.50
Never hinged 14.00
J11 D2 3pf gray ('03) .55 2.50
Never hinged 1.10
On cover 13.50
Pair with gutter between 11.00 37.50
Never hinged 18.00
J12 D2 5pf gray ('03) 1.00 1.75
Never hinged 2.10
On cover 13.50
Pair with gutter between 7.00 37.50
Never hinged 14.00
J13 D2 10pf gray ('03) .60 .90
Never hinged 1.25
On cover 10.00
Pair with gutter between 7.00 37.50
Never hinged 10.50
Nos. J10-J13 (4) 2.75 6.55

Imperf

J10b D2 2pf 55.00
Never hinged 87.50
Pair with gutter between 275.00
Never hinged 440.00
J11c D2 3pf 55.00
Never hinged 87.50
Pair with gutter between 275.00
Never hinged 440.00
J12b D2 5pf 55.00
Never hinged 87.50
Pair with gutter between 275.00
Never hinged 440.00
J13c D2 10pf 55.00
Never hinged 87.50
Pair with gutter between 275.00
Never hinged 450.00

1888

Rose-toned Paper

J10a D2 2pf gray 1.90 4.50
Never hinged 3.75
On cover 13.00

		Pair with gutter between	14.00	44.00
		Never hinged	28.00	
J11a	D2	3pf gray	2.50	2.25
		Never hinged	6.00	
		On cover		13.00
		Pair with gutter between	70.00	
b.		Inverted overprint		2,200.
		On cover		3,500.
J12a	D2	5pf gray	2.50	2.50
		Never hinged	6.00	
		On cover		13.00
		Pair with gutter between	70.00	
J13a	D2	10pf gray	2.50	1.10
		Never hinged	6.00	
		On cover		8.75
		Pair with gutter between	87.50	
b.		As "a," double overprint		2,200.
		On cover		3,500.
		Nos. J10a-J13a (4)	9.40	10.35

No. J13b was used at Pirmasens.

Surcharged in Red in Each Corner

1895

J14 D2 2pf on 3pf gray *44,000.*

At least six copies exist, all used in Aichach.

OFFICIAL STAMPS

Nos. 77-81, 84, 95-96, 98-99, 102 perforated with a large E were issued for official use in 1912-16.

Regular Issue of 1888-1900 Overprinted

1908 Wmk. 95h *Perf. 14½*

O1	A5	3pf dk brown (R)	.75	3.25
O2	A5	5pf dk green (R)	.20	.20
O3	A5	10pf carmine (G)	.20	.20
O4	A5	20pf ultra (R)	.35	.50
O5	A5	50pf maroon	3.25	6.00
		Nos. O1-O5 (5)	4.75	10.15

Nos. O1-O5 were issued for the use of railway officials. "E" stands for "Eisenbahn."

Coat of Arms — O1

1916-17 Typo. *Perf. 11½*

O6	O1	3pf bister brn	.20	.50
O7	O1	5pf yellow grn	.20	.50
O8	O1	7½pf grn, *grn*	.20	.40
O9	O1	7½pf grn ('17)	.20	.35
O10	O1	10pf deep rose	.20	.35
O11	O1	15pf red, *buff*	.30	.40
O12	O1	15pf red ('17)	.20	.50
O13	O1	20pf dp bl, *bl*	1.25	1.90
O14	O1	20pf dp blue ('17)	.20	.35
O15	O1	25pf gray	.20	.40
O16	O1	30pf orange	.20	.40
O17	O1	60pf dark green	.20	.40
O18	O1	1m dl vio, *gray*	.55	1.90
O19	O1	1m maroon ('17)	1.90	450.00
		Nos. O6-O19 (14)	6.00	458.35

Used Values

of Nos. O6-O69 are for postally used stamps. Canceled-to-order stamps, which abound, sell for same prices as unused.

Official Stamps and Type of 1916-17 Overprinted

1918

O20	O1	3pf bister brn	.20	10.00
O21	O1	5pf yellow green	.20	1.00
O22	O1	7½pf gray green	.20	10.00
O23	O1	10pf deep rose	.20	1.00
O24	O1	15pf red	.20	1.00
O25	O1	20pf blue	.20	1.00
O26	O1	25pf gray	.20	1.00
O27	O1	30pf orange	.20	1.00
O28	O1	35pf orange	.20	1.00
O29	O1	50pf olive gray	.20	1.25
O30	O1	60pf dark green	.20	10.00
O31	O1	75pf red brown	.35	2.75
O32	O1	1m dl vio, *gray*	.75	10.00
O33	O1	1m maroon	3.00	325.00
		Nos. O20-O33 (14)	6.30	376.00

O2

O3

O4

1920 Typo. *Perf. 14x14½*

O34	O2	5pf yellow grn	.20	5.00
O35	O2	10pf orange	.20	5.00
O36	O2	15pf carmine	.20	5.00
O37	O2	20pf violet	.20	5.00
O38	O2	30pf dark blue	.20	6.50
O39	O2	40pf bister	.20	6.50

Perf. 14½x14

Wmk. 95v

O40	O3	50pf vermilion	.20	20.00
O41	O3	60pf blue green	.20	8.50
O42	O3	70pf dk violet	.20	22.50
a.		Imperf., pair	26.00	
O43	O3	75pf deep rose	.20	29.00
O44	O3	80pf dull blue	.20	29.00
O45	O3	90pf olive green	.20	40.00
O46	O4	1m dark brown	.20	35.00
a.		Imperf., pair	72.50	
O47	O4	1¼m green	.20	50.00
O48	O4	1½m vermilion	.20	52.50
a.		Imperf. pair	25.00	
O49	O4	2½m deep blue	.20	60.00
a.		Imperf. pair	72.50	
O50	O4	3m dark red	.20	72.50
a.		Imperf. pair	20.00	
O51	O4	5m black	1.50	90.00
a.		Imperf., pair	72.50	
		Nos. O34-O51 (18)	4.90	542.00

Stamps of Preceding Issue Overprinted

1920, Apr. 1

O52	O2	5pf yellow green	.20	2.75
a.		Imperf., pair	26.00	
O53	O2	10pf orange	.20	1.50
O54	O2	15pf carmine	.20	1.50
O55	O2	20pf violet	.20	1.25
O56	O2	30pf dark blue	.20	1.10
O57	O2	40pf bister	.20	1.10
O58	O3	50pf vermilion	.20	1.10
a.		Imperf., pair	26.00	
O59	O3	60pf blue green	.20	1.10
O60	O3	70pf dark violet	1.50	2.25
O61	O3	75pf deep rose	.35	1.10
O62	O3	80pf dull blue	.20	1.10
O63	O3	90pf olive green	1.25	2.75

Similar Ovpt., Words 8mm apart

O64	O4	1m dark brown	.20	1.10
a.		Imperf., pair	26.00	
O65	O4	1¼m green	.20	1.10
O66	O4	1½m vermilion	.20	1.10
O67	O4	2½m deep blue	.20	1.10
a.		Imperf., pair	37.50	
O68	O4	3m dark red	.20	1.10
O69	O4	5m black	8.00	25.00
		Nos. O52-O69 (18)	13.90	49.10

Nos. O52-O69 could be used in all parts of Germany, but were almost exclusively used in Bavaria.

BERGEDORF

LOCATION — A town in northern Germany.

POP. — 2,989 (1861)

Originally Bergedorf belonged jointly to the Free City of Hamburg and the Free City of Lübeck. In 1867 it was purchased by Hamburg.

16 Schillings = 1 Mark

Values for unused stamps are for examples with original gum as defined in the catalogue introduction. Copies without gum sell for about 40% of the figures quoted. Values for used stamps are for examples canceled with parallel bars. Copies bearing dated town postmarks sell for more.

Combined Arms of Lübeck and Hamburg

A1 A2 A3

A4 A5

1861-67 Unwmk. Litho. *Imperf.*

1	A1	½s blk, *pale bl*	37.50	57.50
		Never hinged	65.00	
		No gum	14.50	
		On cover		3,250.
		Pair with gutter between	225.00	
		Never hinged	325.00	
		No gum	87.50	
a.		½s black, *blue* ('67)	110.00	4,500.
		Never hinged	225.00	
		No gum	44.00	
		On cover		26,000.
		Pair with gutter between	500.00	
		Never hinged	875.00	
		No gum	225.00	
2	A3	1s blk, *white*	37.50	300.00
		Never hinged	65.00	
		No gum	14.50	
		On cover		2,400.
		Pair with gutter between	160.00	
		Never hinged	300.00	
		No gum	65.00	
a.		Tête bêche pair, vert.	225.00	
		Never hinged	340.00	
		No gum	87.50	
b.		Tête bêche pair, horiz.	300.00	
		Never hinged	550.00	
		No gum	120.00	
3	A4	1½s blk, *yellow*	17.50	1,100.
		Never hinged	32.50	
		No gum	7.25	
		On cover		4,750.
		Pair with gutter between	175.00	
		Never hinged	300.00	
		No gum	72.50	
a.		Tête bêche pair	*125.00*	
		Never hinged	*225.00*	
		No gum	*55.00*	
		Pair with gutter between	300.00	
		Never hinged	550.00	
		No gum	125.00	
4	A2	3s blue, *pink*	22.50	1,450.
		Never hinged	40.00	
		No gum	7.25	
		On cover		11,000.
		Pair with gutter between	175.00	
		Never hinged	325.00	
		No gum	80.00	
5	A5	4s blk, *brown*	22.50	1,825.
		Never hinged	40.00	
		No gum	7.25	
		On cover		23,500.
		Pair with gutter between	175.00	
		Never hinged	325.00	
		No gum	80.00	

Full margins Nos. 1-3 = 1½mm; No. 4 = ¾mm; No. 5 = 1mm. There are vertical dividing lines between stamps.

Values for pairs

1	A1	½s blk, *pale bl*	87.50	1,800.
		Never hinged	160.00	
a.		½s black, *blue*	300.00	13,000.
		Never hinged	575.00	
2	A3	1s blk, *white*	87.50	1,600.
		Never hinged	160.00	
3	A4	1½s blk, *yellow*	45.00	3,500.
		Never hinged	80.00	
4	A2	3s blue, *pink*	47.50	—
		Never hinged	87.50	
5	A5	4s blk, *brown*	47.50	15,000.
		Never hinged	87.50	

Values for strips of 3

1	A1	½s blk, *pale bl*	150.00	10,000.
		Never hinged	260.00	
a.		½s black, *blue*	500.00	—
		Never hinged	875.00	
2	A3	1s blk, *white*	150.00	8,000.
		Never hinged	260.00	
3	A4	1½s blk, *yellow*	65.00	—
		Never hinged	120.00	
4	A2	3s blue, *pink*	72.50	—
		Never hinged	130.00	
5	A5	4s blk, *brown*	72.50	—
		Never hinged	130.00	

Values for blocks or strips of 4

1	A1	½s blk, *pale bl*	200.00	16,000.
		Never hinged	325.00	
a.		½s black, *blue*	650.00	—
		Never hinged	1,200.	
2	A3	1s blk, *white*	200.00	12,000.
		Never hinged	325.00	
3	A4	1½s blk, *yellow*	87.50	—
		Never hinged	160.00	
4	A2	3s blue, *pink*	110.00	—
		Never hinged	190.00	
5	A5	4s blk, *brown*	110.00	—
		Never hinged	190.00	

Counterfeit cancellations are plentiful.

No. 3 exists in a tête bêche gutter pair. Value, unused $310.

The ½s on violet and 3s on rose, listed previously, as well as a 1s and 1½s on thick paper and 4s on light rose brown, come from proof sheets and were never placed in use. A 1½ "SCHILLINGE" (instead of SCHILLING) also exists only as a proof.

REPRINTS

½ SCHILLING

There is a dot in the upper part of the right branch of "N" of "EIN." The upper part of the shield is blank or almost blank. The horizontal bar of "H" in "HALBER" is generally defective.

1 SCHILLING

The "1" in the corners is generally with foot. The central horizontal bar of the "E" of "EIN" is separated from the vertical branch by a black line. The "A" of "POSTMARKE" has the horizontal bar incomplete or missing. The horizontal bar of the "H" of "SCHILLING" is separated from the vertical branches by a dark line at each side, sometimes the bar is missing.

1½ SCHILLINGE

There is a small triangle under the right side of the tower, exactly over the "R" of "POSTMARKE."

3 SCHILLINGE

The head of the eagle is not shaded. The horizontal bar of the second "E" of "BERGEDORF" is separated from the vertical branch by a thin line. There is generally a colored dot in the lower half of the "S" of "POSTMARKE."

4 SCHILLINGE

The upper part of the shield is blank or has two or three small dashes. In most of the reprints there is a diagonal dash across the wavy lines of the groundwork at the right of "I" and "E" of "VIER."

Reprints, value $1 each.

These stamps were superseded by those of the North German Confederation in 1868.

BREMEN

LOCATION — In northwestern Germany

AREA — 99 sq. mi.

POP. — 122,402 (1871)

Bremen was a Free City and member of the German Confederation. In 1870 it became part of the German Empire.

22 Grote = 10 Silbergroschen.

Coat of Arms — A1

I II III

Type I. The central part of the scroll below the word Bremen is crossed by one vertical line.

Type II. The center of the scroll is crossed by two vertical lines.

Type III. The center of the scroll is crossed by three vertical lines.

1855 Unwmk. Litho. *Imperf.*

Horizontally Laid Paper

1	A1	3gr black, *blue*	175.00	275.00
		Never hinged	375.00	
		No gum	100.00	
		On cover		1,750.

Vertically Laid Paper

1A	A1	3gr black, *blue*	350.00	550.00
		Never hinged	750.00	
		No gum	150.00	
		On cover		2,500.

Full margins = 1½mm.

No. 1 can be found with parts of a papermaker's watermark, consisting of lilies. Value: unused $650; unused , no gum, $375; used $950; on cover $2,600.

See Nos. 9-10.

Values for pairs

1 A1 3gr black, *blue* 500.00 —
Never hinged 875.00
No gum 300.00
1A A1 3gr black, *blue* 1,500. —
Never hinged 2,500.
No gum 1,000.

Values for strips of 3

1 A1 3gr black, *blue* 950.00 —
No gum 500.00
Types I, II and III — —
1A A1 3gr black, *blue* 2,500. —
No gum 1,000.
Types I, II and III — —

Values for blocks of 4

1 A1 3gr black, *blue* *1,450.* —
Never hinged *2,250.*
No gum *800.00*
1A A1 3gr black, *blue* — —

A2

A3

FIVE GROTE

Type I. The shading at the left of the ribbon containing "funf Grote" runs downward from the shield.
Type II. The shading at the left of the ribbon containing "funf Grote" runs upward.

1856-60 Wove Paper

2 A2 5gr blk, *rose* 150.00 *300.00*
Never hinged 290.00
No gum 72.50
On cover 2,900.
a. Printed on both sides
b. "Marken" (not issued) 11.00
Never hinged 18.00
No gum 7.25
3 A2 7gr blk, *yel* ('60) 225.00 *650.00*
Never hinged 440.00
No gum 87.50
On cover *4,500.*
4 A3 5sgr green ('59) 275.00 *300.00*
Never hinged 500.00
No gum 150.00
On cover 2,500.
a. Chalky paper 50.00 *1,500.*
Never hinged 95.00
No gum 30.00
b. 5sgr yellow green 125.00 *300.00*
Never hinged 225.00
No gum 65.00
On cover 2,600.

Full margins: No. 2 = 1¼mm; No. 3 = 1½mm; No. 5 = 1mm. There are vertical dividing lines between stamps.

See Nos. 6, 8, 12-13, 15.

Values for pairs

2 A2 5gr black, *rose* 375.00 *1,500.*
Never hinged 725.00
No gum 225.00
3 A2 7gr black, *yel* 575.00 —
Never hinged 1,050.
No gum 300.00
4 A3 5sgr green 600.00 —
Never hinged 1,200.
No gum 400.00
a. Chalky paper 130.00 —
Never hinged 225.00
No gum 72.50
b. 5sgr yellow green 325.00 *1,500.*
Never hinged 575.00
No gum 175.00

Values for strips of 3

2 A2 5gr black, *rose* 575.00
Never hinged 1,100.
No gum 325.00
3 A2 7gr black, *yel* 1,100.
Never hinged 1,800.
No gum 500.00
4 A3 5sgr green 1,200.
Never hinged 2,000.
No gum 600.00
a. Chalky paper 225.00
Never hinged 375.00
No gum 110.00
b. 5sgr yellow green 575.00
Never hinged 1,100.
No gum 325.00

Values for blocks of 4

2 A2 5gr blk, *rose* 875.00
Never hinged 1,700.
No gum 575.00
3 A2 7gr blk, *yel* 1,450.
Never hinged 2,600.
No gum 650.00
4 A3 5sgr green 1,750.
Never hinged —
No gum 900.00
a. Chalky paper 300.00
Never hinged 500.00
No gum 175.00
b. 5sgr yellow green 800.00
Never hinged 1,450.
No gum 450.00

A4

A5

1861-63 *Serpentine Roulette*

5 A4 2gr orange ('63) 275.00 *1,800.*
No gum 175.00
On cover 5,750.
a. 2gr red orange 700.00 *3,000.*
No gum 400.00
On cover *8,500.*
b. Chalky paper 350.00 *2,800.*
No gum 210.00
On cover 7,000.
c. as "a," chalky paper 700.00 *4,000.*
No gum 400.00
On cover 12,000.
6 A2 5gr blk, *rose* ('62) 200.00 *175.00*
No gum 110.00
On cover 900.00
Two singles on cover *2,500.*
a. Horiz. pair, imperf between —
b. Double impression —
7 A5 10gr black 700.00 *850.00*
No gum 350.00
On cover 2,800.
Two singles on cover *7,000.*
8 A3 5sgr yellow green ('63) 1,100. 175.00
No gum 625.00
On cover 900.00
a. Chalky paper 600.00 425.00
No gum 325.00
On cover 1,400.
b. 5sgr green 925.00 210.00
No gum 550.00
On cover 1,000.

Full margins of No. 5 = 1mm. There are dividing lines between stamps.

See Nos. 11, 14.

Values for pairs

5 A4 2gr orange 900.00 *4,250.*
No gum 550.00
a. 2gr red orange 2,000. —
No gum 1,000.
b. Chalky paper 2,000. —
No gum 1,000.
c. as "a," chalky paper 1,800. —
No gum 1,100.
6 A2 5gr blk, *rose* 1,000. *1,000.*
No gum 600.00
7 A5 10gr black 2,500. *2,450.*
No gum 1,250.
8 A3 5sgr green —
a. Chalky paper —
b. 5sgr yellow green —

Values for strips of 3

5 A4 2gr orange 1,150.
No gum 900.00
a. 2gr red orange —
No gum —
b. Chalky paper —
No gum —
c. as "a," chalky paper 3,000.
No gum 2,000.
6 A2 5gr blk, *rose* —
7 A5 10gr black *5,000.*
8 A3 5sgr green —
a. Chalky paper —
b. 5sgr yellow green —

Values for blocks of 4

5 A4 2gr orange 2,100.
No gum 1,250.
a. 2gr red orange —
No gum —
b. Chalky paper —
No gum —
c. as "a," chalky paper 4,500.
No gum 3,000.
6 A2 5gr blk, *rose* —
7 A5 10gr black — *11,000.*
8 A3 5sgr green —
a. Chalky paper —
b. 5sgr yellow green —

1863

Horizontally (H) or Vertically (V) Laid Paper

9 A1 3gr blk, *blue* (V) 550.00 575.00
No gum 275.00
On cover 2,100.
a. 3gr black, *blue* (H) 2,250. *4,000.*
No gum 1,250.
On cover *12,500.*

Values for pairs

9 A1 3gr blk, *blue* (V) 1,500. *2,500.*
No gum 850.00
a. 3gr black, *blue* (H) —

1866-67 *Perf. 13*

10 A1 3gr black, *blue* 70.00 *275.00*
Never hinged 125.00
No gum 35.00
On cover *1,400.*

Wove Paper

11 A4 2gr orange 62.50 *225.00*
Never hinged 125.00
No gum 32.50
On cover *1,100.*
Pair with gutter between 3,250.
Never hinged 5,000.
No gum 1,400.
a. 2gr red orange 275.00 *500.00*
Never hinged 400.00
No gum 125.00
On cover *1,900.*
b. Horiz. pair, imperf. btwn. 2,800.

12 A2 5gr blk, *rose* 110.00 *275.00*
Never hinged 200.00
No gum 55.00
On cover *3,250.*
a. Horiz. pair, imperf. btwn. 1,250. —
No gum 700.00
13 A2 7gr blk, *yel* ('67) 125.00 *4,000.*
Never hinged 210.00
No gum 70.00
On cover *14,000.*
14 A5 10gr black ('67) 175.00 *1,000.*
Never hinged 325.00
No gum 100.00
On cover *3,500.*
15 A3 5sgr green 125.00 *3,750.*
Never hinged 250.00
No gum 62.50
On cover 35,000.
a. 5sgr yellow green 450.00 175.00
Never hinged 700.00
No gum 250.00
On cover 1,250.
b. As "a," chalky paper 450.00 275.00
Never hinged 800.00
No gum 250.00
On cover 3,250.

Values for pairs

10 A1 3gr black, *blue* 210.00 —
Never hinged 350.00
No gum 110.00
11 A4 2gr orange 175.00 *1,250.*
Never hinged 325.00
No gum 85.00
a. 2gr red orange — —
12 A2 5gr blk, *rose* 275.00 *1,050.*
Never hinged 500.00
No gum 140.00
13 A2 7gr blk, *yel* ('67) 325.00 —
Never hinged 625.00
No gum 175.00
14 A5 10gr black ('67) 425.00 *2,800.*
Never hinged 700.00
No gum 250.00
15 A3 5sgr green 550.00 —
Never hinged 1,000.
No gum 325.00
a. 5sgr yellow green —
b. As "a," chalky paper —

Values for Blocks of 4

10 A1 3gr black, *blue* 700.00
Never hinged 1,250.
No gum 425.00
11 A4 2gr orange 425.00
Never hinged 700.00
No gum 210.00
12 A2 5gr blk, *rose* 625.00
Never hinged 1,050.
No gum 350.00
13 A2 7gr blk, *yel* ('67) 700.00
Never hinged 1,400.
No gum 425.00
14 A5 10gr black ('67) 900.00
Never hinged 1,550.
No gum 575.00
15 A3 5sgr green 1,900.
Never hinged 3,000.
No gum 1,100.

The stamps of Bremen were superseded by those of the North German Confederation on Jan. 1, 1868.

BRUNSWICK

LOCATION — In northern Germany
GOVT. — Former duchy
AREA — 1,417 sq. mi.
POP. — 349,367 (1880)
CAPITAL — Brunswick

Brunswick was a member of the German Confederation and, in 1870 became part of the German Empire.

12 Pfennigs = 1 Gutegroschen
30 Silbergroschen (Groschen) = 24 Gutegroschen = 1 Thaler

Values for unused stamps are for examples with original gum as defined in the catalogue introduction except for Nos. 1-3 which are valued without gum. Nos. 1-3 with original gum sell for much higher prices.

The "Leaping Saxon Horse" — A1

The ½gr has white denomination and "Gr" in right oval.

1852 Unwmk. Typo. *Imperf.*

1 A1 1sgr rose 1,800. 275.00
On cover 1,100.
2 A1 2sgr blue 1,275. 225.00
On cover 875.00
a. Half used as 1sgr on cover —
3 A1 3sgr vermilion 1,300. 225.00
On cover 800.00

Full margins = 1¼mm.

Values for used pairs

1 A1 1sgr rose 1,300.
On cover *1,750.*
2 A1 2sgr blue 2,500.
3 A1 3sgr vermilion 2,500.

Values for used strip of 3

1 A1 1sgr *5,400.*
On cover *8,600.*

See Nos. 4-11, 13-22.

1853-63 Wmk. 102

4 A1 ¼ggr blk, *brn* ('56) 725.00 225.00
No gum 360.00
On cover 875.00
On cover, single franking, local post *13,000.*
5 A1 ⅓sgr black ('56) 125.00 290.00
No gum 50.00
On cover 2,300.
On cover, single franking, local post *7,250.*
6 A1 ½gr blk, *grn* ('63) 21.00 *210.00*
Never hinged 47.50
No gum 8.50
On cover *600.00*
On cover, single franking 1,000.
a. Thin paper (.065mm) 36.00 *360.00*
Never hinged 72.50
No gum 18.00
On cover *600.00*
7 A1 1sgr blk, *orange* 350.00 50.00
No gum 225.00
On cover 150.00
a. 1sgr black, *orange buff* 350.00 57.50
No gum 225.00
On cover 150.00
8 A1 1sgr blk, *yel* ('61) 350.00 45.00
No gum 225.00
On cover 110.00
a. Diagonal half used as ½sgr on cover *18,000.*
9 A1 2sgr blk, *blue* 290.00 50.00
No gum 175.00
On cover 160.00
a. Diagonal half used as 1sgr on cover *8,750.*
b. Vertical half used as 1sgr on cover *18,000.*
c. 2sgr black, *pale blue* — 150.00
On cover 400.00
d. As "c," half used as 1sgr on cover *13,000.*
e. Thick paper (.13mm) — 200.00
On cover 440.00
f. Wmk. inverted *3,600.* *1,450.*
10 A1 3sgr blk, *rose* 450.00 72.50
No gum 290.00
On cover 225.00
11 A1 3sgr rose ('62) 550.00 190.00
No gum 290.00
On cover 440.00
a. 3sgr carmine — 250.00
On cover 500.00

Full margins = 1mm.

Values for pairs

4 A1 ¼ggr blk, *brn* 1,800. 650.00
On cover 1,300.
5 A1 ⅓sgr black 550.00 *1,100.*
On cover 7,250.
6 A1 ½gr blk, *grn* 50.00 *600.00*
No gum 21.50
Never hinged 110.00
On cover *925.00*
7 A1 1sgr blk, *orange* 175.00
On cover 290.00
a. 1sgr black, *orange buff* 1,450. 175.00
On cover 290.00
8 A1 1sgr blk, *yel* 210.00
On cover 360.00
9 A1 2sgr blk, *blue* 725.00 360.00
On cover 725.00
c. 2sgr black, *pale blue* —
e. Thick paper (.13mm) —
10 A1 3sgr blk, *rose* — 325.00
On cover 725.00
11 A1 3sgr rose 1,450. 650.00
No gum 875.00
On cover 1,100.
a. 3sgr carmine 725.00
On cover 1,450.

Values for strips of 3

4 A1 ¼ggr blk, *brn* — 1,100.
On cover 1,600.
5 A1 ⅓sgr black 1,450. *2,000.*
On cover *3,600.*
6 A1 ½gr blk, *grn* 80.00 *1,150.*
No gum 37.50
7 A1 1sgr blk, *orange* — 325.00
On cover 875.00
a. 1sgr black, *orange buff* — 325.00
On cover 875.00
8 A1 1sgr blk, *yel* — 1,100.
9 A1 2sgr blk, *blue* — 1,100.
10 A1 3sgr blk, *rose* — 1,100.
11 A1 3sgr rose — 1,100.
a. 3sgr carmine — 1,100.

Values for blocks or strips of 4

4 A1 ¼ggr blk, *brn* — *1,800.*
On cover *2,500.*
6 A1 ½gr blk, *grn* 110.00 *2,150.*
Never hinged 210.00
No gum 50.00
7 A1 1sgr blk, *orange* — *2,750.*
8 A1 1sgr blk, *yel* 3,250. *2,900.*
No gum 1,800.
9 A1 2sgr blk, *blue* 1,800.
On cover *5,400.*
10 A1 3sgr blk, *rose* *2,200.*
11 A1 3sgr rose *3,600.*
a. 3sgr carmine *5,400.*

A3

A4

1857

12 A3 Four ¼ggr blk, *brn* ('57) 37.50 90.00
No gum 14.00
Single on cover 140.00
Two ¼ggr on cover 100.00
Three ¼ggr on cover 140.00
Four ¼ggr on cover 225.00
Five ¼ggr on cover 290.00
Ten ¼ggr on cover 1,300.
a. Four ¼ggr blk, *yel brown* — 210.00
On cover 440.00

Full margins = 1mm.

Values for pairs

12 A3 Four ¼ggr blk, *brn* 87.50 *290.00*
Never hinged 225.00
No gum 37.50
On cover 700.00
a. Four ¼ggr blk, *yel brown* 600.00

Values for strips of 3

12 A3 Four ¼ggr blk, *brn* 140.00
Never hinged 350.00
No gum 120.00

Values for blocks of 4

12 A3 Four ¼ggr blk, *brn* 290.00
No gum 110.00

Covers: Each multiple corresponds to a rate based on distance and destination. Values are for covers correctly franked.

The bister on white paper was not issued. Value $6.

1864 ***Serpentine Roulette 16***

13 A1 ⅓sgr black 450.00 *2,100.*
No gum 250.00
On cover *4,400.*
14 A1 ½gr blk, *green* 190.00 *3,000.*
No gum 110.00
On cover *11,000.*
15 A1 1sgr blk, *yellow* *2,850.* *1,425.*
No gum 1,800.
On cover *7,250.*
16 A1 1sgr yellow 375.00 125.00
No gum 225.00
On cover 300.00
17 A1 2sgr blk, *blue* 375.00 325.00
No gum 225.00
On cover 900.00
a. Half used as 1sgr on cover *12,000.*
e. Thick paper (.13mm) — 700.00
On cover —
18 A1 3sgr rose 725.00 475.00
No gum 440.00
On cover *1,000.*

Rouletted 12

20 A1 1sgr blk, *yellow* *11,000.*
21 A1 1sgr yellow 600.00 325.00
On cover 875.00
22 A1 3sgr rose — 2,500.

#13, 16, 18, 21-22 are on white paper.
Faked roulettes of Nos. 13-22 exist.

Values for pairs

13 A1 ⅓sgr black *5,400.*
16 A1 1sgr yellow 440.00
On cover 700.00
17 A1 2sgr blk, *blue* 875.00 *1,400.*
No gum 500.00
18 A1 3sgr rose 2,200. 1,500.
No gum 1,400.
21 A1 1sgr yellow 700.00
On cover 1,500.

Values for strips of 3

13 A1 ⅓sgr black *7,250.*
On cover *14,000.*
16 A1 1sgr yellow 700.00
17 A1 2sgr blk, *blue* 1,500.
No gum 825.00
18 A1 3sgr rose *2,400.*
21 A1 1sgr yellow *1,100.*

Values for blocks or strips of 4

13 A1 ⅓sgr black 3,000.
No gum 2,200.
17 A1 2sgr blk, *blue* *3,000.*
18 A1 3sgr rose *3,750.*

Serpentine Roulette

1865 **Embossed** **Unwmk.**

23 A4 ⅓gr black 25.00 *325.00*
Never hinged 50.00
On cover 1,400.
On wrapper or newsprint, single franking 2,800.
24 A4 1gr carmine 2.25 *45.00*
Never hinged 3.75
On cover 125.00
25 A4 2gr ultra 8.25 *110.00*
Never hinged 14.00
On cover 310.00
a. 2gr gray blue 8.25 *110.00*
Never hinged 14.00
On cover 310.00
c. Half used as 1sgr on cover *17,600.*
26 A4 3gr brown 6.50 *125.00*
Never hinged 13.00
On cover 400.00

Faked cancellations of Nos. 5-26 exist.

Values for pairs

23 A4 ⅓gr black 60.00 *800.00*
Never hinged 125.00
24 A4 1gr carmine 5.00 *150.00*
Never hinged 8.75
25 A4 2gr ultra 17.50 *325.00*
Never hinged 32.50
a. 2gr gray blue 17.50 *325.00*
Never hinged 32.50
26 A4 3gr brown 16.00 *440.00*
Never hinged 28.00

Values for strips of 3

23 A4 ⅓gr black 87.50 *1,400.*
Never hinged 190.00
24 A4 1gr carmine 8.25 *310.00*
Never hinged 14.00
25 A4 2gr ultra 26.00 *550.00*
Never hinged 47.50
a. 2gr gray blue 26.00 *550.00*
Never hinged 47.50
26 A4 3gr brown 25.00 *800.00*
Never hinged 42.50

Values for blocks or strips of 4

23 A4 ⅓gr black 140.00 *3,400.*
Never hinged 250.00
24 A4 1gr carmine 11.00
Never hinged 20.00
25 A4 2gr ultra 44.00
Never hinged 65.00
a. 2gr gray blue 44.00
Never hinged 65.00
26 A4 3gr brown 32.50
Never hinged 60.00

Imperf., Pairs

23a A4 ⅓gr 100.00
Never hinged 140.00
24a A4 1gr 30.00
Never hinged 44.00
25b A4 2gr 85.00
Never hinged 140.00
26a A4 3gr 100.00
Never hinged 160.00

Numeral Postmarks

These values are premiums to be added to the used value of the stamp.

The left column has the premium for Nos. 1-22, the right column has the premium to be added for Nos. 23-26.

1 Badenhausen	+120.00	+225.00
2 Bahrdorf	+700.00	
3 Bevern	+225.00	+310.00
4 Blankenburg	+22.50	+310.00
5 Bodenburg	+120.00	+82.50
6 Boerssum	+92.50	+125.00
7 Braunlage	+67.50	+92.50
7 Braunlage (red)	+5,400.	
8 Braunschweig		+9.25
9 Braunschweig, Small 9 ('52-'63)	—	
9 Braunschweig, Large 9 ('63-'67)		+14.00
10 Calvoerde	+92.50	+120.00
11 Delligsen	+140.00	+190.00
12 Eschershausen	+47.50	+70.00
13 Fuerstenberg	+250.00	+375.00
14 Gandersheim	+37.50	+62.50
15 Gittelde	+92.50	+110.00
16 Greene (to 10/10/65)	+225.00	
16 Naensen (after 10/10/65)		+340.00
17 Gross-Winnigstedt	+250.00	+310.00
18 Halle am der Weser	+150.00	+190.00
19 Harzburg	+55.00	+110.00
20 Hasselfelde	+70.00	+100.00
21 Helmstedt	+22.50	+2,000.
22 Hessen	+140.00	+225.00
23 Hohengeiss	+190.00	+225.00
24 Holzminden	+28.00	+82.50
25 Jerxheim	+55.00	+82.50
26 Immendorf (to 12/31/60)	+475.00	
26 Hehlen (from 11/1/62)	+340.00	+460.00
27 Kleine Rheuden (to Oct. '64)	+200.00	
27 Bornum b. Seesen (after Oct. '64)	+225.00	+290.00
28 Koenigslutter	+37.50	+47.50
29 Kreinensen	+55.00	+82.50
30 Langelsheim	+92.50	+125.00
31 Lehre	+190.00	+225.00
32 Lutter a Bge.	+82.50	+110.00
33 Oker	+92.50	+150.00
34 Ottenstein	+225.00	+460.00
35 Ruebeland	+460.00	+625.00
36 Salder, thick lines	+150.00	
36 Salder, thin lines	+92.50	+110.00
37 Schoeningen	+22.50	+55.00
38 Schoeppenstedt	+47.50	+92.50
39 Seesen	+32.50	+47.50
40 Stadtoldendorf	+47.50	+70.00
41 Tanne	+625.00	+825.00
42 Thedinghausen	+140.00	+250.00
43 Vechelde	+70.00	+92.50
44 Velpke	+225.00	+140.00
45 Vorsfelde	+82.50	+110.00
46 Walkenreid	+700.00	
47 Wolfenbuettel		+19.00
48 Zorge	+775.00	+1,100.
49 Mainzholzen (to 10/10/65)	+1,400.	
49 Vorwohle (from 10/10/65)		+1,800.
50 Braunschweig	+8,750.	

Stamps of Brunswick were superseded by those of the North German Confederation on Jan. 1, 1868.

HAMBURG

LOCATION — Northern Germany
GOVT. — A former Free City
AREA — 160 sq. mi.
POP. — 453,869 (1880)
CAPITAL — Hamburg

Hamburg was a member of the German Confederation and became part of the German Empire in 1870.

16 Schillings = 1 Mark

Values for unused stamps are for examples with original gum as defined in the catalogue introduction.

Value Numeral on Arms — A1

1859 **Typo.** **Wmk. 128** ***Imperf.***

1 A1 ½s black 85.00 *550.00*
No gum 47.50
On cover *5,750.*
On cover, single franking *9,250.*
2 A1 1s brown 85.00 *72.50*
No gum 47.50
On cover *800.00*
a. Period betweenn "M" and "B" 210.00 *425.00*
No gum 125.00
3 A1 2s red 85.00 *92.50*
No gum 47.50
On cover *725.00*
4 A1 3s blue 85.00 *110.00*
No gum 47.50
On cover *1,000.*
5 A1 4s yellow green 65.00 *1,300.*
No gum 35.00
On cover *14,250.*
a. 4s green 110.00 *1,150.*
No gum 72.50
On cover *12,750.*
b. Double impression —
6 A1 7s orange 80.00 35.00
No gum 42.50
On cover 290.00
7 A1 9s yellow 175.00 *1,700.*
No gum 110.00
On cover *12,750.*

Full margins = 1¾mm at sides, ¾mm at top and bottom. There are vertical dividing lines between stamps.

See Nos. 13-21.

Values for pairs

1 A1 ½s black 400.00 *1,800.*
2 A1 1s brown 850.00 *300.00*
On cover 1,000.
3 A1 2s red 400.00 *650.00*
On cover 1,450.
4 A1 3s blue 850.00 *725.00*
On cover 2,150.
5 A1 4s yellow green 175.00 *6,500.*
a. 4s green 650.00 *6,500.*
6 A1 7s orange 360.00 175.00
On cover 1,150.
7 A1 9s yellow 650.00 *7,250.*

Values for strips of 3

1 A1 ½s black 540.00
2 A1 1s brown 1,350. *725.00*
3 A1 2s red 540.00 *2,850.*
4 A1 3s blue 1,350. *3,600.*
5 A1 4s yellow green 290.00 —
a. 4s green 925.00 —
6 A1 7s orange 850.00 575.00
7 A1 9s yellow 1,000. *11,500.*

Values for blocks of 4, Unused without gum and used

1 A1 ½s black 360.00
2 A1 1s brown 790.00
3 A1 2s red 360.00
4 A1 3s blue 800.00
5 A1 4s yellow green 225.00
a. 4s green 575.00
6 A1 7s orange 360.00
7 A1 9s yellow 675.00 *18,000.*

A2

A3

1864 **Litho.**

9 A2 1¼s gray 77.50 72.50
No gum 47.50
On cover 290.00
a. 1¼s lilac 150.00 85.00
No gum 80.00
On cover 325.00
b. 1¼s red lilac 125.00 72.50
No gum 65.00
On cover 290.00
c. 1¼s blue 425.00 *850.00*
No gum 275.00
On cover *3,250.*
d. 1¼s greenish gray 110.00 *92.50*
No gum 65.00
On cover 325.00
e. 1¼s mauve(1st printing) 475.00 *850.00*
No gum 260.00
On cover *2,150.*
12 A3 2½s green 125.00 *125.00*
No gum 72.50
On cover *500.00*

Full margins = 1¼mm.

See Nos. 22-23.

The 1¼s and 2½s have been reprinted on watermarked and unwatermarked paper.

Values for pairs

9 A2 1¼s gray 1,200. 225.00
On cover 475.00
a. 1¼s lilac 1,200. 350.00
b. 1¼s red lilac 1,200. 225.00
On cover 425.00
c. 1¼s blue 1,350. —
d. 1¼s greenish gray 425.00 *325.00*
e. 1¼s mauve(1st printing) 1,350. *2,150.*
12 A3 2½s green 500.00 *400.00*

Values for strips of 3

9 A2 1¼s gray 1,800. 725.00
a. 1¼s lilac 1,800. —
b. 1¼s red lilac 1,800. 700.00
c. 1¼s blue —
d. 1¼s greenish gray 650.00 *1,100.*
e. 1¼s mauve(1st printing) 2,250. *4,250.*
12 A3 2½s green 850.00 *1,000.*

Values for unused blocks of 4

9 A2 1¼s gray 2,300.
No gum 1,100.
a. 1¼s lilac 2,300.
No gum 1,100.
b. 1¼s red lilac 2,300.
No gum 1,100.
c. 1¼s blue —
d. 1¼s greenish gray 925.00
No gum 425.00
e. 1¼s mauve(1st printing) 3,600.
No gum 1,800.
12 A3 2½s green 1,450.
No gum 650.00

1864-65 **Typo.** ***Perf. 13½***

13 A1 ½s black 5.50 *10.00*
No gum 2.90
On cover 70.00
a. Horiz. pair, imperf between 65.00
No gum 32.50
14 A1 1s brown 11.00 *15.00*
No gum 6.50
On cover 55.00
a. Half used as ½s on cover *16,000.*
b. Horiz. pair, imperf between 450.00 *650.00*
15 A1 2s red 13.00 *20.00*
No gum 6.25
On cover 87.50
17 A1 3s ultra 32.50 30.00
No gum 22.50
On cover 140.00
a. Imperf., pair 140.00
No gum 70.00
b. Horiz. pair, imperf. vert. —
c. 3s blue 42.50 29.00
No gum 22.50
On cover 140.00
d. 3s Prussian blue 140.00 110.00
No gum 55.00
On cover 540.00
18 A1 4s green 8.75 16.50
No gum 4.00
On cover 175.00
a. 4s blue green 210.00 40.00
No gum 100.00
On cover 175.00
19 A1 7s orange 140.00 100.00
No gum 77.50
On cover 540.00
20 A1 7s vio ('65) 9.25 16.00
No gum 4.50
On cover 87.50
a. Imperf, pair 275.00
No gum 140.00
21 A1 9s yellow 22.50 *1,700.*
No gum 10.50
On cover *19,000.*
a. Vert. pair, imperf btwn. 375.00

Litho.

22 A2 1¼s lilac 72.50 11.00
No gum 44.00
On cover 30.00
a. 1¼s red lilac 72.50 11.00
No gum 44.00
On cover 30.00
b. 1¼s violet 72.50 8.75
No gum 44.00
On cover 26.00
c. As "a," imperf, pair 140.00
No gum 110.00
23 A3 2½s yel grn, blurred printing 110.00 26.00
No gum 55.00
On cover 65.00
a. 2½s blue green, blurred printing 110.00 27.50
No gum 55.00
On cover 65.00
b. 2½s green, fine printing 110.00 28.00
No gum 70.00
On cover 87.50

The 1¼s has been reprinted on watermarked and unwatermarked paper; the 2½s on unwatermarked paper.

Values for used pairs

13 A1 ½s black 37.50
14 A1 1s brown 40.00
15 A1 2s red 65.00
17 A1 3s ultra 100.00
c. 3s blue 110.00
d. 3s Prussian blue 450.00
18 A1 4s green 62.50
a. 4s blue green 110.00
19 A1 7s orange 260.00
20 A1 7s violet 52.50
21 A1 9s yellow *6,600.*
22 A2 1¼s lilac 28.00
a. 1¼s red lilac 28.00
b. 1¼s violet 26.00
23 A3 2½s yel grn 87.50
a. 2½s blue green 110.00

b. 2½s green 125.00

Values for used strips of 3

13 A1 ½s black 87.50
14 A1 1s brown 110.00
15 A1 2s red 140.00
17 A1 3s ultra 225.00
d. 3s Prussian blue 875.00
18 A1 4s green 190.00
a. 4s blue green 375.00
19 A1 7s orange
20 A1 7s violet 140.00
21 A1 9s yellow *9,500.*
22 A2 1¼s lilac 140.00
b. 1¼s violet 140.00
23 A3 2½s yel grn 225.00
b. 2½s green 225.00

Values for Blocks of 4, unused without gum

13 A1 ½s black 15.00 *875.00*
14 A1 1s brown 37.50 *1,600.*
15 A1 2s red 25.00 *1,400.*
17 A1 3s ultra 100.00
c. 3s blue 92.50
d. 3s Prussian blue 440.00
18 A1 4s green 19.00
19 A1 7s orange 550.00
20 A1 7s violet 22.50
21 A1 9s yellow 50.00 *17,500.*
22 A2 1¼s lilac 340.00 *1,500.*
b. 1¼s violet 375.00
23 A3 2½s yel grn 290.00
b. 2½s green 310.00 *1,500.*

A4

A5

Rouletted 10

1866 Unwmk. Embossed

24 A4 1¼s violet 37.50 32.50
No gum 21.00
On cover 110.00
a. 1¼s red violet 72.50 72.50
No gum 37.50
On cover 140.00
25 A5 1½s rose 7.25 *125.00*
No gum 4.00
On cover *550.00*

Values for used pairs

24 A4 1¼s violet 92.50
a. 1¼s red violet 160.00
25 A5 1½s rose *310.00*

Values for used strips of 3

24 A4 1¼s violet 300.00
a. 1¼s red violet 440.00
25 A5 1½s rose *650.00*

Values for unused blocks of 4, without gum

24 A4 1¼s violet 100.00
a. 1¼s red violet 225.00
25 A5 1½s rose 19.00

Reprints:

1¼s: The rosettes between the words of the inscription have a well-defined open circle in the center of the originals, while in the reprints this circle is filled up.

In the upper part of the top of the "g" of "Schilling", there is a thin vertical line which is missing in the reprints.

The two lower lines of the triangle in the upper left corner are of different thicknesses in the originals while in the reprints they are of equal thickness.

The labels at the right and left containing the inscriptions are 2¾mm in width in the originals while they are 2½mm in reprints.

1½s: The originals are printed on thinner paper than the reprints. This is easily seen by turning the stamps over, when on the originals the color and impression will clearly show through, which is not the case in the reprints.

The vertical stroke of the upper part of the "g" in Schilling is very short on the originals, scarcely crossing the top line, while in the reprints it almost touches the center of the "g."

The lower part of the "g" of Schilling in the originals, barely touches the inner line of the frame, in some stamps it does not touch it at all, while in the reprints the whole stroke runs into the inner line of the frame.

A6

1867 Typo. Wmk. 128 *Perf. 13½*

26 A6 2½s dull green 10.00 *65.00*
No gum 4.50
On cover *150.00*
a. 2½s dark green 52.50 *80.00*
No gum 30.00
On cover *225.00*
b. Imperf., pair 225.00
No gum 87.50
c. Horiz. pair, imperf between 92.50
No gum 44.00

Values for used pairs

26 A6 2½s dull green *190.00*
a. 2½s dark green *225.00*

Values for used strips of 3

26 A6 2½s dull green *375.00*
a. 2½s dark green *440.00*

Values for unused blocks of 4, without gum

26 A6 2½s dull green 22.50
a. 2½s dark green 140.00

Forged cancellations exist on almost all stamps of Hamburg, especially on Nos. 4, 7, 21 and 25.

Nos. 1-23 and 26 exist without watermark, but they come from the same sheets as the watermarked stamps.

The stamps of Hamburg were superseded by those of the North German Confederation on Jan. 1, 1868.

HANOVER

LOCATION — Northern Germany
GOVT. — A former Kingdom
AREA — 14,893 sq. mi.
POP. — 3,191,000
CAPITAL — Hanover

Hanover was a member of the German Confederation and became in 1866 a province of Prussia.

10 Pfennigs = 1 Groschen
24 Gute Groschen = 1 Thaler
30 Silbergroschen = 1 Thaler (1858)

Values for unused stamps are for examples with original gum as defined in the catalogue introduction. Copies without gum sell for about 50-60% of the figures quoted.

Coat of Arms
A1 A2

Wmk. Square Frame

1850 Rose Gum Typo. *Imperf.*

1 A1 1g g blk, *gray bl* 3,400. 40.00
On cover, single franking 110.00
On cover, multiple franking 400.00

Full margins = 1mm.

See Nos. 2, 11.

The reprints have white gum and no watermark.

Values for used multiples

1 A1 1g g horiz. pair 130.00
1 A1 1g g vert. pair 3,400. 130.00
On cover *400.00*
1 A1 1g g horiz. strip of 3 *650.00*
1 A1 1g g vert. strip of 3 *1,200.* *650.00*
On cover *1,650.*
1 A1 1g g vert. strip of 4 *4,500.*
1 A1 1g g horiz.. strip of 4 —
On cover *10,000.*
1 A1 1g g block of 4 *7,000.*
On cover *28,500.*

Horizontal multiples are particularly scarce as the stamps were dispensed to the public in vertical strips

The off-cover vert. strip of 4 is unique.

1851-55 Wmk. 130

2 A1 1g g blk, *gray grn* 80.00 5.25
No gum 40.00
On cover, single franking 16.50
On cover, multiple franking 25.00
On cover with #3 *3,250.*
On cover with #3a *3,300.*
On cover with #4 *3,300.*
a. 1g g black, *yellow green* 775.00 26.00
No gum 275.00
On cover, single franking 77.50
On cover, multiple franking 100.00
b. Wmk. inverted *425.00* 200.00
On cover 400.00
c. As "a," wmk inverted 500.00
On cover 1,300.
3 A2 1/30th blk, *salmon* 100.00 42.50
No gum 60.00
On cover, single franking 100.00
On cover, multiple franking 200.00
On cover with other stamps 500.00
a. 1/30th black, *crimson* ('55) 100.00 42.50
No gum 60.00
On cover, single franking 77.50
On cover, multiple franking 200.00
On cover with other stamps 500.00
b. Bisect on cover —
c. Wmk. inverted 1,400.
d. As "a," wmk. inverted 400.00 210.00
On cover 500.00
5 A2 1/15th blk, *gray bl* 150.00 65.00
No gum 77.50
On cover, single franking 165.00
On cover, multiple franking 400.00
On cover with other stamps 490.00
a. Bisect on cover —
b. Wmk inverted *850.00*
On cover *2,300.*
6 A2 1/10th blk, *yellow* 190.00 55.00
No gum 100.00
On cover, single franking 100.00
On cover, multiple franking 490.00
On cover with other stamps 625.00
a. 1/10th black, *orange* 190.00 50.00
No gum 100.00
On cover, single franking 100.00
On cover, multiple franking 490.00
On cover with other stamps 625.00
b. Wmk. inverted 1,300.
c. As "a," wmk. inverted 1,300.

Full margins = 1mm.

Bisects Nos. 3b, 5a, 12a and 13a were used for ½g.

See Nos. 8, 12-13.

The 1/10th has been reprinted on unwatermarked paper, with white gum.

Values for horizontal pairs

2 A1 1g g black, *gray grn* 190.00 20.00
On cover *40.00*
On registered cover *175.00*
a. 1g g black, *yellow green* 100.00
On cover 275.00
On first telegraph form ('52) *20,000.*
On telegraph form ('56) *5,750.*
3 A2 1/30th black, *salmon* 325.00 165.00
No gum 200.00
On cover 525.00
a. 1/30th black, *crimson* 325.00 100.00
No gum 200.00
On cover 225.00
5 A2 1/15th black, *gray bl* 500.00 300.00
No gum 300.00
On cover 1,000.
6 A2 1/10th black, *yellow* 650.00 225.00
No gum 300.00
On cover 850.00
a. 1/10th black, *orange* 650.00 225.00
No gum 300.00
On cover 850.00

Values for vertical pairs

2 A1 1g g black, *gray grn* 180.00 20.00
On cover 40.00
a. 1g g black, *yellow green* 100.00
On cover 260.00
3 A2 1/30th black, *salmon* 400.00 200.00
On cover 650.00
a. 1/30th black, *crimson* 400.00 115.00
On cover 275.00
5 A2 1/15th black, *gray bl* 600.00 375.00
On cover 1,175.
6 A2 1/10th black, *yellow* 825.00 300.00
On cover 1,000.
a. 1/10th black, *orange* 825.00 300.00
On cover 1,000.

Values for horizontal strips of 3

2 A1 1g g black, *gray grn* *475.00* 100.00
On cover 250.00
a. 1g g black, *yellow green* 425.00 400.00
On cover 1,150.
3 A2 1/30th black, *salmon* 600.00 600.00
On cover 1,650.
a. 1/30th black, *crimson* 275.00 260.00
On cover 650.00
5 A2 1/15th black, *gray bl* 2,000. *2,000.*
On cover 5,000.
6 A2 1/10th black, *yellow* 1,300. 1,300.
On cover 2,600.
a. 1/10th black, *orange* 1,300. 1,300.
On cover 2,600.

Values for vertical strips of 3

2 A1 1g g black, *gray grn* *400.00* 85.00
On cover 200.00
a. 1g g black, *yellow green* 350.00 325.00
On cover 850.00
3 A2 1/30th black, *salmon* 750.00 725.00
On cover 2,000.
a. 1/30th black, *crimson* 325.00 350.00
On cover 825.00
5 A2 1/15th black, *gray bl* 2,500. 2,450.
On cover 6,000.
6 A2 1/10th black, *yellow* 1,650. 1,650.
On cover 3,250.
a. 1/10th black, *orange* 1,725. 1,625.
On cover 3,250

Values for vertical strips of 4

2 A1 1g g black, *gray grn* 850.00 *500.00*
On cover *1,300.*
6 A2 1/10th black, *yellow* *3,250.*

Values for vertical strips of 5

2 A1 1g g black, *gray grn* — *1,150.*

Values for blocks of 4

2 A1 1g g black, *gray grn* 1,300. *1,625.*
On cover 6,500.
a. 1g g black, *yellow green* 5,000.
3 A2 1/30th black, *salmon* 1,950.
a. 1/30th black, *crimson* 2,125.
5 A2 1/15th black, *gray bl* 2,600.
6 A2 1/10th black, *yellow* 1,750.
a. 1/10th black, *orange* 1,750.

Crown and Numeral — A3

1853 Wmk. 130

7 A3 3pf rose 400.00 250.00
No gum 250.00
On cover 650.00
a. 3pf dark lilac rose 1,650. 775.00
No gum 725.00
On cover 1,825.

Full margins = 1mm.

See Nos. 9, 16-17, 25.

The reprints of No. 7 have white gum.

Values for horizontal pairs

7 A3 3pf rose 975.00 650.00
On cover 1,300.
a. 3pf dark lilac rose — 2,300.
On cover 3,900.

Values for used vertical pairs

7 A3 3pf rose 650.00
a. 3pf dark lilac rose 2,300.

Values for used horizontal strips of 3

7 A3 3pf rose *1,300.*
a. 3pf dark lilac rose *2,500.*

Values for blocks of 4

7 A3 3pf rose 1,750. *3,250.*
a. 3pf dark lilac rose *6,500.*

Fine Network in Second Color

1855 Unwmk.

8 A2 1/10th blk & org 190.00 125.00
No gum 110.00
On cover 325.00
a. 1/10th black & yellow 325.00 190.00
No gum 195.00
On cover 500.00

Full margins = 1mm.

No. 8 with olive yellow network and other values with fine network are essays.

Values for horizontal pairs

8 A2 1/10th blk & org 650.00 500.00
No gum 400.00
On cover 1,300.
a. 1/10th black & yellow 650.00

Values for vertical pairs

8 A2 1/10th blk & org 490.00
a. 1/10th black & yellow —

Values for strips of 3

8 A2 1/10th blk & org 1,300.
a. 1/10th black & yellow 1,625.

Large Network in Second Color

1856-57

9 A3 3pf rose & blk 250.00 225.00
No gum 85.00
On cover 425.00
a. 3pf rose & gray 325.00 300.00
No gum 115.00
On cover 650.00
11 A1 1g g blk & grn 65.00 6.50
No gum 22.50
On cover 26.00
12 A2 1/30th blk & rose 125.00 26.00
No gum 45.00
On cover 65.00
a. Bisect on cover *13,500.*
b. 1/30th black & carmine 775.00 400.00
No gum 300.00
On cover 775.00
13 A2 1/15th blk & bl 100.00 60.00
No gum 32.50
On cover 165.00
a. Bisect on cover *6,500.*
14 A2 1/10th blk & org ('57) 650.00 45.00
No gum 300.00
On cover 130.00

Full margins = 1mm.

The reprints have white gum, and the network does not cover all the outer margin.

Values for pairs

9 A3 3pf rose & blk 775.00 500.00
On cover 1,100.
a. 3pf rose & gray 1,300. 650.00
On cover 1,300.
11 A1 1g g blk & grn 195.00 40.00
On cover 100.00
12 A2 1/30th blk & rose 325.00 85.00
On cover 165.00
b. 1/30th black & carmine 1,175.
On cover 165.00
13 A2 1/15th blk & bl 225.00 *260.00*
On cover 1,000.
14 A2 1/10th blk & org 225.00
On cover 850.00

Values for horizontal strips of 3

9 A3 3pf rose & blk 850.00
a. 3pf rose & gray 1,175.
11 A1 1g g blk & grn 325.00 200.00
On cover 500.00
12 A2 1/30th blk & rose 775.00 200.00
On cover 500.00
b. 1/30th black & carmine —
13 A2 1/15th blk & bl 400.00 *1,300.*
14 A2 1/10th blk & org 1,300.

Values for blocks of 4

9 A3 3pf rose & blk 1,300. 1,300.
On cover 3,250.
a. 3pf rose & gray 1,475. *1,650.*
On cover *4,000.*
11 A1 1g g blk & grn 800.00 *1,650.*
12 A2 1/30th blk & rose 900.00 *1,250.*
b. 1/30th black & carmine —
13 A2 1/15th blk & bl 1,175. —
14 A2 1/10th blk & org —

Without Network

1859-63

16 A3 3pf pink 110.00 *82.50*
Never hinged 195.00
No gum 52.50

On cover 325.00
a. 3pf carmine rose 65.00 72.50
Never hinged 130.00
No gum 26.00
On cover 200.00
17 A3 3pf grn (Drei Zehntel) ('63) 325.00 775.00
Never hinged 650.00
On cover 2,600.
On cover, single franking, local delivery 3,250.

Full margins = 1mm.

Values for pairs

16 A3 3pf 3pf pink 260.00 400.00
16a A3 3pf carmine rose 140.00 200.00
17 A3 3pf green 775.00 2,000.

Values for horizontal strips of 3

16 A3 3pf 3pf pink 400.00 650.00
16a A3 3pf carmine rose 225.00 400.00
On cover 1,300.
17 A3 3pf green 1,300. 3,250.
On cover 6,500.

Values for blocks of 4

16 A3 3pf 3pf pink 600.00 1,175.
16a A3 3pf carmine rose 325.00 775.00
On cover 5,000.
17 A3 3pf green 2,750. 6,500.

Copies of No. 25 with rouletting trimmed off sometimes pretend to be No. 17. Minimum size of No. 17 acknowledged as genuine: 21½x24½mm.

The reprints of No. 16 have pink gum instead of red; the extremities of the banderol point downward instead of outward.

Crown and Post Horn — A7

King George V — A8

1859-61 *Imperf.*

18 A7 ½g black ('60) 140.00 160.00
Never hinged 300.00
On cover 775.00
a. Rose gum 325.00 275.00
Never hinged 650.00
On cover 725.00
19 A8 1g rose 3.00 2.00
Never hinged 6.00
On cover 5.00
a. 1g vio rose 16.50 16.50
Never hinged 26.00
On cover 40.00
b. 1g carmine 65.00 26.00
Never hinged 115.00
On cover 65.00
c. Half used as ½g on cover 10,000.
20 A8 2g ultra 16.00 26.00
Never hinged 26.00
On cover 77.50
a. Half used as 1g on cover 7,000.
b. 2g dark blue 13.00 35.00
Never hinged 26.00
On cover 100.00
22 A8 3g yellow 200.00 50.00
Never hinged 325.00
On cover 130.00
a. 3g orange yellow 110.00 77.50
Never hinged 200.00
On cover 200.00
23 A8 3g brown ('61) 22.50 40.00
Never hinged 40.00
On cover 100.00
a. One third used as 1g on cover —
b. 3g gray brown ('61) 65.00 200.00
Never hinged 115.00
On cover 400.00
c. 3g black brown ('61) 325.00 325.00
Never hinged 650.00
On cover 650.00
24 A8 10g green ('61) 200.00 725.00
Never hinged 300.00
On cover 4,000.
On cover, single franking 5,000.

Full margins = 1mm.

Reprints of ½g are on thick toned paper with yellowish gum. Originals are on white paper with rose or white gum. Reprints exist tête bêche.

Reprints of 3g yellow and 3g brown have white or pinkish gum. Originals have rose or orange gum.

Values for pairs

18 A7 ½g black 325.00 400.00
On cover 1,050.
a. Rose gum 850.00 650.00
On cover 1,825.
19 A8 1g rose 6.00 6.50
On cover 26.00
a. 1g vio rose 35.00 40.00
On cover 100.00
b. 1g carmine 165.00 65.00
On cover 200.00
20 A8 2g ultra 35.00 85.00
On cover 260.00
b. 2g dark blue 30.00 115.00
On cover 325.00
22 A8 3g yellow 450.00 120.00
On cover 400.00
a. 3g orange yellow 325.00 165.00
On cover 500.00
23 A8 3g brown 45.00 200.00
On cover 600.00
b. 3g gray brown 165.00 500.00
On cover 1,175.
c. 3g black brown 775.00 775.00

24 A8 10g green 425.00 2,250.
On cover 9,750.

Values for horizontal strips of 3

18 A7 ½g black 850.00 1,950.
a. Rose gum 1,300. —
19 A8 1g rose 9.00 40.00
On cover 85.00
a. 1g vio rose 60.00 115.00
On cover 260.00
b. 1g carmine 130.00
On cover 325.00
20 A8 2g ultra 60.00 400.00
b. 2g dark blue 45.00 650.00
22 A8 3g yellow 725.00 200.00
a. 3g orange yellow 600.00 300.00
23 A8 3g brown 72.50 725.00
On cover 1,650.
b. 3g gray brown 275.00 600.00
c. 3g black brown —
24 A8 10g green 650.00 —

Values for blocks of 4

18 A7 ½g black 2,600. 5,250.
a. Rose gum 1,800. 2,900.
19 A8 1g rose 16.50 2,000.
a. 1g vio rose 100.00
b. 1g carmine 85.00 850.00
20 A8 2g ultra 100.00 1,850.
b. 2g dark blue 72.50
22 A8 3g yellow 1,300. 325.00
a. 3g orange yellow 1,175. 450.00
23 A8 3g brown 105.00 2,600.
b. 3g gray brown 400.00 —
c. 3g black brown — —
24 A8 10g green 1,000. 6,000.

1864 White Gum *Perce en Arc 16*

25 A3 3pf grn (Drei Zehntel) 26.00 50.00
Never hinged 50.00
On cover 130.00
26 A7 ½g black 225.00 225.00
Never hinged 400.00
On cover 500.00
27 A8 1g rose 6.50 2.50
Never hinged 13.00
On cover 6.50
28 A8 2g ultra 100.00 50.00
Never hinged 200.00
On cover 140.00
a. Half used as 1g on cover —
29 A8 3g brown 60.00 60.00
Never hinged 105.00
On cover 115.00

Reprints of 3g are percé en arc 13½.

Rose Gum

25a A3 3pf green 65.00 65.00
Never hinged 115.00
On cover 165.00
26a A7 ½g black 400.00 375.00
On cover 850.00
27a A8 1g rose 32.50 20.00
Never hinged 50.00
On cover 40.00
29a A8 3g brown 975.00 975.00
On cover 2,000.

Used examples of Nos. 25a-29a retain the rose color on the reverse after the gum has been removed.

Values for pairs

25 A3 3pf green 65.00 165.00
On cover 325.00
26 A7 ½g black 600.00 500.00
On cover 975.00
27 A8 1g rose 16.50 16.50
On cover 40.00
28 A8 2g ultra 260.00 130.00
On cover 325.00
29 A8 3g brown 130.00 165.00
On cover 325.00

Rose Gum

25a A3 3pf green 200.00 200.00
On cover 450.00
26a A7 ½g black 975.00 850.00
On cover 1,650.
27a A8 1g rose 77.50 50.00
On cover 100.00
29a A8 3g brown 2,600. 3,300.

Values for horizontal strips of 3

25 A3 3pf green 100.00 260.00
26 A7 ½g black 850.00 825.00
27 A8 1g rose 40.00 65.00
On cover 165.00
28 A8 2g ultra 500.00 850.00
On cover 1,300.
29 A8 3g brown 200.00 500.00

Rose Gum

25a A3 3pf green 300.00 325.00
26a A7 ½g black 1,450. 1,600.
27a A8 1g rose 165.00 115.00
On cover 275.00
29a A8 3g brown —

Values for blocks of 4

25 A3 3pf green 130.00 650.00
On cover 1,650.
26 A7 ½g black 1,450. 2,250.
27 A8 1g rose 65.00 1,000.
28 A8 2g ultra 775.00 1,100.
29 A8 3g brown 275.00 1,600.

Rose Gum

25a A3 3pf green 650.00 775.00
On cover 1,650.
26a A7 ½g black 2,600. 2,750.
27a A8 1g rose 300.00 1,300.
29a A8 3g brown 6,000. —

The stamps of Prussia superseded those of Hanover on Oct. 1, 1866.

LUBECK

LOCATION — Situated on an arm of the Baltic Sea between the former German States of Holstein and Mecklenburg.
GOVT. — Former Free City and State
AREA — 115 sq. mi.
POP. — 136,413
CAPITAL — Lubeck

Lubeck was a member of the German Confederation and became part of the German Empire in 1870.

16 Schillings = 1 Mark

Values for Nos. 1-7 unused are for copies without gum. Nos. 6 and 7 with gum sell for about twice the figures quoted. Values for Nos. 8-14 unused are for examples with original gum as defined in the catalogue introduction. Nos. 8-14 without gum sell for about 50-60% of the figures quoted.

Coat of Arms — A1

1859 Litho. Wmk. 148 *Imperf.*

1 A1 ½g gray lilac 400.00 1,700.
With original gum 1,900.
On cover 5,400.
On cover, single franking 8,000.
2 A1 1s orange 400.00 1,700.
With original gum 1,950.
On cover 3,400.
3 A1 2s brown 17.00 200.00
With original gum 90.00
On cover 650.00
a. Value in words reads "ZWEI EIN HALB" 325.00 6,000.
On cover 45,000.
4 A1 2½s rose 35.00 750.00
With original gum 175.00
On cover 1,700.
5 A1 4s green 16.00 500.00
With original gum 65.00
On cover 1,250.
a. 4s yellow green 22.50

Full margins = ¾mm.

Values for pairs

1 A1 ½g gray lilac 1,350. —
2 A1 1s orange 4,750.
On cover 5,500.
3 A1 2s brown 40.00 1,000.
On cover 2,300.
a. Value in words reads "ZWEI EIN HALB" 775.00 —
4 A1 2½s rose 100.00 4,000.
On cover 5,500.
5 A1 4s green 36.00 —
On cover 4,000.
a. 4s yellow green 65.00

Values for blocks of 4

1 A1 ½g gray lilac —
2 A1 1s orange —
3 A1 2s brown 90.00
a. Value in words reads "ZWEI EIN HALB" —
4 A1 2½s rose 260.00
5 A1 4s green 77.50
5a A1 4s yel grn 160.00

1862 Unwmk.

6 A1 ½s lilac 12.00 1,300.
With original gum 26.00
On cover 3,250.
On cover, single franking 6,250.
7 A1 1s yellow orange 21.00 1,300.
With original gum 65.00
On cover 3,250.

Full margins = ¾mm.

The reprints of the 1859-62 issues are unwatermarked and printed in bright colors.

Values for pairs

6 A1 ½s lilac 26.00 4,250.
7 A1 1s yellow orange 52.50 4,250.

Values for strips of 3

6 A1 ½s lilac 42.50
7 A1 1s yellow orange 77.50

Values for blocks of 4

6 A1 ½s lilac 60.00
7 A1 1s yellow orange 105.00

A2

A3

1863 *Rouletted 11½*

Eagle embossed

8 A2 ½s green 32.50 52.50
Never hinged 77.50
No gum 10.00
On cover 325.00
On cover, single franking 325.00
9 A2 1s orange 100.00 125.00
Never hinged 225.00
No gum 65.00
On cover 300.00
a. Rouletted 10 160.00 400.00
Never hinged 400.00
No gum 10.00
On cover 2,600.
10 A2 2s rose 20.00 45.00
Never hinged 50.00
No gum 6.50
On cover 200.00
11 A2 2½s ultra 90.00 325.00
Never hinged 200.00
No gum 45.00
On cover 1,000.
12 A2 4s bister 40.00 85.00
Never hinged 85.00
No gum 15.00
On cover 275.00

The reprints are imperforate and without embossing.

Values for pairs

8 A2 ½s green 85.00 200.00
Never hinged 260.00
On cover 325.00
9 A2 1s orange 260.00 275.00
Never hinged 600.00
a. Rouletted 10 525.00 2,750.
10 A2 2s rose 45.00 130.00
Never hinged 115.00
On cover 225.00
11 A2 2½s ultra 250.00 1,000.
Never hinged 525.00
On cover 2,100.
12 A2 4s bister 90.00 275.00
Never hinged 200.00
On cover 725.00

Values for strips of 3

8 A2 ½s green 130.00 140.00
Never hinged 325.00
On cover 1,000.
9 A2 1s orange 500.00 450.00
Never hinged 1,100.
a. Rouletted 10 850.00 10,000.
10 A2 2s rose 72.50 650.00
Never hinged 175.00
11 A2 2½s ultra 400.00 1,800.
Never hinged 1,100.
12 A2 4s bister 130.00 800.00
Never hinged 325.00

Values for blocks of 4

8 A2 ½s green 180.00 650.00
Never hinged 450.00
On cover 2,000.
9 A2 1s orange 650.00
a. Rouletted 10 1,100.
10 A2 2s rose 100.00
Never hinged 225.00
11 A2 2½s ultra 500.00
12 A2 4s bister 450.00
Never hinged 450.00

1864 Litho. *Imperf.*

13 A3 1¼s dark brown 32.50 72.50
Never hinged 77.50
No gum 13.00
On cover 200.00
a. 1¼s reddish brown 21.00 125.00
Never hinged 45.00
No gum 6.50
On cover 360.00

Values for pairs

13 A3 1¼s dark brown 90.00 325.00
Never hinged 200.00
No gum 32.50
a. 1¼s reddish brown 65.00 600.00
Never hinged 130.00
No gum 23.00

Values for used strips of 3

13 A3 1¼s dark brown 140.00 1,300.
Never hinged 325.00
No gum 60.00
a. 1¼s reddish brown 125.00 2,000.
Never hinged 260.00
No gum 42.50

Values for blocks of 4

13 A3 1¼s dark brown 180.00
No gum 52.50
a. 1¼s reddish brown 180.00
No gum 85.00

A4

1865 *Rouletted 11½*

Eagle embossed

14 A4 1½s red lilac 21.00 65.00
Never hinged 45.00
No gum 8.00
On cover 180.00

Value for pairs

14 A4 1½s red lilac 45.00 240.00
Never hinged 105.00
No gum 18.00

Value for strip of 3

14 A4 1½s red lilac 72.50 800.00
Never hinged 150.00

	No gum	30.00	

Value for block of 4

14	A4 1½s red lilac	105.00	
	Never hinged	225.00	
	No gum	42.50	

The reprints are imperforate and without embossing.

Counterfeit cancellations are found on #1-14.

The stamps of Lübeck were superseded by those of the North German Confederation on Jan. 1, 1868.

MECKLENBURG-SCHWERIN

LOCATION — In northern Germany, bordering on the Baltic Sea.
GOVT. — Grand Duchy
AREA — 5,065 sq. mi. (approx.)
POP. — 674,000 (approx.)
CAPITAL — Schwerin

Mecklenburg-Schwerin was a member of the German Confederation and became part of the German Empire in 1870.

48 Schillings = 1 Thaler

Values for unused stamps are for examples with original gum as defined in the catalogue introduction. Copies without gum sell for about 70% of the figures quoted.

Coat of Arms
A1 A2

1856 Unwmk. Typo. *Imperf.*

1	A1 Four ¼s red	125.00	100.00
	Never hinged	175.00	
	No gum	72.50	
	On cover		200.00
a.	¼s red	12.50	10.00
	No gum	6.75	
	Single on cover		200.00
	Two ¼s on cover		140.00
	Two ¼s on postal envelope		175.00
	Three ¼s on cover		225.00
	Five ¼s on cover		340.00
	Six ¼s on cover		—
	Seven ¼s on cover		—
2	A2 3s yellow	82.50	45.00
	Never hinged	140.00	
	No gum	55.00	
	On cover		175.00
a.	3s orange	67.50	45.00
	Never hinged	120.00	
	No gum	47.50	
	On cover		175.00
3	A2 5s blue	190.00	225.00
	Never hinged	325.00	
	No gum	125.00	
	On cover		875.00

Full margins: #1 = ¾mm; #2-3 = 1¼mm.

Covers: Each multiple of No. 1a corresponds to a rate based on distance and destination. Values are for covers correctly franked.

See Nos. 4, 6-8.

Values for pairs

1	*A1 Four ¼s red*	*675.00*	*340.00*
	No gum	*400.00*	
	On cover		*675.00*
a.	*¼s red*	*27.50*	*20.00*
	No gum	*16.50*	
	On cover		*140.00*
2	*A2 3s yellow*	*275.00*	*260.00*
	No gum	*160.00*	
	On cover		*675.00*
a.	*3s orange*	*275.00*	*260.00*
	No gum	*160.00*	
	On cover		*675.00*
3	*A2 5s blue*	*1,200.*	*1,500.*
	No gum	*725.00*	
	On cover		*3,400.*

A3

1864-67 *Rouletted 11½*

4	A1 Four ¼s red	*2,250.*	*1,500.*
	No gum	1,600.	
	Four ¼s on cover		4,250.
a.	¼s red	140.00	200.00
	No gum	105.00	
	Single on cover		1,350.
b.	Pair of ¼s red		500.00
	On cover		1,650.
	On postal stationery		2,000.
5	A3 Four ¼s red	52.50	42.50
	Never hinged	92.50	
	No gum	30.00	
	Four ¼s on cover		92.50
a.	¼s red	6.75	6.75
	Never hinged	12.00	
	No gum	3.50	
	¼s on cover or postal stationery		95.00
	Two ¼s on cover		100.00
6	A2 2s gray lil ('67)	125.00	*1,350.*
	Never hinged	210.00	
	No gum	57.50	
	On cover		*9,250.*
a.	2s red violet ('66)	200.00	200.00
	Never hinged	325.00	
	No gum	92.50	
	On cover		925.00
7	A2 3s org yel, wide margin ('67)	35.00	*250.00*
	Never hinged	52.50	
	No gum	15.00	
	On cover		800.00
a.	Narrow margin ('65)	140.00	100.00
	Never hinged	225.00	
	No gum	67.50	
	Single on cover		675.00
8	A2 5s bister brn	125.00	*200.00*
	Never hinged	190.00	
	No gum	60.00	
	On cover		1,000.
a.	Thick paper	200.00	*275.00*
	Never hinged	325.00	
	No gum	100.00	
	On cover		1,200.
b.	Ribbed paper	250.00	250.00
	Never hinged	400.00	
	No gum	140.00	
	On cover		1,100.

The overall size of #7, including margin, is 24½x24½mm. That of #7a is 23½x23mm.

Covers: Each multiple of Nos. 4-5 corresponds to a rate based on distance and destination. Values are for covers correctly franked.

The bister on white paper was not issued. Value $12.

Values for pairs

4	*A1 Four ¼s red*		*4,750.*
	On cover		*13,500.*
5	*A3 Four ¼s red*	*120.00*	*110.00*
	Never hinged	*225.00*	
	On cover		*200.00*
6	*A2 2s gray lil ('67)*	*300.00*	*—*
	No gum	*140.00*	
a.	*2s red violet ('66)*	*525.00*	*1,200.*
	No gum	*250.00*	
	On cover		*3,400.*
7	*A2 3s org yel, wide margin ('67)*	*120.00*	*1,150.*
	No gum	*42.50*	
	On cover		*3,000.*
a.	*Narrow margin ('65)*	*600.00*	*300.00*
	No gum	*275.00*	
	On cover		*1,200.*
8	*A2 5s bister brn*	*300.00*	*925.00*
	No gum	*140.00*	
	On cover		*1,350.*
a.	*Thick paper*	*525.00*	*1,150.*
	No gum	*275.00*	
	On cover		*1,450.*
b.	*Ribbed paper*		*—*

Counterfeit cancellations exist on those stamps valued higher used than unused.

These stamps were superseded by those of the North German Confederation on Jan. 1, 1868.

MECKLENBURG-STRELITZ

LOCATION — In northern Germany, divided by Mecklenburg-Schwerin
GOVT. — Grand Duchy
AREA — 1,131 sq. mi.
POP. — 106,347
CAPITAL — Neustrelitz

Mecklenburg-Strelitz was a member of the German Confederation and became part of the German Empire in 1870.

30 Silbergroschen = 48 Schillings = 1 Thaler

Values for unused stamps are for examples with original gum as defined in the catalogue introduction. Copies without gum sell for about 50% of the figures quoted.

Coat of Arms
A1 A2

Rouletted 11½

1864 Unwmk. Embossed

1	A1 ¼sg orange	150.00	*2,000.*
	Never hinged	200.00	
	No gum	67.50	
	On cover		*67,500.*
a.	¼sg yellow orange	275.00	*3,400.*
	Never hinged	500.00	
	No gum	160.00	
	On cover		—
2	A1 ⅓sg green	67.50	*1,150.*
	Never hinged	115.00	
	No gum	27.50	
	On cover		*8,750.*
a.	⅓sg dark green	125.00	*2,000.*
	Never hinged	250.00	
	No gum	62.50	
	On cover		*12,500.*
3	A1 1sch violet	225.00	*2,700.*
	Never hinged	425.00	
	No gum	100.00	
	On cover		*9,000.*
4	A2 1sg rose	125.00	160.00
	Never hinged	225.00	
	No gum	55.00	
	On cover		450.00
5	A2 2sg ultra	35.00	*675.00*
	Never hinged	72.50	
	No gum	15.00	
	On cover		1,700.
6	A2 3sg bister	27.50	*1,100.*
	Never hinged	60.00	
	No gum	12.00	
	On cover		4,000.

Counterfeit cancellations abound.

Values for pairs

1	*A1 ¼sg orange*	*300.00*	*4,750.*
	No gum	*150.00*	
a.	*¼sg yellow orange*	*875.00*	*—*
	No gum	*400.00*	
2	*A1 ⅓sg green*	*150.00*	*2,350.*
	No gum	*67.50*	
	On cover		*9,500.*
a.	*⅓sg dark green*	*300.00*	*5,000.*
	No gum	*150.00*	
	On cover		*12,500.*
3	*A1 1sch violet*	*550.00*	*—*
	No gum	*275.00*	
4	*A2 1sg rose*	*275.00*	*450.00*
	No gum	*120.00*	
	On cover		*875.00*
5	*A2 2sg ultra*	*80.00*	*2,000.*
	Never hinged	*160.00*	
	No gum	*27.50*	
6	*A2 3sg bister*	*60.00*	*3,000.*
	No gum	*27.50*	
	On cover		*16,500.*

These stamps were superseded by those of the North German Confederation in 1868.

OLDENBURG

LOCATION — In northwestern Germany, bordering on the North Sea.
GOVT. — Grand Duchy
AREA — 2,482 sq. mi.
POP. — 483,042 (1910)
CAPITAL — Oldenburg

Oldenburg was a member of the German Confederation and became part of the German Empire in 1870.

30 Silbergroschen = 1 Thaler
30 Groschen = 1 Thaler

Values for unused stamps are for examples with original gum as defined in the catalogue introduction. Copies without gum sell for about 50% of the figures quoted.

A1 A2

1852-55 Unwmk. Litho. *Imperf.*

1	A1 ⅟₃₀th blk, *blue*	325.00	26.00
	No gum	180.00	
	On cover		75.00
2	A1 ⅟₁₅th blk, *rose*	525.00	30.00
	No gum	190.00	
	On cover		75.00
3	A1 ⅟₁₀th blk, *yellow*	750.00	82.50
	No gum	440.00	
	On cover		190.00
4	A2 ⅓sgr blk, *grn* ('55)	1,100.	900.00
	No gum	625.00	
	On newspaper or circular		*1,500.*
	On cover		*5,500.*

Full margins = 1mm.

There are three types of Nos. 1 and 2.

Values for pairs

1	*A1 ⅟₃₀th black, blue*	*1,100.*	*375.00*
	No gum	*600.00*	
	On cover		*900.00*
2	*A1 ⅟₁₅th black, rose*	*7,500.*	*525.00*
	No gum	*4,100.*	
	On cover		*2,200.*
3	*A1 ⅟₁₀th black, yellow*		*825.00*
	On cover		*2,200.*
4	*A2 ⅓sgr black, grn*	*5,600.*	*2,600.*
	No gum	*3,000.*	

Values for strips of 3

1	*A1 ⅟₃₀th black, blue*	*2,200.*	*375.00*
	No gum	*1,250.*	
	On cover		*1,250.*
2	*A1 ⅟₁₅th black, rose*		*2,600.*
3	*A1 ⅟₁₀th black, yellow*		*2,200.*
4	*A2 ⅓sgr black, grn*	*11,000.*	*7,400.*
	No gum	*6,700.*	
	On cover		*14,750.*

Values for blocks of 4

1	*A1 ⅟₃₀th blk, blue*	*3,300.*	*—*
	No gum	*1,900.*	
2	*A1 ⅟₁₅th black, rose*	*—*	*—*
	On cover		*38,500.*
3	*A1 ⅟₁₀th black, yellow*	*—*	*—*
	On cover		*38,500.*
4	*A2 ⅓sgr black, grn*	*21,500.*	
	No gum	*11,000.*	

A3 A4

1859

5	A3 ⅓g blk, *green*	2,200.	*2,650.*
	On cover		*31,500.*
	On newspaper or circular		*18,000.*
6	A3 1g blk, *blue*	600.00	35.00
	On cover		87.50
7	A3 2g blk, *rose*	800.00	500.00
	On cover		*2,300.*
8	A3 3g blk, *yellow*	800.00	500.00
	On cover		*2,100.*
a.	"OLBENBURG"	1,200.	1,000.
	On cover		*2,850.*

Full margins = 1½mm.

See Nos. 10, 13-15.

Values for pairs

5	*A3 ⅓g black, green*		*9,100.*
6	*A3 1g black, blue*		*110.00*
7	*A3 2g black, rose*		*2,200.*
8	*A3 3g black, yellow*		*3,300.*

Values for strips of 3

5	*A3 ⅓g black, green*		*26,000.*
6	*A3 1g black, blue*		*475.00*
7	*A3 2g black, rose*		*13,750.*
8	*A3 3g black, yellow*		*14,250.*

1861

9	A4 ¼g orange	250.00	*3,300.*
	On cover		*20,000.*
10	A3 ⅓g green	375.00	*700.00*
	On cover		*5,000.*
	On cover, single franking		*10,750.*
a.	⅓g bluish green	375.00	*700.00*
	On cover		*5,000.*
	On cover, single franking		*10,750.*
b.	⅓g moss green	1,400.	*2,300.*
	On cover		*9,400.*
	On cover, single franking		*18,250.*
c.	"OLDEIBURG"	*600.00*	*1,000.*
d.	"Dritto"	*600.00*	*1,000.*
e.	"Drittd"	*600.00*	*1,000.*
f.	Printed on both sides		*5,000.*
12	A4 ½g redsh brn	350.00	400.00
	On cover		*2,200.*
a.	½g dark brown	350.00	400.00
	On cover		*2,200.*
13	A3 1g blue	175.00	125.00
	On cover		290.00
a.	1g gray blue	375.00	200.00
	On cover		525.00
b.	Printed on both sides		*3,750.*
14	A3 2g red	350.00	350.00
	On cover		*1,650.*
15	A3 3g yellow	350.00	325.00
	On cover		*2,200.*
a.	"OLDEIBURG"	*600.00*	*600.00*
b.	Printed on both sides		*5,000.*

Full margins = 1mm.

Forged cancellations are found on Nos. 9, 10, 12 and their minor varieties.

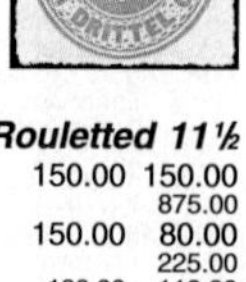

Coat of Arms — A5

1862 Embossed *Rouletted 11½*

16	A5 ⅓g green	150.00	150.00
	On cover		875.00
17	A5 ½g orange	150.00	80.00
	On cover		225.00
a.	½g orange red	190.00	110.00
	On cover		290.00
18	A5 1g rose	92.50	11.50
	On cover		32.50
19	A5 2g ultra	150.00	37.50
	On cover		110.00
20	A5 3g bister	175.00	40.00
	On cover		110.00

1867 *Rouletted 10*

21 A5 ⅓g green 19.00 *450.00*
On cover *1,900.*
22 A5 ½g orange 19.00 *300.00*
On cover *1,250.*
23 A5 1g rose 8.00 *37.50*
On cover *125.00*
a. Half used as ½g on cover —
24 A5 2g ultra 8.00 *325.00*
On cover *1,750.*
25 A5 3g bister 20.00 *250.00*
On cover *1,400.*

Forged cancellations are found on #21-25.

The stamps of Oldenburg were replaced by those of the North German Confederation on Jan. 1, 1868.

PRUSSIA

LOCATION — The greater part of northern Germany.
GOVT. — Independent Kingdom
AREA — 134,650 sq. mi.
POP. — 40,165,219 (1910)
CAPITAL — Berlin

Prussia was a member of the German Confederation and became part of the German Empire in 1870.

12 Pfennigs = 1 Silbergroschen
60 Kreuzer = 1 Gulden (1867)

Values for unused stamps are for examples with original gum as defined in the catalogue introduction. Copies without gum sell for about 50% of the figures quoted.

King Frederick William IV
A1 A2

1850-56 Engr. Wmk. 162 *Imperf.*

Background of Crossed Lines

1 A1 4pf yel grn ('56) 100.00 65.00
On cover 210.00
a. 4pf dark green 150.00 110.00
On cover 290.00
2 A1 6pf (½sg) red org 75.00 45.00
On cover 190.00
3 A2 1sg black, *rose* 75.00 7.50
On cover 20.00
a. 1sg black, *bright red* *18,750.* 400.00
On cover *1,400.*
4 A2 2sg black, *blue* 80.00 11.50
On cover 52.50
a. Half used as 1sg on cover —
5 A2 3sg black, *yellow* 95.00 11.00
On cover 26.00
a. 3sg black, *orange buff* 300.00 30.00
On cover 90.00

Full margins = ½mm.

See Nos. 10-13.

Values for pairs

1 A1 4pf yellow green 225.00 150.00
On cover 375.00
1a A1 4pf dark green 440.00 260.00
On cover 600.00
2 A1 6pf (½ sgr) red orange 225.00 110.00
On cover 375.00
3 A1 1sg black, *rose* 190.00 19.00
On cover 45.00
a. 1sg black, *bright red* 900.00
On cover 2,200.
4 A2 2sg black, *blue* 225.00 55.00
On cover 110.00
5 A2 3sg black, *yellow* 225.00 45.00
On cover 110.00
a. 3sg black, *orange buff* 110.00
On cover 440.00

Reprints exist on watermarked and unwatermarked paper.

A3 A4

Solid Background

1857 Typo. Unwmk.

6 A3 1sg rose 275.00 32.50
On cover 72.50
a. 1sg carmine rose 300.00 40.00
On cover 110.00
7 A3 2sg blue 1,100. 67.50
On cover 225.00
a. 2sg dark blue 1,500. 95.00
On cover 360.00
b. Half used as 1sg on cover —
8 A3 3sg orange 125.00 35.00
On cover 110.00
a. 3sg yellow 1,250. 82.50
On cover 325.00
b. 3sg deep orange 700.00 100.00
On cover 360.00

Full margins = 1¾mm.

The reprints of Nos. 6-8 have a period instead of a colon after "SILBERGR."

Thin translucent paper

6b A3 1sg rose 460.00 80.00
6c A3 1sg carmine rose 460.00 92.50
7c A3 2sg blue 80.00
7d A3 2sg dark blue 1,500. 80.00
8c A3 3sg orange 45.00
8d A3 3sg yellow 190.00
8e A3 3sg deep orange 450.00

Values for pairs

6 A3 1sg rose 600.00 60.00
On cover 180.00
a. 1sg carmine rose 725.00 85.00
On cover 225.00
7 A3 2sg blue 175.00
On cover 550.00
a. 2sg dark blue 360.00
8 A3 3sg orange 360.00 92.50
On cover 300.00
a. 3sg yellow 225.00
On cover 600.00
b. 3sg deep orange 225.00
On cover 725.00

Background of Crossed Lines

1858-60 Typo.

9 A4 4pf green 62.50 27.50
On cover 130.00

Engr.

10 A1 6pf (½sg) org ('59) 160.00 125.00
On cover 525.00
a. 6pf (½sg) brick red 225.00 160.00
On cover 775.00

Typo.

11 A2 1sg rose 27.50 2.00
On cover 11.50
12 A2 2sg blue 95.00 14.00
On cover 60.00
a. 2sg dark blue 125.00 35.00
On cover 130.00
b. Half used as 1sg on cover —
13 A2 3sg orange 82.50 12.00
On cover 52.50
a. 3sg yellow 125.00 14.00
On cover 60.00

Full margins: Nos. 9, 11-13 = ¾mm; No. 10 = ½mm.

Values for pairs

9 A4 4pf green 130.00 52.50
On cover 225.00
10 A1 6pf (½sgr) orange 400.00 260.00
On cover 225.00
a. 6pf (½sgr) brick red 460.00 325.00
On cover 875.00
11 A2 1sg rose 50.00 4.50
On cover 23.00
12 A2 2sg blue 190.00 45.00
On cover 110.00
a. 2sg dark blue 300.00 92.50
On cover 300.00
13 A2 3sg orange 160.00 30.00
On cover 70.00
a. 3sg yellow 250.00 45.00
On cover 92.50

Coat of Arms
A6 A7

1861-67 Embossed *Rouletted 11½*

14 A6 3pf red lilac ('67) 22.50 32.50
On cover 110.00
a. 3pf red violet ('65) 275.00 225.00
On cover 690.00
15 A6 4pf yellow green 8.25 7.00
On cover 50.00
a. 4pf green 35.00 35.00
On cover 130.00
16 A6 6pf orange 8.25 12.00
On cover 52.50
a. 6pf vermilion 100.00 52.50
On cover 150.00
17 A7 1sg rose 2.75 .65
On cover 3.50
18 A7 2sg ultra 8.25 1.25
On cover 8.50
a. 2sg blue 325.00 27.50
On cover 110.00
20 A7 3sg bister 7.75 1.60
On cover 8.00
a. 3sg gray brown ('65) 325.00 27.50
On cover 70.00

Values for pairs

14 A6 3pf red lilac 50.00 *100.00*
On cover 250.00
a. 3pf red violet 600.00 *650.00*
On cover 1,700.
15 A6 4pf yellow green 19.00 *20.00*
On cover 160.00
a. 4pf green 90.00 *90.00*
On cover 300.00
16 A6 6pf orange 21.00 *35.00*
On cover 250.00
a. 6pf vermilion 260.00 150.00
On cover 300.00
17 A7 1sg rose 8.25 2.00
On cover 5.00
18 A7 2sg ultramarine 19.00 3.75
On cover 6.00
a. 2sg blue 775.00 110.00
On cover 350.00
20 A7 3sg bistre 21.00 6.50
On cover 30.00
a. 3sg gray brown 750.00 80.00
On cover 180.00

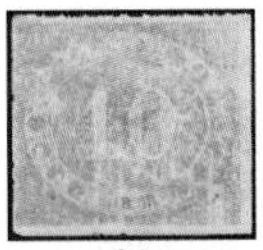

A8 A9

Typographed in Reverse on Paper Resembling Goldbeater's Skin

1866 *Rouletted 10*

21 A8 10sg rose 57.50 *57.50*
On cover —
On cover, single franking 1,300.
On parcel post receipt card 400.00
22 A9 30sg blue 70.00 *110.00*
On cover —
On parcel post receipt card 1,100.

Values for pairs

21 A8 10sg rose 250.00 120.00
On parcel post receipt card 725.00
22 A9 30sg blue 140.00 250.00
On parcel post receipt card 1,900.

Perfect copies of #21-22 are extremely rare.

Covers: Values for Nos. 21-22 on covers and parcel post receipt cards are for stamps used in 1866-1867. Later items are worth considerably less. Covers bearing stamps in perfect condition are extremely rare and are worth much more than the value stated.

See Nos. 4, 6-8.

A10

1867 Embossed *Rouletted 16*

23 A10 1kr green 21.00 *35.00*
On cover 190.00
24 A10 2kr orange 35.00 *77.50*
On cover 450.00
25 A10 3kr rose 17.50 *21.00*
On cover 70.00
26 A10 6kr ultra 17.50 *35.00*
On cover 150.00
27 A10 9kr bister brown 22.50 *37.50*
On cover 150.00

Values for pairs

23 A10 1kr green 45.00 *70.00*
On cover 180.00
24 A10 2kr orange 70.00 *175.00*
On cover 550.00
25 A10 3kr rose 37.50 *60.00*
On cover 225.00
26 A10 6kr ultramarine 37.50 *82.50*
On cover 260.00
27 A10 9kr bister brown 55.00 *77.50*
On cover 360.00

Imperforate stamps of the above sets are proofs.

The stamps of Prussia were superseded by those of the North German Confederation on Jan. 1, 1868.

OFFICIAL STAMPS
See Germany Nos. OL1-OL15.

SAXONY

LOCATION — In central Germany
GOVT. — Kingdom
AREA — 5,787 sq. mi.
POP. — 2,500,000 (approx.)
CAPITAL — Dresden

Saxony was a member of the German Confederation and became a part of the German Empire in 1870.

10 Pfennings = 1 Neu-Groschen
30 Neu-Groschen = 1 Thaler

Values for unused stamps are for examples with original gum as defined in the catalogue introduction. Copies without gum sell for about 50-60% of the figures quoted.

A1

1850 Unwmk. Typo. *Imperf.*

1 A1 3pf brick red *5,500.* *5,250.*
No gum 3,000.
On cover or wrapper *14,750.*
a. 3pf cherry red *8,750.* *13,250.*
No gum 5,600.
On cover or wrapper *30,000.*
b. 3pf brown red *8,750.* *9,000.*
No gum 5,600.
On cover or wrapper *22,500.*

Full margins = 1mm.

There are vertical dividing lines between stamps.

Values for pairs

1 A1 3pf brick red *14,750.* *16,000.*
No gum *8,750.*
On cover or wrapper *28,000.*
1a A1 3pf cherry red *19,000.* *38,000.*
No gum *17,000.*
On cover or wrapper *66,000.*
1b A1 3pf brown red *30,000.* *30,000.*
No gum *17,000.*
On cover or wrapper *60,000.*

Values for strips of 3

1 A1 '3pf brick red *38,000.* *38,000.*

Values for strips of 4 or blocks of 4

1 A1 3pf brick red *137,500.* *165,000.*
1b A1 3pf brown red *165,000.*

Cancellations and usages

1 A1 3pf brick red, *pen cancelled* *5,250.*
On cover, wrapper or circular *15,000.*
1 A1 3pf brick red, *with mute canceller* *5,500.*
On cover, wrapper or circular *19,000.*
1 A1 3pf brick red, *with numeral cancellation,* from *7,100.*
On cover, wrapper or circular —
1 A1 3pf brick red, pair or two singles on local delivery cover *33,000.*

Coat of Arms — A2

Frederick Augustus II — A3

1851

2 A2 3pf green 100.00 72.50
No gum 57.50
On cover 150.00
a. 3pf yellow green 1,350. 600.00
No gum 900.00
On cover 1,350.

Nos. 2 and 2a are valued with the margin just touching the design in one or two places. Copies with margins all around sell considerably higher.

1851-52 Engr.

3 A3 ½ng black, *gray* 52.50 8.25
On cover 32.50
a. ½ng pale blue (error) *19,000.*
5 A3 1ng black, *rose* 82.50 7.00
On cover 22.50
6 A3 2ng black, *pale bl* 200.00 40.00
On cover 130.00
7 A3 2ng blk, *dk bl*('52) 625.00 37.50
On cover 92.50
8 A3 3ng black, *yellow* 125.00 17.50
On cover 60.00

Full margins = ¾mm.

King John I — A4

1855-60

9 A4 ½ng black, *gray* 8.25 2.00
On cover 10.50
a. "1½₂" at left or right — —
On cover 1,300.
10 A4 1ng black, *rose* 8.25 2.00
On cover 10.50
11 A4 2ng black, *dark blue* 17.50 8.25
On cover 35.00
a. 2ng black, *blue* 62.50 26.00
On cover 72.50

12 A4 3ng black, *yellow* 17.50 5.25
On cover 19.00
13 A4 5ng ver ('56) 67.50 50.00
On cover 100.00
a. 5ng orange brown ('60) 200.00 *225.00*
On cover 725.00
b. 5ng deep brown ('57) *625.00* 160.00
On cover 625.00
14 A4 10ng blue ('56) 200.00 200.00
On cover 725.00
On cover, single franking 2,100.

Full margins = 3/4mm.

The 1/2ng is found in 3 types, the 1ng in 2.
In 1861 the 5ng and 10ng were printed on hard, brittle, translucent paper.

A5

A6

Typo.; Arms Embossed

1863 ***Perf. 13***

15 A5 3pf blue green 1.25 *22.50*
On cover 92.50
a. 3pf yellow green 35.00 *50.00*
On cover 130.00
16 A5 1/2ng orange .75 *1.25*
On cover 6.50
a. 1/2ng red orange 17.50 4.00
On cover 10.00
17 A6 1ng rose 1.00 2.00
On cover 6.50
a. Vert. pair, imperf. between *200.00*
b. Horiz. pair, imperf. between *325.00*
18 A6 2ng blue 1.60 4.50
On cover 16.00
a. 2ng dark blue 10.00 22.50
On cover 60.00
19 A6 3ng red brown 2.00 8.25
On cover 22.50
a. 3ng bister brown 17.50 6.25
On cover 16.00
20 A6 5ng dull violet 27.50 *37.50*
On cover 110.00
a. 5ng gray violet 8.25 *275.00*
On cover 550.00
b. 5ng gray blue 14.00 *35.00*
On cover 110.00
c. 5ng slate 21.00 *160.00*
On cover 450.00

The stamps of Saxony were superseded on Jan. 1, 1868, by those of the North German Confederation.

SCHLESWIG-HOLSTEIN

LOCATION — In northern Germany.
GOVT. — Duchies
AREA — 7,338 sq. mi.
POP. — 1,519,000 (approx.)
CAPITAL — Schleswig

Schleswig-Holstein was an autonomous territory from 1848 to 1851 when it came under Danish rule. In 1864, it was occupied by Prussia and Austria, and in 1866 it became a province of Prussia.

16 Schillings = 1 Mark

Values for unused stamps are for examples with original gum as defined in the catalogue introduction. Copies without gum sell for about 50% of the figures quoted.

Coat of Arms — A1

Typographed; Arms Embossed

1850 **Unwmk.** ***Imperf.***

With Silk Threads

1 A1 1s dl bl & grnsh bl 300.00 *5,250.*
No gum 160.00
On cover *9,000.*
a. 1s Prussian blue 650.00
No gum 375.00
b. Double silk thread 1,100.
No gum 750.00
2 A1 2s rose & pink 525.00 *6,500.*
No gum 300.00
On cover *18,750*
On cover, #1 and 2 *55,000.*
a. 2s deep pink & rose 650.00
No gum 325.00
b. Double embossing *2,900.*
No gum 1,500.

Full margins = 1/2mm.

Values for stamps with legible town postmarks

1 A1 1s dull blue & greenish blue, *from* *13,750.*
On cover *22,000.*
2 A1 2s rose & pink, *from* *14,750.*

Values for stamps with legible town cancellations start at the figure above.

Values for pairs

1 A1 1s dull blue & greenish blue 825.00 *11,000.*
No gum 500.00
1a A1 1s prussian blue 1,650.
No gum 900.00
2 A1 2s rose & pink 1,250. *14,750.*
No gum 725.00
2a A1 2s deep pink & rose 1,800.
No gum 1,050.

Values for strips of 3

1 A1 1s dull blue & greenish blue 1,350.
No gum 750.00
1a A1 1s prussian blue 2,400.
No gum 1,500.
2 A1 2s rose & pink 1,850.
No gum 1,200.
2a A1 2s deep pink & rose 2,600.
No gum 1,650.

Values for blocks or strips of 4

1 A1 1s dull blue & greenish blue 1,650.
No gum 1,050.
1a A1 1s prussian blue 3,100.
No gum 2,100.
2 A1 2s rose & pink 2,600.
No gum 1,650.
2a A1 2s deep pink & rose 3,750.
No gum 2,200.

Forged cancellations are found on Nos. 1-2, 5-7, 9, 16 and 19.

A2

A3

1865 **Typo.** ***Rouletted 11 1/2***

3 A2 1/2s rose 27.50 *37.50*
On cover 210.00
On cover, single franking 225.00
4 A2 1 1/4s green 15.00 *19.00*
On cover 32.50
5 A3 1 1/3s red lilac 37.50 *100.00*
On cover 550.00
On cover, single franking *11,000.*
6 A2 2s ultra 37.50 *190.00*
On cover 550.00
7 A3 4s bister 50.00 *1,000.*
On cover *5,900.*

Schleswig

A4

A5

1864 **Typo.** ***Rouletted 11 1/2***

8 A4 1 1/4s green 37.50 17.00
On cover 32.50
9 A4 4s carmine 82.50 *400.00*
On cover 775.00

1865 ***Rouletted 10, 11 1/2***

10 A4 1/2s green 27.50 *47.50*
On cover 210.00
On cover, single franking 225.00
11 A4 1 1/4s red lilac 47.50 21.00
On cover 30.00
a. 1 1/4s gray lilac ('67) 225.00 67.50
On cover 85.00
b. Half of #11a used as 1/2s on cover *30,000.*
12 A5 1 1/3s rose 25.00 *50.00*
On cover 300.00
On cover, single franking 1,900.
13 A4 2s ultra 25.00 *40.00*
On cover 85.00
14 A4 4s bister 27.50 *67.50*
On cover 140.00

Holstein

A6

A7

Type I — Small lettering in frame. Wavy lines in spandrels close together.
Type II — Small lettering in frame. Wavy lines wider apart.
Type III — Larger lettering in frame and no periods after "H R Z G." Wavy lines as II.

1864 **Litho.** ***Imperf.***

15 A6 1 1/4s bl & gray, I 42.50 *47.50*
On cover 140.00
a. Half used as 1/2s on cover *9,250.*
16 A6 1 1/4s bl & gray, II 700.00 *3,000.*
On cover *32,000.*
a. Half used as 1/2s on cover *23,000.*
17 A6 1 1/4s bl & gray, III 37.50 *52.50*
On cover 100.00
With town datestamp 180.00
On cover, with town datestamp 350.00
a. Half used as 1/2s on cover *7,750.*

Full margins = 3/4mm.

1864 **Typo.** ***Rouletted 8***

18 A7 1 1/4s blue & rose 35.00 17.00
On cover 35.00
a. Half used as 1/2s on cover *1,900.*

A8

1865 ***Rouletted 8***

19 A8 1/2s green 50.00 *82.50*
On cover 300.00
On cover, single franking 310.00
20 A8 1 1/4s red lilac 37.50 21.00
On cover 32.50
21 A8 2s blue 42.50 37.50
On cover 110.00

A9

A10

1865-66 ***Rouletted 7 and 8***

22 A9 1 1/4s red lilac ('66) 62.50 22.50
On cover 32.50
a. Half used as 1/2s on cover *23,000.*
23 A10 1 1/3s carmine 52.50 37.50
On cover 290.00
On cover, single franking —
24 A9 2s blue ('66) 125.00 *125.00*
On cover 310.00
25 A10 4s bister 50.00 *67.50*
On cover 140.00

These stamps were superseded by those of North German Confederation on Jan. 1, 1868.

THURN AND TAXIS

A princely house which, prior to the formation of the German Empire, enjoyed the privilege of a postal monopoly. These stamps were superseded on July 1, 1867, by those of Prussia, followed by those of the North German Postal District on Jan. 1, 1868, and later by stamps of the German Empire on Jan. 1, 1872.

Values are for stamps with four complete margins just clear of the framelines. Stamps with margins just touching the framelines on one or two sides are worth approximately 60% of the values quoted. Stamps with four large margins are rare and command premiums of up to 500% over the values quoted.

Values for unused stamps are for examples with original gum as defined in the catalogue introduction. Copies without gum sell for about 50% of the figures quoted.

Northern District

30 Silbergroschen or Groschen = 1 Thaler

A1

A2

1852-58 **Unwmk.** **Typo.** ***Imperf.***

1 A1 1/4sgr blk, *red brn* ('54) 275.00 67.50
On cover 160.00
On cover tied by town datestamp 550.00
On cover, single franking 690.00
On news wrapper, single franking 1,000.
2 A1 1/3sgr blk, *buff* ('58) 125.00 275.00
On cover 690.00
On cover tied by town datestamp 1,350.
3 A1 1/2sgr blk, *green* 750.00 42.50
On cover 160.00
On newspaper wrapper 690.00
a. 1/2sgr black, *olive green* 650.00 27.50
On cover 125.00
On newspaper wrapper 1,350.
4 A1 1sgr blk, *dk bl* 1,375. 160.00
On cover 325.00
5 A1 1sgr blk, *lt bl* ('53) 825.00 25.00
On cover 82.50
6 A1 2sgr blk, *rose* 875.00 37.50
On cover 100.00
a. Half used as 1sgr on cover *6,000.*
7 A1 3sgr blk, *brownish yellow* 1,000. 32.50
On cover 60.00
a. 3sgr blk, *pale orange yellow* 875.00 100.00
On cover 175.00

Full margins = 1/4mm.

Reprints of Nos. 1-12, 15-20, 23-24, were made in 1910. They have "ND" in script on the back. Value, $6.50 each.

1859-60

8 A1 1/4sgr red ('60) 72.50 82.50
Never hinged 125.00
On cover 325.00
9 A1 1/2gr green 275.00 125.00
Never hinged 525.00
On cover 550.00
10 A1 1sgr blue 275.00 57.50
Never hinged 525.00
On cover 160.00
11 A1 2sgr rose ('60) 160.00 110.00
Never hinged 375.00
On cover 410.00
12 A1 3sgr red brn ('60) 160.00 140.00
Never hinged 275.00
On cover 625.00
13 A2 5sgr lilac 1.90 *400.00*
Never hinged 3.50
On cover *2,200.*
14 A2 10sgr orange 2.75 *1,000.*
Never hinged 4.00
On cover *10,250.*
On cover, single franking —

Full margins = 1/4mm.

Excellent forged cancellations exist on Nos. 13 and 14. For reprints, see note after No. 7.

1862-63

15 A1 1/4sgr black ('63) 35.00 *82.50*
Never hinged 57.50
On cover 300.00
On cover, single franking 950.00
Single franking on newspaper 1,100.
16 A1 1/3sgr green ('63) 50.00 *275.00*
Never hinged 82.50
On cover 1,100.
On newsprint, single franking 2,200.
17 A1 1/2sgr org yel 110.00 65.00
Never hinged 160.00
On cover 210.00
18 A1 1sgr rose ('63) 72.50 45.00
Never hinged 110.00
On cover 160.00
19 A1 2sgr blue ('63) 57.50 *125.00*
Never hinged 95.00
On cover 500.00
20 A1 3sgr bister ('63) 27.50 *65.00*
Never hinged 55.00
On cover 190.00

Full margins = 1/4mm.

For reprints, see note after No. 7.

1865 ***Rouletted***

21 A1 1/4sgr black 7.50 *400.00*
Never hinged 11.50
On cover *825.00*
On cover, single franking 2,000.
22 A1 1/3sgr green 11.00 *275.00*
Never hinged 20.00
On cover *600.00*
23 A1 1/2sgr yellow 24.00 *37.50*
Never hinged 32.50
On cover *92.50*
24 A1 1sgr rose 24.00 27.50
Never hinged 32.50
On cover 62.50
25 A1 2sgr blue 1.50 *75.00*
Never hinged 2.25
On cover *140.00*

26 A1 3sgr bister 2.75 *30.00*
Never hinged 3.75
On cover *82.50*

For reprints, see note after No. 7.

1866 *Rouletted in Colored Lines*

27 A1 ¼sgr black 1.10 *1,325.*
Never hinged 2.25
On cover *3,400.*
28 A1 ⅓sgr green 1.10 *600.00*
Never hinged 2.25
On cover *1,900.*
29 A1 ½sgr yellow 1.10 *125.00*
Never hinged 2.25
On cover *290.00*
30 A1 1sgr rose 1.10 *60.00*
Never hinged 2.25
On cover *140.00*
a. Horizontal pair without rouletting between 100.00
b. Half used as ½sgr on cover —
31 A1 2sgr blue 1.10 *600.00*
Never hinged 2.25
On cover *1,350.*
32 A1 3sgr bister 1.10 *160.00*
Never hinged 2.25
On cover *375.00*

Forged cancellations on Nos. 2, 13-14, 15-16, 21-22, 25-32 are plentiful.

Southern District

60 Kreuzer = 1 Gulden

A1

A2

1852-53 Unwmk. *Imperf.*

42 A1 1kr blk, *lt grn* 250.00 21.00
On cover 110.00
On cover, single franking 325.00
On newsprint, single franking 325.00
a. 9kr black, *dull bluish green* 410.00 32.50
On cover 325.00
43 A1 3kr blk, *dk bl* 950.00 65.00
On cover 275.00
44 A1 3kr blk, *bl* ('53) 825.00 21.00
On cover 140.00
45 A1 6kr blk, *rose* 1,325. 14.50
On cover 110.00
46 A1 9kr blk, *brnish yell* 875.00 21.00
On cover 120.00
a. 9kr blk, *pale orange yellow* 850.00 55.00
On cover 160.00

Full margins = ¼mm.

Reprints of Nos. 42-50, 53-56 were made in 1910. Each has "ND" in script on the back. Value, each $6.50.

1859

47 A1 1kr green 25.00 17.50
Never hinged 37.50
On cover 70.00
On cover, single franking 225.00
48 A1 3kr blue 600.00 32.50
Never hinged 1,150.
On cover 160.00
49 A1 6kr rose 600.00 87.50
Never hinged 1,150.
On cover 375.00
50 A1 9kr yellow 600.00 125.00
Never hinged 1,150.
On cover 690.00
51 A2 15kr lilac 2.75 *210.00*
Never hinged 4.00
On cover *1,150.*
52 A2 30kr orange 2.75 *575.00*
Never hinged 4.00
On cover *3,400.*
On cover, single franking —

Forged cancellations exist on Nos. 51 and 52. For reprints, see note after No. 46.

1862

53 A1 3kr rose 14.50 45.00
Never hinged 25.00
On cover 160.00
54 A1 6kr blue 14.50 45.00
Never hinged 25.00
On cover 160.00
55 A1 9kr bister 14.50 45.00
Never hinged 25.00
On cover 190.00

For reprints, see note after No. 46.

1865 *Rouletted*

56 A1 1kr green 10.50 13.00
Never hinged 18.00
On cover 32.50
On cover, single franking 125.00
Single franking on printed matter 125.00
57 A1 3kr rose 17.00 6.50
Never hinged 23.00
On cover 25.00
58 A1 6kr blue 1.25 *20.00*
Never hinged 2.00
On cover 50.00
59 A1 9kr bister 1.90 *22.50*
Never hinged 2.75
On cover 55.00

For reprint of No. 56, see note after No. 46.

1867 *Rouletted in Colored Lines*

60 A1 1kr green 1.10 *22.50*
Never hinged 2.25
On cover 60.00
61 A1 3kr rose 1.10 *20.00*
Never hinged 2.25
On cover 47.50
62 A1 6kr blue 1.10 *32.50*
Never hinged 2.25
On cover 77.50
63 A1 9kr bister 1.10 *32.50*
Never hinged 2.25
On cover 100.00

Forged cancellations exist on Nos. 51-52, 58-63.

The Thurn & Taxis Stamps, Northern and Southern Districts, were replaced on July 1, 1867, by those of Prussia.

WURTTEMBERG

LOCATION — In southern Germany
GOVT. — Kingdom
AREA — 7,530 sq. mi.
POP. — 2,580,000 (approx.)
CAPITAL — Stuttgart

Württemberg was a member of the German Confederation and became a part of the German Empire in 1870. It gave up its postal autonomy on March 31, 1902, but official stamps were issued until 1923.

16 Kreuzer = 1 Gulden
100 Pfennigs = 1 Mark (1875)

Values for unused stamps are for examples with original gum as defined in the catalogue introduction. Unused copies without gum of Nos. 1-46 sell for about 60-70% of the figures quoted. Unused copies without gum of Nos. 47-54 sell for about 50% of the figures quoted.

A1

A1a

1851-52 Unwmk. Typo. *Imperf.*

1 A1 1kr blk, *buff* 1,000. 100.00
On cover 375.00
a. 1kr black, *straw* 3,500. 475.00
On cover 950.00
2 A1 3kr blk, *yellow* 275.00 5.25
On cover 19.00
a. 3kr black, *orange* 3,000. 300.00
On cover 750.00
4 A1 6kr blk, *yel grn* 1,350. 32.50
On cover 82.50
a. 6kr black, *blue green* 2,600. 50.00
On cover 130.00
5 A1 9kr blk, *rose* *4,700.* 32.50
On cover 82.50
6 A1a 18kr blk, *dl vio* ('52) 1,400. 600.00
On cover 1,600.
On cover, single franking 2,600.

Values for Pairs

1	*A1*	*1kr blk, buff*	*375.00*
1a	*A1*	*1kr blk, straw*	*1,650.*
2	*A1*	*3kr blk, yellow*	*60.00*
2a	*A1*	*3kr blk, orange*	*2,200.*
4	*A1*	*6kr blk, yel grn*	*440.00*
4a	*A1*	*6kr blk, yel grn*	*440.00*
5	*A1*	*9kr blk, rose*	*550.00*
6	*A1a*	*18kr blk, dl vio ('52)*	*2,200.*

Full margins = 1mm.

On the "reprints" the letters of "Württemberg" are smaller, especially the first "e"; the right branch of the "r's" of Württemberg runs upward in the reprints and downward in the originals.

Coat of Arms — A2

With Orange Silk Threads

Typographed and Embossed

1857

7 A2 1kr yel brn 500.00 62.50
On cover 160.00
a. 1kr dark brown 1,000. 225.00
On cover 225.00
9 A2 3kr yel org 275.00 6.25
On cover 20.00
10 A2 6kr green 500.00 47.50
On cover 110.00
11 A2 9kr car rose 825.00 47.50
On cover 110.00
a. 9kr dk lilac red 700.00
On cover 1,600.
12 A2 18kr blue 2,400. 1,150.
On cover 2,300.
On cover, single franking 5,600.

Full margins = ¼mm.

Very fine examples of Nos. 7-12 with have one or two margins touching, but not cutting, the frameline.

See Nos. 13-46, 53.

The reprints have red or yellow silk threads and are printed 2mm apart, while the originals are ¾mm apart.

1859 Without Silk Threads

13 A2 1kr brown 525.00 67.50
On cover 300.00
a. 1kr dark brown 1,900. 675.00
On cover 1,300.
15 A2 3kr yel org 225.00 6.25
On cover 23.00
16 A2 6kr green *9,250.* 100.00
On cover 260.00
17 A2 9kr car rose 1,200. 52.50
On cover 120.00
a. 9kr dk reddish lilac 1,000.
On cover 1,900.
18 A2 18kr dark blue 2,900. 1,700.
On cover 4,600.
On cover, single franking 8,900.

Full margins = ¾mm.

The colors of the reprints are brighter; they are also printed 2mm apart instead of 1¼mm.

1860 *Perf. 13½*

19 A2 1kr brown 1,000. 125.00
On cover 450.00
20 A2 3kr yel org 275.00 7.00
On cover 23.00
21 A2 6kr green 2,900. 100.00
On cover 250.00
22 A2 9kr carmine 1,150. 110.00
On cover 300.00
a. 9kr dk lake red 1,500.
On cover 3,900.

1861 Thin Paper

23 A2 1kr brown 525.00 125.00
On cover 300.00
a. 1kr black brown 625.00 140.00
On cover 400.00
25 A2 3kr yel org 62.50 27.50
On cover 60.00
26 A2 6kr green 225.00 52.50
On cover 130.00
27 A2 9kr rose 700.00 125.00
On cover 400.00
a. 9kr claret 775.00 200.00
On cover 475.00
29 A2 18kr dark blue 1,500. 1,200.
On cover 2,600.
On cover, single franking 7,400.

Copies of Nos. 23-29 with all perforations intact sell for considerably more.

1862 *Perf. 10*

30 A2 1kr blk brn 275.00 225.00
On cover 825.00
31 A2 3kr yel org 400.00 27.50
On cover 100.00
32 A2 6kr green 300.00 100.00
On cover 260.00
33 A2 9kr claret 3,000. 625.00
On cover 1,900.

1863

34 A2 1kr yel grn 37.50 10.00
On cover 23.00
a. 1kr green 325.00 82.50
On cover 225.00
36 A2 3kr rose 275.00 3.25
On cover 7.75
a. 3kr dark claret 1,500. 225.00
On cover 550.00
37 A2 6kr blue 125.00 47.50
On cover 110.00
39 A2 9kr yel brn 700.00 140.00
On cover 475.00
a. 9kr red brown 210.00 42.50
On cover 110.00
b. 9kr black brown 1,000. 140.00
On cover 475.00
40 A2 18kr orange 1,000. 325.00
On cover 775.00
On cover, single franking 1,400.

1865-68 *Rouletted 10*

41 A2 1kr yel grn 35.00 7.00
On cover 16.00
a. 1kr dark green 525.00 225.00
On cover 775.00
42 A2 3kr rose 35.00 2.00
On cover 7.00
a. 3kr claret 1,900. 2,250.
On cover 3,900.
43 A2 6kr blue 210.00 42.50
On cover 130.00
44 A2 7kr slate bl ('68) 925.00 125.00
On cover 300.00
45 A2 9kr' bis brn 1,500. 67.50
On cover 190.00
a. 9kr red brown 1,150. 100.00
On cover 150.00
46 A2 18kr orange 1,700. 1,000.
On cover 2,300.
On cover, single franking 3,900.

A3

1869-73 Typo. & Embossed

47 A3 1kr yel grn 24.00 1.60
On cover 6.00
a. 1kr bl grn 190.00 45.00
On cover 100.00
48 A3 2kr orange 140.00 110.00
On cover 400.00
49 A3 3kr rose 12.00 1.00
On cover 3.50
50 A3 7kr blue 52.50 14.00
On cover 35.00
51 A3 9kr lt brn ('73) 67.50 37.50
On cover 190.00
a. 9kr org brn 140.00 110.00
On cover 400.00
52 A3 14kr orange 67.50 37.50
On cover 300.00
On cover, single franking 700.00
a. 14kr lemon yellow 1,400. 1,400.
On cover 3,900.
On cover, single franking 8,500.
b. 14kr dp yel org 175.00 92.50
On cover 450.00
On cover, single franking 1,000.
Nos. 47-52 (6) 363.50 201.60

See No. 54.

1873 *Imperf.*

53 A2 70kr red violet 1,700. 3,750.
On parcel post receipt card *46,000.*
a. 70kr violet 2,900. 5,250.
On parcel post receipt card *50,000.*

Nos. 53 and 53a have single or double lines of fine black dots printed in the gutters between the stamps.

1874 *Perf. 11½x11*

54 A3 1kr yellow green 72.50 29.00
On cover 120.00

A4

A5

1875-1900 Typo.

55 A4 2pf sl gray ('93) 1.60 .75
Never hinged 3.25
On cover 5.25
56 A4 3pf green 17.00 1.25
Never hinged 32.50
On cover 13.00
57 A4 3pf brn ('90) .65 .55
Never hinged 1.60
On cover 1.90
a. Imperf., pair 125.00
Never hinged 260.00
58 A4 5pf violet 7.00 .65
Never hinged 13.50
On cover 1.90
59 A4 5pf grn ('90) 1.25 .55
Never hinged 2.60
On cover 1.60
a. 5pf blue green 250.00 24.00
Never hinged 525.00
On cover 65.00
b. Imperf., pair 125.00
Never hinged 225.00
60 A4 10pf carmine 1.00 .65
Never hinged 1.90
On cover 1.90
a. 10pf rose 67.50 .75
Never hinged 130.00
On cover 5.25
b. Imperf., pair 67.50
Never hinged 140.00
61 A4 20pf ultra 1.00 .65
Never hinged 2.25
On cover 3.25
a. 20pf dull blue 1.00 .65
Never hinged 2.25
On cover 3.25
b. Imperf., pair 125.00
Never hinged 260.00
62 A4 25pf red brn 100.00 8.25
Never hinged 210.00
On cover 45.00
63 A4 25pf org ('90) 2.40 1.00
Never hinged 4.50
On cover 13.00
a. Imperf., pair 125.00
Never hinged 250.00
64 A5 30pf org & blk ('00) 2.75 3.25
Never hinged 5.25
On cover 32.50

65 A5 40pf dp rose & blk ('00) 3.25 4.75
Never hinged 6.00
On cover 80.00
66 A4 50pf gray 700.00 35.00
Never hinged 1,350.
On cover 690.00
On parcel post receipt card 360.00
67 A4 50pf gray grn 52.50 4.00
Never hinged 100.00
On cover 65.00
On parcel post receipt car 23.00
68 A4 50pf pur brn ('90) 2.40 .75
Never hinged 4.50
On cover 65.00
a. 50pf red brown 325.00 42.50
Never hinged 650.00
On cover 775.00
On parcel post receipt card 225.00
b. Imperf., pair 125.00
Never hinged *260.00*
69 A4 2m yellow 775.00 210.00
Never hinged 1,400.
On cover 3,250.
On parcel post receipt card 1,600.
70 A4 2m ver, *buff*('79) 1,900. 110.00
Never hinged —
On cover 3,250.
On parcel post receipt card 2,000.
71 A5 2m org & blk ('86) 7.75 8.25
Never hinged 15.00
Telegraph cancel 3.00
On cover 325.00
On parcel post receipt card 65.00
a. 2m yellow & black 350.00 47.50
Never hinged 700.00
On cover 500.00
On parcel post receipt card 150.00
b. Imperf., pair 125.00
Never hinged 325.00
72 A5 5m bl & blk ('81) 37.50 *140.00*
Never hinged 65.00
Telegraph cancel 67.50
On cover —
On parcel post receipt card 5,250.
a. Double impression of figure of value 160.00
Never hinged 325.00

No. 70 has "Unverkauflich" (not for sale) printed on its back to remind postal clerks that it, like No. 69, was for their use and not to be sold to the public.

The regular postage stamps of Württemberg were superseded by those of the German Empire in 1902. Official stamps were in use until 1923.

WURTTEMBERG OFFICIAL STAMPS

For the Communal Authorities

O1

Perf. 11½x11

1875-1900 Typo. Unwmk.

O1 O1 2pf sl gray ('00) 1.25 .75
Never hinged 3.25
On cover 2.60
O2 O1 3pf brn ('96) 1.25 .65
Never hinged 3.25
On cover 3.25
O3 O1 5pf violet 35.00 1.25
Never hinged 70.00
On cover 10.00
a. Imperf., pair *3,750.*
O4 O1 5pf bl grn ('90) 1.25 .75
Never hinged 3.25
On cover 2.60
a. Imperf., pair 47.50
Never hinged 92.50
O5 O1 10pf rose 7.00 1.25
Never hinged 16.00
On cover 3.75
a. Imperf., pair 82.50
Never hinged 160.00
O6 O1 25pf org ('00) 21.00 4.00
Never hinged 45.00
On cover 8.00
Nos. O1-O6 (6) 66.75 8.65

See Nos. O12-O32. For overprints and surcharges see Nos. O7-O11, O40-O52, O59-O93.

Used Values
When italicized, used values for Nos. O7-O183 are for favor-canceled copies. Postally used copies command a premium.

Stamps of Previous Issues Overprinted in Black

1906, Jan. 30

O7 O1 2pf slate gray 37.50 67.50
Never hinged 70.00
On cover 120.00
O8 O1 3pf dk brown 14.00 10.00
Never hinged 27.50
On cover 15.00
O9 O1 5pf green 4.00 2.75
Never hinged 8.00
On cover 4.50
O10 O1 10pf deep rose 4.00 3.00
Never hinged 8.00
On cover 4.50
O11 O1 25pf orange 42.50 67.50
Never hinged 80.00
On cover 130.00
Nos. O7-O11 (5) 102.00 150.75
Set, C.T.O. 29.00

Centenary of Kingdom of Württemberg.
Nos. O7-O11 also exist imperf but it is doubtful if they were ever issued in that condition.

1906-21 Wmk. 116

O12 O1 2pf slate gray 3.25 *.20*
Never hinged 6.50
On cover 10.00
O13 O1 2½pf gray blk ('16) .55 *.20*
Never hinged 1.00
On cover 1.90
O14 O1 3pf dk brown .65 *.20*
Never hinged 1.30
On cover 1.90
O15 O1 5pf green .65 *.20*
Never hinged 1.30
On cover 1.90
O16 O1 7½pf orange ('16) .55 *.20*
Never hinged 1.00
On cover 1.90
O17 O1 10pf dp rose .65 *.20*
Never hinged 1.30
On cover 1.90
O18 O1 10pf orange ('21) .20 *.20*
Never hinged .35
On cover 1.90
O19 O1 15pf yellow brn ('16) 1.25 *.20*
Never hinged 2.60
On cover 3.75
O20 O1 15pf purple ('17) .65 *.20*
Never hinged 1.30
On cover 3.75
a. 15pf blackish violet ('21) .20 1.00
Never hinged .35
On cover 1.90
O21 O1 20pf dp ultra ('11) 1.25 *.20*
Never hinged 2.60
On cover 3.75
O22 O1 20pf dp green ('21) .20 *.20*
Never hinged .35
On cover 2.60
O23 O1 25pf orange .65 *.20*
Never hinged 1.30
On cover 3.75
O24 O1 25pf brn & blk ('17) .95 *.20*
Never hinged 1.90
On cover 65.00
O25 O1 35pf brown ('19) 1.25 *.65*
Never hinged 2.60
On cover 3.75
O26 O1 40pf rose red ('21) .20 *.20*
Never hinged .35
On cover 1.90
O27 O1 50pf rose lake ('11) 12.00 *.20*
Never hinged 21.00
On cover 23.00
O28 O1 50pf vio brn ('21) .20 *.20*
Never hinged .70
On cover 1.90
O29 O1 60pf olive grn ('21) .35 *.20*
Never hinged 1.00
On cover 2.60
O30 O1 1.25m emerald ('21) .20 *.20*
Never hinged .70
On cover 2.60
O31 O1 2m gray ('21) .20 *.20*
Never hinged .70
On cover 2.60
O32 O1 3m brown ('21) .35 *.20*
Never hinged .65
On cover 2.60
Nos. O12-O32 (21) 26.20 *4.65*

No. O24 contains solid black numerals.
Nos. O12-O32 exist imperf. Value, each pair, $6.50-$17.50.

O3

Perf. 14½x14

1916, Oct. 6 Typo. Unwmk.

O33 O3 2½pf slate 1.25 *1.25*
O34 O3 7½pf orange 1.25 *1.25*
O35 O3 10pf car rose 1.25 *1.25*
O36 O3 15pf yellow brn 1.25 *1.25*
O37 O3 20pf blue 1.25 *1.25*
O38 O3 25pf gray blk 3.25 *1.25*
O39 O3 50pf red brown 7.00 *1.25*
Nos. O33-O39 (7) 16.50 *8.75*

25th year of the reign of King Wilhelm II.

Stamps of 1900-06 Surcharged

Perf. 11½x11

1916, Sept. 10 Wmk. 116

O40 O1 25pf on 25pf orange 2.75 *.65*
a. Without wmk. 27.50

No. O13 Surcharged in Blue

1919 Wmk. 116

O42 O1 2pf on 2½pf gray blk .65 *.40*

Official Stamps of 1906-19 Overprinted

1919

O43 O1 2½pf gray blk .35 *.55*
O44 O1 3pf dk brown 10.00 *.55*
O45 O1 5pf green .35 *.55*
O46 O1 7½pf orange .65 *.55*
O47 O1 10pf rose .35 *.55*
O48 O1 15pf purple .35 *.55*
O49 O1 20pf ultra .35 *.55*
O50 O1 25pf brown & blk .35 *.55*
O51 O1 35pf brown 4.00 *.55*
O52 O1 50pf red brown 4.75 *.55*
Nos. O43-O52 (10) 21.50 *5.50*

Stag — O4

Wmk. 192

1920, Mar. 19 Litho. *Perf. 14½*

O53 O4 10pf maroon 1.00 *1.25*
O54 O4 15pf brown 1.00 *1.25*
O55 O4 20pf indigo 1.00 *1.25*
O56 O4 30pf deep green 1.00 *1.25*
O57 O4 50pf yellow 1.00 *1.25*
O58 O4 75pf bister 2.00 *1.25*
Nos. O53-O58 (6) 7.00 *7.50*

Official Stamps of 1906-19 Overprinted

Perf. 11½x11

1920, Apr. 1 Wmk. 116

O59 O1 5pf green 3.25 8.75
O60 O1 10pf deep rose 2.00 4.00
O61 O1 15pf dp violet 2.00 4.50
O62 O1 20pf ultra 3.25 7.75
a. Wmk. 192 4.00 7.75
O63 O1 50pf red brown 4.00 15.00
Nos. O59-O63 (5) 14.50 40.00

Nos. O59 to O63 were available for official postage throughout all Germany but were used almost exclusively in Württemberg.

Stamps of 1917-21 Surcharged in Black, Red or Blue

1923

O64 O1 5m on 10pf orange .20 *.20*
O65 O1 10m on 15pf dp violet .20 *.20*
O66 O1 12m on 40pf rose red .20 *.20*
O67 O1 20m on 10pf orange .20 *.20*
O68 O1 25m on 20pf green .20 *.20*
O69 O1 40m on 20pf green .20 *.20*
O70 O1 50m on 60pf olive grn .20 *.20*

Surcharged

O71 O1 60m on 1.25m emerald .20 *.20*
O72 O1 100m on 40pf rose red .20 *.20*
O73 O1 200m on 2m gray (R) .20 *.20*
O74 O1 300m on 50pf red brn (Bl) .20 *.20*
O75 O1 400m on 3m brn (Bl) .20 *.20*
O76 O1 1000m on 60pf ol grn .20 *.25*
O77 O1 2000m on 1.25m emerald .20 *.25*
Nos. O64-O77 (14) 2.80 *2.90*

Abbreviations:
Th = (Tausend) Thousand
Mil = (Million) Million
Mlrd = (Milliarde) Billion

Surcharged

1923

O78 O1 5th m on 10pf orange .20 *.35*
O79 O1 20th m on 40pf rose red .20 *.35*
O80 O1 50th m on 15pf violet .20 *.35*
O81 O1 75th m on 2m gray 1.25 *.35*
O82 O1 100th m on 20pf green .20 *.35*
O83 O1 250th m on 3m brown .20 *.35*

Surcharged

O84 O1 1mil m on 60pf ol grn 1.00 *.35*
O85 O1 2mil m on 50pf red brn .20 *.35*
O86 O1 5mil m on 1.25m emer .20 *.35*

Surcharged

O87 O1 4 mlrd m on 50pf red brn 2.40 *.35*
O88 O1 10 mlrd m on 3m brn 2.40 *.35*
Nos. O78-O88 (11) 8.45 *3.85*

No. O23 Surcharged with New Values in Rentenpfennig as

1923, Dec.

O89 O1 3pf on 25pf orange .35 *.35*
O90 O1 5pf on 25pf orange .35 *.35*
O91 O1 10pf on 25pf orange .35 *.35*
O92 O1 20pf on 25pf orange .35 *.35*
O93 O1 50pf on 25pf orange .65 *.35*
Nos. O89-O93 (5) 2.05 *1.75*

For the State Authorities

O6

Perf. 11½x11

1881-1902 Typo. Unwmk.

O94 O6 2pf sl gray ('96) 1.25 1.00
O95 O6 3pf green 21.00 3.25
O96 O6 3pf dk brown ('90) 1.25 .65
O97 O6 5pf violet 5.25 1.25
O98 O6 5pf green ('90) 2.00 .65
O99 O6 10pf rose 3.25 1.00

O100	O6	20pf ultra	.75	1.00
O101	O6	25pf brown	32.50	6.25
O102	O6	25pf orange ('90)	5.25	.75
O103	O6	30pf org & blk ('02)	1.25	1.60
O104	O6	40pf dp rose & blk ('02)	1.25	1.60
O105	O6	50pf gray grn	7.00	7.75
O106	O6	50pf maroon ('91)	1.25	2.75
a.		50pf red brown ('90)	200.00	*1,450.*
O107	O6	1m yellow	62.50	160.00
O108	O6	1m violet ('90)	6.25	14.00
		Nos. O94-O108 (15)	152.00	*203.50*

See #O119-O135. For overprints & surcharges see #O109-O118, O146-O164, O176-O183.

Overprinted in Black

1906

O109	O6	2pf slate gray	27.50	*5.25*
O110	O6	3pf dk brown	5.25	*5.25*
O111	O6	5pf green	4.00	*5.25*
O112	O6	10pf dp rose	4.00	*5.25*
O113	O6	20pf ultra	4.00	*5.25*
O114	O6	25pf orange	8.25	*5.25*
O115	O6	30pf org & blk	8.25	*5.25*
O116	O6	40pf dp rose & blk	32.50	*5.25*
O117	O6	50pf red brown	32.50	*5.25*
O118	O6	1m purple	62.50	*5.25*
		Nos. O109-O118 (10)	188.75	52.50

Cent. of the kingdom of Wűttemberg.

Nos. O109 to O118 are also found imperforate, but it is doubtful if they were ever issued in that condition.

1906-19 **Wmk. 116**

O119	O6	2pf slate gray	.40	*.20*
O120	O6	2½pf gray blk ('16)	.45	*.20*
O121	O6	3pf dk brown	.40	*.20*
O122	O6	5pf green	.40	*.20*
O123	O6	7½pf orange ('16)	.45	*.20*
O124	O6	10pf deep rose	.40	*.20*
O125	O6	15pf yel brn ('16)	.45	*.20*
O126	O6	15pf purple ('17)	.65	*.30*
O127	O6	20pf ultra	.55	*.20*
O128	O6	25pf orange	.40	*.20*
O129	O6	25pf brn & blk ('17)	.35	*.20*
O130	O6	30pf org & blk	.35	*.20*
O131	O6	35pf brown ('19)	1.25	*2.75*
O132	O6	40pf dp rose & blk	.40	*.20*
O133	O6	50pf red brown	.40	*.20*
O134	O6	1m purple	2.00	*.20*
O135	O6	1m sl & blk ('17)	2.00	*.65*
		Nos. O119-O135 (17)	11.30	*6.50*

King Wilhelm II — O8

1916 **Unwmk.** **Typo.** ***Perf. 14***

O136	O8	2½pf slate	.65	*.60*
O137	O8	7½pf orange	.65	*.60*
O138	O8	10pf carmine	.65	*.60*
O139	O8	15pf yellow brn	.65	*.60*
O140	O8	20pf blue	.65	*.60*
O141	O8	25pf gray blk	1.25	*.60*
O142	O8	30pf green	1.25	*.60*
O143	O8	40pf claret	2.00	*.60*
O144	O8	50pf red brn	2.75	*.60*
O145	O8	1m violet	2.75	*.60*
		Nos. O136-O145 (10)	13.25	*6.00*

25th year of the reign of King Wilhelm II.

Stamps of 1890-1906 Surcharged

1916-19 **Wmk. 116** ***Perf. 11½x11***

O146	O6	25pf on 25pf orange	24.00	*.65*
a.		Without watermark	32.50	9,250.
O147	O6	50pf on 50pf red brn	1.25	*.75*
a.		Inverted surcharge	32.50	

Beware of fake cancels on No. O146a.

No. O120 Surcharged in Blue

1919 **Wmk. 116**

O149	O6	2pf on 2½pf gray blk	1.25	*1.25*

Official Stamps of 1890-1919 Overprinted

1919

O150	O6	2½pf gray blk	.45	*.35*
O151	O6	3pf dk brown	7.00	*.65*
a.		Without watermark	47.50	
O152	O6	5pf green	.35	*.35*
O153	O6	7½pf orange	.35	*.35*
O154	O6	10pf rose	.35	*.35*
O155	O6	15pf purple	.35	*.25*
O156	O6	20pf ultra	.35	*.35*
O157	O6	25pf brn & blk	.35	*.35*
a.		Inverted overprint	82.50	*160.00*
O158	O6	30pf org & blk	.65	*.35*
a.		Inverted overprint	225.00	*350.00*
O159	O6	35pf brown	.45	*.35*
O160	O6	40pf rose & blk	.45	*.35*
O161	O6	50pf claret	.65	*.55*
O162	O6	1m slate & blk	.75	*.65*
		Nos. O150-O162 (13)	12.50	*5.25*

Nos. O151, O151a Surcharged in Carmine

1920 **Wmk. 116**

O164	O6	75pf on 3pf dk brn	1.00	*1.00*
a.		Without watermark	67.50	*14.50*

View of Stuttgart O9

10pf, 50pf, 2.50m, 3m, View of Stuttgart. 15pf, 75pf, View of Ulm. 20pf, 1m, View of Tubingen. 30pf, 1.25m, View of Ellwangen.

Wmk. 192

1920, Mar. 25 **Typo.** ***Perf. 14½***

O166	O9	10pf maroon	.55	*1.00*
O167	O9	15pf brown	.55	*1.00*
O168	O9	20pf indigo	.55	*1.00*
O169	O9	30pf blue grn	.55	*1.00*
O170	O9	50pf yellow	.55	*1.00*
O171	O9	75pf bister	.55	*1.00*
O172	O9	1m orange red	.55	*1.00*
O173	O9	1.25m dp violet	.55	*1.00*
O174	O9	2.50m dark ultra	1.25	*1.00*
O175	O9	3m yellow grn	2.00	*1.00*
		Nos. O166-O175 (10)	7.65	*10.00*

Official Stamps of 1906-19 Overprinted

1920 **Wmk. 116** ***Perf. 11½x11***

O176	O6	5pf green	2.00	*3.25*
O177	O6	10pf deep rose	1.25	*2.75*
O178	O6	15pf purple	1.25	*2.75*
O179	O6	20pf ultra	1.25	*1.25*
a.		Wmk. 192	100.00	*275.00*
O180	O6	30pf orange & blk	1.25	*3.25*
O181	O6	40pf dp rose & blk	1.25	*2.75*
O182	O6	50pf red brown	1.25	*3.25*
O183	O6	1m slate & blk	2.00	*7.00*
		Nos. O176-O183 (8)	11.50	*26.25*

The note after No. O63 will also apply to Nos. O176-O183.

NORTH GERMAN CONFEDERATION

Northern District
30 Groschen = 1 Thaler
Southern District
60 Kreuzer = 1 Gulden
Hamburg
16 Schillings = 1 Mark

Values for unused stamps are for examples with original gum as defined in the catalogue introduction. Copies without gum sell for about 50% of the figures quoted.

A1

A2

Rouletted 8½ to 10, 11 to 12½ and Compound

1868 **Typo.** **Unwmk.**

1	A1	¼gr violet	15.00	11.00
		On cover		45.00
		On cover, single franking		150.00
b.		¼gr red lilac	35.00	22.00
		On cover		57.50
		On cover, single franking		150.00
c.		¼gr gray violet	65.00	37.50
		On cover		160.00
		On cover, single franking		550.00
2	A1	⅓gr green	30.00	3.00
		On cover		14.50
3	A1	½gr orange	30.00	2.25
		On cover		7.50
4	A1	1gr rose	15.00	.80
		On cover		4.25
b.		Half used as ½gr on cover		—
5	A1	2gr ultra	75.00	1.50
		On cover		7.50
6	A1	5gr bister	75.00	7.50
		On cover		37.50
7	A2	1kr green	32.50	7.50
		On cover		25.00
8	A2	2kr orange	52.50	42.50
		On cover		140.00
9	A2	3kr rose	32.50	1.90
		On cover		7.50
10	A2	7kr ultra	150.00	9.50
		On cover		30.00
11	A2	18kr bister	32.50	60.00
		On cover		190.00

See Nos. 13-23.

Imperf

1a	A1	¼gr red lilac	190.00	—
2a	A1	⅓gr green	90.00	—
3a	A1	½gr orange	140.00	—
4a	A1	1gr rose	75.00	—
5a	A1	2gr ultra	250.00	—
6a	A1	5gr bister	250.00	—
7a	A2	1kr green	67.50	*110.00*
8a	A2	2kr orange	190.00	90.00
9a	A2	3kr rose	75.00	95.00
10a	A2	7kr ultra	325.00	*625.00*
11a	A2	18kr bister	325.00	*625.00*

A3

1868

12	A3	(½s) lilac brown	75.00	37.50
		On cover		110.00
a.		½gr reddish brown	110.00	55.00
		On cover		110.00
b.		½gr dark carmine brown	130.00	130.00
		On cover		300.00
c.		½gr violet brown	190.00	*190.00*
		On cover		325.00

See No. 24.

1869 ***Perf. 13½x14***

13	A1	¼gr lilac	12.00	11.50
		On cover		40.00
a.		¼gr red violet	21.00	17.00
		On cover		52.50
14	A1	⅓gr green	4.00	1.25
		On cover		8.00
15	A1	½gr orange	4.00	1.25
		On cover		6.50
16	A1	1gr rose	3.25	.65
		On cover		3.75
17	A1	2gr ultra	6.25	1.00
		On cover		6.50
18	A1	5gr bister	7.00	7.00
		On cover		35.00
19	A2	1kr green	10.00	7.00
		On cover		15.00
20	A2	2kr orange	32.50	*82.50*
		On cover		*225.00*
21	A2	3kr rose	6.25	1.25
		On cover		6.00
22	A2	7kr ultra	9.50	7.75
		On cover		26.00
23	A2	18kr bister	125.00	*1,500.*
		On cover		*5,600.*
		On cover, single franking		*8,000.*

Counterfeit cancels exist on No. 23.

1869

24	A3	(½s) dull violet brown	4.00	7.00
		On cover		32.50
a.		½s dark red brown	9.25	*19.00*
		On cover		60.00
b.		½s dark brown	80.00	55.00
		On cover		110.00

A4

A5

Perf. 14x13½

25	A4	10gr gray	275.00	325.00
		Pen cancellation		57.50
		On cover with postmark		1,900.
		On cover with pen cancellation		360.00
26	A5	30gr blue	200.00	*925.00*
		Pen cancellation		*110.00*
		On cover with postmark		*5,900.*
		On cover with pen cancellation		*1,300.*

Counterfeit cancels exist on No. 26.

See Germany designs A2, A3 and A8 for similar stamps.

OFFICIAL STAMPS

O1

1870 **Unwmk.** **Typo.** ***Perf. 14½x14***

O1	O1	¼gr black & buff	21.00	*37.50*
		On cover		*130.00*
O2	O1	⅓gr black & buff	8.25	*17.50*
		On cover		*80.00*
O3	O1	½gr black & buff	2.40	*2.75*
		On cover		*15.00*
O4	O1	1gr black & buff	2.40	.65
		On cover		3.75
O5	O1	2gr black & buff	6.25	3.25
		On cover		15.00
O6	O1	1kr black & gray	27.50	*210.00*
		On cover		*700.00*
O7	O1	2kr black & gray	67.50	*1,250.*
		On cover		*2,200.*
O8	O1	3kr black & gray	21.00	*40.00*
		On cover		*190.00*
O9	O1	7kr black & gray	37.50	*225.00*
		On cover		*700.00*

Counterfeit cancels exist on Nos. O6-O9.

The stamps of the North German Confederation were replaced by those of the German Empire on Jan. 1, 1872.

GERMANY

'jər-mə-nē

LOCATION — In northern Europe bordering on the Baltic and North Seas
AREA — 182,104 sq. mi. (until 1945)
POP. — 67,032,242 (1946)
CAPITAL — Berlin

30 Silbergroschen or Groschen = 1 Thaler
60 Kreuzer = 1 Gulden
100 Pfennigs = 1 Mark (1875)

Watermarks

Wmk. 48 — Diagonal Zigzag Lines

Wmk. 116 — Crosses and Circles

Wmk. 125 — Lozenges

Wmk. 126 — Network

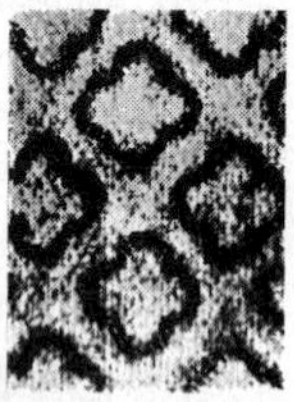

Wmk. 127 — Quatrefoils

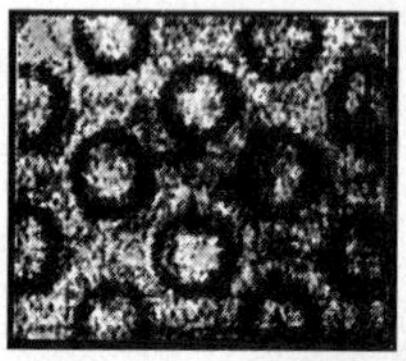

Wmk. 192 — Circles

Wmk. 223 — Eagle

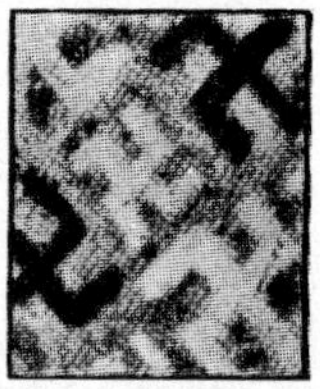

Wmk. 237 — Swastikas

Wmk. 241 — Cross

Empire

Values for unused stamps are for examples with original gum as defined in the catalogue introduction. Any exceptions are specifically mentioned.

Imperial Eagle — A1

Typographed, Center Embossed

1872 Unwmk. *Perf. 13½x14½*

Eagle with small shield

1 A1 ¼gr violet 190.00 85.00
Never hinged 1,300.
On cover 350.00
2 A1 ⅓gr green 425.00 27.50
Never hinged 3,750.
On cover 60.00
a. Imperf. —
3 A1 ½gr red orange 875.00 37.50
Never hinged 3,750.
On cover 60.00
a. ½gr orange yellow 1,000. 45.00
Never hinged 11,500.
On cover 190.00
4 A1 1gr rose 250.00 5.25
Never hinged 1,450.
On cover 11.50
a. Imperf. —
b. Half used as ½gr on cover *45,000.*
5 A1 2gr ultra 1,350. 13.50
Never hinged 10,500.
On cover 27.50
a. Imperf. *8,250.*
6 A1 5gr bister 825.00 82.50
Never hinged 6,900.
On cover 225.00
a. Imperf. *8,250.*
7 A1 1kr green 575.00 50.00
Never hinged 5,000.
On cover 92.50
8 A1 2kr orange 35.00 *150.00*
Never hinged 140.00
On cover 300.00
a. 2kr red orange 525.00 275.00
Never hinged 5,000.
On cover 375.00
9 A1 3kr rose 1,500. 11.50
Never hinged 12,500.
On cover 23.00
10 A1 7kr ultra 2,000. 82.50
Never hinged 13,750.
On cover 140.00
11 A1 18kr bister 450.00 350.00
Never hinged 3,500.
On cover 1,500.

Values for imperforates are for copies postmarked at Leipzig (⅓gr), Coblenz (1gr), Hoengen (2gr) and Leutersdorf (5gr).

A2

A3

1872 Typo. *Perf. 14½x13½*

12 A2 10gr gray 50.00 *1,150.*
Never hinged 125.00
Pen cancellation 70.00
On cover with postmark 3,750.
On cover with pen cancellation 450.00
13 A3 30gr blue 100.00 *2,000.*
Never hinged 225.00
Pen cancellation *500.00*
On cover with postmark 10,750.
On cover with pen cancellation 1,150.

For similar designs see A8, North German Confederation A4, A5.

A4

A5

Center Embossed

1872 *Perf. 13½x14½*

Eagle with large shield

14 A4 ¼gr violet 62.50 82.50
Never hinged 225.00
On cover 375.00
15 A4 ⅓gr yellow green 29.00 12.50
Never hinged 140.00
On cover 37.50
a. ⅓gr blue green 110.00 97.50
Never hinged 450.00
On cover 300.00
16 A4 ½gr orange 35.00 3.75
Never hinged 140.00
On cover 15.00
a. Imperf.
17 A4 1gr rose 42.50 1.90
Never hinged 225.00
On cover 10.00
a. Imperf. *15,500.*
On cover *38,500.*
b. Half used as ½gr on cover *35,000.*
18 A4 2gr ultra 19.00 4.25
Never hinged 75.00
On cover 11.50
19 A4 2½gr orange brn 1,800. 55.00
Never hinged 15,000.
On cover 190.00
a. 2½gr lilac brown *4,000.* 325.00
Never hinged *23,000.*
On cover 750.00
20 A4 5gr bister 29.00 29.00
Never hinged 140.00
On cover 140.00
a. Imperf. *5,750.*
On cover *150,000.*
21 A4 1kr yel grn 32.50 25.00
Never hinged 140.00
On cover 60.00
a. 1kr blue green 350.00 400.00
Never hinged 1,400.
On cover 850.00
22 A4 2kr orange 475.00 *1,900.*
Never hinged 2,300.
On cover *3,500.*
23 A4 3kr rose 22.50 3.50
Never hinged 87.50
On cover 11.00
24 A4 7kr ultra 29.00 *65.00*
Never hinged 140.00
On cover *120.00*
25 A4 9kr red brown 275.00 225.00
Never hinged 1,900.
On cover 450.00
a. 9kr lilac brown 1,400. 450.00
Never hinged 11,500.
On cover 850.00
26 A4 18kr bister 32.50 *1,750.*
Never hinged 110.00
On cover *13,000.*

Values for Nos. 17a and 20a are for copies postmarked at Potsdam (1gr), Damgarten or Anklam (5gr).

#14-26 with embossing inverted are fraudulent.

1874

Brown Surcharge

27 A5 2½gr on 2½gr brn 35.00 40.00
Never hinged 92.50
On cover 150.00
28 A5 9kr on 9kr brown 65.00 *275.00*
Never hinged 160.00
On cover *750.00*

A6

A7

"Pfennige"

1875-77 Typo.

29 A6 3pf blue green 55.00 5.00
Never hinged 450.00
On cover 10.00
a. yellow green 100.00 9.25
Never hinged 850.00
On cover 19.00
30 A6 5pf violet 92.50 2.75
Never hinged 925.00
On cover 5.75

Center Embossed

31 A7 10pf rose 40.00 .85
Never hinged 300.00
On cover 4.00
a. reddish brown ('75) *1,100.* 190.00
Never hinged —
On cover 260.00
32 A7 20pf ultra 450.00 1.10
Never hinged 2,700.
On cover 7.50
a. blue 525.00 30.00
Never hinged 3,850.
On cover 45.00
33 A7 25pf red brown 475.00 16.00
Never hinged 4,500.
On cover 60.00
On cover, single franking 550.00
a. yellow brown 2,300. 100.00
Never hinged *19,000.*
On cover 210.00
b. deep brown ('78) 2,750. 225.00
Never hinged 21,500.
On cover 300.00
On cover, single franking 750.00
34 A7 50pf gray 1,200. 11.00
Never hinged 7,500.
On cover 57.50
On cover, single franking 85.00
a. gray black 2,300. 325.00
Never hinged —
On cover 450.00
On cover, single franking 600.00
35 A7 50pf ol gray ('77) 1,450. 12.00
Never hinged 11,500.
On cover 70.00
a. dk ol green 2,750. 150.00
Never hinged 15,500.
On cover 260.00

See Nos. 37-42. For surcharges see Offices in Turkey Nos. 1-6.

Values for used blocks of 4

29	A6	3pf blue green	425.00
a.		3pf yellow green	450.00
30	A6	5pf violet	30.00
31	A7	10pf rose	22.50
a.		10pf reddish brown	—
32	A7	20pf ultramarine	190.00
a.		20pf blue	300.00
33	A7	25pf red brown	350.00
a.		25pf yellow brown	750.00
b.		25pf deep brown	—
34	A7	50pf gray	150.00
a.		50pf gray black	1,500.
35	A7	50pf olive gray	190.00
a.		50pf dark olive green	1,050.

A8

1875-90 Typo. *Perf. 14½x13½*

36 A8 2m brownish pur ('90) 65.00 2.75
Never hinged 250.00
a. 2m purple ('75) 375.00 125.00
On cover 275.00
b. 2m dull vio pur ('89) 1,500. 60.00
c. 2m pur lilac ('80) *3,000.* 50.00
On cover 225.00

d.	2m rose lilac ('84)	1,250.	13.50
	On cover		160.00
e.	2m carmine lilac ('99)	110.00	42.50
	Never hinged	360.00	

No. 36a used is valued as a stamp with cds cancel dated between Jan. 1875 and November 17, 1884.

Values for Nos. 36a, 36c, 36d on cover are for pencanceled stamps.

Values for used pairs

36	A8 2m brownish pur	9.25
a.	2m pur violet	240.00
b.	2m dull vio pur	140.00
c.	2m pur lilac	150.00
d.	2m rose lilac	42.50
e.	2m carmine lilac	125.00

Value for used strips of 3

36	A8 2m brownish pur	18.00
a.	2m pur violet	390.00
b.	2m dull vio pur	210.00
c.	2m pur lilac	250.00
d.	2m rose lilac	65.00
e.	2m carmine lilac	190.00

Values for used strips of 4

36	A8 2m brownish pur	25.00
a.	2m pur violet	500.00
b.	2m dull vio pur	275.00
c.	2m pur lilac	410.00
d.	2m rose lilac	125.00
e.	2m carmine lilac	300.00

Values for used blocks of 4

36	A8 2m brownish pur	35.00
a.	2m pur violet	—
b.	2m dull vio pur	410.00
c.	2m pur lilac	500.00
d.	2m rose lilac	150.00
e.	2m carmine lilac	325.00

Values for postmarked stamps on parcel post receipt cards

36	A8 2m brownish pur	32.50
a.	2m pur violet	250.00
b.	2m dull vio pur	190.00
c.	2m pur lilac	160.00
d.	2m rose lilac	65.00
e.	2m carmine lilac	160.00

Values for postmarked stamps on registered, insured covers

36	A8 2m brownish pur	65.00
a.	2m pur violet	500.00
b.	2m dull vio pur	390.00
c.	2m pur lilac	325.00
d.	2m rose lilac	140.00
e.	2m carmine lilac	325.00

On cover values are for covers with cancellations falling within the following dates: #36 ('90-'99), #36a ('75-'80, '93-'94), #36b ('89-'90), #36c ('80-Nov. '84), #36d ('84-'89), #36e ('99-'00).

Types of 1875-77, "Pfennig" without final "e"

1880-83 *Perf. 13½x14½*

37	A6 3pf yel green	3.00	.75
	Never hinged	13.50	
	On cover		2.00
a.	Imperf.		—
b.	3pf green (shades)	6.25	.75
	Never hinged	32.50	
	On cover		3.25
38	A6 5pf violet	1.40	.75
	Never hinged	7.75	
	On cover		1.40

Center Embossed

39	A7 10pf red	8.00	.75
	Never hinged	37.50	
	On cover		1.40
a.	Imperf.	*325.00*	
	Never hinged	*575.00*	
b.	10pf rose	20.00	1.40
	Never hinged	72.50	
	On cover		2.25
40	A7 20pf brt ultra	5.75	.75
	Never hinged	15.00	
	On cover		1.80
a.	20pf grayish ultra	110.00	1.10
	Never hinged	575.00	
	On cover		2.50
b.	20pf blue	72.50	7.25
	Never hinged	250.00	
	On cover		13.50
41	A7 25pf dull rose brn	14.50	2.75
	Never hinged	55.00	
	On cover		42.50
a.	25pf red brown, thick paper	190.00	3.75
	Never hinged	1,250.	
	On cover		32.50
b.	25pf orange brown	150.00	4.00
	Never hinged	550.00	
	On cover		32.50
c.	25pf brown ocher	225.00	22.50
	Never hinged	950.00	
	On cover		82.50
42	A7 50pf dp grayish ol grn	7.25	.75
	Never hinged	50.00	
	On cover		12.50
a.	50pf olive green	210.00	1.25
	Never hinged	1,500.	
	On cover		11.00
b.	50pf yellowish ol grn	230.00	30.00
	Never hinged	475.00	
	On cover		65.00
c.	50pf dk green	190.00	17.50
	Never hinged	2,100.	
	On cover		55.00

Values for Nos. 37-42 are for stamps on thin paper. Those on thick paper sell for considerably more.

On cover values are for covers canceled within the following dates: #37-37a ('80-'89), #39 ('87-'89), #39b ('80-'89), #40 ('86-'89), #40a ('80-'84), #40b ('82-'85), #41 ('87-'89), #41a-41b ('83), #41c ('80-'83), #42 ('85-'91), #42a ('80-'86), #42b ('87-'89), #42c ('89).

Values for used blocks of 4

37	A6 3pf yel green	120.00
b.	3pf green (shades)	120.00
38	A6 5pf violet	18.00
39	A7 10pf red	5.50
b.	10pf rose	8.25
40	A7 20pf br ultra	11.00
a.	20pf greyish ultra	32.50
b.	20pf blue	62.50
41	A7 25pf dull rose brn	17.00
a.	25pf red brn, thick paper	37.50
b.	25pf org brn	37.50
c.	25pf brn ocher	160.00
42	A7 50pf grayish ol grn	8.25
a.	50pf ol grn	10.00
b.	50pf yellowish ol grn	190.00
c.	50pf dk grn	125.00

A9

A10

1889-1900 *Perf. 13½x14½*

45	A9 2pf gray ('00)	.50	.65
	Never hinged	1.60	
	On cover		3.25
a.	"REIGHSPOST"	55.00	*140.00*
	Never hinged	175.00	
	On cover		250.00
46	A9 3pf brown	1.50	.75
	Never hinged	9.25	
	On cover		1.60
a.	3pf yellow brown	8.75	.70
	Never hinged	65.00	
	On cover		1.60
b.	Imperf.	160.00	—
	Never hinged	375.00	
c.	3pf reddish brown	50.00	8.00
	Never hinged	390.00	
	On cover		16.50
d.	3pf dark brown	175.00	50.00
	Never hinged	600.00	
	On cover		125.00
e.	3pf olive brown	6.50	2.75
	Never hinged	37.50	
	On cover		6.50
f.	3pf ocher brown	12.50	4.50
	On cover		12.50

On cover values are for covers canceled within the normal period of use: #46 ('91-'97), #46a, 46c ('97-'00), #46d ('89-'90), #46e-46f ('99-'00).

47	A9 5pf blue green	1.25	.70
	Never hinged	7.25	
	On cover		1.60
a.	5pf yellow green	87.50	2.50
	Never hinged	360.00	
	On cover		6.00
b.	5pf gray green	125.00	2.75
	Never hinged	410.00	
	On cover		6.00

On cover values are for covers canceled within the following dates: #47 ('91-'00), #47a ('90-'92), #47b ('89-'92).

48	A10 10pf carmine	1.50	.70
	Never hinged	7.75	
	On cover		1.60
a.	Imperf.	225.00	
	Never hinged	650.00	
b.	10pf brownish rose	8.75	.80
	Never hinged	82.50	
	On cover		1.25
c.	10pf dark carmine	27.50	7.75
	Never hinged	180.00	
	On cover		27.50
d.	10pf brownish red	65.00	6.50
	Never hinged	500.00	
	On cover		25.00
e.	10pf rose carmine	190.00	2.75
	Never hinged	875.00	
	On cover		12.50

On cover values are for covers canceled within the following dates: #48 ('93-'00), #48b ('90-'95), #48c, ('99-'00), #48d ('94-'00), #48e ('89-'90).

49	A10 20pf ultra	7.25	.70
	Never hinged	45.00	
	On cover		1.40
a.	20pf Prus blue	375.00	110.00
	Never hinged	1,650.	
	On cover		190.00
b.	20pf grayish ultra	55.00	3.60
	Never hinged	250.00	
	On cover		7.75
c.	20pf blue (shades)	45.00	1.10
	Never hinged	325.00	
	On cover		3.75

On cover values are for covers canceled within the following dates: #49a ('81-'93), #49b ('92-'94), #49c ('91-'95).

50	A10 25pf orange ('90)	29.00	1.40
	Never hinged	105.00	
	On cover		13.50
	On cover, single franking		110.00
a.	Imperf.	190.00	
	Never hinged	625.00	
b	25pf yellow orange	125.00	6.50
	Never hinged	775.00	
	On cover		35.00
	On cover, single franking		300.00

On cover values are for covers canceled within the following dates: #50 ('91-'00), #51b ('89-'96).

51	A10 50pf chocolate	25.00	.75
	Never hinged	87.50	
	On cover		2.00
a.	50pf copper brown	325.00	10.00
	Never hinged	1,200.	
	On cover		27.50
b.	Imperf.	325.00	
	Never hinged	425.00	
c.	50pf brownish red	1,100.	110.00
	Never hinged	7,200.	
	On cover		325.00
d.	50pf reddish brown	825.00	18.00
	Never hinged	4,800.	
	On cover		37.50
e.	50pf dull rose brown	72.50	2.75
	Never hinged	875.00	
	On cover		15.00

On cover values are for covers canceled within the following dates: #51 ('90-'00), #51a, 51d ('89-'91), #51c ('89-'90), #51e, ('93-'94).

Nos. 45-51 (7)	66.00	5.65
Set, never hinged	265.00	

For surcharges and overprints see Offices in China Nos. 1-6, 16, Offices in Morocco 1-6, Offices in Turkey 8-12.

Values for used blocks of 4

45	A9 2pf gray	4.75
46	A9 3pf brown	45.00
a.	3pf yellow brown	55.00
c.	3pf reddish brown	290.00
e.	3pf olive brown	47.50
f.	3pf ocher brown	57.50
47	A9 5pf blue green	7.25
a.	5pf yellow green	60.00
b.	5pf gray green	60.00
48	A10 10pf carmine	6.50
b.	10pf brownish rose	8.25
c.	10pf dark carmine	160.00
d.	10pf brownish red	160.00
e.	10pf rose carmine	110.00
49	A10 20pf ultra	11.00
a.	20pf Prussian blue	650.00
b.	20pf grayish ultra	60.00
c.	20pf blue (shades)	12.00
50	A10 25pf reddish orange	60.00
b.	25pf yellow orange	190.00
51	A10 50pf chocolate	20.00
a.	50pf copper brown	150.00
c.	50pf brownish red	410.00
d.	50pf reddish brown	250.00
e.	50pf dull rose brown	55.00

Germania — A11

1900, Jan. 1 *Perf. 14*

52	A11 2pf gray	.70	.50
	Never hinged	2.40	
	On cover		3.60
	On cover, single franking		5.50
a.	Imperf.	350.00	
	Never hinged	1,600.	
53	A11 3pf brown	.70	.85
	Never hinged	3.00	
	On cover		1.75
	On cover, single franking		2.25
a.	Imperf.	350.00	
	Never hinged	1,600.	
54	A11 5pf green	1.00	.50
	Never hinged	2.90	
	On cover		2.25
	On cover, single franking		2.25
55	A11 10pf carmine	1.75	.60
	Never hinged	7.25	
	On cover		1.80
	On cover, single franking		2.25
a.	Imperf.	45.00	
	Never hinged	100.00	
56	A11 20pf ultra	7.25	.50
	Never hinged	55.00	
	On cover		3.60
	On cover, single franking		7.75
57	A11 25pf orange & blk, *yel*	12.00	4.50
	Never hinged	72.50	
	On cover		19.00
	On cover, single franking		120.00
58	A11 30pf orange & blk, *sal*	17.50	.70
	Never hinged	140.00	
	On cover		16.00
	On cover, single franking		45.00
59	A11 40pf lake & black	22.50	1.10
	Never hinged	150.00	
	On cover		19.00
	On cover, single franking		65.00
60	A11 50pf pur & blk, *sal*	22.50	.95
	Never hinged	150.00	
	On cover		18.00
	On cover, single franking		65.00
61	A11 80pf lake & blk, *rose*	35.00	2.25
	Never hinged	210.00	
	On cover		45.00
	On cover, single franking		100.00
	Nos. 52-61 (10)	120.90	12.45
	Set, never hinged	795.00	

Early printings of Nos. 57-61 had "REICHSPOST" in taller and thicker letters than on the ordinary stamps.

For surcharges see Nos. 65B, Offices in China 17-32, Offices in Morocco 7-15, 32A, Offices in Turkey 13-20, 25-27.

"REICHSPOST" Larger

57a A11 25pf 1,250. 3,500.
Never hinged 3,500.
58a A11 30pf 1,250. 3,500.
Never hinged 3,500.
59a A11 40pf 1,250. 3,500.
Never hinged 3,500.
60a A11 50pf 1,250. 3,500.
Never hinged 3,500.
61a A11 80pf 1,250. 3,500.
Never hinged 3,500.

General Post Office in Berlin — A12

"Union of North and South Germany" A13

Unveiling Kaiser Wilhelm I Memorial, Berlin — A14

Wilhelm II Speaking at Empire's 25th Anniversary Celebration A15

Two types of 5m:
I — "5" is thick; "M" has slight serifs.
II — "5" thinner; "M" has distinct serifs.

Engr. ***Perf. 14½x14***

62 A12 1m carmine rose 90.00 1.75
Never hinged 375.00
On cover 275.00
On cover, single franking 360.00
a. Imperf. 2,500.
63 A13 2m gray blue 72.50 5.75
Never hinged 450.00
On cover 125.00
On cover, single franking 525.00
64 A14 3m black violet 92.50 45.00
Never hinged 575.00
On cover 1,200.
On cover, single franking 2,300.
65 A15 5m slate & car, I 1,200. 1,800.
Never hinged 3,750.
On cover 4,000.
On cover, single franking, hand painted 3,600.
d. Red and white retouched 325.00 350.00
Never hinged 1,300.
On cover 1,800.
e. White only retouched 575.00 575.00
Never hinged 1,600.
On cover 2,100.
65A A15 5m slate & car, II 325.00 325.00
Never hinged 1,300.
On cover 1,800.
On cover, single franking 3,600.

Nos. 62-65 exist perf. 11½.
The vignette and frame of No. 65 usually did not align perfectly during printing. Red paint was used to retouch the vignette and/or white paint was used to retouch the inner frame.
No. 62a is without gum.
For surcharges see Offices in China Nos. 33-36A, Offices in Morocco 16-19A, Offices in Turkey 21-24B, 28-30.

Half of No. 54 Handstamp Surcharged in Violet **3PF**

1901 ***Perf. 14***

65B A11 3pf on half of 5pf 8,250. 6,500.
Never hinged 22,500.
On newsprint wrapper 15,000.

This provisional was produced aboard the German cruiser Vineta. The purser, with the ship commander's approval, surcharged and bisected 300 5pf stamps so the ship's post office could meet the need for a 3pf (printed matter rate). The crew wanted to send home U.S. newspapers reporting celebrations of the Kaiser's birthday.
Forgeries exist and improper usages as well.

A16

1902 **Typo.**

65C A16 2pf gray 1.40 .50
Never hinged 5.75
On cover 2.50
66 A16 3pf brown .70 .85
Never hinged 2.25
On cover 2.50
a. "DFUTSCHES" 9.25 37.50
Never hinged 29.00
On cover 120.00
b. 3pf yellow brown 160.00 45.00
Never hinged 450.00
On cover 70.00
67 A16 5pf green 2.25 .85
Never hinged 14.00
On cover 1.90
a. 5pf deep blue green 150.00 8.25
Never hinged 510.00
On cover 20.00
68 A16 10pf carmine 7.25 .60
Never hinged 32.50
On cover 1.90
69 A16 20pf ultra 29.00 .85
Never hinged 100.00
On cover 3.75
a. 20pf violet blue 525.00 140.00
Never hinged 2,000.
On cover 160.00
b. 20pf gray blue 775.00 1,000.
Never hinged 5,000.
On cover —
70 A16 25pf org & blk, *yel* 45.00 1.75
Never hinged 160.00
On cover 16.50
71 A16 30pf org & blk, *sal* 50.00 .50
Never hinged 190.00
On cover 16.50
72 A16 40pf lake & blk 65.00 .95
Never hinged 250.00
On cover 16.50
73 A16 50pf pur & blk, *buff* 65.00 1.00
Never hinged 225.00
On cover 22.50
74 A16 80pf lake & blk, *rose* 140.00 2.50
Never hinged 625.00
On cover 37.50
Nos. 65C-74 (10) 405.60 10.35
Set, never hinged 1,600.

Nos. 65C-74 exist imperf. Value, set $2,000.
See Nos. 80-91, 118-119, 121-132, 169, 174, 210. For surcharges see Nos. 133-136, B1, Offices in China 37-42, 47-52, Offices in Morocco 20-28, 33-41, 45-53, Offices in Turkey 31-38, 43-50, 55-59.

A17

A18

A19

A20

Perf. 14¼-14½ (26x17 holes)

Engr.

75 A17 1m carmine rose 225.00 2.50
Never hinged 1,000.
On parcel post receipt card 25.00
On registered letter 50.00
a. Imperf. 875.00 —
Never hinged 2,300.
76 A18 2m gray blue 80.00 92.50
Never hinged 250.00
On parcel post receipt card 300.00
On registered letter 600.00
77 A19 3m black violet 70.00 17.50
Never hinged 1,000.
On parcel post receipt card 275.00
On registered letter 550.00
a. Imperf. 875.00 —
Never hinged 2,500.
78 A20 5m slate & car 210.00 17.50
Never hinged 575.00
On parcel post receipt card 300.00
On registered letter 600.00
a. Imperf. 875.00 —
Never hinged 2,750.

See Nos. 92, 94-95, 102, 111-113. For surcharges see Nos. 115-116, Offices in China 43, 45-46, 53, 55-56, Offices in Morocco 29, 31-32, 42, 44, 54, 56-57, Offices in Turkey 39, 41-42, 51, 53-54.

A21

79 A21 2m gray blue 110.00 4.75
Never hinged 300.00
On parcel post receipt card 65.00
On registered letter 140.00
a. Imperf. 775.00 —
Never hinged 2,250.
Nos. 75-79 (5) 695.00 134.75
Set, never hinged 3,125.

See Nos. 93, 114. For surcharges see Nos. 117, Offices in China 44, 54, Offices in Morocco 30, 43, 55, Offices in Turkey 40, 52.

Perf. 14 (25x16 holes)

75b A17 1m carmine red 460.00 21.00
Never hinged 1,500.
On parcel post receipt card 110.00
On registered letter 225.00
77b A19 3m black violet 60.00 21.00
Never hinged 225.00
On parcel post receipt card 325.00
On registered letter 650.00
78b A20 5m slate & car 8,800. 3,600.
Never hinged 23,750.
On parcel post receipt card 6,000.
On registered letter 12,000.
79b A18 2m gray blue 775.00 24.00
Never hinged 2,200.
On parcel post receipt card 180.00
On registered letter 360.00

1905-19 Typo. Wmk. 125 ***Perf. 14***

Wartime Printing

Stamps with dark colors, indistinct impressions, yellow gum

81 A16 3pf brown .55 1.25
Never hinged 1.00
On cover 1.40
a. 3pf dark brown 13.50 67.50
Never hinged 32.50
On cover 92.50
82 A16 5pf green (shades) .55 1.25
Never hinged 1.00
On cover 1.40
b. Bklt. pane of 5 + label ('11) 225.00 450.00
Never hinged 450.00
c. Bklt. pane of 4 + 2 labels ('10) 350.00 725.00
Never hinged 725.00
d. Bklt. pane of 2 + 4 labels ('12) 225.00 450.00
Never hinged 450.00
e. Bklt. pane, #82 + 5 #83 ('17) 62.50 160.00
Never hinged 160.00
f. Bklt. pane, 2 #82 + 4 #83 ('20) 17.00 42.50
Never hinged 42.50
g. Bklt. pane, 4 #82 + 2 #83 ('19) 17.00 42.50
Never hinged 42.50
83 A16 10pf red .55 1.25
Never hinged 1.40
On cover 1.40
b. Bklt. pane of 5 + label ('10) 300.00 600.00
Never hinged 600.00
c. Bklt. pane of 4 + 2 labels ('12) 275.00 550.00
Never hinged 550.00
d. 10pf carmine red 1.40 1.25
Never hinged 3.50
On cover 1.25
e. 10pf orange red 50.00 160.00
Never hinged 210.00
On cover 230.00
f. 10pf lilac red 230.00 75.00
Never hinged 825.00
On cover 140.00
84 A16 20pf blue vio ('18) .55 1.25
Never hinged 1.60
On cover 1.40
a. 20pf light blue 11.00 3.25
Never hinged 45.00
On cover 8.25
b. 20pf ultramarine 7.25 1.25
Never hinged 37.50
On cover 1.60
c. Imperf. 575.00 2,550.
Never hinged 1,600.
d. Half used as 10pf on cover 625.00

No. 84d was used at Field Post Office No. 107 in 1915, and at Field Post Office No. 766 during 1917.

85 A16 25pf org & blk, *yel* .55 1.25
Never hinged 1.00
On cover 1.40
86 A16 30pf org & blk, *buff* .55 1.25
Never hinged 1.00
On cover 1.40
a. 30pf org & blk, *cr* 22.50 62.50
Never hinged 62.50
On cover 125.00
87 A16 40pf lake & black .85 1.25
Never hinged 3.10
On cover 1.40
88 A16 50pf pur & blk, *buff* .55 1.25
Never hinged 1.10
On cover 1.40
a. 50pf pur & blk, *yel org* 13.50 55.00
Never hinged 35.00
On cover 92.50
89 A16 60pf magenta 1.10 1.25
Never hinged 4.10
On cover 1.60
a. 60pf red violet 11.00 8.25
Never hinged 42.50
On cover 27.50
90 A16 75pf green & blk ('19) .25 1.25
Never hinged .50
On cover 3.75
91 A16 80pf lake & blk, *rose* 1.00 1.60
Never hinged 3.25
On cover 5.00

Perf. 14½ (25x17 holes)

Engr.

92 A17 1m car rose 1.90 1.25
Never hinged 5.50
On cover 3.25
93 A21 2m brt blue 4.50 3.75
Never hinged 11.00
On cover 8.25
a. 2m gray blue ('16) 35.00 25.00
Never hinged 125.00
On cover 32.50
94 A19 3m violet gray 1.90 3.75
Never hinged 4.75
On cover 16.50
b. 3m blk violet 11.00 25.00
Never hinged 25.00
On cover 55.00
95 A20 5m slate & car 1.75 3.00
Never hinged 4.75
On cover 25.00
a. Center inverted 45,000. 65,000.
Set, #80-95, never hinged 48.80

Perf. 14¼-14¾ (26x17 holes)

92a A17 1m car red 110.00 100.00
Never hinged 450.00
On cover 130.00
93b A21 2m bright blue 77.50 45.00
Never hinged 275.00
On cover 72.50
94c A19 3m violet gray 160.00 45.00
Never hinged 600.00
On cover 825.00
95b A20 5m slate & car 55.00 82.50
Never hinged 130.00
On cover 325.00
Nos. 92a-95b (4) 402.50 272.50

Labels in No. 82c contain an "X." The version with advertising is worth 3 times as much. No. 82f has three 10pf stamps in the top row. The version with 3 on the bottom row is worth 4 times as much.

Pre-War Printing

Stamps with bright colors, sharp impressions, high quality (often surfaced) paper, white gum

80 A16 2pf gray ('05) 1.25 2.25
Never hinged 2.75
On cover 8.75
81b A16 3pf dk yellowish brn ('05) 1.40 1.10
Never hinged 3.25
On cover 1.50
82h A16 5pf dk bluish grn 1.20 1.10
Never hinged 5.25
On cover 1.50
82i A16 5pf yel grn ('05) 30.00 11.00
Never hinged 110.00
On cover 30.00
83g A16 10pf red 2.60 1.10
Never hinged 9.25
On cover 1.60
83h A16 10pf rose red ('05) 9.25 1.10
Never hinged 40.00
On cover 1.60
83i A16 10pf carmine 160.00 35.00
Never hinged 600.00
On cover 77.50
83j A16 10pf orange red 130.00 2,650.
Never hinged 450.00
On cover (late '13-14) 4,400.
84e A16 20pf ultra 10.00 1.10
Never hinged 50.00
On cover 1.90
84f A16 20pf light bl ('06) 130.00 4.50
Never hinged 650.00
On cover 10.00
84g A16 20pf vio bl ('06) 225.00 3.60
Never hinged 875.00
On cover 10.00
85a A16 25pf org & blk, *yel* ('06) 32.50 1.75
Never hinged 130.00
On cover 6.50
86b A16 30pf org & blk, *pale yel* ('05) 26.00 1.75
Never hinged 110.00
On cover 5.50
86c A16 30pf org & blk, *yel org* 550.00 55.00
Never hinged 2,000.
On cover 140.00
87a A16 40pf lake & blk ('06) 32.50 1.75
Never hinged 130.00
On cover 10.00
88b A16 50pf pur & blk, *pale yel* ('06) 55.00 1.90
Never hinged 160.00
On cover 10.00

88c A16 50pf pur & blk, *yel org* 550.00 55.00
Never hinged 3,000.
On cover 110.00
89b A16 60pf magenta ('11) 150.00 12.00
Never hinged 575.00
On cover 65.00
89c A16 60pf violet 825.00 725.00
Never hinged 2,500.
On cover 1,650.
91a A16 80pf lake & blk, *rose* ('06) 16.50 2.50
Never hinged 65.00
On cover 10.00

Engr.

Perf. 14¼-14¾ (26x17 holes)

92b A17 1m car red ('06) 60.00 2.25
Never hinged 275.00
On cover 19.00
93c A17 2m brt blue ('06) 55.00 2.25
Never hinged 240.00
On cover 19.00
94a A17 3m brnsh vio ('11) 45.00 23.00
Never hinged 160.00
On cover 100.00
95c A17 5m slate & car ('06) 37.50 19.00
Never hinged 77.50
On cover 110.00

Surcharged and overprinted stamps of designs A16-A22 are listed under Allenstein, Belgium, Danzig, France, Latvia, Lithuania, Marienwerder, Memel, Poland, Romania, Saar and Upper Silesia.

A22

1916-19 **Typo.**

96 A22 2pf lt gray ('18) .25 *3.25*
Never hinged .50
On cover *7.75*
97 A22 2½pf lt gray .25 .95
Never hinged .45
On cover 2.50
98 A22 7½pf red orange .25 1.25
Never hinged .45
On cover 2.25
b. Bklt. pane, 4 #98 + 2 #100 90.00 225.00
Never hinged 225.00
c. Bklt. pane, 2 #98 + 4 #99 77.50 190.00
Never hinged 190.00
d. Bklt. pane, 2 #98 + 4 #100 90.00 225.00
Never hinged 225.00
e. Bklt. pane, 2 #82 + 4 #98 26.00 62.50
Never hinged 62.50
f. 7½pf yellow orange 3.25 1.25
Never hinged 10.00
On cover 2.50
99 A22 15pf yellow brown 2.50 1.25
Never hinged 8.50
On cover 2.25
a. 15pf olive brown 16.50 *19.00*
Never hinged 60.00
On cover 37.50
100 A22 15pf dk violet ('17) .20 *1.25*
Never hinged .60
On cover *2.00*
a. 15pf blue violet 32.50 23.00
Never hinged 100.00
On cover 40.00
b. Bklt. pane, 4 #82 + 2 #100 90.00 225.00
Never hinged 225.00
c. Bklt. pane, 2 #83 + 4 #100 62.50 160.00
Never hinged 160.00
d. 15pf blackish violet 2.75 1.40
Never hinged 7.75
On cover 3.60
101 A22 35pf red brown ('19) .20 *1.25*
Never hinged .50
On cover *3.00*
a. 35pf dk lake brown 20.00 18.00
Never hinged 60.00
On cover 52.50
Nos. 96-101 (6) 3.65 *9.20*
Set, never hinged 11.00

See No. 120. For surcharge see No. B2.
Nos. 98e and 100c have the 2 stamps first in the bottom row.

Type of 1902

1920 Engr. Wmk. 192 ***Perf. 14½***

102 A19 3m black violet 1,600. *3,200.*
Never hinged 3,850.

Republic
National Assembly Issue

A23

A24

Rebuilding Germany — A25

Designs: A23, Live Stump of Tree Symbolizing that Germany will Survive her Difficulties. A24, New Shoots from Oak Stump Symbolical of New Government.

Perf. 13x13½

1919-20 Unwmk. Typo.

105 A23 10pf carmine rose .20 1.25
Never hinged .45
On cover 2.25
106 A24 15pf choc & blue .20 1.25
Never hinged .45
On cover 2.25
107 A25 25pf green & red .20 1.25
Never hinged .45
On cover 2.25
a. "1019" instead of "1919" 82.50 *250.00*
Never hinged 200.00
On cover *325.00*
108 A25 30pf red vio & red ('20) .20 1.25
Never hinged .90
On cover 2.25
a. A25 30pf pale lilac & brownish red 4.10 *13.50*
Never hinged 16.50
On cover *27.50*
b. "1019" instead of "1919" 40.00 *125.00*
Never hinged 100.00
On cover *225.00*
Nos. 105-108 (4) .80 *5.00*
Set, never hinged 2.25

Types of 1902
Perf. 15x14½

1920 Wmk. 125 Offset

111 A17 1m red 1.60 1.40
Never hinged 7.25
On cover 2.75
112 A17 1.25m green 1.40 1.40
Never hinged 5.00
On cover 2.25
113 A17 1.50m yellow brown .20 *1.40*
Never hinged .85
On cover *1.90*
a. 1.50m dark brown 6.00 *16.50*
Never hinged 25.00
On cover *45.00*
b. 1.50m red brown 16.50 12.00
Never hinged 75.00
On cover 25.00
114 A21 2.50m lilac rose .20 *1.10*
Never hinged .85
On cover *2.75*
a. 2.50m magenta 1.50 *1.75*
Never hinged 5.00
On cover 16.50
b. 2.50m brown lilac .45 *1.50*
Never hinged 1.25
On cover *2.75*
Nos. 111-114 (4) 3.40 *5.30*
Set, never hinged 14.00

Nos. 111, 112 and 113 differ from the illustration in many minor respects. The numerals of Nos. 75 and 92 are outlined, with shaded background. Those of No. 111 are plain, with solid background and flags have been added to the top of the building, at right and left.

Types of 1902 Surcharged

1920 Engr. ***Perf. 14½***

115 A17 1.25m on 1m green .40 *5.25*
Never hinged 1.40
On cover *11.00*
116 A17 1.50m on 1m org brn .25 *5.75*
Never hinged 1.40
On cover *11.00*
117 A21 2.50m on 2m lilac rose 8.00 *190.00*
Never hinged 19.00
On cover *300.00*
Nos. 115-117 (3) 8.65 *201.00*
Set, never hinged 21.80

Germania Types of 1902-16

1920 Typo. ***Perf. 14, 14½***

118 A16 5pf brown .20 *1.10*
Never hinged .60
On cover *2.25*
a. 5pf dark brown 1.60 *6.00*
Never hinged 4.10
On cover *10.00*
119 A16 10pf orange .20 *1.10*
Never hinged .45
On cover *1.60*
a. Tête bêche pair .70 *5.00*
Never hinged 1.75
d. Bklt. pane, 4 #119 + 2 #123 2.10 11.00
Never hinged 5.25
120 A22 15pf violet brn .20 *1.10*
Never hinged .45
On cover *2.25*
a. Imperf. 35.00
Never hinged 95.00
b. 15pf pale lake brn 1.25 *5.50*
Never hinged 3.75
On cover *8.25*
c. Bklt. pane, 4 #84 + 2 #120 5.25 12.50
Never hinged 12.50
121 A16 20pf green .20 *1.10*
Never hinged .55
On cover *2.25*
a. Imperf. 225.00
b. 20pf yellow green 1.00 *2.50*
Never hinged 2.75
On cover *6.50*
c. 20pf blue green 30.00 *100.00*
Never hinged 120.00
On cover *140.00*
123 A16 30pf dull blue .20 *1.00*
Never hinged .45
On cover *1.60*
a. Tête bêche pair .70 *5.75*
Never hinged 1.75
d. Bklt. pane, 2 #123 + 4 #124 2.10 11.00
Never hinged 5.25
124 A16 40pf carmine rose .20 *1.10*
Never hinged .45
On cover *1.60*
a. Tête bêche pair .70 *5.00*
Never hinged 1.75
b. Imperf. 140.00 700.00
Never hinged 350.00
d. Bklt. pane, 2 #124 + 4 #126 3.75 35.00
Never hinged 9.75
125 A16 50pf red lilac .45 *1.50*
Never hinged 1.40
On cover *2.75*
126 A16 60pf olive green .20 *1.00*
Never hinged .45
On cover *1.60*
a. Tête bêche pair .60 *8.25*
Never hinged 1.50
c. Imperf. 140.00
Never hinged 350.00
127 A16 75pf red violet .20 *1.00*
Never hinged .65
On cover *2.25*
128 A16 80pf blue violet .20 *1.10*
Never hinged .65
On cover *2.25*
a. Imperf. 140.00
Never hinged 350.00
b. 80pf grayish ultra 13.50 *50.00*
Never hinged 50.00
On cover *65.00*
129 A16 1m violet & grn .20 *1.00*
Never hinged .45
On cover *2.25*
a. Imperf. 77.50
Never hinged 125.00
130 A16 1¼m ver & mag .20 *1.00*
Never hinged .45
On cover *2.25*
131 A16 2m carmine & bl .50 *1.00*
Never hinged 1.10
On cover *2.75*
132 A16 4m black & rose .20 *1.25*
Never hinged .50
On cover *3.25*
Nos. 118-132 (14) 3.35 *15.35*
Set, never hinged 8.60

Stamps of 1920 Surcharged:

No. 133

No. 135

Nos. 134, 136

1921, Aug.

133 A16 1.60m on 5pf .20 1.25
Never hinged .55
On cover 2.50
a. On #118a 65.00 *360.00*
Never hinged 180.00
On cover 425.00
134 A16 3m on 1¼m .20 1.25
Never hinged .55
On cover 2.50
135 A16 5m on 75pf (G) .20 1.25
Never hinged .55
On cover 2.50
136 A16 10m on 75pf .25 1.25
Never hinged .85
On cover 3.00
Nos. 133-136 (4) .85 *5.00*
Set, never hinged 2.50

In 1920 the current stamps of Bavaria were overprinted "Deutsches Reich". These stamps were available for postage throughout Germany, but because they were used almost exclusively in Bavaria, they are listed among the issues of that state.

A26

Iron Workers
A27

Miners
A28

Farmers
A29

Post Horn
A30

Numeral of Value — A31

Plowing A32

Wmk. Lozenges (125)

1921 Typo. *Perf. 14*

137 A26 5pf claret .20 *1.75*
Never hinged .30
On cover *4.10*
138 A26 10pf olive green .20 *1.10*
Never hinged .50
On cover *1.60*
a. Tête bêche pair .70 *20.00*
Never hinged 1.75
b. Bklt. pane, 5 #138 + 1 #141 3.75 52.50
Never hinged 9.75
c. 10pf blackish olive 30.00 *275.00*
Never hinged 140.00
On cover *325.00*
139 A26 15pf grnsh blue .20 *1.10*
Never hinged .35
On cover *2.75*
140 A26 25pf dark brown .20 *1.10*
Never hinged .35
On cover *1.60*
141 A26 30pf blue green .20 *1.10*
Never hinged .35
On cover *2.25*
a. Tête bêche pair .65 *16.00*
Never hinged 1.60
b. Bklt. pane, 2 #124 + 4 #141 4.00 35.00
Never hinged 10.00
142 A26 40pf red orange .20 *1.10*
Never hinged .35
On cover *1.60*
143 A26 50pf violet .30 *1.25*
Never hinged .30
On cover *2.50*
144 A27 60pf red violet .20 *1.10*
Never hinged .35
On cover *1.60*
145 A27 80pf carmine rose .20 *5.00*
Never hinged .35
On cover *13.50*
146 A28 100pf yellow grn .30 *1.60*
Never hinged .90
On cover *5.00*
147 A28 120pf ultra .20 *1.10*
Never hinged .35
On cover *3.25*
148 A29 150pf orange .20 *1.60*
Never hinged .45
On cover *3.25*
149 A29 160pf slate grn .20 *7.25*
Never hinged .35
On cover *16.50*
150 A30 2m dp vio & rose .35 *3.25*
Never hinged 1.25
On cover *6.50*
151 A30 3m red & yel .35 *14.50*
Never hinged 1.25
On cover *27.50*
152 A30 4m dp grn & yel grn .20 *3.25*
Never hinged .85
On cover *5.50*

Engr.

153 A31 5m orange .30 *1.25*
Never hinged 1.00
On cover *2.75*
a. 5m brown orange 13.00 *25.00*
Never hinged 55.00
On cover *40.00*
b. 5m red orange 47.50 *140.00*
Never hinged 175.00
On cover *190.00*
154 A31 10m carmine rose .40 *2.25*
Never hinged 1.10
On cover *4.10*
155 A32 20m indigo & grn .90 *2.50*
Never hinged 3.25
On cover *5.00*
a. Green background inverted 160.00 *775.00*
Never hinged 575.00
On cover *925.00*
b. 20m blk bl & dull grn 30.00 *72.50*
Never hinged 75.00
On cover *125.00*
Nos. 137-155 (19) 5.30 *53.15*
Set, never hinged 13.95

See Nos. 156-209, 211, 222-223, 225, 227. For surcharges and overprints see Nos. 241-245, 247-248, 261-262, 273-276, B6-B7, O24.

1922 Litho. *Perf. 14½x14*

156 A31 100m brown vio, *buff* .20 *1.10*
Never hinged .45
On cover *2.75*
157 A31 200m rose, *buff* .20 *1.10*
Never hinged .45
On cover *2.50*
158 A31 300m green, *buff* .20 *1.10*
Never hinged .45
On cover *2.25*
159 A31 400m bis brn, *buff* .40 *1.90*
Never hinged .95
On cover *6.50*
a. 400m ol brn, *buff* 3.25 *16.50*
Never hinged 12.00
On cover *22.50*
b. 400m red brn, *buff* 20.00 *120.00*
Never hinged 50.00
On cover *160.00*
c. 400m pale brn, *buff* 24.00 *125.00*
Never hinged 72.50
On cover *160.00*
160 A31 500m orange, *buff* .20 *1.10*
Never hinged .35
On cover *2.75*
Nos. 156-160 (5) 1.20 *6.30*
Set, never hinged 2.65

Postally Used vs. CTO

Values quoted for canceled copies of the 1921-1923 issues are for postally used stamps. These bring higher prices than the plentiful canceled-to-order specimens made by applying genuine handstamps to remainders. C.T.O. examples sell for about the same price as unused stamps. Certification of postal usage by competent authorities is necessary.

Perf. 14, 14½

1921-22 Typo. Wmk. 126

161 A26 5pf claret .65 *160.00*
Never hinged 1.50
On cover *300.00*
162 A26 10pf olive grn 3.75 *140.00*
Never hinged 13.00
On cover *250.00*
163 A26 15pf grnsh blue .55 *175.00*
Never hinged 1.10
On cover *300.00*
164 A26 25pf dark brown .20 *3.00*
Never hinged .35
On cover *6.50*
165 A26 30pf blue green .85 *275.00*
Never hinged 1.90
On cover *500.00*
166 A26 40pf red orange .20 *3.75*
Never hinged .45
On cover *8.25*
167 A26 50pf violet ('21) .20 *1.25*
Never hinged .45
On cover *1.60*
168 A27 60pf red violet .20 *19.00*
Never hinged .35
On cover *30.00*
169 A16 75pf red violet .30 *1.90*
Never hinged 1.00
On cover *6.00*
a. 75pf rose lilac 82.50 *120.00*
Never hinged 275.00
On cover *140.00*
170 A26 75pf deep ultra .20 *3.00*
Never hinged .35
On cover *6.50*
171 A27 80pf car rose .40 *52.50*
Never hinged .95
On cover *82.50*
172 A28 100pf olive green .20 *1.25*
Never hinged .45
On cover *1.60*
a. Imperf. 29.00 *625.00*
Never hinged 72.50
b. 100pf bluish green 5.25 *26.00*
Never hinged 13.00
On cover *47.50*
c. 100pf blackish green 6.50 *20.00*
Never hinged 16.50
On cover *26.00*
173 A28 120pf ultra .65 *97.50*
Never hinged 1.60
On cover *160.00*
174 A16 1¼m ver & mag .20 *1.10*
Never hinged .35
On cover *1.90*
175 A29 150pf orange .20 *1.10*
Never hinged .35
On cover *1.60*
a. Imperf. 5.75
Never hinged 15.00
176 A29 160pf slate green .65 *140.00*
Never hinged 1.50
On cover *225.00*
177 A30 2m violet & rose .20 *1.10*
Never hinged .85
On cover *1.60*
178 A30 3m red & yel ('21) .20 *1.10*
Never hinged .65
On cover *2.25*
a. Imperf. 11.50 *300.00*
Never hinged 35.00
179 A30 4m dp grn & yel grn .20 *1.10*
Never hinged .85
On cover *2.50*
180 A30 5m org & yel .20 *1.40*
Never hinged .35
On cover *4.10*
a. Imperf. 140.00
Never hinged 525.00
181 A30 10m car & pale rose .20 *1.10*
Never hinged .35
On cover *2.75*
a. Pale rose (background) omitted 32.50 *825.00*
Never hinged 140.00
182 A30 20m violet & org .20 *1.10*
Never hinged .45
On cover *2.25*
183 A30 30m brown & yel .20 *1.10*
Never hinged .50
On cover *1.60*
184 A30 50m dk grn & vio .20 *1.10*
Never hinged .50
On cover *1.60*
Nos. 161-184 (24) 11.00 *1,084.*
Set, never hinged 30.00

1922-23

SIX MARKS:

Type I — Numerals upright.
Type II — Numerals leaning toward the right and slightly thinner.

EIGHT MARKS:

Type I — Numerals 2½mm wide with thick strokes.
Type II — Numerals 2mm wide with thinner strokes.

185 A30 2m blue violet .20 *1.10*
Never hinged .45
On cover *1.60*
a. Imperf. 140.00
Never hinged 190.00
b. 2m deep reddish vio 1.90 *6.50*
Never hinged 6.50
On cover *13.00*
c. 2m deep violet 16.50 *75.00*
Never hinged 45.00
On cover *120.00*
186 A30 3m red .20 *.95*
Never hinged .45
On cover *1.60*
187 A30 4m dark green .20 *1.10*
Never hinged .60
On cover *1.60*
a. Imperf. 8.25
Never hinged 8.25
188 A30 5m orange .20 *1.10*
Never hinged .60
On cover *1.60*
a. Imperf. 110.00
Never hinged 160.00
189 A30 6m dark blue (II) .20 *1.10*
Never hinged .60
On cover *1.60*
a. Type I .20 *.30*
Never hinged 1.50
On cover *2.50*
b. Imperf. 110.00
Never hinged 160.00
190 A30 8m olive green (I) .20 *1.25*
Never hinged .90
On cover *2.50*
a. Type II .40 *37.50*
Never hinged 1.20
On cover *45.00*
191 A30 20m dk violet ('23) .20 *1.10*
Never hinged .60
On cover *2.25*
192 A30 30m pur brn ('23) .20 *7.25*
Never hinged .50
On cover *12.00*
a. 30m deep brown 1.20 *32.50*
Never hinged 3.25
On cover *57.50*
193 A30 40m lt green .20 *1.50*
Never hinged .90
On cover *2.25*

Engr.

194 A31 5m orange .25 *1.10*
Never hinged 1.10
On cover *2.50*
a. Imperf. 140.00
Never hinged 225.00
b. 5m red orange 25.00 *60.00*
Never hinged 65.00
On cover *90.00*
c. 5m brown orange 35.00 *27.50*
Never hinged 250.00
On cover *50.00*
195 A31 10m carmine rose .55 *1.90*
Never hinged 1.50
On cover *4.00*
196 A32 20m indigo & grn .20 *3.25*
Never hinged .65
On cover *5.00*
a. Imperf. 160.00
Never hinged 225.00
b. Green background inverted 29.00 *375.00*
Never hinged 72.50
c. Green background double 650.00 *3,250.*
Never hinged 2,500.
Nos. 185-196 (12) 2.80 *22.70*
Set, never hinged 8.85

1922-23 Litho. *Perf. 14½x14*

198 A31 50m indigo .20 *1.25*
Never hinged .55
On cover *2.50*
199 A31 100m brn vio, *buff* ('23) .20 *.85*
Never hinged .40
On cover *2.50*
200 A31 200m rose, *buff* ('23) .20 *1.25*
Never hinged .45
On cover *2.25*
a. 200m pale red, *buff* 3.00 *22.50*
Never hinged 10.00
On cover *40.00*
b. 200m reddish lilac, *buff* 20.00 *60.00*
Never hinged 72.50
On cover *92.50*
201 A31 300m grn, *buff* ('23) .20 *.85*
Never hinged .40
On cover *1.60*
202 A31 400m bis brn, *buff* ('23) .20 *.85*
Never hinged .40
On cover *1.60*
203 A31 500m org, *buff* ('23) .20 *.85*
Never hinged .40
On cover *1.60*
204 A31 1000m gray ('23) .20 *.85*
Never hinged .40
On cover *1.60*
205 A31 2000m bl ('23) .35 *1.25*
Never hinged .50
On cover *1.60*
a. 2000m dark blue .60 *5.50*
Never hinged 2.50
On cover *12.00*
206 A31 3000m brn ('23) .20 *2.75*
Never hinged .50
On cover *2.75*
a. 3000m deep yel brn .50 *2.50*
Never hinged 1.60
On cover *4.50*
b. 3000m dk gray brn .85 *4.75*
Never hinged 2.75
On cover *8.75*
c. 3000m blk brn 60.00 *300.00*
Never hinged 160.00
On cover *450.00*
207 A31 4000m vio ('23) .20 *1.25*
Never hinged .40
On cover *3.75*
a. Imperf. 25.00 *140.00*
Never hinged 52.50
208 A31 5000m gray grn ('23) .30 *1.25*
Never hinged .40
On cover *3.25*
a. Imperf. 35.00 *175.00*
Never hinged 92.50
b. 5000m dp bl grn 1.10 *37.50*
Never hinged 3.25
On cover *60.00*
c. 5000m blk grn 5.00 *150.00*
Never hinged 25.00
On cover *250.00*
209 A31 100,000m ver ('23) .20 *.85*
Never hinged .55
On cover *2.75*
a. Imperf. 35.00
Never hinged 92.50
Nos. 198-209 (12) 2.65 *14.10*
Set, never hinged 5.35

1920-22 Wmk. 127 Typo.

210 A16 1¼m ver & mag 450.00 *725.00*
Never hinged 1,150.
On cover *950.00*
211 A30 50m grn & vio ('22) 1.10 *775.00*
Never hinged 3.25
On cover *1,200.*

Wmk. 127 was intended for use only in printing revenue stamps.

Arms of Munich — A33

Wmk. Network (126)

1922, Apr. 22 Typo. *Perf. 13x13½*

212 A33 1¼m claret .20 *1.25*
Never hinged .75
On cover *2.75*
a. 1¼m brn car 2.50 *6.50*
Never hinged 6.50
On cover *13.50*
b. 1¼m pale lilac rose 30.00 *190.00*
Never hinged 82.50
On cover *275.00*
213 A33 2m dark violet .20 *1.25*
Never hinged .75
On cover *2.75*
a. 2m dk red vio 20.00 *110.00*
Never hinged 65.00
On cover *140.00*
214 A33 3m vermilion .20 *1.25*
Never hinged .55
On cover *2.75*
215 A33 4m deep blue .20 *1.25*
Never hinged .55
On cover *2.75*

Wmk. Lozenges (125)

216 A33 10m brown, *buff* .55 *2.50*
Never hinged 2.10
On cover *6.50*
a. 10m vio brn, *buff* 20.00 *70.00*
Never hinged 75.00
On cover *92.50*
217 A33 20m lilac rose, *pink* 3.25 *8.75*
Never hinged 10.00
On cover *20.00*
a. 20m red, *pink* 10.00 *50.00*
Never hinged 35.00
On cover *82.50*
Nos. 212-217 (6) 4.60 *16.25*
Set, never hinged 14.70

Munich Industrial Fair.

Type of 1921 and

Miners — A34

A35

1922-23 Wmk. 126 *Perf. 14*

221 A34 5m orange .20 *13.00*
Never hinged .30
On cover *27.50*
222 A29 10m dull blue ('22) .20 *1.10*
Never hinged .30
On cover *1.60*
223 A29 12m vermilion ('22) .20 *1.10*
Never hinged .30
On cover *3.25*
224 A34 20m red lilac .20 *1.10*
Never hinged .40
On cover *1.60*
a. Wmk. sideways .35 *60.00*
Never hinged 1.40
On cover *92.50*

225 A29 25m olive brown .20 *1.10*
Never hinged .30
On cover *2.75*
226 A34 30m olive green .20 *1.90*
Never hinged .40
On cover *6.50*
a. 30m blk ol grn .50 *37.50*
Never hinged 1.90
On cover *60.00*
227 A29 40m green .20 *1.10*
Never hinged .35
On cover *2.25*
228 A34 50m grnsh blue .35 *110.00*
Never hinged .90
On cover *190.00*
229 A35 100m violet .20 *1.25*
Never hinged .45
On cover *2.25*
a. 100m purple violet .30 *1.20*
Never hinged .45
On cover *2.75*
230 A35 200m carmine rose .20 *1.25*
Never hinged .30
On cover *3.25*
231 A35 300m green .20 *1.10*
Never hinged .30
On cover *2.75*
232 A35 400m dark brown .20 *5.50*
Never hinged .30
On cover *10.00*
233 A35 500m red orange .20 *5.75*
Never hinged .30
On cover *10.00*
234 A35 1000m slate .20 *1.10*
Never hinged .30
On cover *3.25*
Nos. 221-234 (14) 2.95 *146.35*
Set, never hinged 5.50

The 50m was issued only in vertical coils.
Nos. 222-223 exist imperf.
For surcharges and overprints see Nos. 246, 249-260, 263-271, 277, 310, B5, O22-O23, O25-O28.

Wartburg Castle — A36

Cathedral of Cologne — A37

1923 **Engr.**
237 A36 5000m deep blue .20 *2.25*
Never hinged .65
On cover *5.00*
a. Imperf. 250.00 *625.00*
Never hinged 625.00
b. 5000m dk grn bl 5.50 *45.00*
Never hinged 16.50
On cover *65.00*
238 A37 10,000m brn ol .30 *3.50*
Never hinged .70
On cover *10.00*
a. 10,000m ol grn .70 *8.25*
Never hinged 2.50
On cover *15.00*
Set, never hinged 1.35

Abbreviations:
Th = (Tausend) Thousand
Mil = (Million) Million
Mlrd = (Milliarde) Billion

A38

1923 **Typo.**
238A A38 5th m grnsh blue .20 *16.00*
Never hinged .20
On cover *32.50*
b. Imperf. 87.50
Never hinged 225.00
239 A38 50th m bister .20 *1.25*
Never hinged .30
On cover *2.25*
a. Imperf. 11.00 *1,600.*
Never hinged 26.00
240 A38 75th m dark violet .20 *10.00*
Never hinged .20
On cover *16.50*
Set, never hinged .75

For surcharges see Nos. 272, 278.

Stamps and Types of 1922-23 Surcharged in Black, Blue, Green or Brown with Bars over Original Value

Wmk. Lozenges (125)

1923 ***Perf. 14***
241 A26 8th m on 30pf .20 *1.40*
Never hinged .35
On cover *2.25*
a. "8" inverted 17.50 *275.00*
Never hinged 55.00

Wmk. Network (126)

242 A26 5th m on 40pf .20 *1.40*
Never hinged .30
On cover *2.25*
242A A26 8th m on 30pf 14.50 *3,850.*
Never hinged 37.50
On cover *7,000.*
243 A29 15th m on 40m .20 *1.25*
Never hinged .50
On cover *1.90*
244 A29 20th m on 12m .20 *1.40*
Never hinged .30
On cover *2.75*
a. Inverted surcharge 100.00 *875.00*
245 A29 20th m on 25m .20 *2.25*
Never hinged .30
On cover *3.75*
246 A35 20th m on 200m .20 *1.60*
Never hinged .50
On cover *2.25*
a. Inverted surcharge 57.50 625.00
Never hinged 140.00
247 A29 25th m on 25m .20 *14.50*
Never hinged .30
On cover *32.50*
248 A29 30th m on 10m dp bl .20 *1.10*
Never hinged .30
On cover *2.75*
a. Inverted surcharge 65.00
Never hinged 150.00
249 A35 30th m on 200m pale bl (Bl) .20 *1.10*
Never hinged .30
On cover *2.75*
a. Without surcharge 110.00
Never hinged 225.00
250 A35 75th m on 300m yel grn .20 *14.50*
Never hinged .30
On cover *32.50*
a. Imperf. 45.00
Never hinged 90.00
251 A35 75th m on 400m yel grn .20 *1.40*
Never hinged .35
On cover *2.25*
252 A35 75th m on 1000m yel grn .20 *1.60*
Never hinged .50
On cover *2.50*
a. Without surcharge 110.00
Never hinged 225.00
253 A35 100th m on 100m .20 *1.50*
Never hinged .50
On cover *3.25*
a. Double surcharge 125.00
Never hinged 300.00
b. Inverted surcharge 14.50
Never hinged 37.50
254 A35 100th m on 400m bluish grn (G) .20 *1.10*
Never hinged .30
On cover *1.60*
a. Imperf. 50.00 *525.00*
Never hinged 110.00
b. Without surcharge 110.00
Never hinged 225.00
255 A35 125th m on 1000m sal .20 *1.50*
Never hinged .45
On cover *2.75*
256 A35 250th m on 200m .20 *5.25*
Never hinged .30
On cover *12.00*
a. Inverted surcharge 29.00
Never hinged 77.50
b. Double surcharge 45.00
Never hinged 110.00
257 A35 250th m on 300m dp grn .20 *16.00*
Never hinged .30
On cover *27.50*
a. Inverted surcharge 29.00
Never hinged 77.50
258 A35 250th m on 400m .20 *16.00*
Never hinged .30
On cover *27.50*
a. Inverted surcharge 22.50
Never hinged 62.50
259 A35 250th m on 500m pink .20 *1.10*
Never hinged .30
On cover *1.60*
a. Imperf. 50.00
Never hinged 100.00
260 A35 250th m on 500m red org .20 *16.00*
Never hinged .30
On cover *27.50*
a. Double surcharge 26.00
Never hinged 57.50
b. Inverted surcharge 25.00
Never hinged 72.50
261 A26 800th m on 5pf lt grn (G) .20 *3.75*
Never hinged .30
On cover *8.25*
a. Imperf. 29.00 *140.00*
Never hinged 85.00
262 A26 800th m on 10pf lt grn (G) .20 *4.50*
Never hinged .30
On cover *8.25*
a. Imperf. 29.00
Never hinged 85.00
263 A35 800th m on 200m .20 *62.50*
Never hinged .35
On cover *160.00*
a. Double surcharge 72.50
Never hinged 175.00
b. Inverted surcharge 35.00
Never hinged 92.50
264 A35 800th m on 300m lt grn (G) .20 *4.50*
Never hinged .30
On cover *6.50*
a. Black surcharge 42.50
Never hinged 75.00
265 A35 800th m on 400m dk brn .20 *14.50*
Never hinged .30
On cover *37.50*
a. Inverted surcharge 35.00
Never hinged 92.50
b. Double surcharge 45.00
Never hinged 125.00
266 A35 800th m on 400m lt grn (G) .20 *3.75*
Never hinged .30
On cover *6.50*
267 A35 800th m on 500m lt grn (G) .20 *1,250.*
Never hinged .45
On cover *1,650.*
a. 800th m on 500m red org (Bk) 35.00
Never hinged 60.00
268 A35 800th m on 1000m lt grn (G) .20 *1.25*
Never hinged .40
On cover *2.75*
269 A35 2mil m on 200m rose red .20 *1.25*
Never hinged .50
On cover *1.60*
b. 2mil m on 200m car rose (#230) *1,250.*
Never hinged *2,850.*
c. As "b," wmk sideways 1.40 *300.00*
Never hinged 4.10
270 A35 2mil m on 300m dp grn .20 *1.60*
Never hinged .30
On cover *3.25*
a. Inverted surcharge 35.00
Never hinged 92.50
b. Double surcharge 45.00
Never hinged 125.00
271 A35 2mil m on 500m dl rose .20 *6.50*
Never hinged .30
On cover *11.00*
272 A38 2mil m on 5th m dl rose .20 *1.25*
Never hinged .65
On cover *1.60*
b. Imperf. 42.50 *125.00*
Never hinged 85.00

Nos. 264a, 267a were not put in use.

Serrate Roulette 13½

273 A26 400th m on 15pf bis (Br) .20 *4.50*
Never hinged .30
On cover *6.50*
a. Imperf. 45.00 190.00
Never hinged 97.50
274 A26 400th m on 25pf bis (Br) .20 *4.50*
Never hinged .30
On cover *6.50*
a. Imperf. 82.50 *190.00*
Never hinged 140.00
275 A26 400th m on 30pf bis (Br) .20 *4.50*
Never hinged .30
On cover *6.50*
a. Imperf. 32.50
Never hinged 82.50
b. Double surcharge 90.00
Never hinged 175.00
276 A26 400th m on 40pf bis (Br) .20 *4.50*
Never hinged .30
On cover *6.50*
a. Imperf. 32.50
Never hinged 82.50
b. Double surcharge 90.00
Never hinged 175.00
277 A35 2mil m on 200m rose red .45 *125.00*
Never hinged .55
On cover *160.00*
278 A38 2mil m on 5th m dull rose .20 *7.75*
Never hinged .30
On cover *15.50*
Nos. 241-278 (39) 22.35 *5,458.*
Set, never hinged 51.00

Surcharge Omitted

272c A38 2mil m on 5th m 150.00
Never hinged 375.00
273b A26 400th m on 15pf 150.00
Never hinged 375.00
274b A26 400th m on 25pf 150.00
Never hinged 375.00
275c A26 400th m on 30pf 150.00
Never hinged 375.00
276c A26 400th m on 40pf 150.00
Never hinged 375.00

A39

A39a

The stamps of types A39 and A39a usually have the value darker than the rest of the design.

1923 **Wmk. 126** ***Perf. 14***
280 A39 500th m brown .20 *2.50*
Never hinged .30
On cover *6.50*
281 A39 1mil m grnsh bl .20 *1.25*
Never hinged .40
On cover *1.60*
a. Imperf. 45.00 *250.00*
Never hinged 100.00
282 A39 2mil m dull vio .20 *20.00*
Never hinged .40
On cover *35.00*
a. 2mil m deep pur 35.00 *7,200.*
Never hinged 100.00
On cover *8,500.*
284 A39 4mil m yel grn .20 1.40
Never hinged .40
On cover 2.50
a. Value double 57.50
Never hinged 140.00
b. Imperf. 35.00
Never hinged 87.50
285 A39 5mil m rose .20 *1.10*
Never hinged .35
On cover 1.60
286 A39 10mil m red .20 .95
Never hinged .35
On cover 1.60
a. Value double 50.00 *475.00*
Never hinged 125.00
287 A39 20mil m ultra .20 *1.40*
Never hinged .35
On cover 2.50
a. 20mil m blk bl (rotary press) 12.00 *1,500.*
Never hinged 27.50
On cover *1,900.*
288 A39 30mil m red brn .20 *9.25*
Never hinged .35
On cover *16.50*

289 A39 50mil m dull ol grn .20 *1.40*
Never hinged .40
On cover *2.75*
a. Imperf. 45.00 *250.00*
Never hinged 100.00
b. Value inverted 37.50
Never hinged 120.00
c. 50mil m bl grn (rotary press) 1.60 *47.50*
Never hinged 4.50
On cover *100.00*
290 A39 100mil m gray .20 *.95*
Never hinged .35
On cover *2.50*
291 A39 200mil m bis brn .20 *.95*
Never hinged .35
On cover *2.25*
a. Imperf. 19.00
Never hinged 52.50
293 A39 500mil m ol grn .20 *.95*
Never hinged .35
On cover *2.25*
294 A39a 1mlrd m choc .30 *1.25*
Never hinged .35
On cover *2.25*
a. 1mlrd m blk brn (flat press) 450.00 *6,750.*
Never hinged 1,200.
On cover *11,000.*
b. 1mlrd m blk brn (rotary press) 7.75 *77.50*
Never hinged 23.00
On cover *120.00*
295 A39a 2mlrd m pale brn & grn .20 *1.40*
Never hinged .30
On cover *2.50*
296 A39a 5mlrd m yellow & brn .20 *1.25*
Never hinged .30
On cover *2.50*
297 A39a 10mlrd m ap grn & grn .20 *1.25*
Never hinged .30
On cover *2.75*
a. Imperf. 29.00 *225.00*
Never hinged 72.50
298 A39a 20mlrd m bluish grn & brn .20 *1.60*
Never hinged .45
On cover *2.75*
299 A39a 50mlrd m bl & dp bl .20 *32.50*
Never hinged .90
On cover *55.00*
Nos. 280-299 (18) 3.70 *81.35*
Set, never hinged 6.95

Nos. 294, 294a are 21.5x17.7mm. Nos. 287a, 289c, 294b are 22x18mm. Nos. 287, 289 exist from both flat and rotary press printings.

See Nos. 301-309. For surcharges and overprints see Nos. 311-321, O40-O46.

Value Omitted

280a A39 500th m 92.50 *360.00*
Never hinged 190.00
281b A39 1mil m 55.00
Never hinged 140.00
284c A39 4mil m 72.50
Never hinged 140.00
285a A39 5mil m 72.50 *360.00*
Never hinged 140.00
286b A39 10mil m 100.00 *360.00*
Never hinged 160.00
287b A39 20mil m 37.50
Never hinged 65.00
290a A39 100mil m 50.00
Never hinged 82.50
291b A39 200mil m 72.50
Never hinged 120.00
293a A39 500mil m 50.00
Never hinged 82.50
294c A39 1mlrd m 50.00
Never hinged 82.50
296a A39 5mlrd m 50.00
Never hinged 82.50
298a A39 20mlrd m 62.50
Never hinged 120.00
299a A39 50mlrd m 62.50
Never hinged 120.00

Serrate Roulette 13½

301 A39 10mil m red .45 *45.00*
Never hinged 1.40
On cover *72.50*
302 A39 20mil m ultra .45 *275.00*
Never hinged 1.20
On cover *360.00*
303 A39 50mil m dull grn .45 *6.00*
Never hinged 1.20
On cover *11.00*
304 A39 200mil m bis brn .45 *11.50*
Never hinged 1.20
On cover *16.50*
305 A39a 1mlrd m choc .45 *7.00*
Never hinged 1.20
On cover *11.00*
306 A39a 2mlrd m pale brn & grn .45 *3.50*
Never hinged 1.20
On cover *6.50*
307 A39a 5mlrd m yel & brn .65 *2.25*
Never hinged 1.60
On cover *6.00*
308 A39a 20mlrd m bluish grn & brn .65 *11.00*
Never hinged 1.60
On cover *16.50*
309 A39a 50mlrd m bl & dp bl 1.60 *575.00*
Never hinged 5.25
On cover *7775.00*
Nos. 301-309 (9) 5.60 *936.25*
Set, never hinged 15.85

Stamps and Types of 1923 Surcharged with New Values

1923 ***Perf. 14***

A35

310 1mlrd m on 100m vio .20 *27.50*
Never hinged .85
On cover *50.00*
a. Inverted surcharge 95.00
Never hinged 250.00
b. Deep reddish purple 55.00 *3,000.*
Never hinged 140.00
On cover (Munich) *5,250.*

A39

311 5mlrd m on 2mil m .20 *125.00*
Never hinged .85
On cover *160.00*
a. Inverted surcharge 17.50
Never hinged 50.00
b. Double surcharge 45.00
Never hinged 110.00
c. Deep purple 52.50 *9,000.*
Never hinged 150.00
312 5mlrd m on 4mil m .20 *22.50*
Never hinged .55
On cover *37.50*
a. Inverted surcharge 25.00 *775.00*
Never hinged 72.50
b. Double surcharge 35.00
Never hinged 92.50
313 5mlrd m on 10mil m .20 *2.50*
Never hinged .55
On cover *5.00*
a. Inverted surcharge 14.50 *775.00*
Never hinged 47.50
b. Double surcharge 35.00
Never hinged 92.50
314 10mlrd m on 20mil m .20 *2.75*
Never hinged .55
On cover *5.00*
a. Double surcharge 45.00
Never hinged 125.00
b. Inverted surcharge 25.00
Never hinged 72.50
c. Triple surcharge 525.00
d. On #287a 32.50 *1,650.*
Never hinged 92.50
On cover *2,750.*
315 10mlrd m on 50mil m .20 *2.25*
Never hinged .55
On cover *5.00*
a. Inverted surcharge 17.50 *725.00*
Never hinged 50.00
b. Double surcharge 45.00
Never hinged 125.00
c. On #289c 120.00 *1,500.*
Never hinged 400.00
On cover *2,750.*
316 10mlrd m on 100mil m .20 *7.25*
Never hinged .55
On cover *12.00*
a. Inverted surcharge 25.00 *1,100.*
Never hinged 72.50
b. Double surcharge 45.00
Never hinged 125.00
Nos. 310-316 (7) 1.40 *189.75*
Set, never hinged 4.50

No. 310b was issued in Bavaria only and is known as the Hitler provisional. Excellent forgeries exist.

Serrate Roulette 13½

A39

319 5mlrd m on 10mil m 1.60 *175.00*
Never hinged 4.75
On cover *325.00*
a. Inverted surcharge 22.50
Never hinged 65.00
b. Double surcharge 22.50
Never hinged 57.50
320 10mlrd m on 20mil m 5.00 *92.50*
Never hinged 8.75
On cover *160.00*
321 10mlrd m on 50mil m 1.60 *37.50*
Never hinged 4.75
On cover *60.00*
a. Inverted surcharge 22.50
Never hinged 65.00
Nos. 319-321 (3) 8.20 *305.00*
Set, never hinged 18.00

A40

German Eagle — A41

1923 ***Perf. 14***

323 A40 3pf brown .35 .20
Never hinged 1.10
On cover .85
324 A40 5pf dark green .35 .20
Never hinged 1.60
On cover .85
325 A40 10pf carmine .35 .20
Never hinged 1.60
On cover .85
326 A40 20pf deep ultra .95 .35
Never hinged 4.50
On cover 1.10
327 A40 50pf orange 2.50 .85
Never hinged 16.00
On cover 5.00
328 A40 100pf brn vio 8.00 .95
Never hinged 47.50
On cover 6.50
Nos. 323-328 (6) 12.50 2.75
Set, never hinged 72.50

For overprints see Nos. O47-O52.

Imperf

323a A40 3pf 125.00 *225.00*
Never hinged 300.00
324a A40 5pf 65.00 —
Never hinged 150.00
325a A40 10pf 110.00 160.00
Never hinged 260.00
326a A40 20pf 125.00 *225.00*
Never hinged 300.00
327a A40 50pf 140.00 *300.00*
Never hinged 375.00
328a A40 100pf 140.00 —
Never hinged 340.00
Nos. 323a-328a (6) 705.00 *910.00*
Set, never hinged 1,725.

Value Omitted

323b A40 3pf 160.00 *250.00*
Never hinged 375.00
324b A40 5pf 160.00 *250.00*
Never hinged 375.00
325b A40 10pf 160.00
Never hinged 375.00
326b A40 20pf 160.00
Never hinged 375.00
327b A40 50pf 160.00
Never hinged 375.00
328b A40 100pf 160.00
Never hinged 375.00
Nos. 323b-328b (6) 960.00
Set, never hinged 2,250.

1924 **Wmk. 126**

330 A41 3pf lt brown .30 .20
Never hinged 1.50
On cover 1.10
331 A41 5pf lt green .30 .20
Never hinged 2.00
On cover .75
332 A41 10pf vermilion .35 .20
Never hinged 2.50
On cover .75
333 A41 20pf dull blue 1.75 .20
Never hinged 25.00
On cover 2.25
334 A41 30pf rose lilac 1.75 .40
Never hinged 25.00
On cover 3.75
335 A41 40pf olive green 12.00 .60
Never hinged 90.00
On cover 5.50
336 A41 50pf orange 13.00 1.00
Never hinged 125.00
On cover 6.00
Nos. 330-336 (7) 29.45 2.80
Set, never hinged 271.00

The values above 5pf have "Pf" in the upper right corner.

For overprints see Nos. O53-O61.

Imperf.

330a A41 3pf 140.00 *325.00*
Never hinged 340.00
331a A41 5pf 175.00 *325.00*
Never hinged 400.00
332a A41 10pf 225.00
Never hinged 525.00
333a A41 20pf 160.00
Never hinged 375.00
334a A41 30pf 160.00
Never hinged 375.00
335a A41 40pf 190.00
Never hinged 450.00
Nos. 330a-335a (6) 1,050.
Set, never hinged 2,465.

Watermark Sideways

330b A41 3pf 150.00 37.50
Never hinged 300.00
331b A41 5pf 450.00 *550.00*
Never hinged 900.00
332b A41 10pf 37.50 9.00
Never hinged 75.00

Rheinstein Castle — A43

View of Cologne A44

Marienburg Castle — A45

1924 **Engr.** **Wmk. 126**

337 A43 1m green 10.00 2.25
Never hinged 37.50
On cover 9.00
338 A44 2m blue 17.50 1.90
Never hinged 47.50
On cover 30.00
339 A45 3m claret 20.00 5.00
Never hinged 67.50
On cover 60.00
Nos. 337-339 (3) 47.50 9.15
Set, never hinged 152.50

See No. 387.

Dr. Heinrich von Stephan
A46 A47

1924-28 **Typo.**

340 A46 10pf dark green .50 .20
Never hinged 1.50
On cover 1.50
a. Imperf 325.00
341 A46 20pf dark blue 1.25 .50
Never hinged 4.75
On cover 2.25
342 A47 60pf red brown 3.50 .50
Never hinged 19.00
On cover 6.00
a. Chalky paper ('28) 20.00 3.75
Never hinged 105.00
On cover 37.50
343 A47 80pf slate 9.25 1.25
Never hinged 52.50
On cover 32.50
Nos. 340-343 (4) 14.50 2.45
Set, never hinged 77.75

Universal Postal Union, 50th anniversary.

Traffic Wheel — A48

German Eagle Watching Rhine Valley — A49

1925, May 30 ***Perf. 13½x13***

345 A48 5pf deep green 3.00 5.00
Never hinged 19.00
On cover 19.00
346 A48 10pf vermilion 3.50 9.50
Never hinged 19.00
On cover 22.50
Set, never hinged 38.00

German Traffic Exhibition, Munich, May 30-Oct. 11, 1925.

1925 ***Perf. 14***

347 A49 5pf green .40 .30
Never hinged 1.50
On cover .75
348 A49 10pf vermilion .75 .30
Never hinged 3.75
On cover .75
349 A49 20pf deep blue 4.50 1.00
Never hinged 25.00
On cover 4.00
Nos. 347-349 (3) 5.65 1.60
Set, never hinged 30.25

1000 years' union of the Rhineland with Germany.

Speyer Cathedral A50

1925, Sept. 11 **Engr.**

350 A50 5m dull green 32.50 14.50
Never hinged 125.00
On cover 60.00

Johann Wolfgang von Goethe — A51

Designs: 3pf, 25pf, Goethe. 5pf, Friedrich von Schiller. 8pf, 20pf, Ludwig van Beethoven. 10pf, Frederick the Gre©at. 15pf, Immanuel Kant. 30pf, Gotthold Ephraim Lessing. 40pf, Gottfried Wilhelm Leibnitz. 50pf, Johann Sebastian Bach. 80pf, Albrecht Durer.

1926-27 Typo. Perf. 14

351 A51 3pf olive brown .50 .20
Never hinged 4.50
On cover 1.10
352 A51 3pf bister ('27) 1.00 .20
Never hinged 7.50
On cover 1.10
353 A51 5pf dark green 1.00 .20
Never hinged 9.00
On cover .75
b. 5pf light green ('27) 1.00 .20
Never hinged 7.50
On cover 1.10
354 A51 8pf blue grn ('27) 1.00 .20
Never hinged 8.25
On cover 1.10
355 A51 10pf carmine 1.00 .20
Never hinged 6.75
On cover .75
356 A51 15pf vermilion 2.25 .20
Never hinged 12.50
On cover .75
a. Booklet pane of 8 + 2 labels 250.00
Never hinged 600.00
357 A51 20pf myrtle grn 10.00 1.00
Never hinged 125.00
On cover 5.25
a. Wmk. sideways 2,250. 600.00
Never hinged 11,250.
358 A51 25pf blue 3.25 .80
Never hinged 29.00
On cover 5.25
359 A51 30pf olive grn 6.00 .45
Never hinged 45.00
On cover 3.75
360 A51 40pf dp violet 11.00 .50
Never hinged 120.00
On cover 6.00
361 A51 50pf brown 14.00 5.50
Never hinged 120.00
On cover 26.00
362 A51 80pf chocolate 29.00 4.00
Never hinged 375.00
On cover 52.50
Nos. 351-362 (12) 80.00 13.45
Set, never hinged 862.50

Imperf

351a A51 3pf Never hinged 525.
352a A51 3pf Never hinged 525.
353a A51 5pf Never hinged 525.
354a A51 8pf Never hinged 525.
356b A51 15pf Never hinged 525.
357b A51 20pf Never hinged 2,000.

Nos. 354, 356 and 358 Overprinted

1927, Oct. 10

363 A51 8pf blue green 16.00 *55.00*
Never hinged 52.50
On cover 100.00
364 A51 15pf vermilion 16.00 *55.00*
Never hinged 60.00
On cover 100.00
365 A51 25pf blue 16.00 *55.00*
Never hinged 60.00
On cover 140.00
Nos. 363-365 (3) 48.00 165.00
Set, never hinged 172.50

"I.A.A." stands for "Internationales Arbeitsamt," (Intl. Labor Bureau), an agency of the League of Nations. Issued in connection with a meeting of the I.A.A. in Berlin, Oct. 10-15, 1927, they were on sale to the public.

Pres. Friedrich Ebert A60

Pres. Paul von Hindenburg A61

1928-32 Typo. Perf. 14

366 A60 3pf bister .20 .30
Never hinged 2.10
On cover 1.10
367 A61 4pf lt blue ('31) .65 .30
Never hinged 4.00
On cover .60
a. Tête bêche pair 4.50 8.75
Never hinged 8.75
b. Bklt. pane of 9 + label 22.50 55.00
Never hinged 55.00
368 A61 5pf lt green .40 .30
Never hinged 1.50
On cover .75
a. Tête bêche pair 3.50 7.25
Never hinged 7.25
b. Imperf. 125.00
c. Bklt. pane of 6 + 4 labels 17.50 45.00
Never hinged 45.00
d. Bklt. pane, 4 #368 + 6 #369 22.50 55.00
Never hinged 55.00
369 A60 6pf lt olive grn ('32) .70 .20
Never hinged 3.75
On cover .40
a. Bklt. pane, 2 #369 + 8 #373 37.50 92.50
Never hinged 92.50
370 A60 8pf dark green .20 .30
Never hinged 1.40
On cover .75
a. Tête bêche pair 3.50 7.25
Never hinged 7.25
371 A60 10pf vermilion 1.75 1.50
Never hinged 13.00
On cover 5.50
372 A60 10pf red violet ('30) .90 .40
Never hinged 6.00
On cover 1.10
373 A61 12pf orange ('32) 1.10 .20
Never hinged 9.00
On cover .40
a. Tête bêche pair 8.75 17.50
Never hinged 19.50
374 A61 15pf car rose .60 .30
Never hinged 3.50
On cover .75
a. Tête bêche pair 4.50 8.75
Never hinged 8.75
b. Bklt. pane 6 + 4 labels 20.00 50.00
Never hinged 50.00
c. Imperf 350.00
375 A60 20pf Prus green 6.00 3.25
Never hinged 37.50
On cover 6.75
a. Imperf. 300.00
376 A60 20pf gray ('30) 5.75 .40
Never hinged 45.00
On cover 2.25
377 A61 25pf blue 7.25 .50
Never hinged 45.00
On cover 1.90
378 A60 30pf olive green 4.75 .40
Never hinged 35.00
On cover 1.90
379 A61 40pf violet 12.00 .50
Never hinged 160.00
On cover 3.75
380 A60 45pf orange 8.75 2.25
Never hinged 67.50
On cover 6.00
381 A61 50pf brown 8.75 1.40
Never hinged 105.00
On cover 7.50
382 A60 60pf orange brn 11.00 1.90
Never hinged 105.00
On cover 7.50
383 A61 80pf chocolate 20.00 4.50
Never hinged 250.00
On cover 37.50
384 A61 80pf yel bis ('30) 8.75 1.60
Never hinged 67.50
On cover 30.00
Nos. 366-384 (19) 99.50 20.50
Set, never hinged 960.00

Stamps of 1928 Overprinted

1930, June 30

385 A60 8pf dark green 1.00 .50
Never hinged 6.00
On cover 1.00
386 A61 15pf carmine rose 1.00 .50
Never hinged 9.00
On cover 1.00
Set, never hinged 15.00

Issued in commemoration of the final evacuation of the Rhineland by the Allied forces.

View of Cologne A63

1930 Engr. Wmk. 126
Inscribed: "Reichsmark"

387 A63 2m dark blue 29.00 11.50
Never hinged 100.00
On cover 90.00

A type of design A43 in green exists with "Reichsmark" instead of "Mark." It was not issued, though some examples are known in private hands.

Pres. von Hindenburg A64

Frederick the Great A65

1932, Oct. 1 Typo. Wmk. 126

391 A64 4pf blue .50 .35
Never hinged 1.50
On cover 2.25
392 A64 5pf brt green .70 .35
Never hinged 2.25
On cover 2.60
393 A64 12pf dp orange 4.50 .35
Never hinged 18.00
On cover 2.25
394 A64 15pf dk red 3.50 *9.25*
Never hinged 10.50
On cover 52.50
395 A64 25pf ultra 1.10 .55
Never hinged 8.25
On cover 7.50
396 A64 40pf violet 17.50 1.40
Never hinged 75.00
On cover 19.00
397 A64 50pf dk brown 5.75 *11.00*
Never hinged 13.50
On cover 52.50
Nos. 391-397 (7) 33.55 23.25
Set, never hinged 129.00

85th birthday of von Hindenburg.
See Nos. 401-431, 436-441. For surcharges and overprints see France, Luxembourg and Poland.

1933, Apr. 12 Photo.

398 A65 6pf dk green .60 .75
Never hinged 4.50
On cover 1.90
a. Tête bêche pair 5.00 13.00
Never hinged 10.00
399 A65 12pf carmine .60 .75
Never hinged 4.50
On cover 1.90
a. Tête bêche pair 5.00 13.00
Never hinged 10.00
b. Bklt. pane of 5 + label 16.00 37.50
Never hinged 37.50
400 A65 25pf ultra 35.00 20.00
Never hinged 240.00
On cover 37.50
Nos. 398-400 (3) 36.20 21.50
Set, never hinged 249.00

Celebration of Potsdam Day.

Hindenburg Type of 1932

1933 Typo.

401 A64 3pf olive bister 11.50 .45
Never hinged 55.00
On cover 2.25
402 A64 4pf dull blue 3.50 .45
Never hinged 16.00
On cover 1.50
403 A64 6pf dk green 1.75 .40
Never hinged 7.50
On cover 2.25
404 A64 8pf dp orange 5.75 .45
Never hinged 13.00
On cover 2.25
a. Bklt. pane, 3 #404 + 5 #406 62.50 *150.00*
Never hinged 150.00
b. Open "D" 14.50 3.50
Never hinged 32.50
405 A64 10pf chocolate 3.50 .50
Never hinged 22.50
On cover 7.50
406 A64 12pf dp carmine 2.25 .40
Never hinged 15.00
On cover 2.25
a. Bklt. pane, 4 #392 + 4 #406 35.00 *87.50*
Never hinged 87.50
407 A64 15pf maroon 5.00 *22.50*
Never hinged 21.00
On cover 52.50
408 A64 20pf brt blue 6.50 1.90
Never hinged 52.50
On cover 19.00
409 A64 30pf olive grn 6.50 1.25
Never hinged 18.00
On cover 19.00
410 A64 40pf red violet 26.00 2.75
Never hinged 210.00
On cover 35.00
411 A64 50pf dk grn & blk 14.50 2.25
Never hinged 100.00
On cover 62.50
412 A64 60pf claret & blk 26.00 .85
Never hinged 200.00
On cover 57.50
413 A64 80pf dk blue & blk 8.75 1.00
Never hinged 22.50
On cover 82.50
414 A64 100pf orange & blk 24.00 11.00
Never hinged 140.00
On cover 110.00
Nos. 401-414 (14) 145.50 *46.15*
Set, never hinged 893.00

Hindenburg Type of 1932

1933-36 Wmk. 237 Perf. 14

415 A64 1pf black .20 .20
Never hinged .30
On cover .40
a. Bklt. pane, 4 #415, 3 #417, label 3.75 *9.50*
Never hinged 9.50
b. Bklt. pane, 3 #415, 3 #416 + 2 #418 5.25 *13.00*
Never hinged 13.00
c. Bklt. pane, 2 #415, 5 #420, label 7.75 *19.00*
Never hinged 19.00
d. Bklt. pane, 4 #415 + 4 #422 3.00 *7.25*
Never hinged 7.25
416 A64 3pf olive bis ('34) .20 .20
Never hinged .30
On cover .40
a. Bklt. pane, 4 #416 + 4 #418 2.50 *6.25*
Never hinged 6.25
b. Bklt. pane, 4 #416 + 4 #419 2.50 *6.25*
Never hinged 6.25
c. Bklt. pane, 6 #416, 1 #422, label 2.25 *5.50*
Never hinged 5.50
417 A64 4pf dull blue ('34) .20 .20
Never hinged .30
On cover .40
a. Bklt. pane, 3 #417, 4 #422, label 6.25 *16.00*
Never hinged 16.00
418 A64 5pf brt green ('34) .20 .20
Never hinged .30
On cover .40
a. Bklt. pane, 2 #418, 5 #419, label 3.25 *8.25*
Never hinged 8.25
b. Bklt. pane, 2 #418, 3 #419 + 3 #420 4.00 *9.50*
Never hinged 9.75
c. Bklt. pane, 4 #418 + 4 #420 3.25 *8.25*
Never hinged 8.25
419 A64 6pf dk green ('34) .20 .20
Never hinged .30
On cover .40
b. Bklt. pane of 7 + label 7.75 *19.00*
Never hinged 19.00
c. Bklt. pane, 1 #419, 6 #422, label 16.00 *42.50*
Never hinged 40.00
420 A64 8pf dp orange ('34) .20 .20
Never hinged .30
On cover .40
a. Bklt. pane, 3 #420, 4 #422, label 3.25 *8.25*
Never hinged 8.25
b. Open "D" 3.75 3.75
Never hinged 11.00
Never hinged 14.00
421 A64 10pf choc ('34) .20 .20
Never hinged .75
On cover .75
422 A64 12pf dp car ('34) .20 .20
Never hinged .40
On cover .40
a. Bklt. pane of 7 + label 7.75 *19.00*
Never hinged 19.00
423 A64 15pf maroon ('34) .30 .20
Never hinged 1.50
On cover .75
424 A64 20pf brt blue ('34) .40 .20
Never hinged 3.50
On cover .75
425 A64 25pf ultra ('34) .40 .20
Never hinged 3.50
On cover .75
426 A64 30pf olive grn ('34) .65 .20
Never hinged 6.75
On cover .75
427 A64 40pf red violet ('34) .65 .30
Never hinged 9.75
On cover 1.50
428 A64 50pf dk grn & blk ('34) 2.50 .35
Never hinged 14.00
On cover 1.90
429 A64 60pf claret & blk ('34) .65 .35
Never hinged 6.00
On cover 1.90
430 A64 80pf dk bl & blk ('36) 1.90 1.00
Never hinged 6.50
On cover 3.75
431 A64 100pf orange & blk ('34) 2.50 .60
Never hinged 8.25
On cover 5.50
Nos. 415-431 (17) 11.55 5.00
Set, never hinged 62.70

Franz Adolf E. Lüderitz — A66

Swastika, Sun and Nuremberg Castle — A70

Designs: 6pf, Dr. Gustav Nachtigal. 12pf, Karl Peters. 25pf, Hermann von Wissmann.

1934, June 30 Perf. 13x13½

432 A66 3pf brown & choc 2.25 *4.75*
Never hinged 24.00
On cover 19.00
433 A66 6pf dk grn & choc 1.10 .85
Never hinged 9.00
On cover 4.50
434 A66 12pf dk car & choc 1.75 .85
Never hinged 26.00
On cover 4.50
435 A66 25pf brt blue & choc 8.75 *17.00*
Never hinged 90.00
On cover 45.00
Nos. 432-435 (4) 13.85 23.45
Set, never hinged 149.00

Issued in remembrance of the lost colonies of Germany.

Hindenburg Memorial Issue
Type of 1932
With Black Border

1934, Sept. 4 Perf. 14

436 A64 3pf olive bister .70 .35
Never hinged 3.75
On cover 1.50
437 A64 5pf brt green .70 .50
Never hinged 3.75
On cover 1.90
438 A64 6pf dk green 1.40 .30
Never hinged 8.25
On cover .90
439 A64 8pf vermilion 2.25 .30
Never hinged 20.00
On cover 1.50
440 A64 12pf deep carmine 2.25 .30
Never hinged 24.00
On cover .90

441 A64 25pf ultra 6.50 6.25
Never hinged 60.00
On cover 19.00
Nos. 436-441 (6) 13.80 8.00
Set, never hinged 120.00

1934, Sept. 1 **Photo.**
442 A70 6pf dark green 2.75 .30
Never hinged 26.00
On cover 1.50
a. Imperf, never hinged 750.00
443 A70 12pf dark carmine 3.25 .30
Never hinged 37.50
On cover 1.50
a. Imperf, never hinged 750.00
Set, never hinged 63.50

Nazi Congress at Nuremberg.

Allegory "Saar Belongs to Germany" A71

German Eagle A72

1934, Aug. 26 **Typo.** **Wmk. 237**
444 A71 6pf dark green 2.75 .30
Never hinged 26.00
On cover 1.10
445 A72 12pf dark carmine 3.25 .30
Never hinged 37.50
On cover 1.10
Set, never hinged 63.50

Issued to mark the Saar Plebiscite.

Friedrich von Schiller A73

Germania Welcoming Home the Saar A74

1934, Nov. 5
446 A73 6pf green 2.50 .30
Never hinged 25.00
On cover .75
447 A73 12pf carmine 4.50 .30
Never hinged 57.50
On cover .75
Set, never hinged 82.50

175th anniv. of the birth of von Schiller.

1935, Jan. 16 **Photo.**
448 A74 3pf brown .35 1.00
Never hinged 3.00
On cover 2.25
449 A74 6pf dark green .35 .45
Never hinged 3.00
On cover .75
450 A74 12pf lake 1.75 .45
Never hinged 15.00
On cover .90
451 A74 25pf dark blue 7.25 6.25
Never hinged 65.00
On cover 19.00
Nos. 448-451 (4) 9.70 8.15
Set, never hinged 86.00

Return of the Saar to Germany.

German Soldier A75

Wreath and Swastika A76

1935, Mar. 15
452 A75 6pf dark green .65 1.25
Never hinged 7.50
On cover 2.60
453 A75 12pf copper red .65 1.25
Never hinged 8.25
On cover 2.60
Set, never hinged 15.75

Issued to commemorate War Heroes' Day.

1935, Apr. 26 **Unwmk.**
454 A76 6pf dark green .65 1.00
Never hinged 7.50
On cover 3.50
455 A76 12pf crimson .85 1.00
Never hinged 10.50
On cover 3.50
Set, never hinged 18.00

Young Workers' Professional Competitions.

Heinrich Schütz — A77

"The Eagle" — A80

Wmk. Swastikas (237)
1935, June 21 **Engr.** ***Perf. 14***
456 A77 6pf shown .45 .30
Never hinged 4.50
On cover 1.50
457 A77 12pf Bach .65 .30
Never hinged 6.75
On cover 1.50
458 A77 25pf Handel 1.10 .85
Never hinged 11.00
On cover 5.25
Nos. 456-458 (3) 2.20 1.45
Set, never hinged 22.25

Schutz-Bach-Handel celebration.

1935, July 10 ***Perf. 14***

Designs: 12pf, Modern express train. 25pf, "The Hamburg Flyer." 40pf, Streamlined locomotive.

459 A80 6pf dark green .90 .45
Never hinged 6.00
On cover 3.00
a. Imperf 900.00
460 A80 12pf copper red .90 .45
Never hinged 6.00
On cover 3.00
a. Imperf 900.00
461 A80 25pf ultra 5.00 1.50
Never hinged 35.00
On cover 21.00
a. Imperf 1,100.
462 A80 40pf red violet 8.25 1.50
Never hinged 55.00
On cover 22.50
a. Imperf 1,100.
Nos. 459-462 (4) 15.05 3.90
Set, never hinged 102.00

Centenary of railroad in Germany.

Bugler of Hitler Youth Movement A84

Eagle and Swastika over Nuremberg A85

1935, July 25 **Photo.**
463 A84 6pf deep green 1.10 1.90
Never hinged 6.75
On cover 5.25
464 A84 15pf brown lake 1.40 2.25
Never hinged 12.00
On cover 5.50
Set, never hinged 18.75

Hitler Youth Meeting.

1935, Aug. 30 **Engr.**
465 A85 6pf gray green .70 .30
Never hinged 5.25
On cover 1.10
466 A85 12pf dark carmine 1.60 .30
Never hinged 9.75
On cover 1.10
Set, never hinged 15.00

1935 Nazi Congress at Nuremberg.

Nazi Flag Bearer and Feldherrnhalle at Munich — A86

Airplane — A87

1935, Nov. 5 **Photo.** ***Perf. 13½***
467 A86 3pf brown .30 .45
Never hinged 3.00
On cover 1.10
468 A86 12pf dark carmine .40 .45
Never hinged 8.25
On cover 1.10
Set, never hinged 11.25

12th anniv. of the 1st Hitler "Putsch" at Munich, Nov. 9, 1923.

1936, Jan. 6
469 A87 40pf sapphire 4.75 2.25
Never hinged 37.50
On cover 15.00

10th anniv. of the Lufthansa air service.

Gottlieb Daimler — A88

Carl Benz — A89

1936, Feb. 15 ***Perf. 14***
470 A88 6pf dark green .40 .45
Never hinged 5.00
On cover .90
471 A89 12pf copper red .45 .60
Never hinged 6.50
On cover 1.10
Set, never hinged 11.50

The 50th anniv. of the automobile; Intl. Automobile and Motorcycle Show, Berlin.

Otto von Guericke A90

Symbolical of Municipalities A91

1936, May 4
472 A90 6pf dark green .30 .35
Never hinged 1.20
On cover .75

250th anniv. of the death of the German inventor, Otto von Guericke, May 11, 1686.

1936, June 3
473 A91 3pf dark brown .20 .30
Never hinged 1.90
On cover 1.50
474 A91 5pf deep green .20 .30
Never hinged 2.60
On cover 1.50
475 A91 12pf lake .30 .50
Never hinged 3.50
On cover 1.50
476 A91 25pf dark ultra .50 1.00
Never hinged 7.00
On cover 5.50
Nos. 473-476 (4) 1.20 2.10
Set, never hinged 15.00

6th Intl. Cong. of Municipalities, June 7-13.

Allegory of Recreation Congress A92

Salute to Swastika A93

1936, June 30

477 A92 6pf dark green .35 .45
Never hinged 4.00
On cover 2.25
478 A92 15pf deep claret .55 .90
Never hinged 9.00
On cover 3.00
Set, never hinged 13.00

World Congress for Vacation and Recreation held at Hamburg.

1936, Sept. 3 *Perf. 14*

479 A93 6pf deep green .35 .35
Never hinged 4.00
On cover 1.25
480 A93 12pf copper red .45 .45
Never hinged 6.50
On cover 1.25
Set, never hinged 10.50

The 1936 Nazi Congress.

Shield Bearer — A94

German and Austrian Carrying Nazi Flag — A95

1937, Mar. 3 Engr. Unwmk.

481 A94 3pf brown .20 .30
Never hinged 1.90
On cover .75
482 A94 6pf green .20 .30
Never hinged 2.60
On cover .75
483 A94 12pf carmine .50 .45
Never hinged 6.00
On cover 1.10
Nos. 481-483 (3) .90 1.05
Set, never hinged 10.50

The Reich's Air Protection League.

Wmk. Swastikas (237)
1938, Apr. 8 Photo. *Perf. 14x13½*
Size: 23x28mm

484 A95 6pf dark green .20 .35
Never hinged 1.00
On cover .75

Unwmk. *Perf. 12½*
Size: 21½x26mm

485 A95 6pf deep green .20 .50
Never hinged 1.10
On cover 1.10

Union of Austria and Germany.

Cathedral Island A96

Hermann Goering Stadium A97

Town Hall, Breslau — A98

Centennial Hall, Breslau — A99

1938, June 21 Engr. *Perf. 14*

486 A96 3pf dark brown .20 .30
Never hinged 1.10
On cover 1.90
487 A97 6pf deep green .20 .30
Never hinged 1.10
On cover 1.25
488 A98 12pf copper red .30 .30
Never hinged 3.00
On cover 1.25
489 A99 15pf violet brown .60 .65
Never hinged 6.75
On cover 3.75
Nos. 486-489 (4) 1.30 1.55
Set, never hinged 11.95

16th German Gymnastic and Sports Festival held at Breslau, July 23-31, 1938.

Nazi Emblem — A100

1939, Apr. 4 Photo. Wmk. 237

490 A100 6pf dark green 1.10 2.75
Never hinged 7.50
On cover 6.75
491 A100 12pf deep carmine 1.40 2.75
Never hinged 11.00
On cover 6.75
Set, never hinged 18.50

Young Workers' Professional Competitions.

St. Mary's Church — A101

The Krantor, Danzig — A102

1939, Sept. 18

492 A101 6pf dark green .20 .40
Never hinged 1.50
On cover 1.50
493 A102 12pf orange red .30 .55
Never hinged 2.25
On cover 1.50
Set, never hinged 3.00

Unification of Danzig with the Reich.

Johannes Gutenberg and Library at Leipzig — A103

Designs: 6pf, "High House," Leipzig. 12pf, Old Town Hall, Leipzig. 25pf, View of Leipzig Fair.

Inscribed "Leipziger Messe"
Perf. 10½

1940, Mar. 3 Photo. Unwmk.

494 A103 3pf dark brown .20 .35
Never hinged 1.50
On cover 1.50
495 A103 6pf dk gray green .20 .35
Never hinged 1.50
On cover 1.10
496 A103 12pf henna brown .20 .35
Never hinged 1.50
On cover 1.10
497 A103 25pf ultra .45 .95
Never hinged 3.00
On cover 4.50
Nos. 494-497 (4) 1.05 2.00
Set, never hinged 7.50

Leipzig Fair.

SEMI-POSTAL STAMPS

Issues of the Republic

Nos. 83, 83d, 100, 100a, 100d Surcharged

1919, May 1 Wmk. 125 *Perf. 14*

B1 A16 10pf + 5pf on #83d .40 4.50
Never hinged 1.00
On cover 9.00
a. On #83 5.25 140.00
Never hinged 13.50
On cover 240.00
B2 A22 15pf + 5pf on #100 .40 4.50
Never hinged 1.00
On cover 9.00
a. On #100a 15.00 275.00
Never hinged 45.00
On cover 375.00
b. On #100d 15.00 275.00
Never hinged 45.00
On cover 375.00
Set, never hinged 2.00

The surtax was for the war wounded.

"Planting Charity" — SP1

Feeding the Hungry — SP2

1922, Dec. 11 Litho. Wmk. 126

B3 SP1 6m + 4m ultra & brn .20 22.50
Never hinged .75
On cover 37.50
B4 SP1 12m + 8m red org & bl gray .20 22.50
Never hinged .75
On cover 37.50
Set, never hinged 1.50

Nos. 221, 225 and 196 Surcharged

1923, Feb. 19

B5 A34 5m + 100m .20 8.50
Never hinged .45
On cover 19.00
B6 A29 25m + 500m .20 22.50
Never hinged .45
On cover 45.00
a. Inverted surcharge 95.00
Never hinged 160.00
B7 A32 20m + 1000m 2.10 87.50
Never hinged 4.50
On cover 150.00
a. Inverted surcharge 675.00 3,500.
Never hinged 1,750.
b. Green background inverted 175.00 1,150.
Never hinged 400.00
Nos. B5-B7 (3) 2.50 118.50
Set, never hinged 5.40

Note following No. 160 applies to #B1-B7.

1924, Feb. 25 Typo. *Perf. 14½x15*

Designs: 10pf+30pf, Giving drink to the thirsty. 20pf+60pf, Clothing the naked. 50pf+1.50m, Healing the sick.

B8 SP2 5pf + 15pf dk grn 1.10 2.10
Never hinged 5.25
On cover 9.00
B9 SP2 10pf + 30pf ver 1.10 2.10
Never hinged 5.25
On cover 11.00
B10 SP2 20pf + 60pf dk blue 5.75 6.25
Never hinged 22.50
On cover 22.50
B11 SP2 50pf + 1.50m red brn 22.50 52.50
Never hinged 82.50
On cover 110.00
Nos. B8-B11 (4) 30.45 62.95
Set, never hinged 115.50

The surtax was used for emergency aid. See No. B58.

Prussia — SP6

1925, Dec. 15 *Perf. 14*
Inscribed: "1925"

B12 SP6 5pf + 5pf shown .45 1.25
Never hinged 1.90
On cover 7.50
B13 SP6 10pf + 10pf Bavaria 1.00 1.25
Never hinged 5.50
On cover 11.00
B14 SP6 20pf + 20pf Saxony 5.75 12.00
Never hinged 26.00
On cover 35.00
a. Bklt. pane of 2 + 2 labels 175.00 550.00
Never hinged 450.00
Nos. B12-B14 (3) 7.20 14.50
Set, never hinged 33.40

1926, Dec. 1
Inscribed: "1926"

B15 SP6 5pf + 5pf Wurttemberg 1.00 1.25
Never hinged 2.60
On cover 4.50
B16 SP6 10pf + 10pf Baden 1.40 2.10
Never hinged 3.75
On cover 5.50
a. Bklt. pane of 6 + 2 labels 70.00 175.00
Never hinged 175.00
B17 SP6 25pf + 25pf Thuringia 10.50 17.50
Never hinged 29.00
On cover 40.00
B18 SP6 50pf + 50pf Hesse 40.00 70.00
Never hinged 135.00
On cover 120.00
Nos. B15-B18 (4) 52.90 90.85
Set, never hinged 170.00

See Nos. B23-B32.

Pres. Paul von Hindenburg — SP13

1927, Sept. 26 Photo.

B19 SP13 8pf dark green .75 1.25
Never hinged 1.90
On cover 5.50
a. Bklt. pane, 4 #B19, 3 #B20 + label 40.00 100.00
Never hinged 100.00
B20 SP13 15pf scarlet .75 1.90
Never hinged 2.50
On cover 7.50
B21 SP13 25pf deep blue 5.75 17.50
Never hinged 35.00
On cover 40.00
B22 SP13 50pf bister brown 9.25 22.50
Never hinged 40.00
On cover 47.50
Nos. B19-B22 (4) 16.50 43.15
Set, never hinged 79.40

80th birthday of Pres. Hindenburg. The stamps were sold at double face value. The surtax was given to a fund for War Invalids.

Arms Type of 1925

Design: 8pf+7pf, Mecklenberg-Schwerin.

1928, Nov. 15 Typo.
SP6
Inscribed: "1928"

B23 5pf + 5pf Hamburg .50 2.75
Never hinged 1.50
On cover 5.50
B24 8pf + 7pf multi .50 2.75
Never hinged 1.50
On cover 5.50
a. Bklt. pane, 4 #B24, 3 #B25 + label 100.00 250.00
Never hinged 250.00
B25 15pf + 15pf Oldenburg .70 2.75
Never hinged 2.10
On cover 7.50
B26 25pf + 25pf Brunswick 8.75 26.00
Never hinged 47.50
On cover 45.00
B27 50pf + 50pf Anhalt 45.00 75.00
Never hinged 125.00
On cover 120.00
Nos. B23-B27 (5) 55.45 109.25
Set, never hinged 177.60

1929, Nov. 4

Coats of Arms: 8pf+4pf, Lippe-Detmold. 25pf+10pf, Mecklenburg-Strelitz. 50pf+40pf, Schaumburg-Lippe.

Inscribed: "1929"

B28 SP6 5pf + 2pf Bremen .55 1.25
Never hinged 1.90
On cover 3.75
a. Bklt. pane of 6 + 2 labels 11.50 29.00
Never hinged 29.00
B29 SP6 8pf + 4pf multi .55 1.25
Never hinged 1.90
On cover 3.75
a. Bklt. pane, 4 #B29, 3 #B30 + label 35.00 90.00
Never hinged 90.00
B30 SP6 15pf + 5pf Lubeck .65 1.25
Never hinged 3.75
On cover 5.25
B31 SP6 25pf + 10pf multi 11.00 29.00
Never hinged 52.50
On cover 52.50
B32 SP6 50pf + 40pf choc, ocher & red 37.50 70.00
Never hinged 110.00
On cover 110.00
a. "PE" for "PF" 110.00 500.00
Never hinged 140.00
Nos. B28-B32 (5) 50.25 102.75
Set, never hinged 170.00

Cathedral of Aachen — SP24

Brandenburg Gate, Berlin — SP25

Castle of Marienwerder SP26

Statue of St. Kilian and Marienburg Fortress at Würzburg SP27

Souvenir Sheet

Wmk. 223

1930, Sept. 12 Engr. *Perf. 14*

B33 Sheet of 4 325.00 *1,250.*
Never hinged 950.00
On cover *1,800.*
a. SP24 8pf + 4pf dark green 25.00 *67.50*
Never hinged 57.50
b. SP25 15pf + 5pf carmine 25.00 *67.50*
Never hinged 57.50
c. SP26 25pf + 10p dark blue 25.00 *67.50*
Never hinged 57.50
d. SP27 50pf + 40pf dark brown 25.00 *67.50*
Never hinged 57.50
Any single, never hinged 50.00
Any single, on cover 160.00

Intl. Phil. Exhib., Berlin, Sept. 12-21, 1930.

No. B33 is watermarked Eagle on each stamp and "IPOSTA"-"1930" in the margins. Size: approximately 105x150. Each holder of an admission ticket was entitled to purchase one sheet. The ticket cost 1m and the sheet 1.70m (face value 98pf, charity 59pf, special paper 13pf).

The margin of the souvenir sheet is ungummed.

Types of International Philatelic Exhibition Issue

1930, Nov. 1 Wmk. 126

B34 SP24 8 + 4pf dp green .35 *.50*
Never hinged .90
On cover 1.90
Never hinged 40.00
a. Bklt. pane of 7 + label 17.50 45.00
Never hinged 45.00
b. Bklt. pane, 3 #B34, 4 #B35 + label 22.50 55.00
B35 SP25 15 + 5pf car .45 *.75*
Never hinged 1.40
On cover 3.75
B36 SP26 25 + 10pf dk blue 7.00 *19.00*
Never hinged 26.00
On cover 35.00
B37 SP27 50 + 40pf dp brn 19.00 *70.00*
Never hinged 75.00
On cover 110.00
Nos. B34-B37 (4) 26.80 *90.25*
Set, never hinged 103.30

The surtax was for charity.

The Zwinger at Dresden SP28

Breslau City Hall SP29

Heidelberg Castle SP30

Holsten Gate, Lübeck SP31

1931, Nov. 1

B38 SP28 8 + 4pf dk grn .25 *.80*
Never hinged .75
On cover 3.00
a. Bklt. pane of 7 + label 14.00 32.50
Never hinged 35.00
b. Bklt. pane, 3 #B38, 4 #B39 + label 22.50 55.00
Never hinged 55.00
B39 SP29 15 + 5pf carmine .45 *.80*
Never hinged 1.10
On cover 3.75
B40 SP30 25 + 10pf dk blue 7.00 *19.00*
Never hinged 37.50
On cover 37.50
B41 SP31 50 + 40pf dp brown 32.50 *62.50*
Never hinged 120.00
On cover 110.00
Nos. B38-B41 (4) 40.20 *83.10*
Set, never hinged 159.35

The surtax was for charity.

Nos. B38-B39 Surcharged

1932, Feb. 2

B42 SP28 6 + 4pf on 8+4pf 4.50 *8.75*
Never hinged 19.00
On cover 15.00
B43 SP29 12 + 3pf on 15+5pf 5.00 *10.50*
Never hinged 22.50
On cover 22.50
Set, never hinged 37.50

Wartburg Castle — SP32

Stolzenfels Castle — SP33

Nuremberg Castle — SP34

Lichtenstein Castle — SP35

Marburg Castle — SP36

1932, Nov. 1 Engr.

B44 SP32 4 + 2pf lt blue .25 *.45*
Never hinged 1.10
On cover 3.75
a. Bklt. pane, 5 #B44, 5 #B45 10.00 25.00
Never hinged 25.00
B45 SP33 6 + 4pf olive grn .25 *.45*
Never hinged 1.10
On cover 3.50
B46 SP34 12 + 3pf lt red .50 *.80*
Never hinged 1.50
On cover 4.50
b. Bklt. pane of 8 + 2 labels 10.00 25.00
Never hinged 25.00
B47 SP35 25 + 10pf dp blue 7.00 *14.00*
Never hinged 30.00
On cover 30.00
B48 SP36 40 + 40pf brn vio 27.50 *52.50*
Never hinged 100.00
On cover 90.00
Nos. B44-B48 (5) 35.50 *68.20*
Set, never hinged 133.70

The surtax was for charity.

"Tannhäuser" SP37

Designs: 4pf+2pf, "Der Fliegende Hollander." 5pf+2pf, "Das Rheingold." 6pf+4pf, "Die Meistersinger." 8pf+4pf, "Die Walkure." 12pf+3pf, "Siegfried." 20pf+10pf, "Tristan und Isolde." 25pf+15pf, "Lohengrin." 40pf+35pf, "Parsifal."

Wmk. Swastikas (237)

1933, Nov. 1 *Perf. 13½x13*

B49 SP37 3 + 2pf bis brn 1.75 *4.00*
Never hinged 16.00
On cover 9.00
B50 SP37 4 + 2pf dk blue 1.25 *1.60*
Never hinged 13.50
On cover 3.75
b. Bklt. pane, 5 #B50, 5 #B52 57.50 140.00
Never hinged 140.00
B51 SP37 5 + 2pf brt grn 3.25 *5.00*
Never hinged 30.00
On cover 11.00
B52 SP37 6 + 4pf gray grn 1.25 *1.25*
Never hinged 13.50
On cover 3.00
B53 SP37 8 + 4pf dp org 1.60 *2.75*
Never hinged 16.00
On cover 7.50
b. Bklt. pane, 5 #B53, 4 #B54 + label 70.00 175.00
Never hinged 175.00
B54 SP37 12 + 3pf brn red 1.60 *1.50*
Never hinged 16.00
On cover 4.50
B55 SP37 20 + 10pf blue 140.00 140.00
Never hinged 750.00
On cover 300.00
B56 SP37 25 + 15pf ultra 22.50 *32.50*
Never hinged 260.00
On cover 67.50
B57 SP37 40 + 35pf mag 100.00 100.00
Never hinged 700.00
On cover 175.00
Nos. B49-B57 (9) 273.20 288.60
Set, never hinged 1,815.

Perf. 13½x14

B50a SP37 4 + 2pf dark blue 1.00 *2.50*
Never hinged 12.00
On cover 4.50
B52a SP37 6 + 4pf gray grn 1.00 *4.00*
Never hinged 12.00
On cover 7.50
B53a SP37 8 + 4pf dp org 1.90 *3.25*
Never hinged 13.50
On cover 7.50
B54a SP37 12 + 3pf brn red 2.25 *5.25*
Never hinged 15.00
On cover 9.75
B55a SP37 20 + 10pf blue 100.00 82.50
Never hinged 700.00
On cover 125.00
Nos. B50a-B55a (5) 106.15 97.50
Set, never hinged 752.50

Types of Semi-Postal Stamps of 1924 Issue Overprinted "1923-1933" Souvenir Sheet

1933, Nov. 29 Typo. *Perf. 14½*

B58 Sheet of 4 1,150. *7,400.*
Never hinged 4,500.
On cover 11,000.
a. SP2 5 + 15pf dark green 70.00 *250.00*
b. SP2 10 + 30pf vermilion 70.00 *250.00*
c. SP2 20 + 60pf dark blue 70.00 *250.00*
d. SP2 50pf + 1.50m dk brown 65.00 *225.00*
Any single, never hinged 175.00
Any single, on cover 450.00

The Swastika watermark covers the four stamps and above them appears a further watermark "10 Jahre Deutsche Nothilfe" and "1923-1933" below. Sheet size: 208x148mm.

The margin of the souvenir sheet is ungummed.

Businessman SP46

Judge SP54

Designs: 4pf+2pf, Blacksmith. 5pf+2pf, Mason. 6pf+4f, Miner. 8pf+4pf, Architect. 12pf+3pf, Farmer. 20pf+10pf, Agricultural Chemist. 25pf+15pf, Sculptor.

1934, Nov. 5 Engr. *Perf. 13x13½*

B59 SP46 3 + 2pf brown .70 *.90*
Never hinged 6.00
On cover 4.00
B60 SP46 4 + 2pf black .70 *.90*
Never hinged 3.75
On cover 3.75
a. Bklt. pane, 5 #B60, 5 #B62 14.00 35.00
Never hinged 35.00
B61 SP46 5 + 2pf green 5.75 5.75
Never hinged 32.50
On cover 18.00
B62 SP46 6 + 4pf dull grn .45 .45
Never hinged 3.75
On cover 3.75
B63 SP46 8 + 4pf org brn .70 *.90*
Never hinged 6.75
On cover 4.00
a. Bklt. pane, 5 #B63, 4 #B64 + label 26.00 65.00
Never hinged 65.00
B64 SP46 12 + 3pf hn brn .45 .45
Never hinged 2.25
On cover 3.75
B65 SP46 20 + 10pf Prus bl 14.00 *17.50*
Never hinged 80.00
On cover 37.50
B66 SP46 25 + 15pf ultra 14.00 *17.50*
Never hinged 90.00
On cover 37.50
B67 SP54 40 + 35pf plum 45.00 *55.00*
Never hinged 180.00
On cover 100.00
Nos. B59-B67 (9) 81.75 *99.35*
Set, never hinged 405.00

Souvenir Sheet

SP55

1935, June 23 Wmk. 241 *Perf. 14*

B68 SP55 Sheet of 4 700.00 700.00
On cover 825.00
a. 3pf red brown 29.00 32.50
b. 6pf dark green 29.00 32.50
c. 12pf dark carmine 29.00 32.50
d. 25pf dark blue 29.00 32.50
Any single, on cover 100.00

Watermarked cross on each stamp and "OSTROPA 1935" in the margins of the sheet. Size: 148x104mm. 1.70m was the price of a ticket of admission to the Intl. Exhib., Königsberg, June 23-July 3, 1935.

Because the gum on No. B68 contains sulphuric acid and tends to damage the sheet, most collectors prefer to remove it. **Catalogue unused values are for sheet and singles without gum.**

East Prussia SP59

Skating SP69

Designs (Costumes of Various Sections of Germany): 4pf+3pf, Silesia. 5pf+3pf, Rhineland. 6pf+4pf, Lower Saxony. 8pf+4pf, Brandenburg. 12pf+6pf, Black Forest. 15pf+10pf, Hesse. 25pf+15pf, Upper Bavaria. 30pf+20pf, Friesland. 40pf+35pf, Franconia.

Wmk. Swastikas (237)

1935, Oct. 4 *Perf. 14x13½*

B69 SP59 3 + 2pf dk brown .20 *.25*
Never hinged .75
On cover 2.25
a. Bklt. pane, 4 #B69, 5 #B74 + label 11.50 29.00
Never hinged 29.00
B70 SP59 4 + 3pf gray 1.00 *1.25*
Never hinged 5.25
On cover 3.00
B71 SP59 5 + 3pf emerald .20 *.65*
Never hinged .75
On cover 1.90
a. Bklt. pane, 5 #B71, 5 #B72 3.00 7.00
Never hinged 7.00
B72 SP59 6 + 4pf dk green .20 *.25*
Never hinged .45
On cover 1.50
B73 SP59 8 + 4pf yel brn 1.75 1.10
Never hinged 9.00
On cover 5.25
B74 SP59 12 + 6pf dk car .20 *.25*
Never hinged 1.00
On cover .90
B75 SP59 15 + 10pf red brn 4.00 *5.00*
Never hinged 21.00
On cover 19.00
B76 SP59 25 + 15pf ultra 7.00 5.00
Never hinged 37.50
On cover 18.00
B77 SP59 30 + 20pf olive brn 8.75 *16.00*
Never hinged 45.00
On cover 32.50
B78 SP59 40 + 35p plum 8.00 *12.00*
Never hinged 40.00
On cover 32.50
Nos. B69-B78 (10) 31.30 *41.75*
Set, never hinged 160.00

1935, Nov. 25 *Perf. 13½*

12+6pf, Ski jump. 25+15pf, Bobsledding.

B79 SP69 6 + 4pf green .65 .45
Never hinged 4.50
On cover 3.00
B80 SP69 12 + 6pf carmine 1.25 .80
Never hinged 9.00
On cover 4.50
B81 SP69 25 + 15pf ultra 6.00 *7.00*
Never hinged 37.50
On cover 15.00
Nos. B79-B81 (3) 7.90 8.25
Set, never hinged 51.00

Winter Olympic Games held in Bavaria, Feb. 6-16, 1936.

1936, May 8

Designs: 3pf+2pf, Horizontal bar. 4pf+3pf, Diving. 6pf+4pf, Soccer. 8pf+4pf, Throwing javelin. 12pf+6pf, Torch runner. 15pf+10pf,

Fencing. 25pf+15pf, Sculling. 40pf+35pf, Equestrian.

B82 SP69 3 + 2pf brown .20 *.25*
Never hinged 1.00
On cover 1.50
a. Bklt. pane, 5 #B82, 5 #B86 7.00 17.50
Never hinged 17.50
B83 SP69 4 + 3pf indigo .20 *.50*
Never hinged .75
On cover 2.25
a. Bklt. pane, 5 #B83, 5 #B84 7.00 17.50
Never hinged 17.50
B84 SP69 6 + 4pf green .20 *.25*
Never hinged 1.00
On cover 1.90
B85 SP69 8 + 4pf red org 3.00 1.25
Never hinged 18.00
On cover 3.00
B86 SP69 12 + 6pf carmine .25 .25
Never hinged 1.50
On cover 1.50
B87 SP69 15 + 10pf brn vio 4.50 3.00
Never hinged 27.50
On cover 11.00
B88 SP69 25 + 15pf ultra 3.00 *3.25*
Never hinged 18.00
On cover 11.00
B89 SP69 40 + 35pf violet 5.25 *7.00*
Never hinged 32.50
On cover 16.00
Nos. B82-B89 (8) 16.60 *15.75*
Set, never hinged 100.00

Summer Olympic Games, Berlin, 8/1-16/36.
See Nos. B91-B92.

Souvenir Sheet

Horse Race — SP80

1936, June 22 Wmk. 237 *Perf. 14*
B90 SP80 42pf brown 7.00 *13.00*
Never hinged 21.00
On cover 37.50

A surtax of 1.08m was to provide a 100,000m sweepstakes prize. Wmk. 237 appears on the stamp, with "Munchen Riem 1936" watermarked on sheet margin.
For overprint see No. B105.

Types of 1936
Souvenir Sheets

1936, Aug. 1 *Perf. 14x13½*
B91 SP69 Sheet of 4 25.00 *45.00*
Never hinged 90.00
On cover 100.00
B92 SP69 Sheet of 4 25.00 *45.00*
Never hinged 90.00
On cover 100.00
Set, never hinged 180.00

11th Olympic Games, Berlin. No. B91 contains Nos. B82-B84, B89. No. B92 contains Nos. B85-B88.
Wmk. 237 appears on each stamp with "XI Olympische Spiele-Berlin 1936" watermarked on sheet margin. Sold for 1m each.

Frontier Highway, Munich — SP81

Designs: 4pf+3pf, Ministry of Aviation. 5pf+3pf, Nuremberg Memorial. 6pf+4pf, Bridge over the Saale, Saxony. 8pf+4pf, Germany Hall, Berlin. 12pf+6pf, German Alpine highway. 15pf+10pf, Fuhrer House, Munich. 25pf+15pf, Bridge over the Mangfall. 40pf+35pf, Museum of German Art, Munich.

Perf. 13½x14

1936, Sept. 21 Unwmk.
B93 SP81 3pf + 2pf blk brn .20 *.25*
Never hinged .45
On cover 1.10
a. Bklt. pane, 4 #B93 + 5 #B98 + label 9.25 22.50
Never hinged 22.50
B94 SP81 4pf + 3pf black .20 *.55*
Never hinged .60
On cover 1.90
B95 SP81 5pf + 3pf brt grn .20 *.25*
Never hinged .45
On cover 1.10
a. Bklt. pane, 5 #B95, 5 #B96) 3.50 9.25
Never hinged 9.25
B96 SP81 6pf + 4pf dk grn .20 *.25*
Never hinged .45
On cover .75
B97 SP81 8pf + 4pf brown .70 *1.25*
Never hinged 5.25
On cover 2.25
B98 SP81 12pf + 6pf brn car .20 *.25*
Never hinged .45
On cover 1.10
B99 SP81 15pf + 10pf vio brn 2.75 *3.25*
Never hinged 18.00
On cover 7.50
B100 SP81 25pf + 15pf indigo 1.90 *3.25*
Never hinged 12.50
On cover 11.00
B101 SP81 40pf + 35pf rose vio 3.00 *5.00*
Never hinged 21.00
On cover 15.00
Nos. B93-B101 (9) 9.35 *14.30*
Set, never hinged 59.15

Souvenir Sheets

Adolf Hitler — SP90

Wmk. 237
1937, Apr. 5 Photo. *Perf. 14*
B102 SP90 Sheet of 4 15.00 9.25
Never hinged 50.00
On cover 16.50
a. 6pf dark green 1.00 .95
Never hinged 3.50
On cover 5.25

48th birthday of Adolf Hitler. Sold for 1m.
See #B103-B104. For overprint see #B106.

1937, Apr. 16 *Imperf.*
B103 SP90 Sheet of 4 35.00 22.50
Never hinged 150.00
On cover 45.00
a. 6pf dark green 2.25 3.00
Never hinged 7.00
On cover 11.00

German Natl. Phil. Exhib., Berlin, June 16-18, 1937 and the Phil. Exhib. of the Stamp Collectors Group of the Strength Through Joy Organization at Hamburg, Apr. 17-20, 1937. Sold at the Exhib. post offices for 1.50m.

No. B102 with Marginal Inscriptions
Perf. 14 and Rouletted

1937, June 10 Wmk. 237
B104 SP90 Sheet of 4 35.00 *62.50*
Never hinged 175.00
On cover 95.00
a. 6pf dark grn + 25pf label 3.00 5.00
Never hinged 7.00
On cover 18.00

No. B104 inscribed in the margin beside each stamp "25 Rpf. einschliesslich Kultur-spende" in three lines.
The sheets were rouletted to allow for separation of each stamp with its component label. Sold at the post office as individual stamps with labels attached or in complete sheets.

Souvenir Sheet No. B90 Overprinted in Red

1937, Aug. 1 *Perf. 14*
B105 SP80 42pf brown 57.50 *92.50*
Never hinged 140.00
On cover 525.00

4th running of the "Brown Ribbon" horse race at the Munich-Riem Race Course, Aug. 1, 1937.

Souvenir Sheet No. B104 Overprinted in Black on Each Stamp

Perf. 14 and Rouletted

1937, Sept. 3 Wmk. 237
B106 SP90 Sheet of 4 50.00 40.00
Never hinged 175.00
On cover 75.00
a. 6pf dark grn + 25pf label 3.25 3.50
Never hinged 9.25
On cover 18.00

1937 Nazi Congress at Nuremburg.

Lifeboat — SP91

Designs: 4pf+3pf, Lightship "Elbe I." 5pf+3pf, Fishing smacks. 6pf+4pf, Steamer. 8pf+4pf, Sailing vessel. 12pf+6pf, The "Tannenberg." 15pf+10pf, Sea-Train "Schwerin." 25pf+15pf, S. S. Hamburg. 40pf+35pf, S. S. Bremen.

Perf. 13½

1937, Nov. 4 Engr. Unwmk.
B107 SP91 3pf + 2pf dk brwn .20 .25
Never hinged .35
On cover 1.20
a. Bklt. pane, 4 #B107 + 5 #B112 + label 12.00
B108 SP91 4pf + 3pf black 1.00 .70
Never hinged 7.50
On cover 2.50
B109 SP91 5pf + 3pf yel grn .20 *.25*
Never hinged .35
On cover 1.60
a. Bklt. pane, 5 #B109, 5 #B110 5.00
B110 SP91 6pf + 4pf bl grn .20 *.25*
Never hinged .35
On cover 1.20
B111 SP91 8pf + 4pf orange .60 *1.10*
Never hinged 4.50
On cover 2.50
B112 SP91 12pf + 6pf car lake .20 .20
Never hinged .75
On cover 1.20
B113 SP91 15pf + 10pf vio brn 1.25 *3.50*
Never hinged 9.75
On cover 11.00
B114 SP91 25pf + 15pf ultra 3.00 *3.50*
Never hinged 22.50
On cover 9.00
B115 SP91 40pf + 35pf red vio 5.00 *7.00*
Never hinged 37.50
On cover 18.00
Nos. B107-B115 (9) 11.65 *16.75*
Set, never hinged 83.55

No. B115 actually pictures the S.S. Europa.

Youth Carrying Torch and Laurel — SP100

Adolf Hitler — SP101

Wmk. 237
1938, Jan. 28 Photo. *Perf. 14*
B116 SP100 6 + 4pf dk green .70 *1.25*
Never hinged 6.00
On cover 3.00
B117 SP100 12 + 8pf brt car .90 *1.60*
Never hinged 7.50
On cover 3.75
Set, never hinged 13.50

Assumption of power by the Nazis, 5th anniv.

1938, Apr. 13 Engr. Unwmk.
B118 SP101 12 + 38pf copper red 1.40 1.75
Never hinged 9.25
On cover 5.00

Hitler's 49th birthday.

Horsewoman SP102

1938, July 20
B119 SP102 42 + 108pf dp brn 20.00 *45.00*
Never hinged 100.00
On cover 62.50

5th "Brown Ribbon" at Munich.

Adolf Hitler SP103

Theater at Saarbrücken SP104

1938, Sept. 1
B120 SP103 6 + 19pf deep grn 2.25 *3.00*
Never hinged 14.00
On cover 6.00

1938 Nazi Congress at Nuremberg. The surtax was for Hitler's National Culture Fund.

1938, Oct. 9 Photo. Wmk. 237
B121 SP104 6 + 4pf blue grn .90 *1.25*
Never hinged 5.75
On cover 5.00
B122 SP104 12 + 8pf dk car 1.75 *2.00*
Never hinged 8.75
On cover 7.50
Set, never hinged 14.50

Inauguration of the theater of the District of Saarpfalz at Saarbrücken. The surtax was for Hitler's National Culture Fund.

Castle of Forchtenstein SP105

Designs (scenes in Austria and various flowers): 4pf+3pf, Flexenstrasse in Vorarlberg. 5pf+3pf, Zell am See, Salzburg. 6pf+4pf, Grossglockner. 8pf+4pf, Ruins of Aggstein. 12pf+6pf, Prince Eugene Monument, Vienna. 15pf+10pf, Erzberg. 25pf+15pf, Hall, Tyrol. 40pf+35pf, Braunau.

Unwmk.
1938, Nov. 18 Engr. *Perf. 14*
B123 SP105 3 + 2pf olive brn .20 *.25*
Never hinged .60
On cover 1.50
a. Bklt. pane, 4 #B123, 5 #B128 + label 8.75 22.50
Never hinged 22.50
B124 SP105 4 + 3pf indigo 1.50 1.10
Never hinged 8.00
On cover 3.00
B125 SP105 5 + 3pf emerald .20 *.30*
Never hinged .35
On cover 1.90
a. Bklt. pane, 5 #B125, 5 #B126 3.00 7.00
Never hinged 7.00
B126 SP105 6 + 4pf dk grn .20 .20
Never hinged .35
On cover 1.10
B127 SP105 8 + 4pf red org 1.50 1.10
Never hinged 7.00
On cover 2.50
B128 SP105 12 + 6pf dk car .20 *.25*
Never hinged .50
On cover 1.10
B129 SP105 15 + 10pf dp cl 2.75 *3.75*
Never hinged 15.00
On cover 9.00
B130 SP105 25 + 15pf dk blue 2.50 *3.75*
Never hinged 12.50
On cover 7.50
B131 SP105 40 + 35pf plum 5.75 *6.50*
Never hinged 30.00
On cover 15.00
Nos. B123-B131 (9) 14.80 *17.20*
Set, never hinged 74.80

The surtax was for "Winter Help."

Sudeten Couple — SP114

Early Types of Automobiles SP115

1938, Dec. 2 Photo. Wmk. 237

B132 SP114 6 + 4pf blue grn .95 *2.25*
Never hinged 10.00
On cover 6.00
B133 SP114 12 + 8pf dk car 2.25 *3.00*
Never hinged 16.00
On cover 6.00
Set, never hinged 26.00

Annexation of the Sudeten Territory. The surtax was for Hitler's National Culture Fund.

1939

Designs: 12pf+8pf, Racing cars. 25pf+10pf, Modern automobile.

B134 SP115 6 + 4pf dk grn 3.00 3.00
Never hinged 22.50
On cover 7.50
B135 SP115 12 + 8pf brt car 3.00 3.00
Never hinged 22.50
On cover 9.00
B136 SP115 25 + 10pf dp blue 5.00 *5.25*
Never hinged 37.50
On cover 13.50
Nos. B134-B136 (3) 11.00 11.25
Set, never hinged 82.50

Berlin Automobile and Motorcycle Exhibition. The surtax was for Hitler's National Culture Fund. For overprints see #B141-B143.

Adolf Hitler
SP118

Exhibition Building
SP119

Unwmk.

1939, Apr. 13 Engr. *Perf. 14*

B137 SP118 12 + 38pf carmine 1.40 *3.50*
Never hinged 8.25
On cover 9.00

Hitler's 50th birthday. The surtax was for Hitler's National Culture Fund.

1939, Apr. 22 Photo. *Perf. 12½*

B138 SP119 6 + 4pf dk green 1.00 *2.25*
Never hinged 5.25
On cover 6.50
B139 SP119 15 + 5pf dp plum 1.00 *2.25*
Never hinged 7.50
On cover 7.50
Set, never hinged 12.75

Horticultural Exhib. held at Stuttgart. Surtax for Hitler's National Culture Fund.

Adolf Hitler — SP120

Perf. 14x13½

1939, Apr. 28 Wmk. 237

B140 SP120 6 + 19pf black brn 1.75 *3.50*
Never hinged 9.75
On cover 9.00

Day of National Labor. The surtax was for Hitler's National Culture Fund.
See No. B147.

Nos. B134-B136 Overprinted in Black

1939, May 18 *Perf. 14*

B141 SP115 6 + 4pf dk green 16.00 *22.50*
Never hinged 65.00
On cover 55.00
B142 SP115 12 + 8pf brt car 16.00 *22.50*
Never hinged 65.00
On cover 55.00
B143 SP115 25 + 10pf dp blue 16.00 *22.50*
Never hinged 65.00
On cover 55.00
Nos. B141-B143 (3) 48.00 *67.50*
Set, never hinged 195.00

Nurburgring Auto Races, 5/21, 7/23/39.

Racehorse "Investment" and Jockey
SP121

1939, June 18 Engr. Unwmk.

B144 SP121 25 + 50pf ultra 13.00 11.50
Never hinged 55.00
On cover 25.00

70th anniv. of the German Derby. The surtax was divided between Hitler's National Culture Fund and the race promoters.

Man Holding Rearing Horse — SP122

"Venetian Woman" by Albrecht Dürer — SP123

1939, July 12

B145 SP122 42 + 108pf dp brown 13.00 *22.50*
Never hinged 57.50
On cover 35.00

6th "Brown Ribbon" at Munich.

1939, July 12 Photo. Wmk. 237

B146 SP123 6 + 19pf dk grn 5.00 *7.00*
Never hinged 25.00
On cover 15.00

Day of German Art. The surtax was used for Hitler's National Culture Fund.

Hitler Type of 1939
Inscribed "Reichsparteitag 1939"

1939, Aug. 25 *Perf. 14x13½*

B147 SP120 6 + 19pf blk brn 3.25 *7.00*
Never hinged 16.00
On cover 13.50

1939 Nazi Congress at Nuremberg.

Meeting in German Hall, Berlin
SP124

Designs: 4pf+3pf, Meeting of postal and telegraph employees. 5pf+3pf, Professional competitions. 6pf+4pf, 6pf+9pf, Professional camp. 8pf+4pf, 8pf+12pf, Gold flag competitions. 10pf+5pf, Awarding prizes. 12&f+6pf, 12pf+18pf, Automobile race. 15pf+10pf, Sports. 16pf+10pf, 16pf+24pf, Postal police. 20pf+10pf, 20pf+30pf, Glider workshops. 24pf+10pf, 24pf+36pf, Mail coach. 25pf+15pf, Convalescent home, Konigstein.

Perf. 13½x14

1939-41 Unwmk. Photo.

B148 3 + 2pf bister brn 1.50 *4.50*
Never hinged 10.00
On cover 12.50
B149 4 + 3pf slate blue 1.50 *4.50*
Never hinged 10.00
On cover 11.00
B150 5 + 3pf brt bl grn .45 *1.25*
Never hinged 3.00
On cover 4.50
B151 6 + 4pf myrtle grn .55 *1.10*
Never hinged 3.75
On cover 3.75
B151A 6 + 9pf dk grn ('41) .55 *1.25*
Never hinged 3.75
On cover 3.00
B152 8 + 4pf dp org .55 *1.25*
Never hinged 3.75
On cover 3.75
B152A 8 + 12pf hn brn ('41) .80 *1.00*
Never hinged 5.50
On cover 3.75
B153 10 + 5pf dk brown .45 *1.60*
Never hinged 3.00
On cover 3.75
B154 12 + 6pf rose brown .60 *1.60*
Never hinged 4.00
On cover 3.75
B154A 12 + 18pf dk car rose ('41) .80 *1.00*
Never hinged 5.50
On cover 2.50
B155 15 + 10pf dp red lilac .45 *1.60*
Never hinged 3.00
On cover 6.50
B156 16 + 10pf slate grn .45 *1.60*
Never hinged 3.00
On cover 9.00
B156A 16 + 24pf black ('41) .80 *3.25*
Never hinged 5.50
On cover 8.00
B157 20 + 10pf ultra .60 *1.60*
Never hinged 3.75
On cover 11.00
B157A 20 + 30pf ultra ('41) .80 *3.25*
Never hinged 5.50
On cover 11.00
B158 24 + 10pf ol grn 1.50 *3.25*
Never hinged 9.50
On cover 11.00
B158A 24 + 36pf pur ('41) 2.50 *9.00*
Never hinged 18.00
On cover 18.00
B159 25 + 15pf dk blue 1.50 *2.60*
Never hinged 9.50
On cover 12.50
Nos. B148-B159 (18) 16.35 *45.20*
Set, never hinged 110.00

The surtax was used for Hitler's National Culture Fund and the Postal Employees' Fund.
See Nos. B273, B275-B277.

Elbogen Castle — SP136

Buildings: 4pf+3pf, Drachenfels on the Rhine. 5pf+3pf, Kaiserpfalz at Goslar. 6pf+4pf, Clocktower at Graz. 8pf+4pf, Town Hall, Frankfurt. 12pf+6pf, Guild House, Klagenfurt. 15pf+10pf, Ruins of Schreckenstein Castle. 25pf+15pf, Fortress of Salzburg. 40pf+35pf, Castle of Hohentwiel.

1939 Unwmk. Engr. *Perf. 14*

B160 SP136 3 + 2pf dk brn .20 *.35*
Never hinged .45
On cover 1.25
a. Bklt. pane, 4 #B160, 5 #B165 + label 8.75 22.50
Never hinged 22.50
B161 SP136 4 + 3pf gray blk 1.40 *1.60*
Never hinged 6.75
On cover 3.75
B162 SP136 5 + 3pf emerald .20 *.45*
Never hinged .75
On cover 1.25
a. Bklt. pane, 5 #B162, 5 #B163 3.75 9.25
Never hinged 9.25
B163 SP136 6 + 4pf slate grn .20 *.30*
Never hinged .75
On cover 1.10
B164 SP136 8 + 4pf red org 1.40 1.40
Never hinged 6.75
On cover 2.50
B165 SP136 12 + 6pf dk car .20 *.30*
Never hinged .75
On cover .90
B166 SP136 15 + 10pf brn vio 2.10 *4.00*
Never hinged 10.00
On cover 9.00
B167 SP136 25 + 15pf ultra 1.60 *4.00*
Never hinged 8.25
On cover 9.00
B168 SP136 40 + 35pf rose vio 2.25 *5.25*
Never hinged 11.00
On cover 12.50
Nos. B160-B168 (9) 9.55 *17.65*
Set, never hinged 45.00

Hall of Honor at Chancellery, Berlin — SP145

Child Greeting Hitler — SP146

1940, Mar. 28

B169 SP145 24 + 76pf dk grn 5.75 *12.00*
Never hinged 26.00
On cover 22.50

2nd National Stamp Exposition, Berlin.

Perf. 14x13½

1940, Apr. 10 Photo. Wmk. 237

B170 SP146 12 + 38pf cop red 1.40 *5.00*
Never hinged 10.50
On cover 9.00

51st birthday of Adolf Hitler.

Armed Warrior
SP147

Horseman
SP148

1940, Apr. 30 Unwmk. *Perf. 14*

B171 SP147 6 + 4pf sl grn & lt grn .25 *.75*
Never hinged .90
On cover 2.50

Issued to commemorate May Day.

Perf. 14x13½

1940, June 22 Wmk. 237

B172 SP148 25 + 100pf dp ultra 3.25 *8.25*
Never hinged 15.00
On cover 15.00

Blue Ribbon race, Hamburg, June 30, 1940.
Surtax for Hitler's National Culture Fund.

Chariot
SP149

Unwmk.

1940, July 20 Engr. *Perf. 14*

B173 SP149 42 + 108pf brown 14.00 *25.00*
Never hinged 90.00
On cover 37.50

7th "Brown Ribbon" at Munich.
The surtax was for Hitler's National Culture Fund and the promoters of the race.

View of Malmedy
SP150

Design: 12pf+8pf, View of Eupen.

Perf. 14x13½

1940, July 25 Photo. Wmk. 237

B174 SP150 6 + 4pf dk green .60 *2.25*
Never hinged 3.00
On cover 3.75
B175 SP150 12 + 8pf org red .60 *2.25*
Never hinged 3.50
On cover 3.75
Set, never hinged 6.50

Issued on the occasion of the reunion of Eupen-Malmedy with the Reich.

Rocky Cliffs of Heligoland SP152

Artushof in Danzig — SP153

1940, Aug. 9 **Unwmk.**

B176 SP152 6 + 94pf brt bl grn & red org 3.50 *7.00*
Never hinged 20.00
On cover 13.50

Heligoland's 50th year as part of Germany.

1940, Nov. 5 **Engr.** ***Perf. 14***

Buildings: 4pf+3pf, Town Hall, Thorn. 5pf+3pf, Castle at Kaub. 6pf+4pf, City Theater, Poznan. 8pf+4pf, Castle at Heidelberg. 12pf+6pf, Porta Nigra Trier. 15pf+10pf, New German Theater, Prague. 25pf+15pf, Town Hall, Bremen. 40pf+35pf, Town Hall, Munster.

B177 SP153 3 + 2pf dk brn .20 *.30*
Never hinged .35
On cover 1.90
a. Bklt. pane, 4 #B177 + 5 #B182 + label 7.00 17.50
Never hinged 17.50
B178 SP153 4 + 3pf bluish blk .45 *.70*
Never hinged 2.25
On cover 3.00
B179 SP153 5 + 3pf yel grn .20 *.45*
Never hinged .45
On cover 1.25
a. Bklt. pane, 5 #B179, 5 #B180 3.75 9.25
Never hinged 9.25
B180 SP153 6 + 4pf dk grn .20 *.25*
Never hinged .60
On cover .90
B181 SP153 8 + 4pf dp org .90 .75
Never hinged 4.50
On cover 3.00
B182 SP153 12 + 6pf carmine .20 *.25*
Never hinged .60
On cover 1.25
B183 SP153 15 + 10pf dk vio brn .90 *2.25*
Never hinged 4.50
On cover 5.00
B184 SP153 25 + 15pf dp ultra 1.25 *2.25*
Never hinged 6.25
On cover 5.50
B185 SP153 40 + 35pf red lil 2.50 *5.50*
Never hinged 12.50
On cover 11.00
Nos. B177-B185 (9) 6.80 *12.70*
Set, never hinged 32.00

von Behring — SP162

1940, Nov. 26 **Photo.**

B186 SP162 6 + 4pf dp green .45 *1.40*
Never hinged 3.75
On cover 3.00
B187 SP162 25 + 10pf brt ultra .90 *2.25*
Never hinged 6.00
On cover 3.75
Set, never hinged 9.75

Dr. Emil von Behring (1854-1917), bacteriologist.

AIR POST STAMPS

Issues of the Republic

Post Horn with Wings — AP1

Biplane AP2

Perf. 15x14½

1919, Nov. 10 **Typo.** **Unwmk.**

C1 AP1 10pf orange .20 *2.00*
Never hinged .50
On cover 7.50
C2 AP2 40pf dark green .20 *2.50*
Never hinged .50
On cover 7.50
a. Imperf. 1,600.
Set, never hinged 1.00

No. C2a is ungummed.

Carrier Pigeon AP3

German Eagle AP4

1922-23 **Wmk. 126** ***Perf. 14, 14½***

Size: 19x23mm

C3 AP3 25(pf) chocolate .35 *16.00*
Never hinged 1.10
On cover *30.00*
C4 AP3 40(pf) orange .35 *22.50*
Never hinged 1.25
On cover *37.50*
C5 AP3 50(pf) violet .20 *7.75*
Never hinged .60
On cover *17.50*
C6 AP3 60(pf) carmine .45 *17.50*
Never hinged 1.50
On cover *30.00*
C7 AP3 80(pf) blue grn .35 *17.50*
Never hinged 1.20
On cover *30.00*

Perf. 13x13½

Size: 22x28mm

C8 AP3 1m dk grn & pale grn .20 *3.25*
Never hinged .50
On cover *9.00*
C9 AP3 2m lake & gray .20 *3.25*
Never hinged .50
On cover *9.00*
C10 AP3 3m dk blue & gray .20 *4.00*
Never hinged .80
On cover *9.00*
C11 AP3 5m red org & yel .20 *3.25*
Never hinged .50
On cover *9.00*
C12 AP3 10m vio & rose ('23) .20 *10.50*
Never hinged .50
On cover *18.00*
C13 AP3 25m brn & yel ('23) .20 *8.50*
Never hinged .50
On cover *16.00*
C14 AP3 100m ol grn & rose ('23) .20 *7.25*
Never hinged .50
On cover *16.00*
Nos. C3-C14 (12) 3.10 *121.25*
Set, never hinged 9.45

1923

C15 AP3 5m vermilion .20 *45.00*
Never hinged .40
On cover *75.00*
C16 AP3 10m violet .20 *10.50*
Never hinged .40
On cover *20.00*
C17 AP3 25m dark brown .20 *10.50*
Never hinged .40
On cover *18.00*
C18 AP3 100m olive grn .20 *11.00*
Never hinged .40
On cover *16.00*
C19 AP3 200m deep blue .20 *32.50*
Never hinged .40
On cover *65.00*
a. Imperf. 47.50
Never hinged 50.00
Nos. C15-C19 (5) 1.00 109.50
Set, never hinged 2.00

Issued: #C15-C18, June 1. #C19, July 25.
Note following #160 applies to #C1-C19.

1924, Jan. 11 ***Perf. 14***

Size: 19x23mm

C20 AP3 5(pf) yellow grn 1.20 1.20
Never hinged 3.25
On cover 4.50
C21 AP3 10(pf) carmine 1.20 *1.60*
Never hinged 3.25
On cover 6.00
C22 AP3 20(pf) violet blue 5.25 *4.50*
Never hinged 20.00
On cover 10.00
C23 AP3 50(pf) orange 11.00 *21.00*
Never hinged 100.00
On cover 35.00
C24 AP3 100(pf) dull violet 29.00 *47.50*
Never hinged 200.00
On cover 75.00
C25 AP3 200(pf) grnsh blue 55.00 *62.50*
Never hinged 250.00
On cover 300.00
C26 AP3 300(pf) gray 92.50 90.00
Never hinged 550.00
On cover 350.00
a. Imperf. *1,425.*
Nos. C20-C26 (7) 195.15 *228.30*
Set, never hinged 1,127.

1926-27

C27 AP4 5pf green .65 *.80*
Never hinged 3.00
On cover 2.25
C28 AP4 10pf rose red .65 *.80*
Never hinged 5.25
On cover 1.75
b. Tête bêche pair 87.50 190.00
Never hinged 175.00
d. Bklt. pane 10 (6 No. C28 + 4 No. C29) 52.50 140.00
Never hinged 140.00
C29 AP4 15pf lilac rose ('27) 1.40 1.20
Never hinged 16.00
On cover 3.75
a. Double impression *1,375.*
C30 AP4 20pf dull blue 1.40 *1.60*
Never hinged 16.00
On cover 4.50
a. Tête bêche pair 87.50 190.00
Never hinged 175.00
b. Bklt. pane 4 (4 No. C30 + 6 labels) 47.50 110.00
Never hinged 110.00
c. Bklt. pane 5 (5 No. C30 + 5 labels) 190.00 475.00
Never hinged 475.00
C31 AP4 50pf brown org 15.00 4.50
Never hinged 210.00
On cover 16.00
C32 AP4 1m black & salmon 15.00 5.25
Never hinged 90.00
On cover 18.00
C33 AP4 2m black & blue 15.00 *19.00*
Never hinged 120.00
On cover 45.00
C34 AP4 3m black & ol grn 50.00 *67.50*
Never hinged 375.00
On cover 150.00
Nos. C27-C34 (8) 99.10 *100.65*
Set, never hinged 835.00

"Graf Zeppelin" Crossing Ocean — AP5

1928-31 **Photo.**

C35 AP5 1m carmine ('31) 25.00 *32.50*
Never hinged 62.50
On cover 60.00
C36 AP5 2m ultra 37.50 *52.50*
Never hinged 225.00
On cover 90.00
C37 AP5 4m black brown 27.50 *35.00*
Never hinged 95.00
On cover 90.00
Nos. C35-C37 (3) 90.00 *120.00*
Set, never hinged 382.50

Issued: 2m, 4m, Sept. 20. 1m, May 8.
For overprints see Nos. C40-C45.

AP6

1930, Apr. 19 **Wmk. 126**

C38 AP6 2m ultra 230.00 *290.00*
Never hinged 1,250.
On cover 375.00
C39 AP6 4m black brown 230.00 *290.00*
Never hinged 1,300.
On cover 375.00
Set, never hinged 2,550.

First flight of Graf Zeppelin to South America. Nos. C38-C39 exist with watermark vertical or horizontal.
Counterfeits exist of Nos. C38-C45.

Nos. C35-C37 Overprinted in Brown

1931, July 15

C40 AP5 1m carmine 105.00 105.00
Never hinged 400.00
On cover 175.00
C41 AP5 2m ultra 150.00 *190.00*
Never hinged 975.00
On cover 300.00
C42 AP5 4m black brown 375.00 *650.00*
Never hinged 1,600.
On cover 800.00
Nos. C40-C42 (3) 630.00 *945.00*
Set, never hinged 2,975.

Polar flight of Graf Zeppelin.

Nos. C35-C37 Overprinted

1933, Sept. 25

C43 AP5 1m carmine 650.00 *325.00*
Never hinged 2,500.
On cover *400.00*
C44 AP5 2m ultra 65.00 *175.00*
Never hinged 225.00
On cover *260.00*
C45 AP5 4m black brown 65.00 *175.00*
Never hinged 225.00
On cover *600.00*
Nos. C43-C45 (3) 780.00 *675.00*
Set, never hinged 2,950.

Graf Zeppelin flight to Century of Progress International Exhibition, Chicago.

Swastika Sun, Globe and Eagle — AP7

Otto Lilienthal — AP8

Design: 3m, Count Ferdinand von Zeppelin.

Perf. 14, 13½x13

1934, Jan. 21 **Typo.** **Wmk. 237**

C46 AP7 5(pf) brt green .70 .50
Never hinged 3.75
On cover 1.75
C47 AP7 10(pf) brt carmine .70 .65
Never hinged 3.75
On cover 2.25
C48 AP7 15(pf) ultra 1.10 1.10
Never hinged 5.50
On cover 2.25
C49 AP7 20(pf) dull blue 2.20 1.50
Never hinged 12.00
On cover 3.00
C50 AP7 25(pf) brown 3.25 1.40
Never hinged 37.50
On cover 3.00
C51 AP7 40(pf) red violet 6.00 1.00
Never hinged 55.00
On cover 3.00
C52 AP7 50(pf) dk green 9.25 .70
Never hinged 80.00
On cover 5.50
C53 AP7 80(pf) orange yel 3.50 3.50
Never hinged 40.00
On cover 26.00
C54 AP7 100(pf) black 5.75 5.75
Never hinged 50.00
On cover 26.00
C55 AP8 2m green & blk 16.00 *17.50*
Never hinged 90.00
On cover 55.00
C56 AP8 3m blue & blk 29.00 *37.50*
Never hinged 125.00
On cover 75.00
Nos. C46-C56 (11) 77.45 71.10
Set, never hinged 502.50

"Hindenburg" — AP10

Perf. 14, 14½x14

1936, Mar. 16 **Engr.**

C57 AP10 50pf dark blue 15.00 .50
On cover 7.50
C58 AP10 75pf dull green 16.50 .75
On cover 9.00

The note concerning gum after No. B68 also applies to Nos. C57-C58.
Unused values are for stamps without gum.

Count Zeppelin — AP11

Airship Gondola — AP12

1938, July 5 Unwmk. *Perf. 13½*

C59 AP11 25pf dull blue 2.25 .75
Never hinged 16.00
On cover 9.00
C60 AP12 50pf green 3.25 .75
Never hinged 24.00
On cover 9.00
Set, never hinged 40.00

Count Ferdinand von Zeppelin (1838-1917), airship inventor and builder.

OFFICIAL STAMPS

Issues of the Republic

In 1920 the Official Stamps of Bavaria and Wurttemberg then current were overprinted "Deutsches Reich" and made available for official use in all parts of Germany. They were, however, used almost exclusively in the two states where they originated and we have listed them among the issues of those states.

O1

O2

O3

O4

O5

O6

O7

O8

O9

O10

O11

O12

1920-21 Typo. Wmk. 125 *Perf. 14*

O1 O1 5pf deep green .75 *7.00*
Never hinged 2.75
On cover *13.00*
O2 O2 10pf car rose .20 1.05
Never hinged .25
On cover 1.60
O3 O2 10pf orange ('21) .45 *375.00*
Never hinged 2.00
On cover *500.00*
O4 O3 15pf violet brn .20 1.10
Never hinged .25
On cover 1.60
a. Imperf. ('21) 65.00
O5 O4 20pf deep ultra .20 1.05
Never hinged .25
On cover 1.60
O6 O5 30pf org, *buff* .20 1.05
Never hinged .25
On cover 1.60
O7 O6 40pf carmine .20 1.05
Never hinged .30
On cover 1.60
O8 O7 50pf violet, *buff* .20 1.05
Never hinged .25
On cover 1.60
O9 O8 60pf red brown ('21) .20 1.05
Never hinged .75
On cover 1.60
O10 O9 1m red, *buff* .20 1.05
Never hinged .25
On cover 1.60
O11 O10 1.25m dk bl, *yel* .20 1.05
Never hinged .25
On cover 1.90
O12 O11 2m dark blue 3.75 1.90
Never hinged 17.50
On cover 6.50
O13 O12 5m brown, *yel* .20 1.05
Never hinged .55
On cover 1.60
Nos. O1-O13 (13) 6.95 *394.45*
Set, never hinged 25.60

The value of No. O4a is for a copy postmarked at Bautzen.

See No. O15. For surcharges see Nos. O29-O33, O35-O36, O38.

Postally Used vs. CTO

Values quoted for canceled copies of Nos. O1-O46) are for postally used stamps. See note after No. 160.

O13

O14

O15

Wmk. 126, 125 (#O16-O17)

1922-23

O14 O13 75pf dark blue .20 *5.25*
Never hinged .70
On cover *8.25*
O15 O11 2m dark blue .20 *1.00*
Never hinged .25
On cover 1.40
a. Imperf. 92.50
Never hinged 190.00
O16 O14 3m brown, *rose* .20 *1.05*
Never hinged .25
On cover 3.25
O17 O15 10m dk grn, *rose* .20 *1.05*
Never hinged .55
On cover 1.60
O18 O15 10m dk grn, *rose* .20 *7.00*
Never hinged .65
On cover *1.10*
O19 O15 20m dk bl, *rose* .20 *1.00*
Never hinged .25
On cover 1.40
O20 O15 50m vio, *rose* .20 *1.00*
Never hinged .25
On cover 1.40
a. Imperf 75.00
Never hinged 175.00
O21 O15 100m rose red, *rose* .20 *1.00*
Never hinged .25
On cover 1.40
a. Imperf 90.00
Never hinged 225.00
Nos. O14-O21 (8) 1.60 *18.35*
Set, never hinged 3.15

Issue date: #O18-O21, 1923.
Nos. O20-O21 exist imperf.
For surcharges see Nos. O34, O37, O39.

Regular Issue of 1923 Overprinted

a

1923

O22 A34 20m red lilac .20 *7.00*
Never hinged .25
On cover *13.00*
O23 A34 30m olive grn .20 *25.00*
Never hinged .25
On cover *45.00*
O24 A29 40m green .20 *2.75*
Never hinged .60
On cover *4.50*
O25 A35 200m car rose .20 *1.05*
Never hinged .25
On cover *1.60*
O26 A35 300m green .20 *1.05*
Never hinged .25
On cover *1.60*
O27 A35 400m dk brn .20 *1.05*
Never hinged .25
On cover *1.60*
O28 A35 500m red orange .20 *1.05*
Never hinged .45
On cover *1.60*
Nos. O22-O28 (7) 1.40 *38.95*
Set, never hinged 2.30

Official Stamps of 1920-23 Surcharged with New Values

Abbreviations:
Th=(Tausend) Thousand
Mil=(Million) Million
Mlrd=(Milliarde) Billion

1923 Wmk. 125

O29 O12 5th m on 5m .20 *2.75*
Never hinged .20
On cover *5.25*
a. Inverted surcharge 45.00
Never hinged 90.00
O30 O5 20th m on 30pf .20 *2.75*
Never hinged .20
On cover *5.25*
a. Inverted surcharge 50.00
Never hinged 120.00
b. Imperf. 57.50
Never hinged 120.00
O31 O3 100th m on 15pf .20 *2.75*
Never hinged .20
On cover *5.25*
a. Imperf. 57.50
Never hinged 110.00
b. Inverted surcharge 45.00
Never hinged 90.00
O32 O2 250th m on 10pf car rose .20 *2.75*
Never hinged .20
On cover *5.25*
a. Double surcharge 37.50
Never hinged 85.00
O33 O5 800th m on 30pf .60 *230.00*
Never hinged 1.40
On cover *325.00*

Official Stamps and Types of 1920-23 Surcharged with New Values

Wmk. 126

O34 O15 75th m on 50m .20 *2.75*
Never hinged .20
On cover *5.00*
a. Inverted surcharge 45.00
Never hinged 90.00
O35 O3 400th m on 15pf brn .20 *26.50*
Never hinged .25
On cover *32.50*
O36 O5 800th m on 30pf org, *buff* .20 *3.25*
Never hinged .55
On cover *6.50*
O37 O13 1 mil m on 75pf .20 *29.00*
Never hinged .25
On cover *65.00*
O38 O2 2 mil m on 10pf car rose .20 *3.25*
Never hinged .50
On cover *4.50*
a. Imperf. 85.00
Never hinged 160.00
O39 O15 5 mil m on 100m .20 *5.50*
Never hinged .25
On cover *8.25*
Nos. O29-O39 (11) 2.60 *311.25*
Set, never hinged 4.15

The 10, 15 and 30 pfennig are not known with this watermark and without surcharge.

#290-291, 295-299 Overprinted Type "a"

1923

O40 A39 100 mil m .20 *140.00*
Never hinged .60
On cover *275.00*
O41 A39 200 mil m .20 *140.00*
Never hinged .60
On cover *250.00*
O42 A39a 2 mlrd m .20 *105.00*
Never hinged .80
On cover *225.00*
O43 A39a 5 mlrd m .20 *80.00*
Never hinged 1.10
On cover *225.00*
O44 A39a 10 mlrd m 2.75 *120.00*
Never hinged 9.00
On cover *275.00*
O45 A39a 20 mlrd m 3.50 *140.00*
Never hinged 11.00
On cover *275.00*
O46 A39a 50 mlrd m 1.75 *190.00*
Never hinged 5.00
On cover *325.00*
Nos. O40-O46 (7) 8.80 *915.00*
Set, never hinged 28.10

Same Overprint on Nos, 323-328, Values in Rentenpfennig

1923

O47 A40 3pf brown .20 *.30*
Never hinged 1.50
On cover 2.25
O48 A40 5pf dk green .20 *.30*
Never hinged 1.50
On cover .65
a. Inverted overprint 85.00 160.00
Never hinged 175.00
O49 A40 10pf carmine .20 *.30*
Never hinged 1.25
On cover .65
a. Inverted overprint 72.50 160.00
Never hinged 140.00
b. Imperf. 26.00
Never hinged 52.50
O50 A40 20pf dp ultra .55 .35
Never hinged 2.25
On cover 1.40
O51 A40 50pf orange .55 *.70*
Never hinged 2.25
On cover 14.00
O52 A40 100pf brown vio 3.25 *7.00*
Never hinged 15.00
On cover 110.00
Nos. O47-O52 (6) 4.95 *8.95*
Set, never hinged 23.75

Same Overprint On Issues of 1924

1924

O53 A41 3pf lt brown .35 *.80*
Never hinged 1.60
On cover 3.00
a. Inverted overprint 55.00 140.00
Never hinged 105.00
O54 A41 5pf lt green .20 *.30*
Never hinged .80
On cover .65
a. Imperf. 67.50
Never hinged 140.00
b. Inverted overprint 90.00
Never hinged 175.00
O55 A41 10pf vermilion .20 *.30*
Never hinged .80
On cover .65
O56 A41 20pf blue .20 *.30*
Never hinged 1.00
On cover 1.60
O57 A41 30pf rose lilac .70 .35
Never hinged 2.75
On cover 2.50
O58 A41 40pf olive green .70 .40
Never hinged 2.75
On cover 3.25
O59 A41 50pf orange 5.00 2.25
Never hinged 17.50
On cover 8.50
O60 A47 60pf red brown 1.40 *2.60*
Never hinged 5.00
On cover 20.00
O61 A47 80pf slate 6.50 *32.50*
Never hinged 20.00
On cover *250.00*
Nos. O53-O61 (9) 15.25 *39.80*
Set, never hinged 50.00

O16

Swastika — O17

1927-33 *Perf. 14*

O62 O16 3pf bister .30 .20
Never hinged .90
On cover 1.40
O63 O16 4pf lt bl ('31) .30 *.35*
Never hinged .90
On cover 1.10
O64 O16 4pf blue ('33) 5.25 *5.75*
Never hinged 32.50
On cover 10.00
O65 O16 5pf green .20 .20
Never hinged .50
On cover .65
O66 O16 6pf pale ol grn ('32) .30 *.35*
Never hinged 1.75
On cover 1.50
O67 O16 8pf dk grn .30 .20
Never hinged .90
On cover .65
O68 O16 10pf carmine 7.00 5.75
Never hinged 20.00
On cover 20.00
O69 O16 10pf ver ('29), wmk. upright 13.50 *16.00*
Never hinged 37.50
On cover 32.50
a. Wmk. sideways 12.50 *20.00*

Never hinged 52.50
On cover *82.50*
O70 O16 10pf red vio ('30) .30 *.35*
Never hinged 1.10
On cover 1.10
a. Imperf. 95.00
Never hinged 190.00
O71 O16 10pf choc ('33) 2.10 *4.50*
Never hinged 10.50
On cover 8.50
O72 O16 12pf org ('32) .30 *.35*
Never hinged .90
On cover 1.10
O73 O16 15pf vermilion 1.75 .35
Never hinged 3.50
On cover 2.75
O74 O16 15pf car ('29) .40 .35
Never hinged 1.10
On cover 1.90
O75 O16 20pf Prus grn 3.75 1.90
Never hinged 19.00
On cover 6.50
O76 O16 20pf gray ('30) .95 .50
Never hinged 4.50
On cover 1.40
O77 O16 30pf olive grn .80 .35
Never hinged 2.75
On cover 1.40
O78 O16 40pf violet, wmk upright .70 .30
Never hinged 3.00
On cover 2.25
a. Wmk sideways 6.25 *13.50*
Never hinged 15.00
On cover —
O79 O16 60pf red brn ('28) 1.05 *1.10*
Never hinged 3.75
On cover 3.25
Nos. O62-O79 (18) 39.25 38.85
Set, never hinged 145.00

1934, Jan. 18 **Wmk. 237**
O80 O17 3pf bister .30 *.90*
Never hinged 1.10
On cover *1.60*
O81 O17 4pf dull blue .30 *.65*
Never hinged .70
On cover *1.10*
O82 O17 5pf brt green .20 *.45*
Never hinged .50
On cover *1.60*
O83 O17 6pf dk green .20 *.45*
Never hinged .45
On cover *.90*
a. Imperf. 110.00
Never hinged 230.00
O84 O17 8pf vermilion 1.10 *.45*
Never hinged 3.25
On cover *1.10*
O85 O17 10pf chocolate .30 *1.00*
Never hinged 1.10
On cover *2.25*
O86 O17 12pf brt carmine 1.60 *1.10*
Never hinged 5.75
On cover *1.60*
a. Unwmkd. 3.50 *5.00*
Never hinged 11.00
O87 O17 15pf claret .80 *4.50*
Never hinged 3.25
On cover *11.00*
O88 O17 20pf light blue .35 *.80*
Never hinged 1.25
On cover *1.40*
O89 O17 30pf olive grn .65 *.80*
Never hinged 2.00
On cover *2.75*
O90 O17 40pf red violet .65 *.80*
Never hinged 2.00
On cover *5.75*
O91 O17 50pf orange yel .75 *1.00*
Never hinged 2.75
On cover *12.50*
Nos. O80-O91 (12) 7.20 *12.90*
Set, never hinged 24.10

LOCAL OFFICIAL STAMPS

For Use in Prussia

("Nr. 21" refers to the district of Prussia) — LO1

1903 **Unwmk.** **Typo.** ***Perf. 14, 14½***
OL1 LO1 2pf slate .80 *3.75*
Never hinged 2.25
On cover 20.00
OL2 LO1 3pf bister brn .80 *3.75*
Never hinged 2.25
On cover 17.50
OL3 LO1 5pf green .30 *.35*
Never hinged .60
On cover 12.00
OL4 LO1 10pf carmine .30 *.35*
Never hinged .60
On cover 6.50
OL5 LO1 20pf ultra .30 *.35*
Never hinged .60
On cover 6.50
OL6 LO1 25pf org & blk, *yel* .30 *.35*
Never hinged .80
On cover 17.50
OL7 LO1 40pf lake & blk .35 *1.50*
Never hinged 1.10
On cover 25.00
OL8 LO1 50pf pur & blk, *sal* .35 *1.50*
Never hinged .90
On cover 32.50
Nos. OL1-OL8 (8) 3.50 *11.90*
Set, never hinged 9.10

LO2

LO3

LO4

LO5

LO6

LO7

LO8

1920 **Typo.** **Wmk. 125** ***Perf. 14***
OL9 LO2 5pf green .20 *2.40*
Never hinged .80
On cover 5.00
OL10 LO3 10pf carmine .60 *1.40*
Never hinged 2.50
On cover 2.75
OL11 LO4 15pf vio brn .20 *1.05*
Never hinged .45
On cover 2.25
OL12 LO5 20pf dp ultra .20 *1.10*
Never hinged .45
On cover 2.25
OL13 LO6 30pf org, *buff* .20 *1.05*
Never hinged .25
On cover 1.60
OL14 LO7 50pf brn lil, *buff* .30 *1.10*
Never hinged 1.40
On cover 1.90
OL15 LO8 1m red, *buff* 6.50 *3.50*
Never hinged 22.50
On cover 8.25
Nos. OL9-OL15 (7) 8.20 *11.60*
Set, never hinged 28.35

For Use in Baden

LO9

1905 **Unwmk.** **Typo.** ***Perf. 14, 14½***
OL16 LO9 2pf gray blue 50.00 *60.00*
Never hinged 550.00
On cover 120.00
OL17 LO9 3pf brown 5.75 *7.50*
Never hinged 22.50
On cover 32.50
OL18 LO9 5pf green 3.50 *5.75*
Never hinged 16.00
On cover 16.00
OL19 LO9 10pf rose .70 *1.75*
Never hinged 2.75
On cover 15.00
OL20 LO9 20pf blue 1.40 *2.50*
Never hinged 9.25
On cover 16.00
OL21 LO9 25pf org & blk, *yel* 35.00 *50.00*
Never hinged 200.00
On cover 120.00
Nos. OL16-OL21 (6) 96.35 *127.50*
Set, never hinged 800.00

NEWSPAPER STAMPS

Newsboy and Globe — N1

Wmk. Swastikas (237)
1939, Nov. 1 **Photo.** ***Perf. 14***
P1 N1 5pf green .30 *2.30*
Never hinged 1.50
On wrapper or address label 160.00
P2 N1 10pf red brown .30 *2.30*
Never hinged 1.50
On wrapper or address label 160.00
Set, never hinged 3.00

FRANCHISE STAMPS

For use by the National Socialist German Workers' Party

Party Emblem — F1

1938 **Typo.** **Wmk. 237** ***Perf. 14***
S1 F1 1pf black .60 *2.30*
Never hinged 4.50
On cover 5.00
S2 F1 3pf bister .60 *1.40*
Never hinged 4.50
On cover 5.50
S3 F1 4pf dull blue .60 *.90*
Never hinged 4.50
On cover 3.25
S4 F1 5pf brt green .30 *.90*
Never hinged 2.25
On cover 4.75
S5 F1 6pf dk green .30 *.90*
Never hinged 2.25
On cover 3.25
S6 F1 8pf vermilion 2.50 1.10
Never hinged 19.00
On cover 3.25
S7 F1 12pf brt car 4.25 1.10
Never hinged 30.00
On cover 3.25
S8 F1 16pf gray .55 *8.50*
Never hinged 4.00
On cover 27.50
S9 F1 24pf citron .90 *4.25*
Never hinged 7.25
On cover 20.00
S10 F1 30pf olive .90 *4.25*
Never hinged 7.25
On cover 20.00
S11 F1 40pf red violet .90 *8.50*
Never hinged 7.25
On cover 27.50
Nos. S1-S11 (11) 12.40 *34.10*
Set, never hinged 90.00

OCCUPATION STAMPS

100 Centimes = 1 Franc
100 Pfennig = 1 Mark

Issued under Belgian Occupation

Belgian Stamps of 1915-20 Overprinted

Perf. 11½, 14, 14½
1919-21 **Unwmk.**
1N1 A46 1c orange .30 *.45*
Never hinged .70
On parcel post receipt card 67.50
1N2 A46 2c chocolate .30 *.45*
Never hinged .70
On parcel post receipt card 67.50
1N3 A46 3c gray blk ('21) .30 *1.75*
Never hinged 1.40
On parcel post receipt card 100.00
1N4 A46 5c green .60 *.90*
Never hinged 1.50
On parcel post receipt card 67.50
1N5 A46 10c carmine 1.25 *1.75*
Never hinged 4.50
On parcel post receipt card 67.50
1N6 A46 15c purple .60 *.90*
Never hinged 2.00
On parcel post receipt card 67.50
1N7 A46 20c red violet .85 *1.25*
Never hinged 3.00
On parcel post receipt card 67.50
1N8 A46 25c blue 1.10 *1.50*
Never hinged 3.75
On parcel post receipt card 67.50
1N9 A54 25c dp blue ('21) 3.25 *5.75*
Never hinged 10.00
On parcel post receipt card 100.00

Overprinted

1N10 A47 35c brn org & blk 1.10 *1.25*
Never hinged 3.75
On parcel post receipt card 85.00
1N11 A48 40c green & blk 1.10 *1.75*
Never hinged 4.50
On parcel post receipt card 85.00
1N12 A49 50c car rose & blk 5.00 *8.50*
Never hinged 13.50
On parcel post receipt card 85.00
1N13 A56 65c cl & blk ('21) 2.75 *8.50*
Never hinged 6.75
On cover —
1N14 A50 1fr violet 20.00 17.50
Never hinged 55.00
On cover —
1N15 A51 2fr slate 35.00 *37.50*
Never hinged 110.00
On cover —
1N16 A52 5fr deep blue 8.00 *10.00*
Never hinged 30.00
On cover —
1N17 A53 10fr brown 55.00 55.00
Never hinged 115.00
On cover —
Nos. 1N1-1N17 (17) 136.50 *154.70*
Set, never hinged 375.00

Belgian Stamps of 1915 Surcharged

Nos. 1N18-1N22

Nos. 1N23-1N24

Black Surcharge

1920
1N18 A46 5pf on 5c green .40 *.35*
Never hinged 1.10
On cover 14.00
On cover, single franking 45.00
1N19 A46 10pf on 10c car .50 *.45*
Never hinged 1.40
On cover 14.00
On cover, single franking 37.50
1N20 A46 15pf on 15c pur .70 .70
Never hinged 1.60
On cover 14.00
1N21 A46 20pf on 20c red vio .70 *1.00*
Never hinged 1.60
On cover 14.00
On cover, single franking 37.50
1N22 A46 30pf on 25c blue 1.10 *1.25*
Never hinged 2.75
On cover 14.00
On cover, single franking 37.50

Red Surcharge

1N23 A49 75pf on 50c car rose & blk 13.00 *16.00*
Never hinged 35.00
On cover 65.00
1N24 A50 1m25pf on 1fr violet 20.00 *16.00*
Never hinged 52.50
On cover —
Nos. 1N18-1N24 (7) 36.40 *35.75*
Set, never hinged 100.00

EUPEN ISSUE

Belgian Stamps of 1915-20 Overprinted:

Nos. 1N25-1N36

Nos. 1N37-1N41

1920-21 ***Perf. 11½, 14, 14½***
1N25 A46 1c orange .30 *.40*
Never hinged .65
On cover 8.75
1N26 A46 2c chocolate .30 *.40*
Never hinged .65
On cover 8.75
1N27 A46 3c gray blk ('21) .45 *1.40*
Never hinged 1.00
On cover 50.00
1N28 A46 5c green .45 *.90*
Never hinged 1.60
On cover 8.75
On cover, single franking 45.00

1N29 A46 10c carmine	.75	1.25
Never hinged	1.60	
On cover		8.75
On cover, single franking		32.50
1N30 A46 15c purple	1.10	1.25
Never hinged	2.25	
On cover		8.75
1N31 A46 20c red violet	1.25	1.40
Never hinged	2.50	
On cover		8.75
On cover, single franking		50.00
1N32 A46 25c blue	1.10	1.90
Never hinged	2.25	
On cover		10.00
On cover, single franking		27.50
1N33 A54 25c dp blue ('21)	3.50	9.50
Never hinged	7.75	
On cover		45.00
On cover, single franking		50.00
1N34 A47 35c brn org & blk	1.50	1.90
Never hinged	3.25	
On cover		32.50
1N35 A48 40c green & blk	1.75	2.25
Never hinged	3.75	
On cover		32.50
1N36 A49 50c car rose & blk	5.00	7.25
Never hinged	11.00	
On cover		32.50
On cover, single franking		110.00
1N37 A56 65c cl & blk ('21)	2.75	11.00
Never hinged	6.00	
On cover		65.00
1N38 A50 1fr violet	20.00	19.00
Never hinged	40.00	
On cover		65.00
1N39 A51 2fr slate	32.50	30.00
Never hinged	70.00	
On cover		120.00
1N40 A52 5fr deep blue	10.50	11.00
Never hinged	22.50	
On cover		—
1N41 A53 10fr brown	45.00	47.50
Never hinged	100.00	
On cover		—
Nos. 1N25-1N41 (17)	128.20	148.30
Set, never hinged	325.00	

MALMEDY ISSUE

Belgian Stamps of 1915-20 Overprinted:

Nos. 1N42-1N50

Nos. 1N51-1N53

Nos. 1N54-1N58

1920-21

1N42 A46 1c orange	.25	.40
Never hinged	.45	
On cover		8.75
1N43 A46 2c chocolate	.25	.40
Never hinged	.45	
On cover		8.75
1N44 A46 3c gray blk ('21)	.35	1.60
Never hinged	1.10	
On cover		50.00
1N45 A46 5c green	.45	.90
Never hinged	1.10	
On cover		8.75
On cover, single franking		45.00
1N46 A46 10c carmine	.70	1.25
Never hinged	1.60	
On cover		8.75
1N47 A46 15c purple	1.10	1.40
Never hinged	2.50	
On cover		8.75
1N48 A46 20c red violet	1.50	1.90
Never hinged	3.25	
On cover		8.75
On cover, single franking		50.00
1N49 A46 25c blue	1.25	1.90
Never hinged	2.50	
On cover		11.00
On cover, single franking		27.50
1N50 A54 25c dp blue ('21)	3.50	8.75
Never hinged	7.75	
On cover		45.00
On cover, single franking		50.00
1N51 A47 35c brn org & blk	1.50	2.25
Never hinged	3.25	
On cover		32.50
1N52 A48 40c grn & blk	1.50	2.25
Never hinged	3.25	
On cover		32.50
1N53 A49 50c car rose & blk	6.00	7.25
Never hinged	13.00	
On cover		30.00
On cover, single franking		35.00
1N54 A56 65c cl & blk ('21)	2.75	11.00
Never hinged	5.50	
On cover		65.00
1N55 A50 1fr violet	20.00	17.00
Never hinged	40.00	
On cover		65.00
On cover, single franking		100.00
1N56 A51 2fr slate	32.50	30.00
Never hinged	72.50	
On cover		125.00
On cover, single franking		325.00
1N57 A52 5fr deep blue	10.50	17.00
Never hinged	22.50	
On cover		—
1N58 A53 10fr brown	45.00	55.00
Never hinged	100.00	
On cover		—
Nos. 1N42-1N58 (17)	129.10	160.25
Set, never hinged	325.00	

OCCUPATION POSTAGE DUE STAMPS

Belgian Postage Due Stamps of 1919-20, Overprinted

1920 Unwmk. Perf. 14½

1NJ1 D3 5c green	.75	1.10
Never hinged	1.60	
On cover		50.00
On cover, single franking		65.00
1NJ2 D3 10c carmine	1.50	1.90
Never hinged	3.25	
On cover		50.00
1NJ3 D3 20c gray green	3.00	4.50
Never hinged	7.25	
On cover		65.00
1NJ4 D3 30c bright blue	3.00	4.50
Never hinged	7.25	
On cover		65.00
On cover, single franking		100.00
1NJ5 D3 50c gray	15.00	15.00
Never hinged	32.50	
On cover		120.00
Nos. 1NJ1-1NJ5 (5)	23.25	27.00
Set, never hinged	57.50	

Belgian Postage Due Stamps of 1919-20, Overprinted

1NJ6 D3 5c green	1.50	1.10
Never hinged	3.25	
On cover		65.00
On cover, single franking		100.00
1NJ7 D3 10c carmine	3.00	1.90
Never hinged	6.50	
On cover		65.00
a. Inverted overprint	30.00	
1NJ8 D3 20c gray green	10.50	11.50
Never hinged	22.50	
On cover		82.50
1NJ9 D3 30c bright blue	6.00	8.25
Never hinged	13.50	
On cover		100.00
1NJ10 D3 50c gray	12.00	11.00
Never hinged	26.00	
On cover		140.00
Nos. 1NJ6-1NJ10 (5)	33.00	33.75
Set, never hinged	82.50	

GERMAN OFFICES ABROAD

OFFICES IN CHINA

100 Pfennings = 1 Mark
100 Cents = 1 Dollar (1905)

Stamps of Germany, 1889-90, Overprinted in Black at 56 degree Angle

1898 Unwmk. Perf. 13½x14½

1 A9 3pf olive brown	5.75	6.25
Never hinged	19.00	
On cover		27.50
a. 3pf yellow ocher	11.50	14.50
Never hinged	42.50	
On cover		92.50
b. 3pf reddish ocher	22.50	60.00
Never hinged	140.00	
On cover		290.00
2 A9 5pf green	2.25	2.50
Never hinged	10.00	
On cover		19.00
3 A10 10pf carmine	5.75	6.25
Never hinged	19.00	
On cover		17.00
4 A10 20pf ultramarine	17.00	16.00
Never hinged	42.50	
On cover		37.50
5 A10 25pf orange	32.50	30.00
Never hinged	75.00	
On cover		92.50
6 A10 50pf chocolate	16.00	12.50
Never hinged	37.50	
On cover		52.50

Overprinted at 45 degree Angle

1c A9 3pf yellow brown	125.00	23,000.
Never hinged	375.00	
On cover		37,500.
1d A9 3pf reddish ocher	175.00	
Never hinged	1,000.	
e. 3pf gray brown	1,400.	
Never hinged	3,000.	
2a A9 5pf green	11.50	12.50
Never hinged	30.00	
On cover		35.00
3a A10 10pf carmine	14.00	10.50
Never hinged	92.50	
On cover		27.50
4a A10 20pf ultramarine	12.50	10.50
Never hinged	37.50	
On cover		27.50
5a A10 25pf orange	50.00	57.50
Never hinged	190.00	
On cover		160.00
6a A10 50pf chocolate	20.00	16.00
Never hinged	75.00	
On cover		57.50

Value for No. 1c used is for a copy with small 1898 Shanghai cancel. Examples with other cancellations or later Shanghai cancels sell for about half the value quoted.

Covers: Values for Nos. 6, 6a are for over-franked complete covers, usually philatelic.

Foochow Issue

Nos. 3 and 3a Handstamp Surcharged

1900

16 A10 5pf on 10pf, #3	500.00	700.00
Never hinged	1,050.	
On cover		2,000.
a. On No. 3a	575.00	850.00
Never hinged	1,400.	
On cover		1,150.

For similar 5pf surcharges on 10pf carmine, see Tsingtau Issue, Kiauchau.

Tientsin Issue

German Stamps of 1900 Issue Handstamped

1900

17 A11 3pf brown	550.00	625.00
Never hinged	2,100.	
On cover		1,350.
18 A11 5pf green	350.00	325.00
Never hinged	1,350.	
On cover		1,500.
19 A11 10pf carmine	775.00	725.00
Never hinged	4,250.	
On cover		2,250.
20 A11 20pf ultra	700.00	750.00
Never hinged	2,300.	
On cover		2,600.
21 A11 30pf org & blk, *sal*	6,500.	6,500.
Never hinged	13,750.	
On cover		11,500.
22 A11 50pf pur & blk, *sal*	30,000.	16,000.
Never hinged	50,000.	
On cover		26,500.
23 A11 80pf lake & blk, *rose*	4,000.	3,750.
Never hinged	13,500.	
On cover		11,500.

This handstamp is known inverted and double on most values.

Excellent faked handstamps are plentiful.

Covers: Values for Nos. 22-23 are for over-franked complete covers, usually philatelic.

Regular Issue

German Stamps of 1900 Overprinted

A14

A15

Overprinted Horizontally in Black

1901 Perf. 14, 14½

24 A11 3pf brown	1.40	1.40
Never hinged	5.25	
On cover		75.00
a. 3pf light red brown	62.50	75.00
Never hinged	375.00	
On cover		190.00
25 A11 5pf green	1.40	1.00
Never hinged	5.25	
On cover		15.00
26 A11 10pf carmine	2.40	.85
Never hinged	6.00	
On cover		15.00
27 A11 20pf ultra	2.90	1.40
Never hinged	9.00	
On cover		15.00
28 A11 25pf org & blk, *yel*	11.50	15.00
Never hinged	27.50	
On cover		35.00
29 A11 30pf org & blk, *sal*	10.50	12.00
Never hinged	27.50	
On cover		27.50
30 A11 40pf lake & blk	11.00	8.00
Never hinged	27.50	
On cover		27.50
31 A11 50pf pur & blk, *sal*	10.00	8.00
Never hinged	27.50	
On cover		10.00
32 A11 80pf lake & blk, *rose*	12.00	11.50
Never hinged	30.00	
On cover		27.50

Overprinted in Black or Red

33 A12 1m car rose	30.00	30.00
Never hinged	92.50	
On cover		70.00
34 A13 2m gray blue	26.00	27.50
Never hinged	85.00	
On cover		70.00
35 A14 3m blk vio (R)	42.50	62.50
Never hinged	150.00	
On cover		130.00
36 A15 5m slate & car, I	425.00	550.00
Never hinged	850.00	
On cover		1,100.
b. Red and/or white retouched	200.00	290.00
Never hinged	525.00	
On cover		600.00
36A A15 5m slate & car, II	310.00	400.00
Never hinged	525.00	
On cover		600.00
Nos. 24-36A (14)	896.60	1,129.

See note after Germany No. 65A for information on retouches on No. 36. For description of the 5m Type I and Type II, see note above Germany No. 62.

Surcharged on German Stamps of 1902 in Black or Red

a

b

c

1905

37 A16(a) 1c on 3pf	2.90	3.25
Never hinged	6.00	
On cover		22.50
38 A16(a) 2c on 5pf	2.90	1.10
Never hinged	10.00	
On cover		15.00
39 A16(a) 4c on 10pf	6.25	1.10
Never hinged	17.00	
On cover		15.00
40 A16(a) 10c on 20pf	2.90	1.75
Never hinged	9.00	
On cover		15.00
41 A16(a) 20c on 40pf	20.00	7.50
Never hinged	50.00	
On cover		30.00
42 A16(a) 40c on 80pf	32.50	13.00
Never hinged	92.50	
On cover		30.00
43 A17(b) ½d on 1m	14.50	16.00
Never hinged	57.50	
On cover		45.00
44 A21(b) 1d on 2m	17.50	20.00
Never hinged	50.00	
On cover		45.00
45 A19(c) 1½d on 3m (R)	35.00	45.00
Never hinged	45.00	
On cover		85.00
46 A20(b) 2½d on 5m	110.00	290.00
Never hinged	290.00	
On cover		650.00
Nos. 37-46 (10)	244.45	398.70

Surcharged on German Stamps of 1905 in Black or Red

1906-13 **Wmk. 125**

47 A16(a) 1c on 3pf .40 *.70*
Never hinged .75
On cover 15.00
48 A16(a) 2c on 5pf .40 *.70*
Never hinged .75
On cover 15.00
49 A16(a) 4c on 10pf .40 *.70*
Never hinged .75
On cover 15.00
50 A16(a) 10c on 20pf .85 *5.00*
Never hinged 1.75
On cover 15.00
51 A16(a) 20c on 40pf 1.10 *2.50*
Never hinged 1.75
On cover 9.00
52 A16(a) 40c on 80pf 1.10 *35.00*
Never hinged 1.75
On cover 150.00
53 A17(b) ½d on 1m 5.50 *30.00*
Never hinged 15.00
On cover 110.00
54 A21(b) 1d on 2m 6.00 *35.00*
Never hinged 52.50
On cover 85.00
55 A19(c) 1½d on 3m (R) 7.00 *77.50*
Never hinged 57.50
On cover 240.00
56 A20(b) 2½d on 5m 27.50 *42.50*
Never hinged 110.00
On cover 190.00
Nos. 47-56 (10) 50.25 *229.60*

Forged cancellations exist.

OFFICES IN MOROCCO

100 Centimos = 1 Peseta

Stamps of Germany Surcharged in Black

1899 **Unwmk.** ***Perf. 13½x14½***

1 A9 3c on 3pf dk brn 3.00 2.50
Never hinged 7.50
On cover 30.00
2 A9 5c on 5pf green 3.00 2.50
Never hinged 7.50
On cover 22.50
3 A10 10c on 10pf car 7.25 6.25
Never hinged 19.00
On cover 35.00
4 A10 25c on 20pf ultra 15.00 *16.00*
Never hinged 37.50
On cover 60.00
5 A10 30c on 25pf orange 26.00 *30.00*
Never hinged 70.00
On cover 140.00
6 A10 60c on 50pf red brn 20.00 *40.00*
Never hinged 60.00
On cover 92.50

Covers: Value for No. 6 is for overfranked complete covers, usually philatelic.

Before Nos. 1-6 were issued, the same six basic stamps of Germany's 1889-1900 issue were overprinted "Marocco" diagonally without the currency-changing surcharge line, but were not issued. Value, $750 hinged, $1,750. never hinged.

German Stamps of 1900 Surcharged

A12

A13

A14

A15

Black or Red Surcharge

1900 ***Perf. 14, 14½***

7 A11 3c on 3pf 1.25 *1.75*
Never hinged 2.75
On cover 11.50
8 A11 5c on 5pf 1.40 1.10
Never hinged 5.00
On cover 15.00
9 A11 10c on 10pf 2.00 1.10
Never hinged 6.00
On cover 15.00
10 A11 25c on 20pf 2.50 2.50
Never hinged 9.00
On cover 27.50
11 A11 30c on 25pf 10.50 *14.00*
Never hinged 32.50
On cover 35.00
12 A11 35c on 30pf 7.50 6.25
Never hinged 22.50
On cover 30.00
13 A11 50c on 40pf 7.50 6.25
Never hinged 21.00
On cover 30.00
14 A11 60c on 50pf 17.00 *30.00*
Never hinged 50.00
On cover 60.00
15 A11 1p on 80pf 11.50 11.50
Never hinged 42.50
On cover 45.00
16 A12 1p25c on 1m 30.00 *42.50*
Never hinged 100.00
On cover 100.00
17 A13 2p50c on 2m 35.00 *55.00*
Never hinged 100.00
On cover 110.00
18 A14 3p75c on 3m (R) 40.00 *62.50*
Never hinged 170.00
On cover 150.00
19 A15 6p25c on 5m, I 350.00 *460.00*
Never hinged 850.00
On cover 925.00
b. Red and/or white retouched 175.00 *290.00*
Never hinged 525.00
19A A15 6p25c on 5m, II 225.00 *290.00*
Never hinged 450.00
On cover 750.00
Nos. 7-19A (14) 741.15 *984.45*

A 1903 printing of Nos. 8, 16-18 and 19A differs in the "M" and "t" of the surcharge. Values are for 1900 printing: Nos. 8, 16-18. 1903 printing: No. 19A.

See note after Germany No. 65A for information on retouches on No. 19. For description of the 5m Type I and Type II, see note above Germany No. 62.

German Stamps of 1902 Surcharged in Black or Red

a

b

c

1905

20 A16(a) 3c on 3pf 2.90 2.75
Never hinged 7.00
On cover 22.50
21 A16(a) 5c on 5pf 4.50 1.00
Never hinged 11.00
On cover 15.00
22 A16(a) 10c on 10pf 9.25 .80
Never hinged 27.50
On cover 15.00
23 A16(a) 25c on 20pf 20.00 2.90
Never hinged 45.00
On cover 27.50
24 A16(a) 30c on 25pf 6.50 5.25
Never hinged 19.00
On cover 45.00
25 A16(a) 35c on 30pf 9.75 5.25
Never hinged 30.00
On cover 45.00
26 A16(a) 50c on 40pf 9.25 8.50
Never hinged 27.50
On cover 45.00
27 A16(a) 60c on 50pf 29.00 22.50
Never hinged 52.50
On cover 50.00
28 A16(a) 1p on 80pf 29.00 20.00
Never hinged 52.50
On cover 45.00
29 A17(b) 1p25c on 1m 50.00 35.00
Never hinged 200.00
On cover 67.50
30 A21(b) 2p50c on 2m 85.00 *125.00*
Never hinged 270.00
On cover 260.00
31 A19(c) 3p75c on 3m (R) 45.00 *52.50*
Never hinged 110.00
On cover 120.00
32 A20(b) 6p25c on 5m 125.00 *190.00*
Never hinged 325.00
On cover 370.00
Nos. 20-32 (13) 425.15 *471.45*

Surcharged on Germany No. 54

32A A11(a) 5c on 5pf 7.75 *22.50*
Never hinged 18.00
On cover 1,900.

German Stamps of 1905 Surcharged

1906-11 **Wmk. 125**

33 A16(a) 3c on 3pf 8.50 2.00
Never hinged 18.00
On cover 22.50
34 A16(a) 5c on 5pf 8.50 1.00
Never hinged 13.50
On cover 15.00
35 A16(a) 10c on 10pf 8.50 1.00
Never hinged 13.50
On cover 15.00
36 A16(a) 25c on 20pf 17.50 4.25
Never hinged 42.50
On cover 30.00
37 A16(a) 30c on 25pf 20.00 10.50
Never hinged 18.00
On cover 45.00
38 A16(a) 35c on 30pf 17.50 10.50
Never hinged 32.50
On cover 45.00
39 A16(a) 50c on 40pf 37.50 *160.00*
Never hinged 70.00
On cover 275.00
40 A16(a) 60c on 50pf 26.00 14.50
Never hinged 65.00
On cover 35.00
41 A16(a) 1p on 80pf 140.00 *290.00*
Never hinged 325.00
On cover 525.00
42 A17(b) 1p25c on 1m 65.00 *190.00*
Never hinged 160.00
On cover 300.00
43 A21(b) 2p50c on 2m 65.00 *190.00*
Never hinged 160.00
On cover 300.00
44 A20(b) 6p25c on 5m 110.00 *275.00*
Never hinged 325.00
On cover 600.00
Nos. 33-44 (12) 524.00 *1,148.*

Excellent forgeries exist of No. 41.

Surcharge Spelled "Marokko" in Black or Red

1911

45 A16(a) 3c on 3pf .45 *.65*
Never hinged 1.00
On cover 19.00
46 A16(a) 5c on 5pf .45 *.85*
Never hinged 1.00
On cover 15.00
47 A16(a) 10c on 10pf .45 *1.00*
Never hinged 1.10
On cover 15.00
48 A16(a) 25c on 20pf .55 *1.00*
Never hinged 1.10
On cover 22.50
49 A16(a) 30c on 25pf 1.10 *15.00*
Never hinged 2.75
On cover 45.00
50 A16(a) 35c on 30pf 1.10 *8.50*
Never hinged 3.00
On cover 35.00
51 A16(a) 50c on 40pf 1.10 *4.50*
Never hinged 2.75
On cover 22.50
52 A16(a) 60c on 50pf 1.75 *35.00*
Never hinged 3.50
On cover 75.00
53 A16(a) 1p on 80pf 1.60 *27.50*
Never hinged 4.50
On cover 57.50
54 A17(b) 1p25c on 1m 3.00 *62.50*
Never hinged 5.25
On cover 110.00
55 A21(b) 2p50c on 2m 5.25 *50.00*
Never hinged 13.00
On cover 100.00
56 A19(c) 3p75c on 3m (R) 9.75 *175.00*
Never hinged 12.50
On cover 425.00
57 A20(b) 6p25c on 5m 18.00 *260.00*
Never hinged 42.50
On cover 575.00
Nos. 45-57 (13) 44.55 *641.50*

Forged cancellations exist.

OFFICES IN THE TURKISH EMPIRE

Unused values for Nos. 1-6 are for stamps with original gum. Copies without gum sell for about one-third of the figures quoted.

40 Paras = 1 Piaster

A1

A2

German Stamps of 1880-83 Surcharged in Black or Blue

1884 **Unwmk.** ***Perf. 13½x14½***

1 A1 10pa on 5pf dull vio 30.00 27.50
Never hinged 725.00
On cover 375.00
2 A2 20pa on 10pf rose 62.50 *75.00*
Never hinged 1,050.
On cover 300.00
3 A2 1pi on 20pf ultra (Bk) 55.00 4.25
Never hinged 300.00
On cover 92.50
4 A2 1pi on 20pf ultra (Bl) 1,500. 55.00
Never hinged 6,000.
On cover 375.00
5 A2 1¼pi on 25pf org brn 160.00 *200.00*
Never hinged 1,700.
On cover 925.00
a. 1¼ on 25pf choc brn ('91) 125.00 *250.00*
Never hinged 1,100.
6 A2 2½pi on 50pf gray grn 110.00 65.00
Never hinged 1,100.
On cover 925.00
a. 2½pi on 50pf deep olive grn 260.00 190.00
Never hinged 2,300.
On cover 1,100.

There are two types of the surcharge on the 1¼pi and 2½pi stamps, the difference being in the spacing between the figures and the word "PIASTER."

Covers: Values for Nos. 6, 6a are for overfranked complete covers, usually philatelic.

There are re-issues of these stamps which vary only slightly from the originals in overprint measurements.

A3

A4

A5

German Stamps of 1889-1900 Surcharged in Black

1889

8 A3 10pa on 5pf grn 3.50 3.50
Never hinged 23.00
On cover 27.50
9 A4 20pa on 10pf car 7.00 2.25
Never hinged 50.00
On cover 23.00
10 A4 1pi on 20pf ultra 5.25 2.00
Never hinged 30.00
On cover 27.50
11 A5 1¼pi on 25pf org 27.50 17.50
Never hinged 120.00
On cover 100.00
12 A5 2½pi on 50pf choc 35.00 24.00
Never hinged 240.00
On cover 150.00
a. 2½pi on 50pf copper brown 175.00 100.00
Never hinged 390.00
On cover 390.00

Covers: Values for Nos. 12, 12a are for overfranked complete covers, usually philatelic.

German Stamps of 1900 Surcharged

A11

A12

A13

A14

A15

1900 *Perf. 14, 14½*

Black or Red Surcharge

13	A11	10pa on 5pf	1.75	1.75
		Never hinged	5.25	
		On cover		15.00
14	A11	20pa on 10pf	2.25	2.25
		Never hinged	6.00	
		On cover		15.00
15	A11	1pi on 20pf	4.50	1.75
		Never hinged	11.50	
		On cover		15.00
16	A11	1¼pi on 25pf	7.00	4.00
		Never hinged	22.50	
		On cover		19.00
17	A11	1½pi on 30pf	7.00	4.25
		Never hinged	22.50	
		On cover		19.00
18	A11	2pi on 40pf	7.00	4.50
		Never hinged	22.50	
		On cover		19.00
19	A11	2½pi on 50pf	12.50	12.50
		Never hinged	35.00	
		On cover		35.00
20	A11	4pi on 80pf	15.00	12.50
		Never hinged	45.00	
		On cover		35.00
21	A12	5pi on 1m	35.00	35.00
		Never hinged	110.00	
		On cover		100.00
22	A13	10pi on 2m	32.50	*40.00*
		Never hinged	110.00	
		On cover		92.50
23	A14	15pi on 3m (R)	55.00	*90.00*
		Never hinged	160.00	
		On cover		275.00
24	A15	25pi on 5m, I	325.00	*625.00*
		Never hinged	725.00	
		On cover		750.00
a.		Double surcharge		*11,000.*
d.		Red and/or white retouched	160.00	*225.00*
		Never hinged	500.00	
24B	A15	25pi on 5m, II	190.00	*350.00*
		Never hinged	550.00	
		On cover		650.00
c.		Double surcharge	*9,750.*	—
		Nos. 13-24B (13)	694.50	*1,183.*

See note after Germany No. 65A for information on retouches on No. 24. For description of the 5m Type I and Type II, see note above Germany No. 62.

Covers: Values for Nos. 19-24B are for overfranked complete covers, usually philatelic.

German Stamps of 1900 Surcharged in Black

1903-05

25	A11	10pa on 5pf green	14.00	*16.00*
		Never hinged	32.50	
		On cover		75.00
26	A11	20pa on 10pf car	32.50	20.00
		Never hinged	75.00	
		On cover		100.00
27	A11	1pi on 20pf ultra	10.50	8.50
		Never hinged	30.00	
		On cover		60.00

28	A12	5pi on 1m car rose	90.00	80.00
		Never hinged	375.00	
		On cover		290.00
29	A13	10pi on 2m bl ('05)	140.00	*240.00*
		Never hinged	450.00	
		On cover		525.00
30	A15	25pi on 5m sl & car	240.00	*600.00*
		Never hinged	650.00	
		On cover		850.00
a.		Double surcharge	*4,750.*	
		Never hinged	9,250.	
		Nos. 25-30 (6)	527.00	*964.50*

The 1903-05 surcharges may be easily distinguished from those of 1900 by the added bar at the top of the letter "A."

German Stamps of 1902 Surcharged in Black or Red

a

b

1905 **Unwmk.**

31	A16(a)	10pa on 5pf	3.75	2.25
		Never hinged	5.75	
		On cover		15.00
32	A16(a)	20pa on 10pf	8.50	3.00
		Never hinged	19.00	
		On cover		15.00
33	A16(a)	1pi on 20pf	17.50	2.00
		Never hinged	50.00	
		On cover		15.00
34	A16(a)	1¼pi on 25pf	9.75	7.00
		Never hinged	22.50	
		On cover		26.00
35	A16(a)	1½pi on 30pf	18.00	17.00
		Never hinged	70.00	
		On cover		45.00
36	A16(a)	2pi on 40pf	29.00	17.00
		Never hinged	57.50	
		On cover		45.00
37	A16(a)	2½pi on 50pf	11.00	*26.00*
		Never hinged	15.00	
		On cover		57.50
38	A16(a)	4pi on 80pf	30.00	16.00
		Never hinged	70.00	
		On cover		42.50
39	A17(b)	5pi on 1m	37.50	35.00
		Never hinged	140.00	
		On cover		75.00
40	A21(b)	10pi on 2m	37.50	*42.50*
		Never hinged	85.00	
		On cover		110.00
41	A19(b)	15pi on 3m (R)	50.00	*52.50*
		Never hinged	170.00	
		On cover		130.00
42	A20(b)	25pi on 5m	225.00	*425.00*
		Never hinged	500.00	
		On cover		1,000.
		Nos. 31-42 (12)	477.50	*645.25*

German Stamps of 1905 Surcharged in Black or Red

1906-12 **Wmk. 125**

43	A16(a)	10pa on 5pf	1.90	.65
		Never hinged	5.25	
		On cover		15.00
44	A16(a)	20pa on 10pf	2.25	.65
		Never hinged	5.75	
		On cover		15.00
45	A16(a)	1pi on 20pf	3.50	.50
		Never hinged	10.00	
		On cover		15.00
46	A16(a)	1¼pi on 25pf	14.50	11.50
		Never hinged	42.50	
		On cover		37.50
47	A16(a)	1½pi on 30pf	12.50	9.25
		Never hinged	42.50	
		On cover		27.50
48	A16(a)	2pi on 40pf	4.50	1.40
		Never hinged	17.00	
		On cover		19.00
49	A16(a)	2½pi on 50pf	10.50	8.50
		Never hinged	37.50	
		On cover		30.00
50	A16(a)	4pi on 80pf	9.75	*21.00*
		Never hinged	52.50	
		On cover		42.50
51	A17(b)	5pi on 1m	20.00	*32.50*
		Never hinged	92.50	
		On cover		85.00
52	A21(b)	10pi on 2m	20.00	*45.00*
		Never hinged	100.00	
		On cover		110.00
53	A19(b)	15pi on 3m (R)	24.00	*350.00*
		Never hinged	125.00	
		On cover		1,500.
54	A20(b)	25pi on 5m	24.00	*62.50*
		Never hinged	75.00	
		On cover		240.00
		Nos. 43-54 (12)	147.40	*543.45*

German Stamps of 1905 Surcharged Diagonally in Black

1908

55	A16	5c on 5pf	1.40	*1.60*
		Never hinged	3.75	
		On cover		15.00
56	A16	10c on 10pf	3.00	*3.50*
		Never hinged	6.00	
		On cover		22.50
57	A16	25c on 20pf	7.25	*29.00*
		Never hinged	17.00	
		On cover		75.00
58	A16	50c on 40pf	32.50	*70.00*
		Never hinged	85.00	
		On cover		150.00
59	A16	100c on 80pf	60.00	*75.00*
		Never hinged	140.00	
		On cover		210.00
		Nos. 55-59 (5)	104.15	*179.10*

Forged cancellations exist on #37, 53-54, 57-59.

GIBRALTAR

jə-ˈbrol-tər

LOCATION — A fortified promontory, including the Rock, extending from Spain's southeast coast at the entrance to the Mediterranean Sea

GOVT. — British Crown Colony

AREA — 2.5 sq. mi.

POP. — 31,183 (1982)

CAPITAL — Gibraltar

12 Pence = 1 Shilling

20 Shillings = 1 Pound

100 Centimos = 1 Peseta (1889-95)

Catalogue values for unused stamps in this country are for Never Hinged items, beginning with Scott 119 in the regular postage section.

Types of Bermuda Overprinted in Black

1886, Jan. 1 **Wmk. 2** ***Perf. 14***

1	A6	½p green	15.00	8.25
2	A1	1p rose	65.00	5.50
3	A2	2p violet brown	120.00	92.50
4	A8	2½p ultra	160.00	4.25
5	A7	4p orange brn	160.00	100.00
6	A4	6p violet	250.00	210.00
7	A5	1sh bister brn	500.00	400.00
		Nos. 1-7 (7)	1,270.	820.50

Forged overprints of No. 7 are plentiful.

Victoria

A6 A7

A8

A9

1886-98 **Typo.**

8	A6	½p dull green ('87)	11.00	4.50
9	A6	½p gray grn ('98)	6.50	2.00
10	A7	1p rose ('87)	47.50	5.00
11	A7	1p car rose ('98)	7.50	.55
12	A8	2p brn violet	35.00	22.50
13	A8	2p brn vio & ultra ('98)	27.50	2.00
14	A9	2½p brt ultra ('98)	35.00	.60
a.		2½p ultramarine	95.00	3.25
16	A8	4p orange brn	90.00	90.00
17	A8	4p org brn & grn ('98)	21.00	7.50
18	A8	6p violet	125.00	125.00
19	A8	6p vio & car rose ('98)	47.50	25.00
20	A8	1sh bister	225.00	225.00
21	A8	1sh bis & car rose ('98)	47.50	18.00
		Nos. 8-14,16-21 (13)	726.00	527.65

Stamps of 1886 Issue Surcharged in Black

1889, July

22	A6	5c on ½p green	8.75	*22.50*
23	A7	10c on 1p rose	14.50	11.50
24	A8	25c on 2p brn vio	6.00	*8.25*
a.		Small "I" in "CENTIMOS"	140.00	*190.00*
b.		Broken "N"	140.00	*190.00*
25	A9	25c on 2½p ultra	25.00	2.75
a.		Small "I" in "CENTIMOS"	400.00	125.00
b.		Broken "N"	400.00	125.00
26	A8	40c on 4p org brn	62.50	*87.50*
27	A8	50c on 6p violet	67.50	*87.50*
28	A8	75c on 1sh bister	67.50	*82.50*
		Nos. 22-28 (7)	251.75	*302.50*

There are two varieties of the figure "5" in the 5c, 25c, 50c and 75c.

A11

1889-95

29	A11	5c green	5.50	1.00
30	A11	10c rose	5.50	.60
a.		Value omitted	*6,000.*	
31	A11	20c ol green ('95)	14.00	*82.50*
31A	A11	20c ol grn & brn ('95)	50.00	22.50
32	A11	25c ultra	22.50	.90
a		25c deep ultramarine	35.00	.90
33	A11	40c orange brn	4.75	3.25
34	A11	50c violet	4.25	2.50
35	A11	75c olive green	42.50	42.50
36	A11	1p bister	92.50	25.00
36A	A11	1p bis & bl ('95)	6.00	6.00
37	A11	2p blk & car rose ('95)	13.00	*37.50*
38	A11	5p steel blue	52.50	*125.00*
		Nos. 29-38 (12)	313.00	*349.25*

King Edward VII

A12 A13

1903, May 1

39	A12	½p grn & bl grn	12.00	11.00
40	A12	1p violet, *red*	37.50	.70
41	A12	2p grn & car rose	22.50	*30.00*
42	A12	2½p vio & blk, *bl*	6.00	.70
43	A12	6p violet & pur	20.00	*26.00*
44	A12	1sh blk & car rose	32.50	*42.50*
45	A13	2sh green & ultra	175.00	*210.00*
46	A13	4sh vio & green	110.00	*160.00*
47	A13	8sh vio & blk, *bl*	150.00	*160.00*
48	A13	£1 vio & blk, *red*	600.00	*700.00*
		Nos. 39-48 (10)	1,165.	*1,340.*
		Set, ovptd. "SPECIMEN	575.00	

1904-12 **Wmk. 3** **Ordinary Paper**

49A	A12	½p dull grn & br grn	15.00	3.00
50	A12	1p violet, *red*	15.00	.60
a.		Bisected, used as ½p on card		1,600.
51	A12	1p car ('07)	6.50	.70
52	A12	2p grn & car rose ('05)	18.00	7.50
53	A12	2p gray ('10)	10.00	*13.00*
55	A12	2½p ultra ('07)	6.25	1.90
56	A12	6p vio & pur ('06)	47.50	27.50
a.		6p vio & red violet ('12)	160.00	*450.00*
57	A12	1sh blk & car rose ('05)	62.50	17.50
59	A13	2sh grn & ultra ('05)	97.50	*125.00*

Chalky Paper

49	A12	½p blue green ('07)	5.75	2.00
49Ab	A12	½p dull grn & br grn ('04)	13.50	8.00
50b	A12	1p violet, *red* ('05)	5.75	1.00
52a	A12	2p grn & car rose ('07)	9.50	8.00
54	A12	2½p vio & blk, *bl* ('07)	45.00	*110.00*
56b	A12	6p vio & pur ('08)	35.00	15.00
57a	A12	1sh blk & car rose ('06)	572.50	17.50
58	A12	1sh blk, *grn* ('10)	27.50	25.00
59a	A13	2sh grn & ultra ('07)	97.50	*110.00*
60	A13	2sh vio & bl, *bl* ('10)	60.00	*57.50*
61	A13	4sh vio & grn	275.00	350.00

63 A13 8sh vio & grn ('11) 225.00 *250.00*
62 A13 4sh blk & red ('10) 140.00 *175.00*
64 A12 £1 vio & blk, *red* 600.00 *700.00*

No. 56a, used, must have a 1912 cancellation. Stamps used later sell for about the same as unused.

A14

King George V — A15

1912, July 17 Ordinary Paper
66 A14 ½p green 4.00 .80
a. ½p yellow green ('17) 5.75 2.00
67 A14 1p carmine 4.00 .90
a. 1p scarlet ('16) 4.25 1.60
68 A14 2p gray 12.00 1.75
69 A14 2½p ultra 8.25 2.50
a. 2½p pale ultramarine ('17) 8.00 2.25

Chalky Paper
70 A14 6p dl vio & red vio 11.00 *19.00*
71 A14 1sh black, *green* 11.00 4.25
a. 1sh black, *emerald* ('24) 22.50 *100.00*
b. 1sh blk, *bl grn, ol back* ('19) 15.00 *30.00*
c. 1sh blk, *emer, ol back* ('23) 30.00 *82.50*
72 A15 2sh vio & ultra, *bl* 30.00 4.00
73 A15 4sh black & scar 37.50 *65.00*
74 A15 8sh vio & green 90.00 *110.00*
75 A15 £1 vio & blk, *red* 160.00 *230.00*
Nos. 66-75 (10) 367.75 *438.20*
Set, ovptd. "SPECIMEN" 575.00

1921-32 Ordinary Paper Wmk. 4
76 A14 ½p green ('26) 1.60 *1.90*
77 A14 1p rose red 2.25 1.40
78 A14 1½p red brown ('22) 2.25 .60
a. 1½p pale red brown ('24) 2.25 .40
79 A14 2p gray 1.60 1.60
80 A14 2½p ultra 22.50 35.00
81 A14 3p ultra 2.75 1.75
a. 3p br blue ('22) 3.50 4.75

Chalky Paper
82 A14 6p dl vio & red vio ('26) 1.75 *4.00*
a. 6p gray lilac & red violet ('23) 7.00 4.25
83 A14 1sh black, *emer* 12.00 *19.00*
84 A14 1sh ol grn & blk) 17.50 *27.50*
a. 1sh brn olive & black ('32) 17.50 14.00
85 A15 2sh gray vio & ultra, *blue* 21.00 *80.00*
a. 2sh red vio & ultra, *blue* ('25) 8.25 47.50
86 A15 2sh red brn & black 11.00 *35.00*
87 A15 2sh6p green & blk 11.00 *21.00*
88 A15 4sh black & scar 75.00 *125.00*
89 A15 5sh car & black 17.50 *57.50*
90 A15 8sh vio & green 250.00 *425.00*
91 A15 10sh ultra & black 37.50 *80.00*
92 A15 £1 org & black 175.00 *225.00*
93 A15 £5 dl vio & blk 1,750. *4,750.*
Ovptd. "SPECIMEN" 800.00
Nos. 76-92 (17) 662.20 *1,141.*
Nos. 76-92, ovptd. "SPECIMEN" 925.00

Years issued: Nos. 83, 85, 4sh, 8sh, 1924. 2sh6p, 5sh, 10sh, £5, 1925. £1, 1927. Nos. 84, 86, 1929.

Type of 1912 Issue
Inscribed: "THREE PENCE"

1930, Apr. 12 Ordinary Paper
94 A14 3p ultramarine 9.50 2.25
Perf "SPECIMEN" 80.00

Rock of Gibraltar A16

1931-33 Engr. *Perf. 14*
96 A16 1p red 2.25 *3.50*
a. Perf. 13½x14 17.50 6.50
97 A16 1½p red brown 2.75 *3.25*
a. Perf. 13½x14 14.50 5.00
98 A16 2p gray ('32) 8.75 2.25
a. Perf. 13½x14 17.50 2.75
99 A16 3p dk blue ('33) 7.75 4.25
a. Perf. 13½x14 30.00 *32.50*
Nos. 96-99 (4) 21.50 13.25
Set, never hinged 45.00
Set, perf "SPECIMEN" 190.00
Nos. 96a-99a (4) 79.50 46.75
Set, never hinged 150.00

Common Design Types pictured following the introduction.

Silver Jubilee Issue
Common Design Type

1935, May 6 *Perf. 11x12*
100 CD301 2p black & ultra 1.40 *2.50*
101 CD301 3p ultra & brown 3.50 4.00
102 CD301 6p indigo & green 11.50 *15.00*
103 CD301 1sh brown vio & ind 11.50 *12.00*
Nos. 100-103 (4) 27.90 33.50
Set, never hinged 57.50
Set, perf "SPECIMEN" 225.00

Coronation Issue
Common Design Type

1937, May 12 *Perf. 11x11½*
104 CD302 ½p deep green .20 .20
105 CD302 2p gray black .70 *2.10*
106 CD302 3p deep ultra 1.50 *2.10*
Nos. 104-106 (3) 2.40 4.40
Set, never hinged 5.00
Set, perf "SPECIMEN" 150.00

George VI — A17

Rock of Gibraltar A18

Designs: 2p, Rock from north side. 3p, 5p, Europa Point. 6p, Moorish Castle. 1sh, Southport Gate. 2sh, Eliott Memorial. 5sh, Government House. 10sh, Catalan Bay.

Perf. 13, 13½x14 (½p, No. 118), 14 (1½p)

1938-49 Engr. Wmk. 4
107 A17 ½p gray green .20 .35
108 A18 1p red brn ('42) .35 *.55*
a. 1p chestnut, perf. 14 *27.50* 2.75
b. 1p chestnut, perf. 13½ 27.50 2.50
c. Perf. 13½, wmk. sideways ('41) *6.75* *8.25*
109 A18 1½p carmine rose 30.00 .90
b. Perf. 13½ 275.00 45.00
109A A18 1½p gray vio ('43) .25 *1.60*
110 A18 2p dk gray ('42) .35 1.40
a. Perf. 14 27.50 .55
c. Perf. 13½ 1.75 .45
d. Perf. 13½, wmk. sideways ('41) 650.00 52.50
110B A18 2p car rose ('44) .30 .55
111 A18 3p blue ('42) .35 .35
a. Perf. 14 140.00 6.00
b. Perf. 13½ 22.50 1.10
112 A18 5p red org ('47) 1.00 1.25
113 A18 6p dl vio & car rose 3.75 1.90
a. Perf. 14 125.00 1.60
b. Perf. 13½ 50.00 4.00
114 A18 1sh grn & blk ('42) 3.00 *4.50*
a. Perf. 14 45.00 27.50
b. Perf. 13½ 70.00 8.25
115 A18 2sh org brn & blk ('42) 4.00 6.50
a. Perf. 14 70.00 30.00
b. Perf. 13½ 140.00 42.50
116 A18 5sh dk car & blk ('44) 12.50 *21.00*
a. Perf 14 ('38) 100.00 *175.00*
b. Perf. 13½ 40.00 22.50
117 A18 10sh bl & blk ('43) 27.50 27.50
a. Perf. 14 70.00 *150.00*
118 A17 £1 orange 37.50 *37.50*
Nos. 107-118 (14) 121.05 105.85
Set, never hinged 175.00
Set, perf "SPECIMEN" 800.00

Nos. 108c and 110d were issued in coils.
No. 108 (1p, perf. 13) exists with watermark both normal and sideways. Nos. 110 and 110B (both 2p, perf. 13) have watermark sideways.
For overprints see Nos. 127-130.

Catalogue values for unused stamps in this section, from this point to the end of the section, are for Never Hinged items.

Peace Issue
Common Design Type

1946, Oct. 12 *Perf. 13½x14*
119 CD303 ½p bright green .20 .20
120 CD303 3p bright ultra .25 .20
Set, perf "SPECIMEN" 110.00

Silver Wedding Issue
Common Design Types

1948, Dec. 1 Photo. *Perf. 14x14½*
121 CD304 ½p dark green .80 .70

Engr.; Name Typo.
Perf. 11½x11
122 CD305 £1 brown orange 70.00 *87.50*
Set, hinged 55.00

UPU Issue
Common Design Types
Engr.; Name Typo. on 3p, 6p
Perf. 13½, 11x11½

1949, Oct. 10 Wmk. 4
123 CD306 2p rose carmine 1.00 1.25
124 CD307 3p indigo 2.50 1.50
125 CD308 6p rose violet 2.00 2.50
126 CD309 1sh blue green 1.25 4.25
Nos. 123-126 (4) 6.75 9.50

Nos. 110B, 111, 113-114 overprinted in Black or Carmine

1950, Aug. 1 *Perf. 13x12½*
127 A18 2p carmine rose .40 *1.25*
128 A18 3p blue 1.00 *1.25*
129 A18 6p dl vio & car rose 1.25 *1.75*
a. Double overprint 950.00 *1,100.*
130 A18 1sh grn & blk (C) 1.25 *1.75*
Nos. 127-130 (4) 3.90 *6.00*

Adoption of Constitution of 1950.

WAR TAX STAMP

No. 66 Overprinted

1918, Apr. Wmk. 3 *Perf. 14*
MR1 A14 ½p green 1.10 *1.50*
a. Double overprint 900.00

GILBERT AND ELLICE ISLANDS

'gil-bərt ən͵d͵ 'e-ləs 'ī-lənds

LOCATION — Groups of islands in the Pacific Ocean northeast of Australia
GOVT. — British Crown Colony
AREA — 375 sq. mi.
POP. — 57,816 (est. 1973)
CAPITAL — Tarawa

The Gilbert group of which Butaritari, Tarawa and Tamana are the more important, is on the Equator. Ellice Islands, Phoenix Islands, Line Islands (Fanning, Washington and Christmas), and Ocean Island are included in the Colony. The islands were annexed by Great Britain in 1892 and formed into the Gilbert and Ellice Islands Colony in 1915 on request of the native governments.

The colony divided into the Gilbert Islands and Tuvalu, Jan. 1, 1976.

12 Pence = 1 Shilling
20 Shillings = 1 Pound

Catalogue values for unused stamps in this country are for Never Hinged items, beginning with Scott 52.

Stamps and Type of Fiji Overprinted in Black or Red

1911, Jan. 1 Wmk. 3 *Perf. 14*
Ordinary Paper
1 A22 ½p green 8.25 *45.00*
2 A22 1p carmine 35.00 29.00
a. Pair, one without overprint
3 A22 2p gray 8.25 *15.00*
4 A22 2½p ultramarine 17.00 *30.00*

Chalky Paper
5 A22 5p violet & ol grn 30.00 *75.00*
6 A22 6p violet 25.00 *45.00*
7 A22 1sh black, *green* 22.50 60.00
Nos. 1-7 (7) 146.00 *299.00*
Set, ovptd. "SPECIMEN" 300.00

Nos. 1-7 are known with a forged Ocean Island postmark dated "JY 15 11."

Pandanus — A2

1911, Mar. Engr.
Ordinary Paper
8 A2 ½p green 4.00 *16.00*
9 A2 1p carmine 1.75 *7.50*
10 A2 2p gray 1.40 *7.50*
11 A2 2½p ultramarine 4.25 *12.50*
Nos. 8-11 (4) 11.40 *43.50*
Set, ovptd. "SPECIMEN" 160.00

King George V — A3

For description of Dies I and II, see front section of the Catalogue.

Die I

1912-24 Typo.
14 A3 ½p deep green .75 *4.00*
a. ½p yellow green ('14) 5.00 *12.50*
15 A3 1p carmine 2.25 *4.50*
a. 1p scarlet ('15) 4.00 *10.00*
16 A3 2p gray ('16) 15.00 *25.00*
17 A3 2½p ultra ('16) 1.75 *10.00*

Chalky Paper
18 A3 3p vio, *yel*('19) 2.50 *8.00*
19 A3 4p blk & red, *yel* .75 *6.50*
20 A3 5p vio & ol grn 1.75 *6.00*
21 A3 6p vio & red vio 1.25 *6.25*
22 A3 1sh black, *green* 1.25 *4.75*
23 A3 2sh vio & ultra, *bl* 14.50 *25.00*
24 A3 2sh6p blk & red, *bl* 16.00 *21.00*
25 A3 5sh grn & red, *yel* 32.50 *55.00*

Die II

26 A3 £1 vio & blk, *red* ('24) 650.00 *1,550.*
Nos. 14-26 (13) 740.25 *1,726.*
Set, ovptd. "SPECIMEN" 700.00

Die II

1921-27 Ordinary Paper Wmk. 4

27 A3 ½p green 2.25 *2.75*
28 A3 1p deep vio ('27) 5.00 *4.25*
29 A3 1½p scarlet ('24) 5.00 *2.00*
30 A3 2p gray 7.50 *20.00*

Chalky Paper

31 A3 10sh green & red, *emer* ('24) 175.00 *350.00*
Nos. 27-31 (5) 194.75 *379.00*
Set, ovptd. "SPECIMEN" 300.00

Most of Nos. 14-31 are known with the forcged cancellation described in the note following Nos. 1-7.

Common Design Types pictured following the introduction.

Silver Jubilee Issue
Common Design Type

1935, May 6 Engr. *Perf. 11x12*

33 CD301 1p black & ultra 2.00 *9.25*
34 CD301 1½p car & blue 1.50 *3.25*
35 CD301 3p ultra & brn 4.50 *12.50*
36 CD301 1sh brn vio & indigo 25.00 *24.00*
Nos. 33-36 (4) 33.00 *49.00*
Set, never hinged 57.50
Set, perf "SPECIMEN" 160.00

Coronation Issue
Common Design Type

1937, May 12 *Perf. 13½x14*

37 CD302 1p dark purple .20 .20
38 CD302 1½p carmine .25 .25
39 CD302 3p bright ultra .45 .45
Nos. 37-39 (3) .90 .90
Set, never hinged 1.25
Set, perf "SPECIMEN" 100.00

Great Frigate Bird — A4

Pandanus — A5

Designs: 1½p, Canoe crossing reef. 2p, Canoe and boat house. 2½p, Islander's house. 3p, Seascape. 5p, Ellice Islands canoe. 6p, Coconut trees. 1sh, Phosphate loading jetty, Ocean Island. 2sh, Cutter "Nimanoa." 2sh6p, Gilbert Islands canoe. 5sh, Coat of arms of colony.

Perf. 11½x11 (Nos. 40, 43, 50), 12½ (Type A5), 13½ (Nos. 42, 44, 45, 48)

1939, Jan. 14 Engr. Wmk. 4

40 A4 ½p dk grn & sl bl .20 *.65*
41 A5 1p dk vio & brt bl green .20 *1.40*
42 A4 1½p car & black .20 *.80*
43 A4 2p black & brn .25 *.95*
44 A4 2½p dp olive & blk .20 *.65*
a. ½p olive grn & black ('43) 3.00 *5.00*
45 A4 3p ultra & black .20 *.95*
a. Perf. 12 ('55) .25 *2.10*
46 A5 5p dk brn & dp ultra 3.50 1.75
a. 5p dp brn & ultra ('43) 3.75 *8.00*
b. 5p blackish brn & ultra ('44) 3.50 *5.75*
47 A5 6p dl vio & olive .30 *.45*
48 A4 1sh gray bl & blk 2.50 1.60
a. 1sh turq blue & blk ('43) 5.50 3.75
b. Perf. 12 ('51) 2.50 *12.00*
49 A5 2sh red org & ultra 8.75 8.75
50 A4 2sh6p brt bl grn & bl 9.25 *13.00*
51 A5 5sh dp blue & red 10.00 *15.00*
Nos. 40-51 (12) 35.55 *45.95*
Set, never hinged 60.00
Set, perf "SPECIMEN" 375.00

Catalogue values for unused stamps in this section, from this point to the end of the section, are for Never Hinged items.

Peace Issue
Common Design Type

1946, Dec. 16 *Perf. 13½x14*

52 CD303 1p deep magenta .20 .20
53 CD303 3p deep blue .25 .25
Set, perf "SPECIMEN" 90.00

Silver Wedding Issue
Common Design Types

1949, Aug. 29 Photo. *Perf. 14x14½*

54 CD304 1p violet .20 .20

Engraved; Name Typographed
Perf. 11½x11

55 CD305 £1 red 21.00 *22.50*

UPU Issue
Common Design Types

Engr.; Name Typo. on 2p, 3p

1949, Oct. 1 *Perf. 13½, 11x11½*

56 CD306 1p rose violet .65 *1.10*
57 CD307 2p gray black 2.25 2.25
58 CD308 3p indigo .80 *2.40*
59 CD309 1sh blue .80 *2.00*
Nos. 56-59 (4) 4.50 7.75

POSTAGE DUE STAMPS

D1

1940, Aug. Typo. Wmk. 4 *Perf. 12*

J1 D1 1p emerald 5.50 *20.00*
J2 D1 2p dark red 6.00 *22.00*
J3 D1 3p chocolate 8.25 *24.00*
J4 D1 4p deep blue 10.00 *25.00*
J5 D1 5p deep green 13.00 *25.00*
J6 D1 6p brt red vio 13.00 *40.00*
J7 D1 1sh dull violet 22.50 *70.00*
J8 D1 1sh6p turq green 32.50 *100.00*
Nos. J1-J8 (8) 110.75 *326.00*
Set, never hinged 165.00
Set, perf "SPECIMEN" 200.00

WAR TAX STAMP

No. 15a Overprinted

1918 Wmk. 3 *Perf. 14*

MR1 A3 1p scarlet .70 *6.50*
Overprinted "SPECIMEN" 75.00

GOLD COAST

'gōld 'kōst

LOCATION — West Africa between Dahomey and Ivory Coast
GOVT. — Former British Crown Colony
AREA — 91,843 sq. mi.
POP. — 3,089,000 (1952)
CAPITAL — Accra

Attached to the colony were Ashanti and Northern Territories (protectorate). Togoland, under British mandate, was also included for administrative purposes.

12 Pence = 1 Shilling
20 Shillings = 1 Pound

Catalogue values for unused stamps in this country are for Never Hinged items, beginning with Scott 128.

Queen Victoria
A1 A3

Perf. 12½

1875, July Typo. Wmk. 1

1 A1 1p blue 525.00 90.00
2 A1 4p red violet 500.00 140.00
3 A1 6p orange 750.00 75.00
Nos. 1-3 (3) 1,775. 305.00

1876-79 *Perf. 14*

4 A1 ½p bister ('79) 72.50 26.00
5 A1 1p blue 22.50 8.00
a. Half used as ½p on cover *3,750.*
6 A1 2p green ('79) 95.00 11.50
a. Half used as 1p on cover *3,150.*
b. Quarter used as ½p on cover *5,250.*
7 A1 4p red violet 210.00 7.00
a. Quarter used as 1p on cover *5,750.*
b. Half used as 2p on cover *8,000.*
8 A1 6p orange 150.00 22.50
a. One sixth used as 1p on cover *9,000.*
b. Half used as 3p on cover *7,500.*
Nos. 4-8 (5) 550.00 75.00

Handstamp Surcharged "1D" in Black

1883, May

9 A1 1p on 4p red violet

Some experts question the status of No. 9. One canceled copy is in the British Museum. Another copy is supposed to exist (Ferrari).

1883-91 Wmk. 2

10 A1 ½p bister ('83) 210.00 75.00
11 A1 ½p green ('84) 3.25 .95
a. ½p dull green 3.25 1.10
12 A1 1p blue ('83) 1,000. 80.00
13 A1 1p rose ('84) 4.00 .60
a. Half used as ½p on cover *4,500.*
b. 1p carmine 4.00 .60
14 A1 2p gray ('84) 17.00 4.25
a. 2p slate 5.75 .55
b. Half used as 1p on cover *5,000.*
15 A1 2½p bl & org ('91) 4.50 .80
16 A1 3p ol green ('89) 11.00 5.25
a. 3p olive bister 11.00 5.25
17 A1 4p dull vio ('84) 11.00 1.75
a. 4p claret 12.00 3.50
b. Half used as 2p on cover —
18 A1 6p orange ('89) 11.50 6.00
a. One sixth used as 1p on cover —
b. 6p orange brown 11.50 6.00
19 A1 1sh purple ('88) 6.50 1.50
a. 1sh violet 37.50 15.00
20 A1 2sh brown ('84) 52.50 17.50
a. 2sh yellow brown ('88) 90.00 40.00

No. 18 Surcharged in Black

1889, Mar.

21 A1 1p on 6p orange 130.00 55.00
a. Double surcharge *4,000.*

The surcharge exists in two spacings between "PENNY" and bar: 7mm (normal) and 8mm.

No. 21a does not exist unused.

1889

22 A3 5sh lilac & ultra 75.00 17.50
23 A3 10sh lilac & red 87.50 17.50
a. 10sh lilac & carmine 800.00 290.00
24 A3 20sh green & red 3,750. 230.00

1894

25 A3 20sh vio & blk, *red* 190.00 40.00
Nos. 22-25, ovptd. "SPECIMEN" 450.00

1898-1902

26 A3 ½p lilac & green 2.75 1.25
27 A3 1p lil & car rose 2.75 .60
28 A3 2p lil & red ('02) 57.50 *150.00*
29 A3 2½p lilac & ultra 5.75 *6.00*
30 A3 3p lilac & yel 5.75 1.75
31 A3 6p lilac & purple 6.50 1.75
32 A3 1sh gray grn & blk 12.00 *17.50*
33 A3 2sh gray grn & car rose 14.00 *21.00*
34 A3 5sh grn & lil ('00) 60.00 32.50
35 A3 10sh grn & brn ('00) 160.00 60.00
Nos. 26-35 (10) 327.00 *292.35*
Set, ovptd. "SPECIMEN" 210.00

Numerals of 2p, 3p and 6p of type A3 are in color on colorless tablet.

Nos. 29 and 31 Surcharged in Black

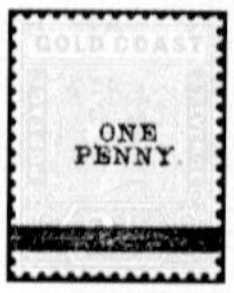

1901, Oct. 6

36 A3 1p on 2½p lil & ultra 3.25 *4.50*
a. "ONE" omitted 1,150.
37 A3 1p on 6p lilac & pur 3.25 4.25
a. "ONE" omitted 325.00 *650.00*

Beware of copies offered as No. 37a that have part of "ONE" showing.

King Edward VII
A5 A6

1902 Wmk. 2

38 A5 ½p violet & green 1.75 *.50*
39 A5 1p vio & car rose 1.75 *.25*
40 A5 2p vio & red org 27.50 *8.50*
41 A5 2½p vio & ultra 5.50 *11.00*
42 A5 3p vio & orange 3.50 1.75
43 A5 6p violet & pur 4.50 1.75
44 A5 1sh green & blk 17.00 4.00
45 A5 2sh grn & car rose 17.50 21.00
46 A5 5sh green & violet 47.50 *100.00*
47 A5 10sh green & brn 65.00 *150.00*
48 A5 20sh vio & blk, *red* 150.00 *180.00*
Nos. 38-48 (11) 341.50 *478.75*
Set, ovptd. "SPECIMEN" 225.00

Numerals of 2p, 3p, 6p and 2sh6p of type A5 are in color on colorless tablet.

1904-07 Wmk. 3

Ordinary Paper

49 A5 ½p vio & grn ('07) 3.00 *8.50*
50 A5 1p vio & car rose 9.00 .40
a. Chalky paper ('06) 11.50 2.25
51 A5 2p vio & red org 5.75 .60
a. Chalky paper ('06) 30.00 2.50
52 A5 2½p vio & ultra ('06) 57.50 57.50
53 A5 3p vio & org ('05) 70.00 7.00
a. Chalky paper ('06) 17.50 .70
54 A5 6p vio & pur ('06) 50.00 1.50
a. Chalky paper ('06) 45.00 2.00
55 A5 2sh6p grn & yel ('06), chalky paper 32.50 *125.00*
Nos. 49-55 (7) 227.75 *200.50*

1907-13 Ordinary Paper

56 A5 ½p green 4.00 .40
a. ½p blue green ('09) 11.00 2.25
57 A5 1p carmine 8.00 .50
58 A5 2p gray ('09) 2.75 .55
59 A5 2½p ultramarine 8.50 2.50

Chalky Paper

60 A5 3p violet, *yel* ('09) 9.50 .65
61 A5 6p dull violet ('08) 19.00 .65
a. 6p dull violet & red violet 4.50 4.25
62 A5 1sh blk, *grn* ('09) 13.00 .65
63 A5 2sh violet & bl, *bl* ('10) 9.50 19.00
a. On ordinary paper 9.25 19.00
64 A5 2sh6p blk & red, *blue* ('11) 32.50 *100.00*
65 A5 5sh grn & red, *yel* ('13) 65.00 *210.00*
Nos. 56-65 (10) 171.75 *334.90*
Set, ovptd. "SPECIMEN" 290.00

1908, Nov. Ordinary Paper

66 A6 1p carmine 3.50 .20
Ovptd. "SPECIMEN" 50.00

King George V
A7 A8

For description of Dies I and II, see front section of the Catalogue.

Die I

1913-21 Ordinary Paper

69 A7 ½p green 2.50 1.25
70 A8 1p carmine 1.40 .20
a. 1p scarlet 1.75 .60
71 A7 2p gray 3.50 3.00
72 A7 2½p ultramarine 6.00 1.25

Chalky Paper

73 A7 3p vio, *yel* ('15) 2.10 1.00
a. Die II ('19) 42.50 6.00
74 A7 6p dull vio & red vio 2.50 *2.75*
75 A7 1sh black, *green* 2.50 *1.50*
a. 1sh black, *emerald* 2.50 2.50
b. 1sh black, *bl grn,* ol back 5.75 .95
c. Die II ('21) 1.75 .60
76 A7 2sh vio & bl, *bl* 10.50 3.25
a. Die II ('21) 175.00 77.50
77 A7 2sh6p blk & red, *bl* 6.00 *16.00*
a. Die II ('21) 27.50 *50.00*
78 A7 5sh grn & red, *yel* 12.00 *60.00*
a. Die II ('21) 35.00 *150.00*
79 A7 10sh grn & red, *grn* ('16) 57.50 *95.00*
a. 10sh grn & red, *emer* 35.00 *150.00*
b. 10sh grn & red, *bl grn,* ol back 22.50 *72.50*
80 A7 20sh vio & blk, *red* ('16) 140.00 95.00

Surface-colored Paper

81 A7 3p violet, *yel* 2.10 1.00
82 A7 5sh grn & red, *yel* 11.50 *60.00*
Nos. 69-82 (14) 260.10 *341.20*

Numerals of 2p, 3p, 6p and 2sh6p of type A7 are in color on plain tablet.

Die II

1921-25 Ordinary Paper Wmk. 4

83 A7 ½p green ('22) 1.00 .60
84 A8 1p brown ('22) .90 .20
85 A7 1½p carmine ('22) 2.10 .20
86 A7 2p gray 2.10 .40
87 A7 2½p orange ('23) .95 *11.00*
88 A7 3p ultra ('22) 2.10 .70

Chalky Paper

89 A7 6p dl vio & red vio ('22) 2.50 *3.50*
90 A7 1sh blk, *emer* ('25) 3.25 *3.75*
91 A7 2sh vio & bl, *bl* ('24) 3.50 *3.75*
92 A7 2sh6p blk & red, *bl* ('25) 8.50 *26.00*
93 A7 5sh grn & red, *yel* ('25) 14.00 *57.50*

Die I

94 A7 15sh dl vio & grn ('21) 150.00 *375.00*
a. Die II ('25) 125.00 *375.00*
95 A7 £2 grn & org 450.00 *1,000.*
Nos. 83-95 (13) 640.90 *1,482.*

Christiansborg Castle — A9

1928, Aug. 1 Photo. *Perf. 13½x14½*

98 A9 ½p green .90 .50
99 A9 1p red brown .90 .20
100 A9 1½p scarlet 1.50 *1.75*
101 A9 2p slate 1.50 .20
102 A9 2½p yellow 1.75 *4.25*
103 A9 3p ultramarine 1.75 .50
104 A9 6p dull vio & blk 1.60 .50
105 A9 1sh red org & blk 3.25 .95
106 A9 2sh purple & black 21.00 6.00
107 A9 5sh ol green & car 57.50 52.50
Nos. 98-107 (10) 91.65 67.35
Set, ovptd. "SPECIMEN" 225.00

Common Design Types pictured following the introduction.

Silver Jubilee Issue
Common Design Type

1935, May 6 Engr. *Perf. 11x12*

108 CD301 1p black & ultra 1.00 .60
109 CD301 3p ultra & brown 3.25 *7.25*
110 CD301 6p indigo & green 8.00 *16.00*
111 CD301 1sh brn vio & indigo 5.50 *19.00*
Nos. 108-111 (4) 17.75 *42.85*
Set, never hinged 29.00
Set, perf "SPECIMEN" 125.00

Coronation Issue
Common Design Type

1937, May 12 *Perf. 11x11½*

112 CD302 1p brown .55 *2.50*
113 CD302 2p dark gray .65 *4.50*
114 CD302 3p deep ultra .80 *2.10*
Nos. 112-114 (3) 2.00 *9.10*
Set, never hinged 3.75
Set, perf "SPECIMEN" 85.00

A10

George VI and Christiansborg Castle — A11

1938-41 Wmk. 4 *Perf. 12*

115 A10 ½p green .35 *.50*
116 A10 1p red brown .35 .20
117 A10 1½p rose red .35 *.50*
118 A10 2p gray black .35 .20
119 A10 3p ultramarine .35 .35
120 A10 4p rose lilac .70 *1.10*
121 A10 6p rose violet .70 .20
122 A10 9p red orange 1.10 .55
123 A11 1sh gray grn & blk 1.40 .55
124 A11 1sh3p turq grn & red brown 1.75 .45
125 A11 2sh dk vio & dp bl 4.75 *11.00*
126 A11 5sh rose car & ol green 9.25 *14.00*
127 A11 10sh purple & black 6.50 *22.50*
Nos. 115-127 (13) 27.90 *52.10*
Set, never hinged 32.50
Set, perf "SPECIMEN" 290.00

Issued: 10sh, July, 1940; 1sh3p, Apr. 12, 1941; others, Apr. 1.

Catalogue values for unused stamps in this section, from this point to the end of the section, are for Never Hinged items.

Peace Issue
Common Design Type

1946, Oct. 14 *Perf. 13½*

128 CD303 2p purple .25 .20
a. Perf. 13½x14 14.00 3.00
129 CD303 4p deep red violet 1.00 *3.25*
a. Perf. 13½x14 2.25 3.50
Set, perf "SPECIMEN" 85.00

A12

A13

½p, Mounted Constable. 1p, Christiansborg Castle. 1½p, Emblem of Joint Provincial Council. 2p, Talking Drums. 2½p, Map. 3p, Manganese mine. 4p, Lake Bosumtwi. 6p, Cacao farmer. 1sh, Breaking cacao pods. 2sh, Trooping the colors. 5sh, Surfboats. 10sh, Forest.

1948, July 1 Engr. *Perf. 12*

130 A12 ½p emerald .20 .35
131 A13 1p deep blue .20 .20
132 A13 1½p red 1.50 .90
133 A12 2p chocolate .65 .20
134 A13 2½p lt brown & red 2.50 *4.25*
135 A13 3p blue 5.00 .60
136 A13 4p dk car rose 4.25 2.50
137 A12 6p org & black .40 .40
138 A13 1sh red org & blk .70 .40
139 A13 2sh rose car & ol brn 4.00 2.50
140 A13 5sh gray & red vio 30.00 7.25
141 A12 10sh ol grn & black 10.00 7.25
Nos. 130-141 (12) 59.40 26.80
Set, perf "SPECIMEN" 290.00

Silver Wedding Issue
Common Design Types

1948, Dec. 20 Photo. *Perf. 14x14½*

142 CD304 1½p scarlet .20 .20

Engraved; Name Typographed
Perf. 11½x11

143 CD305 10sh dk brn olive 17.50 *22.50*

UPU Issue
Common Design Types

Engr.; Name Typo. on 2½p and 3p
1949, Oct. 10 *Perf. 13½, 11x11½*

144 CD306 2p red brown .25 .25
145 CD307 2½p deep orange 1.90 *4.00*
146 CD308 3p indigo .45 *1.75*
147 CD309 1sh blue green .45 .45
Nos. 144-147 (4) 3.05 *6.45*

POSTAGE DUE STAMPS

D1

1923 Typo. Wmk. 4 *Perf. 14*
Yellowish Toned Paper

J1 D1 ½p black 19.00 *125.00*
J2 D1 1p black .95 *1.50*
J3 D1 2p black 3.75 *22.50*
J4 D1 3p black 1.60 *4.00*
Nos. J1-J4 (4) 25.30 *153.00*
Set, ovptd. "SPECIMEN" 85.00

1951-52 Typo. Wmk. 4 *Perf. 14*
Chalk-Surfaced Paper

J5 D1 2p black 3.75 *22.50*
a. Wmk. 4a (error) 425.00
J6 D1 3p black 3.00 *21.00*
a. Wmk. 4a (error) *425.00*
J7 D1 6p black ('52) 2.10 *10.00*
a. Wmk. 4a (error) *1,200.*
J8 D1 1sh black ('52) 2.10 *80.00*
a. Wmk. 4a (error) *900.00*
Nos. J5-J8 (4) 10.95 *133.50*

Issued: #J7-J8, 10/1.

WAR TAX STAMP

Regular Issue of 1913 Surcharged

1918, June Wmk. 3 *Perf. 14*

MR1 A8 1p on 1p scarlet 2.25 .60
Ovpted. "SPECIMEN" 57.50

GRAND COMORO

ˈgrand ˈkä-mə-ˌrō

LOCATION — One of the Comoro Islands in the Mozambique Channel between Madagascar and Mozambique.
GOVT. — French Colony
AREA — 385 sq. mi. (approx.)
POP. — 50,000 (approx.)
CAPITAL — Moroni
See Comoro Islands

100 Centimes = 1 Franc

Navigation and Commerce — A1

Perf. 14x13½

1897-1907 Typo. Unwmk.
Name of Colony in Blue or Carmine

1	A1	1c blk, *lil bl*	.90	.80
2	A1	2c brn, *buff*	1.25	.95
3	A1	4c claret, *lav*	1.75	1.40
4	A1	5c grn, *grnsh*	3.50	2.50
5	A1	10c blk, *lavender*	7.00	4.00
6	A1	10c red ('00)	8.75	7.00
7	A1	15c blue, quadrille paper	17.00	8.00
8	A1	15c gray, *lt gray* ('00)	8.50	7.00
9	A1	20c red, *grn*	10.00	8.00
10	A1	25c blk, *rose*	13.00	10.50
11	A1	25c blue ('00)	16.50	11.00
12	A1	30c brn, *bister*	18.00	12.00
13	A1	35c blk, *yel* ('06)	17.00	11.00
14	A1	40c red, *straw*	18.00	12.00
15	A1	45c blk, *gray grn* ('07)	60.00	50.00
16	A1	50c car, *rose*	30.00	17.50
17	A1	50c brn, *bluish* ('00)	37.50	27.50
18	A1	75c dp vio, *org*	52.50	30.00
19	A1	1fr brnz grn, *straw*	30.00	22.50
		Nos. 1-19 (19)	351.15	243.65

Perf. 13½x14 stamps are counterfeits.

Issues of 1897-1907 Surcharged in Black or Carmine

1912

Spacing between figures of surcharge 1.5mm (5c), 2mm (10c)

20	A1	5c on 2c brn, *buff*	.85	.85
a.		Inverted surcharge	225.00	
b.		Pair, one without surcharge	1,300.	
21	A1	5c on 4c cl, *lav* (C)	.85	.85
a.		Pair, one without surcharge	725.00	
22	A1	5c on 15c blue (C)	.90	.90
23	A1	5c on 20c red, *grn*	.90	.90
24	A1	5c on 25c blk, *rose* (C)	.90	.90
25	A1	5c on 30c brn, *bis* (C)	1.25	1.25
26	A1	10c on 40c red, *straw*	1.25	1.25
27	A1	10c on 45c blk, *gray grn* (C)	1.40	1.40
28	A1	10c on 50c car, *rose*	1.25	1.25
29	A1	10c on 75c dp vio, *org*	1.75	1.75
		Nos. 20-29 (10)	11.30	11.30

Spacing between figures of surcharge 2.25mm (5c), 2.75mm (10c)

20c	A1	5c on 2c brn, *buff*	5.75	5.75
21b	A1	5c on 4c cl, *lav* (C)	7.00	7.00
22a	A1	5c on 15c blue (C)	8.50	8.50
23a	A1	5c on 20c red, *grn*	8.50	8.50
24a	A1	5c on 25c blk, *rose* (C)	9.25	9.25
25a	A1	5c on 30c brn, *bis* (C)	11.50	11.50
26a	A1	10c on 40c red, *straw*	72.50	72.50
27a	A1	10c on 45c blk, *gray grn* (C)	72.50	72.50
28a	A1	10c on 50c car, *rose*	65.00	65.00
29a	A1	10c on 75c dp vio, *org*	110.00	110.00
		Nos. 20c-29a (10)	370.50	370.50

Nos. 20-29 were available for use in Madagascar and the entire Comoro archipelago.

Stamps of Grand Comoro were superseded by those of Madagascar, and in 1950 by those of Comoro Islands.

GREAT BRITAIN

ˈgrāt ˈbri-tᵊn

(United Kingdom)

LOCATION — Northwest of the continent of Europe and separated from it by the English Channel
GOVT. — Constitutional monarchy
AREA — 94,511 sq. mi.
POP. — 55,767,387 (1981)
CAPITAL — London

12 Pence = 1 Shilling
20 Shillings = 1 Pound

The letters in the corners of the early postage issues indicate position in the horizontal and vertical rows in which that particular specimen was placed.

In the case of illustration A1, this stamp came from the 15th horizontal row (O) and was the second stamp (B) from the left in that row. The left corner refers to the horizontal row and the right corner to the vertical row. Thus no two stamps on the plate bore the same combination of letters.

When four corner letters are used (starting in 1858), the lower ones indicate the stamp's position in the sheet and the top ones are the same letters reversed.

Catalogue values for unused stamps in this country are for Never Hinged items, beginning with Scott 264 in the regular postage section, Scott J34 in the postage due section, Scott 10 in British Offices — East Africa Forces, and Scott 93, Scott 246 and Scott 523 in British Offices in Morocco. All of the listings in British Offices — for Use in Eritrea and for Use in Tripolitania are valued as never-hinged.

Watermarks

Wmk. 18 — Small Crown

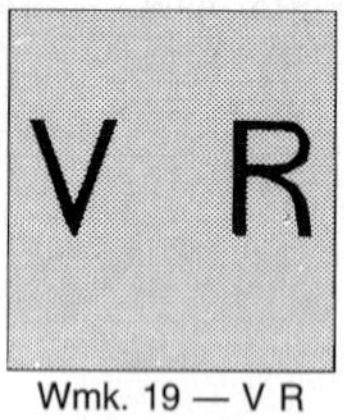

Wmk. 19 — V R

Wmk. 20 — Large Crown

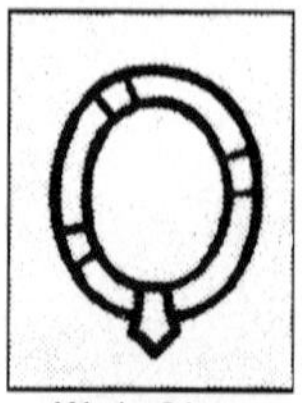

Wmk. 21 — Small Garter

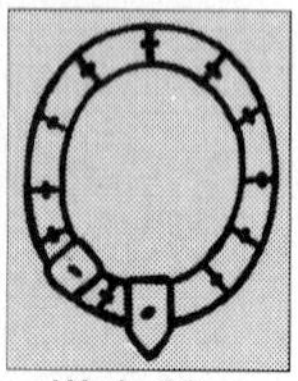

Wmk. 22 — Medium Garter

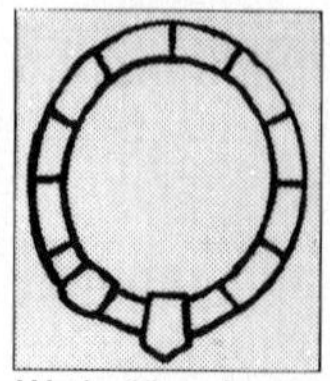

Wmk. 23 — Large Garter

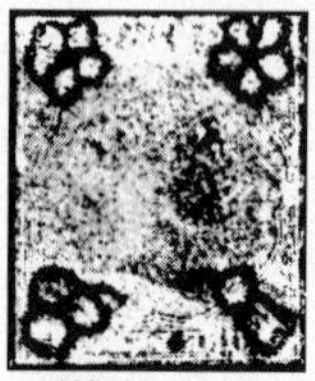

Wmk. 24 — Heraldic Emblems

Wmk. 25 — Spray of Rose

Wmk. 26 — Maltese Cross

Wmk. 27 — "Half Penny" in Script

Wmk. 28 — Anchor

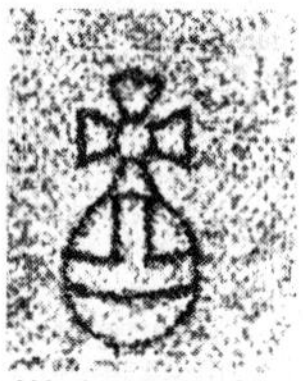

Wmk. 29 — Orb

Wmk. 30 — Imperial Crown

Wmk. 31 — Anchor

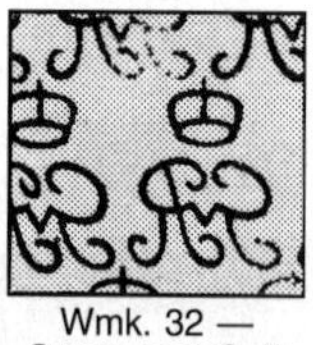

Wmk. 32 — Crown and GvR Multiple

Wmk. 33 — Crown and GvR

Wmk. 33 — In the normal watermark (sometimes termed the "repeated" watermark) the letters "GvR" are extended. The royal cyphers are placed one above the other and usually two appear on each stamp. In the multiple watermark the letters "GvR" are condensed, the cyphers are smaller and are so placed that those in each succeeding row are below the spaces between the cyphers in the row above.

Wmk. 34 — Large Crown and GvR

Wmk. 35 — Crown and Block GvR Multiple

Wmk. 219 — Large Crown and GvR

Wmk. 250 — Crown and E8R Multiple

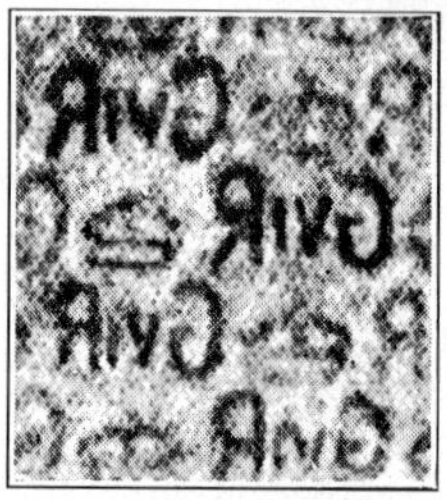

Wmk. 251 — Crown and GviR Multiple

Wmk. 259 — Crown and Large G VI R

Values for unused stamps are for examples with original gum as defined in the catalogue introduction. Very fine examples of Nos. 8-56, 58-73, 78-89, 94-95, and the Official overprints on these designs, will have perforations touching the design on at least one side due to the narrow spacing of the stamps on the plates. Stamps with perfs well clear of the design on all four sides range from scarce to rare and command substantially higher prices.

Cancellations on stamps from the 1847 issue to the 1900 issue, and in many cases beyond, are usually heavy. Values quoted are for stamps with better than average cancellations. Stamps with circular date stamps range from scarce to rare and command higher prices.

Queen Victoria — A1

1840, May Wmk. 18 Engr. *Imperf.*
White Paper

1	A1	1p black	6,000.	275.00
		On cover		475.00
a.		1p intense black	7,500.	375.00

	On cover		550.00
b.	1p gray black (worn plate)	7,500.	400.00
	On cover		550.00
c.	Watermark inverted	11,500.	1,500.
d.	On blued paper (Plates 1-8), *from*		525.00
2	A1 2p blue	13,000.	650.00
	On cover		1,400.
a.	2p pale blue	17,500.	725.00
	On cover		1,450.
b.	2p deep bright blue	17,500.	825.00
	On cover		1,600.
c.	Watermark inverted	21,000.	3,250.

Full margins = ½mm.

No. 1 was printed from 11 plates; No. 2 from 2 plates. The 1p plates 1, 2, 5, 6, 8 and 9 can be found in two or more states.

Stamp and on cover values are for the most common plates.

Issue dates: 1p, May 6; 2p, May 7.

See Nos. 3, 8-9, 11-12, 14, 16, 18, 20, O1. Compare designs A1-A2 with A8, A10.

Values for pairs

1	A1 1p black, *from*	19,000.	825.00
	On cover, *from*		1,050.
2	A1 2p blue, *from*	37,000.	1,600.
	On cover, *from*		2,250.

Values for strips of 3

1	A1 1p black	26,000.	1,200.
	On cover		—
2	A1 2p blue	57,500.	2,250.
	On cover		—

Values for blocks of 4

1	A1 1p black	50,000.	8,250.
	On cover		—
2	A1 2p blue	85,000.	13,750.
	On cover		—

Values for Certified Plated Examples

Stamps from each plate used for Nos. 1-2 can be plated with certainty by experts. Certificates are recommended. Values are for the most common shades of each plate.

1	1p black		
	Plate 1, 1st stage	7,750.	300.
	Plate 1, 2nd stage	6,000.	275.
	Plate 2	6,000.	275.
	Plate 3	8,250.	325.
	Plate 4	6,000.	300.
	Plate 5	6,000.	275.
	Plate 6	6,500.	275.
	Plate 7	6,500.	300.
	Plate 8	8,250.	350.
	Plate 9	8,750.	400.
	Plate 10	11,000.	600.
	Plate 11	10,500.	3,900.
2	2p blue		
	Plate 1	13,000.	650.
	Plate 2	16,500.	700.

Values for cancellations
No. 1, Left Column
No. 2, Right Column

Maltese Cross, red	300.	700.
Maltese Cross, black	275.	650.
Maltese Cross, blue	5,000.	6,000.
Maltese Cross, magenta	1,750.	6,000.
Maltese Cross, yellow	—	
"Penny Post" straight line, black	2,500.	4,500.
Town postmark, black, *from*	3,250.	3,250.
Town postmark, red, *from*	3,250.	—
Town postmark, yellow, *from*	20,000.	
Numeral postmark, 1844 onwards, *from*	775.	1,450.

Maltese Crosses with Numerals in Center, black

No. 1	5,500.	6,000.
No. 2	5,500.	6,000.
No. 3	5,500.	6,000.
No. 4	5,500.	6,000.
No. 5	5,500.	6,000.
No. 6	5,500.	6,000.
No. 7	5,500.	6,000.
No. 8	5,500.	6,000.
No. 9	5,500.	6,000.
No. 10	5,500.	6,000.
No. 11	5,500.	6,000.
No. 12	5,500.	5,500.

Early Dates on Cover

May 6	62,500.	
May 7	7,500.	—
May 8	4,600.	57,500.
May 9	2,800.	
May 10 (Sunday)	25,000.	
May 11-16	1,800.	7,500.
May 17 (Sunday)	10,000.	15,000.
May 18-23	1,700.	7,500.
May 24 (Sunday)	9,500.	15,000.
May 25-30	925.	7,500.
May 31 (Sunday)	9,500.	15,000.

Used in Combination with Mulready Envelopes & Letter Sheets

1d black on U1	5,750.
1p black on U2	15,000.
1p black on U3	5,750.
1p black on U4	15,000.
2p blue on U1	17,500.
2p blue on U2	15,000.
2p blue on U3	17,500.
2p blue on U4	12,500.

A2

1841 Bluish Paper

3	A1 1p red brown	325.00	17.50
	On cover		30.00
a.	1p orange brown	1,000.	140.00
	On cover		175.00
b.	1p lake red	2,750.	550.00
	On cover		750.00
c.	Rouletted 12	8,500.	
d.	"A" missing in lower right corner (position BA, P77)	—	8,750.
4	A2 2p blue	2,750.	85.00
	On cover		260.00
a.	2p pale blue	3,250.	92.50
	On cover		290.00
b.	2p deep bright blue	3,500.	95.00
	On cover		350.00
c.	2p violet blue	16,000.	1,000.
	On cover		—

Full margins = ½mm.

No. 3 exists on silk thread paper, but was not regularly issued.

No. 4 was printed from two plates.

See Nos. 10, 13, 15, 17, 19, 21.

Values for pairs

3	A1 1p red brown	700.00	42.50
	On cover		60.00
4	A2 2p blue	6,000.	175.00
	On cover		400.00

Values for strips of 3

3	A1 1p red brown	1,100.	65.00
	On cover		175.00
4	A2 2p blue	9,000.	260.00
	On cover		600.00

Values for blocks of 4

3	A1 1p red brown	1,600.	240.00
	On cover		475.00
	With Maltese Cross postmarks	350.00	750.00
	On cover		700.00
4	A2 2p blue	12,000.	675.00
	On cover		—

Values for cancellations
No. 3, Left Column
No. 4, Right Column

Maltese Cross, red	3,500.	14,500.
Maltese Cross, black	45.00	210.00
Maltese Cross, blue	500.00	2,750.
"Penny Post" straight line, black	550.00	—
Town postmark, black (from)	500.00	1,100.
Town postmark, red (from)	6,100.	—
Town postmark, yellow (from)	—	—
Town postmark, blue (from)	1,100.	1,750.
Town postmark, green (from)	2,000.	—
Numeral postmark, black (from)	17.50	85.00
Numeral postmark, blue (from)	160.00	650.00
Numeral postmark, red (from)	4,500.	11,000.
Numeral postmark, green (from)	1,400.	2,250.
Numeral postmark, violet (from)	2,000.	—

Maltese Crosses with Numerals in Center, black

No. 1	130.00	450.00
No. 2	130.00	450.00
No. 3	160.00	450.00
No. 4	400.00	410.00
No. 5	130.00	575.00
No. 6	110.00	410.00
No. 7	110.00	775.00
No. 8	110.00	600.00
No. 9	130.00	775.00
No. 10	225.00	875.00
No. 11	225.00	575.00
No. 12	225.00	360.00

Used in Combination with Mulready Envelopes & Letter Sheets

1d red brown on U1	2,750.
1p red brown on U2	9,500.
1p red brown on U3	2,750.
1p red brown on U4	9,500.
2p blue on U1	10,000.
2p blue on U2	10,000.
2p blue on U3	10,000.
2p blue on U4	6,300.

During the reigns of Victoria and Edward VII, many color trials were produced on perfed, gummed and watermarked papers.

A3

A4

With Vertical Silk Threads

1847 Embossed Unwmk.

5	A3 1sh pale green	8,500.	750.00
	On cover		1,000.
	Cut to shape		15.00
a.	1sh green	8,500.	800.00
	On cover		1,000.
	Cut to shape		15.00
b.	1sh deep green	8,750.	750.00
	On cover		1,000.
	Cut to shape		15.00

Die numbers (on base of bust): 1 and 2.

Nos. 5-7 were printed one stamp at a time on the sheet. Space between the stamps usually is very small. Impressions that touch, or even overlap, are numerous.

Stamps with margins ½mm beyond the outer frame are considered as having full margins.

Cover values are for average stamps with complete design but clear, white margins on one or two sides only. Examples with four clear margins sell for much more.

1848

6	A3 10p red brown	5,500.	1,000.
	On cover		1,800.
	Cut to shape		16.00

Die numbers (on base of bust): 1, 2, 3, 4; also without die number.

1854 Wmk. 19

7	A4 6p red violet	6,750.	850.00
	On cover		1,200.
a.	6p dull violet	6,750.	850.00
	On cover		1,200.
b.	6p deep violet	9,000.	2,250.
	On cover		—
c.	6p mauve	6,750.	850.00
	On cover		1,200.
	Cut to shape		13.00

1854-55 Wmk. 18 Engr. *Perf. 16*
Bluish Paper

8	A1 1p red brown	290.00	21.00
	On cover		47.50
a.	1p yellow brown	350.00	45.00
	On cover		50.00
9	A1 1p red brown, re-engraved ('55)	525.00	70.00
	On cover		100.00
a.	Imperf.		—
10	A2 2p blue	2,900.	100.00
	On cover		150.00
a.	2p pale blue	2,900.	100.00
	On cover		150.00

In the re-engraved 1p stamps, the lines of the features are deeper and stronger, the fillet behind the ear more distinct, the shading about the eye heavier, the line of the nostril is turned downward at right and an indentation of color appears between lower lip and chin.

Perf. 14

11	A1 1p red brown ('55)	525.00	70.00
	On cover		125.00
a.	Imperf.		
12	A1 1p red brown, re-engraved ('55)	475.00	52.50
	On cover		85.00
a.	1p org brn, re-engraved	1,400.	150.00
	On cover		210.00
13	A2 2p blue ('55)	5,000.	200.00
	On cover		300.00
a.	Imperf. (P5)		—

Wmk. 20 exists in two types. The first includes two vertical prongs, rising from the top of the crown's headband and extending into each of the two balancing midsections. The second type (illustrated), introduced in 1861, omits these prongs.

1855 Wmk. 20 *Perf. 16*
Bluish Paper

14	A1 1p red brown, re-engraved	800.00	92.50
	On cover		175.00
15	A2 2p blue	7,000.	375.00
	On cover		450.00
a.	Imperf. (P5)		5,750.

1855 Bluish Paper *Perf. 14*

16	A1 1p red brown, re-engraved	210.00	17.50
	On cover		35.00
a.	1p orange brn, re-engraved	425.00	45.00
	On cover		60.00
b.	1p brown rose, re-engraved	290.00	40.00
	On cover		55.00
c.	Imperf.	2,250.	2,000.
17	A2 2p blue	2,000.	57.50
	On cover		150.00

1856-58 White Paper *Perf. 16*

18	A1 1p rose red, re-engraved ('57)	1,450.	70.00
	On cover		150.00
19	A2 2p blue, thin lines ('58)	7,000.	350.00
	On cover		450.00

Perf. 14

20	A1 1p rose red, re-engraved ('57)	47.50	11.00
	On cover		35.00
a.	Imperf.	1,750.	1,400.
b.	1p red brown, re-engraved	800.00	225.00
	On cover		525.00
21	A2 2p blue, thin lines ('57)	2,300.	57.50
	On cover		150.00
a.	Imperf.	—	5,500.
b.	Vertical pair, imperf horiz.		—

#18, 20-21, 24-29, etc., used abroad. See Antigua, Argentina, Bahamas, Bolivia, Brazil, British Guiana, British Honduras, Canada, Cyprus, Dominica, Egypt, Grenada, Jamaica, Malta, Montserrat, Nevis, Newfoundland, Nova Scotia, St. Christopher, St. Lucia, St. Vincent, Tobago, and Virgin Islands for listings of numeral cancels numbered A01-A15, A18, A27-A37, A39-A49, A51-A62, A64-A78, B01-B02, B32, C39, C81-C83, 124, 942, 969, 974, 975, 981, 982.

See Ascension for local cancellations used on Great Britain stamps.

Queen Victoria — A5

1855 Typo. Wmk. 21

22	A5 4p rose, *bluish*	5,000.	400.00
	On cover		600.00
23	A5 4p rose, *white*	—	800.00
	On cover		1,300.

Compare design A5 with A11, A16, A31.

1856 Wmk. 22

24	A5 4p rose, *bluish*	6,000.	450.00
	On cover		600.00
25	A5 4p rose, *white*	4,750.	—
	On cover		—

1857 Wmk. 23

26	A5 4p rose, *white*	1,100.	100.00
	On cover		175.00
a.	4p carmine rose, white paper	1,500.	100.00
	On cover		175.00
b.	Thick glazed paper	3,250.	275.00
	On cover		—

A6

A7

1856 Wmk. 24

27	A6 6p lilac	925.00	100.00
	On cover		175.00
a.	6p deep lilac	1,150.	125.00
	On cover		190.00
b.	Wmk. 3 roses and shamrock		
c.	6p lilac, blued paper	4,500.	725.00
d.	6p lilac, thick paper	2,300.	300.00
28	A7 1sh green	1,250.	290.00
	On cover		425.00
a.	1sh pale green	1,250.	290.00
	On cover		350.00
b.	1sh deep green	2,300.	350.00
	On cover		425.00
c.	1sh green, blued paper		1,300.
d.	1sh green, thick paper		325.00
e.	Imperf		—

Compare design A6 with A13, A18, A22. Compare A7 with A15, A21, A29.

A8

A9

1858-69 Engr. Wmk. 20 *Perf. 14*

29	A8 2p deep blue (P9)	325.00	11.50
a.	2d blue	325.00	11.50
	On cover, #29 or 29a		37.50
	Plate 7	1,200.	52.50
	On cover		75.00
	Plate 8	1,100.	37.50
	On cover		65.00
	Plate 9	325.00	11.50
	On cover		25.00
	Plate 12	1,800.	130.00
	On cover		175.00
b.	Imperf. (P9)		*5,000.*

Lines Above and Below Head Thinner

30	A8 2p blue ('69) (P13)	375.00	22.50
	On cover		35.00
	Plate 14	475.00	29.00
	On cover		42.50
	Plate 15	450.00	29.00
	On cover		42.50
a.	Imperf. (P13)	*6,000.*	

1860-70

31	A9 1½p lilac rose, *bluish* (P1) ('60)	4,500.	
32	A9 1½p dull rose ('70) (P3)	400.00	52.50
a.	1½p lake red	400.00	52.50
	On cover, #32 or 32a		225.00
	"Plate 1"	575.00	75.00
	On cover		375.00
c.	Imperf (P1, 3)	*4,000.*	

The 1½p stamps from Plate 1 carry no plate number. The Plate 3 number is in the border at each side above the lower corner letters.

No. 31 was prepared but not issued.

The "OP-PC" variety is a broken letter.

Queen Victoria — A10

1864

33	A10 1p rose red	17.50	2.25
a.	1p brick red	17.50	2.25
b.	1p lake red	17.50	2.25
	On cover, #33, 33a or 33b		5.75
c.	Imperf. (P116, see footnote)	*1,800.*	*1,400.*

Plate numbers are contained in the scroll work at the sides of the stamp.

Thirty-nine plate numbers besides Plate 116 (No. 33c) are also known imperforate and used. Values for used copies start at $450.

Stamps from plate 177 have been altered and offered as plate 77.

Plate Numbers

Plate 71	40.00	3.50
On cover		5.75
Plate 72	45.00	4.50
Plate 73	45.00	3.50
Plate 74	45.00	2.25
Plate 76	40.00	2.25
Plate 77	*150,000.*	*130,000.*
Plate 78	100.00	2.25
Plate 79	35.00	2.25
Plate 80	50.00	2.25
Plate 81	50.00	2.50
Plate 82	100.00	4.50
Plate 83	125.00	8.00
Plate 84	70.00	2.60
Plate 85	45.00	2.60
Plate 86	57.50	4.50
Plate 87	35.00	2.25
Plate 88	150.00	9.25
Plate 89	45.00	2.25
Plate 90	45.00	2.25
Plate 91	62.50	7.00
Plate 92	40.00	2.25
Plate 93	62.50	2.25
Plate 94	50.00	5.75
Plate 95	45.00	2.25
Plate 96	50.00	2.25
Plate 97	45.00	4.00
Plate 98	57.50	7.00
Plate 99	62.50	5.75
Plate 100	70.00	2.60
Plate 101	70.00	10.50
Plate 102	50.00	2.25
Plate 103	57.50	4.00
Plate 104	85.00	5.75
Plate 105	100.00	8.00
Plate 106	62.50	2.25
Plate 107	70.00	8.00
Plate 108	92.50	2.60
Plate 109	97.50	4.00
Plate 110	70.00	10.50
Plate 111	57.50	2.60
Plate 112	80.00	2.60
Plate 113	57.50	14.00
Plate 114	290.00	14.00
Plate 115	100.00	2.60
Plate 116	85.00	10.50
Plate 117	50.00	2.25
Plate 118	57.50	2.25
Plate 119	50.00	2.25
Plate 120	17.50	2.25
Plate 121	45.00	11.00
Plate 122	17.50	2.25
Plate 123	45.00	2.25
Plate 124	32.50	2.25
Plate 125	45.00	2.25
Plate 127	62.50	2.60
Plate 129	45.00	9.25
Plate 130	62.50	2.60
Plate 131	75.00	18.00
Plate 132	150.00	25.00
Plate 133	125.00	10.50
Plate 134	17.50	2.25
Plate 135	110.00	30.00
Plate 136	100.00	22.50
Plate 137	32.50	2.60
Plate 138	21.00	2.25
Plate 139	70.00	18.00
Plate 140	21.00	2.25
Plate 141	125.00	10.50
Plate 142	80.00	27.50
Plate 143	70.00	17.50
Plate 144	110.00	22.50
Plate 145	35.00	2.60
Plate 146	45.00	7.00
Plate 147	57.50	3.50
Plate 148	45.00	3.50
Plate 149	45.00	7.00
Plate 150	17.50	2.25
Plate 151	65.00	10.50
Plate 152	70.00	6.25
Plate 153	110.00	10.50
Plate 154	57.50	2.25
Plate 155	57.50	2.60
Plate 156	50.00	2.25
Plate 157	57.50	2.25
Plates 158-159	35.00	2.25
Plate 160	35.00	2.25
Plate 161	70.00	8.00
Plate 162	57.50	8.00
Plates 163-164	57.50	3.50
Plate 165	50.00	2.25
Plate 166	50.00	7.00
Plate 167	50.00	2.25
Plate 168	57.50	9.25
Plate 169	70.00	8.00
Plate 170	40.00	2.25
Plate 171	17.50	2.25
Plate 172	35.00	2.25
Plate 173	80.00	10.50
Plate 174	35.00	2.25
Plate 175	70.00	4.00
Plate 176	70.00	2.60
Plate 177	45.00	2.25
Plate 178	70.00	4.00
Plate 179	57.50	2.60
Plate 180	70.00	5.75
Plate 181	50.00	2.25
Plate 182	100.00	5.75
Plate 183	62.50	3.50
Plate 184	35.00	2.60
Plate 185	57.50	3.50
Plate 186	75.00	2.60
Plate 187	57.50	2.25
Plate 188	80.00	11.50
Plate 189	80.00	8.00
Plate 190	57.50	7.00
Plate 191	35.00	8.00
Plate 192	57.50	2.25
Plate 193	35.00	2.25
Plates 194-195	57.50	9.25
Plate 196	57.50	5.75
Plate 197	62.50	10.50
Plate 198	45.00	7.00
Plate 199	62.50	7.00
Plate 200	70.00	2.25
Plate 201	35.00	5.75
Plate 202	70.00	9.25
Plate 203	35.00	*18.00*
Plate 204	62.50	2.60
Plate 205	62.50	3.50
Plate 206	62.50	10.50
Plate 207	70.00	10.50
Plate 208	62.50	18.00
Plate 209	57.50	10.50
Plate 210	75.00	14.00
Plate 211	80.00	22.50
Plate 212	70.00	12.50
Plate 213	70.00	12.50
Plate 214	75.00	21.00
Plate 215	75.00	21.00
Plate 216	80.00	21.00
Plate 217	80.00	8.00
Plate 218	75.00	9.25
Plate 219	100.00	80.00
Plate 220	45.00	8.00
Plate 221	80.00	18.00
Plate 222	92.50	45.00
Plate 223	100.00	70.00
Plate 224	110.00	57.50
Plate 225	2,250.	750.00

Plate Numbers On Cover

Plate 71	7.25
Plate 72	9.00
Plates 73-76, 78-80	7.25
Plate 81	7.00
Plate 82	29.00
Plate 83	42.50
Plate 84	15.00
Plate 85	10.00
Plate 86	9.50
Plate 87	7.25
Plate 88	60.00
Plate 89	7.25
Plate 90	15.00
Plate 91	13.50
Plate 92	7.25
Plate 93	8.75
Plate 94	12.00
Plates 95-96	7.25
Plate 97	10.00
Plate 98	19.00
Plate 99	12.00
Plate 100	42.50
Plate 101	21.00
Plate 102	7.25
Plate 103	15.00
Plate 104	42.50
Plate 105	35.00
Plate 106	8.75
Plate 107	17.50
Plate 108	35.00
Plate 109	30.00
Plate 110	25.00
Plate 111	7.00
Plate 112	25.00
Plate 113	27.50
Plates 114-115	30.00
Plate 116	21.00
Plates 117-120	7.25
Plate 121	22.50
Plates 122-124	7.25
Plates 125, 127	7.50
Plate 129	19.00
Plate 130	7.50
Plate 131	37.50
Plate 132	50.00
Plate 133	60.00
Plate 134	7.25
Plate 135	62.50
Plate 136	45.00
Plate 137	7.50
Plate 138	7.25
Plate 139	42.50
Plate 140	7.25
Plate 141	42.50
Plate 142	55.00
Plate 143	35.00
Plate 144	45.00
Plate 145	7.50
Plate 146	13.50
Plate 147	12.50
Plate 148	7.25
Plate 149	13.50
Plate 150	7.25
Plate 151	25.00
Plate 152	17.50
Plate 153	75.00
Plates 154-155	8.75
Plates 156-160	7.25
Plate 161	35.00
Plate 162	15.00
Plate 163	11.00
Plate 164	17.50
Plate 165	7.25
Plate 166	13.50
Plate 167	7.25
Plate 168	19.00
Plate 169	30.00
Plates 170-172	7.25
Plate 173	25.00
Plate 174	7.25
Plates 175-176	17.50
Plate 177	7.25
Plate 178	30.00
Plate 179	11.00
Plate 180	42.50
Plate 181	7.25
Plate 182	40.00
Plate 183	11.00
Plate 184	25.00
Plate 185	30.00
Plate 186	25.00
Plate 187	11.00
Plate 188	30.00
Plates 189-190	40.00
Plate 191	15.00
Plate 192	7.25
Plate 193	17.50
Plate 194	25.00
Plate 195	19.00
Plate 196	17.50
Plate 197	30.00
Plates 198-199	17.50
Plate 200	25.00
Plate 201	12.00
Plate 202	30.00
Plate 203	37.50
Plate 204	30.00
Plates 205-207	40.00
Plates 208-209	47.50
Plate 210	40.00
Plate 211	150.00
Plates 212-217	90.00
Plate 218	150.00
Plate 219	160.00
Plate 220	90.00
Plate 221	125.00
Plates 222-223	150.00
Plate 224	160.00
Plate 225	2,250.

A11

1862 Typo. Wmk. 23

34	A11 4p vermilion	1,400.	110.00
	On cover		200.00
a.	4p bright red	1,400.	110.00
	On cover		200.00
b.	Hair lines (P4)	1,500.	100.00
	On cover		225.00
c.	As "a," hair lines (P4)	1,500.	92.50
	On cover		225.00
d.	Imperf. (P4)	3,500.	

Hair lines on No. 34a are fine colorless lines drawn diagonally across the corners of the stamp.

A12

A13

A14

A15

1862 Wmk. 24

37	A12 3p pale rose	1,600.	260.00
	On cover		475.00
a.	3p deep rose	3,250.	425.00
	On cover		650.00
b.	With white dots under side ornaments	*21,000.*	*8,000.*
d.	As "b," imperf.	3,750.	
39	A13 6p lilac	1,450.	92.50
	On cover		175.00
a.	6p lilac, blued paper	—	800.00
b.	6p lilac, thick paper	—	225.00
c.	6p lilac, wmk. 3 roses & thistle	—	*8,000.*
d.	6p lilac, hair lines (P4) ('64)	1,850.	185.00
	On cover		300.00
e.	As "d," imperf.	3,000.	
f.	As "d," thick paper	2,250.	225.00
g.	As "d," wmk. 3 roses & shamrock		
h.	6p deep lilac (P3)	1,500.	110.00
	On cover		200.00
40	A14 9p straw	2,900.	310.00
	On cover		475.00
a.	9p straw, blued paper		
b.	9p straw, thick paper	3,750.	450.00
c.	9p straw, wmk. 3 roses & thistle		—
d.	9p bister (P2)	3,250.	400.00
	On cover		700.00
e.	9p bister, hair lines (P3)	*14,000.*	*8,000.*
42	A15 1sh green	1,750	175.00
	On cover		260.00
a.	1sh deep green (P1)	2,500.	350.00
	On cover		450.00
b.	As "c," imperf.	*4,000.*	
c.	1sh deep green, with hair lines (P2)	*21,000.*	

Hair lines on Nos. 39b, 39c, 39e, 40c and 42d are fine colorless lines drawn diagonally across the corners of the stamp.

Compare design A14 with A19.

A16

1865 Wmk. 23

43	A16 4p vermilion (P12)	500.00	57.50
	On cover		125.00
	Plate 10	600.00	100.00
	On cover		150.00
	Plate 11	525.00	57.50
	On cover		125.00
	Plate 14	600.00	92.50

		On cover		150.00
a.		4p dull vermilion (P8)	525.00	62.50
		On cover		125.00
		Plate 7	600.00	100.00
		On cover		160.00
		Plates 9, 13	525.00	62.50
		On cover		125.00
b.		Imperf. (P11,12)	1,800.	

A17

(Hyphen after SIX) — A18

A19

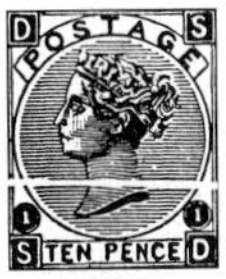

A20

A21

1865 — Wmk. 24

44	A17	3p rose (P4)	1,350.	175.00
		On cover		275.00
a.		Wmk. 3 roses & shamrock	2,900.	900.00
b.		Thick paper	1,350.	200.00
45	A18	6p lilac (P5)	750.00	85.00
		On cover		125.00
a.		6p deep lilac	1,150.	140.00
		On cover		200.00
		Plate 6	2,300.	160.00
		On cover		190.00
b.		Double impression		*11,500.*
c.		Wmk. 3 roses & shamrock (P5)		*800.00*
		As "c," Plate 6		*800.00*
d.		Thick paper	850.00	120.00
46	A19	9p straw (P4)	2,300.	500.00
		On cover		675.00
		Plate 5	*21,000.*	
a.		Wmk. 3 roses & shamrock (P4)	—	*1,150.*
b.		Thick paper	*2,500.*	650.00
47	A20	10p red brn (P1)		*29,000.*
48	A21	1sh green (P4)	1,450.	175.00
		On cover		225.00
a.		Thick paper	1,600.	275.00
b.		Wmk. 3 roses & shamrock		1,150.
c.		Vert. pair, imperf. btwn.		*9,000.*

No. 46, plate 5 is from a proof sheet.

See Nos.49-50, 52-54. Compare design A17 with A27.

(No hyphen after SIX) — A22

A23

1867-80 — Wmk. 25

49	A17	3p rose (P5)	450.00	52.50
		On cover		85.00
a.		3p deep rose	800.00	175.00
		On cover		240.00
		Plate 4	850.00	175.00
		On cover		240.00
		Plate 6	475.00	52.50
		On cover		90.00
		Plate 7	575.00	57.50
		On cover		95.00
		Plate 8	525.00	52.50
		On cover		87.50
		Plate 9	525.00	57.50
		On cover		87.50
		Plate 10	575.00	100.00
		On cover		140.00
b.		Imperf. (P5,6,8,9)	2,750.	
50	A18	6p dull violet (P6)	1,150.	85.00
		On cover		160.00
a.		6p bright violet (P6)	975.00	92.50
		On cover		175.00
51	A22	6p red violet ('69) (P9)	575.00	85.00
		On cover		110.00
a.		6p violet (P9)	575.00	85.00
		On cover		110.00
		Plate 8	525.00	85.00
		On cover		110.00
		Plate 10		*21,500.*
b.		Imperf. (P8, 9)	4,750	3,250.
52	A19	9p bister (P4) ('67)	1,250.	225.00
		On cover		310.00
a.		Imperf. (P4)	5,000.	
53	A20	10p red brown (P1)	2,400.	300.00
		On cover		550.00
		Plate 2	*22,000.*	*8,000.*
a.		10p deep red brown	3,250.	450.00
		On cover		550.00
b.		Imperf. (P1)	5,000.	
54	A21	1sh green (P4)	625.00	37.50
		On cover		60.00
		Plate 5	725.00	40.00
		On cover		60.00
		Plate 6	1,100.	40.00
		On cover		60.00
		Plate 7	1,000.	70.00
		On cover		120.00
a.		1sh deep green	750.00	40.00
		On cover		50.00
b.		Imperf. (P4)	3,250.	1,800.
55	A23	2sh blue (P1)	2,250.	160.00
		On cover		550.00
a.		2sh pale blue	2,900.	210.00
		On cover		550.00
		Plate 3		7,000.
b.		Imperf. (P1)	5,750.	
c.		2sh cobalt blue (P1)	11,500.	2,300.
d.		2sh milky blue (P1)	9,750.	1,350.
56	A23	2sh pale brn (P1) ('80)	*16,000.*	2,900.
		On cover		*11,500.*
a.		Imperf.	13,500.	

No. 51, plate 10 and No. 53, plate 2, are from proof sheets.

A24

1867 — Wmk. 26 — *Perf. 15½x15*

57	A24	5sh rose (P1)	5,250.	625.00
		Plate 2	7,500.	975.00
a.		5sh pale rose	5,250.	625.00
b.		Imperf. (P1)	*9,500.*	

See No. 90. Compare design A24 with A51.

A25

1870 — Engr. — Wmk. 27 — *Perf. 14*

58	A25	½p rose (P5)	100.00	17.50
		On cover		60.00
		Plate 1	225.00	80.00
		On cover		140.00
		Plate 3	175.00	40.00
		On cover		62.50
		Plate 4	140.00	29.00
		On cover		55.00
		Plate 6	100.00	17.50
		On cover		60.00
		Plate 8	280.00	100.00
		On cover		150.00
		Plate 9	4,500.	800.00
		On cover		2,100.
		Plate 10	120.00	17.50
		On cover		60.00
		Plate 11-14	110.00	17.50
		On cover		60.00
		Plate 15	175.00	40.00
		On cover		62.50
		Plate 19	200.00	57.50
		On cover		95.00
		Plate 20	240.00	80.00
		On cover		150.00
a.		Imperf (see footnote)	—	—

Plates 1, 4-6, 8, and 14 are known imperf. Values: from $1,000 unused, $675 used.

A26

A27

A28

A29

Type A28 has a lined background.

1872-73 — Wmk. 25 — Typo.

59	A26	6p brown (P11)	700.00	52.50
		On cover		100.00
		Plate 12		2,900.
a.		6p deep brown (P11)	900.00	90.00
		On cover		140.00
		Plate 12		2,900.
b.		6p pale buff (P11)	625.00	87.50
		On cover		225.00
		Plate 12	2,000.	275.00
		On cover		400.00
60	A26	6p gray (P12) ('73)	1,500.	225.00
		On cover		300.00
a.		Imperf.	*4,000.*	

1873-80

61	A27	3p rose (shades) (P11)	350.00	45.00
		On cover		65.00
		Plates 12, 17, 18	425.00	45.00
		On cover		65.00
		Plate 14	450.00	45.00
		On cover		65.00
		Plates 15-16	350.00	45.00
		On cover		65.00
		Plate 19	350.00	45.00
		On cover		65.00
		Plate 20	500.00	70.00
		On cover		125.00
62	A28	6p gray (P15, 16)	425.00	60.00
		On cover		95.00
		Plates 13, 14	425.00	60.00
		On cover		95.00
		Plate 17	675.00	140.00
		On cover		240.00
63	A28	6p buff (P13)		*14,500.*
64	A29	1sh pale green (P12, 13)	550.00	110.00
		On cover		225.00
		Plates 10, 11	625.00	110.00
		On cover		175.00
		Plate 14		*23,000.*
a.		1sh deep green (P8, 9)	700.00	110.00
		On cover		175.00
65	A29	1sh sal (P13) ('80)	3,300.	550.00
		On cover		750.00

No. 64, plate 14, is from a proof sheet.

See Nos. 83, 86-87. For surcharges see Nos. 94-95. For overprints see Nos. O6, O30.

A30

1875 — Wmk. 28

66	A30	2½p claret (P1, 2)	525.00	85.00
		On cover		140.00
		Plate 3	800.00	125.00
		On cover		190.00
a.		Bluish paper (P1)	725.00	125.00
		On cover		190.00
		Plate 2	*5,750.*	1,350.
		On cover		1,800.
		Plate 3		*4,600.*
		On cover		*11,500.*
b.		Lettered "LH-FL"	*14,500.*	2,000.
		On cover		5,500.

1876-80 — Wmk. 29

67	A30	2½p claret (P4-9, 11-16)	425.00	52.50
		On cover		80.00
		Plate 3	975.00	100.00
		On cover		140.00
		Plate 10	475.00	70.00
		On cover		110.00
		Plate 17	1,250.	250.00
		On cover		375.00
68	A30	2½p ultra ('80) (P19, 20)	400.00	40.00
		On cover		52.50
		Plate 17	400.00	57.50
		On cover		75.00
		Plate 18	425.00	40.00
		On cover		55.00

A31

A32

1876-80 — Wmk. 23

69	A31	4p vermilion (P15)	1,800.	450.00
		On cover		700.00
		Plate 16		*22,500.*
70	A31	4p pale ol grn ('77) (P16)	925.00	260.00
		On cover		400.00
		Plate 15	925.00	275.00
		On cover		425.00
		Plate 17		*15,000.*
a.		Imperf (P15)	—	
71	A31	4p gray brn (P17) ('80)	1,450.	375.00
		On cover		675.00
72	A32	8p brn lilac (P1) ('76)	7,500.	
73	A32	8p org (P1) ('76)	1,150.	325.00
		On cover		410.00

No. 72 was never placed in use.

No. 69, plate 16, is from proof sheets.

A33

A34

1878 — Wmk. 26 — *Perf. 15½x15*

74	A33	10sh slate (P1)	40,000.	2,500.
75	A34	£1 brn lilac (P1)	50,000.	3,750.

See Nos. 91-92. Compare design A34 with A52.

A35

A36

A37

A38

A39

A40

1880-81 — Wmk. 30 — *Perf. 14*

78	A35	½p deep green	45.00	11.50
		On cover		24.00
a.		Imperf.	1,750.	
b.		No watermark	*4,600.*	
c.		½p green	45.00	17.50
79	A36	1p red brown	22.50	11.50
		On cover		21.00
a.		Imperf.	1,800.	
b.		Wmk. 29, error		
80	A37	1½p red brown	175.00	45.00
		On cover		140.00
81	A38	2p lilac rose	225.00	90.00
		On cover		175.00
a.		2p deep rose	225.00	90.00
82	A30	2½p ultra ('81) (P23)	375.00	27.50
		On cover		47.50
		Plate 21	425.00	35.00
		On cover		57.50
		Plate 22	375.00	35.00
		On cover		52.50
a.		Imperf. (P23)	—	
83	A27	3p rose ('81) (P21)	425.00	80.00
		On cover		140.00
		Plate 20	575.00	140.00
		On cover		210.00
84	A31	4p gray brown (P17, 18)	375.00	62.50
		On cover		150.00
85	A39	5p dp indigo ('81)	650.00	110.00
		On cover		225.00
a.		Imperf.	*3,500.*	*2,750.*
86	A28	6p gray (P18)	375.00	70.00
		On cover		110.00
		Plate 17	425.00	70.00
		On cover		110.00
87	A29	1sh salmon (P14) ('81)	475.00	140.00
		On cover		400.00
		Plate 13	575.00	140.00
		On cover		400.00
		Nos. 78-87 (10)	3,142.	648.00

The 1sh in purple was not issued. Value, unused, $4,500.

See No. 98. For overprints see Nos. O2-O3, O37, O45, O55.

Compare design A35 with A54.

1881

88	A40	1p lilac (14 dots in each angle)	220.	32.50
		On cover		52.50
89	A40	1p lilac (16 dots in each angle)	2.90	2.25
		On cover		6.00
a.		Printed on both sides	800.	
b.		Imperf., pair	2,750.	
c.		Unwmkd.	3,500.	
d.		Bluish paper	4,250.	
e.		Printed on the gummed side	750.	

For overprint see No. O4.

1882-83 **Wmk. 31**

90 A24 5sh rose, *bluish*(P4) 19,000. 4,000.
a. White paper 15,000. 3,000.
91 A33 10sh slate, *bluish*(P1) 65,000. 4,750.
a. White paper 65,000. 3,750.
92 A34 £1 brown lilac, *bluish*(P1) 85,000. 8,500.
a. White paper 90,000. 7,500.

A41

1882 **Wmk. Two Anchors (31)**

93 A41 £5 brt orange (P1) 10,000. 4,250.
a. £5 pale dull orange, *bluish* *42,500.* *11,500.*
b. £5 bright orange, *bluish* *42,500.* *11,500.*

The paper of No. 93b is less bluish than that of No. 93a, and it is a later printing.

Types of 1873-80 Surcharged in Carmine

1883 **Wmk. 30**

94 A27 3p on 3p violet 475.00 150.00
On cover 390.00
95 A28 6p on 6p violet 525.00 150.00
On cover 375.00
a. Double surcharge *9,250.*

A44

1883 **Wmk. 31**

96 A44 2sh6p lilac 450.00 140.00
a. Bluish paper *4,250.* *1,150.*

See British Offices Abroad for overprints on types A44-A133.
These overprints include "M.E.F.," "B.A.," "B.M.A.," "E.A.F.," "CHINA," "Morocco Agencies," "TANGIER," "LEVANT," "PARAS," and "PIASTRE(S)."

A45

A46

A47

A48

A49

A50

1883-84 **Wmk. 30**

98 A35 ½p slate blue ('84) 22.50 8.00
On cover 13.50
99 A45 1½p lilac ('84) 100.00 40.00
On cover 110.00
100 A46 2p lilac ('84) 175.00 75.00
On cover 125.00
101 A47 2½p lilac ('84) 80.00 14.00
On cover 27.50
102 A48 3p lilac ('84) 200.00 100.00
On cover 140.00
103 A49 4p green ('84) 450.00 200.00
On cover 290.00
104 A45 5p green ('84) 450.00 200.00
On cover 290.00
105 A46 6p green ('84) 500.00 225.00
On cover 310.00
106 A50 9p green 925.00 425.00
On cover 1,750.
107 A48 1sh green ('84) 1,000. 225.00
On cover 510.00
Nos. 98-107 (10) 3,902. 1,512.

Values are for copies of good color. Faded copies sell for much less.

No. 104 with line instead of period under "d" was not regularly issued. Value, $8,500.

Nos. 98-105 and 107 exist imperf. Values from $950 to $1,150 each for Nos. 98-105, $2,300 for No. 107.

For overprints see Nos. O5, O7, O27-O29.

A51

A52

1884 **Wmk. 31**

108 A51 5sh carmine rose 875.00 210.00
a. Bluish paper 9,500. 3,500.
b. 5sh deep crimson 800.00 210.00
109 A52 10sh ultra 1,725. 525.00
a. 10sh cobalt *25,000.* 7,000.
b. Bluish paper *32,500.* *7,250.*
c. As "a," bluish paper *40,000.* *11,500.*

For overprints see Nos. O8-O9.

A53

1884 **Wmk. 30**

110 A53 £1 brown violet 25,000. 2,400.

See Nos. 123-124. For overprints see Nos. O10, O13, O15.

Queen Victoria Jubilee Issue

A54

A55

A56

A57

A58

A59

A60

A61

A62

A63

A64

A65

Two types of 5p:
I — Squarish dots beside "d."
II — Tiny vertical dashes beside "d."

1887-92 **Wmk. 30**

111 A54 ½p vermilion 1.75 1.10
On cover 7.00
a. Printed on both sides
b. Double impression 11,500.
c. Imperf. 1,850.
d. Printed on gummed side 1,900. 1,500.
112 A55 1½p violet & grn 17.50 8.00
On cover 30.00
a. Double impression of violet 6,900.
113 A56 2p grn & car rose 32.50 13.50
On cover 28.00
a. 2p green & vermilion 400.00 250.00
On cover 975.00
114 A57 2½p violet, *blue* 25.00 3.50
On cover 7.50
a. Imperf. 3,500.
b. Printed on gummed side 3,750.
115 A58 3p violet, *yellow* 25.00 3.75
On cover 35.00
a. 3p violet, *orange* 875.00 550.00
On cover 1,500.
b. Imperf. 5,100.
116 A59 4p brown & grn 35.00 15.00
On cover 40.00
117 A60 4½p car rose & grn ('92) 11.50 47.50
On cover 85.00
118 A61 5p lilac & bl, II 40.00 12.50
On cover 45.00
a. Type I 700.00 85.00
On cover 225.00
119 A62 6p violet, *rose* 35.00 11.50
On cover 85.00
120 A63 9p blue & lilac 70.00 45.00
On cover 225.00
121 A64 10p car rose & lilac ('90) 52.50 42.50
On cover 260.00
a. Imperf. 2,000. *6,900.*
b. 10p scarlet & lilac 70.00 52.50
On cover 120.00
c. 10p dp carmine & red lilac 450.00 225.00
122 A65 1sh green 225.00 70.00
On cover 150.00
Nos. 111-122 (12) 570.75 273.85

See Nos. 125-126. For overprints see Nos. O11-O12, O14, O16-O18, O31-O36, O38, O44, O46-O48, O54, O56-O58, O65-O66.

1888 **Wmk. Three Orbs (29)**

123 A53 £1 brown violet 52,500. 3,750.

1891 **Wmk. 30**

124 A53 £1 green 3,150. 700.00

1900 **Wmk. 30**

125 A54 ½p blue green 2.00 *2.25*
On cover 6.75
a. Imperf *4,000.*
b. Printed on gum side —
126 A65 1sh car rose & green 57.50 *140.00*
On cover 850.00

No. 125 in bright blue is a color changeling.

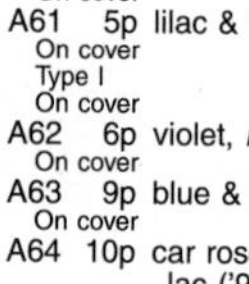

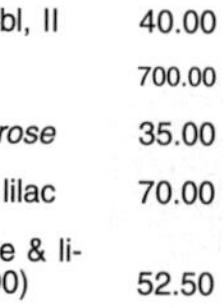

King Edward VII
A66 A67

A68

A69

A70

A71

A72

A73

A74

A75

A76

A77

A78

1902-11 **Wmk. 30** ***Perf. 14***

The stamps of King Edward VII were printed by three contactors. De La Rue (DLR) held the contract from Jan. 1, 1902, through Dec. 31, 1910. De La Rue was replaced by Harrison & Sons (H) on Jan. 1, 1911. From July, 1911, the bi-colored issues were produced by Somerset House (S), while Harrison continued to produce most of the monocolor stamps.

De La Rue printings were made on both ordinary and chalky papers and tend to be more finely printed than those of either of its successors.

The Harrison printings are only on ordinary paper. The stamps perforated 15x14 were only printed by Harrison & Sons and can serve as a comparison to identify printings.

The Somerset House printings are all on ordinary paper, except the 6p bright magenta on chalky paper (#135f) and the 6p dull purple on Dickinson Coated paper (#135j).

ORDINARY PAPER

127 A66 ½p gray green (DLR) 2.25 1.75
Never hinged 3.25
On cover 2.90
a. ½p blue green (DLR) 2.25 1.75
Never hinged 3.25
On cover 2.90
b. ½p deep bluish green '11 (H) 12.50 6.50
Never hinged 18.00
On cover 7.50
c. ½p very pale bluish grn ('11) (H) 45.00 45.00
Never hinged 70.00
On cover 65.00
d. ½p bright green (fine impression; '11) (H) 275.00 160.00
Never hinged 410.00
On cover —
128 A66 1p scarlet (DLR) 2.20 1.60
Never hinged 3.25
On cover 2.90
a. 1p rose red ('11) (H) 9.25 *14.00*
Never hinged 13.50
On cover 19.00
b. 1p rose carmine ('11) (H) 62.50 35.00
Never hinged 95.00
On cover 50.00
c. 1p aniline rose ('11) (H) 210.00 160.00
Never hinged 250.00
On cover —
d. 1p aniline pink ('11) (H) 625.00 350.00

Never hinged 1,000.
On cover —
e. Booklet pane of 6 50.00
f. No watermark ('11) (H) 45.00 45.00
Never hinged 60.00
g. Imperf., pair (DLR) *20,000.*
129 A67 1½p vio & green (DLR) 42.50 20.00
Never hinged 62.50
On cover 32.50
a. 1½p slate purple & green 45.00 20.00
Never hinged 67.50
On cover 32.50
b. 1½p reddish pur & bright grn ('11) (S) 45.00 40.00
Never hinged 75.00
On cover 57.50
c. 1½p dull purple & green ('12) (S) 27.50 *32.50*
Never hinged 40.00
On cover 60.00
130 A68 2p yel grn & car (DLR) 52.50 21.00
Never hinged 82.50
On cover 35.00
a. 2p gray grn & car red '04 (DLR) 55.00 26.00
Never hinged 85.00
On cover 40.00
b. 2p deep grn & red ('11) (S) 29.00 22.50
Never hinged 42.50
On cover 55.00
c. 2p deep grn & car ('11-'12) (S) 29.00 22.50
Never hinged 42.50
On cover 55.00
131 A66 2½p ultra (DLR) 22.50 11.50
Never hinged 32.50
On cover 22.50
a. 2½p pale ultra (DLR) 22.50 11.50
Never hinged 32.50
On cover 22.50
b. 2½p bright blue ('11) (H) 52.50 35.00
Never hinged 95.00
On cover 57.50
132 A69 3p dull pur, *org yel* (DLR) 45.00 14.00
Never hinged 80.00
On cover 35.00
a. 3p deep pur, *org yel* (DLR) 45.00 14.00
Never hinged 80.00
On cover 35.00
b. 3p purple, *lemon* ('11) (H) 75.00 *210.00*
Never hinged 105.00
On cover 575.00
c. 3p gray, *lemon* ('11) (H) *3,500.*
Never hinged *4,200.*
133 A70 4p gray brn & grn (DLR) 57.50 35.00
Never hinged 110.00
On cover 50.00
a. 4p choc brn & green (DLR) 57.50 35.00
Never hinged 100.00
On cover 45.00
134 A71 5p dull pur & ultra (DLR) 64.00 22.50
Never hinged 87.50
On cover 57.50
a. 5p dull reddish pur & brt blue ('11) (S) 35.00 22.50
Never hinged 54.00
On cover 75.00
b. 5p deep reddish pur & brt blue ('11) (S) 35.00 22.50
Never hinged 54.00
On cover 75.00
135 A66 6p pale dull vio (DLR) 40.00 20.00
Never hinged 55.00
On cover 50.00
a. 6p slate purple (DLR) 40.00 20.00
Never hinged 55.00
On cover 50.00
b. 6p red violet ('11) (S) 40.00 30.00
Never hinged 62.50
On cover 60.00
c. 6p dark violet ('12) (S) 40.00 *40.00*
Never hinged 62.50
On cover 65.00
d. 6p deep plum ('13) (S) 32.50 *80.00*
Never hinged 45.00
On cover 140.00
e. 6p royal purple ('11) (S) 57.50 *100.00*
Never hinged 95.00
On cover 190.00
f. 6p dull purple, "Dickinson" coated paper ('13) (S) 160.00 160.00
Never hinged 325.00
On cover —
g. No cross on crown, *from* 575.00
136 A72 9p ultra & dull vio (DLR) 92.50 70.00
Never hinged 175.00
On cover 200.00
a. 9p ultra & slate vio (DLR) 92.50 70.00
Never hinged 175.00
On cover 200.00
b. 9p lt bl & reddish pur ('11) (S) 92.50 85.00
Never hinged 160.00
On cover 200.00
c. 9p deep brt bl & deep dull reddish pur (S) 92.50 85.00
Never hinged 160.00
On cover 200.00
d. 9p blue & dull reddish pur ('11) (S) 70.00 70.00
Never hinged 125.00
On cover 200.00
e. 9p blue & deep plum ('13) (S) 70.00 70.00
Never hinged 125.00
On cover 200.00
f. 9p cobalt bl & slate vio ('11) (S) 110.00 110.00
Never hinged 150.00
On cover 200.00
137 A73 10p car & dull pur (DLR) 92.50 70.00
Never hinged 175.00
On cover 210.00
a. 10p scarlet & dull pur (S) 92.50 85.00
Never hinged 125.00
On cover 210.00
b. 10p aniline pink & dull reddish pur ('11) (S) 290.00 260.00
Never hinged 400.00
On cover 375.00
c. 10p car & dull reddish pur ('12) (S) 80.00 70.00
Never hinged 100.00
On cover 260.00
d. As No. 137, no cross on crown, *from* 350.00 225.00
Never hinged 525.00
138 A74 1sh car & dull grn (DLR) 92.50 40.00
Never hinged 140.00
On cover 140.00
a. 1sh scar & dark green ('11) (S) 92.50 60.00
Never hinged 125.00
On cover 140.00
b. 1sh scar & deep dark grn ('11) (S) 70.00 40.00
Never hinged 105.00
On cover 125.00
c. 1sh car & lt green ('12) (S) 57.50 40.00
Never hinged 90.00
On cover 140.00

Wmk. 31

139 A75 2sh6p lilac (DLR) 250.00 140.00
Never hinged 550.00
On cover 675.00
a. 2sh6p dark violet ('11) (S) 260.00 175.00
Never hinged 550.00
On cover 600.00
b. 2sh6p dull grayish pur ('11) (S) 625.00 400.00
Never hinged 950.00
On cover —
c. 2sh6p dull reddish pur ('11) (S) 225.00 160.00
Never hinged 575.00
On cover 850.00
140 A76 5sh car rose (DLR) 400.00 225.00
Never hinged 600.00
On cover 800.00
a. 5sh deep brt carmine (DLR) 400.00 225.00
Never hinged 600.00
On cover 800.00
b. 5sh carmine (S) 400.00 225.00
Never hinged 600.00
On cover 800.00
141 A77 10sh ultra (DLR) 700.00 525.00
Never hinged 1,250.
On cover —
a. 10sh bright blue ('12) (S) 850.00 575.00
Never hinged 1,500.
On cover —

Wmk. Three Imperial Crowns (30)

142 A78 £1 blue green (DLR) 1,750. 750.00
Never hinged 2,500.
On cover —
b. £1 deep green ('11) (S) 1,750. 800.00
Never hinged 2,400.
On cover —
Nos. 127-138 (12) 605.95 327.35

CHALKY PAPER

129d A67 1½p pale pur & green ('05) (DLR) 45.00 21.00
Never hinged 65.00
On cover 32.50
e. 1½p slate pur & bl grn (DLR) 45.00 19.00
Never hinged 65.00
On cover 35.00
130d A68 2p pale gray grn & car red ('06) (DLR) 55.00 32.50
Never hinged 80.00
On cover 54.00
e. 2p pale gray grn & scar ('09) (DLR) 45.00 27.50
Never hinged 90.00
On cover 50.00
f. 2p dull bl grn & car ('07) (DLR) 80.00 50.00
Never hinged 150.00
On cover 100.00
132d A69 3p dull pur, *org yel* ('06) (DLR) 175.00 80.00
Never hinged 275.00
On cover 100.00
e. 3p pale reddish pur, *org yel* ('06) (DLR) 175.00 70.00
Never hinged 275.00
On cover 90.00
f. 3p dull reddish pur, *yel, lemon back* (DLR) 175.00 *85.00*
Never hinged 275.00
On cover —
g. 3p pale pur, *lemon* (DLR) *40.00* 17.50
Never hinged *57.50*
On cover 35.00
h. 3p purple, *lemon* (DLR) *40.00* 17.50
Never hinged *57.50*
On cover 35.00
133b A70 4p choc brn & grn (DLR) 57.50 35.00
Never hinged 85.00
On cover 85.00
c. 4p choc brn & deep green ('06) (DLR) 45.00 21.00
Never hinged 65.00
On cover 45.00
134c A71 5p dull pur & ultra ('06) (DLR) 62.50 22.50
Never hinged 92.50
On cover 55.00
d. 5p slate pur & ultra ('06) (DLR) 57.50 22.50
Never hinged 85.00
On cover 52.50
135h A66 6p pale dull pur ('06) (DLR) 40.00 21.00
Never hinged 57.50
On cover 52.50
i. 6p dull purple ('06) (DLR) 40.00 21.00
Never hinged 57.50
On cover 52.50
j. 6p bright magenta ('11) (S) 6,000.
Never hinged *7,750.*
136g A72 9p ultra & dull vio ('05) (DLR) 92.50 70.00
Never hinged 150.00
On cover 200.00
h. 9p ultra & slate vio ('05) (DLR) 92.50 70.00
Never hinged 150.00
On cover 210.00
137e A73 10p car & dull pur ('06) (DLR) 92.50 70.00
Never hinged 150.00
On cover 210.00
f. 10p car & slate vio ('06) (DLR) 92.50 70.00
Never hinged 150.00
On cover 210.00
g. 10p scar & dull pur ('10) (DLR) 92.50 70.00
Never hinged 150.00
On cover 210.00
h. Chalky paper, no cross on crown (DLR), *from* 350.00 225.00
Never hinged 600.00
138d A74 1sh car & dull grn ('05) (DLR) 92.50 40.00
Never hinged 150.00
On cover 140.00
e. 1sh scar & dull green ('10) (DLR) 92.50 57.50
Never hinged 150.00
On cover 140.00

Wmk. 31

139d A75 2sh6p pale dull pur ('05) (DLR) 260.00 175.00
Never hinged 500.00
On cover 925.00
e. 2sh6p deep dull pur (DLR) 260.00 175.00
Never hinged 500.00
On cover 925.00

See Nos. 143, 144, 146-150. For overprints see Nos. O19-O26, O39-O43, O49-O53, O59-O64, O67-O83.

See British Offices Abroad for overprints on types A44-A133. These overprints include "M.E.F.," "B.A.," "B.M.A.," "E.A.F.," "CHINA," "Morocco Agencies," "TANGIER," "LEVANT," "PARAS," and "PIASTRE(S)."

1904 **Wmk. 30**

143 A66 ½p pale yel grn (DLR) 2.25 1.75
Never hinged 2.75
On cover 2.90
a. ½p yellow green (DLR) 2.25 1.75
Never hinged 2.75
On cover 2.90
b. Booklet pane of 5 + label (DLR, H) 400.00
c. Booklet pane of 6 (DLR, H) 37.50
d. Double impression (H) *29,000.*
e. Imperf., pair (H) *15,000.*

Edward VII — A79

1909-10

144 A70 4p pale orange (DLR) 22.50 17.50
Never hinged 30.00
On cover 40.00
a. 4p orange red (DLR) 22.50 17.50
Never hinged 32.50
On cover 40.00
b. 4p brown orange (DLR) 175.00 150.00
Never hinged 225.00
On cover —
c. 4p bright orange ('11) (H) 75.00 62.50
Never hinged 110.00
On cover 250.00
145 A79 7p gray ('10) (DLR) 11.50 *21.00*
Never hinged 14.00
On cover 200.00
a. 7p deep gray blk ('10) (DLR) 125.00 *110.00*
Never hinged 160.00
On cover 300.00
b. 7p slate gray ('12) (S) 17.50 *25.00*
Never hinged 25.00
On cover 200.00

1911 ***Perf. 15x14***

146 A66 ½p dull yel green (H) 45.00 *50.00*
Never hinged 65.00
On cover 110.00
a. ½p deep dull green (H) 45.00 *50.00*
Never hinged 65.00
On cover 110.00
147 A66 1p carmine rose (H) 17.50 17.50
Never hinged 30.00
On cover 35.00
a. 1p pale car rose (H) 25.00 17.50
Never hinged 37.50
On cover 35.00
b. 1p rose red (H) 47.50 30.00
Never hinged 70.00
On cover 47.50
148 A66 2½p brt ultra (H) 25.00 17.50
Never hinged 55.00
On cover 32.50
a. 2½p dull blue (H) 25.00 *17.50*
Never hinged 55.00
On cover 32.50
149 A69 3p violet, *yellow* (H) 52.50 17.50
Never hinged 85.00
On cover 45.00
a. 3p gray, *lemon* (H) *3,000.*
Never hinged *3,500.*
150 A70 4p orange (H) 35.00 17.50
Never hinged 55.00
On cover 75.00
Nos. 146-150 (5) 175.00 120.00

King George V
A80 A81

Perf. 15x14

1911, June 22 **Wmk. 30**

Original Die, Type 1

½p: on the right-hand dolphin, the three uppermost scales form a complete triangle.

1p: the ribbon on the wreath at the right of the crown is crossed by two complete lines from top to bottom.

151 A80 ½p yellow green 5.75 4.50
Never hinged 8.25
a. Booklet pane of 6 62.50
b. Perf. 14 (error) *14,000.* 700.00
Never hinged —
c. ½p bluish green 400.00 210.00
Never hinged 550.00
152 A81 1p carmine 5.25 3.00
Never hinged 7.50
a. Booklet pane of 6 62.50
b. Perf. 14 (error) — —
Never hinged —
c. 1p pale carmine 16.00 3.50
Never hinged 25.00
d. As "c," booklet pane of 6 *125.00*
e. As "c," no cross on crown 400.00 250.00
Never hinged —

Original Die, Type 2

½p: on the right-hand dolphin, the three uppermost scales do not complete the triangle, with the line on the left side of the top scale missing entirely.

1p: the ribbon on the wreath at the right of the crown is crossed by one complete line from top to bottom, the other being interrupted.

151d A80 ½p bright green 9.00 1.75
Never hinged 17.50
f. ½p yellow green 13.50 1.75
Never hinged 27.50
g. ½p bluish green 190.00 110.00
Never hinged 300.00
152g A81 1p carmine 8.00 3.50
Never hinged 15.00
h. 1p pale carmine 11.50 4.50
Never hinged 18.00
i. As "h," no cross on crown 450.00 300.00
Never hinged —
j. 1p rose pink 110.00 45.00
Never hinged 160.00
k. 1p scarlet 50.00 21.00
Never hinged 100.00
l. 1p aniline scarlet 200.00 110.00
Never hinged 340.00

1912, Jan. 1 **Re-engraved**

153 A80 ½p yellow green 10.00 4.50
Never hinged 15.00
a. No cross on crown 110.00 57.50
Never hinged 175.00
b. ½p green 10.00 4.50
Never hinged 15.00
c. ½p deep green 17.50 9.25
Never hinged 21.00
154 A81 1p scarlet 6.00 2.25
Never hinged 9.00
a. No cross on crown 92.50 57.50
Never hinged 150.00
b. 1p aniline scarlet 200.00 110.00
Never hinged 240.00
c. As "b," no cross on crown 1,100.

In the re-engraved stamps the lines of the hair and beard are clearer. The re-engraved ½p has 3 lines of shading instead of 4 between the point of neck and frame; in the 1p the body of the lion is nearly covered by lines of shading.

1912, Aug. **Wmk. 33** ***Perf. 15x14***

Die I (Before Re-engraving)

155 A80 ½p yellow green 45.00 45.00
Never hinged 62.50
a. Booklet pane of 6 270.00
Never hinged 525.00
156 A81 1p scarlet 35.00 35.00
Never hinged 50.00
a. Booklet pane of 6 210.00
Never hinged 375.00

Die II (Re-engraved)

157 A80 ½p yellow green 8.00 3.50
Never hinged 17.50
a. No cross on crown 110.00 57.50
Never hinged 160.00
158 A81 1p scarlet 9.25 3.50
Never hinged 15.00
a. No cross on crown 110.00 57.50
Never hinged 160.00

1912-21 **Wmk. 32**

158A A80 ½p yellow green 14.00 9.25
Never hinged 21.00
d. ½p green 14.00 9.25
Never hinged 21.00
e. Imperf., pair 300.00

	Never hinged	400.00	
f.	No cross on crown	110.00	70.00
	Never hinged	225.00	
158B	A81 1p scarlet	20.00	11.50
	Never hinged	30.00	
g.	Imperf., pair	300.00	
	Never hinged	400.00	
f.	No cross on crown	140.00	57.50
	Never hinged	210.00	

A82

A83

A84

A85

A86

A87

A88

A89

King George V — A90

"Britannia Rule the Waves" A91

TWO PENCE:
Die I — Four horizontal lines above the head. Heavy colored lines above and below the bottom tablet. The inner frame line is closer to the central design than it is to the outer frame line.
Die II — Three lines above the head. Thinner lines above and below the bottom tablet. The inner frame line is midway between the central design and the outer frame line.

1912-13 Wmk. 33 *Perf. 15x14*

159	A82 ½p green ('13)	1.10	1.10
	Never hinged	1.60	
a.	Double impression	*22,500.*	
b.	Booklet pane of 6	15.00	
	Never hinged	22.50	
c.	½p deep green	5.50	2.25
	Never hinged	9.00	
d.	½p yellow green	6.50	3.50
	Never hinged	10.00	
e.	½p blue green	45.00	29.00
	Never hinged	57.50	
f.	½p very yellow green ('14)	*4,500.*	
	Never hinged	*6,000.*	
160	A83 1p scarlet	1.10	1.10
	Never hinged	1.90	
a.	Booklet pane of 6	15.00	
	Never hinged	25.00	
b.	Tete beche pair	*67,500.*	
c.	1p vermilion	5.75	2.90
	Never hinged	8.50	
d.	1p pale rose red	17.50	2.90
	Never hinged	24.00	
e.	1p carmine red	12.50	5.75
	Never hinged	20.00	
f.	1p scarlet vermilion	140.00	57.50
	Never hinged	175.00	
161	A84 1½p red brown	4.50	1.75
	Never hinged	7.00	
a.	"PENCF"	210.00	175.00
	Never hinged	210.00	
b.	1½p orange brown	24.00	19.00
	Never hinged	29.00	
c.	1½p chestnut	5.75	1.10
	Never hinged	9.75	
d.	As "c," "PENCF"	125.00	95.00
	Never hinged	160.00	
e.	1½p chocolate brown	10.50	2.25
	Never hinged	17.50	
f.	As "e," Unwmkd.	200.00	125.00
	Never hinged	300.00	
g.	Booklet pane of 6	30.00	
	Never hinged	42.50	
h.	Booklet pane of 4 + 2 labels	525.00	
162	A85 2p deep org (I)	7.00	3.50
	Never hinged	9.00	
a.	2p deep orange (II) ('21)	5.75	4.25
	Never hinged	9.50	
b.	Booklet pane of 6 (I)	67.50	
	Never hinged	100.00	
c.	Booklet pane of 6 (II)	110.00	
	Never hinged	175.00	
d.	2p bright orange (I)	5.75	3.50
	Never hinged	9.50	
e.	2p orange yellow (I)	9.00	3.50
	Never hinged	15.00	
163	A86 2½p ultramarine	14.00	4.50
	Never hinged	24.00	
a.	2½ cobalt blue	14.00	4.50
	Never hinged	24.00	
b.	2½ bright blue ('14)	14.00	4.50
	Never hinged	24.00	
c.	2½ indigo blue ('20)	1,900.	1,100.
	Never hinged	3,250.	
d.	2½ Prussian blue	800.00	700.00
	Never hinged	1,200.	
164	A87 3p bluish violet ('13)	8.00	2.25
	Never hinged	14.00	
a.	3p violet	8.00	3.50
	Never hinged	14.00	
b.	3p reddish violet	14.00	2.25
	Never hinged	21.00	
165	A88 4p slate green	17.50	2.25
	Never hinged	26.00	
a.	4p pale gray green	29.00	5.75
	Never hinged	40.00	
b.	4p deep gray green ('13)	40.00	11.50
	Never hinged	60.00	
166	A89 5p yellow brown	17.50	5.75
	Never hinged	26.00	
a.	Unwmkd.	575.00	
	Never hinged	*850.00*	
b.	5p brown ('13)	17.50	5.75
	Never hinged	26.00	
c.	5p bister brown	125.00	57.50
	Never hinged	215.00	
167	A89 6p rose lilac	17.50	8.00
	Never hinged	30.00	
a.	6p dull violet ('13)	30.00	11.50
	Never hinged	35.00	
b.	Perf. 14	105.00	*125.00*
	Never hinged	125.00	
c.	6p dp reddish purple	30.00	5.75
	Never hinged	50.00	
168	A89 7p ol grn ('13)	22.50	11.50
	Never hinged	32.50	
a.	7p bronze green ('15)	70.00	29.00
	Never hinged	110.00	
b.	7p sage green ('17)	70.00	17.50
	Never hinged	110.00	
169	A89 8p black, *yellow* ('13)	37.50	12.50
	Never hinged	65.00	
a.	8p black, *buff*, granite ('17)	45.00	17.50
	Never hinged	62.50	
170	A90 9p black brown ('13)	22.50	6.75
	Never hinged	32.50	
171	A90 10p light blue ('13)	25.00	22.50
	Never hinged	42.50	
a.	10p bright blue	80.00	29.00
	Never hinged	140.00	
172	A90 1sh bister ('13)	24.00	4.50
	Never hinged	35.00	
a.	1sh bister brown	40.00	14.00
	Never hinged	65.00	
	Nos. 159-172 (14)	219.70	87.95

No. 167 is on chalky paper.
The distinctive yellow green ink used in printing No. 159f, also called "Cyprus" green, is fluorescent under UV light, unlike the inks used in printing other ½p varieties.
See Nos. 177-178, 183, 187-200, 210, 212-220.
Compare design A83 with A97.

See British Offices Abroad for overprints on types A44-A133. These overprints include "M.E.F.," "B.A.," "B.M.A.," "E.A.F.," "CHINA," "Morocco Agencies," "TANGIER," "LEVANT," "PARAS," and "PIASTRE(S)."

Waterlow Brothers & Layton Printing (1913)

Measure 22mm vertically. Perforation holes are larger and evenly spaced.

1913 Engr. Wmk. 34 *Perf. 11x12*

173	A91 2sh6p dark brown	275.00	190.00
	Never hinged	390.00	
b.	2sh6p black brown	260.00	160.00
	Never hinged	375.00	
174	A91 5sh rose car	375.00	310.00
	Never hinged	900.00	
175	A91 10sh indigo blue	625.00	450.00
	Never hinged	1,400.	
176	A91 £1 green	2,100.	1,150.
	Never hinged	4,200.	
a.	£1 dull blue green	2,100.	1,250.
	Never hinged	4,200.	
	Nos. 173-176 (4)	3,375.	2,100.

De La Rue & Co. Printing (1915)

Measure 22mm vertically. Gum tends to be yellowish and patchy. The top right and top left perf teeth are wider than the others. Perforation holes are smaller.

1915 Engr. Wmk. 34 *Perf. 11x12*

173a	A91 2sh6p lt brn (worn plate)	260.00	220.00
	Never hinged	325.00	
173c	A91 2sh6p dp yel brn	290.00	225.00
	Never hinged	500.00	
173d	A91 2sh6p yel brn	260.00	225.00
	Never hinged	450.00	
173e	A91 2sh6p sepia brn	260.00	225.00
	Never hinged	400.00	
174a	A91 5sh br carmine	425.00	350.00
	Never hinged	575.00	
174b	A91 5sh carmine	300.00	250.00
	Never hinged	575.00	
174c	A91 5sh pale carmine (worn plate)	525.00	325.00
	Never hinged	800.00	
175a	A91 10sh light blue	1,800.	800.00
	Never hinged	2,250.	
175b	A91 10sh blue	1,750.	800.00
	Never hinged	2,250.	
175c	A91 10sh deep blue	2,200.	1,000.
	Never hinged	3,000.	

See Nos. 179-181, 222-224.

1913 Wmk. 32 Typo. *Perf. 15x14*
Coil Stamps

177	A82 ½p green	175.00	*210.00*
	Never hinged	250.00	
178	A83 1p scarlet	260.00	*260.00*
	Never hinged	375.00	

Seahorses Types of 1913-15

Bradbury, Wilkinson & Co. Printing (1918-19)

Measure 22.5-23mm vertically. Most examples have a small dot of color at top center, outside of frameline. Perforation holes are larger and evenly spaced.

1919 Engr. Wmk. 34 *Perf. 11x12*

179	A91 2sh6p olive brown	115.00	75.00
	Never hinged	225.00	
a.	2sh6p gray brown	125.00	75.00
	Never hinged	225.00	
b.	2sh6p chocolate brown	140.00	80.00
	Never hinged	260.00	
c.	2sh6p reddish brown	140.00	80.00
	Never hinged	260.00	
180	A91 5sh car rose	290.00	125.00
	Never hinged	325.00	
181	A91 10sh blue	425.00	180.00
	Never hinged	500.00	
	Nos. 179-181 (3)	830.00	380.00

The retouched stamps usually have a dot above the middle of the top frame. They are 22¾mm high, whereas Nos. 173-176 are 22mm high.

Type of 1912-13

1922 Typo. Wmk. 33 *Perf. 15x14*

183	A90 9p olive green	120.00	35.00
	Never hinged	250.00	

British Empire Exhibition Issue

British Lion and George V A92

Wmk. 35

1924, Apr. 23 Engr. *Perf. 14*

185	A92 1p vermilion	11.50	12.50
	Never hinged	17.50	
186	A92 1½p dark brown	17.50	17.50
	Never hinged	26.00	

See Nos. 203-204.

Types of 1912-13 Issue

1924 Typo. *Perf. 15x14*

187	A82 ½p green	1.10	1.10
	Never hinged	1.50	
a.	Wmk. sideways	7.00	3.75
	Never hinged	13.00	
b.	Booklet pane of 6	12.00	
	Never hinged	18.00	
c.	Double impression	*8,750.*	
188	A83 1p scarlet	1.10	1.10
	Never hinged	1.40	
a.	Wmk. sideways	17.50	17.50
	Never hinged	34.00	
b.	Booklet pane of 6	12.50	
	Never hinged	18.50	
189	A84 1½p red brown	1.10	1.10
	Never hinged	1.40	
a.	Tête bêche pair	450.00	*850.00*
	Never hinged	625.00	
b.	Wmk. sideways	10.00	4.00
	Never hinged	21.50	
c.	Booklet pane of 6	12.50	
	Never hinged	18.50	
d.	Bklt. pane of 4 + 2 labels	160.00	
	Never hinged	260.00	
e.	Double impression	*13,500.*	
190	A85 2p dp orange (II)	2.90	2.90
	Never hinged	3.75	
a.	Wmk. sideways	90.00	*90.00*
	Never hinged	160.00	
b.	Unwatermarked	850.00	
	Never hinged	1,300.	
191	A86 2½p ultra	5.75	3.50
	Never hinged	10.00	
a.	Unwatermarked	1,400.	
	Never hinged	1,800.	
192	A87 3p violet	11.50	2.75
	Never hinged	19.00	
193	A88 4p slate green	14.00	2.75
	Never hinged	29.00	
a.	Printed on gummed side	2,000.	
194	A89 5p yel brown	22.50	3.50
	Never hinged	45.00	
195	A89 6p dull violet	3.50	1.75
	Never hinged	5.00	
a.	6p purple, chalky paper	14.00	2.90
198	A90 9p olive green	13.50	4.00
	Never hinged	21.50	
199	A90 10p dull blue	40.00	45.00
	Never hinged	100.00	
200	A90 1sh bister	25.00	3.50
	Never hinged	50.00	
	Nos. 187-200 (12)	141.95	72.95

Nos. 187a, 188a, 189b, 190a issued in coils.
Inverted watermarks on the three lowest values are usually from booklet panes.
Nos. 188-189 were issued also on experimental paper with variety of Wmk. 35: closer spacing; letters shorter, rounder.

British Empire Exhibition Issue

Type of 1924, Dated "1925"

1925, May 9 Engr. *Perf. 14*

203	A92 1p vermilion	17.00	*35.00*
	Never hinged	25.00	
204	A92 1½p brown	45.00	*80.00*
	Never hinged	67.50	

A93

A94

A95

St. George Slaying the Dragon A96

1929, May 10 Typo. *Perf. 15x14*

205	A93 ½p green	2.50	2.50
	Never hinged	3.75	
a.	Wmk. sideways	40.00	40.00
	Never hinged	120.00	
b.	Booklet pane of 6	27.50	
206	A94 1p scarlet	2.50	2.50
	Never hinged	3.75	
a.	Wmk. sideways	70.00	*70.00*
	Never hinged	100.00	
b.	Booklet pane of 6	27.50	
207	A94 1½p dark brown	2.60	2.00
	Never hinged	4.00	
a.	Wmk. sideways	40.00	40.00
	Never hinged	80.00	
b.	Booklet pane of 6	20.00	
c.	Booklet pane of 4 + 2 labels	250.00	
208	A95 2½p deep blue	11.50	11.50
	Never hinged	24.00	
	Nos. 205-208 (4)	19.10	18.50

Nos. 205a, 206a and 207a were issued in coils.

Wmk. 219

Engr. *Perf. 12*

209	A96 £1 black	850.00	625.00
	Never hinged	1,400.	

Universal Postal Union, 9th Congress.

A97

Type A97 designs are re-engraved versions of the types of the 1912-13 issue, with the most obvious difference being the solid appearance of the central field. The backgrounds appear to be solid, although the photoengraving screen can be seen under magnification.

Perf. 14½x14

1934-36 Photo. Wmk. 35

210 A97 ½p dark green .60 .60
Never hinged 1.10
a. Wmk. sideways 8.00 4.00
Never hinged 17.50
b. Booklet pane of 6 11.00
211 A83 1p carmine .60 .60
Never hinged 1.00
a. Wmk. sideways 14.00 7.00
Never hinged 27.50
b. Booklet pane of 6 11.00
c. Imperf., pair *1,400*
d. Pair, imperf. btwn. 2,900.
e. Printed on gummed side *575.00*
212 A97 1½p red brown .60 .60
Never hinged 1.00
a. Imperf., pair 375.00
b. Wmk. sideways 7.00 4.50
Never hinged 10.00
c. Booklet pane of 6 5.50
d. Booklet pane of 4 + 2 labels 110.00
213 A97 2p red org ('35) .85 .85
Never hinged 1.25
a. Imperf., pair *2,300.*
b. Wmk. sideways 100.00 70.00
Never hinged 175.00
214 A97 2½p ultra ('35) 1.75 1.40
Never hinged 2.50
215 A97 3p dk violet ('35) 1.75 1.40
Never hinged 2.50
216 A97 4p dk sl grn ('35) 2.25 1.40
Never hinged 3.50
217 A97 5p yel brown ('36) 7.00 3.00
Never hinged 11.00
218 A97 9p dk ol grn ('35) 14.00 2.75
Never hinged 20.00
219 A97 10p Prus blue ('36) 17.50 11.50
Never hinged 30.00
220 A97 1sh bister brn ('36) 17.50 1.40
Never hinged 35.00
Nos. 210-220 (11) 64.40 25.50

The designs in this set are slightly smaller than the 1912-13 issue.

Nos. 210a, 211a, 212b and 213b were issued in coils.

Britannia Type of 1913-19 Reengraved

1934 Engr. Wmk. 34 *Perf. 11x12*

222 A91 2sh6p brown 80.00 45.00
Never hinged 135.00
223 A91 5sh carmine 180.00 100.00
Never hinged 325.00
224 A91 10sh dark blue 400.00 92.50
Never hinged 650.00
Nos. 222-224 (3) 660.00 237.50

Printed by Waterlow & Sons. Can be distinguished by the crossed lines in background of portrait. Previous issues have horizontal lines only.

Silver Jubilee Issue

A98

Perf. 14½x14

1935, May 7 Photo. Wmk. 35

226 A98 ½p dark green .85 .55
Never hinged 1.25
a. Booklet pane of 4 17.50
227 A98 1p carmine 1.40 *1.75*
Never hinged 2.00
a. Booklet pane of 4 17.50
228 A98 1½p red brown .85 .55
Never hinged 1.25
a. Booklet pane of 4 9.00
229 A98 2½p ultramarine 5.25 *6.25*
Never hinged 7.25
a. 2½p Prussian blue *7,000.* *7,000.*
Never hinged *8,000.*
Nos. 226-229 (4) 8.35 *9.10*

25th anniv. of the reign of George V. Device at right differs on 1½p and 2½p.

Edward VIII — A99

1936 Wmk. 250

230 A99 ½p dark green .20 .20
Never hinged .40
a. Booklet pane of 6 2.00
Never hinged 2.75
231 A99 1p crimson .50 .50
Never hinged .70
a. Booklet pane of 6 3.00
Never hinged 4.50
232 A99 1½p red brown .20 *.35*
Never hinged .40
a. Booklet pane of 6 2.00
Never hinged 2.75
b. Booklet pane of 4 + 2 labels 62.50
Never hinged 85.00
c. Booklet pane of 2 6.00
Never hinged 10.00
233 A99 2½p bright ultra .20 *1.00*
Never hinged .40
Nos. 230-233 (4) 1.10 *2.05*

King George VI and Queen Elizabeth A100

Perf. 14½x14

1937, May 13 Wmk. 251

234 A100 1½p purple brown .25 .25
Never hinged .35

Coronation of George VI and Elizabeth.

See British Offices Abroad for overprints on types A44-A133. These overprints include "M.E.F.," "B.A.," "B.M.A.," "E.A.F.," "CHINA," "Morocco Agencies," "TANGIER," "LEVANT," "PARAS," and "PIASTRE(S)."

A101

A102

King George VI — A103

Nos. 235-240 show face and neck highlighted, background solid.

1937-39

235 A101 ½p deep green .20 .25
Never hinged .25
a. Wmk. sideways .40 .45
Never hinged .55
b. Booklet pane of 6 5.50
Never hinged 7.50
c. Booklet pane of 4 21.00 32.50
Never hinged 42.50
d. Booklet pane of 2 8.50
Never hinged 12.50
236 A101 1p scarlet .20 .20
Never hinged .25
a. Wmk. sideways 8.50 *9.50*
Never hinged 22.50
b. Booklet pane of 6 8.50
Never hinged 12.50
c. Booklet pane of 4 55.00 55.00
Never hinged 110.00
d. Booklet pane of 2 8.50
Never hinged 12.50
237 A101 1½p red brown .20 .20
Never hinged .20
a. Wmk. sideways .80 *1.25*
Never hinged 1.10
b. Booklet pane of 6 8.50
Never hinged 12.50
c. Booklet pane of 4 + 2 labels 45.00
Never hinged 62.50
d. Booklet pane of 2 6.25
Never hinged 9.00
238 A101 2p orange ('38) .50 .50
Never hinged .80
a. Wmk. sideways 50.00 45.00
Never hinged 85.00
b. Booklet pane of 6 25.00
Never hinged 37.50
239 A101 2½p bright ultra .20 .20
Never hinged .35
a. Wmk. sideways 45.00 25.00
Never hinged 80.00
b. Booklet pane of 6 25.00
Never hinged 37.50
c. Tête bêche pair —
240 A101 3p dk purple ('38) 2.40 1.10
Never hinged 4.25
241 A102 4p gray green ('38) .45 .80
Never hinged .70
a. Imperf., pair *4,125.*
Never hinged *5,200.*
b. Horiz. pair, imperf. on 3 sides *4,500.*
Never hinged *6,000.*
242 A102 5p lt brown ('38) 1.60 .90
Never hinged 2.80
a. Imperf., pair *5,000.*
Never hinged *6,300.*
b. Horiz. pair, imperf. on 3 sides *4,300.*
Never hinged *5,500.*
243 A102 6p rose lilac ('39) 1.10 .65
Never hinged 1.40
244 A103 7p emerald ('39) 2.60 .65
Never hinged 5.00
a. Horiz. pair, imperf. on 3 sides *4,400.*
Never hinged *5,700.*
245 A103 8p brt rose ('39) 3.25 .90
Never hinged 5.00
246 A103 9p dp ol green ('39) 3.50 .90
Never hinged 6.50
247 A103 10p royal bl ('39) 3.75 .85
Never hinged 7.00
a. Imperf., pair 5,700.
Never hinged 7,000.
248 A103 1sh brown ('39) 4.25 1.00
Never hinged 8.00
Nos. 235-248 (14) 24.20 9.10
Set, never hinged 42.50

Nos. 235a, 236a, 237a, 238a and 239a were issued in coils.

Nos. 235c and 236c are watermarked sideways.

The 1½p, 1p, 1½p, 2p and 2½p with watermark inverted are from booklet panes.

No. 238 bisects were used in Guernsey from 12/27/40 to 2/24/41. Value, on cover $32.50.

See Nos. 258-263, 266, 280-285.

Oman Surcharges

Various definitive and commemorative stamps between Nos. 243 and 372 were surcharged in annas (a), new paisa (np) and rupees (r) for use in Oman. The surcharges do not indicate where the stamps were used.

King George VI and Royal Arms — A104

King George VI — A105

1939-42 Engr. Wmk. 259 *Perf. 14*

249 A104 2sh6p chestnut 19.00 8.50
Never hinged 42.50
249A A104 2sh6p yel green ('42) 6.00 1.75
Never hinged 13.00
250 A104 5sh dull red 8.50 2.25
Never hinged 22.50
251 A105 10sh indigo 150.00 24.00
Never hinged 325.00
251A A105 10sh ultra ('42) 17.50 5.75
Never hinged 30.00
Nos. 249-251A (5) 201.00 42.25

See No. 275.

Victoria and George VI A106

Perf. 14½x14

1940, May 6 Photo. Wmk. 251

252 A106 ½p deep green .20 .25
Never hinged .30
253 A106 1p scarlet .55 .40
Never hinged 1.10
254 A106 1½p red brown .25 *.85*
Never hinged .55
255 A106 2p orange .60 .85
Never hinged 1.10
256 A106 2½p brt ultra 1.25 .55
Never hinged 2.50
257 A106 3p dark purple 1.90 *4.50*
Never hinged 3.50
Nos. 252-257 (6) 4.75 7.40

Centenary of the postage stamp.

No. 255 bisects were used in Guernsey from 12/27/40 to 2/24/41.

Type of 1937-39, with Background Lightened

1941-42

258 A101 ½p green .20 .20
Never hinged .25
a. Booklet pane of 6 3.00
Never hinged 4.25
b. Booklet pane of 2 1.20
Never hinged 1.50
c. Imperf., pair *3,500.*
Never hinged *5,250.*
d. Tete beche pair *8,000.*
Never hinged *11,500.*
e. Booklet pane of 4
259 A101 1p vermilion .20 .25
Never hinged .25
a. Wmk. sideways ('42) 3.00 5.75
Never hinged 4.50
b. Booklet pane of 2 1.25
Never hinged 1.60
c. Imperf., pair *5,000.*
Never hinged *7,000.*
d. Booklet pane of 4
e. Horiz. pair, imperf on 3 sides *5,000.*
Never hinged *7,000.*
260 A101 1½p lt red brn ('42) .25 .85
Never hinged .50
a. Booklet pane of 2 2.75
Never hinged 4.00
b. Booklet pane of 4
261 A101 2p light orange .25 .50
Never hinged .50
a. Wmk. sideways ('42) 16.50 *21.00*
Never hinged 32.50
b. Booklet pane of 6 6.75
Never hinged 10.00
c. Imperf., pair *4,200.*
Never hinged *5,750.*
d. Tete beche pair *8,250.*
Never hinged *11,500.*
262 A101 2½p ultra .25 .40
Never hinged .35
a. Wmk. sideways ('42) 9.00 *11.00*
Never hinged 17.50
b. Booklet pane of 6 3.75
Never hinged 5.00
c. Imperf., pair *3,250.*
Never hinged *4,500.*
d. Tete beche pair *8,000.*
Never hinged *11,500.*
263 A101 3p violet 1.25 1.10
Never hinged 2.25
Nos. 258-263 (6) 2.40 3.30

Nos. 259a, 261a and 262a were issued in coils.

Nos. 258b, 258e, 259b, 259d, 260a-260b are made from sheets.

Catalogue values for unused stamps in this section, from this point to the end of the section, are for Never Hinged items.

Peace Issue

A107

King George VI and Symbols of Peace and Industry A108

Perf. 14½x14

1946, June 11 Photo. Wmk. 251

264 A107 2½p bright ultra .20 .20
265 A108 3p violet .20 .45

Return to peace at the close of WW II.

George VI Type of 1939

1947, Dec. 29

266 A103 11p violet brown 3.50 *4.00*

A109

King George VI and Queen Elizabeth A110

1948, Apr. 26 *Perf. 14½x14, 14x14½*

267 A109 2½p brt ultra .40 .20
268 A110 £1 dp chalky blue 47.50 47.50

25th anniv. of the marriage of King George VI and Queen Elizabeth.

A111

Vraicking (Gathering Seaweed) A112

1948, May 10 *Perf. 14½x14*

269 A111 1p red .20 .20
270 A112 2½p bright ultra .20 .20

3rd anniversary of the liberation of the Channel Islands from German occupation.

Sold at post offices in the Channel Islands, but valid for postage throughout Great Britain.

A113

A114

A115

A116

1948, July 29

271 A113 2½p bright ultra .25 .20
272 A114 3p deep violet .50 .65
273 A115 6p red violet 1.10 .45
274 A116 1sh dark brown 2.10 1.75
Nos. 271-274 (4) 3.95 3.05

1948 Olympic Games held at Wembley during July and August.

George VI Type of 1939
Wmk. 259

1948, Oct. 1 **Engr.** *Perf. 14*

275 A105 £1 red brown 17.50 *25.00*

A117

A118

A119

A120

Perf. 14½x14

1949, Oct. 10 **Photo.** **Wmk. 251**

276 A117 2½p bright ultra .20 .20
277 A118 3p brt violet .20 .55
278 A119 6p red violet .30 .55
279 A120 1sh brown .70 1.40
Nos. 276-279 (4) 1.40 2.70

UPU, 75th anniversary.

Types of 1937

1950-51 **Wmk. 251** *Perf. 14½x14*

280 A101 ½p light orange .20 .20
a. Booklet pane of 2 1.20
b. Booklet pane of 4 2.00
c. Booklet pane of 6 3.00
d. Imperf., pair *4,500.*
e. Tete beche pair *11,500.*
281 A101 1p ultramarine .20 .20
a. Wmk. sideways 1.25 1.40
b. Booklet pane of 2 1.40
c. Booklet pane of 4 2.10
d. Booklet pane of 6 3.00
e. Booklet pane of 3 + 3 labels 20.00
f. Imperf., pair *3,500.*
282 A101 1½p green .75 .70
a. Wmk. sideways 3.75 *5.75*
b. Booklet pane of 2 2.00
c. Booklet pane of 4 3.75
d. Booklet pane of 6 5.50
283 A101 2p lt red brown .85 .45
a. Wmk. sideways 2.00 *2.25*
b. Booklet pane of 6 9.00
c. Tete beche pair *11,500.*
d. Horiz. pair, imperf on 3 sides *4,600.*
284 A101 2½p vermilion .70 .45
a. Wmk. sideways 2.00 2.00
b. Booklet pane of 6 4.75
c. Tete beche pair
285 A102 4p ultra ('50) 2.25 2.00
a. Double impression *8,000.*
Nos. 280-285 (6) 4.95 4.00

Nos. 281a, 282a, 283a and 284a were issued in coils.

H.M.S. Victory A121

St. George Slaying the Dragon A122

Royal Arms A123

Design: 5sh, White Cliffs, Dover.

Perf. 11x12

1951, May 3 **Engr.** **Wmk. 259**

286 A121 2sh6p green 6.50 1.10
287 A121 5sh dull red 45.00 1.75
288 A122 10sh ultra 16.00 9.75
289 A123 £1 lt red brown 55.00 22.50
Nos. 286-289 (4) 122.50 35.10

Britannia, Symbols of Commerce and Prosperity, King George VI — A124

Festival Symbol A125

Perf. 14½x14

1951, May 3 **Photo.** **Wmk. 251**

290 A124 2½p scarlet .20 .25
291 A125 4p bright ultra .35 .75

Festival of Britain, 1951.

Complete Booklets can be found following the Letter Sheets section.

POSTAGE DUE STAMPS

D1

D2

Perf. 14x14½

1914-24 **Typo.** **Wmk. 33**

J1 D1 ½p emerald .60 .30
Never hinged 1.10
J2 D1 1p rose .60 .30
Never hinged 1.75
a. 1p pale carmine .85 .55
Never hinged 1.75
b. 1p carmine, thick chalky paper ('24) 2.60 *4.00*
Never hinged 4.90
J3 D1 1½p red brown ('22) 55.00 22.50
Never hinged 160.00
J4 D1 2p brown black .60 .30
Never hinged 1.75
J5 D1 3p violet ('18) 5.75 .85
Never hinged 27.50
a. 3p bluish violet ('18) 7.00 3.00
Never hinged 12.50
J6 D1 4p gray green ('21) 20.00 5.75
Never hinged 140.00
J7 D1 5p org brown 7.00 4.00
Never hinged 16.00
J8 D1 1sh blue ('15) 45.00 5.50
Never hinged 150.00
a. 1sh deep bright blue 45.00 5.75
Never hinged 150.00
Nos. J1-J8 (8) 134.55 39.50

1924-30 **Wmk. 35**

J9 D1 ½p emerald 1.40 .85
Never hinged 3.00
J10 D1 1p car rose .70 .30
Never hinged 3.00
J11 D1 1½p red brown 52.50 20.00
Never hinged 150.00
J12 D1 2p black brown 1.10 .30
Never hinged 10.50
J13 D1 3p violet 1.75 .30
Never hinged 11.50
a. Experimental wmk. 45.00 40.00
Never hinged 92.50
b. Printed on the gummed side 87.50
Never hinged 140.00
J14 D1 4p deep green 17.50 3.50
Never hinged 57.50
J15 D1 5p org brown ('30) 37.50 32.50
Never hinged 100.00
J16 D1 1sh blue 11.50 1.10
Never hinged 35.00
J17 D2 2sh6p brown, *yellow* 52.50 2.25
Never hinged 225.00
Nos. J9-J17 (9) 176.45 61.10

The experimental watermark of No. J13a resembles Wmk. 35 but is spaced more closely, with letters short and rounded, crown with flat arch and sides high, lines thicker.

1936-37 **Wmk. 250**

J18 D1 ½p emerald ('37) 4.25 *9.25*
Never hinged 8.50
J19 D1 1p car rose ('37) 1.25 *2.25*
Never hinged 1.75
J20 D1 2p blk brown ('37) 5.25 *12.50*
Never hinged 9.25
J21 D1 3p violet ('37) 1.60 *2.50*
Never hinged 1.75
J22 D1 4p slate green 19.00 *40.00*
Never hinged 40.00
J23 D1 5p bister ('37) 9.00 *26.00*
Never hinged 18.00
a. 5p orange brown 32.50 *29.00*
Never hinged 62.50
J24 D1 1sh blue ('36) 6.50 *10.50*
Never hinged 12.50
J25 D2 2sh6p brn, *yel* ('37) 190.00 10.50
Never hinged 350.00
Nos. J18-J25 (8) 236.85 *113.50*

1938-39 **Wmk. 251**

J26 D1 ½p emerald 5.25 5.75
Never hinged 10.50
J27 D1 1p carmine rose 1.75 .85
Never hinged 3.50
J28 D1 2p black brown 1.50 .85
Never hinged 3.00
J29 D1 3p violet 7.00 1.10
Never hinged 14.00
J30 D1 4p slate green 45.00 15.00
Never hinged 87.50
J31 D1 5p bister ('39) 8.00 .85
Never hinged 16.00
J32 D1 1sh blue 45.00 2.25
Never hinged 87.50
J33 D2 2sh6p brown, *yel* ('39) 45.00 3.00
Never hinged 87.50
Nos. J26-J33 (8) 158.50 29.65

Catalogue values for unused stamps in this section, from this point to the end of the section, are for Never Hinged items.

1951-52

J34 D1 ½p orange 1.10 *3.50*
J35 D1 1p violet blue 1.75 1.75
J36 D1 1½p green ('52) 2.00 *3.50*
J37 D1 4p bright blue 37.50 14.00
J38 D1 1sh olive bister 42.50 16.00
Nos. J34-J38 (5) 84.85 38.75

OFFICIAL STAMPS

A1

Type of Regular Issue of 1840
"V R" in Upper Corners

1840 **Wmk. 18** *Imperf.*

O1 O1 1p black *13,500. 21,000.*
On cover

No. O1 was never placed in use but examples are known used and on covers that passed through the mails by oversight.

Postage stamps perforated with a crown and initials "H.M.O.W.," "O.W.," "B.T." or "S.O.," or with only the initials "H.M.S.O." or "D.S.I.R.," were used for official purposes.

Counterfeits exist of Nos. O2-O83.

Inland Revenue
Regular Issues Overprinted in Black:

a

I. R.
OFFICIAL
b

Type "a" is overprinted on the stamps of ½ penny to 1 shilling inclusive, type "b" on the higher values.

1882-85 **Wmk. 30** *Perf. 14*

O2 A35 ½p green 70.00 22.50
On cover 70.00
O3 A35 ½p slate bl ('85) 70.00 25.00
On cover 100.00
O4 A40 1p lilac 4.50 2.25
On cover 22.50
a. "OFFICIAL" omitted *6,750.*
b. Ovpt. lines transposed
O5 A47 2½p lilac ('85) 350.00 120.00
On cover 1,050.
O6 A28 6p gray 375.00 90.00
On cover —
O7 A48 1sh green ('85) *4,000.* 1,000.
On cover —

Wmk. 31

O8 A51 5sh car rose ('85) 3,500. 1,150.
a. Bluish paper ('85) *7,250.* 2,500.
O9 A52 10sh ultramarine *4,750.* 1,725.
a. 10sh cobalt *15,000.* 4,000.
b. Bluish paper *12,500.* 3,500.

Wmk. Three Imperial Crowns (30)

O10 A53 £1 brown vio *35,000.* *17,500.*

1888-89 **Wmk. 30**
O11 A54 ½p vermilion 9.00 3.50
On cover 70.00
a. "I.R." omitted *3,500.*
O12 A65 1sh green ('89) 500.00 200.00
On cover 2,500.

1890 **Wmk. Three Orbs (29)**
O13 A53 £1 brown vio *52,500. 25,000.*

1891 **Wmk. 30**
O14 A57 2½p violet, *blue* 120.00 11.50
On cover 350.00

Wmk. Three Imperial Crowns (30)

1892
O15 A53 £1 green *7,250.* 1,700.
a. No period after "R" *16,000.* *2,500.*

1901 **Wmk. 30**
O16 A54 ½p blue green 11.50 7.00
On cover 225.00
O17 A62 6p violet, *rose* 350.00 95.00
On cover —
O18 A65 1sh car rose & green 2,300. 600.00
On cover —

1902-04
O19 A66 ½p gray green 25.00 3.50
On cover 125.00
O20 A66 1p carmine 17.00 2.25
On cover 85.00
O21 A66 2½p ultra 575.00 140.00
On cover —
O22 A66 6p dull vio ('04) *140,000. 87,500.*
O23 A74 1sh car rose & green 2,200. 500.00
On cover —

Wmk. 31
O24 A76 5sh car rose *10,000. 5,750.*
O25 A77 10sh ultra *50,000. 25,000.*

Wmk. Three Imperial Crowns (30)
O26 A78 £1 green *40,000. 17,500.*

Nos. O4, O8, O9 and O15 also exist with overprint in blue black.

Government Parcels

Overprinted

1883-86 **Wmk. 30**
O27 A45 1½p lilac ('86) 350.00 67.50
O28 A46 6p green ('86) 1,700. 675.00
O29 A50 9p green 1,400. 575.00
O30 A29 1sh salmon (P13) 800.00 200.00
Plate 14 1,700. 280.00
Nos. O27-O30 (4) 4,250. 1,517.

1887-92
O31 A55 1½p violet & green 80.00 8.00
O32 A56 2p green & car rose ('91) 160.00 24.00
O33 A60 4½p car rose & grn ('92) 260.00 200.00
O34 A62 6p violet, *rose* 160.00 27.50
O35 A63 9p blue & lil ('88) 230.00 40.00
O36 A65 1sh green 400.00 160.00
Nos. O31-O36 (6) 1,290. 459.50

1897
O37 A40 1p lilac 80.00 17.00
a. Inverted overprint 3,750. 1,700.

1900
O38 A65 1sh car rose & grn 400.00 140.00
a. Inverted overprint *8,000.*

1902
O39 A66 1p carmine 35.00 14.00
O40 A68 2p green & car 140.00 35.00
O41 A66 6p dull violet 250.00 35.00
a. Double overprint, one albino *7,500.*
O42 A72 9p ultra & violet 525.00 120.00
O43 A74 1sh car rose & grn 850.00 200.00
Nos. O39-O43 (5) 1,800. 404.00

Office of Works

Overprinted **O.W. OFFICIAL**

1896
O44 A54 ½p vermilion 230.00 120.00
On cover 450.00
O45 A40 1p lilac 400.00 120.00
On cover 575.00

1901-02
O46 A54 ½p blue green 350.00 110.00
On cover —
O47 A61 5p lilac & ultra 2,100. 700.00
On cover —
O48 A64 10p car rose & lil 3,250. 950.00
On cover —

1902
O49 A66 ½p gray green 575.00 175.00
On cover 1,750.
O50 A66 1p carmine 575.00 175.00
On cover 400.00
O51 A68 2p green & car 1,500. 400.00
On cover 2,500.
O52 A66 2½p ultramarine 1,800. 575.00
On cover 4,000.
O53 A73 10p car rose & vio *23,000.* 5,250.
On cover —

Army

Overprinted:

a

b

1896
O54 A54(a) ½p vermilion 4.00 1.75
On cover 45.00
a. "OFFICIAI" 175.00 90.00
O55 A40(a) 1p lilac 4.00 3.00
On cover 75.00
a. "OFFICIAI" 175.00 90.00
O56 A57(b) 2½p violet, *blue* 35.00 22.50
On cover 500.00
Nos. O54-O56 (3) 43.00 27.25

1900
O57 A54(a) ½p blue green 4.50 *8.00*
On cover —

1901
O58 A62(b) 6p violet, *rose* 85.00 45.00
On cover 1,100.

1902
O59 A66(a) ½p gray green 5.75 2.25
On cover 100.00
O60 A66(a) 1p carmine 5.75 2.25
On cover 100.00
a. "ARMY" omitted —
O61 A66(a) 6p dull violet 175.00 80.00
On cover —
Nos. O59-O61 (3) 186.50 84.50

Overprinted

1903
O62 A66 6p dull violet 1,700. 675.00

Royal Household

Overprinted

1902
O63 A66 ½p gray green 350.00 210.00
On cover 1,100.
O64 A66 1p carmine 280.00 170.00
On cover 1,100.

Board of Education

Overprinted

1902
O65 A61 5p lilac & ultra 1,700. 450.00
O66 A65 1sh car rose & grn 5,000. 2,600.

1902-04
O67 A66 ½p gray green 170.00 40.00
On cover 400.00
O68 A66 1p carmine 170.00 40.00
On cover 425.00
O69 A66 2½p ultramarine 2,900. 230.00
On cover —
O70 A71 5p lilac & ultra ('04) 14,000. 4,000.
On cover —
O71 A74 1sh car rose & grn *72,500. 50,000.*

Admiralty

Overprinted

1903
O72 A66 ½p gray green 27.50 14.00
On cover —
O73 A66 1p carmine 17.50 7.00
On cover 310.00
O74 A67 1½p vio & green 200.00 130.00
On cover —
O75 A68 2p green & car 275.00 140.00
On cover —
O76 A66 2½p ultra 350.00 125.00
On cover —
O77 A69 3p violet, *yel* 325.00 140.00
On cover —
Nos. O72-O77 (6) 1,195. 556.00

Overprinted

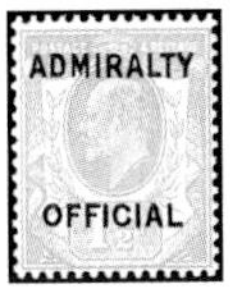

1903
O78 A66 ½p gray green 45.00 22.50
On cover 525.00
O79 A66 1p carmine 45.00 22.50
On cover 140.00
O80 A67 1½p vio & green 675.00 450.00
On cover —
O81 A68 2p green & car 1,000. 500.00
On cover —
O82 A66 2½p ultramarine 1,150. 725.00
On cover —
O83 A69 3p violet, *yel* 900.00 230.00
On cover —

The two types of the "Admiralty Official" overprint differ principally in the shape of the letter "M."

ENVELOPES

Britannia Sending Letters to World (William Mulready, Designer) — E1

Illustration reduced.

1840
U1 E1 1p black 300.00 *375.00*
U2 E1 2p blue 375.00 *1,100.*

LETTER SHEETS

U3 E1 1p black 275.00 *350.00*
U4 E1 2p blue 350.00 *1,100.*

BOOKLETS

Booklets are listed in denomination sequence by reign. Numbers in parenthesis following each listing reflect the number of cover varieties or edition numbers that apply to each cover style.

Values shown for complete booklets are for examples containing most panes having full perforations on two edges of the pane only. Booklets containing most or all panes with very fine, full perforations on all sides are scarce and will sell for more. Also, in booklets where most of the value is contained in only one pane of several, it is assumed that this pane has full perforations on two sides only. If this pane is very fine, the booklet will be worth a considerable premium over the value given.

Sterling Currency

BC1

1904
BK1 BC1 2sh ½p *red,* 4 #128e 300.00

1906-11
BK2 BC1 2sh *red,* 2 #128e, 3 #143c, #143b 900.00
BK3 BC1 2sh *red,* 3 #128e, 1 each #143b-143c (4) 1,100.

Cover inscription on Nos. BK2-BK3 revised to reflect changed contents.

1911
BK4 BC1 2sh *red,* 2#151a, 3 #152a 700.00

BC2

1912-13
BK5 BC2 2sh *red,* 2 #151a, 3 #152a 925.00
BK6 BC2 2sh *red,* 2 #155a, 3 #156a (4) 1,000.

Cover inscription on Nos. BK5-BK6 shows only Inland Postage Rates.

1913
BK7 BC2 2sh *red,* 2 #159b, 3 #160a (35) 450.00
BK8 BC2 2sh *org,* 2 #159b,3 #160a (20) 475.00

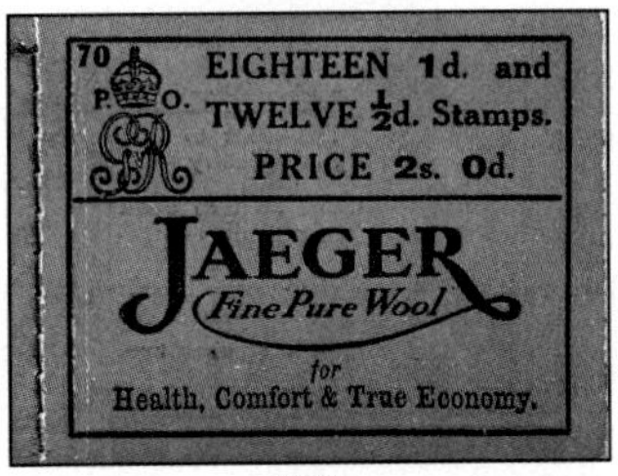

BC3

1917
BK9 BC3 2sh *org,* 2 #159b, 3 #160a (17) 450.00

BC4

1924-34
BK10 BC4 2sh *blue,* #159b, 160a, 161d-161e (2) 1,150.
BK11 BC4 2sh *blue,* #187b, 188b, 189c-189d (277) 425.00

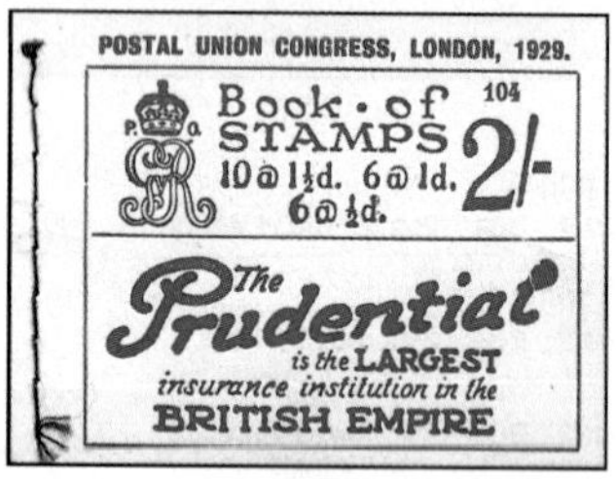

BC5

1929
BK12 BC5 2sh blue, *buff,* #205b-207b, 207c 550.00

1935
BK13 BC4 2sh *blue,* #210b-211b, 212c-212d (58) 450.00

BC6

1935
BK14 BC6 2sh blue, *buff,* #226a-227a, 3 #228a 100.00

1918-19
BK15 BC4 3sh *org,* 2 each #159b, 160a, 161d (11) 575.00
BK16 BC4 3sh *org,* #159b, 160a, 3 #161d (15) 575.00

Cover used for Nos. BK15-BK16 does not have inscription above top line.

1921
BK17 BC4 3sh *blue,* 3 #162b (3) 700.00
BK18 BC4 3sh *blue,* 3 #162c (3) 750.00

1922
BK19 BC4 3sh *scar,* #159b, 160a, 3 #161d (33) 750.00
BK20 BC4 3sh *blue,* 4 #161d (2) 650.00

1924-34
BK21 BC4 3sh *scar,* #187b-188b, 3 #189c (237) 300.00

1929
BK22 BC5 3sh blue, *buff,* #205b-206b, 3 #207b (5) 400.00

1935
BK23 BC4 3sh *scar,* #210b-211b, 3 #212c (27) 325.00

BK24 BC6 3sh red, *buff,* #226a-227a, 5 #228a (4) 100.00

1920
BK25 BC4 3sh6p *org,* #160a, 3 #162b (6) 725.00

Cover used for No. BK25 does not have inscription above top line.

1921
BK26 BC4 3sh6p *org red,* #159b, 160a, 161d, 2 #162b (7) 725.00
BK27 BC4 3sh6p *org red,* #159b, 160a, 161d, 2 #162c (13) 725.00

1931-35
BK28 BC4 5sh *grn,* #187b-188b, 189d, 5 #189c 3,250.
BK29 BC4 5sh *buff,* #187b-188b, 189d, 5 #189c (7) 1,000.
BK30 BC4 5sh *buff,* #210b-211b, 212d, 5 #212c (7) 400.00

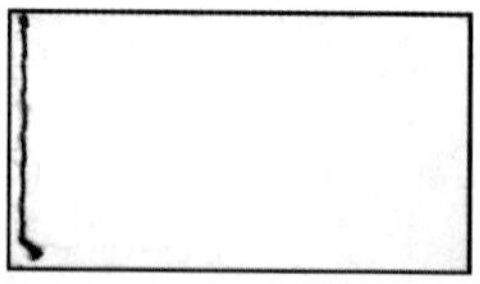
BC7

1936
BK31 BC7 6p *buff,* 2 #232c 70.00

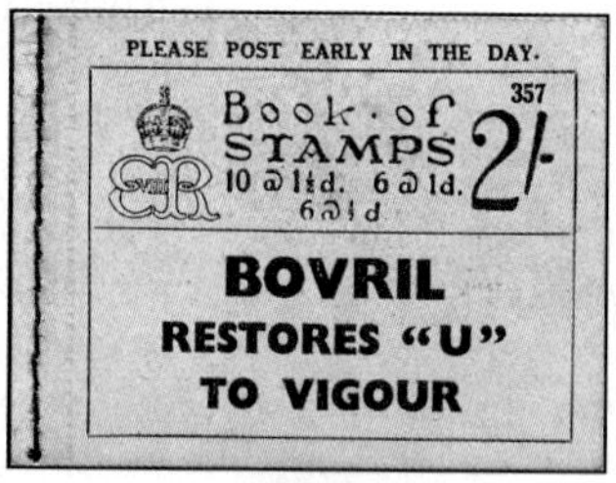

BC8

BK32 BC8 2sh *blue,* #230a-231a, #232a-232b (31) 110.00
BK33 BC8 3sh *scar,* #230a-231a, 3 #232a (12) 100.00
BK34 BC8 5sh *buff,* #230a-231a, 6 #232a (2) 225.00

1938-40
BK35 BC7 6p *buff,* 2 #237d 70.00
BK36 BC7 6p *pink,* #235d-237d 325.00
BK37 BC7 6p *pale grn,* #235c-236c 140.00

No. BK37 is 53x41mm.

1947-51
BK38 BC7 1sh *buff,* 2 each #258b-259b, 260a 27.50
BK39 BC7 1sh *buff,* 2 each #280a, 281b-282b 27.50
BK40 BC7 1sh *buff,* #258e, 259d, 260b 5,250.
BK41 BC7 1sh *buff,* #280b-282b 32.50

Nos. BK40-BK41 are 53x41mm.

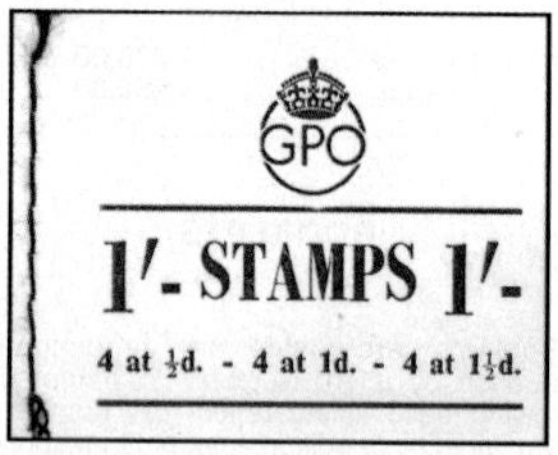

Round GPO Emblem — BC9

1952-53
BK42 BC9 1sh *buff,* #280b, 281c-282c 20.00
a. Inland postage rate corrected in ink on inside booklet cover 22.50

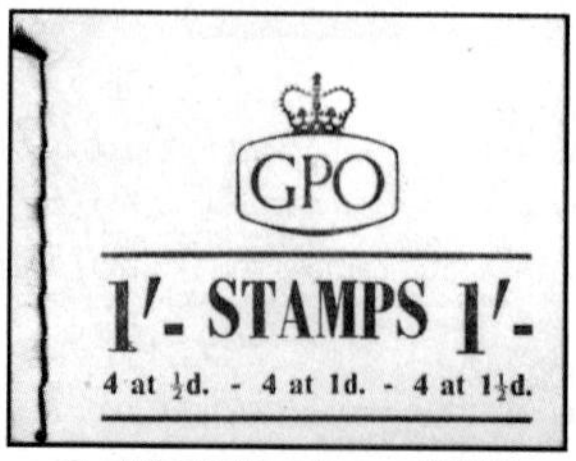

Oval GPO Emblem — BC10

1954
BK43 BC10 1sh *buff,* #280b, 281c-282c 32.50

1937
BK44 BC8 2sh *blue,* #235b-236b, #237b-237c (26) 375.00

BC11

1938
BK45 BC11 2sh *blue,* #235b-236b, #237b-237c (95) 375.00

1940-42

2sh6p Booklets

BK46 BC11 *scar,* #235b, #238b-239b (7) 950.00
BK47 BC11 *blue,* #235b, #238b-239b (6) 950.00

Denomination part of cover of Nos. BK46-BK47 is printed in white on black background.

BK48 BC11 *grn,* #235b, #238b-239b (80) 425.00
BK49 BC11 *grn,* #258a, #261b-262b (120) 450.00

1943
BK50 BC12 *grn,* #258a, #261b-262b (90) 52.50

With booklets issued in August and September 1943, commercial advertising on British booklets was discontinued. Covers and interleaving were used for Post Office slogans. Booklets were no longer numbered, but carried the month and year of issue.

1951-52
BK51 BC12 *grn,* #280c, #283b-284b (10) 40.00
BK52 BC12 *grn,* #280c, 281e, #282d, 284b (15) 37.50

1937-38

3sh Booklets

BK53 BC8 *scar,* #235a-236a, 3 #237b (10) 750.00
BK54 BC11 *scar,* #235a-236a, 3 #237b (34) 750.00

1937-43

5sh Booklets

BK55 BC8 *buff,* #235b-236b, 237c, 5 #237b (3) 850.00
BK56 BC11 *buff,* #235b-236b, 237c, 5 #237b (9) 800.00
BK57 BC11 *buff,* #235b, 238b, 3 #239b (16) 825.00
BK58 BC11 *buff,* #258a, 261b, 3 #262b (20) 800.00

1943-53
BK59 BC12 *tan,* #258a, 261b, 3 #262b (49) 92.50
BK60 BC12 *tan,* #258a, 261b, 3 #262b (20) 1,000.

Cover on No. BK60 has thick horizontal lines separating the GPO emblem and the various inscriptions.

BK61 BC12 *tan,* #280a, 283b, 3 #284b (5) 62.50
BK62 BC12 *tan,* #280c, 281e, 282d, 3 #284b (5) 62.50
BK63 BC12 *tan,* #280c, 281d-282d, 283b, 2 #284b (2) 62.50

BC13

1953-54

2sh6p Booklets

BK64 BC12 *grn,* #280c, 281e, 294c, #296a (6) 29.00
BK65 BC13 *grn,* #280c, 281e, 294c, 296a (7) 32.50
BK66 BC13 *grn,* #281e, 292c, 294c, 296a 500.00

5sh Booklets

BK67 BC12 *brn,* #280c, 281d, 283b, 294c, 2 #296a (3) 40.00
BK68 BC13 *brn,* #280c, 281d, 283b, 294c, 2 #296a (2) 45.00
BK69 BC13 *brn,* #281d, 283b, 292c, 294c, 2 #296a 300.00
BK70 BC13 *brn,* #283b, 292c-294c, 2 #296a 160.00

GUERNSEY OCCUPATION STAMPS

Issued Under German Occupation

OS1

Roulетted 14x7

1941-44	**Typo.**	**Unwmk.**	
N1 OS1	½p light green	4.00	3.00
	Never hinged	5.00	
a.	½p dull green	4.00	4.00
	Never hinged	7.00	
b.	½p pale yellow green	2.50	2.40
	Never hinged	7.00	
c.	½p emerald green	4.00	3.00
	Never hinged	9.00	
d.	½p bluish green	32.50	*35.00*
	Never hinged	40.00	
e.	½p bright green	16.00	15.00
	Never hinged	25.00	
f.	½p olive green	20.00	18.00
	Never hinged	37.50	
g.	Imperf, pair	175.00	
	Never hinged	250.00	
h.	Horiz. pair, imperf between	550.00	
	Never hinged	800.00	
i.	Vert. pair, imperf between	750.00	
	Never hinged	950.00	
N2 OS1	1p red	2.00	2.00
	Never hinged	3.50	
a.	Printed double	90.00	
	Never hinged	125.00	
b.	1p pale vermilion	2.00	*3.00*
	Never hinged	4.00	
c.	1p carmine red	3.00	*4.50*
	Never hinged	5.50	
d.	Imperf, pair	125.00	90.00
	Never hinged	175.00	
e.	Horiz. pair, imperf between	550.00	
	Never hinged	800.00	
f.	Vert. pair, imperf between	750.00	
	Never hinged	950.00	
N3 OS1	2½p ultramarine	5.00	*9.00*
	Never hinged	8.50	
a.	2½p pale ultramarine	5.50	*9.00*
	Never hinged	8.00	
	Nos. N1-N3 (3)	11.00	14.00

Issued: #N1b, 4/7/41; #N1c, 6/41; #N1d, 11/41; #N1e, 2/42; #N1a, 9/42; #N1f, 2/43; #N1, from 7/43; #N2, 2/18/41; #N2a, 7/43; #N2b, 1943; #N3, 4/12/44; #N3a, 7/44.

Additional shades and papers exist. The rouletting is very crude and may not be measurable. This is not a defect.

Wmk. 396 Chain Link Fence

1942 ***Rouletted 14x7***

Bluish French Bank Note Paper

N4 OS1 ½p green	16.00	*21.00*
Never hinged	22.50	
N5 OS1 1p red	8.00	*21.00*
Never hinged	11.50	

Issue dates: ½p, Mar. 11; 1p, Apr. 9.

Nos. N1-N5 remained valid until 4/13/46.

JERSEY OCCUPATION STAMPS

Issued Under German Occupation

OS1

1941-42 Typo. Unwmk. ***Perf. 11***

N1 OS1 ½p bright green	3.00	*5.00*
Never hinged	4.00	
a. Imperf, pair	225.00	
Never hinged	300.00	
b. Vert. pair, imperf between	750.00	
Never hinged	950.00	
c. Horiz. pair, imperf between	600.00	
Never hinged	800.00	
d. On grayish paper	4.00	4.00
Never hinged	6.00	
N2 OS1 1p vermilion	4.00	4.00
Never hinged	5.00	
a. Imperf, pair	240.00	
Never hinged	325.00	
b. Vert. pair, imperf between	750.00	
Never hinged	950.00	
c. Horiz. pair, imperf between	600.00	
Never hinged	800.00	
d. On chalk-surfaced paper	30.00	50.00
Never hinged	40.00	
e. On grayish paper	4.00	*7.00*
Never hinged	6.50	

Issue dates: #N1, 1/29/42; #N1d, 1/43; #N2, 4/1/41; #N2e, 1/43.

Jersey Views — OS2

Designs: ½p, Old Jersey farm; 1p, Portelet Bay; 1½p, Corbiere Lighthouse; 2p, Elizabeth Castle; 2½, Mont Orgueil Castle; 3p, Gathering seaweed.

1943-44 ***Perf. 13½***

N3 OS2 ½p dark green	6.25	*11.00*
Never hinged	10.50	
a. On rough, gray paper	6.00	*7.00*
Never hinged	10.00	
N4 OS2 1p scarlet	1.50	.55
Never hinged	2.50	
a. On newsprint	1.75	.80
Never hinged	2.90	
N5 OS2 1½p brown	4.75	*6.50*
Never hinged	8.00	
N6 OS2 2p orange	4.50	2.40
Never hinged	7.50	
N7 OS2 2½p blue	1.50	1.25
Never hinged	2.50	
a. On newsprint	.75	*2.00*
Never hinged	1.25	
b. On pelure paper	150.00	
Never hinged	250.00	
N8 OS2 3p red violet	.85	*3.50*
Never hinged	1.40	
Nos. N3-N8 (6)	19.35	*25.20*

Issued: ½p, 1p, 6/1/43; 1½p, 2p, 6/8/43; 2½p, 3p, 6/29/43; #N4a, 2/28/44; #N7a, 2/25/44.

Nos. N1-N8 remained valid until 4/13/46.

BRITISH OFFICES ABROAD

Catalogue values for unused stamps in this section are for Never Hinged items, except for Nos. 1a-5c, which are for hinged copies with original gum, except as noted.

OFFICES IN AFRICA MIDDLE EAST FORCES

For use in Ethiopia, Cyrenaica, Eritrea, the Dodecanese and Somalia

Stamps of Great Britain, 1937-42 Overprinted in Black or Blue Black

London Printing — ovpt. 14mm long, square dots

1942-43 Wmk. 251 ***Perf. 14½x14***

1 A101 1p scarlet	2.00	*2.90*
2 A101 2p orange	1.50	*4.00*
3 A101 2½p bright ultra	1.10	*1.40*
4 A101 3p dark purple	.90	.35
a. Double overprint		*4,000.*
5 A102 5p lt brn (Blk)	.80	.35
a. Blue black overprint ('43)	4.25	.20
6 A102 6p rose lilac ('43)	.45	.20
7 A103 9p dp olive grn ('43)	1.00	.20
8 A103 1sh brown ('43)	.55	.20

Wmk. 259

Perf. 14

9 A104 2sh6p yel green ('43)	8.00	1.10
Nos. 1-9 (9)	16.30	10.70

Cairo Printing — ovpt. 13.5mm long, square dots

1a A101 1p scarlet	32.50	15.00
Never hinged	62.50	
2a A101 2p orange	42.50	*110.00*
Never hinged	85.00	
3a A101 2½p bright ultramarine	30.00	8.50
Never hinged	60.00	
4b A101 3p dark purple	70.00	40.00
Never hinged	140.00	
5b A101 5p light brown	225.00	100.00
Never hinged	450.00	

Cairo Printing — ovpt. 13.5mm long, round dots

1b A101 1p scarlet	25.00	10.50
Never hinged	50.00	
2b A101 2p orange	37.50	*95.00*
Never hinged	75.00	
3b A101 2½p bright ultramarine	26.00	8.50
Never hinged	52.50	
4c A101 3p dark purple	62.50	37.50
Never hinged	125.00	
5c A101 5p light brown	210.00	92.50
Never hinged	425.00	

Same Overprint in Blue Black on Nos. 259, 261, 262 and 263

1943, Jan. 1 **Wmk. 251**

10 A101 1p vermilion	1.75	.20
11 A101 2p light orange	1.75	1.40
12 A101 2½p ultramarine	.55	.20
13 A101 3p violet	1.75	.20
Nos. 10-13 (4)	5.80	2.00

There were two printings of Nos. 1-5, both issued Mar. 2, 1942, and both black. Nos. 5a and 6-13 compose a third printing, also made in London. On these stamps, issued Jan. 1, 1943, the overprint is 13½mm wide. The 2sh6p overprint is black, the others blue black.

Same Ovpt. in Black on #250, 251A

1947 **Wmk. 259** ***Perf. 14***

14 A104 5sh dull red	15.00	*20.00*
15 A105 10sh ultramarine	17.50	11.50

In 1950 Nos. 1-15 were declared valid for use in Great Britain. Used values are for copies postmarked in territory of issue. Others sell for about 25 percent less.

POSTAGE DUE STAMPS

Catalogue values for unused stamps in this section are for Never Hinged items.

Postage Due Stamps of Great Britain Overprinted in Blue

1942 **Wmk. 251** ***Perf. 14x14½***

J1 D1 ½p emerald	.35	*14.00*
J2 D1 1p carmine rose	.35	*2.00*
J3 D1 2p black brown	1.40	1.40
J4 D1 3p violet	.55	*4.75*
J5 D1 1sh blue	4.25	*14.00*
Nos. J1-J5 (5)	6.90	*36.15*

No. J1-J5 were used in Eritrea.

FOR USE IN ERITREA

Catalogue values for unused stamps in this section are for Never Hinged items.

100 Cents = 1 Shilling

Stamps of Great Britain 1937-42 Surcharged

a

1948, June **Wmk. 251** ***Perf. 14½x14***

1 A101 5c on ½p green (II)	1.10	.75
2 A101 10c on 1p vermilion (II)	1.10	*2.75*
3 A101 20c on 2p light org (II)	.55	*2.50*
4 A101 25c on 2½p ultra (II)	.80	.70
5 A101 30c on 3p violet (II)	1.40	*5.00*
6 A101 40c on 5p light brown	.55	*4.75*
7 A101 50c on 6p rose lilac	.55	*1.10*
8 A103 75c on 9p deep ol grn	.80	*.85*
9 A103 1sh on 1sh brown	.80	.55

"B. M. A." stands for British Military Administration.

Great Britain Nos. 249A, 250 and 251A Surcharged

1948, June **Wmk. 259** ***Perf. 14***

10 A104 2sh50c on 2sh6p yel grn	9.25	*11.50*
11 A104 5sh on 5sh dl red	9.25	*18.00*
12 A105 10sh on 10sh ultra	25.00	25.00

Great Britain No. 245 Surcharged Type "a"

1949 **Wmk. 251** ***Perf. 14½x14***

13 A103 65c on 8p brt rose	8.00	2.25
Nos. 1-13 (13)	59.15	*75.70*

Stamps of Great Britain 1937-42 Surcharged

c

1950, Feb. 6

14 A101 5c on ½p green (II)	1.40	*9.25*
15 A101 10c on 1p ver (II)	.35	*3.50*
16 A101 20c on 2p lt orange (II)	.35	*.90*
17 A101 25c on 2½p ultra (II)	.35	*.70*
18 A101 30c on 3p violet (II)	.35	*2.50*
19 A102 40c on 5p light brown	.55	*2.00*
20 A102 50c on 6p rose lilac	.35	.25
21 A103 65c on 8p bright rose	2.50	*1.75*
22 A103 75c on 9p dp ol grn	.35	.30
23 A103 1sh on 1sh brown	.35	.20

Great Britain Nos. 249A, 250, 251A Surcharged

Wmk. 259 ***Perf. 14***

24 A104 2sh50c on 2sh6p yel grn	8.00	*5.50*
25 A104 5sh on 5sh dl red	8.00	*14.00*
26 A105 10sh on 10sh ultra	70.00	62.50
Nos. 14-26 (13)	*92.90*	*103.35*

Great Britain Nos. 280, 281, 283 and 284 Surcharged Type "c"

Perf. 14½x14

1951, May 3 **Wmk. 251**

27 A101 5c on ½p lt orange	.35	*.85*
28 A101 10c on 1p ultra	.35	*.85*
29 A101 20c on 2p lt red brown	.35	.35
30 A101 25c on 2½p vermilion	.35	.35

Great Britain Nos. 286-288 Surcharged

Perf. 11x12

1951, May 31 **Wmk. 259**

31 A121 2sh50c on 2sh6p grn	11.50	*26.00*
32 A121 5sh on 5sh dl red	24.00	*26.00*
33 A122 10sh on 10sh ultra	25.00	*26.00*
Nos. 27-33 (7)	61.90	*80.40*

Surcharge arranged to fit the design on #33.

POSTAGE DUE STAMPS

Catalogue values for unused stamps in this section are for Never Hinged items.

Great Britain Nos. J26-J29, J32 Surcharged

1948 **Wmk. 251** ***Perf. 14x14½***

J1 D1 5c on ½p emer	11.00	*25.00*
J2 D1 10c on 1p car rose	11.00	*27.50*
J3 D1 20c on 2p blk brn	8.00	*18.00*
J4 D1 30c on 3p violet	11.00	*18.00*
J5 D1 1sh on 1sh blue	20.00	*35.00*
Nos. J1-J5 (5)	61.00	*123.50*

Great Britain Nos. J26 to J29 and J32 Surcharged

1950, Feb. 6

J6 D1 5c on ½p emer	12.50	*55.00*
J7 D1 10c on 1p car rose	11.50	*17.50*
a. "C" of CENTS omitted	*2,250.*	
J8 D1 20c on 2p blk brn	12.50	*16.00*
J9 D1 30c on 3p violet	15.00	*25.00*
J10 D1 1sh on 1sh blue	17.50	*26.00*
Nos. J6-J10 (5)	69.00	*139.50*

EAST AFRICAN FORCES

FOR USE IN SOMALIA (ITALIAN SOMALILAND)

Catalogue values for unused stamps in this section are for Never Hinged items.

12 Pence = 1 Shilling
100 Cents = 1 Shilling

Stamps of Great Britain 1938-42 Overprinted in Blue

Perf. 14½x14

1943, Jan. 15 **Wmk. 251**

1	A101	1p vermilion	.70	.70
2	A101	2p light orange	1.75	1.40
3	A101	2½p ultramarine	.55	*4.00*
4	A101	3p violet	.90	.20
5	A101	5p light brown	1.10	.45
6	A101	6p rose lilac	.55	*1.40*
7	A103	9p dp olive green	1.10	*2.50*
8	A103	1sh brown	2.50	.20

On Great Britain No. 249A

1946 **Wmk. 259** ***Perf. 14***

9	A104	2sh6p yellow green	11.50	7.50
		Nos. 1-9 (9)	20.65	*18.35*

Stamps of Great Britain, 1937-42 Surcharged

Perf. 14½x14

1948, May 27 **Wmk. 251**

10	A101	5c on ½p grn (II)	1.40	*2.00*
11	A101	15c on 1½p lt red brn (II)	2.00	*17.50*
12	A101	20c on 2p lt org (II)	3.50	*4.75*
13	A101	25c on 2½p ultra (II)	2.50	*5.00*
14	A101	30c on 3p vio (II)	2.50	*10.50*
15	A102	40c on 5p lt brown	1.40	.20
16	A102	50c on 6p rose lilac	.55	*2.25*
17	A103	75c on 9p dp ol grn	2.25	*21.00*
18	A103	1sh on 1sh brown	1.40	.20

Great Britain Nos. 249A and 250 Surcharged

Wmk. 259 ***Perf. 14***

19	A104	2sh50c on 2sh6p yel grn	5.00	*29.00*
20	A104	5sh on 5sh dl red	11.00	*45.00*
		Nos. 10-20 (11)	33.50	*137.40*

Stamps of Great Britain 1937-42 Surcharged

Perf. 14½x14

1950, Jan. 2 **Wmk. 251**

21	A101	5c on ½p grn (II)	.20	*3.50*
22	A101	15c on 1½p lt red brn (II)	.85	*19.00*
23	A101	20c on 2p lt org (II)	.85	*8.50*
24	A101	25c on 2½p ultra (II)	.55	*8.50*
25	A101	30c on 3p violet (II)	1.40	*5.00*
26	A102	40c on 5p light brn	.65	*1.10*
27	A102	50c on 6p rose lilac	.55	*1.10*
28	A103	75c on 9p deep ol grn	2.25	*8.00*
29	A103	1sh on 1sh brown	.70	*1.75*

Great Britain Nos. 249A and 250 Surcharged

Wmk. 259 ***Perf. 14***

30	A104	2sh50c on 2sh 6p yel grn	4.50	*27.50*
31	A104	5sh on 5sh dull red	12.50	*35.00*
		Nos. 21-31 (11)	25.00	*118.95*

FOR USE IN TRIPOLITANIA

Catalogue values for unused stamps in this section are for Never Hinged items.

Stamps of Great Britain, 1937-42, Surcharged

M.A.L.=Military Authority Lire

Perf. 14½x14

1948, July 1 **Wmk. 251**

1	A101	1 l on ½p green (II)	1.00	*1.75*
2	A101	2 l on 1p ver (II)	.35	.20
3	A101	3 l on 1½p lt red brn (II)	.35	*.55*
4	A101	4 l on 2p lt org (II)	.35	*.80*
5	A101	5 l on 2½p ultra (II)	.35	.20
6	A101	6 l on 3p violet (II)	.35	*.45*
7	A102	10 l on 5p lt brown	.35	.20
8	A102	12 l on 6p rose lilac	.35	.20
9	A103	18 l on 9p dp ol grn	.90	*.75*
10	A103	24 l on 1sh brown	.80	*1.75*

Great Britain Nos. 249A, 250 and 251A Surcharged

Wmk. 259 ***Perf. 14***

11	A104	60 l on 2sh6p yel grn	4.00	*9.75*
12	A104	120 l on 5sh dl red	17.50	*21.00*
13	A105	240 l on 10sh ultra	25.00	*110.00*
		Nos. 1-13 (13)	51.65	*147.60*

Stamps of Great Britain 1937-42 Surcharged

Perf. 14½x14

1950, Feb. 6 **Wmk. 251**

14	A101	1 l on ½p green (II)	3.00	*14.00*
15	A101	2 l on 1p ver (II)	2.75	*.45*
16	A101	3 l on 1½p lt red brn (II)	1.10	*14.00*
17	A101	4 l on 2p lt org (II)	1.10	*5.00*
18	A101	5 l on 2½p ultra (II)	.80	*.80*
19	A101	6 l on 3p violet (II)	2.00	*3.75*
20	A102	10 l on 5p lt brown	.55	*4.50*
21	A102	12 l on 6p rose lilac	2.25	.55
22	A103	18 l on 9p dp ol grn	2.50	*2.75*
23	A103	24 l on 1sh brown	2.75	*4.25*

Great Britain Nos. 249A, 250 and 251A Surcharged

Wmk. 259 ***Perf. 14***

24	A104	60 l on 2sh6p yel grn	7.50	*14.00*
25	A104	120 l on 5sh dl red	22.50	*25.00*
26	A105	240 l on 10sh ultra	42.50	*57.50*
		Nos. 14-26 (13)	91.30	*146.55*

Great Britain Nos. 280-284 Surcharged like Nos. 14-23

Perf. 14½x14

1951, May 3 **Wmk. 251**

27	A101	1 l on ½p lt org	.20	*7.00*
28	A101	2 l on 1p ultra	.20	*1.10*
29	A101	3 l on 1½p green	.35	*9.25*
30	A101	4 l on 2p lt red brown	.20	*1.40*
31	A101	5 l on 2½p ver	.30	*8.50*

Great Britain Nos. 286-288 Surcharged

1951, May 3 **Wmk. 259** ***Perf. 11x12***

32	A121	60 l on 2sh6p grn	6.25	*25.00*
33	A121	120 l on 5sh dl red	10.00	*30.00*
34	A122	240 l on 10sh ultra	42.50	*57.50*
		Nos. 27-34 (8)	60.00	*139.75*

Surcharge arranged to fit the design on #34.

POSTAGE DUE STAMPS

Catalogue values for unused stamps in this section are for Never Hinged items.

Great Britain Nos. J26-J29, J32 Surcharged

1948 **Wmk. 251** ***Perf. 14x14½***

J1	D1	1 l on ½p emer	6.25	*57.50*
J2	D1	2 l on 1p car rose	2.75	*30.00*
J3	D1	4 l on 2p blk brn	8.50	*37.50*
J4	D1	6 l on 3p violet	8.50	*24.00*
J5	D1	24 l on 1sh blue	32.50	*110.00*
		Nos. J1-J5 (5)	58.50	*259.00*

Great Britain Nos. J26-J29, J32 Surcharged

1950, Feb. 6

J6	D1	1 l on ½p emer	14.00	*92.50*
J7	D1	2 l on 1p car rose	3.00	*30.00*
J8	D1	4 l on 2p blk brn	4.50	*40.00*
J9	D1	6 l on 3p violet	21.00	*70.00*
J10	D1	24 l on 1sh blue	55.00	*160.00*
		Nos. J6-J10 (5)	97.50	*392.50*

CHINA

100 Cents = 1 Dollar

Stamps of Hong Kong, 1912-14, Overprinted

1917 **Wmk. 3** ***Perf. 14***

Ordinary Paper

1	A11	1c brown	4.50	3.00
2	A11	2c deep green	8.00	.35
3	A12	4c scarlet	6.25	.35
4	A13	6c orange	6.25	.70
5	A12	8c gray	14.00	1.40
6	A11	10c ultramarine	14.00	.35

Chalky Paper

7	A14	12c violet, *yel*	12.50	5.00
8	A14	20c olive grn & vio	14.00	.70
9	A15	25c red vio & dl vio (on #117)	9.25	*17.50*
10	A13	30c orange & violet	40.00	6.25
11	A14	50c black, *emerald*	40.00	6.50
a.		50c blk, *blue green,* ol back	75.00	1.75
b.		50c blk, *emerald,* ol back	50.00	9.75
12	A11	$1 blue & vio, *bl*	80.00	2.90
13	A14	$2 black & red	260.00	62.50
14	A13	$3 violet & grn	625.00	210.00
15	A14	$5 red & grn, *bl grn,* ol back	400.00	290.00
16	A13	$10 blk & vio, *red*	1,000.	550.00
		Nos. 1-16 (16)	2,533.	1,157.

Stamps of Hong Kong, 1921-26, Overprinted

1922-27 **Wmk. 4**

Ordinary Paper

17	A11	1c brown	2.60	*4.25*
18	A11	2c green	4.00	2.60
19	A12	4c scarlet	7.00	2.60
20	A13	6c orange	5.00	4.75
21	A12	8c gray	9.25	*17.50*
22	A11	10c ultramarine	10.00	4.00

Chalky Paper

23	A14	20c ol grn & vio	16.00	5.75
24	A15	25c red violet & dull vio	26.00	*80.00*
25	A14	50c blk, *emerald* ('27)	70.00	*210.00*
26	A11	$1 ultra & vio, *bl*	85.00	*70.00*
27	A14	$2 black & red	225.00	*290.00*
		Nos. 17-27 (11)	459.85	*691.45*

MOROCCO

100 Centimos = 1 Peseta
12 Pence = 1 Shilling
20 Shillings = 1 Pound
100 Centimes = 1 Franc

These stamps were issued for various purposes:

a — For general use at the British Post Offices throughout Morocco.

b — For use in the Spanish Zone of Northern Morocco.

c — For use in the French Zone of Southern Morocco.

d — For use in the International Zone of Tangier.

For convenience these stamps are listed in four groups according to the coinage expressed or surcharged on the stamps, namely:

1 — Value expressed in Spanish currency.
2 — Value in British currency.
3 — Value in French currency.
4 — Stamps overprinted "Tangier."

Spanish Currency

Gibraltar Stamps of 1889-95 Overprinted

1898 **Wmk. 2** ***Perf. 14***

Black Overprint

1	A11	5c green	3.00	*3.00*
		On cover		25.00
2	A11	10c carmine rose	5.00	.85
		On cover		50.00
b.		Double overprint	625.00	
3	A11	20c olive green	11.00	6.25
		On cover		400.00
4	A11	25c ultramarine	4.50	.70
		On cover		300.00
5	A11	40c orange brown	7.00	3.75
		On cover		500.00
6	A11	50c violet	20.00	*26.00*
		On cover		500.00
7	A11	1pe bister & blue	20.00	*30.00*
		On cover		300.00

8 A11 2pe blk & car rose 25.00 *30.00*
On cover 300.00
Nos. 1-8 (8) 95.50 *100.55*

Covers: Values for Nos. 1-6 are for covers bearing stamps paying thr correct rates. Values for Nos. 7-8 are for overfranked covers, usually philatelic.

Dark Blue Overprint

9 A11 40c orange brown *50.00* *35.00*
On cover *500.00*
10 A11 50c violet 14.00 14.00
On cover 500.00
11 A11 1pe bister & blue *175.00* *210.00*
On cover

Inverted "V" for "A"

1a	A11	5c	40.00	*50.00*
2a	A11	10c	260.00	310.00
3a	A11	20c	85.00	*95.00*
4a	A11	25c	140.00	*150.00*
5a	A11	40c	190.00	210.00
6a	A11	50c	290.00	*375.00*
7a	A11	1pe	275.00	*400.00*
8a	A11	2pe	350.00	*400.00*

Overprinted in Black

(Narrower "M," ear of "g" horiz.)

1899

12 A11 5c green .55 *1.10*
On cover 15.00
13 A11 10c carmine rose 2.90 .35
On cover 25.00
14 A11 20c olive green 8.00 .80
On cover 150.00
15 A11 25c ultramarine 12.50 1.00
On cover 100.00
16 A11 40c orange brown 47.50 35.00
On cover 350.00
17 A11 50c violet 11.00 4.00
On cover 350.00
18 A11 1pe bister & blue 32.50 *50.00*
On cover 250.00
19 A11 2pe blk & car rose 62.50 *55.00*
On cover 300.00
Nos. 12-19 (8) 177.45 *147.25*

Covers: Values for Nos. 18-19 are for overfranked covers, usually philatelic.

"M" with long serif

12a	A11	5c	10.00	*15.00*
13a	A11	10c	11.50	*13.50*
14a	A11	20c	40.00	*42.50*
15a	A11	25c	50.00	*55.00*
16a	A11	40c	260.00	*290.00*
17a	A11	50c	125.00	*140.00*
18a	A11	1pe	*175.00*	*290.00*
19a	A11	2pe	375.00	*400.00*

Type of Gibraltar, 1903, with Value in Spanish Currency, Overprinted

1903-05

20 A12 5c gray grn & bl grn 11.00 4.00
21 A12 10c violet, *red* 9.75 .45
22 A12 20c gray grn & car rose ('04) 20.00 *52.50*
23 A12 25c vio & blk, *bl* 9.25 .35
24 A12 50c violet 100.00 *190.00*
25 A12 1pe blk & car rose 47.50 *175.00*
26 A12 2pe black & ultra 57.50 *140.00*
Nos. 20-26 (7) 255.00 *562.30*

"M" with long serif

20a	A12	5c	57.50	*62.50*
21a	A12	10c	50.00	45.00
22a	A12	20c	110.00	*210.00*
23a	A12	25c	57.50	50.00
24a	A12	50c	400.00	*700.00*
25a	A12	1pe	260.00	*575.00*
26a	A12	2pe	300.00	*550.00*

1905-06 Wmk. 3 Chalky Paper

27 A12 5c gray grn & bl grn 11.00 *3.50*
28 A12 10c violet, *red* 12.50 2.25
29 A12 20c gray grn & car rose ('06) 6.25 *35.00*
30 A12 25c violet & blk, *bl* ('06) 45.00 9.75
31 A12 50c violet 8.50 *50.00*
32 A12 1pe blk & car rose 32.50 *92.50*
33 A12 2pe black & ultra 18.00 *40.00*
Nos. 27-33 (7) 133.75 *233.00*

No. 29 is on ordinary paper. Nos. 27 and 28 are on both ordinary and chalky paper.

"M" with long serif

27a	A12	5c	62.50	50.00
28a	A12	10c	62.50	42.50
29a	A12	20c	57.50	*175.00*
30a	A12	25c	350.00	175.00
31a	A12	50c	175.00	*290.00*
32a	A12	1pe	225.00	*375.00*
33a	A12	2pe	210.00	*290.00*

Numerous other minor overprint varieties exist of Nos. 1-33.

British Stamps of 1902-10 Surcharged in Spanish Currency:

#34-42, 46-48

#43-45

1907-10 Wmk. 30

34 A66 5c on ½p pale grn 9.25 .20
35 A66 10c on 1p car 13.50 .20
36 A67 15c on 1½p vio & grn 3.50 .25
a. "1" of "15" omitted 5,400.
37 A68 20c on 2p grn & car 3.00 .25
38 A66 25c on 2½p ultra 2.00 .25
39 A70 40c on 4p brn & grn 1.40 *3.50*
40 A70 40c on 4p org ('10) 1.10 .70
41 A71 50c on 5p lil & ultra 2.25 *3.75*
42 A73 1pe on 10p car rose & vio 25.00 *14.00*

Wmk. 31

43 A75 3pe on 2sh6p vio 24.00 *29.00*
44 A76 6pe on 5sh car rose 40.00 *52.50*
45 A77 12pe on 10sh ultra 85.00 85.00
Nos. 34-45 (12) 210.00 *189.60*

Nos. 36-37, 39-43 are on chalky paper.

Great Britain Nos. 153, 154 and 148 Surcharged

1912 Wmk. 30 Perf. 15x14

46 A80 5c on ½p yel grn 3.50 .20
47 A81 10c on 1p scarlet 1.10 .20
48 A66 25c on 2½p ultra 42.50 30.00
Nos. 46-48 (3) 47.10 30.40

British Stamps of 1912-18 Surcharged in Black or Carmine:

c

d

e

1914-18 Wmk. 33

49 A82(a) 5c on ½p grn .85 .20
50 A83(d) 10c on 1p scar 1.75 .20
51 A84(c) 15c on 1½p red brn('15) 1.10 .25
52 A85(d) 20c on 2p org (I) 1.10 .25
53 A86(d) 25c on 2½p ultra 2.00 .25
54 A90(d) 1pe on 10p lt bl 4.00 *8.00*

Wmk. 34

Perf. 11x12

55 A91(e) 3pe on 2sh6p lt brn 35.00 *160.00*
a. 3pe on 2sh6p dark brown 45.00 *125.00*
56 A91(e) 6pe on 5sh car 32.50 *55.00*
a. 6pe on 5sh light carmine 150.00 *210.00*
57 A91(e) 12pe on 10sh dk bl(C) 110.00 *190.00*
a. 12pe on 10sh blue 100.00 *190.00*
Nos. 49-57 (9) 188.30 *414.15*

Great Britain Nos. 159, 165 Surcharged in Spanish Currency

f

g

1917-23 Wmk. 33 Perf. 15x14

58 A82(f) 3c on ½p green 1.40 *5.00*
59 A88(g) 40c on 4p sl green 3.50 *4.50*

Great Britain Nos. 189, 191, 179 Surcharged in Spanish Currency

1926 Wmk. 35

60 A84(c) 15c on 1½p red brn 8.50 *26.00*
61 A86(d) 25c on 2½p ultra 2.90 *2.90*

Wmk. 34

Perf. 11x12

62 A91(e) 3pe on 2sh6p brn 26.00 *85.00*
Nos. 60-62 (3) 37.40 *113.90*

British Stamps of 1924 Surcharged in Spanish Currency

1929-31 Wmk. 35 Perf. 15x14

63 A82(a) 5c on ½p grn('31) 3.00 *17.50*
64 A83(d) 10c on 1p scar 21.00 *30.00*
65 A85(d) 20c on 2p org (II) ('31) 3.50 *10.00*
66 A88(g) 40c on 4p sl grn ('30) 2.90 2.90
Nos. 63-66 (4) 30.40 *60.40*

Silver Jubilee Issue

Great Britain Nos. 226-229 Surcharged in Blue or Red

1935, May 8 Perf. 14½x14

67 A98 5c on ½p dk grn 1.10 1.10
68 A98 10c on 1p car 3.00 2.50
a. Pair, one reading "CEN-TIMES" 1,600. 1,800.
69 A98 15c on 1½p red brn 6.25 *20.00*
70 A98 25c on 2½p ultra (R) 4.00 2.50
Nos. 67-70 (4) 14.35 *26.10*

25th anniv. of the reign of King George V.

Catalogue values for unused stamps in this section, from this point to the end of the section, are for Never Hinged items.

Great Britain Nos. 210-214, 216, 219 Surcharged in Spanish Currency

1935-37 Photo.

71 A82(a) 5c on ½p dk grn('36) 1.25 *21.00*
72 A97(d) 10c on 1p car 3.25 *11.00*
73 A84(c) 15c on 1½p red brn 7.00 3.75
74 A85(d) 20c on 2p red org ('36) .75 .30
75 A97(d) 25c on 2½p ultra('36) 1.75 *5.00*
76 A88(d) 40c on 4p dk sl grn ('37) .75 *3.50*
77 A90(d) 1pe on 10p Prus bl ('37) 7.00 .35
Nos. 71-77 (7) 21.75 *44.90*

Great Britain Nos. 230-233 Surcharged

"MOROCCO" 14mm

1936 Wmk. 250

78 A99 5c on ½p dk green .20 .20
79 A99 10c on 1p crimson .55 *2.25*
a. "Morocco" 15mm long 4.00 *16.00*
80 A99 15c on 1½p red brown .20 .20
81 A99 25c on 2½p brt ultra .20 .20
Nos. 78-81 (4) 1.15 *2.85*

Great Britain #234 Surcharged in Blue

Perf. 14½x14

1937, May 13 Wmk. 251

82 A100 15c on 1½p purple brn .80 .80

Coronation of George VI and Elizabeth.

Great Britain Nos. 235-237, 239, 241, 244 Surcharged in Blue or Black

h

1937-40

83 A101 5c on ½p dp grn (Bl) 1.40 .35
84 A101 10c on 1p scarlet 1.10 .20
85 A101 15c on 1½p red brown (Bl) 1.40 .30
86 A101 25c on 2½p brt ultra 2.25 1.40
87 A102 40c on 4p gray green ('40) 35.00 15.00
88 A103 70c on 7p emer ('40) 2.00 *16.00*
Nos. 83-88 (6) 43.15 *33.25*

Great Britain Nos. 252-254, 256 Surcharged in Blue or Black

1940, May 6

89 A106 5c on ½p deep grn (Bl) .35 *3.00*
90 A106 10c on 1p scarlet 4.25 *2.90*
91 A106 15c on 1½p red brn (Bl) .80 *2.90*
92 A106 25c on 2½p brt ultra .90 *1.10*
Nos. 89-92 (4) 6.30 *9.90*

Centenary of the postage stamp.

Great Britain Nos. 267 and 268 Surcharged in Black:

i

j

Perf. 14½x14, 14x14½

1948, Apr. 26 Wmk. 251

93 A109(i) 25c on 2½p 1.10 .35
94 A110(j) 45pe on £1 19.00 *25.00*

25th anniv. of the marriage of King George VI and Queen Elizabeth.

Great Britain Nos. 271-274 Surcharged "MOROCCO AGENCIES" and New Value

1948, July 29 Perf. 14½x14

95 A113 25c on 2½p brt ultra .55 *1.40*
96 A114 30c on 3p dp vio .55 *1.40*
97 A115 60c on 6p red vio .55 *1.40*
98 A116 1.20pe on 1sh dk brn .70 *1.40*
a. Double surcharge 925.00
Nos. 95-98 (4) 2.35 *5.60*

1948 Olympic Games, Wembley, July-Aug.

A square of dots obliterates the original denomination on No. 98.

Great Britain Nos. 280-282, 284-285, 247 Surcharged Type "h"

1951-52 Wmk. 251 Perf. 14½x14

99 A101 5c on ½p lt orange 2.25 *5.00*
100 A101 10c on 1p ultra 3.75 *8.50*
101 A101 15c on 1½p green 2.00 *19.00*
102 A101 25c on 2½p ver 2.00 *11.00*
103 A102 40c on 4p ultra ('52) .70 *11.50*
104 A103 1pe on 10p ryl bl ('52) 2.50 *4.00*
Nos. 99-104 (6) 13.20 *59.00*

BRITISH CURRENCY

Stamps of Morocco Agencies were accepted for postage in Great Britain, starting in mid-1950. Copies with contemporaneous Morocco cancellations sell for more.

British Stamps of 1902-11 Overprinted

a

b

Overprint "a" 14½mm long

1907-12 Wmk. 30 *Perf. 14*

Ordinary Paper

201 A66 ½p pale yel grn 2.50 *9.75*
202 A66 1p carmine 11.00 6.25

Chalky Paper

203 A68 2p green & car 11.50 6.25
204 A70 4p brown & grn 4.25 *4.50*
205 A70 4p orange ('12) 11.50 *12.50*
a. Perf. 15x14 25.00 *27.50*
206 A66 6p dull vio 17.00 *21.00*
207 A74 1sh car rose & grn 30.00 *19.00*

Overprinted Type "b"

Wmk. 31

208 A75 2sh6p violet 92.50 *140.00*
Nos. 201-208 (8) 180.25 *219.25*

British Stamps of 1912-18 Overprinted Type "a"

Perf. 14½x14, 15x14

1914-21 Wmk. 33

209 A82 ½p green ('18) 4.00 .55
210 A83 1p scarlet ('17) 1.00 .20
211 A84 1½p red brn ('21) 3.75 *14.00*
212 A85 2p orange ('18) 4.50 .70
213 A87 3p violet ('21) 1.40 .40
214 A88 4p slate grn ('21) 3.75 1.40
215 A89 6p dull vio ('21) 5.50 *17.50*
216 A90 1sh bister ('17) 6.25 1.40

c

Wmk. 34 *Perf. 11x12*

217 A91 2sh6p lt brown 42.50 *57.50*
a. 2sh6p brown 55.00 35.00
b. 2sh6p black brown 52.50 *62.50*
c. Double overprint 1,900. 1,350.
Nos. 209-217 (9) 72.65 *93.65*

Same Overprint on Great Britain Nos. 179-180

1925-31

218 A91 2sh6p gray brown 42.50 29.00
219 A91 5sh car rose ('31) 62.50 *100.00*

British Stamps of 1924 Overprinted Type "a" (14½mm long)

1925-31 Wmk. 35 *Perf. 15x14*

220 A82 ½p green 2.25 .55
221 A84 1½p red brn ('31) 13.50 *15.00*
222 A85 2p dp org (Die II) 2.50 1.10
223 A86 2½p ultra 2.50 *5.75*
224 A89 6p red vio ('31) 2.25 *9.50*
225 A90 1sh bister 19.00 5.75
Nos. 220-225 (6) 42.00 *37.65*

Silver Jubilee Issue

Great Britain Nos. 226-229 Overprinted in Blue or Red

1935, May 8 *Perf. 14½x14*

226 A98 ½p dark green (Bl) 1.40 *7.50*
227 A98 1p carmine (Bl) 1.40 *7.50*
228 A98 1½p red brown (Bl) 2.50 *11.00*
229 A98 2½p ultramarine (R) 2.90 2.90
Nos. 226-229 (4) 8.20 *28.90*

25th anniversary of the reign of King George V.

British Stamps of 1924 Overprinted Type "a" (15½mm long)

1935-36

230 A82 ½p green 9.50 *45.00*
231 A86 2½p ultra *110.00* 35.00
232 A88 4p slate green 8.00 *40.00*
233 A89 6p red violet 1.10 .70
234 A90 1sh bister 62.50 57.50
Nos. 230-234 (5) 191.10 *178.20*

British Stamps of 1934-36 Overprinted "MOROCCO AGENCIES"

1935-36

235 A97 1p carmine 3.50 *16.00*
236 A84 1½p red brn ('36) 3.50 *19.00*
237 A85 2p red org ('36) 1.40 *9.00*
238 A97 2½p ultra ('36) 2.00 *4.75*
239 A87 3p dk violet ('36) .55 .35
240 A88 4p dk slate grn ('36) .55 .35
241 A90 1sh bis brn ('36) .90 *4.00*

Overprinted Type "c"

Wmk. 34

Perf. 11x12

242 A91 2sh6p brown 45.00 *70.00*
243 A91 5sh carmine ('37) 27.50 *110.00*
Nos. 235-243 (9) 84.90 *233.45*

Catalogue values for unused stamps in this section, from this point to the end of the section, are for Never Hinged items.

Great Britain Nos. 231, 233 Overprinted

"MOROCCO" 14mm

1936 Wmk. 250 *Perf. 14½x14*

244 A99 1p crimson .20 .20
a. "Morocco" 15mm long 7.00 *19.00*
245 A99 2½p bright ultra .20 .20
a. "Morocco" 15mm long 1.10 4.75

Great Britain Nos. 258-263, 241-248, 266, 249A-250 Overprinted "MOROCCO AGENCIES" (14½mm long)

1949, Aug. 16 Wmk. 251

246 A101 ½p green 2.00 *8.00*
247 A101 1p vermilion 3.00 *10.00*
248 A101 1½p lt red brown 3.00 *9.50*
249 A101 2p lt orange 3.50 *10.00*
250 A101 2½p ultra 3.75 *11.50*
251 A101 3p violet 1.75 *2.00*
252 A102 4p gray green .55 *1.40*
253 A102 5p lt brown 3.50 *17.00*
254 A102 6p rose lilac 1.75 1.75
255 A103 7p emerald .55 *18.00*
256 A103 8p brt rose 3.50 *7.50*
257 A103 9p dp olive grn .55 *12.50*
258 A103 10p royal blue .55 *7.50*
259 A103 11p violet brn .80 *8.50*
260 A103 1sh brown 3.00 *7.00*

"MOROCCO AGENCIES"

17½mm long

Wmk. 259

Perf. 14

261 A104 2sh6p yellow grn 18.00 *40.00*
262 A104 5sh dull red 32.50 *70.00*
Nos. 246-262 (17) 82.25 *242.15*

Great Britain Nos. 280-284, 286-287 Overprinted "MOROCCO AGENCIES" (14½mm long)

Perf. 14½x14

1951, May 3 Wmk. 251

263 A101 ½p lt orange 2.25 1.10
264 A101 1p ultra 2.25 1.60
265 A101 1½p green 2.25 *3.00*
266 A101 2p lt red brown 2.50 *4.50*
267 A101 2½p vermilion 2.25 *4.75*

"MOROCCO AGENCIES"

17½mm long

Wmk. 259

Perf. 11x12

268 A121 2sh6p green 15.00 *24.00*
269 A121 5sh dull red 15.00 *26.00*
Nos. 263-269 (7) 41.50 *64.95*

French Currency

British Stamps of 1912-22 Surcharged in French Currency in Red or Black:

h

i

Perf. 14½x14, 15x14

1917-24 Wmk. 33

401 A82(h) 3c on ½p green (R) 1.10 *2.90*
402 A82(h) 5c on ½p green .45 1.75
403 A83(h) 10c on 1p scarlet 3.75 .45
404 A84(h) 15c on 1½p red brn 2.90 .20
405 A86(h) 25c on 2½p ultra 2.25 .20
406 A88(h) 40c on 4p slate grn 2.90 1.75
407 A89(h) 50c on 5p yel brn ('23) .90 *3.00*
408 A90(h) 75c on 9p ol grn ('24) 1.10 .85
409 A90(i) 1fr on 10p lt blue 8.00 3.50
Nos. 401-409 (9) *23.35 14.60*

Great Britain No. 179 Surcharged:

k

1924 Wmk. 34 *Perf. 11x12*

410 A91(k) 3fr on 2sh6p brn 8.50 1.75

British Stamps of 1924 Surcharged in French Currency as in 1917-24

1925-26 Wmk. 35 *Perf. 15x14*

411 A82(h) 5c on ½p green .35 *7.50*
412 A83(h) 10c on 1p scarlet .35 *2.25*
413 A84(h) 15c on 1½p red brn 1.10 *2.00*
414 A86(h) 25c on 2½p ultra 1.75 .55
415 A88(h) 40c on 4p sl green .70 *.90*
416 A89(h) 50c on 5p yel brown 1.75 .20
417 A90(h) 75c on 9p ol green 4.00 .20
418 A90(i) 1fr on 10p dl blue 1.40 .20
Nos. 411-418 (8) 11.40 *13.80*

Great Britain Nos. 180, 198 and 200 Surcharged type "k"

1932 Wmk. 34 *Perf. 11x12*

419 A91 6fr on 5sh car rose 42.50 *47.50*

1934 Wmk. 35 *Perf. 14½x14*

420 A90 90c on 9p ol green 18.00 8.50
421 A90 1.50fr on 1sh bister 11.50 2.50

Silver Jubilee Issue

Great Britain Nos. 226-229 Surcharged in Blue or Red

1935, May 8 *Perf. 14½x14*

422 A98 5c on ½p dk green .20 .20
423 A98 10c on 1p carmine 3.00 .85
424 A98 15c on 1½p red brn .40 *.55*
425 A98 25c on 2½p ultra (R) .25 *.35*
Nos. 422-425 (4) 3.85 1.95

25th anniv. of the reign of King George V.

British Stamps of 1934-36 Surcharged Types "h" or "k"

Perf. 14½x14

1935-37 Photo. Wmk. 35

426 A82(h) 5c on ½p dk grn .55 *5.75*
427 A97(h) 10c on 1p car ('36) .40 .35
428 A84(h) 15c on 1½p red brn 5.50 *6.25*
429 A97(h) 25c on 2½p ultra .35 .20
430 A88(h) 40c on 4p dk sl grn .35 .20
431 A89(h) 50c on 5p yel brn .35 .20
432 A90(h) 90c on 9p dk ol grn .40 *2.00*
433 A90(k) 1fr on 10p Prus bl .35 .35
434 A90(h) 1.50fr on 1sh bister brn ('37) .85 *3.75*

Waterlow Printing

Wmk. 34 *Perf. 11x12*

435 A91(k) 3fr on 2sh6p brn 5.50 *14.00*
436 A91(k) 6fr on 5sh car ('36) 7.00 *24.00*
Nos. 426-436 (11) 21.60 *57.05*

Great Britain Nos. 230, 232 Surcharged

1936 Wmk. 250 *Perf. 14½x14*

437 A99 5c on ½p dark green .20 .20
438 A99 15c on 1½p red brown .20 .20

Great Britain No. 234 Surcharged in Blue

1937, May 13 Wmk. 251

439 A100 15c on 1½p purple brn .35 .20

Coronation of George VI and Elizabeth.

Great Britain No. 235 Surcharged in Blue

1937

440 A101 5c on ½p deep green 2.50 *2.90*

For Use in the International Zone of Tangier

Great Britain Nos. 187-190 Overprinted in Black

a

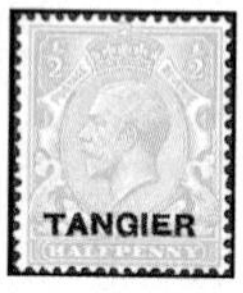

1927 Wmk. 35 *Perf. 15x14*

501 A82 ½p green 3.50 .20
502 A83 1p scarlet 3.50 .30
503 A84 1½p red brown 7.00 4.25
504 A85 2p orange (II) 3.75 .20
Nos. 501-504 (4) 17.75 4.95

Same Overprint on Great Britain Nos. 210-212

1934-35 Photo. *Perf. 14½x14*

505 A82 ½p dark green 1.40 *1.75*
506 A97 1p carmine 4.75 2.75
507 A84 1½p red brown .55 .20
Nos. 505-507 (3) 6.70 *4.70*

Silver Jubilee Issue

Great Britain Nos. 226-228 Overprinted in Blue

b

1935, May 8

508 A98 ½p dark green 1.40 *5.75*
509 A98 1p carmine 16.00 *17.00*
510 A98 1½p red brown 1.40 1.10
Nos. 508-510 (3) 18.80 *23.85*

25th anniv. of the reign of King George V.

Catalogue values for unused stamps in this section, from this point to the end of the section, are for Never Hinged items.

Great Britain Nos. 230-232 Overprinted Type "a"

1936 **Wmk. 250**

511 A99 ½p dark green .20 .20
512 A99 1p crimson .20 .20
513 A99 1½p red brown .20 .20
Nos. 511-513 (3) .60 .60

Great Britain No. 234 Overprinted Type "b" in Blue

1937, May 13 **Wmk. 251**

514 A100 1½p purple brown .55 .55

Coronation of George VI and Elizabeth.

Great Britain Nos. 235-237 Overprinted in Blue or Black

c

1937 ***Perf. 14½x14***

515 A101 ½p deep green (Bl) 2.75 1.75
516 A101 1p scarlet (Bk) 8.00 1.75
517 A101 1½p red brown (Bl) 2.75 .30
Nos. 515-517 (3) 13.50 3.80

Great Britain Nos. 252-254 Ovptd. Type "a" in Blue or Black

1940, May 6

518 A106 ½p deep green (Bl) .35 *5.50*
519 A106 1p scarlet (Bk) .50 *.60*
520 A106 1½p red brown (Bl) 2.25 *5.75*
Nos. 518-520 (3) 3.10 *11.85*

Centenary of the postage stamp.

Great Britain Nos. 258 and 259 Overprinted Type "c" in Blue or Black

1944-45

521 A101 ½p green (Bl) 12.50 5.00
522 A101 1p ver (Bk) ('45) 12.50 3.50

Catalogue values for unused stamps in this section, from this point to the end of the section, are for Never Hinged items.

Great Britain Nos. 264-265 Overprinted:

d

e

1946, June 11

523 A107(d) 2½p bright ultra .75 .75
524 A108(e) 3p violet .75 *2.25*

Return to peace at close of World War II.

Great Britain Nos. 267 and 268 Overprinted Type "a"

1948, Apr. 26 ***Perf. 14½x14, 14x14½***

525 A109 2½p bright ultra .60 .20
a. Pair, one without overprint *5,400.*
526 A110 £1 dp chalky bl 22.50 29.00

25th anniv. of the marriage of King George VI and Queen Elizabeth.

Great Britain Nos. 271 to 274 Overprinted Type "a"

1948, July 29 ***Perf. 14½x14***

527 A113 2½p bright ultra 1.10 *2.25*
528 A114 3p deep violet 1.10 *2.25*
529 A115 6p red violet 1.10 *2.25*
530 A116 1sh dark brown 1.10 *1.40*
Nos. 527-530 (4) 4.40 *8.15*

1948 Olympic Games, Wembley, July-Aug.

Stamps of Great Britain, 1937-47, and Nos. 249A, 250 and 251A Overprinted Type "c"

1949, Jan. 1

531 A101 2p lt org (II) 5.75 *7.00*
532 A101 2½p ultra (II) 2.00 *7.00*
533 A101 3p violet (II) .80 *1.40*
534 A102 4p gray green 12.50 11.50
535 A102 5p light brown 4.25 *22.50*
536 A102 6p rose lilac .80 .35
537 A103 7p emerald 1.40 *15.00*
538 A103 8p bright rose 4.25 *12.50*
539 A103 9p deep ol grn 1.40 *13.50*
540 A103 10p royal blue 1.40 *15.00*
541 A103 11p violet brn 1.75 *12.50*
542 A103 1sh brown 1.40 *3.00*

Wmk. 259

Perf. 14

543 A104 2sh6p yellow grn 5.00 *13.50*
544 A104 5sh dull red 15.00 *42.50*
545 A105 10sh ultra 50.00 *110.00*
Nos. 531-545 (15) 107.70 *287.25*

Great Britain Nos. 276 to 279 Overprinted Type "a"

Perf. 14½x14

1949, Oct. 10 **Wmk. 251**

546 A117 2½p bright ultra .80 *3.00*
547 A118 3p bright violet .80 *2.00*
548 A119 6p red violet .80 *1.40*
549 A120 1sh brown .80 *3.75*
Nos. 546-549 (4) 3.20 *10.15*

Great Britain Nos. 280-288 Overprinted Type "c" or "a" (Shilling Values)

1950-51

550 A101 ½p lt orange 1.00 *1.75*
551 A101 1p ultra 1.10 *3.50*
552 A101 1½p green 1.10 *16.00*
553 A101 2p lt red brn 1.10 *2.90*
554 A101 2½p vermilion 1.10 *5.75*
555 A102 4p ultra ('50) 3.50 3.50

Wmk. 259

Perf. 11x12

556 A121 2sh6p green 11.00 5.75
557 A121 5sh dull red 17.50 *19.00*
558 A122 10sh ultra 22.50 19.00
Nos. 550-558 (9) 59.90 *77.15*

TURKISH EMPIRE

STAMPS OF GREAT BRITAIN USED IN THE TURKISH EMPIRE

Values are for clear cancellations on sound, fault-free stamps, with average to fine centering. In many cases, very fine copies are rare or non-existent.

BEIRUT

British P.O. opened 1873; closed Sept. 30, 1914

No. A24

Stamps of Great Britain, Canceled with barred oval "G06" or circular date stamp "BEYROUT"

1873-80

A1 ½p rose red (#58, P 12-14) 45.00
Plate 19 100.00
Plate 20 140.00
A2 1p rose red (#33, P107, 118, 130, 140, 145, 148, 155, 157, 162, 167, 177, 179, 180, 184-187, 195, 198, 200, 203, 204, 211, 213, 215, 218, 220, 222) *value from* 19.00
A3 1½p lake red (#32, P 3) 300.00
A4 2p blue (#30, P 13-15), *value from* 25.00
A5 2½p claret (#66, P 1-3), *value from* 37.50
a. Bluish paper (#66a, P 1) 87.50
A6 2½p claret (#67, P 3-17), *value from* 30.00
A7 2½p blue (#68, P 17-20), *value from* 19.00
A8 2½p blue (#82, P 21-23), *value from* 13.50
On cover, *value from* *75.00*
A9 3p rose (#49, P 10) —
A10 3p rose (#61, P 12, 15, 16, 18-20), *value from* 47.50
A11 3p rose (#83, P 20, 21) —
A12 4p vermilion (#43, P 11-14), *value from* 45.00
A13 4p vermilion (#69, P 15) 375.00
A14 4p pale olive green (#70, P 15) 250.00
Plate 16 225.00
A15 4p gray brown (#71, P 17) —
A16 4p gray brown (#84, P17, 18), *value from* 55.00
A17 6p violet (#52, P 8, 9) —
A18 6p brown (#59, P 11) 47.50
a. 6p pale buff (#59b, P 11) 100.00
Plate 12 250.00
A19 6p gray (#60, P 12) —
A20 6p gray (#62, P 13-17), *value from* 35.00
A21 8p orange (#73) 425.00
A22 10p red brown (#53) 325.00
A23 1sh green (#54, P 6, 7) *value from* 37.50
A24 1sh green (#64, P 8-10, 12, 13) *value from* 50.00
A25 1sh salmon (#65, P 13) —
A26 1sh salmon (#87, P 13, 14) 60.00
A27 2sh blue (#55) 160.00
A28 5sh rose (#57, P 1) 675.00
Plate 2 850.00

1880

A29 ½p deep green (#78) 12.00
a. ½p green (#78c) 13.00
A30 1p red brown (#79) 16.00
A31 1½p red brown (#80) 175.00
A32 2p lilac rose (#81) 60.00
a. 2p deep lilac rose (#81a) 60.00
A33 5p indigo (#85) 100.00

1881

A34 1p lilac, 14 dots (#88) —
A35 1p lilac, 16 dots (#88) 8.00

1883-84

A36 ½p slate blue (#98) 20.00
A37 1½p lilac (#99) 87.50
A38 2p lilac (#100) 77.50
A39 2½p lilac (#101) 13.50
On cover *75.00*
A41 4p dull green (#103) 200.00
A42 5p dull green (#104) 130.00
A45 1sh dull green (#107) 300.00

1887-92

A46 ½p vermilion 10.00
A53 6p violet, *rose* 27.50
A56 1sh dull green 160.00

1900

A57 ½p blue green 13.50
A58 1sh car rose & grn 200.00

1902-04

A59 ½p blue green 5.75
A60 ½p yellow green 6.00
A61 1p scarlet 5.50
A65 1sh car & dull grn 35.00

CONSTANTINOPLE

British P.O. opened Sept. 1, 1857; closed Sept. 30, 1914; reopened Feb. 4, 1919; closed Sept. 27, 1923

No. A124

Stamps of Great Britain, Canceled with barred oval "C" or circular date stamp "CONSTANTINOPLE"

1857-83

A75 ½p rose red (#58, P 5, 6, 10-15, 20), *value from* 30.00
A76 1p red brown (#8) —
A77 1p red brown (#12) —
A78 1p red brown (#16) 22.50
A79 1p rose red (#20) 8.50
A80 1p rose red (#33, P 71-74, 76, 78-81, 83, 85, 87, 89, 90, 92-97, 99, 101, 102, 105, 106, 108-110, 113, 116, 118-125, 127, 129-131, 134-138, 140, 141, 143-152, 155-167, 170-184, 186-198, 200, 201, 203-208, 210, 212, 214-216, 220, 222, 224) *value from* 10.00
A81 1½p lake red (#32a, P 1) 250.00
A82 2p blue (#17) —
A83 2p blue (#29, P 7) 65.00
Plate 8 55.00
Plate 9 14.00
Plate 12 *200.00*
Plate 13 27.50
Plate 14 37.50
Plate 15 37.50
A84 2½p claret (#66, P 1-3), *value from* 35.00
a. Bluish paper (#66a, P 1, 2) 65.00
b. Lettered "LH-FL" (#66b) —
A85 2½p claret (#67, P 3-17), *value from* 27.50
A86 2½p blue (#68, P 17-20), *value from* 13.50
A87 2½p blue (#82, P 21-23), *value from* 9.00
A88 3p rose (#37) 160.00
A89 3p rose (#44) 87.50
A90 3p rose (#49, P 4-10), *value from* 82.50
A91 3p rose (#61, P 11, 12, 15-18, 19), *value from* 30.00
A92 3p rose (#83, P 21) —
A93 3p on 3p violet (#94)
A94 4p rose (#26) 55.00
a. 4p carmine rose (#26a)
A95 4p vermilion (#34, P 3) 45.00
a. Hairlines (#34c) 60.00
A96 4p vermilion (#43, P 7-14), *value from* 30.00
A97 4p vermilion (#69, P 15) 375.00
A98 4p pale olive green (#70, P 15) 250.00
Plate 16 225.00
A99 4p gray brown (#71, P 17) —
A100 4p gray brown (#84, P17, 18), *value from* 42.50
A101 6p lilac (#27) 70.00
A102 6p lilac (#39, P 3) 75.00
a. 6p lilac, thick paper (#39b, P 4) *200.00*
A103 6p lilac (#45, P 5) 42.50
Plate 6 *175.00*
A104 6p dull violet (#50, P 6) 50.00
A105 6p violet (#51, 6, 8, 9), *value from* 37.50
A106 6p brown (#59, P 11) 35.00
a. 6p pale buff (#59b, P 11) 80.00
Plate 12 225.00
A107 6p gray (#60, P 12) 90.00
A108 6p gray (#62, P 13-16), *value from* 30.00
A109 6p gray (#86, P 17, 18), *value from* 30.00
A110 6p on 6p violet (#95) 100.00
A111 8p orange (#73) 375.00
A112 10p red brown (#47) *17,500.*
A113 10p red brown (#53) 190.00
A114 1sh green (#28) 275.00
a. 1sh green, thick paper (#28d) *275.00*
A115 1sh green (#42) 70.00
A116 1sh green (#48, P 4) 75.00
A117 1sh green (#54, P 4-7), *value from* 20.00
A118 1sh green (#64, P 8-13), *value from* 32.50
A119 1sh salmon (#65, P 13) *240.00*
A120 1sh salmon (#87, P 13, 14), *value from* 55.00
A121 2sh blue (#55) 150.00
A122 5sh rose (#57, P 1) 575.00
Plate 2 850.00
A123 5sh rose, *blue* (#90) *1,200.*
a. White paper (#90a) *1,000.*

1880

A124 ½p deep green (#78) 9.00
a. ½p green (#78c) 11.00
A125 1p red brown (#79) 10.00
A126 2p lilac rose (#81) 50.00
a. 2p deep rose (#81a) 50.00
A127 5p indigo (#85) —

1881

A128 1p lilac, 14 dots (#88) —
A129 1p lilac, 16 dots (#88) 4.00

1883-84

A130 ½p slate blue (#98) 9.00
A131 1½p lilac (#99) —
A132 2p lilac (#100) 75.00
A133 2½p lilac (#101) 10.00
A134 3p lilac (#102) —
A135 4p dull green (#103) —
A136 5p dull green (#104) 130.00
A137 6p dull green (#105) —
A138 9p dull green (#106) —
A139 1sh dull green (#107) 225.00
A140 2sh6p lilac, *bluish* (#90) 600.00
a. White paper (#90a) 100.00
A141 5sh rose (#108) —
a. Bluish paper (#108a)

1887-92

A142 ½p vermilion 4.00
A150 6p violet, *rose* 13.50
A153 1sh dull green 90.00

1900

A154	½p blue green	6.50
A155	1sh car rose & grn	175.00

1902-04

A156	½p blue green	4.50
A157	½p yellow green	5.00
A158	1p scarlet	4.00
A165	6p purple	13.00
A168	1sh car & dull grn	27.50
A169	2sh6p lilac	—
A170	5sh carmine	—

Postal Fiscal stamps of Great Britain are found used in Constantinople. They are rare.

SALONICA

British P.O. opened May 1, 1900; closed October, 1914

Stamps of Great Britain, Canceled with circular date stamp "SALONICA," with single or double circle

1887-92

A197	½p vermilion	20.00
A198	1p lilac	22.50
A199	6p violet, *rose*	30.00
A200	5sh rose (#90a)	950.00

1900

A201	½p blue green	22.50
A202	1sh car rose & grn	200.00

1902-04

A203	½p blue green	27.50
A204	½p yellow green	20.00
A205	1p scarlet	20.00
A206	6p purple	
A207	1sh car & dull grn	50.00

SMYRNA

British P.O. opened 1872; closed Sept. 30, 1914; reopened Mar. 1, 1919; closed Sept., 1922

Stamps of Great Britain, Canceled with barred numeral "F87" or with circular date stamps (various types)

1872-83

A229	½p rose red (#58, P 11-15), *value from*	32.50
A230	1p rose red (#33, P 120, 124, 134, 137-140, 142, 143, 145, 146, 148-153, 155-164, 166-178, 183-188, 193, 195, 196, 198, 200, 201, 204, 210, 212, 215, 217, 218), *value from*	15.00
A231	1½p lake red (#32a, P 1, 3), *value from*	275.00
A232	2p blue (#15)	—
A233	2p blue (#30, P 13-15), *value from*	19.00
A234	2½p claret (#66, P 1-3), *value from*	32.50
a.	Bluish paper (#66a, P 1, 2)	70.00
b.	Lettered "LH-FL" (#66b)	—
A235	2½p claret (#67, P 3-17), *value from*	26.00
A236	2½p blue (#68, P 17-20), *value from*	22.50
A237	2½p blue (#82, P 21-23), *value from*	11.00
A238	3p rose (#49, P 5, 7, 9, 10), *value from*	42.50
A239	3p rose (#61, P 14, 15)	—
A240	4p vermilion (#43, P 12-14), *value from*	30.00
A241	4p vermilion (#69, P 15)	375.00
A242	4p pale olive green (#70, P 15)	250.00
	Plate 16	225.00
A243	4p gray brown (#71, P 17)	—
A244	4p gray brown (#84, P17, 18), *value from*	37.50
A245	6p brown (#59, P 11), *value from*	—
a.	6p pale buff (#59b, P 11)	100.00
	Plate 12	225.00
A246	6p gray (#60, P 12)	95.00
A247	6p gray (#62, P 13-17), *value from*	30.00
A248	6p gray (#86, P 17, 18), *value from*	60.00
A249	6p on 6p violet (#95)	125.00
A250	8p orange (#73)	—
A251	9p bister (#52)	*400.00*
A252	10p red brown (#53)	*275.00*
A253	1sh green (#54, P 6, 7), *value from*	—
A254	1sh green (#64, P 8-13), *value from*	35.00
A255	1sh salmon (#65, P 13)	*250.00*
A256	1sh salmon (#87, P 13, 14), *value from*	60.00
A257	5sh rose (#57, P 2)	—

1880

A258	½p deep green (#78)	10.00
a.	½p green (#78c)	10.00
A259	1p red brown (#79)	14.50
A260	1½p red brown (#80)	110.00
A261	2p lilac rose (#81)	45.00
a.	2p deep rose (#81a)	45.00
A262	5p indigo (#85)	70.00

1881

A263	1p lilac, 16 dots (#88)	6.00

1883-84

A264	½p slate blue (#98)	16.00
A266	2p lilac (#100)	72.50
A267	2½p lilac (#101)	12.00
A269	4p dull green (#103)	—
A270	5p dull green (#104)	140.00
A273	1sh dull green (#107)	275.00

1887-92

A275	½p vermilion	6.00
A282	6p violet, *rose*	22.50
A283	1sh dull green	140.00

1900

A285	½p blue green	8.75
A286	1sh car rose & grn	—

1902-04

A287	½p blue green	5.50
A288	½p yellow green	6.00
A289	1p scarlet	5.50
A296	6p purple	15.00
A299	1sh car & dull grn	30.00
A300	2sh6p lilac	—
A301	5sh carmine	—

STAMBOUL

British P.O. opened Apr. 1, 1884; closed Aug. 25, 1896; reopened Feb. 10, 1908; closed Sept. 30, 1914

Stamps of Great Britain, Canceled with barred "S" or circular date stamps "BRITISH POST OFFICE CONSTANTINOPLE S" or "BRITISH POST OFFICE STAMBOUL

1883-84

A323	½p slate blue (#98)	27.50
A324	2p lilac (#99)	13.50
A325	2p lilac (#100)	—
A326	2½p lilac (#101)	16.00
A327	5p dull green (#104)	160.00

1887-92

A330	½p vermilion	16.00
A338	6p violet, *rose*	37.50
A341	1sh dull green	—

BRITISH STAMPS OVERPRINTED

40 Paras = 1 Piaster
12 Pence = 1 Shilling (1905)

a

b

c

40 PARAS
d

Surcharged on Great Britain Nos. 101, 104, 96

1885, Apr. 1 Wmk. 30 *Perf. 14*

1	A47(a) 40pa on 2½p lil	110.00	1.50
	On cover		10.00
2	A45(b) 80pa on 5p grn	210.00	12.50
	On cover		80.00

Wmk. 31

3	A44(c) 12pi on 2sh6p lilac	52.50	27.50
	On cover		250.00
a.	Bluish paper	400.00	260.00
	On cover		1,600.
	Nos. 1-3 (3)	372.50	41.50

Great Britain Nos. 114, 118 Surcharged

1887 Wmk. 30

4	A57(a) 40pa on 2½p vio, *bl*	4.75	.20
	On cover		5.00
a.	Double surcharge	*2,250.*	*2,900.*
5	A61(b) 80pa on 5p lil & bl	17.50	.35
	On cover		5.00
a.	Small "0" in "80"	225.00	100.00
	On cover		375.00

Great Britain No. 111 Handstamp Surcharged

1893, Feb. 25

6	A54(d) 40pa on ½p ver	*500.00*	*125.00*
	On cover		375.00

No. 6 was a provisional, made and used at Constantinople for five days. Excellent forgeries are known.

Great Britain No. 121 Surcharged

e

1896

7	A64(e) 4pi on 10p car rose & lil	47.50	9.25
	On cover		50.00

British Stamps of 1902 Surcharged

1902-05 Wmk. 30

8	A66(a) 40pa on 2½p ultra	17.50	.20
9	A71(b) 80pa on 5p lil & bl	9.00	2.90
a.	Small "0" in "80"	250.00	210.00
10	A73(e) 4pi on 10p car rose & vio	13.50	4.50

Wmk. 31

11	A75(c) 12pi on 2sh6p vio ('03)	40.00	40.00
12	A76(c) 24pi on 5sh car rose ('05)	35.00	47.50
	Nos. 8-12 (5)	115.00	*95.10*

Great Britain Nos. 131, 134 Surcharged

f

1906 Wmk. 30

13	A66(f) 1pi on 2½p ultra	17.50	.20
14	A71(f) 2pi on 5p lil & ultra	32.50	2.75

Nos. 10, 11, 14 are on both ordinary and chalky paper.

Great Britain Nos. 127-135, 138 Overprinted

g

1905

15	A66 ½p pale green	10.00	.20
16	A66 1p carmine	9.50	.20
17	A67 1½p violet & grn	6.25	2.00
18	A68 2p green & car	3.50	*8.00*
19	A66 2½p ultra	10.00	*22.50*
20	A69 3p violet, *yel*	7.25	*13.50*
21	A70 4p brown & grn	10.00	*50.00*
22	A71 5p lilac & ultra	19.00	*32.50*
23	A66 6p dull violet	15.00	*29.00*
24	A74 1sh car rose & grn	42.50	*57.50*
	Nos. 15-24 (10)	133.00	*215.40*

Nos. 17, 18 and 24 are on both ordinary and chalky paper.

No. 18 Surcharged **1 Piastre**

1906, July 2

25	A68 1pi on 2p grn & car	1,500.	700.00

British Stamps of 1902-09 Surcharged:

j

k

1909

26	A67 30pa on 1½p vio & grn	11.50	1.40
27	A69 1pi10pa on 3p vio, *yel*	13.50	*40.00*
28	A70 1pi30pa on 4p brn & grn	5.75	*19.00*
29	A70 1pi30pa on 4p org	20.00	*70.00*
30	A66 2pi20pa on 6p dl violet	22.50	*70.00*
31	A74 5pi on 1sh car rose & grn	5.00	*11.00*
	Nos. 26-31 (6)	78.25	*211.40*

No. 29 is on ordinary paper, the others are on chalky paper.

Great Britain Nos. 132, 144, 135 Surcharged:

m

n

1910

32	A69(m) 1¼pi on 3p vio, *yel*	.60	*1.25*
33	A70(m) 1¾pi on 4p orange	.60	*.75*
34	A66(n) 2½pi on 6p dl vio	1.60	.80
	Nos. 32-34 (3)	2.80	2.80

There are three different varieties of "4" in the fraction of the 1¾ piastre.

Great Britain Nos. 151-154 Overprinted Type "g"

1911-12 *Perf. 15x14*

35	A80 ½p yellow green	2.25	1.75
36	A81 1p carmine	.55	*7.00*

Re-engraved

37	A80 ½p yel grn ('12)	.90	.20
38	A81 1p scarlet ('12)	.90	*1.75*

Great Britain No. 148 Surcharged

o

39	A66(o) 1pi on 2½p ultra	15.00	3.00
	Nos. 35-39 (5)	19.60	13.70

The surcharge on No. 39 exists in two types with the letters 2½ and 3mm high respectively. The stamp also differs from No. 13 in the perforation.

British Stamps of 1912-13 Surcharged with New Values

1913-14 Wmk. 33

40	A84(j) 30pa on 1½p red brown	4.00	*16.00*
41	A86(o) 1pi on 2½p ultra	8.50	.20
42	A87(m) 1¼pi on 3p vio	5.50	4.75
43	A88(m) 1¾pi on 4p sl grn	3.50	*7.00*
44	A90(o) 4pi on 10p lt bl	9.00	*22.50*
45	A90(o) 5pi on 1sh bis	45.00	*70.00*
	Nos. 40-45 (6)	*75.50*	120.45

British Stamps of 1912-19 Overprinted Type "g"

1913-21

46	A82 ½p green	.45	*1.40*
47	A83 1p scarlet	.35	*5.75*
48	A85 2p orange ('21)	1.40	*32.50*
49	A87 3p violet ('21)	8.50	*11.50*
50	A88 4p sl grn ('21)	5.75	*16.00*
51	A89 5p yel brn ('21)	13.50	*32.50*
52	A89 6p dl vio ('21)	30.00	*10.00*
53	A90 1sh bister ('21)	15.00	*10.00*

Wmk. 34

Perf. 11x12

54	A91 2sh6p brn ('21)	42.50	*100.00*
	Nos. 46-54 (9)	117.45	*219.65*

British Stamps of 1912-19 Surcharged as in 1909-10 and

p

q

1921 Wmk. 33 *Perf. 14½x14*

55	A82(j)	30pa on ½p grn	.90	*13.50*
a.		Inverted surcharge	100.00	
56	A83(p)	1½pi on 1p scar	1.75	1.40
57	A86(p)	3¾pi on 2½p ultra	1.50	.35
58	A87(p)	4½pi on 3p vio	2.25	*4.25*
59	A89(p)	7½p on 5p yel brn	.60	.20
60	A90(p)	15pi on 10p lt bl	.85	.20
61	A90(p)	18¾pi on 1sh bis	5.00	*5.00*

Wmk. 34

Perf. 11x12

62	A91(q)	45pi on 2sh6p brown	22.50	*52.50*
63	A91(q)	90pi on 5sh car rose	30.00	*35.00*
64	A91(q)	180pi on 10sh blue	52.50	45.00
		Nos. 55-64 (10)	117.85	*157.40*

GREECE

'grēs

(Hellas)

LOCATION — Southern part of the Balkan Peninsula in southeastern Europe, bordering on the Ionian, Aegean and Mediterranean Seas
GOVT. — Republic
AREA — 50,949 sq. mi.
POP. — 9,740,417 (1981)
CAPITAL — Athens

In 1923 the reigning king was forced to abdicate and the following year Greece was declared a republic. In 1935, the king was recalled by a "plebiscite" of the people. Greece became a republic in June 1973. The country today includes the Aegean Islands of Chios, Mytilene (Lesbos), Samos, Icaria (Nicaria) and Lemnos, the Ionian Islands (Corfu, etc.) Crete, Macedonia, Western Thrace and part of Eastern Thrace, the Mount Athos District, Epirus and the Dodecanese Islands.

100 Lepta = 1 Drachma

Values for unused stamps are for examples with original gum as defined in the catalogue introduction. Any exceptions will be noted.

Values for Large Hermes Head stamps with double control numbers on the back, Nos. 20e, 21c, 27a, et al, are for examples with two distinct and separate impressions, not for blurred or "slide doubles" caused by paper slippage on the press.

Watermarks

Wmk. 129 — Crown and ET

Wmk. 252 — Crowns

Paris Print

Hermes (Mercury) — A1

Paris Print, Fine Impression

The enlarged illustrations show the head in various states of the plates. The differences are best seen in the shading lines on the cheek and neck.

1861 Unwmk. Typo. *Imperf.*

Without Figures on Back

1	A1	1 l choc, *brnish*	325.00	325.00
		No gum	90.00	
		On cover		850.00
		Single franking on newspaper		1,250.
a.		1 l red brown, *brnish*	450.00	450.00
		No gum	110.00	
		On cover		950.00
		Single franking on newspaper		1,300.
2	A1	2 l ol bis, *straw*	37.50	*45.00*
		No gum	17.50	
		On cover		350.00
a.		2 l brown buff, *buff*	40.00	*45.00*
		No gum	17.50	
		On cover		190.00
3	A1	5 l yel grn, *grnsh*	500.00	92.50
		No gum	140.00	
		On cover		160.00
4	A1	20 l bl, *bluish*	775.00	72.50
		No gum	250.00	
		On cover		125.00
a.		20 l deep blue, *bluish*	1,100.	175.00
		No gum	300.00	
		On cover		—
b.		On pelure paper	1,200.	*225.00*
		On cover		—
5	A1	40 l vio, *bl*	225.00	92.50
		On cover		125.00
6	A1	80 l rose, *pink*	190.00	90.00
		No gum	100.00	
		On cover		300.00
a.		80 l carmine, *pink*	190.00	90.00
		No gum	100.00	
		On cover		300.00

Large Figures, 8mm high, on Back

7	A1	10 l red org, *bl*	600.00	425.00
		No gum	300.00	
		On cover		650.00
a.		"10" on back inverted	—	—
c.		"0" of "10" invtd. on back	—	*1,400.*
d.		"1" of "10" invtd. on back	—	*1,400.*

Full margins = ¾mm.

No. 7 without "10" on back is a proof.

Trial impressions of Paris prints exist in many shades, some being close to those of the issued stamps. The gum used was thin and smooth instead of thick, brownish and crackly as on the issued stamps.

See #8-58. For surcharges see #130, 132-133, 137-139, 141-143, 147-149, 153-154, 157-158.

Values for stamps in pairs

1	A1	1 l choc, *brnish*	850.00	850.00
a.		1 l red brown, *brnish*	950.00	950.00
2	A1	2 l ol bis, *straw*	92.50	110.00
a.		2 l brown buff, *buff*	92.50	110.00
3	A1	5 l yel grn, *grnsh*	1,400.	275.00
4	A1	20 l bl, *bluish*	1,900.	190.00
a.		20 l deep blue, *bluish*	2,300.	410.00
5	A1	40 l vio, *bl*	525.00	410.00
6	A1	80 l rose, *pink*	440.00	325.00
a.		80 l carmine, *pink*	440.00	325.00
7	A1	10 l red org, *bl*	1,500.	1,050.

Values for stamps in strips of 3

1	A1	1 l choc, *brnish*	1,650.	1,750.
2	A1	2 l ol bis, *straw*	125.00	225.00
3	A1	5 l yel grn, *grnsh*	—	650.00
4	A1	20 l bl, *bluish*	—	1,100.
5	A1	40 l vio, *bl*	1,200.	1,350.
6	A1	80 l rose, *pink*	1,050.	925.00
7	A1	10 l red org, *bl*	—	—

Values for stamps in blocks of 4

1	A1	1 l choc, *brnish*	*8,000.*	*8,500.*
		No gum	*1,300.*	
2	A1	2 l ol bis, *straw*	*225.00*	*725.00*
		No gum	*110.00*	
3	A1	5 l yel grn, *grnsh*	*4,400.*	*5,800.*
		No gum	*1,400.*	
4	A1	20 l bl, *bluish*	*8,000.*	
		No gum	*2,500.*	
5	A1	40 l vio, *bl*	*3,000.*	
		No gum	*1,250.*	
6	A1	80 l rose, *pink*	*1,100.*	
		No gum	*650.00*	
7	A1	10 l red org, *bl*	*8,800.*	
		No gum	*2,750.*	

Faint quadrille, horizontal or vertical lines are visible in the background of some Athens print large Hermes head stamps.

Nos. 16, 16a, 16b are the only 1 l stamps that have these lines.

Athens Prints

Athens Print, Typical Clear Impression

Athens Print, Typical Coarse Impression

Figures on Back

5 l:

#11

#18-45

Fine Printing (F)

Fine Printing (F, '62) see footnote

Coarse Printing (C)

1861-62

Without Figures on Back

8	A1	1 l choc, *brnish* (F, '62)	37.50	*55.00*
		On cover		1,100.
a.		1 l dk chocolate, *brnish* (F)	1,100.	1,100.
		On cover		2,500.
b.		1 l chocolate, *brnish* (F)	500.00	500.00
		On cover		1,550.
9	A1	2 l bis brn, *bister* (F)	37.50	*55.00*
		On cover		150.00
a.		2 l dark brown, *straw,* (C)	*4,500.*	—
		On cover		—
b.		2 l bister brown, *bister* (C)	45.00	*62.50*
		On cover		250.00
c.		2 l bister brown, *bister* (F, '62)	47.50	*62.50*
		On cover		260.00
10	A1	20 l dk bl, *bluish* (C)		*10,000.*
		On cover		*50,000.*

With Figures on Back

11	A1	5 l grn, *grnsh* (F)	190.00	80.00
		On cover		190.00
a.		5 l green, *greenish* (C)	210.00	82.50
		On cover		225.00
b.		As "a," double "5" on back (F, C)		*1,400.*
c.		5 l green, *greenish,* bl grn figures on back (F, '62)	225.00	47.50
12	A1	10 l org, *grnsh* (F, '62)	250.00	35.00
		On cover		77.50
a.		10 l orange, *greenish* (C)	625.00	90.00
		On cover		240.00
c.		10 l orange, *greenish* (F)	450.00	82.50
		On cover		190.00
13	A1	20 l blue, *bluish* (F, '62)	*390.00*	47.50
		On cover		77.50
a.		20 l dull blue, *bluish* (C)	*5,000.*	140.00
		On cover		310.00
b.		20 l dark blue, *bluish,* (F)	*2,750.*	67.50
		On cover		150.00
14	A1	40 l red vio, *pale bl* (F, '62)	*1,900.*	110.00
		On cover		250.00
a.		40 l red violet, *blue* (C)	*5,250.*	360.00
		On cover		1,000.
b.		40 l red violet, *blue,* (F)	*3,250.*	250.00
		On cover		650.00
15	A1	80 l carmine, *pink* (F, '62)	77.50	60.00
		On cover		125.00
a.		80 l carmine, *pink* (F)	690.00	90.00
		On cover		250.00
b.		80 l dl rose, *pink* (F)	625.00	87.50
		On cover		250.00

Full margins = ¾mm.

Nos. 8-15 are known as the "Athens Provisionals." The first printings were not very successful, producing the "coarse printings." Later printings used an altered printing method that gave better results (the "fine printings"). All these were issued in the normal manner by the Post Office.

Nos. 8, 9c, 11c, 12, 13, 14, 15 have uninterrupted and even shading lines that do not taper off at the ends. They were produced in May 1862 (F, '62). Other fine printing stamps were produced in Feb.-Apr. 1862 (F).

The numerals on the back are strongly shaded in the right lines with the corresponding left lines being quite thin. The colors of the numerals are generally strong and often show clumps of ink.

Nos. 15a and 15b have vermilion figures on the back, while those of all later printings are carmine.

1862-67

With Figures on Back, Except 1 l, 2 l

16	A1	1 l brn, *brnish* (poor print)	32.50	32.50
		On cover		72.50
a.		1 l red brn, *brnish* (poor print)	65.00	65.00
		On cover		125.00
b.		1 l choc, *brnish*	47.50	47.50
		On cover		92.50
17	A1	2 l bister, *bister*	6.25	*7.25*
		On cover		55.00
a.		2 l brnsh bis, *bister*	9.50	*12.00*
		On cover		55.00
18	A1	5 l grn, *grnsh*	160.00	10.50
		On cover		40.00
a.		5 l yellowish green, *grnsh*	160.00	10.50
		On cover		37.50
19	A1	10 l org, *blue* ('64)	225.00	12.00
		On cover		45.00
a.		10 l yel org, *bluish*	275.00	40.00
		On cover		92.50
b.		As "b," "10" inverted on front of stamp		*11,000.*
c.		10 l red org, *bl* (Dec. '65)	*225.00*	11.00
		On cover		45.00
d.		"01" on back		*110.00*
20	A1	20 l bl, *bluish*	175.00	6.00
		On cover		17.50
a.		20 l lt bl, *bluish* (fine print)	210.00	12.00
		On cover		27.50
b.		20 l dark blue, *bluish*	300.00	19.00
		On cover		82.50
c.		20 l blue, *greenish*	*875.00*	12.00
		On cover		22.50
d.		"80" on back		*1,100.*
e.		Double "20" on back		*825.00*
f.		Without "20" on back		*4,500.*
21	A1	40 l lilac, *bl*	300.00	19.00
		On cover		125.00
a.		40 l grayish lilac, *blue*	1,250.	120.00
		On cover		125.00
b.		40 l lilac brown, *lil gray*	*875.00*	15.00
		On cover		110.00
c.		Double "40" on back		1,100.
22	A1	80 l car, *pale rose*	55.00	11.00
		On cover		110.00
a.		80 l rose, *pale rose*	60.00	12.00
		On cover		110.00
b.		"8" on back inverted	—	250.00

c. "80" on back inverted —
d. "8" only on back 550.00
e. "0" only on back 550.00

Nos. 16-22 represent a series of printings for each value, from 1862 through 1867, until a major cleaning of the plates was done in 1868. **Impressions range from very fine and clear to coarse and blotchy.**

Some printings of Nos. 16, 16a, 16b show faint vertical, horizontal or quadrilled lines in the background. Later 1 l stamps do not show these lines.

Many stamps of this and succeeding issues which are normally imperforate are known privately rouletted, pin-perforated, percé en scie, etc.

1868

From Cleaned Plates
With Figures on Back,
Except 1 l, 2 l

23 A1 1 l gray brn, *brnish* 35.00 *45.00*
On cover 92.50
a. 1 l brown, *brownish* 35.00 *45.00*
On cover 92.50
24 A1 2 l gray bis, *bister* 13.50 *22.50*
On cover 47.50
25 A1 5 l grn, *grnsh* *1,500.* 55.00
On cover 92.50
26 A1 10 l pale org, *bluish* *1,000.* 17.50
On cover 30.00
a. "01" on back —
27 A1 20 l pale bl, *bluish* *1,000.* 7.75
On cover 19.00
a. Double "20" on back *800.00*
28 A1 40 l rose vio, *bl* 225.00 19.00
On cover 125.00
a. "20" on back, corrected to "40" *1,900.* *1,400.*
29 A1 80 l rose car, *pale rose* 140.00 140.00
On cover 325.00

The "0" on the back of No. 29 is printed more heavily than the "8."

1870

With Figures on Back, Except 1 l

30 A1 1 l deep reddish brn, *brnish* 67.50 *125.00*
On cover 200.00
a. 1 l redsh brn, *brnish* 110.00 *140.00*
On cover 300.00
31 A1 20 l lt bl, *bluish* *1,200.* 12.00
On cover 22.50
a. 20 l blue, *bluish* *1,300.* 30.00
On cover 22.50
b. "02" on back 475.00
c. "20" on back inverted 475.00

Nos. 30 and 30a have short lines of shading on cheek. The spandrels of No. 31 are very pale with the lines often broken or missing.

This was an Athens Printing made under supervision of German workmen.

1870

Medium to Thin Paper
Without Mesh
With Figures on Back,
Except 1 l, 2 l

32 A1 1 l brn, *brnish* 115.00 120.00
On cover 160.00
a. 1 l purple brown, *brnish* 150.00 150.00
On cover 250.00
33 A1 2 l sal bis, *bister* 9.00 *17.00*
On cover 62.50
34 A1 5 l grn, *grnsh* *1,750.* 52.50
On cover 92.50
35 A1 10 l lt red org, *grnsh* *1,200.* 47.50
On cover 110.00
a. "01" on back —
b. "10" on back inverted — *600.00*
36 A1 20 l bl, *bluish* *800.00* 7.75
On cover 19.00
a. "02" on back 300.00
b. Double "20" on back 775.00
37 A1 40 l sal, *grnsh* 475.00 60.00
On cover 150.00
a. 40 l lilac, *greenish* —

The stamps of this issue have rather coarse figures on back.

No. 37a is printed in the exact shade of the numerals on the back of No. 37.

1872

Thin Transparent Paper
Showing Mesh
With Figures on Back, Except 1 l

38 A1 1 l grayish brown, *straw* 42.50 *50.00*
On cover 87.50
a. 1 l red brn, *yelsh* 50.00 *60.00*
On cover 120.00
39 A1 5 l grn, *greenish* 410.00 19.00
On cover 37.50
a. 5 l dark green, *grnsh* 600.00 35.00
On cover 50.00
b. Double "5" on back 110.00
40 A1 10 l red org, *grnsh* *650.00* 7.25
On cover 22.50
a. 10 l red orange, *pale lilac* *3,000.* 100.00
On cover 150.00
b. As #40, "10" on back inverted — 50.00
c. Double "10" on back 690.00
d. "0" on back 360.00
e. "01" on back — *1,400.*
41 A1 20 l dp bl, *bluish* 775.00 7.25
On cover 19.00
a. 20 l blue, *bluish* 775.00 24.00
On cover 22.50
b. 20 l dark blue, *blue* 1,000. 22.50
On cover 77.50
42 A1 40 l brn, *bl* 24.00 *32.50*
On cover 92.50
a. 40 l olive brown, *blue* 30.00 *55.00*
On cover 92.50
b. 40 l red violet, *blue* 500.00 50.00
On cover 110.00
c. 40 l gray violet, *blue* 550.00 50.00
On cover 87.50
d. Figures on back bister (#42b, 42c) — 65.00

The mesh is not apparent on Nos. 38, 38a.

1875

On Cream Paper Unless Otherwise Stated
With Figures on Back,
Except 1 l, 2 l

43 A1 1 l gray brn 6.25 4.75
On cover 25.00
a. 1 l dark gray brown 35.00 35.00
On cover 80.00
b. 1 l black brown 47.50 *55.00*
On cover 80.00
c. 1 l red brown 25.00 *30.00*
On cover 80.00
d. 1 l dark red brown 25.00 *35.00*
On cover 80.00
e. 1 l purple brown 37.50 *47.50*
On cover 82.50
44 A1 2 l bister 11.00 *27.50*
On cover 80.00
45 A1 5 l pale yellow green 140.00 15.00
On cover 30.00
a. 5 l dk yel grn 225.00 32.50
On cover 47.50
46 A1 10 l orange 150.00 13.00
On cover 27.50
a. 10 l orange, *yellow* 160.00 13.00
On cover 25.00
c. "00" on back 825.00 80.00
d. "1" on back — 140.00
e. "0" on back — 80.00
f. "01" on back — 250.00
g. Double "10" on back — 300.00
On cover 200.00
47 A1 20 l ultra 92.50 4.50
On cover 11.00
a. 20 l blue 160.00 12.00
On cover 16.00
b. 20 l deep Prussian blue 1,450. 37.50
On cover 82.50
c. "02" on back — 260.00
d. "20" on back inverted — *5,750.*
e. "2" in "20" inverted and broken *75.00*
f. Double "20" on back — 325.00
48 A1 40 l salmon 22.50 *45.00*
On cover 225.00

The back figures are found in many varieties, including "1" and "0" inverted in "10."

Value for No. 47e is for example with "2" of "02" broken (deformed). Also known with unbroken "2"; value used about $600.

1876

Without Figures on Back
Paris Print, Clear Impression

49 A1 30 l ol brn, *yelsh* 175.00 37.50
On cover 375.00
a. 30 l brown, *yellowish* 275.00 72.50
On cover —
50 A1 60 l grn, *grnsh* 27.50 *65.00*
On cover 1,600.

Athens Print, Coarse Impression, Yellowish Paper

51 A1 30 l dark brown 47.50 7.25
On cover 13.50
a. 30 l black brown 47.50 7.25
On cover 13.50
52 A1 60 l green 300.00 42.50
On cover 1,600.

1880-82 **Cream Paper**

Without Figures on Back

53 A1 5 l green 19.00 3.00
On cover 10.00
54 A1 10 l orange 19.00 2.50
On cover 8.75
a. 10 l yellow 19.00 2.50
On cover 8.75
b. 10 l red orange *2,250.* 37.50
On cover 55.00
55 A1 20 l ultra 275.00 110.00
On cover 250.00
56 A1 20 l pale rose (aniline ink) ('82) 5.75 1.90
On cover 10.00
a. 20 l rose (aniline ink) ('82) 6.75 3.00
On cover 11.00
b. 20 l deep carmine *175.00* 8.25
On cover 11.00
57 A1 30 l ultra ('82) 140.00 12.00
On cover 92.50
a. 30 l slate blue 140.00 9.00
On cover 92.50
58 A1 40 l lilac 47.50 9.00
On cover 125.00
a. 40 l violet 52.50 18.00
On cover 160.00

Stamps of type A1 were not regularly issued with perf. 11½ but were freely used on mail.

Hermes — A2

Lepta denominations have white numeral tablets.

Belgian Print, Clear Impression

1886-88 ***Imperf.***

64 A2 1 l brown ('88) 2.10 1.25
65 A2 2 l bister ('88) 7.25 *90.00*
66 A2 5 l yel grn ('88) 9.00 1.75
67 A2 10 l yellow ('88) 12.00 1.75
68 A2 20 l car rose ('88) 25.00 1.10
69 A2 25 l blue 72.50 2.10
70 A2 40 l violet ('88) 57.50 18.00
71 A2 50 l gray grn 3.50 2.10
72 A2 1d gray 85.00 2.75
Nos. 64-72 (9) 273.85 120.80

See Nos. 81-116. For surcharges see Nos. 129, 134, 140, 144, 150, 151-152, 155-156.

1891 ***Perf. 11½***

81 A2 1 l brown 3.00 2.75
82 A2 2 l bister 6.50 —
83 A2 5 l yel grn 14.00 10.00
84 A2 10 l yellow 20.00 10.00
85 A2 20 l car rose 37.50 14.00
86 A2 25 l blue 110.00 19.00
87 A2 40 l violet 100.00 60.00
88 A2 50 l gray grn 17.00 5.00
89 A2 1d gray 110.00 5.50
Nos. 81-89 (9) 418.00 126.25

The Belgian Printings perf. 13½ and most of the values perf. 11½ (Nos. 82-86) were perforated on request of philatelists at the main post office in Athens. While not regularly issued they were freely used for postage.

Athens Print, Poor Impression

Wmk. Greek Words in Some Sheets

1889-95 ***Imperf.***

90 A2 1 l black brn 3.50 1.10
a. 1 l brown 2.50 1.10
91 A2 2 l pale bister 1.40 *1.60*
a. 2 l buff 1.90 *2.25*
92 A2 5 l green 7.75 1.25
a. Double impression *140.00* *275.00*
b. 5 l deep green 9.00 1.75
93 A2 10 l yellow 11.00 1.10
a. 10 l orange 22.50 3.25
b. 10 l dull yellow 32.50 2.25
94 A2 20 l carmine 4.75 1.10
a. 20 l rose 17.50 1.40
95 A2 25 l dull blue 45.00 1.10
a. 25 l indigo 92.50 5.00
b. 25 l ultra 90.00 3.50
c. 25 l brt blue 45.00 2.50
96 A2 25 l lilac 3.75 1.10
a. 25 l red vio ('93) 10.00 2.50
97 A2 40 l red vio ('91) 52.50 25.00
98 A2 40 l blue ('93) 7.25 1.40
99 A2 1d gray ('95) 250.00 5.25

Perf. 13½

100 A2 1 l brown 22.50 22.50
101 A2 2 l buff 1.60 1.60
104 A2 20 l carmine 18.00 5.25
a. 20 l rose 25.00 6.25
105 A2 40 l red violet 77.50 47.50

Other denominations of type A2 were not officially issued with perf. 13½.

Perf. 11½

107 A2 1 l brown 2.50 1.25
a. 1 l black brown 6.25 5.00
108 A2 2 l pale bister 2.25 1.75
a. 2 l buff 2.50 2.50
109 A2 5 l pale green 7.75 1.75
a. 5 l deep green 12.00 2.75
110 A2 10 l yellow 11.00 1.10
a. 10 l dull yellow 30.00 2.25
b. 10 l orange 45.00 5.00
111 A2 20 l carmine 4.75 .65
a. 20 l rose 22.50 1.40
112 A2 25 l dull blue 72.50 3.25
a. 25 l indigo 100.00 19.00
b. 25 l ultra 72.50 47.50
c. 25 l bright blue 52.50 8.00
113 A2 25 l lilac 4.75 1.40
a. 25 l red violet 10.00 2.50
114 A2 40 l red violet 60.00 32.50
115 A2 40 l blue 12.00 2.50
116 A2 1d gray 250.00 9.00

Partly-perforated varieties sell for about twice as much as normal copies.

The watermark on Nos. 90-116 consists of three Greek words meaning Paper for Public Service. It is in double-lined capitals, measures 270x35mm, and extends across three panes.

Boxers — A3

Discobolus by Myron — A4

Vase Depicting Pallas Athene (Minerva) — A5

Chariot Driving A6

Stadium and Acropolis A7

Statue of Hermes by Praxiteles — A8

Statue of Victory by Paeonius — A9

Acropolis and Parthenon A10

Perf. 14x13½, 13½x14

1896 **Unwmk.**

117 A3 1 l ocher 1.00 .50
118 A3 2 l rose 1.50 .50
a. Without engraver's name 11.50 10.50
119 A4 5 l lilac 1.90 1.00
120 A4 10 l slate gray 2.50 1.50
121 A5 20 l red brn 12.00 2.50
122 A6 25 l red 18.00 2.50
123 A5 40 l violet 12.00 6.25
124 A6 60 l black 22.50 12.50
125 A7 1d blue 50.00 10.50
126 A8 2d bister 175.00 60.00
a. Horiz. pair, imperf. btwn.
127 A9 5d green 325.00 275.00
128 A10 10d brown 375.00 *310.00*
Nos. 117-128 (12) 996.40 682.75

1st intl. Olympic Games of the modern era, held at Athens. Counterfeits of Nos. 123-124 and 126-128 exist.

For surcharges see Nos. 159-164.

Preceding Issues Surcharged

1900 ***Imperf.***

129 A2 20 l on 25 l dl bl, #95c 2.75 1.50
a. 20 l on 25 l indigo, #95a 37.50 32.50
b. 20 l on 25 l ultra, #95b 55.00 45.00
c. Double surcharge 45.00 —
d. Triple surcharge 55.00 —
e. Inverted surcharge 45.00 —
f. "20" above word 100.00 —
g. Pair, one without surcharge 160.00 —
h. "20" without word 100.00 —

130 A1 30 l on 40 l vio, *cr,* #58a 4.75 3.75
a. 30 l on 40 l lilac, #58 5.75 5.00
b. Broad "0" in "30" 9.00 5.50
c. First letter of word is "A" 65.00 42.50
d. Double surcharge *275.00 225.00*
132 A1 40 l on 2 l bis, *cr,* #44 5.00 4.50
a. Broad "0" in "40" 8.75 6.50
b. First letter of word is "A" 65.00 50.00
133 A1 50 l on 40 l sal, *cr,* #48 5.00 5.00
a. Broad "0" in "50" 8.75 5.75
b. First letter of word is "A" 65.00 50.00
c. "50" without word 190.00 140.00
d. "50" above word 190.00 140.00
134 A2 1d on 40 l red vio (No. 97) 11.00 4.25
137 A1 3d on 10 l org, *cr,* #54 45.00 45.00
a. 3d on 10 l yellow, #54a 45.00 45.00
138 A1 5d on 40 l red vio, *bl,* #21 87.50 87.50
a. 5d on 40 l red vio, *bl,* #28 100.00 *110.00*
b. "20" on back corrected to "40" *1,100.*
139 A1 5d on 40 l red vio, *bl,* #42b 325.00

Perf. 11½

140 A2 20 l on 25 l dl bl, #112 2.75 2.50
a. 20 l on 25 l indigo, #112a 82.50 50.00
b. 20 l on 25 l ultra, #112b 65.00 45.00
c. Double surcharge 42.50 —
d. Triple surcharge 55.00 —
e. Inverted surcharge 42.50 —
f. "20" above word 100.00 —
141 A1 30 l on 40 l vio, *cr,* #58a 4.75 3.75
a. 30 l on 40 l lilac, #58 8.25 7.75
b. Broad "0" in "30" 7.75 7.75
c. First letter of word "A" 77.50 65.00
d. Double surcharge
142 A1 40 l on 2 l bis, *cr,* #44 6.00 3.75
a. Broad "0" in "40" 8.25 8.25
b. First letter of word "A" 85.00 85.00
143 A1 50 l on 40 l sal, *cr,* #48 6.00 5.00
a. Broad "0" in "50" 10.00 8.25
b. First letter of word "A" 87.50 87.50
c. "50" without word 190.00
144 A2 1d on 40 l red vio, #114 18.00 12.00
147 A1 3d on 10 l yel, *cream,* #54a 42.50 42.50
a. 3d on 10 l org, *cr,* #54 55.00 *60.00*
148 A1 5d on 40 l red vio, *bl,* #21 110.00 110.00
a. 5d on 40 l red vio, *bl,* #28 125.00 *140.00*
149 A1 5d on 40 l red vio, *bl,* #42b 325.00

Perf. 13½

150 A2 2d on 40 l red vio, #105 9.00 *9.50*

The 1d on 40 l perf. 13½ and the 2d on 40 l, both imperf. and perf. 13½, were not officially issued.

Surcharge Including "A M"

"A M" = "Axia Metalliki" or "Value in Metal (gold)."

1900 ***Imperf.***

151 A2 25 l on 40 l vio, #70 5.50 5.50
152 A2 50 l on 25 l bl, #69 22.50 22.50
153 A1 1d on 40 l brn, *bl,* #42b 100.00 100.00
154 A1 2d on 5 l grn, *cr,* #53 14.00 14.00

Perf. 11½

155 A2 25 l on 40 l vio, #87 9.00 8.25
156 A2 50 l on 25 l bl, #86 30.00 *30.00*
157 A1 1d on 40 l brn, *bl,* #42b 125.00 125.00
158 A1 2d on 5 l grn, *cr,* #53 17.00 17.00
Nos. 151-158 (8) 323.00 322.25

Partly-perforated varieties of Nos. 129-158 sell for about two to three times as much as normal copies.

Surcharge Including "A M" on Olympic Issue in Red

1900-01 ***Perf. 14x13½***

159 A7 5 l on 1d blue 8.25 6.00
a. Wrong font "M" with serifs 55.00 *65.00*
b. Double surcharge 190.00 190.00
160 A5 25 l on 40 l vio 55.00 52.50
161 A8 50 l on 2d bister 60.00 45.00
a. Broad "0" in "50" 72.50 47.50
162 A9 1d on 5d grn ('01) 190.00 150.00
a. Greek "D" instead of "A" as 3rd letter 575.00 *650.00*
163 A10 2d on 10d brn ('01) 55.00 *72.50*
a. Greek "D" instead of "A" as 3rd letter 260.00 240.00
Nos. 159-163 (5) 368.25 326.00

Black Surcharge on No. 160

164 A5 50 l on 25 l on 40 l vio (R + Bk) 500.00 475.00
a. Broad "0" in "50" 475.00 *575.00*

Nos. 151-164 and 179-183, gold currency stamps, were generally used for parcel post and foreign money orders. They were also available for use on letters, but cost about 20 per cent more than the regular stamps of the same denomination.

Counterfeit surcharges exist of #159-164.

Giovanni da Bologna's Hermes
A11 A12

A13

FIVE LEPTA.
Type I — Letters of "ELLAS" not outlined at top and left. Only a few faint horizontal lines between the outer vertical lines at sides.
Type II — Letters of "ELLAS" fully outlined. Heavy horizontal lines between the vertical frame lines.

Perf. 11½, 12½, 13½

1901 **Engr.** **Wmk. 129**

165 A11 1 l yellow brn .40 .20
166 A11 2 l gray .60 .20
167 A11 3 l orange .65 .30
168 A12 5 l grn, type I .80 .20
a. 5 l yellow green, type I .60 .20
b. 5 l yellow green, type II .60 .20
169 A12 10 l rose 3.25 .20
170 A11 20 l red lilac 6.50 .20
171 A12 25 l ultra 6.50 .20
172 A11 30 l dl vio 12.00 2.00
173 A11 40 l dk brn 19.00 10.50
174 A11 50 l brn lake 15.50 1.25

Perf. 12½, 14 and Compound

175 A13 1d black 45.00 3.00
a. Horiz. pair, imperf. btwn. 300.00
c. Horiz. pair, imperf. vert. 275.00
d. Vert. pair, imperf. horiz. 275.00

Litho.

Perf. 12½

176 A13 2d bronze 10.00 7.00
177 A13 3d silver 10.00 *7.75*
178 A13 5d gold 13.00 *15.00*
Nos. 165-178 (14) 143.20 48.00
Set, never hinged 225.00

All values1 l through 1d issued on both thick and thin paper. Nos. 173-174 are values for thin paper — values for thick paper are higher.

For overprints and surcharges see Nos. RA3-RA13, N16, N109.

Imperf., Pairs

165a	A11	1 l	11.00
166a	A11	2 l	14.00
167a	A11	3 l	14.00
168c	A12	5 l	11.00
169a	A12	10 l	17.00
170a	A11	20 l	14.00
171a	A12	25 l	14.00
172a	A11	30 l	225.00
173a	A11	40 l	260.00
174a	A11	50 l	55.00
175b	A13	1d	225.00

Nos. 165a-175a were issued on both thick and thin paper. Values are for the less expensive thin paper.

Hermes — A14

1902, Jan. 1 **Engr.** ***Perf. 13½***

179 A14 5 l deep orange 1.50 1.10
a. Imperf., pair 82.50
180 A14 25 l emerald 30.00 3.00
181 A14 50 l ultra 30.00 3.75
a. Imperf., pair 550.00
182 A14 1d rose red 30.00 8.25
183 A14 2d orange brn 52.50 50.00
Nos. 179-183 (5) 144.00 66.10
Set, never hinged 275.00

See note after No. 164. In 1913 remainders of Nos. 179-183 were used as postage dues.

Apollo Throwing Discus
A15

Jumper, with Jumping Weights
A16

Victory — A17

Atlas and Hercules
A18

Struggle of Hercules and Antaeus
A19

Wrestlers
A20

Daemon of the Games
A21

Foot Race
A22

Nike, Priest and Athletes in Pre-Games Offering to Zeus
A23

Wmk. Crown and ET (129)

1906, Mar. **Engr.** ***Perf. 13½, 14***

184 A15 1 l brown .45 .40
a. Imperf., pair *300.00*
185 A15 2 l gray .45 .40
a. Imperf., pair *300.00*
186 A16 3 l orange .45 .40
a. Imperf., pair 300.00
187 A16 5 l green 1.00 .40
a. Imperf., pair 110.00
188 A17 10 l rose red 1.90 .60
a. Imperf., pair *300.00*
189 A18 20 l magenta 3.00 .60
a. Imperf., pair *575.00*
190 A19 25 l ultra 4.25 .85
a. Imperf., pair *575.00*
191 A20 30 l dl pur 3.50 2.75
a. Double impression *1,100.*
192 A21 40 l dk brown 3.50 2.75
193 A18 50 l brn lake 6.50 3.25
194 A22 1d gray blk 65.00 13.00
a. Imperf., pair *1,100.*
195 A22 2d rose 95.00 35.00
196 A22 3d olive yel 155.00 125.00
197 A23 5d dull blue 160.00 140.00
Nos. 184-197 (14) 500.00 325.40
Set, never hinged 1,000.

Greek Special Olympic Games of 1906 at Athens, celebrating the 10th anniv. of the modern Olympic Games.

Surcharged stamps of this issue are revenues.

A24

Iris Holding Caduceus
A25

Hermes Donning Sandals
A26

Hermes Carrying Infant Arcas — A27

Hermes, from Old Cretan Coin — A28

Designs A24 to A28 are from Cretan and Arcadian coins of the 4th Century, B.C.

Serrate Roulette 13½

1911-21 **Engr.** **Unwmk.**

198 A24 1 l green .50 .25
199 A25 2 l car rose .50 .25
200 A24 3 l vermilion .75 .25
201 A26 5 l green 1.50 .25
202 A24 10 l car rose 6.00 .25
203 A25 20 l gray lilac 2.10 .60
204 A25 25 l ultra 7.00 .60
a. Rouletted in black 190.00 140.00
205 A26 30 l car rose 2.75 1.25
206 A25 40 l deep blue 6.00 3.00
207 A26 50 l dl vio 10.50 2.50
208 A27 1d ultra 12.00 .65
209 A27 2d vermilion 17.00 .75
210 A27 3d car rose 17.00 1.00
a. Size 20¼x25½mm ('21) 60.00 30.00
211 A27 5d ultra 27.50 3.00
a. Size 20¼x25½mm ('21) 160.00 25.00
212 A27 10d dp bl ('21) 140.00 70.00
a. Size 20x26½mm ('11) 240.00 125.00
213 A28 25d deep blue 60.00 42.50
Nos. 198-213 (16) 311.10 127.10
Set, never hinged 500.00

The 1921 reissues of the 3d, 5d and 10d measure 20¼x25½mm instead of 20x26½mm.

See Nos. 214-231. For overprints see Nos. 233-248B, N1, N10-N15, N17-N52A, N110-N148, Thrace 22-30, N26-N75.

Imperf., Pairs

198a	A24	1 l		77.50	77.50
200a	A24	3 l		*225.00*	210.00
201a	A26	5 l		22.50	24.00
202a	A24	10 l		45.00	45.00
203a	A25	20 l		190.00	190.00
204b	A25	25 l		250.00	260.00
206a	A25	40 l		300.00	
207a	A26	50 l		290.00	
208a	A27	1d		290.00	
209a	A27	2d		290.00	
210b	A27	3d		290.00	
211b	A27	5d		225.00	
212b	A27	10d	As "a"	*1,400.*	
213a	A28	25d		*2,250.*	

Serrate Roulette 10½x13½, 13½

1913-23 **Litho.**

214 A24 1 l green .20 .20
a. Without period after "Ellas" 77.50 —
215 A25 2 l rose .20 .20
216 A24 3 l vermilion .20 .20
217 A26 5 l green .20 .20
218 A24 10 l carmine .20 .20
219 A25 15 l dl bl ('18) .35 .20
220 A25 20 l slate .35 .20
221 A25 25 l ultra 3.50 .20
a. 25 l blue .20
c. Double impression —
222 A26 30 l rose ('14) .95 .20
223 A25 40 l indigo ('14) 2.10 .70
224 A26 50 l vio brn ('14) 4.25 .35
225 A26 80 l vio brn ('23) 5.25 1.40
226 A27 1d ultra ('19) 7.00 .70
227 A27 2d ver ('19) 6.50 .70
228 A27 3d car rose ('20) 8.50 .80
229 A27 5d ultra ('22) 11.50 1.00

230 A27 10d dp bl ('22) 9.50 1.25
231 A28 25d indigo ('22) 11.50 3.50
Nos. 214-231 (18) 72.25 12.20
Set, never hinged 200.00

Nos. 221, 223 and 226 were re-issued in 1926, printed in Vienna from new plates. There are slight differences in minor details.

The 10 lepta brown, on thick paper, type A28, is not a postage stamp. It was issued in 1922 to replace coins of this denomination during a shortage of copper.

Imperf., Pairs

214b A24 1 l 65.00
215a A25 2 l 110.00
216a A24 3 l 175.00
217a A26 5 l 65.00
218a A24 10 l 82.50
220a A25 20 l 82.50
221b A25 25 l 175.00
222a A26 30 l 175.00
223a A25 40 l 150.00
224a A26 50 l 300.00
225b A26 80 l 92.50
227a A27 2d 100.00
228b A27 3d 300.00
229a A27 5d 360.00

Raising Greek Flag at Suda Bay, Crete A29

1913, Dec. 1 Engr. *Perf. 14½*
232 A29 25 l blue & black 6.75 5.00
Never hinged 10.00
a. Imperf., pair *1,100.*

Union of Crete with Greece. Used only in Crete.

Stamps of 1911-14 Overprinted in Red or Black

Serrate Roulette 13½

1916, Nov. 1 Litho.
233 A24 1 l green (R) .20 .20
234 A25 2 l rose .20 .20
235 A24 3 l vermilion .20 .20
236 A26 5 l green (R) .50 .40
237 A24 10 l carmine .55 .40
238 A25 20 l slate (R) 1.10 .40
239 A25 25 l blue (R) 1.10 .40
a. 25 l ultra 100.00 22.50
240 A26 30 l rose 1.10 .85
a. Pair, one without ovpt.
241 A25 40 l indigo (R) 11.00 3.00
242 A26 50 l vio brn (R) 37.50 2.50

Engr.
243 A24 3 l vermilion .50 .50
244 A26 30 l car rose 1.10 1.10
245 A27 1d ultra (R) 37.50 .75
a. Rouletted in black 325.00 225.00
246 A27 2d vermilion 24.00 3.50
247 A27 3d car rose 14.00 3.50
248 A27 5d ultra (R) 95.00 10.50
248B A27 10d dp bl (R) 24.00 22.50
Nos. 233-248B (17) 249.55 50.90
Set, never hinged 400.00

Most of Nos. 233-248B exist with overprint double, inverted, etc. Minimum value of errors $16. Excellent counterfeits of the overprint varieties exist.

Issued by the Venizelist Provisional Government

Iris — A32

1917, Feb. 5 Litho. *Perf. 14*
249 A32 1 l dp green .25 .20
250 A32 5 l yel grn .25 .20
251 A32 10 l rose .75 .35
252 A32 25 l lt blue 1.10 .35
253 A32 50 l gray vio 9.00 2.50
254 A32 1d ultra 2.25 .75
255 A32 2d lt red 4.50 1.50
256 A32 3d claret 25.00 7.75
257 A32 5d gray bl 5.75 3.00
258 A32 10d dk blue 70.00 20.00
259 A32 25d slate 115.00 *140.00*
Nos. 249-259 (11) 233.85 176.60
Set, never hinged 325.00

The 4d was used only as a revenue stamp.

Imperf., Pairs

249a A32 1 l 9.50
250a A32 5 l 9.50
251a A32 10 l 9.50
252a A32 25 l 17.50
253a A32 50 l 25.00
254a A32 1d 22.50
255a A32 2d 30.00
256a A32 3d 65.00
257a A32 5d 65.00
258a A32 10d 110.00
259a A32 25d 125.00

Stamps of 1917 Surcharged

1923
260 A32 5 l on 10 l rose .25 .25
a. Inverted surcharge 19.00 *27.50*
261 A32 50 l on 50 l gray vio .25 .25
262 A32 1d on 1d ultra .25 .25
a. 1d on 1d gray .25 .25
263 A32 2d on 2d lt red .55 .55
264 A32 3d on 3d claret 1.50 1.50
265 A32 5d on 5d dk bl 1.75 1.75
266 A32 25d on 25d slate 19.00 19.00
Nos. 260-266 (7) 23.55 23.55
Set, never hinged 100.00

Same Surcharge on Occupation of Turkey Stamps, 1913

Perf. 13½
267 O2 5 l on 3 l org .20 .20
a. Inverted surcharge 19.00
268 O1 10 l on 20 l vio 1.00 1.00
a. Inverted surcharge 82.50
269 O2 10 l on 25 l pale bl .25 .25
270 O1 10 l on 30 l gray grn .25 .25
271 O2 10 l on 40 l ind 1.00 1.00
272 O1 50 l on 50 l dk bl .25 .25
a. Inverted surcharge 72.50 37.50
273 O1 2d on 2d gray brn 45.00 45.00
274 O2 3d on 3d dl bl 3.25 3.25
a. Imperf., pair 500.00
275 O1 5d on 5d gray 3.00 3.00
276 O2 10d on 1d vio brn 8.25 8.25
276A O2 10d on 10d car 725.00
Never hinged 1,000.
Nos. 267-276 (10) 62.45 62.45
Set, never hinged 125.00

Dangerous counterfeits of No. 276A exist.

Same Surcharge on Stamps of Crete

Perf. 14

On Crete #50, 52, 59
276B A6 5 l on 1 l red brn 19.00 17.00
277 A8 10 l on 10 l red .20 .20
277B A8 10 l on 25 l bl 87.50 87.50

On Crete #66-69, 71
278 A8 10 l on 25 l blue .20 .20
279 A6 50 l on 50 l lilac .45 *.70*
279A A6 50 l on 50 l ultra 5.50 *8.25*
280 A9 50 l on 1d gray vio 2.25 *3.25*
280A A11 50 l on 5d grn & blk 19.00 19.00

On Crete #77-82
281 A15 10 l on 20 l bl grn 100.00 100.00
282 A16 10 l on 25 l ultra .45 .45
a. Double surcharge 50.00
283 A17 50 l on 50 l yel brn .20 .30
284 A18 50 l on 1d rose car & brn 1.90 1.60
a. Imperf., pair 390.00
285 A19 3d on 3d org & blk 8.75 8.75
286 A20 5d on 5d ol grn & blk 7.75 7.75

On Crete #83-84
287 A21 10 l on 25 l bl & blk .55 .55
a. Imperf., pair
287B A22 50 l on 1d grn & blk 3.25 3.25

On Crete #96
288 A23 10 l on 10 l brn red .20 .20
a. Inverted surcharge 27.50

On Crete #91
288B A17 50 l on 50 l yel brn *725.00*

Dangerous counterfeits of the overprint on No. 288B are plentiful.

On Crete #109
289 A19 3d on 3d org & blk 15.00 15.00

On Crete #111, 113-120
290 A6 5 l on 1 l vio brn .20 .20
a. Inverted surcharge 22.50
291 A13 5 l on 5 l grn .20 .20
a. Inverted surcharge 45.00
292 A23 10 l on 10 l brn red .20 .20
a. Inverted surcharge 45.00
293 A15 10 l on 20 l bl grn .25 .25
a. Inverted surcharge 45.00
294 A16 10 l on 25 l ultra .30 .30
a. Inverted surcharge 45.00
295 A17 50 l on 50 l yel brn .35 .35
296 A18 50 l on 1d rose car & brn 3.00 3.00
a. Inverted surcharge
b. Double surcharge 160.00
c. Double surch., one invtd.
d. Imperf., pair
297 A19 3d on 3d org & blk 8.25 8.25
298 A20 5d on 5d ol grn & blk 140.00 140.00

Dangerous counterfeits of No. 298 exist.

Crete #J2-J9
299 D1 5 l on 5 l red .20 .20
a. Inverted surcharge 37.50 5.50
300 D1 5 l on 10 l red .30 .30
301 D1 10 l on 20 l red 11.00 11.00
a. Inverted surcharge
302 D1 10 l on 40 l red .30 .30
303 D1 50 l on 50 l red .30 *.55*
304 D1 50 l on 1d red .30 .50
a. Double surcharge
305 D1 50 l on 1d on 1d red 7.50 7.50
306 D1 2d on 2d red .85 .85

On Crete #J11-J13
307 D1 5 l on 5 l red 2.75 2.75
308 D1 5 l on 10 l red 1.00 1.00
a. "Ellas" inverted 5.50
309 D1 10 l on 20 l red 35.00 35.00

On Crete #J20-J22, J24-J26
310 D1 5 l on 5 l red .20 .20
311 D1 5 l on 10 l red .20 .20
a. Inverted surcharge 11.00
312 D1 10 l on 20 l red .20 .20
313 D1 50 l on 50 l red .45 .45
314 D1 50 l on 1d red 3.25 3.25
315 D1 2d on 2d red 5.50 5.50

These surcharged Postage Due stamps were intended for the payment of ordinary postage.

Nos. 260 to 315 were surcharged in commemoration of the revolution of 1922.

Nos. 59, 91, 109, 111, 113-120, J11-J13, J20-J22, J24-J26 are on stamps previously overprinted by Crete.

Issues of the Republic

Lord Byron — A33

Byron at Missolonghi — A34

1924, Apr. 16 Engr. *Perf. 12*
316 A33 80 l dark blue .55 .20
317 A34 2d dk vio & blk 1.25 .65
Set, never hinged 2.50

Death of Lord Byron (1788-1824) at Missolonghi.

Tomb of Markos Botsaris — A35

Serrate Roulette 13½

1926, Apr. 24 Litho.
318 A35 25 l lilac .85 .50
Never hinged 1.75

Centenary of the defense of Missolonghi against the Turks.

Corinth Canal A36

Dodecanese Costume A37

Macedonian Costume A38

Monastery of Simon Peter on Mt. Athos A39

White Tower of Salonika A40

Temple of Hephaestus A41

The Acropolis — A42

Cruiser "Georgios Averoff" — A43

Academy of Sciences, Athens — A44

Temple of Hephaestus A45

Acropolis A46

Perf. 12½x13, 13, 13x12½, 13½, 13½x13

1927, Apr. 1 Engr.
321 A36 5 l dark green .20 .20
a. Vert. pair, imperf. horiz. 140.00 92.50
322 A37 10 l orange red .20 .20
a. Horiz. pair, imperf. between 140.00 92.50
c. Double impression 77.50
323 A38 20 l violet .20 .20
324 A39 25 l slate blue .25 .20
a. Imperf., pair 140.00 140.00
b. Vert. pair, imperf. between 150.00 110.00
325 A40 40 l slate blue .25 .20
326 A36 50 l violet .70 .20
327 A36 80 l dk bl & blk .60 .20
a. Imperf., pair 825.00
328 A41 1d dk bl & bis brn (I) .80 .20
a. Imperf., pair 150.00 125.00
b. Center inverted *5,500.*
c. Double impression of center 325.00 225.00
d. Double impression of frame 325.00 225.00
329 A42 2d dk green & blk 6.00 .30
a. Imperf., pair 500.00 *690.00*
330 A43 3d dp violet & blk 5.25 .30
a. Double impression of center 160.00 *210.00*
b. Center inverted *7,750.*
331 A44 5d yellow & blk 12.50 1.40
a. Imperf., pair 825.00 825.00
b. Center inverted 10,000. *3,600.*
c. 5d yellow & green 110.00 37.50
332 A45 10d brn car & blk 37.50 9.50
333 A44 15d brt yel grn & blk 50.00 14.00

334 A46 25d green & blk 95.00 16.00
a. Double impression of center —
Nos. 321-334 (14) 209.45 43.10
Set, never hinged 675.00

See Nos. 364-371 and notes preceding No. 364. For overprints see Nos. RA55, RA57, RA60, RA66, RA70-RA71.

This series as prepared, included a 1 lepton dark brown, type A37, but that value was never issued. Most copies were burned. Value $250.

Gen. Charles N. Fabvier and Acropolis A47

1927, Aug. 1 ***Perf. 12***

335 A47 1d red		.30	.20
336 A47 3d dark blue		2.00	.60
337 A47 6d green		12.00	9.00
Nos. 335-337 (3)		14.30	9.80
Set, never hinged		42.50	

Cent. of the liberation of Athens from the Turks in 1826.

For surcharges see Nos. 376-377.

Bay of Navarino and Pylos A48

Battle of Navarino A49

"Edward" omitted — A50

"Edward" added — A51

Admiral de Rigny — A52

Admiral van der Heyden — A53

Designs: #340-341, Sir Edward Codrington.

Perf. 13½x12½, 12½x13½, 13x12½, 12½x13

1927-28 **Litho.**

338 A48 1.50d gray green	1.60	.25
a. Imperf., pair	275.00	
b. Horiz. pair, imperf. btwn.	875.00	
c. Horiz. pair, imperf. vert.	250.00	
339 A49 4d dk gray bl ('28)	5.25	.85
340 A50 5d dk brn & gray	3.00	*3.50*
a. 5d blk brn & blk ('28)	13.00	6.50
341 A51 5d dk brn & blk ('28)	19.00	9.00
342 A52 5d vio bl & blk ('28)	19.00	9.00
343 A53 5d lake & blk ('28)	12.00	4.75
Nos. 338-343 (6)	59.85	27.35
Set, never hinged	225.00	

Centenary of the naval battle of Navarino.

For surcharges see Nos. 372-375.

Admiral Lascarina Bouboulina A54

Athanasios Diakos A55

Map of Greece in 1830 and 1930 — A56

Sortie from Missolonghi A58

Patriots Declaring Independence — A57

Portraits: 10 l, Constantine Rhigas Ferreos. 20 l, Gregorios V. 40 l, Prince Alexandros Ypsilantis. No. 345, Bouboulina. No. 355, Diakos. No. 346, Theodoros Kolokotronis. No. 356, Konstantinos Kanaris. No.347, Georgios Karaiskakis. No. 357, Markos Botsaris. 2d, Andreas Miaoulis. 3d, Lazaros Koundouriotis. 5d, Count John Capo d'Istria (Capodistria), statesman and doctor. 10d, Petros Mavromichalis. 15d, Dionysios Solomos. 20d, Adamantios Korais.

Various Frames

1930, Apr. 1 **Engr.** ***Perf. 13½, 14***

Imprint of Perkins, Bacon & Co.

344 A55	10 l brown	.20	.20
345 A54	50 l red	.20	.20
346 A54	1d car rose	.20	.20
347 A55	1.50d lt blue	.30	.30
348 A55	2d orange	.45	.45
349 A55	5d purple	1.25	1.25
350 A54	10d gray blk	5.75	5.75
351 A54	15d yellow grn	10.50	10.50
352 A55	20d blue blk	15.00	15.00

Imprint of Bradbury, Wilkinson & Co.

Perf. 12

353 A55	20 l black	.20	.20
354 A55	40 l blue grn	.20	.20
355 A55	50 l brt blue	.20	.20
356 A55	1d brown org	.20	.20
357 A55	1.50d dk red	.30	.30
358 A55	3d dk brown	.55	.55
359 A56	4d dk blue	2.50	2.50
360 A57	25d black	15.00	15.00
361 A58	50d red brn	25.00	*25.00*
	Nos. 344-361 (18)	78.00	*78.00*
	Set, never hinged	225.00	

Greek independence, cent. Some exist imperf.

Arcadi Monastery and Abbot Gabriel (Mt. Ida in Background) A60

1930, Nov. 8 ***Perf. 12***

363 A60 8d deep violet 13.00 1.10
Never hinged 55.00

Issue of 1927 Re-engraved

50 l, Design is clearer, especially "50" and the 10 letters.

Type I

Type II

1d. Type I — Greek letters "L," "A," "D" have sharp pointed tops; numerals "1" are 1½mm wide at the foot, and have a straight slanting serif at top.

1d. Type II — Greek letters "L," "A," "D" have flat tops; numerals "1" are 2mm wide at foot and the serif at top is slightly curved. Perf. 14.

There are many minor differences in the lines of the two designs.

1d. Type III — The "1" in lower left corner has no serif at left of foot. Lines of temple have been deepened, so details stand out more clearly.

2d. On 1927 stamp the Parthenon is indistinct and blurred. On 1933 stamp it is strongly outlined and clear. Between the two pillars at lower right are four blocks of marble. These blocks are clear and distinct on the 1933 stamp but run together on the 1927 issue.

3d. Design is clearer, especially vertical lines of shading in smoke stacks and reflections in the water. Two or more sides perf. 11½.

10d. Background and shading of entire stamp have been lightened. Detail of frame is clearer and more distinct.

15d. Many more lines of shading in sky and foreground. Engraving is sharp and clear, particularly in frame. Two or more sides perf. 11½.

25d. Background has been lightened and foreground reduced until base of larger upright column is removed and fallen column appears nearly submerged.

Sizes in millimeters:
50 l, 1927, 18x24¾. 1933, 18½x24½.
1d, 1927, 24¾x17¾. 1931, 24¾x17¼. 1933, 24½x18¼.
2d, 1927, 24½x17¾. 1933, 24½x18½.

Perf. 11½, 11½x12½, 12½x10, 13, 13x12½, 14

1931-35

364 A36 50 l dk vio ('33)	4.00	1.00
365 A41 1d dk bl & org brn, type II	10.00	1.00
366 A41 1d dk bl & org brn, type III ('33)	5.75	.20
367 A42 2d dk grn & blk ('33)	2.75	.50
368 A43 3d red vio & blk ('34)	3.25	.25
a. Imperf., pair		
369 A45 10d brn car & blk ('35)	47.50	1.50
370 A44 15d pale yel grn & blk ('34)	82.50	17.50
a. Imperf., pair	*1,100.*	
371 A46 25d dk grn & blk ('35)	25.00	17.00
Nos. 364-371 (8)	180.75	38.95
Set, never hinged	440.00	

Nos. 336-337, 340-343 Surcharged in Red

1932 ***Perf. 12½x13½, 12½x13***

372 A52 1.50d on 5d	1.90	.20
373 A53 1.50d on 5d	1.75	.20
a. Double surcharge	110.00	
374 A50 2d on 5d	5.00	.20
375 A51 2d on 5d	7.00	.20

Perf. 12

376 A47 2d on 3d	2.25	.20
a. Double surcharge	125.00	
377 A47 4d on 6d	2.50	1.10
Nos. 372-377 (6)	20.40	2.10
Set, never hinged	50.00	

Adm. Pavlos Koundouriotis and Cruiser "Averoff" — A61

Pallas Athene — A62

Youth of Marathon — A63

1933 ***Perf. 13½x13, 13x13½***

378 A61 50d black & ind	45.00	1.60
a. Imperf., pair	*2,250.*	
379 A62 75d blk & vio brn	92.50	*150.00*
a. Imperf., pair	825.00	
Never hinged	1,700.	
380 A63 100d brn & dull grn	390.00	22.50
a. Imperf., pair	2,750.	
Nos. 378-380 (3)	527.50	*174.10*
Set, never hinged	1,500.	

The imperf pairs are without gum.

For surcharges see Nos. 386-387.

Approach to Athens Stadium A64

Perf. 11½, 11½x10, 13½x11½

1934, Dec. 10

381 A64 8d blue 57.50 2.25
Never hinged 175.00

Perforations on No. 381 range from 10½ to 13, including compounds.

Church of Pantanassa, Mistra — A65

1935, Nov. 1 ***Perf. 13x12½***

382 A65 4d brown	17.00	1.60
Never hinged	42.50	
a. Horiz. pair, imperf. between	650.00	
b. Imperf., pair	650.00	

Issues of the Monarchy

J71, J76, J82, 380, 379 Surcharged in Red or Blue

Nos. 383-385

Nos. 386-387

Serrate Roulette 13½

1935, Nov. 24 **Litho.**

383 D3 50 l on 40 l indigo (R)	.20	.20
a. Double surcharge		27.50
384 D3 3d on 3d car (Bl)	.55	.40

Perf. 13

385 D3 3d on 3d rose red (Bl)	2.75	2.00

Perf. 13x13½

386 A63 5d on 100d (R)	2.25	2.00
387 A62 15d on 75d (Bl)	6.50	6.00
Nos. 383-387 (5)	12.25	10.60
Set, never hinged	30.00	

King Constantine — A66

Center Engr., Frame Litho.
Perf. 12x13½

1936, Nov. 18 **Wmk. 252**

389 A66 3d black & brown .55 .40
  a. Pair, printer's name in Greek 22.50
  b. Pair, printer's name in English 22.50
390 A66 8d black & blue 1.10 .90
  a. Pair, printer's name in Greek 22.50
  b. Pair, printer's name in English 22.50
  Set, never hinged 3.25

Re-burial of the remains of King Constantine and Queen Sophia.

Two printings exist, the first containing varieties "a" and "b" with gray border; second with black border.

King George II — A67

Pallas Athene — A68

1937, Jan. 24 **Engr.** ***Perf. 12½x12***

391 A67 1d green .20 .20
392 A67 3d red brown .25 .20
393 A67 8d dp blue .90 .40
394 A67 100d carmine lake 12.00 12.00
  Nos. 391-394 (4) 13.35 12.80
  Set, never hinged 30.00

For surcharges see Nos. 484-487, 498-500, RA86-RA87, N241-N242.

1937, Apr. 17 **Unwmk.** ***Perf. 11½***

395 A68 3d yellow brown .55 .25
  Never hinged 1.10

Centenary of the University of Athens.

Contest with Bull — A69

Lady of Tiryns — A70

Zeus of Dodona — A71

Coin of Amphictyonic League A72

Diagoras of Rhodes, Victor at Olympics A73

Venus of Melos — A74

Battle of Salamis A75

Chariot of Panathenaic Festival A76

Alexander the Great at Battle of Issos — A77

St. Paul Preaching to Athenians A78

St. Demetrius' Church at Salonika A79

Leo III Victory over Arabs — A80

Allegorical Figure of Glory — A81

Perf. 13½x12, 12x13½

1937, Nov. 1 **Litho.** **Wmk. 252**

396 A69 5 l brn red & bl .20 .20
  a. Double impression of frame 60.00
397 A70 10 l bl & brn red .20 .20
  a. Double impression of frame 60.00
398 A71 20 l black & grn .20 .20
399 A72 40 l green & blk .20 .20
  a. Green impression doubled 60.00
400 A73 50 l brown & blk .20 .20
401 A74 80 l ind & yel brn .20 .20

Engr.

402 A75 2d ultra .20 .20
403 A76 5d red .20 .20
  a. Printer's name omitted 5.50
404 A77 6d olive brn .20 .20
405 A78 7d dk brown .55 .50
406 A79 10d red brown .20 .20
407 A80 15d green .20 .20
408 A81 25d dk blue .20 .20
  Nos. 396-408 (13) 2.95 2.90
  Set, never hinged 4.00

See Nos. 413, 459-466. For overprints and surcharges see Nos. 455-458, 476-477, RA75-RA78, RA83-RA85, N202-N217, N246-N247.

Cerigo, Paxos, Lefkas

Greek stamps with Italian overprints for the islands of Cerigo (Kithyra), Paxos and Lefkas (Santa Maura) are fraudulent.

Royal Wedding Issue

Princess Frederika-Louise and Crown Prince Paul — A82

1938 **Wmk. 252** ***Perf. 13½x12***

409 A82 1d green .20 .20
410 A82 3d orange brn .30 .20
411 A82 8d dark blue .55 .65
  Nos. 409-411 (3) 1.05 1.05
  Set, never hinged 2.75

Arms of Greece, Romania, Yugoslavia and Turkey A83

Statue of King Constantine A84

Perf. 12x12½

1938, Feb. 8 **Litho.** **Unwmk.**

412 A83 6d blue 5.50 1.75
  Never hinged 14.00

Balkan Entente.

Tiryns Lady Type of 1937
Corrected Inscription

1938 **Wmk. 252** ***Perf. 12x13½***

413 A70 10 l blue & brn red .50 *.70*
  Never hinged .85

The first four letters of the third word of the inscription read "TIPY" instead of "TYPI."

Perf. 12x13½

1938, Oct. 8 **Engr.** **Unwmk.**

414 A84 1.50d green .45 .20
415 A84 30d orange brn 2.25 *2.90*
  Set, never hinged 5.50

For overprint see No. N218.

Coats of Arms of Ionian Islands — A85

Fort at Corfu — A86

King George I of Greece and Queen Victoria of England A87

Perf. 12½x12, 13½x12

1939, May 21 **Engr.** **Unwmk.**

416 A85 1d dk blue .85 .25
417 A86 4d green 2.90 1.00
418 A87 20d yellow org 17.00 17.00
419 A87 20d dull blue 17.00 17.00
420 A87 20d car lake 17.00 17.00
  Nos. 416-420 (5) 54.75 52.25
  Set, never hinged 125.00

75th anniv. of the union of the Ionian Islands with Greece.

Runner with Shield — A88

10th Pan-Balkan Games: 3d, Javelin thrower. 6d, Discus thrower. 8d, Jumper.

Perf. 12x13½

1939, Oct. 1 **Litho.** **Unwmk.**

421 A88 50 l slate grn & grn .25 .20
422 A88 3d henna brn & dl rose 1.00 .55
423 A88 6d cop brn & dl org 2.75 2.25
424 A88 8d ultra & gray 2.75 2.50
  Nos. 421-424 (4) 6.75 5.50
  Set, never hinged 18.00

Arms of Greece, Romania, Turkey and Yugoslavia — A92

Perf. 13x12½

1940, May 27 **Wmk. 252**

425 A92 6d blue 8.00 2.25
426 A92 8d blue gray 5.50 2.25
  Set, never hinged 35.00

Balkan Entente.

Emblem of Youth Organization A93

Boy Member — A94

Designs: 3d, 100d, Emblem of Greek Youth Organization. 10d, Girl member. 15d, Javelin Thrower. 20d, Column of members. 25d, Flag bearers and buglers. 30d, Three youths. 50d, Line formation. 75d, Coat of arms.

Perf. 12½, 13½x12½

1940, Aug. 3 **Litho.** **Wmk. 252**

427 A93 3d sil, dp ultra & red .85 *1.25*
428 A94 5d dk bl & blk 6.50 *7.50*
429 A94 10d red org & blk 7.50 *10.00*
430 A94 15d dk grn & blk 30.00 *32.50*
431 A94 20d lake & blk 25.00 25.00
432 A94 25d dk bl & blk 25.00 25.00
433 A94 30d rose vio & blk 25.00 25.00
434 A94 50d lake & blk 30.00 30.00
435 A94 75d dk bl, brn & gold 30.00 32.50
436 A93 100d sil, dp ultra & red 50.00 *37.50*
  Nos. 427-436,C38-C47 (20) 475.55 451.50
  Set, never hinged 1,000.

4th anniv. of the founding of the Greek Youth Organization. The stamps were good for postal duty Aug. 3-5, 1940, only. They remained on sale until Feb. 3, 1941.

For overprints see Nos. N219-N238.

AIR POST STAMPS

Italy-Greece-Turkey-Rhodes Service

Flying Boat off Phaleron Bay — AP1

Flying Boat over Acropolis — AP2

Flying Boat over Map of Southern Europe — AP3

Flying Boat Seen through Colonnade — AP4

Perf. 11½

1926, Oct. 20 Unwmk. Litho.

C1	AP1	2d multicolored	1.60	1.25
a.		Horiz. pair, imperf. vert.	725.00	
C2	AP2	3d multicolored	8.75	8.25
C3	AP3	5d multicolored	1.60	1.25
C4	AP4	10d multicolored	8.25	8.25
		Nos. C1-C4 (4)	20.20	19.00
		Set, never hinged	80.00	

Graf Zeppelin Issue

Zeppelin over Acropolis AP5

1933, May 2 ***Perf. 13½x12½***

C5	AP5	30d rose red	11.00	11.00
C6	AP5	100d deep blue	47.50	47.50
C7	AP5	120d dark brown	47.50	47.50
		Nos. C5-C7 (3)	106.00	106.00
		Set, never hinged	315.00	

Propeller and Pilot's Head AP6

Temple of Apollo, Corinth AP7

Plane over Hermoupolis, Syros — AP8

Allegory of Flight
AP9 AP12

Map of Italy-Greece-Turkey-Rhodes Airmail Route — AP10

Head of Hermes and Airplane — AP11

1933, Oct. 10 Engr. ***Perf. 12***

C8	AP6	50 l green & org	.20	.20
C9	AP7	1d bl & brn org	.30	.25
C10	AP8	3d dk vio & org brn	.50	.50
C11	AP9	5d brn org & dk bl	7.25	4.50
C12	AP10	10d dp red & blk	1.50	1.40
C13	AP11	20d black & grn	7.25	4.00
C14	AP12	50d dp brn & dp bl	45.00	*50.00*
		Nos. C8-C14 (7)	62.00	*60.85*
		Set, never hinged	200.00	

By error the 1d stamp is inscribed in the plural "Draxmai" instead of the singular "Draxmh." This stamp exists bisected, used as a 50 lepta denomination.

All values of this set exist imperforate but were not regularly issued.

For General Air Post Service

Airplane over Map of Greece — AP13

Airplane over Map of Icarian Sea — AP14

Airplane over Acropolis AP15

Perf. 13x13½, 13x12½, 13½x13, 12½x13

1933, Nov. 2

C15	AP13	50 l green	.20	.25
C16	AP13	1d red brown	.30	*.55*
C17	AP14	2d lt violet	.60	*.85*
C18	AP15	5d ultra	3.50	3.50
a.		Imperf., pair	650.00	550.00
b.		Horiz. pair, imperf. vert.	650.00	
C19	AP14	10d car rose	6.50	*7.75*
C20	AP13	25d dark blue	30.00	20.00
C21	AP15	50d dark brown	30.00	*42.50*
a.		Imperf., pair	775.00	650.00
		Nos. C15-C21 (7)	71.10	75.40
		Set, never hinged	225.00	

Helios Driving the Sun Chariot AP16

Iris — AP17

Daedalus Preparing Icarus for Flying — AP18

Pallas Athene Holding Pegasus — AP19

Hermes AP20

Zeus Carrying off Ganymede AP21

Triptolemos, King of Eleusis AP22

Bellerophon and Pegasus — AP23

Phrixos and Helle on the Ram Flying over the Hellespont AP24

Perf. 13x12½, 12½x13

1935, Nov. 10 Engr.

Grayish Paper

Size: 34x23½mm, 23½x34mm

C22	AP16	1d deep red	.50	.50
C23	AP17	2d dull blue	1.10	.65
C24	AP18	5d dk violet	10.00	3.25
C25	AP19	7d blue violet	13.00	6.50
C26	AP20	10d bister brown	2.75	2.75
C27	AP21	25d rose	4.75	*4.50*
C28	AP22	30d dark green	.55	.55
C29	AP23	50d violet	3.90	*4.50*
C30	AP24	100d brown	.75	*1.25*
		Nos. C22-C30 (9)	37.30	*24.45*
		Set, never hinged	125.00	

Re-engraved

1937-39

White Paper

Size: 34¼x24mm, 24x34¼mm

C31	AP16	1d red	.20	.20
C32	AP17	2d gray blue	.20	.20
C33	AP18	5d violet	.20	.20
C34	AP19	7d dp ultra	.20	.20
C35	AP20	10d brn org	1.90	*2.75*
		Nos. C31-C35 (5)	2.70	*3.55*
		Set, never hinged	7.00	

Issued: #C35, 3/1/39; others 8/3/37.

Postage Due Stamp, 1913, Overprinted in Red

Serrate Roulette 13½

1938, Aug. 8 Litho. Unwmk.

C36	D3	50 l violet brown	.20	.20
		Never hinged	.25	
a.		"O" for "P" in word at foot	30.00	30.00

Same Overprint on No. J79 in Red

1939, June 26 ***Perf. 13½x12½***

C37	D3	50 l dark brown	.20	.20
		Never hinged	.20	

Meteora Monasteries, near Trikkala — AP25

Designs: 4d, Simon Peter Monastery. 6d, View of Santorin. 8d, Church of Pantanassa. 16d, Santorin view. 32d, Ponticonissi, Corfu. 45d, Acropolis, Athens. 55d, Erechtheum. 65d, Temple of Nike Apteros. 100d, Temple of the Olympian Zeus, Athens.

Wmk. Crowns (252)

1940, Aug. 3 Litho. ***Perf. 12½***

C38	AP25	2d red org & blk	.65	*1.00*
C39	AP25	4d dk grn & blk	3.00	2.75
C40	AP25	6d lake & blk	5.50	5.00
C41	AP25	8d dk bl & blk	14.05	12.50
C42	AP25	16d rose vio & blk	22.50	19.00
C43	AP25	32d red org & blk	30.00	*35.00*
C44	AP25	45d dk grn & blk	40.00	35.00
C45	AP25	55d lake & blk	40.00	35.00
C46	AP25	65d dk bl & blk	40.00	35.00
C47	AP25	100d rose vio & blk	50.00	45.00
		Nos. C38-C47 (10)	245.70	225.25
		Set, never hinged	550.00	

4th anniv. of the founding of the Greek Youth Organization. The stamps were good for postal duty on Aug. 3-5, 1940, only. They remained on sale until Feb. 3, 1941.

For overprints see Nos. N229-N238.

POSTAGE DUE STAMPS

D1

D2

Perf. 9, 9½, and 10, 10½ and Compound

1875 Litho. Unwmk.

J1	D1	1 l green & black	1.25	1.25
J2	D1	2 l green & black	1.25	1.25
J3	D1	5 l green & black	1.50	1.00
J4	D1	10 l green & black	1.50	1.00
J5	D1	20 l green & black	30.00	15.00
J6	D1	40 l green & black	7.00	4.50
J7	D1	60 l green & black	30.00	16.00
J8	D1	70 l green & black	7.00	7.00
J9	D1	80 l green & black	15.00	12.00
J10	D1	90 l green & black	9.00	9.00

J11 D1 1d green & black 10.00 9.00
J12 D1 2d green & black 11.00 9.00
Nos. J1-J12 (12) 124.50 86.00

Imperforate and part perforated, double and inverted center varieties of Nos. J1-J12 are believed to be printers' waste.

Perf. 12, 13 and 10½x13

J13 D1 1 l green & black 1.50 1.50
J14 D1 2 l green & black 13.00 11.00
J15 D1 5 l green & black 2.50 2.50
J16 D1 10 l green & black 3.00 3.00
J17 D1 20 l green & black 24.00 21.00
J18 D1 40 l green & black 9.00 7.00
J19 D1 60 l green & black 37.50 24.00
J20 D1 70 l green & black 7.00 7.00
J21 D1 80 l green & black 11.00 11.00
J22 D1 90 l green & black 16.00 11.00
J23 D1 1d green & black 24.00 16.00
J24 D1 2d green & black 21.00 16.00
Nos. J13-J24 (12) 169.50 131.00

Redrawn
"Lepton" or "Lepta" in Larger Greek Letters

1876 ***Perf. 9, 9½, and 10, 10½***

J25 D2 1 l green & black 3.75 3.75
J26 D2 2 l dk grn & blk 5.00 4.75
J27 D2 5 l dk grn & blk 300.00 225.00
J28 D2 10 l green & black 2.50 1.75
J29 D2 20 l green & black 3.25 2.50
J30 D2 40 l green & black 27.50 21.00
J31 D2 60 l green & black 22.50 12.50
J32 D2 70 l green & black 18.00 21.00
J33 D2 80 l green & black 15.00 12.50
J34 D2 90 l green & black 15.00 13.00
J35 D2 100 l green & black 18.00 12.50
J36 D2 200 l green & black 18.00 12.50
Nos. J25-J36 (12) 448.50 342.75

Perf. 11½ to 13

J37 D2 1 l yel grn & blk 1.25 .70
J38 D2 2 l yel grn & blk 1.25 .70
J39 D2 5 l yel grn & blk 3.50 .90
J40 D2 10 l yel grn & blk 2.00 1.50
a. Perf. 10-10½x11½-13 3.00
J41 D2 20 l yel grn & blk 2.00 1.50
J42 D2 40 l yel grn & blk 11.00 8.00
J43 D2 60 l yel grn & blk 7.00 7.00
J47 D2 100 l yel grn & blk 9.00 9.00
J48 D2 200 l yel grn & blk 10.00 8.00
Nos. J37-J48 (9) 47.00 37.30

Footnote below #J12 applies also to #J25-J48.

D3

1902 **Engr.** **Wmk. 129** ***Perf. 13½***

J49 D3 1 l chocolate .20 .20
J50 D3 2 l gray .20 .20
J51 D3 3 l orange .20 .20
J52 D3 5 l yel grn .20 .20
J53 D3 10 l scarlet .25 .20
J54 D3 20 l lilac .30 .20
J55 D3 25 l ultra 8.00 4.00
J56 D3 30 l dp vio .30 .30
J57 D3 40 l dk brn .35 .25
J58 D3 50 l red brn .35 .20
J59 D3 1d black .90 .60

Litho.

J60 D3 2d bronze 1.00 1.00
J61 D3 3d silver 2.00 2.00
J62 D3 5d gold 6.00 6.00
Nos. J49-J62 (14) 20.25 15.55

See Nos. J63-J88, J90-J93. For overprints and surcharges see Nos. 383-385, J89, RA56, RA58-RA59, NJ1-NJ31.

Imperf., Pairs

J50a D3 2 l 60.00
J51a D3 3 l 60.00
J52a D3 5 l 60.00
J55a D3 25 l 100.00
J56a D3 30 l 100.00
J58a D3 50 l 100.00
J59a D3 1d 100.00

Serrate Roulette 13½

1913-26 **Unwmk.**

J63 D3 1 l green .20 .20
J64 D3 2 l carmine .20 .20
J65 D3 3 l vermilion .20 .20
J66 D3 5 l green .20 .20
a. Imperf., pair 150.00
b. Double impression 60.00
c. "o" for "p" in lowest word 3.00 3.00
J67 D3 10 l carmine .20 .20
J68 D3 20 l slate .20 .20
J69 D3 25 l ultra .20 .20
J70 D3 30 l carmine .20 .20
J71 D3 40 l indigo .20 .20
J72 D3 50 l vio brn .30 .25
a. "o" for "p" in lowest word 25.00 20.00
J73 D3 80 l lil brn ('24) .40 .20
J74 D3 1d blue 6.00 .80
a. 1d ultramarine 9.00 3.50
J75 D3 2d vermilion 2.00 1.50
J76 D3 3d carmine 4.50 1.50
J77 D3 5d ultra 25.00 8.00
J78 D3 5d gray bl ('26) 4.00 1.50
Nos. J63-J78 (16) 44.00 15.55

In 1922-23 and 1941-42 some postage due stamps were used for ordinary postage.

In 1916 Nos. J52, and J63 to J75 were surcharged for the Mount Athos District (see note after No. N166) but were never issued there. By error some of them were put in use as ordinary postage due stamps in Dec., 1924. In 1932 the balance of them was burned.

Type of 1902 Issue

Perf. 13, 13½x12½, 13½x13

1930 **Litho.**

J79 D3 50 l dk brown .30 .30
J80 D3 1d lt blue .30 .30
J81 D3 2d lt red .30 .30
J82 D3 3d rose red 27.50 25.00
J83 D3 5d gray blue .30 .30
J84 D3 10d gray green .30 .30
J85 D3 15d red brown .30 .30
J86 D3 25d light red .70 .65
Nos. J79-J86 (8) 30.00 27.45

Type of 1902 Issue

1935 **Engr.** ***Perf. 12½x13***

J87 D3 50d orange .30 .30
J88 D3 100d slate green .30 .30

POSTAL TAX STAMPS

"The Tragedy of War" — PT1

Red Cross, Nurses, Wounded and Bearers PT1a

Serrate Roulette 13½

1914 **Litho.** **Unwmk.**

RA1 PT1 2 l red ('18) .20 .20
a. 2 l carmine .35 .25
b. Imperf., pair 200.00
RA2 PT1 5 l blue .50 *.75*
a. Imperf., pair 250.00

1915 ***Serrate Roulette 13***

RA2B PT1a (5 l) dk bl & red 8.00 1.50

The tax was for the Red Cross.

Women's Patriotic League Badge — PT1b

1915, Nov. ***Perf. 11½***

RA2C PT1b (5 l) dk bl & car 1.00 1.00
d. Horiz. pair, imperf. btwn. 50.00

The tax was for the Greek Women's Patriotic League.

Nos. 165, 167, 170, 172-175 Surcharged in Black or Brown:

a

b

In type "b" the letters, especially those in the first line, are thinner than in type "a," making them appear taller.

Perf. 11½, 12½, 13½ and Compound

1917 **Engr.** **Wmk. 129**

RA3 A11(a) 1 l on 1 l 1.50 1.50
a. Double surcharge 5.00
RA4 A11(a) 1 l on 1 l (Br) 20.00 20.00
RA5 A11(a) 1 l on 3 l .30 .30
RA6 A11(b) 1 l on 3 l .30 .30
a. Triple surcharge 5.00
b. Dbl. surch., one invtd. 5.00
c. "K.M." for "K.Π." 20.00
RA7 A11(a) 5 l on 1 l 2.00 2.00
a. Double surcharge 10.00
b. Dbl. surch., one invtd. 10.00
c. Inverted surcharge 10.00
RA8 A11(a) 5 l on 20 l .65 .65
a. Double surcharge 10.00
b. Dbl. surch., one invtd. 10.00
RA9 A11(b) 5 l on 40 l .65 .65
a. Imperf.
RA10 A11(b) 5 l on 50 l .65 .65
a. Double surcharge 25.00
b. Dbl. surch., one invtd. 25.00
RA11 A13(b) 5 l on 1d 2.25 2.25
a. Imperf.
b. Inverted surcharge 50.00
RA12 A11(a) 10 l on 30 l .80 .80
a. Imperf.
b. Double surcharge 20.00
RA13 A11(a) 30 l on 30 l .90 .90
a. Double surcharge 20.00
Nos. RA3-RA13 (11) 30.00 30.00

Same Surcharge On Occupation Stamps of 1912

Serrate Roulette 13½

1917 **Litho.** **Unwmk.**

RA14 O2 (b) 5 l on 25 l pale bl .45 .45
a. Triple surch., one invtd. 6.00
b. Double surcharge 6.00
RA15 O2 (b) 5 l on 40 l indigo .45 .45
a. Double surch., one invtd. 6.00
b. Double surcharge 6.00
RA16 O1 (b) 5 l on 50 l dk bl .45 .45
a. Double surcharge 10.00
b. Inverted surcharge 10.00
Nos. RA14-RA16 (3) 1.35 1.35

There are many wrong font, omitted and misplaced letters and punctuation marks and similar varieties in the surcharges on Nos. RA3 to RA16.

Revenue Stamps Surcharged in Brown

"Victory" — R1

K. Π.
λεπτοῦ
1

1917

RA17 R1 1 l on 10 l blue .60 .60
RA18 R1 1 l on 80 l blue .60 .60
RA19 R1 5 l on 10 l blue 12.00 12.00
RA20 R1 5 l on 60 l blue 4.00 3.00
a. Perf. vert. through middle 4.25 2.50
RA21 R1 5 l on 80 l blue 3.00 3.00
a. Perf. vert. through middle 7.50 4.00
b. Inverted surcharge
RA22 R1 10 l on 70 l blue 14.00 5.00
a. Perf. vert. through middle 4.25 2.00
RA23 R1 10 l on 90 l blue 10.00 8.00
a. Perf. vert. through middle 12.50 11.00
RA24 R1 20 l on 20 l blue 650.00 475.00
RA25 R1 20 l on 30 l blue 4.00 4.00
RA26 R1 20 l on 40 l blue 12.00 10.00
RA27 R1 20 l on 50 l blue 5.00 4.00
RA28 R1 20 l on 60 l blue 350.00 150.00
RA29 R1 20 l on 80 l blue 35.00 22.50
RA30 R1 20 l on 90 l blue 3.00 3.00
a. Inverted surcharge 65.00
Nos. RA17-RA30 (14) 1,103. 700.70

No. RA19 is known only with vertical perforation through the middle.

Counterfeits exist of Nos. RA17-RA43, used.

Surcharged in Brown or Black

RA31 R1 1 l on 50 l vio (Bk) .60 .60
RA32 R1 5 l on 10 l bl (Br) .60 .60
a. Inverted surcharge 60.00
b. Left "5" invert. 60.00
RA33 R1 5 l on 10 l vio (Br) .60 .60
RA34 R1 10 l on 50 l vio (Br) 4.00 4.00
RA35 R1 10 l on 50 l vio (Bk) 22.50 20.00
RA36 R1 20 l on 2d bl (Bk) 6.00 4.00
a. Surcharged "20 lept. 30" 60.00 60.00
b. Horiz. pair, imperf. btwn.
Nos. RA31-RA36 (6) 34.30 29.80

The "t," fourth Greek letter of the denomination in the surcharge ("Lept."), is normally omitted on Nos. RA31, RA34-RA36.

Corfu Issue

Surcharged in Black

1917

RA37 R1 1 l on 10 l blue 1.00 1.00
RA38 R1 5 l on 50 l blue 30.00 30.00
RA39 R1 10 l on 50 l blue 400.00 350.00
RA40 R1 20 l on 50 l blue 1,000. 600.00

Surcharged in Black

RA41 R1 10 l on 50 l blue 7.00 6.00
RA42 R1 20 l on 50 l blue 18.00 12.00
RA43 R1 30 l on 50 l blue 10.00 8.00

Surcharged in Black

RA44 R1 5 l on 10 l vio & red 6.00 1.00
a. "K" with serifs 10.00 3.50

Counterfeits exist of Nos. RA17-RA44.

Similar stamps with denominations higher than 30 lepta were for revenue use.

Wounded Soldier — PT2

1918 ***Serrate Roulette 13½, 11½***

RA45 PT2 5 l bl, yel & red 7.00 1.50

Overprinted

RA46 PT2 5 l blue, yel & red 8.00 1.50

The letters are the initials of Greek words equivalent to "Patriotic Relief Institution." The proceeds were given to the Patriotic League, for the aid of disabled soldiers.

Counterfeits exist of Nos. RA45-RA46.

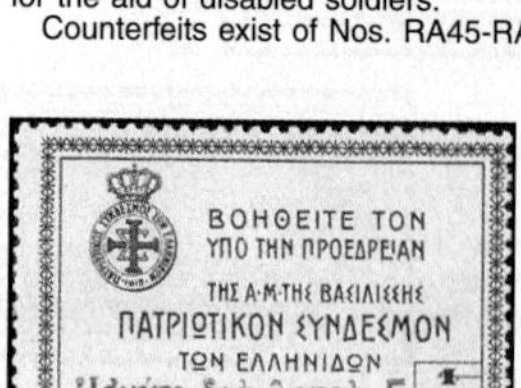
PT3

Surcharge in Red

1922 **Litho.** ***Perf. 11½***

Dark Blue & Red

RA46A PT3 5 l on 10 l *275.00* 5.00
RA46B PT3 5 l on 20 l 50.00 25.00
RA46C PT3 5 l on 50 l 250.00 80.00
RA46D PT3 5 l on 1d 3.25 *35.00*

Counterfeit surcharges exist. Copies of Nos. RA46A-RA46C without surcharge, each 50 cents.

Red Cross Help to Soldier and Family PT3a

St. Demetrius PT4

1924 ***Perf. 11½, 13½ x 12½***

RA47 PT3a 10 l blue, buff & red .70 .25
a. Imperf., pair 40.00
b. Horiz. pair, imperf. btwn. 40.00

Proceeds were given to the Red Cross.

1934 ***Perf. 11½***

RA48 PT4 20 l brown .20 .20
a. Horizontal pair, imperf. between 10.00
b. Vertical pair, imperf. between 15.00
c. Imperf., pair 20.00

No. RA48 was obligatory as a tax on all interior mail, including air post, mailed from Salonika.

For surcharge see No. RA69.

"Health"

PT5 PT6

1934, Dec. 28 ***Perf. 13, 13x13½***

RA49 PT5 10 l bl grn, org & buff .20 .20
a. Vert. pair, imperf. horiz.
RA50 PT5 20 l ultra, org & buff .45 .20
RA51 PT5 50 l grn, org & buff 1.25 .40
Nos. RA49-RA51 (3) 1.90 .80

For surcharge see No. RA67.

1935

RA52 PT6 10 l yel grn, org & buff .20 .20
RA53 PT6 20 l ultra, org & buff .20 .20
RA54 PT6 50 l grn, org & buff .50 .35
Nos. RA52-RA54 (3) .90 .75

The use of #RA49-RA54 was obligatory on all mail during 4 weeks each year including Christmas, the New Year and Easter, and on parcel post packages at all times. For the benefit of the tubercular clerks and officials of the Post, Telephone and Telegraph Service.

See No. RA64. For surcharge see No. RA68.

No. 364 Overprinted in Red

1937, Jan. 20 **Engr.** ***Perf. 13x12½***

RA55 A36 50 l violet 1.25 .20
a. Inverted overprint .75 .20

No. RA55a first appeared as an error, then was issued deliberately in quantity to avoid speculation.

Same Overprint in Blue on No. J67

Litho.

Serrate Roulette 13½

RA56 D3 10 l carmine .20 .20
a. Inverted overprint 50.00

No. RA56 with blue overprint double exists only with additional black overprint of Ionian Islands No. NRA1a.

Same Overprint in Green on No. 364

1937 **Engr.** ***Perf. 13x12½***

RA57 A36 50 l violet .75 .20

Same Overprint, with Surcharge of New Value, on Nos. J66, J68 and 323 in Blue or Black

Serrate Roulette 13½

1938 **Litho.** **Unwmk.**

RA58 D3 50 l on 5 l grn .35 .25
a. "o" for "p" in lowest word 25.00 25.00
b. Vert. pair, imperf. horiz. 50.00
RA59 D3 50 l on 20 l slate .90 .50

Engr. ***Perf. 13x12½***

RA60 A38 50 l on 20 l vio (Bk) .75 .20
Nos. RA58-RA60 (3) 2.00 .95

Surcharge on No. RA60 is 14½x16½mm.

Queens Olga and Sophia PT7

1939, Feb. 1 **Litho.** ***Perf. 13½x12***

RA61 PT7 10 l brt rose, *pale rose* .20 .20
RA62 PT7 50 l gray grn, *pale grn* .20 .20
RA63 PT7 1d dl bl, *lt bl* .20 .20
Nos. RA61-RA63 (3) .60 .60

For overprints and surcharges see Nos. RA65, RA79-RA81A, NRA1-NRA3.

"Health" Type of 1935

1939 ***Perf. 12½***

RA64 PT6 50 l brn & buff .40 .30

No. RA62 Overprinted in Red

1940 ***Perf. 13½x12***

RA65 PT7 50 l gray grn, *pale grn* .25 .25
a. Inverted overprint 35.00
b. Pair, one without surcharge 20.00

Proceeds of #RA64-RA65 were used for the benefit of tubercular clerks and officials of the Post, Telephone and Telegraph Service. #RA65 was used in Albania during the Greek occupation, 1940-41 without additional overprint.

OCCUPATION AND ANNEXATION STAMPS

During the Balkan wars, 1912-13, Greece occupied certain of the Aegean Islands and part of Western Turkey. She subsequently acquired these territories and they were known as the New Greece.

Most of the special issues for the Aegean Islands were made by order of the military commanders.

For Use in the Aegean Islands Occupied by Greece

CHIOS

Greece No. 221 Overprinted in Red

Serrate Roulette 13½

1913 **Litho.** **Unwmk.**

N1 A25 25 l ultramarine 45.00 45.00
a. Inverted overprint 200.00 150.00
b. Greek "L" instead of "D" 200.00 150.00

ICARIA (NICARIA)

Penelope — I1

1912 **Unwmk.** **Litho.** ***Perf. 11½***

N2 I1 2 l orange 1.00 1.50
N3 I1 5 l blue green 1.00 1.50
N4 I1 10 l rose 1.00 1.50
N5 I1 25 l ultra 1.00 1.50
N6 I1 50 l gray lilac 1.25 3.00
N7 I1 1d dark brown 2.00 *9.00*
N8 I1 2d claret 3.00 *15.00*
N9 I1 5d slate 4.50 *22.50*
Nos. N2-N9 (8) 14.75 *55.50*

Counterfeits of Nos. N1-N15 are plentiful.

Stamps of Greece, 1911-23, Overprinted Reading Up

1913 **Engr.**

On Issue of 1911-21

N10 A25 2 l car rose 20.00 20.00
N11 A24 3 l vermilion 20.00 20.00

Litho.

On Issue of 1912-23

N12 A24 1 l green 20.00 20.00
N13 A24 3 l vermilion 20.00 20.00
N14 A26 5 l green 20.00 20.00
N15 A24 10 l carmine 20.00 20.00
Nos. N10-N15 (6) 120.00 120.00

LEMNOS

Regular Issues of Greece Overprinted in Black

On Issue of 1901

1912 **Wmk. 129** **Engr.** ***Perf. 13½***

N16 A11 20 l red lilac 1.40 1.40

On Issue of 1911-21

Unwmk.

Serrate Roulette 13½

N17 A24 1 l green .70 .70
N18 A25 2 l carmine rose .70 .70
N19 A24 3 l vermilion .70 .70
N20 A26 5 l green .70 .70
N21 A24 10 l car rose .70 .70
N22 A25 20 l gray lilac .70 .70
N23 A25 25 l ultra 1.00 1.00
N24 A26 30 l car rose 1.00 1.00
N25 A25 40 l deep blue 2.00 2.00
N26 A26 50 l dl violet 2.00 2.00
N27 A27 1d ultra 3.75 3.75
N28 A27 2d vermilion 15.00 15.00
N29 A27 3d car rose 18.00 18.00
N30 A27 5d ultra 22.50 22.50
N31 A27 10d deep blue 82.50 82.50
N32 A28 25d deep blue 82.50 82.50

On Issue of 1912-23

Litho.

N33 A24 1 l green .30 .30
a. Without period after "Ellas" 125.00 125.00
N34 A26 5 l green .30 .30
N35 A24 10 l carmine .30 .30
N36 A25 25 l ultra 1.50 1.50
Nos. N16-N36 (21) 238.25 238.25

Red Overprint

On Issue of 1911-21

Engr.

N37 A25 2 l car rose .70 .70
N38 A24 3 l vermilion .70 .70
N39 A25 20 l gray lilac 1.75 1.75
N40 A26 30 l car rose 3.00 3.00
N41 A25 40 l deep blue 3.00 3.00
N42 A26 50 l dull violet 3.00 3.00
N43 A27 1d ultra 3.50 3.50
N44 A27 2d vermilion 30.00 30.00
N45 A27 3d car rose 19.00 19.00
N46 A27 5d ultra 35.00 35.00
N47 A27 10d deep blue 85.00 85.00
N48 A28 25d deep blue 85.00 85.00

On Issue of 1912-23

Litho.

N49 A24 1 l green .70 .70
a. Without period after "Ellas" 125.00 125.00
N50 A26 5 l green .30 .30
N51 A24 10 l carmine 1.40 1.40
N52 A25 25 l ultra 1.75 1.75
Nos. N37-N52 (16) 273.80 273.80

The overprint is found inverted or double on many of Nos. N16-N52. There are several varieties in the overprint: Greek "D" for "L," large Greek "S" or "O," and small "O."

No. N49 with Added "Greek Administration" Overprint, as on Nos. N109-N148, in Black

1913

N52A A24 1 l green 22.50 22.50

Counterfeits of #N16-N52A are plentiful.

MYTILENE (LESBOS)

Turkey Nos. 162, 158 Overprinted in Blue

Perf. 12, 13½ and Compound

1912 **Typo.** **Unwmk.**

N53 A21 20pa rose 22.50 22.50
N54 A21 10pi dull red 110.00 110.00

On Turkey Nos. P68, 151-155, 137, 157-158 in Black

N55 A21 2pa olive green 2.00 2.00
N56 A21 5pa ocher 2.00 2.00
N57 A21 10pa blue green 2.00 2.00
N58 A21 20pa rose 2.00 2.00
N59 A21 1pi ultra 4.00 4.00
N60 A21 2pi blue black 22.50 22.50
N61 A19 2½pi dk brown 11.00 11.00
N62 A21 5pi dk violet 22.50 22.50
N63 A21 10pi dull red 110.00 110.00
Nos. N55-N63 (9) 178.00 178.00

On Turkey Nos. 161-163, 145 in Black

N64 A21 10pa blue green 4.00 4.00
a. Double overprint 35.00
N65 A21 20pa rose 4.00 4.00
N66 A21 1pi ultra 4.00 4.00
N67 A19 2pi blue black 47.50 47.50

Nos. N55, N58, N65, N59 Surcharged in Blue or Black

N68 A21 25 l on 2pa 7.50 7.50
a. New value inverted 40.00
N69 A21 50 l on 20pa 10.00 10.00
b. New value inverted 45.00
N70 A21 1d on 20pa (N65) (Bk) 20.00 20.00
a. New value inverted 45.00
N71 A21 2d on 1pi (Bk) 22.50 22.50
a. New value inverted

Same Overprint on Turkey No. J49

N72 A19 1pi blk, *dp rose* 50.00 50.00

The overprint is found on all values reading up or down with inverted "i" in the first word and inverted "e" in the third word.

No. N72 was only used for postage.

Counterfeits of Nos. N53-N72 are plentiful.

SAMOS

Issues of the Provisional Government

Map of Samos OS1

1912 Unwmk. Typo. *Imperf.*

N73	OS1	5 l gray green	20.00	5.50
N74	OS1	10 l red	20.00	5.50
N75	OS1	25 l blue	40.00	20.00
a.		25 l green (error)	*500.00*	*600.00*
		Nos. N73-N75 (3)	80.00	31.00

Nos. N73-N75 exist in tête bêche pairs. Value per set, $500 unused, $250 used.

Counterfeits exist of Nos. N73 to N75.

Hermes — OS2

1912 Litho. *Perf. 11½*

Without Overprint

N76	OS2	1 l gray	3.00	1.50
N77	OS2	5 l lt green	3.75	1.50
N78	OS2	10 l rose	4.00	1.50
b.		Half used as 5 l on cover		15.00
N79	OS2	25 l lt blue	7.00	1.50
N80	OS2	50 l violet brn	12.50	10.00

With Overprint

N81	OS2	1 l gray	1.00	1.10
N82	OS2	5 l blue grn	1.00	1.10
N83	OS2	10 l rose	1.75	1.50
b.		Half used as 5 l on cover		20.00
N84	OS2	25 l blue	2.00	2.00
N85	OS2	50 l violet brn	11.00	6.50
N86	OS2	1d orange	10.00	10.00
		Nos. N76-N86 (11)	57.00	38.20

For overprints and surcharge see Nos. N92-N103.

Imperf., Pairs

Without Overprint

N76a	OS2	1 l	40.00	
N77a	OS2	5 l	40.00	
N78a	OS2	10 l	40.00	
N79a	OS2	25 l	40.00	
N80a	OS2	50 l	40.00	

With Overprint

N81a	OS2	1 l	100.00	
N82a	OS2	5 l	100.00	
N83a	OS2	10 l	100.00	
N85a	OS2	50 l	100.00	100.00

Church in Savior's Name and Fort Ruins OS3

Manuscript Initials in Red or Black

1913

N87	OS3	1d brown (R)	16.00	14.00
N88	OS3	2d deep blue (R)	16.00	14.00
N89	OS3	5d gray grn (R)	30.00	25.00
N90	OS3	10d yellow grn (R)	90.00	80.00
N91	OS3	25d red (Bk)	80.00	67.50
		Nos. N87-N91 (5)	232.00	200.50

Victory of the Greek fleet in 1824 and the union with Greece of Samos in 1912. The manuscript initials are those of Pres. Themistokles Sofulis.

Values the same for copies without initials.

Exist imperf. Counterfeits of Nos. N87-N91 are plentiful.

For overprints see Nos. N104-N108.

Nos. N76 to N80 Overprinted

1914

N92	OS2	1 l gray	4.00	4.00
N93	OS2	5 l lt green	4.00	4.00
N94	OS2	10 l rose	4.25	4.00
a.		Double overprint	60.00	
N95	OS2	25 l lt blue	12.00	12.00
N96	OS2	50 l violet brn	8.00	8.00
a.		Double overprint	100.00	
		Nos. N92-N96 (5)	32.25	32.00

Charity Issues of Greek Administration

Nos. N81 to N86 Overprinted in Red or Black

1915

N97	OS2	1 l gray (R)	20.00	20.00
a.		Black overprint	125.00	
N98	OS2	5 l blue grn (Bk)	.80	.80
a.		Red overprint	125.00	
b.		Double overprint	125.00	
N99	OS2	10 l rose (Bk)	.90	.90
a.		Red overprint	125.00	
b.		Inverted overprint	125.00	
N100	OS2	25 l blue (Bk)	.80	.80
a.		Red overprint	125.00	
N101	OS2	50 l violet brn (Bk)	1.00	1.00
a.		Red overprint	125.00	
N102	OS2	1d orange (R)	2.00	2.00
a.		Inverted overprint	125.00	
b.		Black overprint	100.00	
c.		Double black overprint	150.00	

No. N102 With Additional Surcharge in Black

N103	OS2	1 l on 1d orange	7.00	7.00
a.		Black surcharge double	150.00	
b.		Black surcharge inverted	150.00	
		Nos. N97-N103 (7)	32.50	32.50

Issue of 1913 Overprinted in Red or Black

1915

N104	OS3	1d brown (R)	15.00	15.00
N105	OS3	2d dp blue (R)	20.00	20.00
a.		Double overprint		
N106	OS3	5d gray grn (R)	40.00	40.00
N107	OS3	10d yellow grn (Bk)	45.00	45.00
a.		Inverted overprint		
N108	OS3	25d red (Bk)	600.00	600.00
		Nos. N104-N108 (5)	720.00	720.00

Nos. N97 to N108 inclusive have an embossed control mark, consisting of a cross encircled by a Greek inscription.

Most copies of Nos. N104-N108 lack the initials.

Counterfeits of Nos. N104-N108 are plentiful.

FOR USE IN PARTS OF TURKEY OCCUPIED BY GREECE (NEW GREECE)

Regular Issues of Greece Overprinted

Black Overprint Meaning "Greek Administration"

On Issue of 1901

1912 Wmk. 129 Engr. *Perf. 13½*

N109	A11	20 l red lilac	2.00	2.00

On Issue of 1911-21

Unwmk.

Serrate Roulette 13½

N110	A24	1 l green	.60	.50
N111	A25	2 l car rose	.60	.50
N112	A24	3 l vermilion	.60	.50
N113	A26	5 l green	.60	.50
N114	A24	10 l car rose	1.00	.80
N115	A25	20 l gray lilac	1.50	.80
N116	A25	25 l ultra	2.00	1.00
N117	A26	30 l car rose	2.25	2.25
N118	A25	40 l deep blue	3.25	2.00
N119	A26	50 l dl violet	3.25	2.00
N120	A27	1d ultra	6.50	2.00
N121	A27	2d vermilion	30.00	25.00
N122	A27	3d car rose	30.00	30.00
N123	A27	5d ultra	12.00	10.00
N124	A27	10d deep blue	200.00	200.00
N125	A28	25d dp bl, ovpt. horiz.	125.00	125.00

On Issue of 1913-23

Litho.

N126	A24	1 l green	.60	.60
b.		Without period after "Elias"	100.00	100.00
N127	A26	5 l green	.60	.50
N128	A24	10 l carmine	1.40	.70
N129	A25	25 l blue	3.25	2.00
		Nos. N109-N129 (21)	427.00	408.65

Red Overprint

On Issue of 1911-21

Engr.

N130	A24	1 l green	.80	.80
N131	A25	2 l car rose	6.00	4.00
N132	A24	3 l vermilion	5.00	4.00
N133	A26	5 l green	.90	.70
N134	A25	20 l gray lilac	6.00	1.50
N135	A25	25 l ultra	45.00	45.00
N136	A26	30 l car rose	20.00	15.00
N137	A25	40 l deep blue	3.00	2.25
N138	A26	50 l dl violet	3.00	3.00
N139	A27	1d ultra	12.00	6.00
N140	A27	2d vermilion	45.00	40.00
N141	A27	3d car rose	20.00	17.00
N142	A27	5d ultra	250.00	225.00
N143	A27	10d deep blue	25.00	20.00
N144	A28	25d dp bl, ovpt. horiz.	50.00	50.00
a.		Vertical overprint	200.00	200.00

On Issue of 1913-23

Litho.

N145	A24	1 l green	5.00	5.00
a.		Without period after "Elias"	125.00	
N146	A26	5 l green	.85	.85
N147	A24	10 l carmine	40.00	35.00
N148	A25	25 l blue	2.25	1.75
		Nos. N130-N148 (19)	539.80	476.85

The normal overprint is vertical, reading upward on N109-N124, N126-N143, N145-N148. It is often double or reading downward. There are numerous broken, missing and wrong font letters with a Greek "L" instead of "D" as the first letter of the second word.

Counterfeits exist of Nos. N109-N148.

Cross of Constantine O1

Eagle of Zeus O2

1912 Litho.

N150	O1	1 l brown	.25	.20
N151	O2	2 l red	.25	.20
a.		2 l rose	.30	.20
N153	O2	3 l orange	.30	.20
N154	O1	5 l green	1.25	.20
N155	O1	10 l rose red	5.00	.20
N156	O1	20 l violet	11.00	2.25
N157	O2	25 l pale blue	2.00	.75
N158	O1	30 l gray grn	42.50	2.00
N159	O2	40 l indigo	6.00	4.00
N160	O1	50 l dark blue	3.00	2.50
N161	O2	1d violet brn	4.00	2.50
N162	O1	2d gray brn	40.00	7.00
N163	O2	3d dull blue	100.00	20.00
N164	O1	5d gray	100.00	25.00
N165	O2	10d carmine	100.00	160.00
N166	O1	25d gray blk	100.00	160.00
		Nos. N150-N166 (16)	515.55	387.00

Occupation of Macedonia, Epirus and some of the Aegean Islands.

Sold only in New Greece.

Dangerous forgeries of #N165-N166 exist.

In 1916 some stamps of this issue were overprinted in Greek: "I (era) Koinotis Ag (iou) Orous" for the Mount Athos Monastery District. They were never placed in use and most of them were destroyed.

For surcharges and overprints see Nos. 267-276A, RA14-RA16, Thrace 31-33.

Imperf., Pairs

Without Overprint

N150a	O1	1 l	500.00
N151b	O2	2 l	500.00
N153a	O2	3 l	500.00
N154a	O1	5 l	200.00
N155a	O1	10 l	200.00
N156a	O1	20 l	1,750.
N157a	O2	25 l	1,750.
N158a	O1	30 l	1,750.
N159a	O2	40 l	1,750.
N163a	O2	3d	*2,500.*

CAVALLA

ΕΛΛΗΝΙΚΗ

ΔΙΟΙΚΗΣΙΣ

Bulgaria Nos. 89-97 Surcharged in Red

25 ΛΕΠΤΑ 25

1913 Unwmk. Engr. *Perf. 12*

N167	A20	5 l on 1s myr grn	*13.50*	*13.50*
N169	A25	10 l on 15s brn bis	*50.00*	*50.00*
N170	A26	10 l on 25s ultra & blk	*15.00*	*15.00*
N171	A21	15 l on 2s car & blk	*25.00*	*25.00*
N172	A22	20 l on 3s lake & blk	*25.00*	*25.00*
N173	A23	25 l on 5s grn & blk	*10.50*	*8.50*
N174	A24	50 l on 10s red & blk	*13.50*	*8.50*
N175	A25	1d on 15s brn bis	*80.00*	*60.00*
N176	A27	1d on 30s bl & blk	*60.00*	*30.00*
N177	A28	1d on 50s ocher & blk	*100.00*	*50.00*

Blue Surcharge

N178	A24	50 l on 10s red & blk	*13.50*	*9.00*
		Nos. N167-N178 (11)	*406.00*	*294.50*

The counterfeits and reprints of Nos. N167-N178 are difficult to distinguish from originals. Many overprint varieties exist.

Some specialists question the status of Nos. N167-N178.

DEDEAGATCH

(Alexandroupolis)

ΕΛΛΗΝΙΚΗ

ΔΙΟΙΚΗΣΙΣ

ΔΕΔΕΑΓΑΤΣ

ΔΕΚΑ ΛΕΠΤΑ

D1-(10 lepta)

1913 Unwmk. Typeset *Perf. 11½*

Control Mark in Red

N179	D1	5 l black	35.00	30.00
N180	D1	10 l black	4.00	4.00
N181	D1	25 l black	4.00	4.00
a.		Sheet of 8	100.00	100.00
		Nos. N179-N181 (3)	43.00	38.00

Nos. N179-N181 issued without gum in sheets of 8, consisting of one 5 l, three 10 l normal, one 10 l inverted, three 25 l and one blank. The sheet yields se-tenant pairs of 5 l & 10 l, 10 l & 25 l; tete beche pairs of 5 l & 10 l, 10 l & 25 l and 10 l & 10 l.

Also issued imperf., value $175 unused, $125 canceled.

The 5 l reads "PENTE LEPTA" in Greek letters; the 10 l is illustrated; the 25 l carries the numeral "25."

Bulgaria Nos. 89-90, 92-93, 95 Surcharged

Red Surcharge

1913 *Perf. 12*

N182	A20	5 l on 1s myr grn	60.00	42.50
N183	A26	1d on 25s ultra & blk	60.00	42.50

Blue Surcharge

N184	A24	10 l on 10s red & blk	30.00	25.00
N185	A23	25 l on 5s grn & blk	32.50	25.00
N187	A21	50 l on 2s car & blk	60.00	42.50
		Nos. N182-N185,N187 (5)	242.50	177.50

The surcharges on Nos. N182 to N187 are printed from a setting of eight, which was used for all, with the necessary changes of value. No. 6 in the setting has a Greek "L" instead of "D" for the third letter of the third word of the surcharge.

The 25 l surcharge also exists on 8 copies of the 25s, Bulgaria No. 95.

D2

D3

1913, Sept. 15 Typeset *Perf. 11½*

Control Mark in Blue

N188	D2	1 l blue	65.00
N189	D2	2 l blue	65.00
N190	D2	3 l blue	65.00
N191	D2	5 l blue	65.00
N192	D2	10 l blue	65.00
N193	D2	25 l blue	65.00
N194	D2	40 l blue	65.00
N195	D2	50 l blue	65.00
		Nos. N188-N195 (8)	520.00

Issued without gum in sheets of 8 containing all values.

1913, Sept. 25 Typeset

Control Mark in Blue

N196	D3	1 l blue, *gray blue*	65.00
N197	D3	5 l blue, *gray blue*	65.00
N198	D3	10 l blue, *gray blue*	65.00
N199	D3	25 l blue, *gray blue*	65.00
N200	D3	30 l blue, *gray blue*	65.00
N201	D3	50 l blue, *gray blue*	65.00
		Nos. N196-N201 (6)	390.00

Nos. N196 to N201 were issued without gum in sheets of six containing all values.

Counterfeits of Nos. N182-N201 are plentiful.

FOR USE IN NORTH EPIRUS (ALBANIA)

Greek Stamps of 1937-38 Overprinted in Black

Perf. 13½x12, 12x13½

1940 Litho. Wmk. 252

N202	A69	5 l brn red & bl	.20	.20
a.		Inverted overprint	50.00	
N203	A70	10 l bl & brn red (No. 413)	.20	.20
a.		Double impression of frame	10.00	
N204	A71	20 l blk & grn	.20	.20
a.		Inverted overprint	50.00	
N205	A72	40 l grn & blk	.20	.20
a.		Inverted overprint	50.00	
N206	A73	50 l brn & blk	.20	.20
N207	A74	80 l ind & yel brn	.20	.20
N208	A67	1d green	.20	.20
a.		Inverted overprint	35.00	
N209	A75	2d ultra	.20	.20
N210	A67	3d red brn	.20	.20
N211	A76	5d red	.20	.20
N212	A77	6d ol brn	.20	.20
N213	A78	7d dk brn	.40	.40
N214	A67	8d deep blue	.55	.55
N215	A79	10d red brn	.55	.55
N216	A80	15d green	.95	.95
N217	A81	25d dark blue	1.10	1.10
a.		Inverted overprint	*90.00*	

Engr.

Unwmk.

N218	A84	30d org brn	2.75	2.75
		Nos. N202-N218 (17)	8.50	8.50

Same Overprinted in Carmine on National Youth Issue

1941 Litho. *Perf. 12½, 13½x12½*

N219	A93	3d sil, dp ultra & red	1.00	1.00
N220	A94	5d dk bl & blk	1.60	1.60
N221	A94	10d red org & blk	2.00	2.00
N222	A94	15d dk grn & blk	26.00	26.00
N223	A94	20d lake & blk	3.25	3.25
N224	A94	25d dk bl & blk	6.50	6.50
N225	A94	30d rose vio & blk	6.50	6.50
N226	A94	50d lake & blk	6.50	6.50
N227	A94	75d dk bl, brn & gold	6.50	6.50
N228	A93	100d sil, dp ultra & red	6.50	6.50
a.		Inverted overprint	*175.00*	
		Nos. N219-N228 (10)	66.35	66.35

Same Overprint in Carmine on National Youth Air Post Stamps

N229	AP25	2d red org & blk	.65	.65
a.		Inverted overprint	75.00	
N230	AP25	4d dk grn & blk	3.25	3.25
a.		Inverted overprint	*150.00*	
N231	AP25	6d lake & blk	3.25	3.25
a.		Inverted overprint	*150.00*	
N232	AP25	8d dk bl & blk	3.25	3.25
N233	AP25	16d rose vio & blk	5.00	5.00
N234	AP25	32d red org & blk	5.00	5.00
N235	AP25	45d dk grn & blk	6.50	6.50
N236	AP25	55d lake & blk	6.50	6.50
N237	AP25	65d dk bl & blk	6.50	6.50
N238	AP25	100d rose vio & blk	6.50	6.50
		Nos. N229-N238 (10)	46.40	46.40

Some specialists have questioned the status of Nos. N230a and N231a.

For other stamps issued by Greece for use in occupied parts of Epirus and Thrace, see the catalogue listings of those countries.

POSTAGE DUE STAMPS

FOR USE IN PARTS OF TURKEY OCCUPIED BY GREECE (NEW GREECE)

Postage Due Stamps of Greece, 1902, Overprinted

1912 Wmk. 129 Engr. *Perf. 13½*

Black Overprint

NJ1	D3	1 l chocolate	.40	.40
NJ2	D3	2 l gray	.40	.40
NJ3	D3	3 l orange	.40	.40
NJ4	D3	5 l yel grn	.40	.40
NJ5	D3	10 l scarlet	1.00	1.00
NJ6	D3	20 l lilac	1.00	1.00
NJ7	D3	30 l dp vio	2.00	2.00
NJ8	D3	40 l dk brn	3.50	3.50
NJ9	D3	50 l red brn	5.00	5.00
NJ10	D3	1d black	20.00	20.00
NJ11	D3	2d bronze	15.00	8.00
NJ12	D3	3d silver	42.50	42.50
NJ13	D3	5d gold	85.00	85.00
		Nos. NJ1-NJ13 (13)	176.60	169.60

Red Overprint

NJ14	D3	1 l chocolate	.60	.60
NJ15	D3	2 l gray	.60	.60
NJ16	D3	3 l orange	.40	.40
NJ17	D3	5 l yel grn	.60	.50
NJ18	D3	10 l scar, down	4.00	4.00
NJ19	D3	20 l lilac	.60	.60
NJ20	D3	30 l dp vio	3.50	2.25
NJ21	D3	40 l dk brn	.60	.50
NJ22	D3	50 l red brn	.60	.50
NJ23	D3	1d black	6.00	4.00
NJ24	D3	2d bronze	6.00	6.00
NJ25	D3	3d silver	12.50	12.50
NJ26	D3	5d gold	25.00	25.00
		Nos. NJ14-NJ26 (13)	61.00	57.45

The normal position of the overprint is reading upward but it is often reversed. Some of the varieties of lettering which occur on the postage stamps are also found on the postage due stamps. Double overprints exist on some denominations.

FOR USE IN NORTH EPIRUS (ALBANIA)

Postage Due Stamps of Greece, 1930, Surcharged or Overprinted in Black:

a

b

Perf. 13, 13x12½

1940 Litho. Unwmk.

NJ27	D3(a)	50 l on 25d lt red	.80	.80
NJ28	D3(b)	2d light red	.80	.80
a.		Inverted overprint	40.00	
NJ29	D3(b)	5d blue gray	.80	.80
NJ30	D3(b)	10d green	1.00	1.00
NJ31	D3(b)	15d red brown	.80	.80
		Nos. NJ27-NJ31 (5)	4.20	4.20

POSTAL TAX STAMPS

FOR USE IN NORTH EPIRUS (ALBANIA)

Postal Tax Stamps of Greece, Nos. RA61-RA63, Overprinted Type "b" in Black

1940 Unwmk. Litho. *Perf. 13½x12*

NRA1	PT7	10 l	.20	.20
NRA2	PT7	50 l	.20	.20
a.		Inverted overprint	50.00	
NRA3	PT7	1d	.40	.40
		Nos. NRA1-NRA3 (3)	.80	.80

GREENLAND

ˈgrēn-lənd

LOCATION — North Atlantic Ocean
GOVT. — Danish
AREA — 840,000 sq. mi.
POP. — 52,347 (1984)
CAPITAL — Nuuk (Godthaab)

100 Ore = 1 Krone

Christian X — A1

Polar Bear — A2

Perf. 13x12½

1938-46 Unwmk. Engr.

1	A1	1o olive black	.30	*.30*
2	A1	5o rose lake	1.75	1.40
3	A1	7o yellow green	2.75	*3.25*
4	A1	10o purple	.85	.65
5	A1	15o red	.85	.65
6	A1	20o red ('46)	1.25	1.40
7	A2	30o blue	5.00	*7.00*
8	A2	40o blue ('46)	17.50	7.50
9	A2	1k light brown	5.75	*10.00*
		Nos. 1-9 (9)	36.00	*32.15*
		Set, never hinged	80.00	

Issued: Nov. 1, 1938; Aug. 1, 1946.

For surcharges see Nos. 39-40.

PARCEL POST STAMPS

Arms of Greenland PP1

1905-10 Unwmk. Typo. *Perf. 12¼*

Q1a	PP1	1o ol grn ('05)	775.00	775.00
Q3a	PP1	5o brown ('05-'10)	750.00	*775.00*
Q4a	PP1	10o blue ('05-'10)	950.00	625.00
		Set of 3	1,750.	1,625.

1916-28 *Perf. 11½*

Q1	PP1	1o ol grn ('16-'26)	57.50	*60.00*
Q2	PP1	2o yellow ('16-'24)	325.00	*125.00*
Q3	PP1	5o brown ('18-'28)	125.00	*125.00*
Q4b	PP1	10o blue ('16)	55.00	*65.00*
Q5	PP1	15o violet ('15-'28)	200.00	200.00
Q6	PP1	20o red ('15-'33)	17.00	13.00
		Nos. Q1-Q6 (6)	779.50	*588.00*

1930

Q7a	PP1	70o violet	250.00	225.00
Q8a	PP1	1k yellow	52.50	*65.00*
Q9	PP1	3k brown ('30)	140.00	*175.00*
		Nos. Q7a-Q9 (3)	442.50	*465.00*

1937 Litho. *Perf. 10¾*

Q10	PP1	70o pale violet	42.50	*150.00*
Q11	PP1	1k yellow	40.00	*77.50*
		Nos. Q10-Q11, never hinged	125.00	

1937 Typo.

Q4	PP1	10o blue ('37)	40.00	*72.50*
Q6a	PP1	20o red	40.00	*60.00*
Q7	PP1	70o violet ('37)	40.00	*125.00*
Q8	PP1	1k yellow ('37)	40.00	*140.00*
		Nos. Q4-Q8 (4)	160.00	*397.50*

On lithographed stamps, PAKKE-PORTO is slightly larger, hyphen has rounded ends and lines in shield are fine, straight and evenly spaced.

On typographed stamps, hyphen has squared ends and shield lines are coarse, uneven and inclined to be slightly wavy.

Used values are for stamps postally used from Denmark. Numeral cancels indicate use as postal savings stamps and are worth less. Greenland village cancels are worth more.

Sheets of 25. Certain printings of Nos. Q1-Q2, Q3a, Q4a and Q5-Q6 were issued without sheet margins. Stamps from the outer rows are straight edged. Some of these sheets were reperfed later.

GRENADA

grə-ˈnā-də

LOCATION — Windward Islands, West Indies
GOVT. — Independent nation in the British Commonwealth
AREA — 133 sq. mi.
POP. — 115,000 (est. 1981)
CAPITAL — St. George's

Grenada consists of Grenada Island and the southern Grenadines, including Carriacou. This colony was granted associated statehood with Great Britain in 1967 and became an independent state Feb. 7, 1974.

12 Pence = 1 Shilling
100 Cents = 1 Dollar (1949)

Catalogue values for unused stamps in this country are for Never Hinged items, beginning with Scott 143 in the regular postage section, Scott J15 in the postage due section.

Watermarks

Wmk. 5 — Small Star

Wmk. 6 — Large Star

Wmk. 7 — Large Star with Broad Points

PRE-STAMP POSTAL MARKINGS

Crowned Circle handstamp type I is pictured in the Crowned Circle Handstamps and Great Britain Used Abroad section.

St. George's

1850-58
A2 I "Grenada" crowned circle handstamp in red, on cover 2,250.

In 1846 a Crowned Circle handstamp was issued inscribed "Carriacou." No examples are known.

STAMPS OF GREAT BRITAIN USED IN GRENADA

Numeral cancellation type A is pictured in the Crowned Circle Handstamps and Great Britain Used Abroad section.

1858-60

A15 (St. George's)

A3	A	1p rose red (#20)	500.00
A4	A	2p blue (#29, P7)	1,200.
A5	A	4p rose (#26)	325.00
A6	A	6p lilac (#27)	150.00
A7	A	1sh green (#28)	1,350.

Values for unused stamps are for examples with original gum as defined in the catalogue introduction. Very fine examples of Nos. 1-19, 27-29, and 31-38 will have perforations touching the design on at least one side due to the narrow spacing of the stamps on the plates. Stamps with perfs clear of the design on all four sides are scarce and will command higher prices.

Queen Victoria — A1

Rough Perf. 14 to 16

1861 Engr. Unwmk.

1 A1 1p green 57.50 50.00
 a. 1p blue green 5,250. 350.00
 b. As No. 1, horiz. pair, imperf. btwn.
2 A1 6p rose 1,050. 110.00
 b. 6p lake red, perf. 11-12½ 1,000.

No. 2b was not issued. No. 2 imperf is a proof.

An example the six pence rose (#2), with the barred oval "CANCELLED" handstamp realized $10,450 in a New York auction in 2003.

1863-71 Wmk. 5

3 A1 1p green ('64) 87.50 15.00
 a. 1p yellow green 120.00 30.00
4 A1 6p rose 700.00 20.00
5 A1 6p vermilion ('71) 875.00 20.00
 a. 6p dull red 4,000. 275.00
 g. Double impression 2,350.
 i. 6p orange red ('66) 750.00 14.00

No. 5a always has sideways watermark. Other colors sometimes have sideways watermark.

1873-78 *Clean-Cut Perf. about 15*

5B A1 1p deep green 100.00 45.00
 j. Pair, imperf between 7,000.
 c. 1p blue green ('78) 275.00 45.00
 h. Half used as ½p on cover 11,000.
5D A1 6p vermilion ('75) 925.00 40.00
 e. 6p dull red 950.00 40.00
 f. Double impression 2,350.

1873 Wmk. 6

6 A1 1p blue green 87.50 22.50
 a. Diagonal half used as ½p on cover 11,000.
7 A1 6p vermilion 700.00 35.00

1875 *Perf. 14*

7A A1 1p yellow green 87.50 9.00
 b. Half used as ½p on cover 16,000.
 c. Perf. 15 9,500. 2,600.

A cover bearing one example of the bisected 1p stamp (#7Ab), together with two singles and a 6p stamp, addressed to France, realized $15,400 in a New York auction in 2003.

A2

A2a

Revenue Stamps Surcharged in Black

1875-81 *Perf. 14, 14½*

8 A2 ½p purple ('81) 13.00 7.50
 a. "OSTAGE" 225.00 150.00
 b. Imperf., pair 350.00
 c. "ALF" 4,000.
 d. "PEN"
 e. No hyphen between "HALF" and "PENNY" 225.00 150.00
 f. Double surcharge 350.00 350.00
9 A2a 2½p lake ('81) 70.00 10.00
 a. Imperf., pair 575.00
 b. Imperf. vertically, pair 4,500.
 c. "PENCF" 525.00 225.00
 d. No period after "PENNY" 290.00 90.00
 e. "PENOE" 175.00
10 A2 4p blue ('81) 120.00 10.00

Revenue Stamps Surcharged in Dark Blue

11 A2 1sh purple 750.00 20.00
 a. "SHLLIING" 4,000. 800.00
 b. "NE SHILLING" 3,000.
 c. "OSTAGE" 5,750. 2,300.
 d. Invtd. "S" in "POSTAGE" 4,000. 750.00

See Nos. 27-35.

1881 Wmk. 7

12 A2 2½p lake 200.00 57.50
 a. 2½p claret 500.00 140.00
 b. As No. 12, "PENCF" 875.00 325.00
 c. As No. 12, No period after "PENNY" 650.00 230.00
 d. As "a," "PENCF" 1,850. 825.00
 e. As "a," no period after "PENNY" 1,275. 575.00
13 A2 4p blue 300.00 210.00

A3

A4

A5

A6

Revenue Stamp Overprinted "POSTAGE" in Black

1883 Wmk. 5

Denomination & Crown in 2nd Color

14 A3 ½p orange & grn 900.00 275.00
 a. Unsevered pair 5,000. 1,500.
 b. "POSTAGE" omitted 1,500.
15 A4 ½p orange & grn 325.00 150.00
 a. Unsevered pair 1,7500. 525.00
16 A5 1p orange & grn 375.00 65.00
 a. Inverted overprint 3,250. 2,600.
 b. Double overprint 1,625. 1,275.
 c. Inverted "S" in "Postage" 1,150. 700.00
 d. Diagonal half used as ½p on cover 3,500.

"Postage" in Manuscript, Red or Black

18 A6 1p orange & grn (R) 11,000.
19 A6 1p orange & green — 5,500.

On Nos. 14-19 the words "ONE PENNY" measure from 10-11¼mm in length.

On No. 15, the lower "POSTAGE" is always inverted.

It has been claimed that although Nos. 18 and 19 were used, they were not officially authorized by Grenada's postmaster.

A8

A10

1883 Wmk. 2 *Perf. 14*

20 A8 ½p green 1.50 1.25
 a. Tete beche pair 5.00 17.50
21 A8 1p rose 80.00 4.00
 a. Tete beche pair 260.00 290.00
22 A8 2½p ultra 8.00 1.25
 a. Tete beche pair 30.00 57.50
23 A8 4p slate 5.75 2.25
 a. Tete beche pair 21.00 65.00
24 A8 6p red lilac 5.00 6.50
 a. Tete beche pair 21.00 65.00
25 A8 8p bister 10.50 14.00
 a. Tete beche pair 37.50 87.50
26 A8 1sh violet 140.00 65.00
 a. Tete beche pair 1,650. 1,850.
 Nos. 20-26 (7) 250.75 94.25

Stamps of types A8, A10 and D2 were printed with alternate horizontal rows inverted.

For surcharges see Nos. 36-38, J4-J7.

Revenue Stamps Surcharged

1886 Wmk. 6

27 A2 1p on 1½ org 50.00 35.00
 a. Inverted surcharge 350.00 350.00
 b. Diagonal half used as ½ on cover 2,250.
 c. Double surcharge 575.00 350.00
 d. "HALH" instead of "HALF" 300.00 275.00
28 A2 1p on 1sh org 45.00 35.00
 a. "SHILLNG" instead of "SHILLING" 525.00 450.00
 b. No period after "POSTAGE" 475.00
 c. Half used as ½p on cover 2,350.

Wmk. 5

29 A2 1p on 4p org 190.00 110.00

1887 Wmk. 2

30 A10 1p rose 1.75 1.50
 a. Tete beche pair 3.50 22.50

Revenue Stamps Surcharged:

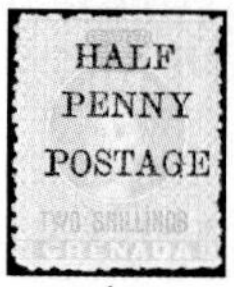

h

i

j

k

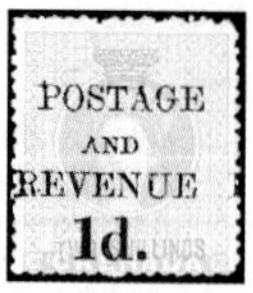

l

1888-91 Wmk. 5 *Perf. 14½*

31 A2 (h) ½p on 2sh org ('89) 14.00 24.00
 a. Double surcharge 350.00 375.00
 b. First "S" in "SHILLINGS" inverted 325.00 350.00
32 A2 (i) 4p on 2sh org 45.00 22.50
 a. "4d" and "POSTAGE" 5mm apart 80.00 35.00
 b. "S" inverted, as in #31b 550.00 400.00
 c. As "a," inverted "S," as in #31b 750.00 650.00

"d" Vertical instead of Slanting

33 A2 (j) 4p on 2sh org 875.00 475.00
34 A2 (k) 1p on 2sh org ('90) 92.50 87.50
 a. Inverted surcharge 875.00 —
 b. "S" inverted 825.00 750.00
35 A2 (l) 1p on 2sh org ('91) 70.00 65.00
 a. Inverted surcharge 450.00 —
 b. No period after "d" 575.00 575.00
 c. "S" inverted

No. 25 Surcharged in Black:

Wmk. 2

36 A8 1p on 8p bister 12.00 15.00
 a. Tete beche pair 50.00 70.00
 b. Inverted surcharge 375.00 325.00
 c. No period after "d" 300.00 300.00

"2" of "½" Upright

37 A8 2½p on 8p bister 10.00 13.00
 a. Tete beche pair 50.00 70.00
 b. Inverted surcharge
 c. Double surcharge 1,000. 925.00
 d. Triple surcharge 1,100.
 e. Double surcharge, one inverted 650.00 575.00

"2" of "½" Italic

38 A8 2½p on 8p bister 10.00 13.00
 Ovptd. "SPECIMEN" 75.00
 a. Tete beche pair 50.00 70.00
 b. Tete beche pair, #37, 38 125.00
 c. Inverted surcharge
 d. Double surcharge 875.00 925.00
 e. Triple surcharge 1,050.
 f. Triple surch., two inverted 1,000.
 g. Double surcharge, one inverted 625.00 575.00

Queen Victoria — A17

1895-99 Wmk. 2 Typo. *Perf. 14*

39 A17 ½p lilac & green 3.00 2.00
40 A17 1p lilac & car rose 5.25 .90
41 A17 2p lilac & brown 47.50 37.50
42 A17 2½p lilac & ultra 7.50 1.75
43 A17 3p lilac & orange 8.00 *18.00*
44 A17 6p lilac & green 14.00 *35.00*
45 A17 8p lilac & black 15.00 *52.50*
46 A17 1sh green & org 22.50 *47.50*
Nos. 39-46 (8) 122.75 *195.15*
Set, ovptd. "SPECIMEN" 175.00

Numerals of ½p, 3p, 8p and 1sh of type A17 are in color on colorless tablet.

Issue dates: 1p, May, 1896; ½p, 2p, Sept. 1899; others, Sept. 5, 1895.

Columbus' Flagship, La Concepcion A18

King Edward VII A19

1898, Aug. 15 Engr. Wmk. 1

47 A18 2½p ultra 16.00 8.00
Ovptd. "SPECIMEN" 100.00
a. Bluish paper 37.50 *47.50*

Discovery of the island by Columbus, Aug. 15th, 1498.

1902 Wmk. 2 Typo.

48 A19 ½p violet & grn 3.75 1.50
49 A19 1p vio & car rose 5.25 .35
50 A19 2p vio & brown 3.50 *11.50*
51 A19 2½p vio & ultra 4.00 3.25
52 A19 3p vio & org 4.50 *10.50*
53 A19 6p vio & green 3.00 *20.00*
54 A19 1sh green & org 5.50 *32.50*
55 A19 2sh grn & ultra 24.00 *65.00*
56 A19 5sh grn & car rose 47.50 *70.00*
57 A19 10sh green & vio 140.00 *300.00*
Nos. 48-57 (10) 241.00 *514.60*
Set, ovptd. "SPECIMEN" 225.00

Numerals of ½p, 3p, 1sh, 2sh and 10sh of type A19 are in color on colorless tablet.

1904-06 Wmk. 3 *Perf. 14*

58 A19 ½p vio & green 20.00 *30.00*
59 A19 1p vio & car rose 11.00 3.00
60 A19 2p vio & brown 65.00 *125.00*
61 A19 2½p vio & ultra 65.00 *75.00*
62 A19 3p vio & org 3.25 *8.00*
63 A19 6p vio & green 6.50 *17.50*
64 A19 1sh green & org 7.00 *30.00*
65 A19 2sh grn & ultra 57.50 *80.00*
66 A19 5sh grn & car rose 75.00 *110.00*
67 A19 10sh green & vio 175.00 *300.00*
Nos. 58-67 (10) 485.25 *778.50*

Nos. 62, 63 and 65 are on both ordinary and chalky paper.

Issued: #58, 60-62, 64, 1905; #63, 65-67, 1906.

Seal of Colony A20

King George V A21

1906-11 Engr.

68 A20 ½p green 5.25 .35
69 A20 1p carmine 7.50 .20
70 A20 2p yellow 3.50 3.50
71 A20 2½p blue 7.00 2.00
a. 2½p ultramarine 9.50 3.75

Typo.

Chalky Paper

Numerals white on dark ground

72 A20 3p vio, *yel* ('08) 5.50 1.90
73 A20 6p violet ('08) 22.50 25.00
74 A20 1sh blk, *grn* ('11) 8.00 5.00
75 A20 2sh vio & blue, *blue* ('08) 22.50 14.00
76 A20 5sh red & green, *yel* ('08) 67.50 *80.00*
Nos. 68-76 (9) 149.25 *131.95*

1908 Wmk. 2

77 A20 1sh black, *green* 32.50 *67.50*
78 A20 10sh red & grn, *grn* 100.00 *210.00*

1913 Ordinary Paper Wmk. 3

79 A21 ½p green 1.10 1.25
80 A21 1p carmine 2.50 .35
a. 1p scarlet ('16) 5.00 1.10
81 A21 2p orange 1.90 .35
82 A21 2½p ultra 2.00 *4.00*

Chalky Paper

83 A21 3p violet, *yel* .75 *1.00*
84 A21 6p dull vio & red vio 1.75 *10.00*
85 A21 1sh black, *green* 1.10 *11.50*
a. 1sh black, *emerald* 1.75 *16.00*
b. 1sh blk, *bl grn,* olive back 52.50 *90.00*
c. As "a," olive back 1.75 *15.00*
86 A21 2sh vio & ultra, *bl* 7.25 *14.00*
87 A21 5sh grn & red, *yel* 20.00 *67.50*
88 A21 10sh grn & red, *grn* 62.50 *100.00*
a. 10sh grn & red, *emer* 60.00 *175.00*
Nos. 79-88 (10) 100.85 *209.95*

1914 Surface-colored Paper

89 A21 3p violet, *yel* .70 *1.60*
90 A21 1sh black, *green* 1.40 *8.50*

1921-29 Ordinary Paper Wmk. 4

91 A21 ½p green 1.40 .35
92 A21 1p rose red .90 .85
93 A21 1p brown ('23) 1.75 .35
94 A21 1½p rose red ('22) 1.75 1.75
95 A21 2p orange 1.40 .35
96 A21 2p gray ('26) 2.75 *3.00*
97 A21 2½p ultramarine 5.25 *10.00*
98 A21 2½p gray ('22) 1.10 *10.00*
99 A21 3p ultra ('22) 1.75 *12.50*

Chalky Paper

100 A21 3p vio, *yel* ('26) 3.50 *5.75*
101 A21 4p blk & red, *yel* ('26) 1.10 *4.25*
102 A21 5p gray vio & ol grn ('22) 1.75 *4.75*
103 A21 6p dl vio & red vio 1.50 *22.50*
104 A21 6p blk & red ('26) 2.50 *2.75*
105 A21 9p gray vio & blk ('22) 2.50 *11.00*
106 A21 1sh blk, *emer* ('23) 3.00 *50.00*
107 A21 1sh org brn ('26) 4.50 *11.00*
108 A21 2sh vio & ultra, *bl* ('22) 7.00 *19.00*
109 A21 2sh6p blk & red, *bl* ('29) 8.00 *22.50*
110 A21 3sh grn & vio ('22) 6.75 *30.00*
111 A21 5sh green & red, *yel* ('23) 14.00 *40.00*
112 A21 10sh green & red, *emer* ('23) 57.50 *150.00*
Nos. 91-112 (22) 131.65 *412.65*

Grand Anse Beach — A22

Seal of the Colony — A23

View of Grand Etang — A24

View of St. George's — A25

1934, Oct. 23 Engr. *Perf. 12½*

114 A22 ½p green .20 *1.25*
a. Perf. 12½x13 ('36) 5.00 *50.00*

Perf. 13½x12½

115 A23 1p blk brn & blk .65 .35
a. Perf 12½ 1.10 3.50

Perf. 12½x13½

116 A24 1½p car & black .90 .45
a. Perf 12½ ('36) 5.25 3.75

Perf. 12½

117 A23 2p org & black 1.10 .80
118 A25 2½p deep blue .55 .55
119 A23 3p ol grn & blk 1.10 *3.25*
120 A23 6p claret & blk 2.250 2.00
121 A23 1sh brown & blk 2.25 *4.50*
122 A23 2sh6p ultra & blk 9.00 *30.00*
123 A23 5sh vio & black 40.00 *55.00*
Nos. 114-123 (10) 60.25 *98.15*
Set, never hinged 125.00

Common Design Types pictured following the introduction.

Silver Jubilee Issue

Common Design Type

1935, May 6 *Perf. 11x12*

124 CD301 ½p green & blk .80 *1.25*
125 CD301 1p black & ultra .80 *1.90*
126 CD301 1½p car & blue .80 *1.90*
127 CD301 1sh brn vio & ind 7.25 *19.00*
Nos. 124-127 (4) 9.65 *24.05*
Set, never hinged 20.00

Coronation Issue

Common Design Type

1937, May 12 Wmk. 4 *Perf. 11x11½*

128 CD302 1p dark purple .25 .25
129 CD302 1½p dark carmine .25 .20
130 CD302 2½p deep ultra .50 .35
Nos. 128-130 (3) 1.00 .80
Set, never hinged 1.60

George VI — A26

Seal of the Colony — A28

Grand Anse Beach — A27

View of Grand Etang — A29

View of St. George's — A30

Seal of the Colony — A31

1937, July 12 Photo. *Perf. 14½x14*

131 A26 ¼p chestnut .50 *.75*

1938, Mar. 16 Engr. *Perf. 12½*

132 A27 ½p green .80 *1.40*
133 A28 1p blk brn & blk .55 .55
134 A29 1½p scarlet & blk .25 *.95*
135 A28 2p orange & blk .20 *.55*
136 A30 2½p ultramarine .20 *.35*
137 A28 3p olive grn & blk .20 *2.10*
138 A28 6p red vio & blk 1.25 .45
139 A28 1sh org brn & blk 2.50 .45
140 A28 2sh ultra & black 10.00 2.00
141 A28 5sh purple & blk 2.25 *2.75*

Perf. 14

142 A31 10sh rose car & gray blue 20.00 13.00
a. 10sh deep car & gray blue, perf. 12 ('43) 300.00 *1,400.*
b. Perf. 12x13 42.50 12.00
Nos. 131-142 (12) 38.70 25.30
Set, never hinged 62.50

1938-42 *Perf. 12½x13½, 13½x12½*

132a A27 ½p 3.00 .90
133a A28 1p .30 .20
134a A29 1½p car & blk 1.25 .40
135a A28 2p 1.40 .75
136a A30 2½p *3,000.* *240.00*
137a A28 3p 2.50 *1.00*
138a A28 6p ('42) 1.25 .35
139a A28 1sh ('42) 2.00 1.50
140a A28 2sh ('41) 12.50 2.00
141a A28 5sh ('47) 1.60 *4.50*

Catalogue values for unused stamps in this section, from this point to the end of the section, are for Never Hinged items.

Peace Issue

Common Design Type

1946, Sept. 25 *Perf. 13½x14*

143 CD303 1½p carmine .20 .20
144 CD303 3½p deep blue .20 .20

Silver Wedding Issue

Common Design Types

1948, Oct. 27 Photo. *Perf. 14x14½*

145	CD304	1½p scarlet	.20	.20

Engr.; Name Typo.

Perf. 11½x11

146	CD305	10sh gray green	14.50	20.00

UPU Issue

Common Design Types

Engr.; Name Typo. on 6c, 12c

Perf. 13½, 11x11½

1949, Oct. 10 Wmk. 4

147	CD306	5c ultra	.25	.25
148	CD307	6c deep olive	1.40	*1.75*
149	CD308	12c red lilac	.30	*.50*
150	CD309	24c red brown	.25	*.55*
		Nos. 147-150 (4)	2.20	3.05

A32

A33

A34

1951, Jan. 8 Engr. *Perf. 11½*

Center in Black

151	A32	½c chestnut	.20	*1.50*
152	A32	1c blue green	.20	*.60*
153	A32	2c dark brown	.20	.20
154	A32	3c carmine	.25	.20
155	A32	4c deep orange	.40	.25
156	A32	5c purple	.50	.30
157	A32	6c olive	.50	.65
158	A32	7c blue	2.00	.30
159	A32	12c red violet	2.25	.75

Perf. 11½x12½

160	A33	25c dark brown	2.50	1.00
161	A33	50c ultra	5.75	.60
162	A33	$1.50 orange	8.25	8.00

Perf. 11½x13

Center in Gray Blue

163	A34	$2.50 deep carmine	7.00	6.50
		Nos. 151-163 (13)	30.00	20.85

See #180-183, 202. For overprints see #166-169.

University Issue

Common Design Types

1951, Feb. 16 *Perf. 14x14½*

164	CD310	3c dp car & gray blk	.55	*1.00*
165	CD311	6c olive & black	.65	.60

Nos. 154-156 and 159 Overprinted in Black or Carmine

1951, Sept. 21 *Perf. 11½*

166	A32	3c carmine & black	.25	*.40*
167	A32	4c dp orange & black	.25	*.40*
168	A32	5c purple & black (C)	.25	*.60*
169	A32	12c red violet & black	.25	*.80*
		Nos. 166-169 (4)	1.00	*2.20*

Adoption of a new constitution for the Windward Islands.

POSTAGE DUE STAMPS

D1

D2

1892 Typo. Wmk. 2 *Perf. 14*

J1	D1	1p black	30.00	2.75
J2	D1	2p black	190.00	3.25
J3	D1	3p black	190.00	4.00
		Nos. J1-J3 (3)	410.00	10.00

Black Surcharge

J4	D2	1p on 6p red lilac	92.50	2.25
a.		Tete beche pair	1,400.	*1,800.*
b.		Double surcharge		190.00
c.		Same as "b," tete beche pair		
J5	D2	1p on 8p bister	875.00	6.00
a.		Tete beche pair	*4,000.*	*1,600.*
J6	D2	2p on 6p red lilac	190.00	4.50
a.		Tete beche pair	*2,000.*	1,275.
J7	D2	2p on 8p bister	3,200.	12.00
a.		Tete beche pair	*7,500.*	3,500.
		Nos. J4-J7 (4)	4,357.	24.75

Nos. J4-J7 were printed with alternate horizontal rows inverted.

1906-11 Wmk. 3

J8	D1	1p black ('11)	3.75	*5.00*
J9	D1	2p black	12.50	3.75
J10	D1	3p black	15.00	6.50
		Nos. J8-J10 (3)	31.25	15.25

D3

1921-22 Wmk. 4

J11	D3	1p black	1.40	*1.40*
J12	D3	1½p black	10.00	*20.00*
J13	D3	2p black	3.00	*4.50*
J14	D3	3p black	3.00	*4.75*
		Nos. J11-J14 (4)	17.40	*30.65*

Issued: 1½p, Dec. 15, 1922, others, Dec. 1921.

Catalogue values for unused stamps in this section, from this point to the end of the section, are for Never Hinged items.

1952, Mar. 1

J15	D3	2c black	.50	*9.00*
a.		Wmk. 4a (error)	25.00	
J16	D3	4c black	.50	*9.00*
a.		Wmk. 4a (error)	25.00	
J17	D3	6c black	.65	*13.00*
a.		Wmk. 4a (error)	42.50	
J18	D3	8c black	.60	*11.00*
a.		Wmk. 4a (error)	50.00	
		Nos. J15-J18 (4)	2.25	*42.00*

WAR TAX STAMPS

Nos. 80a, 80 Overprinted

1916 Wmk. 3 *Perf. 14*

MR1	A21	1p carmine	2.50	2.00
a.		1p scarlet	3.00	3.00
b.		Double overprint	325.00	
c.		Inverted overprint	325.00	

No. 80 Overprinted

MR2	A21	1p scarlet	.30	.20

GRIQUALAND WEST

'gri-kwə-,land 'west

LOCATION — In South Africa west of the Orange Free State and north of the Orange River

GOVT. — Former British Crown Colony

AREA — 15,197 sq. mi.

POP. — 83,375 (1891)

CAPITAL — Kimberley

Originally a territorial division of the Cape of Good Hope Colony, Griqualand West was declared a British Crown Colony in 1873 and together with Griqualand East was annexed to the Cape Colony in 1880.

12 Pence = 1 Shilling

Beware of forgeries.

Stamps of Cape of Good Hope 1864-65 (Type I, 4p, 6p, 1sh) and 1871-76 (Type II, ½p, 1p, 4p, 5sh) Surcharged or Overprinted

Type I — With frame line around stamp.
Type II — Without frame line.

"Hope" — A1

Manuscript Surcharge in Dark Red

1874 Wmk. 1 *Perf. 14*

1	A1	1p on 4p blue (type I)	1,350.	*2,250.*

Overprinted

1877 Black Overprint

2	1p rose	575.00	95.00
a.	Double overprint		*2,250.*

Red Overprint

3	4p blue (type II)	450.00	85.00

Overprinted

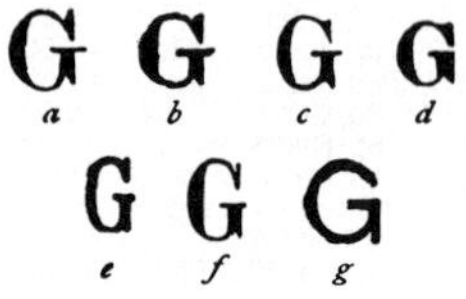

In Black on the One Penny, in Red on the Other Values

4	(a)	½p gray black	21.00	25.00
5	(a)	1p rose	22.50	16.50
6	(a)	4p blue (type I)	210.00	35.00
7	(a)	4p blue (type II)	160.00	22.50
8	(a)	6p dull violet	125.00	25.00
9	(a)	1sh green	150.00	22.50
a.		Inverted overprint		475.00
10	(a)	5sh orange	575.00	27.50
11	(b)	½p gray black	30.00	35.00
12	(b)	1p rose	30.00	22.50
13	(b)	4p blue (type I)	425.00	50.00
14	(b)	4p blue (type II)	275.00	30.00
15	(b)	6p dull violet	200.00	35.00
16	(b)	1sh green	250.00	27.50
17	(b)	5sh orange	800.00	35.00
18	(c)	½p gray black	50.00	*60.00*
19	(c)	1p rose	52.50	35.00
20	(c)	4p blue (type I)	*625.00*	100.00
21	(c)	4p blue (type II)	*475.00*	70.00
22	(c)	6p dull violet	*300.00*	75.00
23	(c)	1sh green	*400.00*	50.00
24	(c)	5sh orange	*1,000.*	55.00
25	(d)	½p gray black	27.50	*32.50*
26	(d)	1p rose	27.50	22.50
27	(d)	4p blue (type I)	425.00	50.00
28	(d)	4p blue (type II)	275.00	32.50
29	(d)	6p dull violet	190.00	35.00
30	(d)	1sh green	250.00	27.50
31	(d)	5sh orange	775.00	32.50
32	(e)	½p gray black	50.00	*62.50*
33	(e)	1p rose	55.00	37.50
34	(e)	4p blue (type I)	600.00	105.00
35	(e)	4p blue (type II)	425.00	67.50
36	(e)	6p dull violet	275.00	72.50
37	(e)	1sh green	375.00	52.50
a.		Inverted overprint		800.00
38	(e)	5sh orange	950.00	57.50
39	(f)	½p gray black	55.00	*72.50*
40	(f)	1p rose	62.50	45.00
41	(f)	4p blue (type I)	725.00	125.00
42	(f)	4p blue (type II)	525.00	85.00
43	(f)	6p dull violet	375.00	90.00
44	(f)	1sh green	450.00	62.50
45	(f)	5sh orange	1,400.	72.50
46	(g)	½p gray black	27.50	27.50
47	(g)	1p rose	22.50	17.50
48	(g)	4p blue (type I)	300.00	47.50
49	(g)	4p blue (type II)	250.00	30.00
50	(g)	6p dull violet	175.00	35.00
51	(g)	1sh green	225.00	25.00
a.		Inverted overprint	—	550.00
52	(g)	5sh orange	725.00	32.50

There are minor varieties of types e and f.

Overprinted in Black

1878

54	(g)	4p blue (type II)	300.00	57.50
55	(g)	6p dull violet	475.00	90.00
56	(i)	1p rose	25.00	17.50
57	(i)	4p blue (type II)	120.00	22.50
58	(i)	6p dull violet	225.00	50.00
a.		Double overprint		*750.00*
59	(k)	1p rose	50.00	30.00
60	(k)	4p blue (type II)	275.00	50.00
61	(k)	6p dull violet	425.00	85.00
62	(l)	1p rose	27.50	20.00
63	(l)	4p blue (type II)	140.00	25.00
64	(l)	6p dull violet	250.00	55.00
65	(m)	1p rose	72.50	65.00

66 (m) 4p blue (type II) 375.00 80.00
67 (m) 6p dull violet 500.00 140.00
68 (n) 1p rose 72.50 65.00
69 (n) 4p blue (type II) 375.00 80.00
70 (n) 6p dull violet 500.00 140.00
a. Double overprint *975.00*
71 (o) 1p rose 57.50 42.50
72 (o) 4p blue (type II) 325.00 62.50
73 (o) 6p dull violet 450.00 95.00
74 (p) 1p rose 67.50 62.50
75 (p) 4p blue (type II) 350.00 72.50
76 (p) 6p dull violet 450.00 125.00
77 (q) 1p rose 110.00 95.00
78 (q) 4p blue (type II) 550.00 160.00
79 (q) 6p dull violet 725.00 225.00
80 (r) 1p rose 375.00 325.00
81 (r) 4p blue (type II) *1,800.* 475.00
82 (r) 6p dull violet *1,800.* 575.00

There are two minor varieties of type i and one of type p.

Overprinted in Red

G G
s *t*

1878

83 (s) ½p gray black 10.00 10.00
a. Double overprint 42.50 57.50
b. Inverted overprint 11.00 11.00
c. Double overprint, inverted 80.00 *100.00*
84 (s) 4p blue (type II) 300.00 100.00
a. Inverted overprint 900.00 75.00
85 (t) ½p gray black 11.00 11.00
a. Double overprint 72.50 72.50
b. Inverted overprint 11.00 *12.50*
86 (t) 4p blue (type II) — 80.00
a. Inverted overprint 325.00 80.00

Black Overprint

87 (s) ½p gray black 180.00 95.00
a. Inverted overprint 190.00 —
b. With 2nd ovpt. *(s)* in red, invtd. 375.00
c. With 2nd ovpt. *(t)* in red, invtd. 105.00
88 (s) 1p rose 10.00 8.50
a. Double overprint 175.00 45.00
b. Inverted overprint 10.00 10.00
c. Double overprint, both inverted 175.00 62.50
d. With second overprint *(s)* in red, both inverted 37.50 37.50
89 (s) 4p blue (type I) 140.00
90 (s) 4p blue (type II) 125.00 26.00
a. Double overprint — 175.00
b. Inverted overprint 190.00 75.00
c. Double overprint, both inverted — 275.00
91 (s) 6p dull violet 125.00 25.00
92 (t) ½p gray black 42.50 42.50
a. Inverted overprint 42.50 42.50
b. With 2nd ovpt. inverted 150.00
93 (t) 1p rose 10.00 10.00
a. Double overprint — 85.00
b. Inverted overprint 77.50 27.50
c. Double overprint, both inverted — 100.00
d. With 2nd ovpt. *(t)* in red, both invtd. 80.00 80.00
94 (t) 4p blue (type I) 140.00
95 (t) 4p blue (type II) 150.00 11.00
a. Double overprint — 200.00
b. Inverted overprint 210.00 27.50
c. Double overprint, both inverted — 250.00
96 (t) 6p dull violet 25.00

Overprinted in Black

97 ½p gray black 15.00 7.25
a. Double overprint 400.00 275.00
98 1p rose 15.00 5.00
a. Double overprint — 150.00
b. Triple overprint — 210.00
c. Inverted overprint — 90.00
99 4p blue (type II) 27.50 5.00
a. Double overprint — 110.00
100 6p brt violet 140.00 8.00
a. Double overprint 625.00 190.00
b. Inverted overprint — 32.50
101 1sh green 110.00 6.00
a. Double overprint 350.00 95.00
102 5sh orange 400.00 10.00
a. Double overprint 525.00 85.00
b. Triple overprint — 300.00

These stamps were declared obsolete in 1880 and the remainders were used in Cape of Good Hope offices as ordinary stamps.

Prices for used stamps are for examples with such cancels.

GUADELOUPE

ˈgwä-dᵊl-ˌüp

LOCATION — In the West Indies lying between Montserrat and Dominica
GOVT. — French colony
AREA — 688 sq. mi.
POP. — 271,262 (1946)
CAPITAL — Basse-Terre

Guadeloupe consists of two large islands, Guadeloupe proper and Grande-Terre, together with five smaller dependencies.

100 Centimes = 1 Franc

FORERUNNERS

Crowned Circle handstamp types are pictured in the Crowned Circle Handstamps and Great Britain Used Abroad section.

BRITISH POST OFFICES IN GUADELOUPE

Guadeloupe

British P.O. opened Oct. 1, 1848; closed 1874

Pre-Stamp Postal Markings

1841

A1 Crowned Circle handstamp Type I, on cover, inscribed "GUADE-LOUPE", *from* *2,100.*

Earliest known use Mar. 9, 1849.

Issues under French Administraion

Stamps of French Colonies Surcharged

1884 Unwmk. *Imperf.*

1 A8 20c on 30c brn, *bis* 52.50 42.50
On cover 1,000.
a. Large "2" 250.00 175.00
2 A8 25c on 35c blk, *org* 42.50 42.50
On cover 625.00
a. Large "2" 250.00 175.00
b. Large "5" 110.00 92.50

The 5c on 4c (French Colonies No. 40) was not regularly issued. Three copies exist. Value $35,000.

The 5c on 4c also exists as an essay, surcharge similar to the issued values. Value $500.

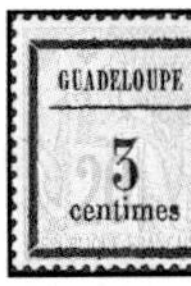
c

d

1889 *Perf. 14x13½*

Surcharged Type c

3 A9 3c on 20c red, *grn* 3.50 3.50
On cover 400.00
4 A9 15c on 20c red, *grn* 21.00 21.00
On cover 400.00
5 A9 25c on 20c red, *grn* 21.00 21.00
On cover 400.00
Nos. 3-5 (3) 45.50 45.50

Surcharged Type d

6 A9 5c on 1c blk, *lil bl* 11.50 11.00
On cover 450.00
a. Inverted surcharge *925.00*
b. Double surcharge *350.00* *350.00*
7 A9 10c on 40c red, *straw* 22.00 22.00
On cover 450.00
a. Double surcharge 325.00 290.00
8 A9 15c on 20c red, *grn* 24.00 22.00
On cover 450.00
a. Double surcharge 325.00 290.00
9 A9 25c on 30c brn, *bis* 35.00 29.00
On cover 450.00
a. Double surcharge 325.00 290.00
Nos. 6-9 (4) 92.50 84.00

The word "centimes" in surcharges "b" and "c" varies from 10 to 12½mm.
Issue dates: No. 6, June 25; others, Mar. 22.

1891

10 A9 5c on 10c blk, *lav* 11.00 8.50
On cover 450.00
11 A9 5c on 1fr brnz grn, *straw* 11.50 9.25
On cover 450.00

Stamps of French Colonies Overprinted in Black

1891 *Imperf.*

12 A7 30c brn, *yelsh* 275.00 250.00
13 A7 80c car, *pnksh* 800.00 *1,000.*

Perf. 14x13½

14 A9 1c blk, *lil bl* 1.25 1.10
On cover —
a. Double overprint 25.00 21.00
b. Inverted overprint 100.00 100.00
15 A9 2c brn, *buff* 1.75 1.50
On cover 450.00
a. Double overprint 29.00 21.00
16 A9 4c claret, *lav* 4.75 4.25
On cover —
17 A9 5c grn, *grnsh* 7.25 5.75
On cover 350.00
a. Double overrinpt 29.00 21.00
b. Inverted overprint 125.00 125.00
18 A9 10c blk, *lavender* 13.00 11.00
On cover 350.00
19 A9 15c blue 40.00 4.25
On cover 175.00
a. Double overprint 70.00
20 A9 20c red, *grn* 32.50 21.00
On cover —
a. Double overprint 175.00 160.00
21 A9 25c blk, *rose* 36.00 3.50
On cover 85.00
a. Double overprint 175.00 160.00
b. Inverted overprint 150.00 150.00
22 A9 30c brn, *bister* 32.50 22.00
On cover —
a. Double overprint 175.00 160.00
23 A9 35c dp vio, *org* 72.50 57.50
On cover —
24 A9 40c red, *straw* 50.00 40.00
On cover 300.00
a. Double overprint 575.00 375.00
25 A9 75c car, *rose* 110.00 95.00
On cover 300.00
26 A9 1fr brnz grn, *straw* 72.50 57.50
On cover —
Nos. 14-26 (13) 474.00 324.35

The following errors may be found in all values: "GNADELOUPE," "GUADELOUEP," "GUADELONPE" and "GUADBLOUPE."

Navigation and Commerce — A7

Perf. 14x13½

1892-1901 Typo. Unwmk.

Colony Name in Blue or Carmine

27 A7 1c blk, *lil bl* 1.10 1.00
28 A7 2c brn, *buff* 1.10 1.00
29 A7 4c claret, *lav* 1.50 1.10
30 A7 5c grn, *grnsh* 3.00 1.10
On cover 17.50
31 A7 5c yel grn ('01) 4.50 1.25
On cover 17.50
32 A7 10c blk, *lavender* 8.50 2.50
On cover 17.50
33 A7 10c red ('00) 6.50 1.75
On cover 17.50
a. Imperf. 80.00
34 A7 15c blue, quadrille paper 14.50 1.50
On cover 17.50
35 A7 15c gray, *lt gray* ('00) 9.50 1.25
On cover 17.50
36 A7 20c red, *grn* 8.50 4.25
On cover 55.00
37 A7 25c blk, *rose* 8.75 2.10
On cover 17.50
38 A7 25c blue ('00) 80.00 80.00
On cover 160.00
39 A7 30c brn, *bister* 18.00 12.50
On cover —
40 A7 40c red, *straw* 18.00 12.50
On cover 100.00
41 A7 50c car, *rose* 25.00 13.50
On cover 100.00
42 A7 50c brn, *az* ('00) 35.00 32.50
On cover 110.00
43 A7 75c dp vio, *org* 25.00 17.50
On cover 110.00
44 A7 1fr brnz grn, *straw* 25.00 24.00
On cover —
Nos. 27-44 (18) 293.45 211.30

Perf. 13½x14 stamps are counterfeits.
For surcharges see Nos. 45-53, 83-85.

Nos. 39-41, 43-44 Surcharged in Black:

f

g

h

1903

45 A7 (f) 5c on 30c 2.75 2.75
On cover 45.00
a. "C" instead of "G" 20.00 20.00
b. Inverted surcharge 25.00 25.00
c. Double surcharge 92.50 92.50
d. Double surch., inverted 110.00
46 A7 (g) 10c on 40c 5.75 5.75
On cover 45.00
a. "C" instead of "G" 21.00 21.00
b. "1" inverted 40.00 40.00
c. Inverted surcharge 30.00 30.00
47 A7 (f) 15c on 50c 8.00 8.00
On cover 45.00
a. "C" instead of "G" 25.00 25.00
b. Inverted surcharge 70.00 70.00
c. "15" inverted 240.00 240.00
48 A7 (g) 40c on 1fr 8.50 8.50
On cover 45.00
a. "C" instead of "G" 25.00 25.00
b. "4" inverted 85.00 85.00
c. Inverted surcharge 70.00 70.00
d. Double surcharge 160.00 160.00
49 A7 (h) 1fr on 75c 29.00 29.00
On cover —
a. "C" instead of "G" 92.50 92.50
b. "1" inverted 110.00 110.00
c. Value above "G & D" 225.00 225.00
d. Inverted surcharge 85.00 85.00
Nos. 45-49 (5) 54.00 54.00

Letters and figures from several fonts were used for these surcharges, resulting in numerous minor varieties.

Nos. 48-49 With Additional Overprint "1903" in a Frame

1904, Mar.

Red Overprint

50 A7 (g) 40c on 1fr 41.00 42.50
On cover 200.00
51 A7 (h) 1fr on 75c 60.00 65.00
On cover 225.00

Blue Overprint

52 A7 (g) 40c on 1fr 32.50 35.00
On cover 175.00
53 A7 (h) 1fr on 75c 57.50 60.00
On cover 200.00
Nos. 50-53 (4) 191.00 202.50

The date "1903" may be found in 19 different positions and type faces within the frame. These stamps may also be found with the minor varieties of Nos. 48-49.

The 40c exists with black overprint. Value, $350 unused or used.

Harbor at Basse-Terre — A8

View of La Soufrière A9

Pointe-à-Pitre, Grand-Terre — A10

1905-27 Typo. *Perf. 14x13½*

54	A8	1c blk, *bluish*	.25	.25
55	A8	2c vio brn, *straw*	.25	.25
56	A8	4c bis brn, *az*	.30	.25
57	A8	5c green	1.75	.50
58	A8	5c dp blue ('22)	.20	.20
59	A8	10c rose	1.60	.40
60	A8	10c green ('22)	1.10	1.10
61	A8	10c red, *bluish* ('25)	.20	.20
62	A8	15c violet	.40	.30
63	A9	20c red, *grn*	.40	.25
64	A9	20c bl grn ('25)	.45	.45
65	A9	25c blue	.75	.30
66	A9	25c ol grn ('22)	.45	.45
67	A9	30c black	3.50	2.10
68	A9	30c rose ('22)	.60	.60
69	A9	30c brn ol, *lav* ('25)	.45	.45
70	A9	35c blk, *yel* ('06)	.50	.50
71	A9	40c red, *straw*	.60	.60
72	A9	45c ol gray, *lil* ('07)	.80	.60
73	A9	45c rose ('25)	.50	.50
74	A9	50c gray grn, *straw*	3.75	2.50
75	A9	50c dp bl ('22)	1.00	1.00
76	A9	50c violet ('25)	.50	.50
77	A9	65c blue ('27)	.50	.50
78	A9	75c car, *bl*	.60	.60
79	A10	1fr blk, *green*	1.25	1.25
80	A10	1fr lt bl ('25)	.75	.75
81	A10	2fr car, *org*	1.50	1.50
82	A10	5fr dp bl, *org*	5.50	5.50
		Nos. 54-82 (29)	30.40	24.35

Nos. 57 and 59 exist imperf. Value, each $45.

For surcharges see #86-95, 167, B1-B2.

Nos. 29, 39 and 40 Surcharged in Carmine or Black

1912, Nov.

Spacing between figures of surcharge 1.5mm (5c), 2mm (10c)

83	A7	5c on 4c claret, *lav* (C)	1.25	1.25
84	A7	5c on 30c brn, *bis* (C)	1.40	1.40
85	A7	10c on 40c red, *straw*	1.50	1.50
		Nos. 83-85 (3)	4.15	4.15

Spacing between figures of surcharge 2.25mm (5c), 2.75mm (10c)

83a	A7	5c on 4c claret, *lav* (C)	125.00	125.00
84a	A7	5c on 30c brn, *bis* (C)	175.00	175.00
85a	A7	10c on 40c red, *straw*	125.00	125.00
		Nos. 83a-85a (3)	425.00	425.00

Stamps and Types of 1905-27 Surcharged with New Value and Bars

1924-27

86	A10	25c on 5fr dp bl, *org*	.60	.60
87	A10	65c on 1fr gray grn	1.00	1.00
88	A10	85c on 1fr gray grn	1.10	1.10
89	A9	90c on 75c dl red	1.00	1.00
90	A10	1.05fr on 2fr ver (Bl)	.75	.75
91	A10	1.25fr on 1fr lt bl (R)	.45	.45
92	A10	1.50fr on 1fr dk bl	.90	.90
93	A10	3fr on 5fr org brn	1.25	1.25
94	A10	10fr on 5fr vio rose, *org*	9.00	9.00
95	A10	20fr on 5fr rose lil, *pnksh*	10.00	10.00
		Nos. 86-95 (10)	26.05	26.05

Years issued: Nos. 87-88, 1925. Nos. 90-91, 1926. Nos. 89, 92-95, 1927.

Sugar Mill — A11

Saints Roadstead A12

Harbor Scene A13

Perf. 14x13½

1928-40 Unwmk. Typo.

96	A11	1c yel & vio	.20	.20
97	A11	2c blk & lt red	.20	.20
98	A11	3c yel & red vio ('40)	.25	.20
99	A11	4c yel grn & org brn	.20	.20
100	A11	5c ver & grn	.20	.20
101	A11	10c bis brn & dp bl	.20	.20
102	A11	15c brn red & blk	.25	.25
103	A11	20c lil & ol brn	.40	.40
104	A12	25c grnsh bl & olvn	.40	.40
105	A12	30c gray grn & yel grn	.25	.25
106	A12	35c bl grn ('38)	.25	.25
107	A12	40c yel & vio	.25	.25
108	A12	45c vio brn & slate	.75	.50
109	A12	45c bl grn & dl grn ('40)	.80	.80
110	A12	50c dl grn & org	.30	.30
111	A12	55c ultra & car ('38)	1.00	1.00
112	A12	60c ultra & car ('40)	.35	.35
113	A12	65c gray blk & ver	.40	.40
114	A12	70c gray blk & ver ('40)	.50	.50
115	A12	75c dl red & bl grn	.50	.50
116	A12	80c car & brn ('38)	.60	.55
117	A12	90c dl red & dl rose	1.50	1.25
118	A12	90c rose red & bl ('39)	.80	.80
119	A13	1fr lt rose & lt bl	4.00	2.10
120	A13	1fr rose red & org ('38)	1.25	1.10
121	A13	1fr bl gray & blk brn ('40)	.50	.50
122	A13	1.05fr lt bl & rose	.95	.95
123	A13	1.10fr lt red & grn	2.75	2.00
124	A13	1.25fr bl gray & blk brn ('33)	.40	.40
125	A13	1.25fr brt rose & red org ('39)	.65	.65
126	A13	1.40fr lt bl & lil rose ('40)	.50	.50
127	A13	1.50fr dl bl & bl	.25	.25
128	A13	1.60fr lil rose & yel brn ('40)	.50	.50
129	A13	1.75fr lil rose & yel brn ('33)	4.00	2.50
130	A13	1.75fr vio bl ('38)	4.50	3.50
131	A13	2fr bl grn & dk brn	.25	.25
132	A13	2.25fr vio bl ('39)	.80	.80
133	A13	2.50fr pale org & grn ('40)	.80	.80
134	A13	3fr org brn & sl	.45	.45
135	A13	5fr dl bl & org	.80	.65
136	A13	10fr vio & ol brn	.80	.65
137	A13	20fr green & mag	1.10	1.10
		Nos. 96-137 (42)	35.80	29.60

Nos. 96-103, 110, 119, 123, 134, 137 exist imperf. Values each $20-$40.

For surcharges see Nos. 161-166.

Common Design Types pictured following the introduction.

Colonial Exposition Issue

Common Design Types

1931, Apr. 13 Engr. *Perf. 12½*

Name of Country in Black

138	CD70	40c deep green	4.50	4.50
139	CD71	50c violet	4.50	4.50
140	CD72	90c red orange	4.50	4.50
141	CD73	1.50fr dull blue	4.50	4.50
		Nos. 138-141 (4)	18.00	18.00

Cardinal Richelieu Establishing French Antilles Co., 1635 — A14

Victor Hugues and his Corsairs — A15

1935 *Perf. 13*

142	A14	40c gray brown	7.75	7.75
143	A14	50c dull red	7.75	7.75
144	A14	1.50fr dull blue	7.75	7.75
145	A15	1.75fr lilac rose	7.75	7.75
146	A15	5fr dark brown	7.75	7.75
147	A15	10fr blue green	7.75	7.75
		Nos. 142-147 (6)	46.50	46.50

Tercentenary of the establishment of the French colonies in the West Indies.

Paris International Exposition Issue

Common Design Types

1937 *Perf. 13*

148	CD74	20c deep violet	1.10	1.10
149	CD75	30c dark green	1.10	1.10
150	CD76	40c car rose	1.50	1.50
151	CD77	50c dk brn & blk	1.50	1.50
152	CD78	90c red	1.50	1.50
153	CD79	1.50fr ultra	1.50	1.50
		Nos. 148-153 (6)	8.20	8.20

Colonial Arts Exhibition Issue

Souvenir Sheet

Common Design Type

1937 *Imperf.*

154	CD75	3fr dark blue	9.50	9.50

New York World's Fair Issue

Common Design Type

1939 Engr. *Perf. 12½x12*

155	CD82	1.25fr car lake	1.00	1.00
156	CD82	2.25fr ultra	1.00	1.00

For surcharges see Nos. 159-160.

SEMI-POSTAL STAMPS

Nos. 59 and 62 Surcharged in Red

1915-17 Unwmk. *Perf. 14 x 13½*

B1	A8	10c + 5c rose	3.50	2.10
		On cover		80.00
B2	A8	15c + 5c violet	3.25	2.10
		On cover		80.00
a.		Double surcharge	140.00	140.00

Curie Issue

Common Design Type

1938, Oct. 24 *Perf. 13*

B3	CD80	1.75fr + 50c brt ultra	11.00	11.00

French Revolution Issue

Common Design Type

Name and Value Typo. in Black

1939, July 5 Photo. *Perf. 13*

B4	CD83	45c + 25c green	8.50	8.50
B5	CD83	70c + 30c brown	8.50	8.50
B6	CD83	90c + 35c red org	8.50	8.50
B7	CD83	1.25fr + 1fr rose pink	8.50	8.50
B8	CD83	2.25fr + 2fr blue	8.50	8.50
		Nos. B4-B8 (5)	42.50	42.50

POSTAGE DUE STAMPS

D1

D2

D3

1876 Unwmk. Typeset *Imperf.*

J1	D1	25c black	1,050.	725.
		On cover		4,500.
J2	D2	40c black, *blue*		28,500.
		On cover		50,000.
J3	D3	40c black	1,250.	925.
		On cover		4,500.

Twenty varieties of each.

Nos. J1 and J3 have been reprinted on thinner and whiter paper than the originals.

D4

D5

1879

J4	D4	15c black, *blue*	40.00	35.00
		On cover		4,500.
a.		Period after "c" omitted	140.00	140.00
J5	D4	30c black	80.00	65.00
		On cover		2,500.
a.		Period after "c" omitted	190.00	175.00

Twenty varieties of each.

1884

J6	D5	5c black	25.00	25.00
		On cover		3,000.
J7	D5	10c black, *blue*	57.50	42.50
		On cover		3,250.
J8	D5	15c black, *violet*	85.00	75.00
		On cover		3,500.
J9	D5	20c black, *rose*	125.00	80.00
		On cover		3,500.
a.		Italic "2" in "20"	700.00	600.00
J10	D5	30c black, *yellow*	125.00	125.00
		On cover		3,750.
J11	D5	35c black, *gray*	45.00	35.00
		On cover		3,250.
J12	D5	50c black, *green*	25.00	20.00
		On cover		3,000.
		Nos. J6-J12 (7)	487.50	402.50

There are ten varieties of the 35c, and fifteen of each of the other values, also numerous wrong font and missing letters.

Postage Due Stamps of French Colonies Surcharged in Black

1903

J13	D1	30c on 60c brn, *cr*	250.	250.
		On cover		2,750.
a.		"3" with flat top	500.	500.
b.		Inverted surcharge	700.	700.
c.		As "a," inverted	1,200.	1,200.
J14	D1	30c on 1fr rose, *cr*	300.	300.
		On cover		2,750.
a.		Inverted surcharge	700.	700.
b.		"3" with flat top	600.	600.
c.		As "b," inverted	1,400.	1,400.

Gustavia Bay — D6

Avenue of Royal Palms — D7

1905-06 Typo. *Perf. 14x13½*

J15	D6	5c blue	.35	.35
		On cover		150.00
J16	D6	10c brown	.45	.45
		On cover		150.00
J17	D6	15c green	.70	.70
		On cover		150.00
J18	D6	20c black, *yel* ('06)	.70	.70
		On cover		150.00
J19	D6	30c rose	.90	.90
		On cover		150.00
J20	D6	50c black	2.75	2.75
		On cover		175.00
J21	D6	60c brown orange	1.50	1.50
		On cover		175.00
J22	D6	1fr violet	2.75	2.75
		On cover		225.00
		Nos. J15-J22 (8)	10.10	10.10

Type of 1905-06 Issue Surcharged

1926-27
J23 D6 2fr on 1fr gray 1.50 1.50
J24 D6 3fr on 1fr ultra ('27) 1.75 1.75

1928, June 18
J25 D7 2c olive brn & lil .20 .20
J26 D7 4c bl & org brn .20 .20
J27 D7 5c gray grn & dk brn .20 .20
J28 D7 10c dl vio & yel .20 .20
J29 D7 15c rose & olive grn .20 .20
J30 D7 20c brn org & ol grn .35 .35
J31 D7 25c brn red & bl grn .35 .35
J32 D7 30c slate & olivine .55 .55
J33 D7 50c ol brn & lt red .55 .55
J34 D7 60c dp bl & blk .55 .55
J35 D7 1fr green & orange 2.25 2.25
J36 D7 2fr bis brn & lt red 1.75 1.75
J37 D7 3fr vio & bl blk .90 .90
Nos. J25-J37 (13) 8.25 8.25

GUATEMALA

ˌgwä-lə-ˈmä-lə

LOCATION — Central America, bordering on Atlantic and Pacific Oceans
GOVT. — Republic
AREA — 42,042 sq. mi.
POP. — 6,577,000 (est. 1984)
CAPITAL — Guatemala City

100 Centavos = 8 Reales = 1 Peso
100 Centavos de Quetzal = 1 Quetzal (1927)

Coat of Arms
A1 A2

Two types of 10c:
Type I — Both zeros in "10" are wide.
Type II — Left zero narrow.

Perf. 14x13½

1871, Mar. 1 Typo. Unwmk.
1 A1 1c ocher .75 *10.00*
a. Imperf., pair 5.00
b. Printed on both sides, imperf. 75.00
2 A1 5c lt bister brn 4.00 *7.50*
a. Imperf. pair 35.00
b. Tête bêche pair 150.00
c. Tête bêche pair, imperf. 2,600.
3 A1 10c blue (I) 5.00 *8.00*
a. Imperf., pair (I) 45.00
b. Type II 8.00 *10.00*
c. Imperf. pair (II) 60.00
4 A1 20c rose 4.00 *7.50*
a. Imperf., pair 45.00
b. 20c blue (error) 125.00 125.00
c. As "b," imperf. *800.00*
Nos. 1-4 (4) 13.75 *33.00*

Forgeries exist. Forged cancellations abound. See No. C458.

1873 Litho. *Perf. 12*
5 A2 4r dull red vio 325.00 85.00
6 A2 1p dull yellow 175.00 115.00

Forgeries exist.

Liberty
A3 A4

A5 A6

1875, Apr. 15 Engr.
7 A3 ¼r black 1.00 *3.50*
8 A4 ½r blue green 1.00 *3.00*
9 A5 1r blue 1.00 *3.00*
a. Half used as ½r on cover *1,700.*
10 A6 2r dull red 1.00 *3.00*
Nos. 7-10 (4) 4.00 *12.50*

Nos. 7-10 normally lack gum. Unused values are for examples without gum.
Forgeries and forged cancellations exist.

Indian Woman — A7

Quetzal — A8

Typographed on Tinted Paper

1878, Jan. 10 *Perf. 13*
11 A7 ½r yellow grn .75 *3.00*
12 A7 2r carmine rose 1.25 *4.00*
13 A7 4r violet 1.25 *4.50*
14 A7 1p yellow 2.00 *9.00*
c. Half used as 4r on cover *2,200.*
Nos. 11-14 (4) 5.25 *20.50*

Some sheets of Nos. 11-14 have papermaker's watermark, "LACROIX FRERES," in double-lined capitals appearing on six stamps.
Part perforate pairs of Nos. 11, 12 and 14 exist. Value for each, about $100.
Forgeries of Nos. 11-14 are plentiful. Forged cancellations exist.
For surcharges see Nos. 18, 20.

Imperf., Pairs
11a A7 ½r yellow green 50.00
12a A7 2r carmine rose 50.00
13a A7 4r violet 50.00
14a A7 1p yellow 50.00

1879 Engr. *Perf. 12*
15 A8 ¼r brown & green 2.50 *2.75*
16 A8 1r black & green 2.50 *3.75*

For similar types see A11, A72, A103, A121, A146. For surcharges see Nos. 17, 19.

Nos. 11, 12, 15, 16 Surcharged in Black

1881 *Perf. 12 and 13*
17 A8 1c on ¼r brn & grn 11.25 *15.00*
a. "ecntavo," 37.50 *45.00*
b. Pair, one without surcharge 200.00
18 A7 5c on ½r yel grn 5.00 *7.50*
a. "ecntavos," 35.00 35.00
b. "5" omitted 100.00
c. Double surcharge 90.00 *110.00*
19 A8 10c on 1r blk & grn 16.00 *22.50*
a. "s" of "centavos" missing 75.00 75.00
b. "ecntavos" 40.00 *45.00*
20 A7 20c on 2r car rose 30.00 *40.00*
a. Horiz. pair, imperf. between 425.00
Nos. 17-20 (4) 62.25 *85.00*

The 5c had three settings.
Surcharge varieties found on Nos. 17-20 include: Period omitted; comma instead of period; "ecntavo." or "ecntavos."; "s" omitted; spaced "centavos."; wider "0" in "20."
Counterfeits of Nos. 17-20 are plentiful.

Quetzal — A11

1881, Nov. 7 Engr. *Perf. 12*
21 A11 1c black & grn 2.75 1.90
22 A11 2c brown & grn 2.75 1.90
a. Center inverted 400.00
23 A11 5c red & grn 5.75 2.50
a. Center inverted *3,000.* 1,300.
24 A11 10c gray vio & grn 2.75 1.90
25 A11 20c yellow & grn 2.75 2.25
a. Center inverted 500.00
Nos. 21-25 (5) 16.75 10.45

Gen. Justo Rufino Barrios — A12

Black Surcharge

Correos Nacionales
25 c. 25 c.
Guatemala.
25 c. 25 c.
25 centavos.

1886, Mar. 6
26 A12 25c on 1p ver .70 .70
a. "centovos" 1.50
b. "centanos" 1.50
c. "255" instead of "25" 150.00
d. Inverted "S" in "Nacionales" 20.00
f. "cen avos" 20.00
h. "Corre cionales" 20.00
i. Inverted surcharge 75.00
27 A12 50c on 1p ver .70 .70
a. "centovos" 1.50
b. "centanos" 1.50
c. "Carreos" 1.50
d. Inverted surcharge 50.00
e. Double surcharge 75.00
f. Inverted "S" in "Nacionales" 10.00
g. "centavo" 20.00
h. "cen avos" 20.00
28 A12 75c on 1p ver .70 .70
a. "centovos" 1.50
b. "centanos" 1.50
c. "Carreos" 1.50
d. "50" for "75" at upper right 2.00
e. Inverted "S" in "Nacionales" 10.00
f. Double surcharge 75.00
g. "ales" inverted 100.00
29 A12 100c on 1p ver 1.40 1.40
a. "110" at upper left and "á" at lower left, instead of "100" 5.00
b. Inverted surcharge 75.00
c. "Guatemala" bolder; 23mm instead of 18½mm wide 2.25
d. Double surcharge, one diagonal 100.00
30 A12 150c on 1p ver 1.40 1.40
a. Inverted "G" 5.00
b. "Guetemala" and italic "5" in upper 4 numerals 5.00
d. Inverted surcharge 90.00
e. Pair, one without surcharge 100.00
f. Double surcharge 100.00
Nos. 26-30 (5) 4.90 4.90

There are many other minor varieties, such as wrong font letters, etc. The surcharge on Nos. 29 and 30 has different letters and ornaments. On No. 29, "Guatemala" normally is 18½mm wide.
Used values of Nos. 26-30 are for canceled to order stamps. Postally used sell for much more.

National Emblem — A13

1886, July 1 Litho. *Perf. 12*
31 A13 1c dull blue 5.00 2.00
32 A13 2c brown 5.00 3.00
33 A13 5c purple 37.50 .75
34 A13 10c red 10.00 .75
35 A13 20c emerald 15.00 1.25
36 A13 25c orange 15.00 1.50
37 A13 50c olive green 10.00 2.00
38 A13 75c carmine rose 10.00 3.00
39 A13 100c red brown 10.00 3.00
40 A13 150c dark blue 15.00 3.75
41 A13 200c orange yellow 17.50 4.75
Nos. 31-41 (11) 150.00 25.75

Used values of Nos. 38-41 are for canceled to order stamps. Postally used sell for more.
See Nos. 43-50, 99-107. For surcharges see Nos. 42, 51-59, 75-85, 97-98, 108-110, 124-130.

No. 32 Surcharged in Black

Two settings:
I — "1886" (no period).
II — "1886." (period).

1886, Nov. 12
42 A13 1c on 2c brown, I 2.00 *2.50*
a. Date inverted, I 75.00
b. Date double, I 75.00
c. Date omitted, I 60.00
d. Date double, one invtd., I 100.00
e. Date triple, one inverted, I 100.00
f. Setting II 1.50 1.00
g. Inverted surcharge, II 4.00
h. Double surcharge, II 100.00

Forgeries exist.

Type I

Type II

Two types of 5c:
I — Thin "5"
II — Larger, thick "5"

1886-95 Engr. *Perf. 12*
43 A13 1c blue .75 .20
44 A13 2c yellow brn 2.25 .20
a. Half used as 1c on cover 100.00
45 A13 5c purple (I) 50.00 1.00
46 A13 5c vio (II) ('88) 1.50 .20
47 A13 6c lilac ('95) .60 .20
48 A13 10c red ('90) 1.50 .20
49 A13 20c green ('93) 3.00 .75
50 A13 25c red org ('93) 7.50 1.25
Nos. 43-44,46-50 (7) 17.10 3.00

The impression of the engraved stamps is sharper than that of the lithographed. On the engraved stamps the top four lines at left are heavier than those below them. (This is also true of the 1c litho., which is distinguished from the engraved only by a slight color difference and the impression.)
The "2" and "5" (I) are more open than the litho. numerals. The "10" of the engraved is wider. The 20c and 25c of the engraved have a vertical line at right end of the "centavos" ribbon.

No. 38 Surcharged in Blue Black

"1894" 14½mm wide

1894, Apr. 25
51 A13 10c on 75c car rose 4.50 4.50
a. Double surcharge 75.00
b. Inverted surcharge 100.00

Same on Nos. 38-41 in Blue or Red
"1894" 14mm wide

1894, June 13
52 A13 2c on 100c 7.50 4.25
53 A13 6c on 150c (R) 7.50 3.50
54 A13 10c on 75c 550.00 500.00
55 A13 10c on 200c 7.50 4.25
c. Inverted surcharge 75.00

Nos. 54-55 exist with thick or thin "1" in new value.

Same on Nos. 39-41 in Black or Red
"1894" 12mm wide

1894, July 14
52a A13 2c on 100c red brn (Bk) 4.00 3.50
b. Vert. pair, one without surcharge 150.00
53a A13 6c on 150c dk bl (R) 4.50 3.50
55a A13 10c on 200c org yel (Bk) 5.00 3.50
d. Inverted surcharge 100.00
e. Vert. pair, one without surcharge 150.00

Nos. 44 and 46 Surcharged in Black, Blue Black, or Red:

b

c

d

e

1894-96

56 A13 (b) 1c on 2c (Bk) .75 .30
a. "Centav" 5.00 5.00
b. Double surcharge 75.00
c. As "a," dbl. surcharge 150.00
d. Blue black surcharge 20.00 20.00
e. Dbl. surch., one inverted 150.00
57 A13 (c) 1c on 5c (R) ('95) .50 .20
a. Inverted surcharge 3.00 3.00
b. "1894" instead of "1895" 3.50 3.00
c. Double surcharge 50.00
58 A13 (d) 1c on 5c (R) ('95) .75 .20
a. Inverted surcharge 50.00 50.00
b. Double surcharge 50.00
59 A13 (e) 1c on 5c (R) ('96) 1.25 .40
a. Inverted surcharge 50.00 50.00
b. Double surcharge 50.00
Nos. 56-59 (4) 3.25 1.10

Nos. 56-58 may be found with thick or thin "1" in the new value.

National Arms and President J. M. Reyna Barrios
A21

1897, Jan. 1 Engr. Unwmk.

60 A21 1c blk, *lil gray* .50 .50
61 A21 2c blk, *grnsh gray* .50 .50
62 A21 6c blk, *brn org* .50 .50
63 A21 10c blk, *dl bl* .50 .50
64 A21 12c blk, *rose red* .50 .50
65 A21 18c blk, *grysh white* 9.25 9.25
66 A21 20c blk, *scarlet* 1.00 1.00
67 A21 25c blk, *bis brn* 1.50 1.00
68 A21 50c blk, *redsh brn* 1.00 1.00
69 A21 75c blk, *gray* 50.00 50.00
70 A21 100c blk, *bl grn* 1.00 1.00
71 A21 150c blk, *dl rose* 100.00 *125.00*
72 A21 200c blk, *magenta* 1.00 1.00
73 A21 500c blk, *yel grn* 1.00 1.00
Nos. 60-73 (14) 168.25 *192.75*

Issued for Central American Exposition.

Stamps often sold as Nos. 65, 69 and 71 are copies with telegraph overprint removed.

Used values for Nos. 60-73 are for canceled-to-order copies. Postally used examples are worth more.

The paper of Nos. 64 and 66 was originally colored on one side only, but has "bled through" on some copies.

No. 64 Surcharged in Violet

1897, Nov.

74 A21 1c on 12c *rose red* 1.00 1.00
a. Inverted surcharge 30.00 30.00
b. Pair, one without surcharge 75.00
c. Dbl. surch., one invtd. 100.00

Stamps of 1886-93 Surcharged in Red

f

g

1898

75 (f) 1c on 5c violet 1.00 1.00
a. Inverted surcharge 75.00
76 (f) 1c on 50c ol grn 1.50 1.25
a. Inverted surcharge 100.00 100.00
77 (f) 6c on 5c violet 4.50 1.50
78 (f) 6c on 150c dk bl 4.50 3.25
79 (g) 10c on 20c emerald 5.00 4.00
a. Double surch., one inverted 125.00 125.00
Nos. 75-79 (5) 16.50 11.00

Black Surcharge

80 (f) 1c on 25c red org 2.00 2.00
81 (f) 1c on 75c car rose 1.50 1.50
a. Double surcharge 100.00
82 (f) 6c on 10c red 10.00 9.00
83 (f) 6c on 20c emer 5.00 4.00
84 (f) 6c on 100c red brn 5.00 4.00
85 (f) 6c on 200c org yel 5.00 4.00
a. Inverted surcharge 50.00 50.00
Nos. 80-85 (6) 28.50 24.50

Information that we have see indicates that No. 77 inverted and double surcharges are counterfeits.

National Emblem
A24 A25

Revenue Stamp Overprinted or Surcharged in Carmine

Perf. 12, 12x14, 14x12

1898, Oct. 8 Litho.

86 A24 1c dark blue 1.40 1.40
a. Inverted overprint 12.50 12.50
87 A24 2c on 1c dk bl 2.25 2.25
a. Inverted surcharge 12.50 12.50

Counterfeits exist.

See type A26.

Revenue Stamps Surcharged in Carmine

1898 Engr. *Perf. 12½ to 16*

88 A25 1c on 10c bl gray .75 .75
a. "ENTAVO" 5.00 5.00
89 A25 2c on 5c pur 1.25 1.00
90 A25 2c on 10c bl gray 6.50 *7.00*
a. Double surch., car & blk 100.00 75.00
91 A25 2c on 50c dp bl 9.25 *9.25*
a. Double surch., car & blk 100.00 100.00
Nos. 88-91 (4) 17.75 *18.00*

Black Surcharge

92 A25 2c on 1c lil rose 3.50 2.00
93 A25 2c on 25c red 7.50 8.00
94 A25 6c on 1p purple 4.00 4.50
95 A25 6c on 5p gray vio 7.50 7.50
96 A25 6c on 10p emer 7.50 7.50
Nos. 92-96 (5) 30.00 29.50

Nos. 88 and 90 are found in shades ranging from Prussian blue to slate blue.

Varieties other than those listed are bogus.

Counterfeits exist of No. 92.

Soaking in water causes marked fading.

See type A27.

No. 46 Surcharged in Red

1899, Sept. *Perf. 12*

97 A13 1c on 5c violet .40 .25
a. Inverted surcharge 7.50 7.50
b. Double surcharge 15.00 15.00
c. Double surcharge, one inverted 15.00 15.00

No. 48 Surcharged in Black

1900, Jan.

98 A13 1c on 10c red .65 .50
a. Inverted surcharge 10.00 10.00
b. Double surcharge 75.00 75.00

Quetzal Type of 1886

1900-02 Engr.

99 A13 1c dark green .60 .25
100 A13 2c carmine .60 .25
101 A13 5c blue (II) 2.25 1.25
102 A13 6c lt green .75 .25
103 A13 10c bister brown 7.50 1.00
104 A13 20c purple 7.50 7.50
105 A13 20c bister brn ('02) 7.50 7.50
106 A13 25c yellow 7.50 7.50
107 A13 25c blue green ('02) 7.50 7.50
Nos. 99-107 (9) 41.70 33.00

No. 49 Surcharged in Black

1901, May

108 A13 1c on 20c green .50 .50
a. Inverted surcharge 22.50 22.50
b. Double surch., one diagonal 50.00
109 A13 2c on 20c green 1.50 1.50

No. 50 Surcharged in Black

1901, Apr.

110 A13 1c on 25c red org .60 .60
a. Inverted surcharge 25.00 25.00
b. Double surcharge 50.00 50.00

A26

A27

Revenue Stamps Surcharged in Carmine or Black

1902, July *Perf. 12, 14x12, 12x14*

111 A26 1c on 1c dk blue 1.10 1.10
a. Double surcharge 20.00
b. Inverted surcharge 20.00
112 A26 2c on 1c dk blue 1.10 1.10
a. Double surcharge 90.00
b. Inverted surcharge 25.00

Perf. 14, 15

113 A27 6c on 25c red (Bk) 2.50 2.50
a. Double surch., one invtd. 75.00 75.00
Nos. 111-113 (3) 4.70 4.70

National Emblem — A28

Statue of Justo Rufino Barrios — A29

"La Reforma" Palace — A30

Temple of Minerva — A31

Lake Amatitlán — A32

Cathedral in Guatemala — A33

Columbus Theater — A34

Artillery Barracks — A35

Monument to Columbus — A36

School for Indians — A37

1902 Engr. *Perf. 12 to 16*

114 A28 1c grn & claret .20 .20
a. Horiz. pair, imperf. vert. 100.00
115 A29 2c lake & blk .20 .20
a. Horiz. or vert. pair, imperf. btwn. 150.00
116 A30 5c blue & blk .30 .20
a. 5c ultra & blk .75 .40
b. Imperf., pair 100.00 100.00
c. Horiz. pair, imperf. vert. 100.00
117 A31 6c bister & grn .30 .20
a. Horiz. pair, imperf. btwn. 150.00
118 A32 10c orange & bl .40 .40
a. Horiz. pair, imperf. vert. 100.00
119 A33 20c rose lil & blk .60 .40
a. Horiz. pair, imperf. vert. 100.00
120 A34 50c red brn & bl .45 .40
a. Vert. pair, imperf. btwn. 350.00
121 A35 75c gray lil & blk .55 .40
a. Horiz. pair, imperf. btwn. 150.00
b. Horiz. pair, imperf. vert. 100.00
122 A36 1p brown & blk .85 .40
a. Horiz. pair, imperf. btwn. 150.00
123 A37 2p ver & blk 1.00 .85
Nos. 114-123 (10) 4.85 3.65

See Nos. 210, 212-214, 219, 223, 239-241, 243. For overprints and surcharges see Nos. 133, 135-139, 144-157, 168, 170-171, 178, 192-194, 298-299, 301, C19, C27, C123.

Issues of 1886-1900 Surcharged in Black or Carmine

1903, Apr. 18 *Perf. 12*

124 A13 25c on 1c dk grn 1.25 .55
a. Inverted surcharge 50.00 50.00
125 A13 25c on 2c carmine 1.50 .55
126 A13 25c on 6c lt grn 2.50 1.75
a. Inverted surcharge 40.00 40.00
127 A13 25c on 10c bis brn 7.50 7.00
128 A13 25c on 75c rose 10.00 10.00
129 A13 25c on 150c dk bl (C) 9.00 9.00
130 A13 25c on 200c yellow 10.00 10.00
Nos. 124-130 (7) 41.75 38.85

Forgeries and bogus varieties exist.

Declaration of Independence
A38

1907, Jan. 1 *Perf. 13½ to 15*

132 A38 12½c ultra & blk .45 .45
a. Horiz. pair, imperf. btwn. 150.00

For surcharge see No. 134.

Nos. 118, 119 and 132 Surcharged in Black or Red

1908, May

133 A32 1c on 10c org & bl .30 .30
a. Double surcharge 25.00
b. Inverted surcharge 15.00 15.00
c. Pair, one without surcharge 50.00
134 A38 2c on 12½c ultra & blk (R) .25 .25
a. Horiz. or vert. pair, imperf. btwn. 100.00
b. Inverted surcharge 15.00 10.00
c. Double surcharge 30.00
135 A33 6c on 20c rose lil & blk .45 .25
a. Inverted surcharge 20.00 20.00
Nos. 133-135 (3) 1.00 .80

Similar Surcharge, Dated 1909, in Red or Black on Nos. 121 and 120

1909, Apr.

136 A35 2c on 75c (R) .55 .55
137 A34 6c on 50c (R) 62.50 62.50
a. Double surcharge 125.00 125.00
138 A34 6c on 50c (Bk) .30 .30
Nos. 136-138 (3) 63.35 63.35

Counterfeits exist of Nos. 137, 137a.

No. 123 Surcharged in Black

139 A37 12½c on 2p ver & blk .30 .30
a. Inverted surcharge 25.00 25.00
b. Period omitted after "1909" 12.50 12.50

Counterfeits exist.

Gen. Miguel García Granados, Birth Cent. (in 1909) — A39

1910, Feb. 11 *Perf. 14*

140 A39 6c bis & indigo .55 .40
a. Imperf., pair 55.00

Some sheets used for this issue contained a two-line watermark, "SPECIAL POSTAGE PAPER / LONDON." For surcharge see No. 143.

General Post Office — A40

Pres. Manuel Estrada Cabrera — A41

1911, June *Perf. 12*

141 A40 25c bl & blk .55 .25
a. Center inverted *1,750.* 900.00
142 A41 5p red & blk .65 .65
a. Center inverted 30.00 27.50

Nos. 116, 118 and 140 Surcharged in Black or Red:

h

i

j

1911 *Perf. 14*

143 A39 (h) 1c on 6c 25.00 9.75
a. Double surcharge 75.00 75.00
144 A30 (i) 2c on 5c (R) 1.60 .85
145 A32 (j) 6c on 10c 1.25 1.25
a. Double surcharge 50.00
Nos. 143-145 (3) 27.85 11.85

See watermark note after No. 140. Forgeries exist.

Nos. 119-121 Surcharged in Black:

k

l

m

1912, Sept.

147 A33 (k) 1c on 20c .40 .40
a. Inverted surcharge 12.50 12.50
b. Double surcharge 15.00 15.00
148 A34 (l) 2c on 50c .40 .40
a. Inverted surcharge 12.50 12.50
b. Double surcharge 12.50
c. Double inverted surcharge 25.00
149 A35 (m) 5c on 75c .80 .80
a. "191" for "1912" 7.50 7.50
b. Double surcharge 15.00 15.00
c. Inverted surcharge 10.00
Nos. 147-149 (3) 1.60 1.60

Forgeries exist.

Nos. 120, 122 and 123 Surcharged in Blue, Green or Black:

n

o

p

1913, July

151 A34 (n) 1c on 50c (Bl) .25 .25
a. Inverted surcharge 10.00
b. Double surcharge 17.50
c. Horiz. pair, imperf. btwn. 100.00
152 A36 (o) 6c on 1p (G) .30 .30
153 A37 (p) 12½c on 2p (Bk) .30 .30
a. Inverted surcharge 15.00 15.00
b. Double surcharge 40.00
c. Horiz. pair, imperf. btwn. 100.00
Nos. 151-153 (3) .85 .85

Forgeries exist.

Nos. 114 and 115 Surcharged in Black:

q

r

s

t

1916-17

154 A28 (q) 2c on 1c ('17) .25 .25
155 A28 (r) 6c on 1c .25 .25
156 A28 (s) 12½c on 1c .250 .25
157 A29 (t) 25c on 2c .25 .25
Nos. 154-157 (4) 3.25 1.00

Numerous errors of value and color, inverted and double surcharges and similar varieties are in the market. They were not regularly issued, but were surreptitiously made and sold.

Counterfeit surcharges abound.

"Liberty" and President Estrada Cabrera — A51

Estrada Cabrera and Quetzal — A52

1917, Mar. 15 *Perf. 14, 15*

158 A51 25c dp blue & brown .25 .20

Re-election of President Estrada Cabrera.

1918 *Perf. 12*

161 A52 1.50p dark blue .30 .25

Radio Station — A54

"Joaquina" Maternity Hospital — A55

"Estrada Cabrera" Vocational School — A56

National Emblem — A57

1919, May 3 *Perf. 14, 15*

162 A54 30c red & blk 2.75 .75
163 A55 60c ol grn & blk .80 .50
164 A56 90c red brn & blk .80 .75
165 A57 3p dp grn & blk 1.75 .50
Nos. 162-165 (4) 6.10 2.50

See Nos. 215, 227. For surcharges see Nos. 166-167, 179-185, 188, 195-198, 245-246, C8-C11, C21-C22.

No. 162 Surcharged

Blue Overprint and Black Surcharge

1920, Jan. **Unwmk.**

166 A54 2c on 30c red & blk .30 .25
a. Inverted surcharge 12.50 12.50
b. "1920" double 10.00 10.00
c. "1920" omitted 15.00 15.00
d. "2 centavos" omitted 20.00
e. Imperf, pair 100.00
f. Pair, imperf. btwn. 100.00

Nos. 123 and 163 Surcharged:

u

v

1920

167 A55 2c on 60c (Bk & R) .25 .25
a. Inverted surcharge 10.00 10.00
b. "1920" inverted 7.50 7.50
c. "1920" omitted 10.00 10.00
d. "1920" only 10.00
e. Double surcharge 25.00
168 A37 25c on 2p (Bk) .30 .25
a. "35" for "25" 10.00 10.00
b. Large "5" in "25" 10.00 10.00
c. Inverted surcharge 15.00 15.00
d. Double surcharge 25.00

A61

1920

169 A61 25c green .25 .20
a. Double overprint 50.00
b. Double overprint, inverted 75.00

See types A65-A66.

No. 119 Surcharged

1921, Apr.

170 A33 12½c on 20c .25 .20
a. Double surcharge 15.00
b. Inverted surcharge 15.00

No. 121 Surcharged

1921, Apr.

171 A35 50c on 75c lil & blk .50 .30
a. Double surcharge 22.50
b. Inverted surcharge 25.00 25.00

Mayan Stele at Quiriguá — A62

Monument to President Granados — A63

"La Penitenciaria" Bridge — A64

1921, Sept. 1 *Perf. 13½, 14, 15*

172 A62 1.50p blue & org .85 .25
173 A63 5p brown & grn 2.75 1.25
174 A64 15p black & ver 22.50 12.50
Nos. 172-174 (3) 26.10 14.00

See Nos. 216, 228, 229. For surcharges see Nos. 186-187, 189-191, 199-201, 207, 231, 247-251, C1-C5, C12, C23-C24.

A65

A66

Telegraph Stamps Overprinted or Surcharged in Black or Red

1921 *Perf. 14*

175 A65 25c green .25 .20
176 A66 12½c on 25c grn (R) .25 .20
177 A66 12½c on 25c grn 15.00 15.00
Nos. 175-177 (3) 15.50 15.40

Nos. 119, 163 and 164 Surcharged in Black or Red:

w

x

1922, Mar.

178 A33(w) 12½c on 20c .25 .25
a. Inverted surcharge 10.00
179 A55(w) 12½c on 60c (R) .50 .50
a. Inverted surcharge 25.00
180 A56(w) 12½c on 90c .50 .50
a. Inverted surcharge 25.00
181 A55(x) 25c on 60c 1.00 1.00
a. Inverted surcharge 20.00
182 A55(x) 25c on 60c (R) 125.00 125.00
183 A56(x) 25c on 90c 1.00 1.00
a. Inverted surcharge 25.00
184 A56(x) 25c on 90c (R) 4.00 4.00
Nos. 178-181,183-184 (6) 7.25 7.25

Counterfeits exist.

Nos. 165, 173-174 Surcharged in Red or Dark Blue

1922, May

185 A57 12½c on 3p grn & blk (R) .25 .25
186 A63 12½c on 5p brn & grn .50 .45
187 A64 12½c on 15p blk & ver .50 .45
Nos. 185-187 (3) 1.25 1.15

Nos. 165, 173-174 Surcharged in Red or Black

1922

188 A57 25c on 3p (I) (R) .20 .20
a. Type II .60 .60
b. Type III .60 .60
c. Type IV .30 .30
d. Inverted surcharge 40.00
e. Horiz. or vert. pair, imperf. btwn. (I) 125.00
189 A63 25c on 5p (I) 1.00 *2.00*
a. Type II 2.00 *3.00*
b. Type III 2.00 *3.00*
c. Type IV 1.00 *2.00*
190 A64 25c on 15p (I) 1.00 *1.50*
a. Type II 2.00 *3.00*
b. Type III 2.00 *3.00*
c. Type IV 1.00 *1.50*
191 A64 25c on 15p (I) (R) 22.50 *30.00*
a. Type II 40.00 *45.00*
b. Type III 45.00 45.00
c. Type IV 30.00 *35.00*
Nos. 188-191 (4) 24.70 *33.70*

Stamps of 1902-21 Surcharged in Dark Blue or Red

1922, Aug. **On Nos. 121-123**

192 A35 25c on 75c (V) .40 .40
a. Type VI .40 .40
b. Type VII 1.75 1.75
c. Type VIII 5.50 4.75
d. Type IX 6.50 6.00
193 A36 25c on 1p (V) .30 .30
a. Type VI .30 .30
b. Type VII 1.25 1.25
c. Type VIII 2.50 2.50
d. Type IX 4.00 3.50
e. Inverted surcharge 40.00
194 A37 25c on 2p (V) .45 .45
a. Type VI .45 .45
b. Type VII 1.25 1.25
c. Type VIII 4.00 4.00
d. Type IX 6.50 6.50

On Nos. 162-165

195 A54 25c on 30c (V) .45 .45
a. Type VI .45 .45
b. Type VII 1.25 1.25
c. Type VIII 5.50 5.50
d. Type IX 6.50 6.50
196 A55 25c on 60c (V) 1.00 *1.50*
a. Type VI 1.25 *1.50*
b. Type VII 6.25 *7.75*
c. Type VIII 8.50 *9.50*
d. Type IX 10.00 *11.00*
197 A56 25c on 90c (V) 1.00 *1.50*
a. Type VI 1.50 *2.00*
b. Type VII 6.00 *6.75*
c. Type VIII 8.50 *9.50*
d. Type IX 10.00 *11.00*
198 A57 25c on 3p (R) (V) .40 .40
a. Type VI .40 .40
b. Type VII 1.25 1.00
c. Type VIII 6.00 4.50
d. Type IX 6.50 6.00
e. Inverted surcharge 50.00

On Nos. 172-174

199 A62 25c on 1.50p (V) .30 .30
a. Type VI .30 .30
b. Type VII 1.25 1.00
c. Type VIII 3.00 3.00
d. Type IX 4.50 4.50
e. Inverted surcharge 40.00
200 A63 25c on 5p (V) .75 *.90*
a. Type VI .80 *1.00*
b. Type VII 3.00 *3.50*
c. Type VIII 5.50 *6.00*
d. Type IX 8.00 *8.50*
201 A64 25c on 15p (V) .85 *.90*
a. Type VI 1.50 1.50
b. Type VII 5.00 *5.50*
c. Type VIII 6.50 6.50
d. Type IX 12.00 12.00
Nos. 192-201 (10) 5.90 7.10

Centenary Palace — A69

National Palace at Antigua — A70

1922 *Perf. 14, 14½*

Printed by Waterlow & Sons

202 A69 12½c green .30 .20
a. Horiz. or vert. pair, imperf. btwn. 100.00
203 A70 25c brown .30 .20

See Nos. 211, 221, 234.

Columbus Theater A71

Quetzal A72

Granados Monument — A73

Litho. by Castillo Bros.

1924, Feb. *Perf. 12*

204 A71 50c rose .50 .20
a. Imperf., pair 7.50
b. Horiz. or vert. pair, imperf. btwn. 25.00
205 A72 1p dark green 2.25 .20
a. Imperf. vertically 15.00
b. Vert. pair, imperf. btwn. 20.00
c. Imperf., pair 7.50
206 A73 5p orange 1.25 .50
a. Imperf., pair 8.50
b. Horiz. pair, imperf. btwn. 20.00
Nos. 204-206 (3) 4.00 .90

For surcharges see Nos. 208-209.

Nos. 172 and 206 Surcharged

1924, July

207 A62 1p on 1.50p bl & org .30 .20
208 A73 1.25p on 5p orange .50 .50
a. "UN PESO 25 Cents." omitted 40.00
b. Horiz. pair, imperf. btwn. 25.00

#208 with two bars over "25 Cents."

1924

209 A73 1p on 5p orange .50 .50

Types of 1902-22 Issues

Engr. by Perkins Bacon & Co.

1924, Aug. **Re-engraved** *Perf. 14*

210 A31 6c bister .20 .20
211 A70 25c brown .20 .20
212 A34 50c red .25 .20
213 A36 1p orange brn .25 .20
214 A37 2p orange .35 .25
215 A57 3p deep green 2.00 .50
216 A64 15p black 5.00 2.75
Nos. 210-216 (7) 8.25 4.30

The designs of the stamps of 1924 differ from those of the 1902-22 issues in many details which are too minute to illustrate. The re-engraved issue may be readily distinguished by the imprint "Perkins Bacon & Co. Ld. Londres."

Pres. Justo Rufino Barrios A74

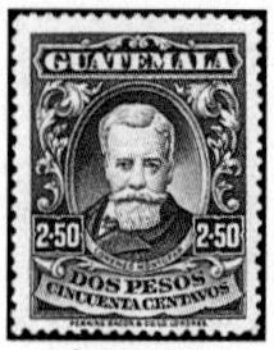
Lorenzo Montúfar A75

1924, Aug.

217 A74 1.25p ultra .20 .20
218 A75 2.50p dk violet 1.00 .25

See Nos. 224, 226. For surcharges see Nos. 232, C6, C20.

Aurora Park — A76

National Post Office — A77

National Observatory A78

Types of 1921-24 Re-engraved and New Designs Dated 1926

Engraved by Waterlow & Sons, Ltd.

1926, July-Aug. *Perf. 12½*

219 A31 6c ocher .20 .20
220 A76 12½c green .20 .20
221 A70 25c brown .20 .20
222 A77 50c red .20 .20
223 A36 1p orange brn .20 .20
224 A74 1.50p dk blue .20 .20
225 A78 2p orange 1.25 1.00
226 A75 2.50p dk violet 1.50 1.25
227 A57 3p dark green .45 .20
228 A63 5p brown vio 1.00 .40
229 A64 15p black 6.00 2.75
Nos. 219-229 (11) 11.40 6.80

These stamps may be distinguished from those of the same designs in preceding issues by the imprint "Waterlow & Sons, Limited, Londres," the date, "1926," and the perforation.

See Nos. 233, 242. For surcharge see No. 230.

Nos. 225-226, 228 Surcharged in Various Colors

1928

230 A78 ½c on 2p (Bl) .65 .50
a. Inverted surcharge 12.50
231 A63 ½c on 5p (Bk) .35 .20
a. Inverted surcharge 10.00 10.00
b. Double surcharge 50.00
c. Blue surcharge 45.00 45.00
d. Blue and black surcharge 50.00 50.00
232 A75 1c on 2.50p (R) .35 .20
b. Double surcharge 50.00
Nos. 230-232 (3) 1.35 .90

Barrios — A79

Montúfar — A80

Granados A81

General Orellana A82

Coat of Arms of Guatemala City — A83

Engraved by T. De la Rue & Co.

1929, Jan. *Perf. 14*

233	A78	½c yellow grn	.75	.20
234	A70	1c dark brown	.25	.20
235	A79	2c deep blue	.25	.20
236	A80	3c dark violet	.20	.20
237	A81	4c orange	.25	.20
238	A82	5c dk carmine	.50	.20
239	A31	10c brown	.40	.20
240	A36	15c ultra	.50	.20
241	A29	25c brown org	1.00	.25
242	A76	30c green	.90	.30
243	A32	50c pale rose	2.00	.60
244	A83	1q black	3.00	.40
		Nos. 233-244 (12)	10.00	3.15

Nos. 233, 234 and 239 to 243 differ from the illustrations in many minor details, particularly in the borders.

See No. 300 for bisect of No. 235. For overprints and surcharges see Nos. 297, C13, C17-C18, C25-C26, C28, E1, RA17-RA18.

No. 227 Surcharged in Black or Red

1929, Dec. 28 *Perf. 12½, 13*

245 A57 3c on 3p dk grn (Bk) 1.25 *1.90*
a. Inverted surcharge 15.00 15.00
246 A57 5c on 3p dk grn (R) 1.25 *1.90*
a. Inverted surcharge 15.00 15.00

Inauguration of the Eastern Railroad connecting Guatemala and El Salvador.

No. 229 Surcharged in Red

1930, Mar. 30 **Unwmk.**

247	A64	1c on 15p black	1.25	*1.40*
248	A64	2c on 15p black	1.25	*1.40*
249	A64	3c on 15p black	1.25	*1.40*
250	A64	5c on 15p black	1.25	*1.40*
251	A64	15c on 15p black	1.25	1.40
		Nos. 247-251 (5)	6.25	*7.00*

Opening of Los Altos electric railway.

Hydroelectric Dam — A85

Los Altos Railway A86

Railroad Station A87

1930, Mar. 30 **Typo.** *Perf. 12*

252 A85 2c brn vio & blk 1.40 *1.90*
a. Horiz. pair, imperf. btwn. 125.00
253 A86 3c dp red & blk 2.75 *2.75*
a. Vert. pair, imperf. btwn. 125.00
254 A87 5c buff & dk bl 2.75 *2.75*
Nos. 252-254 (3) 6.90 *7.40*

Opening of Los Altos electric railway. Exist imperf.

Mayan Stele at Quiriguá — A91

1932, Apr. 8 **Engr.**

258 A91 3c carmine rose 1.90 .40

See Nos. 302-303.

Flag of the Race, Columbus and Tecum Uman A92

1933, Aug. 3 **Litho.** *Perf. 12½*

259	A92	½c dark green	.75	*.75*
260	A92	1c dull brown	1.25	1.10
261	A92	2c deep blue	1.25	1.10
262	A92	3c dull violet	1.25	.75
263	A92	5c rose	1.25	1.10
		Nos. 259-263 (5)	5.75	*4.80*

Day of the Race and 441st anniv. of the sailing of Columbus from Palos, Spain, Aug. 3, 1492, on his 1st voyage to the New World.

The 3c and 5c exist imperf.

Birthplace of Barrios A93

View of San Lorenzo A94

Justo Rufino Barrios A95

National Emblem and Locomotive A96

General Post Office — A97

Telegraph Building and Barrios A98

Military Academy A99

National Police Headquarters — A100

Jorge Ubico and J. R. Barrios A101

1935, July 19 **Photo.**

264	A93	½c yel grn & mag	.40	*.45*
265	A94	1c org red & pck bl	.40	*.45*
266	A95	2c orange & blk	.40	*.55*
267	A96	3c car rose & pck bl	4.50	2.25
268	A97	4c pck bl & org red	4.50	*10.00*
269	A98	5c bl grn & brn	3.25	*4.25*
270	A99	10c slate grn & rose lake	4.50	*5.50*
271	A100	15c ol grn & org brn	4.50	*4.75*
272	A101	25c scarlet & bl	4.50	*4.75*
		Nos. 264-272 (9)	26.95	*32.95*

General Barrios. See Nos. C29-C31.

Lake Atitlán A102

Quetzal A103

Legislative Building — A104

1935, Oct. 10

273	A102	1c brown & crim	.25	.20
274	A103	3c rose car & pck grn	.70	.20
275	A103	3c red org & pck grn	.70	.20
276	A104	4c brt bl & dp rose	.35	.20
		Nos. 273-276 (4)	2.00	.80

See No. 277. For surcharges see Nos. B1-B3.

No. 273 perforated diagonally through the center

1936, June *Perf. 12½x12*

277 A102 (½c) brown & crimson .20 .20
a. Unsevered pair .50 .60

Bureau of Printing — A105

Map of Guatemala A106

1936, Sept. 24 *Perf. 12½*

278 A105 ½c green & pur .25 .20
279 A106 5c blue & dk brn .90 .20

For surcharge see No. B4.

Quetzal A107

Union Park, Quezaltenango A108

Gen. Jorge Ubico on Horseback A109

1c, Tower of the Reformer. 3c, National Post Office. 4c, Government Building, Retalhuleu. 5c, Legislative Palace entrance. 10c, Custom House. 15c, Aurora Airport Custom House. 25c, National Fair. 50c, Residence of Presidential Guard. 1.50q, General Ubico, portrait standing, no cap.

1937, May 20

280	A107	½c pck bl & car rose	.70	*.45*
281	A107	1c ol gray & red brn	.70	.35
282	A108	2c vio & car rose	.60	.35
283	A108	3c brn vio & brt bl	.50	.25
284	A108	4c yel & dl ol grn	2.00	*2.00*
285	A107	5c crim & brt vio	2.10	1.75
286	A107	10c mag & brn blk	3.00	*3.50*
287	A108	15c ultra & cop red	2.50	*3.50*
288	A108	25c red org & vio	3.00	*3.75*
289	A108	50c dk grn & org red	4.50	*5.50*
290	A109	1q magenta & blk	*22.50*	*22.50*
291	A109	1.50q red brn & blk	*22.50*	*22.50*
		Nos. 280-291 (12)	*64.60*	*66.40*

Second term of President Ubico.

Mayan Calendar A119

Natl. Flower (White Nun Orchid) A120

Quetzal — A121

Map of Guatemala A122

1939, Sept. 7 *Perf. 13x12, 12½*

292	A119	½c grn & red brn	*.25*	.20
293	A120	2c bl & gray blk	*1.50*	.30
294	A121	3c red org & turq grn	*2.00*	.55
295	A121	3c ol bis & turq grn	*2.00*	.55
296	A122	5c blue & red	*1.75*	1.75
		Nos. 292-296 (5)	7.50	3.35

For overprints see Nos. 324, C157.

No. 235 Surcharged with New Value in Red

1939, Sept. *Perf. 14*

297 A79 1c on 2c deep blue .25 .20

Stamps of 1929 Surcharged in Blue:

y

z

1940, June

298 A29 (y) 1c on 25c brn org .25 .20
299 A32 (z) 5c on 50c pale rose (bar 10x¾mm) .25 .20
a. Bar 12½x2mm .30 .20
b. Bar 12½x1mm 50.00 5.00

SEMI-POSTAL STAMPS

Regular Issues of 1935-36 Surcharged in Blue or Red similar to illustration

1937, Mar. 15 Unwmk. *Perf. 12½*

B1 A102 1c + 1c brn & crim .75 *1.00*
B2 A103 3c + 1c rose car & pck grn .75 *1.00*
B3 A103 3c + 1c red org & pck grn .75 *1.00*
B4 A106 5c + 1c bl & dk brn (R) .75 *1.00*
Nos. B1-B4 (4) 3.00 *4.00*

1st Phil. Exhib. held in Guatemala, Mar. 15-20.

AIR POST STAMPS

Surcharged in Red on No. 229

1929, May 20 Unwmk. *Perf. 12½*

C1 A64 3c on 15p blk 1.10 *1.40*
C2 A64 5c on 15p blk .55 .45
C3 A64 15c on 15p blk 1.50 .45
a. Double surcharge (G & R) 100.00
C4 A64 20c on 15p blk 2.25 2.25
a. Inverted surcharge 100.00
b. Double surcharge 100.00

Surcharged in Red on No. 216

1929, May 20 *Perf. 14*

C5 A64 5c on 15p black 3.25 2.25
Nos. C1-C5 (5) 8.65 6.80

Surcharged in Black on No. 218

1929, Oct. 9

C6 A75 3c on 2.50p dk vio 1.00 1.00

Airplane and Mt. Agua AP3

1930, June 4 Litho. *Perf. 12½*

C7 AP3 6c rose red .60 .40
a. Double impression 25.00 25.00
b. Imperf., pair 350.00

For overprint see No. C14.

Nos. 227, 229 Surcharged in Black or Red

1930, Dec. 9 *Perf. 12½*

C8 A57 1c on 3p grn (Bk) .40 .40
a. Double surcharge 100.00
C9 A57 2c on 3p grn (Bk) 1.10 *1.50*
C10 A57 3c on 3p grn (R) 1.10 *1.50*
C11 A57 4c on 3p grn (R) 1.10 *1.50*
C12 A64 10c on 15p blk (R) 5.00 *5.00*
a. Double surcharge 125.00
Nos. C8-C12 (5) 8.70 *9.90*

No. 237 Overprinted

1931, May 19 *Perf. 14*

C13 A81 4c orange .40 .30
a. Double overprint 40.00 *50.00*

No. C7 Overprinted

Perf. 12½

C14 AP3 6c rose red 1.50 1.40
a. On No. C7a 30.00 30.00
b. Inverted overprint 7.00 *7.00*

Nos. 240, 242 Overprinted in Red

1931, Oct. 21 *Perf. 14*

C15 A36 15c ultra 2.00 .25
a. Double overprint 125.00 125.00
C16 A76 30c green 3.00 .95
a. Double overprint 75.00 75.00

Nos. 235-236 Overprinted in Red or Green

1931, Dec. 5

C17 A79 2c dp bl (R) 2.50 *3.00*
C18 A80 3c dk vio (G) 2.50 *3.00*

No. 240 Overprinted in Red

C19 A36 15c ultra 2.75 *3.00*

Nos. C17-C19 were issued in connection with the 1st postal flight from Barrios to Miami.

No. 224 Surcharged in Red

1932-33 *Perf. 12½*

C20 A74 2c on 1.50p dk bl .80 .55

Nos. 227, 229 Surcharged in Violet, Red or Blue

C21 A57 3c on 3p grn (V) .80 .25
a. Inverted surcharge 45.00 45.00
b. Vert. pair, imperf. horiz. 900.00
C22 A57 3c on 3p grn (R) .80 .25
C23 A64 10c on 15p blk (R) 7.75 6.25
b. First "I" of "Interior" missing 10.00 10.00
C24 A64 15c on 15p blk (Bl) 9.00 8.50
a. First "I" of "Interior" missing 15.00 15.00
Nos. C20-C24 (5) 19.15 15.80

Issued: #C22, 1/1/33; others, 2/11/32.

No. 237 Overprinted in Green

1933, Jan. 1 *Perf. 14*

C25 A81 4c orange .40 .35
a. Double overprint 40.00 40.00

Nos. 235, 238 and 240 Overprinted in Red or Black

1934, Aug. 7

C26 A82 5c dk car (Bk) 1.50 .25
C27 A36 15c ultra (R) 1.50 .25

Overprinted in Red

C28 A79 2c deep blue .55 .20

View of Port Barrios — AP7

Designs: 15c, Tomb of Barrios. 30c, Equestrian Statue of Barrios.

1935, July 19 Photo. *Perf. 12½*

C29 AP7 10c yel brn & pck grn 6.00 4.50
C30 AP7 15c gray & brn 1.50 *1.75*
C31 AP7 30c car rose & bl vio 1.50 1.25
Nos. C29-C31 (3) 9.00 7.50

Birth cent. of Gen. Justo Rufino Barrios.

Lake Amatitlán AP10

Designs: Nos. C36, C37, C45, C46. Different views of Lake Amatitlan. 3c, Port Barrios. No. C34, C35, Ruins of Port San Felipe. 10c, Port Livingston. No. C39, C40, Port San José. No. C41, C42, View of Atitlan. No. C43, C44, Aurora Airport.

Overprinted with Quetzal in Green

1935-37 Size: 37x17mm

C32 AP10 2c org brn .25 .20
C33 AP10 3c blue .25 .20
C34 AP10 4c black .25 .20
C35 AP10 4c ultra ('37) .25 .20
C36 AP10 6c yel grn .25 .20
C37 AP10 6c blk vio ('37) 4.00 .20
C38 AP10 10c claret .50 .25
C39 AP10 15c red org .65 .40
C40 AP10 15c yel grn ('37) .65 .65
C41 AP10 30c olive grn 6.00 6.50
C42 AP10 30c ol bis ('37) .75 .50
C43 AP10 50c rose vio 17.50 15.00
C44 AP10 50c Prus bl ('36) 4.00 3.00
C45 AP10 1q scarlet 17.50 20.00
C46 AP10 1q car ('36) 4.50 3.00
Nos. C32-C46 (15) 57.30 50.50

Issue dates follow No. C69.

For overprints and surcharges see Nos. C70-C79, CB1-CB2.

Central Park, Antigua AP11

Designs: 1c, Guatemala City. 2c, Central Park, Guatemala City. 3c, Monastery. Nos. C50-C51, Mouth of Dulce River. Nos. C52-C53, Plaza Barrios. Nos. C54-C55, Los Proceres Monument. No. C56, Central Park, Antigua. No. C57, Dulce River. Nos. C58-C59, Quezaltenango. Nos. C60-C61, Ruins at Antigua. Nos. C62-C63, Dock at Port Barrios. Nos. C64-C65, Port San Jose. Nos. C66-C67, Aurora Airport. 2.50q, Island off Atlantic Coast. 5q, Atlantic Coast view.

Overprinted with Quetzal in Green

Size: 34x15mm

C47 AP11 1c yel brn .25 .20
C48 AP11 2c vermilion .25 .20
C49 AP11 3c magenta .50 .25
C50 AP11 4c org yel ('36) 1.75 1.40
C51 AP11 4c car lake ('37) 1.00 .75
C52 AP11 5c dl bl .25 .20
C53 AP11 5c org ('37) .25 .20
C54 AP11 10c red brn .50 .35
C55 AP11 10c ol grn ('37) .50 .30
C56 AP11 15c rose red .25 .20
C57 AP11 15c ver ('37) .25 .20
C58 AP11 20c ultra 2.50 *3.00*
C59 AP11 20c dp cl ('37) .50 .25
C60 AP11 25c gray blk 3.00 *3.50*
C61 AP11 25c bl grn ('37) .45 .25
a. Quetzal omitted *1,100.*
C62 AP11 30c yel grn 1.50 1.50
C63 AP11 30c rose red ('37) 1.00 .20
C64 AP11 50c car rose 7.00 *8.00*
C65 AP11 50c pur ('36) 6.50 *7.50*
C66 AP11 1q dk bl 22.50 *25.00*
C67 AP11 1q dk grn ('36) 7.50 7.50

Size: 46x20mm

C68 AP11 2.50q rose red & ol grn ('36) 5.00 3.00
C69 AP11 5q org & ind ('36) 7.00 4.00
a. Quetzal omitted 1,500. 1,250.
Nos. C47-C69 (23) 70.20 *67.95*

Issued: #C32-C69, 11/1/35; 10/1/36; 1/1/37.

Value for No. C61a is for a sound copy.

For overprints and surcharges see Nos. C80-C91, CB3-CB4.

Types of Air Post Stamps, 1935 Overprinted with Airplane in Blue

2c, Quezaltenango. 3c, Lake Atitlan. 4c, Progressive Colony, Lake Amatitlan. 6c, Carmen Hill. 10c, Relief map. 15c, National University. 30c, Espana Plaza. 50c, Police Station, Aurora Airport. 75c, Amphitheater, Aurora Airport. 1q, Aurora Airport.

1937, May 18

Center in Brown Black

C70 AP10 2c carmine .25 .20
C71 AP10 3c blue 1.00 *1.25*
C72 AP10 4c citron .25 .20
C73 AP10 6c yel grn .35 .25
C74 AP10 10c red vio 2.00 *2.25*
C75 AP10 15c orange 1.50 1.00
C76 AP10 30c ol grn 3.75 3.00
C77 AP10 50c pck bl 5.00 4.25
C78 AP10 75c dk vio 10.00 *11.00*
C79 AP10 1q dp rose 11.00 *12.00*
Nos. C70-C79 (10) 35.10 *35.40*

Overprinted with Airplane in Black

1c, 7th Ave., Guatemala City. 2c, Los Proceres Monument. 3c, Natl. Printing Office. 5c, Natl. Museum. 10c, Central Park. 15c, Escuintla. 20c, Motorcycle Police. 25c, Slaughterhouse, Escuintla. 30c, Exhibition

Hall. 50c, Barrios Plaza. 1q, Polytechnic School. 1.50q, Aurora Airport.

Size: 33x15mm

C80	AP11	1c yel brn & brt bl	.25	.20
C81	AP11	2c crim & dp vio	.25	.20
C82	AP11	3c red vio & red brn	.50	.50
C83	AP11	5c pck grn & cop red	4.00	3.00
C84	AP11	10c car & grn	1.25	1.00
C85	AP11	15c rose & dl ol grn	.50	.25
C86	AP11	20c ultra & blk	3.00	1.75
C87	AP11	25c dk gray & scar	2.50	2.50
C88	AP11	30c grn & dp vio	1.25	1.25
C89	AP11	50c magenta & ultra	10.00	*12.00*

Size: 42x19mm

C90	AP11	1q ol grn & red vio	10.00	*12.00*
C91	AP11	1.50q scar & ol brn	10.00	*12.00*
		Nos. C80-C91 (12)	43.50	*46.65*

Second term of President Ubico.

Souvenir Sheet

AP12

1938, Jan. 10 *Perf. 12½*

C92	AP12	Sheet of 4	3.25	3.25
a.		15c George Washington	.60	.60
b.		4c Franklin D. Roosevelt	.60	.60
c.		4c Map of the Americas	.60	.60
d.		15c Pan American Union Building, Washington, DC	.30	.30

150th anniv. of US Constitution.

President Arosemena, Panama AP13

Flags of Central American Countries — AP19

Designs: 2c, Pres. Cortés Castro, Costa Rica. 3c, Pres. Somoza, Nicaragua. 4c, Pres. Carias Andino, Honduras. 5c, Pres. Martinez, El Salvador. 10c, Pres. Ubico, Guatemala.

1938, Nov. 20 **Unwmk.**

C93	AP13	1c org & ol brn	.25	.20
C94	AP13	2c scar, pale pink & sl grn	.30	.20
C95	AP13	3c grn, buff & ol brn	.40	.30
C96	AP13	4c dk cl, pale lil & brn	.55	.35
C97	AP13	5c bis, pale grn & ol brn	.50	*.60*
C98	AP13	10c ultra, pale bl & brn	1.00	*1.25*
		Nos. C93-C98 (6)	3.00	*2.90*

Souvenir Sheet

C99	AP19	Sheet of 6	2.50	2.50
a.		1c Guatemala	.25	.25
b.		2c El Salvador	.25	.25
c.		3c Honduras	.35	.35
d.		4c Nicaragua	.45	.45
e.		5c Costa Rica	.45	.45
f.		10c Panama	.75	.75

1st Central American Phil. Exhib., Guatemala City, Nov. 20-27.

For overprints see Nos. CO1-CO7.

La Merced Church, Antigua AP20

Designs: 2c, Ruins of Christ School, Antigua. 3c, Aurora Airport. 4c, Drill ground, Guatemala City. 5c, Cavalry barracks. 6c, Palace of Justice. 10c, Customhouse, San José. 15c, Communications Building, Retalhuleu. 30c, Municipal Theater, Quezaltenango. 50c, Customhouse, Retalhuleu. 1q, Departmental Building.

Inscribed "Aéreo Interior" Overprinted with Quetzal in Green

1939, Feb. 14

C100	AP20	1c ol bis & chnt	.20	.20
C101	AP20	2c rose red & sl grn	.20	.20
C102	AP20	3c dl bl & bis	.25	.20
C103	AP20	4c rose pink & yel grn	.25	.20
C104	AP20	5c brn lake & brt ultra	.30	.20
C105	AP20	6c org & gray brn	.35	.20
C106	AP20	10c bis brn & gray blk	.50	.20
C107	AP20	15c dl vio & blk	.75	.20
C108	AP20	30c dp bl & dk car	1.10	.25
C109	AP20	50c org & brt vio	1.50	.40
a.		Quetzal omitted		*1,750.*
C110	AP20	1q yel grn & brt ultra	2.50	1.25
		Nos. C100-C110 (11)	7.90	3.50

See Nos. C111-C122. For overprint and surcharge see No. C124, C132.

1939, Feb. 14

Designs: 1c, Mayan Altar, Aurora Park. 2c, Sanitation Building. 3c, Lake Amatitlan. 4c, Lake Atitlan. 5c, Tamazulapa River bridge. 10c, Los proceres Monument. 15c, Palace of Captains General. 20c, Church on Carmen Hill. 25c, Barrios Park. 30c, Mayan Altar. 50c, Charles III fountain. 1q, View of Antigua.

Inscribed "Aéreo International" or "Aérea Exterior"

Overprinted with Quetzal in Green

C111	AP20	1c ol grn & gldn brn	.20	.20
C112	AP20	2c lt grn & blk	.30	.20
C113	AP20	3c ultra & cob bl	.20	.20
C114	AP20	4c org brn & yel grn	.20	.20
C115	AP20	5c sage grn & red org	.35	.20
C116	AP20	10c lake & sl blk	1.75	.20
C117	AP20	15c ultra & brt rose	1.75	.20
C118	AP20	20c yel grn & ap grn	.60	.20
C119	AP20	25c dl vio & lt ol grn	.60	.20
C120	AP20	30c dl rose & blk	.80	.20
C121	AP20	50c scar & brt yel	1.50	.20
C122	AP20	1q org & yel grn	2.50	.35
		Nos. C111-C122 (12)	10.75	2.55

No. 240 Overprinted in Carmine

1940, Apr. 14 *Perf. 14*

C123	A36	15c ultra	.60	.25

Pan American Union, 50th anniversary.

AIR POST SEMI-POSTAL STAMPS

Air Post Stamps of 1937 Surcharged in Red or Blue

1937, Mar. 15 **Unwmk.** *Perf. 12½*

CB1	AP10	4c + 1c ultra (R)	.90	*1.25*
CB2	AP10	6c + 1c blk vio (R)	.90	*1.25*
CB3	AP11	10c + 1c ol grn (Bl)	.90	*1.25*
CB4	AP11	15c + 1c ver (Bl)	.90	*1.25*
		Nos. CB1-CB4 (4)	3.60	*5.00*

1st Phil. Exhib. held in Guatemala, Mar. 15-20.

AIR POST OFFICIAL STAMPS

Nos. C93-C98 Overprinted in Black

1939, Apr. 29 **Unwmk.** *Perf. 12½*

CO1	AP13	1c org & ol brn	1.10	1.10
CO2	AP13	2c multi	1.10	1.10
CO3	AP13	3c multi	1.10	1.10
CO4	AP13	4c multi	1.10	1.10
CO5	AP13	5c multi	1.10	1.10
CO6	AP13	10c multi	1.10	1.10
		Nos. CO1-CO6 (6)	6.60	6.60

No. C99 with Same Overprint on each Stamp

1939

CO7	AP19	Sheet of 6	.375	3.75
a.		1c yel org, blue & blk	.60	.60
b.		2c lake, org, blue & blk	.60	.60
c.		3c olive, blue & orange	.60	.60
d.		4c dk claret, bl, org & blk	.60	.60
e.		5c grnsh bl, bl, red, org & blk	.60	.60
f.		10c olive bister, red & org	.60	.60

SPECIAL DELIVERY STAMPS

No. 237 Overprinted in Red

1940, June **Unwmk.** *Perf. 14*

E1	A81	4c orange	1.50	.35

No. E1 paid for express service by motorcycle messenger between Guatemala City and Coban.

OFFICIAL STAMPS

O1

National Emblem — O2

1902, Dec. 18 **Typeset** *Perf. 12*

O1	O1	1c green	5.50	3.50
O2	O1	2c carmine	5.50	3.50
O3	O1	5c ultra	5.50	2.75
O4	O1	10c brown violet	7.50	2.75
O5	O1	25c orange	7.50	2.75
a.		Horiz. pair, imperf. between	100.00	
		Nos. O1-O5 (5)	31.50	15.25

Nos. O1-O5 printed on thin paper with sheet watermark "AMERICAN LINEN BOND." Nos. O1-O3 also printed on thick paper with sheet watermark "ROYAL BANK BOND." Values are for copies that do not show the watermark. Counterfeits of Nos. O1-O5 exist.

During the years 1912 to 1926 the Post Office Department perforated the word "OFICIAL" on limited quantities of the following stamps: Nos. 114-123, 132, 141-149, 151-153, 158, 202, 210-229 and RA2. The perforating was done in blocks of four stamps at a time and was of two types.

A rubber handstamp "OFICIAL" was also used during the same period and was applied in violet, red, blue or black to stamps No. 117-118, 121-123, 163-165, 172 and 202-218.

Both perforating and handstamping were done in the post office at Guatemala City and use of the stamps was limited to that city.

1929, Jan. **Engr.** *Perf. 14*

O6	O2	1c pale grnsh bl	.30	.30
O7	O2	2c dark brown	.30	.30
O8	O2	3c green	.30	.30
O9	O2	4c deep violet	.40	.35
O10	O2	5c brown car	.40	.35
O11	O2	10c brown orange	.70	.70
O12	O2	25c dark blue	1.40	1.10
		Nos. O6-O12 (7)	3.80	3.40

POSTAL TAX STAMPS

National Emblem — PT1

Perf. 13½, 14, 15

1919, May 3 **Engr.** **Unwmk.**

RA1	PT1	12½c carmine	.30	.20

Tax for rebuilding post offices.

G. P. O. and Telegraph Building — PT2

1927, Nov. 10 **Typo.** *Perf. 14*

RA2	PT2	1c olive green	.55	.25

Tax to provide a fund for building a post office in Guatemala City.

No. RA2 Overprinted in Green

1936, June 30

RA3	PT2	1c olive green	.70	.55

Liberal revolution, 65th anniversary.

No. RA2 Overprinted in Blue

1936, Sept. 15

RA4	PT2	1c olive green	.55	.55

115th anniv. of the Independence of Guatemala.

No. RA2 Overprinted in Red Brown

1936, Nov. 15
RA5 PT2 1c olive green .55 .45

National Fair.

No. RA2 Overprinted in Red

1937, Mar. 15
RA6 PT2 1c olive green .55 .55

No. RA2 Overprinted in Blue

1938, Jan. 10 ***Perf. 14x14½***
RA7 PT2 1c olive green .30 .25
a. "1937-1939" omitted 110.00

150th anniv. of the US Constitution.

No. RA2 Overprinted in Blue or Red

1938 ***Perf. 14***
RA8 PT2 1c olive green (Bl) .40 .30
RA9 PT2 1c olive green (R) .40 .30

No. RA2 Overprinted in Violet

1938, Nov. 20
RA10 PT2 1c olive green .40 .25

1st Central American Philatelic Exposition.

No. RA2 Overprinted in Green or Black

1939
RA11 PT2 1c olive green (G) .40 .25
RA12 PT2 1c olive green (Bk) .40 .25

No. RA2 Overprinted in Violet or Brown

1940
RA13 PT2 1c olive green (V) .40 .25
RA14 PT2 1c olive green (Br) .40 .25

No. RA2 Overprinted in Red

1940, Apr. 14
RA15 PT2 1c olive green .40 .25

Pan American Union, 50th anniversary.

HAITI

'hā-tē

LOCATION — Western part of Hispaniola
GOVT. — Republic
AREA — 10,700 sq. mi.
POP. — 5,198,000 (est. 1984)
CAPITAL — Port-au-Prince

100 Centimes = 1 Piaster (1906)
100 Centimes = 1 Gourde

Watermark

Wmk. 131 — RH

Liberty Head — A1

A3

A4

On A3 (#18, 19) there are crossed lines of dots on face. On A4 the "5" is 3mm wide, on A1 2½mm wide.

1881 **Unwmk.** **Typo.** ***Imperf.***
1 A1 1c vermilion, *yelsh* 7.00 4.50
2 A1 2c dk violet, *pale lil* 9.00 4.50
3 A1 3c bister, *pale bis* 16.00 5.00
4 A1 5c green, *grnsh* 27.50 8.00
5 A1 7c blue, *grysh* 18.00 3.00
6 A1 20c red brown, *yelsh* 67.50 20.00
Nos. 1-6 (6) 145.00 45.00

Nos. 1-6 were printed from plate I, Nos. 7-13 from plates II and III.

1882 ***Perf. 13½***
7 A1 1c ver, *yelsh* 4.50 1.50
c. Horiz. pair, imperf. btwn. 190.00
d. Vert. pair imperf. btwn. 175.00 150.00
8 A1 2c dk vio, *pale lil* 7.50 2.25
a. 2c dark violet 9.00 5.50
b. 2c red violet, *pale lilac* 6.75 2.60
c. Horiz. pair, imperf. vert. 150.00
d. Vert. pair, imperf. horiz. 150.00
e. Horiz. pair, imperf. between 175.00 175.00
9 A1 3c bister, *pale bis* 9.00 2.50
10 A1 5c grn, *grnsh* 6.50 1.00
a. 5c yellow green, *greenish* 5.50 1.00
b. 5c deep green, *greenish* 5.50 1.00
c. Horiz. pair, imperf. vert. 250.00
d. Horiz. or vert. pair, imperf. btwn. 175.00
11 A1 7c blue, *grysh* 8.25 1.50
a. Horiz. pair, imperf. between
12 A1 7c ultra, *grysh* 13.00 2.50
a. Vert. pair, imperf. between
b. Horiz. pair, imperf. vert.
13 A1 20c pale brn, *yelsh* 6.50 1.40
a. 20c red brown, *yellowish* 13.50 2.25
b. Horiz. pair, imperf. vert 140.00
c. Vert. pair, imperf. horiz. 160.00
d. Horiz. or vert. pair, imperf. btwn. 175.00 160.00
Nos. 7-13 (7) 55.25 12.65

Stamps perf. 14, 16 are postal forgeries.

1886-87 ***Perf. 13½***
18 A3 1c vermilion, *yelsh* 4.50 1.40
a. Horiz. pair, imperf. vert. 175.00
b. Horiz. pair, imperf. between 175.00 175.00
19 A3 2c dk violet, *lilac* 35.00 3.50
20 A4 5c green ('87) 13.50 1.75
Nos. 18-20 (3) 53.00 6.65

General Louis Etienne Félicité Salomon — A5

1887 **Engr.** ***Perf. 14***
21 A5 1c lake .30 .30
22 A5 2c violet .80 .60
23 A5 3c blue .60 .40
24 A5 5c green 3.75 .40
a. Double impression —
Nos. 21-24 (4) 5.45 1.70

Some experts believe the imperfs. of Nos. 21-24 are plate proofs. Value per pair, $30.

No. 23 Handstamp Surcharged in Red

1890
25 A5 2c on 3c blue .50 .40

This surcharge being handstamped is to be found double, inverted, etc. This applies to succeeding surcharged issues.

Coat of Arms A7

Coat of Arms (Leaves Drooping) A9

1891 ***Perf. 13***
26 A7 1c violet .40 .30
27 A7 2c blue .60 .30
28 A7 3c gray lilac .80 .40
a. 3c slate .80 .50
29 A7 5c orange 2.75 .30
30 A7 7c red 6.00 2.25
Nos. 26-30 (5) 10.55 3.55

Nos. 26-30 exist imperf. Value of unused pairs, each $30.
The 2c, 3c and 7c exist imperf. vertically.

No. 28 Surcharged Like No. 25 in Red

1892
31 A7 2c on 3c gray lilac 1.00 .80
a. 2c on 3c slate 1.00 .80

1892-95 **Engr., Litho. (20c)** ***Perf. 14***
32 A9 1c lilac .30 .20
a. Imperf., pair
b. Double impression —
33 A9 2c deep blue .40 .20
34 A9 3c gray .60 .40
35 A9 5c orange 2.00 .30
36 A9 7c red .30 .20
a. Imperf., pair 5.00
37 A9 20c brown 1.40 .85
Nos. 32-37 (6) 5.00 2.15

Nos. 32, 33, 35 exist in horiz. pairs, imperf. vert., Nos. 33, 35, in vert. pairs, imperf. horiz.

1896 **Engr.** ***Perf. 13½***
38 A9 1c light blue .25 *.55*
39 A9 2c red brown .45 *.90*
40 A9 3c lilac brown .25 *.90*
41 A9 5c slate green .25 *.90*
42 A9 7c dark gray .40 *1.25*
43 A9 20c orange .45 *1.75*
Nos. 38-43 (6) 2.05 6.25

Nos. 32-37 are 23¾mm high, Nos. 38-43 23¼mm to 23½mm. The "C" is closed on Nos. 32-37, open on Nos. 38-43. Other differences exist. The stamps of the two issues may be readily distinguished by their colors and perfs.
Nos. 38-43 exist imperf. and in horiz. pairs, imperf. vert. The 1c, 3c, 5c, 7c exist in vert. pairs, imperf. horiz. or imperf. between. The 5c, 7c exist in horiz. pairs, imperf. between. Value of unused pairs, $9 and up.

#37, 43 Surcharged Like #25 in Red

1898
44 A9 2c on 20c brown 1.00 .75
45 A9 2c on 20c orange .60 .50

No. 45 exists in various part perf. varieties.

Coat of Arms — A11

1898 **Wmk. 131** ***Perf. 11***
46 A11 1c ultra 1.10 .75
47 A11 2c brown carmine .40 .20
48 A11 3c dull violet .95 .60
49 A11 5c dark green .40 .25
50 A11 7c gray 2.25 1.60
51 A11 20c orange 2.25 1.60
Nos. 46-51 (6) 7.35 5.00

All values exist imperforate. They are plate proofs.

Pres. T. Augustin Simon Sam — A12

Coat of Arms — A13

1898-99 **Unwmk.** ***Perf. 12***
52 A12 1c ultra .20 .20
53 A13 1c yel green ('99) .20 .20
54 A12 2c deep orange .20 .20
55 A13 2c car lake ('99) .20 .20
56 A12 3c green .20 .20
57 A13 4c red .20 .20
58 A12 5c red brown .20 .20
59 A13 5c pale blue ('99) .20 .20
60 A12 7c gray .20 .20
61 A13 8c carmine .20 .20
62 A13 10c orange red .20 .20
63 A13 15c olive green .50 .35
64 A12 20c black .50 .35
65 A12 50c rose brown .55 .35
66 A12 1g red violet 1.50 1.40
Nos. 52-66 (15) 5.25 4.65

For overprints see Nos. 67-81, 110-124, 169, 247-248.

Stamps of 1898-99 Handstamped in Black

1902
67 A12 1c ultra .45 .40
68 A13 1c yellow green .35 .20
69 A12 2c deep orange .70 .70
70 A13 2c carmine lake .35 .20
71 A12 3c green .35 .35
72 A13 4c red .45 .45
73 A12 5c red brown 1.00 1.00
74 A13 5c pale blue .35 .35
75 A12 7c gray .70 .70
76 A13 8c carmine .70 .70
77 A13 10c orange red .70 .70
78 A13 15c olive green 3.50 2.50
79 A12 20c black 3.50 2.75
80 A12 50c rose brown 8.75 5.50
81 A12 1g red violet 13.50 10.00
Nos. 67-81 (15) 35.35 26.50

Many forgeries exist of this overprint.

Centenary of Independence Issues

Coat of Arms
A14

Pierre D. Toussaint L'Ouverture
A15

Emperor Jean Jacques Dessalines
A16

Pres. Alexandre Sabes Pétion
A17

1904 Engr. *Perf. 13½, 14*

82	A14	1c green	.25	.25

Center Engr., Frame Litho.

83	A15	2c rose & blk	.25	.25
84	A15	5c dull blue & blk	.25	.25
85	A16	7c plum & blk	.25	.25
86	A16	10c yellow & blk	.25	.25
87	A17	20c slate & blk	.25	.25
88	A17	50c olive & blk	.25	.25
		Nos. 82-88 (7)	1.75	1.75

Nos. 82 to 88 exist imperforate.
Nos. 83-88 exist with centers inverted. Some are known with head omitted.
Forgeries exist.

Same Handstamped in Blue

1904

89	A14	1c green	.30	.30
90	A15	2c rose & blk	.30	.30
91	A15	5c dull blue & blk	.30	.30
92	A16	7c plum & blk	.40	.40
93	A16	10c yellow & blk	.40	.40
94	A17	20c slate & blk	.40	.40
95	A17	50c olive & blk	.40	.40
		Nos. 89-95 (7)	2.50	2.50

Two dies were used for the handstamped overprint on Nos. 89-95. Letters and figures are larger on one than on the other. All values exist imperforate.

Pres. Pierre Nord-Alexis — A18

1904 Engr. *Perf. 13½, 14*

96	A18	1c green	.25	.25
97	A18	2c carmine	.25	.25
98	A18	5c dark blue	.25	.25
99	A18	10c orange brown	.25	.25
100	A18	20c orange	.25	.25
101	A18	50c claret	.25	.25
a.		Tête bêche pair	*200.00*	
		Nos. 96-101 (6)	1.50	1.50

Used values are for c-t-o's. Postally used examples are worth more.
Nos. 96-101 exist imperforate.
This issue, and the overprints and surcharges, exist in horiz. pairs, imperf. vert., and in vert. pairs, imperf. horiz.
For overprints and surcharges see Nos. 102-109, 150-161, 170-176, 217-218, 235-238, 240-242, 302-303.
Forgeries of Nos. 96, 101, 101a exist.
Reprints or very accurate imitations of this issue exist, including No. 101a.
Some are printed in very bright colors on very white paper and are found both perforated and imperforate. Generally the original stamps are perf. 13¼, the reprints perf 13½.

Same Handstamped in Blue like #89-95

1904

102	A18	1c green	.50	.50
103	A18	2c carmine	.50	.50
104	A18	5c dark blue	.50	.50
105	A18	10c orange brown	.50	.50
106	A18	20c orange	.50	.50
107	A18	50c claret	.50	.50
		Nos. 102-107 (6)	3.00	3.00

The note after No. 95 applies also to Nos. 102-107. All values exist imperf.
Forgeries exist.

Regular Issue of 1904 Handstamp Surcharged in Black:

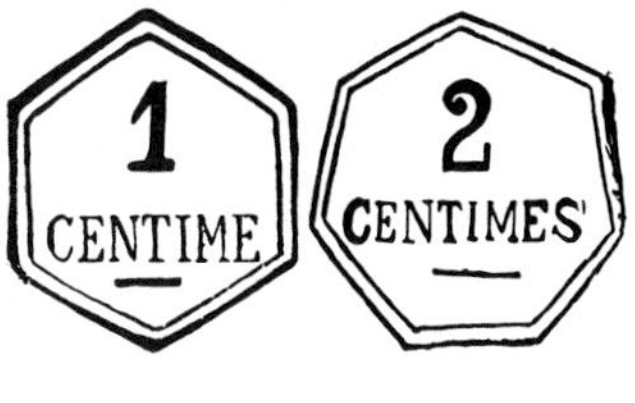

1906, Feb. 20

108	A18	1c on 20c orange	.25	.20
a.		1c on 50c claret	*950.00*	
109	A18	2c on 50c claret	.25	.20

No. 108a is known only with inverted surcharge.
Forgeries exist.

Nos. 52-66 Handstamped in Red

1906

110	A12	1c ultra	.90	.70
111	A13	1c yellow green	.50	.50
112	A12	2c deep orange	1.75	1.75
113	A13	2c carmine lake	1.00	1.00
114	A12	3c green	1.00	1.00
115	A13	4c red	4.25	3.50
116	A12	5c red brown	5.25	4.25
117	A13	5c pale blue	.70	.45
118	A12	7c gray	3.50	3.50
119	A13	8c carmine	.70	.70
120	A13	10c orange red	1.40	.90
121	A13	15c olive green	1.75	1.00
122	A12	20c black	4.25	3.50
123	A12	50c rose brown	4.25	2.75
124	A12	1g red violet	7.00	5.50
		Nos. 110-124 (15)	38.20	31.00

Forgeries of this overprint are plentiful.

Coat of Arms — A19

President Nord-Alexis
A20

Market at Port-au-Prince
A21

Sans Souci Palace — A22

Independence Palace at Gonaives — A23

Entrance to Catholic College at Port-au-Prince
A24

Monastery and Church at Port-au-Prince
A25

Seat of Government at Port-au-Prince
A26

Presidential Palace at Port-au-Prince
A27

For Foreign Postage (centimes de piastre)

1906-13 *Perf. 12*

125	A19	1c de p green	.20	.20
126	A20	2c de p ver	.35	.20
127	A21	3c de p brown	.50	.20
128	A21	3c de p org yel ('11)	5.00	2.75
129	A22	4c de p car lake	.50	.30
130	A22	4c de p lt ol grn ('13)	7.00	4.25
131	A20	5c de p dk blue	1.75	.20
132	A23	7c de p gray	1.40	.70
133	A23	7c de p org red ('13)	21.00	14.00
134	A24	8c de p car rose	1.40	.60
135	A24	8c de p ol grn ('13)	12.00	8.50
136	A25	10c de p org red	.90	.20
137	A25	10c de p red brn ('13)	12.00	8.50
138	A26	15c de p sl grn	1.75	.70
139	A26	15c dp p yel ('13)	5.25	2.75
140	A20	20c de p blue grn	1.75	.70
141	A19	50c de p red	2.75	2.00
142	A19	50c de p org yel ('13)	6.00	4.25
143	A27	1p claret	5.50	3.50
144	A27	1p red ('13)	6.00	5.00
		Nos. 125-144 (20)	93.00	59.50

All 1906 values exist imperf. These are plate proofs.
For overprints and surcharges see Nos. 177-195, 213-216, 239, 245, 249-260, 263, 265-277, 279-284, 286-301, 304.

Nord-Alexis
A28

Coat of Arms — A29

For Domestic Postage (centimes de gourde)

1906-10

145	A28	1c de g blue	.25	.20
146	A29	2c de g org yel	.35	.20
147	A29	2c de g lemon ('10)	.50	.20
148	A28	3c de g slate	.30	.20
149	A29	7c de g green	.90	.35
		Nos. 145-149 (5)	2.30	1.15

For overprints see Nos. 196-197.

Regular Issue of 1904 Handstamp Surcharged in Red like #108-109

1907

150	A18	1c on 5c dk bl	.30	.20
151	A18	1c on 20c org	.25	.20
152	A18	2c on 10c org brn	.25	.20
153	A18	2c on 50c claret	.35	.25

Black Surcharge

154	A18	1c on 5c dk bl	.35	.35
155	A18	1c on 10c org brn	.30	.20
156	A18	2c on 20c org	.25	.25

Brown Surcharge

157	A18	1c on 5c dk bl	.35	.35
158	A18	1c on 10c org brn	.55	.35
159	A18	2c on 20c org	1.75	1.40
160	A18	2c on 50c claret	17.50	16.00

Violet Surcharge

161	A18	1c on 20c org	125.00	

The handstamps are found sideways, diagonal, inverted and double.
Forgeries exist.

A30

President Antoine T. Simon — A31

For Foreign Postage

1910

162	A30	2c de p rose red & blk	.50	.35
163	A30	5c de p bl & blk	10.00	.50
164	A30	20c de p yel grn & blk	7.00	5.50

For Domestic Postage

165	A31	1c de g lake & blk	.20	.20
		Nos. 162-165 (4)	17.70	6.55

For overprint and surcharges see Nos. 198, 262, 278, 285.

A32

A33

Pres. Cincinnatus Leconte — A34

1912

166	A32	1c de g car lake	.25	.25
167	A33	2c de g dp org	.30	.25

For Foreign Postage

168	A34	5c de p dp blue	.55	.25
		Nos. 166-168 (3)	1.10	.75

For overprints see Nos. 199-201.

Stamps of Preceding Issues Handstamped Vertically

1914

On No. 61

169	A13	8c carmine	8.75	7.00

On Nos. 96-101

170	A18	1c green	25.00	21.00
171	A18	2c carmine	25.00	21.00
172	A18	5c dk blue	.45	.25
173	A18	10c orange brn	.45	.25
174	A18	20c orange	.70	.35
175	A18	50c claret	2.00	.90
		Nos. 170-175 (6)	53.60	43.75

Perforation varieties of Nos. 172-175 exist.

No. 175 overprinted "T. M." is a revenue stamp. The letters are the initials of "Timbre Mobile."

On No. 107

176	A18	50c claret	*10,000.*	*10,000.*

Horizontally on Stamps of 1906-13

177	A19	1c de p green	.35	.25
178	A20	2c de p ver	.50	.25
179	A21	3c de p brown	.75	.50
180	A21	3c de p org yel	.35	.25
181	A22	4c de p car lake	.70	.60
182	A22	4c de p lt ol grn	1.75	.95
183	A23	7c de p gray	2.00	2.00
184	A23	7c de p org red	3.75	3.75
185	A24	8c de p car rose	3.50	3.50
186	A24	8c de p ol grn	5.00	5.00
187	A25	10c de p org red	1.00	.50
188	A25	10c de p red brn	2.00	1.25
189	A26	15c de p sl grn	2.75	2.75
190	A26	15c de p yellow	1.75	.95
191	A20	20c de p bl grn	2.50	.90
192	A19	50c de p red	4.25	4.25
193	A19	50c de p org yel	5.75	5.75
194	A27	1p claret	4.25	4.25
195	A27	1p red	6.25	6.25
196	A29	2c de g lemon	.35	.25
197	A28	3c de g slate	.35	.25
		Nos. 177-197 (21)	49.85	44.40

On No. 164

198	A30	20c de p yel grn & blk	2.75	2.75

Vertically on Nos. 166-168

199	A32	1c de g car lake	.30	.25
200	A33	2c de g dp org	.45	.35
201	A34	5c de p dp blue	.70	.25
		Nos. 199-201 (3)	1.45	.85

Two handstamps were used for the overprints on Nos. 169-201. They may be distinguished by the short and long foot of the "L" of "GL" and the position of the first "1" in "1914" with regard to the period above it. Both handstamps are found on all but #176, 294, 295, 306, 308.

Handstamp Surcharged

On Nos. 141 and 143

213	A19	1c de p on 50c de p red	.30	.20
214	A27	1c de p on 1p claret	.45	.40

On Nos. 142 and 144

215	A19	1c de p on 50c de p org yel	.45	.35
216	A27	1c de p on 1p red	.50	.40

Handstamp Surcharged

On Nos. 100 and 101

217	A18	7c on 20c orange	.40	.20
218	A18	7c on 50c claret	.35	.20

The initials on the preceding handstamps are those of Gen. Oreste Zamor; the date is that of his triumphal entry into Port-au-Prince.

Pres. Oreste Zamor

Coat of Arms

Pres. Tancrède Auguste

Owing to the theft of a large quantity of this 1914 issue, while in transit from the printers, the stamps were never placed on sale at post offices. A few copies have been canceled through carelessness or favor. Value, set of 10, $6.

Preceding Issues Handstamp Surcharged in Carmine or Blue

On Nos. 98-101

1915-16

235	A18	1c on 5c dk bl (C)	1.10	1.10
236	A18	1c on 10c org brn	.50	.50
237	A18	1c on 20c orange	.40	.35
238	A18	1c on 50c claret	.40	.40

On No. 132

239	A23	1c on 7c de p gray (C)	.40	.40

On Nos. 106-107

240	A18	1c on 20c orange	.50	.70
241	A18	1c on 50c claret	1.75	.50
242	A18	1c on 50c cl (C)	27.50	21.00
		Nos. 235-242 (8)	32.55	24.95

Nos. 240-242 are known with two types of the "Post Paye" overprint. No. 237 with red surcharge and any stamps with violet surcharge are unofficial.

No. 143 Handstamp Surcharged in Red

1917-19

245	A27	2c on 1p claret	.40	.40

Stamps of 1906-14 Handstamp Surcharged in Various Colors

1c, 5c

On Nos. 123-124

247	A12	1c on 50c (R)	17.50	12.50
248	A12	1c on 1g (R)	21.00	16.00

On #127, 129, 134, 136, 138, 140-141

249	A22	1c on 4c de p (Br)	.40	*.50*
250	A25	1c on 10c de p (Bl)	.40	*.50*
252	A20	1c on 20c de p (R)	.40	*.50*
253	A20	1c on 20c de p (Bk)	.40	*.50*
254	A19	1c on 50c de p (R)	.40	*.50*
255	A19	1c on 50c de p (Bk)	.40	*.50*
256	A21	2c on 3c de p (R)	.40	*.50*
257	A24	2c on 8c de p (R)	.40	*.50*
258	A24	2c on 8c de p (Bk)	.40	*.50*
259	A26	2c on 15c de p (R)	.40	*.50*
260	A20	2c on 20c de p (R)	.40	*.50*
		Nos. 249-260 (11)	4.40	5.50

The 1c on 10c de p stamp in black is actually a blue ink which bled into the stamps.

On Nos. 164, 128

262	A30	1c on 20c de p (Bk)	3.50	3.50
263	A21	2c on 3c de p (R)	.40	.30

On #130, 133, 135, 137, 139, 142, 144

265	A22	1c on 4c de p (R)	.40	.30
266	A23	1c on 7c de p (Br)	.40	.30
267	A26	1c on 15c de p (R)	.40	.30
268	A19	1c on 50c de p (Bk)	.90	.90
269	A27	1c on 1p (Bk)	.90	.90
270	A24	2c on 8c de p (R)	.40	.35
271	A25	2c on 10c de p (Br)	.40	.20
272	A26	2c on 15c de p (R)	.45	.45
273	A25	5c on 10c de p (Bl)	.70	.70
274	A25	5c on 10c de p (VBk)	.45	.45
275	A26	5c on 15c de p (R)	3.50	3.50
		Nos. 265-275 (11)	8.90	8.35

"O. Z." Stamps of 1914 Handstamp Surcharged in Red or Brown

276	A26	1c on 15c de p sl grn	.40	.40
277	A20	1c on 20c de p bl grn	.40	.40
278	A30	1c on 20c de p yel grn & blk	.40	.40
279	A27	1c on 1p claret (Br)	.40	.40
280	A27	1c on 1p claret	1.25	1.25
281	A27	5c on 1p red (Br)	.40	.40
		Nos. 276-281 (6)	3.25	3.25

"O. Z." Stamps of 1914 Handstamp Surcharged in Violet, Green, Red, Magenta or Black

1 ct and 2 cts as in 1917-19 and

1919-20

282	A22	2c on 4c de p car lake (V)	.35	.35
283	A24	2c on 8c de p car rose (G)	.30	.20
284	A24	2c on 8c de p ol grn (R)	.20	.20
285	A30	2c on 20c de p yel grn & blk (R)	.30	.20
286	A19	2c on 50c de p red (G)	.20	.20
288	A19	2c on 50c de p red (R)	.45	.35
289	A19	2c on 50c de p org yel (R)	.25	.20
290	A27	2c on 1pi claret (R)	2.00	1.75
291	A27	2c on 1pi red (R)	1.50	1.50
292	A21	3c on 3c de p brn (R)	.35	.35
293	A23	3c on 7c de p org red (R)	.35	.20
294	A21	5c on 3c de p brn (R)	.40	.20
295	A21	5c on 3c de p org yel (R)	1.40	1.40
296	A22	5c on 4c de p car lake (R)	.45	.45
297	A22	5c on 4c de p ol grn (R)	.25	.25
298	A23	5c on 7c de p gray (V)	.30	.25
299	A23	5c on 7c de p org red (V)	.35	.35
300	A25	5c on 10c de p org red (V)	.25	.25
301	A26	5c on 15c de p yel (M)	.35	.35
		Nos. 282-301 (19)	10.00	9.00

Nos. 217 and 218 Handstamp Surcharged with New Value in Magenta

302	A18	5c on 7c on 20c orange	.35	.35
303	A18	5c on 7c on 50c claret	2.75	2.75

No. 187 Handstamp Surcharged in Magenta

304	A25	5c de p on 10c de p	.45	.45

Postage Due Stamps of 1906-14 Handstamp Surcharged in Black or Magenta (#308)

On Stamp of 1906

305	D2	5c on 50c ol gray	9.00	7.25

On Stamp of 1914

306	D2	5c on 10c violet	.30	.30
307	D2	5c on 50c olive gray	.40	.40
308	D2	5c on 50c ol gray (M)	1.40	1.40
		Nos. 305-308 (4)	11.10	9.35

Nos. 299 with red surcharge and 306-307 with violet are trial colors or essays.

Allegory of Agriculture A40

Allegory of Commerce A41

1920, Apr. **Engr.** ***Perf. 12***

310	A40	3c deep orange	.25	.25
311	A40	5c green	.25	.25
312	A41	10c vermilion	.40	.30
313	A41	15c violet	.35	.25
314	A41	25c deep blue	.40	.30
		Nos. 310-314 (5)	1.65	1.35

Nos. 311-313 overprinted "T. M." are revenue stamps. The letters are the initials of "Timbre Mobile."

President Louis J. Borno — A42

Christophe's Citadel — A43

Old Map of West Indies — A44

Borno — A45

National Capitol — A46

1924, Sept. 3

315	A42	5c deep green	.25	.20
316	A43	10c carmine	.25	.20
317	A44	20c violet blue	.65	.25
318	A45	50c orange & blk	.65	.25
319	A46	1g olive green	1.25	.30
		Nos. 315-319 (5)	3.05	1.20

For surcharges see Nos. 359, C4A.

Coffee Beans and Flowers — A47

1928, Feb. 6

320 A47 35c deep green 2.75 .40

For surcharge see No. 337.

Pres. Louis Borno — A48

1929, Nov. 4

321 A48 10c carmine rose .30 .25

Signing of the "Frontier" treaty between Haiti and the Dominican Republic.

Presidents Salomon and Vincent — A49

Pres. Sténio Vincent — A50

1931, Oct. 16

322	A49	5c deep green	.90	.35
323	A50	10c carmine rose	.90	.35

50th anniv. of Haiti's joining the UPU.

President Vincent — A52

Aqueduct at Port-au-Prince A53

Fort National — A54

Palace of Sans Souci — A55

Christophe's Chapel at Milot — A56

King's Gallery Citadel — A57

Vallières Battery — A58

1933-40

325	A52	3c orange	.20	.20
326	A52	3c dp ol grn ('39)	.20	.20
327	A53	5c green	.20	.20
a.		5c emerald ('38)	.20	.20
b.		5c bright green ('39)	.20	.20
c.		5c brown olive ('40)	.40	.20
329	A54	10c rose car	.40	.20
a.		10c vermilion	.50	.20
330	A54	10c red brn ('40)	.40	.20
331	A55	25c blue	.75	.20
332	A56	50c brown	2.00	.40
333	A57	1g dark green	2.25	.40
334	A58	2.50g olive bister	3.25	.60
		Nos. 325-334 (9)	9.65	2.60

For surcharges see Nos. 357-358, 360.

Alexandre Dumas, His Father and Son — A59

1935, Dec. 29 Litho. *Perf. 11½*

335	A59	10c rose pink & choc	.75	.25
336	A59	25c blue & chocolate	1.25	.30
		Nos. 335-336,C10 (3)	6.00	2.45

Visit of a delegation from France to Haiti.

No. 335 exists imperf and in horiz. pair, imperf. between. #336 exists as pair, imperf horiz.

No. 320 Surcharged in Red

1939, Jan. 24 *Perf. 12*

337 A47 25c on 35c dp grn .70 .30

SEMI-POSTAL STAMPS

Pierre de Coubertin SP1

Engraved & Litho (flag)

1939, Oct. 3 Unwmk. *Perf. 12*

B1	SP1	10c + 10c multi	20.00	20.00
		Nos. B1,CB1-CB2 (3)	50.00	50.00

Pierre de Coubertin, organizer of the modern Olympic Games. The surtax was used to build a Sports Stadium at Port-au-Prince.

AIR POST STAMPS

Plane over Port-au-Prince — AP1

1929-30 Unwmk. Engr. *Perf. 12*

C1	AP1	25c dp grn ('30)	.30	.25
C2	AP1	50c dp vio	.40	.20
C3	AP1	75c red brn ('30)	1.25	1.00
C4	AP1	1g dp ultra	1.40	1.25
		Nos. C1-C4 (4)	3.35	2.70

AP1a

Red Surcharge

1933, July 6

C4A AP1a 60c on 20c blue 40.00 50.00

Non-stop flight of Capt. J. Errol Boyd and Robert G. Lyon from New York to Port-au-Prince.

Plane over Christophe's Citadel — AP2

1933-40

C5	AP2	50c org brn	4.00	.65
C6	AP2	50c ol grn ('35)	3.50	.65
C7	AP2	50c car rose ('37)	2.75	1.25
C8	AP2	50c blk ('38)	2.00	.65
C8A	AP2	60c choc ('40)	.65	.25
C9	AP2	1g ultra	1.50	.40
		Nos. C5-C9 (6)	14.40	3.85

For surcharge see No. C24.

Dumas Type of Regular Issue

1935, Dec. 29 Litho. *Perf. 11½*

C10 A59 60c brt vio & choc 4.00 1.90

Visit of delegation from France to Haiti.

Arms of Haiti and Portrait of George Washington — AP4

1938, Aug. 29 Engr. *Perf. 12*

C11 AP4 60c deep blue .55 .25

150th anniv. of the US Constitution.

AIR POST SEMI-POSTAL STAMPS

Coubertin Semipostal Type of 1939

Unwmk.

1939, Oct. 3 Engr. *Perf. 12*

CB1	SP1	60c + 40c multi	15.00	15.00
CB2	SP1	1.25g + 60c multi	15.00	15.00

POSTAGE DUE STAMPS

D1

D2

1898, May Unwmk. Engr. *Perf. 12*

J1	D1	2c black	.40	.25
J2	D1	5c red brown	.75	.35
J3	D1	10c brown orange	1.10	.50
J4	D1	50c slate	2.10	1.10
		Nos. J1-J4 (4)	4.35	2.20

For overprints see Nos. J5-J9, J14-J16.

Stamps of 1898 Handstamped like #67-81

1902 Black Overprint

J5	D1	2c black	1.10	.80
J6	D1	5c red brown	1.10	.80
J7	D1	10c brown orange	1.40	.80
J8	D1	50c slate	7.00	3.50

Red Overprint

J9	D1	2c black	1.25	1.25
		Nos. J5-J9 (5)	11.85	7.15

1906

J10	D2	2c dull red	.60	.45
J11	D2	5c ultra	1.75	1.75
J12	D2	10c violet	1.75	1.75
J13	D2	50c olive gray	7.50	4.25
		Nos. J10-J13 (4)	11.60	8.20

For surcharges and overprints see Nos. 305-308, J17-J20.

Preceding Issues Handstamped like #169-201

1914 On Stamps of 1898

J14	D1	5c red brown	.60	.45
J15	D1	10c brown orange	.55	.55
J16	D1	50c slate	3.75	2.50
		Nos. J14-J16 (3)	4.90	3.50

On Stamps of 1906

J17	D2	2c dull red	.45	.30
J18	D2	5c ultra	.75	.45
J19	D2	10c violet	3.00	2.50
J20	D2	50c olive gray	5.50	3.50
		Nos. J17-J20 (4)	9.70	6.75

The note after No. 201 applies to Nos. J14-J20 also.

HATAY

hä-'tī

LOCATION — Northwest of Syria, bordering on Mediterranean Sea.
GOVT. — Former semi-independent republic
AREA — 10,000 sq. mi. (approx.)
POP. — 273,350 (1939)
CAPITAL — Antioch

Alexandretta, a semi-autonomous district of Syria under French mandate, was renamed Hatay in 1938 and transferred to Turkey in 1939.

100 Santims = 1 Kurush
40 Paras = 1 Kurush (1939)

Stamps of Turkey, 1931-38, Surcharged in Black:

On A77

On A78

1939 Unwmk. *Perf. 11½x12*

1	A77	10s on 20pa dp org	.80	.35
a.		"Sent" instead of "Sant"	60.00	22.50
2	A78	25s on 1ku dk sl grn	.90	.35
a.		Small "25"	5.00	1.50
3	A78	50s on 2ku dk vio	1.10	.35
a.		Small "50"	5.00	2.00
4	A77	75s on 2½ku green	.80	.40
5	A78	1ku on 4ku slate	6.50	4.25
6	A78	1ku on 5ku rose red	3.50	1.40
7	A78	1½ku on 3ku brn org	1.10	.60
8	A78	2½ku on 4ku slate	2.25	.60
9	A78	5ku on 8ku brt blue	3.00	.90
10	A77	12½ku on 20ku ol grn	4.25	2.00
11	A77	20ku on 25ku Prus bl	8.50	5.00
		Nos. 1-11 (11)	32.70	16.20
		Set, never hinged	80.00	

Map of Hatay — A1

Lions of Antioch A2

Flag of Hatay A3

Post Office A4

1939 Unwmk. Typo. *Perf. 12*

12	A1	10p orange & aqua	1.25	.75
13	A1	30p lt vio & aqua	1.25	.75
14	A1	1½ku olive & aqua	1.25	.75
15	A2	2½ku turq grn	1.50	1.00
16	A2	3ku light blue	1.50	1.00
17	A2	5ku chocolate	1.50	1.00
18	A3	6ku brt blue & car	2.00	1.25
19	A3	7½ku dp green & car	2.25	1.40
20	A3	12ku violet & car	3.00	1.40
21	A3	12½ku dk blue & car	2.50	1.50
22	A4	17½ku brown car	5.00	3.00
23	A4	25ku olive brn	6.00	3.50
24	A4	50ku slate blue	12.50	8.50
		Nos. 12-24 (13)	41.50	25.80
		Set, never hinged	90.00	

Stamps of 1939 Overprinted in Black

1939

25	A1	10p orange & aqua	1.00	.75
a.		Overprint reading up	20.00	
26	A1	30p lt vio & aqua	1.00	.75
27	A1	1½ku ol & aqua	1.25	.80
28	A2	2½ku turq grn	1.25	.80
29	A2	3ku light blue	1.50	.80
30	A2	5ku chocolate	1.75	1.25
a.		Overprint inverted	20.00	
31	A3	6ku brt bl & car	1.75	1.25
32	A3	7½ku dp grn & car	1.75	1.25
33	A3	12ku vio & car	1.75	1.25
34	A3	12½ku dk bl & car	2.00	1.25
35	A4	17½ku brn car	3.00	2.25
a.		Overprint inverted	20.00	
36	A4	25ku olive brn	5.00	4.25
37	A4	50ku slate blue	13.00	10.00
		Nos. 25-37 (13)	36.00	26.65
		Set, never hinged	85.00	

The overprint reads "Date of annexation to the Turkish Republic, June 30, 1939."

On Nos. 25-27, the overprint reads down. On Nos. 28-37, it is horizontal.

POSTAGE DUE STAMPS

Postage Due Stamps of Turkey, 1936, Surcharged or Overprinted in Black

1939 Unwmk. *Perf. 11½*

J1	D6	1ku on 2ku lt bl	1.75	.45
J2	D6	3ku bright violet	2.25	.90
J3	D6	4ku on 5ku Prus bl	2.25	.90
J4	D6	5ku on 12ku brt rose	2.25	.90
J5	D6	12ku bright rose	37.50	27.50
		Nos. J1-J5 (5)	46.00	30.65
		Set, never hinged	100.00	

Castle at Antioch D1

1939 Typo. *Perf. 12*

J6	D1	1ku red orange	2.00	1.00
J7	D1	3ku dk olive brown	2.25	1.00
J8	D1	4ku turqoise green	2.75	1.50
J9	D1	5ku slate black	3.25	2.00
		Nos. J6-J9 (4)	10.25	5.50
		Set, never hinged	25.00	

Nos. J6-J9 Overprinted in Black like Nos. 25-37

1939

J10	D1	1ku red orange	2.00	1.25
J11	D1	3ku dk olive brown	2.25	1.50
J12	D1	4ku turqoise green	2.50	1.75
J13	D1	5ku slate black	4.00	2.00
a.		Overprint inverted	20.00	
		Nos. J10-J13 (4)	10.75	6.50
		Set, never hinged	25.00	

HELIGOLAND

LOCATION — An island in the North Sea near the northern coast of Germany
GOVT. — British Possession
AREA — ¼ sq. mi.
POP. — 2,307 (1900)

Great Britain ceded Heligoland to Germany in 1890. It became part of Schleswig-Holstein province. Stamps of Heligoland were superseded by those of the German Empire.

16 Schillings = 1 Mark
100 Pfennig = 1 Mark = 1 Schilling (1875)

REPRINTS

Most Heligoland issues were extensively reprinted between 1875 and 1895, and these comprise the great majority of Heligoland stamps in the marketplace. Such reprints sell for much less than the originals, usually for $1-$2 each. Expertization of Heligoland issues is strongly recommended by the editors.

Queen Victoria
A1 A2

A3

A4

HALF SCHILLING
A1: Curl below chignon is rounded.
A2: Curl resembles hook or comma.

Typo., Head Embossed

1867-68 Unwmk. *Rouletted*

1	A1	½sch bl grn & rose	290.00	*850.00*
		On cover		*7,250.*
1A	A2	½sch bl grn & rose	675.00	*1,400.*
		On cover		*8,750.*
2	A1	1sch rose & dp grn	160.00	*175.00*
		On cover		*1,600.*
3	A3	2sch rose & pale grn	10.00	*55.00*
		On cover		*550.00*
4	A3	6sch gray grn & rose	12.50	*240.00*
		On cover		*3,000.*

Reprints of No. 2 lack the large curl, those of No. 1A are not in blue green, and those of Nos. 3 and 4 are on slightly porous paper and the colors are either too deep or too bright. The 2sch and 6sch perforated exist only as reprints.

1869-71 *Perf. 13½x14½*

Thick Soft Paper

5	A2	½sch ol grn & car	125.00	*140.00*
		On cover		*1,100.*
a.		½sch blue green & rose	210.00	*225.00*
		On cover		*1,400.*
b.		½sch yellow green & rose	350.00	*325.00*
		On cover		*1,400.*
6	A2	1sch rose & yel grn	175.00	*250.00*
		On cover		*1,500.*

Reprints are on thinner paper and in too dark colors.

1873 Thick Quadrille Paper

7	A4	¼sch pale rose & pale grn	25.00	*2,000.*
		On cover		*6,000.*
a.		¼sch deep rose & pale grn	*250.00*	*2,000.*
		On cover		*6,000.*
8	A4	¾sch yel grn & rose	100.00	*3,250.*
		On cover		*10,500.*
9	A2	½sch brt grn & rose	125.00	*210.00*
		On cover		*1,100.*
10	A4	¾sch gray grn & pale rose	25.00	*1,300.*
		On cover		*3,900.*
a.		¾sch gray green & dp rose	25.00	*1,300.*
		On cover		*3,900.*
11	A2	1sch rose & pale grn	210.00	*350.00*
		On cover		*1,400.*
12	A4	1½sch yel grn & rose	50.00	*275.00*
		On cover		*875.00*

Reprints are never on quadrille paper.

1874 Thin Wove Paper

13	A4	¼sch rose & yel grn	16.00	

Originals have the large curl. The early reprints have the small curl. The later reprints are on thin hard paper with smooth white gum and the colors are too bright.

A5

A6

A7

Coat of Arms — A8

1875 Wove Paper

14	A5	1pf dk rose & dk grn	7.50	*575.00*
		On cover		*1,650.*
15	A5	2pf yel grn & dk rose	8.00	*875.00*
		On cover		*1,900.*
16	A6	5pf dk rose & dk grn	18.00	*21.00*
		On cover		*60.00*
17	A6	10pf blue grn & red	9.00	*37.50*
		On cover		*110.00*
a.		10pf yel green & dark rose	110.00	*27.50*
		On cover		*82.50*
b.		10pf lt green & pale red	140.00	*25.00*
		On cover		*82.50*
18	A7	25pf rose & dk green	11.50	*25.00*
		On cover		*87.50*
a.		25pf dk rose & dk green	11.50	*25.00*
		On cover		*87.50*
19	A7	50pf grn & brick red	14.00	*85.00*
		On cover		*190.00*
a.		50pf dl grn & dk rose	57.50	*30.00*
		On cover		*110.00*

The 1pf and 2pf have been reprinted on very white paper with white gum. The colors are too bright and too light.

1876-88 Typo.

20	A8	3pf dp grn & dl red	225.00	*1,300.*
		On cover		*2,700.*
		On cover, single franking		*8,250.*
a.		3pf green & bright red ('77)	140.00	*950.00*
		On cover		*2,000.*
		On cover, single franking		*8,250.*
21	A8	20pf ver & brt grn ('88)	8.00	*27.50*
		On cover		*92.50*
a.		20pf brn org & grn ('87)	425.00	*42.50*
		On cover		*140.00*
b.		20pf vio car & yel grn ('80)	240.00	*125.00*
		On cover		*360.00*
c.		20pf anil rose & dk grn ('85)	425.00	*65.00*
		On cover		*160.00*
d.		20pf lil rose & dk grn ('76)	240.00	*125.00*
		On cover		*410.00*
e.		20pf rose red & dk grn ('80)	240.00	*125.00*
		On cover		*360.00*

The coat-of-arms on Nos. 20, 21 and sub-varieties is printed in three colors: varying shades of yellow, red and green.

The 3pf has been reprinted. The colors are usually too pale, especially the red, which is either orange or orange red.

A9

A10

1879 Typo.

22	A9	1m dp green & car	200.00	*200.00*
		On cover		*650.00*
a.		1m blue green & salmon	175.00	*210.00*
		On cover		*650.00*
b.		1m dark green & ver	70.00	
23	A10	5m blue grn & sal	125.00	*1,050.*
		On cover		*2,250.*

Perf. 11½

24	A9	1m dp grn & car	1,600.	*5,000.*
25	A10	5m bl grn & rose red	1,300.	*10,500.*
a.		Horiz. pair, imperf. vert.	*3,500.*	

Nos. 13, 20a, 22b, 24 and 25 were never placed in use. Forged cancellations of Nos. 1-23 are plentiful.

Covers: Values for Nos. 22, 22a, 23 are for overfranked complete covers, usually philatelic.

Heligoland stamps were replaced by those of the German Empire in 1890.

HONDURAS

hän-'dur-əs

LOCATION — Central America, between Guatemala on the north and Nicaragua on the south
GOVT. — Republic
AREA — 43,277 sq. mi.
POP. — 4,092,174 (est. 1983)
CAPITAL — Tegucigalpa

8 Reales = 1 Peso
100 Centavos = 1 Peso (1878)
100 Centavos = 1 Lempira (1933)

Values for unused stamps are for examples with original gum as defined in the catalogue introduction. Very fine examples of the locally printed Nos. 95-110, 127, 140, 151-210C, and 218-279 will have margins clear of the perforations but will be noticeably off center.

Watermark

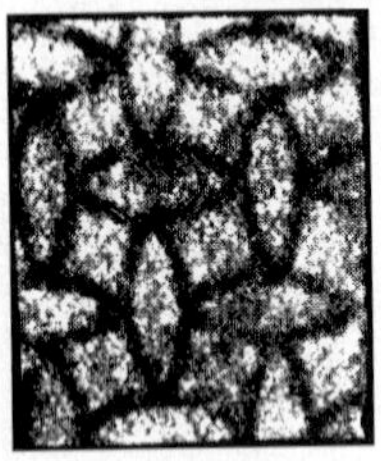

Wmk. 209 — Multiple Ovals

Coat of Arms — A1

1865, Dec. Unwmk. Litho. ***Imperf.***

1	A1	2r black, *green*	.65	—
2	A1	2r black, *pink*	.65	—

Nos. 1 and 2, although inscribed "DOS," were sold for one real.

Most used examples are pen cancelled with cross. Pre-philatelic handstamp cancellations command a premium.

One in 12 stamps has "LOS" for "DOS," and one stamp in each pane of 120 is inscribed "DGS" or "CORRFOS."

No covers are known bearing No. 1. Two covers bearing No. 2 are known.

Comayagua

Tegucigalpa

Medio real = ½ real
Un real = 1 real
Dos reales = 2 reales

Comayagua Issue

1877, May

Red Surcharge

3	A1	½r on 2r blk, *grn*	70.00	

Blue Surcharge

5	A1	2r on 2r blk, *grn*	150.00	—
6	A1	2r on 2r blk, *pink*	*475.00*	—

Black Surcharge

7	A1	1r on 2r blk, *grn*	150.00	
8	A1	2r on 2r blk, *grn*	*800.00*	
9	A1	2r on 2r blk, *pink*	500.00	

No. 5 may exist only as the base for No. 13a.

Tegucigalpa Issue

1877, July

Black Surcharge

13	A1	1r on 2r blk, *grn*	15.00	*35.00*
a.		Surcharged on #5	*1000.*	
14	A1	1r on 2r blk, *pink*	*80.00*	
16	A1	2r on 2r blk, *pink*	—	

Blue Surcharge

18	A1	½r on 2r blk, *grn*	*80.00*	
19	A1	½r on 2r blk, *pink*	*25.00*	
20	A1	1r on 2r blk, *pink*	*35.00*	
23	A1	2r on 2r blk, *pink*	15.00	*25.00*

Red Surcharge

24	A1	½r on 2r blk, *grn*	15.00	*35.00*
25	A1	½r on 2r blk, *pink*	60.00	

Only the stamps valued or dashed used are known to have been postally used. Nos. 3 and 7 may have been postally used, but to date no examples are recorded used. The other listed stamps were sold as remainders. No covers bearing Nos. 13 to 25 are known.

The blue surcharges range from light blue to violet black. The black surcharge has no tinge of blue. The red surcharges range from light to dark carmine. Some exist double or inverted, but genuine errors are rare. Normal cancel is a blue or black 7-bar killer. Target cancels on Nos. 1-24 are forgeries. Surcharges and cancels have been extensively forged.

Regular Issue

President Francisco Morazán — A4

Thin, hard paper, colorless gum
Various Frames

1878, July Engr. ***Perf. 12***

Printed by National Bank Note Co. of N.Y.

30	A4	1c violet	.50	.50
		On cover		*1,000.*
31	A4	2c brown	.50	.50
		On cover		*1,500.*
32	A4	½r black	5.00	.50
		On cover		*350.00*
33	A4	1r green	25.00	.50
		On cover		*450.00*
34	A4	2r deep blue	3.00	*5.00*
		On cover		*3,500.*
35	A4	4r vermilion	5.00	*10.00*
36	A4	1p orange	6.00	*25.00*
		Nos. 30-36 (7)	45.00	*42.00*

Nos. 35 and 36 are not known on cover.

Various counterfeit cancellations exist on Nos. 30-36. Most used copies of Nos. 35-36 offered are actually 35a-36a with fake or favor cancels.

Re-Issue
Soft paper, yellowish gum
Various Frames

1889

Printed by American Bank Note Co. of N.Y.

30a	A4	1c deep violet	*10.00*
31a	A4	2c red brown	.25
32a	A4	½r black	.25
33a	A4	1r blue green	.25
34a	A4	2r ultramarine	*5.00*
35a	A4	4r scarlet vermilion	.25
36a	A4	1p orange yellow	.25
		Nos. 30a-36a (7)	16.25

Although Nos. 30a-36a were not intended for postal use, they were valid, and genuine camcels are known on Nos. 31a-34a.

Arms of Honduras — A5

1890, Jan. 6

40	A5	1c yellow green	.30	.30
41	A5	2c red	.30	.30
42	A5	5c blue	.30	.30
43	A5	10c orange	.35	*.40*
44	A5	20c ocher	.35	*.40*
45	A5	25c rose red	.35	*.40*
46	A5	30c purple	.50	*.60*
47	A5	40c dark blue	.50	*.80*
48	A5	50c brown	.55	*.80*
49	A5	75c blue green	.55	*2.00*
50	A5	1p carmine	.70	*2.25*
		Nos. 40-50 (11)	4.75	*8.55*

The tablets and numerals of Nos. 40 to 50 differ for each denomination.

For overprints see Nos. O1-O11.

Used values of Nos. 1-110 are for stamps with genuine cancellations applied while the stamps were valid. Various counterfeit cancellations exist.

A6

President Luis Bográn — A7

1891, July 31

51	A6	1c dark blue	.30	.30
52	A6	2c yellow brown	.30	.30
53	A6	5c blue green	.30	.30
54	A6	10c vermilion	.30	.30
55	A6	20c brown red	.30	.30
56	A6	25c magenta	.40	*.55*
57	A6	30c slate	.40	*.55*
58	A6	40c blue green	.40	*.55*
59	A6	50c black brown	.50	*.80*
60	A6	75c purple	.50	*1.25*
61	A6	1p brown	.50	*1.60*
62	A7	2p brn & black	1.50	*5.00*
a.		Head inverted	225.00	
63	A7	5p pur & black	1.50	*5.75*
a.		Head inverted	60.00	
64	A7	10p green & blk	1.50	*5.75*
a.		Head inverted	75.00	
		Nos. 51-64 (14)	8.70	*23.30*

#62, 64 exist with papermakers watermark.

For overprints see Nos. O12-O22.

Columbus Sighting Honduran Coast — A8

General Trinidad Cabanas — A9

1892, July 31

65	A8	1c slate	.40	*.45*
66	A8	2c deep blue	.40	*.45*
67	A8	5c yellow green	.40	*.45*
68	A8	10c blue green	.40	*.45*
69	A8	20c red	.40	*.45*
70	A8	25c orange brown	.50	*.55*
71	A8	30c ultramarine	.50	*.60*
72	A8	40c orange	.50	*.90*
73	A8	50c brown	.60	*.85*
74	A8	75c lake	.60	*1.25*
75	A8	1p purple	.60	*1.40*
		Nos. 65-75 (11)	5.30	*7.80*

Discovery of America by Christopher Columbus, 400th anniv.

1893, Aug.

76	A9	1c green	.25	*1.50*
77	A9	2c scarlet	.25	*1.50*
78	A9	5c dark blue	.25	*1.50*
79	A9	10c orange brn	.25	*1.50*
80	A9	20c brown red	.25	*1.50*
81	A9	25c dark blue	.30	*1.50*
82	A9	30c red orange	.45	*1.50*
83	A9	40c black	.45	*1.50*
84	A9	50c olive brn	.45	*1.50*
85	A9	75c purple	.60	*1.50*
86	A9	1p deep magenta	.60	*1.75*
		Nos. 76-86 (11)	4.10	*16.75*

"Justice" A10

President Celio Arias A11

1895, Feb. 15

87	A10	1c vermilion	.30	.30
88	A10	2c deep blue	.30	.30
89	A10	5c slate	.35	*.50*
90	A10	10c brown rose	.45	*.50*
91	A10	20c violet	.45	*.50*
92	A10	30c deep violet	.45	*.85*
93	A10	50c olive brown	.55	*1.25*
94	A10	1p dark green	.60	*1.60*
		Nos. 87-94 (8)	3.45	*5.80*

The tablets and numerals of Nos. 76-94 differ for each denomination.

1896, Jan. 1 Litho. ***Perf. 11½***

95	A11	1c dark blue	.30	*.35*
96	A11	2c yellow brn	.30	*.35*
97	A11	5c purple	1.10	.30
a.		5c red violet	.60	*1.10*
98	A11	10c vermilion	.40	.40
a.		10c red	4.50	*4.50*
99	A11	20c emerald	.75	.50
a.		20c deep green		
100	A11	30c ultramarine	.65	*.70*
101	A11	50c rose	.90	*1.00*
102	A11	1p black brown	1.25	*1.50*
		Nos. 95-102 (8)	5.65	*5.10*

Counterfeits are plentiful. Nos. 95-102 exist imperf. between horiz. or vertically.

Originals of Nos. 95 to 102 are on both thin, semi-transparent paper and opaque paper; reprints are on thicker, opaque paper and usually have a black cancellation "HONDURAS" between horizontal bars.

Railroad Train — A12

1898, Aug. 1

103	A12	1c brown	.50	.20
104	A12	2c rose	.50	.20
105	A12	5c dull ultra	1.00	.25
b.		5c red violet (error)	1.50	.70
106	A12	6c red violet	.90	.25
b.		6c dull rose (error)		
107	A12	10c dark blue	1.00	.30
108	A12	20c dull orange	1.25	.75
109	A12	50c orange red	2.00	1.25
110	A12	1p blue green	4.00	3.00
		Nos. 103-110 (8)	11.15	6.20

Excellent counterfeits of Nos. 103-110 exist.

For overprints see Nos. O23-O27.

Laid Paper

103a	A12	1c	1.00	.50
104a	A12	2c	1.25	.50
105a	A12	5c	1.60	.50
106a	A12	6c	1.60	.75
107a	A12	10c	1.60	1.00
		Nos. 103a-107a (5)	7.05	3.25

General Santos Guardiola A13

President José Medina A14

1903, Jan. 1 Engr. ***Perf. 12***

111	A13	1c yellow grn	.35	.20
112	A13	2c carmine rose	.35	.30
113	A13	5c blue	.35	.30
114	A13	6c dk violet	.35	.30
115	A13	10c brown	.40	.30
116	A13	20c dull ultra	.45	.40
117	A13	50c vermilion	1.25	1.10
118	A13	1p orange	1.25	1.10
		Nos. 111-118 (8)	4.75	4.00

"PERMITASE" handstamped on stamps of 1896-1903 was applied as a control mark by the isolated Pacific Coast post office of Amapala to prevent use of stolen stamps.

1907, Jan. 1 ***Perf. 14***

119	A14	1c dark green	.20	.20
120	A14	2c scarlet	.25	.25
120A	A14	2c carmine	9.00	5.50
121	A14	5c blue	.30	.30
122	A14	6c purple	.35	.30
a.		6c dark violet	.80	.60
123	A14	10c gray brown	.40	.35
124	A14	20c ultra	.90	.85
a.		20c blue violet	110.00	110.00
125	A14	50c deep lake	1.10	1.10
126	A14	1p orange	1.50	1.50
a.		1p orange yellow	—	
		Nos. 119-126 (9)	14.00	10.35

All values of the above set exist imperforate, imperforate horizontally and in horizontal pairs, imperforate between. No. 124a imperf is worth only 10% of the listed perforated variety.

For surcharges see Nos. 128-130.

1909 **Typo.** ***Perf. 11½***

127	A14	1c green	1.25	1.00
a.		Imperf., pair	4.00	4.00
b.		Printed on both sides	7.50	10.00

The 1909 issue is roughly typographed in imitation of the 1907 design. It exists pin perf. 8, 13, etc.

No. 124 Handstamp Surcharged in Black, Green or Red:

1910, Nov. ***Perf. 14***

128	A14	1c on 20c ultra	7.50	6.00
129	A14	5c on 20c ultra (G)	7.50	6.00
130	A14	10c on 20c ultra (R)	7.50	6.00
		Nos. 128-130 (3)	22.50	18.00

As is usual with handstamped surcharges inverts and double exist.

Honduran Scene — A15

1911, Jan. **Litho.** ***Perf. 14, 12 (1p)***

131	A15	1c violet	.35	.20
132	A15	2c green	.35	.20
a.		Perf. 12	5.00	1.25
133	A15	5c carmine	.40	.20
a.		Perf. 12	8.00	3.50
134	A15	6c ultramarine	.50	.30
135	A15	10c blue	.60	.40
136	A15	20c yellow	.60	.50
137	A15	50c brown	2.00	1.75
138	A15	1p olive green	2.50	2.00
		Nos. 131-138 (8)	7.30	5.55

For overprints and surcharges see Nos. 139, 141-147, O28-O47.

No. 132a Overprinted in Red

1911, Sept. 19 ***Perf. 12***

139	A15	2c green	20.00	18.00
a.		Inverted overprint	24.00	22.50

90th anniversary of Independence.

Counterfeit overprints on perf. 14 stamps exist.

President Manuel Bonilla — A16

1912, Feb. 1 **Typo.** ***Perf. 11½***

140	A16	1c orange red	12.00	12.00

Election of Pres. Manuel Bonilla.

Stamps of 1911 Surcharged in Black, Red or Blue:

a

b

1913 **Litho.** ***Perf. 14***

141	A15(a)	2c on 1c violet	1.25	.75
a.		Double surcharge		3.25
b.		Inverted surcharge	4.50	
c.		Double surch., one invtd.	6.75	
d.		Red surcharge	40.00	40.00
142	A15(b)	2c on 1c violet	7.00	5.75
a.		Inverted surcharge	14.00	
143	A15(b)	2c on 10c blue	2.75	2.25
a.		Double surcharge	5.75	5.75
b.		Inverted surcharge		
144	A15(b)	2c on 20c yellow	7.00	6.75
145	A15(b)	5c on 1c violet	2.50	.75
146	A15(b)	5c on 10c bl (Bl)	2.75	1.50
147	A15(b)	6c on 1c violet	2.75	2.25
		Nos. 141-147 (7)	26.00	20.00

Counterfeit surcharges exist.

Terencio Sierra — A17

Bonilla — A18

ONE CENTAVO:
Type I — Solid border at sides below numerals.
Type II — Border of light and dark stripes.

1913-14 **Typo.** ***Perf. 11½***

151	A17	1c dark brn, I	.20	.20
a.		1c brown, type II	.75	.45
152	A17	2c carmine	.25	.20
153	A18	5c blue	.40	.20
154	A18	5c ultra ('14)	.40	.20
155	A18	6c gray vio	.50	.25
156	A18	6c purple ('14)	.40	.25
a.		6c red lilac	.60	.35
157	A17	10c blue	.75	.75
158	A17	10c brown ('14)	1.25	.50
159	A17	20c brown	1.00	.75
160	A18	50c rose	2.00	2.00
161	A18	1p gray green	2.25	2.25
		Nos. 151-161 (11)	9.40	7.55

For overprints and surcharges see Nos. 162-173, O48-O57.

Surcharged in Black or Carmine

1914

162	A17	1c on 2c carmine	.75	.75
163	A17	5c on 2c carmine	1.25	.90
164	A18	5c on 6c gray vio	2.00	2.00
165	A17	10c on 2c carmine	2.00	2.00
166	A18	10c on 6c gray vio	2.00	2.00
a.		Double surcharge	10.00	
167	A18	10c on 6c gray vio (C)	2.00	2.00
168	A18	10c on 50c rose	6.50	5.00
		Nos. 162-168 (7)	16.50	14.65

No. 158 Surcharged with New Value

1915

173	A17	5c on 10c brown	2.50	1.75

Ulua Bridge — A19

Bonilla Theater — A20

1915-16 **Typo.**

174	A19	1c chocolate	.20	.20
175	A19	2c carmine	.20	.20
a.		Tête bêche pair	1.00	1.00
176	A20	5c bright blue	.25	.20
177	A20	6c deep purple	.35	.20
178	A19	10c dull blue	.75	.20
179	A19	20c red brown	1.25	1.00
a.		Tête bêche pair	4.00	4.00
180	A20	50c red	1.50	1.50
181	A20	1p yellow grn	2.50	2.50
		Nos. 174-181 (8)	7.00	6.00

For overprints & surcharges see #183, 231-232, 237, 239-240, 285, 292, C1-C13, C25, C28, C31, C36, C57, CO21, CO30-CO32, CO42, O58-O65.

Imperf., Pairs

174a	A19	1c	2.00	2.00
175b	A19	2c	2.00	2.00
176a	A20	5c	3.50	
178a	A19	10c	3.50	
179b	A19	20c	5.25	
180b	A20	50c	7.00	
181a	A20	1p	8.75	8.75

Francisco Bertrand A21

Statue to Francisco Morazán A22

1916, Feb. 1

182	A21	1c orange	2.00	2.00

Election of Pres. Francisco Bertrand.
Unauthorized reprints exist.

Official Stamp No. O60 Overprinted

1918

183	A20	5c bright blue	2.00	1.50
a.		Inverted overprint	5.00	5.00

1919 **Typo.**

184	A22	1c brown	.20	.20
a.		Printed on both sides	2.00	
b.		Imperf., pair	.70	
185	A22	2c carmine	.25	.20
186	A22	5c lilac rose	.25	.20
187	A22	6c brt violet	.25	.20
188	A22	10c dull blue	.25	.25
189	A22	15c light blue	.75	.20
190	A22	15c dark violet	.60	.20
191	A22	20c orange brn	1.00	.30
a.		20c gray brown	10.00	.30
b.		Imperf., pair	2.75	
192	A22	50c light brown	4.00	2.50
a.		Imperf. pair	15.00	
193	A22	1p yellow green	7.50	*20.00*
a.		Imperf., pair	20.00	
b.		Printed on both sides	9.00	
c.		Tête bêche pair	15.00	
		Nos. 184-193 (10)	15.05	24.25

See note on handstamp following No. 217.
Unauthorized reprints exist.
For overprints and surcharges see Nos. 201-210C, 230, 233, 235-236, 238, 241-243, 287, 289, C58, C61, CO23, CO25, CO33, CO36-CO38, CO39, CO40, O66-O74.

"Dawn of Peace" — A23

1920, Feb. 1

Size: 27x21mm

194	A23	2c rose	2.50	2.50
a.		Tête bêche pair	15.00	12.50
b.		Imperf., pair	15.00	12.50

Size: 51x40mm

195	A23	2c gold	10.00	10.00
196	A23	2c silver	10.00	10.00
197	A23	2c bronze	10.00	10.00
198	A23	2c red	12.00	12.00
		Nos. 194-198 (5)	44.50	44.50

Assumption of power by Gen. Rafael Lopez Gutierrez.
Nos. 195-198 exist imperf.
Unauthorized reprints of #195-198 exist.

Type of 1919, Dated "1920"

1921

201	A22	6c dark violet	10.00	*5.00*
a.		Tête bêche pair	15.00	
b.		Imperf., pair	15.00	

Unauthorized reprints exist.

No. 185 Surcharged in Antique Letters

1922

202	A22	6c on 2c carmine	.40	.40
a.		"ALE" for "VALE"	2.00	2.00
b.		Comma after "CTS"	2.00	2.00
c.		Without period after "CTS"	2.00	2.00
d.		"CT" for "CTS"	2.00	2.00
e.		Double surcharge	4.25	
f.		Inverted surcharge	4.25	

Stamps of 1919 Surcharged in Roman Figures and Antique Letters in Green

1923

203	A22	10c on 1c brown	1.50	1.50
204	A22	50c on 2c carmine	2.00	2.00
a.		Inverted surcharge	10.00	10.00
b.		"HABILTADO"	6.00	6.00

Surcharged in Black or Violet Blue

205	A22	1p on 5c lil rose (Bk)	3.50	3.50
a.		"PSEO"	20.00	20.00
b.		Inverted surcharge	20.00	20.00
206	A22	1p on 5c lil rose (VB)	20.00	20.00
a.		"PSEO"	70.00	

On Nos. 205-206, "Habilitado Vale" is in Antique letters, "Un Peso" in Roman.

No. 185 Surcharged in Roman Letters in Green

207	A22	6c on 2c carmine	3.50	2.75

Nos. 184-185 Surcharged in Roman Letters in Green

208	A22	10c on 1c brown	1.75	1.25
a.		"DIES"	6.00	
b.		"DEIZ"	6.00	
c.		"DEIZ CAS"	6.00	
d.		"TTS" for "CTS"	6.00	
e.		"HABILTADO"	6.00	
f.		"HABILITAD"	6.00	
g.		"HABILITA"	6.00	
h.		Inverted surcharge	30.00	

209 A22 50c on 2c carmine 3.75 2.75
a. "CAT" for "CTA" 10.00
b. "TCA" for "CTA" 10.00
c. "TTS" for "CTS" 10.00
d. "CAS" for "CTS" 10.00
e. "HABILTADO" 10.00

Surcharge on No. 209 is found in two spacings between value and HABILITADO: 5mm (illustrated) and 1½mm.

No. 186 Surcharged in Antique Letters in Black

$ 1.00
HABILITADO
VALE
UN PESO

210 A22 1p on 5c lil rose 25.00 *25.00*
a. "PFSO" 75.00

In the surcharges on Nos. 202 to 210 there are various wrong font, inverted and omitted letters.

No. 184 Surcharged in Large Antique Letters in Green

210C A22 10c on 1c brown 15.00 15.00
d. "DIFZ" 55.00 55.00

Dionisio de Herrera A24

Pres. Miguel Paz Baraona A25

1924, June Litho. ***Perf. 11, 11½***

211 A24 1c olive green .30 .20
212 A24 2c deep rose .35 .20
213 A24 6c red violet .40 .20
214 A24 10c blue .40 .20
215 A24 20c yellow brn .80 .35
216 A24 50c vermilion 1.75 1.10
217 A24 1p emerald 4.00 2.75
Nos. 211-217 (7) 8.00 5.00

In 1924 a facsimile of the signatures of Santiago Herrera and Francisco Caceres, covering four stamps, was handstamped in violet to prevent the use of stamps that had been stolen during a revolution.

Imperfs exist.

For overprints and surcharges see Nos. 280-281, 290-291, C14-C24, C26-C27, C29-C30, C32-C35, C56, C60, C73-C76, CO1-CO5, CO22, CO24, CO28-CO29, CO34-CO35, CO38A, CO39A, CO41, CO43, O75-O81.

1925, Feb. 1 Typo. ***Perf. 11½***

218 A25 1c dull blue 2.00 2.00
a. 1c dark blue 2.00 2.00
219 A25 1c car rose 5.00 5.00
a. 1c brown carmine 5.00 5.00
220 A25 1c olive brn 14.00 14.00
a. 1c orange brown 14.00 14.00
b. 1c dark brown 14.00 14.00
c. 1c black brown 14.00 14.00
221 A25 1c buff 12.00 12.00
222 A25 1c red 60.00 60.00
223 A25 1c green 40.00 40.00
Nos. 218-223 (6) 133.00 133.00

Imperf

225 A25 1c dull blue 5.50 5.50
a. 1c dark blue 5.50 5.50
226 A25 1c car rose 8.75 8.75
a. 1c brown carmine 8.75 8.75
227 A25 1c olive brn 8.75 8.75
a. 1c orange brown 8.75 8.75
b. 1c deep brown 8.75 8.75
c. 1c black brown 8.75 8.75
228 A25 1c buff 8.75 8.75
229 A25 1c red 60.00 60.00
229A A25 1c green 27.50 27.50
Nos. 225-229A (6) 119.25 119.25

Inauguration of President Baraona.
Counterfeits and unauthorized reprints exist.

No. 187 Overprinted in Black and Red

1926, June ***Perf. 11½***

230 A22 6c bright violet 1.50 1.25

Many varieties of this two-part overprint exist: one or both inverted or double, and various combinations. Value, each $10.

Nos. 177 and 187 Overprinted in Black or Red

1926

231 A20 6c deep pur (Bk) 2.00 2.00
a. Inverted overprint 5.50 5.50
b. Double overprint 5.50 5.50
232 A20 6c deep pur (R) 2.50 2.50
a. Double overprint 5.00 5.00
233 A22 6c lilac (Bk) .60 .60
a. 6c violet .75 .75
b. Inverted overprint 5.00 5.00
c. Double overprint 5.00 5.00
d. Double ovpt., one inverted 5.00 5.00
e. "192" 7.50 7.50
f. Double ovpt., both inverted 7.50 7.50

Same Overprint on No. 230

235 A22 6c violet 20.00 20.00
a. "1926" inverted 20.00 20.00
b. "Habilitado" triple, one invtd. 20.00 20.00

No. 188 Surcharged in Red or Black

236 A22 6c on 10c blue (R) .50 .20
c. Double surcharge 5.00 4.00
d. Without bar
e. Inverted surcharge 4.00 3.50
f. "Vale" omitted
g. "6cts" omitted
h. "cts" omitted
k. Black surcharge *55.00 55.00*

Nos. 175 and 185 Overprinted in Green

237 A19 2c carmine .20 .20
a. Tête bêche pair 4.00 4.00
b. Double overprint 2.00 1.40
c. "HARILITADO" 2.00 1.40
d. "1926" only 2.75 2.75
e. Double overprint, one inverted 2.75 2.75
f. "1926" omitted 3.50 3.50
g. Triple overprint, two inverted 5.25 5.25
h. Double on face, one on back 5.25 5.25
238 A22 2c carmine .20 .20
a. "HARILITADO" .90 .90
b. Double overprint 1.40 1.40
c. Inverted overprint 2.00 2.00

No. 177 Overprinted in Red

1926

Large Numerals, 12x5mm

1927

239 A20 6c deep purple 25.00 25.00
a. "1926" over "1927" 35.00 35.00
b. Invtd. ovpt. on face of stamp, normal ovpt. on back 30.00

No. 179 Surcharged

1927

240 A19 6c on 20c brown .75 .75
a. Tête bêche pair 2.75 2.75
c. Interted surcharge 2.50 2.50
d. Double surcharge 8.50 8.50

Nos. 8 and 10 in the setting have no period after "cts" and No. 50 has the "t" of "cts" inverted.

Same Surcharge on Nos. 189-191

241 A22 6c on 15c blue 27.50 27.50
a. "c" of "cts" omitted
242 A22 6c on 15c vio .70 .70
a. Double surcharge 1.75 1.75
b. Double surch., one invtd. 2.00 2.00
c. "L" of "Vale" omitted
243 A22 6c on 20c yel brn .60 .60
a. 6c on 20c deep brown
b. "6" omitted 1.75 1.75
c. "Vale" and "cts" omitted 3.50 3.50
Nos. 240-243 (4) 29.55 29.55

On Nos. 242 and 243 stamps Nos. 12, 16 and 43 in the setting have no period after "cts" and No. 34 often lacks the "s." On No. 243 the "c" of "cts" is missing on stamp No. 38. On No. 241 occur the varieties "ct" or "ts" for "cts." and no period.

Southern Highway — A26

Ruins of Copán — A27

Pine Tree — A28

Presidential Palace — A29

Ponciano Leiva — A30

Pres. M.A. Soto — A31

Lempira — A32

Map of Honduras — A33

President Juan Lindo — A34

Statue of Columbus — A35

1927-29 Typo. Wmk. 209

244 A26 1c ultramarine .30 .20
a. 1c blue .30 .20
245 A27 2c carmine .30 .20
246 A28 5c dull violet .30 .20
247 A28 5c bl gray ('29) 25.00 7.00
248 A29 6c blue black .75 .50
a. 6c gray black .75 .50
249 A29 6c dark bl ('29) .40 .20
a. 6c light blue .40 .20
250 A30 10c blue .70 .20
251 A31 15c deep blue 1.00 .50
252 A32 20c dark blue 1.25 .60
253 A33 30c dark brown 1.50 1.00
254 A34 50c light blue 2.50 1.50
255 A35 1p red 5.00 2.50
Nos. 244-255 (12) 39.00 14.60

In 1929 a quantity of imperforate sheets of No. 249 were stolen from the Litografia Nacional. Some of them were perforated by sewing machine and a few copies were passed through the post. To prevent the use of stolen stamps of the 1927-29 issues they were declared invalid and the stock on hand was overprinted "1929 a 1930."

For overprints and surcharges see Nos. 259-278, CO19-CO20B.

Pres. Vicente Mejia Colindres and Vice-Pres. Rafael Diaz Chávez — A36

President Mejia Colindres — A37

1929, Feb. 25

256 A36 1c dk carmine 3.00 3.00
257 A37 2c emerald 3.00 3.00

Installation of Pres. Vicente Mejia Colindres. Printed in sheets of ten.

Nos. 256 and 257 were surreptitiously printed in transposed colors. They were not regularly issued.

Stamps of 1927-29 Overprinted in Various Colors

1929, Oct.

259 A26 1c blue (R) .20 .20
a. 1c ultramarine (R) .50 .20
b. Double overprint 2.50 1.75
c. As "a", double overprint 2.50 1.75
260 A26 1c blue (Bk) 6.50 6.50
a. 1c ultramarine (Bk)
261 A27 2c car (R Br) 3.50 3.50
a. Double overprint
262 A27 2c car (Bl Gr) 1.00 1.00
a. Double overprint
263 A27 2c car (Bk) 1.00 .50
264 A27 2c car (V) .50 .25
a. Double overprint
b. Double ovpt., one inverted
265 A27 2c org red (V) 1.50
266 A28 5c dl vio (R) .40 .30
a. Double overprint (R+V)
267 A28 5c bl gray (R) 1.00 .75
a. Double overprint (R+Bk)
269 A29 6c gray blk (R) 2.50 2.00
a. Double overprint 6.00 6.00
272 A29 6c dk blue (R) .40 .20
a. 6c light blue (R) .40 .20
b. Double overprint 2.00 2.00
c. Double overprint (R+V)
273 A30 10c blue (R) .40 .20
a. Double overprint 2.50 1.75
274 A31 15c dp blue (R) .50 .25
a. Double overprint 3.50 2.50
275 A32 20c dark bl (R) .50 .35
276 A33 30c dark brn (R) .75 .60
a. Double overprint 3.50 2.50
277 A34 50c light bl (R) 2.00 1.00
278 A35 1p red (V) 5.00 2.50
Nos. 259-278 (17) 27.65

Nos. 259-278 exist in numerous shades. There are also various shades of the red and violet overprints. The overprint may be found reading upwards, downwards, inverted, double, triple, tête bêche or combinations.

Status of both 6c stamps with overprint in black is questioned.

A38

1929, Dec. 10

279 A38 1c on 6c lilac rose .70 .70
- *a.* "1992" for "1929"
- *b.* "9192" for "1929"
- *c.* Surcharge reading down 8.00
- *d.* Dbl. surch., one reading down

Varieties include "1992" reading down and pairs with one surcharge reading down, double or with "1992."

No. 214 Surcharged in Red

Perf. 11, 11½

1930, Mar. 26 **Unwmk.**

280 A24 1c on 10c blue .35 .30
- *a.* "1093" for "1930" 1.40
- *b.* "tsc" for "cts" 1.40

281 A24 2c on 10c blue .35 .30
- *a.* "tsc" for "cts" 2.00
- *b.* "Vale 2" omitted

Official Stamps of 1929 Overprinted in Red or Violet

1930, Mar. **Wmk. 209** ***Perf. 11½***

282 O1 1c blue (R) .50 .50
- *a.* Double overprint 2.00 2.00

284 O1 2c carmine (V) .90 .90

Stamps of 1915-26 Overprinted in Blue

On No. 174

1930, July 19 **Unwmk.**

285 A19 1c chocolate .30 .25
- *a.* Double overprint 1.00 1.00
- *b.* Inverted overprint 1.40 1.40
- *c.* Dbl. ovpt., one inverted 1.40 1.40

On No. 184

287 A22 1c brown 15.00 15.00
- *a.* Double overprint
- *c.* Inverted overprint

On No. 204

289 A22 50c on 2c carmine 100.00 90.00
- *b.* Inverted surcharge

On Nos. 211 and 212

290 A24 1c olive green .20 .20
- *a.* Double overprint 1.75 1.75
- *b.* Inverted overprint 1.75 1.75
- *d.* On No. O75 12.00

291 A24 2c carmine rose .25 .25
- *a.* Double overprint 1.75 1.75
- *b.* Inverted overprint 1.75 1.75

On No. 237

292 A19 2c car (G & Bl) 100.00 100.00

From Title Page of Government Gazette, First Issue — A39

1930, Aug. 11 **Typo.** **Wmk. 209**

295 A39 2c orange .90 .90
296 A39 2c ultramarine .90 .90
297 A39 2c red .90 .90
Nos. 295-297 (3) 2.70 2.70

Publication of the 1st newspaper in Honduras, cent. The stamps were on sale and available for postage on Aug. 11th, 1930, only. Not more than 5 copies of each color could be purchased by an applicant.

Nos. 295-297 exist imperf. and part-perforate. Unauthorized reprints exist.

For surcharges see Nos. CO15-CO18A.

Paz Baraona — A40

Manuel Bonilla — A41

Lake Yojoa — A42

View of Palace at Tegucigalpa A43

City of Amapala A44

Mayan Stele at Copán A45

Christopher Columbus A46

Discovery of America A47

Loarque Bridge A48

Unwmk.

1931, Jan. 2 **Engr.** ***Perf. 12***

298 A40 1c black brown .75 .20
299 A41 2c carmine rose .75 .20
300 A42 5c dull violet 1.00 .20
301 A43 6c deep green 1.00 .20
302 A44 10c brown 1.50 .25
303 A45 15c dark blue 2.00 .30
304 A46 20c black 3.50 .40
305 A47 50c olive green 4.50 1.50
306 A48 1p slate black 9.00 2.50
Nos. 298-306 (9) 24.00 5.75

Regular Issue of 1931 Overprinted in Black or Various Colors

1931

307 A40 1c black brown .40 .30
308 A41 2c carmine rose .60 .30
309 A45 15c dark blue 1.00 .30
310 A46 20c black 2.50 .40

Overprinted

311 A42 5c dull violet .50 .30
312 A43 6c deep green .50 .30
315 A44 10c brown 1.50 .35
316 A47 50c olive green 8.00 5.00
317 A48 1p slate black 10.00 7.50
Nos. 307-317 (9) 25.00 14.75
Nos. 307-317,C51-C55 (14) 50.00 35.75

The overprint is a control mark. It stands for "Tribunal Superior de Cuentas" (Superior Tribunal of Accounts).

Overprint varieties include: inverted; double; double, one or both inverted; on back; pair, one without overprint; differing colors (6c exists with overprint in orange, yellow and red).

President Carías and Vice-President Williams — A49

1933, Apr. 29

318 A49 2c carmine rose .50 .35
319 A49 6c deep green .75 .40
320 A49 10c deep blue 1.00 .50
321 A49 15c red orange 1.25 .75
Nos. 318-321 (4) 3.50 2.00

Inauguration of Pres. Tiburico Carias Andino and Vice-Pres. Abraham Williams, Feb. 1, 1933.

Columbus' Fleet and Flag of the Race — A50

Wmk. 209

1933, Aug. 3 **Typo.** ***Perf. 11½***

322 A50 2c ultramarine 1.00 .65
323 A50 6c yellow 1.00 .65
324 A50 10c lemon 1.40 .85

Perf. 12

325 A50 15c violet 2.00 1.50
326 A50 50c red 4.00 3.50
327 A50 1 l emerald 7.00 7.00
Nos. 322-327 (6) 16.40 14.15

"Day of the Race," an annual holiday throughout Spanish-American countries. Also for the 441st anniv. of the sailing of Columbus to the New World, Aug. 3, 1492.

Masonic Temple, Tegucigalpa — A51

Designs: 2c, President Carias. 5c, Flag. 6c, Tomás Estrada Palma.

Unwmk.

1935, Jan. 12 **Engr.** ***Perf. 12***

328 A51 1c green .40 .20
329 A51 2c carmine .40 .20
330 A51 5c dark blue .40 .25
331 A51 6c black brown .40 .25
- *a.* Vert. pair, imperf. btwn. 20.00 20.00

Nos. 328-331 (4) 1.60 .90
Nos. 328-331,C77-C83 (11) 12.40 5.40

Gen. Carías Bridge — A55

1937, June 4

332 A55 6c car & ol green .75 .35
333 A55 21c grn & violet 1.25 .65
334 A55 46c orange & brn 1.75 1.25
335 A55 55c ultra & black 2.50 2.00
Nos. 332-335 (4) 6.25 4.25

Prolongation of the Presidential term to Jan. 19, 1943.

Seal of Honduras A56

Central District Palace — A57

Designs: 3c, Map of Honduras. 5c, Bridge of Choluteca. 8c, Flag.

1939, Mar. 1 ***Perf. 12½***

336 A56 1c orange yellow .20 .20
337 A57 2c red orange .20 .20
338 A57 3c carmine .30 .20
339 A57 5c orange .30 .20
340 A56 8c dark blue .50 .20
Nos. 336-340 (5) 1.50 1.00
Nos. 336-340,C89-C98 (15) 15.30 8.45

Nos. 336-340 exist imperf.

For overprints see #342-343.

Nos. 336 and 337 Overprinted in Green

1944 ***Perf. 12½***

342 A56 1c orange yellow .30 .30
- *a.* Inverted overprint 5.00 5.00

343 A57 2c red orange 1.25 .75
- *a.* Inverted overprint 5.00 5.00

AIR POST STAMPS

Regular Issue of 1915-16 Overprinted in Black, Blue or Red

1925 **Unwmk.** ***Perf. 11½***

C1 A20 5c lt blue (Bk) 87.50 87.50
C2 A20 5c lt blue (Bl) 300.00 300.00
- *a.* Inverted overprint *400.00*
- *b.* Vertical overprint *600.00*
- *c.* Double overprint *800.00*

C3 A20 5c lt blue (R) *7,250.*

Value for No. C3 is for copy without gum.

C4 A19 10c dk blue (R) 175.00
- *a.* Inverted overprint 325.00
- *b.* Overprint tête bêche, pair *800.00*

C5 A19 10c dk blue (Bk) *1,100.*
C6 A19 20c red brn (Bk) 175.00 175.00
- *a.* Inverted overprint 250.00
- *b.* Tête bêche pair 400.00
- *c.* Overprint tête bêche, pair *725.00*
- *d.* "AFRO" *1,400.*
- *e.* Double overprint *600.00*

C7 A19 20c red brn (Bl) 175.00 175.00
- *a.* Inverted overprint *700.00*
- *b.* Tête bêche pair *1,000*
- *c.* Vertical overprint 900.00

C8 A20 50c red (Bk) 450.00 300.00
- *a.* Inverted overprint *550.00*
- *b.* Overprint tête bêche, pair *900.00*

C9 A20 1p yel grn (Bk) 600.00 600.00

Surcharged in Black or Blue

C10 A19 25c on 1c choc 125.00 125.00
a. Inverted surcharge 700.00
C11 A20 25c on 5c lt bl (Bl) 225.00 225.00
a. Inverted surcharge 700.00
b. Double inverted surcharge *675.00*
C12 A19 25c on 10c dk bl *75,000.*
C13 A19 25c on 20c brn (Bl) 200.00 200.00
a. Inverted surcharge 325.00
b. Tête bêche pair 450.00

Counterfeits of Nos. C1-C13 are plentiful.

Monoplane and Lisandro Garay AP1

1929, June 5 Engr. *Perf. 12*
C13C AP1 50c carmine 2.00 1.75

No. 216 Surcharged in Blue

1929 *Perf. 11, 11½*
C14 A24 25c on 50c ver 5.00 3.50

In the surcharges on Nos. C14 to C40 there are various wrong font and defective letters and numerals, also periods omitted.

Nos. 215-217 Surcharged in Green, Black or Red

1929, Oct.
C15 A24 5c on 20c yel brn (G) 1.40 1.40
a. Double surcharge (R+G) 45.00
C16 A24 10c on 50c ver (Bk) 2.25 1.90
C17 A24 15c on 1p emer (R) 3.50 3.50
Nos. C15-C17 (3) 7.15 6.80

a

b

Nos. 214 and 216 SurchargedVertically in Red or Black

1929, Dec. 10
C18 A24(a) 5c on 10c bl (R) .60 .60
C19 A24(b) 20c on 50c ver 1.00 1.00
a. "1299" for "1929" 190.00
b. "cts. cts." for "cts. oro." 190.00
c. "r" of "Aereo" omitted 2.00
d. Horiz. pair, imperf. btwn. 20.00

Nos. 214, 215 and 180 Surcharged in Various Colors

1930, Feb.
C20 A24 5c on 10c (R) .50 .50
a. "1930" reading down 3.50
b. "1903" for "1930" 3.50
c. Surcharge reading down 10.00
d. Double surcharge 14.00
e. Dbl. surch., one downward 14.00
C21 A24 5c on 10c (Y) *450.00 450.00*
C22 A24 5c on 20c (Bl) 125.00 125.00
C23 A24 10c on 20c (Bk) .70 .70
a. "0" for "10" 3.50
b. Double surcharge 8.75
c. Dbl. surch., one downward 12.00
d. Horiz. pair, imperf. btwn. 70.00
C24 A24 10c on 20c (V) *750.00 750.00*
a. "0" for "10" *1,600.*
C25 A20 25c on 50c (Bk) .95 .95
a. "Internaoicnal" 3.50
b. "o" for "oro" 3.50
c. Inverted surcharge 17.50
d. As "a," invtd. surch. *175.00*
e. As "b," invtd. surch. *175.00*

Surcharge on Nos. C20-C24 are vertical.

Nos. 214, 215 and 180 Surcharged

1930, Apr. 1
C26 A24 5c on 10c blue .50 .50
a. Double surcharge 9.50
b. "Servicioa" 3.50
C27 A24 15c on 20c yel brn .55 .55
a. Double surcharge 7.00
C28 A20 20c on 50c red, surch. reading down .95 .95
a. Surcharge reading up 7.00
Nos. C26-C28 (3) 2.00 2.00

Nos. C22 and C23 Surcharged Vertically in Red

1930
C29 A24 10c on 5c on 20c (Bl+R) .90 .90
a. "1930" reading down 9.00 9.00
b. "1903" for "1930" 9.00 9.00
c. Red surcharge, reading down 14.00
C30 A24 10c on 10c on 20c (Bk+R) 87.50 87.50
a. "0" for "10" 190.00

No. 181 Surcharged as No. C25 and Re-surcharged

C31 A20 50c on 25c on 1p grn 4.25 4.25
a. "Internaoicnal" 7.00
b. "o" for "oro" 7.00
c. 25c surcharge inverted 17.50 17.50
d. 50c surcharge inverted 17.50 17.50
e. As "a" and "c"
f. As "a" and "d"
g. As "b" and "c"
h. As "b" and "d"
Nos. C29-C31 (3) 92.65 92.65

No. 215 Surcharged in Dark Blue

1930, May 22
C32 A24 5c on 20c yel brn 1.25 1.00
a. Double surcharge 5.25 5.25
b. Horiz. pair, imperf. btwn. 60.00 60.00
c. Vertical pair, imperf. between 20.00 20.00

Nos. O78-O80 Surcharged like Nos. C20 to C25 in Various Colors

1930
C33 A24 5c on 10c (R) 450.00 350.00
a. "1930" reading down *875.00*
b. "1903" for "1930" *875.00*
C34 A24 5c on 20c (Bl) 400.00 400.00
C35 A24 25c on 50c (Bk) 225.00 225.00
a. 55c on 50c vermilion 325.00 325.00

No. C35 exists with inverted surcharge.

No. O64 Surcharged like No. C28

C36 A20 20c on 50c red, surcharge reading down *350.00 350.00*
a. Surcharge reading up *350.00 350.00*
b. Dbl. surch., reading down *350.00 350.00*
c. Dbl. surch., reading up *350.00 350.00*

No. O87 Overprinted

1930, Feb. 21 Wmk. 209 *Perf. 11½*
C37 O1 50c yel, grn & blue 1.40 1.25
a. "Internacional" 5.25
b. "luternacional" 5.25
c. Double overprint 5.25

Nos. O86-O88 Overprinted in Various Colors

1930, May 23
C38 O1 20c dark blue (R) 1.10 .85
a. Double overprint 8.75
b. Triple overprint 12.00
C39 O1 50c org, grn & bl (Bk) 1.10 .90
C40 O1 1p buff (Bl) 1.40 1.25
a. Double overprint 10.50
Nos. C38-C40 (3) 3.60 3.00

National Palace AP3

Unwmk.
1930, Oct. 1 Engr. *Perf. 12*
C41 AP3 5c yel orange .50 .30
C42 AP3 10c carmine .75 .60
C43 AP3 15c green 1.00 .75
C44 AP3 20c dull violet 1.25 .60
C45 AP3 1p light brown 4.00 4.00
Nos. C41-C45 (5) 7.50 6.25

Same Overprinted in Various Colors

1931 *Perf. 12*
C51 AP3 5c yel orange (R) *2.00 1.50*
C52 AP3 10c carmine (Bk) *3.00 2.50*
C53 AP3 15c green (Br) *5.00 4.00*
C54 AP3 20c dull vio (O) *5.00 4.25*
C55 AP3 1p lt brown (G) *10.00 8.75*
Nos. C51-C55 (5) *25.00 21.00*

See note after No. 317.

Stamps of Various Issues Surcharged in Blue or Black (#C59)

1931, Oct. *Perf. 11½*

On No. 215

C56 A24 15c on 20c yel brn 3.50 2.75
a. Horiz. pair, imperf. btwn. 42.50
b. Green surcharge 20.00 20.00

On No. O64

C57 A20 15c on 50c red 4.25 3.50
a. Inverted surcharge 10.50 10.50

On No. O72

C58 A22 15c on 20c brn 4.25 4.25
a. Vert. pair, imperf. between 12.00

On Nos. C57 and C58 the word "OFICIAL" is canceled by two bars.

On No. O88
Wmk. 209

C59 O1 15c on 1p buff 4.25 4.25
a. Vert. pair, imperf. horiz. 25.00
b. "Sevricio" 14.00 14.00

The varieties "Vaie" for "Vale," "aereo" with circumflex accent on the first "e" and "Interior" with initial capital "I" are found on #C56, C58-C59. #C57 is known with initial capital in "Interior."

A similar surcharge, in slightly larger letters and with many minor varieties, exists on Nos. 215, O63, O64 and O73. The authenticity of this surcharge is questioned.

Nos. 215, O73, O87-O88 Surcharged in Green, Red or Black

1931, Nov. Unwmk.
C60 A24 15c on 20c (G) 3.50 2.75
a. Inverted surcharge 6.25
b. "XI" omitted 6.25
c. "X" for "XI" 6.25
d. "PI" for "XI" 6.25
C61 A22 15c on 50c (R) 3.50 2.75
a. "XI" omitted 6.75
b. "PI" for "XI" 6.75
c. Double surcharge 20.00 20.00

On No. C61 the word "OFICIAL" is not barred out.

Wmk. 209

C62 O1 15c on 50c (Bk) 2.75 2.50
a. "1391" for "1931" 10.50 10.50
b. Double surcharge 8.75 8.75
C63 O1 15c on 1p (Bk) 2.50 2.25
a. "1391" for "1931" 12.50
b. Surcharged on both sides 7.00

Nos. O76-O78 Surcharged in Black or Red

1932 Unwmk. *Perf. 11, 11½*
C73 A24 15c on 2c .80 .80
a. Double surcharge 5.50
b. Inverted surcharge 4.25
c. "Ae" of "Aero" omitted 1.00
d. On No. 212 (no "Official")
C74 A24 15c on 6c .80 .80
a. Double surcharge 3.50
b. Horiz. pair, imperf. btwn. 17.50
c. "Aer" omitted
d. "A" omitted 1.00
e. Inverted surcharge 3.50
C75 A24 15c on 10c (R) .80 .80
a. Double surcharge 5.50
b. Inverted surcharge 3.50
c. "r" of "Aereo" omitted 1.00

Same Surcharge on No. 214 in Red

C76 A24 15c on 10c dp bl *150.00 100.00*

There are various broken and missing letters in the setting.

A similar surcharge with slightly larger letters exists.

Post Office and National Palace AP4

View of Tegucigalpa — AP5

Designs: 15c, Map of Honduras. 20c, Mayol Bridge. 40c, View of Tegucigalpa. 50c, Owl. 1 l, Coat of Arms.

1935, Jan. 10 *Perf. 12*
C77 AP4 8c blue .20 .20
C78 AP5 10c gray .25 .20
C79 AP5 15c olive gray .40 .20
C80 AP5 20c dull green .50 .20
C81 AP5 40c brown .70 .20
C82 AP4 50c yellow 6.25 1.25
C83 AP4 1 l green 2.50 2.25
Nos. C77-C83 (7) 10.80 4.50

Flags of US and Honduras — AP11

Engr. & Litho.

1937, Sept. 17 **Unwmk.**

C84 AP11 46c multicolored 2.00 1.00

US Constitution, 150th anniv..

Comayagua Cathedral AP12

Founding of Comayagua AP13

Alonzo Cáceres and Pres. Carías — AP14

Lintel of Royal Palace AP15

1937, Dec. 7 **Engr.**

C85	AP12	2c copper red	.20	.20
C86	AP13	8c dark blue	.30	.20
C87	AP14	15c slate black	.50	.50
C88	AP15	50c dark brown	3.00	2.00
		Nos. C85-C88 (4)	4.00	2.90

City of Comayagua founding, 400th anniv.
For surcharges see Nos. C144-C146.

Mayan Stele at Copán AP16

Mayan Temple, Copán AP17

Designs: 15c, President Carias. 30c, José C. de Valle. 40c, Presidential House. 46c, Lempira. 55c, Church of Our Lady of Suyapa. 66c, J. T. Reyes. 1 l, Hospital at Choluteca. 2 l, Ramón Rosa.

1939, Mar. 1 ***Perf. 12½***

C89 AP16	10c orange brn	.20	.20
C90 AP16	15c grnsh blue	.30	.20
C91 AP17	21c gray	.50	.20
C92 AP16	30c dk blue grn	.55	.20
C93 AP17	40c dull violet	1.00	.25
C94 AP16	46c dk gray brn	1.00	.65
C95 AP16	55c green	1.25	1.00
a.	Imperf., pair	22.50	
C96 AP16	66c black	1.75	1.25
C97 AP16	1 l olive grn	3.00	1.00
C98 AP16	2 l henna red	4.25	2.50
	Nos. C89-C98 (10)	13.80	7.45

For surcharges see #C118-C119, C147-C152.

Souvenir Sheets

AP26

14c, Francisco Morazan. 16c, George Washington. 30c, J. C. de Valle. 40c, Simon Bolivar.

1940, Apr. 13 **Engr.** ***Perf. 12***

Centers of Stamps Lithographed

C99 AP26	Sheet of 4	3.00	3.00
a.	14c black, yellow, ultra & rose	.45	.45
b.	16c black, yellow, ultra & rose	.55	.55
c.	30c black, yellow, ultra & rose	.75	.75
d.	40c black, yellow, ultra & rose	.85	.85

Imperf

C100 AP26	Sheet of 4	3.00	3.00
a.	14c black, yellow, ultra & rose	.45	.45
b.	16c black, yellow, ultra & rose	.55	.55
c.	30c black, yellow, ultra & rose	.75	.75
d.	40c black, yellow, ultra & rose	.85	.85

Pan American Union, 50th anniv.
For overprints see Nos. C153-C154, C187.

Air Post Official Stamps of 1939 Overprinted in Red

1940, Oct. 12 ***Perf. 12½***

C101 OA2	2c dp bl & green	.20	.20
C102 OA2	5c dp blue & org	.25	.25
C103 OA2	8c deep bl & brn	.30	.30
C104 OA2	15c dp blue & car	.50	.50
C105 OA2	46c dp bl & ol grn	.80	.80
C106 OA2	50c dp bl & vio	.90	.90
C107 OA2	1 l dp bl & red brn	3.75	3.75
C108 OA2	2 l dp bl & red org	7.50	7.50
	Nos. C101-C108 (8)	14.20	14.20

Erection and dedication of the Columbus Memorial Lighthouse.

AIR POST SEMI-POSTAL STAMPS

No. C13C Surcharged with Plus Sign and Surtax in Black

Unwmk.

1929, June 5 **Engr.** ***Perf. 12***

CB1 AP1	50c + 5c carmine	.50	.30
CB2 AP1	50c + 10c carmine	.60	.35
CB3 AP1	50c + 15c carmine	.85	.55
CB4 AP1	50c + 20c carmine	1.25	.75
	Nos. CB1-CB4 (4)	3.20	1.95

No. C619 Surcharged With New Value in Black and 2000 Sydney Olympics Emblem in Red

2000, Sept. 13 **Litho.** ***Imperf.***

CB5 AP99 48.50 l +1.50 l multi 11.00 11.00

AIR POST OFFICIAL STAMPS

Official Stamps Nos. O78 to O81 Overprinted in Red, Green or Black

1930 ***Perf. 11, 11½***

CO1 A24	10c deep blue (R)	1.25	1.25
CO2 A24	20c yellow brown	1.25	1.25
a.	Vert. pair, imperf. btwn.	14.00	
CO3 A24	50c vermilion (Bk)	1.40	1.40
CO4 A24	1p emerald (R)	1.25	1.25
	Nos. CO1-CO4 (4)	5.15	5.15

OA1

Green Surcharge

CO5 OA1	5c on 6c red vio	1.00	1.00
a.	"1910" for "1930"	2.75	2.75
b.	"1920" for "1930"	2.75	2.75

The overprint exists in other colors and on other denominations but the status of these is questioned.

Official Stamps of 1931 Overprinted

1931 **Unwmk.** ***Perf. 12***

CO6 O2	1c ultra	.35	.35
CO7 O2	2c black brown	.85	.85
CO8 O2	5c olive gray	1.00	1.00
CO9 O2	6c orange red	1.00	1.00
a.	Inverted overprint	24.00	24.00
CO10 O2	10c dark green	1.25	1.25
CO11 O2	15c olive brown	2.00	1.75
a.	Inverted overprint	20.00	20.00
CO12 O2	20c red brown	2.00	1.75
CO13 O2	50c gray violet	1.40	1.40
CO14 O2	1p deep orange	2.00	1.75
	Nos. CO6-CO14 (9)	11.85	11.10

In the setting of the overprint there are numerous errors in the spelling and punctuation, letters omitted and similar varieties.

This set is known with blue overprint. A similar overprint is known in larger type, but its status has not been fully determined.

Postage Stamps of 1918-30 Surcharged Type "a" or Type "b" (#CO22-CO23) in Green, Black, Red and Blue

a

b

1933 **Wmk. 209, Unwmk.**

CO15	A39	20c on 2c #295 (G)	3.25	3.25
CO16	A39	20c on 2c #296 (G)	3.25	3.25
CO17	A39	20c on 2c #297 (G)	3.25	3.25
CO17A	A39	40c on 2c #295	2.00	2.00
CO18	A39	40c on 2c #297 (G)	7.00	7.00
CO18A	A39	40c on 2c #297	4.25	4.25
CO19	A28	40c on 5c #246	4.25	4.25
CO19A	A28	40c on 5c #247	7.00	7.00
CO20	A28	40c on 5c #266	15.00	15.00
CO20A	A28	40c on 5c #267	9.00	9.00
CO20B	A28	40c on 5c #267 (R)	14.00	14.00
CO21	A20	70c on 5c #183	3.00	3.00
CO22	A24	70c on 10c #214 (R)	3.25	3.25
CO23	A22	1 l on 20c #191 (Bl)	3.25	3.25
CO24	A24	1 l on 50c #216 (Bl)	14.00	14.00
CO25	A22	1.20 l on 1p #193 (Bl)	1.00	1.00
		Nos. CO15-CO25 (16)	96.75	96.75

Official Stamps of 1915-29 Surcharged Type "a" or Type "b" (#CO28-CO29, CO33-CO41, CO43) in Black, Red, Green, Orange, Carmine or Blue

CO26	O1	40c on 5c #O84 (Bk)	1.00	1.00
CO27	O1	40c on 5c #O84 (R)	25.00	25.00
CO28	A24	60c on 6c #O77 (Bk)	.70	.70
CO29	A24	60c on 6c #O77 (G)	25.00	25.00
CO30	A20	70c on 5c #O60 (Bk)	5.25	5.25
CO31	A19	70c on 10c #O62 (R)	9.00	9.00
CO32	A19	70c on 10c #O62 (Bk)	7.75	7.75
CO33	A22	70c on 10c #O70 (R)	4.50	4.00
CO34	A24	70c on 10c #O78 (O)	3.50	3.50
CO35	A24	70c on 10c #O78 (C)	4.50	4.50
CO36	A22	70c on 15c #O71 (R)	87.50	87.50
CO37	A22	90c on 10c #O70 (R)	5.25	5.25
CO38	A22	90c on 15c #O71 (R)	8.00	8.00
CO38A	A24	1 l on 2c #O76	1.40	1.40
CO39	A22	1 l on 20c #O72	2.50	2.50
CO39A	A24	1 l on 20c #O79	3.75	3.75
CO40	A22	1 l on 50c #O73	1.90	1.90
CO41	A24	1 l on 50c #O80	4.25	4.25
CO42	A20	1.20 l on 1p #O65	9.00	7.00
CO43	A24	1.20 l on 1p #O81	3.00	3.00
		Nos. CO26-CO43 (20)	212.75	210.25

Varieties of foregoing surcharges exist.

Merchant Flag and Seal of Honduras OA2

1939, Feb. 27 **Unwmk.** ***Perf. 12½***

CO44 OA2	2c dp blue & grn	.20	.20
CO45 OA2	5c dp blue & org	.20	.20
CO46 OA2	8c dp blue & brn	.20	.20
CO47 OA2	15c dp blue & car	.30	.20
CO48 OA2	46c dp blue & ol grn	.40	.30
CO49 OA2	50c dp blue & vio	.50	.30
CO50 OA2	1 l dp blue & red brn	1.75	1.25
CO51 OA2	2 l dp blue & red org	3.75	2.25
	Nos. CO44-CO51 (8)	7.30	4.90

For overprints and surcharges see #C101-C117.

OFFICIAL STAMPS

Type of Regular Issue of 1890 Overprinted in Red

1890 **Unwmk.** ***Perf. 12***

O1 A5	1c pale yellow	.20
O2 A5	2c pale yellow	.20
O3 A5	5c pale yellow	.20
O4 A5	10c pale yellow	.20
O5 A5	20c pale yellow	.20
O6 A5	25c pale yellow	.20
O7 A5	30c pale yellow	.20
O8 A5	40c pale yellow	.20
O9 A5	50c pale yellow	.20
O10 A5	75c pale yellow	.20
O11 A5	1p pale yellow	.20
	Nos. O1-O11 (11)	2.20

Type of Regular Issue of 1891 Overprinted in Red

1891

O12 A6	1c yellow	.20
O13 A6	2c yellow	.20
O14 A6	5c yellow	.20
O15 A6	10c yellow	.20
O16 A6	20c yellow	.20
O17 A6	25c yellow	.20
O18 A6	30c yellow	.20
O19 A6	40c yellow	.20
O20 A6	50c yellow	.20
O21 A6	75c yellow	.20
O22 A6	1p yellow	.20
	Nos. O12-O22 (11)	2.20

Nos. O1 to O22 were never placed in use. Cancellations were applied to remainders. They exist with overprint inverted, double, triple and omitted; also, imperf. and part perf.

Regular Issue of 1898 Overprinted

1898-99 *Perf. 11½*

O23	A12	5c dl ultra	.20
O24	A12	10c dark bl	.20
O25	A12	20c dull org	.30
O26	A12	50c org red	.35
O27	A12	1p blue grn	.60
		Nos. O23-O27 (5)	1.65

Counterfeits of basic stamps and of overprint exist.

Regular Issue of 1911 Overprinted

1911-15 *Perf. 12, 14*

Carmine Overprint

O28	A15	1c violet	1.50	.65
a.		Inverted overprint	2.00	
b.		Double overprint	2.00	
O29	A15	6c ultra	2.50	2.00
a.		Inverted overprint	2.50	
O30	A15	10c blue	1.50	1.25
a.		"OFCAIL"	2.50	
b.		Double overprint	3.50	
O31	A15	20c yellow	15.00	12.00
O32	A15	50c brown	8.00	7.00
O33	A15	1p ol grn	12.00	10.00
		Nos. O28-O33 (6)	40.50	32.90

Black Overprint

O34	A15	2c green	1.00	.70
a.		"CFICIAL"	5.00	
O35	A15	5c carmine	1.50	1.00
a.		Perf. 12	7.50	5.00
O36	A15	6c ultra	4.50	4.50
O37	A15	10c blue	4.00	4.00
O38	A15	20c yellow	5.00	5.00
O39	A15	50c brown	5.50	4.00
		Nos. O34-O39 (6)	21.50	19.20

Counterfeits of overprint of Nos. O28-O39 exist.

With Additional Surcharge

1913-14

O40	A15	1c on 5c car	1.75	1.50
O41	A15	2c on 5c car	2.00	1.50
O42	A15	10c on 1c vio	4.00	3.50
a.		"OFICIAL" inverted	7.50	
O43	A15	20c on 1c vio	3.00	2.50
		Nos. O40-O43 (4)	10.75	9.00

On No. O40 the surcharge reads "1 cent."
Nos. O40-O43 exist with double surcharge.

No. O43 Surcharged Vertically in Black, Yellow or Maroon

1914

O44	A15	10c on 20c on 1c	20.00	20.00
a.		Maroon surcharge	20.00	20.00
O45	A15	10c on 20c on 1c (Y)	40.00	40.00

No. O35 Surcharged **10 c**

1915

O46	A15	10c on 5c car	*20.00*	*20.00*

No. O39 Surcharged

O47	A15	20c on 50c brn	5.00	5.00

Regular Issues of 1913-14 Overprinted in Red or Black

1915 *Perf. 11½*

O48	A17	1c brn (R)	.40	.40
a.		"OFICAIL"	5.00	
O49	A17	2c car (Bk)	.40	.40
a.		"OFICAIL"	5.00	
b.		Double overprint	4.00	
O50	A18	5c ultra (Bk)	.45	.45
a.		"OFIC"	4.00	
O51	A18	5c ultra (R)	1.00	1.00
a.		"OFIC"		
b.		"OFICAIL"	5.00	
O52	A18	6c pur (Bk)	1.50	1.50
a.		6c red lil (Bk)		
O53	A17	10c brn (Bk)	1.25	1.25
O54	A17	20c brn (Bk)	3.00	3.00
O55	A17	20c brn (R)	3.00	3.00
a.		Double overprint (R+Bk)	10.00	
b.		"OFICAIL"	5.00	
O56	A18	50c rose (Bk)	6.00	6.00
		Nos. O48-O56 (9)	17.00	17.00

The 10c blue has the overprint "OFICIAL" in different type from the other stamps of the series. It is stated that forty copies were overprinted for the Postmaster General but the stamp was never put in use or on sale at the post office.

No. 152 Surcharged

O57	A17	1c on 2c car	2.00	2.00
a.		"0.10" for "0.01"	4.25	4.25
b.		"0.20" for "0.01"	4.25	4.25
c.		Double surcharge	8.50	8.50
d.		As "a," double surcharge	77.50	
e.		As "b," double surcharge	77.50	

Regular Issue of 1915-16 Overprinted in Black or Red.

1915-16

O58	A19	1c choc (Bk)	.20	.20
O59	A19	2c car (Bk)	.20	.20
a.		Tête bêche pair	1.25	1.25
b.		Double overprint	2.00	
c.		Double overprint, one inverted	2.00	
d.		"b" and "c" in tête bêche pair		
O60	A20	5c brt blue (R)	.30	.30
a.		Inverted overprint	3.00	
O61	A20	6c deep pur (R)	.40	.40
a.		Black overprint	3.00	
b.		Inverted overprint	2.00	2.00
O62	A19	10c dl bl (R)	.40	.40
O63	A19	20c red brn (Bk)	.60	.60
a.		Tête bêche pair	2.50	
O64	A20	50c red (Bk)	1.75	1.75
O65	A20	1p yel grn (C)	3.75	3.75
		Nos. O58-O65 (8)	7.60	7.60

The 6c, 10c and 1p exist imperf.

Regular Issue of 1919 Overprinted

1921

O66	A22	1c brown	*2.25*	*2.25*
a.		Inverted overprint	3.00	3.00
O67	A22	2c carmine	*6.50*	*6.50*
a.		Inverted overprint	3.00	3.00
O68	A22	5c lilac rose	*6.50*	*6.50*
a.		Inverted overprint	3.00	
O69	A22	6c brt vio	.50	.50
a.		Inverted overprint		
O70	A22	10c dull blue	.60	.60
a.		Double overprint		
O71	A22	15c light blue	.70	.70
a.		Inverted overprint	2.00	
b.		Double ovpt., one inverted	4.00	
O72	A22	20c brown	1.00	1.00
O73	A22	50c light brown	1.50	1.50
O74	A22	1p yellow green	3.00	3.00
		Nos. O66-O74 (9)	22.55	22.55

Regular Issue of 1924 Overprinted

1924 *Perf. 11, 11½*

O75	A24	1c olive brn	.20	.20
O76	A24	2c deep rose	.20	.20
O77	A24	6c red vio	.30	.30
O78	A24	10c deep bl	.45	.45
O79	A24	20c yel brn	.60	.60
O80	A24	50c vermilion	1.25	1.25
O81	A24	1p emerald	2.00	2.00
		Nos. O75-O81 (7)	5.00	5.00

J. C. del Valle — O1

Designs: 2c, J. R. Molina. 5c, Coffee tree. 10c, J. T. Reyes. 20c, Tegucigalpa Cathedral. 50c, San Lorenzo Creek. 1p, Radio station.

1929 Litho. Wmk. 209 *Perf. 11½*

O82	O1	1c blue	.20	.20
O83	O1	2c carmine	.20	.20
a.		2c rose	.20	.20
O84	O1	5c purple	.35	.35
O85	O1	10c emerald	.50	.35
O86	O1	20c dk bl	.60	.60
O87	O1	50c org, grn & bl	1.00	1.00
O88	O1	1p buff	1.75	1.75
		Nos. O82-O88 (7)	4.60	4.45

Nos. O82-O88 exist imperf.

For overprints and surcharges see Nos. 282, 284, C37-C40, C59, C62-C63, CO26-CO27.

View of Tegucigalpa O2

1931 Unwmk. Engr. *Perf. 12*

O89	O2	1c ultra	.30	.20
O90	O2	2c black brn	.30	.20
O91	O2	5c olive gray	.35	.25
O92	O2	6c orange red	.40	.30
O93	O2	10c dark green	.50	.35
O94	O2	15c olive brn	.65	.40
O95	O2	20c red brown	.75	.50
O96	O2	50c gray vio	1.00	.65
O97	O2	1p dp orange	1.75	1.75
		Nos. O89-O97 (9)	6.00	4.60

For overprints see #CO6-CO14, O98-O105.

Official Stamps of 1931 Overprinted in Black

1936-37

O98	O2	1c ultra	.25	.25
O99	O2	2c black brn	.25	.25
a.		Inverted overprint	10.00	
O100	O2	5c olive gray	.30	.30
O101	O2	6c red orange	.40	.40
O102	O2	10c dark green	.40	.40
O103	O2	15c olive brown	.50	.50
a.		Inverted overprint	5.00	
O104	O2	20c red brown	1.00	1.00
a.		"1938-1935"		
O105	O2	50c gray violet	4.00	3.00
		Nos. O98-O105 (8)	7.10	6.10

Double overprints exist on 1c and 2c. No. O97 with this overprint is fraudulent.

HONG KONG

ˈhäŋˌkäŋ

LOCATION — A peninsula and island in southeast China at the mouth of the Canton River
GOVT. — British Crown Colony
AREA — 426 sq. mi.
POP. — 5,313,000 (est. 1983)
CAPITAL — Victoria

100 Cents = 1 Dollar

Catalogue values for unused stamps in this country are for Never Hinged items, beginning with Scott 174 in the regular postage section.

Values for unused stamps are for examples with original gum as defined in the catalogue introduction. Very fine examples of Nos. 1-25, 29-48, 61-66d and 69-70a will have perforations touching the design on at least one side due to the narrow spacing of the stamps on the plates. Stamps with perfs clear of the design on all four sides are scarce and will command higher prices.

Queen Victoria — A1

Unwmk.

1862, Dec. 8 Typo. *Perf. 14*

1	A1	2c pale brown	500.00	100.00
		On cover		500.00
a.		2c deep brown	600.00	125.00
		On cover		575.00
2	A1	8c buff	750.00	80.00
		On cover		500.00
3	A1	12c blue	675.00	67.50
		On cover		425.00
4	A1	18c lilac	675.00	62.50
		On cover		475.00
5	A1	24c green	1,100.	125.00
		On cover		625.00
6	A1	48c rose	3,000.	400.00
		On cover		3,000.
7	A1	96c gray	4,000.	525.00
		On cover		—

1863-80 **Wmk. 1**

8	A1	2c brown ('65)	140.00	8.00
		On cover		50.00
a.		2c deep brown ('64)	300.00	30.00
		On cover		165.00
b.		2c pale yellowish brown	160.00	12.00
		On cover		67.50
9	A1	2c dull rose ('80)	175.00	29.00
		On cover		210.00
a.		2c rose	190.00	30.00
10	A1	4c slate	130.00	8.00
		On cover		50.00
a.		4c greenish grey	350.00	55.00
		On cover		325.00
b.		4c bluish slate	525.00	25.00
		On cover		135.00
11	A1	5c ultra ('80)	525.00	50.00
		On cover		135.00
12	A1	6c lilac	450.00	15.00
		On cover		67.50
a.		6c violet	600.00	15.00
		On cover		75.00
13	A1	8c org buff ('65)	550.00	11.00
		On cover		57.50
a.		8c bright orange	450.00	12.00
		On cover		67.50
b.		8c brownish orange	525.00	12.00
		On cover		75.00
14	A1	10c violet ('80)	650.00	17.50
		On cover		57.50
15	A1	12c light blue	34.00	6.00
		On cover		50.00
a.		12c light greenish blue	1,050.	35.00
		On cover		165.00
b.		12c deep blue	275.00	13.00
		On cover		75.00

16	A1 16c yellow ('77)	2,100.	75.00
	On cover		525.00
17	A1 18c lilac ('66)	7,750.	325.00
	On cover		3,000.
18	A1 24c green ('65)	550.00	11.00
	On cover		100.00
a.	24c deep green	1,000.	30.00
	On cover		125.00
b.	24c pale green	650.00	16.00
	On cover		165.00
19	A1 30c vermilion	825.00	15.00
	On cover		165.00
a.	30c orange vermilion	825.00	16.00
	On cover		165.00
20	A1 30c violet ('71)	275.00	6.00
	On cover		110.00
21	A1 48c rose carmine	1,050.	50.00
	On cover		250.00
a.	48c pale rose	1,100.	55.00
	On cover		290.00
22	A1 48c brown ('80)	1,500.	110.00
	On cover		—
23	A1 96c bister ('65)	*47,500.*	775.00
	On cover		*45,000.*
24	A1 96c gray ('66)	1,600.	60.00
	On cover		*8,250.*
a.	96c brownish black	1,750.	52.50
	On cover		—

Imperfs. are plate proofs.

1874 **Perf. 12½**

25	A1 4c slate	13,500.	300.00
	On cover		3,000.

See #36-49. For surcharges or overprints on stamps of type A1 see #29-35B, 51-56, 61-66, 69-70.

A2

A3

A4

1874 Engr. Wmk. 1 **Perf. 15½x15**

26	A2 $2 sage green	375.00	65.00
	On cover		—
a.	$2 Thin transluscent paper	375.00	65.00
27	A3 $3 violet	275.00	50.00
	On cover		—
a.	$2 Thin transluscent paper	300.00	37.50
28	A4 $10 rose	8,250.	775.00
	On cover		—

Nos. 26-28 are revenues which were used postally. Used values are for postally canceled copies. Black "Paid All" cancels are fiscal usage.

See Nos. 57-59. For surcharges see Nos. 50, 67. For type surcharged see No. 60.

Nos. 17 and 20 Surcharged in Black:

1876 **Perf. 14**

29	A1 16c on 18c lilac	2,500.	185.00
	On cover		2,650.
a.	Wide space btwn. "n" & "t"	8,250.	1,000.
b.	Wide space btwn. "s" & period	8,250.	1,000.
30	A1 28c on 30c violet	1,500.	60.00
	On cover		1,325.

Stamps of 1863-80 Surcharged in Black

1879-80

31	A1 5c on 8c org ('80)	1,100.	110.00
	On cover		1,450.
a.	Inverted surcharge		*18,500.*
b.	Double surcharge		*20,000.*
32	A1 5c on 18c lilac	1,050.	70.00
	On cover		2,500.
33	A1 10c on 12c blue	1,100.	65.00
	On cover		825.00
34	A1 10c on 16c yellow	4,750.	160.00
	On cover		2,500.
a.	Inverted surcharge		*85,000.*
b.	Double surcharge		*85,000.*
35	A1 10c on 24c green ('80)	1,550.	95.00
	On cover		1,650.

Most copies of No. 31a are damaged.

Nos. 16-17, 35B Surcharged in Black

A5

A6

1879

35A	A5 3c on 16c on card	400.00	*2,100.*
	Stamp off card		450.00
d.	White card, red printing	225.	
e.	Yellow card, black printing	250.	
f.	As No. 35A, short "T" in "CENTS"	250.	
35B	A5 5c on 18c on card	400.00	*2,500.*
	Stamp off card		500.00
g.	White card, red printing	250.	
h.	Blue card, white printing	300.	
i.	As No. 35B, short "T" in "CENTS"	275.	
35C	A6 3c on 5c on 18c on card	7,750.	*9,500.*
	Stamp off card	6,500.	*8,250.*
j.	Short "T" in "CENTS"	5,500.	

Nos. 35A-35C were sold affixed to postal cards. Most used copies are found off card so values are given for these.

Type of 1862

1882-1902 **Wmk. 2** **Perf. 14**

36	A1 2c rose lake	175.00	30.00
	On cover		35.00
a.	2c rose pink	225.00	35.00
	On cover		50.00
b.	2c carmine ('84)	42.50	2.00
	On cover		25.00
c.	2c aniline carmine ('84)	42.50	1.75
	On cover		25.00
37	A1 2c green ('00)	30.00	1.00
	On cover		25.00
38	A1 4c slate ('96)	15.00	1.75
	On cover		42.50
39	A1 4c car rose ('00)	21.00	1.00
	On cover		25.00
40	A1 5c ultramarine	30.00	1.00
	On cover		32.50
41	A1 5c yellow ('00)	25.00	7.00
	On cover		82.50
42	A1 10c lilac	775.00	15.00
	On cover		75.00
43	A1 10c green	150.00	1.75
	On cover		25.00
a.	10c blue green	2,000.	42.50
	On cover		1,225.
44	A1 10c vio, *red* ('91)	27.50	1.75
	On cover		25.00
45	A1 10c ultra ('00)	55.00	2.25
	On cover		30.00
46	A1 12c blue ('02)	50.00	*60.00*
	On cover		775.00
47	A1 30c gray grn ('91)	90.00	23.00
	On cover		165.00
a.	30c yellow green	140.00	40.00
	On cover		275.00
48	A1 30c brown ('01)	50.00	24.00
	On cover		275.00
	Nos. 36-48 (13)	1,493.	169.50

No. 47 has fugitive ink. Both colors will turn dull green upon soaking.

The 2c rose, perf 12, is a proof.

No. 28 Surcharged in Black

1880 **Wmk. 1** **Perf. 15½x15**

50	A4 12c on $10 rose	950.00	350.00
	On cover		—

Surcharged in Black

1885-91 **Wmk. 2** **Perf. 14**

51	A1 20c on 30c ver	120.00	7.00
	On cover		250.00
a.	Double surcharge		—
52	A1 20c on 30c gray grn ('91)	200.00	*190.00*
	On cover		1,200.
a.	20c on 30c yellow green	200.00	190.00
53	A1 50c on 48c brown	450.00	35.00
	On cover		400.00
54	A1 50c on 48c lil ('91)	300.00	*325.00*
	On cover		1,650.
55	A1 $1 on 96c ol gray	825.00	80.00
	On cover		1,000.
56	A1 $1 on 96c vio, *red* ('91)	875.00	375.00
	On cover		2,000.

For overprints see Nos. 61-63.

Types of 1874 and

A7

1890-1902 **Wmk. 2** **Perf. 14**

56A	A7 2c dull purple	110.00	29.00
	On cover		125.00

Wmk. 1

57	A2 $2 gray green	450.00	275.00
	On cover		—
58	A3 $3 lilac ('02)	600.00	500.00
	On cover		—
a.	Bluish paper	1,600.	
	On cover		—
59	A4 $10 gray grn ('92)	*12,000.*	*12,000.*
	On cover		—

Due to a shortage of 2c postage stamps, No. 56A was authorized for postal use December 24-30, 1890.

Fake postmarks are known on No. 59. Beware also of fiscal cancels altered to resemble postal cancels.

For surcharge see No. 68.

Type of 1874 Surcharged in Black

1891, Jan. 1 **Wmk. 2**

60	A4 $5 on $10 vio, *red*	350.00	110.00
	On cover		—

Nos. 36b, 44 Overprinted

a

b

1891, Jan. 1

60A	A1 2c carmine (a)	1,050.	425.00
60B	A1 2c carmine (b)	1,050.	425.00
a.	Inverted overprint		6,500.
60C	A1 10c vio, *red* (a)	1,800.	475.00

Nos. 60A-60C were overprinted for use as fiscal stamps, "S.O." denoting "Stamp Office" and "S.D." denoting "Stamp Duty." They were authorized for postal use Jan. 1, 1891-1893. Examples of No. 60A with "O" changed to "D" in manuscript are known.

Forged overprints are often encountered. Expertization is required.

Nos. 52, 54 and 56 Handstamped with Chinese characters

61	A1 (g) 20c on 30c	37.50	8.00
	On cover		165.00
a.	20c on 30c dull green	60.00	10.00
	On cover		130.00
b.	"20 CENTS" double		
62	A1 (h) 50c on 48c	90.00	6.00
	On cover		575.00
63	A1 (i) $1 on 96c	500.00	25.00
	On cover		825.00

No. 61 may be found with Chinese character 2mm, 2½mm or 3mm high.

The handstamped Chinese surcharges on Nos. 61-63 exist in several varieties including inverted, double, triple, misplaced, omitted and (on #63) on both front and back.

Nos. 43 and 20 Surcharged

1891

64	A1 7c on 10c green	82.50	9.00
	On cover		300.00
a.	Double surcharge	*6,500.*	*1,500.*
	On cover		—

Wmk. 1

65	A1 14c on 30c violet	190.00	70.00
	On cover		725.00

Beware of faked varieties.

No. 36 Overprinted in Black

1891, Jan. 22 **Wmk. 2**

66 A1 2c rose *575.00* 130.00
On cover *3,250.*
a. Double overprint *17,500.* *13,000.*
b. "U" of "JUBILEE" shorter *800.00* 200.00
c. "J" of "JUBILEE" shorter *800.00* 200.00
d. Tall "K" in "KONG" *1,300.* 500.00
e. Wide space btwn. "o" & "n" 1,750. 800.00

50th anniversary of the colony.
Beware of faked varieties.

No. 26 Surcharged (Chinese Handstamped)

1897, Sept. **Wmk. 1** ***Perf. 15½x15***

67 A2 $1 on $2 sage green 275.00 140.00
On cover —
a. Without Chinese surcharge 5,000. 4,000.
On cover —

On No. 57

Perf. 14

68 A2 $1 on $2 gray green 275.00 150.00
On cover —
a. Without Chinese surcharge 2,100. 1,750.
On cover —

Handstamp Surcharged in Black

1898 **Wmk. 2**

69 A1 10c on 30c gray grn 55.00 *85.00*
On cover 500.00
a. Large Chinese surcharge 1,250. 1,100.
b. Without Chinese surcharge 600.00 *1,100.*
On cover —
c. As #69, 1½mm between "1" & "0" 800.00 *1,000.*
d. As #69b, 1½mm between "1" & "0" 4,000.
70 A1 $1 on 96c black 190.00 30.00
On cover 1,000.
a. Without Chinese surcharge 3,000. *4,000.*

The Chinese surcharge is added separately.
See notes below Nos. 61-63. The small Chinese surcharge is illustrated.

King Edward VII — A10

1903 **Wmk. 2**

71 A10 1c brown & lilac 2.25 .55
72 A10 2c gray green 12.00 1.60
73 A10 4c violet, *red* 15.00 .45
74 A10 5c org & gray grn 13.00 10.00
75 A10 8c violet & black 12.00 1.75
76 A10 10c ultra & lil, *bl* 45.00 2.00
77 A10 12c red vio & gray grn, *yel* 10.00 5.25
78 A10 20c org brn & blk 52.50 4.00
79 A10 30c blk & gray grn 55.00 24.00
80 A10 50c red vio & gray green 45.00 45.00
81 A10 $1 olive grn & lil 95.00 25.00
82 A10 $2 scar & black 300.00 300.00
83 A10 $3 dp blue & blk 350.00 *375.00*
84 A10 $5 blue grn & lil 550.00 550.00
85 A10 $10 org & blk, *bl* 1,200. 500.00
Nos. 71-85 (15) 2,756. 1,844.

1904-11 **Wmk. 3**

Ordinary or Chalky Paper

86 A10 1c brown ('10) 5.00 1.10
a. Booklet pane of 4
87 A10 2c gray green 9.25 1.50
88 A10 2c deep green 25.00 1.90
a. Booklet pane of 4
b. Booklet pane of 12
89 A10 4c violet, *red* 21.00 .50
90 A10 4c carmine 10.00 .50
a. Booklet pane of 4
b. Booklet pane of 12
91 A10 5c org & gray grn 32.50 10.00
92 A10 6c red vio & org ('07) 27.50 5.25
93 A10 8c vio & blk ('07) 13.00 2.25
94 A10 10c ultra & lil, *bl* 22.50 1.50
95 A10 10c ultramarine 27.50 .50
96 A10 12c red vio & gray grn, *yel* ('07) 15.00 6.00
97 A10 20c org brn & blk 42.50 2.50
98 A10 20c ol grn & vio ('11) 50.00 50.00
99 A10 30c blk & gray grn 47.50 25.00
100 A10 30c org & vio ('11) 60.00 29.00
101 A10 50c red vio & gray green 77.50 10.00
102 A10 50c blk, *grn* ('11) 45.00 18.00
103 A10 $1 ol grn & lil 130.00 29.00
104 A10 $2 scar & black 250.00 130.00
105 A10 $2 blk & car ('10) 325.00 325.00
106 A10 $3 dp bl & blk 275.00 225.00
107 A10 $5 bl grn & lil 450.00 400.00
108 A10 $10 org & blk, *bl* 1,950. 1,200.
Nos. 86-108 (23) 3,910. 2,474.

Nos. 86, 88, 90, 94 and 95 are on ordinary paper only. Nos. 92, 93, 96, 98, 100, 102, 105, 106 and 107 are on chalky paper and the others of the issue are on both papers.

The 4c, 5c, 8c, 12c 20c, 50c, $2 and $5 denominations of type A10 are expressed in colored letters or numerals and letters on a colorless background.

King George V
A11 A12

A13

A14

A15

Type I

Type II

Two Types of 25c:
I: A short vertical stroke crosses the bottom of the top Chinese character in the left label.
II: The vertical stroke is absent from the character.

1912-14 **Ordinary Paper**

109 A11 1c brown 3.00 .60
a. Booklet pane of 12
110 A11 2c deep green 9.00 .40
a. Booklet pane of 12
111 A12 4c carmine 5.00 .40
a. Booklet pane of 12
b. Booklet pane of 4
112 A13 6c orange 5.00 1.10
113 A12 8c gray 26.00 6.00
114 A11 10c ultramarine 37.50 .35

Chalky Paper

115 A14 12c vio, *yel* 6.00 *8.00*
116 A14 20c ol grn & vio 7.00 1.10
117 A15 25c red vio & dl vio (I) 22.50 *25.00*
a. Type II 110.00 50.00
118 A13 30c org & violet 25.00 7.75
119 A14 50c black, *green* 16.00 2.00
a. 50c black, *emerald* 30.00 9.00
b. 50c black, *bl grn,* ol back 1,400. 32.50
c. 50c black, *emer,* ol back 27.50 8.75
120 A11 $1 blue & vio, *bl* 50.00 4.00
121 A14 $2 black & red 150.00 60.00
122 A13 $3 vio & green 225.00 90.00
123 A14 $5 red & grn, *grn* 700.00 425.00
a. $5 red & grn, *bl grn,* ol back 1,200. 350.00
124 A13 $10 blk & vio, *red* 650.00 92.50
Nos. 109-124 (16) 1,937. 724.20

For overprints see British Offices in China #1-27.

1914, May **Surface-colored Paper**

125 A14 12c violet, *yel* 8.00 *15.00*
126 A14 50c black, *green* 16.00 5.00
127 A14 $5 red & grn, *grn* 650.00 325.00
Nos. 125-127 (3) 674.00 345.00

Stamp of 1912-14 Redrawn

 instead of  at upper left.

1919, Sept. **Chalky Paper**

128 A15 25c red vio & dl vio 175.00 65.00

Types of 1912-14 Issue

1921-37 **Wmk. 4**

Ordinary Paper

129 A11 1c brown 1.10 .50
130 A11 2c deep green 3.00 .55
131 A11 2c gray ('37) 21.00 8.00
132 A12 3c gray ('31) 8.00 1.10
133 A12 4c rose red 4.00 1.00
134 A12 5c violet ('31) 11.00 .40
135 A12 8c gray 15.00 *40.00*
136 A12 8c orange 4.75 2.00
137 A11 10c ultramarine 5.00 .45

Chalky Paper

138 A14 12c vio, *yel* ('33) 16.00 2.50
139 A14 20c ol grn & dl vio 6.00 .40
140 A15 25c red vio & dl vio, redrawn 5.50 .75
141 A13 30c yel & violet 12.00 1.75
142 A14 50c blk, *emerald* 16.00 .45
143 A11 $1 ultra & vio, *bl* 40.00 .60
144 A14 $2 black & red 130.00 6.50
145 A13 $3 dl vio & grn ('26) 190.00 65.00
146 A14 $5 red & grn, *emer* ('25) 525.00 80.00
Nos. 129-146 (18) 1,013. 211.95

Common Design Types pictured following the introduction.

Silver Jubilee Issue

Common Design Type

1935, May 6 **Engr.** ***Perf. 11x12***

147 CD301 3c black & ultra 3.00 1.25
148 CD301 5c indigo & grn 10.00 1.25
149 CD301 10c ultra & brn 24.00 4.00
150 CD301 20c brn vio & ind 30.00 8.00
Nos. 147-150 (4) 67.00 14.50
Set, never hinged 175.00

Coronation Issue

Common Design Type

1937, May 12 ***Perf. 11x11½***

151 CD302 4c deep green 4.00 3.00
152 CD302 15c dark carmine 8.75 3.00
153 CD302 25c deep ultra 11.25 2.50
Nos. 151-153 (3) 24.00 8.50
Set, never hinged 40.00

King George VI — A16

1938-48 **Typo.** ***Perf. 14***

Ordinary Paper

154 A16 1c brown .75 .50
155 A16 2c gray 1.00 .20
156 A16 4c orange 2.00 1.50
157 A16 5c green 1.25 .20
157B A16 8c brown red ('41) 1.20 *2.75*
c. Imperf., pair — —
158 A16 10c violet 3.00 .60
159 A16 15c carmine .90 .20
159A A16 20c gray ('46) .60 .20
159B A16 20c rose red ('48) 3.00 .35
160 A16 25c ultramarine 19.00 1.50
160A A16 25c gray ol ('46) 2.25 1.25
161 A16 30c olive bister 125.00 2.00
161B A16 30c lt ultra ('46) 3.00 .20
162 A16 50c red violet 3.25 .60

Chalky Paper

162B A16 80c lilac rose ('48) 2.25 .75
163 A16 $1 lilac & ultra 6.00 2.25
163B A16 $1 dp org & grn ('46) 8.50 .20
164 A16 $2 dp org & grn 60.00 15.00
164A A16 $2 vio & red ('46) 12.50 3.75
165 A16 $5 lilac & red 45.00 45.00
165A A16 $5 grn & vio ('46) 40.00 7.50
166 A16 $10 grn & vio 375.00 95.00
166A A16 $10 vio & ultra ('46) 100.00 35.00
Nos. 154-166A (23) 815.45 216.50
Set, never hinged 1,100.

Coarse Impressions
Ordinary Paper

1941-46 ***Perf. 14½x14***

155a A16 2c gray 1.50 *5.25*
156a A16 4c orange ('46) 3.00 3.25
157a A16 5c green 1.75 *5.25*
158a A16 10c violet 6.00 .20
161a A16 30c dull olive bister 18.00 9.00
162a A16 50c red lilac 20.00 2.00
Nos. 155a-162a (6) 50.25 24.95
Set, never hinged 85.00

A17

1938, Jan. 11 **Wmk. 4**

167 A17 5c green 40.00 20.00
Never hinged 80.00

No. 167 is a revenue stamp officially authorized to be sold and used for postal purposes. Used Jan. 11-20, 1938. The used price is for the stamp on cover. CTO covers exist.

Street Scene — A18

Hong Kong Bank — A22

Liner and Junk — A19

University of Hong Kong — A20

Harbor — A21

China Clipper and Seaplane A23

Perf. 13½x13, 13x13½

1941, Feb. 26 **Engr.** **Wmk. 4**

168 A18 2c sepia & org 4.00 2.00
169 A19 4c rose car & vio 4.00 2.00
170 A20 5c yel grn & blk 2.00 .35
171 A21 15c red & black 4.50 1.25
172 A22 25c dp blue & dk brn 9.00 4.00
173 A23 $1 brn org & brt bl 30.00 12.00
Nos. 168-173 (6) 53.50 21.60
Set, never hinged 95.00

Centenary of British rule.

Catalogue values for unused stamps in this section, from this point to the end of the section, are for Never Hinged items.

Peace Issue

Phoenix Rising from Flames A24

1946, Aug. 29 *Perf. 13x12½*

174	A24 30c car & dp blue	3.00	2.00
175	A24 $1 car & brown	4.00	1.00

Return to peace after WWII.

Silver Wedding Issue

Common Design Types

Perf. 14x14½

1948, Dec. 22 Photo. Wmk. 4

178	CD304 10c purple	2.50	1.00

Engr.; Name Typo.

Perf. 11½x11

179	CD305 $10 rose car	375.00	90.00
	Set, hinged	200.00	

UPU Issue

Common Design Types

Engr.; Name Typo. on 20c & 30c

1949, Oct. 10 *Perf. 13½, 11x11½*

180	CD306 10c violet	4.50	1.00
181	CD307 20c deep car	17.50	3.50
182	CD308 30c indigo	15.00	2.50
183	CD309 80c red violet	35.00	10.00
	Nos. 180-183 (4)	72.00	17.00
	Set, hinged	30.00	

POSTAGE DUE STAMPS

Scales Showing Letter Overweight — D1

1923, Dec. Typo. Wmk. 4 *Perf. 14*

J1	D1 1c brown	2.75	.70
a.	Chalky paper, wmkd. sideways	1.60	*3.50*
J2	D1 2c green	12.00	5.25
J3	D1 4c red	30.00	7.50
J4	D1 6c orange	29.00	15.00
J5	D1 10c ultramarine	25.00	9.00
	Nos. J1-J5 (5)	98.75	37.45
	Set, never hinged	250.00	

No. J1a issued Mar. 21, 1956.

1938-47 *Perf. 14*

J6	D1 2c gray	1.40	*10.00*
J7	D1 4c orange yellow	2.50	*10.00*
J8	D1 6c carmine	10.00	6.00
J9	D1 8c fawn ('46)	6.00	*32.50*
J10	D1 10c violet	15.00	7.50
J11	D1 20c black ('46)	10.00	3.50
J12	D1 50c blue ('47)	35.00	16.00
	Nos. J6-J12 (7)	79.90	85.50
	Set, never hinged	160.00	

Nos. J6-J7 and J10 exist on both ordinary and chalky paper.

OCCUPATION STAMPS

Issued under Japanese Occupation

War Factory Girl — A144

Gen. Maresuke Nogi — A84

Admiral Heihachiro Togo — A86

Stamps of Japan, 1942-43 Surcharged in Black

Wmk. 257

1945, Apr. Typo. *Perf. 13*

N1	A144 1½y on 1s org brn	35.00	30.00
N2	A84 3y on 2s ver	14.00	*25.00*
N3	A86 5y on 5s brn lake	975.00	175.00
	Nos. N1-N3 (3)	1,024.	230.00

No. N1 has eleven characters.

HORTA

ˈhor-tə

LOCATION — An administrative district of the Azores, consisting of the islands of Pico, Fayal, Flores and Corvo

GOVT. — A district of the Republic of Portugal

AREA — 305 sq. mi.

POP. — 49,000 (approx.)

CAPITAL — Horta

1000 Reis = 1 Milreis

STAMPS OF PORTUGAL USED IN HORTA

Barred Numeral "49"

1853 Queen Maria II

A1	5r org brn (#1)	1,200.
A2	25r blue (#2)	60.
A3	50r dp yel grn (#3)	1,100.
a.	50r blue green (#3a)	1,500.
A4	100r lilac (#4)	2,250.

1855 King Pedro V (Straight Hair)

A5	5r red brn (#5)	1,200.
A6	25r blue, type II (#6)	57.50
a.	Type I (#6a)	60.00
A7	50r green (#7)	95.00
A8	100r lilac (#8)	110.00

1856-58

King Pedro V (Curled Hair)

A9	5r red brn (#9)	110.00
A10	25r blue, type II (#10)	70.00
a.	Type I (#10a)	67.50
A11	25r rose, type II (#11; '58)	19.00

1862-64 King Luiz

A12	5r brown (#12)	60.00
A13	10r orange (#13)	67.50
A14	25r rose (#14)	13.50
A15	50r yel green (#15)	90.00
A16	100r lilac (#16; '64)	110.00

1866-67 King Luiz

Imperf.

A17	5r black (#17)	90.00
A18	10r yellow (#18)	140.00
A19	20r bister (#19)	140.00
A20	25r rose (#20; '67)	45.00
A21	50r green (#21)	125.00
A22	80r orange (#22)	125.00
A23	100r dk lilac (#23; '67)	150.00
A24	120r blue (#24)	125.00

Perf. 12½

A28	25r rose (#28)	125.00

Issued under Portuguese Administration

King Carlos

A1 A2

Chalk-surfaced Paper

Perf. 11½, 12½, 13½

1892-93 Typo. Unwmk.

1	A1 5r yellow	2.00	1.50
2	A1 10r reddish violet	2.00	1.75
3	A1 15r chocolate	2.00	2.00
4	A1 20r lavender	3.00	3.00
5	A1 25r dp grn, perf. 11½	4.50	1.00
a.	Perf. 13½	5.00	3.75
6	A1 50r blue	6.25	3.00
a.	Perf. 13½	9.00	5.25
7	A1 75r carmine	6.50	4.00
8	A1 80r yellow green	9.00	8.50
9	A1 100r brn, *yel* ('93)	35.00	17.50
a.	Perf. 12½	125.00	90.00
10	A1 150r car, *rose* ('93)	45.00	32.50
11	A1 200r dk bl, *bl* ('93)	45.00	32.50
12	A1 300r dark blue ('93)	45.00	35.00
	Nos. 1-12 (12)	205.25	142.25

Bisects of No. 1 were used in Aug. 1894. Value $16.

The reprints have shiny white gum and clean-cut perforation 13½. The white paper is thinner than that of the originals. Value unused, $12 each.

1897-1905 *Perf. 11½*

Name and Value in Black Except 500r

13	A2 2½r gray	.50	.30
14	A2 5r orange	.50	.30
15	A2 10r lt green	.50	.30
16	A2 15r brown	5.25	3.00
17	A2 15r gray grn ('99)	1.25	.80
18	A2 20r gray violet	1.75	.85
19	A2 25r sea green	2.25	.45
20	A2 25r car rose ('99)	.90	.50
21	A2 50r blue	3.00	.70
22	A2 50r ultra ('05)	15.00	9.00
23	A2 65r slate blue ('98)	.70	.55
24	A2 75r rose	1.90	.95
25	A2 75r brn, *yel* ('05)	20.00	12.50
26	A2 80r violet	1.25	1.10
27	A2 100r dk blue, *bl*	1.75	.95
28	A2 115r org brn, *pink* ('98)	2.00	1.50
29	A2 130r gray brn, *buff* ('98)	2.00	1.50
30	A2 150r lt brn, *buff*	2.00	1.50
31	A2 180r sl, *pnksh* ('98)	2.00	1.75
32	A2 200r red vio, *pale lil*	5.50	4.00
33	A2 300r dk blue, *rose*	7.50	6.75
34	A2 500r blk & red, *bl*	10.50	8.50
	Nos. 13-34 (22)	88.00	57.75

Stamps of Portugal replaced those of Horta.

HUNGARY

ˈhəŋ-g(ə-)rē

LOCATION — Central Europe

GOVT. — Republic

AREA — 35,911 sq. mi.

POP. — 10,679,000 (est. 1984)

CAPITAL — Budapest

Prior to World War I, Hungary together with Austria comprised the Austro-Hungarian Empire. The Hungarian post became independent on May 1, 1867. During 1850-1871 stamps listed under Austria were also used in Hungary. Copies showing clear Hungarian cancels sell for substantially more.

100 Krajczár (Kreuzer) = 1 Forint
100 Fillér = 1 Korona (1900)
100 Fillér = 1 Pengö (1926)

Catalogue values for unused stamps in this country are for Never Hinged items, beginning with Scott 503 in the regular postage section, Scott B92 in the semi-postal section, Scott C35 in the airpost section, and Scott J130 in the postage due section.

Watermarks

Wmk. 91 — "ZEITUNGS-MARKEN" in Double-lined Capitals across the Sheet

Wmk. 106 — Multiple Star

Wmk. 132 — kr in Oval

Wmk. 133 — Four Double Crosses

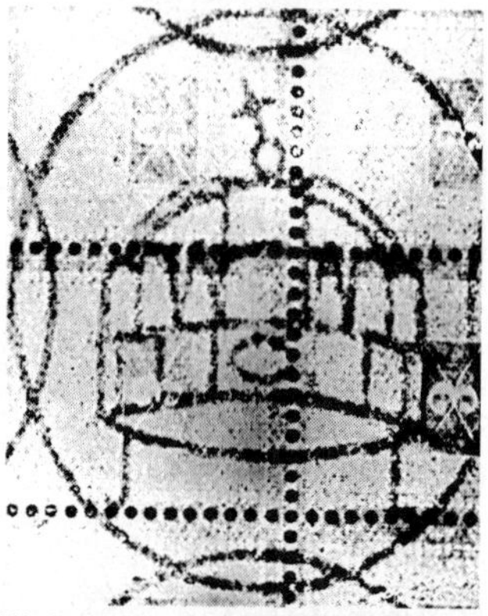

Wmk. 135 — Crown in Oval or Circle, Sideways

Wmk. 136

Wmk. 136a

Wmk. 137 — Double Cross

Wmk. 210 — Double Cross on Pyramid

Watermarks 132, 135, 136 and 136a can be found normal, reversed, inverted, or reversed and inverted.

Values for unused stamps are for examples with original gum as defined in the catalogue introduction. Very fine examples of Nos. 1-12 will have perforations touching the framelines on one or two sides due to imperfect perforating methods. Stamps with perfs clear on all four sides are very scarce and will command substantial premiums.

Issues of the Monarchy

Franz Josef I — A1

1871 Unwmk. Litho. *Perf. 9½*

1 A1 2k orange 225.00 90.00
a. 2k yellow 1,300. 225.00
2 A1 3k lt green 725.00 550.00
3 A1 5k rose 300.00 20.00
a. 5k brick red 600.00 75.00
4 A1 10k blue 700.00 90.00
a. 10k pale blue 950.00 150.00
5 A1 15k yellow brn 750.00 100.00
6 A1 25k violet 750.00 175.00
a. 25k bright violet 850.00 275.00

The first printing of No. 1, in dark yellow, was not issued because of spots on the King's face. A few copies were used at Pest in 1873. Value, $3,500.

1871-72 Engr.

7 A1 2k orange 37.50 7.50
a. 2k yellow 150.00 17.00
b. Bisect on cover —
8 A1 3k green 85.00 25.00
a. 3k blue green 110.00 30.00
9 A1 5k rose 50.00 1.75
a. 5k brick red 125.00 8.00
10 A1 10k deep blue 200.00 10.00
11 A1 15k brown 225.00 15.00
a. 15k copper brown — 900.00
b. 15k black brown 875.00 85.00
12 A1 25k lilac 140.00 40.00
Nos. 7-12 (6) 737.50 99.25

Reprints are perf. 11½ and watermarked "kr" in oval. Value, set $225.

Crown of St. Stephen
A2 A3

Design A3 has an overall burelage of dots. Compare with design N3.

1874-76 *Perf. 13*

13 A2 2k red violet 50.00 4.00
a. 2k violet 60.00 5.00
14 A2 3k yellow green 50.00 4.00
a. 3k blue green 70.00 5.00
15 A2 5k red 15.00 .80
a. 5k brick red 40.00 2.00
b. 5k lilac red 25.00 1.50
c. 5k rose 12.00 .50
16 A2 10k blue 65.00 1.50
17 A2 20k grnsh gray 575.00 14.00
a. 20k gray 600.00 15.00
Nos. 13-17 (5) 755.00 24.30

Perf. 11½

13b A2 2k red violet 70.00 10.00
c. 2k violet 75.00 12.00
d. 2k rose lilac 110.00 9.00
e. 2k gray blue 90.00 9.50
14b A2 3k yellow green 80.00 8.00
c. 3k blue green 90.00 10.00
15d A2 5k red 90.00 2.00
e. 5k rose 80.00 1.50
16a A2 10k blue 110.00 10.00
17b A2 20k gray 1,500. 42.50

Perf. 13x11½

13f A2 2k red violet 150.00 25.00
g. 2k rose lilac 165.00 30.00
14d A2 3k yellow green 100.00 4.25
15f A2 5k lilac red 125.00 12.00
g. 5k rose 150.00 15.00
16b A2 10k blue 200.00 5.75
17c A2 20k gray 600.00 47.50

Perf. 11½x13

13h A2 2k red violet 100.00 4.75
f. 2k rose lilac 165.00 4.00
g. 2k gray blue 125.00 3.50
15h A2 5k red 125.00 1.00
17d A2 20k gray — 95.00

Perf. 9½

14e A2 3k green *3,000. 2,000.*

All examples of the 5k perf 9½ are counterfeit.

1881 Wmk. 132 *Perf. 11½*

18 A2 2k lilac 7.00 .80
a. 2k violet 7.00 .80
b. 2k gray blue 9.00 1.00
19 A2 3k blue green 7.00 .80
a. 3k yellow green 9.00 1.20
20 A2 5k rose 5.00 .30
21 A2 10k blue 12.00 .80
a. 10k pale blue 14.00 1.20
22 A2 20k gray 9.00 1.25
a. 20k greenish gray 10.00 1.50
Nos. 18-22 (5) 40.00 3.95

Perf. 13

18c A2 2k violet 150.00 18.00
d. 2k gray blue 120.00 9.50
19b A2 3k blue green 90.00 3.75
c. 3k yellow green 100.00 5.00
20a A2 5k rose 120.00 3.75
21b A2 10k blue 75.00 4.75
22b A2 20k gray 350.00 15.00

Perf. 13x11½

18e A2 2k violet — 40.00
19d A2 3k blue green 200.00 6.00
e. 3k yellow green — 8.00
20b A2 5k rose — 15.00
21c A2 10k blue — 8.00
22c A2 20k gray 600.00 40.00

Perf. 11½x13

18f A2 2k violet 180.00 9.00
g. 2k gray blue 150.00 7.00
19f A2 3k blue green — 60.00
g. 3k yellow green — 75.00
20c A2 5k rose 75.00 1.00
21d A2 10k blue 1,400. 2.00
22d A2 20k gray — 40.00

Perf. 12x11½

18h A2 2k lilac 1.00 .25
i. 2k violet 12.50 1.20
19h A2 3k blue green 1.00 .25
20d A2 5k rose 2.50 .25
21e A2 10k blue 3.00 .25
22e A2 20k gray 300.00 7.50

1888-98 Typo. *Perf. 11½, 12x11½*

Numerals in Black

22A A3 1k black, one plate .55 .40
c. "1" printed separately 10.50 .90
23 A3 2k red violet .80 .35
a. Perf. 11½ 725.00 50.00
24 A3 3k green 2.00 .50
a. Perf. 11½ 50.00 15.00
25 A3 5k rose 2.00 .30
a. Perf. 11½ 65.00 1.75
26 A3 8k orange 7.00 .80
a. "8" double *150.00*
27 A3 10k blue 5.50 1.40
a. Perf. 11½ 450.00 325.00
28 A3 12k brown & green 14.00 1.00
29 A3 15k claret & blue 11.00 .40
30 A3 20k gray 8.50 2.25
a. Perf. 11½ *1,400. 600.00*
31 A3 24k brn vio & red 25.00 1.25
32 A3 30k ol grn & brn 27.50 .45
33 A3 50k red & org 45.00 1.40

Numerals in Red

34 A3 1fo gray bl & sil 185.00 2.50
a. Perf. 11½ 190.00 3.50
35 A3 3fo lilac brn & gold 18.00 11.00
Nos. 22A-35 (14) 351.85 24.00

Most of Nos. 22A to 103 exist imperforate, but were never so issued.

1898-99 *Perf. 12x11½*

Numerals in Black

Wmk. 135 (Oval)

35A A3 1k black 1.50 .50
36 A3 2k violet 6.00 .50
37 A3 3k green 4.00 .60
38 A3 5k rose 5.00 .40
39 A3 8k orange 17.50 4.00
40 A3 10k blue 5.00 1.00
41 A3 12k red brn & grn 75.00 9.00
42 A3 15k rose & blue 5.00 .75
43 A3 20k gray 35.00 2.00
44 A3 24k vio brn & red 6.00 4.75
45 A3 30k ol grn & brn 40.00 1.50
46 A3 50k dull red & org 100.00 15.00
Nos. 35A-46 (12) 300.00 40.00

Perf. 11½

35Ab A3 1k black 40.00 7.50
36a A3 2k violet 125.00 20.00
37a A3 3k green 100.00 15.00
38a A3 5k rose 140.00 15.00
39a A3 8k orange 250.00 120.00
40a A3 10k blue 150.00 60.00
41a A3 12k red brn & grn 300.00 75.00
42a A3 15k rose & blue 180.00 45.00
43a A3 20k gray 275.00 60.00
44a A3 24k vio brn & red 350.00 140.00
45a A3 30k ol grn & brn 200.00 50.00
46a A3 50k dull red & org 400.00 150.00

Wmk. 135 (Circle)

Perf. 12x11½

35Ac A3 1k black 14.00 7.50
36b A3 2k violet 7.50 .75
37b A3 3k green 8.50 1.25
38b A3 5k rose 10.00 .50
39b A3 8k orange 50.00 15.00
40b A3 10k blue 75.00 3.00
41b A3 12k red brn & grn 60.00 22.50
42b A3 15k rose & blue 200.00 3.00
43b A3 20k gray 5.00 3.50
44b A3 24k vio brn & red 900.00 40.00
45b A3 30k ol grn & brn 5.00 4.00
46b A3 50k dull red & org 15.00 30.00

Perf. 11½

35Ad A3 1k black 50.00 15.00
36c A3 2k violet 200.00 25.00
37c A3 3k green 200.00 40.00
38c A3 5k rose 100.00 15.00
39c A3 8k orange 80.00 12.50
40c A3 10k blue 350.00 80.00
41c A3 12k red brn & grn 550.00 300.00
42c A3 15k rose & blue 375.00 200.00
43c A3 20k gray 1,200. 350.00
44c A3 24k vio brn & red 1,500. 400.00
45c A3 30k ol grn & brn 600.00 150.00
46c A3 50k dull red & org 375.00 275.00

In the watermark with circles, a four-pointed star and "VI" appear four times in the sheet in the large spaces between the intersecting circles. The paper with the circular watermark is often yellowish and thinner than that with the oval watermark.

See note after No. 35.

"Turul" and Crown of St. Stephen — A4

Franz Josef I Wearing Hungarian Crown — A5

1900-04 Wmk. 135 *Perf. 12x11½*

Numerals in Black

47 A4 1f gray .60 .40
a. 1f dull lilac .65 .40
48 A4 2f olive yel .70 .25
49 A4 3f orange .55 .25
50 A4 4f violet .60 .20
a. Booklet pane of 6 60.00
51 A4 5f emerald 2.75 .20
a. Booklet pane of 6 35.00
52 A4 6f claret .95 .60
a. 6f violet brown 1.75 .60
53 A4 6f bister ('01) 12.00 1.20
54 A4 6f olive grn ('02) 4.00 .60
55 A4 10f carmine 3.00 .25
a. Booklet pane of 6 35.00
56 A4 12f violet ('04) 1.50 1.25
57 A4 20f brown ('01) 1.90 .60
58 A4 25f blue 3.25 .65
a. Booklet pane of 6 60.00
59 A4 30f orange brn 22.50 .25
60 A4 35f red vio ('01) 12.50 .40
a. Booklet pane of 6 100.00
61 A4 50f lake 13.00 1.25
62 A4 60f green 44.00 .55
63 A5 1k brown red 45.00 .70
64 A5 2k gray blue ('01) 275.00 22.50
65 A5 3k sea green 85.00 4.50
66 A5 5k vio brown ('01) 85.00 30.00
Nos. 47-66 (20) 613.80 66.60

The watermark on Nos. 47 to 66 is always the circular form of Wmk. 135 described in the note following No. 46.

Pairs imperf between of Nos. 47-49, 51 were favor prints made for an influential Budapest collector. Value, $90 each.

For overprints & surcharges see #B35-B52, 2N1-2N3, 6N1-6N6, 6NB127N1-7N6, 7NB1, 10N1.

See note after No. 35.

Perf. 11½

47b A4 1f gray 90.00 17.50
48a A4 2f olive yel 90.00 12.50
49a A4 3f orange 22.50 2.25
50b A4 4f violet 70.00 1.50
51b A4 5f emerald 5.50 1.40
52b A4 6f claret 110.00 12.50
53a A4 6f bister ('01) 80.00 22.50
54a A4 6f olive grn ('02) 160.00 90.00
55b A4 10f carmine 90.00 3.00
56a A4 12f violet ('04) 70.00 27.50
57a A4 20f brown ('01) 140.00 45.00
58b A4 25f blue 140.00 15.00
59a A4 30f orange brn 150.00 35.00
60b A4 35f red vio ('01) 190.00 80.00
61a A4 50f lake 190.00 80.00
62a A4 60f green 250.00 20.00
63a A5 1k brown red 45.00 3.25
64a A5 2k gray blue ('01) 550.00 120.00
65a A5 3k sea green — *1,500.*
66a A5 5k vio brown ('01) 550.00 225.00

1908-13 Wmk. 136 *Perf. 15*

67 A4 1f slate .35 .20
68 A4 2f olive yellow .30 .20
69 A4 3f orange .35 .20
70 A4 5f emerald .35 .20
c. Booklet pane of 6 100.00
71 A4 6f olive green .35 .20
72 A4 10f carmine .45 .20
c. Booklet pane of 6 100.00
73 A4 12f violet .40 .20
74 A4 16f gray green ('13) .20 .40
75 A4 20f dark brown 3.50 .20
76 A4 25f blue 2.25 .20
77 A4 30f orange brown 2.50 .20
78 A4 35f red violet 3.75 .20
79 A4 50f lake 1.75 .30
80 A4 60f green 4.00 .20
81 A5 1k brown red 7.25 .25
82 A5 2k gray blue 50.00 .55
83 A5 5k violet brown 75.00 7.50
Nos. 67-83 (17) 152.75 11.40

See note after No. 35.

1904-05 Wmk. 136a *Perf. 12x11½*

67a A4 1f slate 1.20 *1.75*
68a A4 2f olive yellow 3.50 .40
69a A4 3f orange .90 .25
70a A4 5f emerald 2.50 .20
71a A4 6f olive green 1.25 .45
72a A4 10f carmine 3.75 .20
73a A4 12f violet 2.25 1.60
75a A4 20f dark brown 12.00 .85
76a A4 25f blue 18.00 .80
77a A4 30f orange brown 4.50 .40
78a A4 35f red violet 14.00 .80
79a A4 50f lake 10.50 2.50
c. 50f magenta .60 *4.00*
80a A4 60f green 200.00 .75
81a A5 1k brown red 150.00 2.00
82a A5 2k gray blue *550.00* 60.00
c. Perf. 11½ *575.00* 87.50
83a A5 5k violet brown 175.00 80.00
Nos. 67a-83a (16) *1,149.* 152.95

1906 *Perf. 15*

67b A4 1f slate .75 .45
68b A4 2f olive yellow .40 .20
69b A4 3f orange .70 .20
70b A4 5f emerald .35 .20
71b A4 6f olive green .90 .20
72b A4 10f carmine .75 .20
73b A4 12f violet 1.10 .20
75b A4 20f dark brown 2.25 .30
76b A4 25f blue 2.75 .20
77b A4 30f orange brown 3.00 .20
78b A4 35f red violet 13.00 .20
79b A4 50f lake 2.25 .50
80b A4 60f green 30.00 .45
81b A5 1k brown red 30.00 .65
82b A5 2k gray blue 100.00 8.00
Nos. 67b-82b (15) 188.20 12.15

1913-16 Wmk. 137 Vert. *Perf. 15*

84 A4 1f slate .30 .20
85 A4 2f olive yellow .20 .20
86 A4 3f orange .20 .20
87 A4 5f emerald .50 .20
88 A4 6f olive green .20 .20
89 A4 10f carmine .20 .20
90 A4 12f violet, *yel* .20 .20
91 A4 16f gray green .35 .50
92 A4 20f dark brown .75 .20
93 A4 25f ultra .85 .20
94 A4 30f orange brown .75 .20
95 A4 35f red violet .75 .20
96 A4 50f lake, *blue* .35 .20
a. Cliché of 35f in plate of 50f 250.00 —
97 A4 60f green 4.25 2.25
98 A4 60f green, *salmon* .60 .30
99 A4 70f red brn, *grn* ('16) .30 .20
100 A4 80f dull violet ('16) .30 .20
101 A5 1k dull red 1.25 .20
102 A5 2k dull blue 2.75 .30
103 A5 5k violet brown 9.00 2.00
Nos. 84-103 (20) 24.05 8.35

See note after No. 35.

For overprints and surcharges see Nos. 2N1-2N3, 6N1-6N6, 6NB12, 7N1-7N6, 7NB1, 10N1.

Wmk. 137 Horiz.

84a A4 1f slate .80 1.25
85a A4 2f olive yellow 2.10 .60
87a A4 5f emerald .50 .60
88a A4 6f olive green 1.00 .60
89b A4 10f carmine 1.10 .35
90a A4 12f violet, *yellow* 2.10 .45
92a A4 20f dark brown 6.25 .50
94a A4 30f orange brown 42.50 .35
95a A4 35f red violet 150.00 .50
96b A4 50f lake, *blue* 10.50 9.50

97a	A4	60f	green	3.75	2.50
98a	A4	60f	green, *salmon*	1.60	.30
101a	A5	1k	dull red	16.00	.50
102a	A5	2k	dull blue	75.00	2.50
			Nos. 84a-102a (14)	313.20	20.50

— A5a

1916, July 1 ***Perf. 15***

103A	A5a	10f	violet brown	.80	.50

Although issued as a postal savings stamp, No. 103A was also valid for postage. Used value is for postal usage.

Exists imperf. Value $10.

For overprints and surcharges see Nos. 2N59, 5N23, 6N50, 8N13, 10N42.

Queen Zita — A6

Charles IV — A7

1916, Dec. 30

104	A6	10f	violet	.75	.60
105	A7	15f	red	.75	.60

Coronation of King Charles IV and Queen Zita on Dec. 30, 1916.

Harvesting (White Numerals) — A8

1916

106	A8	10f	rose	.65	.30
107	A8	15f	violet	.65	.30

For overprints and surcharges see Nos. B56-B57, 2N4-2N5, 5N1.

Harvesting Wheat — A9

Parliament Building at Budapest — A10

1916-18 ***Perf. 15***

108	A9	2f	brown orange	.20	.20
109	A9	3f	red lilac	.20	.20
110	A9	4f	slate gray ('18)	.20	.20
111	A9	5f	green	.20	.20
112	A9	6f	grnsh blue	.20	.20
113	A9	10f	rose red	1.25	.20
114	A9	15f	violet	.20	.20
115	A9	20f	gray brown	.20	.20
116	A9	25f	dull blue	.35	.20
117	A9	35f	brown	.20	.20
118	A9	40f	olive green	.20	.20

Perf. 14

119	A10	50f	red vio & lil	.20	.20
120	A10	75f	brt bl & pale bl	.20	.20
121	A10	80f	grn & pale grn	.20	.20
122	A10	1k	red brn & claret	.20	.20
123	A10	2k	ol brn & bister	.20	.20
124	A10	3k	dk vio & indigo	1.10	.20
125	A10	5k	dk brn & lt brn	1.10	.20
126	A10	10k	vio brn & vio	2.25	.20
			Nos. 108-126 (19)	8.85	3.80

Exist imperf. Value, set $75.

See Nos. 335-377, 388-396. For overprints and surcharges see Nos. 153, 167, C1-C5, J76-J99, 1N1-1N21, 1N26-1N30, 1N33, 1N36-1N39, 2N6-2N27, 2N33-2N38, 2N41, 2N43-2N48, 4N1-4N4, 5N2-5N17, 6N7-6N24, 6N29-6N39, 7N7-7N30, 7N38, 7N41-7N42, 8N1-8N4, 9N1-9N2, 9N4, 10N2-10N16, 10N25-10N29, 10N31, 10N33-10N41, Szeged 1-15, 20-24, 27, 30, 32-33.

During 1921-24 the two center rows of panes of various stamps then current were punched with three holes forming a triangle. These were sold at post offices. Collectors and dealers who wanted the stamps unpunched would have to purchase them through the philatelic agency at a 10% advance over face value.

Charles IV — A11

Queen Zita — A12

1918 ***Perf. 15***

127	A11	10f	scarlet	.20	.20
128	A11	15f	deep violet	.20	.20
129	A11	20f	dark brown	.20	.20
130	A11	25f	brt blue	.20	.20
131	A12	40f	olive green	.20	.20
132	A12	50f	lilac	.20	.20
			Nos. 127-132 (6)	1.20	1.20

Exist imperf. Value, set $25.

For overprints see Nos. 168-173, 1N32, 1N34-1N35, 2N28-2N32, 2N39-2N40, 2N42, 2N49-2N51, 5N18-5N22, 6N25-6N28, 6N40-6N43, 7N31-7N37, 7N39-7N40, 8N5, 9N3, 10N17-10N21, 10N30, 10N32, Szeged 16-19, 25-26, 28-29, 31.

Issues of the Republic

Hungarian Stamps of 1916-18 Overprinted in Black

1918-19 **Wmk. 137** ***Perf. 15, 14***

On Stamps of 1916-18

153	A9	2f	brown orange	.20	.20
154	A9	3f	red lilac	.20	.20
155	A9	4f	slate gray	.20	.20
156	A9	5f	green	.20	.20
157	A9	6f	grnsh blue	.20	.20
158	A9	10f	rose red	.20	.20
159	A9	20f	gray brown	.25	.20
162	A9	40f	olive green	.20	.20
163	A10	1k	red brn & claret	.20	.20
164	A10	2k	ol brn & bis	.20	.20
165	A10	3k	dk violet & ind	.45	.40
166	A10	5k	dk brn & lt brn	1.25	1.50
167	A10	10k	vio brn & vio	.75	.90

On Stamps of 1918

168	A11	10f	scarlet	.20	.20
169	A11	15f	deep violet	.20	.20
170	A11	20f	dark brown	.20	.20
171	A11	25f	brt blue	.25	.20
172	A12	40f	olive green	.25	.20
173	A12	50f	lilac	.25	.20
			Nos. 153-173 (19)	5.85	6.00

Nos. 153-162, 168-173 exist with overprint inverted. Value, each $6.

A13

A14

1919-20 ***Perf. 15***

174	A13	2f	brown orange	.20	.20
176	A13	4f	slate gray	.20	.20
177	A13	5f	yellow grn	.20	.20
178	A13	6f	grnsh blue	.20	.20
179	A13	10f	red	.20	.20
180	A13	15f	violet	.20	.20
181	A13	20f	dark brown	.20	.20
182	A13	20f	green ('20)	.20	.20
183	A13	25f	dull blue	.20	.20
184	A13	40f	olive green	.20	.20
185	A13	40f	rose red ('20)	.20	.20
186	A13	45f	orange	.20	.20

Perf. 14

187	A14	50f	brn vio & pale vio	.20	.20
188	A14	60f	brown & bl ('20)	.20	.20
189	A14	95f	dk bl & bl	.20	.20
190	A14	1k	red brn	.20	.20
191	A14	1k	dk bl & dull bl ('20)	.20	.20
192	A14	1.20k	dk grn & grn	.20	.20
193	A14	1.40k	yellow green	.20	.20
194	A14	2k	ol brn & bis	.20	.20
195	A14	3k	dk vio & ind	.20	.20
196	A14	5k	dk brn & brn	.20	.20
197	A14	10k	vio brn & red vio	.60	.60
			Nos. 174-197 (23)	5.00	5.00

The 3f red lilac, type A13, was never regularly issued without overprint (Nos. 204 and 312). In 1923 a small quantity was sold by the Government at public auction. Value $4.00.

For overprints see Nos. 203-222, 306-330, 1N40, 2N52-2N58, 6N44-6N49, 8N6-8N12, 10N22-10N24, Szeged 34-35.

Issues of the Soviet Republic

Karl Marx — A15

Sándor Petőfi — A16

Ignác Martinovics — A17

György Dózsa — A18

Friedrich Engels — A19

Wmk. 137 Horiz.

1919, June 14 **Litho.** ***Perf. 12½x12***

198	A15	20f	rose & brown	.40	*.50*
199	A16	45f	brn org & dk grn	.40	*.50*
200	A17	60f	blue gray & brn	1.75	*2.00*
201	A18	75f	claret & vio brn	1.75	*2.00*
202	A19	80f	olive db & blk brn	1.75	*2.00*
			Nos. 198-202 (5)	6.05	*7.00*

Used values are for favor cancels.

Exist imperf. Value, Set $100.

Wmk. Vertical

198a	A15	20f		9.00
199a	A16	45f		9.00
200a	A17	60f		9.00
201a	A18	75f		9.00
202a	A19	80f		17.50
			Nos. 198a-202a (5)	53.50

Nos. 198a-202a were not used postally. "Canceled" examples exist. Same values exist.

Stamps of 1919 Overprinted in Red

1919, July 21 **Typo.** ***Perf. 15***

203	A13	2f	brown orange	.20	.20
204	A13	3f	red lilac	.20	.20
205	A13	4f	slate gray	.20	.20
206	A13	5f	yellow green	.20	.20
207	A13	6f	grnsh blue	.20	.20
208	A13	10f	red	.20	.20
209	A13	15f	violet	.20	.20
210	A13	20f	dark brown	.20	.20
211	A13	25f	dull blue	.20	.20
212	A13	40f	olive green	.20	.20
213	A13	45f	orange	.20	.20

Overprinted in Red

Perf. 14

214	A14	50f	brn vio & pale vio	.20	.20
215	A14	95f	dk blue & blue	.20	.20
216	A14	1k	red brown	.20	.20
217	A14	1.20k	dk grn & grn	.20	.20
218	A14	1.40k	yellow green	.20	.20
219	A14	2k	ol brn & bister	.35	.35
220	A14	3k	dk vio & ind	.35	.35
221	A14	5k	dk brn & brn	.35	.35
222	A14	10k	vio brn & red vio	.60	.60
			Nos. 203-222 (20)	4.85	4.85

"Magyar Tanacsköztarsasag" on Nos. 198 to 222 means "Hungarian Soviet Republic."

Issues of the Kingdom

Stamps of 1919 Overprinted in Black

1919, Nov. 16

306	A13	5f	green	.65	.65
307	A13	10f	rose red	.65	.65
308	A13	15f	violet	.65	.65
309	A13	20f	gray brown	.65	.65
310	A13	25f	dull blue	.65	.65
			Nos. 306-310 (5)	3.25	3.25

Issued to commemorate the Romanian evacuation. The overprint reads: "Entry of the National Army-November 16, 1919."

Forged overprints exist.

Nos. 203 to 213 Overprinted in Black

1920, Jan. 26 ***Perf. 15***

311	A13	2f	brown orange	1.10	1.10
312	A13	3f	red lilac	.20	.20
313	A13	4f	slate gray	1.10	1.10
314	A13	5f	yellow green	.20	.20
315	A13	6f	blue green	.30	.30
316	A13	10f	red	.20	.20
317	A13	15f	violet	.20	.20
318	A13	20f	dark brown	.20	.20
319	A13	25f	dull blue	.20	.20
320	A13	40f	olive green	1.40	1.40
321	A13	45f	orange	1.40	1.40

Nos. 214 to 222 Overprinted in Black

Perf. 14

322	A14	50f	brn vio & pale vio	1.40	*1.40*
323	A14	95f	dk bl & bl	1.40	*1.40*
324	A14	1k	red brown	1.40	*1.40*
325	A14	1.20k	dk grn & grn	1.45	*1.45*
326	A14	1.40k	yellow green	1.45	*1.45*
327	A14	2k	ol brn & bis	7.00	*7.00*
328	A14	3k	dk vio & ind	7.00	*7.00*
329	A14	5k	dk brn & brn	.40	*.40*
330	A14	10k	vio brn & red vio	7.00	7.00
			Nos. 311-330 (20)	35.00	35.00

Counterfeit overprints exist.

Types of 1916-18 Issue
Denomination Tablets Without Inner Frame on Nos. 350 to 363

1920-24 Wmk. 137 *Perf. 15*

335	A9	5f brown orange	.20	.20
336	A9	10f red violet	.20	.20
337	A9	40f rose red	.20	.20
338	A9	50f yellow green	.20	.20
339	A9	50f blue vio ('22)	.20	.20
340	A9	60f black	.20	.20
341	A9	1k green ('22)	.20	.20
342	A9	1½k brown vio ('22)	.20	.20
343	A9	2k grnsh blue ('22)	.20	.20
344	A9	2½k dp green ('22)	.20	.20
345	A9	3k brown org ('22)	.20	.20
346	A9	4k lt red ('22)	.20	.20
347	A9	4½k dull violet ('22)	.40	.20
348	A9	5k deep brown ('22)	.20	.20
349	A9	6k dark blue ('22)	.20	.20
350	A9	10k brown ('23)	.20	.20
351	A9	15k slate ('23)	.20	.20
352	A9	20k red vio ('23)	.20	.20
353	A9	25k orange ('23)	.20	.20
354	A9	40k gray grn ('23)	.20	.20
355	A9	50k dark blue ('23)	.20	.20
356	A9	100k claret ('23)	.25	.20
357	A9	150k dark green ('23)	.35	.20
358	A9	200k green ('23)	.35	.20
359	A9	300k rose red ('24)	.50	.20
360	A9	350k violet ('23)	1.25	.20
361	A9	500k dark gray ('24)	1.50	.20
362	A9	600k olive bis ('24)	1.50	.20
363	A9	800k org yel ('24)	2.10	.20

Perf. 14

364	A10	2.50k bl & gray bl	.20	.20
365	A10	3.50k gray	.20	.20
366	A10	10k brown ('22)	.55	.20
367	A10	15k dk gray ('22)	.20	.20
368	A10	20k red vio ('22)	.20	.20
369	A10	25k orange ('22)	.20	.20
370	A10	30k claret ('22)	.20	.20
371	A10	40k gray grn ('22)	.20	.20
372	A10	50k dp blue ('22)	.20	.20
373	A10	100k yel brn ('22)	.20	.20
374	A10	400k turq bl ('23)	.80	.30
375	A10	500k brt vio ('23)	.75	.20
376	A10	1000k lilac ('24)	.85	.20
377	A10	2000k car ('24)	1.75	.20
		Nos. 335-377 (43)	18.70	8.70

Nos. 372 to 377 have colored numerals.

Madonna and Child — A23

1921-25 Typo. *Perf. 12*

378	A23	50k dk brn & bl	.20	.20
379	A23	100k ol bis & yel brn	.30	.20

Wmk. 133

380	A23	200k dk bl & ultra	.30	.20
381	A23	500k vio brn & vio	.60	.25
382	A23	1000k vio & red vio	.80	.30
383	A23	2000k grnsh bl & vio	1.20	.45
384	A23	2500k ol brn & buff	1.40	.35
385	A23	3000k brn red & vio	1.40	.35
386	A23	5000k dk grn & yel grn	1.40	.35
a.		Center inverted	15,000.	8,000.
387	A23	10000k gray vio & pale bl	1.40	1.25
		Nos. 378-387 (10)	9.00	3.90

Nos. 380-387 exist imperf. Value, set of 8 $150.

Issue dates: 50k, 100k, Feb. 27, 1921; 2500k, 10,000k, 1925; others, 1923.

Types of 1916-18
Denomination Tablets Without Inner Frame on Nos. 388-394

1924 Wmk. 133 *Perf. 15*

388	A9	100k claret	.25	.20
389	A9	200k yellow grn	.20	.20
390	A9	300k rose red	.25	.20
391	A9	400k deep blue	.25	.20
392	A9	500k dark gray	.30	.20
393	A9	600k olive bister	.40	.25
a.		"800" in upper right corner	140.00	140.00
394	A9	800k org yel	.45	.20

Perf. 14½x14

395	A10	1000k lilac	1.10	.20
396	A10	2000k carmine	1.60	.20
		Nos. 388-396 (9)	4.80	1.85

Nos. 395 and 396 have colored numerals.

Maurus Jókai (1825-1904), Novelist A24

1925, Feb. 1 Unwmk. *Perf. 12*

400	A24	1000k dp grn & blk brn	2.00	5.50
401	A24	2000k lt brn & blk brn	1.00	.65
402	A24	2500k dk bl & blk brn	2.00	5.50
		Nos. 400-402 (3)	5.00	11.65

Exist imperf. Value, set $50.

Crown of St. Stephen A25

Matthias Cathedral A26

Palace at Budapest — A27

Perf. 14, 15

1926-27 Wmk. 133 Litho.

403	A25	1f dk gray	.35	.20
404	A25	2f lt blue	.40	.20
405	A25	3f orange	.40	.20
406	A25	4f violet	.45	.20
407	A25	6f lt green	.50	.20
408	A25	8f lilac rose	1.10	.20

Typo.

409	A26	10f deep blue	1.40	.20
410	A26	16f dark violet	1.40	.20
411	A26	20f carmine	1.60	.20
412	A26	25f lt brown	1.50	.20

Perf. 14½x14

413	A27	32f dp vio & brt vio	3.50	.20
414	A27	40f dk blue & blue	4.50	.20
		Nos. 403-414 (12)	17.10	2.40

See Nos. 428-436. For surcharges see Nos. 450-456, 466-467.

Madonna and Child — A28

1926-27 Engr. *Perf. 14*

415	A28	1p violet	15.00	.50
416	A28	2p red	15.00	.75
417	A28	5p blue ('27)	15.00	2.75
		Nos. 415-417 (3)	45.00	4.00

Exist imperf. Value, set $250.

Palace at Budapest A29

St. Stephen A30

1926-27 Typo.

418	A29	30f blue grn ('27)	3.00	.20
419	A29	46f ultra ('27)	3.75	.30
420	A29	50f brown blk ('27)	4.25	.20
421	A29	70f scarlet	7.00	.20
		Nos. 418-421 (4)	18.00	.90

For surcharge see No. 480.

1928-29 Engr. *Perf. 15*

422	A30	8f yellow grn	.40	.30
423	A30	8f rose lake ('29)	.40	.30
424	A30	16f orange red	.50	.30
425	A30	16f violet ('29)	.50	.30
426	A30	32f ultra	1.60	1.10
427	A30	32f bister ('29)	1.60	1.10
		Nos. 422-427 (6)	5.00	3.40

890th death anniversary of St. Stephen, the first king of Hungary.
Exist imperf. Value, set $160.

Types of 1926-27 Issue
Perf. 14, 15

1928-30 Typo. Wmk. 210

428	A25	1f black	.25	.20
429	A25	2f blue	.30	.20
430	A25	3f orange	.30	.20
431	A25	4f violet	.30	.20
432	A25	6f blue grn	.40	.20
433	A25	8f lilac rose	.80	.20
434	A26	10f dp blue ('30)	3.25	.20
435	A26	16f violet	1.25	.20
436	A26	20f dull red	1.25	.20
		Nos. 428-436 (9)	8.10	1.80

On #428-433 the numerals have thicker strokes than on the same values of the 1926-27 issue.

Palace at Budapest — A31

Type A31 resembles A27 but the steamer is nearer the right of the design.

1928-31 *Perf. 14*

437	A31	30f emerald ('31)	2.50	.20
438	A31	32f red violet	3.25	.30
439	A31	40f deep blue	4.00	.20
440	A31	46f apple green	3.25	.20
441	A31	50f ocher ('31)	3.25	.20
		Nos. 437-441 (5)	16.25	1.10

Admiral Nicholas Horthy — A32

1930, Mar. 1 Litho. *Perf. 15*

445	A32	8f myrtle green	1.40	.30
446	A32	16f purple	1.40	.35
447	A32	20f carmine	3.75	1.10
448	A32	32f olive brown	3.75	3.75
449	A32	40f dull blue	7.00	1.65
		Nos. 445-449 (5)	17.30	7.15

10th anniv. of the election of Adm. Nicholas Horthy as Regent, Mar. 1, 1920.
Exist imperf. Value, set, $125.

Stamps of 1926-28 Surcharged

1931, Jan. 1 *Perf. 14, 15*

450	A25	2f on 3f orange	1.00	.40
451	A25	6f on 8f magenta	1.00	.20
a.		Perf. 14	25.00	25.00
452	A26	10f on 16f violet	.90	.20

Wmk. 133

453	A25	2f on 3f orange	3.50	3.00
454	A25	6f on 8f magenta	2.75	3.00
a.		Perf. 14	65.00	65.00
455	A26	10f on 16f dk vio	2.25	1.50
456	A26	20f on 25f lt brn	2.25	1.25
a.		Perf. 14	1.60	1.50
		Nos. 450-456 (7)	13.65	9.55

For surcharges see Nos. 466-467.

St. Elizabeth A33

Ministering to Children A34

Wmk. 210

1932, Apr. 21 Photo. *Perf. 15*

458	A33	10f ultra	1.00	.50
459	A33	20f scarlet	1.00	.50

Perf. 14

460	A34	32f deep violet	4.00	2.25
461	A34	40f deep blue	3.00	1.50
		Nos. 458-461 (4)	9.00	4.75

700th anniv. of the death of St. Elizabeth of Hungary.
Exist imperf. Value, set $60.

Madonna, Patroness of Hungary — A35

1932, June 1 *Perf. 12*

462	A35	1p yellow grn	20.00	.85
463	A35	2p carmine	22.50	1.50
464	A35	5p deep blue	85.00	5.00
465	A35	10p olive bister	125.00	30.00
		Nos. 462-465 (4)	252.50	37.35

Exist imperf. Value, set $600.

Nos. 451 and 454 Surcharged

1932, June 14 Wmk. 210 *Perf. 15*

466	A25	2f on 6f on 8f mag	1.50	.40

Wmk. 133

467	A25	2f on 6f on 8f mag	40.00	40.00

Imre Madách — A36

Designs: 2f, Janos Arany. 4f, Dr. Ignaz Semmelweis. 6f, Baron Roland Eotvos. 10f, Count Stephen Szechenyi. 16f, Ferenc Deak. 20f, Franz Liszt. 30f, Louis Kossuth. 32f, Stephen Tisza. 40f, Mihaly Munkacsy. 50f, Alexander Csoma. 70f, Farkas Bolyai.

1932 Wmk. 210 *Perf. 15*

468	A36	1f slate violet	.20	.20
469	A36	2f orange	.20	.20
470	A36	4f ultra	.20	.20
471	A36	6f yellow grn	.20	.20
472	A36	10f Prus green	.20	.20
473	A36	16f dull violet	.25	.20
474	A36	20f deep rose	.20	.20
475	A36	30f brown	.45	.20
476	A36	32f brown vio	.70	.45
477	A36	40f dull blue	.70	.20
478	A36	50f deep green	1.10	.20
479	A36	70f cerise	1.50	.20
		Nos. 468-479 (12)	5.90	2.65
		Set, never hinged	11.50	

Issued in honor of famous Hungarians.
See Nos. 509-510.

No. 421 Surcharged

1933, Apr. 15 Wmk. 133 *Perf. 14*

480	A29	10f on 70f scarlet	2.00	.25
		Never hinged	4.00	

Leaping Stag and Double Cross — A47

Wmk. 210

1933, July 10 Photo. *Perf. 15*

481	A47 10f dk green	.90	1.00
482	A47 16f violet brn	2.50	2.25
483	A47 20f car lake	1.60	1.25
484	A47 32f yellow	3.75	4.00
485	A47 40f deep blue	3.75	4.00
	Nos. 481-485 (5)	12.50	12.50
	Set, never hinged	16.50	

Boy Scout Jamboree at Gödöllö, Hungary, July 20 - Aug. 20, 1933.

Exists imperf. Value, set $150.

Souvenir Sheet

Franz Liszt — A48

1934, May 6 *Perf. 15*

486	A48 20f lake	55.00	100.00
	Never hinged	120.00	

2nd Hungarian Phil. Exhib., Budapest, and Jubilee of the 1st Hungarian Phil. Soc. Sold for 90f, including entrance fee. Size: 64x76mm.

Exists imperf. Value $1,500.

Francis II Rákóczy (1676-1735), Prince of Transylvania A49

1935, Apr. 8 *Perf. 12*

487	A49 10f yellow green	.40	.25
488	A49 16f brt violet	1.50	*1.10*
489	A49 20f dark carmine	.50	.25
490	A49 32f brown lake	2.25	*1.00*
491	A49 40f blue	3.00	2.00
	Nos. 487-491 (5)	7.65	4.60
	Set, never hinged	10.00	

Exists imperf. Value, set $250.

Cardinal Pázmány — A50

Signing the Charter — A51

1935, Sept. 25

492	A50 6f dull green	1.00	1.00
493	A51 10f dark green	.35	.35
494	A50 16f slate violet	1.25	1.25
495	A50 20f magenta	.40	.40
496	A51 32f deep claret	2.75	1.60
497	A51 40f dark blue	2.25	1.60
	Nos. 492-497 (6)	8.00	6.20
	Set, never hinged	11.00	

Tercentenary of the founding of the University of Budapest by Peter Cardinal Pázmány.

Exists imperf. Value, set $250.

Ancient City and Fortress of Buda — A52

Guardian Angel over Buda — A53

Shield of Buda, Cannon and Massed Flags — A54

First Hungarian Soldier to Enter Buda — A55

1936, Sept. 2 *Perf. 11½x12½*

498	A52 10f dark green	.75	.40
499	A53 16f deep violet	2.00	*2.25*
500	A54 20f car lake	.75	.60
501	A55 32f dark brown	2.00	*3.25*
502	A52 40f deep blue	2.00	*4.00*
	Nos. 498-502 (5)	7.50	10.50
	Set, never hinged	14.00	

250th anniv. of the recapture of Budapest from the Turks.

Exists imperf. Value, set $250.

Catalogue values for unused stamps in this section, from this point to the end of the section, are for Never Hinged items.

Budapest International Fair — A56

1937, Feb. 22 *Perf. 12*

503	A56 2f deep orange	.20	.20
504	A56 6f yellow green	.25	.20
505	A56 10f myrtle green	.30	.20
506	A56 20f deep cerise	.50	.25
507	A56 32f dark violet	1.00	.70
508	A56 40f ultra	1.25	.70
	Nos. 503-508 (6)	3.50	2.25

Exist imperf. Value, set $200.

Portrait Type of 1932

5f, Ferenc Kolcsey. 25f, Mihaly Vorosmarty.

1937, May 5 *Perf. 15*

509	A36 5f brown orange	.20	.20
510	A36 25f olive green	.45	.20

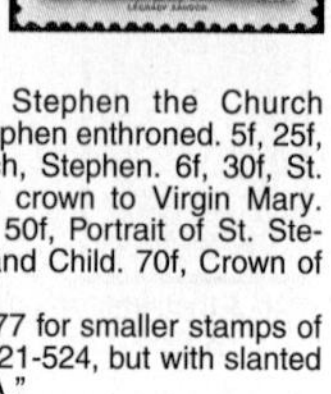

Pope Sylvester II, Archbishop Astrik — A59

Designs: 2f, 16f, Stephen the Church builder. 4f, 20f, St. Stephen enthroned. 5f, 25f, Sts. Gerhardt, Emerich, Stephen. 6f, 30f, St. Stephen offering holy crown to Virgin Mary. 10f, same as 1f. 32f, 50f, Portrait of St. Stephen. 40f, Madonna and Child. 70f, Crown of St. Stephen.

See designs A75-A77 for smaller stamps of designs similar Nos. 521-524, but with slanted "MAGYAR KIR POSTA."

1938, Jan. 1 *Perf. 12*

511	A59 1f deep violet	.20	.20
512	A59 2f olive brown	.20	.20
513	A59 4f brt blue	.20	.20
514	A59 5f magenta	.20	.20
515	A59 6f dp yel grn	.50	.20
516	A59 10f red orange	.60	.20
517	A59 16f gray violet	.60	.25
518	A59 20f car lake	.75	.20
519	A59 25f dark green	1.00	.50
520	A59 30f olive bister	2.00	.20
521	A59 32f dp claret, *buff*	1.00	.90
522	A59 40f Prus green	2.75	.20
523	A59 50f rose vio, *grnsh*	4.00	.20
524	A59 70f ol grn, *bluish*	5.00	.20
	Nos. 511-524 (14)	19.00	3.85

900th anniv. of the death of St. Stephen.

Exists imperf. Value, set $375.

For overprints see Nos. 535-536.

Admiral Horthy — A67

1938, Jan. 1 *Perf. 12½x12*

525	A67 1p peacock green	3.75	.20
526	A67 2p brown	3.75	.25
527	A67 5p sapphire blue	7.00	1.75
	Nos. 525-527 (3)	14.50	2.20

Exist imperf. Value, set $200.

Souvenir Sheet

St. Stephen — A68

1938, May 22 Wmk. 210 *Perf. 12*

528	A68 20f carmine lake	22.50	17.50

3rd Hungarian Phil. Exhib., Budapest. Sheet sold only at exhibition with 1p ticket.

Exists imperf. Value $2,000.

College of Debrecen A69

Three Students — A71

George Marothy — A73

10f, 18th cent. view of College. 20f, 19th cent. view of College. 40f, Stephen Hatvani.

Perf. 12x12½, 12½x12

1938, Sept. 24 Wmk. 210

529	A69 6f deep green	.20	.20
530	A69 10f brown	.20	.20
531	A71 16f brown car	.30	.20
532	A69 20f crimson	.25	.20
533	A73 32f slate green	.80	.45
534	A73 40f brt blue	.90	.30
	Nos. 529-534 (6)	2.65	1.55

Founding of Debrecen College, 400th anniv.

Exists imperf. Value $125.

Types of 1938 Overprinted in Blue (#535) or Carmine (#536):

a

b

1938 *Perf. 12*

535	A59(a) 20f salmon pink	1.25	.50
536	A59(b) 70f brn, *grnsh*	1.40	.50
a.	Overprint omitted	*12,000.*	*8,000.*

Restoration of the territory ceded by Czechoslovakia.

Exists imperf. Value $100.

Forgeries exist of No. 536a.

Crown of St. Stephen A75

St. Stephen A76

Madonna, Patroness of Hungary A77

Coronation Church, Budapest A78

Reformed Church, Debrecen A79

Cathedral, Esztergom A80

Deak Square Evangelical Church, Budapest — A81

Cathedral of Kassa — A82

Wmk. 210

1939, June 1 Photo. *Perf. 15*

537	A75 1f brown car	.20	.20
538	A75 2f Prus green	.20	.20
539	A75 4f ocher	.20	.20
540	A75 5f brown violet	.20	.20
541	A75 6f yellow green	.20	.20
542	A75 10f bister brn	.20	.20
543	A75 16f rose violet	.20	.20
544	A76 20f rose red	.20	.20
545	A77 25f blue gray	.20	.20

Perf. 12

546	A78 30f red violet	.50	.20
547	A79 32f brown	.40	.20
548	A80 40f greenish blue	.50	.20
549	A81 50f olive	.50	.20
550	A82 70f henna brown	.55	.20
	Nos. 537-550 (14)	4.25	2.80

See #521-524, 578-596. For overprints see #559-560.
Exists imperf. Value, set $150.

Girl Scout Sign and Olive Branch — A83

6f, Scout lily, Hungary's shield, Crown of St. Stephen. 10f, Girls in Scout hat & national headdress. 20f, Dove & Scout emblems.

1939, July 20 Photo. *Perf. 12*

551	A83 2f brown orange	.40	.35
552	A83 6f green	.45	.35
553	A83 10f brown	.75	.35
554	A83 20f lilac rose	.90	.70
	Nos. 551-554 (4)	2.50	1.75

Girl Scout Jamboree at Gödöllö.
Exists imperf. Value, set $200.

Admiral Horthy at Szeged, 1919 — A87

Admiral Nicholas Horthy A88

Cathedral of Kassa and Angel Ringing "Bell of Liberty" A89

1940, Mar. 1

555	A87 6f green	.30	.20
556	A88 10f ol blk & ol bis	.30	.20
557	A89 20f brt rose brown	.60	.35
	Nos. 555-557 (3)	1.20	.75

20th anniversary of the election of Admiral Horthy as Regent of Hungary.
Exists imperf. Value, set $75.

Crown of St. Stephen A90

1940, Sept. 5

558	A90 10f dk green & yellow	.20	.20

Issued in commemoration of the recovery of northeastern Transylvania from Romania.
Exists imperf. Value $25.

SEMI-POSTAL STAMPS

Issues of the Monarchy

"Turul" and St. Stephen's Crown — SP1

Franz Josef I Wearing Hungarian Crown — SP2

Wmk. Double Cross (137)

1913, Nov. 20 Typo. *Perf. 14*

B1	SP1	1f slate	.25	.20
B2	SP1	2f olive yellow	.25	.20
B3	SP1	3f orange	.25	.20
B4	SP1	5f emerald	.25	.20
B5	SP1	6f olive green	.25	.20
B6	SP1	10f carmine	.30	.20
B7	SP1	12f violet, *yellow*	.60	.20
B8	SP1	16f gray green	.90	.20
B9	SP1	20f dark brown	2.40	.40
B10	SP1	25f ultra	1.50	.25
B11	SP1	30f orange brown	1.75	.25
B12	SP1	35f red violet	1.75	.25
B13	SP1	50f lake, *blue*	3.00	.60
B14	SP1	60f green, *salmon*	3.00	.50
B15	SP2	1k dull red	26.00	2.00
B16	SP2	2k dull blue	78.00	40.00
B17	SP2	5k violet brown	30.00	30.00
		Nos. B1-B17 (17)	150.45	75.85

Nos. B1-B17 were sold at an advance of 2f over face value, as indicated by the label at bottom. The surtax was to aid flood victims.
For overprints see Nos. 5NB1-5NB10, 6NB1-6NB11.
Exist imperf. Value, set $375.

Semi-Postal Stamps of 1913 Surcharged in Red, Green or Brown:

a

b

1914

B18	SP1(a)	1f slate	.25	.20
B19	SP1(a)	2f olive yel	.25	.20
B20	SP1(a)	3f orange	.25	.20
B21	SP1(a)	5f emerald	.25	.20
B22	SP1(a)	6f olive green	.25	.20
B23	SP1(a)	10f carmine (G)	.35	.20
B24	SP1(a)	12f violet, *yel*	.25	.20
B25	SP1(a)	16f gray green	.30	.20
B26	SP1(a)	20f dark brown	1.00	.20
B27	SP1(a)	25f ultra	1.00	.20
B28	SP1(a)	30f orange brn	1.40	.25
B29	SP1(a)	35f red violet	2.25	.20
B30	SP1(a)	50f lake, *bl*	1.75	.50
B31	SP1(a)	60f green, *salmon*	2.50	.55
B32	SP2(b)	1k dull red (Br)	55.00	25.00
B33	SP2(b)	2k dull blue	40.00	26.00
B34	SP2(b)	5k violet brn	30.00	21.00
		Nos. B18-B34 (17)	137.05	75.50

Exist imperf. Value, set $300.

Regular Issue of 1913 Surcharged in Red or Green:

c

d

1915, Jan. 1

B35	A4(c)	1f slate	.20	.20
B36	A4(c)	2f olive yel	.20	.20
B37	A4(c)	3f orange	.20	.20
B38	A4(c)	5f emerald	.20	.20
B39	A4(c)	6f olive grn	.20	.20
B40	A4(c)	10f carmine (G)	.20	.20
B41	A4(c)	12f violet, *yel*	.20	.20
B42	A4(c)	16f gray green	.25	.25
B43	A4(c)	20f dark brown	.30	.30
B44	A4(c)	25f ultra	.20	.20
B45	A4(c)	30f orange brn	.40	.20
B46	A4(c)	35f red violet	.45	.20
B47	A4(c)	50f lake, *bl*	.65	.25
a.		On No. 96a	*5,500.*	
B48	A4(c)	60f green, *salmon*	.85	.30
B49	A5(d)	1k dull red	1.25	3.00
B50	A5(d)	2k dull blue	3.25	7.50
B51	A5(d)	5k violet brown	9.00	17.50

Surcharged as Type "c" but in Smaller Letters

B52	A4	60f green, *salmon*	2.40	1.00
		Nos. B35-B52 (18)	20.40	32.10

Nos. B18-B52 were sold at an advance of 2f over face value. The surtax to aid war widows and orphans.
Exist imperf. Value, set $100.

Soldiers Fighting
SP3 SP4

Eagle with Sword SP5

Harvesting SP6

1916-17 *Perf. 15*

B53	SP3 10f + 2f rose red	.20	.20
B54	SP4 15f + 2f dull violet	.20	.20
B55	SP5 40f + 2f brn car ('17)	.20	.20
	Nos. B53-B55 (3)	.60	.60

Exist imperf. Value, set $6.50.
For overprints and surcharge see Nos. B58-B60. 1NB1-1NB3, 2NB1-2NB6, 4NJ1, 5NB11-5NB13, 6NB13-6NB15, 7NB2-7NB3, 9NB1, 10NB1-10NB4, Szeged B1-B4.

1917, Sept. 15

Surcharge in Red

B56	SP6 10f + 1k rose	.35	*.50*
B57	SP6 15f + 1k violet	.35	*.50*

Nos. B56 and B57 were issued in connection with the War Exhibition of Archduke Josef.

Issues of the Republic

Semi-Postal Stamps of 1916-17 Overprinted in Black

1918

B58	SP3 10f + 2f rose red	.20	.20
B59	SP4 15f + 2f dull violet	.20	.20
B60	SP5 40f + 2f brown car	.20	.20
	Nos. B58-B60 (3)	.60	.60

Nos. B58-B60 exist with inverted overprint.
Exist imperf. Value, set $6.50.

Postally used copies of Nos. B69-B174 sell for more.

Issues of the Kingdom

Released Prisoner Walking Home — SP7

Prisoners of War — SP8

Homecoming of Soldier — SP9

Wmk. 137 Vert. or Horiz.

1920, Mar. 10 *Perf. 12*

B69	SP7 40f + 1k dull red	1.75	1.75
B70	SP8 60f + 2k gray brown	3.25	3.25
B71	SP9 1k + 5k dk blue	3.25	3.25
	Nos. B69-B71 (3)	8.25	8.25
	Set, never hinged	16.50	

The surtax was used to help prisoners of war return home from Siberia.
Exist imperf. Value, set $50.

Statue of Petöfi — SP10

Griffin — SP11

Sándor Petöfi — SP12

Petöfi Dying — SP13

Petöfi Addressing People — SP14

1923, Jan. 23 *Perf. 14 (10k, 40k), 12*

B72	SP10 10k slate green	.25	*.35*
B73	SP11 15k dull blue	.35	*1.50*
B74	SP12 25k gray brown	.35	*.35*
B75	SP13 40k brown violet	1.50	1.50
B76	SP14 50k violet brown	1.50	1.50
	Nos. B72-B76 (5)	3.95	5.20
	Set, never hinged	8.50	

Birth centenary of the Hungarian poet Sándor Petöfi. The stamps were on sale at double face value, for a limited time and in restricted quantities, after which the remainders were given to a charitable organization.
Exist imperf. Value, set $45.

Child with Symbols of Peace — SP15

Mother and Infant — SP16

Instruction in Archery — SP17

Wmk. 133

1924, Apr. 8 Engr. *Perf. 12*

B77	SP15	300k dark blue	1.50	1.50
a.		Perf. 11½	35.00	30.00
B78	SP16	500k black brown	1.50	1.50
B79	SP17	1000k black green	1.75	1.75
		Nos. B77-B79 (3)	4.75	4.75
		Set, never hinged	9.50	

Each stamp has on the back an inscription stating that it was sold at a premium of 100 per cent over the face value.

Exist imperf. Value, set $40.

Parade of Athletes SP18

Skiing — SP19

Skating — SP20

Diving — SP21

Fencing SP22

Scouts Camping — SP23

Soccer SP24

Hurdling — SP25

Perf. 12, 12½ and Compound

1925 Typo. Unwmk.

B80	SP18	100k bl grn & brn	3.00	*4.00*
B81	SP19	200k lt brn & myr grn	3.50	*5.00*
B82	SP20	300k dark blue	4.00	*6.00*
B83	SP21	400k dp bl & dp grn	5.00	*6.50*
B84	SP22	500k purple brown	6.00	*7.50*
B85	SP23	1000k red brown	7.00	*9.00*
B86	SP24	2000k brown violet	8.00	*10.00*
B87	SP25	2500k olive brown	8.00	*12.00*
		Nos. B80-B87 (8)	44.50	*60.00*
		Set, never hinged	85.00	

These stamps were sold at double face value, plus a premium of 10 per cent on orders sent by mail. They did not serve any postal need and were issued solely to raise funds to aid athletic associations. An inscription regarding the 100 per cent premium is printed on the back of each stamp.

Exist imperf. Value, set $150.

St. Emerich SP26

Sts. Stephen and Gisela SP27

St. Ladislaus SP28

Sts. Gerhardt and Emerich SP29

1930, May 15 Wmk. 210 *Perf. 14*

B88	SP26	8f + 2f deep green	.45	.40
B89	SP27	16f + 4f brt violet	.50	*.70*
B90	SP28	20f + 4f deep rose	1.75	*2.50*
B91	SP29	32f + 8f ultra	2.50	*3.75*
		Nos. B88-B91 (4)	5.20	*7.35*
		Set, never hinged	11.00	

900th anniv. of the death of St. Emerich, son of Stephen I, king, saint and martyr.

Exist imperf. Value, set $30.

Catalogue values for unused stamps in this section, from this point to the end of the section, are for Never Hinged items.

St. Ladislaus — SP30

Holy Sacrament SP31

SP32

1938 May 16 Photo. *Perf. 12*

B92	SP30	16f + 16f dull slate bl	2.50	2.50
B93	SP31	20f + 20f dk car	2.50	2.50

Souvenir Sheet

B94	SP32	Sheet of 7	40.00	32.50
a.		6f + 6f St. Stephen	3.75	3.00
b.		10f + 10f St. Emerich	3.75	3.00
c.		16f + 16f slate blue (B92)	3.75	3.00
d.		20f + 20f dark carmine (B93)	3.75	3.00
e.		32f + 32f St. Elizabeth	3.75	3.00
f.		40f + 40f St. Maurice	3.75	3.00
g.		50f + 50f St. Margaret	3.75	3.00

Printed in sheets measuring 136½x155mm. Nos. B94c and B94d are slightly smaller than B92 and B93.

Eucharistic Cong. in Budapest, May, 1938.

Exist imperf. Value: set $100; souvenir sheet $2,000.

St. Stephen, Victorious Warrior SP33

St. Stephen, Offering Crown SP34

SP35

1938, Aug. 12 *Perf. 12*

B95	SP33	10f + 10f violet brn	3.00	3.00
B96	SP34	20f + 20f red org	3.00	3.00

Souvenir Sheet

B97	SP35	Sheet of 7	30.00	20.00
a.		6f + 6f St. Stephen the Missionary	3.00	2.00
b.		10f + 10f violet brown (B95)	3.00	2.00
c.		16f + 16f Seated Upon Throne	3.00	2.00
d.		20f + 20f red orange (B96)	3.00	2.00
e.		32f + 32f Receives Bishops and Monks	3.00	2.00
f.		40f + 40f St. Gisela, St. Stephen and St. Emerich	3.00	2.00
g.		50f + 50f St. Stephen on Bier	3.00	2.00

Death of St. Stephen, 900th anniversary.

No. B97 is on brownish paper, Nos. B95-B96 on white.

Exist imperf. Value: set $100; souvenir sheet $2,000.

Statue Symbolizing Recovered Territories SP36

Castle of Munkács SP37

Admiral Horthy Entering Komárom SP38

Cathedral of Kassa SP39

Girl Offering Flowers to Soldier — SP40

1939, Jan. 16

B98	SP36	6f + 3f myrtle grn	.60	.35
B99	SP37	10f + 5f olive grn	.25	.20
B100	SP38	20f + 10f dark red	.25	.20
B101	SP39	30f + 15f grnsh blue	1.10	.60
B102	SP40	40f + 20f dk bl gray	1.10	.65
		Nos. B98-B102 (5)	3.30	2.00

The surtax was for the aid of "Hungary for Hungarians" patriotic movement.

Exist imperf. Value, set $125.

Memorial Tablets SP41

Gáspár Károlyi, Translator of the Bible into Hungarian SP42

Albert Molnár de Szenci, Translator of the Psalms SP43

Prince Gabriel Bethlen — SP44

Susanna Lórántffy — SP45

Perf. 12x12½, 12½x12

1939 Photo. Wmk. 210

B103	SP41	6f + 3f green	.70	.55
B104	SP42	10f + 5f claret	.70	.55
B105	SP43	20f + 10f copper red	.80	.75
B106	SP44	32f + 16f bister	1.25	1.00
B107	SP45	40f + 20f chalky blue	1.40	1.00
		Nos. B103-B107 (5)	4.85	3.85

Souvenir Sheets

Perf. 12

B108	SP44	32f olive & vio brn	15.00	15.00

Imperf

B109	SP44	32f bl grn, cop red & gold	15.00	15.00

National Protestant Day. The surtax was used to erect an Intl. Protestant Institute.

The souvenir sheets sold for 1.32p each.

Nos. B103-B107 exist imperf. Value, set $125.

Issue dates: Nos. B103-B107, Oct. 2. Nos. B108-B109, Oct. 27.

Boy Scout Flying Kite — SP47

Allegory of Flight — SP48

Archangel Gabriel from Millennium Monument, Budapest, and Planes — SP49

1940, Jan. 1 ***Perf. 12½x12***

B110	SP47	6f + 6f yellow grn	.75	*.80*
B111	SP48	10f + 10f chocolate	.85	*.95*
B112	SP49	20f + 20f copper red	1.10	*1.25*
		Nos. B110-B112 (3)	2.70	3.00

The surtax was used for the Horthy National Aviation Fund.
Exist imperf. Value, set $100.

SP50

Soldier Protecting Family from Floods SP51

Souvenir Sheet

Wmk. 210

1940, May 6 **Photo.** ***Perf. 12***

B113	SP50	20f + 1p dk blue grn	5.00	5.00

Exist imperf. Value $2,000.

1940, May

B114	SP51	10f + 2f gray brown	.25	.25
B115	SP51	20f + 4f orange red	.25	.25
B116	SP51	20f + 50f red brown	.70	.70
		Nos. B114-B116 (3)	1.20	1.20

The surtax on Nos. B113-B116 was used to aid flood victims.
Exist imperf. Value, set $75.

Hunyadi Coat of Arms SP52

King Matthias SP54

Hunyadi Castle SP53

Equestrian Statue of King Matthias SP55

Corvin Codex — SP56

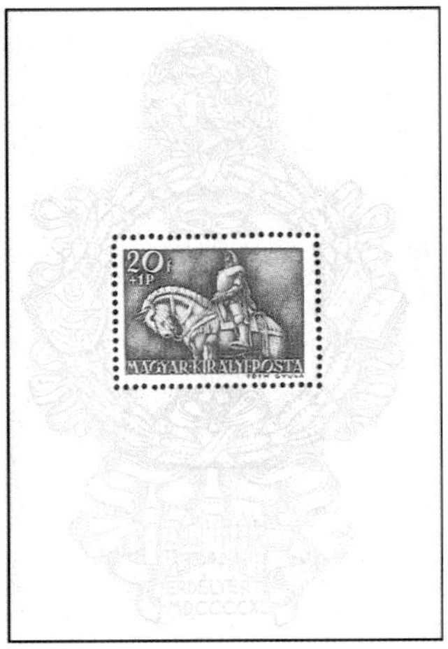

Equestrian Statue of King Matthias — SP57

1940 ***Perf. 12½x12, 12x12½***

B117	SP52	6f + 3f blue grn	.30	.30
B118	SP53	10f + 5f gldn brn	.25	.25
B119	SP54	16f + 8f dk ol bis	.30	.30
B120	SP55	20f + 10f brick red	.50	.40
B121	SP56	32f + 16f dk gray	1.00	.70
		Nos. B117-B121 (5)	2.35	1.95

Souvenir Sheet

B122	SP57	20f + 1p dk bl grn & pale grn	4.50	4.50

King Matthias (1440-1490) at Kolozsvar, Transylvania. The surtax was used for war relief.
Exist imperf. Value: set $75; souvenir sheet $2,000.
Issued: #B117-B121, July 1. #B122. Nov. 7.

Hungarian Soldier — SP58

20f+50f, Virgin Mary and Szekley, symbolizing the return of transylvania. 32f+50f, Szekley Mother Offering Infant Son to the Fatherland.

1940, Dec. 2 **Photo.** ***Perf. 12½x12***

B123	SP58	10f + 50f dk blue grn	.65	.50
B124	SP58	20f + 50f brown car	.65	.50
B125	SP58	32f + 50f yellow brn	.95	.75
		Nos. B123-B125 (3)	2.25	1.75

Occupation of Transylvania. The surtax was for the Pro-Transylvania movement.
Exist imperf. Value, set $100.

Symbol for Drama SP61

Symbol for Sculpture — SP62

Symbols: 16f+16f, Art. 20f+20f, Literature.

1940, Dec. 15 ***Perf. 12x12½, 12½x12***

B126	SP61	6f + 6f dark green	.95	.90
B127	SP62	10f + 10f olive bis	.95	.90
B128	SP62	16f + 16f dk violet	.95	.90
B129	SP61	20f + 20f fawn	.95	.90
		Nos. B126-B129 (4)	3.80	3.60

Souvenir Sheet

1941, Jan. 5 ***Imperf.***

B130		Sheet of 4	4.25	4.25
a.	SP61	6f + 6f olive brown	.80	.80
b.	SP62	10f + 10f henna brown	.80	.80
c.	SP62	16f + 16f dk blue green	.80	.80
d.	SP61	20f + 20f rose violet	.80	.80

Surtax on #B126-B130 was used for the Pension and Assistance Institution for Artists.
Nos. B126-B129 exist imperf. Value, set $40.

AIR POST STAMPS

Issues of the Monarchy

Nos. 120, 123 Surcharged in Red or Blue

Wmk. 137

1918, July 4 **Typo.** ***Perf. 14***

C1	A10	1k 50f on 75f (R)	15.00	*27.50*
C2	A10	4k 50f on 2k (Bl)	15.00	*27.50*

Counterfeits exist.
Exist imperf. Value, set $125.

No. 126 Surcharged

1920, Nov. 7

C3	A10	3k on 10k (G)	.85	*1.25*
C4	A10	8k on 10k (R)	.85	*1.25*
C5	A10	12k on 10k (Bl)	.85	*1.25*
		Nos. C3-C5 (3)	2.55	3.75
		Set, never hinged	6.00	

Icarus — AP3

1924-25 ***Perf. 14***

C6	AP3	100k red brn & red	.50	*1.00*
C7	AP3	500k bl grn & yel grn	.50	*1.00*
C8	AP3	1000k bis brn & brn	.50	*1.00*
C9	AP3	2000k dk bl & lt bl	.50	*1.00*

Wmk. 133

C10	AP3	5000k dl vio & brt vio	.75	*1.50*
C11	AP3	10000k red & dl vio	1.00	*2.00*
		Nos. C6-C11 (6)	3.75	7.50
		Set, never hinged	7.50	

Issue dates: 100k-2000k, Apr. 11, 1924. Others, Apr. 20, 1925.
Exist imperf. Value, set $45.
Forgeries exist.
For surcharges see Nos. J112-J116.

Mythical "Turul" — AP4

"Turul" Carrying Messenger
AP5 AP6

1927-30 **Engr.** ***Perf. 14***

C12	AP4	4f orange ('30)	.30	*.30*
C13	AP4	12f deep green	.30	*.45*
C14	AP4	16f red brown	.30	*.55*
C15	AP4	20f carmine	.30	*.35*
C16	AP4	32f brown vio	1.75	1.50
C17	AP4	40f dp ultra	1.75	.30
C18	AP5	50f claret	1.75	.40
C19	AP5	72f olive grn	2.00	.65
C20	AP5	80f dp violet	2.00	.65
C21	AP5	1p emerald ('30)	4.00	1.25
C22	AP5	2p red ('30)	5.00	3.50
C23	AP5	5p dk blue ('30)	8.00	*25.00*
		Nos. C12-C23 (12)	27.45	34.90
		Set, never hinged	55.00	

Exist imperf. Value, set $125.

1931, Mar. 27

Overprinted

C24	AP6	1p orange (Bk)	30.00	32.50
C25	AP6	2p dull vio (G)	30.00	32.50
		Set, never hinged	120.00	

Exist imperf. Value, set $200.

Monoplane over Danube Valley — AP7

Worker Welcoming Plane, Double Cross and Sun Rays — AP8

Spirit of Flight on Plane Wing AP9

"Flight" Holding Propeller AP10

Wmk. 210

1933, June 20 **Photo.** ***Perf. 15***

C26	AP7	10f blue green	2.90	.20
C27	AP7	16f purple	2.00	.25

Perf. 12½x12

C28	AP8	20f carmine	4.00	.20
C29	AP8	40f blue	3.50	1.25
C30	AP9	48f gray black	4.00	1.50
C31	AP9	72f bister brn	11.00	2.25
C32	AP10	1p yellow grn	20.00	2.00
C33	AP10	2p violet brn	65.00	16.00
C34	AP10	5p dk gray	65.00	*105.00*
		Nos. C26-C34 (9)	177.40	128.65
		Set, never hinged	300.00	

Exist imperf. Value, set $1,500.

Catalogue values for unused stamps in this section, from this point to the end of the section, are for Never Hinged items.

Fokker F VII over Mail Coach AP11

Plane over Parliament AP12

Airplane AP13

1936, May 8 *Perf. 12x12½*

C35	AP11	10f brt green	.50	.20
C36	AP11	20f crimson	.50	.20
C37	AP11	36f brown	.75	.20
C38	AP12	40f brt blue	.75	.20
C39	AP12	52f red org	2.75	.80
C40	AP12	60f brt violet	15.00	1.50
C41	AP12	80f dk sl grn	3.25	.55
C42	AP13	1p dk yel grn	4.25	.35
C43	AP13	2p brown car	6.50	1.50
C44	AP13	5p dark blue	18.50	15.00
		Nos. C35-C44 (10)	52.75	20.50

Exist imperf. Value, set $400.

SPECIAL DELIVERY STAMPS

Issue of the Monarchy

SD1

SD2

1916 Typo. Wmk. 137 *Perf. 15*

E1	SD1	2f gray green & red	.20	.20

Exists imperf. Value $4.

For overprints and surcharges see Nos. 1NE1, 2NE1, 4N5, 5NE1, 6NE1, 7NE1, 8NE1, 10NE1, Szeged E1, J7-J8.

Issue of the Republic

Special Delivery Stamp of 1916 Overprinted

1919

E2	SD1	2f gray green & red	.20	.20

Exists imperf. Value $4.

General Issue

1919

E3	SD2	2f gray green & red	.20	.20

Exists imperf. Value $5.

POSTAGE DUE STAMPS

Issues of the Monarchy

D1

Perf. 11½, 11½x12

1903 Typo. Wmk. 135

J1	D1	1f green & blk	.50	.20
J2	D1	2f green & blk	3.00	1.00
J3	D1	5f green & blk	9.50	4.00
J4	D1	6f green & blk	7.00	3.50
J5	D1	10f green & blk	45.00	2.25
J6	D1	12f green & blk	2.50	1.50
a.		Perf. 11½	80.00	50.00
J7	D1	20f green & blk	11.00	1.50
a.		Perf. 11½	100.00	24.00
J8	D1	50f green & blk	10.50	9.50
a.		Perf. 11½	125.00	110.00
J9	D1	100f green & blk	1.00	.70
		Nos. J1-J9 (9)	90.00	24.15

See Nos. J10-J26, J28-J43. For overprints and surcharges see Nos. J27, J44-J50, 1NJ1-1NJ5, 2NJ1-2NJ16, 4NJ2-4NJ3, 5NJ1-5NJ8, 6NJ1-6NJ9, 7NJ1-7NJ4, 9NJ1-9NJ3, 10NJ1-10NJ6, Szeged J1-J6.

1908-09 Wmk. 136 *Perf. 15*

J10	D1	1f green & black	.45	.45
J11	D1	2f green & black	.30	.30
J12	D1	5f green & black	2.50	1.10
J13	D1	6f green & black	.50	.40
J14	D1	10f green & black	1.50	.40
J15	D1	12f green & black	.50	.40
J16	D1	20f green & black	10.00	.45
c.		Center inverted		4,000.
J17	D1	50f green & black	.95	.95
		Nos. J10-J17 (8)	16.70	4.45

1905 Wmk. 136a *Perf. 11½x12*

J12a	D1	5f green & black	75.00	50.00
J13a	D1	6f green & black	7.50	7.50
J14a	D1	10f green & black	75.00	5.00
J15a	D1	12f green & black	12.50	10.00
J17a	D1	50f green & black	7.50	5.00
J18	D1	100f green & black	2.00	

1906 *Perf. 15*

J11b	D1	2f green & black	2.50	1.90
J12b	D1	5f green & black	2.00	1.75
J13b	D1	6f green & black	2.00	1.25
J14b	D1	10f green & black	10.00	.60
J15b	D1	12f green & black	.60	.60
J16b	D1	20f green & black	15.00	.60
d.		Center inverted	3,000.	3,000.
J17b	D1	50f green & black	1.00	.70
		Nos. J11b-J17b (7)	33.10	7.40

1914 Wmk. 137 Horiz. *Perf. 15*

J19	D1	1f green & black	.20	.20
J20	D1	2f green & black	.20	.20
J21	D1	5f green & black	.40	.40
J22	D1	6f green & black	.60	.60
J23	D1	10f green & black	.70	.70
J24	D1	12f green & black	.35	.35
J25	D1	20f green & black	.35	.35
J26	D1	50f green & black	.40	.40
		Nos. J19-J26 (8)	3.20	3.20

1914 Wmk. 137 Vert.

J20a	D1	2f green & black	57.50	57.50
J21a	D1	5f green & black	7.50	6.25
J22a	D1	6f green & black	16.00	16.00
J25a	D1	20f green & black	2,750.	900.00
J26a	D1	50f green & black	7.50	7.50

No. J9 Surcharged in Red

1915 Wmk. 135

J27	D1	20f on 100f grn & blk	1.25	.90
a.		On No. J18, Wmk. 136a	25.00	20.00

1915-22 Wmk. 137

J28	D1	1f green & red	.20	.20
J29	D1	2f green & red	.20	.20
J30	D1	5f green & red	.20	.20
J31	D1	6f green & red	.20	.20
J32	D1	10f green & red	.20	.20
J33	D1	12f green & red	.20	.20
J34	D1	15f green & red	.20	.20
J35	D1	20f green & red	.20	.20
J36	D1	30f green & red	.20	.20
J37	D1	40f green & red ('20)	.20	.20
J38	D1	50f green & red ('20)	.20	.20
a.		Center inverted	60.00	
J39	D1	120f green & red ('20)	.20	.20
J40	D1	200f green & red ('20)	.20	.20
J41	D1	2k green & red ('22)	.40	.40
J42	D1	5k green & red ('22)	.20	.20
J43	D1	50k green & red ('22)	.20	.20
		Nos. J28-J43 (16)	3.40	3.40

Issues of the Republic

Postage Due Stamps of 1914-18 Overprinted in Black

1918-19

On Issue of 1914

J44	D1	50f green & black	.60	.60

On Stamps and Type of 1915-18

J45	D1	2f green & red	.20	.20
J46	D1	3f green & red	.20	.20
a.		"KOZTARSASAG" omitted	650.00	
J47	D1	10f green & red	.20	.20
J48	D1	20f green & red	.20	.20
J49	D1	40f green & red	.20	.20
a.		Inverted overprint	20.00	20.00
J50	D1	50f green & red	.20	.20
a.		Center and overprint inverted	25.00	25.00
		Nos. J44-J50 (7)	1.80	1.80

Issues of the Kingdom

D3

1919-20 Typo.

J65	D3	2f green & black	.20	.20
a.		Inverted center	1,000.	
J66	D3	3f green & black	.20	.20
J67	D3	20f green & black	.20	.20
J68	D3	40f green & black	.20	.20
J69	D3	50f green & black	.20	.20
		Nos. J65-J69 (5)	1.00	1.00

Postage Due Stamps of this type have been overprinted "Magyar Tancskztarsasag" but have not been reported as having been issued without the additional overprint "heads of wheat."

For overprints see Nos. J70-J75.

New Overprint in Black over "Magyar Tanacskoztarsasag"

1920

J70	D3	2f green & black	.85	1.25
J71	D3	3f green & black	1.25	1.25
J72	D3	10f green & black	1.40	2.25
J73	D3	20f green & black	.85	1.25
J74	D3	40f green & black	.85	1.25
J75	D3	50f green & black	.85	1.25
		Nos. J70-J75 (6)	6.05	8.50

Postage Issues Surcharged

1921-25

Red Surcharge

J76	A9	100f on 15f violet	.20	.20
J77	A9	500f on 15f violet	.20	.20
J78	A9	2½k on 10f red vio	.20	.20
J79	A9	3k on 15f violet	.20	.20
J80	A9	6k on 1½k violet	.20	1.50
J81	A9	9k on 40f ol grn	.20	.20
J82	A9	10k on 2½k green	.20	1.25
J83	A9	12k on 60f blk brn	.20	.20
J84	A9	15k on 1½k vio	.20	.20
J85	A9	20k on 2½k grn	.20	1.10
J86	A9	25k on 1½k vio	.20	.20
J87	A9	30k on 1½k vio	.20	.20
J88	A9	40k on 2½k grn	.20	1.25
J89	A9	50k on 1½k vio	.20	.20
J90	A9	100k on 4½k dl vio	.20	.20
J91	A9	200k on 4½k dl vio	.20	.20
J92	A9	300k on 4½k dl vio	.20	.20
J93	A9	500k on 2k grnsh bl	.30	.20
J94	A9	500k on 3k org brn	.30	.30
J95	A9	1000k on 2k grnsh bl	.30	.20
J96	A9	1000k on 3k org brn	.45	.20
J97	A9	2000k on 2k grnsh bl	.35	.40
J98	A9	2000k on 3k org brn	.70	.35
J99	A9	5000k on 5k brown	.90	1.75
		Nos. J76-J99 (24)	6.70	11.10

Year of issue: 6k, 15k, 25k, 30k, 50k, 1922. 10k, 20k, 40k, 100k - No. J93, Nos. J95, J97, 1923. 5,000k, 1924. Nos. J94, J96, J98, 1925. Others, 1921.

D6

1926 Wmk. 133 Litho. *Perf. 14, 15*

J100	D6	1f rose red	.20	.20
J101	D6	2f rose red	.20	.20
J102	D6	3f rose red	.20	.20
J103	D6	4f rose red	.20	.20
J104	D6	5f rose red	.50	.25
a.		Perf. 15	1.10	.45
J105	D6	8f rose red	.20	.20
J106	D6	10f rose red	.20	.20
J107	D6	16f rose red	.35	.20
J108	D6	32f rose red	.50	.20
J109	D6	40f rose red	.50	.20
J110	D6	50f rose red	.50	.40
J111	D6	80f rose red	1.75	.65
		Nos. J100-J111 (12)	5.30	3.10

Exist imperf. Value, set $100.

See Nos. J117-J123. For surcharges see Nos. J124-J129.

Nos. C7-C11 Surcharged in Red or Green

1926 Wmk. 137 *Perf. 14*

J112	AP3	1f on 500k (R)	.30	.25
J113	AP3	2f on 1000k (G)	.30	.30
J114	AP3	3f on 2000k (R)	.30	.20

Wmk. 133

J115	AP3	5f on 5000k (G)	.65	.55
J116	AP3	10f on 10000k (G)	.45	.35
		Nos. J112-J116 (5)	2.00	1.65

Type of 1926 Issue

1928-32 Wmk. 210 *Perf. 14, 15*

J117	D6	2f rose red	.20	.20
J118	D6	4f rose red ('32)	.20	.20
J119	D6	8f rose red	.20	.20
J120	D6	10f rose red	.20	.20
J121	D6	16f rose red	.20	.20
J122	D6	20f rose red	.30	.20
J123	D6	40f rose red	.70	.20
		Nos. J117-J123 (7)	2.00	1.40

Exist imperf. Value, set $50.

Postage Due Stamps of 1926 Surcharged in Black

1931-33 Wmk. 133

J124	D6	4f on 5f rose red	.35	.20
J125	D6	10f on 16f rose red	1.00	*3.75*
J126	D6	10f on 80f rose red ('33)	.45	.20
J127	D6	12f on 50f rose red ('33)	.45	.20
J128	D6	20f on 32f rose red	.45	.30
		Nos. J124-J128 (5)	2.70	4.65

Surcharged on No. J121

1931 Wmk. 210 *Perf. 15*

J129	D6	10f on 16f rose red	.85	*1.25*

Catalogue values for unused stamps in this section, from this point to the end of the section, are for Never Hinged items.

Figure of Value — D7

1934 Photo. Wmk. 210

J130	D7	2f ultra	.25	.20
J131	D7	4f ultra	.25	.20
J132	D7	6f ultra	.25	.20
J133	D7	8f ultra	.25	.20
J134	D7	10f ultra	.25	.20
J135	D7	12f ultra	.25	.20
J136	D7	16f ultra	.25	.20

J137	D7	20f ultra	.35	.20
J138	D7	40f ultra	.75	.20
J139	D7	80f ultra	1.50	.30
		Nos. J130-J139 (10)	4.35	2.10

Exist imperf. Value, set $60.

OFFICIAL STAMPS

O1

1921-23 Wmk. 137 Typo. *Perf. 15*

O1	O1	10f brn vio & blk	.20	.20
O2	O1	20f ol brn & blk	.20	.20
a.		"HIVATALOS" inverted		*10,000.*
O3	O1	60f blk brn & blk	.20	.20
O4	O1	100f dl rose & blk	.20	.20
O5	O1	250f bl & blk	.20	.20
O6	O1	350f gray & blk	.25	.20
O7	O1	500f lt brn & blk	.25	.20
O8	O1	1000f lil brn & blk	.25	.20
O9	O1	5k brn ('23)	.20	.20
O10	O1	10k choc ('23)	.20	.20
O11	O1	15k gray blk ('23)	.20	.20
O12	O1	25k org ('23)	.20	.20
O13	O1	50k brn & red ('22)	.20	.20
O14	O1	100k bis & red ('22)	.20	.20
O15	O1	150k grn & red ('23)	.20	.20
O16	O1	300k dl red & red ('23)	.25	.20
O17	O1	350k vio & red ('23)	.30	.20
O18	O1	500k org & red ('22)	.30	.20
O19	O1	600k ol bis & red ('23)	.80	.50
O20	O1	1000k bl & red ('22)	.50	.20
		Nos. O1-O20 (20)	5.30	4.30

Counterfeits of No. O2a exist.

Stamps of 1921 Surcharged in Red

1922

O21	O1	15k on 20f ol brn & blk	.20	.20
O22	O1	25k on 60f blk brn & blk	.20	.20

Stamps of 1921 Overprinted in Red

1923

O23	O1	350k gray & blk	.25	.20

With Additional Surcharge of New Value in Red

O24	O1	150k on 100f dl rose & blk	.25	.20
O25	O1	2000k on 250f bl & blk	.60	.40
		Nos. O23-O25 (3)	1.10	.80

1923-24

Paper with Gray Moiré on Face

O26	O1	500k org & red ('23)	.25	.20
O27	O1	1000k bl & red ('23)	.30	.20
O28	O1	3000k vio & red ('24)	.60	*1.25*
O29	O1	5000k bl & red ('24)	.70	*1.50*
		Nos. O26-O29 (4)	1.85	3.15

1924 Wmk. 133

O30	O1	500k orange & red	1.10	1.00
O31	O1	1000k blue & red	1.10	1.00

NEWSPAPER STAMPS

Issues of the Monarchy

St. Stephen's Crown and Post Horn
N1 N2

Litho. (#P1), Typo. (#P2)

1871-72 Unwmk. *Imperf.*

P1	N1	(1k) ver red	50.00	20.00
P2	N2	(1k) rose red ('72)	10.00	2.00
a.		(1k) vermilion	10.00	2.00
b.		Printed on both sides		

Reprints of No. P2 are watermarked. Value, $450.

Letter with Crown and Post Horn — N3

N5

1874

P3	N3	1k orange	3.75	.35

1881 Wmk. "kr" in Oval (132)

P4	N3	1k orange	1.25	.20
a.		1k lemon yellow	16.00	3.50
b.		Printed on both sides		

1898 Wmk. 135

P5	N3	1k orange	1.25	.20

See watermark note after No. 46.

1900 Wmk. Crown in Circle (135)

P6	N5	(2f) red orange	.75	.20

1905 Wmk. Crown (136a)

P7	N5	(2f) red orange	1.00	.20
a.		Wmk. 136 ('08)	1.00	.20

1914-22 Wmk. Double Cross (137)

P8	N5	(2f) orange	.20	.20
a.		Wmk. horiz.	4.50	3.75
P9	N5	(10f) deep blue ('20)	.20	.20
P10	N5	(20f) lilac ('22)	.20	.20
		Nos. P8-P10 (3)	.60	.60

For overprints and surcharges see Nos. 1NJ6-1NJ10, 1NP1, 2NP1, 5NP1, 6NP1, 8NP1, 10NP1, Szeged P1.

NEWSPAPER TAX STAMPS

Issues of the Monarchy

NT1

NT2

NT3

Wmk. 91; Unwmk. from 1871

1868 Typo. *Imperf.*

PR1	NT1	1k blue	5.50	1.50
a.		Pair, one sideways		
PR2	NT2	2k brown	17.50	15.00
a.		2k red brown	275.00	47.50

1868

PR2B	NT3	1k blue	*9,500.*	*6,000.*

No. PR2B was issued for the Military Border District only. All used copies are precanceled (newspaper text printed on the stamp). A similar 2k was not issued.

1889-90 Wmk. "kr" in Oval (132)

PR3	NT1	1k blue	2.00	.80
PR4	NT2	2k brown	5.50	4.00

1898 Wmk. Crown in Oval (135)

PR5	NT1	1k blue	7.50	5.50

These stamps did not pay postage, but represented a fiscal tax collected by the postal authorities on newspapers.

Nos. PR3 and PR5 have a tall "k" in "kr."

OCCUPATION STAMPS

Issued under French Occupation

ARAD ISSUE

The overprints on this issue have been extensively forged. Even the inexpensive values are difficult to find with genuine overprints. Values are for genuine overprints. Collectors should be aware that stamps sold "as is" are likely to be forgeries, and unexpertized collections should be assumed to consist of mostly forged stamps. Education plus working with knowledgeable dealers is mandatory in this collecting area. More valuable stamps should be expertized.

Stamps of Hungary Overprinted in Red or Blue

On Issue of 1916-18

1919 Wmk. 137 *Perf. 15, 14*

1N1	A9	2f brn org (R)	1.60	1.60
1N2	A9	3f red lil (R)	.75	.75
1N3	A9	5f green (R)	20.00	20.00
1N4	A9	6f grnsh bl (R)	1.90	1.90
a.		Inverted overprint	30.00	30.00
1N5	A9	10f rose red	4.00	4.00
1N6	A9	15f violet (R)	1.75	1.75
a.		Double overprint	50.00	50.00
1N7	A9	20f gray brn (R)	50.00	50.00
1N8	A9	35f brown (R)	65.00	65.00
1N9	A9	40f ol grn (R)	37.50	37.50
1N10	A10	50f red vio & lil	6.00	6.00
1N11	A10	75f brt bl & pale bl	2.00	2.00
1N12	A10	80f grn & pale grn	2.75	2.75
1N13	A10	1k red brn & cl	15.00	15.00
1N14	A10	2k ol brn & bis	3.00	3.00
a.		Inverted overprint	50.00	50.00
1N15	A10	3k dk vio & ind	17.50	17.50
1N16	A10	5k dk brn & lt brn	13.50	13.50
1N17	A10	10k vio brn & vio	70.00	70.00
		Nos. 1N1-1N17 (17)	312.25	312.25

With Additional Surcharge:

a

b

c

d

1N18	A9 (a)	45f on 2f brn org	8.00	8.00
1N19	A9 (b)	45f on 2f brn org	8.00	8.00
1N20	A9 (c)	50f on 3f red lil	8.00	8.00
1N21	A9 (d)	50f on 3f red lil	8.00	8.00
		Nos. 1N18-1N21 (4)	32.00	32.00

Overprinted On Issue of 1918

1N22	A11	10f scarlet (Bl)	60.00	60.00
1N23	A11	20f dk brn	.90	.90
1N24	A11	25f brt bl	2.40	2.40
a.		Inverted overprint	30.00	30.00
1N25	A12	40f ol grn	3.25	3.25
		Nos. 1N22-1N25 (4)	66.55	66.55

Ovptd. On Issue of 1918-19, Overprinted "Koztarsasag"

1N26	A9	2f brn org	2.00	2.00
a.		Inverted overprint	50.00	50.00
1N27	A9	4f slate gray	2.00	2.00
1N28	A9	5f green	.60	.60
1N29	A9	6f grnsh bl	12.00	12.00
a.		Inverted overprint	30.00	30.00
1N30	A9	10f rose red (Bl)	60.00	60.00
1N31	A9	20f gray brn	15.00	15.00
1N32	A11	25f brt bl	2.75	2.75
a.		Inverted overprint	30.00	30.00
1N33	A9	40f ol grn	2.00	2.00
1N34	A12	40f ol grn	60.00	60.00
a.		Inverted overprint	125.00	125.00
1N35	A12	50f lilac	8.00	8.00
1N36	A10	1k red brn & cl (Bl)	3.25	3.25
1N37	A10	3k dk vio & ind (Bl)	15.00	15.00
		Nos. 1N26-1N37 (12)	182.60	182.60

No. 1N36 With Additional Surcharge:

e

f

1N38	A10 (e)	10k on 1k	13.50	13.50
1N39	A10 (f)	10k on 1k	13.50	13.50

On Issue of 1919

Inscribed "MAGYAR POSTA"

1N40	A13	10f red (Bl)	6.50	6.50

SEMI-POSTAL STAMPS

Hungarian Semi-Postal Stamps of 1916-17 Overprinted "Occupation francaise" in Blue or Red

1919 Wmk. 137 *Perf. 15*

1NB1	SP3	10f + 2f rose red	65.00	65.00
1NB2	SP4	15f + 2f dl vio (R)	9.50	9.50
1NB3	SP5	40f + 2f brn car	12.50	12.50
		Nos. 1NB1-1NB3 (3)	87.00	87.00

SPECIAL DELIVERY STAMP

Hungarian Special Delivery Stamp of 1916 Overprinted "Occupation francaise"

1919 Wmk. 137 *Perf. 15*

1NE1	SD1	2f gray green & red	.60	.60

POSTAGE DUE STAMPS

Hungarian Postage Due Stamps of 1915 Overprinted "Occupation francaise"

1919 Wmk. 137 *Perf. 15*

1NJ1	D1	2f green & red	7.50	7.50
1NJ2	D1	10f green & red	4.00	4.00
1NJ3	D1	12f green & red	32.50	32.50
1NJ4	D1	15f green & red	42.50	42.50
1NJ5	D1	20f green & red	3.00	3.00

Hungarian Newspaper Stamp of 1914 Surcharged

1NJ6	N5	12f on 2f orange	8.00	8.00
1NJ7	N5	15f on 2f orange	8.00	8.00
1NJ8	N5	30f on 2f orange	8.00	8.00
a.		Double surcharge	50.00	50.00
1NJ9	N5	50f on 2f orange	8.00	8.00
1NJ10	N5	100f on 2f orange	8.00	8.00
		Nos. 1NJ1-1NJ10 (10)	129.50	129.50

NEWSPAPER STAMP

Hungarian Newspaper Stamp of 1914 Overprinted "Occupation francaise"

1919 **Wmk. 137** ***Imperf.***

1NP1 N5 (2f) orange 1.25 1.25

ISSUED UNDER ROMANIAN OCCUPATION

FIRST DEBRECEN ISSUE

The overprints on this issue have been extensively forged. Even the inexpensive values are difficult to find with genuine overprints. The more extensive note before No. 1N1 also applies to Nos. 2N1-2NP16.

Hungarian Stamps of 1913-19 Overprinted in Blue, Red or Black

1919 **Wmk. 137** ***Perf. 15, 14½x14***

On Stamps of 1913

2N1	A4	2f olive yellow	90.00	90.00
2N2	A4	3f orange	125.00	125.00
2N3	A4	6f olive grn (R)	50.00	50.00

On Stamps of 1916

2N4	A8	10f rose	75.00	75.00
2N5	A8	15f violet (Bk)	65.00	65.00

On Stamps of 1916-18

2N6	A9	2f brown org	1.50	1.50
2N7	A9	3f red lilac	.70	.70
2N8	A9	5f green	4.75	4.75
2N9	A9	6f grnsh bl (R)	1.60	1.60
2N10	A9	15f violet (Bk)	.80	.80
a.		Red overprint	75.00	75.00
2N11	A9	20f gray brn	125.00	125.00
2N12	A9	25f dull bl (Bk)	4.50	4.50
2N13	A9	35f brown	60.00	60.00
2N14	A9	40f olive grn	3.75	3.75
2N15	A10	50f red vio & lil	8.25	8.25
2N16	A10	75f brt bl & pale bl (Bk)	2.00	2.00
2N17	A10	80f grn & pale grn (R)	3.50	3.50
2N18	A10	1k red brn & cl	4.75	4.75
2N19	A10	2k ol brn & bis (Bk)	1.75	1.75
2N20	A10	3k dk vio & ind (R)	30.00	30.00
a.		Blue overprint	*65.00*	*65.00*
b.		Black overprint	*250.00*	*250.00*
2N21	A10	5k dk brn & lt brn (Bk)	27.50	27.50
2N22	A10	10k vio brn & vio	*160.00*	*160.00*

With New Value Added

2N23	A9	35f on 3f red lil	2.00	2.00
2N24	A9	45f on 2f brn org	2.00	2.00
2N25	A10	3k on 75f brt bl & pale bl (Bk)	4.00	4.00
2N26	A10	5k on 75f brt bl & pale bl (Bk)	3.75	3.75
2N27	A10	10k on 80f grn & pale grn (R)	3.50	3.50

On Stamps of 1918

2N28	A11	10f scarlet	60.00	60.00
2N28A	A11	15f violet (R)	75.00	75.00
b.		Black overprint	125.00	125.00
2N29	A11	20f dk brown (R)	6.25	6.25
a.		Black overprint	30.00	30.00
b.		Blue overprint	75.00	75.00
2N30	A11	25f brt blue (R)	7.00	7.00
a.		Black overprint	75.00	75.00
2N31	A12	40f olive green	3.00	3.00
2N32	A12	50f lilac	50.00	50.00

On Stamps of 1918-19, Overprinted "Koztarsasag"

2N33	A9	2f brn org	3.00	3.00
2N34	A9	3f red lilac	65.00	65.00
2N35	A9	4f sl gray (R)	1.75	1.75
2N36	A9	5f green	.65	.65
2N37	A9	6f grnsh bl (R)	30.00	30.00
2N38	A9	10f rose red	37.50	37.50
2N39	A11	10f scarlet	25.00	25.00
2N40	A11	15f dp vio (Bk)	45.00	45.00
a.		Red overprint	125.00	125.00
2N41	A9	20f gray brn	3.25	3.25
2N42	A11	20f dk brn (Bk)	37.50	37.50
b.		Red overprint	50.00	50.00
2N43	A9	40f olive grn	1.75	1.75
2N44	A10	1k red brn & cl	2.75	2.75
2N45	A10	2k ol brn & bis (Bk)	60.00	60.00
a.		Blue overprint	125.00	125.00
2N46	A10	3k dk vio & ind (R)	9.75	9.75
a.		Blue overprint	60.00	60.00
b.		Black overprint	*200.00*	*200.00*
2N47	A10	5k dk & lt brn (Bk)	*225.00*	*225.00*
2N48	A10	10k vio brn & vio	*500.00*	*500.00*
2N49	A11	25f brt bl (R)	3.25	3.25
a.		Black overprint	25.00	25.00
2N50	A12	40f olive grn	*125.00*	*125.00*
2N51	A12	50f lilac	2.25	2.25

On Stamps of 1919

2N52	A13	5f green	.50	.50
2N53	A13	6f grnsh bl (Bk)	22.50	22.50
2N54	A13	10f red	.20	.20
2N55	A13	20f dk brown	.20	.20
2N56	A13	25f dl bl (Bk)	1.25	1.25
2N56A	A13	40f olive green	125.00	125.00
2N57	A13	45f orange	15.00	15.00
2N57A	A14	95f dark blue & blue	125.00	125.00
2N57B	A14	1.20k dark green & green	125.00	125.00
2N57C	A14	1.40k yellow green	125.00	125.00
2N58	A14	5k dk brn & brn	3,000.	3,000.

#2N58 is handstamped. Counterfeits exist.

On No. 103A

2N59 A5a 10f violet brn (R) 50.00 50.00

On No. 208

2N60 A13 10f red 75.00 75.00

Nos. 2N1-2N57,2N59-2N60 (61) *2,529.* *2,529.*

SEMI-POSTAL STAMPS

Hungary Nos. B36, B37 Overprinted like Regular Issues in Blue

1919 **Wmk. 137** ***Perf. 14***

2NB1	A4(c)	2f olive yellow	125.00	125.00
2NB1A	A4(c)	3f orange	125.00	125.00

Same Overprint in Blue or Black on Hungary Nos. B53--B55

1919 **Wmk. 137** ***Perf. 15***

2NB1B	SP3	10f + 2f rose red	4.00	4.00
2NB2	SP4	15f + 2f dl vio (Bk)	17.00	17.00
2NB3	SP5	40f + 2f brown car	11.00	11.00
		Nos. 2NB1B-2NB3 (3)	32.00	32.00

Same Overprint on Hungary Nos. B58-B60 (with "Köztarsasag")

1919

2NB4	SP3	10f + 2f rose red	42.50	42.50
2NB5	SP4	15f + 2f dl vio (Bk)	75.00	75.00
2NB6	SP5	40f + 2f brown car	32.50	32.50
		Nos. 2NB4-2NB6 (3)	150.00	150.00

SPECIAL DELIVERY STAMP

Hungarian Special Delivery Stamp of 1916 Overprinted like Regular Issues

1919 **Wmk. 137** ***Perf. 15***

2NE1 SD1 2f gray grn & red (Bl) 3.00 3.00

POSTAGE DUE STAMPS

Hungarian Postage Due Stamps of 1914-19 Overprinted in Black like Regular Issues

1919 **Wmk. 137** ***Perf. 15***

On Stamp of 1914

2NJ1 D1 50f grn & blk *125.00* *125.00*

On Stamps of 1915

2NJ2	D1	1f green & red	62.50	62.50
2NJ3	D1	2f green & red	2.00	2.00
2NJ4	D1	5f green & red	*225.00*	*225.00*
2NJ5	D1	6f green & red	*125.00*	*125.00*
2NJ6	D1	10f green & red	.80	.80
2NJ7	D1	12f green & red	*125.00*	*125.00*
2NJ8	D1	15f green & red	20.00	20.00
2NJ9	D1	20f green & red	4.50	4.50
2NJ10	D1	30f green & red	13.50	13.50

On Stamps of 1918-19, Overprinted "Koztarsasag"

2NJ11	D1	2f green & red	25.00	25.00
2NJ12	D1	3f green & red	30.00	30.00
2NJ13	D1	10f green & red	30.00	30.00
2NJ14	D1	20f green & red	30.00	30.00
2NJ15	D1	40f green & red	30.00	30.00
2NJ16	D1	50f green & red	30.00	30.00
		Nos. 2NJ1-2NJ16 (16)	*878.30*	
		Nos. 2NJ1-2NJ13,2NJ15-2NJ16 (15)		*848.30*

NEWSPAPER STAMP

Hungarian Newspaper Stamp of 1914 Overprinted like Regular Issues

1919 **Wmk. 137** ***Imperf.***

2NP1	N5	(2f) orange (Bl)	.55	.55
a.		Inverted overprint	50.00	50.00
b.		Double overprint	125.00	125.00

SECOND DEBRECEN ISSUE

Complete forgeries exist of this issue and are often found in large multiples or even complete sheets. Values are for genuine stamps.

Mythical "Turul" — OS5

Throwing Lariat OS6

Hungarian Peasant OS7

1920 **Unwmk.** **Typo.** ***Perf. 11½***

3N1	OS5	2f lt brown	2.25	2.25
3N2	OS5	3f red brown	2.25	2.25
3N3	OS5	4f gray	2.25	2.25
3N4	OS5	5f lt green	.50	.50
3N5	OS5	6f slate	2.25	2.25
3N6	OS5	10f scarlet	.50	.50
3N7	OS5	15f dk violet	3.00	3.00
3N8	OS5	20f dk brown	.60	.60
3N9	OS6	25f ultra	1.25	1.25
3N10	OS6	30f buff	.65	.65
3N11	OS6	35f claret	1.25	1.25
3N12	OS6	40f olive grn	.75	.75
3N13	OS6	45f salmon	1.00	1.00
3N14	OS6	50f pale vio	.75	.75
3N15	OS6	60f yellow grn	.90	.90
3N16	OS6	75f Prus blue	.75	.75
3N17	OS7	80f gray grn	.85	.85
3N18	OS7	1k brown red	3.00	3.00
3N19	OS7	2k chocolate	3.00	3.00
3N20	OS7	3k brown vio	2.25	2.25
3N21	OS7	5k bister brn	2.25	2.25
3N22	OS7	10k dull vio	2.25	2.25
		Nos. 3N1-3N22 (22)	34.50	34.50

Thick, Glazed Paper

3N23	OS5	2f lt brown	3.00	3.00
3N24	OS5	3f red brown	3.00	3.00
3N25	OS5	4f gray	3.00	3.00
3N26	OS5	5f lt green	3.00	3.00
3N27	OS5	6f slate	3.00	3.00
3N28	OS5	10f scarlet	.75	.75
3N29	OS5	15f dk vio	3.00	3.00
3N30	OS5	20f dk brown	1.00	1.00
3N31	OS7	80f gray grn	1.50	1.50
3N32	OS7	1k brown red	4.00	4.00
3N33	OS7	1.20k orange	8.00	8.00
3N34	OS7	2k chocolate	4.50	4.50
		Nos. 3N23-3N34 (12)	37.75	37.75

SEMI-POSTAL STAMPS

Carrying Wounded

1920 **Unwmk.** **Typo.** ***Perf. 11½***

3NB1	SP1	20f green	1.25	1.25
3NB2	SP1	50f gray brn	2.25	2.25
3NB3	SP1	1k blue green	2.25	2.25
3NB4	SP1	2k dk green	2.25	2.25

Colored Paper

3NB5	SP1	20f green, *bl*	3.00	3.00
3NB6	SP1	50f brn, *rose*	3.00	3.00
3NB7	SP1	1k dk grn, *grn*	3.00	3.00
		Nos. 3NB1-3NB7 (7)	17.00	17.00

POSTAGE DUE STAMPS

D1

1920 **Typo.** ***Perf. 15***

3NJ1	D1	5f blue green	1.50	1.50
3NJ2	D1	10f blue green	1.50	1.50
3NJ3	D1	20f blue green	.75	.75
3NJ4	D1	30f blue green	.75	.75
3NJ5	D1	40f blue green	1.25	1.25
		Nos. 3NJ1-3NJ5 (5)	5.75	5.75

TEMESVAR ISSUE

Issued under Romanian Occupation

Forgeries exist of the inverted and color error surcharges.

Hungary Nos. 108, 155, 109, 111, E1 Surcharged

1919 **Wmk. 137** ***Perf. 15***

4N1	A9	30f on 2f brn org (Bl)	.40	.40
a.		Red surcharge	2.00	2.00
b.		Inverted surcharge (R)	25.00	25.00
4N2	A9	1k on 4f sl gray (R)	.30	.30
4N3	A9	150f on 3f red lil (Bk)	.20	.20
4N4	A9	150f on 5f grn (Bk)	.40	.40

4N5 SD1 3k on 2f gray grn & red (Bk) 2.00 2.00
a. Blue surcharge .80 .80
Nos. 4N1-4N5 (5) 3.30 3.30

POSTAGE DUE STAMPS

D1

D2

1919 Wmk. 137 *Perf. 15*

4NJ1 D1 40f on 15f + 2f vio (Bk) .50 .50
a. Red surcharge 2.00 2.00
4NJ2 D2 60f on 2f grn & red (Bk) 2.50 2.50
a. Red surcharge 8.00 8.00
4NJ3 D2 60f on 10f grn & red (Bk) 1.25 1.25
a. Red surcharge 4.00 4.00
Nos. 4NJ1-4NJ3 (3) 4.25 4.25

FIRST TRANSYLVANIA ISSUE

Issued under Romanian Occupation

The scarcer values of this issue have been extensively forged. Genuine common values are more easily found.

Issued in Kolozsvar (Cluj)

Hungarian Stamps of 1916-18 Overprinted

1919 Wmk. 137 *Perf. 15, 14*

On Stamp of 1916, White Numerals

5N1 A8 15b violet 4.75 4.75

On Stamps of 1916-18

5N2 A9 2b brown org .20 .25
5N3 A9 3b red lilac .20 .25
5N4 A9 5b green .20 .25
5N5 A9 6b grnsh blue .40 .40
5N5A A9 10b rose red 60.00 60.00
5N6 A9 15b violet .20 .25
5N7 A9 25b dull blue .20 .25
5N8 A9 35b brown .20 .25
5N9 A9 40b olive grn .50 .50
5N10 A10 50b red vio & lil 1.00 1.00
5N11 A10 75b brt bl & pale bl .30 .30
5N12 A10 80b grn & pale grn .20 .25
5N13 A10 1 l red brn & cl .20 .25
5N14 A10 2 l ol brn & bis .60 .60
5N15 A10 3 l dk vio & ind 3.50 3.50
5N16 A10 5 l dk brn & lt brn 2.50 2.50
5N17 A10 10 l vio brn & vio 3.00 3.00

On Stamps of 1918

5N18 A11 10b scarlet 40.00 40.00
5N19 A11 15b dp violet 20.00 20.00
5N20 A11 20b dk brown .25 .25
a. Gold overprint 75.00 75.00
b. Silver overprint 75.00 75.00
5N21 A11 25b brt blue .65 .65
5N22 A12 40b olive grn .30 .30

On No. 103A

5N23 A5a 10b violet brn .35 .35
Nos. 5N1-5N23 (24) 139.70 140.10

SEMI-POSTAL STAMPS

Hungarian Semi-Postal Stamps of 1913-17 Overprinted like Regular Issues

On Issue of 1913

1919 Wmk. 137 *Perf. 14*

5NB1 SP1 1 l on 1f slate 27.50 27.50
5NB2 SP1 1 l on 2f ol yel 70.00 70.00
5NB3 SP1 1 l on 3f org 37.50 37.50
5NB4 SP1 1 l on 5f emer 3.25 3.25
5NB5 SP1 1 l on 10f car 4.50 4.50
5NB6 SP1 1 l on 12f vio,*yel* 16.00 16.00
5NB7 SP1 1 l on 16f gray grn 6.25 6.25
5NB8 SP1 1 l on 25f ultra 60.00 60.00
5NB9 SP1 1 l on 35f red vio 10.00 10.00
5NB10 SP2 1 l on 1k dl red 60.00 60.00

On Issue of 1916-17

Perf. 15

5NB11 SP3 10b + 2b rose red .20 .25
5NB12 SP4 15b + 2b dull vio .20 .25
5NB13 SP5 40b + 2b brn car .20 .25
Nos. 5NB1-5NB13 (13) 295.60 295.75

SPECIAL DELIVERY STAMP

Hungarian Special Delivery Stamp of 1916 Overprinted like Regular Issues

1919 Wmk. 137 *Perf. 15*

5NE1 SD1 2b gray grn & red .30 .30

POSTAGE DUE STAMPS

Hungarian Postage Due Stamps of 1914-18 Overprinted like Regular Issues

On Stamp of 1914

1919 Wmk. 137 *Perf. 15*

5NJ1 D1 50b green & blk 13.00 13.00

On Stamps of 1915

5NJ2 D1 1b green & red *350.00 350.00*
5NJ3 D1 2b green & red .70 .70
5NJ4 D1 5b green & red 60.00 60.00
5NJ5 D1 10b green & red .45 .45
5NJ6 D1 15b green & red 20.00 20.00
5NJ7 D1 20b green & red .40 .40
5NJ8 D1 30b green & red 30.00 30.00
Nos. 5NJ1-5NJ8 (8) *474.55 474.55*

NEWSPAPER STAMP

Hungarian Newspaper Stamp of 1914 Overprinted like Regular Issues

1919 Wmk. 137 *Imperf.*

5NP1 N5 2b orange 3.75 3.75

SECOND TRANSYLVANIA ISSUE

The scarcer values of this issue have been extensively forged. Genuine common values are more easily found.

Issued in Nagyvarad (Oradea)

Hungarian Stamps of 1916-19 Overprinted

1919 Wmk. 137 *Perf. 15, 14*

On Stamps of 1913-16

6N1 A4 2b olive yel 7.00 7.00
6N2 A4 3b orange 13.00 13.00
6N3 A4 6b olive grn 1.75 1.75
6N4 A4 16b gray grn 37.50 37.50
6N5 A4 50b lake, *bl* 1.75 1.75
6N6 A4 70b red brn & grn 26.00 26.00

On Stamp of 1916 (White Numerals)

6N6A A8 15b violet 125.00 125.00

On Stamps of 1916-18

6N7 A9 2b brown org .20 .25
6N8 A9 3b red lilac .20 .25
6N9 A9 5b green .30 .30
6N10 A9 6b grnsh blue 1.60 1.60
6N11 A9 10b rose red 2.10 2.10
6N12 A9 15b violet .20 .25
6N13 A9 20b gray brn 20.00 20.00
6N14 A9 25b dull blue .30 .30
6N15 A9 35b brown .45 .45
6N16 A9 40b olive grn .30 .30
6N17 A10 50b red vio & lil .60 .60
6N18 A10 75b brt bl & pale bl .20 .25
6N19 A10 80b grn & pale grn .30 .30
6N20 A10 1 l red brn & cl .75 .75
6N21 A10 2 l ol brn & bis .20 .25
6N22 A10 3 l dk vio & ind 6.50 6.50
6N23 A10 5 l dk brn & lt brn 3.25 3.25
6N24 A10 10 l vio brn & vio 1.50 1.50

On Stamps of 1918

6N25 A11 10b scarlet 3.25 3.25
6N26 A11 20b dk brown .20 .25
6N27 A11 25b brt blue .75 .75
6N28 A12 40b olive grn 1.10 1.10

On Stamps of 1918-19, Overprinted "Koztarsasag"

6N29 A9 2b brown org 4.00 4.00
6N30 A9 3b red lilac .20 .25
6N31 A9 4b slate gray .20 .25
6N32 A9 5b green .50 .50
6N33 A9 6b grnsh bl 3.00 3.00
6N34 A9 10b rose red 17.50 17.50
6N35 A9 20b gray brn 2.50 2.50
6N36 A9 40b olive grn .50 .50
6N37 A10 1 l red brn & cl .20 .25
6N38 A10 3 l dk vio & ind .75 .75
6N39 A10 5 l dk brn & lt brn 4.50 4.50
6N40 A11 10b scarlet *75.00 75.00*
6N41 A11 20b dk brown 4.50 4.50
6N42 A11 25b brt blue 1.25 1.25
6N43 A12 50b lilac .20 .25

On Stamps of 1919

Inscribed "MAGYAR POSTA"

6N44 A13 5b yellow grn .20 .25
6N45 A13 10b red .20 .25
6N46 A13 20b dk brown .40 .40
6N47 A13 25b dull blue 2.00 2.00
6N48 A13 40b olive grn .65 .65
6N49 A14 5 l dk brn & brn 6.50 6.50

On No. 103A

6N50 A5a 10b violet brn .85 .85
Nos. 6N1-6N50 (51) *381.85 382.45*

SEMI-POSTAL STAMPS

Hungarian Semi-Postal Stamps of 1913-17 Overprinted like Regular Issues

On Stamps of 1913

1919 Wmk. 137 *Perf. 14*

6NB1 SP1 1 l on 1f slate 2.25 2.25
6NB2 SP1 1 l on 2f olive yel 8.50 8.50
6NB3 SP1 1 l on 3f orange 2.75 2.75
6NB4 SP1 1 l on 5f emerald .25 .25
6NB5 SP1 1 l on 6f olive grn 2.25 2.25
6NB6 SP1 1 l on 10f carmine .30 .30
6NB7 SP1 1 l on 12f vio, *yel* 60.00 60.00
6NB8 SP1 1 l on 16f gray grn 2.50 2.50
6NB9 SP1 1 l on 20f dk brn 11.00 11.00
6NB10 SP1 1 l on 25f ultra 7.50 7.50
6NB11 SP1 1 l on 35f red vio 7.75 7.75

On Stamp of 1915

Wmk. 135 *Perf. 11½*

6NB12 A4 5b emerald 20.00 2.00

On Stamps of 1916-17

Wmk. 137 *Perf. 15*

6NB13 SP3 10b + 2b rose red 1.25 1.25
6NB14 SP4 15b + 2b dull vio .45 .45
6NB15 SP5 40b + 2b brown car .20 .25
Nos. 6NB1-6NB15 (15) 126.95 109.00

SPECIAL DELIVERY STAMP

Hungarian Special Delivery Stamp of 1916 Overprinted like Regular Issues

1919 Wmk. 137 *Perf. 15*

6NE1 SD1 2b gray grn & red .40 .40

POSTAGE DUE STAMPS

Hungarian Postage Due Stamps of 1915 Overprinted like Regular Issues

1919 Wmk. 137 *Perf. 15*

6NJ1 D1 1b green & red 30.00 30.00
6NJ2 D1 2b green & red .20 .25
6NJ3 D1 5b green & red 9.75 9.75
6NJ4 D1 6b green & red 6.75 6.75
6NJ5 D1 10b green & red .20 .25
6NJ6 D1 12b green & red 1.50 1.50
6NJ7 D1 15b green & red 1.50 1.50
6NJ8 D1 20b green & red .20 .25
6NJ9 D1 30b green & red 1.60 1.60
Nos. 6NJ1-6NJ9 (9) 51.70 51.85

On Hungary No. J27

Perf. 11½x12

Wmk. 135

6NJ10 D1 20b on 100b grn & blk 350.00 350.00

NEWSPAPER STAMP

Hungarian Newspaper Stamp of 1914 Overprinted like Regular Issues

1919 Wmk. 137 *Imperf.*

6NP1 N5 2b orange .45 .45

FIRST BARANYA ISSUE

Issued under Serbian Occupation

The scarcer values of this issue have been extensively forged. Genuine common values are more easily found.

Hungarian Stamps of 1913-18 Overprinted in Black or Red:

On A4, A9, A11, A12

On A10

1919 Wmk. 137 *Perf. 15*

On Issue of 1913-16

7N1 A4 6f olive grn (R) .90 .90
7N2 A4 50f lake, *bl* .20 .20
7N3 A4 60f grn, *salmon* .75 .75
7N4 A4 70f red brn & grn (R) 2.00 2.00
7N5 A4 70f red brn & grn (Bk) .25 .25
7N6 A4 80f dl vio (R) 3.25 3.25

On Issue of 1916-18

7N7 A9 2f brown org (Bk) 4.25 4.25
7N8 A9 2f brown org (R) .20 .20
7N9 A9 3f red lilac (Bk) .20 .20
7N10 A9 3f red lilac (R) .80 .80
7N11 A9 5f green (Bk) .80 .80
7N12 A9 5f green (R) .20 .20
7N13 A9 6f grnsh bl (Bk) 1.75 1.75
7N14 A9 6f grnsh bl (R) 2.00 2.00
7N15 A9 15f violet .35 .35
7N16 A9 20f gray brn 20.00 20.00
7N17 A9 25f dull blue 3.50 3.50
7N18 A9 35f brown 5.75 5.75
7N19 A9 40f olive grn 20.00 20.00
7N20 A10 50f red vio & lil 2.00 2.00
7N21 A10 75f brt bl & pale bl .40 .40
7N22 A10 80f grn & pale grn .65 .65
7N23 A10 1k red brn & cl .55 .55
7N24 A10 2k ol brn & bis .65 .65
7N25 A10 3k dk vio & ind .65 .65
7N26 A10 5k dk brn & lt brn 1.25 1.25
7N27 A10 10k vio brn & vio 4.00 *4.00*

7N28 A9 45f on 2f brn org .35 .35
7N29 A9 45f on 5f green .20 .20
7N30 A9 45f on 15f violet .20 .20

On Issue of 1918

7N31 A11 10f scarlet (Bk) .20 .20
7N32 A11 20f dk brn (Bk) .20 .20
7N34 A11 25f dp blue (Bk) 1.90 1.90
7N35 A11 25f dp blue (R) 1.10 1.10
7N36 A12 40f olive grn (Bk) 4.50 4.50
7N37 A12 40f olive grn (R) 30.00 30.00

On Issue of 1918-19 (Koztarsasag)

7N38 A9 2f brown org (Bk) 3.50 3.50
7N39 A12 40f ol grn (Bk) *125.00 125.00*
7N40 A12 40f olive grn (R) 20.00 20.00

With New Value Added

7N41 A9 45f on 2f brn org (Bk) 2.00 2.00
7N42 A9 45f on 2f brn org (R) .45 .45

The overprints were set in groups of 25. In each group two stamps have the figures "1" of "1919" with serifs.

SEMI-POSTAL STAMPS

Hungarian Semi-Postal Stamps Overprinted Regular Issue First Type

On Stamp of 1915

1919 Wmk. 137 *Perf. 15*

7NB1 A4 50f + 2f lake, *bl* 16.00 16.00

On Stamps of 1916

7NB2 SP3 10f + 2f rose red .30 .30
7NB3 SP4 15f + 2f dull vio .40 .40
Nos. 7NB1-7NB3 (3) 16.70 16.70

SPECIAL DELIVERY STAMP

SD1

1919 Wmk. 137 *Perf. 15*

7NE1 SD1 105f on 2f gray grn & red 1.25 1.25

POSTAGE DUE STAMPS

Overprinted or Surcharged on Hungary Nos. J29, J32, J35

1919 Wmk. 137 *Perf. 15*

7NJ1 D1 2f green & red 3.75 3.75
7NJ2 D1 10f green & red 1.25 1.25
7NJ3 D1 20f green & red 1.60 1.60

With New Value Added

7NJ4 D1 40f on 2f grn & red 1.50 1.50
Nos. 7NJ1-7NJ4 (4) 8.10 8.10

SECOND BARANYA ISSUE

The scarcer values of this issue have been extensively forged. Genuine common values are more easily found.

Hungarian Stamps of 1916-19 Surcharged in Black and Red

1919 On Stamps of 1916-18

8N1 A9 20f on 2f brn org 4.25 4.25
8N2 A9 50f on 5f green 2.00 2.00
8N3 A9 150f on 15f violet 2.00 2.00
8N4 A10 200f on 75f brt bl & pale bl .75 .75

On Stamp of 1918-19, Overprinted "Koztarsasag"

8N5 A11 150f on 15f dp vio .50 .50

On Stamps of 1919

8N6 A13 20f on 2f brn org .35 .35
8N7 A13 30f on 6f grnsh bl .70 .70
8N8 A13 50f on 5f yel grn .20 .20
8N9 A13 100f on 25f dull bl .25 .25
8N10 A13 100f on 40f ol grn .25 .25
8N11 A13 100f on 45f orange 1.10 1.10
8N12 A13 150f on 20f dk brn 1.40 1.40

On No. 103A

8N13 A5a 10f on 10f vio brn .75 .75
Nos. 8N1-8N13 (13) 14.50 14.50

SPECIAL DELIVERY STAMP

Hungarian Special Delivery Stamp of 1916 Surcharged like Regular Issues

1919 Wmk. 137 *Perf. 15*

8NE1 SD1 10f on 2f gray grn & red .65 .65

NEWSPAPER STAMP

Hungarian Newspaper Stamp of 1914 Surcharged like Regular Issues

1919 Wmk. 137 *Imperf.*

8NP1 N5 10f on 2f orange .80 .80

TEMESVAR ISSUE

Issued under Serbian Occupation

Forgeries exist of the inverted and color error surcharges.

Hungarian Stamps of 1916-18 Surcharged in Black, Blue or Brown:

a

b

1919

9N1 A9(a) 10f on 2f brn org (Bl) .20 .25
a. Black surcharge 15.00 15.00
9N2 A9(b) 30f on 2f brn org .20 .25
a. Inverted surcharge 75.00 75.00
9N3 A11(b) 50f on 20f dk brn (Bl) .20 .25
a. Inverted surcharge
9N4 A9(b) 1k 50f on 15f vio .30 .30
a. Brown surcharge .75 .75
b. Double surcharge (Bk) 50.00 50.00
Nos. 9N1-9N4 (4) .90 1.05

SEMI-POSTAL STAMP

Hungarian Semi-Postal Stamp of 1916 Surcharged in Blue

1919 Wmk. 137 *Perf. 15*

9NB1 SP3 45f on 10f + 2f rose red .20 .25

POSTAGE DUE STAMPS

Hungarian Postage Due Stamps of 1915 Surcharged

1919 Wmk. 137 *Perf. 15*

9NJ1 D1 40f on 2f grn & red .80 .80
9NJ2 D1 60f on 2f grn & red .80 .80
9NJ3 D1 100f on 2f grn & red .80 .80
Nos. 9NJ1-9NJ3 (3) 4.25 4.25

BANAT, BACSKA ISSUE

Issued under Serbian Occupation

Postal authorities at Temesvar applied these overprints. The stamps were available for postage, but were chiefly used to pay postal employees' salaries.

The overprints on this issue have been extensively forged. Even the inexpensive values are difficult to find with genuine overprints. The more extensive note before 1N1 also applies to Nos. 10N1-10NP1.

Hungarian Stamps of 1913-19 Overprinted in Black or Red:

a

b

1919

Type "a" on Stamp of 1913

10N1 A4 50f lake, *blue* 4.00 4.00

Type "a" on Stamps of 1916-18

10N2 A9 2f brown org 4.00 4.00
10N3 A9 3f red lilac 4.00 4.00
10N4 A9 5f green 4.00 4.00
10N5 A9 6f grnsh blue 4.00 4.00
10N6 A9 15f violet 4.00 4.00
10N7 A9 35f brown 35.00 35.00

Type "b"

10N8 A10 50f red vio & lil (R) 30.00 30.00
10N9 A10 75f brt bl & pale bl 4.00 4.00
10N10 A10 80f grn & pale grn 4.00 4.00
a. Red overprint 37.50 37.50
10N11 A10 1k red brn & cl 4.00 4.00
10N12 A10 2k ol brn & bis 4.00 4.00
a. Red overprint 37.50 37.50
10N14 A10 3k dk vio & ind 65.00 65.00
10N15 A10 5k dk brn & lt brn 4.00 4.00
10N16 A10 10k vio brn & vio 4.00 4.00

Type "a" on Stamps of 1918

10N17 A11 10f scarlet 4.00 4.00
10N18 A11 20f dk brown 4.00 4.00
10N19 A11 25f brt blue 4.00 4.00
10N20 A12 40f olive grn 4.00 4.00
10N21 A12 50f lilac 4.00 4.00

Type "a" on Stamps of 1919 Inscribed "Magyar Posta"

10N22 A13 10f red *30.00 30.00*
10N23 A13 20f dk brown *30.00 30.00*
10N24 A13 25f dull blue *37.50 37.50*

Type "a" on Stamps of 1918-19 Overprinted "Koztarsasag"

10N25 A9 4f slate gray 3.50 3.50
10N26 A9 4f sl gray (R) 42.50 42.50
10N27 A9 5f green 4.00 4.00
10N28 A9 6f grnsh blue 4.00 4.00
10N29 A9 10f rose red 30.00 30.00
10N30 A11 15f dp violet 30.00 30.00
10N31 A9 20f gray brn 30.00 30.00
10N32 A11 25f brt blue 30.00 30.00
10N33 A9 40f olive grn 3.50 3.50
10N34 A9 40f ol grn (R) 32.50 32.50

Type "b"

10N35 A10 1k red brn & cl 4.00 4.00
10N36 A10 2k ol brn & bis 30.00 30.00
10N37 A10 3k dk vio & ind 30.00 30.00
10N38 A10 5k dk brn & lt brn 30.00 30.00
10N39 A10 10k vio brn & vio 30.00 30.00

Type "a" on Temesvár Issue

10N40 A9 10f on 2f brn org (Bl & Bk) 4.00 4.00
10N41 A9 1k50f on 15f vio 4.00 4.00

10N42 A5a 50f on 10f vio brn 4.00 4.00
a. Red overprint 75.00 75.00
Nos. 10N1-10N42 (41) 641.50 641.50

SEMI-POSTAL STAMPS

Semi-Postal Stamps of 1916-17 Overprinted Type "a" in Black

1919

10NB1 SP3 10f + 2f rose red 4.00 4.00
10NB2 SP4 15f + 2f dull vio 4.00 4.00
10NB3 SP5 40f + 2f brn car 4.00 4.00

Same Overprint on Temesvar Issue

10NB4 SP3 45f on 10f + 2f rose red (Bl & Bk) 4.00 4.00
Nos. 10NB1-10NB4 (4) 16.00 16.00

SPECIAL DELIVERY STAMP

Hungary No. E1 Surcharged in Black

1919

10NE1 SD1 30f on 2f gray grn & red 4.00 4.00
a. Red overprint 75.00 75.00

POSTAGE DUE STAMPS

Postage Due Stamps of 1914-15 Overprinted Type "a" in Black

1919

10NJ1 D1 2f green & red 4.00 4.00
10NJ2 D1 10f green & red 4.00 4.00
10NJ3 D1 15f green & red 32.50 32.50
10NJ4 D1 20f green & red 4.00 4.00
10NJ5 D1 30f green & red 30.00 30.00
10NJ6 D1 50f green & blk 30.00 30.00
Nos. 10NJ1-10NJ6 (6) 104.50 104.50

NEWSPAPER STAMP

Stamp of 1914 Overprinted Type "a" in Black

1919

10NP1 N5 (2f) orange 4.00 4.00

SZEGED ISSUE

The "Hungarian National Government, Szeged, 1919," as the overprint reads, was an anti-Bolshevist government which opposed the Soviet Republic then in control at Budapest.

The overprints on this issue have been extensively forged. Even the inexpensive stamps are difficult to find with genuine overprints. The more extensive note before No. 1N1 also applies to Szeged Nos. 1-P1.

Hungary Stamps of 1916-19 Overprinted in Green, Red and Blue

On Stamps of 1916-18

1919 *Perf. 15, 14*

11N1 A9 2f brn org (G) 2.25 2.25
11N2 A9 3f red lilac (G) .75 .75
11N3 A9 5f green 2.75 2.75
11N4 A9 6f grnsh blue 32.50 32.50
11N5 A9 15f violet 3.50 3.50
11N6 A10 50f red vio & lil 19.00 19.00
11N7 A10 75f brt bl & pale bl 4.25 4.25
11N8 A10 80f grn & pale grn 18.00 18.00
11N9 A10 1k red brn & cl (G) 2.25 2.25
11N10 A10 2k ol brn & bis 4.75 4.75
11N11 A10 3k dk vio & ind 7.25 7.25
11N12 A10 5k dk brn & lt brn 60.00 60.00
11N13 A10 10k vio brn & vio 60.00 60.00

With New Value Added

11N14	A9	45f on 3f red lil (R & G)	.80	.80
11N15	A10	10k on 1k red brn & cl (Bl & G)	8.00	8.00

On Stamps of 1918

11N16	A11	10f scarlet (G)	2.50	2.50
11N17	A11	20f dk brown	.60	.60
11N18	A11	25f brt blue	22.50	22.50
11N19	A12	40f olive grn	11.00	11.00

On Stamps of 1918-19 Overprinted "Koztarsasag"

11N20	A9	3f red lil (G)	42.50	42.50
11N21	A9	4f slate gray	11.00	11.00
11N22	A9	5f green	25.00	25.00
11N23	A9	6f grnsh blue	15.00	15.00
11N24	A9	10f rose red (G)	32.50	32.50
11N25	A11	10f scarlet)	30.00	30.00
11N26	A11	15f dp violet	10.00	10.00
11N27	A9	20f gray brown	50.00	50.00
11N28	A11	20f dk brown	65.00	65.00
11N29	A11	25f brt blue	20.00	20.00
11N30	A9	40f olive	2.25	2.25
11N31	A12	50f lilac	1.75	1.75
11N32	A10	3k dk vio & ind	37.50	37.50

With New Value Added

11N33	A9	20f on 2f brn org (R & G)	.80	.80

On Stamps of 1919 Inscribed "Magyar Posta"

11N34	A13	20f dk brown	60.00	60.00
11N35	A13	25f dull blue	1.75	1.75
		Nos. 1-35 (35)	667.70	667.70

SEMI-POSTAL STAMPS

Szeged Overprint on Semi-Postal Stamps of 1916-17 in Green or Red

1919

11NB1	SP3	10f + 2f rose red (G)	.85	.85
11NB2	SP4	15f + 2f dl vio (R)	3.75	3.75
11NB3	SP5	40f + 2f brn car (G)	10.00	10.00

With Additional Overprint "Koztarsasag"

11NB4	SP5	40f + 2f brn car (Bk & G)	15.00	15.00
		Nos. B1-B4 (4)	29.60	29.60

SPECIAL DELIVERY STAMP

Szeged Overprint on Special Delivery Stamp of 1916 in Red

1919

11NE1	SD1	2f gray grn & red	11.00	11.00

POSTAGE DUE STAMPS

Szeged Overprint on Stamps of 1915-18 in Red

1919

11NJ1	D1	2f green & red	3.00	3.00
11NJ2	D1	6f green & red	9.75	9.75
11NJ3	D1	10f green & red	3.75	3.75
11NJ4	D1	12f green & red	4.75	4.75
11NJ5	D1	20f green & red	6.00	6.00
11NJ6	D1	30f green & red	9.00	9.00

Red Surcharge

11NJ7	SD1	50f on 2f gray grn & red	2.75	2.75
11NJ8	SD1	100f on 2f gray grn & red	2.75	2.75
		Nos. J1-J8 (8)	41.75	41.75

NEWSPAPER STAMP

Szeged Overprint on Stamp of 1914 in Green

1919 **Wmk. 137** ***Imperf.***

11NP1	N5	(2f) orange	.85	.85

WESTERN HUNGARY

Following World War I, under the terms of the Trianon Treaty of 1920, four districts of western Hungary were transferred to Austrian administration. Three of these districts were German-speaking and joined Austria as the province of Burgenland. In the fourth district, which included the city of Sopron, Hungarian militia resisted incorporation into Austria, and in a plebiscite held Dec. 14-16, 1921, the area's citizens, although mostly German-speaking, overwhelmingly voted for the district to remain a part of Hungary.

During Sept.-Dec., the following stamps were issued by the local authorities and were sold at post offices within the area controlled by the Hungarian partisans.

Overprinted on Hungarian Stamps of 1916-20

1921, Sept. 4

1	A9	10f red violet	12.50	12.50
2	A9	20f gray brown	.65	.65
a.		Inverted overprint	50.00	50.00
3	A9	25f dull blue	75.00	75.00
a.		Inverted overprint	125.00	125.00
4	A9	40f olive green	1.40	1.40
a.		Inverted overprint	50.00	50.00
5	A9	50f yellow green	1.00	1.00
a.		Inverted overprint	50.00	50.00
6	A9	60f black	.90	.90
7	A10	1k red brn & cl	1.60	1.60
a.		Inverted overprint	50.00	50.00
8	A10	2k ol brn & bis	25.00	25.00
a.		Inverted overprint	75.00	75.00
9	A10	2.50k bl & gray bl	60.00	60.00
10	A10	3k dk vio & ind	25.00	25.00
a.		Inverted overprint	125.00	125.00
		Nos. 1-10 (10)	203.05	203.05

This overprint was also applied to 21 other contemporaneous Hungarian stamps, including 5 postage due stamps, but these were not issued. Value, each $10.

Nos. 1-10, and all of the Western Hungary overprints on Hungarian stamps, exist with the three-hole control punch described after Hungary No. 126. Values are for unpunched examples. Stamps with the control punch sell for 20-50 percent more.

1921, Sept. 19

11	A9	5f brown orange	23.00	23.00
12	A9	10f red violet	30.00	30.00
13	A9	15f violet	75.00	75.00
14	A9	20f gray brown	75.00	75.00
15	A9	40f olive green	75.00	75.00
16	A9	50f yellow green	19.00	19.00
a.		Inverted overprint	125.00	125.00
17	A9	60f black	20.00	20.00
18	A10	1k red brn & cl	20.00	20.00
19	A10	2k ol brn & bister	75.00	75.00
		Nos. 11-19 (9)	412.00	412.00

The text overprinted on Nos. 11-19 was machine-overprinted in black. The skull and crossed bones emblem was separately handstamped in red.

1921, Oct. 5

20	A9	10f red violet	.50	.50
21	A9	15f violet	1.00	1.00
22	A9	20f gray brown	.50	.50
23	A9	40f olive green	.50	.50
24	A9	50f yellow green	1.00	1.00
25	A9	60f black	1.00	1.00
26	A10	1k red brn & cl	1.50	1.50
27	A10	2k ol brn & bis	1.00	1.00
28	A9	2.50k on 2f brn org	50.00	50.00
29	A9	2.50k on 5f brn org	1.00	1.00
30	A10	3k dk vio & ind	2.00	2.00
31	A10	5k dk brn & lt brn	2.00	2.00
32	A10	10k vio brn & vio	2.00	2.00
		Nos. 20-32 (13)	64.00	64.00

1921, Oct. 16

33	A9	5f brown orange	2.00	2.00
34	A9	10f red violet	2.00	2.00
35	A9	15f violet	2.00	2.00
36	A9	20f gray brown	2.00	2.00
37	A9	40f olive green	2.00	2.00
38	A9	50f yellow green	2.00	2.00
39	A9	60f black	2.00	2.00
40	A10	1k red brn & cl	2.00	2.00
41	A10	2k ol brn & bis	3.50	3.50
42	A10	2.50k bl & gray bl	7.50	7.50
43	A10	3.50k gray	5.00	5.00
		Nos. 33-43 (11)	32.00	32.00

1921, Oct. 10

44	A9	5f brown orange	60.00	60.00
45	A9	10f red violet	65.00	65.00
46	A9	15f violet	65.00	65.00
47	A9	20f gray brown	65.00	65.00
48	A9	40f olive green	20.00	20.00
49	A9	50f yellow green	4.00	4.00
a.		Inverted overprint	50.00	50.00
50	A9	60f black	4.00	4.00
a.		Inverted overprint	50.00	50.00
51	A10	1k red brn & cl	4.00	4.00
a.		Inverted overprint	50.00	50.00
a.		Double overprint	50.00	50.00
52	A10	2k ol brn & bis	65.00	65.00
53	A10	2.50k bl & gray bl	20.00	20.00
54	A10	3k dk vio & ind	20.00	20.00
55	A10	3.50k gray	20.00	20.00
56	A10	5k dk brn & lt brn	125.00	125.00
57	A10	10k vio brn & vio	125.00	125.00
58	A23	50k dk brn & bl	125.00	125.00
59	A23	100k ol bis & yel brn	125.00	125.00
		Nos. 44-59 (16)	912.00	912.00

See Nos. J1-J3.

A9a

A9b

1921, Oct. 12

60	A9a	20f on 20f gray brn	.40	.40
61	A9a	50f on 50f yel grn	.40	.40
62	A9b	1k on 10f red vio	.40	.40
63	A9b	2k on 40f ol grn	.40	.40
64	A9b	3k on 60f black	.80	.80
65	A9b	5k on 5f brn org	.80	.80
66	A9b	10k on 15f violet	.80	.80
a.		"01" for "10" in surcharge	40.00	40.00
		Nos. 60-66 (7)	4.00	4.00

The large numerals on korona values are surcharged in red.

Arms — A1

M.M. Pronay — A2

Frakno — A3

Németujvár A4

Városszalnak A5

Arms — A6

1921, Nov. 11

67	A1	10f violet brown	.45	*.60*
68	A2	20f green	.50	*.75*
69	A3	40f red brown	.50	*.75*
70	A4	50f green	.45	*.60*
71	A3	60f black	.50	*.75*
a.		Tête bêche pair	25.00	25.00
72	A5	1k vermilion	.40	*.60*
73	A1	2.50k blue	.50	*.75*
74	A4	5k dark brown	.50	*.75*
a.		Tête bêche pair	3.50	3.50
75	A2	10k red violet	.50	*.75*
a.		Tête bêche pair	18.00	18.00
76	A5	50k red violet	.50	*.75*
a.		Tête bêche pair	27.50	27.50
77	A6	100k lilac	.45	*.60*
a.		Tête bêche pair	12.00	12.00
		Nos. 67-77 (11)	5.25	*7.65*

The 10f-40f, 60f, 1k, 2.50k, 50k and 100k exist imperf. Value, each $2. Tête bêche pairs of the 60f, 10k and 50k also exist imperf. Value, each $50.

Nos. 67-77 in different colors are proofs. Value: 10f-50k, each $5; 100k, $20.

See Nos. J4-J9.

1921, Dec. 14

78	A9	10f red violet	1.00	1.00
a.		Inverted overprint	10.00	10.00
79	A9	20f gray brown	1.00	1.00
a.		Inverted overprint	10.00	10.00
80	A9	40f olive green	1.00	1.00
a.		Inverted overprint	10.00	10.00
81	A9	50f yellow green	.50	.50
a.		Inverted overprint	10.00	10.00
82	A9	60f black	.50	.50
a.		Inverted overprint	10.00	10.00
83	A10	1k red brn & claret	.50	.50
a.		Inverted overprint	10.00	10.00
84	A10	2k ol brn & bis	1.00	1.00
a.		Inverted overprint	10.00	10.00
85	A10	2.50k bl & gray bl	1.00	1.00
a.		Inverted overprint	10.00	10.00
86	A10	3.50k gray	1.00	1.00
a.		Inverted overprint	10.00	10.00
87	A10	5k dk brn & lt brn	1.00	1.00
a.		Inverted overprint	10.00	10.00
88	A10	10k vio brn & vio	1.50	1.50
		Nos. 78-88 (11)	10.00	10.00

Six stamps in this design were prepared in 1921 but not issued. Value, each $40.

POSTAGE DUE STAMPS

1921, Oct. 10

J1	D1	2f green & red	75.00	75.00
J2	D1	120f green & red ('20)	30.00	30.00
a.		Inverted overprint	125.00	125.00
J3	D1	200f green & red ('20)	50.00	50.00

D2

1921, Nov. 11

J4	D2	50f green & black	.35	.50
a.		Inverted overprint	75.00	75.00
J5	D2	100f green & black	.35	.50
a.		Inverted overprint	75.00	75.00
J6	D2	200f green & black	.35	.50
a.		Inverted overprint	75.00	75.00
J7	D2	500f green & black	.35	.50
a.		Inverted overprint	75.00	75.00
J8	D2	1000f green & black	.35	.50
a.		Inverted overprint	75.00	75.00
		Nos. J4-J8 (5)	1.75	2.50

Type D2 exists without denomination. Value $50.

Nos. J4-J8 printed in blue are color proofs. Value, each $35.

No. J6 Surcharged in Red

1921, Nov. 11

J9	D2	50f on 200f green & black	30.00	40.00

ICELAND

'is-lənd

LOCATION — Island in the North Atlantic Ocean, east of Greenland
AREA — 39,758 sq. mi.
POP. — 238,175 (1983)
CAPITAL — Reykjavik

Iceland became a republic on June 17, 1944. Formerly this country was united with Denmark under the government of King Christian X who, as a ruling sovereign of both countries, was assigned the dual title of king of each. Although the two countries were temporarily united in certain affairs beyond the king's person, both were acknowledged as sovereign states.

96 Skillings = 1 Rigsdaler
100 Aurar (singular "Eyrir") = 1 Krona (1876)

Watermarks

Wmk. 112 — Crown

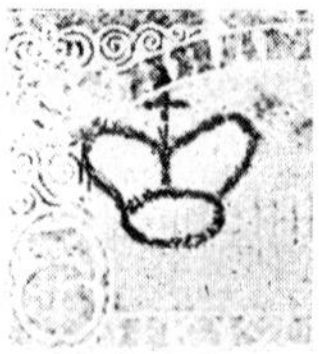

Wmk. 113 — Crown

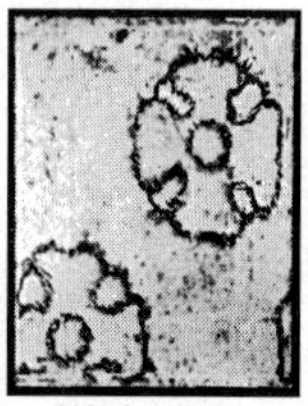

Wmk. 47 — Multiple Rosette

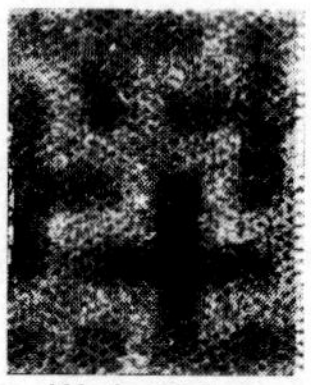

Wmk. 114 — Multiple Crosses

Values for unused stamps are for examples with original gum as defined in the catalogue introduction. Very fine examples of Nos. 1-33A and O1-O12 will have centering with perforations clear of the framelines but with design noticeably off center, and Nos. 1-7 and O1-O3 additionally will have some irregular or shorter perforations. Well centered stamps are quite scarce and will command higher prices.

A1

Perf. 14x13½

1873 Typo. Wmk. 112

1	A1	2s ultra	1,000.	3,000.
		On cover		45,000.
a.		Imperf.	625.	
2	A1	4s dark carmine	175.	1,000.
		On cover		39,000.
a.		Imperf.	625.	—
3	A1	8s brown	300.	1,150.
		On cover		39,000.
a.		Imperf.	350.	
4	A1	16s yellow	1,600.	2,500.
		On cover		—
a.		Imperf.	400.	
		Perf. 12½		
5	A1	3s gray	500.	1,500.
		On cover		—
a.		Imperf.	750.	
6	A1	4s carmine	1,400.	2,100.
		On cover		—
7	A1	16s yellow	110.	625.
		On cover		—

False and favor cancellations are often found on Nos. 1-7. Nos. 1-7 were valid until 7/31/76. Favor cancellations were applied starting in 1882. These cancels have sans-serif letters and dates with lines between the month and day. Values of stamps with favor cancellations range from $75 (#2, 7) to $575 (#4). The imperforate varieties lack gum.

A2

Small "3" — A3

Large "3" — A3a

1876

8	A2	5a blue	400.00	725.00
		On cover		—
		Perf. 14x13½		
9	A2	5a blue	450.00	775.00
		On cover		9,000.
a.		Imperf.	2,000.	
10	A2	6a gray	140.00	30.00
		On cover		1,500.
11	A2	10a carmine	225.00	7.25
		On cover		1,000.
a.		Imperf.	575.00	675.00
12	A2	16a brown	115.00	50.00
		On cover		825.00
13	A2	20a dark violet	35.00	500.00
		On cover		3,000.
14	A2	40a green	100.00	225.00
		On cover		—

Fake and favor cancellations are often found on No. 13, and value is considerably less than that shown.

1882-98

15	A3	3a orange	62.50	20.00
		On cover		650.00
16	A2	5a green	50.00	12.50
		On cover		650.00
17	A2	20a blue	325.00	50.00
		On cover		825.00
a.		20a ultramarine	700.00	290.00
		On cover		1,500.
18	A2	40a red violet	50.00	42.50
		On cover		4,500.
a.		Perf. 13 ('98)	5,000.	
19	A2	50a bl & car ('92)	90.00	100.00
		On cover		1,750.
20	A2	100a brn & vio ('92)	85.00	140.00
		On cover		2,250.
		Nos. 15-20 (6)	662.50	365.00

See note after No. 68.

1896-1901 ***Perf. 13***

21	A3	3a orange ('97)	90.00	11.50
		On cover		500.00
22	A3a	3a yellow ('01)	6.50	21.00
		On cover		1,200.
23	A2	4a rose & gray ('99)	18.00	21.00
		On cover		900.00
24	A2	5a green	3.75	2.90
		On cover		500.00
25	A2	6a gray ('97)	17.50	18.50
		On cover		1,200.
26	A2	10a carmine ('97)	9.00	2.90
		On cover		625.00
27	A2	16a brown	72.50	100.00
		On cover		1,100.
28	A2	20a dull blue ('98)	45.00	37.50
		On cover		775.00
a.		20a dull ultramarine	425.00	42.50
		On cover		1,200.
29	A2	25a yel brown & blue ('00)	20.00	32.50
		On cover		3,000.
30	A2	50a bl & car ('98)	450.00	700.00

Value for No. 30 used is for a canceled-to-order example after the stamp was invalidated in 1902. Stamps genuinely used before invalidation are rare and sell for much more.

See note after No. 68.

For surcharges see Nos. 31-33A, 45-68.

Black and Red Surcharge

Surcharged þrír 3

1897 ***Perf. 13***

31	A2	3a on 5a green	700.	550.
		On cover		700.
a.		Perf. 14x13½	—	4,000.
b.		Inverted surcharge	1,200.	1,000.
		On cover		1,350.
c.		As "a," inverted surcharge		7,500.

Surcharged

32	A2	3a on 5a green	600.	475.
		On cover		550.00
a.		Inverted surcharge	1,150.	900.
		On cover		1,250.
b.		Perf. 14x13½	11,500.	2,300.

All 5 known unused examples of #32b lack gum.

Black Surcharge

Surcharged þrír

33	A2	3a on 5a green	950.	825.
		On cover		850.
b.		Inverted surcharge	1,500.	1,250.

þrır

Surcharged

33A	A2	3a on 5a green	750.	575.
		On cover		625.
c.		Inverted surcharge	1,200.	1,000.

Excellent counterfeits are known.

King Christian IX — A4

1902-04 Wmk. 113 ***Perf. 13***

34	A4	3a orange	6.25	4.00
		On cover		45.00
35	A4	4a gray & rose	4.00	1.40
		On cover		50.00
36	A4	5a yel green	35.00	1.25
		On cover		30.00
37	A4	6a gray brown	21.00	11.50
		On cover		100.00
38	A4	10a car rose	6.25	1.25
		On cover		45.00
39	A4	16a chocolate	9.00	11.50
		On cover		120.00
40	A4	20a deep blue	3.25	5.00
		On cover		40.00
a.		Inscribed "PJONUSTA"	67.50	95.00
		On cover		225.00
41	A4	25a brn & grn	4.50	7.50
		On cover		275.00
42	A4	40a violet	5.00	7.00
		On cover		400.00
43	A4	50a gray & bl blk	6.25	26.00
		On cover		450.00
44	A4	1k sl bl & yel brn	7.50	11.50
		On cover		500.00
44A	A4	2k olive brn & brt blue ('04)	30.00	75.00
		On cover		950.00
44B	A4	5k org brn & slate blue ('04)	150.00	250.00
		On cover		1,350.
		Nos. 34-44B (13)	288.00	412.90

For surcharge see No. 142.

Stamps of 1882-1901 Overprinted

1902-03 Wmk. 112 ***Perf. 13***

Red Overprint

45	A2	5a green	1.00	8.50
a.		Inverted overprint	45.00	70.00
b.		"I" before Gildi omitted	160.00	
c.		'03-'03	275.00	
d.		02'-'03	275.00	
e.		Pair, one without overprint	90.00	
46	A2	6a gray	.90	8.25
a.		Double overprint	55.00	
b.		Inverted overprint	42.50	
c.		'03-'03	325.00	
d.		02'-'03	325.00	
e.		Pair, one with invtd. ovpt.	225.00	
f.		Pair, one without overprint	125.00	
g.		As "f", inverted	175.00	
47	A2	20a dull blue	.80	9.75
a.		Inverted overprint	32.50	50.00
b.		"I" before Gildi omitted	87.50	
c.		02'-'03	275.00	
48	A2	25a yel brn & bl	.90	16.50
a.		Inverted overprint	42.50	55.00
b.		'03-'03	275.00	
c.		02'-'03	275.00	
d.		Double overprint	110.00	

Black Overprint

49	A3	3a orange	190.00	500.00
b.		Inverted overprint	300.00	600.00
c.		"I" before Gildi omitted	400.00	
d.		'03-'03	400.00	
e.		02'-'03	400.00	
50	A3a	3a yellow	1.30	2.00
a.		Double overprint	290.00	
b.		Inverted overprint	45.00	62.50
c.		"I" before Gildi omitted	275.00	
d.		02'-'03	350.00	
51	A2	4a rose & gray	40.00	55.00
a.		Double overprint	175.00	
b.		Inverted overprint	100.00	
c.		Dbl. ovpt., one invtd.	240.00	
d.		"I" before Gildi omitted	230.00	
e.		'03-'03	350.00	
f.		02'-'03	350.00	
g.		Pair, one with invtd. ovpt.	250.00	
52	A2	5a green	350.00	600.00
a.		Inverted overprint	400.00	
b.		Pair, one without overprint	500.00	
c.		As "b", inverted	625.00	
53	A2	6a gray	625.00	950.00
a.		Inverted overprint	725.00	
b.		Pair, one without overprint	725.00	
c.		Double overprint	800.00	
54	A2	10a carmine	1.30	10.50
a.		Inverted overprint	45.00	70.00
b.		Pair, one without overprint	80.00	

55	A2	16a brown	27.50	*40.00*
a.		Inverted overprint	120.00	
b.		"I" before Gildi omitted	225.00	
c.		'03-'03	350.00	
d.		02'-'03	350.00	
56	A2	20a dull blue	*11,000.*	
a.		Inverted overprint	*11,500.*	
57	A2	25 yel brn & bl	*7,250.*	
a.		Inverted overprint	*8,000.*	
58	A2	40a red vio	1.10	*40.00*
a.		Inverted overprint	45.00	
59	A2	50a bl & car	3.50	*67.50*
a.		Double overprint	300.00	
b.		02'-'03	300.00	
c.		'03-'03	225.00	

Perf. 14x13½

Red Overprint

60	A2	5a green	1,750.	—
a.		'03-'03	—	
b.		02'-'03	—	
61	A2	6a gray	1,750.	—
a.		02'-'03	—	
62	A2	20a blue	*4,750.*	—

Black Overprint

63	A3	3a orange	1,150.	*1,850.*
a.		Inverted overprint	1,300.	
b.		02'-'03	1,600.	
c.		'03-'03	1,600.	
64	A2	10a carmine	*7,750.*	—
65	A2	16a brown	1,350.	*1,750.*
a.		Inverted overprint	1,500.	
b.		02'-'03	1,750.	
d.		'03-'03	1,750.	
65C	A2	20a dull blue	*6,500.*	—
66	A2	40a red vio	20.00	*95.00*
a.		Inverted overprint	400.00	—
b.		'03-'03	300.00	
c.		02'-'03	300.00	
67	A2	50a bl & car	40.00	*125.00*
a.		Inverted overprint	175.00	
b.		'03-'03	350.00	
c.		02'-'03	350.00	—
d.		As "c," inverted		
68	A2	100a brn & vio	50.00	*80.00*
a.		Inverted overprint	140.00	
b.		02'-'03	275.00	
c.		'03-'03	275.00	

"I GILDI" means "valid."

In 1904 Nos. 20, 22-30, 45-59 (except 49, 52, 53, 56 and 57) and No. 68 were reprinted for the Postal Union. The reprints are perforated 13 and have watermark type 113. Value $50 each. Without overprint, $100 each.

Kings Christian IX and Frederik VIII — A5

Typo., Center Engr.

1907-08 Wmk. 113 *Perf. 13*

71	A5	1e yel grn & red	1.75	1.10
72	A5	3a yel brn & ocher	4.00	1.60
73	A5	4a gray & red	2.10	1.75
74	A5	5a green	80.00	1.25
75	A5	6a gray & gray brn	50.00	3.50
76	A5	10a scarlet	140.00	1.40
77	A5	15a red & green	7.50	1.25
78	A5	16a brown	8.75	*40.00*
79	A5	20a blue	8.00	6.25
80	A5	25a bis brn & grn	6.50	*12.50*
81	A5	40a claret & vio	6.25	*15.00*
82	A5	50a gray & vio	7.00	*15.00*
83	A5	1k blue & brn	25.00	*65.00*
84	A5	2k dk brn & dk grn	35.00	*75.00*
85	A5	5k brn & slate	190.00	*375.00*
		Nos. 71-85 (15)	571.85	*615.60*

See Nos. 99-107.

For surcharges and overprints see Nos. 130-138, 143, C2, O69.

Jon Sigurdsson A6

Frederik VIII A7

1911 Typo. and Embossed

86	A6	1e olive green	2.40	2.25
87	A6	3a light brown	4.50	*14.00*
88	A6	4a ultramarine	1.60	*1.75*
89	A6	6a gray	11.50	*22.50*
90	A6	15a violet	14.00	1.75
91	A6	25a orange	24.00	*45.00*
		Nos. 86-91 (6)	58.00	*87.25*

Sigurdsson (1811-79), statesman and author.

For surcharge see No. 149.

1912, Feb. 17

92	A7	5a green	32.50	11.50
93	A7	10a red	32.50	11.50
94	A7	20a pale blue	45.00	17.50
95	A7	50a claret	9.25	*35.00*
96	A7	1k yellow	29.00	*72.50*
97	A7	2k rose	27.50	*72.50*
98	A7	5k brown	150.00	*225.00*
		Nos. 92-98 (7)	325.75	*445.50*

For surcharges and overprints see Nos. 140-141, O50-O51.

Type of 1907-08

Typo., Center Engr.

1915-18 Wmk. 114 *Perf. 14x14½*

99	A5	1e yel grn & red	8.00	*17.50*
100	A5	3a bister brn	4.00	2.75
101	A5	4a gray & red	4.00	*9.25*
102	A5	5a green	95.00	1.25
103	A5	6a gray & gray brn	19.00	*125.00*
104	A5	10a scarlet	3.50	1.10
107	A5	20a blue	210.00	22.50
		Nos. 99-107 (7)	343.50	*179.35*

Revenue cancellations consisting of "TOLLUR" boxed in frame are found on stamps used to pay the tax on parcel post packages entering Iceland.

Christian X — A8

1920-22 Typo.

108	A8	1e yel grn & red	.90	*1.10*
109	A8	3a bister brn	8.50	*16.00*
110	A8	4a gray & red	5.00	2.50
111	A8	5a green	2.25	2.00
112	A8	5a ol green ('22)	5.00	1.60
113	A8	6a dark gray	14.00	8.50
114	A8	8a dark brown	8.50	2.25
115	A8	10a red	2.50	*11.50*
116	A8	10a green ('21)	3.50	1.75
117	A8	15a violet	42.50	1.40
118	A8	20a deep blue	2.75	*17.50*
119	A8	20a choc ('22)	60.00	1.60
120	A8	25a brown & grn	17.50	1.75
121	A8	25a red ('21)	17.50	*57.50*
		Revenue cancellation		4.00
122	A8	30a red & green	52.50	3.50
		Revenue cancellation		8.50
123	A8	40a claret	45.00	2.90
		Revenue cancellation		9.00
124	A8	40a dk bl ('21)	80.00	14.00
		Revenue cancellation		10.00
125	A8	50a dk gray & cl	175.00	11.50
		Revenue cancellation		12.50
126	A8	1k dp bl & dk brn	95.00	1.75
		Revenue cancellation		1.60
127	A8	2k ol brn & myr green	230.00	32.50
		Revenue cancellation		3.25
128	A8	5k brn & ind	57.50	17.50
		Revenue cancellation		3.25
		Nos. 108-128 (21)	925.40	*210.60*

See Nos. 176-187, 202.

For surcharges and overprints see Nos.139, 150, C1, C9-C14, O52, O70-O71.

A9

A10

A11

1921-25 Wmk. 113 *Perf. 13*

130	A9	5a on 16a brown	4.00	*29.00*
131	A11	5a on 16a brown	2.25	*8.50*
132	A10	20a on 25a brn & green	8.00	8.00
133	A11	20a on 25a bis brn & green	4.50	*8.00*
134	A9	20a on 40a violet	8.50	*20.00*
135	A11	20a on 40a cl & vio	11.50	*22.50*
137	A9	30a on 50a gray & bl blk ('25)	35.00	*35.00*
		Revenue cancellation		16.00
138	A9	50a on 5k org brn & sl bl ('25)	57.50	55.00
		Revenue cancellation		32.50
		Nos. 130-138 (8)	131.25	*186.00*

No. 111 Surcharged

1922 Wmk. 114 *Perf. 14x14½*

139	A8	10a on 5a green	7.50	3.50

Nos. 95-96, 44A, 85 Surcharged

1924-30 Wmk. 113 *Perf. 13*

140	A7	10k on 50a ('25)	300.00	*450.00*
		Revenue cancellation		35.00
141	A7	10k on 1k	375.00	*625.00*
		Revenue cancellation		70.00
142	A4	10k on 2k ('29)	75.00	32.50
		Revenue cancellation		8.50
143	A5	10k on 5k ('30)	450.00	575.00
		Revenue cancellation		32.50

"Tollur" is a revenue cancellation.

Landing the Mail — A12

Designs: 7a, 50a, Landing the mail. 10a, 35a, View of Reykjavik. 20a, Museum building.

Perf. 14x15

1925, Sept. 12 Typo. Wmk. 114

144	A12	7a yel green	40.00	7.50
145	A12	10a dp bl & brn	40.00	.80
146	A12	20a vermilion	40.00	.80
147	A12	35a deep blue	70.00	9.25
148	A12	50a yel grn & brn	70.00	1.60
		Nos. 144-148 (5)	260.00	19.95

No. 91 Surcharged

1925 Wmk. 113 *Perf. 13*

149	A6	2k on 25a orange	125.00	*140.00*
		Revenue cancellation		17.50

No. 124 Surcharged in Red

1926

150	A8	1k on 40a dark blue	150.00	35.00
		Revenue cancellation		22.50

Parliament Building A15

Designs: 5a, Viking ship in storm. 7a, Parliament meeting place, 1690. 10a, Viking funeral. 15a, Vikings naming land. 20a, The dash for Thing. 25a, Gathering wood. 30a, Thingvalla Lake. 35a, Iceland woman in national costume. 40a, Iceland flag. 50a, First Althing, 930 A.D. 1k, Map of Iceland. 2k, Winter-bound home. 5k, Woman spinning. 10k, Viking Sacrifice to Thor.

Perf. 12½x12

1930, Jan. 1 Litho. Unwmk.

152	A15	3a dull vio & gray vio	3.50	*9.25*
153	A15	5a dk bl & sl grn	3.50	*9.25*
154	A15	7a grn & gray grn	2.90	*9.25*
155	A15	10a dk vio & lilac	9.25	*17.50*
156	A15	15a dp ultra & bl gray	2.25	*9.75*
157	A15	20a rose red & sal	40.00	*80.00*
a.		Double impression	350.00	
158	A15	25a dk brn & lt brown	7.00	*14.00*
159	A15	30a dk grn & sl grn	5.75	*13.00*
160	A15	35a ultra & bl gray	6.50	*12.50*
161	A15	40a dk ultra, red & slate grn	5.75	*13.00*
162	A15	50a red brn & cinnamon	57.50	*140.00*
163	A15	1k ol grn & gray green	57.50	*140.00*
164	A15	2k turq bl & gray green	80.00	*160.00*
165	A15	5k org & yellow	45.00	*125.00*
166	A15	10k mag & dl rose	45.00	*125.00*
		Nos. 152-166 (15)	371.40	*877.50*

Millenary of the "Althing," the Icelandic Parliament, oldest in the world.

Imperfs were privately printed.

For overprints see Nos. O53-O67.

Gullfoss (Golden Falls) — A30

1931-32 Unwmk. Engr. *Perf. 14*

170	A30	5a gray	15.00	1.10
171	A30	20a red	12.50	.25
172	A30	35a ultramarine	25.00	16.00
		Revenue cancellation		1.90
173	A30	60a red lil ('32)	15.00	1.25
174	A30	65a red brn ('32)	2.50	1.25
175	A30	75a grnsh bl ('32)	100.00	35.00
		Revenue cancellation		5.00
		Nos. 170-175 (6)	170.00	54.85

Issued: 5a-35a, Dec. 15; 60a-75a, May 30.

Type of 1920 Christian X Issue Redrawn

Perf. 14x14½

1931-33 Typo. Wmk. 114

176	A8	1e yel grn & red	1.00	*1.25*
177	A8	3a bister brown	15.00	*15.00*
		Revenue cancellation		8.00
178	A8	4a gray & red	2.50	1.40
179	A8	6a dark gray	2.00	*4.00*
180	A8	7a yel grn ('33)	.65	*1.75*
181	A8	10a chocolate	140.00	1.10
182	A8	25a brn & green	17.50	3.50
		Revenue cancellation		3.25
183	A8	30a red & green	29.00	5.75
		Revenue cancellation		7.75
184	A8	40a claret	225.00	21.00
		Revenue cancellation		11.50
185	A8	1k dk bl & lt brn	45.00	7.50
		Revenue cancellation		3.25
186	A8	2k choc & dk grn	275.00	80.00
		Revenue cancellation		8.00
187	A8	10k yel grn & blk	300.00	210.00
		Revenue cancellation		16.00
		Nos. 176-187 (12)	1,052.	352.25

On the redrawn stamps the horizontal lines of the portrait and the oval are closer together than on the 1920 stamps and are crossed by many fine vertical lines.

See No. 202.

Dynjandi Falls — A31

Mount Hekla — A32

Perf. 12½

1935, June 28 Engr. Unwmk.

193	A31	10a blue	22.50	.20
		Never hinged	65.00	
194	A32	1k greenish gray	40.00	.20
		Never hinged	110.00	

Matthias Jochumsson — A33

1935, Nov. 11

195	A33	3a gray green	.70	*4.00*
196	A33	5a gray	14.00	1.25
197	A33	7a yel green	20.00	1.75
198	A33	35a blue	.60	*1.25*
		Nos. 195-198 (4)	35.30	*8.25*
		Set, never hinged	100.00	

Birth cent. of Matthias Jochumsson, poet.

For surcharges see Nos. 212, 236.

King Christian X — A34

1937, May 14 *Perf. 13x12½*
199 A34 10a green 2.30 *22.50*
200 A34 30a brown 2.30 *10.00*
201 A34 40a claret 2.30 *10.00*
Nos. 199-201 (3) 6.90 *42.50*
Set, never hinged 12.00

Reign of Christian X, 25th anniv.

Christian X Type of 1931-33

1937 Unwmk. Typo. *Perf. 11½*
202 A8 1e yel grn & red .80 *2.25*
Never hinged 2.00

Geyser
A35 A36

1938-47 Engr. *Perf. 14*
203 A35 15a dp rose vio 5.75 *11.50*
a. Imperf., pair *625.00*
Never hinged 700.00
204 A35 20a rose red 22.50 .20
205 A35 35a ultra .70 *1.10*
206 A36 40a dk brn ('39) 12.50 *29.00*
207 A36 45a brt ultra ('40) .80 *1.10*
208 A36 50a dk slate grn 21.00 1.10
208A A36 60a brt ultra ('43) 5.75 1.10
c. Perf. 11½ ('47) 2.90 *11.50*
Never hinged (#208Ac) 5.75
208B A36 1k indigo ('45) 1.90 .35
d. Perf. 11½ ('47) 2.90 *11.50*
Never hinged (#208Bd) 5.75
Nos. 203-208B (8) 70.90 *45.45*
Set, never hinged 175.00

University of Iceland A37

1938, Dec. 1 *Perf. 13½*
209 A37 25a dark grn 7.50 *16.00*
210 A37 30a brown 7.50 *16.00*
211 A37 40a brt red vio 7.50 *16.00*
Nos. 209-211 (3) 22.50 *48.00*
Set, never hinged 35.00

20th anniversary of independence.

No. 198 Surcharged with New Value

1939, Mar. 17 *Perf. 12½*
212 A33 5a on 35a blue .80 *1.60*
Never hinged 1.25
a. Double surcharge *250.00*
Never hinged 400.00

Trylon and Perisphere A38

Leif Ericsson's Ship and Route to America A39

Statue of Thorfinn Karlsefni — A40

1939 Engr. *Perf. 14*
213 A38 20a crimson 3.50 *7.00*
214 A39 35a bright ultra 4.00 *8.50*
215 A40 45a bright green 4.25 *10.00*
216 A40 2k dark gray 50.00 *140.00*
Nos. 213-216 (4) 61.75 *165.50*
Set, never hinged 97.50

New York World's Fair.
For overprints see Nos. 232-235.

Codfish — A41

Herring — A42

Flag of Iceland — A43

1939-45 Engr. *Perf. 14, 14x13½*
217 A41 1e Prussian blue .35 *4.50*
a. Perf. 14x13½ 1.60 *5.50*
218 A42 3a dark violet .35 *.90*
a. Perf. 14x13½ 2.25 *8.50*
219 A41 5a dark brown .35 .25
c. Perf. 14x13½ 2.75 1.40
220 A42 7a dark green 5.75 *9.25*
221 A42 10a green ('40) 40.00 .75
b. Perf. 14x13½ 62.50 1.60
Never hinged 180.00
222 A42 10a slate gray ('45) .35 .20
223 A42 12a dk grn ('43) .35 .55
224 A41 25a brt red ('40) 27.50 .20
b. Perf. 14x13½ 57.50 2.10
Never hinged (#224b) 170.00
225 A41 25a hn brn ('45) .35 .20
226 A42 35a carmine ('43) .50 .35
227 A41 50a dk bl grn ('43) .60 .20

Typo.
228 A43 10a car & ultra 2.25 1.25
Nos. 217-228 (12) 78.70 *18.60*
Set, never hinged 190.00

Statue of Thorfinn Karlsefni — A44

1939-45 Engr. *Perf. 14*
229 A44 2k dark gray 2.90 .20
230 A44 5k dk brn ('43) 22.50 .45
231 A44 10k brn yel ('45) 11.50 1.75
Nos. 229-231 (3) 36.90 2.40
Set, never hinged 85.00

1947

Perf. 11½
229a A44 2k 7.75 1.60
230a A44 5k 29.00 2.00
231a A44 10k 11.50 *45.00*
Nos. 229a-231a (3) 48.25 *48.60*
Set, never hinged 145.00

New York World's Fair Issue of 1939 Overprinted "1940" in Black

1940, May 11 *Perf. 14*
232 A38 20a crimson 8.00 *29.00*
233 A39 35a bright ultra 8.00 *29.00*
234 A40 45a bright green 8.00 *29.00*
235 A40 2k dark gray 100.00 *425.00*
Nos. 232-235 (4) 124.00 *512.00*
Set, never hinged 230.00

SEMI-POSTAL STAMPS

Shipwreck and Rescue by Breeches Buoy SP1

Children Gathering Rock Plants SP2

Old Fisherman at Shore SP3

Unwmk.

1933, Apr. 28 Engr. *Perf. 14*
B1 SP1 10a + 10a red brown 1.90 *6.25*
B2 SP2 20a + 20a org red 1.90 *6.25*
B3 SP1 35a + 25a ultra 1.90 *6.25*
B4 SP3 50a + 25a blue grn 1.90 *6.25*
Nos. B1-B4 (4) 7.60 *25.00*
Set, never hinged 12.00

Receipts from the surtax were devoted to a special fund for use in various charitable works especially those indicated on the stamps: "Slysavarnir" (Rescue work), "Barnahaeli" (Asylum for scrofulous children), "Ellhaeli" (Asylum for the Aged).

Souvenir Sheets

King Christian X — SP4

1937, May 15 **Typo.**
B5 SP4 Sheet of 3 40.00 *290.00*
Never hinged 75.00
a. 15a violet 9.25 *50.00*
b. 25a red 9.25 *50.00*
c. 50a blue 9.25 *50.00*

Reign of Christian X, 25th anniv. Sheet sold for 2kr.

SP5

Designs: 30a, 40a, Ericsson statue, Reykjavik. 60a, Iceland's position on globe.

1938, Oct. 9 Photo. *Perf. 12*
B6 SP5 Sheet of 3 4.50 *27.50*
Never hinged 9.00
a. 30a scarlet 1.10 *11.00*
b. 40a purple 1.10 *11.00*
c. 60a deep green 1.10 *11.00*

Leif Ericsson Day, Oct. 9, 1938.

AIR POST STAMPS

No. 115 Overprinted

Perf. 14x14½

1928, May 31 Wmk. 114
C1 A8 10a red 1.40 *11.50*
Never hinged 1.25

Same Overprint on No. 82

1929, June 29 Wmk. 113 *Perf. 13*
C2 A5 50a gray & violet 57.50 *110.00*
Never hinged 140.00

Gyrfalcon AP1

Perf. 12½x12

1930, Jan. 1 Litho. Unwmk.
C3 AP1 10a dp ultra & gray blue 22.50 *67.50*
Never hinged 45.00

Imperfs were privately printed.
For overprint see No. CO1.

Snaefellsjokull, Extinct Volcano — AP2

Parliament Millenary: 20a, Fishing boat. 35a, Iceland pony. 50a, Gullfoss (Golden Falls). 1k, Ingolfour Arnarson Statue.

Wmk. 47

1930, June 1 Typo. *Perf. 14*
C4 AP2 15a org brn & dl bl 30.00 *60.00*
C5 AP2 20a bis brn & sl bl 30.00 *60.00*
C6 AP2 35a olive grn & brn 55.00 *125.00*
C7 AP2 50a dp grn & dp bl 55.00 *125.00*
C8 AP2 1k olive grn & dk red 55.00 *125.00*
Nos. C4-C8 (5) 225.00 *495.00*
Set, never hinged 425.00

Regular Issue of 1920 Overprinted

Perf. 14x14½

1931, May 25 Wmk. 114
C9 A8 30a red & green 40.00 *150.00*
C10 A8 1k dp bl & dk brn 12.50 *150.00*
C11 A8 2k ol brn & myr grn 57.50 *150.00*
Nos. C9-C11 (3) 110.00 *450.00*
Set, never hinged 210.00

Nos. 185, 128 and 187 Overprinted in Red

1933, June 16
C12 A8 1k dk bl & lt brn 150.00 *575.00*
Never hinged 325.00
C13 A8 5k brn & indigo 500. *1,375.*
Never hinged 1,050.
C14 A8 10k yel grn & blk 1,100. *2,750.*
Never hinged 2,400.

Excellent counterfeit overprints exist.
Visit of the Italian Flying Armada en route from Rome to Chicago; also for the payment of the charges on postal matter sent from Iceland to the US via the Italian seaplanes.

Plane over Thingvalla Lake — AP7

10a-20a, Plane over Thingvalla Lake. 25a-50a, Plane and Aurora Borealis. 1k-2k, Map of Iceland.

Perf. 12½x14

1934, Sept. 1 Engr. Unwmk.
C15 AP7 10a blue 2.30 *2.75*
C16 AP7 20a emerald 4.50 *6.50*
a. Perf. 14 22.50 19.00
C17 AP7 25a dark violet, perf. 14 11.50 *17.50*
Revenue cancellation 22.50
a. Perf. 12½x14 22.50 *30.00*
C18 AP7 50a red vio, perf. 14 4.00 *7.75*
C19 AP7 1k dark brown 22.50 *32.50*
Revenue cancellation 22.50
C20 AP7 2k red orange 11.50 *13.50*
Nos. C15-C20 (6) 56.30 *80.50*
Set, never hinged 110.00

AIR POST OFFICIAL STAMPS

No. C3 Overprinted In Red

1930, Jan. 1 Unwmk. *Perf. 12½x12*

CO1 AP1 10a dp ultra & gray blue 22.50 *125.00*
Never hinged 45.00

Imperfs were privately printed.

OFFICIAL STAMPS

For Nos. O1-O12, see note on condition before No. 1.

O1

O2

O3

Perf. 14x13½

1873 Typo. Wmk. 112

O1 O1 4s green *7,500.* *7,500.*
a. Imperf. 135.
O2 O1 8s red lilac 500. *650.*
On cover —
a. Imperf. 600.

Perf. 12½

O3 O1 4s green 85. *400.*
On cover *15,000.*

False and favor cancellations are often found on Nos. O1-O37. Nos. O1-O3 were valid until 7/31/76. Favor cancellations were applied starting in 1882. These cancels have sans-serif letters and dates with lines between the month and day. Values of stamps with favor cancellations range from $60 (#O3) to $1,250 (#O1). The imperforate varieties lack gum.

1876-95 *Perf. 14x13½*

O4 O2 3a yellow 35.00 *55.00*
On cover *6,000.*
O5 O2 5a brown 9.00 *15.00*
On cover *4,500.*
a. Imperf. 300.00
O6 O2 10a blue 67.50 15.00
On cover *4,500.*
a. 10a ultramarine 400.00 55.00
On cover —
O7 O2 16a carmine 22.50 *50.00*
On cover —
O8 O2 20a yellow green 22.50 *40.00*
On cover *4,500.*
O9 O2 50a rose lilac ('95) 67.50 *85.00*
Nos. O4-O9 (6) 224.00 *260.00*

1898-1902 *Perf. 13*

O10 O2 3a yellow 13.50 *32.50*
O11 O2 4a gray ('01) 32.50 *40.00*
On cover —
O12 O2 10a ultra ('02) 62.50 *110.00*
Nos. O10-O12 (3) 108.50 *182.50*

A 5a brown, perf. 13, Wmk. 112, exists. It was not regularly issued.
See note after No. O30.
For overprints see Nos. O20-O30.

1902 Wmk. 113 *Perf. 13*

O13 O3 3a buff & black 4.00 2.75
On cover 375.00
O14 O3 4a dp grn & blk 4.00 2.25
On cover 375.00
O15 O3 5a org brn & blk 3.00 *4.00*
On cover 375.00
O16 O3 10a ultra & black 3.50 *4.00*
On cover 350.00
O17 O3 16a carmine & blk 3.00 *14.50*
On cover 375.00
O18 O3 20a green & blk 15.00 7.75
On cover 450.00
O19 O3 50a violet & blk 7.00 *11.00*
On cover 450.00
Nos. O13-O19 (7) 39.50 *46.25*

Stamps of 1876-1901 Overprinted in Black

1902-03 Wmk. 112 *Perf. 13*

O20 O2 3a yellow 1.00 *2.40*
a. "I" before Gildi omitted 90.00
b. Inverted overprint 17.00 *22.50*
c. As "a," invtd. 225.00
d. Pair, one with invtd. ovpt. 90.00
e. '03-'03 225.00
f. 02'-'03 225.00
O21 O2 4a gray 1.00 *2.25*
a. "I" before Gildi omitted 100.00
b. Inverted overprint 29.00 *40.00*
e. '03-'03 290.00 *150.00*
f. 02'-'03 290.00
g. Pair, one without ovpt. 90.00
h. Pair, one with invtd. ovpt. 1,000.
i. "L" only of "I GILDI" inverted 175.00
O22 O2 5a brown .80 *2.25*
O23 O2 10a ultramarine .80 *2.25*
a. "I" before Gildi omitted 29.00
b. Inverted overprint 22.50 *32.50*
c. '03-'03 230.00
d. 02'-'03 230.00
e. "L" only of "I GILDI" 25.00
f. As "e," inverted 110.00
g. "IL" only of "I GILDI" 55.00
O24 O2 20a yel green .80 *25.00*
Nos. O20-O24 (5) 4.40 *34.15*

Perf. 14x13½

O25 O2 3a yellow 325.00 *1,100.*
a. "02'-'03" 625.00
b. '03-'03 625.00
O26 O2 5a brown 8.00 *125.00*
a. Inverted overprint 55.00
b. '03-'03 225.00
c. 02'-'03 225.00
d. "L" only of "I GILDI" inverted 225.00
O27 O2 10a blue 425.00 *850.00*
a. "I" before Gildi omitted 750.00
b. Inverted overprint 600.00 *900.00*
c. '03-'03 850.00
d. 02'-'03 850.00
O28 O2 16a carmine 17.00 *70.00*
a. "I" before Gildi omitted 225.00
b. Double overprint 110.00
c. Dbl. ovpt., one inverted 350.00
d. Inverted overprint 100.00 *140.00*
e. '03-'03 325.00
O29 O2 20a yel green 22.50 *80.00*
a. Inverted overprint 100.00 *140.00*
b. '03-'03 290.00
c. 02'-'03 290.00
O30 O2 50a red lilac 6.50 *60.00*
a. "I" before Gildi omitted 45.00
b. Inverted overprint 90.00
Nos. O25-O30 (6) 804.00 *2,285.*

Nos. O10-O12, O20-O24, O28 and O30 were reprinted in 1904. They have the watermark of 1902 (type 113) and are perf. 13. Value $60 each. Without overprint $80 each.

Christian IX, Frederik VIII — O4

Christian X — O5

Engraved Center

1907-08 Wmk. 113 *Perf. 13*

O31 O4 3a yellow & gray 6.75 *8.00*
O32 O4 4a green & gray 3.50 *8.50*
O33 O4 5a brn org & gray 10.00 4.00
O34 O4 10a deep bl & gray 2.25 *3.00*
O35 O4 15a lt blue & gray 4.50 *8.50*
O36 O4 16a carmine & gray 4.50 *29.00*
O37 O4 20a yel grn & gray 12.50 5.50
O38 O4 50a violet & gray 7.25 *10.00*
Nos. O31-O38 (8) 51.25 *76.50*

1918 Wmk. 114 *Perf. 14x14½*

O39 O4 15a lt bl & gray 14.00 *35.00*

1920-30 Typo.

O40 O5 3a yellow & gray 4.50 *3.50*
O41 O5 4a dp grn & gray 1.10 *3.25*
O42 O5 5a orange & gray 1.10 1.10
O43 O5 10a dk bl & gray 10.00 1.10
O44 O5 15a lt blue & gray .60 *.90*
O45 O5 20a yel grn & gray 45.00 4.00
O46 O5 50a violet & gray 40.00 2.00
O47 O5 1k car & gray 40.00 2.50
O48 O5 2k bl & blk ('30) 7.00 *19.00*
O49 O5 5k brn & blk ('30) 35.00 *50.00*
Nos. O40-O49 (10) 184.30 87.35

See No. O68.

Nos. 97 and 98 Overprinted

1922, May Wmk. 113 *Perf. 13*

O50 A7 2k rose, larger letters, no period 29.00 *55.00*
a. Smaller letters, with period 85.00 60.00
O51 A7 5k brown 225.00 *250.00*

No. 115 Surcharged

1923 Wmk. 114 *Perf. 14x14½*

O52 A8 20a on 10a red 25.00 2.25

Parliament Millenary Issue

#152-166 Overprinted in Red or Blue

1930, Jan. 1 Unwmk. *Perf. 12½x12*

O53 A15 3a (R) 14.00 *40.00*
O54 A15 5a (R) 14.00 *40.00*
O55 A15 7a (R) 14.00 *40.00*
O56 A15 10a (Bl) 14.00 *40.00*
O57 A15 15a (R) 14.00 *40.00*
O58 A15 20a (Bl) 14.00 *40.00*
O59 A15 25a (Bl) 14.00 *40.00*
O60 A15 30a (R) 14.00 *40.00*
O61 A15 35a (R) 14.00 *40.00*
O62 A15 40a (Bl) 14.00 *40.00*
O63 A15 50a (Bl) 140.00 *350.00*
O64 A15 1k (R) 140.00 *350.00*
O65 A15 2k (R) 175.00 *375.00*
O66 A15 5k (Bl) 140.00 *350.00*
O67 A15 10k (Bl) 140.00 *350.00*
Nos. O53-O67 (15) 875.00 *2,175.*

Type of 1920 Issue Redrawn

1931 Wmk. 114 Typo.

O68 O5 20a yel grn & gray 37.50 3.25

For differences in redrawing see note after No. 187.

No. 82 Overprinted in Black

Overprint 15mm long

1936, Dec. 7 Wmk. 113 *Perf. 13*

O69 A5 50a gray & vio 22.50 *25.00*

Same Overprint on Nos. 180 and 115

Perf. 14x14½

Wmk. 114

O70 A8 7a yellow green 2.90 *29.00*
O71 A8 10a red 10.00 2.00
Nos. O69-O71 (3) 35.40 *56.00*

INDIA

ˈin-dē-ə

LOCATION — Southern, central Asia
GOVT. — Republic
AREA — 1,266,732 sq. mi.
POP. — 683,810,051 (1981)
CAPITAL — New Delhi

On August 15, 1947, India was divided into two self-governing dominions: Pakistan and India. India became a republic in 1950.

The stamps of pre-partition India fall into three groups:

1) Issues inscribed simply "East India" (to 1881) and "India" (from 1882), for use mainly in British India proper, but available and valid throughout the country;

2) Issues as above and overprinted with one of the names of the six "Convention" states (Chamba, Faridkot, Gwalior, Jind, Nabha and Patiala) which had a postal convention with British India, for use in these states.

3) Issues of the feudatory states, over which the British India government exercised little internal control, valid for use only within the states issuing them.

12 Pies = 1 Anna
16 Annas = 1 Rupee

Catalogue values for unused stamps in this country are for Never Hinged items, beginning with Scott 168 in the regular postage section, Scott 51 in Hyderabad regular issues, Scott O54 in Hyderabad officials, Scott 49 in Jaipur regular issues, Scott O30 in Jaipur officials, Scott 39 in Soruth regular issues and Scott O19 in Soruth official

All of the values are for Never Hinged for all of the items in the sections for Jasdan, Rajasthan, and Travancore-Cochin.

Watermarks

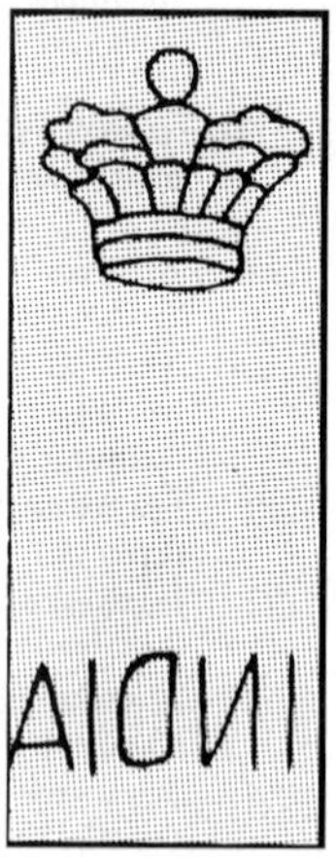

Wmk. 36 — Crown and INDIA

Wmk. 37 — Coat of Arms in Sheet. (Reduced illustration. Watermark covers a large section of the sheet.)

Wmk. 38 — Elephant's Head

Wmk. 39 — Star

Wmk. 40

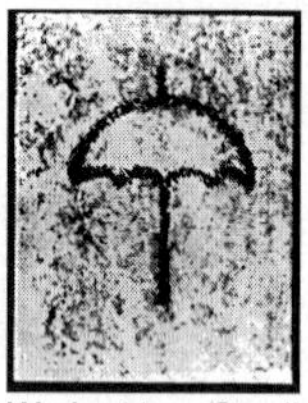

Wmk. 41 — Small Umbrella

Wmk. 42 — Urdu Characters

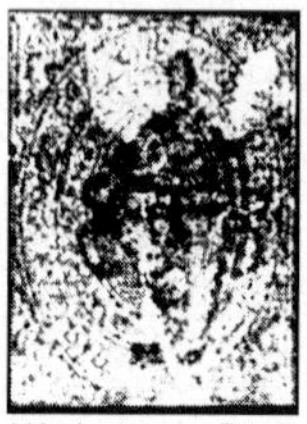

Wmk. 43 — Shell

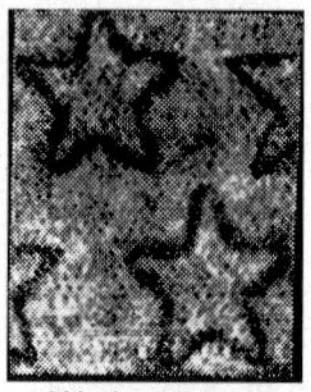

Wmk. 196 — Multiple Stars

Wmk. 211 — Urdu Characters

Wmk. 294 — Letters and Ornaments in Sheet (size reduced)

SCINDE DISTRICT POST

A1

1852, July 1 Embossed *Imperf.*

A1	A1	½a *white*	3,750.	825.
		On cover		12,000.
A2	A1	½a blue	*10,000.*	3,750.
		On cover		22,500.
A3	A1	½a *red*	—	8,250.
		On cover		—

Obsolete October, 1854.

Nos. A1-A3 were issued without gum. No. A3 is embossed on red wafer. It is usually found with cracks and these examples are worth somewhat less than the values given, depending on the degree of cracking.

Two examples of No. 3 are known unused, three on cover or part of cover.

Covers: On cover values are for very fine examples. Average to fine examples sell for approximately 40% of the values given.

GENERAL ISSUES

Unused stamps of India are valued with original gum as defined in the catalogue introduction except for Nos. 1-7 which are valued without gum.

Queen Victoria
A1 A2

A3

A4

A5

East India Company

Litho.; Typo. (#5)

1854 Wmk. 37 *Imperf.*

1	A1	½a red	825.00	
2	A2	½a blue	57.50	16.00
		On cover		100.00
		On cover, pair		250.00
a.		½a deep blue	75.00	22.50
b.		Printed on both sides		*8,500.*
4	A3	1a red	65.00	35.00
		On cover		200.00
		On cover, pair		500.00
a.		1a scarlet	130.00	45.00
5	A4	2a green	90.00	25.00
		On cover		240.00
		On cover, pair		600.00
a.		Half used as ½a on cover		*200,000.*
6	A5	4a red & blue	4,500.	450.00
		On cover		625.00
		On cover, pair		1,500.
a.		4a deep red & blue	4,500.	550.00
		Cut to shape		14.00
c.		Head inverted		*90,000.*
		As "c," cut to shape		*35,000.*
e.		Double impression of head		*6,250.*

No. 1 was not placed in use.

Nos. 2, 4, 5 and 6 are known with unofficial perforation.

There are 3 dies of No. 2, and 2 dies of No. 4, showing slight differences.

There are 4 dies of the head and 2 dies of the frame of No. 6.

Beware of forgeries.

A6

1855

7	A6	1a red	850.00	150.00
		On cover		525.00

No. 7 was printed from a lithographic transfer made from the original die retouched. The lines of the bust at the lower left are nearly straight and meet in a point.

Beware of forgeries.

Nos. 9-35 are normally found with very heavy cancelations, and values are for stamps so canceled. Lightly canceled copies are seldom seen. The same holds true for Nos. O1-O26.

Diadem includes Maltese Crosses — A7

1855-64 Unwmk. Typo. *Perf. 14*

Blue Glazed Paper

9	A7	4a black	475.00	16.00
		On cover		125.00
a.		Imperf., pair	*3,250.*	*3,250.*
b.		Half used as 2a on cover		*8,000.*
10	A7	8a rose	450.00	15.00
		On cover		175.00
a.		Imperf., pair	1,900.	—
b.		Half used as 4a on cover		*67,500.*

1855-64 White Paper

11	A7	½a blue	60.00	1.75
a.		Imperf., pair	365.00	*1,000.*
12	A7	1a brown	55.00	2.50
a.		Imperf., pair	800.00	*1,400.*
b.		Vert. pair, imperf between		
c.		Half used as ½a on cover		*75,000.*
13	A7	2a dull rose	475.00	30.00
a.		Imperf., pair	2,000.	2,000.
14	A7	2a yellow green	725.00	825.00
a.		Imperf., pair	2,000.	
15	A7	2a buff	250.00	30.00
a.		2a orange	450.00	32.50
b.		Imperf., pair	1,750.	—
16	A7	4a black	275.00	7.00
a.		Imperf., pair	2,000.	2,000.
b.		Diagonal half used as 2a on cover		*27,500.*
17	A7	4a green ('64)	1,000.	40.00
18	A7	8a rose	300.00	22.50
a.		Half used as 4a on cover		*67,500.*

No. 14 was not regularly issued. See note after No. 25.

Many stamps of types A7-A90 are overprinted "Service" or "On H. M. S." For these, see listings of Official stamps.

Crown Colony

Queen Victoria — A8

1860-64 Unwmk. *Perf. 14*

19	A8	8p lilac	42.50	6.00
a.		Diagonal half used as 4p on cover		*75,000.*
b.		Imperf., pair	2,100.	*3,250.*
19C	A8	8p lilac, *bluish*	210.00	90.00

1865-67 Wmk. 38

20	A7	½a blue	6.50	.35
a.		Imperf., pair		1,400.
21	A8	8p lilac	9.00	9.00
22	A7	1a brown	3.00	.40
23	A7	2a brownish orange	27.50	1.60
a.		2a yellow	80.00	4.00
b.		Imperf., pair		3,000.
24	A7	4a green	375.00	22.50
25	A7	8a rose	1,250.	80.00

No. 21 was variously surcharged locally, "NINE" or "NINE PIE," to indicate that it was being sold for 9 pies (the soldier's letter rate had been raised from 8 to 9 pies). These surcharges were made without government authorization.

Stamps of types A7 and A9 overprinted with crown and surcharged with new values were for use in Straits Settlements.

A9

A10

Diadem: Rows of pearls & diamonds — A11

FOUR ANNAS

Type I — Slanting line at corner of mouth extends downward only. Shading about mouth and chin. Pointed chin.

Type II — Line at corner of mouth extends both up and down. Upper lip and chin are defined by a colored line. Rounded chin.

1866-68

26	A9	4a green, type I	70.00	3.50
26B	A9	4a blue grn, type II	22.50	2.50
27	A10	6a8p slate	50.00	22.50
a.		Imperf., pair	2,000.	
28	A11	8a rose ('68)	30.00	6.00
		Nos. 26-28 (4)	172.50	34.50

Type A11 is a redrawing of type A7. Type A7 has Maltese crosses in the diadem, while type A11 has shaded lozenges.

A12

SIX ANNAS
Type I — "POSTAGE" 3½mm high
Type II — "POSTAGE" 2½mm high

Blue Glazed Paper
Green Overprint
Perf. 14 Vert.

1866, June 28 **Wmk. 36**

29	A12	6a violet, type I	625.00	125.00
		On cover		700.
a.		Inverted overprint		*9,500.*
30	A12	6a violet, type II	1,200.	150.00
		On cover		1,000.

Nos. 29 and 30 were made from revenue stamps with the labels at top and bottom cut off. Most and sometimes all of the watermark was removed with the labels.

These stamps are often found with cracked surface or scuffs. Such examples sell for somewhat less.

A13

A14

A15

A16

1873-76 **Wmk. 38** ***Perf. 14***

31	A7	½a blue, redrawn	4.50	.55
32	A13	9p lilac ('74)	15.00	15.00
33	A14	6a bister ('76)	6.00	1.60
34	A15	12a red brown ('76)	8.50	*21.00*
35	A16	1r slate ('74)	42.50	25.00
		Nos. 31-35 (5)	76.50	63.15

In the redrawn ½ anna the lines of the mouth are more deeply cut, making the lips appear fuller and more open, and the nostril is defined by a curved line.

Victorian and Edwardian stamps overprinted "Postal Service" and new denominations were customs fee due stamps, not postage stamps.

Empire

A17

A18

A19

A20

A21

A22

A23

A24

A25

A26

A27

1882-87 **Wmk. 39**

36	A17	½a green	4.00	.20
a.		Double impression	425.00	525.00
37	A18	9p rose	1.10	*2.00*
38	A19	1a maroon	4.00	.35
a.		1a violet brown	4.00	.35
39	A20	1a6p bister brown	1.10	*1.40*
40	A21	2a ultra	4.00	.35
a.		Double impression	875.00	*1,150.*
41	A22	3a brown org	8.25	1.10
a.		3a orange	15.00	6.25
42	A23	4a olive green	15.00	1.10
43	A24	4a6p green	19.00	5.00
44	A25	8a red violet	24.00	2.25
a.		8a rose lilac	22.50	2.25
45	A26	12a violet, *red*	7.50	3.50
46	A27	1r gray	16.00	5.50
		Nos. 36-46 (11)	103.95	22.75

A 6a bister and a 12a Venetian red were prepared but not issued. A postal counterfeit exists of No. 46. Examples are scarce.

No. 40a used value is for copy with postal cancellation.

See Nos. 56-58. For surcharges see Nos. 47, 53 and British East Africa No. 59. For overprints see Nos. M2-M4, M6-M9, Gwalior Nos. O1-O5.

Beginning with the 1882-87 issue, higher denomination stamps exist used for telegrams. The telegraph cancellation has concentric circles. These for 10-15% of the postally used values.

No. 43 Surcharged

1891, Jan. 1

47	A24	2½a on 4a6p green	3.25	.65

A28

A29

1892

48	A28	2a6p green	2.75	.45
49	A29	1r aniline car & grn	11.00	2.25
a.		1r carmine rose & green	20.00	5.00

See No. 59. For overprints see Nos. M5, M10 and Gwalior No. O6.

Queen Victoria
A30 A31

1895, Sept. 1

50	A30	2r brown & rose	37.50	12.50
51	A30	3r green & brown	27.50	11.00
52	A30	5r violet & ultra	40.00	27.50
		Nos. 50-52 (3)	105.00	51.00

Used high values such as Nos. 50-52, 71-76, 95-98, 124-125, as well as similar high value official issues are for postally used examples. Stamps bearing telegraph or revenue cancellations sell for much lower prices. Most telegraph cancellations on issues of Edward VII and George V can be recognized by the appearance of "T," "TEL" or "GTO" or if they contain the concentric circles of a target.

No. 36 Surcharged

1898

53	A17	¼a on ½a green	.20	*.55*
a.		Double surcharge	190.00	
b.		Double impression of stamp	250.00	

For #61, 81 with this overprint see #77, 105.

1899

54	A31	3p carmine rose	.45	.20

For overprint see No. M1, Gwalior No. O11.

1900

55	A31	3p gray	.80	*1.10*
56	A17	½a light green	1.75	.50
57	A19	1a carmine rose	2.00	.20
58	A21	2a violet	3.50	2.00
59	A28	2a6p ultramarine	3.50	4.25
		Nos. 55-59 (5)	11.55	8.05

For overprints see Nos. M11, Gwalior O7-O10.

Edward VII — A32

A33

A34

A35

A36

A37

A38

A39

A40

A41

A42

A43

1902-09

60	A32	3p gray	1.10	.20
61	A33	½a green	1.10	.20
a.		Booklet pane of 6 ('04)	32.50	
62	A34	1a carmine rose	1.60	.20
a.		Booklet pane of 6 ('04)	92.50	

63 A35 2a violet 4.25 .45
64 A36 2a6p ultra 5.00 .65
65 A37 3a brown org 5.00 .65
66 A38 4a olive green 3.25 .65
67 A39 6a bister 11.00 4.75
68 A40 8a red violet 8.75 1.10
69 A41 12a violet, *red* 9.00 2.25
70 A42 1r car rose & grn 6.75 .75
a. 1r rose & green ('11) 40.00 4.50
71 A43 2r brown & rose 27.50 4.50
72 A43 3r green & brn ('04) 27.50 20.00
73 A43 5r violet & ultra ('04) 60.00 40.00
74 A43 10r carmine rose & green ('09) 110.00 30.00
75 A43 15r olive gray & ultra ('09) 140.00 45.00
76 A43 25r ultra & org brown 825.00 850.00
Telegraph cancel 300.00
Nos. 60-75 (16) 421.80 151.35

For overprints see Nos. M12-M20, Gwalior Nos. O12-O18.

No. 61 Surcharged Like No. 53

1905

77 A33 ¼a on ½a green .60 .20
a. Inverted surcharge 850.00

A44

A45

1906

78 A44 ½a green 3.25 .20
a. Booklet pane of 4 17.50
79 A45 1a carmine rose 1.90 .20
a. Booklet pane of 4 25.00

For overprints see Gwalior Nos. O19-O20.

A46

A47

A48

A49

A50

A51

A52

A53

A54

A55

George V — A56

1911-23 **Wmk. 39**

80 A46 3p gray 1.50 .20
a. Booklet pane of 4 25.00
81 A47 ½a green 1.60 .20
a. Double impression 175.00
b. Booklet pane of 4 21.00
82 A48 1a carmine rose 2.75 .20
a. Printed on both sides
b. Booklet pane of 4 35.00
83 A48 1a dk brown ('22) .85 .20
a. Booklet pane of 4 42.50
84 A49 2a dull violet 3.50 .40
a. Booklet pane of 4 42.50
85 A50 2a6p ultramarine 2.90 *3.25*
86 A51 3a brown org 4.25 .20
87 A51 3a ultra ('23) 13.00 .65
88 A52 4a olive green 8.00 .55
89 A53 6a yel bister 4.25 1.40
90 A53 6a bister ('15) 4.25 1.10
91 A54 8a red violet 6.25 1.25
92 A55 12a claret 6.50 2.40
93 A56 1r grn & red brn 16.00 1.60
94 A56 2r brn & car rose 22.50 1.90
95 A56 5r vio & ultra 55.00 7.00
96 A56 10r car rose & grn 75.00 12.50
97 A56 15r ol grn & ultra 95.00 25.00
98 A56 25r ultra & brn org 175.00 37.50
Nos. 80-98 (19) 498.10 97.50

See Nos. 106-125. For type surcharged see No. 104. For overprints see Nos. M23-M25, M27, M29-M37, M39-M43, Gwalior No. O29.

Nos. 93-98 also were used to pay for radio licenses, and stamps so used include "WIRELESS" in the cancel. Used values so canceled are worth 10-15% of the values shown, which are for postally used examples.

A57

1913-26

99 A57 2a6p ultramarine 2.90 .25
100 A57 2a6p brown org ('26) 6.00 6.00

See #112. For overprints see #M28, M38.

"One and Half" — A58

"One and a Half" — A59

1919

101 A58 1½a chocolate 3.25 .35
a. Booklet pane of 4 35.00

For overprint see No. M26.

1921-26

102 A59 1½a chocolate 3.50 *4.25*
103 A59 1½a rose ('26) 3.25 .35

See No. 109.

Type of 1911-26 Surcharged

1921

104 A48 9p on 1a rose .90 .35
a. Surcharged "NINE-NINE" 80.00 *140.00*
b. Surcharged "PIES-PIES" 80.00 *140.00*
c. Double surcharge 160.00 *190.00*
e. Booklet pane of 4 27.50

Forgeries exist of Nos. 104a-104c.

No. 81 Surcharged Like No. 53

1922

105 A47 ¼a on ½a green .55 .40
a. Inverted surcharge 10.00
b. Pair, one without surcharge 225.00

Types of 1911-26 Issues

1926-36 **Wmk. 196**

106 A46 3p slate .35 .20
107 A47 ½a green 1.40 .20
108 A48 1a dark brown .55 .20
a. Tete beche pair 1.50 *11.00*
b. Booklet pane of 4 16.00
109 A59 1½a car rose ('29) 2.25 .20
110 A49 2a dull violet 1.50 .20
a. Booklet pane of 4 32.50
111 A49 2a ver ('34) 4.00 .55
a. Small die ('36) 5.00 .35

112 A57 2a6p buff 1.90 .20
113 A51 3a ultramarine 9.00 1.25
114 A51 3a blue ('30) 9.00 .20
115 A51 3a car rose ('32) 6.25 .20
116 A52 4a olive green 1.60 .20
117 A53 6a bister ('35) 8.00 2.00
118 A54 8a red violet 4.25 .20
119 A55 12a claret 5.25 .35
120 A56 1r green & brown 5.25 .50
121 A56 2r brn org & car rose 12.50 .85
122 A56 5r dk vio & ultra 25.00 1.40
123 A56 10r carmine & grn 50.00 3.25
124 A56 15r ol grn & ultra 25.00 32.50
125 A56 25r blue & ocher 100.00 40.00
Nos. 106-125 (20) 273.05 84.65

No. 111 measures 19x22½mm, while the small die, No. 111a, measures 18½x22mm.

For overprints see Gwalior #O30-O39, O44-O45.

A60

A61

1926-32 **Typo.**

126 A60 2a dull violet .55 .20
a. Tete beche pair 10.00 37.50
b. 2a rose violet .45 .20
c. Booklet pane of 4 19.00
127 A60 2a vermilion ('32) 11.00 7.00
128 A61 4a olive green 6.25 .20
Nos. 126-128 (3) 17.80 7.40

For overprints see Gwalior Nos. O33-O34.

Fortress of Purana Qila — A62

George V Flanked by Dominion Columns A67

½a, War Memorial Arch. 1a, Council Building. 2a, Viceroy's House. 3a, Parliament Building.

Wmk. 196 Sideways

1931, Feb. 9 **Litho.** ***Perf. 13½x14***

129 A62 ¼a brown & ol grn 2.50 3.75
130 A62 ½a green & violet 1.50 .50
131 A62 1a choc & red vio 1.50 .25
132 A62 2a blue & green 1.90 1.25
133 A62 3a car & choc 4.50 2.50
134 A67 1r violet & green 11.00 *25.00*
Nos. 129-134 (6) 22.90 33.25

Change of the seat of Government from Calcutta to New Delhi.

A68

A69

A70

Wmk. 196

1932, Apr. 22 **Litho.** ***Perf. 14***

135 A68 9p dark green 1.90 .20
136 A69 1a3p violet .65 .20
137 A70 3a6p deep blue 4.25 .20
Nos. 135-137 (3) 6.80 .60

No. 135 exists both litho. and typo.
For overprints see Gwalior #O41 and O43.

A71

A72

1934 **Typo.**

138 A71 ½a green 4.25 .20
139 A72 1a dark brown 2.25 .20

For overprints see Gwalior #O40 and O42.

Silver Jubilee Issue

Gateway of India, Bombay A73

Designs: 9p, Victoria Memorial, Calcutta. 1a, Rameswaram Temple, Madras. 1¼a, Jain Temple, Calcutta. 2½a, Taj Mahal, Agra. 3½a, Golden Temple, Amritsar. 8a, Pagoda, Mandalay.

Wmk. 196 Sideways

1935 **Litho.** ***Perf. 13½x14***

142 A73 ½a lt green & black .75 .20
143 A73 9p dull green & blk .50 .20
144 A73 1a brown & black .50 .20
145 A73 1¼a violet & black .50 .20
146 A73 2½a brown org & blk 1.75 .40
147 A73 3½a blue & black 3.50 1.00
148 A73 8a rose lilac & blk 4.00 2.25
Nos. 142-148 (7) 11.50 4.45

25th anniv. of the reign of George V.

A80

A82

King George VI

Dak Runner A81

Mail transport: 2a6p, Dak bullock cart. 3a, Dak tonga. 3a6p, Dak camel. 4a, Mail train. 6a, Mail steamer. 8a, Mail truck. 12a, 14a, Mail plane.

Perf. 13½x14 or 14x13½

1937-40 **Typo.** **Wmk. 196**

150 A80 3p slate .35 .20
151 A80 ½a brown .90 .20
152 A80 9p green 2.50 .25
153 A80 1a carmine .30 .20
a. Tete beche pair .55 1.75
b. Booklet pane of 4 4.50
154 A81 2a scarlet 1.75 .30
155 A81 2a6p purple .55 .25
156 A81 3a yellow green 3.25 .30
157 A81 3a6p ultramarine 2.10 .50
158 A81 4a dark brown 8.50 .25
159 A81 6a peacock blue 8.50 .80
160 A81 8a blue violet 5.00 .50
161 A81 12a car lake 11.00 1.10
161A A81 14a rose vio ('40) 12.50 1.25
162 A82 1r brown & slate .75 .20
163 A82 2r dk brn & dk violet 2.75 .35
164 A82 5r dp ultra & dk green 12.00 .60
165 A82 10r rose car & dk violet 12.00 1.00
166 A82 15r dk green & dk brown 60.00 *75.00*
167 A82 25r dk vio & blue violet 85.00 20.00
Nos. 150-167 (19) 229.70 *103.25*

The King's portrait is larger on No. 161A than on other stamps of type A81.

For overprints see Gwalior Nos. O48-O51.

Catalogue values for unused stamps in this section, from this point to the end of the section, are for Never Hinged items.

A83

A84

A85

Perf. 13½x14

1941-43 Typo. Wmk. 196

168	A83	3p slate ('42)	.35	.20
169	A83	½a rose vio ('42)	1.25	.20
170	A83	9p light green	1.25	.20
171	A83	1a car rose ('43)	1.25	.20
172	A84	1a3p bister	1.25	.20
172A	A84	1½a dark pur ('42)	1.50	.20
173	A84	2a scarlet	1.90	.20
174	A84	3a violet	3.75	.20
175	A84	3½a ultramarine	1.25	.30
176	A85	4a chocolate	.90	.20
177	A85	6a peacock blue	4.25	.20
178	A85	8a blue violet	1.90	.30
179	A85	12a carmine lake	3.75	.50
		Nos. 168-179 (13)	24.55	3.10

Early printings of the 1½a and 3a were lithographed.

For surcharge see No. 199.

For stamps with this overprint, or a smaller type, see Oman (Muscat).

Symbols of Victory A86

1946, Jan. 2 Litho. *Perf. 13*

195	A86	9p green	.50	.60
196	A86	1½a dull purple	.30	.25
197	A86	3½a ultramarine	.70	.50
198	A86	12a brown lake	1.75	.75
		Nos. 195-198 (4)	3.25	2.10

Victory of the Allied Nations in WWII.

No. 172 Surcharged With New Value and Bars

1946, Aug. 8 *Perf. 13½x14*

199	A84	3p on 1a3p bister	.20	.20

AIR POST STAMPS

De Havilland Hercules over Lake AP1

Wmk. 196 Sideways

1929-30 Typo. *Perf. 14*

C1	AP1	2a dull green	.55	.30
C2	AP1	3a deep blue	.80	.55
C3	AP1	4a gray olive	2.25	1.10
a.		4a olive green ('30)	2.75	1.10
C4	AP1	6a bister	2.75	.70
C5	AP1	8a red violet	3.25	3.25
C6	AP1	12a brown red	9.75	9.75
		Nos. C1-C6 (6)	19.35	15.65

MILITARY STAMPS

China Expeditionary Force

Regular Issues of India, 1882-99, Overprinted

1900 Wmk. 39 *Perf. 14*

M1	A31	3p carmine rose	.30	.75
M2	A17	½a dark green	.60	.90
M3	A19	1a maroon	3.25	1.00
M4	A21	2a ultra	2.50	5.75
M5	A28	2a6p green	10.00	18.00
M6	A22	3a orange	2.25	15.00
M7	A23	4a olive green	2.25	6.50
M8	A25	8a red violet	2.25	10.00
M9	A26	12a violet, *red*	12.00	15.00
M10	A29	1r car rose & grn	12.00	12.50
a.		Double overprint		
		Nos. M1-M10 (10)	47.40	85.40

The 1a6p of this set was overprinted, but not issued. Value $250.

Overprinted on 1900 Issue of India

1904, Feb. 27

M11	A19	1a carmine rose	20.00	7.00

Overprinted on 1902-09 Issue of India

1904

M12	A32	3p gray	2.40	3.25
M13	A34	1a carmine rose	4.25	.60
M14	A35	2a violet	11.00	1.50
M15	A36	2a6p ultra	2.50	3.50
M16	A37	3a brown org	3.00	3.25
M17	A38	4a olive green	6.75	9.00
M18	A40	8a red violet	6.25	6.75
M19	A41	12a violet, *red*	8.50	15.00
M20	A42	1r car rose & grn	10.00	21.00
		Nos. M12-M20 (9)	54.65	63.85

Overprinted on 1906 Issue of India

1909

M21	A44	½a green	1.50	1.00
M22	A45	1a carmine rose	1.50	.40

Overprinted on 1911-19 Issues of India

1913-21

M23	A46	3p gray	2.60	10.00
M24	A47	½a green	1.90	2.00
M25	A48	1a carmine rose	2.40	1.25
M26	A58	1½a chocolate	18.00	42.50
M27	A49	2a violet	8.25	30.00
M28	A57	2a6p ultra	6.75	15.00
M29	A51	3a brown org	19.00	100.00
M30	A52	4a olive green	15.00	100.00
M31	A54	8a red violet	15.00	200.00
M32	A55	12a claret	15.00	82.50
M33	A56	1r grn & red brn	47.50	150.00
		Nos. M23-M33 (11)	151.40	733.25

Issue dates: No. M23, 1913; others, 1921.

Indian Expeditionary Force

Regular Issues of India, 1911-13, Overprinted

1914 Wmk. 39 *Perf. 14*

M34	A46	3p gray	.20	.20
a.		Double overprint	30.00	25.00
M35	A47	½a green	.20	.20
M36	A48	1a carmine rose	.20	.20
M37	A49	2a violet	.30	.25
M38	A57	2a6p ultra	.30	.25
M39	A51	3a brown org	.60	.60
M40	A52	4a olive green	.65	.65
M41	A54	8a red violet	1.00	1.00
M42	A55	12a claret	1.75	1.75
a.		Double overprint		
M43	A56	1r grn & red brn	3.25	3.50
		Nos. M34-M43 (10)	8.45	8.60

OFFICIAL STAMPS

Nos. O1-O26 are normally found with very heavy cancellations, and values are for stamps so canceled. Lightly canceled copies are seldom seen.

Regular Issues Overprinted in Black

1866, Aug. 1 Unwmk. *Perf. 14*

O1	A7	½a blue	1,100.	140.00
a.		Inverted overprint		
O3	A7	1a brown		140.00
O4	A7	8a rose	22.50	50.00

The 8p lilac unwatermarked (No. 19) with "Service" overprint was not officially issued.

Wmk. 38

O5	A7	½a blue	225.00	12.50
a.		Inverted overprint		
b.		Without period		210.00
O6	A8	8p lilac	20.00	52.50
O7	A7	1a brown	190.00	15.00
a.		Inverted overprint		
O8	A7	2a yellow	175.00	85.00
a.		Imperf.		
b.		Inverted overprint		
O9	A7	4a green	200.00	80.00
a.		Inverted overprint		
O10	A9	4a green (I)	1,000.	250.00

Reprints were made of #O5, O7, O10 (type II).

Revenue Stamps Surcharged or Overprinted

Queen Victoria — O1

Blue Glazed Paper
Black Surcharge

1866 Wmk. 36 *Perf. 14 Vertically*

O11	O1	2a violet	350.00	250.00

The note after No. 30 will apply here also.

No. O10 is often found with cracked surface or scuffs. Such examples sell for somewhat less.

Reprints of No. O11 are surcharged in either black or green, and have the word "SERVICE" 16½x2½mm, instead of 16½x2¾mm and "TWO ANNAS" 18x3mm, instead of 20x3¼mm.

O2

O3

O4

1866

Green Overprint

O12	O2	2a violet	825.	325.
O13	O3	4a violet	4,500.	1,250.
O14	O4	8a violet	5,000.	5,000.

The note after No. 30 will apply here also.

These stamps are often found with cracked surface or scuffs. Such examples sell for somewhat less.

Reprints of No. O12 have the overprint in sans-serif letters 2¼mm high, instead of Roman letters 2½mm high. On the reprints of No. O13 "SERVICE" measures 16½x2¼mm, instead of 20¼x3mm and "POSTAGE" 18x2¼mm, instead of 22x3mm.

On No. O14 "SERVICE" is 20½mm long, instead of 20mm and "POSTAGE" is 23mm long, instead of 22mm. All three overprints are in a darker green than on the original stamps.

O5

Green Overprint

1866 Wmk. 40 *Perf. 15½x15*

Lilac Paper

O15	O5	½a violet	425.00	85.00
a.		Double overprint	3,000.	

Regular Issues Overprinted in Black

1866-73 Wmk. 38 *Perf. 14*

O16	A7	½a blue	30.00	.35
O17	A7	½a bl, re-engraved	140.00	67.50
a.		Double overprint		
O18	A7	1a brown	32.50	.40
O19	A7	2a orange	4.50	2.00
a.		2a yellow	20.00	2.25
O20	A9	4a green (I)	2.75	1.50
O21	A11	8a rose	3.00	1.50
		Nos. O16-O21 (6)	212.75	73.25

The 6a8p with this overprint was not issued. Value $25.

Overprinted in Black

1874-82

O22	A7	½a blue, re-engraved	8.00	.20
a.		Blue overprint	350.00	45.00
O23	A7	1a brown	12.50	.20
a.		Blue overprint	550.00	120.00
O24	A7	2a orange	40.00	17.50
O25	A9	4a green (I)	12.50	2.75
O26	A11	8a rose	4.25	4.00
		Nos. O22-O26 (5)	77.25	24.65

1883-97 Wmk. 39

O27	A17	½a green	.40	.20
a.		Pair, one without overprint		
b.		Double overprint		1,150.
O28	A19	1a maroon	.35	.20
a.		Inverted overprint	350.00	475.00
b.		Double overprint		1,150.
c.		1a violet brown	2.25	.35
O29	A21	2a ultramarine	4.50	.50
O30	A23	4a olive green	15.00	.40
O31	A25	8a red violet	7.00	.40
O32	A29	1r car rose & grn	11.00	.40
		Nos. O27-O32 (6)	38.25	2.10

1899

O33	A31	3p carmine rose	.20	.20

1900

O34	A17	½a light green	1.25	.30
O35	A19	1a carmine rose	2.50	.20
a.		Double overprint		1,350.
b.		Inverted overprint		1,400.
O36	A21	2a violet	27.50	.50
		Nos. O34-O36 (3)	31.25	1.00

1902-09

O37	A32	3p gray	.85	.20
O38	A33	½a green	1.00	.20
O39	A34	1a carmine rose	.85	.20
O40	A35	2a violet	2.50	.20
O41	A38	4a olive green	4.25	.20
O42	A39	6a bister	2.25	.20
O43	A40	8a red lilac	5.25	.50
O44	A42	1r car rose & green ('05)	4.50	.20
		Nos. O37-O44 (8)	21.45	1.90

1906-07

O45	A44	½a green	1.00	.20
O46	A45	1a carmine rose	1.75	.20
a.		Pair, one without overprint		
b.		Overprint on back		—

1909

O47	A43	2r brown & rose	*6.50*	.90
O48	A43	5r violet & ultra	*11.00*	1.00
O49	A43	10r car rose & grn	*21.00*	8.50
a.		10r red & green	52.50	6.00
O50	A43	15r ol gray & ultra	52.50	30.00
O51	A43	25r ultra & org brn	130.00	50.00
		Nos. O47-O51 (5)	221.00	90.40

For surcharges see Nos. O67-O69.

Regular Issues Overprinted in Black

1912-22

O52	A46	3p gray	.25	.20
O53	A47	½a green	.25	.20
a.		Double overprint	110.00	
O54	A48	1a carmine rose	.75	.20
a.		Double overprint		950.00
O55	A48	1a dark brown ('22)	1.00	.20
a.		Imperf., pair	75.00	
O56	A49	2a violet	.50	.20
O57	A52	4a olive green	.75	.20
O58	A53	6a bister	1.25	*1.75*
O59	A54	8a red violet	1.75	.75

Overprinted in Black

O60	A56	1r green & red brn	2.00	.80
O61	A56	2r yel brn & car rose	2.50	*3.50*
O62	A56	5r violet & ultra	10.50	*13.50*
O63	A56	10r car rose & grn	35.00	32.50
O64	A56	15r ol grn & ultra	80.00	*95.00*
O65	A56	25r ultra & brn org	180.00	150.00
		Nos. O52-O65 (14)	316.50	299.00

For surcharge see No. O69b.

O6

O7

1921 **Black Surcharge**

O66	O6	9p on 1a rose	.75	.60

For overprint see Gwalior No. O28.

Official Stamps of 1909 Surcharged

1925

O67	A43	1r on 15r ol gray & ultra	4.00	3.00
O68	A43	1r on 25r ultra & org brn	20.00	*60.00*
O69	A43	2r on 10r red & grn	3.50	3.50
a.		2r on 10r car rose & green	210.00	55.00
b.		Surcharge on #O63 (error)	800.00	

Official Stamps of 1912-13 Surcharged

O70	A56	1r on 15r ol grn & ultra	19.00	*65.00*
a.		Inverted surcharge		
O71	A56	1r on 25r ultra & brn org	5.00	*9.00*
a.		Inverted surcharge	600.00	
		Nos. O67-O71 (5)	51.50	*140.50*

1926

O73	O7	1a on 6a bister	.40	.40

Regular Issues of 1911-26 Surcharged

O74	A48	1a on 1a dk brn (error)	180.00	180.00
O75	A58	1a on 1½a choc	.20	.20
O76	A59	1a on 1½a choc	1.75	*4.00*
b.		Double surcharge	30.00	
O77	A57	1a on 2a6p ultra	.50	.50
		Nos. O73-O77 (5)	182.85	185.10

Nos. O74, O75 and O76 have short bars over the numerals in the upper corners.

Regular Issues of 1926-35 Overprinted

1926-35 **Wmk. 196**

O78	A46	3p slate ('29)	.20	.20
O79	A47	½a green ('31)	5.00	.40
O80	A48	1a dark brown	.20	.20
a.		Overprint as on No. O55	100.00	4.75
O81	A49	2a vermilion ('35)	1.00	1.00
a.		Small die	.85	.20
O82	A60	2a dull violet	.20	.20
O83	A60	2a vermilion ('32)	.90	2.00
O84	A57	2a6p buff ('32)	.25	.20
O85	A52	4a olive green ('35)	1.00	.20
O86	A61	4a olive green	.35	.20
O87	A53	6a bister('35)	18.00	9.00
O88	A54	8a red violet	.50	.20
O89	A55	12a claret	.50	*1.75*

Overprinted

O90	A56	1r green & brn ('30)	2.25	.90
O91	A56	2r brn org & car rose ('30)	6.00	6.00
O92	A56	10r car & green ('31)	70.00	50.00
		Nos. O78-O92 (15)	106.35	72.45

Regular Issues of 1932-34 Overprinted Type "a"

1932-35

O93	A71	½a green ('35)	.60	.20
O94	A68	9p dark green	.25	.20
O95	A72	1a dark brown ('35)	1.90	.20
O96	A69	1a3p violet	.25	.20
		Nos. O93-O96 (4)	3.00	.80

Regular Issue of 1937 Overprinted Type "a"

1937-39 ***Perf. 13½x14***

O97	A80	½a brown ('38)	10.00	.25
O98	A80	9p green	11.50	.35
O99	A80	1a carmine	2.10	.20

Type "b" Overprint

O100	A82	1r brown & slate ('38)	.30	.30
O101	A82	2r dk brown & dk vio ('38)	.85	*1.90*
O102	A82	5r dp ultra & dk green ('38)	1.50	*4.25*
O103	A82	10r rose car & dark violet ('39)	8.50	3.75
		Nos. O97-O103 (7)	34.75	11.00

No. 136 Surcharged in Black

1939, May **Wmk. 196** ***Perf. 14***

O104	A69	1a on 1a3p violet	*10.00*	1.75

King George VI — O8

1939-43 **Typo.** ***Perf. 13½x14***

O105	O8	3p slate	.20	.20
O106	O8	½a brown	3.75	.20
O106A	O8	½a dk rose vio ('43)	.20	.20
O107	O8	9p green	.20	.20
O108	O8	1a car rose	.20	.20
O108A	O8	1a3p bister ('41)	*3.25*	*.65*
O108B	O8	1½a dull pur ('43)	.20	.20
O109	O8	2a scarlet	.20	.20
O110	O8	2½a purple	.20	.20
O111	O8	4a dark brown	.20	.20
O112	O8	8a blue violet	.30	.20
		Nos. O105-O112 (11)	*8.90*	*2.65*

For overprints see Gwalior Nos. O52-O61. Stamps overprinted "Postal Service" or "I. P. N." were not used as postage stamps.

CONVENTION STATES OF THE BRITISH EMPIRE IN INDIA

CHAMBA

'chəm-bə

LOCATION — A State of India located in the north Punjab, south of Kashmir.
AREA — 3,127 sq. mi.
POP. — 168,908 (1941)
CAPITAL — Chamba

The varieties with small letters in the overprint are not listed as the letters are merely broken and not from another font of type.

Indian Stamps Overprinted in Black

1886-95 **Wmk. 39** ***Perf. 14***

1	A17	½a green	.30	*.35*
a.		"CHMABA"	*350.00*	*425.00*
c.		Double overprint	600.00	
2	A19	1a violet brown	.75	*.90*
a.		"CHMABA"	*525.00*	600.00
3	A20	1a6p bis brown ('95)	.85	*6.75*
4	A21	2a ultramarine	.95	*1.00*
a.		"CHMABA"	*2,100.*	
5	A28	2a6p green ('95)	24.00	*52.50*
6	A22	3a brn org	1.00	*2.75*
a.		3a orange	5.00	*12.50*
b.		Inverted overprint		
c.		"CHMABA"	4,750.	
7	A23	4a olive green	2.75	*4.50*
a.		"CHMABA"	*1,500.*	
8	A25	8a red violet	4.00	*9.00*
a.		"CHMABA"	*4,250.*	4,250.
9	A26	12a vio, *red* ('90)	3.50	*6.75*
a.		"CHMABA"	*7,250.*	
b.		1st "T" of "STATE" invtd.	6,000.	
10	A27	1r gray	25.00	*72.50*
a.		"CHMABA"	*9,600.*	
11	A29	1r car rose & grn ('95)	4.75	*7.50*
12	A30	2r brown & rose ('95)	62.50	*210.00*
13	A30	3r grn & brown ('95)	65.00	*160.00*
14	A30	5r vio & bl ('95)	72.50	*300.00*

Wmk. 38

15	A14	6a bister ('90)	2.25	*9.00*
		Nos. 1-15 (15)	270.10	*843.50*

1900 **Wmk. 39**

15B	A31	3p carmine rose	.30	.20

1902-04

16	A31	3p gray ('04)	.30	.20
a.		Inverted overprint	67.50	
17	A17	½a light green	.30	.20
18	A19	1a carmine rose	.30	.20
19	A21	2a violet ('03)	6.25	*15.00*
		Nos. 16-19 (4)	7.15	*15.60*

1903-05

20	A32	3p gray	.30	*.55*
21	A33	½a green	.30	.20
22	A34	1a carmine rose	.55	.20
23	A35	2a violet	.65	*1.40*
24	A37	3a brown org ('05)	1.90	*2.40*
25	A38	4a olive green ('04)	2.50	*8.75*
26	A39	6a bister ('05)	2.25	*11.00*
27	A40	8a red violet ('04)	3.00	*10.00*
28	A41	12a violet, *red*	3.50	*13.00*
29	A42	1r car rose & grn ('05)	4.25	*12.50*
		Nos. 20-29 (10)	19.20	*60.00*

1907

30	A44	½a green	.30	*2.00*
31	A45	1a carmine rose	.50	*2.50*

1913-24

32	A46	3p gray	.30	*.40*
33	A47	½a green	.30	*.60*
34	A48	1a carmine rose	2.50	*2.75*
35	A48	1a dark brown ('22)	.80	*1.50*
36	A49	2a violet	1.10	*3.25*
37	A51	3a brown orange	1.25	*2.25*
38	A51	3a ultra ('24)	1.40	*7.50*
39	A52	4a olive green	1.00	*1.50*
40	A53	6a bister	.95	*1.50*
41	A54	8a red violet	1.75	*4.00*
42	A55	12a claret	1.60	*5.00*
43	A56	1r green & red brown	7.25	*9.75*
		Nos. 32-43 (12)	20.20	*40.00*

India No. 104 Overprinted

1921

44	A48	9p on 1a rose	.90	*14.00*

India Stamps of 1913-26 Overprinted

1922-27

45	A58	1½a chocolate	18.00	*55.00*
46	A59	1½a chocolate	.90	*2.50*
47	A59	1½a rose	.60	*8.50*
48	A57	2a6p ultramarine	.50	*1.75*
49	A57	2a6p brown orange	1.00	*7.25*
		Nos. 45-49 (5)	21.00	*75.00*

India Stamps of 1926 Overprinted

1927-28 **Wmk. 196**

50	A46	3p slate	.30	*.50*
51	A47	½a green	.30	*.75*
52	A48	1a dark brown	1.40	.25
53	A60	2a dull violet	1.00	.85
54	A51	3a ultramarine	.80	*7.75*
55	A61	4a olive green	.70	*1.90*
57	A54	8a red violet	1.10	*4.50*
58	A55	12a claret	1.10	*5.00*

Overprinted

59	A56	1r green & brown	3.50	*11.00*
		Nos. 50-55,57-59 (9)	10.20	*32.50*

India Stamps of 1926-35 Overprinted

1932-37

60 A71 ½a green .60 *3.25*
61 A68 9p dark green .30 *4.75*
62 A72 1a dark brown .35 .25
63 A69 1a3p violet .30 *2.00*
64 A59 1½a carmine rose .30 *4.00*
65 A49 2a vermilion .40 *9.00*
a. Small die 125.00 125.00
66 A57 2a6p buff .30 *6.00*
67 A51 3a carmine rose .65 *3.75*
68 A52 4a olive green ('36) 3.25 *5.00*
69 A53 6a bister ('37) 45.00 *65.00*
Nos. 60-69 (10) 51.45 *103.00*

Same Overprint on India Stamps of 1937

1938 **Wmk. 196** ***Perf. 13½x14***

70 A80 3p slate .60 *1.25*
71 A80 ½a brown .30 .30
72 A80 9p green .70 *1.90*
73 A80 1a carmine .70 .60

Overprinted

74 A81 2a scarlet .40 *2.50*
75 A81 2a6p purple .30 *5.00*
76 A81 3a yellow green 3.00 *8.00*
77 A81 3a6p ultra 1.25 *4.50*
78 A81 4a dark brown 1.40 *4.50*
79 A81 6a peacock blue 6.25 *15.00*
80 A81 8a blue violet 1.25 *4.50*
81 A81 12a carmine lake 2.50 *10.00*

Overprinted

82 A82 1r brown & slate 25.00 *25.00*
83 A82 2r dk brn & dk vio 35.00 *125.00*
84 A82 5r dp ultra & dk green 65.00 *240.00*
85 A82 10r rose car & dk vio 110.00 *350.00*
86 A82 15r dk grn & dk brown 225.00 *325.00*
87 A82 25r dk vio & bl vio 275.00 *525.00*
Nos. 70-87 (18) 753.65 *1,648.*

India Nos. 151 and 153 Overprinted

1942

87B A80 ½a brown 22.50 *12.50*
88 A80 1a carmine 27.50 *18.00*

Same Ovpt. on India Stamps of 1941-42

1942-44

89 A83 3p slate .50 *2.00*
90 A83 ½a rose violet ('43) .50 *1.10*
91 A83 9p lt green ('43) .75 *4.50*
92 A83 1a car rose ('43) .75 *1.25*
93 A84 1½a dk purple ('44) .75 *3.25*
94 A84 2a scarlet ('43) 2.25 *4.00*
95 A84 3a violet ('43) 7.00 *13.00*
96 A84 3½a ultra ('43) 3.75 *20.00*
97 A85 4a chocolate ('43) 5.25 4.50
98 A85 6a pck blue ('43) 13.00 *30.00*
99 A85 8a blue violet ('43) 11.50 *35.00*
100 A85 12a car lake ('43) 22.50 *45.00*
Nos. 89-100 (12) 68.50 *163.60*

India Nos. 162-167 Overprinted

1943 **Wmk. 196** ***Perf. 13½x14***

101 A82 1r brown & slate 19.00 *25.00*
102 A82 2r dk brown & dk vio 25.00 *95.00*
103 A82 5r dp ultra & dk grn 55.00 *125.00*
104 A82 10r rose car & dk vio 85.00 *275.00*
105 A82 15r dk grn & dk brn 160.00 *475.00*
106 A82 25r dk vio & bl vio 300.00 *525.00*
Nos. 101-106 (6) 644.00 *1,520.*

India No. 161A Overprinted

1948

107 A81 14a rose violet 6.50 *2.75*

OFFICIAL STAMPS

Indian Stamps Overprinted in Black

1886-98 **Wmk. 39** ***Perf. 14***

O1 A17 ½a green .30 .20
a. "CHMABA" 210.00 210.00
c. "SERV CE"
O2 A19 1a violet brown .80 .30
a. "CHMABA" 400.00 350.00
c. "SERV CE" *2,100.*
d. "SERVICE" double *1,250.* *1,250.*
O3 A21 2a ultra .80 .75
a. "CHMABA" *1,075.* *1,500.*
O4 A22 3a brown orange 1.50 *5.50*
a. 3a orange — —
b. "CHMABA" *2,400.* *2,500.*
O5 A23 4a olive green 1.40 *2.00*
a. "CHMABA" *1,075.* *1,500.*
c. "SERV CE" *2,750.*
O6 A25 8a red violet .80 *1.00*
a. "CHMABA" *5,500.* *5,500.*
O7 A26 12a vio, *red* ('90) 5.75 *17.50*
a. "CHMABA" *6,000.*
b. 1st "T" of "STATE" invtd.
O8 A27 1r gray ('90) 10.00 *52.50*
a. "CHMABA" *4,750.*
O9 A29 1r car rose & grn ('98) 4.75 *15.00*

Wmk. 38

O10 A14 6a bister 3.00 *5.25*
Nos. O1-O10 (10) 29.10 100.00

1902-04 **Wmk. 39**

O11 A31 3p gray ('04) .30 *.30*
O12 A17 ½a light green .30 *1.75*
O13 A19 1a carmine rose .35 .25
O14 A21 2a violet 7.25 *15.00*
Nos. O11-O14 (4) 8.20 *17.30*

1903-05

O15 A32 3p gray .30 *.35*
O16 A33 ½a green .30 .20
O17 A34 1a carmine rose .45 .20
O18 A35 2a violet .65 .25
O19 A38 4a olive green ('05) 2.75 *7.00*
O20 A40 8a red violet ('05) 3.00 *6.50*
O21 A42 1r car rose & grn ('05) 1.40 *3.50*
Nos. O15-O21 (7) 8.85 *18.00*

1907

O22 A44 ½a green .25 *.75*
a. Inverted overprint *4,500.* *4,500.*
O23 A45 1a carmine rose 1.50 *1.00*

1913

O24 A49 2a violet 10.00
O25 A52 4a olive green 12.00

India No. 63 Overprinted

O26 A35 2a violet 60.00

No. O26 was never placed in use.

India Stamps of 1911-29 Overprinted:

a

b

1913-25

O27 A46 (a) 3p gray .30 .20
O28 A47 (a) ½a green .30 .20
O29 A48 (a) 1a carmine rose 2.40 .20
O30 A48 (a) 1a dk brown ('25) 1.10 .25
O31 A49 (a) 2a violet ('14) .65 *5.00*
O32 A52 (a) 4a olive green .65 *6.00*
O33 A54 (a) 8a red violet 1.10 *6.50*
O34 A56 (b) 1r grn & red brn 2.40 *11.00*
Nos. O27-O34 (8) 8.90 29.35

India No. O66 Overprinted

1921

O35 O6 9p on 1a rose .20 *3.00*

India Stamps of 1926-35 Overprinted

1927-39 **Wmk. 196**

O36 A46 3p slate .45 .20
O37 A47 ½a green .30 .20
O38 A68 9p dark green ('32) 1.50 *4.75*
O39 A48 1a dark brown .20 .20
O40 A69 1a3p violet ('32) 4.50 .40
O41 A60 2a dull violet .90 *.40*
O42 A61 4a olive green .90 .85
O43 A54 8a red violet 3.00 *4.75*
O44 A55 12a claret 2.00 *11.50*

Overprinted

O45 A56 1r green & brown 9.75 *20.00*
O45A A56 2r brn org & car rose ('39) 19.00 *150.00*
O45B A56 5r dk vio & ultra ('39) 35.00 *210.00*
O45C A56 10r car & grn ('39) 47.50 *210.00*
Nos. O36-O45C (13) 125.00 613.25

India Stamps of 1926-35 Overprinted

1935-36

O46 A71 ½a green 1.75 *.30*
O47 A72 1a dark brown 2.00 .40
O48 A49 2a vermilion 2.75 .80
a. Small die 2.00 *10.00*
O49 A52 4a olive grn ('36) 3.50 2.50
Nos. O46-O49 (4) 10.00 *4.00*

Same Overprint on India Stamps of 1937

1938 ***Perf. 13½x14***

O50 A80 9p green 7.50 *25.00*
O51 A80 1a carmine 6.00 1.50

India Stamps of 1937 Overprinted

1940-41

O51A A82 1r brn & sl ('41) 725.00 *825.00*
O52 A82 2r dk brn & dk vio 47.50 *175.00*
O53 A82 5r dp ultra & dk grn 85.00 *300.00*
O54 A82 10r rose car & dk vio 150.00 *475.00*

India Official Stamps of 1939-43 Overprinted

1941-46 **Wmk. 196**

O55 O8 3p slate ('44) .30 *.65*
O56 O8 ½a brown 11.00 1.50
O57 O8 ½a dk rose vio ('44) .30 *1.60*
O58 O8 9p green .30 *5.50*
O59 O8 1a carmine rose .30 *1.25*
O60 O8 1a3p bister ('46) 50.00 12.50
O61 O8 1½a dull pur ('46) .85 *4.50*
O62 O8 2a scarlet ('44) 1.25 *3.75*
O63 O8 2½a purple ('44) 1.75 *14.50*
O64 O8 4a dark brown ('44) 3.00 *6.75*
O65 O8 8a blue vio ('41) 4.25 *37.50*
Nos. O55-O65 (11) 73.30 *90.00*

India Nos. 162-165 Overprinted

1944

O66 A82 1r brown & slate 27.50 *110.00*
O67 A82 2r dk brn & dk vio 35.00 *160.00*
O68 A82 5r dp ultra & dk grn 90.00 *225.00*
O69 A82 10r rose car & dk vio 125.00 *375.00*
Nos. O66-O69 (4) 277.50 *870.00*

FARIDKOT

fe-'rēd-,kōt

LOCATION — A State of India lying northeast of Nabha in the central Punjab.
AREA — 638 sq. mi.
POP. — 164,364
CAPITAL — Faridkot

Previous stamp issues are listed under Feudatory States. Stamps of Faridkot were superseded by those of India in 1901.

The varieties with small letters in the overprint are not listed as the letters are merely broken and not from another font.

India Stamps Overprinted in Black

1887-93 **Wmk. 39** ***Perf. 14***

4 A17 ½a green .95 .95
a. "ARIDKOT"
5 A19 1a violet brown .95 *1.90*
6 A21 2a ultramarine 2.50 *3.50*

7	A22	3a orange	4.75	*7.50*
8	A23	4a olive green	5.25	*12.50*
a.		"ARIDKOT"	1,075.	
9	A25	8a red violet	9.00	*27.50*
a.		"ARIDKOT"	2,400.	
10	A27	1r gray	35.00	*325.00*
a.		"ARIDKOT"	*2,400.*	
11	A29	1r car rose & grn ('93)	30.00	*75.00*

Wmk. 38

12	A14	6a bister	1.60	*11.00*
a.		"ARIDKOT"	1,600.	
		Nos. 4-12 (9)	90.00	*464.85*

1900 Wmk. Star. (39)

13	A31	3p car rose	.75	*35.00*
14	A26	12a violet, *red*	30.00	*350.00*

OFFICIAL STAMPS

India Stamps Overprinted in Black

1886 Wmk. 39 *Perf. 14*

O1	A17	½a green	.20	*.50*
a.		"SERV CE"	1,600.	
O2	A19	1a violet brown	.50	*1.10*
a.		"SERV CE"	2,100.	
O3	A21	2a ultramarine	1.60	*7.00*
a.		"SERV CE"	2,100.	
O4	A22	3a orange	1.25	*3.50*
O5	A23	4a olive green	4.50	*6.00*
a.		"SERV CE"	2,100.	
O6	A25	8a red lilac	4.50	*20.00*
a.		"SERV CE"	2,400.	
O7	A27	1r gray	37.50	*150.00*

Wmk. 38

O8	A14	6a bister	22.50	*60.00*
a.		"ARIDKOT"	1,250.	
b.		"SERVIC"	2,100.	
		Nos. O1-O8 (8)	72.55	*248.10*

1896 Wmk. 39

O9	A29	1r car rose & green	75.00	*425.00*

Obsolete March 31, 1901.

GWALIOR

ˈgwäl-ē-ˌo̦ə̦r

LOCATION — One of the Central Provinces of India
AREA — 26,008 sq. mi.
POP. — 4,006,159 (1941)
CAPITAL — Lashkar

The varieties with small letters in the overprint are not listed as the letters are merely broken and not from another font.

India Stamps Overprinted in Black

Lines Spaced 16-17mm

1885 Wmk. 39 *Perf. 14*

1	A17	½a green	35.00	20.00
2	A19	1a violet brown	40.00	*25.00*
3	A20	1a6p bister brown	55.00	
4	A21	2a ultramarine	40.00	12.00
5	A25	8a red lilac	55.00	
6	A27	1r gray	55.00	

Wmk. 38

7	A9	4a green	60.00	
8	A14	6a bister	60.00	
		Nos. 1-8 (8)	400.00	57.00

The Hindi overprint measures 13½-14x2mm and 15-15½x2½mm.

The two sizes are found in the same sheet in the proportion of one of the smaller to three of the larger.

The ½a, 1a, 2a, also exist with lines 13mm apart and the short Hindi overprint.

Reprints of the ½a and 1a have the 13mm spacing, the short Hindi overprint and usually carry the overprint "Specimen."

India Stamps Overprinted

Red Overprint

1885 Wmk. 39

9	A17	½a green	.50	.25
10	A21	2a ultramarine	8.50	*10.00*
11	A27	1r gray	6.00	*16.00*

Wmk. 38

12	A9	4a green	15.00	8.75
		Nos. 9-12 (4)	30.00	35.00

Nos. 9-12 have been reprinted. They have the short Hindi overprint. Most copies bear the word "Reprint." Those without it cannot be distinguished from the originals.

Black Overprint

1885-91 Wmk. 39

13	A17	½a green	.30	.20
a.		"GWALICR"	85.00	*125.00*
b.		Double overprint	—	
14	A18	9p rose	30.00	*50.00*
15	A19	1a violet brown	.70	.20
16	A20	1a6p bister brown	.50	1.00
17	A21	2a ultramarine	.60	.20
18	A22	3a orange	3.00	.20
19	A23	4a olive green	3.50	.75
20	A25	8a red violet	4.50	1.00
21	A26	12a violet, *red*	3.00	.75
22	A27	1r gray	2.50	1.10

Wmk. 38

23	A14	6a bister	1.50	6.00
		Nos. 13-23 (11)	50.10	*61.40*

The Hindi overprint measures 13½-14x2mm and 15-15½x2½mm as in the preceding issue.

1896 Wmk. 39

24	A28	2a6p green	5.50	*16.00*
a.		"GWALICR"	475.00	
25	A29	1r car rose & grn	3.00	2.75
a.		"GWALICR"	725.00	*900.00*
26	A30	2r bis brn & rose	5.50	3.00
27	A30	3r green & brown	7.00	3.50
28	A30	5r violet & blue	14.00	6.50
		Nos. 24-28 (5)	35.00	31.75

The Hindi inscription varies from 13 to 15½mm long.

1899

29	A31	3p carmine rose	.30	.20
a.		Inverted overprint	900.00	475.00

1901-04

30	A31	3p gray ('04)	5.50	*50.00*
31	A17	½a light green	.30	*.95*
32	A19	1a carmine rose	.60	.30
33	A21	2a violet	.85	3.25
34	A28	2a6p ultra ('03)	.85	4.00
		Nos. 30-34 (5)	8.10	*58.50*

1903-08

35	A32	3p gray	.50	.20
36	A33	½a green	.30	.20
37	A34	1a carmine rose	.30	.20
38	A35	2a violet	.50	.50
39	A36	2a6p ultra ('05)	.75	*4.75*
40	A37	3a brown org ('04)	1.10	.25
41	A38	4a olive green	1.00	.35
42	A39	6a bister ('06)	1.90	1.90
43	A40	8a red violet	2.25	1.00
44	A41	12a vio, *red* ('05)	2.75	2.40
45	A42	1r car rose & grn ('05)	1.60	1.25
46	A43	2r brown & rose	6.75	8.50
47	A43	3r grn & brn ('08)	19.00	*32.50*
48	A43	5r vio & bl ('08)	14.00	*21.00*
		Nos. 35-48 (14)	52.70	*75.00*

There are two settings of the overprint on Nos. 35, 37-46. In the first (1903), "GWALIOR" is 14mm long and lines are spaced 1¾mm. In the second (1908), "GWALIOR" is 13mm long and lines are 2¾mm apart. No. 36 exists only with first overprint, Nos. 47-48 only with second.

1907

49	A44	½a green	.30	*.70*
50	A45	1a carmine rose	1.25	.25

No. 49 exists with both settings of overprint. See note below No. 48.

1912-23

51	A46	3p gray	.30	.20
52	A47	½a green	.30	.20
a.		Inverted overprint		*450.00*
53	A48	1a car rose	.30	.20
a.		Double overprint	37.50	
54	A48	1a dk brown ('23)	.40	.20
55	A49	2a violet	.35	.20
56	A51	3a brown orange	.40	.20
57	A52	4a olive grn ('13)	.50	.50
58	A53	6a bister	.80	.80
59	A54	8a red vio ('13)	.95	.50
60	A55	12a claret ('14)	1.00	*2.10*
61	A56	1r green & red brn	4.25	.65
62	A56	2r brn & car rose	3.75	3.75
63	A56	5r violet & ultra	16.00	5.50
		Nos. 51-63 (13)	29.30	15.00

India No. 104 Overprinted

1921

64	A48	9p on 1a rose	.20	.20
a.		Inverted overprint	—	

India Stamps of 1911-26 Overprinted

Hindi Overprint 15mm Long

1923-27

66	A59	1½a choc ('25)	1.25	.40
67	A59	1½a rose ('27)	.30	.20
a.		Inverted overprint	—	—
68	A57	2a6p ultra ('25)	1.25	*1.50*
69	A57	2a6p brown org ('27)	.30	*.40*
70	A51	3a ultra ('24)	1.00	.50
		Nos. 66-70 (5)	4.10	3.00

Similar Ovpt. on India Stamps of 1926-35
Hindi Overprint 13½mm Long

1928-32 Wmk. 196

71	A46	3p slate ('32)	.65	.20
72	A47	½a green ('30)	1.25	.20
73	A48	1a dark brown	.65	.20
74	A60	2a dull violet	.65	.30
75	A51	3a ultramarine	.85	.40
76	A61	4a olive green	.85	.85
77	A54	8a red violet	1.10	1.10
78	A55	12a claret	1.25	*2.50*

Overprinted

79	A56	1r green & brown	1.75	*2.75*
80	A56	2r brn org & car rose	5.00	4.00
81	A56	5r dk vio & ultra ('29)	13.50	*21.00*
82	A56	10r car & grn ('30)	37.50	29.00
83	A56	15r olive green & ultra ('30)	60.00	52.50
84	A56	25r bl & ocher ('30)	150.00	125.00
		Nos. 71-84 (14)	275.00	240.00

India Stamps of 1932-35 Overprinted in Black

Hindi Overprint 13½mm Long

1933-36

85	A71	½a green ('36)	.40	.20
86	A68	9p dk green ('33)	1.75	.30
87	A72	1a dk brown ('36)	.30	.20
88	A69	1a3p violet ('36)	.40	.20
89	A49	2a vermilion ('36)	1.25	1.10
		Nos. 85-89 (5)	4.10	2.00

Same Ovpt. on India Stamps of 1937

1938-40 *Perf. 13½x14*

90	A80	3p slate ('40)	2.50	.25
91	A80	½a brown	2.75	.20
92	A80	9p green ('40)	18.00	10.00
93	A80	1a carmine	2.50	.20
94	A81	3a yel green ('39)	7.00	2.00
95	A81	4a dark brown	21.00	5.00
96	A81	6a pck blue ('39)	1.25	*2.00*
		Nos. 90-96 (7)	55.00	19.65

Same Overprinted on India Stamps of 1941-43

1942-49

100	A83	3p slate ('44)	.30	.20
101	A83	½a rose vio ('46)	.30	.20
102	A83	9p light green	.30	.20
103	A83	1a car rose ('44)	.30	.20
104	A84	1½a dk purple ('44)	.45	.20
105	A84	2a scarlet ('44)	.30	.20
106	A84	3a violet ('44)	.25	.20
108	A85	4a choc ('44)	.25	.20
109	A85	6a pck blue ('48)	12.00	*18.00*
110	A85	8a blue violet	2.50	*2.50*
111	A85	12a carmine lake	5.50	*16.00*

India Nos. 162-167 Overprinted

Perf. 13½x14

112	A82	1r brn & sl ('45)	4.50	1.60
113	A82	2r dk brn & dk vio ('49)	27.50	9.00
114	A82	5r dp ultra & dk grn ('49)	40.00	35.00
115	A82	10r rose car & dk vio ('49)	35.00	*42.50*
116	A82	15r dk grn & dk brn ('48)	110.00	*160.00*
117	A82	25r dk vio & blue vio ('48)	110.00	*125.00*
		Nos. 100-106,108-117 (17)	349.45	411.20

India Stamps of 1941-43 Overprinted

1949

118	A83	3p slate	.60	.45
119	A83	½a rose violet	.50	.45
120	A83	1a carmine rose	.50	.50
121	A84	2a scarlet	11.00	1.60
122	A84	3a violet	27.50	20.00
123	A85	4a chocolate	2.40	2.00
124	A85	6a pck blue	25.00	*37.50*
125	A85	8a blue violet	57.50	37.50
126	A85	12a carmine lake	275.00	125.00
		Nos. 118-126 (9)	400.00	225.00

OFFICIAL STAMPS

India Stamps Overprinted in Black

1895 Wmk. 39 *Perf. 14*

O1	A17	½a green	.30	.20
a.		Double overprint		900.00
O2	A19	1a maroon	.55	.20
O3	A21	2a ultramarine	1.00	.35
O4	A23	4a olive green	1.50	.75
O5	A25	8a red violet	1.00	.75
O6	A29	1r car rose & grn	3.75	2.50
		Nos. O1-O6 (6)	8.10	4.75

Nos. O1 to O6 inclusive are known with the last two characters of the lower word transposed.

1901-04

O7	A31	3p gray ('04)	1.10	*1.90*
O8	A17	½a light green	.30	.20
O9	A19	1a carmine rose	3.25	.20
O10	A21	2a violet ('03)	.45	*1.25*
		Nos. O7-O10 (4)	5.10	*3.55*

1902

O11	A31	3p carmine rose	.25	.25

1903-05

O12	A32	3p gray	.30	.20
O13	A33	½a green	1.75	.20
O14	A34	1a carmine rose	.45	.20
O15	A35	2a violet	1.75	.20
O16	A38	4a olive grn ('05)	3.00	.60
O17	A40	8a red violet	3.50	.30
O18	A42	1r car rose & grn ('05)	2.75	.75
		Nos. O12-O18 (7)	13.50	2.45

1907

O19	A44	½a green	.75	.20
O20	A45	1a carmine rose	4.00	.20

Two spacings of the overprint lines, 10mm and 8mm, are found on Nos. O12-O20.

1913

O21	A46	3p gray	.30	.20
O22	A47	½a green	.30	.20
O23	A48	1a carmine rose	.30	.20
a.		Double overprint	57.50	

O24	A49	2a violet	.50	.25
O25	A52	4a olive green	.50	*.75*
O26	A54	8a red violet	.75	*1.00*
O27	A56	1r grn & red brn	17.50	15.00
		Nos. O21-O27 (7)	20.15	17.60

India No. O66 Overprinted

1921

O28	O6	9p on 1a rose	.30	.20

India No. 83 Overprinted

1923

O29	A48	1a dark brown	2.50	.20

Similar Ovpt. on India Stamps of 1926-35

1927-35 **Wmk. 196**

O30	A46	3p slate	.30	.20
O31	A47	½a green	.30	.20
O32	A48	1a dark brown	.30	.20
O33	A60	2a dull violet	.30	.20
O34	A61	4a olive green	.40	.30
O35	A54	8a red violet	.40	*.65*

Overprinted

O36	A56	1r green & brown	.85	*1.50*
O37	A56	2r brn org & car rose ('35)	7.00	*8.25*
O38	A56	5r dk vio & ultra ('32)	10.50	*150.00*
O39	A56	10r car & grn ('32)	80.00	*300.00*
		Nos. O30-O39 (10)	100.35	*461.50*

India Stamps of 1926-35 Overprinted

1933-37 ***Perf. 13½x14, 14***

O40	A71	½a green ('36)	.35	.25
O41	A68	9p dk green ('35)	.30	.25
O42	A72	1a dk brown ('36)	.30	.20
O43	A69	1a3p violet ('33)	.50	.20
O44	A49	2a ver ('36)	.30	*.40*
a.		Small die ('36)	1.75	1.00
O45	A52	4a olive green ('37)	.40	*.50*
		Nos. O40-O45 (6)	2.15	1.80

For surcharge see No. O62.

Same Overprint on India Stamps

1938 ***Perf. 13½x14***

O46	A80	½a brown	2.00	.25
O47	A80	1a carmine	2.00	.20

India Nos. 162-165 Overprinted

1945-48 **Wmk. 196** ***Perf. 13½x14***

O48	A82	1r brown & slate	1.50	*12.00*
O49	A82	2r dk brn & dk vio	15.00	*60.00*
O50	A82	5r dp ultra & dk grn ('46)	45.00	*325.00*
O51	A82	10r rose car & dk vio ('48)	72.50	*650.00*
		Nos. O48-O51 (4)	134.00	*1,047.*

India Official Stamps of 1939-43 Overprinted

1940-44 **Wmk. 196** ***Perf. 13½x14***

O52	O8	3p slate	.30	.20
O53	O8	½a brown	1.50	.25
O54	O8	½a dk rose vio ('43)	.30	.20
O55	O8	9p green ('43)	.30	.30
O56	O8	1a car rose ('41)	1.00	.20
O57	O8	1a3p bister ('42)	14.00	1.50
O58	O8	1½a dull purple ('43)	.50	.30
O59	O8	2a scarlet ('41)	.50	.30
O60	O8	4a dark brown ('44)	.55	*1.50*
O61	O8	8a blue vio ('44)	1.25	*5.75*
		Nos. O52-O61 (10)	20.20	10.50

Gwalior No. O43 with Additional Surcharge in Black

1942

O62	A69	1a on 1a3p violet	10.50	2.75

JIND

'jind

(Jhind)

LOCATION — A State of India in the north Punjab.
AREA — 1,299 sq. mi.
POP. — 361,812 (1941)
CAPITAL — Sangrur

Previous stamp issues are listed under Feudatory States.

The varieties with small letters are not listed as the letters are merely broken and not from another font.

India Stamps Overprinted in Black — JHIND STATE

1885 **Wmk. 39** ***Perf. 14***

33	A17	½a green	.75	.75
a.		Overprint reading down	52.50	52.50
34	A19	1a violet brown	15.00	*20.00*
a.		Overprint reading down	600.00	
35	A21	2a ultra	4.25	4.25
a.		Overprint reading down	725.00	
36	A25	8a red lilac	350.00	
a.		Overprint reading down	*10,500.*	
37	A27	1r gray	550.00	
a.		Overprint reading down	*12,000.*	

Wmk. 38

38	A9	4a green	19.00	*26.00*
		Nos. 33-38 (6)	939.00	51.00

On the reprints of Nos. 33 to 38 "Jhind" measures 8mm instead of 9mm and "State" 9mm instead of 9½mm.

India Stamps Overprinted in Red or Black — JEEND STATE

1885 **Wmk. 39**

39	A17	½a green (R)	60.00
40	A19	1a violet brown	60.00
41	A21	2a ultra (R)	125.00
42	A25	8a red lilac	180.00
43	A27	1r gray (R)	185.00

Wmk. 38

44	A9	4a green (R)	175.00
		Nos. 39-44 (6)	785.00

India Stamps Overprinted — JHIND STATE

Red Overprint

1886 **Wmk. 39**

45	A17	½a green	10.50
a.		"JEIND"	1,400.
46	A21	2a ultramarine	12.50
a.		"JEIND"	1,600.
47	A27	1r gray	27.50
a.		"JEIND"	2,400.

Wmk. 38

48	A9	4a green	25.00
		Nos. 45-48 (4)	75.50

Nos. 46, 47 and 48 were not placed in use.

Black Overprint

1886-98 **Wmk. 39**

49	A17	½a green ('88)	.30	.20
a.		Inverted overprint	175.00	
50	A19	1a violet brown	.30	.20
a.		"JEIND"	600.00	
51	A20	1a6p bister brn ('97)	.75	.75
52	A21	2a ultra	.30	.25
53	A22	3a orange	.30	.20
54	A23	4a olive green	.35	.30
55	A25	8a red violet	.60	*.75*
a.		"JEIND"	2,400.	
56	A26	12a vio, *red* ('97)	.60	*.75*
57	A27	1r gray ('91)	13.00	*8.75*
58	A29	1r car rose & green ('98)	10.00	*7.50*
59	A30	2r brn & rose ('97)	325.00	*160.00*
60	A30	3r grn & brn ('97)	525.00	*160.00*
61	A30	5r vio & bl ('97)	575.00	*275.00*

Wmk. 38

62	A14	6a bister	.90	*1.00*
		Nos. 49-62 (14)	1,452.	*615.65*

1900 **Wmk. 39**

63	A31	3p carmine rose	.30	.20

1902-04

64	A31	3p gray ('04)	.30	.20
65	A17	½a light green	.30	*.30*
66	A19	1a carmine rose	.30	*.35*
		Nos. 64-66 (3)	.90	*.85*

1903-09

67	A32	3p gray	.30	.20
a.		Double overprint		
68	A33	½a green	.30	.20
69	A34	1a car rose ('09)	.30	.20
a.		Double overprint		
70	A35	2a violet ('06)	.30	.20
70A	A36	2a6p ultra ('09)	.30	*.35*
71	A37	3a brown orange	.30	.25
a.		Double overprint	87.50	
72	A38	4a olive green	.30	.35
73	A39	6a bister ('05)	.40	*.50*
74	A40	8a red violet	.40	*.50*
75	A41	12a vio, *red* ('05)	.60	*.75*
76	A42	1r car rose & grn ('05)	.75	*.90*
		Nos. 67-76 (11)	4.25	4.40

1907

77	A44	½a green	.30	.20
78	A45	1a carmine rose	.30	.20

1913

80	A46	3p gray	.30	.20
81	A47	½a green	.30	.20
82	A48	1a carmine rose	.30	.20
83	A49	2a violet	.30	.25
84	A51	3a brown orange	.85	*1.00*
85	A53	6a bister	2.00	*2.25*
		Nos. 80-85 (6)	4.05	*4.10*

India Stamps of 1911-26 Overprinted

1913-14

88	A46	3p gray	.20	.20
89	A47	½a green	.20	.20
90	A48	1a carmine rose	.20	.20
91	A49	2a violet	.20	.20
92	A51	3a brown orange	.20	.20
93	A52	4a olive green	.20	.20
94	A53	6a bister	.20	.20
95	A54	8a red violet	.25	.25
96	A55	12a claret	.30	*.35*
97	A56	1r grn & red brn	.50	.50
		Nos. 88-97 (10)	2.45	2.50

India No. 104 Overprinted

1921

98	A48	9p on 1a rose	2.00	*2.25*

India Stamps of 1913-19 Overprinted

1922

99	A58	1½a chocolate	.70	*.80*
100	A57	2a6p ultramarine	.40	*.45*

Same Overprint on India Stamps of 1911-26

1924

101	A48	1a dark brown	.30	.20
102	A59	1½a chocolate	.40	*.45*

Same Overprint on India No. 87

1925

103	A51	3a ultramarine	.30	*.25*

Same Overprint on India Stamps of 1911-26

1927

104	A59	1½a rose	.30	.20
105	A57	2a6p brown orange	.30	.20
106	A56	2r yel brn & car rose	6.00	*6.25*
107	A56	5r violet & ultra	35.00	*27.50*
		Nos. 104-107 (4)	41.60	*34.15*

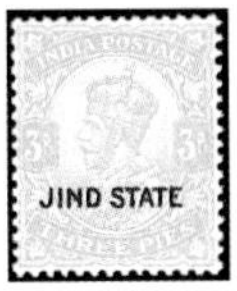

India Stamps of 1926-35 Overprinted

1927-32 **Wmk. 196**

108	A46	3p slate	.30	.20
109	A47	½a green	.30	.20
110	A68	9p dark green ('32)	.40	.55
111	A48	1a dark brown	.30	.20
112	A69	1a3p violet ('32)	.30	.40
113	A59	1½a carmine rose	.30	.30
114	A60	2a dull violet	.30	.20
115	A57	2a6p buff	.30	.20
116	A51	3a ultramarine	.40	.45
117	A61	4a olive green	.30	.30
118	A54	8a red violet	1.25	*1.60*
119	A55	12a claret	.75	*1.90*

Overprinted

120	A56	1r green & brown	4.00	*2.50*
121	A56	2r buff & car rose	25.00	*15.00*
122	A56	5r dk vio & ultra	15.00	*17.50*
123	A56	10r car rose & grn	17.50	*35.00*
124	A56	15r ol grn & blue	65.00	*125.00*
125	A56	25r blue & ocher	100.00	*160.00*
		Nos. 108-125 (18)	231.70	*361.50*

India Stamps of 1926-35 Overprinted

1934-37

126	A71	½a green	.20	.20
127	A72	1a dark brown	.20	.20
128	A49	2a vermilion	.20	.20
129	A51	3a carmine rose	.20	.20
130	A70	3a6p deep blue ('37)	.20	.20
131	A52	4a olive green	.25	.25
132	A53	6a bister ('37)	.25	.25
		Nos. 126-132 (7)	1.50	1.50

Same Overprint on India Stamps of 1937

1937-38 **Wmk. 196** ***Perf. 13½x14***

133	A80	3p slate ('38)	.20	*.25*
134	A80	½a brown ('38)	.20	*.30*
135	A80	9p green	.30	.30
136	A80	1a carmine	.20	.20
137	A81	2a scarlet ('38)	.20	.20
138	A81	2a6p purple ('38)	.20	.20
139	A81	3a yel grn ('38)	.20	.20
140	A81	3a6p ultra ('38)	.30	*.35*
141	A81	4a dk brown ('38)	.30	*.35*
142	A81	6a pck blue ('38)	.35	*.60*
143	A81	8a blue vio ('38)	.45	*1.75*
144	A81	12a car lake ('38)	.65	*2.50*

Overprinted

1938

145 A82 1r brown & slate 11.00 *11.00*
146 A82 2r dk brn & dk violet 17.00 *18.00*
147 A82 5r dp ultra & dk green 45.00 *60.00*
148 A82 10r rose car & dk violet 90.00 *110.00*
149 A82 15r dk grn & dk brown 175.00 *350.00*
150 A82 25r dk vio & bl vio 350.00 *425.00*
Nos. 133-150 (18) 691.55 *981.20*

India Stamps of 1937 Overprinted

1942-43 Wmk. 196 *Perf. 13½x14*

155 A80 3p slate 2.75 2.75
156 A80 ½a brown 2.75 2.75
157 A80 9p green 2.75 2.75
158 A80 1a carmine 2.75 2.75
159 A82 1r brn & slate 3.00 *8.25*
160 A82 2r dk brn & dk violet 9.25 *15.00*
161 A82 5r dp ultra & dk green 40.00 *62.50*
162 A82 10r rose car & dk vio ('43) 52.50 *125.00*
163 A82 15r dk grn & dk brn ('43) 120.00 *160.00*
164 A82 25r dk vio & bl vio 85.00 *275.00*
Nos. 155-164 (10) 320.75 *656.75*

Same Overprint on India Stamps of 1941-43

165 A83 3p slate .30 .30
166 A83 ½a rose vio ('43) .20 .20
167 A83 9p light green .20 .20
168 A83 1a car rose ('43) .20 .20
169 A84 1a3p bister ('43) .45 .45
170 A84 1½a dark purple 1.90 1.90
171 A84 2a scarlet .20 .20
172 A84 3a violet ('43) 1.10 1.10
173 A84 3½a ultramarine .40 .40
174 A85 4a chocolate .40 .40
175 A85 6a peacock blue .45 .40
176 A85 8a blue violet 1.90 *2.25*
177 A85 12a carmine lake 7.50 5.25
Nos. 165-177 (13) 15.20 *13.25*

OFFICIAL STAMPS

India Stamps Overprinted in Black

1885 Wmk. 39 *Perf. 14*

O1 A17 ½a green .30 .20
a. "JHIND STATE" reading down 85.00 32.50
O2 A19 1a violet brown .30 .20
a. "JHIND STATE" reading down 7.00 7.00
O3 A21 2a ultra 17.50 17.50
a. "JHIND STATE" reading down *1,250.*
Nos. O1-O3 (3) 18.10 17.90

The reprints may be distinguished by the same measurements as the reprints of the corresponding regular issue.

India Stamps Overprinted in Red or Black

SERVICE

JEEND STATE

1885

O4 A17 ½a green (R) 50.00
O5 A19 1a violet brown 50.00
O6 A21 2a ultra (R) 50.00
Nos. O4-O6 (3) 150.00

India Stamps Overprinted

1886

Red Overprint

O7 A17 ½a green 14.00
a. "JEIND" *725.00*
b. "ERVICE"
O8 A21 2a ultramarine 14.00
a. "JEIND" *900.00*
b. "ERVICE"

No. O8 was not placed in use.

1886-96

Black Overprint

O9 A17 ½a green ('88) .35 .25
O10 A19 1a violet brown 2.25 .25
a. "JEIND" *600.00*
b. "ERVICE"
O11 A21 2a ultramarine .30 .25
O12 A23 4a olive green .65 .40
O13 A25 8a red violet 1.90 1.90
O14 A29 1r car rose & grn ('96) 6.00 *10.50*
Nos. O9-O14 (6) 11.45 *13.55*

1902

O15 A17 ½a light green .30 .25

1903-06

O16 A32 3p gray .30 .20
O17 A33 ½a green 1.25 .20
a. "HIND" 210.00
O18 A34 1a carmine rose 1.75 .20
a. "HIND" 210.00
O19 A35 2a violet .30 .20
O20 A38 4a olive green .60 .35
O21 A40 8a red violet 2.50 2.00
O22 A42 1r car rose & grn ('06) 2.75 2.50
Nos. O16-O22 (7) 9.45 5.65

1907

O23 A44 ½a green .30 .20
O24 A45 1a carmine rose .30 .20

Indian Stamps of 1911-26 Overprinted

1914-27

O25 A46(a) 3p gray .30 .20
O26 A47(a) ½a green .40 .20
O27 A48(a) 1a car rose .40 .20
O28 A49(a) 2a violet .30 .20
O29 A52(a) 4a olive green .30 .20
a. Double overprint
O30 A54(a) 8a red violet .40 .40
O31 A56(b) 1r grn & red brn 1.25 .40
O32 A56(b) 2r yel brn & car rose ('27) 12.00 *10.50*
O33 A56(b) 5r vio & ultra ('27) 20.00 *21.00*
Nos. O25-O33 (9) 35.35 *33.30*

India Nos. 83 and 89 Overprinted Type "a"

1924-27

O34 A48 1a dark brown .30 .20
O35 A53 6a bister ('27) .30 .30

India Stamps of 1926-35 Overprinted

1927-32

O36 A46 3p slate .20 .20
O37 A47 ½a green .20 .20
O38 A68 9p dark green ('32) .20 .20
O39 A48 1a dark brown .20 .20
O40 A69 1a3p violet ('32) .20 .25
O41 A60 2a dull violet .20 .20
O42 A61 4a olive green .20 .20
O43 A54 8a red violet .25 .25
O44 A55 12a claret .30 .40

Overprinted

O45 A56 1r green & brown 1.75 *1.90*
O46 A56 2r buff & car rose 5.75 *6.50*
O47 A56 5r dk vio & ultra 12.50 *13.00*
O48 A56 10r car rose & grn 27.50 *26.00*
Nos. O36-O48 (13) 49.45 *49.50*

India Stamps of 1926-35 Overprinted Type "c"

1934-37

O49 A71 ½a green .30 .20
O50 A72 1a dark brown .30 .20
O51 A49 2a vermilion .30 .20
O52 A57 2a6p buff ('37) 1.10 1.10
O53 A52 4a olive green 1.25 1.25
O54 A53 6a bister ('37) 1.25 1.25
Nos. O49-O54 (6) 4.50 4.20

India Nos. 151-153 Overprinted Type "c"

1937-42 *Perf. 13½x14*

O55 A80 ½a brown ('42) 32.50 .45
O56 A80 9p green .40 .20
O57 A80 1a carmine .40 .20

India Nos. 162-165 Overprinted Type "d"

O58 A82 1r brn & sl ('40) 19.00 13.00
O59 A82 2r dk brn & dk vio ('40) 30.00 *45.00*
O60 A82 5r dp ultra & dk grn ('40) 77.50 *80.00*
O61 A82 10r rose car & dk vio ('40) 125.00 *125.00*
Nos. O55-O61 (7) 284.80 263.85

India Official Stamps of 1939-43 Overprinted

1940-43

O62 O8 3p slate .20 .20
O63 O8 ½a brown 2.50 1.25
O64 O8 ½a dk rose vio ('43) .25 .20
O65 O8 9p green .20 .20
O66 O8 1a car rose .20 .20
O67 O8 1½a dull pur ('43) .90 .75
O68 O8 2a scarlet .20 .20
O69 O8 2½a purple .25 .25
O70 O8 4a dark brown .25 .20
O71 O8 8a blue violet .90 .90

India Nos. 162-165 Overprinted

1942 Wmk. 196 *Perf. 13½x14*

O72 A82 1r brown & slate 14.00 *22.50*
O73 A82 2r dk brn & dk violet 27.50 *40.00*
O74 A82 5r dp ultra & dk green 62.50 *125.00*
O75 A82 10r rose car & dk violet 125.00 *210.00*
Nos. O62-O75 (14) 234.85 *401.85*

NABHA

ˈnäb-hə

LOCATION — A State of India in the eastern and southeastern Punjab
AREA — 966 sq. mi.
POP. — 340,044 (1941)
CAPITAL — Nabha

The varieties with small letters in the overprint are not listed as the letters are merely broken and not from another font.

Indian Stamps Overprinted in Black

1885 Wmk. 39 *Perf. 14*

1 A17 ½a green .45 *.55*
2 A19 1a violet brown 19.00 *30.00*
3 A21 2a ultramarine 9.50 *11.00*
4 A25 8a red lilac 350.00
5 A27 1r gray 375.00

Wmk. 38

6 A9 4a green 37.50 *45.00*

On the reprints "Nabha" and "State" each measure 9½mm. On the originals they measure 11 and 10mm respectively.

Indian Stamps Overprinted

Red Overprint

1885 Wmk. 39

7 A17 ½a green .50 .50
8 A21 2a ultramarine .80 .85
9 A27 1r gray 80.00 *80.00*

Wmk. 38

10 A9 4a green 17.50 *32.50*

Black Overprint

1885-97 Wmk. 39

11 A17 ½a green .25 .20
12 A18 9p rose ('92) .75 .85
13 A19 1a violet brown .30 .20
14 A20 1a6p bister brn .60 .60
a. "ABHA" 240.00
15 A21 2a ultramarine .60 .50
16 A22 3a orange 1.75 1.75
17 A23 4a olive green .75 .50
18 A25 8a red lilac 1.75 1.75
19 A26 12a vio, *red* ('89) 1.10 *1.50*
20 A27 1r gray 12.50 *25.00*
21 A29 1r car rose & grn ('93) 5.00 2.50
a. "N BHA" —
22 A30 2r brn & rose ('97) 100.00 *150.00*
23 A30 3r grn & brn ('97) 100.00 *150.00*
24 A30 5r vio & blk ('97) 125.00 *160.00*

Wmk. 38

25 A14 6a bister ('89) 2.00 *2.50*
Nos. 11-25 (15) 352.35 *497.85*

Nos. 7, 8, 9, 10, 13, and 18 have been reprinted. They usually bear the overprint "Specimen."

1900 Wmk. 39

26 A31 3p carmine rose .30 .20

1903-09

27 A32 3p gray .30 .20
28 A33 ½a green .30 .25
a. "NABH"
29 A34 1a car rose .40 .35
30 A35 2a violet .40 .40
30A A36 2a6p ultra 27.50 *42.50*
31 A37 3a brown orange .70 .70
32 A38 4a olive green .70 .70
33 A39 6a bister .90 .90
34 A40 8a red violet .70 *.90*
35 A41 12a violet, *red* 1.75 *1.90*
36 A42 1r car rose & grn 1.75 *1.90*
Nos. 27-36 (11) 35.40 *50.70*

1907

37 A44 ½a green .30 .20
38 A45 1a carmine rose .30 .20

1913

40 A46 3p gray .30 .20
41 A47 ½a green .30 .20
42 A48 1a carmine rose .30 .20
43 A49 2a violet .30 .20
44 A51 3a brown orange .30 .20
45 A52 4a olive green .30 .30
46 A53 6a bister .30 *.25*
47 A54 8a red violet .30 .30

48 A55 12a claret .35 *.40*
49 A56 1r green & red brn 1.50 1.50
Nos. 40-49 (10) 4.25 3.75

1924
50 A48 1a dark brown .30 .20

India Stamps of 1926-35 Overprinted

1927-32 **Wmk. 196**
51 A46 3p slate ('32) .20 .20
52 A47 ½a green .20 .20
53 A48 1a dark brown .20 .20
54 A60 2a dull violet ('32) .20 .20
55 A57 2a6p buff ('32) .25 .25
56 A51 3a blue ('30) .25 .25
57 A61 4a olive green ('32) .80 .80

Overprinted

58 A56 2r brown org & car rose ('32) 22.50 *7.75*
59 A56 5r dk violet & ultra ('32) 70.00 *27.50*
Nos. 51-59 (9) 94.60 *37.35*

India Stamps of 1926-35 Overprinted

1936-37
63 A71 ½a green .20 .20
64 A68 9p dark green ('37) .20 .20
65 A72 1a dark brown .20 .20
66 A69 1a3p violet ('37) .20 .20
67 A51 3a car rose ('37) .50 *.55*
68 A52 4a olive green ('37) .50 *.65*
Nos. 63-68 (6) 1.80 *2.00*

Same Overprint in Black on 1937 Stamps of India

1938-39 ***Perf. 13½x14***
69 A80 3p slate 3.75 1.25
70 A80 ½a brown .50 .60
71 A80 9p green 15.00 11.00
72 A80 1a carmine .30 *.30*
73 A81 2a scarlet .30 *.25*
74 A81 2a6p purple .30 *.30*
75 A81 3a yel green .50 *.75*
76 A81 3a6p ultramarine .45 *.60*
77 A81 4a dark brown 1.40 *2.00*
78 A81 6a peacock blue 1.40 *3.00*
79 A81 8a blue violet 2.75 *3.75*
80 A81 12a car lake 3.50 *5.00*

Overprinted

81 A82 1r brown & slate 8.00 *11.00*
82 A82 2r dk brn & dk vio 20.00 *27.50*
83 A82 5r dp ultra & dk green 55.00 *77.50*
84 A82 10r rose car & dk vio ('39) 87.50 *125.00*
85 A82 15r dk grn & dk brn ('39) 150.00 *275.00*
86 A82 25r dk vio & blue vio ('39) 200.00 *300.00*
Nos. 69-86 (18) 550.65 *844.80*

India Stamps of 1937 Overprinted in Black

1942 ***Perf. 13½x14***
87 A80 3p slate 22.50 4.00
88 A80 ½a brown 42.50 17.50
89 A80 9p green 17.50 4.50
90 A80 1a carmine 17.50 2.50
Nos. 87-90 (4) 100.00 28.50

Same on India Nos. 168-179

1942-46 **Wmk. 196**
100 A83 3p slate .35 .35
101 A83 ½a rose vio ('43) .45 .45
102 A83 9p lt green ('43) .45 .45
103 A83 1a car rose ('46) .45 .45
104 A84 1a3p bister ('44) .45 .45
105 A84 1½a dark pur ('43) .55 .55
106 A84 2a scarlet ('44) .80 .80
107 A84 3a violet ('44) 1.25 1.25
108 A84 3½a ultramarine 2.00 2.00
109 A85 4a choc ('43) 2.00 2.00
110 A85 6a pck blue ('44) 2.00 2.00
111 A85 8a blue vio ('44) 2.50 2.50
112 A85 12a car lake ('44) 5.00 5.00
Nos. 100-112 (13) 18.25 18.25

OFFICIAL STAMPS

Indian Stamps Overprinted in Black

1885 **Wmk. 39** ***Perf. 14***
O1 A17 ½a green .60 .60
O2 A19 1a violet brown .40 .40
O3 A21 2a ultra 50.00 *57.50*
Nos. O1-O3 (3) 51.00 *58.50*

The reprints have the same measurements as the reprints of the regular issue of the same date.

Indian Stamps Overprinted

1885

Red Overprint
O4 A17 ½a green .70 *.95*
O5 A21 2a ultramarine .50 *.55*

1885-97

Black Overprint
O6 A17 ½a green .30 .20
a. Period after "SERVICE" 85.00 1.75
O7 A19 1a violet brown .30 .20
a. "NABHA STATE" double *240.00*
b. Period after "SERVICE" 4.50 1.75
O8 A21 2a ultra .75 .20
O9 A22 3a orange 9.50 *27.50*
O10 A23 4a olive green .90 .30
O11 A25 8a red vio ('89) .65 .60
O12 A26 12a vio, *red* ('89) 3.25 *8.00*
O13 A27 1r gray ('89) 30.00 *125.00*
O14 A29 1r car rose & grn ('97) 24.00 *35.00*

Wmk. 38
O15 A14 6a bister ('89) 8.00 *9.50*
Nos. O6-O15 (10) 77.65 *206.50*

Nos. O4, O5, and O7 have been reprinted. They usually bear the overprint "Specimen."

1903-06 **Wmk. 39**
O16 A32 3p gray ('06) .30 .20
O17 A33 ½a green .30 .20
O18 A34 1a carmine rose .30 .20
O19 A35 2a violet .30 .30
O20 A38 4a olive green .30 .25
a. Double overprint
O21 A40 8a red violet .50 .40
O22 A42 1r car rose & grn 1.25 1.00
Nos. O16-O22 (7) 3.25 2.55

1907
O23 A44 ½a green .30 .20
O24 A45 1a carmine rose .30 .20

1913
O25 A52 4a olive green 17.50
O26 A56 1r grn & red brn 92.50

Indian Stamps of 1911-26 Overprinted:

1913
O27 A46(a) 3p gray .30 .20
O28 A47(a) ½a green .30 .20
O29 A48(a) 1a carmine rose .30 .20
O30 A49(a) 2a violet .30 .20
O31 A52(a) 4a olive green .30 .20
O32 A54(a) 8a red violet .30 .25
O33 A56(b) 1r grn & red brn .50 .50
Nos. O27-O33 (7) 2.30 1.75

India Stamps of 1926-35 Overprinted

Perf. 13½x14, 14

1932-45 **Wmk. 196**
O34 A46 3p slate .30 .20
O35 A72 1a dark brown ('35) .30 .20
O36 A52 4a olive green ('45) 7.00 1.75
O37 A54 8a red violet ('37) .70 .85
Nos. O34-O37 (4) 8.30 3.00

Same Overprint in Black on India Stamps of 1937

1938
O38 A80 9p green 2.25 2.25
O39 A80 1a carmine .65 .65

Official Stamps of India 1939-43 Overprinted in Black

1942-44 ***Perf. 13½x14***
O40 O8 3p slate .30 .20
O41 O8 ½a brown ('43) .30 .20
O42 O8 ½a dk rose vio ('44) 2.25 2.25
O43 O8 9p green ('43) .30 .20
O44 O8 1a car rose ('43) .30 .20
O45 O8 1½a dull purple ('43) .35 .35
O46 O8 2a scarlet ('43) .30 .20
O47 O8 4a dark brown ('43) 1.90 *2.75*
O48 O8 8a blue violet ('43) 1.90 *2.75*

India Nos. 162-164 Overprinted in Black

O49 A82 1r brown & slate 15.00 *30.00*
O50 A82 2r dk brn & dk vio 45.00 *110.00*
O51 A82 5r dp ultra & dk green 240.00 *240.00*
Nos. O40-O51 (12) 307.90 *389.10*

PATIALA

ˌpət-ē-ˈäl-ə

LOCATION — A State of India in the central Punjab
AREA — 5,942 sq. mi.
POP. — 1,936,259 (1941)
CAPITAL — Patiala

The varieties with small letters in the overprint are not listed as the letters are merely broken and not from another font.

Indian Stamps Overprinted in Red

1884 **Wmk. 39** ***Perf. 14***
1 A17 ½a green .85 *.90*
a. Double ovpt., one horiz. 1,750. 475.00
2 A19 1a violet brown 14.00 14.00
a. Double overprint
b. Double ovpt., one in black 600.00
c. Pair, one as "b," one without overprint
3 A21 2a ultra 5.25 5.75
4 A25 8a red lilac 300.00 *475.00*
a. Double ovpt., one in black 50.00
c. Overprint reversed
d. Pair like "a," one with overprint reversed
5 A27 1r gray 125.00 *125.00*

Wmk. 38
6 A9 4a green 14.00 16.00
Nos. 1-6 (6) 459.10 *636.65*

Indian Stamps Overprinted in Red

1885 **Wmk. 39**
7 A17 ½a green .40 .35
a. "AUTTIALLA" 8.50
c. "STATE" only
8 A21 2a ultra .85 .45
a. "AUTTIALLA" 15.00
9 A27 1r gray 5.00 *10.50*
a. "AUTTIALLA" 475.00

Wmk. 38
10 A9 4a green 1.10 1.10
a. Double overprint, one in black 240.00
b. Pair, one as "a," one with black overprint

Same, Overprinted in Black

Wmk. 39
11 A19 1a violet brown .30 .25
a. "AUTTIALLA" 35.00
c. Double overprint, one in red 4.00
d. Pair, one as "c," one without overprint
12 A25 8a red lilac 4.50 4.50
a. "AUTTIALLA" 240.00
Nos. 7-12 (6) 12.15 *17.15*

Nos. 7-12 have been reprinted. Most of them bear the word "Reprint." The few copies that escaped the overprint cannot be distinguished from the originals.

The error "AUTTIALLA" has been reprinted in entire sheets, in red on the ½, 2, 4a and 1r and in black on the ½, 1, 2, 4, 8a and 1r. "STATE" is 7¾mm long, instead of 8½mm. Most copies are overprinted "Reprint."

Same, Overprinted in Black

1891-96
13 A17 ½a green .30 .20
14 A18 9p rose .30 .30
15 A19 1a violet brown .30 .20
a. "STATE" only 175.00 *300.00*
16 A20 1a6p bister brown .35 .40
17 A21 2a ultra .55 .20
18 A22 3a orange .30 .30
19 A23 4a olive grn ('96) .30 .20
a. "STATE" only 400.00 210.00
20 A25 8a red violet ('96) .55 .55
21 A26 12a violet, *red* .45 .55
22 A29 1r car rose & grn ('96) 4.25 *7.00*
23 A30 2r brn & rose ('95) 100.00
24 A30 3r grn & brn ('95) 125.00
25 A30 5r vio & bl ('95) 150.00

Wmk. 38
26 A14 6a bister .35 .30
Nos. 13-26 (14) 383.00

1899 **Wmk. 39**
27 A31 3p carmine rose .30 .20
a. Pair, one without overprint 2,500.

1902
28 A17 ½a light green .30 .20
29 A19 1a carmine rose .30 .20

1903-06
31 A32 3p gray .30 .20
32 A33 ½a green .30 .20
33 A34 1a carmine rose .30 .20
a. Pair, one without overprint 1,250.
34 A35 2a violet .30 .20
35 A37 3a brown orange .30 .25
36 A38 4a olive green ('06) .75 .40
37 A39 6a bister ('05) .55 .50
38 A40 8a red violet ('06) .45 .40
39 A41 12a vio, *red* ('06) 1.25 1.25
40 A42 1r car rose & grn ('05) 2.00 .75
Nos. 31-40 (10) 6.50 4.35

1908
41 A44 ½a green .30 .20
42 A45 1a carmine rose .30 .20

1912-14
43 A46 3p gray .20 .20
44 A47 ½a green .20 .20
45 A48 1a carmine rose .20 .20
46 A49 2a violet .20 .20
47 A51 3a brown orange .25 .25
48 A52 4a olive green .25 .20
49 A53 6a bister .30 .30
50 A54 8a red violet .45 .25
51 A55 12a claret .65 .40
52 A56 1r green & red brn 3.50 2.50
Nos. 43-52 (10) 6.20 4.70

1922-26
53 A48 1a dk brown ('23) .30 .20
54 A58 1½a chocolate .30 .30
55 A51 3a ultra ('26) .30 .25
56 A56 2r yel brn & car rose ('26) 10.00 *7.25*
57 A56 5r vio & ultra ('26) 20.00 *15.00*
Nos. 53-57 (5) 30.90 23.00

India Stamps of 1926-35 Overprinted

1928-34 **Wmk. 196**
60 A46 3p slate .20 .20
61 A47 ½a green .20 .20
62 A68 9p dark green .20 .20
63 A48 1a dark brown .20 .20
64 A69 1a3p violet .20 .20
65 A60 2a dull violet .20 .20
66 A57 2a6p buff 1.50 1.50
67 A51 3a blue .90 .90
68 A61 4a olive green .25 .30
69 A54 8a red violet .40 .40

Overprinted

70 A56 1r green & brown 3.00 *1.25*
71 A56 2r buff & car rose 5.00 *2.00*
Nos. 60-71 (12) 12.25 7.55

India Stamps of 1926-35 Overprinted Like Nos. 60-69

1935-37 ***Perf. 14***
75 A71 ½a green ('37) .20 .20
76 A72 1a dk brown ('36) .20 .20
77 A49 2a ver ('36) .20 .20
78 A51 3a car rose ('37) 1.50 1.50
79 A52 4a olive green .50 .50
Nos. 75-79 (5) 2.60 2.60

Same Overprint in Black on Stamps of India, 1937

1937-38 ***Perf. 13½x14***
80 A80 3p slate ('38) 16.00 2.50
81 A80 ½a brown ('38) 3.50 .70
82 A80 9p green 1.25 .45
83 A80 1a carmine .80 .25
84 A81 2a scarlet ('38) 1.00 .25
85 A81 2a6p purple ('38) 1.25 .25
86 A81 3a yel green ('38) 1.25 .25
87 A81 3a6p ultra ('38) 1.60 .40
88 A81 4a dark brown ('38) 12.00 .35
89 A81 6a pck blue ('38) 12.00 .45
90 A81 8a blue violet ('38) 16.00 1.10
91 A81 12a car lake ('38) 14.00 1.10

Overprinted Like Nos. 70-71

1938
92 A82 1r brown & slate 17.50 10.00
93 A82 2r dk brn & dk vio 22.50 19.00
94 A82 5r dp ultra & dk green 32.50 *37.50*
95 A82 10r rose car & dk vio 50.00 *85.00*
96 A82 15r dk grn & dk brn 95.00 *150.00*
97 A82 25r dk vio & bl vio 125.00 *210.00*
Nos. 80-97 (18) 423.15 *519.55*

India Nos. 150-153 Overprinted in Black

1942-43 ***Perf. 13½x14***
98 A80 3p slate 12.00 1.50
99 A80 ½a brown ('43) 5.50 1.10
100 A80 9p green ('43) 150.00 3.75
101 A80 1a carmine 15.00 1.50
Nos. 98-101 (4) 182.50 7.85

India Stamps of 1941-43 with same Overprint in Black

1942-47 ***Perf. 13½x14***
102 A83 3p slate .35 .20
103 A83 ½a rose violet ('43) .35 .20
104 A83 9p lt green ('43) .35 .20
a. Pair, one without overprint *2,750.*
105 A83 1a car rose ('46) .35 .20
106 A84 1a3p bister ('43) 1.10 *1.60*
107 A84 1½a dk purple ('43) 2.25 .80
108 A84 2a scarlet ('46) 2.25 .20
109 A84 3a violet ('46) 1.25 .55
110 A84 3½a ultra ('46) 6.50 *15.00*
111 A85 4a choc ('46) 1.60 .55
112 A85 6a pck blue ('46) 1.25 *8.50*
113 A85 8a blue vio ('46) 1.60 *4.00*
114 A85 12a car lake ('45) 4.00 *27.50*

India No. 162 Overprinted in Black

115 A82 1r brown & slate ('47) 10.00 *47.50*
Nos. 102-115 (14) 33.20 *107.00*

OFFICIAL STAMPS

Indian Stamps Overprinted in Black and Red

1884 **Wmk. 39** ***Perf. 14***
O1 A17 ½a green 6.00 .25
O2 A19 1a vio brown .45 .20
a. "SERVICE" double 1,000. 475.00
b. "SERVICE" inverted 1,000.
c. "PUTTIALLA STATE" dbl. 90.00
d. "PUTTIALLA STATE" invtd. 1,000. 90.00
O3 A21 2a ultra *2,500.* 200.00

Same, Overprinted in Red or Black:

a

b

1885-90
O4 A17(a) ½a green (R & Bk) .55 .20
a. "AUTTIALLA" 45.00 15.00
d. "SERVICE" double 725.00
O5 A17(b) ½a green (Bk) .45 .20
O6 A19(a) 1a vio brn (Bk) .25 .20
a. "AUTTILLA" 600.00 37.50
c. "SERVICE" dble., one invtd. 600.00
d. "SERVICE" double 1,250. 225.00
O7 A21(b) 2a ultra (R) .30 .20
c. "SERVICE" dbl., one invtd. 40.00
Nos. O4-O7 (4) 1.55 .80

There are reprints of Nos. O4, O6 and O7. That of No. O4 has "SERVICE" overprinted in red in large letters and that of No. O6 has the same overprint in black. The originals have the word in small black letters. The reprints of No. O7, except those overprinted "Reprint," cannot be distinguished from the originals. These three reprints also exist with the error "AUTTIALLA."

Same, Overprinted in Black

1891-1900
O8 A17 ½a green ('95) .30 .20
b. "SERVICE" inverted 67.50
O9 A19 1a vio brown ('00) 2.25 .20
a. "SERVICE" inverted 72.50
O10 A21 2a ultramarine .95 .45
a. "SERVICE" inverted 72.50
O11 A22 3a orange .35 .25
O12 A23 4a olive green .30 .20
O13 A25 8a red violet .30 .25
O14 A26 12a violet, *red* .50 .30
O15 A27 1r gray .55 .30

Wmk. 38
O16 A14 6a bister .45 .40
Nos. O8-O16 (9) 5.95 2.55

1902 **Wmk. 39**
O17 A19 1a carmine rose .25 .20

1903
O18 A29 1r car rose & green 5.25 5.50

1903-09
O19 A32 3p gray .30 .20
O20 A33 ½a green .30 .20
O21 A34 1a carmine rose .30 .20
O22 A35 2a violet .30 .20
O23 A37 3a brown orange .75 .75
O24 A38 4a olive green ('05) .30 .20
O25 A40 8a red violet .30 .20
O26 A42 1r car rose & grn ('06) .85 .85
Nos. O19-O26 (8) 3.40 2.80

1907
O27 A44 ½a green .30 .20
O28 A45 1a carmine rose .30 .20

India Stamps of 1911-26 Overprinted:

a

b

1913-26
O29 A46(a) 3p gray .30 .20
O30 A47(a) ½a green 1.10 .20
O31 A48(a) 1a car rose .30 .20
O32 A49(a) 2a violet .30 .20
O33 A52(a) 4a olive green .30 .20
O34 A54(a) 8a red violet .30 .20
O35 A56(b) 1r grn & red brn 1.25 .45
O36 A56(b) 2r yel brn & car rose ('26) 10.00 *9.25*
O37 A56(b) 5r vio & ultra ('26) 11.00 *22.50*
Nos. O29-O37 (9) 24.85 *33.40*

Same Overprint on India Nos. 83 and 89

1925-26
O38 A48(a) 1a dark brown .30 .20
O39 A53(a) 6a bister ('26) .30 .20

India Stamps of 1926-35 Overprinted

1927-36 **Wmk. 196**
O40 A46 3p slate .20 .20
O41 A47 ½a green .20 .20
O42 A48 1a dark brown .20 .20
O43 A69 1a3p violet .20 .20
O44 A60 2a dull violet .20 .20
O45 A60 2a vermilion .20 .20
O46 A57 2a6p buff .20 .20
O47 A61 4a olive green .20 .20
O48 A54 8a red violet .25 .25

Overprinted

O49 A56 1r green & brown 1.50 .30
O50 A56 2r brn org & car rose ('36) 5.00 *3.25*
Nos. O40-O50 (11) 8.35 *5.40*

India Stamps of 1926-34 Overprinted

1935-36
O51 A71 ½a green ('36) .20 .20
O52 A72 1a dark brown ('36) .20 .20
O53 A49 2a vermilion .30 .20
a. Small die .25 .20
O54 A52 4a olive green ('36) .30 .20
Nos. O51-O54 (4) 1.00 *.80*

Same Overprint on India #151-153

1938-39 ***Perf. 13½x14***
O55 A80 ½a brown ('39) .60 .20
O56 A80 9p green ('39) 21.00 *27.50*
O57 A80 1a carmine .60 .20
Nos. O55-O57 (3) 22.20 *27.90*

India No. 136 Surcharged in Black

1939 ***Perf. 14***
O58 A69 1a on 1a3p violet 2.00 .70
"SERVICE" measures 9¼mm.

No. 64 Surcharged in Black 1A SERVICE 1A

1940
O59 A69 1a on 1a3p violet 2.00 1.40
"SERVICE" measures 8½mm.

India Nos. 162-164 Overprinted

Perf. 13½x14
O60 A82 1r brown & slate 3.50 3.50
O61 A82 2r dk brn & dk vio 17.00 17.00
O62 A82 5r dp ultra & dk grn 32.50 32.50

India Official Stamps of 1939-43 Overprinted

1940-45
O63 O8 3p slate ('41) .20 .20
O64 O8 ½a brown .20 .20
O65 O8 ½a dk rose vio ('43) .20 .20
O66 O8 9p green .20 .20
O67 O8 1a carmine rose .25 .20
O68 O8 1a3p bister ('41) .20 .20
O69 O8 1½a dull purple ('45) .40 .20
O70 O8 2a scarlet ('41) .20 .20
O71 O8 2½a purple ('41) .20 .20
O72 O8 4a dk brown ('45) .30 .30
O73 O8 8a blue violet ('45) .90 *1.25*

India Nos. 162-164 Overprinted in Black

O74 A82 1r brn & slate ('43) 9.00 6.50
O75 A82 2r dk brn & dk vio ('45) 16.00 *37.50*
O76 A82 5r dp ultra & dk grn ('45) 24.00 *60.00*
Nos. O63-O76 (14) 52.25 *107.35*

NATIVE FEUDATORY STATES

ALWAR

ˈəl-wər

LOCATION — A Feudatory State of India, lying southwest of Delhi in the Jaipur Residency.
AREA — 3,158 sq. mi.
POP. — 749,751.
CAPITAL — Alwar

Katar (Indian Dagger) — A1

1877 Unwmk. Litho. *Rouletted*

1 A1 ¼a ultramarine 1.00 .75
  a. ¼a blue 1.00 .75
  b. Horiz. pair, imperf. vert. 32.50
2 A1 1a brown 1.00 1.00
  a. 1a yellow brown 1.00 1.00
  b. 1a red brown 1.00 1.00
  c. Horiz. pair, imperf. vert. 55.00 55.00

Redrawn

1899-1901 *Pin-perf. 12*

3 A1 ¼a sl blue, wide margins 6.00 3.50
4 A1 ¼a yel grn, narrow margins ('01) 5.25 3.50
  a. Horiz. pair, imperf. btwn. 325.00
  b. ¼a emer, wide margins ('99) 600.00
  c. ¼a emer, narrow margins 5.25 4.75

Nos. 3 and 4b are printed farther apart in the sheet.

On Nos. 3 and 4, the shading of the left border line is missing.

Nos. 1 to 4 occasionally show portions of the papermaker's watermark, W. T. & Co.

Alwar stamps became obsolete in 1902.

BAMRA

ˈbäm-rə

LOCATION — A Feudatory State in the Eastern States, Orissa States Agency, Bengal.
AREA — 1,988 sq. mi.
POP. — 151,259
CAPITAL — Deogarh

Stamps of Bamra were issued without gum.

A1

A2

1888 Unwmk. Typeset *Imperf.*

1 A1 ¼a black, *yellow* 80.00
  a. "g" inverted *2,400.*
2 A1 ½a black, *rose* 52.50
  a. "g" inverted *2,100.*
3 A1 1a black, *blue* 32.50
  a. "g" inverted *1,600.*
  b. "postge"
4 A1 2a black, *green* 45.00
  a. "postge" *2,100.*
5 A1 4a black, *yellow* 32.50
  a. "postge" *1,750.*
6 A1 8a black, *rose* 30.00
  a. "postge" *1,600.*
  Nos. 1-6 (6) 272.50

All values may be found with the scroll inverted, and with the long end of the scroll pointing to the right or left.

On No. 5 the last character on the 3rd line is a vertical line. On No. 1 it is not vertical.

On No. 2 the last character on the 3rd line looks like a backwards "R" with a bent leg. On No. 6 it looks like an apostrophe.

Nos. 1 and 2 have been reprinted in blocks of 8 and Nos. 1-6 in blocks of 20. In the reprints the 4th character of the native inscription often has the curved upper line broken at the left, but in many instances comparison with photographic reproductions of the original settings is the only certain test.

1890

7 A2 ¼a black, *rose lilac* 1.00 1.00
  a. "Quatrer" 10.00 10.00
  b. "e" of "Postage" inverted 10.00 10.00
  c. "Eeudatory" 10.00 10.00
8 A2 ½a black, *green* 1.40 1.40
  a. "Eeudatory" 16.00 16.00
  b. "postage" with small "p" 1.40 1.40
  c. First "a" of "anna" inverted 14.00
9 A2 1a black, *yellow* 3.25 3.25
  a. "Eeudatory" 35.00 *40.00*
  b. "postage" with small "p" 2.00 2.00
  c. "annas" 65.00 65.00
10 A2 2a black, *rose lilac* 4.75 4.75
  a. "Eeudatory" 60.00 *67.50*
11 A2 4a black, *rose lilac* 35.00 35.00
  a. "Eeudatory" 175.00 175.00
12 A2 8a black, *rose lilac* 10.00 10.00
  a. "BAMBA" 125.00 125.00
  b. "Foudatory" & "Postage" 125.00 125.00
  c. "postage" with small "p" 10.00 10.00
13 A2 1r black, *rose lilac* 32.50 32.50
  a. "BAMBA" 160.00 160.00
  b. "Eeudatory" 175.00 175.00
  c. "postage" with small "p" 32.50 32.50
  Nos. 7-13 (7) 87.90 87.90

1893

14 A2 ¼a black, *rose* .90 .90
  a. "postage" with small "p" .90 .90
15 A2 ¼a black, *magenta* .90 .90
  a. "postage" with small "p" .90 .90
  b. "AM" of "BAMRA" invtd.
  c. "M" OF "BAMRA" invtd.
  d. "AMRA" of "BAMRA" inverted 22.50
  e. "M" and 2nd "A" of "BAMRA" inverted 52.50 52.50
  f. First "a" of "anna" inverted 27.50 27.50
16 A2 2a black, *rose* 1.40 1.40
  a. "postage" with small "p" 1.40 1.40
17 A2 4a black, *rose* 3.25 3.25
  a. "postage" with small "p" 3.25 3.25
  b. "BAMBA" 250.00 250.00
18 A2 8a black, *rose* 5.00 5.00
  a. "postage" with small "p" 5.00 5.00
19 A2 1r black, *rose* 18.00 20.00
  a. "postage" with small "p" 30.00 30.00
  Nos. 14-19 (6) 29.45 31.45

The central ornament varies in size and may be found in various positions.

Bamra stamps became obsolete Dec. 31, 1894.

BARWANI

bər-ˈwän-ē

LOCATION — A Feudatory State of Central India, in the Malwa Agency.
AREA — 1,178 sq. mi.
POP. — 141,110
CAPITAL — Barwani

The stamps of Barwani were all typographed and normally issued in booklets containing panes of four. Exceptions are noted (Nos. 14-15, 20-25). The majority were completely perforated, but some of the earlier printings were perforated only between the stamps, leaving one or two sides imperf. Nos. 1-25 were issued without gum. Many shades exist.

Rana Ranjit Singh
A1 A2

1921, April (?) Unwmk. *Pin-Perf 7*
Toned Medium Wove Paper
Clear Impression

1 A1 ¼a dull Prus green 75.00 *275.00*
2 A1 ½a dull blue 210.00 *425.00*

1921 *Coarse Perf. 7 x Imperf.*
White Thin Wove Paper
Blurred Impression

3 A1 ¼a dull green 17.50 *75.00*
4 A1 ½a pale blue 15.00 *125.00*

1921 Toned Laid Paper *Imperf.*

5 A1 ¼a light green 15.00
6 A1 ½a light green 3.00
  a. Perf. 11, top or bottom only 2.50

1921 *Coarse Perf. 7, 7 x Imperf.*
Thick Wove Paper
Very Blurred Impression

7 A1 ¼a dull blue 15.00
8 A1 ½a dull green 22.50

In 1927 #7-8 were printed on thin hard paper.

1922 *Perf. 7 x Imperf.*
Thick Glazed Paper

9 A1 ¼a dull ultra 50.00

Rough Perf. 11 x Imperf.

10 A2 1a vermilion 2.00 *18.00*
11 A2 2a violet 2.00 *20.00*
  a. Double impression *275.00*
  Nos. 9-11 (3) 54.00 38.00

Shades of No. 11 include purple. No. 11 was also printed on thick dark toned paper.

1923-26 *Perf.*
Wove, Laid Paper

12 A1 ¼a grayish ultra, perf. 8½ 1.60 *30.00*
13 A1 ¼a black, perf. 7 x imperf. 55.00 *175.00*
14 A1 ¼a dull rose, perf. 11½-12 1.25 *7.50*
15 A1 ¼a dk bl, perf. 11 ('26) 1.25 *7.50*
16 A1 ½a grn, perf. 11ximperf. 1.25 *15.00*
  Nos. 12-16 (5) 60.35 235.00

No. 12 was also printed on pale gray thin toned paper.

No. 14 was printed on horizontally laid paper in horizontal sheets of 12 containing three panes of 4.

No. 15 was printed on vertically laid paper in horizontal sheets of 8.

Rana Ranjit Singh — A3

1927-28 *Perf. 7*
Thin Wove Paper

17 A3 4a dull orange 55.00 *300.00*

No. 17 was also printed in light brown on thick paper, pin-perf. 6, and in orange brown on thick paper, rough perf. 7.

1928 *Coarse Perf. 7*
Thick Glazed Paper

18 A1 ¼a bright blue 9.00
19 A1 ½a bright yel green 18.00

1928, Nov. *Rough Perf. 10½*

20 A1 ¼a deep ultra 3.25
  a. Tête bêche pair 8.50
21 A1 ½a yellow green 4.00
  a. Tête bêche pair 7.50

1929-31 *Perf. 11*

22 A1 ¼a blue 2.00 *7.50*
  a. ¼a ultramarine 1.50 *10.00*
23 A1 ½a emerald green 2.50 *10.00*
24 A2 1a car pink ('31) 10.00 *25.00*
25 A3 4a salmon 40.00 *150.00*
  Nos. 22-25 (4) 54.50 192.50

Nos. 20-25 were printed in sheets of 8 (4x2).

No. 22 had five printings in various shades (bright to deep blue) in horizontal or vertical format.

No. 23 also printed in dark myrtle green.

Rana Devi Singh
A4 A5

1932-48 *Perf. 11, 12*
Glazed Paper

26 A4 ¼a dark gray 1.40 *9.50*
27 A4 ½a blue green 1.40 *9.50*
28 A4 1a brown 1.50 *9.00*
  a. 1a chocolate, perf. 8½ ('48) 10.00 30.00
29 A4 2a deep red violet 2.75 *15.00*
  a. Perf. 12x11
  b. 2a red lilac 12.50
30 A4 4a olive green 8.50 *17.00*
  Nos. 26-30 (5) 15.55 *60.00*

Types of 1921-27

1934-48 *Perf. 11*

31 A1 ¼a slate gray 2.25 *17.50*
32 A1 ½a green 3.50 *22.50*
33 A2 1a dark brown 9.00 *17.50*
  a. 1a brown, perf. 8½ ('48) 9.00 *25.00*
34 A2 2a brt purple ('38) 60.00 *175.00*
35 A2 2a rose car ('46) 20.00 *75.00*
36 A3 4a olive green 20.00 *37.50*
  Nos. 31-36 (6) 114.75 345.00

In the nine printings of Nos. 26-36, several plate settings spaced the cliches from 2 to 9mm apart. Hence the stamps come in different overall sizes. Not all values were in each printing. Values are for the commonest varieties.

No. 36 was also printed in pale sage green.

1938

37 A5 1a dark brown 22.50 *40.00*
  a. Booklet pane of 4 50.00

Stamps of type A5 in red are revenues.

Barwani stamps became obsolete July 1, 1948.

BHOPAL

bō-ˈpäl

LOCATION — A Feudatory State of Central India, in the Bhopal Agency.
AREA — 6,924 sq. mi.
POP. — 995,745
CAPITAL — Bhopal

Inscription in Urdu in an octagon embossed on Nos. 1-83, in a circle embossed on Nos. 84-90. On designs A1-A3, A7, A11-A12, A14-A15, A19-A21 the embossing makes up the central part of the design.

The embossing may be found inverted or sideways.

Expect irregular perfs on the perforated stamps, Nos. 19-77, due to a combination of imperfect perforating methods and the fragility of the papers.

Nos. 1-90 issued without gum.

A1

A2

Double Lined Frame

1876 Unwmk. Litho. *Imperf.*

1 A1 ¼a black 350.00 300.00
a. "EGAM" 1,250. 1,250.
b. "BFGAM" 1,250. 1,250.
c. "BEGAN" 775.00 775.00
2 A1 ½a red 17.50 17.50
a. "EGAM" 50.00 *90.00*
b. "BFGAM" 50.00 *90.00*
c. "BEGAN" 35.00 *60.00*

Single Lined Frame

1877

3 A2 ¼a black *4,000.*
a. "NWAB"
4 A2 ½a red 20.00 *37.50*
a. "NWAB" 125.00 *175.00*

A3

A4

1878

5 A3 ¼a black 5.00 *8.50*
a. "J" diagonal, plate II 5.00 *10.00*

All stamps of type A3 are lettered "EEGAM" for "BEGAM."

1878

6 A4 ½a pale red 4.50 *10.00*
a. ½a brown red 20.00 27.50
b. "NWAB" 15.00
c. "JAHN" 24.00
d. "EECAM" 24.00

A5

A6

1879-80

7 A5 ¼a green 9.00 *15.00*
8 A5 ½a red 10.00 *15.00*

Perf.

9 A5 ¼a green 7.00 *10.00*
10 A5 ½a red 10.00
Nos. 7-10 (4) 36.00 *40.00*

Nos. 7 and 9 have the value in parenthesis; Nos. 8 and 10 are without parenthesis.

1881 *Imperf.*

11 A6 ¼a green 5.00
a. "NAWA" 20.00
b. "CHAH" 50.00

Perf.

12 A6 ¼a green 7.00
a. "NAWA" 27.50
b. "CHAH" 75.00

A7

1881-89 *Imperf.*

13 A7 ¼a black 4.00 *10.00*
a. "NWAB" 8.00
14 A7 ½a red 3.00 *7.50*
a. "NWAB" 7.00
15 A7 1a brown 2.75 *8.00*
a. "NWAB" 6.50
16 A7 2a blue 1.50 *8.00*
a. "NWAB" 4.00
17 A7 4a yellow 10.00 *32.50*
a. "NWAB" 25.00
Nos. 13-17 (5) 21.25 *66.00*

A8

A9

1884 *Perf.*

19 A8 ¼a green 125.00 *160.00*
a. "JAN" 125.00 *160.00*
b. "BEGM" 400.00
c. "NWAB" 650.00
d. "SHAHAN" 650.00
e. "JN" 450.00
f. "JAHA" 300.00
20 A9 ¼a green 3.00 *8.50*
a. "ANAWAB" 10.00

On type A9 there is a dash at the left of "JA" of "JAHAN" instead of a character like a comma as on types A5 and A6.

Imitations of No. 19 were printed about 1904 in black on wove paper and in red on laid paper, both imperf. and pin-perf.

A10

1884 Laid Paper *Imperf.*

21 A10 ¼a blue green 90.00 *125.00*
a. "NWAB" 300.00
b. "NAWAJANAN" 300.00
c. "SAH" 300.00
22 A10 ½a black 1.60 1.25
a. "NWAB" 7.00
b. "NAWAJANAN" 7.00
c. "SAH" 7.00

Perf.

23 A10 ¼a blue green .50 *2.50*
a. "NWAB" 3.00
b. "NAWAJANAN" 3.00
c. "SAH" 3.00
24 A10 ½a black .40 *1.75*
a. "NWAB" 2.75
b. "NAWAJANAN" 2.75
c. "SAH" 2.75
Nos. 21-24 (4) 92.50 130.50

Type Redrawn

1886 Wove Paper *Imperf.*

25 A10 ¼a grayish green .35 *2.00*
a. ¼a green .35 *2.00*
b. "NWAB" 2.00
c. "NAWA" 1.50
d. "NAWAA" 2.00
e. "NAWABABEGAAM" 2.00
f. "NWABA" 2.00
26 A10 ½a red .30 .30
a. "SAH" 3.00
b. "NAWABA" 2.75

Perf.

27 A10 ¼a green 1.50 *2.50*
a. "NWAB" 8.00
b. "NAWA" 8.00
c. "NAWAA" 8.00
d. "NAWABABEGAAM" 8.00
e. "NWABA" 8.00
28 A10 ½a red 2.50 2.50
a. "SAH" 12.00
b. "NAWABA" 12.00
Nos. 25-28 (4) 4.65 7.30

On Nos. 25-28 the inscriptions are closer to the value than on Nos. 21-24.

A11

A12

1886 *Imperf.*

29 A11 ½a red 1.40 6.00
a. "BEGAM" 7.50
b. "NWAB" 7.50

Laid Paper

30 A12 4a yellow 6.00
a. "EEGAM" 10.00
b. Wove paper 600.00
c. As "a," wove paper *775.00*

Perf.

31 A12 4a yellow 2.50 *10.00*
a. "EEGAM" 5.00 *15.00*
Nos. 29-31 (3) 9.90

A13

A14

1889 Wove Paper *Imperf.*

32 A13 ¼a green .50 .75
a. "SAH" 3.00 *4.75*
b. "NAWA" 3.00 *4.75*
33 A14 ¼a black 1.10 1.25
a. "EEGAN" 7.25

Perf.

34 A13 ¼a green .50 *1.25*
a. "SAH" 3.25
b. "NAWA" 3.25
c. Imperf. vertically
35 A14 ¼a black 1.00 *3.00*
a. "EEGAN" 9.00 *20.00*
b. Horiz. pair, imperf. between 210.00
Nos. 32-35 (4) 3.10 6.25

Type A13 has smaller letters in the upper corners than Type A10.

A15

A16

1890 *Imperf.*

36 A15 ¼a black 1.00 .80
37 A15 1a brown .90 *3.00*
a. "EEGAM" 10.00 *15.00*
b. "BBGAM" 10.00 *15.00*
38 A7 2a greenish blue .80 1.00
a. "BBEGAM" 6.50 *9.00*
b. "NAWAH" 6.50 *9.00*
39 A7 4a yellow 1.00 *2.10*
40 A16 8a blue 30.00 *57.50*
a. "HAH" 45.00
b. "JABAN" 45.00
Nos. 36-40 (5) 33.70 64.40

An imperf. imitation of Nos. 36 and 41 was printed about 1904 in black on wove paper.

Perf.

41 A15 ¼a black 1.25 *2.10*
a. Pair, imperf. between 7.50
42 A15 1a brown .90 *3.00*
a. "EECAM" 17.50 *20.00*
b. "BBGAM" 17.50 *20.00*
43 A7 2a greenish blue .85 *1.50*
a. "BBEGAM" 6.00 *12.00*
b. "NAWAH" 6.00 *12.00*
44 A7 4a yellow 1.50 *4.00*
45 A16 8a blue 32.50 *60.00*
a. "HAH" 45.00
b. "JABAN" 45.00
Nos. 41-45 (5) 37.00 70.60

Nos. 40 and 45 have a frame line around each stamp.

Imperf

46 A12 ½a red (BECAM) .90 1.10
47 A13 ½a red (NWAB) .75 .60
a. Inverted "N"
b. "SAH" 7.50

Perf.

48 A12 ½a red (BECAM) .60 .60
a. Without embossing
49 A13 ½a red (NWAB) .75 .85
a. Inverted "N"
b. "SAH" 7.50
Nos. 46-49 (4) 3.00 3.15

1891-93 Laid Paper *Imperf.*

50 A16 8a deep green 40.00 *75.00*
a. "HAH" 55.00
b. "JABAN" 55.00

Perf.

51 A16 8a deep green 40.00 *75.00*
a. "HAH" 60.00
b. "JABAN" 60.00

For overprint, see No. 83.

1894 Redrawn *Imperf.*

53 A10 ¼a green .60 .60
a. "NAWAH" 5.00 *6.00*
54 A11 ½a brick red 1.00 .75
55 A16 8a blue black 15.00 15.00
a. Laid paper 27.50

Perf.

56 A10 ¼a green 1.60 1.25
a. "NAWAH" 7.50 7.50
57 A11 ½a brick red .60 *1.00*
58 A16 8a blue black 20.00 *24.00*
Nos. 53-58 (6) 38.80 42.60

The ¼a redrawn has letters in corners larger; value in very small characters.

The 8a redrawn has no frame to each stamp but a frame to the sheet.

1898 *Imperf.*

60 A16 8a black 24.00 *35.00*
b. "E" of "BEGAM" inverted 55.00

A17

A18

A19

A20

A21

1895

Laid Paper

61 A17 ¼a green 1.50 1.50
62 A18 ¼a red 1.75 1.75
63 A19 ¼a black .75 .75
a. "NAWB" 4.25 4.25
64 A20 ½a black .75 .75
65 A21 ½a red .90 1.10

Perf.

66 A17 ¼a green 3.25 3.25
67 A18 ¼a red 1.60 1.60
68 A19 ¼a black 2.50 2.50
a. "NAWB" 18.00
69 A20 ½a black 1.60 1.60
70 A21 ½a red
Nos. 61-69 (9) 14.60 14.80

Imperf. imitations of Nos. 65 and 70 were printed about 1904 in deep red on laid paper and in black on wove paper.

Wove Paper

Small Pin-perf.

71 A16 8a blue black

A22

A23

1898 *Imperf.*

72 A22 ¼a black .30 .30
a. "SHAN" 2.50
73 A22 ¼a green .35 .35
a. "SHAN" 2.50
74 A23 ¼a black 1.50 .50
Nos. 72-74 (3) 2.15 1.15

1899

75 A13 ½a black ("NWAB") 2.25 *3.00*
a. "SHN" 14.00 *17.50*
b. "NWASBAHJAHNJ" 14.00 *17.50*
c. "SIIAN" 7.00 *8.50*
d. "SBAH" 14.00 *17.50*
e. "SBAN" 14.00 *17.50*
f. "NWIB" 14.00 *17.50*
g. "BEIAM" 14.00 *17.50*

A24

Coat of Arms — A25

1902

76 A24 ¼a red 1.10 *2.25*
77 A24 ½a black 1.60 *2.75*
a. Printed on both sides 425.00

78 A24 1a brown 2.75 *6.75*
79 A24 2a blue 4.00 *5.50*
80 A24 4a orange 32.50 *47.50*
81 A24 8a violet 50.00 *80.00*
82 A24 1r rose 150.00 *175.00*
Nos. 76-82 (7) 241.95 *319.75*

No. 50 Overprinted in Red

1903
83 A16 8a deep green 75.00 75.00
a. Inverted overprint 190.00 190.00

There are two types of the overprint which is the Arabic S, initial of the Begum.

Inscription in Circle
Embossed on Each Stamp

1903
84 A24 ¼a red .35 *1.75*
85 A24 ½a black .45 *2.25*
86 A24 1a brown .55 *2.75*
87 A24 2a blue 1.50 *10.50*
88 A24 4a orange 16.00 *24.00*
89 A24 8a violet 27.50 *57.50*
90 A24 1r rose 35.00 *77.50*
Nos. 84-90 (7) 81.35 176.25

The embossing in a circle, which was first used in 1903, has been applied to many early stamps and impressions from redrawn plates of early issues. So far as is now known, these should be classed as reprints.

1908 **Engr.** ***Perf. 13½***
99 A25 1a yellow green 3.00 3.00
a. Printed on both sides 90.00

OFFICIAL STAMPS

O1

Size: 20½x25mm

Overprinted

1908 **Unwmk.** **Engr.** ***Perf. 13½***
O1 O1 ½a yellow green 1.50 .20
a. Pair, one without ovpt. 350.00
b. Inverted overprint 125.00
c. Double ovpt., one invtd. 125.00
O2 O1 1a carmine 2.75 .20
a. Inverted overprint 60.00
O3 O1 2a blue 16.00 .20
O4 O1 4a red brown 7.25 .20
Nos. O1-O4 (4) 27.50 .80

Overprinted

O5 O1 ½a yellow green 2.50 .20
O6 O1 1a carmine 6.00 .90
O7 O1 2a blue 3.00 .20
a. Inverted overprint 20.00
O8 O1 4a red brown 45.00 .20
a. Inverted overprint 17.50 *50.00*
Nos. O5-O8 (4) 56.50 1.50

The difference in the two overprints is in the shape of the letters, most noticeable in the "R."

Type of 1908 Issue
Size: 25½x30½mm

Overprinted

1930-31 **Litho.** ***Perf. 14***
O9 O1 ½a gray green ('31) 5.25 .70
O10 O1 1a carmine 6.00 .20
O11 O1 2a blue 5.75 .20
O12 O1 4a brown 5.25 .40
Nos. O9-O12 (4) 22.25 1.50

½a, 2a, 4a are inscribed "POSTAGE" on the left side; 1a "POSTAGE AND REVENUE."

Similar to Type O1
Size: 21x25mm
"POSTAGE" at left
"BHOPAL STATE" at right

1932-33 ***Perf. 11½, 13, 13½, 14***
O13 O1 ¼a orange yellow 1.75 .20
a. Pair, one without overprint 85.00
b. Perf. 13½ 5.25 2.75
c. Perf. 14 10.00 .20

"BHOPAL GOVT." at right
Perf. 13½

O14 O1 ½a yellow green 3.00 .20
O15 O1 1a brown red 5.50 .20
O16 O1 2a blue 5.50 .20
O17 O1 4a brown 4.25 .50
Nos. O13-O17 (5) 20.00 1.30

No. O14, O16-O17 Surcharged in Red, Violet, Black or Blue:

a

b

c

1935-36 ***Perf. 13½***
O18 O1(a) ¼a on ½a (R) 17.00 9.00
a. Inverted surcharge 150.00 60.00
O19 O1(b) 3p on ½a (R) 2.10 *2.50*
O20 O1(a) ¼a on 2a (R) 17.00 11.50
a. Inverted surcharge 125.00 50.00
O21 O1(b) 3p on 2a (R) 3.00 2.75
a. Inverted surcharge 45.00 27.50
O22 O1(a) ¼a on 4a (R) 700.00 190.00
O23 O1(a) ¼a on 4a (Bk) ('36) 45.00 16.00
O24 O1(b) 3p on 4a (R) 67.50 32.50
O25 O1(b) 3p on 4a (Bk) ('36) 2.10 2.25
O26 O1(c) 1a on ½a (V) 2.50 1.25
a. Inverted surcharge 50.00 35.00
O27 O1(c) 1a on 2a (R) 1.90 1.50
a. Inverted surcharge 50.00 50.00
O28 O1(c) 1a on 2a (Bk) ('36) .60 *.90*
O29 O1(c) 1a on 4a (Bl) 3.25 *3.50*
Nos. O18-O29 (12) 861.95 273.65

Nos. O18-O25 are arranged in composite sheets of 100. The 2 top horizontal rows of each value are surcharged "a" and the next 5 rows as "b." The next 3 rows as "b" but in a narrower setting.

Various errors of spelling or inverted letters are found on Nos. O18-O29.

Arms of Bhopal — O2

1935 **Litho.**
O30 O2 1a3p claret & blue 2.50 .20
a. Overprint omitted 45.00 45.00

Inscribed: "Bhopal State Postage"
Ovptd. "SERVICE" 11mm long

1937 ***Perf. 12***
O31 O2 1a6p dk claret & blue 1.50 .25
a. Overprint omitted 90.00 75.00

See Nos. O42, O45.

Arms of Bhopal — O3

Brown or Black Overprint

1936-38 **Typo.**
O32 O3 ¼a orange (Br) .60 .20
a. Black overprint 7.50 .50
c. Inverted overprint — 240.00
d. As "a," inverted — 210.00
O32B O3 ¼a yellow (Br) ('38) 2.00 .50
O33 O3 1a carmine 1.10 .20
Nos. O32-O33 (3) 3.70 .90

Moti Mahal O4

Overprinted "SERVICE"

1936 ***Perf. 11½***
O34 O4 ½a green & chocolate .50 .40
a. Double impression of stamp .75 12.50

Moti Masjid — O5

4a, Taj Mahal and Be-Nazir Palaces.

Overprinted "SERVICE"

1937 ***Perf. 11½***
O35 O5 2a dk blue & brown 1.25 .20
a. Inverted overprint 210.00 210.00
O36 O5 4a bister brn & blue 2.50 .30

Types of 1937
Overprinted "SERVICE" in Black or Brown

Designs: 4a, Taj Mahal. 8a, Ahmadabad Palace. 1r, Rait-Ghat.

1938-44
O37 O4 ½a dp green & brown .50 .20
O38 O5 2a violet & dp grn 5.00 .20
O39 O5 4a red brn & brt bl 2.00 .35
O40 O5 8a red vio & blue 3.00 .75
a. "SERAICE" 275.00 *350.00*
b. Overprint omitted — 125.00
c. Double overprint — 125.00
O41 O5 1r bl & red vio (Br) 9.50 3.50
a. Black overprint ('44) 12.00 3.50
b. "SREVICE" 125.00 150.00
c. Overprint omitted 450.00
d. Double overprint 55.00 55.00
Nos. O37-O41 (5) 20.00 5.00

#O39 measures 36½x22½mm, #O40 39x24mm, #O41 45½x27¾mm.

Type of 1935

1939 ***Perf. 12***
O42 O2 1a6p dark claret 4.00 .50

Tiger — O6

Design: 1a, Deer.

1940 **Typo.** ***Perf. 11½***
O43 O6 ¼a ultramarine 2.50 .75
O44 O6 1a red violet 14.00 1.00

Type of 1935
Inscribed: "Bhopal State Postage"

1941
O45 O2 1a3p emerald .75 .85

Moti Palace — O7

Coat of Arms — O8

2a, Moti Mosque. 4a, Be-Nazir Palaces.

Perf. 11½, 12
1944-46 **Unwmk.** **Typo.**
O46 O8 3p ultramarine .30 .30
O47 O7 ½a light green .50 .45
O48 O8 9p orange brn ('46) 4.25 1.60
a. Imperf., pair 60.00
O49 O8 1a brt red vio ('45) 2.25 .80
O50 O8 1½a deep plum .70 .35
O51 O7 2a red violet ('45) 3.50 2.00
O52 O8 3a yellow ('46) 4.50 *6.00*
a. Imperf., pair 60.00
O53 O7 4a brown ('45) 2.25 1.00
O54 O8 6a brt rose ('46) 6.75 *22.50*
a. Imperf., pair 75.00
Nos. O46-O54 (9) 25.00 35.00

For surcharges see Nos. O58-O59.

1946-47 **Unwmk.** ***Perf. 11½***
O55 O8 1a violet 5.75 1.75
O56 O7 2a violet ('47) 8.75 9.75
O57 O8 3a deep orange 60.00 47.50
a. Imperf., pair — 150.00
Nos. O55-O57 (3) 74.50 59.00

No. O50 Surcharged "2 As." and Bars

1949 ***Perf. 12***
O58 O8 2a on 1½a dp plum 2.00 *4.50*
a. Inverted surcharge
b. Double surcharge
c. Imperf., pair 160.00 *175.00*

Same Surcharged "2 As." and Rosettes

1949 ***Perf. 12, Imperf.***
O59 O8 2a on 1½a dp plum 550.00 550.00

Three or more types of "2" in surcharge. Bhopal stamps became obsolete in 1950.

BHOR

'bō͵ə͵r

LOCATION — A Feudatory State in the Kolhapur Residency and Deccan States Agency.
AREA — 910 sq. mi.
POP. — 141,546
CAPITAL — Bhor

A1

A2

Handstamped
1879 **Unwmk.** ***Imperf.***
Without Gum

1 A1 ½a carmine 1.75 *2.00*
2 A2 1a carmine 1.75 *2.00*

Pant Sachiv Shankarrao — A3

1901 **Typo.**

Without Gum

3	A3	½a red	5.50	*27.50*

BIJAWAR

bi-'jä-wər

LOCATION — A Feudatory State in the Bundelkhand Agency of Central India.
AREA — 973 sq. mi.
POP. — 115,852
CAPITAL — Bijawar

A1

Maharaja Sir Sawant Singh — A2

1935-36 Typo. Unwmk. *Perf. 10½*

1	A1	3p brown	2.50	1.50
a.		Imperf., pair	7.00	
b.		Rouletted 7 ('36)	.95	*2.00*
2	A1	6p carmine	2.25	1.50
a.		Rouletted 7 ('36)	2.25	2.50
3	A1	9p purple	2.25	1.50
a.		Rouletted 7 ('36)	4.00	4.00
4	A1	1a dark blue	2.75	1.75
a.		Rouletted 7 ('36)	4.25	4.25
5	A1	2a slate green	2.75	2.00
a.		Rouletted 7 ('36)	4.25	7.50

1937 ***Perf. 9***

6	A2	4a red orange	4.75	*7.00*
7	A2	6a yellow	4.75	*14.00*
8	A2	8a emerald	5.25	*16.00*
9	A2	12a turquoise blue	5.75	*14.00*
10	A2	1r purple	25.00	*35.00*
a.		"1Rs" instead of "1R"	45.00	*67.50*
		Nos. 1-10 (10)	58.00	*94.25*

Bijawar stamps became obsolete in 1939.

BUNDI

'bün-dē

LOCATION — A Feudatory State in the Rajputana Agency of India.
AREA — 2,220 sq. mi.
POP. — 216,722
CAPITAL — Bundi

Katar (Indian Dagger) — A1

A2

A3

Laid Paper

1894 Unwmk. Litho. *Imperf.*

Without Gum

Gutters between Stamps

1	A1	½a slate	3,250.	*2,400.*

Redrawn; Blade Does Not Touch Oval

No Gutters between Stamps

Wove Paper

1A	A1	½a slate	15.00	13.00
b.		Value above, name below	210.00	210.00
c.		Top right ornament omitted	600.00	600.00

On No. 1A, the dagger is thinner and its point does not touch the oval inner frame.

1896

Laid Paper

Without Gum

2	A2	½a slate	5.00	5.25

1897-98 **Without Gum**

3	A3	1a red	6.50	6.00
4	A3	2a yellow green	8.00	*10.00*
5	A3	4a yellow green	17.00	*18.00*
6	A3	8a red	32.50	*40.00*
7	A3	1r yellow, *blue*	50.00	*52.50*
		Nos. 3-7 (5)	114.00	*126.50*

A4

A5

Redrawn; Blade Wider and Diamond-shaped

1898-1900 **Without Gum**

8	A3	½a slate	.40	.40
9	A3	1a red	.75	.60
10	A3	2a emerald	4.50	4.50
a.		1st 2 characters of value omitted	350.00	350.00
11	A3	4a emer (value above)	8.00	8.00
12	A4	8a red	8.00	*9.50*
13	A5	1r yellow, *blue*	5.00	*10.00*
a.		Wove paper	8.50	8.50
		Nos. 8-13 (6)	26.65	*33.00*

On Nos. 9-10, the blade is wider and nearly diamond-shaped.

Point of Dagger to Left

14	A3	4a green	5.00	5.00

Maharao Rajah with Symbols of Spiritual and Temporal Power — A6

Rouletted 11 to 13 in Color

1915 **Typo.**

Without Gum

"Bundi" in 3 Characters (word at top right)

15	A6	¼a blue	.60	.60
a.		Laid paper	7.25	6.25
16	A6	½a black	.85	.85
17	A6	1a vermilion	1.10	1.10
a.		Laid paper	9.25	9.25
18	A6	2a emerald	1.25	1.25
19	A6	2½a yellow	3.50	*4.25*
20	A6	3a brown	2.00	*4.25*
21	A6	4a yel green	4.25	4.25
23	A6	6a ultramarine	8.50	*21.00*
a.		6a deep blue	8.50	
24	A6	8a orange	6.25	6.25
25	A6	10a olive	7.75	7.75
26	A6	12a dark green	11.50	11.50
27	A6	1r violet	27.50	*35.00*
28	A6	2r car brn & blk	35.00	*42.50*
29	A6	3r blue & brown	85.00	*150.00*
30	A6	4r pale grn & red brown	275.00	*300.00*
31	A6	5r ver & pale grn	300.00	*425.00*
		Nos. 15-31 (16)	770.05	*1,015.*

Minor differences in lettering in top and bottom panels may be divided into 8 types, but not all values come in each type. In one subtype the top appears as one word. Nos. 30-31 have an ornamental frame around the design.

For overprints see Nos. O1-O39.

1941 ***Perf. 11***

"Bundi" in 4 Characters (word at top right)

32	A6	¼a light blue	4.50	4.50
33	A6	½a black	37.50	37.50
34	A6	1a carmine	17.50	*27.50*
35	A6	2a yellow green	32.50	
		Nos. 32-35 (4)	92.00	69.50

The 4-character spelling of "Bundi" is found also on stamps rouletted in color: on ½a and 4a in small characters, and on ¼a, ½a, 1a, 4a, 4r and 5r in large characters like those on Nos. 32-35.

For overprints see Nos. O41-O48.

Arms of Bundi — A7

1941-45 Typo. *Perf. 11*

36	A7	3p bright ultra	.20	*.30*
37	A7	6p indigo	.30	*.50*
38	A7	1a red orange	.50	*1.00*
39	A7	2a fawn	4.75	*8.00*
a.		2a brown ('45)	4.75	*10.50*
40	A7	4a brt yel green	5.25	*12.00*
41	A7	8a dull green	9.00	*19.00*
42	A7	1r royal blue	11.00	*30.00*
		Nos. 36-42 (7)	31.00	*70.80*

The 1st printing of Nos. 36-42 was gummed. All later printings were without gum. **Values are for copies without gum.**

For overprints see Nos. O49-O55.

A8

Maj. Maharao Rajah Bahadur Singh — A9

View of Bundi — A10

1947 ***Perf. 11***

43	A8	¼a deep green	.30
44	A8	½a purple	.30
45	A8	1a yellow green	.30
46	A9	2a red	.50
47	A9	4a deep orange	1.50
48	A10	8a violet blue	2.50
49	A10	1r chocolate	5.50
		Nos. 43-49 (7)	10.90

For overprints see Rajasthan Nos. 1-14.

OFFICIAL STAMPS

Regular Issue of 1915 Handstamped in Black, Red or Green

a

Rouletted 11 to 13 in Color

1918 **Unwmk.**

Without Gum

O1	A6	¼a dark blue	.45
O2	A6	½a black	2.50
O3	A6	1a vermilion	1.10
O4	A6	2a emerald	2.50
O5	A6	2½a yellow	3.00
O6	A6	3a brown	3.00
O7	A6	4a yel green	6.00
O8	A6	6a blue	4.75
O9	A6	8a orange	9.00
O10	A6	10a olive green	9.00
O11	A6	12a dark green	11.00
O12	A6	1r violet	15.00
O13	A6	2r car brn & blk	90.00
O14	A6	3r blue & brown	175.00
O15	A6	4r pale grn & red brn	325.00
O16	A6	5r ver & pale grn	325.00
		Nos. O1-O16 (16)	982.30

All values come with black handstamp and most exist in red. The overprint is found in various positions, double, inverted, etc.

Several denominations exist in two or more types. See notes following Nos. 31 and 35.

Regular Issue of 1915 Handstamped in Black, Red or Green

b

1919 **Without Gum**

O17	A6	¼a dark blue	1.50
O18	A6	½a black	3.00
O19	A6	1a vermilion	3.50
O20	A6	2a emerald	6.00
O21	A6	2½a yellow	15.00
O22	A6	3a brown	21.00
O23	A6	4a yel green	15.00
O24	A6	6a blue	15.00
O25	A6	8a orange	30.00
O26	A6	10a olive green	35.00
O27	A6	12a dark green	35.00
O28	A6	1r violet	30.00
O29	A6	2r car brn & blk	125.00
O30	A6	3r blue & brown	190.00
O31	A6	4r pale grn & red brn	400.00
O32	A6	5r ver & pale grn	400.00
		Nos. O17-O32 (16)	1,325.

Note following No. O16 applies to this issue.

Regular Issue of 1915 Handstamped in Carmine or Black

c

1919 ***Rouletted in Color***

Without Gum

O33	A6	¼a blue	5.00	5.00
O34	A6	½a black	3.50	
O35	A6	1a vermilion	7.50	
O36	A6	2a yel green	9.00	
O37	A6	8a orange	45.00	
O38	A6	10a olive	45.00	
O39	A6	12a dark green	75.00	
		Nos. O33-O39 (7)	190.00	

Nos. 33 and 35 Handstamped Type "a" in Black or Carmine

1941 ***Perf. 11***

O41	A6	½a black	55.00
O42	A6	2a yellow green	55.00

Nos. 32 and 35 Handstamped Type "b" in Black or Carmine

O43	A6	¼a light blue	47.50
O44	A6	2a yellow green	80.00

Nos. 32-35 Handstamped Type "c" in Black or Carmine

1941

O45	A6	¼a light blue	65.00
O46	A6	½a black	65.00
O47	A6	1a carmine	75.00
O48	A6	2a yellow green	27.50
		Nos. O45-O48 (4)	232.50

Nos. 36 to 42 Overprinted in Black or Carmine

1941 *Perf. 11*

O49	A7	3p brt ultra (C)	1.25	1.75
O50	A7	6p indigo (C)	3.00	3.50
O51	A7	1a red orange	3.50	4.75
O52	A7	2a fawn	6.00	9.00
O53	A7	4a brt yel green	24.00	30.00
O54	A7	8a dull green	35.00	45.00
O55	A7	1r royal blue (C)	45.00	60.00
		Nos. O49-O55 (7)	117.75	154.00

BUSSAHIR

'bus-ə-ˌhiˌəˌr

(Bashahr)

LOCATION — A Feudatory State in the Punjab Hill States Agency
AREA — 3,439 sq. mi.
POP. — 100,192
CAPITAL — Bashahr

Tiger

A1 A2

A3

A4

A5

A6

A7

A8

Overprinted "R S" in Violet, Rose, or Blue Green (BG)

Laid Paper

1895 Unwmk. Litho. *Imperf.*

1	A1	¼a pink (V)	1,000.	
2	A2	½a slate (R)	300.00	
3	A3	1a red (V)	125.00	
4	A4	2a yellow (V,R)	30.00	125.00
5	A5	4a violet (V,R)	60.00	
6	A6	8a brown (V,BG)	60.00	150.00
a.		Without overprint	175.00	
7	A7	12a green (R)	175.00	
8	A8	1r ultra (R)	50.00	
		Nos. 1-8 (8)	1,800.	

Perf. 7 to 14

9	A1	¼a pink (V,BG)	27.50	60.00
10	A2	½a slate (R)	13.00	67.50
11	A3	1a red (V)	13.00	55.00
a.		Pin-perf.	65.00	125.00
12	A4	2a yel (V,R,BG)	19.00	60.00
a.		Pin-perf. (V,R)	25.00	50.00
13	A5	4a vio (V,R,BG)	13.00	65.00
a.		Pin-perf. (R)	50.00	
14	A6	8a brown (V,BG)	13.50	67.50
15	A7	12a green (V,R)	40.00	82.50
a.		Pin-perf. (R)	65.00	
b.		Without overprint	47.50	
16	A8	1r ultra (V,R)	21.00	67.50
a.		Pin-perf. (R)	65.00	
		Nos. 9-16 (8)	160.00	525.00

"R. S." are the initials of Tika Raghunath Singh, son of the Raja.

A9

A10

A11

A12

A13

A14

Overprinted "R S" Like Nos. 1-16
Wove Paper

1896 Engr. *Pin-perf.*

17	A9	¼a dk gray vio (R)	—	650.00
18	A10	½a blue gray (R)	475.00	150.00

1900 Litho. *Imperf.*

19	A9	¼a red (V,BG)	2.50	5.50
20	A9	¼a violet (V,R)	3.75	
21	A10	½a blue (V,R)	6.00	15.00
22	A11	1a olive (R)	8.75	20.00
23	A11	1a red (V,BG)	2.50	7.50
24	A12	2a yellow (V)	26.00	
a.		2a ocher (R)	26.00	
25	A13	2a yellow (V)	26.00	
a.		2a ocher (V)	26.00	
26	A14	4a brn vio (V,R,BG)	27.50	75.00
		Nos. 19-26 (8)	103.00	

Pin-perf.

27	A9	¼a red (V,BG)	2.40	5.50
28	A9	¼a violet (R)	12.00	11.00
29	A10	½a blue (V,R)	7.75	20.00
30	A11	1a olive (V,R)	14.50	
31	A11	1a red (V)	—	175.00
32	A11	1a vermilion (BG)	3.75	7.50
33	A12	2a yellow (BG)	400.00	425.00
34	A13	2a yellow (V,R)	27.50	47.50
a.		2a ocher (V)	35.00	
35	A14	4a brn vio (V,R,BG)	37.50	
		Nos. 27-35 (8)	505.40	

Obsolete March 31, 1901.

Stamps overprinted with the monogram above (RNS) or with the monogram "PS" were never issued for postal purposes. They are either reprints or remainders to which this overprint has been applied. Many other varieties have appeared since the stamps became obsolete. It is probable that all or nearly all of them are reprints.

CHARKHARI

chər-'kär-ē

LOCATION — A Feudatory State in the Bundelkhand Agency in Central India.
AREA — 880 sq. mi.
POP. — 120,351
CAPITAL — Maharajnagar

A1

Thin White or Blue Wove Paper

1894 Unwmk. Typo. *Imperf.*
Value in the Plural
Without Gum

1	A1	1a green	1,750.	2,400.
2	A1	2a green	2,000.	
3	A1	4a green	1,250.	

1897

Value in the Singular
Without Gum

3A	A1	¼a rose	1,000.	775.00
4	A1	¼a purple	2.50	2.25
5	A1	½a purple	2.50	2.25
6	A1	1a green	5.00	4.50
7	A1	2a green	7.00	6.25
8	A1	4a green	7.00	6.25
		Nos. 4-8 (5)	24.00	21.50

In a later printing, the numerals of Nos. 4-8 are smaller or of different shape.

Proofs are known on paper of various colors.

A2

A3

Size: 19½x23mm

1909 Litho. *Perf. 11*

9	A2	1p red brown	2.10	32.50
10	A2	1p pale blue	.90	.60
11	A2	½a scarlet	1.25	.85
12	A2	1a light green	1.40	1.75
13	A2	2a ultra	2.10	2.75
14	A2	4a deep green	2.10	2.75
15	A2	8a brick red	5.00	13.00
16	A2	1r red brown	8.75	24.00
		Nos. 9-16 (8)	23.60	78.20

See #22-27, 39-43. For surcharges see #37-38A.

1919 Handstamped *Imperf.*
Without Gum

21	A3	1p violet	6.50	4.50
c.		Double frameline	27.50	

The 1p black, type A3, is a proof.

A3a

Wove Paper

1922 Handstamped *Imperf.*
Without Gum

21A	A3a	1a violet	57.50	65.00
b.		Perf. 11, laid paper	57.50	90.00

Type of 1909 Issue Redrawn
Size: 20x23½mm

1930-40 **Typo.**
Without Gum

22	A2	1p dark blue	.30	11.50
23	A2	½a olive green	.85	11.50
23A	A2	½a cop brown ('40)	4.00	19.00
24	A2	1a light green	.60	11.50
25	A2	1a chocolate	5.50	19.00
25A	A2	1a dull red ('40)	65.00	47.50
26	A2	2a light blue	1.00	14.00
a.		Tête bêche pair	60.00	
27	A2	4a carmine	2.75	16.00
a.		Tête bêche pair	11.00	
		Nos. 22-27 (8)	80.00	150.00

Guesthouse of Raja at Charkhari Reservoir — A4

Imlia Palace — A5

Industrial School — A6

View of City — A7

Maharajnagar Fort, Charkhari City — A8

Guesthouse A9

Palace Gate — A10

Temples at Rampur — A11

Govordhan Temple — A12

1931 *Perf. 11, 11½, 12*

28	A4	½a dull green	.70	.20
29	A5	1a black brown	.80	.20
30	A6	2a purple	.50	.20
31	A7	4a olive green	.70	.20
32	A8	8a magenta	.80	.20
33	A9	1r rose & green	1.25	.20
34	A10	2r brown & red	2.25	.20
35	A11	3r bl grn & choc	5.50	.20
36	A12	5r violet & blue	5.50	.20
		Nos. 28-36 (9)	18.00	1.80

Size range of A4-A12: 30-31x19½-24mm.

Many errors of perforation and printing exist.

Used values are for canceled to order copies.

Nos. 15-16 Surcharged in Black

1940 *Perf. 11*
37 A2 ½a on 8a brick red 22.50 *125.00*
a. Surcharge inverted 240.00
b. "1" of "½" inverted 225.00
38 A2 1a on 1r red brown 65.00 *325.00*
b. Surcharge inverted 275.00
38A A2 "1 ANNA" on 1r red brown 400.00 *450.00*

Type of 1930

1943 Unwmk. Typo. ***Imperf.***
Size: 20x23½mm
39 A2 1p violet 12.50 *95.00*
a. Tête bêche pair 50.00
40 A2 1p apple green 37.50 *150.00*
41 A2 ½a orange red 15.00 *30.00*
42 A2 ½a black 42.50 *125.00*
43 A2 2a grayish green 32.50 *40.00*
a. Tête bêche pair 65.00
Nos. 39-43 (5) 140.00 *440.00*

COCHIN

kō-'chin

LOCATION — A Feudatory State in the Madras States Agency in Southern India.
AREA — 1,480 sq. mi.
POP. — 1,422,875 (1941)
CAPITAL — Ernakulam

See the United State of Travancore and Cochin.

6 Puttans = 5 Annas
12 Pies = 1 Anna
16 Annas = 1 Rupee

State Seal
A1 A1a

1892 Unwmk. Typo. ***Perf. 12***
1 A1 ½p yellow 2.25 2.25
a. Imperf., pair — —
b. Laid paper 425.00 200.00
2 A1 1p red violet 2.25 1.60
a. 1p purple (error) 175.00 125.00
3 A1 2p purple 1.75 1.75
a. Imperf.
Nos. 1-3 (3) 6.25 5.60

Nos. 1 to 3 sometimes have watermark large umbrella in the sheet.

Wmk. Coat of Arms and Inscription in Sheet

1896
4 A1a 1p violet 65.00 *65.00*

Wmk. 43
4A A1a 1p violet 17.50 *30.00*

Originally intended for revenue use, Nos. 4-4A were later authorized for postal use.

1894 **Wmk. 41**
Thin Paper
5 A1 ½p orange 1.25 1.25
a. Imperf., pair
6 A1 1p magenta 5.50 4.25
7 A1 2p purple 3.00 3.00
a. Imperf., pair — 1,000.
Nos. 5-7 (3) 9.75 8.50

A2

A3 A4

A5

Thin (1898) or Thick (1903) Paper

1898-1903
8 A2 3p ultra .20 .20
9 A3 ½p gray green .55 .20
a. Pair, one sideways 775.00 775.00
10 A4 1p rose 1.40 .25
a. Laid paper 1,750.
b. Tete beche pair 3,000. 2,400.
c. As "a," tete beche pair *7,750.*
11 A5 2p purple 2.00 .35
a. Double impression 850.00 300.00
Nos. 8-11 (4) 4.15 1.00

Type of 1898 Surcharged

1909
13 A2 2p on 3p red violet .40 .35
a. Inverted surcharge 72.50 72.50
b. Pair, stamps tete beche 125.00 *150.00*
c. Pair, stamps & surch. tete beche 160.00 *175.00*

The surcharge is also known in a thin "2" measuring 5½x7mm, with curving foot. Value $250.

Sri Rama Varma I — A6

1911-13 Engr. ***Perf. 14***
14 A6 2p brown .20 .20
a. Imperf., pair
15 A6 3p blue .40 .20
a. Perf. 14x12½ 25.00 2.50
16 A6 4p yel green 1.10 .20
17 A6 9p car rose .80 .20
18 A6 1a orange buff 2.00 .20
19 A6 1½a lilac 4.00 .50
20 A6 2a gray 5.50 .50
21 A6 3a vermilion 26.00 26.00
Nos. 14-21 (8) 40.00 28.00

For surcharge and overprints see Nos. 34, O2-O9, O23-O24, O27.

Sri Rama Varma II
A7 A8

1918-23 Engr. ***Perf. 14***
23 A7 2p brown 4.50 .20
24 A7 4p green .80 .20
25 A7 6p red brown ('22) 1.90 .20
26 A7 8p black brown ('23) 1.25 .20
27 A7 9p carmine rose 12.00 .25
28 A7 10p deep blue 1.90 .20
29 A8 1a brown orange 9.75 .90
30 A7 1½a red violet ('21) 1.90 .20
31 A7 2a gray 3.50 .20
32 A7 2¼a yel green ('22) 3.50 2.50
33 A7 3a vermilion 9.00 .35
Nos. 23-33 (11) 50.00 5.40

The 1a is found in two types, the difference lying in the first of the three characters directly above the maharaja's head.

For surcharges and overprints see Nos. 36-40, 52-53, O10-O22, O25-O26, O28-O36, O71A.

No. 15 Surcharged

Type I — Numeral 8mm high. Curved foot. Top begins with a ball. (As illustrated.)
Type II — Numeral 9mm high. Curved foot. Top begins with a curved line.
Type III — Numeral 6mm high. Straight foot. "Two pies" 15mm wide.
Type IV — "2" as in type III. Capital "P" in "Pies." "Two Pies" 13mm wide.
Type V — Heavy gothic numeral. Capital "P" in "Pies."

1922-29
34 A6 2p on 3p blue (Type I) .40 .20
a. Type II 2.00 .90
b. Type III 3.25 .25
c. Type IV .30 .20
d. Type V 80.00 *125.00*
e. Double surcharge, I 350.00 350.00
f. Double surcharge II 600.00

Types II and III exist with a capital "P" in "Pies." It occurs once in each sheet of the second and third settings. There are four settings.

Type V is the first stamp, fourth row, of the fourth setting.

No. 32 Surcharged

1928
36 A7 1a on 2¼a yel green 4.50 *10.50*
a. Double surcharge *425.00* *425.00*

Nos. 24, 26 and 28 Surcharged in Black

1932-33
38 A7 3p on 4p green .95 .70
39 A7 3p on 8p black brown .95 *1.90*
40 A7 9p on 10p deep blue 1.10 *2.40*
Nos. 38-40 (3) 3.00 5.00

Sri Rama Varma III
A9 A10

1933-38 Engr. ***Perf. 13x13½***
41 A9 2p brown ('36) .55 .20
42 A9 4p green 1.40 .20
43 A9 6p red brown .95 .20
44 A10 1a brown org ('34) .48 .20
45 A9 1a8p rose red 5.25 3.00
46 A9 2a gray black ('38) 1.25 .55
47 A9 2¼a yellow green 1.25 .20
48 A9 3a red org ('38) 2.25 1.10
49 A9 3a4p violet 1.10 1.10
50 A9 6a8p black brown 3.50 7.25
51 A9 10a deep blue 3.50 8.50
Nos. 41-51 (11) 21.48 22.50

See Nos. 55-58. For overprints and surcharges see Nos. 54, 59-62, 73A-74, 76-77, 89, O37-O57, O70-O71, O72-O77A, O89.

Nos. 26 and 28 Surcharged in Red

1934 ***Perf. 13½***
52 A7 6p on 8p black brown 2.25 .75
53 A7 6p on 10p dark blue 2.25 2.25

No. 44 Overprinted in Black

a

1939 **Engr.**
54 A10 1a brown orange 2.25 .50

Types of 1933-38

1938-41 Litho. ***Perf. 11, 13***
55 A9 2p dull brown .80 .40
56 A9 4p dull green ('41) .85 .20
57 A9 6p red brown 1.90 .20
c. Perf. 13 *3,000.*
57A A10 1a brown orange 55.00 *67.50*
58 A10 2¼a yellow green 5.25 .20
Nos. 55-58 (5) 63.80 *68.50*

Type of 1934 Overprinted in Black Type "a" or

b

1941-42 ***Perf. 11 (#59), 13 (#60)***
59 A10(a) 1a brown orange 240.00 1.00
a. Perf. 13 300.00
60 A10(b) 1a brown org ('42) 10.00 .75
a. Perf. 11 2.50 2.50

No. 45 Surcharged in Black

c

1943-44 Engr. ***Perf. 13x13½***
61 A9 3p on 1a8p rose red ('44) 2.50 *6.50*
62 A9 1a3p on 1a8p rose red 1.60 .20

Maharaja Sri Kerala Varma
A11 A12

1943 Litho. Wmk. 294 ***Perf. 11, 13***
63 A11 2p dull gray brn, wmk. 41 1.00 *1.60*
a. Wmk. 294 22.50 2.00
64 A11 4p gray green 3.00 2.75
a. Wmk. 41 600.00 300.00
65 A11 6p red brown 8.00 1.10
66 A11 9p ultramarine 24.00 .80
67 A12 1a brown orange 19.00 32.50
a. Wmk. 41 90.00 90.00
68 A11 2¼a lt ol green 20.00 1.75
Nos. 63-68 (6) 75.00 40.50

For surcharges and overprints see Nos. 69-73, 75, 78, 78B, O58-O69.

No. 64 Surcharged Type "c"
69 A11 3p on 4p gray green 2.75 .20
a. Wmk. 41 55.00 15.00

Nos. 64, 64a and 65 Surcharged in Black

d

1944-48 **Wmk. 294**
70 A11 2p on 6p red brown .70 *2.10*
71 A11 3p on 4p gray green 3.25 .20
72 A11 3p on 6p red brown .80 .20
73 A11 4p on 6p red brown 2.75 *7.50*
Nos. 70-73 (4) 7.50 10.00

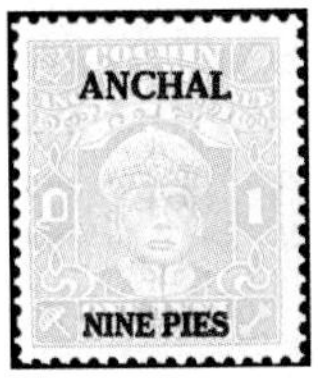

Nos. 57A, 67a Surcharged in Black

1944 **Litho.** **Wmk. 41**
73A A10 6p on 1a brown org *240.00* 150.00
74 A10 9p on 1a brown org 225.00 32.50
75 A12 9p on 1a brown org 4.50 2.00
Nos. 73A-75 (3) *469.50* 184.50

No. 56 Surcharged Type "c" in Black
76 A9 3p on 4p dull green 5.50 3.75

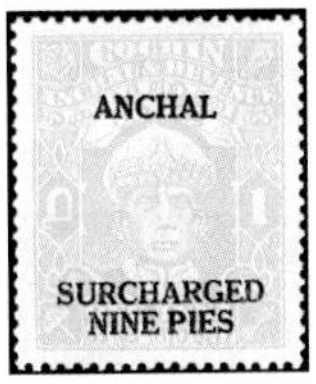

Nos. 57A, 67a Surcharged in Black

1944
77 A10 9p on 1a brown orange 12.50 4.00
78 A12 9p on 1a brown orange 4.00 2.25

No. 67a Surcharged Type "c"
1944 **Wmk. 41**
78B A12 1a3p on 1a brn org 3,250.

Maharaja Ravi Varma
A13 A15

1944-46 **Wmk. 294** ***Perf. 13***
79 A13 9p ultra ('46) 5.50 7.75
a. Perf. 11 10.00 2.00
80 A13 1a3p magenta 4.00 4.75
81 A13 1a9p ultra ('46) 6.50 7.25
Nos. 79-81 (3) 16.00 19.75

For overprints and surcharges see Nos. O78-O80, Travancore 12, 14, O10.

1946-50 **Litho.** ***Perf. 13***
82 A15 2p dull brown 1.10 .20
a. Perf. 11 13.00 .75
b. Perf. 11x13 300.00 80.00
83 A15 3p carmine rose .45 .20
83A A15 4p gray green ('50) *3,000.* 65.00
84 A15 6p red brown ('47) 16.00 3.00
a. Perf. 11 150.00 .20
85 A15 9p ultramarine .45 .20
86 A15 1a dp orange ('47) 4.50 *24.00*
a. Perf. 11 450.00
87 A15 2a gray ('47) 62.50 7.00
a. Perf. 11 95.00 .20
88 A15 3a vermilion 40.00 .40
Nos. 82-83,84-88 (7) 125.00 35.00

For surcharges and overprints see Nos. 98-99, O81-O88, Travancore 8, 13, 15-15A, O11.

No. 45 Surcharged Type "d"
Perf. 13x13½
1947-48 **Wmk. 41** **Engr.**
89 A9 6p on 1a8p rose red 2.75 18.00

Maharaja Sri Kerala Varma II — A16

1948-49 **Wmk. 294** ***Perf. 11***
90 A16 2p olive brown 1.10 .20
91 A16 3p car ('49) .55 .20
92 A16 4p gray green 7.50 1.50
a. Horiz. pair, imperf. vert. 425.00
93 A16 6p red brown 9.25 .20
94 A16 9p ultra ('49) 1.60 .20
95 A16 2a black 32.50 .50
96 A16 3a ver ('49) 37.50 .50
97 A16 3a4p violet ('49) 60.00 350.00
Nos. 90-97 (8) 150.00 353.30

For overprints see Nos. O90-O97, Travancore 9-11, O8-O9.

No. 86 Surcharged Type "d" in Black
1949
98 A15 6p on 1a dp orange 55.00 *125.00*
99 A15 9p on 1a dp orange 75.00 *125.00*

Dutch Palace A17

Design: 2a, Chinese fishing net.

1949 **Unwmk.** ***Perf. 11***
100 A17 2a gray 2.50 *5.50*
a. Imperf. vert., horiz. pair 500.00
101 A17 2¼a gray green 2.50 *5.00*
a. Imperf. vert., horiz. pair 500.00 500.00

See Travancore-Cochin for succeeding issues.

OFFICIAL STAMPS

Stamps and Type of 1911-14 Overprinted

h

1913-14 **Wmk. 41** **Engr.** ***Perf. 14***
O2 A6 4p yel green 8.00 .20
a. Inverted overprint — 300.00
b. Double inverted overprint
O3 A6 9p car rose 82.50 .20
O4 A6 1½a red violet 32.50 .20
a. Double overprint 450.00
O5 A6 2a gray 12.00 .20
O6 A6 3a vermilion 42.50 .35
O7 A6 6a violet 37.50 1.60
O8 A6 12a blue 35.00 4.75
O9 A6 1½r deep green 25.00 *42.50*
Nos. O2-O9 (8) 275.00 50.00

Stamps and Type of 1918-23 Overprinted

i

1918-34
O10 A7 4p green 4.75 .20
a. Double overprint — 425.00
O11 A7 6p red brn ('22) 4.75 .20
a. Double overprint — 400.00
O12 A7 8p blk brn ('26) 7.50 .20
O13 A7 9p carmine rose 19.00 .20
O14 A7 10p dp blue ('23) 8.00 .20
O16 A7 1½a red vio ('21) 5.00 .20
a. Double overprint 240.00
O17 A7 2a gray 30.00 .20
O18 A7 2¼a yel grn ('22) 7.50 .20
b. Double overprint 350.00
O19 A7 3a ver ('22) 18.00 .20
a. Double overprint 400.00
O20 A7 6a violet ('22) 22.50 .40
O21 A7 12a blue ('29) 25.00 2.40
O22 A7 1½r dk green ('34) 27.50 *70.00*
Nos. O10-O22 (12) *179.50* *74.60*

On Nos. O2-O22, width of overprint varies from 14¾mm to 16½mm.

No. 15 Overprinted in Red

j

1921
O23 A6 3p blue 100.00 .75

Nos. O3 and O13 Surcharged with New Values
1923-29
O24 A6 8p on 9p car rose 240.00 1.25
O25 A7 8p on 9p car rose 70.00 .20
a. Double surcharge 300.00
O26 A7 10p on 9p car rose ('25) 60.00 .50
a. Double surcharge 350.00
O27 A6 10p on 9p car rose ('29) 350.00 13.00
Nos. O24-O27 (4) 720.00 14.95

Regular Issue of 1918-23 Overprinted

k

1933-34
O28 A7 4p green 17.00 1.10
O29 A7 6p red brown ('34) 10.50 .20
O30 A7 8p black brown 5.50 .20
O31 A7 10p deep blue 4.75 .20
O32 A7 2a gray ('34) 21.00 .20
O33 A7 3a vermilion 6.25 .20
O34 A7 6a dk violet ('34) 60.00 2.40
Nos. O28-O34 (7) 125.00 4.50

Same with Additional Surcharge on Type of Regular Issue of 1918-23 in Red

O35 A7 6p on 8p black brown 1.75 .20
O36 A7 6p on 10p dk blue ('34) 4.00 .20

Regular Issue of 1933 Overprinted Type "k" in Black as in 1933-34
1933-35 ***Perf. 13x13½***
O37 A9 4p green .90 .20
O38 A9 6p red brown 1.10 .20
O39 A10 1a brown orange 7.50 .20
O40 A9 1a8p rose red 2.50 .25
O41 A9 2a gray 7.50 .20
O42 A9 2¼a yellow green 3.50 .20
O43 A9 3a vermilion 35.00 .20
O44 A9 3a4p violet 3.25 .20
O45 A9 6a8p black brown 3.25 .20
O46 A9 10a deep blue 3.25 .40
Nos. O37-O46 (10) 67.75 2.25

Regular Stamps of 1934-38 Overprinted in Black

m

1939-41 ***Perf. 11, 13x13½***
O47 A10 1a brown orange 32.50 .50
O48 A9 2a gray black 18.00 1.25
O49 A9 3a red orange 9.50 1.25
Nos. O47-O49 (3) 60.00 3.00

Similar Overprint on Types of 1933-36
Perf. 11, 13x13½
1939-41 **Litho.** **Wmk. 294**
O50 A9 4p dull green ('41) 32.50 12.00
Wmk. 41
O51 A9 6p red brown ('41) 4.50 2.25
a. Wmk. 294 32.50 1.10
O52 A10 1a brown orange .50 .20
a. Wmk. 294 2.25 .30
O53 A9 3a orange ('40) 1.50 .80
b. Wmk. 294 10.00 1.50
Nos. O50-O53 (4) 39.00 15.25

Similar Overprint in Narrow Serifed Capitals on No. 57
Wmk. 41 ***Perf. 11***
O53A A9 6p red brown 850.00 325.00

Type of 1933-36 Overprinted in Black

o

Perf. 10½, 11, 13x13½
O54 A9 4p dull green ('41) 12.50 1.75
O55 A9 6p red brown ('41) 11.00 .45
O56 A9 2a gray black 9.00 .80
Nos. O54-O56 (3) 32.50 3.00

Type of 1934 Overprinted in Black

p

1941 ***Perf. 11***
O57 A10 1a brown orange 190.00 2.50

Stamps and Types of 1944 Overprinted in Black

q

Perf. 11, 13x13½
1944-48 **Wmk. 294**
O58 A11 4p gray green 11.00 3.25
a. Perf. 11 60.00 5.00
O59 A11 6p red brown .75 .20
O60 A11 2a gray black 2.00 .45
O61 A11 2¼a dull yel green 1.25 .60
a. Additional ovpt. on back 75.00
O62 A11 3a red orange 3.00 .50
Nos. O58-O62 (5) 18.00 5.00

Same Overprint with Additional Surcharge

O63	A11	3p on 4p gray green	1.25	.20
a.		Additional overprint on back		
O64	A12	3p on 1a brown org	8.25	3.75
O65	A11	9p on 6p red brown	3.50	1.90
O66	A12	1a3p on 1a brown org	3.00	1.25
		Nos. O63-O66 (4)	16.00	7.10

Same Overprint in Black on Types of 1944 Surcharged Type "c"

O67	A11	3p on 4p gray green	2.75	.30
O68	A11	9p on 6p red brown	.20	.20
O69	A12	1a3p on 1a brown org	3.50	.20
		Nos. O67-O69 (3)	6.45	.70

Nos. O52 and O16 Surcharged Type "d"

1944 Wmk. 41 *Perf. 11, 13x13½, 14*

O70	A10	3p on 1a brown org	1.25	*2.50*
O71	A10	9p on 1a brown org	125.00	30.00

Engr.

O71A	A7	9p on 1½a red vio	240.00	17.50

No. O52 Surcharged Type "c"

O72	A10	1a3p on 1a brn org	300.00	80.00

No. 76 Overprinted in Black

Perf. 13

O72A	A9	3p on 4p dull green	125.00	50.00

No. 45 Overprinted Type "k" and Surcharged Type "d"

1944-48 Wmk. 41 *Perf. 13x13½*

O73	A9	9p on 1a8p rose red	125.00	20.00
O74	A9	1a9p on 1a8p rose red	1.75	1.25

No. 45 Overprinted Type "k" and Surcharged Type "c"

O75	A9	3p on 1a8p rose red	2.75	1.10
O76	A9	1a9p on 1a8p rose red	1.00	.20

Type of 1939-41 Overprinted in Black

1946 Wmk. 294 *Perf. 11*

O77	A9	2a gray	50.00	1.00
O77A	A9	2¼a yellow green	900.00	15.00

Same Overprint in Black on #79-81

1946 Litho. *Perf. 13*

O78	A13	9p ultramarine	2.10	.20
O79	A13	1a3p magenta	1.25	.20
a.		Double overprint	24.00	18.00
O80	A13	1a9p ultramarine	.30	*.70*
		Nos. O78-O80 (3)	3.65	1.10

Types and Stamps of 1946-48 Overprinted Type "h"

1946-48

O81	A15	3p car rose	.60	.20
O82	A15	4p gray green	24.00	4.50
O83	A15	6p red brown	5.50	.70
O84	A15	9p ultra	.75	.20
O85	A15	1a3p magenta	2.25	.50
O86	A15	1a9p ultra	1.90	.40
O87	A15	2a gray black	13.00	2.75
O88	A15	2¼a olive green	17.00	2.75
		Nos. O81-O88 (8)	65.00	12.00

No. 56 Overprinted Type "q" and Surcharged Type "d"

1947 Wmk. 41 Engr. *Perf. 13x13½*

O89	A9	3p on 4p dull green	18.00	5.50

Stamps and Type of 1948-49 Overprinted Type "o"

1948-49 Wmk. 294 Litho. *Perf. 11*

O90	A16	3p carmine ('49)	1.00	.20
O91	A16	4p gray green	.90	.30
O92	A16	6p red brown	2.00	.20
O93	A16	9p ultramarine	2.00	.20
O94	A16	2a black ('49)	1.00	.20
O95	A16	2¼a lt ol green ('49)	2.75	*4.50*
O96	A16	3a vermilion ('49)	.90	.40
O97	A16	3a4p deep pur ('49)	26.00	22.50
		Nos. O90-O97 (8)	36.55	28.50

See Travancore-Cochin for succeeding issues.

DHAR

ˈdär

LOCATION — A Feudatory State in the Malwa Agency in Central India.
AREA — 1,800 sq. mi.
POP. — 243,521
CAPITAL — Dhar

A1

Arms of Dhar — A2

The stamps of type A1 have an oval control mark handstamped in black.

Unwmk.

1897-1900 Typeset *Imperf.*

Without Gum

1	A1	½p black, *red*	2.25	*2.50*
a.		Characters for "pice" transposed	15.00	
b.		Five characters in first word	.75	
c.		Without control mark	82.50	
2	A1	¼a black, *org red* ('00)	2.25	*3.00*
a.		Without control mark	125.00	
3	A1	½a black, *lil rose*	3.50	*4.00*
4	A1	1a black, *bl grn*	7.00	*10.50*
5	A1	2a black, *yel* ('00)	25.00	*35.00*
		Nos. 1-5 (5)	40.00	*55.00*

1898-1900 Typo. *Perf. 11½*

6	A2	½a red	.85	.85
7	A2	½a rose ('00)	1.50	1.50
a.		Imperf., pair	35.00	
8	A2	1a maroon	1.00	1.00
9	A2	1a violet ('00)	1.25	1.25
10	A2	1a claret ('00)	1.00	1.00
11	A2	2a dark green ('00)	3.25	*5.00*
		Nos. 6-11 (6)	8.85	*10.60*

Obsolete Mar. 31, 1901.

DUNGARPUR

LOCATION — A princely state in Rajasthan, in northwestern India.
AREA — 1,447 sq. mi.
POP. — 100,103 (1901)
CAPITAL — Dungarpur

Arms of Dungarpur — A1

1933-1947 Unwmk. Litho. *Perf. 11*

1	A1	¼a bister yellow	2,000.	400.00
		On cover		1,000.
a.		¼a lemon yellow ('34)	2,500.	500.00
		On cover		1,250.
2	A1	¼a salmon ('35)	5,000.	1,000.
		On cover		2,500.
a.		¼a red brown ('36)	3,750.	750.00
		On cover		1,900.
b.		¼a orange red ('38)	6,250.	1,250.
		On cover		3,100.
3	A1	1a pale turquoise blue	1,500.	300.00
		On cover		750.00
a.		1a turquoise blue	2,000.	400.00
		On cover		1,000.
4	A1	1a3p deep red violet ('35)	3,000.	600.00
		On cover		2,400.
5	A1	2a deep dull green ('47)	3,750.	750.00
		On cover		3,000.
6	A1	4a dull rose red	6,250.	1,250.
		On cover		5,000.
a.		4a rose red ('34)	7,000.	1,400.
		On cover		5,500.

A2

A3

A4

A5

A6

A7

A8

A9

A10

Maharawal Lakshman Singh

1934-38 Typo. *Perf. 12*

7	A2	¼a org buff ('36)	1,750.	200.00
		On cover		450.00
8	A3	½a vermilion, Die I	500.00	125.00
		On cover		350.00
9	A4	1a blue		
a.		Perf 11½ ('38)	750.00	125.00
		On cover		350.00
10	A5	4a gray brown	2,000.	650.00
		On cover		2,000.

There are three dies of the ½ anna: Die I measures 21x25½mm, and width of turban is 7½mm; Die II measures 20x20½mm; Die III measures 21x25½mm, and width of turban is 6½mm. There are 4 distinct cliches of Die III, printed in a block of 4, differing in the space between the top of the turban and the frame: Pos. 1 = 2mm; Pos. 2 = 2.5mm; Pos. 3 = 1mm; Pos. 4 = 1.5mm.

1940-41 *Perf. 11, 11½ (#15)*

11	A2	¼a dull org('41)	1,500.	150.00
		On cover		300.00
12	A3	½a carmine, Die I	500.00	150.00
		On cover		450.00
13	A4	1a blue	500.00	100.00
		On cover		250.00
14	A6	2a bright green	2,500.	900.00
		On cover		2,500.
15	A5	4a gray brown	1,800.	450.00
		On cover		1,350.

1943 *Pin-Perf 11½*

16	A6	2a bright green	2,500.	900.00
		On cover		2,500.

1943-44 *Perf. 10½*

17	A2	¼a dull org('44)	1,500.	150.00
		On cover		300.00
18	A3	½a vermilion, Die I ('44)	600.00	175.00
		On cover		550.00
19	A7	½a vermilion, Die II ('44)	600.00	175.00
		On cover		550.00
a.		Horiz. pair, #18 + #19	1,300.	450.
		On cover		1,000.
b.		Vert. pair, imperf between		5,000.
20	A4	1a blue ('44)	500.00	100.00
		On cover		250.00
21	A8	1a3p mauve	2,000.	450.00
		On cover		1,500.
22	A5	4a pale brown ('44)	2,400.	650.00
		On cover		2,000.

1945 *Perf. 10*

23	A2	¼a orange	2,000.	150.00
		On cover		300.00
24	A9	½a vermilion, Die III ('44)	800.00	100.00
		On cover		250.00
25	A4	1a blue	500.00	100.00
		On cover		250.00
26	A8	1a3p bright mauve	2,000.	450.00
		On cover		1,500.
27	A10	1½a deep violet	2,000.	450.00
		On cover		1,350.
28	A5	4a brown	1,600.	400.00
		On cover		1,000.

The stamps of Dungarpur became obsolete in Sept. 1949.

DUTTIA

ˈdət-ē-ə

(Datia)

LOCATION — A Feudatory State in the Bundelkhand Agency in Central India.
AREA — 912 sq. mi.
POP. — 158,834
CAPITAL — Datia

Ganesh, Elephant-headed God

A1 A2

All Duttia stamps have a circular control mark, about 23mm in diameter, handstamped in blue or black. All were issued without gum.

1893 Typeset Unwmk. *Imperf.*

1	A1	¼a black, *org red*	3,000.
2	A1	½a blk, *grysh grn*	7,250.
3	A2	1a black, *red*	2,400.
4	A1	2a black, *yellow*	2,100.
5	A1	4a black, *rose*	1,500.

Type A2 with Frameline around God, Rosettes in Lower Corners

1896 (?)

5A	A2	½ black, *green*	*3,500.*
5C	A2	2a dk blue, *lemon*	*2,400.*

A 1a in this revised type has been reported.

1897

6	A2	½a black, *green*	18.00	*175.00*
7	A2	1a black	70.00	*210.00*
a.		Laid paper	15.00	
8	A2	2a black, *yellow*	22.50	*190.00*
9	A2	4a black, *rose*	18.00	*150.00*
		Nos. 6-9 (4)	128.50	*725.00*

A3

A4

10 A3 ½a black, *green* 60.00
11 A3 1a black 125.00
12 A3 2a black, *yellow* 67.50
13 A3 4a black, *rose* 62.50
Nos. 10-13 (4) 315.00

1899-1900
Rouletted in Colored Lines on 2 or 3 Sides

14 A4 ¼a red (shades) 2.40
b. Tete beche pair *3,000.*
15 A4 ½a black, *green* 2.50
16 A4 1a black 2.75
17 A4 2a black, *yellow* 2.50
18 A4 4a black, *rose red* 3.50
a. Tete beche pair
Nos. 14-18 (5) 13.65

1904 ***Imperf.***

22 A4 ¼a carmine 3.00
23 A4 ½a black, *green* 16.00
24 A4 1a black 11.50
Nos. 22-24 (3) 30.50

1911 ***Perf. 13½***

25 A4 ¼a carmine 5.50 *25.00*

1916 ***Imperf.***

26 A4 ¼a dull blue 5.00 *17.50*
27 A4 ½a green 5.00 *20.00*
28 A4 1a violet 4.50 *20.00*
a. Tete beche pair 20.00
29 A4 2a brown 12.00 *24.00*
29A A4 4a brick red 67.50
Nos. 26-29A (5) 94.00 81.50

1918

31 A4 ½a ultramarine 3.50 12.50
32 A4 1a rose 3.00 14.00
33 A4 2a violet 5.25 *25.00*

Perf. 12

34 A4 ¼a black 4.25 20.00
Nos. 31-34 (4) 16.00 71.50

1920 ***Rouletted***

35 A4 ¼a blue 2.00 10.00
36 A4 ½a rose 2.75 14.00

Perf. 7

37 A4 ½a dull red 10.00 25.00
Nos. 35-37 (3) 14.75 49.00

Duttia stamps became obsolete in 1921.

FARIDKOT

fe-ˈrēd-ˌkōt

LOCATION — A Feudatory State in the Punjab Agency of India.
AREA — 638 sq. mi.
POP. — 164,364
CAPITAL — Faridkot

4 Folus or Paisas = 1 Anna

A1

A2

A3

Handstamped

1879-86 **Unwmk.** ***Imperf.***
Without Gum

1 A1 1f ultramarine 1.50 *3.00*
a. Laid paper 16.00 16.00
b. Tete beche pair 240.00
2 A2 1p ultramarine 2.50 *7.50*
a. Laid paper 50.00 *75.00*
3 A3 1p ultramarine 1.25
a. Tete beche pair 210.00
Nos. 1-3 (3) 5.25 10.50

Several other varieties exist, but it is believed that only the stamps listed here were issued for postal use. They became obsolete Dec. 31, 1886. See Faridkot under Convention States for issues of 1887-1900.

HYDERABAD (DECCAN)

ˈhīd-ə-rə-ˌbad

LOCATION — Central India
AREA — 82,313 sq. mi.
POP. — 16,338,534 (1941)
CAPITAL — Hyderabad

This independent princely state was occupied and annexed by India in 1948.

Catalogue values for unused stamps in this State are for Never Hinged items, beginning with Scott 51 in the regular postage section, and Scott O54 in the officials section.

Expect irregular perfs on the Nos. 1-14 and O1-O20 due to the nature of the paper.

A1

A2

1869-71 **Engr.** **Unwmk.** ***Perf. 11½***

1 A1 ½a brown ('71) 5.50 6.00
2 A2 1a olive green 10.00 5.50
a. Imperf. horiz., pair 125.00 85.00
3 A1 2a green ('71) 27.50 24.00
Nos. 1-3 (3) 43.00 35.50

For overprints see Nos. O1-O3, O11-O13.
The reprints are perforated 12½.

A3

A4

Wove Paper

1871-1909 ***Perf. 12½***

4 A3 ½a orange brown .20 .20
a. ½a red brown .20 .20
b. ½a magenta (error) 25.00 11.00
c. Perf. 11½ 15.00 15.00
d. ½a rose .20 .20
e. ½a bright vermilion .20 .20
5 A3 1a dark brown .50 .40
a. Imperf., pair 25.00
b. Pair, imperf. between 50.00
c. Perf. 11½ 37.50 37.50
6 A3 1a black ('09) .95 .20
7 A3 2a green .20 .20
a. 2a olive green ('09) .20 .20
b. Perf. 11½ 125.00
8 A3 3a yellow brown .30 .20
a. Perf. 11½ 22.50 22.50
9 A3 4a slate .40 .30
a. Imperf. horiz., pair 240.00 240.00
b. Perf. 11½ 50.00 50.00
10 A3 4a deep green .80 .45
a. 4a olive green 2.50 2.25
11 A3 8a bister brown .95 .55
a. Perf. 11½
12 A3 12a blue 1.40 1.40
a. Perf. 11½ 95.00 95.00
b. 12a slate green 1.25 1.25
Nos. 4-12 (9) 5.70 3.90

For overprints see Nos. 13, O4-O10, O14-O20, O25-O26.

Surcharged

1900

13 A3 ¼a on ½a brt ver 1.00 1.10
a. Inverted surcharge 27.50 19.00

1902

14 A4 ¼a blue 2.00 1.90

Seal of the Nizam
A5 A6

Engraved by A. G. Wyon

1905 **Wmk. 42**

17 A5 ¼a blue 2.00 .20
18 A5 ½a red 4.75 .20
19 A5 ½a orange 4.75 .20
Nos. 17-19 (3) 11.50 .60

For overprints see Nos. O21-O23.

Perf. 11, 11½, 12½, 13½ and Compound

1908-11

20 A5 ¼a gray .40 .20
21 A5 ½a green .85 .20
22 A5 1a carmine .50 .20
23 A5 2a lilac .35 .20
24 A5 3a brn orange ('09) .85 .20
25 A5 4a olive green ('09) .85 .25
26 A5 8a violet ('11) .50 .20
27 A5 12a blue green ('11) 6.00 2.75
Nos. 20-27 (8) 10.30 4.20

For overprints see Nos. O24, O27-O38.

Engr. by Bradbury, Wilkinson & Co.

1912

28 A5 ¼a brown violet .20 .20
29 A5 ½a deep green 2.00 .20
a. Imperf., pair 20.00

The frame of type A5 differs slightly in each denomination.

Nos. 20-21 measure 19½x20½mm.

Nos. 28-29 measure 20x21½mm.

For overprints see Nos 37, O39-O40, O44.

1915-16

30 A6 ½a green .60 .20
31 A6 1a carmine rose .60 .20
32 A6 1a red 6.00 .20
Nos. 30-32 (3) 7.20 .60

Unless used, imperf. stamps of types A5 and A6 are from plate proof sheets.

See #58. For overprints see #38, O41-O43, O45.

A7

1927 **Wmk. 211** ***Perf. 13½***

36 A7 1r yellow 6.00 5.75

Stamps of 1912-16 Surcharged in Red

(4 pies)

(8 pies)

1930

37 A5 4p on ¼a brown violet .20 .20
a. Perf. 11 125.00
b. Double surcharge
38 A6 8p on ½a green .20 .20
a. Perf. 11 150.00 90.00

For overprints see Nos. O44-O45.

Seal of Nizam — A8

Char Minar — A9

High Court of Justice A10

Reservoir for City of Hyderabad A11

Bidar College — A13

Entrance to Ajanta Caves A12

Victory Tower at Daulatabad A14

Wmk. 211

1931-48 **Engr.** ***Perf. 13½***

39 A8 4p black .20 .20
a. Laid paper ('47) 5.25 3.25
39B A8 6p car lake ('48) 1.00 .60
40 A8 8p green .20 .20
a. 8p yel grn, laid paper ('47) 5.25 3.25
b. Imperf., pair 47.50
41 A9 1a dark brown .20 .20
42 A10 2a dark violet .25 .20
a. Imperf., pair 125.00
43 A11 4a ultramarine .60 .20
a. Imperf., pair 150.00
44 A12 8a deep orange 1.00 .60
45 A13 12a scarlet 2.00 *2.50*
46 A14 1r yellow 2.75 2.75
Nos. 39-46 (9) 8.20 7.45

On No. 39B, "POSTAGE" has been moved to ribbon at bottom of design.

Nos. 39a and 40a are printed from worn plates. The background of the design is unshaded.

See #59. For overprints see #O46-O53, O56.

Unani General Hospital A15

Osmania General Hospital A16

Osmania University A17

Osmania Jubilee Hall — A18

Perf. 13½x14

1937, Feb. 13 Litho. Unwmk.

47 A15 4p violet & black .20 .20
48 A16 8p brown & black .20 .20
49 A17 1a dull orange & gray .20 .20
50 A18 2a dull green & gray .50 .50
Nos. 47-50 (4) 1.10 1.10

The Nizam's Silver Jubilee.

Catalogue values for unused stamps in this section, from this point to the end of the section, are for Never Hinged items.

Returning Soldier — A19

1946 Typo. *Perf. 13½*

51 A19 1a dark blue .20 .20

Wmk. 211

52 A19 1a blue .20 .20

Wmk. Nizam's Seal in Sheet

Laid Paper

53 A19 1a dark blue .50 .35
Nos. 51-53 (3) .90 .75

Victory of the Allied Nations in WW II.

Town Hall, Hyderabad A20

1947, Feb. 17 Litho. Wove Paper

54 A20 1a black .20 .20

Inauguration of the Reformed Legislature, Feb. 17th, 1947.

Power House, Hyderabad A21

Designs: 3a, Kaktyai Arch, Warangal Fort. 6a, Golkunda Fort.

Perf. 13½x14

1947-49 Typo. Wmk. 211

55 A21 1a4p dark green .20 .20
56 A21 3a blue .20 .20
57 A21 6a olive brown 4.00 4.00
a. 6a red brown ('49) 35.00 35.00
b. Imperf., pair 90.00
Nos. 55-57 (3) 4.40 4.40

Seal Type of 1915

1947 Engr. *Perf. 13½*

58 A6 ½a rose lake .35 .20

For overprint see No. O54.

Seal Type of 1931

1949 Litho.

59 A8 2p brown 1.25 .20

For overprint see No. O55.

OFFICIAL STAMPS

Regular Issues of 1869-71 Overprinted

1873 Unwmk. *Perf. 11½, 12½*

Red Overprint

O1 A1 ½a brown 21.00
O2 A2 1a olive green 50.00 25.00
O3 A1 2a green 35.00
O4 A3 ½a red brown 3.50 3.50
O5 A3 1a dark brown 6.50 4.25
O6 A3 2a green 6.50 4.00
O7 A3 3a yel brown 8.50 7.00
O8 A3 4a slate 7.00 6.25
O9 A3 8a bister 8.50 8.50
O10 A3 12a blue 11.00 9.00

Black Overprint

O11 A1 ½a brown 15.00
O12 A2 1a olive green 20.00
O13 A1 2a green 27.50
O14 A3 ½a red brown 3.00 1.75
O15 A3 1a dark brown 2.00 1.75
O16 A3 2a green 2.25 .60
O17 A3 3a yel brown 2.00 1.00
O18 A3 4a slate 2.75 2.75
O19 A3 8a bister 5.00 5.00
O20 A3 12a blue 8.00 8.00

The above official stamps became obsolete in August, 1878. Since that date the "Official" overprint has been applied to the reprints and probably to original stamps. Two new varieties of the overprint have also appeared, both on the reprints and on the current stamps. These are overprinted in various colors, positions and combinations.

Same Ovpt. On Regular Issues of 1905-11

1908 Wmk. 42

O21 A5 ½a green 2.00 .20
O22 A5 1a carmine 2.00 .20
O23 A5 2a lilac 3.25 .20
Nos. O21-O23 (3) 7.25 .60

Perf. 11, 11½, 12½, 13½ and Compound

1909-11

O24 A5 ½a red 1.75 .20
O25 A3 1a black 1.00 .20
O26 A3 2a olive green 1.75 .30
O27 A5 3a brown orange 10.00 5.00
O28 A5 4a olive green ('11) 1.50 .30
O29 A5 8a violet ('11) 1.75 .35
O30 A5 12a blue green ('11) 2.50 .35
Nos. O24-O30 (7) 20.25 6.70

Regular Issue of 1908-11 Overprinted

1911-12

O31 A5 ¼a gray .20 .20
O32 A5 ½a green .30 .20
O33 A5 1a carmine .20 .20
O34 A5 2a lilac .20 .20
O35 A5 3a brown orange 1.00 .20
O36 A5 4a olive green .75 .20
O37 A5 8a violet 1.00 .20
O38 A5 12a blue green 2.25 .50
Nos. O31-O38 (8) 5.90 1.90

Same Overprint on Regular Issue of 1912

1912

O39 A5 ¼a brown violet .20 .20
a. ¼a gray violet .20 .20
O40 A5 ½a deep green .20 .20

Same Ovpt. On Regular Issue of 1915-16

1917

O41 A6 ½a green .60 .20
O42 A6 1a carmine rose 1.00 .20
O43 A6 1a red 1.00 .20
Nos. O41-O43 (3) 2.60 .60

Same Overprint on Nos. 37 and 38

1930

O44 A5 4p on ¼a brown violet .80 .20
O45 A6 8p on ½a green .80 .20

Same Overprint on Regular Issue of 1931

1934-47 Wmk. 211 *Perf. 13½*

O46 A8 4p black .20 .20
a. Laid paper ('47) .30
b. Imperf., pair 50.00
O47 A8 8p green .20 .20
a. 8p yel grn, laid paper ('47) 2.00 .30
b. Inverted overprint 175.00 175.00
O48 A9 1a dark brown .25 .20
O49 A10 2a dark violet .25 .20
O50 A11 4a ultramarine .65 .20
O51 A12 8a deep orange 2.00 .20
O52 A13 12a scarlet 2.00 .25
O53 A14 1r yellow 2.75 .30
Nos. O46-O53 (8) 8.30 1.75

Catalogue values for unused stamps in this section, from this point to the end of the section, are for Never Hinged items.

Same Overprint on Nos. 58-59, 39B

1947-50 *Perf. 13½*

O54 A6 ½a rose lake 3.25 1.00
O55 A8 2p brown ('49) 2.50 1.25
O56 A8 6p car lake ('50) 4.00 3.00
Nos. O54-O56 (3) 9.75 5.25

IDAR

ˈē-dər

LOCATION — A Feudatory State in the Western India States Agency.
AREA — 1,669 sq. mi.
POP. — 262,660
CAPITAL — Himmatnagar

Stamps of Idar are in booklet panes of four. All stamps have one or two straight edges.

Maharaja Shri Himatsinhji
A1 A2

1939 Unwmk. Typo. *Perf. 11*

1 A1 ½a light green 2.75 *14.00*

1941 Same Redrawn

2 A1 ½a green 4.50

The panels containing denomination and name of state are shaded.

1944 Unwmk. *Perf. 12*

3 A2 ½a green .75 *14.00*
4 A2 1a purple .40
a. Imperf., pair 160.00
5 A2 2a blue .45
6 A2 4a red 1.40
Nos. 3-6 (4) 3.00

INDORE

in-ˈdō̤ər

(Holkar)

LOCATION — A Feudatory State in the Indore Agency in Central India.
AREA — 9,902 sq. mi.
POP. — 1,513,966
CAPITAL — Indore

Maharaja Tukoji Rao II — A1

A2

1886 Unwmk. Litho. *Perf. 15*

1 A1 ½a lilac 2.00 2.00

1889 Handstamped *Imperf.*

3 A2 ¼a black, *rose* 1.75 *1.90*

No. 3 exists in two types.

The originals of this stamp are printed in water color. The reprints are in oil color and on paper of a deeper shade of rose.

Maharaja Shivaji Rao — A3

1889-92 Engr. *Perf. 15*

4 A3 ¼a orange .20 .20
5 A3 ½a brown violet .20 .20
6 A3 1a green .50 .50
7 A3 2a vermilion 1.25 .65
Nos. 4-7 (4) 2.15 1.55

For overprint see No. 14.

Maharaja Tukoji Rao III
A4 A5

1904-08 *Perf. 13½, 14*

8 A4 ¼a orange .20 .20
9 A5 ½a lake ('08) 5.00 .20
a. Imperf., pair 17.50
10 A5 1a green ('07) 3.75 .20
a. Imperf., pair 125.00
11 A5 2a brown ('05) 2.50 .20
a. Imperf., pair 62.50
12 A5 3a violet 2.25 .45
13 A5 4a ultramarine 2.50 .45
Nos. 8-13 (6) 16.20 1.70

For overprints see Nos. O1-O7.

No. 5 Surcharged

1905 *Perf. 15*

14 A3 ¼a on ½a brown violet 1.75 1.60

Maharaja Yeshwant Rao II
A6 A7

1928-38 Engr. *Perf. 13½*

15 A6 ¼a orange .20 .20
16 A6 ½a claret .20 .20
17 A6 1a green .20 .20
18 A6 1¼a green ('33) .35 .20
19 A6 2a dark brown .90 .65
20 A6 2a Prus blue ('36) .50 .30
21 A6 3a dull violet .90 .90
22 A6 3½a dull violet ('34) 1.00 1.00
23 A6 4a ultramarine 1.00 1.00
24 A6 4a bister ('38) 1.75 .50
25 A6 8a gray 2.00 2.00
26 A6 8a red orange ('38) 7.50 3.25
27 A6 12a rose red ('34) 7.00 7.00

Perf. 14

28	A7	1r lt blue & black	11.00	*15.00*
29	A7	2r car lake & black	22.50	*25.00*
30	A7	5r org brn & black	30.00	30.00
		Nos. 15-30 (16)	87.00	87.40

Imperforates of types A6 and A7 were used with official sanction at Indore City during a stamp shortage in 1938. They were from sheets placed by the printers (Perkins, Bacon) on top of packets of 100 perforated sheets as identification.

Stamps of 1929-33 Surcharged in Black

1940 *Perf. 13, 14*

31	A7	¼a on 5r org brn & blk	.65	.20
a.		Dbl. surch., black over green		225.00
32	A7	½a on 2r car lake & blk	1.00	.20
33	A6	1a on 1¼a green	1.10	.20
a.		Inverted surcharge	75.00	
		Nos. 31-33 (3)	2.75	.60

Stamps with green surcharge only are proofs.

A8

1941-47 **Typo.** *Perf. 11*

34	A8	¼a orange	.20	.20
35	A8	½a rose lilac	.50	.20
36	A8	1a dk olive green	.65	.20
37	A8	1¼a yellow green	.75	.20
a.		Imperf., pair	150.00	
38	A8	2a turquoise blue	6.00	1.75
39	A8	4a bister ('47)	16.00	16.00

Size: 23x28¼mm

40	A8	2r car lake & blk ('47)	12.50	*25.00*
41	A8	5r brn org & blk	14.00	*30.00*
		Nos. 34-41 (8)	50.60	*73.55*

OFFICIAL STAMPS

Stamps and Type of 1904-08 Overprinted

1904-06 *Perf. 13½, 14*

O1	A5	½a lake	.20	.20
a.		Inverted overprint	14.00	
b.		Double overprint	14.00	
c.		Imperf., pair	20.00	
O2	A5	1a green	.20	.20
O3	A5	2a brown ('05)	.20	.20
O4	A5	3a violet ('06)	.75	.75
a.		Imperf., pair	125.00	
O5	A5	4a ultra ('05)	1.25	1.25
		Nos. O1-O5 (5)	2.60	2.60

Same Overprint on No. 8

1907

O6	A4	¼a orange	.20	.20

No. 9 Overprinted

O7	A5	½a lake	.20	.20

#O1, O7 differ mainly in the shape of the "R."

JAIPUR

ˈjī-ˌpu̇ər

LOCATION — A Feudatory State in the Jaipur Residency of India.
AREA — 15,610 sq. mi.
POP. — 3,040,876
CAPITAL — Jaipur

Catalogue values for unused stamps in this State are for Never Hinged items, beginning with Scott 49 in the regular postage section, and Scott O30 in the officials section.

Chariot of Surya, Sun God — A1a

A1

Pin-perf. 14x14½

1904 **Typo.** **Unwmk.**

1	A1	½a ultramarine	6.25	6.25
a.		½a pale blue	16.00	16.00
b.		½a gray blue		300.00
c.		As "b," imperf.	400.00	*450.00*
1D	A1a	½a blue	1.75	2.00
e.		½a ultramarine	1.75	2.00
f.		Imperf.		
2	A1	1a dull red	1.75	1.90
a.		1a chestnut	12.50	12.50
3	A1	2a pale green	2.75	2.75
a.		2a emerald	4.25	4.50
		Nos. 1-3 (4)	12.50	12.90

No. 1 has 36 varieties (on 2 plates), differing in minor details. Nos. 1b and 1c are from plate II. No. 1D has 24 varieties (one plate).

Chariot of Surya — A2

Perf. 12½x12 and 13½

1904-06 **Engr.**

4	A2	¼a olive green ('06)	.20	.20
5	A2	½a deep blue	.20	.20
6	A2	1a carmine	.40	.30
7	A2	2a dark green	.75	.65
8	A2	4a red brown	3.75	2.00
9	A2	8a violet	2.50	1.90
10	A2	1r yellow	3.75	4.00
		Nos. 4-10 (7)	11.55	9.25

For overprints see Nos. 21-22.

A3

A4

1911 **Typo.** *Imperf.*
Without Gum

11	A3	¼a yellow green	1.50	*1.75*
a.		¼a olive green	1.50	*1.75*
b.		"¼" inverted	2.00	2.00
12	A3	¼a olive yellow	.20	.20
b.		¼a blue (error)		
13	A3	½a ultramarine	.20	.20
a.		½a dull blue	.20	.20
b.		"⅓" for "½"	5.00	
14	A3	1a carmine	.30	.30
15	A3	2a deep green	2.50	*2.75*
a.		2a gray green	2.50	*2.75*
		Nos. 11-15 (5)	4.70	*5.20*

There are six types for each value and several settings of the ¼a and ½a in the 1911 issue.

Wmk. "Dorling & Co., London" in Sheet

1913-18 ***Perf. 11***

16	A4	¼a olive bister	.20	.20
a.		Pair, imperf. between	75.00	75.00
17	A4	½a ultramarine	.20	.20
18	A4	1a carmine ('18)	.20	.20
a.		1a scarlet	.20	.20
b.		Vertical pair, imperf. between	87.50	87.50
19	A4	2a green ('18)	2.00	2.00
20	A4	4a red brown	.60	.60
		Nos. 16-20 (5)	3.20	3.20

For overprints see Nos. O1-O6, O9-O10.

Stamps of 1904-06 Surcharged

1926 **Unwmk.** **Engr.** ***Perf. 13½***

21	A2	3a on 8a violet	.75	.85
a.		Inverted surcharge	150.00	150.00
22	A2	3a on 1r yellow	.75	.85
a.		Inverted surcharge	150.00	150.00

Wmk. "Overland Bank" in Sheet

1928 **Typo.** ***Perf. 12***

17a	A4	½a ultramarine	4.75	4.75
18c	A4	1a rose red	12.50	7.50
18d	A4	1a scarlet	12.50	7.50
19a	A4	2a green	24.00	18.00
20a	A4	4a pale brown		
23	A4	8a violet		
23A	A4	1r red orange	150.00	150.00

Durbar Commemorative Issue

Chariot of Surya, Sun God — A5

Maharaja Man Singh II — A6

Elephant with Standard — A7

Sowar in Armor — A8

Blue Peafowl — A9

Royal Bullock Carriage — A10

Royal Elephant Carriage — A11

Albert Museum — A12

Sireh-Deorhi Gate — A13

Chandra Palace — A14

Amber Palace — A15

Rajas Jai Singh II and Man Singh II — A16

Perf. 13½x14, 14, 14x13½

1931, Mar. 14 **Typo.** **Unwmk.**

24	A5	¼a red brown & blk	.25	.20
25	A6	½a dull vio & blk	.40	.20
26	A7	1a blue & black	1.90	.90
27	A8	2a ocher & black	1.90	.90
28	A9	2½a rose & black	8.50	*15.00*
29	A10	3a dk green & blk	8.50	*14.00*
30	A11	4a dull grn & blk	5.50	*11.50*
31	A12	6a dk blue & blk	5.50	*11.50*
32	A13	8a brown & black	6.50	*14.00*
33	A14	1r olive & black	10.00	*22.50*
34	A15	2r lt green & blk	10.00	*27.50*
35	A16	5r violet & black	14.00	*32.50*
		Nos. 24-35 (12)	72.95	*150.70*

Investiture of the Maharaja Man Singh II with full ruling powers.

Eighteen sets of this issue were overprinted in red "INVESTITURE—MARCH 14, 1931" for presentation to distinguished personages.

For surcharges see Nos. 47, 48, 58. For overprints see Nos. O12-O16, Rajasthan 16.

Man Singh II Type of 1931 and

Raja Man Singh II — A18

1932-46 ***Perf. 14***

36	A6	¼a red brn & blk	.20	.20
36A	A6	¾a brn orange & black ('43)	.20	.20
37	A18	1a blue & black	.20	.20
37A	A6	1a blue & black	.50	.20
38	A18	2a ocher & black	.20	.20
38A	A6	2a ocher & blk ('45)	.75	.20

39	A6	2½a dk car & blk	.20	.20
40	A6	3a green & black	.25	.20
41	A18	4a gray grn & blk	.75	.75
41A	A6	4a gray green & blk ('45)	1.25	.75
42	A6	6a blue & black	.65	.65
43	A18	8a choc & black	.65	.65
43A	A6	8a choc & blk ('45)	2.00	*3.00*
44	A18	1r bis & gray blk	7.50	*10.00*
44A	A6	1r bis & gray blk ('46)	7.50	*10.00*
45	A18	2r yel grn & blk	37.50	*50.00*
		Nos. 36-45 (16)	60.30	*77.40*

For overprints see Nos. O17-O30, Rajasthan Nos. 15, 17-25.

Stamps of 1931-32 Surcharged in Red or Black

1936 ***Perf. 14x13½, 13½x14***

46	A18	1r on 2r yel grn & blk (R)	2.25	*3.75*
47	A16	1r on 5r violet & blk	2.00	*3.75*

No. 25 Surcharged in Red

1938 ***Perf. 14x13½***

48	A6	¼a on ½a dull vio & blk	2.25	2.25

Catalogue values for unused stamps in this section, from this point to the end of the section, are for Never Hinged items.

Amber Palace A19

Designs: ¼a, Palace gate. ¾a, Map of Jaipur. 1a, Observatory. 2a, Palace of the Winds. 3a, Arms of the Raja. 4a, Gate of Amber Fort. 8a, Chariot of the Sun. 1r, Raja Man Singh II.

1947-48 Unwmk. Engr. ***Perf. 14***

49	A19	¼a dk green & red brn ('48)	.20	.20
50	A19	½a blue vio & dp grn	.20	.20
51	A19	¾a dk car & blk ('48)	.20	*.25*
52	A19	1a dp ultra & chioc	.25	*.35*
53	A19	2a car & blue vio	.20	*.35*
54	A19	3a dk gray & grn ('48)	.30	*.50*
55	A19	4a choc & dp ultra	.40	*.70*
56	A19	8a dk brown & red	.50	*.70*
57	A19	1r dk red vio & bl grn ('48)	1.25	*2.25*
		Nos. 49-57 (9)	3.50	*5.50*

25th anniv. of the enthronement of Raja Man Singh II.

No. 25 Surcharged in Carmine with New Value and Bars

1947

58	A6	3p on ½a	15.00	15.00
a.		"3 PIE"	50.00	50.00
b.		Inverted surcharge	52.50	52.50
c.		Double surch., one inverted	125.00	125.00
d.		As "a," inverted surcharge	225.00	225.00

For overprint see No. O31.

OFFICIAL STAMPS

Regular Issue of 1913-22 Overprinted in Black or Red

1929 Unwmk. ***Perf. 12½x12, 11***

O1	A4	¼a olive green	.35	.20
O2	A4	½a ultramarine	.35	.20
a.		Inverted overprint		90.00
O3	A4	½a ultra (R)	.35	.20
O4	A4	1a red	.50	.20
O5	A4	2a green	.45	.25
O6	A4	4a red brown	2.25	.90
O7	A4	8a purple (R)	18.00	18.00
O8	A4	1r red orange	35.00	35.00
		Nos. O1-O8 (8)	57.25	54.95

The 8a and 1r not issued without overprint. For overprint see No. O11.

Regular Issue of 1913-22 Overprinted in Black or Red

b

1931 ***Perf. 11, 12½x12***

O9	A4	½a ultra	75.00	.20
O10	A4	½a ultra (R)	90.00	.20
O10A	A4	8a purple	240.00	240.00
O10B	A4	1r red orange	240.00	240.00
		Nos. O9-O10B (4)	645.00	480.40

No. O5 Surcharged

1932

O11	A4	½a on 2a green	150.00	.25

Regular Issue of 1931 Overprinted in Red

1931-37 ***Perf. 13½x14, 14***

O12	A6	¼a red brn & blk ('36)	.20	.20
O13	A6	½a dull vio & blk	.20	.20
O14	A7	1a blue & black	210.00	1.50
O15	A8	2a ocher & blk ('36)	.90	.45
O16	A11	4a dl grn & blk ('37)	7.50	3.00

For overprint see No. O32.

Same on Regular Issue of 1932 in Red

1932-37 ***Perf. 14***

O17	A18	1a blue & black	3.00	.30
O18	A18	2a ocher & black	3.00	.30
O19	A18	4a gray grn & blk ('37)	*240.00*	*13.50*
O20	A18	8a choc & black	2.75	1.00
O21	A18	1r bister & gray blk	20.00	20.00
		Nos. O17-O21 (5)	*268.75*	*35.10*

No. 36 Overprinted Type "b" in Black

1939 ***Perf. 14***

O22	A6	¼a red brown & blk	45.00	35.00

Nos. 36A, 38A, 39, 41A, 43A, 44A and Type of 1931 Overprinted in Carmine

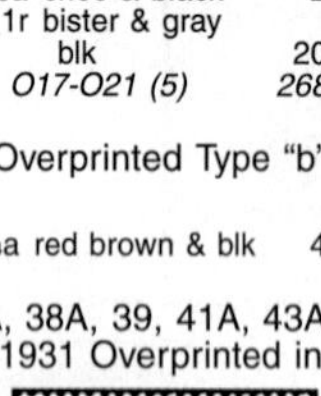

1941-46 Unwmk. ***Perf. 13½, 14***

O23	A6	¾a brn org & blk ('43)	.20	.20
O24	A6	1a blue & blk ('41)	.30	.20
O25	A6	2a ocher & black	.45	.20
O26	A6	2½a dk car & blk ('46)	1.25	*4.50*
O27	A6	4a gray grn & blk ('46)	.60	.30
O28	A6	8a choc & black	1.25	.60
O29	A6	1r bis & gray blk	*175.00*	
		Nos. O23-O28 (6)	4.05	*6.00*

Catalogue values for unused stamps in this section, from this point to the end of the section, are for Never Hinged items.

No. O24 Surcharged with New Value and Bars in Carmine

1947 ***Perf. 13½***

O30	A6	9p on 1a blue & blk	.25	.25

No. 58 Overprinted in Red "SERVICE"

Perf. 14

O31	A6	3p on ½a	3.50	*5.00*
a.		Inverted surcharge	1,400.	1,250.
b.		Double surch., one inverted	65.00	65.00
c.		"3 PIE"	350.00	350.00

No. O13 Surcharged "Three-quarter Anna" in Devanagari, similar to surcharge on No. 48, and Bars in Carmine

1949 ***Perf. 14x13½***

O32	A6	¾a on ½a dl vio & blk	10.00	6.00

For later issues see Rajasthan.

JAMMU AND KASHMIR

'jəm-ü and 'kash-mi(ə)r

LOCATION — A Feudatory State in the Kashmir Residency in the extreme north of India.
AREA — 82,258 sq. mi.
POP. — 4,021,616 (1941)
CAPITAL — Srinagar

All stamps of Jammu and Kashmir were issued without gum.

½ Anna — A1

1 Anna — A2

¼ Rupee — A3

Native Grayish Laid Paper

Handstamped

1866-67 Unwmk. ***Imperf.***

Printed in Water Colors

1	A1	½a gray black	275.00	125.00
		Cut to shape	25.00	20.00
2	A2	1a dull blue	475.00	125.00
a.		1a ultramarine	475.00	125.00
b.		1a royal blue	650.00	450.00
		Cut to shape	40.00	15.00
3	A2	1a gray black	1,500.	1,250.
		Cut to shape	75.00	75.00
4	A3	¼r dull blue	*1,100.*	*475.00*
a.		¼r ultramarine	*1,100.*	*475.00*
b.		¼r indigo	*2,500.*	*1,250.*
		Cut to shape	1,100.	475.00
5	A3	¼r gray black	1,600.	—
		Cut to shape	1,600.	—
		Nos. 1-5 (5)	4,950.	1,975.

It has now been proved by the leading authorities on Indian stamps that all stamps of ½ anna and 1 anna printed from the so-called Die A are forgeries and that no such die was ever in use.

See Nos. 24-59.

JAMMU

A part of the Feudatory State of Jammu & Kashmir, both being ruled by the same sovereign.

½ Anna — A4

1 Anna — A5

Printed in blocks of four, three types of the ½a and one of the 1a.

Native Grayish Laid Paper

Printed in Water Colors

1867-77 Unwmk. ***Imperf.***

6	A4	½a black	125.00	150.00
7	A4	½a indigo	300.00	240.00
a.		½a deep ultramarine	240.00	175.00
b.		½a deep violet blue	175.00	75.00
8	A4	½a red	2.25	1.90
a.		½a orange red	32.50	16.00
b.		½a orange	47.50	47.50
9	A5	1a black	1,400.	950.00
10	A5	1a indigo	600.00	325.00
a.		1a deep ultramarine	600.00	325.00
b.		1a deep violet blue	600.00	325.00
11	A5	1a red	2.75	2.75
a.		1a orange red	16.00	17.50
b.		1a orange		425.00

1876

12	A4	½a emerald	1,500.	950.00
13	A4	½a bright blue	1,250.	275.00
14	A5	1a emerald	2,750.	1,600.
15	A5	1a bright blue	300.00	*325.00*

Native Grayish Laid Paper

1877 **Printed in Oil Colors**

16	A4	½a red	8.00	7.00
a.		½a brown red	—	35.00
17	A4	½a black		900.00
18	A5	1a red	25.00	20.00
a.		1a brown red	—	125.00
19	A5	1a black		*1,900.*

The formerly listed ½a dark blue, ½a dark green, 1a dark blue and 1a dark green are believed to be reprints.

European White Laid Paper

20	A4	½a red	—	*950.00*
a.		Thin laid bâtonné paper		*1,250.*
21	A5	1a red	*375.00*	
a.		Thin laid bâtonné paper	*4,250.*	

European White Wove Paper

22	A4	½a red		*450.00*
23	A5	1a red		

RE-ISSUES

For Jammu Only

Native Grayish Laid Paper

Printed in Water Colors

1869-76 ***Imperf.***

24	A1	½a deep black	*16.50*	*175.00*
25	A1	½a bright blue	275.00	*350.00*
26	A1	½a orange red	210.00	55.00
a.		½a orange	90.00	*125.00*
b.		½a red	110.00	*350.00*
27	A1	½a emerald	75.00	*210.00*
28	A1	½a yellow	550.00	*900.00*
29	A2	1a deep black	240.00	
30	A2	1a bright blue	85.00	*325.00*
31	A2	1a orange red	175.00	*240.00*
b.		1a red	200.00	*325.00*
32	A2	1a emerald	75.00	210.00
33	A2	1a yellow	725.00	
34	A3	¼r deep black	240.00	—
35	A3	¼r bright blue	160.00	
a.		¼r indigo	1,100.	650.00
36	A3	¼r orange red	125.00	190.00
a.		¼r orange		—
b.		¼r red	110.00	*150.00*
37	A3	¼r emerald	210.00	350.00
38	A3	¼r yellow	350.00	

Native Grayish Laid Paper

1877 **Printed in Oil Colors**

39	A1	½a red	25.00	*45.00*
40	A1	½a black	25.00	*45.00*
41	A1	½a slate blue	125.00	*210.00*
42	A1	½a sage green	125.00	
43	A2	1a red	30.00	*175.00*
45	A2	1a slate blue	20.00	*240.00*
46	A2	1a sage green	125.00	
47	A3	¼r red	210.00	*475.00*
50	A3	¼r sage green	125.00	

European White Laid Paper

51	A1	½a red		775.00
52	A1	½a black	20.00	*42.50*
53	A1	½a slate blue	32.50	*240.00*
54	A1	½a yellow	*125.00*	
56	A2	1a slate blue	42.50	*425.00*
57	A3	¼r red	425.00	425.00
58	A3	¼r sage green	*1,250.*	

European Brownish Wove Paper

59	A1	½a red		*1,000.*

It is probable that the issues of 1876, 1877 and the re-issues of the circular stamps were made to supply the demands of philatelists more than for postal needs. They were, however, available for postage.

There exist also reprints, printed in a variety of colors, on native and European thin wove paper. Collectors are warned against official imitations, which are very numerous. They are printed on several kinds of paper and in a great variety of colors.

A5a

Handstamped in Oil Color

1877, Nov.

60	A5a	(½a) red	*950.00*

This provisional, made with a canceling device, was used only in Nov. 1877, at Jammu city.

KASHMIR

A part of the Feudatory State of Jammu & Kashmir, both being ruled by the same sovereign.

½ Anna — A6

Printed in Water Colors
Native Grayish Laid Paper
Printed from a Single Die

1866 Unwmk. *Imperf.*

62	A6	½a black	*2,400.*	350.00

¼ Anna — A7

½ Anna — A8

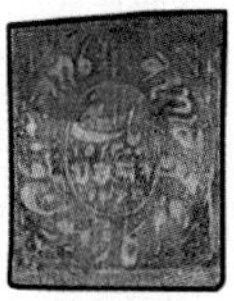
1 Anna
A9

2 Annas
A10

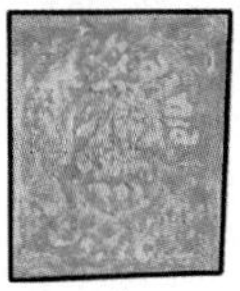
4
Annas — A11

8
Annas — A12

The ¼a, 1a and 2a are printed in strips of five varieties, the ½a in sheets of twenty varieties and the 4a and 8a from single dies.

1866-70

63	A7	¼a black	2.00	2.00
64	A8	½a black	*1,250.*	*160.00*
65	A8	½a ultra	2.00	1.25
a.		½a blue	3.75	1.50
66	A9	1a black	2,100.	425.00
67	A9	1a red orange	7.50	7.50
68	A9	1a Venetian red	11.00	8.00
69	A9	1a orange brown	10.00	7.50
70	A9	1a ultra	*3,000.*	*1,400.*
71	A10	2a olive yellow	10.00	*12.50*
72	A11	4a emerald	27.50	26.00
73	A12	8a red	27.50	27.50

All the stamps printed in oil colors are reprints.

As in Jammu, official imitations are numerous and are found in many colors and on various papers.

JAMMU & KASHMIR

¼
Anna — A13

½
Anna — A14

1
Anna — A15

2
Annas — A16

4
Annas — A17

8
Annas — A18

Laid Paper

Printed in Oil Colors

1878 *Rough Perf. 10-14*

74	A13	¼a red	—	—
75	A14	½a red	12.50	*15.00*
a.		Wove paper		*210.00*
76	A14	½a slate blue	75.00	50.00
77	A15	1a red	1,250.	
78	A15	1a bright violet	—	—

1878-80 *Imperf.*

79	A13	¼a red	17.50	12.50
80	A14	½a red	7.50	7.50
81	A14	½a slate	13.00	12.50
82	A15	1a red	7.50	7.50
83	A15	1a violet	20.00	20.00
a.		1a dull purple	30.00	30.00
84	A16	2a red	60.00	60.00
85	A16	2a bright violet	27.50	25.00
86	A16	2a dull ultra	*75.00*	75.00
87	A17	4a red	175.00	150.00

Thick Wove Paper

88	A14	½a red	22.50	*45.00*
89	A15	1a red	40.00	17.50
90	A16	2a red	15.00	17.50

Thin Toned Wove Paper

1879-80

91	A13	¼a red	2.50	*2.75*
92	A14	½a red	.50	.50
93	A15	1a red	2.00	*2.50*
94	A16	2a red	2.75	3.50
95	A17	4a red	6.25	6.25
96	A18	8a red	6.50	7.00
		Nos. 91-96 (6)	20.50	22.50

Thin Laid Bâtonné Paper

1880 Printed in Water Color

97	A13	¼a ultramarine	800.00	475.00

Thin Toned Wove Paper

1881 Printed in Oil Colors

98	A13	¼a orange	7.00	*8.50*
99	A14	½a orange	16.00	11.00
100	A15	1a orange	15.00	8.00
101	A16	2a orange	12.50	8.00
102	A17	4a orange	25.00	*35.00*
103	A18	8a orange	50.00	*55.00*
		Nos. 98-103 (6)	125.50	125.50

⅛ Anna — A19

Thin White or Yellowish Wove Paper

1883-94

104	A19	⅛a yellow brown	.70	*1.00*
a.		⅛a yellow	.70	*1.00*
105	A13	¼a brown	.55	.50
a.		Double impression	1,250.	
106	A14	½a red	1.00	.35
a.		½a rose	1.10	.60
106B	A19	½a bright blue	35.00	
c.		½a dull blue	4.00	
107	A15	1a bronze green	.75	.50
108	A15	1a yel green	.75	.50
109	A15	1a blue green	1.00	
110	A15	1a bister	—	
111	A17	4a green	2.75	2.75
112	A17	4a olive green	2.50	*3.25*
113	A18	8a deep blue	7.50	*8.50*
114	A18	8a dark ultra	6.75	*8.00*
115	A18	8a gray violet	9.00	*14.50*

Printed in Water Color

116	A18	8a gray blue	125.00	90.00

Printed in Oil Colors

Yellow Pelure Paper

117	A16	2a red	2.25	2.25

Yellow Green Pelure Paper

118	A16	2a red	2.00	*2.50*

Deep Green Pelure Paper

119	A16	2a red	10.00	10.00

Coarse Yellow Wove Paper

120	A16	2a red	1.50	.90
		Nos. 104-120 (17)	209.00	145.50

Thin Creamy Laid Paper

1886-94

121	A19	⅛a yellow	35.00	*45.00*
122	A13	¼a brown	8.00	*5.50*
123	A14	½a vermilion	6.00	4.50
124	A14	½a rose red		55.00
125	A15	1a green	90.00	90.00
126	A17	4a green	—	—

Printed in Water Color

127	A18	8a gray blue	160.00	150.00
		Nos. 121-127 (6)	354.00	350.00

Impressions of types A13 to A19 in colors other than the issued stamps are proofs. Forgeries to defraud the post exist, and some are common.

1/4 Anna

Stamps of the above type, printed in red or black, were never placed in use.

OFFICIAL STAMPS

Same Types as Regular Issues
White Laid Paper

1878 Unwmk. *Rough Perf. 10-14*

O1	A14	½a black		*1,100.*

Imperf

O3	A14	½a black	80.00	80.00
O4	A15	1a black	50.00	50.00
O5	A16	2a black	45.00	42.50
		Nos. O3-O5 (3)	175.00	172.50

Thin White or Yellowish Wove Paper

1880

O6	A13	¼a black	.65	*.75*
O7	A14	½a black	.20	*.30*
O8	A15	1a black	.20	*.50*
O9	A16	2a black	.30	*.45*
O10	A17	4a black	.40	*.75*
O11	A18	8a black	1.25	1.00
		Nos. O6-O11 (6)	3.00	3.75

Thin Creamy Laid Paper

1890-91

O12	A13	¼a black	4.50	4.50
O13	A14	½a black	3.00	*3.50*
O14	A15	1a black	1.40	*3.00*
O15	A16	2a black	40.00	
O16	A17	4a black	45.00	45.00
O17	A18	8a black	30.00	*45.00*
		Nos. O12-O17 (6)	123.90	101.00

Obsolete October 31, 1894.

JASDAN

LOCATION — A Feudatory State in the Kathiawar Agency in Western India.
AREA — 296 sq. mi.
POP. — 34,056 (1931)
CAPITAL — Jasdan

In 1948 Jasdan was incorporated in the United State of Saurashtra (see Soruth).

Catalogue values for all unused stamps in this state are for Never Hinged items.

Sun — A1

Perf. 8½ to 10½

1942 Unwmk. Typo.

1	A1	1a green	2.75

Issued in booklet panes of 4 and 8.
The 1a carmine is a revenue stamp.
Jasdan's stamp became obsolete Feb. 15, 1948.

JHALAWAR

ˈjäl-ə-ˌwär

LOCATION — A Feudatory State in the Rajputana Agency of India.
AREA — 813 sq. mi.
POP. — 107,890
CAPITAL — Jhalrapatan

Apsaras, Hindu Nymph
A1 A2

Laid Paper

1887-90 Unwmk. *Imperf.*

Without Gum

1	A1	1p yellow green	2.00	3.25
2	A2	¼a green	.75	1.25

Obsolete October 31, 1900.

JIND

ˈjind

(Jhind)

LOCATION — A State of India in the north Punjab.
AREA — 1,299 sq. mi.
POP. — 361,812 (1941)
CAPITAL — Sangrur

A1

A2

A3

A4

A5

1874 Unwmk. Litho. *Imperf.*

Thin White Wove Paper

Without Gum

1	A1	½a blue	5.50	3.50
2	A2	1a lilac	7.50	7.50
3	A3	2a yellow	1.25	1.25
4	A4	4a green	27.50	5.50
5	A5	8a dark violet	175.00	40.00
		Nos. 1-5 (5)	216.75	57.75

1875

Thick Blue Laid Paper

Without Gum

6	A1	½a blue	.25	.25
7	A2	1a red violet	.50	.50
8	A3	2a brown orange	.75	.75
9	A4	4a green	.85	.85
10	A5	8a purple	4.25	4.25
		Nos. 6-10 (5)	6.60	6.60

1885 Without Gum *Perf. 12*

11	A1	½a blue	4.25	4.25

A6

A7

A8

A9

A10

A11

1882-84 Without Gum *Imperf.*

Thin Yellowish Wove Paper

12	A6	¼a buff	.20	.20
a.		Double impression		
13	A7	½a yellow	.55	.55
14	A8	1a brown	1.40	1.40
15	A9	2a blue	.55	.55
16	A10	4a green	.65	.65
17	A11	8a red	2.00	1.40
		Nos. 12-17 (6)	5.35	4.75

Perf. 12

18	A6	¼a buff	.30	.30
19	A7	½a yellow	.40	.40
20	A8	1a brown	.85	.85
21	A9	2a blue	1.50	1.75
22	A10	4a green	2.75	2.75
23	A11	8a red	6.75	6.75
a.		Thick white paper	6.75	6.75
		Nos. 18-23 (6)	12.55	12.80

Laid Paper

Imperf

24	A6	¼a buff	3.50	3.50
25	A7	½a yellow	1.00	1.00
26	A8	1a brown	1.00	1.00
27	A9	2a blue	55.00	55.00
28	A11	8a red	3.75	3.75
		Nos. 24-28 (5)	64.25	64.25

Perf. 12

29	A6	¼a buff	11.00	11.00
30	A7	½a yellow	15.00	11.00
31	A8	1a brown	3.75	3.75
32	A11	8a red	5.00	5.00
		Nos. 29-32 (4)	34.75	30.75

As postage stamps these issues became obsolete in July, 1885, but some possibly remained in use as revenue stamps.

For later issues see Jind under Convention States.

KISHANGARH

'kish-ən-ˌgär

LOCATION — A Feudatory State in the Jaipur Residency of India.
AREA — 858 sq. mi.
POP. — 85,744
CAPITAL — Kishangarh

Kishangarh was incorporated in Rajasthan in 1947-49.

Stamps were issued without gum except Nos. 27-35.

Coat of Arms — A1

1899-1900 Unwmk. Typo. *Imperf.*

Soft Porous Paper

1	A1	1a green	21.00	21.00
2	A1	1a blue ('00)	*550.00*	

Pin-perf.

3	A1	1a green	47.50	47.50

A2

A3

Coat of Arms — A4

Maharaja Sardul Singh — A5

A6

A7

Coat of Arms—A9
A8

Thin Wove Paper

1899-1900 Handstamped *Imperf.*

4	A2	¼a carmine	.45	.45
5	A2	¼a green	150.00	
6	A3	½a blue	.90	.60
7	A3	½a green	13.00	13.00
8	A3	½a carmine	13.00	13.00
9	A3	½a violet	30.00	*35.00*
10	A4	1a gray violet	.60	.45
a.		1a gray	.60	.45
11	A4	1a rose	60.00	*65.00*
11A	A5	2a orange	4.00	4.00
12	A6	4a chocolate	1.90	1.90
a.		Laid paper	45.00	45.00
13	A7	1r dull green	18.00	
13A	A7	1r light brown	50.00	45.00
14	A8	2r brown red	70.00	
a.		Laid paper	55.00	
15	A9	5r violet	45.00	
a.		Laid paper	75.00	

Pin-perf

16	A2	¼a magenta	.25	.25
a.		¼a rose	.25	
17	A2	¼a green	*175.00*	65.00
a.		Imperf. vertically	300.00	300.00
18	A3	½a blue	.30	.30
a.		½a dark blue	.60	.60
19	A3	½a green	12.00	12.00
a.		Imperf. vert., pair	60.00	60.00
20	A4	1a gray violet	.55	.45
a.		1a gray	.75	.75
b.		1a red lilac		6.00
d.		As "b," laid paper	30.00	22.50
20E	A4	1a rose	40.00	27.50
21	A5	2a orange	7.00	4.50
21B	A6	4a pale red brown	1.50	1.25
c.		4a chocolate	1.50	1.25
22	A7	1r dull green	14.00	*19.00*
b.		Laid paper	125.00	
23	A8	2r brown red	42.50	42.50
b.		Laid paper	60.00	
24	A9	5r red violet	32.50	
d.		Laid paper	90.00	

Nos. 4-24 exist tête bêche and sell for a slight premium.

For overprints see #O1-O11, Rajasthan #26-28, 30-32.

A9a

A9b

Soft Porous Paper

1901 Typo.

24A	A9a	½a rose	10.00	10.00
24B	A9b	1a dull violet	18.00	18.00

For overprint see No. O12.

A10

A11

1903 Stout Hard Paper *Imperf.*

25	A10	½a pink	6.50	5.25
a.		Printed on both sides		*1,250.*

1904 Thin Wove Paper *Pin-perf.*

25B	A11	8a gray	6.50	6.50

Exists tête bêche. Slight premium.

For overprints see #O13, O33, Rajasthan #29.

A11a

Maharaja Sardul Singh — A12

25D	A11a	1r green	27.50	27.50

For overprint see No. O13A.

1903 *Imperf.*

Stout Hard Paper

26	A12	2a yellow	4.50	4.50

For overprints see Nos. O14, O34.

Maharaja Madan Singh
A13 A14

1904-05 Engr. *Perf. 12½, 13½*

27	A13	¼a carmine	.35	.20
28	A13	½a chestnut	.35	.20
29	A13	1a deep blue	1.50	.50
30	A13	2a orange	13.50	13.50
31	A13	4a dark brown	4.00	4.00
32	A13	8a purple ('05)	8.00	8.00
33	A13	1r dark green	11.00	11.00
34	A13	2r lemon yellow	17.00	*27.50*
35	A13	5r purple brown	22.50	*42.50*
		Nos. 27-35 (9)	78.20	*107.40*

For overprints see Nos. O15-O22, O35-O38, Rajasthan Nos. 33-39.

Thin Wove Paper

1913 Typo. *Rouletted 9½*

37	A14	2 "ANNA" violet	2.50	2.50

Exists tete beche. Slight premium.

See #40-50. For overprint see Rajasthan #43.

Maharaja Madan Singh
A15 A16

Thick, Chalk-surfaced Paper

1913 *Rouletted 6½, 12*

38	A15	¼a pale blue	.20	.20
a.		"Kishangahr"	3.25	3.25
b.		Imperf., pair	4.50	
39	A16	2a purple	13.00	13.00
a.		"Kishangahr"	85.00	85.00

For overprint see No. O23.

1913-16 *Rouletted 12, 14½*

40	A14	¼a pale blue	.20	.20
41	A14	½a green ('15)	.20	.20
a.		Printed on both sides	250.00	
42	A14	1a carmine	.90	.90
43	A14	2 "ANNAS" purple	2.75	*3.50*
44	A14	4a ultramarine	5.75	*9.00*
45	A14	8a brown	5.75	*12.00*
46	A14	1r rose lilac	12.00	*24.00*
47	A14	2r dark green	30.00	*35.00*
48	A14	5r brown	45.00	*60.00*
		Nos. 40-48 (9)	102.55	*144.80*

On Nos. 40-48 the halftone screen covers the entire design.

Nos. 41-48 have ornaments on both sides of value in top panel.

For overprints see Nos. O24-O30, O39-O43, Rajasthan Nos. 40-42, 44-48.

Type of 1913-16 Redrawn

1918 *Rouletted*

50	A14	1a rose red	.90	.90

The redrawn stamp is 24¾mm wide instead of 26mm. There is a white oval around the portrait with only traces of the red line. There is less shading outside the wreath.

For overprint see No. O44.

Maharaja Jagjanarajan Singh
A17 A18

Thick Glazed Paper

1928-29 *Pin-perf. 14½ to 16*

52	A17	¼a light blue	.20	.20
53	A17	½a lt yellow green	.30	.30
a.		Imperf., pair	35.00	35.00
54	A18	1a carmine rose	.55	.55
55	A18	2a red violet	2.00	2.00
56	A17	4a yellow brown	1.50	1.50
57	A17	8a purple	4.00	4.00
58	A17	1r green	4.00	4.00
59	A17	2r lemon	15.00	*24.00*
60	A17	5r red brown	30.00	*35.00*
a.		Imperf., pair	125.00	
		Nos. 52-60 (9)	57.55	*71.55*

Thick Soft Unglazed Paper

1945-47

52a	A17	¼a gray blue	1.25	1.25
b.		¼a greenish blue ('47)	1.25	1.25
53b	A17	½a deep green	1.25	1.25
54a	A18	1a dull carmine	2.50	2.50
b.		1a dark violet blue		
55a	A18	2a deep red violet	5.00	5.00
b.		2a violet brown, imperf.	20.00	
56a	A17	4a brown	25.00	25.00
57a	A17	8a violet	32.50	*40.00*
58a	A17	1r deep green	40.00	*55.00*

The 2r and 5r exist on same paper.

For overprints see Rajasthan Nos. 49-58.

For later issues see Rajasthan.

OFFICIAL STAMPS

Used values are for CTO copies.

Regular Issues of 1899-1916 Handstamped

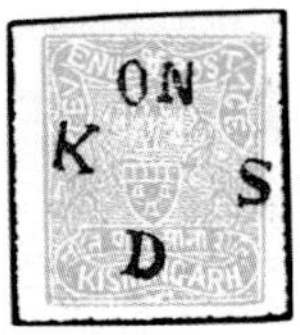

Black Handstamp
On Issue of 1899-1900

1918 Unwmk. *Imperf.*

O1 A2 ¼a carmine 8.50
O2 A4 1a gray violet 3.50 2.25
O3 A6 4a chocolate 17.00 17.00

Pin-perf

O4 A2 ¼a carmine .50 .50
O4A A2 ¼a green 40.00
O4B A3 ½a blue 27.50
O6 A4 1a gray violet 3.50 1.50
O7 A5 2a orange
O8 A6 4a chocolate 15.00 15.00
O9 A7 1r dull green 60.00 60.00
O10 A8 2r brown red 125.00 125.00
O11 A9 5r red violet 175.00 175.00

See tete beche note after No. 24.

On Issue of 1901

O12 A9b 1a dull violet

On Issue of 1904

O13 A11 8a gray 32.50 32.50
O13A A11a 1r green

Imperf.

O14 A12 2a yellow 17.00 17.00

On Issue of 1904-05

Perf. 12½, 13

O15 A13 ¼a carmine 15.00 12.50
O16 A13 ½a chestnut .60 .50
O17 A13 1a deep blue 9.25 4.00
O18 A13 2a orange
O19 A13 4a dark brown 15.00 15.00
O20 A13 8a purple 60.00 50.00
O21 A13 1r dark green 250.00 250.00
O22 A13 5r purple brn

On Issue of 1913

Rouletted

O23 A15 ¼a pale blue 8.50

On Issue of 1913-16

O24 A14 ¼a pale blue .75 .35
O25 A14 ½a green 1.40 .60
O26 A14 1a carmine 1.40 .65
O27 A14 2a purple 2.00 2.00
O28 A14 4a ultra 22.50 22.50
O29 A14 8a brown 42.50 42.50
O30 A14 1r rose lilac 85.00 85.00
O31 A14 2r dark green 300.00
O32 A14 5r brown 425.00

Red Handstamp

On Issue of 1904

Pin-perf

O33 A11 8a gray 42.50 42.50

Imperf

O34 A12 2a yellow 35.00 35.00

On Issue of 1904-05

Perf. 12½, 13

O35 A13 1a deep blue 12.00 12.00
O36 A13 4a dark brown 15.00 15.00
O37 A13 8a purple 25.00 *35.00*
O38 A13 1r dark green 45.00 *72.50*

On Issue of 1913-16

Rouletted

O39 A14 ¼a pale blue 8.50 8.50
O40 A14 ½a green 8.50 8.50
O41 A14 2a purple 22.50 22.50
O42 A14 4a ultra 42.50 42.50
O43 A14 8a brown 42.50 42.50

On Issue of 1918

Redrawn

O44 A14 1a rose red

The overprint on Nos. O1 to O44 is handstamped and, as usual with that style of overprint, is found inverted, double, etc. In this instance there is evidence that many of the varieties were deliberately made.

LAS BELA

ləs ˈbāl-ə

LOCATION — A Feudatory State in the Baluchistan District.
AREA — 7,132 sq. mi.
POP. — 63,008
CAPITAL — Bela

A1

A2

1897-98 Unwmk. Typo. *Perf. 12*

1 A1 ½a black, *white* 9.75 9.75
2 A1 ½a black, *gray* 2.75 2.50
3 A1 ½a black, *blue* ('98) 5.50 5.50
Nos. 1-3 (3) 18.00 17.75

1901

4 A2 1a black, *red orange* 9.75 9.75

1904 *Pin-perf*

5 A1 ½a black, *lt blue* 6.00 6.00

Granite Paper

6 A1 ½a black, *greenish gray* 3.75 3.75

Las Bela stamps became obsolete in Mar. 1907.

MORVI

ˈmor-vē

LOCATION — A Feudatory State in the Kathiawar Agency, Western India.
AREA — 822 sq. mi.
POP. — 113,023
CAPITAL — Morvi

In 1948 Morvi was incorporated in the United State of Saurashtra (see Soruth).

Sir Lakhdhirji Waghji The Thakur Sahib of Morvi — A1

1931 Unwmk. Typo. *Perf. 12*
Size: 21½x26½mm

1 A1 3p red .95 *1.10*
a. 3p deep blue (error) 6.00
2 A1 ½a deep blue 1.50 1.25
3 A1 1a red brown 2.00 *2.50*
4 A1 2a yellow brown 4.00 *4.75*
Nos. 1-4 (4) 8.45 *9.60*

Nos. 1-4 and 1a were printed in two blocks of four, with stamps 5½mm apart, and perforated on four sides. Nos. 1 and 2 were also printed in blocks of four, with stamps 10mm apart, and perforated on two or three sides.

A2

A3

1932 Size: 21x25½mm *Perf. 11*

5 A2 3p rose .35 *.75*
6 A2 6p gray green 1.25 *1.50*
7 A2 6p emerald 1.25 *2.50*
8 A2 1a ultramarine 1.10 *1.60*
9 A2 2a violet 7.25 *9.00*
Nos. 5-9 (5) 11.20 *15.35*

1934-48 *Perf. 14, Rough Perf. 11*

10 A3 3p carmine rose .25 *.30*
a. 3p red .30 .30
11 A3 6p emerald .30 *.60*
a. 6p green .30 *.60*
12 A3 1a red brown 1.10 *1.50*
a. 1a brown 1.25 1.75
13 A3 2a violet 1.10 *1.50*
Nos. 10-13 (4) 2.75 *3.90*

The 1934 London printing of Nos. 10-13 is perf. 14; the later Morvi Press printing is rough perf. 11.

Morvi stamps became obsolete Feb. 15, 1948.

NANDGAON

ˈnän͵d͵-͵gaun

LOCATION — A Feudatory State in the Chhattisgarh States Agency in Central India.
AREA — 871 sq. mi.
POP. — 182,380
CAPITAL — Rajnandgaon

A1

A2

White Paper

1892, Feb. Unwmk. Typo. *Imperf.*
Without Gum

1 A1 ½a blue 2.50
2 A1 2a rose 12.00

Some authorities claim that No. 2 was a revenue stamp.

For overprints see Nos. O1-O2.

1893 Without Gum

4 A2 ½a green 9.00
5 A2 2a rose 10.50

For overprint see No. O5.

Same Redrawn

1894 Without Gum

6 A2 ½a yellow green 13.00 9.50
7 A2 1a rose 30.00 30.00
a. Laid paper 125.00

The redrawn stamps have smaller value characters and wavy lines between the stamps.

For overprints see Nos. O3-O4.

OFFICIAL STAMPS

Regular Issues Handstamped in Violet

1893-94 Unwmk. *Imperf.*
Without Gum

O1 A1 ½a blue *50.00*
O2 A1 2a red *65.00*
O3 A2 ½a yellow green .55 .55
O4 A2 1a rose 2.00
a. Laid paper 6.50
O5 A2 2a rose 3.00 3.00

Some authorities believe that this handstamp was used as a control mark, rather than to indicate a stamp for official mail.

The 1 anna has been reprinted in brown and in blue.

Nandgaon stamps became obsolete in July, 1895.

NOWANUGGUR

͵nau-ə-ˈnəg-ər

(Navanagar)

LOCATION — A Feudatory State in the Kathiawar Agency, Western India.
AREA — 3,791 sq. mi.
POP. — 402,192
CAPITAL — Navanagar

Stamps of Nowanuggur were superseded by those of India.

6 Dokra = 1 Anna
16 Annas = 1 Rupee

Kandjar (Indian Dagger) — A1

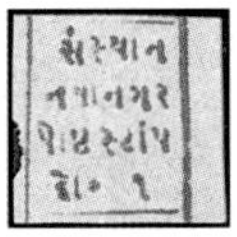

A2

1877 Unwmk. Typo. *Imperf.*
Without Gum
Laid Paper

1 A1 1d dull blue .50 *10.00*
a. 1d ultramarine .50 *10.00*
b. Tete beche pair 1,100.

Perf. 12½

2 A1 1d slate 65.00 65.00
a. Tete beche pair 1,900.
b. Wove paper

1877-88 *Imperf.*
Without Gum
Wove Paper

3 A2 1d black, *red violet* .45 *.90*
a. 1d black, *rose* .45 *.90*
b. Characters at beginning of 3rd line read "4102" instead of "418"
4 A2 2d black, *green* .60 *.90*
a. 2d black, *blue green* .75 *1.25*
b. "4102" instead of "418"
5 A2 3d black, *yellow* 1.10 *1.50*
a. 3d black, *orange yellow* 1.25 *1.75*
b. "4102" instead of "418"
c. Laid paper 32.50
d. 2d black, *yellow* (error in sheet of 3d) 400.00
Nos. 3-5 (3) 2.15 *3.30*

Nos. 3-5 range in width from 14 to 19mm.

Seal of the State — A3

1893 Thick Paper *Imperf.*
Without Gum

6 A3 1d black 60.00

Perf. 12

7 A3 1d black 7.50
8 A3 3d orange 4.50

Imperf
Thin Paper

9 A3 1d black 50.00
10 A3 2d dark green 50.00
11 A3 3d orange 42.50
Nos. 9-11 (3) 142.50

Perf. 12

12	A3	1d black	.20	.30
13	A3	2d green	.45	.45
14	A3	3d orange	.60	.60
a.		Imperf. vert., pair		
		Nos. 12-14 (3)	1.25	1.35

Obsolete at end of 1895.

ORCHHA

'or-chə

(Orcha)

LOCATION — A Feudatory State in the Bundelkhand Agency in Central India.
AREA — 2,080 sq. mi.
POP. — 314,661
CAPITAL — Tikamgarh

Seal of Orchha — A1

1913-17 Unwmk. Litho. *Imperf.*
Without Gum

1	A1	¼a ultra ('15)	.20	.25
2	A1	½a emerald ('14)	.20	.30
a.		Background of arms unshaded	20.00	30.00
3	A1	1a carmine ('14)	1.60	2.25
a.		Background of arms unshaded	20.00	
4	A1	2a brown ('17)	4.50	5.50
5	A1	4a orange ('14)	7.50	8.25
		Nos. 1-5 (5)	14.00	16.55

Essays similar to Nos. 2-5 are in different colors.

Maharaja Singh Dev
A2 A3

1939-40 *Perf. 13½, 13½x14*

6	A2	¼a chocolate	.25	10.00
7	A2	½a yellow green	.25	8.50
8	A2	¾a ultramarine	.25	13.00
9	A2	1a rose red	.25	8.50
10	A2	1¼a deep blue	.25	13.00
11	A2	1½a lilac	.25	12.50
12	A2	2a vermilion	1.25	10.00
13	A2	2½a turq green	1.60	8.50
14	A2	3a dull violet	1.60	12.00
15	A2	4a blue gray	2.50	13.00
16	A2	8a rose lilac	6.00	30.00
17	A3	1r sage green	10.00	40.00
18	A3	2r lt violet ('40)	25.00	65.00
19	A3	5r yel org ('40)	80.00	190.00
20	A3	10r blue	190.00	300.00
		Nos. 6-20 (15)	319.45	734.00

POONCH

'pünch

LOCATION — A Feudatory State in the Kashmir Residency in India.
AREA — 1,627 sq. mi.
POP. — 287,000 (estimated)
CAPITAL — Poonch

Poonch was feudatory to Jammu and Kashmir. Cancellations of Jammu and Kashmir are found on Poonch stamps, which became obsolete in 1894. The stamps are all printed in watercolor and handstamped from single dies. They may be found on various papers, including wove, laid, wove batonne, laid batonne and ribbed, in various colors and tones. Nearly all Poonch stamps exist tete beche and impressed sideways. Issued without gum.

A1

White Paper
Handstamped
1876 Unwmk. *Imperf.*
Size: 22x21mm

1	A1	6p red	125.

1877
Size: 19x17mm

1A	A1	½a red	5,500.	1,500.

1879
Size: 21x19mm

1B	A1	½a red	775.

A2

A3

A4

A5

A6

1880-88
White Paper

2	A2	1p red ('84)	12.00	10.50
3	A3	½a red	4.75	3.00
4	A4	1a red	4.25	4.25
5	A5	2a red	10.50	10.50
6	A6	4a red	10.50	

Yellow Paper

7	A2	1p red	1.50	1.50
8	A3	½a red	1.90	1.50
9	A4	1a red	3.75	3.50
10	A5	2a red	1.90	2.75
11	A6	4a red	1.10	1.10

Blue Paper

12	A2	1p red	7.75	7.75
13	A4	1a red	2.00	2.00

Orange Paper

14	A2	1p red	.30	.30
15	A3	½a red	4.75	4.75
16	A5	2a red	10.50	10.50
17	A6	4a red	6.50	6.50

Green Paper

18	A3	½a red	5.50	5.50
19	A4	1a red	2.75	2.75
20	A5	2a red	2.50	3.75
21	A6	4a red	10.00	12.00

Lavender Paper

22	A2	1p red	24.00	24.00
23	A4	1a red	12.00	12.00
24	A5	2a red	.90	.90

OFFICIAL STAMPS

White Paper
Handstamped
1888 Unwmk. *Imperf.*

O1	A2	1p black	.35	.60
O2	A3	½a black	.50	.75
O3	A4	1a black	.75	.75
O4	A5	2a black	1.00	1.00
O5	A6	4a black	1.50	1.50
		Nos. O1-O5 (5)	4.10	4.60

1890
Yellowish Paper

O6	A2	1p black	1.10	
O7	A3	½a black	4.25	4.25
O8	A4	1a black	10.00	7.00
O9	A5	2a black	3.50	3.75
O10	A6	4a black	10.00	
		Nos. O6-O10 (5)	28.85	

Obsolete since 1894.

RAJASTHAN

'rä-jə-ˌstän

(Greater Rajasthan Union)

AREA — 128,424 sq. miles
POP. — 13,085,000

The Rajasthan Union was formed in 1947-49 by 14 Indian States, including the stamp-issuing States of Bundi, Jaipur and Kishangarh.

Catalogue values for all unused stamps in this state are for Never Hinged items.

Bundi Nos. 43 to 49 Overprinted

a

1948 Unwmk. *Perf. 11*
Handstamped in Black, Violet or Blue

1	A8	¼a deep green (Bk, V)	3.50	
a.		Blue overprint	20.00	
2	A8	½a purple (Bk, V)	2.25	
a.		Blue overprint	20.00	
3	A8	1a yel green (Bk)	3.50	
4	A9	2a red (Bk)	6.00	
5	A9	4a dp orange (V)	16.00	
a.		Black overprint	25.00	
6	A10	8a vio bl (Bk, V)	3.50	
7	A10	1r chocolate (Bl)	55.00	
a.		Black overprint		
b.		Violet overprint	140.00	
		Nos. 1-7 (7)	89.75	

Typo. in Black

12	A9	4a deep orange	2.00	
13	A10	8a violet blue	55.00	
14	A10	1r chocolate	7.50	
		Nos. 12-14 (3)	64.50	

Stamps of Jaipur, 1931-47, Overprinted in Blue or Carmine

1949 Center in Black *Perf. 14*

15	A6	¼a red brown (Bl)	3.00	2.50
16	A6	½a dull violet	3.00	2.50
17	A6	¾a brown org (Bl)	4.00	2.50
18	A6	1a blue	3.50	3.25
19	A6	2a ocher	4.00	3.25
20	A6	2½a rose (Bl)	5.75	3.25
21	A6	3a green	6.25	4.00
22	A6	4a gray green	6.25	4.75
23	A6	6a blue	7.00	6.50
24	A6	8a chocolate	9.50	20.00
25	A6	1r bister	10.50	27.50
		Nos. 15-25 (11)	62.75	80.00

Kishangarh Stamps and Types of 1899-1904 Handstamped Type "a" in Rose

1949 *Pin-perf., Rouletted*

26	A3	½a blue (#18)	25.00
27	A4	1a dull lilac (#20)	14.00
28	A6	4a pale red brown (#21B)	15.00
29	A11	8a gray (#25B)	27.50
30	A7	1r dull green (#22)	22.50
31	A8	2r brown red (#23)	25.00
32	A9	5r red violet (#24)	30.00
		Nos. 26-32 (7)	159.00

Kishangarh Nos. 28, 31-36 Handstamped Type "a" in Rose or Green

1949 Engr. *Perf. 13½, 12½*

33	A13	½a chestnut (R)	10.50
34	A13	4a dark brown (G)	13.00
35	A13	4a dark brown (R)	13.00
36	A13	8a purple (R)	13.00
37	A13	1r dark green (R)	21.00
38	A13	2r lemon yellow (R)	21.00
39	A13	5r purple brown (R)	25.50
		Nos. 33-39 (7)	117.00

Kishangarh Nos. 40-42, 37, 43, 46-48 Handstamped Type "a" in Rose

1949 Typo. *Rouletted*

40	A14	¼a pale blue	8.00	8.00
41	A14	½a green	8.00	8.00
42	A14	1a carmine	7.50	7.50
43	A14	2 "anna" violet	7.50	7.50
44	A14	2 "annas" purple	7.50	7.50
45	A14	8a brown	7.50	7.50
46	A14	1r rose lilac	9.00	9.00
47	A14	2r dark green	12.50	12.50
48	A14	5r brown	32.50	32.50
		Nos. 40-48 (9)	100.00	100.00

Kishangarh Stamps and Types of 1928-29 Handstamped Type "a" in Rose

1949 *Pin-perf*

49	A17	¼a greenish blue	13.00	13.00
50	A17	½a yel green	6.50	6.50
51	A18	1a car rose	9.00	9.00
52	A18	2a red violet	12.00	12.00
53	A17	4a yel brown	2.50	2.50
54	A17	8a purple	9.00	7.25
55	A17	1r deep green	7.50	7.50
56	A17	2r lemon	24.00	24.00
57	A17	5r red brown	25.00	25.00
		Nos. 49-57 (9)	108.50	106.75

Type of Kishangarh 1928-29, Handstamped Type "a" in Rose

1949 *Pin-perf*

58	A18	1a dark violet blue

No. 58 exists imperf.

Rajasthan stamps became obsolete Apr. 1, 1950.

RAJPEEPLA

räj-'pē-plə

(Rajpipla)

LOCATION — A Feudatory State near Bombay in the Gujarat States Agency in India.
AREA — 1,517 sq. mi.
POP. — 206,086
CAPITAL — Nandod

4 Paisas = 1 Anna

Kandjar (Indian Daggers) — A1

A2

A3

1880 Unwmk. Litho. *Perf. 11, 12½*
Without Gum

1	A1	1pa ultramarine	1.00	4.75
2	A2	2a green	6.25	6.75
a.		Horiz. pair, imperf. btwn.	750.00	750.00
3	A3	4a red	4.50	4.50
		Nos. 1-3 (3)	11.75	16.00

The stamps of Rajpeepla have been obsolete since 1886.

SIRMOOR

sir-ˈmu̦ə̦r

(Sirmur)

LOCATION — A Feudatory State in the Punjab District of India.
AREA — 1,046 sq. mi.
POP. — 148,568
CAPITAL — Nahan

A1

Raja Sir Shamsher Prakash — A2

1879 Unwmk. *Perf. 11½*

Wove Paper

1	A1	1p green	6.00	6.00
a.		Imperf., pair		

Laid Paper

2	A1	1p blue	3.00	*30.00*
a.		Imperf., pair		

1885-88 Litho. *Perf. 14 and 14½.*

3	A2	3p brown	.20	.20
4	A2	3p orange	.20	.20
5	A2	6p green	.60	.60
6	A2	1a blue	.45	.45
7	A2	2a carmine	2.00	2.00
		Nos. 3-7 (5)	3.45	3.45

There are several printings, dies and minor variations of this issue.

For overprints see Nos. O1-O16.

A3

Elephant — A4

1893 *Perf. 11½*

9	A3	1p yellow green	.30	.30
a.		1pa dark blue green	.30	.30
10	A3	1p ultramarine	.50	.50
b.		Imperf., pair	60.00	

Nos. 9 and 10 are re-issues, which were available for postage.

The printed perforation, which is a part of the design, is in addition to the regular perforation.

1895-99 Engr. *Perf. 14*

11	A4	3p orange	.60	.20
12	A4	6p green	.90	.25
13	A4	1a dull blue	1.10	.30
14	A4	2a dull red	1.10	.45
15	A4	3a yellow green	2.00	2.00
16	A4	4a dark green	2.00	2.00
17	A4	8a deep blue	5.50	*7.50*
18	A4	1r vermilion	7.50	*9.00*
		Nos. 11-18 (8)	20.70	*21.70*

Sir Surendar Bikram Prakash — A5

1899

19	A5	3a yellow green	2.75	*6.00*
20	A5	4a dark green	3.50	*7.25*
21	A5	8a blue	4.00	*7.75*
22	A5	1r vermilion	6.50	*15.00*
		Nos. 19-22 (4)	16.75	*36.00*

OFFICIAL STAMPS

Regular Stamps Overprinted

Black Overprint

1890-91 Unwmk. *Perf. 14, 14½*

O1	A2	3p orange	1.40	
O2	A2	6p green	1.40	.90
a.		Double overprint		
b.		Double ovpt., one in red	1,250.	
O3	A2	1a blue	12.00	12.00
O4	A2	2a carmine	9.00	9.00
		Nos. O1-O4 (4)	23.80	

1890-92

Red Overprint

O5	A2	6p green	4.50	4.00
O6	A2	1a blue	17.00	9.00

O7	A2	6p green	2.50	1.60
a.		Double overprint		
b.		Inverted overprint		
O8	A2	1a blue	6.00	2.00
a.		Inverted overprint		240.00
b.		Double overprint		240.00

1892

Black Overprint

O9	A2	3p orange	.20	.20
a.		Inverted overprint	75.00	
O10	A2	6p green	.75	.75
O11	A2	1a blue	3.25	3.25
a.		Double overprint	150.00	
O12	A2	2a carmine	2.50	2.50
a.		Inverted overprint	150.00	125.00
		Nos. O9-O12 (4)	6.70	6.70

Black Overprint

O13	A2	3p orange	3.25	1.50
a.		Inverted overprint		
O14	A2	6p green	2.75	.50
O15	A2	1a blue	1.90	.75
O16	A2	2a carmine	4.75	4.25
		Nos. O13-O16 (4)	12.65	7.00

There are several settings of some of these overprints, differing in the sizes and shapes of the letters, the presence or absence of the periods, etc.

The overprints on Nos. O1-O16 are press printed. In addition, nine varieties of handstamped overprints were applied in 1894-96. Most of the handstamps are very similar to the press printed overprints.

Obsolete Mar. 31, 1901.

SORUTH

(Sorath)

(Junagarh)

(Saurashtra)

LOCATION — A Feudatory State near Bombay in the Western India States Agency in India.
AREA — 3,337 sq. mi.
POP. — 670,719
CAPITAL — Junagarh

The United State of Saurashtra (area 31,885 sq. mi.; population 2,900,000) was formed in 1948 by 217 States, including the stamp-issuing States of Jasdan, Morvi, Nowanuggur and Wadhwan.

Nos. 1-27 were issued without gum.

Catalogue values for unused stamps in this State are for Never Hinged items, beginning with Scott 39 in the regular postage section, and Scott O19 in the officials section.

Junagarh

A1

A2

Handstamped in Watercolor

1864 Unwmk. *Imperf.*

Laid Paper

1	A1	(1a) black, *bluish*	425.00	24.00
a.		Wove paper		80.00
1B	A1	(1a) black, *gray*	425.00	24.00

Wove Paper

2	A1	(1a) black, *cream*		125.00

1868 Typo. *Imperf.*

Wove Paper

3	A2	1a black, *yellowish*		
4	A2	1a red, *green*		1,400.
5	A2	1a red, *blue*		1,400.
6	A2	1a black, *pink*	210.00	42.00
7	A2	2a black, *yellow*		2,100.

Laid Paper

8	A2	1a black, *blue*	25.00	10.00
a.		Left character, 3rd line, omitted		
9	A2	1a red	20.00	20.00
a.		Left character, 3rd line, omitted		
10	A2	4a black	125.00	*150.00*
a.		Left character, 3rd line, omitted		

A 1a black on white laid paper exists in type A2.

In 1890 official imitations of 1a and 4a stamps, type A2, were printed in sheets of 16 and 4. Original sheets have 20 stamps. Four of these imitations are perf. 12, six are imperf.

A3

A4

1877-86 Laid Paper *Imperf.*

11	A3	1a green	.20	.20
a.		Printed on both sides	250.00	
12	A4	4a vermilion	.75	.75
a.		Printed on both sides	250.00	
13	A4	4a scarlet, *bluish*	.90	.90
		Nos. 11-13 (3)	1.85	1.85

Perf. 12

14	A3	1a green	.20	.20
a.		1a blue (error)	425.00	425.00
c.		Imperf., pair	6.50	6.50
d.		Wove paper	.75	.75
e.		As "a," wove paper	425.00	425.00
f.		As "d," imperf. btwn., pair	10.50	10.50
15	A3	1a green, *bluish*	.80	.80
a.		Pair, imperf. btwn.	42.50	42.50
16	A4	4a red	.90	.90
a.		4a carmine	.90	.90
c.		Wove paper	1.75	1.75
d.		As "c," imperf., pair	12.00	12.00
17	A4	4a scarlet, *bluish*	1.50	1.50
		Nos. 14-17 (4)	3.40	3.40

Nos. 14d and 16c Surcharged

1913-14 *Perf. 12*

18	A3	3p on 1a green	.20	.20
a.		Laid paper		30.00
b.		Inverted surcharge	20.00	
c.		Imperf., pair		
19	A4	1a on 4a red	1.00	1.00
a.		Laid paper	5.00	5.00
b.		Imperf., pair		
c.		Double surcharge	175.00	

A5

A6

1914 *Perf. 12*

20	A5	3p green	.50	.50
a.		Imperf., pair	1.00	1.00
21	A6	1a rose carmine	.50	.60
a.		Imperf., pair	4.00	4.00
b.		Laid paper	20.00	15.00

Nawab Mahabat Khan III

A7 A8

1923-29 Wove Paper *Perf. 12*

22	A7	3p violet	.45	.45
a.		Imperf.		
b.		Laid paper ('29)	.75	.75
c.		As "b," imperf. ('29)	1.40	1.40
d.		As "b," horiz. pair, imperf btwn.	30.00	
23	A8	1a red	1.50	1.50
a.		Imperf., pair		
b.		Laid paper	2.00	2.00

Surcharged with New Value

27	A8	3p on 1a red	1.50	1.50

Two types of surcharge.

Junagarh City and The Girnar A9

Gir Lion — A10

Nawab Mahabat Khan III — A11

Kathi Horse A12

1929 *Perf. 14*

30	A9	3p dk green & blk	1.00	.20
31	A10	½a dk blue & blk	3.75	.20
32	A11	1a claret & blk	2.25	.60
33	A12	2a org buff & blk	9.00	.35
34	A9	3a car rose & blk	2.50	.25
35	A10	4a dull vio & blk	10.50	.30
36	A12	8a apple grn & blk	12.00	*8.75*
37	A11	1r dull blue & blk	3.50	*7.00*
		Nos. 30-37 (8)	44.50	*17.65*

For surcharges see Nos. 40-42, O20-O25. For overprints see Nos. O1-O14.

Type of 1929

Inscribed "Postage and Revenue"

1937

38	A11	1a claret & black	2.00	.50

For overprint see No. O15.

Catalogue values for unused stamps in this section, from this point to the end of the section, are for Never Hinged items.

United State of Saurashtra

A13

Bhavnagar Court Fee Stamp Overprinted in Black "U.S.S. Revenue & Postage Saurashtra"

1949 Unwmk. Typo. *Perf. 11*

39 A13 1a deep claret 1.75 1.75
a. "POSTAGE" omitted 125.00 125.00
b. Double overprint 125.00 125.00
c. "REVENUE & POSTAGE" omitted 125.00 125.00

Nos. 30, 31 Surcharged in Black or Carmine "POSTAGE & REVENUE ONE ANNA"

1949-50 *Perf. 14*

40 A9 1a on 3p dk grn & blk (bl) ('50) 10.00 10.00
a. "OSTAGE" 125.00 125.00
41 A10 1a on ½a dk bl & blk (C) 7.00 1.40
a. Double surcharge 125.00 125.00

For overprint see No. O19.

No. 33 Surcharged in Green "Postage & Revenue ONE ANNA"

1949

42 A12 1a on 2a org buff & blk 5.75 2.00

For overprint see No. O26.

OFFICIAL STAMPS

Regular Issue of 1929 Overprinted in Red

a

1929 Unwmk. *Perf. 14*

O1 A9 3p dk green & black .20 .20
O2 A10 ½a dk blue & black .40 .20
O3 A11 1a claret & black .20 .20
O4 A12 2a org buff & black .75 .20
O5 A9 3a car rose & black .40 .20
O6 A10 4a dull violet & blk .75 .20
O7 A12 8a apple green & blk 1.25 .20
O8 A11 1r dull blue & blk 1.90 2.00
Nos. O1-O8 (8) 5.85 3.40

For surcharges see Nos. O20-O24.

Regular Issue of 1929 Overprinted in Red

b

1933-49

O9 A9 3p dk grn & black ('49) 175.00 4.25
O10 A10 ½a dk bl & black ('49) 250.00 4.25
O11 A9 3a car rose & blk 9.50 4.50
O12 A10 4a dull vio & blk 22.50 13.00
O13 A12 8a apple grn & blk 22.50 15.00
O14 A11 1r dull blue & blk 25.00 20.00

The 3p is also known with ms. "SARKARI" overprint in carmine.
For surcharge see No. O25.

No. 38 Overprinted Type "a" in Red

1938

O15 A11 1a claret & black 2.50 .50

Catalogue values for unused stamps in this section, from this point to the end of the section, are for Never Hinged items.

United State of Saurashtra

No. 41 with Manuscript "Service" in Carmine

1949

O19 A10 1a on ½a dk bl & blk (C) 27.50

No. 42 is also known with carmine ms. "Service" overprint in English or Gujarati.

Nos. O4-O8 and O14 Surcharged "ONE ANNA" in Blue or Black

1949

Surcharge 2¼mm high

O20 A12 1a on 2a (Bl) 1,000. 24.00
O21 A9 1a on 3a 1,000. 24.00
O22 A10 1a on 4a 150.00 22.50
O23 A12 1a on 8a 150.00 22.50

Surcharge 4mm High, Handstamped

O24 A11 1a on 1r (#O8) 250.00 15.00
O25 A11 1a on 1r (#O14) 125.00 27.50
Nos. O20-O25 (6) 2,675. 135.50

No. 42 Overprinted Type "b" in Carmine

1949 Unwmk. *Perf. 14*

O26 A12 1a on 2a 20.00 6.75

TRAVANCORE

'trav-ən-ˌkō̦ə̦r

LOCATION — A Feudatory State in the Madras States Agency, on the extreme southwest coast of India.
AREA — 7,662 sq. mi.
POP. — 6,070,018 (1941)
CAPITAL — Trivandrum

16 Cash = 1 Chuckram
2 Chuckrams = 1 Anna

Conch Shell (State Seal)
A1 A2

1888 Unwmk. Typo. *Perf. 12*
Laid Paper

1 A1 1ch ultramarine 6.00 4.50
2 A1 2ch orange red 5.50 4.75
3 A1 4ch green 22.50 22.50
Nos. 1-3 (3) 34.00 31.75

The frame and details of the central medallion differ slightly on each denomination of type A1.
Laid paper printings of Nos. 1-3, 5-7 in completely different colors are essays.

1889-99 Wmk. 43
Wove Paper

4 A1 ½ch violet .20 .20
5 A1 1ch ultramarine .20 .20
a. Vertical pair, imperf. between
6 A1 2ch scarlet .90 .20
a. Horiz. pair, imperf. between 100.00
7 A1 4ch dark green 1.25 .30
Nos. 4-7 (4) 2.55 .90

Shades exist for each denomination.
For surcharges see #10-11. For type surcharged see #20. For overprints see #O1-O2, O4, O6, O18, O24-O25, O27B, O32-O33, O42.

1901-32

8 A2 ¾ch black 1.25 .20
9 A2 ¾ch brt violet ('32) 1.25 .20
a. Horizontal pair, imperf. between

For overprints see Nos. O26-O27, O44, O52.

No. 4 Surcharged

1906

10 A1 ¼ch on ½ch violet .45 .20
a. Inverted surcharge 35.00 35.00
11 A1 ⅜ch on ½ch violet .20 .20
a. Pair, one without surcharge
b. Inverted surcharge
c. Double surcharge

A3 A4

1908-11

12 A3 4ca rose .20 .20
13 A1 6ca red brown ('10) .90 .20
a. Printed on both sides
14 A4 3ch purple ('11) .75 .20
Nos. 12-14 (3) 1.85 .60

For surcharge & overprints see #19, O3, O5, O8, O13, O15, O20, O22, O30-O31, O53.

A5 A6

1916

15 A5 7ch red violet 1.90 .30
16 A6 14ch orange 4.00 2.50

For overprints see Nos. O11-O12, O34-O35.

A7 A8

1920-33

17 A7 1¼ch claret 1.25 .20
18 A7 1½ch light red ('33) 1.25 .20

For surcharges see Nos. 27-28. For overprints see Nos. O7, O17, O28-O29, O38, O56.

No. 12 and Type of 1888 Surcharged

1921

19 A3 1ca on 4ca rose .20 .20
a. Inverted surcharge 10.50 6.50
20 A1 5ca on 1ch dull bl (R) .20 .20
a. Inverted surcharge 13.00 4.00
b. Double surcharge 18.00 13.00

1921-32

21 A8 5ca bister .20 .20
22 A8 5ca brown ('32) 1.25 .20
23 A8 10ca rose .20 .20
Nos. 21-23 (3) 1.65 .60

For surcharges & overprints see #29-30, O9-O10, O14, O16, O19, O21, O23, O36-O37.

Sri Padmanabha Shrine at Trivandrum
A9

State Chariot — A10

Maharaja Sir Bala Rama Varma — A11

1931, Nov. 6

24 A9 6ca emerald & black .50 .30
25 A10 10ca ultra & black .50 .30
26 A11 3ch violet & black 2.00 .55
Nos. 24-26 (3) 3.00 1.15

Investiture of Sir Bala Rama Varma with full ruling powers.

No. 17 Surcharged

1932, Jan. 14

27 A7 1ca on 1¼ch claret .20 .20
a. Inverted surcharge 5.00 5.00
b. Double surcharge 16.00 16.00
28 A7 2ca on 1¼ch claret .20 .20
a. Inverted surcharge 5.00 5.00
b. Double surcharge 16.00 16.00
c. Pair, one without surcharge 150.00 150.00

Type of 1932 and No. 23 Surcharged like Nos. 19-20

1932, Mar. 5

29 A8 1ca on 5ca vio brown .20 .20
a. Inverted surcharge 13.00 12.00
b. Double surcharge 13.00 13.00
c. Pair, one without surcharge 55.00
30 A8 2ca on 10ca rose .30 .20
a. Inverted surcharge 9.00 9.00
b. Double surcharge 21.00 21.00

Untouchables Entering Temple and Maharaja — A12

Designs: Different temples and frames.

Perf. 11½, 12½

1937, Mar. 29 Litho.

32 A12 6ca carmine .20 .20
33 A12 12ca ultramarine .20 .20
34 A12 1½ch light green .20 .20
35 A12 3ch purple .30 .20
Nos. 32-35 (4) .90 .80

Temple Entry Bill.

Lake Ashtamudi
A13

A14 A15

Sir Bala Rama Varma — A16

Sri Padmanabha Shrine — A17

View of Cape Comerin A18

Pachipara Reservoir A19

Perf. 11, 12, 12½ or Compound

1939, May 9			**Litho.**	
36	A13	1ch yellow green	.20	.20
37	A14	1½ch carmine	.45	.20
a.		Perf. 13½	18.00	18.00
38	A15	2ch orange	.20	.20
39	A16	3ch chocolate	.25	.20
40	A17	4ch henna brown	.30	.20
41	A18	7ch light blue	1.50	1.10
42	A19	14ch turq green	3.00	2.00
		Nos. 36-42 (7)	5.90	4.10

27th birthday of Maharaja Sir Bala Rama Varma.

For surcharges and overprints see Nos. 45, O45-O51, Travancore-Cochin 3-7, O3-O7.

Maharaja Sir Bala Rama Varma and Aruvikara Falls A20

Maharaja and Marthanda Varma Bridge, Alwaye A21

1941, Oct. 20			**Typo.**	
43	A20	6ca violet black	3.50	.20
44	A21	¾ch dull brown	3.00	.20

29th birthday of the Maharaja, Oct. 20, 1941.

For overprints & surcharges see #46-47, 49, O54-O55, Travancore-Cochin 1, O1.

Stamps and Types of 1939-41 Surcharged in Black

Perf. 11, 12½

1943, Sept. 17			**Wmk. 43**	
45	A14	2ca on 1½ch carmine	.90	.20
46	A21	4ca on ¾ch dull brown	1.50	.20
47	A20	8ca on 6ca red	2.00	.20
		Nos. 45-47 (3)	4.40	.60

For overprints see Nos. O57-O59.

Maharaja Sir Bala Rama Varma — A22

1946, Oct. 24		**Typo.**	***Perf. 11, 12***	
48	A22	8ca rose red	1.25	.50

For overprint see No. O60. For surcharges see Travancore-Cochin Nos. 2, O2.

No. O54 Overprinted "SPECIAL" Vertically in Orange

1946			***Perf. 12½***	
49	A20	6ca violet black	6.50	6.00

OFFICIAL STAMPS

Nos. O1-O60 were issued without gum.

Regular Issues of 1889-1911 Overprinted in Red or Black

Perf. 12, 12½

1911, Aug. 16			**Wmk. 43**	
O1	A1	1ch indigo (R)	.40	.20
a.		Inverted overprint	8.75	5.50
b.		"nO" for "On"	50.00	50.00
c.		Double overprint	37.50	37.50
O2	A1	2ch scarlet	.50	.20
a.		Inverted overprint	11.00	10.00
O3	A4	3ch purple	.40	.20
a.		Inverted overprint	11.00	10.00
b.		Double overprint	40.00	40.00
O4	A1	4ch dark green	.50	.20
a.		Inverted overprint	12.50	11.00
b.		Double overprint	40.00	40.00
		Nos. O1-O4 (4)	1.80	.80

Same Ovpt. on Regular Issues of 1889-1920

1918-20				
O5	A3	4ca rose	.20	.20
a.		Imperf., pair	37.50	37.50
b.		Inverted overprint	12.50	7.50
c.		Double overprint	17.50	5.50
O6	A1	½ch violet (R)	.20	.20
a.		Inverted overprint	7.00	3.50
O7	A7	1¼ch claret	.30	.20
a.		Inverted overprint	12.50	7.50
b.		Double overprint	21.00	17.50
		Nos. O5-O7 (3)	.70	.60

Same Ovpt. on Regular Issues of 1909-21

1921				
O8	A1	6ca red brown	.25	.20
a.		Inverted overprint	8.75	7.50
O9	A8	10ca rose	.50	.20
a.		Inverted overprint	22.50	12.50
b.		Double overprint	27.50	17.50

Same Overprint on Regular Issue of 1921

1922				
O10	A8	5ca bister	.20	.20
a.		Inverted overprint	7.00	3.50

For surcharge see No. O39B.

Same Overprint on Regular Issue of 1916

1925				
O11	A5	7ch plum	1.10	.20
O12	A6	14ch orange	1.60	.20

Same Overprint in Blue on Regular Issues of 1889-1921

O13	A3	4ca rose	15.00	1.40
O14	A8	5ca bister		
O15	A1	6ca red brown	8.50	1.40
O16	A8	10ca rose	21.00	4.50
O17	A7	1¼ch claret	24.00	6.50
O18	A1	4ch dark green	35.00	9.00

Some authorities question the authenticity of No. O14.

1930

Black Overprint

O19	A8	5ca brown	.20	.20

Regular Issues of 1889-1932 Overprinted in Black or Red

1930-34				
O20	A3	4ca rose	8.00	6.00
O21	A8	5ca brown	18.00	13.00
a.		Inverted overprint	90.00	90.00
O22	A1	6ca org brown	.20	.20
O23	A8	10ca rose	1.90	.25
O24	A1	½ch violet ('34)	.35	.20
O25	A1	½ch purple (R)	.20	.20
O26	A2	¾ch black (R) ('32)	.60	.20
O27	A2	¾ch brt vio ('33)	.20	.20
O27B	A1	1ch gray blue (R) ('33)	.75	.20
O28	A7	1¼ch claret	1.50	.45
O29	A7	1½ch dull red ('32)	.30	.20
O30	A4	3ch purple ('33)	1.50	.20
O31	A4	3ch purple (R)	.65	.20
O32	A1	4ch deep green (R)	1.25	.20
O33	A1	4ch deep green	2.75	1.40
O34	A5	7ch maroon	1.75	.20
O35	A6	14ch orange ('31)	2.50	.40
		Nos. O20-O35 (17)	42.40	23.70

The overprint on Nos. O22, O26 and O28 is smaller than the illustration. There are two sizes of the overprint on No. O27.

For surcharges see Nos. O39, O40-O41.

Type of 1921-32 and No. 17 Surcharged and Overprinted

1932				
O36	A8	6ca on 5ca dk brown	.20	.20
O36A	A8	6ca on 5ca bister	.75	.20
O37	A8	12ca on 10a rose	.35	.20
a.		New value inverted	8.50	8.50
O38	A7	1ch8ca on 1¼ch cl	.45	.20
		Nos. O36-O38 (4)	1.75	.80

Nos. O21, O10, O23 and O28 Surcharged in Black

O39	A8	6ca on 5ca dk brown	.25	.20
a.		New value inverted		
O39B	A8	6ca on 5ca bis	.60	.20
O40	A8	12ca on 10ca rose	.40	.20
a.		New value inverted	8.50	8.50
b.		"On S S" inverted		
c.		Ovpt. & surch. inverted	21.00	21.00
O41	A7	1ch8ca on 1¼ch cl	.60	.20
a.		New value inverted		
		Nos. O39-O41 (4)	1.85	.80

Regular Issue of 1889-94 Overprinted

1933				
O42	A1	½ch violet	1.75	1.25

Regular Issue of 1901 Overprinted in Red

1933				
O44	A2	¾ch black	.35	.20

Regular Issue of 1939 Overprinted in Black

a 

1939			***Perf. 11, 12, 12½***	
O45	A13	1ch yellow green	.20	.20
a.		Inverted overprint	15.00	15.00
b.		Double overprint	15.00	15.00
O46	A14	1½ch carmine	.35	.20
a.		"SESVICE"	85.00	100.00
O47	A15	2ch orange	.45	.20
a.		"SESVICE"	60.00	75.00
O48	A16	3ch chocolate	.35	.20
a.		"SESVICE"	150.00	30.00
O49	A17	4ch henna brown	.75	.25
O50	A18	7ch light blue	1.75	.40
O51	A19	14ch turq green	3.00	.50
		Nos. O45-O51 (7)	6.85	1.95

27th birthday of Maharaja Sir Bala Rama Varma.

No. 9 Overprinted

b 

1939		**Wmk. 43**	***Perf. 12.***	
O52	A2	¾ch violet	1.75	.20

No. 13 Overprinted Type "b"

1941				
O53	A1	6ca red brown	.50	.20

Nos. 43-44 Overprinted Type "a"

1941			***Perf. 12½***	
O54	A20	6ca violet black	.30	.20
O55	A21	¾ch dull brown	.30	.20

29th birthday of the Maharaja, Oct. 20, 1941.

For overprint see No. 49.

No. 18 Overprinted Type "b"

1945			***Perf. 12***	
O56	A7	1½ch light red	.65	.20

Nos. 45-48 Overprinted Type "a"

1945-49			***Perf. 11, 12***	
O57	A14	2ca on 1½ch car	.20	.20
O58	A21	4ca on ¾ch dull brn	.30	.20
O59	A20	8ca on 6ca red	.25	.20
O60	A22	8ca rose red ('49)	1.25	.80
a.		Double impression of stamp	30.00	30.00
		Nos. O57-O60 (4)	2.00	1.40

Travancore stamps became obsolete June 30, 1949.

TRAVANCORE-COCHIN

'trav-ən-ˌkō̤ə̤r kō-'chin

LOCATION — Southern India
AREA — 9,155 sq. mi.
POP. — 7,492,000

The United State of Travancore-Cochin was established July 1, 1949.

Catalogue values for all unused stamps in this state are for Never Hinged items.

Travancore Stamps of 1939-47 Surcharged in Red or Black

a 

Perf. 11, 12, 12½

1949, July 1 **Wmk. 43**

1	A20	2p on 6ca vio blk (R)	1.10	.70
2	A22	4p on 8ca rose red	.50	.20
3	A13	½a on 1ch yel grn	1.40	.20
a.		Inverted surcharge	7.00	7.00
b.		"NANA"	125.00	70.00
4	A15	1a on 2ch orange	1.50	.20
5	A17	2a on 4ch hn brn	1.25	.45
a.		Inverted surcharge	—	250.00
6	A18	3a on 7ch lt blue	4.50	2.75
7	A19	6a on 14ch turq grn	6.00	*13.00*
		Nos. 1-7 (7)	16.25	17.50

For overprints see Nos. O1-O7, O12-O17. For types overprinted see Nos. O18-O23.

Cochin Nos. 80, 91 and Types of 1944-46 Surcharged in Black or Carmine

b 

1949-50 **Wmk. 294** ***Perf. 11, 13***

8	A15	3p on 9p ultra	6.75	*14.00*
9	A16	3p on 9p ultra	1.75	1.75
10	A16	3p on 9p ultra (C)	2.75	2.00
11	A16	6p on 9p ultra (C)	.75	.30
12	A13	6p on 1a3p mag ('50)	3.25	*3.50*
13	A15	6p on 1a3p magenta	11.00	*12.00*
14	A13	1a on 1a9p ultra (C)	.80	*1.00*
15	A15	1a on 1a9p ultra (C)	3.00	1.75
		Nos. 8-15 (8)	30.05	36.30

The surcharge exists with line of Hindi characters varying from 16½ to 23mm wide.
For overprints see Nos. O10-O11, O24.

Cochin No. 86 Overprinted 

1949

15A	A15	1a deep orange	4.00	*.40*

Conch Shell — A23

View of River — A24

Wmk. 196

1950, Oct. **Litho.** ***Perf. 14***

16	A23	2p rose red	1.40	1.40
17	A24	4p ultramarine	2.00	*10.00*

Cochin No. 86 and Type of 1948-50 Overprinted in Black 

1950, Apr. 1 **Wmk. 294** ***Perf. 13, 11***

18	A15	1a deep orange	5.50	*40.00*
19	A16	1a deep orange		

The existence of No. 19 has been questioned.

No. 18 Surcharged in Black 

20	A15	6p on 1a deep orange	2.50	*32.50*
21	A15	9p on 1a deep orange	2.00	*25.00*

OFFICIAL STAMPS

Travancore Stamps of 1939-46 Surcharged Type "a" in Red or Black and Overprinted

c 

1949 **Wmk. 43** ***Perf. 11, 12, 12½***

O1	A20	2p on 6ca vio blk (R)	.75	.20
O2	A22	4p on 8ca rose red	1.75	.50
O3	A13	½a on 1ch yel grn	.35	.20
O4	A15	1a on 2ch orange	13.00	4.00
O5	A17	2a on 4ch hn brn	.90	.60
O6	A18	3a on 7ch lt blue	3.25	1.25
O7	A19	6a on 14ch turq grn	9.00	5.25
		Nos. O1-O7 (7)	29.00	12.00

Cochin Nos. O90-O91 Surcharged Type "b" in Black

1950 **Wmk. 294** ***Perf. 11***

O8	A16	6p on 3p carmine	.75	.50
a.		Double surcharge	—	300.00
O9	A16	9p on 4p gray grn	.50	*1.50*

No. O9 exists with Hindi characters varying from 18 to 22mm wide.

Travancore-Cochin Nos. 14-15 Overprinted "ON C G S"

Perf. 13

O10	A13	1a on 1a9p ultra	.60	.40
O11	A15	1a on 1a9p ultra	17.50	13.00

Nos. 2-7 Overprinted in Black

d 

1949-51 **Wmk. 43** ***Perf. 11, 12½***

O12	A22	4p on 8ca rose red	.20	.20
O13	A13	½a on 1ch yel green	.25	.20
O14	A15	1a on 2ch orange	.20	.20
O15	A17	2a on 4ch hn brn	1.25	.70
O16	A18	3a on 7ch lt blue	2.50	.95
O17	A19	6a on 14ch turq grn	.60	2.75
		Nos. O12-O17 (6)	5.00	5.00

Types of 1949 Overprinted Type "d"

1951 **Wmk. 294**

O18	A13	½a on 1ch yel green	.35	.35
O19	A15	1a on 2ch orange	.40	.35

Type of 1949 Overprinted Type "c"

Unwmk.

O20	A22	4p on 8ca rose red	1.40	1.10

No. O20 is not from an unwatermarked part of sheet with wmk. 294 but is printed on paper entirely without watermark.

Nos. 1, 3 and 5 Overprinted Type "c"

Wmk. 294

O21	A13	½a on 1ch yel green	1.10	.50
O22	A20	2p on 6ca violet black	.20	*1.00*
O23	A17	2a on 4ch henna brn	1.10	.75
		Nos. O21-O23 (3)	2.40	2.25

No. 9 Overprinted in Black 

1951

O24	A16	3p on 9p ultra	.60	.55

WADHWAN

wə-'dwän

LOCATION — A Feudatory State in Kathiawar Agency, Western India.
AREA — 242 sq. mi.
POP. — 44,259
CAPITAL — Wadhwan

Coat of Arms — A1

1888 **Litho.** **Unwmk.** ***Pin-perf.***

Thin Paper

1	A1	½p black	27.50

Perf. 12½

2	A1	½p black	8.00	*30.00*

1889 ***Perf. 12 and 12½***

Thick Paper

3	A1	½p black	5.50	*6.00*
		Nos. 1-3 (3)	41.00	

INDO-CHINA

ˌin-ˌdō-'chī-nə

LOCATION — French possessions on the Cambodian Peninsula in south-eastern Asia, bordering on the South China Sea and the Gulf of Siam
GOVT. — Former French Colony and Protectorate
AREA — 280,849 sq. mi.
POP. — 27,030,000 (estimated 1949)
CAPITAL — Hanoi

100 Centimes = 1 Franc
100 Cents = 1 Piaster (1918)

Stamps of French Colonies Surcharged in Black or Red:

a

b

1889 **Unwmk.** ***Perf. 14x13½***

1	A9(a)	5c on 35c dp vio, *org*	9.25	*8.50*
		On cover		1,000.
a.		Date in smaller type	200.00	175.00
2	A9(b)	5c on 35c dp vio, *org* (R)	70.00	67.50
		On cover		1,200.
a.		Date in smaller type	160.00	160.00
b.		Inverted surcharge, #2	1,400.	1,400.
c.		Inverted surcharge, #2a	2,100.	2,100.

Issue dates: No. 1, Jan. 8; No. 2, Jan. 10.
"R" is is the Colonial Governor, P. Richaud, "D" is the Saigon P.M. General P. Demars.

For other overprints on designs A3-A27a see various issues of French Offices in China.

Navigation & Commerce A3

France A4

Name of Colony in Blue or Carmine

1892-1900 **Typo.** ***Perf. 14x13½***

3	A3	1c blk, *lil bl*	.85	.75
		On cover		25.00
4	A3	2c brn, *buff*	1.25	1.10
		On cover		25.00
5	A3	4c claret, *lav*	1.25	1.10
		On cover		25.00
6	A3	5c grn, *grnsh*	1.75	.90
		On cover		10.00
7	A3	5c yel grn ('00)	1.00	.75
		On cover		10.00
8	A3	10c blk, *lavender*	6.00	1.25
		On cover		10.00
9	A3	10c red ('00)	2.50	1.40
		On cover		10.00
10	A3	15c blue, quadrille paper	29.00	1.40
		On cover		10.00
11	A3	15c gray ('00)	6.75	1.40
		On cover		20.00
12	A3	20c red, *grn*	8.50	4.75
		On cover		35.00
13	A3	25c blk, *rose*	13.50	2.75
		On cover		15.00
a.		"INDO-CHINE" omitted	*6,000.*	*6,000.*
14	A3	25c blue ('00)	15.00	2.50
		On cover		15.00
15	A3	30c brn, *bis*	20.00	5.75
		On cover		35.00
16	A3	40c red, *straw*	20.00	9.00
		On cover		35.00
17	A3	50c car, *rose*	37.50	11.00
		On cover		50.00
18	A3	50c brn, *az* ('00)	22.50	5.75
		On cover		75.00
19	A3	75c dp vio, *org*	19.00	12.50
		On cover		80.00
a.		"INDO-CHINE" inverted	*6,000.*	*6,000.*
20	A3	1fr brnz grn, *straw*	42.50	25.00
		On cover		100.00
a.		"INDO-CHINE" double	850.00	925.00
21	A3	5fr red lil, *lav* ('96)	110.00	82.50
		On cover		600.00
		Nos. 3-21 (19)	358.85	171.55

Perf. 13½x14 stamps are counterfeits.
For surcharges and overprints see Nos. 22-23, Q2-Q4.

Nos. 11 and 14 Surcharged in Black

1903

22	A3	5c on 15c gray	1.00	.85
		On cover		20.00
23	A3	15c on 25c blue	1.25	.90
		On cover		30.00

Issue dates: No. 22, Dec. 4; No. 23, Aug. 8.

1904-06

24	A4	1c olive grn	.50	.50
		On cover		20.00
25	A4	2c vio brn, *buff*	.75	.50
		On cover		20.00
26	A4	4c claret, *bluish*	.60	.50
		On cover		20.00
27	A4	5c deep green	1.00	.35
		On cover		8.00
28	A4	10c carmine	1.25	.50
		On cover		8.00
29	A4	15c org brn, *bl*	1.25	.70
		On cover		8.00
30	A4	20c red, *grn*	2.75	1.25
		On cover		15.00
31	A4	25c deep blue	12.00	1.25
		On cover		10.00
32	A4	30c pale brn	4.75	2.25
		On cover		30.00
33	A4	35c blk, *yel* ('06)	16.00	2.25
		On cover		40.00
34	A4	40c blk, *bluish*	5.00	1.10
		On cover		40.00
35	A4	50c bister brn	8.00	2.25
		On cover		40.00
36	A4	75c red, *org*	37.50	22.50
		On cover		60.00
37	A4	1fr pale grn	17.50	6.00
		On cover		35.00
38	A4	2fr brn, *org*	45.00	30.00
		On cover		80.00
39	A4	5fr dp vio, *lil*	190.00	135.00
		On cover		400.00

40	A4	10fr org brn, *grn*	180.00	135.00
		On cover		600.00
		Nos. 24-40 (17)	523.85	341.90

For surcharges see Nos. 59-64.

Annamite Girl — A5

Cambodian Girl — A6

Cambodian Woman — A7

Annamite Women — A8

Hmong Woman — A9

Laotian Woman — A10

Cambodian Woman — A11

1907 ***Perf. 14x13½***

41	A5	1c ol brn & blk	.55	.20
42	A5	2c yel brn & blk	.20	.20
43	A5	4c blue & blk	.75	.75
44	A5	5c grn & blk	1.75	.65
45	A5	10c red & blk	1.75	.40
46	A5	15c vio & blk	1.25	.90
47	A6	20c vio & blk	2.75	1.50
48	A6	25c bl & blk	6.00	.90
49	A6	30c brn & blk	8.50	4.50
50	A6	35c ol grn & blk	2.25	1.50
51	A6	40c yel brn & blk	4.00	1.40
52	A6	45c org & blk	8.00	4.50
53	A6	50c car & blk	12.00	4.25

Perf. 13½x14

54	A7	75c ver & blk	10.00	6.00
55	A8	1fr car & blk	45.00	16.00
56	A9	2fr grn & blk	13.00	11.50
57	A10	5fr blue & blk	40.00	32.50
58	A11	10fr pur & blk	82.50	70.00
		Nos. 41-58 (18)	240.25	157.65

For surcharges see Nos. 65-93, B1-B7.

Stamps of 1904-06 Surcharged in Black or Carmine

There are two settings of surcharge. Type 1: 2½mm between numerals. Type II: 3mm between numerals.

1912, Nov. ***Perf. 14x13½***

Spacing between figures of surcharge 1.5mm (5c), 2mm (10c)

59	A4	5c on 4c cl, *bluish*	4.50	4.50
60	A4	5c on 15c org brn, *bl* (C)	1.00	1.00
61	A4	5c on 30c pale brn	1.10	1.10
62	A4	10c on 40c blk, *bluish* (C)	1.10	1.10
63	A4	10c on 50c bis brn (C)	1.10	1.10
64	A4	10c on 75c red, *org*	4.25	4.25
		Nos. 59-64 (6)	13.05	13.05

Spacing between figures of surcharge 2.25mm (5c), 2.75mm (10c)

59a	A4	5c on 4c cl, *bluish*	725.00	725.00
60a	A4	5c on 15c org brn, *bl* (C)	27.50	27.50
61a	A4	5c on 30c pale brn	70.00	70.00
62a	A4	10c on 40c blk, *bluish* (C)	57.50	57.50
63a	A4	10c on 50c bis brn (C)	60.00	60.00
64a	A4	10c on 75c red, *org*	100.00	100.00
		Nos. 59a-64a (6)	1,040.	1,040.

Nos. 41-58 Surcharged with New Values in Cents or Piasters in Black, Red or Blue

1919, Jan.

65	A5	⅖c on 1c	1.75	.40
66	A5	⅘c on 2c	1.50	.65
67	A5	1⅗c on 4c (R)	2.00	.55
68	A5	2c on 5c	1.50	.20
a.		Inverted surcharge	85.00	
69	A5	4c on 10c (Bl)	1.25	.40
a.		Closed "4"	6.00	1.75
b.		Double surcharge	90.00	
70	A5	6c on 15c	4.50	.75
a.		Inverted surcharge	90.00	
71	A6	8c on 20c	4.00	1.40
72	A6	10c on 25c	3.75	.70
73	A6	12c on 30c	7.00	.70
74	A6	14c on 35c	3.75	.50
a.		Closed "4"	8.50	4.50
75	A6	16c on 40c	5.75	1.40
76	A6	18c on 45c	7.00	2.10
77	A6	20c on 50c (Bl)	9.50	.70
78	A7	30c on 75c (Bl)	13.00	1.75
79	A8	40c on 1fr (Bl)	21.00	2.10
80	A9	80c on 2fr (R)	19.00	6.00
a.		Double surcharge	240.00	190.00
81	A10	2pi on 5fr (R)	85.00	67.50
82	A11	4pi on 10fr (R)	130.00	110.00
		Nos. 65-82 (18)	321.25	197.80

Types of 1907 Issue Surcharged with New Values in Black or Red

Nos. 88-92

No. 93

1922

88	A5	1c on 5c ocher & blk	1.00	
89	A5	2c on 10c gray grn & blk	1.75	
90	A6	6c on 30c lt red & blk	2.00	
91	A6	10c on 50c lt bl & blk	2.00	
92	A6	11c on 55c vio & blk, *bluish*	2.25	
93	A6	12c on 60c lt bl & blk, *pnksh* (R)	2.10	
		Nos. 88-93 (6)	11.10	

Nos. 88-93 were sold officially in Paris but were never placed in use in the colony.

Nos. 88-93 exist without surcharge but were not regularly issued in that condition. Value, Nos. 88-89, each $140; Nos. 90-91, each $110; Nos. 92-93, each $75.

A12

A13

"CENTS" below Numerals

1922-23 ***Perf. 14x13½***

94	A12	⅒c blk & sal ('23)	.20	.20
a.		Double impression of frame		
95	A12	⅕c blue & blk	.20	.20
96	A12	⅖c ol brn & blk	.25	.20
a.		Head and value doubled	175.00	175.00
97	A12	⅘c rose & blk, *lav*	.40	.20
98	A12	1c yel brn & blk	.75	.20
99	A12	2c gray grn & blk	.70	.50
100	A12	3c vio & blk	.50	.20
101	A12	4c org & blk	1.00	.20
a.		Head and value doubled	125.00	125.00
102	A12	5c car & blk	.40	.20
a.		Head and value doubled	225.00	225.00
103	A13	6c dl red & blk	.80	.30
104	A13	7c grn & blk	1.50	.50
105	A13	8c blk, *lav*	2.00	1.25
106	A13	9c ocher & blk, *grnsh*	1.50	.70
107	A13	10c bl & blk	.90	.50
108	A13	11c vio & blk	1.25	.50
109	A13	12c brn & blk	1.50	.35
a.		Head and value double (11c+12c)	350.00	350.00
110	A13	15c org & blk	2.25	.50
111	A13	20c bl & blk, *straw*	2.50	.50
112	A13	40c ver & blk, *bluish*	3.00	1.25
113	A13	1pi bl grn & blk, *grnsh*	6.75	5.00
114	A13	2pi vio brn & blk, *pnksh*	12.50	9.50
		Nos. 94-114 (21)	40.85	22.95

For overprints see Nos. O17-O32.

Plowing near Tower of Confucius A14

Bay of Along A15

Angkor Wat, Cambodia A16

Carving Wood A17

That Luang Temple, Laos A18

Founding of Saigon A19

1927, Sept. 26

115	A14	⅒c lt olive grn	.20	.20
116	A14	⅕c yellow	.20	.20
117	A14	⅖c light blue	.20	.20
118	A14	⅘c dp brn	.35	.35
119	A14	1c orange	.50	.20
120	A14	2c blue grn	.90	.35
121	A14	3c indigo	1.00	.20
122	A14	4c lil rose	1.60	1.00
123	A14	5c dp vio	.80	.20
a.		Booklet pane of 10	*140.00*	
124	A15	6c deep red	1.90	.65
a.		Booklet pane of 10	*140.00*	
125	A15	7c lt brn	1.25	.55
126	A15	8c gray green	1.50	.75
127	A15	9c red vio	1.25	.75
128	A15	10c light blue	1.50	.90
129	A15	11c orange	1.50	.90
130	A15	12c myrtle grn	1.25	.70
131	A16	15c dl rose & ol brn	6.75	6.25
132	A16	20c vio & slate	3.00	1.75
133	A17	25c org brn & lil rose	7.00	4.75
134	A17	30c dp bl & ol gray	3.75	2.75
135	A18	40c ver & lt bl	6.00	2.10
136	A18	50c lt grn & slate	8.00	2.25
137	A19	1pi dk bl, blk & yel	21.00	6.50
a.		Yellow omitted	175.00	
138	A19	2pi red, dp bl & org	24.00	11.50
		Nos. 115-138 (24)	95.40	45.95

Common Design Types pictured following the introduction.

Colonial Exposition Issue

Common Design Types Surcharged with New Values

1931, Apr. 13 **Engr.** ***Perf. 12½***

Name of Country in Black

140	CD71	4c on 50c violet	1.90	1.90
141	CD72	6c on 90c red org	2.00	2.00
142	CD73	10c on 1.50fr dl bl	2.75	2.75
		Nos. 140-142 (3)	6.65	6.65

Junk — A20

Tower at Ruins of Angkor Thom — A21

Planting Rice — A22

Apsaras, Celestial Dancer A23

1931-41 **Photo.** ***Perf. 13½x13***

143	A20	⅒c Prus blue	.20	.20
144	A20	⅕c lake	.20	.20
145	A20	⅖c org red	.20	.20
146	A20	½c red brn	.20	.20
147	A20	⅘c dk vio	.20	.20
148	A20	1c blk brn	.20	.20
149	A20	2c dk grn	.20	.20
150	A21	3c dp brn	.20	.20
151	A21	3c dk grn ('34)	4.50	1.25
152	A21	4c dk bl	.90	.35
153	A21	4c dk grn ('38)	.65	.35
153A	A21	4c yel org ('40)	.20	.20
154	A21	5c dp vio	.20	.20
154A	A21	5c dp grn ('41)	.30	.30
155	A21	6c org red	.20	.20
a.		Bklt. pane 5 + 1 label		
156	A21	7c blk ('38)	.20	.20
157	A21	8c rose lake ('38)	.20	.20
157A	A21	9c blk, *yel* ('41)	.55	.55
158	A22	10c dark blue	.50	.35
158A	A22	10c ultra, *pink* ('41)	.40	.40
159	A22	15c dk brn	4.00	1.00
160	A22	15c dk bl ('33)	.20	.20
161	A22	18c blue ('38)	.50	.35
162	A22	20c rose	.20	.20
163	A22	21c olive grn	.20	.20
164	A22	22c dk grn ('38)	.20	.20
165	A22	25c dp vio	2.60	1.10
165A	A22	25c dk bl ('41)	.40	.40
166	A22	30c org brn ('32)	.35	.20

Perf. 13½

167	A23	50c dk brn	.60	.20
168	A23	60c dl vio ('32)	.60	.20
168A	A23	70c lt bl ('41)	.45	.40
169	A23	1pi yel grn	.80	.50
170	A23	2pi red	1.00	.50
		Nos. 143-170 (34)	22.50	11.80

Nos. 166, 167, 169 and 170 were issued without the letters "RF" in 1943, by the Vichy Government.

For surcharge & overprints see #214A, O1-O16.

Emperor Bao-Dai A24

King Sisowath Monivong A25

For Use in Annam

1936, Nov. 20 **Engr.** ***Perf. 13***

171	A24	1c brown	.75	.75
172	A24	2c green	.75	.75
173	A24	4c violet	.75	.75
174	A24	5c red brn	.95	.95
175	A24	10c lil rose	1.50	1.50
176	A24	15c ultra	2.00	2.00
177	A24	20c scarlet	2.00	2.00
178	A24	30c plum	2.75	2.75
179	A24	50c slate grn	2.75	2.75

No.	Type	Description	Unused	Used
180	A24	1pi rose vio	3.75	3.75
181	A24	2pi black	4.50	4.50
		Nos. 171-181 (11)	22.45	22.45

For Use in Cambodia

No.	Type	Description	Unused	Used
182	A25	1c brown	.75	.75
183	A25	2c green	.75	.75
184	A25	4c violet	.80	.80
185	A25	5c red brn	.80	.80
186	A25	10c lil rose	2.00	2.00
187	A25	15c ultra	2.50	2.50
188	A25	20c scarlet	2.10	2.10
189	A25	30c plum	2.50	2.50
190	A25	50c slate grn	2.50	2.50
191	A25	1pi rose vio	3.00	3.00
192	A25	2pi black	4.50	4.50
		Nos. 182-192 (11)	22.20	22.20

Paris International Exposition Issue

Common Design Types

1937, Apr. 15

No.	Type	Description	Unused	Used
193	CD74	2c dp vio	.80	.80
194	CD75	3c dk grn	.80	.80
195	CD76	4c car rose	.80	.80
196	CD77	6c dk brn	.90	.90
197	CD78	9c red	.90	.90
198	CD79	15c ultra	.95	.95
		Nos. 193-198 (6)	5.15	5.15

Colonial Arts Exhibition Issue

Souvenir Sheet

Common Design Type

1937, Apr. 15 ***Imperf.***

No.	Type	Description	Unused	Used
199	CD79	30c dull violet	7.25	*9.25*

Governor-General Paul Doumer — A26

1938, June 8 Photo. *Perf. 13½x13*

No.	Type	Description	Unused	Used
200	A26	5c rose car	.75	.50
201	A26	6c brown	.85	.55
202	A26	18c brt bl	.85	.55
		Nos. 200-202,C18 (4)	2.95	1.80

Trans-Indo-Chinese Railway, 35th anniv.

New York World's Fair Issue

Common Design Type

1939, May 10 Engr. *Perf. 12½x12*

No.	Type	Description	Unused	Used
203	CD82	13c car lake	.50	.50
204	CD82	23c ultra	.75	.75

Mot Cot Pagoda, Hanoi — A27

1939, June 12 ***Perf. 13***

No.	Type	Description	Unused	Used
205	A27	6c blk brn	.75	.75
206	A27	9c vermilion	.75	.75
207	A27	23c ultra	.75	.75
208	A27	39c rose vio	.85	.85
		Nos. 205-208 (4)	3.10	3.10

Golden Gate International Exposition.

SEMI-POSTAL STAMPS

No. 45 Surcharged

Perf. 14x13½

1914, Oct. 28 **Unwmk.**

No.	Type	Description	Unused	Used
B1	A5	10c +5c red & blk	1.10	1.00

Nos. 44-46 Surcharged

1915-17

No.	Type	Description	Unused	Used
B2	A5	5c + 5c grn & blk ('17)	1.00	1.00
a.		Double surcharge	160.00	160.00
B3	A5	10c + 5c red & blk	1.90	1.25
B4	A5	15c + 5c vio & blk ('17)	1.90	1.25
a.		Triple surcharge	140.00	
b.		Quadruple surcharge	140.00	
		Nos. B2-B4 (3)	4.80	3.50

Nos. B2-B4 Surcharged with New Values in Blue or Black

1918-19

No.	Type	Description	Unused	Used
B5	A5	4c on 5c + 5c (Bl)	4.00	*4.00*
a.		Closed "4"	160.00	
B6	A5	6c on 10c + 5c	3.25	*4.00*
B7	A5	8c on 15c + 5c ('19)	12.50	10.00
a.		Double surcharge	160.00	
		Nos. B5-B7 (3)	19.75	18.00

France Nos. B5-B10 Surcharged

1918 (?)

No.	Type	Description	Unused	Used
B8	SP5	10c on 15c + 10c	1.00	1.00
B9	SP5	16c on 25c + 15c	3.25	3.25
B10	SP6	24c on 35c + 25c	5.50	5.50
a.		Double surcharge	575.00	
B11	SP7	40c on 50c + 50c	9.75	9.75
B12	SP8	80c on 1fr + 1fr	21.00	21.00
B13	SP8	4pi on 5fr + 5fr	185.00	185.00
		Nos. B8-B13 (6)	225.50	225.50

Curie Issue

Common Design Type

Inscription and Date in Upper Margin

1938, Oct. 24 Engr. ***Perf. 13***

No.	Type	Description	Unused	Used
B14	CD80	18c + 5c brt ultra	8.50	8.50

French Revolution Issue

Common Design Type

Name and Value Typo. in Black

1939, July 5 **Photo.**

No.	Type	Description	Unused	Used
B15	CD83	6c + 2c green	9.25	9.25
B16	CD83	7c + 3c brown	9.25	9.25
B17	CD83	9c + 4c red org	9.25	9.25
B18	CD83	13c + 10c rose pink	9.25	9.25
B19	CD83	23c + 20c blue	9.25	9.25
		Nos. B15-B19 (5)	46.25	46.25

AIR POST STAMPS

Airplane AP1

1933-41 Unwmk. Photo. ***Perf. 13½***

No.	Type	Description	Unused	Used
C1	AP1	1c ol brn	.20	.20
C2	AP1	2c dk grn	.20	.20
C3	AP1	5c yel grn	.20	.20
C4	AP1	10c red brn	.50	.20
C5	AP1	11c rose car ('38)	.55	.20
C6	AP1	15c dp bl	.55	.20
C6A	AP1	16c brt pink ('41)	.20	.20
C7	AP1	20c grnsh gray	.35	.35
C8	AP1	30c org brn	.20	.20
C9	AP1	36c car rose	1.50	.20
C10	AP1	37c ol grn ('38)	.55	.20
C10A	AP1	39c dk ol grn ('41)	.20	.20
C11	AP1	60c dk vio	.20	.20
C12	AP1	66c olive grn	.35	.20
C13	AP1	67c brt bl ('38)	.90	.70
C13A	AP1	69c brt ultra ('41)	.50	.50
C14	AP1	1pi black	.50	.20
C15	AP1	2pi yel org	.75	.20
C16	AP1	5pi purple	1.50	.35
C17	AP1	10pi deep red	3.00	.80
		Nos. C1-C17 (20)	12.90	5.70

See Nos. C27-C28.

Issue dates: 11c, 37c, June 8; 67c, Oct. 5; 16c, 39c, 69c, Feb. 5; others, June 1, 1933.

Stamps of type AP1 without "RF" monogram were issued in 1942 and 1943 by the Vichy Government. On the Vichy stamps, the figure of value has been moved to the lower left corner of the vignette.

Trans-Indo-Chinese Railway Type

1938, June 8

No.	Type	Description	Unused	Used
C18	A26	37c red orange	.50	.20

AIR POST SEMI-POSTAL STAMP

French Revolution Issue

Common Design Type

Unwmk.

1939, July 5 Photo. ***Perf. 13***

Name and Value Typo. in Orange

No.	Type	Description	Unused	Used
CB1	CD83	39c + 40c brn blk	19.00	19.00

POSTAGE DUE STAMPS

French Colonies No. J21 Surcharged

1904, June 26 Unwmk. ***Imperf.***

No.	Type	Description	Unused	Used
J1	D1	5c on 60c brn, *buff*	10.00	9.25
		On cover		800.00

French Colonies Nos. J10-J11 Surcharged in Carmine

1905, July 22

No.	Type	Description	Unused	Used
J2	D1	5c on 40c black	22.50	11.00
		On cover		500.00
J3	D1	10c on 60c black	22.50	14.50
		On cover		500.00
J4	D1	30c on 60c black	22.50	14.50
		On cover		500.00
		Nos. J2-J4 (3)	67.50	40.00

Dragon from Steps of Angkor Wat

D1 D2

1908 Typo. ***Perf. 14x13½***

No.	Type	Description	Unused	Used
J5	D1	2c black	1.10	.85
J6	D1	4c dp bl	1.10	.85
J7	D1	5c bl grn	1.25	.85
J8	D1	10c carmine	2.25	.85
J9	D1	15c violet	3.00	2.00
J10	D1	20c chocolate	1.40	.95
		On cover		80.00
J11	D1	30c ol grn	1.40	.95
J12	D1	40c claret	6.50	5.25
J13	D1	50c grnsh bl	5.25	1.10
		On cover		80.00
J14	D1	60c orange	9.00	6.75
J15	D1	1fr gray	18.00	12.00
J16	D1	2fr yel brn	18.00	12.00
J17	D1	5fr red	29.00	29.00
		Nos. J5-J17 (13)	97.25	73.40

Surcharged with New Values in Cents or Piasters

1919

No.	Type	Description	Unused	Used
J18	D1	⅘c on 2c blk	1.25	.85
J19	D1	1⅗c on 4c dp bl	1.25	.85
J20	D1	2c on 5c bl grn	2.25	1.40
J21	D1	4c on 10c car	3.00	.70
J22	D1	6c on 15c vio	6.75	2.00
J23	D1	8c on 20c choc	4.50	1.75
J24	D1	12c on 30c ol grn	6.75	1.60
J25	D1	16c on 40c cl	6.75	1.50
J26	D1	20c on 50c grnsh bl	8.50	4.50
J27	D1	24c on 60c org	2.25	1.40
a.		Closed "4"	14.00	11.50
J28	D1	40c on 1fr gray	3.50	1.10
a.		Closed "4"	14.00	11.50
J29	D1	80c on 20c yel brn	32.50	14.00
J30	D1	2pi on 5fr red	45.00	32.50
a.		Double surcharge	160.00	125.00
b.		Triple surcharge	160.00	125.00
		Nos. J18-J30 (13)	124.25	64.15

"CENTS" below Numerals

1922, Oct.

No.	Type	Description	Unused	Used
J31	D2	⅖c black	.20	.20
J32	D2	⅘c red	.20	.20
J33	D2	1c buff	.35	.30
J34	D2	2c gray grn	.50	.35
J35	D2	3c violet	.55	.55
J36	D2	4c orange	.55	.35
a.		"4 CENTS" omitted	450.00	
b.		"4 CENTS" double	65.00	65.00
J37	D2	6c ol grn	1.25	.40
J38	D2	8c blk, *lav*	.85	.40
J39	D2	10c dp bl	1.75	.65
J40	D2	12c ocher, *grnsh*	1.00	.80
J41	D2	20c dp bl, *straw*	1.25	.65
J42	D2	40c red, *bluish*	1.25	.80
J43	D2	1pi brn vio, *pnksh*	4.25	2.75
		Nos. J31-J43 (13)	13.95	8.40

Pagoda of Mot Cot, Hanoi — D3

Dragon of Annam — D4

Perf. 14x13½, 13½x14

1927, Sept. 26

No.	Type	Description	Unused	Used
J44	D3	⅖c vio brn & org	.20	.20
J45	D3	⅘c vio & blk	.20	.20
J46	D3	1c brn red & sl	.65	.65
J47	D3	2c grn & brn ol	.75	.75
J48	D3	3c red brn & bl	1.00	1.00
J49	D3	4c ind & brn	1.00	1.00
J50	D3	6c dp red & ver	1.25	1.00
J51	D3	8c ol brn & vio	1.10	.85
J52	D4	10c dp bl	1.75	.65
J53	D4	12c olive	4.00	3.50
J54	D4	20c rose	2.75	1.40
J55	D4	40c bl grn	2.75	2.50
J56	D4	1pi red org	13.00	13.00
		Nos. J44-J56 (13)	30.40	26.70

D5

Value Surcharged in Black or Blue

1931-41 ***Perf. 13***

No.	Type	Description	Unused	Used
J57	D5	⅒c red, *org* ('38)	.20	.20
J58	D5	⅖c red, *org*	.20	.20
J59	D5	⅘c red, *org*	.20	.20
J60	D5	1c red, *org*	.20	.20
J61	D5	2c red, *org*	.20	.20
J62	D5	2.5c red, *org* ('40)	.20	.20
J63	D5	3c red, *org* ('38)	.20	.20
J64	D5	4c red, *org*	.20	.20
J65	D5	5c red, *org* ('38)	.20	.20
J66	D5	6c red, *org*	.20	.20
J67	D5	10c red, *org*	.20	.20
J68	D5	12c red, *org*	.35	.20
J69	D5	14c red, *org* ('38)	.35	.20
J70	D5	18c red, *org* ('41)	.35	.20
J71	D5	20c red, *org*	.35	.20
J72	D5	50c red, *org*	.60	.35
J72A	D5	1pi red, *org*	7.00	6.50
J73	D5	1pi red, *org* (Bl)	1.75	.95
		Nos. J57-J73 (18)	12.95	10.80

OFFICIAL STAMPS

Regular Issues of 1931-32 Overprinted in Blue or Red

Overprinted

Perf. 13, 13½

1933, Feb. 27 **Unwmk.**

No.	Type	Description	Unused	Used
O1	A20	1c black brown (Bl)	.55	.55
O2	A20	2c dark green (Bl)	.65	.35

Overprinted

No.	Type	Description	Unused	Used
O3	A21	3c deep brown (Bl)	.85	.50
a.		Inverted overprint	110.00	
O4	A21	4c dark blue (R)	1.10	.65
a.		Inverted overprint	110.00	
O5	A21	5c deep violet (Bl)	1.75	.70
O6	A21	6c orange red (Bl)	1.75	.80

Overprinted

No.	Type	Description	Unused	Used
O7	A22	10c dk blue (R)	.70	.65
O8	A22	15c dk brown (Bl)	2.10	1.40
O9	A22	20c rose (Bl)	2.25	.55

O10 A22 21c olive grn (Bl) 2.10 1.25
O11 A22 25c dp violet (Bl) 1.10 .35
O12 A22 30c orange brn (Bl) 2.25 .55

Overprinted

O13 A23 50c dark brown (Bl) 8.50 2.75
O14 A23 60c dull violet (Bl) 2.00 1.75
O15 A23 1pi yellow green (Bl) 21.00 7.00
O16 A23 2pi red (Bl) 8.00 7.00
Nos. O1-O16 (16) 56.65 26.80

Type of Regular Issue, 1922-23 Overprinted diagonally in Black or Red "SERVICE"

1934, Oct. 4 ***Perf. 14x13***

O17 A13 1c olive green .80 .55
O18 A13 2c brown orange .80 .55
O19 A13 3c yellow green 1.00 .45
O20 A13 4c cerise 1.75 .90
O21 A13 5c yellow 1.00 .55
O22 A13 6c orange red 4.25 4.00
O23 A13 10c gray grn (R) 2.50 1.75
O24 A13 15c ultra 1.60 1.25
O25 A13 20c gray black (R) 1.40 1.10
O26 A13 21c light violet 7.75 6.50
O27 A13 25c rose lake 9.25 7.75
O28 A13 30c lilac gray 1.25 1.00
O29 A13 50c brt violet 5.75 5.00
O30 A13 60c gray 10.50 8.25
O31 A13 1pi blue (R) 21.00 18.00
O32 A13 2pi deep red 32.50 27.50
Nos. O17-O32 (16) 103.10 85.10

The value tablet has colorless numeral and letters on solid background.

PARCEL POST STAMPS

French Colonies No. 50 Overprinted

1891 **Unwmk.** ***Perf. 14x13½***

Q1 A9 10c black, *lavender* 16.00 5.75
On parcel post receipt card 400.00

The overprint on No. Q1 was also handstamped in shiny ink. Value unused, $600.

Indo-China No. 8 Overprinted

1898

Q2 A3 10c black, *lavender* 19.50 *25.00*
On parcel post receipt card 400.00

Nos. 8 and 9 Overprinted

1902

Q3 A3 10c black, *lavender* 42.50 22.50
On parcel post receipt card 400.00
a. Inverted overprint 82.50 37.50
Q4 A3 10c red 50.00 27.50
On parcel post receipt card 400.00
a. Inverted overprint 70.00 40.00
b. Double overprint 70.00 40.00

INHAMBANE

ˌin-yəm-ˈban-ə

LOCATION — East Africa
GOVT. — A district of Mozambique, former Portuguese colony
AREA — 21,000 sq. mi. (approx.)
POP. — 248,000 (approx.)

CAPITAL — Inhambane

1000 Reis = 1 Milreis
100 Centavos = 1 Escudo (1913)

Stamps of Mozambique Overprinted

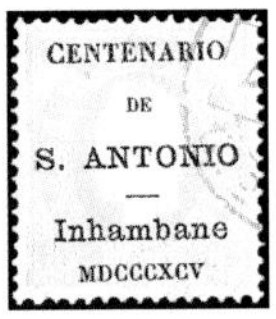

On 1886 Issue

1895, July 1 **Unwmk.** ***Perf. 12½***

Without Gum

1 A2 5r black 37.50 30.00
2 A2 10r green 35.00 25.00
a. Perf. 13½ 80.00 75.00
3 A2 20r rose 60.00 30.00
4 A2 25r lilac *400.00 250.00*
5 A2 40r chocolate 55.00 40.00
6 A2 50r blue 55.00 32.50
a. Perf. 13½ 50.00 50.00
7 A2 100r yellow brown *500.00 400.00*
8 A2 200r gray violet 50.00 40.00
9 A2 300r orange 50.00 40.00
Nos. 1-9 (9) *1,242. 887.50*

On 1894 Issue

Perf. 11½

10 A3 50r lt blue 42.50 35.00
a. Perf. 12½ 55.00 42.50
11 A3 75r rose 55.00 40.00
12 A3 80r yellow green 45.00 37.50
13 A3 100r brown, *buff* 140.00 60.00
14 A3 150r carmine, *rose* 50.00 45.00
Nos. 10-14 (5) 332.50 217.50

700th anniv. of the birth of St. Anthony of Padua.

The status of Nos. 4 and 7 is questionable. No. 3 is always discolored.

Forged overprints exist. Genuine overprints are 21mm high.

King Carlos — A1

1903, Jan. 1 **Typo.** ***Perf. 11½***

Name and Value in Black except 500r

15 A1 2½r gray .30 .30
16 A1 5r orange .30 .30
17 A1 10r lt green .60 .40
18 A1 15r gray green 1.00 .75
19 A1 20r gray violet .85 .55
20 A1 25r carmine .70 .55
21 A1 50r brown 1.75 1.25
22 A1 65r dull blue 17.50 15.00
23 A1 75r lilac 2.00 1.40
24 A1 100r dk blue, *blue* 2.75 1.25
25 A1 115r org brn, *pink* 5.00 5.00
26 A1 130r brown, *straw* 5.00 5.00
27 A1 200r red vio, *pink* 5.00 4.25
28 A1 400r dull bl, *straw* 8.25 7.50
29 A1 500r blk & red, *bl* 16.00 12.00
30 A1 700r gray blk, *straw* 16.00 13.00
Nos. 15-30 (16) 83.00 68.50

For surcharge & overprints see #31-47, 88-101.

No. 22 Surcharged in Black

1905

31 A1 50r on 65r dull blue 2.75 2.00

Nos. 15-21, 23-30 Overprinted in Carmine or Green

1911

32 A1 2½r gray .20 .20
33 A1 5r orange .20 .20
34 A1 10r lt green .20 .20
35 A1 15r gray green .30 .30
36 A1 20r gray violet .30 .30
37 A1 25r carmine (G) .70 .50
38 A1 50r brown .50 .50
39 A1 75r lilac .50 .50
40 A1 100r dk blue, *bl* .50 .50
41 A1 115r org brn, *pink* 1.00 .95
42 A1 130r brown, *straw* 1.00 .95
43 A1 200r red vio, *pink* 1.00 .95
44 A1 400r dull bl, *straw* 1.25 1.00
45 A1 500r blk & red, *bl* 1.50 1.00
46 A1 700r gray blk, *straw* 1.75 1.50
Nos. 32-46 (15) 10.90 9.55

No. 31 Overprinted in Red

1914

47 A1 50r on 65r dull blue 1.75 1.25
a. "Republica" inverted 25.00 25.00

Vasco da Gama Issue of Various Portuguese Colonies

Common Design Types CD20-CD27 Surcharged

1913

On Stamps of Macao

48 CD20 ¼c on ½a bl grn 1.25 1.25
49 CD21 ½c on 1a red 1.25 1.25
50 CD22 1c on 2a red vio 1.25 1.25
a. Inverted surcharge 35.00 35.00
51 CD23 2½c on 4a yel grn 1.25 1.25
52 CD24 5c on 8a dk bl 1.25 1.25
53 CD25 7½c on 12a vio brn 2.25 2.25
54 CD26 10c on 16a bis brn 1.75 1.75
55 CD27 15c on 24a bis 1.75 1.75
Nos. 48-55 (8) 12.00 12.00

On Stamps of Portuguese Africa

56 CD20 ¼c on 2½r bl grn 1.00 1.00
57 CD21 ½c on 5r red 1.00 1.00
58 CD22 1c on 10r red vio 1.00 1.00
59 CD23 2½c on 25r yel grn 1.00 1.00
60 CD24 5c on 50r dk bl 1.00 1.00
61 CD25 7½c on 75r vio brn 2.00 2.00
62 CD26 10c on 100r bis brn 1.50 1.50
63 CD27 15c on 150r bis 1.50 1.50
Nos. 56-63 (8) 10.00 10.00

On Stamps of Timor

64 CD20 ¼c on ½a bl grn 1.25 1.25
a. Inverted surcharge 35.00 35.00
65 CD21 ½c on 1a red 1.25 1.25
66 CD22 1c on 2a red vio 1.25 1.25
67 CD23 2½c on 4a yel grn 1.25 1.25
68 CD24 5c on 8a dk bl 1.25 1.25
69 CD25 7½c on 12a vio brn 2.50 2.50
70 CD26 10c on 16a bis brn 1.75 1.75
71 CD27 15c on 24a bis 1.75 1.75
Nos. 64-71 (8) 12.25 12.25
Nos. 48-71 (24) 34.25 34.25

Ceres — A2

1914 **Typo.** ***Perf. 15x14***

Name and Value in Black

72 A2 ¼c olive brown .50 .50
73 A2 ½c black .50 .50
a. Imperf.
74 A2 1c blue green .50 .50
75 A2 1½c lilac brown .50 .50
76 A2 2c carmine .50 .50
77 A2 2½c lt violet .35 .35
78 A2 5c deep blue .80 .80
79 A2 7½c yellow brown 1.25 1.25
80 A2 8c slate 1.25 1.25
81 A2 10c orange brown 1.10 1.10
82 A2 15c plum 2.00 1.60
83 A2 20c yellow green 2.00 1.60
84 A2 30c brown, *grn* 3.00 2.50
85 A2 40c brown, *pink* 3.00 2.75
86 A2 50c orange, *sal* 5.00 4.50
87 A2 1e green, *blue* 6.00 5.00
Nos. 72-87 (16) 28.25 25.20

No. 31 Overprinted in Carmine

1915 ***Perf. 11½***

88 A1 50c on 65r dull blue 8.00 6.00

Nos. 15-21, 23-30 Overprinted Locally

1917

89 A1 2½r gray 25.00 25.00
90 A1 5r orange 25.00 25.00
91 A1 15r gray green 2.50 2.50
92 A1 20r gray violet 2.00 2.00
93 A1 50r brown 2.00 2.00
94 A1 75r lilac 2.00 2.00
95 A1 100r blue, *blue* 3.00 2.50
96 A1 115r org brn, *pink* 3.00 2.50
97 A1 130r brn, *straw* 3.00 2.50
98 A1 200r red vio, *pink* 3.00 2.50
99 A1 400r dull bl, *straw* 6.00 3.00
100 A1 500r blk & red, *bl* 5.00 3.00
101 A1 700r gray blk, *straw* 14.00 8.00
Nos. 89-101 (13) 95.50 82.50

The stamps of Inhambane have been superseded by those of Mozambique.

ININI

ˌē-ni-ˈnē

LOCATION — In northeastern South America, adjoining French Guiana
GOVT. — Former territory of French Guiana
AREA — 30,301 sq. mi.
POP. — 5,024 (1946)
CAPITAL — St. Elie

Inini was separated from French Guiana in 1930 and reunited with it in when the colony became an integral part of the Republic, acquiring the same status as the departments of Metropolitan France, under a law effective Jan. 1, 1947.

100 Centimes = 1 Franc

Used values are for canceled-to-order copies.

Stamps of French Guiana, 1929-40, Overprinted in Black, Red or Blue:

Nos. 1-9

Nos. 10-26

Nos. 27-40

1932-40 Unwmk. *Perf. 13½x14*

1	A16	1c gray lil & grnsh bl	.30	*.35*
		On cover, *from*		250.00
2	A16	2c dk red & bl grn	.30	*.35*
		On cover, *from*		250.00
3	A16	3c gray lil & grnsh bl ('40)	.45	*.50*
		On cover, *from*		250.00
4	A16	4c ol brn & red vio ('38)	.45	*.50*
		On cover, *from*		250.00
5	A16	5c Prus bl & red org	.45	*.50*
		On cover, *from*		250.00
6	A16	10c magenta & brn	.30	*.35*
		On cover, *from*		250.00
7	A16	15c yel brn & red org	.30	*.35*
		On cover, *from*		250.00
8	A16	20c dk bl & ol grn	.30	*.35*
		On cover, *from*		250.00
9	A16	25c dk red & dk brn	.75	*.80*

Perf. 14x13½

10	A17	30c dl grn & lt grn	1.60	*1.75*
		On cover, *from*		250.00
11	A17	30c grn & brn ('40)	.45	*.50*
		On cover, *from*		250.00
12	A17	35c Prus grn & ol ('38)	.80	*1.00*
		On cover, *from*		250.00
13	A17	40c org brn & ol gray	.65	*.80*
		On cover, *from*		250.00
14	A17	45c ol grn & lt grn ('40)	1.10	*1.25*
		On cover, *from*		250.00
15	A17	50c dk bl & ol gray	.50	*.60*
		On cover, *from*		250.00
16	A17	55c vio bl & car ('38)	3.75	*4.00*
		On cover, *from*		250.00
17	A17	60c sal & grn ('40)	.50	*.55*
		On cover, *from*		250.00
18	A17	65c sal & grn ('38)	1.40	*1.50*
		On cover, *from*		250.00
19	A17	70c ind & sl bl ('40)	.60	*.75*
		On cover, *from*		250.00
20	A17	75c ind & sl bl (Bl)	2.00	*2.50*
		On cover, *from*		250.00
21	A17	80c blk & vio bl (R) ('38)	.75	*.80*
		On cover, *from*		250.00
22	A17	90c dk red & ver	1.25	*1.40*
		On cover, *from*		250.00
23	A17	90c red vio & brn ('39)	.60	*.65*
		On cover, *from*		250.00
24	A17	1fr lt vio & brn	13.00	*13.50*
		On cover, *from*		*500.00*
25	A17	1fr car & lt red ('38)	1.10	*1.25*
		On cover, *from*		250.00
26	A17	1fr blk & vio bl ('40)	.75	*1.00*
		On cover, *from*		250.00
27	A18	1.25fr blk brn & bl grn ('33)	.85	*1.00*
		On cover, *from*		250.00
28	A18	1.25fr rose & lt red ('39)	.75	*.80*
		On cover, *from*		250.00
29	A18	1.40fr ol brn & red vio ('40)	.75	*.80*
		On cover, *from*		250.00
30	A18	1.50fr dk bl & lt bl	.75	*.80*
		On cover, *from*		250.00
31	A18	1.60fr ol brn & bl grn ('40)	.75	*.80*
		On cover, *from*		250.00
32	A18	1.75fr brn, red & blk brn ('33)	15.00	*16.00*
		On cover, *from*		*500.00*
33	A18	1.75fr vio bl ('38)	1.25	*1.50*
		On cover, *from*		250.00
34	A18	2fr dk grn & rose red	.90	*.95*
		On cover, *from*		250.00
35	A18	2.25fr vio bl ('39)	.75	*.80*
		On cover, *from*		250.00
36	A18	2.50fr cop red & brn ('40)	.75	*.80*
		On cover, *from*		250.00
37	A18	3fr brn red & red vio	.90	*1.00*
		On cover, *from*		250.00
38	A18	5fr dl vio & yel grn	.90	*1.00*
		On cover, *from*		250.00
39	A18	10fr ol gray & dp ultra (R)	1.25	*1.40*
		On cover, *from*		250.00
40	A18	20fr indigo & ver	1.25	*1.40*
		On cover, *from*		*400.00*
		Nos. 1-40 (40)	61.20	*66.90*

Cover values are for examples bearing stamps used to pay correct postage rates.

Common Design Types pictured following the introduction.

Colonial Arts Exhibition Issue

Souvenir Sheet
Common Design Type

1937 ***Imperf.***

41	CD75	3fr red brown	13.00	*16.00*

New York World's Fair Issue

Common Design Type

1939, May 10 Engr. *Perf. 12½x12*

42	CD82	1.25fr car lake	3.00	3.00
43	CD82	2.25fr ultra	3.00	3.00

SEMI-POSTAL STAMPS

Common Design Type

Photo.; Name & Value Typo. in Black

1939, July 5 Unwmk. *Perf. 13*

B1	CD83	45c + 25c green	11.50	11.50
B2	CD83	70c + 30c brown	11.50	11.50
B3	CD83	90c + 35c red org	11.50	11.50
B4	CD83	1.25fr + 1fr rose pink	11.50	11.50
B5	CD83	2.25fr + 2fr blue	11.50	11.50
		Nos. B1-B5 (5)	57.50	57.50

POSTAGE DUE STAMPS

Cover values are for examples bearing stamps used to pay correct postage due rates.

Postage Due Stamps of French Guiana, 1929, Overprinted in Black

1932, Apr. 7 Unwmk. *Perf. 13½x14*

J1	D3	5c indigo & Prus bl	.20	.20
		On cover		*1,250.*
J2	D3	10c bis brn & Prus grn	.50	.50
		On cover		*1,250.*
J3	D3	20c grn & rose red	.50	.50
		On cover		*1,250.*
J4	D3	30c ol brn & rose red	.50	.50
		On cover		*1,250.*
J5	D3	50c vio & ol brn	.80	.80
		On cover		*1,250.*
J6	D3	60c brn red & ol brn	1.00	1.00
		On cover		*1,250.*

Overprinted in Black or Red

J7	D4	1fr dp bl & org brn	.95	.95
		On cover		*1,250.*
J8	D4	2fr brn red & bluish grn	1.25	1.25
		On cover		*1,250.*
J9	D4	3fr vio & blk (R)	6.25	*9.00*
		On cover		*1,250.*
J10	D4	3fr vio & blk	2.75	2.75
		On cover		*1,250.*
		Nos. J1-J10 (10)	14.70	17.45

IONIAN ISLANDS

ī-ˈō-nē-ən ˈī-ləndz

LOCATION — A group of seven islands, of which six-Corfu, Paxos Lefkas (Santa Maura), Cephalonia, Ithaca and Zante-are in the Ionian Sea west of Greece, and a seventh-Kythera (Cerigo)-is in the Mediterranean south of Greece.
GOVT. — British Protectorate
AREA — 752 sq. mi.
POP. — 251,000 (approx.)

These islands were acquired by Great Britain in 1815 but in 1864 were ceded to Greece on request of the inhabitants.

10 Oboli = 1 Penny
12 Pence = 1 Shilling

Watermarks

Wmk. 138 — "2"

Wmk. 139 — "1"

Queen Victoria — A1

1859 Unwmk. Engr. *Imperf.*

1	A1	(½p) orange	85.00	*575.00*

Wmk. 138

2	A1	(1p) blue	22.50	*210.00*

Wmk. 139

3	A1	(2p) lake	17.50	*210.00*
		Nos. 1-3 (3)	125.00	*995.00*

Full margins = ¼mm at sides, ¾mm at top and bottom.

Forged cancellations are plentiful.

IRAN

i-ˈrän

(Persia)

LOCATION — Western Asia, bordering on the Persian Gulf and the Gulf of Oman
GOVT. — Islamic republic
AREA — 636,000 sq. mi.
POP. — 43,830,000 (est. 1984)
CAPITAL — Tehran

20 Shahis (or Chahis) = 1 Kran
10 Krans = 1 Toman
100 Centimes = 1 Franc = 1 Kran (1881)
100 Dinars = 1 Rial (1933)
100 Rials = 1 Pahlavi

Values of early stamps vary according to condition. Quotations for Nos. 1-20, 33-40 are for fine copies. Very fine to superb specimens sell at much higher prices, and inferior or poor copies sell at reduced prices, depending on the condition of the individual specimen.
Cracked gum on unused stamps does not detract from the value.

Beware of forgeries and/or reprints of most Iran stamps between the years 1870-1925. Scott values are for genuine stamps. Collectors should be aware that forgeries of many issues outnumber genuine examples by factors of 10 or 20 to one. Failing specialized knowledge on the part of the collector, these stamps should be examined or authenticated by acknowledged experts before purchase.

Watermark

Wmk. 161 — Lion

Many issues have handstamped surcharges. As usual with such surcharges there are numerous inverted, double and similar varieties.

Coat of Arms
A1 A2

Design A2 has value numeral below lion.

1870 Unwmk. Typo. *Imperf.*

1	A1	1s dull violet	175.00
2	A1	2s green	125.00
3	A1	4s greenish blue	125.00
4	A1	8s red	125.00
		Nos. 1-4 (4)	550.00

Values for used copies of Nos. 1-4 are omitted, since this issue was only pen canceled. After 1875, postmarked remainders were sold to collectors. Values same as unused.
Printed in blocks of 4. Many shades exist. Forgeries exist.

Printed on Both Sides

1a	A1	1s	1,300.
2a	A1	2s	900.
3a	A1	4s	2,000.
4a	A1	8s	1,200.

Vertically Rouletted 10½ on 1 or 2 Sides

1875	**Thick Wove Paper**		
11	A2 1s black	150.00	50.00
a.	Imperf., pair	*400.00*	*400.00*
12	A2 2s blue	125.00	50.00
a.	Tête bêche pair	*10,000.*	
b.	Imperf., pair	*575.00*	*575.00*
13	A2 4s vermilion	200.00	60.00
a.	Imperf., pair	*625.00*	*625.00*
b.	4s bright red, thin paper, imperf.	525.00	
14	A2 8s yellow green	100.00	60.00
a.	Tête bêche pair	*12,500.*	*7,500.*
b.	Imperf., pair	*70.00*	*70.00*
	Nos. 11-14 (4)	575.00	220.00

Four varieties of each.

Nos. 11-14 were printed in horizontal strips of 4 with 3-10mm spacing between stamps. The strips were then cut very close all around (generally touching or cutting the outer framelines). Then they were hand-rouletted between the stamps. Values are for stamps with rouletting on both sides and margins clear at top and bottom. Stamps showing the rouletting on only one side sell for considerably less.

Nos. 11 to 14 also exist pin-perforated and percé en scie.

No. 13b has spacing of 2-3mm.

See Nos. 15-20, 33-40.

Medium to Thin White or Grayish Paper

1876		**Imperf.**	
14A	A2 1s black	200.00	*300.00*
15	A2 1s gray black	37.50	*75.00*
a.	Printed on both sides	*1,000.*	
b.	Laid paper	500.00	
16	A2 2s gray blue	375.00	*450.00*
a.	Printed on both sides	—	
17	A2 2s black	600.00	
	Pair	6,000.	
a.	Tête bêche pair	*5,750.*	
18	A2 4s vermilion	200.00	60.00
a.	Printed on both sides	800.00	450.00
19	A2 1k rose	600.00	50.00
a.	Printed on both sides		350.00
b.	Laid paper	*2,000.*	225.00
c.	1k yellow (error)	*9,500.*	
d.	Tête bêche pair		*15,000.*
20	A2 4k yellow	1,000.	70.00
a.	Printed on both sides		*825.00*
b.	Laid paper	*1,000.*	110.00
c.	Tête bêche pair		*18,000.*

Nos. 15-16, 18-20 were printed in blocks of 4, and Nos. 14A and 17 in vertical strips of 4, with spacing of 2mm or less.

Nos. 14A and 17 are on medium to thick grayish wove paper. Forgeries exist.

Official reprints of the 1s and 4s are on thick coarse white paper without gum. Value, each $350.

Unofficial Reprints:

1875 and 1876 issues.

The reprints of the 1s and 1k stamps are readily told; the pearls of the circle are heavier, the borders of the circles containing the Persian numeral of value are wider and the figure "1" below the lion is always Roman.

The reprints of the 2s have the outer line of the frame at the left and at the bottom broken and on some specimens entirely missing.

A distinguishing mark by which to tell the 4s and 4k stamps is the frame, the outer line of which is of the same thickness as the inner line, while on the originals the inner line is very thin and the outer line thick; another feature of most of the reprints is a gash in the lower part of the circle below the figure "4."

In the reprints of the 8s stamps the small scroll nearest to the circles with Persian numerals at the bottom of the stamp touches the frame below it; the inner and outer lines of the frame are of equal thickness, while in the originals the outer line is much heavier than the inner one.

All reprints are found canceled to order.

Nasser-eddin Shah Qajar — A3

Perf. 10½, 11, 12, 13, and Compounds

1876		**Litho.**	
27	A3 1s lilac & blk	20.00	6.00
28	A3 2s green & blk	25.00	7.50
29	A3 5s rose & blk	25.00	4.00
30	A3 10s blue & blk	40.00	8.00
	Nos. 27-30 (4)	110.00	25.50

Bisects of the 5s and 1s, the latter used with 2s stamps, were used to make up the 2½ shahis postcard rate. Bisects of the 10s were used in the absence of 5s stamps to make up the letter rate.

The 10s was bisected and surcharged "5 Shahi" or "5 Shahy" for local use in Azerbaijan province and Khoy in 1877.

"Imperfs" of the 5s are envelope cutouts.

Forgeries and official reprints exist.

Very fine examples will have perforations cutting the background net on one side. Genuine stamps withs perfs clear of net on all four sides are very scarce.

1878	**Typo.**	**Imperf.**	
33	A2 1k car rose	300.00	90.00
34	A2 1k red, *yellow*	*2,000.*	90.00
a.	Tête bêche pair		*5,250.*
35	A2 4k ultramarine	275.00	100.00
36	A2 5k violet	850.00	200.00
37	A2 5k gold	*3,500.*	450.00
38	A2 5k red bronze	*7,500.*	1,500.
39	A2 5k vio bronze	*25,000.*	2,000.
40	A2 1t bronze, *bl*	*55,000.*	*5,500.*

Four varieties of each except for 4k which has 3.

Nos. 33 and 34 are printed from redrawn clichés. They have wide colorless circles around the corner numerals.

Nasser-eddin Shah Qajar — A6

Sun — A7

Perf. 10½, 12, 13, and Compounds

1879		**Litho.**	
41	A6 1k brown & blk	200.00	7.00
a.	Imperf., pair		—
b.	Inverted center		*3,500.*
42	A6 5k blue & blk	400.00	5.00
a.	Imperf., pair	—	*450.00*
b.	Inverted center		1,350.
c.	Inverted center, imperf		1,350.

1880			
43	A6 1s red & black	50.00	15.00
b.	Pair, imperf between	*2,000.*	
44	A6 2s yellow & blk	85.00	10.00
45	A6 5s green & blk	350.00	2.00
46	A6 10s violet & blk	550.00	25.00
	Nos. 43-46 (4)	1,035.	52.00

Forgeries and official reprints exist.

The 2, 5 and 10sh of this issue and the 1 and 5kr of the 1879 issue have been reprinted from a new die which resembles the 5 shahi envelope. The aigrette is shorter than on the original stamps and touches the circle above it.

Imperf., Pair

43a	A6 1s	1,500.	
44a	A6 2s	—	*750.00*
46a	A6 10s	—	600.00

1881	**Litho.**	***Perf. 12, 13, 12x13***	
47	A7 5c dull violet	30.00	10.00
48	A7 10c rose	30.00	10.00
49	A7 25c green	4,000.	75.00
	Nos. 47-49 (3)	4,060.	95.00

1882	**Engr., Border Litho.**		
50	A7 5c blue vio & vio	40.00	40.00
51	A7 10c dp pink & rose	40.00	40.00
52	A7 25c deep grn & grn	500.00	20.00
	Nos. 50-52 (3)	580.00	100.00

Very fine examples of Nos. 50-52 will have perforations cutting the outer colored border but clear of the inner framelines.

Counterfeits of Nos. 50-52, 53, 53a are plentiful and have been used to create forgeries of Nos. 66, 66a, 70 and 70a. They usually have a strong, complete inner frameline at right. On genuine stamps that line is weak or missing.

A8

Shah Nasr-ed-Din
A9 A10

A11

Type I

Type II (error)

Type I: Three dots at right end of scroll.
Type II: Two dots at right end of scroll.

1882-84		**Engr.**	
53	A8 5s green, type I	35.00	1.50
a.	5s green, type II	75.00	10.00
54	A9 10s buff, org & blk	75.00	10.00
55	A10 50c buff, org & blk	400.00	55.00
56	A10 50c gray & blk ('84)	125.00	65.00
57	A10 1fr blue & black	150.00	10.00
58	A10 5fr rose red & blk	125.00	10.00
59	A11 10fr buff, red & blk	150.00	30.00
	Nos. 53-59 (7)	1,060.	181.50

Crude forgeries of Nos. 58-59 exist. Halves of the 10s, 50c and 1fr surcharged with Farsi characters in red or black are frauds. The 50c and 1fr surcharged with a large "5" surrounded by rays are also frauds.

No. 59 used is valued for c-t-o.

For overprints and surcharges see #66-72.

Very fine examples of Nos. 53-59 will have perforations cutting the outer colored border but clear of the inner framelines.

A12

A13

Perf. 12-12½, 13

1885, March-May		**Litho.**	
59A	A12 5c blue	400.00	35.00
a.	5c violet blue	400.00	50.00
b.	5c ultramarine	400.00	50.00
c.	5c dp reddish lilac	650.00	100.00
d.	As "a," imperf	3,000.	

No. 59A was issued because of an urgent need for 5c stamps, pending the arrival of No. 62 in July. No. 59A has 88 sunrays instead of the 124 sunrays on the typographed stamp, No. 62.

1885-86		**Typo.**	
60	A12 1c green	15.00	1.50
61	A12 2c rose	15.00	1.50
62	A12 5c dull blue	40.00	.75
63	A13 10c brown	15.00	1.50
64	A13 1k slate	40.00	2.00
65	A13 5k dull vio ('86)	700.00	35.00
	Nos. 60-65 (6)	825.00	42.25

Nos. 53, 54, 56 and 58 Surcharged in Black:

a

b

c

d

e

f

1885			
66	(a) 6c on 5s grn, type I	125.00	30.00
a.	6c on 5s green, type II	200.00	100.00
67	(b) 12c on 50c gray & blk	125.00	30.00
68	(c) 18c on 10s buff, org & black	125.00	30.00
69	(d) 1t on 5fr rose red & black	125.00	30.00
	Nos. 66-69 (4)	500.00	120.00

1887			
70	(e) 3c on 5s grn, type I	125.00	30.00
a.	3c on 5s green, type II	200.00	100.00
71	(a) 6c on 10s buff, org & blk	125.00	30.00
72	(f) 8c on 50c gray & blk	125.00	30.00
	Nos. 70-72 (3)	375.00	90.00

The word "OFFICIEL" indicated that the surcharged stamps were officially authorized.

Surcharges on the same basic stamps of values other than those listed are believed to be bogus.

Counterfeits of Nos. 66-72 abound.

Very fine examples of Nos. 66-72 will have perforations cutting the outer colored border but clear of the inner framelines.

A14

A15

1889 Typo. *Perf. 11, 13½, 11x13½*

73	A14	1c pale rose	2.50	.75
74	A14	2c pale blue	2.50	.75
75	A14	5c lilac	1.50	.50
76	A14	7c brown	7.50	1.50
77	A15	10c black	2.50	.75
78	A15	1k red orange	4.50	.75
79	A15	2k rose	40.00	6.00
80	A15	5k green	25.00	6.00
		Nos. 73-80 (8)	86.00	17.00

All values exist imperforate.
Canceled to order copies of No. 76 abound.
For surcharges see Nos. 622-625.
Nos. 73-80 with average centering, faded colors and/or toned paper sell for much less.

A16

A17

1891 *Perf. 10½, 11½*

81	A16	1c black	2.50	1.00
82	A16	2c brown	2.50	1.00
83	A16	5c deep blue	2.50	.20
84	A16	7c gray	350.00	12.00
85	A16	10c rose	2.50	.50
86	A16	14c orange	2.50	1.50
87	A17	1k green	25.00	2.00
88	A17	2k orange	700.00	25.00
89	A17	5k ocher yellow	8.00	*30.00*
		Nos. 81-89 (9)	1,095.	73.20

For surcharges see Nos. 626-629.

A18

Nasser-eddin Shah Qajar — A19

1894 *Perf. 12½*

90	A18	1c lilac	1.00	.20
91	A18	2c blue green	1.00	.20
92	A18	5c ultramarine	1.00	.20
93	A18	8c brown	1.00	.20

Perf. 11½x11

94	A19	10c orange	1.25	.75
95	A19	16c rose	25.00	50.00
96	A19	1k red & yellow	3.00	.75
97	A19	2k brn org & pale bl	4.00	1.00
98	A19	5k violet & silver	5.00	1.50
99	A19	10k red & gold	15.00	10.00
100	A19	50k green & gold	30.00	10.00
		Nos. 90-100 (11)	87.25	74.80

Canceled to order copies sell for one-third of listed values.
Reprints exist. They are hard to distinguish from the originals. Value, set $15.
See Nos. 104-112, 136-144. For overprints see Nos. 120-128, 152-167, 173-181. For surcharges see Nos. 101-103, 168, 206, 211.

Nos. 93, 98 With Violet or Magenta Surcharge

a

b

1897 *Perf. 12½, 11½x11*

101	A18(a)	5c on 8c brown (V)	25.00	4.00
102	A19(b)	1k on 5k vio & sil (V)	35.00	15.00
103	A19(b)	2k on 5k vio & sil (M)	50.00	30.00
		Nos. 101-103 (3)	110.00	49.00

Forgeries exist.

Lion Type of 1894 and

Mozaffar-eddin Shah Qajar — A22

1898 Typo. *Perf. 12½*

104	A18	1c gray	1.50	.35
105	A18	2c pale brown	1.50	.35
106	A18	3c dull violet	5.00	3.00
107	A18	4c vermilion	5.00	3.00
108	A18	5c yellow	5.00	.25
109	A18	8c orange	10.00	7.00
110	A18	10c light blue	4.00	.50
111	A18	12c rose	3.00	1.00
112	A18	16c green	12.50	7.00
113	A22	1k ultramarine	6.00	1.00
114	A22	2k pink	5.00	2.00
115	A22	3k yellow	5.00	3.00
116	A22	4k gray	8.00	5.00
117	A22	5k emerald	8.00	6.00
118	A22	10k orange	25.00	15.00
119	A22	50k bright vio	40.00	25.00
		Nos. 104-119 (16)	144.50	79.45

Unauthorized reprints of Nos. 104-119 were made from original clichés. Paper shows a vertical mesh. These abound unused and canceled to order. Value unused, hinged, $16.
See Nos. 145-151. For overprints see Nos. 129-135, 182-188. For surcharges see Nos. 169, 171, 207, 209, 215.

Reprints have been used to make counterfeits of Nos. 120-135, 152-167.

Stamps of 1898 Handstamped in Violet:

a

b

c

d

e

f

g

h

1899

120	(a)	1c gray	5.00	5.00
121	(b)	2c pale brown	5.00	*8.00*
122	(b)	3c dull violet	12.00	*15.00*
123	(c)	4c vermilion	18.00	*30.00*
124	(c)	5c yellow	10.00	3.00
125	(d)	8c orange	15.00	*40.00*
126	(d)	10c light blue	6.50	*8.00*
127	(d)	12c rose	15.00	8.00
128	(d)	16c green	25.00	*30.00*
129	(e)	1k ultramarine	25.00	10.00
130	(f)	2k pink	30.00	25.00
131	(f)	3k yellow	80.00	*200.00*
132	(g)	4k gray	100.00	*200.00*
133	(g)	5k emerald	30.00	*40.00*
134	(h)	10k orange	60.00	60.00
135	(h)	50k brt violet	120.00	*150.00*
		Nos. 120-135 (16)	556.50	832.00

The handstamped control marks on Nos. 120-135 exist sideways, inverted and double. Counterfeits are plentiful.

Types of 1894-98

1899 Typo. *Perf. 12½*

136	A18	1c gray, *green*	2.50	.75
137	A18	2c brown, *green*	2.50	.75
138	A18	3c violet, *green*	7.00	5.00
139	A18	4c red, *green*	7.00	5.00
140	A18	5c yellow, *green*	2.50	.30
141	A18	8c orange, *green*	7.00	5.00
142	A18	10c pale blue, *grn*	5.00	.50
143	A18	12c lake, *green*	6.00	1.25
144	A18	16c green, *green*	17.50	5.00
145	A22	1k red	10.00	1.25
146	A22	2k deep green	20.00	8.50
147	A22	3k lilac brown	25.00	17.00
148	A22	4k orange red	25.00	17.00
149	A22	5k gray brown	25.00	17.00
150	A22	10k deep blue	400.00	100.00
151	A22	50k brown	60.00	30.00
		Nos. 136-151 (16)	622.00	214.30

Canceled to order copies abound.
Unauthorized reprints of Nos. 136-151 were made from original clichés. Paper is chalky and has white gum. The design can be seen through the back of the reprints. Value unused, hinged, $30.
For surcharges and overprints see Nos. 171, 173-188, 206-207, 209, 211, 215.

Nos. 104-111 Handstamped in Violet

(Struck once on every two stamps.)

1900

152	A18	1c gray	35.00	15.00
153	A18	2c pale brown	45.00	20.00
154	A18	3c dull violet	70.00	50.00
155	A18	4c vermilion	80.00	50.00
156	A18	5c yellow	20.00	10.00
158	A18	10c light blue	—	—
159	A18	12c rose	80.00	50.00
		Nos. 152-159 (6)	330.00	195.00

Values are for single authenticated copies. Pairs sell for much more.
This control mark, in genuine state, was not applied to the 8c orange (Nos. 109, 125).

Same Overprint Handstamped on Nos. 120-127 in Violet

(Struck once on each block of 4.)

160	A18	1c gray	75.00	50.00
163	A18	4c vermilion	200.00	140.00
164	A18	5c yellow	35.00	20.00
166	A18	10c light blue	300.00	175.00
167	A18	12c rose	80.00	50.00
		Nos. 160-167 (5)	690.00	435.00

Values are for single authenticated copies. Blocks are rare and worth much more.
Counterfeits exist of Nos. 152-167.

No. 93 Surcharged in Violet

1900

168	A18	5c on 8c brown	35.00	2.50

No. 145 Surcharged in Violet

1901

169	A22	12c on 1k red	100.00	100.00
a.		Blue surcharge	125.00	125.00

Counterfeits exist.
Some specialists state that No. 169 with black surcharge was made for collectors.

A23

1902 Violet Surcharge

171	A23	5k on 50k brown	200.00	80.00
a.		Blue surcharge	200.00	90.00

Counterfeits exist. See No. 207.

Nos. 136-151 Overprinted in Black

1902

173	A18	1c gray, *green*	15.00	10.00
174	A18	2c brown, *green*	15.00	10.00
175	A18	3c violet, *green*	15.00	10.00
176	A18	4c red, *green*	75.00	15.00
177	A18	5c yellow, *green*	10.00	5.00
178	A18	8c orange, *green*	20.00	15.00
179	A18	10c pale blue, *grn*	20.00	10.00
180	A18	12c lake, *green*	20.00	10.00
181	A18	16c green, *green*	50.00	25.00
182	A22	1k red	75.00	25.00
183	A22	2k deep green	100.00	50.00
188	A22	50k brown	120.00	75.00

Overprinted on No. 168

206	A18	5c on 8c brown	100.00	50.00

Overprinted on Nos. 171 and 171a

207	A23	5k on 50k brown	200.00	100.00
a.		On #171a	250.00	100.00

Overprinted on Nos. 169 and 169a

209	A22	12c on 1k red	100.00	50.00
a.		On #169a	100.00	50.00

Counterfeits of the overprint of Nos. 173-183, 188, 206-207, 209 are plentiful. Practically all examples with overprint sideways, inverted, double and double with one inverted are frauds.

Nos. 142 and 145 Surcharged in Violet

1902

211	A18	5c on 10c pale bl, *grn*	50.00	20.00

Surcharges in different colors were made for collectors.

Initials of Victor Castaigne, Postmaster of Meshed — A24

1902 Typo. *Imperf.*

222	A24	1c black	—	450.00
a.		Inverted frame		—
b.		Inverted center	—	*3,000.*
223	A24	2c black	—	450.00
a.		Inverted frame		—
b.		"2" in right upper corner	*3,000.*	*1,750.*
c.		Frame printed on both sides	1,000.	—
224	A24	3c black	—	1,000.
225	A24	5c violet	—	200.00
a.		"5" in right upper corner		—
b.		Frame printed on both sides	*2,250.*	*1,000.*
c.		Inverted center		—
226	A24	5c black	—	350.00
a.		Persian "5" in lower left corner		—
b.		Inverted center		—
227	A24	12c dull blue	—	1,250.
a.		Inverted frame		—
b.		Inverted center		—
228	A24	1k rose	—	3,000.

The design of No. 228 differs slightly from the illustration.
Nos. 222-228 were printed in three operations. Inverted centers have frames and

numerals upright. Inverted frames have centers and numerals upright.

Pin-perforated

234 A24 12c dull blue	—	1,500.

The post office at Meshed having exhausted its stock of stamps, the postmaster issued the above series provisionally. The center of the design is the seal of the postmaster who also wrote his initials upon the upper part, using violet ink for the 1k and red for the others.

Unauthorized reprints, including pinperforated examples of Nos. 222-226, and forgeries exist.

Expert knowledge or certificates of authenticity are required.

A25

TWO TYPES:

Type I — "CHAHI" or "KRANS" are in capital letters.

Type II — Only "C" of "Chahi" or "K" of "Krans" is a capital.

The 3c and 5c sometimes have a tall narrow figure in the upper left corner. The 5c is also found with the cross at the upper left broken or missing. These varieties are known with many of the overprints.

Stamps of Design A25 have a faint fancy background in the color of the stamp. All issued stamps have handstamped controls as listed.

Handstamp Overprinted in Black

1902 **Typeset** ***Imperf.***

Type I

235 A25 1c gray & buff	*150.00*	100.00
236 A25 2c brown & buff	*150.00*	100.00
237 A25 3c green & buff	*175.00*	110.00
238 A25 5c red & buff	*100.00*	75.00
239 A25 12c ultra & buff	*200.00*	150.00
Nos. 235-239 (5)	*775.00*	535.00

Counterfeits abound. Type II stamps with this overprint are forgeries.

The 3c with violet overprint is believed not to have been regularly issued.

Handstamp Overprinted in Rose

1902 **Type I**

247 A25 1c gray & buff	20.00	2.00
a. With Persian numerals "2"	100.00	*100.00*
248 A25 2c brown & buff	20.00	2.00
249 A25 3c dp grn & buff	20.00	2.00
250 A25 5c red & buff	20.00	.75
251 A25 10c ol yel & buff	40.00	3.00
252 A25 12c ultra & buff	60.00	5.00
253 A25 1k violet & bl	50.00	6.00
254 A25 2k ol grn & bl	90.00	12.50
256 A25 10k dk bl & bl	150.00	30.00
257 A25 50k red & blue	750.00	600.00
Nos. 247-257 (10)	1,220.	663.25

A 5k exists but its' status is doubtful.

Nos. 247-257 and the 12c on brown paper and on blue paper with blue quadrille lines are known without overprint but are not believed to have been regularly issued in this condition.

The 1c to 10k, A25 type I, with violet overprint are believed not to have been regularly issued. Five denominations also exist with overprint in blue, black or green.

Type II

280 A25 1c gray & yellow	100.00	100.00
281 A25 2c brown & yel	100.00	100.00
282 A25 3c dk grn & yel	150.00	150.00
a. "Persans"	60.00	60.00
283 A25 5c red & yellow	35.00	15.00
284 A25 10c ol yel & yel	75.00	15.00
285 A25 12c blue & yel	100.00	25.00
290 A25 50k org red & bl	850.00	600.00

The 3c, inscribed "Persans," is not believed to have been regularly issued.

The same overprint in violet was applied to nine denominations of the Type II stamps, but these, too, are believed not to have been regularly issued. The overprint also exists in blue, black and green.

Reprints, counterfeits, counterfeit overprints, with or without cancellations, re plentiful for Nos. 247-257, 280-290.

Five stamps of type A25, type II, in high denominations (10, 20, 25, 50 and 100 tomans), with "Postes 1319" lion overprint in blue, were used only on money orders, not for postage. They are usually numbered on the back in red, blue or black.

Handstamp Surcharged in Black

1902

Type I

308 A25 5k on 5k ocher & bl	*175.00*	*50.00*

Counterfeits of No. 308 abound.

This surcharge in rose, violet, blue or green is considered bogus.

This surcharge on 50k orange red and blue, and on 5k ocher and blue, type II, is considered bogus.

Handstamp Overprinted Diagonally in Black

1902

Type I

315 A25 2c brown & buff	175.00	60.00
a. Rose overprint	250.00	125.00

Type II

316 A25 2c brown & yel	—	—
a. Rose overprint	—	—

"P. L." stands for "Poste Locale."

Counterfeits of Nos. 315-316 exist.

Some specialists believe that Type II stamps were not used officially for this overprint.

Handstamp Overprinted in Black or Rose

1902 **Type II**

317 A25 2c brn & yellow	175.00	60.00
318 A25 2c brown & yel (R)	250.00	125.00

Counterfeits of Nos. 317-318 exist.

Overprinted in Blue

1903

Type I

321 A25 1k violet & blue	60.00	60.00

Type II

336 A25 1c gray & yellow	40.00	40.00
337 A25 2c brown & yellow	40.00	40.00
338 A25 5c red & yellow	35.00	35.00
339 A25 10c olive yel & yel	50.00	50.00
340 A25 12c blue & yellow	55.00	55.00
Nos. 321-340 (6)	280.00	280.00

The overprint also exists in violet and black, but it is doubtful whether such items were regularly issued.

Forgeries of Nos. 321, 336-340 abound. Genuine unused examples are seldom found.

Arms of Persia — A26

Mozaffar-eddin Shah Qajar — A27

1903-04 **Typo.** ***Perf. 12½***

351 A26 1c violet	2.00	.20
352 A26 2c gray	2.00	.20
353 A26 3c green	2.00	.20
354 A26 5c rose	2.00	.20
355 A26 10c yellow brn	3.00	1.50
356 A26 12c blue	4.00	.50

Engr.

Perf. 11½x11

357 A27 1k violet	12.00	.50
358 A27 2k ultramarine	20.00	1.25
359 A27 5k orange brn	30.00	2.00
360 A27 10k rose red	30.00	4.00
361 A27 20k orange ('04)	35.00	5.00
362 A27 30k green ('04)	60.00	12.50
363 A27 50k green	400.00	100.00
Nos. 351-363 (13)	602.00	128.05

No. 355 exists with blue diagonal surcharge "1 CHAHI"; its status is questioned.

A government decree in November, 1903, required that all picture postcards be censored by the Central Post Office, which would apply a control mark on each card to show that the 2c tax for this service had been paid. No. 352 was overprinted "Controle" in several styles, for this purpose. Value: unused $100; used, from $25.

See Nos. 428-433. For surcharges and overprints see #364-420, 446-447, 464-469, O8-O28, P1.

No. 353 Surcharged in Violet or Blue

1903

364 A26 1c on 3c green (V)	17.50	12.50
365 A26 2c on 3c green (Bl)	17.50	12.50

A 2c surcharge on No. 354 exists, but its status is dubious.

No. 360 Surcharged in Blue

366 A27 12c on 10k rose red	75.00	40.00
a. Black surcharge		40.00
b. Violet surcharge		40.00
Nos. 364-366 (3)	110.00	65.00

Used values for Nos. 366a-366b are for c-t-o copies.

No. 363 Surcharged in Blue or Black

1903

368 A27 2t on 50k grn (Bl)	150.00	55.00
a. Rose surcharge	175.00	100.00
b. Black surcharge	175.00	100.00
370 A27 3t on 50k grn (Bk)	150.00	55.00
a. Violet surcharge	175.00	55.00
b. Rose surcharge	200.00	125.00

No. 363 Surcharged in Blue or Black

1904

372 A27 2t on 50k grn (Bl)	160.00	55.00
375 A27 3t on 50k grn (Bk)	160.00	55.00

The 2t on 50k also exists with surcharge in rose, violet, black and magenta; the 3t on 50k in rose, violet and blue. Values about the same unused; about 50 percent higher used.

No. 352 Overprinted in Violet

1904 ***Perf. 12½***

393 A26 2c gray	50.00	25.00
a. Black overprint	50.00	25.00
b. Rose overprint	50.00	25.00

This overprint also exists in blue, violet blue, maroon and gray, but these were not regularly issued.

Stamps of 1903 Surcharged in Black:

a

b

c

1904

400 A26(a) 3c on 5c rose	20.00	.75
401 A26(b) 6c on 10c brown	20.00	.75
402 A27(c) 9c on 1k violet	35.00	3.50
Nos. 400-402 (3)	75.00	5.00

Stamps of 1903 Surcharged in Black, Magenta or Violet:

1905-06

404 A26 1c on 3c green ('06)	35.00	15.00
405 A27 1c on 1k violet	35.00	15.00
406 A27 2c on 5k orange brn	40.00	25.00
407 A26 1c on 3c grn (M) ('06)	15.00	5.00
408 A27 1c on 1k violet (M)	20.00	10.00
409 A27 2c on 5k org brn (V)	30.00	15.00
Nos. 404-409 (6)	175.00	85.00

Nos. 355 and 358 Surcharged in Violet

419 A26 1c on 10c brown	*150.00*	*300.00*
420 A27 2c on 2k ultra	*250.00*	*500.00*

Forgeries of Nos. 419-420 are common. Forgeries of No. 420, especially, are hard to distinguish since the original handstamp was used. Genuine used copies may, in some cases, be identified by the cancellation.

A28

Typeset; "Provisoire" Overprint Handstamped in Black

1906 *Imperf.*

No.	Type	Description	Unused	Used
422	A28	1c violet	5.00	1.00
a.		Irregular pin perf. or perf. 10½	40.00	15.00
423	A28	2c gray	7.50	5.00
424	A28	3c green	5.00	1.00
425	A28	6c red	7.50	.75
426	A28	10c brown	60.00	45.00
427	A28	13c blue	35.00	10.00
		Nos. 422-427 (6)	120.00	62.75

Stamps of type A28 have a faint background pattern of tiny squares within squares, an ornamental frame and open rectangles for the value corners.

The 3c and 6c also exist perforated.

Nos. 422-427 are known without overprint but were probably not issued in that condition. Nearly all values are known with overprint inverted and double.

Forgeries are plentiful.

Lion Type of 1903 and

Mohammed-Ali Shah Qajar
A29 A30

1907-09 **Typo.** *Perf. 12½*

No.	Type	Description	Unused	Used
428	A26	1c vio, *blue*	2.00	.25
429	A26	2c gray, *blue*	2.00	.25
430	A26	3c green, *blue*	2.00	.25
431	A26	6c rose, *blue*	2.00	.25
432	A26	9c org, *blue*	2.00	.30
433	A26	10c brown, *blue*	3.00	1.00

Engr.

Perf. 11, 11½

No.	Type	Description	Unused	Used
434	A29	13c dark blue	4.00	2.00
435	A29	1k red	6.50	1.50
436	A29	26c red brown	5.00	2.00
437	A29	2k deep grn	12.50	1.50
438	A29	3k pale blue	15.00	1.00
439	A29	4k brt yellow	300.00	10.00
440	A29	4k bister	15.00	3.00
441	A29	5k dark brown	15.00	3.00
442	A29	10k pink	20.00	3.00
443	A29	20k gray black	20.00	10.00
444	A29	30k dark violet	20.00	15.00
445	A30	50k gold, ver & black ('09)	100.00	25.00
		Nos. 428-445 (18)	546.00	79.30

Frame of No. 445 lithographed. Nos. 434-444 were issued in 1908.

Remainders canceled to order abound. Used values for Nos. 437-445 are for c-t-os.

Nos. 428-429 Overprinted in Black

1909 *Perf. 12½*

No.	Type	Description	Unused	Used
446	A26	1c violet, *blue*	60.00	30.00
447	A26	2c gray, *blue*	60.00	30.00

Counterfeits of Nos. 446-447 exist.

Coat of Arms — A31

1909 **Typo.** *Perf. 12½x12*

No.	Type	Description	Unused	Used
448	A31	1c org & maroon	.50	.35
449	A31	2c vio & maroon	.50	.35
450	A31	3c yel grn & mar	.50	.35
451	A31	6c red & maroon	.50	.25
452	A31	9c gray & maroon	.50	.35
453	A31	10c red vio & mar	.50	.35
454	A31	13c dk blue & mar	.50	2.00
455	A31	1k sil, vio & bis brown	1.00	2.00
456	A31	26c dk grn & mar	1.00	3.00
457	A31	2k sil, dk grn & bis brown	1.00	2.00
458	A31	3k sil, gray & bis brown	1.00	3.50
459	A31	4k sil, by & bis brn	1.00	3.50
460	A31	5k gold, brn & bis brown	2.50	3.50
461	A31	10k gold, org & bis brown	5.00	10.00
462	A31	20k gold, ol grn & bister brn	7.00	20.00
463	A31	30k gold, car & bis brown	12.00	20.00
		Nos. 448-463 (16)	35.00	71.50

Unauthorized reprints of Nos. 448-463 abound. Originals have clean, bright colors, centers stand out clearly, and paper is much thinner. Nos. 460-463 originals have gleaming gold margins; reprint margins appear as blackish yellow. Centers of reprints of Nos. 448-454, 456 are brown.

Values above are for unused reprints and for authenticated used stamps. Original unused stamps sell for much higher prices.

For surcharges & overprints see #516-519, 541-549. 582-585, 588-594, 597, 601-606, 707-722, C1-C16, O31-O40.

Nos. 428-444, Imperf., Surcharged in Red or Black:

1910 **Blue Paper** *Imperf.*

No.	Type	Description	Unused	Used
464	A26	1c on 1c violet	160.00	110.00
465	A26	1c on 2c gray	160.00	110.00
466	A26	1c on 3c green	160.00	110.00
467	A26	1c on 6c rose (Bk)	160.00	110.00
468	A26	1c on 9c orange	160.00	110.00
469	A26	1c on 10c brown	160.00	110.00

White Paper

No.	Type	Description	Unused	Used
470	A29	2c on 13c dp bl	160.00	110.00
471	A29	2c on 26c red brown (Bk)	160.00	110.00
472	A29	2c on 1k red (Bk)	160.00	110.00
473	A29	2c on 2k dp grn	160.00	110.00
474	A29	2c on 3k pale bl	160.00	110.00
475	A29	2c on 4k brt yel	160.00	110.00
476	A29	2c on 4k bister	160.00	110.00
477	A29	2c on 5k dk brn	160.00	110.00
478	A29	2c on 10k pink (Bk)	160.00	110.00
479	A29	2c on 20k gray blk	160.00	110.00
480	A29	2c on 30k dk vio	160.00	110.00
		Nos. 464-480 (17)	2,720.	1,870.

Nos. 464-480 were prepared for use on newspapers, but nearly the entire printing was sold to stamp dealers. The issue is generally considered speculative. Counterfeit surcharges exist on trimmed stamps.

Used values are for c-t-o.

Ahmad Shah Qajar — A32

Perf. 11½, 11½x11, 11½x12
Engr. center, Typo. frame

1911-13

No.	Type	Description	Unused	Used
481	A32	1c green & org	.50	.20
482	A32	2c red & sepia	.50	.20
483	A32	3c gray brn & grn	.50	.20
a.		3c bister brown & green	.50	1.00
484	A32	5c brn & car ('13)	.50	.75
485	A32	6c gray & car	.50	.20
486	A32	6c grn & red brown ('13)	.50	.20
487	A32	9c yel brn & vio	.75	.20
488	A32	10c red & org brn	.75	.20
489	A32	12c grn & ultra ('13)	.50	.50
490	A32	13c violet & ultra	1.00	2.00
491	A32	1k ultra & car	1.00	.50
492	A32	24c vio & grn ('13)	1.00	1.00
493	A32	26c ultra & green	1.00	5.00
494	A32	2k grn & red vio	2.00	1.00
495	A32	3k violet & blk	2.00	1.50
496	A32	4k ultramarine & gray ('13)	2.00	20.00
497	A32	5k red & ultra	3.00	2.00
498	A32	10k ol bis & cl	5.00	3.00
499	A32	20k vio brn & bis	6.00	4.00
500	A32	30k red & green	7.00	5.00
		Nos. 481-500 (20)	36.00	47.65

Values for Nos. 481-500 unused are for reprints, which cannot be distinguished from the late printings of the stamps. These are perf 11½ (11½x12 for the 4k) with the distance between the inner lines of the inscription tablets at top and bottom of the portrait being 19mm. Unused stamps with other perfs or a shorter vignette sell for much higher prices.

The reprints include inverted centers for some denominations.

For surcharges and overprints see Nos. 501-515, 520-540, 586-587, 595, 598, 600, 607-609, 630-634, 646-666.

Stamps of 1911 Overprinted in Black

1911

No.	Type	Description	Unused	Used
501	A32	1c grn & orange	20.00	3.00
502	A32	2c red & sepia	20.00	3.00
503	A32	3c gray brn & grn	20.00	3.00
504	A32	6c gray & carmine	20.00	3.00
505	A32	9c yel brn & vio	20.00	3.00
506	A32	10c red & org brn	30.00	3.00
507	A32	13c vio & ultra	30.00	5.00
508	A32	1k ultra & car	70.00	7.00
509	A32	26c ultra & green	50.00	10.00
510	A32	2k grn & red vio	70.00	10.00
511	A32	3k vio & black	100.00	10.00
512	A32	5k red & ultra	150.00	15.00
513	A32	10k ol bis & claret	300.00	30.00
514	A32	20k vio brn & bis	300.00	30.00
515	A32	30k red & green	400.00	40.00
		Nos. 501-515 (15)	1,600.	175.00

The "Officiel" overprint does not signify that the stamps were intended for use on official correspondence but that they were issued by authority. It was applied to the stocks in Tabriz and all post offices in the Tabriz region after a large quantity of stamps had been stolen during the Russian occupation of Tabriz.

The "Officiel" overprint has been counterfeited.

Stamps of 1909-11 Overprinted in Black

On #449-451, 454

1911, Oct.

No.	Type	Description	Unused	Used
516	A31	2c vio & maroon	100.00	50.00
517	A31	3c yel grn & mar	100.00	50.00
518	A31	6c red & maroon	100.00	50.00
519	A31	13c dk blue & mar	125.00	75.00

On #482-483, 485, 490

No.	Type	Description	Unused	Used
520	A32	2c red & sepia	100.00	50.00
521	A32	3c gray brn & grn	100.00	50.00
522	A32	6c gray & car	100.00	50.00
523	A32	13c violet & ultra	125.00	75.00

Stamps were sold at a 10% discount to stagecoach station keepers on the Tehran-Recht route. To prevent speculation, these stamps were overprinted "Stagecoach Stations" in French and Farsi.

Forgeries exist, usually overprinted on reprints of the 1909 issue and used copies of the 1911 issue. Values are for authenticated copies.

In 1912 this overprint, reading "Sultan Mohammad Ali-Shah Kajar," was handstamped on outgoing mail in the Persian Kurdistan region occupied by the forces of the former Shah Mohammed-Ali. It was applied after the stamps were on cover and is found on 8 of the Ahmad Shah Qajar stamps of 1911 (1c, 2c, 3c, 6c, 9c, 13c, 1k and 26c). Some specialists add the 10c. Forgeries are abundant.

Nos. 490 and 493 Surcharged:

a

b

1914

No.	Type	Description	Unused	Used
535	A32(a)	1c on 13c	17.50	2.00
536	A32(b)	3c on 26c	17.50	4.00

In 1914 a set of 19 stamps was prepared as a coronation issue. The 10 lower values each carry a different portrait; the 9 higher values show buildings and scenes. The same set printed with black centers was overprinted in red "SERVICE." The stamps were never placed in use, but were sold to stamp dealers in 1923.

Nos. 484 and 489 Surcharged in Black or Violet:

c

d

1915

No.	Type	Description	Unused	Used
537	A32(c)	1c on 5c	15.00	2.00
538	A32(c)	2c on 5c (V)	15.00	2.00
539	A32(c)	2c on 5c	125.00	40.00
540	A32(d)	6c on 12c	20.00	2.00
		Nos. 537-540 (4)	175.00	46.00

Nos. 455, 454 Surcharged:

e

f

1915 *Perf. 12½x12*

No.	Type	Description	Unused	Used
541	A31(e)	5c on 1k multi	27.50	5.00
542	A31(f)	12c on 13c multi	32.50	7.00

Counterfeit surcharges on reprints abound.

Nos. 448-453, 455 Overprinted

1915

543	A31	1c org & maroon	15.00	2.00
544	A31	2c vio & maroon	15.00	2.00
545	A31	3c grn & maroon	15.00	2.00
546	A31	6c red & maroon	15.00	2.00
547	A31	9c gray & maroon	15.00	3.00
548	A31	10c red vio & mar	50.00	5.00
549	A31	1k sil, vio & bis brn	75.00	5.00
		Nos. 543-549 (7)	200.00	21.00

This overprint ("1333") also exists on the 2k, 10k, 20k and 30k, but they were not issued.

Counterfeit overprints, usually on reprints, abound.

Imperial Crown — A33

King Darius, Farohar overhead — A34

Ruins of Persepolis — A35

Perf. 11½ or Compound 11x11½

Engr., Typo.

1915, Mar. **Wmk. 161**

560	A33	1c car & indigo	.20	*2.00*
561	A33	2c bl & carmine	.20	*2.00*
562	A33	3c dark green	.20	*2.00*
a.		Inverted center		—
564	A33	5c red	.20	*2.50*
565	A33	6c olive grn & car	.20	*2.00*
a.		Inverted center		—
566	A33	9c yel brn & vio	.20	*2.00*
567	A33	10c bl grn & yel brn	.20	*2.00*
568	A33	12c ultramarine	.20	*2.00*
569	A34	1k sil, yel brn & gray	.65	*5.00*
570	A33	24c yel brn & dk brn	.25	*5.00*
571	A34	2k silver, bl & rose	.65	*5.00*
572	A34	3k sil, vio & brn	.65	*5.00*
573	A34	5k sil, brn & green	.65	*7.00*
574	A35	1t gold, pur & blk	.65	*10.00*
575	A35	2t gold, grn & brn	1.00	*10.00*
576	A35	3t gold, cl & red brn	1.00	*10.00*
577	A35	5t gold, blue & ind	1.00	*10.00*
		Nos. 560-577 (17)	8.10	*83.50*

Coronation of Shah Ahmed.

Nos. 560-568, 570 are engraved. Nos. 569, 571-573 are engraved except for silver margins. Nos. 574-577 have centers engraved, frames typographed.

The 3c and 6c with inverted centers are considered genuine errors. Unauthorized reprints exist of these varieties and of other denominations with inverted centers. **Values unused for Nos. 560-577 are for reprints.**

For surcharges and overprints see Nos. 610-616, 635-646, O41-O57, Q19-Q35.

Nos. 455, 461-463 Overprinted

1915 Unwmk. Typo. ***Perf. 12½x12***

582	A31	1k sil, vio & bis brn	*2.00*	*20.00*
583	A31	10k multicolored	*5.00*	*30.00*
584	A31	20k multicolored	*7.00*	*100.00*
585	A31	30k multicolored	*12.00*	*60.00*
		Nos. 582-585 (4)	*26.00*	*210.00*

Genuine unused examples are rare. Most unused copies offered in the marketplace are reprints, and the unused values above are for reprints. Used values for for authenticated copies.

Forgeries abound of Nos. 582-585.

No. 491 Surcharged

1917 ***Perf. 11½***

586	A32	12c on 1k multi	*1,200.*	*850.00*
587	A32	24c on 1k multi	*700.00*	*475.00*

Issued during the Turkish occupation of Kermanshah. Forgeries exist.

Values for unused stamps are for reprints. Unused examples of the original stamps are rare, and most copies offered in the marketplace are reprints.

No. 448 Overprinted "1335" in Persian Numerals

1917 ***Perf. 12½x12***

588	A31	1c org & maroon	*350.00*	250.00

Overprint on No. 588 is similar to date in "k" and "l" surcharges. Forgeries exist.

Nos. 449, 452-453, 456 Surcharged:

k

l

1917

589	A31(k)	1c on 2c	20.00	3.00
590	A31(k)	1c on 9c	25.00	4.00
591	A31(k)	1c on 10c	20.00	3.00
592	A31(l)	3c on 9c	25.00	4.00
593	A31(l)	3c on 10c	20.00	3.00
594	A31(l)	3c on 26c	30.00	5.00

Same Surcharge on No. 488

595	A32(k)	1c on 10c	37.50	1.50
596	A32(l)	3c on 10c	37.50	1.50

Nos. 454 & 491 Surcharged Type "e"

597	A31	5c on 13c	25.00	5.00
598	A32	5c on 1k	20.00	2.00

Counterfeit surcharges on "canceled" reprints of Nos. 449, 452-454, 456 abound.

No. 489 Surcharged

600	A32	6c on 12c grn & ultra	65.00	15.00

No. 457 Overprinted

1918

601	A31	2k multi	55.00	10.00

Nos. 459-460 Surcharged:

1918

602	A31	24c on 4k multi	62.50	10.00
603	A31	10k on 5k multi	100.00	15.00

The surcharges of Nos. 602-603 have been counterfeited.

Nos. 457-463 Overprinted

1918

603A	A31	2k multicolored	*3.00*	*65.00*
604	A31	3k multicolored	*3.00*	*15.00*
604A	A31	4k multicolored	*5.00*	*150.00*
604B	A31	5k multicolored	*5.00*	*75.00*
605	A31	10k multicolored	*8.00*	*50.00*
605A	A31	20k multicolored	*20.00*	*200.00*
606	A31	30k multicolored	*15.00*	*100.00*
		Nos. 603A-606 (7)	*59.00*	*655.00*

Genuine unused examples are rare. Most unused copies offered in the marketplace are reprints, and the unused values above are for reprints. Used values for for authenticated copies.

Forgeries abound of Nos. 603A-606.

Nos. 489, 488 and 491 Surcharged:

m

n

607	A32(m)	3c on 12c	50.00	1.50
608	A32(n)	6c on 10c	35.00	1.50
609	A32(m)	6c on 1k	35.00	1.50
		Nos. 607-609 (3)	120.00	4.50

Genuine unused examples are rare. Most unused copies offered in the marketplace are reprints, and the unused values above are for reprints.

Nos. 571-577 Overprinted in Black or Red

1918 **Wmk. 161**

610	A34	2k sil, blue & rose	10.00	10.00
611	A34	3k sil, vio & brn (R)	10.00	10.00
612	A34	5k sil, brn & grn (R)	10.00	10.00
613	A35	1t gold, pur & black (R)	15.00	15.00
614	A35	2t gold, grn & brn	15.00	15.00
615	A35	3t gold, cl & red brn	15.00	15.00
616	A35	5t gold, bl & ind (R)	15.00	20.00
		Nos. 610-616 (7)	90.00	95.00

The overprint commemorates the end of World War I. Counterfeits of this overprint are plentiful.

A36

Color Litho., Black Typo.

1919 **Unwmk.** ***Perf. 11½***

617	A36	1c yel & black	15.00	1.00
618	A36	3c green & black	15.00	1.00
619	A36	5c rose & black	35.00	3.00
620	A36	6c vio & black	25.00	1.00
621	A36	12c blue & black	60.00	10.00
		Nos. 617-621 (5)	150.00	16.00

Nos. 617-621 exist imperf., in colors other than the originals, with centers inverted and double impressions. Some specialists call them fraudulent, others call them reprints.

This issue has been extensively counterfeited, and most examples in the marketplace are forgeries.

Counterfeits having double line over "POSTES" abound.

Nos. 75, 85-86 Surcharged in Various Colors

1919 ***Perf. 10½, 11, 11½, 13½***

622	A14	2k on 5c lilac (Bk)	7.50	7.50
623	A14	3k on 5c lilac (Br)	7.50	7.50
624	A14	4k on 5c lilac (G)	7.50	7.50
625	A14	5k on 5c lilac (V)	7.50	7.50
626	A16	10k on 10c rose (Bl)	20.00	20.00
627	A16	20k on 10c rose (G)	20.00	20.00
628	A16	30k on 10c rose (Br)	20.00	20.00
629	A16	50k on 14c org (V)	20.00	20.00
		Nos. 622-629 (8)	110.00	110.00

Nos. 622-629 exist with inverted and double surcharge. Some specialists consider these fraudulent.

Nos. 486, 489 Handstamp Surcharged

1921 ***Perf. 11½, 11½x11***

630	A32	10c on 6c	75.00	15.00
631	A32	1k on 12c	75.00	15.00

Counterfeits exist.

No. 489 Surcharged

632	A32	6c on 12c	225.00	15.00

Nos. 486, 489 Surcharged in Violet:

1921

633	A32	10c on 6c	120.00	40.00
a.		Surcharge handstamped in black	350.00	350.00
634	A32	1k on 12c	120.00	40.00
a.		Surcharge handstamped in black	350.00	350.00

Counterfeits exist.

Coronation Issue of 1915 Overprinted

1921, May **Wmk. 161** ***Perf. 11, 11½***

635	A33	3c dark grn	15.00	
a.		Center and overprint inverted		—
636	A33	5c red	15.00	
637	A33	6c olive grn & car	15.00	
638	A33	10c bl grn & yel brn	15.00	
639	A33	12c ultramarine	15.00	
640	A34	1k sil, yel brn & gray	20.00	
641	A34	2k sil, blue & rose	20.00	
642	A34	5k sil, brn & green	20.00	
643	A35	2t gold, grn & brn	25.00	

No.	Type	Description	Unused	Used
644	A35	3t gold, cl & red brn	30.00	
645	A35	5t gold, blue & ind	30.00	
		Nos. 635-645 (11)	220.00	

Counterfeits of this Feb. 21, 1921, overprint are plentiful. Inverted overprints exist on all values; some specialists consider them fraudulent.

Stamps of 1911-13 Overprinted

1922 Unwmk. *Perf. 11½, 11½x11*

No.	Type	Description	Unused	Used
646	A32	1c grn & orange	3.00	.20
a.		Inverted overprint	—	
647	A32	2c red & sepia	3.00	.20
648	A32	3c brn & green	*3.00*	.20
a.		3c bister brown & green	8.00	.20
649	A32	5c brown & car	75.00	25.00
650	A32	6c grn & red brn	5.00	.20
651	A32	9c yel brn & vio	5.00	.20
652	A32	10c red & org brn	6.00	.20
a.		Double ovpt., one inverted		
653	A32	12c green & ultra	10.00	.50
654	A32	1k ultra & car	15.00	1.00
655	A32	24c vio & green	15.00	1.00
656	A32	2k grn & red vio	40.00	1.00
657	A32	3k vio & black	45.00	1.50
658	A32	4k ultra & gray	60.00	20.00
659	A32	5k red & ultra	50.00	2.00
660	A32	10k ol bis & cl	*275.00*	5.00
661	A32	20k vio brn & bis	*300.00*	7.00
662	A32	30k red & green	*425.00*	10.00
		Nos. 646-662 (17)	*1,335.*	75.20

The status of inverted overprints on 5c and 12c is dubious. Unlisted inverts on other denominations are generally considered fraudulent. Counterfeits of this overprint exist.

Nos. 653, 655 Surcharged

1922

No.	Type	Description	Unused	Used
663	A32	3c on 12c	55.00	1.00
664	A32	6c on 24c	55.00	2.00

Nos. 661-662 Surcharged:

1923

No.	Type	Description	Unused	Used
665	A32	10c on 20k	80.00	10.00
666	A32	1k on 30k	110.00	15.00

Ahmed Shah Qajar — A37

Perf. 11½, 11x11½, 11½x11

1924-25 Engr.

No.	Type	Description	Unused	Used
667	A37	1c orange	2.50	.20
668	A37	2c magenta	2.50	.20
669	A37	3c orange brown	2.50	.20
670	A37	6c black brown	2.50	.20
671	A37	9c dark green	2.00	.75
672	A37	10c dark violet	2.00	.30
673	A37	12c red	2.00	.30
674	A37	1k dark blue	2.00	.35
675	A37	2k indigo & red	2.00	1.00
a.		Center inverted	6,500.	*3,000.*
676	A37	3k dk vio & red brown	17.00	2.00
677	A37	5k red & brown	20.00	*30.00*
678	A37	10k choc & lilac	15.00	25.00
679	A37	20k dk grn & brn	30.00	30.00
680	A37	30k org & blk brn	40.00	40.00
		Nos. 667-680 (14)	142.00	130.50

For overprints see Nos. 703-706.

A38

SIX CHAHIS

Type I

Type II

Dated 1924

Color Litho., Black Typo.

1924 *Perf. 11*

No.	Type	Description	Unused	Used
681	A38	1c yel brn & blk	3.00	1.00
682	A38	2c gray & blk	3.00	1.00
683	A38	3c dp rose & blk	3.00	1.00
684	A38	6c orange & blk (I)	5.00	1.50
a.		6c orange & blk (II)	5.00	2.00
		Nos. 681-684 (4)	14.00	4.50

The 1c was surcharged "Chahis" by error. Later the "s" was blocked out in black.

Counterfeits having double line over "POSTES" are plentiful.

Dated 1925

1925

No.	Type	Description	Unused	Used
686	A38	2c yel grn & blk	3.00	.50
687	A38	3c red & blk	3.00	.50
689	A38	6c chalky bl & blk	3.00	.50
690	A38	9c lt brn & blk	12.00	1.00
691	A38	10c gray & blk	20.00	3.00
694	A38	1k emer & blk	40.00	7.00
695	A38	2k lilac & blk	110.00	25.00
		Nos. 686-695 (7)	191.00	37.50

Counterfeits having double line over "POSTES" are plentiful.

A39

Gold Overprint on Treasury Department Stamps

1925

No.	Type	Description	Unused	Used
697	A39	1c red	7.00	4.00
698	A39	2c yellow	7.00	4.00
699	A39	3c yellow green	7.00	4.00
700	A39	5c dark gray	30.00	20.00
701	A39	10c deep orange	15.00	5.00
702	A39	1k ultramarine	15.00	10.00
		Nos. 697-702 (6)	81.00	47.00

Deposition of Ahmad Shah Qajar and establishment of provisional government of Reza Shah Pahlavi.

#697-702 have same center (Persian lion in sunburst) with 6 different frames. Overprint reads: "Post / Provisional Government / of Pahlavi / 9th Abanmah / 1304 / 1925."

Nos. 667-670 Overprinted

1926 *Perf. 11½, 11x11½, 11½x11*

No.	Type	Description	Unused	Used
703	A37	1c orange	3.00	1.50
704	A37	2c magenta	3.00	2.00
705	A37	3c orange brown	3.00	1.50
706	A37	6c black brown	75.00	75.00
		Nos. 703-706 (4)	84.00	80.00

Overprinted to commemorate the Pahlavi dynasty, dated 16 December 1925. Counterfeits exist.

Nos. 448-463 Overprinted

1926 *Perf. 11½, 12½x12*

No.	Type	Description	Unused	Used
707	A31	1c org & maroon	7.00	.25
a.		Inverted overprint	500.00	
708	A31	2c vio & maroon	7.00	.25
709	A31	3c yel grn & mar	7.00	.25
a.		Inverted overprint	500.00	
710	A31	6c red & maroon	7.00	.25
711	A31	9c gray & maroon	7.00	.25
712	A31	10c red vio & mar	7.00	.35
713	A31	13c dk bl & mar	15.00	.35
714	A31	1k multi	30.00	.35
715	A31	26c dk grn & mar	15.00	.35
716	A31	2k multi	30.00	.50
717	A31	3k multi	70.00	.50
718	A31	4k sil, bl & bis brn	500.00	10.00
719	A31	5k multi	150.00	8.00
720	A31	10k multi	400.00	8.50
721	A31	20k multi	500.00	10.00
722	A31	30k multi	500.00	12.00
		Nos. 707-722 (16)	2,252.	52.15

Overprinted to commemorate the Pahlavi government in 1926.

Values for Nos. 707-722 are for stamps perf. 11½, on thick paper. Copies perf. 12½x12 on thin paper are worth substantially more.

Forgeries exist perf. 12½x12, with either machine overprints or handstamps. Most of these fakes can be identified by the absence of the top serif of the "1" in "1926."

A40

Reza Shah Pahlavi — A41

1926-29 Typo. *Perf. 11*

No.	Type	Description	Unused	Used
723	A40	1c yellow green	4.00	.20
724	A40	2c gray violet	4.00	.20
725	A40	3c emerald	4.00	.20
727	A40	6c magenta	5.00	.25
728	A40	9c rose	10.00	.50
729	A40	10c bister brown	20.00	5.00
730	A40	12c deep orange	25.00	3.00
731	A40	15c pale ultra	30.00	2.00
733	A41	1k dull bl ('27)	50.00	10.00
734	A41	2k brt vio ('29)	150.00	50.00
		Nos. 723-734 (10)	302.00	71.35

1928 Redrawn

No.	Type	Description	Unused	Used
740	A40	1c yellow green	25.00	.25
741	A40	2c gray violet	25.00	.25
742	A40	3c emerald	25.00	.25
743	A40	6c rose	25.00	.50
		Nos. 740-743 (4)	100.00	1.25

On the redrawn stamps much of the shading of the face, throat, collar, etc., has been removed.

The letters of "Postes Persanes" and those in the circle at upper right are smaller. The redrawn stamps measure 20¼x25¾mm instead of 19¾x25¼mm.

A42

Reza Shah Pahlavi — A43

Perf. 11½, 12, 12½, Compound

1929 Photo.

No.	Type	Description	Unused	Used
744	A42	1c yel grn & cer	2.00	.25
745	A42	2c scar & brt blue	2.00	.25
746	A42	3c mag & myr grn	2.00	.25
747	A42	6c yel brn & ol grn	2.00	.25
748	A42	9c Prus bl & ver	3.00	.25
749	A42	10c bl grn & choc	4.00	.25
750	A42	12c gray blk & pur	6.00	.30
751	A42	15c citron & ultra	7.00	.30
752	A42	1k dull bl & blk	10.00	.50
753	A42	24c ol grn & red brn	7.00	.50

Engr.

Perf. 11½

No.	Type	Description	Unused	Used
754	A42	2k brn org & dk vio	100.00	1.50
755	A42	3k dark grn & dp rose	125.00	2.00
756	A42	5k red brn & dp green	50.00	2.00
757	A42	1t ultra & dp rose	50.00	5.00
758	A42	2t carmine & blk	75.00	15.00

Engr. and Typo.

No.	Type	Description	Unused	Used
759	A43	3t gold & dp vio	125.00	25.00
		Nos. 744-759 (16)	570.00	53.60

For overprints see Nos. 810-817.

Reza Shah Pahlavi — A44

1931-32 Litho. *Perf. 11*

No.	Type	Description	Unused	Used
760	A44	1c ol brn & ultra	3.00	.20
761	A44	2c red brn & blk	3.00	.20
762	A44	3c lilac rose & ol	3.00	.20
763	A44	6c red org & vio	3.00	.20
764	A44	9c ultra & red org	10.00	.40
765	A44	10c ver & gray	20.00	1.00
766	A44	11c bl & dull red	30.00	20.00
767	A44	12c turq blue & lil rose	40.00	.70
768	A44	16c black & red	40.00	1.75
769	A44	1k car & turq bl	80.00	1.75
770	A44	27c dk gray & dl bl	70.00	1.75
		Nos. 760-770 (11)	302.00	28.15

For overprints see Nos. 818-826.

A45

Reza Shah Pahlavi — A46

1933-34

No.	Type	Description	Unused	Used
771	A45	5d olive brown	1.50	.25
772	A45	10d blue	1.50	.25
773	A45	15d gray	1.50	.25
774	A45	30d emerald	1.50	.25
775	A45	45d turq blue	2.00	.50
776	A45	50d magenta	3.00	.50
777	A45	60d green	4.00	.50
778	A45	75d brown	7.00	1.00
779	A45	90d red	8.00	1.50
780	A46	1r dk rose & blk	20.00	1.00
781	A46	1.20r gray blk & rose	25.00	1.00
782	A46	1.50 citron & bl	30.00	1.00
783	A46	2r lt bl & choc	40.00	1.00
784	A46	3r mag & green	55.00	2.00
785	A46	5r dk brn & red org	200.00	35.00
		Nos. 771-785 (15)	400.00	46.00

For overprints see Nos. 795-809.

"Justice"
A47

"Education"
A49

Ruins of Persepolis
A48

Tehran Airport
A50

Sanatorium at Sakhtessar — A51

Cement Factory, Chah-Abdul-Azim — A52

Gunboat "Palang"
A53

Railway Bridge over Karun River
A54

Post Office and Customs Building, Tehran
A55

1935, Feb. 21 Photo. *Perf. 12½*

786	A47	5d red brn & grn	1.00	.75
787	A48	10d red org & gray black	1.00	.75
788	A49	15d mag & Prus bl	1.50	.75
789	A50	30d black & green	1.50	.75
790	A51	45d ol grn & red brn	2.00	.75
791	A52	75d grn & dark brn	6.00	1.25
792	A53	90d blue & car rose	20.00	5.00
793	A54	1r red brn & pur	50.00	20.00
794	A55	1½r violet & ultra	25.00	10.00
		Nos. 786-794 (9)	108.00	40.00

Reign of Riza Shah Pahlavi, 10th anniv.

Stamps of 1933-34 Overprinted in Black

1935 *Perf. 11*

795	A45	5d olive brown	1.50	.50
796	A45	10d blue	1.50	.50
797	A45	15d gray	2.00	.50
798	A45	30d emerald	2.00	.50
799	A45	45d turq blue	7.00	1.75
800	A45	50d magenta	4.00	.50
801	A45	60d green	4.00	.50
802	A45	75d brown	7.50	5.00
803	A45	90d red	25.00	25.00
804	A46	1r dk rose & blk	75.00	*100.00*
805	A46	1.20r gray black & rose	10.00	1.50
806	A46	1.50r citron & bl	10.00	1.50
807	A46	2r lt bl & choc	30.00	1.50
808	A46	3r mag & green	50.00	7.00
809	A46	5r dk brn & red org	250.00	250.00
		Nos. 795-809 (15)	479.50	396.25

Same Overprint on Stamps of 1929

1935 *Perf. 12, 12x12½*

810	A42	1c yel green & cer	425.00	*600.00*
811	A42	2c scar & brt blue	275.00	*400.00*
812	A42	3c mag & myr grn	175.00	*200.00*
813	A42	6c yel brn & ol grn	140.00	*150.00*
814	A42	9c Prus bl & ver	85.00	80.00

Perf. 11½

815	A42	1t ultra & dp rose	42.50	30.00
816	A42	2t carmine & blk	50.00	40.00
817	A43	3t gold & dp vio	70.00	50.00
		Nos. 810-817 (8)	1,262.	1,550.

No. 817 is overprinted vertically.
Forged overprints exist.

Same Ovpt. on Stamps of 1931-32

1935 *Perf. 11*

818	A44	1c ol brn & ultra	340.00	325.00
819	A44	2c red brn & blk	125.00	125.00
820	A44	3c lilac rose & ol	90.00	100.00
821	A44	6c red org & vio	175.00	175.00
822	A44	9c ultra & red org	200.00	225.00
823	A44	11c blue & dull red	12.50	3.50
824	A44	12c turq bl & lil rose	375.00	500.00
825	A44	16c black & red	15.00	5.00
826	A44	27c dk gray & dull bl	19.00	5.00
		Nos. 818-826 (9)	1,351.	1,463.

Forged overprints exist.

Reza Shah Pahlavi — A56

1935 Photo. *Perf. 11*

Size: 19x27mm

827	A56	5d violet	2.00	.20
828	A56	10d lilac rose	2.00	.20
829	A56	15d turquoise bl	2.00	.20
830	A56	30d emerald	2.00	.20
831	A56	45d orange	2.00	.20
832	A56	50d dull lt brn	2.75	.30
833	A56	60d ultramarine	10.00	.65
834	A56	75d red orange	10.00	.75
835	A56	90d rose	12.50	.75

Size: 21½x31mm

836	A56	1r dull lilac	25.00	.50
837	A56	1.50r blue	25.00	2.00
838	A56	2r dk olive grn	40.00	.75
839	A56	3r dark brown	45.00	2.00
840	A56	5r slate black	250.00	15.00
		Nos. 827-840 (14)	430.25	23.70

Reza Shah Pahlavi
A57 A58

1936-37 Litho. *Perf. 11*

Size: 20x27mm

841	A57	5d bright vio	2.00	.20
842	A57	10d magenta	2.00	.20
843	A57	15d bright ultra	2.00	.20
844	A57	30d yellow green	2.00	.20
845	A57	45d vermilion	3.00	.20
846	A57	50d black brn ('37)	3.00	.20
847	A57	60d brown orange	3.00	.20
848	A57	75d rose lake	3.00	.25
849	A57	90d rose red	5.00	.35

Size: 23x31mm

850	A57	1r turq green	15.00	.25
851	A57	1.50r deep blue	15.00	.35
852	A57	2r bright blue	20.00	.35
853	A57	3r violet brown	25.00	.80
854	A57	5r slate green	40.00	1.25
855	A57	10r dark brown & ultra ('37)	200.00	20.00
		Nos. 841-855 (15)	340.00	25.00

1938-39 *Perf. 11*

Size: 20x27mm

856	A58	5d light violet	2.00	.20
857	A58	10d magenta	2.00	.20
858	A58	15d violet blue	2.00	.20
859	A58	30d bright green	2.00	.20
860	A58	45d vermilion	3.00	.20
861	A58	50d black brown	3.00	.20
862	A58	60d brown orange	3.00	.20
863	A58	75d rose lake	3.00	.20
864	A58	90d rose red ('39)	5.00	.25

Size: 22½x30mm

865	A58	1r turq green	10.00	.25
866	A58	1.50r deep blue	15.00	.30
867	A58	2r lt blue ('39)	20.00	.30
868	A58	3r violet brown	30.00	.70
869	A58	5r gray grn ('39)	50.00	1.25
870	A58	10r dark brown & ultra ('39)	150.00	7.50
		Nos. 856-870 (15)	300.00	12.15

Reza Shah Pahlavi — A58a

1939, Mar. 15 *Perf. 13*

870A	A58a	5d gray blue	2.00	2.00
870B	A58a	10d brown	2.00	2.00
870C	A58a	30d green	2.00	2.00
870D	A58a	60d dark brown	2.00	2.00
870E	A58a	90d red	4.00	4.00
870F	A58a	1.50r blue	15.00	10.00
870G	A58a	5r lilac	25.00	25.00
870H	A58a	10r carmine	45.00	45.00
		Nos. 870A-870H (8)	97.00	92.00

60th birthday of Riza Shah Pahlavi. Printed in sheets of 4, perf. 13 and imperf. The imperf. sell for 50% more. The 1r violet and 2r orange were not available to the public. Value unused $15 each.

Crown Prince and Princess Fawziya
A59

1939, Apr. 25 Photo. *Perf. 11½*

871	A59	5d red brown	.50	.30
872	A59	10d bright violet	.50	.30
873	A59	30d emerald	1.50	.35
874	A59	90d red	12.00	2.00
875	A59	1.50r bright blue	20.00	4.00
		Nos. 871-875 (5)	34.50	6.95

Wedding of Crown Prince Mohammad Reza Pahlavi to Princess Fawziya of Egypt.

AIR POST STAMPS

Type of 1909 Overprinted

1927 Unwmk. Typo. *Perf. 11½*

C1	A31	1c org & maroon	2.50	1.00
C2	A31	2c vio & maroon	2.50	1.00
C3	A31	3c grn & maroon	2.50	1.00
C4	A31	6c red & maroon	2.50	1.00
C5	A31	9c gray & maroon	4.00	1.00
C6	A31	10c red vio & mar	6.00	1.00
C7	A31	13c dk bl & mar	8.00	2.50
C8	A31	1k sil, vio & bis brown	8.00	2.50
C9	A31	26c dk grn & mar	8.00	2.50
C10	A31	2k sil, dk grn & bis brown	15.00	3.00
C11	A31	3k sil, gray & bis brown	25.00	6.00
C12	A31	4k sil, bl & bis brown	40.00	15.00
C13	A31	5k gold, brn & bis brown	40.00	10.00
C14	A31	10k gold, org & bis brown	250.00	250.00
C15	A31	20k gold, ol grn & bis brn	250.00	250.00
C16	A31	30k gold, car & bis brown	250.00	250.00
		Nos. C1-C16 (16)	914.00	797.50

Counterfeit overprints are plentiful. They are found on Nos. 448-463, perf. 12½x12 instead of 11½.

Exist without overprint. Value, set $4,000.

AP1

AP2

AP3

AP4

AP5

Airplane, Value and "Poste aérièn" Surcharged on Revenue Stamps

1928 *Perf. 11*

C17	AP1	3k yellow brn	125.00	40.00
C18	AP2	5k dark brown	30.00	10.00
C19	AP3	1t gray vio	30.00	10.00
C20	AP4	2t olive bister	30.00	10.00
C21	AP5	3t deep green	35.00	15.00
		Nos. C17-C21 (5)	250.00	85.00

AP6

AP7

"Poste aerienne"

1928-29

C22	AP6	1c emerald	1.00	.50
a.		1c yellow green	1.00	.50
b.		Double overprint	35.00	
C23	AP6	2c light blue	1.00	.20
C24	AP6	3c bright rose	1.00	.20
C25	AP6	5c olive brn	1.00	.20
a.		"5" omitted	650.00	*750.00*
b.		Horiz. pair, imperf. btwn.	*250.00*	
C26	AP6	10c dark green	1.00	.20
a.		"10" omitted	30.00	
b.		"1" inverted	50.00	
C27	AP7	1k dull vio	2.00	1.00
a.		"1" inverted	65.00	
C28	AP7	2k orange	5.00	2.00
a.		"S" for "s" in "Krs"	100.00	
		Nos. C22-C28 (7)	12.00	4.30

Counterfeits exist.

Revenue Stamps Similar to Nos. C17 to C21, Overprinted like Nos. C22 to C28: "Poste aerienne"

1929

C29	AP1	3k yellow brn	100.00	25.00
C30	AP2	5k dark brn	20.00	5.00
C31	AP3	10k violet	25.00	10.00
C32	AP4	20k olive grn	30.00	10.00
C33	AP5	30k deep grn	40.00	15.00
		Nos. C29-C33 (5)	215.00	65.00

Riza Shah Pahlavi and Eagle — AP8

1930, July 6 Photo. *Perf. 12½x11½*

C34	AP8	1c ol bis & brt bl	.50	.50
C35	AP8	2c blue & gray blk	.50	.50
C36	AP8	3c ol grn & dk vio	.50	.50
C37	AP8	4c dk vio & pck bl	.50	.50
C38	AP8	5c lt grn & mag	.50	.50
C39	AP8	6c mag & bl grn	.50	.50
C40	AP8	8c dk gray & dp violet	.50	.50
C41	AP8	10c dp ultra & ver	.50	.50
C42	AP8	12c slate & org	.50	.50
C43	AP8	15c org brn & ol green	.50	.50
C44	AP8	1k Prus bl & scar	5.00	2.50
		Engr.		
C45	AP8	2k black & ultra	5.00	2.50
C46	AP8	3k dk brn & gray green	6.50	3.00
C47	AP8	5k dp red & gray black	6.50	4.00
C48	AP8	1t orange & vio	25.00	8.00
C49	AP8	2t dk grn & red brown	25.00	10.00
C50	AP8	3t brn vio & sl bl	175.00	50.00
		Nos. C34-C50 (17)	253.00	85.00

Same Overprinted in Black

1935 Photo.

C51	AP8	1c ol bis & brt bl	.50	.50
C52	AP8	2c blue & gray blk	.50	.50
C53	AP8	3c ol grn & dk vio	.50	.50
C54	AP8	4c dk vio & pck bl	.50	.50
C55	AP8	5c lt grn & mag	.50	.50
C56	AP8	6c mag & bl grn	.50	.50
C57	AP8	8c dk gray & dp violet	.50	.50
C58	AP8	10c dp ultra & ver	.50	.50
C59	AP8	12c slate & org	.50	.50
C60	AP8	15c org brn & ol green	.50	.50
C61	AP8	1k Prus bl & scar	25.00	*30.00*
		Engr.		
C62	AP8	2k blk & ultra	20.00	*25.00*
C63	AP8	3k dk brn & gray green	25.00	15.00
C64	AP8	5k dp red & gray black	10.00	10.00
C65	AP8	1t orange & vio	225.00	175.00
C66	AP8	2t dk grn & red brown	25.00	20.00
C67	AP8	3t brn vio & sl bl	35.00	20.00
		Nos. C51-C67 (17)	370.00	300.00

OFFICIAL STAMPS

Four bicolored stamps of this design (1s, 2s, 5s, 10s), with centers embossed, exist, but were never issued or used in Iran. Value $40. They are known imperforate and in many trial colors.

Shah Muzaffar-ed-Din O1

No. 145 Surcharged in Black

1902 *Perf. 12½*

O5	O1	5c on 1k red	30.00	30.00
O6	O1	10c on 1k red	30.00	30.00
O7	O1	12c on 1k red	40.00	40.00
		Nos. O5-O7 (3)	100.00	100.00

Nos. 351-363 Overprinted in Black

1903-06

O8	A26	1c violet	2.50	.20
O9	A26	2c gray	2.50	.20
O10	A26	3c green	2.50	.20
O11	A26	5c rose	2.50	.20
O12	A26	10c yel brown	5.00	.20
O13	A26	12c blue	7.00	.20
		Perf. 11½x11		
O14	A27	1k violet	8.00	1.50
O15	A27	2k ultra	8.00	2.00
a.		Violet overprint	50.00	
O16	A27	5k org brown	22.50	2.50
O17	A27	10k rose red	22.50	3.50
a.		Violet overprint		50.00
O18	A27	20k orange ('06)	60.00	7.00
O19	A27	30k green ('06)	80.00	20.00
O20	A27	50k green	250.00	100.00
		Nos. O8-O20 (13)	473.00	137.70

Overprinted on Nos. 368, 370a

O21	A27	2t on 50k grn (Bl)	175.00	75.00
O22	A27	3t on 50k grn (V)	175.00	75.00

Overprinted on Nos. 372, 375, New Value Surcharged in Blue or Black

1905

O23	A27	2t on 50k grn (Bl)	175.00	75.00
O28	A27	3t on 50k grn (Bk)	175.00	75.00

The 2t on 50k also exists with surcharge in black and magenta; the 3t on 50k in violet and magenta. Values about the same.

Regular Issue of 1909 Overprinted

There is a space between the word "Service" and the Persian characters.

1911 *Perf. 12½x12*

O31	A31	1c org & maroon	8.00	6.00
O32	A31	2c vio & maroon	8.00	6.00
O33	A31	3c yel grn & mar	8.00	6.00
O34	A31	6c red & maroon	8.00	6.00
O35	A31	9c gray & maroon	17.50	11.00
O36	A31	10c multicolored	17.50	12.00
O38	A31	1k multicolored	45.00	35.00
O40	A31	2k multicolored	125.00	80.00
		Nos. O31-O40 (8)	237.00	162.00

The 13c, 26c and 3k to 30k denominations were not regularly issued with this overprint. Dangerous counterfeits exist, usually on reprints.

Regular Issue of 1915 Overprinted

1915 Wmk. 161 *Perf. 11, 11½*

O41	A33	1c car & indigo	2.50	2.50
O42	A33	2c bl & carmine	2.50	2.50
O43	A33	3c dark green	2.50	2.50
O44	A33	5c red	2.50	2.50
O45	A33	6c ol grn & car	2.50	2.50
O46	A33	9c yel brn & vio	2.50	2.50
O47	A33	10c multicolored	2.50	2.50
O48	A33	12c ultramarine	3.00	3.00
O49	A34	1k multicolored	7.00	7.00
O50	A33	24c multicolored	3.50	3.50
O51	A34	2k sil, bl & rose	7.00	7.00
O52	A34	3k sil, vio & brn	7.00	7.00
O53	A34	5k multicolored	7.50	7.50
O54	A35	1t gold, pur & blk	10.00	10.00
O55	A35	2t gold, grn & brn	10.00	10.00
O56	A35	3t multicolored	12.50	12.50
O57	A35	5t gold, bl & ind	15.00	15.00
		Nos. O41-O57 (17)	100.00	100.00

Coronation of Shah Ahmed.

Reprints have dull rather than shiny overprint. **Value, set, $17.50.**

NEWSPAPER STAMP

No. 429 Overprinted

1909 Typo. Unwmk. *Perf. 12½*

P1	A26	2c gray, *blue*	45.00	20.00

PARCEL POST STAMPS

Regular issues of 1907-08 (types A26, A29) with the handstamp above in blue, black or green are of questionable status as issued stamps. The handstamp probably is a cancellation.

No. 436 Overprinted in Black

1909 Engr. *Perf. 11½*

Q18	A29	26c red brown	20.00	15.00

The overprint is printed.

Regular Issue of 1915 Overprinted in Black

1915 Wmk. 161 *Perf. 11, 11½*

Q19	A33	1c car & indigo	*2.50*	*2.50*
Q20	A33	2c bl & carmine	*2.50*	*2.50*
Q21	A33	3c dark green	*2.50*	*2.50*
Q22	A33	5c red	*2.50*	*2.50*
Q23	A33	6c ol green & car	*2.50*	*2.50*
Q24	A33	9c yel brn & vio	*2.50*	*2.50*
Q25	A33	10c bl grn & yel brn	*2.50*	*2.50*
Q26	A33	12c ultramarine	*3.00*	*3.00*
Q27	A34	1k multicolored	*7.00*	*7.00*
Q28	A33	24c multicolored	*3.50*	*3.50*
Q29	A34	2k multicolored	*7.00*	*7.00*
Q30	A34	3k multicolored	*7.00*	*7.00*
Q31	A34	5k multicolored	*7.50*	*7.50*
Q32	A35	1t multicolored	*10.00*	*10.00*
Q33	A35	2t gold, grn & brn	*10.00*	*10.00*
Q34	A35	3t multicolored	*12.50*	*12.50*
Q35	A35	5t multicolored	*15.00*	*15.00*
		Nos. Q19-Q35 (17)	100.00	*100.00*

Coronation of Shah Ahmed.

Reprints have dull rather than shiny overprint. **Value, set, $16.**

IRAQ

i-räk

LOCATION — In western Asia, bounded on the north by Syria and Turkey, on the east by Iran, on the south by Saudi Arabia, and on the west by Jordan

GOVT. — Republic

AREA — 167,925 sq. mi.

POP. — 12,029,700 (est. 1982)

CAPITAL — Baghdad

Iraq, formerly Mesopotamia, a province of Turkey, was mandated to Great Britain in 1920. The mandate was terminated in 1932. For earlier issues, see Mesopotamia.

16 Annas = 1 Rupee.

1000 Fils = 1 Dinar (1932)

Issues under British Mandate

Sunni Mosque — A1

Gufas on the Tigris — A2

Assyrian Winged Bull — A4

Ctesiphon Arch — A5

Motif of Assyrian Origin — A3

Colors of the Dulaim Camel Corps — A6

Golden Shiah Mosque of Kadhimain — A7

Conventionalized Date Palm or "Tree of Life" — A8

1923-25	Engr.	Wmk. 4	Perf. 12	
1	A1	½a olive grn	.60	.25
2	A2	1a brown	.90	.25
3	A3	1½a car lake	.50	.25
4	A4	2a brown org	.50	.25
5	A5	3a dp blue	1.00	.25
6	A6	4a dull vio	1.90	.35
7	A7	6a blue grn	1.25	.35
8	A6	8a olive bis	2.00	.75
9	A8	1r grn & brn	4.25	.90
10	A1	2r black	17.50	8.00
11	A1	2r bister ('25)	47.50	4.00
12	A6	5r orange	42.50	15.00
13	A7	10r carmine	55.00	22.50
		Nos. 1-13 (13)	175.40	53.10

For overprints see Nos. O1-O24, O42, O47, O51-O53.

King Faisal I — A9

1927

14	A9	1r red brown	9.50	1.25

See No. 27. For overprint and surcharges see Nos. 43, O25, O54.

King Faisal I

A10 A11

1931				
15	A10	½a green	.70	.30
16	A10	1a chestnut	.70	.30
17	A10	1½a carmine	1.10	.45
18	A10	2a orange	.90	.20
19	A10	3a light blue	1.00	.20
20	A10	4a pur brown	1.50	*1.75*
21	A10	6a Prus blue	2.00	.80
22	A10	8a dark green	2.25	2.00
23	A11	1r dark brown	4.50	1.75
24	A11	2r yel brown	6.75	5.00
25	A11	5r dp orange	25.00	*35.00*
26	A11	10r red	77.50	*85.00*
27	A9	25r violet	650.00	*800.00*
		Nos. 15-27 (13)	773.90	*932.75*

See Nos. 44-60. For overprints see Nos. O26-O41, O43-O46, O48-O50, O54-O71.

Issues of the Kingdom

Nos. 6, 15-27 Surcharged in "Fils" or "Dinars" in Red, Black or Green:

a

b

c

دينار ١
1 Dinar

d

1932, Apr. 1				
28	A10(a)	2f on ½a (R)	.30	.20
29	A10(a)	3f on ½a	.30	.20
a.		Double surcharge	*160.00*	
b.		Inverted surcharge	*160.00*	
30	A10(a)	4f on 1a (G)	1.25	.35
31	A10(a)	5f on 1a	.40	.20
a.		Double surcharge	*275.00*	
b.		Inverted Arabic "5"	*35.00*	*40.00*
32	A10(a)	8f on 1½a	.55	.50
a.		Inverted surcharge	*160.00*	
33	A10(a)	10f on 2a	.60	.20
34	A10(a)	15f on 3a	1.25	1.50
35	A10(a)	20f on 4a	2.00	1.50
36	A6(b)	25f on 4a	3.50	3.75
a.		"Flis" for "Fils"	*350.00*	*425.00*
b.		Inverted Arabic "5"	*425.00*	*550.00*
37	A10(a)	30f on 6a	2.25	.75
38	A10(a)	40f on 8a	3.25	2.75
39	A11(c)	75f on 1r	3.00	2.75
40	A11(c)	100f on 2r	9.00	4.75
41	A11(c)	200f on 5r	20.00	*24.00*
42	A11(d)	½d on 10r	77.50	*95.00*
a.		Bar in "½" omitted	*800.00*	*925.00*
43	A9(d)	1d on 25r	150.00	*200.00*
		Nos. 28-43 (16)	275.15	*338.40*

King Faisal I

A12 A13

A14

Values in "Fils" and "Dinars"

1932, May 9			Engr.	
44	A12	2f ultra	.25	.20
45	A12	3f green	.25	.20
46	A12	4f vio brown	.25	.20
47	A12	5f gray green	.30	.20
48	A12	8f deep red	.40	.20
49	A12	10f yellow	.50	.20
50	A12	15f deep blue	.80	.20
51	A12	20f orange	.95	.55
52	A12	25f rose lilac	.95	.55
53	A12	30f olive grn	2.00	.20
54	A12	40f dark violet	1.25	1.00
55	A13	50f deep brown	1.25	.30
56	A13	75f lt ultra	2.75	2.00
57	A13	100f deep green	4.50	1.25
58	A13	200f dark red	15.00	7.00
59	A14	½d gray blue	45.00	37.50
60	A14	1d claret	90.00	*95.00*
		Nos. 44-60 (17)	166.40	146.75

For overprints see Nos. O55-O71.

A15

A16

King Ghazi — A17

1934-38			Unwmk.	
61	A15	1f purple ('38)	.50	.25
62	A15	2f ultra	.30	.25
63	A15	3f green	.30	.25
64	A15	4f pur brown	.30	.25
65	A15	5f gray green	.30	.25
66	A15	8f deep red	.50	.25
67	A15	10f yellow	.65	.25
68	A15	15f deep blue	.65	.25
69	A15	20f orange	.65	.25
70	A15	25f brown vio	1.25	.35
71	A15	30f olive grn	.90	.25
72	A15	40f dark vio	1.00	.25
73	A16	50f deep brown	2.50	.25
74	A16	75f ultra	2.25	.40
75	A16	100f deep green	2.75	.50
76	A16	200f dark red	4.50	1.00
77	A17	½d gray blue	12.50	9.25
78	A17	1d claret	50.00	15.00
		Nos. 61-78 (18)	81.80	29.50

For overprints see Nos. 226, O72-O89.

OFFICIAL STAMPS

British Mandate

Regular Issue of 1923 Overprinted:

k

l

1923		Wmk. 4	Perf. 12	
O1	A1(k)	½a olive grn	.90	.50
O2	A2(k)	1a brown	1.00	.20
O3	A3(l)	1½a car lake	2.75	.75
O4	A4(k)	2a brown org	1.75	.30
O5	A5(k)	3a deep blue	3.50	.75
O6	A6(l)	4a dull violet	3.50	.50
O7	A7(k)	6a blue green	5.25	1.40
O8	A6(l)	8a olive bister	5.75	1.30
O9	A8(l)	1r green & brn	6.50	1.40
O10	A1(k)	2r black (R)	20.00	9.00
O11	A6(l)	5r orange	60.00	27.50
O12	A7(k)	10r carmine	85.00	60.00
		Nos. O1-O12 (12)	195.90	103.60

Regular Issue of 1923-25 Overprinted:

m

n

1924-25				
O13	A1(m)	½a olive green	1.25	.30
O14	A2(m)	1a brown	1.00	.30
O15	A3(n)	1½a car lake	1.00	.30
O16	A4(m)	2a brown org	1.75	.30
O17	A5(m)	3a deep blue	2.25	.30
O18	A6(n)	4a dull violet	5.00	.30
O19	A7(m)	6a blue green	2.10	.30
O20	A6(n)	8a olive bister	5.00	.40
O21	A8(n)	1r green & brn	11.00	1.00
O22	A1(m)	2r bister ('25)	37.50	4.50
O23	A6(n)	5r orange	60.00	50.00
O24	A7(m)	10r brown red	85.00	52.50
		Nos. O13-O24 (12)	212.85	110.50

For overprint see Nos. O42, O47, O51-O53.

No. 14 Overprinted Type "n"

1927

O25	A9	1r red brown	8.00	2.00

Regular Issue of 1931 Overprinted Vertically

o

1931				
O26	A10	½a green	.20	3.00
O27	A10	1a chestnut	.20	.20
O28	A10	1½a carmine	7.50	16.00
O29	A10	2a orange	.70	.20
O30	A10	3a light blue	1.25	.70
O31	A10	4a purple brown	1.40	.90
O32	A10	6a Pruss blue	5.00	12.50
O33	A10	8a dark green	5.00	12.50

Overprinted Horizontally

p

O34	A11	1r dark brown	9.50	12.50
O35	A11	2r yellow brown	20.00	45.00
O36	A11	5r deep orange	47.50	*85.00*
O37	A11	10r red	85.00	*140.00*
		Nos. O26-O37 (12)	183.25	328.50

Overprinted Vertically Reading Up

O38	A9(p)	25r violet	900.00	*1,200.*

For overprints see Nos. O39-O41, O43-O46, O48-O50, O54.

Kingdom

Nos. O15, O19, O22-O24, O26-O31, O33-O35, O38 Surcharged with New Values in Fils and Dinars, like Nos. 28-43

1932, Apr. 1				
O39	A10	3f on ½a	4.00	4.00
O40	A10	4f on 1a (G)	2.75	.20
O41	A10	5f on 1a	2.75	.20
a.		Inverted Arabic "5"	*52.50*	*35.00*
O42	A3	8f on 1½a	6.25	.60
O43	A10	10f on 2a	3.50	.20
O44	A10	15f on 3a	4.75	2.75
O45	A10	20f on 4a	4.75	2.75
O46	A10	25f on 4a	5.00	2.25
O47	A7	30f on 6a	5.25	2.00
O48	A10	40f on 8a	4.50	4.00
a.		"Flis" for "Fils"	*300.00*	*450.00*
O49	A11	50f on 1r	6.25	4.00
O50	A11	75f on 1r	7.00	7.00
O51	A1	100f on 2r	20.00	4.00
O52	A6	200f on 5r	26.00	26.00
O53	A7	½d on 10r	75.00	*100.00*
a.		Bar in "½" omitted	*850.00*	*975.00*
O54	A9	1d on 25r	140.00	*210.00*
		Nos. O39-O54 (16)	317.75	369.95

Regular Issue of 1932 Overprinted Vertically like Nos. O26-O33

1932, May 9				
O55	A12	2f ultramarine	1.00	.20
O56	A12	3f green	1.00	.20
O57	A12	4f violet brn	1.25	.20
O58	A12	5f gray	1.25	.20
O59	A12	8f deep red	1.25	.20
O60	A12	10f yellow	2.25	.20
O61	A12	15f deep blue	2.75	.20
O62	A12	20f orange	2.75	.20
O63	A12	25f rose lilac	2.75	.40
O64	A12	30f olive grn	4.00	.40
O65	A12	40f dark violet	5.75	.40

Overprinted Horizontally Like Nos. O34 to O37

O66	A13	50f deep brown	3.75	.50
O67	A13	75f lt ultra	2.75	1.00
O68	A13	100f deep green	12.50	1.50
O69	A13	200f dark red	22.50	8.75

Overprinted Vertically like No. O38

O70	A14	½d gray blue	15.00	22.50
O71	A14	1d claret	70.00	*100.00*
		Nos. O55-O71 (17)	152.50	*137.05*

Regular Issue of 1934-38 Overprinted Type "o" Vertically Reading up in Black

1934-38			Unwmk.	
O72	A15	1f purple ('38)	1.10	.50
O73	A15	2f ultramarine	1.10	.20
O74	A15	3f green	.65	.20
O75	A15	4f purple brn	1.10	.20
O76	A15	5f gray green	1.00	.20
O77	A15	8f deep red	4.50	.20
O78	A15	10f yellow	.45	.20
O79	A15	15f deep blue	10.00	1.50
O80	A15	20f orange	1.00	.20
O81	A15	25f brown violet	20.00	6.25
O82	A15	30f olive green	4.50	.20
O83	A15	40f dark violet	5.75	.40

Overprinted Type "p"

O84	A16	50f deep brown	1.00	.65
O85	A16	75f ultramarine	6.75	.90
O86	A16	100f deep green	1.75	1.00
O87	A16	200f dark red	4.50	2.75

Overprinted Type "p" Vertically Reading Up

O88	A17	½d gray blue	11.00	*18.00*
O89	A17	1d claret	45.00	*55.00*
		Nos. O72-O89 (18)	121.15	88.55

IRELAND

'īr-lənd

(Eire)

LOCATION — Comprises the entire island of Ireland, except 5,237 square miles at the extreme north
GOVT. — Republic
AREA — 27,136 sq. mi.
POP. — 3,443,405 (1981)
CAPITAL — Dublin

12 Pence = 1 Shilling

Catalogue values for unused stamps in this country are for Never Hinged items, beginning with Scott 99 in the regular postage section, and Scott J5 in the postage due section.

Watermarks

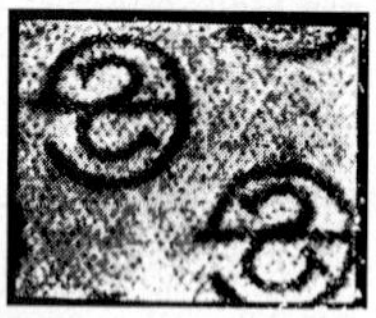

Wmk. 44 — SE in Monogram

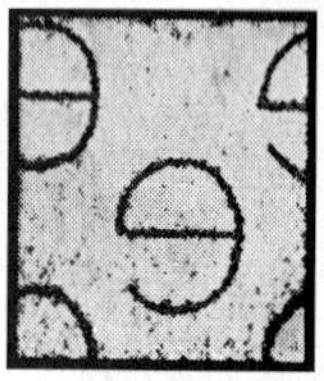

Wmk. 262 — Multiple "e"

Overprinted by Dollard, Ltd.

Great Britain Nos. 159-167, 170-172, 179-181 Overprinted

Overprint measures 15x17½mm

This overprint means "Provisional Government of Ireland."

Black or Gray Black Overprint

1922, Feb. 17 Wmk. 33 *Perf. 15x14*

1 A82 ½p green .90 *1.00*
Never hinged 1.50
a. Inverted overprint 500.00 *700.00*
Never hinged 750.00
2 A83 1p scarlet 1.00 *1.00*
Never hinged 1.75
a. Inverted overprint 300.00 *550.00*
b. Double overprint —
3 A86 2½p ultra 1.75 *6.50*
Never hinged 4.25
4 A87 3p violet 7.00 *10.00*
Never hinged 12.50
5 A88 4p slate green 4.50 *15.00*
Never hinged 10.00
6 A89 5p yel brown 5.50 *16.00*
Never hinged 13.00
7 A90 9p black brown 16.00 *30.00*
Never hinged 40.00
8 A90 10p light blue 11.00 *25.00*
Never hinged 20.00
Nos. 1-8 (8) 47.65 *104.50*

The ½p with red overprint is a proof.

Red or Carmine Overprint

1922, Apr.-July

9 A86 2½p ultra 1.90 *7.00*
Never hinged 3.75
10 A88 4p slate green (R) 12.50 *21.00*
Never hinged 25.00
10A A88 4p slate green (C) 65.00 *90.00*
Never hinged 125.00
11 A90 9p black brown 20.00 *30.00*
Never hinged 50.00
Nos. 9-11 (4) 99.40 *148.00*

Overprinted in Black

Overprint measures 21½x14mm

There is a variation that is 21x14mm. The "h" and "é" are 1mm apart. See Nos. 36-38.

1922, Feb. 17 Wmk. 34 *Perf. 11x12*

12 A91 2sh6p brown 40.00 *90.00*
Never hinged 100.00
13 A91 5sh car rose 85.00 *160.00*
Never hinged 200.00
14 A91 10sh gray blue 175.00 *350.00*
Never hinged 375.00
Nos. 12-14 (3) 300.00 *600.00*

Overprinted by Alex. Thom & Co.

Overprinted in Black

Overprint measures 14½x16mm

TWO PENCE

Die I — Four horizontal lines above the head. Heavy colored lines above and below the bottom tablet. The inner frame line is closer to the central design than it is to the outer frame line.

Die II — Three lines above the head. Thinner lines above and below the bottom tablet. The inner frame line is midway between the central design and the outer frame line.

1922, Feb. 17 Wmk. 33 *Perf. 15x14*

15 A84 1½p red brown 1.50 *1.75*
Never hinged 4.00
a. "PENCF" 400.00 *350.00*
16 A85 2p orange (II) 2.75 1.25
Never hinged 6.00
a. Inverted overprint (II) 400.00 *500.00*
b. 2p orange (I) 2.75 1.25
As "b," never hinged 6.00
c. Inverted overprint (I) 210.00 *300.00*
17 A89 6p red violet 11.00 *8.00*
Never hinged 25.00
18 A90 1sh bister 19.00 17.50
Never hinged 40.00
Nos. 15-18 (4) 34.25 28.50

Important: see Nos. 25-26, 31, 35.

Overprinted by Harrison & Sons

Coil Stamps

Overprinted in Black in Glossy Black Ink

Overprint measures 15¼x17mm

1922, June

19 A82 ½p green 3.50 *8.00*
Never hinged 6.50
20 A83 1p scarlet 3.50 *6.50*
Never hinged 5.00
21 A84 1½p red brown 6.50 *45.00*
Never hinged 10.00
22 A85 2p orange (I) 20.00 *37.50*
Never hinged 35.00
a. 2p orange (II) 18.00 *42.50*
Never hinged 30.00
Nos. 19-22 (4) 33.50 *97.00*

In Harrison overprint, "i" of "Rialtas" extends below the base of the other letters.

The Harrison stamps were issued in coils, either horizontal or vertical. The paper is double where the ends of the strips were overlapped. Mint pairs with the overlap sell for about three times the price of a single. The perforations are often clipped.

Overprinted by Alex. Thom & Co.

Stamps of Great Britain, 1912-22 Overprinted as Nos. 15 to 18, in Shiny to Dull Blue Black, or Red

Overprint measures 14½x16mm

Note: The blue black overprints can best be distinguished from the black by use of 50-power magnification with a light source behind the stamp.

1922, July-Nov. *Perf. 15x14*

23 A82 ½p green 2.00 1.35
Never hinged 4.50
24 A83 1p scarlet 1.00 1.75
Never hinged 3.00
25 A84 1½p red brown 6.00 *7.00*
Never hinged 11.00
26 A85 2p orange (II) 3.00 1.00
Never hinged 4.75
a. Inverted overprint (II) 275.00 *500.00*
b. 2p orange (I) 20.00 2.00
Never hinged 40.00
27 A86 2½p ultra (R) 10.00 *24.00*
Never hinged 15.00
28 A87 3p violet 2.50 *4.00*
Never hinged 5.00
29 A88 4p slate green (R) 4.50 *4.75*
Never hinged 7.00
30 A89 5p yellow brown 8.50 *12.00*
Never hinged 14.00
31 A89 6p red violet 8.00 5.00
Never hinged 15.00
32 A90 9p blk brn (R) 14.00 *17.00*
Never hinged 30.00
33 A90 9p ol grn (R) 7.50 *32.50*
Never hinged 15.00
34 A90 10p light blue 26.00 *50.00*
Never hinged 50.00
35 A90 1sh bister 12.50 *11.00*
Never hinged 25.00
Nos. 23-35 (13) 105.50 *171.35*

Nos. 23, 24, 28, 34 overprinted in dull black, rather than the normal blue-black, are believed to be proofs, pressed into use when supplies of the issued values ran low.

Overprinted as Nos. 12 to 14 in Blue Black (Shiny to Dull)

Overprint measures 21x13½mm

The "h" and "é" are ½mm apart.

1922 Wmk. 34 *Perf. 11x12*

36 A91 2sh6p gray brown 200. *325.*
Never hinged 400.
37 A91 5sh car rose 225. *375.*
Never hinged 450.
38 A91 10sh gray blue 1,500. *1,800.*
Never hinged 2,500.
Nos. 36-38 (3) 1,925. *2,500.*

Overprinted in Blue Black

Overprint measures 15¾x16mm

1922, Dec. Wmk. 33 *Perf. 15x14*

39 A82 ½p green 1.50 *2.00*
Never hinged 2.25
40 A83 1p scarlet 1.50 *4.00*
Never hinged 6.00
41 A84 1½p red brown 2.75 *12.50*
Never hinged 6.00
42 A85 2p orange (II) 10.00 10.00
Never hinged 17.50
43 A90 1sh bister 35.00 *47.50*
Never hinged 55.00
Nos. 39-43 (5) 50.75 *76.00*

Stamps of Great Britain, 1912-22, Overprinted in Shiny to Dull Blue Black or Red

This overprint means "Irish Free State"

Overprint measures 15x8½mm
"1922" is 6¼mm long

The inner loop of the "9" is an upright oval.

The measurement of "1922" is made across the bottom of the numerals and does not include the serif at the top of the "1."

There were 5 plates for printing the overprint on Nos. 44-55. In the impressions from plate I the 12th stamp in the 15th row has no accent on the 2nd "A" of "SAORSTAT." To correct this an accent was inserted by hand, sometimes this was in a reversed position.

On Nos. 56-58 the accent was omitted on the 2nd stamp in the 3rd and 8th rows. Damage to the plate makes the accent look reversed on the 4th stamp in the 7th row. The top of the "t" slants down in a line with the so-called accent.

1922-23 Wmk. 33 *Perf. 15x14*

44 A82 ½p green .60 .75
Never hinged 1.25
a. Accent omitted 1,300. *1,000.*
b. Accent added 125.00 *150.00*
45 A83 1p scarlet .60 .75
Never hinged 1.25
a. Accent omitted *8,750.* *6,500.*
b. Accent added 150.00 *175.00*
c. Accent and final "t" omitted *7,750.* *5,500.*
d. Accent and final "t" added 250.00 *300.00*
46 A84 1½p red brown 3.00 *12.50*
Never hinged 7.00
47 A85 2p orange (II) 1.75 *3.00*
Never hinged 5.00
48 A86 2½p ultra (R) 2.75 *7.50*
Never hinged 6.00
a. Accent omitted 160.00 *200.00*
49 A87 3p violet 8.00 *10.00*
Never hinged 15.00
a. Accent omitted 325.00 *350.00*
50 A88 4p sl green (R) 3.75 *6.00*
Never hinged 7.00
a. Accent omitted 225.00 *300.00*
51 A89 5p yel brown 3.00 *7.00*
Never hinged 7.00
52 A89 6p dull violet 2.75 2.25
Never hinged 6.00
a. Accent added *900.00* *900.00*
53 A90 9p ol green (R) 3.50 *9.00*
Never hinged 8.50
a. Accent omitted 275.00 *350.00*
54 A90 10p lt blue 20.00 *40.00*
Never hinged 40.00
55 A90 1sh bister 12.50 *11.00*
Never hinged 32.50
a. Accent omitted *7,000.* *8,000.*
b. Accent added *825.00* *900.00*

Perf. 11x12

Wmk. 34

56 A91 2sh6p lt brown 45.00 *80.00*
Never hinged 95.00
a. Accent omitted 450.00 *500.00*
57 A91 5sh car rose 90.00 *160.00*
Never hinged 175.00
a. Accent omitted 550.00 *650.00*
58 A91 10sh gray blue 190.00 *375.00*
Never hinged 400.00
a. Accent omitted *2,750.* *3,250.*
Nos. 44-58 (15) 387.20 *724.75*

Overprinted by Harrison & Sons

Coil Stamps

Same Ovpt. in Black or Blue Black

1923 Wmk. 33 *Perf. 15x14*

59 A82 ½p green 2.00 *12.00*
Never hinged 4.00
a. Tall "1" 8.00 45.00
Never hinged 20.00
60 A83 1p scarlet 4.50 *16.00*
Never hinged 10.00
a. Tall "1" 35.00 140.00
Never hinged 80.00
61 A84 1½p red brown 5.00 *40.00*
Never hinged 15.00
a. Tall "1" 80.00 200.00
Never hinged 150.00
62 A85 2p orange (II) 6.00 *12.00*
Never hinged 11.00
a. Tall "1" 10.00 *45.00*
Never hinged 25.00
Nos. 59-62 (4) 17.50 *80.00*

These stamps were issued in coils, made by joining horizontal or vertical strips of the stamps. See 2nd paragraph after #22. In some strips there were two stamps with the "1" of "1922" 2½mm high and with serif at foot.

In this setting the middle "e" of "eireann" is a trifle above the line of the other letters, making the word appear slightly curved. The lower end of the "1" of "1922" is rounded on #59-62 instead of flat as on #44-47.

The inner loop of the "9" is round.

See Nos. 77b, 78b and 79b.

Booklet Panes

For very fine the perforation holes at top or bottom of the pane should be visible, though not necessarily perfect half circles.

"Sword of Light" — A1

Map of Ireland — A2

Coat of Arms — A3

Celtic Cross — A4

Perf. 15x14

1922-23 Typo. Wmk. 44

65 A1 ½p emerald .40 .40
Never hinged .85
a. Booklet pane of 6 *300.00*
66 A2 1p car rose .40 .40
Never hinged 1.50
a. Booklet pane of 6 *350.00*
b. Booklet pane of 3 + 3 labels *250.00*
67 A2 1½p claret 1.50 *2.25*
Never hinged 5.00

68 A2 2p deep green .40 .40
Never hinged 1.00
a. Booklet pane of 6 *275.00*
b. Perf. 15 horiz. ('35) *12,500.* *1,500.*

No. 68b is valued in the grade of fine.

69 A3 2½p chocolate 1.50 *4.50*
Never hinged 6.00
70 A4 3p ultra 1.50 *2.00*
Never hinged 6.00
71 A3 4p slate 2.25 *3.50*
Never hinged 7.50
72 A1 5p deep violet 11.00 10.00
Never hinged 45.00
73 A1 6p red violet 4.00 4.00
Never hinged 10.00
74 A3 9p violet 18.00 17.50
Never hinged 100.00
75 A4 10p brown 9.00 *20.00*
Never hinged 42.50
76 A1 1sh light blue 22.50 12.50
Never hinged 90.00
Nos. 65-76 (12) 72.45 77.45

The 2p was issued in 1922; other denominations in 1923.
No. 68b is a vertical coil stamp.
See Nos. 87, 91-92, 105-117, 137-138, 225-226, 326. For types overprinted see Nos. 118-119.

Overprinted by the Government Printing Office, Dublin Castle and British Board of Inland Revenue at Somerset House, London

Great Britain Nos. 179-181 Ovptd. in Black or Gray Black

"1922" is 5½mm long

The measurement of "1922" is made across the bottom of the numerals and does not include the serif at the top of the "1."

1925 Wmk. 34 *Perf. 11x12*
77 A91 2sh6p gray brown 50.00 *120.00*
Never hinged 100.00
78 A91 5sh rose red 60.00 *210.00*
Never hinged 125.00
79 A91 10sh gray blue 160.00 *425.00*
Never hinged 375.00
Nos. 77-79 (3) 270.00 *755.00*

In 1927 the 2sh6p, 5sh and 10sh stamps were overprinted from a plate in which the Thom and Castle clichés were combined, thus including wide and narrow "1922" in the same setting.

Overprinted by British Board of Inland Revenue at Somerset House, London

Pair with "1922" Wide and Narrow

1927
77a A91 2sh6p 325.
Never hinged 500.
78a A91 5sh 500.
Never hinged 850.
79a A91 10sh 1,500.
Never hinged 2,250.
Nos. 77a-79a (3) 2,325.

Wide "1922"
"1922" is 6¼mm long

1927-28
77b A91 2sh6p 50.00 *50.00*
Never hinged 90.00
78b A91 5sh ('28) 90.00 *100.00*
Never hinged 175.00
79b A91 10sh ('28) 225.00 *325.00*
Never hinged 400.00
Nos. 77b-79b (3) 365.00 475.00

Daniel O'Connell — A5

Perf. 15x14
1929, June 22 Wmk. 44
80 A5 2p dark green .50 .40
Never hinged .75
81 A5 3p dark blue 5.00 *10.00*
Never hinged 14.00
82 A5 9p dark violet 6.00 *9.50*
Never hinged 15.00
Nos. 80-82 (3) 11.50 *19.90*

Catholic Emancipation in Ireland, centenary.

Shannon River Hydroelectric Station — A6

1930, Oct. 15
83 A6 2p black brown .50 *1.00*
Never hinged 3.00

Opening of the hydroelectric development of the River Shannon.

Farmer with Scythe
A7

Cross of Cong and Chalice
A8

1931, June 12
84 A7 2p pale blue .70 .50
Never hinged 1.50

Bicentenary of Royal Dublin Society.

1932, May 12
85 A8 2p dark green .80 .50
Never hinged 2.50
86 A8 3p bright blue 2.00 *4.75*
Never hinged 6.00

International Eucharistic Congress.

Coil Stamp
Type of 1922-23 Issue

1933-34 *Perf. 15 Horizontally*
87 A2 1p rose ('34) 25.00 *30.00*
Never hinged 40.00
a. 1p carmine rose 125.00 *175.00*
Never hinged 200.00

No. 87a has a single perforation at each side near the top, while No. 87 is perforated top and bottom only.
See No. 68b.

Adoration of the Cross
A9

Hurling
A10

1933, Sept. 18 *Perf. 15x14*
88 A9 2p slate green .40 .40
Never hinged 1.00
89 A9 3p deep blue 2.25 *5.00*
Never hinged 7.00

Holy Year.

1934, July 27
90 A10 2p green .90 .75
Never hinged 2.00

50th anniv. of the Gaelic Athletic Assoc.

Coil Stamps
Types of 1922-23
Wmk. 44 Sideways

1934 *Perf. 14 Vertically*
91 A1 ½p green 32.50 *37.50*
Never hinged 50.00
92 A2 2p gray green 55.00 *70.00*
Never hinged 100.00

Overprinted by Harrison & Sons

Great Britain Nos. 222-224 Overprinted in Black

1935 Wmk. 44 *Perf. 11x12*
93 A91 2sh6p brown 50.00 *62.50*
Never hinged 125.00
94 A91 5sh carmine 175.00 *210.00*
Never hinged 375.00
95 A91 10sh dark blue 500.00 *650.00*
Never hinged 1,300.
Nos. 93-95 (3) 725.00 922.50

Waterlow printing can be distinguished by the crossed lines in the background of portrait. Previous issues have horizontal lines only.

St. Patrick and Paschal Fire — A11

1937, Sept. 8 Wmk. 44 *Perf. 14x15*
96 A11 2sh6p bright green 70.00 60.00
Never hinged 225.00
97 A11 5sh brown violet 120.00 100.00
Never hinged 275.00
98 A11 10sh dark blue 70.00 70.00
Never hinged 225.00
Nos. 96-98 (3) 260.00 *230.00*

See Nos. 121-123.

Catalogue values for unused stamps in this section, from this point to the end of the section, are for Never Hinged items.

Allegory of Ireland and Constitution
A12

1937, Dec. 29 *Perf. 15x14*
99 A12 2p plum 1.00 *6.00*
100 A12 3p deep blue 6.00 6.00

Constitution Day.
See Nos. 169-170.

Father Theobald Mathew
A13

1938, July 1
101 A13 2p black brown 1.00 .25
102 A13 3p ultramarine 9.50 6.50

Temperance Crusade by Father Mathew, centenary.

Washington, US Eagle and Harp — A14

1939, Mar. 1
103 A14 2p bright carmine 1.00 .30
104 A14 3p deep blue 11.00 9.50

US Constitution, 150th anniv.

Coil Stamp
Type of 1922-23

1940-46 Wmk. 262 *Perf. 15 Horiz.*
105 A2 1p car rose ('46) 50.00 15.00
a. Perf. 14 horiz. 45.00 50.00

Types of 1922-23

1940-42 *Perf. 15x14*
Size: 18x22mm
106 A1 ½p emerald ('41) 1.50 .50
a. Booklet pane of 6 *350.00*
107 A2 1p car rose ('41) .40 .40
a. Booklet pane of 6 6.00
b. Bklt. pane of 3 + 3 labels *1,250.*
108 A2 1½p claret ('41) 12.00 .75
a. Booklet pane of 6 140.00
109 A2 2p deep green .40 .40
a. Booklet pane of 6 12.50
110 A3 2½p choc ('41) 12.00 .75
a. Booklet pane of 6 95.00
111 A4 3p dull blue ('41) .40 .40
a. Booklet pane of 6 40.00
112 A3 4p slate .40 .40
a. Booklet pane of 6 65.00
113 A1 5p deep violet .40 .40
114 A1 6p red violet ('42) .75 .40
115 A3 9p violet .75 *.90*
116 A4 10p olive brown 1.00 .90
117 A1 1sh blue 120.00 20.00
Nos. 106-117 (12) 150.00 26.20

POSTAGE DUE STAMPS

D1

1925 Typo. Wmk. 44 *Perf. 14x15*
J1 D1 ½p emerald 20.00 30.00
Never hinged 90.00
J2 D1 1p carmine 12.00 9.00
Never hinged 40.00
J3 D1 2p dark green 22.50 11.00
Never hinged 80.00
J4 D1 6p plum 7.50 10.00
Never hinged 30.00
Nos. J1-J4 (4) 62.00 60.00

Catalogue values for unused stamps in this section, from this point to the end of the section, are for Never Hinged items.

1940-70 Wmk. 262
J5 D1 ½p emerald ('43) 27.50 22.50
J6 D1 1p brt carmine ('41) 1.10 .50
J7 D1 1½p vermilion ('52) 2.25 *5.00*
J8 D1 2p dark green 1.25 .55
J9 D1 3p blue ('52) 2.25 2.00
J10 D1 5p royal purple ('43) 3.50 *7.50*
J11 D1 6p plum ('60) 4.00 1.75
J12 D1 8p orange ('62) 7.50 7.50
J13 D1 10p red lilac ('65) 8.50 7.00
J14 D1 1sh lt yel grn ('69) 25.00 9.00
Nos. J5-J14 (10) 82.85 63.30

ITALIAN COLONIES

ə-ˈtal-yən ˈkä-lə-nēz

General Issues for all Colonies

100 Centesimi = 1 Lira

Used values in italics are for postaly used stamps. CTO's or stamps with fake cancels sell for about the same as unused, hinged stamps.

Type of Italy, Dante Alighieri Society Issue, in New Colors and Overprinted in Red or Black

1932, July 11 Wmk. 140 *Perf. 14*

No.	Type	Description	Unused	Used
1	A126	10c gray blk	.75	*2.25*
		Never hinged	1.90	
		On cover		50.00
2	A126	15c olive brn	.75	*2.25*
		Never hinged	1.90	
		On cover		72.50
3	A126	20c slate grn	.75	1.40
		Never hinged	1.90	
		On cover		50.00
4	A126	25c dk grn	.75	1.40
		Never hinged	1.90	
		On cover		50.00
5	A126	30c red brn (Bk)	.75	1.40
		Never hinged	1.90	
		On cover		95.00
6	A126	50c bl blk	.75	.75
		Never hinged	1.90	
		On cover		42.50
7	A126	75c car rose (Bk)	1.40	3.75
		Never hinged	3.75	
		On cover		72.50
8	A126	1.25 l dk bl	1.40	*6.00*
		Never hinged	3.75	
		On cover		125.00
9	A126	1.75 l violet	1.40	*8.75*
		Never hinged	3.75	
		On cover		250.00
10	A126	2.75 l org (Bk)	1.40	*18.00*
		Never hinged	3.75	
		On cover		325.00
11	A126	5 l + 2 l ol grn	1.40	*21.00*
		Never hinged	3.75	
		On cover		—
12	A126	10 l + 2.50 l dp bl	1.40	*32.50*
		Never hinged	3.75	
		On cover		—
		Nos. 1-12,C1-C6 (18)	*24.70*	*185.20*
		Nos. 1-12, set on overfranked philatelic cover		250.00

Types of Italy, Garibaldi Issue, in New Colors and Inscribed: "POSTE COLONIALI ITALIANE"

1932, July 1 Photo.

No.	Type	Description	Unused	Used
13	A138	10c green	2.75	*11.00*
		Never hinged	7.25	
		On cover		115.00
14	A138	20c car rose	2.75	6.00
		Never hinged	7.25	
		On cover		87.50
15	A138	25c green	2.75	6.00
		Never hinged	7.25	
		On cover		87.50
16	A138	30c green	2.75	11.00
		Never hinged	7.25	
		On cover		115.00
17	A138	50c car rose	2.75	6.00
		Never hinged	7.25	
		On cover		72.50
18	A141	75c car rose	2.75	*13.00*
		Never hinged	7.25	
		On cover		130.00
19	A141	1.25 l deep blue	2.75	*13.00*
		Never hinged	7.25	
		On cover		160.00
20	A141	1.75 l + 25c dp bl	5.00	*18.00*
		Never hinged	12.50	
		On cover		325.00
21	A144	2.55 l + 50c ol brn	5.00	*32.50*
		Never hinged	12.50	
		On cover		—
22	A145	5 l + 1 l dp bl	5.00	*40.00*
		Never hinged	12.50	
		On cover		—
		Nos. 13-22,C8-C12 (15)	*57.75*	*257.00*
		Nos. 13-22, set on overfranked philatelic cover		360.00

See Nos. CE1-CE2.

Plowing with Oxen — A1

Pack Camel — A2

Lioness — A3

1933, Mar. 27 Wmk. 140

No.	Type	Description	Unused	Used
23	A1	10c ol brn	7.25	*11.00*
		Never hinged	18.00	
		On cover		100.00
24	A2	20c dl vio	7.25	*11.00*
		Never hinged	18.00	
		On cover		72.50
25	A3	25c green	7.25	11.00
		Never hinged	18.00	
		On cover		100.00
26	A1	50c purple	7.25	11.00
		Never hinged	18.00	
		On cover		72.50
27	A2	75c carmine	7.25	*14.50*
		Never hinged	18.00	
		On cover		130.00
28	A3	1.25 l blue	7.25	*14.50*
		Never hinged	18.00	
		On cover		175.00
29	A1	2.75 l red orange	11.00	21.00
		Never hinged	27.50	
		On cover		400.00
30	A2	5 l + 2 l gray grn	16.00	*47.50*
		Never hinged	40.00	
		On cover		—
31	A3	10 l + 2.50 l org brn	16.00	*47.50*
		Never hinged	40.00	
		On cover		—
		Nos. 23-31,C13-C19 (16)	*169.50*	*395.50*
		Nos. 23-31, set on overfranked philatelic cover		450.00

Annexation of Eritrea by Italy, 50th anniv.

Agricultural Implements A4

Arab and Camel — A5

"Eager with New Life" — A7

Steam Roller — A6

1933 Photo. *Perf. 14*

No.	Type	Description	Unused	Used
32	A4	5c orange	6.00	*8.75*
		Never hinged	14.50	
		On cover		110.00
33	A5	25c green	6.00	*8.75*
		Never hinged	14.50	
		On cover		87.50
34	A6	50c purple	6.00	*8.75*
		Never hinged	14.50	
		On cover		72.50
35	A4	75c carmine	6.00	*14.50*
		Never hinged	14.50	
		On cover		110.00
36	A5	1.25 l deep blue	6.00	*14.50*
		Never hinged	14.50	
		On cover		140.00
37	A6	1.75 l rose red	6.00	*14.50*
		Never hinged	14.50	
		On cover		180.00
38	A4	2.75 l dark blue	6.00	*22.00*
		Never hinged	14.50	
		On cover		240.00
39	A5	5 l brnsh blk	8.75	*32.50*
		Never hinged	22.50	
		On cover		—
40	A6	10 l bluish blk	8.75	*35.00*
		Never hinged	22.50	
		On cover		—
41	A7	25 l gray black	13.00	*50.00*
		Never hinged	32.50	
		On cover		—
		Nos. 32-41,C20-C27 (18)	*144.00*	*413.75*
		Nos. 32-41, set on overfranked philatelic cover		450.00

10th anniversary of Fascism. Each denomination bears a different inscription.

Issue dates: 25 l, Dec. 26; others, Oct. 5.

Mercury and Fasces — A8

Soccer Kickoff — A10

Scoring a Goal — A9

1934, Apr. 18

No.	Type	Description	Unused	Used
42	A8	20c red orange	1.40	*5.00*
		Never hinged	3.75	
		On cover		100.00
43	A8	30c slate green	1.40	*5.00*
		Never hinged	3.75	
		On cover		130.00
44	A8	50c indigo	1.40	*5.00*
		Never hinged	3.75	
		On cover		110.00
45	A8	1.25 l blue	1.40	*5.00*
		Never hinged	3.75	
		On cover		250.00
		Nos. 42-45 (4)	*5.60*	*20.00*
		Nos. 42-45, set on overfranked philatelic cover		120.00

15th annual Trade Fair, Milan.

1934, June 5

No.	Type	Description	Unused	Used
46	A9	10c olive green	21.00	*32.50*
		Never hinged	55.00	
		On cover		240.00
47	A9	50c purple	40.00	21.00
		Never hinged	100.00	
		On cover		210.00
48	A9	1.25 l blue	40.00	*80.00*
		Never hinged	100.00	
		On cover		400.00
49	A10	5 l brown	55.00	*215.00*
		Never hinged	140.00	
		On cover		—
50	A10	10 l gray blue	55.00	*215.00*
		Never hinged	140.00	
		On cover		—
		Nos. 46-50,C29-C35 (12)	*412.00*	*1,126.*
		Nos. 46-50, set on overfranked philatelic cover		1,250.

2nd World Soccer Championship.

SEMI-POSTAL STAMPS

Many issues of Italy and Italian Colonies include one or more semi-postal denominations. To avoid splitting sets, these issues are generally listed as regular postage, airmail, etc., unless all values carry a surtax.

AIR POST STAMPS

Italian Air Post Stamps for Dante Alighieri Society Issue in New Colors and Overprinted in Red or Black Like #1-12

1932, July 11 Wmk. 140 *Perf. 14*

No.	Type	Description	Unused	Used
C1	AP10	50c gray blk (R)	1.40	*6.00*
		Never hinged	3.75	
		On cover		65.00
C2	AP11	1 l indigo (R)	1.40	*6.00*
		Never hinged	3.75	
		On cover		80.00
C3	AP11	3 l gray (R)	2.25	*8.75*
		Never hinged	5.50	
		On cover		250.00
C4	AP11	5 l ol brn (R)	2.25	*14.50*
		Never hinged	5.50	
		On cover		325.00
C5	AP10	7.70 l + 2 l car rose	2.25	*18.00*
		Never hinged	5.50	
		On cover		—
C6	AP11	10 l + 2.50 l org	2.25	*32.50*
		Never hinged	5.50	
		On cover		—
		Nos. C1-C6 (6)	*11.80*	*85.75*
		Nos. C1-C6, set on flown cover		180.00

Leonardo da Vinci — AP1

1932, Sept. 7 Photo. *Perf. 14½*

No.	Type	Description	Unused	Used
C7	AP1	100 l dp grn & brn	11.50	*80.00*
		Never hinged	30.00	
		On cover		400.00

Types of Italian Air Post Stamps, Garibaldi Issue, in New Colors and Inscribed: "POSTE AEREA COLONIALE ITALIANA"

1932, July 1

No.	Type	Description	Unused	Used
C8	AP13	50c car rose	2.75	*13.00*
		Never hinged	7.25	
		On cover		110.00
C9	AP14	80c green	2.75	*13.00*
		Never hinged	7.25	
		On cover		87.50
C10	AP13	1 l + 25c ol brn	6.00	*21.00*
		Never hinged	14.50	
		On cover		87.50
C11	AP13	2 l + 50c ol brn	6.00	*21.00*
		Never hinged	14.50	
		On cover		110.00
C12	AP14	5 l + 1 l ol brn	6.00	*32.50*
		Never hinged	14.50	
		On cover		72.50
		Nos. C8-C12 (5)	*23.50*	*100.50*
		Nos. C8-C12, set on flown cover		300.00

Eagle AP2

Savoia Marchetti 55 — AP3

Savoia Marchetti 55 Over Map of Eritrea AP4

1933 *Perf. 14*

No.	Type	Description	Unused	Used
C13	AP2	50c org brn	6.00	*11.00*
		Never hinged	14.50	
		On cover		87.50
C14	AP2	1 l blk vio	6.00	*11.00*
		Never hinged	14.50	
		On cover		110.00
C15	AP3	3 l carmine	11.50	*21.00*
		Never hinged	29.00	
		On cover		250.00
C16	AP3	5 l olive brn	11.50	*21.00*
		Never hinged	29.00	
		On cover		325.00
C17	AP2	7.70 l + 2 l slate	16.00	*47.50*
		Never hinged	40.00	
		On cover		—
C18	AP3	10 l + 2.50 l dp bl	16.00	*47.50*
		Never hinged	40.00	
		On cover		—
C19	AP4	50 l dk vio	16.00	*47.50*
		Never hinged	40.00	
		On cover		—
		Nos. C13-C19 (7)	*83.00*	*206.50*
		Nos. C13-C19, set on flown cover		450.00

50th anniv. of Italian Government of Eritrea. Issue dates: 50 l, June 1; others, Mar. 27.

Macchi-Costoldi Seaplane — AP5

Savoia S73 — AP6

Winding Propeller AP7

"More Efficient Machinery" AP8

1933-34

C20	AP5	50c org brn	7.25	11.50
		Never hinged	18.00	
		On cover		95.00
C21	AP6	75c red vio	7.25	11.50
		Never hinged	18.00	
		On cover		110.00
C22	AP5	1 l bis brn	7.25	11.50
		Never hinged	18.00	
		On cover		140.00
C23	AP6	3 l olive gray	7.25	*25.00*
		Never hinged	18.00	
		On cover		200.00
C24	AP5	10 l dp vio	7.25	*25.00*
		Never hinged	18.00	
		On cover		—
C25	AP6	12 l bl grn	7.25	*35.00*
		Never hinged	18.00	
		On cover		—
C26	AP7	20 l gray blk	10.00	*45.00*
		Never hinged	25.00	
		On cover		—
C27	AP8	50 l blue ('34)	18.00	*40.00*
		Never hinged	45.00	
		On cover		—
		Nos. C20-C27 (8)	71.50	*204.50*
		Nos. C20-C27, set on flown cover		450.00

Tenth anniversary of Fascism.
Issue dates: 50 1, Dec. 26; others, Oct. 5.

Natives Hailing Dornier Wal — AP9

1934, Apr. 24

C28	AP9	25 l brown olive	21.00	*115.00*
		Never hinged	55.00	
		On flown cover		275.00
		On flown cover, single franking		240.00

Issued in honor of Luigi Amadeo, Duke of the Abruzzi (1873-1933).

Airplane over Stadium AP10

Goalkeeper Leaping — AP11

Seaplane and Soccer Ball AP12

1934, June

C29	AP10	50c yel brn	13.00	*32.50*
		Never hinged	32.50	
		On cover		200.00
C30	AP10	75c dp vio	13.00	*32.50*
		Never hinged	32.50	
		On cover		250.00
C31	AP11	5 l brn blk	35.00	*72.50*
		Never hinged	90.00	
		On cover		475.00
C32	AP11	10 l red org	35.00	*72.50*
		Never hinged	90.00	
		On cover		—
C33	AP10	15 l car rose	35.00	*72.50*
		Never hinged	90.00	
		On cover		—
C34	AP11	25 l green	35.00	140.00
		Never hinged	90.00	
		On cover		—
C35	AP12	50 l bl grn	35.00	140.00
		Never hinged	90.00	
		On flown cover, single franking		200.00
		Nos. C29-C35 (7)	201.00	*562.50*
		Nos. C29-C35, set on flown cover		1,250.

World Soccer Championship Games, Rome. Issued: 50 l, June 21; others, June 5.

AIR POST SPECIAL DELIVERY STAMPS

Garibaldi Type of Italy
Wmk. 140

1932, Oct. 6 Photo. *Perf. 14*

CE1	APSD1	2.25 l + 1 l dk vio & sl	6.00	*21.00*
		Never hinged	14.50	
		On cover		—
CE2	APSD1	4.50 l + 1.50 l dk brn & grn	6.00	—
		Never hinged	14.50	
		On cover		—
		Nos. CE1-CE2, set on flown cover		250.00

ITALIAN EAST AFRICA

ə-ˈtal-yən ˈēst ˈa-fri-kə

LOCATION — In eastern Africa, bordering on the Red Sea and Indian Ocean
GOVT. — Italian Colony
AREA — 665,977 sq. mi. (estimated)
POP. — 12,100,000 (estimated)
CAPITAL — Asmara

This colony was formed in 1936 and included Ethiopia and the former colonies of Eritrea and Italian Somaliland. For previous issues see listings under these headings.

100 Centesimi = 1 Lira

Used values in italics are for postaly used stamps. CTO's or stamps with fake cancels sell for about the same as unused, hinged stamps.

Grant's Gazelle — A1

Eagle and Lion — A2

Victor Emmanuel III — A3

Fascist Legionary — A5

Statue of the Nile — A4

Desert Road — A6

Wmk. 140

1938, Feb. 7 Photo. *Perf. 14*

1	A1	2c red orange	1.10	*.90*
		Never hinged	2.75	
		On cover		25.00
2	A2	5c brown	1.10	.20
		Never hinged	2.75	
		On cover		18.00
3	A3	7½c dk violet	1.40	*2.90*
		Never hinged	3.75	
		On cover		95.00
4	A4	10c olive brown	2.25	.20
		Never hinged	5.50	
		On cover		8.75
5	A5	15c slate green	1.10	.20
		Never hinged	2.75	
		On cover		25.00
6	A3	20c crimson	1.10	.20
		Never hinged	2.75	
		On cover		18.00
7	A6	25c green	2.25	.20
		Never hinged	5.50	
		On cover		8.75
8	A1	30c olive brown	1.40	8.00
		Never hinged	3.75	
		On cover		18.00
9	A2	35c sapphire	2.25	*7.25*
		Never hinged	5.50	
		On cover		110.00
10	A3	50c purple	1.10	.20
		Never hinged	2.75	
		On cover		5.00

Engr.

11	A5	75c carmine lake	2.25	.35
		Never hinged	5.50	
		On cover		42.50
12	A6	1 l olive green	1.40	.20
		Never hinged	3.75	
		On cover		5.75
13	A3	1.25 l deep blue	2.25	.35
		Never hinged	5.50	
		On cover		18.00
14	A4	1.75 l orange	14.50	.20
		Never hinged	35.00	
		On cover		5.75
15	A2	2 l cerise	2.25	.35
		Never hinged	5.50	
		On cover		18.00
16	A6	2.55 l dark brown	11.00	*21.00*
		Never hinged	27.50	
		On cover		210.00
17	A1	3.70 l purple	35.00	35.00
		Never hinged	90.00	
		On cover		325.00
18	A5	5 l purple	8.75	3.75
		Never hinged	22.50	
		On cover		250.00
19	A2	10 l henna brown	13.00	14.50
		Never hinged	32.50	
		On cover		325.00
20	A4	20 l dull green	21.00	21.00
		Never hinged	55.00	
		On cover		—
		Nos. 1-20,C1-C11,CE1-CE2 (33)	259.10	201.35
		Nos. 1-20, set on overfranked philatelic cover		500.00

Augustus Caesar (Octavianus) A7

Goddess Abundantia A8

1938, Apr. 25 Photo. *Perf. 14*

21	A7	5c bister brn	.75	*1.75*
		Never hinged	1.75	
		On cover		110.00
22	A8	10c copper red	.75	*1.10*
		Never hinged	1.75	
		On cover		42.50
23	A7	25c deep green	1.10	*1.10*
		Never hinged	2.75	
		On cover		65.00
24	A8	50c purple	1.10	*.75*
		Never hinged	2.75	
		On cover		35.00
25	A7	75c crimson	1.10	2.50
		Never hinged	2.75	
		On cover		125.00
26	A8	1.25 l deep blue	1.10	7.25
		Never hinged	2.75	
		On cover		210.00
		Nos. 21-26,C12-C13 (8)	7.40	*21.70*
		Nos. 21-26, set on overfranked philatelic cover		180.00

Bimillenary of the birth of Augustus Caesar (Octavianus), first Roman emperor.

Rome-Berlin Axis.

Four stamps of type AP8, without "Posta Aerea," were prepared in 1941, but not issued. Value, each $1,900.

Native Boat — A9

Native Soldier — A10

Statue Suggesting Italy's Conquest of Ethiopia — A11

1940, May 11 Wmk. 140

27	A9	5c olive brown	.75	*.75*
		Never hinged	1.75	
		On cover		87.50
28	A10	10c red orange	1.10	*.75*
		Never hinged	2.75	
		On cover		42.50
29	A11	25c green	1.10	1.40
		Never hinged	2.75	
		On cover		57.50
30	A9	50c purple	1.10	.75
		Never hinged	2.75	
		On cover		42.50
31	A10	75c rose red	1.10	*3.75*
		Never hinged	2.75	
		On cover		180.00
32	A11	1.25 l dark blue	1.10	2.75
		Never hinged	2.75	
		On cover		210.00
33	A10	2 l + 75c carmine	1.10	*14.50*
		Never hinged	2.75	
		On cover		—
		Nos. 27-33,C14-C17 (11)	12.35	*33.15*
		Nos. 27-33, set on overfranked philatelic cover		225.00

Issued in connection with the first Triennial Overseas Exposition held at Naples.

SEMI-POSTAL STAMPS

Many issues of Italy and Italian Colonies include one or more semi-postal denominations. To avoid splitting sets, these issues are generally listed as regular postage, airmail, etc., unless all values carry a surtax.

AIR POST STAMPS

Plane Flying over Mountains AP1

Mussolini Carved in Stone Cliff — AP2

Airplane over Lake Tsana AP3

Bataleur Eagle — AP4

Eagle Attacking Serpent — AP5

Wmk. Crowns (140)

1938, Feb. 7 Photo. *Perf. 14*

C1 AP1 25c slate green 2.75 *3.75*
Never hinged 7.25
On cover 42.50
C2 AP2 50c olive brown 50.00 .20
Never hinged 125.00
On cover 4.50
C3 AP3 60c red orange 2.10 *8.75*
Never hinged 5.50
On cover 125.00
C4 AP1 75c orange brn 2.75 2.10
Never hinged 7.25
On cover 18.00
C5 AP4 1 l slate blue 8.25 .20
Never hinged 21.00
On cover 4.50

Engr.

C6 AP2 1.50 l violet 1.40 .35
Never hinged 3.75
On cover 18.00
C7 AP3 2 l slate blue 1.40 1.40
Never hinged 3.75
On cover 35.00
C8 AP1 3 l carmine lake 2.10 6.00
Never hinged 5.50
On cover 87.50
C9 AP4 5 l red brown 35.00 21.00
Never hinged 90.00
On cover 210.00
C10 AP2 10 l violet brn 1.40 1.40
Never hinged 3.75
On cover 325.00
C11 AP1 25 l slate blue 18.00 21.00
Never hinged 45.00
On cover —
Nos. C1-C11 (11) 125.15 66.15
Nos. C1-C11, set on overfranked philatelic flown cover 225.00

1938, Apr. 25 Photo.

C12 AP5 50c bister brown .75 2.50
Never hinged 1.90
On cover 42.50
C13 AP5 1 l purple .75 *4.75*
Never hinged 1.90
On cover 80.00
Nos. C12-C13, set on overfranked philatelic flown cover 72.50

Bimillenary of the birth of Augustus Caesar (Octavianus), first Roman emperor.

Triennial Overseas Exposition Type

#C14, C16, Tractor. #C15, C17, Plane over city.

1940, May 11

C14 A10 50c olive gray 1.10 *4.25*
Never hinged 2.75
On cover —
C15 A9 1 l purple 1.10 *4.25*
Never hinged 2.75
On cover —
C16 A10 2 l + 75c gray blue 1.40 —
Never hinged 3.75
On cover —
C17 A9 5 l + 2.50 l red brn 1.40 —
Never hinged 3.75
On cover —
Nos. C14-C17 (4) 5.00 *8.50*
Nos. C14-C17, set on overfranked philatelic flown cover 225.00

AIR POST SPECIAL DELIVERY STAMPS

Plow and Airplane — APSD1

Wmk. 140

1938, Feb. 7 Engr. *Perf. 14*

CE1 APSD1 2 l slate blue 3.75 *7.25*
Never hinged 9.00
On cover 500.00
CE2 APSD1 2.50 l dark brown 3.75 *11.00*
Never hinged 9.00
On cover —

SPECIAL DELIVERY STAMPS

Victor Emmanuel III — SD1

Wmk. 140

1938, Apr. 16 Engr. *Perf. 14*

E1 SD1 1.25 l dark green 3.75 6.00
Never hinged 9.00
On cover 180.00
E2 SD1 2.50 l dark carmine 3.75 *15.00*
Never hinged 9.00
On cover —

ITALIAN STATES

ə-ˈtal-yən ˈstāts

Watermarks

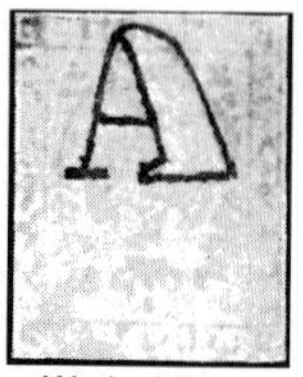

Wmk. 157 — Large Letter "A"

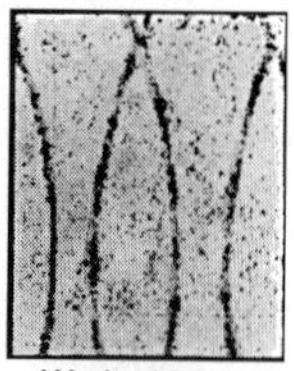

Wmk. 184 — Interlaced Wavy Lines

Wmk. 184 has double lined letters diagonally across the sheet readiing: "II R R POSTE TOSCANE."

Wmk. 185 — Crowns in the sheet

The watermark consists of twelve crowns, arranged in four rows of three, with horizontal and vertical lines between them. Only parts of the watermark appear on each stamp.
(Reduced illustration.)

Wmk. 186 — Fleurs-de-Lis in Sheet

MODENA

LOCATION — In northern Italy
GOVT. — Duchy
AREA — 1,003 sq. mi.
POP. — 448,000 (approx.)
CAPITAL — Modena

In 1852, when the first postage stamps were issued, Modena was under the rule of Duke Francis V of the House of Este-Lorraine. In June, 1859, he was overthrown and the Duchy was annexed to the Kingdom of Sardinia which on March 17, 1861, became the Kingdom of Italy.

100 Centesimi = 1 Lira

Values of Modena stamps vary tremendously according to condition. Values are for very fine examples, and values for unused stamps are for examples with original gum as defined in the catalogue introduction. Extremely fine or superb copies sell at much higher prices, and fine or poor copies sell at greatly reduced prices.

Coat of Arms
A1 A2

1852 Unwmk. Typo. *Imperf.*

Without Period After Figures of Value

1 A1 5c blk, *green* 2,300. 140.00
No gum 575.00
On cover 500.00
a. Pair, #1, 6 2,750. *2,000.*
No gum 925.00
On cover *8,000.*
2 A1 10c blk, *rose* 575.00 90.00
No gum 140.00
On cover 340.00
a. "EENT. 10" *7,250.* *2,500.*
No gum 1,800.
On cover *12,750.*
b. "1" of "10" inverted *7,250.* *2,500.*
No gum 1,800.
On cover *12,750.*
c. "CNET" *1,450.* *1,800.*
No gum 375.00
On cover *7,250.*
d. No period after "CENT" *2,175.* 875.00
No gum 550.00
On cover *3,500.*
e. Pair, #2, 7 1,200. *2,500.*
No gum 550.00
On cover *10,500.*
f. Frame below figure of value omitted 1,800.
On cover *9,000.*
3 A1 15c blk, *yellow* 57.50 35.00
No gum 14.50
On cover 180.00
a. "CETN 15." *7,250.* *1,100.*
No gum 1,800.
On cover *4,400.*
b. No period after "CENT" 290.00 *575.00*
No gum 110.00
On cover *2,900.*
4 A1 25c blk, *buff* 72.50 42.50
No gum 18.00
On cover 240.00
a. No period after "CENT" 650.00 *1,100.*
No gum 180.00
On cover *4,400.*
b. "ENT.25" omitted *1,000.* —
No gum 290.00
c. 25c black, *green* (error) 2,900. 2,000.
d. "N" of "CENT" omitted 725.00 1,800.
No gum 240.00
On cover *7,250.*
e. Raised period after "CENT" 1,450. —
5 A1 40c blk, *blue* 440.00 125.00
No gum 110.00
On cover 575.00
a. 40c black, *pale blue* *14,500.* 1,350.
On cover 6,500.
b. No period after "CENT" *1,800.* *1,800.*
No gum 650.00
On cover *7,250.*
c. As "a," no period after "CENT" — —
d. Pair, #5, 8 725.00 *2,500.*
No gum 290.00
On cover *10,500.*

Full margins = 1mm.
There are dividing lines between stamps.

Unused examples of No. 5a lack gum.
Used examples of No. 4c have a green administrative cancellation.
See Nos. PR3-PR4.

Values for pairs

1 A1 5c black, *green* 4,750. 325.00
On cover 1,300.
2 A1 10c black, *rose* 1,250. 300.00
On cover 1,450.
3 A1 15c black, *yellow* 125.00 *210.00*
On cover 1,350.
4 A1 25c black, *buff* 160.00 *440.00*
On cover 2,200.
5 A1 40c black, *blue* 925.00 500.00
On cover 2,500.
5a A1 40c black, *pale blue* — *13,500.*

With Period After Figures of Value

6 A1 5c blk, *green* 35.00 *47.50*
No gum 9.00
On cover 190.00
Single franking, on newspaper 2,200.
a. 5c black, *olive green* 440.00 140.00
No gum 30.00
On cover 500.00
b. "ENT" — *2,500.*
On cover *12,750.*
c. "CNET" *4,250.* *3,600.*
No gum 1,250.
On cover *14,500.*
d. As "a," "CNET" *2,200.* *2,200.*
No gum 725.00
On cover *8,750.*
e. "E" of "CENT" sideways — *5,750.*
No gum —
On cover *17,500.*
f. As "a," "CEN1" *2,500.* *2,500.*
No gum 800.00
On cover *10,000.*
g. As "a," no period after "5" 650.00 575.00
No gum 210.00
On cover *2,350.*
h. Double impression, no gum *1,200.* —
i. As "a," double impression *1,200.* —
No gum 130.00
j. Pair, #6a, 6g 1,200. *2,350.*
No gum 130.00
On cover 9,750.
k. No space between "T" and "5" 10,000. 5,750.
On cover *17,500.*
7 A1 10c blk, *rose* 440.00 325.00
No gum 110.00
On cover 1,100.
On cover, single franking 4,400.
a. "CENE" 1,450. *1,800.*
No gum 440.00
On cover *7,250.*
b. "CNET" 650.00 *900.00*
No gum 200.00
On cover 3,600.
c. "CE6T" 1,450. *1,800.*
No gum 440.00
On cover *7,250.*
d. "N" of "CENT" sideways *10,000.* *4,350.*
No gum 3,100.
On cover *17,500.*
e. Double impression 1,500. *4,400.*
No gum 365.00
f. Raised period after "10" 1,450. 1,800.
No gum 440.00
On cover *7,250.*
8 A1 40c blk, *blue* 50.00 *125.00*
No gum 12.50
On cover 575.00
a. "CNET" 290.00 *900.00*
No gum 90.00
On cover 3,600.

b. "CENE" 650.00 *1,800.*
No gum 200.00
On cover *7,250.*
c. "CE6T" 650.00 *1,800.*
No gum 200.00
On cover *7,250.*
d. "49" 290.00 *900.00*
No gum 90.00
On cover 3,600.
e. "4C" 650.00 *1,800.*
No gum 125.00
On cover *7,250.*
f. "CEN.T" *32,500.* —
No gum *20,000.*
g. Space between "T" and period 290.00 *925.00*
No gum 90.00
On cover *8,500.*

Values for pairs

6 A1 5c black, *green* 80.00 *130.00*
On cover 650.00
6a A1 5c black, *olive green* 925.00 325.00
On cover 1,300.
7 A1 10c black, *rose* 925.00 725.00
On cover 2,500.
8 A1 40c black, *blue* 110.00 *500.00*
On cover 2,500.
9 A1 1L black 125.00 *11,000.*
On cover *27,500.*

Wmk. 157

9 A1 1 l black 57.50 *2,150.*
No gum 14.50
On cover *9,000.*
On cover, single franking *55,000.*
a. With period after "LIRA" 160.00 *4,000.*
No gum 47.50
On cover *16,000.*
b. No period after "1" 150.00 *3,250.*
No gum 47.50
On cover *13,000.*

Full margins = 1mm.
There are dividing lines between stamps.

Provisional Government

1859 **Unwmk.**

10 A2 5c green 1,450. *700.00*
No gum 360.00
On cover 3,250.
On cover, single franking *23,500.*
a. 5c emerald 1,525. *800.00*
No gum 375.00
On cover 3,600.
b. 5c dark green 1,525. 800.00
No gum 375.00
On cover 3,600.
11 A2 15c brown 2,350. *4,000.*
No gum 575.00
On cover *25,000.*
a. 15c gray brown 325.00
No gum 80.00
b. 15c black brown 2,600. 5,000.
No gum 800.00
On cover *36,000.*
c. No period after "15" *2,900.* *4,750.*
No gum 900.00
d. Period before "CENT" *4,000.* *6,500.*
No gum 1,000.
e. Double impression (#11a) *1,450.*
No gum 440.00
f. As #11a, no period after "15" 400.00
No gum 110.00
g As #11a, period before "CENT" 650.00
No gum 210.00
12 A2 20c lilac 65.00 *1,200.*
No gum 18.00
On cover 5,000.
a. 20c violet 4,000. 160.00
No gum 1,000.
On cover 875.00
b. 20c blue violet 2,200. 160.00
No gum 550.00
On cover 875.00
c. As #12, no period after "20" 100.00 *1,450.*
No gum 32.50
On cover 5,750.
d. As #12, "ECNT" 250.00 *3,100.*
No gum 72.50
On cover *15,500.*
e. As #12, "N" inverted 200.00 *2,200.*
No gum 65.00
On cover 11,000.
f. Double impression (#12b) — *5,750.*
No gum
g. As #12b, no period after "20" 3,100. 725.00
13 A2 40c carmine 190.00 *1,275.*
No gum 47.50
On cover 9,000.
On cover, single franking *23,500.*
a. 40c brown rose 190.00 *1,275.*
No gum 47.50
On cover *9,000.*
b. No period after "40" 360.00 *2,275.*
No gum 110.00
On cover —
c. Period before "CENT" 360.00 *2,275.*
No gum 110.00
On cover —
d. Inverted "5" before the "C", no gum *32,500.* *44,000.*
14 A2 80c buff 190.00 *19,000.*
No gum 47.50
On cover *125,000.*
On cover, single franking *160,000.*
a. 80c brown orange 190.00 *19,000.*
No gum 37.50
On cover *125,000.*
b. "CENT 8" 360.00 —
No gum 115.00
c. "CENT 0" 1,200. —
No gum 360.00
d. No period after "80" 360.00 —
No gum 115.00
e. "N" inverted 360.00 —
No gum 115.00

Full margins = 1mm.
There are dividing lines between stamps.

Values for pairs

10 A2 5c green 3,100. 1,500.
On cover *7,250.*
11 A2 15c brown 5,250. *12,000.*
On cover —
11a A2 15c gray brown 675.00 —
On cover —
12 A2 20c lilac 140.00 *6,000.*
On cover —
12b A2 20c blue violet 4,750. 1,600.
On cover *6,500.*
13 A2 40c carmine 400.00 *16,500.*
On cover *50,000.*
14 A2 80c buff 400.00
On cover

The reprints of the 1859 issue have the word "CENT" and the figures of value in different type from the originals. There is no frame line at the bottom of the small square in the lower right corner.

NEWSPAPER TAX STAMPS

NT1

NT2

B. G. CEN. 9
Type I

B. G. CEN. 9.
Type II

1853 **Unwmk.** **Typo.** ***Imperf.***

PR1 NT1 9c blk, *violet* (I) — *3,100.*
No gum *14,500.*
On newspaper *11,000.*
PR2 NT1 9c blk, *violet* (II) 725.00 80.00
No gum 180.00
On newspaper 210.00
a. No period after "9" 1,100. 275.00
No gum 275.00
On newspaper 1,100.

Full margins = 1mm.
There are dividing lines between stamps.

All known unused examples of #PR1 lack gum.

1855-57

PR3 A1 9c blk, *violet* 3.65
No gum .90
a. No period after "9" 7.25
No gum 1.80
b. No period after "CENT" 11.00
No gum 2.75
c. Large period after "9" 8.75
No gum 3.00
PR4 A1 10c blk, *gray vio* ('57) 72.50 *250.00*
No gum 18.00
On newspaper 1,600.
On newspaper, uncanceled 40.00
a. "CEN1" 360.00 *1,450.*
No gum 100.00
On newspaper 5,750.
b. Frameline under value tablet missing 360.00 *1,450.*
No gum 100.00
On newspaper 5,750.

Full margins = 1mm.
There are dividing lines between stamps.

No. PR3 was never placed in use.

1859

PR5 NT2 10c black 1,150. *2,200.*
No gum 290.00
On newspaper 8,250.
On newspaper, uncancelled 725.00
a. Double impression *16,500.* *20,000.*
b. Vert. guidelines between stamps 1,150.
No gum 290.00
c. Blurred and shifted impression 1,700. *3,100.*
On newspaper 11,750.

Full margins = 1½mm.
No. PR5 has horizontal guide lines between stamps. No. PR5b is a second printing, which was not issued.

Values for unused pairs

PR5 NT2 10c black 2,750.
PR5b NT2 10c black 2,750.

Values for unused blocks

PR5 NT2 10c black *8,000.*
PR5b NT2 10c black *8,000.*

These stamps did not pay postage, but were a fiscal tax collected by the postal authorities on newspapers arriving from foreign countries.
The stamps of Modena were superseded by those of Sardinia in February, 1860.

PARMA

LOCATION — Comprising the present provinces of Parma and Piacenza in northern Italy.
GOVT. — Independent Duchy
AREA — 2,750 sq. mi. (1860)
POP. — 500,000 (1860)
CAPITAL — Parma

Parma was annexed to Sardinia in 1860.

100 Centesimi = 1 Lira

Values of Parma stamps vary tremendously according to condition. Values are for very fine examples, and values for unused stamps are for examples with original gum as defined in the catalogue introduction except for No. 8 which is known only without gum. Extremely fine or superb copies sell at much higher prices, and fine or poor copies sell at greatly reduced prices.

Crown and Fleur-de-lis
A1 A2

1852 **Unwmk.** **Typo.** ***Imperf.***

1 A1 5c blk, *yellow* 125.00 *140.00*
No gum 32.50
On cover 450.00
On cover, single franking 4,300.
2 A1 10c blk, *white* 125.00 *140.00*
No gum 32.50
On cover 450.00
On cover, single franking *9,000.*
3 A1 15c blk, *pink* 3,600. 72.50
No gum 900.00
On cover 180.00
a. Tête bêche pair, horiz. *100,000.*
On cover *200,000.*
Tête bêche pair, vert., on cover *240,000.*
b. Double impression *4,250.*
4 A1 25c blk, *violet* *14,500.* 215.00
No gum 3,600.
On cover 725.00
5 A1 40c blk, *blue* 2,900. 400.00
No gum 725.00
On cover 1,450.
a. 40c black, *pale blue* — 525.00
No gum 5,400.
On cover 2,400.

Full margins = ½mm.

Values for pairs

1 A1 5c black, *yellow* 260.00 *325.00*
On cover 1,100.
2 A1 10c black 275.00 *325.00*
On cover 1,300.
3 A1 15c black, *pink* 8,000. 210.00
On cover 850.00
4 A1 25c black, *violet* *32,500.* *9,750.*
On cover *28,500.*
5 A1 40c black, *blue* 6,250. 1,200.
On cover 4,100.
5a A1 40c black, *pale blue* *14,250.* 1,600.
On cover 5,500.

1854-55

6 A1 5c org yel *8,600.* 875.00
No gum 2,100.
On cover 2,000.
On cover or newspaper, single franking *20,000.*
a. 5c lemon yellow *11,500.* 1,100.
No gum 2,900.
On cover 2,700.
b. Double impression *18,000.*
7 A1 15c red *10,000.* 215.00
No gum 2,500.
On cover 425.00
8 A1 25c red brn ('55) *7,500.* 425.00
On cover 1,150.
a. Double impression *36,000.*

Full margins = ½mm.

No. 8 unused is without gum.

Values for pairs

6 A1 5c orange yellow — 1,600.
On cover 4,500.

6a A1 5c lemon yellow —
On cover —
7 A1 15c red 23,500. 475.00
On cover 1,100.
8 A1 25c red brown 20,000.
On cover 55,000.

1857-59

9 A2 15c red ('59) 360.00 360.00
No gum 90.00
On cover 1,100.
10 A2 25c red brown 575.00 215.00
No gum 140.00
On cover 500.00
11 A2 40c bl, wide "0" ('58) 80.00 500.00
No gum 20.00
On cover 2,000.
a. Narrow "0" in "40" 85.00 550.00
No gum 21.50
On cover 2,350.
b. Pair, #11, 11a 210.00 1,600.
No gum 72.50
On cover 6,500.

Full margins = 1mm.

Values for pairs

9 A2 15c red 790.00 850.00
On cover 2,150.
10 A2 25c red brown 2,500. 4,500.
On cover 18,000.
11 A2 40c blue 360.00 1,100.
On cover 4,250.

Provisional Government

A3

1859

12 A3 5c yel grn 650.00 23,000.
No gum 160.00
On cover —
a. 5c blue green 2,900. 4,250.
No gum 725.00
On cover 27,000.
13 A3 10c brown 1,325. 650.00
No gum 325.00
On cover 3,250.
a. 10c deep brown 1,325. 650.00
No gum 325.00
On cover 3,250.
b. "1" of "10" inverted 2,700. 5,400.
No gum 725.00
On cover 37,500.
c. Thick "0" in "10" 2,700. 5,500.
No gum 725.00
On cover 37,500.
14 A3 20c pale blue 1,325. 200.00
No gum 325.00
On cover 875.00
a. 20c deep blue 1,325. 240.00
No gum 325.00
On cover 1,100.
b. Thick "0" in "20" 1,550. 250.00
No gum 425.00
On cover 1,300.
15 A3 40c red 725.00 8,750.
No gum 175.00
On cover 46,500.
a. 40c brown red 23,000. 12,500.
No gum 6,750.
On cover 42,500.
b. Thick "0" in "40" (#15) 825.00 10,500.
No gum 225.00
On cover 54,000.
c. Thick "0" in "40," (#15a) 25,000. 14,500.
No gum 8,600.
On cover 50,000.
16 A3 80c olive yellow 8,000. 230,000.
No gum 2,400.
a. 80c orange yellow 11,000. —
No gum 3,000.
b. 80c bister 8,600.
No gum 2,900.
c. 80c orange bister 9,750.
No gum 3,000.
d. Thick "0" in "80" (#16) 8,500.
No gum 2,900.
e. Thick "0" in "80," (#16a) 11,500.
No gum 4,000.

Full margins = 1¼mm.

Nos. 12-16 exist in two other varieties: with spelling "CFNTESIMI" and with small "A" in "STATI." These are valued about 50 per cent more than normal stamps.

See Nos. PR1-PR2.

Values for pairs

12 A3 5c yellow green 1,450. 48,500.
On cover 100,000.
12a A3 5c blue green 6,750. 10,000.
On cover 55,000.
13 A3 10c brown 2,900. 1,450.
On cover 6,750.
14 A3 20c pale blue 2,900. 5,000.
On cover 30,000.
15 A3 40c red 1,600.
15a A3 40c brown red 55,000.
16 A3 80c orange yellow 18,000.
16a A3 80c olive yellow 27,500.

NEWSPAPER TAX STAMPS

Type of 1859

1853-57 Unwmk. Typo. *Imperf.*

Normal Paper ('53)

PR1 A3 6c black, *deep rose* 2,300. 325.00
No gum 575.00
On newspaper 14,500.
On newspaper, uncanceled 850.00
PR2 A3 9c black, *blue* 1,275. 15,500.
No gum 325.00
On newspaper 42,500.
On newspaper, uncanceled 475.00

Full margins = 1¼mm.

Thin, Semitransparent Paper ('57)

PR1a A3 6c black, *rose* ('57) 140.00
No gum 35.00
PR2a A3 9c black, *blue* 72.50
No gum 18.00

These stamps belong to the same class as the Newspaper Tax Stamps of Modena, Austria, etc.

Note following #16 also applies to #PR1-PR2.

Nos. PR1a-PR2a were not issued.

The stamps of Parma were superseded by those of Sardinia in 1860.

ROMAGNA

LOCATION — Comprised the present Italian provinces of Forli, Ravenna, Ferrara and Bologna.
GOVT. — One of the Roman States
AREA — 5,626 sq. mi.
POP. — 1,341,091 (1853)
CAPITAL — Ravenna

Postage stamps were issued when a provisional government was formed pending the unification of Italy. In 1860 Romagna was annexed to Sardinia and since 1862 the postage stamps of Italy have been used.

100 Bajocchi = 1 Scudo

Values of Romagna stamps vary tremendously according to condition. Values are for very fine examples, and values for unused stamps are for examples with original gum as defined in the catalogue introduction. Extremely fine or superb copies sell at much higher prices, and fine or poor copies sell at greatly reduced prices.

A1

1859 Unwmk. Typo. *Imperf.*

1 A1 ½b blk, *straw* 35.00 325.00
No gum 9.00
On cover 1,800.
On newspaper, single franking 14,500.
a. Half used as ¼b on cover 14,750.
As "a," single franking 115,000.
2 A1 1b blk, *drab* 35.00 160.00
No gum 9.00
On cover 800.00
3 A1 2b blk, *buff* 50.00 175.00
No gum 13.00
On cover 1,000.
a. Half used as 1b on cover 6,400.
4 A1 3b blk, *dk grn* 57.50 350.00
No gum 15.00
On cover 2,250.
5 A1 4b blk, *fawn* 650.00 160.00
No gum 200.00
On cover 900.00
a. Half used as 2b on cover 32,500.
6 A1 5b blk, *gray vio* 72.50 400.00
No gum 18.00
On cover 4,000.
7 A1 6b blk, *yel grn* 475.00 8,000.
No gum 120.00
On cover 87,500.
a. Half used as 3b on cover 145,000.
8 A1 8b blk, *rose* 225.00 1,800.
No gum 65.00
On cover 19,000.
a. Half used as 4b on cover 145,000.
9 A1 20b blk, *gray grn* 225.00 2,500.
No gum 65.00
On cover 23,500.

Full margins = 1mm.
There are dividing lines between stamps.

Forged cancellations are plentiful.
Bisects used Oct. 12, 1859 to Mar. 1, 1860.

Values for pairs

1 A1 ½b black, *straw* 80.00 725.00
On cover 3,650.
2 A1 1b black, *drab* 80.00 625.00
On cover 2,500.
3 A1 2b black, *buff* 110.00 550.00
On cover 2,200.
4 A1 3b black, *dark green* 125.00 2,000.
On cover 10,000.
5 A1 4b black, *fawn* 1,500. 2,500.
On cover 12,750.
6 A1 5b black, *gray violet* 160.00
7 A1 6b black, *yellow green* 1,000.
8 A1 8b black, *rose* 475.00
9 A1 20b black, *gray green* 475.00

Values for blocks of 4

1 A1 ½b black, *straw* 160.00 —
2 A1 1b black, *drab* 160.00
3 A1 2b black, *buff* 225.00
4 A1 3b black, *dark green* 250.00
5 A1 4b black, *fawn* 2,900.
6 A1 5b black, *gray violet* 325.00
7 A1 6b black, *yellow green* 2,200.
8 A1 8b black, *rose* 975.00
9 A1 20b black, *gray green* 975.00

These stamps have been reprinted several times. The reprints usually resemble the originals in the color of the paper but there are impressions on incorrect colors and also in colors on white paper. They often show broken letters and other injuries. The Y shaped ornaments between the small circles in the corners are broken and blurred and the dots outside the circles are often missing or joined to the circles.

The stamps of Romagna were superseded by those of Sardinia in February, 1860.

ROMAN STATES

LOCATION — Comprised most of the central Italian Peninsula, bounded by the former Kingdom of Lombardy-Venetia and Modena on the north, Tuscany on the west, and the Kingdom of Naples on the southeast.
GOVT. — Under the direct government of the See of Rome.
AREA — 16,000 sq. mi.
POP. — 3,124,758 (1853)
CAPITAL — Rome

Upon the formation of the Kingdom of Italy, the area of the Roman States was greatly reduced and in 1870 they disappeared from the political map of Europe. Postage stamps of Italy have been used since that time.

100 Bajocchi = 1 Scudo
100 Centesimi = 1 Lira (1867)

Values of Roman States stamps vary tremendously according to condition. Values are for very fine examples, and values for unused stamps are for examples with original gum as defined in the catalogue introduction. Extremely fine or superb copies sell at much higher prices, and fine or poor copies sell at greatly reduced prices.

Papal Arms
A1 A2

A3

A4

A5

A6

A7

A8

A9

A10

A11

1852 Unwmk. Typo. *Imperf.*

1 A1 ½b black, *dull violet* 57.50 125.00
No gum 14.00
On cover 540.00
On cover, single franking 1,050.
a. ½b black, *gray blue* 725.00 95.00
No gum 180.00
On cover 300.00
On cover, single franking 600.00
b. ½b black, *gray lilac* 725.00 325.00
No gum 180.00
On cover 1,450.
On cover, single franking 2,900.
c. ½b black, *gray* 725.00 92.50
No gum 180.00
On cover 300.00
On cover, single franking 625.00
d. ½b black, *reddish violet* 3,600. 1,800.
No gum 900.00
On cover 9,000.
e. ½b black, *dark violet* 275.00 275.00
No gum 72.50
On cover 1,300.
f. Tête bêche pair 32,500.
On cover 97,500.
h. As "a," half used as ¼b on wrapper, pen canceled 65,000.
i. As #1, double impression — 5,750.
j. Impression on both sides — 13,000.
k. As #1a, double impression 6,000.
2 A2 1b black, *gray green* 290.00 11.00
No gum 72.50
On cover 30.00
a. 1b black, *blue green* 850.00 57.50
No gum 210.00
On cover 175.00
b. As "a," half used as ½b on cover 550.00
c. Grayish greasy ink 1,075. 40.00
No gum 575.00
On cover 120.00
d. Double impression 6,000.
On cover 18,000.
e. Impression on both sides — 13,000.
3 A3 2b black, *greenish white* 14.00 72.50
No gum 3.50
On cover 200.00
a. 2b black, *yellow green* 215.00 15.00
No gum 52.50
On cover 42.50
b. As #3, half used as 1b on cover 6,500.
c. As "a," half used as 1b on cover 475.00
d. Grayish greasy ink 1,075. 40.00
No gum 650.00
On cover 120.00
e. No period after "BAJ" 150.00 42.50
No gum 42.50
On cover 130.00
f. As "a" and "e" 425.00 27.50
No gum 110.00
On cover 85.00
g. Double impression 5,500.
4 A4 3b black, *brown* 175.00 65.00
No gum 45.00
On cover 200.00
a. 3b black, *light brown* 5,250. 125.00
No gum 1,350.
On cover 500.00
b. 3b black, *yellow brown* 2,500. 50.00
No gum 625.00
On cover 125.00
c. 3b black, *yellow buff* 2,500. 50.00
No gum 625.00
On cover 125.00
d. 3b black, *chrome yellow* 42.50 200.00
No gum 11.00
On cover 575.00
e. One-third used as 1b on circular 3,600.
f. Two-thirds used as 2b on circular 11,500.
g. Grayish greasy ink 5,250. 215.00
No gum 3,600.
On cover 725.00
h. Impression on both sides — 13,000.
i. Double impression — 6,000.
j. Half used as 1½b on cover 14,250.

5 A5 4b black, *lemon* 250.00 85.00
No gum 62.50
On cover 210.00
a. 4b black, *yellow* 250.00 85.00
No gum 62.50
On cover 210.00
b. 4b black, *rose brown* 10,000. 125.00
No gum 2,900.
On cover 400.00
c. 4b black, *gray brown* 7,750. 87.50
No gum 2,100.
On cover 210.00
d. Half used as 2b on cover 2,700.
e. One-quarter used as 1b on cover *25,000.*
f. Impression on both sides — *13,000.*
g. Ribbed paper 300.00 75.00
No gum 80.00
On cover 225.00
h. Grayish greasy ink 16,000. 350.00
No gum 11,000.
On cover 1,100.
i. As "a," half used as 2b on cover 4,250.
j. As "a," one-quarter used as 1b on cover *23,500.*

6 A6 5b black, *rose* 250.00 16.00
No gum 62.50
On cover 55.00
a. 5b black, *pale rose* 260.00 18.00
No gum 67.50
On cover 57.50
c. Impression on both sides *13,000.*
d. Double impression *6,000.*
On cover *25,000.*
e. Grayish greasy ink 1,500. 47.50
No gum 850.00
On cover 140.00
f. Half used as 2½b on cover *72,500.*

7 A7 6b black, *greenish gray* 1,000. 85.00
No gum 250.00
On cover 200.00
a. 6b black, *gray* 1,600. 92.50
No gum 310.00
On cover 240.00
b. 6b black, *grayish lilac* 1,400. 225.00
No gum 350.00
On cover 800.00
c. Grayish greasy ink 4,250. 250.00
No gum 2,150.
On cover 850.00
d. Double impression — *6,000.*
On cover *18,000.*
e. Half used as 3b on cover 5,750.
f. One-third used as 2b on cover *21,500.*

8 A8 7b black, *blue* 1,425. 80.00
No gum 350.00
On cover 290.00
On cover, single franking 4,100.
a. Half used as 3¼b on cover *36,000.*
b. Double impression — 5,500.
On cover *13,000.*
c. Grayish greasy ink 4,300. 160.00
No gum 2,150.
On cover 650.00

9 A9 8b black 650.00 47.50
No gum 160.00
On cover 140.00
a. Half used as 4b on cover 9,500.
b. Quarter used as 2b on cover *90,000.*
c. Double impression — —
d. Grayish greasy ink 2,650. 250.00
No gum 1,300.
On cover 700.00

10 A10 50b dull blue *16,000.* 1,800.
No gum 4,000.
On cover 6,750.
On cover, single franking 28,000.
a. 50b deep blue (worn impression) *23,000.* 2,900.
No gum 5,750.
On cover (from an 1864 printing) 42,500.

11 A11 1sc rose *4,000.* *3,600.*
No gum 1,000.
On cover, with grill cancellation 48,000.
On cover, single franking, with c.d.s. 67,500.

Full margins: Nos. 1-2, 4-5, 10-11 = ½mm; Nos. 3, 6-8 = ¾mm; No. 9 = 1¼mm. There are double dividing lines between stamps on Nos. 1-2, 4-5, 9.

Counterfeits exist of Nos. 10-11. Fraudulent cancellations are found on No. 11.

Covers: Values for Nos. 1-2, 4-5, 9 are for covers bearing stamps with at least one frameline complete on each side; for Nos. 3, 6-8, 10-11, stamps are cut square clear of the design. Covers bearing stamps with framelines missing are worth much less; covers with stamps showing all 8 framelines intact are worth much more.

Nos. 1, 8, 10-11 single frankings are worth much more. Nos. 10-11 with circular datestamps are worth 10-20% more.

Grayish greasy ink stamps are from specific 1854 printings. Covers usually are dated 1854.

A12

A13

A14

A15

A16

A17

A18

1867 ***Imperf.***

Glazed Paper

12 A12 2c black, *green* 115.00 *275.00*
No gum 29.00
On cover 800.00
On cover, single franking 975.00
a. No period after "Cent" 140.00 *290.00*
No gum 35.00
On cover 850.00

13 A13 3c black, *gray* 1,275. *7,750.*
No gum 325.00
On cover *90,000.*
a. 3c black, *lilac gray* 3,200. *2,500.*
No gum 800.00
On cover 18,500.

14 A14 5c black, *light blue* 175.00 *250.00*
No gum 45.00
On cover 500.00
On cover, single franking 1,500.
a. No period after "5" 350.00 *500.00*
No gum 90.00
On cover 1,000.

15 A15 10c black, *vermilion* 1,575. 92.50
No gum 400.00
On cover 210.00
a. Double impression 7,250.
On cover *32,000.*

16 A16 20c black, *copper red* (unglazed) 200.00 115.00
No gum 55.00
On cover 260.00
a. No period after "20" 650.00 325.00
No gum 160.00
On cover 950.00
b. No period after "CENT" 650.00 315.00
No gum 160.00
On cover 950.00

17 A17 40c black, *yellow* 225.00 *215.00*
No gum 57.50
On cover 575.00
a. No period after "40" 290.00 275.00
No gum 72.50
On cover 850.00

18 A18 80c black, *lilac rose* 200.00 *525.00*
No gum 36.00
On cover 2,100.
On cover, single franking 4,100.
a. No period after "80" 350.00 *850.00*
No gum 90.00
On cover 3,000.

Values for stamps in pairs

12 A12 2c black, *green* 575.00
On cover 1,700.
13 A13 3c black, *gray* 21,500.
On cover —
13a A13 3c black, *lilac gray* 9,000.
On cover —
14 A14 5c black, *light blue* 540.00
On cover 1,100.
15 A15 10c black, *vermilion* 290.00
On cover 1,150.
16 A16 20c black, *copper red* (unglazed) 725.00
On cover 1,800.
17 A17 40c black, *yellow* *900.00*
On cover 3,600.
18 A18 80c black, *lilac rose* *1,250.*
On cover 5,000.

Full margins: No. 12 = 2mm; Nos. 13, 17 = 1¼mm; Nos. 14, 18 = 1½mm at sides, 1mm at top and bottom;
No. 15 = 2½mm at sides, 1mm at top and bottom; No. 16 = 1½mm at sides, ¼mm at top and bottom.
There are double dividing lines between stamps.

Imperforate stamps on unglazed paper, or in colors other than listed, are unfinished remainders of the 1868 issue.

Fraudulent cancellations are found on Nos. 13, 14, 17, 18.

Covers: Values for Nos. 12-18 are for covers bearing stamps with at least one frameline complete on each side.

Covers bearing stamps with framelines missing are worth much less; covers with stamps showing all 8 framelines intact are worth much more.

1868 **Glazed Paper** ***Perf. 13***

19 A12 2c black, *green* 10.50 *72.50*
No gum 2.75
On cover 200.00
On newspaper, single franking 425.00
a. No period after "CENT" 12.50 *90.00*
No gum 3.25
On cover 260.00
b. Figure "2" omitted *17,000.* *19,000.*
c. Vert. pair, imperf horiz. 425.00
d. Horiz. pair, imperf vert. 425.00
e. Horiz. pair, imperf between 800.00

20 A13 3c black, *gray* 47.50 *3,200.*
No gum 12.00
On cover *25,750.*
a. 3c black, *lilac gray* *9,000.* *20,000.*
No gum 2,250.
On cover *145,000.*

21 A14 5c black, *light blue* 29.00 *57.50*
No gum 7.25
On cover 140.00
On cover, single franking 1,300.
a. No period after "5" 32.50 *72.50*
No gum 9.00
On cover 175.00
b. No period after "Cent" 110.00 *290.00*
No gum 32.50
On cover 850.00
c. 5c black, *lt bl* (unglazed, imperf., without gum) 90.00 —
d. Horiz. pair, imperf vert. 425.00
e. Horiz. pair, imperf between 800.00 *4,250.*

22 A15 10c black, *orange ver* 3.50 *12.50*
No gum .90
On cover 30.00
a. 10c black, *vermilion* 72.50 14.00
No gum 18.00
On cover 45.00
b. 10c black, *ver* (unglazed) 1.00 —
No gum —
c. 10c black, *ver* (unglazed, imperf., without gum) 1.00 —
d. As #22, vert. pair, imperf horiz. 240.00
e. As "a," vert. pair, imperf horiz. 500.00
f. As #22, horiz. pair, imperf vert. 275.00
g. As "a," horiz. pair, imperf vert. 400.00
h. As #22, horiz. pair, imperf between 425.00
i. As "a," horiz. pair, imperf between 900.00 *4,750.*
j. As "a," vert. pair, imperf between 1,100. *5,000.*

23 A16 20c black, *deep crimson* 5.75 *26.50*
No gum 1.50
On cover 90.00
a. 20c black, *magenta* 7.25 *42.50*
No gum 1.80
On cover 125.00
b. 20c black, *magenta* (unglazed) 350.00 *35.00*
No gum 90.00
On cover 110.00
c. 20c black, *magenta* (imperf., without gum) 2.90 —
d. 20c black, *copper red* (unglazed) 1,800. 50.00
No gum 450.00
On cover 125.00
e. 20c black, *deep crimson* (imperf., without gum) 2.90 —
f. No period after "20" (*copper red*) *2,500.* 350.00
No gum 650.00
On cover 1,100.
g. No period after "20" (*mag*) 29.00 *215.00*
No gum 7.25
On cover 650.00
h. No period after "20" (*deep crimson*) 29.00 *215.00*
No gum 7.25
On cover 650.00
i. No period after "CENT" (*copper red*) *2,500.* 350.00
No gum 650.00
On cover 1,100.
j. No period after "CENT" (*magenta*) 29.00 *215.00*
No gum 7.25
On cover 650.00
k. No period after "CENT" (*deep crimson*) 29.00 *215.00*
No gum 7.25
On cover 650.00
l. Horiz. pair, imperf vert. 275.00
m. As #23, horiz. pair, imperf between 425.00
n. As "d," horiz. pair, imperf between 5,000. *9,500.*
o. As #23, vert. pair, imperf between 550.00
p. As "d," vert. pair, imperf between —

24 A17 40c black, *greenish yellow* 10.00 *140.00*
No gum 2.50
On cover 425.00
a. 40c black, *yellow* 250.00 *90.00*
No gum 65.00
On cover 260.00
b. 40c black, *orange yellow* 110.00 *900.00*
No gum 27.50
On cover 2,700.
c. No period after "40" 14.50 *115.00*
No gum 3.75
On cover 350.00
d. Vert. pair, imperf horiz. 400.00
e. Horiz. pair, imperf vert. 400.00

25 A18 80c black, *rose lilac* 250.00 *360.00*
No gum 60.00
On cover 1,750.
a. 80c black, *bright rose* *5,750.* *45,000.*
No gum 850.00
On cover *215,000.*
b. 80c black, *rose* (unglazed) 57.50 —
No gum 11.50
c. No period after "80" (*rose lilac*) 110.00 *500.00*
No gum 27.50
On cover —
d. 80c black, *pale rose lilac* (unglazed) 85.00 —
e. 80c black, *pale rose* 50.00 350.00
No gum 6.50
On cover 1,750.
f. As "e," no period after "80" 65.00 600.00
No gum 16.00
On cover 3,000.
g. As "a," no period after "80" 6,750. —
No gum 1,800.
h. As "e," double impression — —
i. As "e," vert. pair, imperf horiz. 400.00
j. As #25, vert. pair, imperf horiz. 1,100.
k. As "b," vert. pair, imperf horiz. 500.00
l. As "b," horiz. pair, imperf vert. 575.00
m. As "e,"horiz. pair, imperf vert. 425.00
n. As "b," horiz. pair, imperf between —
o. As #25, vert. pair, imperf between 1,450.
p. As "e," vert. pair, imperf between 1,000.

Values for stamps in pairs

19 A12 2c black, *green* 24.00 *150.00*
On cover 425.00
20 A13 3c black, *gray* 100.00 *8,250.*
On cover *65,000.*
20a A13 3c black, *lilac gray* 20,000.
21 A14 5c black, *light blue* 65.00 *125.00*
On cover 260.00
22 A15 10c black, *orange vermilion* 8.25 *32.50*
On cover 100.00
23 A16 20c black, *deep crimson* 12.50 *290.00*
On cover 1,150.
23d A16 20c black, *copper red* (unglazed) 3,750. 290.00
On cover 1,150.
24 A17 40c black, *greenish yellow* 22.00 *325.00*
On cover 1,350.
25a A18 80c black, *bright rose* 12,500.
25b A18 80c black, *rose lilac* (unglazed) 145.00
25c A18 80c black, *pale rose* 100.00 *900.00*
On cover 3,600.

All values except the 3c are known imperforate vertically or horizontally.

Double impressions are known of the 5c, 10c, 20c (all three colors), 40c and 80c.

Covers: Nos. 21, 25 single frankings are worth much more.

Fraudulent cancellations are found on Nos. 20, 24 and 25.

The stamps of the 1867 and 1868 issues have been privately reprinted; many of these reprints are well executed and it is difficult to distinguish them from the originals. Most reprints show more or less pronounced defects of the design. On the originals the horizontal lines between stamps are unbroken, while on most of the reprints these lines are broken. Most of the perforated reprints gauge 11½.

Roman States stamps were replaced by those of Italy in 1870.

SARDINIA

LOCATION — An island in the Mediterranean Sea off the west coast of Italy and a large area in northwestern Italy, including the cities of Genoa, Turin and Nice.

GOVT. — Kingdom

As a result of war and revolution, most of the former independent Italian States were joined to the Kingdom of Sardinia in 1859 and 1860. On March

17, 1861, the name was changed to the Kingdom of Italy.

100 Centesimi = 1 Lira

Values of Sardinia stamps vary tremendously according to condition. Values are for very fine examples, and values for unused stamps are for examples with original gum as defined in the catalogue introduction. Extremely fine or superb copies sell at much higher prices, and fine or poor copies sell at greatly reduced prices.

King Victor Emmanuel II

A1 A2

A3

A4

1851 Unwmk. Litho. *Imperf.*

1	A1 5c gray black	10,000.	2,150.
	No gum	2,500.	
	On cover		7,250.
	On cover, single franking		20,000.
a.	5c black	10,000.	2,150.
	No gum	2,500.	
	On cover		7,250.
	On cover, single franking		20,000.
2	A1 20c blue	8,250.	215.00
	No gum	2,000.	
	On cover		650.00
a.	20c deep blue	8,250.	215.00
	No gum	2,000.	
	On cover		650.00
b.	20c pale blue	8,250.	360.00
	No gum	2,100.	
	On cover		1,100.
c.	20c deep sky blue	11,750.	875.00
	No gum	3,250.	
	On cover		5,400.
3	A1 40c rose	17,250.	4,250.
	No gum	4,300.	
	On cover		16,000.
a.	40c violet rose	17,250.	7,250.
	No gum	4,300.	
	On cover		21,500.

Full margins = ½mm.

Values of pairs

1a	A1 5c black	21,500.	4,650.
	On cover		14,500.
2	A1 20c blue	17,500.	1,100.
	On cover		4,250.
3	A1 40c rose	42,500.	10,750.
	On cover		42,500.

Values of blocks of 4

1a	A1 5c black	57,500.	
2	A1 20c blue	77,500.	
3	A1 40c rose	120,000.	

Vignette & Inscriptions Embossed

1853

4	A2 5c *blue green*	16,000.	1,325.
	No gum	4,000.	
	On cover		4,000.
	On cover, single franking		8,000.
a.	Double embossing		3,250.
	On cover		9,500.
5	A2 20c *dull blue*	17,250.	175.00
	No gum	4,300.	
	On cover		575.00
a.	Double embossing		1,400.
	On cover		4,250.
6	A2 40c *pale rose*	10,750.	1,100.
	No gum	2,700.	
	On cover		3,750.
a.	40c *rose*	14,250.	1,800.
	No gum	3,600.	
	On cover		6,250.
b.	Double embossing		2,500.
	On cover		9,000.

Full margins = ¾mm.

Values for pairs

4	A2 5c *blue green*	36,000.	2,750.
	On cover		7,800.
5	A2 20c *dull blue*	40,000.	900.00
	On cover		2,700.
6	A2 40c *pale rose*	25,000.	2,700.
	On cover		10,750.

Values for blocks of 4

4	A2 5c *blue green*		72.500.
5	A2 20c *dull blue*		
6	A2 40c *pale rose*	57,500.	60,000.

Lithographed Frame in Color, Colorless Embossed Vignette

1854

7	A3 5c yellow green	32,500.	650.00
	No gum	12,750.	
	On cover		2,900.
	On cover, single franking		5,750.
a.	Double embossing		1,450.
	On cover		5,750.
b.	5c grayish green	3,250.	—
	No gum	800.00	
c.	5c deep green	3,250.	—
8	A3 20c blue	18,000.	140.00
	No gum	5,400.	
	On cover		500.00
a.	Double embossing		550.00
	On cover		1,800.
b.	20c indigo	900.00	—
	No gum	225.00	
9	A3 40c rose	90,000.	3,250.
	No gum	40,000.	
	On cover		9,750.
a.	Double embossing		5,750.
	On cover		18,000.
b.	40c brown rose	215.00	—
	No gum	55.00	

Full margins = ¾mm.

Values for pairs

7	A3 5c yellow green		1,450.
	On cover		5,750.
b.	5c grayish green	7,250.	
8	A3 20c blue		725.00
	On cover		2,150.
b.	20c indigo	2,150.	
9	A3 40c rose		8,250.
	On cover		28,500.
b.	40c brown rose	500.00	

Values for blocks of 4

7	A3 5c yellow green		110,000.
b.	5c grayish green	14,250.	—
8	A3 20c blue		—
b.	20c indigo	4,000.	
9	A3 40c rose		—
b.	40c brown rose	1,000.	

Nos. 7b, 8b and 9b, differing in shade from the original stamps, were prepared but not issued.

Typographed Frame in Color, Colorless Embossed Vignette

1855-63 Unwmk. *Imperf.*

Stamps of this issue vary greatly in color, paper and sharpness of embossing as between the early (1855-59) printings and the later (1860-63) ones. Year dates after each color name indicate whether the stamp falls into the Early or Late printing group.

As a rule, early printings are on smooth thick paper with sharp embossing, while later printings are usually on paper varying from thick to thin and of inferior quality with embossing less distinct and printing blurred. The outer frame shows a distinct design on the early printings, while this design is more or less blurred or even a solid line on the later printings.

10	A4 5c green ('62-63)	5.75	14.50
	No gum	1.50	
	On cover		57.50
	On cover, single franking		100.00
a.	5c yellow green ('62-63)	35.00	21.00
	No gum	9.00	
	On cover		85.00
	On cover, single franking		110.00
b.	5c olive green ('60-61)	425.00	275.00
	No gum	90.00	
	On cover		1,150.
	On cover, single franking		1,400.
c.	5c yellow green ('55-59)	1,000.	200.00
	No gum	250.00	
	On cover		800.00
	On cover, single franking		1,000.
d.	5c myrtle green ('57)	5,000.	500.00
	No gum	1,250.	
	On cover		2,000.
	On cover, single franking		2,400.
e.	5c emerald ('55-57)	3,600.	425.00
	No gum	900.00	
	On cover		2,150.
	On cover, single franking		1,500.
f.	Head inverted	—	3,250.
	On cover		29,000.
g.	Double head, one inverted	—	3,250.
11	A4 10c bister ('63)	5.75	21.00
	No gum	1.50	
	On cover		65.00
a.	10c ocher ('62)	105.00	21.00
	No gum	27.00	
	On cover		65.00
b.	10c olive bister ('62)	175.00	27.50
	No gum	45.00	
	On cover		85.00
c.	10c olive green ('61)	250.00	37.50
	No gum	62.50	
	On cover		110.00
d.	10c reddish brown ('61)	1,250.	140.00
	No gum	310.00	
	On cover		425.00
e.	10c gray brown ('61)	175.00	50.00
	No gum	45.00	
	On cover		150.00
f.	10c olive gray ('60-61)	350.00	72.50
	No gum	90.00	
	On cover		210.00
g.	10c gray ('60)	1,275.	225.00
	No gum	325.00	
	On cover		700.00
h.	10c grayish brown ('59)	125.00	215.00
	No gum	32.50	
	On cover		650.00
i.	10c violet brown ('59)	650.00	275.00
	No gum	160.00	
	On cover		850.00
j.	10c dark brown ('58)	775.00	400.00
	No gum	200.00	
	On cover		1,150.
k.	Head inverted	—	4,000.
	On cover		32,000.
l.	Double head, one inverted	—	4,000.
	On cover		32,000.
m.	Pair, one without embossing	2,500.	—
n.	Half used as 5c on cover (15c rate)		100,000.
o.	Half used as 5c on cover (5c rate)		155,000.
12	A4 20c indigo ('62)	115.00	50.00
	No gum	29.00	
	On cover		150.00
a.	20c blue ('61)	215.00	21.00
	No gum	55.00	
	On cover		65.00
b.	20c light blue ('60-61)	215.00	21.00
	No gum	55.00	
	On cover		65.00
c.	20c Prussian bl ('59-60)	725.00	35.00
	No gum	180.00	
	On cover		110.00
d.	20c indigo ('57-58)	540.00	50.00
	No gum	140.00	
	On cover		150.00
e.	20c sky blue ('55-56)	5,000.	215.00
	No gum	1,250.	
	On cover		650.00
f.	20c cobalt ('55)	2,850.	125.00
	No gum	725.00	
	On cover		400.00
g.	Head inverted	2,850.	1,425.
	No gum	1,425.	
	On cover		10,750.
h.	Double head, one inverted	—	—
i.	Pair, one without embossing	1,425.	—
	No gum	725.00	
j.	Half used as 10c on cover		125,000.
13	A4 40c red ('63)	22.50	50.00
	No gum	5.75	
	On cover		150.00
a.	40c rose ('61-62)	180.00	72.50
	No gum	45.00	
	On cover		210.00
b.	40c carmine ('60)	725.00	425.00
	No gum	180.00	
	On cover		1,250.
c.	40c light red ('57)	3,250.	140.00
	No gum	800.00	
	On cover		425.00
d.	40c vermilion ('55-57)	5,000.	425.00
	No gum	1,250.	
	On cover		1,750.
e.	Head inverted	—	5,500.
	On cover		32,500.
f.	Double head, one inverted	—	5,500.
g.	Pair, one without embossing	2,150.	—
	No gum	1,075.	
h.	Half used as 20c on cover		72,500.
14	A4 80c orange yellow ('62)	27.50	500.00
	No gum	7.25	
	On cover		3,600.
a.	80c yellow ('60-61)	32.50	400.00
	No gum	8.50	
	On cover		2,350.
b.	80c yellow ocher ('59)	900.00	725.00
	No gum	225.00	
	On cover		5,000.
c.	80c ocher ('58)	225.00	575.00
	No gum	57.50	
	On cover		4,000.
d.	80c brown orange ('58)	225.00	575.00
	No gum	57.50	
	On cover		4,000.
e.	Head inverted	—	20,000.
	On cover		77,500.
f.	Half used as 40c on cover		—
15	A4 3 l bronze, thin paper ('61)	500.00	3,250.
	No gum	125.00	
	On cover		120,000.
	On cover, single franking		180,000.
a.	Thick, opaque paper	600.00	3,250.
	No gum	200.00	
	On cover		120,000.
	On cover, single franking		180,000.

Full margins = 1mm.

Values for pairs

10	A4 5c green	11.50	30.00
	On cover		130.00
a.	5c yellow green	72.50	45.00
	On cover		175.00
b.	5c olive green	850.00	190.00
	On cover		725.00
c.	5c yellow green	2,000.	425.00
	On cover		1,575.
d.	5c myrtle green	10,000.	1,100.
	On cover		4,000.
e.	5c emerald	7,250.	900.00
	On cover		4,300.
11	A4 10c bister	11.50	55.00
	On cover		160.00
a.	10c ocher	210.00	55.00
	On cover		160.00
b.	10c olive bister	360.00	80.00
	On cover		210.00
c.	10c olive green	500.00	200.00
	On cover		600.00
f.	10c olive gray	700.00	200.00
	On cover		600.00
h.	10c grayish brown	250.00	475.00
	On cover		1,425.
j.	10c dark brown	1,550.	875.00
	On cover		3,100.
12	A4 20c indigo	230.00	140.00
	On cover		500.00
b.	20c light blue	430.00	62.50
	On cover		260.00
c.	20c prussian blue	1,450.	110.00
	On cover		400.00
d.	20c indigo	1,100.	200.00
	On cover		800.00
f.	20c cobalt	5,750.	375.00
	On cover		1,300.
13	A4 40c red	45.00	160.00
	On cover		575.00
a.	40c rose	360.00	240.00
	On cover		800.00
b.	40c carmine	1,450.	650.00
	On cover		2,000.
c.	40c light red	6,500.	325.00
	On cover		975.00
d.	40c vermilion	10,000.	975.00
	On cover		3,750.
14	A4 80c orange yellow	57.50	1,150.
	On cover		7,900.
a.	80c yellow	65.00	975.00
	On cover		9,250.
b.	80c yellow ocher	1,800.	1,600.
	On cover		11,000.
c.	80c ocher	475.00	1,275.
	On cover		9,000.
d.	80c brown orange	475.00	1,300.
	On cover		9,000.
15	A4 3 l bronze, thin paper	1,000.	10,750.
a.	Thick opaque paper	1,200.	10,750.

Forgeries of the inverted and double head varieties have been made by applying a faked head embossing to printer's waste without head. These forgeries are plentiful.

Fraudulent cancellations are found on #13-15.

The 5c, 20c and 40c have been reprinted; the embossing of the reprints is not as sharp as that of the originals,the colors are dull and blurred.

NEWSPAPER STAMPS

N1

Typographed and Embossed

1861 Unwmk. *Imperf.*

P1	N1 1c black	8.00	14.00
	No gum	2.00	
	On newspaper or cover		40.00
a.	Numeral "2"	725.00	2,500.
	No gum	650.00	
	On newspaper or cover		14,250.
b.	Figure of value inverted	2,150.	34,000.
c.	Double impression		—
	No gum	—	
P2	N1 2c black	160.00	115.00
	No gum	42.50	
	On newspaper or cover		210.00
a.	Numeral "1"	11,000.	32,500.
	No gum	5,400.	
b.	Figure of value inverted	2,150.	34,000.
	No gum	725.00	

Full margins = 1mm.

Values for pairs

P1	N1 1c black	16.00	30.00
	On newspaper or cover		80.00
P2	N1 2c black	400.00	260.00
	On newspaper or cover		525.00

Forgeries of the varieties of the embossed numerals have been made from printer's waste without numerals.

See Italy No. P1 for 2c buff.

The stamps of Sardinia were superseded in 1862 by those of Italy, which were identical with the 1855 issue of Sardinia, but perforated. Until 1863, imperforate and perforated stamps were issued simultaneously.

TUSCANY

LOCATION — In the north central part of the Apennine Peninsula.
GOVT. — Grand Duchy
AREA — 8,890 sq. mi.
POP. — 2,892,000 (approx.)
CAPITAL — Florence

Tuscany was annexed to Sardinia in 1860.

60 Quattrini = 20 Soldi = 12 Crazie = 1 Lira

100 Centesimi = 1 Lira (1860)

Values of Tuscany stamps vary tremendously according to condition. Values are for very fine examples, and values for unused stamps are for examples with original gum as defined in the catalogue introduction. Extremely fine or superb copies sell at much higher prices, and fine or poor copies sell at greatly reduced prices.

Covers: Values are for covers bearing stamps with four margins. Covers with stamps lacking four margins are worth much less.

Dangerous counterfeits exist of #1-PR1c.

Lion of Tuscany — A1

1851-52 Typo. Wmk. 185 *Imperf.*

Blue, Grayish Blue or Gray Paper

1	A1 1q black ('52)	12,000.	1,750.
	No gum	3,000.	
	On cover		5,250.
	On newspaper, single franking		9,500.
	On circular, single franking		14,000.
a.	1q black, *bluish* ('51)	14,000.	2,000.
	No gum	3,500.	
	On cover		5,850.
	On newspaper, single franking		10,250.
	On circular, single franking		15,600.
2	A1 1s ocher, *grayish*	14,000.	2,000.
	No gum	3,500.	
	On cover		5,850.
a.	1s orange, *grayish*	15,500.	2,000.
	No gum	3,900.	
	On cover		7,000.
b.	1s yellow, *bluish*	18,000.	2,100.
	No gum	4,600.	
	On cover		8,500.
c.	1s yellow bister, *bluish*	10,000.	1,400.
	No gum	4,600.	
	On cover		8,500.
d.	1s golden yellow, *bluish*	17,000.	1,500.
	No gum	4,750.	
	On cover		9,000.
e.	1s bister orange, *grayish*	8,250.	1,400.
	No gum	6,850.	
	On cover		9,400.
3	A1 2s scarlet	47,500.	6,750.
	No gum	11,750.	
	On cover		16,500.
4	A1 1cr carmine	7,750.	115.00
	No gum	1,950.	
	On cover		400.00
a.	1cr brown carmine	9,500.	115.00
	No gum	2,400.	
	On cover		400.00
5	A1 2cr blue	4,650.	125.00
	No gum	1,200.	
	On cover		500.00
a.	2cr greenish blue	5,000.	160.00
	No gum	1,250.	
	On cover		625.00
6	A1 4cr green	7,750.	175.00
	No gum	1,950.	
	On cover		575.00
a.	4cr bluish green	7,750.	175.00
	No gum	1,950.	
	On cover		575.00
7	A1 6cr slate blue	8,500.	275.00
	No gum	2,150.	
	On cover		950.00
a.	6cr blue	7,750.	275.00
	No gum	1,950.	
	On cover		950.00
b.	6cr indigo	8,500.	275.00
	No gum	2,150.	
	On cover		950.00
8	A1 9cr gray lilac	18,500.	215.00
	No gum	4,750.	
	On cover		1,000.
a.	9cr deep violet	18,500.	215.00
	No gum	4,750.	
	On cover		1,000.
9	A1 60cr red ('52)	77,500.	22,500.
	No gum	19,500.	
	On cover		130,000.

Values for Pairs

1	A1 1q black ('52)	25,500.	3,900.
	On cover		11,750.
2	A1 1s ocher, *grayish*	31,000.	4,250.
	On cover		21,500.
3	A1 2s scarlet		14,000.
	On cover		35,000.
4	A1 1cr carmine		275.00
	On cover		950.00
5	A1 2cr blue		400.00
	On cover		2,500.
6	A1 4cr green	17,500.	775.00
	On cover		3,200.
7a	A1 6cr blue	17,500.	1,100.
	On cover		4,250.
8a	A1 9cr deep violet		650.00
	On cover		2,500.
9	A1 60cr red ('52)		78,000.

Full margins = ¼mm.

The first paper was blue, later paper more and more grayish. Stamps on distinctly blue paper sell about 20 percent higher, except Nos. 3 and 9 which were issued on blue paper only. Examples without watermark are proofs.

Reprints of Nos. 3 and 9 have re-engraved value labels, color is too brown and impressions blurred and heavy. Paper same as originals.

1857-59 Wmk. 184

White Paper

10	A1 1q black	1,575.	950.00
	No gum	390.00	
	On cover		2,750.
	On newspaper, single franking		5,750.
	On circular, single franking		11,000.
11	A1 1s yellow	42,500.	5,500.
	No gum	10,750.	
	On cover		25,000.
12	A1 1cr carmine	11,000.	575.00
	No gum	2,750.	
	On cover		1,400.
13	A1 2cr blue	3,100.	125.00
	No gum	775.00	
	On cover		500.00
a.	2cr greenish blue	3,400.	325.00
	No gum	775.00	
	On cover		500.00
b.	2cr yellowish gray green	3,400.	140.00
	No gum	775.00	
	On cover		500.00
14	A1 4cr blue green	7,750.	175.00
	No gum	2,000.	
	On cover		575.00
15	A1 6cr deep blue	9,750.	275.00
	No gum	2,500.	
	On cover		950.00
16	A1 9cr gray lilac ('59)	39,000.	5,500.
	No gum	9,750.	
	On cover		27,500.

Full margins = ¼mm.

Values for pairs

10	A1 1q black	3,500.	2,000.
	On cover		5,750.
11	A1 1s yellow		16,500.
	On cover		57,500.
12	A1 1cr carmine	25,000.	1,250.
	On cover		2,800.
13	A1 2cr blue	7,000.	400.00
	On cover		2,000.
14	A1 4cr blue green	17,500.	750.00
	On cover		3,750.
15	A1 6cr deep blue	42,500.	1,100.
	On cover		4,250.
16	A1 9cr gray lilac		15,500.
	On cover		62,500.

Provisional Government

Coat of Arms — A2

1860

17	A2 1c brn lilac	2,750.	850.00
	No gum	675.00	
	On cover		2,750.
	On newspaper or wrapper, single franking		4,000.
	On circular, single franking		6,000.
a.	1c red lilac	3,500.	975.00
	No gum	875.00	
	On cover		3,000.
	On newspaper or wrapper, single franking		6,000.
	On circular, single franking		6,250.
b.	1c gray lilac	2,750.	850.00
	No gum	675.00	
	On cover		2,750.
	On newspaper or wrapper, single franking		4,100.
	On circular, single franking		6,000.
18	A2 5c green	11,750.	225.00
	No gum	3,000.	
	On cover		675.00
	On cover, single franking		19,500.
a.	5c olive green	13,500.	250.00
	No gum	3,350.	
	On cover		750.00
b.	5c yellow green	16,000.	325.00
	No gum	4,000.	
	On cover		1,050.
19	A2 10c deep brown	4,000.	55.00
	No gum	1,000.	
	On cover		175.00
a.	10c gray brown	3,150.	55.00
	No gum	775.00	
	On cover		175.00
b.	10c purple brown	3,150.	55.00
	No gum	775.00	
	On cover		175.00
20	A2 20c blue	9,750.	175.00
	No gum	2,500.	
	On cover		700.00
a.	20c deep blue	9,750.	190.00
	No gum	2,500.	
	On cover		850.00
b.	20c gray blue	10,500.	190.00
	No gum	2,650.	
	On cover		850.00
21	A2 40c rose	14,000.	275.00
	No gum	3,500.	
	On cover		1,550.
a.	40c carmine	14,000.	275.00
	No gum	3,500.	
	On cover		1,550.
b.	Half used as 20c on cover		155,000.
22	A2 80c pale red brn	27,500.	1,275.
	No gum	6,800.	
	On cover		7,000.
	On cover, single franking		10,500.
a.	80c brown orange	27,500.	1,275.
	No gum	6,750.	
	On cover		7,000.
	On cover, single franking		10,500.
23	A2 3 l ocher	195,000.	85,000.
	No gum	77,500.	

Full margins = ¼mm.

Values for pairs

17b	A2 1c gray lilac	6,000.	1,850.
	On cover	—	5,750.
18	A2 5c green		500.00
	On cover		1,400.
19a	A2 10c deep brown	7,000.	140.00
	On cover		550.00
20	A2 20c blue	21,500.	500.00
	On cover		2,500.
21a	A2 40c carmine	31,500.	2,000.
	On cover		8,250.
22	A2 80c pale red brown		4,000.
	On cover		19,500.

NEWSPAPER TAX STAMP

NT1

1854 Unwmk. Typo. *Imperf.*

Yellowish Pelure Paper

PR1	NT1 2s black	77.50	
	No gum	20.00	
	On newsprint, uncanceled		275.00
a.	Tête bêche pair	700.00	
b.	As "a," one stamp on back	700.00	
c.	Double impression	550.00	

Full margins = 10mm.

This stamp represented a fiscal tax on newspapers coming from foreign countries. It was not canceled when used.

The stamps of Tuscany were superseded by those of Sardinia in 1861.

TWO SICILIES

LOCATION — Formerly comprised the island of Sicily and the lower half of the Apennine Peninsula.

GOVT. — Independent Kingdom

CAPITAL — Naples

The Kingdom was annexed to Sardinia in 1860.

200 Tornesi = 100 Grana = 1 Ducat

Values of Two Sicilies stamps vary tremendously according to condition. Values are for very fine examples, and values for unused stamps are for examples with original gum as defined in the catalogue introduction. Extremely fine or superb copies sell at much higher prices, and fine or poor copies sell at greatly reduced prices.

Naples

Coat of Arms
A1 A2

A3

A4

A5

A6

A7

1858 Engr. Wmk. 186 *Imperf.*

1	A1 ½g pale lake	2,000.	360.00
	No gum	500.00	
	On cover		1,000.
	Single franking on newspaper or wrapper		1,500.
	Single franking on circular		2,000.
a.	½g rose lake	2,000.	360.00
	No gum	525.00	
	On cover		1,000.
	Single franking on newspaper or wrapper		1,500.
	Single franking on circular		2,000.
b.	½g lake	2,600.	550.00
	No gum	650.00	
	On cover		1,450.
	Single franking on newspaper or wrapper		2,200.
	Single franking on circular		2,900.
c.	½g carmine lake	3,250.	800.00
	No gum	825.00	
	On cover		2,400.
	Single franking on newspaper or wrapper		3,500.
	Single franking on circular		4,750.
d.	Half used as ¼g on newspaper		215,000.
2	A2 1g pale lake	1,000.	50.00
	No gum	250.00	
	On cover		120.00
a.	1g rose lake	575.00	50.00
	No gum	140.00	
	On cover		120.00
b.	1g brown lake	1,450.	110.00
	No gum	375.00	
	On cover		275.00
c.	1g carmine lake	900.00	87.50
	No gum	240.00	
	On cover		215.00
d.	Printed on both sides		2,000.
e.	Printed on both sides, one inverted		900.00
	On cover		3,600.
3	A3 2g pale lake	400.00	16.00
	No gum	100.00	
	On cover		36.00
a.	2g rose lake	400.00	16.00
	No gum	100.00	
	On cover		36.00
b.	2g lake	650.00	29.00
	No gum	160.00	
	On cover		72.50
c.	2g carmine lake	900.00	25.00
	No gum	200.00	
	On cover		65.00
d.	Impression of 1g on reverse		1,800.
e.	Double impression		11,000.
	On cover		32,750.
f.	Printed on both sides		2,000.
4	A4 5g brown lake	3,100.	60.00
	No gum	800.00	
	On cover		190.00
a.	5g rose lake	2,600.	60.00
	No gum	650.00	
	On cover		190.00
b.	5g carmine lake	4,000.	65.00
	No gum	1,000.	
	On cover		200.00
d.	Printed on both sides		5,000.
e.	5g rose carmine	5,500.	175.00
	No gum	1,400.	
	On cover		440.00
f.	5g bright carmine	6,000.	215.00
	No gum	1,500.	
	On cover		650.00
g.	5g dark carmine	7,000.	325.00
	No gum	1,750.	
	On cover		1,000.
5	A5 10g rose lake	5,750.	215.00
	No gum	1,450.	
	On cover		575.00
a.	10g lake	6,200.	290.00
	No gum	1,550.	
	On cover		1,000.
b.	10g carmine lake	6,100.	290.00
	No gum	1,550.	
	On cover		1,000.
c.	Printed on both sides		16,000.
d.	Double impression		18,000.
	On cover		55,000.
6	A6 20g rose lake	5,100.	650.00
	No gum	1,300.	
	On cover		2,750.
a.	20g lake	5,100.	725.00
	No gum	1,300.	
	On cover		3,250.
b.	Double impression	72,500.	
c.	20g pale rose	7,250.	1,500.

No gum 1,800.
On cover 5,500.
d. 20g pale car rose *8,500.* 1,750.
No gum 2,100.
On cover 7,000.
7 A7 50grose lake *11,500.* 2,900.
No gum 2,900.
On cover 29,000.
a. 50g lake *11,500.* 2,900.
No gum 2,900.
On cover 29,000.

Values for pairs

1	A1 ½g pale lake	4,200.	750.00
	On cover		*2,200.*
1b	A1 ½g pale lake	5,500.	1,150.
	On cover		*3,100.*
2	A2 1g pale lake	2,200.	110.00
	On cover		*275.00*
2a	A2 1g rose lake	1,300.	110.00
	On cover		*275.00*
3	A3 2g pale lake	875.00	40.00
	On cover		*100.00*
3a	A3 2g rose lake	875.00	40.00
	On cover		*100.00*
4a	A4 5g rose lake	5,400.	440.00
	On cover		*1,300.*
4e	A4 5g rose carmine	11,500.	1,100.
	On cover		*3,250.*
5	A5 10g rose lake	12,750.	1,750.
	On cover		*5,250.*
5b	A5 10g carmine lake	13,250.	2,550.
	On cover		*7,600.*
6	A6 20g rose lake	11,000.	4,000.
	On cover		*16,000.*
6c	A6 20g pale car rose	16,250.	5,800.
	On cover		*20,000.*
7	A7 50g rose lake	*25,000.*	14,500.
	On cover		*72,500.*

Values for strips of 3

1	A1 ½g pale lake	1,300.
	On cover	*3,250.*
1b	A1 ½g pale lake	1,800.
	On cover	*4,500.*
2	A2 1g pale lake	360.00
	On cover	*900.00*
2a	A2 1g rose lake	360.00
	On cover	*900.00*
3	A3 2g pale lake	160.00
	On cover	*500.00*
3a	A3 2g rose lake	160.00
	On cover	*500.00*
4a	A4 5g rose lake	1,800.
	On cover	*7,250.*
4e	A4 5g rose carmine	3,250.
	On cover	*13,000.*
5	A5 10g rose lake	7,250.
	On cover	*22,000.*
5b	A5 10g carmine lake	12,750.
	On cover	—
6	A6 20g rose lake	23,500.
	On cover	—
6c	A6 20g pale car rose	35,000.
	On cover	—
7	A7 50g rose lake	50,000.
	On cover	—

Full margins = 1mm at sides, 1½mm at top and bottom.

Covers: Single frankings of Nos. 1, 2, 7 on newspapers, wrappers or circulars are worth much more.

Only one example of No. 6b is known.

As a secret mark, the engraver, G. Masini, placed a minute letter of his name just above the lower outer line of each stamp. There were three plates of the 2g, one plate of the 50g, and two plates of each of the other values.

Nos. 1-2, 4-7 have been reprinted in bright rose and Nos. 1, 7 in dull brown. The reprints are on thick unwatermarked paper. Value $8 each.

Provisional Government

A8

A9

1860

8 A8 ½t deep blue 180,000. 11,500.
No gum 60,000.
On newspaper 20,000.
On circular 21,500.
On official document 27,500.
9 A9 ½t blue 44,000. 3,800.
No gum 14,500.
On newspaper 12,750.
On circular 26,000.
On official document 16,500.
a. ½t deep blue 44,000. 3,800.
No gum 12,000.
On newspaper 12,750.
On circular 26,000.
On official document 16,500.

Full margins = 1¼mm at sides, 2mm at top and bottom.

100 varieties of each.

No. 8 was made from the plate of No. 1, which was altered by changing the "G" to "T."

No. 9 was made from the same plate after a second alteration erasing the coat of arms and inserting the Cross of Savoy. Dangerous counterfeits exist of Nos. 8-9.

Covers: Nos. 8-10 on official documents are worth more than on newspapers.

Sicily

Ferdinand II — A10

1859 Unwmk. Engr. *Imperf.*
Soft Porous Paper, Brownish Gum
(Naples consignment)

10 A10 ½g orange 800.00 800.00
No gum 200.00
On cover 3,600.
On circular, single franking 8,000.
On newspaper, single franking 5,500.
a. ½g yellow 8,750. 2,500.
No gum 2,100.
On cover 12,750.
On circular, single franking 25,500.
On newspaper, single franking 24,000.
b. ½g olive yellow — 40,000.
On cover 90,000.
On circular, single franking —
On newspaper, single franking 145,000.
c. Printed on both sides — *40,000.*
d. ½g brownish yellow 11,500. 6,000.
No gum 5,000.
On cover *44,000.*
e. ½g deep orange 1,300. *3,250.*
No gum 325.00
On cover 15,000.
f. ½g reddish orange 16,500.

A newspaper with single franking ½ grana orange, No. 10e, sold for the equivalent of U.S. $14,750 at a Turin auction in 2004.

11 A10 1g dark brown 17,500. 700.00
No gum 5,250.
On cover 3,500.
On cover, single franking 18,250.
a. 1g olive brown (I) 40,000. 875.00
No gum 10,500.
On cover 4,500.
On cover, single franking 18,250.
12 A10 1g olive green (III) 1,800. 240.00
No gum 500.00
On cover 725.00
On cover, single franking 6,500.
a. 1g grysh olive grn (II) 3,650. 175.00
No gum 925.00
On cover 550.00
On cover, single franking 5,500.
b. 1g olive brown (II) 1,100. 125.00
No gum 300.00
On cover 400.00
On cover, single franking 5,500.
c. Double impression 4,400. 4,400.
On cover 32,500.
13 A10 2g blue 3,250. 115.00
No gum 925.00
On cover 275.00
On cover, single franking 4,000.
a. 2g deep blue *5,500.* 440.00
No gum 1,300.
On cover 1,100.
On cover, single franking 1,100.
b. Printed on both sides — 26,000.
c. 2g greenish blue 1,100. 140.00
No gum 275.00
On cover 375.00
d. 2g ultramarine 11,000. 875.00
No gum 2,750.
On cover 2,200.
e. 2g cobalt 4,400. 190.00
No gum 1,100.
On cover 450.00
f. 2g dark cobalt 11,000. 500.00
No gum 2,750.
On cover 1,300.
14 A10 5g deep rose 725.00 600.00
No gum 200.00
On cover 3,600.
On cover, single franking 8,500.
a. 5g carmine 725.00 600.00
No gum 190.00
On cover 3,500.
On cover, single franking 8,500.
b. 5g brick red 13,000. 6,500.
No gum 3,250.
On cover 25,000.
c. 5g dark carmine 3,650. 1,000.
No gum 925.00
On cover 6,250.
d. 5g blood red 2,500. 1,100.
No gum 640.00
On cover 6,500.
15 A10 5g vermilion 600.00 *1,600.*
No gum 175.00
On cover 12,000.
On cover, single franking 26,000.
a. 5g orange vermilion 400.00 *1,825.*
No gum 80.00
On cover 13,500.
On cover, single franking 18,000.
b. 5g bright vermilion 440.00 *2,200.*
No gum 110.00
On cover 17,500.
16 A10 10g dark blue 800.00 375.00
No gum 240.00
On cover 2,800.
On cover, single franking 2,800.
a. 10g indigo 875.00 400.00
No gum 240.00
On cover 2,800.
On cover, single franking 2,800.
b. 10g indigo black 3,600. 1,800.
No gum 800.00
On cover 11,000.
17 A10 20g dk gray vio 800.00 625.00
No gum 225.00
On cover 4,250.
On cover, single franking 13,500.
a. 20g slate black 3,000. 1,800.
No gum 925.00
On cover 11,000.
b. 20g slate violet 3,250. *3,750.*
No gum 1,100.
On cover 22,000.
18 A10 50g dk brn red 800.00 *4,750.*
No gum 240.00
On cover 90,000.
On cover, single franking —
a. 50g dark purple lake 2,200. —

Hard White Paper, White Gum
(Palermo consignment)

10g A10 ½g orange 575.00 *4,000.*
No gum 175.00
On cover —
10h A10 ½g bright orange 575.00 *5,000.*
No gum 175.00
On cover —
12g A10 1g grayish olive (!!) 650.00 140.00
No gum 200.00
On cover 400.00
12h A10 1g pale olive green (III) 200.00 *180.00*
No gum 60.00
On cover 600.00
12i A10 1g olive green (III) 200.00 180.00
No gum 60.00
On cover 600.00
13g A10 2g blue 180.00 120.00
No gum 55.00
On cover 275.00
13h A10 2g pale blue 180.00 120.00
No gum 55.00
On cover 275.00

Full margins = 1mm.

Covers: Single frankings of Nos. 11, 12, 15, 17 on newspapers or covers are worth more.

Fraudulent cancellations are known on Nos. 10, 15, 15a and 18.

There were three plates each for the 1g and 2g, two each for the ½g and 5g and one plate each for the other values.

Nos. 10a, 10b, 11, 11a, 14, 14a, 14b and 15 are printed from Plate I on which the stamps are 2 to 2½mm apart. On almost all stamps from Plate I, the S and T of POSTA touch.

Nos. 12a, and 15a are from Plate II and No. 12 is from Plate III. On both Plates II and III stamps are spaced 1½mm apart. Most stamps from Plate II have a white line about 1mm long below the beard.

The ½g blue is stated to be a proof of which two copies are known used on cover.

Neapolitan Provinces

King Victor Emmanuel II — A11

Lithographed, Center Embossed
1861 Unwmk. *Imperf.*

19 A11 ½t green 18.00 *225.00*
No gum 4.50
On cover 360.00
On newspaper, single franking 360.00
On circular, single franking 800.00
a. ½t yellow green 500.00 290.00
No gum 125.00
On cover 575.00
On circular, single franking 950.00
b. ½t emerald 5,750. 900.00
No gum 1,450.
On cover 1,800.
On circular, single franking 3,100.
c. ½t black (error) *47,500.* *57,500.*
No gum *23,500.*
d. Head inverted (green) 240.00
No gum 65.00
e. Head inverted (yel grn) 11,500.
On cover 36,000.
f. Printed on both sides 29,000.
g. ½t olive green 3,250. 575.00
No gum 825.00
On cover 1,450.
20 A11 ½g bister 175.00 *225.00*
No gum 45.00
On cover 475.00
On cover, single franking 2,900.
a. ½g brown 175.00 *250.00*
No gum 45.00
On cover 640.00
On cover, single franking 3,100.
b. ½g gray brown 215.00 *225.00*
No gum 55.00
On cover 475.00
On cover, single franking 2,900.
c. Head inverted 1,800. —
No gum 725.00
21 A11 1g black 350.00 32.50
No gum 90.00
On cover 110.00
On cover, single franking 1,000.
a. Head inverted *1,800.*
On cover 9,000.
b. 1g silver gray 14,500. 1,800.
On cover 5,500.
22 A11 2g blue 115.00 12.50
No gum 29.00
On cover 32.50
a. 2g deep blue 115.00 12.50
No gum 29.00
On cover 32.50
b. Head inverted *400.00* *900.00*
No gum 110.00
On cover 5,750.
c. 2g black (error) *60,000.*
d. 2g sky blue 2,900. 29.00
No gum 725.00
On cover 72.50
e. 2g slate blue 4,400. 180.00
No gum 1,100.
On cover 550.00
f. 2g indigo 5,000. 440.00
No gum 1,300.
On cover 1,300.
23 A11 5g car rose 215.00 125.00
No gum 55.00
On cover 400.00
a. 5g vermilion 215.00 175.00
No gum 55.00
On cover 550.00
b. 5g lilac rose 250.00 290.00
No gum 62.50
On cover 875.00
c. Head inverted 1,100. *8,000.*
No gum 360.00
e. Printed on both sides 18,000.
f. 5g lilac 290.00 *440.00*
No gum 72.50
On cover 1,300.
g. 5g dark lilac 725.00 625.00
No gum 180.00
On cover 1,800.
25 A11 10g orange 110.00 *275.00*
No gum 27.50
On cover 725.00
a. 10g ocher *1,300.* 725.00
No gum 325.00
On cover 2,200.
b. 10g bister 125.00 *275.00*
No gum 30.00
On cover 725.00
c. 10g olive bister 650.00 *900.00*
No gum 160.00
On cover 2,750.
26 A11 20g yellow 500.00 *2,500.*
No gum 125.00
On cover 10,000.
a. Head inverted 36,000.
b. 20g orange yellow 550.00 *2,900.*
No gum 140.00
On cover 11,500.
27 A11 50g gray 35.00 *9,000.*
No gum 9.00
On cover *125,000.*
On cover, single franking *160,000.*
a. 50g slate 42.50 *9,000.*
No gum 11.00
On cover *12,750.*
b. 50g slate blue 50.00 *11,500.*
No gum 13.00
On cover *175,000.*
c. 50g blackish gray 160.00
No gum 40.00

Full margins = 1mm.

Counterfeits of the inverted head varieties of this issue are plentiful. See note on forgeries after Sardinia No. 15.

Values for pairs

19	A11 ½t green	40.00	*525.00*
	On cover		1,500.
20	A11 ½t bister	400.00	*500.00*
	On cover		1,000.
21	A11 1g black	825.00	72.50
	On cover		240.00
22	A11 2g blue	250.00	55.00
	On cover		275.00
23	A11 5g carmine rose	500.00	*550.00*
	On cover		2,200.
25	A11 10g orange	240.00	*2,200.*
	On cover		8,750.
26	A11 20g yellow	1,100.	*6,250.*
	On cover		32,000.
27	A11 50g gray	85.00	*27,500.*

Values for blocks of 4

19	A11 ½t green	80.00	*22,000.*
20	A11 ½t bister	800.00	*25,000.*
21	A11 1g black	1,600.	*15,000.*
22	A11 2g blue	500.00	*15,750.*
23	A11 5g carmine rose	1,000.	—
25	A11 10g orange	500.00	—
26	A11 20g yellow	2,250.	—
27	A11 50g gray	160.00	

Fraudulent cancellations are found on Nos. 19-20, 23-27.

Stamps similar to those of Sardinia 1855-61, type A4 but with inscriptions in larger, clearer lettering, were prepared in 1861 for the Neapolitan Provinces. They were not officially issued although a few are known postally used. Denominations: 5c, 10c, 20c, 40c and 80c.

Stamps of Two Sicilies were replaced by those of Italy in 1862.

ITALY

'i-tᵊl-ē

LOCATION — Southern Europe
GOVT. — Republic
AREA — 119,764 sq. mi.
POP. — 56,929,101 (est. 1983)
CAPITAL — Rome

Kngdom

100 Centesimi = 1 Lira

Watermarks

Wmk. 87 — Honeycomb

Wmk. 140 — Crown

Values of Italy stamps vary tremendously according to condition. Quotations are for very fine examples, and values for unused stamps are for examples with original gum as defined in the catalogue introduction. Extremely fine or superb copies sell at much higher prices, and fine or poor copies sell at greatly reduced prices.

Very fine examples of Nos. 17-21, 24-75, J2-J27, O1-O8 and Q1-Q6 will have perforations barely clear of the frameline or design due to the narrow spacing of the stamps on the plates.

Values for never hinged stamps are for examples centered clear of perfs. Premiums do not apply to stamps with perforations cutting the design.

King Victor Emmanuel II

A4 A5

Typographed; Head Embossed

1862 Unwmk. *Perf. 11½x12*

17 A4	10c bister	6,500.	290.00
	No gum	2,500.	
	Never hinged	10,000.	
	On cover		575.00
a.	10c yellow brown	9,000.	360.00
	No gum	3,500.	
	On cover		725.00
b.	10c brown	15,000.	400.00
	No gum	5,500.	
	On cover		1,000.
c.	10c dk olive brn	22,000.	875.00
	No gum	8,000.	
	On cover		2,200.
d.	10c dark brown	25,000.	875.00
	No gum	8,500.	
	On cover		2,200.
e.	10c olive bister	19,000.	475.00
	No gum	7,250.	
	On cover		1,200.
f.	10c reddish org	19,000.	875.00
	No gum	7,250.	
	On cover		2,200.
g.	Vert. half used as 5c on cover		100,000.
19 A4	20c dark blue	19.00	35.00
	No gum	12.00	
	Never hinged	47.50	
	On cover		125.00
a.	20c blue	725.00	725.00
	No gum	325.00	
	On cover		2,500.
b.	20c pale blue	13,000.	3,250.
	No gum	5,750.	
	On cover		13,000.
c.	20c pale milky blue	19,000.	6,000.
	No gum	8,750.	
	On cover		23,000.
d.	20c gray blue	575.00	650.00
	No gum	300.00	
	On cover		2,250.
e.	20c dp dk blue	11,500.	3,250.
	No gum	5,500.	
	On cover		13,000.
f.	Vert. half used as 10c on cover		110,000.
20 A4	40c red	290.00	160.00
	No gum	65.00	
	Never hinged	575.00	
	On cover		350.00
a.	40c pale rose	575.00	290.00
	No gum	150.00	
	On cover		875.00
b.	40c brt car red	325.00	190.00
	On cover		360.00
c.	40c deep car red	325.00	190.00
	On cover		360.00
21 A4	80c orange	65.00	1,600.
	No gum	32.50	
	Never hinged	130.00	
	On cover		6,500.
a.	80c bright yellow	65.00	1,600.
	No gum	32.50	
	On cover		6,500.
b.	80c dark yellow	72.50	1,600.
	No gum	35.00	
	On cover		6,500.
c.	80c olive yellow	6,500.	
	No gum	3,000.	
	On cover		

The outer frame shows a distinct design on the early printings, while this design is more or less blurred, or even a solid line, on the later printings.

The 20c and 40c exist perf. 11½. These are remainders of Sardinia with forged perforations.

Counterfeit cancellations are often found on No. 21.

Values for pairs

17 A4	10c bister	13,500.	625.00
	On cover		1,250.
19 A4	20c dark blue	40.00	90.00
	On cover		375.00
20 A4	40c red	625.00	725.00
	On cover		3,000.
21 A4	80c orange	140.00	4,750.
	On cover		29,000.

Values for strips of 3

17 A4	10c bister	—	1,150.
	On cover		5,750.
19 A4	20c dark blue	60.00	375.00
	On cover		1,800.
20 A4	40c red	1,000.	3,600.
	On cover		21,500.
21 A4	80c orange	225.00	—
	On cover		—

Values for strips of 4

17 A4	10c bister	—	4,750.
	On cover		23,500.
19 A4	20c dark blue	85.00	1,800.
	On cover		12,750.
20 A4	40c red	—	—
	On cover		—
21 A4	80c orange	—	—
	On cover		—

Values for blocks of 4

17 A4	10c bister	40,000.	—
	On cover		—
19 A4	20c dark blue	140.00	15,500.
	On cover		—
20 A4	40c red	1,900.	—
	On cover		—
21 A4	80c orange	425.00	—
	On cover		—

Values for strips of 5

17 A4	10c bister	—	—
	On cover		—
19 A4	20c dark blue	—	7,250.
	On cover		26,000.
20 A4	40c red	—	—
	On cover		—
21 A4	80c orange	—	—
	On cover		—

Lithographed; Head Embossed

1863 *Imperf.*

22 A4	15c blue	87.50	50.00
	No gum	32.50	
	Never hinged	175.00	
	On cover		1,100.
a.	Head inverted		65,000.
	On cover		165,000.
b.	Double head	1,125.	80.00
	No gum	65.00	
	On cover		200.00
c.	Head omitted	290.00	42,000.
	On cover		100,000.
d.	15c deep blue	87.50	50.00
	No gum	32.50	
	Never hinged	175.00	
	On cover		140.00
e.	15c pale blue	87.50	50.00
	No gum	32.50	
	Never hinged	175.00	
	On cover		140.00
f.	15c milky blue	200.00	800.00
	No gum	72.50	
	On cover		2,350.
g.	15c sky blue	500.00	1,000.
	No gum	180.00	
	On cover		3,100.
h.	15c violet indigo	180.00	215.00
	No gum	65.00	
	On cover		650.00
i.	15c gray blue	1,300.	725.00
	No gum	550.00	
	On cover		2,200.

See note after Sardinia No. 15.

No. 22c is valued with original gum only.

Values for a pair of stamps

22 A4	15c blue	180.00	160.00
	On cover		500.00

Values for used strip of 3

22 A4	15c blue		725.00
	On cover		2,900.

Values for used strip of 4

22 A4	15c blue		4,400.
	On cover		21,750.

Values for blocks of 4

22 A4	15c blue	560.00	25,500.
	On cover		64,000.

Two types of No. 23:

Type I — First "C" in bottom line nearly closed.

Type II — "C" open. Line broken below "Q."

1863 Litho.

23 A5	15c blue, Type II	7.25	11.50
	No gum	2.90	
	Never hinged	13.50	
	On cover		30.00
a.	Type I	360.00	25.00
	No gum	44.00	
	Never hinged	725.00	
	On cover		62.50
b.	15c slate blue (II)	11.00	18.00
	No gum	4.40	
	On cover		45.00
c.	As "a," double impression		4,750.
	On cover		18,250.
d.	15c pale blue (I)	360.00	25.00
	No gum	350.00	
	On cover		62.50
e.	15c pale blue (II)	7.25	13.00
	No gum	2.90	
	On cover		32.50

Values for pairs

23 A5	15c blue (II)	14.50	26.00
	On cover		65.00
a.	Type I	800.00	57.50
	On cover		140.00

Values for used strips of 3

23 A5	15c blue (II)		100.00
	On cover		400.00
a.	Type I		160.00
	On cover		650.00

Values for used strips of 4

23 A5	15c blue (II)		400.00
	On cover		2,000.
a.	Type I		825.00
	On cover		3,250.

Values for blocks of 4

23 A5	15c blue (II)	55.00	13,750.
	On cover		42,000.
a.	Type I	2,550.	13,750.
	On cover		42,000.

Values for used strips of 5

23 A5	15c blue (II)		1,600.
	On cover		8,000.
a.	Type I		3,250.
	On cover		16,500.

Values for Nos. 24-33 are for well-centered stamps with perforations clear of frameline. Values for used stamps are for stamps canceled with legible circular date stamps. Copies with numeral and other cancellations sell for somewhat less.

Values for never hinged mint stamps are for examples with very fine centering. Never hinged premiums over hinged original gum values do not apply to stamps with perforations cutting into the design. This applies to all 19th century issues.

A6

A7

A8

A13

1863-77 Typo. Wmk. 140 *Perf. 14*

Turin Printing

24 A6	1c gray green	7.25	3.50
	No gum	1.80	
	Never hinged	18.00	
	On cover		7.25
a.	Imperf., pair		12,000.
	On cover		37,500.
25 A7	2c org brn ('65)	25.00	2.00
	No gum	4.25	
	Never hinged	62.50	
	On cover		5.00
a.	Imperf., pair	225.00	325.00
	Imperf single, on cover		500.00
26 A8	5c slate grn	1,700.	4.00
	No gum	250.00	
	Never hinged	3,350.	
	On cover		8.00
27 A8	10c buff	2,750.	5.00
	No gum	375.00	
	Never hinged	5,500.	
a.	10c orange brown	2,725.	5.00
	No gum	375.00	
	Never hinged	5,500.	
	On cover, #27 or 27a		10.00
28 A8	10c blue ('77)	5,500.	6.00
	No gum	800.00	
	Never hinged	11,000.	
	On cover		14.50
29 A8	15c blue	2,250.	3.50
	No gum	290.00	
	Never hinged	4,350.	
	On cover		14.50
a.	Imperf, single		5,500.
	On cover		43,500.
30 A8	30c brown	11.00	11.00
	No gum	2.25	
	Never hinged	27.50	
	On cover		32.50
a.	Imperf, single		—
	Imperf single, on cover		—
31 A8	40c carmine	5,500.	5.75
	No gum	800.00	
	Never hinged	11,000.	
a.	40c rose	5,500.	5.75
	No gum	800.00	
	Never hinged	11,000.	
	On cover, #31 or 31a		24.00
32 A8	60c lilac	11.00	16.00
	No gum	2.25	
	Never hinged	27.50	
	On cover		65.00
33 A13	2 l vermilion	25.00	100.00
	No gum	14.50	
	Never hinged	62.50	
	On cover		2,500.
	On cover, single franking		4,000.

Nos. 26 to 32 have the head of type A8 but with different corner designs for each value.

Early printings of Nos. 24-27, 29-33 were made in London by De La Rue, later printings in Turin. Used examples can be determined by cancellation date. Unused singles cannot be distinguished.

For overprints see Italian Offices Abroad Nos. 1-5, 8-11.

De La Rue Printing

Stamps from De La Rue printing are distinguished by legible datestamps with dates between Dec. 1863 and Dec. 1865.

24	A6	1c	18.00
		On cover	36.00
		On cover, single franking	215.00
25	A7	2c	110.00
		On cover	160.00
26	A8	5c	18.00
		On cover	36.00
27	A8	10c	18.00
a.		10c	18.00
		On cover, #27 or 27a	36.00
		On cover, single franking, #27 or 27a	300.00
29	A8	15c	3.60
		On cover	14.50
30	A8	30c	90.00
		On cover	275.00
31	A8	40c	18.00
a.		40c	18.00
		On cover, #31 or 31a	55.00
32	A8	60c	42.50
		On cover	175.00
33	A13	2 l	360.00
		On cover	*9,000.*
		On cover, single franking	*11,500.*

Values for blocks of 4
Turin Printing

24	A6	1c	55.00	22.00
		On cover		75.00
25	A7	2c	200.00	25.00
		On cover		100.00
26	A8	5c	11,000.	57.50
		On cover		350.00
27	A8	10c	18,000.	125.00
a.		10c	18,000.	125.00
		On cover, #27 or 27a		900.00
28	A8	10c	38,000	440.00
		On cover		2,200.
30	A8	30c	80.00	*550.00*
		On cover		3,800.
31	A8	40c	36,500.	550.00
a.		40c	36,500.	550.00
		On cover, #31 or 31a		3,800.
32	A8	60c	80.00	*1,800.*
		On cover		11,000.
33	A13	2 l	200.00	*4,000.*

Values for blocks of 4
De La Rue Printing

24	A6	1c	180.00
		On cover	1,100.
26	A8	5c	180.00
		On cover	1,100.
27	A8	10c	400.00
		On cover	2,750.
29	A8	15c	1,750.
		On cover	11,000.
30	A8	30c	*5,750.*
		On cover	23,000.
31	A8	40c	2,200.
		On cover	15,000.

Watermark Inverted
De La Rue Printing

24b	A6	1c	140.00
		On cover	575.00
25b	A7	2c	650.00
		On cover	—
29b	A8	15c	140.00
		On cover	575.00

Turin Printing

24c	A6	1c	50.00	29.00
		On cover		140.00
25c	A7	2c	87.50	87.50
		On cover		525.00
26a	A8	5c	—	110.00
		On cover		550.00
27b	A8	10c	—	87.50
		On cover		525.00
28a	A8	10c	—	87.50
		On cover		210.00
30b	A8	30c	100.00	290.00
		On cover		—
31b	A8	40c	—	180.00
		On cover		900.00
32a	A8	60c	—	250.00
		On cover		1,300.
33a	A13	2 l	—	575.00
		On cover		—

No. 29 Surcharged in Brown

1865

Type I — Dots flanking stars in oval, and dot in eight check-mark ornaments in corners.
Type II — Dots in oval, none in corners.
Type III — No dots.

34	A8	20c on 15c bl (I)	625.00	4.25
		No gum	90.00	
		Never hinged	1,250.	
		On cover		11.00
a.		Type II	7,250.	18.00
		No gum	1,200.	
		Never hinged	14,500.	
		On cover		45.00
b.		Type III	1,600.	7.25
		No gum	325.00	
		Never hinged	3,250.	
		On cover		18.00
c.		Inverted surcharge (I)		*57,500.*

A15

1867-77 Typo.

35	A15	20c blue	650.00	1.45
		No gum	110.00	
		Never hinged	1,300.	
		On cover		2.90
36	A15	20c orange ('77)	4,000.	3.50
		No gum	575.00	
		Never hinged	8,000.	
		On cover		9.00

For overprints see Italian Offices Abroad #9-10.

Official Stamps Surcharged in Blue

1877

37	O1	2c on 2c lake	200.00	29.00
		No gum	25.00	
		Never hinged	400.00	
		On cover		57.50
38	O1	2c on 5c lake	250.00	35.00
		No gum	40.00	
		Never hinged	500.00	
		On cover		72.50
39	O1	2c on 20c lake	900.00	4.25
		No gum	140.00	
		Never hinged	1,800.	
		On cover		8.75
40	O1	2c on 30c lake	800.00	14.50
		No gum	87.50	
		Never hinged	1,600.	
		On cover		29.00
41	O1	2c on 1 l lake	625.00	4.25
		No gum	80.00	
		Never hinged	1,250.	
		On cover		8.75
42	O1	2c on 2 l lake	615.00	11.00
		No gum	80.00	
		Never hinged	1,250.	
		On cover		22.00
43	O1	2c on 5 l lake	875.00	14.50
		No gum	100.00	
		Never hinged	1,750.	
		On cover		29.00
44	O1	2c on 10 l lake	625.00	18.00
		No gum	80.00	
		Never hinged	1,250.	
		On cover		36.00

Inverted Surcharge

37a	O1	2c on 2c		1,600.
		On cover		*16,250.*
38a	O1	2c on 5c		1,250.
		On cover		*13,000.*
39a	O1	2c on 20c	*36,000.*	875.00
		On cover		*8,750.*
40a	O1	2c on 30c		1,300.
		On cover		*13,000.*
41a	O1	2c on 1 l	*43,500.*	1,200.
		On cover		*13,000.*
42a	O1	2c on 2 l	*43,500.*	1,300.
		On cover		*13,000.*
43a	O1	2c on 5 l		1,300.
		On cover		*13,000.*
44a	O1	2c on 10 l		1,300.
		On cover		*13,000.*

Values for blocks of 4

37	O1	2c on 2c lake	1,300.	200.00
		On cover		*1,000.*
38	O1	2c on 5c lake	1,700.	250.00
		On cover		*1,300.*
39	O1	2c on 20c lake	6,000.	65.00
		On cover		*325.00*
40	O1	2c on 30c lake	5,250.	110.00
		On cover		*550.00*
41	O1	2c on 1 l lake	4,000.	65.00
		On cover		*325.00*
42	O1	2c on 2 l lake	4,000.	140.00
		On cover		*725.00*
43	O1	2c on 5 l lake	5,750.	180.00
		On cover		*900.00*
44	O1	2c on 10 l lake	4,000.	225.00
		On cover		*1,100.*

King Humbert I — A17

1879 Typo. *Perf. 14*

45	A17	5c blue green	8.75	1.40
		No gum	2.25	
		Never hinged	22.00	
		On cover		4.50
46	A17	10c claret	500.00	1.60
		No gum	80.00	
		Never hinged	1,000.	
		On cover		4.75
47	A17	20c orange	475.00	1.40
		No gum	72.50	
		Never hinged	950.00	
		On cover		4.50
48	A17	25c blue	875.00	7.25
		No gum	120.00	
		Never hinged	1,750.	
		On cover		22.00
49	A17	30c brown	175.00	*1,900.*
		No gum	110.00	
		Never hinged	360.00	
		On cover		*12,750.*
50	A17	50c violet	21.00	21.00
		No gum	6.25	
		Never hinged	55.00	
		On cover		65.00
51	A17	2 l vermilion	57.50	*325.00*
		No gum	32.50	
		Never hinged	115.00	
		On cover		*95,000.*

Values for blocks of 4

45	A17	5c blue green	65.00	55.00
		On cover		180.00
46	A17	10c claret	3,500.	80.00
		On cover		400.00
47	A17	20c orange	3,100.	200.00
		On cover		1,200.
48	A17	25c blue	5,800.	625.00
49	A17	30c brown	1,200.	
50	A17	50c violet	175.00	*1,800.*
51	A17	2 l vermilion	375.00	*20,000.*

Nos. 45-51 have the head of type A17 with different corner designs for each value.

Beware of forged cancellations on No. 49, on or off cover.

No. 51 on complete commercial covers is very rare. On large pieces or cover fronts, it is worth $1,500-$15,000, depending on the usage and on the individual piece.

For surcharges and overprints see Nos. 64-66, Italian Offices Abroad 12-17.

Arms of Savoy — A24

Humbert I — A25

A26

A27

A28

A29

1889

52	A24	5c dark green	900.00	3.00
		No gum	100.00	
		Never hinged	1,800.	
		On cover		7.25
53	A25	40c brown	13.00	18.00
		No gum	5.75	
		Never hinged	32.50	
		On cover		110.00
54	A26	45c gray green	2,000.	8.75
		No gum	500.00	
		Never hinged	6,000.	
		On cover		26.00
55	A27	60c violet	17.50	*35.00*
		No gum	7.25	
		Never hinged	44.00	
		On cover		440.00
		On cover, single franking		2,000.
56	A28	1 l brown & yel	17.50	18.00
		No gum	7.25	
		Never hinged	44.00	
		On cover		140.00
		On cover, single franking		1,000.
a.		1 l brown & orange	19.00	21.00
		No gum	8.00	
		Never hinged	47.50	
		On cover		175.00
		On cover, single franking		1,000.
57	A29	5 l grn & claret	30.00	*800.00*
		No gum	14.50	
		Never hinged	80.00	
		On cover		*135,000.*

Values for blocks of 4

52	A24	5c dark green	6,000.	65.00
		On cover		325.00
53	A25	40c brown	100.00	*1,300.*
		On cover		6,500.
54	A26	45c gray green	23,500.	1,800.
		On cover		9,000.
55	A27	60c violet	140.00	*3,600.*
		On cover		14,500.
56	A28	1 l brown & yel	140.00	*650.00*
		On cover		6,500.
57	A29	5 l grn & claret	250.00	

Forged cancellations exist on #51, 57.

No. 57 on complete commercial covers is very rare. On large pieces or cover fronts, it is worth $2,850-$20,000, depending on the usage and on the individual piece.

Parcel Post Stamps of 1884-86 Surcharged in Black

1890

58	PP1	2c on 10c ol gray	5.50	6.50
		No gum	3.25	
		Never hinged	22.00	
		On cover		27.50
a.		Inverted surcharge	440.00	*2,750.*
59	PP1	2c on 20c blue	5.50	6.50
		No gum	3.25	
		Never hinged	22.00	
		On cover		27.50
60	PP1	2c on 50c claret	57.50	42.50
		No gum	25.00	
		Never hinged	225.00	
		On cover		110.00
a.		Inverted surcharge		*32,500.*
61	PP1	2c on 75c blue grn	5.50	*6.50*
		No gum	3.25	
		Never hinged	22.00	
		On cover		27.50
62	PP1	2c on 1.25 l org	50.00	32.50
		No gum	20.00	
		Never hinged	200.00	
		On cover		100.00
a.		Inverted surcharge	*60,000.*	*30,000.*
63	PP1	2c on 1.75 l brn	22.50	*55.00*
		No gum	13.00	
		Never hinged	95.00	
		On cover		140.00

Values for blocks of 4

58	PP1	2c on 10c ol gray	65.00	65.00
		On cover		300.00
59	PP1	2c on 20c blue	65.00	65.00
		On cover		300.00
60	PP1	2c on 50c claret	650.00	325.00
		On cover		1,000.
61	PP1	2c on 75c blue grn	65.00	65.00
		On cover		300.00
62	PP1	2c on 1.25 l org	575.00	250.00
		On cover		1,000.
63	PP1	2c on 1.75 l brn	275.00	*325.00*
		On cover		1,200.

Covers: Single frankings of Nos. 58-63 on newspapers or circulars are worth more.

Stamps of 1879 Surcharged

1890-91

64	A17	2c on 5c bl grn ('91)	20.00	50.00
		No gum	14.50	
		Never hinged	50.00	
		On cover		100.00
a.		"2" with thin tail	125.00	290.00
		On cover		1,200.
65	A17	20c on 30c brown	440.00	9.00
		No gum	72.50	
		Never hinged	875.00	
		On cover		27.50
66	A17	20c on 50c violet	500.00	42.50
		No gum	80.00	
		Never hinged	1,000.	
		On cover		125.00

Values for blocks of 4

64	A17	2c on 5c bl grn ('91)	150.00	*250.00*
		On cover		500.00
65	A17	20c on 30c brown	3,000.	4,250.
		On cover		13,000.
66	A17	20c on 50c violet	3,400.	*3,600.*
		On cover		11,000.

On Nos. 65-66 the period is omitted in the surcharge.

Arms of Savoy — A33

Humbert I — A34

A35

A36

A37

A38

1891-96 **Typo.**

67	A33	5c green	575.00	2.10
		No gum	80.00	
		Never hinged	1,200.	
		On cover		6.50
68	A34	10c claret ('96)	8.75	2.10
		No gum	2.25	
		Never hinged	22.00	
		On cover		4.50
69	A35	20c orange ('95)	8.75	2.10
		No gum	2.10	
		Never hinged	22.00	
		On cover		4.50
70	A36	25c blue	8.75	9.00
		No gum	2.10	
		Never hinged	22.00	
		On cover		35.00
71	A37	45c ol grn ('95)	8.75	9.00
		No gum	2.10	
		Never hinged	22.00	
		On cover		35.00
72	A38	5 l blue & rose	87.50	*175.00*
		No gum	35.00	
		Never hinged	175.00	
		On cover		*18,000.*

Values for blocks of 4

67	A33	5c green	3,750.	35.00
		On cover		210.00
68	A34	10c claret ('96)	65.00	35.00
		On cover		250.00
69	A35	20c orange ('95)	65.00	*160.00*
		On cover		1,600.
70	A36	25c blue	65.00	*300.00*
		On cover		3,000.
71	A37	45c ol grn ('95)	65.00	*550.00*
		On cover		5,500.
72	A38	5 l blue & rose	575.00	*2,350.*

Value of No. 72 on cover is for a complete cover. Stamps on piece or cover fronts are more common and worth much less.

Arms of Savoy — A39

A40

A41

1896-97

73	A39	1c brown	10.00	7.25
		No gum	3.00	
		Never hinged	25.00	
		On cover		11.00
a.		Half used as ½c on cover		1,350.
74	A40	2c orange brown	10.00	1.75
		No gum	2.00	
		Never hinged	25.00	
		On cover		3.50
75	A41	5c green ('97)	35.00	1.75
		No gum	7.25	
		Never hinged	90.00	
		On cover		3.50

Values for blocks of 4

73	A39	1c brown	75.00	35.00
		On cover		110.00
74	A40	2c orange brown	77.50	18.00
		On cover		110.00
75	A41	5c green ('97)	275.00	30.00
		On cover		175.00

A42

Coat of Arms
A43 A44

Victor Emmanuel III
A45 A46

1901-26

76	A42	1c brown	1.40	.35
		Never hinged	3.50	
		On cover		1.10
a.		Imperf, single	360.00	*550.00*
77	A43	2c org brn	1.40	.35
		Never hinged	3.50	
		On cover		1.10
a.		Double impression	100.00	*175.00*
b.		Imperf, single	110.00	*140.00*
78	A44	5c blue grn	72.50	.55
		Never hinged	180.00	
		On cover		1.40
a.		Imperf, single	1,750.	
		Never hinged	2,000.	
79	A45	10c claret	95.00	1.10
		Never hinged	240.00	
		On cover		4.50
a.		Imperf, single	—	*7,250.*
80	A45	20c orange	21.00	1.10
		Never hinged	55.00	
		On cover		4.50
81	A45	25c ultra	175.00	3.50
		Never hinged	450.00	
		On cover		32.50
a.		25c dp blue	175.00	3.50
		Never hinged	450.00	
		On cover		32.50
82	A46	25c grn & pale grn ('26)	.75	.30
		Never hinged	1.90	
		On cover		1.25
83	A45	40c brown	625.00	8.75
		Never hinged	1,550.	
		On cover		50.00
84	A45	45c olive grn	10.00	.35
		Never hinged	25.00	
		On cover		10.00
a.		Imperf, single	125.00	*190.00*
85	A45	50c violet	725.00	14.50
		Never hinged	1,800.	
		On cover		175.00
86	A46	75c dk red & rose ('26)	4.25	.30
		Never hinged	11.00	
		On cover		2.50
87	A46	1 l brown & grn	4.25	.35
		Never hinged	11.00	
		On cover		3.50
a.		Imperf, single	65.00	*100.00*
b.		Floral design (green) omitted	140.00	
c.		Double impression of vignette (brown)	65.00	*90.00*
88	A46	1.25 l bl & ultra ('26)	11.00	.30
		Never hinged	27.50	
		On cover		1.75
89	A46	2 l dk grn & org ('23)	21.00	6.00
		Never hinged	55.00	
		On cover		55.00
90	A46	2.50 l dk grn & org ('26)	50.00	7.25
		Never hinged	125.00	
		On cover		62.50
91	A46	5 l blue & rose	30.00	5.75
		Never hinged	72.50	
		On cover		200.00
		Nos. 76-91 (16)	1,847.	50.80

Values for Blocks of 4

76	A42	1c brown	11.00	2.40
77	A43	2c org brn	11.00	2.25
78	A44	5c blue grn	560.00	9.75
79	A45	10c claret	725.00	12.00
80	A45	20c orange	160.00	14.50
81	A45	25c ultra	1,400.	72.50
81a	A45	25c deep blue	1,400.	72.50
82	A46	25c grn & pale grn ('26)	7.25	.30
83	A45	40c brown	4,750.	325.00
84	A45	45c olive grn	80.00	18.00
85	A45	50c violet	5,600.	475.00
86	A46	75c dk red & rose ('26)	47.50	.30
87	A46	1 l brown & grn	32.50	2.50
88	A46	1.25 l bl & ultra ('26)	125.00	.30
89	A46	2 l dk grn & org ('23)	240.00	100.00
90	A46	2.50 l dk grn & org ('26)	560.00	32.50
91	A46	5 l blue & rose	210.00	72.50

Nos. 83, 85, unused, are valued in fine condition.

The borders of Nos. 79-81, 83-85, 87, 89 and 91 differ slightly for each denomination.

On Nos. 82, 86, 88 and 90, the value is expressed as "Cent. 25," etc.

See No. 87b in set following No. 174G.

For surcharges and overprints see Nos. 148-149, 152, 158, 174F-174G, B16; Austria N20-N21, N27, N30, N52-N53, N58, N60, N64-N65, N71, N74; Dalmatia 1, 6-7.

Overprints & Surcharges
See Offices in China, Crete, Africa, Turkish Empire (Albania to Valona) and Aegean Islands for types A36-A58 overprinted or surcharged.

No. 80 Surcharged in Black

1905

92	A45	15c on 20c org	52.50	1.25
		Never hinged	130.00	
		Block of 4	725.00	1.25
		On cover		8.00
a.		Double surcharge		*3,300.*

A47

No. 93

No. 111

No. 123

1906 **Unwmk.** **Engr.** ***Perf. 12***

93	A47	15c slate	65.00	.90
		Never hinged	160.00	
		Block of 4	725.00	
		On cover		5.50
a.		Vert. pair, imperf horiz.	160.00	*175.00*
b.		Horiz. pair, imperf vert.	160.00	*175.00*
c.		Booklet pane of 6		—
		Cplt. bklt., 4 #93b	*11,000.*	

A48

A49

1906-19 **Wmk. 140** **Typo.** ***Perf. 14***

94	A48	5c green	1.10	.30
		Never hinged	3.25	
		Block of 4	14.00	
		On cover		.75
a.		Imperf, single	35.00	*35.00*
b.		Printed on both sides	215.00	
		Never hinged	325.00	
95	A48	10c claret	2.50	.30
		Never hinged	7.75	
		Block of 4	32.00	
		On cover		.75
a.		Imperf, single	35.00	*35.00*
96	A48	15c slate ('19)	1.40	.35
		Never hinged	3.75	
		Block of 4	16.50	
		On cover		1.40
a.		Imperf, single	125.00	*200.00*
		Nos. 94-96 (3)	5.00	.95

The frame of #95 differs in several details.

See Nos. 96b-96d following No. 174G.

For overprints and surcharge see Nos. 142A-142B, 150, 174A, B5, B9-B10; Austria N22-N23, N31, N54-N55, N61-N62, N66-N67; Dalmatia 2-5.

1908-27

97	A49	20c brn org ('25)	1.40	.90
		Never hinged	3.60	
		On cover		4.50
98	A49	20c green ('25)	.20	.20
		Never hinged	.45	
		On cover		.90
99	A49	20c lil brn ('26)	2.10	.30
		Never hinged	5.50	
		On cover		1.10
100	A49	25c blue	2.10	.30
		Never hinged	5.50	
		On cover		.90
a.		Imperf., pair	65.00	*65.00*
b.		Printed on both sides	175.00	*275.00*
101	A49	25c lt grn ('27)	5.75	*13.00*
		Never hinged	14.50	
		On cover		47.50

102 A49 30c org brn ('22) 2.10 .75
Never hinged 5.50
On cover 4.50
a. Imperf, single 200.00 —
103 A49 30c gray ('25) 4.25 .20
Never hinged 11.00
On cover 2.90
104 A49 40c brown 3.75 .30
Never hinged 9.00
On cover .90
a. Imperf., pair 200.00 —
105 A49 50c violet 1.40 .30
Never hinged 3.75
On cover .90
a. Imperf., pair 190.00 —
106 A49 55c dl vio ('20) 8.75 14.50
Never hinged 22.00
On cover 110.00
107 A49 60c car ('17) 2.10 .35
Never hinged 5.50
On cover 2.10
108 A49 60c blue ('23) 6.00 *50.00*
Never hinged 14.50
On cover 250.00
On postal card 150.00
109 A49 60c brn org ('26) 8.75 .55
Never hinged 22.00
On cover 7.25
110 A49 85c red brn ('20) 14.50 8.75
Never hinged 36.00
On cover 65.00
Nos. 97-110 (14) 63.15 *90.40*

Values for Mint Never Hinged and Used Blocks of 4

97	A49	20c brn org ('25)	16.00	
98	A49	20c green ('25)	2.00	
99	A49	20c lil brn ('26)	24.00	
100	A49	25c blue	24.00	
101	A49	25c lt grn ('27)	62.50	*180.00*
102	A49	30c org brn ('22)	22.50	16.00
103	A49	30c gray ('25)	45.00	14.00
104	A49	40c brown	75.00	
105	A49	50c violet	16.00	
106	A49	55c dl vio ('20)	95.00	
107	A49	60c car ('17)	24.00	
108	A49	60c blue ('23)	62.50	*600.00*
109	A49	60c brn org ('26)	95.00	
110	A49	85c red brn ('20)	150.00	

Hinged blocks of Nos. 97-110 do not command a premium above the value of the single stamps that comprise them. Similarly, used blocks not valued above are worth the combined value of 4 singles.

The upper panels of Nos. 104 and 105 are in solid color with white letters. A body of water has been added to the background.

See Nos. 100c-105j following No. 174G.

For overprints & surcharges see #142C-142D,147, 151, 153-157, 174B-174E, B7-B8, B12-B15A; Austria N24-N26, N28-N29, N32, N56-N57, N59, N63, N68-N70, N72-N73.

A50

A51

Redrawn

Perf. 13x13½, 13½x14

1909-17 Typo. Unwmk.

111 A50 15c slate black 250.00 2.10
Never hinged 625.00
Block of 4 2,750.
On cover 8.00
112 A50 20c brown org ('16) 57.50 4.25
Never hinged 140.00
Block of 4 625.00
On cover 14.50

No. 111 is similar to No. 93, but the design has been redrawn and the stamp is 23mm high instead of 25mm. There is a star at each side of the coat collar, but one is not distinct. See illustrations next to A47.

For overprints see Nos. B6, B11.

Wmk. 140 ***Perf. 14***

113 A50 20c brn org ('17) 7.25 .35
Never hinged 18.00
Block of 4 80.00
On cover 1.40
a. Imperf., pair 30.00 *30.00*

Stamps overprinted "Prestito Nazionale, 1917," or later dates, are Thrift or Postal Savings Stamps.

1910, Nov. 1

114 A51 10 l gray grn & red 72.50 25.00
Never hinged 180.00
Block of 4 180.00
On cover 1,450.
On cover, single franking *4,000.*
a. Red inverted *4,500.*

For surcharge see Dalmatia No. 8.

Giuseppe Garibaldi
A52 A53

Perf. 14x13½

1910, Apr. 15 Unwmk.

115 A52 5c green 25.00 *25.00*
Never hinged 100.00
Block of 4 500.00
On cover 100.00
116 A52 15c claret 50.00 *50.00*
Never hinged 200.00
Block of 4 1,000.
On cover 200.00

50th anniversary of freedom of Sicily.

1910, Dec. 1

117 A53 5c claret 110.00 110.00
Never hinged 500.00
Block of 4 650.00
On cover 440.00
118 A53 15c green 225.00 175.00
Never hinged 950.00
Block of 4 1,200.
On cover 725.00
#115-118, set of 2 commem covers 875.00

50th anniversary of the plebiscite of the southern Italian provinces in 1860.

Used values in italics are for postally used stamps. CTO's sell for about the same as unused, hinged stamps.

Symbols of Rome and Turin — A54

Symbol of Valor — A55

Genius of Italy — A56

Glory of Rome — A57

1911, May 1 Engr. ***Perf. 14x13½***

119 A54 2c brown 2.75 *5.75*
Never hinged 7.25
Block of 4 32.50
On cover 20.00
a. Vert. pair, imperf horiz. 87.50 87.50
b. Horiz. pair, imperf vert. 87.50 87.50
c. Perf. 13½ 45.00 45.00
120 A55 5c deep green 35.00 *32.50*
Never hinged 90.00
Block of 4 400.00
On cover 72.50
a. Perf. 13½ 150.00 87.50
121 A56 10c carmine 29.00 *42.50*
Never hinged 72.50
Block of 4 325.00
On cover 110.00
a. Vert. pair, imperf horiz. —
b. Horiz. pair, imperf vert. 180.00 180.00
c. Perf 13½ —
122 A57 15c slate 32.50 *65.00*
Never hinged 80.00
Block of 4 360.00
On cover 160.00
Nos. 119-122 (4) 99.25 *145.75*
Set on commem cover 290.00

50th anniv. of the union of Italian States to form the Kingdom of Italy.

Nos. 115 to 122 were sold at a premium over their face value.

For surcharges see Nos. 126-128.

Victor Emmanuel III
A58

Campanile, Venice
A59

1911, Oct. Re-engraved ***Perf. 13½***

123 A58 15c slate 29.00 1.10
Never hinged 72.50
Block of 4 310.00
On cover 2.90
a. Imperf., pair 200.00
b. Printed on both sides 325.00 *475.00*
c. Bklt. pane of 6 —
Cplt. bklt., 4 #123c *4,400.*

The re-engraved stamp is 24mm high. The stars at each side of the coat collar show plainly and the "C" of "Cent" is nearer the frame than in No. 93. See illustrations next to A47.

For surcharge see No. 129.

1912, Apr. 25 ***Perf. 14x13½***

124 A59 5c indigo 8.75 *13.00*
Never hinged 22.00
Block of 4 95.00
On cover 35.00
125 A59 15c dk brn 50.00 *55.00*
Never hinged 125.00
Block of 4 560.00
On cover 140.00
Set on commem cover 130.00

Re-erection of the Campanile at Venice.

Nos. 120-121 Surcharged in Black

1913, Mar. 1

126 A55 2c on 5c dp grn 2.10 *6.00*
Never hinged 5.50
Block of 4 23.00
On cover 35.00
a. On #120a 35.00 *55.00*
127 A56 2c on 10c car 2.10 *6.00*
Never hinged 5.50
Block of 4 23.00
On cover 35.00

No. 122 Surcharged in Violet

128 A57 2c on 15c slate 2.10 *6.00*
Never hinged 5.50
Block of 4 23.00
On cover 35.00
Nos. 126-128 (3) 6.30 *18.00*
Set, never hinged 15.00
Set on commem cover 80.00

No. 123 Surcharged

1916

129 A58 20c on 15c slate 16.00 1.10
Never hinged 40.00
Block of 4 160.00
On cover 2.90
a. Bklt. pane of 6 —
Cplt. bklt., 4 #129a *2,200.*
b. Inverted surcharge 300.00 300.00
c. Double surcharge 190.00 190.00
d. Surcharge on reverse 175.00
e. Vert. pair, one without surcharge 1,000.
Never hinged 1,300.
f. Horiz. strip of 3, 2 without surcharge 1,100.
Never hinged 1,350.
g. Imperf, single 145.00 *180.00*
h. Pair, one stamp with albino surcharge 500.00

Old Seal of Republic of Trieste
A60

Allegory of Dante's Divine Comedy
A61

Italy Holding Laurels for Dante — A62

Dante Alighieri — A63

Wmk. 140

1921, June 5 Litho. ***Perf. 14***

130 A60 15c blk & rose 6.50 *35.00*
Never hinged 16.00
Block of 4 65.00
On cover 400.00
a. Horiz. pair, imperf btwn. 575.00
131 A60 25c bl & rose 6.50 *35.00*
Never hinged 16.00
Block of 4 65.00
On cover 400.00
132 A60 40c brn & rose 6.50 *35.00*
Never hinged 16.00
Block of 4 65.00
On cover 400.00
Nos. 130-132 (3) 19.50 *105.00*
Set, never hinged 10.50
Set on commem cover 375.00

Reunion of Venezia Giulia with Italy.

1921, Sept. 28 Typo.

133 A61 15c vio brn 6.00 *20.00*
Never hinged 14.50
Block of 4 65.00
On cover 80.00
a. Imperf, pair 70.00
Imperf, single 32.50 32.50
134 A62 25c gray grn 6.00 *20.00*
Never hinged 14.50
Block of 4 65.00
On cover 80.00
a. Imperf, pair 70.00
Imperf, single 32.50 32.50
135 A63 40c brown 6.00 *20.00*
Never hinged 14.50
Block of 4 65.00
On cover 80.00
a. Imperf, pair 70.00
Imperf, single 32.50 32.50
Nos. 133-135 (3) 18.00 *60.00*
Set, never hinged 43.50
Set on commem cover —

600th anniversary of the death of Dante.

A 15c gray was not issued. Value: hinged $45, never hinged $92.50.

Nos. 133-135 exist in part perforate pairs.

"Victory" — A64

1921, Nov. 1 Engr. ***Perf. 14***

136 A64 5c olive green 1.10 *1.75*
Never hinged 2.75
Block of 4 11.00
On cover 11.00
137 A64 10c red 1.40 *2.10*
Never hinged 3.60
Block of 4 14.50
On cover 22.00
138 A64 15c slate green 2.75 *8.75*
Never hinged 7.25
Block of 4d 29.00
On cover 36.00

139 A64 25c ultra 1.40 *5.75*
Never hinged 3.60
Block of 4 14.50
On cover 25.00
Nos. 136-139 (4) 6.65 *18.35*
Set, never hinged 15.50
Set on commem cover 55.00

Perf. 14x13¼

136a A64 5c 2.10 *2.90*
Never hinged 5.50
137a A64 10c 2.90 *3.60*
Never hinged 7.25
138a A64 15c 7.25 *13.00*
Never hinged 18.00
139a A64 25c 2.90 *7.25*
Never hinged 7.25

Perf. 13½

137b A64 10c 110.00 *160.00*
139b A64 25c 160.00 *200.00*

Imperf Singles

136b A64 5c 210.00 210.00
Never hinged *325.00*
137c A64 10c 210.00 *425.00*
Never hinged *325.00*
139c A64 25c 160.00 160.00
Never hinged *240.00*
d. Double impression 550.00 —
Never hinged 825.00

Unwmk.

136c A64 5c 4.75 *8.75*
Never hinged 12.00
137d A64 10c 11.00 *18.00*
Never hinged 27.50
138b A64 15c 25.00 *40.00*
Never hinged 62.50
139e A64 25c 11.00 *18.00*
Never hinged 27.50

Wmk. Small Cross

136d A64 5c 18.00 *29.00*
Never hinged 45.00
137e A64 10c 36.00 *65.00*
Never hinged 90.00
138c A64 15c 90.00 *140.00*
Never hinged 225.00
139f A64 25c 36.00 *65.00*
Never hinged 90.00

3rd anniv. of the victory on the Piave.
For surcharges see Nos. 171-174.

Flame of Patriotism Tempering Sword of Justice — A65

Giuseppe Mazzini — A66

Mazzini's Tomb A67

1922, Sept. 20 Typo. *Perf. 14*

140 A65 25c maroon 11.50 *29.00*
Never hinged 29.00
Block of 4 110.00
On cover 180.00
141 A66 40c vio brn 21.00 *35.00*
Never hinged 55.00
Block of 4 210.00
On cover 200.00
142 A67 80c dk bl 11.50 *45.00*
Never hinged 29.00
Block of 4 110.00
On cover 250.00
Nos. 140-142 (3) 44.00 *109.00*
Set, never hinged 102.00
Set on commem cover 210.00

Mazzini (1805-1872), patriot and writer.

Nos. 95, 96, 100 and 104 Overprinted in Black

1922, June 4 Wmk. 140 *Perf. 14*

142A A48 10c claret 400.00 325.00
Never hinged 1,000.
On cover 900.00
142B A48 15c slate 250.00 250.00
Never hinged 640.00
On cover 875.00
142C A49 25c blue 225.00 250.00
Never hinged 575.00
On cover 875.00
142D A49 40c brown 350.00 290.00
Never hinged 900.00
On cover 900.00
Nos. 142A-142D (4) 1,225. 1,115.
Set, never hinged 2,825.
Set on commem postal card 1,300.
Set on commem cover 1,350.

Values for mint never hinged and used blocks of 4

142A A48 10c claret 4,600. 3,500.
142B A48 15c slate 2,900. 2,700.
142C A49 25c blue 2,700. 2,700.
142D A49 40c brown 4,200. 3,100.

9th Italian Philatelic Congress, Trieste. Counterfeits exist.

Christ Preaching The Gospel — A68

Portrait at upper right and badge at lower right differ on each value. Portrait at upper left is of Pope Gregory XV. Others: 20c, St. Theresa. 30c, St. Dominic. 50c, St. Francis of Assisi. 1 l, St. Francis Xavier.

1923, June 11

143 A68 20c ol grn & brn org 4.25 *100.00*
Never hinged 11.00
Block of 4 45.00
On cover 575.00
144 A68 30c claret & brn org 4.25 *100.00*
Never hinged 11.00
Block of 4 45.00
On cover 575.00
145 A68 50c vio & brn org 4.25 *100.00*
Never hinged 11.00
Block of 4 45.00
On cover 575.00
146 A68 1 l bl & brn org 4.25 *100.00*
Never hinged 11.00
Block of 4 45.00
On cover 575.00
Nos. 143-146 (4) 17.00 *400.00*
Set, never hinged 45.00
Set on commem cover 800.00

Forged cancellations exist on Nos. 143-146.

Imperf Singles

143a A68 20c 290.00 *360.00*
144a A68 30c 290.00 *360.00*
145a A68 50c 290.00 *360.00*
146a A68 1 l 290.00 *360.00*

Perf. 14 Horiz., Singles

144b A68 30c 87.50 *180.00*
145b A68 50c 87.50 *180.00*
146b A68 1 l 87.50 *180.00*

Horiz. Pairs, Imperf Between

144c A68 30c 725.00 *800.00*
Never hinged 900.00
145c A68 50c 950.00 *1,100.*
Never hinged 1,200.
146c A68 1 l 725.00 *800.00*
Never hinged 900.00

Vert. Pairs, Imperf Between

143b A68 20c 725.00 *800.00*
Never hinged 900.00
144d A68 30c 725.00 *800.00*
Never hinged 900.00
145d A68 50c 725.00 *800.00*
Never hinged 900.00
146d A68 1 l 725.00 *800.00*
Never hinged 900.00

300th anniv. of the Propagation of the Faith. Practically the entire issue was delivered to speculators.

Stamps of Previous Issues, Surcharged:

a

b

c

d

Lire 1,75
e

Two types of 7½c surcharge:
Type I: Base of "1" level with top of "2."
Type II: Base of "1" higher than top of "2," fraction bar longer.

Two types of 25c on 60c surcharge:
Type I: Bars of obliterator long and widely spaced.
Type II: Bars shorter and narrowly spaced.

1923-25

147 A49(a) 7½c on 85c (I) .20 *1.10*
Never hinged .45
On cover 22.00
On cover, single franking 32.50
a. Double surcharge — *1,150.*
b. Type II 9.50 *50.00*
Never hinged 23.00
On cover 160.00
On cover, single franking 240.00
c. As "b," double surcharge 360.00 —
148 A42(b) 10c on 1c .20 *.30*
Never hinged .45
On cover 2.90
a. Inverted surcharge 22.00 *35.00*
149 A43(b) 10c on 2c .20 *.30*
Never hinged .45
On cover 2.90
a. Inverted surcharge 55.00 *87.50*
b. Vert. pair, one without surcharge *725.00* —
150 A48(c) 10c on 15c .20 *.30*
Never hinged .45
On cover 2.90
a. Vert. pair, one without surcharge *575.00*
151 A49(a) 20c on 25c .20 *.55*
Never hinged .45
On cover 2.90
152 A45(d) 25c on 45c .35 *13.00*
Never hinged .90
On cover 80.00
a. Vert. pair, one without surcharge *575.00*
153 A49(a) 25c on 60c (I) 1.40 .90
Never hinged 3.50
On cover 18.00
a. Vert. pair, one without surcharge *575.00* —
b. Type II 18.00 *55.00*
Never hinged 45.00
On cover 310.00
On cover, single franking 440.00
c. As "a," Type II *575.00*

Single franked covers bearing No. 153b were canceled between 2/15/25 and 3/16/25.

154 A49(a) 30c on 50c .20 *.30*
Never hinged .45
On cover 14.50
On cover, single franking 47.50
155 A49(a) 30c on 55c .75 .30
Never hinged 1.80
On cover 35.00
On cover, single franking 80.00
156 A49(a) 50c on 40c 4.50 .35
Never hinged 11.00
On cover 4.25
a. Inverted surcharge 180.00 *275.00*
b. Double surcharge 110.00 *125.00*
157 A49(a) 50c on 55c 20.00 11.00
Never hinged 50.00
On cover 25.00
a. Inverted surcharge 875.00 *1,450.*
Never hinged 1,100.
158 A51(e) 1.75 l on 10 l 10.00 *22.00*
Never hinged 25.00
On cover 290.00
On cover, single franking 800.00
a. Vert. pair, one without surcharge *950.00*
Never hinged 1,200.
Nos. 147-158 (12) 38.20 50.40
Set, never hinged 95.00

Values for mint never hinged blocks of 4

147 A49(a) 7½c on 85c (I) 2.00
147b A49(a) 7½c on 85c (II) 100.00
148 A42(b) 10c on 1c 2.00
149 A43(b) 10c on 2c 2.00
150 A48(c) 10c on 15c 2.00
151 A49(a) 20c on 25c 2.00
152 A45(d) 25c on 45c 3.75
153 A49(a) 25c on 60c (I) 15.00
153b A49(a) 25c on 60c (II) 190.00
154 A49(a) 30c on 50c 2.00
155 A49(a) 30c on 55c 7.50
156 A49(a) 50c on 40c 45.00
157 A49(a) 50c on 55c 210.00
158 A51(e) 1.75 l on 10 l 100.00

Years of issue: Nos. 148-149, 156-157, 1923; Nos. 147, 152-153, 1924; others, 1925.

Emblem of the New Government A69

Wreath of Victory, Eagle and Fasces A70

Symbolical of Fascism and Italy — A71

Unwmk.

1923, Oct. 24 Engr. *Perf. 14*

159 A69 10c dark green 4.50 *8.75*
Never hinged 11.00
On cover 25.00
a. Imperf., single 725.00 *725.00*
Never hinged 900.00
160 A69 30c dark violet 4.50 *8.75*
Never hinged 11.00
On cover 25.00
161 A69 50c brown carmine 7.25 *14.50*
Never hinged 18.00
On cover 57.50

Wmk. 140 Typo.

162 A70 1 l blue 11.00 14.50
Never hinged 27.50
On cover 80.00
163 A70 2 l brown 14.50 18.00
Never hinged 35.00
On cover 130.00
164 A71 5 l blk & bl 22.00 *50.00*
Never hinged 55.00
On cover 325.00
a. Imperf., single 290.00 —
Nos. 159-164 (6) 63.75 *114.50*
Set, never hinged 160.00
Set on commem cover 415.00

Values for mint never hinged blocks of 4

159 A69 10c dark green 45.00
160 A69 30c dark violet 45.00
161 A69 50c brown carmine 75.00
162 A70 1 l blue 110.00
163 A70 2 l brown 150.00
164 A71 5 l blk & bl 225.00

Anniv. of the March of the Fascisti on Rome.

Fishing Scene A72

Designs: 15c, Mt. Resegone. 30c, Fugitives bidding farewell to native mountains. 50c, Part of Lake Como. 1 l, Manzoni's home, Milan. 5 l, Alessandro Manzoni. The first four designs show scenes from Manzoni's work "I Promessi Sposi."

1923, Dec. 29 *Perf. 14*

165 A72 10c brn red & blk 14.50 *87.50*
Never hinged 35.00
On cover 440.00
166 A72 15c bl grn & blk 14.50 *87.50*
Never hinged 35.00
On cover 440.00
167 A72 30c blk & slate 14.50 *87.50*
Never hinged 35.00
On cover 440.00
a. Imperf, pair —
As "a," single 2,400.
Never hinged 2,900.
168 A72 50c org brn & blk 14.50 *87.50*
Never hinged 35.00
On cover 440.00
169 A72 1 l blue & blk 110.00 *475.00*
Never hinged 290.00
On cover 1,450.
a. Imperf, pair, without gum —
As "a," single 140.00 *575.00*
170 A72 5 l vio & blk 625.00 *2,650.*
Never hinged 1,900.
On cover —
a. Imperf, pair —
As "a," single 725.00
Never hinged 1,800.
Nos. 165-170 (6) 793.00 *3,475.*
Set, never hinged 2,500.
Set on commem cover *8,750.*

Values for mint never hinged blocks of 4

165	A72	10c brn red & blk	160.00
166	A72	15c bl grn & blk	160.00
167	A72	30c blk & slate	160.00
168	A72	50c org brn & blk	160.00
169	A72	1 l blue & blk	1,300.
170	A72	5 l vio & blk	6,750.

50th anniv. of the death of Alessandro Manzoni.

Values are for stamps with perforations clear of the design. Very fine centered examples command a 50% premium.

Nos. 136-139 Surcharged

1924, Feb. ***Perf. 14***

171 A64 1 l on 5c ol grn 16.00 *140.00*
Never hinged 40.00
On cover 875.00
172 A64 1 l on 10c red 10.00 *140.00*
Never hinged 25.00
On cover 725.00
173 A64 1 l on 15c slate grn 16.00 *140.00*
Never hinged 40.00
On cover 875.00
174 A64 1 l on 25c ultra 10.00 *140.00*
Never hinged 25.00
On cover 725.00
Nos. 171-174 (4) 52.00 *560.00*
Set, never hinged 130.00
Set on commem cover *2,750.*

Surcharge forgeries exist.

Perf. 14x13½

171a A64 1 l on 5c 32.50 *180.00*
Never hinged 65.00
172a A64 1 l on 10c 18.00 *180.00*
Never hinged 35.00
173a A64 1 l on 15c 32.50 *180.00*
Never hinged 65.00
174h A64 1 l on 25c 18.00 *180.00*
Never hinged 35.00
Nos. 171a-174h (4) 101.00 *720.00*
Set, never hinged 200.00

Perf. 13½

171b A64 1 l on 5c 160.00 *500.00*
Never hinged *325.00*
174i A64 1 l on 25c 160.00 —
Never hinged *325.00*

Unwmk.

171c A64 1 l on 5c 72.50 —
Never hinged 250.00
172b A64 1 l on 10c 47.50 —
Never hinged 150.00
173b A64 1 l on 15c 72.50 —
Never hinged 250.00
174j A64 1 l on 25c 47.50 —
Never hinged 150.00

Nos. 95, 102, 105, 108, 110, 87 and 89 Overprinted in Black or Red

1924, Feb. 16

174A A48 10c claret 1.40 *21.00*
Never hinged 3.60
On cover 130.00
174B A49 30c org brn 1.40 *21.00*
Never hinged 3.60
On cover 130.00
174C A49 50c violet 1.40 *21.00*
Never hinged 3.60
On cover 130.00
174D A49 60c bl (R) 11.50 *72.50*
Never hinged 29.00
On cover 275.00
174E A49 85c choc (R) 6.00 *72.50*
Never hinged 14.50
On cover 275.00
174F A46 1 l brn & grn 40.00 *290.00*
Never hinged 100.00
On cover 1,450.
174G A46 2 l dk grn & org 29.00 *290.00*
Never hinged 72.50
On cover 2,000.
Nos. 174A-174G (7) 90.70 *788.00*
Set, never hinged 225.00
Set on commem cover 2,750.

Values for mint never hinged blocks of 4

174A	A48	10c claret	15.00
174B	A49	30c org brn	15.00
174C	A49	50c violet	15.00
174D	A49	60c bl (R)	120.00
174E	A49	85c choc (R)	60.00
174F	A46	1 l brn & grn	400.00
174G	A46	2 l dk grn & org	300.00

These stamps were sold on an Italian warship which made a cruise to South American ports in 1924.

Overprint forgeries exist of #174D-174G.

Stamps of 1901-22 with Advertising Labels Attached

Perf. 14 all around, Imperf. between

1924-25

96b A48 15c + Bitter Campari 2.90 *18.00*
Never hinged 5.75
On cover 87.50
96c A48 15c + Cordial Campari 2.90 *6.00*
Never hinged 16.00
On cover 87.50
96d A48 15c + Columbia 45.00 35.00
Never hinged 87.50
On cover 210.00
100c A49 25c + Abrador 87.50 87.50
Never hinged 175.00
On cover 625.00
100d A49 25c + Coen 200.00 45.00
Never hinged 400.00
On cover 275.00
100e A49 25c + Piperno 1,450. 625.00
Never hinged 2,200.
On cover 2,500.
100f A49 25c + Reinach 87.50 65.00
Never hinged 175.00
On cover 400.00
100g A49 25c + Tagliacozzo 650.00 610.00
Never hinged 1,300.
On cover 2,100.
102b A49 30c + Columbia 29.00 *32.50*
Never hinged 57.50
On cover *140.00*
105b A49 50c + Coen 1,450. 65.00
Never hinged 2,200.
On cover 275.00
105c A49 50c + Columbia 18.00 13.00
Never hinged 35.00
On cover 62.50
105d A49 50c + De Montel 2.90 13.00
Never hinged 5.75
On cover 225.00
105e A49 50c + Piperno 1,800. 210.00
Never hinged 2,600.
On cover 650.00
105f A49 50c + Reinach 200.00 50.00
Never hinged 400.00
On cover 250.00
105g A49 50c + Siero Casali 22.00 *32.50*
Never hinged 45.00
On cover 200.00
105h A49 50c + Singer 2.90 *7.25*
Never hinged 6.00
On cover 32.50
105i A49 50c + Tagliacozzo *2,200.* 450.00
Never hinged 3,250.
On cover 1,600.
105j A49 50c + Tantal 290.00 110.00
Never hinged 575.00
On cover 450.00
87b A46 1 l + Columbia 650.00 650.00
Never hinged 1,300.
On cover 3,250.
Nos. 96b-87b (19) 9,190. 3,124.
Set, never hinged 8,300.

No. 113 with Columbia label and No. E3 with Cioccolato Perugina label were prepared but not issued. Values: Columbia, unused $47.50, never hinged $95; Cioccolato, unused $15, never hinged $30.

King Victor Emmanuel III — A78

1925-26 Engr. Unwmk. *Perf. 11*

175 A78 60c brn car .75 .75
Never hinged 1.80
On cover 1.80
a. Perf. 13½ 5.75 2.10
Never hinged 14.50
On cover 5.75
b. Imperf., pair 250.00 —
Never hinged 375.00
c. Perf. 11x13½ 500.00 290.00
Never hinged 750.00
d. Perf. 13½x11 500.00 290.00
Never hinged 750.00
176 A78 1 l dk bl .75 .75
Never hinged 1.80
On cover 2.50
a. Perf. 13½ 13.00 7.25
Never hinged 32.50
On cover 18.00
b. Imperf., pair 250.00 —
Never hinged 375.00
c. Perf. 11x13½ 440.00 210.00
Never hinged 650.00
d. Perf. 13½x11 440.00 210.00
Never hinged 650.00

Perf. 13½

177 A78 1.25 l dk bl ('26) 3.50 2.10
Never hinged 9.00
On cover 22.00
a. Perf. 11 87.50 72.50
Never hinged 210.00
On cover 210.00
b. Imperf., pair 550.00 —
Never hinged 825.00
c. Perf. 11x13½ 725.00 340.00
Never hinged 900.00
d. Perf. 13½x11 725.00 340.00
Never hinged 900.00
Nos. 175-177 (3) 5.00 3.60
Set, never hinged 12.50

25th year of the reign of Victor Emmanuel III.

Nos. 175 to 177 exist with sideways watermark of fragments of letters or a crown, which are normally on the sheet margin.

St. Francis and His Vision A79

Monastery of St. Damien A80

Assisi Monastery A81

St. Francis' Death A82

St. Francis — A83

1926, Jan. 30 Wmk. 140 *Perf. 14*

178 A79 20c gray grn .75 *.90*
Never hinged 1.80
On cover 4.00
a. Imperf single 725.00 725.00
Never hinged 900.00
179 A80 40c dk vio .75 *.90*
Never hinged 1.80
On cover 4.00
180 A81 60c red brn .75 *.90*
Never hinged 1.80
On cover 4.00
a. Imperf single 400.00 400.00
Never hinged 600.00

Unwmk. *Perf. 11*

181 A83 30c slate blk .75 *.90*
Never hinged 1.80
On cover 4.00
a. Perf. 13½ 22.00 13.00
Never hinged 55.00
On cover 32.50
b. Perf. 13½x11 400.00
c. Perf. 11x13½ 400.00
182 A82 1.25 l dark blue 3.60 .90
Never hinged 9.00
On cover 8.75
a. Perf. 13½ 440.00 25.00
Never hinged 1,100.
On cover 87.50

Perf. 13½

183 A83 5 l + 2.50 l dk brn 10.00 *87.50*
Never hinged 25.00
On cover —
Nos. 178-183 (6) 16.60 *92.00*
Set, never hinged 40.00

700th anniv. of the death of St. Francis of Assisi.

Alessandro Volta — A84

1927 Wmk. 140 Typo. *Perf. 14*

188 A84 20c dk car 1.50 1.10
Never hinged 3.60
On cover 10.00
189 A84 50c grnsh blk 2.10 .75
Never hinged 5.40
On cover 8.75
190 A84 60c chocolate 4.25 *4.40*
Never hinged 11.00
On cover 42.50
191 A84 1.25 l ultra 10.00 7.25
Never hinged 25.00
On cover 65.00
Nos. 188-191 (4) 17.85 13.50
Set, never hinged 45.00

Cent. of the death of Alessandro Volta. The 20c in purple is Cyrenaica No. 25a.

A85

A86

1927-29 Size: 17½x22mm *Perf. 14*

192 A85 50c brn & slate 2.10 .35
Never hinged 5.50
On cover 1.25
a. Imperf, pair — —
As "a," single 210.00 290.00
Never hinged 325.00

Unwmk.
Engr. *Perf. 11*
Size: 19x23mm

193 A85 1.75 l dp brn 2.90 .30
Never hinged 5.50
On cover 1.25
a. Perf. 13½ ('29) *30,000.* *2,400.*
Never hinged *44,000.*
On cover 7,000.
b. Perf. 11x13½ ('29) — 1,600.
c. Perf. 13½x11 ('29) — 1,600.
d. Imperf, single *2,000.*
Never hinged 3,000.
194 A85 1.85 l black 1.50 .65
Never hinged 3.60
On cover 36.00
195 A85 2.55 l brn car 3.25 *8.75*
Never hinged 8.25
On cover 150.00
196 A85 2.65 l dp vio 4.00 *57.50*
Never hinged 10.00
On cover 875.00
On cover, single franking 1,450.
a. Imperf, single 1,400.
Never hinged 2,000.
Nos. 192-196 (5) 13.75 *67.55*
Set, never hinged 35.00

1928-29 Wmk. 140 Typo. *Perf. 14*

197 A86 7½c lt brown 2.90 *11.00*
Never hinged 7.25
On cover 29.00
On cover, single franking 110.00
198 A86 15c brown org ('29) 2.10 .30
Never hinged 5.50
On cover 5.75
199 A86 35c gray blk ('29) 5.50 11.00
Never hinged 13.50
On cover 50.00
On cover, single franking 400.00
200 A86 50c dull violet 11.50 .30
Never hinged 29.00
On cover .90
a. Imperf single 210.00
Never hinged 325.00
Nos. 197-200 (4) 22.00 *22.60*
Set, never hinged 55.00

Emmanuel Philibert, Duke of Savoy — A87

Statue of Philibert, Turin — A88

Philibert and Italian Soldier of 1918 — A89

1928 *Perf. 11, 14*

201 A87 20c red brn & ultra 7.25 *11.00*
Never hinged 18.00
On cover 29.00
a. Perf. 13½ 145.00 145.00
Never hinged 360.00
On cover 400.00
202 A87 25c dp red & bl grn 7.25 *11.00*
Never hinged 18.00
On cover 29.00
a. Perf. 13½ 57.50 42.50
Never hinged 145.00
On cover 145.00

203 A87 30c bl grn & red brn 14.00 *21.00*
Never hinged 36.00
On cover 55.00
a. Center inverted *50,000.* *5,500.*
No gum *40,000.*
b. Perf. 13½ 29.00 29.00
Never hinged 72.50
On cover 90.00
204 A89 50c org brn & bl 3.60 1.10
Never hinged 9.00
On cover 5.00
205 A89 75c dp red 4.40 3.60
Never hinged 11.00
On cover 18.00
206 A88 1.25 l bl & blk 4.40 3.60
Never hinged 11.00
On cover 20.00
207 A89 1.75 l bl grn 29.00 21.00
Never hinged 72.50
On cover 55.00
208 A87 5 l vio & bl grn 26.00 *90.00*
Never hinged 65.00
On cover 400.00
209 A89 10 l blk & pink 32.50 *180.00*
Never hinged 80.00
On cover *5,750.*
210 A88 20 l vio & blk 62.50 *625.00*
Never hinged 150.00
On cover 9,750.
Nos. 201-210 (10) 190.90 *967.30*
Set, never hinged 470.00

400th anniv. of the birth of Emmanuel Philibert, Duke of Savoy; 10th anniv. of the victory of 1918; Turin Exhibition.

She-wolf Suckling Romulus and Remus
A90 A95a

Julius Caesar
A91

Augustus Caesar
A92

"Italia" — A93

A94

A95

1929-42 Wmk. 140 Photo. *Perf. 14*
213 A90 5c olive brn 1.40 .20
Never hinged 3.60
On cover .35
214 A91 7½c deep vio .20 .20
Never hinged .45
On cover 20.00
215 A92 10c dark brown .20 .20
Never hinged .45
On cover .35
216 A93 15c slate grn .20 .20
Never hinged .45
On cover .35
217 A91 20c rose red .20 .20
Never hinged .45
On cover .35
218 A94 25c dp green .20 .20
Never hinged .45
On cover .35
219 A95 30c olive brn .20 .20
Never hinged .45
On cover .35
a. Imperf., pair 875.00
Never hinged 1,750.
220 A93 35c dp blue .20 .20
Never hinged .45
On cover 29.00
221 A95 50c purple .20 .20
Never hinged .45
On cover .35
a. Imperf., pair 525.00 *550.00*
Never hinged 1,050.
222 A94 75c rose red .20 .20
Never hinged .45
On cover .35
222A A91 1 l dk pur ('42) .20 .20
Never hinged .45
On cover 18.00
223 A94 1.25 l dp blue .20 .20
Never hinged .45
On cover .35
224 A92 1.75 l red org .20 .20
Never hinged .45
On cover .35
225 A93 2 l car lake .20 .20
Never hinged .45
On cover .35
226 A95a 2.55 l slate grn .20 .20
Never hinged .45
On cover 29.00
226A A95a 3.70 l pur ('30) .20 .20
Never hinged .45
On cover 50.00
227 A95a 5 l rose red .20 .20
Never hinged .45
On cover 18.00
228 A93 10 l purple 3.60 3.60
Never hinged 9.00
On cover 60.00
229 A91 20 l lt green 4.25 *11.00*
Never hinged 11.00
On cover 240.00
230 A92 25 l bluish sl 10.00 *32.50*
Never hinged 25.00
On cover 18.00
231 A94 50 l dp violet 11.50 *36.00*
Never hinged 29.00
On cover 1,800.
Nos. 213-231 (21) 33.95 *86.50*
Set, never hinged 85.00

Stamps of the 1929-42 issue overprinted "G.N.R." are 1943 local issues of the Guardia Nazionale Republicana.

See Nos. 427-438, 441-459.

For surcharge and overprints see Nso. 460, M1-M13, 1N10-1N13, 1LN1-1LN1A, 1LN10; Italian Social Republic 1-5A; Yugoslavia-Ljubljana N36-N54.

Courtyard of Monte Cassino
A96

Monks Laying Cornerstone — A98

St. Benedict of Nursia — A100

Designs: 25c, Fresco, "Death of St. Benedict." 75c+15c, 5 l+1 l, Monte Cassino Abbey.

1929, Aug. 1 Photo. Wmk. 140
232 A96 20c red orange 1.40 1.40
Never hinged 3.50
On cover 7.25
233 A96 25c dk green 1.40 1.40
Never hinged 3.50
On cover 7.25
234 A98 50c + 10c ol brn 3.50 *14.50*
Never hinged 9.00
On cover 42.50
235 A98 75c + 15c crim 4.25 *21.00*
Never hinged 11.00
On cover 57.50
236 A96 1.25 l + 25c saph 5.75 *23.00*
Never hinged 14.50
On cover 65.00
237 A98 5 l + 1 l dk vio 8.75 *80.00*
Never hinged 21.00
On cover 290.00

Unwmk.
Engr.
238 A100 10 l + 2 l slate grn 13.00 *160.00*
Never hinged 32.50
On cover 1,600.
Nos. 232-238 (7) 38.05 *301.30*
Set, never hinged 95.00
Set on overfranked philatelic cover 575.00

14th cent. of the founding of the Abbey of Monte Cassino by St. Benedict in 529 A.D. The premium on some of the stamps was given to the committee for the celebration of the centenary.

Prince Humbert and Princess Marie José
A101

1930, Jan. 8 Photo. Wmk. 140
239 A101 20c orange red .70 .55
Never hinged 1.80
On cover 3.50
240 A101 50c + 10c ol brn 2.10 *3.50*
Never hinged 5.50
On cover 8.75
241 A101 1.25 l + 25c dp bl 5.00 *11.50*
Never hinged 12.50
On cover 29.00
Nos. 239-241 (3) 7.80 *15.55*
Set, never hinged 20.00
Set on overfranked philatelic cover 32.50

Marriage of Prince Humbert of Savoy with Princess Marie José of Belgium.

The surtax on Nos. 240 and 241 was for the benefit of the Italian Red Cross Society.

The 20c in green is Cyrenaica No. 35a.

Ferrucci Leading His Army
A102

Fabrizio Maramaldo Killing Ferrucci
A103

Francesco Ferrucci — A104

1930, July 10
242 A102 20c rose red .70 .70
Never hinged 1.80
On cover 8.50
243 A103 25c deep green 1.25 .70
Never hinged 3.10
On cover 8.50
244 A103 50c purple .70 .35
Never hinged 1.80
On cover 4.25
245 A103 1.25 l deep blue 10.00 4.25
Never hinged 25.00
On cover 50.00
246 A104 5 l + 2 l org red 20.00 *110.00*
Never hinged 50.00
On cover 475.00
Nos. 242-246 (5) 32.65 *116.00*
Set, never hinged 80.00
Set on overfranked philatelic cover 440.00
Nos. 242-246,C20-C22 (8) 54.15 *256.50*
Set, never hinged 135.00

4th cent. of the death of Francesco Ferrucci, Tuscan warrior.

Overprints
See Aegean Islands for types A103-A145 Overprinted.

Helenus and Aeneas
A106

Designs: 20c, Anchises and Aeneas watch passing of Roman Legions. 25c, Aeneas feasting in shade of Albunea. 30c, Ceres and her children with fruits of Earth. 50c, Harvesters at work. 75c, Woman at loom, children and calf. 1.25 l, Anchises and his sailors in sight of Italy. 5 l+1.50 l, Shepherd piping by fireside. 10 l+2.50 l, Aeneas leading his army.

1930, Oct. 21 Photo. *Perf. 14*
248 A106 15c olive brn 2.10 2.10
Never hinged 5.50
On cover 13.00
249 A106 20c orange 2.10 1.40
Never hinged 5.50
On cover 7.25
250 A106 25c green 2.75 1.40
Never hinged 7.25
On cover 7.25
251 A106 30c dull vio 8.50 3.60
Never hinged 21.00
On cover 16.00
252 A106 50c violet 14.50 .70
Never hinged 36.00
On cover 3.60
253 A106 75c rose red 3.60 *7.25*
Never hinged 9.00
On cover 36.00
254 A106 1.25 l blue 3.60 *7.25*
Never hinged 9.00
On cover 50.00

Unwmk. Engr.
255 A106 5 l +1.50 l red brn 55.00 *250.00*
Never hinged 140.00
On cover 725.00
256 A106 10 l +2.50 l gray grn 55.00 *325.00*
Never hinged 140.00
On cover *2,350.*
Nos. 248-256 (9) 147.15 *598.70*
Set, never hinged 365.00
Set on overfranked philatelic cover 1,800.
Nos. 248-256,C23-C26 (13) 296.65 *1,235.*
Set, never hinged 750.00

Bimillenary of the birth of Virgil. Surtax on Nos. 255-256 was for the National Institute Figli del Littorio.

Arms of Italy (Fascist Emblems Support House of Savoy Arms) — A115

1930, Dec. 16 Photo. Wmk. 140
257 A115 2c deep orange 1.40 .20
Never hinged 3.60
On cover 11.00

St. Anthony being Installed as a Franciscan
A116

Olivares Hermitage, Portugal
A118

St. Anthony Freeing Prisoners
A120

St. Anthony's Death
A121

St. Anthony Succoring the Poor — A122

Designs: 25c, St. Anthony preaching to the fishes. 50c, Basilica of St. Anthony, Padua.

Wmk. 140
1931, Mar. 9 Photo. *Perf. 14*
258 A116 20c dull violet 3.60 1.10
Never hinged 9.00
On cover 4.40
259 A116 25c gray green 2.10 1.10
Never hinged 5.50
On cover 4.40
260 A118 30c brown 5.75 2.10
Never hinged 14.50
On cover 11.00
261 A118 50c violet 1.75 .70
Never hinged 4.50
On cover 3.25
262 A120 1.25 l blue 18.00 8.75
Never hinged 45.00
On cover 36.00

Unwmk. Engr.

263 A121 75c brown red 8.50 *14.50*
Never hinged 21.00
On cover 57.50
a. Perf. 12 90.00 *210.00*
Never hinged 180.00
On cover 500.00
264 A122 5 l + 2.50 l ol grn 36.00 *180.00*
Never hinged 90.00
On cover 475.00
Nos. 258-264 (7) 75.70 *208.25*
Set, never hinged 370.00
Set on overfranked philatelic cover 440.00

7th centenary of the death of Saint Anthony of Padua.

Tower of Meloria — A123

Training Ship "Amerigo Vespucci" A124

Cruiser "Trento" A125

1931, Nov. 29 Photo. Wmk. 140

265 A123 20c rose red 8.00 1.75
Never hinged 31.00
On cover 8.50
266 A124 50c purple 8.00 1.40
Never hinged 31.00
On cover 7.25
267 A125 1.25 l dk bl 21.00 4.25
Never hinged 85.00
On cover 32.50
Nos. 265-267 (3) 37.00 7.40
Set, never hinged 150.00
Set on overfranked philatelic cover 37.50

Royal Naval Academy at Leghorn (Livorno),50th anniv.

Giovanni Boccaccio A126

Designs: 15c, Niccolo Machiavelli. 20c, Paolo Sarpi. 25c, Count Vittorio Alfieri. 30c, Ugo Foscolo. 50c, Count Giacomo Leopardi. 75c, Giosue Carducci. 1.25 l, Carlo Giuseppe Botta. 1.75 l, Torquato Tasso. 2.75 l, Francesco Petrarca. 5 l+2 l, Ludovico Ariosto. 10 l+2.50 l, Dante Alighieri.

1932, Mar. 14 *Perf. 14*

268 A126 10c olive brn 2.90 1.40
Never hinged 7.25
On cover 11.00
269 A126 15c slate green 2.90 1.80
Never hinged 7.25
On cover 25.00
270 A126 20c rose red 2.90 1.40
Never hinged 7.25
On cover 7.25
271 A126 25c dp green 2.90 1.10
Never hinged 7.25
On cover 5.75
272 A126 30c olive brn 3.60 1.40
Never hinged 9.00
On cover 18.00
273 A126 50c violet 2.10 .70
Never hinged 5.50
On cover 3.25
274 A126 75c car rose 14.50 7.25
Never hinged 36.00
On cover 36.00
275 A126 1.25 l dp blue 4.25 3.60
Never hinged 11.00
On cover 29.00
276 A126 1.75 l orange 11.00 7.25
Never hinged 27.00
On cover 42.50
277 A126 2.75 l gray 21.00 *29.00*
Never hinged 55.00
On cover 125.00
278 A126 5 l + 2 l car rose 26.00 *130.00*
Never hinged 65.00
On cover 575.00
279 A126 10 l + 2.50 l ol grn 32.50 *210.00*
Never hinged 80.00
On cover *1,750.*
Nos. 268-279 (12) 126.55 *394.90*
Set, never hinged 330.00
Set on overfranked philatelic cover 1,000.
Nos. 268-279,C28-C33,C34 (19) 209.20 *1,146.*
Set, never hinged 420.00

Dante Alighieri Society, a natl. literary association founded to promote development of the Italian language and culture. The surtax was added to the Society funds to help in its work.

View of Caprera A138

Garibaldi Carrying His Dying Wife A141

Garibaldi Memorial A144

Giuseppe Garibaldi A145

Designs: 20c, 30c, Garibaldi meeting Victor Emmanuel II. 25c, 50c, Garibaldi at Battle of Calatafimi. 1.25 l, Garibaldi's tomb. 1.75 l+25c, Rock of Quarto.

1932, Apr. 6

280 A138 10c gray blk 2.10 1.40
Never hinged 5.50
On cover 8.75
281 A138 20c olive brn 2.10 1.10
Never hinged 5.50
On cover 7.25
282 A138 25c dull grn 2.90 1.40
Never hinged 7.25
On cover 5.75
283 A138 30c orange 2.90 2.10
Never hinged 7.25
On cover 25.00
284 A138 50c violet 1.40 .35
Never hinged 3.50
On cover 2.90
285 A141 75c rose red 14.50 8.75
Never hinged 35.00
On cover 29.00
286 A141 1.25 l dp blue 29.00 3.50
Never hinged 72.50
On cover 25.00
287 A141 1.75 l + 25c bl gray 35.00 *80.00*
Never hinged 90.00
On cover 290.00
288 A144 2.55 l + 50c red brn 29.00 *110.00*
Never hinged 72.50
On cover 325.00
289 A145 5 l + 1 l cop red 20.00 *110.00*
Never hinged 72.50
On cover 475.00
Nos. 280-289 (10) 138.90 *318.60*
Set, never hinged 375.00
Set on overfranked philatelic cover 725.00
Nos. 280-289,C35-C39,CE1-CE2 (17) 192.65 *541.35*
Set, never hinged 485.00

50th anniv. of the death of Giuseppe Garibaldi, patriot.

Plowing with Oxen and Tractor A146

10c, Soldier guarding mountain pass. 15c, Marine, battleship & seaplane. 20c, Head of Fascist youth. 25c, Hands of workers & tools. 30c, Flags, Bible & altar. 35c, "New roads for the new Legions." 50c, Mussolini statue, Bologna. 60c, Hands with spades. 75c, Excavating ruins. 1 l, Steamers & galleons. 1.25 l, Italian flag, map & points of compass. 1.75 l, Flag, athlete & stadium. 2.55 l, Mother & child. 2.75 l, Emblems of drama, music, art & sport. 5 l+2.50 l, Roman emperor.

1932, Oct. 27 Photo.

290 A146 5c dk brown 2.10 1.10
Never hinged 5.50
On cover 18.00
291 A146 10c dk brown 2.10 .70
Never hinged 5.50
On cover 8.75
292 A146 15c dk gray grn 2.10 1.10
Never hinged 5.50
On cover 11.00
293 A146 20c car rose 2.10 .55
Never hinged 5.50
On cover 2.90
294 A146 25c dp green 2.10 .35
Never hinged 5.50
On cover 2.90
295 A146 30c dk brown 2.90 1.10
Never hinged 7.25
On cover 14.50
296 A146 35c dk blue 7.25 *8.75*
Never hinged 18.00
On cover 65.00
297 A146 50c purple 1.40 .35
Never hinged 3.50
On cover 1.75
298 A146 60c orange brn 11.00 7.25
Never hinged 27.50
On cover 42.50
299 A146 75c car rose 3.50 3.50
Never hinged 9.00
On cover 18.00
300 A146 1 l black vio 14.50 5.75
Never hinged 35.00
On cover 35.00
301 A146 1.25 l dp blue 3.50 1.40
Never hinged 9.00
On cover 18.00
302 A146 1.75 l orange 21.00 1.80
Never hinged 55.00
On cover 18.00
303 A146 2.55 l dk gray 26.00 *35.00*
Never hinged 65.00
On cover 110.00
304 A146 2.75 l slate grn 26.00 *35.00*
Never hinged 65.00
On cover 140.00
305 A146 5 l + 2.50 l car rose 35.00 *250.00*
Never hinged 90.00
On cover *1,100.*
Nos. 290-305 (16) 162.55 *353.70*
Set, never hinged 410.00
Set on overfranked philatelic cover 975.00
Nos. 290-305,C40-C41,E16-E17 (20) 181.20 *522.95*
Set, never hinged 450.00

10th anniv. of the Fascist government and the March on Rome.

Statue of Athlete — A162

Cross in Halo, St. Peter's Dome — A163

1933, Aug. 16 *Perf. 14*

306 A162 10c dk brown .70 .70
Never hinged 1.80
On cover 5.75
307 A162 20c rose red .70 .70
Never hinged 1.80
On cover 7.25
308 A162 50c purple .70 .35
Never hinged 1.80
On cover 4.25
309 A162 1.25 l blue 4.25 *5.75*
Never hinged 11.00
On cover 32.50
Nos. 306-309 (4) 6.35 7.50
Set, never hinged 16.50
Set on overfranked philatelic cover 42.50

Intl. University Games at Turin, Sept., 1933.

1933, Oct. 23

Designs: 25c, 50c, Angel with cross. 1.25 l, as 20c. 2.55 l, + 2.50 l, Cross with doves.

310 A163 20c rose red 4.25 1.10
Never hinged 11.00
On cover 7.25
311 A163 25c green 11.00 1.40
Never hinged 27.00
On cover 7.25
312 A163 50c purple 4.25 .35
Never hinged 11.00
On cover 2.75
313 A163 1.25 l dp blue 11.00 4.25
Never hinged 27.50
On cover 32.50
314 A163 2.55 l + 2.50 l blk 7.25 *90.00*
Never hinged 18.00
On cover *400.00*
Nos. 310-314 (5) 37.75 *97.10*
Set, never hinged 95.00
Set on overfranked philatelic cover 325.00
Nos. 310-314,CB1-CB2 (7) 41.40 *128.10*
Set, never hinged 100.00

Issued at the solicitation of the Order of the Holy Sepulchre of Jerusalem to mark the Holy Year.

Anchor of the "Emanuele Filiberto" A166

Antonio Pacinotti A172

Designs: 20c, Anchor. 50c, Gabriele d'Annunzio. 1.25 l, St. Vito's Tower. 1.75 l, Symbolizing Fiume's annexation. 2.55 l+2 l, Victor Emmanuel III arriving aboard "Brindisi." 2.75 l+2.50 l, Galley, gondola and battleship.

1934, Mar. 12

315 A166 10c dk brown 5.75 3.50
Never hinged 14.50
On cover *18.00*
316 A166 20c rose red 1.40 1.40
Never hinged 3.50
On cover *8.75*
317 A166 50c purple 1.40 1.40
Never hinged 3.50
On cover *7.25*
318 A166 1.25 l blue 1.40 *5.75*
Never hinged 3.50
On cover *36.00*
319 A166 1.75 l + 1 l indigo 1.40 *32.50*
Never hinged 3.50
On cover *290.00*
320 A166 2.55 l + 2 l dull vio 1.40 *50.00*
Never hinged 3.50
On cover *400.00*
321 A166 2.75 l + 2.50 l ol grn 1.40 *50.00*
Never hinged 3.50
On cover *425.00*
Nos. 315-321 (7) 14.15 *144.55*
Set, never hinged 35.00
Set on overfranked philatelic cover 725.00
Nos. 315-321,C56-C61,CE5-CE7 (16) 22.95 *279.65*
Set, never hinged 45.00

10th anniversary of annexation of Fiume.

1934, May 23

322 A172 50c purple .70 .35
Never hinged 1.80
On cover *3.50*
323 A172 1.25 l sapphire 1.10 *2.50*
Never hinged 2.75
On cover *25.00*
Set, never hinged 4.50
Set on overfranked philatelic cover 25.00

75th anniv. of invention of the dynamo by Antonio Pacinotti (1841-1912), scientist.

Guarding the Goal — A173

Players — A175

Soccer Players A174

1934, May 23

324 A173 20c red orange 5.75 *7.25*
Never hinged 14.50
On cover 35.00
325 A174 25c green 5.75 2.10
Never hinged 14.50
On cover 25.00
326 A174 50c purple 5.75 1.10
Never hinged 14.50
On cover 18.00

327 A174 1.25 l blue 14.00 14.50
Never hinged 35.00
On cover 110.00
328 A175 5 l + 2.50 l brn 80.00 *360.00*
Never hinged 200.00
On cover *2,200.*
Nos. 324-328 (5) 111.25 *384.95*
Set, never hinged 275.00
Set on overfranked philatelic cover *2,000.*
Nos. 324-328,C62-C65 (9) 219.25 *934.95*
Set, never hinged 550.00

2nd World Soccer Championship.
For overprints see Aegean Islands Nos. 31-35.

Luigi Galvani — A176

1934, Aug. 16
329 A176 30c brown, *buff* .90 .70
Never hinged 2.40
On cover 5.75
330 A176 75c carmine, *rose* 1.25 2.75
Never hinged 3.10
On cover 25.00
Set, never hinged 5.50
Set on overfranked philatelic cover 27.50

Intl. Congress of Electro-Radio-Biology.

Carabinieri Emblem — A177

Cutting Barbed Wire A178

Designs: 20c, Sardinian Grenadier and soldier throwing grenade. 25c, Alpine Infantry. 30c, Military courage. 75c, Artillery. 1.25 l, Acclaiming the Service. 1.75 l+1 l, Cavalry. 2.55 l+2 l, Sapping Detail. 2.75 l+2 l, First aid.

1934, Sept. 6 Photo. Wmk. 140
331 A177 10c dk brown 2.10 2.10
Never hinged 5.50
On cover 14.50
332 A178 15c olive grn 2.10 *3.50*
Never hinged 5.50
On cover 18.00
333 A178 20c rose red 2.10 1.50
Never hinged 5.50
On cover 10.00
334 A177 25c green 3.50 1.50
Never hinged 9.00
On cover 10.00
335 A178 30c dk brown 3.50 *7.25*
Never hinged 9.00
On cover 29.00
336 A178 50c purple 2.10 .70
Never hinged 5.50
On cover 3.50
337 A178 75c car rose 35.00 11.00
Never hinged 90.00
On cover 40.00
338 A178 1.25 l dk blue 35.00 7.25
Never hinged 90.00
On cover 29.00
339 A177 1.75 l + 1 l red org 16.00 *45.00*
Never hinged 40.00
On cover 360.00
340 A178 2.55 l + 2 l dp cl 16.00 *62.50*
Never hinged 40.00
On cover 460.00
341 A178 2.75 l + 2 l vio 19.00 *65.00*
Never hinged 47.50
On cover 625.00
Nos. 331-341 (11) 136.40 *207.30*
Set, never hinged 350.00
Nos. 331-341,C66-C72 (18) 179.75 *339.80*
Set, never hinged 460.00
Set on overfranked philatelic cover 975.00

Centenary of Military Medal of Valor.
For overprints see Aegean Islands Nos. 36-46.

Man Holding Fasces A187

Standard Bearer, Bayonet Attack A188

Design: 30c, Eagle and soldier.

1935, Apr. 23 ***Perf. 14***
342 A187 20c rose red .70 .70
Never hinged 1.80
On cover 7.25
343 A187 30c dk brown 4.25 *5.75*
Never hinged 11.00
On cover 29.00
344 A188 50c purple .70 .35
Never hinged 1.80
On cover 5.75
Nos. 342-344 (3) 5.65 6.80
Set, never hinged 14.00
Set on overfranked philatelic cover 30.00

Issued in honor of the University Contests.

Fascist Flight Symbolism A190

Leonardo da Vinci — A191

1935, Oct. 1
345 A190 20c rose red 14.50 1.80
Never hinged 57.50
On cover 20.00
346 A190 30c brown 29.00 5.75
Never hinged 110.00
On cover 65.00
347 A191 50c purple 57.50 1.10
Never hinged 225.00
On cover 14.50
348 A191 1.25 l dk blue 65.00 6.50
Never hinged 260.00
On cover 85.00
Nos. 345-348 (4) 166.00 15.15
Set, never hinged 650.00
Set on overfranked philatelic cover 140.00

International Aeronautical Salon, Milan.

Vincenzo Bellini — A192

Bellini's Villa — A194

Bellini's Piano A193

1935, Oct. 15
349 A192 20c rose red 14.00 3.50
Never hinged 35.00
On cover 14.50
350 A192 30c brown 21.00 11.00
Never hinged 55.00
On cover 21.00
351 A192 50c violet 21.00 1.50
Never hinged 55.00
On cover 8.75
352 A192 1.25 l dk blue 36.00 14.50
Never hinged 90.00
On cover 57.50
353 A193 1.75 l + 1 l red org 32.50 *150.00*
Never hinged 80.00
On cover 425.00
354 A194 2.75 l + 2 l ol blk 57.50 *160.00*
Never hinged 150.00
On cover 550.00
Nos. 349-354 (6) 182.00 *340.50*
Set, never hinged 460.00
Set on overfranked philatelic cover 725.00
Nos. 349-354,C79-C83 (11) 220.10 *594.75*
Set, never hinged 550.00

Bellini (1801-35), operatic composer.

Map of Italian Industries A195

Designs: 20c, 1.25 l, Map of Italian Industries. 30c, 50c, Cogwheel and plow.

1936, Mar. 23
355 A195 20c red .70 .35
Never hinged 1.80
On cover 4.25
356 A195 30c brown .70 1.10
Never hinged 1.80
On cover 10.75
357 A195 50c purple .70 .30
Never hinged 1.80
On cover 2.75
358 A195 1.25 l blue 4.25 2.75
Never hinged 11.00
On cover 18.00
Nos. 355-358 (4) 6.35 4.50
Set, never hinged 16.00
Set on overfranked philatelic cover 800.00

The 17th Milan Trade Fair.

Flock of Sheep A197

Ajax Defying the Lightning A199

Bust of Horace A200

Designs: 20c, 1.25 l+1 l, Countryside in Spring. 75c, Capitol. 1.75 l+1 l, Pan piping. 2.55 l+1 l, Dying warrior.

Wmk. Crowns (140)
1936, July 1 Photo. *Perf. 14*
359 A197 10c dp green 5.75 1.10
Never hinged 14.50
On cover 8.75
360 A197 20c rose red 4.25 .70
Never hinged 11.00
On cover 7.25
361 A199 30c olive brn 5.75 2.10
Never hinged 14.00
On cover 18.00
362 A200 50c purple 5.75 .35
Never hinged 14.00
On cover 4.25
363 A197 75c rose red 14.50 8.50
Never hinged 35.00
On cover 29.00
364 A197 1.25 l + 1 l dk bl 25.00 *92.50*
Never hinged 62.50
On cover 275.00
365 A199 1.75 l + 1 l car rose 29.00 *140.00*
Never hinged 72.50
On cover 290.00
366 A197 2.55 l + 1 l sl blk 35.00 *150.00*
Never hinged 90.00
On cover 440.00
Nos. 359-366 (8) 125.00 *395.25*
Set, never hinged 310.00
Set on overfranked philatelic cover 800.00
Nos. 359-366,C84-C88 (13) 162.25 *668.00*
Set, never hinged 400.00

2000th anniv. of the birth of Quintus Horatius Flaccus (Horace), Roman poet.

Child Holding Wheat — A204

Child Giving Salute — A205

Child and Fasces — A206

"Il Bambino" by della Robbia — A207

1937, June 28
367 A204 10c yellow brn 2.75 1.40
Never hinged 7.25
On cover 14.50
368 A205 20c car rose 2.75 1.10
Never hinged 7.25
On cover 5.75
369 A204 25c green 2.75 1.75
Never hinged 7.25
On cover 18.00
370 A206 30c dk brown 4.25 3.50
Never hinged 11.00
On cover 21.00
371 A205 50c purple 2.75 .35
Never hinged 7.25
On cover 3.50
372 A207 75c rose red 14.50 14.50
Never hinged 35.00
On cover 55.00
373 A205 1.25 l dk blue 18.00 14.50
Never hinged 45.00
On cover 50.00
374 A206 1.75 l + 75c org 36.00 *100.00*
Never hinged 90.00
On cover 425.00
375 A207 2.75 l + 1.25 l dk bl grn 29.00 *110.00*
Never hinged 72.50
On cover 550.00
376 A205 5 l + 3 l bl gray 35.00 *160.00*
Never hinged 90.00
On cover 1,100.
Nos. 367-376 (10) 147.75 *407.10*
Set, never hinged 375.00
Set on overfranked philatelic cover 1,150.
Nos. 367-376,C89-C94 (16) 211.00 *763.85*
Set, never hinged 415.00

Summer Exhibition for Child Welfare. The surtax on Nos. 374-376 was used to support summer camps for children.

Rostral Column — A208

15c, Army Trophies. 20c, Augustus Caesar (Octavianus) offering sacrifice. 25c, Cross Roman Standards. 30c, Julius Caesar and Julian Star. 50c, Augustus receiving acclaim. 75c, Augustus Caesar. 1.25 l, Symbolizing maritime glory of Rome. 1.75 l+1 l, Sacrificial Altar. 2.55 l+2 l, Capitol.

1937, Sept. 23
377 A208 10c myrtle grn 2.90 .70
Never hinged 7.25
On cover 5.75
378 A208 15c olive grn 2.90 1.10
Never hinged 7.25
On cover 14.50
379 A208 20c red 2.90 .55
Never hinged 7.25
On cover 4.50
380 A208 25c green 2.90 .55
Never hinged 7.25
On cover 4.50
381 A208 30c olive bis 3.50 .70
Never hinged 9.00
On cover 11.00
382 A208 50c purple 2.90 .30
Never hinged 7.25
On cover 3.25

383 A208 75c scarlet 2.90 4.25
Never hinged 7.25
On cover 21.00
384 A208 1.25 l dk blue 7.00 5.00
Never hinged 18.005
On cover 22.50
385 A208 1.75 l + 1 l plum 35.00 *100.00*
Never hinged 90.00
On cover 275.00
386 A208 2.55 l + 2 l sl blk 45.00 *130.00*
Never hinged 120.00
On cover 360.00
Nos. 377-386 (10) 107.90 *243.15*
Set, never hinged 150.00
Set on overfranked philatelic cover 575.00
Nos. 377-386,C95-C99 (15) 197.90 *459.15*
Set, never hinged 390.00

Bimillenary of the birth of Emperor Augustus Caesar (Octavianus) on the occasion of the exhibition opened in Rome by Mussolini, Sept. 22, 1937.
For overprints see Aegean Islands #47-56.

Gasparo Luigi Pacifico Spontini A218

Antonius Stradivarius A219

Count Giacomo Leopardi A220

Giovanni Battista Pergolesi A221

Giotto di Bondone — A222

1937, Oct. 25

387 A218 10c dk brown 1.40 .70
Never hinged 3.50
On cover 5.75
388 A219 20c rose red 1.40 .70
Never hinged 3.50
On cover 4.25
389 A220 25c dk green 1.40 .70
Never hinged 3.50
On cover 4.25
390 A221 30c dk brown 1.40 1.40
Never hinged 3.50
On cover 14.50
391 A220 50c purple 1.40 .70
Never hinged 3.50
On cover 2.90
392 A221 75c crimson 2.10 *4.25*
Never hinged 5.25
On cover 29.00
393 A222 1.25 l dp blue 2.90 *4.25*
Never hinged 7.25
On cover 29.00
394 A218 1.75 l dp orange 2.90 *4.25*
Never hinged 7.25
On cover 29.00
395 A219 2.55 l + 2 l gray grn 14.50 *120.00*
Never hinged 35.00
On cover 360.00
396 A222 2.75 l + 2 l red brn 14.50 *140.00*
Never hinged 35.00
On cover 400.00
Nos. 387-396 (10) 43.90 *276.95*
Set, never hinged 110.00
Set on overfranked philatelic cover 575.00

Centennials of Spontini, Stradivarius, Leopardi, Pergolesi and Giotto.
For overprints see Aegean Islands #57-58.

Guglielmo Marconi A223

Augustus Caesar (Octavianus) A224

1938, Jan. 24

397 A223 20c rose pink 2.90 .70
Never hinged 7.25
On cover 6.50
398 A223 50c purple .70 .30
Never hinged 1.75
On cover 4.25
399 A223 1.25 l blue 2.90 5.00
Never hinged 7.25
On cover 29.00
Nos. 397-399 (3) 6.50 6.00
Set, never hinged 16.00
Set on overfranked philatelic cover 29.00

Guglielmo Marconi (1874-1937), electrical engineer, inventor of wireless telegraphy.

1938, Oct. 28

10c, Romulus Plowing. 25c, Dante. 30c, Columbus. 50c, Leonardo da Vinci. 75c, Victor Emmanuel II and Garibaldi. 1.25 l, Tomb of Unknown Soldier, Rome. 1.75 l, Blackshirts' March on Rome, 1922. 2.75 l, Map of Italian East Africa and Iron Crown of Monza. 5 l, Victor Emmanuel III.

400 A224 10c brown 1.75 .90
Never hinged 4.50
On cover 6.25
401 A224 20c car rose 1.75 .90
Never hinged 4.50
On cover 8.00
402 A224 25c dk green 1.75 .90
Never hinged 4.50
On cover 10.00
403 A224 30c olive brn 1.75 1.75
Never hinged 4.50
On cover 12.50
404 A224 50c lt violet 1.75 .90
Never hinged 5.50
On cover 4.50
405 A224 75c rose red 2.75 1.75
Never hinged 6.25
On cover 27.50
406 A224 1.25 l dp blue 5.50 1.75
Never hinged 14.00
On cover 27.50
407 A224 1.75 l vio blk 7.25 2.75
Never hinged 18.00
On cover 30.00
408 A224 2.75 l slate grn 18.00 *32.50*
Never hinged 45.00
On cover 160.00
409 A224 5 l lt red brn 32.50 *45.00*
Never hinged 82.50
On cover 275.00
Nos. 400-409 (10) 74.75 *89.10*
Set, never hinged 190.00
Set on overfranked philatelic cover 475.00
Nos. 400-409,C100-C105 (16) 103.50 *208.85*
Set, never hinged 265.00

Proclamation of the Empire.

Wood-burning Engine and Streamlined Electric Engine — A234

1939, Dec. 15 Photo. *Perf. 14*

410 A234 20c rose red .70 .55
Never hinged 1.80
On cover 7.25
411 A234 50c brt violet 1.40 .70
Never hinged 3.50
On cover 5.75
412 A234 1.25 l dp blue 2.90 3.50
Never hinged 7.25
On cover 25.00
Nos. 410-412 (3) 5.00 4.75
Set, never hinged 12.50
Set on overfranked philatelic cover 30.00

Centenary of Italian railroads.

SEMI-POSTAL STAMPS

Many issues of Italy and Italian Colonies include one or more semi-postal denominations. To avoid splitting sets, these issues are generally listed as regular postage, airmail, etc., unless all values carry a surtax.

Italian Flag — SP1

Italian Eagle Bearing Arms of Savoy — SP2

1915-16 Typo. Wmk. 140 *Perf. 14*

B1 SP1 10c + 5c rose 7.25 3.75
Never hinged 18.00
On cover *12.50*
B2 SP2 15c + 5c slate 6.00 3.00
Never hinged 14.50
On cover 11.50
B3 SP2 20c + 5c orange 29.00 20.00
Never hinged 72.50
On cover 45.00
Nos. B1-B3 (3) 42.25 *26.75*
Set, never hinged 105.00

No. B2 Surcharged

1916

B4 SP2 20c on 15c + 5c 18.00 11.50
Never hinged 45.00
On cover 62.50
a. Double overprint 500.00 —
Never hinged 775.00
b. Inverted overprint 500.00 450.00
Never hinged 775.00
c. Pair, one without surcharge 1,200.
Never hinged 1,450.

Regular Issues of 1906-16 Overprinted in Blue or Red

1921

B5 A48 10c claret (Bl) 1,000. 1,000.
No gum 360.00
Never hinged 1,500.
On BLP envelope 440.00 *4,000.*
a. Double overprint 1,200.
Never hinged 1,750.
B6 A50 20c brn org (Bl) 1,450. 325.00
No gum 475.00
Never hinged 2,200.
On BLP envelope 550.00 900.00
B7 A49 25c blue (R) 200.00 110.00
No gum 80.00
Never hinged 400.00
On BLP envelope 95.00 *440.00*
a. Double overprint 325.00
B8 A49 40c brn (Bl) 80.00 16.00
No gum 30.00
Never hinged 160.00
On BLP envelope 32.50 *55.00*
a. Inverted overprint 130.00 115.00
b. Violet ovpt. 140.00 *22.00*
No gum 35.00
Never hinged 290.00
On BLP envelope 45.00 87.50
c. Maroon ovpt. 110.00 20.00
No gum 32.50
Never hinged 225.00
On BLP envelope 40.00 80.00
d. Blue black ovpt. 200.00 62.50
No gum 57.50
Never hinged 400.00
On BLP envelope 72.50 240.00
Nos. B5-B8 (4) *2,730.* 1,451.
Set, never hinged 4,250.

Regular Issues of 1901-22 Overprinted in Black, Blue, Brown or Red

1922-23

Typographed Ovpt.

B9 A48 10c cl ('23) (Bk) 87.50 57.50
No gum 30.00
Never hinged 175.00
On BLP envelope 35.00 *650.00*
a. Blue ovpt. 87.50 62.50
No gum 30.00
Never hinged 175.00
On BLP envelope 62.50 *800.00*
b. Brown ovpt. 87.50 62.50
No gum 30.00
Never hinged 175.00
On BLP envelope 40.00 1,200.
d. Blk ovpt. double 130.00
e. As "b," ovpt. double 140.00
B10 A48 15c slate (Org) 360.00 *400.00*
No gum 140.00
Never hinged 725.00
On BLP envelope 200.00 *6,500.*
b. Red overprint 360.00 *400.00*
No gum 110.00
Never hinged 575.00
On BLP envelope 200.00 *5,500.*
B11 A50 20c brn org (Bk) 325.00 *360.00*
No gum 120.00
Never hinged 650.00
On BLP envelope 140.00 *1,800.*
B12b A49 25c bl ('23) (R) 290.00 *360.00*
No gum 110.00
Never hinged 575.00
On BLP envelope 140.00 —
c. Orange ovpt. 290.00 360.00
No gum 110.00
Never hinged 575.00
On BLP envelope 140.00 —
B12A A49 30c org brn (Bk) 210.00 140.00
No gum 72.50
Never hinged 440.00
On BLP envelope 95.00 *2,900.*
B15A A49 85c choc (Bk) 290.00 *360.00*
No gum 110.00
Never hinged 575.00
On BLP envelope 140.00 *11,000.*

Litho. Ovpt.

B9c A48 10c Blk ovpt. 110.00 80.00
No gum 40.00
Never hinged 230.00
On BLP envelope 45.00 *240.00*
B10a A48 15c Blue ovpt. 800.00 725.00
No gum 275.00
Never hinged 1,600.
On BLP envelope 400.00 *5,750.*
c. Blk ovpt. 5,100. —
Never hinged 6,350.
B11a A50 20c Blue ovpt. 650.00 325.00
No gum 240.00
Never hinged 1,300.
On BLP envelope 250.00 *1,000.*
b. Blk ovpt. 650.00 550.00
No gum 240.00
Never hinged 1,300.
On BLP envelope 250.00 *1,200.*
B12 A49 25c blue (Bk) 110.00 87.50
No gum 35.00
Never hinged 210.00
On BLP envelope 47.50 *725.00*
B13 A49 40c brn (Bl) 160.00 87.50
No gum 55.00
Never hinged 325.00
On BLP envelope 65.00 *725.00*
a. Black ovpt. 160.00 87.50
No gum 55.00
Never hinged 325.00
On BLP envelope 65.00 *725.00*
b. As "a," invtd. ovpt. 140.00 —
B14 A49 50c vio ('23) (Bk) 575.00 500.00
No gum 200.00
Never hinged 1,200.
On BLP envelope 250.00 1,800.
a. Blue overprint —
B15 A49 60c car (Bk) 2,200. 1,900.
No gum 800.00
Never hinged 3,250.
On BLP envelope 1,000. 6,500.
B16 A46 1 l brn & grn ('23) (Bk) 3,600. 2,200.
No gum 1,450.
Never hinged 5,500.
On BLP envelope 1,750. *4,400.*
a. Inverted overprint *4,000.*
Never hinged *6,000.*
Set, #B9-B16, B12A, B15A, never hinged 13,000.

The stamps overprinted "B. L. P." were sold by the Government below face value to the National Federation for Assisting War Invalids. Most of them were affixed to special envelopes (Buste Lettere Postali) which bore advertisements. The Federation was permitted to sell these envelopes at a reduction of 5c from the face value of each stamp. The profits for the war invalids were derived from the advertisements.
The overprint on Nos. B9-B16 is wider (13½mm) than that on Nos. B5-B8 (11mm).
Counterfeits of the B.L.P. overprints exist.

Administering Fascist Oath — SP3

1923, Oct. 29 *Perf. 14x14½*

B17 SP3 30c + 30c brown 30.00 *87.50*
Never hinged 72.50
On cover 275.00
B18 SP3 50c + 50c violet 30.00 *87.50*
Never hinged 72.50
On cover 275.00
a. Horiz. pair, imperf between 1,000.

B19 SP3 1 l + 1 l gray 30.00 *87.50*
Never hinged 72.50
On cover *275.00*
Nos. B17-B19 (3) 90.00 *262.50*
Set, never hinged 220.00
Set on commem cover 440.00

The surtax was given to the Benevolent Fund of the Black Shirts (the Italian National Militia).
Anniv. of the March of the Fascisti on Rome.

St. Maria Maggiore SP4

Pope Opening Holy Door SP8

Designs: 30c+15c, St. John Lateran. 50c+25c, St. Paul's Church. 60c+30c, St. Peter's Basilica. 5 l+2.50 l, Pope closing Holy Door.

1924, Dec. 24 *Perf. 12*
B20 SP4 20c + 10c dk grn & brn 3.60 *11.00*
Never hinged 9.00
On cover 35.00
B21 SP4 30c + 15c dk brn & brn 3.60 *11.00*
Never hinged 9.00
On cover 35.00
B22 SP4 50c + 25c vio & brn 3.60 *11.00*
Never hinged 9.00
On cover 42.50
B23 SP4 60c + 30c dp rose & brn 3.60 *32.50*
Never hinged 9.00
On cover 72.50
B24 SP8 1 l + 50c dp bl & vio 5.75 *32.50*
Never hinged 14.50
On cover 130.00
B25 SP8 5 l + 2.50 l org brn & vio 7.25 *65.00*
Never hinged 18.00
On cover 325.00
Nos. B20-B25 (6) 27.40 *163.00*
Set, never hinged 57.50
Set on commem cover 325.00

The surtax was contributed toward the Holy Year expenses.

Castle of St. Angelo SP10

Victor Emmanuel II — SP14

Designs: 50c+20c, 60c+30c, Aqueduct of Claudius. 1.25 l+50c, 1.25 l+60c, Capitol, Roman Forum. 5 l+2 l, 5 l+2.50 l, People's Gate.

Unwmk.
1926, Oct. 26 **Engr.** *Perf. 11*
B26 SP10 40c + 20c dk brn & blk 2.90 *14.50*
Never hinged 7.25
On cover 57.50
B27 SP10 60c + 30c brn red & ol brn 2.90 *14.50*
Never hinged 7.25
On cover 57.50
B28 SP10 1.25 l + 60c bl grn & blk 2.90 *45.00*
Never hinged 7.25
On cover 130.00
B29 SP10 5 l + 2.50 l dk bl & blk 4.50 *130.00*
Never hinged 11.00
On cover 400.00
Nos. B26-B29 (4) 13.20 *204.00*
Set, never hinged 32.50
Set on commem cover 400.00

Stamps inscribed "Poste Italiane" and "Fiere Campionaria di Tripoli" are listed in Libya.

1928, Mar. 1
B30 SP10 30c + 10c dl vio & blk 10.00 *29.00*
Never hinged 25.00
On cover 72.50
B31 SP10 50c + 20c ol grn & sl 17.50 *29.00*
Never hinged 45.00
On cover 60.00
B32 SP10 1.25 l + 50c dp bl & blk 22.00 *57.50*
Never hinged 55.00
On cover 175.00
B33 SP10 5 l + 2 l brn red & blk 47.50 *210.00*
Never hinged 110.00
On cover 550.00
Nos. B30-B33 (4) 97.00 *325.50*
Set, never hinged 235.00
Set on commem cover 650.00

The tax on Nos. B26 to B33 was devoted to the charitable work of the Voluntary Militia for National Defense.
See Nos. B35-B38.

1929, Jan. 4 **Photo.** ***Perf. 14***
B34 SP14 50c + 10c ol grn 3.50 *8.00*
Never hinged 9.00
On cover 40.00

50th anniv. of the death of King Victor Emmanuel II. The surtax was for veterans.

Type of 1926 Issue

Designs in same order.

1930, July 1 **Engr.**
B35 SP10 30c + 10c dk grn & vio 2.10 *22.00*
Never hinged 5.50
On cover 65.00
B36 SP10 50c + 10c dk grn & bl grn 2.90 *18.00*
Never hinged 7.25
On cover 45.00
B37 SP10 1.25 l + 30c ind & grn 7.25 *42.50*
Never hinged 18.00
On cover 130.00
B38 SP10 5 l + 1.50 l blk brn & ol brn 14.50 *175.00*
Never hinged 35.00
On cover 700.00
Nos. B35-B38 (4) 26.75 *257.50*
Set, never hinged 55.00
Set on commem cover 650.00

The surtax was for the charitable work of the Voluntary Militia for National Defense.

Militiamen at Ceremonial Fire with Quotation from Leonardo da Vinci — SP15

Symbolical of Pride for Militia — SP16

Symbolical of Militia Guarding Immortality of Italy SP17

Militia Passing Through Arch of Constantine SP18

1935, July 1 **Photo.** **Wmk. 140**
B39 SP15 20c + 10c rose red 8.75 *10.00*
Never hinged 22.00
On cover 55.00
B40 SP16 25c + 15c green 8.75 *16.00*
Never hinged 22.00
On cover 55.00
B41 SP17 50c + 30c purple 8.75 *20.00*
Never hinged 22.00
On cover 200.00
B42 SP18 1.25 l + 75c blue 8.75 *30.00*
Never hinged 22.00
On cover 325.00
Nos. B39-B42 (4) 35.00 *76.00*
Set, never hinged 87.50
Set on commemorative cover 300.00
Nos. B39-B42,CB3 (5) 42.25 *103.50*
Set, never hinged 105.00

The surtax was for the Militia.

AIR POST STAMPS

Used values for this section are for postally used stamps with legible cancellations. Forged cancels on Nos. C1-C105 abound, and expertization is srongly recommended.

Special Delivery Stamp No. E1 Overprinted

1917, May **Wmk. 140** ***Perf. 14***
C1 SD1 25c rose red 14.50 *32.50*
Never hinged 35.00
On flown colored postcard 80.00
On flown white postcard *1,000.*

Type of SD3 Surcharged in Black

1917, June 27
C2 SD3 25c on 40c violet 17.50 *40.00*
Never hinged 45.00
On flown cover or postcard 80.00

Type SD3 was not issued without surcharge.

AP2

1926-28 **Typo.**
C3 AP2 50c rose red ('28) 16.00 11.00
Never hinged 40.00
On commercial cover 35.00
C4 AP2 60c gray 4.50 *11.00*
Never hinged 11.00
On commercial cover 35.00
C5 AP2 80c brn vio & brn ('28) 29.00 *95.00*
Never hinged 72.50
On commercial cover 290.00
C6 AP2 1 l blue 10.00 *11.00*
Never hinged 25.00
On commercial cover 35.00
C7 AP2 1.20 l brn ('27) 25.00 *100.00*
Never hinged 62.50
On commercial cover 210.00
C8 AP2 1.50 l buff 16.00 29.00
Never hinged 40.00
On commercial cover 85.00
C9 AP2 5 l gray grn 35.00 *92.50*
Never hinged 90.00
On commercial cover 275.00
Nos. C3-C9 (7) 135.50 *349.50*
Set, never hinged 340.00
Nos. C4, C6, C8, C9 on overfranked philatelic cover (Mar. 1926) 475.00

Nos. C4 and C6 Surcharged

1927, Sept. 16
C10 AP2 50c on 60c gray 17.50 *50.00*
Never hinged 45.00
On commercial cover 85.00
a. Pair, one without surcharge 1,300.
Never hinged 1,600.
C11 AP2 80c on 1 l blue 50.00 *200.00*
Never hinged 125.00
On commercial cover 410.00
Set, never hinged 170.00
On overfranked commem. cover 500.00

Pegasus AP3

Wings AP4

Spirit of Flight — AP5

Arrows AP6

1930-32 **Photo.** **Wmk. 140**
C12 AP4 25c dk grn ('32) .20 .20
Never hinged .45
On commercial cover 13.00
C13 AP3 50c olive brn .20 .20
Never hinged .45
On commercial cover 1.40
C14 AP5 75c org brn ('32) .35 .20
Never hinged .90
On commercial cover 21.00
C15 AP4 80c org red .20 *.70*
Never hinged .45
On commercial cover 50.00
C16 AP5 1 l purple .20 .20
Never hinged .45
On commercial cover 1.40
C17 AP6 2 l deep blue .35 .20
Never hinged .90
On commercial cover 25.00
C18 AP3 5 l dk green .70 *1.40*
Never hinged 1.75
On commercial cover 42.50
C19 AP3 10 l dp car 1.40 *5.75*
Never hinged 3.50
On commercial cover 80.00
Nos. C12-C19 (8) 3.60 8.85
Set, never hinged 9.00

The 50c, 1 l and 2 l were reprinted in 1942 with labels similar to those of Nos. 427-438, but were not issued. Value, set of 3, $100.
For overprints see Nos. MC1-MC5. For overprints and surcharges on design AP6 see Nos. C52-C55; Yugoslavia-Ljubljana NB9-NB20, NC11-NC17.

Ferrucci Type of Postage

Staue of Ferrucci.

1930, July 10
C20 A104 50c purple 3.50 *14.50*
Never hinged 9.00
On commercial cover 72.50
C21 A104 1 l orange brn 3.50 *16.00*
Never hinged 9.00
On commercial cover 97.50
C22 A104 5 l + 2 l brn vio 14.50 *110.00*
Never hinged 35.00
On commercial cover 500.00
Nos. C20-C22 (3) 21.50 *140.50*
Set, never hinged 52.50
Set, on flown overfranked commem. cover 325.00

For overprinted types see Aegean Islands Nos. C1-C3.

Virgil Type of Postage

Jupiter sending forth his eagle.

1930, Oct. 21 **Photo.** **Wmk. 140**
C23 A106 50c lt brown 21.00 *29.00*
Never hinged 55.00
On commercial cover 72.50
C24 A106 1 l orange 21.00 *32.50*
Never hinged 55.00
On commercial cover 130.00

Engr.
Unwmk.
C25 A106 7.70 l + 1.30 l vio brn 50.00 *275.00*
Never hinged 125.00
On commercial cover 1,250.

C26 A106 9 l + 2 l indigo 57.50 *300.00*
Never hinged 140.00
On commercial cover 1,800.
Nos. C23-C26 (4) 149.50 *636.50*
Set, never hinged 375.00
Set, on flown overfranked commem. cover 1,250.

The surtax on Nos. C25-C26 was for the National Institute Figli del Littorio.

For overprinted types see Aegean Islands Nos. C4-C7.

Trans-Atlantic Squadron — AP9

1930, Dec. 15 Photo. Wmk. 140

C27 AP9 7.70 l Prus bl & gray 350.00 *1,100.*
Never hinged 725.00
On flown cover *1,450.*
a. Seven stars instead of six 1,150. —
Never hinged 2,300.
On flown cover *20,000.*

Flight by Italian aviators from Rome to Rio de Janeiro, Dec. 1930-Jan. 12, 1931.

Leonardo da Vinci's Flying Machine AP10

Leonardo da Vinci AP11

Leonardo da Vinci — AP12

1932

C28 AP10 50c olive brn 4.40 *5.75*
Never hinged 11.00
On commercial cover 45.00
C29 AP11 1 l violet 5.75 *7.25*
Never hinged 14.50
On commercial cover 72.50
C30 AP11 3 l brown red 7.25 *25.00*
Never hinged 18.00
On commercial cover 125.00
C31 AP11 5 l dp green 11.50 *29.00*
Never hinged 29.00
On commercial cover 175.00
C32 AP10 7.70 l + 2 l dk bl 8.75 *85.00*
Never hinged 21.00
On commercial cover *1,100.*
C33 AP11 10 l + 2.50 l blk brn 10.00 *125.00*
Never hinged 25.00
On commercial cover *1,250.*
Nos. C28-C33 (6) 47.65 *277.00*
Set, never hinged 110.00
Set, on flown overfranked commem. cover 650.00

Engr.
Unwmk.

C34 AP12 100 l brt bl & grnsh blk 35.00 *475.00*
Never hinged 90.00
On flown cover *1,450.*
a. Thin paper 160.00 *875.00*
Never hinged 325.00

Dante Alighieri Soc. and especially Leonardo da Vinci, to whom the invention of a flying machine has been attributed. Surtax was for the benefit of the Society.

Inscription on No. C34: "Man with his large wings by beating against the air will be able to dominate it and lift himself above it".

Issued: #C28-C33, Mar. 14; #C34, Aug. 6.

For overprinted types see Aegean Islands Nos. C8-C13.

Garibaldi's Home at Caprera AP13

Farmhouse where Anita Garibaldi Died AP14

50c, 1 l+25c, Garibaldi's home, Caprera. 2 l+50c, Anita Garibaldi. 5 l+1 l, Giuseppe Garibaldi.

1932, Apr. 6 Photo. Wmk. 140

C35 AP13 50c copper red 4.50 *7.25*
Never hinged 11.00
On commercial cover 40.00
C36 AP14 80c deep green 4.50 *11.50*
Never hinged 11.00
On commercial cover 90.00
C37 AP13 1 l + 25c red brn 7.25 *29.00*
Never hinged 18.00
On commercial cover 110.00
C38 AP13 2 l + 50c dp bl 11.50 *40.00*
Never hinged 29.00
On commercial cover 175.00
C39 AP14 5 l + 1 l dp grn 11.50 *45.00*
Never hinged 29.00
On commercial cover 450.00
Nos. C35-C39 (5) 39.25 *132.75*
Set, never hinged 80.00
Set, on flown overfranked commem. cover 300.00

50th anniv. of the death of Giuseppe Garibaldi, patriot. The surtax was for the benefit of the Garibaldi Volunteers.

For overprinted types see Aegean Islands Nos. C15-C19.

March on Rome Type of Postage

50c, Eagle sculpture and airplane. 75c, Italian buildings from the air.

1932, Oct. 27 ***Perf. 14***

C40 A146 50c dark brown 2.90 *8.50*
Never hinged 7.25
On cover 35.00
C41 A146 75c orange brn 8.50 *29.00*
Never hinged 21.00
On cover 90.00
Set, never hinged 27.50
Set, on flown overfranked commem. cover 115.00

Graf Zeppelin Issue

Zeppelin over Pyramid of Caius Cestius AP19

5 l, Tomb of Cecilia Metlella. 10 l, Stadium of Mussolini. 12 l, St. Angelo Castle and Bridge. 15 l, Roman Forum. 20 l, Imperial Avenue.

1933, Apr. 24

C42 AP19 3 l black & grn 19.00 *72.50*
Never hinged 47.50
On flown cover 210.00
C43 AP19 5 l green & brn 19.00 *92.50*
Never hinged 47.50
On flown cover 290.00
C44 AP19 10 l car & dl bl 19.00 *210.00*
Never hinged 19.00
On flown cover 615.00
C45 AP19 12 l dk bl & red org 19.00 *350.00*
Never hinged 19.00
On flown cover 865.00
C46 AP19 15 l dk brn & gray 19.00 *440.00*
Never hinged 19.00
On flown cover 1,200.
C47 AP19 20 l org brn & bl 19.00 *460.00*
Never hinged 19.00
On flown cover 1,300.
a. Vertical pair, imperf. between 7,250.
Never hinged 11,000.
Nos. C42-C47 (6) 114.00 *1,625.*
Set, never hinged 285.00
Set, on flown overfranked commem. cover 3,750.

Balbo's Trans-Atlantic Flight Issue

Italian Flag

King Victor Emmanuel III

Allegory "Flight" — AP25

#C49, Colosseum at Rome, Chicago skyline. #C48-C49 consist of 3 parts; Italian flag, Victor Emmanuel III, & scene arranged horizontally.

1933, May 20

C48 AP25 5.25 l + 19.75 l red, grn & ultra 110.00 *1,600.*
Never hinged 210.00
On flown cover 2,900.
a. Left stamp without ovpt. *20,000.*
Never hinged *30,000.*
C49 AP25 5.25 l + 44.75 l grn, red & ultra 140.00 *1,600.*
Never hinged 290.00
On flown cover 2,500.

Transatlantic Flight, Rome-Chicago, of 24-seaplane squadron led by Gen. Italo Balbo. Center and right sections paid postage. At left is registered air express label overprinted "APPARECCHIO" and abbreviated pilot's name. Twenty triptychs of each value differ in name overprint.

No. C49 overprinted "VOLO DI RITORNO/ NEW YORK-ROMA" was not issued; flight canceled. Value never hinged, $40,000.

For overprints see Nos. CO1, Aegean Islands C26-C27.

Type of Air Post Stamp of 1930 Surcharged in Black

1934, Jan. 18

C52 AP6 2 l on 2 l yel 6.50 *57.50*
Never hinged 16.00
On flight cover 100.00
C53 AP6 3 l on 2 l yel grn 6.50 *85.00*
Never hinged 16.00
On flight cover 120.00
C54 AP6 5 l on 2 l rose 6.50 *175.00*
Never hinged 16.00
On flight cover 400.00
C55 AP6 10 l on 2 l vio 6.50 *250.00*
Never hinged 16.00
On flight cover 550.00
Nos. C52-C55 (4) 26.00 *567.50*
Set, never hinged 65.00
Set, on overfranked flown cover 1,050.

For use on mail carried on a special flight from Rome to Buenos Aires.

Annexation of Fiume Type

25c, 75c, View of Fiume Harbor. 50c, 1 l+50c, Monument to the Dead. 2 l+1.50 l, Venetian Lions. 3 l+2 l, Julian wall.

1934, Mar. 12

C56 A166 25c green .70 *3.50*
Never hinged 1.75
On cover 47.50
C57 A166 50c brown .70 *2.10*
Never hinged 1.75
On cover 32.50
C58 A166 75c org brn .70 *8.50*
Never hinged 1.75
On cover 115.00
C59 A166 1 l + 50c dl vio .70 *14.50*
Never hinged 1.75
On cover 160.00
C60 A166 2 l + 1.50 l dl bl .70 *19.00*
Never hinged 1.75
On cover 250.00
C61 A166 3 l + 2 l blk brn .70 *20.00*
Never hinged 1.75
On cover 360.00
Nos. C56-C61 (6) 4.20 *67.60*
Set, never hinged 10.50
Nos. C56-C61, CE6-CE7 on overfranked commem. cover 550.00
No. CE5 on commem. cover (July 1934) 575.00

Airplane and View of Stadium AP32

Soccer Player and Plane AP33

Airplane and Stadium Entrance AP35

Airplane over Stadium AP34

1934, May 24

C62 AP32 50c car rose 8.50 *21.00*
Never hinged 8.50
On cover 92.50
C63 AP33 75c gray blue 14.50 *29.00*
Never hinged 35.00
On cover 140.00
C64 AP34 5 l + 2.50 l ol grn 42.50 *210.00*
Never hinged 110.00
On cover *1,000.*
C65 AP35 10 l + 5 l brn blk 42.50 *290.00*
Never hinged 110.00
On cover *2,000.*
Nos. C62-C65 (4) 108.00 *550.00*
Set, never hinged 275.00
Set, on overfranked commem. cover 2,000.

2nd World Soccer Championships.

For overprinted types see Aegean Islands Nos. C28-C31.

Zeppelin under Fire AP36

Air Force Memorial — AP40

Designs: 25c, 80c, Zeppelin under fire. 50c, 75c, Motorboat patrol. 1 l+50c, Desert infantry. 2 l+1 l, Plane attacking troops.

1934, Apr. 24

C66 AP36 25c dk green 2.90 *5.75*
Never hinged 7.25
On cover 35.00
C67 AP36 50c gray 2.90 *7.25*
Never hinged 7.25
On cover 32.50
C68 AP36 75c dk brown 2.90 *8.50*
Never hinged 7.25
On cover 100.00
C69 AP36 80c slate blue 2.90 *11.00*
Never hinged 7.25
On cover 130.00

C70 AP36 1 l + 50c red brn	7.25	*27.50*
Never hinged	7.25	
On cover		210.00
C71 AP36 2 l + 1 l brt bl	10.00	*32.50*
Never hinged	7.25	
On cover		360.00
C72 AP40 3 l + 2 l brn blk	14.50	*40.00*
Never hinged	7.25	
On cover		400.00
Nos. C66-C72 (7)	43.35	*132.50*
Set, never hinged	110.00	
Nos. C66-C72, CE8-CE9 on overfranked commem. cover		725.00

Cent. of the institution of the Military Medal of Valor.

For overprinted types see Aegean Islands Nos. C32-C38.

King Victor Emmanuel III — AP41

1934, Nov. 5

C73 AP41 1 l purple	2.90	*45.00*
Never hinged	7.25	
On cover		130.00
C74 AP41 2 l brt blue	2.90	*55.00*
Never hinged	7.25	
On cover		160.00
C75 AP41 4 l red brown	6.50	*180.00*
Never hinged	16.00	
On cover		360.00
C76 AP41 5 l dull green	6.50	*250.00*
Never hinged	16.00	
On cover		440.00
C77 AP41 8 l rose red	20.00	*325.00*
Never hinged	50.00	
On cover		725.00
C78 AP41 10 l brown	23.00	*440.00*
Never hinged	57.50	
On cover		875.00
Nos. C73-C78 (6)	61.80	*1,295.*
Set, never hinged	150.00	
Set, on overfranked commem. cover		2,150.

65th birthday of King Victor Emmanuel III and the nonstop flight from Rome to Mogadiscio.

For overprint see No. CO2.

Muse Playing Harp AP42

Angelic Dirge for Bellini AP43

Scene from Bellini Opera, La Sonnambula — AP44

1935, Sept. 24

C79 AP42 25c dull yellow	1.80	*6.25*
Never hinged	4.50	
On cover		30.00
C80 AP42 50c brown	1.80	*4.50*
Never hinged	4.50	
On cover		30.00
C81 AP42 60c rose carmine	4.50	*11.00*
Never hinged	11.00	
On cover		67.50
C82 AP43 1 l + 1 l purple	12.00	*92.50*
Never hinged	27.50	
On cover		290.00
C83 AP44 5 l + 2 l green	18.00	*140.00*
Never hinged	42.50	
On cover		540.00
Nos. C79-C83 (5)	38.10	*254.25*
Set, never hinged	90.00	
Set, on overfranked commem. cover		550.00

Vincenzo Bellini, (1801-35), operatic composer.

Quintus Horatius Flaccus Type

25c, Seaplane in Flight. 50c, 1 l+1 l, Monoplane over valley. 60c, Oak and eagle. 5 l+2 l, Ruins of ancient Rome.

1936, July 1

C84 A197 25c dp green	2.75	*6.25*
Never hinged	6.25	
On cover		45.00
C85 A197 50c dk brown	3.50	*5.50*
Never hinged	8.00	
On cover		45.00
C86 A197 60c scarlet	4.50	*11.00*
Never hinged	11.00	
On cover		90.00
C87 A197 1 l + 1 l vio	10.50	*100.00*
Never hinged	27.50	
On cover		290.00
C88 A197 5 l + 2 l slate bl	16.00	*150.00*
Never hinged	37.50	
On cover		600.00
Nos. C84-C88 (5)	37.25	*272.75*
Set, never hinged	90.00	
Set, on overfranked commem. cover		725.00

Child of the Balilla AP49

Heads of Children AP50

1937, June 28

C89 AP49 25c dk bl grn	7.25	9.00
Never hinged	18.00	
On cover		72.50
C90 AP50 50c brown	7.25	6.25
Never hinged	18.00	
On cover		50.00
C91 AP49 1 l purple	7.25	*9.00*
Never hinged	18.00	
On cover		72.50
C92 AP50 2 l + 1 l dk bl	11.00	*82.50*
Never hinged	25.00	
On cover		325.00
C93 AP49 3 l + 2 l org	14.50	*110.00*
Never hinged	35.00	
On cover		550.00
C94 AP50 5 l + 3 l rose lake	16.00	*140.00*
Never hinged	45.00	
On cover		900.00
Nos. C89-C94 (6)	63.25	*356.75*
Set, never hinged	150.00	
Set, on overfranked commem. cover		1,000.

Summer Exhibition for Child Welfare. The surtax on Nos. C92-C94 was used to support summer camps for poor children.

Prosperous Italy AP51

50c, Prolific Italy. 80c, Apollo's steeds. 1 l+1 l, Map & Roman Standard. 5 l+1 l, Augustus Caesar.

1937, Sept. 23

C95 AP51 25c red vio	5.50	*8.00*
Never hinged	14.00	
On cover		45.00
C96 AP51 50c olive brn	5.50	*6.25*
Never hinged	14.00	
On cover		45.00
C97 AP51 80c orange brn	12.50	*9.25*
Never hinged	30.00	
On cover		90.00
C98 AP51 1 l + 1 l dk bl	29.00	*72.50*
Never hinged	75.00	
On cover		225.00
C99 AP51 5 l + 1 l dl vio	37.50	*120.00*
Never hinged	100.00	
On cover		400.00
Nos. C95-C99 (5)	90.00	*216.00*
Set, never hinged	230.00	
Set, on overfranked commem. cover		575.00

Bimillenary of the birth of Augustus Caesar (Octavianus) on the occasion of the exhibition opened in Rome by Mussolini on Sept. 22nd, 1937.

For overprinted types see Aegean Islands Nos. C39-C43.

King Victor Emmanuel III — AP56

25c, 3 l, King Victor Emmanuel III. 50c, 1 l, Dante Alighieri. 2 l, 5 l, Leonardo da Vinci.

1938, Oct. 28

C100 AP56 25c dull green	2.75	5.50
Never hinged	6.25	
On cover		35.00
C101 AP56 50c dk yel brn	2.75	5.50
Never hinged	6.25	
On cover		30.00
C102 AP56 1 l violet	3.50	*6.25*
Never hinged	9.00	
On cover		35.00
C103 AP56 2 l royal blue	4.50	*25.00*
Never hinged	11.00	
On cover		80.00
C104 AP56 3 l brown car	7.25	*32.50*
Never hinged	18.00	
On cover		160.00
C105 AP56 5 l dp green	8.00	*45.00*
Never hinged	21.00	
On cover		225.00
Nos. C100-C105 (6)	28.75	*119.75*
Set, never hinged	75.00	
Set, on overfranked commem. cover		375.00

Proclamation of the Empire.

AIR POST SEMI-POSTAL STAMPS

Holy Year Type of Postage

Dome of St. Peter's, dove with olive branch, Church of the Holy Sepulcher.

Wmk. 140

1933, Oct. 23 Photo. *Perf. 14*

CB1 A163 50c + 25c org brn	.90	*11.00*
Never hinged	3.50	
On cover		50.00
CB2 A163 75c + 50c brn vio	2.75	*20.00*
Never hinged	5.50	
On cover		100.00
Set, never hinged	9.00	

Symbolical of Military Air Force — SPAP2

1935, July 1

CB3 SPAP2 50c + 50c brown	7.25	*27.50*
Never hinged	20.00	
On cover		160.00

The surtax was for the Militia.

AIR POST SPECIAL DELIVERY STAMPS

Garibaldi, Anita Garibaldi, Plane APSD1

Wmk. 140

1932, June 2 Photo. *Perf. 14*

CE1 APSD1 2.25 l + 1 l	7.25	*45.00*
Never hinged	20.00	
On cover		275.00
CE2 APSD1 4.50 l + 1.50 l	7.25	*45.00*
Never hinged	21.00	
On cover		360.00
Set, never hinged	40.00	

Death of Giuseppe Garibaldi, 50th anniv.

For overprinted types see Aegean Islands Nos. CE1-CE2.

Airplane and Sunburst APSD2

1933-34

CE3 APSD2 2 l gray blk ('34)	.20	*2.00*
Never hinged	.45	
On cover		40.00
CE4 APSD2 2.25 l gray blk	5.50	*140.00*
Never hinged	11.50	
On cover		725.00
Set, never hinged	12.00	

For overprint and surcharge see Nos. MCE1; Yugoslavia-Ljubljana NCE1.

Annexation of Fiume Type

Flag raising before Fascist headquarters.

1934, Mar. 12

CE5 A166 2 l + 1.25 l	1.10	*22.50*
Never hinged	1.75	
On cover		575.00
CE6 A166 2.25 l + 1.25 l	1.75	*22.50*
Never hinged	2.75	
On cover		425.00
CE7 A166 4.50 l + 2 l	1.75	*22.50*
Never hinged	2.75	
On cover		500.00
Nos. CE5-CE7 (3)	4.60	*67.50*
Set, never hinged	7.25	

Triumphal Arch in Rome APSD4

1934, Aug. 31

CE8 APSD4 2 l + 1.25 l brown	6.25	*35.00*
Never hinged	18.00	
On cover		525.00
CE9 APSD4 4.50 l + 2 l cop red	7.25	*35.00*
Never hinged	22.50	
On cover		525.00
Set, never hinged	40.00	

Centenary of the institution of the Military Medal of Valor.

For overprinted types see Aegean Islands Nos. CE3-CE4.

AIR POST OFFICIAL STAMPS

Balbo Flight Type of Air Post Stamp of 1933 Overprinted

SERVIZIO DI STATO

1933 Wmk. 140 *Perf. 14*

CO1 AP25 5.25 l + 44.75 l red, grn & red vio	2,500.	*11,000.*
Never hinged	4,250.	

Type of Air Post Stamp of 1934 Overprinted in Gold Crown and "SERVIZIO DI STATO"

1934

CO2 AP41 10 l blue blk	725.00	*10,500.*
Never hinged	1,450.	

65th birthday of King Victor Emmanuel III and the non-stop flight from Rome to Mogadiscio.

PNEUMATIC POST STAMPS

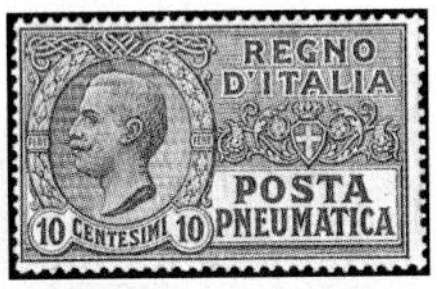

PN1

1913-28 Wmk. 140 Typo. *Perf. 14*

D1 PN1 10c brown	2.75	*16.00*
D2 PN1 15c brn vio ('28)	3.50	*11.00*
a. 15c dull violet ('21)	2.75	*18.00*
D3 PN1 15c rose red ('28)	3.50	*18.00*
D4 PN1 15c claret ('28)	3.50	*11.00*
D5 PN1 20c brn vio ('25)	13.50	*30.00*
D6 PN1 30c blue ('23)	11.00	*30.00*
D7 PN1 35c rose red ('27)	16.00	*190.00*
D8 PN1 40c dp red ('26)	22.50	*175.00*
Nos. D1-D8 (8)	76.25	*541.00*

Nos. D1, D2a, D5-D6, D8 Surcharged Like Nos. C10-C11

1924-27

D9 PN1 15c on 10c	3.50	*20.00*
D10 PN1 15c on 20c ('27)	9.00	*35.00*
D11 PN1 20c on 10c ('25)	7.25	*32.50*
D12 PN1 20c on 15c ('25)	9.00	*20.00*

D13 PN1 35c on 40c ('27) 18.00 *150.00*
D14 PN1 40c on 30c ('25) 9.00 *140.00*
Nos. D9-D14 (6) 55.75 *397.50*

Dante Alighieri PN2

Galileo Galilei PN3

1933, Mar. 29 Photo.
D15 PN2 15c dark violet .25 *1.40*
D16 PN3 35c rose red .25 *2.25*

Similar to Types of 1933, Without "REGNO"

1945, Oct. 22 Wmk. 277
D17 PN2 60c dull brown .20 *1.75*
D18 PN3 1.40 l dull blue .20 *1.75*

SPECIAL DELIVERY STAMPS

Victor Emmanuel III — SD1

1903-26 Typo. Wmk. 140 *Perf. 14*
E1 SD1 25c rose red 40.00 1.40
a. Imperf., pair 450.00 450.00
E2 SD1 50c dl red ('20) 1.75 1.75
E3 SD1 60c dl red ('22) 4.50 .90
E4 SD1 70c dl red ('25) .45 .35
E5 SD1 1.25 l dp bl ('26) .45 .20
Nos. E1-E5 (5) 47.15 4.60

No. E1 is almost always found poorly centered, and it is valued thus.

For overprints and surcharges see Nos. C1, E11, E13, Austria NE1-NE2, Dalmatia E1, Offices in Crete, Offices in Africa, Offices in Turkish Empire.

Victor Emmanuel III — SD2

1908-26
E6 SD2 30c blue & rose .90 *3.50*
E7 SD2 2 l bl & red ('25) 3.50 *50.00*
E8 SD2 2.50 l bl & red ('26) 2.75 *5.50*
Nos. E6-E8 (3) 7.15 *59.00*

The 1.20 lire blue and red (see No. E12) was prepared in 1922, but not issued. Value $175.

For surcharges and overprints see Nos. E10, E12, Austria MNE3, Dalmatia E2, Offices in China, Offices in Africa, Offices in Turkish Empire.

SD3

1917, Nov.
E9 SD3 25c on 40c violet 17.50 *40.00*

Type SD3 not issued without surcharge. For surcharge see No. C2.

No. E6 Surcharged

1921, Oct.
E10 SD2 1.20 l on 30c .90 *16.00*
a. Comma in value omitted 12.50 *35.00*
b. Double surcharge 27.50

No. E2 Surcharged

1922, Jan. 9
E11 SD1 60c on 50c dull red 29.00 2.00
a. Inverted surcharge 250.00 *250.00*
b. Double surcharge *750.00*
c. Imperf., pair 450.00 *450.00*

Type of 1908 Surcharged

1924, May
E12 SD2 1.60 l on 1.20 l bl & red 1.40 *50.00*
a. Double surch., one inverted 310.00 *290.00*

No. E3 Surcharged like No. E11

1925, Apr. 11
E13 SD1 70c on 60c dull red .90 .90
a. Inverted surcharge 300.00 *325.00*

Victor Emmanuel III — SD4

1932-33 Photo.
E14 SD4 1.25 l green .20 .20
E15 SD4 2.50 l dp org ('33) .25 *3.75*

For overprints and surcharges see Nos. ME1, Italian Social Republic E1-E2, Yugoslavia-Ljubljana NB5-NB8, NE1.

March on Rome Type of Postage

1.25 l Ancient Pillars and Entrenchments. 2.50 l, Head of Mussolini, trophies of flags, etc.

1932, Oct. 27
E16 A146 1.25 l deep green 1.75 *1.75*
E17 A146 2.50 l deep orange 5.50 *130.00*
Set, never hinged 18.00

AUTHORIZED DELIVERY STAMPS

For the payment of a special tax for the authorized delivery of correspondence privately instead of through the post office.

AD1

Coat of Arms — AD2

1928 Wmk. 140 Typo. *Perf. 14*
EY1 AD1 10c dull blue 2.75 .50
a. Perf. 11 16.00 5.00

1930 Photo. *Perf. 14*
EY2 AD2 10c dark brown .20 .20

For surcharge and overprint see Nos. EY3, Italian Social Republic EY1.

POSTAGE DUE STAMPS

Unused values for Postage Due stamps are for examples with full original gum. Stamps with part gum or privately gummed sell for much less.

D1

D2

1863 Unwmk. Litho. *Imperf.*
J1 D1 10c yellow 1,400. 110.00
No gum 62.50
Never hinged 3,000.
On cover 375.00
On cover, uncanceled 87.50
a. 10c yellow orange 1,400. 140.00
No gum 70.00
Never hinged 3,000.
On cover 500.00
On cover, uncanceled 95.00

1869 Wmk. 140 Typo. *Perf. 14*
J2 D2 10c buff 3,000. 20.00
No gum 425.00
Never hinged 5,250.
On cover 90.00

D3

D4

1870-1925
J3 D3 1c buff & mag 2.50 5.50
No gum .65
Never hinged 5.00
On cover 70.00
J4 D3 2c buff & mag 9.00 12.50
No gum 1.75
Never hinged 17.50
On cover 120.00
J5 D3 5c buff & mag .30 .30
No gum .20
Never hinged .80
On cover 2.25
J6 D3 10c buff & mag ('71) .35 .30
No gum .20
Never hinged 1.00
On cover 2.25
b. Imperf, single *1,200.*
J7 D3 20c buff & mag ('94) 2.00 .30
No gum .50
Never hinged 5.00
On cover 1.75
a. Imperf., pair 92.50 *125.00*
J8 D3 30c buff & mag 1.40 .45
No gum .30
Never hinged 3.50
On cover 4.50
b. Imperf, pair *8,750.* 875.00
J9 D3 40c buff & mag 1.75 .90
No gum .30
Never hinged 3.50
On cover 18.00
J10 D3 50c buff & mag 1.40 .40
No gum .30
Never hinged 3.50
On cover 4.50
b. Imperf., single *950.00*
J11 D3 60c buff & mag 95.00 1.75
No gum 16.00
Never hinged 250.00
On cover 37.50
J12 D3 60c buff & brn ('25) 12.50 3.75
Never hinged 25.00
On cover 22.50
J13 D3 1 l lt bl & brn 3,750. 7.25
No gum 450.00
Never hinged 6,800.
On cover 65.00
J14 D3 1 l bl & mag ('94) 3.75 .40
No gum .75
Never hinged 10.00
On cover 3.75
a. Imperf., pair 92.50 100.00
J15 D3 2 l lt bl & brn 3,750. 14.00
No gum 450.00
Never hinged 6,800.
On cover 600.00
J16 D3 2 l bl & mag ('03) 20.00 1.25
Never hinged 40.00
On cover 130.00
J17 D3 5 l bl & brn ('74) 210.00 17.00
No gum 30.00
Never hinged 400.00
On cover *15,000.*
J18 D3 5 l bl & mag ('03) 90.00 7.25
Never hinged 175.00
On cover 325.00
J19 D3 10 l bl & brn ('74) *5,000.* 17.00
No gum 700.00
Never hinged 9,500.
On cover —
J20 D3 10 l bl & mag ('94) 67.50 2.75
No gum 10.00
Never hinged 150.00
On cover 1,500.

Early printings of 5c, 10c, 30c, 40c, 50c and 60c were in buff and magenta, later ones (1890-94) in stronger shades. The earlier, paler shades and their inverted-numeral varieties sell for considerably more than those of the later shades. Values are for the later shades.

Covers: Covers bearing Nos. J5-J6, J8-J11 dated between Jan. 1870 and Dec. 1889 have stamps from early printings and are worth more.

For surcharges and overprints see Nos. J25-J27, Offices in China, Offices in Turkish Empire.

Numeral Inverted

J3a	D3	1c	3,000.	1,800.
J4a	D3	2c	*7,000.*	3,000.
		On cover		*27,500.*
J5a	D3	5c	2.00	2.00
J6a	D3	10c	3.25	3.25
		On cover		*150.00*
J7b	D3	20c	13.50	14.00
J8a	D3	30c	4.50	*7.75*
		On cover		*13,000.*
J9a	D3	40c	300.00	*350.00*
J10a	D3	50c	32.50	35.00
J11a	D3	60c	190.00	190.00
J13a	D3	1 l		*18,000.*
J14b	D3	1 l	2,000.	1,500.
		On cover		*6,000.*
J15a	D3	2 l		*1,750.*
J16a	D3	2 l	*1,725.*	*1,600.*
J17a	D3	5 l		950.00
J19a	D3	10 l		275.00

1884-1903
J21 D4 50 l green 27.50 30.00
No gum 12.50
Never hinged 70.00
J22 D4 50 l yellow ('03) 40.00 21.00
Never hinged 72.50
J23 D4 100 l claret 27.50 11.00
No gum 5.00
Never hinged 70.00
J24 D4 100 l blue ('03) 32.50 10.00
Never hinged 55.00
Nos. J21-J24 (4) 127.50 72.00

Nos. J21-J24 were used for Post Office internal accounting purposes and are not known used on cover.

Nos. J3 & J4 Surcharged in Black

1890-91
J25 D3 10c on 2c 62.50 17.00
No gum 11.50
Never hinged 125.00
On cover 105.00
J26 D3 20c on 1c 275.00 12.50
No gum 40.00
Never hinged 550.00
On cover 82.50
a. Inverted surcharge *5,500.*
J27 D3 30c on 2c 900.00 4.50
No gum 140.00
Never hinged 1,900.
On cover 60.00
a. Inverted surcharge *1,500.*
Nos. J25-J27 (3) 1,237. 34.00

Coat of Arms
D6 D7

1934 Photo.
J28 D6 5c brown .35 .20
J29 D6 10c blue .35 .20
J30 D6 20c rose red .35 .20
J31 D6 25c green .35 .20
J32 D6 30c red org .35 .20
J33 D6 40c blk brn .35 *1.10*
J34 D6 50c violet .35 .20
J35 D6 60c slate blk .35 *3.50*
J36 D7 1 l red org .35 .20
J37 D7 2 l green .35 .20
J38 D7 5 l violet .75 .45

J39	D7	10 l blue	2.25	1.10
J40	D7	20 l car rose	3.50	*7.00*
		Nos. J28-J40 (13)	10.00	14.75

For overprints and surcharges see Italian Social Republic #J1-J13, Yugoslavia-Ljubljana NJ14-NJ22.

OFFICIAL STAMPS

O1

1875 Wmk. 140 Typo. *Perf. 14*

O1	O1	2c lake	.65	*1.25*
		No gum	.25	
		Never hinged	1.00	
		On cover		4.00
O2	O1	5c lake	.65	*1.25*
		No gum	.25	
		Never hinged	1.00	
		On cover		5.50
O3	O1	20c lake	.25	*.40*
		No gum	.25	
		Never hinged	.55	
		On cover		1.25
O4	O1	30c lake	.25	*.50*
		No gum	.25	
		Never hinged	.55	
		On cover		1.75
O5	O1	1 l lake	1.40	*4.25*
		No gum	.50	
		Never hinged	2.50	
		On cover		62.50
O6	O1	2 l lake	8.50	*17.00*
		No gum	2.50	
		Never hinged	15.00	
		On cover		190.00
O7	O1	5 l lake	55.00	*82.50*
		No gum	14.00	
		Never hinged	87.50	
		On cover		1,400.
O8	O1	10 l lake	100.00	55.00
		No gum	22.50	
		Never hinged	160.00	
		On cover		3,250.
		Nos. O1-O8 (8)	166.70	*162.15*

Covers: Values for Nos. O7-O8 are for over-franked covers.

For surcharges see Nos. 37-44.

Stamps inscribed "Servizio Commissioni" were used in connection with the postal service but not for the payment of postage.

NEWSPAPER STAMP

N1

Typographed, Numeral Embossed

1862 Unwmk. *Imperf.*

P1	N1	2c buff	27.50	*75.00*
		No gum	14.00	
		Never hinged	55.00	
		On newspaper or cover		190.00
a.		Numeral double	300.00	*1,000.*
		On newspaper or cover		*4,000.*
b.		Printed on gummed side	275.00	

Black 1c and 2c stamps of similar type are listed under Sardinia.

PARCEL POST STAMPS

King Humbert I — PP1

1884-86 Wmk. 140 Typo. *Perf. 14*

Various Frames

Q1	PP1	10c olive gray	90.00	27.50
		No gum	15.00	
		Never hinged	250.00	
		On parcel post receipt card		*1,300.*
Q2	PP1	20c blue	150.00	45.00
		No gum	25.00	
		Never hinged	460.00	
		On parcel post receipt card		*3,250.*
Q3	PP1	50c claret	6.00	5.50
		No gum	1.50	
		Never hinged	15.00	
		On parcel post receipt card		*1,750.*
Q4	PP1	75c blue grn	5.50	5.50
		No gum	1.50	
		Never hinged	15.00	
		On parcel post receipt card		*1,750.*
Q5	PP1	1.25 l orange	13.00	14.00
		No gum	3.25	
		Never hinged	37.50	
		On parcel post receipt card		*2,250.*
Q6	PP1	1.75 l brown	16.00	*67.50*
		No gum	7.50	
		Never hinged	45.00	
		On parcel post receipt card		—

For surcharges see Nos. 58-63.

Parcel Post stamps from No. Q7 onward were used by affixing them to the waybill so that one half remained on it following the parcel, the other half staying on the receipt given the sender. Most used halves are right halves. Complete stamps were and are obtainable canceled, probably to order.

Both unused and used values are for complete stamps.

PP2

1914-22 Wmk. 140 *Perf. 13*

Q7	PP2	5c brown	1.00	*2.25*
Q8	PP2	10c deep blue	1.00	*2.25*
Q9	PP2	20c black ('17)	2.00	*2.25*
Q10	PP2	25c red	3.00	*2.25*
Q11	PP2	50c orange	3.00	*3.00*
Q12	PP2	1 l violet	4.00	1.25
Q13	PP2	2 l green	5.00	2.25
Q14	PP2	3 l bister	6.25	4.00
Q15	PP2	4 l slate	10.50	4.00
Q16	PP2	10 l rose lil ('22)	30.00	7.25
Q17	PP2	12 l red brn ('22)	95.00	*140.00*
Q18	PP2	15 l ol grn ('22)	95.00	*140.00*
Q19	PP2	20 l brn vio ('22)	67.50	*150.00*
		Nos. Q7-Q19 (13)	323.25	*460.75*

Halves Used

Q7-Q15	.20
Q16	.20
Q17-Q19	.75

Imperfs exist. Value per pair: 20c, 25c, 50c, 2 l, 4 l, 10 l, $50 each; 3 l, $60; 12 l, 15 l, 20 l, $200 each.

No. Q7 Surcharged

Q20	PP2	30c on 5c brown	.60	*2.75*
		Half stamp		.20
Q21	PP2	60c on 5c brown	.95	*2.75*
		Half stamp		.20
Q22	PP2	1.50 l on 5c brown	3.00	*20.00*
		Half stamp		.25
a.		Double surcharge	25.00	

No. Q16 Surcharged

LIRE 3 LIRE 3

Q23	PP2	3 l on 10 l rose lilac	3.00	*11.00*
		Half stamp		.20
		Nos. Q20-Q23 (4)	7.55	*36.50*

PP3

1927-39 Wmk. 140

Q24	PP3	5c brn ('38)	.45	*.50*
Q25	PP3	10c dp bl ('39)	.45	*.50*
Q26	PP3	25c red ('32)	.45	*.50*
Q27	PP3	30c ultra	.45	*.75*
Q28	PP3	50c org ('32)	.45	*.50*
Q29	PP3	60c red	.45	*.75*
Q30	PP3	1 l lilac ('31)	.45	*.50*
Q31	PP3	1 l brn vio ('36)	12.50	12.50
Q32	PP3	2 l grn ('32)	.45	*.75*
Q33	PP3	3 l bister	.45	*1.50*
a.		Printed on both sides	15.00	
Q34	PP3	4 l gray	.45	*1.50*
Q35	PP3	10 l rose lil ('34)	1.25	*4.25*
Q36	PP3	20 l lil brn ('33)	1.75	*7.25*
		Nos. Q24-Q36 (13)	20.00	*31.75*

Value of used halves, Nos. Q24-Q36, each 20 cents.

For overprints see Italian Social Republic Nos. Q1-Q12.

OCCUPATION STAMPS

Issued under Austrian Occupation

Emperor Karl of Austria

OS1 OS2

Austria #M49-M67 Surcharged in Black

1918 Unwmk. *Perf. 12½*

N1	OS1	2c on 1h grnsh bl	.35	*.70*
N2	OS1	3c on 2h red org	.35	*.70*
N3	OS1	4c on 3h ol gray	.35	*.70*
N4	OS1	6c on 5h ol grn	.35	*.70*
N5	OS1	7c on 6h vio	.35	*.70*
a.		Perf. 12½x11½	28.00	*65.00*
N6	OS1	11c on 10h org brn	.35	*.70*
N7	OS1	13c on 12h blue	.35	*.70*
N8	OS1	16c on 15h brt rose	.35	*.70*
N9	OS1	22c on 20h red brn	.35	*.70*
a.		Perf. 11½	14.00	*30.00*
N10	OS1	27c on 25h ultra	.50	*1.00*
N11	OS1	32c on 30h slate	.35	*.70*
N12	OS1	43c on 40h ol bis	.35	*.70*
a.		Perf. 11½	14.00	*30.00*
N13	OS1	53c on 50h dp grn	.35	*.70*
N14	OS1	64c on 60h rose	.35	*.70*
N15	OS1	85c on 80h dl bl	.35	*.70*
N16	OS1	95c on 90h dk vio	.35	*.70*
N17	OS2	2 l 11c on 2k rose, *straw*	.35	.70
N18	OS2	3 l 16c on 3k grn, *bl*	1.00	2.00
N19	OS2	4 l 22c on 4k rose, *grn*	1.00	2.00
		Nos. N1-N19 (19)	8.10	*16.20*

Emperor Karl — OS3

Austria #M69-M81 Surcharged in Black

1918

N20	OS3	2c on 1h grnsh bl	6.00
N21	OS3	3c on 2h orange	6.00
N22	OS3	4c on 3h ol gray	6.00
N23	OS3	6c on 5h yel grn	6.00
N24	OS3	11c on 10h dk brn	6.00
N25	OS3	22c on 20h red	6.00
N26	OS3	27c on 25h blue	6.00
N27	OS3	32c on 30h bister	6.00
N28	OS3	48c on 45h dk sl	6.00
N29	OS3	53c on 50h dp grn	6.00
N30	OS3	64c on 60h violet	6.00
N31	OS3	85c on 80h rose	6.00
N32	OS3	95c on 90h brn vio	6.00
N33	OS3	1 l 6c on 1k ol grn, *grnish*	6.00
		Nos. N20-N33 (14)	84.00

Nos. N20 to N33 inclusive were never placed in use in the occupied territory. They were, however, on sale at the Post Office in Vienna for a few days before the Armistice.

OCCUPATION SPECIAL DELIVERY STAMPS

Bosnia #QE1-QE2 Surcharged

1918 Unwmk. *Perf. 12½*

NE1	SH1	3c on 2h ver	5.50	*12.00*
NE2	SH1	6c on 5h dp grn	5.50	*12.00*

Nos. NE1-NE2 are on yellowish paper. Reprints on white paper sell for about 70 cents a set.

OCCUPATION POSTAGE DUE STAMPS

Bosnia #J16, J18-J19, J21-J24 Surcharged Like Nos. NE1-NE2

1918 Unwmk. *Perf. 12½*

NJ1	D2	6c on 5h red	1.90	*3.75*
a.		Perf. 11½	5.50	*12.00*
NJ2	D2	11c on 10h red	1.90	*3.75*
a.		Perf. 11½	5.50	*12.00*
NJ3	D2	16c on 15h red	.90	*1.90*
NJ4	D2	27c on 25h red	.90	*1.90*
NJ5	D2	32c on 30h red	.90	*1.90*
NJ6	D2	43c on 40h red	.90	*1.90*
NJ7	D2	53c on 50h red	.90	*1.90*
		Nos. NJ1-NJ7 (7)	8.30	*17.00*

OCCUPATION NEWSPAPER STAMPS

Austrian #MP1-MP4 Surcharged

1918 Unwmk. *Perf. 12½*

NP1	MN1	3c on 2h blue	.20	*.25*
a.		Perf. 11½	2.75	*6.00*
NP2	MN1	7c on 6h org	.45	*.90*
NP3	MN1	11c on 10h car	.45	*.90*
NP4	MN1	22c on 20h brn	.35	*.70*
a.		Perf. 11½	15.00	*32.50*
		Nos. NP1-NP4 (4)	1.45	*2.75*

ITALIAN OFFICES ABROAD

Stamps listed under this heading were issued for use in the Italian Post Offices which, for various reasons, were maintained from time to time in foreign countries.

100 Centesimi = 1 Lira

GENERAL ISSUE

Values of Italian Offices Abroad stamps vary tremendously according to condition. Quotations are for very fine examples, and values for unused stamps are for examples with original gum as defined in the catalogue introduction. Extremely fine or superb copies sell at much higher prices, and fine or poor copies sell at greatly reduced prices. In addition, unused copies without gum are discounted severely.

Very fine examples of Nos. 1-17 will have perforations barely clear of the frameline or design due to the narrow spacing of the stamps on the plates.

Italian Stamps with Corner Designs Slightly Altered and Overprinted

1874-78 Wmk. 140 *Perf. 14*

1	A6	1c ol grn	2.50	*7.50*
		No gum	.75	
		Never hinged	25.00	
		On cover		*450.00*
		On newspaper, single franking		1,500.
a.		Inverted overprint	*13,750.*	
c.		2 dots in lower right corner	15.00	*90.00*
d.		Three dots in upper right corner	140.00	*650.00*
e.		Without overprint	26,000.	
f.		1c gray green	20.00	
		On cover		*500.00*

2 A7 2c org brn 3.00 *10.00*
No gum .90
Never hinged 30.00
On cover *450.00*
a. Without overprint 26,000. 37,000.
3 A8 5c slate grn 275.00 9.00
No gum 50.00
Never hinged 1,100.
On cover *275.00*
On newspaper, single franking 850.00
a. Lower right corner not altered *7,900.* 1,000.
4 A8 10c buff 675.00 17.50
No gum 140.00
Never hinged 2,800.
On cover *250.00*
On newspaper, single franking —
a. Upper left corner not altered *9,500.* 525.00
b. None of the corners altered — *30,000.*
c. Lower corners not altered *2,400.*
5 A8 10c blue ('78) 125.00 5.00
No gum 25.00
Never hinged 550.00
On cover *325.00*
6 A15 20c blue 625.00 9.50
No gum 120.00
Never hinged 2,500.
On cover *150.00*
On newspaper, single franking *1,000.*
7 A15 20c org ('78) 2,500. 4.50
No gum 500.00
Never hinged *7,250.*
On cover *325.00*
8 A8 30c brown 1.00 *5.75*
No gum .40
Never hinged 3.50
On cover *110.00*
a. None of the corners altered *18,000.*
b. Right lower corner not altered — —
c. Double overprint —
9 A8 40c rose 1.00 *4.50*
No gum .40
Never hinged 3.50
On cover *100.00*
10 A8 60c lilac 2.00 *30.00*
No gum .75
Never hinged 12.50
On cover *2,100.*
a. 60c pale lilac 27.50 *30.00*
On cover 3,500.
11 A13 2 l vermilion 45.00 *225.00*
No gum 17.50
Never hinged 225.00
On cover *14,000.*

Values for stamps in pairs

1 A6 1c gray green 21.00 *45.00*
On cover *900.00*
2 A7 2c org brn 25.00 *50.00*
On cover *1,050.*

3 A8 5c slate grn 1,125. 50.00
On cover 650.00
4 A8 10c buff 2,800. 100.00
On cover 650.00
5 A8 10c blue 575.00 37.50
On cover 700.00
6 A15 20c blue 2,500. 60.00
On cover 325.00
7 A15 20c orange 10,000. 77.50
On cover 1,850.
8 A8 30c brown 3.00 *100.00*
On cover *775.00*
9 A8 40c rose 3.00 *32.50*
On cover *950.00*
10 A8 60c lilac 10.00 *250.00*
On cover *4,500.*
11 A13 2 l vermilion 225.00 *1,300.*
On cover —

1881

12 A17 5c green 1.50 *3.50*
No gum .65
Never hinged 25.00
On cover 210.00
On cover, single franking 775.00
13 A17 10c claret 1.50 *2.75*
No gum .65
Never hinged 17.50
On cover *275.00*
14 A17 20c orange 1.50 *2.00*
No gum .65
Never hinged 17.50
On cover *125.00*
a. Double overprint, on piece —
15 A17 25c blue 1.50 *3.50*
No gum .65
Never hinged 17.50
On cover *875.00*
16 A17 50c violet 3.50 *22.50*
No gum 1.00
Never hinged 35.00
On cover *2,000.*
17 A17 2 l vermilion 7.50 —
No gum 1.75
Never hinged 52.50

Values for Stamps in Pairs

12 A17 5c green — *26.50*
On cover 450.00
13 A17 10c claret — *20.00*
On cover 625.00
14 A17 20c orange — *25.00*
On cover 700.00
15 A17 25c blue — *55.00*
On cover 1,900.
16 A17 50c violet — *140.00*
On cover *4,500.*

The "Estero" stamps were used in various parts of the world, South America, Africa, Turkey, etc.

Forged cancellations exist on Nos. 1-2, 9-11, 16.

OFFICES IN CHINA

100 Cents = 1 Dollar

PEKING

Italian Stamps of 1901-16 Handstamped **PECHINO 2 CENTS**

Wmk. 140, Unwmk.

1917 ***Perf. 12, 13½, 14***

1 A48 2c on 5c green 95.00 52.50
Never hinged 150.00
On cover 200.00
a. Inverted surcharge 95.00 47.50
Never hinged 150.00
b. Double surcharge, one inverted 200.00 150.00
c. 4c on 5c green *3,100.*
Never hinged 4,000.
d. 8c on 5c green —
e. Pair, one with "PECHINO", one "TIENTSIN" 3,000.
Never hinged 3,750.
3 A48 4c on 10c claret (No. 95) 190.00 100.00
Never hinged 290.00
On cover 300.00
a. Inverted surcharge 190.00 95.00
Never hinged 290.00
b. Double surcharge, one inverted 400.00 225.00
c. 4c on 10c claret (No. 79) —
5 A58 6c on 15c slate 375.00 225.00
Never hinged 600.00
On cover 550.00
b. 8c on 15c slate 1,800. 1,425.
Never hinged 2,250.
c. Pair, one without surcharge —
d. Pair, one with "PECHINO", one "TIENTSIN" 4,500.
Never hinged 5,750.
7 A58 8c on 20c on 15c slate 2,300. 1,050.
Never hinged 2,750.
On cover 1,900.
a. Inverted surcharge 2,200. 950.00
Never hinged 2,750.
8 A50 8c on 20c brn org (No. 112) *3,500.* 1,200.
Never hinged *4,400.*
On cover 2,000.
a. Inverted surcharge *3,300.* *1,100.*
Never hinged 4,400.
9 A49 20c on 50c vio *19,500.* *12,000.*
Never hinged *23,000.*
a. Inverted surcharge *18,500.* *11,000.*
Never hinged *23,000.*
b. 40c on 50c violet *7,000.* *6,500.*
Never hinged 8,250.

c. As "b," inverted surcharge *6,600.* *6,000.*
Never hinged *8,250.*
11 A46 40c on 1 l brn & grn *126,000.* *17,000.*
a. Inverted surcharge 95,000. 12,750.

Excellent forgeries exist of the higher valued stamps of Offices in China.

Italian Stamps of 1901-16 Overprinted

1917-18

12 A42 1c brown 8.75 *13.00*
Never hinged 13.50
On cover 275.00
13 A43 2c orange brown 8.75 *13.00*
Never hinged 13.50
On cover 275.00
a. Double overprint 160.00
14 A48 5c green 2.60 *3.50*
Never hinged 4.00
On cover 150.00
a. Double overprint 95.00
15 A48 10c claret 2.60 *3.50*
Never hinged 4.00
On cover 150.00
16 A50 20c brn org (No. 112) 85.00 *72.50*
Never hinged 125.00
17 A49 25c blue 2.60 *6.50*
Never hinged 4.00
On cover 150.00
18 A49 50c violet 2.60 *7.25*
Never hinged 4.00
On cover 200.00
19 A46 1 l brown & grn 5.25 *12.00*
Never hinged 8.00
On cover 350.00
20 A46 5 l blue & rose 8.75 *19.00*
Never hinged 13.50
21 A51 10 l gray grn & red 85.00 *190.00*
Never hinged 125.00
Nos. 12-21 (10) 211.90 *340.25*

Italy No. 113, the watermarked 20c brown orange, was also overprinted "Pechino," but not issued. Value $10, $19 never hinged.

Italian Stamps of 1901-16 Surcharged:

a

2
dollari

Pechinc
b

TWO DOLLARS:
Type I — Surcharged "2 dollari" as illustration "b."
Type II — Surcharged "2 DOLLARI."
Type III — Surcharged "2 dollari." "Pechino" measures 11½mm wide, instead of 13mm.

1918-19 ***Perf. 14***

22 A42 ½c on 1c brown 80.00 *75.00*
Never hinged 120.00
a. Surcharged "1 cents" 275.00 *325.00*
23 A43 1c on 2c org brn 2.50 *4.50*
Never hinged 3.50
On cover 175.00
a. Surcharged "1 cents" 160.00 *175.00*
24 A48 2c on 5c green 2.50 *4.50*
Never hinged 3.50
On cover 140.00
25 A48 4c on 10c claret 2.50 *4.50*
Never hinged 3.50
On cover 140.00
26 A50 8c on 20c brn org (No. 112) 12.50 *9.50*
Never hinged 19.00
On cover 225.00
a. "8 CENTS" doubled 175.00 175.00
27 A49 10c on 25c blue 6.00 *9.50*
Never hinged 8.75
On cover 225.00
a. "10 CENTS" doubled 175.00 175.00
28 A49 20c on 50c violet 7.00 *9.50*
Never hinged 11.00
On cover 300.00
29 A46 40c on 1 l brown & green 95.00 *125.00*
Never hinged 140.00
30 A46 $2 on 5 l bl & rose (type I) 175.00 *300.00*
Never hinged 275.00
a. Type II *34,500.* *29,750.*
Never hinged *35,000.*
b. Type III *5,000.* *3,750.*
Never hinged *6,000.*
Nos. 22-30 (9) 383.00 *542.00*

Italy No. 100 Surcharged

1919

32 A49 10c on 25c blue 3.00 *9.00*
Never hinged 6.00
On cover 175.00

PEKING SPECIAL DELIVERY STAMPS

Italian Special Delivery Stamp 1908 Overprinted Like Nos. 12-21

1917 **Wmk. 140** ***Perf. 14***

E1 SD2 30c blue & rose 5.25 *17.00*
Never hinged 10.50
On cover 625.00

No. E1 Surcharged

1918

E2 SD2 12c on 30c bl & rose 37.50 *140.00*
Never hinged 82.50
On cover 850.00

PEKING POSTAGE DUE STAMPS

Italian Postage Due Stamps Overprinted Like Nos. 12-21

1917 **Wmk. 140** ***Perf. 14***

J1 D3 10c buff & magenta 2.10 *5.75*
Never hinged 4.25
a. Double overprint 175.00
J2 D3 20c buff & magenta 2.10 *5.75*
Never hinged 4.25
J3 D3 30c buff & magenta 2.10 *5.75*
Never hinged 4.25
J4 D3 40c buff & magenta 4.00 *5.75*
Never hinged 8.25
Nos. J1-J4 (4) 10.30 *23.00*

Nos. J1-J4 Surcharged Like No. E2

1918

J5 D3 4c on 10c *35,000.* *30,000.*
Never hinged *36,000.*
J6 D3 8c on 20c 11.00 *17.00*
Never hinged 15.00
a. Pair, one without surcharge 550.00
J7 D3 12c on 30c 37.50 *50.00*
Never hinged 55.00
J8 D3 16c on 40c 210.00 *300.00*
Never hinged 320.00

In 1919, the same new values were surcharged on Italy Nos. J6-J9 in a different style: four lines to cancel the denomination, and "-PECHINO- 4 CENTS." These were not issued. Value $4.50 each, never hinged $9 each.

TIENTSIN

Italian Stamps of 1906 Handstamped **TIENTSIN 2 CENTS**

Wmk. 140, Unwmk.

1917 ***Perf. 12, 13½, 14***

1 A48 2c on 5c green 190.00 160.00
Never hinged 290.00
On cover 425.00
a. Surcharge inverted 190.00 150.00
b. Double surcharge 210.00 140.00
c. 4c on 5c green *4,250.*
Never hinged *5,250.*
d. Double surcharge, one inverted 210.00 140.00
2 A48 4c on 10c claret 325.00 210.00
Never hinged 475.00
On cover 600.00
a. Surcharge inverted 325.00 190.00
b. Double surcharge 360.00 210.00
c. Double surcharge, one inverted 4,000. 225.00
4 A58 6c on 15c slate 775.00 550.00
Never hinged 950.00
On cover 1,000.
a. Surcharge inverted 775.00 500.00
Never hinged 950.00
b. 4c on 15c slate 2,300. 1,925.
Never hinged 3,200.
Nos. 1-4 (3) 1,290. 920.00

Italian Stamps of 1901-16 Overprinted

1917-18

5 A42 1c brown 8.75 *13.00*
Never hinged 13.50
On cover 275.00
a. Inverted overprint 160.00 175.00
6 A43 2c orange brn 8.75 *13.00*
Never hinged 13.50
On cover 275.00
7 A48 5c green 2.75 *3.50*
Never hinged 4.00
On cover 175.00
8 A48 10c claret 2.75 *3.50*
Never hinged 4.00
On cover 175.00
a. Double overprint 190.00
9 A50 20c brn org (#112) 85.00 *72.50*
Never hinged 125.00
10 A49 25c blue 2.75 *6.50*
Never hinged 4.00
On cover 175.00
11 A49 50c violet 2.75 *7.25*
Never hinged 4.00
On cover 275.00
12 A46 1 l brown & grn 5.50 *11.00*
Never hinged 8.00
On cover 400.00
13 A46 5 l blue & rose 8.75 *19.00*
Never hinged 13.50
14 A51 10 l gray grn & red 85.00 *190.00*
Never hinged 125.00
Nos. 5-14 (10) 212.75 *339.25*

Italy No. 113, the watermarked 20c brown orange was also overprinted "Tientsin," but not issued. Value $10, $19 never hinged.

Italian Stamps of 1901-16 Surcharged:

a

b

TWO DOLLARS:
Type I — Surcharged "2 Dollari" as illustration "b".
Type II — Surcharged "2 dollari".
Type III — Surcharged "2 Dollari". "Tientsin" measures 10mm wide instead of 13mm.

1918-21 ***Perf. 14***

15 A42 ½c on 1c brown 80.00 *75.00*
Never hinged 120.00
a. Inverted surcharge 190.00 *210.00*
b. Surcharged "1 cents" 300.00 *300.00*
c. Vertical fraction bar 1,900.
16 A43 1c on 2c org brn 2.25 *4.50*
Never hinged 4.00
On cover 175.00
a. Surcharged "1 cents" 190.00 *210.00*
b. Inverted surcharge 175.00 190.00
17 A48 2c on 5c green 2.25 *4.50*
Never hinged 4.00
On cover 140.00
18 A48 4c on 10c claret 2.25 *4.50*
Never hinged 4.00
On cover 140.00
19 A50 8c on 20c brn org (#112) 12.50 *9.50*
Never hinged 19.00
On cover 225.00
20 A49 10c on 25c blue 6.00 *9.50*
Never hinged 9.00
On cover 200.00
21 A49 20c on 50c violet 7.25 *9.50*
Never hinged 11.00
On cover 300.00
22 A46 40c on 1 l brn & grn 95.00 *125.00*
Never hinged 140.00
23 A46 $2 on 5 l bl & rose (type I) 175.00 *325.00*
Never hinged 275.00
a. Type II *5,500.* *4,400.*
Never hinged *6,500.*
b. Type III ('21) *5,000.* *3,750.*
Never hinged *6,000.*
Nos. 15-23 (9) 382.50 *567.00*

SPECIAL DELIVERY STAMPS

Italian Special Delivery Stamp of 1908 Overprinted

1917 **Wmk. 140** ***Perf. 14***

E1 SD2 30c blue & rose 5.25 *17.00*
Never hinged 10.50
On cover 625.00

No. E1 Surcharged

1918

E2 SD2 12c on 30c bl & rose 37.50 *140.00*
Never hinged 75.00
On cover 875.00

POSTAGE DUE STAMPS

Italian Postage Due Stamps Overprinted

1917 **Wmk. 140** ***Perf. 14***

J1 D3 10c buff & magenta 2.10 *5.75*
Never hinged 4.25
a. Double overprint 160.00
J2 D3 20c buff & magenta 2.10 *5.75*
Never hinged 4.25
J3 D3 30c buff & magenta 2.10 *5.75*
Never hinged 4.25
a. Double overprint 160.00
J4 D3 40c buff & magenta 4.25 *5.75*
Never hinged 8.25
Nos. J1-J4 (4) 10.55 *23.00*

Nos. J1-J4 Surcharged

1918

J5 D3 4c on 10c *1,525.* *1,925.*
Never hinged *2,250.*
a. "4 CENTS" handstamped *4,000.* *4,000.*
Never hinged *5,250.*
J6 D3 8c on 20c 11.00 *17.00*
Never hinged 15.00
a. "8 CENTS" double 850.00
Never hinged 1,100.
J7 D3 12c on 30c 37.50 *50.00*
Never hinged 55.00
J8 D3 16c on 40c 210.00 *300.00*
Never hinged 320.00

In 1919, the same new values were surcharged on Italy Nos. J6-J9 in a different style: four lines to cancel the denomination, and "-TIENTSIN- 4 CENTS." These were not issued. Value $4.50 each, never hinged $9 each.

OFFICES IN CRETE

40 Paras = 1 Piaster
100 Centesimi = 1 Lira (1906)

Italy Nos. 70 and 81 Surcharged in Red or Black

a

b

1900-01 **Wmk. 140** ***Perf. 14***

1 A36(a) 1pi on 25c blue 4.50 *30.00*
Never hinged 17.50
On cover 1,400.
2 A45(b) 1pi on 25c dp bl (Bk) ('01) 2.25 *55.00*
Never hinged 8.75
On cover 325.00

Values for pairs

1 A36(a) 1pi on 25c blue 14.00 *120.00*
2 A45(b) 1pi on 25c dp bl (Bk) ('01) 7.00

Italian Stamps Overprinted

1906
On Nos. 76-79, 92, 81, 83-85, 87, 91

3 A42 1c brown .45 *1.10*
Never hinged .90
On cover 160.00
a. Pair, one without ovpt. 400.00
4 A43 2c org brn .45 *1.10*
Never hinged .90
On cover 140.00
a. Imperf., pair 825.00
b. Double overprint 175.00
5 A44 5c bl grn .90 *1.40*
Never hinged 1.75
On cover 77.50
6 A45 10c claret 82.50 65.00
Never hinged 175.00
7 A45 15c on 20c org 1.10 *1.50*
Never hinged 2.10
On cover 160.00
8 A45 25c blue 4.50 4.50
Never hinged 9.00
On cover 225.00
9 A45 40c brown 4.00 *4.50*
Never hinged 8.25
On cover 375.00
10 A45 45c ol grn 3.50 *4.50*
Never hinged 7.25
On cover 550.00
11 A45 50c violet 4.50 *6.50*
Never hinged 9.00
On cover 700.00
12 A46 1 l brn & grn 26.00 *29.00*
Never hinged 50.00
13 A46 5 l bl & rose 140.00 *150.00*
Never hinged 260.00
Nos. 3-13 (11) 267.90 *269.10*
Set on overfranked philatelic cover 675.00

Values for blocks of four

6 A45 10c claret 1,000. 425.00
13 A46 5 l bl & rose 1,400. *875.00*

On Nos. 94-95, 100, 104-105

1907-10

14 A48 5c green .75 *1.10*
Never hinged 1.50
On cover 77.50
a. Inverted overprint 190.00
15 A48 10c claret .75 *1.10*
Never hinged 1.50
On cover 100.00
16 A49 25c blue 1.50 *3.50*
Never hinged 3.00
On cover 125.00
17 A49 40c brown 15.00 *19.00*
Never hinged 30.00
On cover 225.00
18 A49 50c violet 1.50 *3.50*
Never hinged 3.00
On cover 275.00
Nos. 14-18 (5) 19.50 *28.20*

On No. 111 in Violet

1912 **Unwmk.** ***Perf. 13x13½***

19 A50 15c slate black 1.50 *2.75*
Never hinged 3.00
On cover 140.00
Nos. 14-19 on overfranked philatelic cover 100.00

SPECIAL DELIVERY STAMP

Special Delivery Stamp of Italy Overprinted

1906 **Wmk. 140** ***Perf. 14***

E1 SD1 25c rose red 4.00 *8.50*
Never hinged 7.50
On cover 390.00

Some sheets from the first printing have a second, albino overprint.

OFFICES IN AFRICA

40 Paras = 1 Piaster
100 Centesimi = 1 Lira (1910)

BENGASI

Italy No. 81 Surcharged in Black

1901 **Wmk. 140** ***Perf. 14***

1 A45 1pi on 25c dp bl 22.50 *77.50*
Never hinged 45.00
On cover 250.00

Same Surcharge on Italy No. 100

1911

1A A49 1pi on 25c blue 25.00 *77.50*
Never hinged 47.50
On cover 325.00

TRIPOLI

Italian Stamps of 1901-09 Overprinted in Black or Violet

1909 **Wmk. 140**

2 A42 1c brown 2.50 *2.25*
Never hinged 5.00
On cover 175.00
a. Inverted overprint 160.00
3 A43 2c orange brn .90 *1.25*
Never hinged 1.75
On cover 140.00
4 A48 5c green 55.00 4.50
On cover 55.00
a. Double overprint 175.00
5 A48 10c claret 1.75 *1.25*
Never hinged 3.50
On cover 57.50
a. Double overprint 140.00 *150.00*
6 A49 25c blue 1.50 *1.25*
Never hinged 3.00
On cover 125.00
7 A49 40c brown 3.75 *3.00*
Never hinged 7.50
On cover 240.00
8 A49 50c violet 5.25 *4.00*
Never hinged 10.50
On cover 275.00

Perf. 13½x14
Unwmk.

9 A50 15c slate blk (V) 2.25 *2.25*
Never hinged 4.50
On cover 150.00
Nos. 2-9 (8) 72.90 *19.75*

Italian Stamps of 1901 Overprinted

1909 **Wmk. 140** ***Perf. 14***

10 A46 1 l brown & grn 65.00 45.00
Never hinged 125.00
On cover 550.00
11 A46 5 l blue & rose 17.50 125.00
Never hinged 35.00
Set of 10 on overfranked, philatelic cover 400.00

Same Overprint on Italy Nos. 76-77

1915

12 A42 1c brown 1.50
Never hinged 3.00
13 A43 2c orange brown 1.50
Never hinged 3.00

Nos. 12-13 were prepared but not issued.

SPECIAL DELIVERY STAMPS

Italy Nos. E1, E6 Overprinted Like Nos. 10-11

1909 **Wmk. 140** ***Perf. 14***

E1 SD1 25c rose red 3.00 *6.50*
Never hinged 6.00
On cover 190.00
E2 SD2 30c blue & rose 8.75 *9.50*
Never hinged 17.50
On cover 375.00

Tripoli was ceded by Turkey to Italy in Oct., 1912, and became known as the Colony of Libia. Later issues will be found under Libya.

OFFICES IN TURKISH EMPIRE

40 Paras = 1 Piaster

Various powers maintained post offices in the Turkish Empire before World War I by authority of treaties which ended with the signing of the Treaty of Lausanne in 1923. The foreign post offices were closed Oct. 27, 1923.

GENERAL ISSUE

Italian Stamps of 1906-08 Surcharged

Printed at Turin

1908 Wmk. 140

1 A48 10pa on 5c green .90 *.90*
Never hinged 1.75
On cover 45.00
2 A48 20pa on 10c claret .90 *.90*
Never hinged 1.75
On cover 60.00
3 A49 40pa on 25c blue 1.75 *1.50*
Never hinged 3.50
On cover 40.00
4 A49 80pa on 50c violet 2.75 *2.10*
Never hinged 5.50
On cover 70.00

See Janina Nos. 1-4.

Surcharged in Violet

Unwmk.

5 A47 30pa on 15c slate 1.25 *1.50*
Never hinged 2.50
On cover 45.00
Nos. 1-5 (5) 7.55 *6.90*

Nos. 1, 2, 3 and 5 were first issued in Janina, Albania, and subsequently for general use. They can only be distinguished by the cancellations.

Italian Stamps of 1901-08 Surcharged:

Nos. 6-8

1 PIASTRA
No. 9

2 PIASTRE
Nos. 10-12

Printed at Constantinople

1908 First Printing

6 A48 10pa on 5c green 110. 100.
Never hinged 160.
On cover 150.
a. Vert. pair, one without surcharge 1,050.
Never hinged 1,300.
7 A48 20pa on 10c claret 110. 100.
Never hinged 160.
On cover 190.
8 A47 30pa on 15c slate 325. 300.
Never hinged 475.
On cover 450.
9 A49 1pi on 25c blue 325. 300.
Never hinged 475.
On cover 575.
a. "PIASTRE" 450.
10 A49 2pi on 50c violet 1,050. 1,050.
Never hinged 1,600.
11 A46 4pi on 1 l brn & grn *5,000.* *4,000.*
Never hinged *6,000.*
12 A46 20pi on 5 l bl & rose *13,000.* *8,500.*
Never hinged *17,000.*

On Nos. 8, 9 and 10 the surcharge is at the top of the stamp. No. 11 has the "4" closed at the top. No. 12 has the "20" wide.

Second Printing

Surcharged:

Nos. 13-15

No. 16

Nos. 17-19

13 A48 10pa on 5c green 3.00 *4.25*
Never hinged 6.00
On cover 95.00
14 A48 20pa on 10c claret 3.00 *4.25*
Never hinged 6.00
On cover 95.00
15 A47 30pa on 15c slate 12.00 *12.00*
Never hinged 24.00
On cover 150.00
a. Double surcharge 80.00 87.50
b. Triple surcharge 160.00 175.00
16 A49 1pi on 25c blue 3.00 *3.25*
Never hinged 6.00
On cover 170.00
a. "PIPSTRA" 65.00 72.50
b. "1" omitted 65.00 72.50
17 A49 2pi on 50c violet 27.50 *30.00*
Never hinged 55.00
a. Surcharged "20 PIASTRE" 700.00 775.00
Never hinged 900.00
b. "20" with "0" scratched out 210.00 225.00
c. "2" 5mm from "PIASTRE" 140.00 150.00
18 A46 4pi on 1 l brn & grn 525.00 450.00
Never hinged 800.00
19 A46 20pi on 5 l bl & rose 2,000. 1,375.
Never hinged 2,600.
Nos. 13-19 (7) 2,573. 1,878.

On No. 18 the "4" is open at the top.

Third Printing

Surcharged in Red

20 A47 30pa on 15c slate 1.50 *1.60*
Never hinged 3.00
On cover 60.00
a. Double surcharge 140.00 150.00

Fourth Printing

Surcharged:

20 20
PIASTRE

20B A46 4pi on 1 l brn & grn 29.00 30.00
Never hinged 57.50
c. Inverted "S" 82.50 90.00
20D A46 20pi on 5 l bl & rose 95.00 *110.00*
Never hinged 190.00
i. Inverted "S" 225.00 250.00

Fifth Printing

Surcharged

20 20
PIASTRE

20E A46 4pi on 1 l brn & grn 27.50 35.00
Never hinged 52.50
f. Surch. "20 PIASTRE" 850.00
Never hinged 950.00
20G A46 20pi on 5 l bl & rose 27.50 35.00
Never hinged 55.00
On cover 150.00
h. Double surcharge 650.00 *700.00*

Italian Stamps of 1906-19 Surcharged

1921

21 A48 1pi on 5c green 82.50 *175.00*
Never hinged 160.00
22 A48 2pi on 15c slate 3.00 *5.50*
Never hinged 6.00
On cover 130.00
23 A50 4pi on 20c brn org (No. 113) 35.00 *32.50*
Never hinged 70.00
24 A49 5pi on 25c blue 35.00 *32.50*
Never hinged 70.00
a. Double surcharge 175.00
25 A49 10pi on 60c carmine 1.50 *2.75*
Never hinged 3.00
Nos. 21-25 (5) 157.00 *248.25*
Set of 5 on overfranked philatelic cover 350.00

No. 21 is almost always found poorly centered, and it is valued thus.

On No. 25 the "10" is placed above "PIASTRE."

Italian Stamps of 1901-19 Surcharged

n

o

1922

26 A42(n) 10pa on 1c brown 1.25 *1.75*
Never hinged 2.40
27 A43(n) 20pa on 2c org brn 1.25 *1.75*
Never hinged 2.40
28 A48(n) 30pa on 5c green 2.40 *3.00*
Never hinged 4.75
29 A48(o) 1pi20pa on 15c slate 3.50 *1.75*
Never hinged 7.25
30 A50(n) 3pi on 20c brn org (#113) 4.25 *9.00*
Never hinged 8.25
31 A49(o) 3pi30pa on 25c blue 1.75 *1.75*
Never hinged 3.50
32 A49(o) 7pi20pa on 60c carmine 3.50 *3.00*
Never hinged 7.25
33 A46(n) 15pi on 1 l brn & grn 15.00 *27.50*
Never hinged 32.50
Nos. 26-33 (8) 32.90 *49.50*
Set of 5 on overfranked philatelic cover 110.00

No No. 32, the distance between the two lines is 2mm. See note after No. 58A.

Italy No. 100 Surcharged

34 A49 3.75pi on 25c blue 1.50 1.75
Never hinged 3.00

Italian Stamps of 1901-20 Surcharged:

q

r

1922

35 A48 30pi on 5c green 3.00 *6.50*
Never hinged 4.50
On cover 160.00
36 A49 1.50pi on 25c blue 1.40 *3.00*
Never hinged 2.00
On cover 45.00
37 A49 3.75pi on 40c brown 1.90 *3.50*
Never hinged 3.00
On cover 40.00
a Double surcharge 130.00
38 A49 4.50pi on 50c violet 5.25 *11.00*
Never hinged 7.75
On cover 45.00
39 A49 7.50pi on 60c carmine 4.50 *8.25*
Never hinged 6.50
On cover 55.00
a Double surcharge 190.00
b Pair, one without surcharge 450.00
40 A49 15pi on 85c red brn 7.50 *17.00*
Never hinged 11.00
On cover 70.00
41 A46 18.75pi on 1 l brn & grn 3.75 *13.00*
Never hinged 5.50
On cover 150.00

On No. 40 the numerals of the surcharge are above "PIASTRE."

On No. 42 the figure "4" is open at top. See note after No. 61.

On No. 43 the figure "9" has a curved or arched bottom. See note after No. 62.

Surcharged

45
PIASTRE

42 A46 45pa on 5 l bl & rose 225.00 *300.00*
Never hinged 360.00
43 A51 90pa on 10 l gray grn & red 250.00 *325.00*
Never hinged 400.00

Italian Stamps of 1901-17 Surcharged Type "q" or:

44 A43 30pa on 2c org brn 1.40 *1.60*
Never hinged 1.95
On cover 110.00
45 A50 1.50pi on 20c brn org (#113) 1.40 *1.40*
Never hinged 1.95
On cover 55.00
Nos. 35-45 (11) 505.10 *690.25*

Italian Stamps of 1901-20 Surcharged in Black or Red

46 A48 30pa on 5c green .90 *1.75*
Never hinged 1.75
On cover 175.00
a. RARA" instead of "PARA" 10.00 10.00
47 A48 1½pi on 10c claret 1.25 *1.75*
Never hinged 2.50
On cover 95.00
48 A49 3pi on 25c blue 8.75 4.50
Never hinged 17.50
On cover 120.00
49 A49 3¾pi on 40c brown 1.60 *1.75*
Never hinged 3.50
On cover 150.00
50 A49 4½pi on 50c violet 26.00 25.00
Never hinged 52.50
On cover 190.00
51 A49 7½pi on 85c red brn 4.50 *5.75*
Never hinged 8.75
On cover 90.00
a. "PIASIRE" 30.00 *32.50*
52 A46 7½pi on 1 l brn & grn (R) 5.25 *7.25*
Never hinged 11.00
On cover 120.00
a. Double surcharge 110.00 125.00
b. "PIASIRE" 35.00 *37.50*
53 A46 15pi on 1 l brn & grn 40.00 *100.00*
Never hinged 82.50
54 A46 45pi on 5 l blue & rose 70.00 *62.50*
Never hinged 140.00
55 A51 90pi on 10 l gray grn & red 57.50 *100.00*
Never hinged 120.00
Nos. 46-55 (10) 215.75 *310.25*
Set of 10on overfranked philatelic cover 425.00

Italian Stamps of 1901-20 Surcharged Type "o" or:

No. 58

No. 59

Nos. 61-62

1923

56 A49 1pi20pa on 25c blue 6.50
Never hinged 13.50
57 A49 3pi30pa on 40c brown 6.50
Never hinged 13.50
58 A49 4pi20pa on 50c violet 6.50
Never hinged 37.50
58A A49 7pi20pa on 60c car 19.00
Never hinged 37.50
59 A49 15pi on 85c red brn 6.50
Never hinged 13.50
60 A46 18pi30pa on 1 l brn & grn 6.50
Never hinged 13.50
a. Double surcharge *175.00*
61 A46 45pi on 5 l bl & rose 19.00
Never hinged 37.50
62 A51 90pi on 10 l gray grn & red 17.50
Never hinged 35.00
Nos. 56-62 (8) 88.00

On No. 58A the distance between the lines is 1.5mm. On No. 61 the figure "4" is closed at top. On No. 62 the figure "9" is nearly rectilinear at bottom.

Nos. 56-62 were not issued.

SPECIAL DELIVERY STAMPS

Italian Special Delivery Stamps Surcharged

Surcharged 

1908 Wmk. 140 *Perf. 14*

E1 SD1 1pi on 25c rose red 1.75 *2.10*
Never hinged 3.50
On cover 210.00

Surcharged 

1910

E2 SD2 60pa on 30c blue & rose 2.75 *3.25*
Never hinged 5.50
On cover *600.00*

Surcharged 

1922

E3 SD2 15pi on 1.20 l on 30c bl & rose 13.00 *30.00*
Never hinged 27.50
On cover 360.00

On No. E3, lines obliterate the first two denominations.

Surcharged **15 PIASTRE**

1922

E4 SD2 15pi on 30c bl & rose 175.00 *325.00*
Never hinged 360.00

Surcharged 

1923

E5 SD2 15pi on 1.20 l blue & red 7.50
Never hinged 15.00

No. E5 was not regularly issued.

ALBANIA

Stamps of Italy Surcharged in Black 

1902 Wmk. 140 *Perf. 14*

1 A44 10pa on 5c green 1.90 *.90*
Never hinged 3.75
On cover 90.00

2 A45 35pa on 20c orange 3.25 *2.50*
Never hinged 6.50
On cover 190.00

3 A45 40pa on 25c blue 6.50 2.50
Never hinged 13.50
On cover 340.00
Nos. 1-3 (3) 11.65 *5.90*
Set of 3 on overfranked philatelic cover 190.00

Nos. 1-3 with red surcharges are proofs.

1907

4 A48 10pa on 5c green 25.00 *32.50*
Never hinged 47.50
On cover 120.00

5 A48 20pa on 10c claret 14.50 *14.00*
Never hinged 29.00
On cover 95.00

6 A45 80pa on 50c violet 14.50 *14.00*
Never hinged 29.00
On cover 260.00
Nos. 4-6 (3) 54.00 *60.50*
Set of 3 on overfranked philatelic cover 150.00

No. 5 is almost always found poorly centered, and it is valued thus.

CONSTANTINOPLE

Stamps of Italy Surcharged in Black or Violet 

Wmk. 140, Unwmk. (#3)

1909-11 *Perf. 14, 12*

1 A48 10pa on 5c green .90 *1.40*
Never hinged 1.75
On cover 60.00

2 A48 20pa on 10c claret .90 *1.40*
Never hinged 1.75
On cover 60.00

3 A47 30pa on 15c slate (V) .90 *1.40*
Never hinged 1.75
On cover 95.00

4 A49 1pi on 25c blue .90 *1.40*
Never hinged 1.75
On cover 95.00
a. Double surcharge 140.00 *150.00*

5 A49 2pi on 50c violet 1.25 *1.60*
Never hinged 2.40
On cover 140.00

Surcharged 

6 A46 4pi on 1 l brn & grn 1.50 *1.90*
Never hinged 3.00

7 A46 20pi on 5 l bl & rose 32.50 32.50
Never hinged 65.00

8 A51 40pi on 10 l gray grn & red 2.75 *17.00*
Never hinged 5.50
Nos. 1-8 (8) 41.60 *58.60*
Set of 8 on overfranked philatelic cover 120.00

Italian Stamps of 1901-19 Surcharged:

Nos. 10, 12-13

Nos. 9, 11

1922

9 A48 20pa on 5c green 10.00 *14.50*
Never hinged 20.00
On cover 475.00

10 A48 1pi20pa on 15c slate 1.00 *1.50*
Never hinged 2.00
On cover 140.00

11 A49 3pi on 30c org brn 1.00 *1.50*
Never hinged 2.00
On cover 57.50

12 A49 3pi30pa on 40c brown 1.00 *1.50*
Never hinged 2.00
On cover 110.00

13 A46 7pi20pa on 1 l brn & grn 1.00 *1.50*
Never hinged 2.00
On cover 120.00
Nos. 9-13 (5) 14.00 *20.50*
Set of 8 on overfranked philatelic cover 140.00

Italian Stamps of 1901-20 Surcharged 

1923

14 A48 30pa on 5c green 1.50 *1.60*
Never hinged 3.00
On cover 240.00

15 A49 1pi20pa on 25c blue 1.50 *1.60*
Never hinged 3.00
On cover 95.00

16 A49 3pi30pa on 40c brown 1.50 *1.40*
Never hinged 3.00
On cover 95.00

17 A49 4pi20pa on 50c violet 1.50 *1.40*
Never hinged 3.00
On cover 75.00

18 A49 7pi20pa on 60c car 1.50 *1.40*
Never hinged 3.00
On cover 110.00

19 A49 15pi on 85c red brn 1.50 *2.50*
Never hinged 3.00
On cover 175.00

20 A46 18pi30pa on 1 l brn & grn 2.25 *5.50*
Never hinged 3.00
On cover 240.00

21 A46 45pi on 5 l bl & rose 2.25 *5.50*
Never hinged 4.50

22 A51 90pi on 10 l gray grn & red 2.25 *6.00*
Never hinged 4.50
Nos. 14-22 (9) 15.75 *26.90*
Set of 9 on overfranked philatelic cover 110.00

CONSTANTINOPLE SPECIAL DELIVERY STAMP

Unissued Italian Special Delivery Stamp of 1922 Surcharged in Black 

1923 Wmk. 140 *Perf. 14*

E1 SD2 15pi on 1.20 l bl & red 3.75 *17.00*
Never hinged 7.50
On cover *460.00*

CONSTANTINOPLE POSTAGE DUE STAMPS

Italian Postage Due Stamps of 1870-1903 Overprinted 

1922 Wmk. 140 *Perf. 14*

J1 D3 10c buff & mag 22.50 *35.00*
Never hinged 32.50

J2 D3 30c buff & mag 22.50 *35.00*
Never hinged 32.50

J3 D3 60c buff & mag 22.50 *35.00*
Never hinged 32.50

J4 D3 1 l blue & mag 22.50 *35.00*
Never hinged 32.50

J5 D3 2 l blue & mag 600.00 *1,000.*
Never hinged 950.00

J6 D3 5 l blue & mag 210.00 *350.00*
Never hinged 300.00
Nos. J1-J6 (6) 900.00 *1,490.*

A circular control mark with the inscription "Poste Italiane Constantinopoli" and with the arms of the Kingdom of Italy (Savoy Cross) in the center was applied to each block of four of these stamps in black. Value, set of 6 blocks of four with control marks, $7,500.

Without Control Mark

J1a D3 10c buff & mag 950.00
Never hinged 1,200.

J2a D3 30c buff & mag 950.00
Never hinged 1,200.

J3a D3 60c buff & mag 950.00
Never hinged 1,200.

J4a D3 1 l blue & mag 950.00
Never hinged 1,200.

J5a D3 2 l blue & mag 950.00
Never hinged 1,200.

J6a D3 5 l blue & mag 950.00
Never hinged 1,200.
Nos. J1a-J6a (6) 5,700.

DURAZZO

Stamps of Italy Surcharged in Black or Violet 

Wmk. 140, Unwmk. (#3)

1909-11 *Perf. 14, 12*

1 A48 10pa on 5c green .45 *.90*
Never hinged .90
On cover 60.00

2 A48 20pa on 10c claret .45 *.90*
Never hinged .90
On cover 60.00

3 A47 30pa on 15c slate (V) 21.00 1.75
Never hinged 42.50
On cover 120.00

4 A49 1pi on 25c blue .75 *1.25*
Never hinged 1.50
On cover 120.00

5 A49 2pi on 50c violet .75 *1.25*
Never hinged 1.50
On cover 200.00

Surcharged 

6 A46 4pi on 1 l brn & grn 1.75 *1.50*
Never hinged 3.50
On cover 275.00

7 A46 20pi on 5 l bl & rose 110.00 110.00
Never hinged 225.00

8 A51 40pi on 10 l gray grn & red 5.00 *52.50*
Never hinged 9.50
Nos. 1-8 (8) 140.15 170.05
Set of 8 stamps on overfranked philatelic cover 350.00

No. 3 Surcharged 

1916 Unwmk. *Perf. 12*

9 A47 20c on 30pa on 15c slate 2.50 *12.00*
Never hinged 5.00
On cover 95.00

JANINA

Stamps of Italy Surcharged 

1902-07 Wmk. 140 *Perf. 14*

1 A44 10pa on 5c green 4.25 1.40
Never hinged 8.00
On cover 55.00

2 A45 35pa on 20c orange 2.50 *1.60*
Never hinged 5.00
On cover 95.00

3 A45 40pa on 25c blue 14.50 4.00
Never hinged 29.00
On cover 150.00

4 A45 80pa on 50c vio ('07) 32.50 *27.50*
Never hinged 65.00
On cover 240.00
Nos. 1-4 (4) 53.75 *34.50*
Nos. 1-3 on overfranked philatelic cover 82.50

Surcharged in Black or Violet 

Wmk. 140, Unwmk. (#7)

1909-11 *Perf. 14, 12*

No.	Type	Description	Unused	Used
5	A48	10pa on 5c green	.40	*.45*
		Never hinged	.80	
		On cover		67.50
6	A48	20pa on 10c claret	.40	*.45*
		Never hinged	.80	
		On cover		67.50
7	A47	30pa on 15c slate (V)	.45	*.60*
		Never hinged	.90	
		On cover		120.00
8	A49	1pi on 25c blue	.45	*.60*
		Never hinged	.90	
		On cover		120.00
9	A49	2pi on 50c violet	.90	*.80*
		Never hinged	1.75	
		On cover		200.00

Surcharged

No.	Type	Description	Unused	Used
10	A46	4pi on 1 l brn & grn	.90	*.90*
		Never hinged	1.75	
		On cover		300.00
11	A46	20pi on 5 l bl & rose	140.00	160.00
		Never hinged	275.00	
12	A51	40pi on 10 l gray grn & red	6.00	*47.50*
		Never hinged	12.00	
		Nos. 5-12 (8)	149.50	211.30
		Set of 8 on overfranked philatelic cover		350.00

JERUSALEM

Stamps of Italy Surcharged in Black or Violet

Wmk. 140, Unwmk. (#3)

1909-11 *Perf. 14, 12*

No.	Type	Description	Unused	Used
1	A48	10pa on 5c green	1.90	*4.00*
		Never hinged	3.00	
		On cover		200.00
2	A48	20pa on 10c claret	1.90	*4.00*
		Never hinged	3.00	
		On cover		200.00
3	A47	30pa on 15c slate (V)	1.90	*5.75*
		Never hinged	3.00	
		On cover		340.00
4	A49	1pi on 25c blue	1.90	*4.00*
		Never hinged	3.00	
		On cover		500.00
5	A49	2pi on 50c violet	8.75	*10.50*
		Never hinged	13.50	
		On cover		775.00

Surcharged

No.	Type	Description	Unused	Used
6	A46	4pi on 1 l brn & grn	12.00	*19.00*
		Never hinged	18.00	
		On cover		2,250.
7	A46	20pi on 5 l bl & rose	500.00	*325.00*
		Never hinged	725.00	
8	A51	40pi on 10 l gray grn & red	16.00	*175.00*
		Never hinged	25.00	
		Nos. 1-8 (8)	544.35	*547.25*
		Set of 8 on overfranked philatelic cover		3,000.

Forged cancellations exist on Nos. 1-8.

SALONIKA

Stamps of Italy Surcharged in Black or Violet

Wmk. 140, Unwmk. (#3)

1909-11 *Perf. 14, 12*

No.	Type	Description	Unused	Used
1	A48	10pa on 5c green	.45	*.55*
		Never hinged	.90	
		On cover		60.00
2	A48	20pa on 10c claret	.45	*.55*
		Never hinged	.90	
		On cover		60.00
3	A47	30pa on 15c slate (V)	.75	*.90*
		Never hinged	1.50	
		On cover		110.00
4	A49	1pi on 25c blue	.75	*.90*
		Never hinged	1.50	
		On cover		90.00
5	A49	2pi on 50c violet	.90	*1.10*
		Never hinged	1.75	
		On cover		175.00

Surcharged

No.	Type	Description	Unused	Used
6	A46	4pi on 1 l brn & grn	1.25	*1.40*
		Never hinged	2.50	
		On cover		275.00
7	A46	20pi on 5 l bl & rose	210.00	225.00
		Never hinged	360.00	
8	A51	40pi on 10 l gray grn & red	6.00	*37.50*
		Never hinged	12.00	
		Nos. 1-8 (8)	220.55	267.90
		Set of 8 on overfranked philatelic cover		550.00

SCUTARI

Stamps of Italy Surcharged in Black or Violet

Wmk. 140, Unwmk. (#3)

1909-11 *Perf. 14, 12*

No.	Type	Description	Unused	Used
1	A48	10pa on 5c green	.35	*.75*
		Never hinged	.70	
		On cover		60.00
2	A48	20pa on 10c claret	.35	*.75*
		Never hinged	.70	
		On cover		60.00
3	A47	30pa on 15c slate (V)	13.00	3.00
		Never hinged	26.00	
		On cover		140.00
4	A49	1pi on 25c blue	.35	*1.25*
		Never hinged	.70	
		On cover		95.00
5	A49	2pi on 50c violet	.60	*1.50*
		Never hinged	1.20	
		On cover		275.00

Surcharged

No.	Type	Description	Unused	Used
6	A46	4pi on 1 l brn & grn	.75	*1.75*
		Never hinged	1.50	
		On cover		375.00
7	A46	20pi on 5 l bl & rose	15.00	*22.50*
		Never hinged	30.00	
8	A51	40pi on 10 l gray grn & red	35.00	*90.00*
		Never hinged	70.00	
		Nos. 1-8 (8)	65.40	*121.50*
		Set of 8 on overfranked philatelic cover		225.00

Surcharged like Nos. 1-5

1915

No.	Type	Description	Unused	Used
9	A43	4pa on 2c orange brn	1.50	*3.00*
		Never hinged	3.00	
		On cover		82.50

No. 3 Surcharged

1916 **Unwmk.** *Perf. 12*

No.	Type	Description	Unused	Used
10	A47	20c on 30pa on 15c slate	3.50	*14.50*
		Never hinged	7.00	
		On cover		190.00

SMYRNA

Stamps of Italy Surcharged in Black or Violet

Wmk. 140, Unwmk. (#3)

1909-11 *Perf. 14, 12*

No.	Type	Description	Unused	Used
1	A48	10pa on 5c green	.35	*.55*
		Never hinged	.70	
		On cover		60.00
2	A48	20pa on 10c claret	.35	*.55*
		Never hinged	.70	
		On cover		60.00
3	A47	30pa on 15c slate (V)	1.10	*1.25*
		Never hinged	2.10	
		On cover		140.00
4	A49	1pi on 25c blue	1.10	*1.25*
		Never hinged	2.10	
		On cover		95.00
5	A49	2pi on 50c violet	1.50	*1.75*
		Never hinged	3.00	
		On cover		240.00

Surcharged

No.	Type	Description	Unused	Used
6	A46	4pi on 1 l brn & grn	1.75	*2.25*
		Never hinged	3.50	
		On cover		275.00
7	A46	20pi on 5 l bl & rose	90.00	100.00
		Never hinged	175.00	
8	A51	40pi on 10 l gray grn & red	8.75	*62.50*
		Never hinged	17.50	
		Nos. 1-8 (8)	104.90	*170.10*
		Set of 8 on overfranked philatelic cover		300.00

Italian Stamps of 1901-22 Surcharged:

Nos. 10, 12-13

Nos. 9, 11

1922

No.	Type	Description	Unused	Used
9	A48	20pa on 5c green	15.00	
		Never hinged	30.00	
10	A48	1pi20pa on 15c slate	.40	
		Never hinged	.80	
11	A49	3pi on 30c org brn	.40	
		Never hinged	.80	
12	A49	3pi30pa on 40c brown	.75	
		Never hinged	1.50	
13	A46	7pi20pa on 1 l brn & grn	.75	
		Never hinged	1.50	
		Nos. 9-13 (5)	17.30	

Nos. 9-13 were not issued.

VALONA

Stamps of Italy Surcharged in Black or Violet

Wmk. 140, Unwmk. (#3)

1909-11 *Perf. 14, 12*

No.	Type	Description	Unused	Used
1	A48	10pa on 5c green	.20	*.90*
		Never hinged	.45	
		On cover		60.00
2	A48	20pa on 10c claret	.20	*.90*
		Never hinged	.45	
		On cover		60.00
3	A47	30pa on 15c slate (V)	10.50	3.00
		Never hinged	21.00	
		On cover		125.00
4	A49	1pi on 25c blue	.75	*1.10*
		Never hinged	1.50	
		On cover		100.00
5	A49	2pi on 50c violet	.75	*1.40*
		Never hinged	1.50	
		On cover		225.00

Surcharged

No.	Type	Description	Unused	Used
6	A46	4pi on 1 l brn & grn	1.10	*1.75*
		Never hinged	2.10	
		On cover		350.00
7	A46	20pi on 5 l bl & rose	29.00	35.00
		Never hinged	57.50	
8	A51	40pi on 10 l gray grn & red	32.50	*92.50*
		Never hinged	65.00	
		Nos. 1-8 (8)	75.00	*136.55*
		Set of 8 on overfranked philatelic cover		250.00

Italy No. 123 Surcharged in Violet or Red Violet

1916

No.	Type	Description	Unused	Used
9	A58	30pa on 15c slate (V)	3.00	*8.25*
		Never hinged	6.00	
		On cover		140.00
a.		Red violet surcharge	6.00	*17.00*

No. 9 Surcharged

No.	Type	Description	Unused	Used
10	A58	20c on 30pa on 15c slate	1.25	*9.50*
		Never hinged	2.50	
		On cover		140.00

AEGEAN ISLANDS

(Dodecanese)

A group of islands in the Aegean Sea off the coast of Turkey. They were occupied by Italy during the Tripoli War and were ceded to Italy by Turkey in 1924 by the Treaty of Lausanne. Stamps of Italy overprinted with the name of the island were in use at the post offices maintained in the various islands.

Rhodes, on the island of the same name, was capital of the entire group.

100 Centesimi = 1 Lira

GENERAL ISSUE

Italian Stamps of 1907-08 Overprinted

1912 **Wmk. 140** *Perf. 14*

No.	Type	Description	Unused	Used
1	A49	25c blue	26.00	*17.00*
		Never hinged	52.50	
		On cover		62.50
a.		Inverted overprint	190.00	*210.00*
2	A49	50c violet	26.00	*17.00*
		Never hinged	52.50	
		On cover		95.00
a.		Inverted overprint	190.00	*210.00*
		Set on overfranked philatelic cover		75.00

Virgil Issue

Types of Italian Stamps of 1930 Overprinted in Red or Blue

1930 Photo. Wmk. 140 *Perf. 14*

3 A106 15c vio blk .90 *5.75*
Never hinged 1.75
On cover 67.50
4 A106 20c org brn .90 *5.75*
Never hinged 1.75
On cover 62.50
5 A106 25c dk green .90 *2.25*
Never hinged 1.75
On cover 47.50
6 A106 30c lt brown .90 *2.25*
Never hinged 1.75
On cover 62.50
7 A106 50c dull vio .90 *2.25*
Never hinged 1.75
On cover 47.50
8 A106 75c rose red .90 *5.75*
Never hinged 1.75
On cover 95.00
9 A106 1.25 l gray bl .90 *8.25*
Never hinged 1.75
On cover 140.00

Engr.
Unwmk.

10 A106 5 l + 1.50 l dk vio 2.10 *15.00*
Never hinged 4.25
On cover 13.50
11 A106 10 l + 2.50 l ol brn 2.10 *15.00*
Never hinged 4.25
On cover 13.50
Nos. 3-11,C4-C7 (13) *18.00* 128.75
Set on overfranked philatelic cover 240.00

St. Anthony of Padua Issue

Types of Italian Stamps of 1931 Overprinted in Blue or Red

1932 Photo. Wmk. 140 *Perf. 14*

12 A116 20c black brn 13.00 *9.00*
Never hinged 26.00
On cover 90.00
13 A116 25c dull grn 13.00 9.00
Never hinged 26.00
On cover 82.50
14 A118 30c brown org 13.00 *10.50*
Never hinged 26.00
On cover 90.00
15 A118 50c dull vio 13.00 7.25
Never hinged 26.00
On cover 75.00
16 A120 1.25 l gray bl 13.00 12.00
Never hinged 26.00
On cover 140.00

Engr.
Unwmk.

17 A121 75c lt red 13.00 *14.00*
Never hinged 26.00
On cover 200.00
18 A122 5 l + 2.50 l dp org 13.00 *52.50*
Never hinged 26.00
On cover —
Nos. 12-18 (7) 91.00 *114.25*
Set on overfranked philatelic cover 275.00

Types of Italian Stamps of 1932 Overprinted

1932 Photo. Wmk. 140

19 A126 10c grnsh gray .85 *2.10*
Never hinged 1.75
On cover 47.50
20 A126 15c black vio .85 *2.10*
Never hinged 1.75
On cover 57.50
21 A126 20c brown org .85 *2.10*
Never hinged 1.75
On cover 47.50
22 A126 25c dp green .85 2.10
Never hinged 1.75
On cover 42.50
23 A126 30c dp org .85 *2.10*
Never hinged 1.75
On cover 55.00
24 A126 50c dull vio .85 .90
Never hinged 1.75
On cover 42.50
25 A126 75c rose red .85 *2.60*
Never hinged 1.75
On cover 82.50
26 A126 1.25 l blue .85 *2.10*
Never hinged 1.75
On cover 90.00
27 A126 1.75 l ol brn .95 *2.60*
Never hinged 1.90
On cover 160.00
28 A126 2.75 l car rose 1.00 *2.60*
Never hinged 2.00
On cover 200.00
29 A126 5 l + 2 l dp vio 1.10 *9.00*
Never hinged 2.25
On cover —
30 A126 10 l + 2.50 l dk brn 1.10 *13.00*
Never hinged 2.25
On cover —
Nos. 19-30 (12) 10.95 *43.30*
Set of on overfranked philatelic cover 200.00

See Nos. C8-C14.

Soccer Issue

Types of Italy, "Soccer" Issue, Overprinted in Black or Red

1934

31 A173 20c brn rose (Bk) 35.00 37.50
Never hinged 87.50
On cover 275.00
32 A174 25c green (R) 35.00 37.50
Never hinged 87.50
On cover 240.00
33 A174 50c violet (R) 150.00 19.00
Never hinged 340.00
On cover 200.00
34 A174 1.25 l gray bl (R) 35.00 *82.50*
Never hinged 87.50
On cover *350.00*
35 A175 5 l +2.50 l bl (R) 35.00 *210.00*
Never hinged 87.50
On cover —
Nos. 31-35 (5) 290.00 *386.50*
Set on overfranked philatelic cover 950.00

See Nos. C28-C31.

Same Overprint on Types of Medal of Valor Issue of Italy, in Red or Black

1935

36 A177 10c sl gray (R) 26.00 *27.50*
Never hinged 52.50
On cover 120.00
37 A178 15c brn (Bk) 26.00 *27.50*
Never hinged 52.50
On cover 120.00
38 A178 20c red org (Bk) 26.00 *27.50*
Never hinged 52.50
On cover 120.00
39 A177 25c dp grn (R) 26.00 *27.50*
Never hinged 52.50
On cover 120.00
40 A178 30c lake (Bk) 26.00 *27.50*
Never hinged 52.50
On cover 120.00
41 A178 50c ol grn (Bk) 26.00 *27.50*
Never hinged 52.50
On cover 120.00
42 A178 75c rose red (Bk) 26.00 *27.50*
Never hinged 52.50
On cover 200.00
43 A178 1.25 l dp bl (R) 26.00 *27.50*
Never hinged 52.50
On cover 250.00
44 A177 1.75 l + 1 l pur (R) 17.00 *27.50*
Never hinged 32.50
On cover —
45 A178 2.55 l + 2 l dk car (Bk) 17.00 *27.50*
Never hinged 32.50
On cover —
46 A178 2.75 l + 2 l org brn (Bk) 17.00 *27.50*
Never hinged 32.50
On cover —
Nos. 36-46 (11) 259.00 *302.50*
Set on overfranked philatelic cover 1,250.

See Nos. C32-C38, CE3-CE4.

Dante Alighieri Society Issue

Types of Italy, 1937, Overprinted in Blue or Red

1938 Wmk. 140 *Perf. 14*

47 A208 10c dk brn (Bl) 1.75 2.50
Never hinged 3.50
On cover 95.00
48 A208 15c pur (R) 1.75 2.50
Never hinged 3.50
On cover 90.00
49 A208 20c yel bis (Bl) 1.75 2.50
Never hinged 3.50
On cover 62.50
50 A208 25c myr grn (R) 1.75 2.50
Never hinged 3.50
On cover 75.00
51 A208 30c dp cl (Bl) 1.75 2.50
Never hinged 3.50
On cover 95.00
52 A208 50c sl grn (R) 1.75 4.50
Never hinged 3.50
On cover 62.50
53 A208 75c rose red (Bl) 1.75 4.50
Never hinged 3.50
On cover 125.00
54 A208 1.25 l dk bl (R) 1.75 4.50
Never hinged 3.50
On cover 200.00
55 A208 1.75 l + 1 l dp org (Bl) 2.50 *9.00*
Never hinged 5.00
On cover —
56 A208 2.55 l + 2 l ol brn (R) 2.50 *9.00*
Never hinged 5.00
On cover —
Nos. 47-56 (10) 19.00 44.00
Set on overfranked philatelic cover 275.00

Bimillenary of birth of Augustus Caesar (Octavianus), first Roman emperor.
See Nos. C39-C43.

Same Overprint of Type of Italy, 1937, in Red

1938

57 A222 1.25 l deep blue .85 *1.50*
Never hinged 1.65
On cover 60.00
58 A222 2.75 l + 2 l brown 1.00 *6.50*
Never hinged 2.00
On cover 200.00
Set on overfranked philatelic cover 55.00

600th anniversary of the death of Giotto di Bondone, Italian painter.

Statue of Roman Wolf — A1

Arms of Rhodes — A2

Dante's House, Rhodes A3

1940 Photo.

59 A1 5c lt brown .20 .55
Never hinged .40
On cover 90.00
60 A2 10c pale org .20 .55
Never hinged .40
On cover 67.50
61 A3 25c blue grn .55 1.00
Never hinged 1.10
On cover 60.00
62 A1 50c rose vio .55 1.00
Never hinged 1.10
On cover 60.00
63 A2 75c dull ver .55 1.40
Never hinged 1.10
On cover 110.00
64 A3 1.25 l dull blue .55 1.60
Never hinged 1.10
On cover 175.00
65 A2 2 l + 75c rose .55 9.50
Never hinged 1.10
Nos. 59-65,C44-C47 (11) 6.15 28.05
Nos. 59-65 on overfranked philatelic cover 67.50

Triennial Overseas Exposition, Naples.

AIR POST STAMPS

Ferrucci Issue

Types of Italian Air Post Stamps of 1930 Overprinted in Blue or Red Like Nos. 12-18

1930 Wmk. 140 *Perf. 14*

C1 A104 50c brn vio (Bl) 4.50 *9.50*
Never hinged 9.00
On cover 90.00
C2 A104 1 l dk bl (R) 4.50 *9.50*
Never hinged 9.00
On cover 150.00
C3 A104 5 l + 2 l dp car (Bl) 9.75 *27.50*
Never hinged 19.00
On cover —
Nos. C1-C3 (3) 18.75 *46.50*
Set on overfranked philatelic flown cover 175.00

Nos. C1-C3 were sold at Rhodes only.

Virgil Issue

Types of Italian Air Post Stamps of 1930 Overprinted in Red or Blue Like Nos. 3-11

1930 Photo.

C4 A106 50c dp grn (R) 1.25 *11.50*
Never hinged 2.50
On cover 82.50
C5 A106 1 l rose red (Bl) 1.25 *13.00*
Never hinged 2.50
On cover 140.00

Engr.
Unwmk.

C6 A106 7.70 l + 1.30 l dk brn (R) 2.50 *17.00*
Never hinged 5.00
On cover —
C7 A106 9 l + 2 l gray (R) 2.50 *25.00*
Never hinged 5.00
On cover —
Nos. C4-C7 (4) 7.50 *66.50*
Set on overfranked philatelic flown cover 175.00

Dante Alighieri Society Issue

Types of Italian Air Post Stamps of 1932 Overprinted Like Nos. 19-30

1932 Wmk. 140

C8 AP10 50c car rose .90 *2.10*
Never hinged 1.75
On cover 75.00
C9 AP11 1 l dp grn .90 *2.10*
Never hinged 1.75
On cover 82.50
C10 AP11 3 l dl vio .90 *2.25*
Never hinged 1.75
On cover 175.00
C11 AP11 5 l dp org .90 *2.25*
Never hinged 1.75
On cover 190.00
C12 AP10 7.70 l + 2 l ol brn 1.25 *6.50*
Never hinged 2.50
On cover —
C13 AP11 10 l + 2.50 l dk bl 1.25 *11.50*
Never hinged 2.50
On cover —
Nos. C8-C13 (6) 6.10 *26.70*
Set on overfranked philatelic flown cover 140.00

Leonardo da Vinci — AP12

1932 Photo. *Perf. 14½*

C14 AP12 100 l dp bl & grnsh gray 13.00 *65.00*
Never hinged 26.00
On flown cover *500.00*

Garibaldi Types of Italian Air Post Stamps of 1932 Overprinted in Red or Blue Like Nos. 12-18

1932

C15 AP13 50c deep green 22.50 *50.00*
Never hinged 45.00
On cover 125.00
C16 AP14 80c copper red 22.50 *50.00*
Never hinged 45.00
On cover 175.00

C17 AP13 1 l + 25c dl bl 22.50 *50.00*
Never hinged 45.00
On cover 240.00
C18 AP13 2 l + 50c red brn 22.50 *50.00*
Never hinged 45.00
On cover 275.00
C19 AP14 5 l + 1 l bluish sl 22.50 *50.00*
Never hinged 45.00
On cover —
Nos. C15-C19 (5) 112.50 *250.00*
Set on overfranked philatelic flown cover 275.00

See Nos. CE1-CE2.

Graf Zeppelin over Rhodes AP17

1933 ***Perf. 14***
C20 AP17 3 l olive brn 27.50 *87.50*
Never hinged 55.00
On cover 240.00
C21 AP17 5 l dp vio 27.50 *100.00*
Never hinged 55.00
On cover 425.00
C22 AP17 10 l dk green 27.50 *190.00*
Never hinged 55.00
On cover 500.00
C23 AP17 12 l dk blue 27.50 *210.00*
Never hinged 55.00
On cover 575.00
C24 AP17 15 l car rose 27.50 *210.00*
Never hinged 55.00
On cover 700.00
C25 AP17 20 l gray blk 27.50 *210.00*
Never hinged 55.00
On cover 700.00
Nos. C20-C25 (6) 165.00 *1,007.*
Set on overfranked philatelic flown cover 2,750.
Set of 6 flown covers 3,000.

Balbo Flight Issue

Types of Italian Air Post Stamps of 1933 Overprinted

1933 **Wmk. 140** ***Perf. 14***
C26 AP25 5.25 l + 19.75 l grn, red & bl gray 21.00 *72.50*
Never hinged 42.50
On cover 2,250.
C27 AP25 5.25 l + 44.75 l red, grn & bl gray 21.00 *72.50*
Never hinged 42.50
On cover 2,250.
Set on overfranked philatelic flown cover 4,250.

Soccer Issue

Types of Italian Air Post Stamps of 1934 Overprinted in Black or Red Like #31-35

1934
C28 AP32 50c brown (R) 4.00 *25.00*
Never hinged 9.25
On cover 240.00
C29 AP33 75c rose red) 4.00 *25.00*
Never hinged 9.25
On cover 300.00
C30 AP34 5 l + 2.50 l red org 11.00 *50.00*
Never hinged 27.50
On cover —
C31 AP35 10 l + 5 l grn (R) 11.00 *82.50*
Never hinged 27.50
On cover —
Nos. C28-C31 (4) 30.00 *182.50*
Set on overfranked philatelic flown cover 825.00

Types of Medal of Valor Issue of Italy Overprinted in Red or Black Like #31-35

1935
C32 AP36 25c dp grn 32.50 *45.00*
Never hinged 65.00
On cover 190.00
C33 AP36 50c blk brn (R) 32.50 *45.00*
Never hinged 65.00
On cover 175.00
C34 AP36 75c rose 32.50 *45.00*
Never hinged 65.00
On cover 190.00
C35 AP36 80c dk brn 32.50 *45.00*
Never hinged 65.00
On cover
C36 AP36 1 l + 50c ol grn 26.00 *45.00*
Never hinged 52.50
On cover —
C37 AP36 2 l + 1 l dp bl (R) 26.00 *45.00*
Never hinged 52.50
On cover

C38 AP40 3 l + 2 l vio (R) 26.00 *45.00*
Never hinged 52.50
On cover
Nos. C32-C38 (7) 208.00 *315.00*
Nos. C32-C38, CE3-CE4 on overfranked philatelic flown cover 825.00

Types of Italy Air Post Stamps, 1937, Overprinted in Blue or Red Like #47-56

1938 **Wmk. 140** ***Perf. 14***
C39 AP51 25c dl gray vio (R) 1.90 2.25
Never hinged 3.75
On cover 125.00
C40 AP51 50c grn (R) 1.90 2.25
Never hinged 3.75
On cover 75.00
C41 AP51 80c brt bl (R) 1.90 7.25
Never hinged 3.75
On cover 140.00
C42 AP51 1 l + 1 l rose lake 2.75 10.50
Never hinged 5.50
On cover —
C43 AP51 5 l + 1 l rose red 5.00 *22.50*
Never hinged 10.00
On cover —
Nos. C39-C43 (5) 13.45 44.75
Set on overfranked philatelic flown cover 300.00

Bimillenary of the birth of Augustus Caesar (Octavianus).

Statues of Stag and Roman Wolf AP18

Plane over Government Palace, Rhodes — AP19

1940 **Photo.**
C44 AP18 50c olive blk .75 1.60
Never hinged 1.50
On cover 110.00
C45 AP19 1 l dk vio .75 1.60
Never hinged 1.50
On cover 125.00
C46 AP18 2 l + 75c dk bl .75 3.25
Never hinged 1.50
On cover —
C47 AP19 5 l + 2.50 l cop brn .75 6.00
Never hinged 1.50
On cover —
Nos. C44-C47 (4) 3.00 12.45
Set on overfranked philatelic flown cover 90.00

Triennial Overseas Exposition, Naples.

AIR POST SPECIAL DELIVERY STAMPS

Type of Italian Garibaldi Air Post Special Delivery Stamps Overprinted in Blue or Ocher Like Nos. 12-18

1932 **Wmk. 140** ***Perf. 14***
CE1 APSD1 2.25 l + 1 l bl & rose & (Bl) 30.00 *72.50*
Never hinged 60.00
On cover —
CE2 APSD1 4.50 l + 1.50 l ocher & gray (O) 30.00 *72.50*
Never hinged 60.00
On cover —

Type of Medal of Valor Issue of Italy, Overprinted in Black Like Nos. 31-35

1935
CE3 APSD4 2 l + 1.25 l dp bl 26.00 *45.00*
Never hinged 52.50
CE4 APSD4 4.50 l + 2 l grn 26.00 *45.00*
Never hinged 52.50

ISSUES FOR THE INDIVIDUAL ISLANDS

Italian Stamps of 1901-20 Overprinted with Names of Various Islands as

a

b

c

The 1912-22 issues of each island have type "a" overprint in black on all values except 15c (type A58) and 20c on 15c, which have type "b" overprint in violet.

The 1930-32 Ferruci and Garibaldi issues are types of the Italian issues overprinted type "c."

CALCHI

Overprinted "Karki" in Black or Violet

1912-22 **Wmk. 140** ***Perf. 13½, 14***
1 A43 2c orange brn 4.25 4.00
Never hinged 8.50
On cover 67.50
a. Double overprint 225.00
2 A48 5c green 1.40 *4.00*
Never hinged 2.75
On cover 35.00
3 A48 10c claret .35 *4.00*
Never hinged .70
On cover 35.00
4 A48 15c slate ('22) 2.50 *25.00*
Never hinged 5.00
On cover 300.00
a. Double overprint 225.00
5 A50 20c brn org ('21) 2.50 *22.50*
Never hinged 5.00
On cover 240.00
6 A49 25c blue .35 *4.00*
Never hinged .70
On cover 70.00
7 A49 40c brown .35 *4.00*
Never hinged .70
On cover 140.00
8 A49 50c violet .35 *7.25*
Never hinged .70
On cover 175.00

Unwmk.

9 A58 15c slate (V) 19.00 8.25
Never hinged 37.50
On cover 110.00
10 A50 20c brn org ('17) 80.00 *100.00*
Never hinged 160.00
On cover 450.00
Nos. 1-10 (10) 111.05 *183.00*
Nos. 1-3, 6-9 on overfranked philatelic cover 82.50

No. 9 Surcharged

1916 ***Perf. 13½***
11 A58 20c on 15c slate 1.10 *14.50*
Never hinged 2.25

Ferrucci Issue

Overprinted in Red or Blue

1930 **Wmk. 140** ***Perf. 14***
12 A102 20c vio (R) 1.25 *2.50*
Never hinged 2.50
On cover 82.50
13 A103 25c dk grn (R) 1.25 *2.50*
Never hinged 2.50
On cover 100.00
14 A103 50c blk (R) 1.25 *4.25*
Never hinged 2.50
On cover 75.00
15 A103 1.25 l dp bl (R) 1.25 *4.25*
Never hinged 2.50
On cover 175.00
16 A104 5 l + 2 l dp car (Bl) 1.90 *7.25*
Never hinged 3.75
On cover —
Nos. 12-16 (5) 6.90 *20.75*
Set on overfranked philatelic cover 82.50

Garibaldi Issue

Overprinted "CARCHI" in Red or Blue

1932
17 A138 10c brown 5.25 *9.50*
Never hinged 10.50
On cover 120.00
18 A138 20c red brn (Bl) 5.25 *9.50*
Never hinged 10.50
On cover 82.50
19 A138 25c dp grn 5.25 *9.50*
Never hinged 10.50
On cover 82.50
20 A138 30c bluish sl 5.25 *9.50*
Never hinged 10.50
On cover 110.00
21 A138 50c red vio (Bl) 5.25 *9.50*
Never hinged 10.50
On cover 70.00
22 A141 75c cop red (Bl) 5.25 *9.50*
Never hinged 10.50
On cover 200.00
23 A141 1.25 l dl bl 5.25 *9.50*
Never hinged 10.50
On cover 275.00
24 A141 1.75 l + 25c brn 5.25 *9.50*
Never hinged 10.50
On cover —
25 A144 2.55 l + 50c org (Bl) 5.25 *9.50*
Never hinged 10.50
On cover —
26 A145 5 l + 1 l dl vio 5.25 *9.50*
Never hinged 10.50
On cover —
Nos. 17-26 (10) 52.50 *95.00*
Set on overfranked philatelic cover 325.00

CALINO

Overprinted "Calimno" in Black or Violet

1912-21 **Wmk. 140** ***Perf. 13½, 14***
1 A43 2c orange brn 4.25 4.00
Never hinged 8.50
On cover 67.50
2 A48 5c green 1.25 *4.00*
Never hinged 2.50
On cover 35.00
3 A48 10c claret .35 *4.00*
Never hinged .70
On cover 35.00
4 A48 15c slate ('21) 2.25 *25.00*
Never hinged 5.00
On cover 275.00
5 A50 20c brn org ('21) 2.25 *25.00*
Never hinged 5.00
On cover 200.00
6 A49 25c blue 3.75 *4.00*
Never hinged 7.25
On cover 67.50
7 A49 40c brown .35 *4.00*
Never hinged .70
On cover 140.00
8 A49 50c violet .35 *7.25*
Never hinged .70
On cover 175.00

Unwmk.

9 A58 15c slate (V) 16.00 8.25
Never hinged 32.50
On cover 110.00
10 A50 20c brn org ('17) 62.50 *100.00*
Never hinged 120.00
On cover 275.00
Nos. 1-10 (10) 93.30 *185.50*
Nos. 1-3, 6-9 on overfranked philatelic cover 82.50

No. 9 Surcharged Like Calchi No. 11

1916 ***Perf. 13½***
11 A58 20c on 15c slate 8.75 *17.00*
Never hinged 17.50

Ferrucci Issue

Overprinted in Red or Blue

1930 **Wmk. 140** ***Perf. 14***
12 A102 20c violet (R) 1.25 *2.50*
Never hinged 2.50
On cover 82.50
13 A103 25c dk green (R) 1.25 *2.50*
Never hinged 2.50
On cover 100.00
14 A102 50c black (R) 1.25 *4.25*
Never hinged 2.50
On cover 75.00
15 A102 1.25 l dp bl (R) 1.25 *4.25*
Never hinged 2.50
On cover 175.00
16 A104 5 l + 2 l dp car (Bl) 1.90 *7.25*
Never hinged 3.75
On cover —
Nos. 12-16 (5) 6.90 *20.75*
Set on overfranked philatelic cover 50.00

Garibaldi Issue

Overprinted in Red or Blue

1932
17 A138 10c brown 5.25 *9.50*
Never hinged 9.50
On cover 120.00
18 A138 20c red brn (Bl) 5.25 *9.50*
Never hinged 9.50
On cover 82.50
19 A138 25c dp grn 5.25 *9.50*
Never hinged 10.50
On cover 82.50

20 A138 30c bluish sl 5.25 *9.50*
Never hinged 10.50
On cover 110.00
21 A138 50c red vio (Bl) 5.25 *9.50*
Never hinged 10.50
On cover 67.50
22 A141 75c cop red (Bl) 5.25 *9.50*
Never hinged 10.50
On cover 200.00
23 A141 1.25 l dull blue 5.25 *9.50*
Never hinged 10.50
On cover 275.00
24 A141 1.75 l + 25c brn 5.25 *9.50*
Never hinged 10.50
On cover —
25 A144 2.55 l + 50c org (Bl) 5.25 *9.50*
Never hinged 9.50
On cover —
26 A145 5 l + 1 l dl vio 5.25 *9.50*
Never hinged 9.50
On cover —
Nos. 17-26 (10) 52.50 *95.00*
Set on overfranked philatelic cover 325.00

CASO

Overprinted "Caso" in Black or Violet

1912-21 Wmk. 140 *Perf. 13½, 14*

1 A43 2c orange brn 4.25 4.00
Never hinged 8.50
On cover 70.00
2 A48 5c green 1.40 *4.00*
Never hinged 2.75
On cover 42.50
3 A48 10c claret .35 *4.00*
Never hinged .70
On cover 42.50
4 A48 15c slate ('21) 2.25 *25.00*
Never hinged 5.00
On cover 275.00
5 A50 20c brn org ('20) 1.75 *19.00*
Never hinged 3.50
On cover 225.00
6 A49 25c blue .35 *4.00*
Never hinged .70
On cover 67.50
7 A49 40c brown .35 *4.00*
Never hinged .70
On cover 140.00
8 A49 50c violet .35 *7.25*
Never hinged .70
On cover 175.00

Unwmk.

9 A58 15c slate (V) 19.00 *8.25*
Never hinged 37.50
On cover 110.00
10 A50 20c brn org ('17) 80.00 *100.00*
Never hinged 160.00
On cover 325.00
Nos. 1-10 (10) 110.05 *179.50*
Nos. 1-3, 6-9 on overfranked philatelic cover 82.50

No. 9 Surcharged Like Calchi No. 11

1916 *Perf. 13½*

11 A58 20c on 15c slate .55 *11.50*
Never hinged 1.10
On cover 95.00

Ferrucci Issue

Overprinted in Red or Blue

1930 Wmk. 140 *Perf. 14*

12 A102 20c violet (R) 1.25 *2.50*
Never hinged 2.50
On cover 82.50
13 A103 25c dk green (R) 1.25 *2.50*
Never hinged 2.50
On cover 100.00
14 A102 50c black (R) 1.25 *4.25*
Never hinged 2.50
On cover 75.00
15 A102 1.25 l dp bl (R) 1.25 *4.25*
Never hinged 2.50
On cover 175.00
16 A104 5 l + 2 l dp car (Bl) 1.90 *7.25*
Never hinged 3.75
On cover —
Nos. 12-16 (5) 6.90 *20.75*
Set on overfranked philatelic cover 82.50

Garibaldi Issue

Overprinted in Red or Blue

1932

17 A138 10c brown 5.25 *9.50*
Never hinged 10.50
On cover 120.00
18 A138 20c red brn (Bl) 5.25 *9.50*
Never hinged 10.50
On cover 82.50
19 A138 25c dp grn 5.25 *9.50*
Never hinged 10.50
On cover 82.50
20 A138 30c bluish sl 5.25 *9.50*
Never hinged 10.50
On cover 110.00
21 A138 50c red vio (Bl) 5.25 *9.50*
Never hinged 10.50
On cover 67.50
22 A141 75c cop red (Bl) 5.25 *9.50*
Never hinged 10.50
On cover 190.00
23 A141 1.25 l dull blue 5.25 *9.50*
Never hinged 10.50
On cover 275.00
24 A141 1.75 l + 25c brn 5.25 *9.50*
Never hinged 10.50
On cover —
25 A144 2.55 l + 50c org (Bl) 5.25 *9.50*
Never hinged 10.50
On cover —
26 A145 5 l + 1 l dl vio 5.25 *9.50*
Never hinged 10.50
On cover —
Nos. 17-26 (10) 52.50 *95.00*
Set on overfranked philatelic cover 325.00

COO

(Cos, Kos)

Overprinted "Cos" in Black or Violet

1912-22 Wmk. 140 *Perf. 13½, 14*

1 A43 2c orange brn 4.25 4.00
Never hinged 8.50
On cover 67.50
2 A48 5c green 42.50 4.00
Never hinged 80.00
On cover 35.00
3 A48 10c claret 1.90 *4.00*
Never hinged 3.75
On cover 35.00
4 A48 15c slate ('22) 2.50 *32.50*
Never hinged 5.00
On cover 275.00
5 A50 20c brn org ('21) 1.75 *19.00*
Never hinged 3.50
On cover 200.00
6 A49 25c blue 16.00 4.00
Never hinged 32.50
On cover 70.00
7 A49 40c brown .35 *4.00*
Never hinged .70
On cover 150.00
8 A49 50c violet .35 *7.25*
Never hinged .70
On cover 175.00

Unwmk.

9 A58 15c slate (V) 19.00 8.25
Never hinged 37.50
On cover 110.00
10 A50 20c brn org ('17) 25.00 *100.00*
Never hinged 50.00
On cover 275.00
Nos. 1-10 (10) 113.60 *187.00*
Nos. 1-3, 6-9 on overfranked philatelic cover 82.50

No. 9 Surcharged Like Calchi No. 11

1916 *Perf. 13½*

11 A58 20c on 15c slate 8.75 *19.00*
Never hinged 17.50
On cover 82.50

Ferrucci Issue

Overprinted in Red or Blue

1930 Wmk. 140 *Perf. 14*

12 A102 20c violet (R) 1.25 *2.50*
Never hinged 2.50
On cover 82.50
13 A103 25c dk green (R) 1.25 *2.50*
Never hinged 2.50
On cover 100.00
14 A102 50c black (R) 1.25 *4.25*
Never hinged 2.50
On cover 75.00
15 A102 1.25 l dp bl (R) 1.25 *4.25*
Never hinged 2.50
On cover 175.00
16 A104 5 l + 2 l dp car (Bl) 1.90 7.25
Never hinged 3.75
On cover —
Nos. 12-16 (5) 6.90 *20.75*
Set on overfranked philatelic cover 82.50

Garibaldi Issue

Overprinted in Red or Blue

1932

17 A138 10c brown 5.25 *9.50*
Never hinged 10.50
On cover 120.00
18 A138 20c red brn (Bl) 5.25 *9.50*
Never hinged 10.50
On cover 82.50
19 A138 25c dp grn 5.25 *9.50*
Never hinged 10.50
On cover 82.50
20 A138 30c bluish sl 5.25 *9.50*
Never hinged 10.50
On cover 110.00
21 A138 50c red vio (Bl) 5.25 *9.50*
Never hinged 10.50
On cover 70.00
22 A141 75c cop red (Bl) 5.25 *9.50*
Never hinged 10.50
On cover 200.00
23 A141 1.25 l dull blue 5.25 *9.50*
Never hinged 10.50
On cover 275.00
24 A141 1.75 l + 25c brn 5.25 *9.50*
Never hinged 10.50
On cover —
25 A144 2.55 l + 50c org (Bl) 5.25 *9.50*
Never hinged 10.50
On cover —
26 A145 5 l + 1 l dl vio 5.25 *9.50*
Never hinged 10.50
On cover —
Nos. 17-26 (10) 52.50 *95.00*
Set on overfranked philatelic cover 325.00

LERO

Overprinted "Leros" in Black or Violet

1912-22 Wmk. 140 *Perf. 13½, 14*

1 A43 2c orange brn 4.25 4.00
Never hinged 8.50
On cover 67.50
2 A48 5c green 3.00 *4.00*
Never hinged 6.00
On cover 35.00
3 A48 10c claret .60 *4.00*
Never hinged 1.25
On cover 35.00
4 A48 15c slate ('22) 2.50 *21.00*
Never hinged 5.00
On cover 225.00
5 A50 20c brn org ('21) 100.00 67.50
Never hinged 200.00
On cover 250.00
6 A49 25c blue 17.50 4.00
Never hinged 35.00
On cover 70.00
7 A49 40c brown 2.50 *4.00*
Never hinged 5.00
On cover 150.00
8 A49 50c violet .35 *7.25*
Never hinged .70
On cover 175.00

Unwmk.

9 A58 15c slate (V) 32.50 8.25
Never hinged 65.00
On cover 110.00
10 A50 20c brn org ('17) 25.00 *100.00*
Never hinged 50.00
On cover 275.00
Nos. 1-10 (10) 188.20 *224.00*
Nos. 1-3, 6-9 on overfranked philatelic cover 82.50

No. 9 Surcharged Like Calchi No. 11

1916 *Perf. 13½*

11 A58 20c on 15c slate 8.75 *17.00*
Never hinged 17.50
On cover 82.50

Ferrucci Issue

Overprinted in Red or Blue

1930 *Perf. 14*

12 A102 20c violet (R) 1.25 *2.50*
Never hinged 2.50
On cover 82.50
13 A103 25c dk green (R) 1.25 *2.50*
Never hinged 2.50
On cover 100.00
14 A102 50c black (R) 1.25 *4.25*
Never hinged 2.50
On cover 75.00
15 A102 1.25 l dp bl (R) 1.25 *4.25*
Never hinged 2.50
On cover 175.00
16 A104 5 l + 2 l dp car (Bl) 1.90 *7.25*
Never hinged 3.75
On cover —
Nos. 12-16 (5) 6.90 *20.75*
Set on overfranked philatelic cover 82.50

Garibaldi Issue

Overprinted in Red or Blue

1932

17 A138 10c brown 5.25 *9.50*
Never hinged 9.50
On cover 120.00
18 A138 20c red brn (Bl) 5.25 *9.50*
Never hinged 9.50
On cover 82.50
19 A138 25c dp grn 5.25 *9.50*
Never hinged 9.50
On cover 82.50
20 A138 30c bluish sl 5.25 *9.50*
Never hinged 10.50
On cover 110.00
21 A138 50c red vio (Bl) 5.25 *9.50*
Never hinged 10.50
On cover 70.00
22 A141 75c cop red (Bl) 5.25 *9.50*
Never hinged 10.50
On cover 190.00
23 A141 1.25 l dull blue 5.25 *9.50*
Never hinged 10.50
On cover 275.00
24 A141 1.75 l + 25c brn 5.25 *9.50*
Never hinged 10.50
On cover —
25 A144 2.55 l + 50c org (Bl) 5.25 *9.50*
Never hinged 10.50
On cover —
26 A145 5 l + 1 l dl vio 5.25 *9.50*
Never hinged 9.50
On cover —
Nos. 17-26 (10) 52.50 *95.00*
Set on overfranked philatelic cover 325.00

LISSO

Overprinted "Lipso" in Black or Violet

1912-22 Wmk. 140 *Perf. 13½, 14*

1 A43 2c orange brn 4.25 *4.00*
Never hinged 8.50
On cover 67.50
2 A48 5c green 1.60 *4.00*
Never hinged 3.25
On cover 35.00
3 A48 10c claret .75 *4.00*
Never hinged 1.50
On cover 35.00
4 A48 15c slate ('22) 2.50 *21.00*
Never hinged 5.00
On cover 200.00
5 A50 20c brn org ('21) 2.50 *25.00*
Never hinged 5.00
On cover 300.00
6 A49 25c blue .35 *4.00*
Never hinged .70
On cover 70.00
7 A49 40c brown 1.10 *4.00*
Never hinged 2.25
On cover 175.00
8 A49 50c violet .35 *7.25*
Never hinged .70
On cover 175.00

Unwmk.

9 A58 15c slate (V) 17.50 8.25
Never hinged 35.00
On cover 110.00
10 A50 20c brn org ('17) 40.00 *100.00*
Never hinged 75.00
On cover 300.00
Nos. 1-10 (10) 70.90 *181.50*
Nos. 1-3, 6-9 on overfranked philatelic cover 82.50

No. 9 Surcharged Like Calchi No. 11

1916 *Perf. 13½*

11 A58 20c on 15c slate .65 *15.00*
Never hinged 1.40
On cover 92.50

Ferrucci Issue

Overprinted in Red or Blue

1930 Wmk. 140 *Perf. 14*

12 A102 20c violet (R) 1.25 *2.50*
Never hinged 2.50
On cover 82.50
13 A103 25c dk green (R) 1.25 *2.50*
Never hinged 2.50
On cover 100.00
14 A102 50c black (R) 1.25 *4.25*
Never hinged 2.50
On cover 75.00
15 A102 1.25 l dp bl (R) 1.25 *4.25*
Never hinged 2.50
On cover 175.00
16 A104 5 l + 2 l dp car (Bl) 1.90 *7.25*
Never hinged 3.75
On cover —
Nos. 12-16 (5) 6.90 *20.75*
Set on overfranked philatelic cover 82.50

Garibaldi Issue

Overprinted "LIPSO" in Red or Blue

1932

17 A138 10c brown 5.25 *9.50*
Never hinged 10.50
On cover 120.00
18 A138 20c red brn (Bl) 5.25 *9.50*
Never hinged 10.50
On cover 82.50
19 A138 25c dp grn 5.25 *9.50*
Never hinged 10.50
On cover 82.50
20 A138 30c bluish sl 5.25 *9.50*
Never hinged 10.50
On cover 110.00
21 A138 50c red vio (Bl) 5.25 *9.50*
Never hinged 10.50
On cover 70.00
22 A141 75c cop red (Bl) 5.25 *9.50*
Never hinged 10.50
On cover 190.00
23 A141 1.25 l dull blue 5.25 *9.50*
Never hinged 10.50
On cover 275.00
24 A141 1.75 l + 25c brn 5.25 *9.50*
Never hinged 10.50
On cover —
25 A144 2.55 l + 50c org (Bl) 5.25 *9.50*
Never hinged 10.50
On cover —
26 A145 5 l + 1 l dl vio 5.25 *9.50*
Never hinged 10.50
On cover —
Nos. 17-26 (10) 52.50 *95.00*
Set on overfranked philatelic cover 325.00

NISIRO

Overprinted "Nisiros" in Black or Violet

1912-22 Wmk. 140 *Perf. 13½, 14*

1 A43 2c orange brn 4.25 *4.00*
Never hinged 8.50
On cover 82.50
2 A48 5c green 1.40 *4.00*
Never hinged 2.75
On cover 45.00

3 A48 10c claret .35 4.00
Never hinged .70
On cover 45.00
4 A48 15c slate ('22) 12.00 22.50
Never hinged 25.00
On cover 225.00
5 A50 20c brn org ('21) 62.50 77.50
Never hinged 125.00
On cover 300.00
6 A49 25c blue 1.25 4.00
Never hinged 2.50
On cover 67.50
7 A49 40c brown .35 4.00
Never hinged .70
On cover 160.00
8 A49 50c violet 2.50 7.25
Never hinged 5.00
On cover 175.00

Unwmk.

9 A58 15c slate (V) 16.00 8.25
Never hinged 32.50
On cover 30.00
10 A50 20c brn org ('17) 80.00 100.00
Never hinged 160.00
On cover 125.00
Nos. 1-10 (10) 180.60 *235.50*
Nos. 1-3, 6-9 on over-franked philatelic cover 82.50

No. 9 Surcharged Like Calchi No. 11

1916 ***Perf. 13½***
11 A58 20c on 15c slate .65 15.00
Never hinged 1.40
On cover 110.00

Ferrucci Issue

Overprinted in Red or Blue

1930 Wmk. 140 *Perf. 14*
12 A102 20c violet (R) 1.25 2.50
Never hinged 2.50
On cover 82.50
13 A103 25c dk green (R) 1.25 2.50
Never hinged 2.50
On cover 100.00
14 A102 50c black (R) 1.25 4.25
Never hinged 2.50
On cover 75.00
15 A102 1.25 l dp bl (R) 1.25 4.25
Never hinged 2.50
On cover 175.00
16 A104 5 l + 2 l dp car (Bl) 1.90 7.25
Never hinged 3.75
On cover —
Nos. 12-16 (5) 6.90 *20.75*
Set on overfranked philatelic cover 82.50

Garibaldi Issue

Overprinted in Red or Blue

1932
17 A138 10c brown 5.25 9.50
Never hinged 10.50
On cover 120.00
18 A138 20c red brn (Bl) 5.25 9.50
Never hinged 10.50
On cover 82.50
19 A138 25c dp grn 5.25 9.50
Never hinged 10.50
On cover 82.50
20 A138 30c bluish sl 5.25 9.50
Never hinged 10.50
On cover 110.00
21 A138 50c red vio (Bl) 5.25 9.50
Never hinged 10.50
On cover 70.00
22 A141 75c cop red (Bl) 5.25 9.50
Never hinged 10.50
On cover 190.00
23 A141 1.25 l dull blue 5.25 9.50
Never hinged 10.50
On cover 275.00
24 A141 1.75 l + 25c brn 5.25 9.50
Never hinged 10.50
On cover —
25 A144 2.55 l + 50c org (Bl) 5.25 9.50
Never hinged 10.50
On cover —
26 A145 5 l + 1 l dl vio 5.25 9.50
Never hinged 10.50
On cover —
Nos. 17-26 (10) 52.50 *95.00*
Set on overfranked philatelic cover 325.00

PATMO

Overprinted "Patmos" in Black or Violet

1912-22 Wmk. 140 *Perf. 13½, 14*
1 A43 2c orange brn 4.25 4.00
Never hinged 8.50
On cover 67.50
2 A48 5c green 1.40 4.00
Never hinged 2.75
On cover 37.50
3 A48 10c claret 1.25 4.00
Never hinged 2.50
On cover 37.50
4 A48 15c slate ('22) 2.50 25.00
Never hinged 5.00
On cover 225.00
5 A50 20c brn org ('21) 100.00 100.00
Never hinged 200.00
On cover 325.00
6 A49 25c blue .45 4.00
Never hinged .90
On cover 70.00
7 A49 40c brown 2.25 4.00
Never hinged 4.50
On cover 160.00
8 A49 50c violet .35 4.00
Never hinged .70
On cover 175.00

Unwmk.

9 A58 15c slate (V) 16.00 8.25
Never hinged 32.50
On cover 110.00
10 A50 20c brn org ('17) 40.00 100.00
Never hinged 75.00
On cover 300.00
Nos. 1-10 (10) 168.45 *257.25*
Nos. 1-3, 6-9 on over-franked philatelic cover 82.50

No. 9 Surcharged Like Calchi No. 11

1916 ***Perf. 13½***
11 A58 20c on 15c slate 8.75 19.00
Never hinged 17.50
On cover 110.00

Ferrucci Issue

Overprinted in Red or Blue

1930 Wmk. 140 *Perf. 14*
12 A102 20c violet (R) 1.25 2.50
Never hinged 2.50
On cover 82.50
13 A103 25c dk green (R) 1.25 2.50
Never hinged 2.50
On cover 100.00
14 A102 50c black (R) 1.25 4.25
Never hinged 2.50
On cover 75.00
15 A102 1.25 l dp bl (R) 1.25 4.25
Never hinged 2.50
On cover 175.00
16 A104 5 l + 2 l dp car (Bl) 1.90 7.25
Never hinged 3.75
On cover —
Nos. 12-16 (5) 6.90 *20.75*
Set on overfranked philatelic cover 82.50

Garibaldi Issue

Overprinted in Red or Blue

1932
17 A138 10c brown 5.25 9.50
Never hinged 10.50
On cover 120.00
18 A138 20c red brn (Bl) 5.25 9.50
Never hinged 10.50
On cover 82.50
19 A138 25c dp grn 5.25 9.50
Never hinged 10.50
On cover 82.50
20 A138 30c bluish sl 5.25 9.50
Never hinged 10.50
On cover 110.00
21 A138 50c red vio (Bl) 5.25 9.50
Never hinged 10.50
On cover 70.00
22 A141 75c cop red (Bl) 5.25 9.50
Never hinged 10.50
On cover 190.00
23 A141 1.25 l dull blue 5.25 9.50
Never hinged 10.50
On cover 275.00
24 A141 1.75 l + 25c brn 5.25 9.50
Never hinged 10.50
On cover —
25 A144 2.55 l + 50c org (Bl) 5.25 9.50
Never hinged 10.50
On cover —
26 A145 5 l + 1 l dl vio 5.25 9.50
Never hinged 10.50
On cover —
Nos. 17-26 (10) 52.50 *95.00*
Set on overfranked philatelic cover 325.00

PISCOPI

Overprinted "Piscopi" in Black or Violet

1912-21 Wmk. 140 *Perf. 13½, 14*
1 A43 2c orange brn 4.25 4.00
Never hinged 8.50
On cover 82.50
2 A48 5c green 1.40 4.00
Never hinged 2.75
On cover 37.50
3 A48 10c claret .35 4.00
Never hinged .70
On cover 37.50
4 A48 15c slate ('21) 8.75 25.00
Never hinged 17.50
On cover 240.00
5 A50 20c brn org ('21) 25.00 35.00
Never hinged 50.00
On cover 325.00
6 A49 25c blue .35 4.00
Never hinged .70
On cover 70.00
7 A49 40c brown .35 4.00
Never hinged .70
On cover 160.00
8 A49 50c violet .35 7.25
Never hinged .70
On cover 175.00

Unwmk.

9 A58 15c slate (V) 19.00 8.25
Never hinged 37.50
On cover 110.00
10 A50 20c brn org ('17) 40.00 100.00
Never hinged 75.00
On cover 300.00
Nos. 1-10 (10) 99.80 *195.50*
Nos. 1-3, 6-9 on over-franked philatelic cover 82.50

No. 9 Surcharged Like Calchi No. 11

1916 ***Perf. 13½***
11 A58 20c on 15c slate .65 14.50
Never hinged 1.40
On cover 110.00

Ferrucci Issue

Overprinted in Red or Blue

1930 Wmk. 140 *Perf. 14*
12 A102 20c violet (R) 1.25 2.50
Never hinged 2.50
On cover 82.50
13 A103 25c dk green (R) 1.25 2.50
Never hinged 2.50
On cover 100.00
14 A102 50c black (R) 1.25 4.25
Never hinged 2.50
On cover 75.00
15 A102 1.25 l dp bl (R) 1.10 4.25
Never hinged 2.50
On cover 175.00
16 A104 5 l + 2 l dp car (Bl) 1.90 7.25
Never hinged 3.75
On cover —
Nos. 12-16 (5) 6.75 *20.75*
Set on overfranked philatelic cover 82.50

Garibaldi Issue

Overprinted in Red or Blue

1932
17 A138 10c brown 5.25 9.50
Never hinged 10.50
On cover 120.00
18 A138 20c red brn (Bl) 5.25 9.50
Never hinged 10.50
On cover 82.50
19 A138 25c dp grn 5.25 9.50
Never hinged 10.50
On cover 82.50
20 A138 30c bluish sl 5.25 9.50
Never hinged 10.50
On cover 110.00
21 A138 50c red vio (Bl) 5.25 9.50
Never hinged 10.50
On cover 70.00
22 A141 75c cop red (Bl) 5.25 9.50
Never hinged 10.50
On cover 190.00
23 A141 1.25 l dull blue 5.25 9.50
Never hinged 10.50
On cover 275.00
24 A141 1.75 l + 25c brn 5.25 9.50
Never hinged 10.50
On cover —
25 A144 2.55 l + 50c org (Bl) 5.25 9.50
Never hinged 10.50
On cover —
26 A145 5 l + 1 l dl vio 5.25 9.50
Never hinged 10.50
On cover —
Nos. 17-26 (10) 52.50 *95.00*
Set on overfranked philatelic cover 325.00

RHODES

(Rodi)

Overprinted "Rodi" in Black or Violet

1912-24 Wmk. 140 *Perf. 13½, 14*
1 A43 2c org brn .35 4.00
Never hinged .70
On cover 47.50
2 A48 5c green 1.25 4.00
Never hinged 2.50
On cover 32.50
a. Double overprint 175.00
3 A48 10c claret .35 4.00
Never hinged .70
On cover 32.50
4 A48 15c slate ('21) 75.00 35.00
Never hinged 150.00
On cover 275.00
5 A45 20c org ('16) 1.75 3.75
Never hinged 3.50
On cover 110.00
6 A50 20c brn org ('19) 4.00 9.50
Never hinged 8.00
On cover 160.00
a. Double overprint 60.00
7 A49 25c blue 1.25 4.00
Never hinged 2.50
On cover 67.50
8 A49 40c brown 1.90 4.00
Never hinged 3.75
On cover 150.00
9 A49 50c violet .35 6.50
Never hinged .70
On cover 175.00
10 A49 85c red brn ('22) 35.00 57.50
Never hinged 72.50
On cover 240.00
11 A46 1 l brn & grn ('24) 1.75
Never hinged 3.50

No. 11 was not regularly issued.

Unwmk.

12 A58 15c slate (V) 21.00 8.25
Never hinged 42.50
On cover 110.00
13 A50 20c brn org ('17) 87.50 82.50
Never hinged 175.00
On cover 300.00
Nos. 1-13 (13) 231.45 223.00
Nos. 1-3, 7-9, 12 on over-franked philatelic cover *250.00*

No. 12 Surcharged Like Calchi No. 11

1916 ***Perf. 13½***
14 A58 20c on 15c slate 65.00 77.50
Never hinged 130.00
On cover 175.00

Windmill, Rhodes — A1

Medieval Galley — A2

Christian Knight — A3

Crusader Kneeling in Prayer — A4

Crusader's Tomb — A5

No Imprint

1929 Unwmk. Litho. *Perf. 11*
15 A1 5c magenta 3.00 .90
Never hinged 7.50
On cover 27.50
16 A2 10c olive brn 3.00 .75
Never hinged 7.50
On cover 10.00
17 A3 20c rose red 3.00 .20
Never hinged 7.50
On cover 7.00
18 A3 25c green 3.00 .20
Never hinged 7.50
On cover 7.00
19 A4 30c dk blue 3.00 .35
Never hinged 7.50
On cover 20.00
20 A5 50c dk brown 3.00 .20
Never hinged 7.50
On cover 5.00
21 A5 1.25 l dk blue 3.00 .90
Never hinged 7.50
On cover 27.50
22 A4 5 l magenta 32.50 45.00
Never hinged 82.50
On cover 500.00
23 A4 10 l olive brn 100.00 140.00
Never hinged 225.00
On cover 1,700.
Nos. 15-23 (9) 153.50 *188.50*
Set on overfranked philatelic cover *925.00*

Visit of the King and Queen of Italy to the Aegean Islands. The stamps are inscribed "Rodi" but were available for use in all the Aegean Islands.

Nos. 15-23 and C1-C4 were used in eastern Crete in 1941-42 with Greek postmarks.

See Nos. 55-63.

Ferrucci Issue

Overprinted in Red or Blue

1930 Wmk. 140 *Perf. 14*
24 A102 20c violet (R) 1.25 2.50
Never hinged 2.50
On cover 82.50
25 A103 25c dk green (R) 1.25 2.50
Never hinged 2.50
On cover 100.00
26 A103 50c black (R) 1.25 4.25
Never hinged 2.50
On cover 75.00
27 A103 1.25 l dp blue (R) 1.25 4.25
Never hinged 2.50
On cover 175.00

28 A104 5 l + 2 l dp car (Bl) 1.90 *7.25*
Never hinged 3.75
On cover —
Nos. 24-28 (5) 6.90 *20.75*
Set on overfranked philatelic cover *82.50*

Hydrological Congress Issue

Rhodes Issue of 1929 Overprinted

1930 Unwmk. *Perf. 11*

29 A1 5c magenta 8.75 *8.25*
Never hinged 17.50
On cover 200.00
30 A2 10c olive brn 10.50 *8.25*
Never hinged 21.00
On cover 175.00
31 A3 20c rose red 17.50 *7.25*
Never hinged 35.00
On cover 175.00
32 A3 25c green 22.50 7.25
Never hinged 45.00
On cover 190.00
33 A4 30c dk blue 10.50 *8.25*
Never hinged 21.00
On cover 200.00
34 A5 50c dk brown 400.00 27.50
Never hinged 800.00
On cover 175.00
35 A5 1.25 l dk blue 300.00 42.50
Never hinged 600.00
On cover 300.00
36 A4 5 l magenta 160.00 *225.00*
Never hinged 325.00
On cover —
37 A4 10 l olive grn 160.00 *250.00*
Never hinged 325.00
On cover —
Nos. 29-37 (9) 1,089. *584.25*
Set on overfranked philatelic cover 1,550.

Rhodes Issue of 1929 Overprinted in Blue or Red

1931

38 A1 5c mag (Bl) 3.00 *5.75*
Never hinged 6.00
On cover 125.00
39 A2 10c ol brn (R) 3.00 *5.75*
Never hinged 6.00
On cover 95.00
40 A3 20c rose red (Bl) 3.00 *9.00*
Never hinged 6.00
On cover 95.00
41 A3 25c green (R) 3.00 *9.00*
Never hinged 6.00
On cover 125.00
42 A4 30c dk blue (R) 3.00 *9.00*
Never hinged 6.00
On cover 150.00
43 A5 50c dk brown (R) 25.00 21.00
Never hinged 50.00
On cover 175.00
44 A5 1.25 l dk bl (R) 19.00 *37.50*
Never hinged 37.50
On cover 275.00
Nos. 38-44 (7) 59.00 97.00
Set on overfranked philatelic cover 275.00

Italian Eucharistic Congress, 1931.

Garibaldi Issue

Overprinted in Red or Blue

1932 Wmk. 140 *Perf. 14*

45 A138 10c brown 5.25 *9.50*
Never hinged 10.50
On cover 120.00
46 A138 20c red brn (Bl) 5.25 *9.50*
Never hinged 10.50
On cover 82.50
47 A138 25c dp grn 5.25 *9.50*
Never hinged 10.50
On cover 82.50
48 A138 30c bluish sl 5.25 *9.50*
Never hinged 10.50
On cover 110.00
49 A138 50c red vio (Bl) 5.25 *9.50*
Never hinged 10.50
On cover 70.00
50 A141 75c cop red (Bl) 5.25 *9.50*
Never hinged 10.50
On cover 190.00
51 A141 1.25 l dl bl 5.25 *9.50*
Never hinged 10.50
On cover 275.00
52 A141 1.75 l + 25c brn 5.25 *9.50*
Never hinged 10.50
On cover —
53 A144 2.55 l + 50c org (Bl) 5.25 *9.50*
Never hinged 10.50
On cover —
54 A145 5 l + 1 l dl vio 5.25 *9.50*
Never hinged 10.50
On cover —
Nos. 45-54 (10) 52.50 *95.00*
Set on overfranked philatelic cover 325.00

Types of Rhodes Issue of 1929
Imprint: "Officina Carte-Valori Roma"

1932

55 A1 5c rose lake .75 .20
Never hinged 1.50
On cover 12.50
56 A2 10c dk brn .75 .20
Never hinged 1.50
On cover 5.00
57 A3 20c red .75 .20
Never hinged 1.50
On cover 3.50
58 A3 25c dl grn .75 .20
Never hinged 1.50
On cover 3.50
59 A4 30c dl bl .75 .20
Never hinged 1.50
On cover 3.50
60 A5 50c blk brn .75 .20
Never hinged 1.50
On cover 2.00
61 A5 1.25 l dp bl .75 .20
Never hinged 1.50
On cover 5.00
62 A4 5 l rose lake .75 1.10
Never hinged 1.50
On cover 240.00
63 A4 10 l ol brn 1.50 *2.50*
Never hinged 3.00
On cover 600.00
Nos. 55-63 (9) 7.50 5.00

Aerial View of Rhodes A6

Map of Rhodes — A7

Deer and Palm — A8

1932 Wmk. 140 Litho. *Perf. 11*

Shield in Red

64 A6 5c blk & grn 4.50 *8.25*
Never hinged 6.50
On cover 190.00
65 A6 10c blk & vio bl 4.50 *4.50*
Never hinged 6.50
On cover 110.00
66 A6 20c blk & dl yel 4.50 *4.50*
Never hinged 6.50
On cover 110.00
67 A6 25c lil & blk 4.50 *4.50*
Never hinged 6.50
On cover 140.00
68 A6 30c blk & pink 4.50 *4.50*
Never hinged 6.50
On cover 175.00

Shield and Map Dots in Red

69 A7 50c blk & gray 4.50 *4.50*
Never hinged 6.50
On cover 110.00
70 A7 1.25 l red brn & gray 4.50 *11.00*
Never hinged 6.50
On cover 240.00
71 A7 5 l dk bl & gray 13.00 *32.50*
Never hinged 20.00
On cover —
72 A7 10 l dk grn & gray 37.50 *67.50*
Never hinged 55.00
On cover —
73 A7 25 l choc & gray 300.00 *750.00*
Never hinged 450.00
On cover —
Nos. 64-73 (10) 382.00 *891.75*
Set on overfranked philatelic cover *1,550.*

20th anniv. of the Italian occupation and 10th anniv. of Fascist rule.

1935, Apr. Photo. Wmk. 140

74 A8 5c orange 7.50 *12.00*
Never hinged 15.00
On cover 200.00
75 A8 10c brown 7.50 *12.00*
Never hinged 15.00
On cover 110.00
76 A8 20c car rose 7.50 *13.00*
Never hinged 15.00
On cover 125.00
77 A8 25c green 7.50 *13.00*
Never hinged 15.00
On cover 140.00
78 A8 30c purple 7.50 *14.50*
Never hinged 15.00
On cover 160.00
79 A8 50c red brn 7.50 *14.50*
Never hinged 15.00
On cover 110.00
80 A8 1.25l blue 7.50 *35.00*
Never hinged 15.00
On cover 200.00
81 A8 5 l yellow 100.00 *190.00*
Never hinged 200.00
On cover —
Nos. 74-81 (8) 152.50 *304.00*
Set on overfranked philatelic cover 550.00

Holy Year.

RHODES AIR POST STAMPS

Symbolical of Flight — AP18

Wmk. 140 Upright

1935 Typo. *Perf. 14*

C1 AP18 50c black & yellow .20 .20
Never hinged .35
On cover 1.75
C2 AP18 80c black & mag 2.75 *2.50*
Never hinged 6.00
On cover 50.00
C3 AP18 1 l black & green 1.50 .20
Never hinged .90
On cover 3.50
C4 AP18 5 l black & red vio 5.00 *2.75*
Never hinged 10.00
On cover 170.00
Nos. C1-C4 (4) 9.45 *5.65*

Wmk. 140 Sideways

1937-38 Typo. *Perf. 14*

C1a AP18 50c black & yellow .20 .20
Never hinged .35
On cover 1.75
C2a AP18 80c black & mag .65 *1.50*
Never hinged 1.25
On cover 50.00
C3a AP18 1 l black & green .45 .20
Never hinged 3.00
On cover 3.50
C4a AP18 5 l black & red vio 1.10 *2.75*
Never hinged 2.10
On cover 180.00
Nos. C1a-C4a (4) 2.40 *4.65*

RHODES SPECIAL DELIVERY STAMPS

Stag — SD1

1936 Photo. Wmk. 140 *Perf. 14*

E1 SD1 1.25 l green 1.50 1.25
Never hinged 3.00
On cover 90.00
E2 SD1 2.50 l vermilion 2.25 *2.50*
Never hinged 4.50
On cover 275.00

RHODES POSTAGE DUE STAMPS

Maltese Cross PD1

Immortelle PD2

1934 Photo. Wmk. 140 *Perf. 13*

J1 PD1 5c vermilion .75 .90
Never hinged 1.50
On cover *190.00*
J2 PD1 10c carmine .75 .90
Never hinged 1.50
On cover 125.00
J3 PD1 20c dk grn .75 .55
Never hinged 1.50
On cover 120.00
J4 PD1 30c purple .75 .75
Never hinged 1.50
On cover 125.00
J5 PD1 40c dk bl .75 1.90
Never hinged 1.50
On cover *190.00*
J6 PD2 50c vermilion .75 .55
Never hinged 1.50
On cover 100.00
J7 PD2 60c carmine .75 3.00
Never hinged 1.50
On cover *190.00*
J8 PD2 1 l dk grn .75 3.00
Never hinged 1.50
On cover *150.00*
J9 PD2 2 l purple .75 1.90
Never hinged 1.50
On cover *240.00*
Nos. J1-J9 (9) 6.75 13.45

RHODES PARCEL POST STAMPS

Both unused and used values are for complete stamps.

PP1

PP2

1934 Photo. Wmk. 140 *Perf. 13*

Q1 PP1 5c vermilion 1.40 1.40
Never hinged 2.75
Q2 PP1 10c carmine 1.40 1.40
Never hinged 2.75
Q3 PP1 20c dk green 1.40 1.40
Never hinged 2.75
Q4 PP1 25c purple 1.40 1.40
Never hinged 2.75
Q5 PP1 50c dk blue 1.40 1.40
Never hinged 2.75
Q6 PP1 60c black 1.40 1.40
Never hinged 2.75
Q7 PP2 1 l vermilion 1.40 1.40
Never hinged 2.75
Q8 PP2 2 l carmine 1.40 1.40
Never hinged 2.75
Q9 PP2 3 l dk green 1.40 1.40
Never hinged 2.75
Q10 PP2 4 l purple 1.40 1.40
Never hinged 2.75
Q11 PP2 10 l dk blue 1.40 1.40
Never hinged 2.75
Nos. Q1-Q11 (11) 15.40 15.40

Value of used halves, Nos. Q1-Q11, each 20 cents.

See note preceding No. Q7 of Italy.

SCARPANTO

Overprinted "Scarpanto" in Black or Violet

1912-22 Wmk. 140 *Perf. 13½, 14*

1 A43 2c org brn 4.25 4.00
Never hinged 8.50
On cover 92.50
2 A48 5c green 1.40 *4.00*
Never hinged 2.75
On cover 45.00
3 A48 10c claret .35 *4.00*
Never hinged .70
On cover 45.00
4 A48 15c slate ('22) 8.75 *17.50*
Never hinged 17.50
On cover 225.00
5 A50 20c brn org ('21) 25.00 27.50
Never hinged 50.00
On cover 240.00
6 A49 25c blue 4.25 4.00
Never hinged 8.00
On cover 92.50
7 A49 40c brown .35 *4.00*
Never hinged .70
On cover 160.00
8 A49 50c violet 1.25 *7.25*
Never hinged 2.50
On cover 200.00

Unwmk.

9 A58 15c slate (V) 15.00 8.25
Never hinged 30.00
On cover 110.00
10 A50 20c brn org ('17) 80.00 *100.00*
Never hinged 160.00
On cover 3.00
Nos. 1-10 (10) 140.60 *180.50*
Nos. 1-3, 6-9 on overfranked philatelic cover 82.50

No 9 Surcharged Like Calchi No. 11

1916 *Perf. 13½*

11 A58 20c on 15c slate .65 *17.00*
Never hinged 1.40
On cover 110.00

Ferrucci Issue
Overprinted in Red or Blue

1930 Wmk. 140 *Perf. 14*

12 A102 20c violet (R) 1.25 *2.50*
Never hinged 2.50
On cover 82.50
13 A103 25c dk green (R) 1.25 *2.50*
Never hinged 2.50
On cover 100.00
14 A102 50c black (R) 1.25 *4.25*
Never hinged 2.50
On cover 3.75
15 A102 1.25 l dp bl (R) 1.25 *4.25*
Never hinged 2.50
On cover 3.75
16 A104 5 l + 2 l dp car (Bl) 1.90 *7.25*
Never hinged 3.75
On cover 175.00
Nos. 12-16 (5) 6.90 *20.75*
Set on overfranked philatelic cover 82.50

Garibaldi Issue
Overprinted in Red or Blue

1932

17 A138 10c brown 5.25 *9.50*
Never hinged 10.50
On cover 120.00
18 A138 20c red brn (Bl) 5.25 *9.50*
Never hinged 10.50
On cover 82.50
19 A138 25c dp grn 5.25 *9.50*
Never hinged 10.50
On cover 82.50
20 A138 30c bluish sl 5.25 *9.50*
Never hinged 10.50
On cover 110.00
21 A138 50c red vio (Bl) 5.25 *9.50*
Never hinged 10.50
On cover 67.50
22 A141 75c cop red (Bl) 5.25 *9.50*
Never hinged 10.50
On cover 190.00
23 A141 1.25 l dull blue 5.25 *9.50*
Never hinged 10.50
On cover 200.00
24 A141 1.75 l + 25c brn 5.25 *9.50*
Never hinged 10.50
On cover —
25 A144 2.55 l + 50c org (Bl) 5.25 *9.50*
Never hinged 10.50
On cover —
26 A145 5 l + 1 l dl vio 5.25 *9.50*
Never hinged 10.50
On cover —
Nos. 17-26 (10) 52.50 *95.00*
Set on overfranked philatelic cover 325.00

SIMI

Overprinted "Simi" in Black or Violet

1912-21 Wmk. 140 *Perf. 13½, 14*

1 A43 2c org brn 4.25 4.00
Never hinged 8.50
On cover 82.50
2 A48 5c green 12.50 4.00
Never hinged 25.00
On cover 42.50
3 A48 10c claret .35 4.00
Never hinged .70
On cover 42.50
4 A48 15c slate ('21) 80.00 35.00
Never hinged 130.00
On cover 225.00
5 A50 20c brn org ('21) 32.50 21.00
Never hinged 65.00
On cover 200.00
6 A49 25c blue 1.60 4.00
Never hinged 3.25
On cover 92.50
7 A49 40c brown .35 4.00
Never hinged .70
On cover 160.00
8 A49 50c violet .35 *7.25*
Never hinged .70
On cover 180.00

Unwmk.

9 A58 15c slate (V) 25.00 8.25
Never hinged 50.00
On cover 110.00
10 A50 20c brn org ('17) 32.50 *72.50*
Never hinged 72.50
On cover 225.00
Nos. 1-10 (10) 189.40 *164.00*
Nos. 1-3, 6-9 on overfranked philatelic cover 82.50

No. 9 Surcharged Like Calchi No. 11

1916 *Perf. 13½*

11 A58 20c on 15c slate 5.25 *13.00*
Never hinged 10.50
On cover 92.50

Ferrucci Issue
Overprinted in Red or Blue

1930 Wmk. 140 *Perf. 14*

12 A102 20c violet (R) 1.25 *2.50*
Never hinged 2.50
On cover 82.50
13 A103 25c dk green (R) 1.25 *2.50*
Never hinged 2.50
On cover 100.00
14 A102 50c black (R) 1.25 *4.25*
Never hinged 2.50
On cover 75.00
15 A102 1.25 l dp bl (R) 1.25 *4.25*
Never hinged 2.50
On cover 180.00
16 A104 5 l + 2 l dp car (Bl) 1.90 *7.25*
Never hinged 3.75
On cover —
Nos. 12-16 (5) 6.90 *20.75*
Set on overfranked philatelic cover 82.50

Garibaldi Issue
Overprinted in Red or Blue

1932

17 A138 10c brown 5.25 *9.50*
Never hinged 10.50
On cover 120.00
18 A138 20c red brn (Bl) 5.25 *9.50*
Never hinged 10.50
On cover 82.50
19 A138 25c dp grn 5.25 *9.50*
Never hinged 10.50
On cover 82.50
20 A138 30c bluish sl 5.25 *9.50*
Never hinged 10.50
On cover 110.00
21 A138 50c red vio (Bl) 5.25 *9.50*
Never hinged 10.50
On cover 67.50
22 A141 75c cop red (Bl) 5.25 *9.50*
Never hinged 10.50
On cover 190.00
23 A141 1.25 l dull blue 5.25 *9.50*
Never hinged 10.50
On cover 275.00
24 A141 1.75 l + 25c brn 5.25 *9.50*
Never hinged 10.50
On cover —
25 A144 2.55 l + 50c org (Bl) 5.25 *9.50*
Never hinged 10.50
On cover —
26 A145 5 l + 1 l dl vio 5.25 *9.50*
Never hinged 10.50
On cover —
Nos. 17-26 (10) 52.50 *95.00*
Set on overfranked philatelic cover 325.00

STAMPALIA

Overprinted "Stampalia" in Black or Violet

1912-21 Wmk. 140 *Perf. 13½, 14*

1 A43 2c org brn 4.25 *4.00*
Never hinged 8.50
On cover 82.50
2 A48 5c green .35 *4.00*
Never hinged .70
On cover 45.00
3 A48 10c claret .35 *4.00*
Never hinged .70
On cover 45.00
4 A48 15c slate ('21) 6.00 *17.50*
Never hinged 12.50
On cover 200.00
5 A50 20c brn org ('21) 25.00 *27.50*
Never hinged 50.00
On cover 225.00
6 A49 25c blue .45 *4.00*
Never hinged .90
On cover 100.00
7 A49 40c brown 1.90 *4.00*
Never hinged 3.75
On cover 175.00
8 A49 50c violet .35 *7.25*
Never hinged .70
On cover 200.00

Unwmk.

9 A58 15c slate (V) 19.00 8.25
Never hinged 37.50
On cover 110.00
10 A50 20c brn org ('17) 42.50 *72.50*
Never hinged 85.00
On cover 250.00
Nos. 1-10 (10) 100.15 *153.00*
Nos. 1-3, 6-9 on overfranked philatelic cover 82.50

No. 9 Surcharged Like Calchi No. 11

1916 *Perf. 13½*

11 A58 20c on 15c slate .55 *11.50*
Never hinged 1.10
On cover 92.50

Ferrucci Issue
Overprinted in Red or Blue

1930 Wmk. 140 *Perf. 14*

12 A102 20c violet (R) 1.25 *2.50*
Never hinged 2.50
On cover 82.50
13 A103 25c dk green (R) 1.25 *2.50*
Never hinged 2.50
On cover 100.00
14 A102 50c black (R) 1.25 *4.25*
Never hinged 2.50
On cover 75.00
15 A102 1.25 l dp bl (R) 1.25 *4.25*
Never hinged 2.50
On cover 180.00
16 A104 5 l + 2 l dp car (Bl) 1.90 *7.25*
Never hinged 3.75
On cover —
Nos. 12-16 (5) 6.90 *20.75*
Set on overfranked philatelic cover 82.50

Garibaldi Issue
Overprinted in Red or Blue

1932

17 A138 10c brown 5.25 *9.50*
Never hinged 10.50
On cover 120.00
18 A138 20c red brn (Bl) 5.25 *9.50*
Never hinged 10.50
On cover 82.50
19 A138 25c dp grn 5.25 *9.50*
Never hinged 10.50
On cover 82.50
20 A138 30c bluish sl 5.25 *9.50*
Never hinged 10.50
On cover 110.00
21 A138 50c red vio (Bl) 5.25 *9.50*
Never hinged 10.50
On cover 67.50
22 A141 75c cop red (Bl) 5.25 *9.50*
Never hinged 10.50
On cover 190.00
23 A141 1.25 l dull blue 5.25 *9.50*
Never hinged 10.50
On cover 275.00
24 A141 1.75 l + 25c brn 5.25 *9.50*
Never hinged 10.50
On cover —
25 A144 2.55 l + 50c org (Bl) 5.25 *9.50*
Never hinged 10.50
On cover —
26 A145 5 l + 1 l dl vio 5.25 *9.50*
Never hinged 10.50
On cover —
Nos. 17-26 (10) 52.50 *95.00*
Set on overfranked philatelic cover 325.00

IVORY COAST

'iv-rē 'kōst

LOCATION — West coast of Africa, bordering on Gulf of Guinea
GOVT. — French Colony
AREA — 127,520 sq. mi.
POP. — 13,107,000 (est. 1991)
CAPITAL — Yamoussoukro

100 Centimes = 1 Franc

Navigation and Commerce — A1

Perf. 14x13½

1892-1900 Typo. Unwmk.

Colony Name in Blue or Carmine

1 A1 1c black, *lil bl* 1.40 1.40
On cover 50.00
2 A1 2c brown, *buff* 2.00 1.75
On cover 50.00
3 A1 4c claret, *lav* 3.50 2.50
On cover 50.00
4 A1 5c green, *grnsh* 9.00 5.75
On cover 15.00
5 A1 10c black, *lavender* 13.00 9.25
On cover 17.50
6 A1 10c red ('00) 95.00 72.50
On cover —
7 A1 15c blue, quadrille paper 21.00 9.25
On cover 15.00
8 A1 15c gray ('00) 13.00 3.50
On cover 25.00
9 A1 20c red, *green* 14.00 11.00
On cover 75.00
10 A1 25c black, *rose* 16.00 3.50
On cover 20.00
11 A1 25c blue ('00) 25.00 21.00
On cover 40.00
12 A1 30c brown, *bister* 22.50 17.00
On cover 80.00
13 A1 40c red, *straw* 17.50 10.00
On cover 80.00
14 A1 50c car, *rose* 62.50 47.50
On cover 80.00
15 A1 50c brn, *azure* ('00) 25.00 17.50
On cover 90.00
16 A1 75c deep vio, *org* 25.00 20.00
On cover 110.00
17 A1 1fr brnz grn, *straw* 40.00 27.50
On cover —
Nos. 1-17 (17) 405.40 280.90

Perf. 13½x14 stamps are counterfeits.
For surcharges see Nos. 18-20, 37-41.

Nos. 12, 16-17 Surcharged in Black

1904

18 A1 0,05c on 30c brn, *bis* 65.00 65.00
On cover 110.00
19 A1 0,10c on 75c vio, *org* 13.00 13.00
On cover 45.00
20 A1 0,15c on 1fr brnz grn, *straw* 16.00 16.00
On cover 55.00
Nos. 18-20 (3) 94.00 94.00

Gen. Louis Faidherbe A2

Oil Palm — A3

Dr. N. Eugène Ballay A4

1906-07

Name of Colony in Red or Blue

21 A2 1c slate 1.25 1.25
22 A2 2c chocolate 1.25 1.25
23 A2 4c choc, *gray bl* 1.75 1.75
a. Name double 140.00
24 A2 5c green 2.90 1.90
25 A2 10c carmine (B) 6.50 4.25
26 A3 20c black, *azure* 7.00 6.50
27 A3 25c bl, *pinkish* 6.50 4.00
28 A3 30c choc, *pnksh* 8.50 6.00
30 A3 35c black, *yel* 9.25 4.25
31 A3 45c choc, *grnsh* 13.00 8.25
32 A3 50c deep violet 12.00 8.50
33 A3 75c blue, *org* 12.00 8.50
34 A4 1fr black, *azure* 29.00 26.00
35 A4 2fr blue, *pink* 40.00 35.00
36 A4 5fr car, *straw* (B) 70.00 67.50
Nos. 21-36 (15) 220.90 184.90

Stamps of 1892-1900 Surcharged in Carmine or Black

1912

Spacing between figures of surcharge 1.5mm (5c), 2mm (10c)

37 A1 5c on 15c gray (C) 1.00 1.00
38 A1 5c on 30c brn, *bis* (C) 1.10 1.10
39 A1 10c on 40c red, *straw* 1.75 1.75
a. Pair, one without surcharge 62.50
40 A1 10c on 50c brn, *az* (C) 2.50 2.50
41 A1 10c on 75c dp vio, *org* 6.50 6.50
Nos. 37-41 (5) 12.85 12.85

Spacing between figures of surcharge 2.25mm (5c), 2.75mm (10c)

37a A1 5c on 15c gray (C) 8.50 8.50
38a A1 5c on 30c brn, *bis* (C) 8.50 8.50

39b	A1	10c on 40c red, *straw*	50.00	50.00
40a	A1	10c on 50c brn, *az* (C)	92.50	92.50
41a	A1	10c on 75c dp vio, *org*	200.00	200.00
		Nos. 37a-41a (5)	359.50	359.50

River Scene A5

1913-35

42	A5	1c vio brn & vio	.20	.20
43	A5	2c brown & blk	.20	.20
44	A5	4c vio & vio brn	.20	.20
45	A5	5c yel grn & bl grn	.70	.35
46	A5	5c choc & ol brn ('22)	.20	.20
47	A5	10c red org & rose	1.25	.70
48	A5	10c yel grn & bl grn ('22)	.35	.35
49	A5	10c car rose, *bluish* ('26)	.20	.20
50	A5	15c org & rose ('17)	.70	.35
51	A5	20c black & gray	.50	.35
52	A5	25c ultra & bl	8.00	5.50
53	A5	25c blk & vio ('22)	.35	.35
54	A5	30c choc & brn	1.40	1.25
55	A5	30c red org & rose ('22)	2.00	2.00
56	A5	30c lt bl & rose red ('26)	.35	.35
57	A5	30c dl grn & grn ('27)	.35	.35
58	A5	35c vio & org	.55	.50
59	A5	40c gray & bl grn	1.10	.55
60	A5	45c red org & choc	.70	.50
61	A5	45c dp rose & mar ('34)	4.75	3.75
62	A5	50c black & vio	3.50	2.50
63	A5	50c ultra & bl ('22)	1.10	1.10
64	A5	50c ol grn & bl ('25)	.50	.50
65	A5	60c vio, *pnksh* ('25)	.50	.50
66	A5	65c car rose & ol grn ('26)	1.25	1.25
67	A5	75c brn & rose	.70	.55
68	A5	75c ind & ultra ('34)	3.25	3.25
69	A5	85c red vio & blk ('26)	1.25	1.25
70	A5	90c brn red & rose ('30)	11.00	10.00
71	A5	1fr org & black	.80	.70
72	A5	1.10fr dl grn & dk brn ('28)	4.75	4.75
73	A5	1.50fr lt bl & dp bl ('30)	7.25	5.75
74	A5	1.75fr lt ultra & mag ('35)	11.00	7.50
75	A5	2fr brn & blue	3.50	1.40
76	A5	3fr red vio ('30)	7.25	5.75
77	A5	5fr dk bl & choc	5.75	4.00
		Nos. 42-77 (36)	87.40	68.95

Nos. 45, 47, 50 and 58 exist on both ordinary and chalky paper.

For surcharges see Nos. 78-91, B1.

Nos. 45, 47 and 52, pasted on cardboard and overprinted "Valeur d'echange" and value of basic stamp, were used as emergency currency in 1920.

Stamps and Type of 1913-34 Surcharged

1922-34

78	A5	50c on 45c dp rose & maroon ('34)	3.00	2.10
79	A5	50c on 75c indigo & ultra ('34)	1.90	1.50
80	A5	50c on 90c brn red & rose ('34)	1.90	1.90
81	A5	60c on 75c vio, *pnksh*	.40	.40
82	A5	65c on 15c orange & rose ('25)	.85	.85
83	A5	85c on 75c brown & rose ('25)	1.25	.85
		Nos. 78-83 (6)	9.30	7.60

Stamps and Type of 1913 Surcharged with New Value and Bars

1924-27

84	A5	25c on 2fr (R)	.80	.80
85	A5	25c on 5fr	.80	.80
86	A5	90c on 75c brn red & cer ('27)	1.10	.95
87	A5	1.25fr on 1fr dk bl & ultra (R) ('26)	.80	.80
88	A5	1.50fr on 1fr lt bl & dk blue ('27)	1.10	1.10
89	A5	3fr on 5fr brn red & bl grn ('27)	4.25	4.00
90	A5	10fr on 5fr dl red & rose lil ('27)	13.00	12.00
91	A5	20fr on 5fr bl grn & ver ('27)	16.00	14.50
		Nos. 84-91 (8)	37.85	34.95

Common Design Types pictured following the introduction.

Colonial Exposition Issue
Common Design Types
Name of Country in Black

1931 Engr. Perf. 12½

92	CD70	40c deep green	2.75	2.75
93	CD71	50c violet	4.50	4.50
94	CD72	90c red orange	3.50	3.50
95	CD73	1.50fr dull blue	4.50	4.50
		Nos. 92-95 (4)	15.25	15.25

Stamps of Upper Volta 1928, Overprinted

1933 Perf. 13½x14

96	A5	2c brown & lilac	.20	.20
97	A5	4c blk & yellow	.20	.20
98	A5	5c ind & gray bl	.50	.35
99	A5	10c indigo & pink	.35	.35
100	A5	15c brown & blue	.95	.70
101	A5	20c brown & green	.95	.70
102	A6	25c brn & yellow	1.60	1.40
103	A6	30c dp grn & brn	1.90	1.50
104	A6	45c brown & blue	6.25	5.00
105	A6	65c indigo & bl	2.40	2.00
106	A6	75c black & lilac	3.25	2.00
107	A6	90c brn red & lil	2.40	2.40

Overprinted

108	A7	1fr brown & green	3.25	2.40
109	A7	1.50fr ultra & grysh	3.25	2.40

Surcharged

110	A6	1.25fr on 40c blk & pink	2.00	1.90
111	A6	1.75fr on 50c blk & green	3.50	2.50
		Nos. 96-111 (16)	32.95	26.00

Baoulé Woman — A6

Rapids on Comoe River — A9

Mosque at Bobo-Dioulasso — A7

Coastal Scene A8

1936-44 Perf. 13

112	A6	1c carmine rose	.20	.20
113	A6	2c ultramarine	.20	.20
114	A6	3c dp grn ('40)	.20	.20
115	A6	4c chocolate	.20	.20
116	A6	5c violet	.20	.20
117	A6	10c Prussian bl	.20	.20
118	A6	15c copper red	.20	.20
119	A7	20c ultramarine	.20	.20
120	A7	25c copper red	.30	.20
121	A7	30c blue green	.20	.20
122	A7	30c brown ('40)	.20	.20
123	A6	35c dp grn ('38)	.60	.35
124	A7	40c carmine rose	.30	.20
125	A7	45c brown	.50	.50
126	A7	45c blue grn ('40)	.20	.20
127	A7	50c plum	.35	.35
128	A7	55c dark vio ('38)	.35	.35
129	A8	60c car rose ('40)	.30	.30
130	A8	65c red brown	.50	.35
131	A8	70c red brn ('40)	.35	.35
132	A8	75c dark violet	.95	.55
133	A8	80c blk brn ('38)	1.00	.70
134	A8	90c carmine rose	7.25	4.50
135	A8	90c dk grn ('39)	.50	.50
136	A8	1fr dark green	3.75	2.25
137	A8	1fr car rose ('38)	1.00	.55
138	A8	1fr dk vio ('40)	.35	.35
139	A8	1.25fr copper red	.35	.20
140	A8	1.40fr ultra ('40)	.35	.35
141	A8	1.50fr ultramarine	.35	.20
141A	A8	1.50fr grnsh blk ('44)	1.50	1.50
142	A8	1.60fr blk brn ('40)	.80	.80
143	A9	1.75fr carmine rose	.35	.20
144	A9	1.75fr dull bl ('38)	.75	.60
145	A9	2fr ultramarine	.50	.35
146	A9	2.25fr dark bl ('39)	.90	.90
147	A9	2.50fr rose red ('40)	1.10	1.10
148	A9	3fr green	.65	.35
149	A9	5fr chocolate	.65	.35
150	A9	10fr violet	1.00	.75
151	A9	20fr copper red	1.75	1.50
		Nos. 112-151 (41)	31.55	23.70

Stamps of types A7-A9 without "RF" were issued in 1944, but were not placed on sale in the colony.

For surcharges see Nos. B8-B11.

Paris International Exposition Issue
Common Design Types

1937 Perf. 13

152	CD74	20c deep violet	1.10	1.10
153	CD75	30c dark green	1.10	1.10
154	CD76	40c carmine rose	1.25	1.25
155	CD77	50c dk brn & bl	1.25	1.25
156	CD78	90c red	1.25	1.25
157	CD79	1.50fr ultra	1.40	1.40
		Nos. 152-157 (6)	7.35	7.35

Colonial Arts Exhibition Issue
Souvenir Sheet
Common Design Type

1937 Imperf.

158	CD76	3fr sepia	7.00	*7.50*

Louis Gustave Binger A10

1937 Perf. 13

159	A10	65c red brown	.35	.35

Death of Governor General Binger; 50th anniv. of his exploration of the Niger.

Caillie Issue
Common Design Type

1939 Engr. Perf. 12½x12

160	CD81	90c org brn & org	.55	.55
161	CD81	2fr bright violet	.80	.80
162	CD81	2.25fr ultra & dk bl	.95	.95
		Nos. 160-162 (3)	2.30	2.30

New York World's Fair Issue
Common Design Type

1939

163	CD82	1.25fr carmine lake	1.00	1.00
164	CD82	2.25fr ultramarine	1.00	1.00

SEMI-POSTAL STAMPS

No. 47 Surcharged in Red

1915 Unwmk. Perf. 14x13½

B1	A5	10c + 5c	1.00	1.00
a.		Double surcharge	52.50	52.50

Issued on ordinary and chalky paper.

Curie Issue
Common Design Type

1938 Perf. 13

B2	CD80	1.75fr + 50c brt ultra	7.75	6.50

French Revolution Issue
Common Design Type

1939 Photo.
Name and Value Typo. in Black

B3	CD83	45c + 25c grn	5.75	5.75
B4	CD83	70c + 30c brn	5.75	5.75
B5	CD83	90c + 35c red org	5.75	5.75
B6	CD83	1.25fr + 1fr rose pink	5.75	5.75
B7	CD83	2.25fr + 2fr blue	5.75	5.75
		Nos. B3-B7 (5)	28.75	28.75

AIR POST STAMPS

Common Design Type

1940 Unwmk. Engr. Perf. 12½x12

C1	CD85	1.90fr ultramarine	.20	.20
C2	CD85	2.90fr dark red	.20	.20
C3	CD85	4.50fr dk gray grn	.50	.50
C4	CD85	4.90fr yel bister	.70	.70
C5	CD85	6.90fr deep orange	1.25	1.25
		Nos. C1-C5 (5)	2.85	2.85

POSTAGE DUE STAMPS

Natives — D1

D2

Perf. 14x13½
1906-07 Unwmk. Typo.

J1	D1	5c grn, *greenish*	2.90	2.90
J2	D1	10c red brown	2.90	2.90
J3	D1	15c dark blue	4.25	4.25
J4	D1	20c blk, *yellow*	6.50	6.50
J5	D1	30c red, *straw*	6.50	6.50
J6	D1	50c violet	5.00	5.00
J7	D1	60c black, *buff*	24.00	24.00
J8	D1	1fr blk, *pinkish*	26.00	26.00
		Nos. J1-J8 (8)	78.05	78.05

1914

J9	D2	5c green	.20	.20
J10	D2	10c rose	.20	.20
J11	D2	15c gray	.20	.20
J12	D2	20c brown	.35	.35
J13	D2	30c blue	.35	.35
J14	D2	50c black	.55	.55
J15	D2	60c orange	.80	.80
J16	D2	1fr violet	1.10	1.10
		Nos. J9-J16 (8)	3.75	3.75

Type of 1914 Issue Surcharged

1927

J17 D2 2fr on 1fr lilac rose	1.75	1.75
J18 D2 3fr on 1fr org brown	1.75	1.75

PARCEL POST STAMPS

Postage Due Stamps of French Colonies Overprinted

Overprinted in Black

1903 **Unwmk.** ***Imperf.***

Q1 D1 50c lilac	42.50	40.00
Q2 D1 1fr rose, *buff*	42.50	40.00

Overprinted in Black

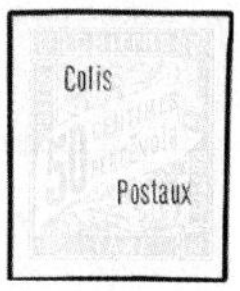

Q3 D1 50c lilac	*2,750.*	*3,000.*
Q4 D1 1fr rose, *buff*	*2,750.*	*3,000.*

Accents on "O" of "COTE"
Nos. Q7-Q8, Q11-Q12, Q15, Q17-Q18, Q21-Q22, Q24-Q25 exist with or without accent.

Overprinted

Red Overprint

Q5 D1 50c lilac	110.00	110.00
a. Inverted overprint	325.00	325.00

Blue Black Overprint

Q6 D1 1fr rose, *buff*	80.00	80.00
a. Inverted overprint	260.00	260.00

Surcharged in Black

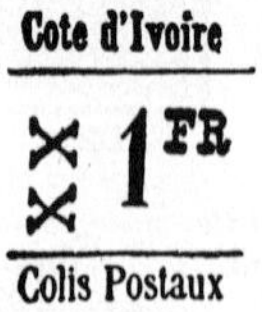

a

b

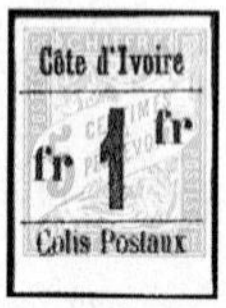

c

d

e

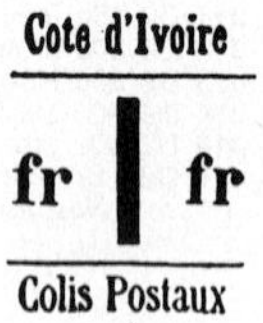

f

g

h

1903

Q7 D1 50c on 15c pale grn	15.00	14.00
a. Inverted surcharge	140.00	140.00
Q8 D1 50c on 60c brn, *buff*	35.00	32.50
a. Inverted surcharge	140.00	140.00
Q9 (a) 1fr on 5c blue	*3,250.*	*2,750.*
Q10 (b) 1fr on 5c blue	*3,250.*	*2,000.*
Q11 (c) 1fr on 5c blue	18.00	14.00
a. Inverted surcharge	200.00	200.00
Q12 (d) 1fr on 5c blue	20.00	16.00
Q13 (e) 1fr on 5c blue	*3,900.*	*3,250.*
Q14 (f) 1fr on 5c blue	*10,000.*	*7,500.*
Q15 (g) 1fr on 5c blue	100.00	100.00
Q16 (h) 1fr on 5c blue	*2,750.*	*3,000.*
Q17 (c) 1fr on 10c gray brn	25.00	21.50
a. Inverted surcharge	325.00	325.00
Q18 (d) 1fr on 10c gray brn	40.00	36.00
a. Inverted surcharge	325.00	325.00
Q19 (g) 1fr on 10c gray brn	*3,250.*	*3,000.*
Q20 (h) 1fr on 10c gray brn	*39,000.*	

Some authorities regard Nos. Q9 and Q10 as essays. A sub-type of type "a" has smaller, bold "XX" without serifs.

Surcharged in Black:

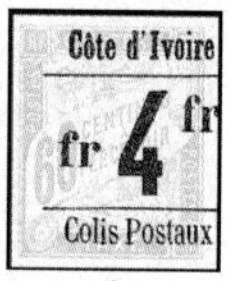

j

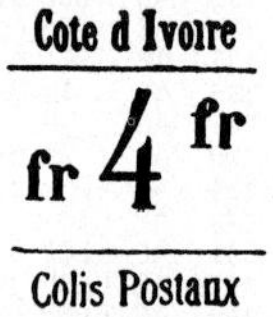

k

l

Q21 (i) 4fr on 60c brn, *buff*	120.00	120.00
a. Double surcharge		—
Q22 (k) 4fr on 60c brn, *buff*	325.00	325.00
Q23 (l) 4fr on 60c brn, *buff*	850.00	700.00

Surcharged in Black

Q24 D1 4fr on 15c green	175.00	175.00
a. One large star	300.00	300.00
b. Two large stars	300.00	300.00
Q25 D1 4fr on 30c rose	175.00	175.00
a. One large star	300.00	300.00
b. Two large stars	300.00	300.00

Overprinted in Black

1904

Q26 D1 50c lilac	35.00	35.00
a. Inverted overprint		
Q27 D1 1fr rose, *buff*	35.00	35.00
a. Inverted overprint		

Overprinted in Black

Q28 D1 50c lilac	35.00	35.00
a. Inverted overprint	160.00	160.00
Q29 D1 1fr rose, *buff*	35.00	35.00
a. Inverted overprint	175.00	175.00

Surcharged in Black

Q30 D1 4fr on 5c blue	240.00	240.00
Q31 D1 8fr on 15c green	240.00	240.00

Overprinted in Black

1905

Q32 D1 50c lilac	80.00	80.00
Q33 D1 1fr rose, *buff*	80.00	80.00

Surcharged in Black

Q34 D1 2fr on 1fr rose, *buff*	225.00	225.00
Q35 D1 4fr on 1fr rose, *buff*	225.00	225.00
a. Italic "4"	1,600.	1,400.
Q36 D1 8fr on 1fr rose, *buff*	550.00	550.00

JAMAICA

jə-'mā-kə

LOCATION — Caribbean Sea, about 90 miles south of Cuba
GOVT. — Independent state in the British Commonwealth
AREA — 4,411 sq. mi.
POP. — 2,230,000 (est. 1982)
CAPITAL — Kingston

Jamaica administered two dependencies: Cayman Islands and Turks and Caicos Islands.

12 Pence = 1 Shilling
20 Shillings = 1 Pound

Catalogue values for unused stamps in this country are for Never Hinged items, beginning with Scott 129 in the regular postage section.

Watermark

Wmk. 45 — Pineapple

STAMPS OF GREAT BRITAIN USED IN JAMAICA

For information on these cancels, see the Crowned Circle Handstamps and Great Britain Used Abroad section.

A01 (Kingston)

Type A Cancel

Short letter and numbers.

1858-60

A1 A 1p rose red, perf. 16 (#18)	375.00
A2 A 1p rose red, perf. 14 (#20)	50.00
A3 A 4p rose (#26)	50.00
A4 A 6p lilac (#27)	50.00
A5 A 1sh green (#28)	190.00

See note after No. A13.

Duplex cancel

Tall letter and numbers.

1859-60

A6 1p rose red (#20)	225.00
A7 4p rose (#26)	55.00
A8 6p lilac (#27)	55.00
A9 1sh green (#28)	440.00

Double Numeral cancel

As type A but bolder letter and numbers.

A10 1p rose red (#20)	300.00
A11 4p rose (#26)	175.00
a. Thick glazed paper (#26b)	500.00
A12 6p lilac (#27)	175.00
A13 1sh green (#28)	—

Single examples of Nos. A10-A12 can be difficult to distinguish from Nos. A2-A4.

A27 (Alexandria)	
A14 A 1p rose red (#20)	575.00
A15 A 2p blue (#21)	700.00
A16 A 4p rose (#26)	225.00
A17 A 6p lilac (#27)	525.00
A28 (Anotto Bay)	
A18 A 1p rose red (#20)	400.00
A19 A 4p rose (#26)	100.00
A20 A 6p lilac (#27)	325.00
A29 (Bath)	
A21 A 1p rose red (#20)	175.00
A22 A 4p rose (#26)	110.00
A23 A 6p lilac (#27)	525.00
A30 (Black River)	
A24 A 1p rose red (#20)	175.00
A25 A 4p rose (#26)	82.50
A26 A 6p lilac (#27)	175.00
A31 (Brown's Town)	
A27 A 1p rose red (#20)	225.00
A28 A 4p rose (#26)	225.00
A29 A 6p lilac (#27)	225.00
A32 (Buff Bay)	
A30 A 1p rose red (#20)	175.00
A31 A 4p rose (#26)	210.00
A32 A 6p lilac (#27)	175.00
A33 (Chapelton)	
A33 A 1p rose red (#20)	225.00
A34 A 4p rose (#26)	150.00
A35 A 6p lilac (#27)	225.00
A34 (Claremont)	
A36 A 1p rose red (#20)	400.00
A37 A 4p rose (#26)	200.00
A38 A 6p lilac (#27)	400.00
A35 (Clarendon)	
A39 A 1p rose red (#20)	350.00
A40 A 4p rose (#26)	150.00
A41 A 6p lilac (#27)	225.00
A36 (Dry Harbour)	
A42 A 1p rose red (#20)	525.00
A43 A 4p rose (#26)	440.00
A44 A 6p lilac (#27)	375.00
A37 (Duncans)	
A45 A 1p rose red (#20)	—
A46 A 4p rose (#26)	525.00
A47 A 6p lilac (#27)	375.00
A39 (Falmouth)	
A48 A 1p rose red (#20)	110.00
A49 A 4p rose (#26)	70.00
A50 A 6p lilac (#27)	90.00
A51 A 1sh green (#28)	825.00
A40 (Flint River)	
A52 A 1p rose red (#20)	210.00
A53 A 4p rose (#26)	150.00
A54 A 6p lilac (#27)	210.00

A55 A 1sh green (#28) 825.00

A41 (Gayle)

A56 A 1p rose red (#20) 575.00
A57 A 4p rose (#26) 175.00
A58 A 6p lilac (#27) 190.00
A59 A 1sh green (#28) 440.00

A42 (Golden Spring)

A60 A 1p rose red (#20) 240.00
A61 A 4p rose (#26) 210.00
A62 A 6p lilac (#27) 525.00
A63 A 1sh green (#28) 825.00

A43 (Gordon Town)

A64 A 1p rose red (#20) —
A65 A 4p rose (#26) —
A66 A 6p lilac (#27) 575.00

A44 (Goshen)

A67 A 1p rose red (#20) 175.00
A68 A 4p rose (#26) 160.00
A69 A 6p lilac (#27) 82.50

A45 (Grange Hill)

A70 A 1p rose red (#20) 210.00
A71 A 4p rose (#26) 70.00
A72 A 6p lilac (#27) 87.50
A73 A 1sh green (#28) 700.00

A46 (Green Island)

A74 A 1p rose red (#20) 410.00
A77 A 4p rose (#26) 210.00
A76 A 6p lilac (#27) 350.00
A77 A 1sh green (#28) 825.00

A47 (Highgate)

A78 A 1p rose red (#20) 240.00
A79 A 4p rose (#26) 160.00
A80 A 6p lilac (#27) 240.00

A48 (Hope Bay)

A81 A 1p rose red (#20) 525.00
A82 A 4p rose (#26) 210.00
A83 A 6p lilac (#27) 525.00

A49 (Lilliput)

A84 A 1p rose red (#20) 210.00
A85 A 4p rose (#26) 210.00
A86 A 6p lilac (#27) 105.00

A51 (Lucea)

A87 A 1p rose red (#20) 325.00
A88 A 4p rose (#26) 82.50
A89 A 6p lilac (#27) 210.00

A52 (Manchioneal)

A90 A 1p rose red (#20) 400.00
A91 A 4p rose (#26) 225.00
A92 A 6p lilac (#27) —

A53 (Mandeville)

A93 A 1p rose red (#20) 225.00
A94 A 4p rose (#26) 82.50
A95 A 6p lilac (#27) 200.00

A54 (May Hill)

A96 A 1p rose red (#20) 120.00
A97 A 4p rose (#26) 110.00
A98 A 6p lilac (#27) 82.50

A55 (Mile Gulley)

A99 A 1p rose red (#20) 350.00
A100 A 4p rose (#26) 210.00
A101 A 6p lilac (#27) 210.00

A56 (Moneague)

A102 A 1p rose red (#20) 210.00
A103 A 4p rose (#26) 265.00
A104 A 6p lilac (#27) 525.00

A57 (Montego Bay)

A105 A 1p rose red (#20) 225.00
A106 A 4p rose (#26) 70.00
A107 A 6p lilac (#27) 82.50
A108 A 1sh green (#28) 825.00

A58 (Montpelier)

A109 A 1p rose red (#20) —
A110 A 4p rose (#26) —
A111 A 6p lilac (#27) 875.00

A59 (Morant Bay)

A112 A 1p rose red (#20) 400.00
A113 A 4p rose (#26) 82.50
A114 A 6p lilac (#27) 87.50

A60 (Ocho Rios)

A115 A 1p rose red (#20) —
A116 A 4p rose (#26) 110.00
A117 A 6p lilac (#27) 200.00

A61 (Old Harbour)

A118 A 1p rose red (#20) 210.00
A119 A 4p rose (#26) 165.00
A120 A 6p lilac (#27) 165.00

A62 (Plantain Garden River)

A121 A 1p rose red (#20) 165.00
A122 A 4p rose (#26) 110.00
A123 A 6p lilac (#27) 165.00

A64 (Port Antonio)

A124 A 1p rose red (#20) 500.00
A125 A 4p rose (#26) 325.00
A126 A 6p lilac (#27) 325.00

A65 (Port Morant)

A127 A 1p rose red (#20) 325.00
A128 A 4p rose (#26) 120.00
A129 A 6p lilac (#27) 325.00

A66 (Port Maria)

A130 A 1p rose red (#20) 210.00
A131 A 4p rose (#26) 87.50
A132 A 6p lilac (#27) 325.00

A67 (Port Royal)

A133 A 1p rose red (#20) 400.00
A134 A 2p blue (#27, P9) —
A135 A 4p rose (#26) 400.00
A136 A 6p lilac (#27) 400.00

A68 (Porus)

A137 A 1p rose red (#20) 210.00
A138 A 4p rose (#26) 105.00
A139 A 6p lilac (#27) 410.00

A69 (Ramble)

A140 A 1p rose red (#20) 210.00
A141 A 4p rose (#26) 210.00
a. Thick glazed paper (#26b) 500.00
A142 A 6p lilac (#27) 325.00

A70 (Rio Bueno)

A143 A 1p rose red (#20) —
A144 A 4p rose (#26) 200.00
A145 A 6p lilac (#27) 130.00

A71 (Rodney Hall)

A146 A 1p rose red (#20) 175.00
A147 A 4p rose (#26) 120.00
A148 A 6p lilac (#27) 150.00

A72 (St. David's)

A149 A 1p rose red (#20) 210.00
A150 A 4p rose (#26) 400.00
A151 A 6p lilac (#27) —

A73 (St. Ann's Bay)

A152 A 1p rose red (#20) 210.00
A153 A 4p rose (#26) 110.00
A154 A 6p lilac (#27) 210.00

A74 (Salt Gut)

A155 A 1p rose red (#20) 200.00
A156 A 4p rose (#26) —
A157 A 6p lilac (#27) 210.00

A75 (Savannah-la-Mar)

A158 A 1p rose red (#20) 120.00
A159 A 4p rose (#26) 75.00
A160 A 6p lilac (#27) 210.00
A161 A 1sh green (#28) 700.00

A76 (Spanish Town)

A162 A 1p rose red (#20) 130.00
A163 A 4p rose (#26) 70.00
A164 A 6p lilac (#27) 120.00
A165 A 1sh green (#28) 525.00

A77 (Stewart Town)

A166 A 1p rose red (#20) 525.00
A167 A 4p rose (#26) 350.00
A168 A 6p lilac (#27) 210.00

A78 (Vere)

A169 A 1p rose red (#20) 325.00
A170 A 4p rose (#26) 105.00
A171 A 6p lilac (#27) 75.00
A172 A 1sh green (#28) 750.00

Cancels A38 (Ewarton) and A50 (Little River) were received after the post offices were closed. The numbers were reallocated in 1862 to Falmouth and Malvern, respectively. Cancel A63 (Pear Tree Grove) has not been found canceling stamps of Great Britain, even though its allocation is well documented.

Issued under British Administration

Values for unused stamps are for examples with original gum as defined in the catalogue introduction. Very fine examples of Nos. 1-12 will have perforations touching the design on at least one side due to the narrow spacing of the stamps on the plates. Stamps with perfs clear on all four sides are scarce and will command higher prices.

Queen Victoria
A1 A2

A3

A4

A5

A6

1860-63 Typo. Wmk. 45 *Perf. 14*

1 A1 1p blue 65.00 15.00
a. Diagonal half used as ½p on cover 825.00
b. 1p deep blue 140.00 35.00
c. 1p pale blue 77.50 19.00
d. 1p pale greenish blue 100.00 24.00
2 A2 2p rose 160.00 65.00
a. 2p deep rose 240.00 65.00
3 A3 3p green ('63) 160.00 32.50
4 A4 4p brown org 250.00 62.50
a. 4p orange 250.00 27.50
5 A5 6p lilac 225.00 27.50
a. 6p deep lilac 1,050. 65.00
b. 6p gray lilac 350.00 40.00
6 A6 1sh brown 225.00 35.00
a. 1sh lilac brown 700.00 30.00
b. 1sh yellow brown 575.00 32.50

All except No. 3 exist imperforate.

1870-71 Wmk. 1

7 A1 1p blue 70.00 .90
a. 1p deep blue 70.00 1.60
8 A2 2p rose 75.00 .85
a. 2p brownish rose 87.50 1.10
9 A3 3p green 110.00 9.25
10 A4 4p brown org ('72) 210.00 12.00
a. 4p red orange 450.00 6.50
11 A5 6p lilac ('71) 75.00 6.00
12 A6 1sh brown ('73) 27.50 9.50
Nos. 7-12 (6) 567.50 38.50

The 1p and 4p exist imperf.
See Nos. 17-23, 40, 43, 47-53.

A7

A8

A9

A10

1872, Oct. 29

13 A7 ½p claret 16.00 3.75
a. ½p deep claret 18.00 6.00

Exists imperf. See No. 16.

1875, Aug. 27 *Perf. 12½*

14 A8 2sh red brown 45.00 20.00
15 A9 5sh violet 97.50 *150.00*

Exist imperf.
See Nos. 29-30, 44, 54.

1883-90 Wmk. 2 *Perf. 14*

16 A7 ½p blue green ('85) 3.75 1.10
a. ½p gray green 1.10 .20
17 A1 1p blue ('84) 350.00 6.00
18 A1 1p carmine ('85) 42.50 .65
a. 1p rose 70.00 .95
19 A2 2p rose ('84) 215.00 4.50
20 A2 2p slate ('85) 87.50 .55
a. 2p gray 115.00 4.25
21 A3 3p ol green ('86) 2.75 1.40
a. 3p sage green ('86) 3.50 .90
22 A4 4p red brown 2.25 .40
a. 4p orange brown 440.00 24.00
23 A5 6p orange yel ('90) 6.00 5.00
a. 6p yellow 26.00 8.00
Nos. 16-23 (8) 709.75 19.60

Nos. 18 and 20 exist imperf. Perf. 12 stamps are considered to be proofs.
For surcharge, see No. 27.

#16-26, O1-O4 used in Cayman Islands.

See Cayman Islands for stamps with Grand Cayman and Cayman Brac cancellations.

1889-91

24 A10 1p lilac & red vio 4.75 .20
25 A10 2p deep green 8.00 *6.50*
a. 2p green 21.00 3.75
26 A10 2½p lilac & ultra ('91) 6.00 .75
Nos. 24-26 (3) 18.75 *7.45*

Unused copies of No. 25 may be distinguished from No. 25a by their brown gum.

No. 22 Surcharged in Black

1890, June

27 A4 2½p on 4p red brn 30.00 10.50
a. 1.5mm btw lines of surcharge 37.50 19.00
b. Double surcharge 350.00 250.00
d. "PFNNY" 100.00 70.00
f. As "d," double surcharge

Three settings of surcharge.

1897

28 A6 1sh brown 5.50 *6.50*
29 A8 2sh red brown 30.00 22.50
30 A9 5sh violet 60.00 *87.50*
Nos. 28-30 (3) 95.50 *116.50*

The 2sh exists imperf.

Llandovery Falls
A12

Arms of Jamaica
A13

1900, May 1 Engr. Wmk. 1

31 A12 1p red 4.25 .25

1901, Sept. 25

32 A12 1p red & black 3.75 .20
a. Pair, imperf. horiz. 9,750.
b. Bluish paper 120.00 110.00

1903-04 Typo. Wmk. 2

33 A13 ½p green & black 1.60 .30
b. "SERv ET" for "SERVIET" 45.00 *47.50*
34 A13 1p car & black ('04) 1.90 .20
b. "SERv ET" for "SERVIET" 35.00 37.50
35 A13 2½p ultra & black 3.75 .45
a. "SERv ET" for "SERVIET" 65.00 *80.00*
36 A13 5p yel & black ('04) 16.00 *25.00*
a. "SERv ET" for "SERVIET" 800.00 *1,050.*
Nos. 33-36 (4) 23.25 *25.95*
Set, overprinted "SPECIMEN" 87.50

1905-11 Chalky Paper Wmk. 3

37 A13 ½p green & black 5.00 .20
b. "SERv ET" for "SERVIET" 32.50 *45.00*
38 A13 1p car & black 20.00 .55
39 A13 2½p ultra & blk ('07) 3.25 4.50
40 A4 4p black, *yel* ('10) 8.00 *45.00*
Overprinted "SPECIMEN" 37.50
41 A13 5p yel & black ('07) 65.00 *75.00*
a. "SERv ET" for "SERVIET" 1,100. *1,300.*
42 A13 6p red vio & vio ('11) 14.00 13.00
Overprinted "SPECIMEN" 37.50
43 A6 1sh black, *green* ('10) 4.75 *9.25*
Overprinted "SPECIMEN" 37.50
44 A8 2sh vio, *blue* ('10) 7.00 3.75
Overprinted "SPECIMEN" 37.50
45 A13 5sh vio & black 47.50 45.00
Overprinted "SPECIMEN" 37.50
Nos. 37-45 (9) 174.50 196.25

1905-11 Ordinary Paper

46 A13 2½p ultra ('10) 3.00 1.40
a. 2½p deep ultramarine 2.75 1.90
Overprinted "SPECIMEN" 37.50
47 A3 3p sage green ('07) 6.50 4.00
a. 3p olive green ('07) 5.50 3.25

48 A3 3p pale purple, *yel* ('10) 5.00 3.75
Overprinted "SPECIMEN" 37.50
a. 3p vio, *yel* ('10) 2.10 1.60
49 A4 4p red brn ('08) 75.00 80.00
50 A4 4p red, *yel* ('11) 1.60 *8.50*
Overprinted "SPECIMEN" 37.50
51 A5 6p dull vio ('09) 30.00 *45.00*
Overprinted "SPECIMEN" 37.50
a. 6p purple, chalky paper ('10) 11.00 *20.00*
52 A5 6p org yel ('09) 26.50 *55.00*
a. 6p orange ('06) 17.00 27.50
53 A6 1sh brown ('06) 20.00 *32.50*
a. 1sh deep brown 30.00 *47.50*
54 A8 2sh red brn ('08) 110.00 *160.00*
Nos. 46-54 (9) 277.60 *390.15*

Nos. 48 and 51 also come on chalky paper.

A14

A15

1906

58 A14 ½p green 4.00 .25
a. Booklet pane of 6
b. ½p yellow green 9.25 .55
Overprinted "SPECIMEN" 37.50
c. ½p deep green 5.00 .25
59 A15 1p carmine 1.60 .20
Overprinted "SPECIMEN" 40.00

For overprints see Nos. MR1, MR4, MR7, MR10.

Edward VII
A16

George V
A17

1911, Feb. 3

60 A16 2p gray 3.50 *14.00*
Overprinted "SPECIMEN" 37.50

1912-20

61 A17 1p scarlet ('16) 2.00 .80
a. 1p carmine ('12) 1.75 .20
b. Booklet pane of 6
62 A17 1½p brown org ('16) 1.10 .70
a. 1½p yellow orange 15.00 1.25
63 A17 2p gray 2.25 *2.00*
64 A17 2½p dp br blue .75 *1.25*
a. 2"1/2)p ultra ('13) 1.75 .20

Chalky Paper

65 A17 3p violet, *yel* .60 .50
a. 3p violet, *lemon* ('16) 4.25 1.75
66 A17 4p scar & blk, *yel* ('13) .60 *4.00*
a. 4p scar & blk, *lemon* ('16) 26.00 21.00
b. 4p scar & blk, *pale yel* ('19) 24.00 17.00
67 A17 6p red vio & dl vio 4.00 2.50
a. 6p dull purple & bright purple ('12) 5.25 *10.50*
b. 6p dull purple & bright magenta ('20) 4.00 *2.50*
68 A17 1sh black, *green* 2.50 2.25
a. 1sh blk, *bl grn*, olive back ('20) 2.50 *6.25*
69 A17 2sh ultra & vio, *blue* ('19) 15.00 *29.00*
70 A17 5sh scarlet & green, *yel* ('19) 62.50 *100.00*
a. 5sh scarlet & green, *pale yellow* ('20) 62.50 *100.00*
b. 5sh scarlet & green, *orange buff* ('20) 140.00 *190.00*

Surface-colored Paper

71 A17 3p violet, *yel* ('13) .65 .45
72 A17 4p scar & black, *yel* ('14) 1.00 *4.50*
73 A17 1sh black, *green* ('15) 1.50 *5.50*
Nos. 61-73 (13) 94.45 *153.45*

See Nos. 101-102. For overprints see Nos. MR2-MR3, MR5-MR6, MR8-MR9, MR11.

Exhibition Buildings of 1891 — A18

Arawak Woman Preparing Cassava — A19

World War I Contingent Embarking for Overseas Duty — A20

King's House, Spanish Town — A21

Return of Overseas Contingent, 1919 — A22

Columbus Landing in Jamaica — A23

Cathedral in Spanish Town — A24

Statue of Queen Victoria — A26

Memorial to Admiral Rodney — A27

Monument to Sir Charles Metcalfe — A28

Woodland Scene — A29

King George V — A30

1919-21 Typo. Wmk. 3 *Perf. 14*

Chalky Paper

75 A18 ½p ol grn & dk grn ('20) 1.10 1.10
76 A19 1p org & car ('21) 2.40 2.00

Engr.

Ordinary Paper

77 A20 1½p green .45 1.10
78 A21 2p grn & bl ('21) 1.25 *4.50*
79 A22 2½p blue & dk blue ('21) 15.00 3.50
80 A23 3p blue & grn ('21) 1.75 *2.75*
81 A24 4p green & dk brown ('21) 2.75 *10.00*
83 A26 1sh brt org & org ('20) 4.25 *9.00*
a. Frame inverted *24,000.* *18,000.*
As "a," revenue cancel *3,000.*
84 A27 2sh brn & bl ('20) 15.00 *30.00*
85 A28 3sh org & violet ('20) 22.50 *92.50*
86 A29 5sh ocher & blue ('21) 62.50 *92.50*
87 A30 10sh dk myrtle grn ('20) 85.00 *175.00*
Nos. 75-87 (12) 213.95 *423.95*

See note after No. 100.

A 6p stamp depicting the abolition of slavery was sent to the Colony but was not issued. "Specimen" copies exist with wmk. 3 or 4. Value $1,500 each.

Without "Specimen," value $24,000.

Port Royal in 1853
A31

1921-23 Typo. Wmk. 4 *Perf. 14*

Chalky Paper

88 A18 ½p ol grn & dk grn ('22) .60 .60
a. Booklet pane of 4
89 A19 1p orange & car ('22) 1.75 .20
a. Booklet pane of 6

Engr.

Ordinary Paper

90 A20 1½p green 1.00 .50
91 A21 2p grn & blue 7.50 .90
92 A22 2½p bl & dk bl 6.25 2.00
93 A23 3p bl & grn ('22) 2.75 .80
94 A24 4p grn & dk brn 1.10 .35
95 A31 6p bl & blk ('22) 14.00 2.25
96 A26 1sh brn org & dl org 2.00 .90
97 A27 2sh brn & bl ('22) 3.75 .75
98 A28 3sh org & violet 12.50 10.50
99 A29 5sh ocher & bl ('23) 32.50 29.00
a. 5sh orange & blue 30.00 26.00
100 A30 10sh dk myrtle green ('22) 57.50 80.00
Nos. 88-100 (13) 143.20 128.75
Set, never hinged 260.00

No. 89 differs from No. 76 in having the words "Postage and Revenue" at the bottom.

On No. 79 the horizontal bar of the flag at the left has a broad white line below the colored line. On No. 92 this has been corrected and the broad white line placed above the colored line.

Watermark is sideways on #76-77, 87, 89-90.

Type of 1912-19 Issue

1921-27 Typo. Wmk. 4

101 A17 ½p green ('27) 2.00 .20
a. Booklet pane of 6
102 A17 6p red vio & dl vio 9.25 4.50

No. 102 is on chalky paper.

A32

Type I

Type II

Type II — Cross shading beneath "Jamaica."

1929-32 Engr. *Perf. 13½x14, 14*

103 A32 1p red, type I 2.50 .20
a. 1p red, type II ('32) 5.25 .20
b. Booklet pane of 6, type II
104 A32 1½p brown 2.25 .20
105 A32 9p violet brown 3.75 1.25
Nos. 103-105 (3) 8.50 1.65
Set, never hinged 14.00

The frames on Nos. 103 to 105 differ.

Coco Palms at Columbus Cove — A33

Scene near Castleton, St. Andrew — A34

Priestman's River, Portland Parish — A35

1932 *Perf. 12½*

106 A33 2p grn & gray blk 15.00 3.25
a. Vertical pair, imperf. between *6,250.*
107 A34 2½p ultra & sl blue 3.25 1.75
a. Vertical pair, imperf. between *12,500.* *12,500.*
108 A35 6p red vio & gray black 14.00 2.00
Nos. 106-108 (3) 32.25 7.00
Set, never hinged 40.00

Common Design Types pictured following the introduction.

Silver Jubilee Issue

Common Design Type

1935, May 6 *Perf. 11x12*

109 CD301 1p car & blue .45 .25
a. Booklet pane of 6 *175.00*
110 CD301 1½p black & ultra .70 *1.75*
111 CD301 6p indigo & grn 6.25 *16.00*
112 CD301 1sh brn vio & ind 5.25 *9.25*
Nos. 109-112 (4) 12.65 27.25
Set, never hinged 20.00

Coronation Issue

Common Design Type

1937, May 12 *Perf. 13½x14*

113 CD302 1p carmine .20 .20
114 CD302 1½p gray black .20 .20
115 CD302 2½p bright ultra .40 .50
Nos. 113-115 (3) .80 .90
Set, never hinged 1.75

King George VI — A36

Coco Palms at Columbus Cove — A37

Scene near Castleton, St. Andrew — A38

Bananas A39

Citrus Grove A40

Priestman's River, Portland Parish — A41

Kingston Harbor A42

Sugar Industry A43

Bamboo Walk — A44

Woodland Scene — A45

King George VI — A46

1938-51 ***Perf. 13½x14***

116	A36	½p dk blue grn	1.25	.20
a.		Booklet pane of 6	9.00	
b.		Wmkd. sideways		
117	A36	1p carmine	.90	.20
a.		Booklet pane of 6	13.00	
118	A36	1½p brown	.90	.20

Perf. 12½, 13x13½, 13½x13, 12½x13

119	A37	2p grn & gray blk, perf. 12½	.90	.90
a.		Perf. 13x13½ ('39)	1.90	.55
b.		Perf. 12½x13 ('51)	.90	.20
120	A38	2½p ultra & sl bl	2.10	*2.00*
121	A39	3p grn & lt ultra	.55	*1.75*
122	A40	4p grn & yel brn	.30	.20
123	A41	6p red vio & gray blk, perf. 13½x13 ('50)	1.50	.20
a.		Perf. 12½	2.50	.35
124	A42	9p rose lake	.30	.55
125	A43	1sh dk brn & brt grn	4.25	.20
126	A44	2sh brn & brt bl	14.50	1.10

Perf. 13, 14

127	A45	5sh ocher & bl, perf. 13 ('50)	4.50	4.25
a.		Bluish paper, perf. 13 ('49)	4.50	3.50
b.		Perf. 14	10.00	3.75
128	A46	10sh dk myrtle grn, perf. 14	8.00	*10.50*
a.		Perf. 13 ('50)	6.50	*8.00*
		Nos. 116-128 (13)	39.95	22.25
		Set, never hinged	80.00	

See Nos. 140, 148, 149, 152.

Catalogue values for unused stamps in this section, from this point to the end of the section, are for Never Hinged items.

Courthouse, Falmouth A47

Kings Charles II and George VI A48

House of Assembly, 1762-1869 A50

Institute of Jamaica — A49

Allegory of Labor and Learning — A51

Constitution and Flag of Jamaica A52

Perf. 12½

1945, Aug. 20 **Engr.** **Wmk. 4**

129	A47	1½p brown	.20	.20
a.		Booklet pane of 4	37.50	
b.		Perf. 12½x13½ ('46)	3.50	.60
130	A48	2p dp grn, perf. 12½x13½	.35	*.55*
a.		Perf. 12½	7.25	.90
131	A49	3p bright ultra	.20	*.55*
a.		Perf. 13 ('46)	1.75	*3.00*
132	A50	4½p slate black	.35	.35
a.		Perf. 13 ('46)	2.40	*2.75*
133	A51	2sh chocolate	.35	.55
134	A52	5sh deep blue	1.25	1.10
135	A49	10sh green	.95	*2.40*
		Nos. 129-135 (7)	3.65	*5.70*

Granting of a new Constitution in 1944.

Peace Issue

Common Design Type

1946, Oct. 14 **Wmk. 4** ***Perf. 13½***

136	CD303	1½p black brown	.20	.20
a.		Perf. 13½x14	2.40	.20

Perf. 13½x14

137	CD303	3p deep blue	.60	.60
a.		Perf. 13½	.40	*4.25*

Silver Wedding Issue

Common Design Types

1948, Dec. 1 **Photo.** ***Perf. 14x14½***

138	CD304	1½p red brown	.25	.25

Engr.; Name Typo.

Perf. 11½x11

139	CD305	£1 red	27.50	*47.50*

Type of 1938 and

Tobacco Industry A53

1949, Aug. 15 **Engr.** ***Perf. 12½***

140	A39	3p ultra & slate blue	1.25	1.25
141	A53	£1 purple & brown	37.50	32.50

UPU Issue

Common Design Types

Perf. 13½, 11x11½

1949, Oct. 10 **Wmk. 4**

142	CD306	1½p red brown	.20	.20
143	CD307	2p dark green	1.25	.95
144	CD308	3p indigo	.40	*.65*
145	CD309	6p rose violet	.55	*1.25*
		Nos. 142-145 (4)	2.40	3.05

University Issue

Common Design Types

1951, Feb. 16 ***Perf. 14x14½***

146	CD310	2p brown & gray blk	.30	.20
147	CD311	6p rose lilac & gray blk	.60	.35

George VI Type of 1938

1951, Oct. 25 ***Perf. 13½x14***

148	A36	½p orange	.60	.25
a.		Booklet pane of 6	9.00	
149	A36	1p blue green	.90	.20
a.		Booklet pane of 6	18.00	

Boy Scout Emblem with Map — A54

Map and Emblem A55

Perf. 13½x13, 13x13½

1952, Mar. 5 **Typo.** **Wmk. 4**

150	A54	2p blk, yel grn & blue	.20	.20
151	A55	6p blk, yel grn & dk red	.30	*.60*

1st Caribbean Boy Scout Jamboree, 1952.

Banana Type of 1938

1952, July 1 **Engr.** ***Perf. 12½***

152	A39	3p rose red & green	1.50	.25

SEMI-POSTAL STAMPS

Native Girl — SP1

Native Boy — SP2

Native Boy and Girl — SP3

1923, Nov. 1 **Engr.** ***Perf. 12***

B1	SP1	½p green & black	.70	*6.25*
B2	SP2	1p car & black	2.00	*11.50*
B3	SP3	2½p blue & black	9.75	*20.00*
		Nos. B1-B3 (3)	12.45	*37.75*

Each stamp was sold for ½p over face value. The surtax benefited the Child Saving League of Jamaica.

WAR TAX STAMPS

Regular Issues of 1906-19 Overprinted

WAR STAMP.

1916 **Wmk. 3** ***Perf. 14***

MR1	A14	½p green	.20	.40
a.		Without period	11.00	*27.50*
b.		Double overprint	110.00	*140.00*
c.		Inverted overprint	100.00	*125.00*
d.		As "c," without period	350.00	
MR2	A17	3p violet, *yel*	1.10	*20.00*
a.		Without period	25.00	*85.00*

Surface-colored Paper

MR3	A17	3p violet, *yel*	12.50	*30.00*
		Nos. MR1-MR3 (3)	13.80	*50.40*

Regular Issues of 1906-18 Overprinted

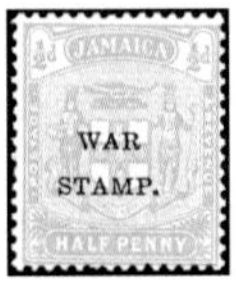

MR4	A14	½p green	.20	.30
a.		Without period	12.50	*37.50*
b.		Pair, one without ovpt.	2,750.	2,500.
c.		"R" inserted by hand	800.00	750.00
d.		"WAR" only	125.00	
MR5	A17	1½p orange	.20	.20
a.		Without period	5.75	*8.50*
b.		"TAMP"	150.00	*160.00*
c.		"S" inserted by hand	275.00	
d.		"R" omitted	1,400.	1,250.
e.		"R" inserted by hand	800.00	700.00
MR6	A17	3p violet, *yel*	1.40	1.10
a.		Without period	32.50	*62.50*
b.		"TAMP"	425.00	400.00
c.		"S" inserted by hand	200.00	200.00
d.		Inverted overprint	325.00	175.00
e.		As "a," inverted		
		Nos. MR4-MR6 (3)	1.80	1.60

Regular Issues of 1906-19 Overprinted

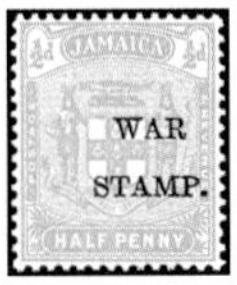

1917, Mar.

MR7	A14	½p green	.60	.35
a.		Without period	9.25	*22.50*
b.		Overprinted on back instead of face	200.00	
c.		Inverted overprint	14.00	40.00
MR8	A17	1½p orange	.20	.20
a.		Without period	4.00	*19.00*
b.		Double overprint	92.50	*100.00*
c.		Inverted overprint	92.50	85.00
d.		As "a," inverted		
MR9	A17	3p violet, *yel*	.60	1.60
a.		Without period	17.00	*40.00*
b.		Vertical overprint	350.00	350.00
c.		Inverted overprint	160.00	
d.		As "a," inverted		
		Nos. MR7-MR9 (3)	1.40	2.15

There are many minor varieties of Nos. MR1-MR9.

Regular Issues of 1906-19 Overprinted in Red

1919, Oct. 4

MR10	A14	½p green	.20	.20
MR11	A17	3p violet, *yel*	4.00	3.50

OFFICIAL STAMPS

No. 16 Overprinted in Black

Type I — Word 15 to 16mm long.
Type II — Word 17 to 17½mm long.

1890 **Wmk. 2** ***Perf. 14***

O1	A7	½p green (II)	9.75	1.25
a.		Type I	29.00	25.00
b.		Inverted overprint (II)	75.00	*80.00*
c.		Double overprint (II)	80.00	*90.00*
d.		Dbl. ovpt., one invtd. (II)	400.00	400.00
e.		Dbl. ovpt., one vert. (II)	1,100.	
f.		Double overprint (I)	575.00	
g.		Missing "O"	550.00	
h.		Missing "L"	700.00	700.00
i.		Missing both "I"s	625.00	625.00

No. 16 and Type of 1889 Overprinted

1890-91

O2	A7	½p green	9.25	.70
O3	A10	1p carmine rose	5.25	.90
O4	A10	2p slate	11.00	1.25
		Nos. O2-O4 (3)	25.50	2.85

JAPAN

jə-'pan

LOCATION — North Pacific Ocean, east of China
GOVT. — Constitutional monarchy
AREA — 142,726 sq. mi.
POP. — 120,020,000 (est. 1984)
CAPITAL — Tokyo

1000 Mon = 10 Sen
100 Sen = 1 Yen (or En)
10 Rin = 1 Sen

Watermarks

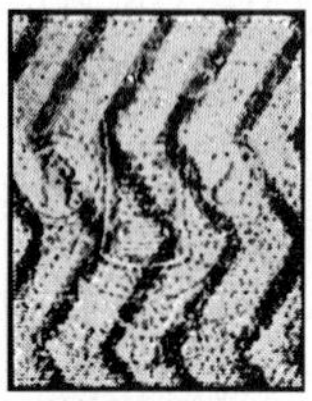
Wmk. 141 — Zigzag Lines

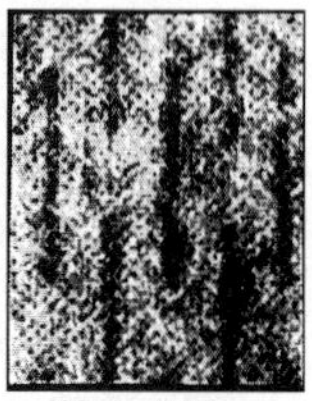
Wmk. 142 — Parallel Lines

Wmk. 257 — Curved Wavy Lines

Counterfeits of Nos. 1-71 are plentiful. Some are excellent and deceive many collectors.

Nos. 1-54A were printed from plates of 40 with individually engraved subjects. Each stamp in the sheet is slightly different.

Pair of Dragons Facing Characters of Value — A1

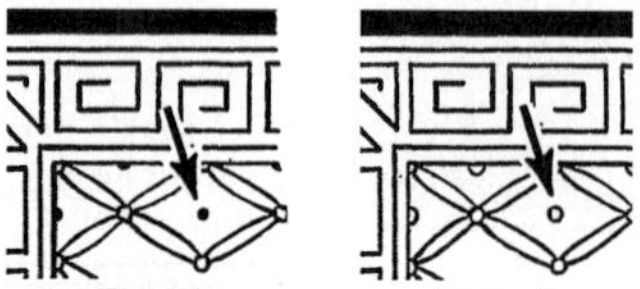
Plate I Plate II

48 mon:
Plate I — Solid dots in inner border.
Plate II — Tiny circles replace dots.

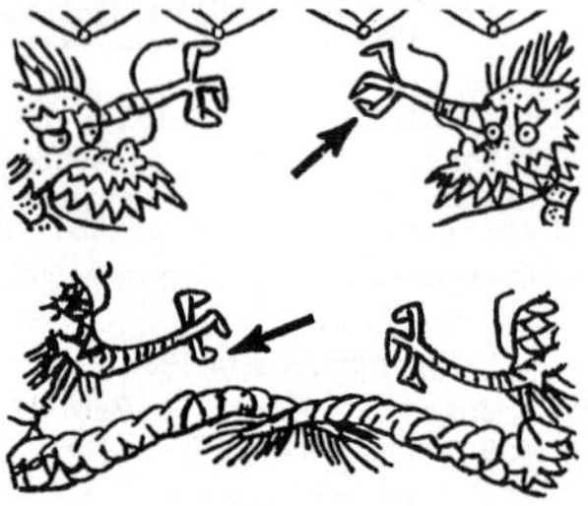
Plate I

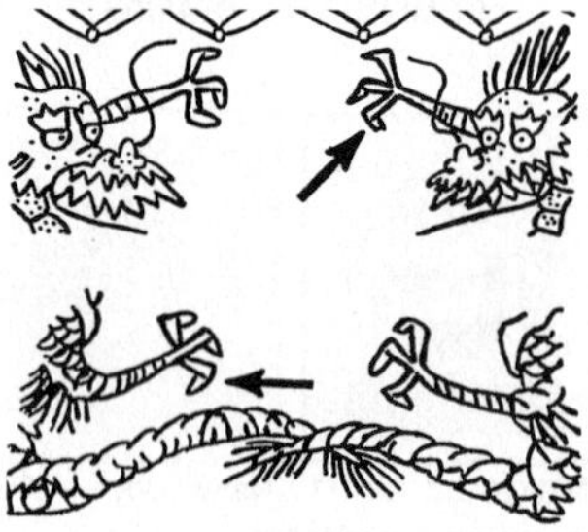
Plate II

100 mon:
Plate I — Lowest dragon claw at upper right and at lower left point upward.
Plate II — Same two claws point downward.

Plate I Plate II

200 mon:
Plate I — Dot in upper left corner.
Plate II — No dot. (Some Plate I copies show dot faintly; these can be mistaken for Plate II.)

Plate I Plate II

500 mon:
Plate I — Lower right corner of Greek-type border incomplete
Plate II — Short horizontal line completes corner border pattern.

Unwmk.

1871, Apr. 20 Engr. *Imperf.*

Native Laid Paper Without Gum
Denomination in Black

1	A1	48m brown (I)	225.	275.
a.		48m red brown (I)	225.	275.
b.		Wove paper (I)	240.	275.
c.		48m brown (II)	260.	285.
d.		Wove paper (II)	260.	285.
2	A1	100m blue (I)	200.	225.
a.		Wove paper (I)	260.	260.
b.		Plate II	475.	450.
c.		Wove paper (II)	625.	625.
3	A1	200m vermilion (I)	350.	300.
a.		Wove paper (I)	375.	325.
b.		Plate II	1,700.	1,500.
c.		Wove paper (II)		*3,000.*
4	A1	500m blue green (I)	425.	425.
a.		500m greenish blue (I)	475.	425.
b.		500m green (I)	1,000.	950.
c.		500m yellow green (I)	1,050.	1,000.
d.		Wove paper (I)	525.	475.
e.		500m blue green (II)	450.	*2,600.*
f.		500m greenish blue (II)	450.	*2,600.*
g.		Wove paper (II)	1,700.	*3,250.*
h.		Denomination inverted (I)		*85,000.*

Perforations, Nos. 5-8

Perforations on Nos. 5-8 generally are rough and irregular due to the perforating equipment used and the quality of the paper. Values are for stamps with rough perfs that touch the frameline on one or more sides.

Dragons and Denomination — A1a

½ sen:
Plate I — Same as 48m Plate II. Measures not less than 19.8x19.8mm. Some subjects on this plate measure 20.3x20.2mm.
Plate II — Same as 48m Plate II. Measures not more than 19.7x19.3mm. Some subjects measure 19.3x18.7mm.

Plate I & II Plate III

1 sen:
Plate I — Same as 100m Plate I. Narrow space between frameline and Greek-type border.
Plate II — Same as 100m Plate II. Same narrow space between frameline and border.
Plate III — Space between frameline and border is much wider. Frameline thinner. Shading on dragon heads heavier than on Plates I and II.

Native Laid Paper
With or Without Gum

1872 *Perf. 9-12 & compound*

Denomination in Black

5	A1a	½s brown (II)	75.00	80.00
a.		½s red brown (II)	75.00	80.00
b.		½s gray brown (II)	75.00	80.00
c.		Wove paper (II)	700.00	625.00
d.		½s brown (I)	100.00	150.00
e.		½s red brown (I)	100.00	150.00
f.		½s gray brown (I)	100.00	150.00
g.		Wove paper (I)	150.00	210.00
6	A1a	1s blue (II)	225.00	240.00
a.		Wove paper (II)	475.00	475.00
b.		Plate I	900.00	*1,800.*
c.		Wove paper (I)	*4,250.*	
d.		Plate III	*7,000.*	1,500.
e.		Wove paper (III)		*4,000.*
7	A1a	2s vermilion	375.00	375.00
a.		Wove paper	400.00	400.00
8	A1a	5s blue green	500.00	500.00
a.		5s yellow green	500.00	475.00
b.		Wove paper	675.00	675.00

In 1896 the government made imperforate imitations of Nos. 6-7 to include in a presentation book.

Expect perforations on Nos. 9-71 to be rough and irregular.

Imperial Crest and Branches of Kiri Tree — A2

Dragons and Chrysanthemum Crest — A3

Imperial Chrysanthemum Crest — A4

Imperial Crest and Branches of Kiri Tree — A5

Perf. 9 to 13 and Compound

1872-73

Native Wove or Laid Paper of Varying Thickness

9	A2	½s brown, *wove*	21.00	21.00
a.		Upper character in left label has 2 diagonal top strokes missing	1,600.	1,250.
b.		Laid paper	67.50	—
c.		As "a," laid paper	1,900.	—

Nos. 9, 9a are on stiff, brittle wove paper. Nos. 9b, 9c on a soft, fibrous paper. Nos. 9b and 9c probably were never put in use.

10	A2	1s blue, *wove*	47.50	26.00
a.		Laid paper	50.00	27.50
11	A2	2s ver, *wove*	100.00	50.00
12	A2	2s dull rose, *laid*	75.00	35.00
a.		Wove paper	100.00	47.50
13	A2	2s yel, *laid* ('73)	75.00	21.00
a.		Wove paper ('73)	175.00	26.00
14	A2	4s rose, *laid* ('73)	67.50	25.00
a.		Wove paper ('73)	210.00	32.00
15	A3	10s blue grn, *wove*	260.00	160.00
16	A3	10s yel grn, *laid*	475.00	325.00
a.		Wove paper ('73)	525.00	500.00
17	A4	20s lilac, *wove*	350.00	300.00
a.		20s violet, *wove*	350.00	300.00
b.		20s red violet, *laid*		—
18	A5	30s gray, *wove*	450.00	350.00

See Nos. 24-25, 30-31, 37-39, 51-52.

1874

Foreign Wove Paper

24	A2	4s rose	600.	200.
25	A5	30s gray	—	*5,000.*

A6

A7

A8

Design A6 differs from A2 by the addition of a syllabic character in a box covering crossed kiri branches above SEN. Stamps of design A6 differ for each value in border and spandrel designs.

In design A7, the syllabic character appears just below the buckle. In design A8, it appears in an oval frame at bottom center below SE of SEN.

With Syllabic Characters

イ	ロ	ハ	ニ	ホ	ヘ	ト	チ
i	ro	ha	ni	ho	he	to	chi
1	2	3	4	5	6	7	8
リ	ヌ	ル	ヲ	ワ	カ	ヨ	タ
ri	nu	ru	wo	wa	ka	yo	ta
9	10	11	12	13	14	15	16
レ	ソ	ツ	子	ナ	ラ	ム	
re	so	tsu	ne	na	ra	mu	
17	18	19	20	21	22	23	

Perf. 9½ to 12½ and Compound

1874

Native Laid or Wove Paper

28 A6 2s yellow 175.00 275.00

Unused value is for copies with syll. 16, used value for copies with syll. 1.

29 A7 6s vio brn (Syll. 1) 1,100. 325.
Syllabic 2 1,300. 325.
Syllabic 3 850.
Syllabic 4,5,7 425.
Syllabic 6 525.
Syllabic 8 400.
Syllabic 9 475.
Syllabic 10 2,900.
Syllabic 11 2,600.
Syllabic 12 1,500.
30 A4 20s red vio (Syll. 3) *6,750.*
Syllabic 2 *7,000.*
31 A5 30s gray (Syll. 1) 2,600. 2,850.
a. Very thin laid paper 2,600. 2,850.

No. 30, syll. 1, comes only with specimen dot. Value $20,000.

Perf. 11 to 12½ and Compound

1874

Foreign Wove Paper

32 A6 ½s brown (Syll. 1) 22.50 15.00
Syllabic 2 35.00 30.00
33 A6 1s blue (Syll. 4,6,9) 135.00 30.00
Syllabic 1,2,3 150.00 30.00
Syllabic 5 425.00 100.00
Syllabic 7 190.00 80.00
Syllabic 8 135.00 30.00
Syllabic 10 150.00 42.50
Syllabic 11 150.00 80.00
Syllabic 12 160.00 42.50
34 A6 2s yel (Syll. 2-4, 9, 15, 17, 20) 110.00 26.00
Syllabic 1 210.00 26.00
Syllabic 5 300.00 26.00
Syllabic 6 1,700. 37.50
Syllabic 7 1,700. 18.00
Syllabic 8 110.00 29.00
Syllabic 10 *2,250.* 40.00
Syllabic 11 110.00 18.00
Syllabic 12,22 *2,400.* 18.00
Syllabic 13 *1,900.* 18.00
Syllabic 14 *2,400.* 29.00
Syllabic 16 *1,900.* 18.00
Syllabic 18,19 110.00 18.00
Syllabic 21 190.00 18.00
Syllabic 23 200.00 18.00
35 A6 4s rose (Syll. 1) 1,900. 275.00
36 A7 6s vio brn (Syll. 16) 110.00 45.00
Syllabic 10 425.00 475.00
Syllabic 11 375.00
Syllabic 13 *4,500.*
Syllabic 14 240.00 190.00
Syllabic 15 *2,400.*
Syllabic 17 150.00 67.50
Syllabic 18 210.00 85.00
37 A3 10s yel grn (Syll. 2) 72.50 42.50
Syllabic 1 240.00 75.00
Syllabic 3 550.00 300.00
38 A4 20s violet (Syll. 5) 200.00 65.00
Syllabic 4 200.00 65.00
39 A5 30s gray (Syll. 1) 200.00 57.50

1875 ***Perf. 9 to 13 and Compound***

40 A6 ½s gray (Syll. 2, 3) 17.00 16.00
Syllabic 4 25.00
41 A6 1s brn (Syll. 15-17) 30.00 15.00
Syllabic 5 300.00 42.50
Syllabic 7 225.00
Syllabic 8 *13,500.* 210.00
Syllabic 12 500.00 150.00
Syllabic 13 40.00 15.00
Syllabic 14 42.50 15.00
42 A6 4s green (Syll. 1) 85.00 20.00
Syllabic 2 125.00 19.00
Syllabic 3 110.00 19.00
43 A7 6s orange (Syll. 16,17) 75.00 19.00
Syllabic 10 150.00 42.50
Syllabic 11 125.00 32.50
Syllabic 13 125.00 29.00
Syllabic 14 160.00 32.50
Syllabic 15
44 A8 6s orange (Syll. 20) 72.50 17.00
Syllabic 19 75.00 15.00
Syllabic 21 95.00 19.00
Syllabic 22 3,500. 1,500.

Dragons
A9

Wild Goose
A10

Wagtail — A11

Imperial Crest — A11a

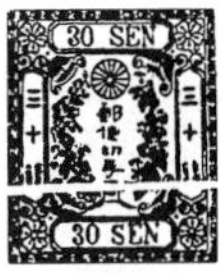
Kiri Branches
A11b

Goshawk
A12

45 A9 10s ultra (Syll. 4) 100.00 17.50
Syllabic 5 *3,250.* 300.00
46 A10 12s rose (Syll. 1) 210.00 100.00
Syllabic 2 225.00 125.00
Syllabic 3 *3,000.* 400.00
47 A11 15s lilac (Syll. 1) 210.00 125.00
Syllabic 2 210.00 125.00
Syllabic 3 225.00 140.00
48 A11a 20s rose (Syll. 8) 62.50 15.00
49 A11b 30s vio (Syll. 2-4) 115.00 50.00
50 A12 45s lake (Syll. 1) 250.00 125.00
Syllabic 2 1,250. 425.00
Syllabic 3 1,200. 350.00

Issued: #46, syll. 2, 1882; #46, syll. 3, 1883; others, 1875.

The 1s brown on laid paper, type A6, formerly listed as No. 50A, is one of several stamps of the preceding issue which exist on a laid type paper. They are difficult to identify and mainly of interest to specialists.

Without Syllabic Characters

1875

51 A2 1s brown *5,250.* 550.00
52 A2 4s green 275.00 70.00

Branches of Kiri Tree Tied with Ribbon
A13

Imperial Crest and Kiri Branches
A14

1875-76

53 A13 1s brown 55.00 13.00
54 A13 2s yellow 100.00 16.00
54A A14 5s green ('76) 200.00 90.00
Nos. 53-54A (3) 355.00 119.00

A15

A16

Imperial Crest, Star and Kiri Branches
A17

Sun, Kikumon and Kiri Branches
A18

Imperial Crest and Kiri Branches
A19

Kikumon
A20

Perf. 8 to 14 and Compound

1876-77 **Typo.**

55 A15 5r slate 16.00 10.00
56 A16 1s black 37.50 4.25
a. Horiz. pair, imperf. btwn.
57 A16 2s brown ol 52.50 3.00
58 A16 4s blue grn 42.50 4.00
a. 4s green 42.50 4.00
59 A17 5s brown 65.00 22.50
60 A17 6s orange ('77) 160.00 57.50
61 A17 8s vio brn ('77) 67.50 6.00
62 A17 10s blue ('77) 55.00 2.50
63 A17 12s rose ('77) 210.00 150.00
64 A18 15s yel grn ('77) 150.00 2.50
65 A18 20s dk blue ('77) 160.00 12.00
66 A18 30s violet ('77) 210.00 110.00
a. 30s red violet 210.00 110.00
67 A18 45s carmine ('77) 625.00 525.00

1879

68 A16 1s maroon 15.00 1.25
69 A16 2s dk violet 40.00 2.00
70 A16 3s orange 60.00 24.00
71 A18 50s carmine 210.00 12.50
Nos. 68-71 (4) 325.00 39.75

1883

72 A16 1s green 11.50 .60
73 A16 2s car rose 15.00 .25
74 A17 5s ultra 22.50 .50
Nos. 72-74 (3) 49.00 1.35

1888-92

75 A15 5r gray blk ('89) 5.00 .45
76 A16 3s lilac rose ('92) 15.00 .45
77 A16 4s olive bis 13.00 .45
78 A17 8s blue lilac 19.00 1.60
79 A17 10s brown org 17.00 .45
80 A18 15s purple 57.50 .50
81 A18 20s orange 75.00 1.50
a. 20s yellow 75.00 1.50
82 A19 25s blue green 150.00 1.50
83 A18 50s brown 100.00 3.25
84 A20 1y carmine 160.00 4.25
Nos. 75-84 (10) 611.50 14.40

Stamps of types A16-A18 differ for each value, in backgrounds and ornaments.

Nos. 58, 61-62, 64-65, 71-84 are found with telegraph or telephone office cancellations. These sell at considerably lower prices than postally used copies.

Cranes and Imperial Crest — A21

Perf. 11½ to 13 and Compound

1894, Mar. 9

85 A21 2s carmine 22.50 3.00
86 A21 5s ultra 35.00 11.00

25th wedding anniv. of Emperor Meiji (Mutsuhito) and Empress Haru.

Gen. Yoshihisa Kitashirakawa
A22 A23

Field Marshal Akihito Arisugawa
A24 A25

1896, Aug. 1 **Engr.**

87 A22 2s rose 26.00 2.75
88 A23 5s deep ultra 52.50 2.75
89 A24 2s rose 26.00 2.75
90 A25 5s deep ultra 52.50 2.75
Nos. 87-90 (4) 157.00 11.00

Victory in Chinese-Japanese War (1894-95).

A26

A27

A28

A29

Perf. 11½ to 14 and Compound

1899-1907 **Typo.**

91 A26 5r gray 5.50 1.00
92 A26 ½s gray ('01) 3.00 .20
93 A26 1s lt red brn 3.50 .20
94 A26 1½s ultra ('00) 12.00 .85
95 A26 1½s violet ('06) 9.00 .25
96 A26 2s lt green 9.00 .20
97 A26 3s violet brn 8.50 .25
a. Double impression
98 A26 3s rose ('06) 5.00 .25
99 A26 4s rose 6.00 1.25
a. 4s pink ('06) 7.00 1.75
100 A26 5s orange yel 17.00 .25
101 A27 6s maroon ('07) 29.00 3.50
102 A27 8s olive grn 30.00 5.00
103 A27 10s deep blue 11.00 .20
104 A27 15s purple 40.00 2.00
105 A27 20s red orange 21.00 .25
106 A28 25s blue green 60.00 1.00
107 A28 50s red brown 60.00 2.00
108 A29 1y carmine 70.00 3.00
Nos. 91-108 (18) 399.50 21.65

For overprints see Nos. M1, Offices in China, 1-18, Offices in Korea, 1-14.

Boxes for Rice Cakes and Marriage Certificates
A30

Symbols of Korea and Japan
A31

Perf. 11½ to 12½ and Compound

1900, May 10

109 A30 3s carmine 28.00 1.00

Wedding of the Crown Prince Yoshihito and Princess Sadako.

For overprints see Offices in China No. 19, Offices in Korea, 15.

1905, July 1

110 A31 3s rose red 77.50 19.00

Issued to commemorate the amalgamation of the postal services of Japan and Korea. Korean stamps were withdrawn from sale June 30, 1905, but remained valid until Aug. 31. No. 110 was used in the Korea and China Offices of Japan, as well as in Japan proper.

Field-piece and Japanese Flag — A32

Empress Jingo — A33

1906, Apr. 29

111 A32 1½s blue 26.00 4.00
112 A32 3s carmine rose 55.00 16.00

Triumphal military review following the Russo-Japanese War.

1908 **Engr.**

113 A33 5y green 750.00 5.00
114 A33 10y dark violet 1,000. 7.50

The frame of No. 114 differs slightly from the illustration.

See Nos. 146-147.

For overprints see Offices in China Nos. 20-21, 48-49.

A34

A35

A36

Perf. 12, 12x13, 13x13½

1913 **Typo.** **Unwmk.**

115 A34 ½s brown 6.00 .85
116 A34 1s orange 12.00 .85
117 A34 1½s lt blue 16.00 1.25
a. Booklet pane of 6 175.00
118 A34 2s green 17.00 .85
119 A34 3s rose 24.00 .45
a. Booklet pane of 6 175.00
120 A35 4s red 26.00 10.50
121 A35 5s violet 30.00 1.25
122 A35 10s deep blue 95.00 .60
123 A35 20s claret 95.00 1.25
124 A35 25s olive green 95.00 2.60
125 A36 1y yel grn & mar 650.00 24.00
Nos. 115-125 (11) 1,066. 44.45

1914-25 **Wmk. 141** **Granite Paper**

Size: 19x22½mm ("Old Die")

127 A34 ½s brown 2.10 .20
128 A34 1s orange 2.10 .20
129 A34 1½s blue 2.10 .20
a. Booklet pane of 6 72.50
d. As "a," imperf.
130 A34 2s green 4.25 .20
a. Booklet pane of 6 72.50
131 A34 3s rose 1.60 .20
a. Booklet pane of 6 60.00
132 A35 4s red 14.00 1.00
a. Booklet pane of 6 72.50
133 A35 5s violet 13.00 .45
134 A35 6s brown ('19) 18.00 2.40
136 A35 8s gray ('19) 15.00 9.00
137 A35 10s deep blue 15.00 .20
a. Booklet pane of 6 72.50
138 A35 13s olive brn ('25) 35.00 1.90
139 A35 20s claret 72.50 .60
140 A35 25s olive grn 12.00 .85
141 A36 30s orange brn ('19) 18.00 .50
143 A36 50s dk brown ('19) 26.00 1.00
145 A36 1y yel grn & mar 140.00 1.50
b. Imperf., pair
146 A33 5y green 425.00 4.00
147 A33 10y violet 625.00 6.00
Nos. 127-147 (18) 1,440. 30.40

1924-33

"New Die" Size: 18½x22mm (Flat Plate)

or 18½x22½mm (Rotary)

127a A34 ½s brown 1.75 .95
128a A34 1s orange 1.75 .95
129b A34 1½s blue 2.75 .30
c. Bklt. pane of 6 ('30) 19.00
131b A34 3s rose 1.10 .20
c. Bklt. pane of 6 ('28) 45.00
133a A35 5s violet 15.00 .20
135 A35 7s red org ('30) 7.75 .20
138a A35 13s bister brn ('25) 6.00 .20
140a A35 25s olive green 45.00 .20
142 A36 30s org & grn ('29) 17.00 .30
144 A36 50s yel brn & dk bl ('29) 12.00 .50
145a A36 1y yel grn & mar 67.50 1.00
Nos. 127a-145a (11) 177.60 5.00

See Nos. 212-213, 239-241, 243, 245, 249-252, 255. For overprints see Nos. C1-C2, M2-M5, Offices in China, 22-47.

Ceremonial Cap — A37

Imperial Throne — A38

Enthronement Hall, Kyoto — A39

Perf. 12½

1915, Nov. 10 **Typo.** **Unwmk.**

148 A37 1½s red & blk 2.00 .55
149 A38 3s orange & vio 2.50 .80

Engr.

Perf. 12x12½

150 A39 4s carmine rose 12.00 10.00
151 A39 10s ultra 24.00 16.00
Nos. 148-151 (4) 40.50 27.35

Enthronement of Emperor Yoshihito.

Mandarin Duck — A40

Ceremonial Cap — A41

1916, Nov. 3 **Typo.** ***Perf. 12½***

152 A40 1½s green, red & yel 2.00 1.00
153 A40 3s red & yellow 3.75 1.25
154 A41 10s ultra & dk blue 625.00 225.00

Nomination of the Prince Heir Apparent, later Emperor Hirohito.

A42

Dove and Olive Branch — A43

Perf. 12, 12½, 13½x13

1919, July 1 **Engr.**

155 A42 1½s dark brown 2.00 .60
156 A43 3s gray green 2.50 1.00
157 A42 4s rose 5.50 3.75
158 A43 10s dark blue 23.00 12.00
Nos. 155-158 (4) 33.00 17.35

Restoration of peace after World War I.

Census Officer, A.D. 652 — A44

Meiji Shrine, Tokyo — A45

Perf. 12½

1920, Sept. 25 **Typo.** **Unwmk.**

159 A44 1½s red violet 6.50 2.60
160 A44 3s vermilion 7.00 2.60

Taking of the 1st modern census in Japan. Not available for foreign postage except to China.

1920, Nov. 1 **Engr.**

161 A45 1½s dull violet 2.50 1.10
162 A45 3s rose 2.50 1.10

Dedication of the Meiji Shrine. Not available for foreign postage except to China.

National and Postal Flags — A46

Ministry of Communications Building, Tokyo — A47

Typographed (A46), Engraved (A47)

1921, Apr. 20 ***Perf. 12½, 13x13½***

163 A46 1½s gray grn & red 1.60 .90
164 A47 3s violet brn 2.10 1.00
165 A46 4s rose & red 30.00 17.00
166 A47 10s dark blue 175.00 125.00
Nos. 163-166 (4) 208.70 143.90

50th anniv. of the establishment of postal service and Japanese postage stamps.

Battleships "Katori" and "Kashima" — A48

1921, Sept. 3 **Litho.** ***Perf. 12½***

167 A48 1½s violet 2.00 1.00
168 A48 3s olive green 2.25 1.00
169 A48 4s rose red 22.50 15.00
170 A48 10s deep blue 25.00 18.00
Nos. 167-170 (4) 51.75 35.00

Return of Crown Prince Hirohito from his European visit.

Mount Fuji — A49

Mt. Niitaka, Taiwan — A50

Perf. 13x13½

1930-37 **Typo.** **Wmk. 141**

Granite Paper

Size: 18½x22mm ("New Die")

171 A49 4s green ('37) 2.40 .35
172 A49 4s orange 5.50 .25
174 A49 8s olive green 8.50 .20
175a A49 20s blue ('37) 19.00 26.00
176 A49 20s brown violet 26.00 .20
Nos. 171-176 (5) 61.40 27.00

1922-29

Size: 19x22½mm ("Old Die")

171a A49 4s green 7.50 2.60
172a A49 4s orange ('29) 75.00 7.50
173 A49 8s rose 15.00 5.25
174a A49 8s olive green ('29) 210.00 67.50
175 A49 20s deep blue 17.00 .50
176a A49 20s brown vio ('29) 75.00 1.25
Nos. 171a-176a (6) 399.50 84.60

See Nos. 242, 246, 248.

Perf. 12½

1923, Apr. 16 **Unwmk.** **Engr.**

177 A50 1½s orange 8.50 6.75
178 A50 3s dark violet 13.00 5.75

1st visit of Crown Prince Hirohito to Taiwan. The stamps were sold only in Taiwan, but were valid throughout the empire.

Cherry Blossoms
A51

Sun and Dragonflies
A52

Empress Jingo — A53

1923 **Wmk. 142** **Litho.** ***Imperf.***

Without Gum; Granite Paper

179 A51 ½s gray 4.50 2.25
180 A51 1½s lt blue 5.00 1.00
181 A51 2s red brown 4.50 1.00
182 A51 3s brt rose 3.25 .80
183 A51 4s gray green 35.00 12.00
184 A51 5s dull violet 15.00 1.00
185 A51 8s red orange 55.00 21.00
186 A52 10s deep brown 27.50 1.00
187 A52 20s deep blue 30.00 1.25
Nos. 179-187 (9) 179.75 41.30

#179-187 exist rouletted and with various perforations. These were made privately.

Perf. 12, 13x13½

1924 **Engr.** **Wmk. 141**

Granite Paper

188 A53 5y gray green 210.00 3.00
189 A53 10y dull violet 325.00 2.00

See Nos. 253-254.

Cranes — A54

Phoenix — A55

Perf. 10½ to 13½ and Compound

1925, May 10 Litho. Unwmk.

190	A54	1½s gray violet	2.00	1.00
191	A55	3s silver & brn org	2.60	1.50
a.		Vert. pair, imperf. btwn.	425.00	
192	A54	8s light red	20.00	11.00
193	A55	20s silver & gray grn	45.00	35.00
		Nos. 190-193 (4)	69.60	48.50

25th wedding anniv. of the Emperor Yoshihito (Taisho) and Empress Sadako.

Mt. Fuji — A56

Yomei Gate, Nikko — A57

Nagoya Castle — A58

Perf. 13½x13

1926-37 Typo. Wmk. 141

Granite Paper

194	A56	2s green	1.60	.20
195	A57	6s carmine	6.00	.20
196	A58	10s dark blue	7.00	.20
197	A58	10s carmine ('37)	8.00	7.00
		Nos. 194-197 (4)	22.60	7.60

See Nos. 244, 247. For surcharges see People's Republic of China No. 2L5-2L6.

Baron Hisoka Maejima — A59

Map of World on Mollweide's Projection — A60

Perf. 12½, 13x13½

1927, June 20 Unwmk.

198	A59	1½s lilac	2.50	1.00
199	A59	3s olive green	2.50	1.00
200	A60	6s carmine rose	50.00	45.00
201	A60	10s blue	62.50	45.00
		Nos. 198-201 (4)	117.50	92.00

50th anniv. of Japan's joining the UPU. Baron Maejima (1835-1919) organized Japan's modern postal system and was postmaster general.

Phoenix — A61

Enthronement Hall, Kyoto — A62

1928, Nov. 10 Engr. *Perf. 12½*

Yellow Paper

202	A61	1½s deep green	1.00	.50
203	A62	3s red violet	1.00	.50
204	A61	6s carmine rose	2.10	1.60
205	A62	10s deep blue	3.00	2.10
		Nos. 202-205 (4)	7.10	4.70

Enthronement of Emperor Hirohito.

Great Shrines of Ise — A63

Map of Japanese Empire — A64

1929, Oct. 2 *Perf. 12½*

206	A63	1½s gray violet	1.00	1.00
207	A63	3s carmine	1.50	1.10

58th rebuilding of the Ise Shrines.

1930, Sept. 25 Unwmk.

208	A64	1½s deep violet	2.00	1.25
209	A64	3s deep red	2.25	1.50

2nd census in the Japanese Empire.

Meiji Shrine — A65

1930, Nov. 1 Litho.

210	A65	1½s green	1.50	.85
211	A65	3s brown org	2.00	1.00

10th anniv. of dedication of Meiji Shrine.

Coil Stamps

Wmk. Zigzag Lines (141)

1933 Typo. *Perf. 13 Horiz.*

212	A34	1½s light blue	13.00	17.00
213	A34	3s rose	14.00	21.00

Japanese Red Cross Badge — A66

Red Cross Building, Tokyo — A67

Perf. 12½

1934, Oct. 1 Engr. Unwmk.

214	A66	1½s green & red	1.50	1.00
215	A67	3s dull vio & red	1.75	1.25
216	A66	6s dk car & red	8.00	5.00
217	A67	10s blue & red	12.00	8.00
		Nos. 214-217 (4)	23.25	15.25

15th International Red Cross Congress. Sheets of 20 with commemorative marginal inscription. One side of sheet is perf. 13.

White Tower of Liaoyang and Warship "Hiei" — A68

Akasaka Detached Palace, Tokyo — A69

1935, Apr. 2

218	A68	1½s olive green	1.00	.60
219	A69	3s red brown	1.50	1.00
220	A68	6s carmine	6.25	3.00
221	A69	10s blue	9.00	6.00
		Nos. 218-221 (4)	17.75	10.60

Visit of Emperor Kang Teh of Manchukuo (Henry Pu-yi) to Tokyo, April 6, 1935. Sheets of 20 with commemorative marginal inscription. One side of sheet is perf. 13.

Mt. Fuji — A70

1935 Typo. *Perf. 13x13½*

Granite Paper

222	A70	1½s rose carmine	10.00	.75
a.		Miniature sheet of 20	600.00	500.00

Issued to pay postage on New Year's cards from Dec. 1-31, 1935. After Jan. 1, 1936, used for ordinary letter postage. No. 222 was issued in sheets of 100.

Mt. Fuji A71

Fuji from Lake Ashi A72

Fuji from Lake Kawaguchi — A73

Fuji from Mishima A74

1936, July 10 Photo. Wmk. 141

Granite Paper

223	A71	1½s red brown	3.00	2.00
224	A72	3s dark green	4.50	3.00
225	A73	6s carmine rose	10.00	8.00
226	A74	10s dark blue	12.00	10.00
		Nos. 223-226 (4)	29.50	23.00

Fuji-Hakone National Park.

Dove, Map of Manchuria and Kwantung — A75

Shinto Shrine, Port Arthur — A76

Headquarters of Kwantung Government A77

1936, Sept. 1 Litho. *Perf. 12½*

Granite Paper

227	A75	1½s gray violet	18.00	10.00
228	A76	3s red brown	14.00	12.00
229	A77	10s dull green	150.00	130.00
		Nos. 227-229 (3)	182.00	152.00

30th anniv. of Japanese administration of Kwangtung Leased Territory and the South Manchuria Railway Zone.

Imperial Diet Building A78

Grand Staircase A79

1936, Nov. 7 Engr. *Perf. 13*

230	A78	1½s green	2.00	1.00
231	A79	3s brown vio	3.00	1.50
232	A79	6s carmine	6.00	4.00
233	A78	10s blue	10.00	5.75
		Nos. 230-233 (4)	21.00	12.25

Opening of the new Diet Building, Tokyo.

"Wedded Rocks," Futamigaura — A80

1936, Dec. 10 Photo.

234	A80	1½s rose carmine	3.50	.20

Issued to pay postage on New Year's greeting cards.

Types of 1913-26

Perf. 13½x13, 13x13½

1937 Typo. Wmk. 257

239	A34	½s brown	1.90	1.00
240	A34	1s orange yel	2.75	1.25
241	A34	3s rose	1.00	.20
242	A49	4s green	3.75	.20
243	A35	5s violet	5.00	.20
244	A57	6s crimson	8.00	.95
245	A35	7s red org	8.00	.25
246	A49	8s olive bister	8.50	.50
247	A58	10s carmine	6.75	.25
248	A49	20s blue	12.00	.50
249	A35	25s olive grn	35.00	2.00
250	A36	30s org & grn	25.00	.50
251	A36	50s brn org & dk bl	100.00	2.00
252	A36	1y yel grn & mar	55.00	1.50
		Nos. 239-252 (14)	272.65	11.30

Engr.

253	A53	5y gray green	250.00	3.25
254	A53	10y dull violet	375.00	3.00

For overprint see People's Republic of China No. 2L6.

Coil Stamp

1938 Typo. *Perf. 13 Horiz.*

255	A34	3s rose	4.00	4.00

New Year's Decoration — A81

1937, Dec. 15 Photo. *Perf. 13*

256	A81	2s scarlet	6.75	.20

Issued to pay postage on New Year's cards, later for ordinary use.

Trading Ship A82

Rice Harvest A83

Gen. Maresuke Nogi — A84

Power Plant — A85

Admiral Heihachiro Togo A86

Mount Hodaka A87

Garambi Lighthouse, Taiwan — A88

Diamond Mountains, Korea — A89

Meiji Shrine, Tokyo — A90

Yomei Gate, Nikko — A91

Plane and Map of Japan — A92

Kasuga Shrine, Nara — A93

Mount Fuji and Cherry Blossoms A94

Horyu Temple, Nara A95

Miyajima Torii, Itsukushima Shrine — A96

Golden Pavilion, Kyoto — A97

Great Buddha, Kamakura A98

Kamatari Fujiwara A99

Plum Blossoms — A100

Typographed or Engraved

1937-45 Wmk. 257 *Perf. 13*

257	A82	½s purple	.50	.30
258	A83	1s fawn	1.50	.25
259	A84	2s crimson	.35	.20
a.		Booklet pane of 20	42.50	
b.		2s pink, perf. 12 ('45)	1.25	.85
c.		2s vermilion ('44)	2.10	1.60
260	A85	3s green ('39)	.35	.20
261	A86	4s dark green	.75	.20
a.		Booklet pane of 20	13.00	
262	A87	5s dark ultra ('39)	.75	.20
263	A88	6s orange ('39)	1.50	.60
264	A89	7s deep green ('39)	.50	.20
265	A90	8s dk pur & pale vio ('39)	.45	.20
266	A91	10s lake ('38)	2.40	.20
267	A92	12s indigo ('39)	.50	.30
268	A93	14s rose lake & pale rose ('38)	.50	.25
269	A94	20s ultra ('40)	.50	.20
270	A95	25s dk brn & pale brn ('38)	.50	.20
271	A96	30s pck blue ('39)	1.10	.20
a.		Imperf., pair	400.00	
272	A97	50s ol & pale ol ('39)	.60	.20
a.		Pale olive (forest) omitted		
273	A98	1y brn & pale brn ('39)	3.00	1.00
274	A99	5y dp gray grn ('39)	20.00	2.00
275	A100	10y dk brn vio ('39)	14.00	1.50
		Nos. 257-275 (19)	49.75	8.40

Nos. 257-261, 265, 268, 270, 272- 273 are typographed; the others are engraved.

Coil Stamps

1938-39 Typo. *Perf. 13 Horiz.*

276	A82	½s purple ('39)	2.75	*4.00*
277	A84	2s crimson	3.25	*4.25*
278	A86	4s dark green	3.75	*4.25*
279	A93	14s rose lake & pale rose	80.00	70.00
		Nos. 276-279 (4)	89.75	82.50

See Nos. 329, 331, 333, 341, 351, 360 and 361. For surcharges see Nos. B4-B5, Burma 2N4-2N27, China-Taiwan, 8-9, People's Republic of China 2L3, 2L7, 2L9-2L10, 2L39, Korea 55-56. For overprints see Ryukyu Islands (US Specialized) Nos. 2X1-2X2, 2X4-2X7, 2X10, 2X13-2X14, 2X17, 2X20, 2X23, 2X27, 2X29, 2X33-2X34, 3X2-3X7, 3X10-3X11, 3X14, 3X17, 3X19, 3X21, 3X23, 3X26-3X30, 5X1-5X3, 5X5-5X8, 5X10.

Mount Nantai — A101

Kegon Falls — A102

Sacred Bridge, Nikko A103

Mount Hiuchi A104

Unwmk.

1938, Dec. 25 Photo. *Perf. 13*

280	A101	2s brown orange	1.00	.50
281	A102	4s olive green	1.00	.50
282	A103	10s deep rose	6.00	3.75
283	A104	20s dark blue	6.00	3.75
a.		Souvenir sheet of 4, #280-283	65.00	75.00
		Never hinged	100.00	
		Nos. 280-283 (4)	14.00	8.50
		Set, never hinged	35.00	

Nikko National Park. No. 283a sold for 50s.

Many souvenir sheets were sold in folders. Values are for sheets without folders.

Mount Daisen A106

Yashima Plateau, Inland Sea A107

Abuto Kwannon Temple A108

Tomo Bay, Inland Sea A109

1939, Apr. 20

285	A106	2s lt brown	1.00	.50
286	A107	4s yellow grn	1.60	1.00
287	A108	10s dull rose	7.00	4.00
288	A109	20s blue	7.00	4.00
a.		Souvenir sheet of 4, #285-288	27.50	40.00
		Never hinged	60.00	
		Nos. 285-288 (4)	16.60	9.50
		Set, never hinged	35.00	

Daisen and Inland Sea National Parks. No. 288a sold for 50s.

View from Kuju Village, Kyushu A111

Mount Naka A112

Crater of Mount Naka A113

Volcanic Cones of Mt. Aso A114

1939, Aug. 15

290	A111	2s olive brown	1.00	.50
291	A112	4s yellow green	3.00	2.00
292	A113	10s carmine	17.50	9.00
293	A114	20s sapphire	24.00	10.00
a.		Souvenir sheet of 4, #290-293	85.00	100.00
		Never hinged	140.00	
		Nos. 290-293 (4)	45.50	21.50
		Set, never hinged	90.00	

Aso National Park. No. 293a sold for 50s.

Globe — A116

Tsunetami Sano — A117

1939, Nov. 15 ***Perf. 12½***

Cross in Carmine

295 A116 2s brown 1.50 .90
296 A117 4s yellow green 1.60 1.00
297 A116 10s crimson 8.00 7.00
298 A117 20s sapphire 8.00 7.00
Nos. 295-298 (4) 19.10 15.90
Set, never hinged 35.00

Intl. Red Cross Society founding, 75th anniv.

Sacred Golden Kite — A118

Mount Takachiho — A119

Five Ayu Fish and Sake Jar — A120

Kashiwara Shrine — A121

1940 **Engr.** ***Perf. 12***

299 A118 2s brown orange 1.00 1.00
300 A119 4s dark green .75 .65
301 A120 10s dark carmine 3.75 3.25
302 A121 20s dark ultra 1.00 1.00
Nos. 299-302 (4) 6.50 5.90
Set, never hinged 7.50

2,600th anniv. of the legendary date of the founding of Japan.

Mt. Hokuchin, Hokkaido A122

Mt. Asahi, Hokkaido A123

Sounkyo Gorge — A124

Tokachi Mountain Range A125

1940, Apr. 20 **Photo.** ***Perf. 13***

303 A122 2s brown 1.00 1.00
304 A123 4s yellow green 3.00 2.00
305 A124 10s carmine 7.00 6.00
306 A125 20s sapphire 7.00 6.25
a. Souvenir sheet of 4, #303-306 160.00 200.00
Never hinged 275.00
Nos. 303-306 (4) 18.00 15.25
Set, never hinged 35.00

Daisetsuzan National Park. No. 306a sold for 50s.

Mt. Karakuni, Kyushu A127

Mt. Takachiho A128

Torii of Kirishima Shrine A129

Lake of the Six Kwannon A130

1940, Aug. 21

308 A127 2s brown 1.00 .75
309 A128 4s green 2.00 1.50
310 A129 10s carmine 7.00 5.00
311 A130 20s deep ultra 8.00 6.00
a. Souvenir sheet of 4, #308-311 160.00 210.00
Never hinged 275.00
Nos. 308-311 (4) 18.00 13.25
Set, never hinged 40.00

Kirishima National Park.
No. 311a sold for 50s.

Education Minister with Rescript on Education A132

Characters Signifying Loyalty and Filial Piety A133

1940, Oct. 25 **Engr.** ***Perf. 12½***

313 A132 2s purple 1.00 1.00
314 A133 4s green 1.25 1.25
Set, never hinged 2.25

50th anniv. of the imperial rescript on education, given by Emperor Meiji to clarify Japan's educational policy.

SEMI-POSTAL STAMPS

Douglas Plane over Japan Alps — SP1

Wmk. Zigzag Lines (141)

1937, June 1 **Photo.** ***Perf. 13***

B1 SP1 2s + 2s rose carmine 1.75 .75
B2 SP1 3s + 2s purple 1.75 1.25
B3 SP1 4s + 2s green 2.50 1.00
Nos. B1-B3 (3) 6.00 3.00
Set, never hinged 8.00

The surtax was for the Patriotic Aviation Fund to build civil airports.

AIR POST STAMPS

Regular Issue of 1914 Overprinted in Red or Blue

Wmk. Zigzag Lines (141)

1919, Oct. 3 ***Perf. 13x13½***

Granite Paper

C1 A34 1½s blue (R) 260.00 72.50
C2 A34 3s rose (Bl) 450.00 210.00

Excellent counterfeits exist.

Passenger Plane over Lake Ashi — AP1

1929-34 **Engr.** ***Perf. 13½x13***

Granite Paper

C3 AP1 8½s orange brn 27.50 14.00
C4 AP1 9½s rose 9.00 3.75
C5 AP1 16½s yellow grn 9.00 4.00
C6 AP1 18s ultra 10.00 3.75
C7 AP1 33s gray 20.00 3.25
Nos. C3-C7 (5) 75.50 28.75
Set, never hinged 190.00

Souvenir Sheet

C8 AP1 Sheet of 4, #C4-C7 1,400. 1,250.
Never hinged 2,200.

Issued: 9½s, 3/1/34; #C8, 4/20/34; others, 10/6/29. #C8 for Communications Commemoration Day (1st observance of establishment of the postal service and issuance of #1-4). Sold only at Phil. Exhib. p.o., Tokyo, 4/20-27. Size: 110x100mm.

MILITARY STAMPS

Nos. 98, 119, 131 Overprinted

1910-14 **Unwmk.** ***Perf. 11½ to 13½***

M1 A26 3s rose 225.00 35.00
M2 A34 3s rose ('13) 350.00 140.00

Wmk. 141

M3 A34 3s rose ('14) 35.00 16.00
Nos. M1-M3 (3) 610.00 191.00

Nos. M1-M3 overprint type I has 3.85mm between characters; type II, 4-4.5mm (movable type).

1921 **On Offices in China No. 37**

M4 A34 3s rose *5,750.* *4,750.*

No. M4 is a provisional military stamp issued at the Japanese Post Office, Tsingtao, China. The overprint differs from the illustration, being 12mm high with thicker characters. Counterfeits are plentiful.

Overprint 16mm High

1924 **On No. 131**

M5 A34 3s rose 100.00 72.50
a. 3s rose (#131b) 100.00 75.00

Excellent forgeries exist of Nos. M1-M5.

JAPANESE OFFICES ABROAD

Offices in China

Regular Issues of Japan Overprinted in Red or Black

Perf. 11½, 12, 12½, 13½, 13x13½

1900-06 **Unwmk.**

1 A26 5r gray (R) 3.50 2.75
2 A26 ½s gray (R) ('01) 2.10 .70
3 A26 1s lt red brn (R) 2.10 .70
4 A26 1½s ultra 9.50 2.10
5 A26 1½s vio ('06) 5.25 .95
6 A26 2s lt grn (R) 5.25 .70
7 A26 3s violet brn 5.75 .70
8 A26 3s rose ('06) 4.25 .50
9 A26 4s rose 4.75 1.25
10 A26 5s org yel (R) 9.50 1.25
11 A27 6s maroon ('06) 18.00 12.00
12 A27 8s ol grn (R) 9.50 6.00
13 A27 10s deep blue 9.50 1.00
14 A27 15s purple 20.00 1.75
15 A27 20s red org 18.00 1.00
16 A28 25s blue grn (R) 37.50 4.00
17 A28 50s red brown 40.00 3.00
18 A29 1y carmine 60.00 3.00
Nos. 1-18 (18) 264.45 43.35

No. 6 with black overprint is bogus.
Nos. 5, 6, 8, 9 and 13 exist as booklet panes of 6, made from sheet stamps. They are rare.

1900

19 A30 3s carmine 27.50 15.00

Wedding of Crown Prince Yoshihito and Princess Sadako.

1908

20 A33 5y green 375.00 47.50
21 A33 10y dark violet 650.00 110.00

On #20-21 the space between characters of the overprint is 6½mm instead of 1½mm.

1913 ***Perf. 12, 12x13, 13x13½***

22 A34 ½s brown 15.00 15.00
23 A34 1s orange 16.00 16.00
24 A34 1½s lt blue 42.50 19.00
25 A34 2s green 50.00 21.00
26 A34 3s rose 24.00 8.00
27 A35 4s red 70.00 70.00
28 A35 5s violet 70.00 55.00
29 A35 10s deep blue 70.00 22.50
30 A35 20s claret 275.00 150.00
31 A35 25s olive green 100.00 22.50
32 A36 1y yel grn & mar 825.00 550.00
Nos. 22-32 (11) 1,557. 949.00

Nos. 24, 25, 26, 27 and 29 exist in booklet panes of 6, made from sheet stamps. The No. 26 pane is very rare.

1914-21 **Wmk. 141**

Granite Paper

33 A34 ½s brown 3.25 .80
34 A34 1s orange 3.75 .80
35 A34 1½s blue 4.25 .80
36 A34 2s green 2.75 .95
37 A34 3s rose 2.40 .80
38 A35 4s red 10.50 4.75
39 A35 5s violet 19.00 1.75
40 A35 6s brown ('20) 32.50 19.00
41 A35 8s gray ('20) 40.00 21.00
42 A35 10s dp blue 13.50 1.25
43 A35 20s claret 45.00 3.25
44 A35 25s olive grn 55.00 3.50
45 A36 30s org brn ('20) 80.00 29.00
46 A36 50s dk brn ('20) 95.00 32.50
47 A36 1y yel grn & mar ('18) 140.00 6.75
48 A33 5y green 1,900. 550.00
49 A33 10y violet ('21) 2,700. 1,700.
Nos. 33-49 (17) 5,146. 2,376.

On Nos. 48-49 the space between characters of overprint is 4½mm, instead of 6½mm on Nos. 20-21 and 1½mm on all lower values. See No. M4.
No. 42 exists as a booklet pane of 6, made from sheet stamps. It is very rare.
Counterfeit overprints exist of Nos. 1-49.

Offices in Korea

Regular Issue of Japan Overprinted in Red or Black

1900 Unwmk. *Perf. 11½, 12, 12½*

1	A26	5r gray (R)	19.00	8.75
2	A26	1s lt red brn (R)	20.00	5.00
3	A26	1½s ultra	250.00	130.00
4	A26	2s lt green (R)	19.00	10.00
5	A26	3s violet brn	17.00	4.75
6	A26	4s rose	65.00	27.50
7	A26	5s org yel (R)	67.50	27.50
8	A27	8s ol grn (R)	250.00	120.00
9	A27	10s deep blue	35.00	9.00
10	A27	15s purple	62.50	6.00
11	A27	20s red orange	62.50	5.00
12	A28	25s blue grn (R)	220.00	55.00
13	A28	50s red brown	175.00	18.00
14	A29	1y carmine	475.00	14.00
		Nos. 1-14 (14)	1,737.	440.50

1900

15	A30	3s carmine	100.00	55.00

Wedding of Crown Prince Yoshihito and Princess Sadako.

Counterfeit overprints exist of Nos. 1-15.

JORDAN

'jor-dᵊn

Trans-Jordan

LOCATION — In the Near East, separated from the Mediterranean Sea by Israel
GOVT. — Kingdom
AREA — 38,400 sq. mi.
POP. — 3,750,000 (est. 1982)
CAPITAL — Amman

The former Turkish territory was mandated to Great Britain following World War I. It became an independent state in 1946.

10 Milliemes = 1 Piaster
1000 Mils = 1 Palestine Pound (1930)

British Mandate

Stamps and Type of Palestine 1918 Overprinted in Black or Silver

Perf. 14, 15x14

1920, Nov. Wmk. 33

1	A1	1m dark brown	.70	*1.50*
a.		Inverted overprint	140.00	250.00
b.		Perf. 14	1.60	1.60
c.		As "b," inverted overprint	160.00	
2	A1	2m blue green	.80	.80
a.		Perf. 15x14	9.50	*10.00*
3	A1	3m light brown	1.25	1.25
a.		Perf. 14	19.50	17.50
4	A1	4m scarlet	1.10	*1.25*
a.		Perf. 14	19.00	*21.00*
5	A1	5m orange	2.50	.90
a.		Perf. 15x14	2.50	1.25
6	A1	1pi dark blue (S)	1.75	*1.90*
a.		Perf. 15x14	*2,250.*	
7	A1	2pi olive green	3.50	3.25
a.		Perf. 15x14	4.50	*6.00*
8	A1	5pi plum	3.00	*6.50*
a.		Perf. 15x14	29.00	*35.00*
9	A1	9pi bister	4.50	*25.00*
a.		Perf. 15x14	1,000.	*1,500.*
10	A1	10pi ultramarine	5.00	*25.00*
11	A1	20pi gray	10.50	*40.00*
		Nos. 1-11 (11)	34.60	*107.35*

The overprint reads "Sharqi al-ardan" (East of Jordan).

For overprints see Nos. 12-63, 83A.

Stamps of 1920 Issue Handstamp Surcharged "Ashir el qirsh" (tenth of piaster) and numeral in Black, Red or Violet

1922

12	A1	1/10pi on 1m dk brn	25.00	*30.00*
13	A1	1/10pi on 1m dk brn (R)	70.00	67.50
13A	A1	1/10pi on 1m dk brn (V)	77.50	70.00
14	A1	2/10pi on 2m bl grn	30.00	29.00
a.		3/10pi on 2m bl grn (error)	125.00	100.00
15	A1	2/10pi on 2m bl grn (R)	87.50	80.00
16	A1	2/10pi on 2m bl grn (V)	100.00	100.00
17	A1	3/10pi on 3m lt brn	11.00	10.00
17A	A1	3/10pi on 3m lt brn (V)	160.00	150.00
18	A1	4/10pi on 4m scar	55.00	50.00
19	A1	5/10pi on 5m org	200.00	100.00
c.		Perf. 15x14	190.00	100.00
19A	A1	5/10pi on 5m dp org (R)	225.00	
19B	A1	5/10pi on 5m org (V)	300.00	

For overprints see No. 83B.

Handstamp Surcharged "El qirsh" (piaster) and numeral in Black, Red or Violet

20	A1	1pi dk bl (R)	190.00	60.00
20A	A1	1pi dk bl (V)	400.00	
21	A1	2pi ol grn (Bk)	275.00	75.00
22	A1	2pi ol grn (R)	325.00	80.00
22A	A1	2pi ol grn (V)	325.00	90.00
23	A1	5pi plum (Bk)	50.00	*70.00*
23A	A1	5pi plum (V)	*275.00*	
24	A1	9pi bister (Bk)	325.00	*350.00*
25	A1	9pi bister (R)	150.00	140.00
a.		Perf. 14	600.00	600.00
26	A1	10pi ultra (Bk)	925.00	*1,000.*
27	A1	20pi gray (Bk)	750.00	*850.00*
27A	A1	20pi gray (V)	1,000.	950.00

Same Surcharge in Black on Palestine Nos. 13-14

28	A1	10pi on 10pi ultra	*2,000.*	*2,500.*
29	A1	20pi on 20pi gray	*2,600.*	*3,000.*

For overprints see Nos. 86, 88, 94, 97, 98.

Stamps of 1920 Handstamped in Violet, Black or Red

1922, Dec. *Perf. 15x14, 14*

30	A1	1m dk brn (V)	24.00	20.00
31	A1	1m dk brn (Bk)	20.00	18.00
32	A1	1m dk brn (R)	13.50	*15.00*
33	A1	2m bl grn (V)	9.00	8.00
34	A1	2m bl grn (Bk)	11.00	10.00
35	A1	2m bl grn (R)	27.50	25.00
36	A1	3m lt brn (V)	7.75	7.00
37	A1	3m lt brn (Bk)	8.75	8.00
38	A1	3m lt brn (R)	45.00	40.00
39	A1	4m scar (V)	50.00	50.00
39A	A1	4m scar (Bk)	50.00	50.00
40	A1	4m scar (R)	50.00	50.00
41	A1	5m orange (V)	17.00	10.00
42	A1	5m orange (R)	37.50	*10.00*
a.		Perf. 14	325.00	75.00
43	A1	1pi dk blue (V)	17.00	9.00
44	A1	1pi dk blue (R)	27.50	15.00
45	A1	2pi ol grn (V)	22.50	15.00
a.		Perf. 14	82.50	80.00
46	A1	2pi ol grn (Bk)	13.50	10.00
47	A1	2pi ol grn (R)	60.00	40.00
48	A1	5pi plum (V)	65.00	*80.00*
a.		Perf. 14	110.00	*110.00*
49	A1	5pi plum (R)	100.00	*100.00*
50	A1	9pi bister (V)	225.00	*250.00*
50A	A1	9pi bister (Bk)	72.50	*80.00*
50B	A1	9pi bister (R)	450.00	*450.00*
51	A1	10pi ultra (V)	1,250.	*1,600.*
51A	A1	10pi ultra (R)	*2,000.*	*1,900.*
52	A1	20pi gray (V)	1,250.	*1,800.*
52A	A1	20pi gray (R)	*1,750.*	*2,000.*

The overprint reads "Hukumat al Sharqi al Arabia" (Arab Government of the East) and date, 1923. The surcharges or overprints on Nos. 12 to 52A inclusive are handstamped and, as usual, are found inverted and double.

Ink pads of several colors were in use at the same time and the surcharges and overprints frequently show a mixture of two colors.

For overprints see #84, 87, 89, 92-93, 95-96.

Stamps of 1920 Overprinted in Gold

1923, Mar. 1 *Perf. 14, 15x14*

53	A1	1m dark brn (G)	17.50	*24.00*
a.		Perf. 15x14	1,600.	*1,800.*
54	A1	2m blue grn (G)	16.00	18.00
a.		Double overprint	300.00	
b.		Inverted overprint	375.00	350.00
55	A1	3m lt brn (G)	13.50	*15.00*
a.		Black overprint	82.50	*85.00*
56	A1	4m scarlet (Bk)	11.00	*12.00*
57	A1	5m orange (Bk)	11.00	12.00
a.		Perf. 15x14	55.00	45.00
58	A1	1pi dk blue (G)	11.00	*14.00*
a.		Double overprint	500.00	*475.00*
b.		Black overprint	*875.00*	*850.00*
59	A1	2pi ol grn (G)	17.00	*15.00*
a.		Black overprint	275.00	250.00
b.		Overprint on back	175.00	
60	A1	5pi plum (G)	65.00	*80.00*
a.		Inverted overprint	250.00	
b.		"922" for "921"		
61	A1	9pi bister (Bk)	82.50	*100.00*
a.		Perf. 15x14	*200.00*	*200.00*
62	A1	10pi ultra (G)	77.50	*100.00*
63	A1	20pi gray (G)	77.50	*100.00*
a.		Inverted overprint	400.00	
b.		Double overprint	475.00	
c.		Double ovpt., one inverted	475.00	

The overprint reads "Hukumat al Sharqi al Arabia, Nissan Sanat 921" (Arab Government of the East, April, 1921).

For overprints see Nos. 85, 99, 100, 102.

Stamps of Hejaz, 1922, Overprinted in Black

Coat of Arms (Hejaz A7)

1923, Apr. Unwmk. *Perf. 11½*

64	A7	1/8pi orange brn	2.25	*1.75*
a.		Double overprint	225.00	
65	A7	½pi red	2.25	1.75
a.		Inverted overprint	125.00	
66	A7	1pi dark blue	1.60	1.00
a.		Inverted overprint	140.00	140.00
67	A7	1½pi violet	1.60	*1.75*
a.		Double overprint	160.00	
68	A7	2pi orange	2.25	*6.00*
a.		Inverted overprint		
b.		Pair, one without overprint		
69	A7	3pi olive brn	3.25	*8.50*
a.		Inverted overprint	250.00	
b.		Double overprint	250.00	250.00
c.		Pair, one without overprint	*400.00*	
70	A7	5pi olive green	5.50	*9.50*
		Nos. 64-70 (7)	18.70	*30.25*

The overprint is similar to that on the preceding group but is differently arranged. There are numerous varieties in the Arabic letters.

For overprints see Nos. 71-72, 91, J1-J5.

With Additional Surcharge of New Value in Arabic:

a

b

71	A7(a)	1/4pi on 1/8pi	4.50	*5.50*
a.		Inverted surcharge	175.00	
72	A7(b)	10pi on 5pi	17.00	*22.50*

Independence Issue

Palestine Stamps and Type of 1918 Overprinted Vertically in Black or Gold

1923, May Wmk. 33 *Perf. 15x14*

73	A1	1m dark brn (Bk)	19.00	*17.00*
a.		Double ovpt., one reversed	725.00	650.00
73B	A1	1m dark brn (G)	175.00	175.00
c.		Double ovpt., one reversed	1,000.	
74	A1	2m blue grn	30.00	*35.00*
75	A1	3m lt brown	11.00	*12.00*
76	A1	4m scarlet	11.00	*12.00*
77	A1	5m orange	55.00	*60.00*
78	A1	1pi dk blue (G)	55.00	*60.00*
a.		Double overprint	*650.00*	*650.00*
79	A1	2pi olive grn	55.00	*70.00*
80	A1	5pi plum (G)	65.00	*70.00*
a.		Double overprint	*725.00*	
81	A1	9pi bis, perf. 14	55.00	*60.00*
82	A1	10pi ultra, perf. 14	65.00	*80.00*
83	A1	20pi gray	77.50	*90.00*
		Nos. 73-83 (12)	673.50	741.00

The overprint reads, "Arab Government of the East (abbreviated), Souvenir of Independence, 25th, May, 1923 ('923')."

There were printed 480 complete sets and a larger number of the 1, 2, 3 and 4m. A large number of these sets were distributed to high officials. The overprint was in a setting of twenty-four and the error "933" instead of "923" occurs once in the setting.

The overprint exists reading downward on all values, as illustrated, and reading upward on all except the 5m and 2pi.

Forged overprints exist.

For overprint see No. 101.

Stamps of Preceding Issues, Handstamp Surcharged

83A	A1	2½ 10pi on 5m dp org	175.00	*175.00*
83B	A1	5/10pi on 3m (#17)	—	
84	A1	5/10pi on 3m (#36)	20.00	20.00
85	A1	5/10pi on 3m (#55)	8.75	8.75
86	A1	5/10pi on 5pi (#23)	42.50	42.50
87	A1	5/10pi on 5pi (#48)	4.00	4.00
88	A1	1pi on 5pi (#23)	42.50	42.50
89	A1	1pi on 5pi (#48)	*1,900.*	

Same Surcharge on Palestine Stamp of 1918

90	A1	5/10pi on 3m lt brn	*10,000.*	

No. 90 is valued in the grade of fine-very fine. Very fine examples are not known.

As is usual with handstamped surcharges these are found double, inverted, etc.

No. 67 Surcharged by Handstamp

Unwmk. *Perf. 11½*

91	A7	½pi on 1½pi vio	3.50	*3.75*
a.		Surcharge typographed	30.00	*32.50*

The surcharge reads: "Nusf el qirsh" (half piastre). See note after No. 90.

Stamps of Preceding Issues Surcharged by Handstamp

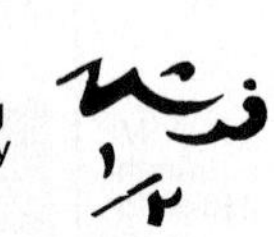

Perf. 14, 15x14

1923, Nov. Wmk. 33

92	A1	½pi on 2pi (#45)	45.00	45.00
93	A1	½pi on 2pi (#47)	87.50	87.50
94	A1	½pi on 5pi (#23)	27.50	27.50
95	A1	½pi on 5pi (#48)	2,750.	2,000.
96	A1	½pi on 5pi (#49)	1,800.	2,750.
97	A1	½pi on 9pi (#24)	*6,500.*	
98	A1	½pi on 9pi (#25)	87.50	87.50
99	A1	½pi on 9pi (#61)	160.00	160.00

Surcharged by Handstamp

100	A1	1pi on 10pi (#62)	*2,000.*	*2,000.*
101	A1	1pi on 10pi (#82)	*3,000.*	*3,000.*
102	A1	2pi on 20pi (#63)	22.50	*24.00*

Of the 25 copies made of No. 100, a few were handstamped in violet.

Stamp of Hejaz, 1922, Overprinted by Handstamp

1923, Dec. **Unwmk.** ***Perf. 11½***

103	A7	½pi	red	3.00	*3.25*

Stamp of Hejaz, 1922, Overprinted

1924

104	A7	½pi	red	3.25	*3.75*

King Hussein Issue

Stamps of Hejaz, 1922, Overprinted

1924

Gold Overprint

105	A7	½pi	red	1.25	1.25
106	A7	1pi	dark blue	1.75	1.75
107	A7	1½pi	violet	1.50	1.50
108	A7	2pi	orange	2.00	2.00

Black Overprint

109	A7	½pi	red	.65	.65
110	A7	1pi	dark blue	.75	.75
111	A7	1½pi	violet	.90	.90
112	A7	2pi	orange	1.00	1.00
			Nos. 105-112 (8)	9.80	9.80

The overprint reads: "Arab Government of the East. In commemoration of the visit of H. M. the King of the Arabs, 11 Jemad el Than i 1342 (17th Jan. 1924)." The overprint was in a setting of thirty-six and the error "432" instead of "342" occurs once in the setting and is found on all values.

Stamps of Hejaz, 1922-24, Overprinted in Black or Red

Coat of Arms (Hejaz A8)

1924

113	A7	⅛pi	red brown	.50	.20
114	A7	¼pi	yellow green	.20	.20
a.			Tête bêche pair	2.00	2.00
115	A7	½pi	red	.20	.20
116	A7	1pi	dark blue	4.25	4.25
117	A7	1½pi	violet	3.75	3.75
118	A7	2pi	orange	3.25	3.25
119	A7	3pi	red brown	2.40	2.40
120	A7	5pi	olive green	3.00	*3.75*
121	A8	10pi	vio & dk brn (R)	6.75	*7.50*
a.			Pair, one without overprint		
			Nos. 113-121 (9)	24.30	25.50

The overprint reads: "Hukumat al Sharqi al Arabia, 1342." (Arab Government of the East, 1924).

Stamps of Hejaz, 1925, Overprinted in Black or Red

(Hejaz A9)

(Hejaz A10)

(Hejaz A11)

1925, Aug.

122	A9	⅛pi	chocolate	.60	.60
123	A9	¼pi	ultramarine	.60	.60
124	A9	½pi	carmine rose	.60	.20
125	A10	1pi	yellow green	.60	.20
126	A10	1½pi	orange	1.40	*2.50*
127	A10	2pi	deep blue	2.00	*3.00*
128	A11	3pi	dark green (R)	2.50	*4.50*
129	A11	5pi	orange brn	4.00	*8.00*
			Nos. 122-129 (8)	12.30	*19.60*

The overprint reads: "Hukumat al Sharqi al Arabi. 1343 Sanat." (Arab Government of the East, 1925). Nos. 122-129 exist imperforate, and with overprint inverted or double.

Type of Palestine, 1918

1925, Nov. 1 **Wmk. 4** ***Perf. 14***

130	A1	1m	dark brown	.20	.20
131	A1	2m	yellow	.20	.20
132	A1	3m	Prussian bl	.20	.20
133	A1	4m	rose	.20	.20
134	A1	5m	orange	.20	.20
135	A1	6m	blue green	.20	.20
136	A1	7m	yel brown	.20	.20
137	A1	8m	red	.20	.20
138	A1	1pi	gray	.35	.35
139	A1	13m	ultramarine	.45	*.75*
140	A1	2pi	olive green	.75	*.90*
141	A1	5pi	plum	3.75	*4.50*
142	A1	9pi	bister	7.50	*8.25*
143	A1	10pi	light blue	12.50	*15.00*
144	A1	20pi	violet	26.00	*27.50*
			Nos. 130-144 (15)	52.90	*58.85*

This overprint reads: "Sharqi al-ardan" (East of Jordan).

For overprints see Nos. J12-J23.

Perf. 15x14

142a	A1	9pi	860.00	*1,425.*
143a	A1	10pi	100.00	*110.00*
144a	A1	20pi	1,375.	1,275.
		Nos. 142a-144a (3)	2,335.	*2,810.*

Amir Abdullah ibn Hussein
A1 A2

1927-29 **Engr.** ***Perf. 14***

145	A1	2(m)	Prus blue	.20	*.35*
146	A1	3(m)	rose	.55	1.40
147	A1	4(m)	green	1.10	*2.75*
148	A1	5(m)	orange	.55	*.35*
149	A1	10(m)	red	1.10	*1.40*
150	A1	15(m)	ultra	1.10	.35
151	A1	20(m)	olive grn	1.40	1.40
152	A2	50(m)	claret	3.75	*5.50*
153	A2	90(m)	bister	9.75	*15.00*
154	A2	100(m)	lt blue	10.50	16.00
155	A2	200(m)	violet	24.50	*35.00*
156	A2	500(m)	dp brn ('29)	87.50	*110.00*
157	A2	1000(m)	gray ('29)	175.00	*210.00*
			Nos. 145-157 (13)	317.00	*399.50*

For overprints see Nos. 158-168, B1-B12, J24-J29.

Stamps of 1927 Overprinted in Black

1928, Sept. 1

158	A1	2(m)	Prus blue	1.00	*1.90*
159	A1	3(m)	rose	1.15	*2.50*
160	A1	4(m)	green	1.25	*2.50*
161	A1	5(m)	orange	1.25	*1.60*
162	A1	10(m)	red	1.90	*4.50*
163	A1	15(m)	ultra	1.90	1.90
164	A1	20(m)	olive grn	5.00	*10.00*
165	A2	50(m)	claret	7.75	*11.50*
166	A2	90(m)	bister	17.00	*32.50*
167	A2	100(m)	lt blue	32.50	*50.00*
168	A2	200(m)	violet	85.00	*125.00*
			Nos. 158-168 (11)	155.70	*243.90*

The overprint is the Arabic word "Dastour," meaning "Constitution." The stamps were in commemoration of the enactment of the law setting forth the Constitution.

A3

"MILS" or "L. P." at lower right and Arabic equivalents at upper left.

1930-36 **Engr.** ***Perf. 14***

Size: 17¾x21mm

169	A3	1m	red brn ('34)	.20	*.95*
170	A3	2m	Prus blue	.20	*.55*
171	A3	3m	rose	.55	*.80*
172	A3	3m	green ('34)	1.40	*1.25*
173	A3	4m	green	.90	*2.10*
174	A3	4m	rose ('34)	2.25	1.75
175	A3	5m	orange	.50	.20
a.			Perf. 13½x14 (coil) ('36)	16.00	10.00
176	A3	10m	red	.95	.20
177	A3	15m	ultra	.95	.20
a.			Perf. 13½x14 (coil) ('36)	16.00	10.00
178	A3	20m	olive grn	1.75	.55

Size: 19¾x23½mm

179	A3	50m	red violet	2.50	2.10
180	A3	90m	bister	4.50	*5.75*
181	A3	100m	light blue	5.75	*5.75*
182	A3	200m	violet	14.00	*17.00*
183	A3	500m	deep brown	26.00	*52.50*
184	A3	£1	gray	82.50	*125.00*
			Nos. 169-184 (16)	144.90	*216.65*

See Nos. 199-220, 230-235. For overprint see No. N15a.

1939 ***Perf. 13½x13***

Size: 17¾x21mm

169a	A3	1m	red brown	4.00	3.00
170a	A3	2m	Prussian blue	10.25	3.00
172a	A3	3m	green	17.00	6.25
174a	A3	4m	rose	75.00	20.00
175b	A3	5m	orange	80.00	4.75
176a	A3	10m	red	110.00	6.25
177b	A3	15m	ultramarine	42.50	5.50
178a	A3	20m	olive green	65.00	19.00
			Nos. 169a-178a (8)	403.75	67.75

For overprint see No. N3a.

Mushetta — A4

Nymphaeum, Jerash — A5

Kasr Kharana — A6

Kerak Castle — A7

Temple of Artemis, Jerash — A8

Aijalon Castle — A9

Khazneh, Rock-hewn Temple, Petra — A10

Allenby Bridge, River Jordan — A11

Amir Abdullah ibn Hussein — A13

Ancient Threshing Floor — A12

1933, Feb. 1 ***Perf. 12***

185	A4	1m	dk brn & blk	.65	*.95*
186	A5	2m	claret & blk	.75	*.75*
187	A6	3m	blue green	.90	*1.25*
188	A7	4m	bister & blk	1.40	*1.90*
189	A8	5m	orange & blk	1.60	*1.60*
190	A9	10m	brown red	1.90	*2.75*
191	A10	15m	dull blue	2.75	1.60
192	A11	20m	ol grn & blk	4.50	*5.50*
193	A12	50m	brn vio & blk	10.50	*11.50*
194	A6	90m	yel & black	15.00	*22.50*
195	A8	100m	blue & blk	18.00	*22.50*
196	A9	200m	dk vio & blk	55.00	*70.00*
197	A10	500m	brn & ver	160.00	*225.00*
198	A13	£1	green & blk	575.00	*825.00*
			Nos. 185-198 (14)	847.95	*1,192.*

Nos. 194-197 are larger than the lower values in the same designs.

SEMI-POSTAL STAMPS

Locust Campaign Issue

Nos. 145-156 Overprinted

1930, Apr. 1 **Wmk. 4** ***Perf. 14***

B1	A1	2(m)	Prus blue	1.60	*3.50*
a.			Inverted overprint	200.00	
B2	A1	3(m)	rose	1.60	*3.50*
B3	A1	4(m)	green	1.75	*4.75*
B4	A1	5(m)	orange	18.00	16.75
a.			Double overprint	300.00	
B5	A1	10(m)	red	1.90	*3.50*
B6	A1	15(m)	ultra	1.90	*3.50*
a.			Inverted overprint	200.00	
B7	A1	20(m)	olive grn	1.90	*5.00*
B8	A2	50(m)	claret	6.75	*11.50*
B9	A2	90(m)	bister	15.00	*45.00*
B10	A2	100(m)	lt blue	18.00	*47.50*
B11	A2	200(m)	violet	42.50	*110.00*

B12	A2	500(m) brown	125.00	*160.00*
a.		"C" of "Locust" omitted	750.00	
		Nos. B1-B12 (12)	235.90	*414.50*

These stamps were issued to raise funds to help combat a plague of locusts.

POSTAGE DUE STAMPS

Stamps of Regular Issue (Nos. 69, 66-68 Surcharged with New Value like No. 91) Overprinted

This overprint reads: "Mustahaq" (Tax or Due)

1923 Unwmk. *Perf. 11½*

Typo. Ovpt. "Mustahaq" 10mm long

J1	A7	½pi on 3pi ol brn	45.00	*55.00*
a.		Inverted overprint	175.00	175.00
b.		Double overprint	175.00	175.00

Handstamped Overprint 12mm long

J2	A7	½pi on 3pi ol brn	12.50	*15.00*
J3	A7	1pi dark blue	8.00	*9.00*
J4	A7	1½pi violet	8.00	*9.00*
J5	A7	2pi orange	9.00	*10.00*
		Nos. J1-J5 (5)	82.50	*98.00*

These overprints are found double, inverted, etc. as is usual with handstamps.

Stamps of Hejaz Handstamped

J6	A7	½pi red	1.00	*1.25*
J7	A7	1pi dark blue	1.10	*1.75*
J8	A7	1½pi violet	1.40	*2.25*
J9	A7	2pi orange	2.00	*3.00*
J10	A7	3pi olive brown	3.00	*5.50*
J11	A7	5pi olive green	5.50	*8.00*
		Nos. J6-J11 (6)	14.00	*21.75*

Type of Palestine, 1918, Overprinted

1925 Wmk. 4 *Perf. 14*

J12	A1	1m dark brown	1.75	*5.00*
J13	A1	2m yellow	2.50	*3.25*
J14	A1	4m rose	4.25	*5.00*
J15	A1	8m red	5.00	*8.50*
J16	A1	13m ultramarine	6.75	*8.50*
J17	A1	5pi plum	7.75	*11.50*
a.		Perf. 15x14	67.50	*77.50*
		Nos. J12-J17 (6)	28.00	*41.75*

The overprint reads: "Mustahaq. Sharqi al'Ardan." (Tax. Eastern Jordan).

Stamps of Palestine, 1918, Surcharged

1926

J18	A1	1m on 1m dk brn	3.50	*5.00*
J19	A1	2m on 1m dk brn	3.50	*5.00*
J20	A1	4m on 3m Prus bl	3.50	*6.75*
J21	A1	8m on 3m Prus bl	3.75	*7.50*
J22	A1	13m on 13m ultra	3.75	*8.50*
J23	A1	5pi on 13m ultra	5.00	*10.50*
		Nos. J18-J23 (6)	23.00	*43.25*

The surcharge reads "Tax—Eastern Jordan" and New Value.

Stamps of Regular Issue, 1927, Overprinted

1929

J24	A1	2m Prussian bl	1.25	*3.75*
J25	A1	10m red	2.00	*3.75*
J26	A2	50m claret	7.75	*16.00*
		Nos. J24-J26 (3)	11.00	*23.50*

With Additional Surcharge

J27	A1	1(m) on 3(m) rose	1.25	*4.25*
J28	A1	4(m) on 15(m) ultra	2.00	*4.25*
a.		Inverted surch. and ovpt.	95.00	
J29	A2	20(m) on 100(m) lt bl	5.75	*13.00*
		Nos. J27-J29 (3)	9.00	*21.50*

D1

1929 Engr. *Perf. 14*

Size: 17¼x21mm

J30	D1	1m brown	.75	*3.25*
a.		Perf. 13½x13	90.00	45.00
J31	D1	2m orange	.75	*3.75*
J32	D1	4m green	.75	*4.25*
J33	D1	10m carmine	2.00	*4.75*
J34	D1	20m olive green	7.75	*15.00*
J35	D1	50m blue	9.50	*19.00*
		Nos. J30-J35 (6)	21.50	*50.00*

See Nos. J39-J43 design with larger type. For surcharge see No. J52. For overprints see Nos. NJ1a, NJ3, NJ5a, NJ6-NJ7.

OFFICIAL STAMP

Saudi Arabia No. L34 Overprinted

1924, Jan. Typo. *Perf. 11½*

O1	A7	½pi red	275.00	100.00

Overprint reads: "(Government) the Arabian East 1342."

KARELIA

kə-ˈrē-lə-ə

LOCATION — In northwestern Soviet Russia.
GOVT. — An autonomous republic of the Soviet Union.
AREA — 55,198 sq. mi. (approx.).
POP. — 270,000 (approx.).
CAPITAL — Petrozavodsk (Kalininsk).

In 1921 the Karelians rebelled and for a short period a form of sovereignty independent of Russia was maintained.

100 Pennia = 1 Markka

Bear — A1

1922 Unwmk. Litho. *Perf. 11½, 12*

1	A1	5p dark gray	8.00	*40.00*
2	A1	10p light blue	8.00	*40.00*
3	A1	20p rose red	8.00	*40.00*
4	A1	25p yellow brown	8.00	*40.00*
5	A1	40p magenta	8.00	*40.00*
6	A1	50p gray green	8.00	*40.00*
7	A1	75p orange yellow	8.00	*40.00*
8	A1	1m pink & gray	8.00	*40.00*
9	A1	2m yel grn & gray	22.50	*90.00*
10	A1	3m lt blue & gray	22.50	*110.00*
11	A1	5m red lil & gray	22.50	*140.00*
12	A1	10m lt brn & gray	22.50	*200.00*
13	A1	15m green & car	22.50	*200.00*
14	A1	20m rose & green	22.50	*200.00*
15	A1	25m yellow & blue	22.50	*200.00*
		Nos. 1-15 (15)	221.50	*1,460.*
		Set, never hinged	400.00	

Nos. 1-15 were valid Jan. 31-Feb. 16, 1922. Use probably ended Feb. 3, although cancellations of the 4th and 5th exist.
Counterfeits abound.

KENYA, UGANDA, TANGANYIKA

ˈke-nyə, ü-ˈgan-də, ˌtan-zə-ˈnē-ə

LOCATION — East Africa, bordering on the Indian Ocean
GOVT. — States in British Commonwealth
AREA — 679,802 sq. mi.
POP. — 42,760,000 (est. 1977)
CAPITAL — Nairobi (Kenya), Kampala (Uganda), Dar es Salaam (Tanzania)

Kenya became a crown colony in 1906, including the former East Africa Protectorate leased from the Sultan of Zanzibar and known as the Kenya Protectorate.

The inland Uganda Protectorate, lying west of Kenya Colony, was declared a British Protectorate in 1894.

Tanganyika, a trust territory larger than Kenya or Uganda, was grouped with them postally from 1935 under the East African Posts & Telecommunications Admin.

100 Cents = 1 Rupee
100 Cents = 1 Shilling (1922)
20 Shillings = 1 Pound

Catalogue values for unused stamps in this country are for Never Hinged items, beginning with Scott 90.

East Africa and Uganda Protectorates

King George V
A1 A2

1921 Typo. Wmk. 4 *Perf. 14*

Ordinary Paper

1	A1	1c black	.50	*1.25*
2	A1	3c green	6.00	*7.50*
3	A1	6c rose red	5.00	*10.00*
4	A1	10c orange	9.50	1.25
5	A1	12c gray	5.50	*125.00*
6	A1	15c ultramarine	9.50	*17.50*

Chalky Paper

7	A1	50c gray lilac & blk	15.00	*110.00*
8	A2	2r blk & red, *blue*	80.00	*175.00*
9	A2	3r green & violet	135.00	*200.00*
10	A2	5r gray lil & ultra	150.00	*275.00*
11	A2	50r gray grn & red	2,200.	*4,500.*
		Nos. 1-10 (10)	416.00	*922.50*

The name of the colony was changed to Kenya in August, 1920, but stamps of the East Africa and Uganda types were continued in use. Stamps of types A1 and A2 watermarked Multiple Crown and C A (3) are listed under East Africa and Uganda Protectorates.

For stamps of Kenya and Uganda overprinted "G. E. A." used in parts of former German East Africa occupied by British forces, see Tanganyika Nos. 1-9.

Kenya and Uganda

King George V
A3 A4

1922-27 Wmk. 4

18	A3	1c brown	1.00	*2.25*
19	A3	5c violet	3.75	.75
20	A3	5c green ('27)	2.25	.45
21	A3	10c green	1.75	.35
22	A3	10c black ('27)	4.50	.20
23	A3	12c black	4.50	*27.50*
24	A3	15c car rose	1.40	.20
25	A3	20c orange	3.50	.20
26	A3	30c ultra	2.25	.50
27	A3	50c gray	2.75	.20
28	A3	75c ol bister	5.00	*10.00*
29	A4	1sh green	4.50	2.75
30	A4	2sh gray lilac	10.00	10.00
31	A4	2sh50c brown ('25)	22.50	*80.00*
32	A4	3sh gray black	19.00	7.00
33	A4	4sh gray ('25)	22.50	*90.00*
34	A4	5sh carmine	25.00	25.00
35	A4	7sh50c org ('25)	80.00	*160.00*
36	A4	10sh ultra	55.00	52.50
37	A4	£1 org & blk	175.00	*250.00*
38	A4	£2 brn vio & grn ('25)	725.00	*1,150.*
39	A4	£3 yel & dl vio ('25)	1,100.	—
40	A4	£4 rose lil & blk ('25)	1,850.	—
41	A4	£5 blue & blk	2,000.	—
		Revenue cancel		55.00
41A	A4	£10 grn & blk	*9,000.*	
41B	A4	£20 grn & red ('25)	*17,500.*	
41C	A4	£25 red & blk	*21,500.*	
41D	A4	£50 brn & blk	*27,500.*	
41E	A4	£75 gray & purple	*70,000.*	
41F	A4	£100 blk & red	*72,500.*	
		Nos. 18-37 (20)	446.15	*719.85*

High face value stamps are known with revenue cancellations removed and forged postal cancellations added.

Common Design Types pictured following the introduction.

Kenya, Uganda, Tanganyika
Silver Jubilee Issue
Common Design Type

1935, May Engr. *Perf. 13½x14*

42	CD301	20c ol grn & lt bl	1.25	.20
43	CD301	30c blue & brown	2.25	*3.00*
44	CD301	65c indigo & green	1.50	*2.75*
45	CD301	1sh brt vio & indigo	1.90	*2.50*
		Nos. 42-45 (4)	6.90	*8.45*
		Set, never hinged	12.50	

Kavirondo Cranes — A5

Dhow on Lake Victoria — A6

Lion — A7

Mount Kilimanjaro — A8

Jinja Bridge by Ripon Falls — A9

Mount Kenya — A10

Lake Naivasha A11

FIVE CENTS
Type I — Left rope does not touch sail.
Type II — Left rope touches sail.

Perf. 13, 14, 11½x13, 13x11½
Engr.; Typo. (10c, £1)

1935, May 1

46	A5	1c red brn & blk	.75	*1.00*
47	A6	5c grn & blk (I)	1.75	.50
a.		Type II	*22.50*	5.00
b.		Perf. 13x11½ (I)	*3,750.*	*600.00*
c.		Perf. 13x11½ (II)	*675.00*	*200.00*
48	A7	10c black & yel	3.50	.65
49	A8	15c red & black	2.75	.20
50	A5	20c red org & blk	3.25	.20
51	A9	30c dk ultra & blk	2.25	.80
52	A6	50c blk & red vio	1.75	.20
53	A10	65c yel brn & blk	3.00	*2.00*
54	A11	1sh grn & black	1.60	.80
a.		Perf. 13x11½ ('36)	*1,350.*	125.00
55	A8	2sh red vio & rose brn	5.50	4.25
56	A11	3sh blk & ultra	7.25	*15.00*
a.		Perf. 13x11½	*2,150.*	
57	A9	5sh car & black	19.00	*30.00*
58	A5	10sh ultra & red vio	70.00	*95.00*
59	A7	£1 blk & scar	160.00	*200.00*
		Nos. 46-59 (14)	282.35	350.60
		Set, never hinged	600.00	

Coronation Issue
Common Design Type

1937, May 12 Engr. _Perf. 13½x14_

60	CD302	5c deep green	.20	.20
61	CD302	20c deep orange	.30	.20
62	CD302	30c brt ultra	.40	.25
		Nos. 60-62 (3)	.90	.65
		Set, never hinged	2.00	

Kavirondo Cranes — A12

Dhow on Lake Victoria — A13

Lake Naivasha — A14

Jinja Bridge, Ripon Falls — A16

Mt. Kilimanjaro A15

Lion — A17

FIFTY CENTS:
Type I — Left rope does not touch sail.
Type II — Left rope touches sail.

1938-54 Engr. _Perf. 13x13½_

66	A12	1c vio brn & blk	.25	*.35*
a.		1c red brown & gray black, perf. 13 ('42)	1.50	.45

Perf. 13x11½

67	A13	5c grn & blk	3.00	.25
68	A13	5c red org & brn ('49)	.40	*2.25*
a.		Perf. 13x12½ ('50)	1.60	*3.00*
69	A14	10c org & brn	2.00	.20
a.		Perf. 14 ('41)	90.00	7.25
70	A14	10c grn & blk ('49)	.25	*.75*
a.		Perf. 13x12½ ('50)	1.75	.20

Perf. 13x12½

71	A14	10c gray & red brn ('52)	.80	*.55*

Perf. 13½x13, 13x13½

72	A15	15c car & gray blk ('43)	3.25	*2.75*
a.		Booklet pane of 4	14.00	
b.		Perf. 13	17.00	.50
73	A15	15c grn & blk ('52)	1.60	*4.00*
74	A12	20c org & gray blk ('42)	5.75	.20
a.		Booklet pane of 4	24.00	
b.		Imperf., pair		
c.		Perf. 13	*35.00*	.30
d.		Perf. 14 ('41)	*50.00*	12.50

Perf. 13x12½

75	A13	25c car & blk ('52)	1.25	*2.25*

Perf. 13x13½

76	A16	30c dp bl & gray blk ('42)	2.00	.35
a.		Perf. 14 ('41)	*130.00*	12.50
b.		Perf. 13	*40.00*	.40
77	A16	30c brn & pur ('52)	1.25	.40
78	A12	40c brt bl & gray blk ('52)	1.50	*3.50*

Perf. 13x12½

79	A13	50c gray blk & red vio (II) ('49)	5.75	.60
a.		Perf. 13x11½ (II)	14.00	1.10
b.		Perf. 13x11½ (I)	175.00	*250.00*

Perf. 13x11½

80	A14	1sh yel brn & gray blk	18.00	.25
a.		Perf. 13x12½ ('49)	10.00	.60

Perf. 13½x13

81	A15	2sh red vio & org brn ('44)	22.50	.30
a.		Perf. 13	*100.00*	2.25
b.		Perf. 14 ('41)	*62.50*	2.25

Perf. 13x12½

82	A14	3sh gray blk & ultra ('50)	27.50	3.00
a.		Perf. 13x11½	35.00	4.00

Perf. 13x13½

83	A16	5sh car rose & gray blk ('44)	27.50	1.40
a.		Perf. 13	*125.00*	17.50
b.		Perf. 14 ('41)	*35.00*	2.25
84	A12	10sh ultra & red vio ('44)	40.00	4.25
a.		Perf. 13	110.00	22.50
b.		Perf. 14 ('41)	32.50	20.00

Typo.
Perf. 14

85	A17	£1 blk & scar ('41)	22.50	*17.50*
a.		Perf. 11½x13	275.00	130.00
b.		Perf. 12½ ('54)	12.00	*32.50*
		Nos. 66-85 (20)	187.05	*45.10*
		Set, never hinged	250.00	

See Nos. 98-99.

South Africa Nos. 48, 57, 60 and 62 Surcharged

Basic stamps of Nos. 86-89 are inscribed alternately in English and Afrikaans.

1941-42 Wmk. 201 _Perf. 15x14, 14_

86	A6	5c on 1p car & gray, pair	1.00	*1.50*
a.		Single, English	.20	.20
b.		Single, Afrikaans	.20	.20
87	A17	10c on 3p ultra, pair	2.50	*3.75*
a.		Single, English	.30	.35
b.		Single, Afrikaans	.30	.35
88	A7	20c on 6p org & grn, pair	2.25	*2.50*
a.		Single, English	.20	.25
b.		Single, Afrikaans	.20	.25
89	A11	70c on 1sh lt bl & ol brn, pair	15.00	*11.00*
a.		Single, English	.50	.45
b.		Single, Afrikaans	.50	.45
		Nos. 86-89 (4)	20.75	18.75
		Set, never hinged	30.00	

Issued: #86-88, 7/1/41; #89, 4/20/42.

Catalogue values for unused stamps in this section, from this point to the end of the section, are for Never Hinged items.

Peace Issue
Common Design Type
Perf. 13½x14

1946, Nov. 11 Engr. Wmk. 4

90	CD303	20c red orange	.20	.20
91	CD303	30c deep blue	.40	.30

Silver Wedding Issue
Common Design Types

1948, Dec. 1 Photo. _Perf. 14x14½_

92	CD304	20c orange	.20	.20

Engr.; Name Typo.
Perf. 11½x11

93	CD305	£1 red	35.00	*52.50*

UPU Issue
Common Design Types
Engr.; Typo. on Nos. 95 and 96

1949, Oct. 10 _Perf. 13, 11x11½_

94	CD306	20c red orange	.20	.20
95	CD307	30c indigo	1.50	1.10
96	CD308	50c gray	.40	.20
97	CD309	1sh red brown	.50	.35
		Nos. 94-97 (4)	2.60	1.85

Type of 1949 with Added Inscription: "Royal Visit 1952"

1952, Feb. 1 Engr. _Perf. 13x12½_

98	A14	10c green & black	.20	*1.25*
99	A14	1sh yel brn & gray blk	.30	*2.00*

Visit of Princess Elizabeth, Duchess of Edinburgh, and the Duke of Edinburgh, 1952.

POSTAGE DUE STAMPS

Kenya and Uganda

D1

D2

Perf. 14½x14

1928-33 Typo. Wmk. 4

J1	D1	5c deep violet	3.00	1.00
J2	D1	10c orange red	3.00	1.00
J3	D1	20c yel green	3.00	4.00
J4	D1	30c ol brn ('31)	22.50	16.00
J5	D1	40c dull blue	8.50	*16.00*
J6	D1	1sh grnsh gray ('33)	72.50	*125.00*
		Nos. J1-J6 (6)	112.50	*163.00*
		Set, never hinged	175.00	

Kenya, Uganda, Tanganyika

1935, May 1 _Perf. 13½x14_

J7	D2	5c violet	3.50	2.25
J8	D2	10c red	.35	.65
J9	D2	20c green	.55	.65
J10	D2	30c brown	1.00	*.90*
J11	D2	40c ultramarine	2.00	*4.00*
J12	D2	1sh gray	25.00	*25.00*
		Nos. J7-J12 (6)	32.40	*33.45*
		Set, never hinged	45.00	

KIAUCHAU

(Kiautschou)

LOCATION — A district of China on the south side of the Shantung peninsula.
GOVT. — A former German colony.
AREA — 200 sq. mi.
POP. — 192,000 (approx. 1914).

The area was seized by Germany in 1897 and through negotiations that followed was leased to Germany by China.

100 Pfennig = 1 Mark
100 Cents = 1 Dollar (1905)

STAMPS OF GERMAN OFFICES IN CHINA USED IN KIAUCHAU

Type A

Type B

Type C

Stamps of 1898 canceled Type B or Type C

1898

56 degree Angle

A1	A9	3pf dark brown (#1)	17.50
		On cover	37.50
a.		3pf yellow brown (#1a)	15.00
		On cover	30.00
b.		3pf reddish brown (#1b)	95.00
		On cover	95.00
A2	A9	5pf green (#2)	8.75
		On cover	15.00
A3	A10	10pf carmine (#3)	15.00
		On cover	22.50
A4	A10	20pf ultramarine (#4)	175.00
		On cover	265.00
A5	A10	25pf orange (#5)	75.00
		On cover	150.00
A6	A10	50pf red brown (#6)	75.00
		On cover	225.00

Canceled Type A
45 degree Angle

A7	A9	3pf yellow brown (#1c)	*11,000.*
		On cover	—
A8	A9	5pf green (#2a)	19.00
		On cover	26.00
A9	A10	10pf carmine (#3a)	19.00
		On cover	22.50
A10	A10	20pf ultramarine (#4a)	15.00
		On cover	30.00
A11	A10	25pf orange (#5a)	75.00
		On cover	150.00
A12	A10	50pf red brown (#6a)	65.00
		On cover	200.00

Cancellations other than Types A-C are scarce and command premiums.

TSINGTAU ISSUES

Stamps of Germany, Offices in China 1898, with Additional Surcharge:

a

b

c

On Nos. 1-9, a blue or violet line is drawn through "PF. 10 PF." All exist without this line. All copies of Nos. 1b, 2b and 3b lack the colored line.

The three surcharge types can most easily be distinguished by the differences in the lower loop of the "5."

1900

"China" Overprint at 56 degree Angle

1 A10(a) 5pfg on 10pf car 40.00 47.50
Never hinged 125.00
On cover 190.00
c. Dbl. surch., one inverted 325.00
Never hinged 725.00
2 A10(b) 5pfg on 10pf car 40.00 47.50
Never hinged 125.00
On cover 190.00
c. Dbl. surch., one inverted 325.00
Never hinged 725.00
3 A10(c) 5pfg on 10pf car 40.00 47.50
Never hinged 125.00
On cover 190.00
c. Dbl. surch., one inverted 325.00
Never hinged 725.00

"China" Overprint at 45 degree Angle

1a A10(a) 5pfg on 10pf car 125.00 *115.00*
Never hinged 325.00
On cover 300.00
b. Double surcharge 400.00 *525.00*
Never hinged 875.00
2a A10(b) 5pfg on 10pf car 125.00 *115.00*
Never hinged 325.00
On cover 300.00
b. Double surcharge 400.00 *525.00*
Never hinged 875.00
3a A10(c) 5pfg on 10pf car 125.00 *115.00*
Never hinged 325.00
On cover 300.00
b. Double surcharge 400.00 *525.00*
Never hinged 875.00

Surcharged:

5 Pf. *d* **5 Pf.** *e* **5 Pf.** *f*

"China" Overprint at 48 degree Angle on Nos. 4-9

4 A10(d) 5pf on 10pf car 2,000. 2,750.
Never hinged 3,400.
On cover *5,000.*
a. Double surcharge *6,750. 13,500.*
On cover *24,000.*
5 A10(e) 5pf pn 10pf car *2,000. 2,750.*
Never hinged 3,400.
On cover 5,000.
a. Double surcharge *6,750. 13,500.*
On cover *24,000.*
6 A10(f) 5pf on 10pf car *2,000. 2,750.*
Never hinged 3,400.
On cover 5,000.
a. Double surcharge *6,750. 15,000.*
On cover *24,000.*
b. 5fP *15,000.*
On cover —
c. As "b," double surcharge — —

5

With Additional Handstamp

7 A10(d) 5pf on 10pf car *34,000. 40,000.*
Never hinged *47,500.*
On cover *75,000.*
8 A10(f) 5pf on 10pf car *34,000. 40,000.*
Never hinged *47,500.*
On cover *75,000.*
a. On No. 6b — —

With Additional Handstamp **5 Pf.**

9 A10(f) 5pf on 10pf car *6,750. 8,750.*
Never hinged 11,000.
On cover *17,500.*
a. Double surcharge *32,500.*

b. On No. 6a
c. On No. 6b
d. On No. 6c

On Nos. 1-9, a blue or violet line is drawn through "PF. 10 PF." All exist without this line. All copies of Nos. 1b, 2b and 3b lack the colored line.

Kaiser's Yacht "Hohenzollern"
A1 A2

1901, Jan. Unwmk. Typo. *Perf. 14*

10 A1 3pf brown 1.75 1.75
Never hinged 4.40
On cover 37.50
11 A1 5pf green 4.25 1.40
Never hinged 4.40
On cover 14.50
12 A1 10pf carmine 2.25 1.90
Never hinged 5.75
On cover 15.00
13 A1 20pf ultra 6.50 7.25
Never hinged 18.00
On cover 22.50
14 A1 25pf org & blk, *yel* 11.50 *14.50*
Never hinged 29.00
On cover 45.00
15 A1 30pf org & blk, *sal* 11.50 *14.00*
Never hinged 29.00
On cover 47.50
16 A1 40pf lake & blk 14.00 *17.50*
Never hinged 37.50
On cover 47.50
17 A1 50pf pur & blk, *sal* 14.00 *20.00*
Never hinged 37.50
On cover 47.50
18 A1 80pf lake & blk, *rose* 25.00 *47.50*
Never hinged 62.50
On cover 100.00

Engr. *Perf. 14½x14*

19 A2 1m carmine 45.00 *80.00*
Never hinged 125.00
On cover 145.00
20 A2 2m blue 65.00 *95.00*
Never hinged 175.00
On cover 160.00
21 A2 3m blk vio 65.00 *175.00*
Never hinged 175.00
On cover 325.00
22 A2 5m slate & car 175.00 *575.00*
Never hinged 525.00
On cover 1,100.
Nos. 10-22 (13) 440.75 *1,050.*
Set, never hinged 1,225.
Set, ovptd. "SPECIMEN" 950.00
Set, ovptd. "SPECIMEN," never hinged 1,900.

Covers: Values for Nos. 17-22 are for overfranked complete covers, usually philatelic.

A3

A4

1905 Typo.

23 A3 1c brown 1.10 1.50
Never hinged 3.75
On cover 17.50
24 A3 2c green 1.60 1.10
Never hinged 4.40
On cover 14.50
25 A3 4c carmine 3.75 1.25
Never hinged 8.75
On cover 14.50
26 A3 10c ultra 7.25 4.75
Never hinged 17.50
On cover 22.50
27 A3 20c lake & blk 30.00 17.50
Never hinged 87.50
On cover 47.50
28 A3 40c lake & blk, *rose* 70.00 *85.00*
Never hinged 225.00
On cover 175.00

Engr.

29 A4 $½ carmine 62.50 *72.50*
Never hinged 140.00
On cover 175.00
30 A4 $1 blue, 26x17 holes 160.00 85.00
Never hinged 440.00
On cover 190.00
a. $1 blue, 25x16 holes 130.00 120.00
Never hinged 325.00
On cover 190.00
31 A4 $1½ blk vio 1,000. *1,475.*
Never hinged 2,250.
On cover 2,400.
32 A4 $2½ slate & car, 26x17 holes 1,325. *4,400.*
Never hinged 3,650.
On cover 6,600.
a. $2½ slate & car, 25x16 holes 1,900. *3,500.*
Never hinged 4,400.
On cover 4,750.
Nos. 23-32 (10) 2,661. *6,143.*
Set, never hinged 6,800.

Values for Nos. 27-32 on cover are for overfranked, usually philatelic, covers.

1905-09 Wmk. 125 Typo.

33 A3 1c brown ('06) 1.10 1.50
Never hinged 3.00
On cover 30.00
a. 1c yellow brown ('16) .45 —
Never hinged 1.90
34 A3 2c green ('09) 1.00 *1.10*
Never hinged 2.50
On cover 14.50
a. 2c dark green ('14) .45 *1.90*
Never hinged 2.50
On cover 18.00
35 A3 4c carmine ('09) .75 *1.10*
Never hinged 1.90
On cover 14.50
36 A3 10c ultra ('09) .95 *3.25*
Never hinged 2.40
On cover 20.00
a. 10c blue 11.00 4.50
Never hinged 25.00
On cover 15.00
37 A3 20c lake & blk ('08) 2.50 *14.50*
Never hinged 5.50
On cover 52.50
a. 20c red & black ('18) 1.40
Never hinged 3.75
38 A3 40c lake & blk, *rose* 2.75 *47.50*
Never hinged 7.25
On cover 120.00

Engr.

39 A4 $½ carmine, 26x17 holes ('07) 5.75 *57.50*
Never hinged 22.50
On cover 140.00
a. $½ pale rose, 25x17 holes ('18) 4.75
Never hinged 18.00
40 A4 $1 blue, 26x17 holes ('06) 7.25 *62.50*
Never hinged 30.00
On cover 150.00
a. $1 bright blue, 25x17 holes ('18) 5.75
Never hinged 22.50
41 A4 $1½ blk violet 6.50 *660.00*
Never hinged 22.50
On cover —
a. $1½ gray violet, 25x17 holes ('18) 9.50
Never hinged 45.00
42 A4 $2½ slate & car 17.50 *440.00*
Never hinged 80.00
On cover 825.00
Nos. 33-42 (10) 46.05 1,288.
Set, never hinged 175.00

Nos. 37a, 39a, 40a and 41a were not placed in use.

KIONGA

ˈkyoŋ-gə

LOCATION — Southeast Africa and northeast Mozambique, on Indian Ocean south of Rovuma River
GOVT. — Part of German East Africa
AREA — 400 sq. mi.

This territory, occupied by Portuguese troops during World War I was allotted to Portugal by the Treaty of Versailles. Later it became part of Mozambique.

100 Centavos = 1 Escudo

Lourenco Marques No. 149 Surcharged in Red — 1srch

1916, May 29 Unwmk. *Perf. 11½*

1 A2 ½c on 100r bl, *bl* 24.00 20.00
2 A2 1c on 100r bl, *bl* 22.50 17.00
3 A2 2½c on 100r bl, *bl* 22.50 17.00
4 A2 5c on 100r bl, *bl* 22.50 17.00
Nos. 1-4 (4) 91.50 71.00

Most of the stock of Lourenço Marques #149 used for these surcharges lacked gum. Unused examples with original gum are worth approximately 50% more than the values shown.

KOREA

kə-'rē-ə

(Corea)

(Chosen, Tyosen, Tae Han)

LOCATION — Peninsula extending from Manchuria between the Yellow Sea and the Sea of Japan
GOVT. — Republic
AREA — 38,221 sq. mi.
POP. — 39,950,743 (1983)
CAPITAL — Seoul

Korea (or Corea) an independent monarchy for centuries under Chinese influence, came under Japanese influence in 1895. Japanese stamps were used there as early as 1875. Administrative control was assumed by Japan in 1904 and annexation followed in 1910. Postage stamps of Japan were used in Korea from 1905 to early 1946.

100 Mon = 1 Tempo
5 Poon = 1 Cheun
100 Sen = 1 Yen
1000 Re = 100 Cheun = Weun

Stylized Yin Yang
A1 A2

Perf. 8½ to 11½

1884 Typo. Unwmk.

1	A1 5m rose	50.00	
2	A2 10m blue	10.00	

Reprints and counterfeits of Nos. 1-2 exist.

These stamps were never placed in use. Values: 25 and 50 mon, each $7; 100 mon $10.
Counterfeits exist.

Yin Yang — A6

Two types of 50p:
I — No period after "50."
II — Period after "50."

Perf. 11½, 12, 12½, 13 and Compound

1895 Litho.

6	A6 5p green	20.00	14.00
a.	5p pale yellow green	27.50	17.00
b.	Vert. pair, imperf horiz.	50.00	50.00
c.	Horiz. pair, imperf. vert.	50.00	50.00
d.	Vertical pair, imperf. between	55.00	55.00
e.	Horiz. pair, imperf. btwn.	55.00	55.00
7	A6 10p deep blue	29.00	15.00
a.	Horiz. pair, imperf. between	72.50	72.50
b.	Vert. pair, imperf. horiz.	57.50	57.50
8	A6 25p maroon	45.00	25.00
a.	Horiz. pair, imperf. between	92.50	92.50
b.	Vert. pair, imperf. horiz.	90.00	90.00
9	A6 50p purple (II)	18.00	10.00
a.	Horiz. pair, imperf. between	70.00	70.00
b.	Vert, pair, imperf. horiz.	40.00	40.00
c.	Horiz. pair, imperf. vert.	40.00	40.00
d.	Type I	22.50	16.00
	Nos. 6-9 (4)	112.00	64.00

For overprints and surcharges see Nos. 10-17C, 35-38.
Counterfeits exist of Nos. 6-9 and all surcharges and overprints.

Overprinted "Tae Han" in Korean and Chinese Characters

1897

Red Overprint

10	A6 5p green	90.00	10.00
a.	5p pale yellow green	200.00	150.00
b.	Inverted overprint	150.00	150.00
c.	Without ovpt. at bottom	125.00	125.00
d.	Without overprint at top	125.00	125.00
f.	Double overprint at top	140.00	140.00
g.	Overprint at bottom in blk	160.00	160.00
h.	Pair, one without overprint	450.00	450.00
i.	Double overprint at top, inverted at bottom	525.00	
11	A6 10p deep blue	100.00	15.00
a.	Without ovpt. at bottom	140.00	140.00
b.	Without overprint at top	140.00	140.00
c.	Double overprint at top	150.00	150.00
d.	Bottom overprint inverted	140.00	140.00
e.	Top ovpt. dbl., one in blk	210.00	210.00
f.	Top overprint omitted, bottom overprint inverted	400.00	
12	A6 25p maroon	110.00	17.00
a.	Overprint at bottom invtd.	140.00	140.00
b.	Overprint at bottom in blk	210.00	210.00
c.	Bottom overprint omitted	140.00	140.00
e.	Top ovpt. dbl., one in blk	225.00	225.00
f.	Top and bottom overprints double, one of each in blk	250.00	250.00
g.	Pair, one without overprint	425.00	425.00
13	A6 50p purple	90.00	12.00
a.	Without ovpt. at bottom	110.00	110.00
b.	Without overprint at top	110.00	110.00
c.	Bottom overprint double	100.00	100.00
e.	Pair, one without overprint	275.00	275.00
	Nos. 10-13 (4)	390.00	54.00

1897

Black Overprint

13F	A6 5p green	300.00	80.00
13G	A6 10p deep blue	300.00	100.00
h.	Without ovpt. at bottom	350.00	
14	A6 25p maroon	300.00	100.00
a.	Without ovpt. at bottom	325.00	
b.	Without overprint at top	325.00	
c.	Double overprint at bottom	325.00	
15	A6 50p purple	300.00	80.00
a.	Without ovpt. at bottom	325.00	
	Nos. 13F-15 (4)	1,200.	

These stamps with black overprint, also No. 16A, are said not to have been officially authorized.

Nos. 6, 6a and 8 Surcharged in Red or Black

1900

15B	A6 1p on 5p grn (R)	*3,500.*	*750.00*
c.	Yellow green		
16	A6 1p on 25p mar	95.00	55.00

Same Surcharge in Red or Black on Nos. 10, 10a, 12, 12c and 14

16A	A6 1p on 5p grn (R)	950.00	
b.	1p on 5p pale yellow green	950.00	
17	A6 1p on 25p (#12)	45.00	20.00
a.	Figure "1" omitted	80.00	
b.	On #12c	70.00	70.00
17C	A6 1p on 25p (#14)	750.00	160.00

Counterfeit overprints and surcharges of Nos. 10-17C exist. See note after No. 15.

A8

A9

A10

A11

A12

A13

A14

A15

A16

A17

A18

A19

A20

A21

1900-01 Typo. *Perf. 11*

18	A8 2re gray	5.00	3.50
19	A9 1ch yellow grn	10.50	4.00
20B	A11 2ch pale blue	12.00	8.00
21	A12 3ch orange red	12.00	4.50
a.	Vert. pair, imperf. horiz.	175.00	175.00
22	A13 4ch carmine	35.00	14.00
23	A14 5ch pink	15.00	8.00
24	A15 6ch dp blue	16.00	6.50
25	A16 10ch purple ('01)	32.50	10.00
26	A17 15ch gray vio	27.50	10.00
27	A18 20ch red brown	37.50	14.00
31	A19 50ch ol grn & pink	290.00	100.00
32	A20 1wn rose, blk & bl	775.00	160.00
33	A21 2wn pur & yel grn	1,300.	250.00
	Nos. 18-33 (13)	2,568.	592.50

Nos. 22, 23, 25, 26, 33 exist imperf.
Some examples of Nos. 18-27 exist with forged Tae Han overprints in red. It is believed that Nos. 18 and 21 exist with genuine Tae Han overprints.
Reprints of No. 24 were made in light blue, perf. 12x13, in 1905 for a souvenir booklet. See note after No. 54.
See Nos. 52-54.

Perf. 10

18a	A8 2re	8.00	3.50
19a	A9 1ch	10.00	4.50
20	A10 2ch blue	35.00	18.00
a.	Horiz. pair, imperf. btwn.	*725.00*	
20Ba	A11 2ch pale blue	50.00	45.00
21b	A12 3ch	14.00	4.50
22a	A13 4ch	45.00	17.50
23a	A14 5ch	20.00	9.00
24a	A15 6ch	22.50	11.00
26a	A17 15ch	150.00	125.00
27a	A18 20ch	200.00	175.00
	Nos. 18a-27a (10)	554.50	413.00

Emperor's Crown — A22

1902, Oct. 18 *Perf. 11½*

34	A22 3ch orange	40.00	18.50

40th year of the reign of Emperor Kojong.
An imperf. single was part of the 1905 souvenir booklet. See note following No. 54.
Counterfeits exist.

Nos. 8 and 9 Handstamp Surcharged in Black

1ch

2ch

3ch

Perf. 11½, 12, 12½, 13 and Compound

1902

35	A6 1ch on 25p maroon	25.00	6.00
b.	Horiz. pair, imperf. btwn.	80.00	
c.	Imperf.	50.00	
d.	Vert. pair, imperf. horiz.	50.00	
e.	On No. 12	90.00	90.00

36 A6 2ch on 25p maroon 27.50 7.00
b. Imperf. 45.00
d. On No. 12 90.00 90.00
36E A6 2ch on 50p purple 160.00 150.00
f. Character "cheun" unabbreviated (in two rows instead of one) 250.00 175.00
37 A6 3ch on 50p purple 25.00 7.00
b. With character "cheun" unabbreviated (in two rows instead of one) 2,100. 800.00
d. Horiz. pair, imperf. btwn. 60.00
e. Vert. pair, imperf. btwn. 60.00
g. On No. 13 60.00 60.00
38 A6 3ch on 25p maroon 60.00 60.00
Nos. 35-38 (5) 297.50 230.00

There are several sizes of these surcharges. Being handstamped, inverted and double surcharges exist.

Counterfeit surcharges exist.

Falcon — A23

1903 *Perf. 13½x14*

39	A23	2re slate		6.50	6.25
40	A23	1ch violet brn		8.00	7.50
41	A23	2ch green		12.50	7.50
42	A23	3ch orange		10.00	7.50
43	A23	4ch rose		19.00	9.50
44	A23	5ch yellow brn		19.00	11.00
45	A23	6ch lilac		25.00	12.50
46	A23	10ch blue		32.50	16.00
47	A23	15ch red, *straw*		45.00	22.50
48	A23	20ch vio brn, *straw*		62.50	32.50
49	A23	50ch red, *grn*		200.00	110.00
50	A23	1wn vio, *lav*		525.00	290.00
51	A23	2wn vio, *org*		525.00	290.00
		Nos. 39-51 (13)		1,490.	822.75

Values are for copies with perfs touching the design.

Types of 1901

1903 *Perf. 12½*

Thin, Semi-Transparent Paper

52	A19	50ch pale ol grn & pale pink	*275.00*	*140.00*
53	A20	1wn rose, blk & bl	*550.00*	*175.00*
54	A21	2wn lt vio & lt grn	*700.00*	*225.00*
		Nos. 52-54 (3)	*1,525.*	540.00

No. 24, perf. 12x13, No. 34 imperf. and most examples of Nos. 52-54 unused are from souvenir booklets made up in 1905 when the Japanese withdrew all Korean stamps from circulation.

KUWAIT

ku-'wāt

LOCATION — Northwestern coast of the Persian Gulf
GOVT. — Sheikdom under British Protection
AREA — 7,000 sq. mi.
POP. — 1,910,856 (est. 1985)
CAPITAL — Kuwait

16 Annas = 1 Rupee

Catalogue values for unused stamps in this country are for Never Hinged items, beginning with Scott 72 in the regular postage section.

There was a first or trial setting of the overprint with the word "Koweit." Twenty-four sets of regular and official stamps were printed with this spelling. Value for set, $10,000.

Catalogue values for Nos. 1-71 used, are for postally used examples. Stamps with telegraph cancellations are worth less.

Stamps of India, 1911-23, Overprinted

a

b

1923-24 **Wmk. 39** *Perf. 14*

1	A47(a)	½a green	3.25	*6.50*
2	A48(a)	1a dk brown	3.00	*3.00*
3	A58(a)	1½a chocolate	2.25	*4.75*
4	A49(a)	2a violet	4.00	*5.00*
5	A57(a)	2a6p ultra	2.75	*10.00*
6	A51(a)	3a brown org	4.75	*22.50*
7	A51(a)	3a ultra ('24)	9.50	*3.00*
8	A52(a)	4a ol green	8.50	*27.50*
9	A53(a)	6a bister	10.00	*16.00*
10	A54(a)	8a red violet	9.75	*38.00*
11	A55(a)	12a claret	17.50	*47.50*
12	A56(b)	1r grn & red brown	25.00	*30.00*
13	A56(b)	2r brn & car rose	47.50	*100.00*
14	A56(b)	5r vio & ultra	110.00	*240.00*
15	A56(b)	10r car & green	150.00	*375.00*
		Nos. 1-15 (15)	407.75	*928.75*

Overprint "a" on India No. 102 is generally considered unofficial.

Nos. 1-4, 6-7 exist with inverted overprint. None of these are believed to have been sold at the Kuwait post office.

For overprints see Nos. O1-O13.

Stamps of India, 1926-35, Overprinted type "a"

1929-37 **Wmk. 196**

17	A47	½a green	3.00	1.75
18	A71	½a green ('34)	5.50	1.75
19	A48	1a dark brown	9.00	1.90
20	A72	1a dk brown ('34)	6.00	1.25
21	A60	2a dk violet	3.75	1.25
22	A60	2a vermilion	27.50	*95.00*
23	A49	2a ver ('34)	25.00	6.75
a.		Small die	5.00	2.50
24	A51	3a ultramarine	4.00	2.00
25	A51	3a car rose ('34)	7.00	*4.50*
26	A61	4a olive green	29.00	*82.50*
27	A52	4a ol green ('34)	8.00	*14.50*
28	A53	6a bister ('37)	22.50	*65.00*
29	A54	8a red violet	10.00	17.50
30	A55	12a claret	25.00	*47.50*

Overprinted

c

31	A56	1r green & brown	15.00	*30.00*
32	A56	2r buff & car rose	16.00	*72.50*
33	A56	5r dk vio & ultra ('37)	100.00	*275.00*
34	A56	10r car & grn ('34)	210.00	*450.00*
35	A56	15r ol grn & ultra ('37)	650.00	*900.00*
		Nos. 17-35 (19)	1,176.	*2,070.*

For overprints see Nos. O15-O25.

Stamps of India, 1937, Overprinted type "a" (A80, A81) or "c" (A82)

1939 **Wmk. 196** *Perf. 13½x14*

45	A80	½a brown	1.00	*1.50*
46	A80	1a carmine	1.00	*1.50*
47	A81	2a scarlet	2.00	*2.50*
48	A81	3a yel green	3.00	*2.50*
49	A81	4a dark brown	4.50	*15.00*
50	A81	6a peacock blue	4.50	*9.00*
51	A81	8a blue violet	10.00	*35.00*
52	A81	12a car lake	8.50	*50.00*
53	A82	1r brown & slate	3.00	*4.00*
54	A82	2r dk brown & dk violet	11.50	*14.00*
55	A82	5r dp ultra & dk green	15.00	*22.50*
56	A82	10r rose car & dk violet	72.50	90.00
a.		Double overprint	350.00	350.00
57	A82	15r dk green & dk brown	90.00	*180.00*
		Nos. 45-57 (13)	226.50	*427.50*
		Set, never hinged	350.00	

Stamps of India 1940-43, Overprinted in Black

1945 **Wmk. 196** *Perf. 13½x14*

59	A83	3p slate	1.75	*3.75*
60	A83	½a rose violet	1.00	*2.75*
61	A83	9p lt green	2.50	*8.75*
62	A83	1a car rose	1.25	*2.00*
63	A84	1½a dark purple	1.75	*8.50*
64	A84	2a scarlet	2.00	*3.50*
65	A84	3a violet	3.25	*5.00*
66	A84	3½a ultramarine	4.25	*8.50*
67	A85	4a chocolate	3.25	*3.75*
68	A85	6a peacock blue	12.50	10.00
69	A85	8a blue violet	6.50	4.00
70	A85	12a car lake	7.00	4.25
71	A81	14a rose violet	12.50	*20.00*
		Nos. 59-71 (13)	59.50	*84.75*
		Set, never hinged	85.00	

Catalogue values for unused stamps in this section, from this point to the end of the section, are for Never Hinged items.

British Postal Administration

See Oman (Muscat) for similar stamps with surcharge of new value only.

Great Britain Nos. 258 to 263, 243 and 248 Surcharged in Black

1948-49 **Wmk. 251** *Perf. 14½x14*

72	A101	½a on ½p grn	1.50	*1.75*
73	A101	1a on 1p ver	1.50	*1.75*
74	A101	1½a on 1½p lt red brown	2.25	1.75
75	A101	2a on 2p lt org	1.75	*1.75*
76	A101	2½a on 2½p ultra	2.25	1.00
77	A101	3a on 3p violet	1.50	.85
a.		Pair, one without surcharge	—	
78	A102	6a on 6p rose lil	1.50	.75
79	A103	1r on 1sh brown	3.75	2.00

Great Britain Nos. 249A, 250 and 251A Surcharged in Black

Wmk. 259 *Perf. 14*

80	A104	2r on 2sh6p yel grn	4.00	*4.50*
81	A104	5r on 5sh dull red	7.00	4.50
81A	A105	10r on 10sh ultra	35.00	7.50
		Nos. 72-81A (11)	62.00	28.10

Issued: #72-81, Apr., 1948; 10r, July 4, 1949.

Bars of surcharge at bottom on No. 81A.

Silver Wedding Issue

Great Britain Nos. 267 and 268 Surcharged in Black

Perf. 14½x14, 14x14½

1948 **Wmk. 251**

82	A109	2½a on 2½p brt ultra	1.25	1.00
83	A110	15r on £1 deep chalky blue	35.00	35.00

Three bars obliterate the original denomination on No. 83.

Olympic Games Issue

Great Britain Nos. 271 to 274 Surcharged "KUWAIT" and New Value in Black

1948 *Perf. 14½x14*

84	A113	2½a on 2½p brt ultra	1.25	1.25
85	A114	3a on 3p dp violet	1.25	1.25
86	A115	6a on 6p red violet	1.50	1.50
87	A116	1r on 1sh dk brown	1.50	1.50
		Nos. 84-87 (4)	5.50	5.50

A square of dots obliterates the original denomination on No. 87.

UPU Issue

Great Britain Nos. 276 to 279 Surcharged "KUWAIT", New Value and Square of Dots in Black

1949, Oct. 10 **Photo.**

89	A117	2½a on 2½p brt ultra	1.00	1.00
90	A118	3a on 3p brt vio	1.25	1.25
91	A119	6a on 6p red vio	1.75	*2.50*
92	A120	1r on 1sh brown	2.00	1.50
		Nos. 89-92 (4)	6.00	6.25

Great Britain Nos. 280-285 Surcharged Like Nos. 72-79 in Black

1950-51 **Wmk. 251** *Perf. 14½x14*

93	A101	½a on ½p lt org	2.00	1.75
94	A101	1a on 1p ultra	2.00	1.75
95	A101	1½a on 1½p green	2.00	*2.50*
96	A101	2a on 2p lt red brown	2.25	1.75
97	A101	2½a on 2½p ver	2.25	*2.50*
98	A102	4a on 4p ultra ('50)	2.00	1.50

Great Britain Nos. 286-288 Surcharged in Black

Perf. 11x12

Wmk. 259

99	A121	2r on 2sh6p green	15.00	5.00
100	A121	5r on 5sh dl red	22.50	6.00
101	A122	10r on 10sh ultra	30.00	8.50
		Nos. 93-101 (9)	80.00	31.25

Longer bars, at lower right, on No. 101.
Issued: 4a, 10/2/50; others, 5/3/51.

Stamps of Great Britain, 1952-54 Surcharged "KUWAIT" and New Value in Black or Dark Blue

1952-54 **Wmk. 298** *Perf. 14½x14*

102	A126	½a on ½p red org ('53)	.20	.40
103	A126	1a on 1p ultra ('53)	.20	.20
104	A126	1½a on 1½p green	.20	.25
105	A126	2a on 2p red brn ('53)	.20	.20
106	A127	2½a on 2½p scarlet	.20	.25
107	A127	3a on 3p dk pur (Dk Bl) ('54)	.30	.20
108	A128	4a on 4p ultra ('53)	1.10	.40
109	A129	6a on 6p lilac rose ('54)	1.10	.20
111	A132	12a on 1sh6p dk green ('53)	3.50	1.00
112	A131	1r on 1sh6p dk blue ('53)	3.00	.20
		Nos. 102-112 (10)	10.00	3.30

Coronation Issue

Great Britain Nos. 313-316 Surcharged "KUWAIT" and New Value in Black

1953, June 3

113	A134	2½a on 2½p scarlet	2.25	1.25
114	A135	4a on 4p brt ultra	2.25	1.25
115	A136	12a on 1sh3p dk grn	3.25	2.00
116	A137	1r on 1sh6p dk blue	2.75	.50
		Nos. 113-116 (4)	10.50	5.00

Squares of dots obliterate the original denominations on Nos. 115 and 116.

Great Britain Stamps of 1955-56 Surcharged "KUWAIT" and New Value in Black

1955 **Wmk. 308** **Engr.** *Perf. 11x12*

117	A133	2r on 2sh6p dk brown	6.25	1.50
118	A133	5r on 5sh crimson	6.75	4.25
119	A133	10r on 10sh dp ultra	7.00	4.25
		Nos. 117-119 (3)	20.00	10.00

The surcharge on #117-119 exists in two types.

AIR POST STAMPS

Air Post Stamps of India, 1929-30, Overprinted type "c"

1933-34 Wmk. 196 *Perf. 14*

C1	AP1	2a dull green	12.00	*17.00*
C2	AP1	3a deep blue	2.25	*2.75*
C3	AP1	4a gray olive	110.00	*150.00*
C4	AP1	6a bister ('34)	4.50	*5.00*
		Nos. C1-C4 (4)	128.75	*174.75*

Counterfeits of Nos. C1-C4 exist.

OFFICIAL STAMPS

Stamps of India, 1911-23, Overprinted

Nos. O1-O9

Nos. O10-O14

1923-24 Wmk. 39 *Perf. 14*

O1	A47	½a green	2.50	*10.00*
O2	A48	1a brown	3.00	*9.00*
O3	A58	1½a chocolate	3.50	*20.00*
O4	A49	2a violet	6.00	*17.50*
O5	A57	2a6p ultra	5.25	*30.00*
O6	A51	3a brown org	5.50	*40.00*
O7	A51	3a ultra ('24)	5.75	*30.00*
O8	A52	4a olive grn	4.75	*45.00*
O9	A54	8a red violet	7.50	*55.00*
O10	A56	1r grn & brn	22.50	*80.00*
O11	A56	2r brn & car rose	25.00	*125.00*
O12	A56	5r vio & ultra	92.50	*325.00*
O13	A56	10r car & grn	175.00	*350.00*
O14	A56	15r ol grn & ultra	240.00	*500.00*
		Nos. O1-O14 (14)	598.75	*1,636.*

Stamps of India, 1926-30, Overprinted

Nos. O15-O20

Nos. O21-O25

1929-33 Wmk. 196

O15	A48	1a dk brown	4.50	*20.00*
O16	A60	2a violet	62.50	*150.00*
O17	A51	3a blue	5.00	*30.00*
O18	A61	4a ol green	5.75	*65.00*
O19	A54	8a red violet	6.50	*85.00*
O20	A55	12a claret	32.50	*150.00*
O21	A56	1r green & brn	6.50	*170.00*
O22	A56	2r buff & car rose	10.00	*250.00*
O23	A56	5r dk vio & ultra	34.00	*375.00*
O24	A56	10r car & green	67.50	*500.00*
O25	A56	15r olive grn & ultra	150.00	*1,000.*
		Nos. O15-O25 (11)	384.75	*2,795.*

LABUAN

lə-'bü-ən

LOCATION — An island in the East Indies, about six miles off the northwest coast of Borneo

GOVT. — A British possession, administered as a part of the North Borneo Colony

AREA — 35 sq. mi.

POP. — 8,963 (estimated)

CAPITAL — Victoria

The stamps of Labuan were replaced by those of Straits Settlements in 1906.

100 Cents = 1 Dollar

Covers: there are no known covers bearing Nos. 1-4. Except for Nos. 19, 19a, 29, 29a covers bearing Nos. 5-32 are very rare. Values for listed covers are for properly franked commercial covers or postal cards. Philatelic covers also exist and sell for much less.

Watermark

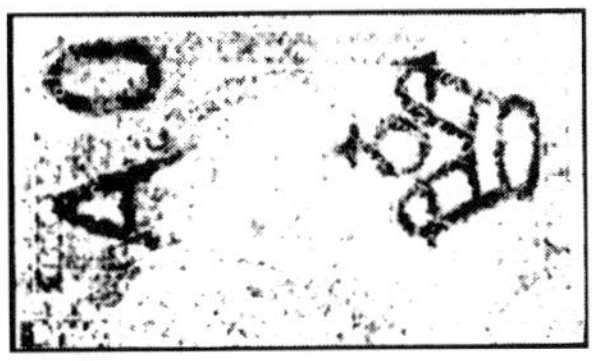
Wmk. 46 — C A over Crown

Queen Victoria — A1

On Nos. 1, 2, 3, 4 and 11 the watermark is 32mm high. It is always placed sideways and extends over two stamps.

1879, May Engr. Wmk. 46 *Perf. 14*

1	A1	2c green	1,150.	850.00
2	A1	6c orange	225.00	190.00
3	A1	12c carmine	1,725.	750.00
4	A1	16c blue	70.00	*140.00*
		Nos. 1-4 (4)	3,170.	1,930.

Covers: Covers bearing Nos. 1-4 are not known.

See Nos. 5-10, 16-24, 33-39, 42-48. For surcharges see Nos. 12-15, 25, 31, 40-41.

1880-82 Wmk. 1

5	A1	2c green	24.00	*34.00*
6	A1	6c orange	115.00	*125.00*
7	A1	8c carmine ('82)	115.00	*115.00*
8	A1	10c yel brown	175.00	*100.00*
9	A1	12c carmine	275.00	*375.00*
10	A1	16c blue ('81)	92.50	92.50
		Nos. 5-10 (6)	796.50	*841.50*

Covers: Covers bearing Nos. 5-10 are very rare.

A2

A3

A3a

A4

1880-83 Wmk. 46

11	A2	6c on 16c blue (with additional "6" across original value) R)	2,500.	1,000.
a.		One "6"		

Wmk. 1

12	A2	8c on 12c carmine	1,700.	1,100.
a.		Original value not obliterated	2,200.	1,500.
b.		Additional surcharge "8" across original value	1,800.	1,300.
c.		"8" inverted	1,800.	1,200.
d.		As "a," "8" inverted	—	—
13	A3	8c on 12c car ('81)	375.00	425.00
14	A3a	8c on 12c car ('81)	125.00	140.00
a.		"Eighr"	*18,500.*	
b.		Inverted surcharge	11,500.	
c.		Double surcharge	1,850.	1,800.
15	A4	$1 on 16c blue (R) ('83)	*3,750.*	

Covers: Covers bearing Nos. 11-15 are very rare.

On No. 12 the original value is obliterated by a pen mark in either black or red.

1883-86 Wmk. 2

16	A1	2c green	21.00	*30.00*
a.		Horiz. pair, imperf. btwn.	9,750.	
17	A1	2c rose red ('85)	3.50	*11.50*
a.		2c pale rose red ('86)	3.00	*10.50*
18	A1	8c carmine	275.00	110.00
19	A1	8c dk violet ('85)	25.00	8.00
		On cover		*1,200.*
a.		8c mauve ('86)	29.00	9.25
		On cover		*1,200.*
20	A1	10c yellow brn	35.00	*45.00*
21	A1	10c black brn ('86)	11.00	*45.00*
22	A1	16c blue	110.00	*210.00*
23	A1	16c gray blue ('86)	140.00	
24	A1	40c ocher	19.00	*110.00*
		Nos. 16-24 (9)	639.50	*569.50*

Covers: Covers bearing Nos. 16-18, 20-24 are very rare.

Nos. 1-10, 16-24 are in sheets of 10.

For surcharges see Nos. 26-30, 32.

A5

A6

A7

A8

1885 Wmk. 1

25	A5	2c on 16c blue	1,100.	*975.00*

Wmk. 2

26	A5	2c on 8c car	250.00	*450.00*
a.		Double surcharge		—
27	A6	2c on 16c blue	125.00	*190.00*
a.		Double surcharge		*5,000.*
28	A7	2c on 8c car	75.00	*115.00*

Covers: Covers bearing Nos. 25-28 are very rare.

1891

Black or Red Surcharge

29	A8	6c on 8c violet	10.50	9.25
		On cover		*1,350.*
a.		6c on 8c dark violet	140.00	110.00
		On cover		*1,650.*
b.		Double surcharge	375.00	—
c.		As "a," "Cents" omitted	475.00	500.00
d.		Inverted surcharge	75.00	*75.00*
e.		Dbl. surch., one inverted	850.00	—
f.		Dbl. surch., both inverted	850.00	—
g.		"6" omitted	500.00	
h.		Pair, one without surcharge	1,400.	1,400.
i.		Invt. surcharge, "Cents" omitted	525.00	—
j.		As "d," one without surcharge	1,600.	1,600.
k.		As "a," inverted surcharge	225.00	200.00
m.		As "a," double surcharge	550.00	—
n.		As "a," double surcharge, one inverted	975.00	
p.		As "a," pair, one inverted, one omitted	1,600.	—
q.		As "a," horiz. pair, imperf,. btwn.	—	—
30	A8	6c on 8c dk vio (R)	975.00	475.00
a.		Inverted surcharge	1,400.	675.00

Wmk. 46

31	A8	6c on 16c blue	2,300.	2,100.
a.		Inverted surcharge	8,750.	6,400.

Wmk. 2

32	A8	6c on 40c ocher	9,250.	5,000.
a.		Inverted surcharge	8,000.	7,500.

Covers: Covers bearing Nos. 30-32 are very rare. Values for Nos. 29 and 29a on cover are for properly franked commercial covers or postal cards. Philatelic covers exist and sell for much less.

1892 Engr. Unwmk.

33	A1	2c rose	6.00	4.25
		On cover		*725.00*
34	A1	6c yellow green	10.00	5.75
		On cover		*800.00*
35	A1	8c violet	6.50	10.50
		On cover		*1,050.*
a.		8c pale violet ('93)	4.25	*8.00*
		On cover		*1,050.*
36	A1	10c brown	14.00	10.00
		On cover		*1,150.*
a.		10c dk sepia brown('93)	11.50	*17.50*
		On cover		—
37	A1	12c deep ultra	7.50	*8.50*
		On cover		*975.00*
38	A1	16c gray	7.50	*11.50*
		On cover		*1,200.*
39	A1	40c ocher	32.50	*34.00*
		On cover		—
a.		40c brown buff('93)	47.50	30.00
		On cover		—
		Nos. 33-39 (7)	84.00	84.50

The 2c, 8c and 10c are in sheets of 30; others in sheets of 10.

Values for covers are for properly franked commercial usages. Philatelic covers exist and sell for lower prices.

Remainders of the 1892 issue were canceled to order, but in most cases cannot be distinguished from postally used examples.

Nos. 39 and 38 Surcharged

1893

40	A1	2c on 40c ocher	210.00	110.00
		On cover		*1,550.*
a.		Inverted surcharge	425.00	*600.00*
41	A1	6c on 16c gray	400.00	175.00
		On cover		*2,100.*
a.		Inverted surcharge	550.00	350.00
b.		Surcharge sideways	575.00	350.00
c.		"Six" omitted	—	—
d.		"Cents" omitted	—	—
e.		Handstamped "Six Cents"	*2,200.*	

Surcharges on Nos. 40-41 each exist in 10 types. Counterfeits exist.

No. 41e was handstamped on copies of No. 41 on which the surcharge failed to print or was printed partially or completely albino.

Values for covers are for properly franked commercial usages.

From Jan. 1, 1890, to Jan. 1, 1906, Labuan was administered by the British North Borneo Co. Late in that period, unused remainders of Nos. 42-83, 53a, 63a, 64a, 65a, 66a, 68a, 85-86, 96-118, 103a, 107a, J1-J9, J3a and J6a were canceled to order by bars forming an oval. Values for these stamps used are for those with this form of cancellation, unless described as postally used, which are for stamps with dated town cancellations. Nos. 63b, 64b, 65b, 104a, J6a, and possibly others, only exist c.t.o.

1894, Apr. Litho.

42	A1	2c bright rose	1.90	.65
		Postally used		15.50
		On cover		*1,000.*
43	A1	6c yellow green	14.50	.65
		Postally used		35.00
		On cover		*2,100.*
a.		Horiz. pair, imperf. btwn.	*7,000.*	
44	A1	8c bright violet	15.00	.65
		Postally used		35.00
		On cover		*2,100.*
45	A1	10c brown	47.50	.65
		Postally used		50.00
		On cover		*3,100.*
46	A1	12c light ultra	22.50	.80
		Postally used		72.50
		On cover		*4,250.*
47	A1	16c gray	30.00	.65
		Postally used		47.50
		On cover		—
48	A1	40c orange	57.50	.65
		Postally used		47.50
		On cover		—
		Nos. 42-48 (7)	188.90	4.70

Counterfeits exist.

Values for covers are for properly franked commercial usages. Philatelic covers exist and sell for lower prices.

Dyak Chieftain — A9

Malayan Sambar — A10

Sago Palm A11

Argus Pheasant A12

Arms of North Borneo — A13

Dhow — A14

Saltwater Crocodile — A15

Mt. Kinabalu — A16

Arms of North Borneo — A17

1894, May-1896 Engr. *Perf. 14½-15*
49 A9 1c lilac & black 2.00 .65
Postally used 10.50
On cover 210.00
a. Vert. pair, imperf. between 975.00 350.00
50 A10 2c blue & black 3.50 .65
Postally used 10.50
On cover 210.00
a. Imperf., pair 825.00
51 A11 3c bister & black 5.25 .65
Postally used 21.00
On cover 350.00
52 A12 5c green & black 42.50 1.10
Postally used 30.00
On cover 500.00
a. Horiz. pair, imperf. between 1,800.
53 A13 6c brn red & blk 3.50 .65
Postally used 17.50
On cover 310.00
a. Imperf., pair 725.00 425.00
54 A14 8c rose & black 9.75 .65
Postally used 30.00
On cover 500.00
a. 8c red & black 18.00 .45
Postally used 30.00
On cover 575.00
55 A15 12c orange & black 37.50 .65
Postally used 70.00
On cover —
56 A16 18c ol brn & blk 29.00 .65
Postally used 77.50
On cover —
a. 18c olive bister & black 67.50 .55
Postally used 95.00
On cover —
b. Vert. pair, imperf. between 1,250.
57 A17 24c lilac & blue 18.00 .65
Postally used 60.00
On cover 1,050.
a. 24c mauve & blue 25.00 .55
Postally used 75.00
On cover —
Nos. 49-57 (9) 151.00 6.30

Perf. 13½-14
49b A9 1c lilac & black 11.50
Postally used 12.00
On cover 240.00
50b A10 2c blue & black 5.75
Postally used 10.50
On cover 240.00
51a A11 3c bister & black 10.00 47.50
Postally used 12.50
On cover 290.00
52b A12 5c green & black 22.50 .40
Postally used 17.50
On cover 310.00
53b A13 6c brn red & blk 2.10
54b A14 8c rose & black 35.00 .70
Postally used 45.00
On cover 800.00
54c A14 8c red & black 30.00
Postally used 50.00
On cover 975.00
55a A15 12c orange & black 85.00 2.90
Postally used 100.00
On cover —
56c A16 18c ol brn & blk 80.00
56d A16 18c ol bister & blk 35.00
Postally used 95.00
On cover —
57b A17 24c lilac & blue 18.00 .70
Postally used 60.00
On cover —
57c A17 24c mauve & blue 26.00
Postally used 70.00
On cover —

Perf. 13½-14 compound 14½-15
49c A9 1c lilac & black 30.00
50c A10 2c blue & black 35.00
51b A11 3c bister & black —
53c A13 6c brn red & blk 2.10

Perf. 13½-14 compound 12-13
49d A9 1c lilac & black 30.00 1.40
Postally used 14.00
On cover 310.00
50d A10 2c blue & black —
51c A11 3c bister & black 47.50
52c A12 5c green & black 70.00
53d A13 6c brown red & blk —
55b A15 12c orange & black —
Postally used 110.00
On cover —
56e A16 18c ol bister & blk —

Perf. 12-13
49e A9 1c lilac & black —
50e A10 2c blue & black 100.00
51d A11 3c bister & black —
52d A12 5c green & black 125.00
53e A13 6c brown red & blk —
55c A15 12c orange & black —

Values for covers are for properly franked commercial usages.

For overprints see Nos. 66-71.

A18

A19

A20

A21

1895, June Litho.
58 A18 4c on $1 red 1.40 .50
Postally used 2.90
59 A18 10c on $1 red 5.00 .50
Postally used 2.10
60 A18 20c on $1 red 35.00 .50
Postally used 14.00
61 A18 30c on $1 red 37.50 .60
Postally used 50.00
62 A18 40c on $1 red 35.00 .60
Postally used 40.00
Nos. 58-62 (5) 113.90 2.70
Set, optd "SPECIMEN" 92.50

1896
63 A19 25c blue green 32.50 1.10
Postally used 40.00
a. Imperf, pair 82.50
b. Without overprint 25.00 2.75
c. As "a," imperf, pair 50.00
64 A20 50c claret 32.50 1.10
Postally used 40.00
a. Imperf, pair 82.50
b. Without overprint 25.00 2.75
c. As "a," imperf, pair 50.00
65 A21 $1 dark blue 70.00 1.10
Postally used 70.00
a. Imperf, pair 82.50
b. Without overprint 37.50 2.50
c. As "a," imperf, pair 55.00
Nos. 63-65 (3) 135.00 3.30

For surcharges and overprint see #93-95, 116-118, 120.

Nos. 49-54 Overprinted

1896 *Perf. 14½-15*
66 A9 1c lilac & black 22.50 1.10
Postally used 29.00
a. "JEBILEE" 1,250. 350.00
Postally used 700.00
b. "JUBILE" 2,200.
c. Orange overprint 225.00 27.50
Postally used 240.00
67 A10 2c blue & black 45.00 1.10
Postally used 26.00
a. Vert. pair, imperf. btwn. 825.00
Postally used 1,050.
b. "JEBILEE" 1,400.
Postally used 1,400.
c. "JUBILE" 2,500.
d. Vert. strip of 3, imperf between 8,000.
68 A11 3c bister & black 42.50 1.10
Postally used 30.00
a. "JEBILEE" 925.00
Postally used 1,600.
b. "JUBILE" —
69 A12 5c green & black 65.00 1.40
Postally used 22.50
a. Double overprint 625.00
Postally used 600.00
70 A13 6c brown red & blk 32.50 1.10
Postally used 29.00
a. Double overprint 800.00
Postally used 600.00
b. "JUBILE" 2,500.
71 A14 8c rose & black 50.00 1.10
Postally used 17.50
a. Double overprint —
Postally used 2,900.
Nos. 66-71 (6) 257.50 6.90

Perf. 13½-14
66d A9 1c lilac & black 25.00
Postally used 30.00
e. Double overprint 350.00 400.00
Postally used 400.00
f. Orange overprint 290.00
Postally used 290.00
67e A10 2c blue & black 45.00
Postally used 21.00
68c A11 3c bister & black 55.00 1.40
Postally used 37.50
d. Triple overprint 1,150.
69b A12 5c green & black 72.50 1.40
Postally used 30.00
70c A13 6c brown red & blk —
Postally used 92.50
71b A14 8c rose & black 47.50 1.40
Postally used 15.00

Perf. 13½-14 compound 14½-15
67f A10 2c blue & black —
Postally used 55.00
68e A11 3c bister & black —
70d A13 6c brown red & blk —
71c A14 8c rose & black 72.50
Postally used 24.00

Perf. 13½-14 compound 12-13
66g A9 1c lilac & black —
Postally used 24.00
h. Orange overprint —
Postally used 290.00
67g A10 2c blue & black —
68f A11 3c bister & black —
Postally used 450.00
g. Double overprint 290.00 175.00
h. Triple overprint 975.00
69c A12 5c green & black —

Perf. 12-13
66i A9 1c lilac & black —

Cession of Labuan to Great Britain, 50th anniv.

Dyak Chieftain A22

Malayan Sambar A23

Sago Palm A24

Argus Pheasant A25

A26

Dhow — A27

Saltwater Crocodile — A28

Mt. Kinabalu "Postal Revenue" — A29

Coat of Arms — A30

1897-1900 Engr. *Perf. 14½-15*
72 A22 1c lilac & black 5.50 .65
Postally used 7.25
72A A22 1c red brn & blk 4.00 .90
73 A23 2c blue & black 27.50 .90
a. Vert. pair, imperf between 750.00
b. Horiz. pair, imperf between 825.00
75 A24 3c bister & blk 11.50 .65
Postally used 8.50
a. Vert. pair, imperf between 925.00 625.00
76 A25 5c green & blk 57.50 .90
Postally used 72.50
78 A26 6c brn red & blk 8.50 .65
Postally used 29.00
a. Vert. pair, imperf between 700.00
79 A27 8c red & black 25.00 .65
Postally used 17.50
80 A28 12c red & black 45.00 1.10
Postally used 72.50
82 A30 24c gr lilac & bl 18.00 .65
Postally used 70.00

Perf. 13½-14
72Ab A22 1c red brn & blk 17.50 .90
Postally used 22.50
73c A23 2c blue & black 17.50 .90
Postally used 6.25
74 A23 2c grn & blk ('00) 5.25 .45
Postally used 3.50
a. Horiz. pair, imperf between 2,600.
75b A24 3c bister & blk 17.50 .65
Postally used 30.00
76b A25 5c green & blk 62.50 .90
Postally used 72.50
77 A25 5c lt bl & blk ('00) 40.00 .90
Postally used 29.00
78b A26 6c brn red & blk 11.50 .65
Postally used 42.50
79a A27 8c red & black 60.00 .65
79b A27 8c vermilion & black 20.00 .65
80a A28 12c red & black 92.50 1.00
Postally used 110.00
81 A29 18c ol bis & blk 22.50 .65
Postally used 90.00
82a A30 24c gr lilac & bl 45.00 .85
Postally used 92.50

Perf. 13½-14 compound 14½-15
72c A22 1c lilac & black —

Perf. 13½-14 compound 12-13
73d A23 2c blue & black 45.00
Postally used 24.00
74b A23 2c grn & blk ('00) —
75c A24 3c bister & blk 35.00
Postally used 42.50
76c A25 5c green & blk —
Postally used 110.00
77a A25 5c lt bl & blk ('00) —
78c A26 6c brn red & blk 7.25
79c A27 8c red & black 42.50 4.25

Perf. 16
72Ad A22 1c red brn & blk 20.00
Postally used 18.00
73e A23 2c blue & black 9.25
79d A27 8c red & black 42.50 4.25
81a A29 18c ol bis & blk 6.00
Postally used 62.50
b. Vert. pair, imperf between —

For surcharges see Nos. 87-89, 110-112.

"Postage & Revenue" — A31

"Postage & Revenue" — A32

1897, Nov. *Perf. 14½-15*
83 A31 18c bister & black 110.00 2.75
Postally used 77.50
84 A32 24c brn lilac & blue 42.50 3.00
Postally used 72.50
Overprinted "SPECIMEN" 30.00

a. 24c ocher & blue 32.50 2.50

Perf. 13½-14

83a A31 18c bister & black —
84b A32 24c brn lilac & blue 40.00 *2.90*
Postally used 72.50

Perf. 13½-14 compound 12-13

84c A32 24c brn lilac & blue —
Postally used 95.00

Perf. 16

83b A31 18c bister & black 10.50
84d A32 24c brn lilac & blue 40.00

No. 84a only exists cto.
For surcharges see Nos. 92, 115.

"Postage & Revenue" — A33

"Postage & Revenue" — A34

1898, Mar. Perf. 14½-15

85 A33 12c red & black 57.50 4.25
Postally used 72.50
86 A34 18c bister & black 35.00 3.50
Postally used 92.50

Perf. 13½-14

85a A33 12c red & black 4.25
Postally used —
86a A34 18c bister & black 35.00 3.50
Postally used 85.00

Perf. 13½-14 compound 14½-15

85b A33 12c red & black —

Perf. 13½-14 compound 12-13

86b A34 18c bister & black 57.50
Postally used 77.50

Perf. 12-13

86c A34 18c bister & black —

Perf. 16

85c A33 12c red & black 72.50
Postally used 77.50

For surcharges see Nos. 90-91, 113-114.

Regular Issue Surcharged in Black

1899 Perf. 14½-15

87 A25 4c on 5c grn & blk 45.00 37.50
88 A26 4c on 6c brn red & blk 27.50 27.50
89 A27 4c on 8c red & blk 72.50 57.50
90 A33 4c on 12c red & blk 55.00 52.50
91 A34 4c on 18c bis & blk 35.00 25.00
a. Double surcharge 525.00 *575.00*
92 A32 4c on 24c lil & bl 35.00 *42.50*

Perf. 14

93 A19 4c on 25c blue grn 8.50 *10.50*
94 A20 4c on 50c claret 8.50 *10.50*
95 A21 4c on $1 dk blue 8.50 *10.50*
Nos. 87-95 (9) 295.50 *274.00*
Set, ovptd. "SPECIMEN" 160.00

Perf. 13½-14

88a A26 4c on 6c brn red & blk 40.00 *50.00*
89a A27 4c on 8c red & blk 40.00 *45.00*
90a A33 4c on 12c red & blk 55.00 50.00
92a A32 4c on 24c lil & bl 27.50 *37.50*

Perf. 13½-14 compound 12-13

88b A26 4c on 6c brn red & blk 70.00 *80.00*
89b A27 4c on 8c red & blk 40.00 *50.00*
90b A33 4c on 12c red & blk 77.50 *92.50*

92b A32 4c on 24c lil & bl 40.00 *42.50*

Perf. 12-13

89c A27 4c on 8c red & blk —

Perf. 16

90c A33 4c on 12c red & blk 55.00 55.00
92c A32 4c on 24c lil & bl 60.00 *70.00*

Orangutan A35

Sun Bear A36

Railroad Train — A37

Crown — A38

1899-1901 Perf. 13½-14

96 A35 4c yel brown & blk 8.50 .85
Postally used 55.00
a. Vert. pair, imperf. btwn. 1,150.
b. Perf 13½-14 compound 12-13 40.00
97 A35 4c car & blk ('00) 16.00 1.10
Postally used 4.25
a. Perf 14½-15 8.50 .70
Postally used 11.50
b. Perf 13½-14 compound 12-13 40.00 1.10
Postally used 11.50
c. Perf 16 —
98 A36 10c gray vio & dk brn ('01) 70.00 .85
Postally used 110.00
99 A37 16c org brn & grn (G) ('01) 70.00 3.50
Postally used 140.00
a. Perf 14½-15 140.00
b. Perf 13½-14 compound 12-13 40.00
Postally used *175.00*
c. Perf 12-13 240.00
Nos. 96-99 (4) 164.50 6.30
Set, ovptd. "SPECIMEN" 175.00

1902-03 Engr. Perf. 13½-14

99A A38 1c vio & black 5.25 .70
Postally used 10.00
100 A38 2c green & blk 5.25 .45
Postally used 6.25
100A A38 3c sepia & blk 4.25 .45
Postally used 14.50
101 A38 4c car & black 4.25 .45
Postally used 5.00
102 A38 8c org & black 11.50 .70
Postally used 14.50
103 A38 10c sl blue & brn 4.25 .45
Postally used 14.50
a. Vert. pair, imperf. between 825.00
104 A38 12c yel & black 8.25 .45
Postally used 17.50
a. Vert. strip of 3, imperf. horiz. *4,500.*
105 A38 16c org brn & grn 7.00 .45
Postally used 21.00
a. Vert. pair, imperf. between —
106 A38 18c bis brn & blk 5.25 .45
Postally used 29.00
107 A38 25c grnsh bl & grn 9.75 .70
Postally used 24.00
a. 25c greenish blue & black 575.00
108 A38 50c gray lil & vio 14.50 1.10
Postally used 57.50
109 A38 $1 org & red brn 11.50 1.10
Postally used 70.00
Nos. 99A-109 (12) 91.00 7.45
Set, optd "SPECIMEN" 240.00

Perf. 14½-15

99Ab A38 1c vio & black 110.00
Postally used 10.50
100b A38 2c green & blk —
Postally used 8.50
101a A38 4c car & black 7.75
Postally used 11.50
102a A38 8c org & black 9.25
103b A38 10c sl blue & brn 6.25
107b A38 25c grnsh bl & grn 21.00 .75
Postally used 42.50

109a A38 $1 org & red brn 14.00 .90

Perf. 13½-14 compound 12-13

99Ac A38 1c vio & black 110.00
Postally used 11.00
Postally used 72.50
101b A38 4c car & black 85.00
Postally used 72.50
108a A38 50c gray lil & vio 26.00
Postally used 72.50

Perf. 16

104b A38 12c yel & black 7.25
Postally used 26.00

Line Through "B" of "LABUAN"

Perf. 13½-14

99Ad A38 1c vio & black 60.00 8.50
Postally used 100.00
100c A38 2c green & blk 60.00 8.50
Postally used 82.50
100Ac A38 3c sepia & blk 60.00 8.50
Postally used 100.00
101c A38 4c car & black 60.00 8.50
Postally used 70.00
102b A38 8c org & black 85.00 8.50
Postally used 110.00
103c A38 10c sl blue & brn 57.50 8.50
Postally used 120.00
104c A38 12c yel & black 70.00 8.50
Postally used 140.00
105b A38 16c org brn & grn 82.50 8.50
Postally used 160.00
106a A38 18c bis brn & blk 70.00 8.50
Postally used 200.00
107c A38 25c grnsh bl & grn 100.00 8.50
Postally used 200.00
108b A38 50c gray lil & vio 200.00 12.50
Postally used 425.00
109b A38 $1 org & red brn 140.00 14.00
Postally used 425.00
Nos. 99Ad-109b (12) 1,045. 111.50

There are 3 known examples of No. 104a, all cto.

The "line through B" variety is a constant plate flaw in position R5/10.

Regular Issue of 1896-97 Surcharged in Black

1904 Perf. 14½x15

110 A25 4c on 5c green & blk 55.00 19.00
Postally used 57.50
111 A26 4c on 6c brown red & black 16.00 *19.00*
Postally used 55.00
112 A27 4c on 8c red & blk 30.00 19.00
Postally used 57.50
113 A33 4c on 12c red & blk 25.00 19.00
Postally used 57.50
a. Perf 16 35.00
Postally used 62.50
114 A34 4c on 18c bis & blk 37.50
Postally used 62.50
a. Perf 13½-14, comp. 12-13 35.00
Postally used 62.50
b. Perf 12-13 —
115 A32 4c on 24c brn lil & bl 22.50 19.00
Postally used 70.00
a. Perf 13½-14 30.00
Postally used 55.00
b. Perf 13½-14, comp. 12-13 42.50
Postally used 70.00
c. Perf 16 40.00 20.00
Postally used 57.50

Perf. 14

116 A19 4c on 25c blue green 11.50 *19.00*
Postally used 35.00
117 A20 4c on 50c claret 11.50 *19.00*
Postally used 35.00
a. Double surcharge 375.00
118 A21 4c on $1 dark blue 11.50 *19.00*
Postally used 35.00
Nos. 110-118 (9) 220.50 152.00

Stamps of North Borneo, 1893, and Labuan No. 65a Overprinted in Black:

a

b

c

1905

119 A30(a) 25c slate blue 1,275. 1,100.
120 A21(c) $1 blue 950.00
121 A33(b) $2 gray green 3,250.
Postally used 3,900.
122 A34(c) $5 red violet *6,000.* 1,200.
Postally used *8,250.*
a. $5 dull purple —
123 A35(c) $10 brown *22,000.* *8,500.*

Nos. 119, 120 and 123 do not exist postally used. No. 120 exists only cto.

POSTAGE DUE STAMPS

Regular Issues Overprinted

1901 Unwmk. Perf. 14

J1 A23 2c green & black 20.00 .70
Postally used 29.00
a. Double overprint 425.00
J2 A24 3c bister & black 70.00 1.10
Postally used 100.00
J3 A35 4c car & black 85.00 .80
a. Double overprint 650.00
J4 A25 5c lt blue & black 100.00 1.10
Postally used 140.00
J5 A26 6c brown red & blk 85.00 1.10
Postally used 120.00
J6 A27 8c red & black 80.00 1.40
Postally used 110.00
a. Center inverted, ovpt. reading down *10,250.*
d. 8c rose red & blk 77.50
Postally used 125.00
J7 A33 12c red & black 95.00 4.25
a. Overprint reading down *825.00*
J9 A32 24c brown lil & bl 90.00 4.00
Postally used 125.00
c. 24c ocher & blue 72.50 1.75
Nos. J1-J9 (8) 625.00 14.45

Perf. 14½-15

J3b A35 4c car & black 35.00 .60
Postally used 100.00
J4a A25 5c lt blue & black 1.40
J5a A26 6c brown red & blk 45.00
Postally used 100.00
J6b A27 8c red & black 77.50 1.10
Postally used 140.00
J6e A27 8c rose red & blk 9.75
J7b A33 12c red & black 100.00 15.00
Postally used 125.00
J8 A34 18c ol bister & blk 100.00 2.10
Postally used 125.00
J9a A32 24c brown lil & bl 40.00

Perf. 14½-15, Compound 12-13

J1b A23 2c green & black 77.50 12.50
Postally used 92.50
J2a A24 3c bister & black 77.50 2.90
J4b A25 5c lt blue & black 77.50
Postally used 175.00

Perf. 16

J5b A26 6c brown red & blk 50.00 .90
J6c A27 8c red & black 77.50
Postally used 100.00
J9d A32 24c ocher & blue 50.00
Postally used 100.00

Perf. 13½-14, Compound 12-13

J9b A32 24c brown lil & bl 77.50

See note after No. 41.

The stamps of Labuan were superseded by those of Straits Settlements in 1906.

LAGOS

'lā-ˌgäs

LOCATION — West Africa, bordering on the former Southern Nigeria Colony
GOVT. — British Crown Colony and Protectorate
AREA — 3,460 sq. mi. (approx.)
POP. — 1,500,000 (1901)
CAPITAL — Lagos

This territory was purchased by the British in 1861 and placed under the Governor of Sierra Leone. In 1874 it was detached and formed part of the Gold Coast Colony until 1886 when the Protectorate of Lagos was established. It was chartered to the Royal Niger Company until 1899 when all territories of this Company were surrendered to the Crown of Great Britain and formed into the Northern and Southern Nigeria Protectorates. In 1906 Lagos and Southern Nigeria were united to form the Colony and Protectorate of Southern Nigeria.

12 Pence = 1 Shilling

Queen Victoria — A1

1874-75 Typo. Wmk. 1 *Perf. 12½*

1	A1	1p lilac	65.00	37.50
2	A1	2p blue	65.00	32.50
3	A1	3p red brown ('75)	97.50	47.50
4	A1	4p rose	97.50	45.00
5	A1	6p blue green	110.00	14.00
6	A1	1sh orange ('75)	325.00	70.00
a.		Value 15½mm instead of 16½mm long	525.00	160.00
		Nos. 1-6 (6)	760.00	246.50

1876 *Perf. 14*

7	A1	1p lilac	45.00	21.00
8	A1	2p blue	47.50	15.00
9	A1	3p red brown	110.00	21.00
a.		3p chestnut	125.00	40.00
10	A1	4p rose	210.00	12.50
11	A1	6p green	110.00	7.00
12	A1	1sh orange	675.00	95.00
		Nos. 7-12 (6)	1,197.	171.50

The 4p exists with watermark sideways.

#19, 43a, 53a

#19b, 43, 53

1882-1902 Wmk. 2

13	A1	½p green ('86)	2.25	.95
14	A1	1p lilac	22.00	11.50
15	A1	1p car rose	2.25	.95
16	A1	2p blue	175.00	5.50
17	A1	2p gray	67.50	6.50
18	A1	2p lil & bl ('87)	4.00	3.25
19	A1	2½p ultra ('91)	4.50	2.00
a.		2½p blue	90.00	57.50
b.		As No. 19, larger letters of value	25.00	19.00
20	A1	3p orange brn	17.50	5.75
21	A1	3p lilac & brn orange ('91)	3.00	*3.75*
22	A1	4p rose	160.00	14.00
23	A1	4p violet	115.00	9.50
24	A1	4p lil & blk ('87)	2.50	2.00
25	A1	5p lil & grn ('94)	3.00	*12.50*
26	A1	6p olive green	9.00	*45.00*
27	A1	6p lilac & red violet ('87)	5.50	3.50
28	A1	6p lilac & car rose ('02)	5.75	*13.50*
29	A1	7½p lilac & car rose ('94)	2.50	*35.00*
30	A1	10p lil & yel ('94)	3.75	*15.00*
31	A1	1sh orange ('85)	8.00	*22.50*
32	A1	1sh yellow green & blk ('87)	6.50	*27.50*
a.		1sh blue green & black	5.75	*29.00*
33	A1	2sh6p ol brn ('86)	375.00	325.00
34	A1	2sh6p green & car rose ('87)	27.50	*92.50*
35	A1	5sh blue ('86)	650.00	500.00
36	A1	5sh green & ultra ('87)	47.50	*175.00*
37	A1	10sh brn vio ('86)	1,700.	1,150.
38	A1	10sh grn & brn ('87)	90.00	*225.00*

Excellent forgeries exist of Nos. 33, 35 and 37 on paper with genuine watermark.

No. 24 Surcharged in Black

1893

39	A1	½p on 4p lilac & blk	5.00	3.00
a.		Double surcharge	62.50	62.50
b.		Triple surcharge	140.00	
c.		½p on 2p lilac & blue (#18)		20,000.

Four settings of surcharge.

Only one used example is known of No. 39c. The two unused examples are in museums.

King Edward VII — A3

1904, Jan. 22

40	A3	½p grn & bl grn	1.75	*6.25*
41	A3	1p vio & blk, *red*	1.10	.20
42	A3	2p violet & ultra	6.75	7.00
43	A3	2½p vio & ultra, *bl*	1.25	*1.75*
a.		Smaller letters of value	5.00	*9.75*
44	A3	3p vio & org brn	2.50	2.00
45	A3	6p vio & red vio	40.00	11.50
46	A3	1sh green & blk	40.00	*47.50*
47	A3	2sh6p grn & car rose	105.00	*230.00*
48	A3	5sh grn & ultra	150.00	*325.00*
49	A3	10sh green & brn	325.00	*850.00*
		Nos. 40-49 (10)	673.35	*1,481.*
		Set, ovptd. "SPECIMEN"	200.00	

1904-05 Wmk. 3

Ordinary Paper

50	A3	½p grn & bl grn	8.50	3.00
51	A3	1p vio & blk, *red*	8.00	.20
52	A3	2p violet & ultra	2.50	2.25
53	A3	2½p vio & ultra, *bl*, smaller letters of value	62.50	*140.00*
54	A3	3p vio & org brn	4.00	1.50
55	A3	6p vio & red vio	7.50	2.50
56	A3	1sh green & blk	15.00	2.75
57	A3	2sh6p grn & car rose	18.50	*62.50*
58	A3	5sh grn & ultra	25.00	*110.00*
59	A3	10sh green & brn	67.50	*225.00*
		Nos. 50-59 (10)	219.00	*549.70*

Chalky Paper

50a	A3	½p grn & bl grn	11.50	2.00
51a	A3	1p vio & blk, *red*	1.75	.20
52a	A3	2p violet & ultra	15.00	11.50
53a	A3	2½p vio & ultra, *bl*	2.00	*18.50*
54a	A3	3p vio & org brn	17.50	2.00
55a	A3	6p vio & red vio	5.00	1.75
56a	A3	1sh green & blk	26.00	2.50
57a	A3	2sh6p grn & car rose	40.00	*57.50*
58a	A3	5sh grn & ultra	75.00	*190.00*
59a	A3	10sh green & brn	85.00	*225.00*
		Nos. 50a-59a (10)	278.75	*510.95*

The stamps of Lagos were superseded by those of Southern Nigeria.

LATAKIA

ˌla-tə-'kē-ə

LOCATION — A division of Syria in Western Asia
GOVT. — French Mandate
AREA — 2,500 sq. mi.
POP. — 278,000 (approx. 1930)
CAPITAL — Latakia

This territory, included in the Syrian Mandate to France under the Versailles Treaty, was formerly known as Alaouites. The name Latakia was adopted in 1930. See Alaouites and Syria.

100 Centimes = 1 Piaster

Stamps of Syria Overprinted in Black or Red

Perf. 12x12½, 13½

1931-33 Unwmk.

1	A6	10c red violet	.70	.70
2	A6	10c vio brn ('33)	.95	.95
3	A7	20c dk blue (R)	.70	.70
4	A7	20c brown org ('33)	.95	.95
5	A8	25c gray grn (R)	.70	.70
6	A8	25c dk bl gray (R) ('33)	1.00	1.00
7	A9	50c violet	1.60	1.60
8	A15	75c org red ('32)	1.75	1.75
9	A10	1p green (R)	1.60	1.60
10	A11	1.50p bis brn (R)	2.25	2.25
11	A11	1.50p dp grn ('33)	2.25	2.25
12	A12	2p dk vio (R)	2.25	2.25
13	A13	3p yel grn (R)	4.00	4.00
14	A14	4p orange	4.00	4.00
15	A15	4.50p rose car	4.25	4.25
16	A16	6p grnsh blk (R)	4.25	4.25
17	A17	7.50p dl blue (R)	3.25	3.25
18	A18	10p dp brown (R)	7.25	7.25
19	A19	15p dp green (R)	7.25	7.25
20	A20	25p violet brn	14.50	14.50
21	A21	50p dk brown (R)	13.00	13.00
22	A22	100p red orange	35.00	35.00
		Nos. 1-22 (22)	113.45	113.45

AIR POST STAMPS

Air Post Stamps of Syria, 1931, Overprinted in Black or Red

1931-33 Unwmk. *Perf. 13½*

C1	AP2	50c ocher	.70	.70
a.		Inverted overprint	875.00	875.00
C2	AP2	50c blk brn (R) ('33)	1.75	1.75
C3	AP2	1p chestnut brn	1.75	1.75
C4	AP2	2p Prus blue (R)	2.75	2.75
C5	AP2	3p blue grn (R)	3.50	3.50
C6	AP2	5p red violet	4.50	4.50
C7	AP2	10p slate grn (R)	6.00	6.00
C8	AP2	15p orange red	8.50	8.50
C9	AP2	25p orange brn	16.00	16.00
C10	AP2	50p black (R)	27.50	27.50
C11	AP2	100p magenta	27.50	27.50
		Nos. C1-C11 (11)	100.45	100.45

POSTAGE DUE STAMPS

Postage Due Stamps of Syria, 1931, Overprinted like Regular Issue

1931 Unwmk. *Perf. 13½*

J1	D7	8p blk, *gray bl* (R)	16.50	16.50
J2	D8	15p blk, *dl rose* (R)	15.00	15.00

Stamps of Latakia were superseded in 1937 by those of Syria.

LATVIA

'lat-vē-ə

(Lettonia, Lettland)

LOCATION — Northern Europe, bordering on the Baltic Sea and the Gulf of Riga
GOVT. — Independent Republic
AREA — 25,395 sq. mi.
POP. — 1,994,506 (estimated 1939)
CAPITAL — Riga

Latvia was created a sovereign state following World War I and was admitted to the League of Nations in 1922. In 1940 it became a republic in the Union of Soviet Socialist Republics.

100 Kapeikas = 1 Rublis
100 Santims = 1 Lat (1923)

Catalogue values for unused stamps in this country are for Never Hinged items, beginning with Scott 1 in the regular postage section, Scott B1 in the semi-postal section, Scott C1 in the air post section, Scott CB1 in the air post semi-postal section, and Scott 2N45 in the Russian Occupation section.

Catalogue values for unused stamps in this section are for Never Hinged items.

Watermarks

Wmk. 108 — Honeycomb

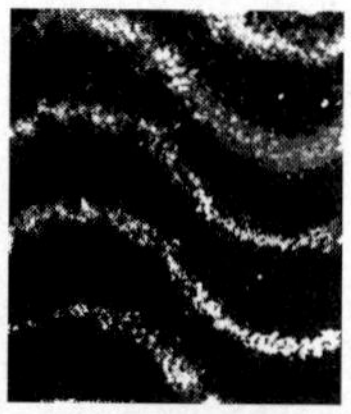

Wmk. 145 — Wavy Lines

Wmk. 181 — Wavy Lines

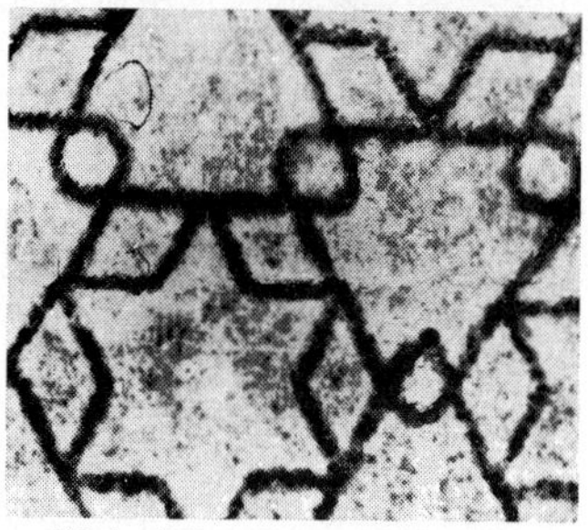

Wmk. 197 — Star and Triangles

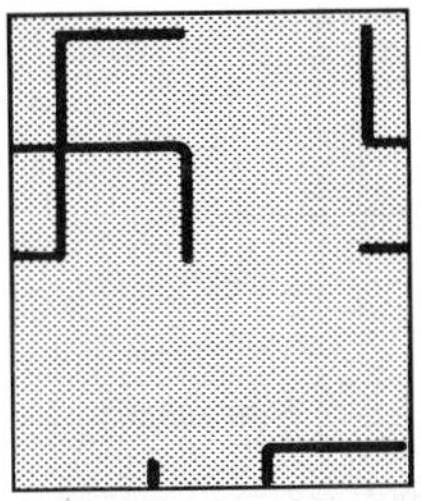

Wmk. 212 — Multiple Swastikas

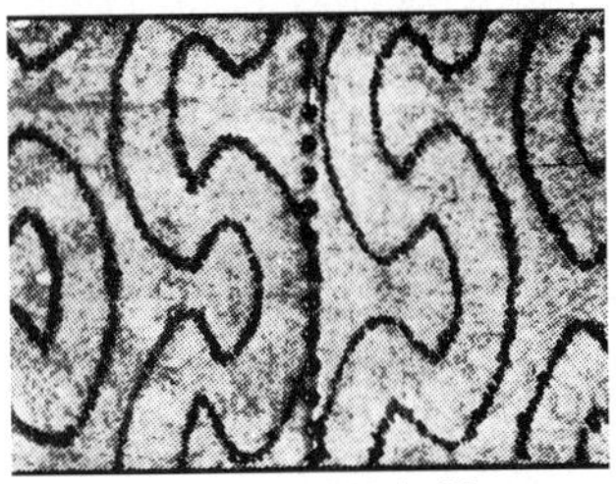

Wmk. 265 — Multiple Waves

Arms — A1

Printed on the Backs of German Military Maps

Unwmk.

1918, Dec. 18 Litho. *Imperf.*

1	A1	5k carmine	1.25	1.25

Perf. 11½

2	A1	5k carmine	1.25	1.25

Values given are for stamps where the map on the back is printed in brown and black. Maps printed only in black are valued at $3.50 each mint or used. Stamps with no printing on the back are from the outer rows of some sheets.

Redrawn

Paper with Ruled Lines

1919 *Imperf.*

3	A1	5k carmine	.50	.25
4	A1	10k dark blue	.50	.25
5	A1	15k green	.50	.25

Perf. 11½

6	A1	5k carmine	2.75	2.75
7	A1	10k dark blue	2.75	2.75
8	A1	15k deep green	7.75	7.75
		Nos. 3-8 (6)	14.75	14.00

In the redrawn design the wheat heads are thicker, the ornament at lower left has five points instead of four, and there are minor changes in other parts of the design.

The sheets of this and subsequent issues were usually divided in half by a single line of perforation gauging 10. Thus stamps are found with this perforation on one side.

1919 Pelure Paper *Imperf.*

9	A1	3k lilac	7.00	6.00
10	A1	5k carmine	.20	.20
11	A1	10k deep blue	.20	.20
12	A1	15k dark green	.20	.20
13	A1	20k orange	.20	.20
13A	A1	25k gray	42.50	37.50
14	A1	35k dark brown	.25	.25
15	A1	50k purple	.25	.25
16	A1	75k emerald	5.00	5.00
		Nos. 9-16 (9)	55.80	49.80

Perf. 11½, 9½

17	A1	3k lilac	35.00	25.00
18	A1	5k carmine	1.00	.80
19	A1	10k deep blue	4.00	3.00
20	A1	15k dark green	3.00	3.00
21	A1	20k orange	3.75	3.75
22	A1	35k dark brown	4.50	4.50
23	A1	50k purple	6.00	6.00
24	A1	75k emerald	15.00	15.00
		Nos. 17-24 (8)	72.25	61.05

Values are for perf 11½. Examples Perf 9½ sell for more.

Nos. 17-24 are said to be unofficially perforated varieties of Nos. 9-16.

1919 Wmk. 108 *Imperf.*

25	A1	3k lilac	.30	.20
26	A1	5k carmine	.30	.20
27	A1	10k deep blue	.30	.20
28	A1	15k deep green	.35	.20
29	A1	20k orange	.40	.25
30	A1	25k gray	.80	.50
31	A1	35k dark brown	.40	.25
32	A1	50k purple	.40	.25
33	A1	75k emerald	.50	.25
		Nos. 25-33 (9)	3.75	2.30

The variety "printed on both sides" exists for 3k, 10k, 15k, 20k and 35k. Value, $20 each.

See #57-58, 76-82. For surcharges and overprints see #86, 132-133, 2N1-2N8, 2N12-2N19.

Liberation of Riga — A2

Rising Sun — A4

1919 Wmk. 108

43	A2	5k carmine	.50	.25
44	A2	15k deep green	.50	.25
45	A2	35k brown	.70	.45
		Nos. 43-45 (3)	1.70	.95

Unwmk.

Pelure Paper

49	A2	5k carmine	15.00	9.50
50	A2	15k deep green	15.00	9.50
51	A2	35k brown	30.00	9.50
		Nos. 49-51 (3)	60.00	28.50

For surcharge and overprints see Nos. 87, 2N9-2N11, 2N20-2N22.

1919 *Imperf.*

55	A4	10k gray blue	.85	.60

Perf. 11½

56	A4	10k gray blue	1.50	1.50

Type of 1918

1919 Laid Paper *Perf. 11½*

57	A1	3r slate & org	1.60	1.00
58	A1	5r gray brn & org	2.50	1.00

Independence Issue

Allegory of One Year of Independence A5

1919, Nov. 18 Unwmk.

Wove Paper

Size: 33x45mm

59	A5	10k brown & rose	1.25	1.00

Laid Paper

60	A5	10k brown & rose	1.25	1.00

Size: 28x38mm

61	A5	10k brown & rose	.30	.25
a.		Imperf.	45.00	
62	A5	35k indigo & grn	.30	.20
a.		Vert. pair, imperf. btwn.	45.00	40.00

Wmk. 197

Thick Wove Paper

Blue Design on Back

63	A5	1r green & red	.90	.75
		Nos. 59-63 (5)	4.00	3.20

There are two types of Nos. 59 and 60. In type I the trunk of the tree is not outlined. In type II it has a distinct white outline.

No. 63 was printed on the backs of unfinished 5r bank notes of the Workers and Soldiers Council, Riga.

For surcharges see Nos. 83-85, 88, 94.

Warrior Slaying Dragon — A6

1919-20 Unwmk. *Perf. 11½*

Wove Paper

64	A6	10k brown & car	.50	.20
a.		Horiz. pair, imperf. btwn.	50.00	40.00
65	A6	25k ind & yel grn	.60	.30
a.		Pair, imperf. btwn.	50.00	40.00
66	A6	35k black & bl ('20)	.75	.30
a.		Horiz. pair, imperf. btwn.	50.00	40.00
67	A6	1r dk grn & brn ('20)	1.50	.60
a.		Horiz. pair, imperf. vert.	50.00	40.00
b.		Horiz. pair, imperf. btwn.	50.00	40.00
		Nos. 64-67 (4)	3.35	1.40

Issued in honor of the liberation of Kurzeme (Kurland). The paper sometimes shows impressed quadrille lines.

For surcharges see Nos. 91-93.

Latgale Relief Issue

Latvia Welcoming Home Latgale Province — A7

1920, Mar.

Brown and Green Design on Back

68	A7	50k dk green & rose	1.00	.40
a.		Horiz. pair, imperf. vert.	50.00	
69	A7	1r slate grn & brn	1.10	.45
a.		Horiz. pair, imperf. vert.	50.00	

No. 68-69 were printed on the backs of unfinished bank notes of the government of Colonel Bermondt-Avalov and on the so-called German "Ober-Ost" money.

For surcharges see Nos. 95-99.

First National Assembly Issue

Latvia Hears Call to Assemble — A8

1920

70	A8	50k rose	.85	.30
a.		Imperf., pair	10.00	6.00
71	A8	1r blue	.85	.20
a.		Vert. pair, imperf. btwn.	45.00	45.00
b.		Imperf., pair	20.00	15.00
72	A8	3r dk brn & grn	.85	.75
73	A8	5r slate & vio brn	2.25	.80
		Nos. 70-73 (4)	4.80	2.05

For surcharges see Nos. 90, 134.

Type of 1918 Issue

Wove Paper

1920-21 Unwmk. *Perf. 11½*

76	A1	5k carmine	.20	.20
78	A1	20k orange	.20	.20
79	A1	40k lilac ('21)	.60	.20
80	A1	50k violet	.60	.20
81	A1	75k emerald	.60	.20
82	A1	5r gray brn & org ('21)	3.75	.20
		Nos. 76-82 (6)	5.95	1.20

No. 63 Surcharged in Black, Brown or Blue

1920, Sept. 1

83	A5	10r on 1r grn & red (Bk)	2.50	1.50
84	A5	20r on 1r grn & red (Br)	4.75	3.00
85	A5	30r on 1r grn & red (Bl)	7.50	5.00
		Nos. 83-85 (3)	14.75	9.50

Types of 1919 Surcharged

1920-21 Wmk. 108 *Perf. 11½*

86	A1	2r on 10k dp blue	3.00	*4.00*
87	A2	2r on 35k brown	.95	*3.75*

No. 62 Surcharged in Red

Unwmk.

88	A5	2r on 35k ind & grn	.70	.50

No. 70 Surcharged in Blue

1921

90	A8	2r on 50k rose	.90	.60

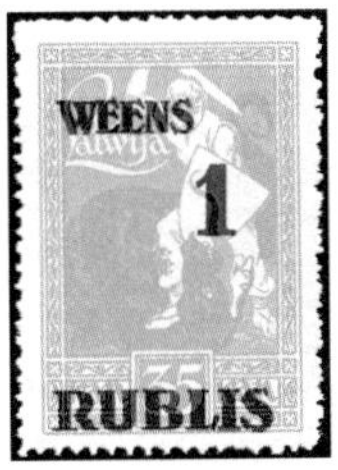

Nos. 64-66 Surcharged in Red or Blue

1920-21

91	A6	1r on 35k blk & bl (R)	.55	.30
92	A6	2r on 10k brn & rose (Bl)	1.00	.60
93	A6	2r on 25k ind & grn (R)	.65	.35
a.		Imperf.	—	
		Nos. 91-93 (3)	2.20	1.25

On Nos. 92 and 93 the surcharge reads "DIVI 2 RUBLI."

No. 83 with Added Surcharge

1921 Wmk. 197

94	A5	10r on 10r on 1r	2.50	1.00

Latgale Relief Issue of 1920 Surcharged in Black or Blue

1921, May 31 — **Unwmk.**

95	A7	10r on 50k	2.10	1.00
a.		Imperf.	—	
96	A7	20r on 50k	6.75	3.00
97	A7	30r on 50k	8.50	2.50
98	A7	50r on 50k	15.00	5.00
99	A7	100r on 50k (Bl)	32.50	12.00
		Nos. 95-99 (5)	64.85	23.50

Excellent counterfeits exist.

Arms and Stars for Vidzeme, Kurzeme & Latgale — A10

Coat of Arms — A11

Type I, slanting cipher in value.
Type II, upright cipher in value.

Perf. 10, 11½ and Compound
Wmk. Similar to 181

1921-22 — **Typo.**

101	A10	50k violet (II)	1.00	.30
102	A10	1r orange yel	.60	.30
103	A10	2r deep green	.40	.20
104	A10	3r brt green	1.25	.45
105	A10	5r rose	1.40	.20
106	A10	6r dp claret	2.10	.75
107	A10	9r orange	1.50	.40
108	A10	10r blue (I)	1.50	.20
109	A10	15r ultra	3.50	.60
a.		Printed on both sides	*45.00*	
110	A10	20r dull lilac (II)	22.50	4.00

1922, Aug. 21 — ***Perf. 11½***

111	A11	50r dk brn & pale brn (I)	35.00	4.50
112	A11	100r dk bl & pale bl (I)	40.00	6.00
		Nos. 101-112 (12)	110.75	17.90

#101-131 sometimes show letters of a paper maker's watermark "PACTIEN LIGAT MILLS."
See Nos. 126-131, 152-154.

A12

2 SANTIMS
Type A, tail of "2" ends in an upstroke.
Type B, tail of "2" is nearly horizontal.

1923-25 — ***Perf. 10, 11, 11½***

113	A12	1s violet	1.00	.20
114	A12	2s org yel (A)	1.75	.25
115	A12	4s dark green	1.50	.20
a.		Horiz. pair, imperf. btwn.	50.00	45.00
116	A12	5s lt green ('25)	4.50	.40
117	A12	6s grn, *yel* ('25)	6.00	.20
118	A12	10s rose red (I)	3.00	.20
a.		Horiz. pair, imperf. btwn.	50.00	30.00
119	A12	12s claret	.45	.25
120	A12	15s brn, *sal*	6.00	.20
a.		Horiz. pair, imperf. btwn.	50.00	30.00
121	A12	20s dp blue (II)	3.50	.20
122	A12	25s ultra ('25)	.85	.20
123	A12	30s pink (I) ('25)	9.00	.25
124	A12	40s lilac (I)	3.50	.20
125	A12	50s lil gray (II)	6.50	.25
126	A11	1 l dk brn & pale brn	21.00	.60
127	A11	2 l dk blue & blue	34.00	1.00
130	A11	5 l dp grn & pale grn	100.00	5.00
131	A11	10 l car rose & pale rose (I)	6.00	6.00
		Nos. 113-131 (17)	208.55	15.60

Value in "Santims" (1s); "Santimi" (2s-6s) or "Santimu" (others).
See note after No. 110.
See Nos. 135-151, 155-157. For overprints and surcharges see Nos. 164-167, B21-B23.

Nos. 79-80 Surcharged

No. 72 Surcharged

1927 — **Unwmk.** — ***Perf. 11½***

132	A1	15s on 40k lilac	.90	.30
133	A1	15s on 50k violet	2.50	1.00
134	A8	1 l on 3r brn & grn	21.00	6.50
		Nos. 132-134 (3)	24.40	7.80

Types of 1923-25 Issue

1927-33 — **Wmk. 212** — ***Perf. 10, 11½***

135	A12	1s dull violet	.25	.20
136	A12	2s org yel (A)	1.50	.20
137	A12	2s org yel (B) ('33)	1.00	.20
138	A12	3s org red ('31)	.25	.20
139	A12	4s dk green ('29)	6.50	1.40
140	A12	5s lt green ('31)	.85	.20
141	A12	6s grn, *yel*	.20	.20
142	A12	7s dk green ('31)	1.25	.20
143	A12	10s red (I)	4.25	.40
144	A12	10s grn, *yel* (I) ('32)	16.00	.20
145	A12	15s brn, *sal*	7.50	.20
146	A12	20s pink (I)	9.00	.20
147	A12	20s pink (II)	8.00	.20
148	A12	30s lt blue (I)	3.50	.20
149	A12	35s dk blue ('31)	2.50	.20
150	A12	40s dl lil (I) ('29)	3.75	.20
151	A12	50s gray (II)	5.00	.25
152	A11	1 l dk brn & pale brn	14.00	.30
153	A11	2 l dk bl & bl ('31)	50.00	1.25
154	A11	5 l grn & pale grn ('33)	225.00	30.00
		Nos. 135-154 (20)	360.30	36.40

The paper of Nos. 141, 144 and 145 is colored on the surface only.
See note above No. 113 for types A and B, and note above No. 101 for types I and II.

Type of 1927-33 Issue
Paper Colored Through

1931-33 — ***Perf. 10***

155	A12	6s grn, *yel*	.20	.20
156	A12	10s grn, *yel* (I) ('33)	30.00	.20
157	A12	15s brn, *salmon*	8.00	.20
		Nos. 155-157 (3)	38.20	.60

View of Rezekne — A13

Designs (Views of Cities): 15s, Jelgava. 20s, Cesis (Wenden). 30s, Liepaja (Libau). 50s, Riga. 1 l, Riga Theater.

1928, Nov. 18 — **Litho.** — ***Perf. 10, 11½***

158	A13	6s dp grn & vio	1.75	.30
159	A13	15s dk brn & ol grn	1.75	.30
160	A13	20s cerise & bl grn	2.10	.40
161	A13	30s ultra & vio brn	2.50	.30
162	A13	50s dk gray & plum	2.50	1.00
163	A13	1 l blk brn & brn	6.50	1.50
		Nos. 158-163 (6)	17.10	3.80

10th anniv. of Latvian Independence.

Riga Exhibition Issue

Stamps of 1927-33 Overprinted

Latvijas ražojumu izstāde Rigā, 1932.g.10.–18.IX.

1932, Aug. 30 — ***Perf. 10, 11***

164	A12	3s orange	1.75	1.10
165	A12	10s green, *yel*	3.25	.35
166	A12	20s pink (I)	3.75	1.00
167	A12	35s dark blue	5.00	2.25
		Nos. 164-167 (4)	13.75	4.70

Riga Castle — A19

Arms and Shield — A20

Allegory of Latvia — A21

Ministry of Foreign Affairs — A22

1934, Dec. 15 — **Litho.** — ***Perf. 10½, 10***

174	A19	3s red orange	.25	.20
175	A20	5s yellow grn	.25	.20
176	A20	10s gray grn	2.00	.20
177	A21	20s deep rose	2.00	.20
178	A22	35s dark blue	.60	.20
179	A19	40s brown	.60	.20
		Nos. 174-179 (6)	5.70	1.20

Atis Kronvalds A23

A. Pumpurs A24

Juris Maters A25

Mikus Krogzemis (Auseklis) A26

1936, Jan. 4 — **Wmk. 212** — ***Perf. 11½***

180	A23	3s vermilion	2.75	*3.75*
181	A24	10s green	2.75	*3.75*
182	A25	20s rose pink	2.75	*3.75*
183	A26	35s dark blue	2.75	*3.75*
		Nos. 180-183 (4)	11.00	15.00

President Karlis Ulmanis — A27

1937, Sept. 4 — **Litho.** — ***Perf. 10, 11½***

184	A27	3s org red & brn org	.50	.90
185	A27	5s yellow grn	.50	.90
186	A27	10s dk sl grn	.75	.90
187	A27	20s rose lake & brn lake	1.00	.60
188	A27	25s black vio	1.75	.90
189	A27	30s dark blue	1.60	1.00
190	A27	35s indigo	1.75	2.50
191	A27	40s lt brown	1.75	2.00
192	A27	50s olive blk	1.75	2.50
		Nos. 184-192 (9)	11.35	12.20

60th birthday of President Ulmanis.

Independence Monument, Rauna (Ronneburg) A28

Independence Monument, Jelgava — A30

Monument Entrance to Cemetery at Riga A29

War Memorial, Valka — A31

Independence Monument, Iecava — A32

Independence Monument, Riga — A33

Tomb of Col. Kalpaks — A34

Unwmk.
1937, July 12 — **Litho.** — ***Perf. 10***
Thick Paper

193	A28	3s vermilion	.75	.80
194	A29	5s yellow grn	.75	.80
195	A30	10s deep grn	.75	.80
196	A31	20s carmine	1.75	1.00
197	A32	30s lt blue	2.00	2.00

Wmk. 212
Engr. — ***Perf. 11½***
Thin Paper

198	A33	35s dark blue	2.00	2.00
199	A34	40s brown	3.50	3.00
		Nos. 193-199 (7)	11.50	10.40

View of Vidzeme — A35

General J. Balodis A37

President Karlis Ulmanis A38

Views: 5s, Latgale. 30s, Riga waterfront. 35s, Kurzeme. 40s, Zemgale.

1938, Nov. 17 ***Perf. 10, 10½x10***

200	A35	3s brown org	.40	.20
a.		Booklet pane of 4	40.00	
201	A35	5s yellow grn	.50	.20
a.		Booklet pane of 4	40.00	
202	A37	10s dk green	.60	.20
a.		Booklet pane of 2	40.00	
203	A38	20s red lilac	.40	.20
a.		Booklet pane of 2	40.00	
204	A35	30s deep blue	1.50	.20
205	A35	35s indigo	1.50	.20
a.		Booklet pane of 2	40.00	
206	A35	40s rose violet	2.50	.25
		Nos. 200-206 (7)	7.40	1.45

The 20th anniversary of the Republic.

School, Riga — A42

Independence Monument, Riga — A45

President Karlis Ulmanis A49

Designs: 5s, Castle of Jelgava. 10s, Riga Castle. 30s, Symbol of Freedom. 35s, Community House Daugavpils. 40s, Powder Tower and War Museum, Riga.

1939, May 13 **Photo.** ***Perf. 10***

207	A42	3s brown orange	.60	.75
208	A42	5s deep green	.90	.75
209	A42	10s dk slate grn	1.25	.75
210	A45	20s dk car rose	2.75	1.25
211	A42	30s brt ultra	1.75	.75
212	A42	35s dark blue	2.50	1.75
213	A45	40s brown violet	3.50	1.50
214	A49	50s grnsh black	6.00	1.50
		Nos. 207-214 (8)	19.25	9.00

5th anniv. of National Unity Day.

Harvesting Wheat — A50

Apple — A51

1939, Oct. 8

215	A50	10s slate green	1.25	.60
216	A51	20s rose lake	1.75	.65

8th Agricultural Exposition held near Riga.

Arms and Stars for Vidzeme, Kurzeme and Latgale — A52

1940

217	A52	1s dk vio brn	.45	.40
218	A52	2s ocher	.75	.60
219	A52	3s red orange	.20	.20
220	A52	5s dk olive brn	.20	.20
221	A52	7s dk green	.45	.40
222	A52	10s dk blue grn	1.25	.25
224	A52	20s rose brown	1.25	.25
225	A52	30s dp red brn	1.75	.40
226	A52	35s brt ultra	.20	.50
228	A52	50s dk slate grn	2.50	.75
229	A52	1 l olive green	6.00	2.25
		Nos. 217-229 (11)	15.00	6.20

SEMI-POSTAL STAMPS

Catalogue values for unused stamps in this section are for Never Hinged items.

"Mercy" Assisting Wounded Soldier — SP1

1920 **Unwmk.** **Typo.** ***Perf. 11½***

Brown and Green Design on Back

B1	SP1	20(30)k dk brn & red	1.25	*1.25*
B2	SP1	40(55)k dk bl & red	1.25	*1.25*
B3	SP1	50(70)k dk grn & red	1.00	*1.50*
B4	SP1	1(1.30)r dl sl & red	1.50	*2.50*

Wmk. Star and Triangles (197)

Blue Design on Back

B5	SP1	20(30)k dk brn & red	1.25	*1.25*
B6	SP1	40(55)k dk bl & red	1.25	*1.25*
a.		Vert. pair, imperf. btwn.	40.00	
B7	SP1	50(70)k dk grn & red	1.00	*1.50*
B8	SP1	1(1.30)r dk sl & red	2.00	*2.50*

Wmk. Similar to 145

Pink Paper ***Imperf.***

Brown, Green and Red Design on Back

B9	SP1	20(30)k dk brn & red	1.75	*2.50*
B10	SP1	40(55)k dk bl & red	1.75	*2.50*
B11	SP1	50(70)k dk grn & red	1.75	*2.50*
B12	SP1	1(1.30)r dk sl & red	3.50	*4.25*
		Nos. B1-B12 (12)	19.25	*24.75*

These semi-postal stamps were printed on the backs of unfinished bank notes of the Workers and Soldiers Council, Riga, and the Bermondt-Avalov Army. Blocks of stamps showing complete banknotes on reverse are worth approximately three times the catalogue value of the stamps.

Nos. B1-B8 Surcharged

1921 **Unwmk.** ***Perf. 11½***

Brown and Green Design on Back

B13	SP1	20k + 2r dk brn & red	3.00	*4.00*
B14	SP1	40k + 2r dk bl & red	3.00	*4.00*
B15	SP1	50k + 2r dk grn & red	3.00	*4.00*
B16	SP1	1r + 2r dk sl & red	3.00	*4.00*

Wmk. Star and Triangles (197)

Blue Design on Back

B17	SP1	20k + 2r dk brn & red	30.00	*30.00*
B18	SP1	40k + 2r dk bl & red	30.00	*30.00*
B19	SP1	50k + 2r dk grn & red	30.00	*30.00*
B20	SP1	1r + 2r dk sl & red	30.00	*30.00*
		Nos. B13-B20 (8)	132.00	*136.00*

Regular Issue of 1923-25 Surcharged in Blue

1923 **Wmk. Similar to 181** ***Perf. 10***

B21	A12	1s + 10s violet	1.00	1.00
B22	A12	2s + 10s yellow	1.00	1.00
B23	A12	4s + 10s dk green	1.00	1.00
		Nos. B21-B23 (3)	3.00	3.00

The surtax benefited the Latvian War Invalids Society.

Lighthouse and Harbor, Liepaja (Libau) SP2

Church at Liepaja — SP5

Coat of Arms of Liepaja — SP6

Designs: 15s (25s), City Hall, Liepaja. 25s (35s), Public Bathing Pavilion, Liepaja.

1925, July 23 ***Perf. 11½***

B24	SP2	6s (12s) red brown & deep blue	4.25	3.50
B25	SP2	15s (25s) dk bl & brn	2.50	*2.75*
B26	SP2	25s (35s) violet & dark green	4.00	2.00
B27	SP5	30s (40s) dark blue & lake	7.50	*8.50*
B28	SP6	50s (60s) dark grn & violet	11.00	*11.00*
		Nos. B24-B28 (5)	29.25	*27.75*

Tercentenary of Liepaja (Libau). The surtax benefited that city. Exist imperf. Value, unused set $450.

President Janis Cakste — SP7

1928, Apr. 18 **Engr.**

B29	SP7	2s (12s) red orange	4.00	3.00
B30	SP7	6s (16s) deep green	4.00	3.00
B31	SP7	15s (25s) red brown	4.00	3.00
B32	SP7	25s (35s) deep blue	4.25	3.50
B33	SP7	30s (40s) claret	4.25	3.50
		Nos. B29-B33 (5)	20.50	16.00

The surtax helped erect a monument to Janis Cakste, 1st pres. of the Latvian Republic.

Venta River — SP8

Allegory, "Latvia" — SP9

View of Jelgava SP10

National Theater, Riga — SP11

View of Cesis (Wenden) SP12

Riga Bridge and Trenches SP13

Perf. 11½, Imperf.

1928, Nov. 18 **Wmk. 212** **Litho.**

B34	SP8	6s (16s) green	4.00	2.75
B35	SP9	10s (20s) scarlet	4.00	2.75
B36	SP10	15s (25s) maroon	4.00	2.75
B37	SP11	30s (40s) ultra	4.25	2.75
B38	SP12	50s (60s) dk gray	4.50	3.00
B39	SP13	1 l (1.10 l) choc	4.75	3.50
		Nos. B34-B39 (6)	25.50	17.50

The surtax was given to a committee for the erection of a Liberty Memorial.

Z. A. Meierovics SP14

1929, Aug. 22 ***Perf. 11½, Imperf.***

B46	SP14	2s (4s) orange	5.75	3.75
B47	SP14	6s (12s) dp grn	5.75	3.75
B48	SP14	15s (25s) red brown	5.75	3.75
B49	SP14	25s (35s) deep blue	6.00	3.75
B50	SP14	30s (40s) ultra	6.50	3.75
		Nos. B46-B50 (5)	29.75	18.75

The surtax was used to erect a monument to Z. A. Meierovics, Latvian statesman.

Tuberculosis Cross — SP15

Allegory of Hope for the Sick — SP16

Gustavs Zemgals — SP17

Riga Castle — SP18

Daisies and Double-barred Cross — SP20

Tuberculosis Sanatorium, near Riga — SP22

Cakste, Kviesis and Zemgals SP23

Designs: No. B61, Janis Cakste, 1st pres. of Latvia. No. B63, Pres. Alberts Kviesis.

1930, Dec. 4 Typo. *Perf. 10, 11½*

B56	SP15	1s (2s) dk vio & red orange	1.40	1.40
B57	SP15	2s (4s) org & red orange	1.40	1.40
a.		Cliché of 1s (2s) in plate of 2s (4s)	*650.00*	*650.00*
B58	SP16	4s (8s) dk grn & red	1.75	1.75
B59	SP17	5s (10s) brt grn & dk brown	1.75	1.75
B60	SP18	6s (12s) ol grn & bister	1.75	1.75
B61	SP17	10s (20s) dp red & black	2.25	2.25
B62	SP20	15s (30s) mar & dl green	1.90	2.25
B63	SP17	20s (40s) rose lake & ind	2.75	2.25
B64	SP22	25s (50s) multi	6.00	6.00
B65	SP23	30s (60s) multi	6.00	6.00
		Nos. B56-B65 (10)	26.95	26.80

Surtax for the Latvian Anti-Tuberculosis Soc. For surcharges see Nos. B72-B81.

J. Rainis and New Buildings, Riga SP24

Character from Play and Rainis SP25

Characters from Plays — SP26

Rainis and Lyre SP27

Flames, Flag and Rainis SP28

1930, May 23 Wmk. 212 *Perf. 11½*

B66	SP24	1s (2s) dull violet	1.25	1.00
B67	SP25	2s (4s) yellow org	1.25	1.00
B68	SP26	4s (8s) dp green	1.25	1.00
B69	SP27	6s (12s) yel grn & red brown	1.25	1.00
B70	SP28	10s (20s) dark red	32.50	*35.00*
B71	SP27	15s (30s) red brn & yellow green	35.00	*40.00*
		Nos. B66-B71 (6)	72.50	*79.00*

Sold at double face value, surtax going to memorial fund for J. Rainis (Jan Plieksans, 1865-1929), writer and politician.

Exist imperf. Value twice that of perf. stamps.

9

Nos. B56 to B65 Surcharged in Black

1931, Aug. 19 *Perf. 10, 11½*

B72	SP18	9s on 6s (12s)	1.75	1.10
B73	SP15	16s on 1s (2s)	21.00	15.00
B74	SP15	17s on 2s (4s)	2.10	1.40
B75	SP16	19s on 4s (8s)	6.50	6.00
B76	SP17	20s on 5s (10s)	4.25	*6.00*
B77	SP20	23s on 15s (30s)	2.00	2.00
B78	SP17	25s on 10s (20s)	4.25	3.00
B79	SP17	35s on 20s (40s)	6.50	3.75
B80	SP22	45s on 25s (50s)	22.50	*25.00*
B81	SP23	55s on 30s (60s)	27.50	*30.00*
		Nos. B72-B81 (10)	98.35	93.25

The surcharge replaces the original total price, including surtax.

Nos. B73-B81 have no bars in the surcharge. The surtax aided the Latvian Anti-Tuberculosis Society.

Lacplesis, the Deliverer SP29

Designs: 1s, Kriva telling stories under Holy Oak. 2s, Enslaved Latvians building Riga under knight's supervision. 4s, Death of Black Knight. 5s, Spirit of Lacplesis over freed Riga.

Inscribed: "AIZSARGI" (Army Reserve)

1932, Feb. 10 *Perf. 10½, Imperf.*

B82	SP29	1s (11s) vio brn & bluish	3.25	3.25
B83	SP29	2s (17s) ocher & ol green	3.25	3.25
B84	SP29	3s (23s) red brn & org brown	3.25	3.25
B85	SP29	4s (34s) dk green & green	3.50	3.50
B86	SP29	5s (45s) green & emerald	4.00	4.00
		Nos. B82-B86 (5)	17.25	17.25

Surtax aided the Militia Maintenance Fund.

Marching Troops SP30

Infantry in Action SP31

Nurse Binding Soldier's Wound — SP32

Army Soup Kitchen — SP33

Gen. J. Balodis — SP34

1932, May *Perf. 10½, Imperf.*

B87	SP30	6s (25s) ol brn & red violet	7.00	6.00
B88	SP31	7s (35s) dk bl grn & dark blue	7.00	6.00
B89	SP32	10s (45s) ol green & black brown	7.00	6.00
B90	SP33	12s (55s) lake & ol green	7.50	6.50
B91	SP34	15s (75s) red org & brown violet	8.50	8.50
		Nos. B87-B91 (5)	37.00	33.00

The surtax aided the Latvian Home Guards.

Symbolical of Unified Latvia — SP35

Aid to the Sick — SP37

Symbolical of the Strength of the Latvian Union SP36

"Charity" SP38

Wmk. Multiple Swastikas (212)

1936, Dec. 28 Litho. *Perf. 11½*

B92	SP35	3s orange red	2.50	*4.00*
B93	SP36	10s green	2.50	*4.00*
B94	SP37	20s rose pink	2.50	*4.50*
B95	SP38	35s blue	2.50	*4.50*
		Nos. B92-B95 (4)	10.00	*17.00*

Souvenir Sheets

SP39

1938, May 12 Wmk. 212 *Perf. 11*

B96	SP39	Sheet of 2	15.00	*20.00*
a.		35s Justice Palace, Riga	4.50	*5.00*
b.		40s Power Station, Kegums	4.50	*5.00*

Sold for 2 l. The surtax of 1.25 l was for the National Reconstruction Fund.

No. B96 exists imperf.

Overprinted in Blue with Dates 1934 1939 and "15" over "V"

1939

B97	SP39	Sheet of 2	30.00	*40.00*

5th anniv. of Natl. Unity Day. Sold for 2 lats. Surtax for the Natl. Reconstruction Fund.

AIR POST STAMPS

Catalogue values for unused stamps in this section are for Never Hinged items.

Blériot XI — AP1

Wmk. Wavy Lines Similar to 181

1921, July 30 Litho. *Perf. 11½*

C1	AP1	10r emerald	5.00	4.00
a.		Imperf.	12.00	*13.00*
C2	AP1	20r dark blue	5.00	4.00
a.		Imperf.	12.00	*13.00*

1928, May 1

C3	AP1	10s deep green	5.00	1.50
C4	AP1	15s red	3.00	1.50
C5	AP1	25s ultra	6.00	3.50
a.		Pair, imperf. btwn.	30.00	
		Nos. C3-C5 (3)	14.00	6.50

Nos. C1-C5 sometimes show letters of a paper maker's watermark "PACTIEN LIGAT MILLS."

1931-32 Wmk. 212 *Perf. 11, 11½*

C6	AP1	10s deep green	1.75	.90
C7	AP1	15s red	2.50	1.40
C8	AP1	25s deep blue ('32)	14.00	1.60
		Nos. C6-C8 (3)	18.25	3.90

Type of 1921 Overprinted or Surcharged in Black

1933, May 26 Wmk. 212 *Imperf.*

C9	AP1	10s deep green	22.50	22.50
C10	AP1	15s red	22.50	22.50
C11	AP1	25s deep blue	30.00	30.00
C12	AP1	50s on 15s red	225.00	225.00
C13	AP1	100s on 25s dp blue	225.00	225.00
		Nos. C9-C13 (5)	525.00	525.00

Honoring and financing a flight from Riga to Bathurst, Gambia. The plane crashed at Neustettin, Germany.

Counterfeits exist of Nos. C1-C13.

AIR POST SEMI-POSTAL STAMPS

Catalogue values for unused stamps in this section are for Never Hinged items.

Durbes Castle, Rainis Birthplace — SPAP1

Wmk. 212

1930, May 26 Litho. *Perf. 11½*

CB1 SPAP1	10s (20s) red & olive green	10.00	*12.00*
CB2 SPAP1	15s (30s) dk yel green & copper red	10.00	*12.00*

Surtax for the Rainis Memorial Fund.

Imperf.

CB1a SPAP1	10s (20s)	17.50	*17.50*
CB2a SPAP1	15s (30s)	17.50	*17.50*

Nos. C6-C8 Surcharged in Magenta, Blue or Red

SPAP2

1931, Dec. 5

CB3 AP1	10s + 50s deep green (M)	13.00	*14.00*
CB4 AP1	15s + 1 l red (Bl)	13.00	*14.00*
CB5 AP1	25s + 1.50 l deep blue	13.00	*14.00*
	Nos. CB3-CB5 (3)	39.00	*42.00*

Surtax for the Latvian Home Guards.

Imperf.

CB3a AP1	10s + 50s	13.50	*14.50*
CB4a AP1	15s + 1 l	13.50	*14.50*
CB5a AP1	25s + 1.50 l	13.50	*14.50*
	Nos. CB3a-CB5a (3)	40.50	*43.50*

1932, June 17 *Perf. 10½*

CB6 SPAP2	10s (20s) dk sl grn & green	18.50	*19.00*
CB7 SPAP2	15s (30s) brt red & buff	18.50	*19.00*
CB8 SPAP2	25s (50s) dp bl & gray	18.50	*19.00*
	Nos. CB6-CB8 (3)	55.50	*57.00*

Surtax for the Latvian Home Guards.

Imperf.

CB6a SPAP2	10s (20s)	20.00	20.00
CB7a SPAP2	15s (30s)	20.00	20.00
CB8a SPAP2	25s (50s)	20.00	20.00
	Nos. CB6a-CB8a (3)	60.00	*60.00*

Icarus — SPAP3

Leonardo da Vinci — SPAP4

Charles Balloon — SPAP5

Wright Brothers Biplane SPAP6

Bleriot Monoplane SPAP7

1932, Dec. *Perf. 10, 11½*

CB9 SPAP3	5s (25s) ol bister & green	21.00	21.00
CB10 SPAP4	10s (50s) ol brn & gray grn	21.00	21.00
CB11 SPAP5	15s (75s) red brown & gray grn	21.00	21.00
CB12 SPAP6	20s (1 l) gray grn & lil rose	21.00	21.00
CB13 SPAP7	25s (1.25 l) brn & bl	21.00	21.00
	Nos. CB9-CB13 (5)	105.00	105.00

Issued to honor pioneers of aviation. The surtax of four times the face value was for wounded Latvian aviators.

Imperf.

CB9a SPAP3	5s (25s)	22.00	*24.00*
CB10a SPAP4	10s (50s)	22.00	*24.00*
CB11a SPAP5	15s (75s)	22.00	*24.00*
CB12a SPAP6	20s (1 l)	22.00	*24.00*
CB13a SPAP7	25s (1.25 l)	22.00	*24.00*
	Nos. CB9a-CB13a (5)	110.00	120.00

Icarus Falling SPAP8

Monument to Aviators SPAP9

Proposed Tombs for Aviators
SPAP10 SPAP11

1933, Mar. 15 *Perf. 11½*

CB14 SPAP8	2s (52s) blk & ocher	16.00	*20.00*
CB15 SPAP9	3s (53s) blk & red org	16.00	*20.00*
CB16 SPAP10	10s (60s) blk & dk yel green	16.00	*20.00*
CB17 SPAP11	20s (70s) blk & cerise	16.00	*20.00*
	Nos. CB14-CB17 (4)	64.00	*80.00*

50s surtax for wounded Latvian aviators.

Imperf.

CB14a SPAP8	2s (52s)	19.00	21.00
CB15a SPAP9	3s (53s)	19.00	21.00
CB16a SPAP10	10s (60s)	19.00	21.00
CB17a SPAP11	20s (70s)	19.00	21.00
	Nos. CB14a-CB17a (4)	76.00	84.00

Monoplane Taking Off SPAP12

Designs: 7s (57s), Biplane under fire at Riga. 35s (1.35 l), Map and planes.

1933, June 15 Wmk. 212 *Perf. 11½*

CB18 SPAP12	3s (53s) org & sl blue	37.50	*40.00*
CB19 SPAP12	7s (57s) sl bl & dk brn	37.50	*40.00*
CB20 SPAP12	35s (1.35 l) dp ultra & ol black	37.50	*40.00*
	Nos. CB18-CB20 (3)	112.50	*120.00*

Surtax for wounded Latvian aviators. Counterfeits exist.

Imperf.

CB18a SPAP12	3s (53s)	39.00	*42.50*
CB19a SPAP12	7s (57s)	39.00	*42.50*
CB20a SPAP12	35s (1.35 l)	39.00	*42.50*
	Nos. CB18a-CB20a (3)	117.00	*127.50*

American Gee-Bee SPAP13

English Seaplane S6B SPAP14

Graf Zeppelin over Riga SPAP15

DO-X SPAP16

1933, Sept. 5 *Perf. 11½*

CB21 SPAP13	8s (68s) brn & gray black	70.00	*70.00*
CB22 SPAP14	12s (1.12 l) brn car & ol green	70.00	*70.00*
CB23 SPAP15	30s (1.30 l) blue & gray black	82.50	*85.00*
CB24 SPAP16	40s (1.90 l) brn vio & indigo	75.00	*70.00*
	Nos. CB21-CB24 (4)	297.50	295.00

Surtax for wounded Latvian aviators.

Imperf.

CB21a SPAP13	8s (68s)	85.00	85.00
CB22a SPAP14	12s (1.12 l)	85.00	85.00
CB23a SPAP15	30s (1.30 l)	95.00	95.00
CB24a SPAP16	40s (1.90 l)	90.00	90.00
	Nos. CB21a-CB24a (4)	355.00	*355.00*

OCCUPATION STAMPS

Issued under German Occupation

German Stamps of 1905-18 Handstamped

1919 Wmk. 125 *Perf. 14, 14½*

Red Overprint

1N1	A22	2½pf gray	225.00	225.00
1N2	A16	5pf green	175.00	90.00
1N3	A22	15pf dk vio	275.00	90.00
1N4	A16	20pf blue vio	110.00	40.00
1N5	A16	25pf org & blk, *yel*	375.00	275.00
1N6	A16	50pf pur & blk, *buff*	375.00	275.00

Blue Overprint

1N7	A22	2½pf gray	225.00	225.00
1N8	A16	5pf green	110.00	60.00
1N9	A16	10pf carmine	92.50	35.00
1N10	A22	15pf dk vio	275.00	150.00
1N11	A16	20pf bl vio	110.00	35.00
1N12	A16	25pf org & blk, *yel*	375.00	275.00
1N13	A16	50pf pur & blk, *buff*	375.00	275.00
		Nos. 1N1-1N13 (13)	3,097.	2,050.

Inverted and double overprints exist, as well as counterfeit overprints.

Some experts believe that Nos. 1N1-1N7 were not officially issued. All used copies are canceled to order.

OCCUPATION STAMPSISSUED UNDER RUSSIAN OCCUPATION

Fake overprints/surcharges exist on Nos. 2N1-2N36.

The following stamps were issued at Mitau during the occupation of Kurland by the West Russian Army under Colonel Bermondt-Avalov.

Stamps of Latvia Handstamped

1919 Wmk. 108 *Imperf.*

On Stamps of 1919

2N1	A1	3k lilac	12.50	*17.50*
2N2	A1	5k carmine	12.50	*17.50*
2N3	A1	10k dp blue	67.50	*92.50*
2N4	A1	20k orange	12.50	*17.50*
2N5	A1	25k gray	12.50	*17.50*
2N6	A1	35k dk brown	12.50	*17.50*
2N7	A1	50k purple	12.50	*17.50*
2N8	A1	75k emerald	15.00	*22.50*

On Riga Liberation Stamps

2N9	A2	5k carmine	7.50	*12.50*
2N10	A2	15k dp green	7.50	*12.50*
2N11	A2	35k brown	7.50	*12.50*

Stamps of Latvia Overprinted

On Stamps of 1919

2N12	A1	3k lilac	5.00	*7.50*
2N13	A1	5k carmine	5.00	*7.50*
2N14	A1	10k dp blue	60.00	*92.50*
2N15	A1	20k orange	10.00	*15.00*
2N16	A1	25k gray	17.50	*35.00*
2N17	A1	35k dk brown	12.50	*17.50*
2N18	A1	50k purple	12.50	*17.50*
2N19	A1	75k emerald	12.50	*17.50*

On Riga Liberation Stamps

2N20	A2	5k carmine	4.00	*6.00*
2N21	A2	15k dp green	4.00	*6.00*
2N22	A2	35k brown	4.00	*6.00*
a.		Inverted overprint	*110.00*	
		Nos. 2N1-2N22 (22)	327.00	*485.50*

The letters "Z. A." are the initials of "Zapadnaya Armiya"-i.e. Western Army.

Russian Stamps of 1909-17 Surcharged

Perf. 14, 14½x15

Unwmk.

On Stamps of 1909-12

2N23	A14	10k on 2k grn	4.00	*5.00*
a.		Inverted surcharge	*30.00*	
2N24	A15	30k on 4k car	3.50	*4.50*
2N25	A14	40k on 5k cl	3.50	*4.50*
2N26	A15	50k pn 10k dk bl	3.50	*4.50*
2N27	A11	70k on 15k red brn & bl	3.50	*4.50*
a.		Inverted surcharge	*50.00*	
2N28	A8	90k on 20k bl & car	3.50	*4.50*
2N29	A11	1r on 25k grn & vio	3.50	4.50
2N30	A11	1½r on 35k red brn & grn	22.50	37.50
2N31	A8	2r on 50k vio & grn	4.50	6.50
a.		Inverted surcharge	*35.00*	
2N32	A11	4r on 70k brn & org	12.50	15.00

Perf. 13½

2N33	A9	6r on 1r pale brn, brn & org	12.50	15.00

On Stamps of 1917
Imperf

2N34 A14 20k on 3k red 4.50 *5.00*
2N35 A14 40k on 5k claret 32.50 *42.50*
2N36 A12 10r on 3.50r mar & lt grn 32.50 *42.50*
a. Inverted surcharge *100.00*
Nos. 2N23-2N36 (14) 146.50 *196.00*

Eight typographed stamps of this design were prepared in 1919, but never placed in use. They exist both perforated and imperforate. Value, set, imperf. $1, perf. $2.

Reprints and counterfeits exist.

Catalogue values for unused stamps in this section, from this poit to the end of the section, are for Never Hinged items.

Arms of Soviet Latvia — OS1

1940 Typo. Wmk. 265 ***Perf. 10***

2N45 OS1 1s dk violet .20 .20
2N46 OS1 2s orange yel .20 .20
2N47 OS1 3s orange ver .20 .20
2N48 OS1 5s dk olive grn .20 .20
2N49 OS1 7s turq green .20 .20
2N50 OS1 10s slate green 1.40 .20
2N51 OS1 20s brown lake .85 .20
2N52 OS1 30s light blue 2.10 .25
2N53 OS1 35s brt ultra .20 .20
2N54 OS1 40s chocolate 1.40 .20
2N55 OS1 50s lt gray 2.00 .20
2N56 OS1 1 l lt brown 2.75 .25
2N57 OS1 5 l brt green 20.00 7.50
Nos. 2N45-2N57 (13) 31.70 10.00

Used values of #2N45-2N57 are for CTOs. Commercially use are worth three times as much.

LEBANON

'le-bə-nən

(Grand Liban)

LOCATION — Asia Minor, bordering on the Mediterranean Sea
GOVT. — Republic
AREA — 4,036 sq. mi.
POP. — 3,500,000 (est. 1984)
CAPITAL — Beirut

Formerly a part of the Syrian province of Turkey, Lebanon was occupied by French forces after World War I. It was mandated to France after it had been declared a separate state. Limited autonomy was granted in 1927 and full independence achieved in 1941. The French issued two sets of occupation stamps (with T.E.O. overprint) for Lebanon in late 1919. The use of these and later occupation issues (of 1920-24, with overprints "O.M.F." and "Syrie-Grand Liban") was extended to Syria, Cilicia, Alaouites and Alexandretta. By custom, these are all listed under Syria.

100 Centimes = 1 Piaster
100 Piasters = 1 Pound

Issued under French Mandate

Stamps of France 1900-21 Surcharged

1924 Unwmk. ***Perf. 14x13½***

1 A16 10c on 2c vio brn .75 .35
a. Inverted surcharge 30.00 27.50
2 A22 25c on 5c orange .75 .30
3 A22 50c on 10c green .75 .30
4 A20 75c on 15c sl grn 1.25 .65
5 A22 1p on 20c red brn .85 .25
a. Double surcharge 32.50 27.50
b. Inverted surcharge 35.00 32.50
6 A22 1.25p on 25c blue 2.25 .80
7 A22 1.50p on 30c org 1.25 .75
8 A22 1.50p on 30c red 1.25 .75
9 A20 2.50p on 50c dl bl 1.00 .35
a. Inverted surcharge 27.50 27.50

Surcharged

10 A18 2p on 40c red & pale bl 2.50 1.25
a. Inverted surcharge 27.50 27.50
11 A18 3p on 60c violet & ultra 4.00 2.25
12 A18 5p on 1fr cl & ol green 4.75 2.50
13 A18 10p on 2fr org & pale bl 8.00 4.00
a. Inverted surcharge 50.00 50.00
14 A18 25p on 5fr dk bl & buff 12.00 6.50
a. Inverted surcharge 85.00 85.00
Nos. 1-14 (14) 41.35 21.00

Broken and missing letters and varieties of spacing are numerous in these surcharges.

For overprints see Nos. C1-C4.

Stamps of France, 1923, (Pasteur) Surcharged "GRAND LIBAN" and New Values

15 A23 50c on 10c green 1.00 .25
a. Inverted surcharge 35.00 25.00
16 A23 1.50p on 30c red 1.25 .50
17 A23 2.50p on 50c blue 1.00 .25
a. Inverted surcharge 30.00 27.50
Nos. 15-17 (3) 3.25 1.00

Commemorative Stamps of France, 1924, (Olympic Games) Surcharged "GRAND LIBAN" and New Values

18 A24 50c on 10c gray grn & yel grn 17.50 *20.00*
a. Inverted surcharge 350.00
19 A25 1.25p on 25c rose & dk rose 17.50 *20.00*
a. Inverted surcharge 350.00
20 A26 1.50p on 30c brn red & blk 17.50 *20.00*
a. Inverted surcharge 350.00
21 A27 2.50p on 50c ultra & dk bl 17.50 *20.00*
a. Inverted surcharge 350.00
Nos. 18-21 (4) 70.00 80.00

Stamps of France, 1900-24, Surcharged

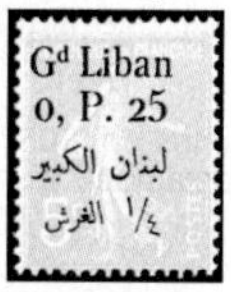

1924-25

22 A16 10c on 2c vio brn .30 .20
23 A22 25c on 5c orange .45 .25
24 A22 50c on 10c green .85 .35
25 A20 75c on 15c gray grn .65 .25
26 A22 1p on 20c red brn .55 .20
27 A22 1.25p on 25c blue 1.00 .40
28 A22 1.50p on 30c red .80 .35
29 A22 1.50p on 30c orange 35.00 22.50
30 A22 2p on 35c vio ('25) 1.00 .45
31 A20 3p on 60c lt vio ('25) 1.25 .50
32 A20 4p on 85c ver 1.50 .90

Surcharged

33 A18 2p on 40c red & pale bl 1.00 .50
a. 2nd line of Arabic reads "2 Piastre" (singular) 2.00 .50
34 A18 2p on 45c green & blue ('25) 13.50 10.00
35 A18 3p on 60c violet & ultra 1.50 .55
36 A18 5p on 1fr cl & ol green 2.00 .90
37 A18 10p on 2fr org & pale bl 5.00 2.50
38 A18 25p on 5fr dk bl & buff 8.00 3.50
Nos. 22-38 (17) 74.35 44.30

Last line of surcharge on No. 33 has four characters, with a 9-like character between the third and fourth in illustration. Last line on No. 33a is as illustrated.

The surcharge may be found inverted on most of Nos. 22-38, and double on some values.

For overprints see Nos. C5-C8.

Stamps of France 1923-24 (Pasteur) Surcharged as Nos. 22-32

39 A23 50c on 10c green .60 .30
a. Inverted surcharge 35.00 25.00
b. Double surcharge 40.00 21.00
40 A23 75c on 15c green .70 .50
41 A23 1.50p on 30c red .85 .50
a. Inverted surcharge 35.00 25.00
42 A23 2p on 45c red 1.75 1.25
a. Inverted surcharge 35.00 21.00
43 A23 2.50p on 50c blue .60 .35
a. Inverted surcharge 35.00 21.00
b. Double surcharge 40.00 21.00
44 A23 4p on 75c blue 1.75 1.25
Nos. 39-44 (6) 6.25 4.15

France Nos. 198 to 201 (Olympics) Surcharged as Nos. 22-32

45 A24 50c on 10c 17.50 *20.00*
46 A25 1.25p on 25c 17.50 *20.00*
47 A26 1.50p on 30c 17.50 *20.00*
48 A27 2.50p on 50c 17.50 *20.00*
Nos. 45-48 (4) 70.00 80.00

France No. 219 (Ronsard) Surcharged as Nos. 22-32

49 A28 4p on 75c bl, *bluish* 1.50 1.00
a. Inverted surcharge 65.00 50.00

Cedar of Lebanon — A1

Crusader Castle, Tripoli — A3

View of Beirut A2

Designs: 50c, Crusader Castle, Tripoli. 75c, Beit-ed-Din Palace. 1p, Temple of Jupiter, Baalbek. 1.25p, Mouktara Palace. 1.50p, Harbor of Tyre. 2p, View of Zahle. 2.50p, Ruins at Baalbek. 3p, Square at Deir-el-Kamar. 5p, Castle at Sidon. 25p, Square at Beirut.

1925 Litho. ***Perf. 12½, 13½***

50 A1 10c dark violet .50 .20

Photo.

51 A2 25c olive black .60 .20
52 A2 50c yellow grn .50 .20
53 A2 75c brn orange .50 .20
54 A2 1p magenta 1.25 .30
55 A2 1.25p deep green 1.50 .50
56 A2 1.50p rose red .60 .20
57 A2 2p dark brown .75 .20
58 A2 2.50p peacock bl 1.25 .30
59 A2 3p orange brn 1.75 .40
60 A2 5p violet 2.00 .50
61 A3 10p violet brn 6.00 .80
62 A2 25p ultramarine 17.50 4.50
Nos. 50-62 (13) 34.70 8.50

For surcharges and overprints see Nos. 63-107, B1-B12, C9-C38, CB1-CB4.

Stamps of 1925 with Bars and Surcharged

1926

63 A2 3.50p on 75c brn org .75 .75
64 A2 4p on 25c ol blk 1.25 1.25
65 A2 6p on 2.50p pck bl 1.00 1.00
66 A2 12p on 1.25p dp grn 1.00 1.00
67 A2 20p on 1.25p dp grn 4.00 4.00

Stamps of 1925 with Bars and Surcharged

68 A2 4.50p on 75c brn org 1.50 1.50
69 A2 7.50p on 2.50p pck bl 1.50 1.50
70 A2 15p on 25p ultra 1.50 1.50
Nos. 63-70 (8) 12.50 12.50

No. 51 with Bars and Surcharged

1927

71 A2 4p on 25c ol blk 1.25 1.25

Issues of Republic under French Mandate

Stamps of 1925 Issue Overprinted in Black or Red

1927

72 A1 10c dark vio (R) .30 .20
a. Black overprint 35.00
73 A2 50c yellow grn .30 .20
74 A2 1p magenta .30 .20
75 A2 1.50p rose red .50 .30
76 A2 2p dark brown .75 .45
77 A2 3p orange brn .60 .20
78 A2 5p violet 1.25 .50
79 A3 10p violet brn 1.50 .55
80 A2 25p ultramarine 17.50 4.00
Nos. 72-80 (9) 23.00 6.60

On Nos. 72 and 79 the overprint is set in two lines. On all stamps the double bar obliterates GRAND LIBAN.

Same Overprint on Provisional Issues of 1926-27

15 PIASTERS ON 25 PIASTERS

TYPE I — "République Libanaise" at foot of stamp.

TYPE II — "République Libanaise" near top of stamp.

81 A2 4p on 25c ol blk .50 .20
82 A2 4.50p on 75c brn org .60 .20
83 A2 7.50p on 2.50p pck bl .75 .20
84 A2 15p on 25p ultra (I) 6.00 2.50
a. Type II 5.50 3.75
Nos. 81-84 (4) 7.85 3.10

Most of Nos. 72-84 are known with overprint double, inverted or on back as well as face.

Stamps of 1927 Overprinted in Black or Red

1928

86 A1 10c dark vio (R) .50 .50
a. French overprint omitted, on #50
87 A2 50c yel grn (Bk) 1.25 1.25
a. Arabic overprint inverted 35.00 25.00
88 A2 1p magenta (Bk) .60 .60
a. Inverted overprint 35.00 25.00
89 A2 1.50p rose red (Bk) 1.25 1.25
90 A2 2p dark brown (R) 1.75 1.75
90A A2 2p dk brn (Bk+R) 90.00 90.00
91 A2 3p org brown (Bk) 1.00 1.00

92 A2 5p violet (Bk+R) 2.25 2.25
93 A2 5p violet (R) 2.00 2.00
a. French ovpt. below Arabic 30.00 14.00
94 A3 10p vio brn (Bk) 3.50 3.50
a. Double overprint 100.00 90.00
b. Double overprint inverted
c. Inverted overprint 100.00 70.00
95 A2 25p ultra (Bk+R) 9.00 9.00
95A A2 25p ultra (R) 11.00 11.00
Nos. 86-95A (12) 124.10 124.10

On all stamps the double bar with Arabic overprint obliterates Arabic inscription.

Same Overprint on Nos. 81-84

96 A2 4p on 25c (Bk+R) 1.25 1.25
97 A2 4.50p on 75c (Bk) 1.25 1.25
98 A2 7.50p on 2.50p (Bk+R) 3.00 3.00
99 A2 7.50p on 2.50p (R) 5.00 5.00
100 A2 15p on 25p (II) (Bk+R) 8.00 8.00
a. Arabic overprint inverted
101 A2 15p on 25p (I) (R) 10.00 10.00
Nos. 96-101 (6) 28.50 28.50

The new values are surcharged in black. The initials in ( ) refer to the colors of the overprints.

Stamps of 1925 Surcharged in Red or Black

1928-29 *Perf. 13½*

102 A2 50c on 75c brn org (Bk) ('29) 1.00 1.00
103 A2 2p on 1.25p dp grn 1.00 1.00
104 A2 4p on 25c ol blk 1.00 1.00
a. Double surcharge 35.00 25.00
105 A2 7.50p on 2.50p pck bl 1.50 1.50
a. Double surcharge 40.00 25.00
b. Inverted surcharge 55.00 25.00
106 A2 15p on 25p ultra 17.50 5.25
Nos. 102-106 (5) 22.00 9.75

On Nos. 103, 104 and 105 the surcharged numerals are 3¼mm high, and have thick strokes.

No. 86 Surcharged in Red

1928

107 A1 5c on 10c dk vio 1.25 .30

Silkworm, Cocoon and Moth — A4

1930, Feb. 11 **Typo.** *Perf. 11*

108 A4 4p black brown 11.00 9.50
109 A4 4½p vermilion 11.00 9.50
110 A4 7½p dark blue 11.00 9.50
111 A4 10p dk violet 11.00 9.50
112 A4 15p dark green 11.00 9.50
113 A4 25p claret 11.00 9.50
Nos. 108-113 (6) 66.00 57.00

Sericultural Congress, Beirut. Presentation imperfs exist.

Pigeon Rocks, Ras Beirut — A5

View of Bickfaya A8

Beit-ed-Din Palace A10

Crusader Castle, Tripoli A11

Ruins of Venus Temple, Baalbek A12

Ancient Bridge, Dog River A13

Belfort Castle A14

Afka Falls — A19

20c, Cedars of Lebanon. 25c, Ruins of Bacchus Temple, Baalbek. 1p, Crusader Castle, Sidon Harbor. 5p, Arcade of Beit-ed-Din Palace. 6p, Tyre Harbor. 7.50p, Ruins of Sun Temple, Baalbek. 10p, View of Hasbeya. 25p, Government House, Beirut. 50p, View of Deir-el-Kamar. 75c, 100p, Ruins at Baalbek.

1930-35 **Litho.** *Perf. 12½, 13½*

114 A5 10c brown orange .30 .20
115 A5 20c yellow brn .30 .20
116 A5 25c deep blue .40 .30

Photo.

117 A8 50c orange brn 2.00 1.00
118 A11 75c ol brn ('32) .90 .70
119 A8 1p deep green 1.00 .80
120 A8 1p brn vio ('35) 1.75 .70
121 A10 1.50p violet brn 2.00 1.25
122 A10 1.50p dp grn ('32) 2.25 1.00
123 A11 2p Prussian bl 3.00 1.10
124 A12 3p black brown 3.00 1.10
125 A13 4p orange brn 3.00 1.10
126 A14 4.50p carmine 3.25 1.10
127 A14 5p greenish blk 2.00 1.00
128 A13 6p brn violet 3.50 1.90
129 A10 7.50p deep blue 3.25 1.10
130 A10 10p dk ol grn 6.00 1.10
131 A19 15p blk violet 9.00 2.40
132 A19 25p blue green 14.00 4.00
133 A8 50p apple grn 40.00 10.50
134 A11 100p black 40.00 12.50
Nos. 114-134 (21) 140.90 45.05

See Nos. 135, 144, 152-155. For surcharges see Nos. 147-149, 161, 173-174.

Pigeon Rocks Type of 1930-35 Redrawn

1934 **Litho.** *Perf. 12½x12*

135 A5 10c dull orange 3.50 1.50

Lines in rocks and water more distinct. Printer's name "Hélio Vaugirard, Paris," in larger letters.

Cedar of Lebanon A23

President Emile Eddé A24

Dog River Panorama A25

1937-40 **Typo.** *Perf. 14x13½*

137 A23 10c rose car .30 .20
137A A23 20c aqua ('40) .30 .20
137B A23 25c pale rose lilac ('40) .30 .20
138 A23 50c magenta .30 .20
138A A23 75c brown ('40) .30 .20

Engr.

Perf. 13

139 A24 3p dk violet 2.00 .30
140 A24 4p black brown .35 .20
141 A24 4.50p carmine .50 .20
142 A25 10p brn carmine 1.00 .20
142A A25 12½p dp ultra ('40) .50 .20
143 A25 15p dk grn ('38) 2.00 .30
143A A25 20p chestnut ('40) .60 .20
143B A25 25p crimson ('40) .75 .25
143C A25 50p dk vio ('40) 3.00 .65
143D A25 100p sepia ('40) 2.00 .90
Nos. 137-143D (15) 14.20 4.40

Nos. 137A, 137B, 138A, 142A, 143A, 143B, 143C, and 143D exist imperforate.

For surcharges see Nos. 145-146A, 150-151, 160, 162, 175-176.

View of Bickfaya A26

Type A8 Redrawn

1935 (?) **Photo.** *Perf. 13½*

144 A26 50c orange brown 6.00 3.50

Arabic inscriptions more condensed.

Stamps of 1930-37 Surcharged in Black or Red

1937-42 *Perf. 13, 13½*

145 A24 2p on 3p dk vio .75 .75
146 A24 2½p on 4p blk brn .75 .75
146A A24 2½p on 4p black brown (R) ('42) .75 .75
147 A10 6p on 7.50p dp bl (R) 2.25 2.25

Stamps of 1930-35 and Type of 1937-40 Surcharged in Black or Red

Perf. 13½, 13

148 A8 7.50p on 50p ap grn 1.25 1.25
149 A11 7.50p on 100p blk (R) 1.25 1.25
150 A25 12.50p on 7.50p dk bl (R) 2.75 2.75

Type of 1937-40 Surcharged in Red with Bars and

1939 **Engr.** *Perf. 13*

151 A25 12½p on 7.50p dk bl 1.00 1.00
Nos. 145-151 (8) 10.75 10.75

Type of 1930-35 Redrawn
Imprint: "Beiteddine-Imp.-Catholique-Beyrouth-Liban."

1939 **Litho.** *Perf. 11½*

152 A10 1p dk slate grn 1.00 .20
153 A10 1.50p brn violet 1.00 .35
154 A10 7.50p carmine lake 1.00 .45
Nos. 152-154 (3) 3.00 1.00

Bridge Type of 1930-35
Imprint: "Degorce" instead of "Hélio Vaugirard"

1940 **Engr.** *Perf. 13*

155 A13 5p grnsh blue .75 .20

Exists imperforate.

SEMI-POSTAL STAMPS

Regular Issue of 1925 Surcharged in Red or Black

1926 **Unwmk.** *Perf. 14x13½*

B1 A2 25c + 25c ol blk 2.00 2.00
B2 A2 50c + 25c yellow green (B) 2.00 2.00
B3 A2 75c + 25c brown orange (B) 2.00 2.00
B4 A2 1p + 50c mag 2.00 2.00
B5 A2 1.25p + 50c dp grn 2.25 2.25
B6 A2 1.50p + 50c rose red (B) 2.25 2.25
a. Double surcharge 40.00 30.00
B7 A2 2p + 75c dk brn 2.00 2.00
B8 A2 2.50p + 75c pck bl 2.25 2.25
B9 A2 3p + 1p org brn 2.25 2.25
B10 A2 5p + 1p vio (B) 2.25 2.25
B11 A3 10p + 2p violet brown (B) 2.25 2.25
B12 A2 25p + 5p ultra 2.25 2.25
Nos. B1-B12 (12) 25.75 25.75

On No. B11 the surcharge is set in six lines to fit the shape of the stamp. All values of this series exist with inverted surcharge. Value each, $14.

See Nos. CB1-CB4.

AIR POST STAMPS

#10-13 with Additional Overprint

1924 **Unwmk.** *Perf. 14x13½*

C1 A18 2p on 40c 8.00 *8.00*
a. Double surcharge
C2 A18 3p on 60c 8.00 *8.00*
C3 A18 5p on 1fr 8.00 *8.00*
a. Dbl. surch. and ovpt.
C4 A18 10p on 2fr 8.00 *8.00*
a. Invtd. surch. and ovpt. 95.00
Nos. C1-C4 (4) 32.00 *32.00*

Nos. 33, 35-37 Overprinted

C5	A18	2p on 40c	9.00	5.00
C6	A18	3p on 60c	9.00	5.00
C7	A18	5p on 1fr	9.00	5.00
a.		Overprint reversed	40.00	
C8	A18	10p on 2fr	9.00	5.00
a.		Overprint reversed	40.00	
b.		Double surcharge	40.00	
		Nos. C5-C8 (4)	36.00	20.00

Nos. 57, 59-61 Overprinted in Green

1925

C9	A2	2p dark brown	2.50	2.50
C10	A2	3p orange brown	2.50	2.50
C11	A2	5p violet	2.50	2.50
a.		Inverted overprint		
C12	A3	10p violet brown	2.50	2.50
		Nos. C9-C12 (4)	10.00	10.00

Nos. 57, 59-61 Overprinted in Red

c

1926

C13	A2	2p dark brown	2.50	2.50
C14	A2	3p orange brown	2.50	2.50
C15	A2	5p violet	2.50	2.50
C16	A3	10p violet brown	2.50	2.50
		Nos. C13-C16 (4)	10.00	10.00

Airplane poited down on No. C16.

Exist with inverted overprint. Value, each $15.

Issues of Republic under French Mandate

Nos. C13-C16 Overprinted

d

1927

C17	A2	2p dark brown	3.25	3.25
C18	A2	3p orange brown	3.25	3.25
C19	A2	5p violet	3.25	3.25
C20	A3	10p violet brown	3.25	3.25
		Nos. C17-C20 (4)	13.00	13.00

On No. C19 "Republique Libanaise" is above the bars. Overprint set in two lines on No. C20.

Nos. C17-C20 with Additional Overprint

e

1928

Black Overprint

C21	A2	2p brown	9.00	4.00
a.		Double overprint	25.00	
b.		Inverted overprint	25.00	
C22	A2	3p orange brown	9.00	4.00
a.		Double overprint	25.00	
C23	A2	5p violet	9.00	4.00
a.		Double overprint	15.00	
C24	A3	10p violet brown	9.00	4.00
a.		Double overprint	15.00	
		Nos. C21-C24 (4)	36.00	16.00

On Nos. C21-C24 the airplane is always in red.

Nos. 52, 54, 57, 59-62 Overprinted in Red or Black (No. C34)

f

1928

C25	A2	2p dark brown	2.50	.85
C26	A2	3p orange brown	2.50	.85
C27	A2	5p violet	2.50	.85
C28	A3	10p violet brown	3.00	.85

1929

C33	A2	50c yellow green	.50	.40
a.		Inverted overprint	35.00	15.00
C34	A2	1p magenta (Bk)	.75	.50
a.		Inverted overprint	35.00	15.00
C35	A2	25p ultra	175.00	100.00
a.		Inverted overprint	350.00	250.00
		Nos. C25-C34 (6)	11.75	4.30
		Nos. C25-C35 (7)	186.75	104.30

On Nos. C25-C28 the airplane is always in red.

On No. C28 the overprinted orientation is horizontal. The bars covering the old country names are at the left.

The red overprint of a silhouetted plane and "Republique Libanaise," as on Nos. C25-C27, was also applied to Nos. C9-C12. These are believed to have been essays, and were not regularly issued.

No. 62 with Surcharge Added in Red

Two types of surcharge:

I — The "5" of "15 P." is italic. The "15" is 4mm high. Arabic characters for "Lebanese Republic" and for "15 P." are on same line in that order.

II — The "5" is in Roman type (upright) and smaller; "15" is 3½mm high. Arabic for "Lebanese Republic" is centered on line by itself, with Arabic for "15 P." below right end of line.

C36	A2	15p on 25p ultra (I)	200.00	175.00
a.		Type II (#106)	*600.00*	*600.00*

Nos. 102 Overprinted Type "c" in Blue

C37	A2	50c on 75c	.50	.30
a.		Airplane inverted	45.00	
b.		French and Arabic surch. invtd.		
c.		"P" omitted		
d.		Airplane double	50.00	

No. 55 Surcharged in Red

1930

C38	A2	2p on 1.25p dp green	1.25	1.00
a.		Inverted surcharge	30.00	15.00

Airplane over Racheya AP2

Designs: 1p, Plane over Broumana. 2p, Baalbek. 3p, Hasroun. 5p, Byblos. 10p, Kadicha River. 15p, Beirut. 25p, Tripoli. 50p, Kabeljas. 100p, Zahle.

1930-31 Photo. *Perf. 13½*

C39	AP2	50c dk violet ('31)	.20	.20
C40	AP2	1p yellow grn ('31)	.20	.20
C41	AP2	2p dp orange ('31)	.50	.40
C42	AP2	3p magenta ('31)	.50	.40
C43	AP2	5p indigo	.50	.40
C44	AP2	10p orange red	1.25	.65
C45	AP2	15p orange brn	.75	.60
C46	AP2	25p gray vio ('31)	1.10	1.00
C47	AP2	50p dp claret	4.00	3.25
C48	AP2	100p olive brown	5.00	4.00
		Nos. C39-C48 (10)	14.00	11.10

Nos. C39 to C48 exist imperforate.

Tourist Publicity Issue

Skiing in Lebanon AP12

Bay of Jounie AP13

1936, Oct. 12

C49	AP12	50c slate grn	1.60	1.60
C50	AP13	1p red orange	2.00	2.00
C51	AP12	2p black violet	2.00	2.00
C52	AP13	3p yellow grn	2.00	2.00
C53	AP12	5p brown car	2.00	2.00
C54	AP13	10p orange brn	2.00	2.00
C55	AP13	15p dk carmine	25.00	25.00
C56	AP12	25p green	85.00	85.00
		Nos. C49-C56 (8)	121.60	121.60

Nos. C49 to C56 exist imperforate.

Lebanese Pavilion at Exposition AP14

1937, July 1 *Perf. 13½*

C57	AP14	50c olive black	.50	.50
C58	AP14	1p yellow green	.50	.50
C59	AP14	2p dk red orange	.50	.50
C60	AP14	3p dk olive grn	.50	.50
C61	AP14	5p deep green	.65	.65
C62	AP14	10p carmine lake	3.50	3.50
C63	AP14	15p rose lake	3.75	3.75
C64	AP14	25p orange brn	6.50	6.50
		Nos. C57-C64 (8)	16.40	16.40

Paris International Exposition.

Arcade of Beit-ed-Din Palace AP15

Ruins of Baalbek AP16

1937-40 Engr. *Perf. 13*

C65	AP15	50c ultra ('38)	.20	.20
C66	AP15	1p henna brn ('40)	.20	.20
C67	AP15	2p sepia ('40)	.20	.20
C68	AP15	3p rose ('40)	.95	.35
C69	AP15	5p lt green ('40)	.20	.20
C70	AP16	10p dull violet	.20	.20
C71	AP16	15p turq bl ('40)	.75	.50
C72	AP16	25p violet ('40)	1.90	1.40
C73	AP16	50p yellow grn ('40)	3.50	2.00
C74	AP16	100p brown ('40)	1.90	1.00
		Nos. C65-C74 (10)	10.00	6.25

Nos. C65-C74 exist imperforate.

Medical College of Beirut AP17

1938, May 9 Photo. *Perf. 13*

C75	AP17	2p green	.75	*1.00*
C76	AP17	3p orange	.75	*1.00*
C77	AP17	5p lilac gray	1.50	*2.00*
C78	AP17	10p lake	3.00	*5.00*
		Nos. C75-C78 (4)	6.00	*9.00*

Medical Congress.

Maurice Noguès and View of Beirut — AP18

1938, July 15 *Perf. 11*

C79	AP18	10p brown carmine	3.00	1.50
a.		Souv. sheet of 4, perf. 13½	35.00	20.00
b.		Perf. 13½	7.50	4.00

10th anniversary of first Marseille-Beirut flight, by Maurice Noguès.

No. C79a has marginal inscriptions in French and Arabic. Exists imperf.; value $250.

AIR POST SEMI-POSTAL STAMPS

#C13-C16 Surcharged Like #B1-B12

1926 *Perf. 13½*

CB1	A2	2pi + 1pi dark brown	3.00	2.25
CB2	A2	3pi + 2pi orabge brown	3.00	2.25
CB3	A2	5pi + 3pi violet	3.00	2.25
CB4	A3	10pl + 5pi violet brown	3.00	2.25
		Nos. CB1-CB4 (4)	12.00	9.00

These stamps were sold for their combined values, original and surcharged. The latter represented their postal franking value and the former was a contribution to the relief of refugees from the Djebel Druze War.

POSTAGE DUE STAMPS

Postage Due Stamps of France, 1893-1920, Surcharged like Regular Issue

1924 Unwmk. *Perf. 14x13½*

J1	D2	50c on 10c choc	2.75	2.00
J2	D2	1p on 20c ol grn	2.75	2.00
J3	D2	2p on 30c red	2.75	2.00
J4	D2	3p on 50c vio brn	2.75	2.00
J5	D2	5p on 1fr red brn, *straw*	2.75	2.00
		Nos. J1-J5 (5)	13.75	10.00

Postage Due Stamps of France, 1893-1920, Surcharged

1924

J6	D2	50c on 10c choc	3.50	2.00
J7	D2	1p on 20c ol grn	3.50	2.00
J8	D2	2p on 30c red	3.50	2.00
J9	D2	3p on 50c vio brn	3.50	2.00
J10	D2	5p on 1fr red brn, *straw*	3.50	2.00
		Nos. J6-J10 (5)	17.50	10.00

Ancient Bridge across Dog River — D3

Designs: 1p, Village scene. 2p, Pigeon Rocks, near Beirut. 3p, Belfort Castle. 5p, Venus Temple at Baalbek.

1925 Photo. *Perf. 13½*

J11	D3	50c brown, *yellow*	.30	.20
J12	D3	1p violet, *rose*	.50	.25
J13	D3	2p black, *blue*	.80	.40
J14	D3	3p black, *red org*	1.50	.75
J15	D3	5p black, *bl grn*	2.75	1.40
		Nos. J11-J15 (5)	5.85	3.00
		Set, never hinged	40.00	

Nos. J11 to J15 Overprinted

1927

J16	D3	50c brown, *yellow*	.40	.20
J17	D3	1p violet, *rose*	.65	.30
J18	D3	2p black, *blue*	.90	.45
J19	D3	3p black, *red org*	2.50	1.40
J20	D3	5p black, *bl grn*	3.00	1.60
		Nos. J16-J20 (5)	7.45	3.95
		Set, never hinged	11.00	

Nos. J16 to J20 with Additional Overprint

1928

J21	D3	50c brn, *yel* (Bk+R)	1.00	.50
J22	D3	1p vio, *rose* (Bk)	1.00	.50
J23	D3	2p blk, *bl* (Bk+R)	2.00	1.00
J24	D3	3p blk, *red org* (Bk)	4.00	2.00
J25	D3	5p blk, *bl grn* (Bk+R)	4.50	2.25
		Nos. J21-J25 (5)	12.50	6.25
		Set, never hinged	65.00	

No. J23 has not the short bars in the upper corners.

Postage Due Stamps of 1925 Overprinted in Red like Nos. J21-J25

1928

J26	D3	50c brn, *yel* (R)	.50	.20
J27	D3	2p blk, *bl* (R)	2.50	1.50
J28	D3	5p blk, *bl grn* (R)	7.00	4.00
		Nos. J26-J28 (3)	10.00	5.70
		Set, never hinged	19.00	

No. J28 has not the short bars in the upper corners.

D4

Bas-relief of a Ship — D5

D6

D7

D8

Bas-relief from Sarcophagus of King Ahiram — D9

D10

1930-40 Photo.; Engr. (No. J35)

J29	D4	50c black, *rose*	.30	.25
J30	D5	1p blk, *gray bl*	.60	.40
J31	D6	2p blk, *yellow*	.80	.60
J32	D7	3p blk, *bl grn*	.80	.60
J33	D8	5p blk, *orange*	3.75	2.50
J34	D9	8p blk, *lt rose*	2.50	1.75
J35	D8	10p dk green ('40)	4.00	2.25
J36	D10	15p black	3.25	1.50
		Nos. J29-J36 (8)	16.00	9.85
		Set, never hinged	60.00	

Nos. J29-J36 exist imperf.

LEEWARD ISLANDS

'lē-wərd 'ī-lənds

LOCATION — A group of islands in the West Indies, southeast of Puerto Rico
GOVT. — British Colony
AREA — 423 sq. mi.
POP. — 108,847 (1946)
CAPITAL — St. John

While stamps inscribed "Leeward Islands" were in use, 1890-1956, the colony consisted of the presidencies (now colonies) of Antigua, Montserrat, St. Christopher (St. Kitts) with Nevis and Anguilla, the British Virgin Islands and Dominica (which became a separate colony in 1940).

Each presidency issued its own stamps, using them along with the Leeward Islands general issues.

12 Pence = 1 Shilling
20 Shillings = 1 Pound

Catalogue values for unused stamps in this country are for Never Hinged items, beginning with Scott 116.

Queen Victoria — A1

1890 Typo. Wmk. 2 *Perf. 14*

1	A1	½p lilac & green	3.75	1.40
2	A1	1p lilac & car	4.00	.20
3	A1	2½p lilac & ultra	5.00	.30
4	A1	4p lilac & org	5.00	8.25
5	A1	6p lilac & brown	12.00	13.00
6	A1	7p lilac & slate	4.75	12.00
7	A1	1sh green & car	21.00	52.50
8	A1	5sh green & ultra	135.00	275.00
		Nos. 1-8 (8)	190.50	362.65
		Set, ovptd. "SPECIMEN"	225.00	

Denomination of Nos. 7-8 are in color on plain tablet: "ONE SHILLING" or "FIVE SHILLINGS."

For overprints and surcharges see Nos. 9-19.

Jubilee Issue

Regular Issue of 1890 Handstamp Overprinted

1897, July 22

9	A1	½p lilac & green	4.50	15.00
10	A1	1p lilac & car	5.25	15.00
11	A1	2½p lilac & ultra	5.50	15.00
12	A1	4p lilac & org	40.00	80.00
13	A1	6p lilac & brown	55.00	105.00
14	A1	7p lilac & slate	55.00	105.00
15	A1	1sh green & car	130.00	220.00
16	A1	5sh green & ultra	525.00	850.00
		Nos. 9-16 (8)	820.25	1,405.

Double Overprints

9a	A1	½p	1,350.
10a	A1	1p	1,150.
	b.	Triple overprint	3,750.
11a	A1	2½p	1,350.
12a	A1	4p	1,350.
13a	A1	6p	1,600.
14a	A1	7p	1,600.
15a	A1	1sh	2,100.
16a	A1	5sh	5,750.

60th year of Queen Victoria's reign. Excellent counterfeits of Nos. 9-16 exist.

Stamps of 1890 Surcharged in Black or Red:

b

c

1902, Aug.

17	A1(b)	1p on 4p lilac & org	3.25	5.25
a.		Tall narrow "O" in "One"	37.50	72.50
18	A1(b)	1p on 6p lilac & brn	4.25	11.50
a.		Tall narrow "O" in "One"	52.50	125.00
19	A1(c)	1p on 7p lilac & sl	3.75	7.25
		Nos. 17-19 (3)	11.25	24.00

King Edward VII — A4

Numerals of ¼p, 2p, 3p and 2sh6p of type A4 are in color on plain tablet. The 1sh and 5sh denominations are expressed as "ONE SHILLING" and "FIVE SHILLINGS" on plain tablet.

1902

20	A4	½p violet & green	6.00	1.10
21	A4	1p vio & car rose	7.50	.20
22	A4	2p violet & bister	3.00	4.50
23	A4	2½p violet & ultra	6.00	2.50
24	A4	3p violet & black	5.00	8.00
25	A4	6p violet & brown	2.75	8.50
26	A4	1sh grn & car rose	3.75	20.00
27	A4	2sh6p green & blk	29.00	75.00
28	A4	5sh green & ultra	50.00	80.00
		Nos. 20-28 (9)	113.00	199.80
		Set, ovptd. "SPECIMEN"	160.00	

1905-11 Wmk. 3

Chalky Paper

29	A4	½p vio & grn ('06)	3.75	2.25
30	A4	1p vio & car rose	9.00	.90
31	A4	2p vio & bis ('08)	5.25	15.00
32	A4	2½p vio & ultra	65.00	35.00
33	A4	3p violet & black	13.00	42.50
34	A4	3p violet, *yel* ('10)	3.75	8.00
35	A4	6p vio & brn ('08)	42.50	75.00
36	A4	6p violet & red violet ('11)	9.00	7.50
37	A4	1sh grn & car rose ('08)	45.00	110.00
38	A4	1sh blk, *grn* ('11)	6.00	22.50
39	A4	2sh6p blk & red, *blue* ('11)	42.50	50.00
40	A4	5sh grn & red, *yel* ('11)	45.00	70.00
		Nos. 29-40 (12)	289.75	438.65

Nos. 29 and 33 are valued on ordinary paper. Values on chalky paper; No. 29, $20 unused, $12 unused; No. 33, $42.50 unused, *$75* used.

1907-11

Ordinary Paper

41	A4	¼p brown ('09)	3.00	1.90
42	A4	½p green	3.75	1.40
43	A4	1p red	11.00	.85
a.		1p rose carmine	40.00	3.75
44	A4	2p gray ('11)	3.75	8.00
45	A4	2½p ultramarine	7.50	4.50
		Nos. 41-45 (5)	29.00	16.65

A5

King George V — A6

For description of dies I and II, see "Dies of British Colonial Stamps" in Table of Contents.

The ½p, 1p, 2½p and 6p denominations of type A5 show the numeral on horizontally-lined tablet. The 1sh and 5sh denominations are expressed as "ONE SHILLING" and "FIVE SHILLINGS" on plain tablet.

Die I

1912

Ordinary Paper

46	A5	¼p brown	1.90	1.10
47	A5	½p green	5.25	1.75
48	A5	1p carmine	5.25	1.10
a.		1p scarlet	6.75	1.10
49	A5	2p gray	4.25	5.75
50	A5	2½p ultramarine	3.50	7.25
		Nos. 46-50 (5)	20.15	16.95

1912-22

Chalky Paper

51	A5	3p violet, *yel*	1.90	11.00
52	A5	4p blk & red, *yel* (Die II) ('22)	4.00	22.50
53	A5	6p vio & red vio	3.25	8.50
54	A5	1sh blk, *bl grn, ol back*	9.50	8.50
a.		1sh black, *green*	3.25	8.50
55	A5	2sh vio & ultra, *bl* (Die II) ('22)	9.00	57.50
56	A5	2sh6p black & red, *blue* ('14)	13.00	40.00
57	A5	5sh green & red, *yellow* ('14)	55.00	100.00
		Nos. 46-57 (12)	115.80	264.95
		Set, ovptd. "SPECIMEN"	300.00	

1914

Surface-colored Paper

58	A5	3p violet, *yel*	67.50	125.00
59	A5	1sh black, *green*	55.00	40.00
60	A5	5sh green & red, *yel*	45.00	85.00
		Nos. 58-60 (3)	167.50	250.00

Die II

1921-32 Wmk. 4

Ordinary Paper

61	A5	¼p dk brown ('22)	2.50	1.10
a.		¼p dark brown (I) ('32)	6.25	17.00
62	A5	½p green	1.10	.80
a.		½p green (I) ('32)	27.50	32.50
63	A5	1p carmine	2.50	.60
a.		1p rose red (I) ('32)	26.00	.55
64	A5	1p dp violet ('22)	2.50	1.10
65	A5	1½p rose red ('26)	3.50	2.10
66	A5	1½p red brn ('29)	1.40	.20
a.		1½p red brown (I) ('32)	4.50	3.00
68	A5	2p gray ('22)	2.10	.85
69	A5	2½p orange ('23)	6.75	52.50
70	A5	2½p ultra ('27)	3.75	1.40
a.		Die I ('32)	7.50	3.75
71	A5	3p ultra ('23)	5.00	27.50

Chalky Paper

72	A5	3p violet, *yel*	1.60	6.75
73	A5	4p black & red, *yel* ('23)	3.25	22.50
74	A5	5p vio & olive grn ('22)	2.75	4.50
75	A5	6p vio & red vio ('23)	20.00	85.00
a.		Die I ('32)	6.75	8.50
76	A5	1sh blk, *emerald* ('23)	6.75	8.50
a.		1sh black, *green* (I) ('32)	52.50	80.00
77	A5	2sh vio & ultra, *bl* ('22)	17.50	42.50
78	A5	2sh6p blk & red, *bl* ('23)	6.75	24.00
79	A5	3sh green & vio	12.50	26.00
80	A5	4sh black & scar	12.50	42.50
81	A5	5sh grn & red, *yel*	40.00	75.00
82	A6	10sh red & grn, *emer* ('28)	60.00	90.00

Wmk. 3

83	A6	£1 black & vio, *red* ('28)	240.00	275.00
		Nos. 61-66,68-83 (22)	454.70	790.40

Common Design Types pictured following the introduction.

Silver Jubilee Issue
Common Design Type

Perf. 11x12

1935, May 6 Engr. Wmk. 4

96	CD301	1p car & dk blue	1.00	2.00
97	CD301	1½p blk & ultra	2.00	1.00
98	CD301	2½p ultra & brn	3.00	3.00
99	CD301	1sh brn vio & ind	7.50	11.00
		Nos. 96-99 (4)	13.50	17.00
		Set, never hinged	24.00	
		Set, perf "SPECIMEN"	105.00	

Coronation Issue
Common Design Type

1937, May 12 ***Perf. 13½x14***

100	CD302	1p carmine	.20	.20
101	CD302	1½p brown	.20	.25
102	CD302	2½p bright ultra	.45	.35
		Nos. 100-102 (3)	.85	.80
		Set, never hinged	1.75	
		Set, perf "SPECIMEN"	80.00	

King George VI

A7 A8

1938-51 Typo. ***Perf. 14***

103	A7	¼p brown	.20	.65
104	A7	½p green	.35	.35
105	A7	1p carmine	.55	2.75
a.		1p scarlet ('42)	.95	.95
106	A7	1½p red brown	.70	.25
107	A7	2p gray	1.40	.75
108	A7	2½p ultramarine	.35	*.85*
109	A7	3p dl org ('42)	.25	*.75*
a.		3p brown orange	22.50	2.50
110	A7	6p vio & red vio	2.75	2.10
111	A7	1sh blk, *emerald*	3.00	1.00
112	A7	2sh vio & ultra, *bl*	5.50	1.40
113	A7	5sh grn & red, *yel*	22.50	*15.00*
114	A8	10sh red & grn, *emer*	70.00	65.00

Two dies were used for the 1p, differing in thickness of shading line at base of "1."

Wmk. 3 ***Perf. 13***

115	A8	£1 blk & vio, *scar* ('51)	32.50	*40.00*
a.		£1 black & brown purple, *red*, perf. 14	225.00	175.00
		Never hinged	350.00	
b.		£1 black & purple, *carmine*, perf. 14 ('41)	30.00	22.50
		Never hinged	55.00	
c.		£1 black & brown purple, *salmon*, perf. 14 ('43)	27.50	27.50
		Never hinged	40.00	
d.		Wmkd. sideways (as #115, perf. 13)	*2,200.*	
		Never hinged	3,300.	
		Nos. 103-115 (13)	140.05	130.85
		Set, never hinged	225.00	

The 3p-£1 were issued on chalky paper in 1938 and on ordinary paper in 1942. Values are for the most common varieties.

Issued: #115, 12/13/51; others, 11/25/38.

See Nos. 120-125.

Catalogue values for unused stamps in this section, from this point to the end of the section, are for Never Hinged items.

Peace Issue
Common Design Type

Perf. 13½x14

1946, Nov. 1 Wmk. 4 Engr.

116	CD303	1½p brown	.25	.25
117	CD303	3p deep orange	.25	.25
		Set, perf "SPECIMEN"	75.00	

Silver Wedding Issue
Common Design Types

1949, Jan. 2 Photo. ***Perf. 14x14½***

118	CD304	2½p bright ultra	.20	.20

Perf. 11½x11

Engr.; Name Typographed

119	CD305	5sh green	5.25	4.50

George VI Type of 1938

1949, July 1 Typo. ***Perf. 13½x14***

120	A7	½p gray	.25	.65
121	A7	1p green	.55	.20
122	A7	1½p orange & black	.55	.20
123	A7	2p crimson rose	1.40	.65
124	A7	2½p black & plum	.55	.20
125	A7	3p ultramarine	.65	.20
		Nos. 120-125 (6)	3.95	2.10

UPU Issue
Common Design Types

Engr.; Name Typo. on 3p and 6p

1949, Oct. 10 ***Perf. 13½, 11x11½***

126	CD306	2½p slate	.20	.65
127	CD307	3p indigo	1.60	.90
128	CD308	6p red lilac	.65	.90
129	CD309	1sh blue green	.75	.90
		Nos. 126-129 (4)	3.20	3.35

University Issue
Common Design Types

Perf. 14x14½

1951, Feb. 16 Engr. Wmk. 4

130	CD310	3c gray black & org	.35	.45
131	CD311	12c lilac & rose car	1.00	.90

LIBERIA

lī-'bir-ē-ə

LOCATION — West coast of Africa, between Ivory Coast and Sierra Leone
GOVT. — Republic
AREA — 43,000 sq. mi.
POP. — 1,900,000 (est. 1984)
CAPITAL — Monrovia

100 Cents = 1 Dollar

Values for unused stamps are for examples with original gum as defined in the catalogue introduction. Any exceptions will be noted. Very fine examples of Nos. 1-3, 13-21 and 157-159 will have perforations just clear of the design due to the narrow spacing of the stamps on the plates and/or imperfect perforating methods.

Watermarks

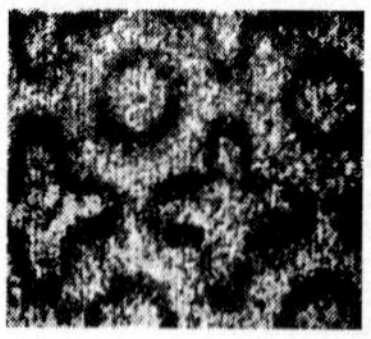

Wmk. 116 — Crosses and Circles

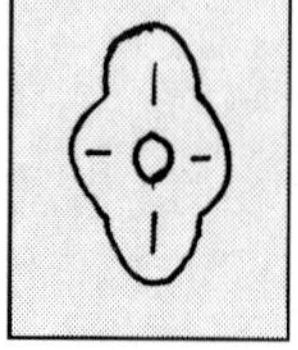

Wmk. 143

"Liberia" — A1

1860 Unwmk. Litho. ***Perf. 12***

Thick Paper

1	A1	6c red	400.00	*300.00*
a.		Imperf, pair	500.00	
2	A1	12c deep blue	22.50	*50.00*
a.		Imperf, pair	250.00	
3	A1	24c green	50.00	*50.00*
a.		Imperf, pair	300.00	
		Nos. 1-3 (3)	472.50	*400.00*

Stamps set very close together. Copies of the 12c occasionally show traces of a frame line around the design.

Medium to Thin Paper

With a single-line frame around each stamp, about 1mm from the border

1864 ***Perf. 11, 12***

7	A1	6c red	62.50	*77.50*
a.		Imperf, pair	200.00	
8	A1	12c blue	72.50	*87.50*
a.		Imperf, pair	200.00	
9	A1	24c lt green	82.50	*95.00*
a.		Imperf, pair	200.00	
		Nos. 7-9 (3)	217.50	*260.00*

Stamps set about 5mm apart. Margins large and perforation usually outside the frame line.

Without Frame Line

1866-69

13	A1	6c lt red	20.00	30.00
14	A1	12c lt blue	20.00	30.00
15	A1	24c lt yellow grn	20.00	30.00
		Nos. 13-15 (3)	60.00	90.00

Stamps set 2-2½mm apart with small margins. Stamps are usually without frame line but those from one transfer show broken and irregular parts of a frame.

With Frame Line

1880 ***Perf. 10½***

16	A1	1c ultra	5.00	7.50
17	A1	2c rose	5.00	*5.25*
a.		Imperf, pair	175.00	
18	A1	6c violet	5.00	5.25
19	A1	12c yellow	5.00	*5.25*
20	A1	24c rose red	5.00	5.25
		Nos. 16-20 (5)	25.00	28.50

Unused values for Nos. 16-20 are for copies without gum.

For surcharges see Nos. 157-159.

Counterfeits

Counterfeits exist of Nos. 1-28, 32 and 64.

From Arms of Liberia — A2

1881

21	A2	3c black	10.00	10.00

Unused value is for copies without gum.

A3

A4

1882 ***Perf. 11½, 12, 14***

22	A3	8c blue	50.00	10.00
23	A4	16c red	8.00	5.00

On No. 22 the openings in the figure "8" enclose a pattern of slanting lines. Compare with No. 32.

Canceled to Order

Beginning with the issue of 1885, values in the used column are for "canceled to order" stamps. Postally used copies sell for much more.

A5

A6

From Arms of Liberia — A7

A8

Perf. 10½, 11, 12, 11½x10½, 14, 14½

1885

24	A5	1c carmine	2.00	2.00
a.		1c rose	2.00	2.00
25	A5	2c green	2.00	2.00
26	A5	3c violet	2.00	2.00
27	A5	4c brown	2.00	2.00
28	A5	6c olive gray	2.00	2.00
29	A6	8c bluish gray	4.00	4.00
a.		8c lilac	7.00	7.00
30	A6	16c yellow	12.00	12.00
31	A7	32c deep blue	29.00	29.00
		Nos. 24-31 (8)	55.00	55.00

In the 1885 printing, the stamps are spaced 2mm apart and the paper is medium. In the 1892 printing, the stamps are 4½mm apart.

For surcharges see Nos. J1-J2.

Imperf., Pair

24b	A5	1c	3.00	
25a	A5	2c	4.25	
26a	A5	3c	5.00	
27a	A5	4c	5.00	
28a	A5	6c	4.25	4.25
29b	A6	8c	12.50	
30a	A6	16c	15.00	
31a	A7	32c	30.00	

Imperf. pairs with 2mm spacing sell for higher prices.

1889 ***Perf. 12, 14***

32	A8	8c blue	4.25	4.25
a.		Imperf., pair	20.00	

The openings in the figure "8" are filled with network. See No. 22.

A9

Elephant — A10

Oil Palm — A11

Pres. Hilary R. W. Johnson — A12

Vai Woman in Full Dress — A13

Coat of Arms — A14

Liberian Star — A15

Coat of Arms — A16

Hippopotamus
A17

Liberian
Star — A18

President
Johnson — A19

1892-96 Wmk. 143 Engr. *Perf. 15*

33 A9 1c vermilion .50 .40
a. 1c blue (error) 40.00
34 A9 2c blue .50 .40
a. 2c vermilion (error) 40.00
35 A10 4c green & blk 1.75 1.00
a. Center inverted 100.00
36 A11 6c blue green .70 .50
37 A12 8c brown & blk .95 .95
a. Center inverted 450.00 450.00
b. Center sideways 450.00
38 A12 10c chrome yel & indigo ('96) .95 .65
39 A13 12c rose red .95 .65
40 A13 15c slate ('96) .95 .65
41 A14 16c lilac 3.50 1.75
a. 16c deep greenish blue (error) 110.00
42 A14 20c vermilion ('96) 3.50 1.75
43 A15 24c ol grn, *yel* 2.00 1.10
44 A15 25c yel grn ('96) 2.00 1.40
45 A16 30c steel bl ('96) 6.25 4.50
46 A16 32c grnsh blue 3.50 2.75
a. 32c lilac (error) *110.00*
47 A17 $1 ultra & blk 10.00 9.00
a. $1 blue & black 11.00 11.00
48 A18 $2 brown, *yel* 9.00 8.00
49 A19 $5 carmine & blk 10.00 10.00
a. Center inverted 325.00 325.00
Nos. 33-49 (17) 57.00 45.45

Many imperforates, part-perforated and misperforated varieties exist.

The 1c, 2c and 4c were issued in sheets of 60; 6c, sheet of 40; 8c, 10c, sheets of 30; 12c, 15c, 24c, 25c, sheets of 20; 16c, 20c, 30c, sheets of 15; $1, $2, $5, sheets of 10.

For overprints & surcharges see #50, 64B-64F, 66, 71-77, 79-81, 85-93, 95-100, 160, O1-O13, O15-O25, O37-O41, O44-O45.

No. 36 Surcharged:

a

5 5

Five
Cents
b

1893

50 A11 (a) 5c on 6c blue grn 1.75 1.10
a. "5" with short flag 6.00 6.00
b. Both 5's with short flags 5.00 5.00
c. "i" dot omitted 19.00 19.00
d. Surcharge "b" 30.00 30.00

"Commerce," Globe and
Krumen — A22

1894 Unwmk. Engr. *Imperf.*

52 A22 5c carmine & blk 5.00 5.00

Rouletted

53 A22 5c carmine & blk 10.00 7.50

For overprints see Nos. 69, O26-O27.

Oil Palm
A23

Hippopotamus
A24

Elephant — A25

Liberty — A26

1897-1905 Wmk. 143 *Perf. 14 to 16*

54 A23 1c lilac rose 1.00 .65
a. 1c violet 1.00 .65
55 A23 1c deep green ('00) 1.25 .95
56 A23 1c lt green ('05) 3.00 1.60
57 A24 2c bister & blk 2.50 1.60
58 A24 2c org red & blk ('00) 5.00 2.10
59 A24 2c rose & blk ('05) 2.50 1.60
60 A25 5c lake & black 2.50 1.60
a. 5c lilac rose & black 2.50 1.60
61 A25 5c gray bl & blk ('00) 5.00 5.00
62 A25 5c ultra & blk ('05) 3.50 2.75
a. Center inverted 700.00
63 A26 50c red brn & blk 3.25 3.50
Nos. 54-63 (10) 29.50 21.35

For overprints & surcharges see #65, 66A-68. 70, 78, 82-84, M1, O28-O36, O42, O92.

A27

Two types:
I — 13 pearls above "Republic Liberia."
II — 10 pearls.

1897 Unwmk. Litho. *Perf. 14*

64 A27 3c red & green (I) .25 *.60*
a. Type II *10.00* .20

No. 64a is considered a reprint, unissued. "Used" copies are CTO.

For surcharge see No. 128.

Official Stamps
Handstamped in Black ORDINARY

1901-02 Wmk. 143

On Nos. O7-O8, O10-O12

64B A14 16c lilac *500.00 500.00*
64C A15 24c ol grn, *yel* *400.00 400.00*
64D A17 $1 blue & blk *2,000. 2,000.*
64E A18 $2 brown, *yel*
64F A19 $5 carmine & blk

On Stamps with "O S" Printed

65 A23 1c green *35.00 40.00*
66 A9 2c blue *95.00 100.00*
66A A24 2c bister & blk — *150.00*
67 A24 2c org red & blk *40.00 40.00*
68 A25 5c gray bl & blk *35.00 35.00*
69 A22 5c vio & grn (No. O26) *275.00 300.00*
70 A25 5c lake & blk *225.00 225.00*
71 A12 10c yel & blue blk *35.00 60.00*
a. "O S" omitted
72 A13 15c slate *35.00 60.00*
73 A14 16c lilac *300.00 300.00*
74 A14 20c vermilion *40.00 50.00*
75 A15 24c ol grn,*yel* *50.00 50.00*
76 A15 25c yellow grn *40.00 50.00*
a. "O S" omitted
77 A16 30c steel blue *40.00 40.00*
78 A26 50c red brn & blk *47.50 52.50*
79 A17 $1 ultra & blk *275.00 275.00*
a. "O S" omitted
80 A18 $2 brn, *yel* *1,800. 1,800.*
81 A19 $5 car & blk *2,000. 2,000.*
a. "O S" omitted *2,750. 2,750.*

On Stamps with "O S" Handstamped

82 A23 1c deep green 62.50
83 A24 2c org red & blk 75.00
84 A25 5c lake & blk 125.00
85 A12 10c yel & bl blk 110.00
86 A14 20c vermilion 125.00
87 A15 24c ol grn, *yel* 125.00
88 A15 25c yel grn 150.00
89 A16 30c steel blue 500.00
90 A16 32c grnsh blue 200.00

Varieties of Nos. 65-90 include double and inverted overprints.

Nos. 47, O10, O23a
Surcharged in
Carmine

1902

91 A17 75c on $1 #47 15.00 13.00
a. Thin "C" and comma 19.00 19.00
b. Inverted surcharge 62.50 62.50
c. As "a," inverted
92 A17 75c on $1 #O10 *2,500.*
a. Thin "C" and comma *3,500.*
93 A17 75c on $1 #O23a *2,700.*
a. Thin "C" and comma *3,500.*

Liberty — A29

1903 Unwmk. Engr. *Perf. 14*

94 A29 3c black .30 .20
a. Printed on both sides 45.00
b. Perf. 12 20.00 6.00

For overprint see No. O43.

Stamps of 1892 Surcharged in Blue

a

b

1903 Wmk. 143

95 A14 (a) 10c on 16c lilac 3.00 4.00
96 A15 (b) 15c on 24c ol grn, *yel* 4.50 5.50
97 A16 (b) 20c on 32c grnsh bl 6.25 7.75
Nos. 95-97 (3) 13.75 17.25

Nos. 50, O3 and 45 Surcharged in
Black or Red

1904

98 A11 1c on 5c on 6c bl grn .60 .55
a. "5" with short flag 4.25 4.25
b. Both 5's with short flags 8.75 8.75
c. "i" dot omitted 10.00 10.00
d. Surcharge on #50d 12.50 12.50
e. Inverted surcharge 6.75 6.75
99 A10 2c on 4c grn & blk 1.50 2.75
a. Pair, one without surcharge 35.00
b. Double surcharge
c. Double surcharge, red and blk 62.50
d. Surcharged on back also 19.00
e. "Official" overprint missing 30.00
100 A16 2c on 30c stl bl (R) 8.75 14.00
Nos. 98-100 (3) 10.85 17.30

African
Elephant — A33

Mercury — A34

Chimpanzee
A35

Great Blue
Touraco — A36

Agama — A37

Egret — A38

Head of Liberty
From Coin — A39

A40

Liberian
Flag — A41

Pygmy
Hippopotamus
A42

Liberty with Star
of Liberia on
Cap — A43

Mandingos — A44

Executive Mansion and Pres. Arthur Barclay — A45

1906 Unwmk. Engr. *Perf. 14*

101	A33	1c green & blk	1.25	.40
102	A34	2c carmine & blk	.25	.20
103	A35	5c ultra & blk	2.25	.55
104	A36	10c red brn & blk	3.50	.55
105	A37	15c pur & dp grn	12.00	2.50
106	A38	20c orange & blk	8.50	1.75
107	A39	25c dull blue & gray	.75	.20
108	A40	30c deep violet	.85	.20
109	A41	50c dp green & blk	.85	.20
110	A42	75c brown & blk	10.00	1.75
111	A43	$1 rose & gray	2.50	.20
112	A44	$2 dp green & blk	3.75	.30
113	A45	$5 red brown & blk	7.75	.40
		Nos. 101-113 (13)	54.20	9.20

For surcharges see Nos. 114, 129, 130, 141, 145-149, 161, M2, M5, O72-O73, O82-O85, O96. For overprints see Nos. O46-O58.

Center Inverted

101a	A33	1c	37.50	37.50
102a	A34	2c	27.50	27.50
103a	A35	5c	125.00	125.00
104a	A36	10c	57.50	57.50
105a	A37	15c	125.00	125.00
106b	A38	20c	125.00	125.00
107a	A39	25c	55.00	55.00
109b	A41	50c	55.00	55.00
110b	A42	75c	92.50	92.50
111a	A43	$1	75.00	75.00
112a	A44	$2	72.50	72.50

Imperf., Pairs

101b	A33	1c	11.00	
102b	A34	2c	4.50	
106a	A38	20c	17.00	
107b	A39	25c	45.00	45.00
109a	A41	50c	17.00	
110a	A42	75c	17.00	
113a	A45	$5	22.50	

No. 104 Surcharged in Black

1909

114 A36 3c on 10c red brn & blk 4.50 4.50

Coffee Plantation — A46

Pres. Barclay — A47

S. S. Pres. Daniel E. Howard, former Gunboat Lark — A48

Commerce with Caduceus — A49

Vai Woman Spinning Cotton — A50

Blossom and Fruit of Pepper Plants — A51

Circular House — A52

President Barclay — A53

Men in Canoe — A54

Liberian Village — A55

1909-12 ***Perf. 14***

115	A46	1c yel grn & blk	.45	.35
116	A47	2c lake & blk	.45	.35
117	A48	5c ultra & blk	.45	.35
118	A49	10c plum & blk, perf. 12½ ('12)	.45	.35
a.		Imperf., pair	12.00	
b.		Perf 14 ('12)	1.40	1.40
c.		As "b," pair, imperf between	18.00	
d.		Perf 12½x14	1.75	1.40
119	A50	15c indigo & blk	2.25	.40
120	A51	20c rose & grn	2.75	.40
b.		Imperf.		
121	A52	25c dk brn & blk	.90	.40
a.		Imperf.		
122	A53	30c dark brown	2.75	.40
123	A54	50c green & blk	2.75	.40
124	A55	75c red brn & blk	2.75	.40
		Nos. 115-124 (10)	15.95	3.80

Rouletted

125 A49 10c plum & blk .75 .45

For surcharges see Nos. 126-127E, 131-133, 136-140, 142-144, 151-156, 162, B1-B2, M3-M4, M6-M7, O70-O1, O74-O81, O86-O91, O97.

For overprints see Nos. O59-O69.

Center Inverted

116a	A47	2c	70.00	60.00
117a	A48	5c	62.50	55.00
119a	A50	15c	47.50	47.50
120a	A51	20c	70.00	55.00
121b	A52	25c	47.50	42.50
123a	A54	50c	75.00	62.50

Stamps and Types of 1909-12 Surcharged in Blue or Red

1910-12 ***Rouletted***

126	A49	3c on 10c plum & blk (Bl)	.40	.25
a.		"3" inverted		
126B	A49	3c on 10c blk & ultra (R)	30.00	5.00

#126B is roulette 7. It also exists in roulette 13.

Perf. 12½, 14, 12½x14

127	A49	3c on 10c plum & blk (Bl) ('12)	.40	.25
a.		Imperf., pair	22.50	
b.		Double surcharge, one invtd.	22.50	
c.		Double vertical surcharge		
127E	A49	3c on 10c blk & ultra (R) ('12)	17.00	.55
		Nos. 126-127E (4)	47.80	6.05

Nos. 64, 64a Surcharged in Dark Green

1913

128	A27	8c on 3c red & grn (I)	.30	.20
a.		Surcharge on No. 64a	3.00	.20
b.		Double surcharge	6.25	
c.		Imperf., pair	20.00	
d.		Inverted surcharge	25.00	

Stamps of Preceding Issues Surcharged

a

b

1914

On Issue of 1906

129	A39 (a)	2c on 25c dl bl & gray	7.50	2.25
130	A40 (b)	5c on 30c dp violet	7.50	2.25

On Issue of 1909

131	A52 (a)	2c on 25c brn & blk	7.50	2.25
132	A53 (b)	5c on 30c dk brown	7.50	2.25
133	A54 (a)	10c on 50c grn & blk	7.50	2.25
		Nos. 129-133 (5)	37.50	11.25

Liberian House A57

Providence Island, Monrovia Harbor A58

1915 Engr. Wmk. 116 *Perf. 14*

134	A57	2c red	.20	.20
135	A58	3c dull violet	.20	.20

For overprints see Nos. 196-197, O113-O114, O128-O129.

Nos. 109, 111-113, 119-124 Surcharged with New Values in Dark Blue, Black or Red:

c

d

e

f

g

1915-16 Unwmk.

136	A50 (c)	2c on 15c (R)	.90	.90
137	A52 (d)	2c on 25c (R)	8.00	8.00
138	A51 (e)	5c on 20c (Bk)	1.10	5.75
139	A53 (f)	5c on 30c (R)	4.50	4.50
a.		Double surcharge	14.00	14.00
140	A53 (g)	5c on 30c (R)	40.00	40.00

h

i

141	A41 (h)	10c on 50c (R)	8.00	8.00
a.		Double surch., one invtd.		
142	A54 (i)	10c on 50c (R)	14.00	14.00
a.		Double surcharge red & blk	35.00	35.00
b.		Blue surcharge	35.00	35.00
143	A54 (i)	10c on 50c (Bk)	20.00	15.00

j

k

144	A55 (j)	20c on 75c (Bk)	3.50	5.75
145	A43 (k)	25c on $1 (Bk)	42.50	42.50

l

50

Cents

m

146	A44 (l)	50c on $2 (R)	11.00	11.00
a.		"Ceuts"	22.50	22.50
147	A44 (m)	50c on $2 (R)	800.00	800.00

n

1

=

148	A45	$1 on $5 (Bk)	65.00	65.00
a.		Double surcharge	90.00	90.00

o

149 A45 $1 on $5 (R) 52.50 52.50

The color of the red surcharge varies from light dull red to almost brown.

Handstamped Surcharge, Type "i"

150 A54 10c on 50c (Dk Bl) 14.00 14.00

No. 119 Surcharged in Black

2

151 A50 2c on 15c 400.00 400.00

No. 119 Surcharged in Red

152 A50 2c on 15c 45.00 40.00
a. Double surcharge 92.50

Nos. 116-117 Surcharged in Black or Red

a1: 1
b1: 1c
c1: one cemt
d1: 1ct
e1: one one
f1: 1c (inverted)
g1: 1cent * * * * * *
h1: 1 c 1
i1: one c one
j1: 1cts
k2: Two cemts
l2: Two cents
m2: 2cents
n2: Two cts (inverted)
o2: 2c

p2: 2. 2.
q2: two c two
r2: 2 2
s2: two
t2: 2cent

153 A47 1c on 2c lake & blk 2.50 2.50
a. Strip of 10 types 35.00
154 A48 2c on 5c ultra & blk (R) 2.50 2.50
a. Black surcharge 14.00 14.00
b. Strip of 10 types (R) 35.00
c. Strip of 10 types (Bk) 165.00

The 10 types of surcharge are repeated in illustrated sequence on 1c on 2c in each horiz. row and on 2c on 5c in each vert. row of sheets of 100 (10x10).

No. 116 and Type of 1909 Surcharged:

one ct.

155 A47 1c on 2c lake & blk 190.00 190.00

2ct

156 A48 2c on 5c turq & blk 140.00 140.00

Nos. 18-20 Surcharged

1916

157 A1 3c on 6c violet 42.50 42.50
a. Inverted surcharge 75.00 75.00
158 A1 5c on 12c yellow 3.00 3.00
a. Inverted surcharge 12.50 12.50
b. Surcharge sideways 12.50
159 A1 10c on 24c rose red 2.75 3.00
a. Inverted surcharge 15.00 15.00
b. Surcharge sideways
Nos. 157-159 (3) 48.25 48.50

Unused values for Nos. 157-159 are for copies without gum.

Nos. 44 and 108 Surcharged

p

1917 FIVE II CENTS

r

1917 **Wmk. 143**

160 A15 (p) 4c on 25c yel grn 11.00 11.00
a. "OUR" 25.00 25.00
b. "FCUR" 25.00 25.00

Unwmk.

161 A40 (r) 5c on 30c dp vio 90.00 90.00

No. 118 Surcharged in Red

1918

162 A49 3c on 10c plum & blk 2.25 2.25
a. "3" inverted 9.25 9.25

Bongo Antelope — A59

Symbols of Liberia — A61

Two-spot Palm Civet A60

A62

Palm-nut Vulture — A66

Oil Palm — A63

Mercury — A64

Traveler's Tree — A65

"Mudskipper" or Bommi Fish — A67

Mandingos A68

"Liberia" A71

Coast Scene A69

Liberia College A70

1918 **Engr.** ***Perf. 12½, 14***

163	A59	1c dp grn & blk	.55	.20
164	A60	2c rose & blk	.70	.20
165	A61	5c gray bl & blk	.20	.20
166	A62	10c dark green	.20	.20
167	A63	15c blk & dk grn	2.50	.20
168	A64	20c claret & blk	.30	.20
169	A65	25c dk grn & grn	2.75	.20
170	A66	30c red vio & blk	12.50	.70
171	A67	50c ultra & blk	22.50	3.00
172	A68	75c ol bis & blk	.75	.20
173	A69	$1 yel brn & bl	6.00	.20
174	A70	$2 lt vio & blk	5.50	.20
175	A71	$5 dark brown	5.75	.35
		Nos. 163-175 (13)	60.20	6.05

For surcharges see Nos. 176-177, 228-229, 248-270, B3-B15, O111-O112, O155-O157.
For overprints see Nos. O98-O110.

Nos. 163-164, F10-F14 Surcharged

1920

176 A59 3c on 1c grn & blk 1.00 1.00
a. "CEETS" 17.00 17.00
b. Double surcharge 10.00 10.00
c. Triple surcharge 15.00 15.00
177 A60 4c on 2c rose & blk 1.00 1.00
a. Inverted surcharge 20.00 20.00
b. Double surcharge 10.00 10.00
c. Double surcharge, one invtd. 18.00
d. Triple surcharge, one inverted 25.00 25.00
e. Quadruple surcharge 30.00 30.00
f. Typewritten surcharge
g. Same as "f" but inverted
h. Printed and typewritten surcharges, both inverted
178 R6 5c on 10c bl & blk 2.50 2.50
a. Inverted surcharge 10.00 10.00
b. Double surcharge 10.00 10.00
c. Double surcharge, one invtd. 15.00 15.00
d. Typewritten surcharge ("five") 100.00
e. Printed and typewritten surcharges 100.00
179 R6 5c on 10c org red & blk 2.50 2.50
a. 5c on 10c orange & black 4.00 2.75
b. Inverted surcharge 15.00
c. Double surcharge 15.00
d. Double surcharge, one invtd. 18.00 15.00
e. Typewritten surch. in violet 100.00 100.00
f. Typewritten surch. in black
g. Printed and typewritten surcharges 100.00
180 R6 5c on 10c grn & blk 2.50 2.50
a. Double surcharge 10.00 10.00
b. Double surcharge, one invtd. 18.00 18.00
c. Inverted surcharge 18.00
d. Quadruple surcharge 25.00 25.00
e. Typewritten surcharge 100.00
f. Printed and typewritten surcharges
181 R6 5c on 10c vio & blk (Monrovia) 4.00 4.00
a. Double surcharge, one invtd. 25.00 25.00
182 R6 5c on 10c mag & blk (Robertsport) 2.00 2.00
a. Double surcharge 15.00 15.00
b. Double surcharge, one invtd. 15.00 15.00
c. Double surcharge, both invtd. 25.00
Nos. 176-182 (7) 15.50 15.50

Cape Mesurado A75

Pres. Daniel E. Howard — A76

Arms of Liberia — A77

Crocodile A78

Pepper Plant A79

Leopard A80

Village Scene A81

Krumen in Dugout A82

Rapids in St. Paul's River A83

Bongo Antelope A84

Hornbill A85

Elephant A86

1921 Wmk. 116 *Perf. 14*

183	A75	1c green	.20	.20
184	A76	5c dp bl & blk	.20	.20
185	A77	10c red & dl bl	.20	.20
186	A78	15c dl vio & grn	4.00	.30
187	A79	20c rose red & grn	1.75	.20
188	A80	25c org & blk	4.75	.30
189	A81	30c grn & dl vio	.25	.20
190	A82	50c org & ultra	.30	.20
191	A83	75c red & blk brn	.50	.20
a.		Center inverted		70.00
192	A84	$1 red & blk	20.00	1.10
193	A85	$2 yel & ultra	6.50	.45
194	A86	$5 car rose & vio	20.00	.60
		Nos. 183-194 (12)	58.65	4.15

For overprints see Nos. 195, 198-208, O115-O127, O130-O140.

Nos. 134-135, 183-194 Overprinted "1921"

195	A75	1c green	16.00	.30
196	A57	2c red	16.00	.30
197	A58	3c dull violet	22.50	.30
198	A76	5c dp bl & blk	3.50	.30
199	A77	10c red & dull bl	35.00	.30
200	A78	15c dull vio & grn	16.00	1.00
201	A79	20c rose red & grn, ovpt. invtd.	7.25	.75
202	A80	25c orange & blk	16.00	1.00
203	A81	30c grn & dull vio	2.50	.30
204	A82	50c orange & ultra	3.50	.30
205	A83	75c red & blk brn	4.75	.30
206	A84	$1 red & blk	45.00	1.50
207	A85	$2 yellow & ultra	16.00	1.50
208	A86	$5 car rose & vio	42.50	2.00
		Nos. 195-208 (14)	246.50	10.15

Overprint exists inverted in Nos. 195-208 and normal on No. 201.

First Settlers Landing at Cape Mesurado from U. S. S. Alligator A87

1923 Litho.

209	A87	1c lt blue & blk	14.00	.25
210	A87	2c claret & ol gray	20.00	.25
211	A87	5c ol grn & ind	20.00	.25
212	A87	10c bl grn & vio	.75	.25
213	A87	$1 rose & brn	2.50	.25
		Nos. 209-213 (5)	57.25	1.25

Centenary of founding of Liberia.

Memorial to J. J. Roberts, 1st Pres. — A88

Hall of Representatives, Monrovia — A89

Liberian Star — A90

A91

Pres. Charles Dunbar Burgess King — A92

Hippopotamus — A93

Antelope A94

West African Buffalo A95

Grebos Making Dumboy A96

Pineapple A97

Carrying Ivory Tusk A98

Rubber Planter's House — A99

Stockton Lagoon — A100

Grebo Houses — A101

1923 *Perf. 13½x14½, 14½x13½*

White Paper

214	A88	1c yel grn & dp grn	5.00	.80
215	A89	2c claret & brn	5.00	.20
216	A90	3c lilac & blk	.35	.20
217	A91	5c bl vio & blk	75.00	.20
218	A92	10c slate & brn	.35	.20
219	A93	15c bister & bl	22.50	.35
220	A94	20c bl grn & vio	2.50	.35
221	A95	25c org red & brn	110.00	.40
222	A96	30c dk brn & vio	.60	.20
223	A97	50c dull vio & org	1.25	.20
224	A98	75c gray & bl	1.90	.40
225	A99	$1 dp red & dk vio	30.00	.60
226	A100	$2 orange & blue	5.00	.55
227	A101	$5 dp grn & brn	30.00	.55
		Nos. 214-227 (14)	289.45	5.20

Brownish Paper

222a	A96	30c dk brn & vio	.60	.20
223a	A97	50c dull vio & org	1.00	.20
224a	A98	75c gray & bl	1.90	.45
225a	A99	$1 dp red & dk vio	4.50	.60
226a	A100	$2 orange & blue	5.75	.60
227a	A101	$5 dp grn & brn	12.00	.50

Nos. 222-227 also exist on a light buff paper. Values are the same as for copies on brownish paper.

For overprints see Nos. O141-O154.

No. 163 Surcharged

1926 Unwmk. *Perf. 14*

228	A59	2c on 1c dp grn & blk	2.50	2.50
a.		Surcharge with ornamental design as on #O155	10.50	

No. 163 Surcharged in Red

1927

No.	Type	Description	Unused	Used
229	A59	2c on 1c dp grn & blk	7.00	7.00
a.		"Ceuts"	10.00	
b.		"Vwo"	10.00	
c.		"Twc"	10.00	
d.		Double surcharge	20.00	
e.		Wavy lines omitted	12.50	

Palms A102

Map of Africa — A103

President King — A104

1928 **Engr.** ***Perf. 12***

No.	Type	Description	Unused	Used
230	A102	1c green	.55	.35
231	A102	2c dark violet	.35	.25
232	A102	3c bister brn	.35	.25
233	A103	5c ultra	.75	.40
234	A104	10c olive gray	1.00	.40
235	A103	15c dull violet	4.50	1.65
236	A103	$1 red brown	55.00	19.00
		Nos. 230-236 (7)	62.50	22.30

For surcharges & overprints see Nos. 288A, 289A, 290A-291, 292A, C1-C3, O158-O165.

Nos. 164-168, 170-175 Surcharged in Various Colors and Styles, "1936" and New Values

1936 ***Perf. 12½, 14***

No.	Type	Description	Unused	Used
248	A60	1c on 2c (Bl)	.25	*2.50*
249	A61	3c on 5c (Bl)	.20	*2.00*
250	A62	4c on 10c (Br)	.20	*2.00*
251	A63	6c on 15c (Bl)	.25	*2.50*
252	A64	8c on 20c (V)	.20	*2.00*
253	A66	12c on 30c (V)	.45	*4.50*
254	A67	14c on 50c (Bl)	.50	*5.00*
255	A68	16c on 75c (Br)	.25	*2.50*
256	A69	18c on $1 (Bk)	.25	*2.50*
a.		22c on $1 yellow brown & blue	3.75	
257	A70	22c on $2 (V)	.35	*3.50*
258	A71	24c on $5 (Bk)	.45	*4.50*
		Nos. 248-258 (11)	3.35	33.50

Official Stamps, Nos. O99-O110, Surcharged or Overprinted in various colors and styles with 6 pointed star and "1936"

1936

No.	Type	Description	Unused	Used
259	A60	1c on 2c (Bl)	.20	*4.00*
260	A61	3c on 5c (Bl)	.20	*4.00*
261	A62	4c on 10c (Bl)	.20	*4.00*
262	A63	6c on 15c (Bl)	.20	*4.00*
263	A64	8c on 20c (V)	.20	*4.00*
264	A66	12c on 30c (V)	.35	*10.00*
a.		"193" instead of "1936"	9.50	
265	A67	14c on 50c (Bl)	.45	*11.00*
266	A68	16c on 75c (Bk)	.25	*6.00*
267	A69	18c on $1 (Bk)	.25	*6.00*
268	A70	22c on $2 (Bl)	.30	*7.50*
269	A71	24c on $5 (Bk)	.35	*8.50*
270	A65	25c (Bk)	.45	*11.00*
		Nos. 259-270 (12)	3.40	80.00

Hornbill — A106

Designs: 2c, Bushbuck. 3c, West African dwarf buffalo. 4c, Pygmy hippopotamus. 5c, Lesser egret. 6c, Pres. E. J. Barclay.

Perf. Compound of 11½, 12, 12½, 14

1937, Apr. 10 **Engr.** **Unwmk.**

No.	Type	Description	Unused	Used
271	A106	1c green & blk	.55	.30
272	A106	2c carmine & blk	.55	.20
273	A106	3c violet & blk	.55	.30
274	A106	4c orange & blk	.85	.50
275	A106	5c blue & blk	.85	.35
276	A106	6c green & blk	.30	.20
		Nos. 271-276 (6)	3.65	1.85

Coast Line of Liberia, 1839 — A107

Seal of Liberia, Map and Farming Scenes — A108

Thomas Buchanan and Residence at Bassa Cove — A109

1940, July 29 **Engr.** ***Perf. 12***

No.	Type	Description	Unused	Used
277	A107	3c dark blue	.20	.20
278	A108	5c dull red brn	.20	.20
279	A109	10c dark green	.20	.20
		Nos. 277-279 (3)	.60	.60

100th anniv. of the founding of the Commonwealth of Liberia.

For overprints & surcharges see Nos. 280-282, B16-B18, C14-C16, CB1-CB3, CE1, CF1, E1, F35 in the Scott Standard Catalogue, Vol. 4.

SEMI-POSTAL STAMPS

No. 127 Surcharged in Red

1915 **Unwmk.** ***Perf. 14***

No.	Type	Description	Unused	Used
B1	A49	2c + 3c on 10c	1.00	*3.50*
a.		Double red surcharge		
b.		Double blue surcharge		
c.		Both surcharges double		
d.		Pair, one without "2c"		

Same Surcharge On Official Stamp of 1912

No.	Type	Description	Unused	Used
B2	A49	2c + 3c on 10c blk & ultra	1.00	*3.50*
a.		Double surcharge		

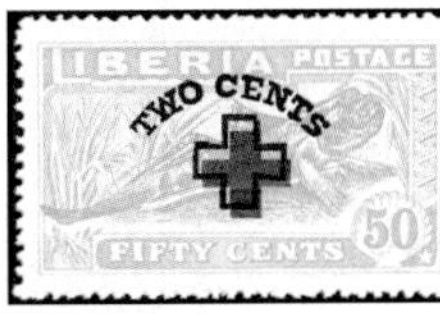

Regular Issue of 1918 Surcharged in Black and Red

1918 ***Perf. 12½, 14***

No.	Type	Description	Unused	Used
B3	A59	1c + 2c dp grn & blk	.65	*5.00*
B4	A60	2c + 2c rose & blk	.65	*5.00*
a.		Double surch., one inverted		
b.		Invtd. surch., cross double		
c.		Invtd. surch., cross omitted	17.00	
B5	A61	5c + 2c gray bl & blk	.30	*1.50*
a.		Imperf., pair	9.25	
B6	A62	10c + 2c dk green	.60	*1.50*
a.		Inverted surcharge	5.75	27.50
B7	A63	15c + 2c blk & dk grn	2.50	5.00
B8	A64	20c + 2c claret & blk	1.00	*4.00*
B9	A65	25c + 2c dk grn & grn	2.00	*7.50*
B10	A66	30c + 2c red vio & blk	5.00	*5.00*
B11	A67	50c + 2c ultra & blk	4.00	*8.00*
B12	A68	75c + 2c ol bis & blk	1.75	*15.00*
B13	A69	$1 + 2c yel brn & bl	3.00	*27.50*
B14	A70	$2 + 2c lt vio & blk	4.00	*38.50*
B15	A71	$5 + 2c dk brown	9.50	*95.00*
		Nos. B3-B15 (13)	34.95	*218.50*

Used values are for postally canceled stamps.

AIR POST STAMPS

Regular Issue of 1928 Surcharged in Black "AIR MAIL" and New Values

1936, Feb. 28 **Unwmk.** ***Perf. 12***

No.	Type	Description	Unused	Used
C1	A102	6c on 2c violet	150.00	*175.00*
C2	A102	6c on 3c bis brn	150.00	*175.00*

Same Surcharge on Official Stamp of 1928

No.	Type	Description	Unused	Used
C3	A102	6c on 1c green	150.00	*175.00*
m.		On No. 230 (error)	*750.00*	
		Nos. C1-C3 (3)	450.00	525.00

Values are for stamps with disturbed gum. Many counterfeits exist.

Waco Plane — AP1

1936, Sept. 30 **Engr.** ***Perf. 14***

No.	Type	Description	Unused	Used
C3A	AP1	1c yellow grn & blk	.20	.20
C3B	AP1	2c carmine & blk	.20	.20
C3C	AP1	3c purple & blk	.20	.20
C3D	AP1	4c orange & blk	.20	.20
C3E	AP1	5c blue & blk	.20	.20
C3F	AP1	6c green & blk	.20	.20
		Nos. C3A-C3F (6)	1.20	1.20

Liberia's 1st air mail service of Feb. 28, 1936.

Nos. C3A-C3F exist in pairs imperf. between (value, $50 each) and in pairs imperf. (value $15 each).

Eagle in Flight — AP2

Sikorsky Amphibian — AP5

Trimotor Plane AP3

Egrets — AP4

Designs: 3c, 30c, Albatross.

1938, Sept. 12 **Photo.** ***Perf. 12½***

No.	Type	Description	Unused	Used
C4	AP2	1c green	.20	.20
C5	AP3	2c red orange	.30	.20
C6	AP3	3c olive green	.40	.20
C7	AP4	4c orange	.45	.20
C8	AP4	5c brt blue grn	.75	.20
C9	AP3	10c violet	.75	.20
C10	AP5	20c magenta	1.10	.20
C11	AP3	30c gray black	1.75	.20
C12	AP2	50c brown	2.25	.20
C13	AP5	$1 blue	4.00	.20
		Nos. C4-C13 (10)	11.95	2.00

For surcharges see Nos. C17-C36, C45-C46, C47-C48, C49-C50.

REGISTRATION STAMPS

R1

1893 **Unwmk.** **Litho.** ***Perf. 14, 15***

Without Value Surcharged

No.	Type	Description	Unused	Used
F1	R1	(10c) blk (Buchanan)	250.	250.
F2	R1	(10c) blk (Greenville)	*2,250.*	*2,250.*
F3	R1	(10c) blk (Harper)	*2,250.*	*2,250.*
F4	R1	(10c) blk (Monrovia)	30.	30.
F5	R1	(10c) blk (Robertsport)	1,000.	1,000.

Types of 1893 Surcharged in Black

1894 ***Perf. 14***

No.	Type	Description	Unused	Used
F6	R1	10c bl, *pink* (Buchanan)	5.00	5.25
F7	R1	10c grn, *buff* (Harper)	5.00	5.25
F8	R1	10c red, *yel* (Monrovia)	5.00	5.25
F9	R1	10c rose, *bl* (Robertsport)	5.00	5.25
		Nos. F6-F9 (4)	20.00	21.00

Exist imperf or missing one 10. Value, each $10.

President Garretson W. Gibson — R6

1903 **Engr.** ***Perf. 14***

No.	Type	Description	Unused	Used
F10	R6	10c bl & blk (Buchanan)	1.10	.20
a.		Center inverted	100.00	
F11	R6	10c org red & blk ("Grenville")	1.10	
a.		Center inverted	100.00	
b.		10c orange & black	1.90	.20
F12	R6	10c grn & blk (Harper)	1.10	.20
a.		Center inverted	100.00	

F13 R6 10c vio & blk (Monrovia) 1.10 .20
a. Center inverted 100.00
b. 10c lilac & black 1.90
F14 R6 10c mag & blk (Robertsport) 1.10 .20
a. Center inverted 100.00
Nos. F10-F14 (5) 5.50
Nos. F10, F11b, F12-F14 .75

For surcharges see Nos. 178-182.

S.S. Quail on Patrol — R7

1919 Litho. *Serrate Roulette 12*
F15 R7 10c blk & bl (Buchanan) .50 1.00

Serrate Roulette 12, Perf. 14
F16 R7 10c ocher & blk ("Grenville") .50 1.00
F17 R7 10c grn & blk (Harper) .50 1.00
F18 R7 10c vio & bl (Monrovia) .50 1.00
F19 R7 10c rose & blk (Robertsport) .50 1.00
Nos. F15-F19 (5) 2.50 5.00

Gabon Viper — R8

Wmk. Crosses and Circles (116)
1921 Engr. *Perf. 13x14*
F20 R8 10c cl & blk (Buchanan) 60.00 1.50
F21 R8 10c red & blk (Greenville) 15.00 1.50
F22 R8 10c ultra & blk (Harper) 15.00 1.50
F23 R8 10c org & blk (Monrovia) 15.00 1.50
a. Imperf., pair 150.00
F24 R8 10c grn & blk (Robertsport) 15.00 1.50
a. Imperf., pair 150.00
Nos. F20-F24 (5) 120.00 7.50

Preceding Issue Overprinted "1921"
F25 R8 10c (Buchanan) 15.00 3.00
F26 R8 10c (Greenville) 15.00 3.00
F27 R8 10c (Harper) 15.00 3.00
F28 R8 10c (Monrovia) 15.00 3.00
F29 R8 10c (Robertsport) 15.00 3.00
Nos. F25-F29 (5) 75.00 15.00

Nos. F25-F29 exist with "1921" inverted. Value same as normal.

Passengers Going Ashore from Ship — R9

Designs: No. F31, Transporting merchandise, shore to ship (Greenville). No. F32, Sailing ship (Harper). No. F33, Ocean liner (Monrovia). No. F34, Canoe in surf (Robertsport).

1924 Litho. *Perf. 14*
F30 R9 10c gray & carmine 3.50 .30
F31 R9 10c gray & blue grn 3.50 .30
F32 R9 10c gray & orange 3.50 .30
F33 R9 10c gray & blue 3.50 .30
F34 R9 10c gray & violet 3.50 .30
Nos. F30-F34 (5) 17.50 1.50

POSTAGE DUE STAMPS

Nos. 26, 28 Surcharged

1892 Unwmk. *Perf. 11*
J1 A5 3c on 3c violet 2.50 2.75
a. Imperf., pair 15.00
b. Inverted surcharge 45.00 45.00
c. As "a," inverted surcharge 110.00

Perf. 12
J2 A5 6c on 6c olive gray 7.50 9.00
a. Imperf., pair 22.50
b. Inverted surcharge 52.50 35.00

D2

Engr.; Figures of Value Typographed in Black
1893 Wmk. 143 *Perf. 14, 15*
J3 D2 2c org, *yel* 1.40 .75
J4 D2 4c rose, *rose* 1.40 .75
J5 D2 6c brown, *buff* 1.40 .90
J6 D2 8c blue, *blue* 1.40 .90
J7 D2 10c grn, *lil rose* 1.60 1.10
J8 D2 20c vio, *gray* 1.60 1.10
a. Center inverted 110.00 110.00
J9 D2 40c ol brn, *grnsh* 3.25 2.25
Nos. J3-J9 (7) 12.05 7.75

All values of the above set exist imperforate.

MILITARY STAMPS

"LFF" are the initials of "Liberian Frontier Force." Nos. M1-M7 were issued for the use of troops sent to guard the frontier.

Issues of 1905, 1906 and 1909 Surcharged

1916 Wmk. 143
M1 A23 1c on 1c lt grn 175.00 175.00
a. 2nd "F" inverted 250.00 250.00
b. "FLF" 250.00 250.00
c. Inverted surcharge 250.00 250.00

Unwmk.
M2 A33 1c on 1c grn & blk 500.00 500.00
a. 2nd "F" inverted 550.00 550.00
b. "FLF" 550.00 550.00
M3 A46 1c on 1c yel grn & blk 3.75 4.50
a. 2nd "F" inverted 7.50 7.50
b. "FLF" 7.50 7.50
M4 A47 1c on 2c lake & blk 3.75 4.50
a. 2nd "F" inverted 7.50 7.50
b. "FLF" 7.50 7.50

Surcharge exists sideways on Nos. M2, M5; double on Nos. M1-M4; inverted on Nos. M2-M4.

Nos. O46, O59-O60 Surcharged

M5 A33 1c on 1c 400.00 400.00
a. 2nd "F" inverted 550.00 550.00
b. "FLF" 550.00 550.00
M6 A46 1c on 1c 3.75 4.50
a. 2nd "F" inverted 7.50 7.50
b. "FLF" 7.50 7.50
c. "LFF 1c" inverted 10.00 10.00
d. As "a" and "1c" inverted 14.00
e. "FLF 1c" inverted 14.00
M7 A47 1c on 2c 2.75 3.25
a. 2nd "F" inverted 5.75 5.75
b. "FLF" 5.75 5.75
c. Pair, one without "LFF 1c"

OFFICIAL STAMPS

Types of Regular Issues Overprinted "OFFICIAL" in Various Colors

Perf. 12½ to 15 and Compound
1892 Wmk. 143
O1 A9 1c vermilion .50 .50
O2 A9 2c blue .50 .50
O3 A10 4c grn & blk .50 .50
O4 A11 6c bl grn .50 .50
O5 A12 8c brn & blk .50 .50
O6 A13 12c rose red 1.25 1.25
O7 A14 16c red lilac 1.25 1.25
O8 A15 24c ol grn, *yel* 1.25 1.25
O9 A16 32c grnsh bl 1.25 1.25
O10 A17 $1 bl & blk 25.00 10.00
O11 A18 $2 brn, *yel* 10.50 7.25
O12 A19 $5 car & blk 15.00 6.50
Nos. O1-O12 (12) 58.00 31.25

1893
O13 A11 (a) 5c on 6c bl grn (No. 50) .95 .95
a. "5" with short flag 5.00 5.00
b. Both 5's with short flags 5.00 5.00
c. "i" dot omitted 19.00 19.00
d. Overprinted on #50d 45.00 45.00

1894
Overprinted "O S" in Various Colors
O15 A9 1c vermilion .50 .25
O16 A9 2c blue .60 .30
a. Imperf.
O17 A10 4c grn & blk .70 .40
O18 A12 8c brn & blk .70 .40
O19 A13 12c rose red 1.00 .45
O20 A14 16c red lilac 1.00 .45
O21 A15 24c ol grn, *yel* 1.00 .50
O22 A16 32c grnsh bl 2.00 .60
O23 A17 $1 bl & blk 20.00 15.00
a. $1 ultra & black 20.00 15.00
O24 A18 $2 brn, *yel* 20.00 15.00
O25 A19 $5 car & blk 92.50 62.50
Nos. O15-O25 (11) 140.00 95.85

Unwmk.
Imperf
O26 A22 5c vio & grn 3.00 1.90

Rouletted
O27 A22 5c vio & grn 3.00 1.90

Regular Issue of 1896-1905 Overprinted "O S" in Black or Red

1898-1905 Wmk. 143 *Perf. 14, 15*
O28 A23 1c lil rose .65 .65
O29 A23 1c dp grn ('00) .65 .65
O30 A23 1c lt grn (R) ('05) .65 .65
O31 A24 2c bis & blk 1.25 .45
a. Pair, one without overprint 62.50
O32 A24 2c org red & blk ('00) 2.10 1.10
O33 A24 2c rose & blk ('05) 3.25 2.10
O34 A25 5c lake & blk 2.10 1.10
O35 A25 5c gray bl & blk ('00) 2.60 1.10
O36 A25 5c ultra & blk (R) ('05) 4.25 2.75
O37 A12 10c chr yel & ind 1.25 1.25
O38 A13 15c slate 1.25 1.25
O39 A14 20c vermilion 2.25 1.50
O40 A15 25c yel grn 1.25 1.25
O41 A16 30c steel blue 3.25 2.10
O42 A26 50c red brn & blk 3.25 2.10
Nos. O28-O42 (15) 30.00 20.00

For surcharge see No. O92.

Official stamps overprinted "ORDINARY" or with a bar with an additional surcharge are listed as Nos. 64B-90, 92-93, 99.

Red Overprint

1903 Unwmk. *Perf. 14*
O43 A29 3c green .20 .20
a. Overprint omitted 5.00
b. Inverted overprint

Two overprint types: I — Thin, sharp, dark red. II — Thick, heavier, orange red. Same value.

On No. 50

O3

1904 Black Surcharge Wmk. 143
O44 A11 1c on 5c on 6c bl grn 1.25 1.50
a. "5" with short flag 4.25
b. Both "5s" with straight flag 8.00 8.00

Red Surcharge
O45 O3 2c on 30c steel blue 8.00 8.00
a. Double surcharge, red and black
b. Surcharge also on back

Types of Regular Issue Overprinted in Various Colors — a

1906 Unwmk.
O46 A33 1c grn & blk (R) .45 .30
O47 A34 2c car & blk (Bl) .20 .20
a. Center and overprint inverted 20.00 11.00
b. Inverted overprint 6.00
O48 A35 5c ultra & blk (Bk) .45 .30
a. Inverted overprint 15.00 15.00
b. Center and overprint invtd. 40.00
O49 A36 10c dl vio & blk (R) .55 .40
a. Inverted overprint 10.00 10.00
b. Center and overprint invtd. 40.00
O50 A37 15c brn & blk (Bk) 2.25 .40
a. Inverted overprint 4.50
b. Overprint omitted 12.00 6.00
c. Center and overprint invtd. 50.00
O51 A38 20c dp grn & blk (R) .55 .40
a. Overprint omitted 15.00
O52 A39 25c plum & gray (Bl) .35 .20
a. With 2nd ovpt. in blue, invtd. 15.00
O53 A40 30c dk brn (Bk) .40 .20
O54 A41 50c org brn & dp grn (G) .55 .20
a. Inverted overprint 5.00 4.00
O55 A42 75c ultra & blk (Bk) 1.00 .70
a. Inverted overprint 9.50 5.75
b. Overprint omitted 22.50
O56 A43 $1 dp grn & gray (R) .65 .20
a. Inverted overprint
O57 A44 $2 plum & blk (Bl) 1.90 .20
a. Overprint omitted 22.50 15.00
O58 A45 $5 org & blk (Bk) 4.00 .20
a. Overprint omitted 11.00
b. Inverted overprint 12.00 8.00
Nos. O46-O58 (13) 13.30 3.90

Nos. O52, O54, O55, O56 and O58 are known with center inverted.

For surcharges see Nos. O72, O82-O85, O96.

1909-12
O59 A46 1c emer & blk (R) .25 .20
O60 A47 2c car rose & brn (Bl) .25 .20
a. Overprint omitted
O61 A48 5c turq & blk (Bk) .30 .20
a. Double overprint, one inverted 7.50
O62 A49 10c blk & ultra (R) ('12) .40 .20
O63 A50 15c cl & blk (Bl) .40 .30
O64 A51 20c bis & grn (Bk) .75 .35
O65 A52 25c ultra & grn (Bk) .75 .35
a. Double overprint 4.75 4.75
O66 A53 30c dk bl (R) .55 .20
O67 A54 50c brn & grn (Bk) .90 .25
a. Center inverted 27.50
b. Inverted overprint 4.00 2.75
O68 A55 75c pur & blk (R) 1.00 .20
Nos. O59-O68 (10) 5.55 2.45

Nos. O63, O64, O67 and O68 are known without overprint and with center inverted.

For surcharges see Nos. O74-O81, O86-O90, O97.

Rouletted

O69 A49 10c blk & ultra (R) .70 .70

Nos. 126B and 127E Overprinted type "a" ("OS") in Red

1910-12 ***Rouletted***

O70 A49 3c on 10c blk & ultra .60 1.00

Perf. 12½, 14, 12½x14

O71 A49 3c on 10c blk & ultra ('12) .60 .30
- *a.* Pair, one without surch., the other with dbl. surch., one invtd.
- *b.* Double surcharge, one inverted 3.75

Stamps of Preceding Issues Surcharged with New Values like Regular Issue and

c 

1914

On Nos. O52 and 110

O72 A39 (a) 2c on 25c plum & gray 17.00 7.00
O73 A42 (c) 20c on 75c brn & blk 5.75 3.50

On Nos. O66 and O68

O74 A53 (b) 5c on 30c dk bl 5.75 3.50
O75 A55 (c) 20c on 75c pur & blk (R) 8.50 3.50
Nos. O72-O75 (4) 37.00 17.50

Official Stamps of 1906-09 Surcharged Like Regular Issues of Same Date

1915-16

O76 A50 (c) 2c on 15c (Bk) .75 .50
O77 A52 (d) 2c on 25c (Bk) 4.25 4.25
O78 A51 (e) 5c on 20c (Bk) .75 .50
O79 A53 (g) 5c on 30c (R) 7.00 7.00
O80 A54 (i) 10c on 50c (Bk) 4.50 2.75
O81 A55 (j) 20c on 75c (R) 2.25 2.25
O82 A43 (k) 25c on $1 (R) 16.00 16.00
- *a.* "25" double 22.50
- *b.* "OS" inverted 22.50

O83 A44 (l) 50c on $2 (Bk) 50.00 50.00
- *a.* "Ceuts" 70.00 70.00

O84 A44 (m) 50c on $2 (Br) 18.00 18.00
O85 A45 (n) $1 on $5 (Bk) 17.00 17.00

Handstamped Surcharge

O86 A54 (i) 10c on 50c (Bk) 8.50 8.50

Nos. O60-O61 Surcharged like Nos. 153-154 in Black or Red

O87 A47 1c on 2c 2.25 2.25
Strip of 10 types 25.00
O88 A48 2c on 5c (R) 2.25 2.25
Strip of 10 types (R) 25.00
- *a.* Black surcharge 8.50 8.50
Strip of 10 types (Bk) 125.00

See note following Nos. 153-154.

#O60-O61 Surcharged like #155-156

O90 A47 1c on 2c 125.00 125.00
O91 A48 2c on 5c 100.00 100.00

No. O42 Surcharged 

O92 A26 10c on 50c (Bk) 11.00 11.00

No. O53 Surcharged like No. 161

1917

O96 A40 5c on 30c dk brn 17.00 17.00
- *a.* "FIV" 27.50 27.50

The editors consider the 1915-17 issues unnecessary and speculative.

#O62 Surcharged in Red like #162

1918

O97 A49 3c on 10c blk & ultra 1.90 1.90

Types of Regular Issue of 1918 Overprinted Type "a" ("OS") in Black, Blue or Red

1918 **Unwmk.** ***Perf. 12½, 14***

O98 A59 1c dp grn & red brn (Bk) .40 .20
O99 A60 2c red & blk (Bl) .40 .20
O100 A61 5c ultra & blk (R) .75 .20
O101 A62 10c ultra (R) .40 .20
O102 A63 15c choc & dk grn (Bl) 1.90 .40
O103 A64 20c gray lil & blk (R) .55 .20
O104 A65 25c choc & grn (Bk) 3.50 .45
O105 A66 30c brt vio & blk (R) 4.25 .45
O106 A67 50c mar & blk (Bl) 5.25 .45
- *a.* Overprint omitted 11.00

O107 A68 75c car brn & blk (Bl) 2.00 .20
O108 A69 $1 ol bis & turq bl (Bk) 4.00 .20
O109 A70 $2 ol bis & blk (R) 6.25 .20
O110 A71 $5 yel grn (Bk) 8.00 .25
Nos. O98-O110 (13) 37.65 3.60

For surcharges see Nos. 259-269, O111-O112, O155-O157. For overprint see No. 270.

Official Stamps of 1918 Surcharged like Regular Issue

1920

O111 A59 3c on 1c grn & red brn .90 .55
- *a.* "CEETS" 15.00 15.00
- *b.* Double surcharge 8.00 8.00
- *c.* Double surch., one invtd. 15.00 15.00
- *d.* Triple surcharge 20.00 20.00

O112 A60 4c on 2c red & blk .55 .55
- *a.* Inverted surcharge 12.00 12.00
- *b.* Double surcharge 12.00 12.00
- *c.* Double surch., one invtd. 10.00 10.00
- *d.* Triple surcharge 15.00 15.00

Types of Regular Issues of 1915-21 Overprinted 

1921 **Wmk. 116** ***Perf. 14***

O113 A57 2c rose red 5.50 .20
O114 A58 3c brown 1.10 .20
O115 A79 20c brn & ultra 1.50 .25

Same, Overprinted "O S"

O116 A75 1c dp grn 1.10 .20
O117 A76 5c dp bl & brn 1.10 .20
O118 A77 10c red vio & blk .55 .20
O119 A78 15c blk & grn 3.25 .40
- *a.* Double overprint

O120 A80 25c org & grn 4.25 .40
O121 A81 30c brn & red 1.10 .20
O122 A82 50c grn & blk 1.10 .20
- *a.* Overprinted "S" only

O123 A83 75c bl & vio 2.25 .20
O124 A84 $1 bl & blk 15.00 .45
O125 A85 $2 grn & org 8.00 .65
O126 A86 $5 grn & bl 9.00 1.40
Nos. O113-O126 (14) 54.80 5.15

Preceding Issues Overprinted "1921"

1921

O127 A75 1c dp grn 4.75 .20
O128 A57 2c rose red 4.75 .20
O129 A58 3c brown 4.75 .20
O130 A76 5c dp bl & brn 2.75 .20
O131 A77 10c red vio & blk 4.75 .20
O132 A78 15c blk & grn 5.25 .20
O133 A79 20c brn & ultra 5.25 .25
O134 A80 25c org & grn 6.00 .50
O135 A81 30c brn & red 4.75 .20
O136 A82 50c grn & blk 5.50 .20
O137 A83 75c bl & vio 3.50 .20
O138 A84 $1 bl & blk 9.50 1.25
O139 A85 $2 org & grn 12.00 1.40
O140 A86 $5 grn & bl 9.50 2.00
Nos. O127-O140 (14) 83.00 7.20

Types of Regular Issue of 1923 Overprinted "O S"

1923 ***Perf. 13½x14½, 14½x13½***

White Paper

O141 A88 1c bl grn & blk 5.75 .20
O142 A89 2c dl red & yel brn 5.75 .20
O143 A90 3c gray bl & blk 5.75 .20
O144 A91 5c org & dk grn 5.75 .20
O145 A92 10c ol bis & dk vio 5.75 .20
O146 A93 15c yel grn & bl .75 .25
O147 A94 20c vio & ind .75 .25
O148 A95 25c brn & red brn 22.50 .25
O149 A96 30c dp ultra & brn 1.50 .20
O150 A97 50c dl bis & red brn 1.50 .40
O151 A98 75c gray & grn 1.50 .20
O152 A99 $1 red org & grn 3.00 .45
- *a.* Overprint omitted 11.00

O153 A100 $2 red lil & ver 4.00 .20
O154 A101 $5 bl & brn vio 5.00 1.50
Nos. O141-O154 (14) 69.25 4.70

Brownish Paper

O149a A96 30c dp ultra & brn .75 .30
- *b.* Overprint omitted 2.00

O150a A97 50c dl bis & red brn 1.50 .30
O151a A98 75c gray & grn 1.50 .30
O152a A99 $1 red org & grn 1.50 .45
- *b.* Overprint omitted 11.00

O153a A100 $2 red lil & ver 2.50 1.00
O154a A101 $5 bl & brn vio 3.00 1.50

Nos. O149-O154 also exist on a light buff paper. Values are the same as for copies on brownish paper.

No. O98 Surcharged in Red Brown 

1926 **Unwmk.** ***Perf. 14***

O155 A59 2c on 1c 2.25 2.25
- *a.* "Gents" 7.25
- *b.* Surcharged in black 5.75
- *c.* As "b," "Gents" 9.50

No. O98 Surcharged in Black 

1926

O156 A59 2c on 1c .85 .85
- *a.* Inverted surcharge 20.00
- *b.* "Gents" 10.00

No. O98 Surcharged in Red 

1927

O157 A59 2c on 1c 25.00 25.00
- *a.* "Ceuts" 40.00
- *b.* "Vwo" 40.00
- *c.* "Twc" 40.00

Regular Issue of 1928 Overprinted in Red or Black 

1928 ***Perf. 12***

O158 A102 1c grn (R) .80 .40
O159 A102 2c gray vio (R) 2.50 1.50
O160 A102 3c bis brn (Bk) 2.75 3.00
O161 A103 5c ultra (R) .80 .40
O162 A104 10c ol gray (R) 2.50 1.25
O163 A103 15c dl vio (R) 2.50 .75
O164 A103 $1 red brn (Bk) 55.00 19.00
Nos. O158-O164 (7) 66.85 26.30

For surcharges see Nos. C3, O165.

LIBYA

'li-bē-ə

(Libia)

LOCATION — North Africa, bordering on the Mediterranean Sea
GOVT. — Republic
AREA — 679,358 sq. mi.
POP. — 3,500,000 (est. 1982)
CAPITAL — Tripoli

In 1939, the four northern provinces of Libya, a former Italian colony, were incorporated in the Italian national territory. Included in the territory is the former Turkish Vilayet of Tripoli, annexed in 1912. See Cyrenaica and Tripolitania.

100 Centesimi = 1 Lira

Watermarks

Wmk. 140 — Crown

Used values in italics are for postally used stamps. CTO's sell for about the same as unused, hinged stamps.

Stamps of Italy Overprinted in Black

Libia Type I — **Libia** Type II

Two types of overprint. Type I: bold letters, dots close within letter "i." Type II: thinner letters, dots further away within letter "i."

1912-22 Wmk. 140 *Perf. 14*

Type I

1 A42 1c brown ('15) 1.50 .90
Never hinged 3.75
On cover 20.00
a. Double overprint 225.00 215.00
Never hinged 325.00
2 A43 2c orange brn 1.50 .50
Never hinged 3.75
On cover 20.00
3 A48 5c green 1.50 .35
Never hinged 3.75
On cover 7.50
a. Double overprint 87.50 87.50
Never hinged 130.00
b. Imperf., pair 325.00
Never hinged 440.00
c. Inverted overprint —
d. Pair, one without overprint 325.00 325.00
Never hinged 500.00
4 A48 10c claret 11.00 .20
Never hinged 27.50
On cover 7.50
a. Pair, one without overprint 325.00 325.00
Never hinged 500.00
b. Double overprint 150.00 140.00
Never hinged 225.00
5 A48 15c slate ('22) 3.75 *5.00*
Never hinged 9.25
On cover 65.00
6 A45 20c orange ('15) 3.75 .20
Never hinged 9.25
On cover 19.00
a. Double overprint 180.00 *190.00*
Never hinged 275.00
b. Pair, one without overprint 600.00 600.00
Never hinged 875.00
7 A50 20c brn org ('18) 3.75 *5.25*
Never hinged 9.25
On cover 47.50
8 A49 25c blue 3.75 .20
Never hinged 9.25
On cover 40.00
9 A49 40c brown 11.00 .50
Never hinged 27.50
On cover 150.00
10 A45 45c ol grn ('17) 26.00 *24.00*
Never hinged 65.00
On cover 80.00
a. Inverted overprint 440.00
Never hinged 660.00
11 A49 50c violet 22.50 1.40
Never hinged 65.00
On cover 200.00
12 A49 60c brn car ('18) 14.00 *20.00*
Never hinged 37.50
On cover 110.00
13 A46 1 l brown & green ('15) 65.00 1.75
Never hinged 160.00
On cover 80.00
14 A46 5 l bl & rose ('15) 325.00 *275.00*
Never hinged 825.00
On cover *2,500.*
15 A51 10 l gray green & red ('15) 35.00 *125.00*
Never hinged 90.00
Nos. 1-15 (15) 529.00 *460.25*

Type II

1b A42 1c brown ('15) 1.50 1.90
Never hinged 3.50
On cover 70.00
3e A48 5c green 1.50 .85
Never hinged 3.50
On cover 15.00
f. Double overprint 80.00 80.00
Never hinged 110.00
g. Imperf., pair 300.00
Never hinged 385.00
h. Pair, one without overprint 300.00 300.00
Never hinged 385.00
4c A48 10c claret 13.00 .20
Never hinged 21.00
On cover 14.00
d. Pair, one without overprint 290.00 290.00
Never hinged 375.00
e. Double overprint 140.00 140.00
Never hinged 210.00
6c A45 20c orange ('15) 3.50 1.50
Never hinged 7.50
On cover 30.00
8a A49 25c blue 3.75 .60
Never hinged 8.50
On cover 80.00
b. Double overprint, both type II *140.00* *150.00*
Never hinged *225.00*
11a A49 50c violet 80.00 1.40
Never hinged 175.00
On cover 275.00
13a A46 1 l brown & green ('15) 70.00 3.50
Never hinged 150.00
On cover 100.00
14a A46 5 l bl & rose ('15) 325.00 *275.00*
Never hinged 725.00
On cover *2,300.*
15a A51 10 l gray green & red ('15) 2,400.
Never hinged 4,500.

For surcharges see Nos. 37-38.

Overprinted in Violet

1912 Unwmk.

16 A58 15c slate 175.00 1.90
Never hinged 450.00
On cover 47.50
a. Blue black overprint *14,500.* 30.00
Never hinged *18,500.*
On cover 110.00

No. 16 Surcharged — CENT 20

1916, Mar. Unwmk.

19 A58 20c on 15c slate 32.50 8.75
Never hinged 80.00
On cover 30.00
a. Blue-black surcharge 47.50 19.00
Never hinged 120.00
On cover 50.00

Roman Legionary — A1

Diana of Ephesus — A2

Ancient Galley Leaving Tripoli — A3

"Victory" — A4

1921 Engr. Wmk. 140 *Perf. 14*

20 A1 1c blk & gray brn 3.00 5.75
Never hinged 7.25
On cover 65.00
21 A1 2c blk & red brn 3.00 5.75
Never hinged 7.25
On cover 65.00
22 A1 5c black & green 3.50 .75
Never hinged 9.25
On cover 2.25
a. 5c black & red brown (error) 1,475.
Never hinged 1,800.
b. Center inverted 55.00 80.00
Never hinged 110.00
c. Imperf., pair 475.00 550.00
Never hinged 950.00
23 A2 10c blk & rose 3.75 .75
Never hinged 9.25
On cover 2.25
a. Center inverted 55.00 80.00
Never hinged 110.00
24 A2 15c blk brn & brn org 87.50 3.00
Never hinged 225.00
On cover 18.00
a. Center inverted 115.00 *225.00*
Never hinged 240.00
25 A2 25c dk bl & bl 3.75 .20
Never hinged 9.25
On cover 2.25
a. Center inverted 18.00 25.00
Never hinged 37.50
b. Imperf., pair 650.00 725.00
Never hinged 1,300.
26 A3 30c blk & blk brn 21.00 75.00
Never hinged 55.00
On cover 3.75
a. Center inverted 1,900. 1,900.
Never hinged 2,400.
27 A3 50c blk & ol grn 11.00 .20
Never hinged 22.50
On cover 2.25
a. 50c black & brown (error) 400.00
Never hinged 800.00
b. Center inverted *2,750.*
28 A3 55c black & vio 11.00 18.00
Never hinged 27.50
On cover 300.00
29 A4 1 l dk brn & brn 35.00 .20
Never hinged 90.00
On cover 2.25
30 A4 5 l blk & dk blue 21.00 21.00
Never hinged 55.00
On cover 650.00
31 A4 10 l dk bl & ol grn 225.00 125.00
Never hinged 550.00
On cover *1,300.*
Nos. 20-31 (12) 428.50 255.60

Nos. 20-31 also exist perf. 14x13. Values substantially higher.
See #47-61. For surcharges see #102-121.

Italy Nos. 136-139 Overprinted

1921, Apr.

33 A64 5c olive green 1.75 *6.50*
Never hinged 4.50
On cover 87.50
a. Double overprint 290.00 300.00
Never hinged 440.00
34 A64 10c red 1.85 *6.50*
Never hinged 4.50
On cover 140.00
a. Double overprint 300.00 300.00
Never hinged 440.00
b. Inverted overprint 450.00 450.00
Never hinged 660.00
35 A64 15c slate green 1.75 *10.00*
Never hinged 4.50
On cover 160.00
36 A64 25c ultramarine 1.75 *10.00*
Never hinged 4.50
On cover 200.00
Nos. 33-36 (4) 7.10 *33.00*

3rd anniv. of the victory of the Piave.

Nos. 11, 8 Surcharged

1922, June 1

37 A49 40c on 50c violet 2.25 2.25
Never hinged 5.50
On cover 60.00
38 A49 80c on 25c blue 2.25 *6.50*
Never hinged 5.50
On cover 225.00

Libyan Sibyl — A6

1924-31 Unwmk. *Perf. 14½x14*

39 A6 20c deep green .75 .20
Never hinged 1.90
On cover 1.90
c. Vert. pair, imperf between and top 1,325.
Never hinged 1,650.
d. Horiz. pair, imperf between and at right 1,325.
Never hinged 1,650.
e. Horiz. pair, imperf between and at left 1,325.
Never hinged 1,650.
40 A6 40c brown 1.50 .75
Never hinged 3.75
On cover 14.50
b. Imperf single 250.00 *325.00*
Never hinged 375.00
41 A6 60c deep blue .75 .20
Never hinged 1.90
On cover 18.50
b. Imperf single 240.00
Never hinged 350.00
42 A6 1.75 l orange ('31) .30 .20
Never hinged .75
On cover 4.50
b. Imperf single 240.00 *275.00*
Never hinged 350.00
43 A6 2 l carmine 3.00 1.10
Never hinged 7.25
On cover 22.50
44 A6 2.55 l violet ('31) 5.00 11.00
Never hinged 12.50
On cover 130.00
Nos. 39-44 (6) 11.30 13.45

1926-29 *Perf. 11*

39a A6 20c 30.00 .30
Never hinged 75.00
On cover 8.75
40a A6 40c 22.50 2.50
Never hinged 57.50
On cover 19.00
41a A6 60c 22.50 .50
Never hinged 57.50
On cover 37.50
43a A6 2 l ('29) 11.50 5.50
Never hinged 30.00
On cover 45.00
Nos. 39a-43a (4) 86.50 8.80

Type of 1921

1924-40 Unwmk. *Perf. 13½ to 14*

47 A1 1c blk & gray brown 3.00 6.00
Never hinged 7.50
On cover 110.00
48 A1 2c blk & red brn 3.00 6.00
Never hinged 7.50
On cover 110.00
49 A1 5c blk & green 3.75 .75
Never hinged 9.25
On cover 2.25
50 A1 7½c blk & brown ('31) .35 7.50
Never hinged .90
On cover 65.00
51 A2 10c blk & dl red 3.00 .30
Never hinged 7.50
On cover 2.25
b. Center inverted 160.00
Never hinged 240.00
c. 10c blk & carmine 3.00 .30
Never hinged 7.50
On cover 2.25
52 A2 15c blk brn & org 6.75 1.10
Never hinged 14.50
On cover 16.00
b. Center inverted, perf. 11 *2,350.* *3,650.*
Never hinged *2,900.*
53 A2 25c dk bl & bl 42.50 .55
Never hinged 110.00
On cover 2.25
a. Center inverted 225.00 250.00
Never hinged 350.00
54 A3 30c blk & blk brn 3.00 .55
Never hinged 7.50
On cover 3.75
55 A3 50c blk & ol grn 3.00 .30
Never hinged 7.50
On cover 2.25
b. Center inverted 2,200.
Never hinged 2,750.
56 A3 55c black & vio 375.00 475.00
Never hinged 950.00
57 A4 75c violet & red ('31) 3.00 .20
Never hinged 7.50
On cover 14.50
58 A4 1 l dk brn & brn 7.50 .35
Never hinged 19.00
On cover 3.00
59 A3 1.25 l indigo & ultra ('31) .30 .20
Never hinged .75
On cover 11.00

60 A4 5 l blk & dark blue ('40) 110.00 100.00
Never hinged 275.00
On cover 800.00
Nos. 47-60 (14) 564.15 598.80

Perf. 11

47a A1 1c 225.00
Never hinged 550.00
48a A1 2c 225.00
Never hinged 550.00
49a A1 5c 65.00 2.50
Never hinged 160.00
On cover 22.50
51a A2 10c 45.00 6.00
Never hinged 110.00
On cover 15.00
52a A2 15c 300.00 30.00
Never hinged 750.00
On cover 87.50
54a A3 30c 125.00 2.25
Never hinged 325.00
On cover 7.50
55a A3 50c 650.00 .20
Never hinged 1,650.
On cover 2.25
58a A4 1 l 250.00 .35
Never hinged 650.00
On cover 13.00
60a A4 5 l ('37) *2,000.* 300.00
Never hinged 3,100.
On cover 875.00
61 A4 10 l dk bl & olive grn ('37) 440.00 375.00
Never hinged 875.00
On cover *1,450.*

Nos. 47a and 48a were not sent to the colony. A few philatelically inspired covers exist.

Italy #197 and 88 Overprinted Like #1-15

1929 Wmk. 140 *Perf. 14*

62 A86 7½c light brown 5.75 *35.00*
Never hinged 14.50
On cover 200.00
a. Double overprint — —
63 A46 1.25 l blue & ultra 40.00 20.00
Never hinged 100.00
On cover 110.00
a. Inverted overprint 2,000.
Never hinged 2,600.

Italy #193 Overprinted Like #33-36

1929 Unwmk. *Perf. 11*

64 A85 1.75 l deep brown 50.00 2.10
Never hinged 125.00
On cover 47.50
h. Perf 13¾ *6,600.*
On cover —

No. 64a is not known unused and is very rare on cover.

Water Carriers A7

Man of Tripoli — A8

Designs: 25c, Minaret. 30c, 1.25 l, Tomb of Holy Man near Tagiura. 50c, Statue of Emperor Claudius at Leptis. 75c, Ruins of gardens.

1934, Feb. 17 Photo. *Perf. 14*

64A A7 10c brown 4.25 *14.50*
Never hinged 11.00
On cover 120.00
64B A8 20c carmine rose 4.25 *13.00*
Never hinged 11.00
On cover 130.00
64C A8 25c green 4.25 *13.00*
Never hinged 11.00
On cover 140.00
64D A7 30c dark brown 4.25 *13.00*
Never hinged 11.00
On cover 160.00
64E A8 50c purple 4.25 *11.00*
Never hinged 11.00
On cover 130.00
64F A7 75c rose 4.25 *21.00*
Never hinged 11.00
On cover 225.00
64G A7 1.25 l blue 42.50 *65.00*
Never hinged 110.00
On cover 400.00
Nos. 64A-64G (7) 68.00 *150.50*
Nos. 64A-64G,C14-C18 (12) 357.50 *655.50*
Nos. 64A-64G on overfranked philatelic cover *1,500.*

8th Sample Fair, Tripoli.

Bedouin Woman — A15

Highway Memorial Arch — A16

1936, May 11 Wmk. 140 *Perf. 14*

65 A15 50c purple 1.50 *3.00*
Never hinged 3.50
On cover 30.00
66 A15 1.25 l deep blue 1.50 *8.00*
Never hinged 3.50
On cover 110.00
Nos. 65-66 on overfranked philatelic cover 50.00

10th Sample Fair, Tripoli.

1937, Mar. 15

67 A16 50c copper red 2.10 *4.25*
Never hinged 5.50
On cover 120.00
68 A16 1.25 l sapphire 2.10 *10.00*
Never hinged 5.50
On cover 180.00
Nos. 67-68,C28-C29 (4) 8.40 *28.75*

Coastal road to the Egyptian frontier, opening.

Nos. 67-68 Overprinted in Black

1937, Apr. 24

69 A16 50c copper red 13.00 *32.50*
Never hinged 32.50
On cover 125.00
70 A16 1.25 l sapphire 13.00 *32.50*
Never hinged 32.50
On cover 225.00
Nos. 69-70,C30-C31 (4) 52.00 *130.00*

11th Sample Fair, Tripoli.

Roman Wolf and Lion of St. Mark A17

View of Fair Buildings A18

1938, Mar. 12

71 A17 5c brown .25 1.10
Never hinged .55
On cover 55.00
72 A18 10c olive brown .25 .75
Never hinged .55
On cover 30.00
73 A17 25c green .50 1.25
Never hinged 1.25
On cover 50.00
74 A18 50c purple .60 .55
Never hinged 1.50
On cover 22.50
75 A17 75c rose red 1.10 *2.10*
Never hinged 2.75
On cover 120.00
76 A18 1.25 l dark blue 1.10 *5.00*
Never hinged 3.00
On cover 150.00
Nos. 71-76,C32-C33 (8) 6.00 *17.85*
Nos. 71-76 on overfranked philatelic cover 90.00

12th Sample Fair, Tripoli.

Augustus Caesar (Octavianus) A19

Goddess Abundantia A20

1938, Apr. 25

77 A19 5c olive brown .20 1.50
Never hinged .55
On cover 130.00
78 A20 10c brown red .20 1.50
Never hinged .55
On cover 47.50
79 A19 25c dk yel green .50 .65
Never hinged 1.20
On cover 65.00
80 A20 50c dk violet .50 .50
Never hinged 1.20
On cover 40.00
81 A19 75c orange red 1.50 *1.75*
Never hinged 3.75
On cover 150.00
82 A20 1.25 l dull blue 1.50 *3.00*
Never hinged 3.75
On cover 190.00
Nos. 77-82,C34-C35 (8) 5.85 *14.65*
Nos. 77-82 on overfranked philatelic cover 130.00

Birth bimillenary of Augustus Caesar (Octavianus), first Roman emperor.

Desert City — A21

View of Ghadames A22

1939, Apr. 12 Photo.

83 A21 5c olive brown .35 1.10
Never hinged .90
On cover 47.50
84 A22 20c red brown .75 1.10
Never hinged 1.90
On cover 30.00
85 A21 50c rose violet .75 1.10
Never hinged 1.90
On cover 14.50
86 A22 75c scarlet .75 *2.10*
Never hinged 1.90
On cover 80.00
87 A21 1.25 l gray blue .75 *3.25*
Never hinged 1.90
On cover 130.00
Nos. 83-87,C36-C38 (8) 5.05 *14.25*
Nos. 83-87 on overfranked philatelic cover 55.00

13th Sample Fair, Tripoli.

Modern City — A23

Oxen and Plow A24

Mosque — A25

1940, June 3 Wmk. 140 *Perf. 14*

88 A23 5c brown .30 1.10
Never hinged .75
On cover 57.50
89 A24 10c red orange .30 .75
Never hinged .75
On cover 47.50
90 A25 25c dull green .65 *1.10*
Never hinged 1.60
On cover 50.00
91 A23 50c dark violet .65 *.75*
Never hinged 1.60
On cover 26.00
92 A24 75c crimson .75 *3.00*
Never hinged 1.90
On cover 150.00
93 A25 1.25 l ultramarine 1.10 *4.25*
Never hinged 2.75
On cover 225.00
94 A24 2 l + 75c rose lake 1.10 *14.50*
Never hinged 2.75
On cover 400.00
Nos. 88-94,C39-C42 (11) 8.05 *43.60*
Nos. 88-94 on overfranked philatelic cover 190.00

Triennial Overseas Exposition, Naples.

SEMI-POSTAL STAMPS

Many issues of Italy and Italian Colonies include one or more semipostal denominations. To avoid splitting sets, these issues are generally listed as regular postage, semipostals or airmails, etc.

Semi-Postal Stamps of Italy Overprinted

1915-16 Wmk. 140 *Perf. 14*

B1 SP1 10c + 5c rose 3.50 *14.50*
Never hinged 9.25
On cover 87.50
a. Double overprint 525.00
Never hinged 775.00
B2 SP2 15c + 5c slate 14.50 *26.00*
Never hinged 37.50
On cover 150.00
B3 SP2 20c + 5c org ('16) 4.25 *30.00*
Never hinged 11.00
On cover 240.00
a. Double overprint, one albino 325.00
Never hinged 500.00
Nos. B1-B3 (3) 22.25 *70.50*
Set on overfranked philatelic cover *240.00*

No. B2 with Additional Surcharge

1916, Mar.

B4 SP2 20c on 15c + 5c slate 14.50 *30.00*
Never hinged 37.50
On cover 240.00
a. Double surcharge 525.00
Never hinged 775.00

View of Port, Tripoli SP1

Designs: B5, B6, View of port, Tripoli. B7, B8, Arch of Marcus Aurelius. B9, B10, View of Tripoli.

1927, Feb. 15 Litho.

B5 SP1 20c + 5c brn vio & black 3.50 13.50
Never hinged 9.25
On cover 110.00
B6 SP1 25c + 5c bl grn & black 3.50 13.50
Never hinged 9.25
On cover 150.00
B7 SP1 40c + 10c blk brn & black 3.50 13.50
Never hinged 9.25
On cover 150.00

B8 SP1 60c + 10c org brn & black 3.50 13.50
Never hinged 9.25
On cover 175.00
B9 SP1 75c + 20c red & black 3.50 13.50
Never hinged 9.25
On cover 225.00
B10 SP1 1.25 l + 20c bl & blk 18.00 32.50
Never hinged 45.00
On cover 450.00
Nos. B5-B10 (6) 35.50 100.00
Set on overfranked philatelic cover 300.00

First Sample Fair, Tripoli. Surtax aided fair. See Nos. EB1-EB2.

View of Tripoli — SP2

Knights of Malta Castle SP3

Designs: 50c+20c, Date palm. 1.25 l+20c, Camel riders. 2.55 l+50c, View of Tripoli. 5 l+1 l, Traction well.

1928, Feb. 20 Wmk. 140 *Perf. 14*
B11 SP2 30c + 20c mar & blk 3.00 14.50
Never hinged 7.25
On cover 110.00
B12 SP2 50c + 20c bl grn & blk 3.00 14.50
Never hinged 7.25
On cover 130.00
B13 SP2 1.25 l + 20c red & blk 3.00 14.50
Never hinged 7.25
On cover 190.00
B14 SP3 1.75 l + 20c bl & blk 3.00 14.50
Never hinged 7.25
On cover 250.00
B15 SP3 2.55 l + 50c brn & blk 4.25 18.00
Never hinged 11.00
On cover 325.00
B16 SP3 5 l + 1 l pur & blk 7.25 30.00
Never hinged 18.00
On cover —
Nos. B11-B16 (6) 23.50 106.00
Set on overfranked philatelic cover 300.00

2nd Sample Fair, Tripoli, 1928. The surtax was for the aid of the Fair.

Olive Tree — SP4

Herding SP5

Designs: 50c+20c, Dorcas gazelle. 1.25 l+20c, Peach blossoms. 2.55 l+50c, Camel caravan. 5 l+1 l, Oasis with date palms.

1929, Apr. 7
B17 SP4 30c + 20c mar & blk 8.75 18.00
Never hinged 22.50
On cover 175.00
B18 SP4 50c + 20c bl grn & blk 8.75 18.00
Never hinged 22.50
On cover 160.00
B19 SP4 1.25 l + 20c scar & blk 8.75 18.00
Never hinged 22.50
On cover 300.00
B20 SP5 1.75 l + 20c bl & blk 8.75 18.00
Never hinged 22.50
On cover 475.00
B21 SP5 2.55 l + 50c yel brn & blk 8.75 18.00
Never hinged 22.50
On cover 575.00
B22 SP5 5 l + 1 l pur & blk 110.00 215.00
Never hinged 275.00
On cover —
Nos. B17-B22 (6) 153.75 305.00
Set on overfranked philatelic cover 1,100.

3rd Sample Fair, Tripoli, 1929. The surtax was for the aid of the Fair.

Harvesting Bananas — SP6

Water Carriers SP7

Designs: 50c, Tobacco plant. 1.25 l, Venus of Cyrene. 2.55 l+45c, Black bucks. 5 l+1 l, Motor and camel transportation. 10 l+2 l, Rome pavilion.

1930, Feb. 20 Photo.
B23 SP6 30c dark brown 2.10 11.00
Never hinged 5.50
On cover 160.00
B24 SP6 50c violet 2.10 11.00
Never hinged 5.50
On cover 150.00
B25 SP6 1.25 l deep blue 2.10 11.00
Never hinged 5.50
On cover 240.00
B26 SP7 1.75 l + 20c scar 3.75 18.00
Never hinged 9.25
On cover 300.00
B27 SP7 2.55 l + 45c dp grn 11.50 25.00
Never hinged 29.00
On cover 500.00
B28 SP7 5 l + 1 l dp org 11.50 35.00
Never hinged 29.00
On cover —
B29 SP7 10 l + 2 l dk vio 11.50 40.00
Never hinged 29.00
On cover —
Nos. B23-B29 (7) 44.55 151.00
Set on overfranked philatelic cover 440.00

4th Sample Fair at Tripoli, 1930. The surtax was for the aid of the Fair.

Statue of Ephebus — SP8

Exhibition Pavilion SP9

Designs: 25c, Arab musician. 50c, View of Zeughet. 1.25 l, Snake charmer. 1.75 l+25c, Windmill. 2.75 l+45c, "Zaptie." 5 l+1 l, Mounted Arab.

1931, Mar. 8
B30 SP8 10c black brown 3.75 7.50
Never hinged 9.25
On cover 150.00
B31 SP8 25c green 3.75 7.50
Never hinged 9.25
On cover 160.00
B32 SP8 50c purple 3.75 7.50
Never hinged 9.25
On cover 150.00
B33 SP8 1.25 l blue 3.75 11.50
Never hinged 9.25
On cover 240.00
B34 SP8 1.75 l + 25c car rose 3.75 14.50
Never hinged 9.25
On cover —
B35 SP8 2.75 l + 45c org 11.00 18.00
Never hinged 27.50
On cover —
B36 SP8 5 l + 1 l dl vio 11.00 25.00
Never hinged 27.50
On cover —
B37 SP9 10 l + 2 l brn 35.00 55.00
Never hinged 92.50
On cover —
Nos. B30-B37 (8) 75.75 146.50
Nos. B30-B37,C3,EB3 (10) 83.00 182.00
Nos. B30-B37 on overfranked philatelic cover 650.00

Fifth Sample Fair, Tripoli. Surtax aided fair.

Papaya Tree SP10

Dorcas Gazelle SP12

Ar Tower, Mogadiscio SP11

Designs: 10c, 50c, Papaya tree. 20c, 30c, Euphorbia abyssinica. 25c, Fig cactus. 75c, Mausoleum, Ghirza. 1.75 l+25c, Lioness. 5 l+1 l, Bedouin with camel.

1932, Mar. 8
B38 SP10 10c olive brn 4.25 11.50
Never hinged 11.00
On cover 100.00
B39 SP10 20c brown red 4.25 11.50
Never hinged 11.00
On cover 80.00
B40 SP10 25c green 4.25 11.50
Never hinged 11.00
On cover 100.00
B41 SP10 30c olive blk 4.25 11.50
Never hinged 11.00
On cover 150.00
B42 SP10 50c dk violet 4.25 11.50
Never hinged 11.00
On cover 80.00
B43 SP10 75c carmine 5.75 11.50
Never hinged 14.50
On cover 225.00
B44 SP11 1.25 l dk blue 5.75 16.00
Never hinged 14.50
On cover 275.00
B45 SP11 1.75 l + 25c ol brn 25.00 50.00
Never hinged 62.50
On cover 400.00
B46 SP11 5 l + 1 l dp bl 25.00 110.00
Never hinged 62.50
On cover —
B47 SP12 10 l + 2 l brn violet 80.00 215.00
Never hinged 200.00
On cover —
Nos. B38-B47 (10) 162.75 460.00
Nos. B38-B47,C4-C7 (14) 250.25 637.50
Nos. B38-B47 on overfranked philatelic cover 1,500.

Sixth Sample Fair, Tripoli. Surtax aided fair.

Ostrich — SP13

Arab Musician SP14

Designs: 25c, Incense plant. 30c, Arab musician. 50c, Arch of Marcus Aurelius. 1.25 l, African eagle. 5 l+1 l, Leopard. 10 l+2.50 l, Tripoli skyline and fasces.

1933, Mar. 2 Photo. Wmk. 140
B48 SP13 10c dp violet 25.00 15.00
Never hinged 62.50
On cover 160.00
B49 SP13 25c dp green 13.00 26.00
Never hinged 32.50
On cover 130.00
B50 SP14 30c orange brn 13.00 26.00
Never hinged 32.50
On cover 160.00
B51 SP13 50c purple 11.50 26.00
Never hinged 29.00
On cover 130.00
B52 SP13 1.25 l dk blue 30.00 47.50
Never hinged 75.00
On cover 375.00
B53 SP14 5 l + 1 l ol brn 65.00 110.00
Never hinged 160.00
On cover —
B54 SP13 10 l + 2.50 l car 65.00 160.00
Never hinged 160.00
On cover —
Nos. B48-B54 (7) 222.50 410.50
Nos. B48-B54,C8-C13 (13) 275.50 514.50
Nos. B48-B54 on overfranked philatelic cover 1,500.

Seventh Sample Fair, Tripoli. Surtax aided fair.

Pomegranate Tree — SP15

Designs: 50c+10c, 2 l+50c, Musician. 75c+15c, 1.25 l+25c, Tribesman.

1935, Feb. 16
B55 SP15 10c + 10c brown 1.10 4.00
Never hinged 2.75
On cover 130.00
B56 SP15 20c + 10c rose red 1.10 4.00
Never hinged 2.75
On cover 150.00
B57 SP15 50c + 10c purple 1.10 4.00
Never hinged 2.75
On cover 130.00
B58 SP15 75c + 15c car 1.10 4.00
Never hinged 2.75
On cover 180.00
B59 SP15 1.25 l + 25c dl blue 1.10 4.00
Never hinged 2.75
On cover 300.00
B60 SP15 2 l + 50c ol grn 1.10 7.25
Never hinged 2.75
On cover —
Nos. B55-B60 (6) 6.60 27.25
Nos. B55-B60,C19-C24 (12) 17.60 76.50
Nos. B55-B60 on overfranked philatelic cover 550.00

Ninth Sample Fair, Tripoli. Surtax aided fair.

AIR POST STAMPS

Italy Nos. C3 and C5 Overprinted

1928-29 Wmk. 140 *Perf. 14*
C1 AP2 50c rose red 8.75 14.50
Never hinged 22.50
On cover 80.00
C2 AP2 80c brn vio & brn ('29) 27.50 50.00
Never hinged 70.00
On cover 250.00

Airplane AP1

1931, Mar. 8 Photo. Wmk. 140
C3 AP1 50c blue 1.50 13.00
Never hinged 3.75
On flown cover 165.00

See note after No. B37.

Seaplane over Bedouin Camp
AP2

Designs: 50c, 1 l, Seaplane over Bedouin camp. 2 l+1 l, 5 l+2 l, Seaplane over Tripoli.

1932, Mar. 1 ***Perf. 14***

C4 AP2 50c dark blue 8.75 *30.00*
Never hinged 22.50
On cover *145.00*
C5 AP2 1 l org brown 8.75 *30.00*
Never hinged 22.50
On cover *165.00*
C6 AP2 2 l + 1 l dk gray 20.00 *62.50*
Never hinged 50.00
On cover —
C7 AP2 5 l + 2 l car 50.00 *55.00*
Never hinged 200.00
On cover —
Nos. C4-C7 (4) 87.50 *177.50*
Set on overfranked philatelic cover 475.00

See note after No. B47.

Seaplane Arriving at Tripoli
AP3

Designs: 50c, 2 l+50c, Seaplane arriving at Tripoli. 75c, 10 l+2.50 l, Plane over Tagiura. 1 l, 5 l+1 l, Seaplane leaving Tripoli.

1933, Mar. 1

C8 AP3 50c dp green 5.00 *7.50*
Never hinged 16.00
On cover *145.00*
C9 AP3 75c carmine 5.00 *7.50*
Never hinged 16.00
On cover *180.00*
C10 AP3 1 l dk blue 5.00 *7.50*
Never hinged 16.00
On cover *225.00*
C11 AP3 2 l + 50c pur 10.00 *14.00*
Never hinged 30.00
On cover —
C12 AP3 5 l + 1 l org brn 14.00 *22.50*
Never hinged 55.00
On cover —
C13 AP3 10 l + 2.50 l gray blk 14.00 *45.00*
Never hinged 55.00
On cover —
Nos. C8-C13 (6) 53.00 *104.00*
Set on overfranked philatelic cover 575.00

See note after No. B54.

Seaplane over Tripoli Harbor
AP4

Airplane and Camel — AP5

Designs: 50c, 5 l+1 l, Seaplane over Tripoli harbor. 75c, 10 l+2 l, Plane and minaret.

1934, Feb. 17 **Photo.** **Wmk. 140**

C14 AP4 50c slate bl 7.25 *20.00*
Never hinged 18.00
On cover *180.00*
C15 AP4 75c red org 7.25 *20.00*
Never hinged 18.00
On cover *225.00*
C16 AP4 5 l + 1 l dp grn 87.50 *140.00*
Never hinged 225.00
On cover —
C17 AP4 10 l + 2 l dl vio 87.50 *150.00*
Never hinged 225.00
On cover —
C18 AP5 25 l + 3 l org brn 100.00 *175.00*
Never hinged 250.00
On cover —
Nos. C14-C18 (5) 289.50 *505.00*
Set on overfranked philatelic cover 1,100.

Eighth Sample Fair, Tripoli. Surtax aided fair. See Nos. CE1-CE2.

Plane and Ancient Tower — AP6

Camel Train
AP7

Designs: 25c+10c, 3 l+1.50 l, Plane and ancient tower. 50c+10c, 2 l+30c, Camel train. 1 l+25c, 10 l+5 l, Arab watching plane.

1935, Apr. 12

C19 AP6 25c + 10c green .75 *4.25*
Never hinged 1.90
On cover *165.00*
C20 AP7 50c + 10c slate bl .75 *4.25*
Never hinged 1.90
On cover *165.00*
C21 AP7 1 l + 25c blue .75 *4.25*
Never hinged 1.90
On cover *225.00*
C22 AP7 2 l + 30c rose red .75 *5.75*
Never hinged 1.90
On cover —
C23 AP6 3 l + 1.50 l brn .75 *5.75*
Never hinged 1.90
On cover —
C24 AP7 10 l + 5 l dl vio 7.25 *25.00*
Never hinged 18.00
On cover —
Nos. C19-C24 (6) 11.00 *49.25*
Set on overfranked philatelic cover 260.00

See note after No. B60.

Cyrenaica No. C6 Overprinted in Black

1936, Oct.

C25 AP2 50c purple 5.75 .35
Never hinged 14.50
On cover 2.25

Same on Tripolitania Nos. C8 and C12

1937

C26 AP1 50c rose carmine .35 .20
Never hinged .90
On cover 2.00
C27 AP2 1 l deep blue 1.75 .90
Never hinged 4.50
On cover 5.00
Set, never hinged 5.40

See Nos. C45-C50.

Ruins of Odeon Theater, Sabrata
AP8

1937, Mar. 15 **Photo.**

C28 AP8 50c dark violet 2.10 *5.75*
Never hinged 5.50
On cover 100.00
C29 AP8 1 l vio black 2.10 *8.75*
Never hinged 5.50
On cover 180.00
Set, never hinged 11.00
Set on overfranked philatelic cover 110.00

Opening of a coastal road to the Egyptian frontier.

Nos. C28-C29 Overprinted "XI FIERA DI TRIPOLI"

1937, Mar. 15

C30 AP8 50c dark violet 13.00 *32.50*
Never hinged 32.50
On cover 80.00
C31 AP8 1 l violet blk 13.00 *32.50*
Never hinged 32.50
On cover 165.00
Set, never hinged 65.00
Set on overfranked philatelic cover 240.00

11th Sample Fair, Tripoli.

View of Tripoli
AP9

Eagle Attacking Serpent
AP10

1938, Mar. 12 ***Perf. 14***

C32 AP9 50c dk olive grn 1.10 *2.10*
Never hinged 2.75
On cover 42.50
C33 AP9 1 l slate blue 1.10 *5.00*
Never hinged 2.75
On cover 80.00
Set, never hinged 5.50

12th Sample Fair, Tripoli.

1938, Apr. 25 **Wmk. 140**

C34 AP10 50c olive brown .35 *1.75*
Never hinged .90
On cover 40.00
C35 AP10 1 l brn violet 1.10 *4.00*
Never hinged 2.75
On cover 80.00
Set, never hinged 3.75

Birth bimillenary Augustus Caesar (Octavianus), first Roman emperor.

Arab and Camel
AP11

Design: 50c, Fair entrance.

1939, Apr. 12 **Photo.**

C36 AP11 25c green .35 *1.75*
Never hinged .90
On cover 50.00
C37 AP11 50c olive brown .60 *1.75*
Never hinged 1.50
On cover 40.00
C38 AP11 1 l rose violet .75 *2.10*
Never hinged 1.90
On cover 100.00
Nos. C36-C38 (3) 1.70 *5.60*
Set, never hinged 4.00

13th Sample Fair, Tripoli.

Plane Over Modern City
AP12

Design: 1 l, 5 l+2.50 l, Plane over oasis.

1940, June 3

C39 AP12 50c brn blk .50 *.90*
Never hinged 1.25
On cover *50.00*
C40 AP12 1 l brn vio .50 *1.75*
Never hinged 1.25
On cover *87.50*
C41 AP12 2 l + 75c indigo 1.10 *5.50*
Never hinged 2.75
On cover —
C42 AP12 5 l + 2.50 l copper brn 1.10 *10.00*
Never hinged 2.75
On cover —
Nos. C39-C42 (4) 3.20 *18.15*
Set, never hinged 8.00
Set on overfranked philatelic cover 130.00

Triennial Overseas Exposition, Naples.

AIR POST SPECIAL DELIVERY STAMPS

APSD1

Wmk. 140

1934, Feb. 17 **Photo.** ***Perf. 14***

CE1 APSD1 2.25 l olive blk 25.00 *42.50*
Never hinged 62.50
On cover *1,200.*
CE2 APSD1 4.50 l + 1 l gray blk 25.00 *42.50*
Never hinged 62.50
On cover —
Set, never hinged 125.00
Set, on overfranked flown cover *1,100.*

8th Sample Fair at Tripoli. The surtax was for the aid of the Fair.

SPECIAL DELIVERY STAMPS

Special Delivery Stamps of Italy Overprinted

Two types of overprint. See note preceding No. 1 for descriptions.

1915-16. **Wmk. 140** ***Perf. 14***

E1 SD1 25c rose red, ovpt. type I 21.00 20.00
Never hinged 55.00
On cover 110.00
a. Overprinted type II 21.00 20.00
Never hinged 55.00
On cover 55.00
E2 SD2 30c blue & rose, ovpt. type I 5.75 *40.00*
Never hinged 14.50
On cover 375.00
a. Overprinted type II 5.75 40.00
Never hinged 52.50
On cover 300.00
Set, never hinged 70.00

Issued: Nos. E1, E2, Nov. 1915; Nos. E1a, E2a, Dec. 1916.
For surcharges see Nos. E7-E8.

"Italia"
SD3

1921-23 **Engr.** ***Perf. 13½***

E3 SD3 30c blue & rose 2.10 *6.50*
Never hinged 5.50
On cover 100.00
E4 SD3 50c rose red & brn 3.00 *10.00*
Never hinged 7.25
On cover 120.00
E5 SD3 60c dk red & brn ('23) 7.25 *16.00*
Never hinged 18.00
On cover 165.00
E6 SD3 2 l dk bl & red ('23) 10.00 *30.00*
Never hinged 25.00
On cover 325.00
Nos. E3-E6 (4) 22.35 *62.50*
Set, never hinged 55.00

30c, 2 l inscribed "EXPRES."
For surcharges see Nos. E9-E12.

Nos. E1-E2 Surcharged

1922, June 1

E7 SD1 60c on 25c rose red 11.50 *16.00*
Never hinged 30.00
On cover 190.00
E8 SD2 1.60 l on 30c bl & rose 13.00 *32.50*
Never hinged 32.50
On cover 425.00
Set, never hinged 62.50

Nos. E5-E6 Surcharged in Blue or Red:

No. E9

Nos. E10, E12

No. E11

1926-36

E9 SD3 70c on 60c 7.25 *16.00*
Never hinged 18.00
On cover 145.00
E10 SD3 2.50 l on 2 l (R) 10.00 *30.00*
Never hinged 25.00
On cover 475.00

Perf. 11

E11 SD3 1.25 l on 60c 5.25 1.75
Never hinged 13.00
On cover 16.50
a. Perf. 14 ('36) 19.00 3.50
Never hinged 47.50
On cover 100.00
b. Black surcharge *95,000.* *8,750.*
Never hinged *117,500.*
On cover *20,000.*
E12 SD3 2.50 l on 2 l (R) 115.00 *440.00*
Never hinged 290.00
On cover *1,800.*
Nos. E9-E12 (4) 137.50 *487.75*
Set, never hinged 300.00

Issued: #E9-E10, July 1926; #E11-E12, 1927.

SEMI-POSTAL SPECIAL DELIVERY STAMPS

Camel Caravan SPSD1

Wmk. 140

1927, Feb. 15 Litho. *Perf. 14*

EB1 SPSD1 1.25 l + 30c pur & blk 8.75 32.50
Never hinged 22.50
On cover 225.00
EB2 SPSD1 2.50 l + 1 l yel & blk 8.75 32.50
Never hinged 22.50
On cover —
Set, never hinged 45.00

See note after No. B10.
No. EB2 is inscribed "EXPRES."

War Memorial SPSD2

1931, Mar. 8 Photo.

EB3 SPSD2 1.25 l + 20c car rose 5.75 *22.50*
Never hinged 14.50

See note after No. B37.

AUTHORIZED DELIVERY STAMPS

Italy No. EY1 Overprinted in Black

1929, May 11 Wmk. 140 *Perf. 14*

EY1 AD1 10c dull blue 25.00 35.00
Never hinged 62.50
On cover 440.00
a. Perf. 11 87.50 125.00
Never hinged 225.00
On cover 375.00

Italy No. EY2 Overprinted in Black

1941, May *Perf. 14*

EY2 AD2 10c dark brown 10.00 18.00
Never hinged 25.00
On cover 375.00

A variety of No. EY2, with larger "LIBIA" and yellow gum, was prepared in 1942, but not issued. Value 35 cents, never hinged $1.90.

AD1

1942 Litho. Wmk. 140

EY3 AD1 10c sepia .75
Never hinged 1.90

No. EY3 was not issued.

POSTAGE DUE STAMPS

Italian Postage Due Stamps, 1870-1903 Overprinted in Black

1915, Nov. Wmk. 140 *Perf. 14*

J1 D3 5c buff & magenta 2.25 *7.25*
Never hinged 3.25
On cover 225.00
J2 D3 10c buff & magenta 2.25 *3.75*
Never hinged 3.25
On cover 130.00
J3 D3 20c buff & magenta 3.00 *5.75*
Never hinged 4.40
On cover 130.00
a. Double overprint 440.00
Never hinged 650.00
b. Inverted overprint 440.00
Never hinged 675.00
J4 D3 30c buff & magenta 3.75 *7.50*
Never hinged 5.50
On cover 165.00
J5 D3 40c buff & magenta 5.75 *8.75*
Never hinged 8.75
On cover 225.00
a. "40" in black *4,100.*
Never hinged *5,100.*
J6 D3 50c buff & magenta 3.75 *5.75*
Never hinged 5.50
On cover 130.00
J7 D3 60c buff & magenta 5.75 *11.00*
Never hinged 8.75
On cover 225.00
J8 D3 1 l blue & magenta 3.75 11.00
Never hinged 5.50
On cover 240.00
a. Double overprint *5,250.* *6,000.*
J9 D3 2 l blue & magenta 55.00 *65.00*
Never hinged 82.50
On cover —
J10 D3 5 l blue & magenta 65.00 *100.00*
Never hinged 100.00
On cover —
Nos. J1-J10 (10) 150.25 *225.75*

1926

J11 D3 60c buff & brown 87.50 *125.00*
Never hinged 130.00
On cover 250.00

Postage Due Stamps of Italy, 1934, Overprinted in Black

1934

J12 D6 5c brown .25 *3.00*
Never hinged .55
On cover 190.00
J13 D6 10c blue .25 *3.00*
Never hinged .55
On cover 100.00
J14 D6 20c rose red 1.40 1.50
Never hinged 3.60
On cover 100.00
J15 D6 25c green 1.40 1.50
Never hinged 3.60
On cover 87.50
J16 D6 30c red orange 1.40 *5.75*
Never hinged 3.60
On cover 165.00
J17 D6 40c black brn 1.40 *3.75*
Never hinged 3.60
On cover 180.00
J18 D6 50c violet 1.75 .35
Never hinged 4.50
On cover 80.00
J19 D6 60c black 1.75 *14.50*
Never hinged 4.50
On cover 240.00
J20 D7 1 l red orange 1.40 .35
Never hinged 3.75
On cover 100.00
J21 D7 2 l green 40.00 14.50
Never hinged 100.00
On cover 240.00
J22 D7 5 l violet 72.50 32.50
Never hinged 180.00
On cover —
J23 D7 10 l blue 11.00 *42.50*
Never hinged 27.50
On cover —
J24 D7 20 l carmine 11.00 *57.50*
Never hinged 27.50
On cover —
Nos. J12-J24 (13) 145.50 *180.70*

PARCEL POST STAMPS

These stamps were used by affixing them to the way bill so that one half remained on it following the parcel, the other half staying on the receipt given the sender. Most used halves are right halves. Complete stamps were obtainable canceled, probably to order. Both unused and used values are for complete stamps.

Italian Parcel Post Stamps, 1914-22, Overprinted

1915-24 Wmk. 140 *Perf. 13½*

Q1 PP2 5c brown 2.10 *8.75*
Never hinged 3.25
a. Double overprint 325.00
Never hinged *500.00*
Q2 PP2 10c deep blue 2.10 *8.75*
Never hinged 3.25
Q3 PP2 20c blk ('18) 3.00 *8.75*
Never hinged 4.40
Q4 PP2 25c red 3.00 *8.75*
Never hinged 4.40
Q5 PP2 50c orange 4.25 *8.75*
Never hinged 6.75
Q6 PP2 1 l violet 4.25 *11.00*
Never hinged 6.75
Q7 PP2 2 l green 5.75 *11.00*
Never hinged 8.75
Q8 PP2 3 l bister 7.25 *11.00*
Never hinged 11.00
Q9 PP2 4 l slate 7.25 *11.00*
Never hinged 11.00
Q10 PP2 10 l rose lil ('24) 57.50 *72.50*
Never hinged 87.50
Q11 PP2 12 l red brn ('24) 110.00 *175.00*
Never hinged 165.00
Q12 PP2 15 l ol grn ('24) 110.00 *250.00*
Never hinged 165.00
Q13 PP2 20 l brn vio ('24) 210.00 *300.00*
Never hinged 325.00
Nos. Q1-Q13 (13) 526.45 *885.25*

Halves Used

Q1-Q6	.20
Q7-Q9	.30
Q10	2.00
Q11	3.50
Q12	8.00
Q13	9.00

Same Overprint on Parcel Post Stamps of Italy, 1927-36

1927-38

Q14 PP3 10c dp bl ('36) 3.50 *6.00*
Never hinged 5.50
Q15 PP3 25c red ('36) 3.50 *6.00*
Never hinged 5.50
Q16 PP3 30c ultra ('29) 1.40 *3.00*
Never hinged 2.25
Q17 PP3 50c orange 65.00 175.00
Never hinged 100.00
a. Overprint 8¾x2mm ('31) 110.00 *250.00*
Never hinged 165.00
Q18 PP3 60c red ('29) 1.50 *3.00*
Never hinged 2.25
Q19 PP3 1 l lilac ('36) 30.00 *87.50*
Never hinged 42.50
Q20 PP3 2 l grn ('38) 32.50 *87.50*
Never hinged 50.00
Q21 PP3 3 l bister 2.10 *7.25*
Never hinged 3.25
Q22 PP3 4 l gray 2.10 *11.50*
Never hinged 3.25
Q23 PP3 10 l rose lil ('36) 250.00 360.00
Never hinged 390.00
Q24 PP3 20 l brn vio ('36) 300.00 *440.00*
Never hinged 440.00
Nos. Q14-Q24 (11) 691.60 *1,186.*

Halves Used

Q14, Q16, Q18	.25
Q15	.35
Q17	9.00
Q19-Q20	1.50
Q21-Q22	.50
Q23	18.00
Q24	19.00

The overprint measures 10x1½mm on No. Q17.

Same Overprint on Italy No. Q24

1939

Q25 PP3 5c brown *11,750.*
Never hinged *15,000.*

The overprint was applied to the 5c in error. Few copies exist.

LIECHTENSTEIN

ˈlik-tən-ˌshtin

LOCATION — Central Europe southeast of Lake Constance, between Austria and Switzerland
GOVT. — Principality
AREA — 61.8 sq. mi.
POP. — 4,896 (est. 1984)
CAPITAL — Vaduz

The Principality of Liechtenstein is a sovereign state consisting of the two counties of Schellenberg and Vaduz. Since 1921 the post office has been administered by Switzerland.

100 Heller = 1 Krone
100 Rappen = 1 Franc (1921)

Watermark

Greek Cross — Wmk. 183

Austrian Administration of the Post Office

Prince Johann II — A1

Perf. 12½x13

1912, Feb. 1 Unwmk. Typo.

Thick Chalky Paper

1 A1 5h yellow green 35.00 13.00
Never hinged 140.00
On cover 22.50
2 A1 10h rose 70.00 13.00
Never hinged 325.00
On cover 22.50
3 A1 25h dark blue 70.00 40.00
Never hinged 260.00
On cover 150.00
Nos. 1-3 (3) 175.00 66.00
Set, never hinged 725.00
First day cover, #1-3 325.00

Nos. 1-3 exist imperf. Value set, $440 unused with original gum, $1,350 never hinged.

Values for blocks of 4 (NH, used)

1	A1	5h yellow green	600.00	77.50
2	A1	10h rose	1,300.	77.50
3	A1	25h dark blue	1,050.	275.00

1915

Thin Unsurfaced Paper

1a A1 5h yellow green 12.00 *15.00*
Never hinged 35.00
On cover 24.00
2a A1 10h rose 75.00 22.50
Never hinged 260.00
On cover 45.00
3a A1 25h dark blue 575.00 150.00
Never hinged 2,200.
On commercial cover, single franking 440.00
b. 25h ultramarine 350.00 350.00
Never hinged 1,300.
On commercial cover, single franking *7,750.*
#1a-3a, never hinged 2,500.

Nos. 1a-3a exist imperf. Value set, $875 unused with original gum, $2,500 never hinged.

Values for blocks of 4 (NH, used)

1a	A1	5h yellow green	140.00	77.50
2a	A1	10h rose	1,050.	130.00
3a	A1	25h dark blue	8,800.	775.00
b.		25h ultramarine	5,200.	2,300.

Coat of Arms — A2

Prince Johann II — A3

1917-18

4 A2 3h violet 1.40 1.50
Never hinged 6.25
On cover 21.00
5 A2 5h yellow green 1.40 1.50
Never hinged 6.25
On cover 17.00
6 A3 10h claret 1.40 1.50
Never hinged 6.25
On cover 17.00
7 A3 15h dull red 1.40 1.50
Never hinged 6.25
On cover 25.00
8 A3 20h dark green 1.40 1.50
Never hinged 6.25
On cover 25.00
9 A3 25h deep blue 1.40 1.50
Never hinged 6.25
On cover 27.50
Nos. 4-9 (6) 8.40 9.00
Set, never hinged 37.50
Nos. 4-7, 9, set of 5 on fdc (6/14/17) 750.00

Exist imperf. Value set unused original gum, $350.
For surcharges see Nos. 11-16.

Prince Johann II — A4

1918, Nov. 12

Dates in Upper Corners

10 A4 20h dark green .45 *2.00*
Never hinged 3.25
On cover *27.50*
First day cover 110.00

Accession of Prince Johann II, 60th anniv. Exists imperf. Value $150.

National Administration of the Post Office

Stamps of 1917-18 Overprinted or Surcharged

a

b

c

1920

11 A2(a) 5h yellow green 1.90 *7.50*
Never hinged 8.25
On cover *425.00*
On cover, overfranked 140.00
a. Inverted overprint 75.00 *175.00*
Never hinged 200.00
b. Double overprint 15.00 *100.00*
Never hinged 40.00
On cover *500.00*
12 A3(a) 10h claret 1.90 *7.50*
Never hinged 8.25
On cover *425.00*
On cover, overfranked 140.00
a. Inverted overprint 75.00 175.00
Never hinged 200.00
b. Double overprint 15.00 *100.00*
Never hinged 40.00
On cover *600.00*
c. Overprint type "c" 15.00 *100.00*
Never hinged 35.00
On cover *450.00*
13 A3(a) 25h deep blue 1.90 *7.50*
Never hinged 8.25
On cover *425.00*
On cover, overfranked 140.00
a. Inverted overprint 75.00 *175.00*
Never hinged 200.00
b. Double overprint 15.00 *100.00*
Never hinged 35.00
On cover *600.00*
14 A2(b) 40h on 3h violet 1.90 *7.50*
Never hinged 8.25
On cover *425.00*
On cover, overfranked 140.00
a. Inverted surcharge 75.00 *175.00*
Never hinged 200.00
15 A3(c) 1k on 15h dull red 1.90 *7.50*
Never hinged 8.25
On cover *425.00*
On cover, overfranked 140.00
a. Inverted surcharge 75.00 *175.00*
Never hinged 200.00
b. Overprint type "a" 67.50 *150.00*
Never hinged 250.00
On cover *750.00*
16 A3(c) 2½k on 20h dk grn 1.90 *7.50*
Never hinged 8.25
On cover *425.00*
On cover, overfranked 140.00
a. Inverted surcharge 75.00 *175.00*
Never hinged 200.00
Nos. 11-16 (6) 11.40 *45.00*
Set, never hinged 50.00

Coat of Arms A5

Chapel of St. Mamertus A6

Coat of Arms with Supporters A15

Designs: 40h, Gutenberg Castle. 50h, Courtyard, Vaduz Castle. 60h, Red Tower, Vaduz. 80h, Old Roman Tower, Schaan. 1k, Castle at Vaduz. 2k, View of Bendern. 5k, Prince Johann I. 7½k, Prince Johann II.

1920 Engr. *Imperf.*

18 A5 5h olive bister .25 5.75
Never hinged .55
On cover 105.00
19 A5 10h deep orange .25 5.75
Never hinged .55
On cover 92.50
20 A5 15h dark blue .25 5.75
Never hinged .55
On cover 105.00
21 A5 20h deep brown .25 5.75
Never hinged .80
On cover 70.00
22 A5 25h dark green .25 5.75
Never hinged .80
On cover 80.00
23 A5 30h gray black .25 5.75
Never hinged 1.10
On cover 105.00
24 A5 40h dark red .25 5.75
Never hinged 1.10
On cover 70.00
25 A6 1k blue .25 5.75
Never hinged 2.00
On cover 105.00
#18-25, set of 8 on fdc (5/5/20) 1,100.

Perf. 12½

32 A5 5h olive bister .25 *.50*
Never hinged .55
On cover *82.50*
33 A5 10h deep orange .25 *.50*
Never hinged .55
On cover *70.00*
34 A5 15h deep blue .25 *.50*
Never hinged .55
On cover *82.50*
35 A5 20h red brown .25 *.50*
Never hinged .55
On cover *55.00*
36 A6 25h olive green .25 *.50*
Never hinged .55
On cover *70.00*
37 A5 30h dark gray .25 *.50*
Never hinged .55
On cover *92.50*
38 A6 40h claret .25 *.50*
Never hinged .55
On cover *82.50*
39 A6 50h yellow green .25 *.50*
Never hinged .55
On cover *82.50*
40 A6 60h red brown .25 *.505*
Never hinged .55
On cover *100.00*
41 A6 80h rose .25 *.50*
Never hinged .55
On cover *50.00*
42 A6 1k dull violet .45 *.90*
Never hinged 1.10
On cover *82.50*
43 A6 2k light blue .45 *1.00*
Never hinged 1.60
On cover 105.00
44 A6 5k black .45 *1.10*
Never hinged 2.90
On cover *275.00*
45 A6 7½k slate .45 *1.50*
Never hinged 3.25
On cover *350.00*
46 A15 10k ocher .45 *1.50*
Never hinged 8.00
On cover *400.00*
Nos. 18-46 (23) 6.75 *61.55*
Set, never hinged 27.50

Used values for Nos. 18-46 are for canceled to order stamps. Value with postal cancels approximately $45.
Many denominations of Nos. 32-46 are found imperforate, imperforate vertically and imperforate horizontally.
For surcharges see Nos. 51-52.

Madonna and Child — A16

1920, Oct. 5

47 A16 50h olive green .45 *1.40*
Never hinged 2.50
On cover *140.00*
48 A16 80h brown red .45 *1.40*
Never hinged 2.50
On cover *140.00*
49 A16 2k dark blue .45 *2.10*
Never hinged 2.50
On cover *140.00*
Nos. 47-49 (3) 1.35 *4.90*
Set, never hinged 7.50
Set of 3 on fdc 105.00
Set of 3 on overfranked cover 17.50

80th birthday of Prince Johann II.

Imperf., Singles

47a A16 50h 6.00 —
Never hinged 8.00
48a A16 80h 6.00 —
Never hinged 8.00
49a A16 2k 6.00 —
Never hinged 8.00
Set of 3 singles on fdc 1,600.

On 1/31/21 the Swiss took over the Post Office administration. Previous issues were demonitized and remainders of Nos. 4-49 were sold.

Swiss Administration of the Post Office

No. 19 Surcharged

No. 51

No. 52

1921 Unwmk. Engr. *Imperf.*

51 A5 2rp on 10h dp org .90 *27.50*
Never hinged 3.50
On cover *450.00*
First day cover (2/1/21) *1,000.*
a. Double surcharge 97.50 *140.00*
Never hinged 160.00
On cover *550.00*
b. Inverted surcharge 80.00 *140.00*
Never hinged 140.00
On cover *550.00*
c. Double surch., one inverted 100.00 *87.50*
Never hinged 175.00
On cover *550.00*
d. Comma after "Rp" 52.50 *100.00*
Never hinged 100.00
On cover *550.00*
e. Inverted comma after "Rp" 52.50 *100.00*
Never hinged 100.00
On cover *550.00*
52 A5 2rp on 10h dp org .60 *20.00*
Never hinged 1.40
On cover *400.00*
First day cover (2/27/21) *750.00*
a. Double surcharge 80.00 *175.00*
Never hinged 140.00
On cover *550.00*
b. Inverted surcharge 80.00 *175.00*
Never hinged 140.00
On cover *550.00*

c.		Double surch., one inverted	92.50	*190.00*
		Never hinged	160.00	
		On cover		*550.00*

Arms with Supporters A19

Chapel of St. Mamertus A20

View of Vaduz A21

Designs: 25rp, Castle at Vaduz. 30rp, View of Bendern. 35rp, Prince Johann II. 40rp, Old Roman Tower at Schaan. 50rp, Gutenberg Castle. 80rp, Red Tower at Vaduz.

1921 *Perf. 12½, 9½ (2rp, 10rp, 15rp)*

Surface Tinted Paper (#54-61)

54	A19	2rp lemon	1.00	*10.00*
		Never hinged	3.75	
		On cover		*21.00*
55	A19	2½rp black	1.10	*11.00*
		Never hinged	4.00	
		On cover		*12.50*
a.		Perf. 9½	1.25	*57.50*
		Never hinged	2.75	
		On cover		*450.00*
56	A19	3rp orange	1.10	*10.00*
		Never hinged	2.90	
		On cover		*22.50*
a.		Perf. 9½	140.00	*3,750.*
		Never hinged	350.00	
		On cover		*4,400.*
57	A19	5rp olive green	11.50	1.75
		Never hinged	32.50	
		On cover		7.00
a.		Perf. 9½	67.50	*13.00*
		Never hinged	200.00	
		On cover		*27.50*
58	A19	7½rp dark blue	6.75	*35.00*
		Never hinged	19.00	
		On cover		*62.50*
a.		Perf. 9½	275.00	*875.00*
		Never hinged	675.00	
		On cover		*1,250.*
59	A19	10rp yellow green	26.00	8.75
		Never hinged	95.00	
		On cover		18.00
a.		Perf. 12½	35.00	6.00
		Never hinged	90.00	
		On cover		14.00
60	A19	13rp brown	8.25	*77.50*
		Never hinged	22.50	
		On cover		*92.50*
a.		Perf. 9½	95.00	*2,150.*
		Never hinged	300.00	
		On cover		*3,450.*
b.		Perf. 12½x9½	125.00	—
		Never hinged	400.00	
61	A19	15rp dark violet	22.50	20.00
		Never hinged	37.50	
		On cover		40.00
a.		Perf. 12½	21.00	*24.00*
		Never hinged	67.50	
		On cover		*72.50*
62	A20	20rp dull vio & blk	67.50	1.90
		Never hinged	175.00	
		On cover		7.00
63	A20	25rp rose red & blk	3.50	3.00
		Never hinged	8.00	
		On cover		12.00
64	A20	30rp dp grn & blk	75.00	17.00
		Never hinged	200.00	
		On cover		35.00
65	A20	35rp brn & blk, *straw*	6.50	*13.50*
		Never hinged	13.50	
		On cover		*27.50*
66	A20	40rp dk blue & blk	9.75	5.50
		Never hinged	24.00	
		On cover		14.00
67	A20	50rp dk grn & blk	17.00	6.75
		Never hinged	32.50	
		On cover		18.00
68	A20	80rp gray & blk	30.00	*67.50*
		Never hinged	57.50	
		On cover		*105.00*
69	A21	1fr dp claret & blk	57.50	45.00
		Never hinged	120.00	
		On cover		92.50
		Nos. 54-69 (16)	344.95	*334.15*
		Set, never hinged	1,150.	

Nos. 54-69 exist imperforate; Nos. 54-61, partly perforated. See Nos. 73, 81. For surcharges see Nos. 70-71.

Nos. 58, 60a Surcharged in Red

1924 ***Perf. 12½, 9½***

70	A19	5rp on 7½rp	1.25	*2.00*
		Never hinged	3.50	
		On cover		*27.50*
a.		Perf. 9½	15.00	6.75
		Never hinged	45.00	
		On cover		55.00
71	A19	10rp on 13rp	.70	*15.00*
		Never hinged	2.00	
		On cover		*27.50*
a.		Perf. 12½	19.00	*40.00*
		Never hinged	35.00	
		On cover		*175.00*

Type of 1921

1924 **Wmk. 183** ***Perf. 11½***

Granite Paper

73	A19	10rp green	14.00	2.00
		Never hinged	65.00	
		On cover		21.00

Peasant A28

Government Palace and Church at Vaduz A30

10rp, 20rp, Courtyard, Vaduz Castle.

1924-28 **Typo.** ***Perf. 11½***

74	A28	2½rp ol grn & red vio ('28)	1.25	*5.00*
		Never hinged	3.75	
		On cover		*14.00*
75	A28	5rp brown & blue	2.25	.75
		Never hinged	6.50	
		On cover		3.25
76	A28	7½rp bl grn & brn ('28)	1.90	*5.50*
		Never hinged	3.75	
		On cover		*11.50*
77	A28	15rp red brn & bl grn ('28)	8.75	*27.50*
		Never hinged	19.00	
		On cover		*45.00*

Engr.

78	A28	10rp yellow grn	11.50	.60
		Never hinged	27.50	
		On cover		3.25
79	A28	20rp deep red	37.50	.90
		Never hinged	85.00	
		On cover		4.50
80	A30	1½fr blue	82.50	*87.50*
		Never hinged	210.00	
		On cover		*275.00*
		Nos. 74-80 (7)	145.65	*127.75*
		Set, never hinged	350.00	

Bendern Type of 1921

1925

81	A20	30rp blue & blk	11.50	2.00
		Never hinged	55.00	
		On cover		21.00

Prince Johann II — A31

Prince Johann II as Boy and Man A32

1928, Nov. 12 **Typo.** **Wmk. 183**

82	A31	10rp lt brn & ol grn	4.50	5.00
		Never hinged	11.00	
		On cover		11.50
83	A31	20rp org red & ol grn	6.75	10.00
		Never hinged	22.50	
		On cover		18.00
84	A31	30rp sl bl & ol grn	22.50	17.50
		Never hinged	85.00	
		On cover		45.00
85	A31	60rp red vio & ol grn	45.00	*75.00*
		Never hinged	160.00	
		On cover		*140.00*

Engr.

Unwmk.

86	A32	1.20fr ultra	37.50	*87.50*
		Never hinged	110.00	
		On cover		*275.00*
87	A32	1.50fr black brown	67.50	*190.00*
		Never hinged	210.00	
		On cover		*450.00*
88	A32	2fr deep car	67.50	*190.00*
		Never hinged	210.00	
		On cover		*450.00*
89	A32	5fr dark green	67.50	*225.00*
		Never hinged	210.00	
		On cover		*1,000.*
		Nos. 82-89 (8)	318.75	*800.00*
		Set, never hinged	1,000.	
		Set of 8 on fdc		1,800.

70th year of the reign of Prince Johann II.

Prince Francis I, as a Child — A33

Prince Francis I as a Man — A34

Princess Elsa — A35

Prince Francis and Princess Elsa — A36

1929, Dec. 2 **Photo.**

90	A33	10rp olive green	.35	*3.00*
		Never hinged	1.10	
		On cover		*7.00*
91	A34	20rp carmine	.55	*5.00*
		Never hinged	1.75	
		On cover		*11.50*
92	A35	30rp ultra	.90	*17.50*
		Never hinged	2.75	
		On cover		*35.00*
93	A36	70rp brown	16.00	*100.00*
		Never hinged	55.00	
		On cover		*140.00*
		Nos. 90-93 (4)	17.80	*125.50*
		Set, never hinged	55.00	
		Set of 4 on fdc		400.00

Values for used blocks of 4

90	A33	10rp olive green	*14.00*
91	A34	20rp carmine	*22.50*
92	A35	30rp ultra	*77.50*
93	A36	70rp brown	*450.00*

Accession of Prince Francis I, Feb. 11, 1929.

Grape Girl — A37

Chamois Hunter — A38

Mountain Cattle — A39

Courtyard, Vaduz Castle — A40

Mt. Naafkopf — A41

Chapel at Steg — A42

Rofenberg Chapel — A43

Chapel of St. Mamertus — A44

Alpine Hotel, Malbun — A45

Gutenberg Castle — A46

Schellenberg Monastery — A47

Castle at Vaduz — A48

Mountain Cottage — A49

Prince Francis and Princess Elsa — A50

1930 *Perf. 10½*

94	A37	3rp brown lake	.70	2.00
		Never hinged	2.75	
		On cover		7.50
95	A38	5rp deep green	1.90	5.00
		Never hinged	11.00	
		On cover		7.50
96	A39	10rp dark violet	1.60	5.00
		Never hinged	11.00	
		On cover		10.00
97	A40	20rp dp rose red	27.50	5.00
		Never hinged	82.50	
		On cover		110.00
98	A41	25rp black	5.50	*32.50*
		Never hinged	22.50	
		On cover		*50.00*
99	A42	30rp dp ultra	5.50	7.50
		Never hinged	22.50	
		On cover		15.00
103	A46	60rp olive blk	67.50	30.00
		Never hinged	225.00	
		On cover		50.00
104	A47	90rp violet brn	67.50	*250.00*
		Never hinged	250.00	
		On cover		*375.00*
105	A48	1.20fr olive brn	82.50	*275.00*
		Never hinged	275.00	
		On cover		*375.00*
106	A49	1.50fr black violet	45.00	55.00
		Never hinged	140.00	
		On cover		150.00
107	A50	2fr gray grn & red brn	55.00	*100.00*
		Never hinged	160.00	
		On cover		*150.00*

Perf. 11½

95a	A38	5rp dp grn	.75	.65
		Never hinged	11.00	
		On cover		5.00
96b	A39	10rp dp vio	.85	.35
		Never hinged	11.00	
		On cover		5.00
97a	A40	20rp dp rose red	19.00	.45
		Never hinged	60.00	
		On cover		6.00
98a	A41	25rp blk	67.50	*250.00*
		Never hinged	275.00	
		On cover		*375.00*
99b	A42	30rp dp ultra	5.00	.85
		Never hinged	19.00	
		On cover		12.50
100a	A43	35rp dk grn	*5,750.*	*10,000.*
		Never hinged	*10,500.*	
102a	A45	50rp blk brn	110.00	175.00
		Never hinged	400.00	
		On cover		*250.00*
103a	A46	60rp olive blk	57.50	11.00
		Never hinged	210.00	
		On cover		50.00
104a	A47	90rp vio brn	65.00	65.00
		Never hinged	275.00	
		On cover		200.00
105b	A48	1.20fr ol brn	75.00	*125.00*
		Never hinged	300.00	
		On cover		*300.00*
106a	A49	1.50fr blk vio	32.50	35.00
		Never hinged	110.00	
		On cover		150.00
107b	A50	2fr gray grn & red brn	52.50	*65.00*
		Never hinged	175.00	
		On cover		*160.00*

Perf. 11½x10½

96a	A39	10rp dk violet	6.75	*75.00*
		Never hinged	19.00	
		On cover		*100.00*
99a	A42	30rp dp ultra	675.00	*1,800.*
		Never hinged	1,700.	
		On cover		*4,000.*
100	A43	35rp dark green	6.75	*15.00*
		Never hinged	25.00	
		On cover		*37.50*
101	A44	40rp lt brown	6.75	6.00
		Never hinged	25.00	
		On cover		22.50
102	A45	50rp black brown	67.50	15.00
		Never hinged	240.00	
		On cover		30.00
105a	A48	1.20fr ol brn	*5,750.*	*10,000.*
		Never hinged	10,500.	
107a	A50	2fr ol grn & red brn	2,500.	*5,500.*
		Never hinged	*5,250.*	
		On cover		*7,500.*
		Set, never hinged	1,500.	

For overprints see Nos. O1-O8.

Values for used blocks of 4

Perf. 10½

94	A37	3rp brn lake	9.25
95	A38	5rp dp grn	22.50
96	A39	10rp dk vio	22.50
97	A40	20rp dp rose red	22.50
98	A41	25rp blk	*140.00*
99	A42	30rp dp ultra	32.50
103	A46	60rp ol blk	110.00
104	A47	90rp vio brn	*1,000.*
105	A48	1.20fr ol brn	*1,150.*
106	A49	1.50fr blk vio	250.00
107	A50	2fr ol grn & red brn	*450.00*

Perf. 11½

95a	A38	5rp dp grn	9.25
96b	A39	10rp dk vio	9.25
97a	A40	20rp dp rose red	14.00
98a	A41	25rp blk	*1,250.*
99b	A42	30rp dp ultra	22.50
100a	A43	35rp dk grn	—
102a	A45	50rp blk brn	*750.00*
103a	A46	60rp ol blk	110.00
104a	A47	90rp vio brn	450.00
105b	A48	1.20fr ol brn	*925.00*
106a	A49	1.50fr blk vio	225.00
107b	A50	2fr ol grn & red brn	*450.00*

Perf. 11½x10½

96a	A39	10rp dk vio	*325.00*
99a	A42	30rp dp ultra	*7,250.*
100	A43	35rp dk grn	*70.00*
101	A44	40rp lt brn	37.50
102	A45	50rp blk brn	82.50
105a	A48	1.20fr ol brn	—
107a	A50	2fr ol grn & red brn	—

Mt. Naafkopf A51

Gutenberg Castle A52

Vaduz Castle — A53

1933, Jan. 23 *Perf. 14½*

108	A51	25rp red orange	175.00	62.50
		Never hinged	550.00	
		On cover		82.50
109	A52	90rp dark green	6.75	*75.00*
		Never hinged	16.00	
		On cover		*140.00*
110	A53	1.20fr red brown	91.00	*250.00*
		Never hinged	250.00	
		On cover		*350.00*
		Nos. 108-110 (3)	272.75	*387.50*
		Set, never hinged	825.00	
		Set of 3 on fdc		2,100.

For overprints see Nos. O9-O10.

Values for used blocks of 4

108	A51	25rp red org	350.00
109	A52	90rp dk grn	*350.00*
110	A53	1.20fr red brn	*1,200.*

Prince Francis I

A54 A55

1933, Aug. 28 *Perf. 11*

111	A54	10rp purple	18.00	*35.00*
		Never hinged	55.00	
		On cover		*45.00*
112	A54	20rp brown carmine	18.00	*35.00*
		Never hinged	55.00	
		On cover		*45.00*
113	A54	30rp dark blue	18.00	*35.00*
		Never hinged	55.00	
		On cover		*45.00*
		Nos. 111-113 (3)	54.00	*105.00*
		Set, never hinged	165.00	
		Set of 3 on fdc		125.00

Values for used blocks of 4

111	A54	10rp pur	*140.00*
112	A54	20rp brn car	*140.00*
113	A54	30rp dk bl	*140.00*

80th birthday of Prince Francis I.

1933, Dec. 15 **Engr.** *Perf. 12½*

114	A55	3fr violet blue	82.50	*175.00*
		Never hinged	225.00	
		On cover		*450.00*
		First day cover		*2,100.*

See No. 152.

Agricultural Exhibition Issue

Souvenir Sheet

Arms of Liechtenstein — A56

1934, Sept. 29 *Perf. 12*

Granite Paper

115	A56	5fr brown	*1,200.*	*2,100.*
		Never hinged	*2,450.*	
		On cover		*3,250.*
		First day cover		*2,750.*
		Single stamp	*850.00*	*1,700.*
		Never hinged	*1,600.*	
		On cover		*3,000.*
		First day cover		*3,250.*

See No. 131.

Coat of Arms A57

"Three Sisters" (Landmark) A58

Church of Schaan A59

Bendern A60

Rathaus, Vaduz — A61

Samina Valley — A62

Samina Valley in Winter A63

Ruin at Schellenberg — A64

Government Palace — A65

Vaduz Castle A66

Gutenberg Castle A68

Alpine Hut — A69

Princess Elsa — A70

Coat of Arms — A71

60rp, Vaduz castle, diff. 1.50fr, Valuna.

1934-35 **Photo.** *Perf. 11½*

116	A57	3rp copper red	.25	.50
		Never hinged	.55	
		On cover		1.75
117	A58	5rp emerald	3.25	1.50
		Never hinged	11.00	
		On cover		1.75
118	A59	10rp deep violet	.45	1.00
		Never hinged	1.75	
		On cover		9.00
119	A60	15rp red org	.25	1.00
		Never hinged	1.10	
		On cover		4.50
120	A61	20rp red	.45	1.00
		Never hinged	1.75	
		On cover		2.25
121	A62	25rp brown	18.00	*47.50*
		Never hinged	55.00	
		On cover		*60.00*
122	A63	30rp dk blue	3.75	1.50
		Never hinged	12.00	
		On cover		4.00
123	A64	35rp gray grn	.90	*6.00*
		Never hinged	2.75	
		On cover		*11.50*
124	A65	40rp brown	1.10	*5.00*
		Never hinged	3.25	
		On cover		*9.25*
125	A66	50rp lt brown	16.00	15.00
		Never hinged	60.00	
		On cover		27.50
126	A66	60rp claret	1.40	*6.50*
		Never hinged	4.50	
		On cover		*14.00*
127	A68	90rp deep green	5.50	*21.00*
		Never hinged	16.00	
		On cover		*35.00*
128	A69	1.20fr deep blue	2.25	*21.00*
		Never hinged	8.00	
		On cover		*35.00*
129	A69	1.50fr brn car	2.75	*25.00*
		Never hinged	11.00	
		On cover		*45.00*
		Nos. 116-129 (14)	56.30	*153.50*
		Set, never hinged	190.00	
		#125-128 on fdc (6/18/34)		375.00
		#116-118 on fdc (12/17/34)		450.00
		#120-121 on fdc (1/3/35)		450.00
		#119, 122-124, 129 on fdc (12/9/35)		550.00

Engr.

Perf. 12½

130	A70	2fr henna brn ('35)	55.00	*175.00*
		Never hinged	110.00	
		On cover		*350.00*
131	A71	5fr dk vio ('35)	275.00	*850.00*
		Never hinged	525.00	
		On cover		*1,800.*

No. 131 has the same design as the 5fr in the souvenir sheet, No. 115. See #226, B14. For overprints see Nos. O11-O20.

Bridge at Malbun A72

Labor: 20rp, Constructing Road to Triesenberg. 30rp, Binnen Canal. 50rp, Bridge near Planken.

1937, June 30 **Photo.**

132	A72	10rp brt violet	1.10	1.50
		Never hinged	4.00	
		On cover		3.75
133	A72	20rp red	1.10	*2.00*
		Never hinged	4.00	
		On cover		*3.75*
134	A72	30rp brt blue	1.10	*2.50*
		Never hinged	4.00	
		On cover		*5.50*

135 A72 50rp yellow brown 1.10 *3.00*
Never hinged 4.00
On cover *7.00*
Nos. 132-135 (4) 4.40 9.00
Set, never hinged 16.00
Set of 4 on fdc 110.00

Ruin at Schalun — A76

Peasant in Rhine Valley A77

Ruin at Schellenberg — A78

Knight and Gutenberg Castle A79

Baron von Brandis and Vaduz Castle A80

Designs: 5rp, Chapel at Masescha. 10rp, Knight and Vaduz Castle. 15rp, Upper Valüna Valley. 20rp, Wooden Bridge over Rhine, Bendern. 25rp, Chapel at Steg. 90rp, "The Three Sisters". 1fr, Frontier stone. 1.20fr, Gutenberg Castle and Harpist. 1.50fr, Alpine View of Lawena and Schwartzhorn.

1937-38

136 A76 3rp yellow brown .25 *.50*
Never hinged .55
On cover 1.40

Pale Buff Shading

137 A76 5rp emerald .25 .25
Never hinged .55
On cover 1.40
138 A76 10rp violet .25 .25
Never hinged .55
On cover 1.40
139 A76 15rp dk slate grn .25 *.50*
Never hinged .55
On cover 1.90
140 A76 20rp brn org .25 .50
Never hinged .55
On cover 1.90
141 A76 25rp chestnut .45 *2.50*
Never hinged 1.40
On cover 5.00
142 A77 30rp blue & gray 2.75 1.00
Never hinged 9.50
On cover 2.75
144 A78 40rp dark green 1.90 2.00
Never hinged 5.50
On cover 5.50
145 A79 50rp dark brown .70 *2.50*
Never hinged 2.25
On cover *4.50*
146 A80 60rp dp claret ('38) 1.90 *2.50*
Never hinged 5.50
On cover *7.00*
147 A80 90rp gray vio ('38) 9.25 *15.00*
Never hinged 27.50
On cover *27.50*
148 A80 1fr red brown 1.90 *12.50*
Never hinged 5.50
On cover *21.00*
149 A80 1.20fr dp brn ('38) 6.75 *22.50*
Never hinged 21.00
On cover *42.50*
a. Imperf, single *800.00* *3,250.*
Never hinged *1,400.*
On cover *5,750.*
150 A80 1.50fr slate bl ('38) 2.75 *22.50*
Never hinged 10.00
On cover *42.50*
Nos. 136-150 (14) 29.60 *85.00*
Set, never hinged 90.00

For overprints see Nos. O21-O29.

Souvenir Sheet

Josef Rheinberger — A91

1938, July 30 **Engr.** ***Perf. 12***
151 Sheet of 4 18.00 20.00
Never hinged 55.00
a. A91 50rp slate gray 2.25 3.75
Never hinged 5.50

Third Philatelic Exhibition of Liechtenstein. Sheet size: 99¾x135mm.
See No. 153.

Francis Type of 1933
Thick Wove Paper

1938, Aug. 15 ***Perf. 12½***
152 A55 3fr black, *buff* 9.25 *80.00*
Never hinged 19.00

Issued in memory of Prince Francis I, who died July 25, 1938. Sheets of 20.

Josef Gabriel Rheinberger (1839-1901), German Composer and Organist — A92

1939, Mar. 31
153 A92 50rp slate green .70 *4.50*
Never hinged 1.90

Issued in sheets of 20. See No. 151.

Scene of Homage, 1718 — A93

1939, May 29
154 A93 20rp green lake .90 2.00
155 A93 30rp slate blue .90 1.50
156 A93 50rp gray green .90 2.00
Nos. 154-156 (3) 2.70 5.50
Set, never hinged 11.00

Honoring Prince Franz Joseph II. Sheets of 20.

Cantonal Coats of Arms — A94

Prince Franz Joseph II — A96

Design: 3fr, Arms of Principality.

1939
157 A94 2fr dk green, *buff* 6.75 *37.50*
158 A94 3fr indigo, *buff* 4.50 *37.50*
159 A96 5fr brown, *buff* 13.50 *25.00*
a. Sheet of 4 85.00 *140.00*
Never hinged 150.00
Nos. 157-159 (3) 24.75 *100.00*
Set, never hinged 60.00

2fr, 3fr issued in sheets of 12; 5fr in sheets of 4.

Prince Johann as a Child A100

Memorial Tablet A101

Prince Johann II — A102

30rp, Prince Johann and Tower at Vaduz. 50rp, Prince Johann and Gutenberg Castle. 1fr, Prince Johann in 1920 and Vaduz Castle.

1940 **Photo.** ***Perf. 11½.***
160 A100 20rp henna brown .45 *2.00*
161 A100 30rp indigo .45 *3.00*
162 A100 50rp dk slate grn .90 *10.00*
163 A100 1fr brown vio 6.75 *65.00*
164 A101 1.50fr violet blk 6.50 *60.00*
165 A102 3fr brown 3.25 *20.00*
Nos. 160-165 (6) 18.30 *160.00*
Set, never hinged 45.00

Birth centenary of Prince Johann II.
Nos. 160-164 issued in sheets of 25; No. 165 in sheets of 12.
Issue dates: 3fr, Oct. 5; others Aug. 10.

SEMI-POSTAL STAMPS

Prince Johann II — SP1

Coat of Arms — SP2

Wmk. 183

1925, Oct. 5 **Engr.** ***Perf. 11½***
B1 SP1 10rp yellow green 27.50 14.00
B2 SP1 20rp deep red 20.00 14.00
B3 SP1 30rp deep blue 6.00 4.50
Nos. B1-B3 (3) 53.50 32.50
Set, never hinged 150.00

85th birthday of the Prince Regent. Sold at a premium of 5rp each, the excess being devoted to charities.

1927, Oct. 5 **Typo.**
B4 SP2 10rp multicolored 6.75 *15.00*
B5 SP2 20rp multicolored 6.75 *15.00*
B6 SP2 30rp multicolored 5.00 *12.50*
Nos. B4-B6 (3) 18.50 *42.50*
Set, never hinged 50.00

87th birthday of Prince Johann II.
These stamps were sold at premiums of 5, 10 and 20rp respectively. The money thus obtained was devoted to charity.

Railroad Bridge Demolished by Flood SP3

Designs: 10rp+10rp, Inundated Village of Ruggel. 20rp+10rp, Austrian soldiers rescuing refugees. 30rp+10rp, Swiss soldiers salvaging personal effects.

1928, Feb. 6 **Litho.** **Unwmk.**
B7 SP3 5rp + 5rp brn vio & brn 11.00 20.00
B8 SP3 10rp + 10rp bl grn & brn 15.00 22.50
B9 SP3 20rp + 10rp dl red & brn 15.00 22.50
B10 SP3 30rp + 10rp dp bl & brn 12.50 22.50
Nos. B7-B10 (4) 53.50 87.50
Set, never hinged 180.00

The surtax on these stamps was used to aid the sufferers from the Rhine floods.

Coat of Arms — SP7

Princess Elsa — SP8

Design: 30rp, Prince Francis I.

1932, Dec. 21 **Photo.**
B11 SP7 10rp (+ 5rp) olive grn 15.00 *25.00*
B12 SP8 20rp (+ 5rp) rose red 15.00 *25.00*
B13 SP8 30rp (+ 10rp) ultra 20.00 *30.00*
Nos. B11-B13 (3) 50.00 *80.00*
Set, never hinged 125.00

The surtax was for the Child Welfare Fund.

Postal Museum Issue
Souvenir Sheet

SP10

1936, Oct. 24 **Litho.** ***Imperf.***
B14 SP10 Sheet of 4 12.50 *37.50*
Never hinged 37.50

Sheet contains 2 each, #120, 122. Sold for 2fr.

AIR POST STAMPS

Airplane over Snow-capped Mountain Peaks — AP1

Airplane above Vaduz Castle — AP2

Airplane over Rhine Valley — AP3

Perf. 10½, 10½x11½

1930, Aug. 12 Photo. Unwmk.

Gray Wavy Lines in Background

C1	AP1	15rp dark brown	6.00	*8.00*
C2	AP1	20rp slate	14.00	11.50
C3	AP2	25rp olive brown	8.00	*21.00*
C4	AP2	35rp slate blue	12.00	*20.00*
C5	AP3	45rp olive green	27.50	*40.00*
C6	AP3	1fr lake	32.50	30.00
		Nos. C1-C6 (6)	*100.00*	130.50
		Set, never hinged	350.00	

For surcharge see No. C14.

Zeppelin over Naafkopf, Falknis Range AP4

Design: 2fr, Zeppelin over Valüna Valley.

1931, June 1 *Perf. 11½*

C7	AP4	1fr olive black	37.50	*75.00*
C8	AP4	2fr blue black	72.50	*200.00*
		Set, never hinged	325.00	

Golden Eagle — AP6

15rp, Golden Eagle in flight, diff. 20rp, Golden Eagle in flight, diff. 30rp, Osprey. 50rp, Eagle.

1934-35

C9	AP6	10rp brt vio ('35)	4.50	13.00
C10	AP6	15rp red org ('35)	12.00	30.00
C11	AP6	20rp red ('35)	14.00	30.00
C12	AP6	30rp brt bl ('35)	14.00	30.00
C13	AP6	50rp emerald	8.00	21.00
		Nos. C9-C13 (5)	52.50	124.00
		Set, never hinged	150.00	

No. C6 Surcharged with New Value

1935, June 24 *Perf. 10½x11½*

C14	AP3	60rp on 1fr lake	25.00	37.50
		Never hinged	75.00	

Airship "Hindenburg" AP11

Design: 2fr, Airship "Graf Zeppelin."

1936, May 1 *Perf. 11½*

C15	AP11	1fr rose carmine	30.00	62.50
C16	AP11	2fr violet	20.00	62.50
		Set, never hinged	125.00	

AP13

10rp, Barn swallows. 15rp, Black-headed Gulls. 20rp, Gulls. 30rp, Eagle. 50rp, Northern Goshawk. 1fr, Lammergeier. 2fr, Lammergeier.

1939, Apr. 3 Photo.

C17	AP13	10rp violet	.30	.20
C18	AP13	15rp red orange	.80	1.65
C19	AP13	20rp dark red	1.00	.45
C20	AP13	30rp dull blue	1.00	.80
C21	AP13	50rp brt green	2.75	1.65
C22	AP13	1fr rose car	2.75	*12.00*
C23	AP13	2fr violet	2.00	*12.00*
		Nos. C17-C23 (7)	10.60	*28.75*
		Set, never hinged	20.00	

POSTAGE DUE STAMPS

National Administration of the Post Office

D1

1920 Unwmk. Engr. *Perf. 12½*

J1	D1	5h rose red	.20	.20
J2	D1	10h rose red	.20	.20
J3	D1	15h rose red	.20	.20
J4	D1	20h rose red	.20	.20
J5	D1	25h rose red	.20	.20
J6	D1	30h rose red	.20	.20
J7	D1	40h rose red	.20	.20
J8	D1	50h rose red	.20	.20
J9	D1	80h rose red	.20	.20
J10	D1	1k dull blue	.20	.40
J11	D1	2k dull blue	.20	.40
J12	D1	5k dull blue	.20	.40
		Nos. J1-J12 (12)	2.40	3.00
		Set, never hinged	3.00	

Nos. J1-J12 exist imperf. and part perf.

Swiss Administration of the Post Office

D2

Post Horn — D3

1928 Litho. Wmk. 183 *Perf. 11½*

Granite Paper

J13	D2	5rp purple & orange	.70	*1.75*
J14	D2	10rp purple & orange	.85	*1.75*
J15	D2	15rp purple & orange	1.40	*8.50*
J16	D2	20rp purple & orange	1.40	*2.50*
J17	D2	25rp purple & orange	1.40	*5.00*
J18	D2	30rp purple & orange	4.00	*7.50*
J19	D2	40rp purple & orange	4.75	*8.50*
J20	D2	50rp purple & orange	5.50	*12.50*
		Nos. J13-J20 (8)	20.00	*48.00*
		Set, never hinged	57.50	

Engraved; Value Typographed in Dark Red

1940 Unwmk. *Perf. 11½*

J21	D3	5rp gray blue	1.00	*2.10*
J22	D3	10rp gray blue	.50	.40
J23	D3	15rp gray blue	.75	*2.10*
J24	D3	20rp gray blue	.75	*1.25*
J25	D3	25rp gray blue	1.25	*2.50*
J26	D3	30rp gray blue	2.00	*3.25*
J27	D3	40rp gray blue	2.00	*3.25*
J28	D3	50rp gray blue	2.00	*3.75*
		Nos. J21-J28 (8)	10.25	*18.60*
		Set, never hinged	25.00	

OFFICIAL STAMPS

Regular Issue of 1930 Overprinted in Various Colors with Crown and:

Perf. 10½, 11½, 11½x10½

1932 Unwmk.

O1	A38	5rp dk grn (Bk)	5.50	9.00
O2	A39	10rp dark vio (R)	37.50	7.50
a.		Perf. 11½x10½	*600.00*	*1,000.*
O3	A40	20rp dp rose red (Bl)	50.00	7.50
a.		Perf. 10½	160.00	40.00
O4	A42	30rp ultra (R)	10.00	10.00
a.		Perf. 10½	15.00	17.50
O5	A43	35rp dp grn (Bk)	8.00	20.00
a.		Perf. 11½	*3,750.*	*6,000.*
O6	A45	50rp blk brn (Bl)	37.50	12.50
a.		Perf. 11½	90.00	140.00
O7	A46	60rp olive blk (R)	7.50	32.50
O8	A48	1.20fr olive brn (G)	82.50	275.00
		Nos. O1-O8 (8)	238.50	374.00

Nos. 108, 110 Overprinted in Black

1933 *Perf. 14½*

O9	A51	25rp red orange	30.00	35.00
O10	A53	1.20fr red brown	60.00	*175.00*

Same Overprint in Various Colors on Regular Issue of 1934-35

1934-36 *Perf. 11½*

O11	A58	5rp emerald (R)	.50	1.25
O12	A59	10rp dp vio (Bk)	.60	1.10
O13	A60	15rp red org (V)	.30	1.10
O14	A61	20rp red (Bk)	.35	1.10
O15	A62	25rp brown (R)	27.50	*65.00*
O16	A62	25rp brown (Bk)	1.50	*6.75*
O17	A63	30rp dark bl (R)	1.90	3.50
O18	A66	50rp lt brown (V)	.90	1.25
O19	A68	90rp dp grn (Bk)	5.50	*20.00*
O20	A70	1.50fr brown car (Bl)	27.50	*110.00*
		Nos. O11-O20 (10)	66.55	*211.05*

Regular Issue of 1937-38 Overprinted in Black, Red or Blue

1937-41

O21	A76	5rp emerald (Bk)	.20	.20
O22	A76	10rp vio & buff (R)	.20	.25
O23	A76	20rp brown org (Bl)	.95	1.00
O24	A76	20rp brn org (Bk) ('41)	.95	1.00
O25	A76	25rp chestnut (Bk)	.50	1.25
O26	A77	30rp blue & gray (Bk)	.75	.50
O27	A79	50rp dk brn & buff (R)	.45	1.00
O28	A80	1fr red brown (Bk)	.85	*4.25*
O29	A80	1.50fr slate bl (Bk) ('38)	2.75	*7.25*
		Nos. O21-O29 (9)	7.60	*16.70*
		Set, never hinged	15.00	

LITHUANIA

ˌli-thə-ˈwā-nē-ə

(Lietuva)

LOCATION — Northern Europe bordering on the Baltic Sea
GOVT. — Independent republic
AREA — 22,959 sq. mi.
POP. — 2,879,070 (1940)
CAPITAL — Vilnius

Lithuania was under Russian rule when it declared its independence in 1918. The League of Nations recognized it in 1922. In 1940 it became a republic in the Union of Soviet Socialist Republics.

100 Skatiku = 1 Auksinas
100 Centai = 1 Litas (1922)

Catalogue values for unused stamps in this country are for Never Hinged items, beginning with Scott 30, Scott B43 in the semi-postal section, Scott C1 in the air post section, Scott CB1 in the air post semi-postal section and Scott 2N9 in the Russian occupation section.

Nos. 1-26 were printed in sheets of 20 (5x4) which were imperf. at the outer sides, so that only 6 stamps in each sheet were fully perforated. Values are for the stamps partly imperf. The stamps fully perforated sell for at least double these values. There was also a printing of Nos. 19-26 in a sheet of 160, composed of blocks of 20 of each stamp. Pairs or blocks with different values se-tenant sell for considerably more than the values for the stamps singly.
Nos. 1-26 are without gum.

Watermarks

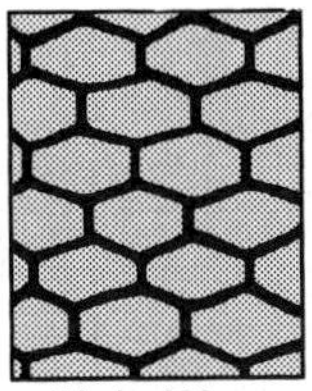

Wmk. 109 — Webbing

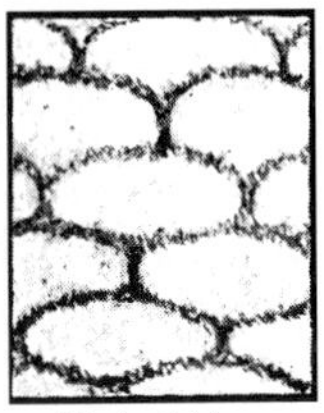

Wmk. 144 — Network

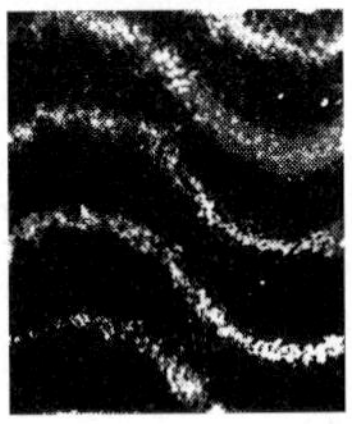

Wmk. 145 — Wavy Lines

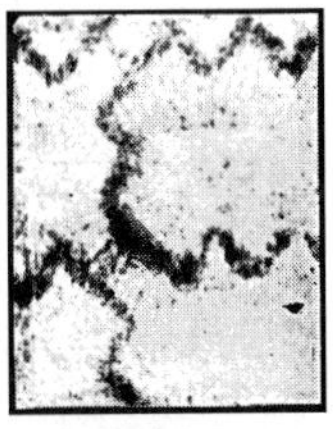

Wmk. 146 — Zigzag Lines Forming Rectangles

Wmk. 147 — Parquetry

Wmk. 198 — Intersecting Diamonds

Wmk. 209 — Multiple Ovals

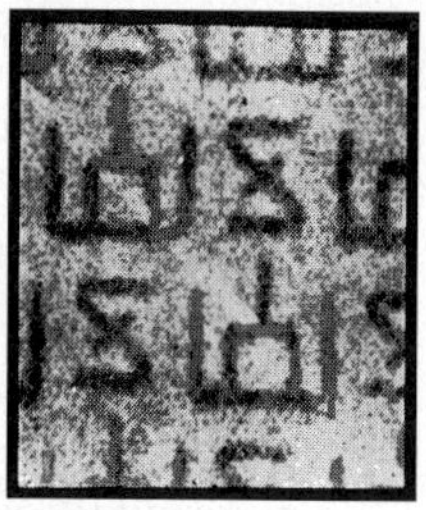

Wmk. 238 — Multiple Letters

A1

A2

Perf. 11½

1918, Dec. 27 Unwmk. Typeset

First Vilnius Printing

Thin Figures

1	A1	10sk black	100.00	100.00
2	A1	15sk black	100.00	100.00

1918, Dec. 31

Second Vilnius Printing

Thick Figures

3	A1	10sk black	70.00	55.00
4	A1	15sk black	70.00	55.00
5	A1	20sk black	18.00	15.00
6	A1	30sk black	20.00	15.00
7	A1	40sk black	25.00	15.00
8	A1	50sk black	20.00	15.00
		Nos. 3-8 (6)	223.00	170.00

First Kaunas Issue

1919, Jan. 29

9	A2	10sk black	8.00	5.50
10	A2	15sk black	8.00	5.50
a.		"5" for "15"	90.00	70.00
11	A2	20sk black	8.00	5.50
12	A2	30sk black	8.00	5.50
		Nos. 9-12 (4)	32.00	22.00

A3

A4

Second Kaunas Issue

1919, Feb. 18

13	A3	10sk black	3.00	1.75
14	A3	15sk black	3.00	1.75
15	A3	20sk black	3.00	1.75
a.		"astas" for "pastas"	65.00	55.00
16	A3	30sk black	3.00	1.75
17	A3	40sk black	3.00	1.75
18	A3	50sk black	3.00	1.75
19	A3	60sk black	3.00	1.75
		Nos. 13-19 (7)	21.00	12.25

Third Kaunas Issue

1919, Mar. 1

20	A4	10sk black	3.00	1.75
21	A4	15sk black	3.00	1.75
22	A4	20sk black	3.00	1.75
23	A4	30sk black	3.00	1.75
24	A4	40sk black	3.00	1.75
25	A4	50sk black	3.00	1.75
26	A4	60sk black	3.00	1.75
		Nos. 20-26 (7)	21.00	12.25

Catalogue values for unused stamps in this section, from this point to the end of the section, are for Never Hinged items.

The White Knight "Vytis"

A5 A6

A7 A8

Perf. 10½ to 14 & Compound

1919 Litho. Wmk. 144

Gray Granite Paper

30	A5	10sk deep rose	1.00	.25
a.		Wmk. vert.	17.50	10.00
31	A5	15sk violet	1.00	.25
a.		Wmk. vert.	17.50	10.00
32	A5	20sk dark blue	1.25	.30
33	A5	30sk deep orange	1.25	.30
a.		Wmk. vert.	17.50	10.00
34	A5	40sk dark brown	1.25	.30
35	A6	50sk blue green	1.25	.50
36	A6	75sk org & dp rose	1.25	.25
37	A7	1auk gray & rose	2.50	.50
38	A7	3auk bis brn & rose	2.50	.50
39	A7	5auk blue grn & rose	2.50	.65
		Nos. 30-39 (10)	15.75	3.80

Nos. 30a, 31a and 33a are from the first printing with watermark vertical showing points to left; various perforations.

Nos. 30-39 exist imperf. Value in pairs, $50.

Issued: #30a, 31a, 33a, 2/17/19; #30-36, 3/20/19.

1919 Wmk. 145

Thick White Paper

40	A5	10sk dull rose	.35	.20
41	A5	15sk violet	.35	.20
42	A5	20sk dark blue	.35	.20
43	A5	30sk orange	.35	.20
44	A5	40sk red brown	.35	.20
45	A6	50sk green	.35	.20
46	A6	75sk yel & dp rose	.35	.20
47	A7	1auk gray & rose	.90	.20
48	A7	3auk yellow brn & rose, perf. 12½	.55	.25
49	A7	5auk bl grn & rose	.90	.35
		Nos. 40-49 (10)	4.80	2.20

Nos. 40-49 exist imperf. Value in pairs, $42.50.

Perf. 10½ to 14 & Compound

1919, May 8

Thin White Paper

50	A5	10sk red	.35	.20
51	A5	15sk lilac	.35	.20
52	A5	20sk dull blue	.35	.20
53	A5	30sk buff	.35	.20
54	A5	40sk gray brn	.35	.20
55	A6	50sk lt green	.35	.20
56	A6	60sk violet & red	.35	.20
57	A6	75sk bister & red	.35	.20
58	A8	1auk gray & red	.35	.20
59	A8	3auk lt brown & red	.35	.20
60	A8	5auk blue grn & red	.35	.20
		Nos. 50-60 (11)	3.85	2.20

Nos. 50-60 exist imperf. Value, pairs $70.

See Nos. 93-96. For surcharges see Nos. 114-115, 120-139, 149-150.

"Lithuania" Receiving Benediction — A9

The Spirit of Lithuania Rises — A10

"Lithuania" with Chains Broken — A11

White Knight — A12

1920, Feb. 16 Wmk. 146 *Perf. 11½*

70	A9	10sk dp rose	3.50	2.00
71	A9	15sk lt violet	3.50	2.00
72	A9	20sk gray blue	3.50	2.00
73	A10	30sk yellow brn	3.50	2.00
74	A11	40sk brown & grn	3.50	2.00
75	A10	50sk deep rose	3.50	2.00
76	A10	60sk lt violet	3.50	2.00
77	A11	80sk purple & red	3.50	2.00
78	A11	1auk green & red	3.50	2.00
79	A12	3auk brown & red	3.50	2.00
80	A12	5auk green & red	3.50	2.00
a.		Right "5" dbl., grn and red	90.00	90.00
		Nos. 70-80 (11)	38.50	22.00

Anniv. of natl. independence. The stamps were on sale only 3 days in Kaunas. The stamps were available in other cities after that. Only a limited number of stamps was sold at post offices but 40,000 sets were delivered to the bank of Kaunas.

All values exist imperforate.

White Knight — A13

Grand Duke Vytautas — A14

Grand Duke Gediminas A15

Sacred Oak and Altar A16

1920, Aug. 25

81	A13	10sk rose	.85	.40
a.		Imperf., pair	35.00	
82	A13	15sk dark violet	.85	.40
83	A14	20sk grn & lt grn	.85	.40
84	A13	30sk brown	.85	.40
a.		Pair, #82, 84	35.00	
85	A15	40sk gray grn & vio	.85	.40
86	A14	50sk brn & brn org	2.25	1.00
87	A14	60sk red & org	1.50	1.00
88	A15	80sk blk, db & red	1.50	1.00
89	A16	1auk orange & blk	1.50	1.00
90	A16	3auk green & blk	1.50	1.00
91	A16	5auk gray vio & blk	3.50	1.00
		Nos. 81-91 (11)	16.00	8.00

Opening of Lithuanian National Assembly. On sale for three days.

1920

92	A14	20sk green & lilac	150.00
92A	A15	40sk gray grn, buff & vio	150.00
92B	A14	50sk brown & gray lil	150.00
92C	A14	60sk red & green	150.00
92D	A15	80sk black, grn & red	150.00
		Nos. 92-92D (5)	750.00

Nos. 92 to 92D were trial printings. By order of the Ministry of Posts, 2,000 copies of each were placed on sale at post offices.

Type of 1919 Issue

1920 Unwmk. *Perf. 11½*

93	A5	15sk lilac	6.00	2.00
94	A5	20sk deep blue	6.00	2.00

Wmk. 109

95	A5	20sk deep blue	5.25	2.00
96	A5	40sk gray brown	12.00	3.00
		Nos. 93-96 (4)	29.25	9.00

Watermark horizontal on Nos. 95-96.

No. 96 exists perf. 10½x11½.

Imperf., Pairs

93a	A5	15sk	32.00	32.00
94a	A5	20sk	32.00	32.00
95a	A5	20sk	17.00	17.00
96a	A5	40sk	48.00	48.00

Sower A17

Peasant Sharpening Scythe A18

Prince Kestutis A19

Black Horseman A20

Perf. 11, 11½ and Compound

1921-22

97	A17	10sk brt rose	.85	.55
98	A17	15sk violet	.35	*.70*
99	A17	20sk ultra	.25	.20
100	A18	30sk brown	2.50	*1.10*
101	A19	40sk red	.25	.20
102	A18	50sk olive	.35	.20
103	A18	60sk grn & vio	2.50	*1.65*
104	A19	80sk brn org & car	.35	.20
105	A19	1auk brown & grn	.35	.20
106	A19	2auk gray bl & red	.35	.20
107	A20	3auk yel brn & dk bl	1.00	.40
108	A17	4auk yel & dk bl ('22)	.45	.20
109	A20	5auk gray blk & rose	1.00	*1.50*
110	A17	8auk grn & blk ('22)	.45	.20
111	A20	10auk rose & vio	1.00	.55
112	A20	25auk bis brn & grn	1.25	.85
113	A20	100auk dl red & gray blk	12.50	8.00
		Nos. 97-113 (17)	25.75	16.90

Imperf., Pairs

97a	A17	10sk	—	
98a	A17	15sk	—	
99a	A17	20sk	—	
100a	A18	30sk	—	
101a	A19	40sk	24.00	
102a	A18	50sk	24.00	
103a	A18	60sk	—	
104a	A19	80sk	—	
105a	A19	1auk	—	
106a	A19	2auk	120.00	
107a	A20	3auk	120.00	
109a	A20	5auk	120.00	
110a	A17	8auk	8.50	8.50
111a	A20	10auk	50.00	
112a	A20	25auk	50.00	
113a	A20	100auk	50.00	

For surcharges see Nos. 140-148, 151-160.

No. 57 Surcharged

Perf. 12½x11½

1922, May Wmk. 145

114	A6	4auk on 75sk bis & red	.90	.20
a.		Inverted surcharge	30.00	30.00

Same with Bars over Original Value

115	A6	4auk on 75sk bis & red	4.00	*8.00*
a.		Double surcharge	30.00	30.00

Povilas Luksis — A20a

Justinas Staugaitis, Antanas Smetona, Stasys Silingas — A20b

Portraits: 40s, Lt. Juozapavicius. 50s, Dr. Basanavicius. 60s, Mrs. Petkeviciute. 1auk, Prof. Voldemaras. 2auk, Pranas Dovidaitis. 3auk, Dr. Slezevicius. 4auk, Dr. Galvanauskas. 5auk, Kazys Grinius. 6auk, Dr. Stulginskis. 8auk, Pres. Smetona.

1922 Litho. Unwmk.

116	A20a	20s blk & car rose	1.25	.90
116A	A20a	40s bl grn & vio	1.25	.90
116B	A20a	50s plum & grnsh bl	1.25	.90
117	A20a	60s pur & org	1.25	.90
117A	A20a	1auk car & lt bl	1.25	.90
117B	A20a	2auk dp bl & yel brn	1.25	.90
c.		Center inverted	100.00	100.00
118	A20a	3auk mar & ultra	1.25	.90
118A	A20a	4auk dk grn & red vio	1.25	.90
118B	A20a	5auk blk brn & dp rose	1.25	.90
119	A20a	6auk dk bl & grnsh bl	1.25	.90
a.		Cliché of 8auk in sheet of 6auk	100.00	100.00
119B	A20a	8auk ultra & bis	1.25	.90
119C	A20b	10auk dk vio & bl grn	1.25	.90
		Nos. 116-119C (12)	15.00	10.80

League of Nations' recognition of Lithuania. Sold only on Oct. 1, 1922.

Forty sheets of the 6auk each included eight copies of the 8auk.

Stamps of 1919-22 Surcharged in Black, Carmine or Green

On Nos. 37-39

1922 Wmk. 144 *Perf. 11½x12*

Gray Granite Paper

120	A7	3c on 1auk	175.00	110.00
121	A7	3c on 3auk	175.00	110.00
122	A7	3c on 5auk	110.00	65.00
		Nos. 120-122 (3)	460.00	285.00

White Paper

Wmk. 145

Perf. 14, 11½, 12½x11½

123	A5	1c on 10sk red	2.75	1.50
124	A5	1c on 15sk lilac	4.00	1.50
125	A5	1c on 20sk dull bl	2.50	1.50
126	A5	1c on 30sk orange	100.00	100.00
127	A5	1c on 30sk buff	.40	.40
128	A5	1c on 40sk gray brn	2.00	1.50
129	A6	2c on 50sk green	3.00	1.50
130	A6	2c on 60sk vio & red	.20	.20
131	A6	2c on 75sk bis & red	2.00	1.50
132	A8	3c on 1auk gray & red	.45	.45
133	A8	3c on 3auk brn & red	.25	.20
134	A8	3c on 5auk bl grn & red	.25	.20
		Nos. 123-125,127-134 (11)	17.80	10.45

On Stamps of 1920

1922 Unwmk. *Perf. 11*

136	A5	1c on 20sk dp bl (C)	4.00	2.00

Wmk. Webbing (109)

Perf. 11, 11½

138	A5	1c on 20sk dp bl (C)	3.75	2.00
139	A5	1c on 40sk gray brn (C)	8.00	1.25

On Stamps of 1921-22

140	A18	1c on 50sk ol (C)	.25	.20
a.		Imperf., pair	45.00	
b.		Inverted surcharge	40.00	
c.		Double surch., one invtd.		
141	A17	3c on 10sk	12.00	8.00
142	A17	3c on 15sk	.25	.20
143	A17	3c on 20sk	.45	1.50
144	A18	3c on 30sk	17.50	12.00
145	A19	3c on 40sk	.45	.45
a.		Imperf., pair		
146	A18	5c on 50sk	.20	.20
147	A18	5c on 60sk	17.50	15.00
148	A19	5c on 80sk	.60	.50
a.		Imperf., pair	35.00	15.00

Wmk. Wavy Lines (145)

Perf. 12½x11½

149	A6	5c on 4auk on 75sk (No. 114) (G)	1.75	10.00
150	A6	5c on 4auk on 75sk (No. 115) (G)	17.50	17.50

Wmk. Webbing (109)

Perf. 11, 11½

151	A19	10c on 1auk	.85	.20
a.		Inverted surcharge	50.00	
152	A19	10c on 2auk	.25	.20
a.		Inverted surcharge	45.00	
b.		Imperf., pair	40.00	
153	A17	15c on 4auk	.25	.20
a.		Inverted surcharge	40.00	
154	A20	25c on 3auk	17.50	17.50
155	A20	25c on 5auk	12.00	5.00
156	A20	25c on 10auk	2.50	1.50
a.		Imperf., pair	40.00	
157	A17	30c on 8auk (C)	1.25	.35
a.		Inverted surcharge	40.00	20.00
158	A20	50c on 25auk	4.00	2.50
160	A20	1 l on 100auk	4.25	2.50
		Nos. 136-160 (23)	127.05	100.75

A21

Ruin — A22

Seminary Church, Kaunas — A23

1923 Litho. Wmk. 109 *Perf. 11*

165	A21	10c violet	6.75	.20
166	A21	15c scarlet	2.50	.20
167	A21	20c olive brown	2.50	.20
168	A21	25c deep blue	2.50	.20
169	A22	50c yellow green	2.50	.20
170	A22	60c red	2.50	.20
171	A23	1 l orange & grn	11.00	.20
172	A23	3 l red & gray	15.00	.45
173	A23	5 l brown & blue	22.50	1.00
		Nos. 165-173 (9)	67.75	2.85

See Nos. 189-209, 281-282. For surcharges see Nos. B1-B42.

Memel Coat of Arms — A24

Lithuanian Coat of Arms — A25

Biruta Chapel — A26

Kaunas, War Memorial A27

Trakai Ruins A28

Memel Lighthouse — A29

Memel Harbor A30

Perf. 11, 11½, 12

1923, Aug. Unwmk.

176	A24	1c rose, grn & blk	2.25	1.60
177	A25	2c dull vio & blk	2.25	1.60
178	A26	3c yellow & blk	2.25	1.60
179	A24	5c bl, buff & blk	2.75	1.90
180	A27	10c orange & blk	2.75	1.90
181	A27	15c green & blk	3.00	2.50
182	A28	25c brt vio & blk	3.00	2.50
183	A25	30c red vio & blk	4.00	3.00
184	A29	60c ol grn & blk	3.75	2.75
185	A30	1 l bl grn & blk	3.75	2.75
186	A26	2 l red & black	8.50	7.00
187	A28	3 l blue & black	8.50	7.00
188	A29	5 l ultra & black	9.00	7.00
		Nos. 176-188 (13)	55.75	43.10

This series was issued ostensibly to commemorate the incorporation of Memel with Lithuania.

Type of 1923 Issue

1923 Unwmk. *Perf. 11*

189	A21	5c pale green	3.00	.20
190	A21	10c violet	4.00	.20
a.		Imperf., pair	45.00	
191	A21	15c scarlet	4.50	.20
a.		Imperf., pair	45.00	
193	A21	25c blue	7.50	.20
		Nos. 189-193 (4)	19.00	.80

1923 Wmk. 147

196	A21	2c pale brown	1.25	.25
197	A21	3c olive bister	1.40	.20
198	A21	5c pale green	1.40	.20
199	A21	10c violet	3.25	.20
202	A21	25c deep blue	7.00	.20
a.		Imperf., pair	40.00	
204	A21	36c orange brown	10.50	.50
		Nos. 196-204 (6)	24.80	1.55

Perf. 11½, 14½, 11½x14½

1923-25 Wmk. 198

207	A21	25c deep blue	450.00	300.00
208	A22	50c deep green ('25)	3.25	.40
209	A22	60c carmine ('25)	4.00	.40

Double- barred Cross A31

Dr. Jonas Basanavicius A32

1927, Jan. *Perf. 11½, 14½*

210	A31	2c orange	1.75	.20
211	A31	3c deep brown	1.75	.20
212	A31	5c green	2.50	.20
a.		Imperf., pair	20.00	
213	A31	10c violet	4.00	.20
214	A31	15c red	3.50	.20
a.		Imperf., pair	20.00	
215	A31	25c blue	4.50	.20
		Nos. 210-215 (6)	18.00	1.20

1927-29 Wmk. 147 *Perf. 14½*

216	A31	5c green	30.00	35.00
217	A31	30c blue ('30)	27.50	5.00

See Nos. 233-240, 278-280.

1927 Unwmk. *Perf. 11½, 14½x11½*

219	A32	15c claret & blk	2.50	1.25
220	A32	25c dull blue & blk	2.50	1.25
221	A32	50c dk green & blk	2.50	1.25
222	A32	60c dk violet & blk	5.00	2.00
		Nos. 219-222 (4)	12.50	5.75

Dr. Jonas Basanavicius (1851-1927), patriot and folklorist.

National Arms — A33

1927, Dec. 23 Wmk. 109 *Perf. 14½*

223	A33	1 l blue grn & gray	2.25	.60
224	A33	3 l vio & pale grn	5.75	.60
225	A33	5 l brown & gray	6.75	1.00
		Nos. 223-225 (3)	14.75	2.20

Pres. Antanas Smetona — A34

Decade of Independence A35

Dawn of Peace — A36

1928, Feb. Wmk. 109

226	A34	5c org brn & grn	1.00	.30
227	A34	10c violet & blk	1.25	.30
228	A34	15c orange & brn	1.25	.30
229	A34	25c blue & indigo	1.25	.30
230	A35	50c ultra & dl vio	1.50	.30
231	A35	60c carmine & blk	1.50	.55
232	A36	1 l blk brn & drab	2.00	.70
		Nos. 226-232 (7)	9.75	2.75

10th anniv. of Lithuanian independence.

Type of 1926 Issue

1929-31

233	A31	2c orange ('31)	16.50	1.00
234	A31	5c green	3.75	.20
235	A31	10c violet ('31)	12.00	1.00
237	A31	15c red	4.50	.20
a.		Tête bêche pair	40.00	30.00
239	A31	30c dark blue	7.00	.20

Unwmk.

240	A31	15c red ('30)	12.50	.60
		Nos. 233-240 (6)	56.25	3.20

Grand Duke Vytautas A37

Grand Duke, Mounted A38

1930, Feb. 16 *Perf. 14*

242	A37	2c yel brn & dk brn	.45	.20
243	A37	3c dk brn & vio	.45	.20
244	A37	5c yel grn & dp org	.45	.20
245	A37	10c vio & emer	.45	.20
246	A37	15c dp rose & vio	.45	.20
247	A37	30c dk bl & brn vio	.85	.20
248	A37	36c brn vio & ol blk	1.25	.20
249	A37	50c dull grn & ultra	.85	.30
250	A37	60c dk blue & rose	.85	.35
251	A38	1 l bl grn, db & red brn	3.50	.40
252	A38	3 l dk brn, sal & dk vio	4.75	1.00
253	A38	5 l ol brn, gray & red	10.00	1.25
254	A38	10 l multicolored	27.50	9.00
255	A38	25 l multicolored	60.00	30.00
		Nos. 242-255 (14)	111.80	43.70

5th cent. of the death of the Grand Duke Vytautas.

Kaunas, Railroad Station A39

Cathedral at Vilnius — A39a

Designs: 15c, 25c, Landscape on the Neman River. 50c, Main Post Office, Kaunas.

Perf. 14, Imperf.

1932, July 21 **Wmk. 238**

256	A39	10c dk red brn & ocher	.45	.45
257	A39	15c dk brown & ol	.80	.80
258	A39	25c dk blue & ol	1.25	1.25
259	A39	50c gray blk & ol	2.50	2.50
260	A39a	1 l dk blue & ol	5.00	5.00
261	A39a	3 l red brn & gray grn	6.50	6.50
		Wmk. 198		
262	A39	5c vio bl & ocher	.45	.45
263	A39a	60c grnsh blk & lil	5.00	5.00
		Nos. 256-263 (8)	21.95	21.95

Issued for the benefit of Lithuanian orphans.

In September, 1935, a red overprint was applied to No. 259: "ORO PASTAS / LITUANICA II / 1935 / NEW YORK-KAUNAS." Value, $250.

Vytautas Fleeing from Prison, 1382 A40

Designs: 15c, 25c, Conversion of Ladislas II Jagello and Vytautas (1386). 50c, 60c, Battle at Tannenberg (1410). 1 l, 3 l, Meeting of the Nobles (1429).

1932 **Wmk. 209** *Perf. 14, Imperf.*

264	A40	5c red & rose lake	.75	.35
265	A40	10c ol bis & org brn	.85	.35
266	A40	15c rose lil & ol grn	1.00	.50
267	A40	25c dk vio brn & ocher	2.25	1.25
268	A40	50c dp grn & bis brn	2.25	1.75
269	A40	60c ol grn & brn car	5.50	2.50
270	A40	1 l ultra & ol grn	6.00	3.00
271	A40	3 l dk brn & dk grn	6.50	4.00
		Nos. 264-271 (8)	25.10	13.70

15th anniversary of independence.

A. Visteliauskas A41

Mother and Child — A42

Designs: 15c, 25c, Petras Vileisis. 50c, 60c, Dr. John Sliupas. 1 l, 3 l, Jonas Basanavicius.

1933 *Perf. 14, Imperf.*

272	A41	5c yel grn & car	.60	.30
273	A41	10c ultra & car	.80	.40
274	A41	15c orange & red	1.00	.50
275	A41	25c dk bl & blk brn	1.50	.90
276	A41	50c ol gray & dk bl	2.50	1.50
277	A41	60c org brn & chnt	8.00	4.00
277A	A41	1 l red & vio brn	10.00	4.75
277B	A41	3 l turq grn & vio brn	11.00	6.00
		Nos. 272-277B (8)	35.40	18.35

50th anniv. of the 1st newspaper, "Ausra," in lithuanian language.

1933, Sept. *Perf. 14, Imperf.*

Designs: 15c, 25c, Boy reading. 50c, 60c, Boy playing with blocks. 1 l, 3 l, Woman and boy at the Spinning Wheel.

277C	A42	5c dp yel grn & org brn	.25	.20
277D	A42	10c rose brn & ultra	.35	.20
277E	A42	15c ol grn & plum	.45	.25
277F	A42	25c org & gray blk	1.50	.75
277G	A42	50c ol grn & car	1.75	1.25
277H	A42	60c blk & yel org	5.75	3.00
277I	A42	1 l dk brn & ultra	6.75	3.25
277K	A42	3 l rose lil & ol grn	7.25	*5.00*
		Nos. 277C-277K (8)	24.05	*13.90*

Issued for the benefit of Lithuanian orphans.

Types of 1923-26 Issues

1933-34 **Wmk. 238** *Perf. 14*

278	A31	2c orange	32.00	4.00
279	A31	10c dark violet	40.00	6.00
280	A31	15c red	32.00	3.00
281	A22	50c green	32.00	7.00
282	A22	60c red	32.00	6.00
		Nos. 278-282 (5)	168.00	26.00

Pres. Antanas Smetona, 60th Birthday — A43

1934 **Unwmk.** **Engr.** *Perf. 11½*

283	A43	15c red	7.50	.20
284	A43	30c green	10.00	.25
285	A43	60c blue	12.50	.40
		Nos. 283-285 (3)	30.00	.85

A44

A47

Arms — A45

Knight A48

Girl with Wheat — A46

Wmk. 198; Wmk. 209 (35c, 10 l)

1934-35 **Litho.** *Perf. 14*

286	A44	2c rose & dull org	1.25	.20
287	A44	5c bl grn & grn	1.25	.20
288	A45	10c chocolate	2.75	.20
289	A46	25c dk brn & emer	4.50	.20
290	A45	35c carmine	4.50	.20
291	A46	50c dk blue & blue	5.75	.20
292	A47	1 l sl & mar	60.00	.20
293	A47	3 l grn & gray grn	.35	.20
294	A48	5 l maroon & gray bl	.55	.45
295	A48	10 l choc & yel	3.00	1.50
		Nos. 286-295 (10)	83.90	3.55

No. 290 exists imperf. Value, pair $35.

For overprint see No. 2N9.

1936-37 **Wmk. 238** *Perf. 14*

Size: 17½x23mm

296	A44	2c orange ('37)	.25	.20
297	A44	5c green	.30	.20

Pres. Smetona A49

Arms A50

1936-37 **Unwmk.**

298	A49	15c carmine	9.00	.20
299	A49	30c green ('37)	12.00	.20
300	A49	60c ultra ('37)	11.00	.20
		Nos. 298-300 (3)	32.00	.60

1937-39 **Wmk. 238** *Perf. 14*

Paper with Gray Network

301	A50	10c green	1.60	.20
302	A50	25c magenta	.25	.20
303	A50	35c red	.85	.20
304	A50	50c brown	.40	.20
305	A50	1 l dp vio bl ('39)	.45	.45
		Nos. 301-305 (5)	3.55	1.25

No. 304 exists in two types:

I — "50" is fat and broad, with "0" leaning to right.

II — "50" is thinner and narrower, with "0" straight.

For overprint see No. 2N10.

Jonas Basanavicius Reading Act of Independence A51

President Antanas Smetona A52

Perf. 13x13½

1939, Jan. 15 **Engr.** **Unwmk.**

306	A51	15c dark red	.50	.30
307	A52	30c deep green	.85	.30
308	A51	35c red lilac	1.25	.45
309	A52	60c dark blue	1.25	.60
a.		Souvenir sheet of 2, #308-309	10.00	15.00
b.		As "a," imperf.	60.00	60.00
		Nos. 306-309 (4)	3.85	1.65

20th anniv. of Independence.

Nos. 309a, 309b sold for 2 l.

Same Overprinted in Blue

1939

310	A51	15c dark red	.85	.90
311	A52	30c deep green	.90	.90
312	A51	35c red lilac	2.00	1.00
313	A52	60c dark blue	2.25	1.00
		Nos. 310-313 (4)	6.00	3.80

Recovery of Vilnius.

View of Vilnius A53

Gediminas — A54

Trakai Ruins A55

Unwmk.

1940, May 6 **Photo.** *Perf. 14*

314	A53	15c brn & pale brn	.45	.25
315	A54	30c dk grn & lt grn	.85	.85
316	A55	60c dk bl & lt bl	1.75	1.00
a.		Souv. sheet of 3, #314-316, imperf.	12.00	16.00
		Nos. 314-316 (3)	3.05	2.10

Return of Vilnius to Lithuania, Oct. 10, 1939. Exist imperf.

No. 316a has simulated perforations in gold. Sold for 2 l.

White Knight — A56

Angel — A57

Woman Releasing Dove A58

Mother and Children A59

Liberty Bell — A60

Mythical Animal — A61

1940

317	A56	5c brown carmine	.20	.20
318	A57	10c green	.85	.35
319	A58	15c dull orange	.20	.20
320	A59	25c light brown	.20	.20
321	A60	30c Prussian green	.20	.20
322	A61	35c red orange	.25	.25
		Nos. 317-322 (6)	1.90	1.40

Nos. 317-322 exist imperf.
For overprints see Nos. 2N11-2N16.

SEMI-POSTAL STAMPS

Regular Issue of 1923-24 Surcharged in Blue, Violet or Black:

On A21

On A22

On A23

1924, Feb. Wmk. 147 ***Perf. 11***

B1	A21	2c + 2c pale brn (Bl)	1.25	1.50
B2	A21	3c + 3c ol bis (Bl)	1.25	1.50
B3	A21	5c + 5c pale grn (V)	1.25	1.50
B4	A21	10c + 10c vio (Bk)	3.00	3.00
B5	A21	36c + 34c org brn (V)	6.50	10.00

Wmk. Webbing (109)

B6	A21	10c + 10c vio (Bk)	6.50	7.50
B7	A21	15c + 15c scar (V)	1.50	1.50
B8	A21	20c + 20c ol brn (Bl)	3.00	3.50
B9	A21	25c + 25c bl (Bk)	16.50	16.50
B10	A22	50c + 50c yel grn (V)	6.75	8.00
B11	A22	60c + 60c red (V)	7.00	10.00
B12	A23	1 l + 1 l org & grn (V)	8.00	11.00
B13	A23	3 l + 2 l red & gray (V)	12.00	15.00
B14	A23	5 l + 3 l brn & bl (V)	16.00	20.00

Unwmk.

B15	A21	25c + 25c dp bl (Bk)	5.00	6.00
		Nos. B1-B15 (15)	95.50	116.50

For War Invalids

Semi-Postal Stamps of 1924 Surcharged

Surcharged in Gold or Copper

1926, Dec. 3 Wmk. 147

B16	A21	1 + 1c on #B1	1.00	1.25
a.		Inverted surcharge	35.00	
B17	A21	2 + 2c on #B2 (C)	1.00	1.25
B19	A21	2 + 2c on #B3	1.00	1.25
a.		Double surch., one inverted	35.00	
B20	A21	5 + 5c on #B4	1.75	2.00
B21	A21	14 + 14c on #B5	6.00	7.00

Wmk. Webbing (109)

B22	A21	5 + 5c on #B6	10.00	10.00
B23	A21	5 + 5c on #B7	2.00	2.00
B24	A21	10 + 10c on #B8	2.00	2.00
B25	A21	10 + 10c on #B9	65.00	65.00

Unwmk.

B26	A21	10 + 10c on #B15	4.00	5.00

Surcharged in Copper or Silver:

On A22

On A23

Wmk. Webbing (109)

B27	A22	20 + 20c on #B10	4.00	5.00
B28	A22	25 + 25c on #B11	6.00	7.00
B29	A23	30 + 30c on #B12 (S)	9.00	11.00
		Nos. B16-B29 (13)	112.75	119.75

For War Orphans

Surcharged in Gold

1926, Dec. 3 Wmk. 147

B30	A21	1 + 1c on #B1	.90	.90
B31	A21	2 + 2c on #B2	.90	.90
a.		Inverted surcharge	25.00	
B32	A21	2 + 2c on #B3	.90	.90
a.		Inverted surcharge	25.00	
B33	A21	5 + 5c on #B4	2.00	2.25
B34	A21	19 + 19c on #B5	4.00	5.00

Wmk. Webbing (109)

B35	A21	5 + 5c on #B6	9.50	9.50
B36	A21	10 + 10c on #B7	1.75	2.00
B37	A21	15 + 15c on #B8	2.00	2.25
B38	A21	15 + 15c on #B9	60.00	60.00

Unwmk.

B39	A21	15 + 15c on #B15	2.75	2.75

Surcharged in Gold:

On A22

On A23

Wmk. 109

B40	A22	25c on #B10	5.00	6.00
B41	A22	30c on #B11	8.00	7.00
B42	A23	50c on #B12	10.00	11.00
		Nos. B30-B42 (13)	107.70	110.45

Catalogue values for unused stamps in this section, from this point to the end of the section, are for Never Hinged items.

Javelin throwing — SP1

Natl. Olympiad, July 15-20: 5c+5c, Archery. 30c+10c, Diving. 60c+15c, Running.

Unwmk.

1938, July 13 Photo. ***Perf. 14***

B43	SP1	5c + 5c grn & dk grn	6.50	6.50
B44	SP1	15c + 5c org & red org	6.50	6.50
B45	SP1	30c + 10c bl & dk bl	12.00	12.00
B46	SP1	60c + 15c tan & brn	16.00	16.00
		Nos. B43-B46 (4)	41.00	41.00

Same Overprinted in Red, Blue or Black:

Nos. B47, B50

Nos. B48-B49

1938, July 13

B47	SP1	5c + 5c (R)	12.00	7.50
B48	SP1	15c + 5c (Bl)	12.00	7.50
B49	SP1	30c + 10c (R)	15.00	7.50
B50	SP1	60c + 15c (Bk)	20.00	12.50
		Nos. B47-B50 (4)	59.00	35.00

National Scout Jamboree, July 12-14. Forged cancellations exist.

Basketball Players
SP6 SP7

Flags of Competing Nations and Basketball — SP8

1939 Photo. ***Perf. 14***

B52	SP6	15c + 10c copper brn & brn	6.50	6.50
B53	SP7	30c + 15c myrtle grn & grn	6.50	6.50
B54	SP8	60c + 40c blue vio & gray vio	12.00	12.00
		Nos. B52-B54 (3)	25.00	25.00

3rd European Basketball Championships held at Kaunas. The surtax was used for athletic equipment. Nos. B52-B54 exist imperf. Value, each pair, $175.

AIR POST STAMPS

Catalogue values for unused stamps in this section are for Never Hinged items.

Winged Posthorn AP1

Airplane over Neman River — AP2

Air Squadron AP3

Plane over Gediminas Castle — AP4

1921 Litho. Wmk. 109 ***Perf. 11½***

C1	AP1	20sk ultra	1.60	.75
C2	AP1	40sk red orange	1.40	.75
C3	AP1	60sk green	1.40	.75
a.		Imperf., pair	40.00	
C4	AP1	80sk lt rose	1.40	.75
a.		Horiz. pair, imperf. vert.	45.00	35.00
C5	AP2	1auk green & red	1.60	.50
a.		Imperf., pair	35.00	35.00
C6	AP3	2auk brown & blue	1.75	.75
C7	AP4	5auk slate & yel	2.75	1.25
		Nos. C1-C7 (7)	11.90	5.50

For surcharges see Nos. C21-C26, C29.

Allegory of Flight — AP5

1921, Nov. 6

C8	AP5	20sk org & gray bl	2.50	1.50
C9	AP5	40sk dl bl & lake	2.50	1.50
C10	AP5	60sk vio bl & ol grn	2.50	1.50
C11	AP5	80sk ocher & dp grn	2.50	1.50
a.		Vert. pair, imperf. btwn.	30.00	25.00
C12	AP5	1auk bl grn & bl	2.50	1.50
C13	AP5	2auk gray & brn org	2.50	1.50
C14	AP5	5auk dl lil & Prus bl	2.50	1.50
		Nos. C8-C14 (7)	17.50	10.50

Opening of airmail service.

Plane over Kaunas — AP6

Black Overprint

1922, July 16 ***Perf. 11, 11½***

C15	AP6	1auk ol brn & red	2.75	2.75
a.		Imperf., pair	55.00	
C16	AP6	3auk violet & grn	2.75	2.75
C17	AP6	5auk dp blue & yel	2.75	4.00
		Nos. C15-C17 (3)	8.25	9.50

Nos. C15-C17, without overprint, were to be for the founding of the Air Post service but they were not put in use at that time. Subsequently the word "ZENKLAS" (stamp) was overprinted over "ISTEIGIMAS" (founding) and the date "1921, VI, 25" was obliterated by short vertical lines.

For surcharge see No. C31.

Plane over Gediminas Castle — AP7

1922, July 22

C18	AP7	2auk blue & rose	1.50	.85
C19	AP7	4auk brown & rose	1.50	.85
C20	AP7	10auk black & gray bl	1.75	1.40
		Nos. C18-C20 (3)	4.75	3.10

For surcharges see Nos. C27-C28, C30.

Nos. C1-C7, C17-C20 Surcharged like Regular Issues in Black or Carmine

1922

C21	AP1	10c on 20sk	5.75	2.50
C22	AP1	10c on 40sk	3.00	1.50
C23	AP1	10c on 60sk	3.00	1.50
a.		Inverted surcharge	40.00	

C24	AP1 10c on 80sk	3.00	1.50
C25	AP2 20c on 1auk	12.00	6.00
C26	AP3 20c on 2auk	15.00	7.50
a.	Without "CENT"	175.00	125.00
C27	AP7 25c on 2auk	1.75	1.00
a.	Inverted surcharge	40.00	35.00
C28	AP7 30c on 4auk (C)	1.75	1.00
a.	Double surcharge	45.00	40.00
C29	AP4 50c on 5auk	3.00	1.50
C30	AP7 50c on 10auk	1.75	1.00
a.	Inverted surcharge	45.00	40.00
C31	AP6 1 l on 5auk	25.00	15.00
a.	Double surcharge	45.00	
	Nos. C21-C31 (11)	75.00	40.00

Airplane and Carrier Pigeons AP8

"Flight" AP9

1924, Jan. 28 Wmk. 147 *Perf. 11*

C32	AP8 20c yellow	1.75	.75
C33	AP8 40c emerald	1.75	.75
a.	Horiz. or vert. pair, imperf. between	55.00	
C34	AP8 60c rose	1.75	.75
a.	Imperf., pair	75.00	
C35	AP9 1 l dk brown	3.50	.75
	Nos. C32-C35 (4)	8.75	3.00

Most copies, if not all, of the "unwatermarked" varieties show faint traces of watermark, according to experts.

For surcharges see Nos. CB1-CB4.

Swallow — AP10

1926, June 17 Wmk. 198 *Perf. 14½*

C37	AP10 20c carmine rose	1.25	.75
a.	Horiz. or vert. pair, imperf. between	50.00	
C38	AP10 40c violet & red org	1.25	.75
a.	Horiz. or vert. pair, imperf. between	50.00	
C39	AP10 60c blue & black	2.50	.75
a.	Horiz. or vert. pair, imperf. between	50.00	
c.	Center inverted	225.00	150.00
	Nos. C37-C39 (3)	5.00	2.25

Juozas Tubelis — AP11

Vytautas and Airplane over Kaunas AP12

Vytautas and Antanas Smetona AP13

1930, Feb. 16 Wmk. 109 *Perf. 14*

C40	AP11 5c blk, bis & brn	.70	.30
C41	AP11 10c dk bl, db & blk	.70	.30
C42	AP11 15c mar, gray & bl	.70	.30
C43	AP12 20c dk brn, org & dl red	.70	.50
C44	AP12 40c dk bl, lt bl & vio	1.25	.50
C45	AP13 60c bl grn, lil & blk	2.00	.55
C46	AP13 1 l dl red, lil & blk	3.75	1.00
	Nos. C40-C46 (7)	9.80	3.45

5th cent. of the death of the Grand Duke Vytautas.

Map of Lithuania, Klaipeda and Vilnius — AP14

15c, 20c, Airplane over Neman. 40c, 60c, City Hall, Kaunas. 1 l, 2 l, Church of Vytautas, Kaunas.

Wmk. Multiple Letters (238)

1932, July 21 *Perf. 14, Imperf.*

C47	AP14 5c ver & ol grn	.85	.60
C48	AP14 10c dk red brn & ocher	.85	.60
C49	AP14 15c dk bl & org yel	.85	.60
C50	AP14 20c sl blk & org	3.50	.75
C51	AP14 60c ultra & ocher	5.00	3.00
C52	AP14 2 l dk bl & yel	6.50	4.00

Wmk. 198

C53	AP14 40c vio brn & yel	4.50	2.75
C54	AP14 1 l vio brn & grn	8.50	5.00
	Nos. C47-C54 (8)	30.55	17.30

Issued for the benefit of Lithuanian orphans.

Mindaugas in the Battle of Shauyai, 1236 — AP15

15c, 20c, Coronation of Mindaugas (1253). 40c, Grand Duke Gediminas and his followers. 60c, Founding of Vilnius by Gediminas (1332). 1 l, Gediminas capturing the Russian Fortifications. 2 l, Grand Duke Algirdas before Moscow (1368).

Perf. 14, Imperf.

1932, Nov. 28 Wmk. 209

C55	AP15 5c grn & red lil	.90	.75
C56	AP15 10c emer & rose	.90	.75
C57	AP15 15c rose vio & bis brn	.90	.75
C58	AP15 20c rose red & blk brn	3.50	.50
C59	AP15 40c choc & dk gray	5.50	1.10
C60	AP15 60c org & gray blk	6.00	3.00
C61	AP15 1 l rose vio & grn	7.00	5.00
C62	AP15 2 l dp bl & brn	8.00	7.50
	Nos. C55-C62 (8)	32.70	19.35

Anniv. of independence.

Nos. C58-C62 exist with overprint "DARIUS-GIRENAS / NEW YORK-1933- KAUNAS" below small plane. The overprint was applied in New York with the approval of the Lithuanian consul general. Lithuanian postal authorities seem not to have been involved in the creation or release of these overprints.

Trakai Castle, Home of the Grand Duke Kestutis — AP16

Designs: 15c, 20c, Meeting of Kestutís and the Hermit Birute. 40c, 60c, Hermit Birute. 1 l, 2 l, Kestutis and his Brother Algirdas.

1933, May 6 *Perf. 14, Imperf.*

C63	AP16 5c ol gray & dp bl	.80	.60
C64	AP16 10c gray vio & org brn	.80	.60
C65	AP16 15c dp blue & lilac	.80	.60
C66	AP16 20c org brn & lilac	2.50	1.00
C67	AP16 40c lt ultra & lilac	3.50	*1.75*
C68	AP16 60c brown & lt ultra	5.00	*3.50*
C69	AP16 1 l ol gray & dp bl	7.00	*4.00*
C70	AP16 2 l vio gray & yel grn	10.00	*8.00*
	Nos. C63-C70 (8)	30.40	*20.05*

Reopening of air service to Berlin-Kaunas-Moscow, and 550th anniv. of the death of Kestutis.

Joseph Maironis — AP17

Joseph Tumas-Vaizgantas — AP17a

Designs: 40c, 60c, Vincas Kudirka. 1 l, 2 l, Julia A. Zemaite.

1933, Sept. 15 *Perf. 14, Imperf.*

C71	AP17 5c crim & dp bl	.65	.65
C72	AP17 10c bl vio & grn	.65	.65
C73	AP17a 15c dk grn & choc	.65	.65
C74	AP17a 20c brn car & ultra	.90	.90
C75	AP17 40c red brn & ol grn	1.50	1.50
C76	AP17 60c dk bl & choc	2.50	2.50
C77	AP17 1 l citron & indigo	3.50	3.50
C78	AP17 2 l dp grn & red brn	5.75	5.75
	Nos. C71-C78 (8)	16.10	16.10

Issued for the benefit of Lithuanian orphans.

Capts. Steponas Darius and Stas. Girenas AP18

Ill-Fated Plane "Lituanica" AP19

The Dark Angel of Death — AP20

"Lituanica" over Globe — AP21

"Lituanica" and White Knight — AP22

Perf. 11½

1934, May 18 Unwmk. Engr.

C79	AP18 20c scarlet & blk	.20	.20
C80	AP19 40c dp rose & bl	.20	.20
C81	AP18 60c dk vio & blk	.20	.20
C82	AP20 1 l black & rose	.35	.20
C83	AP21 3 l gray grn & org	.90	.50
C84	AP22 5 l dk brn & bl	3.50	3.25
	Nos. C79-C84 (6)	5.35	4.55

Death of Capts. Steponas Darius and Stasys Girenas on their New York-Kaunas flight of 1933.

No. C80 exists with diagonal overprint: "F. VAITKUS / nugalejo Atlanta / 21-22-IX-1935." Value $300.

Felix Waitkus and Map of Transatlantic Flight — AP23

Wmk. 238

1936, Mar. 24 Litho. *Perf. 14*

C85	AP23 15c brown lake	2.25	.75
C86	AP23 30c dark green	3.25	.75
C87	AP23 60c blue	4.25	2.00
	Nos. C85-C87 (3)	9.75	3.50

Transatlantic Flight of the Lituanica II, Sept. 21-22, 1935.

AIR POST SEMI-POSTAL STAMPS

Catalogue values for unused stamps in this section are for Never Hinged items.

Nos. C32-C35 Surcharged like Nos. B1-B9 (No. CB1), Nos. B10-B11 (Nos. CB2-CB3), and Nos. B12-B14 (No. CB4) in Red, Violet or Black

1924 Wmk. 147 *Perf. 11*

CB1	AP8 20c + 20c yellow (R)	16.00	8.00
CB2	AP8 40c + 40c emerald (V)	16.00	8.00
CB3	AP8 60c + 60c rose (V)	16.00	8.00
CB4	AP9 1 l + 1 l dk brown	16.00	8.00
	Nos. CB1-CB4 (4)	64.00	32.00

Surtax for the Red Cross. See note following No. C35.

SOUTH LITHUANIA

GRODNO DISTRICT

Russian Stamps of 1909-12 Surcharged in Black or Red

1919 Unwmk. *Perf. 14, 14½x15*

L1	A14 50sk on 3k red	55.00	40.00
a.	Double surcharge		
L2	A14 50sk on 5k claret	55.00	40.00
a.	Imperf., pair	300.00	275.00
L3	A15 50sk on 10k dk bl (R)	55.00	40.00
L4	A11 50sk on 15k red brn & bl	55.00	40.00
a.	Imperf., pair	350.00	325.00
L5	A11 50sk on 25k grn & gray vio (R)	55.00	40.00
L6	A11 50sk on 35k red brn & grn	55.00	40.00
L7	A8 50sk on 50k vio & grn	55.00	40.00
L8	A11 50sk on 70k brn & org	55.00	40.00
	Nos. L1-L8 (8)	440.00	320.00

Excellent counterfeits are plentiful.

This surcharge exists on Russia No. 119, the imperf. 1k orange of 1917. Value, unused $90, used $60.

OCCUPATION STAMPS

ISSUED UNDER GERMAN OCCUPATION

German Stamps Overprinted in Black

On Stamps of 1905-17

1916-17 Wmk. 125 Perf. 14, 14½

1N1	A22	2½pf gray	.65	*1.00*
1N2	A16	3pf brown	.25	.20
1N3	A16	5pf green	.65	*1.00*
1N4	A22	7½pf orange	.65	*1.00*
1N5	A16	10pf carmine	.65	*1.00*
1N6	A22	15pf yel brn	3.00	2.00
1N7	A22	15pf dk vio ('17)	.65	*1.00*
1N8	A16	20pf ultra	1.00	1.00
1N9	A16	25pf org & blk, *yel*	.50	*.50*
1N10	A16	40pf lake & blk	1.00	*3.75*
1N11	A16	50pf vio & blk, *buff*	1.00	*1.50*
1N12	A17	1m car rose	12.00	3.50
		Nos. 1N1-1N12 (12)	22.00	*17.45*
		Set, never hinged	40.00	

These stamps were used in the former Russian provinces of Suvalki, Vilnius, Kaunas, Kurland, Estland and Lifland.

ISSUED UNDER RUSSIAN OCCUPATION

Catalogue values for unused stamps in this section are for Never Hinged items.

Lithuanian Stamps of 1937-40 Overprinted in Red or Blue

1940 Wmk. 238 Perf. 14

2N9	A44	2c orange (Bl)	.30	.40
2N10	A50	50c brown (Bl)	.75	.50

Unwmk.

2N11	A56	5c brown car (Bl)	.30	.40
2N12	A57	10c green (R)	5.00	5.00
2N13	A58	15c dull orange (Bl)	.30	.40
2N14	A59	25c lt brown (R)	.30	.40
2N15	A60	30c Prus green (R)	.65	.50
2N16	A61	35c red orange (Bl)	.90	1.00
		Nos. 2N9-2N16 (8)	8.50	8.60

Values for used stamps are for CTOs. Postally used examples are considerably more.

The Lithuanian Soviet Socialist Republic was proclaimed July 21, 1940.

LOURENCO MARQUES

lə-ˈren͵t͵-͵ō-͵mär-ˈkes

LOCATION — In the southern part of Mozambique in Southeast Africa
GOVT. — Part of Portuguese East Africa Colony
AREA — 28,800 sq. mi. (approx.)
POP. — 474,000 (approx.)
CAPITAL — Lourenço Marques

Stamps of Mozambique replaced those of Lourenço Marques in 1920. See Mozambique.

1000 Reis = 1 Milreis
100 Centavos = 1 Escudo (1913)

King Carlos — A1

Perf. 11½, 12½, 13½

1895 Typo. Unwmk.

1	A1	5r yellow	.75	.25
2	A1	10r redsh violet	.75	.35
3	A1	15r chocolate	1.00	.50
4	A1	20r lavender	1.00	.50
5	A1	25r blue green	1.00	.30
a.		Perf. 11½	3.00	.85
6	A1	50r light blue	2.00	.60
a.		Perf. 13½	10.00	3.75
b.		Perf. 11½		
7	A1	75r rose	1.50	1.25
8	A1	80r yellow grn	4.50	2.75
9	A1	100r brn, *yel*	3.00	1.00
a.		Perf. 12½	5.00	3.25
10	A1	150r car, *rose*	5.00	3.00
11	A1	200r dk bl, *bl*	6.00	3.00
12	A1	300r dk bl, *sal*	7.50	4.00
		Nos. 1-12 (12)	34.00	17.50

For surcharges and overprints see Nos. 29, 58-69, 132-137, 140-143, 156-157, 160.

Saint Anthony of Padua Issue

Regular Issues of Mozambique, 1886 and 1894, Overprinted in Black

1895 Without Gum Perf. 12½

On 1886 Issue

13	A2	5r black	17.00	10.00
14	A2	10r green	25.00	10.00
15	A2	20r rose	35.00	11.00
16	A2	25r lilac	40.00	14.00
17	A2	40r chocolate	21.00	12.00
18	A2	50r bl, perf. 13½	30.00	10.00
a.		Perf. 12½	50.00	27.50
19	A2	100r yellow brn	60.00	27.50
20	A2	200r gray vio	40.00	22.50
21	A2	300r orange	40.00	30.00

On 1894 Issue

Perf. 11½

22	A3	5r yellow	35.00	25.00
23	A3	10r redsh vio	40.00	15.00
24	A3	50r light blue	40.00	20.00
a.		Perf. 12½	40.00	35.00
25	A3	75r rose, perf. 12½	40.00	25.00
26	A3	80r yellow grn	60.00	40.00
27	A3	100r brown, *buff*	350.00	100.00
28	A3	150r car, *rose*, perf. 12½	25.00	18.00
		Nos. 13-28 (16)	898.00	390.00

No. 12 Surcharged in Black

1897, Jan. 2

29	A1	50r on 300r	175.00	75.00

Most copies of No. 29 were issued without gum.

King Carlos — A2

1898-1903 Perf. 11½

Name, Value in Black except 500r

30	A2	2½r gray	.20	.20
31	A2	5r orange	.20	.20
32	A2	10r lt green	.20	.20
33	A2	15r brown	1.00	.85
34	A2	15r gray green ('03)	.55	.35
a.		Imperf.		
35	A2	20r gray violet	.55	.20
a.		Imperf.		
36	A2	25r sea green	.70	.30
a.		Perf. 13½	25.00	6.75
b.		25r light green (error)	*32.50*	*32.50*
c.		Perf. 12½	*20.00*	50.00
37	A2	25r car ('03)	.30	.20
a.		Imperf.		
38	A2	50r blue	2.00	.40
39	A2	50r brown ('03)	.80	.70
40	A2	65r dull bl ('03)	14.00	8.00
41	A2	75r rose	1.75	1.40
42	A2	75r lilac ('03)	1.10	.95
a.		Imperf.		
43	A2	80r violet	2.50	1.25
44	A2	100r dk blue, *blue*	1.75	.65
a.		Perf. 13½	14.00	4.75
45	A2	115r org brn, *pink* ('03)	7.00	5.00
46	A2	130r brn, *straw* ('03)	7.00	5.00
47	A2	150r brn, *straw*	2.00	1.40
48	A2	200r red lil, *pnksh*	2.75	1.25
49	A2	300r dk bl, *rose*	3.00	1.25
50	A2	400r dl bl, *straw* ('03)	8.00	5.00
51	A2	500r blk & red, *bl* ('01)	6.00	3.00
52	A2	700r vio, *yelsh* ('01)	10.00	6.00
		Nos. 30-52 (23)	73.35	43.75

For surcharges and overprints see Nos. 57, 71-74, 76-91, 138, 144-155.

Coat of Arms — A3

Surcharged On Upper and Lower Halves of Stamp

1899 Imperf.

53	A3	5r on 10r grn & brn	20.00	6.00
54	A3	25r on 10r grn & brn	20.00	6.00
55	A3	50r on 30r grn & brn	30.00	11.00
a.		Inverted surcharge		
56	A3	50r on 800r grn & brn	40.00	15.00
		Nos. 53-56 (4)	110.00	38.00

The lower half of No. 55 can be distinguished from that of No. 56 by the background of the label containing the word "REIS." The former is plain, while the latter is formed of white intersecting curved horizontal lines over vertical shading of violet brown.

Values are for undivided stamps. Halves sell for ¼ as much.

Most copies of Nos. 53-56 were issued without gum. Values are for copies without gum.

No. 41 Surcharged in Black

1899 Perf. 11½

57	A2	50r on 75r rose	5.00	2.50

Most copies of No. 57 were issued without gum. Values are for copies without gum.

Surcharged in Black

On Issue of 1895

1902 Perf. 11½, 12½

58	A1	65r on 5r yellow	4.00	2.50
59	A1	65r on 15r choc	4.00	2.50
60	A1	65r on 20r lav	5.00	2.50
a.		Perf. 12½	25.00	15.00
61	A1	115r on 10r red vio	5.00	3.00
62	A1	115r on 200r bl, *bl*	5.00	3.00
63	A1	115r on 300r bl, *sal*	5.00	3.00
64	A1	130r on 25r grn, perf. 12½	2.00	2.00
a.		Perf. 11½	30.00	22.50
65	A1	130r on 80r yel grn	3.00	3.00
66	A1	130r on 150r car, *rose*	4.00	3.00
67	A1	400r on 50r lt bl	8.00	6.00
68	A1	400r on 75r rose	8.00	6.00
69	A1	400r on 100r brn, *buff*	7.00	6.00

On Newspaper Stamp of 1893

70	N1	65r on 2½ brn	4.00	2.00
		Nos. 58-70 (13)	64.00	44.50

Surcharge exists inverted on Nos. 61, 70.

Nos. 64, 67 and 68 have been reprinted on thin white paper with shiny white gum and clean-cut perforation 13½. Value $6 each.

For overprints see Nos. 132-137, 140-143, 156-157, 160.

Issue of 1898-1903 Overprinted in Black

1903 Perf. 11½

71	A2	15r brown	2.00	.85
72	A2	25r sea green	1.50	.85
73	A2	50r blue	2.50	.85
74	A2	75r rose	3.00	1.40
a.		Inverted overprint	50.00	50.00
		Nos. 71-74 (4)	9.00	3.95

Surcharged in Black

1905

76	A2	50r on 65r dull blue	1.75	1.50

Regular Issues Overprinted in Carmine or Green

1911

77	A2	2½r gray	.20	.20
78	A2	5r orange	.20	.20
a.		Double overprint	10.00	10.00
b.		Inverted overprint	10.00	10.00
79	A2	10r lt grn	.30	.25
80	A2	15r gray grn	.30	.25
a.		Inverted overprint	10.00	10.00
81	A2	20r dl vio	.60	.40
82	A2	25r car (G)	.30	.25
83	A2	50r brown	.60	.40
84	A2	75r lilac	.60	.40
85	A2	100r dk bl, *bl*	.80	.40
86	A2	115r org brn, *pink*	5.50	2.00
87	A2	130r brn, *straw*	.80	.60
88	A2	200r red lil, *pnksh*	.75	.50
89	A2	400r dl bl, *straw*	1.00	.80
90	A2	500r blk & red, *bl*	1.10	.85
91	A2	700r vio, *yelsh*	1.40	1.00
		Nos. 77-91 (15)	14.45	8.50

Vasco da Gama Issue of Various Portuguese Colonies Common Design Types Surcharged

1913 Perf. 12½-16

On Stamps of Macao

92	CD20	¼c on ½a bl grn	2.25	2.25
93	CD21	½c on la red	2.25	2.25
94	CD22	1c on 2a red vio	2.25	2.25
95	CD23	2½c on 4a yel grn	2.25	2.25
96	CD24	5c on 8a dk bl	2.25	2.25
97	CD25	7½c on 12a vio brn	4.25	4.25
98	CD26	10c on 16a bis brn	3.50	3.50
a.		Inverted surcharge	40.00	40.00
99	CD27	15c on 24a bister	3.75	3.75
		Nos. 92-99 (8)	22.75	22.75

On Stamps of Portuguese Africa

100	CD20	¼c on 2½r bl grn	1.40	1.40
101	CD21	½c on 5r red	1.40	1.40
102	CD22	1c on 10r red vio	1.40	1.40
103	CD23	2½c on 25r yel grn	1.40	1.40
104	CD24	5c on 50r dk bl	1.40	1.40
105	CD25	7½c on 75r vio brn	3.50	3.50
106	CD26	10c on 100r bis brn	2.50	2.50
107	CD27	15c on 150r bis	2.50	2.50
		Nos. 100-107 (8)	15.50	15.50

On Stamps of Timor

108	CD20	¼c on ½a bl grn	1.75	1.75
109	CD21	½c on 1a red	1.75	1.75
110	CD22	1c on 2a red vio	1.75	1.75
111	CD23	2½c on 4a yel grn	1.75	1.75
112	CD24	5c on 8a dk bl	2.00	1.75
113	CD25	7½c on 12a vio brn	3.50	3.50
114	CD26	10c on 16a bis brn	2.75	2.75
115	CD27	15c on 24a bister	2.75	2.75
		Nos. 108-115 (8)	18.00	17.75
		Nos. 92-115 (24)	56.25	56.00

Ceres — A4

1914 Typo. ***Perf. 15x14***

Name and Value in Black

116	A4	¼c olive brn	.20	.20
117	A4	½c black	.20	.20
a.		Value omitted	15.00	
118	A4	1c blue grn	.20	.20
119	A4	1½c lilac brn	.20	.20
a.		Imperf.		
120	A4	2c carmine	.20	.20
121	A4	2½c lt vio	.20	.20
122	A4	5c dp blue	.20	.20
123	A4	7½c yellow brn	.20	.20
124	A4	8c slate	.20	.20
125	A4	10c orange brn	1.50	.85
126	A4	15c plum	1.00	.35
127	A4	20c yellow grn	2.50	.50
128	A4	30c brown, *green*	3.50	1.00
129	A4	40c brown, *pink*	9.00	4.00
130	A4	50c orange, *sal*	8.00	3.00
131	A4	1e green, *blue*	10.00	3.00
		Nos. 116-131 (16)	37.30	14.50

Values of Nos. 116-124 are for stamps on ordinary paper. Those on chalky paper sell for 8 to 12 times as much. Nos. 127-131 issued only on chalky paper.

For surcharges see Nos. 139, 159, 161-162, B1-B12.

In 1921 Nos. 117 and 119 were surcharged 10c and 30c respectively, for use in Mozambique as Nos. 230 and 231. These same values, surcharged 5c and 10c respectively, with the addition of the word "PORTEADO," were used in Mozambique as postage dues, Nos. J44 and J45.

Provisional Issue of 1902 Overprinted Locally in Carmine

1914 ***Perf. 11½, 12½***

132	A1	115r on 10r red vio	1.00	.45
a.		"Republica" inverted	20.00	
133	A1	115r on 200r bl, *bl*	1.00	.45
134	A1	115r on 300r bl, *sal*	1.10	.45
a.		Double overprint	40.00	40.00
135	A1	130r on 25r grn	1.50	.70
a.		Perf. 12½	3.25	1.60
136	A1	130r on 80r yel grn	1.10	.35
137	A1	130r on 150r car, *rose*	1.10	.35
		Nos. 132-137 (6)	6.80	2.75

No. 135a was issued without gum.

Nos. 78 and 117 Perforated Diagonally and Surcharged in Carmine

1915 ***Perf. 11½***

138	A2	¼c on half of 5r org, pair	5.00	5.00
a.		Pair without dividing perfs.	20.00	20.00

Perf. 15x14

139	A4	¼c on half of ½c blk, pair	9.00	9.00

The added perforation on Nos. 138-139 runs from lower left to upper right corners, dividing the stamp in two. Values are for pairs, both halves of the stamp.

Provisional Issue of 1902 Overprinted in Carmine

1915 ***Perf. 11½, 12½***

140	A1	115r on 10r red vio	.55	.40
141	A1	115r on 200r bl, *bl*	.55	.40
142	A1	115r on 300r bl, *sal*	.55	.40
143	A1	130r on 150r car, *rose*	.55	.40
		Nos. 140-143 (4)	2.20	1.60

Nos. 34 and 80 Surcharged

1915

On Issue of 1903

144	A2	2c on 15r gray grn	.75	.70

On Issue of 1911

145	A2	2c on 15r gray grn	.75	.70
a.		New value inverted	22.50	

Regular Issues of 1898-1903 Overprinted Locally in Carmine

1916

146	A2	15r gray grn	1.50	1.00
147	A2	50r brown	3.50	2.00
a.		Inverted overprint		
148	A2	75r lilac	3.50	2.00
149	A2	100r blue, *bl*	3.00	1.00
150	A2	115r org brn, *pink*	2.50	1.00
151	A2	130r brown, *straw*	10.00	5.00
152	A2	200r red lil, *pnksh*	7.00	2.00
153	A2	400r dull bl, *straw*	12.00	4.00
154	A2	500r blk & red, *bl*	7.00	3.00
155	A2	700r vio, *yelsh*	12.00	5.00
		Nos. 146-155 (10)	62.00	26.00

Same Overprint on Nos. 67-68

1917

156	A1	400r on 50r lt blue	1.25	.65
a.		Perf. 13½	11.50	9.00
157	A1	400r on 75r rose	2.50	1.00

No. 69 exists with this overprint. It was not officially issued.

Type of 1914 Surcharged in Red

1920 ***Perf. 15x14***

159	A4	4c on 2½c violet	1.00	.30

Stamps of 1914 Surcharged in Green or Black

a

b

1921

160	A1(a)	¼c on 115r on 10r red vio (G)	.80	.80
161	A4(b)	1c on 2½c vio (Bk)	.60	.40
a.		Inverted surcharge	40.00	
162	A4(b)	1½c on 2½c vio (Bk)	.80	.60
		Nos. 160-162 (3)	2.20	1.80

Nos. 159-162 were postally valid throughout Mozambique.

SEMI-POSTAL STAMPS

Regular Issue of 1914 Overprinted or Surcharged:

a

b

c

1918 ***Perf. 15x14½***

B1	A4(a)	¼c olive brn	2.00	*3.00*
B2	A4(a)	½c black	2.00	*4.00*
B3	A4(a)	1c bl grn	2.00	*4.00*
B4	A4(a)	2½c violet	4.00	4.00
B5	A4(a)	5c blue	4.00	*6.00*
B6	A4(a)	10c org brn	5.00	*7.00*
B7	A4(b)	20c on 1½c lil brn	5.00	*8.00*
B8	A4(a)	30c brn, *grn*	5.00	*9.00*
B9	A4(b)	40c on 2c car	5.00	*10.00*
B10	A4(b)	50c on 7½c bis	8.00	*12.00*
B11	A4(b)	70c on 8c slate	10.00	*15.00*
B12	A4(c)	$1 on 15c mag	10.00	*15.00*
		Nos. B1-B12 (12)	62.00	*97.00*

Nos. B1-B12 were used in place of ordinary postage stamps on Mar. 9, 1918.

NEWSPAPER STAMPS

Numeral of Value — N1

Perf. 11½

1893, July 28 Typo. Unwmk.

P1	N1	2½r brown	.25	.65
a.		Perf. 12½	20.00	17.50

For surcharge see No. 70.

Saint Anthony of Padua Issue

Mozambique No. P6 Overprinted

1895, July 1 ***Perf. 11½, 13½***

P2	N3	2½r brown	20.00	17.50
a.		Inverted overprint	30.00	30.00

LUXEMBOURG

'lək-səm-ˌbərg

LOCATION — Western Europe between southern Belgium, Germany and France

GOVT. — Grand Duchy

AREA — 998 sq. mi.

POP. — 365,800 (est. 1984)

CAPITAL — Luxembourg

12½ Centimes = 1 Silbergroschen
100 Centimes = 1 Franc

Watermarks

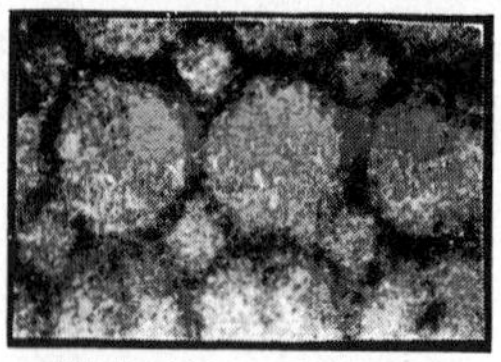
Wmk. 110 — Octagons

Wmk. 149 — W

Wmk. 213 — Double Wavy Lines

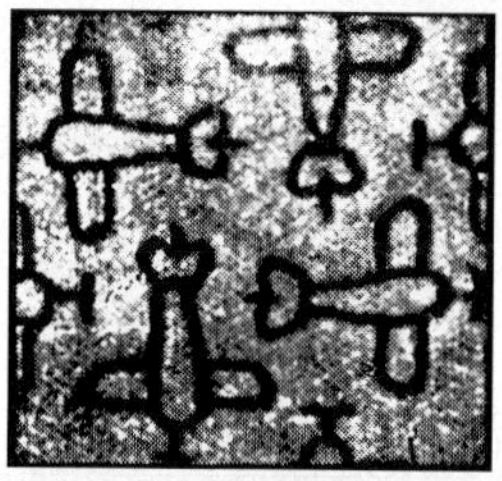
Wmk. 216 — Multiple Airplanes

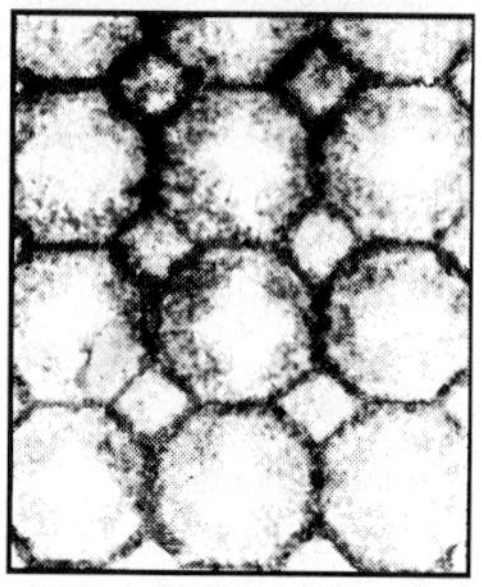
Wmk. 246 — Multiple Cross Enclosed in Octagons

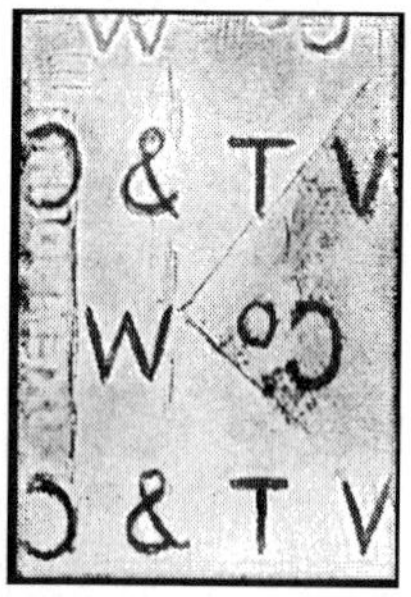
Wmk. 247 — Multiple Letters

Unused values of Nos. 1-47 are for stamps without gum. Though these stamps were issued with gum, most examples offered are without gum. Stamps with original gum sell for more.

Grand Duke William III — A1

Luxembourg Print

Wmk. 149

1852, Sept. 15 Engr. ***Imperf.***

1	A1	10c gray black	*2,500.*	60.00
		With gum	*4,400.*	
		On cover		425.00
a.		10c greenish black ('53)	*2,600.*	72.50
		With gum	*5,250.*	
		On cover		800.00
b.		10c intense black ('54)	*3,250.*	150.00
		With gum	—	
		On cover		1,400.
2	A1	1sg brown red ('53)	1,700.	110.00
		With gum	—	
		On cover		—
a.		1sg brick red	1,700.	110.00
		With gum	*3,000.*	
		On cover		1,000.
b.		1sg orange red ('54)	1,700.	110.00
		With gum	*3,000.*	
		On cover		1,000.
c.		1sg blood red	3,000.	575.00
		With gum	—	
		On cover		1,850.
3	A1	1sg rose ('55)	1,600.	100.00
		With gum	*3,000.*	
		On cover		750.00
a.		1sg carmine rose ('56)	1,600.	110.00

With gum 3,000.
On cover 850.00
b. 1sg dark carmine rose, thin paper ('59) 1,800. 300.00
With gum 4,250.
On cover 2,000.
Nos. 1-3 (3) 270.00

Full margins = 1mm.

Reprints of both values exist on watermarked paper. Some of the reprints show traces of lines cancelling the plates, but others can be distinguished only by an expert.

See Nos. 278-279, 603.

Values for pairs

1 A1 10c gray black — 110.00
On cover 1,100.
2b A1 1sg orange red — 250.00
On cover 1,750.
3 A1 1sg rose — 300.00
On cover 1,750.

Values for strips of 3

1 A1 10c gray black — 525.00
On cover 1,450.
2b A1 1sg orange red — —
On cover —
3 A1 1sg rose — 450.00
On cover 1,850.

Values for strips of 4

1 A1 10c gray black — 1,100.
On cover 1,900.
2b A1 1sg orange red — —
On cover —
3 A1 1sg rose — 1,600.
On cover 3,250.

Values for blocks of 4

1 A1 10c gray black — 5,200.
On cover 9,000.
2b A1 1sg orange red — —
On cover —
3 A1 1sg rose — 6,500.
On cover 11,000.

Coat of Arms
A2 A3

No. 26

No. 39

Frankfurt Print

1859-64 Typo. Unwmk.

4 A2 1c buff ('63) 140.00 450.00
With gum 200.00
On cover 2,000.
5 A2 2c black ('60) 110.00 575.00
With gum 160.00
On cover 2,400.
6 A2 4c yellow ('64) 200.00 190.00
With gum 275.00
On cover 2,000.
a. 4c orange ('64) 210.00 210.00
With gum 300.00
On cover 2,200.
7 A3 10c blue 200.00 21.00
With gum 290.00
On cover 200.00
a. 10c dark blue 1,350. 35.00
With gum 1,900.
On cover 225.00
8 A3 12½c rose 300.00 160.00
With gum 425.00
On cover 1,000.
9 A3 25c brown 400.00 300.00
With gum 550.00
On cover 2,000.
10 A3 30c rose lilac 375.00 250.00
With gum 450.00
On cover 1,800.
11 A3 37½c green 350.00 210.00
With gum 475.00
On cover 1,200.
12 A3 40c red orange 925.00 250.00
With gum 1,350.
On cover 1,100.

Full margins = ½mm.

Counterfeits of Nos. 1-12 exist.

See Nos. 13-25, 27-38, 40-47. For surcharges and overprints see Nos. 26, 39, O1-O51.

Values for pairs

4 A2 1c buff 325.00 1,350.
On cover 9,000.
5 A2 2c black 575.00 1,700.
On cover 8,500.
6 A2 4c yellow 650.00 640.00
On cover 7,000.
a. 4c orange 675.00 650.00
On cover 7,000.
7 A3 10c blue 850.00 225.00
On cover 1,050.
a. 10c dark blue 3,000. 90.00
On cover —
8 A3 12½c rose 800.00 475.00
On cover 3,350.
9 A3 25c brown 1,400. 1,200.
On cover 4,250.
10 A3 30c rose lilac 1,150. 725.00
On cover 8,250.
11 A3 37½c green 1,400. 925.00
On cover 6,750.
12 A3 40c red orange 3,200. 750.00
On cover 3,600.

1865-71 *Rouletted*

13 A2 1c red brown 200.00 300.00
With gum 300.00
On cover 1,400.
14 A2 2c black ('67) 22.50 16.00
With gum 35.00
On cover 475.00
15 A2 4c yellow ('67) 675.00 200.00
With gum 1,050.
On cover 2,000.
16 A2 4c green ('71) 40.00 27.50
With gum 60.00
On cover 250.00
Nos. 13-16 (4) 937.50 543.50

Values for pairs

13 A2 1c red brown 425.00 750.00
On cover 2,500.
14 A2 2c black ('67) 55.00 55.00
On cover 700.00
15 A2 4c yellow ('67) 2,300. 750.00
On cover 2,750.
16 A2 4c green ('71) 100.00 100.00
On cover 625.00

Values for strips of 3

13 A2 1c red brown 700.00 1,450.
On cover 3,600.
14 A2 2c black ('67) 140.00 190.00
On cover 1,200.
15 A2 4c yellow ('67) — 1,750.
On cover —
16 A2 4c green ('71) 250.00 300.00
On cover 1,000.

1865-74 *Rouletted in Color*

17 A2 1c red brn ('72) 45.00 5.50
With gum 52.50
On cover 120.00
18 A2 1c orange ('69) 37.50 7.25
With gum 45.00
On cover 140.00
a. 1c brown orange ('67) 140.00 45.00
With gum 155.00
On cover —
b. 1c red orange ('69) 1,650. 450.00
With gum 2,100.
On cover —
19 A3 10c rose lilac 140.00 2.50
With gum 175.00
On cover 30.00
a. 10c lilac 150.00 2.50
With gum 175.00
On cover 30.00
b. 10c gray lilac 140.00 2.50
With gum 175.00
On cover 35.00
20 A3 12½c carmine ('71) 190.00 6.00
With gum 250.00
On cover 110.00
a. 12½c rose 250.00 8.50
With gum 290.00
On cover 160.00
21 A3 20c gray brown ('72) 150.00 5.00
With gum 175.00
On cover 210.00
a. 20c yellow brown ('69) 175.00 8.50
With gum 210.00
On cover 250.00
22 A3 25c blue ('72) 900.00 12.00
With gum 1,100.
On cover 275.00
22A A3 25c ultra ('65) 900.00 12.00
With gum 1,100.
On cover 275.00
23 A3 30c lilac rose 925.00 85.00
With gum 1,150.
On cover 1,600.
24 A3 37½c bister ('66) 900.00 300.00
With gum 1,100.
On cover 3,250.
25 A3 40c pale orange ('74) 45.00 100.00
With gum 55.00
On cover 1,050.
a. 40c orange red ('66) 1,200. 72.50
With gum 1,500.
On cover 1,000.
26 A4 1fr on 37½c bis ('73) 1,100. 85.00
With gum 1,300.
On cover 1,300.
a. Surcharge inverted 3,600.

Luxembourg Print

1874 Typo. *Imperf.*

27 A2 4c green 110.00 110.00
With gum 150.00
On cover 700.00

1875-79 *Perf. 13*

Narrow Margins

29 A2 1c red brown ('78) 37.50 5.00
With gum 45.00
On cover 175.00
30 A2 2c black 150.00 29.00
With gum 175.00
On cover 275.00
31 A2 4c green 1.50 9.25
With gum 1.75
On cover 350.00
32 A2 5c yellow ('76) 190.00 29.00
With gum 250.00
On cover 225.00
a. 5c orange yellow 750.00 150.00
With gum 875.00
On cover 1,200.
b. Imperf. 750.00 1,200.
With gum 875.00
33 A3 10c gray lilac 550.00 1.50
With gum 600.00
On cover 19.00
b. 10c lilac 1,650. 37.50
With gum 1,900.
On cover 300.00
c. Imperf. 2,000. 2,750.
With gum 2,500.
34 A3 12½c lilac rose ('76) 750.00 25.00
With gum 875.00
On cover 210.00
35 A3 12½c car rose ('77) 500.00 25.00
With gum 600.00
On cover 210.00
36 A3 25c blue ('77) 1,000. 17.00
With gum 1,200.
On cover 490.00
37 A3 30c dull rose ('78) 900.00 550.00
With gum 1,100.
On cover 1,800.
38 A3 40c orange ('79) 1.25 9.50
With gum 1.60
On cover 1,200.
39 A5 1fr on 37½c bis ('79) 8.50 29.00
With gum 10.00
On cover 1,200.
a. "Pranc" 6,000. 7,500.
With gum 7,250.
b. Without surcharge 600.00
With gum 725.00
c. As "b," imperf. 600.00
With gum 700.00
As "c," pair 1,200.
With gum 1,450.

In the Luxembourg print the perforation is close to the border of the stamp. Excellent forgeries of No. 39a are plentiful, as well as faked cancellations on Nos. 31, 38 and 39.

Nos. 32b and 33c are said to be essays; Nos. 39b and 39c printer's waste.

Haarlem Print

Perf. 12½x12, 13½ (5c, 12½c)

1880-81

Wide Margins

40 A2 1c yel brn ('81) 9.50 6.00
With gum 11.00
On cover 175.00
a. Perf. 11½x12 16.00 12.00
With gum 21.00
b. Perf. 13½ 11.50 6.50
With gum 15.00
On cover 190.00
41 A2 2c black 8.50 1.75
With gum 10.00
On cover 190.00
a. Perf. 11½x12 16.00 10.00
With gum 19.00
b. Perf. 13½ 11.00 1.75
With gum 13.00
On cover 190.00
42 A2 5c yellow ('81) 250.00 110.00
With gum 290.00
On cover 350.00
b. Perf. 12½x12 950.00 490.00
With gum 1,200.
On cover —
c. Perf. 11½x12 1,200. 725.00
With gum 1,450.
43 A3 10c gray lilac 190.00 1.00
With gum 225.00
On cover 19.00
b. Perf. 11½x12 225.00 6.00
With gum 275.00
c. Perf. 13½ 210.00 2.10
With gum 275.00
On cover 30.00
44 A3 12½c rose ('81) 225.00 225.00
With gum 290.00
On cover 825.00
b. Perf. 12½x12 250.00 225.00
With gum 290.00
On cover 825.00
c. Perf. 11½x12 290.00 250.00
With gum 350.00
45 A3 20c gray brown ('81) 55.00 19.00
With gum 65.00
On cover 250.00
a. Perf. 11½x12 65.00 32.50
With gum 80.00
b. Perf. 13½ 60.00 21.00
With gum 70.00
On cover 300.00
46 A3 25c blue 300.00 5.00
With gum 350.00
On cover 160.00
b. Perf. 11½x12 350.00 25.00
With gum 450.00
c. Perf. 13½ 325.00 6.00
With gum 400.00
On cover 210.00
47 A3 30c dull rose ('81) 4.00 22.50
With gum 5.25
On cover 750.00
a. Perf. 11½x12 10.00 40.00
With gum 12.50

Gray Yellowish Paper

Perf. 12½

42a A2 5c 7.25
With gum 8.75
43a A3 10c 3.50
With gum 4.50
44a A3 12½c 9.50
With gum 11.50
46a A3 25c 5.00
With gum 5.75
Nos. 42a-46a (4) 25.25

Nos. 42a-46a were not regularly issued.

"Industry" and "Commerce"
A6

Grand Duke Adolphe
A7

1882, Dec. 1 Typo. *Perf. 12½*

48 A6 1c gray lilac .20 .40
Never hinged .50
On cover 6.00
49 A6 2c olive gray .20 .40
Never hinged .40
On cover 5.00
d. 2c olive brown .90 .50
Never hinged 2.50
On cover 11.00
50a A6 4c olive bister .60 2.75
Never hinged 1.50
On cover 8.50
51 A6 5c lt green .50 .40
Never hinged 1.75
On cover 6.00
52 A6 10c rose 6.00 .40
Never hinged 50.00
On cover 5.00
53 A6 12½c slate 1.75 30.00
Never hinged 9.50
On cover 60.00
54 A6 20c orange 3.00 1.90
Never hinged 12.00
On cover 25.00
55 A6 25c ultra 190.00 1.90
Never hinged 1,000.
On cover 27.50
57 A6 50c bister brown .75 11.00
Never hinged 3.00
On cover 60.00
d. 50c gray brown 25.00 9.50
Never hinged 50.00
On cover 60.00

For overprints see Nos. O52-O64.

Perf. 12½x12

48a A6 1c gray lilac .30 .60
Never hinged .80
49a A6 2c olive gray .45 .80
Never hinged 1.00
50 A6 4c olive bister .25 2.50
Never hinged 1.40
51a A6 5c lt green .85 1.50
Never hinged 2.50
52a A6 10c rose 7.00 1.00
Never hinged 50.00
53a A6 12½c slate 1.75 30.00
Never hinged 5.50
54a A6 20c orange 5.00 5.00
Never hinged 16.00
55a A6 25c ultra 175.00 1.90
Never hinged 1,000.
56a A6 30c gray green 19.00 14.00
Never hinged 90.00
57a A6 50c bister brown 1.50 12.00
Never hinged 6.00
58 A6 1fr pale violet .75 30.00
Never hinged 3.50
59a A6 5fr brown orange 37.50 190.00
Never hinged 65.00

Perf. 11½x12

48b A6 1c gray lilac 1.20 6.00
Never hinged 3.00
49b A6 2c olive gray 1.20 6.00
Never hinged 3.00
50b A6 4c olive bister 1.20 5.00
Never hinged 3.00
51b A6 5c lt green 5.00 7.00
Never hinged 12.00
52b A6 10c rose 12.00 7.00
Never hinged 60.00
53b A6 12½c slate 5.50 40.00
Never hinged 14.00
54b A6 20c orange 8.00 12.00
Never hinged 25.00
55b A6 25c ultra 175.00 6.00
Never hinged 1,000.
56b A6 30c gray green 25.00 35.00
Never hinged 95.00
57b A6 50c bister brown 5.00 14.50
Never hinged 14.50
58b A6 1fr pale violet 2.50 35.00
Never hinged 7.00
59b A6 5fr brown orange 90.00 225.00
Never hinged 150.00

Perf. 13½

48c A6 1c gray lilac 9.00 1.20
Never hinged 17.50
49c A6 2c olive gray 1.75 2.50
Never hinged 3.50
50c A6 4c olive bister 1.20 3.00
Never hinged 3.00
51c A6 5c lt green 1.75 1.75
Never hinged 5.00
52c A6 10c rose 9.50 4.00
Never hinged 55.00
53c A6 12½c slate 3.50 30.00
Never hinged 9.50
54c A6 20c orange 6.00 6.00
Never hinged 17.50
55c A6 25c ultra 175.00 3.00
Never hinged 1,000.
56 A6 30c gray green 19.00 14.50
Never hinged 85.00
57c A6 50c bister brown 1.90 12.00
Never hinged 7.00
58c A6 1fr pale violet 3.50 30.00
Never hinged 12.00
59 A6 5fr brown orange 37.50 190.00
Never hinged 60.00

Perf. 11, 11½x11, 12½

1891-93 Engr.

60 A7 10c carmine .20 .40
Never hinged .70
On cover 5.50
a. Sheet of 25, perf. 11½ 100.00

b. 10c dark carmine 9.50 1.75
Never hinged 19.00
On cover 30.00

61 A7 12½c slate grn ('93) .50 .70
Never hinged 2.50
On cover 11.00

62 A7 20c orange ('93) 12.00 .70
Never hinged 50.00
On cover 22.50
a. 20c brown, perf. 11½ 110.00 300.00
Never hinged 190.00

63 A7 25c blue .70 .60
Never hinged 3.00
On cover 8.75
a. Sheet of 25, perf. 11½ 1,000.
Never hinged 1,750.

64 A7 30c olive grn ('93) 1.40 1.25
Never hinged 3.00
On cover 27.50

65 A7 37½c green ('93) 2.75 2.50
Never hinged 6.00
On cover 37.50

66 A7 50c brown ('93) 7.25 3.00
Never hinged 25.00
On cover 37.50

67 A7 1fr dp violet ('93) 14.50 6.50
Never hinged 65.00
On cover 85.00
c. 1fr reddish violet 55.00 11.00
Never hinged 110.00
On cover 150.00
d. 1fr bluish violet 65.00 11.00
Never hinged 130.00
On cover 175.00

68 A7 2½fr black ('93) 1.50 25.00
Never hinged 3.00
On cover 290.00

69 A7 5fr lake ('93) 37.50 80.00
Never hinged 85.00
On cover 850.00
Nos. 60-69 (10) 78.30 120.65

No. 62a was never on sale at any post office, but exists postally used.

Covers: Cover values are for postally used and correctly franked covers. Low denomination stamps on ordinary postcards sell for somewhat less. Overfranked philatelic covers sell for much less.

For overprints see Nos. O65-O74.

Grand Duke Adolphe — A8

1895, May 4 Typo. *Perf. 12½*

70 A8 1c pearl gray 2.10 .50
Never hinged 12.00
On cover 8.50

71 A8 2c gray brown .20 .20
Never hinged 1.20
On cover 4.00

72 A8 4c olive bister .20 .50
Never hinged 1.75
On cover 8.50

73 A8 5c green 2.10 .20
Never hinged 30.00
On cover 6.00

74 A8 10c carmine 8.25 .20
Never hinged 50.00
On cover 5.00
Nos. 70-74 (5) 12.85 1.60

For overprints see Nos. O75-O79.

Coat of Arms — A9

Grand Duke William IV — A10

1906-26 Typo. *Perf. 12½*

75 A9 1c gray ('07) .20 .20
Never hinged .25
On cover 2.50

76 A9 2c olive brn ('07) .20 .20
Never hinged .25
On cover 2.50

77 A9 4c bister ('07) .20 .40
Never hinged .40
On cover 3.00

78 A9 5c green ('07) .20 .20
Never hinged 1.20
On cover 2.50

79 A9 5c lilac ('26) .20 .20
Never hinged .25
On cover 2.25

80 A9 6c violet ('07) .20 .50
Never hinged 1.00
On cover 5.00

81 A9 7½c orange ('19) .20 3.50
Never hinged .25
On cover 25.00

Engr.

Perf. 11, 11½x11

82 A10 10c scarlet 1.50 .20
Never hinged 2.50
On cover 11.00
a. Souvenir sheet of 10 450.00 1,200.
Never hinged 700.00
On cover 1,650.

b. Perf. 11 2.25 25.00
Never hinged 12.00
On cover —

83 A10 12½c slate grn ('07) 1.75 .60
Never hinged 8.50
On cover 6.00

84 A10 15c orange brn ('07) 1.75 .70
Never hinged 7.00
On cover 9.50

85 A10 20c orange ('07) 2.50 .70
Never hinged 14.50
On cover 9.50

86 A10 25c ultra ('07) 60.00 .50
Never hinged 325.00
On cover 9.50

87 A10 30c olive grn ('08) 1.00 .70
Never hinged 2.50
On cover 9.50

88 A10 37½c green ('07) 1.00 .80
Never hinged 3.00
On cover 16.50
a. Perf. 12½ 30.00 14.50
Never hinged 210.00
On cover 90.00

89 A10 50c brown ('07) 5.00 1.25
Never hinged 17.50
On cover 16.50

90 A10 87½c dk blue ('08) 1.75 11.00
Never hinged 6.00
On cover 65.00

91 A10 1fr violet ('08) 6.00 2.10
Never hinged 25.00
On cover 40.00
a. 1fr deep violet 14.00 3.25
Never hinged 60.00
On cover 65.00

92 A10 2½fr vermilion ('08) 55.00 92.50
Never hinged 160.00
On cover 45.00

93 A10 5fr claret ('08) 9.50 60.00
Never hinged 25.00
On cover 250.00
Nos. 75-93 (19) 148.15 176.25

No. 82a for accession of Grand Duke William IV to the throne.

Set of 12 stamps, imperf on thick paper $1,200.

For surcharges and overprints see Nos. 94-96, 112-117, O80-O98.

Nos. 90, 92-93 Surcharged in Red or Black

1912-15

94 A10 62½c on 87½c (R) 1.75 2.50
Never hinged 6.50
On cover 60.00

95 A10 62½c on 2½fr (Bk) ('15) 2.50 5.00
Never hinged 6.00
On cover 17.50

96 A10 62½c on 5fr (Bk) ('15) .70 3.50
Never hinged 2.50
On cover 7.00
Nos. 94-96 (3) 4.95 11.00

Grand Duchess Marie Adelaide A11

Grand Duchess Charlotte A12

1914-17 Engr. *Perf. 11½, 11½x11*

97 A11 10c lake .20 .20
Never hinged .25
On cover 1.20

98 A11 12½c dull green .20 .20
Never hinged .25
On cover 1.75

99 A11 15c sepia .20 .20
Never hinged .25
On cover 3.00

100 A11 17½c dp brown ('17) .20 .60
Never hinged .40
On cover 8.50

101 A11 25c ultra .20 .20
Never hinged .40
On cover 1.75

102 A11 30c bister .20 .70
Never hinged .70
On cover 4.00

103 A11 35c dark blue .20 .60
Never hinged .50
On cover 3.00

104 A11 37½c black brn .20 .60
Never hinged .50
On cover 4.00

105 A11 40c orange .20 .50
Never hinged .70
On cover 4.00

106 A11 50c dark gray .20 .70
Never hinged 1.75
On cover 7.00

107 A11 62½c blue green .40 3.50
Never hinged 1.50
On cover 25.00

108 A11 87½c orange ('17) .30 3.50
Never hinged 1.50
On cover 25.00

109 A11 1fr orange brown 2.50 1.00
Never hinged 14.00
On cover 25.00

110 A11 2½fr red .60 3.50
Never hinged 1.20
On cover 90.00

111 A11 5fr dark violet 9.50 55.00
Never hinged 45.00
On cover 190.00
Nos. 97-111 (15) 15.30 71.00

For surcharges and overprints see Nos. 118-124, B7-B10, O99-O113. Nos. 97, 98, 101, 107, 109 and 111 overprinted "Droits de statistique" are revenue stamps.

Stamps of 1906-19 Surcharged with New Value and Bars in Black or Red

1916-24

112 A9 2½c on 5c ('18) .20 .20
Never hinged .40
On cover 1.75
a. Double surcharge 75.00
Never hinged 90.00

113 A9 3c on 2c ('21) .20 .20
Never hinged .40
On cover 1.75

114 A9 5c on 1c ('23) .20 .20
Never hinged .40
On cover 1.75

115 A9 5c on 4c ('23) .20 .60
Never hinged .40
On cover 2.50

116 A9 5c on 7½c ('24) .20 .20
Never hinged .40
On cover 2.50

117 A9 6c on 2c (R) ('22) .20 .25
Never hinged .50
On cover 2.50

118 A11 7½c on 10c ('18) .20 .20
Never hinged .40
On cover 1.75

119 A11 17½c on 30c .20 .60
Never hinged .40
On cover 6.00

120 A11 20c on 17½c ('21) .20 .20
Never hinged .40
On cover 2.50

121 A11 25c on 37½c ('23) .20 .20
Never hinged .40
On cover 2.50
a. Double surcharge 90.00
Never hinged 120.00

122 A11 75c on 62½c (R) ('22) .20 .20
Never hinged .40
On cover 3.50

123 A11 80c on 87½c ('22) .20 .20
Never hinged .40
On cover 5.00

124 A11 87½c on 1fr .60 7.25
Never hinged 1.75
On cover 30.00
Nos. 112-124 (13) 3.00 10.50

1921, Jan. 6 Engr. *Perf. 11½*

125 A12 15c rose .20 .40
Never hinged .40
On cover 3.00
a. Sheet of 5, perf 11 150.00 250.00
Never hinged 350.00
Perf. 11, single 6.00 12.00
Never hinged 9.50
b. Sheet of 25, perf. 11½, 11x11½, 12x11½ 5.50 17.00
Never hinged 7.00

Birth of Prince Jean, first son of Grand Duchess Charlotte, Jan. 5 (No. 125a). No. 125 was printed in sheets of 100.

See Nos. 131-150. For surcharges and overprints see Nos. 154-158, O114-O131, O136.

Vianden Castle — A13

Foundries at Esch — A14

Adolphe Bridge — A15

1921-34 *Perf. 11½*

126 A13 1fr carmine .20 .45
Never hinged .50
On cover 15.00
a. Perf. 11x11½ .25 1.20
Never hinged .25
On cover 35.00

127 A13 1fr dk blue ('26) .20 .55
Never hinged .60
On cover 17.50

Perf. 11½x11; 11½ (#129, 130)

128 A14 2fr indigo .20 .65
Never hinged .70
On cover 30.00

129 A14 2fr dk brown ('26) 2.50 2.25
Never hinged 15.00
On cover 60.00

130 A15 5fr dk violet 8.75 8.75
Never hinged 50.00
On cover 150.00
a. Perf. 12½ ('34) 14.00 11.00
Never hinged 70.00
On cover 175.00
b. Perf. 11½x11 12.00 12.00
Never hinged 60.00
On cover 175.00
Nos. 126-130 (5) 11.85 12.65

For overprints see Nos. O132-O135, O137-138, O140.

See No. B85.

Charlotte Type of 1921

1921-26 *Perf. 11½*

131 A12 2c brown .20 .20
Never hinged .25
On cover 3.00

132 A12 3c olive green .20 .20
Never hinged .25
On cover 3.00
a. Sheet of 25 10.00 25.00
Never hinged 25.00

133 A12 6c violet .20 .20
Never hinged .25
On cover 3.00
a. Sheet of 25 10.00 25.00
Never hinged 25.00

134 A12 10c yellow grn .20 .40
Never hinged .25
On cover 3.00

135 A12 10c olive brn ('24) .20 .20
Never hinged .25
On cover 3.00

136 A12 15c brown olive .20 .20
Never hinged .40
On cover 3.00

137 A12 15c pale green ('24) .20 .20
Never hinged .50
On cover 3.00

138 A12 15c dp orange ('26) .20 .40
Never hinged .40
On cover 3.00

139 A12 20c dp orange .20 .20
Never hinged .40
On cover 3.00
a. Sheet of 25 60.00 110.00
Never hinged 95.00

140 A12 20c yellow grn ('26) .20 .40
Never hinged .40
On cover 3.00

141 A12 25c dk green .20 .20
Never hinged .40
On cover 1.75

142 A12 30c carmine rose .20 .20
Never hinged .40
On cover 3.00

143 A12 40c brown orange .20 .20
Never hinged .40
On cover 3.00

144 A12 50c deep blue .20 .60
Never hinged 1.00
On cover 5.50

145 A12 50c red ('24) .20 .40
Never hinged .40
On cover 3.00

146 A12 75c red .20 1.50
Never hinged .60
On cover 12.00
a. Sheet of 25 325.00
Never hinged 450.00

147 A12 75c deep blue ('24) .20 .40
Never hinged .40
On cover 6.00

148 A12 80c black .20 1.25
Never hinged 1.60
On cover 15.00
a. Sheet of 25 325.00
Never hinged 450.00
Nos. 131-148 (18) 3.60 7.35

For surcharges and overprints see Nos. 154-158, O114-O131, O136.

Philatelic Exhibition Issue

1922, Aug. 27 *Imperf.*

Laid Paper

149 A12 25c dark green 1.50 5.50
Never hinged 4.50

150 A12 30c carmine rose 1.50 5.50
Never hinged 4.50

Nos. 149 and 150 were sold exclusively at the Luxembourg Phil. Exhib., Aug. 1922.

Souvenir Sheet

View of Luxembourg — A16

1923, Jan. 3 ***Perf. 11***
151 A16 10fr dp grn, sheet 1,100. *1,800.*
Never hinged 1,750.

Birth of Princess Elisabeth.

1923, Mar. ***Perf. 11½***
152 A16 10fr black 7.25 *12.50*
Never hinged 22.50
a. Perf. 12½ ('34) 7.25 *11.00*
Never hinged 15.00

For overprint see No. O141.

The Wolfsschlucht near Echternach — A17

1923-34 ***Perf. 11½***
153 A17 3fr dk blue & blue 1.10 1.10
Never hinged 5.50
a. Perf. 12½ ('34) .90 .65
Never hinged 5.00

For overprint see No. O139.

Stamps of 1921-26 Surcharged with New Values and Bars

1925-28
154 A12 5c on 10c yel grn .20 .20
Never hinged .30
155 A12 15c on 20c yel grn ('28) .20 .20
Never hinged .25
a. Bars omitted
156 A12 35c on 40c brn org ('27) .20 .20
Never hinged .25
157 A12 60c on 75c dp bl ('27) .25 .20
Never hinged .60
158 A12 60c on 80c blk ('28) .40 .35
Never hinged .60
Nos. 154-158 (5) 1.25 1.15

Grand Duchess Charlotte — A18

1926-35 **Engr.** ***Perf. 12***
159 A18 5c dk violet .20 .20
Never hinged .25
160 A18 10c olive grn .20 .20
Never hinged .25
161 A18 15c black ('30) .25 .25
Never hinged .50
162 A18 20c orange .40 .20
Never hinged .60
163 A18 25c yellow grn .50 .20
Never hinged 1.00
164 A18 25c vio brn ('27) .45 .20
Never hinged 1.00
165 A18 30c yel grn ('27) .45 .50
Never hinged .85
166 A18 30c gray vio ('30) .50 .40
Never hinged .85
167 A18 35c gray vio ('28) .25 .20
Never hinged .50
168 A18 35c yel grn ('30) .20 .20
Never hinged .40
169 A18 40c olive gray .20 .20
Never hinged .25
170 A18 50c red brown .20 .20
Never hinged .25
171 A18 60c blue grn ('28) .25 .20
Never hinged .50
172 A18 65c black brn .25 .50
Never hinged .60
173 A18 70c blue vio ('35) .20 .20
Never hinged .25
174 A18 75c rose .25 .25
Never hinged .60
175 A18 75c bis brn ('27) .20 .20
Never hinged .25
176 A18 80c bister brn .25 .60
Never hinged .60
177 A18 90c rose ('27) 1.50 .90
Never hinged 4.00
178 A18 1fr black 1.25 .60
Never hinged 3.50
179 A18 1fr rose ('30) .60 .50
Never hinged 1.50
180 A18 1¼fr dk blue .20 .45
Never hinged .40
181 A18 1¼fr yellow ('30) 7.25 .90
Never hinged 17.50
182 A18 1¼fr blue grn ('31) .60 .20
Never hinged 2.50
183 A18 1¼fr rose car ('34) 12.00 1.40
Never hinged 40.00
184 A18 1½fr dp blue ('27) 2.50 .90
Never hinged 7.00
185 A18 1¾fr dk blue ('30) .40 .50
Never hinged 1.50
Nos. 159-185 (27) 31.50 11.25
Set, never hinged 90.00

For surcharges and overprints see Nos. 186-193, N17-N29, O142-O178.

Stamps of 1926-35, Surcharged with New Values and Bars

1928-39
186 A18 10(c) on 30c yel grn ('29) .50 .20
Never hinged 1.00
187 A18 15c on 25c yel grn .40 .30
Never hinged .90
187A A18 30c on 60c bl grn ('39) .20 1.00
Never hinged .50
188 A18 60c on 65c blk brn .25 .25
Never hinged .50
189 A18 60c on 75c rose .25 .25
Never hinged .50
190 A18 60c on 80c bis brn .45 .50
Never hinged .60
191 A18 70(c) on 75c bis brn ('35) 6.00 .20
Never hinged 14.50
192 A18 75(c) on 90c rose ('29) 1.75 .20
Never hinged 4.00
193 A18 1¾(fr) on 1½fr dp bl ('29) 3.50 1.60
Never hinged 7.50
Nos. 186-193 (9) 13.30 4.50
Set, never hinged 30.00

The surcharge on No. 187A has no bars.

View of Clervaux A19

1928-34 ***Perf. 12½***
194 A19 2fr black ('34) 1.00 .50
Never hinged 3.50
a. Perf. 11½ ('28) 1.25 .60
Never hinged 6.00

See No. B66. For overprint see No. O179.

Coat of Arms — A20

1930, Dec. 20 **Typo.** ***Perf. 12½***
195 A20 5c claret .40 .20
196 A20 10c olive green .60 .20
Set, never hinged 3.00

View of the Lower City of Luxembourg A21

Gate of "Three Towers" A22

1931, June 20 **Engr.**
197 A21 20fr deep green 3.25 9.50
Never hinged 5.50

For overprint see No. O180.

1934, Aug. 30 ***Perf. 14x13½***
198 A22 5fr blue green 1.25 3.50
Never hinged 3.25

For surcharge and overprint see Nos. N31, O181.

Castle From Our Valley A23

1935, Nov. 15 ***Perf. 12½x12***
199 A23 10fr green 2.10 5.75
Never hinged 4.50

For surcharge and overprint see Nos. N32, O182.

Municipal Palace — A24

1936, Aug. 26 **Photo.** ***Perf. 11½***
Granite Paper
200 A24 10c brown .20 .20
201 A24 35c green .20 .50
202 A24 70c red orange .20 *.70*
203 A24 1fr carmine rose 1.25 *5.50*
204 A24 1.25fr violet 2.10 *7.00*
205 A24 1.75fr brt ultra 1.25 *6.00*
Nos. 200-205 (6) 5.20 *19.90*
Set, never hinged 13.00

11th Cong. of Intl. Federation of Philately.

Arms of Luxembourg A25

William I A26

Designs: 70c, William II. 75c, William III. 1fr, Prince Henry. 1.25fr, Grand Duke Adolphe. 1.75fr, William IV. 3fr, Regent Marie Anne. 5fr, Grand Duchess Marie Adelaide. 10fr, Grand Duchess Charlotte.

1939, May 27 **Engr.** ***Perf. 12½x12***
206 A25 35c brt green .25 .20
207 A26 50c orange .25 .25
208 A26 70c slate green .20 .20
209 A26 75c sepia .65 *1.25*
210 A26 1fr red 1.60 *3.25*
211 A26 1.25fr brown violet .20 .20
212 A26 1.75fr dark blue .20 .20
213 A26 3fr lt brown .25 .50
214 A26 5fr gray black .50 *1.00*
215 A26 10fr copper red .75 *2.75*
Nos. 206-215 (10) 4.85 *9.80*
Set, never hinged 7.75

Centenary of Independence.

Allegory of Medicinal Baths — A35

1939, Sept. 18 **Photo.** ***Perf. 11½***
216 A35 2fr brown rose .50 1.40
Never hinged 1.00

Elevation of Mondorf-les-Bains to town status.
See No. B104. For surcharge see No. N30.

Souvenir Sheet

A36

1939, Dec. 20 **Engr.** ***Perf. 14x13***
217 A36 Sheet of 3 35.00 *90.00*
Sheet, never hinged 90.00
a. 2fr vermilion, *buff* 5.75 *22.50*
b. 3fr dark green, *buff* 5.75 *22.50*
c. 5fr blue, *buff* 5.75 *22.50*

20th anniv. of the reign of Grand Duchess Charlotte (Jan. 15, 1919) and her marriage to Prince Felix (Nov. 6, 1919).
See Nos. B98-B103.

SEMI-POSTAL STAMPS

Clervaux Monastery SP1

Designs: 15c+10c, View of Pfaffenthal. 25c+10c, View of Luxembourg.

Engr.; Surcharge Typo. in Red
1921, Aug. 2 **Unwmk.** ***Perf. 11½***
B1 SP1 10c + 5c green .20 *4.50*
B2 SP1 15c + 10c org red .20 *5.75*
B3 SP1 25c + 10c dp grn .20 *4.50*
Nos. B1-B3 (3) .60 *14.75*
Set, never hinged 2.25

The amount received from the surtax on these stamps was added to a fund for the erection of a monument to the soldiers from Luxembourg who died in World War I.

Nos. B1-B3 with Additional Surcharge in Red or Black

1923, May 27
B4 SP1 25c on #B1 (R) 1.10 *14.50*
B5 SP1 25c on #B2 1.10 *17.50*
B6 SP1 25c on #B3 1.10 *14.50*
Nos. B4-B6 (3) 3.30 *46.50*
Set, never hinged 8.75

Unveiling of the monument to the soldiers who died in World War I.

Regular Issue of 1914-15 Surcharged in Black or Red

1924, Apr. 17 ***Perf. 11½x11***
B7 A11 12½c + 7½c grn .20 *2.75*
B8 A11 35c + 10c dk bl (R) .20 *2.75*
B9 A11 2½fr + 1fr red 1.10 *27.50*
B10 A11 5fr + 2fr dk vio .55 *17.50*
Nos. B7-B10 (4) 2.05 *50.50*
Set, never hinged 3.50

Nurse and Patient
SP4

Prince Jean
SP5

1925, Dec. 21 Litho. *Perf. 13*

B11 SP4 5c (+ 5c) dl vio .20 .70
B12 SP4 30c (+ 5c) org .20 3.00
B13 SP4 50c (+ 5c) red brn .20 *5.50*
B14 SP4 1fr (+ 10c) dp bl .40 *14.00*
Nos. B11-B14 (4) 1.00 *23.20*
Set, never hinged 1.75

1926, Dec. 15 Photo. *Perf. 12½x12*

B15 SP5 5c (+ 5c) vio & blk .20 .55
B16 SP5 40c (+ 10) grn & blk .20 .90
B17 SP5 50c (+ 15c) lem & blk .20 .95
B18 SP5 75c (+ 20c) lt red & blk .25 *11.00*
B19 SP5 1.50fr (+ 30c) gray bl & blk .35 *12.00*
Nos. B15-B19 (5) 1.20 *25.40*
Set, never hinged 2.50

Grand Duchess Charlotte and Prince Felix — SP6

1927, Sept. 4 Engr. *Perf. 11½*

B20 SP6 25c dp vio 1.10 *10.00*
B21 SP6 50c green 1.50 *16.00*
B22 SP6 75c rose lake 1.10 *10.00*
B23 SP6 1fr gray blk 1.10 *10.00*
B24 SP6 1½fr dp bl 1.10 *10.00*
Nos. B20-B24 (5) 5.90 *56.00*
Set, never hinged 17.00

Introduction of postage stamps in Luxembourg, 75th anniv. These stamps were sold exclusively at the Luxembourg Philatelic Exhibition, September 4-8, 1927, at a premium of 3 francs per set, which was donated to the exhibition funds.

Princess Elisabeth
SP7

Princess Marie Adelaide
SP8

1927, Dec. 1 Photo. *Perf. 12½*

B25 SP7 10c (+ 5c) turq bl & blk .20 *.55*
B26 SP7 50c (+ 10c) dk brn & blk .20 *.95*
B27 SP7 75c (+ 20c) org & blk .20 *1.50*
B28 SP7 1fr (+ 30c) brn lake & blk .25 *11.00*
B29 SP7 1½fr (+ 50c) ultra & blk .20 *11.00*
Nos. B25-B29 (5) 1.05 *25.00*
Set, never hinged 2.25

The surtax was for Child Welfare societies.

1928, Dec. 12 *Perf. 12½x12*

B30 SP8 10c (+ 5c) ol grn & brn vio .20 *1.10*
B31 SP8 60c (+ 10c) brn & ol grn .40 *2.75*
B32 SP8 75c (+ 15c) vio rose & bl grn .70 *7.25*
B33 SP8 1fr (+ 25c) dk grn & brn 1.75 *22.50*
B34 SP8 1½fr (+ 50c) cit & bl 1.75 *22.50*
Nos. B30-B34 (5) 4.80 *56.10*
Set, never hinged 11.00

Princess Marie Gabrielle
SP9

Prince Charles
SP10

1929, Dec. 14 *Perf. 13*

B35 SP9 10c (+ 10c) mar & dp grn .20 *1.10*
B36 SP9 35c (+ 15c) dk grn & red brn 1.50 *7.25*
B37 SP9 75c (+ 30c) ver & blk 1.75 *9.00*
B38 SP9 1¼fr (+ 50c) mag & bl grn 2.25 *22.50*
B39 SP9 1¾fr (+ 75c) Prus bl & sl 2.75 *27.50*
Nos. B35-B39 (5) 8.45 *67.35*
Set, never hinged 20.00

The surtax was for Child Welfare societies.

1930, Dec. 10 *Perf. 12½*

B40 SP10 10c (+ 5c) bl grn & ol brn .20 1.10
B41 SP10 75c (+ 10c) vio brn & bl grn 1.10 *4.75*
B42 SP10 1fr (+ 25c) car rose & vio 2.50 *17.50*
B43 SP10 1¼fr (+ 75c) ol bis & dk brn 4.00 *22.50*
B44 SP10 1¾fr (+ 1.50fr) ultra & red brn 4.50 *22.50*
Nos. B40-B44 (5) 12.30 *68.35*
Set, never hinged 50.00

The surtax was for Child Welfare societies.

Princess Alix
SP11

Countess Ermesinde
SP12

1931, Dec. 10

B45 SP11 10c (+ 5c) brn org & gray .40 1.10
B46 SP11 75c (+ 10c) claret & bl grn 4.00 *14.50*
B47 SP11 1fr (+ 25c) dp grn & gray 7.25 *29.00*
B48 SP11 1¼fr (+ 75c) dk vio & bl grn 7.25 *29.00*
B49 SP11 1¾fr (+ 1.50fr) bl & gray 11.00 *55.00*
Nos. B45-B49 (5) 29.90 *128.60*
Set, never hinged 110.00

The surtax was for Child Welfare societies.

1932, Dec. 8

B50 SP12 10c (+ 5c) ol bis .40 1.10
B51 SP12 75c (+ 10c) dp vio 2.75 *14.50*
B52 SP12 1fr (+ 25c) scar 11.00 *32.50*
B53 SP12 1¼fr (+ 75c) red brn 11.00 *32.50*
B54 SP12 1¾fr (+ 1.50fr) dp bl 11.00 *32.50*
Nos. B50-B54 (5) 36.15 *113.10*
Set, never hinged 92.50

The surtax was for Child Welfare societies.

Count Henry VII — SP13

John the Blind — SP14

1933, Dec. 12

B55 SP13 10c (+ 5c) yel brn .40 1.10
B56 SP13 75c (+ 10c) dp vio 4.75 *14.50*
B57 SP13 1fr (+ 25c) car rose 11.00 *35.00*
B58 SP13 1¼fr (+ 75c) org brn 14.50 *47.50*
B59 SP13 1¾fr (+ 1.50fr) brt bl 14.50 *50.00*
Nos. B55-B59 (5) 45.15 *148.10*
Set, never hinged 125.00

1934, Dec. 5

B60 SP14 10c (+ 5c) dk vio .20 1.10
B61 SP14 35c (+ 10c) dp grn 2.50 *9.00*
B62 SP14 75c (+ 15c) rose lake 2.50 *9.00*
B63 SP14 1fr (+ 25c) dp rose 14.50 *47.50*
B64 SP14 1¼fr (+ 75c) org 14.50 *47.50*
B65 SP14 1¾fr (+ 1.50fr) brt bl 14.50 *47.50*
Nos. B60-B65 (6) 48.70 *161.60*
Set, never hinged 125.00

Teacher
SP15

Sculptor and Painter — SP16

Journalist
SP17

Engineer
SP18

Scientist
SP19

Lawyer — SP20

Savings Bank and Adolphe Bridge — SP21

Surgeon
SP22

1935, May 1 Unwmk. *Perf. 12½*

B65A SP15 5c violet .20 *1.10*
B65B SP16 10c brn red .25 *1.10*
B65C SP17 15c olive .40 *1.75*
B65D SP18 20c orange .55 *3.50*
B65E SP19 35c yel grn .70 *3.25*
B65F SP20 50c gray blk .95 *4.75*
B65G SP21 70c dk green 1.40 *5.50*
B65H SP22 1fr car red 1.75 *7.25*
B65J SP19 1.25fr turq 7.25 *50.00*
B65K SP18 1.75fr blue 9.00 *52.50*
B65L SP16 2fr lt brown 27.50 *110.00*
B65M SP17 3fr dk brown 37.50 *150.00*
B65N SP20 5fr lt blue 65.00 *275.00*
B65P SP15 10fr red vio 160.00 *450.00*
B65Q SP22 20fr dk green 175.00 *550.00*
Nos. B65A-B65Q (15) 487.45 *1,665.*
Set, never hinged 1,000.

Sold at double face, surtax going to intl. fund to aid professional people.

Philatelic Exhibition Issue

Type of Regular Issue of 1928

Wmk. 246

1935, Aug. 15 Engr. *Imperf.*

B66 A19 2fr (+ 50c) blk 4.75 *16.00*
Never hinged 13.00

Philatelic exhibition held at Esch-sur-Alzette.

Charles I — SP23

Perf. 11½

1935, Dec. 2 Photo. Unwmk.

B67 SP23 10c (+ 5c) vio .20 .40
B68 SP23 35c (+ 10c) grn .40 *.55*
B69 SP23 70c (+ 20c) dk brn .95 *1.50*
B70 SP23 1fr (+ 25c) rose lake 14.50 *37.50*
B71 SP23 1.25fr (+ 75c) org brn 14.50 *37.50*
B72 SP23 1.75fr (+ 1.50fr) bl 14.50 *47.50*
Nos. B67-B72 (6) 45.05 *124.95*
Set, never hinged 110.00

Wenceslas I, Duke of Luxembourg — SP24

1936, Dec. 1 *Perf. 11½x13*

B73 SP24 10c + 5(c) blk brn .20 .25
B74 SP24 35c + 10(c) bl grn .20 *.55*
B75 SP24 70c + 20(c) blk .40 *.90*
B76 SP24 1fr + 25(c) rose car 2.50 *14.50*
B77 SP24 1.25fr + 75(c) vio 2.25 *29.00*
B78 SP24 1.75fr + 1.50(fr) saph 1.60 *17.50*
Nos. B73-B78 (6) 7.15 *62.70*
Set, never hinged 32.50

Wenceslas II — SP25

1937, Dec. 1 *Perf. 11½x12½*

B79 SP25 10c + 5c car & blk .20 .40
B80 SP25 35c + 10c red vio & grn .20 .55
B81 SP25 70c + 20c ultra & red brn .25 .55
B82 SP25 1fr + 25c dk grn & scar 1.60 *17.00*
B83 SP25 1.25fr + 75c dk brn & vio 2.25 *17.00*
B84 SP25 1.75fr + 1.50fr blk & ultra 2.75 *17.50*
Nos. B79-B84 (6) 7.25 *53.00*
Set, never hinged 17.50

Souvenir Sheet

SP26

Wmk. 110

1937, July 25 **Engr.** ***Perf. 13***

B85 SP26 Sheet of 2		4.00	*11.50*
	Never hinged	11.00	
a.	2fr red brown, single stamp	1.50	*5.50*

National Philatelic Exposition at Dudelange on July 25-26.

Sold for 5fr per sheet, of which 1fr was for the aid of the exposition.

Portrait of St. Willibrord — SP28

St. Willibrord, after a Miniature SP29

Abbey at Echternach — SP30

Designs: No, B87, The Rathaus at Echternach. No. B88, Pavilion in Abbey Park, Echternach. No. B91, Dancing Procession in Honor of St. Willibrord.

Perf. 14x13, 13x14

1938, June 5 **Engr.** **Unwmk.**

B86	SP28	35c + 10c dk bl grn	.40	*.55*
B87	SP28	70c + 10c ol gray	.70	*.55*
B88	SP28	1.25fr + 25c brn car	1.50	*2.50*
B89	SP29	1.75fr + 50c sl bl	2.50	*2.75*
B90	SP30	3fr + 2fr vio brn	5.50	*9.00*
B91	SP30	5fr + 5fr dk vio	6.50	*7.25*
		Nos. B86-B91 (6)	17.10	22.60
		Set, never hinged	60.00	

12th centenary of the death of St. Willibrord. The surtax was used for the restoration of the ancient Abbey at Echternach.

Duke Sigismond SP32

Prince Jean SP33

1938, Dec. 1 **Photo.** ***Perf. 11½***

B92	SP32	10c + 5c lil & blk	.20	.40
B93	SP32	35c + 10c grn & blk	.20	.55
B94	SP32	70c + 20c buff & blk	.25	*.55*
B95	SP32	1fr + 25c red org & blk	1.90	*14.50*
B96	SP32	1.25fr + 75c gray bl & blk	1.90	*14.50*
B97	SP32	1.75fr + 1.50fr bl & blk	3.25	*22.50*
		Nos. B92-B97 (6)	7.70	53.00
		Set, never hinged	22.50	

1939, Dec. 1 **Litho.** ***Perf. 14x13***

Designs: Nos. B99, B102, Prince Felix. Nos. B100, B103, Grand Duchess Charlotte.

B98	SP33	10c + 5c red brn, *buff*	.20	.40
B99	SP33	35c + 10c sl grn, *buff*	.20	1.10
B100	SP33	70c + 20c blk, *buff*	.95	*1.50*
B101	SP33	1fr + 25c red org, *buff*	4.00	*32.50*
B102	SP33	1.25fr + 75c vio brn, *buff*	4.75	*50.00*
B103	SP33	1.75fr + 1.50fr lt bl, *buff*	5.50	*65.00*
		Nos. B98-B103 (6)	15.60	*150.50*
		Set, never hinged	45.00	

See No. 217 (souvenir sheet).

Allegory of Medicinal Baths — SP36

1940, Mar. 1 **Photo.** ***Perf. 11½***

B104 SP36 2fr + 50c gray, blk & slate grn		1.10	*20.00*
	Never hinged	4.00	

AIR POST STAMPS

Airplane over Luxembourg — AP1

1931-33 **Unwmk.** **Engr.** ***Perf. 12½***

C1	AP1	50c green ('33)	.55	*1.10*
C2	AP1	75c dark brown	.55	*1.50*
C3	AP1	1fr red	.55	*1.50*
C4	AP1	1¼fr dark violet	.55	*1.50*
C5	AP1	1¾fr dark blue	.55	*1.50*
C6	AP1	3fr gray black ('33)	1.10	*6.00*
		Nos. C1-C6 (6)	3.85	*13.10*
		Set, never hinged	8.25	

POSTAGE DUE STAMPS

Coat of Arms — D1

1907 **Unwmk.** **Typo.** ***Perf. 12½***

J1	D1	5c green & black	.20	*.25*
J2	D1	10c green & black	1.40	*.25*
J3	D1	12½c green & black	.45	*.90*
J4	D1	20c green & black	.70	*.80*
J5	D1	25c green & black	17.50	1.50
J6	D1	50c green & black	.65	*4.25*
J7	D1	1fr green & black	.35	*3.50*
		Nos. J1-J7 (7)	21.25	11.45

See Nos. J10-J22.

Nos. J3, J5 Surcharged

1920

J8	D1	15c on 12½c	2.25	*7.25*
J9	D1	30c on 25c	2.25	*9.00*

Arms Type of 1907

1921-35

J10	D1	5c green & red	.20	*.40*
J11	D1	10c green & red	.20	*.35*
J12	D1	20c green & red	.20	*.35*
J13	D1	25c green & red	.20	*.35*
J14	D1	30c green & red	.55	*.60*
J15	D1	35c green & red ('35)	.55	.35
J16	D1	50c green & red	.55	*.60*
J17	D1	60c green & red ('28)	.45	*.50*
J18	D1	70c green & red ('35)	.55	.35
J19	D1	75c green & red ('30)	.55	.25
J20	D1	1fr green & red	.55	*1.10*
J21	D1	2fr green & red ('30)	.55	*6.50*
J22	D1	3fr green & red ('30)	1.60	*18.00*
		Nos. J10-J22 (13)	6.70	29.70
		Set, never hinged	27.50	

OFFICIAL STAMPS

Forged overprints on Nos. O1-O64 abound.

Unused values of Nos. O1-O51 are for stamps without gum. Though these stamps were issued with gum, most examples offered are without gum. Stamps with original gum sell for somewhat more.

Regular Issues Overprinted Reading Diagonally Up or Down

Frankfurt Print

Rouletted in Color except 2c

1875 **Unwmk.**

O1	A2	1c red brown	27.50	37.50
O2	A2	2c black	27.50	37.50
O3	A3	10c lilac	2,100.	2,100.
O4	A3	12½c rose	475.00	575.00
O5	A3	20c gray brn	37.50	57.50
O6	A3	25c blue	250.00	140.00
O7	A3	25c ultra	1,900.	1,400.
O8	A3	30c lilac rose	32.50	*75.00*
O9	A3	40c pale org	160.00	225.00
a.		40c org red, thick paper	250.00	325.00
c.		As "a," thin paper	1,650.	1,400.
O10	A4	1fr on 37½c bis	150.00	22.50

Double overprints exist on Nos. O1-O6, O8-O10.

Overprints reading diagonally down sell for more.

Inverted Overprint

O1a	A2	1c	190.00	225.00
O2a	A2	2c	190.00	225.00
O3a	A3	10c	2,500.	2,500.
O4a	A3	12½c	650.00	925.00
O5a	A3	20c	55.00	75.00
O6a	A3	25c	1,100.	1,300.
O7a	A3	25c	2,100.	1,500.
O8a	A3	30c	650.00	925.00
O9b	A3	40c pale orange	325.00	450.00
O10a	A4	1fr on 37½c	175.00	75.00

Luxembourg Print

1875-76 ***Perf. 13***

O11	A2	1c red brown	11.00	27.50
O12	A2	2c black	14.00	32.50
O13	A2	4c green	100.00	190.00
O14	A2	5c yellow	65.00	85.00
a.		5c orange yellow	75.00	110.00
O15	A3	10c gray lilac	92.50	100.00
O16	A3	12½c rose	85.00	100.00
O17	A3	12½c lilac rose	225.00	275.00
O18	A3	25c blue	11.00	*32.50*
O19	A5	1fr on 37½c bis	42.50	65.00
		Nos. O11-O19 (9)	646.00	907.50

Double overprints exist on Nos. O11-O15.

Inverted Overprint

O11a	A2	1c	92.50	*110.00*
O12a	A2	2c	150.00	190.00
O13a	A2	4c	160.00	190.00
O14b	A2	5c	500.00	650.00
O15a	A3	10c	500.00	190.00
O16a	A3	12½c	400.00	550.00
O17a	A3	12½c	450.00	525.00
O18a	A3	25c	125.00	175.00
O19a	A5	1fr on 37½c	200.00	250.00
		Nos. O11a-O19a (9)	2,567.	2,830.

Haarlem Print

1880 ***Perf. 11½x12, 12½x12, 13½***

O22 A3 25c blue		2.25	2.75

Overprinted

Frankfurt Print

1878 ***Rouletted in Color***

O23	A2	1c red brown	140.00	160.00
O25	A3	20c gray brn	190.00	225.00
O26	A3	30c lilac rose	750.00	575.00
O27	A3	40c orange	325.00	450.00
O28	A4	1fr on 37½c bis	550.00	110.00
		Nos. O23-O28 (5)	1,955.	1,520.

Inverted Overprint

O23a	A2	1c	225.00	300.00
O25a	A3	20c	325.00	400.00
O26a	A3	30c	925.00	700.00
O27a	A3	40c	875.00	925.00
O28a	A4	1fr on 37½c	650.00	1540.00

Luxembourg Print

1878-80 ***Perf. 13***

O29	A2	1c red brown	750.00	925.00
O30	A2	2c black	190.00	225.00
O31	A2	4c green	190.00	225.00
O32	A2	5c yellow	375.00	450.00
O33	A3	10c gray lilac	375.00	400.00
O34	A3	12½c rose	65.00	110.00
O35	A3	25c blue	525.00	550.00
		Nos. O29-O35 (7)	2,470.	2,885.

Inverted Overprint

O29a	A2	1c	140.00	160.00
O30a	A2	2c	14.50	27.50
O31a	A2	4c	150.00	190.00
O32a	A2	5c	1,500.	1,500.
O33a	A3	10c	92.50	110.00
O34a	A3	12½c	525.00	600.00
O35a	A3	25c	850.00	1,000.

Overprinted

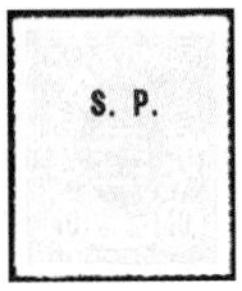

Frankfurt Print

1881 ***Rouletted in Color***

O39 A3 40c orange		37.50	65.00
a.	Inverted overprint	210.00	275.00

"S.P." are initials of "Service Public."

Luxembourg Print

Perf. 13

O40	A2	1c red brown	140.00	160.00
O41	A2	4c green	210.00	210.00
a.		Inverted overprint	250.00	
O42	A2	5c yellow	600.00	750.00
O43	A5	1fr on 37½c bis	32.500	47.50
		Nos. O40-O43 (4)	987.00	1,167.

Haarlem Print

Perf. 11½x12, 12½x12, 13½

O44	A2	1c yellow brn	8.50	9.25
O45	A2	2c black	9.25	9.25
O46	A2	5c yellow	140.00	190.00
a.		Inverted overprint	225.00	
O47	A3	10c gray lilac	125.00	160.00
O48	A3	12½c rose	225.00	250.00
O49	A3	20c gray brown	65.00	92.50
O50	A3	25c blue	72.50	92.50
O51	A3	30c dull rose	75.00	110.00
		Nos. O44-O51 (8)	720.25	913.50

Stamps of the 1881 issue with the overprint of the 1882 issue shown below were never issued.

Overprinted

Perf. 11½x12, 12½x12, 12½, 13½

1882

O52	A6	1c gray lilac	.25	.50
O53	A6	2c ol gray	.25	.50
a.		"S" omitted	110.00	
O54	A6	4c ol bister	.35	.650
O55	A6	5c lt green	.55	.80
O56	A6	10c rose	12.00	20.00
O57	A6	12½c slate	1.90	4.75
O58	A6	20c orange	1.90	4.00
O59	A6	25c ultra	19.00	27.50
O60	A6	30c gray grn	4.25	10.00
O61	A6	50c bis brown	1.10	2.75

O62 A6 1fr pale vio 1.10 2.75
O63 A6 5fr brown org 12.00 27.50
Nos. O52-O63 (12) 54.65 107.55

Nos. O52-O63 exist without one or both periods, also with varying space between "S" and "P." Nine denominations exist with double overprint, six with inverted overprint.

Overprinted **S. P.**

1883 ***Perf. 13½***
O64 A6 5fr brown org *2,200. 2,200.*

Overprinted

1891-93 ***Perf. 11, 11½, 11½x11, 12½***
O65 A7 10c carmine .20 .50
a. Sheet of 25 55.00
O66 A7 12½c slate grn 6.50 8.75
O67 A7 20c orange 12.00 8.50
O68 A7 25c blue .35 .50
a. Sheet of 25 65.00
O69 A7 30c olive grn 8.25 8.50
O70 A7 37½c green 8.25 10.00
O71 A7 50c brown 6.50 10.00
O72 A7 1fr dp vio 6.50 11.50
O73 A7 2½fr black 37.50 72.50
O74 A7 5fr lake 32.50 55.00
Nos. O65-O74 (10) 118.55 185.75

1895 ***Perf. 12½***
O75 A8 1c pearl gray 1.90 1.90
O76 A8 2c gray brn 1.40 1.90
O77 A8 4c olive bis 1.40 1.90
O78 A8 5c green 4.00 5.00
O79 A8 10c carmine 32.50 35.00
Nos. O75-O79 (5) 41.20 45.70

Nos. O66-O79 exist without overprint and perforated "OFFICIEL" through the stamp. Value for set, $25.

Nos. O65a and O68a were issued to commemorate the coronation of Grand Duke Adolphe.

Regular Issue of 1906-26 Overprinted

1908-26 ***Perf. 11x11½, 12½***
O80 A9 1c gray .20 .20
a. Inverted overprint 125.00
O81 A9 2c olive brn .20 .20
O82 A9 4c bister .20 .20
a. Double overprint 140.00
O83 A9 5c green .20 .20
O84 A9 5c lilac ('26) .20 .20
O85 A9 6c violet .20 .20
O86 A9 7½c org ('19) .20 .20
O87 A10 10c scarlet .25 .45
O88 A10 12½c slate grn .25 *.55*
O89 A10 15c orange brn .40 *.70*
O90 A10 20c orange .40 *.70*
O91 A10 25c ultra .40 *.70*
O92 A10 30c olive grn 4.00 *6.50*
O93 A10 37½c green .65 .65
O94 A10 50c brown 1.10 *1.50*
O95 A10 87½c dk blue 2.75 *3.25*
O96 A10 1fr violet 3.25 *4.00*
O97 A10 2½fr vermilion 65.00 65.00
O98 A10 5fr claret 55.00 47.50
Nos. O80-O98 (19) 134.85 132.90

On Regular Issue of 1914-17

1915-17
O99 A11 10c lake .35 *.65*
O100 A11 12½c dull grn .35 *.65*
O101 A11 15c olive blk .35 *.65*
O102 A11 17½c dp brn ('17) .35 .65
O103 A11 25c ultra .35 *.65*
O104 A11 30c bister 1.40 *5.00*
O105 A11 35c dk blue .35 *1.10*
O106 A11 37½c blk brn .35 *1.50*
O107 A11 40c orange .45 *1.10*
O108 A11 50c dk gray .45 *.95*
O109 A11 62½c blue grn .45 *1.50*
O110 A11 87½c org ('17) .45 *1.75*
O111 A11 1fr orange brn .45 *1.50*
O112 A11 2½fr red .45 *2.75*
O113 A11 5fr dk violet .45 *3.25*
Nos. O99-O113 (15) 7.00 23.65

On Regular Issues of 1921-26 in Black

1922-26 ***Perf. 11½, 11½x11, 12½***
O114 A12 2c brown .20 .20
O115 A12 3c olive grn .20 .20
O116 A12 6c violet .20 .20
O117 A12 10c yellow grn .20 .35
O118 A12 10c ol grn ('24) .20 .35
O119 A12 15c brown ol .20 .35
O120 A12 15c pale grn ('24) .20 .35
O121 A12 15c dp org ('26) .20 .25
O122 A12 20c dp orange .20 .35
O123 A12 20c yel grn ('26) .20 .25
O124 A12 25c dk green .20 .35
O125 A12 30c car rose .20 .35
O126 A12 40c brown org .20 .35
O127 A12 50c dp blue .20 .45
O128 A12 50c red ('24) .20 .35
O129 A12 75c red .20 .45
O130 A12 75c dp bl ('24) .20 .45
O131 A12 80c black 4.75 11.00
O132 A13 1fr carmine .40 .90
O133 A14 2fr indigo 3.00 6.50
O134 A14 2fr dk brn ('26) 1.75 5.00
O135 A15 5fr dk vio 17.50 42.50
Nos. O114-O135 (22) 30.80 71.50

On Regular Issues of 1921-26 in Red

1922-34 ***Perf. 11, 11½, 11½x11, 12½***
O136 A12 80c blk, perf. 11½ .20 .35
O137 A13 1fr dk bl, perf. 11½ ('26) .20 .55
O138 A14 2fr ind, perf. 11½x11 .45 1.25
O139 A17 3fr dk bl & bl, perf. 11 2.75 2.75
a. Perf. 11½ .90 1.40
b. Perf. 12½ 1.60 2.25
O140 A15 5fr dk vio, perf. 11½x11 4.00 7.50
a. Perf. 12½ ('34) 27.50 27.50
O141 A16 10fr blk, perf. 11½ 10.00 21.00
a. Perf. 12½ 27.50 27.50
Nos. O136-O141 (6) 17.60 33.40

On Regular Issue of 1926-35

1926-27 ***Perf. 12***
O142 A18 5c dk violet .20 .20
O143 A18 10c olive grn .20 .20
O144 A18 20c orange .20 .20
O145 A18 25c yellow grn .20 .20
O146 A18 25c blk brn ('27) .35 .55
O147 A18 30c yel grn ('27) .65 1.10
O148 A18 40c olive gray .20 .20
O149 A18 50c red brown .20 .20
O150 A18 65c black brn .20 .20
O151 A18 75c rose .20 .20
O152 A18 75c bis brn ('27) .45 .70
O153 A18 80c bister brn .20 .40
O154 A18 90c rose ('27) .35 .55
O155 A18 1fr black .20 .40
O156 A18 1¼fr dk blue .20 .20
O157 A18 1½fr dp blue ('27) .55 .95
Nos. O142-O157 (16) 4.55 6.45

Type of Regular Issue, 1926-35, Overprinted

1928-35 **Wmk. 213**
O158 A18 5c dk violet .20 .20
O159 A18 10c olive grn .20 .20
O160 A18 15c black ('30) .20 .65
O161 A18 20c orange .45 .65
O162 A18 25c violet brn .45 .65
O163 A18 30c yellow grn .50 .70
O164 A18 30c gray vio ('30) .20 .65
O165 A18 35c yel grn ('30) .20 .65
O166 A18 35c gray vio .50 .70
O167 A18 40c olive gray .50 .70
O168 A18 50c red brown .45 .65
O169 A18 60c blue grn .45 .65
O170 A18 70c blue vio ('35) 3.50 7.25
O171 A18 75c bister brn .45 .65
O172 A18 90c rose .50 .70
O173 A18 1fr black .50 .70
O174 A18 1fr rose ('30) .20 .65
O175 A18 1¼fr yel ('30) 1.75 4.50
O176 A18 1¼fr bl grn ('31) 1.75 4.50
O177 A18 1½fr deep blue .50 .70
O178 A18 1¾fr dk blue ('30) .20 .65
Nos. O158-O178 (21) 13.65 27.35

Type of Regular Issues of 1928-31 Overprinted Like Nos. O80-O98

1928-31 **Wmk. 216** ***Perf. 11½***
O179 A19 2fr black .50 1.00

Wmk. 110 ***Perf. 12½***
O180 A21 20fr dp green ('31) 2.25 5.00

No. 198 Overprinted Like Nos. O80-O98

1934 **Unwmk.** ***Perf. 14x13½***
O181 A22 5fr blue green 2.25 3.25

Type of Regular Issue of 1935 Overprinted Like Nos. O158-O178 in Red

1935 **Wmk. 247** ***Perf. 12½x12***
O182 A23 10fr green 1.60 4.00

OCCUPATION STAMPS

Issued under German Occupation

Stamps of Germany, 1933-36, Overprinted in Black

1940, Oct. 1 **Wmk. 237** ***Perf. 14***
N1 A64 3pf olive bis .25 *.50*
N2 A64 4pf dull blue .25 *.55*
N3 A64 5pf bright green .25 *.50*
N4 A64 6pf dark green .25 *.50*
N5 A64 8pf vermilion .25 *.50*
N6 A64 10pf chocolate .25 *.50*
N7 A64 12pf deep carmine .25 *.50*
N8 A64 15pf maroon .25 *.70*
a. Inverted overprint *450.00 1,300.*
N9 A64 20pf bright blue .25 *1.25*
N10 A64 25pf ultra .35 *1.75*
N11 A64 30pf olive green .35 *1.75*
N12 A64 40pf red violet .50 *1.90*
N13 A64 50pf dk green & blk .50 *2.00*
N14 A64 60pf claret & blk .50 *2.75*
N15 A64 80pf dk blue & blk 1.00 *3.75*
N16 A64 100pf orange & blk 1.25 *5.75*
Nos. N1-N16 (16) 6.70 *25.15*
Set, never hinged 16.00

Nos. 159-162, 164, 168-171, 173, 175, 179, 182, 216, 198-199 Surcharged in Black

b

a

c

d

Perf. 12, 14x13½, 12½x12, 11½
1940, Dec. 5 **Unwmk.**
N17 A18(a) 3rpf on 15c .20 *.35*
N18 A18(a) 4rpf on 20c .20 *.40*
N19 A18(a) 5rpf on 35c .20 *.40*
N20 A18(a) 6rpf on 10c .20 *.40*
N21 A18(a) 8rpf on 25c .20 *.40*
N22 A18(a) 10rpf on 40c .20 *.40*
N23 A18(a) 12rpf on 60c .20 *.40*
N24 A18(a) 15rpf on 1fr rose .20 *.40*
N25 A18(a) 20rpf on 50c .20 *.75*
N26 A18(a) 25rpf on 5c .20 *1.25*
N27 A18(a) 30rpf on 70c .20 *.60*
N28 A18(a) 40rpf on 75c .20 *1.00*
N29 A18(a) 50rpf on 1¼fr .20 *.60*
N30 A35(b) 60rpf on 2fr 1.40 *12.50*
N31 A22(c) 80rpf on 5fr .40 *2.25*
N32 A23(d) 100rpf on 10fr .50 *3.00*
Nos. N17-N32 (16) 4.90 *25.10*
Set, never hinged 7.00

OCCUPATION SEMI-POSTAL STAMPS

Semi-Postal Stamps of Germany, 1940 Overprinted in Black

1941, Jan. 12 **Unwmk.** ***Perf. 14***
NB1 SP153 3pf + 2pf dk brn .20 *.85*
NB2 SP153 4pf + 3pf bluish blk .20 *.85*
NB3 SP153 5pf + 3pf yel grn .20 *.85*
NB4 SP153 6pf + 4pf dk grn .20 *.85*
NB5 SP153 8pf + 4pf dp org .20 *.85*
NB6 SP153 12pf + 6pf carmine .20 *.85*
NB7 SP153 15pf + 10pf dk vio brn .30 *1.90*
NB8 SP153 25pf + 15pf dp ultra .85 *3.75*
NB9 SP153 40pf + 35pf red lil 1.50 *6.25*
Nos. NB1-NB9 (9) 3.85 *17.00*
Set, never hinged 7.50

MACAO

mə-'kau

LOCATION — Off the Chinese coast at the mouth of the Canton River
GOVT. — Portuguese Overseas Territory
AREA — 6 sq. mi.
POP. — 261,680 (1981)
CAPITAL — Macao

The territory includes the two small adjacent islands of Coloane and Taipa.

1000 Reis = 1 Milreis
78 Avos = 1 Rupee (1894)
100 Avos = 1 Pataca (1913)

Watermark

Wmk. 232 — Maltese Cross

Portuguese Crown — A1

1884-85 **Typo.** **Unwmk.** ***Perf. 13½***
1 A1 5r black 13.00 6.50
2a A1 10r orange 25.00 9.00
3a A1 10r green ('85) 82.50 60.00
4 A1 20r bister 32.50 17.00
5 A1 20r rose ('85) 45.00 14.00
6 A1 25r rose 22.50 5.00
7a A1 25r violet ('85) 140.00 60.00
8 A1 40r blue 87.50 25.00
9a A1 40r yellow ('85) 140.00 60.00
10 A1 50r green 250.00 75.00
11a A1 50r blue ('85) 225.00 70.00
12 A1 80r gray ('85) 57.50 30.00
13 A1 100r red lilac 37.50 15.00
a. 100r lilac 37.50 15.00
14 A1 200r orange 70.00 20.00
15a A1 300r chocolate 250.00 100.00

Perf. 12½
1a A1 5r black 20.00 10.00
2 A1 10r orange 25.00 9.00
3 A1 10r green ('85) 30.00 8.00
4a A1 20r bister 40.00 25.00
6a A1 25r rose 30.00 7.50
7 A1 25r violet ('85) 30.00 10.00
8a A1 40r blue 140.00 45.00

9 A1 40r yellow ('85) 42.50 20.00
10a A1 50r green 450.00 150.00
11 A1 50r blue ('85) 57.50 25.00
12a A1 80r gray ('85) 75.00 40.00
13b A1 100r red lilac 40.00 15.00
c. 100r lilac 40.00 15.00
14a A1 200r orange 125.00 40.00
15 A1 300r chocolate 100.00 25.00

The reprints of the 1885 issue are printed on smooth, white chalky paper, ungummed and on thin white paper with shiny white gum and clean-cut perforation 13½.

For surcharges see Nos. 16-28, 108-109.

Nos. 13a, 13c Surcharged in Black

1884 *Perf. 12½*

Without Gum

16 A1 80r on 100r lilac 90.00 30.00
a. Inverted surcharge *175.00 60.00*
b. Without accent on "e" of "reis" 80.00 32.50
c. Perf. 13½ 125.00 30.00
d. As "b," perf. 13½ 140.00 55.00

Nos. 6, 6a, 10, 10a Surcharged in Black, Blue or Red:

b

c

1885

Without Gum

17 A1(b) 5r on 25r rose, perf. 12½ (Bk) 21.00 6.50
a. With accent on "e" of "Reis" 35.00 12.00
b. Double surcharge 200.00 150.00
c. Inverted surcharge 175.00 110.00
d. Perf. 13½ 125.00 100.00
e. As "d," inverted surcharge *175.00 125.00*
f. Thin bar 21.00 6.50
g. As "a," thin bar 22.50 15.00
h. As "c," thin bar *225.00 175.00*
18 A1(b) 10r on 25r rose (Bl) 47.50 12.00
a. Accent on "e" of "Reis"
b. Pair, one without surcharge —
19 A1(b) 10r on 50r grn, perf. 13½ (Bl) 175.00 55.00
a. Perf. 12½ 300.00 80.00
20 A1(b) 20r on 50r green, perf. 12½ (Bk) 47.50 10.00
a. Double surcharge 150.00
b. Accent on "e" of "Reis"
c. Perf. 13½ 50.00 12.50
21 A1(b) 40r on 50r grn, perf. 12½ (R) 175.00 50.00
a. Perf. 13½ 240.00 50.00
Nos. 17-21 (5) 466.00 133.50

1885

Without Gum

22 A1(c) 5r on 25r rose (Bk) 32.50 11.00
a. Original value not obliterated
23 A1(c) 10r on 50r green (Bk) 32.50 11.00
a. Inverted surcharge
b. Perf. 12½ 32.50 11.00
c. Thin bar *100.00 100.00*
d. As "b," thin bar *125.00 125.00*

Nos. 12, 12a, 13, 13a, 14, 14a Surcharged in Black

1887 *Perf. 13½, 12½*

Without Gum

24 A1 5r on 80r gray 32.50 6.00
a. "R" of "Reis" 4mm high 125.00 50.00
b. Perf. 12½ 150.00 45.00
25 A1 5r on 100r lilac 125.00 25.00
a. Perf. 12½ 95.00 27.50
26 A1 10r on 80r gray 65.00 13.00
a. "R" 4mm high 140.00 47.50
27 A1 10r on 200r orange 140.00 35.00
a. "R" 4mm high, "e" without accent 200.00 50.00
b. Perf. 13½ 140.00 35.00
28 A1 20r on 80r gray 100.00 22.50
a. "R" 4mm high 175.00 47.50
b. Perf. 12½ 50.00
c. "R" 4mm high, "e" without accent 160.00 47.50
Nos. 24-28 (5) 462.50 101.50

The surcharges with larger "R" (4mm) have accent on "e." Smaller "R" is 3mm high.

Occasionally Nos. 24, 26 and 28 may be found with original gum. Values the same.

Coat of Arms — A6

Red Surcharge

1887, Oct. 20 *Perf. 12½*

Without Gum

32 A6 5r green & buff 14.00 5.50
a. With labels, 5r on 10r 77.50 65.00
b. With labels, 5r on 20r 90.00 65.00
c. With labels, 5r on 60r 77.50 65.00
33 A6 10r green & buff 14.00 8.00
a. With labels, 10r on 10r 95.00 75.00
b. With labels, 10r on 60r 110.00 75.00
34 A6 40r green & buff 14.00 *12.00*
a. With labels, 40r on 20r 150.00 *110.00*
Nos. 32-34 (3) 42.00 25.50

Nos. 32-34 were local provisionals, created by perforating contemporary revenue stamps to remove the old value inscriptions and then surcharging the central design portion. The unused portion of the design was normally removed prior to use. For simplicity's sake, we refer to these extraneous portions of the original revenue stamps as "labels."

The 10r also exists with 20r labels, and 40r with 10r labels. Value, $250 each.

King Luiz — A7

King Carlos — A9

Typographed and Embossed

1888, Jan. *Perf. 12½, 13½*

Chalk-surfaced Paper

35 A7 5r black 21.00 4.00
36 A7 10r green 21.00 6.00
a. Perf. 13½ 75.00 25.00
37 A7 20r carmine 35.00 6.00
38 A7 25r violet 35.00 6.00
39 A7 40r chocolate 35.00 6.00
a. Perf. 13½ 60.00 15.00
40 A7 50r blue 60.00 10.00
41 A7 80r gray 95.00 15.00
a. Imperf., pair —
42 A7 100r brown 45.00 10.00
43 A7 200r gray lilac 90.00 16.00
44 A7 300r orange 72.50 15.00
Nos. 35-44 (10) 509.50 94.00

Nos. 37-44 were issued without gum.

For surcharges and overprints see Nos. 45, 58-66B, 110-118, 164-170, 239.

No. 43 Surcharged in Red

1892 *Perf. 13½*

Without Gum

45 A7 30r on 200r gray lilac 60.00 20.00
a. Inverted surcharge 250.00 75.00
b. Perf. 12½ 60.00 20.00

1894, Nov. 15 Typo. *Perf. 11½*

46 A9 5r yellow 8.25 2.50
47 A9 10r redsh violet 8.25 2.50
48 A9 15r chocolate 12.50 3.50
49 A9 20r lavender 14.00 4.00
50 A9 25r green 35.00 8.00
51 A9 50r lt blue 37.50 8.00
a. Perf. 13½ 325.00 200.00
52 A9 75r carmine 70.00 20.00
53 A9 80r yellow green 37.50 15.00
54 A9 100r brown, *buff* 40.00 15.00
55 A9 150r carmine, *rose* 45.00 15.00
56 A9 200r dk blue, *blue* 62.50 20.00
57 A9 300r dk blue, *sal* 82.50 25.00
Nos. 46-57 (12) 453.00 138.50

Nos. 49-57 were issued without gum, No. 49 with or without gum.

For surcharges and overprints see Nos. 119-130, 171-181, 183-186, 240, 251, 257-258.

Stamps of 1888 Surcharged in Red, Green or Black

1894 Without Gum *Perf. 12½*

58 A7 1a on 5r black (R) 11.00 3.00
a. Short "1" 9.50 3.00
b. Inverted surcharge 35.00 27.50
c. Double surcharge *150.00*
d. Surch. on back instead of face 35.00 35.00
59 A7 3a on 20r carmine (G) 19.00 4.00
a. Inverted surcharge
60 A7 4a on 25r violet (Bk) 19.00 5.50
a. Inverted surcharge 60.00 50.00
61 A7 6a on 40r choc (Bk) 19.00 5.50
a. Perf. 13½ 25.00 12.00
62 A7 8a on 50r blue (R) 55.00 12.00
a. Double surch., one inverted
b. Inverted surcharge 125.00 60.00
c. Perf. 13½ 60.00 27.50
63 A7 13a on 80r gray (Bk) 22.50 6.25
a. Double surcharge
64 A7 16a on 100r brown (Bk) 45.00 8.00
a. Inverted surcharge
b. Perf. 13½ 115.00 110.00
65 A7 31a on 200r gray lil (Bk) 72.50 11.00
a. Inverted surcharge 150.00 75.00
b. Perf. 13½ 75.00 12.00
66 A7 47a on 300r orange (G) 72.50 11.00
a. Double surcharge
Nos. 58-66 (9) 335.50 66.25

The style of type used for the word "PROVISORIO" on Nos. 58 to 66 differs for each value.

A 2a on 10r green was unofficially surcharged and denounced by the authorities.

On No. 45

66B A7 5a on 30r on 200r 150.00 50.00
c. Perf. 13½ 150.00 50.00

Vasco da Gama Issue

Common Design Types

1898, Apr. 1 Engr. *Perf. 12½ to 16*

67 CD20 ½a blue green 10.00 2.25
68 CD21 1a red 10.00 2.25
69 CD22 2a red violet 10.00 2.25
70 CD23 4a yellow green 10.00 2.25
71 CD24 8a dark blue 19.00 3.00
72 CD25 12a violet brown 30.00 4.50
73 CD26 16a bister brown 26.00 3.00
74 CD27 24a bister 30.00 7.50
Nos. 67-74 (8) 145.00 27.00

For overprints and surcharges see Nos. 187-194.

King Carlos — A11

1898-1903 Typo. *Perf. 11½*

Name and Value in Black except #103

75 A11 ½a gray 4.50 .80
a. Perf. 12½ 15.00 3.50
76 A11 1a orange 4.50 .80
a. Perf. 12½ 15.00 3.50
77 A11 2a yellow green 5.75 1.50
78 A11 2a gray green ('03) 6.25 1.50
79 A11 2½a red brown 7.50 1.65
80 A11 3a gray violet 7.50 2.00
81 A11 3a slate ('03) 6.25 1.65
82 A11 4a sea green 9.00 2.25
83 A11 4a carmine ('03) 6.25 1.50
84 A11 5a gray brn ('00) 14.00 2.50
85 A11 5a pale yel brn ('03) 9.00 2.25
86 A11 6a red brown ('03) 10.00 2.00
87 A11 8a blue 12.50 2.25
88 A11 8a gray brn ('03) 15.00 4.00
89 A11 10a slate blue ('00) 15.00 2.25
90 A11 12a rose 15.00 4.50
91 A11 12a red lilac ('03) 62.50 15.00
92 A11 13a violet 18.00 4.50
93 A11 13a gray lilac ('03) 22.50 4.50
94 A11 15a pale ol grn ('00) 90.00 10.00
95 A11 16a dk blue, *bl* 17.00 4.50
96 A11 18a org brn, *pink* ('03) 32.50 10.00
97 A11 20a brn, *yelsh* ('00) 45.00 4.75
98 A11 24a brown, *buff* 27.50 6.00
99 A11 31a red lilac 27.50 9.00
100 A11 31a red lil, *pink* ('03) 32.50 10.50
101 A11 47a dk blue, *rose* 50.00 11.00
102 A11 47a dull bl, *straw* ('03) 60.00 13.00
103 A11 78a blk & red, *bl* ('00) 77.50 12.50
Nos. 75-103 (29) 710.50 148.65

Issued without gum: Nos. 76a, 77, 79-80, 82, 84, 89, 94, 97 and 103.

For surcharges and overprints see Nos. 104-107, 132-136, 141, 147-157D, 159-161, 182, 195-209, 253-255, 258A.

Nos. 92, 95, 98-99 Surcharged in Black

1900

Without Gum

104 A11 5a on 13a violet 20.00 2.75
105 A11 10a on 16a dk bl, *bl* 22.50 4.00
106 A11 15a on 24a brn, *buff* 22.50 4.00
107 A11 20a on 31a red lilac 25.00 6.50

Regular Issues Surcharged

On Stamps of 1884-85

1902 *Perf. 11½*

Black Surcharge

108 A1 6a on 10r orange 30.00 5.50
a. Double surcharge 140.00 75.00
109 A1 6a on 10r green 21.00 5.00

On Stamps of 1888

Red Surcharge

Perf. 12½, 13½

110 A7 6a on 5r black 10.00 2.00
a. Inverted surcharge 110.00 60.00

Black Surcharge

111 A7 6a on 10r green 8.25 2.25
112 A7 6a on 40r choc 8.25 2.25
a. Double surcharge 125.00 50.00
b. Perf. 13½ 30.00 6.50
113 A7 18a on 20r rose 17.00 4.50
a. Double surcharge 160.00 70.00
b. Inverted surcharge 175.00 —
114 A7 18a on 25r violet 175.00 50.00
115 A7 18a on 80r gray 190.00 60.00
a. Double surcharge 225.00 175.00
116 A7 18a on 100r brown 30.00 8.00
a. Perf. 13½ 90.00 35.00
117 A7 18a on 200r gray lil 175.00 60.00
a. Perf. 12½ 190.00 60.00
118 A7 18a on 300r orange 30.00 10.00
a. Perf. 13½ 57.50 25.00

Issued without gum: Nos. 110-118.

Nos. 109 to 118 inclusive, except No. 111, have been reprinted. The reprints have white gum and clean-cut perforation 13½ and the colors are usually paler than those of the originals.

On Stamps of 1894

1902-10 *Perf. 11½, 13½*

119 A9 6a on 5r yellow 7.75 2.25
a. Inverted surcharge 77.50 50.00
120 A9 6a on 10r red vio 26.00 5.00
121 A9 6a on 15r choc 26.00 5.00
122 A9 6a on 25r green 7.75 2.25
123 A9 6a on 80r yel grn 7.75 2.25
124 A9 6a on 100r brn, *buff* 15.00 3.00
a. Perf. 11½ 26.00 8.00
125 A9 6a on 200r bl, *bl* 10.00 2.25
a. Vert. half used as 3a on cover ('10)
126 A9 18a on 20r lavender 21.00 4.00
127 A9 18a on 50r lt blue 26.00 4.00
a. Perf. 13½ 77.50 14.00
128 A9 18a on 75r carmine 21.00 4.00
129 A9 18a on 150r car, *rose* 21.00 4.00
130 A9 18a on 300r bl, *salmon* 26.00 4.00

On Newspaper Stamp of 1893

Perf. 12½

131 N3 18a on 2½r brown 10.00 3.25
a. Perf. 13½ 27.50 7.00
b. Perf. 11½ 45.00 14.00
Nos. 108-131 (24) 919.75 254.75

Issued without gum: Nos. 122-130, 131b.

Stamps of 1898-1900 Overprinted in Black

1902 **Perf. 11½**

132 A11 2a yellow green 21.00 4.00
133 A11 4a sea green 21.00 4.00
134 A11 8a blue 21.00 4.00
135 A11 10a slate blue 26.00 5.00
136 A11 12a rose 70.00 7.00
Nos. 132-136 (5) 159.00 24.00

Issued without gum: Nos. 133, 135.
Reprints of No. 133 have shiny white gum and clean-cut perforation 13½. Value $1.

No. 91 Surcharged

1905

Without Gum

141 A11 10a on 12a red lilac 30.00 12.50

Nos. J1-J3 Overprinted

1910, Oct. **Perf. 11½x12**

144 D1 ½a gray green 12.50 4.00
a. Inverted overprint 30.00 25.00
b. Double overprint 40.00 40.00
145 D1 1a yellow green 12.50 4.00
a. Inverted overprint 30.00 25.00
146 D1 2a slate 15.00 4.00
a. Inverted overprint 35.00 25.00
Nos. 144-146 (3) 40.00 12.00

No. 144 issued without gum, Nos. 145-146 with and without gum.

Stamps of 1898-1903 Overprinted in Carmine or Green

Lisbon Overprint

Overprint 24½mm long. "A" has flattened top.

1911, Apr. 2 **Perf. 11½**

147 A11 ½a gray 2.10 .75
a. Inverted overprint 20.00 20.00
147B A11 1a orange 2.00 .75
c. Inverted overprint 20.00 20.00
148 A11 2a gray green 2.00 .75
a. Inverted overprint 5.00 5.00
149 A11 3a slate 6.25 .75
a. Inverted overprint 12.50 5.00
150 A11 4a carmine (G) 6.25 2.00
a. 4a pale yel brn (error) *55.00* *50.00*
b. As No. 150, inverted overprint 25.00 25.00
151 A11 5a pale yel brn 6.25 4.00
152 A11 6a red brown 6.25 4.00
153 A11 8a gray brown 6.25 4.00
154 A11 10a slate blue 6.25 4.00
155 A11 13a gray lilac 10.00 5.00
a. Inverted overprint 60.00 60.00
156 A11 16a dk blue, *bl* 10.00 5.00
a. Inverted overprint 60.00 60.00
157 A11 18a org brn, *pink* 16.00 6.00
157A A11 20a brown, *straw* 16.00 6.00
157B A11 31a red lil, *pink* 30.00 8.00
157C A11 47a dull bl, *straw* 50.00 10.00
157D A11 78a blk & red, *bl* 82.50 12.00
Nos. 147-157D (16) 258.10 73.00

Issued without gum: Nos. 151, 153-157D.

Coat of Arms — A14

1911 **Perf. 11½x12**

Red Surcharge

158 A14 1a on 5r brn & buff 32.50 12.50
a. "1" omitted 67.50 50.00
b. Inverted surcharge 45.00 25.00
c. Larger "1" 35.00 30.00

Stamps of 1900-03 Surcharged

Diagonal Halves

1911 **Without Gum** **Perf. 11½**

Black Surcharge

159 A11 2a on half of 4a car 32.50 32.50
a. "2" omitted 80.00 80.00
b. Inverted surcharge 65.00 65.00
d. Entire stamp 65.00 65.00
159C A11 5a on half of 10a sl bl (#89) *4,000.* —
e. Entire stamp —

Red Surcharge

160 A11 5a on half of 10a sl bl (#89) *1,000* *1,000*
a. Inverted surcharge *750.00* *750.00*
b. Entire stamp — —
161 A11 5a on half of 10a sl bl (#135) 125.00 80.00
a. Inverted surcharge 250.00 165.00
b. Entire stamp 275.00 165.00

A15

1911 **Perf. 12x11½**

Laid or Wove Paper

162 A15 1a black 475.00 —
a. "Corrieo" 1,900. —
163 A15 2a black 575.00 —
a. "Corrieo" 1,900. —

The vast majority of used stamps were not canceled.

Surcharged Stamps of 1902 Overprinted in Red or Green

Local Overprint

Overprint 23mm long. "A" has pointed top.

1913 **Without Gum** **Perf. 11½**

164 A1 6a on 10r green (R) 37.50 12.00
a. "REPUBLICA" double 65.00 65.00

Perf. 12½, 13½

165 A7 6a on 5r black (G) 15.00 3.50
166 A7 6a on 10r green (R) 31.00 8.00
167 A7 6a on 40r choc (R) 10.50 3.00
a. Perf. 13½ 50.00 20.00
168 A7 18a on 20r car (G) 21.00 6.00
169 A7 18a on 100r brown (R) 125.00 40.00
a. Perf. 13½ 100.00 50.00
170 A7 18a on 300r org (R) 32.50 9.00
a. Perf. 13½ 50.00 10.00
Nos. 164-170 (7) 272.50 81.50

"REPUBLICA" Inverted

164b A1 6a on 10r green (R) 65.00 65.00
165a A7 6a on 5r black (G) 65.00 60.00
166a A7 6a on 10r green (R) 65.00 60.00
167b A7 6a on 40r choc (R) 65.00 60.00
168a A7 18a on 20r car (G) 66.00 60.00
169b A7 18a on 100r brown (R) 95.00 60.00
170b A7 18a on 300r org (R) 65.00 60.00

1913 **Without Gum** **Perf. 11½, 13½**

171 A9 6a on 10r red vio (G) 14.50 3.00
172 A9 6a on 10r red vio (R) 175.00 26.00
173 A9 6a on 15r choc (R) 14.50 4.00
174 A9 6a on 25r green (R) 16.00 4.00
175 A9 6a on 80r yel grn (R) 14.50 4.00
176 A9 6a on 100r brn, *buff*(R) 30.00 7.00
a. Perf. 11½ 32.50 8.00
177 A9 18a on 20r lav (R) 19.00 4.00
178 A9 18a on 50r lt bl (R) 19.00 4.00
a. Perf. 13½ 21.00 5.00
179 A9 18a on 75r car (G) 19.00 4.50
180 A9 18a on 150r car, *rose* (G) 21.00 5.00
181 A9 18a on 300r dk bl, *buff* (R) 32.50 10.00

On No. 141

182 A11 10a on 12a red lil (R) 13.00 3.50
Nos. 171-182 (12) 388.00 79.00

"REPUBLICA" Inverted

171a A9 6a on 10r red vio (G) 65.00 60.00
172a A9 6a on 10r red vio (R) 65.00 60.00
174a A9 6a on 25r green (R) 65.00 60.00
175a A9 6a on 80r yel grn (R) 65.00 60.00
176b A9 6a on 100r brn, *buff*(R) 65.00 60.00
177a A9 18a on 20r lav (R) 65.00 60.00
178b A9 18a on 50r lt bl (R) 65.00 60.00
179a A9 18a on 75r car (G) 65.00 60.00
180a A9 18a on 150r car, *rose* (G) 65.00 60.00
181a A9 18a on 300r dk bl, *buff* (R) 65.00 60.00

Stamps of Preceding Issue Surcharged

1913 **Without Gum** **Perf. 11½**

183 A9 2a on 18a on 20r (R) 10.00 4.00
184 A9 2a on 18a on 50r (R) 10.00 4.00
a. Perf. 13½ 11.00 4.25
185 A9 2a on 18a on 75r (G) 10.00 4.00
186 A9 2a on 18a on 150r (G) 10.00 4.00
Nos. 183-186 (4) 40.00 16.00

"REPUBLICA" Inverted

183b A9 2a on 18a on 20r (R) 20.00 —
184b A9 2a on 18a on 50r (R) 20.00 —
185b A9 2a on 18a on 75r (G) 20.00 —
186b A9 2a on 18a on 150r (G) 20.00 —

"2" Surcharge Inverted

183c A9 2a on 18a on 20r (R) 30.00 32.50
184c A9 2a on 18a on 50r (R) 30.00 32.50
185c A9 2a on 18a on 75r (G) 30.00 32.50
186c A9 2a on 18a on 150r (G) 30.00 32.50

"2" Surcharge Double

183d A9 2a on 18a on 20r (R) 30.00 27.50
184d A9 2a on 18a on 50r (R) 30.00 30.00
185d A9 2a on 18a on 75r (G) 32.50 35.00
186d A9 2a on 18a on 150r (G) 35.00 40.00

Vasco da Gama Issue Overprinted or Surcharged:

j

k

187 CD20 (j) ½a blue green 7.75 2.00
188 CD21 (j) 1a red 8.50 2.00
189 CD22 (j) 2a red violet 8.50 2.00
a. Double ovpt., one inverted 100.00
190 CD23 (j) 4a yellow grn 7.75 2.00
191 CD24 (j) 8a dk blue 13.00 2.00
192 CD25 (k) 10a on 12a vio brn 24.00 5.00
193 CD26 (j) 16a bister brn 17.00 4.00
194 CD27 (j) 24a bister 27.50 5.00
Nos. 187-194 (8) 114.00 24.00

Stamps of 1898-1903 Overprinted in Red or Green

1913 **Without Gum** **Perf. 11½**

195 A11 4a carmine (G) 250.00 100.00
196 A11 5a yellow brn 27.50 20.00
a. Inverted overprint *50.00* *40.00*
197 A11 6a red brown 77.50 40.00
198 A11 8a gray brown 625.00 300.00
198A A11 10a dull blue —
199 A11 13a violet 77.50 32.50
a. Inverted overprint 95.00
200 A11 13a gray lilac 37.50 20.00
201 A11 16a blue, *bl* 45.00 20.00
202 A11 18a org brn, *pink* 45.00 20.00
203 A11 20a brown, *yelsh* 45.00 20.00
204 A11 31a red lil, *pink* 67.50 30.00
205 A11 47a dull bl, *straw* 100.00 40.00

Only 20 copies of No. 198A were sold by the Post Office.

Stamps of 1911-13 Surcharged

On Stamps of 1911 With Lisbon "Republica"

1913

206 A11 ½a on 5a yel brn (R) 15.00 3.00
a. "½ Avo" inverted 125.00 70.00
207 A11 4a on 8a gray brn (R) 30.00 4.00
a. "4 Avos" inverted 150.00 70.00

On Stamps of 1913 With Local "Republica"

208 A11 1a on 13a violet (R) 125.00 30.00
209 A11 1a on 13a gray lil (R) 15.00 3.00
Nos. 206-209 (4) 185.00 40.00

Issued without gum: Nos. 207-209.

"Ceres" — A16

1913-24 **Perf. 12x11½, 15x14**

Name and Value in Black

210 A16 ½a olive brown 1.75 .20
a. Inscriptions inverted 50.00
211 A16 1a black 1.75 .20
a. Inscriptions inverted 50.00
b. Inscriptions double 50.00
212 A16 1½a yel grn ('24) 1.75 .20
213 A16 2a blue green 1.75 .20
a. Inscriptions inverted 40.00
214 A16 3a orange ('23) 10.00 3.00
215 A16 4a carmine 6.75 1.00
216 A16 4a lemon ('24) 14.00 2.25
217 A16 5a lilac brown 7.75 3.00
218 A16 6a lt violet 7.75 3.00
219 A16 6a gray ('23) 47.50 7.50
220 A16 8a lilac brown 7.75 3.00
221 A16 10a deep blue 7.75 3.00
222 A16 10a pale blue ('23) 27.50 6.00
223 A16 12a yellow brn 11.00 3.00
224 A16 14a lilac ('24) 42.50 12.00
225 A16 16a slate 20.00 5.00
226 A16 20a orange brn 20.00 5.00
227 A16 24a slate grn ('23) 25.00 7.00
228 A16 32a orange brn ('24) 25.00 8.00
229 A16 40a plum 21.00 5.00
230 A16 56a dull rose ('24) 50.00 15.00
231 A16 58a brown, *grn* 35.00 12.00
232 A16 72a brown ('23) 67.50 20.00
233 A16 76a brown, *pink* 50.00 14.00
234 A16 1p orange, *sal* 67.50 20.00
235 A16 1p orange ('24) 200.00 30.00
236 A16 3p green, *bl* 200.00 50.00
237 A16 3p pale turq ('24) 425.00 60.00
238 A16 5p car rose ('24) 350.00 75.00
Nos. 210-238 (29) 1,753.
Nos. 210-221,223-238 (28) 367.55

For surcharges see Nos. 256, 259-267.

Preceding Issues and No. P4 Overprinted in Carmine

On Stamps of 1902

Perf. 11½, 12, 12½, 13½, 11½x12

1915

239 A7 6a on 10r green 14.50 2.00
240 A9 6a on 5r yellow 14.50 2.00
241 A9 6a on 10r red vio 14.50 2.00
242 A9 6a on 15r choc 12.50 1.50
243 A9 6a on 25r green 12.00 1.50
244 A9 6a on 80r yel grn 12.00 1.50
245 A9 6a on 100r brn, *buff* 21.00 3.00
246 A9 6a on 200r bl, *bl* 11.00 2.00
247 A9 18a on 20r lav 21.00 4.00
248 A9 18a on 50r lt bl 45.00 4.00
249 A9 18a on 75r car 40.00 4.00
250 A9 18a on 150r car, *rose* 45.00 4.00
251 A9 18a on 300r bl, *sal* 40.00 4.00
252 N3 18a on 2½r brn 32.50 2.00

With Additional Overprint

253 A11 8a blue 14.50 3.00
254 A11 10a slate blue 14.50 3.00
a. "Provisorio" double 110.00

On Stamp of 1905

255 A11 10a on 12a red lilac 14.50 3.00
Nos. 239-255 (17) 379.00 46.50

Issued without gum: Nos. 243-251 and 255.

No. 217 Surcharged

1919-20

Without Gum

256 A16 ½a on 5a lilac brn 100.00 25.00

Nos. 243 and 244 Surcharged

2

257 A9 2a on 6a on 25r green 500.00 75.00
258 A9 2a on 6a on 80r yel grn 100.00 30.00

No. 152 Surcharged

258A A11 2a on 6a red brown 175.00 60.00
Nos. 256-258A (4) 875.00 190.00

Issued without gum: Nos. 256-258A.

Stamps of 1913-24 Surcharged

1931-33

259 A16 1a on 24a slate grn ('33) 14.50 4.00
260 A16 2a on 32a org brn ('33) 14.50 4.00
261 A16 4a on 12a bis brn ('33) 14.50 4.00
262 A16 5a on 6a lt gray ('33) 57.50 20.00
263 A16 5a on 6a lt vio ('33) 30.00 11.00
264 A16 7a on 8a lil brn 24.00 5.00
265 A16 12a on 14a lil 24.00 5.00
266 A16 15a on 16a dk gray ('33) 24.00 5.00
267 A16 20a on 56a dl rose ('33) 50.00 11.00
Nos. 259-267 (9) 253.00 69.00

"Portugal" and Vasco da Gama's Flagship "San Gabriel" — A17

Wmk. 232

1934, Feb. 1 Typo. *Perf. 11½*

268 A17 ½a bister .45 .40
269 A17 1a olive brown .45 .20
270 A17 2a blue green 1.10 .50
271 A17 3a violet 1.40 .50
272 A17 4a black 1.75 .50
273 A17 5a gray 1.75 .80
274 A17 6a brown 1.75 .80
275 A17 7a brt rose 3.25 1.00
276 A17 8a brt blue 3.25 1.00
277 A17 10a red orange 7.25 2.00
278 A17 12a dark blue 7.25 2.00
279 A17 14a olive green 7.25 2.00
280 A17 15a maroon 7.25 2.00
281 A17 20a orange 7.25 2.00
282 A17 30a apple green 14.00 3.50
283 A17 40a violet 14.00 3.50
284 A17 50a olive bister 21.00 5.00
285 A17 1p lt blue 110.00 27.50
286 A17 2p brown org 140.00 35.00
287 A17 3p emerald 225.00 40.00
288 A17 5p dark violet 350.00 87.50
Nos. 268-288 (21) 925.40 217.70

See Nos. 316-323. For overprints and surcharges see Nos. 306-315, C1-C6, J43-J49.

Common Design Types

Perf. 13½x13

1938, Aug. 1 Engr. Unwmk.

Name and Value in Black

289 CD34 1a gray green 1.00 .35
290 CD34 2a orange brown 1.25 .55
291 CD34 3a dk vio brn 1.25 .55
292 CD34 4a brt green 1.25 .55
293 CD35 5a dk carmine 1.25 .55
294 CD35 6a slate 1.25 .55
295 CD35 8a rose violet 2.10 2.25
296 CD36 10a brt red vio 2.50 2.25
297 CD36 12a red 3.25 2.60
298 CD36 15a orange 3.25 2.60
299 CD37 20a blue 16.50 2.90
300 CD37 40a gray black 16.50 3.50
301 CD37 50a brown 16.50 3.75
302 CD38 1p brown car 50.00 7.25
303 CD38 2p olive green 100.00 11.00
304 CD38 3p blue violet 125.00 22.50
305 CD38 5p red brown 250.00 37.50
Nos. 289-305 (17) 592.85 101.20

For surcharge see No. 315A.

AIR POST STAMPS

Stamps of 1934 Overprinted or Surcharged in Black

a

b

1936 Wmk. 232 *Perf. 11½*

C1 A17 (a) 2a blue green 2.50 .75
C2 A17 (a) 3a violet 4.25 .75
C3 A17 (b) 5a on 6a brown 4.25 .75
C4 A17 (a) 7a brt rose 4.25 .75
C5 A17 (a) 8a brt blue 7.00 1.00
C6 A17 (a) 15a maroon 27.50 4.00
Nos. C1-C6 (6) 49.75 8.00

Common Design Type

Name and Value in Black

Perf. 13½x13

1938, Aug. 1 Engr. Unwmk.

C7 CD39 1a scarlet .90 .50
C8 CD39 2a purple 1.10 .50
C9 CD39 3a orange 1.60 .90
C10 CD39 5a ultra 3.25 1.25
C11 CD39 10a lilac brn 5.50 1.25
C12 CD39 20a dk green 11.00 3.00
C13 CD39 50a red brown 18.00 4.00
C14 CD39 70a rose car 22.50 5.00
C15 CD39 1p magenta 45.00 18.00
Nos. C7-C15 (9) 108.85 34.40

No. C13 exists with overprint "Exposicao Internacional de Nova York, 1939-1940" and Trylon and Perisphere.

POSTAGE DUE STAMPS

Numeral of Value — D1

Perf. 11½x12

1904, July Typo. Unwmk.

Name and Value in Black

J1 D1 ½a gray green 1.50 1.25
a. Name & value inverted 42.50 22.50
J2 D1 1a yellow grn 1.90 1.25
J3 D1 2a slate 1.90 1.25
J4 D1 4a pale brown 1.90 1.25
J5 D1 5a red orange 3.50 2.00
J6 D1 8a gray brown 3.75 2.00
J7 D1 12a red brown 5.00 2.00
J8 D1 20a dull blue 8.25 4.50
J9 D1 40a carmine 10.50 6.00
J10 D1 50a orange 19.00 12.00
J11 D1 1p gray violet 37.50 25.00
Nos. J1-J11 (11) 94.70 58.50

Issued without gum: Nos. J7-J11. Issued with or without gum: No. J4. Others issued with gum.

For overprints see Nos. 144-146, J12-J32.

Issue of 1904 Overprinted in Carmine or Green

Lisbon Overprint

Overprint 24½mm long. "A" has flattened top.

1911

J12 D1 ½a gray green .30 .20
J13 D1 1a yellow green .30 .20
J14 D1 2a slate .30 .20
J15 D1 4a pale brown .40 .20
J16 D1 5a orange .40 .20
J17 D1 8a gray brown .50 .20
J18 D1 12a red brown 1.25 .40
J19 D1 20a dull blue 2.50 .85
J20 D1 40a carmine (G) 8.50 1.25
J21 D1 50a orange 15.00 2.50
J22 D1 1p gray violet 30.00 3.50
Nos. J12-J22 (11) 59.45 9.70

Issued without gum: Nos. J19-J22.

Issue of 1904 Overprinted in Red or Green

Local Overprint

Overprint 23mm long. "A" has pointed top.

1914

J22A D1 ½a gray green *1,500. 600.00*
J23 D1 1a yellow green 3.00 .35
J24 D1 2a slate 3.00 .35
J25 D1 4a pale brown 3.00 .35
J26 D1 5a orange 3.50 .35
J27 D1 8a gray brown 3.50 .35
J28 D1 12a red brown 3.50 .35
J29 D1 20a dull blue 12.50 2.00
J30 D1 40a car (G) 35.00 4.00
a. Double ovpt., red and green 100.00 22.50
J31 D1 50a orange 35.00 4.00
J32 D1 1p gray violet 70.00 8.00
Nos. J23-J32 (10) 172.00 20.10

Issued without gum: Nos. J28, J30-J32.

WAR TAX STAMPS

Victory WT1

1919, Aug. 11 Unwmk. *Perf. 15x14*

Overprinted in Black or Carmine

MR1 WT1 2a green 2.25 1.00
MR2 WT1 11a green (C) 3.50 1.40

Nos. MR1-MR2 were also for use in Timor.

A 9a value was issued for revenue use. Value $10.

NEWSPAPER STAMPS

Nos. P1-P2

No. P3

Typographed and Embossed

1892-93 Unwmk. *Perf. 12½*

Black Surcharge

Without Gum

P1 A7 2½r on 40r choc 4.00 2.50
a. Inverted surcharge 40.00 30.00
b. Perf. 13½ 4.50 4.50
P2 A7 2½r on 80r gray 4.00 2.50
a. Inverted surcharge 40.00 35.00
b. Double surcharge
c. Perf. 13½ 40.00 35.00
P3 A7 2½r on 10r grn ('93) 4.00 2.50
a. Double surcharge
b. Perf. 13½ 5.00 4.50
Nos. P1-P3 (3) 12.00 7.50

N3

N4

1893-94 Typo. *Perf. 11½*

P4 N3 2½r brown 3.25 2.00
a. Perf. 11½ 3.25 2.25
b. Perf. 13½ 3.50 2.00
P5 N4 ½a on 2½r brn (Bk) ('94) 3.25 2.25
a. Double surcharge

For surcharges see Nos. 131, 252.

POSTAL TAX STAMPS

Pombal Commemorative Issue

Common Design Types

Perf. 12½

1925, Nov. 3 Engr. Unwmk.

RA1 CD28 2a red org & blk 3.25 .70
RA2 CD29 2a red org & blk 3.25 .70
RA3 CD30 2a red org & blk 3.25 .70
Nos. RA1-RA3 (3) 9.75 2.10

Symbolical of Charity — PT1

1930, Dec. 25 Litho. *Perf. 11*

RA4 PT1 5a dk brown, *yel* 7.00 5.00

POSTAL TAX DUE STAMPS

Pombal Commemorative Issue

Common Design Types

1925 Unwmk. *Perf. 12½*

RAJ1	CD28	4a red orange & blk	3.25	.70
RAJ2	CD29	4a red orange & blk	3.25	.70
RAJ3	CD30	4a red orange & blk	3.25	.70
		Nos. RAJ1-RAJ3 (3)	9.75	2.10

MADAGASCAR

ˌma-də-ˈgas-kər

LOCATION — Large island off the coast of southeastern Africa
GOVT. — French colony.
AREA — 226,658 sq. mi.
POP. — 3,797,936 (est. 1940)
CAPITAL — Antananarivo

Madagascar became a French protectorate in 1885 and a French colony in 1896 following several years of dispute among France, Great Britain, and the native government. The colony administered the former protectorates of Anjouan, Grand Comoro, Mayotte, Diego-Suarez, Nossi-Be and Sainte-Marie de Madagascar. Previous issues of postage stamps are found under these individual headings.

12 Pence = 1 Shilling
100 Centimes = 1 Franc

British Consular Mail stamps of Madagascar were gummed only in one corner. Unused values are for stamps without gum. Examples having the original corner gum will command higher prices. Most used examples of these stamps have small faults and values are for stamps in this condition. Used stamps without faults are scarce and are worth more. Used stamps are valued with the commonly used crayon or pen cancellations.

"B C M" and Arms
A1

Handstamped "British Vice-Consulate"

1884 Unwmk. Typo. *Rouletted*

Black Seal Handstamped

1	A1	1p violet	500.	400.
b.		Seal omitted	5,500.	5,500.
2	A1	2p violet	325.	290.
3	A1	3p violet	350.	300.
4	A1	4p violet 1 oz.	4,250.	4,250.
a.		"1 oz." corrected to "4 oz." in mss.	800.	700.
b.		Seal omitted	*4,850.*	4,850.
5	A1	6p violet	450.	*500.*
6	A1	1sh violet	425.	*475.*
7	A1	1sh6p violet	500.	
8	A1	2sh violet	700.	
9	A1	1p on 1sh vio		
10	A1	4½ on 1sh vio		
11	A1	6p red	750.	625.

1886

Violet Seal Handstamped

12	A1	4p violet	1,350.	—
13	A1	6p violet	2,400.	—

Handstamped "British Consular Mail" as on A3

Black Seal Handstamped

14	A1	4p violet	1,850.	—

Violet Seal Handstamped

15	A1	4p violet	5,000.	—

The 1, 2, 3 and 4 pence are inscribed "POSTAL PACKET," the other values of the series are inscribed "LETTER."

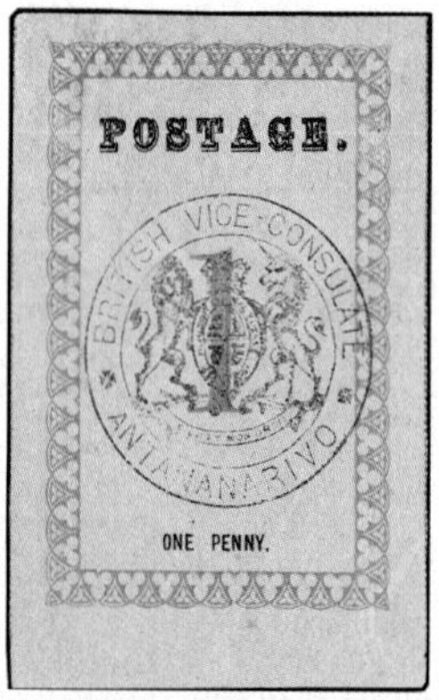

"British Vice-Consulate" — A2

Three types of A2 and A3:
I — "POSTAGE" 29½mm. Periods after "POSTAGE" and value.
II — "POSTAGE" 29½mm. No periods.
III — "POSTAGE" 24½mm. Period after value.

1886

Violet Seal Handstamped

16	A2	1p rose, I	325.	—
a.		Type II	1,050.	—
17	A2	1½p rose, I	1,050.	*875.*
a.		Type II	1,950.	—
18	A2	2p rose, I	350.	—
19	A2	3p rose, I	450.	*375.*
a.		Type II	1,150.	—
20	A2	4p rose, III	500.	—
21	A2	4½p rose, I	550.	*350.*
a.		Type II	1,750.	—
22	A2	6p rose, II	1,350.	—
23	A2	8p rose, I	1,250.	*1,250.*
a.		Type III	600.	—
24	A2	9p rose	1,000.	—
24A	A2	1sh rose, III		—
24B	A2	1sh6p rose, III	4,250.	—
25	A2	2sh rose, III	2,600.	—

Black Seal Handstamped

Type I

26	A2	1p rose	125.	*150.*
27	A2	1½p rose	1,500.	*1,150.*
28	A2	2p rose	160.	—
29	A2	3p rose	1,500.	*1,100.*
30	A2	4½p rose	1,050.	*575.*
31	A2	8p rose	2,600.	2,600.
32	A2	9p rose	3,250.	2,900.
32A	A2	2sh rose, III	—	—

"British Consular Mail" — A3

1886

Violet Seal Handstamped

33	A3	1p rose, II	110.	—
34	A3	1½p rose, II	175.	—
35	A3	2p rose, II	185.	—
36	A3	3p rose, II	160.	—
37	A3	4p rose, III	475.	—
38	A3	4½p rose, II	160.	—
39	A3	6p rose, II	375.	—
40	A3	8p rose, III	650.	—
a.		Type I	1,500.	—
41	A3	9p rose, I	300.	—
42	A3	1sh rose, III	1,350.	—
43	A3	1sh6p rose, III	1,500.	—
44	A3	2sh rose, III	1,750.	—

Black Seal Handstamped

45	A3	1p rose, I	90.	—
a.		Type II	90.	*140.*
46	A3	1½p rose, I	90.	—
a.		Type II	80.	110.
47	A3	2p rose, I	115.	—
a.		Type II	82.50	130.
48	A3	3p rose, I	110.	*110.*
a.		Type II	95.	*140.*
49	A3	4p rose, III	225.	—
50	A3	4½p rose, I	110.	*150.*
a.		Type II	95.	*140.*
51	A3	6p rose, II	95.	*140.*
52	A3	8p rose, I	140.	—
a.		Type III	750.	—
53	A3	9p rose, I	150.	*210.*
54	A3	1sh rose, III	525.	—
55	A3	1sh6p rose, III	625.	—
56	A3	2sh rose, III	700.	—

Seal Omitted

45b	A3	1p rose, II	2,850.
46b	A3	1½p rose, II	2,850.
48b	A3	3p rose, II	4,000.
49a	A3	4p rose, III	3,250.
50b	A3	4½p rose, II	4,250.
51a	A3	6p rose, II	4,250.
52b	A3	8p rose, III	3,500.
53a	A3	9p rose, I	3,750.
54a	A3	1sh rose, III	4,000.
55a	A3	1sh6p rose, III	3,750.
56a	A3	2sh rose, III	4,000.

Some students of these issues doubt that the 1886 "seal omitted" varieties were regularly issued.

Red Seal Handstamped

57	A3	3p rose, I	*10,500.*	
58	A3	4½p rose, I	*5,750.*	

FRENCH OFFICES IN MADAGASCAR

The general issues of French Colonies were used in these offices in addition to the stamps listed here.

Stamps of French Colonies Surcharged in Black:

a

b

c

1889 Unwmk. *Perf. 14x13½*

Overprint Type "a"

1	A9	05c on 10c blk, *lav*	*650.*	*190.*
a.		Inverted surcharge	*1,500.*	*1,100.*
b.		Vertical surcharge	*925.00*	*875.*
c.		05c and 25c on 10c blk, *lav*	*2,000.*	*1,100.*
d.		Pair, one without surcharge		*2,000.*
2	A9	05c on 25c blk, *rose*	*650.*	*190.*
a.		Inverted surcharge	*1,500.*	*1,100.*
b.		25c on 10c lav (error)	*9,000.*	*7,250.*
c.		Double surcharge	*1,100.*	*1,000.*
3	A9	25c on 40c red, *straw*	*575.*	*160.*
		On cover		*900.*
a.		Inverted surcharge	*1,200.*	*925.*
b.		Double surcharge	*1,450.*	*1,150.*
c.		Vertical surcharge		*1,150.*

Covers: Values are for commercial covers paying correct rates. Philatelic covers sell for less.

1891

Overprint Type "b"

4	A9	05c on 40c red, *straw*	*200.00*	*90.00*
a.		Double "5" in surcharge	*625.00*	*625.00*
5	A9	15c on 25c blk, *rose*	*200.00*	*100.00*
a.		Surcharge vertical	*210.00*	*125.00*

Overprint Type "c"

b.		Double surcharge	625.00	575.00
6	A9	5c on 10c blk, *lav*	*225.00*	*110.00*
a.		Double surcharge	*750.00*	*725.00*
7	A9	5c on 25c blk, *rose*	*240.00*	*125.00*

See Senegal Nos. 4, 8 for similar surcharge on 20c, 30c.

Forgeries of Nos. 1-7 exist.

A4

1891 Type-set *Imperf.*

Without Gum

8	A4	5c blk, *green*	150.00	30.00
9	A4	10c blk, *lt bl*	100.00	30.00
		On cover		575.00
10	A4	15c ultra, *pale bl*	100.00	32.50
		On cover		575.00
11	A4	25c brn, *buff*	21.00	14.00
		On cover		400.00
12	A4	1fr blk, *yellow*	1,000.	275.00
13	A4	5fr vio & blk, *lil*	2,000.	1,000.

Ten varieties of each. Nos. 12-13 have been extensively forged.

Most copies of Nos. 12-13 are defective due to the frail paper. Thinned examples sell for about 25% of the values quoted which are for copies without damage.

Stamps of France 1876-90, Overprinted in Red or Black

1895 *Perf. 14x13½*

14 A15 5c grn, *grnsh* (R) 15.00 7.25
On cover 175.00
15 A15 10c blk, *lav* (R) 47.50 28.00
On cover 175.00
16 A15 15c bl (R) 70.00 18.00
On cover 175.00
17 A15 25c blk, *rose* (R) 100.00 20.00
On cover 140.00
18 A15 40c red, *straw* (Bk) 80.00 28.00
On cover 240.00
19 A15 50c rose, *rose* (Bk) 100.00 42.50
On cover 240.00
20 A15 75c dp vio, *org* (R) 110.00 50.00
On cover 400.00
21 A15 1fr brnz grn, *straw* (Bk) 130.00 65.00
On cover 450.00
22 A15 5fr vio, *lav* (Bk) 175.00 80.00
On cover —
Nos. 14-22 (9) 827.50 338.75

Majunga Issue

Stamps of France, 1876-86, Surcharged with New Value

1895

Manuscript Surcharge in Red

22A A15 0,15c on 25c blk, *rose* *6,500.*
22B A15 0,15c on 1fr brnz grn, *straw* *5,250.*

Handstamped in Black

22C A15 15c on 25c blk, *rose* *6,000.*
22D A15 15c on 1fr brnz grn, *straw* *5,500.*

On most of #22C and all of #22D the manuscript surcharge of #22A-22B was washed off. Three types of "15" were used for No. 22C.

Stamps of France, 1876-84, Surcharged with New Value

1896

23 A15 5c on 1c blk, *bl* *5,500.* *2,100.*
On cover *5,500.*
24 A15 15c on 2c brn, *buff* *2,100.* *875.*
On cover *3,250.*
25 A15 25c on 3c gray, *grysh* *2,750.* *950.*
On cover *3,250.*
26 A15 25c on 4c cl, *lav* *5,500.* *1,600.*
On cover *5,500.*
27 A15 25c on 40c red, *straw* *1,350.* *700.*
On cover *2,750.*

The oval of the 5c and 15c surcharges is smaller than that of the 25c, and it does not extend beyond the edges of the stamp as the 25c surcharge does.

Excellent counterfeits of the surcharges on Nos. 22A to 27 exist.

Issues of the Colony

Navigation and Commerce — A7

1896-1906 Typo. *Perf. 14x13½*

Colony Name in Blue or Carmine

28 A7 1c blk, *lil bl* 1.00 .80
On cover 45.00
a. Name double 300.00
29 A7 2c brn, *buff* 1.75 .95
On cover 45.00
a. Name in blue black 3.75 3.75
30 A7 4c claret, *lav* 1.90 1.25
On cover 45.00
31 A7 5c grn, *grnsh* 6.50 1.25
On cover 11.00
32 A7 5c yel grn ('01) 1.60 .70
On cover 11.00
33 A7 10c blk, *lav* 6.50 1.75
On cover 11.00
34 A7 10c red ('00) 2.50 .70
On cover 11.00
35 A7 15c blue, quadrille paper 12.50 1.25
On cover 16.00
36 A7 15c gray ('00) 2.25 1.25
On cover 16.00
37 A7 20c red, *grn* 6.25 1.60
On cover 55.00
38 A7 25c blk, *rose* 9.00 4.00
On cover 16.00
39 A7 25c blue ('00) 21.50 20.00
On cover *100.00*
40 A7 30c brn, *bis* 8.00 3.00
On cover 55.00
41 A7 35c blk, *yel* ('06) 36.00 6.00
On cover 65.00
a. Name inverted 15,000.
42 A7 40c red, *straw* 9.50 4.75
On cover 55.00
43 A7 50c car, *rose* 11.50 2.40
On cover 55.00
44 A7 50c brn, *az* ('00) 27.50 25.00
On cover 87.50
45 A7 75c dp vio, *org* 5.00 3.75
On cover 92.50
a. Thin, transluscent paper 3.50 2.25
46 A7 1fr brnz grn, *straw* 12.50 2.25
On cover 110.00
a. Name in blue ('99) 24.00 18.50
47 A7 5fr red lil, *lav* ('99) 32.50 27.50
On cover —
Nos. 28-47 (20) 215.75 110.15

Perf. 13½x14 stamps are counterfeits.

For surcharges see Nos. 48-55, 58-60, 115-118, 127-128.

Nos. 32, 43, 44 and 46, affixed to pressboard with animals printed on the back, were used as emergency currency in the Comoro Islands in 1920.

Surcharged in Black

1902

48 A7 05c on 50c car, *rose* 6.00 4.00
On cover 45.00
a. Inverted surcharge 90.00 90.00
49 A7 10c on 5fr red lil, *lav* 19.50 14.50
On cover 55.00
a. Inverted surcharge 110.00 110.00
50 A7 15c on 1fr ol grn, *straw* 8.00 6.00
On cover 45.00
a. Inverted surcharge 97.50 97.50
b. Double surcharge 290.00 290.00
Nos. 48-50 (3) 33.50 24.50

Surcharged in Black

51 A7 0,01 on 2c brn, *buff* 8.00 8.00
On cover 65.00
a. Inverted surcharge 57.50 57.50
b. "00,1" instead of "0,01" 115.00 115.00
c. As "b" inverted — —
d. Comma omitted 160.00 160.00
e. Name in blue black 8.25 8.25
52 A7 0,05 on 30c brn, *bis* 8.50 8.50
On cover 45.00
a. Inverted surcharge 57.50 57.50
b. "00,5" instead of "0,05" 72.50 72.50
c. As "b" inverted 350.00 350.00
d. Comma omitted 160.00 160.00
53 A7 0,10 on 50c car, *rose* 8.00 8.00
On cover 45.00
a. Inverted surcharge 57.50 57.50
b. Comma omitted 160.00 160.00
54 A7 0,15 on 75c vio, *org* 6.25 6.25
On cover 45.00
a. Inverted surcharge 62.50 62.50
b. Comma omitted 160.00 160.00
c. As "b," inverted 550.00 550.00
55 A7 0,15 on 1fr ol grn, *straw* 12.50 12.50
On cover 50.00
a. Inverted surcharge 80.00 80.00
b. Comma omitted 1,050. 1,050.

Surcharged On Stamps of Diego-Suarez

56 A11 0,05 on 30c brn, *bis* 132.50 110.00
On cover 400.00
a. "00,5" instead of "0,05" 775.00 775.00
b. Inverted surcharge 1,050. 1,050.
57 A11 0,10 on 50c car, *rose* *4,100.* *4,100.*
Nos. 51-55 (5) 43.25 43.25

Counterfeits of Nos. 56-57 exist with surcharge both normal and inverted.

Surcharged in Black

58 A7 0,01 on 2c brn, *buff* 8.00 8.00
On cover 65.00
a. Inverted surcharge 57.50 57.50
b. Comma omitted 160.00 160.00
59 A7 0,05 on 30c brn, *bis* 7.25 7.25
On cover 45.00
a. Inverted surcharge 57.50 57.50
b. Comma omitted 160.00 160.00
60 A7 0,10 on 50c car, *rose* 6.25 6.25
On cover 45.00
a. Inverted surcharge 57.50 57.50
b. Comma omitted 160.00 160.00
Nos. 58-60 (3) 21.50 21.50

Surcharged On Stamps of Diego-Suarez

61 A11 0,05 on 30c brn, *bis* 110.00 110.00
On cover 375.00
a. Inverted surcharge 1,050. 1,050.
62 A11 0,10 on 50c car, *rose* *4,100.* *4,100.*

Se-tenant Pairs

51g	0,01 #51 + #58	20.00	—
52g	0,05 #52 + #59	22.50	—
53g	0,10 #53 + #60	20.00	—
56g	0,05 #56 + #62	350.00	—
57g	0,10 #57 + #63	—	—

BISECTS

During alleged stamp shortages at several Madagascar towns in 1904, it is claimed that bisects were used. After being affixed to letters, these bisects were handstamped "Affranchissement — exceptionnel — (faute de timbres)" and other inscriptions of similar import. The stamps bisected were 10c, 20c, 30c and 50c denominations of Madagascar type A7 and Diego-Suarez type A11. The editors believe these provisionals were unnecessary and speculative.

Zebu, Traveler's Tree and Lemur — A8

Transportation by Sedan Chair — A9

1903 Engr. *Perf. 11½*

63 A8 1c dk violet 1.00 1.00
a. On bluish paper 6.75 5.50
64 A8 2c olive brn 1.00 1.00
65 A8 4c brown 1.10 1.10
66 A8 5c yellow grn 5.75 1.40
67 A8 10c red 10.00 1.00
68 A8 15c carmine 14.00 1.25
a. On bluish paper *140.00* *140.00*
69 A8 20c orange 4.75 2.25
70 A8 25c dull blue 25.00 4.25
71 A8 30c pale red 36.00 13.50
72 A8 40c gray vio 25.00 5.00
73 A8 50c brown org 45.00 24.00
74 A8 75c orange yel 55.00 25.00
75 A8 1fr dp green 55.00 26.00
76 A8 2fr slate 70.00 27.50
77 A8 5fr gray black 72.50 *80.00*
Nos. 63-77 (15) 421.10 214.25

Nos. 63-77 exist imperf. Value of set, $600.

For surcharges see Nos. 119-124, 129.

1908-28 Typo. *Perf. 13½x14*

79 A9 1c violet & ol .20 .20
80 A9 2c red & ol .20 .20
81 A9 4c ol brn & brn .20 .20
82 A9 5c bl grn & ol .85 .20
83 A9 5c blk & rose ('22) .20 .20
84 A9 10c rose & brown .85 .20
85 A9 10c bl grn & ol grn ('22) .50 .30
86 A9 10c org brn & vio ('25) .20 .20
87 A9 15c dl vio & rose ('16) .20 .20
88 A9 15c dl grn & lt grn ('27) .40 .35
89 A9 15c dk bl & rose red ('28) 1.40 .80
90 A9 20c org & brn .45 .25
91 A9 25c blue & blk 2.50 .60
92 A9 25c vio & blk ('22) .25 .20
93 A9 30c brown & blk 2.50 1.10
94 A9 30c rose red & brn ('22) .45 .30
95 A9 30c grn & red vio ('25) .40 .20
96 A9 30c dp grn & yel grn ('27) 1.25 .80
97 A9 35c red & black 1.75 .90
98 A9 40c vio brn & blk 1.00 .50
99 A9 45c bl grn & blk .80 .50
100 A9 45c red & ver ('25) .40 .35
101 A9 45c gray lil & mag ('27) 1.25 .80
102 A9 50c violet & blk .85 .50
103 A9 50c blue & blk ('22) .75 .50
104 A9 50c blk & org ('25) .80 .20
105 A9 60c vio, *pnksh* ('25) .60 .50
106 A9 65c black & bl ('25) .80 .70
107 A9 75c rose red & blk .80 .50
108 A9 85c grn & ver ('25) 1.25 .80
109 A9 1fr brown & ol .80 .50
110 A9 1fr dull blue ('25) .95 .95
111 A9 1fr rose & grn ('28) 5.25 4.25
112 A9 1.10fr bis & bl grn ('28) 1.75 1.75
113 A9 2fr blue & olive 3.50 1.40
114 A9 5fr vio & vio brn 12.00 5.25
Nos. 79-114 (36) 48.30 27.35

75c violet on pinkish stamps of type A9 are No. 138 without surcharge.

For surcharges and overprints see Nos. 125-126, 130-146, 178-179, B1, 212-214.

Preceding Issues Surcharged in Black or Carmine

1912, Nov. *Perf. 14x13½*

115 A7 5c on 15c gray (C) 1.00 1.00
a. Wide spacing in surcharge 7.75 7.75

116 A7 5c on 20c red, *grn* .90 .90
a. Inverted surcharge 125.00
b. As #116, wide spacing in surcharge 6.50 6.50
c. As #116a, wide spacing in surcharge 2,000.
117 A7 5c on 30c brn, *bis* (C) 1.00 1.00
a. Wide spacing in surcharge 9.25 9.25
118 A7 10c on 75c vio, *org* 8.50 8.50
a. Double surcharge 250.00
b. As #118, wide spacing in surcharge 190.00 190.00
c. As #118a, wide spacing in surcharge 2,700.
119 A8 5c on 2c ol brn (C) .50 .50
120 A8 5c on 20c org .80 .80
121 A8 5c on 30c pale red 1.00 1.00
122 A8 10c on 40c gray vio (C) 1.40 1.40
123 A8 10c on 50c brn org 2.75 2.75
124 A8 10c on 75c org yel 5.25 5.25
a. Inverted surcharge 190.00
Nos. 115-124 (10) 23.10 23.10

Two spacings between the surcharged numerals are found on Nos. 115 to 118: Narrow spacing between figures of surcharge 1.5mm (5c), 2mm (10c); Wide spacing between figures of surcharge 2.25mm (5c), 2.75mm (10c). Values for Nos. 115-118 are for stamps with narrow spacing.

Stamps of Anjouan, Grand Comoro Island, Mayotte and Mohéli with similar surcharges were also available for use in Madagascar and the entire Comoro archipelago.

Preceding Issues Surcharged in Red or Black

g

h

1921

On Nos. 98 & 107

125 A9 (g) 30c on 40c (R) 1.75 1.75
126 A9 (g) 60c on 75c 2.75 2.75

On Nos. 45 & 47

127 A7 (g) 60c on 75c (R) 6.50 6.50
a. Inverted surcharge 175.00 175.00
128 A7 (h) 1fr on 5fr .75 .75

On No. 77

129 A8 (h) 1fr on 5fr (R) 70.00 70.00
Nos. 125-129 (5) 81.75 81.75

Stamps and Type of 1908-16 Surcharged in Black or Red

130 A9 1c on 15c dl vio & rose .70 .70
131 A9 25c on 35c red & blk 5.00 5.00
132 A9 25c on 35c red & blk (R) 15.00 15.00
133 A9 25c on 40c brn & blk 4.25 4.25
134 A9 25c on 45c grn & blk 2.75 2.75
Nos. 130-134 (5) 27.70 27.70
Nos. 125-134 (10) 109.45 109.45

Stamps and Type of 1908-28 Surcharged with New Value and Bars

1922-27

135 A9 25c on 15c dl vio & rose .25 .20
a. Double surcharge 72.50
136 A9 25c on 2fr bl & ol .30 .20
137 A9 25c on 5fr vio & vio brn .25 .20
138 A9 60c on 75c vio, *pnksh* .45 .35
139 A9 65c on 75c rose red & blk .80 .80
140 A9 85c on 45c bl grn & blk 1.25 1.00
141 A9 90c on 75c dl red & rose red .80 .80
142 A9 1.25fr on 1fr lt bl (R) .60 .25
143 A9 1.50fr on 1fr dp bl & dl bl .60 .25
144 A9 3fr on 5fr grn & vio 1.60 1.00
145 A9 10fr on 5fr org & rose lil 7.50 4.75
146 A9 20fr on 5fr rose & sl bl 8.50 6.75
Nos. 135-146 (12) 22.90 16.55

Years of issue: #138, 1922; #136, 137, 1924; #135, 139-140, 1925; #142, 1926; #141, 142-146, 1927.

See Nos. 178-179.

Sakalava Chief — A10

Hova Woman — A12

Hova with Oxen A11

Bétsiléo Woman A13

Perf. 13½x14, 14x13½

1930-44 **Typo.**

147 A11 1c dk bl & bl grn ('33) .20 .20
148 A10 2c brn red & dk brn .20 .20
149 A10 4c dk brn & vio .20 .20
150 A11 5c lt grn & red .25 .20
151 A12 10c ver & dp grn .40 .20
152 A13 15c dp red .25 .20
153 A11 20c yel brn & dk bl .25 .20
154 A12 25c vio & dk brn .25 .20
155 A13 30c Prus blue .65 .45
156 A10 40c grn & red .75 .50
157 A13 45c dull violet .90 .55
158 A11 65c ol grn & vio 1.10 .80
159 A13 75c dk brown .85 .50
160 A11 90c brn red & dk red 1.40 .90
161 A12 1fr yel brn & dk bl 1.75 1.10
162 A12 1fr dk red & car rose ('38) .95 .90
163 A12 1.25fr dp bl & dk brn ('33) 1.60 .90
164 A10 1.50fr dk & dp bl 5.50 1.10
165 A10 1.50fr brn & dk red ('38) .75 .50
165A A10 1.50fr dk red & brn ('44) .50 .50
166 A10 1.75fr dk brn & dk red ('33) 4.25 1.60
167 A10 5fr vio & dk brn 1.25 .70
168 A10 20fr yel brn & dk bl 2.00 1.75
Nos. 147-168 (23) 26.20 14.35

For surcharges and overprints see #211, 215, 217-218, 222-223, 228-229, 233, 235, 239, 257 and note after #B10.

Common Design Types pictured following the introduction.

Colonial Exposition Issue

Common Design Types

1931 **Engr.** ***Perf. 12½***

Name of Country in Black

169 CD70 40c deep green 1.40 1.00
170 CD71 50c violet 2.00 1.25
171 CD72 90c red orange 2.00 1.25
172 CD73 1.50fr dull blue 2.50 1.50
Nos. 169-172 (4) 7.90 5.00

General Joseph Simon Galliéni — A14

1931 **Engr.** ***Perf. 14***

Size: 21½x34½mm

173 A14 1c ultra .50 .45
174 A14 50c orange brn 1.40 .35
175 A14 2fr deep red 5.75 4.25
176 A14 3fr emerald 4.75 2.50
177 A14 10fr dp orange 4.00 2.50
Nos. 173-177 (5) 16.40 10.05

See Nos. 180-190. For overprints and surcharges see Nos. 216, 219, 221, 224, 232, 258.

Nos. 113 and 109 Surcharged

1932 ***Perf. 13½x14***

178 A9 25c on 2fr bl & ol .75 .50
179 A9 50c on 1fr brn & ol .75 .50

No. 178 has numerals in thick block letters. No. 136 has thin shaded numerals.

Galliéni Type of 1931

1936-40 **Photo.** ***Perf. 13½, 13x13½***

Size: 21x34mm

180 A14 3c sapphire ('40) .25 .20
181 A14 45c brt green ('40) .50 .40
182 A14 50c yellow brown .25 .20
183 A14 60c brt red lil ('40) .40 .20
184 A14 70c brt rose ('40) .60 .40
185 A14 90c copper brn ('39) .50 .40
186 A14 1.40fr org yel ('40) .90 .50
187 A14 1.60fr purple ('40) .90 .60
188 A14 2fr dk carmine .50 .20
189 A14 3fr green 4.50 2.25
190 A14 3fr olive blk ('39) .90 .70
Nos. 180-190 (11) 10.20 6.05

For overprint see note after #B10.

Paris International Exposition Issue

Common Design Types

1937, Apr. 15 **Engr.** ***Perf. 13***

191 CD74 20c dp violet .95 .95
192 CD75 30c dk green .95 .95
193 CD76 40c car rose 1.00 1.00
194 CD77 50c dk brn & blk 1.40 1.40
195 CD78 90c red 1.40 1.40
196 CD79 1.50fr ultra 1.40 1.40
Nos. 191-196 (6) 7.10 7.10

Colonial Arts Exhibition Issue

Common Design Type

Souvenir Sheet

1937 ***Imperf.***

197 CD74 3fr orange red 5.00 *5.50*

Jean Laborde A15

1938-40 ***Perf. 13***

198 A15 35c green .65 .40
199 A15 55c dp purple .65 .40
200 A15 65c orange red .90 .40
201 A15 80c violet brn .65 .40
202 A15 1fr rose car .90 .35
203 A15 1.25fr rose car ('39) .40 .20
204 A15 1.75fr dk ultra 1.75 .70
205 A15 2.15fr yel brn 2.50 1.75
206 A15 2.25fr dk ultra ('39) .60 .50
207 A15 2.50fr blk brn ('40) .65 .50
208 A15 10fr dk green ('40) 1.25 .90
Nos. 198-208 (11) 10.90 6.50

Nos. 198-202, 204, 205 commemorate the 60th anniv. of the death of Jean Laborde, explorer.

For overprints and surcharges see Nos. 220, 225-227, 230-231, 234, 236-237.

New York World's Fair Issue

Common Design Type

1939, May 10 **Engr.** ***Perf. 12½x12***

209 CD82 1.25fr car lake 1.00 1.00
210 CD82 2.25fr ultra 1.10 1.10

For surcharge see No. 240.

SEMI-POSTAL STAMPS

No. 84 Surcharged in Red

1915, Feb. **Unwmk.** ***Perf. 13½x14***

B1 A9 10c + 5c rose & brn 1.25 1.25

Curie Issue

Common Design Type

1938, Oct. 24 ***Perf. 13***

B2 CD80 1.75fr + 50c brt ultra 9.00 9.00

French Revolution Issue

Common Design Type

Name and Value Typographed in Black

1939, July 5 **Photo.**

B3 CD83 45c + 25c grn 8.00 8.00
B4 CD83 70c + 30c brn 8.00 8.00
B5 CD83 90c + 35c red org 8.00 8.00
B6 CD83 1.25fr + 1fr rose pink 8.00 8.00
B7 CD83 2.25fr + 2fr blue 8.00 8.00
Nos. B3-B7 (5) 40.00 40.00

AIR POST STAMPS

Airplane and Map of Madagascar — AP1

Perf. 13x13½

1935-41 **Photo.** **Unwmk.**

C1 AP1 50c yel grn & red .60 .45
C2 AP1 90c yel grn & red ('41) .45
C3 AP1 1.25fr claret & red .50 .50
C4 AP1 1.50fr brt bl & red .50 .50
C5 AP1 1.60fr brt bl & red ('41) .20 .20
C6 AP1 1.75fr org & red 8.75 3.75
C7 AP1 2fr Prus bl & red .85 .45
C8 AP1 3fr dp org & red ('41) .20 .20
C9 AP1 3.65fr ol blk & red ('38) .85 .50
C10 AP1 3.90fr pck grn & red ('41) .20 .20
C11 AP1 4fr rose & red 40.00 2.75
C12 AP1 4.50fr blk & red 23.50 1.75
C13 AP1 5.50fr ol blk & red ('41) .25 .20
C14 AP1 6fr rose lil & red ('41) .35 .20
C15 AP1 6.90fr dl vio & red ('41) .20 .20
C16 AP1 8fr rose lil & red 1.50 .90
C17 AP1 8.50fr grn & red 1.50 1.10
C18 AP1 9fr ol grn & red ('41) .35 .35
C19 AP1 12fr vio brn & red .80 .55
C20 AP1 12.50fr dl vio & red 1.90 .90
C21 AP1 15fr org yel & red ('41) .80 .55
C22 AP1 16fr ol grn & red 1.75 1.10
C23 AP1 20fr dk brn & red 2.50 1.10

C24	AP1 50fr brt ultra & red ('38)	4.00	3.25
	Nos. C1,C3-C24 (23)	92.05	21.65

According to some authorities the 90c was not placed on sale in Madagascar.

AIR POST SEMI-POSTAL STAMPS

French Revolution Issue
Common Design Type
Unwmk.
1939, July 5 Photo. *Perf. 13*
Name and Value in Orange

CB1	CD83 4.50fr + 4fr brn blk	14.50	14.50

POSTAGE DUE STAMPS

D1

Governor's Palace — D2

Postage Due Stamps of French Colonies Overprinted in Red or Blue

1896 Unwmk. *Imperf.*

J1	D1 5c blue (R)	9.75	8.00
	On cover		*300.00*
J2	D1 10c brown (R)	9.00	6.50
	On cover		*300.00*
J3	D1 20c yellow (Bl)	8.00	6.00
	On cover		*300.00*
J4	D1 30c rose red (Bl)	8.00	7.00
	On cover		*300.00*
J5	D1 40c lilac (R)	65.00	42.50
	On cover		—
J6	D1 50c gray vio (Bl)	12.00	8.25
	On cover		*400.00*
J7	D1 1fr dk grn (R)	70.00	57.50
	On cover		—
	Nos. J1-J7 (7)	181.75	135.75

1908-24 Typo. *Perf. 13½x14*

J8	D2 2c vio brn	.20	.20
J9	D2 4c violet	.20	.20
J10	D2 5c green	.20	.20
J11	D2 10c deep rose	.20	.20
J12	D2 20c olive green	.40	.40
J13	D2 40c brn, *straw*	.45	.45
J14	D2 50c brn, *bl*	.60	.60
J15	D2 60c orange ('24)	.60	.60
J16	D2 1fr dark blue	1.10	1.10
	Nos. J8-J16 (9)	3.95	3.95

Type of 1908 Issue Surcharged

1924-27

J17	D2 60c on 1fr org	1.90	1.90

Surcharged

J18	D2 2fr on 1fr lil rose ('27)	.90	.90
J19	D2 3fr on 1fr ultra ('27)	.90	.90

MADEIRA

mə-'dir-ə

LOCATION — A group of islands in the Atlantic Ocean northwest of Africa
GOVT. — Part of the Republic of Portugal
AREA — 314 sq. mi.
POP. — 150,574 (1900)
CAPITAL — Funchal

These islands are considered an integral part of Portugal and since 1898 postage stamps of Portugal have been in use.

1000 Reis = 1 Milreis
100 Centavos = 1 Escudo (1925)

STAMPS OF PORTUGAL USED IN MADEIRA

Barred Numeral "51"

1853 Queen Maria II

A1	5r org brn (#1)	1,500.
A2	25r blue (#2)	110.
A3	50r dp yel grn (#3)	1,500.
A4	100r lilac (#4)	3,500.

1855 King Pedro V (Straight Hair)

A5	5r red brn (#5)	1,900.
A6	25r blue, type II (#6)	85.00
	On cover	400.00
a.	Type I (#6a)	95.00
	On cover	300.00
A7	50r green (#7)	125.00
A8	100r lilac (#8)	150.00

1856-58
King Pedro V (Curled Hair)

A9	5r red brn (#9)	190.00
A10	25r blue, type II (#10)	150.00
	On cover	400.00
a.	Type I (#10a)	125.00
	On cover	375.00
A11	25r rose, type II (#11; '58)	45.00
	On cover	225.00

1862-64 King Luiz

A12	5r brown (#12)	150.00
A13	10r orange (#13)	150.00
A14	25r rose (#14)	42.50
	On cover	140.00
A15	50r yel green (#15)	140.00
	On cover	400.00
A16	100r lilac (#16; '64)	175.00

1866-67 King Luiz
Imperf.

A17	5r black (#17)	175.00
A18	10r yellow (#18)	200.00
A19	20r bister (#19)	200.00
A20	25r rose (#20)	150.00
	On cover	300.00
A21	50r green (#21)	200.00
	On cover	400.00
A22	80r orange (#22)	200.00
	On cover	*500.00*
A23	100r dk lilac (#23; '67)	300.00
A24	120r blue (#24)	150.00
	On cover	*500.00*

Perf. 12½

A28	25r rose (#28)	150.00

Issued under Portuguese Administration

It is recommended that the rare overprinted 1868-81 stamps be purchased accompanied by certificates of authenticity from competent experts.

King Luiz
A1 A2

Stamps of Portugal Overprinted

1868, Jan. 1 Unwmk. *Imperf.*
Black Overprint

2	A1 20r bister	200.00	100.00
a.	Inverted overprint		—
b.	Rouletted		—
3	A1 50r green	200.00	100.00
4	A1 80r orange	225.00	100.00
a.	Double overprint		—
5	A1 100r lilac	225.00	100.00
	Nos. 2-5 (4)	850.00	400.00

The 5r black does not exist as a genuinely imperforate original.

Reprints of 1885 are on stout white paper, ungummed. (Also, 5r, 10r and 25r values were overprinted.) Reprints of 1905 are on ordinary white paper with shiny gum and have a wide "D" and "R." Value, $12 each.

Lozenge Perf.

2c	A1	20r	—
3a	A1	50r	—
4b	A1	80r	—
5a	A1	100r	—

Overprinted in Red or Black

1868-70 *Perf. 12½*

6	A1 5r black (R)	55.00	37.50
8	A1 10r yellow	90.00	80.00
9	A1 20r bister	140.00	110.00
10	A1 25r rose	57.50	12.00
a.	Inverted overprint		—
11	A1 50r green	175.00	140.00
a.	Inverted overprint		—
12	A1 80r orange	175.00	140.00
13	A1 100r lilac	175.00	140.00
a.	Inverted overprint		—
14	A1 120r blue	110.00	80.00
15	A1 240r violet ('70)	500.00	400.00
	Nos. 6-15 (9)	1,477.	1,139.

Two types of 5r differ in the position of the "5" at upper right.

The reprints are on stout white paper, ungummed, with rough perforation 13½, and on thin white paper with shiny white gum and clean-cut perforation 13½. The overprint has the wide "D" and "R" and the first reprints included the 5r with both black and red overprint. Value $10 each.

Overprinted in Red or Black

1871-80 *Perf. 12½, 13½*

16	A2 5r black (R)	8.50	6.00
a.	Inverted overprint		—
b.	Double overprint	55.00	55.00
c.	Perf. 14	90.00	55.00
18	A2 10r yellow	30.00	22.50
19	A2 10r bl grn ('79)	140.00	110.00
a.	Perf. 13½	160.00	140.00
20	A2 10r yel grn ('80)	65.00	52.50
21	A2 15r brn ('75)	19.00	11.50
22	A2 20r bister	30.00	22.50
23	A2 25r rose	11.00	4.50
a.	Inverted overprint	32.50	32.50
b.	Double overprint	32.50	32.50
24	A2 50r green ('72)	62.50	30.00
a.	Double overprint		—
b.	Inverted overprint	160.00	160.00
25	A2 50r blue ('80)	125.00	55.00
26	A2 80r orange ('72)	77.50	67.50
27	A2 100r pale lil ('73)	82.50	40.00
a.	Perf. 14	200.00	85.00
b.	Perf. 13½	110.00	57.50
28	A2 120r blue	110.00	80.00
29	A2 150r blue ('76)	160.00	140.00
a.	Perf. 13½	175.00	150.00
30	A2 150r yel ('79)	275.00	240.00
31	A2 240r vio ('74)	700.00	500.00
32	A2 300r vio ('76)	75.00	67.50
	Nos. 16-32 (16)	1,971.	1,449.

There are two types of the overprint, the second one having a broad "D."

The reprints have the same characteristics as those of the 1868-70 issues.

King Luiz
A3 A4

1880-81

33	A3 5r black	32.50	21.00
34	A4 25r pearl gray	32.50	21.00
a.	Inverted overprint	52.50	52.50
35	A5 25r lilac	40.00	11.00
a.	25r purple brown	30.00	11.00
b.	25r gray	32.50	10.00
	Nos. 33-35 (3)	105.00	53.00

Nos. 33, 34 and 35 have been reprinted on stout white paper, ungummed, and the last three on thin white paper with shiny white gum. The perforations are as previously described.

Common Design Types pictured following the introduction.

Vasco da Gama Issue
Common Design Types

1898, Apr. 1 Engr. *Perf. 14-15*

37	CD20	2½r blue grn	2.40	1.25
38	CD21	5r red	2.40	1.25
39	CD22	10r red violet	3.00	1.50
40	CD23	25r yel green	2.75	1.25
41	CD24	50r dk blue	8.50	3.25
42	CD25	75r vio brown	10.00	7.00
43	CD26	100r bister brn	10.00	7.00
44	CD27	150r bister	15.00	11.50
		Nos. 37-44 (8)	54.05	34.00

Nos. 37-44 with "REPUBLICA" overprint and surcharges are listed as Portugal Nos. 199-206.

Ceres — A6

1928, May 1 Engr. *Perf. 13½*
Value Typographed in Black

45	A6	3c deep violet	.30	*.60*
46	A6	4c orange	.30	*.60*
47	A6	5c light blue	.30	*.60*
48	A6	6c brown	.30	*.60*
49	A6	10c red	.30	*.60*
50	A6	15c yel green	.30	*.60*
51	A6	16c red brown	.35	*.60*
52	A6	25c violet rose	.75	.60
53	A6	32c blue grn	.75	.60
54	A6	40c yel brown	1.50	*1.75*
55	A6	50c slate	1.50	*1.75*
56	A6	64c Prus blue	1.50	*3.00*
57	A6	80c dk brown	1.50	*5.00*
58	A6	96c carmine rose	7.50	*3.00*
59	A6	1e black	1.25	3.00
a.		Value omitted	42.50	*45.00*
		Never hinged	75.00	
60	A6	1.20e light rose	1.25	*3.00*
61	A6	1.60e ultra	1.25	*3.00*
62	A6	2.40e yellow	2.00	*3.50*
63	A6	3.36e dull green	3.00	*5.75*
64	A6	4.50e brown red	4.00	*9.00*
65	A6	7e dark blue	5.00	*17.50*
		Nos. 45-65 (21)	34.90	*64.65*

It was obligatory to use these stamps in place of those in regular use on May 1, June 5, July 1 and Dec. 31, 1928, Jan. 1 and 31, May 1 and June 5, 1929. The amount obtained from this sale was donated to a fund for building a museum.

Less than very fine examples sell for much less.

NEWSPAPER STAMP

Numeral of Value — N1

Newspaper Stamp of Portugal Overprinted in Black
Perf. 12½, 13½

1876, July 1 Unwmk.

P1	N1 2½r olive	8.50	4.25
a.	Inverted overprint	30.00	

The reprints have the same papers, gum, perforations and overprint as the reprints of the regular issues.

POSTAL TAX STAMPS

Pombal Commemorative Issue
Common Design Types

1925 Unwmk. Engr. *Perf. 12½*

RA1	CD28 15c gray & black	.60	.65
RA2	CD29 15c gray & black	.60	.65
RA3	CD30 15c gray & black	.60	.65
	Nos. RA1-RA3 (3)	1.80	1.95

POSTAL TAX DUE STAMPS

Pombal Commemorative Issue
Common Design Types

1925 Unwmk. *Perf. 12½*

RAJ1	CD28 30c gray & black	.85	3.50
RAJ2	CD29 30c gray & black	.85	3.50
RAJ3	CD30 30c gray & black	.85	3.50
	Nos. RAJ1-RAJ3 (3)	2.55	10.50

MALAYA

mə-'lā-ə

Federated Malay States

LOCATION — Malay peninsula
GOVT. — British Protectorate
AREA — 27,585 sq. mi.
CAPITAL — Kuala Lumpur

The Federated Malay States consisted of the sultanates of Negri Sembilan, Pahang, Perak and Selangor.

Stamps of the Federated Malay States replaced those of the individual states and were used until 1935, when individual issues were resumed.

100 Cents = 1 Dollar

Catalogue values for unused stamps in this country are for Never Hinged items, beginning with Scott J20 in the postage due section, Scott 128 in Johore, Scott 55 in Kedah, Scott 44 in Kelantan, Scott 1 in Malacca, Scott 36 in Negri Sembilan, Scott 44 in Pahang, Scott 1 in Penang, Scott 99 in Perak, Scott 1 in Perlis, Scott 74 in Selangor, and Scott 47 in Trengganu.

Watermarks

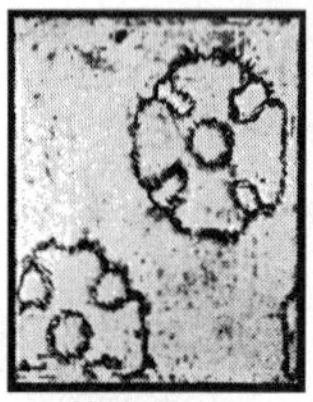
Wmk. 47 — Multiple Rosettes

Wmk. 71 — Rosette

Stamps of Straits Settlements overprinted "BMA MALAYA" are listed in Straits Settlements.

Stamps and Type of Negri Sembilan Overprinted in Black

1900 **Wmk. 2** ***Perf. 14***

1	A2	1c lilac & green	3.50	*8.00*
2	A2	2c lilac & brown	35.00	*75.00*
3	A2	3c lilac & black	3.00	*4.75*
4	A2	5c lilac & olive	80.00	*190.00*
5	A2	10c lilac & org	8.00	*30.00*
6	A2	20c green & olive	100.00	*110.00*
7	A2	25c grn & car rose	250.00	*400.00*
8	A2	50c green & black	100.00	*150.00*
		Nos. 1-8 (8)	579.50	*967.75*
		Set, ovptd. "SPECIMEN"	210.00	

Overprinted on Perak Nos. 51, 53, 57-58, 60-61

1900

9	A9	5c lilac & olive	16.00	*65.00*
10	A9	10c lilac & org	80.00	*75.00*

Wmk. 1

11	A10	$1 green & lt grn	190.00	275.00
12	A10	$2 green & car rose	160.00	275.00
13	A10	$5 green & ultra	400.00	*575.00*
		Revenue cancel		70.00
13A	A10	$25 green & org	*8,750.*	
		Revenue cancel		250.00
		Overprinted "SPECIMEN"	375.00	
		Nos. 9-13 (5)	846.00	*1,265.*

No. 10 with bar omitted is an essay.

Elephants and Howdah — A3

Tiger — A4

Stamps of type A4 are watermarked sideways.

1900 **Typo.**

14	A3	$1 green & lt green	125.	140.
15	A3	$2 grn & car rose	140.	150.
16	A3	$5 green & ultra	250.	300.
a.		$5 green & pale ultramarine	250.	250.
		Revenue cancel		15.
17	A3	$25 grn & orange	2,250.	1,300.
		Revenue cancel		*75.*
		Overprinted "SPECIMEN"	260.	
		Nos. 14-17 (4)	2,765.	1,890.
		Nos. 14-16, ovpted. "SPECIMEN"	160.00	

High values with revenue cancellations are plentiful and inexpensive.

1901 **Wmk. 2**

18	A4	1c blue grn & blk	7.50	7.50
a.		1c green & gray	3.75	1.10
b.		1c green & gray brown	11.00	.40
19	A4	3c brown & gray	6.25	.40
a.		3c brown & black	10.50	4.25
b.		3c brown & gray brown	5.00	.25
20	A4	4c rose & black	18.00	7.00
a.		4c carmine & gray	7.50	4.25
b.		4c carmine & gray brown	25.00	2.75
21	A4	5c scar & grn, *yel*	2.75	3.50
22	A4	8c ultra & blk	50.00	18.00
a.		8c ultramarine & gray	24.00	6.50
b.		8c ultramarine & gray brown	30.00	4.25
23	A4	10c violet & blk	110.00	37.50
a.		10c violet & gray	87.50	8.75
b.		10c purple & black	150.00	35.00
c.		10c purple & gray	92.50	11.50
d.		10c purple & gray brown	95.00	8.00
24	A4	20c black & gray vio	26.00	11.50
25	A4	50c brn org & black	175.00	150.00
a.		50c brown orange & gray	110.00	57.50
b.		50c brown orange & gray brown	100.00	50.00
		Nos. 18-25 (8)	395.50	235.40
		Set, ovptd. "SPECIMEN"	210.00	

1904-10 **Wmk. 3 Sideways**

26	A4	1c green & black	80.00	9.75
a.		1c green & gray brown	40.00	.80
27	A4	3c brown & gray	67.50	1.10
a.		3c brn & gray brn ('05)	45.00	2.00
b.		As "a," chalky paper ('05)	45.00	3.25
28	A4	4c rose & black	5.75	.90
a.		Chalky paper	20.00	2.25
b.		4c scarlet & black	25.00	3.00
c.		4c scarlet & gray brown	40.00	3.75
d.		4c scarlet & gray	47.50	4.00
29	A4	5c scar & grn, *yel*	10.00	2.00
a.		Chalky paper	30.00	5.25
b.		5c carmine & deep green, *yel*	11.50	2.50
c.		5c car & dp grn, *org buff* ('21)	16.00	6.75
d.		5c car & dp grn, *pale yel* ('22)	11.50	5.25
30	A4	8c ultra & black ('05)	80.00	21.00
a.		8c ultra & gr brn ('05)	21.50	4.75
b.		As "a," chalky paper	62.50	15.00
c.		As "b," wmk upright ('07)	9.25	5.50
31	A4	10c violet & black	92.50	5.75
a.		10c claret & gray brown	80.00	6.75
b.		As "a," chalky paper ('05)	97.50	9.75
c.		10c claret & black	27.50	.75
d.		10c purple & gray brown ('05)	80.00	3.75
e.		10c purple & black	27.50	3.25
32	A4	20c blk & gray vio ('05)	11.50	1.50
a.		Chalky paper	15.00	3.50
33	A4	50c brn org & blk ('05)	100.00	17.50
a.		50c orange & gray ('05)	80.00	9.25
b.		50c org brn & gray brn ('06)	52.50	9.25
c.		As "b," chalky paper	57.50	8.75
d.		50c org brn & jet blk ('14)	125.00	10.75
e.		50c orange brown & gray	67.50	9.25

The 1c and 4c are on ordinary paper, the other values on both ordinary and chalky papers.

Chalky Paper

34	A3	$1 green & lt green ('07)	67.50	50.00
35	A3	$2 green & car rose ('06)	85.00	125.00
36	A3	$5 grn & ultra ('06)	190.00	*150.00*
		Revenue cancellation		20.00
37	A3	$25 grn & org ('10)	1,400.	825.00
		Revenue cancellation		40.00
		Nos. 26-36 (11)	789.75	*384.50*

High values with revenue cancellations are plentiful and inexpensive.

1906-22 **Ordinary Paper**

Two dies for Nos. 38 and 44:
I — Thick line under "Malay."
II — Thin line under "Malay."

38	A4	1c dull grn, die II	6.00	.20
b.		Die I	15.00	.55
39	A4	1c brown ('19)	3.50	1.50
40	A4	2c green ('19)	2.50	.55
41	A4	3c brown	10.50	.20
42	A4	3c carmine ('09)	3.50	.20
43	A4	3c dp gray ('19)	2.25	.20
44	A4	4c scar, die II	2.25	.20
b.		Die I ('19)	3.75	5.50
45	A4	6c orange ('19)	3.50	3.00
46	A4	8c ultra ('09)	21.00	1.60
47	A4	10c ultra ('19)	10.50	2.25
48	A4	35c red, *yellow*	9.00	*20.00*
		Nos. 38-48 (11)	74.50	29.90

1922-32 **Wmk. 4**

Ordinary Paper

49	A4	1c brown ('22)	2.75	3.00
50	A4	1c black ('23)	.85	.25
51	A4	2c dk brown ('25)	5.75	3.00
52	A4	2c green ('26)	.95	.20
53	A4	3c dp gray ('23)	4.25	7.00
54	A4	3c green ('24)	3.50	2.75
55	A4	3c brown ('27)	.95	.50
56	A4	4c scar (II) ('23)	3.50	.60
57	A4	4c orange ('26)	.80	.20
c.		Unwatermarked	*475.00*	*300.00*
58	A4	5c vio, *yel* ('22)	1.25	.20
59	A4	5c dk brown ('32)	2.40	.20
60	A4	6c orange ('22)	.80	.55
61	A4	6c scarlet ('26)	1.25	.20
62	A4	10c ultra ('23)	1.90	*7.75*
63	A4	10c ultra & blk ('23)	2.75	.80
64	A4	10c vio, *yel* ('31)	9.00	.55
65	A4	12c ultra ('22)	1.90	.20
66	A4	20c blk & vio ('23)	7.00	.25

Chalky Paper

67	A4	25c red vio & ol vio ('29)	3.50	1.25
68	A4	30c yel & dl vio ('29)	4.75	2.40
69	A4	35c red, *yel* ('28)	9.00	*21.00*
70	A4	35c dk vio & car ('31)	19.00	17.50
71	A4	50c org & blk ('24)	19.00	5.75
72	A4	50c blk, *bl grn* ('31)	6.25	1.90
73	A3	$1 gray grn & yel grn ('26)	19.00	*42.50*
a.		$1 green & blue green	24.00	*60.00*
74	A3	$2 grn & car ('26)	24.00	*87.50*
75	A3	$5 grn & ultra ('25)	95.00	*160.00*
76	A3	$25 grn & org ('28)	1,200.	875.00
		Nos. 49-75 (27)	251.05	*368.00*

#64 is on chalky paper; #66 exists on both ordinary and chalky paper; #69 is on ordinary paper.

1931-34

77	A4	$1 red & blk, *blue*	17.50	4.75
78	A4	$2 car & green, *yel* ('34)	55.00	50.00
79	A4	$5 car & green, *emer* ('34)	225.00	*240.00*
		Nos. 77-79 (3)	297.50	*294.75*

POSTAGE DUE STAMPS

D1

D2

Perf. 14½x14

1924-26 **Typo.** **Wmk. 4**

J1	D1	1c violet	4.25	7.75
J2	D1	2c black	2.50	3.50
J3	D1	4c green ('26)	4.75	*12.00*
J4	D1	8c red	8.75	*19.00*
J5	D1	10c orange	10.00	*17.50*
J6	D1	12c ultramarine	14.50	*25.00*
		Nos. J1-J6 (6)	44.75	*84.75*

1936-38 ***Perf. 14½x14***

J7	D2	1c dk violet ('38)	5.75	1.25
J8	D2	4c yellow green	16.00	1.60
J9	D2	8c scarlet	7.50	*6.25*
J10	D2	10c yel orange	10.00	.55
J11	D2	12c blue violet	12.50	*19.00*
J12	D2	50c black ('38)	40.00	*10.00*
		Nos. J7-J12 (6)	91.75	*38.65*

#J7-J12 were also used in Straits Settlements.

For overprints see #NJ1-NJ20, Malacca #NJ1-NJ6.

1945-49

J13	D2	1c reddish violet	4.00	2.40
J14	D2	3c yel green	9.25	16.00
J15	D2	5c org scarlet	9.25	*19.00*
J16	D2	8c yel org ('49)	25.00	16.00
J17	D2	9c yel orange	77.50	55.00
J18	D2	15c blue vio	225.00	55.00
J19	D2	20c dk blue ('48)	14.50	19.00
		Nos. J13-J19 (7)	364.50	182.40

For surcharge see No. J34.

Catalogue values for unused stamps in this section, from this point to the end of the section, are for Never Hinged items.

1951-62 **Wmk. 4** ***Perf. 14***

J20	D2	1c dull violet ('52)	.35	1.60
J21	D2	2c dk gray ('53)	.85	2.10
J22	D2	3c green ('52)	22.50	12.00
J23	D2	4c dk brown ('53)	.45	4.50
J24	D2	5c vermilion	47.50	12.00
J25	D2	8c yel orange	2.25	4.25
J26	D2	12c magenta ('54)	1.10	6.00
J27	D2	20c deep blue	3.50	6.25
		Nos. J20-J27 (8)	78.50	48.70

Nos. J13-J27 were used throughout the Federation and in Singapore, later in Malaysia.

1957-62 ***Perf. 12½***

J21a	D2	2c ('60)	.50	*12.00*
J23a	D2	4c ('60)	.95	*16.00*
J26a	D2	12c ('62)	2.25	*26.00*
J27a	D2	20c	8.25	*32.50*
		Nos. J21a-J27a (4)	11.95	*86.50*

OCCUPATION STAMPS

Issued Under Japanese Occupation

Malayan Fruit and Fronds
OS1

Tin Dredging
OS2

Monument to Japanese War Dead
OS3

Malayan Plowman
OS4

1943 **Unwmk.** **Litho.** ***Perf. 12½***

N30	OS1	2c emerald	.20	.20
a.		Rouletted	1.75	1.75
b.		Imperf., pair	5.00	5.00
N31	OS2	4c rose red	.25	.20
a.		Rouletted	1.75	1.75
b.		Imperf., pair	5.00	5.00
N32	OS3	8c dull blue	.20	.20
		Nos. N30-N32 (3)	.65	.60

1943, Sept. 1

N33	OS4	8c violet	8.50	3.25
N34	OS4	15c carmine red	7.50	3.25

Publicity for Postal Savings which had reached a $10,000,000 total in Malaya.

Rubber Tapping
OS5

Seaside Houses
OS6

Japanese Shrine, Singapore
OS7

Sago Palms
OS8

Johore Bahru and Strait of Johore
OS9

Malay Mosque, Kuala Lumpur
OS10

1943, Oct. 1

N35	OS5	1c gray green	.30	.60
N36	OS5	3c olive gray	.30	.25
N37	OS6	10c red brown	.30	.25
N38	OS7	15c violet	.55	1.50
N39	OS8	30c olive green	.55	.55
N40	OS9	50c blue	1.25	1.25
N41	OS10	70c dull blue	17.00	14.00
		Nos. N35-N41 (7)	20.25	18.40

Rice Planting and Map of Malaysia — OS11

1944, Feb. 15

N42	OS11	8c carmine	7.50	3.50
N43	OS11	15c violet	4.50	3.50

Issued on the anniversary of the fall of Singapore to commemorate the "Birth of New Malaya".

OCCUPATION POSTAGE DUE STAMPS

Stamps and Type of Postage Due Stamps of 1936-38 Handstamped in Black, Red or Brown

1942 Wmk. 4 *Perf. 14½x14*

NJ1	D2	1c violet	11.50	*20.00*
NJ2	D2	3c yellow green	47.50	*52.50*
NJ3	D2	4c yellow green	32.50	25.00
NJ4	D2	8c red	65.00	55.00
NJ5	D2	10c yellow orange	21.00	*32.50*
NJ6	D2	12c blue violet	21.00	*40.00*
NJ7	D2	50c black	52.50	*65.00*
		Nos. NJ1-NJ7 (7)	251.00	290.00

Overprinted in Black

DAI NIPPON
2602
MALAYA

1942

NJ8	D2	1c violet	1.50	*8.00*
NJ9	D2	3c yel green	11.00	*16.00*
NJ10	D2	4c yel green	10.00	*10.50*
NJ11	D2	8c red	14.00	*14.50*
NJ12	D2	10c yel orange	1.50	*10.50*
NJ13	D2	12c blue violet	1.50	*22.50*
		Nos. NJ8-NJ13 (6)	39.50	82.00

The 9c and 15c with this overprint were not regularly issued.

Postage Due Stamps of 1936-45 Overprinted

1943

NJ14	D2	1c reddish vio	1.00	*3.00*
NJ15	D2	3c yel green	1.00	*3.00*
NJ15A	D2	4c yel green	37.50	*40.00*
NJ16	D2	5c scarlet	1.00	*3.75*
NJ17	D2	9c yel orange	.70	*5.25*
NJ18	D2	10c yel orange	.80	*5.25*
NJ19	D2	12c blue violet	1.25	*10.50*
NJ20	D2	15c blue violet	1.25	*5.25*
		Nos. NJ14-NJ20 (8)	44.50	76.00

#NJ15A is said to have been extensively forged.

ISSUED UNDER THAI OCCUPATION

For use in Kedah, Kelantan, Perlis and Trengganu

War Memorial — OS1

Perf. 12½

1943, Dec. Unwmk. Litho.

2N1	OS1	1c pale yellow	32.50	*35.00*
2N2	OS1	2c buff	12.50	*22.50*
2N3	OS1	3c pale green	21.00	*40.00*
	a.	Imperf., pair	750.00	
2N4	OS1	4c dull lilac	15.00	*30.00*
2N5	OS1	8c rose	15.00	*22.50*
2N6	OS1	15c lt blue	40.00	*65.00*
		Nos. 2N1-2N6 (6)	136.00	*215.00*

These stamps, in cent denominations, were for use only in the four Malayan states ceded to Thailand by the Japanese. The states reverted to British rule in September, 1945.

JOHORE

jə-'hōr

LOCATION — At the extreme south of the Malay Peninsula.
AREA — 7,330 sq. mi.
POP. — 1,009,649 (1960)
CAPITAL — Johore Bahru

Stamps of the Straits Settlements Overprinted in Black

Overprinted 

1876 Wmk. 1 *Perf. 14*

1	A2 2c brown	11,500.	5,000.
b.	Double overprint		—

Overprinted 

Overprint 13 to 14mm Wide

1884-86 Wmk. 2

1A	A2 2c rose	200.00	*210.00*
c.	Double overprint	1,150.	

Without Period

Overprint 16¾x2mm ("H" & "E" wide)

2	A2 2c rose	1,600.	625.00
a.	Double overprint		1,850.
b.	"J" raised	1,600.	625.00
c.	As "b," double overprint	3,500.	1,850.
d.	"H" & "E" narrow, ovpt. 16mm	1,950.	750.00
e.	As "d," double overprint	—	—
f.	All ovpt. letters narrow	*5,500.*	

Overprinted 

Overprint 11x2½mm

3	A2 2c rose ('86)	100.00	*110.00*

Overprinted JOHORE

Overprint 17½x2¾mm

4	A2 2c rose ('85)	*2,900.*	—

Overprinted 

Overprint 12½ to 15x2¾mm

5	A2 2c rose	12.50	*20.00*
a.	"H" wide ('85)	100.00	100.00

Overprinted 

Overprint 9x2½mm

6	A2 2c brown		
7	A2 2c rose ('86)	65.00	*65.00*
a.	Double overprint	875.00	

Overprinted 

Overprint 9x3mm

8	A2 2c rose ('86)	45.00	47.50

Overprinted 

Overprint 14 to 15x3mm

9	A2 2c rose	12.50	8.75
a.	2c bright rose ('90)	12.50	*12.50*

Tall "J" 3½mm high

10	A2 2c rose	140.00	125.00
a.	2c bright rose ('90)	150.00	135.00

Overprinted 

1888

Overprint 15 to 15½x3mm

11	A2 2c rose	150.00	65.00
a.	Tall "J" in "Johor"	750.00	400.00
b.	Double overprint	800.00	

Overprinted 

1890-91

Overprint 12½ to 13x2½mm

12	A2 2c rose	16.00	16.00

Overprint 12x2¾mm

13	A2 2c rose ('91)	*8,750.*	

Surcharged in Black:

a

b

c

d

1891

14	A3(a) 2c on 24c green	45.00	*65.00*
15	A3(b) 2c on 24c green	150.00	150.00
a.	Thin, narrow "J"	425.00	425.00
16	A3(c) 2c on 24c green	29.00	45.00
a.	"CENST"	975.00	500.00
17	A3(d) 2c on 24c green	140.00	140.00
	Nos. 14-17 (4)	364.00	400.00

Sultan Abubakar — A5

1891-94 Typo. Unwmk.

18	A5	1c lilac & vio ('94)	.60	.60
19	A5	2c lilac & yellow	.60	*1.75*
20	A5	3c lilac & car rose ('94)	.65	.60
21	A5	4c lilac & black	3.25	*18.00*
22	A5	5c lilac & green	8.00	*24.00*
23	A5	6c lilac & blue	9.25	*24.00*
24	A5	$1 green & car rose	87.50	*190.00*
		Nos. 18-24 (7)	109.85	*258.95*

For surcharges and overprints see #26-36.

Stamps of 1892-94 Surcharged in Black

1894

26	A5	3c on 4c lilac & blk	3.00	.65
a.		No period after "Cents"	92.50	75.00
27	A5	3c on 5c lilac & grn	2.00	3.75
a.		No period after "Cents"	110.00	150.00
28	A5	3c on 6c lilac & bl	3.50	4.25
a.		No period after "Cents"	175.00	200.00
29	A5	3c on $1 green & car	11.50	75.00
a.		No period after "Cents"	425.00	750.00
		Nos. 26-29 (4)	20.00	83.65

Coronation Issue

Stamps of 1892-94 Overprinted "KEMAHKOTAAN"

1896

30	A5	1c lilac & violet	.70	1.25
31	A5	2c lilac & yellow	.60	1.40
32	A5	3c lilac & car rose	1.60	1.40
33	A5	4c lilac & black	1.40	3.00
34	A5	5c lilac & green	7.75	10.00
35	A5	6c lilac & blue	7.25	*8.75*
36	A5	$1 green & car rose	55.00	100.00
		Nos. 30-36 (7)	74.30	125.80

Overprinted "KETAHKOTAAN"

30a	A5	1c	4.25	*5.50*
31a	A5	2c	2.40	*5.50*
32a	A5	3c	6.25	*9.25*
33a	A5	4c	4.00	*9.25*
34a	A5	5c	5.00	*10.50*
35a	A5	6c	5.50	*8.75*
36a	A5	$1	42.50	*110.00*
		Nos. 30a-36a (7)	69.90	*158.75*

Coronation of Sultan Ibrahim.

Sultan Ibrahim — A7

1896-99 Typo. Wmk. 71

37	A7	1c green	.95	.60
38	A7	2c green & blue	.55	.50
39	A7	3c green & vio	1.60	1.10
40	A7	4c green & car rose	.60	.70
41	A7	4c yel & red ('99)	1.00	.70
42	A7	5c green & brn	1.00	1.90
43	A7	6c green & yel	1.10	2.75
44	A7	10c green & black	10.50	*55.00*
45	A7	25c green & vio	11.50	*42.50*
46	A7	50c grn & car rose	21.00	*55.00*
47	A7	$1 lilac & green	30.00	*77.50*
48	A7	$2 lilac & car rose	30.00	*77.50*
49	A7	$3 lilac & blue	40.00	*110.00*
50	A7	$4 lilac & brn	42.50	*92.50*
51	A7	$5 lilac & orange	92.50	*140.00*
		Nos. 37-51 (15)	284.80	*658.25*

On Nos. 44-46 the numerals are on white tablets. Numerals of Nos. 48-51 are on tablets of solid color.

Stamps of 1896-1926 with revenue cancellations sell for a fraction of those used postally.

For surcharges see Nos. 52-58.

Nos. 40-41 Surcharged in Black

1903

52	A7	3c on 4c yel & red	1.25	1.25
a.		Without bars	4.00	*6.50*
53	A7	10c on 4c grn & car rose	3.50	4.75
a.		Without bars	35.00	*55.00*

Bars on Nos. 52-53 were handruled with pen and ink.

Surcharged

54	A7	50c on $3 lilac & blue	35.00	*87.50*

Surcharged

55	A7	$1 on $2 lilac & car rose	75.00	*140.00*
a.		Inverted "e" in "one"	1,600.	

Surcharged

1904

56	A7	10c on 4c yel & red	29.00	42.50
a.		Double surcharge	*9,800.*	
57	A7	10c on 4c grn & car rose	10.50	*40.00*
58	A7	50c on $5 lil & org	65.00	125.00
		Nos. 56-58 (3)	104.50	207.50

Sultan Ibrahim — A8

The 10c, 21c, 25c, 50c, and $10 to $500 denominations of type A8 show the numerals on white tablets. The numerals of the 8c, 30c, 40c, and $2 to $5 demoninations are shown on tablets of solid colors.

1904-08 Typo. Wmk. 71

59	A8	1c violet & green	.80	.20
60	A8	2c violet & brn org	1.50	2.40
61	A8	3c violet & black	1.50	.25
62	A8	4c violet & red	9.25	1.50
63	A8	5c violet & ol grn	1.10	3.00
64	A8	8c violet & blue	3.00	6.25
65	A8	10c violet & black	40.00	11.00
66	A8	25c violet & green	4.00	*24.00*
67	A8	50c violet & red	40.00	17.50
68	A8	$1 green & vio	19.00	*72.50*
69	A8	$2 green & car	27.50	*62.50*
70	A8	$3 green & blue	325.00	*87.50*
71	A8	$4 green & brn	35.00	*125.00*
72	A8	$5 green & org	47.50	*100.00*
73	A8	$10 green & blk	65.00	*150.00*
74	A8	$50 green & blue	*225.00*	*300.00*
75	A8	$100 green & scar	*425.00*	*625.00*
		Revenue cancel		47.50
		Nos. 59-73 (15)	620.15	*663.60*

The 1c, 2c and 10c also exist on chalky paper.

Nos. 74 and 75 were theoretically available for postage but were mostly used for revenue purposes.

For surcharge see No. 86.

1910-18 Wmk. 47

Chalky Paper

76	A8	1c violet & green	.25	.20
77	A8	2c violet & orange	5.50	.80
78	A8	3c violet & black	4.00	.80
79	A8	4c violet & red	3.00	.95
80	A8	5c violet & ol grn	2.75	.80
81	A8	8c violet & blue	5.00	5.50
82	A8	10c violet & black	30.00	3.00
83	A8	25c violet & green	5.50	*27.50*
84	A8	50c violet & red	72.50	*92.50*
85	A8	$1 green & vio	77.50	*87.50*
		Nos. 76-85 (10)	206.00	*219.55*

#78-79, 82 exist with horizontal watermark.

No. 64 Surcharged

1912 Wmk. 71

86	A8	3c on 8c vio & blue	2.40	4.75
a.		"T" of "CENTS" omitted	475.00	

1918-19 Typo. Wmk. 3

Chalky Paper

87	A8	2c violet & orange	.95	1.90
88	A8	2c violet & grn ('19)	.60	.85
89	A8	4c violet & red	.70	.20
90	A8	5c vio & olive grn ('19)	1.90	2.75
91	A8	10c violet & blue	1.90	1.90
92	A8	21c violet & orange	3.50	5.50
93	A8	25c vio & grn ('19)	10.00	19.00
94	A8	50c vio & red ('19)	24.00	40.00
95	A8	$1 grn & red vio	14.00	55.00
96	A8	$2 green & scar	30.00	55.00
97	A8	$3 green & blue	35.00	92.50
98	A8	$4 green & brn	55.00	125.00
99	A8	$5 green & org	72.50	125.00
100	A8	$10 green & blk	150.00	*240.00*
		Nos. 87-100 (14)	400.05	*764.60*

1921-40 Wmk. 4

101	A8	1c violet & black	.20	.20
102	A8	2c violet & brn	.85	1.60
103	A8	2c green & dk grn ('28)	.20	.20
104	A8	3c green ('25)	2.25	4.25
105	A8	3c dull vio & brn ('28)	1.40	1.50
106	A8	4c vio & red	2.25	.20
107	A8	5c vio & ol grn	.50	.20
108	A8	6c vio & red brown	.25	.20
109	A8	10c vio & blue	24.00	40.00
110	A8	10c vio & yel ('22)	.50	.20
111	A8	12c vio & blue	1.50	1.90
111A	A8	12c ultra ('40)	42.50	7.75
112	A8	21c dull vio & org ('28)	3.50	3.50
113	A8	25c vio & green	4.25	1.25
114	A8	30c dull vio & org ('36)	3.50	3.00
115	A8	40c dull vio & brn ('36)	3.50	*5.00*
116	A8	50c violet & red	3.50	1.50
117	A8	$1 grn & red violet	3.50	1.10
118	A8	$2 grn & red	7.75	5.50
119	A8	$3 grn & blue	55.00	72.50
120	A8	$4 grn & brn ('26)	92.50	150.00
121	A8	$5 grn & org	62.50	*72.50*
122	A8	$10 grn & blk	190.00	*240.00*
123	A8	$50 grn & ultra	775.00	
124	A8	$100 grn & red	1,900.	
125	A8	$500 ultra & org brn ('26)	*26,500.*	
		Revenue cancel		190.00
		Nos. 101-122 (23)	505.90	*614.05*

Nos. 123, 124 and 125 were available for postage but were probably used only fiscally.

A9

A10

1935, May 15 Engr. *Perf. 12½*

126	A9	8c Sultan Ibrahim, Sultana	5.00	1.50

1940, Feb. *Perf. 13½*

127	A10	8c Sultan Ibrahim	12.00	.25

Catalogue values for unused stamps in this section, from this point to the end of the section, are for Never Hinged items.

Silver Wedding Issue

Common Design Types

Inscribed: "Malaya Johore"

Perf. 14x14½

1948, Dec. 1 Wmk. 4 Photo.

128	CD304	10c purple	.20	.20

Perf. 11½x11

Engr.; Name Typo.

129	CD305	$5 green	32.50	47.50

Common Design Types Pictured following the introduction.

Sultan Ibrahim — A11

1949-55 Wmk. 4 Typo. *Perf. 18*

130	A11	1c black	.40	.25
131	A11	2c orange	.40	.25
132	A11	3c green	1.10	.60
133	A11	4c chocolate	.40	.25
134	A11	5c rose vio ('52)	.50	.25
135	A11	6c gray	.65	.25
a.		Wmk. 4a (error)	425.00	
136	A11	8c rose red	2.10	1.50
137	A11	8c green ('52)	1.10	1.75
138	A11	10c plum	.65	.25
a.		Imperf., pair	*850.00*	
139	A11	12c rose red ('52)	1.25	3.25
140	A11	15c ultra	2.10	.85
141	A11	20c dk grn & blk	2.10	1.10
142	A11	20c ultra ('52)	1.40	.35
143	A11	25c org & rose lil	1.60	.25
144	A11	30c plum & rose red ('55)	4.25	2.75
145	A11	35c dk vio & rose red ('52)	3.25	2.50
146	A11	40c dk vio & rose red	4.00	8.00
147	A11	50c ultra & blk	3.00	.35
148	A11	$1 vio brn & ultra	5.75	2.25
149	A11	$2 rose red & emer	21.00	7.25
150	A11	$5 choc & emer	42.50	15.00
		Nos. 130-150 (21)	99.50	49.25

UPU Issue

Common Design Types

Inscribed: "Malaya-Johore"

Engr.; Name Typo. on 15c, 25c

1949, Oct. 10 *Perf. 13½, 11x11½*

151	CD306	10c rose violet	.45	.20
152	CD307	15c indigo	1.25	1.00
153	CD308	25c orange	.90	1.60
154	CD309	50c slate	1.60	2.25
		Nos. 151-154 (4)	4.20	5.05

POSTAGE DUE STAMPS

D1

Perf. 12½

1938, Jan. 1 Typo. Wmk. 4

J1	D1	1c rose red	10.50	*40.00*
J2	D1	4c green	40.00	*50.00*
J3	D1	8c dull yellow	42.50	*160.00*
J4	D1	10c bister brown	42.50	*62.50*
J5	D1	12c rose violet	62.50	*150.00*
		Nos. J1-J5 (5)	198.00	*462.50*

OCCUPATION POSTAGE DUE STAMPS

Issued under Japanese Occupation

Johore Nos. J1-J5 Overprinted in Black, Brown or Red

1942 Wmk. 4 *Perf. 12½*

NJ1	D1	1c rose red	55.00	90.00
NJ2	D1	4c green	72.50	90.00
NJ3	D1	8c dull yellow	85.00	100.00

NJ4	D1	10c bister brown	20.00	60.00
NJ5	D1	12c rose violet	32.50	60.00
		Nos. NJ1-NJ5 (5)	265.00	400.00

Johore Nos. J1-J5 Overprinted in Black

1943

NJ6	D1	1c rose red	2.50	13.00
NJ7	D1	4c green	2.50	13.00
NJ8	D1	8c dull yellow	9.00	16.00
NJ9	D1	10c bister brown	6.50	20.00
NJ10	D1	12c rose violet	6.50	26.00
		Nos. NJ6-NJ10 (5)	27.00	88.00

Nos. NJ6-NJ10 exist with second character sideways.

KEDAH

'ke-də

LOCATION — On the west coast of the Malay Peninsula.
AREA — 3,660 sq. mi.
POP. — 752,706 (1960)
CAPITAL — Alor Star

Sheaf of Rice — A1

Native Plowing — A2

Council Chamber — A3

1912-21 Engr. Wmk. 3 *Perf. 14*

1	A1	1c green & black	.70	.30
2	A1	1c brown ('19)	.65	.55
3	A1	2c green ('19)	.60	.35
4	A1	3c car & black	5.25	.35
5	A1	3c dk violet ('19)	.75	1.10
6	A1	4c slate & car	11.50	.30
7	A1	4c scarlet ('19)	4.50	.25
8	A1	5c org brown & grn	2.50	3.50
9	A1	8c ultra & blk	4.50	4.00
10	A2	10c black brn & bl	2.50	1.00
11	A2	20c yel grn & blk	5.50	4.75
12	A2	21c red vio & vio ('19)	6.50	65.00
13	A2	25c red vio & bl ('21)	2.00	27.50
14	A2	30c car & black	3.50	12.50
15	A2	40c lilac & blk	4.00	16.00
16	A2	50c dull bl & brn	10.50	15.00
17	A3	$1 scar & blk, *yel*	18.00	25.00
18	A3	$2 dk brn & dk grn	25.00	100.00
19	A3	$3 dk bl & blk, *bl*	85.00	200.00
20	A3	$5 car & black	85.00	190.00
		Nos. 1-20 (20)	278.45	667.45
		Set, ovptd. "SPECIMEN"	525.00	

There are two types of No. 7, one printed from separate plates for frame and center, the other printed from a single plate.
Overprints are listed after No. 45.

Stamps of 1912 Surcharged

1919

21	A3	50c on $2 dk brn & dk grn	80.00	85.00
a.		"C" of ovpt. inserted by hand	1,350.	1,500.
22	A3	$1 on $3 dk bl & blk, *blue*	22.50	100.00

1921-36 Wmk. 4

Two types of 1c:
I — The 1's have rounded corners, small top serif. Small letters "c."
II — The 1's have square-cut corners, large top serif. Large letters "c."

Two types of 2c:
I — The 2's have oval drops. Letters "c" are fairly thick and rounded.
II — The 2's have round drops. Letters "c" thin and slightly larger.

23	A1	1c brown	.60	.20
24	A1	1c blk (I) ('22)	.25	.20
a.		1c black (II) ('39)	42.50	6.50
25	A1	2c green (I)	.70	.20
a.		2c green (II) ('40)	90.00	13.00
26	A1	3c dk violet	1.10	.95
27	A1	3c green ('22)	1.90	1.10
28	A1	4c carmine	7.00	.20
29	A1	4c dull vio ('26)	1.25	.20
30	A1	5c yellow ('22)	1.90	.20
31	A1	6c scarlet ('26)	.95	.90
32	A1	8c gray ('36)	12.50	.20
33	A2	10c blk brn & bl	2.40	1.10
34	A2	12c dk ultra & blk ('26)	3.00	5.75
35	A2	20c green & blk	3.50	3.00
36	A2	21c red vio & vio	3.00	18.00
37	A2	25c red vio & bl	3.00	5.75
38	A2	30c red & blk ('22)	4.00	4.00
39	A2	35c claret ('26)	7.00	35.00
40	A2	40c red vio & blk	4.00	30.00
41	A2	50c dp blue & brn	3.00	6.50
42	A3	$1 scar & blk, *yel* ('22)	9.00	10.50
43	A3	$2 brn & green	18.00	100.00
44	A3	$3 dk bl & blk, *bl*	50.00	77.50
45	A3	$5 car & black	65.00	150.00
		Nos. 23-45 (23)	203.05	451.45

For overprints see Nos. N1-N6.

Stamps of 1912-21 Overprinted in Black: "MALAYA-BORNEO EXHIBITION." in Three Lines

1922 Wmk. 3

3a	A1	2c green	9.25	27.50
12a	A2	21c red vio & vio	32.50	110.00
13a	A2	25c red vio & blue	32.50	125.00
b.		Inverted overprint	1,200.	
16a	A2	50c dull blue & brn	35.00	150.00

Wmk. 4

23a	A1	1c brown	3.25	22.50
26a	A1	3c dark violet	4.75	42.50
28a	A1	4c carmine	4.75	42.50
33a	A2	10c blk brn & blue	9.25	57.50
		Nos. 3a-33a (8)	131.25	577.50

Industrial fair at Singapore, Mar. 31-Apr. 15, 1922.
On Nos. 12a, 13a and 16a, "BORNEO" exists both 14mm and 15mm wide.

Sultan of Kedah, Sir Abdul Hamid Halim Shah — A4

1937, July Wmk. 4 *Perf. 12½*

46	A4	10c sepia & ultra	3.25	.60
47	A4	12c gray vio & blk	27.50	14.50
48	A4	25c brn vio & ultra	9.00	5.50
49	A4	30c dp car & yel grn	10.00	11.50
50	A4	40c brn vio & blk	3.25	16.00
51	A4	50c dp blue & sepia	4.75	5.50
52	A4	$1 dk green & blk	3.50	12.00
53	A4	$2 dk brn & yel grn	125.00	95.00
54	A4	$5 dp car & black	42.50	100.00
		Nos. 46-54 (9)	228.75	260.60

For overprints see Nos. N7-N15.

Catalogue values for unused stamps in this section, from this point to the end of the section, are for Never Hinged items.

Silver Wedding Issue
Common Design Types
Inscribed: "Malaya Kedah"

1948, Dec. 1 Photo. *Perf. 14x14½*

55	CD304	10c purple	.20	.25

Perf. 11½x11

Engraved; Name Typographed

56	CD305	$5 rose car	35.00	45.00

UPU Issue
Common Design Types
Inscribed: "Malaya-Kedah"

Engr.; Name Typo. on 15c, 25c

1949, Oct. 10 *Perf. 13½, 11x11½*

57	CD306	10c rose violet	.20	.20
58	CD307	15c indigo	1.60	1.40
59	CD308	25c orange	.95	1.40
60	CD309	50c slate	1.50	2.00
		Nos. 57-60 (4)	4.25	5.00

Sheaf of Rice A5

Sultan Tungku Badlishah A6

1950-55 Wmk. 4 Typo. *Perf. 18*

61	A5	1c black	.30	.20
62	A5	2c orange	.30	.20
63	A5	3c green	.70	.55
64	A5	4c chocolate	.30	.20
65	A5	5c rose vio ('52)	.30	.20
66	A5	6c gray	.30	.20
67	A5	8c rose red	1.00	1.75
68	A5	8c green ('52)	.70	1.75
69	A5	10c plum	.30	.20
70	A5	12c rose red ('52)	.55	3.75
71	A5	15c ultramarine	2.10	1.25
72	A5	20c dk green & blk	2.10	3.75
73	A5	20c ultra ('52)	.90	.30
74	A6	25c org & rose lilac	1.10	.65
75	A6	30c plum & rose red ('55)	4.50	1.25
76	A6	35c dk vio & rose red ('52)	1.40	2.40
77	A6	40c dk vio & rose red	2.75	8.50
78	A6	50c ultra & black	1.50	.20
79	A6	$1 yel brown & ultra	10.50	2.40
80	A6	$2 rose red & emer	37.50	32.50
81	A6	$5 choc & emerald	50.00	42.50
		Nos. 61-81 (21)	119.10	104.70

Issued Under Japanese Occupation

Stamps of Kedah 1922-36, Overprinted in Red or Black

1942, May 13 Wmk. 4 *Perf. 14*

N1	A1	1c black (R)	2.40	2.75
N2	A1	2c green (R)	40.00	55.00
N3	A1	4c dull violet (R)	3.25	4.00
N4	A1	5c yellow (R)	3.00	4.00
a.		Black overprint	350.00	400.00
N5	A1	6c scarlet (Bk)	2.40	4.75
N6	A1	8c gray (R)	3.75	3.75

Nos. 46 to 54 Overprinted in Red

Perf. 12½

N7	A4	10c sepia & ultra	6.75	7.50
N8	A4	12c gray vio & blk	17.50	20.00
N9	A4	25c brn vio & ultra	8.75	11.00
a.		Black overprint	140.00	140.00
N10	A4	30c dp car & yel grn	80.00	87.50
N11	A4	40c brn vio & blk	35.00	40.00
N12	A4	50c dp blue & sep	35.00	35.00
N13	A4	$1 dk grn & blk	160.00	160.00
a.		Inverted overprint	350.00	350.00
N14	A4	$2 dk brn & yel green	275.00	190.00
N15	A4	$5 dp car & blk	125.00	125.00
a.		Black overprint	300.00	300.00
		Nos. N1-N15 (15)	797.80	750.25

KELANTAN

kə-'lan-ˌtan

LOCATION — On the eastern coast of the Malay Peninsula.
AREA — 5,750 sq. mi.
POP. — 545,620 (1960)
CAPITAL — Kota Bharu

Symbols of Government — A1

1911-15 Typo. Wmk. 3 *Perf. 14*

Ordinary Paper

1	A1	1c gray green	7.00	1.00
a.		1c green	5.50	.35
2	A1	3c rose red	5.00	.20
3	A1	4c black & red	1.75	.20
4	A1	5c grn & red, *yel*	11.50	1.00
5	A1	8c ultramarine	6.25	1.25
6	A1	10c black & violet	35.00	.90

Chalky Paper

7	A1	30c violet & red	12.50	3.00
8	A1	50c black & org	9.25	3.00
9	A1	$1 green & emer	55.00	55.00
10	A1	$1 grn & brn ('15)	55.00	2.20
11	A1	$2 grn & car rose	1.75	4.75
12	A1	$5 green & ultra	4.75	8.75
13	A1	$25 green & org	50.00	92.50
		Nos. 1-13 (13)	254.75	173.75
		Set, ovptd. "SPECIMEN"	325.00	

For overprints see listings after No. 26. For surcharges see Nos. N20-N22.

1921-28 Wmk. 4

Ordinary Paper

14	A1	1c green	6.50	.90
15	A1	1c black ('23)	.70	.70
16	A1	2c brown	6.50	5.75
17	A1	2c green ('26)	1.50	.60
18	A1	3c brown ('27)	4.00	2.25
19	A1	4c black & red	1.25	.20
20	A1	5c grn & red, *yel*	1.10	.20
21	A1	6c claret	3.50	3.00
22	A1	6c rose red ('28)	6.00	8.00
23	A1	10c black & violet	3.00	.20

Chalky Paper

24	A1	30c dull vio & red ('26)	6.00	8.00
25	A1	50c black & orange	7.25	57.50
26	A1	$1 green & brown	42.50	90.00
		Nos. 14-26 (13)	89.80	177.30

Stamps of 1911-21 Overprinted in Black: "MALAYA BORNEO EXHIBITION" in Three Lines

1922 Wmk. 3

3a	A1	4c black & red	4.50	42.50
4a	A1	5c green & red, *yel*	7.00	45.00
7a	A1	30c violet & red	9.00	80.00
8a	A1	50c black & orange	11.50	90.00
10a	A1	$1 green & brown	35.00	125.00
11a	A1	$2 green & car rose	90.00	225.00
12a	A1	$5 green & ultra	225.00	550.00

Wmk. 4

14a	A1	1c green	3.25	42.50
23a	A1	10c black & violet	7.75	72.50
		Nos. 3a-23a (9)	393.00	1,272.

Industrial fair at Singapore. Mar. 31-Apr. 15, 1922.

Sultan Ismail
A2 A2a

1928-33 Engr. *Perf. 12*

Size: 21½x30mm

27	A2	$1 ultramarine	14.00	35.00

Perf. 14

28	A2	$1 blue ('33)	50.00	47.50

1937-40 *Perf. 12*

Size: 22½x34½mm

29	A2a	1c yel & ol green	.20	.65
30	A2a	2c deep green	1.50	.20
31	A2a	4c brick red	3.00	.80
32	A2a	5c red brown	3.00	.20
33	A2a	6c car lake	7.75	5.75
34	A2a	8c gray green	3.00	.20
35	A2a	10c dark violet	14.50	4.00
36	A2a	12c deep blue	1.90	6.00
37	A2a	25c vio & red org	3.00	5.50
38	A2a	30c scar & dk vio	27.50	24.00
39	A2a	40c blue grn & org	5.75	32.50
40	A2a	50c org & ol grn	35.00	7.25

41	A2a	$1 dp grn & dk violet	32.50	*18.00*
42	A2a	$2 red & red brn ('40)	275.00	*275.00*
43	A2a	$5 rose lake & org ('40)	450.00	*650.00*
		Nos. 29-43 (15)	863.60	*1,030.*

For overprints see Nos. N1-N19.

Catalogue values for unused stamps in this section, from this point to the end of the section, are for Never Hinged items.

Silver Wedding Issue
Common Design Types
Inscribed: "Malaya Kelantan"
Perf. 14x14½

1948, Dec. 1 Wmk. 4 Photo.

44	CD304	10c purple	.30	.40

Perf. 11½x11
Engraved; Name Typographed

45	CD305	$5 rose car	35.00	*65.00*

Common Design Types pictured following the introduction.

UPU Issue
Common Design Types
Inscribed: "Malaya-Kelantan"
Engr.; Name Typo. on 15c, 25c
1949, Oct. 10 *Perf. 13½, 11x11½*

46	CD306	10c rose violet	.40	.40
47	CD307	15c indigo	1.60	.80
48	CD308	25c orange	.65	2.00
49	CD309	50c slate	1.50	2.00
		Nos. 46-49 (4)	4.15	5.20

Sultan Ibrahim — A3

Perf. 18
1951, July 11 Wmk. 4 Typo.

50	A3	1c black	.25	.30
51	A3	2c orange	.75	.30
52	A3	3c green	4.75	1.60
53	A3	4c chocolate	.25	.25
54	A3	6c gray	.25	.25
55	A3	8c rose red	1.10	*3.75*
56	A3	10c plum	.25	.25
57	A3	15c ultramarine	4.00	.75
58	A3	20c dk green & blk	.70	5.50
59	A3	25c orange & plum	.80	.75
60	A3	40c vio brn & rose red	6.25	12.00
61	A3	50c dp ultra & blk	1.60	.45
62	A3	$1 vio brown & ultra	9.50	4.75
63	A3	$2 rose red & emer	35.00	26.00
64	A3	$5 choc & emer	75.00	55.00

1952-55

65	A3	5c rose violet	.70	.50
66	A3	8c green	1.10	*2.40*
67	A3	12c rose red	1.10	*3.25*
68	A3	20c ultramarine	1.25	*.25*
69	A3	30c plum & rose red ('55)	1.90	2.40
70	A3	35c dk vio & rose red	1.40	*1.90*
		Nos. 50-70 (21)	147.90	122.60

Compare with Pahang A8, Perak A16, Selangor A15, Trengganu A5.

Issued Under Japanese Occupation

Kelantan No. 35 Handstamped in Black

1942 Wmk. 4 *Perf. 12*

N1	A2a	10c dark violet	400.00	500.00

Some authorities believe No. N1 was not regularly issued.

Kelantan Nos. 29-40 Surcharged in Black or Red and Handstamped with Oval Seal "a" in Red

1 Cents

Sunakawa — a

Handa — b

1942

N2	1c on 50c org & ol green	200.00	200.00
a.	With "b" seal	65.00	65.00
N3	2c on 40c bl grn & orange	350.00	350.00
a.	With "b" seal	55.00	65.00
N4	5c on 12c dp bl (R)	200.00	200.00
N5	8c on 5c red brn (R)	225.00	225.00
a.	With "b" seal (R)	160.00	190.00
N6	10c on 6c car lake	95.00	150.00
a.	With "b" seal	95.00	150.00
N7	12c on 8c gray green (R)	60.00	140.00
N8	30c on 4c brick red	1,100.	1,200.
N9	40c on 2c dp grn (R)	60.00	100.00
N10	50c on 1c yel & ol green	850.00	800.00

Kelantan Nos. 29-40, 19-20, 22 Surcharged in Black or Red and Handstamped with Oval Seal "a" in Red

2 CENTS

N10A	1c on 50c org & ol green	125.00	110.00
N11	2c on 40c bl grn & orange	125.00	125.00
N11A	4c on 30c scar & dark vio	1,200.	1,200.
N12	5c on 12c dp bl (R)	200.00	200.00
N13	6c on 25c vio & red org	200.00	200.00
N14	8c on 5c red brown (R)	110.00	87.50
N15	10c on 6c car lake	110.00	125.00
N16	12c on 8c gray grn (R)	225.00	250.00
a.	With "b" seal (R)	75.00	100.00
N17	25c on 10c dk vio	1,200.	*1,250.*
N17A	30c on 4c brick red	1,600.	*1,800.*
N18	40c on 2c dp grn (R)	60.00	100.00
N19	50c on 1c yel & ol green	*1,200.*	1,100.

Perf. 14

N20	$1 on 4c blk & red (R)	65.00	87.50
N21	$2 on 5c grn & red, *yel*	65.00	87.50
N22	$5 on 6c rose red	65.00	87.50

Examples of Nos. N2-N22 without handstamped seal are from the remainder stocks sent to Singapore after Kelantan was ceded to Thailand. Some authorities believe stamps without seals were used before June 1942.

ISSUED UNDER THAI OCCUPATION

OS1

1943, Nov. 15 *Perf. 11*

2N1	OS1	1c violet & black	*225.00*	*350.00*
2N2	OS1	2c violet & black	*275.00*	*275.00*
2N3	OS1	4c violet & black	*275.00*	*350.00*
2N4	OS1	8c violet & black	*275.00*	*275.00*
2N5	OS1	10c violet & black	*350.00*	*450.00*
		Nos. 2N1-2N5 (5)	*1,400.*	*1,700.*

Stamps with centers in red are revenues.

MALACCA

mə-ˈla-kə

Melaka

LOCATION — On the west coast of the Malay peninsula.
AREA — 640 sq. mi.
POP. — 318,110 (1960)
CAPITAL — Malacca

Catalogue values for unused stamps in this section are for Never Hinged items.

Silver Wedding Issue
Common Design Types
Inscribed: "Malaya Malacca"
Perf. 14x14½

1948, Dec. 1 Wmk. 4 Photo.

1	CD304	10c purple	.35	*2.10*

Engraved; Name Typographed
Perf. 11½x11

2	CD305	$5 lt brown	32.50	*47.50*

Type of Straits Settlements, 1937-41, Inscribed "Malacca"
Perf. 18

1949, Mar. 1 Wmk. 4 Typo.

3	A29	1c black	.35	*.80*
4	A29	2c orange	.95	.50
5	A29	3c green	.35	*2.00*
6	A29	4c chocolate	.35	.20
7	A29	6c gray	.90	*1.00*
8	A29	8c rose red	.90	*7.00*
9	A29	10c plum	.35	.20
10	A29	15c ultramarine	3.00	.70
11	A29	20c dk green & blk	.55	*.80*
12	A29	25c org & rose lil	.55	.80
13	A29	40c dk vio & rose red	1.40	*12.50*
14	A29	50c ultra & black	1.10	*1.40*
15	A29	$1 vio brn & ultra	9.75	*22.50*
16	A29	$2 rose red & emer	24.00	*24.00*
17	A29	$5 choc & emer	50.00	*40.00*
		Nos. 3-17 (15)	94.50	*114.40*

See Nos. 22-26.

UPU Issue
Common Design Types
Inscribed: "Malaya-Malacca"
Engr.; Name Typo. on 15c, 25c
Perf. 13½, 11x11½

1949, Oct. 10 Wmk. 4

18	CD306	10c rose violet	.35	*.55*
19	CD307	15c indigo	2.25	*2.00*
20	CD308	25c orange	.50	*5.50*
21	CD309	50c slate	1.25	*5.50*
		Nos. 18-21 (4)	4.35	*13.55*

Type of Straits Settlements, 1937-41, Inscribed "Malacca"

1952, Sept. 1 Wmk. 4 *Perf. 18*

22	A29	5c rose violet	.65	*1.60*
23	A29	8c green	1.10	*4.75*
24	A29	12c rose red	2.10	*.75*
25	A29	20c ultramarine	3.25	2.75
26	A29	35c dk vio & rose red	1.60	*3.25*
		Nos. 22-26 (5)	8.70	*13.10*

Issued Under Japanese Occupation
Stamps of Straits Settlements, 1937-41 Handstamped in Carmine

The handstamp covers four stamps. Values are for single stamps. Blocks of four showing complete handstamp sell for six times the price of singles.

1942 Wmk. 4 *Perf. 14*

N1	A29	1c black	100.00	80.00
N2	A29	2c brown orange	90.00	75.00
N3	A29	3c green	100.00	80.00
N4	A29	5c brown	140.00	150.00
N5	A29	8c gray	210.00	150.00
N6	A29	10c dull violet	100.00	100.00
N7	A29	12c ultramarine	100.00	125.00
N8	A29	15c ultramarine	80.00	100.00
N9	A29	30c org & vio	*1,900.*	—
N10	A29	40c dk vio & rose red	800.00	700.00
N11	A29	50c blk, *emerald*	975.00	975.00
N12	A29	$1 red & blk, *bl*	1,050.	975.00
N13	A29	$2 rose red & gray grn	*1,900.*	—
N14	A29	$5 grn & red, *grn*	*1,900.*	—

Some authorities believe Nos. N9, N13, and N14 were not regularly issued.

OCCUPATION POSTAGE DUE STAMPS

Malaya Postage Due Stamps and Type of 1936-38, Handstamped Like Nos. N1-N14 in Carmine

1942 Wmk. 4 *Perf. 14½x14*

NJ1	D2	1c violet	*225.00*	*210.00*
NJ2	D2	4c yel green	*250.00*	*250.00*
NJ3	D2	8c red	*2,300.*	*1,850.*
NJ4	D2	10c yel orange	*500.00*	*425.00*
NJ5	D2	12c blue violet	*700.00*	*575.00*
NJ6	D2	50c black	*2,100.*	*1,600.*
		Nos. NJ1-NJ6 (6)	*6,075.*	*4,910.*

Pricing note above No. N1 also applies to Nos. NJ1-NJ6.

NEGRI SEMBILAN

ˈne-grē səm-ˈbē-lən

LOCATION — South of Selangor on the west coast of the Malay Peninsula, bordering on Pahang on the east and Johore on the south.
AREA — 2,580 sq. mi.
POP. — 401,742 (1960)
CAPITAL — Seremban

Stamps of the Straits Settlements Overprinted in Black

1891 Wmk. 2 *Perf. 14*
Overprint 14½ to 15mm Wide

1	A2	2c rose	3.50	*5.75*

Tiger — A1

Tiger Head — A2

1891-94 Typo.

2	A1	1c green ('93)	3.50	1.10
3	A1	2c rose	3.75	*8.75*
4	A1	5c blue ('94)	35.00	*45.00*
		Nos. 2-4 (3)	42.25	*54.85*
		Set, ovptd. "SPECIMEN"	92.50	

1895-99

5	A2	1c lilac & green	11.00	5.75
6	A2	2c lilac & brown	40.00	*125.00*
7	A2	3c lilac & car rose	16.00	1.10
8	A2	5c lilac & olive	9.75	9.25
9	A2	8c lilac & blue	35.00	18.00
10	A2	10c lilac & orange	30.00	16.00
11	A2	15c green & vio	47.50	*85.00*
12	A2	20c grn & ol ('99)	75.00	*45.00*
13	A2	25c grn & car rose	80.00	*100.00*
14	A2	50c green & black	80.00	75.00
		Nos. 5-14 (10)	424.25	*480.10*
		Set, ovptd. "SPECIMEN"	210.00	

For surcharges see Nos. 15-16, 19-20.

Stamps of 1891-99 Surcharged

1899 Green Surcharge

15	A2	4c on 8c lil & blue	5.50	5.00
a.		Double surcharge	2,100.	2,100.
b.		Pair, one without surcharge	5,250.	4,000.
c.		Double surcharge, 1 green, 1 red	925.00	975.00

Black Surcharge

16	A2	4c on 8c lil & blue	1,275.	*1,375.*

Same Surcharge and Bar in Black

17	A1	4c on 1c green	2.25	*17.50*
18	A1	4c on 5c blue	1.50	*17.50*
19	A2	4c on 3c lil & car rose	3.50	*18.00*
a.		Double surcharge	2,100.	1,150.
b.		Pair, one without surcharge	6,250.	*4,600.*
c.		Bar omitted	925.00	750.00
d.		Bar double		925.00
e.		"FOUR" double (at right)	2,100.	1,850.
f.		"CENTS" double (at left)	2,100.	1,850.
g.		Inverted surcharge	1,750.	1,400.
h.		As "g," one surcharge albino	—	—

Bar at bottom on #17-18, at top on #19.

No. 11 Surcharged in Black

One cent.

1900

20	A2	1c on 15c grn & vio	110.00	*210.00*
a.		Inverted period	425.00	*750.00*

Arms of Negri Sembilan
A4 A5

1935-41 Typo. Wmk. 4

21	A4	1c black ('36)	1.25	.20
22	A4	2c dp green ('36)	.80	.20
22A	A4	2c brown org ('41)	.20	*45.00*
22B	A4	3c green ('41)	.20	*6.50*
23	A4	4c brown orange	.80	.20
24	A4	5c chocolate	.80	.20
25	A4	6c rose red	4.50	1.10
25A	A4	6c gray ('41)	3.00	*80.00*
26	A4	8c gray	1.90	.25
27	A4	10c dull vio ('36)	1.90	.20
28	A4	12c ultra ('36)	2.40	.70
28A	A4	15c ultra ('41)	3.25	*57.50*
29	A4	25c rose red & dull vio ('36)	2.40	2.40
30	A4	30c org & dull vio ('36)	3.25	4.50
31	A4	40c dull vio & car	1.50	*5.75*
32	A4	50c blk, *emer* ('36)	6.00	1.50
33	A4	$1 red & blk, *bl* ('36)	2.40	3.25
34	A4	$2 rose red & grn ('36)	32.50	42.50
35	A4	$5 brn red & grn, *emer* ('36)	24.00	*57.50*
		Nos. 21-35 (19)	93.05	*309.45*

For overprints see Nos. N1-N31.

Catalogue values for unused stamps in this section, from this point to the end of the section, are for Never Hinged items.

Silver Wedding Issue
Common Design Types
Inscribed: "Malaya Negri Sembilan"

1948, Dec. 1 Photo. *Perf. 14x14½*

36	CD304	10c purple	.25	.30

Perf. 11½x11

Engraved; Name Typographed

37	CD305	$5 green	26.00	37.50

Common Design Types pictured following the introduction.

1949-55 Wmk. 4 Typo. *Perf. 18*

38	A5	1c black	.20	.20
39	A5	2c orange	.20	.20
40	A5	3c green	.50	.40
41	A5	4c chocolate	.20	.20
42	A5	5c rose violet	.20	.20
43	A5	6c gray	.40	.20
44	A5	8c rose red	.75	.80
45	A5	8c green	2.75	2.75
46	A5	10c plum	.40	.20
47	A5	12c rose red	2.75	2.75
48	A5	15c ultramarine	2.00	.55
49	A5	20c dk green & blk	1.10	1.10
50	A5	20c ultramarine	1.40	.40
51	A5	25c org & rose lilac	.60	.25
52	A5	30c plum & rose red ('55)	3.25	2.00
53	A5	35c dk vio & rose red	1.40	2.75
54	A5	40c dk vio & rose red	1.50	*5.50*
55	A5	50c ultra & black	1.50	.55
56	A5	$1 vio brn & ultra	3.25	1.40
57	A5	$2 rose red & emer	13.50	11.00
58	A5	$5 choc & emerald	60.00	40.00
		Nos. 38-58 (21)	97.85	73.40

UPU Issue
Common Design Types
Inscribed: "Malaya-Negri Sembilan"
Engr.; Name Typo. on 15c, 25c

1949, Oct. 10 *Perf. 13½, 11x11½*

59	CD306	10c rose violet	.20	.20
60	CD307	15c indigo	.55	.55
61	CD308	25c orange	1.00	1.00
62	CD309	50c slate	2.00	3.00
		Nos. 59-62 (4)	3.75	4.75

Issued under Japanese Occupation

Stamps and Type of Negri Sembilan, 1935-41, Handstamped in Red, Black, Brown or Violet

1942 Wmk. 4 *Perf. 14*

N1	A4	1c black	25.00	16.00
N2	A4	2c brown org	16.00	17.50
N3	A4	3c green	21.00	21.00
N4	A4	5c chocolate	29.00	27.50
N5	A4	6c rose red	600.00	600.00
N6	A4	6c gray	150.00	150.00
N7	A4	8c gray	87.50	87.50
N8	A4	8c rose red	55.00	47.50
N9	A4	10c dark violet	110.00	110.00
N10	A4	12c ultramarine	900.00	900.00
N11	A4	15c ultramarine	20.00	11.00
N12	A4	25c rose red & dk vio	35.00	40.00
N13	A4	30c org & dk vio	175.00	190.00
N14	A4	40c dk vio & car	750.00	750.00
N15	A4	$1 red & blk, *bl*	140.00	140.00
N16	A4	$5 brn red & grn, *emerald*	325.00	350.00

The 8c rose red is not known to have been issued without overprint.
Some authorities believe Nos. N5 and N7 were not regularly issued.

Stamps of Negri Sembilan, 1935-41, Overprinted in Black

N17	A4	1c black	1.40	1.40
a.		Inverted overprint	17.00	27.50
b.		Dbl. ovpt., one invtd.	47.50	*67.50*
N18	A4	2c brown orange	1.60	1.40
N19	A4	3c green	1.40	1.00
N20	A4	5c chocolate	.90	.90
N21	A4	6c gray	2.00	2.00
a.		Inverted overprint		*1,000.*
N22	A4	8c rose red	2.75	2.75
N23	A4	10c dk violet	5.50	5.50
N24	A4	15c ultramarine	8.00	4.75
N25	A4	25c rose red & dk vio	2.00	*6.75*
N26	A4	30c org & dk vio	4.00	*5.00*
N27	A4	$1 red & blk, *bl*	140.00	175.00
		Nos. N17-N27 (11)	169.55	206.45

The 8c rose red is not known to have been issued without overprint.

Negri Sembilan, Nos. 21, 24 and 29, Overprinted or Surcharged in Black:

a

b

c

1943

N28	A4	1c black	.65	.65
a.		Inverted overprint	17.00	24.00
N29	A4	2c on 5c choc	.55	.65
N30	A4	6c on 5c choc	.65	.90
a.		"6 cts." inverted	350.00	*400.00*
N31	A4	25c rose red & dk violet	2.00	2.75
		Nos. N28-N31 (4)	3.85	4.95

The Japanese characters read: "Japanese Postal Service."

PAHANG

pə-'haŋ

LOCATION — On the east coast of the Malay Peninsula.
AREA — 13,820 sq. mi.
POP. — 338,210 (1960)
CAPITAL — Kuala Lipis

Stamps of the Straits Settlements Overprinted in Black

Overprinted

Overprint 16x2¾mm

1889 Wmk. 2 *Perf. 14*

1	A2	2c rose	110.00	57.50
2	A3	8c orange	1,950.	1,725.
3	A7	10c slate	275.00	300.00

Overprinted

Overprint 12½x2mm

4	A2	2c rose	5.25	*9.25*
a.		Antique letters	875.00	
b.		2c pale rose	13.50	*18.00*

Overprinted **PAHANG**

1890 Overprint 15x2½mm

5	A2	2c rose	5,250.	1,600.

Overprinted

Overprint 16x2¾mm

6	A2	2c rose	110.00	16.00

Surcharged in Black:

PAHANG
Two
CENTS

a

b

c

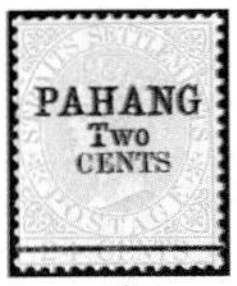

d

1891

7	A3 (a)	2c on 24c green	800.00	*875.00*
8	A3 (b)	2c on 24c green	300.00	*325.00*
9	A3 (c)	2c on 24c green	175.00	*190.00*
10	A3 (d)	2c on 24c green	800.00	*875.00*
		Nos. 7-10 (4)	2,075.	2,265.

A5

A6

1892-95 Typo.

11	A5	1c green	5.00	4.50
12	A5	2c rose	5.25	3.75
13	A5	5c blue	12.50	*45.00*
		Nos. 11-13 (3)	22.75	*53.25*
		Set, ovptd. "SPECIMEN"	85.00	

For surcharges see Nos. 21-22.

1895-99

14	A6	3c lilac & car rose	7.50	3.25
14A	A6	4c lil & car rose ('99)	20.00	14.00
15	A6	5c lilac & olive	29.00	*24.00*
		Nos. 14-15 (3)	56.50	*41.25*
		Set of 3, ovptd. "SPECIMEN"	75.00	

For surcharge see No. 28.

Stamps of Perak, 1895-99, Overprinted

1898-99

16	A9	10c lilac & orange	21.00	*29.00*
17	A9	25c green & car rose	100.00	*175.00*
18	A9	50c green & black	400.00	*425.00*
18A	A9	50c lilac & black	210.00	275.00

Overprinted

Wmk. 1

19	A10	$1 green & lt grn	400.00	500.00
20	A10	$5 green & ultra	1,300.	1,850.
		Nos. 16-20 (6)	2,431.	3,254.

No. 13 Cut in Half Diagonally and Surcharged in Red With New Value and Initials "J. F. O." in ms.

1897, Aug. 2 Wmk. 2

Red Surcharge

21	A5	2c on half of 5c blue	*1,950.*	*450.00*
a.		Black surcharge	*8,750.*	*3,500.*
b.		Bisected horizontally		*1,850.*
22	A5	3c on half of 5c blue	*1,500.*	*450.00*
a.		Black surcharge	*8,750.*	*3,500.*
b.		Bisected horizontally	*5,500.*	*1,850.*
c.		Unsevered pair, #21, 22	*11,000.*	*4,500.*
d.		Se-tenant pair, #21, 22	*4,500.*	*1,150.*

Used at Kuala Lipis. No. 22c consists a complete, unsevered, stamp. No. 22d consists of halves of two separate stamps perfed between.

Perak No. 52 Surcharged

1898

25	A9	4c on 8c lilac & blue	4.50	*6.50*
a.		Double surcharge	875.00	
b.		Inverted surcharge	3,250.	1,500.

Same Surcharge on pieces of White Paper

1898 Without Gum *Imperf.*

26		4c black		3,500.
27		5c black	2,250.	

Pahang No. 15 Surcharged

1899				***Perf. 14***
28	A6	4c on 5c lilac & olive	18.00	*65.00*

Sultan Abu Bakar
A7 A8

1935-41		**Typo. Wmk. 4**		***Perf. 14***
29	A7	1c black ('36)	.20	.20
30	A7	2c dp green ('36)	1.50	.20
30A	A7	3c green ('41)	.20	*5.50*
31	A7	4c brown orange	.80	.20
32	A7	5c chocolate	.95	.20
33	A7	6c rose red ('36)	3.50	*9.50*
34	A7	8c gray	2.40	.20
34A	A7	8c rose red ('41)	.80	*25.00*
35	A7	10c dk violet ('36)	.80	.20
36	A7	12c ultra ('36)	3.25	3.00
36A	A7	15c ultra ('41)	1.90	*32.50*
37	A7	25c rose red & pale vio ('36)	2.40	1.10
38	A7	30c org & dk vio ('36)	1.50	1.60
39	A7	40c dk vio & car	1.90	2.40
40	A7	50c black, *emer* ('36)	8.00	2.25
41	A7	$1 red & blk, *blue* ('36)	4.50	6.00
42	A7	$2 rose red & green ('36)	40.00	*72.50*
43	A7	$5 brn red & grn, *emer* ('36)	14.50	*72.50*
		Nos. 29-43 (18)	89.10	*235.05*

The 3c was printed on both ordinary and chalky paper; the 15c only on ordinary paper; other values only on chalky paper.

A 2c brown orange and 6c gray, type A7, exist, but are not known to have been regularly issued.

For overprints see Nos. N1-N21.

Catalogue values for unused stamps in this section, from this point to the end of the section, are for Never Hinged items.

Silver Wedding Issue

Common Design Types
Inscribed: "Malaya Pahang"

Perf. 14x14½

1948, Dec. 1		**Photo.**		**Wmk. 4**
44	CD304	10c purple	.25	.30
		Perf. 11½x11		
		Engraved; Name Typopgraphed		
45	CD305	$5 green	32.50	55.00

UPU Issue

Common Design Types
Inscribed: "Malaya-Pahang"

Engr.; Name Typo. on 15c, 25c

1949, Oct. 10		***Perf. 13½, 11x11½***		
46	CD306	10c rose violet	.20	.20
47	CD307	15c indigo	.40	.40
48	CD308	25c orange	1.10	1.10
49	CD309	50c slate	1.90	1.90
		Nos. 46-49 (4)	3.60	3.60

Perf. 18

1950, June 1		**Wmk. 4**		**Typo.**
50	A8	1c black	.25	.30
51	A8	2c orange	.25	.30
52	A8	3c green	.25	.60
53	A8	4c chocolate	.25	.30
54	A8	6c gray	.25	.30
55	A8	8c rose red	.25	*3.00*
56	A8	10c plum	.25	.30
57	A8	15c ultramarine	.30	.30
58	A8	20c dk green & blk	.30	*3.00*
59	A8	25c org & rose lilac	.30	.30
60	A8	40c dk vio & rose red	1.25	*11.00*
61	A8	50c dp ultra & black	1.10	.30
62	A8	$1 vio brn & ultra	3.50	3.00
63	A8	$2 rose red & emer	19.00	30.00
64	A8	$5 choc & emer	60.00	*47.50*
1952-55				
65	A8	5c rose violet	.25	.30
66	A8	8c green	1.25	1.25
67	A8	12c rose red	1.25	2.10
68	A8	20c ultramarine	1.10	.30
69	A8	30c plum & rose red ('55)	1.75	.60
70	A8	35c dk vio & rose red	.90	.35
		Nos. 50-70 (21)	94.00	*105.40*

Issued under Japanese Occupation

Stamps of Pahang, 1935-41, Handstamped in Black, Red, Brown or Violet

1942		**Wmk. 4**		***Perf. 14***
N1	A7	1c black	35.00	40.00
N1A	A7	3c green	125.00	140.00
N2	A7	5c chocolate	15.00	9.50
N3	A7	8c rose red	26.00	11.00
N3A	A7	8c gray	240.00	240.00
N4	A7	10c dk violet	60.00	60.00
N5	A7	12c ultramarine	1,200.	1,200.
N6	A7	15c ultramarine	87.50	87.50
N7	A7	25c rose red & pale vio	21.00	37.50
N8	A7	30c org & dk vio	17.00	32.50
N9	A7	40c dk vio & car	17.50	35.00
N10	A7	50c blk, *emerald*	300.00	350.00
N11	A7	$1 red & blk, *bl*	100.00	125.00
N12	A7	$5 brown red & grn, *emer*	575.00	625.00

Some authorities claim the 2c green, 4c brown orange, 6c rose red and $2 rose red and green were not regularly issued with this overprint.

Stamps of Pahang, 1935-41, Overprinted in Black

N13	A7	1c black	2.00	1.10
N14	A7	5c chocolate	2.00	2.00
N15	A7	8c rose red	35.00	3.75
N16	A7	10c violet brown	20.00	9.00
N17	A7	12c ultramarine	2.00	3.00
N18	A7	25c rose red & pale vio	7.50	*10.50*
N19	A7	30c org & dk vio	2.75	*5.50*
		Nos. N13-N19 (7)	71.25	*34.85*

Pahang No. 32 Overprinted and Surcharged in Black

e

f

1943				
N20	A7(e)	6c on 5c chocolate	1.40	1.40
N21	A7(f)	6c on 5c chocolate	2.00	1.50

The Japanese characters read: "Japanese Postal Service."

PENANG

pə-naŋ

LOCATION — An island off the west coast of the Malay Peninsula, plus a coastal strip called Province Wellesley.
AREA — 400 sq. mi.
POP. — 616,254 (1960)
CAPITAL — Georgetown

Catalogue values for unused stamps in this section are for Never Hinged items.

Common Design Types pictured following the introduction.

Silver Wedding Issue

Common Design Types
Inscribed: "Malaya Penang"

Perf. 14x14½

1948, Dec. 1		**Wmk. 4**		**Photo.**
1	CD304	10c purple	.50	.25
		Perf. 11½x11		
		Engraved; Name Typographed		
2	CD305	$5 lt brown	37.50	35.00

Type of Straits Settlements, 1937-41, Inscribed "Penang"

1949-52				***Perf. 18***
3	A29	1c black	.25	.25
4	A29	2c orange	1.00	.25
5	A29	3c green	.25	1.25
6	A29	4c chocolate	.25	.20
7	A29	5c rose vio ('52)	2.40	3.25
8	A29	6c gray	.35	.25
9	A29	8c rose red	.75	*3.75*
10	A29	8c green ('52)	1.75	2.00
11	A29	10c plum	.25	.20
12	A29	12c rose red ('52)	2.40	5.75
13	A29	15c ultramarine	.60	*.35*
14	A29	20c dk grn & blk	.60	1.10
15	A29	20c ultra ('52)	.65	1.40
16	A29	25c org & rose lilac	2.00	.25
17	A29	35c dk vio & rose red ('52)	1.10	1.50
18	A29	40c dk vio & rose red	1.75	*12.50*
19	A29	50c ultra & black	3.00	.25
20	A29	$1 vio brn & ultra	19.00	2.40
21	A29	$2 rose red & emer	25.00	2.40
22	A29	$5 choc & emerald	55.00	3.50
		Nos. 3-22 (20)	118.35	*42.80*

UPU Issue

Common Design Types
Inscribed: "Malaya-Penang"

Engr.; Name Typo. on 15c, 25c

1949, Oct. 10		***Perf. 13½, 11x11½***		
23	CD306	10c rose violet	.25	.20
24	CD307	15c indigo	2.40	*3.25*
25	CD308	25c orange	.70	*3.25*
26	CD309	50c slate	1.75	*4.00*
		Nos. 23-26 (4)	5.10	10.70

Issued under Japanese Occupation

Stamps of Straits Settlements, 1937-41, Overprinted in Red or Black

1942		**Wmk. 4**		***Perf. 14***
N1	A29	1c black (R)	5.00	3.50
N2	A29	2c brown orange	5.00	4.75
N3	A29	3c green (R)	5.50	4.25
N4	A29	5c brown (R)	3.25	7.50
N5	A29	8c gray (R)	2.75	1.60
N6	A29	10c dull vio (R)	2.00	2.50
N7	A29	12c ultra (R)	4.25	*16.00*
N8	A29	15c ultra (R)	2.00	3.50
N9	A29	40c dk vio & rose red	5.50	*16.00*
N10	A29	50c black, *emer* (R)	5.25	*27.50*
N11	A29	$1 red & blk, *bl*	14.00	*37.50*
N12	A29	$2 rose red & gray grn	57.50	*92.50*
N13	A29	$5 grn & red, *grn*	550.00	625.00
		Nos. N1-N13 (13)	662.00	842.10

Stamps of Straits Settlements Handstamped in Red

Okugawa Seal

1942		**Wmk. 4**		***Perf. 14***
N14	A29	1c black	14.00	12.50
N15	A29	2c brown orange	27.50	25.00
N16	A29	3c green	22.50	25.00
N17	A29	5c brown	35.00	29.00
N18	A29	8c gray	30.00	37.50
N19	A29	10c dull violet	57.50	57.50
N20	A29	12c ultramarine	35.00	55.00
N21	A29	15c ultramarine	57.50	57.50
N22	A29	40c dk vio & rose red	125.00	125.00
N23	A29	50c blk, *emerald*	225.00	250.00
N24	A29	$1 red & blk, *bl*	225.00	300.00
N25	A29	$2 rose red & gray grn	700.00	700.00
N26	A29	$5 grn & red, *grn*	2,100.	1,725.
		Nos. N14-N26 (13)	3,654.	3,399.

Handstamped in Red

Uchibori Seal

N14a	A29	1c	160.00	125.00
N15a	A29	2c	160.00	110.00
N16a	A29	3c	110.00	110.00
N17a	A29	5c	2,100.	2,100.
N18a	A29	8c	92.50	100.00
N19a	A29	10c	150.00	150.00
N20a	A29	12c	100.00	125.00
N21a	A29	15c	110.00	125.00
		Nos. N14a-N21a (8)	2,982.	2,945.

PERAK

'per-ə-ˌak

LOCATION — On the west coast of the Malay Peninsula.
AREA — 7,980 sq. mi.
POP. — 1,327,120 (1960)
CAPITAL — Taiping

Straits Settlements No. 10 Handstamped in Black

1878		**Wmk. 1**		***Perf. 14***
1	A2	2c brown	1,850.	1,350.

Overprinted

Overprint 17x3½mm Wide

1880-81				
2	A2	2c brown	32.50	*65.00*

Overprinted

Overprint 10 to 14½mm Wide

3	A2	2c brown, ovpt. 12-13.5mm ('81)	150.00	*160.00*
	a.	"R" narrow, "A" wide	150.00	*175.00*
	b.	"R" narrow, "A" narrow	225.00	*240.00*
	c.	"P" wide, "K" wide	525.00	500.00
	d.	2c brown, ovpt. 10.25mm ('80)	800.00	625.00
	e.	2c brown, ovpt. 11mm ('80)	1,600.	750.00
	f.	2c brown, ovpt. 14.5mm ('80)	1,850.	850.00

Same Overprint on Straits Settlements Nos. 40, 41a

1883				**Wmk. 2**
4	A2	2c brown	22.50	*55.00*
	a.	Double overprint	700.00	
5	A2	2c rose	26.00	*47.50*
	a.	"A" wide	26.00	*75.00*
	b.	"E" wide	26.00	*57.50*
	c.	Double overprint	750.00	
	d.	As "b," double overprint	750.00	

Overprinted

Overprint 14 to 15½mm Wide

6	A2	2c rose	3.50	2.50
	a.	Inverted overprint	425.00	550.00
	b.	Double overprint	675.00	675.00
	c.	"E" in overprint narrow	75.00	75.00
	d.	As "c," inverted overprint	1,500.	*1,600.*

For surcharge, see No. 19E

Overprinted

Overprint 12¾ to 14mm Wide

1886-90

7 A2 2c rose 1.90 6.25
a. "FERAK" corrected by pen 400.00 475.00
b. 2c pale rose 175.00 32.50

Overprinted

Overprint 10x1¾mm

8 A2 2c rose 16.00 52.50

Overprinted

Overprint 12-12½x2¾mm

10 A2 2c rose 5.75 24.00
a. Double overprint 1,600.

Overprinted

Overprint 10½-10¾x2½mm

11 A2 2c rose 110.00 125.00

Straits Settlements Nos. 11, 41a, 42 Surcharged in Black or Blue

q

r

s

t

12 A2(q) 2c on 4c rose, as #3 ('83) 625.00 300.00
a. 2c on 4c rose, as #5b ('83) 1,100. 450.00
b. 2c on 4c rose, Sts. Setts. #42 (q) 3,250.
c. 2c on 4c rose, Sts. Setts. #11 (q) 10,000.
13 A2(t) 1c on 2c rose 250.00 150.00
a. Without period after "CENT" ('90) — 300.00
14 A2(r) 1c on 2c rose 75.00 100.00
a. Without period after "PERAK" 625.00 675.00
b. Double surcharge 1,050.
c. Both "N"'s wide ('86) 110.00 140.00
15 A2(s) 1c on 2c rose (Bl) 45.00 57.50
15A A2(s) 1c on 2c rose (Bk) 2,100. 1,500.

In type "r" PERAK is 11½ to 14mm wide.

No. 12 was first overprinted with the type of No. 3 and then surcharged "TWO CENTS." No. 12a was first overprinted with the type of No. 5c and subsequently surcharged "TWO CENTS." Nos. 12b and 12c were surcharged and overprinted in one operation.

Nos. 13 and 13a were created in two operations, surcharging No. 6.

Nos. 14, 14a, 15 and 15A were overprinted in one operation.

Surcharged in Black

16 A2 1c on 2c rose 140.00 150.00
a. Double surcharge 1,850. 1,850.

Surcharged

I
CENT
PERAK

17 A2 1c on 2c rose

Some authorities question the status of No. 17.

Surcharged

1
CENT
PERAK

18 A2 1c on 2c rose 2,100. 2,200.
b. Double surcharge, one inverted
c. "PREAK"

Surcharged

I
CENT
PERAK

18A A2 1c on 2c rose 675.00 700.00

Surcharged

19 A2 1c on 2c rose 2.75 10.00
a. Double surcharge, one inverted
b. Inverted surcharge
c. "One" inverted 3,200.
d. Double surcharge 1,250.

No. 6 surcharged "1 CENT" in Italic Serifed Capital Letters

1886

19E A2 1c on 2c rose 2,500. 2,300.

Straits Settlements No. 41a Surcharged

u

v

w

x

y

z

h

1889-90

20 A2(u) 1c on 2c rose 2.25 5.75
a. Italic Roman "K" in "PERAK" 350.00 450.00
b. Double surcharge 1,250.
c. 2c bright rose 2.50 2.50
21 A2(v) 1c on 2c rose 675.00 850.00
23 A2(w) 1c on 2c rose 12.50 40.00
a. "PREAK" 575.00 675.00
b. 2c bright rose 18.50 40.00
c. As "b," "PREAK" 800.00 950.00
24 A2(x) 1c on 2c rose 140.00 160.00
25 A2(y) 1c on 2c rose 7.50 15.00
a. 2c bright rose 5.25 15.00
26 A2(z) 1c on 2c rose 9.25 17.50
a. 2c bright rose 5.25 17.50
27 A2(h) 1c on 2c rose 17.50 35.00
a. 2c bright rose 17.50 30.00

Straits Settlements Nos. 41a, 48, 54 Surcharged in Black:

a

b

c

d

e

f

g

1891 **Wmk. 2**

28 A2(a) 1c on 2c rose 1.10 4.50
a. Bar omitted 210.00
29 A2(a) 1c on 6c violet 57.50 42.50
30 A3(b) 2c on 24c green 13.00 13.00
31 A2(c) 1c on 2c rose 7.00 19.00
a. Bar omitted 950.00
32 A2(d) 1c on 2c rose 1.40 5.75
a. Bar omitted 240.00
33 A2(d) 1c on 6c violet 95.00 95.00
34 A3(d) 2c on 24c green 47.50 42.50
35 A2(e) 1c on 2c rose 8.00 18.00
a. Bar omitted 950.00
36 A2(e) 1c on 6c violet 175.00 210.00
37 A3(e) 2c on 24c green 125.00 80.00
38 A2(f) 1c on 6c violet 175.00 75.00
39 A3(f) 2c on 24c green 125.00 95.00
40 A2(g) 1c on 6c violet 160.00 175.00
41 A3(g) 2c on 24c green 125.00 95.00
Nos. 28-41 (14) 1,115. 970.25

A7

1892-95 **Typo.** **Perf. 14**

42 A7 1c green 3.00 .70
43 A7 2c rose 2.25 .70
44 A7 2c orange ('95) .90 5.50
45 A7 5c blue 5.50 4.75
Nos. 42-45 (4) 11.65 11.65
Set, ovptd. "SPECIMEN" 110.00

For overprint see No. O10.

Type of 1892 Surcharged in Black

1895

46 A7 3c on 5c rose .60 2.75
Overprinted "SPECIMEN" 35.00

A9

A10

1895-99 **Wmk. 2** **Perf. 14**

47 A9 1c lilac & green 1.40 .60
48 A9 2c lilac & brown 1.10 .60
49 A9 3c lilac & car rose 3.00 .25
50 A9 4c lil & car rose ('99) 10.50 7.00
51 A9 5c lilac & olive 3.50 .80
52 A9 8c lilac & blue 45.00 .80
53 A9 10c lilac & orange 12.00 .65
54 A9 25c grn & car rose ('96) 150.00 16.00
55 A9 50c lilac & black 45.00 45.00
56 A9 50c grn & blk ('99) 100.00 100.00

Wmk. 1

57 A10 $1 green & lt grn 125.00 125.00
58 A10 $2 grn & car rose ('96) 175.00 175.00
59 A10 $3 green & ol ('96) 225.00 225.00
60 A10 $5 green & ultra 475.00 450.00
61 A10 $25 grn & org ('96) 6,600. 2,000.
Overprinted "SPECIMEN" 225.00
Nos. 47-57 (11) 496.50 296.70
Nos. 47-60 ovptd. "SPECIMEN" 450.00

For surcharges and overprint see #62-68, O11, Malaya 9-13A.

Stamps of 1895-99 Surcharged in Black:

i

k

m

1900 **Wmk. 2**

62 A9(i) 1c on 2c lilac & brown .70 2.25
63 A9(k) 1c on 4c lilac & car rose .80 6.50
a. Double surcharge 1,100.
64 A9(i) 1c on 5c lilac & ol 1.10 8.00
65 A9(i) 3c on 8c lilac & blue 3.25 3.25
a. No period after "Cent" 140.00 160.00
b. Double surcharge 475.00 475.00
66 A9(i) 3c on 50c green & black 1.90 5.75
a. No period after "Cent" 110.00 175.00

Wmk. 1

67 A10(m) 3c on $1 grn & lt green 60.00 125.00
a. Double surcharge 1,400.
68 A10(m) 3c on $2 grn & car rose 30.00 87.50
Nos. 62-68 (7) 97.75 238.25

Sultan Iskandar
A14 A15

1935-37 **Typo.** **Wmk. 4**

Chalky Paper

69 A14 1c black ('36) .20 .20
70 A14 2c dp green ('36) .20 .20
71 A14 4c brown orange .25 .20
72 A14 5c chocolate .20 .20
73 A14 6c rose red ('37) 4.75 3.00
74 A14 8c gray 3.25 .50
75 A14 10c dk vio ('36) .90 .20
76 A14 12c ultra ('36) 4.00 1.40
77 A14 25c rose red & pale vio ('36) 1.90 1.50
78 A14 30c org & dark vio ('36) 1.90 2.40

79 A14 40c dk vio & car 6.50 5.50
80 A14 50c blk, *emerald* ('36) 4.00 2.25
81 A14 $1 red & blk, *bl* ('36) 3.25 2.40
82 A14 $2 rose red & green ('36) 25.00 14.00
83 A14 $5 brn red & grn, *emer* ('36) 55.00 32.50
Nos. 69-83 (15) 111.30 66.45

1938-41

84 A15 1c black ('39) 3.00 .20
85 A15 2c dp green ('39) 1.90 .20
85A A15 2c brn org ('41) .70 *1.90*
85B A15 3c green ('41) 1.25 .50
86 A15 4c brn org ('39) 20.00 .20
87 A15 5c choc ('39) 1.90 .20
88 A15 6c rose red ('39) 20.00 .20
89 A15 8c gray 20.00 .20
89A A15 8c rose red ('41) .80 *6.50*
90 A15 10c dk violet 20.00 .20
91 A15 12c ultramarine 20.00 3.00
91A A15 15c ultra ('41) 1.75 *18.00*
92 A15 25c rose red & pale vio ('39) 72.50 4.00
93 A15 30c org & dk vio 10.50 2.50
94 A15 40c dk vio & rose red 47.50 2.50
95 A15 50c blk, *emerald* 24.00 .65
96 A15 $1 red & blk, *bl* ('40) 110.00 19.00
97 A15 $2 rose red & grn ('40) 110.00 80.00
98 A15 $5 red, *emer* ('40) 190.00 *325.00*
Nos. 84-98 (19) 675.80 *464.95*

For overprints see Nos. N1-N40.

Catalogue values for unused stamps in this section, from this point to the end of the section, are for Never Hinged items.

Silver Wedding Issue
Common Design Types
Inscribed: "Malaya Perak"

1948, Dec. 1 Photo. *Perf. 14x14½*
99 CD304 10c purple .25 .20

Perf. 11½x11
Engraved; Name Typographed
100 CD305 $5 green 27.50 35.00

Common Design Types pictured following the introduction.

UPU Issue
Common Design Types
Inscribed: "Malaya-Perak"
Engr.; Name Typo. on 15c, 25c
Perf. 13½, 11x11½

1949, Oct. 10 Wmk. 4
101 CD306 10c rose violet .20 .20
102 CD307 15c indigo .60 .55
103 CD308 25c orange .90 1.10
104 CD309 50c slate 2.00 2.40
Nos. 101-104 (4) 3.70 4.25

Sultan Yussuf Izuddin Shah — A16

1950, Aug. 17 Typo. *Perf. 18*
105 A16 1c black .25 .40
106 A16 2c orange .25 .40
107 A16 3c green 2.00 1.40
108 A16 4c chocolate .25 .40
109 A16 6c gray .25 .40
110 A16 8c rose red .30 1.10
111 A16 10c plum .25 .40
112 A16 15c ultramarine .30 .50
113 A16 20c dk grn & blk .30 1.25
114 A16 25c org & plum .30 .40
115 A16 40c vio brn & rose red 2.00 6.75
116 A16 50c dp ultra & blk .75 .40
117 A16 $1 vio brn & ultra 10.00 1.10
118 A16 $2 rose red & emer 19.00 6.75
119 A16 $5 choc & emerald 40.00 21.00

1952-55
120 A16 5c rose violet .50 .40
121 A16 8c green 1.60 1.40
122 A16 12c rose red 1.60 3.25
123 A16 20c ultramarine 1.10 .40
124 A16 30c plum & rose red ('55) 1.90 .40
125 A16 35c dk vio & rose red 1.00 .50
Nos. 105-125 (21) 83.90 49.00

OFFICIAL STAMPS

Stamps and Types of Straits Settlements Overprinted in Black

1890 Wmk. 1 *Perf. 14*
O1 A3 12c blue 190.00 240.00
O2 A3 24c green 700.00 *725.00*

Wmk. 2
O3 A2 2c rose 3.00 4.50
a. No period after "S" 65.00 65.00
b. Double overprint 1,800. 1,800.
O4 A2 4c brown 10.50 24.00
a. No period after "S" 125.00 *160.00*
O5 A2 6c violet 25.00 55.00
O6 A3 8c orange 35.00 90.00
O7 A7 10c slate 90.00 95.00
O8 A3 12c vio brown 240.00 300.00
O9 A3 24c green 125.00 *175.00*

P.G.S. stands for Perak Government Service.

Perak No. 45 Overprinted

1894
O10 A7 5c blue 60.00 1.25
a. Inverted overprint 900.00 650.00

Same Overprint on No. 51

1897
O11 A9 5c lilac & olive 1.50 .35
a. Double overprint 400.00 425.00

OCCUPATION STAMPS

Issued under Japanese Occupation

Stamps of Perak, 1938-41, Handstamped in Black, Red, Brown or Violet

1942 Wmk. 4 *Perf. 14*
N1 A15 1c black 50.00 35.00
N2 A15 2c brn orange 35.00 21.00
N3 A15 3c green 35.00 37.50
N4 A15 5c chocolate 11.50 11.00
N5 A15 8c gray 55.00 37.50
N6 A15 8c rose red 25.00 35.00
N7 A15 10c dk violet 22.50 27.50
N8 A15 12c ultramarine 150.00 150.00
N9 A15 15c ultramarine 30.00 35.00
N10 A15 25c rose red & pale vio 27.50 30.00
N11 A15 30c org & dk vio 35.00 40.00
N12 A15 40c dk vio & rose red 175.00 190.00
N13 A15 50c blk, *emerald* 57.50 *60.00*
N14 A15 $1 red & blk, *bl* 275.00 300.00
N15 A15 $2 rose red & grn *1,500.* *1,500.*
N16 A15 $5 red, *emerald* 750.00 750.00

Some authorities claim No. N6 was not regularly issued. This overprint also exists on No. 85

Stamps of Perak, 1938-41, Overprinted in Black

N16A A15 1c black 40.00 40.00
N17 A15 2c brn org 1.60 1.60
a. Inverted overprint 27.50 29.00
N18 A15 3c green 1.25 1.40
a. Inverted overprint 27.50 30.00
N18B A15 5c chocolate 40.00
N19 A15 8c rose red 1.25 .65
a. Inverted overprint 10.00 10.00
b. Dbl. ovpt., one invtd. 250.00 275.00
c. Pair, one without ovpt. 500.00 475.00
N20 A15 10c dk violet 8.50 9.50
N21 A15 15c ultramarine 6.00 6.75
N21A A15 30c org & dk vio 35.00 35.00
N22 A15 50c blk, *emerald* 4.00 6.00
N23 A15 $1 red & blk, *bl* 350.00 *375.00*
N24 A15 $5 red, *emerald* 60.00 67.50
a. Inverted overprint 350.00 *400.00*

Some authorities claim Nos. N16A, N18B and N21A were not regularly issued.

Overprinted on Perak No. 87 and Surcharged in Black "2 Cents"
N25 A15 2c on 5c chocolate 2.00 1.40

Perak Nos. 84 and 89A Overprinted in Black

N26 A15 1c black 3.25 4.00
a. Inverted overprint 35.00 40.00
N27 A15 8c rose red 3.25 2.00
a. Inverted overprint 20.00 24.00

Overprinted on Perak No. 87 and Surcharged in Black "2 Cents"
N28 A15 2c on 5c chocolate 5.00 5.00
a. Inverted overprint 35.00 47.50
b. As "a," "2 Cents" omitted 50.00 57.50

Stamps of Perak, 1938-41, Overprinted or Surcharged in Black:

n

No. N31

No. N32

1943
N29 A15 1c black .65 .65
N30 A15 2c brn orange 35.00 35.00
N31 A15 2c on 5c choc 1.00 1.00
a. "2 Cents" inverted 35.00 40.00
b. Entire surcharge inverted 35.00 40.00
N32 A15 2c on 5c choc 1.40 1.40
a. Vertical characters invtd. 35.00 40.00
b. Entire surcharge inverted 35.00 40.00
N33 A15 3c green 37.50 37.50
N34 A15 5c chocolate 1.00 1.00
a. Inverted overprint 50.00 60.00
N35 A15 8c gray 35.00 35.00
N36 A15 8c rose red 1.00 1.00
a. Inverted overprint 35.00 40.00
N37 A15 10c dk violet 1.25 1.25
N38 A15 30c org & dk vio 2.75 4.00
N39 A15 50c blk, *emerald* 5.50 9.50
N40 A15 $5 red, *emerald* 75.00 85.00
Nos. N29-N40 (12) 197.05 212.30

No. N34 was also used in the Shan States of Burma. The Japanese characters read: "Japanese Postal Service."
Some authorities claim Nos. N30, N33 and N35 were not regularly issued.

PERLIS

'per-ləs

LOCATION — On the west coast of the Malay peninsula, adjoining Siam and Kedah.
AREA — 310 sq. mi.
POP. — 97,645 (1960)
CAPITAL — Kangar

Catalogue values for unused stamps in this section are for Never Hinged items.

Silver Wedding Issue
Common Design Types
Inscribed: "Malaya Perlis"
Perf. 14x14½

1948, Dec. 1 Photo. Wmk. 4
1 CD304 10c purple .35 *3.25*

Engraved; Name Typographed
Perf. 11½x11
2 CD305 $5 lt brown 32.50 *52.50*

UPU Issue
Common Design Types
Inscribed: "Malaya-Perlis"
Engr.; Name Typo. on 15c, 25c

1949, Oct. 10 *Perf. 13½, 11x11½*
3 CD306 10c rose violet .35 *1.40*
4 CD307 15c indigo 1.40 *3.75*
5 CD308 25c orange .85 *2.25*
6 CD309 50c slate 1.90 *4.25*
Nos. 3-6 (4) 4.50 11.65

SELANGOR

sə-'laŋ-ər

LOCATION — South of Perak on the west coast of the Malay Peninsula.
AREA — 3,160 sq. mi.
POP. — 1,012,891 (1960)
CAPITAL — Kuala Lumpur

Stamps of the Straits Settlements Overprinted

Handstamped in Black or Red

1878 Wmk. 1 *Perf. 14*
1 A2 2c brown (Bk) 325.00
2 A2 2c brown (R)

The authenticity of Nos. 1-2 and the 2c brown, watermarked Crown and CA, is questioned.

S.

Overprinted in Black

1882 Wmk. 2
3 A2 2c brown — 2,900.
4 A2 2c rose

Overprinted

Overprint 16 to 16¾mm Wide

1881 Wmk. 1
5 A2 2c brown 110.00 110.00
a. Double overprint
b. "S" inverted 525.00 *550.00*
c. "S" wide 190.00 *200.00*
d. "N" wide *6,250.* *2,300.*
e. "SE" and "AN" wide ('82) 225.00 *225.00*
f. "SEL" and "N" wide ('82) 225.00 *225.00*
g. "SELAN" wide ('82) 225.00 *225.00*

Overprint 16 to 17mm Wide

1882-83 Wmk. 2
6 A2 2c brown 175.00 140.00
7 A2 2c rose 140.00 100.00

Overprinted

Overprint 14¼x3mm

8 A2 2c rose 11.50 *24.00*
a. Double overprint 975.00 850.00

Overprinted 

Overprint 14½ to 15½mm Wide

1886-89

9 A2 2c rose 37.50 *45.00*

Overprinted 

Overprint 16½x1¾mm

9A A2 2c rose 57.50 57.50
b. Double overprint 800.00

Overprinted 

Overprint 15½ to 17mm Wide With Period

10 A2 2c rose 100.00 75.00

Without Period

11 A2 2c rose 10.50 3.25

Same Overprint, but Vertically

12 A2 2c rose 18.00 *30.00*

Overprinted 

12A A2 2c rose 125.00 3.50

Overprinted *Selangor*

Overprint 17mm Wide

13 A2 2c rose 1,250. *1,400.*

Overprinted *SELANGOR*

14 A2 2c rose 375.00 175.00

Overprinted Vertically 

1889

15 A2 2c rose 550.00 30.00

Overprinted Vertically 

Overprint 19 to 20¾mm Wide

16 A2 2c rose 210.00 92.50

Similar Overprint, but Diagonally

17 A2 2c rose 2,100.

Overprinted Vertically 

18 A2 2c rose 80.00 7.00

Same Overprint Horizontally

18A A2 2c rose 3,750.

Surcharged in Black:

a

b

SELANGOR
Two
CENTS

c

d

e

1891

19 A3 (a) 2c on 24c green 30.00 *75.00*
20 A3 (b) 2c on 24c green 190.00 *250.00*
21 A3 (c) 2c on 24c green 190.00 *250.00*
22 A3 (d) 2c on 24c green 100.00 *150.00*
23 A3 (e) 2c on 24c green 190.00 *250.00*
Nos. 19-23 (5) 700.00 975.00

A6

1891-95 Typo. Wmk. 2

24 A6 1c green 1.75 .30
25 A6 2c rose 4.00 1.10
26 A6 2c orange ('95) 3.00 1.00
27 A6 5c blue 27.50 5.50
Nos. 24-27 (4) 36.25 7.90
Set, ovptd. "SPECIMEN" 100.00

Type of 1891 Surcharged 

1894

28 A6 3c on 5c rose 4.00 .55
Overprinted "SPECIMEN" in black 40.00

A8

A9

1895-99 Wmk. 2 *Perf. 14*

29 A8 3c lilac & car rose 3.25 .20
30 A8 5c lilac & olive .70 .25
31 A8 8c lilac & blue 55.00 8.00
32 A8 10c lilac & orange 10.50 .80
33 A8 25c grn & car rose 65.00 30.00
34 A8 50c lilac & black 45.00 20.00
35 A8 50c green & black 190.00 60.00

Wmk. 1

36 A9 $1 green & lt grn 70.00 90.00
37 A9 $2 grn & car rose 150.00 150.00
38 A9 $3 green & olive 325.00 210.00
39 A9 $5 green & ultra 190.00 210.00
40 A9 $10 grn & brn vio 550.00 425.00
41 A9 $25 green & org 1,400.

High values with revenue cancellations are plentiful and inexpensive.

Surcharged in Black:

1900 Wmk. 2

42 A8 1c on 5c lilac & olive 80.00 *125.00*
43 A8 1c on 50c grn & blk 1.60 1.90
a. Double surcharge 1,900.
44 A8 3c on 50c grn & blk 10.50 *16.00*
Nos. 42-44 (3) 92.10 *142.90*

Mosque at Klang
A12

Sultan Sulaiman
A13

1935-41 Typo. Wmk. 4 *Perf. 14*

45 A12 1c black ('36) .25 .20
46 A12 2c dp green ('36) .80 .20
46A A12 2c org brn ('41) 3.25 1.60
46B A12 3c green ('41) 1.10 *1.90*
47 A12 4c orange brown .25 .20
48 A12 5c chocolate .80 .20
49 A12 6c rose red 6.50 .20
50 A12 8c gray .70 .20
51 A12 10c dk violet ('36) .70 .20
52 A12 12c ultra ('36) 1.90 .20
52A A12 15c ultra ('41) 10.50 *32.50*
53 A12 25c rose red & pale vio ('36) 1.90 *.90*
54 A12 30c org & dk vio ('36) 1.75 *1.40*
55 A12 40c dk vio & car 2.40 1.60
56 A12 50c blk, *emer* ('36) 1.90 .70
57 A13 $1 red & black, *blue* ('36) 7.00 1.10
58 A13 $2 rose red & green ('36) 25.00 7.00
59 A13 $5 brn red & grn, *emer* ('36) 70.00 *42.50*
Nos. 45-59 (18) 136.70 *92.80*

Nos. 46A-46B were printed on both ordinary and chalky paper; 15c only on ordinary paper; other values only on chalky paper.

An 8c rose red was prepared but not issued.

For overprints see #N1-N15, N18A-N24, N26-N39.

Sultan Hisam-ud-Din Alam Shah
A14 A15

1941

72 A14 $1 red & blk, *blue* 10.50 5.50
73 A14 $2 car & green 65.00 *27.50*

A $5 stamp of type A14, issued during the Japanese occupation with different overprints (Nos. N18, N25A, N42), also exists without overprint. The unoverprinted stamp was not issued. Value $125.

For overprints see #N16-N17, N24A, N25, N40-N41.

Catalogue values for unused stamps in this section, from this point to the end of the section, are for Never Hinged items.

Silver Wedding Issue

Common Design Types

Inscribed: "Malaya Selangor"

Perf. 14x14½

1948, Dec. 1 Photo. Wmk. 4

74 CD304 10c purple .20 .20

Perf. 11½x11

Engraved; Name Typographed

75 CD305 $5 green 25.00 24.00

Common Design Types pictured following the introduction.

UPU Issue

Common Design Types

Inscribed: "Malaya-Selangor"

Engr.; Name Typo. on Nos. 77 & 78

1949, Oct. 10 *Perf. 13½, 11x11½*

76 CD306 10c rose violet .40 .40
77 CD307 15c indigo .55 .55
78 CD308 25c orange .90 .90
79 CD309 50c slate 1.90 1.90
Nos. 76-79 (4) 3.75 3.75

1949, Sept. 12 Typo. *Perf. 18*

80 A15 1c black .25 .35
81 A15 2c orange .25 .35
82 A15 3c green .55 1.75
83 A15 4c chocolate .25 .35
84 A15 6c gray .35 .35
85 A15 8c rose red .55 1.75
86 A15 10c plum .25 .35
87 A15 15c ultramarine 1.50 .35
88 A15 20c dk grn & black 2.50 1.00
89 A15 25c orange & rose lil 1.40 .35
90 A15 40c dk vio & rose red 3.25 7.25
91 A15 50c ultra & black .90 .35
92 A15 $1 vio brn & ultra 3.75 .35
93 A15 $2 rose red & emer 11.00 1.75
94 A15 $5 choc & emerald 60.00 2.75

1952-55

95 A15 5c rose violet .25 .35
96 A15 8c green .35 .35
97 A15 12c rose red .90 .75
98 A15 20c ultramarine 2.00 .35
99 A15 30c plum & rose red ('55) 2.50 .75
100 A15 35c dk vio & rose red 1.50 1.00
Nos. 80-100 (21) 94.25 22.95

Issued under Japanese Occupation

Stamps of Selangor 1935-41 Handstamped Vertically or Horizontally in Black, Red, Brown or Violet 

1942, Apr. 3 Wmk. 4 *Perf. 14*

N1 A12 1c black 15.00 21.00
N2 A12 2c deep green 600.00 600.00
N3 A12 2c orange brown 55.00 55.00
N4 A12 3c green 35.00 17.00
N5 A12 5c chocolate 10.00 10.00
N6 A12 6c rose red 200.00 200.00
N7 A12 8c gray 27.50 27.50
N8 A12 10c dark violet 22.50 27.50
N9 A12 12c ultramarine 47.50 47.50
N10 A12 15c ultramarine 17.00 20.00
N11 A12 25c rose red & pale vio 80.00 95.00
N12 A12 30c org & dk vio 15.00 30.00
N13 A12 40c dk vio & car 100.00 140.00
N14 A12 50c blk, *emerald* 40.00 47.50
N15 A13 $5 brn red & grn, *emer* 275.00 275.00

Some authorities believe No. N15 was not issued regularly.

Handstamped Vertically on Stamps and Type of Selangor 1941 in Black or Red

N16 A14 $1 red & blk, *bl* 67.50 80.00
N17 A14 $2 car & green 80.00 110.00
N18 A14 $5 brn red & grn, *emer* 110.00 110.00

Stamps and Type of Selangor, 1935-41, Overprinted in Black 

1942, May

N18A A12 1c black 110.00 110.00
N19 A12 3c green 1.00 1.00
N19A A12 5c chocolate 110.00 110.00
N20 A12 10c dark violet 35.00 35.00
N21 A12 12c ultramarine 2.75 5.00
N22 A12 15c ultramarine 5.50 4.00
N23 A12 30c org & dk vio 35.00 35.00
N24 A12 40c dk vio & car 4.00 4.00
N24A A14 $1 red & blk, *bl* 35.00 35.00
N25 A14 $2 car & green 24.00 30.00
N25A A14 $5 red & grn, *emer* 55.00 55.00
Nos. N18A-N25A (11) 417.25 424.00

Overprint is horizontal on $1, $2, $5.

On Nos. N18A and N19 the overprint is known reading up, instead of down.

Some authorities claim Nos. N18A, N19A, N20, N23, N24A and N25A were not regularly issued.

Selangor No. 46B Overprinted in Black

DAI NIPPON YUBIN

1942, Dec.

N26	A12	3c green	400.00	400.00

Stamps and Type of Selangor, 1935-41, Overprinted or Surcharged in Black or Red:

i

k

l

m

1943

N27	A12(i)	1c black	1.40	1.40
N28	A12(k)	1c black (R)	.90	.90
N29	A12(l)	2c on 5c choc (R)	.90	.90
N30	A12(i)	3c green	1.00	1.00
N31	A12(l)	3c on 5c choc	.65	1.00
N32	A12(k)	5c choc (R)	.65	1.00
N33	A12(l)	6c on 5c choc	.25	*.90*
N34	A12(m)	6c on 5c choc	.25	*1.00*
N35	A12(i)	12c ultra	1.40	1.60
N36	A12(i)	15c ultra	6.75	10.00
N37	A12(k)	15c ultra	13.50	13.50
N38	A12(m)	$1 on 10c dk vio	.50	*1.40*
N39	A12(m)	$1.50 on 30c org & dk vio	.50	*1.40*
N40	A14(i)	$1 red & blk, *blue*	6.75	8.50
N41	A14(i)	$2 car & grn	24.00	24.00
N42	A14(i)	$5 brn red & grn, *emer*	50.00	55.00
		Nos. N27-N42 (16)	109.40	123.50

The "i" overprint is vertical on Nos. N40-N42 and is also found reading in the opposite direction on Nos. N30, N35 and N36.

The overprint reads: "Japanese Postal Service."

Singapore is listed following Sierra Leone.

SUNGEI UJONG

'suŋ ü-juŋ

Formerly a nonfederated native state on the Malay Peninsula, which in 1895 was consolidated with the Federated State of Negri Sembilan.

Stamps of the Straits Settlements Overprinted in Black

Overprinted

1878 Wmk. 1 *Perf. 14*

2	A2	2c brown	2,600.	3,000.

Overprinted SUNGEI UJONG

4	A2	2c brown	325.00	
5	A2	4c rose	*900.00*	

No. 5 is no longer recognized by some experts.

Overprinted

1882-83 Wmk. 2

6	A2	2c brown	350.00	—
7	A2	4c rose	3,200.	3,500.

This overprint on the 2c brown, wmk. 1, is probably a trial printing.

Overprinted

11	A2	2c brown	325.00	*375.00*

Overprinted

1881-84

14	A2	2c brown	725.00	450.00
15	A2	2c rose	125.00	125.00
a.		"Ujong" printed sideways		
b.		"Sungei" printed twice		
16	A2	4c brown	300.00	400.00
17	A3	8c orange	1,900.	1,400.
18	A7	10c slate	625.00	625.00

Overprinted

19	A2	2c brown	55.00	*125.00*

Overprinted

1885-90

Without Period

20	A2	2c rose	35.00	*77.50*

With Period

21	A2	2c rose	125.00	90.00
a.		"UNJOG"	5,500.	3,500.

Overprinted

22	A2	2c rose	95.00	110.00
a.		Double overprint	725.00	725.00

Overprinted

23	A2	2c rose	125.00	*150.00*

Overprinted

24	A2	2c rose	14.50	*40.00*
a.		Double overprint		

Overprinted

25	A2	2c rose	100.00	*110.00*

Overprinted

26	A2	2c rose	175.00	175.00
c.		Double overprint		

Overprinted

Overprint 14-16x3mm

26A	A2	2c rose	9.00	13.00

Overprinted

26B	A2	2c rose	40.00	18.00

Stamp of 1883-91 Surcharged:

a

SUNGEI
UJONG
Two
CENTS

b

c

SUNGEI
UJONG
Two
CENTS

d

1891

27	A3	(a) 2c on 24c green	175.00	*190.00*
28	A3	(b) 2c on 24c green	850.00	*925.00*
29	A3	(c) 2c on 24c green	325.00	*350.00*
30	A3	(d) 2c on 24c green	850.00	*900.00*
		Nos. 27-30 (4)	2,200.	2,365.

On Nos. 27-28, SUNGEI is 14½mm, UJONG 12¾x2½mm.

A3

A4

1891-94 Typo. *Perf. 14*

31	A3	2c rose	40.00	35.00
32	A3	2c orange ('94)	2.25	5.50
33	A3	5c blue ('93)	6.50	7.75
		Nos. 31-33 (3)	48.75	48.25

Type of 1891 Surcharged in Black

1894

34	A3	1c on 5c green	1.40	.90
35	A3	3c on 5c rose	3.25	*6.00*

1895

36	A4	3c lilac & car rose	9.25	3.00

Stamps of Sungei Ujong were superseded by those of Negri Sembilan in 1895.

TRENGGANU

treŋ'gä-ˌnü

LOCATION — On the eastern coast of the Malay Peninsula.
AREA — 5,050 sq. mi.
POP. — 302,171 (1960)
CAPITAL — Kuala Trengganu

Sultan Zenalabidin
A1 A2

1910-19 Typo. Wmk. 3 *Perf. 14*

Ordinary Paper

1	A1	1c gray green	3.25	1.50
a.		1c blue green	2.00	1.10
2	A1	2c red vio & brn ('15)	1.10	1.00
3	A1	3c rose red	2.50	2.50
4	A1	4c brn orange	4.00	*6.25*
5	A1	4c grn & org brn ('15)	2.40	*5.75*
6	A1	4c scarlet ('19)	1.40	*2.00*
7	A1	5c gray	1.50	*3.75*
8	A1	5c choc & gray ('15)	2.75	2.25
9	A1	8c ultramarine	1.50	10.00
10	A1	10c red & grn, *yel* ('15)	1.50	2.50

Chalky Paper

11	A1	10c violet, *yel*	5.75	15.00
a.		10c violet, *pale yel*	3.75	5.75
12	A1	20c red vio & vio	4.00	*4.75*
13	A1	25c dl vio & grn ('15)	9.25	*37.50*
14	A1	30c blk & dl vio ('15)	7.75	*62.50*
15	A1	50c blk & sep, *grn*	5.50	*9.75*
16	A1	$1 red & blk, *blue*	20.00	*27.50*
17	A1	$3 red & grn, *grn* ('15)	190.00	*375.00*
18	A2	$5 lil & blue grn	190.00	*525.00*
19	A2	$25 green & car	1,100.	
		Revenue Cancel		300.00
		Overprinted "SPECIMEN"	290.00	
		Nos. 1-18 (18)	454.15	*1,094.*
		Nos. 1-18 ovptd. "SPECIMEN"	625.00	

On No. 19 the numerals and Arabic inscriptions at top, left and right are in color on a colorless background.

Overprints are listed after No. 41. For surcharges see Nos. B1-B4.

A3

Sultan Badaru'l-alam
A4

1921-38 Wmk. 4 *Perf. 14*

Chalky Paper

20	A3	1c black ('25)	2.00	1.75
21	A3	2c deep green	1.50	2.40
22	A3	3c dp grn ('25)	2.25	1.10
23	A3	3c lt brn ('38)	27.50	*16.00*
24	A3	4c rose red	1.75	1.40
25	A3	5c choc & gray	2.40	5.75
26	A3	5c vio, *yel* ('25)	2.00	1.40
27	A3	6c orange ('24)	4.25	.60
28	A3	8c gray ('38)	30.00	6.75
29	A3	10c ultramarine	2.40	1.10
30	A3	12c ultra ('25)	5.00	*5.25*
31	A3	20c org & dl vio	2.50	*1.75*
32	A3	25c dk vio & grn	2.75	*3.50*
33	A3	30c blk & dl vio	4.00	4.25
34	A3	35c red, *yel* ('25)	5.50	*9.00*
35	A3	50c car & green	8.50	3.75
36	A3	$1 ultra & vio, *bl* ('29)	11.00	4.25
37	A3	$3 red & green, *emer* ('25)	62.50	*175.00*
38	A4	$5 red & grn, *yel* ('38)	350.00	*2,000.*
39	A4	$25 blue & lil	750.00	*1,250.*
		Overprinted "SPECIMEN"	160.00	
40	A4	$50 org & green	1,850.	*3,200.*
		Overprinted "SPECIMEN"	350.00	
41	A4	$100 red & green	5,750.	7,500.
		Overprinted "SPECIMEN"	625.00	
		Nos. 20-37 (18)	177.80	*245.00*
		Nos. 20-38 ovptd. or perf "SPECIMEN"	800.00	

On Nos. 39 to 41 the numerals and Arabic inscriptions at top, left and right are in color on a colorless background.

A 2c orange, 6c gray, 8c rose red and 15c ultramarine, type A3, exist, but are not known to have been regularly issued.

For surcharges and overprints see Nos. 45-46, N1-N60.

Stamps of 1910-21 Overprinted in Black: "MALAYA BORNEO EXHIBITION" in THREE LINES

1922, Mar. Wmk. 3

8a	A1	5c chocolate & gray	4.00	*32.50*
10a	A1	10c red & green, *yel*	4.00	*32.50*
12a	A1	20c red vio & violet	3.50	*42.50*
13a	A1	25c dull vio & green	3.50	*42.50*
14a	A1	30c black & dull vio	3.50	*42.50*
15a	A1	50c blk & sepia, *grn*	3.50	*42.50*
16a	A1	$1 red & blk, *blue*	16.00	*80.00*
17a	A1	$3 red & grn, *green*	175.00	*475.00*
18a	A2	$5 lil & blue green	240.00	*475.00*

Wmk. 4

21a	A3	2c deep green	2.40	*40.00*
24a	A3	4c rose red	6.50	*40.00*
		Nos. 8a-24a (11)	461.90	*1,345.*

Industrial fair at Singapore, Mar. 31-Apr. 15.

1921 Wmk. 3

Chalky Paper

42	A3	$1 ultra & vio, *bl*	19.00	*27.50*
43	A3	$3 red & grn, *emer*	110.00	*110.00*
44	A4	$5 red & green, *yel*	110.00	*100.00*
		Nos. 42-44 (3)	239.00	*237.50*

Types of 1921-25 Surcharged in Black

1941, May 1 Wmk. 4 *Perf. 13½x14*

45	A3	2c on 5c magenta, *yel*	8.00	*6.50*
46	A3	8c on 10c lt ultra	13.00	*6.50*

For overprints see #N30-N33, N46-N47, N59-N60.

Catalogue values for unused stamps in this section, from this point to the end of the section, are for Never Hinged items.

Silver Wedding Issue

Common Design Types

Inscribed: "Malaya Trengganu"

1948, Dec. 1 Photo. *Perf. 14x14½*

47	CD304	10c purple	.20	.20

Engraved; Name Typographed

Perf. 11½x11

48	CD305	$5 rose car	35.00	52.50

Common Design Types pictured following the introduction.

UPU Issue

Common Design Types

Inscribed: "Malaya-Trengganu"

Engr.; Name Typo. on 15c, 25c

Perf. 13½, 11x11½

1949, Oct. 10 Wmk. 4

49	CD306	10c rose violet	.60	.60
50	CD307	15c indigo	.70	1.90
51	CD308	25c orange	1.25	3.25
52	CD309	50c slate	1.90	3.25
		Nos. 49-52 (4)	4.45	9.00

Sultan Ismail Nasiruddin Shah — A5

1949, Dec. 27 Typo. *Perf. 18*

53	A5	1c black	.30	.45
54	A5	2c orange	.30	.45
55	A5	3c green	1.00	1.40
56	A5	4c chocolate	.50	.45
57	A5	6c gray	1.00	1.10
58	A5	8c rose red	1.40	1.75
59	A5	10c plum	.50	.45
60	A5	15c ultramarine	1.50	1.50
61	A5	20c dk grn & black	2.00	4.50
62	A5	25c org & rose lilac	1.90	3.00
63	A5	40c dk vio & rose red	3.75	25.00
64	A5	50c dp ultra & black	2.40	2.50
65	A5	$1 vio brn & ultra	4.50	9.00
66	A5	$2 rose red & emer	25.00	22.50
67	A5	$5 choc & emerald	67.50	62.50

1952-55

68	A5	5c rose violet	.30	.45
69	A5	8c green	1.40	3.00
70	A5	12c rose red	1.40	*6.25*
71	A5	20c ultramarine	1.40	1.40
72	A5	30c plum & rose red ('55)	2.50	6.25
73	A5	35c dk vio & rose red	3.00	6.25
		Nos. 53-73 (21)	123.55	160.15

SEMI-POSTAL STAMPS

Nos. 3, 4 and 9 Surcharged

1917, Oct. Wmk. 3 *Perf. 14*

B1	A1	3c + 2c rose red	.60	*3.50*
	a.	"CSOSS"	65.00	*100.00*
	b.	Comma after "2c"	4.00	*10.50*
	c.	Pair, one without surcharge	2,900.	*2,900.*
B2	A1	4c + 2c brn org	.90	*5.50*
	a.	"CSOSS"	275.00	*275.00*
	b.	Comma after "2c"	16.00	*42.50*
B3	A1	8c + 2c ultra	1.50	*10.50*
	a.	"CSOSS"	175.00	*210.00*
	b.	Comma after "2c"	13.00	*45.00*
		Nos. B1-B3 (3)	3.00	*19.50*

Same Surcharge on No. 5

1918

B4	A1	4c + 2c grn & org brn	1.90	*10.50*
	a.	Pair, one without surcharge	*2,300.*	

POSTAGE DUE STAMPS

D1

Perf. 14

1937, Aug. 10 Typo. Wmk. 4

J1	D1	1c rose red	7.50	*62.50*
		Never hinged	11.50	
J2	D1	4c green	8.00	*67.50*
		Never hinged	11.50	
J3	D1	8c lemon	45.00	*375.00*
		Never hinged	67.50	
J4	D1	10c light brown	87.50	*110.00*
		Never hinged	125.00	
		Nos. J1-J4 (4)	148.00	*615.00*
		Set, perf "SPECIMEN"	160.00	

For overprints see Nos. NJ1-NJ4.

OCCUPATION STAMPS

Issued under Japanese Occupation

Stamps of Trengganu, 1921-38, Handstamped in Black or Brown

1942 Wmk. 4 *Perf. 14*

N1	A3	1c black	110.00	110.00
N2	A3	2c deep green	190.00	275.00
N3	A3	3c lt brown	140.00	110.00
N4	A3	4c rose red	275.00	190.00
N5	A3	5c violet, *yel*	17.50	19.00
N6	A3	6c orange	13.50	20.00
N7	A3	8c gray	17.50	25.00
N8	A3	10c ultramarine	13.50	27.50
N9	A3	12c ultramarine	15.00	25.00
N10	A3	20c org & dl vio	15.00	22.50
N11	A3	25c dk vio & grn	13.50	27.50
N12	A3	30c blk & dl vio	13.50	25.00
N13	A3	35c red, *yel*	22.50	27.50
N14	A3	50c car & grn	125.00	95.00
N15	A3	$1 ultra & vio, *blue*	1,650.	1,750.
N16	A3	$3 red & grn, *emerald*	125.00	140.00
N17	A4	$5 red & grn, *yellow*	240.00	240.00
N17A	A4	$25 blue & lil	1,500.	
N17B	A4	$50 org & grn	*8,800.*	
N17C	A4	$100 red & grn	950.00	

Handstamped in Red

N18	A3	1c black	275.00	225.00
N19	A3	2c dp green	140.00	160.00
N20	A3	5c violet, *yel*	35.00	20.00
N21	A3	6c orange	20.00	20.00
N22	A3	8c gray	275.00	240.00
N23	A3	10c ultramarine	275.00	275.00
N24	A3	12c ultramarine	55.00	55.00
N25	A3	20c org & dl vio	35.00	35.00
N26	A3	25c dk vio & grn	40.00	40.00
N27	A3	30c blk & dl vio	35.00	35.00
N28	A3	35c red, *yellow*	35.00	20.00
N29	A3	$3 red & grn, *emerald*	100.00	40.00
N29A	A3	$25 blue & lil	500.00	500.00

Handstamped on Nos. 45 and 46 in Black or Red

N30	A3	2c on 5c (Bk)	140.00	140.00
N31	A3	2c on 5c (R)	100.00	100.00
N32	A3	8c on 10c (Bk)	25.00	35.00
N33	A3	8c on 10c (R)	35.00	40.00

Stamps of Trengganu, 1921-38, Overprinted in Black

1942

N34	A3	1c black	15.00	17.00
N35	A3	2c deep green	100.00	*140.00*
N36	A3	3c light brown	16.00	29.00
N37	A3	4c rose red	15.00	20.00
N38	A3	5c violet, *yel*	10.00	20.00
N39	A3	6c orange	10.00	17.00
N40	A3	8c gray	67.50	20.00
N41	A3	12c ultramarine	10.00	13.50
N42	A3	20c org & dl vio	13.50	25.00
N43	A3	25c dk vio & grn	13.50	17.00
N44	A3	30c blk & dl vio	13.50	20.00
N45	A3	$3 red & grn, *emer*	100.00	140.00

Overprinted on Nos. 45 and 46 in Black

N46	A3	2c on 5c mag, *yel*	13.50	17.00
N47	A3	8c on 10c lt ultra	11.50	20.00
		Nos. N34-N47 (14)	409.00	*515.50*

Stamps of Trengganu, 1921-38, Overprinted in Black

1943

N48	A3	1c black	13.50	19.00
N49	A3	2c deep green	13.50	27.50
N50	A3	5c violet, *yel*	11.50	27.50
N51	A3	6c orange	15.00	27.50
N52	A3	8c gray	95.00	67.50
N53	A3	10c ultramarine	100.00	175.00
N54	A3	12c ultramarine	19.00	*35.00*
N55	A3	20c org & dl vio	20.00	*35.00*
N56	A3	25c dl vio & grn	19.00	*35.00*
N57	A3	30c blk & dl vio	20.00	*35.00*
N58	A3	35c red, *yellow*	20.00	*40.00*

Overprinted on Nos. 45 and 46 in Black

N59	A3	2c on 5c mag, *yel*	11.00	*35.00*
N60	A3	8c on 10c lt ultra	27.50	*25.00*
		Nos. N48-N60 (13)	385.00	*584.00*

The Japanese characters read: "Japanese Postal Service."

OCCUPATION POSTAGE DUE STAMPS

Trengganu Nos. J1-J4 Handstamped in Black or Brown

1942 Wmk. 4 *Perf. 14*

NJ1	D1	1c rose red	67.50	*95.00*
NJ2	D1	4c green	125.00	*125.00*
NJ3	D1	8c lemon	25.00	*67.50*
NJ4	D1	10c light brown	25.00	*50.00*
		Nos. NJ1-NJ4 (4)	242.50	*337.50*

The handstamp reads: "Seal of Post Office of Malayan Military Department."

MALDIVE ISLANDS

'mol-ˌdīv 'ī-ləndz

LOCATION — A group of 2,000 islands in the Indian Ocean about 400 miles southwest of Ceylon.
GOVT. — Republic
AREA — 115 sq. mi.
POP. — 168,000 (est. 1983)
CAPITAL — Male

Maldive Islands was a British Protectorate as a dependency of Ceylon.

100 Cents = 1 Rupee

Stamps of Ceylon, 1904-05, Overprinted

1906, Sept. 9 Wmk. 3 *Perf. 14*

1	A36	2c orange brown	16.00	*25.00*
2	A37	3c green	17.50	*25.00*
3	A37	4c yellow & blue	32.50	*60.00*
4	A38	5c dull lilac	5.00	*6.50*
5	A40	15c ultramarine	62.50	*100.00*
6	A40	25c bister	72.50	*100.00*
		Nos. 1-6 (6)	206.00	*316.50*

Minaret of Juma Mosque, near Male — A1

1909 Engr. Wmk. 47

7	A1	2c orange brown	2.00	2.25
8	A1	3c green	.50	.70
9	A1	5c red violet	.30	.30
10	A1	10c carmine	7.50	.80
		Nos. 7-10 (4)	10.30	4.05

Type of 1909 Issue Redrawn

Perf. 14½x14

1933 Photo. Wmk. 233

11	A1	2c gray	2.75	1.75
12	A1	3c yellow brown	.75	1.50
13	A1	5c brown lake	17.50	10.00
14	A1	6c brown red	1.75	5.00
15	A1	10c green	1.00	.50
16	A1	15c gray black	6.50	11.00
17	A1	25c red brown	6.50	11.00

18 A1 50c red violet 6.50 11.00
19 A1 1r blue black 12.50 5.00
Nos. 11-19 (9) 55.75 56.75

On the 6c, 15c, 25c and 50c, the right hand panel carries only the word "CENTS."

Nos. 11-19 exist with watermark vert. or horiz. The 5c with vert. watermark sells for twice the price of the horiz. watermark.

MALTA

'mol-tə

LOCATION — A group of islands in the Mediterranean Sea off the coast of Sicily
GOVT. — Republic within the British Commonwealth
AREA — 122 sq. mi.
POP. — 329,189 (1983)
CAPITAL — Valletta

The former colony includes the islands of Malta, Gozo, and Comino.

4 Farthings = 1 Penny
12 Pence = 1 Shilling
20 Shillings = 1 Pound

Catalogue values for unused stamps in this country are for Never Hinged items, beginning with Scott 206 in the regular postage section.

FORERUNNERS

Values are for clear cancellations on sound, fault-free stamps, with average to fine centering. In many cases, very fine copies are rare or non-existent.

STAMPS OF GREAT BRITAIN USED IN MALTA

Canceled with seven-line wavy obliterator

1855-56

A1 1p red brown, Die I (#8) 950.00
A2 1p red brown, Die II (#12) 925.00
A3 1p red brown, Die II (#14) 950.00
A4 1p red brown, Die II (#16) 925.00
A5 2p blue (#17) —
A6 6p red violet (#7) *4,750.*
A7 1sh green (#5) *5,250.*

Cancelled with oval barred "M" obliterator

1857-59

A8 1p red brown (#3) *1,900.*
A9 1p red brown, Die I (#8) 150.00
A10 1p red brown, Die II (#9) 1,050.
A11 1p red brown, Die II (#12) 265.00
A12 1p red brown, Die II (#16) 87.50
A13 1p rose red (#20) 24.00
A14 2p blue (#4) *3,500.*
A15 2p blue (#10) 875.00
A16 2p blue (#17) 65.00
A17 2p blue (#19) 350.00
A18 2p blue, Plate 7 (#29) 67.50
Plate 8 57.50
Plate 9 47.50
A19 4p rose (#26) 50.00
a. Thick glazed paper (#26b) 210.00
A20 6p red violet (#7) *4,150.*
A21 6p lilac (#27) 60.00
a. Thick paper (#27d) 240.00
b. Bluish paper (#27c) 1,000.
A22 1sh green (#28) 140.00
a. Thick paper (#28d) 210.00

Cancelled 'A25' in barred oval

1860-84

A23 ½p rose red, plates 4-6, 8-15, 19 (#58), *value from* 27.50
A24 1p red brown (#3) *3,250.*
A25 1p red brown, Die I (#8) 375.00
A26 1p red brown, Die I (#16) 87.50
A27 1p rose red (#20) 9.00
A28 1p rose red, (#33), plates 71-74, 76, 78-125, 127, 129-224 *value from* 17.50
A29 1½p lake red, plates 1, 3 (#32), *value from* 525.00
A30 2p blue (#4) *4,750.*
A31 2p blue (#17) 82.50
A32 2p blue, plates 7, 8, 9, 12 (#29), *value from* 17.50
A33 2p blue, plates 13, 14, 15 (#30), *value from* 17.50
A34 2½p claret, plates 1, 2, 3 (#66), *value from* 37.50
a. Bluish paper, plates 1, 2 (#66a), *value from* 82.50
b. Lettered "LH-FL" (#66b) *2,750.*
A35 2½p claret, plates 3-17 (#67), *value from* 19.00
A36 2½p blue plates 17-20 (#68), *value from* 22.50
A37 2½p blue plates 21-23 (#82), *value from* 12.50
A38 3p rose (#37) 140.00
A39 3p rose (#44) 87.50
A40 3p rose, plates 4-10 (#49), *value from* 27.50
A41 3p rose, plates 11-20 (#61), *value from* 37.50
A42 3p rose, plates 20, 21 (#83), *value from* 1,050.
A43 3p on 3d violet (#94) 550.00
A44 4p rose (#26) 45.00
a. Thick glazed paper (#26b) 175.00
A45 4p vermilion, plate 3 (#34) 45.00
a. Hair lines (#34c) 55.00
A46 4p vermilion, plates 7-14 (#43), *value from* 27.50
A47 4p vermilion, plate 15 (#69) 210.00
A48 4p pale olive green, plate 15 (#70) 175.00
Plate 16 (#70) 175.00
A49 4p gray brown, plate 17 (#71) 240.00
A50 4p gray brown, plate 17, 18 (#84), *value from* 57.50
A51 6p red violet (#7) *3,000.*
A52 6p lilac (#27) 55.00
a. Thick paper (#27d) —
A53 6p lilac, plate 3 (#39) 45.00
a. Hairlines, plate 4 (#39b) 100.00
A54 6p lilac (#45) 45.00
Plate 6 (#45) 100.00
a. Wmk. 3 (#45c) *1,400.*
Plate 6 (#45c) —
A55 6p dull violet, plate 6 (#50) 50.00
A56 6p violet, plates 6, 8, 9 (#51) 40.00
A57 6p brown plate 11 (#59), *value from* 37.50
a. 6p pale buff, plate 11 (#59b) 120.00
Plate 12 (#59b) 140.00
A58 6p gray, plate 12 (#60) 140.00
A59 6p gray, plates 13-17 (#62), *value from* 37.50
A60 6p gray, plates 17, 18 (#86), *value from* 72.50
A61 6p on 6p violet (#95) 140.00
A62 8p orange (#73) 440.00
A63 9p straw (#40) 700.00
a. 9p bister (#40a) 650.00
A64 9p straw (#46) 650.00
A65 9p bister (#52) 825.00
A66 10p red brown (#53) 190.00
A67 1sh green (#5) *3,250.*
A68 1sh green (#28) 160.00
a. Thick paper (#28d) 325.00
A69 1sh green (#42) 95.00
A70 1sh green (#48) 95.00
A71 1sh green, plates 4-7 (#54), *value from* 32.50
A72 1sh green, plates 8-13 (#64), *value from* 47.50
A73 1sh salmon, plate 13 (#65) 300.00
A74 1sh salmon, plates 13, 14 (#87), *value from* 90.00
A75 2sh blue (#55) 165.00
A76 2sh brown (#56) *3,000.*
A77 5sh rose, plate 1 (#57) 475.00
Plate 2 (#57) 575.00
A78 5sh rose, *bluish* (#90) *2,000.*
a. White paper (#90a) *1,750.*
A79 10sh gray green (#74) *3,250.*

1880

A80 ½p deep green (#78) 15.00
a. ½p green (#78c) 15.00
A81 1p red brown (#79) 14.00
A82 1½p red brown (#80) 475.00
A83 2p lilac rose (#81) 45.00
a. 2p deep lilac rose (#81a) 45.00
A84 5p indigo (#85) 77.50

1881

A85 1p lilac, 14 dots (#88) 30.00
A86 1p lilac, 16 dots (#89) 10.00

1883-84

A87 ½p slate blue (#98) 16.50
A88 1½p lilac (#99) —
A89 2p lilac (#100) 100.00
A90 2½p lilac (#101) 14.00
A91 3p lilac (#102) —
A92 4p dull green (#103) 190.00
A93 5p dull green (#104) 165.00
A94 6p dull green (#105) —
A95 9p dull green (#106) —
A96 1sh dull green (#107) —
A97 5sh rose, white paper (#108) 1,150.
a. Bluish paper (#108a) *1,900.*

Postal Fiscal stamps of Great Britain are found used in Malta. They are rare.

STAMPS OF FRANCE USED IN MALTA

1853-60

A98 5c green (#13) —
On cover —
A99 10c bister (#14) 125.00
On cover *1,400.*
A100 20c blue (#15) 115.00
On cover *1,300.*
A101 40c orange (#18) 92.50
On cover *1,050.*
A102 80c lake, *yellowish* (#19) 145.00
On cover *1,650.*
A103 80c rose, *pinkish* (#20) 145.00
On cover *1,650.*

1862-67

A104 5c green (#23) 57.50
On cover *1,250.*
A105 10c bister (#25) 37.50
On cover *975.00*
A106 20c blue (#26) 92.50
On cover *1,175.*
A107 40c orange (#27) 100.00
On cover *1,300.*
A108 80c rose, *pinkish* (#28) 150.00
On cover *1,550.*
a. 80c carmine rose (#28b) 175.00
On cover *1,600.*

1863-70

A109 10c bister (#32) 80.00
On cover *1,500.*
A110 20c blue (#33) 57.50
On cover *1,350.*
A111 30c brown, *yellowish* (#34) 80.00
On cover *1,650.*
A112 40c orange, *yellowish* (#35) 100.00
On cover *1,500.*
A113 80c rose, *pinkish* (#36) 150.00

Stamps of Italy, and occasionally those of other Mediterranean countries, are found obliterated by the A25 cancellations, usually originating in ship mail.

Issued under British Administration

Values for unused stamps are for examples with original gum as defined in the catalogue introduction. Very fine examples of Nos. 1-7 will have perforations touching the frameline on one or more sides due to the narrow spacing of the stamps on the plate. Stamps with perfs clear of the frameline are scarce and will command higher prices.

Queen Victoria
A1 A2

A3 A4

1860-61 Unwmk. Typo. *Perf. 14*

1 A1 ½p buff ('63) 775.00 375.00
On cover *1,650.*
a. ½p pale buff ('63) 775.00 375.00
On cover *1,650.*
b. ½p brown orange ('61) 1,050. 440.00
On cover *1,750.*
2 A1 ½p buff, *bluish* 1,100. 550.00
On cover *2,400.*
a. Imperf. (single) *11,750.*

1863-80 Wmk. 1

3 A1 ½p yellow buff ('75) 75.00 65.00
a. ½p buff 100.00 65.00
b. ½p brown orange ('67) 375.00 105.00
c. ½p orange yellow ('80) 200.00 105.00
d. ½p bright orange ('64) 560.00 165.00
e. ½p dull orange ('70) 240.00 82.50
f. ½p orange buff ('72) 165.00 70.00
g. ½p pale buff ('77) 190.00 65.00
h. ½p yellow ('81) 110.00 65.00
4 A1 ½p golden yel (aniline) ('74) 325.00 375.00

1865 *Perf. 12½*

5 A1 ½p buff 150.00 110.00
a. ½p yellow buff 325.00 190.00

1878 *Perf. 14x12½*

6 A1 ½p buff 190.00 100.00
a. Perf. 12½x14 950.00
b. ½p yellow ('79) 210.00 105.00

1882 Wmk. 2 *Perf. 14*

7 A1 ½p reddish orange ('84) 20.00 *55.00*
a. ½p orange 42.50 40.00

1885, Jan. 1

8 A1 ½p green 3.25 .60
9 A2 1p car rose 5.75 .40
a. 1p rose 100.00 30.00
10 A3 2p gray 6.50 1.75
11 A4 2½p ultramarine 47.50 1.25
a. 2½p bright ultramarine 47.50 1.25
b. 2½p dull blue 65.00 3.00
12 A3 4p brown 13.00 3.50
a. Imperf., pair *6,000.* *6,000.*
13 A3 1sh violet 45.00 11.00
a. 1sh pale dull violet ('90) 70.00 22.50
Nos. 8-13 (6) 121.00 18.50
Set of 6, overprinted "SPECIMEN" *4,000.*

Do not confuse faded examples of No. 13 for No. 13a.

For surcharge see No. 20.

Queen Victoria within Maltese Cross — A5

1886 Wmk. 1

14 A5 5sh rose 125.00 95.00
Overprinted "SPECIMEN" 700.00

Gozo Fishing Boat — A6 Ancient Galley — A7

1899, Feb. 4 Engr. Wmk. 2

15 A6 4½p black brown 21.00 15.00
16 A7 5p brown red 40.00 17.50

See Nos. 42-45.

"Malta" — A8

St. Paul after Shipwreck — A9

1899 **Wmk. 1**
17 A8 2sh6p olive gray 47.50 14.00
18 A9 10sh blue black 105.00 75.00

See No. 64. For overprint see No. 85.

Valletta Harbor — A10

1901, Jan. 1 **Wmk. 2**
19 A10 1f red brown 1.75 .55
a. 1f brown 5.25 3.00

See Nos. 28-29.

No. 11 Surcharged in Black

1902, July 4
20 A4 1p on 2½p dull blue 1.25 1.60
a. "Pnney" 32.50 *65.00*
b. Double surcharge 17,500. *4,500.*
d. 1p on 2½p bright ultra 1.10 *2.00*
e. As "d," "Pnney" 35.00 *65.00*
Overprinted "SPECIMEN" 82.50

King Edward VII — A12

1903-04 **Typo.**
21 A12 ½p dark green 10.00 1.00
22 A12 1p car & black 17.50 .50
23 A12 2p gray & red vio 32.50 7.00
24 A12 2½p ultra & brn vio 27.50 5.25
25 A12 3p red vio & gray 2.00 .60
26 A12 4p brown & blk ('04) 30.00 19.00
27 A12 1sh violet & gray 22.50 8.25
Nos. 21-27 (7) 142.00 41.60
Set of 7 ovptd "SPECIMEN" 175.00

1904-11 **Wmk. 3**
28 A10 1f red brown ('05) 7.00 .95
29 A10 1f dk brown ('10) 3.50 .20
30 A12 ½p green 6.00 .35
31 A12 1p car & blk ('05) 11.00 .25
32 A12 1p carmine ('07) 3.00 .20
33 A12 2p gray & red vio ('05) 12.00 2.50
34 A12 2p gray ('11) 3.75 6.50
35 A12 2½p ultra & brn vio 25.00 .70
36 A12 2½p ultra ('11) 6.50 3.75
37 A12 4p brn & blk ('06) 13.00 6.50
38 A12 4p scar & blk, *yel* ('11) 4.75 4.00
39 A12 1sh violet & gray 57.50 2.40
40 A12 1sh blk, *grn* ('11) 8.75 3.75
41 A12 5sh scar & grn, *yel* ('11) 75.00 87.50

Engr.
42 A6 4½p black brn ('05) 32.50 6.50
43 A6 4½p orange ('11) 5.25 4.00
44 A7 5p red ('04) 32.50 5.75
45 A7 5p ol green ('10) 5.00 4.00
a. 5p deep sage green ('14) 13.00 *16.00*
Nos. 28-45 (18) 312.00 139.80

A13

A15

King George V — A16

1914-21 **Typo.**

Ordinary Paper
49 A13 ¼p brown 1.25 .20
50 A13 ½p green 2.50 .35
51 A13 1p scarlet ('15) 1.75 .45
a. 1p carmine ('14) 1.75 .20
52 A13 2p gray ('15) 11.00 4.75
53 A13 2½p ultramarine 2.50 .60

Chalky Paper
54 A15 3p vio, *yel* 3.00 *11.50*
a. 3p violet, *orange yellow,* 70.00 50.00
58 A13 6p dull vio & red vio 13.00 *21.00*
59 A15 1sh black, *green* 14.00 *20.00*
a. 1sh black, *bl grn,* ol back 22.50 27.50
b. 1sh black, *emerald* ('21) 37.50 *82.50*
c. As "b," olive back 10.00 *27.50*
60 A16 2sh ultra & dl vio, *bl* 57.50 35.00
61 A16 5sh scar & grn, *yel* 105.00 *115.00*

Surface-colored Paper
62 A15 1sh blk, *grn* ('15) 16.00 *30.00*
Nos. 49-54,58-62 (11) 227.50 238.85

See Nos. 66-68, 70-72. For overprints see Nos. 77-82, 84.

Valletta Harbor — A17

1915 **Engr.**

Ordinary Paper
63 A17 4p black 17.50 4.75

St. Paul A18

George V A19

1919
64 A8 2sh6p olive green 70.00 *95.00*
65 A18 10sh black 3,500. *4,400.*
Revenue cancel 85.00
Overprinted "SPECIMEN" 950.00

For overprint see No. 83.

1921-22 **Typo.** **Wmk. 4**

Ordinary Paper
66 A13 ¼p brown 2.75 *32.50*
67 A13 ½p green 3.50 *22.50*
68 A13 1p rose red 3.25 1.90
69 A19 2p gray 5.25 2.00
70 A13 2½p ultramarine 4.25 *32.50*

Chalky Paper
71 A13 6p dull vio & red vio 32.50 80.00
72 A16 2sh ultra & dull vio, *bl* 70.00 *225.00*

Engr.

Ordinary Paper
73 A18 10sh black 400.00 *750.00*
Nos. 66-73 (8) 521.50 1,146.

For overprints and surcharge see Nos. 86-93, 97.

Stamps of 1914-19 Overprinted in Red or Black

1922 **Wmk. 3**

Ordinary Paper

Overprint 21mm
77 A13 ½p green 1.10 2.00
78 A13 2½p ultra 9.75 32.50

Chalky Paper
79 A15 3p violet, *yel* 3.50 19.00
80 A13 6p dull lil & red vio 2.75 18.00
81 A15 1sh black, *emer* 4.00 18.00

Overprint 28mm
82 A16 2sh ultra & dull vio, *bl* (R) 250.00 525.00

Ordinary Paper
83 A8 2sh6p olive grn 25.00 52.50

Chalky Paper
84 A16 5sh scar & grn, *yel* 57.50 92.50
Nos. 77-84 (8) 353.60 759.50

Wmk. 1

Ordinary Paper
85 A9 10sh blue black (R) 225.00 *400.00*

Same Overprint on Stamps of 1921

1922 **Ordinary Paper** **Wmk. 4**

Overprint 21mm
86 A13 ¼p brown .35 *.85*
87 A13 ½p green 2.25 *7.00*
88 A13 1p rose red 1.10 .20
89 A19 2p gray 2.50 .50
90 A13 2½p ultramarine 1.25 1.10

Chalky Paper
91 A13 6p dull vio & red vio 12.50 *37.50*

Overprint 28mm
92 A16 2sh ultra & dull vio, *bl* (R) 45.00 *100.00*

Ordinary Paper
93 A18 10sh black (R) 160.00 *225.00*
Nos. 86-93 (8) 224.95 372.15

No. 69 Surcharged

1922, Apr. 15
97 A19 1f on 2p gray .75 .50

"Malta" — A20

Britannia and Malta — A21

1922-26 **Typo.**

Chalky Paper
98 A20 ¼p brown 3.00 .70
99 A20 ½p green 3.00 .20
100 A20 1p buff & plum 3.75 .20
101 A20 1p violet ('24) 3.75 .90
102 A20 1½p org brn ('23) 4.75 .20
103 A20 2p ol brn & turq 3.25 1.40
104 A20 2½p ultra ('26) 3.25 *8.00*
105 A20 3p ultramarine 4.25 1.75
a. 3p blue 3.75 1.75
106 A20 3p blk, *yel* ('26) 3.50 *15.00*
107 A20 4p yel & ultra 2.25 *2.75*
108 A20 6p ol grn & vio 3.75 2.50
109 A21 1sh ol brn & blue 8.00 2.75
110 A21 2sh ultra & ol brn 11.50 11.50
111 A21 2sh6p blk & red vio 12.50 *17.50*
112 A21 5sh ultra & org 24.00 *47.50*
113 A21 10sh ol brn & gray 62.50 *175.00*

Engr.

Ordinary Paper
114 A20 £1 car red & blk ('25) 140.00 *350.00*
a. £1 rose car & blk ('22) 140.00 *350.00*
Nos. 98-114 (17) 297.00 637.85

No. 114a has watermark sideways.

For overprints and surcharges see Nos. 115-129.

No. 105 Surcharged

1925, Dec.
115 A20 2½p on 3p ultramarine 2.00 *4.00*

Stamps of 1922-26 Overprinted

1926
116 A20 ¼p brown .80 *4.50*
117 A20 ½p green .80 .20
118 A20 1p violet 1.10 .25
119 A20 1½p orange brown 1.10 .70
120 A20 2p ol brn & turq .85 1.10
121 A20 2½p ultramarine 1.40 .90
122 A20 3p black, *yel* .85 .90
a. Inverted overprint 200.00 *550.00*
123 A20 4p yel & ultra 8.00 *20.00*
124 A20 6p ol grn & vio 3.25 4.00
125 A21 1sh ol brn & bl 6.25 12.50
126 A21 2sh ultra & ol brown 57.50 *160.00*
127 A21 2sh6p blk & red vio 15.00 *40.00*
128 A21 5sh ultra & org 10.50 *40.00*
129 A21 10sh ol brn & gray 8.00 *21.00*
Nos. 116-129 (14) 115.40 306.05

George V — A22

Valletta Harbor — A23

St. Publius — A24

Notabile (Mdina) — A25

Gozo Fishing Boat — A26

Statue of Neptune — A27

Ruins at Mnaidra — A28

St. Paul — A29

1926-27 **Typo.** ***Perf. 14½x14***
131 A22 ¼p brown .90 .20
132 A22 ½p green .70 .20
133 A22 1p red 3.50 1.10
134 A22 1½p orange brn 2.25 .20
135 A22 2p gray 5.25 *11.00*
136 A22 2½p blue 4.50 1.10
137 A22 3p dark violet 5.00 3.00
138 A22 4p org red & blk 3.75 *11.00*
139 A22 4½p yel buff & vio 4.00 3.25
140 A22 6p red & violet 5.00 4.25

Engr. ***Perf. 12½***
Inscribed: "Postage"

141	A23	1sh	black	7.50	5.25
142	A24	1sh6p	green & blk	7.50	*15.00*
143	A25	2sh	dp vio & blk	7.50	*17.00*
144	A26	2sh6p	ver & black	17.00	*55.00*
145	A27	3sh	blue & blk	20.00	*35.00*
146	A28	5sh	green & blk	25.00	*70.00*
147	A29	10sh	car & blk	62.50	*110.00*
			Nos. 131-147 (17)	181.85	*342.55*

See #167-183. For overprints see #148-166.

Stamps and Type of 1926-27 Overprinted in Black

1928 ***Perf. 14½x14***

148	A22	¼p	brown	1.75	.20
149	A22	½p	green	1.75	.20
150	A22	1p	red	2.00	*3.75*
151	A22	1p	orange brown	5.25	.20
152	A22	1½p	yel brown	2.25	1.00
153	A22	1½p	red	5.00	.20
154	A22	2p	gray	5.00	*10.50*
155	A22	2½p	blue	2.25	.20
156	A22	3p	dark violet	2.25	1.00
157	A22	4p	org red & blk	2.25	2.00
158	A22	4½p	yel & violet	2.50	1.10
159	A22	6p	red & violet	2.50	1.75

Overprinted in Red

Perf. 12½

160	A23	1sh	black	6.25	3.00
161	A24	1sh6p	green & blk	7.50	*11.00*
162	A25	2sh	dp vio & blk	27.50	*62.50*
163	A26	2sh6p	ver & black	20.00	*26.00*
164	A27	3sh	ultra & blk	22.50	*35.00*
165	A28	5sh	yel grn & blk	32.50	*75.00*
166	A29	10sh	car rose & black	62.50	*100.00*
			Nos. 148-166 (19)	213.50	334.60

Issued: Nos. 151, 153, Dec. 5; others, Oct. 1.

Types of 1926-27 Issue

1930, Oct. 20 Typo. ***Perf. 14½x14***
Inscribed: "Postage & Revenue"

167	A22	¼p	brown	.70	.20
168	A22	½p	green	.70	.20
169	A22	1p	yel brown	.70	.20
170	A22	1½p	red	.80	.20
171	A22	2p	gray	1.40	.60
172	A22	2½p	blue	2.25	.20
173	A22	3p	dark violet	1.75	.20
174	A22	4p	org red & blk	1.40	*4.50*
175	A22	4½p	yel & violet	3.75	1.40
176	A22	6p	red & violet	3.25	1.40

Engr. ***Perf. 12½***

177	A23	1sh	black	11.00	16.00
178	A24	1sh6p	green & blk	9.75	22.50
179	A25	2sh	dp vio & blk	11.00	22.50
180	A26	2sh6p	ver & black	20.00	55.00
181	A27	3sh	ultra & blk	30.00	62.50
182	A28	5sh	yel grn & blk	37.50	75.00
183	A29	10sh	car rose & blk	65.00	140.00
			Nos. 167-183 (17)	200.95	402.60

Common Design Types pictured following the introduction.

Silver Jubilee Issue

Common Design Type

1935, May 6 ***Perf. 11x12***

184	CD301	½p	green & blk	.35	.50
185	CD301	2½p	ultra & brn	2.40	*4.00*
186	CD301	6p	ol grn & lt bl	6.25	4.00
187	CD301	1sh	brn vio & ind	10.00	14.00
			Nos. 184-187 (4)	19.00	22.50
			Set, never hinged	27.50	

Coronation Issue

Common Design Type

1937, May 12 Wmk. 4 ***Perf. 13½x14***

188	CD302	½p	deep green	.20	.20
189	CD302	1½p	carmine	.25	.20
190	CD302	2½p	bright ultra	.55	.50
			Nos. 188-190 (3)	1.00	.90
			Set, never hinged	1.50	

Valletta Harbor — A30

Fort St. Angelo — A31

Verdala Palace — A32

Neolithic Ruins — A33

Victoria and Citadel, Gozo — A34

De l'Isle Adam Entering Mdina — A35

St. John's Co-Cathedral A36

Mnaidra Temple — A37

Statue of Antonio Manoel de Vilhena — A38

Woman in Faldetta — A39

St. Publius — A40

Mdina Cathedral A41

Palace Square — A43

Statue of Neptune — A42

St. Paul — A44

1938-43 Wmk. 4 ***Perf. 12½***

191	A30	1f	brown	.20	.20
192	A31	½p	green	.40	.20
192A	A31	½p	chnt ('43)	.20	.20
193	A32	1p	chestnut	3.50	.20
193A	A32	1p	grn ('43)	.20	.20
194	A33	1½p	rose red	.25	.20
194A	A33	1½p	dk gray ('43)	.20	.20
195	A34	2p	dark gray	.90	.75
195A	A34	2p	rose red ('43)	.40	.25
196	A35	2½p	blue	.90	.60
196A	A35	2½p	violet ('43)	.35	.35
197	A36	3p	violet	.75	.55
197A	A36	3p	blue ('43)	.40	.20
198	A37	4½p	ocher & ol green	.30	.30
199	A38	6p	rose red & ol green	.60	.30
200	A39	1sh	black	.60	.55
201	A40	1sh6p	sage grn & black	7.50	1.00
202	A41	2sh	dk bl & lt grn	1.10	1.10
203	A42	2sh6p	rose red & black	5.00	4.00
204	A43	5sh	bl grn & blk	4.75	4.75
205	A44	10sh	dp rose & blk	12.50	12.50
			Nos. 191-205 (21)	41.00	28.60
			Never hinged	50.00	

See #236a. For overprints see #208-222.

Catalogue values for unused stamps in this section, from this point to the end of the section, are for Never Hinged items.

Peace Issue

Common Design Type
Inscribed: "Malta" and Crosses

Perf. 13½x14

1946, Dec. 3 Engr. Wmk. 4

206	CD303	1p	bright green	.20	.20
207	CD303	3p	dark ultra	.35	.90

Stamps of 1938-43 Overprinted in Black or Carmine

a

1948, Nov. 25 ***Perf. 12½***

208	A30	1f	brown	.35	.20
209	A31	½p	chestnut	.35	.20
210	A32	1p	green	.35	.20
211	A33	1½p	dk gray (C)	1.40	.20
212	A34	2p	rose red	1.40	.30
213	A35	2½p	violet (C)	.90	.30
214	A36	3p	blue (C)	1.40	.20
215	A37	4½p	ocher & ol grn	2.25	1.75
216	A38	6p	rose red & ol green	3.50	.45
217	A39	1sh	black	3.25	.70
218	A40	1sh6p	sage grn & blk	2.75	1.25
219	A41	2sh	dk bl & lt grn (C)	5.75	2.75
220	A42	2sh6p	rose red & blk	14.00	2.75
221	A43	5sh	bl grn & blk (C)	22.50	5.00
222	A44	10sh	dp rose & blk	22.50	25.00
			Nos. 208-222 (15)	82.65	41.25

The overprint is smaller on No. 208. It reads from lower left to upper right on Nos. 209 and 221.

See Nos. 235-240.

Silver Wedding Issue

Common Design Types
Inscribed: "Malta" and Crosses

1949, Jan. 4 Photo. ***Perf. 14x14½***

223	CD304	1p	dark green	.55	.20

Perf. 11½x11
Engr.

224	CD305	£1	dark blue	45.00	40.00

UPU Issue

Common Design Types
Inscribed: "Malta" and Crosses

Perf. 13½, 11x11½

1949, Oct. 10 Engr. Wmk. 4

225	CD306	2½p	violet	.35	.20
226	CD307	3p	indigo	3.50	1.25
227	CD308	6p	dp carmine	.70	1.10
228	CD309	1sh	slate	.70	*2.75*
			Nos. 225-228 (4)	5.25	5.30

Princess Elizabeth — A45

Madonna and Child — A46

1950, Dec. 1 Engr. ***Perf. 12x11½***

229	A45	1p	emerald	.20	.20
230	A45	3p	bright blue	.25	.25
231	A45	1sh	gray black	.75	1.40
			Nos. 229-231 (3)	1.20	1.85

Visit of Princess Elizabeth.

1951, July 12

232	A46	1p	green	.20	.20
233	A46	3p	purple	.55	.20
234	A46	1sh	slate black	1.25	1.00
			Nos. 232-234 (3)	2.00	1.40

700th anniv. of the presentation of the scapular to St. Simon Stock.

Types of 1938-43 Overprinted Type "a" in Red or Black

1953, Jan. 8 Wmk. 4 ***Perf. 12½***

235	A32	1p	gray (R)	.35	.20
236	A33	1½p	green	.35	.20
a.			Overprint omitted		*11,500.*
237	A34	2p	ocher	.35	.20
238	A35	2½p	rose red	.60	*1.75*
239	A36	3p	violet (R)	.60	.20
240	A37	4½p	ultra & ol grn (R)	.65	*1.00*
			Nos. 235-240 (6)	2.90	3.55

AIR POST STAMPS

No. 140 Overprinted

Perf. 14½x14

1928, Apr. 1 Typo. Wmk. 4

C1	A22	6p red & violet	5.50	6.75

POSTAGE DUE STAMPS

D1

Maltese Cross — D2

1925 Typeset Unwmk. *Imperf.*

J1	D1	½p	black, *white*	1.40	8.00
J2	D1	1p	black, *white*	3.75	3.50
J3	D1	1½p	black, *white*	3.50	4.25
J4	D1	2p	black, *white*	8.50	*15.00*
J5	D1	2½p	black, *white*	3.25	3.25
a.			"2" of "½" omitted	1,200.	1,400.
J6	D1	3p	black, *gray*	10.50	*17.00*
J7	D1	4p	black, *orange*	5.75	*11.00*
J8	D1	6p	black, *orange*	5.75	*20.00*
J9	D1	1sh	black, *orange*	8.50	*25.00*
J10	D1	1sh6p	black, *orange*	16.00	*62.50*
			Nos. J1-J10 (10)	66.90	*169.50*

These stamps were typeset in groups of 42. In each sheet there were four impressions of a group, two of them being inverted and making tete beche pairs.

Forged examples of No. J5a are known.

Wmk. 4 Sideways

1925 Typo. *Perf. 12*

J11	D2	½p	blue green	1.40	.70
J12	D2	1p	violet	1.40	.50
J13	D2	1½p	yellow brown	1.75	1.00
J14	D2	2p	gray	12.50	1.25
J15	D2	2½p	orange	2.25	1.40
J16	D2	3p	dark blue	4.00	1.40
J17	D2	4p	olive green	14.00	*18.00*
J18	D2	6p	claret	3.50	4.75
J19	D2	1sh	gray black	7.50	*14.00*
J20	D2	1sh6p	deep rose	9.75	*32.50*
			Nos. J11-J20 (10)	58.05	*75.50*

In 1953-57 six values (½p-2p, 3p, 4p) were reissued on chalky paper in slightly different colors.

WAR TAX STAMPS

Nos. 50, 25 Overprinted

1918 Wmk. 3 *Perf. 14*

MR1	A13	½p green	.30	.30

Wmk. 2

MR2	A12	3p red violet & gray	3.00	4.00

MANCHUKUO

ˈman-ˈchü-ˈkwō

LOCATION — Covering Manchuria, or China's three northeastern provinces — Fengtien, Kirin and Heilungkiang — plus Jehol province.
GOVT. — Independent state under Japanese influence
AREA — 503,013 sq. mi. (estimated)
POP. — 43,233,954 (est. 1940)
CAPITAL — Hsinking (Changchun)

Manchukuo was formed in 1932 with the assistance of Japan. In 1934 Henry Pu-yi, Chief Executive, was enthroned as Emperor Kang Teh.

100 Fen = 1 Yuan

Watermarks

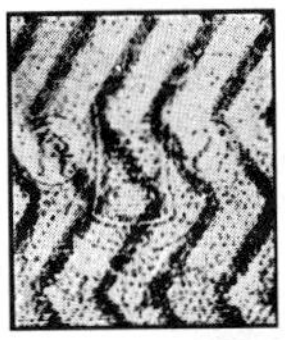

Wmk. 141 — Horizontal Zigzag Lines

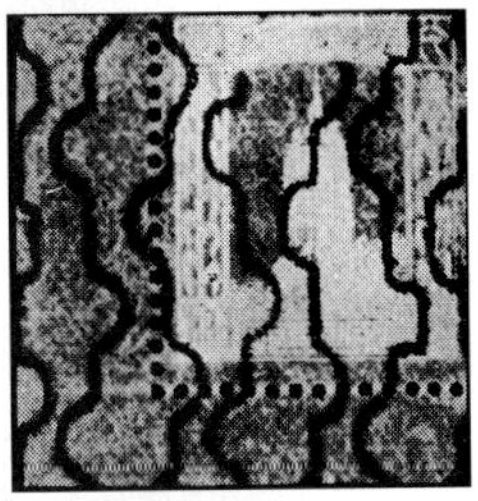

Wmk. 239 — Curved Wavy Lines

Wmk. 242 — Characters

Pagoda at Liaoyang A1

Chief Executive Henry Pu-yi A2

Five characters in top label. Inscription reads "Manchu State Postal Administration."

Lithographed
Perf. 13x13½

1932, July 26 Unwmk.

White Paper

1	A1	½f	gray brown	1.10	.70
2	A1	1f	dull red	1.60	.35
3	A1	1½f	lilac	5.50	5.00
4	A1	2f	slate	6.00	1.00
5	A1	3f	dull brown	7.50	7.50
6	A1	4f	olive green	2.25	.50
7	A1	5f	green	3.00	.55
8	A1	6f	rose	9.50	3.50
9	A1	7f	gray	3.00	1.00
10	A1	8f	ocher	15.00	12.50
11	A1	10f	orange	5.50	.50
12	A2	13f	dull brown	11.00	7.00
13	A2	15f	rose	20.00	3.00
14	A2	16f	turquoise grn	27.50	9.00
15	A2	20f	gray brown	8.00	1.75
16	A2	30f	orange	8.50	2.25
17	A2	50f	olive green	16.00	3.25
18	A2	1y	violet	37.50	9.00
			Nos. 1-18 (18)	188.45	68.35
			Set, never hinged	275.00	

A local provisional overprint of a horizontal line of four characters in red or black, reading "Chinese Postal Administration," was applied to Nos. 1-18 by followers of Gen. Su Ping-wen, who rebelled against the Manchukuo government in September, 1932. Many counterfeits exist.

See #23-31. For surcharges see #36, 59-61.

See note on local handstamps at end of the Manchukuo listings.

Flags, Map and Wreath — A3

Old State Council Building — A4

1933, Mar. 1 *Perf. 12½*

19	A3	1f	orange	4.00	4.00
20	A4	2f	dull green	12.00	12.00
21	A3	4f	light red	4.50	4.50
22	A4	10f	deep blue	30.00	30.00
			Nos. 19-22 (4)	50.50	50.50
			Set, never hinged	75.00	

1st anniv. of the establishing of the State. Nos. 19-22 were printed in sheets of 100 with a special printing in sheets of 20.

Type of 1932
Perf. 13x13½

1934, Feb. Engr. Wmk. 239

Granite Paper

23	A1	½f	dark brown	1.75	1.65
24	A1	1f	red brown	1.75	.90
25	A1	1½f	dark violet	5.50	3.00
26	A1	2f	slate	4.00	1.50
27	A1	3f	brown	2.50	.60
28	A1	4f	olive brown	25.00	5.00
29	A1	10f	deep orange	9.00	1.00
30	A2	15f	rose	450.00	200.00
31	A2	1y	violet	25.00	10.00
			Nos. 23-31 (9)	524.50	223.65

For surcharge see No. 60.

Emperor's Palace — A5

Phoenix — A6

1934, Mar. 1 *Perf. 12½*

32	A5	1½f	orange brown	3.75	3.75
33	A6	3f	carmine	3.25	1.75
34	A5	6f	green	7.50	7.50
35	A6	10f	dark blue	20.00	17.50
			Nos. 32-35 (4)	34.50	30.50
			Set, never hinged	47.50	

Enthronement of Emperor Kang Teh. Nos. 32-35 were printed in sheets of 100, with a special printing in sheets of 20.

No. 6 Surcharged in Black

Perf. 13x13½

1934 Unwmk. White Paper

36	A1	1f on 4f olive grn	5.50	2.50
a.		Brown surcharge	37.50	37.50
b.		Upper left character of surcharge omitted		
c.		Inverted surcharge	110.00	110.00

Pagoda at Liaoyang A7

Emperor Kang Teh A8

Six characters in top label instead of five as in 1932-34 issues.

Inscription reads "Manchu Empire Postal Administration."

Perf. 13x13½

1934-36 Wmk. 239 Engr.

Granite Paper

37	A7	½f	brown	.50	.35
38	A7	1f	red brown	1.00	.30
39	A7	1½f	dk violet	1.00	.50
a.			Booklet pane of 6	60.00	
41	A7	3f	brown ('35)	.50	.35
a.			Booklet pane of 6	65.00	
42	A7	5f	dk blue ('35)	10.00	2.00
43	A7	5f	gray ('36)	5.00	2.00
44	A7	6f	rose ('35)	3.00	.60
45	A7	7f	dk gray ('36)	2.50	2.00
47	A7	9f	red orange ('35)	2.50	.75
50	A8	15f	ver ('35)	2.50	.85
51	A8	18f	Prus grn ('35)	25.00	5.00
52	A8	20f	dk brown ('35)	4.00	.90
53	A8	30f	orange brn ('35)	4.50	.90
54	A8	50f	ol grn ('35)	6.00	2.00
55	A8	1y	dk violet ('35)	20.00	6.00
a.			1y violet	20.00	8.00
			Nos. 37-55 (15)	88.00	24.50
			Set, never hinged	110.00	

4f and 8f, type A7, were prepared but not issued. Values $45 and $15, respectively.

1935 Wmk. 242 *Perf. 13x13½*

57	A7	10f	deep blue	8.00	1.00
58	A8	13f	light brown	10.00	5.00
			Set, never hinged	25.00	

Nos. 6 and 28 Surcharged in Black

1935 White Paper Unwmk.

59	A1	3f on 4f ol grn	65.00	60.00
		Never hinged	90.00	

1935 Granite Paper Wmk. 239

60	A1	3f on 4f olive brn	8.00	4.00
		Never hinged	15.00	

Similar Surcharge on No. 14

1935 White Paper Unwmk.

61	A2	3f on 16f turq grn	14.00	9.00
		Never hinged	18.00	
		Nos. 59-61 (3)	87.00	73.00

Orchid Crest of Manchukuo A9

Sacred White Mountains and Black Waters A10

1935, Jan. 1 Litho. Wmk. 141
Granite Paper

62	A9	2f green	5.00	1.75
63	A10	4f dull ol grn	2.00	1.50
64	A9	8f ocher	4.00	4.00
65	A10	12f brown red	16.00	*17.50*
		Nos. 62-65 (4)	27.00	24.75
		Set, never hinged	27.50	

Nos. 62-65 exist imperforate.

1935 Wmk. 242

66	A9	2f yellow green	3.50	.75
68	A9	8f ocher	5.00	6.00
70	A10	12f brown red	11.00	15.00
		Nos. 66-70 (3)	19.50	21.75
		Set, never hinged	29.00	

Nos. 62-70 issued primarily to pay postage to China, but valid for any postal use.

See Nos. 75-78, 113, 115, 158. For surcharges see Nos. 101, 103-104, 106-109, People's Republic of China No. 2L19.

Mt. Fuji — A11

Phoenix — A12

Perf. 11, 12½ and Compound
1935, Apr. 1 Engr. Wmk. 242

71	A11	1½f dull green	2.25	1.50
72	A12	3f orange	2.25	2.00
a.		3f red orange	6.00	5.00
73	A11	6f dk carmine	5.50	4.75
a.		Horiz. pair, imperf. btwn.	250.00	
b.		Perf. 11x12½	30.00	27.50
74	A12	10f dark blue	5.50	6.00
a.		Perf. 12½x11	22.50	25.00
b.		Perf. 12½	22.50	25.00
		Nos. 71-74 (4)	15.50	14.25
		Set, never hinged	22.00	

Visit of the Emperor of Manchukuo to Tokyo.

Orchid Crest — A13

Types of A9 & A10
Redrawn and Engraved
1936 Wmk. 242 *Perf. 13x13½*

75	A13	2f lt green	.75	.30
76	A10	4f olive green	2.75	.55
77	A13	8f ocher	1.75	.75
78	A10	12f orange brn	37.50	27.50
		Nos. 75-78 (4)	42.75	29.10
		Set, never hinged	57.50	

Unbroken lines of shading in the background of Nos. 76 and 78. Shading has been removed from right and left of the mountains. Nearly all lines have been removed from the lake. There are numerous other alterations in the design.

Issued primarily to pay postage to China, but valid for any postal use.

See #112. For surcharges see #102-106.

Wild Goose over Sea of Japan — A14

Communications Building at Hsinking — A15

Perf. 12x12½, 12½x12
1936, Jan. 26 Wmk. 242

79	A14	1½f black brown	2.25	2.00
80	A15	3f rose lilac	2.25	.55
81	A14	6f carmine rose	5.25	5.25
82	A15	10f blue	6.25	6.00
		Nos. 79-82 (4)	16.00	13.80
		Set, never hinged	40.00	

Postal convention with Japan.

New State Council Building A16

Carting Soybeans A17

North Mausoleum at Mukden A18

Summer Palace at Chengteh A19

1936-37 Wmk. 242 *Perf. 13x13½*

83	A16	½f brown	.40	.20
84	A16	1f red brown	.40	.20
85	A16	1½f violet	3.25	2.75
a.		Booklet pane of 6	80.00	
86	A17	2f lt green ('37)	.40	.20
a.		Booklet pane of 6	20.00	
87	A16	3f chocolate	.40	.20
a.		Booklet pane of 6	200.00	
88	A18	4f lt ol grn ('37)	.40	.20
a.		Booklet pane of 6	25.00	
89	A16	5f gray black	19.00	7.50
90	A17	6f carmine	.45	.20
91	A18	7f brown blk	.60	.30
92	A18	9f red orange	.65	.35
93	A19	10f blue	.70	.20
94	A18	12f dp orange ('37)	.55	.20
95	A18	13f brown	30.00	35.00
96	A18	15f carmine	1.10	.35
97	A17	20f dk brown	1.10	.35
98	A19	30f chestnut brn	1.10	.35
99	A17	50f olive green	1.40	.50
100	A19	1y violet	2.75	.60
		Nos. 83-100 (18)	64.65	49.65
		Set, never hinged	105.00	

Nos. 83, 84, 86, 88 and 93 are known imperforate but were not regularly issued.

See Nos. 159-163. For overprints see Nos. 140-141, 148-151. For surcharges see People's Republic of China Nos. 2L1-2L2, 2L11-2L18, 2L20-2L37, 2L40-2L52.

a

b

c

d

1937

Surcharged on No. 66

101	A9 (a)	2½f on 2f	1.75	1.50

Surcharged on Nos. 75, 76 and 78

102	A13 (a)	2½f on 2f	1.75	1.50
103	A10 (b)	5f on 4f	3.00	3.00
104	A10 (c)	13f on 12f	9.00	9.00

Surcharged in Black on Nos. 75, 76 and 70
Space between bottom characters of surcharge 4½mm

105	A13 (d)	2½f on 2f	1.75	1.50
a.		Inverted surcharge	110.00	85.00
b.		Vert. pair, one without surch.	95.00	
106	A10 (b)	5f on 4f	2.50	1.50
107	A10 (c)	13f on 12f	9.00	8.00

Surcharged on No. 70
Space between characters 6½mm

108	A10 (c)	13f on 12f	175.00	175.00

Same Surcharge on No. 63
Space between characters 4½mm
Wmk. 141

109	A10 (b)	5f on 4f	6.00	5.00
		Nos. 101-109 (9)	209.75	206.00
		Set, never hinged	300.00	

Nos. 101-109 were issued primarily to pay postage to China, but were valid for any postal use.

Rising Sun over Manchurian Plain — A20

Composite Picture of Manchurian City — A21

Perf. 12½
1937, Mar. 1 Litho. Unwmk.

110	A20	1½f carmine rose	2.25	3.00
111	A21	3f blue green	2.40	1.00
		Set, never hinged	6.50	

5th anniv. of the founding of the State of Manchukuo.

Types of 1936
Perf. 13x13½
1937 Wmk. 242 Engr.

112	A13	2½f dk violet	.60	.25
113	A10	5f black	.20	.20
115	A10	13f dk red brown	.60	.30
		Nos. 112-115 (3)	1.40	.75
		Set, never hinged	1.80	

Issued primarily to pay postage to China, but were valid for any postal use.

Pouter Pigeon — A22

National Flag and Buildings — A23

Perf. 12x12½
1937, Sept. 16 Unwmk.

116	A22	2f dark violet	1.50	1.50
117	A23	4f rose carmine	1.50	1.00
118	A22	10f dark green	3.25	1.90
119	A23	20f dark blue	4.75	4.75
		Nos. 116-119 (4)	11.00	9.15
		Set, never hinged	15.00	

Completion of the national capital, Hsinking, under the first Five-Year Construction Plan.

Map — A24

Dept. of Justice Building — A27

Japanese Residents' Association Building — A25

Postal Administration Building — A26

Perf. 12x12½, 13
1937, Dec. 1 Litho. Unwmk.

121	A24	2f dark carmine	1.00	.80
122	A25	4f green	1.75	1.10
123	A25	8f orange	4.00	3.25
124	A26	10f blue	4.00	3.50
125	A27	12f lt violet	5.00	4.50
126	A26	20f lilac brown	7.00	6.00
		Nos. 121-126 (6)	22.75	19.15
		Set, never hinged	27.50	

Issued in commemoration of the abolition of extraterritorial rights within Manchukuo.

New Year Greetings — A28

Map and Cross — A29

1937, Dec. 15 Engr. *Perf. 12x12½*

127	A28	2f dk blue & red	1.90	.55
		Never hinged	2.40	
a.		Double impression of border	12.50	

Issued to pay postage on New Year's greeting cards.

Wmk. 242
1938, Oct. 15 Litho. *Perf. 13*

128	A29	2f lake & scarlet	.60	.55
129	A29	4f slate grn & scar	.60	.55
		Set, never hinged	1.60	

Founding of the Red Cross Soc. in Manchukuo.

Network of State Railroads in Manchukuo A30

Express Train "Asia" A31

1939, Oct. 21

130	A30	2f dk org, blk & dp bl	.80	.70
131	A31	4f dp blue & indigo	.80	.70
		Set, never hinged	2.25	

Attainment of 10,000 kilometers in the railway mileage in Manchuria.

Stork Flying above Mast of Imperial Flagship — A32

1940 Photo. Unwmk.

132	A32	2f brt red violet	.20	.20
133	A32	4f brt green	.25	.25
		Set, never hinged	.55	

Second visit of Emperor Kang Teh to Emperor Hirohito of Japan.

Census Taker and Map of Manchukuo A33

Census Form A34

1940, Sept. 10 Litho. Wmk. 242

134 A33 2f vio brn & org .20 .20
135 A34 4f black & green .30 .25
a. Double impression of green 50.00
Set, never hinged .55

National census starting Oct. 1.

Message of Congratulation from Premier Chang Ching-hui — A35

Dragon Dance A36

1940, Sept. 18 Engr.

136 A35 2f carmine .20 .20
137 A36 4f indigo .30 .30
a. Imperf., pair 90.00
Set, never hinged .55

2600th anniversary of the birth of the Japanese Empire.

AIR POST STAMPS

Sheep Grazing AP1

Railroad Bridge AP2

Wmk. Characters (242)

1936-37 Engr. *Perf. 13x13½*

Granite Paper

C1 AP1 18f green 12.50 12.50
C2 AP1 19f blue green ('37) 3.00 3.50
C3 AP2 38f blue 12.50 15.00
C4 AP2 39f deep blue ('37) 1.50 1.75
Nos. C1-C4 (4) 29.50 32.75
Set, never hinged 35.00

With the end of World War II and the collapse of Manchukuo, the Northeastern Provinces reverted to China. In many Manchurian towns and cities, the Manchukuo stamps were locally handstamped in ideograms: "Republic of China," "China Postal Service" or "Temporary Use for China." A typical example is shown above. Many of these local issues also were surcharged.

MARIANA ISLANDS

ˌmar-ē-ˈa-nə ˈī-ləndz

LOCATION — A group of 14 islands in the West Pacific Ocean, about 1500 miles east of the Philippines.
GOVT. — Possession of Spain, then of Germany
AREA — 246 sq. mi.
POP. — 44,025 (1935)
CAPITAL — Saipan

Until 1899 this group belonged to Spain but in that year all except Guam were ceded to Germany.

100 Centavos = 1 Peso
100 Pfennig = 1 Mark (1899)

Values for unused stamps are for examples with original gum as defined in the catalogue introduction. Very fine examples of Nos. 1-6 will have perforations touching or just cutting into the design. Stamps with perfs clear on all sides and well centered are rare and sell for substantially more.

Issued under Spanish Dominion

King Alfonso XIII — A1

Stamps of the Philippines Handstamped Vertically in Blackish Violet Reading Up or Down

1899, Sept. Unwmk. *Perf. 14*

1 A1 2c dark blue green 675.00 250.00
On cover *2,500.*
2 A1 3c dark brown 525.00 165.00
On cover *2,500.*
3 A1 5c car rose 775.00 275.00
On cover *3,000.*
4 A1 6c dark blue *5,000.* 3,750.
On cover *6,500.*
5 A1 8c gray brown 375.00 150.00
On cover *2,500.*
6 A1 15c slate green 1,900. 1,000.
On cover *5,000.*

Overprint forgeries of Nos. 1-6 exist.

Issued under German Dominion

Stamps of Germany, 1889-90, Overprinted in Black at 56 degree Angle

1900, May Unwmk. *Perf. 13½x14½*

11 A9 3pf dark brown 12.00 *25.00*
Never hinged 21.00
On cover *67.50*
12 A9 5pf green 15.00 *26.00*
Never hinged 27.00
On cover *67.50*
13 A10 10pf carmine 17.00 *37.50*
Never hinged 32.50
On cover *80.00*
14 A10 20pf ultra 21.50 *100.00*
Never hinged 50.00
On cover *225.00*
15 A10 25pf orange 52.50 *125.00*
Never hinged 140.00
On cover *400.00*
b. Inverted overprint *2,000.*
Never hinged *3,400.*
16 A10 50pf red brn 52.50 *180.00*
Never hinged 140.00
On cover *450.00*
Nos. 11-16 (6) 170.50 *493.50*

Forged cancellations exist on Nos. 11-16, 17-29.

Covers: Value for No. 16 on cover is for overfranked complete cover, usually philatelic.

Stamps of Germany, 1889-90, Overprinted in Black at 48 degree Angle

1899, Nov. 18

11a A9 3pf light brown *1,500. 1,500.*
Never hinged 2,700.
On cover *4,750.*
12a A9 5pf green *2,300. 1,250.*
Never hinged 4,000.
On cover *1,700.*
13a A10 10pf carmine 160.00 *175.00*
Never hinged 450.00
On cover 350.00
14a A10 20pf ultra 160.00 *175.00*
Never hinged 450.00
On cover 350.00
15a A10 25pf orange *2,850. 2,500.*
Never hinged 8,250.
On cover *5,500.*
16a A10 50pf red brown *2,850. 2,500.*
Never hinged 8,250.
On cover *4,500.*

Covers: Value for No. 16a on cover is for overfranked complete cover, usually philatelic.

Kaiser's Yacht "Hohenzollern"
A4 A5

1901, Jan. Typo. *Perf. 14*

17 A4 3pf brown 1.00 *1.40*
Never hinged 1.90
On cover 8.50
18 A4 5pf green 1.00 *1.50*
Never hinged 1.90
On cover 7.00
19 A4 10pf carmine 1.00 *3.00*
Never hinged 1.90
On cover *13.50*
20 A4 20pf ultra 1.25 *5.75*
Never hinged 2.40
On cover *27.50*
21 A4 25pf org & blk, *yel* 1.50 *10.50*
Never hinged 3.50
On cover *55.00*
22 A4 30pf org & blk, *sal* 1.50 *11.00*
Never hinged 3.50
On cover *55.00*
23 A4 40pf lake & blk 1.50 *11.00*
Never hinged 3.75
On cover *55.00*
24 A4 50pf pur & blk, *sal* 1.60 *12.50*
Never hinged 4.25
On cover *47.50*
25 A4 80pf lake & blk, *rose* 2.00 *21.00*
Never hinged 5.75
On cover *82.50*

Engr.
Perf. 14½x14

26 A5 1m carmine 2.75 *57.50*
Never hinged 15.00
On cover *150.00*
27 A5 2m blue 4.50 *75.00*
Never hinged 19.00
On cover *190.00*
28 A5 3m blk vio 5.75 *110.00*
Never hinged 26.00
On cover *290.00*
29 A5 5m slate & car 110.00 *425.00*
Never hinged 340.00
On cover *825.00*
Nos. 17-29 (13) 135.35 *745.15*

Covers: Values for Nos. 24-29 on cover are for overfranked complete covers, usually philatelic.

Wmk. Lozenges (125)

1916-19 Typo. *Perf. 14*

30 A4 3pf brown ('19) .80
Never hinged 1.60

Engr.
Perf. 14½x14

31 A5 5m slate & carmine, 25x17 holes 20.00
Never hinged 175.00
a. 5m slate & carmine, 26x17 holes 35.00
Never hinged 210.00

Nos. 30 and 31 were never placed in use.

MARIENWERDER

mä-ˈrē-ən-ˌve̦ə̦rd-ər

LOCATION — Northeastern Germany, bordering on Poland
GOVT. — District of West Prussia

By the Versailles Treaty the greater portion of West Prussia was ceded to Poland but the district of Marienwerder was allowed a plebiscite which was held in 1920 and resulted in favor of Germany.

100 Pfennig = 1 Mark

Plebiscite Issues

Symbolical of Allied Supervision of the Plebiscite — A1

1920 Unwmk. Litho. *Perf. 11½*

1 A1 5pf green .75 .95
Never hinged 1.50
On cover 3.75
2 A1 10pf rose red .75 .80
Never hinged 1.50
On cover 3.75
3 A1 15pf gray .75 1.25
Never hinged 1.50
On cover 3.75
4 A1 20pf brn org .75 .85
Never hinged 1.50
On cover 3.75
5 A1 25pf deep blue .75 .85
Never hinged 1.50
On cover 7.50
6 A1 30pf orange .90 .75
Never hinged 1.90
On cover 9.25
7 A1 40pf brown .75 .70
Never hinged 1.50
On cover 6.00
8 A1 50pf violet .75 .75
Never hinged 1.50
On cover 6.00
9 A1 60pf red brown 4.00 2.50
Never hinged 7.50
On cover 19.00
10 A1 75pf chocolate .90 .90
Never hinged 1.90
On cover 11.50
11 A1 1m brn & grn .75 .90
Never hinged 1.50
On cover 11.50
12 A1 2m dk vio 2.00 2.25
Never hinged 3.75
On cover 35.00
13 A1 3m red 4.75 4.00
Never hinged 10.00
On cover 37.50
14 A1 5m blue & rose 22.50 21.00
Never hinged 50.00
On cover 80.00
a. 5m ultramarine & pale red 22.50 *21.00*
Never hinged 50.00
Nos. 1-14 (14) 41.05 38.45
Set, never hinged 90.00

These stamps occasionally show parts of two papermakers' watermarks, consisting of the letters "O. B. M." with two stars before and after, or "P. & C. M."

Nos. 1-14 exist imperf.; value for set, $700. Nearly all exist part perf.

Stamps of Germany, 1905-19, Overprinted

1920 Wmk. 125 *Perf. 14, 14½*

24 A16 5pf green 15.00 *27.50*
Never hinged 29.00
On cover 60.00
a. Inverted overprint 110.00
Never hinged 190.00
26 A16 20pf bl vio 5.50 *24.00*
Never hinged 15.00
On cover 37.50
a. Inverted overprint 57.50
Never hinged 110.00
b. Double overprint 75.00
Never hinged 140.00
28 A16 50pf vio & blk, *buff* 350.00 *700.00*
Never hinged 750.00
On cover *1,500.*
a. 50pf vio & blk, *pale yel org* 750.00 *2,750.*
Never hinged *2,750.*
On cover *3,500.*
29 A16 75pf grn & blk 4.00 *7.25*
Never hinged 7.50
On cover 19.00
a. Inverted overprint 57.50
Never hinged 110.00
30 A16 80pf lake & blk, *rose* 72.50 *110.00*
Never hinged 140.00
On cover 290.00
31 A17 1m car rose 80.00 *150.00*
Never hinged 150.00
On cover 375.00
a. Inverted overprint 375.00
Never hinged 750.00
Nos. 24-31 (6) 527.00 *1,018.*
Set, never hinged 1,100.

Trial impressions were made in red, green and lilac, and with 2½mm instead of 3mm space between the lines of the overprint. These were printed on the 75pf and 80pf. The 1 mark was overprinted with the same words in 3 lines of large sans-serif capitals. All these are essays. Some were passed through the post, apparently with speculative intent.

Stamps of Germany, 1905-18, Surcharged

32	A22 1m on 2pf gray	20.00	*42.50*
	Never hinged	45.00	
	On cover		75.00
33	A22 2m on 2½pf gray	8.00	*16.00*
	Never hinged	22.50	
	On cover		75.00
a.	Inverted surcharge	50.00	*92.50*
	Never hinged	92.50	
34	A16 3m on 3pf brown	11.00	*17.00*
	Never hinged	22.50	
	On cover		92.50
a.	Double surcharge	50.00	*92.50*
	Never hinged	92.50	
b.	Inverted surcharge	50.00	*92.50*
	Never hinged	92.50	
35	A22 5m on 7½pf org	8.00	*20.00*
	Never hinged	22.50	
	On cover		110.00
a.	Inverted surcharge	50.00	*92.50*
	Never hinged	92.50	
b.	Double surcharge	50.00	*92.50*
	Never hinged	92.50	
	Nos. 32-35 (4)	47.00	*95.50*
	Set, never hinged	110.00	

There are two types of the letters "M," "C," "i" and "e" and of the numerals "2" and "5" in these surcharges.

Counterfeits exist of Nos. 24-35.

Stamps of Germany, 1920, Overprinted

1920, July ***Perf. 15x14½***

36	A17 1m red	2.50	*3.50*
	Never hinged	5.25	
	On cover		57.50
37	A17 1.25m green	3.25	*4.25*
	Never hinged	7.00	
	On cover		57.50
38	A17 1.50m yellow brown	4.00	*5.50*
	Never hinged	9.25	
	On cover		57.50
39	A21 2.50m lilac rose	2.50	*4.25*
	Never hinged	6.00	
	On cover		75.00
	Nos. 36-39 (4)	12.25	*17.50*
	Set, never hinged	27.50	

A2

1920 **Unwmk.** ***Perf. 11½***

40	A2 5pf green	2.10	1.40
	Never hinged	5.00	
	On cover		11.50
41	A2 10pf rose red	2.10	1.40
	Never hinged	5.00	
	On cover		15.00
42	A2 15pf gray	10.50	9.00
	Never hinged	22.50	
	On cover		37.50
43	A2 20pf brn org	1.10	1.40
	Never hinged	3.00	
	On cover		11.50
44	A2 25pf dp bl	12.00	*15.00*
	Never hinged	27.50	
	On cover		37.50
45	A2 30pf orange	1.00	.70
	Never hinged	2.25	
	On cover		6.00
46	A2 40pf brown	.80	.80
	Never hinged	1.50	
	On cover		6.00
47	A2 50pf violet	1.50	1.00
	Never hinged	3.00	
	On cover		7.50
48	A2 60pf red brn	6.00	3.50
	Never hinged	11.50	
	On cover		19.00
49	A2 75pf chocolate	6.00	4.50
	Never hinged	12.50	
	On cover		27.00
50	A2 1m brn & grn	.80	.55
	Never hinged	2.25	
	On cover		11.50
51	A2 2m dk vio	1.10	1.00
	Never hinged	2.75	
	On cover		27.00
52	A2 3m light red	1.40	.85
	Never hinged	3.75	
	On cover		45.00
53	A2 5m blue & rose	2.75	1.10
	Never hinged	5.25	
	On cover		75.00
	Nos. 40-53 (14)	49.15	42.20
	Set, never hinged	100.00	

MARSHALL ISLANDS

ˈmär-shəl ˈī-lənds

LOCATION — Two chains of islands in the West Pacific Ocean, northwest of the Gilbert and Ellice group
GOVT. — German possession
AREA — 176 sq. mi.
POP. — 15,179 (1913)
CAPITAL — Jaluit

100 Pfennig = 1 Mark

Watermark

Wmk. 125 — Lozenges

Issued under German Dominion

A1

A2

Stamps of Germany Overprinted "Marschall-Inseln" in Black

Two printings of Nos. 1-4: Berlin printing, white, smooth shiny gum; Jaluit printing, yellowish, dull gum.

1897 **Unwmk.** ***Perf. 13½x14½***

1	A1 3pf dark brown (Berlin)	125.00	*600.00*
	Never hinged	525.00	
	On cover		950.00
a.	3pf light yellowish brown (Jaluit)	*3,600.*	*2,000.*
	Never hinged	8,000.	
	On cover		*12,000.*
b.	3pf reddish ochre (Jaluit)	3,600.	2,100.
	Never hinged	7,200.	
	On cover		*12,000.*
2	A1 5pf green (Berlin)	110.00	*450.00*
	Never hinged	325.00	
	On cover		800.00
a.	5pf green (Jaluit)	525.00	440.00
	Never hinged	1,300.	
	On cover		*950.00*
3	A1 10pf carmine (Berlin)	45.00	*110.00*
	Never hinged	140.00	
	On cover		2.50
a.	Vertical half used as 5pf on postcard		*27,500.*
b.	As "a," on newspaper wrapper		*34,000.*
c.	10pf carmine (Jaluit)	60.00	*85.00*
	Never hinged	175.00	
	On cover		240.00
4	A2 20pf ultra (Berlin)	45.00	*110.00*
	Never hinged	140.00	
	On cover		250.00
a.	20pf ultra (Jaluit)	60.00	*95.00*
	Never hinged	175.00	
	On cover		275.00
5	A2 25pf orange (Berlin)	125.00	*700.00*
	Never hinged	475.00	
	On cover		*2,400.*
6	A2 50pf red brown (Berlin)	125.00	*700.00*
	Never hinged	475.00	
	On cover		*2,000.*

Nos. 5 and 6 were not placed in use, but canceled copies and covers exist.

Value for No. 6 on cover is for complete, overfranked covers, usually philatelic.

Forged cancellations are found on almost all Marshall Islands stamps.

Overprinted "Marshall-Inseln"

1899-1900

7	A1 3pf dk brn ('00)	4.50	*5.25*
	Never hinged	12.00	
	On cover		20.00
a.	3pf light brown	240.00	*725.00*
	Never hinged	600.00	
	On cover		—
8	A1 5pf green	9.00	*12.00*
	Never hinged	24.00	
	On cover		20.00
9	A2 10pf car ('00)	9.50	*15.00*
	Never hinged	27.50	
	On cover		30.00
a.	Half used as 5pf on postcard		*8,000.*
10	A2 20pf ultra ('00)	15.00	*24.00*
	Never hinged	40.00	
	On cover		42.50
11	A2 25pf orange	17.50	*40.00*
	Never hinged	55.00	
	On cover		70.00
12	A2 50pf red brown	28.00	*45.00*
	Never hinged	80.00	
	On cover		95.00
a.	Half used as 25pf on cover		*35,000.*
	Nos. 7-12 (6)	83.50	*141.25*

Values for Nos. 9a and 12a are for properly used items, addressed and sent to Germany.

Kaiser's Yacht "Hohenzollern"
A3 A4

1901 **Unwmk.** **Typo.** ***Perf. 14***

13	A3 3pf brown	.65	1.60
	Never hinged	1.40	
	On cover		45.00
14	A3 5pf green	.65	1.60
	Never hinged	1.40	
	On cover		17.50
15	A3 10pf carmine	.65	*5.00*
	Never hinged	1.40	
	On cover		25.00
16	A3 20pf ultra	.90	*9.00*
	Never hinged	1.40	
	On cover		40.00
17	A3 25pf org & blk, *yel*	1.00	*15.00*
	Never hinged	2.00	
	On cover		85.00
18	A3 30pf org & blk, *sal*	1.00	*15.00*
	Never hinged	2.00	
	On cover		80.00
19	A3 40pf lake & blk	1.00	*15.00*
	Never hinged	2.00	
	On cover		80.00
20	A3 50pf pur & blk, *sal*	1.40	*22.50*
	Never hinged	4.00	
	On cover		60.00
21	A3 80pf lake & blk, *rose*	2.40	*32.50*
	Never hinged	12.00	
	On cover		80.00

Engr.

Perf. 14½x14

22	A4 1m carmine	3.50	*80.00*
	Never hinged	16.00	
	On cover		*125.00*
23	A4 2m blue	5.25	*110.00*
	Never hinged	20.00	
	On cover		*190.00*
24	A4 3m blk vio	8.00	*190.00*
	Never hinged	27.50	
	On cover		*300.00*
25	A4 5m slate & car	120.00	*475.00*
	Never hinged	475.00	
	On cover		*875.00*
	Nos. 13-25 (13)	146.40	972.20

Covers: Values for Nos. 20-25 on cover are for overfranked complete covers, usually philatelic.

Wmk. Lozenges (125)

1916 **Typo.** ***Perf. 14***

26	A3 3pf brown	.80	
	Never hinged	1.90	

Engr.

Perf. 14½x14

27	A4 5m slate & carmine, 25x17 holes	32.00	
	Never hinged	120.00	
a.	5m slate & carmine, 26x17 holes	32.00	
	Never hinged	140.00	

Nos. 26 and 27 were never placed in use.

The stamps of Marshall Islands overprinted "G. R. I." and new values in British currency were all used in New Britain and are listed among the issues for that country.

MARTINIQUE

ˌmär-tᵊn-ˈēk

LOCATION — Island in the West Indies, southeast of Puerto Rico
GOVT. — French Colony
AREA — 385 sq. mi.
POP. — 261,595 (1946)
CAPITAL — Fort-de-France

100 Centimes = 1 Franc

Stamps of French Colonies 1881-86 Surcharged in Black

Nos. 1, 7

No. 2

No. 3

No. 4

Nos. 5-6, 8

Nos. 9-20

1886-91 **Unwmk.** ***Perf. 14x13½***

1	A9 5 on 20c	45.00	37.50
	On cover		625.00
a.	Double surcharge	*550.00*	*550.00*
2	A9 5c on 20c	*12,000.*	*12,000.*
3	A9 15c on 20c ('87)	210.00	175.00
	On cover		800.00
a.	Inverted surcharge	*1,800.*	*1,800.*
4	A9 15c on 20c ('87)	80.00	72.50
	On cover		500.00
a.	Inverted surcharge	*1,100.*	*1,100.*
5	A9 01 on 20c ('88)	16.00	13.00
	On cover		500.00
a.	Inverted surcharge	*275.00*	*260.00*
6	A9 05 on 20c	11.00	8.50
	On cover		500.00
7	A9 15 on 20c ('88)	150.00	140.00
	On cover		500.00
c.	Inverted surcharge	*600.00*	*600.00*
8	A9 015 on 20c ('87)	46.50	*46.50*
	On cover		500.00
a.	Inverted surcharge	*625.00*	*625.00*
9	A9 01c on 2c ('88)	2.90	2.00
	On cover		500.00
a.	Double surcharge	*375.00*	*375.00*
10	A9 01c on 4c ('88)	11.00	3.25
	On cover		375.00
11	A9 05c on 4c ('88)	1,100.	1,100.
12	A9 05c on 10c ('90)	92.50	57.50
	On cover		450.00
a.	Slanting "5"	*225.00*	*175.00*
13	A9 05c on 20c ('88)	22.00	14.50
	On cover		375.00
a.	Slanting "5"	*110.00*	*85.00*
b.	Inverted surcharge	*300.00*	*275.00*
14	A9 05c on 30c ('91)	26.00	18.00
	On cover		375.00
a.	Slanting "5"	*110.00*	*92.50*
15	A9 05c on 35c ('91)	13.50	12.00
	On cover		375.00
a.	Slanting "5"	*100.00*	*92.50*
b.	Inverted surcharge	*225.00*	*200.00*
16	A9 05c on 40c ('91)	50.00	35.00
	On cover		425.00
a.	Slanting "5"	*175.00*	*110.00*
17	A9 15c on 4c ('88)	*9,000.*	*8,250.*
18	A9 15c on 20c ('87)	110.00	82.50
	On cover		375.00
a.	Slanting "5"	*400.00*	*300.00*
b.	Double surcharge	*525.00*	*525.00*
19	A9 15c on 25c ('90)	25.00	13.50
	On cover		425.00
a.	Slanting "5"	*110.00*	*100.00*
b.	Inverted surcharge	*250.00*	*225.00*
20	A9 15c on 75c ('91)	140.00	115.00
	On cover		550.00
a.	Slanting "5"	*425.00*	*350.00*

French Colonies No. 47 Surcharged

1891

21	A9 01c on 2c brn, *buff*	8.00	8.00
	On cover		375.00

French Colonies Nos. J5-J9 Surcharged

1891-92 **Black Surcharge** ***Imperf.***

22	D1 05c on 5c blk ('92)	12.50	11.50
	On cover		375.00
a.	Slanting "5"	*52.50*	*45.00*
23	D1 05c on 15c blk	11.50	11.00
	On cover		375.00
b.	Slanting "5"	*52.50*	*45.00*
24	D1 15c on 20c blk	14.50	11.00
	On cover		375.00
a.	Inverted surcharge	*210.00*	*210.00*
b.	Double surcharge	*210.00*	*210.00*

25 D1 15c on 30c blk 14.50 11.00
On cover 375.00
a. Inverted surcharge 210.00 210.00
b. Slanting "5" 57.50 45.00
Nos. 22-25 (4) 53.00 44.50

Red Surcharge

26 D1 05c on 10c blk 10.00 8.50
On cover 375.00
a. Inverted surcharge 210.00 210.00
27 D1 05c on 15c blk 11.00 11.00
On cover 375.00
28 D1 15c on 20c blk 40.00 29.00
On cover 375.00
a. Inverted surcharge 300.00 300.00
Nos. 26-28 (3) 61.00 48.50

French Colonies No. 54 Surcharged in Black

j

k

1892 ***Perf. 14x13½***

29 A9 (j) 05c on 25c 50.00 50.00
On cover 325.00
a. Slanting "5" 210.00 210.00
30 A9 (j) 15c on 25c 28.00 28.00
On cover 325.00
a. Slanting "5" 200.00 200.00
31 A9 (k) 05c on 25c 42.50 40.00
On cover 325.00
a. "1882" instead of "1892" 500.00 450.00
b. "95" instead of "05" 600.00 550.00
c. Slanting "5" 200.00 200.00
32 A9 (k) 15c on 25c 25.00 24.00
On cover 325.00
a. "1882" instead of "1892" 450.00 425.00
b. Slanting "5" 110.00 110.00
Nos. 29-32 (4) 145.50 142.00

Navigation and Commerce — A15

1892-1906 Typo. *Perf. 14x13½*
"MARTINIQUE" Colony in Carmine or Blue

33 A15 1c blk, *lil bl* 1.25 1.00
a. "MARTINIQUE" in blue 725.00 725.00
34 A15 2c brn, *buff* 1.25 1.10
35 A15 4c claret, *lav* 1.40 1.10
36 A15 5c grn, *grnsh* 1.75 1.10
On cover 20.00
37 A15 5c yel grn ('99) 2.50 .85
On cover 20.00
38 A15 10c blk, *lav* 8.50 1.40
On cover 20.00
39 A15 10c red ('99) 4.00 1.10
On cover 20.00
40 A15 15c blue, quadrille paper 32.50 6.00
On cover 37.50
41 A15 15c gray ('99) 11.00 1.60
On cover 37.50
42 A15 20c red, *grn* 16.00 7.25
43 A15 25c blk, *rose* 18.00 2.50
On cover 20.00
44 A15 25c blue ('99) 12.00 12.00
On cover 37.50
45 A15 30c brn, *bis* 24.00 14.00
46 A15 35c blk, *yel* ('06) 12.00 7.25
On cover 65.00
47 A15 40c red, *straw* 26.50 14.00
On cover 65.00
48 A15 50c car, *rose* 30.00 18.50
On cover 65.00
49 A15 50c brn, *az* ('99) 30.00 26.00
On cover 85.00
50 A15 75c dp vio, *org* 24.00 15.00
On cover 100.00
51 A15 1fr brnz grn, *straw* 24.00 16.00
On cover 125.00
52 A15 2fr vio, *rose* ('04) 72.50 62.50
On cover
53 A15 5fr lil, *lav* ('03) 82.50 75.00
On cover
Nos. 33-53 (21) 435.65 285.25

Perf. 13½x14 stamps are counterfeits.
For surcharges see Nos. 54-61, 101-104.

Stamps of 1892-1903 Surcharged in Black

1904

54 A15 10c on 30c brn, *bis* 10.00 10.00
On cover 50.00
a. Double surcharge 400.00 400.00
55 A15 10c on 5fr lil, *lav* 11.00 11.00
On cover 50.00

Surcharged

56 A15 10c on 30c brn, *bis* 17.00 17.00
On cover 65.00
57 A15 10c on 40c red, *straw* 17.00 17.00
On cover 65.00
a. Double surcharge 325.00 325.00
58 A15 10c on 50c car, *rose* 20.00 20.00
On cover 65.00
59 A15 10c on 75c dp vio, *org* 14.00 14.00
On cover 65.00
60 A15 10c on 1fr brnz grn, *straw* 14.00 14.00
On cover 65.00
a. Double surcharge 190.00 190.00
61 A15 10c on 5fr lil, *lav* 210.00 210.00
On cover —
Nos. 54-61 (8) 313.00 313.00

Martinique Woman — A16

Girl Bearing Pineapple in Cane Field — A18

View of Fort-de-France — A17

1908-30 Typo.

62	A16	1c red brn & brn	.20	.20
63	A16	2c ol grn & brn	.25	.20
64	A16	4c vio brn & brn	.25	.20
65	A16	5c grn & brn	.75	.20
66	A16	5c org & brn ('22)	.30	.20
67	A16	10c car & brn	.90	.40
68	A16	10c bl grn & grn ('22)	.40	.20
69	A16	10c brn vio & rose ('25)	.40	.20
70	A16	15c brn vio & rose ('17)	.45	.20
71	A16	15c bl grn & gray grn ('25)	.30	.30
72	A16	15c dp bl & red org ('27)	1.25	1.25
73	A16	20c vio & brn	1.10	.80
74	A17	25c bl & brn	1.60	.80
75	A17	25c org & brn ('22)	.65	.40
76	A17	30c brn org & brn	1.60	.80
77	A17	30c dl red & brn ('22)	.50	.50
78	A17	30c rose & ver ('24)	.45	.45
79	A17	30c ol brn & brn ('25)	.45	.45
80	A17	30c sl bl & bl grn ('27)	1.25	1.25
81	A17	35c vio & brn	.60	.50
82	A17	40c gray grn & brn	.60	.40
83	A17	45c dk brn & brn	.60	.40
84	A17	50c rose & brn	1.60	.80
85	A17	50c bl & brn ('22)	1.10	1.10
86	A17	50c org & grn ('25)	.60	.20
87	A17	60c dk bl & lil rose ('25)	.60	.50
88	A17	65c vio & ol brn ('27)	1.40	1.40
89	A17	75c slate & brn	1.00	.60
90	A17	75c ind & dk bl ('25)	.60	.50
91	A17	75c org brn & lt bl ('27)	2.00	2.00
92	A17	90c brn red & brt red ('30)	4.25	4.25
93	A18	1fr dl bl & brn	.90	.60
94	A18	1fr dk bl ('25)	.75	.60
95	A18	1fr ver & ol grn ('27)	1.60	1.60
96	A18	1.10fr vio & dk brn ('28)	2.50	2.50
97	A18	1.50fr ind & ultra ('30)	4.25	4.25
98	A18	2fr gray & brn	3.25	1.40
99	A18	3fr red vio ('30)	7.25	7.25
100	A18	5fr org red & brn	8.00	6.00
		Nos. 62-100 (39)	56.50	45.85

For surcharges see Nos. 105-128, B1.

Nos. 41, 43, 47 and 53 Surcharged in Carmine or Black

1912, Aug.
Spacing between figures of surcharge 1.5mm (5c), 2mm (10c)

101 A15 5c on 15c gray (C) .80 .80
102 A15 5c on 25c blk, *rose* (C) 1.25 1.25
103 A15 10c on 40c red, *straw* 1.75 1.75
104 A15 10c on 5fr lil, *lav* 2.25 2.25
Nos. 101-104 (4) 6.05 6.05

Spacing between figures of surcharge 2.25mm (5c), 2.75mm (10c)

101a A15 5c on 15c gray (C) 37.50 37.50
102a A15 5c on 25c blk, *rose* (C) 77.50 77.50
103a A15 10c on 40c red, *straw* 125.00 125.00
104a A15 10c on 5fr lil, *lav* 77.50 77.50
Nos. 101a-104a (4) 317.50 317.50

Nos. 62, 63, 70 Surcharged

1920, June 15

105 A16 5c on 1c 1.60 1.60
a. Double surcharge 32.50 32.50
b. Inverted surcharge 21.00 21.00
106 A16 10c on 2c 1.60 1.60
a. Inverted surcharge 29.00 29.00
107 A16 25c on 15c 1.40 1.40
a. Double surcharge 42.50 42.50
b. Inverted surcharge 42.50 42.50
Nos. 105-107 (3) 4.60 4.60

No. 70 Surcharged in Various Colors

1922, Dec.

108 A16 1c on 15c (Bk) .35 .35
109 A16 2c on 15c (Bl) .35 .35
110 A16 5c on 15c (R) .50 .50
a. Imperf., pair 100.00
Nos. 108-110 (3) 1.20 1.20

Types of 1908-30 Surcharged

1923-25

111 A17 60c on 75c bl & rose .45 .45
112 A17 65c on 45c ol brn & brn ('25) 1.00 1.00
113 A17 85c on 75c blk & brn (R) ('25) 1.25 1.25
Nos. 111-113 (3) 2.70 2.70

Nos. 63, 73, 76-77, 84-85 Surcharged in Brown

Surcharge is horiz. on #114-115, vert. reading up on #116, 119 and down on #117-118.

1924, Feb. 14

114 A16 1c on 2c 2.10 2.10
a. Double surcharge 260.00 260.00
b. Inverted surcharge 55.00 55.00
115 A16 5c on 20c 3.00 3.00
a. Inverted surcharge 50.00 50.00
116 A17 15c on 30c (#76) 11.50 11.50
a. Surcharge reading down 32.50 32.50
117 A17 15c on 30c (#77) 16.00 16.00
a. Surcharge reading up 50.00 50.00
118 A17 25c on 50c (#84) 210.00 210.00
119 A17 25c on 50c (#85) 7.25 7.25
a. Surcharge reading down 25.00 25.00
Nos. 114-119 (6) 249.85 249.85

Stamps and Types of 1908-30 Surcharged with New Value and Bars

1924-27

120 A16 25c on 15c brn vio & rose ('25) .40 .40
121 A18 25c on 2fr gray & brn .30 .30
122 A18 25c on 5fr org red & brn (Bl) 1.75 1.40
123 A17 90c on 75c brn red & red ('27) 3.00 2.10
124 A18 1.25fr on 1fr dk bl ('26) .85 .70
125 A18 1.50fr on 1fr dk bl & ultra ('27) 1.40 .85
126 A18 3fr on 5fr dl red & grn ('27) 2.10 2.10
127 A18 10fr on 5fr dl grn & dp red ('27) 9.00 9.00
128 A18 20fr on 5fr org brn & red vio ('27) 14.00 13.50
Nos. 120-128 (9) 32.80 30.35

Common Design Types pictured following the introduction.

Colonial Exposition Issue
Common Design Types

1931, Apr. 13 Engr. *Perf. 12½*
Name of Country in Black

129 CD70 40c deep green 4.00 4.00
130 CD71 50c violet 4.00 4.00
131 CD72 90c red orange 4.00 4.00
132 CD73 1.50fr dull blue 4.00 4.00
Nos. 129-132 (4) 16.00 16.00

Village of Basse-Pointe — A19

Government Palace, Fort-de-France — A20

Martinique Women A21

1933-40 Photo. *Perf. 13½*

133	A19	1c red, *pink*	.20	.20
134	A20	2c dull blue	.20	.20
135	A20	3c sepia ('40)	.20	.20
136	A19	4c olive grn	.20	.20
137	A20	5c dp rose	.25	.25
138	A19	10c blk, *pink*	.25	.25
139	A20	15c blk, *org*	.25	.25
140	A21	20c org brn	.25	.25
141	A19	25c brn vio	.25	.25
142	A20	30c green	.40	.40
143	A20	30c lt ultra ('40)	.25	.25
144	A21	35c dl grn ('38)	.65	.60
145	A21	40c olive brn	.50	.40
146	A20	45c dk brn	1.60	1.40
147	A20	45c grn ('40)	.45	.45
148	A20	50c red	.40	.20
149	A19	55c brn red ('38)	1.10	.80
150	A19	60c lt bl ('40)	.70	.70
151	A21	65c red, *grn*	.40	.40
152	A21	70c brt red vio ('40)	.50	.50
153	A19	75c dk brn	.85	.65
154	A20	80c vio ('38)	.60	.50
155	A19	90c carmine	1.40	1.25
156	A19	90c brt red vio ('39)	.70	.70
157	A20	1fr blk, *grn*	1.60	1.00
158	A20	1fr rose red ('38)	.60	.50
159	A21	1.25fr dk vio	.50	.50
160	A21	1.25fr dp rose ('39)	.60	.60
161	A19	1.40fr lt ultra ('40)	.60	.60
162	A20	1.50fr dp bl	.50	.40

163	A20	1.60fr chnt ('40)	.60	.60
164	A21	1.75fr ol grn	6.50	3.50
165	A21	1.75fr dp bl ('38)	.50	.50
166	A19	2fr dk bl, *grn*	.40	.30
167	A21	2.25fr blue ('39)	.60	.60
168	A19	2.50fr sepia ('40)	.75	.75
169	A21	3fr brn vio	.50	.45
170	A21	5fr red, *pink*	.95	.80
171	A19	10fr dk bl, *bl*	.75	.60
172	A20	20fr red, *yel*	1.10	.70
		Nos. 133-172 (40)	29.60	23.65

For surcharges see Nos. 190-195.

Landing of Bélain d'Esnambuc — A22

Freed Slaves Paying Homage to Victor Schoelcher A23

1935, Oct. 22 **Engr.** ***Perf. 13***

173	A22	40c blk brn	2.10	2.10
174	A22	50c dl red	2.10	2.10
175	A22	1.50fr ultra	9.50	9.50
176	A23	1.75fr lil rose	9.75	9.75
177	A23	5fr brown	9.75	9.75
178	A23	10fr blue grn	7.25	7.25
		Nos. 173-178 (6)	40.45	40.45

Tercentenary of French possessions in the West Indies.

Colonial Arts Exhibition Issue

Common Design Type

Souvenir Sheet

1937 ***Imperf.***

179	CD74	3fr brt grn	6.50	*7.75*

Paris International Exposition Issue

Common Design Types

1937, Apr. 15 ***Perf. 13***

180	CD74	20c dp vio	1.25	1.25
181	CD75	30c dk grn	1.40	1.40
182	CD76	40c car rose	1.40	1.40
183	CD77	50c dk brn & blk	1.40	1.40
184	CD78	90c red	1.50	1.50
185	CD79	1.50fr ultra	1.50	1.50
		Nos. 180-185 (6)	8.45	8.45

New York World's Fair Issue

Common Design Type

1939, May 10 ***Perf. 12½x12***

186	CD82	1.25fr car lake	.80	.80
187	CD82	2.25fr ultra	.95	.95

SEMI-POSTAL STAMPS

Regular Issue of 1908 Surcharged in Red

Perf. 13½x14

1915, May 15 **Unwmk.**

B1	A16	10c + 5c car & brn	1.75	1.25
		On cover		100.00

Curie Issue

Common Design Type

1938, Oct. 24 ***Perf. 13***

B2	CD80	1.75fr + 50c brt ultra	10.00	10.00

French Revolution Issue

Common Design Type

Photo.; Name & Value Typo. in Black

1939, July 5

B3	CD83	45c + 25c grn	8.00	8.00
B4	CD83	70c + 30c brn	8.00	8.00
B5	CD83	90c + 35c red org	8.00	8.00
B6	CD83	1.25fr + 1fr rose pink	8.00	8.00
B7	CD83	2.25fr + 2fr blue	8.00	8.00
		Nos. B3-B7 (5)	40.00	40.00

POSTAGE DUE STAMPS

The set of 14 French Colonies postage due stamps (Nos. J1-J14) overprinted "MARTINIQUE" diagonally in red in 1887 was not an official issue.

Postage Due Stamps of France, 1893-1926 Overprinted

1927, Oct. 10 ***Perf. 14x13½***

J15	D2	5c light blue	1.25	1.25
		On cover		—
J16	D2	10c brown	1.40	1.40
		On cover		125.00
J17	D2	20c olive green	1.60	1.60
		On cover		—
J18	D2	25c rose	1.90	1.90
		On cover		—
J19	D2	30c red	2.25	2.25
		On cover		125.00
J20	D2	45c green	3.75	3.75
J21	D2	50c brn violet	4.75	4.75
J22	D2	60c blue green	4.75	4.75
J23	D2	1fr red brown	6.75	6.75
J24	D2	2fr bright vio	8.25	8.25
J25	D2	3fr magenta	9.50	9.50
		Nos. J15-J25 (11)	46.15	46.15

Tropical Fruit — D3

1933, Feb. 15 **Photo.** ***Perf. 13½***

J26	D3	5c dk bl, *green*	.35	.35
J27	D3	10c orange brown	.35	.35
J28	D3	20c dk blue	.70	.70
J29	D3	25c red, *pink*	.80	.80
J30	D3	30c dk vio	.80	.80
J31	D3	45c red, *yel*	.60	.60
J32	D3	50c dk brn	1.00	1.00
J33	D3	60c dl grn	1.00	1.00
J34	D3	1fr blk, *org*	1.00	1.00
J35	D3	2fr dp rose	1.00	1.00
J36	D3	3fr dk blue, *bl*	1.00	1.00
		Nos. J26-J36 (11)	8.60	8.60

PARCEL POST STAMP

Postage Due Stamp of French Colonies Surcharged in Black

TIMBRE POSTE
5 F.
MARTINIQUE
COLIS POSTAUX

1903, Oct. **Unwmk.** ***Imperf.***

Q1	D1	5fr on 60c brn, *buff*	475.00	*550.00*
a.		Inverted surcharge	*600.00*	*625.00*

MAURITANIA

mor-ə-ta-nē-ə

LOCATION — Northwestern Africa, bordering on the Atlantic Ocean
GOVT. — French Colony
AREA — 398,000 sq. mi.
POP. — 1,834,500 (est. 1984)
CAPITAL — Nouakchott

100 Centimes = 1 Franc

General Louis Faidherbe A1

Oil Palms — A2

Dr. Noel Eugène Ballay A3

Perf. 14x13½

1906-07 **Typo.** **Unwmk.**

"Mauritanie" in Red or Blue

1	A1	1c slate	.60	.60
		On cover		60.00
2	A1	2c chocolate	1.10	.75
		On cover		60.00
3	A1	4c choc, *gray bl*	1.75	1.25
		On cover		60.00
4	A1	5c green	.85	.70
		On cover		40.00
5	A1	10c carmine (B)	10.00	4.00
		On cover		60.00
7	A2	20c black, *azure*	18.50	13.00
		On cover		80.00
8	A2	25c blue, *pnksh*	6.25	5.00
		On cover		50.00
9	A2	30c choc, *pnksh*	95.00	50.00
		On cover		150.00
10	A2	35c black, *yellow*	6.75	4.00
		On cover		130.00
11	A2	40c car, *az* (B)	7.25	5.75
		On cover		130.00
12	A2	45c choc, *grnsh* ('07)	8.00	6.00
		On cover		130.00
13	A2	50c deep violet	7.25	5.50
		On cover		130.00
14	A2	75c blue, *org*	6.50	6.00
		On cover		150.00
15	A3	1fr black, *azure*	18.50	18.50
		On cover		200.00
16	A3	2fr blue, *pink*	45.00	45.00
		On cover		400.00
17	A3	5fr car, *straw*(B)	115.00	115.00
		On cover		800.00
		Nos. 1-17 (16)	348.30	281.05

Crossing Desert A4

1913-38

18	A4	1c brn vio & brn	.25	.20
19	A4	2c black & blue	.30	.20
20	A4	4c violet & blk	.30	.20
21	A4	5c yel grn & bl grn	.85	.50
22	A4	5c brn vio & rose ('22)	.20	.20
23	A4	10c rose & red org	1.90	1.25
24	A4	10c yel grn & bl grn ('22)	.45	.40
25	A4	10c lil rose, *bluish* ('25)	.35	.35
26	A4	15c dk brn & blk ('17)	.45	.35
27	A4	20c bis brn & org	.45	.35
28	A4	25c blue & vio	1.10	.95
29	A4	25c grn & rose ('22)	.20	.20
30	A4	30c bl grn & rose	1.10	1.00
31	A4	30c rose & red org ('22)	1.25	1.25
32	A4	30c black & yel ('26)	.20	.20
33	A4	30c bl grn & yel grn ('28)	.95	.95
34	A4	35c brown & vio	.65	.50
35	A4	35c dp grn & lt grn ('38)	1.00	1.00
36	A4	40c gray & bl grn	2.25	1.75
37	A4	45c org & bis brn	1.25	.95
38	A4	50c brn vio & rose	.95	.95
39	A4	50c dk bl & ultra ('22)	.40	.40
40	A4	50c gray grn & dp bl ('26)	.70	.70
41	A4	60c vio, *pnksh* ('26)	.50	.50
42	A4	65c yel brn & lt bl ('26)	.70	.70
43	A4	75c ultra & brown	.70	.65
44	A4	85c myr grn & lt brn ('26)	.80	.80
45	A4	90c brn red & rose ('30)	1.75	1.50
46	A4	1fr rose & black	.80	.80
47	A4	1.10fr vio & ver ('28)	9.00	9.00
48	A4	1.25fr dk bl & blk brn ('33)	1.75	1.75
49	A4	1.50fr lt bl & dp bl ('30)	1.00	1.00
50	A4	1.75fr bl grn & brn red ('33)	1.60	1.50
51	A4	1.75fr dk bl & ultra ('38)	1.60	1.10
52	A4	2fr red org & vio	1.60	1.25
53	A4	3fr red violet ('30)	1.60	1.50
54	A4	5fr violet & blue	2.75	2.10
		Nos. 18-54 (37)	43.65	38.95

Cover values for this issue start at $30.
For surcharges see Nos. 55-64, B1-B2.

Stamp and Type of 1913-38 Surcharged

1922-25

55	A4	60c on 75c violet, *pnksh*	.70	.70
56	A4	65c on 15c dk brn & blk ('25)	1.40	1.40
57	A4	85c on 75c ultra & brn ('25)	1.40	1.40
		Nos. 55-57 (3)	3.50	3.50

Stamp and Type of 1913-38 Surcharged with New Value and Bars

1924-27

58	A4	25c on 2fr red org & vio	.80	.80
59	A4	90c on 75c brn red & cer ('27)	1.90	1.90
60	A4	1.25fr on 1fr dk bl & ultra ('26)	.45	.45
61	A4	1.50fr on 1fr bl & dp bl ('27)	1.25	1.25
62	A4	3fr on 5fr ol brn & red vio ('27)	5.50	5.50
63	A4	10fr on 5fr mag & bl grn ('27)	5.50	5.50
64	A4	20fr on 5fr bl vio & dp org ('27)	6.50	6.50
		Nos. 58-64 (7)	21.90	21.90

Common Design Types pictured following the introduction.

Colonial Exposition Issue

Common Design Types

Engr.; Name of Country Typo. in Black

1931, Apr. 13 ***Perf. 12½***

65	CD70	40c deep green	6.00	6.00
66	CD71	50c violet	4.00	4.00
67	CD72	90c red orange	4.00	4.00
68	CD73	1.50fr dull blue	4.00	4.00
		Nos. 65-68 (4)	18.00	18.00

Paris International Exposition Issue

Common Design Types

1937, Apr. 15 ***Perf. 13***

69	CD74	20c deep violet	.95	.95
70	CD75	30c dark green	1.10	1.10
71	CD76	40c carmine rose	1.10	1.10
72	CD77	50c dk brn & blk	1.10	1.10
73	CD78	90c red	1.10	1.10
74	CD79	1.50fr ultra	1.10	1.10
		Nos. 69-74 (6)	6.45	6.45

Colonial Arts Exhibition Issue

Common Design Type

Souvenir Sheet

1937 ***Imperf.***

75	CD76	3fr dark blue	6.00	*7.50*

Camel Rider — A5

Mauri Couple — A8

Mauris on Camels A6

Family before Tent — A7

1938-40 ***Perf. 13***

76	A5	2c violet blk	.20	.20
77	A5	3c dp ultra	.20	.20
78	A5	4c rose violet	.20	.20
79	A5	5c orange red	.20	.20
80	A5	10c brown car	.30	.30
81	A5	15c dk violet	.30	.30
82	A6	20c red	.30	.30
83	A6	25c deep ultra	.30	.30
84	A6	30c deep brown	.20	.20
85	A6	35c Prus green	.60	.60
86	A6	40c rose car ('40)	.25	.25
87	A6	45c Prus grn ('40)	.25	.25
88	A6	50c purple	.35	.35
89	A7	55c rose violet	.80	.80
90	A7	60c violet ('40)	.35	.35
91	A7	65c deep green	.80	.80
92	A7	70c red ('40)	.60	.60
93	A7	80c deep blue	1.10	1.10
94	A7	90c rose violet ('39)	.65	.65
95	A7	1fr red	1.75	1.75
96	A7	1fr dp green ('40)	.65	.65
97	A7	1.25fr rose car ('39)	1.25	1.25
98	A7	1.40fr dp blue ('40)	.65	.65
99	A7	1.50fr violet	.75	.75
99A	A7	1.50fr red brn ('40)	82.50	82.50
100	A7	1.60fr black brn ('40)	1.40	1.40
101	A8	1.75fr deep ultra	1.10	1.10
102	A8	2fr rose violet	.70	.70
103	A8	2.25fr dull ultra ('39)	.60	.60
104	A8	2.50fr black brn ('40)	.75	.75
105	A8	3fr deep green	.60	.60
106	A8	5fr scarlet	.80	.80
107	A8	10fr deep brown	1.40	1.40
108	A8	20fr brown car	1.50	1.50
		Nos. 76-108 (34)	104.35	104.35

Nos. 91 and 109 surcharged with new values are listed under French West Africa.

For surcharges see Nos. B9-B12.

Caillie Issue

Common Design Type

1939, Apr. 5 **Engr.** ***Perf. 12½x12***

109	CD81	90c org brn & org	.95	.95
110	CD81	2fr brt violet	.95	.95
111	CD81	2.25fr ultra & dk bl	1.00	1.00
		Nos. 109-111 (3)	2.90	2.90

New York World's Fair Issue

Common Design Type

1939, May 10

112	CD82	1.25fr carmine lake	.55	.55
113	CD82	2.25fr ultra	.55	.55

SEMI-POSTAL STAMPS

Nos. 23 and 26 Surcharged in Red

1915-18 **Unwmk.** ***Perf. 14x13½***

B1	A4	10c + 5c rose & red org	1.40	1.40
		On cover		60.00
B2	A4	15c + 5c dk brn & blk ('18)	1.60	1.60
		On cover		60.00

Curie Issue

Common Design Type

1938, Oct. 24 ***Perf. 13***

B3	CD80	1.75fr + 50c brt ultra	7.25	7.25

French Revolution Issue

Common Design Type

Photo.; Name and Value Typographed in Black

1939, July 5 **Unwmk.**

B4	CD83	45c + 25c grn	8.00	8.00
B5	CD83	70c + 30c brn	8.00	8.00
B6	CD83	90c + 35c red org	8.00	8.00
B7	CD83	1.25fr + 1fr rose pink	8.00	8.00
B8	CD83	2.25fr + 2fr bl	8.00	8.00
		Nos. B4-B8 (5)	40.00	40.00

AIR POST STAMPS

Common Design Type

Perf. 12½x12

1940, Feb. 8 **Engr.** **Unwmk.**

C1	CD85	1.90fr ultra	.45	.45
C2	CD85	2.90fr dk red	.45	.45
C3	CD85	4.50fr dk gray grn	.50	.50
C4	CD85	4.90fr yel bister	.85	.85
C5	CD85	6.90fr deep org	1.00	1.00
		Nos. C1-C5 (5)	3.25	3.25

POSTAGE DUE STAMPS

D1

D2

Perf. 14x13½

1906-07 **Unwmk.** **Typo.**

J1	D1	5c grn, *grnsh*	2.25	2.25
		On cover		200.00
J2	D1	10c red brn	3.50	3.25
		On cover		200.00
J3	D1	15c dk bl	7.25	6.00
		On cover		200.00
J4	D1	20c blk, *yellow*	8.75	7.25
		On cover		200.00
J5	D1	30c red, *straw*	9.50	8.00
		On cover		200.00
J6	D1	50c violet	14.50	14.50
		On cover		200.00
J7	D1	60c blk, *buff*	11.00	9.25
		On cover		200.00
J8	D1	1fr blk, *pinkish*	16.00	14.50
		On cover		200.00
		Nos. J1-J8 (8)	72.75	65.00

Issue dates: 20c, 1906; others 1907.

Regular postage stamps canceled "T" in a triangle were used for postage due.

1914

J9	D2	5c green	.20	.20
		On cover		150.00
J10	D2	10c rose	.20	.20
		On cover		150.00
J11	D2	15c gray	.35	.35
		On cover		150.00
J12	D2	20c brown	.35	.35
		On cover		150.00
J13	D2	30c blue	.65	.65
		On cover		150.00
J14	D2	50c black	1.25	1.25
		On cover		150.00
J15	D2	60c orange	1.00	1.00
		On cover		150.00
J16	D2	1fr violet	1.00	1.00
		On cover		150.00
		Nos. J9-J16 (8)	5.00	5.00

Type of 1914 Issue Surcharged

1927, Oct. 10

J17	D2	2fr on 1fr lil rose	2.25	2.25
J18	D2	3fr on 1fr org brn	2.60	2.60

MAURITIUS

mo-'ri-sh,ē-,əs

LOCATION — Island in the Indian Ocean about 550 miles east of Madagascar
GOVT. — British Colony
AREA — 720 sq. mi.
POP. — 969,191 (est. 1983)
CAPITAL — Port Louis

12 Pence = 1 Shilling
100 Cents = 1 Rupee (1878)

Nos. 1-6, 14-17 unused are valued without gum.

Nos. 3a-8, 14-15 are printed on fragile paper with natural irregularities which might be mistaken for faults.

Very fine examples of Nos. 22-58 will have perforations touching the design on one or more sides. Examples with perfs clear on four sides are scarce and will sell for more. Inferior copies will sell for much reduced prices.

Catalogue values for unused stamps in this country are for Never Hinged items, beginning with Scott 223 in the regular postage section, Scott J1 in the postage due section.

Queen Victoria
A1 A2

1847 **Unwmk.** **Engr.** ***Imperf.***

1	A1	1p orange	*1,100,000.*	*600,000.*
2	A1	2p dark blue		*675,000.*

Nos. 1 and 2 were engraved and printed in Port Louis. There is but one type of each value. The initials "J. B." on the bust are those of the engraver, J. Barnard.

All unused copies of the 2p are in museums. There is one unused copy of the 1p in private hands.

1848

Earliest Impressions

Thick Yellowish Paper

3	A2	1p orange	*42,500.*	*15,750.*
4	A2	2p dark blue	*35,000.*	*18,000.*
d.		"PENOE"	*70,000.*	*27,500.*

Early Impressions

Yellowish White Paper

3a	A2	1p orange	*17,500.*	*6,500.*
4a	A2	2p blue	*20,000.*	*7,250.*
e.		"PENOE"	*32,500.*	*11,750.*

Bluish Paper

5	A2	1p orange	*17,500.*	*6,750.*
6	A2	2p blue	*20,000.*	*7,250.*
c.		"PENOE"	*32,500.*	*11,500.*

Intermediate Impressions

Yellowish White Paper

3b	A2	1p red orange	*9,250.*	2,400.
4b	A2	2p blue	*12,500.*	3,500.
f.		"PENOE"	*16,000.*	*5,750.*

Bluish Paper

5a	A2	1p red orange	*9,250.*	2,400.
6a	A2	2p blue	*9,250.*	2,750.
d.		"PENOE"	*15,500.*	*5,750.*
f.		Double impression		—

Worn Impressions

Yellowish White Paper

3c	A2	1p orange red	3,000.	550.
d.		1p brownish red	3,000.	550.
4c	A2	2p blue	3,250.	1,000.
g.		"PENOE"	*4,000.*	1,700.

Bluish Paper

5b	A2	1p orange red	2,250.	475.
c.		1p brownish red	2,100.	475.
d.		Pair, double impression		
6b	A2	2p blue	3,250.	950.
e.		"PENOE"	*4,000.*	1,600.

Latest Impressions

Yellowish or Grayish Paper

3e	A2	1p orange red	1,900.	450.
f.		1p brownish red	1,900.	450.
4h	A2	2p blue	2,400.	650.
i.		"PENOE"	*4,500.*	1,200.

Bluish Paper

5e	A2	1p orange red	1,800.	450.
f.		1p brownish red	1,800.	450.
6g	A2	2p blue	2,500.	650.
h.		"PENOE"	4,500.	1,200.

These stamps were printed in sheets of twelve, four rows of three, and each position differs in details. The "PENOE" error is the most pronounced variety on the plates and is from position 7.

The stamps were in use until 1859. Earliest impressions, Nos. 3-4, show the full background of diagonal and vertical lines with the diagonal lines predominant. Early impressions, Nos. 3a-4a, 5-6, show the full background with the vertical lines predominating. As the plate became worn the vertical lines disappeared, giving the intermediate impressions, Nos. 3b-4b, 5a-6a.

Worn impressions, Nos. 3c-4c, 5b-6b, have little background remaining, and latest impressions, Nos. 3e-4h, 5e-6g, have also lost details of the frame and head. The paper of the early impressions is usually rather thick, that of the worn impressions rather thin. Expect natural fibrous inclusions in the paper of all impressions.

"Britannia"
A3 A4

1849-58

7	A3	red brown, *blue*	17.00
8	A3	blue ('58)	4.25

Nos. 7-8 were never placed in use.

1858-59

9	A3	(4p) green, *bluish*	500.00	240.00
10	A3	(6p) red	40.00	*75.00*
11	A3	(9p) magenta ('59)	650.00	240.00
a.		Used as 1p ('62)		190.00

No. 11 was re-issued in Nov. 1862, as a 1p stamp (No. 11a). When used as such it is always canceled "B53."

1858 **Black Surcharge**

12 A4 4p green, *bluish* 1,150. 450.00

Queen Victoria — A5

Early Impressions

1859, Mar.

14 A5 2p blue, *grayish* 6,500. 2,250.
a. 2p deep blue, *grayish* 6,250. 2,150.
14B A5 2p blue, *bluish* 5,500. 2,000.
c. Intermediate impression 3,500. 800.00
d. Worn impression 1,750. 525.00

Type A5 was engraved by Lapirot, in Port Louis, and was printed locally. There were twelve varieties in the sheet.

Early impressions have clear and distinct background lines. In the intermediate impressions, the lines are somewhat blurred, and white patches appear. In the worn impressions, the background lines are discontinuous, with many white patches. Analogous wear is also obvious in the background of the inscriptions on all four sides. Values depend on the state of wear. One should expect natural fibrous inclusions in the paper on all printings.

A6

A7

1859, Oct.

15 A6 2p blue, *bluish* *120,000.* 4,750.

No. 15 was printed from the plate of the 1848 issue after it had been entirely re-engraved by Sherwin. It is commonly known as the "fillet head." The plate of the 1p, 1848, was also re-engraved but was never put in use.

1859, Dec. **Litho.**

Laid Paper

16 A7 1p vermilion 4,250. 925.
a. 1p deep red *7,500.* 1,800.
b. 1p red *5,500.* 1,700.
17 A7 2p pale blue 2,250. 525.
a. 2p slate blue 4,500. 850.
b. 2p blue 2,600. 625.

Lithographed locally by Dardenne.

"Britannia" — A8

1859 **Wove Paper** **Engr.** ***Imperf.***

18 A8 6p blue 725.00 42.50
19 A8 1sh vermilion 2,400. 52.50

1861

20 A8 6p gray violet 26.00 *47.50*
21 A8 1sh green 575.00 140.00

1862 ***Perf. 14 to 16***

22 A8 6p slate 25.00 *70.00*
a. Horiz. pair, imperf between *6,000.*
23 A8 1sh deep green 2,250. 400.00

Following the change in currency in 1878, a number of issues denominated in sterling were overprinted "CANCELLED" in serifed type and sold as remainders.

A9

A10

1860-63 **Typo.** ***Perf. 14***

24 A9 1p brown lilac 210.00 22.50
25 A9 2p blue 250.00 42.50
26 A9 4p rose 250.00 32.50
27 A9 6p green ('62) 750.00 140.00
28 A9 6p lilac ('63) 275.00 100.00
29 A9 9p dull lilac 125.00 50.00
Overprinted "CANCELLED" 95.00
30 A9 1sh buff ('62) 300.00 95.00
31 A9 1sh green ('63) 625.00 175.00

For surcharges see Nos. 43-45.

1863-72 **Wmk. 1**

32 A9 1p lilac brown 75.00 12.50
Overprinted "CANCELLED" 60.00
a. 1p bister brown 125.00 10.50
b. 1p brown 95.00 8.00
33 A9 2p blue 87.50 9.25
Overprinted "CANCELLED" 70.00
a. Imperf., pair 1,600. 2,300.
34 A9 3p vermilion 57.50 12.50
Overprinted "CANCELLED" 42.50
a. 3p deep red 160.00 27.50
35 A9 4p rose 100.00 4.25
Overprinted "CANCELLED" 80.00
36 A9 6p lilac ('64) 225.00 32.50
37 A9 6p blue grn ('65) 150.00 5.75
Overprinted "CANCELLED" 110.00
a. 6p yellow green ('65) 175.00 15.00
38 A9 9p green ('72) 150.00 *240.00*
39 A9 1sh org yel ('64) 225.00 25.00
Overprinted "CANCELLED" 165.00
a. 1sh yellow 210.00 15.00
40 A9 1sh blue ('70) 175.00 22.50
41 A9 5sh red violet 190.00 65.00
Overprinted "CANCELLED" 145.00
a. 5sh bright violet 250.00 65.00
Overprinted "CANCELLED" 180.00
Nos. 32-41 (10) 1,435. 429.25

For surcharges see Nos. 48-49, 51-58, 87.

1872

42 A10 10p claret 275.00 42.50
Overprinted "CANCELLED" 190.00

For surcharges see Nos. 46-47.

No. 29 Surcharged in Black or Red:

a

b

1876 **Unwmk.**

43 A9(a) ½p on 9p 11.00 *17.50*
Overprinted "CANCELLED" 10.00
a. Inverted surcharge *550.00*
b. Double surcharge *1,750.*
44 A9(b) ½p on 9p *2,750.*
Overprinted "CANCELLED" 300.00
45 A9(b) ½p on 9p (R) *1,900.*
Overprinted "CANCELLED" 125.00

Nos. 44 and 45 were never placed in use. No. 45 is valued with perfs cutting into the design.

Stamps of 1863-72 Surcharged in Black:

c

d

1876-77 **Wmk. 1**

46 A10(a) ½p on 10p claret 2.25 *20.00*
47 A10(c) ½p on 10p cl ('77) 4.75 *37.50*
Overprinted "CANCELLED" 3.00
48 A9(d) 1p on 4p rose ('77) 12.00 17.50
49 A9(d) 1sh on 5sh red vio ('77) 300.00 110.00
Overprinted "CANCELLED" 45.00
a. 1sh on 5sh violet ('77) 250.00 125.00
Overprinted "CANCELLED" 45.00
Nos. 46-49 (4) 319.00 *185.00*

A16

Black Surcharge

1878

50 A16 2c claret 8.50 5.75

Stamps and Type of 1863-72 Surcharged in Black

e

51 A9 4c on 1p bister brn 17.50 6.00
52 A9 8c on 2p blue 80.00 2.00
53 A9 13c on 3p org red 15.00 32.50
54 A9 17c on 4p rose 200.00 2.75
55 A9 25c on 6p sl blue 225.00 6.00
56 A9 38c on 9p violet 27.50 *70.00*
57 A9 50c on 1sh green 110.00 3.25
58 A9 2r50c on 5sh violet 17.50 *17.50*
Nos. 50-58 (9) 701.00 *145.75*

For surcharge see No. 87.

A18

A19

A20

A21

A22

A23

A24

A25

A26

1879-80 **Wmk. 1**

59 A18 2c red brn ('80) 45.00 16.00
60 A19 4c orange 75.00 4.50
61 A20 8c blue ('80) 19.00 3.00
62 A21 13c slate ('80) 150.00 200.00
63 A22 17c rose ('80) 65.00 6.00
64 A23 25c bister 350.00 10.00
65 A24 38c violet ('80) 200.00 250.00
66 A25 50c green ('80) 4.75 3.50
67 A26 2r50c brn vio ('80) 40.00 *70.00*
Nos. 59-67 (9) 948.75 563.00

Nos. 59-67 are known imperforate.

For surcharges & overprints see #76-78, 83-86, 122-123.

1882-93 **Wmk. 2**

68 A18 1c violet ('93) 2.00 .55
Overprinted "SPECIMEN" 60.00
69 A18 2c red brown 37.50 6.00
70 A18 2c green ('85) 2.50 .70
Overprinted "SPECIMEN" 60.00
71 A19 4c orange 75.00 3.50
72 A19 4c rose ('85) 3.25 .80
Overprinted "SPECIMEN" 60.00
73 A20 8c blue ('91) 2.25 1.10
74 A23 25c bister ('83) 5.50 2.25
75 A25 50c dp orange ('87) 35.00 10.00
Overprinted "SPECIMEN" 60.00
Nos. 68-75 (8) 163.00 24.90

For surcharges and overprint see #88-89, 121.

Nos. 63 and Type of 1882 Surcharged in Black:

f

g

1883 **Wmk. 1**

Surcharge Measures 14x3½mm

76 A22(f) 16c on 17c rose 175.00 65.00
a. Double surcharge 2,000.

Surcharge Measures 15½x3½mm

77 A22(f) 16c on 17c rose 190.00 65.00

Surcharge Measures 15½x2¾mm

78 A22(f) 16c on 17c rose *350.00* *125.00*

Wmk. 2

79 A22(g) 16c on 17c rose 87.00 1.75
Nos. 76-79 (4) *802.00* *256.75*

Queen Victoria — A29

1885-94

80 A29 15c orange brown ('92) 5.00 1.50
81 A29 15c blue ('94) 7.00 1.10
82 A29 16c orange brown 5.00 1.25
Nos. 80-82 (3) 17.00 3.85
Set of 3, ovptd "SPECIMEN" 180.00

For surcharges see Nos. 90, 116.

Various Stamps Surcharged in Black or Red:

h

j

1885-87 **Wmk. 1**

83 A24(h) 2c on 38c violet 110.00 42.50
a. Inverted surcharge 750.00 700.00
b. Double surcharge 800.00
c. Without bar 190.00
84 A21(j) 2c on 13c sl (R) ('87) 55.00 *100.00*
a. Inverted surcharge 190.00 *190.00*
b. Double surcharge 650.00
c. As "b," one on back *750.00*

k

l

1891

85 A22(k) 2c on 17c rose 110.00 *125.00*
a. Inverted surcharge 400.00 —
b. Double surcharge 700.00 700.00
86 A24(h) 2c on 38c vio 4.50 5.75
a. Double surcharge 190.00 190.00
b. Dbl. surch., one invtd. 190.00 190.00
c. Inverted surcharge 800.00 —
87 A9(e+l) 2c on 38c on 9p vio 3.25 4.50
a. Double surcharge 700.00 700.00
b. Inverted surcharge 375.00 —
c. Dbl. surch., one invtd. 150.00 175.00

Wmk. 2

88 A19(k) 2c on 4c rose 1.75 .70
a. Double surcharge 95.00 87.50
b. Inverted surcharge 87.50 —
c. Dbl. surch., one invtd. 95.00 87.50
Nos. 85-88 (4) 119.50 135.95

m

n

1893, Jan.

89 A18(m) 1c on 2c violet 1.50 .65
Overprinted "SPECIMEN" 30.00

90 A29(n) 1c on 16c org brown 1.50 *3.25*

Coat of Arms — A38

1895-1904 Wmk. 2

91 A38 1c lilac & ultra .90 1.75
92 A38 1c gray blk & black .60 .25
93 A38 2c lilac & orange 3.50 .60
94 A38 2c dull lil & vio 1.25 .20
95 A38 3c lilac .90 .60
96 A38 3c grn & scar, *yel* 4.75 1.50
97 A38 4c lilac & green 4.75 .60
98 A38 4c dull lil & car, *yel* 1.75 .50
99 A38 4c gray green & pur 1.25 *2.40*
100 A38 4c black & car, *blue* 7.50 .70
101 A38 5c lilac & vio, *buff* 8.00 *62.50*
102 A38 5c lilac & blk, *buff* 3.00 3.00
103 A38 6c grn & rose 5.50 4.75
104 A38 6c violet & scar, *red* 2.10 .95
105 A38 8c gray grn & blk, *buff* 2.40 *8.75*
106 A38 12c black & car rose 2.10 *2.75*
107 A38 15c grn & org 14.00 *7.50*
108 A38 15c blk & ultra, *blue* 60.00 1.50
109 A38 18c gray grn & ultra 11.00 4.75
110 A38 25c grn & car, *grn*, chalky paper 11.00 *27.50*
a. Ordinary paper ('02) 9.25 *22.50*
111 A38 50c green, *yel* 20.00 *47.50*
Nos. 91-111 (21) 166.25 *180.55*
Set of 21, ovptd "SPECIMEN" 350.00

The 25c is on both ordinary and chalky paper. Ornaments in lower panel omitted on #106-111.

Year of issue: #103, 107, 1899; #92, 94, 98, 1900; #96, 99, 101-102, 104-106, 110-111, 1902; #100, 108, 1904; others, 1895.

See #128-135. For surcharges and overprints see #113, 114, 117-120.

Diamond Jubilee Issue

Arms A39

1898, May 23 Wmk. 46

112 A39 36c brown org & ultra 14.00 20.00
Overprinted "SPECIMEN" 50.00

60th year of Queen Victoria's reign.
For surcharges see Nos. 114 and 127.

No. 109 Surcharged in Red

1899 Wmk. 2

113 A38 6c on 18c 1.25 1.25
a. Inverted surcharge 500.00 250.00

No. 112 Surcharged in Blue

Wmk. 46

114 A39 15c on 36c 1.75 2.10
a. Without bar 350.00

Admiral Mahe de La Bourdonnais A40

1899, Dec. Engr. Wmk. 1

115 A40 15c ultra 14.00 4.00
Overprinted "SPECIMEN" 80.00

Birth bicent. of Admiral Mahe de La Bourdonnais, governor of Mauritius, 1734-46.

No. 82 Surcharged in Black

1900 Wmk. 2

116 A29 4c on 16c orange brown 3.75 15.00

No. 109 Surcharged in Black

r

1902

117 A38 12c on 18c grn & ultra 2.40 *6.00*

Preceding Issues Overprinted in Black

1902

118 A38 4c lilac & car, *yel* 1.50 .35
119 A38 6c green & rose 1.50 *3.25*
120 A38 15c green & orange 2.75 .85
121 A23 25c bister 3.75 3.25

Wmk. 1

122 A25 50c green 5.25 3.50
123 A26 2r50c brown violet 100.00 *150.00*
Nos. 118-123 (6) 114.75 161.20

Coat of Arms — A41

1902 Wmk. 1

124 A41 1r blk & car rose 60.00 60.00

Wmk. 2 Sideways

125 A41 2r50c grn & blk, *bl* 21.00 *100.00*
126 A41 5r blk & car, *red* 75.00 *100.00*
Nos. 124-126 (3) 156.00 *260.00*
Set of 3, ovptd "SPECIMEN" 85.00

No. 112 Surcharged type "r" but with longer bar

1902 Wmk. 46

127 A39 12c on 36c 1.50 1.75
a. Inverted surcharge 550.00 400.00

Arms Type of 1895-1904

1904-07 Wmk. 3

Chalky Paper

128 A38 1c gray blk & black ('07) 10.00 4.25
129 A38 2c dl lil & vio ('05) 24.00 2.10
130 A38 3c grn & scar, *yel* 27.50 11.00
131 A38 4c blk & car, *blue* 18.00 1.75
132 A38 6c vio & scar, *red* ('06) 10.50 .35
133 A38 15c blk & ultra, *bl* 5.00 .40
135 A38 50c green, *yel* 2.25 *2.75*
136 A41 1r black & car rose ('07) 26.00 *55.00*
Nos. 128-136 (8) 123.25 *77.60*

The 2c, 4c, 6c also exist on ordinary paper.

Ornaments in lower panel omitted on 15c and 50c.

Arms — A42

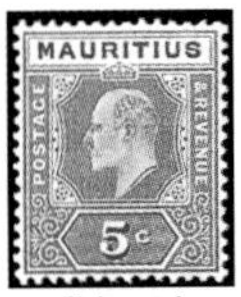

Edward VII — A43

1910 Wmk. 3

Ordinary Paper

137 A42 1c black 3.25 .35
138 A42 2c brown 3.25 .20
139 A42 3c green 3.50 .20
140 A42 4c ol grn & rose 4.25 .20
141 A43 5c gray & rose 3.25 *3.50*
142 A42 6c carmine 2.75 .20
143 A42 8c brown orange 3.50 *1.50*
144 A43 12c gray 2.40 *3.25*
145 A42 15c ultramarine 19.00 .20

Chalky Paper

146 A43 25c blk & scar, *yel* 2.50 *15.00*
147 A43 50c dull vio & blk 2.50 *22.50*
148 A43 1r blk, *green* 8.00 *15.00*
149 A43 2r50c blk & car, *bl* 16.00 *87.50*
150 A43 5r grn & car, *yel* 35.00 *125.00*
151 A43 10r grn & car, *grn* 110.00 *225.00*
Nos. 137-151 (15) 219.15 *499.60*

Numerals of 12c, 25c and 10r of type A43 are in color on plain tablet.

See Nos. 161-178.

King George V — A44

Die I

For description of dies I and II see front section of the Catalogue.

Numeral tablet of 5c, 50c, 1r, 2.50r and 5r of type A44 has lined background with colorless denomination.

1912-22 Wmk. 3

Ordinary Paper

152 A44 5c gray & rose 2.10 *4.25*
153 A44 12c gray 5.00 1.10

Chalky Paper

154 A44 25c blk & red, *yel* .50 1.75
a. 25c gray black & red, *yellow*, Die II .90 *2.00*
Overprinted "SPECIMEN" 40.00
155 A44 50c dull vio & blk 50.00 *92.50*
156 A44 1r black, *emerald*, die II 2.75 *8.50*
Overprinted "SPECIMEN" 40.00
a. 1r black, *emer, olive back*, die I ('21) 9.25 *60.00*
b. blk, *bl grn*, olive back, die I 4.25 *19.00*
157 A44 2r50c blk & red, *bl* 22.50 *62.50*
158 A44 5r grn & red, *yel* 100.00 *150.00*
a. Die II ('22) 55.00 *175.00*
159 A44 10r grn & red, *emer*, die II ('21) 35.00 *100.00*
Overprinted "SPECIMEN" 47.50
a. 10r grn & red, *bl grn*, *olive back*, die I 950.00
b. 10r green & red, *emer*, die I 50.00 *150.00*
c. 10r grn & red, *emer*, *olive back*, die I 87.50 *175.00*
d. 10r grn & red, *grn*, die I 75.00 *140.00*

Surface-colored Paper

160 A44 25c blk & red, *yel* ('16) .50 *14.50*
Nos. 152-160 (9) 218.35 *435.10*

1921-26 Wmk. 4

Ordinary Paper

161 A42 1c black 1.25 1.25
162 A42 2c brown 1.25 .20
163 A42 2c violet, *yel* ('25) 1.10 .35
164 A42 3c green ('25) 3.25 1.40
165 A42 4c ol grn & rose 1.75 *2.10*
166 A42 4c green 1.25 .20
167 A42 4c brown ('25) 3.25 1.90
168 A42 6c rose red 15.00 8.00
169 A42 6c violet 1.50 .20
170 A42 8c brown org ('25) 2.75 *19.00*
171 A42 10c gray ('22) 2.50 *4.25*
172 A42 10c rose red ('25) 4.75 1.90
173 A42 12c rose red 1.90 .50
174 A42 12c gray ('25) 2.10 *4.25*
175 A42 15c ultramarine 7.00 6.00
176 A42 15c dull blue ('25) 1.75 .25
177 A42 20c ultra ('22) 2.40 .95
178 A42 20c dull vio ('25) 10.50 *12.50*
Nos. 161-178 (18) 65.25 *65.20*

Ornaments in lower panel omitted on #171-178.

For surcharges see Nos. 201-203.

Die II

1922-34

Ordinary Paper

179 A44 1c black .95 *1.50*
180 A44 2c brown .90 .20
181 A44 3c green .90 .50
182 A44 4c olive grn & red ('27) .70 .35
a. Die I ('32) 7.50 *50.00*
183 A44 4c green, die I ('33) 7.00 .55
184 A44 5c gray & car 1.10 .20
a. Die I ('32) 7.50 7.50
185 A44 6c olive brn ('28) 1.50 .70
186 A44 8c orange .90 *12.50*
187 A44 10c rose red ('26) 1.50 .20
a. Die I ('32) 7.50 *10.00*
188 A44 12c gray, small "c" ('22) 1.75 *17.00*
189 A44 12c gray, "c" larger & thinner ('34) 6.25 .20
190 A44 12c rose red .35 *4.25*
191 A44 15c dk blue ('28) 1.25 .20
192 A44 20c dull vio .80 .50
193 A44 20c dk blue ('34) 15.00 1.00
a. Die I ('27) 12.00 1.10
194 A44 25c black & red, *yel* .35 .20
a. Die I ('32) 3.25 *40.00*

Chalky Paper

195 A44 50c dull vio & blk 9.25 4.25
196 A44 1r blk, *emerald* 4.50 .60
a. Die I ('32) 20.00 *40.00*
197 A44 2r50c blk & red, *bl* 25.00 7.50
198 A44 5r green & red, *yel* 35.00 *80.00*
199 A44 10r green & red, *emer* ('28) 87.50 *210.00*
Nos. 179-199 (21) 202.45 *342.40*

A45

1924

200 A45 50r lilac & green 900.00 *1,600.*
Overprinted "SPECIMEN" 225.00

Nos. 166, 173, 177 Surcharged

1925

201 A42 3c on 4c green 3.50 *4.75*
202 A42 10c on 12c rose red .35 *.60*
203 A42 15c on 20c ultra .65 .60
Nos. 201-203 (3) 4.50 5.95

Common Design Types pictured following the introduction.

Silver Jubilee Issue

Common Design Type

1935, May 6 Engr. *Perf. 13½x14*

204 CD301 5c gray black & ultra .60 .20
205 CD301 12c indigo & green 5.50 .20
206 CD301 20c blue & brown 7.00 .25
207 CD301 1r brt vio & indigo 35.00 *50.00*
Nos. 204-207 (4) 48.10 50.65

Coronation Issue

Common Design Type

1937, May 12 Wmk. 4 *Perf. 13½x14*

208 CD302 5c dark purple .20 .20
209 CD302 12c carmine .20 .20
210 CD302 20c bright ultra .25 .25
Nos. 208-210 (3) .65 .65
Set, never hinged 1.40

King George VI — A46

1938-43 Typo. *Perf. 14*

211 A46 2c gray .20 .20
a. Perf. 15x14 ('43) .85 .20
212 A46 3c rose vio & car 1.50 1.40
213 A46 4c green .70 *1.40*
214 A46 5c violet 1.60 .55
a. Perf. 15x14 ('43) 50.00 .20
215 A46 10c carmine 1.60 .20
a. Perf. 15x14 ('43) 30.00 .60
216 A46 12c salmon pink .70 .20
a. Perf. 15x14 ('43) 50.00 .60
217 A46 20c blue .70 .20
218 A46 25c maroon 3.25 .20
219 A46 1r brown black 11.00 1.40
220 A46 2.50r pale violet 18.00 8.75
221 A46 5r olive green 19.00 17.00
222 A46 10r rose violet 7.25 *22.50*
Nos. 211-222 (12) 65.50 54.00
Set, never hinged 100.00

Catalogue values for unused stamps in this section, from this point to the end of the section, are for Never Hinged items.

Peace Issue
Common Design Type
Perf. 13½x14
1946, Nov. 20 Engr. Wmk. 4
223 CD303 5c lilac .20 .20
224 CD303 20c deep blue .20 .20

"Post Office" Stamp of 1847 — A47

1948, Mar. 22 *Perf. 11½*
225 A47 5c red vio & orange .20 .20
226 A47 12c green & orange .20 .20
227 A47 20c blue & dp blue .20 .20
228 A47 1r lt red brn & dp blue .35 .35
Nos. 225-228 (4) .95 .95

Cent. of the 1st Mauritius postage stamps.

Silver Wedding Issue
Common Design Types
1948, Oct. 25 Photo. *Perf. 14x14½*
229 CD304 5c violet .25 .25
Perf. 11½x11
Engraved; Name Typographed
230 CD305 10r lilac rose 12.00 27.50

UPU Issue
Common Design Types
Engr.; Name Typo. on 20c, 35c
Perf. 13½, 11x11½
1949, Oct. 10 Wmk. 4
231 CD306 12c rose carmine .65 .70
232 CD307 20c indigo 1.40 1.50
233 CD308 35c rose violet .65 .70
234 CD309 1r sepia .65 .25
Nos. 231-234 (4) 3.35 3.15

Sugar Factory — A48

Aloe Plant — A49

Designs: 2c, Grand Port. 4c, Tamarind Falls. 5c, Rempart Mountain. 10c, Transporting cane. 12c, Map and dodo. 20c, "Paul et Virginie." 25c, Statue of Mahe La Bourdonnais. 35c, Government House. 50c, Pieter Both Mountain. 1r, Sambar. 2.50r, Port Louis. 5r, Beach scene. 10r, Arms.

Perf. 13½x14½, 14½x13½
1950, July 1 Photo.
235 A48 1c red violet .25 .55
236 A48 2c cerise .25 .25
237 A49 3c yel green .70 *2.75*
238 A49 4c green .25 *1.40*
239 A48 5c greenish blue .25 .25
240 A48 10c red .30 *.75*
241 A48 12c olive green 1.50 *2.25*
242 A49 20c brt ultra .70 .25
243 A49 25c vio brown 1.50 .45
244 A48 35c rose violet .30 .25
245 A49 50c emerald 2.25 .55
246 A48 1r sepia 4.75 .25
247 A48 2.50r orange 13.00 6.75
248 A48 5r red brown 16.00 15.00
249 A48 10r gray blue 16.00 *20.00*
Nos. 235-249 (15) 58.00 51.70

SPECIAL DELIVERY STAMPS

SD1

1903 Wmk. 1 *Perf. 14*
Red Surcharge
E1 SD1 15c on 15c ultra 9.00 22.50

SD2

SD3

EXPRESS
DELIVERY
(INLAND)
15 c

New Setting with Smaller "15c" without period — SD3a

1904
E2 SD2 15c on 15c ultra 45.00 62.50
a. "INLAND" inverted 2,600.
b. Inverted "A" in "INLAND" 1,250. 925.00
E3 SD3 15c on 15c ultra 8.50 3.50
a. Double surcharge, both inverted 1,500. 1,500.
b. Inverted surcharge 850.00 *550.00*
c. Vert. pair, imperf between *4,000.*
E3F SD3a 15c on 15c ultra 575.00 550.00
g. Inverted surcharge 1,400.
h. Double surcharge 2,900.
i. Double surcharge, both inverted — 4,250.
j. "c" omitted 2,000.

To make No. E2 the word "INLAND" was printed on No. E1. For Nos. E3 and E3F, new settings of the surcharge were made with different spacing between the words.

SD4

SD5

E4 SD4 15c green & red 4.75 4.75
a. Double surcharge 525.00 550.00
b. Inverted surcharge 750.00 625.00
c. "LNIAND." —
d. As "c," double surcharge *625.00* 575.00
E5 SD5 18c green & black 3.00 27.50
a. Exclamation point (!) instead of "I" in "FOREIGN" 550.00

POSTAGE DUE STAMPS

Catalogue values for unused stamps in this section are for Never Hinged items.

Numeral — D1

Perf. 14½x14
1933-54 Typo. Wmk. 4
J1 D1 2c black 1.40 .60
On cover *500.00*
J2 D1 4c violet .60 .75
On cover *500.00*
J3 D1 6c red .70 *.90*
On cover *500.00*
J4 D1 10c green .80 *1.40*
On cover *500.00*
J5 D1 20c ultramarine .60 *1.75*
On cover *600.00*
J6 D1 50c dp red lilac ('54) .65 *18.00*
On cover *800.00*
J7 D1 1r orange ('54) .80 *18.00*
On cover *900.00*
Nos. J1-J7 (7) 5.55 *41.40*

Covers: Values are for properly franked commercial covers. Philatelic covers sell for less.

MAYOTTE

mä-'yät

LOCATION — One of the Comoro Islands situated in the Mozambique Channel midway between Madagascar and Mozambique (Africa)
GOVT. — French Colony
AREA — 140 sq. mi.
POP. — 13,783 (1914)
CAPITAL — Dzaoudzi
See Comoro Islands

100 Centimes = 1 Franc

Stamps of Mayotte were replaced successively by those of Madagascar, Comoro Islands and France.

Navigation and Commerce — A1

Perf. 14x13½
1892-1907 Typo. Unwmk.
Name of Colony in Blue or Carmine
1 A1 1c blk, *lil bl* .85 .75
2 A1 2c brn, *buff* 1.25 1.10
a. Name double 350.00 300.00
3 A1 4c claret, *lav* 1.90 1.10
4 A1 5c grn, *grnsh* 4.00 2.10
5 A1 10c blk, *lavender* 6.50 3.25
6 A1 10c red ('00) 52.50 40.00
7 A1 15c blue, quadrille paper 12.00 7.25
8 A1 15c gray ('00) 95.00 82.50
9 A1 20c red, *grn* 8.00 7.25
10 A1 25c blk, *rose* 10.00 6.00
11 A1 25c blue ('00) 10.00 9.00
12 A1 30c brn, *bis* 15.00 10.00
13 A1 35c blk, *yel* 7.25 5.75
14 A1 40c red, *straw* 15.00 10.00
15 A1 45c blk, *gray grn* ('07) 15.00 14.00
16 A1 50c carmine, *rose* 22.50 16.00
17 A1 50c brn, *az* ('00) 22.50 22.50
18 A1 75c dp vio, *org* 20.00 14.00
19 A1 1fr brnz grn, *straw* 24.00 15.00
20 A1 5fr red lil, *lav* ('99) 100.00 95.00
Nos. 1-20 (20) 443.25 362.55

Perf. 13½x14 stamps are counterfeits.

Issues of 1892-1907 Surcharged in Black or Carmine

1912
Spacing between figures of surcharge 1.5mm (5c), 2mm (10c)
22 A1 5c on 2c brn, *buff* 2.10 2.10
23 A1 5c on 4c cl, *lav* (C) 1.50 1.50
24 A1 5c on 15c bl (C) 1.50 1.50
25 A1 5c on 20c red, *grn* 1.25 1.25
26 A1 5c on 25c blk, *rose* (C) 1.40 1.40
a. Double surcharge 200.00
b. Pair, one stamp without surcharge $700
27 A1 5c on 30c brn, *bis* (C) 1.50 1.50
28 A1 10c on 40c red, *straw* 1.50 1.50
a. Double surcharge 225.00
29 A1 10c on 45c blk, *gray grn* (C) 1.50 1.50
a. Double surcharge 200.00 *225.00*
30 A1 10c on 50c car, *rose* 3.25 3.25
31 A1 10c on 75c dp vio, *org* 1.60 1.60
32 A1 10c on 1fr brnz grn, *straw* 2.10 2.10
Nos. 22-32 (11) 19.20 19.20

Spacing between figures of surcharge 2.25mm (5c), 2.75mm (10c)
22a A1 5c on 2c brn, *buff* 13.00 13.00
23a A1 5c on 4c cl, *lav* (C) 10.00 10.00
24a A1 5c on 15c bl (C) 10.00 10.00
25a A1 5c on 20c red, *grn* 10.00 10.00
26c A1 5c on 25c blk, *rose* (C) 10.00 10.00
d. Double surcharge 2,500. 2,400.
27a A1 5c on 30c brn, *bis* (C) 10.00 10.00
28b A1 10c on 40c red, *straw* 52.50 52.50
c. Double surcharge 3,000. 2,700.
29b A1 10c on 45c blk, *gray grn* (C) 50.00 50.00
c. Double surcharge 3,000. *2,700.*
30a A1 10c on 50c car, *rose* 70.00 70.00
31a A1 10c on 75c dp vio, *org* 65.00 65.00
32a A1 10c on 1fr brnz grn, *straw* 125.00 125.00
Nos. 22a-32a (11) 425.50 425.50

Nos. 22-32 were available for use in Madagascar and the entire Comoro archipelago.

MEMEL

ˈmā-məl

LOCATION — In northern Europe, bordering on the Baltic Sea
GOVT. — Special commission (see below)
AREA — 1099 sq. mi.
POP. — 151,960

Following World War I this territory was detached from Germany and by Treaty of Versailles assigned to the government of a commission of the Allied and Associated Powers (not the League of Nations), which administered it until January, 1923, when it was forcibly occupied by Lithuania. In 1924 Memel became incorporated as a semi-autonomous district of Lithuania with the approval of the Allied Powers and the League of Nations.

100 Pfennig = 1 Mark
100 Centu = 1 Litas (1923)

Excellent counterfeits of all Memel stamps exist.

Stamps of Germany, 1905-20, Overprinted

Wmk. Lozenges (125)

1920, Aug. 1 ***Perf. 14, 14½***

1	A16	5pf green	.80	*3.25*
2	A16	10pf car rose	2.25	*9.00*
3	A16	10pf orange	.25	*1.50*
4	A22	15pf violet brown	2.40	*8.00*
5	A16	20pf blue violet	.80	*3.25*
6	A16	30pf org & blk, *buff*	1.75	*4.00*
7	A16	30pf dull blue	.40	*1.60*
8	A16	40pf lake & blk	.25	*1.60*
9	A16	50pf pur & blk, *buff*	.25	*1.60*
10	A16	60pf olive green	1.00	*4.50*
11	A16	75pf grn & blk	2.40	*9.50*
12	A16	80pf blue violet	1.50	*4.75*

Overprinted

13	A17	1m car rose	.40	*1.50*
14	A17	1.25m green	10.50	*47.50*
15	A17	1.50m yel brn	4.00	*15.00*
16	A21	2m blue	2.00	*6.50*
17	A21	2.50m red lilac	12.00	*27.50*
		Nos. 1-17 (17)	42.95	*150.55*

Stamps of France, Surcharged in Black

On A22

On A18

1920 **Unwmk.** ***Perf. 14x13½***

18	A22	5pf on 5c green	.20	*.55*
19	A22	10pf on 10c red	.20	*1.00*
20	A22	20pf on 25c blue	.20	*.55*
21	A22	30pf on 30c org	.40	*1.00*
22	A22	40pf on 20c red brn	.20	*.55*
23	A22	50pf on 35c vio	.20	*.55*
24	A18	60pf on 40c red & pale bl	.35	*1.00*
25	A18	80pf on 45c grn & bl	.55	*1.60*
26	A18	1m on 50c brn & lav	.20	*1.60*
27	A18	1m 25pf on 60c vio & ultra	1.25	*4.50*
28	A18	2m on 1fr cl & ol grn	.35	*.75*
29	A18	3m on 5fr bl & buff	18.50	*32.50*
		Nos. 18-29 (12)	22.60	*46.15*

For stamps with additional surcharges and overprints see Nos. 43-49, C1-C4.

French Stamps of 1900-20 Surcharged like Nos. 24 to 29 in Red or Black

4
Type I

4
Type II

Four Marks

1920-21 **Unwmk.** ***Perf. 14x13½***

30	A18	3m on 2fr org & pale bl	12.00	*32.50*
31	A18	4m on 2fr org & pale bl (I) (Bk)	.25	*.65*
a.		Type II	80.00	*125.00*
32	A18	10m on 5fr bl & buff	2.50	*7.25*
33	A18	20m on 5fr bl & buff	30.00	*95.00*
		Nos. 30-33 (4)	44.75	*135.40*

For stamps with additional overprints see Nos. C5, C19.

New Value with Initial Capital

1921

39	A18	60Pf on 40c red & pale bl	4.25	*10.50*
40	A18	3M on 60c vio & ultra	2.10	*4.00*
41	A18	10M on 5fr bl & buff	1.60	*3.50*
42	A18	20M on 45c grn & bl	6.50	*25.00*
		Nos. 39-42 (4)	14.45	*43.00*

The surcharged value on No. 40 is in italics.
For stamps with additional overprints see Nos. C6-C7, C18.

Stamps of 1920 Surcharged with Large Numerals in Dark Blue or Red

1921-22

43	A22	15pf on 10pf on 10c	.40	*.80*
a.		Inverted surcharge	60.00	*125.00*
44	A22	15pf on 20pf on 25c	.35	*.80*
a.		Inverted surcharge	60.00	*82.50*
45	A22	15pf on 50pf on 35c (R)	.25	*.50*
a.		Inverted surcharge	60.00	*82.50*
46	A22	60pf on 40pf on 20c	.25	*.60*
a.		Inverted surcharge	60.00	*125.00*
47	A18	75pf on 60pf on 40c	.60	*1.00*
48	A18	1.25m on 1m on 50c	.20	*.50*
49	A18	5.00m on 2m on 1fr	.65	*2.00*
a.		Inverted surcharge	160.00	*550.00*
		Nos. 43-49 (7)	2.70	*6.20*

Stamps of France Surcharged in Black or Red

On A20, A22

1922

50	A22	5pf on 5c org	.20	*.50*
51	A22	10pf on 10c red	.80	*3.50*
52	A22	10pf on 10c grn	.20	*.50*
53	A22	15pf on 10c grn	.20	*.60*
54	A22	20pf on 20c red brn	6.50	*25.00*
55	A22	20pf on 25c bl	7.25	*25.00*
56	A22	25pf on 5c org	.20	*.60*
57	A22	30pf on 30c red	.80	*3.25*
58	A22	35pf on 35c vio	.20	*.40*
59	A20	50pf on 50c dl bl	.20	*.50*
60	A20	75pf on 15c grn	.20	*.40*
61	A22	75pf on 35c vio	.20	*.50*
62	A22	1m on 25c blue	.20	*.40*
63	A22	1¼m on 30c red	.20	*.40*
64	A22	3m on 5c org	.20	*2.10*
65	A20	6m on 15c grn (R)	.35	*2.00*
66	A22	8m on 30c red	.40	*6.50*

On A18

67	A18	40pf on 40c red & pale bl	.20	*.50*
68	A18	80pf on 45c grn & bl	.20	*.50*
69	A18	1m on 40c red & pale bl	.20	*.50*
70	A18	1.25m on 60c vio & ultra (R)	.20	*.50*
71	A18	1.50m on 45c grn & bl (R)	.20	*.50*
72	A18	2m on 45c grn & bl	.50	*1.00*
73	A18	2m on 1fr cl & ol grn	.20	*.50*
74	A18	2¼m on 40c red & pale bl	.20	*.35*
75	A18	2½m on 60c vio & ultra	.35	*.75*
76	A18	3m on 60c vio & ultra (R)	.60	*1.60*
77	A18	4m on 45c grn & bl	.20	*.25*
78	A18	5m on 1fr cl & ol grn	.25	*.50*
79	A18	6m on 60c vio & ultra	.20	*.35*
80	A18	6m on 2fr org & pale bl	.25	*.50*
81	A18	9m on 1fr cl & ol grn	.20	*.50*
82	A18	9m on 5fr bl & buff (R)	.35	*1.60*
83	A18	10m on 45c grn & bl (R)	.40	*2.10*
84	A18	12m on 40c red & pale bl	.20	*1.00*
85	A18	20m on 40c red & pale bl	.40	*2.50*
86	A18	20m on 2fr org & pale bl	.20	1.00
87	A18	30m on 60c vio & ultra	.40	*2.10*
88	A18	30m on 5fr dk bl & buff	3.50	*10.00*
89	A18	40m on 1fr cl & ol grn	.50	*2.75*
90	A18	50m on 2fr org & pale bl	8.00	*25.00*
91	A18	80m on 2fr org & pale bl (R)	.50	*2.75*
92	A18	100m on 5fr bl & buff	.50	*5.50*
		Nos. 50-92 (43)	37.20	*137.25*

A 500m on 5fr dark blue and buff was prepared, but not officially issued. Value, $800.
For stamps with additional surcharges and overprints see Nos. 93-99, C8-C17, C20-29C.

Nos. 52, 54, 67, 59 Surcharged "Mark"

1922-23

93	A22	10m on 10pf on 10c	.75	*4.50*
a.		Double surcharge	100.00	*240.00*
94	A22	20m on 20pf on 20c	.40	*2.00*
95	A18	40m on 40pf on 40c ('23)	.60	*2.50*
96	A20	50m on 50pf on 50c	1.60	*7.25*
		Nos. 93-96 (4)	3.35	16.25

Nos. 72, 61, 70 Surcharged with New Values in Red or Black

1922-23

97	A18	10m on 2m on 45c	1.60	*7.25*
98	A22	25m on 1m on 25c	1.60	*7.25*
99	A18	80m on 1.25m on 60c (Bk) ('23)	1.25	*4.00*
		Nos. 97-99 (3)	4.45	18.50

For No. 99 with additional surcharges see Nos. N28-N30.

AIR POST STAMPS

Nos. 24-26, 28, 31, 39-40 Overprinted in Dark Blue

1921, July 6 **Unwmk.** ***Perf. 14x13½***

C1	A18	60pf on 40c	35.00	*80.00*
C2	A18	80pf on 45c	2.50	*8.00*
C3	A18	1m on 50c	2.50	*4.75*
C4	A18	2m on 1fr	2.50	*7.50*
a.		"Flugpost" inverted	175.00	*325.00*
C5	A18	4m on 2fr (I)	3.75	*13.00*
a.		Type II	100.00	*225.00*

New Value with Initial Capital

C6	A18	60Pf on 40c	3.50	*8.00*
a.		"Flugpost" inverted	175.00	*350.00*
C7	A18	3M on 60c	3.00	*8.00*
a.		"Flugpost" inverted	175.00	*350.00*
		Nos. C1-C7 (7)	52.75	*129.25*

The surcharged value on No. C7 is in italics.

Nos. 67-71, 73, 76, 78, 80, 82 Overprinted in Dark Blue

1922, May 12

C8	A18	40pf on 40c	.35	*2.00*
C9	A18	80pf on 45c	.35	*2.00*
C10	A18	1m on 40c	.35	*2.00*
C11	A18	1.25m on 60c	.65	*2.10*
C12	A18	1.50m on 45c	.65	*2.50*
C13	A18	2m on 1fr	.65	*2.50*
C14	A18	3m on 60c	.65	*2.50*
C15	A18	5m on 1fr	.80	*2.60*
C16	A18	6m on 2fr	.80	*2.60*
C17	A18	9m on 5fr	.80	*2.60*

Same Overprint On Nos. 40, 31

C18	A18	3m on 60c	80.00	*1,000.*
C19	A18	4m on 2fr	.65	*2.50*
		Nos. C8-C17,C19 (11)	6.70	25.90

Nos. 67, 69-71, 73, 76, 78, 80, 82 Overprinted in Black or Red

1922, Oct. 17

C20	A18	40pf on 40c	1.20	*8.00*
C21	A18	1m on 40c	1.20	*8.00*
C22	A18	1.25m on 60c (R)	1.20	*8.00*
C23	A18	1.50m on 45c (R)	1.20	*8.00*
C24	A18	2m on 1fr	1.20	*8.00*
C25	A18	3m on 60c (R)	1.20	*8.00*
C26	A18	4m on 2fr	1.20	*8.00*
C27	A18	5m on 1fr	1.20	*8.00*
C28	A18	6m on 2fr	1.20	*8.00*
C29	A18	9m on 5fr (R)	1.20	*8.00*
		Nos. C20-C29 (10)	12.00	*80.00*

No. C26 is not known without the "FLUGPOST" overprint.

OCCUPATION STAMPS

Issued under Lithuanian Occupation

Surcharged in Various Colors on Unissued Official Stamps of Lithuania Similar to Type O4

On Nos. N1-N6

On Nos. N7-N11

Memel Printing

1923 **Unwmk.** **Litho.** ***Perf. 11***

N1	O4	10m on 5c bl (Bk)	.80	4.75
a.		"Memel" and bars omitted	5.75	*47.50*
N2	O4	25m on 5c bl (R)	.80	4.75
N3	O4	50m on 25c red (Bk)	.80	5.00
N4	O4	100m on 25c red (G)	.80	5.00
N5	O4	400m on 1 l brn (R)	1.25	8.00
N6	O4	500m on 1 l brn (Bl)	1.25	8.00
		Nos. N1-N6 (6)	5.70	35.50

Nos. N1 and N3-N6 exist with double surcharge. Value $50 each.

Kaunas Printing

Black Surcharge

N7	O4	10m on 5c blue	.50	3.25
N8	O4	25m on 5c blue	.50	3.25
N9	O4	50m on 25c red	.50	3.25
N10	O4	100m on 25c red	.65	3.25
N11	O4	400m on 1 l brn	1.10	6.00
		Nos. N7-N11 (5)	3.25	19.00

No. N8 has the value in "Markes," others of the group have it in "Markiu."
For additional surcharge see No. N87.

Surcharged in Various Colors on Unissued Official Stamps of Lithuania Similar to Type O4

1923

N12	O4	10m on 5c bl (R)	1.60	5.75
a.		"Markes" instead of "Markiu"	14.50	65.00
N13	O4	20m on 5c bl (R)	1.60	5.75
N14	O4	25m on 25c red (Bl)	1.60	8.00
N15	O4	50m on 25c red (Bl)	3.25	8.00
a.		Inverted surcharge	40.00	160.00
N16	O4	100m on 1 l brn (Bk)	3.25	10.50
a.		Inverted surcharge	40.00	160.00
N17	O4	200m on 1 l brn (Bk)	4.00	10.50
		Nos. N12-N17 (6)	15.30	48.50

No. N14 has the value in "Markes," others of the group have it in "Markiu."

"Vytis"
O4 O5

1923, Mar.

N18	O4	10m lt brown	.40	3.50
N19	O4	20m yellow	.40	3.50
N20	O4	25m orange	.40	3.50
N21	O4	40m violet	.40	3.50
N22	O4	50m yellow grn	.80	3.50
N23	O5	100m carmine	.50	3.50
N24	O5	300m olive grn	4.00	80.00
N25	O5	400m olive brn	1.25	3.75
N26	O5	500m lilac	4.00	80.00
N27	O5	1000m blue	1.10	4.50
		Nos. N18-N27 (10)	13.25	189.25

No. N20 has the value in "Markes."
For surcharges see Nos. N44-N69, N88-N114.

No. 99 Surcharged in Green

1923, Apr. 13

N28	A18	100m on No. 99	5.00	21.00
N29	A18	400m on No. 99	5.00	21.00
N30	A18	500m on No. 99	5.00	21.00
		Nos. N28-N30 (3)	15.00	63.00

The normal position of the green surcharge is sideways, with the top at the left. It exists reversed on the three stamps.

Ship — O7

Seal — O8

Lighthouse — O9

1923, Apr. 12 **Litho.**

N31	O7	40m olive grn	3.25	22.50
N32	O7	50m brown	3.25	22.50
N33	O7	80m green	3.25	22.50
N34	O7	100m red	3.25	22.50
N35	O8	200m deep blue	3.25	22.50
N36	O8	300m brown	3.25	22.50
N37	O8	400m lilac	3.25	22.50
N38	O8	500m orange	3.25	22.50
N39	O8	600m olive grn	3.25	22.50
N40	O9	800m deep blue	3.25	22.50
N41	O9	1000m lilac	3.25	22.50
N42	O9	2000m red	3.25	22.50
N43	O9	3000m green	3.25	22.50
		Nos. N31-N43 (13)	42.25	292.50

Union of Memel with Lithuania. Forgeries exist.
For surcharges see Nos. N70-N86.

Nos. N20, N24, N26 Surcharged in Various Colors

1923

Thin Figures

N44	O5	2c on 300m (R)	6.50	9.00
N45	O5	3c on 300m (R)	7.00	12.00
N46	O4	10c on 25m (Bk)	7.00	9.00
a.		Double surcharge	47.50	190.00
N47	O4	15c on 25m (Bk)	7.00	9.00
N48	O5	20c on 500m (Bl)	9.50	17.50
N49	O5	30c on 500m (Bk)	7.25	9.00
N50	O5	50c on 500m (G)	20.00	22.50
a.		Inverted surcharge	65.00	240.00
		Nos. N44-N50 (7)	64.25	88.00

Nos. N19, N21-N27 Surcharged:

N51	O4	2c on 20m yellow	3.25	14.00
N52	O4	2c on 50c yel grn	3.25	9.50
N53	O4	3c on 40m violet	4.00	10.50
a.		Double surcharge	60.00	175.00
N54	O5	3c on 300m ol grn	2.50	5.00
a.		Double surcharge	95.00	325.00
N55	O5	5c on 100m carmine	5.75	5.00
N56	O5	5c on 300m ol grn (R)	3.50	10.00
N57	O5	10c on 400m ol brn	8.00	14.50
N58	O5	30c on 500m lilac	5.50	17.50
N59	O5	1 l on 1000m blue	16.00	45.00
		Nos. N51-N59 (9)	51.75	131.00

There are several types of the numerals in these surcharges. Nos. N56 and N58 have "CENT" in short, thick letters, as on Nos. N44 to N50.

Nos. N18-N23, N25, N27 Surcharged

Thick Figures

N60	O4	2c on 10m lt brn	3.00	10.00
N61	O4	2c on 20m yellow	10.00	110.00
N62	O4	2c on 50m yel grn	3.00	11.00
N63	O4	3c on 10m lt brn	3.00	11.00
a.		Double surcharge	60.00	200.00
N64	O4	3c on 40m violet	18.00	125.00
N65	O5	5c on 100m car	3.00	12.00
a.		Double surcharge	60.00	200.00
N66	O5	10c on 400m ol brn	90.00	525.00
N67	O4	15c on 25m orange	90.00	525.00
N68	O5	50c on 1000m blue	5.00	8.00
a.		Double surcharge	60.00	200.00
N69	O5	1 l on 1000m blue	6.00	16.00
a.		Double surcharge	90.00	200.00
		Nos. N60-N69 (10)	231.00	1,353.

No. N69 is surcharged like type "b" in the following group.

Nos. N31-N43 Surcharged:

a

b

N70	O7(a)	15c on 40m ol grn	5.50	17.50
N71	O7(a)	30c on 50m brown	5.00	9.00
N72	O7(a)	30c on 80m green	5.00	20.00
N73	O7(a)	30c on 100m red	5.50	8.00
N74	O8(a)	50c on 200m dp blue	6.00	17.50
N75	O8(a)	50c on 300m brn	5.00	8.00
N76	O8(a)	50c on 400m lilac	5.50	14.50
N77	O8(a)	50c on 500m org	5.50	8.00
N78	O8(b)	1 l on 600m ol grn	5.50	22.00
N79	O9(b)	1 l on 800m dp blue	6.50	19.00
N80	O9(b)	1 l on 1000m lil	6.00	19.00
N81	O9(b)	1 l on 2000m red	6.00	20.00
N82	O9(b)	1 l on 3000m grn	6.50	20.00
		Nos. N70-N82 (13)	73.50	202.50

These stamps are said to have been issued to commemorate the institution of autonomous government.
Double or inverted surcharges exist on Nos. N71, N75-N77. Value, each $60.

Nos. N32, N34, N36, N38 Surcharged in Green

1923

N83	O7	15c on 50m brn	275.	2,000.
N84	O7	25c on 100m red	150.	1,200.
N85	O8	30c on 300m brn	250.	1,300.
N86	O8	60c on 500m org	150.	1,200.

Surcharges on Nos. N83-N86 are of two types, differing in width of numerals. Values are for stamps with narrow numerals, as illustrated. Stamps with wide numerals sell for two to four times as much.

Nos. N8, N10-N11, N3 Surcharged in Red or Green

N87	O4	10c on 25m on 5c bl (R)	35.00	47.50
N88	O4	15c on 100m on 25c red (G)	35.00	175.00
a.		Inverted surcharge	150.00	350.00
N89	O4	30c on 400m on 1 l brn (R)	17.50	30.00
N90	O4	60c on 50m on 25c red (G)	35.00	190.00
		Nos. N87-N90 (4)	122.50	442.50

Nos. N18-N22 Surcharged in Green or Red

N91	O4	15c on 10m	8.00	24.00
N92	O4	15c on 20m	3.50	20.00
N93	O4	15c on 25m	4.00	20.00
N94	O4	15c on 40m	3.50	20.00
N95	O4	15c on 50m (R)	3.50	12.00
N96	O4	25c on 10m	4.25	22.50
N97	O4	25c on 20m	3.50	17.50
N98	O4	25c on 25m	4.00	20.00
N99	O4	25c on 40m	4.00	23.00
N100	O4	25c on 50m (R)	2.60	12.00
N101	O4	30c on 10m	6.50	30.00
N102	O4	30c on 20m	3.50	19.00
N103	O4	30c on 25m	5.00	22.50
N104	O4	30c on 40m	3.75	17.50
N105	O4	30c on 50m (R)	3.00	15.00
		Nos. N91-N105 (15)	62.60	295.00

Nine stamps between Nos. N95 and N114 exist with inverted surcharge. No. N102 exists with double surcharge.

Nos. N23, N25, N27 Surcharged in Green or Red

N106	O5	15c on 100m	2.50	12.00
N107	O5	15c on 400m	2.50	10.00
N108	O5	15c on 1000m (R)	60.00	325.00
N109	O5	25c on 100m	2.50	12.00
N110	O5	25c on 400m	2.50	9.50
N111	O5	25c on 1000m (R)	65.00	350.00
N112	O5	30c on 100m	3.00	13.00
N113	O5	30c on 400m	3.00	13.00
N114	O5	30c on 1000m (R)	65.00	360.00
		Nos. N106-N114 (9)	206.00	1,104.

Nos. N96 to N100 and N109 to N111 are surcharged "Centai," the others "Centu."

MESOPOTAMIA

ˌme-sə-pə-ˈtā-mē-ə

LOCATION — In Western Asia, bounded on the north by Syria and Turkey, on the east by Persia, on the south by Saudi Arabia and on the west by Trans-Jordan.
GOVT. — A former Turkish Province
AREA — 143,250 (1918) sq. mi.
POP. — 2,849,282 (1920)
CAPITAL — Baghdad

During World War I this territory was occupied by Great Britain. It was recognized as an independent state and placed under British Mandate but in 1932 the Mandate was terminated and the country admitted to membership in the League of Nations as the Kingdom of Iraq. Postage stamps of Iraq are now in use.

16 Annas = 1 Rupee

Watermark

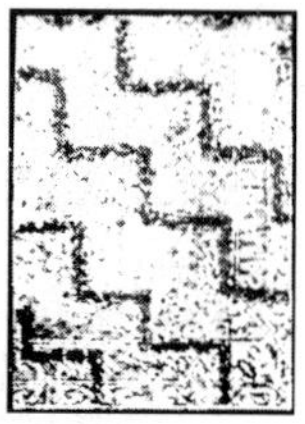

Wmk. 48 — Diagonal Zigzag Lines

Issued under British Occupation

Baghdad Issue
Stamps of Turkey 1901-16 Surcharged

N1

N2

N3

N4

N5

The surcharges were printed from slugs which were arranged to fit the various shapes of the stamps.

1917 Unwmk. *Perf. 12, 13½*

On Turkey Nos. 254, 256, 258-260

N1 ¼a on 2pa red lil 140.00 170.00
a. "IN BRITISH" omitted 6,500.
N2 ¼a on 5pa vio brown 100.00 110.00
a. "¼ An" omitted 6,000.
N3 ½a on 10pa green 650.00 775.00
N4 1a on 20pa red 400.00 450.00
a. "BAGHDAD" double 1,525.
N5 2a on 1pi blue 170.00 200.00
Nos. N1-N5 (5) 1,460. 1,705.

On Turkey No. 249

N6 A22 2a on 1pi ultra 375.00 525.00
a. "IN BRITISH" omitted 7,000.

On Turkey No. 251

N7 A23 ½a on 10pa green 1,100. 1,300.

On Turkey Nos. 272-273

N8 A29 1a on 20pa red 250. 300.
a. "OCCUPATION" omitted 5,500.
b. "BAGHDAD" double 1,525.
N9 A30 2a on 1pi blue 4,000. 4,100.

On Turkey Nos. 346-348

N10 A41 ½a on 10pa car, perf 12½ 450.00 475.00
a. Perf 13½ 875.00 950.00
N11 A41 1a on 20pa ultra, perf 12½ 950.00 1,100.
a. "1 An" omitted 7,750.
b. Perf 13½ 3,750.
N12 A41 2a on 1pi vio & black, perf 13½ 100.00 110.00
a. "BAGHDAD" omitted 5,250.
b. Perf 12½ 200.00 210.00

On Turkey Nos. 297, 300

N13 A17 ¼a on 5pa purple 5,000.
N14 A17 2a on 1pi blue 225.00 300.00
a. "OCCUPATION" omitted —

On Turkey No. 306

N15 A18 1a on 20pa car 450.00 475.00
a. Value omitted 7,000.

On Turkey Nos. 329-331

N16 A22 ½a on 10pa bl grn 100.00 110.00
N17 A22 1a on 20pa car rose 400.00 450.00
a. "1 An" omitted 4,500. 4,500.
b. With additional "Behie" 5,250. 5,250.
N18 A22 2a on 1pi ultra 140.00 125.00
a. "BAGHDAD" omitted —

On Turkey No. 337

N19 A22 1a on 20pa car rose 4,000. 4,750.

On Turkey No. P125

N20 A17 1a on 20pa car 5,000.

On Turkey Nos. B1, B8

Inscription in crescent is obliterated by another crescent handstamped in violet black on Nos. N21-N27.

N21 A18 ½a on 10pa dull grn 120.00 140.00
a. "OCCUPATION" omitted 5,500.
N22 A21 1a on 20pa car rose 400.00 475.00

On Semi-Postal Stamps of 1916

On Turkey No. B29

N23 A21 2a on 1pi ultra 1,550. 1,750.

On Turkey Nos. B33-B34

N24 A22 1a on 20pa car rose 120.00 140.00
N25 A22 2a on 1pi ultra 175.00 190.00
a. "OCCUPATION" omitted 6,000.
b. "BAGHDAD" omitted 6,000.

On Turkey No. B42

N26 A41 ½a on 10pa car, perf 12½ 180.00 200.00
a. "BAGHDAD" double 2,500.
b. Perf 13½ 350.00 375.00

On Turkey No. B38

N27 A11 1a on 10pa on 20pa vio brn 200.00 200.00
a. "OCCUPATION" omitted 6,000. 6,000.

Iraq Issue

N28

N29

N30

N31

N32

N33

N34

N35

N36

N37

N38

N39

N40

N41

Turkey Nos. 256, 258-269 Surcharged

1918-20 *Perf. 12*

N28 ¼a on 5pa vio brn .25 .60
N29 ½a on 10pa grn .25 .20
N30 1a on 20pa red .25 .20
N31 1½a on 5pa vio brn 3.00 .40
N32 2½a on 1pi blue .95 .20
a. Inverted surcharge 4,000.
N33 3a on 1½pi car & black .85 .20
a. Double surcharge, red & blk 2,100.
N34 4a on 1¾pi slate & red brn .85 .20
a. Center inverted 12,000.
N35 6a on 2pi grn & black 1.60 .90
N36 8a on 2½pi org & ol grn .90 .40
N37 12a on 5pi dl vio 1.75 1.75
N38 1r on 10pi red brown 2.25 1.10
N39 2r on 25pi ol grn 7.75 2.40
N40 5r on 50pi car 20.00 15.00
N41 10r on 100pi dp blue 45.00 12.00
Nos. N28-N41 (14) 85.65 35.55

See #N50-N53. For overprints see #NO1-NO21.

Mosul Issue

A13

A14

A15

A16

A17

A18

A19

1919 Unwmk. *Perf. 11½, 12*

N42 A13 ½a on 1pi grn & brn red 2.40 1.75
N43 A14 1a on 20pa *rose* 1.50 1.75
a. "POSTAGE" omitted
N44 A15 1a on 20pa *rose* 4.50 4.50
a. Double surcharge

Turkish word at right of tughra ("reshad") is large on No. N43, small on No. N44.

Wmk. Turkish Characters

Perf. 12½

N45 A16 2½a on 1pi vio & yel 1.50 1.50
N46 A17 3a on 20pa grn & yel 35.00 55.00

Wmk. 48

N47 A17 3a on 20pa green 1.75 3.50
N48 A18 4a on 1pi dull vio 3.50 3.50
a. Double surcharge 900.00
b. "4" omitted 1,700.
c. As "b," double surcharge
N49 A19 8a on 10pa claret 3.00 2.40
a. Double surcharge 600.00 725.00
b. Inverted surcharge 725.00 850.00
c. 8a on 1pi dull violet 1,800.
Nos. N42-N49 (8) 53.15 73.90

Value for No. 49c is for copies with the perfs cutting into the design.

Iraq Issue

Types of 1918-20 Issue

1921		Wmk. 4	*Perf. 12*	
N50	A28	½a on 10pa green	.90	.25
N51	A26	1½a on 5pa dp brn	.90	.25
N52	A37	2r on 25pi ol grn	13.00	12.00
		Nos. N50-N52 (3)	14.80	12.50

Type of 1918-20 without "Reshad"

1922			**Unwmk.**	
N53	A36	1r on 10pi red brn	100.00	20.00

"Reshad" is the small Turkish word at right of the tughra in circle at top center.

For overprint see No. NO22.

OFFICIAL STAMPS

Nos. N29-N41 Overprinted:

1920		Unwmk.	*Perf. 12*	
NO1	A28	½a on 10pa grn	3.00	.60
NO2	A29	1a on 20pa red	1.40	.35
NO3	A26	1½a on 5pa vio brown	7.25	1.50
NO4	A30	2½a on 1pi blue	1.50	1.60
NO5	A31	3a on 1½pi car & black	7.75	.55
NO6	A32	4a on 1¾pi sl & red brn	8.50	1.75
NO7	A33	6a on 2pi grn & black	11.00	3.00
NO8	A34	8a on 2½pi org & ol grn	9.50	1.75
NO9	A35	12a on 5pi dull vio	7.25	3.00
NO10	A36	1r on 10pi red brown	8.50	2.75
NO11	A37	2r on 25pi ol green	16.00	9.50
NO12	A38	5r on 50pi car	30.00	19.00
NO13	A39	10r on 100pi dp blue	50.00	35.00
		Nos. NO1-NO13 (13)	161.65	80.35

Same Overprint on Types of Regular Issue of 1918-20

1921-22			**Wmk. 4**	
NO14	A28	½a on 10pa grn	.70	.70
NO15	A29	1a on 20pa red	1.60	.70
NO16	A26	1½a on 5pa dp brn	1.60	.50
NO17	A32	4a on 1¾pi gray & red brn	1.60	.90
NO18	A33	6a on 2pi grn & black	9.50	*50.00*
NO19	A34	8a on 2½pi org & yel grn	2.75	1.90
NO20	A35	12a on 5pi dl vio	12.00	*42.50*
NO21	A37	2r on 25pi ol grn	42.50	*55.00*
		Nos. NO14-NO21 (8)	72.25	*152.20*

Same Overprint on No. N53

1922			**Unwmk.**	
NO22	A36	1r on 10pi red brn	14.00	5.00

MEXICO

ˈmek-si-ˌkō

LOCATION — Extreme southern part of the North American continent, south of the United States
GOVT. — Republic
AREA — 756,198 sq. mi.
POP. — 76,791,819 (est. 1984)
CAPITAL — Mexico, D.F

8 Reales = 1 Peso
100 Centavos = 1 Peso

District Overprints

Nos. 1-149 are overprinted with names of various districts, and sometimes also with district numbers and year dates. Some of the district overprints are rare and command high prices. Values given for Nos. 1-149 are for the more common district overprints.

Watermarks

Wmk. 150 — PAPEL SELLADO in Sheet

Wmk. 151 — R. P. S. in the Sheet (R.P.S. stands for "Renta Papel Sellado")

Wmk. 152 — "CORREOS E U M" on Every Horizontal Line of Ten Stamps

Wmk. 153 — "R M" Interlaced

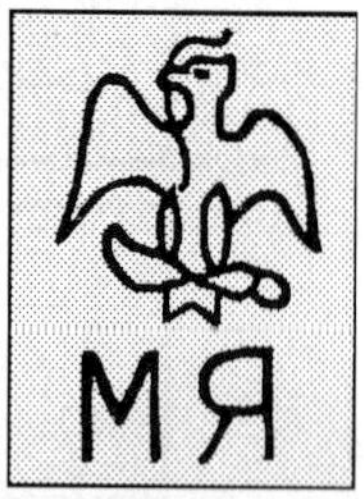

Wmk. 154 — Eagle and R M

Wmk. 155 — SERVICIO POSTAL DE LOS ESTADOS UNIDOS MEXICANOS

Wmk. 156 — CORREOS MEXICO

Wmk. 248 — SECRETARIA DE HACIENDA MEXICO

Wmk. 260 — Lines and SECRETARIA DE HACIENDA MEXICO

Miguel Hidalgo y Costilla — A1

Handstamped with District Name

1856		Unwmk. Engr.	*Imperf.*	
1	A1	½r blue	45.00	35.00
	b.	Without overprint	40.00	40.00
	c.	Double impression		150.00
2	A1	1r yellow	27.50	4.50
	b.	Half used as ½r on cover		*10,000.*
	c.	Without overprint	22.50	27.50
	d.	1r green (error)		
3	A1	2r yellow grn	25.00	3.00
	a.	2r blue green	275.00	40.00
	b.	2r emerald	250.00	50.00
	c.	Half used as 1r on cover		600.00
	d.	Without overprint	35.00	20.00
	e.	As "a," without overprint	250.00	40.00
	f.	As "b," without overprint		75.00
	g.	Printed on both sides (yel green)	300.00	
4	A1	4r red	150.00	100.00
	a.	Half used as 2r on cover		250.00
	b.	Quarter used as 1r on cover		700.00
	c.	Without overprint	125.00	*150.00*
	d.	Three quarters used as 3r on cover		*12,000.*
5	A1	8r red lilac	300.00	175.00
	a.	8r violet	250.00	175.00
	b.	Without overprint	200.00	200.00
	c.	Eighth used as 1r on cover		*11,000.*
	d.	Quarter used as 2r on cover		225.00
	e.	Half used as 4r on cover		900.00
		Nos. 1-5 (5)	547.50	317.50

The 1r and 2r were printed in sheets of 60 with wide spacing between stamps, and in sheets of 190 or 200 with narrow spacing.

All values, except the 1r, have been reprinted, some of them several times. The reprints usually show signs of wear and the impressions are often smudgy. The paper is usually thicker than that of the originals. Reprints are usually on very white paper. Reprints are found with and without overprints and with cancellations made both from the original handstamps and from forged ones.

Counterfeits exist.

See Nos. 6-12. For overprints see Nos. 35-45.

1861				
6	A1	½r black, *buff*	45.00	40.00
	a.	Without overprint	30.00	57.50
7	A1	1r black, *green*	17.50	5.00
	a.	Impression of 2r on back		450.00
	b.	Without overprint	5.00	20.00
	d.	As "b," blk, *pink* (error)	8,000	*9,000.*
	f.	Double impression		150.00
8	A1	2r black, *pink*	13.00	4.00
	a.	Impression of 1r on back	2,000.	
	b.	Half used as 1r on cover		750.00
	c.	Without overprint	3.00	20.00
	d.	Printed on both sides		2,250.
	e.	Double impression		100.00
	f.	As "e," without overprint	—	
9	A1	4r black, *yellow*	175.00	90.00
	a.	Half used as 2r on cover		190.00
	b.	Without overprint	45.00	90.00
	c.	Quarter used as 1r on cover		700.00
	d.	Three-quarters used as 3r on cover		*35,000.*
10	A1	4r dull rose, *yel*	175.00	65.00
	a.	Half used as 2r on cover		*950.00*
	b.	Without overprint	100.00	125.00
	c.	Printed on both sides		*9,000.*
	d.	Quarter used as 1r on cover		*10,000.*
11	A1	8r black, *red brn*	325.00	225.00
	b.	Quarter used as 2r on cover		200.00
	c.	Half used as 4r on cover		750.00
	d.	Without overprint	100.00	210.00
	e.	Three quarters used as 6r on cover		*45,000.*
12	A1	8r grn, *red brn*	450.00	210.00
	a.	Half used as 4r on cover		30,000.
	b.	Without overprint	125.00	175.00
	c.	Quarter used as 2r on cover		40,000.
	d.	Printed on both sides	*12,500.*	*12,500.*
		Nos. 6-12 (7)	1,200.	639.00

Nos. 6, 9, 10, 11 and 12 have been reprinted. Most reprints of the ½r, 4r and 8r are on vertically grained paper. Originals are on horizontally grained paper. The original ½r stamps are much worn but the reprints are unworn. The paper of the 4r is too deep and rich in color and No. 10 is printed in too bright red.

Reprints of the 8r can only be told by experts. All these reprints are found in fancy colors and with overprints and cancellations as in the 1856 issue.

Counterfeits exist.

Hidalgo — A3

Coat of Arms — A4

With District Name

1864			*Perf. 12*	
14	A3	1r red	*750.*	*3,000.*
	a.	Without District Name	.75	
15	A3	2r blue	*550.*	*1,000.*
	a.	Without District Name	.75	
16	A3	4r brown	*1,250.*	*2,400.*
	a.	Without District Name	1.25	
	b.	Vert. pair, imperf. between		
17	A3	1p black	*3,250.*	*22,500.*
	a.	Without District Name	2.00	

Nos. 14 to 17 were issued with district overprints of Saltillo or Monterrey on the toned paper of 1864. Overprints on the 1867 white paper are fraudulent. Counterfeits and counterfeit cancellations are plentiful. The 1r red with "½" surcharge is bogus.

Overprint of District Name, etc.

1864-66 *Imperf.*

Five types of overprints:
I — District name only.
II — District name, consignment number and "1864" in large figures.
III — District name, number and "1864" in small figures.
IV — District name, number and "1865."
V — District name, number and "1866."

18	A4	3c brn (IV, V)	1,200.	*2,500.*
	a.	Without overprint	650.00	
	b.	Laid paper	*4,500.*	*6,000.*
19	A4	½r brown (I)	350.00	225.00
	a.	Type II	2,200.	2,250.
	b.	Without overprint	175.00	*600.00*
20	A4	½r lilac (IV)	55.00	50.00
	a.	Type III	130.00	72.50
	b.	Type II	200.00	200.00
	c.	Type V		*3,000.*
	d.	½r gray (V)	65.00	75.00
	e.	Without overprint	4.00	
	f.	½r gray lilac	250.00	100.00
21	A4	1r blue (IV, V)	13.00	8.00
	a.	Type III	75.00	35.00
	b.	Without overprint	2.00	
	c.	Half used as ½r on cover		*3,000.*
22	A4	1r ultra (I, II)	100.00	27.50
	a.	Type III	75.00	35.00
	b.	Without overprint	140.00	125.00
	c.	Half used as ½r on cover		*7,250.*
23	A4	2r org (III, IV, V)	8.75	3.25
	a.	Type II	17.50	4.25
	b.	Type I	47.50	6.00
	c.	2r dp org, without ovpt., early plate	175.00	65.00
	d.	Without ovpt., late plate	1.50	
	e.	Half used as 1r on cover		*6,000.*
24	A4	4r grn (III, IV, V)	85.00	45.00
	a.	Types I, II	160.00	77.50
	b.	4r dk grn, without ovpt.	3.50	*1,700.*
	d.	Half used as 2r on cover		*700.00*

25 A4 8r red (IV, V) 125.00 80.00
a. Types II, III 150.00 110.00
b. Type I 400.00 175.00
c. 8r dk red, without ovpt. 5.25 *500.00*
f. Quarter used as 2r on cover *15,000.*
g. Three-quarters used as 6r on cover

The 2r printings from the early plates are 25½mm high; those from the late plate, 24½mm.

Varieties listed as "Without overprint" in unused condition are remainders.

Besides the overprints of district name, number and date, Nos. 18-34 often received, in the district offices, additional overprints of numbers and sometimes year dates. Copies with these "sub-consignment numbers" sell for more than stamps without them.

Genuine copies of No. 20c should bear Mexico district name overprint, together with consignment numbers 1-1866 or 17-1866. Gray lilac copies of other consignments are examples of No. 20f.

Value unused for No. 18 is for an example without gum. Copies with original gum sell for more. Copies of No. 18a on laid paper are forgeries.

No. 25g does not exist on fuul cover.

Faked quarterlings and bisects of 1856-64 are plentiful.

The 3c has been reprinted from a die on which the words "TRES CENTAVOS," the outlines of the serpent and some of the background lines have been retouched.

Emperor Maximilian — A5

Overprinted with District Name, Number and Date 1866 or 866; also with Number and Date only, or with Name only

1866 **Litho.**
26 A5 7c lilac gray 65.00 125.00
a. 7c deep gray 85.00 140.00
27 A5 13c blue 35.00 35.00
a. Half used as 7c on cover —
b. 13c cobalt blue 25.00 25.00
c. Without overprint 2,500.
28 A5 25c buff 12.50 9.00
a. Half used as 13c on cover —
b. Without overprint 2,500.
29 A5 25c orange 12.00 12.00
a. 25c red orange 20.00 27.50
b. 25c red brown 85.00 47.50
c. 25c brown *110.00* 85.00
30 A5 50c green 25.00 30.00
Nos. 26-30 (5) 149.50 211.00

Litho. printings have round period after value numerals.

Overprinted with District Name, Number and Date 866 or 867; also with Number and Date only
Engr.

31 A5 7c lilac 450.00 *5,500.*
a. Without overprint 3.50
32 A5 13c blue 12.00 12.00
a. Without overprint 1.25
33 A5 25c orange brown 12.00 11.00
a. Without overprint 1.25
34 A5 50c green 700.00 70.00
a. Without overprint 2.50

See "sub-consignment" note after No. 25.

Engraved printings have square period after value numerals.

Varieties listed as "Without overprint" in unused condition are remainders.

Stamps of 1856-61 Overprinted

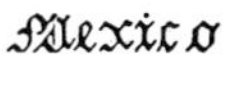

1867
35 A1 ½r blk, *buff* 2,500. *4,000.*
36 A1 1r blk, *green* 60.00 10.00
37 A1 2r blk, *pink* 22.50 5.00
a. Printed on both sides 140.00
38 A1 4r red, *yel* 625.00 50.00
a. Printed on both sides 175.00
39 A1 4r red *6,000.* *3,250.*
40 A1 8r blk, *red brn* 3,500. 275.00
41 A1 8r grn, *red brn* *4,000.*

Dangerous counterfeits exist of the "Mexico" overprint.

Copies of No. 38 with yellow removed are offered as No. 39.

Same Overprint
Thin Gray Blue Paper
Wmk. 151

42 A1 ½r gray 275.00 190.00
a. Without overprint 175.00 175.00
43 A1 1r blue 400.00 65.00
b. Without overprint 300.00 125.00
44 A1 2r green 200.00 30.00
a. Printed on both sides 6,000. 3,500.
b. Without overprint 300.00 50.00
45 A1 4r rose 3,000. 75.00
a. Without overprint *5,000.* 225.00

Most copies of Nos. 42-45 do not show the watermark. Values are such copies. Examples showing the watermark sell for more.

Reprints of the ½r and 4r exist on watermarked paper. Reprints of ½r and 8r also exist in gray on thick grayish wove paper, unwatermarked.

Hidalgo — A6

Thin Figures of Value, without Period after Numerals

6 CENT. 12 CENT.
25 CENT. 50 CENT.
100 CENT.

Overprinted with District Name, Number and Abbreviated Date

1868 **Unwmk.** **Litho.** ***Imperf.***
46 A6 6c blk, *buff* 40.00 20.00
47 A6 12c blk, *green* 45.00 20.00
a. Period after "12" 65.00 55.00
48 A6 25c bl, *pink* 75.00 20.00
a. Without overprint 125.00
49 A6 50c blk, *yellow* 600.00 60.00
50 A6 100c blk, *brown* 775.00 140.00
51 A6 100c brn, *brn* 1,750. 500.00

Perf.

52 A6 6c blk, *buff* 35.00 35.00
a. Without overprint 150.00
b. Period after "6" 100.00 75.00
53 A6 12c blk, *green* 35.00 12.00
a. Period after "12" 85.00 30.00
b. Very thick paper 50.00 25.00
c. Without overprint 110.00
54 A6 25c blue, *pink* 55.00 10.00
b. Without overprint 150.00
55 A6 50c blk, *yellow* 325.00 45.00
56 A6 100c blk, *brown* 375.00 110.00
c. Without overprint 350.00
57 A6 100c brn, *brn* 1,000. 375.00
a. Printed on both sides 1,250. 1,000.

Four kinds of perforation are found in the 1868 issue: serrate, square, pin and regular. The narrow spacing between stamps was inadequate for some of these perforation types.

Thick Figures of Value, with Period after Numerals

6. CENT. 12. CENT
25. CENT. 50. CENT.
100. CENT

Overprinted with District Name, Number and Abbreviated Date
Imperf

58 A6 6c blk, *buff* 9.50 4.50
59 A6 12c blk, *green* 4.25 1.25
a. Very thick paper 10.00
c. 12c black, *buff* (error) 575.00 575.00
d. Printed on both sides *3,000.*
e. No period after "12" —
61 A6 25c blue, *pink* 8.00 1.25
a. No period after "25" 90.00
c. Very thick paper 25.00 6.00
d. "85" for "25" 75.00 50.00
e. "35" for "25" 75.00
f. Printed on both sides —
62 A6 50c blk, *yellow* 125.00 15.00
a. No period after "50" 225.00 35.00
b. 50c blue, *lt pink* (error) *3,000.* *2,000.*
c. Half used as 25c on cover 1,000.
d. Very thick paper 50.00
64 A6 100c blk, *brown* 150.00 90.00
a. No period after "100" 175.00 100.00
b. Very thick paper 75.00
c. Quarter used as 25c on cover *2,000.*
Nos. 58-64 (5) 296.75 112.00

Perf.

65 A6 6c blk, *buff* 40.00 20.00
a. Very thick paper 60.00 35.00
66 A6 12c blk, *green* 5.50 5.50
a. Very thick paper 20.00 15.00
b. 12c black, *buff* (error) 575.00 575.00
c. No period after "12" —
68 A6 25c blue, *pink* 20.00 2.50
a. No period after "25" 80.00 80.00
c. Thick paper 30.00 15.00
d. "85" for "25" 80.00 40.00
69 A6 50c blk, *yellow* 200.00 25.00
a. No period after "50" 200.00 30.00
b. 50c blue, *lt pink* (error) *2,500.* *1,500.*
c. Thick paper 60.00
70 A6 100c blk, *brown* 200.00 60.00
a. No period after "100" 200.00 65.00
b. Very thick paper 80.00
Nos. 65-70 (5) 465.50 113.00

Postal forgeries of Nos. 58-70 were printed from original plates with district name overprints forged. These include the pelure paper varieties and some thick paper varieties. The "Anotado" handstamp was applied to some of the confiscated forgeries and they were issued, including Nos. 73a and 78a.

Stamps of 1868 Handstamped

Overprinted with District Name, Number and Abbreviated Date Thick Figures with Period

1872 ***Imperf.***
71 A6 6c blk, *buff* 650.00 675.00
72 A6 12c blk, *green* 85.00 75.00
73 A6 25c bl, *pink* 40.00 45.00
a. Pelure paper 55.00 65.00
b. "85" for "25" 125.00
74 A6 50c blk, *yellow* 850.00 475.00
a. No period after "50" 900.00 475.00
75 A6 100c blk, *brown* 1,250. 1,000.
a. No period after "100" 1,100.

Perf.

76 A6 6c blk, *buff* 750.00
77 A6 12c blk, *green* 90.00 80.00
78 A6 25c blue, *pink* 35.00 42.50
a. Pelure paper 65.00 90.00
79 A6 50c blk, *yellow* 850.00 600.00
a. No period after "50" 550.00
80 A6 100c blk, *brown* 1,200.

Counterfeit "Anotado" overprints abound. Genuine cancellations other than Mexico City or of the Diligencias de Puebla are unknown. It is recommended that these be purchased accompanied by certificates of authenticity from competent experts.

The stamps of the 1872 issue are found perforated with square holes, pin-perf. 13, 14 or 15, and with serrate perforation.

Counterfeits of the 1868 6c, 12c buff, 50c and 100c (both colors) from new plates have clear, sharp impressions and more facial shading lines than the originals. These counterfeits are found perf. and imperf., with thick and thin numerals, and with the "Anotado" overprint.

Hidalgo — A8

Moiré on White Back Overprinted with District Name, Number and Abbreviated Date White Wove Paper

1872 **Litho.** **Wmk. 150** ***Imperf.***
81 A8 6c green 75.00 60.00
82 A8 12c blue 50.00 35.00
a. Laid paper 1,000. 175.00
83 A8 25c red 125.00 25.00
a. Laid paper 1,000. 175.00
84 A8 50c yellow 475.00 250.00
a. 50c blue (error) 1,500.
b. Laid paper 2,000.
c. As "a," without ovpt. 65.00
86 A8 100c gray lilac 350.00 200.00
Nos. 81-86 (5) 1,075. 570.00

Wmk. "LA + F"

81a A8 6c green 240.00 125.00
82b A8 12c blue 160.00 62.50
83b A8 25c red 210.00 47.50
c. Without overprint 250.00
84d A8 50c yellow 1,500. 950.00
86a A8 100c gray lilac 900.00 600.00

1872 **Wmk. 150** ***Pin-perf.***
87 A8 6c green 425.00 425.00
88 A8 12c blue 62.50 50.00
89 A8 25c red 140.00 45.00
b. Laid paper 500.00
90 A8 50c yellow 650.00 325.00
a. 50c blue (error) *500.00* *625.00*
b. As "a," without overprint 100.00
92 A8 100c gray lilac 375.00 300.00
Nos. 87-92 (5) 1,652. 1,145.

Wmk. "LA + F"

87a A8 6c green 475.00 450.00
88a A8 12c blue 160.00 175.00
89a A8 25c red 450.00 110.00
90c A8 50c yellow 1,300. 1,100.
92a A8 100c gray lilac 1,000. 675.00

The watermark "LA+F" stands for La Croix Frères, the paper manufacturers, and is in double-lined block capitals 13mm high. A single stamp will show only part of this watermark.

Values for Nos. 87-92a are for examples with visible perfs on all sides.

1872 **Unwmk.** ***Imperf.***
93 A8 6c green 12.50 12.50
a. Without moiré on back, without overprint 60.00 65.00
b. Vertically laid paper 3,000. 1,300.
c. Bottom label retouched 100.00 90.00
d. Very thick paper 37.50 37.50
94 A8 12c blue 2.00 1.75
a. Without moiré on back, without overprint 30.00 35.00
b. Vertically laid paper 350.00 210.00
c. Thin gray bl paper of 1867 (Wmk 151) 2,000.
95 A8 25c red 8.50 2.00
a. Without moiré on back, without overprint 30.00 35.00
b. Vertically laid paper 450.00 500.00
c. Thin gray bl paper of 1867 (Wmk 151) 1,500.
96 A8 50c yellow 140.00 35.00
a. 50c orange 140.00 35.00
b. Without moiré on back, without overprint 50.00 70.00
c. Vertically laid paper 2,000.
d. 50c blue (error) 650.00
e. As "d," without overprint 45.00
f. As "e," without moiré on back 65.00
g. Half used as 25c on cover *5,000.*
98 A8 100c gray lilac 90.00 50.00
a. 100c lilac 100.00 42.50
b. Without moiré on back, without overprint 50.00 110.00
c. Vertically laid paper 1,250.
Nos. 93-98 (5) 253.00 101.25

Counterfeits of these stamps are 24½mm high instead of 24mm. The printing is sharper and more uniform than the genuine. Forged district names and consignment numbers exist.

Pin-perf. and Serrate Perf.

99 A8 6c green 90.00 75.00
100 A8 12c blue 3.50 3.00
a. Vertically laid paper 350.00
b. Horiz. pair, imperf. vert. 100.00 100.00
c. Vert. pair, imperf. between 150.00
101 A8 25c red 3.25 1.50
a. Vertically laid paper 500.00
b. Horiz. pair, imperf. vert. 100.00 100.00
102 A8 50c yellow 175.00 50.00
a. 50c orange 160.00 50.00
b. 50c blue (error) 475.00 500.00
c. As "b," without overprint 45.00
104 A8 100c lilac 150.00 80.00
a. 100c gray lilac 125.00 80.00
Nos. 99-104 (5) 421.75 209.50

Values for Nos. 99-104a are for examples with visible perfs on all sides.

Hidalgo
A9 A10

A11 A12

A13 A14

Overprinted with District Name and Number and Date; also with Number and Date only
Thick Wove Paper, Some Showing Vertical Ribbing

1874-80 **Unwmk.** **Engr.** ***Perf. 12***
105 A9 4c org ('80) 12.50 12.00
a. Vert. pair, imperf. btwn. 60.00
b. Without overprint 6.50 12.50
c. Half used as 2c on cover 1,000.
106 A10 5c brown 4.50 3.00
a. Horizontally laid paper 100.00 55.00
b. Imperf., pair 60.00
c. Horiz. pair, imperf. btwn. 50.00 300.00
d. Vert. pair, imperf. btwn. 110.00 110.00
e. Without overprint 37.50 37.50
f. As "a," wmkd. "LACROIX" 350.00 200.00

107 A11 10c black 2.00 1.25
a. Horizontally laid paper 2.50 2.50
b. Horiz. pair, imperf. btwn. 75.00 75.00
c. Without overprint 35.00 27.50
d. Half used as 5c on cover 2,000.
e. Imperf., pair
f. As "a," wmkd. "LACROIX" 60.00 45.00
108 A11 10c org ('78) 2.00 1.25
a. 10c yellow bister 7.50 4.25
b. Imperf., pair
c. Without overprint 55.00 55.00
d. Half used as 5c on cover 100.00
109 A12 25c blue .85 .70
b. Horizontally laid paper 2.25 1.75
c. Imperf., pair 50.00 25.00
d. Without overprint 35.00 20.00
e. Horiz. pair, imperf. btwn. 125.00
f. As "b," horiz. pair, imperf. vert. 200.00
g. As "b," wmkd. "LACROIX" 50.00 40.00
h. Printed on both sides 1,500.
i. Half used as 10c on cover 2,000.
110 A13 50c green 13.00 13.00
a. Without overprint 50.00
b. Half used as 25c on cover 2,500.
111 A14 100c carmine 18.00 15.00
a. Imperf., pair 200.00 200.00
b. Without overprint 50.00
c. Quarter used as 25c on cover 3,000.
Nos. 105-111 (7) 52.85 46.20

The "LACROIX" watermark is spelled out "LACROIX FRERES" in 2 lines of block capitals without serifs once to a sheet of horiz. laid paper.6-12 stamps may have a portion of the wmk.

1875-77 Wmk. 150

112 A10 5c brown 55.00 35.00
113 A11 10c black 55.00 35.00
114 A12 25c blue 55.00 32.50
115 A13 50c green 300.00 200.00
116 A14 100c carmine 275.00 175.00
Nos. 112-116 (5) 740.00 477.50

1881 Unwmk. Thin Wove Paper

117 A9 4c orange 70.00 70.00
a. Without overprint 20.00 20.00
118 A10 5c brown 10.00 6.50
a. Without overprint .50 20.00
b. As "a," vert. pair, imperf. horiz. 1,000.
119 A11 10c orange 6.00 3.50
a. Imperf., pair
b. Vert. pair, imperf. horiz.
c. Without overprint .75 4.50
d. Vert. pair, imperf. btwn.
e. Half used as 5c on cover 1,500.
120 A12 25c blue 4.00 2.25
a. Imperf., pair 100.00
b. Without overprint .50 8.00
c. Double impression 65.00
d. Printed on both sides *1,500.*
121 A13 50c green 45.00 40.00
a. Without overprint 4.00 30.00
122 A14 100c carmine 50.00 50.00
a. Without overprint 6.00 300.00

The stamps of 1874-81 are found with number and date wide apart, close together or omitted, and in various colors.

The thin paper is fragile and easily damaged. Values for Nos. 117-122 are for undamaged, fine examples.

Benito Juárez — A15

Overprinted with District Name and Number and Date; also with Number and Date only

1879 *Perf. 12*

Thick Wove Paper, Some Showing Vertical Ribbing

123 A15 1c brown 4.00 4.00
a. Without overprint 75.00 140.00
b. 1c gray 20.00 15.00
124 A15 2c dk violet 4.00 4.50
a. Without overprint 75.00 150.00
b. Printed on both sides
c. 2c dark gray 20.00 14.00
125 A15 5c orange 2.25 1.50
a. Without overprint 75.00 90.00
b. Double impression *500.00*
126 A15 10c blue 3.00 2.50
a. Without overprint 75.00 150.00
b. 10c ultra 160.00 160.00
127 A15 25c rose 8.00 30.00
a. Without overprint 1.75 150.00
128 A15 50c green 15.00 50.00
a. Without overprint 1.25 150.00
b. Printed on both sides 165.00
129 A15 85c violet 20.00 250.00
a. Without overprint 2.50
130 A15 100c black 25.00 75.00
a. Without overprint 3.00 150.00
Nos. 123-130 (8) 81.25 417.50

Used values for Nos. 127-130 are for copies with postal cancellations. Pen cancelled copies are worth the same as unused stamps.

Forged cancellations on Nos. 127-130 are plentiful.

1882

Thin Wove Paper

131 A15 1c brown 40.00 37.50
a. Without overprint 125.00
132 A15 2c dk violet 27.50 24.00
a. 2c slate 47.50 50.00
b. Without overprint 110.00
c. Half used as 1c on cover
133 A15 5c orange 9.00 6.00
a. Without overprint 1.25
b. Half used as 2c on cover
c. As "a," vert. pair, imperf. btwn.
134 A15 10c blue 9.00 6.00
a. Without overprint 1.25
b. Half used as 5c on cover
135 A15 10c brown 9.00
a. Imperf., pair 3.00
136 A15 12c brown 7.50 8.00
a. Without overprint 2.50 22.50
b. Imperf., pair 75.00
c. Half used as 6c on cover
137 A15 18c orange brn 9.00 15.00
a. Horiz. pair, imperf. btwn. 100.00
b. Without overprint 2.25 18.00
138 A15 24c violet 9.00 11.00
a. Without overprint 2.25 17.50
139 A15 25c rose 45.00 250.00
a. Without overprint 4.50
140 A15 25c orange brn 5.50
141 A15 50c green 45.00 75.00
a. Without overprint 6.25
142 A15 50c yellow 80.00 350.00
a. Without overprint 150.00
143 A15 85c red violet 55.00
144 A15 100c black 75.00 *250.00*
a. Without overprint 5.00
b. Vert. pair, imperf. btwn. 165.00 165.00
145 A15 100c orange 95.00 400.00
a. Without overprint 175.00
Nos. 131-145 (15) 520.50 1,432.

No. 135, 140 and 143 exist only without overprint. They were never placed in use.

Used values for Nos. 139, 141, 142, 144 and 145 are for postally used copies. Forged cancellations are plentiful. Pen cancelled copies are worth the same as unused stamps.

See note on thin paper after No. 122.

A16

Overprinted with District Name, Number and Abbreviated Date

1882-83

146 A16 2c green 11.00 8.00
a. Without overprint 27.50 20.00
147 A16 3c car lake 11.00 8.00
a. Without overprint 5.25 8.50
148 A16 6c blue ('83) 30.00 40.00
a. Without overprint 30.00 50.00
149 A16 6c ultra 6.00 8.50
a. Without overprint 3.50 6.00
b. As "a," imperf pair 50.00
Nos. 146-149 (4) 58.00 64.50

See note on thin paper after No. 122.

Hidalgo — A17

1884 Wove or Laid Paper *Perf. 12*

150 A17 1c green 4.00 .75
a. Imperf., pair 32.50
b. 1c blue (error) 500.00 475.00
151 A17 2c green 0.75 2.00
a. Imperf., pair 60.00 55.00
b. Half used as 1c on cover
152 A17 3c green 12.50 2.00
a. Imperf., pair 110.00 90.00
b. Horiz. pair, imperf. vert. 125.00 125.00
153 A17 4c green 16.00 2.00
a. Imperf., pair 75.00 65.00
b. Half used as 2c on cover 200.00
154 A17 5c green 17.50 1.50
a. Imperf., pair 110.00 90.00
155 A17 6c green 15.00 1.50
a. Imperf., pair 75.00 65.00
156 A17 10c green 16.00 .75
a. Imperf., pair 75.00 70.00
157 A17 12c green 30.00 3.50
a. Vert. pair, imperf. between 75.00 60.00
b. Half used as 6c on cover 125.00
158 A17 20c green 90.00 2.50
a. Diagonal half used as 10c on cover 200.00
b. Imperf., pair 160.00 125.00
159 A17 25c green 140.00 5.00
a. Imperf., pair 250.00 200.00
160 A17 50c green .60 *5.00*
a. Imperf., pair 25.00 20.00
161 A17 1p blue .60 *11.00*
a. Imperf., pair 60.00 45.00
b. Vert. pair, imperf. between 100.00
162 A17 2p blue .60 *22.50*
a. Imperf., pair 75.00 60.00
163 A17 5p blue 350.00 200.00
164 A17 10p blue 500.00 225.00
Nos. 150-162 (13) 349.55 *60.00*

Imperforate varieties should be purchased in pairs or larger. Single imperforates are usually trimmed perforated stamps.

Beware of copies of No. 150 that have been chemically changed to resemble No. 150b.

Forged cancels on Nos. 161-162 are plentiful.

Some values exist perf. 11.

See Nos. 165-173, 230-231.

1885

165 A17 1c pale green 30.00 7.00
166 A17 2c carmine 25.00 3.50
a. Diagonal half used as 1c on cover 100.00
167 A17 3c orange brn 25.00 6.00
a. Imperf., pair 100.00 100.00
168 A17 4c red orange 40.00 17.50
169 A17 5c ultra 25.00 3.50
170 A17 6c dk brown 30.00 6.00
a. Half used as 3c on cover 210.00
171 A17 10c orange 25.00 1.50
a. 10c yellow 27.50 1.50
b. Horiz. pair, imperf. btwn. 100.00 100.00
172 A17 12c olive brn 55.00 9.00
173 A17 25c grnsh blue 200.00 20.00
Nos. 165-173 (9) 455.00 74.00

Numeral of Value — A18

1886 *Perf. 12*

174 A18 1c yellow green 2.25 .75
a. 1c blue grn 5.50 4.50
b. Horiz. pair, imperf. btwn. 75.00 60.00
c. Perf. 11 45.00 45.00
175 A18 2c carmine 2.60 .90
a. Horiz. pair, imperf. btwn. 80.00 75.00
b. Vert. pair, imperf. between 75.00 75.00
c. Perf. 11 45.00 45.00
d. Half used as 1c on cover 100.00
176 A18 3c lilac 12.00 7.50
177 A18 4c lilac 18.00 5.25
a. Perf. 11 50.00 *55.00*
178 A18 5c ultra 2.25 1.00
a. 5c blue 2.25 .75
179 A18 6c lilac 30.00 7.50
180 A18 10c lilac 22.50 1.10
a. Perf. 11 125.00
181 A18 12c lilac 25.00 14.00
182 A18 20c lilac 160.00 100.00
183 A18 25c lilac 70.00 17.50
Nos. 174-183 (10) 344.60 155.50

Nos. 175, 191, 194B, 196, 202 exist with blue or black surcharge "Vale 1 Cvo." These were made by the Colima postmaster.

1887

184 A18 3c scarlet 1.90 .60
a. Imperf., pair 75.00
185 A18 4c scarlet 7.50 2.25
186 A18 6c scarlet 12.50 2.25
a. Horiz. pair, imperf. btwn. 75.00
187 A18 10c scarlet 2.75 .60
a. Imperf., pair 75.00
b. Horiz. pair, imperf. btwn. 45.00
188 A18 20c scarlet 18.00 1.50
a. Horiz. pair, imperf. btwn. 75.00
189 A18 25c scarlet 15.00 4.00
Nos. 184-189 (6) 57.65 11.20

Perf. 6

190 A18 1c blue grn 45.00 45.00
191 A18 2c brown car 22.50 42.00
192 A18 5c ultra 15.00 4.50
a. 5c blue 15.00 4.50
193 A18 10c lilac 15.00 4.25
193A A18 10c brown lilac 15.00 3.00
194 A18 10c scarlet 35.00 15.00

Perf. 6x12

194A A18 1c blue grn 62.50 42.50
194B A18 2c brown car 85.00 75.00
194C A18 3c scarlet 300.00 350.00
194D A18 5c ultra 60.00 45.00
194E A18 10c lilac 90.00 75.00
194F A18 10c scarlet 80.00 60.00
194G A18 10c brown lilac 90.00 75.00

Many shades exist.

Paper with colored ruled lines on face or reverse of stamp

1887 *Perf. 12*

195 A18 1c green 75.00 45.00
196 A18 2c brown car 190.00 47.50
198 A18 5c ultra 110.00 30.00
199 A18 10c scarlet 110.00 25.00

Perf. 6

201 A18 1c green 60.00 20.00
202 A18 2c brown car 60.00 24.00
204 A18 5c ultra 50.00 12.00
205 A18 10c brown lil 42.50 10.00
206 A18 10c scarlet 250.00 40.00
Nos. 201-206 (5) 462.50 106.00

Perf. 6x12

207 A18 1c green 225.00 140.00
208 A18 2c brown car 325.00 140.00
209 A18 5c ultra 225.00 140.00
210 A18 10c brown lil 275.00 125.00
211 A18 10c scarlet 325.00 200.00
Nos. 207-211 (5) 1,375. 745.00

The existence of No. 196A is questioned.

1890-95 Wmk. 152 *Perf. 11 & 12*

Wove or Laid Paper

212 A18 1c yellow grn .75 .35
a. 1c blue green .75 .35
b. Horiz. pair, imperf. btwn. 35.00 35.00
c. Laid paper 2.50 2.50
d. Horiz. pair, imperf. vert. 35.00 35.00
213 A18 2c carmine 1.50 .75
a. 2c brown car 1.25 1.00
b. Vert. pair, imperf. btwn. 150.00
c. Imperf., pair 200.00
214 A18 3c vermilion 1.00 .60
b. Horiz. pair, imperf. btwn. 80.00
215 A18 4c vermilion 3.25 2.10
a. Horiz. pair, imperf. btwn. 80.00
216 A18 5c ultra .60 .50
a. 5c dull blue 1.00 .50
217 A18 6c vermilion 3.75 2.75
a. Horiz. pair, imperf. btwn. 45.00
218 A18 10c vermilion .50 .35
b. Horiz. or vert. pair, imperf. btwn. 45.00 45.00
c. Vert. pair, imperf. horiz. 45.00
d. Imperf., pair 50.00
219 A18 12c ver ('95) 14.00 18.00
220 A18 20c vermilion 3.50 1.50
220A A18 20c dk violet 150.00 *175.00*
221 A18 25c vermilion 5.00 2.50
Nos. 212-220,221 (10) 33.85 29.40

No. 219 has been reprinted in slightly darker shade than the original.

1892

222 A18 3c orange 4.00 2.00
223 A18 4c orange 4.25 3.00
224 A18 6c orange 5.75 2.00
225 A18 10c orange 27.50 2.00
226 A18 20c orange 50.00 6.00
227 A18 25c orange 16.00 4.50
Nos. 222-227 (6) 107.50 19.50

1892

228 A18 5p carmine 1,250. 900.
229 A18 10p carmine 1,900. 1,250.
230 A17 5p blue green 3,500. 1,200.
231 A17 10p blue green *7,000. 2,700.*

1894 *Perf. 5½, 6*

232 A18 1c yellow grn 3.00 3.00
233 A18 3c vermilion 9.00 9.00
234 A18 4c vermilion 40.00 37.50
235 A18 5c ultra 12.50 5.00
236 A18 10c vermilion 7.50 3.00
236A A18 20c vermilion 110.00 110.00
237 A18 25c vermilion 62.50 62.50
Nos. 232-237 (7) 244.50 230.00

Perf. 5½x11, 11x5½, Compound and Irregular

238 A18 1c yellow grn 7.00 7.00
238A A18 2c brown car 16.00 16.00
238B A18 3c vermilion 47.50 32.50
238C A18 4c vermilion 55.00 55.00
239 A18 5c ultra 17.50 12.50
a. 5c blue 12.50 12.50
239C A18 6c vermilion 75.00 75.00
240 A18 10c vermilion 20.00 7.00
240A A18 20c vermilion 200.00 200.00
241 A18 25c vermilion 62.50 62.50
Nos. 238-241 (9) 500.50 467.50

The stamps of the 1890 to 1895 issues are also to be found unwatermarked, as part of the sheet frequently escaped the watermark.

Letter Carrier — A20

Mounted Courier with Pack Mule — A21

Statue of Cuauhtémoc A22

Mail Coach A23

Mail Train — A24

Regular or Pin Perf. 12

1895 Wmk. 152

Wove or Laid Paper

242	A20	1c	green	3.00	.75
a.			Vert. pair, imperf. horiz.	100.00	
d.			Watermarked sideway ('97)	125.00	15.00
243	A20	2c	carmine	3.75	1.00
a.			Half used as 1c on cover		50.00
c.			Watermarked sideways ('97)	80.00	10.00
244	A20	3c	orange brown	3.75	1.00
a.			Vert. pair, imperf. horiz.		80.00
d.			Watermarked sideways ('97)	125.00	10.00
246	A21	4c	orange	12.50	1.50
a.			4c orange red	7.50	1.25
247	A22	5c	ultra	7.00	.35
a.			Imperf., pair	50.00	50.00
b.			Horiz. or vert. pair, imperf. between	65.00	50.00
e.			Half used as 2c on cover		60.00
f.			Watermarked sideways ('97)	15.00	5.00
248	A23	10c	lilac rose	4.50	1.00
a.			Horiz. or vert. pair, imperf. between		75.00
b.			Half used as 5c on cover		60.00
249	A21	12c	olive brown	50.00	12.50
251	A23	15c	brt blue	27.50	3.00
b.			Watermarked sideways ('97)		100.00
252	A23	20c	brown rose	32.50	3.00
b.			Half used as 10c on cover		60.00
c.			Watermarked sideways ('97)	1,000.	750.00
253	A23	50c	purple	70.00	16.00
a.			Half used as 25c on cover		100.00
254	A24	1p	brown	90.00	35.00
a.			Watermarked sideways ('97)	750.00	*900.00*
255	A24	5p	scarlet	300.00	190.00
256	A24	10p	deep blue	650.00	350.00
			Nos. 242-256 (13)	1,254.	615.10

No. 248 exists in perf. 11.

Nos. 242d, 243c, 244d, 247f, 251b, 252c and 254a was a special printing, made in Jan. 1897. The watermark is sideways, the grain of the paper is horizontal (rather than vertical, as appears on Nos. 242-256, and the design is somewhat shorter than the other stamps in this series. The sideways orientation of the watermark is the most easily identifable feature of this printing.

Important: For unwatermarked examples of Nos. 242-256, see the footnote after No. 291.

Perf. 6

242b	A20	1c	green	60.00	35.00
243b	A20	2c	carmine	125.00	60.00
244b	A20	3c	orange brown	90.00	50.00
247c	A22	5c	ultra	90.00	50.00
248c	A23	10c	lilac rose	125.00	55.00
249a	A21	12c	olive brown	100.00	50.00

Perf. 6x12, 12x6 & Compound or Irregular

242c	A20	1c	green	30.00	20.00
244c	A20	3c	orange brown	35.00	20.00
246b	A21	4c	orange	75.00	50.00
247d	A22	5c	ultra	75.00	50.00
248d	A23	10c	lilac rose	35.00	20.00
249b	A21	12c	olive brown	50.00	25.00
251a	A23	15c	brt blue	60.00	40.00
252a	A23	20c	brown rose	100.00	70.00
253b	A23	50c	purple	150.00	100.00

See Nos. 257-291. For overprints see Nos. O10-O48A.

"Irregular" Perfs. Some copies perf. 6x12, 12x6, 5½x11 and 11x5½ have both perf. 6 and 12 or perf. 5½ and 11 on one or more sides of the stamp. These are known as irregular perfs.

1896-97 Wmk. 153 *Perf. 12*

257	A20	1c	green	12.00	1.00
c.			Imperf., pair		250.00
258	A20	2c	carmine	15.00	1.25
a.			Horiz. pair, imperf. vert.		
259	A20	3c	orange brn	17.50	1.25
260	A21	4c	orange	27.50	1.50
c.			4c deep orange	25.00	5.00
261	A22	5c	ultra	7.00	1.00
a.			Imperf., pair	50.00	
b.			Vert. pair, imperf. btwn.	100.00	
262	A21	12c	olive brn	140.00	70.00
263	A23	15c	brt blue	175.00	11.00
264	A23	20c	brown rose	700.00	250.00
265	A23	50c	purple	140.00	95.00
266	A24	1p	brown	250.00	200.00
267	A24	5p	scarlet	750.00	500.00
268	A24	10p	dp blue	850.00	450.00
			Nos. 257-268 (12)	3,084.	1,582.

Perf. 6

257a	A20	1c	green	35.00	25.00
259a	A20	3c	orange brown	35.00	20.00
260a	A21	4c	orange	40.00	25.00
261c	A22	5c	ultra	110.00	70.00
263a	A23	15c	bright blue	75.00	35.00

Perf. 6x12, 12x6 and Compound or Irregular

257b	A20	1c	green	25.00	20.00
258b	A20	2c	carmine	50.00	25.00
259b	A20	3c	orange brown	40.00	20.00
260b	A21	4c	orange	45.00	20.00
261d	A22	5c	ultra	40.00	20.00
262a	A21	12c	olive brown	125.00	80.00
263b	A23	15c	bright blue	250.00	125.00
264a	A23	20c	brown rose		
265a	A23	50c	purple		

1897-98 Wmk. 154 *Perf. 12*

269	A20	1c	green	18.00	2.25
270	A20	2c	scarlet	30.00	3.75
271	A21	4c	orange	47.50	3.00
a.			Horizontal pair, imperf. vertical		—
272	A22	5c	ultra	45.00	3.00
a.			Imperf., pair	75.00	
273	A21	12c	olive brown	160.00	42.50
275	A23	15c	brt blue	225.00	75.00
276	A23	20c	brown rose	140.00	12.00
277	A23	50c	purple	325.00	65.00
278	A24	1p	brown	375.00	165.00
278A	A24	5p	scarlet	—	—
			Nos. 269-278 (9)	1,365.	371.50

Perf. 6

269a	A20	1c	green	45.00	25.00
270a	A20	2c	scarlet	45.00	25.00
272b	A22	5c	ultra	60.00	25.00
273a	A21	12c	olive brown	110.00	60.00
276a	A23	20c	brown rose		*650.00*

Perf. 6x12, 12x6 and Compound or Irregular

269b	A20	1c	green	25.00	15.00
270b	A20	2c	scarlet	30.00	22.50
271b	A21	4c	orange	65.00	12.50
272c	A22	5c	ultra	50.00	15.00
273b	A21	12c	olive brown	125.00	65.00
275a	A23	15c	bright blue	125.00	65.00
276b	A23	20c	brown rose	240.00	30.00
277a	A23	50c	purple	125.00	50.00

1898 Unwmk. *Perf. 12*

279	A20	1c	green	3.00	.50
a.			Horiz. pair, imperf. vert	300.00	
b.			Imperf., pair	100.00	
280	A20	2c	scarlet	6.25	.75
a.			2c green (error)	*475.00*	
281	A20	3c	orange brn	6.00	.75
a.			Imperf., pair	150.00	150.00
b.			Pair, imperf. between	80.00	80.00
282	A21	4c	orange	30.00	3.00
b.			4c deep orange	37.50	7.00
283	A22	5c	ultra	2.00	.50
a.			Imperf., pair	50.00	50.00
b.			Pair, imperf. between	125.00	
284	A23	10c	lilac rose	500.00	175.00
285	A21	12c	olive brn	75.00	27.50
a.			Imperf., pair	200.00	
286	A23	15c	brt blue	160.00	8.00
287	A23	20c	brown rose	35.00	3.00
a.			Imperf., pair	200.00	
288	A23	50c	purple	140.00	42.50
289	A24	1p	brown	160.00	75.00
290	A24	5p	carmine rose	500.00	400.00
291	A24	10p	deep blue	750.00	550.00
			Nos. 279-291 (13)	2,367.	1,286.

Warning: Sheets of Nos. 242-256 (watermarked "CORREOS E U M") have a column of stamps without watermarks, because the watermark did not fit the sheet size. As a result, be careful not to confuse unwatermarked examples of Nos. 242-256 with Nos. 279-291. This is especialy important for No. 284. Nos. 242-256 have a vertical grain or mesh to the paper. Nos. 279-291 have a horizontal grain or mesh to the paper.

Perf. 6

279c	A20	1c	green	85.00	35.00
280b	A20	2c	scarlet	75.00	30.00
281c	A20	3c	orange brown	50.00	35.00
283c	A22	5c	ultra	65.00	30.00
287b	A23	20c	brown rose	125.00	75.00
291a	A24	10p	deep blue		

Perf. 6x12, 12x6 and Compound or Irregular

279d	A20	1c	green	25.00	20.00
280c	A20	2c	scarlet	25.00	20.00
281d	A20	3c	orange brown	30.00	20.00
282a	A21	4c	orange	40.00	25.00
283d	A22	5c	ultra	20.00	10.00
284a	A23	10c	lilac rose	125.00	85.00
285b	A21	12c	olive brown	90.00	60.00
286a	A23	15c	bright blue	75.00	50.00
287c	A23	20c	brown rose	100.00	50.00
288a	A23	50c	purple	575.00	575.00

Forgeries of the 6 and 6x12 perforations of 1895-98 are plentiful.

Coat of Arms

A25 A26

A27

A28

A29

A30

A31

Juanacatlán Falls — A32

View of Mt. Popocatépetl A33

Cathedral, Mexico, D. F. — A34

1899, Nov. 1 Wmk. 155 *Perf. 14, 15*

294	A25	1c	green	1.75	.35
295	A26	2c	vermilion	4.25	.35
296	A27	3c	orange brn	2.75	.35
297	A28	5c	dark blue	4.50	.35
298	A29	10c	violet & org	5.75	.35
299	A30	15c	lav & claret	7.50	.35
300	A31	20c	rose & dk bl	8.50	.40
301	A32	50c	red lil & blk	32.50	2.25
a.			50c lilac & black	40.00	2.25
302	A33	1p	blue & blk	75.00	3.50
303	A34	5p	carmine & blk	250.00	12.00
			Nos. 294-303 (10)	392.50	20.25

See Nos. 304-305, 307-309. For overprints see Nos. 420-422, 439-450, 452-454, 482-483, 515-516, 539, 550, O49-O60, O62-O66, O68-O74, O101.

A35

1903

304	A25	1c	violet	1.40	.35
a.			Booklet pane of 6	55.00	
305	A26	2c	green	1.90	.35
a.			Booklet pane of 6	82.50	
306	A35	4c	carmine	4.50	.45
307	A28	5c	orange	1.10	.35
a.			Booklet pane of 6	82.50	
308	A29	10c	blue & org	4.50	.35
309	A32	50c	carmine & blk	72.50	6.00
			Nos. 304-309 (6)	85.90	7.85

For overprints see Nos. 451, O61, O67.

Independence Issue

Josefa Ortiz — A36

Leona Vicario — A37

López Rayón — A38

Juan Aldama — A39

Miguel Hidalgo — A40

Ignacio Allende — A41

Epigmenio González A42

Mariano Abasolo A43

Declaration of Independence A44

Mass on the Mount of Crosses A45

Capture of Granaditas A46

1910 *Perf. 14*

310	A36	1c	dull violet	.35	.35
a.			Booklet pane of 4	40.00	
311	A37	2c	green	.35	.35
a.			Booklet pane of 8	40.00	
312	A38	3c	orange brn	.60	.35
313	A39	4c	carmine	2.25	.45
314	A40	5c	orange	.35	.35
a.			Booklet pane of 8	27.50	
315	A41	10c	blue & org	1.40	.35
316	A42	15c	gray bl & cl	7.50	.50
317	A43	20c	red & bl	4.50	.40
318	A44	50c	red brn & blk	11.00	1.60
319	A45	1p	blue & blk	13.50	1.90
320	A46	5p	car & blk	55.00	15.00
			Nos. 310-320 (11)	96.80	21.60
			Set, never hinged	125.00	

Independence of Mexico from Spain, cent.

For overprints and surcharges see Nos. 370-380, 423-433, 455-465, 484-494, 517-

538, 540-549, 551-558, 577-590, O75-O85, O102-O112, O191-O192, O195, RA13, Merida 1.

CIVIL WAR ISSUES

During the 1913-16 Civil War, provisional issues with various handstamped overprints were circulated in limited areas.

Sonora

A47

Seal

Typeset in a row of five varieties. Two impressions placed tête bêche (foot to foot) constitute a sheet. The settings show various wrong font and defective letters, "!" for "1" in "1913," etc. The paper occasionally has a manufacturer's watermark.

a *b* *c* *d*

Four Types of the Numerals.
a — Wide, heavy-faced numerals.
b — Narrow Roman numerals.
c — Wide Roman numerals.
d — Gothic or sans-serif numerals.

Nos. 321-346 Issued Without Gum

Embossed "CONSTITUCIONAL"

1913 Typeset Unwmk. *Perf. 12*

321 A47 (a) 5c black & red 4,250. 800.00
a. "CENTAVOB" *4,750. 850.00*

Colorless Roulette

322 A47(b) 1c black & red 20.00 24.00
a. With green seal *1,500. 1,250.*
323 A47(a) 2c black & red 19.00 14.00
a. With green seal *2,000. 2,000.*
324 A47(c) 2c black & red 85.00 70.00
a. With green seal *5,000. 5,000.*
325 A47(a) 3c black & red 95.00 75.00
a. With green seal *750.00 750.00*
326 A47(a) 5c black & red 175.00 75.00
a. "CENTAVOB" 200.00 50.00
327 A47(d) 5c black & red 1,200. 350.00
a. With green seal *1,000.*
328 A47(b) 10c black & red 32.50 35.00

Black Roulette

329 A47(d) 5c black & red 275.00 125.00
a. "MARO" 85.00 50.00

Stamps are known with the embossing double or omitted.

The varieties with green seal are from a few sheets embossed "Constitucional" which were in stock at the time the green seal control was adopted.

Without Embossing
With Green Seal
Colorless Roulette

336 A47(b) 1c black & red 15.00 10.00
337 A47(a) 3c black & red 14.50 9.00
a. Imperf. *350.00*
338 A47(a) 5c black & red 750.00 250.00
a. "CENTAVOB" *800.00* 275.00
339 A47(b) 10c black & red 8.00 7.50

Colored Roulette

340 A47(d) 5c brnsh blk & red 25.00 6.00
a. 5c lilac brown & red 75.00 22.50
b. Double seal *1,250.*
c. Red printing omitted *1,000.*

1913-14 *Black Roulette*
With Green Seal

341 A47(a) 1c black & red 4.00 4.00
b. "erano" ('14) 100.00 60.00
342 A47(d) 2c black & red 4.50 4.00
a. "erano" ('14) 30.00 35.00
343 A47(a) 3c black & red 4.75 4.00
a. "CENTAVO" 25.00 25.00
b. "erano" ('14) 35.00 35.00
344 A47(d) 5c black & red 4.75 4.00
b. Heavy black penetrating roulette 2.75 1.75
c. As "b," "MARO" 10.50 5.00
Nos. 341-344 (4) 18.00 16.00

Stamps without seal are unfinished remainders.

On Nos. 341-344 the rouletting cuts the paper slightly or not at all. On Nos. 344b-344c the rouletting is heavy, cutting deeply into the paper.

1914

345 A47(a) 5c black & red 5.00 5.00
346 A47(b) 10c black & red 4.25 5.00

Coat of Arms — A49

Revenue Stamps Used for Postage

1913 Litho. *Rouletted 14, 14x7*

347 A49 1c yellow grn 2.00 *2.50*
Never hinged 2.50
a. With coupon 7.00 6.00
Never hinged 10.00
348 A49 2c violet 3.50 *4.00*
Never hinged 5.00
a. With coupon 17.50 14.50
Never hinged 25.00
349 A49 5c brown .60 *.75*
Never hinged .75
a. With coupon 2.00 1.50
Never hinged 3.00
350 A49 10c claret 2.50 *3.50*
Never hinged 4.00
a. With coupon 15.00 12.00
Never hinged 30.00
351 A49 20c gray grn 3.00 *3.50*
Never hinged 4.00
a. With coupon 20.00 18.00
Never hinged 50.00
352 A49 50c ultra 10.00 *15.00*
Never hinged 15.00
a. With coupon 60.00 47.50
Never hinged 90.00
353 A49 1p orange 42.50 *50.00*
Never hinged 60.00
a. With coupon 150.00 110.00
Never hinged 200.00
Nos. 347-353 (7) 64.10 79.25

For a short time these stamps (called "Ejercitos") were used for postage with coupon attached. Later this was required to be removed unless they were to be used for revenue. Stamps overprinted with district names are revenues. Values above 1p were used for revenue. Imperfs exist of all values, but were not issued.

Many copies do not have gum because of a flood.

Use of typeset Sonora revenue stamps for postage was not authorized or allowed.

Coat of Arms
A50 A51

5c (A50): "CINCO CENTAVOS" 14x2mm

1914 *Rouletted 9½x14*

354 A50 1c deep blue .45 .45
355 A50 2c yellow grn .60 .35
a. 2c green 3.00 1.75
356 A50 4c blue vio 11.00 2.50
a. Horiz. pair, imperf. btwn. 250.00
357 A50 5c gray grn 11.00 3.00
a. Horiz. pair imperf. btwn. 250.00
358 A50 10c red .45 .45
359 A50 20c yellow brn .60 .60
a. 20c deep brown 2.25 2.25
b. Horiz. pair, imperf. btwn. 250.00
360 A50 50c claret 2.50 3.50
a. Horiz. pair, imperf. btwn. 250.00
361 A50 1p brt violet 14.00 16.00
a. Horiz. pair, imperf. btwn. 250.00
Nos. 354-361 (8) 40.60 26.85
Set, never hinged 60.00

Nos. 354-361 (called "Transitorios") exist imperf. but were not regularly issued.

Many copies do not have gum because of a flood.

See Note after No. 465.

See No. 369. For overprints see Nos. 362-368, 559-565.

Overprinted in Black

1914

362 A50 1c deep blue 200.00 175.00
Never hinged 200.00
363 A50 2c yellow green 225.00 200.00
Never hinged 225.00
364 A50 4c blue violet 250.00 300.00
Never hinged 300.00
365 A50 5c gray green 35.00 50.00
Never hinged 25.00
a. Horiz. pair, imperf. btwn. 550.00
366 A50 10c red 150.00 150.00
Never hinged 125.00
367 A50 20c yellow brn *2,500. 2,500.*
368 A50 50c claret *3,500. 3,500.*

Values are for copies with design close to, or just touching, the perfs.

Excellent counterfeits of this overprint exist.

Redrawn
"CINCO CENTAVOS" 16x2½mm

1914 *Perf. 12*

369 A51 5c gray green 1.00 .35
Never hinged .25

Imperfs are printers' waste.

Regular Issue of 1910 Overprinted in Violet, Magenta, Black or Green

1914 Wmk. 155 *Perf. 14*

370 A36 1c dull violet 1.50 .60
a. Booklet pane of 4 75.00
371 A37 2c green 3.00 1.25
a. Booklet pane of 8 75.00
372 A38 3c orange brn 3.00 1.25
373 A39 4c carmine 5.00 2.00
374 A40 5c orange 1.00 .35
a. Booklet pane of 8 60.00
375 A41 10c blue & org 6.00 2.00
376 A42 15c gray bl & cl 10.00 3.00
377 A43 20c red & blue 20.00 6.00
378 A44 50c red brn & blk 24.00 8.00
379 A45 1p blue & blk 50.00 10.00
380 A46 5p carmine & blk 175.00 150.00
Nos. 370-380 (11) 298.50 184.45
Set, never hinged 275.00

Overprinted On Postage Due Stamps of 1908

381 D1 1c blue 25.00 30.00
382 D1 2c blue 25.00 30.00
383 D1 4c blue 25.00 30.00
384 D1 5c blue 25.00 30.00
385 D1 10c blue 25.00 30.00
Nos. 381-385 (5) 125.00 150.00
Set, never hinged 110.00

This overprint is found double, inverted, sideways and in pairs with and without the overprint.

There are two or more types of this overprint.

The Postage Due Stamps and similar groups of them which follow were issued and used as regular postage stamps.

Values are for copies where the overprint is clear enough to be expertised.

Counterfeits abound.

A52

A53

1914 Unwmk. Litho. *Perf. 12*

386 A52 1c pale blue .35 .50
387 A52 2c light green .35 .45
388 A52 3c orange .50 .50
389 A52 5c deep rose .50 .35
390 A52 10c rose .70 .85
391 A52 15c rose lilac 1.20 1.75
392 A52 50c yellow 2.00 2.50
a. 50c ocher 1.75
393 A52 1p violet 8.50 12.00
Nos. 386-393 (8) 14.10 18.90
Set, never hinged 18.00

Nos. 386-393, are known imperforate.

This set is usually called the Denver Issue because it was printed there.

See Note after No. 465.

For overprints and surcharges see Nos. 566-573, 591-592.

Revenue Stamps Used for Postage

1914, July *Perf. 12*

393A A53 1c rose 40.00
393B A53 2c lt green 35.00
393C A53 3c lt orange 75.00
393D A53 5c red 15.00
393E A53 10c gray green 70.00
Nos. 393A-393E (5) 235.00

Nos. 393A-393E were used in the northeast. Values are for examples with postal cancellations.

Unused copies are to be considered as revenues.

Pres. Madero

Stamps in this design, featuring Pres. Madero, within a frame very similar to that of the Denver Issue (Nos. 386-393), were ordered in 1915 by Francisco Villa, to be used by the Constitutionalist government. Five values (1c green, 2c brown, 3c carmine, 5c blue, and 10c yellow) were printed by Ellis Brothers & Co., El Paso, Texas. By the time of the stamps' arrival in Mexico City, the Constitutionalist regime had fallen, and the new Conventionist government returned them to the printer, who later sold the unissued stamps within the philatelic market. Value, set $10.

Background as A55 — A54

A55

Nos. 394-410 Issued Without Gum

1914 *Imperf.*

Values and Inscriptions in Black

Inscribed "SONORA"

394 A54 1c blue & red .35 .35
a. Double seal
b. Without seal 20.00
395 A54 2c green & org .35 .35
a. Without seal 100.00
396 A54 5c yellow & grn .35 .35
a. 5c orange & green 1.50 1.25
b. Without seal *300.00*
397 A54 10c lt bl & red 3.50 1.75
a. 10c blue & red 40.00 15.00
398 A54 20c yellow & grn 1.75 2.00
399 A54 20c orange & bl 15.00 17.50
400 A54 50c green & org 1.25 1.25
Nos. 394-400 (7) 22.55 23.55

Shades. Stamps of type A54 are usually termed the "Coach Seal Issue."

Inscribed "DISTRITO SUR DE LA BAJA CAL"

401 A54 1c yellow & blue 2.00 *30.00*
a. Without seal 50.00
402 A54 2c gray & ol grn 2.50 *25.00*
403 A54 5c olive & rose 2.00 *20.00*
a. Without seal 50.00
404 A54 10c pale red & dl vio 2.00 *20.00*
a. Without seal 50.00
Nos. 401-404 (4) 8.50 95.00

Counterfeit cancellations exist.

Inscribed "SONORA"

405 A55 1c blue & red 6.00
a. Without seal 50.00
406 A55 2c green & org .50
407 A55 5c yellow & grn .50 *2.50*
a. Without seal 75.00
408 A55 10c blue & red .50 *2.50*
409 A55 20c yellow & grn 75.00 *15.00*
a. Without seal 95.00
b. Double seal *80.00*
Nos. 405-409 (5) *82.50 20.00*

With "PLATA" added to the inscription

410 A55 1c blue & red 1.00
a. "PLATA" inverted 60.00
b. Pair, one without "PLATA" 15.00
411 A55 10c blue & red 1.00
412 A55 20c yellow & grn 2.50
a. "PLATA" double 50.00
413 A55 50c gray grn & org 1.75
a. Without seal 1.00
b. As "a," "P" of "PLATA" missing 150.00
Nos. 410-413 (4) 6.25

Stamps of type A55 are termed the "Anvil Seal Issue".
Nos. 394-413 were issued without gum.
Nos. 410-413 were not placed in use.

Oaxaca

Coat of Arms — A56

5c:
Type I — Thick numerals, 2mm wide.
Type II — Thin numerals, 1½mm wide.

Perf. 8½ to 14

1915 Typo. Unwmk.

414 A56 1c dull violet 2.00 1.25
415 A56 2c emerald 3.00 2.25
a. Inverted numeral 30.00
e. Numeral omitted 35.00
416 A56 3c red brown 4.00 3.50
b. Inverted numeral 30.00
417 A56 5c org (type I) 75.00 75.00
a. Tête bêche pair 175.00 175.00
418 A56 5c org (type II) .50 .75
a. Types I and II in pair 70.00
419 A56 10c blue & car 4.00 4.00
Nos. 414-419 (6) 88.50 86.75
Set, never hinged 35.00

Many printing errors, imperfs and part perfs exist. Mostly these are printers' waste, private reprints or counterfeits.
Nos. 414-419 printed on backs of post office receipt forms.

Regular Issues of 1899-1910 Overprinted in Black

1914 Wmk. 155 *Perf. 14*

On Issues of 1899-1903

420 A28 5c orange
421 A30 15c lav & claret 250.00 250.00
Never hinged 200.00
422 A31 20c rose & dk bl *1,000.* 500.00

Counterfeits exist.

The listing of No. 420 is being re-evaluated. The Catalogue Editors would appreciate any information on the stamp.

On Issue of 1910

423 A36 1c dull violet .35 .35
424 A37 2c green .35 .35
425 A38 3c orange brown .40 .40
426 A39 4c carmine .50 .50
427 A40 5c orange .35 .35
428 A41 10c blue & orange .35 .35
429 A42 15c gray bl & claret .70 .60
430 A43 20c red & blue .75 .70

Overprinted

431 A44 50c red brn & blk 1.75 1.50
432 A45 1p blue & blk 7.50 5.00
433 A46 5p carmine & blk 40.00 30.00
Nos. 423-433 (11) 53.00 40.10
Set, never hinged 75.00

In the first setting of the overprint on 1c to 20c, the variety "GONSTITUCIONALISTA" occurs 4 times in each sheet of 100. In the second setting it occurs on the last stamp in each row of 10.
The overprint exists reading downward on Nos. 423-430; inverted on Nos. 431-433; double on Nos. 423-425, 427.

See Note after No. 465.

Postage Due Stamps of 1908 Overprinted

434 D1 1c blue 4.75 5.00
435 D1 2c blue 6.00 5.00
436 D1 4c blue 25.00 25.00
437 D1 5c blue 25.00 25.00
438 D1 10c blue 5.50 5.00
a. Double overprint
Nos. 434-438 (5) 66.25 65.00
Set, never hinged 50.00

Preceding Issues Overprinted

This is usually called the "Villa" monogram. Counterfeits abound.

1915

On Issue of 1899

439 A25 1c green *210.00*
440 A26 2c vermilion *210.00*
441 A27 3c orange brn *175.00*
442 A28 5c dark blue *210.00*
443 A29 10c violet & org *210.00*
444 A30 15c lav & claret *750.00* 750.00
445 A31 20c rose & bl *1,000.* —
446 A32 50c red lil & blk *500.00* —
447 A33 1p blue & blk *500.00*
448 A34 5p car & blk *750.00* —
Nos. 439-448 (10) *4,515.*

On Issue of 1903

449 A25 1c violet *200.00*
450 A26 2c green *200.00*
451 A35 4c carmine *200.00*
452 A28 5c orange 45.00
a. Inverted overprint *75.00*
453 A29 10c blue & org *750.00* —
454 A32 50c car & blk —
Nos. 449-454 (5) *1,395.*

In Sept. 1915 Postmaster Hinojosa ordered a special printing of Nos. 439-454 (as valued) for sale to collectors. Earlier a small quantity of Nos. 444-445, 448 and 452-454 was regularly issued. They are hard to distinguish and sell for much more. Counterfeits abound.

On Issue of 1910

455 A36 1c dull violet .85 1.00
456 A37 2c green .40 .60
457 A38 3c orange brown .60 .75
458 A39 4c carmine 4.00 4.50
459 A40 5c orange .35 .35
460 A41 10c blue & orange 7.00 7.50
461 A42 15c gray bl & cl 3.00 4.00
462 A43 20c red & blue 5.50 7.00
463 A44 50c red brn & blk 13.00 14.00
464 A45 1p blue & blk 17.00 20.00
465 A46 5p carmine & blk *150.00*
Never hinged 300.00
Nos. 455-464 (10) 51.70 59.70
Nos. 455-464, never hinged 75.00

Nos. 455-465 are known with overprint inverted, double and other variations. Most were ordered by Postmaster General Hinojosa for philtelic purposes. They were sold at a premium. This applies to Nos. 354-361, 386-393, 431-433 with this monogram as well.

Overprinted On Postage Due Stamps of 1908

466 D1 1c blue 15.00 20.00
467 D1 2c blue 15.00 20.00
468 D1 4c blue 15.00 20.00
469 D1 5c blue 15.00 20.00
470 D1 10c blue 15.00 20.00
Nos. 466-470 (5) 75.00 100.00
Set, never hinged 60.00

Nos. 466 to 470 are known with inverted overprint. All other values of the 1899 and 1903 issues exist with this overprint. See note after No. 465.

Issues of 1899-1910 Overprinted

This is called the "Carranza" or small monogram. Counterfeits abound.

On Issues of 1899-1903

482 A28 5c orange 30.00 20.00
Never hinged 25.00
483 A30 15c lav & claret 125.00 80.00
Never hinged 125.00

On Issue of 1910

484 A36 1c dull violet .70 .70
485 A37 2c green .70 .60
486 A38 3c orange brn .75 .75
487 A39 4c carmine 2.00 2.00
488 A40 5c orange .35 .35
489 A41 10c blue & org 1.50 1.50
a. Double ovpt., one invtd. 25.00
490 A42 15c gray bl & cl 1.50 1.50
491 A43 20c red & blue 1.50 1.50
492 A44 50c red brn & blk 10.00 10.00
493 A45 1p blue & blk 15.00 15.00
494 A46 5p car & blk 150.00 *150.00*
Nos. 484-494 (11) 184.00 *183.90*
Set, never hinged 250.00

All values exist with inverted overprint; all but 5p with double overprint.

Overprinted On Postage Due Stamps of 1908

495 D1 1c blue 20.00 25.00
496 D1 2c blue 20.00 25.00
497 D1 4c blue 20.00 25.00
498 D1 5c blue 20.00 25.00
499 D1 10c blue 20.00 25.00
Nos. 495-499 (5) 100.00 125.00
Set, never hinged 75.00

Nos. 495-499 exist with inverted overprint.
It is stated that, in parts of Mexico occupied by the revolutionary forces, instructions were given to apply a distinguishing overprint to all stamps found in the post offices. This overprint was usually some arrangement or abbreviation of "Gobierno Constitucionalista". Such overprints as were specially authorized or were in general use in large sections of the country are listed. Numerous other handstamped overprints were used in one town or locality. They were essentially military faction control marks necessitated in most instances by the chaotic situation following the split between Villa and Carranza. The fact that some were often struck in a variety of colors and positions suggests the influence of philatelists.

Coat of Arms A57

Statue of Cuauhtémoc A58

Ignacio Zaragoza A59

José María Morelos A60

Francisco Madero — A61

Benito Juárez — A62

1915 Unwmk. Litho. *Rouletted 14*

500 A57 1c violet .20 .20
501 A58 2c green .25 .20
502 A59 3c brown .50 .25
503 A60 4c carmine .50 .25
504 A61 5c orange .75 .25
505 A62 10c ultra .35 .30
Nos. 500-505 (6) 2.55 1.45
Set, never hinged 3.00

Nos. 500-505 exists imperf.; some exist imperf. vertically or horizontally; some with rouletting and perforation combined. These probably were not regularly issued in these forms.
See Nos. 506-511. For overprints see Nos. O86-O97.

Map of Mexico — A63

Veracruz Lighthouse A64

Post Office, Mexico, D.F. — A65

TEN CENTAVOS:
Type I — Size 19½x24mm. Crossed lines on coat.
Type II — Size 19x23½mm. Diagonal lines only on coat.

1915-16 *Perf. 12*

506 A57 1c violet .40 .25
507 A58 2c green .40 .30
508 A59 3c brown .50 .30
509 A60 4c carmine .50 .35
a. "CEATRO" 7.50 7.50
510 A61 5c orange .75 .35
511 A62 10c ultra, type I 1.00 .35
a. 10c ultra, type II .50 .25

Engr.

512 A63 40c slate .75 .35
513 A64 1p brown & blk 1.00 .75
a. Inverted center 200.00
514 A65 5p cl & ultra ('16) 10.00 4.00
a. Inverted center 400.00
Nos. 506-514 (9) 15.30 7.00
Set, never hinged 20.00

Nos. 507-508, 510-514, exist imperf; Nos. 513-514 imperf with inverted center. These varieties were not regularly issued.
See Nos. 626-628, 647. For overprints see Nos. O92-O100, O121-O123, O132-O133, O142-O144, O153-O154, O162-O164, O174, O188, O193, O207, O222.

Issues of 1899-1910 Overprinted in Blue, Red or Black

1916 Wmk. 155 *Perf. 14*

On Issues of 1899-1903

515 A28 5c orange (Bl) 125.00 175.00
Never hinged 150.00
516 A30 15c lav & cl (Bl) 475.00 475.00
Never hinged 600.00

On Issue of 1910

517 A36 1c dull vio (R) 10.00 *10.00*
518 A37 2c green (R) .50 .35
519 A38 3c orange brn (Bl) .55 .40
a. Double overprint 500.00
520 A39 4c carmine (Bl) 6.00 *8.00*
521 A40 5c orange (Bl) .25 .25
a. Double overprint 75.00
522 A41 10c blue & org (R) 1.25 1.50
523 A42 15c gray bl & cl (Bk) 1.75 3.00
524 A43 20c red & bl (Bk) 1.75 3.00
525 A44 50c red brn & blk (R) 8.50 5.00
526 A45 1p blue & blk (R) 15.00 6.50
527 A46 5p car & blk (R) 175.00 175.00
Nos. 517-527 (11) 220.55 213.00
Nos. 517-527, never hinged 275.00

Nos. 519-524 exist with this overprint (called the "Corbata") reading downward and Nos. 525-527 with it inverted. Of these varieties only Nos. 519-521 were regularly issued.

On Nos. 423-430

528 A36 1c dull vio (R) 2.50 4.00
529 A37 2c green (R) .75 .60
530 A38 3c orange brn (Bl) .60 .60
531 A39 4c carmine (Bl) .60 .60
532 A40 5c orange (Bl) 1.00 .30

533 A41 10c blue & org (R) .75 .60
534 A42 15c gray bl & cl (Bk) .80 .80
535 A43 20c red & bl (Bk) .80 .80

On Nos. 431-433 in Red

536 A44 50c red brn & blk 7.50 6.00
537 A45 1p blue & blk 16.00 16.00
538 A46 5p carmine & blk 150.00 140.00
a. Tablet inverted 300.00
Nos. 528-538 (11) 181.30 170.30
Nos. Set, never hinged 250.00

Nos. 529 to 535 are known with the overprint reading downward and Nos. 536 to 538 with it inverted.

On No. 482

539 A28 5c orange (Bl) 225.00 *225.00*

On Nos. 484-494

540 A36 1c dull vio (R) 5.00 *5.00*
541 A37 2c green (R) .60 .60
a. Monogram inverted 80.00
542 A38 3c orange brn (Bl) .50 .60
543 A39 4c carmine (Bl) 7.50 9.00
544 A40 5c orange (Bl) .90 .25
545 A41 10c blue & org (R) 1.50 2.00
546 A42 15c gray bl & cl (Bk) 1.25 .60
a. Tablet double *500.00 500.00*
b. Monogram double *500.00*
547 A43 20c red & bl (Bk) 1.25 1.10
548 A44 50c red brn & blk (R) 7.50 9.00
a. Monogram inverted 65.00
b. Tablet inverted 75.00
549 A45 1p blue & blk (R) 11.00 12.00
a. Tablet double 175.00
b. Monogram inverted 60.00
Nos. 539-549 (11) 262.00 *265.15*
Set, never hinged 150.00

Nos. 541-547 exist with overprint reading downward. A few 5p were overprinted for the Post Office collection.

On No. 453

550 A28 5c orange (Bl) 125.00 *125.00*
Never hinged 200.00

On Nos. 455-462

551 A36 1c dull vio (R) 11.00 *15.00*
552 A37 2c green (R) 1.50 .90
553 A38 3c org brn (Bl) 3.25 *4.50*
554 A39 4c carmine (Bl) 13.00 *15.00*
555 A40 5c orange (Bl) 4.50 *6.00*
556 A41 10c bl & org (R) 12.00 *14.00*
a. Monogram inverted *250.00*
557 A42 15c gray bl & cl (Bk) 12.00 *14.00*
a. Monogram inverted *250.00*
558 A43 20c red & bl (Bk) 12.00 *14.00*
a. Monogram inverted *250.00*
Nos. 550-558 (9) 194.25 *208.40*
Set, never hinged 325.00

Stamps of 50c, 1p and 5p were overprinted for the Post Office collection but were not regularly issued.

Issues of 1914 Overprinted

On "Transitorio" Issue

Rouletted 9½x14

Unwmk.

559 A50 1c dp blue (R) 24.00 24.00
Never hinged 500.00
560 A50 2c yellow grn (R) 12.00 18.00
Never hinged 18.00
561 A50 4c blue vio (R) 425.00 375.00
Never hinged 500.00
562 A50 10c red (Bl) 2.00 6.00
Never hinged 2.50
a. Vertical overprint 125.00
663 A50 20c yellow brn (Bl) 3.00 6.00
Never hinged 5.00
564 A50 50c claret (Bl) 15.00 20.00
Never hinged 30.00
565 A50 1p violet (Bl) 24.00 24.00
Never hinged 75.00
a. Horiz. pair, imperf. btwn.
Nos. 559-565 (7) 505.00 473.00

Overprinted in Blue On "Denver" Issue

Perf. 12

566 A52 1c pale blue 3.75
567 A52 2c lt green 3.75
568 A52 3c orange .45 *5.00*
569 A52 5c deep rose .45 *5.00*
570 A52 10c rose .45 *5.00*
571 A52 15c rose lilac .45 *5.00*
572 A52 50c yellow 1.10 *15.00*
573 A52 1p violet 9.50 *25.00*
Nos. 566-573 (8) 19.90
Set, never hinged 25.00

Many of the foregoing stamps exist with the "G. P. DE M." overprint printed in other colors than those listed. These "trial color" stamps were not regularly on sale at post offices but were available for postage and used copies are known.

There appears to have been speculation in Nos. 516, 517, 520, 528, 539, 540, 543, 566, and 567. A small quantity of each of these stamps was sold at post offices but subsequently they could be obtained only from officials or their agents at advanced prices.

Venustiano Carranza A66

Coat of Arms A67

1916, June 1 Engr. *Perf. 12*

574 A66 10c blue 1.50 1.00
a. Imperf., pair 25.00
575 A66 10c lilac brown 14.00 15.00
a. Imperf., pair 50.00
Nos. 574-575, never hinged 20.00

Entry of Carranza into Mexico, D.F.

Stamps of type A66 with only horizontal lines in the background of the oval are essays.

1916

576 A67 1c lilac .35 .25
Never hinged .25

Issue of 1910 Surcharged in Various Colors

This overprint is called the "Barril."

1916 Wmk. 155 *Perf. 14*

577 A36 5c on 1c dl vio (Br) .50 .50
a. Vertical surcharge 1.25 1.25
b. Double surcharge 150.00
578 A36 10c on 1c dl vio (Bl) .50 .50
a. Double surcharge 100.00
579 A40 20c on 5c org (Br) .50 .50
a. Double surcharge 90.00
580 A40 25c on 5c org (G) .40 .50
581 A37 60c on 2c grn (R) 25.00 20.00
Nos. 577-581 (5) 26.90 22.00
Set, never hinged 30.00

On Nos. 423-424, 427

582 A36 5c on 1c (Br) .50 .50
a. Double tablet, one vertical 100.00
b. Inverted tablet 250.00 250.00
583 A36 10c on 1c (Bl) 1.00 1.00
584 A40 25c on 5c (G) .50 .50
a. Inverted tablet 225.00 225.00
585 A37 60c on 2c (R) 425.00 *425.00*
Never hinged 350.00
Nos. 582-584, never hinged 3.00

No. 585 was not regularly issued.

The variety "GONSTITUCIONALISTA" is found on Nos. 582 to 585.

On No. 459

586 A40 25c on 5c org (G) .25 .25
Never hinged .30

On Nos. 484-485, 488

587 A36 5c on 1c (Br) 15.00 20.00
a. Vertical tablet 100.00 125.00
588 A36 10c on 1c (Bl) 5.00 7.50
589 A40 25c on 5c (G) 1.00 1.50
a. Inverted tablet 225.00
590 A37 60c on 2c (R) 450.00
Never hinged 400.00
Nos. 587-589, never hinged 30.00

No. 590 was not regularly issued.

Surcharged on "Denver" Issue of 1914

1916 Unwmk. *Perf. 12*

591 A52 60c on 1c pale bl (Br) 3.00 6.00
592 A52 60c on 2c lt grn (Br) 3.00 6.00
a. Inverted surcharge *1,250.*
Set, never hinged 10.00

Postage Due Stamps Surcharged Like Nos. 577-581

1916 Wmk. 155 *Perf. 14*

593 D1 5c on 1c blue (Br) 2.50
594 D1 10c on 2c blue (V) 2.50
595 D1 20c on 4c blue (Br) 2.50
596 D1 25c on 5c blue (G) 2.50
597 D1 60c on 10c blue (R) 1.50
598 D1 1p on 1c blue (C) 1.50
599 D1 1p on 2c blue (C) 1.50
600 D1 1p on 4c blue (C) .80 .80
601 D1 1p on 5c blue (C) 2.50
602 D1 1p on 10c blue (C) 2.50
Nos. 593-602 (10) 20.30
Set, never hinged 40.00

There are numerous "trial colors" and "essays" of the overprints and surcharges on Nos. 577 to 602. They were available for postage though not regularly issued.

Postage Due Stamps Surcharged

1916

603 D1 2.50p on 1c blue 1.25 1.25
604 D1 2.50p on 2c blue 10.00
605 D1 2.50p on 4c blue 10.00 250.00
606 D1 2.50p on 5c blue 10.00
607 D1 2.50p on 10c blue 10.00
Nos. 603-607 (5) 41.25
Set, never hinged 100.00

Regular Issue

Ignacio Zaragoza A68

Ildefonso Vázquez A69

J. M. Pino Suárez A70

Jesús Carranza A71

Maclovio Herrera — A72

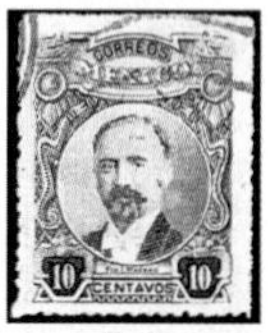

F. I. Madero — A73

Belisario Domínguez A74

Aquiles Serdán A75

Rouletted 14½

1917-20 Engr. Unwmk.

Thick Paper

608 A68 1c dull violet 2.00 1.00
Never hinged 2.50
609 A68 1c lilac gray ('20) 5.00 .75
Never hinged 2.00
a. 1c gray ('20) 5.00 5.00
610 A69 2c gray green 1.50 .50
Never hinged 3.00
611 A70 3c bister brn 1.50 1.00
Never hinged 3.00
612 A71 4c carmine 2.50 1.00
Never hinged 7.50
613 A72 5c ultra 2.50 .50
Never hinged 3.25
a. Horiz. pair, imperf. btwn. 75.00
b. Imperf., pair 35.00 75.00
614 A73 10c blue 4.00 .50
Never hinged 5.00
a. Without imprint 7.50 1.00
Never hinged 12.00
615 A74 20c brown rose 40.00 2.00
Never hinged 60.00
a. 20c rose 40.00 2.00
Never hinged 70.00
616 A75 30c gray brown 90.00 3.00
Never hinged 200.00
617 A75 30c gray blk ('20) 100.00 4.00
Never hinged 250.00
Nos. 608-617 (10) 249.00 14.25

Perf. 12

Thick or Medium Paper

618 A68 1c dull violet 35.00 25.00
Never hinged 100.00
619 A69 2c gray green 10.00 6.00
Never hinged 15.00
620 A70 3c bis brn ('17) 200.00 200.00
Never hinged 250.00
622 A72 5c ultra 5.00 .25
Never hinged 8.00
623 A73 10c blue ('17) 5.00 .25
Never hinged 7.00
a. Without imprint ('17) 20.00 15.00
Never hinged 35.00
624 A74 20c rose ('20) 140.00 3.00
Never hinged 350.00
625 A75 30c gray blk ('20) 140.00 2.00
Never hinged 350.00

Thin or Medium Paper

626 A63 40c violet 65.00 1.00
Never hinged 200.00
627 A64 1p blue & blk 50.00 1.50
Never hinged 150.00
a. With center of 5p 450.00
b. 1p bl & dark blue (error) 500.00 20.00
c. Vert. pair, imperf. btwn. 250.00
628 A65 5p green & blk 1.50 *10.00*
Never hinged 1.75
a. With violet or red control number 25.00 10.00
b. With center of 1p 450.00

The 1, 2, 3, 5 and 10c are known on thin paper perforated. It is stated they were printed for Postal Union and "specimen" purposes.

All values exist imperf; these are not known to have been regularly issued. Nos. 627a and 628b were not regularly issued.

All values except 3c have an imprint.

For overprints and surcharges see Nos. B1-B2, O113-O165.

Meeting of Iturbide and Guerrero A77

Entering City of Mexico A78

1921

632 A77 10c blue & brn 22.50 3.00
Never hinged 75.00
a. Center inverted *25,000.*
633 A78 10p black brn & blk 20.00 35.00
Never hinged 25.00

Commemorating the meeting of Augustin de Iturbide and Vicente Guerrero and the entry into City of Mexico in 1821.

For overprint see No. O194.

"El Salto de Agua," Public Fountain A79

Pyramid of the Sun at Teotihuacán A80

Chapultepec Castle A81

Columbus Monument A82

Juárez Colonnade, Mexico, D. F. A83

Monument to Josefa Ortiz de Dominguez A84

Cuauhtémoc Monument — A85

1923 Unwmk. *Rouletted 14½*

634	A79	2c scarlet	2.00	.20
635	A80	3c bister brn	2.00	.25
636	A81	4c green	2.50	.75
637	A82	5c orange	5.00	.20
638	A83	10c brown	3.75	.20
639	A85	10c claret	3.50	.20
640	A84	20c dk blue	50.00	1.75
641	A85	30c dk green	32.50	2.00
		Nos. 634-641 (8)	101.25	5.55
		Set, never hinged	150.00	

See Nos. 642-646, 650-657, 688-692, 727A, 735A-736. For overprints see Nos. O166-O173, O178-O181, O183-O187, O196-O197, O199-O206, O210, O212-O214, O217-O222.

Communications Building — A87

Palace of Fine Arts (National Theater) A88

Two types of 1p:
I — Eagle on palace dome.
II — Without eagle.

1923 Wmk. 156 *Perf. 12*

642	A79	2c scarlet	10.00	10.00
643	A81	4c green	1.40	.30
644	A82	5c orange	10.00	7.00
645	A85	10c brown lake	12.50	6.00
646	A83	30c dark green	.95	.20
647	A63	40c violet	1.25	.25
648	A87	50c olive brn	1.00	.25
649	A88	1p red brn & bl (I)	1.00	1.00
a.		Type II	3.00	*10.00*
		Nos. 642-649 (8)	38.10	25.00
		Set, never hinged	45.00	

Most of Nos. 642-649 are known imperforate or part perforate but probably were not regularly issued.
For overprints see Nos. O175-O176, O189-O190, O208-O209, O223.

1923-34 *Rouletted 14½*

650	A79	2c scarlet	.25	.20
651	A80	3c bis brn ('27)	.25	.20
652	A81	4c green	45.00	35.00
653	A82	4c green ('27)	.25	.20
654	A82	5c orange	.25	.20
655	A85	10c lake	.25	.20
656	A84	20c deep blue	.75	.30
657	A83	30c dk green ('34)	.75	.30
		Nos. 650-657 (8)	47.75	36.60
		Set, never hinged	110.00	

Nos. 650 to 657 inclusive exist imperforate.

Medallion A90

Map of Americas A91

Francisco García y Santos — A92

Post Office, Mexico, D. F. — A93

1926 *Perf. 12*

658	A90	2c red	2.50	1.00
659	A91	4c green	2.50	1.00
660	A90	5c orange	2.50	.75
661	A91	10c brown red	4.00	1.00
662	A92	20c dk blue	4.00	1.25
663	A92	30c dk green	7.00	4.00
664	A92	40c violet	12.50	3.00
665	A93	1p brown & blue	25.00	10.00
a.		1p red & blue	35.00	15.00
		Nos. 658-665 (8)	60.00	22.00
		Set, never hinged	90.00	

Pan-American Postal Congress.
Nos. 658-665 were also printed in black, on unwatermarked paper, for presentation to delegates to the Universal Postal Congress at London in 1929. Remainders were overprinted in 1929 for use as airmail official stamps, and are listed as Nos. CO3-CO10.
For overprints see Nos. 667-674, 675A-682, CO3-CO10.

Benito Juárez — A94

1926 *Rouletted 14½*

666	A94	8c orange	.30	.20
		Never hinged	.40	

For overprint see No. O182.

Nos. 658-665 Overprinted

1930 *Perf. 12*

667	A90	2c red	4.00	2.25
a.		Reading down	15.00	15.00
668	A91	4c green	4.00	2.50
a.		Reading down	15.00	15.00
669	A90	5c orange	4.00	2.00
a.		Reading down	15.00	35.00
b.		Double overprint	75.00	*75.00*
670	A91	10c brown red	7.50	2.50
671	A92	20c dk blue	9.50	3.50
672	A92	30c dk green	8.50	4.00
a.		Reading down	10.00	12.00
673	A92	40c violet	12.50	8.50
a.		Reading down	47.50	50.00
674	A93	1p red brn & bl	11.00	7.00
a.		Double overprint	250.00	
b.		Triple overprint	200.00	
		Nos. 667-674 (8)	61.00	32.25
		Set, never hinged	125.00	

Overprint horizontal on 1p.

Arms of Puebla — A95

1931, May 1 Engr.

675	A95	10c dk bl & dk brn	3.00	.50
		Never hinged	5.00	

400th anniversary of Puebla.

Nos. 658-665a Overprinted

1931

676	A91	4c green	65.00	70.00
677	A90	5c orange	12.00	17.00
678	A91	10c brown red	12.00	14.00
679	A92	20c dk blue	12.00	18.00
680	A92	30c dk green	21.00	25.00
681	A92	40c violet	30.00	35.00
682	A93	1p brown & bl	27.50	35.00
a.		1p red & blue	40.00	45.00
		Nos. 676-682 (7)	179.50	214.00
		Set, never hinged	350.00	

Overprint horizontal on 1p.
Nos. 676 and 682 are not known to have been sold to the public through post offices.
Forgeries of overprint exist.

Bartolomé de las Casas A96

Emblem of Mexican Society of Geography and Statistics A97

1933, Mar. 3 Engr. *Rouletted 14½*

683	A96	15c dark blue	.30	.20
		Never hinged	.25	

For overprint see No. O215.

1933, Oct. *Rouletted 14½*

684	A97	2c deep green	1.50	.60
685	A97	5c dark brown	1.75	.50
686	A97	10c dark blue	.75	.20
687	A97	1p dark violet	95.00	65.00
		Nos. 684-687 (4)	99.00	66.30
		Set, never hinged	75.00	

XXI Intl. Congress of Statistics and the 1st centenary of the Mexican Society of Geography and Statistics.

Types of 1923 and PT1

1934 *Perf. 10½, 11 (4c)*

687A	PT1	1c brown	1.00	.30
688	A79	2c scarlet	.35	.20
689	A82	4c green	.35	.20
690	A85	10c brown lake	.35	.20
691	A84	20c dark blue	.75	.75
692	A83	30c dk blue grn	1.00	1.25
		Nos. 687A-692 (6)	3.80	2.90
		Set, never hinged	4.50	

See 2nd note after Postal Tax stamp No. RA3.

Indian Archer — A99

Indian — A100

Woman Decorating Pottery A101

Peon A102

Potter A103

Sculptor A104

Craftsman A105

Offering to the Gods A106

Worshiper — A107

1934, Sept. 1 Wmk. 156 *Perf. 10½*

698	A99	5c dk green	3.75	1.00
699	A100	10c brown lake	5.00	1.50
700	A101	20c ultra	12.00	8.00
701	A102	30c black	24.00	20.00
702	A103	40c black brn	35.00	25.00
703	A104	50c dull blue	70.00	70.00
704	A105	1p brn lake & blk	140.00	70.00
705	A106	5p brn blk & red brn	290.00	290.00
706	A107	10p brown & vio	1,000.	1,100.
a.		Unwatermarked	*3,250.*	
		Never hinged	5,000.	
		Nos. 698-706 (9)	1,579.	1,585.
		Set, never hinged	1,650.	

National University.
The design of the 1p is wider than the rest of the set. Values are for copies with perfs just touching the design.
See Nos. C54-C61, RA13B.

Yalalteca Indian — A108

Tehuana Indian — A109

Arch of the Revolution A110

Tower of Los Remedios A111

Cross of Palenque A112

Independence Monument A113

Independence Monument, Puebla
A114

Monument to the Heroic Cadets
A115

Stone of Tizoc — A116

Ruins of Mitla — A117

Coat of Arms
A118

Charro
A119

Imprint: "Oficina Impresora de Hacienda-Mexico"

1934-40 Wmk. 156 *Perf. 10½*
Size: 20x26mm

707 A108 1c orange .65 .20
a. Unwmkd. —
708 A109 2c green .65 .20
a. Unwmkd. 3.75 3.75
709 A110 4c carmine .90 .20
710 A111 5c olive brn .65 .20
a. Unwmkd. 400.00 350.00
711 A112 10c dk blue .80 .20
712 A112 10c violet ('35) 1.25 .20
a. Unwmkd. 200.00 40.00
713 A113 15c lt blue 4.00 .30
714 A114 20c gray green 1.90 .20
a. 20c olive green 2.00 .20
715 A114 20c ultra ('35) 1.40 .20
a. Unwmkd. 150.00
716 A115 30c lake .90 .20
a. Unwmkd. 350.00
716B A115 30c lt ultra ('40) 1.00 .20
717 A116 40c red brown 1.00 .20
718 A117 50c grnsh black .90 .20
a. Imperf., pair 110.00
b. Unwmkd. 375.00
719 A118 1p dk brn & org 2.50 .20
a. Imperf., pair 350.00
720 A119 5p org & vio 7.75 .75
Nos. 707-720 (15) 26.25 3.65
Set, never hinged 355.00

No. 718a was not regularly issued.
The existence of No. 707a has been questioned.
See Nos. 729-733, 733B, 735, 784-788, 795A-800A, 837-838, 840-841, 844, 846-851.
For overprints see Nos. 728, O224-O232.

Tractor — A120

1935, Apr. 1 Wmk. 156 *Perf. 10½*
721 A120 10c violet 4.00 .50
Never hinged 5.00

Industrial census of Apr. 10, 1935.

Arms of Chiapas
A121

Emiliano Zapata
A122

1935, Sept. 14
722 A121 10c dark blue .50 .20
Never hinged .75
a. Unwmkd. 125.00 100.00

The 111th anniversary of the joining of the state of Chiapas with the federal republic of Mexico. See No. 734.

1935, Nov. 20 Wmk. 156
723 A122 10c violet .75 .20
Never hinged 1.00

25th anniversary of the Plan of Ayala.

US and Mexico Joined by Highways
A123

Matalote Bridge
A124

View of Nuevo Laredo Highway — A125

1936 Wmk. 248 *Perf. 14*
725 A123 5c blue grn & rose .35 .25
726 A124 10c slate bl & blk .50 .25
727 A125 20c brn & dk grn 1.50 1.00
Nos. 725-727,C77-C79 (6) 3.60 2.40
Set, never hinged 4.50

Opening of the Mexico City - Nuevo Laredo Highway.

Monument Type of 1923

1936 Wmk. 248 Engr. *Perf. 10½*
727A A85 10c brown lake *2,500.* 650.00

No. 712 Overprinted in Green

1936, Dec. 15 Wmk. 156
728 A112 10c violet .60 .50
Never hinged .75

1st National Congress of Industrial Hygiene and Medicine.

Type of 1934
Redrawn size: 17½x21mm
Imprint: "Talleres de Imp. de Est. y Valores-Mexico"

1937 Photo. Wmk. 156 *Perf. 14*
729 A108 1c orange .60 .20
a. Imperf., pair 12.50 12.50
Never hinged 25.00
730 A109 2c dull green .60 .20
a. Imperf., pair 12.50 12.50
Never hinged 30.00
731 A110 4c carmine .90 .20
a. Imperf., pair 12.50 12.50
Never hinged 30.00
732 A111 5c olive brn .80 .20
a. Unwmkd. *300.00*
733 A112 10c violet .70 .20
a. Imperf., pair 10.00 12.50
Never hinged 12.00
Nos. 729-733 (5) 3.60 1.00
Set, never hinged 4.25

The imperfs were not regularly issued.

Never hinged 2,000.

Types of 1934-35

1937 Wmk. 260
Size: 17½x21mm
733B A111 5c olive brown *3,200.* 250.00

1937 Engr. *Perf. 10½*
734 A121 10c dark blue 35.00 35.00
Never hinged 20.00

1937
Size: 20x26mm
735 A112 10c violet 350.00 55.00

Types of 1923

1934-37 Wmk. 260 *Perf. 10½*
735A A79 2c scarlet *4,000.*
735B A85 10c brown lake

Forged perforations exist.
The listing of No. 735B is being re-evaluated. The Catalogue Editors would appreciate any information on the stamp.

Rouletted 14½
736 A85 10c claret *4,500. 175.00*

Blacksmith
A126

Revolutionary Soldier
A127

Revolutionary Envoy — A128

Wmk. 156
1938, Mar. 26 Photo. *Perf. 14*
737 A126 5c black & brn .80 .20
738 A127 10c red brown .35 .25
739 A128 20c maroon & org 6.00 1.00
Nos. 737-739,C82-C84 (6) 13.15 4.90
Set, never hinged 20.00

Plan of Guadalupe, 25th anniv.

Arch of the Revolution
A129

Independence Monument
A131

Design: 10c, National Theater.

1938, July 1
740 A129 5c bister brn 4.25 .60
741 A129 5c red brown 25.00 2.25
742 A129 10c orange 15.00 11.00
743 A129 10c chocolate 1.00 .20
744 A131 20c brown lake 6.00 4.00
745 A131 20c black 18.00 15.00
Nos. 740-745 (6) 69.25 33.05
Nos. 740-745,C85-C90 (12) 129.60 63.30
Set, never hinged 125.00

16th Intl. Congress of Planning & Housing.

Arch of the Revolution
A132

1939, May 1
746 A132 10c Prus blue .65 .20
Nos. 746,C91-C93 (4) 4.75 2.95
Set, never hinged 9.75

New York World's Fair.

Indian — A133

1939, May 17
747 A133 10c red orange .45 .20
Nos. 747,C94-C96 (4) 5.55 2.75
Set, never hinged 12.10

Tulsa World Philatelic Convention.

Juan Zumárraga
A134

First Printing Shop in Mexico, 1539
A135

Design: 10c, Antonio de Mendoza.

1939, Sept. 1 Engr. *Perf. 10½*
748 A134 2c brown blk .75 .25
749 A135 5c green .75 .20
750 A134 10c red brown .25 .20
Nos. 748-750,C97-C99 (6) 3.75 1.75
Set, never hinged 4.75

400th anniversary of printing in Mexico.

View of Taxco
A137

Allegory of Agriculture
A138

10c, Two hands holding symbols of commerce.

1939, Oct. 1 Photo. *Perf. 12x13*
751 A137 2c dark carmine 1.25 .20
752 A138 5c sl grn & gray grn .25 .20
753 A138 10c org brn & buff .25 .20
Nos. 751-753,C100-C102 (6) 6.25 1.80
Set, never hinged 8.00

Census Taking.

"Penny Black" of 1840
A140

Roadside Monument
A141

1940, May *Perf. 14*
754 A140 5c black & lemon .90 .50
755 A140 10c dark violet .25 .20
756 A140 20c lt blue & car .25 .20
757 A140 1p gray & red org 7.00 4.00
758 A140 5p black & Prus bl 50.00 50.00
Nos. 754-758,C103-C107 (10) 141.00 115.90
Set, never hinged 210.00

Postage stamp centenary.

1940 **Wmk. 156**

759 A141 6c deep green	.50	.25
Never hinged	.70	

Opening of the highway between Mexico, D. F., and Guadalajara. See Nos. 789, 842.

Vasco de Quiroga — A142

Melchor Ocampo — A143

College Seal — A144

1940, July 15 **Engr.** ***Perf. 10½***

760 A142 2c violet	1.30	.50
761 A143 5c copper red	.80	.20
762 A144 10c olive bister	.80	.30
a. Imperf., pair	150.00	
Nos. 760-762,C108-C110 (6)	5.10	2.50
Set, never hinged	9.00	

Founding of the National College of San Nicolas de Hidalgo, 400th anniv.

Coat of Arms of Campeche A145

1940, Aug. 7 **Photo.** ***Perf. 12x13***

763 A145 10c bis brn & dk car	5.00	1.25
Never hinged	5.00	
Nos. 763,C111-C113 (4)	12.60	6.70
Set, never hinged	26.00	

400th anniversary of the founding of Campeche.

Man at Helm A146

1940, Dec. 1

764 A146 2c red org & blk	1.60	.60
765 A146 5c peacock bl & red brn	8.00	3.50
766 A146 10c slate grn & dk brn	4.00	.85
Nos. 764-766,C114-C116 (6)	21.00	9.45
Set, never hinged	45.00	

Inauguration of Pres. Manuel Avila Camacho.

SEMI-POSTAL STAMPS

Nos. 622, 614 Surcharged in Red

1918, Dec. 25 **Unwmk.** **Engr.** ***Perf. 12***

B1 A72 5c + 3c ultra	20.00	25.00

Rouletted 14½

B2 A73 10c + 5c blue	25.00	25.00
Set, never hinged	40.00	

AIR POST STAMPS

Eagle AP1

Unwmk.

1922, Apr. 2 **Engr.** ***Perf. 12***

C1 AP1 50c blue & red brn	67.50	50.00
Never hinged	75.00	
a. 50c dark blue & claret ('29)	90.00	90.00
Never hinged	125.00	

See #C2-C3. For overprints and surcharges see #C47-C48, CO1-CO2B, CO18-CO19, CO29.

1927, Oct. 13 **Wmk. 156**

C2 AP1 50c dk bl & red brn	.75	.25
Never hinged	1.00	
a. 50c dark blue & claret ('29)	.75	.25
Never hinged	1.25	
b. Vert. strip of 3, imperf. btwn.	*7,500.*	

The vignettes of Nos. C1a and C2a fluoresce a bright rose red under UV light.

1928

C3 AP1 25c brn car & gray brn	.45	.20
C4 AP1 25c dk grn & gray brn	.45	.20

On May 3, 1929, certain proofs or essays were sold at the post office in Mexico, D. F. They were printed in different colors from those of the regularly issued stamps. There were 7 varieties perf. and 2 imperf. and a total of 225 copies. They were sold with the understanding that they were for collections but the majority of them were used on air mail sent out that day.

Capt. Emilio Carranza and his Airplane "México Excelsior" AP2

1929, June 19

C5 AP2 5c ol grn & sepia	1.10	.65
C6 AP2 10c sep & brn red	1.25	.70
C7 AP2 15c vio & dk grn	3.00	1.25
C8 AP2 20c brown & blk	1.25	.75
C9 AP2 50c brn red & blk	7.50	5.00
C10 AP2 1p black & brn	15.00	10.00
Nos. C5-C10 (6)	29.10	18.35
Set, never hinged	50.00	

1st anniv. of death of Carranza (1905-28). For overprints see Nos. C29-C36, C40-C44.

Coat of Arms and Airplane AP3

1929-34 ***Perf. 11½, 12***

C11 AP3 10c violet	.35	.20
C12 AP3 15c carmine	1.35	.20
C13 AP3 20c brown olive	37.50	1.25
C14 AP3 30c gray black	.20	.20
C15 AP3 35c blue green	.35	.25
a. Imperf., pair	1,200.	
C16 AP3 50c red brn ('34)	1.25	.65
C17 AP3 1p blk & dk bl	1.25	.65
C18 AP3 5p claret & dp bl	4.00	3.50
C19 AP3 10p vio & ol brn	6.00	7.00
Nos. C11-C19 (9)	52.25	13.90
Set, never hinged	60.00	

1930-32 ***Rouletted 13, 13½***

C20 AP3 5c lt blue ('32)	.35	.20
C21 AP3 10c violet	.35	.20
C22 AP3 15c carmine	.35	.20
a. 15c rose carmine	.40	.20
C23 AP3 20c brown olive	1.50	.20
a. 20c brown	.50	.20
b. 20c yellow brown	.50	.20
c. Horiz. pair, imperf. btwn.		
C24 AP3 25c violet	.95	.80
C25 AP3 50c red brown	.90	.75
Nos. C20-C25 (6)	4.40	2.35
Set, never hinged	5.50	

Trial impressions of No. C20 were printed in orange but were never sold at post offices.

See Nos. C62-C64, C75. For overprints and surcharges see Nos. C28, C38-C39, C46, C49-C50, CO17, CO20-CO28, CO30.

Plane over Plaza, Mexico City — AP4

1929, Dec. 10 **Wmk. 156** ***Perf. 12***

C26 AP4 20c black violet	1.25	1.00
C27 AP4 40c slate green	85.00	75.00
Set, never hinged	125.00	

Aviation Week, Dec. 10-16.
For overprint see No. CO11.

No. C21 Overprinted in Red

1930, Apr. 20 ***Rouletted 13, 13½***

C28 AP3 10c violet	2.00	1.25
Never hinged	2.25	

National Tourism Congress at Mexico, D. F., Apr. 20-27, 1930.

Nos. C5 and C7 Overprinted

1930, Sept. 1 ***Perf. 12***

C29 AP2 5c ol grn & sepia	5.50	4.50
a. Double overprint	225.00	*250.00*
C30 AP2 15c violet & dk grn	9.00	7.75
Set, never hinged	45.00	

Nos. C5-C10 Overprinted

1930, Dec. 18

C31 AP2 5c ol grn & sepia	7.00	6.50
C32 AP2 10c sep & brn red	3.50	4.00
a. Double overprint	50.00	50.00
C33 AP2 15c vio & dk grn	7.50	7.00
C34 AP2 20c brown & blk	7.00	5.50
C35 AP2 50c brn red & blk	14.00	10.00
C36 AP2 1p black & brn	4.00	2.75
Nos. C31-C36 (6)	43.00	35.75
Set, never hinged	125.00	

Plane over Flying Field AP5

1931, May 15 **Engr.** ***Perf. 12***

C37 AP5 25c lake	4.00	4.50
Never hinged	4.50	
a. Imperf., pair	80.00	72.50
Never hinged	100.00	

Aeronautic Exhibition of the Aero Club of Mexico. Of the 25c, 15c paid air mail postage and 10c went to a fund to improve the Mexico City airport.

For surcharge see No. C45.

Nos. C13 and C23 Surcharged in Red

1931

C38 AP3 15c on 20c brn ol	32.50	35.00
Never hinged	40.00	

Rouletted 13, 13½

C39 AP3 15c on 20c brn ol	.30	.20
Never hinged	.35	
a. Inverted surcharge	150.00	
b. Double surcharge	150.00	
c. Pair, one without surcharge	350.00	

Nos. C5 to C9 Overprinted

1932, July 13 ***Perf. 12***

C40 AP2 5c ol grn & sep	6.00	5.00
a. Imperf., pair	50.00	50.00
C41 AP2 10c sep & brn red	5.00	3.00
a. Imperf., pair	50.00	50.00
C42 AP2 15c vio & bk grn	6.00	4.00
a. Imperf., pair	50.00	50.00
C43 AP2 20c brn & blk	5.00	2.75
a. Imperf., pair	50.00	50.00
C44 AP2 50c brn red & blk	35.00	35.00
a. Imperf., pair	50.00	50.00
Nos. C40-C44 (5)	57.00	49.75
Set, never hinged	125.00	
Set, C40a-C44a never hinged	300.00	

Death of Capt. Emilio Carranza, 4th anniv.

No. C37 Surcharged

1932

C45 AP5 20c on 25c lake	.70	.30
Never hinged	2.00	
a. Imperf., pair	72.50	72.50
Never hinged	90.00	

No. C13 Surcharged

C46 AP3 30c on 20c brn ol	30.00	30.00
Never hinged	40.00	

Similar Surcharge on Nos. C3 and C4

C47 AP1 40c on 25c (#C3)	.90	.90
Never hinged	1.25	
a. Inverted surcharge	*11,000.*	
C48 AP1 40c on 25c (#C4)	50.00	50.00
Never hinged	50.00	

Surcharged on Nos. C23 and C24
Rouletted 13, 13½

C49 AP3 30c on 20c brn ol	.35	.20
Never hinged	.40	
a. Inverted surcharge		*2,750.*
C50 AP3 80c on 25c dl vio	1.75	1.25
Never hinged	2.50	
Nos. C45-C50 (6)	83.70	82.65

Palace of Fine Arts — AP6

1933, Oct. 1 Engr. *Perf. 12*

C51 AP6 20c dk red & dl vio 3.50 1.40
C52 AP6 30c dk brn & dl vio 6.75 6.00
C53 AP6 1p grnsh blk & dl vio 70.00 70.00
Nos. C51-C53 (3) 80.25 77.40
Set, never hinged 175.00

21st Intl. Cong. of Statistics and the cent. of the Mexican Soc. of Geography and Statistics.

National University Issue

Nevado de Toluca AP7

Pyramids of the Sun and Moon AP8

View of Ajusco AP9

Volcanoes Popocatepetl and Iztaccíhuatl — AP10

Bridge over Tepecayo AP11

Chapultepec Fortress — AP12

Orizaba Volcano (Citlaltépetl) — AP13

Mexican Girl and Aztec Calendar Stone AP14

1934, Sept. 1 Wmk. 156 *Perf. 10½*

C54 AP7 20c orange 5.00 5.00
C55 AP8 30c red lilac & vio 9.00 9.00
C56 AP9 50c ol grn & bis brn 11.00 *12.00*
C57 AP10 75c blk & yel grn 12.00 *15.00*
C58 AP11 1p blk & pck bl 15.00 15.00
C59 AP12 5p bis brn & dk bl 75.00 *95.00*
C60 AP13 10p indigo & mar 240.00 175.00
C61 AP14 20p brn & brn lake 1,250. *1,300.*
Nos. C54-C61 (8) 1,617. 1,626.
Set, never hinged 1,750.

Type of 1929-34

1934-35 *Perf. 10½, 10½x10*

C62 AP3 20c olive green .35 .20
a. 20c slate 500.00 500.00
Never hinged 600.00
C63 AP3 30c slate .40 .40
C64 AP3 50c red brn ('35) 2.00 2.00
Nos. C62-C64 (3) 2.75 2.60
Set, never hinged 3.50

Symbols of Air Service AP15

Tláloc, God of Water (Quetzalcóatl Temple) — AP16

Orizaba Volcano (Citlaltépetl) — AP17

"Eagle Man" AP18

Symbolical of Flight AP19

Aztec Bird-Man — AP20

Allegory of Flight and Pyramid of the Sun AP21

"Eagle Man" and Airplanes AP22

Natives Looking at Airplane and Orizaba Volcano — AP23

Imprint: "Oficina Impresora de Hacienda-Mexico"

Perf. 10½x10, 10x10½

1934-35 Wmk. 156

C65 AP15 5c black .45 .20
a. Imperf., pair
C66 AP16 10c red brown .90 .20
C67 AP17 15c gray green 1.25 .20
a. Imperf., pair 400.00
C68 AP18 20c brown car 3.00 .20
a. 20c lake 4.00 .20
b. Imperf., pair
C69 AP19 30c brown olive .70 .20
C70 AP20 40c blue ('35) 1.25 .20
C71 AP21 50c green 2.50 .20
a. Imperf., pair 275.00
C72 AP22 1p gray grn & red brn 3.50 .20
C73 AP23 5p dk car & blk 7.25 .70
Nos. C65-C73 (9) 20.80 2.30
Set, never hinged 30.00

See Nos. C76A, C80, C81, C132-C140, C170-C177A. For overprint see No. C74.

No. C68 Overprinted in Violet

1935, Apr. 16

C74 AP18 20c lake *3,250. 4,000.*
Never hinged 5,000.

Amelia Earhart's goodwill flight to Mexico.

Arms-Plane Type of 1929-34

1935 Wmk. 248 *Perf. 10½x10*

C75 AP3 30c slate 3.00 5.00
Never hinged 3.50

Francisco I. Madero AP24

1935, Nov. 20 Wmk. 156

C76 AP24 20c scarlet .30 .25
Never hinged .45

Plan of San Luis, 25th anniv. See No. C76B.

Eagle Man Type of 1934-35

1936 Wmk. 260

C76A AP18 20c lake *4,500.* 60.00
Never hinged 6,000.

Madero Type of 1935

C76B AP24 20c scarlet *12,500.*

Tasquillo Bridge AP25

Corona River Bridge AP26

Bridge on Nuevo Laredo Highway AP27

Wmk. 248

1936, July 1 Photo. *Perf. 14*

C77 AP25 10c slate bl & lt bl .35 .20
C78 AP26 20c dl vio & org .35 .20
C79 AP27 40c dk bl & dk grn .55 .50
Nos. C77-C79 (3) 1.25 .90
Set, never hinged 1.75

Opening of Nuevo Laredo Highway.

Eagle Man Type of 1934-35

Perf. 10½x10

1936, June 18 Engr. Unwmk.

C80 AP18 20c brown carmine 10.00 7.00
Never hinged 15.00

Imprint: "Talleres de Imp. de Est. y Valores-Mexico"

1937 Wmk. 156 Photo. *Perf. 14*

C81 AP18 20c rose red 1.25 .20
Never hinged 1.50
a. 20c brown carmine 1.50 .20
Never hinged 2.00
b. 20c dark carmine 2.00 .20
Never hinged 4.50
c. Imperf., pair 37.50 50.00
Never hinged 60.00

There are two sizes of watermark 156. No. C81c was not regularly issued.

Cavalryman AP28

Early Biplane over Mountains AP29

Venustiano Carranza on Horseback AP30

1938, Mar. 26

C82 AP28 20c org red & bl .50 .20
C83 AP29 40c bl & org red .75 *1.00*
C84 AP30 1p bl & bis brn 4.75 2.25
Nos. C82-C84 (3) 6.00 3.45
Set, never hinged 18.00

Plan of Guadalupe, 25th anniversary.

Reconstructed edifices of Chichén Itzá — AP31

Designs: Nos. C85, C86, The Zócalo and Cathedral, Mexico City. Nos. C89, C90, View of Acapulco.

1938, July 1

C85 AP31 20c carmine rose .35 .25
C86 AP31 20c purple 20.00 10.00
C87 AP31 40c brt green 10.00 5.00
C88 AP31 40c dark green 10.00 5.00
C89 AP31 1p light blue 10.00 5.00
C90 AP31 1p slate blue 10.00 5.00
Nos. C85-C90 (6) 60.35 30.25
Set, never hinged 125.00

16th Intl. Cong. of Planning & Housing.

Statue of José María Morelos — AP34

1939 Engr. *Perf. 10½*

C91 AP34 20c green .70 .50
Never hinged 1.00
C92 AP34 40c red violet 2.00 1.25
Never hinged 5.00

C93 AP34 1p vio brn & car 1.40 1.00
Never hinged 1.75
Nos. C91-C93 (3) 4.10 2.75
Set, never hinged 7.75

New York World's Fair. Released in New York May 2, in Mexico May 24.

Type of 1939 Overprinted in Cerise

1939, May 23
C93A AP34 20c blue & red 200.00 400.00
Never hinged 450.00

Issued for the flight of Francisco Sarabia from Mexico City to New York on May 25.

Statue of Pioneer Woman, Ponca City, OK — AP35

1939, May 17
C94 AP35 20c gray brown 1.00 .40
C95 AP35 40c slate green 2.50 1.25
C96 AP35 1p violet 1.60 .90
Nos. C94-C96 (3) 5.10 2.55
Set, never hinged 11.50

Tulsa World Philatelic Convention.

First Engraving Made in Mexico, 1544 — AP36

First Work of Legislation Printed in America, 1563 — AP37

Designs: 1p, Reproduction of oldest preserved Mexican printing.

1939, Sept. 7 **Wmk. 156**
C97 AP36 20c slate blue .25 .20
a. Unwmkd. 50.00
C98 AP37 40c slate green .65 .20
a. Imperf., pair 700.00
C99 AP37 1p dk brn & car 1.10 .70
Nos. C97-C99 (3) 2.00 1.10
Set, never hinged 2.50

400th anniversary of printing in Mexico.

Alternated Perforations
Nos. 763-766, 774-779, 792-795, 801-804, 806-811, 813-818, C100-C102, C111-C116, C123-C128, C143-C162, C430-C431 have alternating small and large perforations.

Transportation — AP39

Designs: 40c, Finger counting and factory. 1p, "Seven Censuses."

Perf. 12x13, 13x12
1939, Oct. 2 **Photo.**
C100 AP39 20c dk bl & bl 1.00 .20
C101 AP39 40c red org & org .75 .25
C102 AP39 1p ind & vio bl 2.75 .75
Nos. C100-C102 (3) 4.50 1.20
Set, never hinged 6.00

National Census of 1939-40.

Penny Black Type of Regular Issue, 1940

1940, May ***Perf. 14***
C103 A140 5c blk & dk grn .65 .55
C104 A140 10c bis brn & dp bl .55 .25
C105 A140 20c car & bl vio .40 .20
C106 A140 1p car & choc 6.00 5.00
C107 A140 5p gray grn & red brn 75.00 55.00
Nos. C103-C107 (5) 82.60 61.00
Set, never hinged 110.00

Issue dates: 5c-1p, May 2; 5p, May 15.

Part of Original College at Pátzcuaro AP43

College at Morelia (18th Century) — AP44

College at Morelia (1940) AP45

1940, July 15 **Engr.** ***Perf. 10½***
C108 AP43 20c brt green .45 .20
C109 AP44 40c orange .50 .30
C110 AP45 1p dp pur, red brn & org 1.25 1.00
Nos. C108-C110 (3) 2.20 1.50
Set, never hinged 5.00

400th anniv. of the founding of the National College of San Nicolas de Hidalgo.

Pirate Ship AP46

Designs: 40c, Castle of San Miguel. 1p, Temple of San Francisco.

Perf. 12x13, 13x12
1940, Aug. 7 **Photo.**
C111 AP46 20c red brn & bis brn 1.10 .70
C112 AP46 40c blk & sl grn 1.50 .75
C113 AP46 1p vio bl & blk 5.00 4.00
Nos. C111-C113 (3) 7.60 5.45
Set, never hinged 21.00

400th anniversary of Campeche.

Inauguration Type of Regular Issue, 1940

1940, Dec. 1 ***Perf. 12x13***
C114 A146 20c gray blk & red org 1.90 1.00
C115 A146 40c chnt brn & dk sl 2.00 1.50
C116 A146 1p brt vio bl & rose 3.50 2.00
Nos. C114-C116 (3) 7.40 4.50
Set, never hinged 20.00

AIR POST OFFICIAL STAMPS

Nos. C4 and C3 Overprinted in Black or Red

1929 **Wmk. 156** ***Perf. 12***
CO1 AP1 25c dk grn & gray brn 4.50 3.25
a. Without period 20.00 20.00
CO2 AP1 25c dk grn & gray brn (R) 4.00 *5.00*
a. Without period 21.00 21.00
CO2B AP1 25c brn car & gray brn 10.00 *12.50*
c. Without period 25.00 25.00
Nos. CO1-CO2B (3) 18.50 20.75
Set, never hinged 27.50

Types of Regular Issue of 1926 Overprinted in Red

1929, Oct. 15 **Unwmk.**
CO3 A90 2c black 75.00 *90.00*
CO4 A91 4c black 75.00 *90.00*
CO5 A90 5c black 75.00 *90.00*
CO6 A91 10c black 75.00 *90.00*
CO7 A92 20c black 75.00 *90.00*
CO8 A92 30c black 75.00 *90.00*
CO9 A92 40c black 75.00 *90.00*
Nos. CO3-CO9 (7) 525.00 630.00
Set, never hinged 675.00

Horizontal Overprint
CO10 A93 1p black *2,250.* *2,250.*
Set, never hinged 2,000.

#CO3-CO9 also exist with overprint reading up.

No. C26 Overprinted in Black

1930 **Wmk. 156**
CO11 AP4 20c black violet 1.10 *1.75*
Never hinged 1.30
a. Without period 20.00 *20.00*
b. Inverted overprint 18.00 *18.00*
c. As "a," inverted overprint 210.00 210.00

No. CO11 with red overprint is believed not to have been issued for postal purposes.

Plane over Mexico City OA1

1930 **Engr.**
CO12 OA1 20c gray black 6.00 6.00
CO13 OA1 35c lt violet 1.10 *1.90*
CO14 OA1 40c ol brn & dp bl 1.25 *1.75*
CO15 OA1 70c vio & ol gray 1.25 *1.75*
Nos. CO12-CO15 (4) 9.60 *11.40*
Set, never hinged 17.50

No. CO12 Surcharged in Red

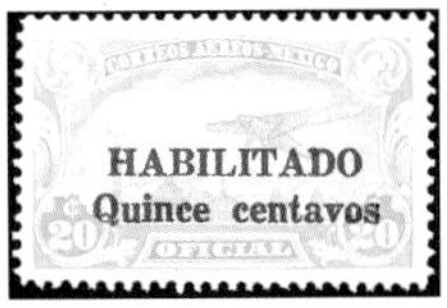

1931
CO16 OA1 15c on 20c .85 *1.40*
Never hinged 1.20
a. Inverted surcharge 140.00
b. Double surcharge 140.00

No. C20 Overprinted

1932 ***Rouletted 13, 13½***
CO17 AP3 5c light blue .80 *.90*
Never hinged 1.10

Air Post Stamps of 1927-32 Overprinted

On No. C1a
1932 **Unwmk.** ***Perf. 12***
CO18 AP1 50c dk bl & cl 1,000. 1,000.
Never hinged 1,600.

On Nos. C2, C2a
Wmk. 156
CO19 AP1 50c dk bl & red brn 1.25 *1.50*
Never hinged 1.25
a. 50c dark blue & claret 1.40 *1.60*

See note after No. C2.

On Nos. C11 and C12
1932 ***Perf. 12***
CO20 AP3 10c violet 22.50 *25.00*
Never hinged 26.00
CO21 AP3 15c carmine 350.00 *375.00*
Never hinged 400.00

On Nos. C21 to C23
Rouletted 13, 13½
CO22 AP3 10c violet .35 *.55*
CO23 AP3 15c carmine 1.40 *2.00*
CO24 AP3 20c brn olive 1.40 *2.00*

Nos. C20, C21 C23 and C25 Overprinted

1933-34 ***Rouletted 13½***
CO25 AP3 5c light blue .30 *.55*
CO26 AP3 10c violet ('34) .30 *.90*
CO27 AP3 20c brown olive .75 *1.25*
CO28 AP3 50c red brn ('34) 1.25 *1.90*

On No. C2
Perf. 12
CO29 AP1 50c dk bl & red brn 1.10 *2.00*
a. 50c dark blue & claret 1.60 *2.50*

On No. C11
Perf. 12

CO30	AP3	10c violet ('34)	140.00	*175.00*
a.		Double overprint		*325.00*

Forgeries exist.

SPECIAL DELIVERY STAMPS

Motorcycle Postman SD1

1919 Unwmk. Engr. *Perf. 12*

E1	SD1	20c red & black	70.00	2.75

1923 Wmk. 156

E2	SD1	20c blk car & blk	.30	.25

For overprint see No. E7

Messenger with Quipu — SD2

1934

E3	SD2	10c brn red & blue	.30	.50

Indian Archer — SD3

Imprint: "Oficina Impresora de Hacienda Mexico."

1934 *Perf. 10x10½*

E4	SD3	10c black violet	1.50	.50

See Nos. E5-E6, E8-E9.

Redrawn
Imprint: "Talleres de Imp. de Est. y Valores-Mexico."

1938-41 Photo. *Perf. 14*

E5	SD3	10c slate violet	.75	.25
a.		Unwatermarked	50.00	
E6	SD3	20c orange red ('41)	.50	.15

Imperforate copies of No. E6 were not regularly issued.

No. E2 Overprinted "1940" in Violet

1940 Engr. *Perf. 12*

E7	SD1	20c red & black	.40	.20

INSURED LETTER STAMPS

Insured Letters — IL1

Registered Mailbag — IL2

Safe — IL3

1935 Engr. Wmk. 156 *Perf. 10½*

G1	IL1	10c vermilion	1.75	.75
a.		Perf. 10x10½		
G2	IL2	50c dk bl	10.00	.60
G3	IL3	1p turq grn	1.25	.85
		Nos. G1-G3 (3)	13.00	2.20

Nos. G1 and G4 were issued both with and without imprint.

POSTAGE DUE STAMPS

D1

1908 Engr. Wmk. 155 *Perf. 14*

J1	D1	1c blue	1.00	*3.00*
J2	D1	2c blue	1.00	*3.00*
J3	D1	4c blue	1.00	*3.00*
J4	D1	5c blue	1.00	*3.00*
J5	D1	10c blue	1.00	*3.00*
		Nos. J1-J5 (5)	5.00	*15.00*

For overprints and surcharges see Nos. 381-385, 434-438, 466-470, 495-499, 593-607.

PORTE DE MAR STAMPS

These stamps were used to indicate the amount of cash to be paid to the captains of the mail steamers taking outgoing foreign mail.

PM2

PM3

1875 Unwmk. Litho. *Imperf.*

JX9	PM2	2c black	.60	*50.00*
a.		"5" added to make 25c	12.00	*100.00*
JX10	PM2	10c black	.80	*30.00*
JX11	PM2	12c black	.80	*50.00*
JX12	PM2	20c black	1.00	*50.00*
JX13	PM2	25c black	3.25	*50.00*
JX14	PM2	35c black	3.25	*60.00*
JX15	PM2	50c black	3.00	*60.00*
JX16	PM2	60c black	3.00	*75.00*
JX17	PM2	75c black	3.50	*75.00*
JX18	PM2	85c black	3.25	*100.00*
JX19	PM2	100c black	4.00	*100.00*
		Nos. JX9-JX19 (11)	26.45	700.00

Same, Numerals Larger

JX20	PM2	5c black	1.00	*50.00*
JX21	PM2	25c black	1.65	*50.00*
JX22	PM2	35c black	250.00	
JX23	PM2	50c black	1.00	*50.00*
JX24	PM2	60c black	125.00	
JX25	PM2	100c black	.60	*100.00*
		Nos. JX20-JX25 (6)	379.25	

In Nos. JX9-JX19 the figures of value are 7mm high and "CENTAVOS" is 7½mm long. On Nos. JX20-JX25 the figures of value are 8mm high and "CENTAVOS" is 9½mm long.

Nos. JX9-JX25 exist with overprints of district names.

Counterfeits exist of Nos. JX9-JX31.

1879

JX26	PM3	2c brown	.50	
JX27	PM3	5c yellow	.50	
JX28	PM3	10c red	.50	
JX29	PM3	25c blue	.50	
JX30	PM3	50c green	.50	
JX31	PM3	100c violet	.50	
		Nos. JX26-JX31 (6)	3.00	

Nos. JX26-JX31 were never put in use.

Nos. JX26-JX31 were printed on paper watermarked "ADMINISTRACION GENERAL DE CORREOS MEXICO." Aprroximately ¾ of the stamps do not show any of the watermark.

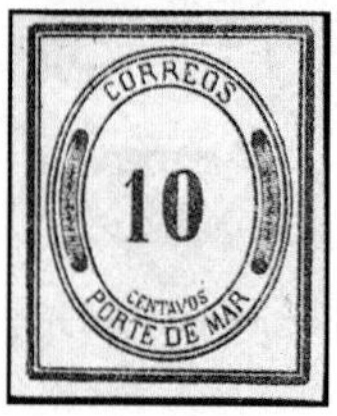

Stamps of this design were never issued. Copies appeared on the market in 1884. Value, set, $22.

All were printed in same sheet of 49 (7x7). Sheet consists of 14 of 10c; 7 each of 25c, 35c, 50c; 4 each of 60c, 85c; 3 each of 75c, 100c. There are four varieties of 10c, two of 25c, 35c and 50c.

OFFICIAL STAMPS

Hidalgo — O1

Wove or Laid Paper

1884-93 Unwmk. Engr. *Perf. 12*

O1	O1	red	1.40	1.00
a.		Vert. pair, imperf. betwn.	100.00	
O1B	O1	scarlet ('85)	1.40	1.00
O2	O1	olive brn ('87)	.90	.70
a.		Horiz. pair, imperf. betwn.	—	
b.		Blue ruled lines on paper		
O3	O1	orange ('88)	2.50	.90
a.		Vert. pair, imperf. betwn.	90.00	
b.		Perf. 11	15.00	12.00
O4	O1	blue grn ('93)	1.40	.80
a.		Imperf., pair	15.00	12.00
b.		Perf. 11	15.00	12.00
		Nos. O1-O4 (5)	7.60	4.40

Pin-perf. 6

O5	O1	olive brown ('87)	80.00	20.00

Wmk. "Correos E U M" on every Vertical Line of Ten Stamps (152)

1894 *Perf. 5½*

O6	O1	ultra	3.00	2.75
a.		Vert. pair, imperf. horiz.	35.00	
b.		Imperf., pair	45.00	

Perf. 11, 12

O7	O1	ultra	1.75	1.60

Perf. 5½x11, 11x5½

O9	O1	ultra	12.00	8.00
		Nos. O6-O9 (3)	16.75	12.35

Regular Issues with Handstamped Overprint in Black

1895 *Perf. 12*

O10	A20	1c green	17.50	6.00
O11	A20	2c carmine	20.00	6.00
O12	A20	3c orange brn	17.50	6.00
O13	A21	4c red orange	26.00	12.00
a.		4c orange	42.50	14.00
O14	A22	5c ultra	35.00	12.00
O15	A23	10c lilac rose	32.50	3.00
O16	A21	12c olive brn	70.00	30.00
O17	A23	15c brt blue	42.50	18.00
O18	A23	20c brown rose	42.50	18.00
O19	A23	50c purple	90.00	42.50
O20	A24	1p brown	200.00	90.00
O21	A24	5p scarlet	475.00	250.00
O22	A24	10p deep blue	750.00	500.00
		Nos. O10-O22 (13)	1,818.	993.50

Similar stamps with red overprint were not officially placed in use.

Black Overprint

1896-97 Wmk. 153

O23	A20	1c green	60.00	10.00
O24	A20	2c carmine	60.00	12.00
O25	A20	3c orange brn	60.00	12.00
O26	A21	4c red orange	60.00	12.00
a.		4c orange	75.00	22.50
O27	A22	5c ultra	60.00	12.00
O28	A21	12c olive brn	80.00	30.00
O29	A23	15c brt blue	100.00	30.00
O29A	A23	50c purple	650.00	650.00
		Nos. O23-O29A (8)	1,130.	768.00

Black Overprint

1897 Wmk. 154

O30	A20	1c green	100.00	30.00
O31	A20	2c scarlet	90.00	35.00
O33	A21	4c orange	125.00	60.00
O34	A22	5c ultra	100.00	35.00
O35	A21	12c olive brn	125.00	42.50
O36	A23	15c brt blue	160.00	42.50
O37	A23	20c brown rose	110.00	18.00
O38	A23	50c purple	150.00	30.00
O39	A24	1p brown	375.00	125.00
		Nos. O30-O39 (9)	1,335.	418.00

Black Overprint

1898 Unwmk.

O40	A20	1c green	35.00	9.50
O41	A20	2c scarlet	35.00	9.50
O42	A20	3c orange brn	35.00	9.50
O43	A21	4c orange	60.00	12.00
O44	A22	5c ultra	60.00	20.00
O45	A23	10c lilac rose	650.00	500.00
O46	A21	12c olive brn	125.00	30.00
O47	A23	15c brt blue	125.00	30.00
O48	A23	20c brown rose	225.00	75.00
O48A	A23	50c purple	375.00	150.00
O48B	A24	10p deep blue		—
		Nos. O40-O48A (10)	1,725.	845.50

Black Overprint

1900 Wmk. 155 *Perf. 14, 15*

O49	A25	1c green	37.50	2.50
O50	A26	2c vermilion	50.00	4.00
O51	A27	3c yellow brn	50.00	2.50
O52	A28	5c dark blue	50.00	4.50
O53	A29	10c violet & org	65.00	5.50
O54	A30	15c lavender & cl	65.00	5.50
O55	A31	20c rose & dk bl	75.00	2.50
O56	A32	50c red lil & blk	150.00	25.00
O57	A33	1p blue & blk	300.00	25.00
O58	A34	5p carmine & blk	575.00	75.00
		Nos. O49-O58 (10)	1,417.	152.00

Black Overprint

1903

O59	A25	1c violet	35.00	4.00
O60	A26	2c green	35.00	4.00
O61	A35	4c carmine	65.00	2.50
O62	A28	5c orange	65.00	13.00
O63	A29	10c blue & org	70.00	4.00
O64	A32	50c carmine & blk	200.00	25.00
		Nos. O59-O64 (6)	470.00	52.50

Regular Issues Overprinted

On Issues of 1899-1903

1910

O65	A26	2c green	175.00	6.50
O66	A27	3c orange brn	175.00	4.00
O67	A35	4c carmine	200.00	10.00
O68	A28	5c orange	225.00	50.00
O69	A29	10c blue & org	200.00	4.00
O70	A30	15c lav & claret	225.00	6.50
O71	A31	20c rose & dk bl	275.00	3.00
O72	A32	50c carmine & blk	375.00	35.00
O73	A33	1p blue & blk	575.00	125.00
O74	A34	5p carmine & blk	200.00	125.00
		Nos. O65-O74 (10)	2,625.	369.00

On Issue of 1910

1911

O75	A36	1c violet	5.00	5.00
O76	A37	2c green	3.75	2.25
O77	A38	3c orange brn	5.00	2.50
O78	A39	4c carmine	5.50	2.25
O79	A40	5c orange	12.50	7.00
O80	A41	10c blue & org	5.50	2.50
O81	A42	15c gray bl & cl	13.00	8.50
O82	A43	20c red & blue	10.00	2.50
O83	A44	50c red brn & blk	35.00	15.00
O84	A45	1p blue & blk	60.00	25.00
O85	A46	5p carmine & blk	300.00	125.00
		Nos. O75-O85 (11)	455.25	197.50

Nos. 500 to 505 Overprinted

1915 Unwmk. *Rouletted 14½*

O86 A57 1c violet 1.00 *2.00*
O87 A58 2c green 1.00 *2.00*
O88 A59 3c brown 1.25 *2.00*
O89 A60 4c carmine 1.00 *2.00*
O90 A61 5c orange 1.00 *2.00*
O91 A62 10c ultra 1.25 *2.00*
Nos. O86-O91 (6) 6.50 12.00

All values are known with inverted overprint. All values exist imperforate and part perforate but were not regularly issued in these forms.

On Nos. 506 to 514

1915-16 *Perf. 12*

O92 A57 1c violet 1.50 *2.00*
O93 A58 2c green 1.50 *2.00*
O94 A59 3c brown 1.50 *2.00*
O95 A60 4c carmine 1.50 *2.00*
a. "CEATRO" 21.00 *30.00*
O96 A61 5c orange 1.50 *2.00*
O97 A62 10c ultra, type II 1.50 *2.00*
a. Double overprint *475.00*
O98 A63 40c slate 8.00 *14.50*
a. Inverted overprint 24.00 *25.00*
b. Double overprint 40.00
O99 A64 1p brown & blk 10.00 *14.50*
a. Inverted overprint 27.50 27.50
O100 A65 5p claret & ultra 60.00 *60.00*
a. Inverted overprint 80.00
Nos. O92-O100 (9) 87.00 101.00

Nos. O98 and O99 exist imperforate but probably were not issued in that form.

Preceding Issues Overprinted in Red, Blue or Black

On No. O74

1916 Wmk. 155

O101 A34 5p carmine & blk 900.00

On Nos. O75 to O85

O102 A36 1c violet 6.50
O103 A37 2c green 1.25
O104 A38 3c orange brn (Bl) 1.75
O105 A39 4c carmine (Bl) 7.00
O106 A40 5c orange (Bl) 1.75
O107 A41 10c blue & org 1.75
O108 A42 15c gray bl & cl (Bk) 1.75
O109 A43 20c red & bl (Bk) 1.90
O110 A44 50c red brn & blk 200.00
O111 A45 1p blue & blk 11.00
O112 A46 5p carmine & blk *3,250.*
Nos. O102-O111 (10) 234.65

No. O102 with blue overprint is a trial color. Counterfeits exist of Nos. O110, O112.

Nos. 608, 610 to 612, 615 and 616 Overprinted Vertically in Red or Black

Thick Paper

1918 Unwmk. *Rouletted 14½*

O113 A68 1c violet (R) 60.00 35.00
O114 A69 2c gray grn (R) 65.00 35.00
O115 A70 3c bis brn (R) 60.00 35.00
O116 A71 4c carmine (Bk) 60.00 35.00
O117 A74 20c rose (Bk) 125.00 90.00
O118 A75 30c gray brn (R) 190.00 175.00

On Nos. 622-623
Medium Paper
Perf. 12

O119 A72 5c ultra (R) 40.00 40.00
O120 A73 10c blue (R) 35.00 25.00
a. Double overprint 400.00 *400.00*
Nos. O113-O120 (8) 635.00 470.00

Overprinted Horizontally in Red

On Nos. 626-628
Thin Paper

O121 A63 40c violet (R) 35.00 27.50
O122 A64 1p bl & blk (R) 85.00 700.00
O123 A65 5p grn & blk (R) *575.00 600.00*
Nos. O121-O123 (3) 695.00 1,327.

Nos. 608 and 610 to 615 Overprinted Vertically Up in Red or Black

Thick Paper

1919 *Rouletted 14½*

O124 A68 1c dull vio (R) 6.00 6.00
a. "OFICIAN" 70.00 *80.00*
O125 A69 2c gray grn (R) 9.50 3.50
a. "OFICIAN" 70.00 *80.00*
O126 A70 3c bis brn (R) 14.00 6.00
a. "OFICIAN" 95.00 *100.00*
O127 A71 4c car (Bk) 29.00 13.00
c. "OFICIAN" —
O127A A72 5c ultra 200.00 125.00
b. "OFICIAN" *500.00*
O128 A73 10c blue (R) 9.50 2.50
a. "OFICIAN" 85.00 60.00
O129 A74 20c rose (Bk) 60.00 47.50
a. "OFICIAN" 140.00

On Nos. 618, 622
Perf. 12

O130 A68 1c dull violet (R) 47.50 47.50
a. "OFICIAN" 140.00 100.00
O131 A72 5c ultra (R) 47.50 22.50
a. "OFICIAN" 140.00 100.00

Overprinted Horizontally
On Nos. 626-627
Thin Paper

O132 A63 40c violet (R) 47.50 35.00
O133 A64 1p bl & blk (R) 60.00 50.00
Nos. O124-O133 (11) 530.50 358.50

Nos. 608 to 615 and 617 Overprinted Vertically down in Black, Red or Blue

Size: 17½x3mm

1921 *Rouletted 14½*

O134 A68 1c gray (Bk) 30.00 12.00
a. 1c dull violet (Bk) 17.00 7.00
O135 A69 2c gray grn (R) 5.00 3.00
O136 A70 3c bis brn (R) 8.50 4.50
O137 A71 4c carmine (Bk) 27.50 21.00
O138 A72 5c ultra (R) 25.00 12.00
O139 A73 10c bl, reading down (R) 32.50 12.00
a. Overprint reading up 60.00 60.00
O140 A74 20c rose (Bl) 47.50 27.50
O141 A75 30c gray blk (R) 25.00 25.00

Overprinted Horizontally
On Nos. 626-628
Perf. 12

O142 A63 40c violet (R) 32.50 32.50
O143 A64 1p bl & blk (R) 25.00 25.00
O144 A65 5p grn & blk (Bk) *600.00 600.00*
Nos. O134-O144 (11) 858.50 774.50

Nos. 609 to 615 Overprinted Vertically Down in Black

1921-30 *Rouletted 14½*

O145 A68 1c gray 5.00 2.50
a. 1c lilac gray 1.00 .70
O146 A69 2c gray green 1.75 .70
O147 A70 3c bister brn .80 .70
a. "OFICAL" 47.50 25.00
b. "OIFCIAL" 47.50 25.00
c. Double overprint 140.00
O148 A71 4c carmine 22.50 2.50
O149 A72 5c ultra 1.00 .70
O150 A73 10c blue 1.00 .70
a. "OIFCIAL" 50.00
O151 A74 20c brown rose 9.00 *9.50*
a. 20c rose 5.00 2.50

On No. 625
Perf. 12

O152 A75 30c gray black 7.25 2.50

Overprinted Horizontally
On Nos. 626, 628

O153 A63 40c violet 7.00 5.00
a. "OFICAL" 60.00 60.00
b. "OICIFAL" 60.00 60.00
c. Inverted overprint 90.00 *125.00*
O154 A65 5p grn & blk ('30) 375.00 *375.00*
Nos. O145-O154 (10) 430.30 399.80

Overprinted Vertically Down in Red On Nos. 609, 610, 611, 613 and 614

1921-24 *Rouletted 14½*

O155 A68 1c lilac 1.60 1.00
O156 A69 2c gray green 1.50 .90
O157 A70 3c bister brown 4.00 1.00
O158 A72 5c ultra 1.60 .80
O159 A73 10c blue 35.00 3.50
a. Double overprint

On Nos. 624-625
Perf. 12

O160 A74 20c rose 7.25 1.60
O161 A75 30c gray black 19.00 5.00

Overprinted Horizontally
On Nos. 626-628

O162 A63 40c violet 14.00 7.50
a. Vert. pair, imperf. btwn.
O163 A64 1p blue & blk 35.00 25.00
O164 A65 5p green & blk 300.00 *300.00*

Overprinted Vertically Down in Blue on No. 612
Rouletted 14½

O165 A71 4c carmine 7.00 3.50
Nos. O155-O165 (11) 425.95 *349.80*

Same Overprint Vertically Down in Red on Nos. 635 and 637

1926-27 *Rouletted 14½*

O166 A80 3c bis brn, ovpt. horiz. 12.00 12.00
a. Period omitted 30.00 30.00
O167 A82 5c orange 27.50 *30.00*

Same Overprint Vertically Down in Blue or Red On Nos. 650, 651, 655 and 656
Wmk. 156

O168 A79 2c scarlet (Bl) 20.00 20.00
a. Overprint reading up 30.00 30.00
O169 A80 3c bis brn, ovpt. horiz. (R) 5.00 5.00
a. Inverted overprint 60.00
O170 A85 10c claret (Bl) 35.00 16.00
O171 A84 20c deep blue (R) 14.00 12.00
a. Overprint reading up 14.00 12.00

Overprinted Horizontally in Red
On Nos. 643, 646-649
Perf. 12

O172 A81 4c green 6.00 6.00
O173 A83 30c dk grn 6.00 6.00
O174 A63 40c violet 16.00 16.00
a. Inverted overprint 80.00
O175 A87 50c olive brn 1.50 1.50
a. 50c yellow brown 18.00 18.00
O176 A88 1p red brn & bl 15.00 15.00
Nos. O168-O176 (9) 118.50 97.50

Same Overprint Horizontally on No. 651, Vertically Up on Nos. 650, 653-656, 666, RA1

1927-31 *Rouletted 14½*

O177 PT1 1c brown ('31) .70 *1.00*
O178 A79 2c scarlet .70 *1.00*
a. "OFICAIL" 30.00 30.00
b. Overprint reading down 1.50 *2.00*
O179 A80 3c bis brn 2.00 1.50
a. "OFICAIL" 40.00 30.00
O180 A82 4c green 1.50 1.00
a. "OFICAIL" 40.00 40.00
b. Overprint reading down 10.00 2.00
O181 A82 5c orange 4.00 3.00
a. Overprint reading down 4.00 2.50
O182 A94 8c orange 12.00 8.00
a. Overprint reading down 7.00 6.00
O183 A85 10c lake 2.00 2.00
a. Overprint reading down 2.00 2.00
O184 A84 20c dark blue 10.00 4.00
a. "OFICAIL" 40.00 40.00
b. Overprint reading down 20.00 20.00
Nos. O177-O184 (8) 32.90 21.50

Overprinted Vertically Up on #O186, Horizontally On Nos. 643 and 645 to 649

1927-33 *Perf. 12*

O185 A81 4c green 6.00 5.00
a. Inverted overprint 30.00 30.00
O186 A85 10c brown lake 55.00 45.00
O187 A83 30c dark green 1.40 1.00
a. Inverted overprint 30.00 30.00
b. Pair, tête bêche overprints 35.00 35.00
c. "OFICAIL" 35.00 35.00
O188 A63 40c violet 12.00 8.00
O189 A87 50c olive brn ('33) 3.25 *4.00*
O190 A88 1p red brn & bl 24.00 20.00
Nos. O185-O190 (6) 101.65 83.00

The overprint on No. O186 is vertical.

Nos. 320, 628, 633 Overprinted Horizontally

On Stamp No. 320

1927-28 Wmk. 155 *Perf. 14, 15*

O191 A46 5p car & blk (R) 175.00 *250.00*
O192 A46 5p car & blk (Bl) 175.00 *250.00*

Unwmk. *Perf. 12*

O193 A65 5p grn & blk (Bk) 375.00 *500.00*
a. Inverted overprint — —
O194 A78 10p blk brn & blk (Bl) 200.00 *300.00*

No. 320 Overprinted Horizontally

Wmk. 155 *Perf. 14*

O195 A46 5p carmine & blk 300.00

Nos. 650 and 655 Overprinted Horizontally

1928-29 Wmk. 156 *Rouletted 14½*
Size: 16x2½mm

O196 A79 2c dull red 18.00 12.00
O197 A85 10c rose lake 27.50 12.00

Nos. RA1, 650-651, 653-656 Overprinted

1932-33

O198 PT1 1c brown .70 *1.00*
O199 A79 2c dull red .80 *1.00*
O200 A80 3c bister brn 3.00 3.00
O201 A82 4c green 10.00 8.00
O202 A82 5c orange 12.00 8.00
O203 A85 10c rose lake 3.25 3.00
O204 A84 20c dark blue 15.00 10.00
a. Double overprint *200.00 90.00*
Nos. O198-O204 (7) 44.75 34.00

Nos. 651, 646-649 Overprinted Horizontally

1933 *Rouletted 14½*

O205 A80 3c bister brn 3.00 3.00

Perf. 12

O206 A83 30c dk green 8.00 3.00
O207 A63 40c violet 15.00 6.00
O208 A87 50c olive brn 2.50 3.00
a. "OFICIAL OFICIAL" 50.00 50.00

O209 A88 1p red brn & bl, type I 3.00 3.00
a. Type II 2.75 *3.50*

Overprinted Vertically On No. 656
Rouletted 14½

O210 A84 20c dark blue 18.00 10.00
Nos. O205-O210 (6) 49.50 28.00

Nos. RA1, 651, 653, 654, 683 Overprinted Horizontally

1934-37 ***Rouletted 14½***
Size: 13x2mm

O211 PT1 1c brown 5.00 *6.00*
O212 A80 3c bister brn .70 .70
O213 A82 4c green 12.00 10.00
O214 A82 5c orange .70 .70
O215 A96 15c dk blue ('37) 1.00 1.00
Nos. O211-O215 (5) 19.40 18.40

See No. O217a.

Same Overprint on Nos. 687A-692

1934-37 ***Perf. 10½***

O216 PT1 1c brown ('37) 1.00 *1.25*
O217 A79 2c scarlet 1.00 *1.50*
a. On No. 650 (error) 350.00
b. Double overprint 275.00
O218 A82 4c green ('35) 1.40 1.60
O219 A85 10c brown lake 1.00 1.00
O220 A84 20c dk blue ('37) 1.25 1.25
O221 A83 30c dk bl grn ('37) 2.00 2.00

On Nos. 647 and 649
Perf. 12, 11½x12

O222 A63 40c violet 3.00 3.50
O223 A88 1p red brn & bl (I) 5.00 *6.00*
a. Type II 4.00 4.00
Nos. O216-O223 (8) 15.65 18.10

On Nos. 707 to 709, 712, 715, 716, 717, 718 and 719

O224 A108 1c orange 2.00 *4.00*
O225 A109 2c green 1.25 *2.00*
O226 A110 4c carmine 1.25 *1.40*
O227 A112 10c violet 1.25 *2.50*
O228 A114 20c ultra 1.60 *2.50*
O229 A115 30c lake 2.00 *4.00*
O230 A116 40c red brown 2.50 *4.00*
O231 A117 50c black 2.75 *2.75*
O232 A118 1p dk brn & org 8.00 *12.00*
Nos. O224-O232 (9) 22.60 *35.15*

POSTAL TAX STAMPS

Morelos Monument — PT1

Rouletted 14½

1925 **Engr.** **Wmk. 156**

RA1 PT1 1c brown .35 .20
a. Imperf. 30.00

1926 ***Perf. 12***

RA2 PT1 1c brown .75 *5.00*
a. Booklet pane of 2 12.00

1925 **Unwmk.** ***Rouletted 14½***

RA3 PT1 1c brown 75.00 19.00

It was obligatory to add a stamp of type PT1 to the regular postage on every article of domestic mail matter. The money obtained from this source formed a fund to combat a plague of locusts.

In 1931, 1c stamps of type PT1 were discontinued as Postal Tax stamps. It was subsequently used for the payment of postage on drop letters (announcement cards and unsealed circulars) to be delivered in the city of cancellation. See No. 687A.

For overprints see Nos. O177, O198, O211, O216, RA4.

PT2

Mother and Child — PT3

Red Overprint

1929 **Wmk. 156**

RA4 PT1 1c brown .35 .20
a. Overprint reading down 75.00 75.00

There were two settings of this overprint. They may be distinguished by the two lines being spaced 4mm or 6mm apart.

The money from sales of this stamp was devoted to child welfare work.

1929 **Litho.** ***Rouletted 13, 13½***

RA5 PT3 1c violet .35 .20

PT4

PT5

1929 **Unwmk.**
Size: 18x24½mm

RA6 PT4 2c deep green .40 .20
RA7 PT4 5c brown .40 .20
a. Imperf., pair 60.00 60.00

For surcharges see Nos. RA10-RA11.

1929 **Size: 19x25¼mm**

Two types of 1c:

Type I — Background lines continue through lettering of top inscription. Denomination circle hangs below second background line. Paper and gum white.

Type II — Background lines cut away behind some letters. Circle rests on second background line. Paper and gum yellowish.

RA8 PT5 1c violet, type I .35 .20
a. Booklet pane of 4 10.00
b. Booklet pane of 2 18.00
c. Type II .40 .20
d. Imperf., pair 50.00 50.00
RA9 PT5 2c deep green .65 .20
a. Imperf., pair 12.00

The use of these stamps, in addition to the regular postage, was compulsory. The money obtained from their sale was used for child welfare work.

For surcharge see No. RA12.

Nos. RA6, RA7, RA9 Surcharged

1930

RA10 PT4 1c on 2c dp grn .75 .40
RA11 PT4 1c on 5c brown 1.00 .60
RA12 PT5 1c on 2c dp grn 2.00 1.00
Nos. RA10-RA12 (3) 3.75 2.00

Used stamps exist with surcharge double or reading down.

No. 423 Overprinted

1931, Jan. 30 **Wmk. 155** ***Perf. 14***

RA13 A36 1c dull violet .40 .40
a. "PRO INFANCIA" double 50.00

Indian Mother and Child — PT6

Mosquito Attacking Man — PT7

Wmk. 156

1934, Sept. 1 **Engr.** ***Perf. 10½***

RA13B PT6 1c dull orange .30 .20

1939 **Photo.** **Wmk. 156** ***Perf. 14***

RA14 PT7 1c Prus blue 1.50 .20
a. Imperf. 3.00 3.00

This stamp was obligatory on all mail, the money being used to aid in a drive against malaria.

See Nos. RA16, RA19.

PROVISIONAL ISSUES

During the struggle led by Juarez to expel the Emperor Maximilian, installed June, 1864 by Napoleon III and French troops, a number of towns when free of Imperial forces issued provisional postage stamps. Maximilian was captured and executed June 19, 1867, but provisional issues continued current for a time pending re-establishment of Republican Government.

Campeche

A southern state in Mexico, comprising the western part of the Yucatan peninsula.

A1

White Paper
Numerals in Black

1876 **Handstamped** ***Imperf.***

1 A1 5c gray blue & blue *2,000.*
2 A1 25c gray blue & blue *1,100.*
3 A1 50c gray blue & blue *4,500.*

The stamps printed in blue-black and blue on yellowish paper, formerly listed as issued in 1867, are now known to be an unofficial production of later years. They are reprints, but produced without official sanction.

Chiapas

A southern state in Mexico, bordering on Guatemala and the Pacific Ocean.

A1

1866 **Typeset**

1 A1 ½r blk, *gray bl* 2,000. *1,300.*
2 A1 1r blk, *lt grn* *850.*
3 A1 2r blk, *rose* *900.*
4 A1 4r blk, *lt buff* *2,000.*
a. Vertical half used as 2r on cover *3,000.*
5 A1 8r blk, *rose* *15,000.*
a. Quarter used as 2r on cover *4,000.*
b. Half used as 4r on cover *5,000.*

Chihuahua

A city of northern Mexico and capital of the State of Chihuahua.

A1

1872 **Handstamped**

1 A1 12(c) black *1,200.*
2 A1 25(c) black *1,000.*

Specialists question the authenticity of these stamps. The Catalogue Editors would appreciate any information on this issue.

Cuautla

A town in the state of Morelos.

A1

1867 **Handstamped**

1 A1 (2r) black *7,000.*

All known examples on cover are uncanceled. Examples are known without the "73" inside the oval.

Cuernavaca

A city of Mexico, just south of the capital, and the capital of the State of Morelos.

A1

1867 **Handstamped**

1 A1 (1r) black *1,750.*
2 A1 (2r) black *40,000.*

No. 1 was canceled at Cuernavaca with the district name overprint. Supplies of overprinted stamps were sent to the Tetecala and Yquala sub-offices, where they were canceled with the usual local postmarks.

No. 2 was created by doubling the impression of the basic stamp and applying the district name overprint twice.

Unused examples of Nos. 1 and 2 do not exist.

Counterfeits exist.

Guadalajara

A city of Mexico and capital of the State of Jalisco.

A1

Dated "1867"
1st Printing
Medium Wove Paper

1867 **Handstamped** ***Imperf.***

1 A1 Medio r blk, *white* 350.00 250.00
2 A1 un r blk, *gray bl* 200.00
3 A1 un r blk, *dk bl* 450.00

4	A1	un r blk, *white*		150.00
5	A1	2r blk, *dk grn*	80.00	21.00
6	A1	2r blk, *white*		125.00
7	A1	4r blk, *rose*	250.00	*300.00*
a.		Half used as 2r on cover		500.00
8	A1	4r blk, *white*		500.00
9	A1	un p blk, *lilac*	250.00	*300.00*

Serrate Perf.

10	A1	un r blk, *gray bl*		400.00
11	A1	2r blk, *dk grn*		250.00
12	A1	4r blk, *rose*		350.00

2nd Printing

No Period after "2" or "4"

Thin Quadrille Paper

Imperf

13	A1	2r blk, *green*	30.00	20.00
a.		Half used as 1r on cover		400.00

Serrate Perf.

14	A1	2r blk, *green*		150.00

Thin Laid Batonné Paper

Imperf

15	A1	2r blk, *green*	45.00	24.00

Serrate Perf.

16	A1	2r blk, *green*		150.00

3rd Printing

Capital "U" in "Un" on 1r, 1p

Period after "2" and "4"

Thin Wove Paper

Imperf

16A	A1	Un r blk, *white*		125.00
17	A1	Un r blk, *blue*		90.00
17A	A1	Un r blk, *lilac*	100.00	
18	A1	2r blk, *rose*		50.00
18A	A1	4r blk, *blue*	500.00	*1,000.*

Serrate Perf.

19	A1	Un r blk, *blue*		300.00

Thin Quadrille Paper

Imperf

20	A1	2r blk, *rose*	42.50	42.50
21	A1	4r blk, *blue*	15.00	30.00
22	A1	4r blk, *white*	90.00	
23	A1	Un p blk, *lilac*	15.00	60.00
24	A1	Un p blk, *rose*	65.00	

Serrate Perf.

25	A1	Un p blk, *lilac*	750.00	300.00
25A	A1	Un p blk, *rose*		300.00

Thin Laid Batonné Paper

Imperf

26	A1	Un r blk, *green*	22.50	17.50
27	A1	2r blk, *rose*	27.50	22.50
27A	A1	2r blk, *green*		47.50
28	A1	4r blk, *blue*	17.50	42.50
29	A1	4r blk, *white*	100.00	
30	A1	Un p blk, *lilac*	30.00	52.50
31	A1	Un p blk, *rose*	65.00	

Serrate Perf.

32	A1	Un r blk, *green*	65.00	
33	A1	2r blk, *rose*	70.00	*200.00*
34	A1	4r blk, *blue*		250.00

Thin Oblong Quadrille Paper

Imperf

35	A1	Un r blk, *blue*	250.00	22.50
36	A1	4r blk, *blue*		600.00

Serrate Perf.

37	A1	Un r blk, *blue*		300.00

4th Printing

Dated "1868"

Wove Paper

1868 ***Imperf.***

38	A1	2r blk, *lilac*	30.00	14.00
a.		Half used as 1r on cover		500.00
39	A1	2r blk, *rose*	52.50	65.00

Serrate Perf.

40	A1	2r blk, *lilac*		52.50
41	A1	2r blk, *rose*		95.00

Laid Batonné Paper

Imperf

42	A1	un r blk, *green*	12.50	12.50
a.		"nu" instead of "un"		300.00
43	A1	2r blk, *lilac*	12.50	12.50

Serrate Perf.

44	A1	un r blk, *green*	250.00	200.00

Quadrille Paper.

Imperf

45	A1	2r blk, *lilac*	25.00	14.00

Serrate Perf.

46	A1	2r blk, *lilac*	300.00	300.00

Laid Paper

Imperf

47	A1	un r blk, *green*	13.00	17.00
a.		"nu" instead of "un"		70.00
48	A1	2r blk, *lilac*	32.50	32.50
49	A1	2r blk, *rose*	37.50	37.50

Serrate Perf.

50	A1	un r blk, *green*		55.00
51	A1	2r blk, *rose*	110.00	

Counterfeits of Nos. 1-51 abound.

Merida

A city of southeastern Mexico, capital of the State of Yucatan.

Mexico No. 521 Surcharged **25**

1916 **Wmk. 155** ***Perf. 14***

1	A40	25(c) on 5c org, on cover		*500.00*

The G.P.DE.M. overprint reads down.

Authorities consider the Monterrey, Morelia and Patzcuaro stamps to be bogus.

Tlacotalpan

A village in the state of Veracruz.

A1

Handstamped Monogram, Value in Manuscript

1856, Oct.

1	A1	½(r) black		*30,000.*

REVOLUTIONARY ISSUES

SINALOA

A northern state in Mexico, bordering on the Pacific Ocean. Stamps were issued by a provisional government.

Coat of Arms — A1

1929 **Unwmk.** **Litho.** ***Perf. 12***

1	A1	10c blk, red & bl	5.00	
a.		Tête bêche pair	35.00	
2	A1	20c blk, red & gray	5.00	

Just as Nos. 1 and 2 were ready to be placed on sale the state was occupied by the Federal forces and the stamps could not be used. At a later date a few copies were canceled by favor.

A recent find included a number of errors or printer's waste.

YUCATAN

A southeastern state of Mexico.

Chalchiuitlicue, Nahuatl Water Goddess — A1

"Casa de Monjas" A2

Temple of the Tigers A3

Without Gum

1924 **Unwmk.** **Litho.** ***Imperf.***

1	A1	5c violet	10.00	15.00
2	A2	10c carmine	40.00	50.00
3	A3	50c olive green	175.00	

Perf. 12

4	A1	5c violet	50.00	60.00
5	A2	10c carmine	50.00	75.00
6	A3	50c olive green	200.00	

Nos. 3 and 6 were not regularly issued.

MIDDLE CONGO

'mi-dᵊl 'käŋ-ₒgō

LOCATION — Western Africa at the Equator, bordering on the Atlantic Ocean
GOVT. — French Colony
AREA — 166,069
POP. — 746,805 (1936)
CAPITAL — Brazzaville

In 1910 Middle Congo, formerly a part of French Congo, was declared a separate colony. It was grouped with Gabon and the Ubangi-Shari and Chad Territories and officially designated French Equatorial Africa. This group became a single administrative unit in 1934. See Gabon.

100 Centimes = 1 Franc

Leopard A1

Bakalois Woman — A2

Coconut Grove — A3

Perf. 14x13½

1907-22 **Typo.** **Unwmk.**

1	A1	1c ol gray & brn	.30	.30
2	A1	2c vio & brn	.30	.30
3	A1	4c blue & brn	.65	.60
4	A1	5c dk grn & bl	.65	.35
5	A1	5c yel & bl ('22)	.75	.35
6	A1	10c car & bl	.65	.60
7	A1	10c dp grn & bl grn ('22)	2.75	2.75
8	A1	15c brn vio & rose	1.75	.65
9	A1	20c brown & bl	2.25	2.10
10	A2	25c blue & grn	1.10	.80
11	A2	25c bl grn & gray ('22)	.80	.80
12	A2	30c scar & grn	1.75	1.25
13	A2	30c dp rose & rose ('22)	1.40	1.40
14	A2	35c vio brn & bl	1.50	1.00
15	A2	40c dl grn & brn	1.50	1.00
16	A2	45c violet & red	4.50	3.00
17	A2	50c bl grn & red	1.75	1.50
18	A2	50c bl & grn ('22)	1.50	1.50
19	A2	75c brown & bl	5.75	4.00
20	A3	1fr dp grn & vio	8.50	6.50
21	A3	2fr vio & gray grn	9.50	5.75
22	A3	5fr blue & rose	26.50	21.00
		Nos. 1-22 (22)	76.10	57.50

For stamps of types A1-A3 in changed colors, see Chad and Ubangi-Shari. French Congo A4-A6 are similar but inscribed "Congo Francais."

For overprints and surcharges see Nos. 23-60, B1-B2.

Stamps and Types of 1907-22 Overprinted in Black, Blue or Red

1924-30

23	A1	1c ol gray & brn	.25	.20
24	A1	2c violet & brn	.25	.20
25	A1	4c blue & brn	.25	.20
26	A1	5c yellow & bl	.35	.20
27	A1	10c grn & bl grn (R)	.80	.20
28	A1	10c car & gray ('25)	.30	.30
29	A1	15c brn vio & rose (Bl)	.60	.35
a.		Double surcharge	85.00	
30	A1	20c brown & blue	.50	.45
31	A1	20c bl grn & yel grn ('26)	.30	.30
32	A1	20c dp brn & rose lil ('27)	1.10	.40

Overprinted

33	A2	25c bl grn & gray	.75	.35
34	A2	30c rose & pale rose (Bl)	1.10	.40
35	A2	30c gray & bl vio (R) ('25)	.60	.50
36	A2	30c dk grn & grn ('27)	1.25	.95
37	A2	35c choc & bl	.50	.50
38	A2	40c ol grn & brn	1.25	.80
39	A2	45c vio & pale red (Bl)	1.25	.80
a.		Inverted overprint	100.00	100.00
40	A2	50c blue & grn (R)	1.10	.60
41	A2	50c org & blk ('25)	.65	.50
a.		Without overprint	125.00	
42	A2	65c org brn & bl ('27)	2.00	1.40
43	A2	75c brown & blue	.95	.80
44	A2	90c brn red & pink ('30)	3.50	2.75
45	A3	1fr green & vio	1.25	1.00
a.		Double overprint	175.00	140.00
46	A3	1.10fr vio & brn ('28)	3.25	2.50
47	A3	1.50fr ultra & bl ('30)	4.75	3.50
48	A3	2fr vio & gray grn	1.25	1.00
49	A3	3fr red violet ('30)	5.50	4.25
50	A3	5fr blue & rose	3.75	2.50
		Nos. 23-50 (28)	39.35	27.90

Nos. 48 and 50 Surcharged with New Values

1924

51	A3	25c on 2fr vio & gray grn	.85	.85
52	A3	25c on 5fr bl & rose (Bl)	.85	.85

Types of 1924-27 Surcharged with New Values in Black or Red

1925-27

53	A3	65c on 1fr red org & ol brn	.80	.80
54	A3	85c on 1fr red org & ol brn	.80	.80
55	A2	90c on 75c brn red & rose red ('27)	1.40	1.25
56	A3	1.25fr on 1fr dl bl & ultra (R)	.60	.60
57	A3	1.50fr on 1fr ultra & bl ('27)	1.40	1.25
a.		New value omitted	100.00	
58	A3	3fr on 5fr org brn & dl red ('27)	3.00	2.00
a.		New value omitted	225.00	
59	A3	10fr on 5fr ver & bl grn ('27)	9.50	8.00
60	A3	20fr on 5fr org brn & vio ('27)	10.00	8.00
		Nos. 53-60 (8)	27.50	22.70

Bars cover old values on Nos. 56-60.

Common Design Types pictured following the introduction.

Colonial Exposition Issue
Common Design Types

1931 **Engr.** ***Perf. 12½***

Name of Country in Black

61	CD70	40c deep green	3.25	2.75
62	CD71	50c violet	2.50	2.00
63	CD72	90c red orange	2.50	2.50
64	CD73	1.50fr dull blue	4.00	3.25
		Nos. 61-64 (4)	12.25	10.50

Viaduct at Mindouli A4

Pasteur Institute at Brazzaville A5

Government Building, Brazzaville — A6

1933 **Photo.** ***Perf. 13½***

65	A4	1c lt brown	.20	.20
66	A4	2c dull blue	.20	.20
67	A4	4c olive grn	.25	.20
68	A4	5c red violet	.45	.20
69	A4	10c slate	.45	.20
70	A4	15c dk violet	.95	.50
71	A4	20c red, *pink*	7.25	4.25
72	A4	25c orange	.95	.70
73	A4	30c yellow grn	1.75	1.10
74	A5	40c orange brn	2.00	.95
75	A5	45c blk, *green*	1.10	.95
76	A5	50c black violet	.75	.60
77	A5	65c brn red, *grn*	1.25	.60
78	A5	75c black, *pink*	11.00	5.75
79	A5	90c carmine	1.40	.70
80	A5	1fr dark red	.95	.55
81	A5	1.25fr Prus blue	1.75	.75
82	A5	1.50fr dk blue	8.00	2.75
83	A6	1.75fr dk violet	1.90	.80
84	A6	2fr grnsh blk	1.90	.90
85	A6	3fr orange	4.00	2.75
86	A6	5fr slate blue	13.50	10.00
87	A6	10fr black	45.00	23.50
88	A6	20fr dark brown	26.00	19.00
		Nos. 65-88 (24)	132.95	78.10

SEMI-POSTAL STAMPS

No. 6 Surcharged in Black

1916 **Unwmk.** ***Perf. 14x13½***

B1	A1	10c + 5c car & blue	1.10	1.00
a.		Double surcharge	95.00	95.00
b.		Inverted surcharge	85.00	85.00

A printing with the surcharge placed lower and more to the left was made and used in Ubangi.

No. 6 Surcharged in Red

B2	A1	10c + 5c car & blue	1.00	1.00

POSTAGE DUE STAMPS

Postage Due Stamps of France Overprinted

1928 **Unwmk.** ***Perf. 14x13½***

J1	D2	5c light blue	.35	.35
J2	D2	10c gray brn	.60	.60
J3	D2	20c olive grn	.80	.80
J4	D2	25c brt rose	1.00	1.00
J5	D2	30c lt red	1.10	1.10
J6	D2	45c blue grn	1.10	1.10
J7	D2	50c brown vio	1.25	1.25
J8	D2	60c yellow brn	2.00	2.00
J9	D2	1fr red brn	2.00	2.00
J10	D2	2fr orange red	2.75	2.75
J11	D2	3fr brt violet	4.50	4.50
		Nos. J1-J11 (11)	17.45	17.45

Village on Ubangi, Dance Mask — D3

Steamer on Ubangi River — D4

1930 **Typo.**

J12	D3	5c dp bl & ol	.60	.60
J13	D3	10c dp red & brn	.90	.90
J14	D3	20c green & brn	2.10	2.10
J15	D3	25c lt bl & brn	3.00	3.00
J16	D3	30c bis brn & Prus bl	4.00	4.00
J17	D3	45c Prus bl & ol	4.75	4.75
J18	D3	50c red vio & brn	4.75	4.75
J19	D3	60c gray lil & bl blk	5.25	5.25
J20	D4	1fr bis brn & bl blk	9.00	9.00
J21	D4	2fr violet & brn	9.75	9.75
J22	D4	3fr dk red & brn	9.75	9.75
		Nos. J12-J22 (11)	53.85	53.85

Rubber Trees and Djoué River — D5

1933 **Photo.** ***Perf. 13½***

J23	D5	5c apple green	.60	.60
J24	D5	10c dk bl, *bl*	.60	.60
J25	D5	20c red, *yel*	1.10	1.10
J26	D5	25c chocolate	1.10	1.10
J27	D5	30c orange red	1.60	1.60
J28	D5	45c dk violet	1.60	1.60
J29	D5	50c gray black	2.10	2.10
J30	D5	60c blk, *orange*	3.25	3.25
J31	D5	1fr brown rose	4.75	4.75
J32	D5	2fr orange yel	5.75	5.75
J33	D5	3fr Prus blue	9.25	9.25
		Nos. J23-J33 (11)	31.70	31.70

MOHELI

mo-'ā-lē

LOCATION — One of the Comoro Islands, situated in the Mozambique Channel midway between Madagascar and Mozambique (Africa)
GOVT. — French Colony
AREA — 89 sq. mi.
POP. — 4,000
CAPITAL — Fomboni
See Comoro Islands

100 Centimes = 1 Franc

Navigation and Commerce — A1

Perf. 14x13½

1906-07 **Typo.** **Unwmk.**

Name of Colony in Blue or Carmine

1	A1	1c blk, *lil bl*	2.50	1.50
2	A1	2c brn, *buff*	1.25	1.00
3	A1	4c claret, *lav*	2.25	1.75
4	A1	5c yellow grn	2.75	1.75
5	A1	10c carmine	3.50	1.75
6	A1	20c red, *green*	9.25	5.25
7	A1	25c blue	9.25	4.25
8	A1	30c brn, *bister*	13.00	10.00
9	A1	35c blk, *yellow*	7.50	3.25
10	A1	40c red, *straw*	13.00	9.25
11	A1	45c blk, *gray grn* ('07)	57.50	42.50
12	A1	50c brn, *az*	18.00	11.00
13	A1	75c dp vio, *org*	20.00	18.00
14	A1	1fr brnz grn, *straw*	18.00	12.00
15	A1	2fr vio, *rose*	26.50	26.50
16	A1	5fr lil, *lavender*	105.00	100.00
		Nos. 1-16 (16)	309.25	249.75

Perf. 13½x14 stamps are counterfeits.

No. 12, affixed to pressboard with animals printed on the back, was used as emergency currency in the Comoro Islands in 1920.

Issue of 1906-07 Surcharged in Carmine or Black

1912

Spacing between figures of surcharge 1.5mm (5c), 2mm (10c)

17	A1	5c on 4c cl, *lav* (C)	1.25	1.25
18	A1	5c on 20c red, *grn*	2.50	2.50
19	A1	5c on 30c brn, *bis* (C)	1.50	1.50
20	A1	10c on 40c red, *straw*	1.50	1.50
21	A1	10c on 45c blk, *gray grn* (C)	1.25	1.25
a.		"Moheli" double	350.00	
b.		"Moheli" triple	350.00	
22	A1	10c on 50c brn, *az* (C)	2.50	2.50
		Nos. 17-22 (6)	10.50	10.50

Spacing between figures of surcharge 2.25mm (5c), 2.75mm (10c)

17a	A1	5c on 4c cl, *lav* (C)	13.00	13.00
18a	A1	5c on 20c red, *grn*	42.50	42.50
19a	A1	5c on 30c brn, *bis* (C)	42.50	42.50
20a	A1	10c on 40c red, *straw*	130.00	130.00
21c	A1	10c on 45c blk, *gray grn* (C)	60.00	60.00
22a	A1	10c on 50c brn, *az* (C)	125.00	125.00
		Nos. 17a-22a (6)	413.00	413.00

The stamps of Mohéli were supposed to have been superseded by those of Madagascar, January, 1908. However, Nos. 17-22 were surcharged in 1912 to use up remainders. These were available for use in Madagascar and the entire Comoro archipelago. In 1950 stamps of Comoro Islands came into use.

MONACO

'mä-nə-ˌkō

LOCATION — Southern coast of France, bordering on the Mediterranean Sea
GOVT. — Principality
AREA — 481 acres
POP. — 27,063 (1982)
CAPITAL — Monaco

100 Centimes = 1 Franc

STAMPS OF SARDINIA

CANCELLED WITH SARDINIAN "MENTONE" C.D.S.

1851

A1	20c blue (#2) on cover, stamp pen cancelled	*7,500.*

No. A1 is unique.

1853

A2	20c blue (#5)	—

1854

A3	20c blue (#8)	—

1855-60

A4	5c yellow green (#10a)	925.00
	On cover	—
A5	10c bister (#11)	450.00
	On cover	—
A6	20c light blue (#12b)	450.00
	On cover	*8,100.*
A7	40c red (#13)	600.00
	On cover	—
A8	80c orange yellow (#14)	2,750.
	On cover	—

With French Small Figures "4220" for Menton

A9	10c bister (#11)	*1,500.*
A10	80c orange yellow (#14)	*5,100.*

STAMPS OF SARDINIA CANCELLED WITH SARDINIAN "MONACO" C.D.S.

1853

A12	20c blue (#5) on cover	*9,000.*

One cover and four singles of No. A12 are known.

1854

A13	20c blue (#8) on cover	—

One example of No. A12 is known.

1855-60

A14	5c yellow green (#10a)	1,900.
	On cover	*21,500.*
A15	10c bister (#11)	900.00
	On cover, from	*16,250.*
A16	20c light blue (#12b)	750.00
	On cover, from	*10,800.*
A17	40c red (#13)	1,200.
	On cover, from	*16,250.*
A18	80c orange yellow (#14)	5,400.
	On cover	*21,500.*

With French Small Figures "4222" for Monaco

A19	10c bister (#11)	*2,200.*
A20	20c blue (#12a)	*1,800.*
A21	40c red (#13)	*2,900.*
A22	80c orange yellow (#14)	*4,000.*

STAMPS OF FRANCE CANCELLED WITH SARDINIAN "MENTONE" C.D.S.

A23	10c bister (#14)	875.00
	On cover, from	*4,800.*
A24	20c blue(#15)	425.00
	On cover, from	*3,000.*
A25	40c orange(#18)	1,450.
	On cover, from	*10,000.*
A26	80c carmine(#19)	1,450.
	On cover, from	*10,000.*

STAMPS OF FRANCE CANCELLED WITH SARDINIAN "MONACO" C.D.S.

A27	10c bister (#14)	1,325.
	On cover, from	*11,000.*
A28	20c blue(#15)	725.00
	On cover, from	*11,000.*
A29	40c orange(#18)	1,600.
A30	80c carmine(#19)	2,900.

STAMPS OF FRANCE CANCELLED WITH VARIOUS FRENCH POSTMARKS OF MONACO "4222" SMALL FIGURES

Empire, Imperf

1853-60

A31	1c olive green (#12)	1,600.
A32	5c green (#13)	1,325.
A33	10c bister (#14)	550.
	On cover, from	*5,750.*
A34	20c blue (#15)	375.
	On cover, from	*3,300.*
A35	40c orange (#18)	1,100.
	On cover, from	*13,800.*
A36	80c carmine(#19)	1,750.
A37	20c blue (#26)	*16,500.*

Empire, Imperf

1853-60 **1853-60**

"2387" LARGE FIGURES

A38	1c olive green (#12)	—
A39	5c yellow green (#13)	1,000.
A40	10c bister (#14)	550.00
A41	20c blue (#15)	450.00
A42	40c orange (#18)	1,000.
A43	80c carmine(#19)	—

1862-71 ***Empire, Perforated***

A44	1c olive green (#22)	725.00
A45	5c yellow green (#23)	300.00
	On cover, from	*2,600.*
A46	10c bister (#25)	60.00
	On cover, from	725.00

A47 20c blue (#26) 110.00
On cover, from 300.00
A48 40c orange (#27) 210.00
On cover, from *3,600.*
A49 80c rose (#28) 850.00
On cover, from *10,800.*

1863-70 ***Empire, "Laureated"***

A50 1c bronze green, *pale blue* (#29) 210.00
On cover, from *3,000.*
A51 2c red brown, *yellowish* (#30) 290.00
A52 4c gray (#31) 325.00
On cover, from *3,300.*
A53 10c bister, *yellowish* (#32) 110.00
On cover, from 725.00
A54 20c blue, *bluish* (#33) 70.00
On cover, from 290.00
A55 30c brown, *yelsh* (#34) 160.00
On cover, from *1,450.*
A56 40c orange, *yelsh* (#35) 140.00
On cover, from *1,200.*
A57 80c rose, *pinkish* (#36) 210.00
On cover, from *1,900.*
A58 5fr gray lilac, *lav* (#37) 1,900.

1870-71 ***Bordeaux Issue***

A59 1c olive green, *pale blue* (#38) 450.00
A60 2c red brown, *yellowish* (B) (#39) 1,000.
A61 4c gray (#40) 1,000.
A62 5c green, *greenish* (#41) 400.00
On cover, from 400.00
A63 10c bister, *yellowish* (A) (#42) 290.00
On cover, from 2,150.
A64 20c blue, *bluish* (#43) 8,400.
A65 20c blue, *bluish* (#44) 290.00
On cover, from *2,200.*
A66 20c blue, *bluish* (#45) 290.00
On cover, from *2,150.*
A67 30c brown, *yelsh* (#46) 550.00
A68 40c orange, *yelsh* (#47) 450.00
A69 80c rose, *pinkish* (#48) 600.00

1870-73 ***Ceres***

A70 1c olive green, *pale blue* (#50) 210.00
A71 2c red brown, *yellowish* (#51) 300.00
A72 4c gray (#52) 240.00
A73 5c yellow green, *pale blue* (#53) 140.00
On cover, from 1,600.
A74 10c bister, *yellowish* (#54) 700.00
A75 10c bister, *rose* ('73) (#55) 150.00
On cover, from 1,400.
A76 15c bister, *yellowish* ('71) (#56) 110.00
On cover, from 1,100.
A77 20c dull blue, *bluish* (#57) 200.00
On cover, from 1,950.
A78 40c orange, *yelsh* (I) (#59) 110.00
On cover, from 1,100.

Ceres, Larger Figures of Value

1872-75

A79 10c bister, *rose* ('75) (#60) 150.00
On cover, from 1,500.
A80 15c bister ('73) (#61) 140.00
On cover, from 1,600.
A81 30c brown, *yellowish* (#62) 150.00
On cover, from 1,900.
A82 80c rose, *pinkish* (#63) 210.00
On cover, from 1,900.

Empire, Imperf

1862-71 **1862-71**

"2387" SMALL FIGURES

A83 10c bister (#25) 725.00
On cover, from *16,500.*
A84 20c blue (#26) 450.00
On cover, from *7,200.*
A85 40c orange (#27) 450.00
On cover, from *7,200.*

1863-70 ***Empire, "Laureated"***

A86 20c blue, *bluish* (#33) 600.00
On cover, from *8,400.*
A87 30c brown, *yelsh* (#34) 450.00
On cover, from *6,600.*
A88 40c orange, *yelsh* (#35) 240.00
On cover, from *4,900.*
A89 80c rose, *pinkish* (#36) 290.00
A90 5fr gray lilac, *lav* (#37) 2,100.

1870-71 ***Bordeaux Issue***

A91 5c green, *greenish* (#41) 925.00
A92 10c bister, *yellowish* (A) (#42) 325.00
On cover 7,200.
A93 20c blue, *bluish* (#43) 1,100.
A94 20c blue, *bluish* ('71) (#45) 1,100.
A95 30c brown, *yelsh* (#46) 1,100.
On cover 7,200.
A96 40c orange, *yelsh* (#47) 500.00
On cover *6,300.*
A97 80c rose, *pinkish* (#48) 600.00
On cover 1,600.

Ceres, Larger Figures of Value

1872-75

A98 30c brown, *yellowish* (#62) 400.00
A99 80c rose, *pinkish* (#63) —

"MONACO / (87)" DOUBLE CIRCLE DATESTAMP, DATE IN 3 LINES, WITHOUT TIME INDICIA

Empire, Imperf

1853-60

A100 1c olive green (#12) 210.00
A101 5c yellow green (#13) 325.00
A102 10c bister (#14) 275.00
A103 20c blue (#15) 275.00
A104 40c orange (#18) —

1862-71 ***Empire, Perforated***

A105 1c olive green (#22) 200.00
A106 5c yellow green (#23) 200.00
On cover, from 425.00
A107 5c green, *pale blue* ('71) (I) (#24) —
A108 10c bister (#25) 160.00
A109 20c blue (#26) 290.00
On cover, from 2,900.
A110 40c orange (#27) 200.00
On cover, from 2,900.
A111 80c rose (#28) 650.00

1863-70 ***Empire, "Laureated"***

A112 1c bronze green, *pale blue* (#29) —
A113 2c red brown, *yellowish* (#30) 87.50
On cover, from *1,600.*
A114 4c gray (#31) 87.50
On cover, from *1,400.*
A115 10c bister, *yellowish* (#32) 140.00
A116 20c blue, *bluish* (#33) 290.00
On cover, from *2,200.*
A117 30c brown, *yelsh* (#34) —
A118 40c orange, *yelsh* (#35) —
A119 80c rose, *pinkish* (#36) —
A120 5fr gray lilac, *lav* (#37) 1,900.

"MONACO / (87)" SINGLE CIRCLE DATESTAMP, DATE IN 3 LINES, WITH TIME INDICIA

Empire, Perforated

1862-71

A121 10c bister (#25) 400.00

1863-70 ***Empire, "Laureated"***

A122 1c brnz grn, *pale blue* (#29) 160.00
A123 2c red brn, *yelsh* (#30) 130.00
A124 4c gray (#31) 130.00
A125 10c bister, *yellowish* (#32) 400.00
A126 20c blue, *bluish* (#33) 325.00

1870-71 ***Bordeaux Issue***

A127 5c green, *greenish* (#41) 500.00

1870-73 ***Ceres***

A128 1c ol grn, *pale blue* (#50) 290.00
A129 2c red brn, *yelsh* (#51) 290.00
A130 4c gray (#52) 290.00
A131 5c yel grn, *pale blue* (#53) 290.00

"MONACO / (87)" DOUBLE CIRCLE DATESTAMP, DATE IN 3 LINES, WITH TIME INDICIA

Empire, Perforated

1862-71

A132 1c olive green (#22) 200.00
A133 5c yellow green (#23) 200.00
On cover, from 450.00
A134 5c green, *pale blue* ('71) (I) (#24) 210.00
A135 10c bister (#25) 200.00
A136 20c blue (#26) 300.00
A137 40c orange (#27) —
A138 80c rose (#28) —

1863-70 ***Empire, "Laureated"***

A139 1c brnz grn, *pale blue* (#29) 125.00
A140 2c red brn, *yelsh* (#30) 85.00
On cover, from *1,000.*
A141 4c gray (#31) 110.00
On cover, from *1,100.*
A142 10c bister, *yellowish* (#32) 125.00
A143 20c blue, *bluish* (#33) 240.00
On cover, from *3,000.*
A144 30c brown, *yelsh* (#34) 325.00
A145 40c orange, *yelsh* (#35) 240.00
A146 80c rose, *pinkish* (#36) 325.00
A147 5fr gray lilac, *lav* (#37) 1,900.

1870-71 ***Bordeaux Issue***

A148 1c ol grn, *pale blue* (#38) 325.00
On cover, from *3,250.*
A149 2c red brn, *yelsh* (B) (#39) 450.00
A150 4c gray (#40) 725.00
On cover, from *4,900.*
A151 5c green, *greenish* (#41) 400.00
On cover —
A152 10c bister, *yelsh* (A) (#42) 210.00
On cover —
A153 20c blue, *bluish* (#44) 210.00
On cover, from *4,400.*
A154 20c blue, *bluish* (#45) 210.00
On cover, from *3,800.*
A155 30c brown, *yelsh* (#46) 725.00
A156 40c orange, *yelsh* (#47) 325.00
A157 80c rose, *pinkish* (#48) 500.00

1870-73 ***Ceres***

A158 1c ol grn, *pale blue* (#50) 110.00
A159 2c red brn, *yelsh* (#51) 110.00
On cover, from *1,600.*
A160 4c gray (#52) 110.00
A161 5c yel grn, *pale blue* (#53) 72.50
On cover, from *1,200.*
A162 10c bister, *rose* ('73) (#55) 140.00
On cover 1,200.
A163 15c bister, *yelsh* ('71) (#56) 92.50
On cover, from 1,400.
A164 20c dull blue, *bluish* (#57) 160.00
A165 25c blue, *bluish* ('71) (#58) 92.50
On cover, from *725.00*
A166 40c orange, *yelsh* (I) (#59) 190.00
On cover, from 2,100.

Ceres, Larger Figures of Value

1872-75

A167 10c bister, *rose* ('75) (#60) 140.00
On cover, from *1,200.*
A168 15c bister ('73) (#61) 92.50
On cover, from *1,400.*
A169 30c brown, *yellowish* (#62) 140.00
On cover, from 1,800.
A170 80c rose, *pinkish* (#63) 290.00
On cover —

"MONACO / PRINCIPAUTE" DOUBLE CIRCLE DATESTAMP, DATE IN 3 LINES, WITH TIME INDICIA

Empire, "Laureated"

1863-70

A171 5fr gray lilac, *lav* (#37) 1,600.

1870-73 ***Ceres***

A172 1c ol grn, *pale blue* (#50) 110.00
A173 2c red brn, *yelsh* (#51) 110.00
On cover, from *1,600.*
A174 4c gray (#52) 110.00
A175 5c yel grn, *pale blue* (#53) 85.00
On cover, from *1,200.*
A176 15c bister, *yelsh* ('71) (#56) 140.00
On cover, from —
A177 20c dull blue, *bluish* (#57) —
A178 25c blue, *bluish* ('71) (#58) 85.00
On cover, from *725.00*
A179 40c orange, *yelsh* (I) (#59) 290.00
On cover —

Ceres, Larger Figures of Value

1872-75

A180 10c bister, *rose* ('75) (#60) 140.00
On cover, from *1,200.*
A181 15c bister ('73) (#61) 85.00
On cover, from *1,400.*
A182 30c brown, *yellowish* (#62) 140.00
On cover, from *1,800.*
A183 80c rose, *pinkish* (#63) 290.00
On cover —

"MONACO / PRINCIPAUTE" DOUBLE CIRCLE DATESTAMP, DATE IN 3 LINES, WITH TIME INDICIA IN SANS SERIF CHARACTERS

Peace & Commerce Issue, Type I ("N" under "B")

1876-78

A184 1c green, *greenish* (#64) 290.00
On cover —
A185 2c green, *greenish* (#65) 1,200.
On cover —
A186 4c green, *greenish* (#66) 210.00
On cover —
A187 5c green, *greenish* (#67) 210.00
On cover *6,600.*
A188 10c green, *greenish* (#68) 2,100.
On cover —
A189 15c gray lilac, *grayish* (#69) 160.00
On cover *875.00*
A190 20c red brown, *straw* (#70) 210.00
On cover —
A191 25c ultramarine, *bluish* (#72) 210.00
On cover *1,200.*
A192 30c brown, *yellowish* (#73) 140.00
On cover *875.00*
A193 40c red, *straw* (#74) 150.00
On cover *1,200.*
A194 75c carmine, *rose* (#75) 210.00
On cover 550.00
A195 1fr bronze green, *straw* (#76) 110.00
On cover *2,100.*

Peace & Commerce Issue, Type II ("N" under "U")

1876-90

A196 2c green, *greenish* (#77) 210.00
On cover —
A197 5c green, *greenish* (#78) 40.00
On cover 500.00
A198 10c green, *greenish* (#79) 725.00
On cover —
A199 15c gray lilac, *grayish* (#80) 42.50
On cover 325.00
A200 25c ultramarine, *bluish* (#81) 42.50
On cover 210.00
A201 25c blue, *bluish* (#81a) 55.00
On cover 290.00
A202 30c yel brn, *yelsh* (#82) 110.00
On cover —
A203 75c car, *rose* ('77) (#83) —
On cover —
A204 1fr brnz grn, *straw* ('77) (#84) 110.00
On cover 1,400.
A205 1c black, *lilac blue*(#86) 210.00
On cover *2,800.*
A206 2c brown, *straw* (#88) 160.00
On cover —
A207 3c yellow, *straw* ('78) (#89) 210.00
On cover —
A208 4c claret, *lavender* (#90) 72.50
On cover 1,600.
A209 10c black, *lavender* (#91) 72.50
On cover 1,100.
A210 15c blue ('78) (#92) 40.00
On cover 210.00
A211 25c black, *red* ('78) (#93) 85.00
On cover *1,300.*
A212 35c black, *yellow* ('78) (#94) 725.00
On cover —
A213 40c red, *straw* ('80) (#95) 65.00
On cover 850.00
A214 5fr violet, *lavender* (#96) 290.00
On cover *7,200.*
A215 3c gray, *grayish* ('80) (#97) 160.00
On cover —
A216 20c red, *yellow green* (#98) 110.00
On cover —
A217 25c yellow, *straw* (#99) 42.50
On cover *425.00*

"MONACO / ALPES-MARITIMES" DOUBLE CIRCLE DATESTAMP, DATE IN 3 LINES, WITH TIME INDICIA

Ceres

1870-73

A218 4c gray (#52) 1,900.
A219 5c yel grn, *pale blue* (#53) 1,900.
A220 25c blue, *bluish* ('71) (#58) 1,100.
On cover *10,000.*

"MONTE-CARLO / PTE. DE MONACO" DOUBLE CIRCLE DATESTAMP, DATE IN 3 LINES, WITH TIME INDICIA

Peace & Commerce Issue, Type II ("N" under "U")

1876-90

A221 2c green, *greenish* (#77) —
A222 5c green, *greenish* (#78) 72.50
A223 10c green, *greenish* (#79) —
A224 15c gray lilac, *grayish* (#80) —
A225 25c ultramarine, *bluish* (#81) —
A226 25c blue, *bluish* (#81a) —
A227 30c yel brn, *yelsh* (#82) 190.00

A228 75c carm, *rose* ('77) (#83) —
A229 1fr brnz grn, *straw* ('77) (#84) 110.00
A230 1c black, *lilac blue*(#86) 110.00
A231 2c brown, *straw* (#88) 72.50
A232 3c yellow, *straw* ('78) (#89) —
A233 4c claret, *lavender* (#90) 72.50
A234 10c black, *lavender* (#91) 72.50
A235 15c blue ('78) (#92) 65.00
On cover 875.00
A236 25c black, *red* ('78) (#93) 85.00
On cover 1,100.
A237 35c black, *yellow* ('78) (#94) —
A238 40c red, *straw* ('80) (#95) 110.00
A239 5fr violet, *lavender* (#96) 475.00
A240 3c gray, *grayish* ('80) (#97) 110.00
A241 20c red, *yellow green* (#98) 110.00
A242 25c yellow, *straw* (#99) 72.50

Other "Monte-Carlo" cancelations exist, used at mail transit offices.

POSTAGE DUE STAMPS OF FRANCE "MONACO / PRINCIPAUTE" DOUBLE CIRCLE DATESTAMP, DATE IN 3 LINES, WITH TIME INDICIA

Empire, "Laureated"

1859-95

AJ1 10c black (#J3) —
AJ2 15c black ('63) (#J4) 900.00
AJ3 25c black ('71) (#J6) 1,300.
AJ4 30c black ('78) (#J7) 1,300.
AJ5 1c black (#J11) 42.50
On cover 300.00
AJ6 2c black (#J12) 72.50
On cover 875.00
AJ7 3c black (#J13) 72.50
On cover 950.00
AJ8 4c black (#J14) 110.00
On cover —
AJ9 5c black (#J15) 35.00
On cover 290.00
AJ10 10c black (#J16) 35.00
On cover 290.00
AJ11 15c black (#J17) 55.00
On cover 325.00
AJ12 20c black (#J18) 160.00
On cover —
AJ13 30c black (#J19) 55.00
On cover 290.00
AJ14 40c black (#J20) 140.00
On cover —
AJ15 50c black ('92) (#J21) 160.00
On cover 1,100.
AJ16 60c black ('84) (#J22) 130.00
On cover 725.00
AJ17 2fr black ('84) (#J24) 850.00
AJ18 5fr black ('84) (#J25) 1,400.
AJ19 1fr brown (#J26) 475.00
AJ20 2fr brown (#J27) 475.00
AJ21 5fr brown (#J28) 725.00
AJ22 5c blue ('94) (#J29) 29.00
On cover 72.50
AJ23 10c brown (#J30) 29.00
On cover 90.00
AJ24 15c light green ('94) (#J31) 29.00
On cover 110.00
AJ25 30c red ('94) (#J34) 29.00
On cover 90.00
AJ26 50c brn violet ('95) (#J38) 35.00
On cover 140.00

"MONTE-CARLO / PTE. DE MONACO" DOUBLE CIRCLE DATESTAMP, DATE IN 3 LINES, WITH TIME INDICIA

1882-95

AJ27 1c black (#J11) 42.50
On cover 290.00
AJ28 2c black (#J12) 72.50
On cover 950.00
AJ29 3c black (#J13) 85.00
AJ30 4c black (#J14) —
AJ31 5c black (#J15) 55.00
On cover 325.00
AJ32 10c black (#J16) 55.00
On cover 290.00
AJ33 15c black (#J17) 32.50
On cover 290.00
AJ34 20c black (#J18) 240.00
On cover —
AJ35 30c black (#J19) 55.00
On cover 325.00
AJ36 40c black (#J20) 160.00
On cover —
AJ37 50c black ('92) (#J21) 160.00
On cover 875.00
AJ38 60c black ('84) (#J22) —
AJ39 1fr brown (#J26) 360.00
AJ40 2fr brown (#J27) —
AJ41 5fr brown (#J28) 475.00
AJ42 5c blue ('94) (#J29) 21.00
On cover 55.00
AJ43 10c brown (#J30) 29.00
On cover 85.00
AJ44 15c light green ('94) (#J31) 29.00
On cover 85.00
AJ45 30c red ('94) (#J34) 21.00
On cover 55.00
AJ46 50c brn violet ('95) (#J38) 35.00
On cover 110.00

Other "Monte-Carlo" cancelations exist, used at mail transit offices.

Issues of the Principality

Values for unused stamps are for examples with original gum as defined in the catalogue introduction. Very fine examples of Nos. 1-181, B1-B50, C1 and J1-J27 will have perforations clear of the design and/or frameline. Very well centered are worth more than the values quoted.

Prince Charles III — A1

Prince Albert I — A2

1885 Unwmk. Typo. *Perf. 14x13½*

1 A1 1c olive green 25.00 16.00
Never hinged 37.50
On cover with other values 290.00
On postal stationery to upgrade rate 525.00
a. 1c bronze green 30.00 21.00
Never hinged 45.00
2 A1 2c dull lilac 57.50 25.00
Never hinged 72.50
On cover with other values 290.00
On postal stationery to upgrade rate 525.00
a. 2c slate violet 62.50 32.50
Never hinged 80.00
3 A1 5c blue 70.00 35.00
Never hinged 85.00
On cover with other values 175.00
On postal stationery to upgrade rate 290.00
4 A1 10c brown, *straw* 82.50 35.00
Never hinged 120.00
On cover with other values 225.00
On postal stationery to upgrade rate 225.00
5 A1 15c rose 350.00 17.50
Never hinged 475.00
On cover 175.00
6 A1 25c green 700.00 65.00
Never hinged 925.00
On cover 350.00
7 A1 40c slate, *rose* 85.00 42.50
Never hinged 110.00
On cover 225.00
On cover, single franking 400.00
8 A1 75c black, *rose* 275.00 110.00
Never hinged 400.00
On cover 800.00
On cover, single franking *1,150.*
9 A1 1fr black, *yellow* 1,750. 450.00
Never hinged 2,300.
On cover *4,000.*
Philatelic cover, single franking *2,900.*
10 A1 5fr rose, *green* 3,000. 1,850.
Never hinged 4,400.
On registered cover *11,500.*
On money letter *10,500.*
Philatelic cover, single franking *7,750.*

Values for blocks of 4

1 A1 1c olive green 125.00 92.50
Never hinged 190.00
On cover 160.00
2 A1 2c dull lilac 260.00 260.00
Never hinged 350.00
On cover 375.00
3 A1 5c blue 400.00 225.00
Never hinged 600.00
On cover 575.00
4 A1 10c brown, *straw* 400.00 225.00
Never hinged 600.00
On cover 550.00
5 A1 15c rose 2,200. 150.00
Never hinged 2,750.
6 A1 25c green 5,500. 700.00
Never hinged 7,000.
7 A1 40c slate, *rose* 425.00 350.00
Never hinged 525.00
On cover 1,300.
8 A1 75c black, *rose* 1,700. 690.00
Never hinged 2,400.
9 A1 1fr black, *yellow* *12,000.* *9,500.*
Never hinged

No blocks of No. 10 are known. A few pairs do exist. Values: unused $14,500; used $5,750.

1891-1921

11 A2 1c olive green .70 .70
Never hinged 1.10
On cover 8.50
On printed matter 175.00
12 A2 2c dull violet .80 .80
Never hinged 1.25
On cover 8.50
On printed matter 115.00
13 A2 5c blue 45.00 5.75
Never hinged 85.00
On cover 24.00
On cover, single franking 90.00
14 A2 5c yellow grn ('01) .35 .35
Never hinged .65
On cover 7.00
On cover, single franking 57.50
15 A2 10c brown, *straw* 100.00 14.00
Never hinged 160.00
On cover 85.00
On cover, with #13 (15c rate) 175.00
On cover, single franking —
a. 10c dark brown, *yellow* 110.00 17.50
Never hinged 175.00
16 A2 10c carmine ('01) 2.75 .70
Never hinged 6.25
On cover 29.00
On postcard 29.00
a. 10c rose 3.50 .60
Never hinged 7.00
On cover 29.00
17 A2 15c rose 175.00 7.75
Never hinged 275.00
On cover 30.00
On cover, single franking 85.00
a. Double impression *1,300.*
18 A2 15c vio brn, *straw* ('01) 2.75 1.00
Never hinged 6.25
On cover 30.00
19 A2 15c gray green ('21) 1.75 *2.25*
Never hinged 2.90
On cover 18.00
On cover, single franking 30.00
20 A2 25c green 250.00 29.00
Never hinged 400.00
On cover 90.00
On cover, single franking 175.00
21 A2 25c deep blue ('01) 14.00 4.50
Never hinged 26.00
On cover 57.50
22 A2 40c slate, *rose* ('94) 3.50 2.10
Never hinged 5.50
On cover 57.50
On cover, single franking 85.00
23 A2 50c violet brown (shades), *orange* 6.50 4.25
Never hinged 11.50
On cover 29.00
On cover, single franking 57.50
a. 50c brown, *orange* 12.50 12.50
Never hinged 21.00
On cover 35.00
24 A2 75c vio brn, *buff* ('94) 27.50 17.00
Never hinged 50.00
On cover 140.00
On cover, single franking 290.00
a. 75c lilac brown, *buff* 36.00 27.50
Never hinged 62.50
On cover 50.00
25 A2 75c ol brn, *buff* ('21) 18.00 *19.00*
Never hinged 40.00
On cover 115.00
On cover, single franking —
26 A2 1fr black, *yellow* 15.00 9.75
Never hinged 30.00
On cover 115.00
On cover, single franking —
a. 1fr black, *pale yel straw* 15.00 11.50
Never hinged 30.00
On cover 125.00
27 A2 5fr rose, *grn* 85.00 80.00
Never hinged 175.00
On cover 975.00
Philatelic cover, overfranked 350.00
a. 5fr carmine rose, *green* 160.00 120.00
Never hinged 350.00
Philatelic cover, overfranked 350.00
b. Perf 11 *2,000.*
28 A2 5fr dull violet ('21) 175.00 *200.00*
Never hinged 310.00
On cover *1,400.*
Philatelic cover, overfranked 850.00
29 A2 5fr dark green ('21) 19.00 *25.00*
Never hinged 37.50
On cover 290.00
Philatelic cover, overfranked 115.00
a. 5fr pale green ('21) 400.00 275.00
Never hinged 575.00
Nos. 11-29 (19) 942.60 423.90

The handstamp "OL" in a circle of dots is a cancellation, not an overprint.

On cover values for Nos. 27-29 are for overfranked philatelic covers.

See No. 1782. For overprints and surcharges see Nos. 30-35, 57-59, B1.

Stamps of 1901-21 Overprinted or Surcharged:

1921, Mar. 5

30 A2 5c lt green .60 *.60*
Never hinged 1.05
On cover 40.00
31 A2 75c brown, *buff* 4.00 *5.75*
Never hinged 8.00
On cover 70.00
32 A2 2fr on 5fr dull vio 27.50 *52.50*
Never hinged 52.50
On cover 85.00
On cover, single franking© 225.00
Nos. 30-32 (3) 32.10 *58.85*

Issued to commemorate the birth of Princess Antoinette, daughter of Princess Charlotte and Prince Pierre, Comte de Polignac.

Stamps and Type of 1891-1921 Surcharged

1922

33 A2 20c on 15c gray green 1.10 *1.40*
Never hinged 2.00
On cover 17.50
34 A2 25c on 10c rose .70 *.90*
Never hinged 1.10
On cover 17.50
35 A2 50c on 1fr black, *yel* 5.00 *5.75*
Never hinged 9.50
On cover 35.00
Nos. 33-35 (3) 6.80 *8.05*

Prince Albert I — A5

Oceanographic Museum — A6

"The Rock" of Monaco — A7

Royal Palace — A8

1922-24 Engr. *Perf. 11*

40 A5 25c deep brown 3.00 *3.90*
Never hinged 5.75
On cover 5.75
a. 25c olive brown 11.50 11.50
Never hinged 19.00
On cover 22.50
41 A6 30c dark green .90 .90
Never hinged 1.75
On cover 11.50
a. 30c gray green 2.75 2.75
Never hinged 4.00
On cover 14.00
42 A6 30c scarlet ('23) .50 .45
Never hinged .75
On cover 1.15
a. 30c salmon .75 1.75
Never hinged 1.25
On cover 1.15
43 A6 50c ultra 3.50 3.50
Never hinged 7.00
On cover 5.75
a. 50c pale ultra 4.90 *5.25*
Never hinged 8.50
On cover 9.00
b. 50c greenish blue 4.75 4.75
Never hinged 8.00
On cover —
44 A7 60c black brown .35 .35
Never hinged .50
On cover 1.15
a. 60c pale gray .70 .70
Never hinged 1.10
On cover 1.50
45 A7 1fr black, *yellow* .25 .25
Never hinged .40
On cover 1.15
a. 1fr gray black, *yellow* .40 .25
Never hinged .70
On cover 1.15
46 A7 2fr scarlet ver .50 .45
Never hinged .85
On cover 2.50
a. 2fr carmine 2.50 *3.00*
Never hinged 4.50
On cover 5.75
47 A8 5fr red brown 30.00 *35.00*
Never hinged 52.50
On cover 75.00
a. 5fr deep brown 52.50 *60.00*
Never hinged 90.00
On cover 150.00
48 A8 5fr green, *bluish* 9.25 *9.25*
Never hinged 20.00
On cover 30.00
a. 5fr dk green, *lil* ('24) 10.50 *21.00*
Never hinged 21.00
On cover 35.00
49 A8 10fr carmine 12.00 16.00
Never hinged 26.00
On cover 29.00
a. 10fr rose 47.50 *57.50*

		Never hinged	80.00	
		On cover		85.00
		Nos. 40-49 (10)	60.25	*70.05*

Nos. 40-49 exist imperf.

Prince Louis II
A9 A10

St. Dévote Viaduct ("Bridge of Suicides") A11

1923-24 **Engr.**

No.	Type	Description	Unused	Used
50	A9	10c deep green	.35	*.55*
		Never hinged	.55	
		On cover		1.15
51	A9	15c car rose ('24)	.45	*.70*
		Never hinged	.70	
		On cover		1.15
52	A9	20c red brown	.35	*.55*
		Never hinged	.65	
		On cover		1.15
53	A9	25c violet	.25	*.45*
		Never hinged	.45	
		On cover		1.15
a.		Without engraver's name	22.50	22.50
		Never hinged	30.00	
		On cover		—
54	A11	40c orange brn ('24)	.60	.50
		Never hinged	.85	
		On cover		1.15
55	A10	50c ultra	.35	*.45*
		Never hinged	.50	
		On cover		1.15
		Nos. 50-55 (6)	2.35	*3.20*

The 25c comes in 2 types, one with larger "5" and "c" touching frame of numeral tablet.

Stamps of the 1922-24 issues sometimes show parts of the letters of a papermaker's watermark.

The engraved stamps of type A11 measure 31x21½mm. The typographed stamps of that design measure 36x21½mm.

See #86-88. For surcharges see #95-96.

Stamps and Type of 1891-1921 Surcharged

1924, Aug. 5 ***Perf. 14x13½***

No.	Type	Description	Unused	Used
57	A2	45c on 50c brn ol, *buff*	.50	*.70*
		Never hinged	.75	
		On cover		1.15
		On cover, single franking		2.25
a.		Double surcharge	700.00	700.00
		Never hinged	925.00	
58	A2	75c on 1fr blk, *yel*	.50	*.70*
		Never hinged	.75	
		On cover		1.15
		On cover, single franking		2.25
a.		Double surcharge	425.00	*425.00*
		Never hinged	500.00	
59	A2	85c on 5fr dk green	.50	*.70*
		Never hinged	.75	
		On cover		1.15
		On cover, single franking		2.25
a.		Double surcharge	*575.00*	*575.00*
		Never hinged	700.00	
		Nos. 57-59 (3)	1.50	2.10
		Set, never hinged	2.25	

Grimaldi Family Coat of Arms — A12

Prince Louis II — A13

Louis II — A14

View of Monaco A15

1924-33 **Typo.**

No.	Type	Description	Unused	Used
60	A12	1c gray black	.20	.20
61	A12	2c red brown	.20	.20
62	A12	3c brt violet ('33)	2.40	1.75
63	A12	5c orange ('26)	.35	.30
64	A12	10c blue	.20	.20
65	A13	15c apple green	.20	.20
66	A13	15c dull vio ('29)	2.25	1.40
67	A13	20c violet	.20	.20
68	A13	20c rose	.35	.25
69	A13	25c rose	.20	.20
70	A13	25c red, *yel*	.20	*.25*
71	A13	30c orange	.20	.20
72	A13	40c black brown	.25	.20
73	A13	40c lt bl, *bluish*	.35	.35
74	A13	45c gray black ('26)	.70	.55
75	A14	50c myrtle grn ('25)	.20	*.25*
76	A13	50c brown, *org*	.20	.20
77	A14	60c yellow brn ('25)	.20	*.25*
78	A13	60c ol grn, *grnsh*	.20	*.25*
79	A13	75c ol grn, *grnsh* ('26)	.70	.35
80	A13	75c car, *straw* ('26)	.35	.20
81	A13	75c slate	.90	.55
82	A13	80c red, *yel* ('26)	.40	.30
83	A13	90c rose, *straw* ('27)	1.75	1.25
84	A13	1.25fr bl, *bluish* ('26)	.20	.20
85	A13	1.50fr bl, *bluish* ('27)	3.50	1.75
		Size: 36x21½mm		
86	A11	1fr blk, *orange*	.20	*.25*
87	A11	1.05fr red violet ('26)	.20	*.25*
88	A11	1.10fr blue grn ('27)	7.50	5.75
89	A15	2fr vio & ol brn ('25)	1.50	.65
90	A15	3fr rose & ultra, *yel* ('27)	21.00	10.00
91	A15	5fr green & rose ('25)	7.00	5.00
92	A15	10fr yel brn & bl ('25)	21.00	17.50
		Nos. 60-92 (33)	75.25	51.40
		Set, never hinged	140.00	

Nos. 60 to 74 and 76 exist imperforate.

For surcharges see Nos. 93-94, 97-99, C1.

Type of 1924-33 Surcharged with New Value and Bars

1926-31

No.	Type	Description	Unused	Used
93	A13	30c on 25c rose	.30	.25
94	A13	50c on 60c ol grn, *grnsh* ('28)	1.10	.35
95	A11	50c on 1.05fr red vio ('28)	.75	.70
a.		Double surcharge		
96	A11	50c on 1.10fr bl grn ('31)	10.50	7.25
97	A13	50c on 1.25fr bl, *bluish* (R) ('28)	1.25	.55
98	A13	1.25fr on 1fr bl, *bluish*	.55	.50
99	A15	1.50fr on 2fr vio & ol brn ('28)	5.50	4.50
		Nos. 93-99 (7)	19.95	14.10
		Set, never hinged	40.00	

Princes Charles III, Louis II and Albert I A17

1928, Feb. 18 **Engr.** ***Perf. 11***

No.	Type	Description	Unused	Used
100	A17	50c dull carmine	2.25	*4.50*
101	A17	1.50fr dark blue	2.25	*4.50*
102	A17	3fr dark violet	2.25	*4.50*
		Nos. 100-102 (3)	6.75	13.50
		Set, never hinged	13.50	

Nos. 100-102 were sold exclusively at the Intl. Phil. Exhib. at Monte Carlo, Feb., 1928. One set was sold to each purchaser of a ticket of admission to the exhibition which cost 5fr. Exist imperf. Value, set $22.50.

Old Watchtower A20

Royal Palace A21

Church of St. Dévote — A22

Prince Louis II — A23

"The Rock" of Monaco A24

Gardens of Monaco A25

Fortifications and Harbor — A26

1932-37 ***Perf. 13, 14x13½***

No.	Type	Description	Unused	Used
110	A20	15c lilac rose	.80	.25
111	A20	20c orange brn	.80	.25
112	A21	25c olive blk	1.10	.35
113	A22	30c yellow grn	1.40	.35
114	A23	40c dark brown	2.90	1.40
115	A24	45c brown red	3.00	1.10
a.		45c red	390.00	390.00
116	A23	50c purple	2.90	.85
117	A25	65c blue green	3.00	.55
118	A26	75c deep blue	4.00	1.75
119	A23	90c red	8.50	2.75
120	A22	1fr red brown ('33)	24.00	6.75
121	A26	1.25fr rose lilac	5.50	3.25
122	A23	1.50fr ultra	35.00	9.25
123	A21	1.75fr rose lilac	31.00	8.50
124	A21	1.75fr car rose ('37)	19.00	12.50
125	A24	2fr dark blue	10.50	4.50
126	A20	3fr purple	16.00	7.75
127	A21	3.50fr orange ('35)	42.50	27.50
128	A22	5fr violet	22.50	17.00
129	A21	10fr deep blue	110.00	65.00
130	A25	20fr black	150.00	125.00
		Nos. 110-130 (21)	494.40	296.60
		Set, never hinged	950.00	

Postage Due Stamps of 1925-32 Surcharged or Overprinted in Black:

1937-38 ***Perf. 14x13***

No.	Type	Description	Unused	Used
131	D3	5c on 10c violet	.75	.75
132	D3	10c violet	.75	.75
133	D3	15c on 30c bister	.75	.75
134	D3	20c on 30c bister	.75	.75
135	D3	25c on 60c red	1.10	1.10
136	D3	30c bister	2.00	1.75
137	D3	40c on 60c red	1.90	1.75
138	D3	50c on 60c red	2.40	2.25
139	D3	65c on 1fr lt bl	2.00	2.00
140	D3	85c on 1fr lt bl	4.75	4.25
141	D3	1fr light blue	6.75	6.75
142	D3	2.15fr on 2fr dl red	6.75	6.75
143	D3	2.25fr on 2fr dl red ('38)	16.00	16.00
144	D3	2.50fr on 2fr dl red ('38)	25.00	25.00
		Nos. 131-144 (14)	71.65	70.60
		Set, never hinged	140.00	

Grimaldi Arms — A27

Prince Louis II — A28

1937-43 **Engr.**

No.	Type	Description	Unused	Used
145	A27	1c dk vio brn ('38)	.20	.20
146	A27	2c emerald	.20	.20
147	A27	3c brt red violet	.20	.20
148	A27	5c red	.20	.20
149	A27	10c ultra	.20	.20
149A	A27	10c black ('43)	.20	.20
150	A27	15c violet ('39)	1.50	1.40
150A	A27	30c dull green ('43)	.20	.20
150B	A27	40c rose car ('43)	.20	.20
150C	A27	50c brt violet ('43)	.20	.20
151	A28	55c red brown ('38)	5.00	2.00
151A	A27	60c Prus blue ('43)	.20	.20
152	A28	65c violet ('38)	24.00	11.00
153	A28	70c red brown ('39)	.35	.35
153A	A27	70c red brown ('43)	.20	.20
154	A28	90c violet ('39)	.35	.30
155	A28	1fr rose red ('38)	15.00	8.50
156	A28	1.25fr rose red ('39)	.35	.35
157	A28	1.75fr ultra ('38)	15.00	9.00
158	A28	2.25fr ultra ('39)	.35	.25
		Nos. 145-158 (20)	64.10	35.35
		Set, never hinged	110.00	

#151, 152, 155, 157 exist imperf.

Souvenir Sheet

Prince Louis II — A29

1938, Jan. 17 **Unwmk.** ***Imperf.***

No.	Type	Description	Unused	Used
159	A29	10fr magenta	55.00	55.00
		Never hinged	150.00	

"Fête Nationale" 1/17/38. Size: 99x120mm.

Cathedral of Monaco — A30

St. Nicholas Square — A31

Palace Gate — A32

Palace of Monaco — A34

Panorama of Monaco A33

Harbor of Monte Carlo A35

1939-46 *Perf. 13*

160	A30	20c	rose lilac	.25	.25
161	A31	25c	gldn brown	.45	.30
162	A32	30c	dk blue grn	.35	.30
162A	A32	30c	brown red ('40)	.35	.25
163	A31	40c	henna brn	.70	.50
164	A33	45c	brt red vio	.50	.50
165	A34	50c	dk blue grn	.35	.25
166	A32	60c	rose carmine	.40	.35
166A	A32	60c	dk green ('40)	.90	.70
166B	A35	70c	brt red vio ('41)	.40	.25
167	A35	75c	dark green	.40	.25
167A	A30	80c	dull green ('43)	.20	*.25*
168	A34	1fr	brown black	.40	.25
168A	A33	1fr	claret ('43)	.20	.20
168B	A35	1.20fr	ultra ('46)	.25	*.35*
168C	A34	1.30fr	brown blk ('41)	.40	.35
168D	A31	1.50fr	ultra ('46)	.40	.40
169	A31	2fr	rose violet	.40	.30
169A	A35	2fr	lt ultra ('43)	.20	.20
169B	A34	2fr	green ('46)	.35	.25
170	A33	2.50fr	red	22.50	13.50
171	A33	2.50fr	dp blue ('40)	1.10	1.10
172	A35	3fr	brown red	.45	.35
172A	A31	3fr	black ('43)	.20	.20
172B	A30	4fr	rose lilac ('46)	1.10	.45
172C	A34	4.50fr	brt violet ('43)	.20	.20
173	A30	5fr	Prus blue	4.00	3.50
173A	A32	5fr	deep green ('43)	.20	.20
173B	A34	6fr	lt violet ('46)	.70	.55
174	A33	10fr	green	1.00	*1.25*
174A	A30	10fr	deep blue ('43)	.20	*.25*
174B	A35	15fr	rose pink ('43)	.40	*.25*
175	A32	20fr	brt ultra	1.60	1.10
175A	A33	20fr	sepia ('43)	.40	.25
175B	A35	25fr	blue green ('46)	1.40	1.00
			Nos. 160-175B (35)	43.30	30.60
			Set, never hinged	65.00	

See Nos. 214-221, 228-232, 274-275, 319-320, 407-408, 423, 426, 428-429, B36-B50.

Louis II Stadium A36

1939, Apr. 23 **Engr.**

176	A36	10fr dark green	92.50	*95.00*
		Never hinged	140.00	

Inauguration of Louis II Stadium.

Louis II Stadium A37

1939, Aug. 15

177	A37	40c dull green	1.10	1.10
178	A37	70c brown black	1.50	1.50
179	A37	90c dark violet	1.75	1.75
180	A37	1.25fr copper red	2.75	2.75
181	A37	2.25fr dark blue	3.25	3.25
		Nos. 177-181 (5)	10.35	10.35
		Set, never hinged	17.00	

8th International University Games.

Imperforates

Nearly all Monaco stamps from 1940 onward exist imperforate. Officially 20 sheets, ranging from 25 to 100 subjects, were left imperforate.

SEMI-POSTAL STAMPS

No. 16 Surcharged in Red

1914, Oct. **Unwmk.** *Perf. 14x13½*

B1 A2 10c + 5c carmine	6.75	*6.75*
Never hinged	15.00	
On cover, 10c rate		57.50

View of Monaco — SP2

1919, Sept. 20 **Typo.**

B2 SP2 2c + 3c lilac	32.50	*32.50*
Never hinged	60.00	
On Cover		50.00
B3 SP2 5c + 5c green	17.50	*18.00*
Never hinged	35.00	
On Cover		35.00
B4 SP2 15c + 10c rose	17.50	*18.00*
Never hinged	35.00	
On Cover		35.00
B5 SP2 25c + 15c blue	39.00	*40.00*
Never hinged	65.00	
On Cover		55.00
B6 SP2 50c + 50c brn, *buff*	175.00	*160.00*
Never hinged	325.00	
On Cover		210.00
B7 SP2 1fr + 1fr blk, *yel*	275.00	*340.00*
Never hinged	525.00	
On Cover		460.00
B8 SP2 5fr + 5fr dull red	925.00	*1,050.*
Never hinged	1,750.	
On Cover		1,750.
Nos. B2-B8 (7)	1,481.	*1,658.*

Nos. B4-B8 Surcharged

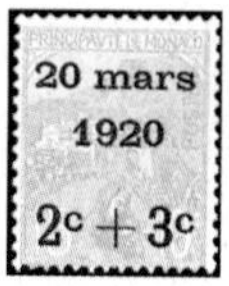

1920, Mar. 20

B9 SP2 2c + 3c on #B4	40.00	*40.00*
Never hinged	72.50	
On Cover		70.00
a. "c" of "3c" inverted	*1,500.*	*1,600.*
Never hinged	2,400.	
b. Pair, Nos. 9, 9a	2,250.	*2,600.*
Never hinged	3,000.	
B10 SP2 2c + 3c on #B5	40.00	*40.00*
Never hinged	72.50	
On Cover		70.00
a. "c" of "3c" inverted	*1,500.*	*1,600.*
Never hinged	2,400.	
b. Pair, Nos. 10, 10a	2,250.	*2,600.*
Never hinged	*3,000.*	
B11 SP2 2c + 3c on #B6	40.00	*40.00*
Never hinged	72.50	
On Cover		70.00
a. "c" of "3c" inverted	*1,500.*	*1,600.*
Never hinged	*2,400.*	
b. Pair, Nos. 11, 11a	2,250.	*2,600.*
Never hinged	*3,000.*	
B12 SP2 5c + 5c on #B7	40.00	*40.00*
Never hinged	72.50	
On Cover		70.00
B13 SP2 5c + 5c on #B8	40.00	*40.00*
Never hinged	72.50	
On Cover		70.00

Overprinted

B14 SP2 15c + 10c rose	25.00	25.00
Never hinged	50.00	
On Cover		35.00
B15 SP2 25c + 15c blue	14.00	14.00
Never hinged	24.00	
On Cover		21.00
B16 SP2 50c + 50c brown, *buff*	50.00	50.00
Never hinged	95.00	
On Cover		105.00
B17 SP2 1fr + 1fr black, *yel*	70.00	70.00
Never hinged	125.00	
On Cover		275.00
B18 SP2 5fr + 5fr red	6,000.	6,000.
Never hinged	9,250.	
On Cover		—
Nos. B9-B17 (9)	359.00	359.00

Marriage of Princess Charlotte to Prince Pierre, Comte de Polignac.

Palace Gardens SP3

"The Rock" of Monaco SP4

Bay of Monaco SP5

Prince Louis II — SP6

1937, Apr. **Engr.** *Perf. 13*

B19	SP3	50c + 50c green	2.25	2.25
B20	SP4	90c + 90c car	2.25	2.25
B21	SP5	1.50fr + 1.50fr blue	5.00	5.00
B22	SP6	2fr + 2fr violet	10.50	10.50
B23	SP6	5fr + 5fr brn red	90.00	90.00
		Nos. B19-B23 (5)	110.00	110.00
		Set, never hinged	210.00	

The surtax was used for welfare work.

Pierre and Marie Curie — SP7

Monaco Hospital, Date Palms SP8

1938, Nov. 15 *Perf. 13*

B24	SP7	65c + 25c dp bl grn	9.50	9.50
B25	SP8	1.75fr + 50c dp ultra	10.50	10.50
		Set, never hinged	35.00	

B24 and B25 exist imperforate.

The surtax was for the International Union for the Control of Cancer.

Lucien — SP9

Honoré II — SP10

Louis I — SP11

Charlotte de Gramont — SP12

Antoine I — SP13

Marie de Lorraine — SP14

Jacques I SP15

Louise-Hippolyte SP16

Honoré III — SP17

"The Rock," 18th Century SP18

1939, June 26

B26	SP9	5c + 5c brown blk	1.90	1.10
B27	SP10	10c + 10c rose vio	1.90	1.10
B28	SP11	45c + 15c brt green	6.75	5.00
B29	SP12	70c + 30c brt red vio	10.00	9.00
B30	SP13	90c + 35c vio	10.00	9.00
B31	SP14	1fr + 1fr ultra	25.00	24.00
B32	SP15	2fr + 2fr brn org	25.00	24.00
B33	SP16	2.25fr + 1.25fr Prus bl	30.00	30.00
B34	SP17	3fr + 3fr dp rose	40.00	*42.50*
B35	SP18	5fr + 5fr red	75.00	*77.50*
		Nos. B26-B35 (10)	225.55	223.20
		Set, never hinged	400.00	

Types of Regular Issue, 1939 Surcharged in Red

1940, Feb. 10 **Engr.** *Perf. 13*

B36	A30	20c + 1fr violet	2.75	2.75
B37	A31	25c + 1fr dk grn	2.75	2.75
B38	A32	30c + 1fr brn red	2.75	2.75
B39	A31	40c + 1fr dk blue	2.75	2.75
B40	A33	45c + 1fr rose car	2.75	2.75
B41	A34	50c + 1fr brown	2.75	2.75
B42	A32	60c + 1fr dk grn	3.50	3.50
B43	A35	75c + 1fr brn blk	3.50	3.50
B44	A34	1fr + 1fr scarlet	4.50	4.50
B45	A31	2fr + 1fr indigo	4.50	4.50
B46	A33	2.50fr + 1fr dk grn	11.00	11.00
B47	A35	3fr + 1fr dk blue	11.00	11.00
B48	A30	5fr + 1fr brn blk	15.00	15.00
B49	A33	10fr + 5fr lt blue	28.00	28.00
B50	A32	20fr + 5fr brn vio	29.00	29.00
		Nos. B36-B50 (15)	126.50	126.50
		Set, never hinged	275.00	

The surtax was used to purchase ambulances for the French government.

AIR POST STAMPS

No. 91 Surcharged in Black

Perf. 14x13½

1933, Aug. 22 **Unwmk.**

C1	A15	1.50fr on 5fr	21.00	22.50
a.		Imperf., pair	350.00	

POSTAGE DUE STAMPS

D1

Prince Albert I — D2

Perf. 14x13½

1905-43 **Unwmk.** **Typo.**

J1	D1	1c olive green	.45	.55
J2	D1	5c green	.45	.55
		On cover		57.50
J3	D1	10c rose	.45	.55
		On cover		57.50
J4	D1	10c brn ('09)	290.00	125.00
		On cover		175.00
J5	D1	15c vio brn, *straw*	3.50	1.75
J6	D1	20c bis brn, *buff* ('26)	.35	.35
J7	D1	30c blue	.45	.55
		On cover		57.50
J8	D1	40c red vio ('26)	.35	.35
J9	D1	50c brn, *org*	4.50	4.00
		On cover		57.50
J10	D1	50c blue grn ('27)	.35	.35
J11	D1	60c gray blk ('26)	.35	.65
J12	D1	60c brt vio ('34)	20.00	25.00
J13	D1	1fr red brn, *straw* ('26)	.35	.25
J14	D1	2fr red org ('27)	1.00	1.50
J15	D1	3fr mag ('27)	1.00	1.50
J15A	D1	5fr ultra ('43)	.80	1.00
		Nos. J1-J15A (16)	324.35	163.90

For surcharge see No. J27.

1910

J16	D2	1c olive green	.25	.45
J17	D2	10c light violet	.45	.60
J18	D2	30c bister	190.00	160.00

In January, 1917, regular postage stamps overprinted "T" in a triangle were used as postage due stamps.

Nos. J17 and J18 Surcharged

1918

J19	D2	20c on 10c lt vio	4.00	6.75
a.		Double surcharge	*1,000.*	
J20	D2	40c on 30c bister	4.50	7.50

D3

1925-32

J21	D3	1c gray green	.40	.45
J22	D3	10c violet	.40	.55
J23	D3	30c bister	.45	.70
J24	D3	60c red	.70	.75
J25	D3	1fr lt bl ('32)	70.00	60.00
J26	D3	2fr dull red ('32)	70.00	70.00
		Nos. J21-J26 (6)	141.95	132.45

Nos. J25 and J26 have the numerals of value double-lined.

"Recouvrements" stamps were used to recover charges due on undelivered or refused mail which was returned to the sender.

No. J9 Surcharged

1925

J27	D1	1fr on 50c brn, *org*	.80	.55
a.		Double surcharge	*700.00*	

MONGOLIA

män-'gōl-yə

(Outer Mongolia)

LOCATION — Central Asia, bounded on the north by Siberia, on the west by Sinkiang, on the south and east by China proper and Manchuria
GOVT. — Republic
AREA — 604,250 sq. mi.
POP. — 1,820,000 (est. 1984)
CAPITAL — Ulan Bator

Outer Mongolia, which had long been under Russian influence although nominally a dependency of China, voted at a plebescite on October 20, 1945, to sever all ties with China and become an independent nation. See Tannu Tuva.

100 Cents = 1 Dollar
100 Mung = 1 Tugrik (1926)

Watermark

Wmk. 170 — Greek Border and Rosettes

Scepter of Indra — A1

A2

1924 **Litho.** **Unwmk.** *Perf. 10, 13½*

Surface Tinted Paper

1	A1	1c multi, *bister*	4.50	4.50
2	A1	2c multi, *brnsh*	5.50	3.75
a.		Perf. 13½	37.50	32.50
3	A1	5c multi	27.50	22.50
a.		Perf. 10	37.50	32.50
4	A1	10c multi, *gray bl*	10.00	7.75
a.		Perf. 10	20.00	13.00
5	A1	20c multi, *gray*	20.00	11.00
6	A1	50c multi, *salmon*	32.50	20.00
7	A1	$1 multi, *yellow*	50.00	30.00
b.		Perf. 10	650.00	190.00
		Nos. 1-7 (7)	150.00	99.50

These stamps vary in size from 19x25mm (1c) to 30x39mm ($1). They also differ in details of the design.

Errors of perforating and printing exist.

Some quantities of Nos. 1-2, 4-7 were defaced with horizontal perforation across the center.

The 5c exists perf 11½. Value, $325 unused, hinged, $190 used.

Revenue Stamps Handstamp Overprinted "POSTAGE" in Violet

Sizes: 1c to 20c: 22x36mm
50c, $1: 26x43½mm
$5: 30x45½mm

1926 *Perf. 11*

16	A2	1c blue	11.00	11.00
17	A2	2c orange	11.00	11.00
18	A2	5c plum	15.00	13.00
19	A2	10c green	20.00	17.00
20	A2	20c yel brn	22.50	19.00
21	A2	50c brn & ol grn	*190.00*	*175.00*
22	A2	$1 brn & salmon	*550.00*	*475.00*
23	A2	$5 red, yel & gray	*650.00*	—
		Nos. 16-23 (8)	*1,469.*	*721.00*

Black Overprint

16a	A2	1c blue	20.00	13.00
17a	A2	2c orange	24.00	15.00
18a	A2	5c plum	27.50	17.50
19a	A2	10c green	37.50	20.00
20a	A2	20c yellow brown	50.00	45.00
21a	A2	50c brown & olive grn	*500.00*	*140.00*
22a	A2	$1 brown & salmon	*450.00*	*350.00*
23a	A2	$5 red, yellow & gray		
		Nos. 16a-22a (7)	*1,109.*	*600.50*

Red Overprint

16b	A2	1c blue
17b	A2	2c orange
18b	A2	5c plum
19b	A2	10c green
20b	A2	20c yellow brown

The preceding handstamped overprints may be found inverted, double, etc. Counterfeits abound.

For overprints and surcharges see #48-61.

Yin Yang and other Symbols
A3 A4

TYPE I — The pearl above the crescent is solid. The devices in the middle of the stamp are not outlined.

TYPE II — The pearl is open. The devices and panels are all outlined in black.

1926-29 *Perf. 11*

Type I

Size: 22x28mm

32	A3	5m lilac & blk	5.00	5.00
33	A3	20m blue & blk	4.50	4.50

Type II

Size: 22x29mm

34	A3	1m yellow & blk	1.50	.90
35	A3	2m brn org & blk	1.75	1.00
36	A3	5m lilac & blk	2.75	1.50
37	A3	10m lt blue & blk	1.75	1.25
a.		Imperf, pair		
38	A3	20m dp bl & blk ('29)	15.00	9.00
a.		Imperf, pair	250.00	250.00
39	A3	25m yel grn & blk	4.50	1.90
a.		Imperf, pair	125.00	110.00

Size: 26x34mm

40	A3	40m lemon & blk	6.25	2.25
41	A3	50m buff & blk	7.75	3.50

Size: 28x37mm

42	A4	1t brown, grn & blk	20.00	8.50
43	A4	3t red, yel & blk	42.50	32.50
44	A4	5t brn vio, rose & blk	65.00	52.50
		Nos. 32-44 (13)	178.25	124.30

In 1929 a change was made in the perforating machine. Every fourth pin was removed, which left the perforation holes in groups of three with blank spaces between the groups. Nos. 38 and 44A-44D have only this interrupted perforation. Nos. 37 and 39 are found with both perforations.

For overprints and surcharges see #45-47.

Yin Yang and other Symbols — A5

1929, July ***Interrupted Perf 11***

44A	A5	5m lilac & black	25.00	20.00
44B	A5	10mlt grnish blue & black	100.00	65.00
a.		imperf, pair	—	
44C	A5	20mblue & black	35.00	25.00
a.		imperf, pair	—	
b.		Horiz. pair, imperf btwn.		—
44D	A5	25myel grn & black	27.50	22.50
a.		imperf, pair	—	

See note after No. 44.

Nos. 34, 35, 40 Handstamped With New Values in Black

1930

45	A3	10m on 1m	32.50	30.00
46	A3	20m on 2m	45.00	40.00
47	A3	25m on 40m	50.00	45.00
		Nos. 45-47 (3)	127.50	115.00

Symbols of Government
A6 A7

Violet Overprint, Handstamped

1931

48	A6	1c blue	19.00	9.00
a.		Blue overprint	87.50	37.50
49	A6	2c orange	20.00	6.50
50	A6	5c brown vio	27.50	6.50
a.		Blue overprint	65.00	22.50
51	A6	10c green	22.50	6.50
a.		Blue overprint	65.00	37.50
52	A6	20c bister brn	35.00	9.25
53	A6	50c brown & ol yel	—	—
54	A6	$1 brown & salmon	—	—
		Nos. 48-54 (5)	124.00	37.75

Revenue Stamps Surcharged in Black, Red or Blue

1931

59	A7	5m on 5c brn vio (Bk)	32.50	12.50
a.		Inverted surcharge		35.00
b.		Imperf., pair	225.00	225.00
60	A7	10m on 10c green (R)	47.50	27.50
a.		Inverted surcharge	90.00	50.00
b.		Imperf., pair	225.00	225.00

61	A7	20m on 20c bis brn (Bl)	60.00	35.00
a.		Inverted surcharge		55.00
b.		Imperf., pair	225.00	225.00
		Nos. 59-61 (3)	140.00	75.00

On Nos. 59-61, "Postage" is always diagonal, and may read up or down.

Weaver at Loom — A8

Telegrapher A9

Sukhe Bator A10

Lake and Mountains — A11

Designs: 5m, Mongol at lathe. 10m, Government building, Ulan Bator. 15m, Young Mongolian revolutionary. 20m, Studying Latin alphabet. 25m, Mongolian soldier. 50m, Monument to Sukhe Bator. 3t, Sheep shearing. 5t, Camel caravan. 10t, Chasing wild horses.

Perf. 12½x12

1932 Photo. Wmk. 170

62	A8	1m	brown	1.90	1.25
63	A9	2m	red violet	1.90	1.25
64	A8	5m	indigo	.65	.30
65	A8	10m	dull green	.65	.30
66	A9	15m	dp brown	.65	.30
67	A9	20m	rose red	.65	.30
68	A9	25m	dull violet	.90	.30
69	A10	40m	gray black	.90	.35
70	A10	50m	dull blue	.65	.40

Perf. 11x12

71	A11	1t	dull green	1.10	.55
72	A11	3t	dull violet	3.50	1.40
73	A11	5t	brown	15.00	8.50
74	A11	10t	ultra	22.50	14.50
			Nos. 62-74 (13)	50.95	29.70

Used values are for c-t-o's.

MONTENEGRO

ˌmän-tə-ˈnē-ˌgrō

LOCATION — Southern Europe, bordering on the Adriatic Sea
GOVT. — Kingdom
AREA — 5,603 sq. mi.
POP. — 516,000 (estimated)
CAPITAL — Cetinje

This kingdom, formerly a Turkish Protectorate, later became independent. On December 1, 1918, Montenegro united with Serbia, Bosnia and Herzegovina, Croatia, Dalmatia and Slovenia to form the Kingdom of the Serbs, Croats and Slovenes which became Yugoslavia in 1929.

100 Novcic = 1 Florin
100 Helera = 1 Kruna (1902)
100 Para = 1 Kruna (1907)
100 Para = 1 Perper (1910)

Canceled to Order

Used values for Nos. 1-110, H1-H5, J1-J26, are for canceled to order stamps. Postally used specimens sell for considerably more.

Watermark

Wmk. 91 — "BRIEF-MARKEN" (#1-14) or "ZEITUNGS-MARKEN" (#15-21) in Double-lined Capitals once across sheet

Prince Nicholas I — A1

1874 Typo. Wmk. 91

Early Printings

Perf. 10½ Large Holes, pointed teeth

Narrow Spacing (2-2½mm)

1	A1	2n	yellow	30.00	30.00
2	A1	3n	green	40.00	30.00
3	A1	5n	rose red	37.50	27.50
4	A1	7n	lt lilac	37.50	25.00
5	A1	10n	blue	100.00	65.00
6	A1	15n	yel bister	125.00	97.50
7	A1	25n	lilac gray	225.00	150.00
			Nos. 1-7 (7)	595.00	425.00

Middle Printings (1879)

Perf. 12, 12½, 13 and Compound

Narrow spacing

8	A1	2n	yellow	10.00	7.00
a.			Perf. 12-13x10½	65.00	65.00
9	A1	3n	green	7.50	5.50
10	A1	5n	red	7.50	5.50
11	A1	7n	rose lilac	7.50	5.50
a.			7n lilac	19.00	14.00
12	A1	10n	blue	13.00	11.00
a.			Perf. 12-13x10½	65.00	52.50
13	A1	15n	bister brn	19.00	11.00
14	A1	25n	gray lilac	25.00	16.00
			Nos. 8-14 (7)	89.50	61.50

Late Printings (1893?)

Perf. 10½, 11½ Small holes, broad teeth (Perf. 11½ also with pointed teeth)

Narrow and wide spacing (2¾-3½mm)

15	A1	2n	yellow	3.00	1.60
a.			Perf. 11 ('94)	27.50	17.50
16	A1	3n	green	3.00	2.00
17	A1	5n	red	3.25	1.50
18	A1	7n	rose	2.50	1.25
a.			Perf. 11 ('94)	12.00	9.00
19	A1	10n	blue	3.00	2.10
20	A1	15n	brown	3.00	2.40
21	A1	25n	brown violet	3.25	2.50
			Nos. 15-21 (7)	21.00	13.35

Dates of issue of the late printings are still being researched.

Types of 1874-93 Overprinted in Black or Red

1893 ***Perf. 10½, 11½***

22	A1	2n	yellow	35.00	6.50
a.			Perf. 11	*35.00*	*35.00*
23	A1	3n	green	2.40	1.40
24	A1	5n	red	1.60	.85
25	A1	7n	rose	4.00	2.50
a.			Perf. 12	60.00	50.00
b.			7n rose lilac	5.00	3.00
c.			7n lilac, perf. 12	*125.00*	
d.			Perf. 11	*40.00*	*30.00*
26	A1	10n	blue	2.50	2.00
27	A1	10n	blue (R)	4.00	3.25
28	A1	15n	brown	3.00	1.60
a.			Perf. 12	50.00	42.50
29	A1	15n	brown (R)	*1,250.*	*1,100.*
30	A1	25n	brown violet	2.75	2.00
31	A1	25n	brn vio (R)	4.00	3.00
a.			Perf. 12½		*225.00*
			Nos. 22-28,30-31 (9)	59.25	23.10

Introduction of printing to Montenegro, 400th anniversary.

This overprint had many settings. Several values exist with "1494" or "1495" instead of "1493", or with missing letters or numerals due to wearing of the clichés. Double and inverted overprints exist. Some printings were made after 1893 to supply a philatelic demand, but were available for postage.

The 7n with red overprint was not issued.

1894-98 Wmk. 91 ***Perf. 10½, 11½***

32	A1	1n	gray blue	.20	.20
33	A1	2n	emerald ('98)	.20	.20
34	A1	3n	carmine rose ('98)	.20	.20
35	A1	5n	orange ('98)	1.50	.40
36	A1	7n	gray lilac ('98)	.30	.30
37	A1	10n	magenta ('98)	.30	.30
38	A1	15n	red brown ('98)	.25	.25
39	A1	20n	brown orange	.25	.20
40	A1	25n	dull blue ('98)	.25	.25
41	A1	30n	maroon	.25	.20
42	A1	50n	ultra	.30	.25
43	A1	1fl	deep green	.50	.50
44	A1	2fl	red brown	.75	.75
			Nos. 32-44 (13)	5.25	4.00

Monastery at Cetinje (Royal Mausoleum) A3

Perf. 10½, 11½

1896, Sept. 1 Litho. Unwmk.

45	A3	1n	dk blue & bis	.20	.20
46	A3	2n	magenta & yel	.25	.25
47	A3	3n	org brn & yel grn	.25	.25
48	A3	5n	bl grn & bis	.25	.25
49	A3	10n	yellow & ultra	.25	.25
50	A3	15n	dk blue & grn	.25	.25
a.			Perf. 11½	30.00	30.00
51	A3	20n	bl grn & ultra	.25	.25
a.			Perf. 11½	27.50	27.50
52	A3	25n	dk blue & yel	.25	.25
53	A3	30n	magenta & bis	.25	.25
54	A3	50n	red brn & gray bl	.25	.25
55	A3	1fl	rose & gray bl	.40	.40
56	A3	2fl	brown & black	.40	.40
			Nos. 45-56 (12)	3.25	3.25

Bicentenary of the ruling dynasty, founded by the Vladika, Danilo Petrovich of Nyegosh.

Inverted centers and other errors exist, but experts believe these to be printer's waste.

Perf. 11½ counterfeits are common.

Prince Nicholas I
A4 A5

Perf. 13x13½, 13x12½ (2h, 5h, 50h, 2k, 5k), 12½ (1h, 25h)

1902, July 12

57	A4	1h	ultra	.20	.20
58	A4	2h	rose lilac	.20	.20
59	A4	5h	green	.20	.20
60	A4	10h	rose	.20	.20
61	A4	25h	dull blue	.25	.25
62	A4	50h	gray green	.40	.40
63	A4	1k	chocolate	.35	.35
64	A4	2k	pale brown	.45	.45
65	A4	5k	buff	.60	.60
			Nos. 57-65 (9)	2.85	2.85

The 2h black brown and 25h indigo were not issued. The 25h, perf. 12½, probably was never issued.

Constitution Issue

Same Overprinted in Red or Black "Constitution" 15mm

1905, Dec. 5

66	A4	1h	ultra (R)	.20	.20
67	A4	2h	rose lilac	.20	.20
68	A4	5h	green (R)	.20	.20
69	A4	10h	rose	.20	.20
70	A4	25h	dull blue (R)	.20	.20
71	A4	50h	gray green (R)	.20	.20
72	A4	1k	chocolate (R)	.25	.25
73	A4	2k	pale brown (R)	.40	.40
74	A4	5k	buff	.50	.50
			Nos. 66-74 (9)	2.35	2.35

Overprints in other colors are proofs.

1906

"Constitution" 16½mm

66a	A4	1h	ultra (R)	.20	.20
67a	A4	2h	rose lilac	.20	.20
68a	A4	5h	green (R)	.20	.20
69a	A4	10h	rose	.20	.20
70a	A4	25h	dull blue (R)	.20	.20
71a	A4	50h	gray green (R)	.20	.20
72a	A4	1k	chocolate (R)	.20	.20
73a	A4	2k	pale brown (R)	.25	.25
74a	A4	5k	buff	.50	.50
			Nos. 66a-74a (9)	2.15	2.15

Three settings of Nos. 66a-74a containing four types of "YCTAB": I, 9¾mm, II, 11¼mm, III, 10¼mm, IV, 8½mm. Type IV occurs only in one setting, at two positions. Nos. 67a, 69a-74a, H3a exist in type IV.

Two errors occur: "Constitutton" and "Coustitution." Many other varieties including reversed color overprints exist.

Values are for types I and II.

1907, June 1 Engr. ***Perf. 12½***

75	A5	1pa	ocher	.20	.20
76	A5	2pa	black	.20	.20
77	A5	5pa	yellow green	.25	.20
78	A5	10pa	rose red	.25	.20
79	A5	15pa	ultra	.20	.20
80	A5	20pa	red orange	.20	.20
81	A5	25pa	indigo	.20	.20
82	A5	35pa	bister brown	.20	.20
83	A5	50pa	dull violet	.30	.20
84	A5	1kr	carmine rose	.30	.25
85	A5	2kr	green	.30	.30
86	A5	5kr	red brown	.40	.35
			Nos. 75-86 (12)	3.00	2.70

Many Montenegro stamps exist imperforate or part perforate. Experts believe these to be printer's waste.

King Nicholas I as a Youth — A6

King Nicholas I and Queen Milena — A7

King Nicholas I — A11

Prince Nicholas — A12

5pa, 10pa, 25pa, 35pa, Nicholas in 1910. 15pa, Nicholas in 1878. 20pa, King and Queen, diff.

1910, Aug. 28 Engr.

87	A6	1pa	black	.20	.20
88	A7	2pa	purple brown	.20	.20
89	A6	5pa	dark green	.20	.20
90	A6	10pa	carmine	.20	.20
91	A6	15pa	slate blue	.20	.20
92	A7	20pa	olive green	.20	.20
93	A6	25pa	deep blue	.20	.20
94	A6	35pa	chestnut	.20	.20
95	A11	50pa	violet	.25	.20
96	A11	1per	lake	.25	.20
97	A11	2per	yellow green	.50	.30
98	A12	5per	pale blue	.65	.40
			Nos. 87-98 (12)	3.25	2.70

Proclamation of Montenegro as a kingdom, the 50th anniv. of the reign of King Nicholas and the golden wedding celebration of the King and Queen.

King Nicholas I — A13

1913, Apr. 1 Typo.

99	A13	1pa	orange	.20	.20
100	A13	2pa	plum	.20	.20
101	A13	5pa	deep green	.20	.20
102	A13	10pa	deep rose	.20	.20
103	A13	15pa	blue gray	.20	.20
104	A13	20pa	dark brown	.20	.20

105	A13	25pa deep blue	.20	.20
106	A13	35pa vermilion	.25	.25
107	A13	50pa pale blue	.20	.20
108	A13	1per yellow brown	.20	.20
109	A13	2per gray violet	.20	.20
110	A13	5per yellow green	.20	.20
		Nos. 99-110 (12)	2.45	2.45

ACKNOWLEDGMENT OF RECEIPT STAMPS

Prince Nicholas I
AR1 AR2

Perf. 10½, 11½

1895 Litho. Wmk. 91

H1	AR1	10n ultra & rose	.50	.50

1902 Unwmk. *Perf. 12½*

H2	AR2	25h orange & carmine	.50	.50

Constitution Issue

#H2 Overprinted in Black Like #66-74

1905

H3	AR2	25h orange & carmine	.50	.50
a.		"Constitution" 16½mm ('06)	.50	.50

See note after 74a.

AR3

Nicholas I — AR4

1907 Engr.

H4	AR3	25pa olive	.25	.25

1913 Typo.

H5	AR4	25pa olive green	.25	.25

POSTAGE DUE STAMPS

D1

D2

Perf. 10½, 11, 11½

1894 Litho. Wmk. 91

J1	D1	1n red	1.50	1.00
J2	D1	2n yellow green	.50	.30
J3	D1	3n orange	.40	.30
J4	D1	5n olive green	.25	.20
J5	D1	10n violet	.25	.20
J6	D1	20n ultra	.25	.20
J7	D1	30n emerald	.25	.20
J8	D1	50n pale gray grn	.25	.20
		Nos. J1-J8 (8)	3.65	2.60

1902 Unwmk. *Perf. 12½*

J9	D2	5h orange	.20	.20
J10	D2	10h olive green	.20	.20
J11	D2	25h dull lilac	.20	.20
J12	D2	50h emerald	.20	.20
J13	D2	1k pale gray green	.20	.20
		Nos. J9-J13 (5)	1.00	1.00

Constitution Issue

Postage Due Stamps of 1902 Overprinted in Black or Red Like Nos. 66-74

1905

J14	D2	5h orange	.20	.20
J15	D2	10h olive green (R)	.20	.20
J16	D2	25h dull lilac	.20	.20
J17	D2	50h emerald	.20	.20
J18	D2	1k pale gray green	.20	.20
		Nos. J14-J18 (5)	1.00	1.00

The 10h with "Constitution" 16½mm is not known used. It is an unissued stamp.

D3

D4

1907 Typo. *Perf. 13x13½*

J19	D3	5pa red brown	.20	.20
J20	D3	10pa violet	.20	.20
J21	D3	25pa rose	.20	.20
J22	D3	50pa green	.20	.20
		Nos. J19-J22 (4)	.80	.80

1913 *Perf. 12½*

J23	D4	5pa gray	.20	.20
J24	D4	10pa violet	.20	.20
J25	D4	25pa blue gray	.20	.20
J26	D4	50pa lilac rose	.20	.20
		Nos. J23-J26 (4)	.80	.80

ISSUED UNDER AUSTRIAN OCCUPATION

Austrian Military Stamps of 1917 Overprinted

1917 Unwmk. *Perf. 12½*

1N1	M1	10h blue	5.75	3.50
1N2	M1	15h car rose	5.75	3.50

Austrian Military Stamps of 1917 Overprinted in Black

1918

1N3	M1	10h blue	35.00
1N4	M1	15h car rose	1.90

Nos. 1N3-1N4 were never placed in use.

This overprint exists on other stamps of Austria and Bosnia and Herzegovina, and in blue or red.

MONTSERRAT

ˌmän‚t‚-sə-ˈrat

LOCATION — West Indies southeast of Puerto Rico
GOVT. — British Crown Colony
AREA — 39 sq. mi.
POP. — 12,074 (1980)
CAPITAL — Plymouth

Montserrat was one of the four presidencies of the former Leeward Islands colony until it became a colony itself in 1956.

Montserrat stamps were discontinued in 1890 and resumed in 1903. In the interim, stamps of Leeward Islands were used. In 1903-56, stamps of Montserrat and Leeward Islands were used concurrently.

12 Pence = 1 Shilling
20 Shillings = 1 Pound
100 Cents = 1 Dollar (1951)

Catalogue values for unused stamps in this country are for Never Hinged items, beginning with Scott 104 in the regular postage section.

PRE-STAMP POSTAL MARKINGS

Crowned Circle handstamp type VI is pictured in the Crowned Circle Handstamps and Great Britain Used Abroad section.

Plymouth

1852-58

A1	VI	"Montserrat" crowned circle handstamp in red, on cover	4,500.

The handstamp was used, in black, as a provisional in 1886.

STAMPS OF GREAT BRITAIN USED IN MONTSERRAT

Numeral cancellation type A is pictured in the Crowned Circle Handstamps and Great Britain Used Abroad section.

1858-60

A08 (Plymouth)

A2	A	1p rose red (#20)	1,300.
A3	A	4p rose (#26)	—
A4	A	6p lilac (#27)	550.00
A5	A	1sh green (#28)	1,800.

Issued under British Administration

Values for unused stamps are for examples with original gum as defined in the catalogue introduction. Very fine examples of Nos. 1-2, 6 and 11 will have perforations touching the design on at least one side due to the narrow spacing of the stamps on the plates. Stamps with perfs clear of the framelines on all four sides are scarce and will command higher prices.

Stamps of Antigua Overprinted in Black

a

1876 Engr. Wmk. 1 *Perf. 14*

1	A1	1p red	27.50	19.00
a.		Vert. or diag. half used as ½p on cover		1,650.
c.		"S" inverted	1,250.	875.00
2	A1	6p green	75.00	50.00
a.		Vertical half used as 3p on cover		—
b.		Vertical third used as 2p on cover		6,000.
c.		"S" inverted	1,450.	1,350.
d.		6p blue green	1,350.	
e.		As "d," "S" inverted	*9,000.*	

Some experts consider Nos. 2d, 2e to be from a trial printing.

Queen Victoria — A2

1880 Typo.

3	A2	2½p red brown	300.00	225.00
4	A2	4p blue	160.00	47.50

See Nos. 5, 7-10.

1884 Wmk. 2

5	A2	½p green	1.25	*8.75*

Antigua No. 18 Overprinted type "a"

1884 Engr.

6	A1	1p rose red	19.00	20.00
a.		Vert. half used as ½p on cover		1,550.
b.		"S" inverted	1,100.	1,100.

Type of 1880

1884-85 Typo.

7	A2	2½p red brown	275.00	77.50
8	A2	2½p ultra ('85)	25.00	22.50
9	A2	4p blue	2,100.	300.00
10	A2	4p red lilac ('85)	6.00	3.50

Antigua No. 20 Overprinted type "a"

1884 Engr. *Perf. 12*

11	A1	1p red	82.50	65.00
a.		"S" inverted	2,350.	1,550.
b.		Vert. half used as ½p on cover		1,900.

Symbol of the Colony — A3

King Edward VII — A4

1903 Wmk. 2 Typo. *Perf. 14*

12	A3	½p gray green	.90	17.00
13	A3	1p car & black	.90	.50
14	A3	2p brown & black	6.50	35.00
15	A3	2½p ultra & black	1.75	2.10
16	A3	3p dk vio & brn orange	5.00	35.00
17	A3	6p ol grn & vio	5.75	57.50
18	A3	1sh vio & gray grn	12.00	20.00

19 A3 2sh brn org & gray green 30.00 20.00
20 A3 2sh6p blk & gray grn 22.50 45.00

Wmk. 1

21 A4 5sh car & black 125.00 175.00
Nos. 12-21 (10) 210.30 407.10
Set of 10, ovptd "SPECIMEN" 190.00

1904-08 **Wmk. 3**

Chalky Paper

22 A3 ½p grn & gray grn 5.50 2.25
23 A3 1p car & blk ('08) 17.00 30.00
24 A3 2p brown & black 2.50 1.40
25 A3 2½p ultra & blk ('06) 3.00 7.75
26 A3 3p dk vio & brn orange 11.00 2.75
27 A3 6p ol grn & vio 11.00 6.50
28 A3 1sh violet & gray grn ('08) 11.50 8.50
29 A3 2sh brn org & gray grn ('08) 35.00 52.50
30 A3 2sh6p blk & gray grn ('08) 50.00 57.50
31 A4 5sh car & blk ('07) 110.00 125.00
Nos. 22-31 (10) 256.50 294.15
Set of 10, ovptd "SPECIMEN" 300.00

The ½, 2, 3 and 6p are also on ordinary paper.

1908-13

Ordinary Paper

31A A3 ½p deep green 8.25 1.10
32 A3 1p carmine 1.75 .35
33 A3 2p gray 2.00 18.00
34 A3 2½p ultramarine 2.50 4.25

Chalky Paper

35 A3 3p vio, *yellow* 1.10 22.50
36 A3 6p red vio & gray vio 7.75 60.00
37 A3 1sh blk, *green* 10.00 55.00
38 A3 2sh bl & vio, *bl* 35.00 67.50
39 A3 2sh 6p car & blk, *blue* 35.00 87.50
40 A4 5sh grn & scar, *yel* 60.00 92.50

Surface-colored Paper

41 A3 3p vio, *yel* ('13) 4.50 35.00
Overprinted "SPECIMEN" 26.00
Nos. 31A-41 (11) 167.85 443.70
#31A-40, ovptd "SPECIMEN" 250.00

King George V
A5 A6

1913

Chalky Paper

42 A5 5sh green & scar, *yel* 80.00 110.00
Overprinted "SPECIMEN" 85.00

1916-22 **Wmk. 3** ***Perf. 14***

Ordinary Paper

43 A6 ½p green .65 2.75
44 A6 1p scarlet 1.10 .90
45 A6 2p gray 2.25 5.00
46 A6 2½p ultramarine 3.50 21.00

Chalky Paper

47 A6 3p violet, *yel* 1.40 9.75
48 A6 4p blk & red, *yel* ('22) 6.50 42.50
49 A6 6p dl vio & red violet 3.50 24.00
50 A6 1sh blk, *bl grn*, ol back 3.50 26.00
51 A6 2sh vio & ultra, *bl* 17.00 35.00
52 A6 2sh 6p blk & red, *bl* 26.00 60.00
53 A6 5sh grn & red, *yel* 45.00 60.00
Nos. 43-53 (11) 110.40 286.90
Set of 11, ovptd "SPECIMEN" 200.00

For overprints see Nos. MR1-MR3.

1922-29 **Wmk. 4**

Ordinary Paper

54 A6 ¼p brown .35 6.25
55 A6 ½p green ('23) .20 .25
56 A6 1p dp violet ('23) .80 .70
57 A6 1p carmine ('29) 1.10 1.75
58 A6 1½p orange 3.50 11.00
59 A6 1½p rose red ('23) .60 4.25
60 A6 1½p fawn ('29) 2.00 .55
61 A6 2p gray .80 2.25
62 A6 2½p ultramarine 9.25 18.00
63 A6 2½p orange ('23) 2.75 21.00
64 A6 3p ultra ('23) .80 18.00

Chalky Paper

65 A6 3p vio, *yel* ('26) 2.00 5.50
66 A6 4p black & red, *yel* ('23) 1.75 14.00
67 A6 5p dull vio & ol grn 4.50 11.00
68 A6 6p dull vio & red vio ('23) 3.50 8.50
69 A6 1sh blk, *emer* ('23) 3.50 8.00
70 A6 2sh vio & ultra, *bl* 8.00 16.00
71 A6 2sh 6p blk & red, *bl* ('23) 14.00 57.50
72 A6 3sh green & vio 14.00 21.00
73 A6 4sh black & scar 17.50 42.50
74 A6 5sh grn & red, *yel* ('23) 30.00 47.50
Nos. 54-74 (21) 120.90 315.50
Set of 21, ovptd or perforated "SPECIMEN" 350.00

Tercentenary Issue

New Plymouth and Harbor
A7

1932, Apr. 18 **Engr.**

75 A7 ½p green .85 7.75
76 A7 1p red .85 6.50
77 A7 1½p orange brown 1.40 2.75
78 A7 2p gray 1.90 19.00
79 A7 2½p ultra 1.40 18.00
80 A7 3p orange 1.90 19.00
81 A7 6p violet 2.50 32.50
82 A7 1sh olive green 14.50 42.50
83 A7 2sh6p lilac rose 52.50 87.50
84 A7 5sh dark brown 115.00 200.00
Nos. 75-84 (10) 192.80 435.50
Set, never hinged 325.00
Set of 10, perforated "SPECIMEN" 250.00

300th anniv. of the colonization of Montserrat.

Common Design Types pictured following the introduction.

Silver Jubilee Issue

Common Design Type

1935, May 6 ***Perf. 11x12***

85 CD301 1p car & dk blue 1.25 4.25
86 CD301 1½p gray blk & ultra 1.90 3.75
87 CD301 2½p ultra & brn 2.75 4.25
88 CD301 1sh brn vio & ind 4.25 18.00
Nos. 85-88 (4) 10.15 30.25
Set, never hinged 19.00
Set, perforated "SPECIMEN" 100.00

Coronation Issue

Common Design Type

1937, May 12 ***Perf. 13½x14***

89 CD302 1p carmine .20 .35
90 CD302 1½p brown .25 .25
91 CD302 2½p bright ultra .25 .70
Nos. 89-91 (3) .70 1.30
Set, never hinged 1.10

Carr's Bay — A8

Sea Island Cotton — A9

Botanic Station
A10

1941-48 ***Perf. 14***

92 A8 ½p dk grn ('42) .20 .20
93 A9 1p car ('42) .40 .35
94 A9 1½p rose vio ('42) .40 .55
95 A10 2p red orange 1.20 .80
96 A9 2½p brt ultra ('43) .40 .35
97 A8 3p brown ('42) 1.50 .45
98 A10 6p dull vio ('42) 2.00 .70
99 A8 1sh brn lake ('42) 1.75 .35
100 A10 2sh6p slate bl ('43) 13.50 3.00
101 A8 5sh car rose ('42) 16.00 3.50

Perf. 12

102 A10 10sh blue ('48) 10.00 30.00
103 A8 £1 black ('48) 10.00 30.00
Nos. 92-103 (12) 57.35 70.25
Set, never hinged 85.00

1938, Aug. 2 ***Perf. 13***

92a A8 ½p 2.50 4.25
93a A8 1p 2.50 4.25
94a A9 1½p 10.00 16.00
95a A10 2p 10.00 16.00
96a A9 2½p .85 1.50
97a A8 3p 2.00 3.25
98a A10 6p 10.00 16.00
99a A8 1sh 10.00 16.00
100a A10 2sh6p 17.50 27.50
101a A8 5sh 21.00 35.00
Nos. 92a-101a (10) 86.35 139.75
Set, never hinged 140.00

Catalogue values for unused stamps in this section, from this point to the end of the section, are for Never Hinged items.

Peace Issue

Common Design Type

1946, Nov. 1 **Engr.** ***Perf. 13½x14***

104 CD303 1½p deep magenta .20 .20
105 CD303 3p brown .20 .20

Silver Wedding Issue

Common Design Types

1949, Jan. 3 **Photo.** ***Perf. 14x14½***

106 CD304 2½p brt ultra .20 .20

Engraved; Name Typographed

Perf. 11½x11

107 CD305 5sh rose carmine 7.75 11.50

UPU Issue

Common Design Types

Engr.; Name Typo. on 3p and 6p

Perf. 13½, 11x11½

1949, Oct. 10 **Wmk. 4**

108 CD306 2½p ultramarine .45 .45
109 CD307 3p chocolate .65 .65
110 CD308 6p lilac .75 .75
111 CD309 1sh rose violet 1.10 1.10
Nos. 108-111 (4) 2.95 2.95

University Issue

Common Design Types

1951, Feb. 16 **Engr.** ***Perf. 14x14½***

112 CD310 3c rose lil & gray blk .25 .25
113 CD311 12c violet & black .80 .80

Government House
A11

Designs (portrait at right on 12c, 24c and $2.40): 2c, $1.20, Cotton field. 3c, Map of Presidency. 4c, 24c, Picking tomatoes. 5c, 12c, St. Anthony's Church. 6c, $4.80, Badge of Presidency. 8c, 60c, Cotton ginning.

Perf. 11½x11

1951, Sept. 17 **Engr.** **Wmk. 4**

114 A11 1c gray .20 .20
115 A11 2c green .20 .20
116 A11 3c orange brown .20 .20
117 A11 4c rose carmine .20 .20
118 A11 5c red violet .20 .20
119 A11 6c dark brown .30 .30
120 A11 8c dark blue .45 .45
121 A11 12c red brn & blue .90 .90
122 A11 24c emer & rose carmine 1.25 1.25
123 A11 60c rose car & gray black 2.50 2.50
124 A11 $1.20 dp bl & emer 8.25 8.25
125 A11 $2.40 dp grn & gray black 10.00 12.00
126 A11 $4.80 pur & gray blk 20.00 26.00
Nos. 114-126 (13) 44.65 52.65

WAR TAX STAMPS

No. 43 Overprinted in Red or Black

1917-18 **Wmk. 3** ***Perf. 14***

MR1 A6 ½p green (R) .20 1.75
MR2 A6 ½p green ('18) .20 2.25

Type of Regular Issue of 1919 Overprinted

1918

MR3 A6 1½p orange & black .30 .35
Set of 10, ovptd "SPECIMEN" 90.00

Denomination on No. MR3 in black on white ground. Two dots under "d."

MOROCCO

mə-ˈrä-ˌkō

LOCATION — Northwest coast of Africa
GOVT. — Kingdom
AREA — Approx. 170,000 sq. mi.
POP. — 4,442,000 (1912 est.)
CAPITAL — Rabat

In 1892 the Sultan of Morocco established a postal service for most of the country's chief towns and cities. This service, utilizing handstuck franks, carried official correspondence, as well as some private correspondence. With French guidance, it was reorganized as the *Administration Cherifienne des Postes, Telegraphes et Telephones* in Sept. 1911. In 1912 Morocco became a French protectorate, and on Oct. 1, 1913, the Cherifian PTT was merged with the French *Administration des Postes et Telegraphes.*

Stamps were issued by the Moroccan post office in 1912, and these remained in use throughout the country until 1915 and in Tangier until 1919.

400 Moussonats = 1 Rial

Aissaouas Mosque, Tangier — A1a

On White Paper

1912, May 25 **Litho.** ***Perf. 11***

Narrow Margins

A1 A1a 1m light gray 8.00 7.00
A2 A1a 2m lilac 8.50 8.00
A3 A1a 5m blue green 11.00 7.00
A4 A1a 10m vermilion 17.00 7.00
A5 A1a 20m blue 25.00 21.00
A6 A1a 50m violet 35.00 30.00
Nos. A1-A6 (6) 104.50 80.00

On Nos. A1-A12, the 5m and 10m values always have the name of the engraver beneath the design, while the 1m, 20m and 50m always lack name, and the 2m value exists both with and without name.

Aissaouas Mosque, Tangier — A1b

On Lightly Tinted Paper

1913, Feb.

Wide Margins

A7	A1b	1m gray	.95	.95
A8	A1b	2m brown lilac	.95	.95
A9	A1b	5m blue green	1.40	1.40
A10	A1b	10m vermilion	1.40	1.40
A11	A1b	20m blue	3.00	3.00
A12	A1b	50m gray violet	3.50	3.50
		Nos. A7-A12 (6)	11.20	11.20

No. A6 Surcharged with New Values

1913, Nov.

A13	A1a	.05 on 50c violet	1,400.	*1,600.*
A14	A1a	.10 on 50c violet	1,400.	*1,600.*

MOZAMBIQUE

mō-zəm-ˈbēk

LOCATION — Southeastern Africa, bordering on the Mozambique Channel
GOVT. — Portuguese Colony
AREA — 308,642 sq. mi.
POP. — 14,140,000 (est. 1983)
CAPITAL — Maputo

Mozambique, or Portuguese East Africa, was divided into eight districts: Lourenco Marques, Inhambane, Quelimane, Tete, Mozambique, Zambezia, Nyassa and the Manica and Sofala region formerly administered by the Mozambique Company. At various times the districts issued their own stamps which were eventually replaced by those inscribed "Mocambique."

1000 Reis = 1 Milreis
100 Centavos = 1 Escudo (1913)

Portuguese Crown — A1

King Luiz — A2

Perf. 12½, 13½

1877-85 Typo. Unwmk.

1	A1	5r black	2.00	1.00
a.		Perf. 13½	3.00	1.60
2	A1	10r yellow	15.00	4.50
3	A1	10r green ('81)	1.50	.60
4	A1	20r bister	1.50	.75
a.		Perf. 13½	3.00	2.00
5	A1	20r rose ('85)	350.00	150.00
6	A1	25r rose	1.00	.35
a.		Perf. 13½	6.75	1.60
7	A1	25r violet ('85)	3.00	2.00
8	A1	40r blue	25.00	15.00
9	A1	40r yel buff ('81)	2.00	1.60
a.		Perf. 12½	3.50	3.00
10	A1	50r green	70.00	25.00
a.		Perf. 13½	125.00	60.00
11	A1	50r blue ('81)	.75	.40
12	A1	100r lilac	1.00	.50
13	A1	200r orange	2.00	1.40
a.		Perf. 12½	5.25	4.50
14	A1	300r chocolate	2.25	2.00
		Nos. 1-4,6-14 (13)	127.00	55.10

The reprints of the 1877-85 issues are printed on a smooth white chalky paper, ungummed, with rough perforation 13½, also on thin white paper, with shiny white gum and clean-cut perforation 13½.

Typographed and Embossed

1886 ***Perf. 12½***

15	A2	5r black	1.50	.60
16	A2	10r green	1.50	.70
17	A2	20r rose	2.00	1.50
18	A2	25r dull lilac	9.00	1.40
19	A2	40r chocolate	1.75	.85
20	A2	50r blue	2.25	.50
21	A2	100r yellow brn	2.50	.50
22	A2	200r gray violet	4.25	1.75
23	A2	300r orange	4.50	2.00
		Nos. 15-23 (9)	29.25	9.80

Perf. 13½

15a	A2	5r	4.00	2.75
16a	A2	10r	4.25	2.75
17a	A2	20r	13.00	6.00
18a	A2	25r	13.00	6.00
19a	A2	40r	15.00	9.50
20a	A2	50r	16.00	4.50
22a	A2	200r	15.00	12.50
		Nos. 15a-22a (7)	80.25	44.00

Nos. 15, 18, 19, 20, 21 and 23 have been reprinted. The reprints have shiny white gum and clean-cut perforation 13½. Many of the colors are paler than those of the originals.

For surcharges and overprints see Nos. 23A, 36-44, 46-48, 72-80, 192, P1-P5.

No. 19 Surcharged in Black

PROVISORIO

5 5

1893, Jan. ***Perf. 12½***

Without Gum

23A	A2	5r on 40r choc	125.00	50.00

There are three varieties of No. 23A:
I — "PROVISORIO" 19mm long, numerals 4½mm high.
II — "PROVISORIO" 19½mm long, numerals 5mm high.
III — "PROVISORIO" 19½mm long, numerals of both sizes.

King Carlos I — A3

1894 Typo. ***Perf. 11½, 12½***

24	A3	5r yellow	.50	.45
25	A3	10r red lilac	.50	.35
26	A3	15r red brown	1.25	.75
27	A3	20r gray lilac	1.25	.50
28	A3	25r blue green	1.25	.20
29	A3	50r lt blue	5.00	1.50
a.		Perf. 12½	7.50	2.00
30	A3	75r rose	1.75	1.25
31	A3	80r yellow grn	2.00	1.00
32	A3	100r brown, *buff*	1.75	1.25
33	A3	150r car, *rose*	8.00	4.00
a.		Perf. 11½		
34	A3	200r dk blue, *blue*	5.00	3.00
35	A3	300r dk blue, *salmon*	7.00	3.00
		Nos. 24-35 (12)	35.25	17.25

Nos. 28 and 31-33 have been reprinted with shiny white gum and clean-cut perf. 13½.

For surcharges and overprints see Nos. 45, 81-92, 193-198, 201-205, 226-228, 238-239.

Stamps of 1886 Overprinted in Red or Black

CENTENARIO 1195 1895 ANTONINO

1895, July 1 ***Perf. 12½***

Without Gum

36	A2	5r black (R)	11.00	5.50
37	A2	10r green	12.50	6.50
38	A2	20r rose	14.00	6.00
39	A2	25r violet	16.00	6.50
a.		Double overprint		
40	A2	40r chocolate	17.50	7.50
41	A2	50r blue	17.50	7.50
a.		Perf. 13½	80.00	55.00
42	A2	100r yellow brown	17.50	8.25
43	A2	200r gray violet	27.50	13.00
a.		Perf. 13½	100.00	65.00
44	A2	300r orange	37.50	17.50
		Nos. 36-44 (9)	171.00	78.25

Birth of Saint Anthony of Padua, 7th cent.

No. 35 Surcharged in Black

50
réis

1897, Jan. 2 ***Perf. 12½***

Without Gum

45	A3	50r on 300r dk bl, *sal*	150.00	40.00

Nos. 17, 19 Surcharged

MOCAMBIQUE
2 ½
REIS

a

MOCAMBIQUE
2½
RÉIS

b

c

1898

Without Gum

46	A2 (a)	2½r on 20r rose	42.50	11.00
47	A2 (b)	2½r on 20r rose	27.50	10.00
a.		Inverted surcharge	55.00	45.00
48	A2 (c)	5r on 40r choc	35.00	10.00
a.		Inverted surcharge	90.00	45.00
		Nos. 46-48 (3)	105.00	31.00

King Carlos I — A4

1898-1903 Typo. ***Perf. 11½***

Name and Value in Black except 500r

49	A4	2½r gray	.20	.20
50	A4	5r orange	.20	.20
51	A4	10r lt green	.25	.20
52	A4	15r brown	3.00	1.50
53	A4	15r gray grn ('03)	.70	.55
54	A4	20r gray violet	.85	.40
55	A4	25r sea green	.85	.40
56	A4	25r carmine ('03)	.70	.30
57	A4	50r dark blue	1.50	.50
58	A4	50r brown ('03)	2.00	1.50
59	A4	65r dull blue ('03)	15.00	12.00
60	A4	75r rose	7.00	2.75
61	A4	75r red lilac ('03)	3.00	1.75
62	A4	80r violet	6.00	3.25
63	A4	100r dk blue, *bl*	2.00	1.00
64	A4	115r org brn, *pink* ('03)	10.00	5.00
65	A4	130r brown, *straw* ('03)	10.00	5.00
66	A4	150r brown, *straw*	10.00	2.75
67	A4	200r red lilac, *pnksh*	2.00	1.40
68	A4	300r dk blue, *rose*	8.00	3.25
69	A4	400r dl bl, *straw* ('03)	13.00	7.50
70	A4	500r blk & red, *bl* ('01)	20.00	8.00
71	A4	700r vio, *yelsh* ('01)	25.00	9.00
		Nos. 49-71 (23)	141.25	68.40

For overprints and surcharges see Nos. 94-113, 200, 207-220.

Stamps of 1886-94 Surcharged

1902 ***Perf. 12½, 13½***

On Stamps of 1886

Red Surcharge

72	A2	115r on 5r blk	5.00	2.00

Black Surcharge

73	A2	65r on 20r rose	5.00	2.50
a.		Double surcharge	50.00	50.00
74	A2	65r on 40r choc	6.00	4.00
75	A2	65r on 200r violet	5.00	1.75
76	A2	115r on 50r blue	2.00	1.00
77	A2	130r on 25r red vio	3.00	.90
78	A2	130r on 300r orange	3.00	.90
79	A2	400r on 10r green	7.50	3.25
80	A2	400r on 100r yel brn	40.00	25.00
		Nos. 72-80 (9)	76.50	41.30

The reprints of Nos. 74, 75, 76, 77, 79 and 80 have shiny white gum and clean-cut perforation 13½.

On Stamps of 1894

Perf. 11½

81	A3	65r on 10r red lil	3.50	2.00
82	A3	65r on 15r red brn	3.50	2.00
a.		Pair, one without surcharge		
83	A3	65r on 20r gray lil	3.75	2.00
84	A3	115r on 5r yel	4.00	2.00
a.		Inverted surcharge		
85	A3	115r on 25r bl grn	3.50	2.00
86	A3	130r on 75r rose	4.00	2.25
87	A3	130r on 100r brn, *buff*	6.00	5.00
88	A3	130r on 150r car, *rose*	4.00	2.00
89	A3	130r on 200r bl, *bl*	5.00	3.50
90	A3	400r on 50r lt bl	1.00	1.40
91	A3	400r on 80r yel grn	1.00	1.40
92	A3	400r on 300r bl, *sal*	1.00	1.40

On Newspaper Stamp of 1893

Perf. 13½

93	N3	115r on 2½r brn	2.00	2.25
		Nos. 81-93 (13)	42.25	29.20

Reprints of No. 87 have shiny white gum and clean-cut perforation 13½.

Overprinted in Black

On Stamps of 1898

Perf. 11½

94	A4	15r brown	2.00	.85
95	A4	25r sea green	2.50	.85
96	A4	50r blue	3.00	1.75
97	A4	75r rose	5.00	2.00
		Nos. 94-97 (4)	12.50	5.45

No. 59 Surcharged in Black

1905

98	A4	50r on 65r dull blue	3.00	2.00

Stamps of 1898-1903 Overprinted in Carmine or Green

1911

99	A4	2½r gray	.30	.20
a.		Inverted overprint	15.00	15.00
100	A4	5r orange	.30	.20
101	A4	10r lt green	2.00	.50
102	A4	15r gray grn	.30	.20
103	A4	20r gray vio	2.00	.40
104	A4	25r carmine (G)	.30	.20
a.		25r gray violet (error)		
105	A4	50r brown	.50	.20
106	A4	75r red lilac	1.00	.50
107	A4	100r dk blue, *bl*	1.00	.50
108	A4	115r org brn, *pink*	1.50	.85
109	A4	130r brown, *straw*	1.50	.85
a.		Double overprint		
110	A4	200r red lil, *pnksh*	3.00	.70
111	A4	400r dull bl, *straw*	3.50	.85
112	A4	500r blk & red, *bl*	4.00	.85
113	A4	700r vio, *straw*	4.50	.85
		Nos. 99-113 (15)	25.70	7.85

King Manoel — A5

Overprinted in Carmine or Green

1912 ***Perf. 11½x12***

114	A5	2½r violet	.20	.20
115	A5	5r black	.20	.20
116	A5	10r gray grn	.20	.20
117	A5	20r carmine (G)	.55	.40
118	A5	25r vio brn	.20	.20
119	A5	50r dp blue	.50	.35
120	A5	75r bis brn	.50	.35
121	A5	100r brn, *lt grn*	.50	.35
122	A5	200r dk grn, *salmon*	1.00	.70
123	A5	300r black, *azure*	1.00	.70

Perf. 14x15

124	A5	500r ol grn & vio brn	2.00	1.25
		Nos. 114-124 (11)	6.85	4.90

Vasco da Gama Issue of Various Portuguese Colonies Common Design Types Surcharged

1913

On Stamps of Macao

125	CD20	¼c on ½a bl grn	1.50	1.50
126	CD21	½c on 1a red	1.50	1.50
127	CD22	1c on 2a red vio	1.50	1.50
128	CD23	2½c on 4a yel grn	1.50	1.50
a.		Double surcharge	50.00	50.00
129	CD24	5c on 8a dk bl	2.50	2.50
130	CD25	7½c on 12a vio brn	2.00	2.00
131	CD26	10c on 16a bis brn	1.75	1.50
132	CD27	15c on 24a bis	1.50	1.50
		Nos. 125-132 (8)	13.75	13.50

On Stamps of Portuguese Africa

133	CD20	¼c on 2½r bl grn	1.25	1.25
134	CD21	½c on 5r red	1.25	1.25
135	CD22	1c on 10r red vio	1.25	1.25
a.		Inverted surcharge	45.00	45.00
136	CD23	2½c on 25r yel grn	1.25	1.25
137	CD24	5c on 50r dk bl	1.25	1.25
138	CD25	7½c on 75r vio brn	1.75	1.75
139	CD26	10c on 100r bis brn	1.50	1.50
140	CD27	15c on 150r bis	1.50	1.50
		Nos. 133-140 (8)	11.00	11.00

On Stamps of Timor

141	CD20	¼c on ½a bl grn	1.50	1.50
142	CD21	½c on 1a red	1.50	1.50
143	CD22	1c on 2a red vio	1.50	1.50
144	CD23	2½c on 4a yel grn	1.50	1.50
145	CD24	5c on 8a dk bl	1.50	1.50
146	CD25	7½c on 12a vio brn	3.00	3.00
147	CD26	10c on 16a bis brn	1.50	1.50
148	CD27	15c on 24a bis	2.00	2.00
		Nos. 141-148 (8)	14.00	14.00
		Nos. 125-148 (24)	38.75	38.50

Ceres — A6

1914-26 Typo. *Perf. 15x14, 12x11½*

Name and Value in Black

149	A6	¼c olive brown	.20	.20
150	A6	½c black	.20	.20
151	A6	1c blue green	.20	.20
152	A6	1½c lilac brown	.20	.20
153	A6	2c carmine	.20	.20
154	A6	2c gray ('26)	.20	.20
155	A6	2½c lt vio	.20	.20
156	A6	3c org ('21)	.20	.20
157	A6	4c pale rose ('21)	.20	.20
158	A6	4½c gray ('21)	.20	.20
159	A6	5c deep blue	.20	.20
160	A6	6c lilac ('21)	.20	.20
a.		Name and value printed twice		
161	A6	7c ultra ('21)	.20	.20
162	A6	7½c yel brn	.20	.20
163	A6	8c slate	.20	.20
164	A6	10c org brn	.20	.20
165	A6	12c gray brn ('21)	.25	.20
166	A6	12c blue grn ('22)	.20	.20
167	A6	15c plum	1.40	1.00
a.		Perf. 12x11½ ('30)	.65	.35
168	A6	15c brn rose ('22)	.20	.20
169	A6	20c yel grn	.20	.20
170	A6	24c ultra ('26)	4.50	2.00
171	A6	25c choc ('26)	1.50	1.25
172	A6	30c brown, *grn*	1.50	1.10
173	A6	30c deep green ('21)	1.00	.20
174	A6	30c gray bl, *pink* ('21)	1.50	1.25
175	A6	40c brn, *pink*	1.25	.85
176	A6	40c turq blue ('22)	1.00	.30
177	A6	50c org, *salmon*	2.75	3.00
178	A6	50c lt violet ('26)	.50	.20
179	A6	60c red brn, *pink* ('21)	1.00	.85
180	A6	60c dk blue ('22)	1.00	.30
181	A6	60c rose ('26)	1.10	.25
182	A6	80c dk brn, *bl* ('21)	1.10	.85
183	A6	80c brt rose ('22)	1.00	.25
184	A6	1e grn, *bl*, perf. 12x11½ ('21)	1.40	.60
a.		Perf. 15x14	6.00	2.00
185	A6	1e rose ('21)	1.60	.50
186	A6	1e blue ('26)	1.60	.65
187	A6	2e brt vio, *pink* ('21)	1.40	.60
188	A6	2e dk violet ('22)	1.00	.35
189	A6	5e buff ('26)	7.25	2.50
190	A6	10e pink ('26)	12.00	5.00
191	A6	20e pale turq ('26)	35.00	17.50
		Nos. 149-191 (43)	87.40	45.35

For surcharges see Nos. 232-234, 236-237, 249-250, J46-50.

Stamps of 1902 Overprinted Locally in Carmine

1915

On Provisional Stamps of 1902

192	A2	115r on 5r black	150.00	100.00
193	A3	115r on 5r yellow	1.25	.75
194	A3	115r on 25r bl grn	1.25	.75
195	A3	130r on 75r rose	1.25	.75
196	A3	130r on 100r brn, *buff*	1.25	.75
197	A3	130r on 150r car, *rose*	1.25	.75
198	A3	130r on 200r bl, *bl*	1.25	.75
199	N3	115r on 2½r brn	.80	.40

On No. 97

200	A4	75r rose	1.50	1.10
		Nos. 192-200 (9)	159.80	106.00

Stamps of 1902-05 Overprinted in Carmine

1915

On Provisional Stamps of 1902

201	A3	115r on 5r yellow	.80	.50
202	A3	115r on 25r bl grn	.80	.55
203	A3	130r on 75r rose	.80	.55
204	A3	130r on 150r car, *rose*	1.00	.50
205	A3	130r on 200r bl, *bl*	1.00	.50
206	N3	115r on 2½r brn	1.00	.50

On No. 96

207	A4	50r blue	1.00	.50

On No. 98

208	A4	50r on 65r dull blue	1.00	.50
		Nos. 201-208 (8)	7.40	4.10

Stamps of 1898-1903 Overprinted Locally in Carmine Like Nos. 192-200

1917

209	A4	2½r gray	20.00	17.50
210	A4	15r gray grn	15.00	12.50
211	A4	20r gray vio	15.00	12.50
212	A4	50r brown	14.00	11.00
213	A4	75r red lilac	32.50	25.00
214	A4	100r blue, *bl*	6.00	2.50
215	A4	115r org brn, *pink*	8.00	3.00
216	A4	130r brown, *straw*	7.50	3.00
217	A4	200r red lil, *pnksh*	7.50	2.50
218	A4	400r dull bl, *straw*	7.50	3.00
219	A4	500r blk & red, *bl*	7.00	2.50
220	A4	700r vio, *yelsh*	15.00	6.00
		Nos. 209-220 (12)	155.00	101.00

War Tax Stamps of 1916-18 Surcharged

1918 ***Rouletted 7***

221	WT2	2½c on 5c rose	2.50	1.50

Perf. 11, 12

222	WT2	2½c on 5c red	1.10	.70
a.		"PETRIA"	2.00	2.00
b.		"PEPUBLICA"	2.00	2.00
c.		"1910" for "1916"	9.00	4.00

War Tax Stamps of 1916-18 Surcharged

1919 ***Perf. 11***

224	WT1	1c on 1c gray grn	.75	.40
a.		"PEPUBLICA"	4.75	4.00
b.		Rouletted 7	300.00	100.00

Perf. 12

225	WT2	1½c on 5c red	.40	.35
a.		"PETRIA"	3.00	2.00
b.		"PEPUBLICA"	3.00	2.50
c.		"1910" for "1916"	7.50	3.75

Stamps of 1902 Overprinted Locally in Carmine Like Nos. 192-200

1920

226	A3	400r on 50r lt blue	1.25	1.25
227	A3	400r on 80r yel grn	1.25	1.25
228	A3	400r on 300r bl, *sal*	1.25	1.25
		Nos. 226-228 (3)	3.75	3.75

War Tax Stamp of 1918 Surcharged in Green

1920 ***Perf. 12***

229	WT2	6c on 5c red	.60	.48
a.		"1910" for "1916"	8.00	5.00
b.		"PETRIA"	2.50	2.00
c.		"PEPUBLICA"	2.50	2.00

Lourenco Marques Nos. 117, 119 Surcharged in Red or Bue

1921 ***Perf. 15x14***

230	A4	10c on ½c blk (R)	.75	.40
231	A4	30c on 1½c brn (Bl)	1.25	.70

Same Surcharge on Mozambique Nos. 150, 152, 155 in Red, Blue or Green

232	A6	10c on ½c blk (R)	1.00	.85
233	A6	30c on 1½c brn (Bl)	1.10	.70
234	A6	60c on 2½c vio (G)	1.50	.80
		Nos. 230-234 (5)	5.60	3.45

War Tax Stamp of 1918 Surcharged in Green

1921 ***Perf. 12***

235	WT2	2e on 5c red	1.00	.50
a.		"PETRIA"	2.50	2.25
b.		"PEPUBLICA"	4.25	2.50
c.		"1910" for "1916"	8.00	6.50

No. 157 Surcharged

1923 ***Perf. 12x11½***

236	A6	50c on 4c pale rose	1.00	.55

No. 183 Overprinted in Green

1924

237	A6	80c bright rose	1.00	.60

4th centenary of the death of Vasco da Gama.

Nos. 90 and 91 Surcharged

1925 ***Perf. 11½***

238	A3	40c on 400r on 50r	.70	.70
239	A3	40c on 400r on 80r	.60	.50
a.		"a" omitted	42.50	42.50

Postage Due Stamp of 1917 Overprinted in Black and Bars in Red

1929, Jan. ***Perf. 12***

247	D1	50c gray	.85	.55

No. 188 Surcharged

1931 ***Perf. 11½***

249	A6	70c on 2e dk vio	1.00	.50
250	A6	1.40e on 2e dk vio	1.50	.50

"Portugal" Holding Volume of the "Lusiads" — A7

Wmk. Maltese Cross (232)

1933, July 13 Typo. *Perf. 14*

Value in Red or Black

251	A7	1c bister brn (R)	.20	.20
252	A7	5c black brn	.20	.20
253	A7	10c dp violet	.20	.20
254	A7	15c black (R)	.20	.20
255	A7	20c light gray	.20	.20
256	A7	30c blue green	.20	.20
257	A7	40c orange red	.20	.20
258	A7	45c brt blue	.40	.20
259	A7	50c dk brown	.30	.20
260	A7	60c olive grn	.25	.20
261	A7	70c orange brn	.20	.20
262	A7	80c emerald	.20	.20
263	A7	85c deep rose	1.00	.50
264	A7	1e red brown	.75	.25
265	A7	1.40e dk blue (R)	7.00	1.10
266	A7	2e dk violet	2.00	.35
267	A7	5e apple green	3.00	.50
268	A7	10e olive bister	7.00	1.00
269	A7	20e orange	22.50	2.00
		Nos. 251-269 (19)	46.00	8.10

See Nos. 298-299.

Common Design Types pictured following the introduction.

Common Design Types

Perf. 13½x13

1938, Aug. Engr. Unwmk.

Name and Value in Black

270	CD34	1c gray green	.20	.20
271	CD34	5c orange brn	.20	.20
272	CD34	10c dk carmine	.20	.20
273	CD34	15c dk vio brn	.20	.20
274	CD34	20c slate	.20	.20
275	CD35	30c rose vio	.20	.20
276	CD35	35c brt green	.30	.20
277	CD35	40c brown	.40	.20
278	CD35	50c brt red vio	.40	.20
279	CD36	60c gray black	.50	.20
280	CD36	70c brown vio	.50	.20
281	CD36	80c orange	.75	.20
282	CD36	1e red	.70	.20
283	CD37	1.75e blue	1.75	.30
284	CD37	2e brown car	1.50	.30
285	CD37	5e olive green	3.50	.50
286	CD38	10e blue vio	9.00	1.00
287	CD38	20e red brown	22.50	1.40
		Nos. 270-287 (18)	43.00	6.10

For surcharges see Nos. 297, 301.

No. 258 Surcharged in Black

1938, Jan. 16 Wmk. 232 *Perf. 14*

288	A7	40c on 45c brt blue	2.50	1.40

Map of Africa — A7a

Perf. 11½x12

1939, July 17 Litho. Unwmk.

289	A7a	80c vio, *pale rose*	1.50	1.25
290	A7a	1.75e bl, *pale bl*	4.00	2.75
291	A7a	3e grn, *yel grn*	6.00	4.00
292	A7a	20e brn, *buff*	*30.00*	*50.00*
		Nos. 289-292 (4)	*41.50*	*58.00*

Presidential visit.

SEMI-POSTAL STAMPS

"History" Pointing out to "the Republic" Need for Charity SP1

Nurse Leading Wounded Soldiers SP2

Veteran Relating Experiences — SP3

Perf. 11½

1920, Dec. 1 Litho. Unwmk.

B1	SP1	¼c olive	3.50	3.50
B2	SP1	½c olive blk	3.50	3.50
B3	SP1	1c dp bister	3.50	3.50
B4	SP1	2c lilac brn	3.50	3.50
B5	SP1	3c lilac	3.50	3.50
B6	SP1	4c green	3.50	3.50
B7	SP2	5c grnsh blue	3.50	3.50
B8	SP2	6c light blue	3.50	3.50
B9	SP2	7½c red brown	3.50	3.50
B10	SP2	8c lemon	3.50	3.50
B11	SP2	10c gray lilac	3.50	3.50
B12	SP2	12c pink	3.50	3.50
B13	SP3	18c rose	3.50	3.50
B14	SP3	24c vio brn	3.50	3.50
B15	SP3	30c pale ol grn	3.50	3.50
B16	SP3	40c dull red	3.50	3.50
B17	SP3	50c yellow	3.50	3.50
B18	SP3	1e ultra	3.50	3.50
		Nos. B1-B18 (18)	63.00	63.00

Nos. B1-B18 were used Dec. 1, 1920, in place of ordinary stamps. The proceeds were for war victims.

AIR POST STAMPS

Common Design Type

Perf. 13½x13

1938, Aug. Engr. Unwmk.

Name and Value in Black

C1	CD39	10c scarlet	.30	.20
C2	CD39	20c purple	.30	.20
C3	CD39	50c orange	.30	.20
C4	CD39	1e ultra	.40	.30
C5	CD39	2e lilac brn	1.00	.30
C6	CD39	3e dk green	1.75	.40
C7	CD39	5e red brown	2.00	.70
C8	CD39	9e rose car	4.25	.75
C9	CD39	10e magenta	5.50	1.10
		Nos. C1-C9 (9)	15.80	4.15

No. C7 exists with overprint "Exposicao Internacional de Nova York, 1939-1940" and Trylon and Perisphere.

POSTAGE DUE STAMPS

D1

1904 Unwmk. Typo. *Perf. 11½x12*

Name and Value in Black

J1	D1	5r yellow grn	.40	.20
J2	D1	10r slate	.40	.20
J3	D1	20r yellow brn	.40	.25
J4	D1	30r orange	.75	.60
J5	D1	50r gray brn	.70	.40
J6	D1	60r red brown	3.25	1.60
J7	D1	100r red lilac	2.75	1.60
J8	D1	130r dull blue	1.25	.85
J9	D1	200r carmine	1.75	1.00
J10	D1	500r violet	2.25	1.00
		Nos. J1-J10 (10)	13.90	7.70

See J34-J43. For overprints see Nos. 247, J11-J30.

Same Overprinted in Carmine or Green

1911

J11	D1	5r yellow green	.20	.20
J12	D1	10r slate	.20	.20
J13	D1	20r yellow brn	.30	.20
J14	D1	30r orange	.30	.20
J15	D1	50r gray brown	.40	.30
J16	D1	60r red brown	.50	.35
J17	D1	100r red lilac	.55	.45
J18	D1	130r dull blue	1.10	.80
J19	D1	200r carmine (G)	1.10	.90
J20	D1	500r violet	1.25	.85
		Nos. J11-J20 (10)	5.90	4.45

Nos. J1-J10 Overprinted Locally in Carmine

1916

J21	D1	5r yellow grn	3.75	3.00
J22	D1	10r slate	5.00	1.75
J23	D1	20r yellow brn	75.00	52.50
J24	D1	30r orange	20.00	11.00
J25	D1	50r gray brown	75.00	52.50
J26	D1	60r red brown	60.00	40.00
J27	D1	100r red lilac	75.00	50.00
J28	D1	130r dull blue	2.25	2.00
J29	D1	200r carmine	2.50	2.75
J30	D1	500r violet	5.25	4.50
		Nos. J21-J30 (10)	323.75	220.00

War Tax Stamps of 1916 Overprinted Diagonally

1918 *Rouletted 7*

J31	WT1	1c gray green	.85	.70
J32	WT2	5c rose	.85	.70
	a.	Inverted overprint	8.25	7.50

Perf. 11

J33	WT1	1c gray green	.85	.70
	a.	"PEPUBLICA"	50.00	40.00
		Nos. J31-J33 (3)	2.55	2.10

Type of 1904 Issue With Value in Centavos

1917 *Perf. 12*

J34	D1	½c yellow green	.20	.20
J35	D1	1c slate	.20	.20
J36	D1	2c orange brown	.20	.20
J37	D1	3c orange	.20	.20
J38	D1	5c gray brown	.20	.20
J39	D1	6c pale brn	.20	.20
J40	D1	10c red violet	.20	.20
J41	D1	13c deep blue	.20	.20
J42	D1	20c rose	.20	.20
J43	D1	50c gray	.20	.20
		Nos. J34-J43 (10)	2.00	2.00

Lourenco Marques Nos. 117, 119 Surcharged in Red

1921

J44	A4	5c on ½c blk	1.50	.70
J45	A4	10c on 1½c brn	1.50	.70

Same Surcharge on Mozambique Nos. 151, 155, 157 in Red or Green

J46	A6	6c on 1c bl grn (R)	1.50	.85
J47	A6	20c on 2½c vio (R)	1.00	.70
J48	A6	50c on 4c rose (G)	1.00	.70
		Nos. J44-J48 (5)	6.50	3.65

Regular Issues of 1921-22 Surcharged in Black or Red

1924 *Perf. 12x11½*

J49	A6	20c on 30c ol grn (Bk)	1.00	.40
	a.	Perf. 15x14	19.00	4.50
J50	A6	50c on 60c dk bl (R)	1.00	.55

WAR TAX STAMPS

Coats of Arms of Portugal and Mozambique on Columns, Allegorical Figures of History of Portugal and the Republic Holding Scroll with Date of Declaration of War — WT1

Prow of Galley of Discoveries. Left, "Republic" Teaching History of Portugal; Right "History" with Laurels (Victory) and Sword (Symbolical of Declaration of War) — WT2

1916 Unwmk. Litho. *Rouletted 7*

MR1	WT1	1c gray green	2.00	.50
	a.	Imperf., pair	15.00	
MR2	WT2	5c rose	2.00	.50
	a.	Imperf., pair	15.00	

1918 *Perf. 11, 12*

MR3	WT1	1c gray green	.50	.50
	a.	"PEPUBLICA"	8.50	4.75
MR4	WT2	5c red	.70	.60
	a.	"PETRIA"	2.25	2.25
	b.	"PEPUBLICA"	2.50	2.25
	c.	"1910" for "1916"	10.00	5.00
	d.	Imperf., pair		
		Nos. MR1-MR4 (4)	5.20	2.10

For surcharges and overprints see Nos. 221-225, 229, 235, J31-J33.

NEWSPAPER STAMPS

No. 19 Surcharged in Black, Red or Blue:

JORNAES JORNAES

2 ½ REIS 2½ 2½

a b

1893 Unwmk. *Perf. 11½, 12½, 13½*

P1	A2 (a)	2½r on 40r	200.00	90.00
P2	A2 (a)	5r on 40r	175.00	90.00
P3	A2 (a)	5r on 40r (R)	150.00	75.00
P4	A2 (a)	5r on 40r (Bl)	180.00	75.00
P5	A2 (b)	2½r on 40r	22.50	16.00
		Nos. P1-P5 (5)	727.50	346.00

Nos. P1-P5 exist with double surcharge, Nos. P2-P4 with inverted surcharge.

N3

1893 Typo. *Perf. 11½, 13½*

P6	N3	2½r brown	.35	.30

For surcharge and overprint see Nos. 93, 199, 206.

No. P6 has been reprinted on chalk-surfaced paper with clean-cut perforation 13½. Value, 50 cents.

POSTAL TAX STAMPS

Pombal Commemorative Issue

Common Design Types

1925 Engr. *Perf. 12½*

RA1	CD28	15c brown & black	.30	.25
RA2	CD29	15c brown & black	.30	.25
RA3	CD30	15c brown & black	.30	.25
		Nos. RA1-RA3 (3)	.90	.75

Seal of Local Red Cross Society
PT7 PT8

Surcharged in Various Colors

1925 Typo. *Perf. 11½*

RA4	PT7	50c slate & yel (Bk)	1.40	1.40

1926

RA5	PT8	40c slate & yel (Bk)	3.00	3.00
RA6	PT8	50c slate & yel (R)	3.00	3.00
RA7	PT8	60c slate & yel (V)	3.00	3.00
RA8	PT8	80c slate & yel (Br)	3.00	3.00
RA9	PT8	1e slate & yel (Bl)	3.00	3.00
RA10	PT8	2e slate & yel (G)	3.00	3.00
		Nos. RA5-RA10 (6)	18.00	18.00

Obligatory on mail certain days of the year. The tax benefited the Cross of the Orient Society.

Type of 1926 Issue

1927

Black Surcharge

RA11 PT8 5c red & yel 3.00 3.00
RA12 PT8 10c green & yel 3.00 3.00
RA13 PT8 20c gray & yel 3.00 3.00
RA14 PT8 30c lt bl & yel 3.00 3.00
RA15 PT8 40c vio & yel 3.00 3.00
RA16 PT8 50c car & yel 3.00 3.00
RA17 PT8 60c brown & yel 3.00 3.00
RA18 PT8 80c blue & yel 3.00 3.00
RA19 PT8 1e olive & yel 3.00 3.00
RA20 PT8 2e yel brn & yel 3.00 3.00
Nos. RA11-RA20 (10) 30.00 30.00

See note after No. RA10.

PT9

1928 **Litho.**

RA21 PT9 5c grn, yel & blk 4.00 4.00
RA22 PT9 10c sl bl, yel & blk 4.00 4.00
RA23 PT9 20c gray blk, yel & blk 4.00 4.00
RA24 PT9 30c brn rose, yel & blk 4.00 4.00
RA25 PT9 40c cl brn, yel & blk 4.00 4.00
RA26 PT9 50c red org, yel & blk 4.00 4.00
RA27 PT9 60c brn, yel & blk 4.00 4.00
RA28 PT9 80c dk brn, yel & blk 4.00 4.00
RA29 PT9 1e gray, yel & blk 4.00 4.00
RA30 PT9 2e red, yel & blk 4.00 4.00
Nos. RA21-RA30 (10) 40.00 40.00

See note after RA10.

Mother and Children PT10

Mousinho de Albuquerque PT11

1929 **Photo.** ***Perf. 14***

RA31 PT10 40c ultra, cl & blk 2.50 2.50

The use of this stamp was compulsory on all correspondence to Portugal and Portuguese Colonies for eight days beginning July 24, 1929.

See Nos.RA39-RA47.

1930-31 ***Perf. 14½x14***

Inscribed: "MACONTENE"

RA32 PT11 50c lake, red & gray 3.50 4.00

Inscribed: "COOLELA"

RA33 PT11 50c red vio, red brn & gray 3.50 4.00

Inscribed: "MUJENGA"

RA34 PT11 50c org red, red & gray 3.50 4.00

Inscribed: "CHAIMITE"

RA35 PT11 50c dp grn, bl grn & gray 3.50 4.00

Inscribed: "IBRAHIMO"

RA36 PT11 50c dk bl, blk & gray 3.50 4.00

Inscribed: "MUCUTO-MUNO"

RA37 PT11 50c ultra, blk & gray 3.50 4.00

Inscribed: "NAGUEMA"

RA38 PT11 50c dk vio, lt vio & gray 3.50 4.00
Nos. RA32-RA38 (7) 24.50 28.00

The portrait is that of Mousinho de Albuquerque, the celebrated Portuguese warrior, and the names of seven battles in which he took part appear at the foot of the stamps. The stamps were issued for the memorial fund bearing his name and their use was obligatory on all correspondence posted on eight specific days in the year.

Type of 1929 Issue
Denominations in Black
No. RA40 Without Denomination

1931 ***Perf. 14***

RA39 PT10 40c rose & vio 4.00 3.25
RA40 PT10 40c ol grn & vio ('32) 5.00 4.00
RA41 PT10 40c bis brn & rose ('33) 5.00 4.00
RA42 PT10 bl grn & rose ('34) 3.50 2.75
RA43 PT10 40c org & ultra ('36) 5.00 4.00
RA44 PT10 40c choc & ultra ('37) 5.00 4.00
RA45 PT10 40c grn & brn car ('38) 7.00 5.00
RA46 PT10 40c yel & blk ('39) 7.00 5.00
RA47 PT10 40c gray brn ('40) 7.00 5.00
Nos. RA39-RA47 (9) 48.50 37.00

POSTAL TAX DUE STAMPS

Pombal Commemorative Issue
Common Design Types

1925 **Unwmk.** ***Perf. 12½***

RAJ1 CD28 30c brown & black .50 .60
RAJ2 CD29 30c brown & black .50 .60
RAJ3 CD30 30c brown & black .50 .60
Nos. RAJ1-RAJ3 (3) 1.50 1.80

MOZAMBIQUE COMPANY

mō-zəm-'bēk 'kəmp-nē

LOCATION — Comprises the territory of Manica and Sofala of the Mozambique Colony in southeastern Africa
GOVT. — A part of the Portuguese Colony of Mozambique
AREA — 51,881 sq. mi.
POP. — 368,447 (1939)
CAPITAL — Beira

The Mozambique Company was chartered by Portugal in 1891 for 50 years. The territory was under direct administration of the Company until July 18, 1941

1000 Reis = 1 Milreis
100 Centavos = 1 Escudo (1916)

Mozambique Nos. 15-23 Overprinted in Carmine or Black

1892 **Unwmk.** ***Perf. 12½, 13½***

1 A2 5r black (C) 1.25 .25
a. Pair, one without overprint 50.00 22.50
2 A2 10r green 1.25 .25
3 A2 20r rose 1.25 .25
a. Perf. 13½ 45.00 30.00
4 A2 25r violet 1.50 .35
a. Double overprint 27.50
5 A2 40r chocolate 1.25 .30
a. Double overprint 20.00
6 A2 50r blue 1.50 .25
7 A2 100r yellow brown 1.25 .35
8 A2 200r gray violet 2.50 .45
9 A2 300r orange 3.50 .70
Nos. 1-9 (9) 15.25 3.15

Nos. 1 to 6, 8-9 were reprinted in 1905. These reprints have white gum and clean-cut perf. 13½ and the colors are usually paler than those of the originals.

Company Coat of Arms — A2

Perf. 11½, 12½, 13½

1895-1907 **Typo.**

Black or Red Numerals

10 A2 2½r olive yellow .25 .25
11 A2 2½r gray ('07) 1.50 1.50
12 A2 5r orange .25 .20
a. Value omitted 15.00
b. Perf. 13½ 2.00 1.10
13 A2 10r red lilac .40 .30
14 A2 10r yel grn ('07) 2.50 .40
a. Value inverted at top of stamp 20.00 20.00
15 A2 15r red brown 1.00 .30
16 A2 15r dk green ('07) 2.50 .40
17 A2 20r gray lilac 1.50 .30
18 A2 25r green .75 .30
a. Perf. 13½ 1.90 1.25
19 A2 25r carmine ('07) 2.50 .60
a. Value omitted 15.00 10.00
20 A2 50r blue .90 .30
21 A2 50r brown ('07) 2.50 .60
a. Value omitted 15.00
22 A2 65r slate blue ('02) .75 .35
23 A2 75r rose .55 .30
24 A2 75r red lilac ('07) 5.00 1.00
25 A2 80r yellow green .35 .30
26 A2 100r brown, *buff* .40 .30
27 A2 100r dk bl, *bl* ('07) 4.00 1.00
28 A2 115r car, *pink* ('04) 1.00 .70
29 A2 115r org brn, *pink* ('07) 6.00 1.40
30 A2 130r grn, *pink* ('04) 1.50 .70
31 A2 130r brn, *yel* ('07) 6.00 1.40
32 A2 150r org brn, *pink* .35 .35
33 A2 200r dk blue, *bl* .35 .35
a. Perf. 13½ 2.00 1.60
34 A2 200r red lil, *pink* ('07) 7.00 1.40
35 A2 300r dk bl, *salmon* .50 .30
a. Perf. 13½ 2.50 1.40
36 A2 400r brn, *bl* ('04) 2.50 .70
37 A2 400r dl bl, *yel* ('07) 8.00 1.90
38 A2 500r blk & red .55 .40
39 A2 500r blk & red, *bl* ('07) 8.00 1.90
a. 500r pur & red, *yel* (error)
40 A2 700r slate, *buff* ('04) 8.50 2.00
41 A2 700r pur, *yel* ('07) 5.00 2.00
42 A2 1000r violet & red .90 .40
Nos. 10-42 (33) 83.75 24.60

#12b, 18a, 33a, 35a were issued without gum.

For overprints & surcharges see #43-107, B1-B7.

Nos. 25 and 6 Surcharged or Overprinted in Red:

PROVISORIO
25
b

PROVISORIO
c

1895 ***Perf. 12½, 13½***

43 A2(b) 25r on 80r yel grn 22.50 15.00
44 A2(c) 50r blue 9.00 4.00

Overprint "c" on No. 44 also exists reading from upper left to lower right.

Stamps of 1895 Overprinted in Bister, Orange, Violet, Green, Black or Brown

1898 ***Perf. 12½, 13½***

Without Gum

45 A2 2½r olive yel (Bi) 5.00 1.50
a. Double overprint 40.00 25.00
b. Red overprint 60.00 50.00
46 A2 5r orange (O) 7.00 1.50
47 A2 10r red lilac (V) 7.00 1.50
48 A2 15r red brown (V) 10.00 3.00
a. Red overprint
49 A2 20r gray lilac (V) 10.00 3.00
50 A2 25r green (G) 12.00 3.00
a. Inverted overprint 65.00 40.00
51 A2 50r blue (Bk) 12.00 4.00
a. Inverted overprint 60.00 40.00
52 A2 75r rose (V) 12.50 5.00
a. Inverted overprint 75.00 40.00
b. Red overprint
53 A2 80r yellow grn (G) 17.50 5.00
a. Inverted overprint
54 A2 100r brn, *buff* (Br) 17.50 5.00
55 A2 150r org brn, *pink* (O) 17.50 5.00
a. Inverted overprint 75.00 30.00
b. Double overprint
56 A2 200r dk blue, *bl* (Bk) 16.00 7.50
57 A2 300r dk blue, *sal* (Bk) 20.00 10.00
a. Inverted overprint 60.00 50.00
b. Green overprint
Nos. 45-57 (13) 164.00 55.00

Vasco da Gama's discovery of route to India, 400th anniversary.
No. 57b was prepared but not issued.

Nos. 45 and 49 were also issued with gum.
The "Centenario" overprint on stamps perf. 11½ is forged.

Nos. 23, 12, 17 Surcharged in Black, Carmine or Violet

25
PROVISORIO
e

25
Réis
f

50
RÉIS
g

1899 ***Perf. 12½***

59 A2(e) 25r on 75r rose (Bk) 4.00 2.00

1900 ***Perf. 12½, 12½x11½***

60 A2(f) 25r on 5r org (C) 1.75 1.25
61 A2(g) 50r on half of 20r gray lil (V) 2.00 1.00
b. Entire stamp 15.00 9.00

No. 61b is perf. 11½ vertically through center.

Stamps of 1895-1907 Overprinted Locally in Carmine or Green

1911 ***Perf. 11½, 13½***

61A A2 2½r gray (C) 7.00 3.00
62 A2 5r orange (G) 6.00 3.00
63 A2 10r yellow grn (C) .70 .50
64 A2 15r dk green (C) .90 .50
a. Double overprint 40.00 20.00
65 A2 20r gray lilac (G) 1.25 .50
a. Perf. 13½ 1.40 .80
66 A2 25r carmine (G) 1.25 .60
67 A2 50r brown (G) .70 .45
68 A2 75r red lilac (G) 1.10 .45
69 A2 100r dk bl, *bl* (C) 1.25 .50
70 A2 115r org brn, *pink* (G) 2.00 .60
71 A2 130r brn, *yel* (G) 3.00 .60
72 A2 200r red lil, *pink* (G) 3.00 .60
73 A2 400r dull bl, *yel* (C) 3.00 .60
74 A2 500r blk & red, *bl* (C) 4.00 .95
75 A2 700r pur, *yel* (G) 4.00 .95
Nos. 61A-75 (15) 39.15 13.80

Nos. 63, 67 and 71 exist with inverted overprint; Nos. 63, 72 and 75 with double overprint.

Overprinted in Lisbon in Carmine or Green

1911 ***Perf. 11½, 12½***

75B A2 2½r gray .30 .20
76 A2 5r orange .30 .20
77 A2 10r yellow grn .25 .20
78 A2 15r dark green .35 .20
79 A2 20r gray lilac .40 .20
80 A2 25r carmine (G) .35 .20
a. Value inverted at top of stamp 18.00
81 A2 50r brown .70 .20
82 A2 75r red lilac .70 .20
a. Value omitted 15.00
83 A2 100r dk blue, *bl* 1.00 .20
84 A2 115r org brn, *pink* 2.50 .30
85 A2 130r brown, *yel* 3.00 .35
a. Double overprint 30.00
86 A2 200r red lil, *pink* 3.00 .25
87 A2 400r dull bl, *yel* 5.00 .30
88 A2 500r blk & red, *bl* 7.50 .30
89 A2 700r pur, *yel* 5.00 .50
Nos. 75B-89 (15) 30.35 3.80

Nos. 75B-89 Surcharged

1916 — *Perf. 11½*

90	A2	¼c on 2½r gray	.20	.20
91	A2	½c on 5r org	.20	.20
a.		"½c" double	20.00	
92	A2	1c on 10r yel grn	.40	.20
93	A2	1½c on 15r dk grn	.40	.20
a.		Imperf., pair	35.00	
94	A2	2c on 20r gray lil	.50	.20
95	A2	2½c on 25r car	1.00	.25
96	A2	5c on 50r brn	.40	.20
a.		Imperf., pair	40.00	
97	A2	7½c on 75r red lil	.65	.20
98	A2	10c on 100r dk bl, *bl*	1.25	.30
a.		Inverted surcharge	40.00	40.00
99	A2	11½c on 115r org brn, *pink*	3.50	.35
a.		Inverted surcharge	50.00	50.00
100	A2	13c on 130r brn, *yel*	6.50	.30
101	A2	20c on 200r red lil, *pink*	5.50	.30
102	A2	40c on 400r dl bl, *yel*	6.50	.35
103	A2	50c on 500r blk & red, *bl* (R)	8.00	.70
104	A2	70c on 700r pur, *yel*	8.00	.75
		Nos. 90-104 (15)	43.00	4.70

Nos. 87 to 89 Surcharged

1918 — *Perf. 11½*

105	A2	½c on 700r pur, *yel*	2.50	.95
106	A2	2½c on 500r blk & red, *bl* (Bl)	3.50	.95
107	A2	5c on 400r dl bl, *yel*	4.50	.95
		Nos. 105-107 (3)	10.50	2.85

Native and Village — A9

Man and Ivory Tusks — A10

Corn — A11

Tapping Rubber Tree — A12

Sugar Refinery — A13

Buzi River Scene — A14

Tobacco Field — A15

View of Beira — A16

Coffee Plantation A17

Orange Tree A18

Cotton Field A19

Sisal Plantation A20

Scene on Beira R. R. — A21

Court House at Beira — A22

Coconut Palm A23

Mangroves A24

Cattle — A25

Company Arms — A26

1918-31 — **Engr.** — *Perf. 14, 15, 12½*

108	A9	¼c brn & yel grn	.25	.20
109	A9	¼c ol grn & blk ('25)	.20	.20
110	A10	½c black	.25	.20
111	A11	1c green & blk	.25	.20
112	A12	1½c black & grn	.25	.25
113	A13	2c carmine & blk	.25	.20
114	A13	2c ol blk & blk ('25)	.25	.25
115	A14	2½c lilac & blk	.20	.20
116	A11	3c ocher & blk ('23)	.25	.20
117	A15	4c grn & brn ('21)	.25	.20
118	A15	4c red & blk ('25)	.20	.20
119	A9	4½c gray & blk ('23)	.20	.20
120	A16	5c blue & blk	.20	.20
121	A17	6c claret & bl ('21)	.80	.30
122	A17	6c lilac & blk ('25)	.25	.20
123	A21	7c ultra & blk ('23)	1.00	.50
124	A18	7½c orange & grn	.75	.30
125	A19	8c violet & blk	.20	.20
126	A20	10c red org & blk	.20	.20
128	A19	12c brn & blk ('23)	1.00	.35
129	A19	12c bl grn & blk ('25)	2.00	.35
130	A21	15c carmine & blk	.40	.30
131	A22	20c dp green & blk	.35	.20
132	A23	30c red brn & blk	3.50	.70
133	A23	30c gray grn & blk ('25)	2.00	.25
134	A23	30c bl grn & blk ('31)	3.50	.40
135	A24	40c yel grn & blk	.85	.45
136	A24	40c grnsh bl & blk ('25)	.70	.30
137	A25	50c orange & blk	2.25	.75
138	A25	50c lt vio & blk ('25)	2.25	.45
139	A25	60c rose & brn ('23)	1.50	.50
140	A20	80c ultra & brn ('23)	4.00	.70
141	A20	80c car & blk ('25)	1.00	.35
142	A26	1e dk green & blk	2.25	.45
143	A26	1e blue & blk ('25)	2.25	.35
144	A16	2e rose & vio ('23)	5.00	.70
145	A16	2e lilac & blk ('25)	4.00	.45
		Nos. 108-145 (37)	45.00	12.40

Shades exist of several denominations.
For surcharges see Nos. 146-154, RA1.

Nos. 132, 142, 115, 120, 131, 135, 125, 137 Surcharged with New Values in Red, Blue, Violet or Black:

h

i

j

1920 — *Perf. 14, 15*

146	A23(h)	½c on 30c (Bk)	6.00	4.50
147	A26(h)	½c on 1e (R)	6.00	4.50
148	A14(h)	1½c on 2½c (Bl)	4.00	2.25
149	A16(h)	1½c on 5c (V)	4.00	3.50
150	A14(h)	2c on 2½c (R)	1.75	1.75
151	A22(i)	4c on 20c (V)	7.50	4.50
152	A24(i)	4c on 40c (V)	8.50	5.00
153	A19(j)	6c on 8c (R)	8.00	5.50
154	A25(j)	6c on 50c (Bk)	9.00	5.50
		Nos. 146-154 (9)	54.75	37.00

The surcharge on No. 148 is placed vertically between two bars. On No. 154 the two words of the surcharge are 13mm apart.

Native — A27

View of Beira — A28

Tapping Rubber Tree — A29

Picking Tea — A30

Zambezi River — A31

1925-31 — **Engr.** — *Perf. 12*

155	A27	24c ultra & blk	1.00	.50
156	A28	25c choc & ultra	1.00	.50
157	A27	85c brn red & blk ('31)	.85	.45
158	A28	1.40e dl bl & blk ('31)	.85	.45
159	A29	5e yel brn & ultra	1.25	.30
160	A30	10e rose & blk	1.75	.75
161	A31	20e green & blk	1.75	.75
		Nos. 155-161 (7)	8.45	3.70

Ivory Tusks — A32

Panning Gold — A33

1931 — **Litho.** — *Perf. 14*

162	A32	45c lt blue	2.00	.85
163	A33	70c yellow brn	1.40	.35

Zambezi Railroad Bridge A34

1935 — **Engr.** — *Perf. 12½*

164	A34	1e dk blue & blk	2.00	1.40

Opening of a new bridge over the Zambezi River.

Airplane over Beira — A35

1935

165	A35	5c blue & blk	.45	.35
166	A35	10c red org & blk	.45	.35
a.		Square pair, imperf. between	50.00	
167	A35	15c red & blk	.45	.35
a.		Square pair, imperf. between	50.00	
168	A35	20c yel grn & blk	.45	.35
169	A35	30c green & blk	.45	.35
170	A35	40c gray bl & blk	.45	.35
171	A35	45c blue & blk	.45	.35
172	A35	50c violet & blk	.45	.35
a.		Square pair, imperf. btwn.	60.00	
173	A35	60c carmine & brn	.60	.35
174	A35	80c carmine & blk	.60	.35
		Nos. 165-174 (10)	4.80	3.50

Issued to commemorate the opening of the Blantyre-Beira Salisbury air service.

Giraffe — A36

Thatched Huts — A37

Rock Python — A41

Coconut Palms A50

Zambezi Railroad Bridge A52

Sena Gate — A53

Company Arms — A54

Designs: 10c, Dhow. 15c, St. Caetano Fortress, Sofala. 20c, Zebra. 40c, Black rhinoceros. 45c, Lion. 50c, Crocodile. 60c, Leopard. 70c, Mozambique woman. 80c, Hippopotami. 85c, Vasco da Gama's flagship. 1e, Man in canoe. 2e, Greater kudu.

1937, May 16 ***Perf. 12½***

175	A36	1c yel grn & vio	.20	*.20*
176	A37	5c blue & yel grn	.20	*.20*
177	A36	10c ver & ultra	.20	*.20*
178	A37	15c carmine & blk	.20	*.20*
179	A36	20c green & ultra	.20	*.20*
180	A41	30c dk grn & ind	.20	*.30*
181	A41	40c gray bl & blk	.20	*.30*
182	A41	45c blue & brn	.20	*.30*
183	A41	50c dk vio & emer	.20	*.30*
184	A37	60c carmine & bl	.20	*.20*
185	A36	70c yel brn & pale grn	.20	*.20*
186	A37	80c car & pale grn	.40	.30
187	A41	85c org red & blk	.40	.40
188	A41	1e dp bl & blk	.30	.20
189	A50	1.40e dk bl & pale grn	.30	.20
190	A41	2e pale lilac & brn	.70	.20
191	A52	5e yel brn & bl	1.00	*.70*
192	A53	10e carmine & blk	2.00	1.40
193	A54	20e grn & brn vio	2.50	2.75
		Nos. 175-193 (19)	9.80	8.75

Stamps of 1937 Overprinted in Red or Black

1939, Aug. 28

194	A41	30c dk grn & ind (R)	1.50	.85
195	A41	40c gray bl & blk (R)	1.50	.85
196	A41	45c blue & brn (Bk)	1.50	.85
197	A41	50c dk vio & emer (R)	2.00	1.00
198	A41	85c org red & blk (Bk)	2.00	1.00
199	A41	1e dp bl & blk (R)	1.75	1.25
200	A41	2e pale lil & brn (Bk)	2.50	1.60
		Nos. 194-200 (7)	12.75	7.40

Visit of the President of Portugal to Beira in 1939.

King Alfonso Henriques
A55

King John IV
A56

1940, Feb. 16 Typo. ***Perf. 11½x12***

201	A55	1.75e blue & lt blue	.70	.70

800th anniv. of Portuguese independence.

1941 Engr. ***Perf. 12½***

202	A56	40c gray grn & blk	.30	.20
203	A56	50c dk vio & brt grn	.30	.20
204	A56	60c brt car & dp bl	.30	.20
205	A56	70c brn org & dk grn	.30	.20
206	A56	80c car & dp grn	.30	.20
207	A56	1e dk bl & blk	.30	.20
		Nos. 202-207 (6)	1.80	1.20

300th anniv. of the restoration of the Portuguese Monarchy.

Mozambique Company's charter terminated July 18th, 1941 after which date its stamps were superseded by those of the territory of Mozambique.

SEMI-POSTAL STAMPS

Lisbon Issue of 1911 Overprinted in Red

1917 Unwmk. ***Perf. 11½***

B1	A2	2½r gray	7.50	*10.50*
a.		Double overprint	75.00	*75.00*
B2	A2	10r yellow grn	8.75	*15.00*
B3	A2	20r gray lilac	12.00	*20.00*
B4	A2	50r brown	20.00	*25.00*
B5	A2	75r red lilac	65.00	*70.00*
B6	A2	100r dk blue, *bl*	65.00	*70.00*
B7	A2	700r purple, *yel*	160.00	*225.00*
		Nos. B1-B7 (7)	338.25	*435.50*

Nos. B1-B7 were used on July 31, 1917, in place of ordinary stamps. The proceeds were given to the Red Cross.

AIR POST STAMPS

Airplane over Beira — AP1

1935 Unwmk. Engr. ***Perf. 12½***

C1	AP1	5c blue & blk	.20	.20
C2	AP1	10c org red & blk	.20	.20
C3	AP1	15c red & blk	.20	.20
C4	AP1	20c yel grn & blk	.20	.20
C5	AP1	30c green & blk	.20	.20
C6	AP1	40c gray bl & blk	.20	.20
C7	AP1	45c blue & blk	.20	.20
C8	AP1	50c dk vio & blk	.40	.20
C9	AP1	60c car & brn	.40	.20
C10	AP1	80c car & blk	.50	.20
C11	AP1	1e blue & blk	.50	.20
C12	AP1	2e mauve & blk	1.25	.25
C13	AP1	5e bis brn & bl	1.25	.40
C14	AP1	10e car & blk	1.40	.60
C15	AP1	20e bl grn & blk	2.75	.85
		Nos. C1-C15 (15)	9.85	4.30

POSTAGE DUE STAMPS

D1

1906 Unwmk. Typo. ***Perf. 11½x12***

Denominations in Black

J1	D1	5r yellow grn	.70	.30
J2	D1	10r slate	.70	.30
J3	D1	20r yellow brn	1.25	.30
J4	D1	30r orange	1.50	1.00
J5	D1	50r gray brown	1.50	1.00
J6	D1	60r red brown	22.50	9.00
J7	D1	100r red lilac	4.00	2.50
J8	D1	130r dull blue	32.50	12.00
J9	D1	200r carmine	13.00	4.00
J10	D1	500r violet	18.00	5.00
		Nos. J1-J10 (10)	95.65	35.40

Nos. J1-J10 Overprinted in Carmine or Green

1911

J11	D1	5r yellow grn	.20	.20
J12	D1	10r slate	.20	.20
J13	D1	20r yellow brn	.20	.20
J14	D1	30r orange	.20	.20
J15	D1	50r gray brown	.30	.20
J16	D1	60r red brown	.40	.30
J17	D1	100r red lilac	.40	.30
J18	D1	130r dull blue	2.00	1.00
J19	D1	200r carmine (G)	1.25	.85
J20	D1	500r violet	2.50	1.00
		Nos. J11-J20 (10)	7.65	4.45

D2

Company Arms — D3

1916 **Typo.**

With Value in Centavos in Black

J21	D2	½c yellow grn	.30	.20
J22	D2	1c slate	.30	.20
J23	D2	2c orange brn	.30	.20
J24	D2	3c orange	.60	.25
J25	D2	5c gray brown	.60	.25
J26	D2	6c pale brown	.60	.25
J27	D2	10c red lilac	.60	.30
J28	D2	13c gray blue	.90	.55
J29	D2	20c rose	1.25	.65
J30	D2	50c gray	3.00	.85
		Nos. J21-J30 (10)	8.45	3.70

1919 Engr. ***Perf. 12½, 13½, 14, 15***

J31	D3	½c green	.20	.20
J32	D3	1c slate	.20	.20
J33	D3	2c red brown	.20	.20
J34	D3	3c orange	.20	.20
J35	D3	5c gray brown	.20	.20
J36	D3	6c lt brown	.45	.45
J37	D3	10c lilac rose	.45	.45
J38	D3	13c dull blue	.45	.45
J39	D3	20c rose	.45	.45
J40	D3	50c gray	.45	.45
		Nos. J31-J40 (10)	3.25	3.25

NEWSPAPER STAMP

Newspaper Stamp of Mozambique Overprinted Like Nos. 1-9

1894 Unwmk. ***Perf. 11½***

P1	N3	2½r brown	.50	.40
a.		Inverted overprint	30.00	30.00
b.		Perf. 12½	.85	.50

Reprints are on stout white paper with clean-cut perf. 13½. Value $1.

POSTAL TAX STAMPS

No. 116 Surcharged in Black

1932 ***Perf. 12½***

RA1	A11	2c on 3c org & blk	1.40	*2.00*

Charity — PT2

1933 Litho. ***Perf. 11***

RA2	PT2	2c magenta & blk	1.00	*2.00*

PT3

PT4

1940 Unwmk. ***Perf. 10½***

RA3	PT3	2c black & ultra	15.00	*16.00*

1941

RA4	PT4	2c black & brt red	15.00	*16.00*

NATAL

nə-'tal

LOCATION — Southern coast of Africa, bordering on the Indian Ocean
GOVT. — British Crown Colony
AREA — 35,284 sq. mi.
POP. — 1,206,386 (1908)
CAPITAL — Pietermaritzburg

Natal united with Cape of Good Hope, Orange Free State and the Transvaal in 1910 to form the Union of South Africa.

12 Pence = 1 Shilling
20 Shillings = 1 Pound

Values for Nos. 1-7 are for examples with complete margins and free from damage. Unused values for No. 8 on are for stamps with original gum as defined in the catalogue introduction. Very fine examples of Nos. 8-49, 61-63 and 79 will have perforations touching the design on one or more sides due to the narrow spacing of the stamps on the plates. Stamps with perfs clear of the design on all four sides are scarce and will command higher prices.

Watermark

Wmk. 5 — Small Star

Crown and V R (Victoria Regina)
A1 A2

Crown and Laurel — A3

A4

A5

Colorless Embossing

1857 Unwmk. ***Imperf.***

1	A1	3p *rose*	550.
a.		Tete beche pair	*45,000.*
2	A2	6p *green*	1,400.
a.		Diagonal half used as 3p on cover	*11,000.*
3	A3	9p *blue*	*9,000.*
4	A4	1sh *buff*	*7,500.*

1858

5	A5	1p *blue*	1,400.
6	A5	1p *rose*	2,200.
a.		No. 1 embossed over No. 6	—
7	A5	1p *buff*	1,275.

Reprints: The paper is slightly glazed, the embossing sharper and the colors as follows: 1p pale blue, deep blue, carmine rose or yellow; 3p pale rose or carmine rose; 6p bright green or yellow green; 1sh pale buff or pale yellow. Bogus cancellations are found on the reprints.

The stamps printed on surface-colored paper are revenue stamps with trimmed perforations.

Queen Victoria
A6 A7

1860 Engr. *Perf. 14*

8	A6	1p rose	160.00	90.00
9	A6	3p blue	200.00	55.00
a.		Vert. pair, imperf betwn.		*9,750.*

1863 *Perf. 13*

10	A6	1p red	110.00	35.00
a.		1p carmine lake	110.00	35.00

1861 *Clean-cut Perf. 14 to 16*

11	A6	3p blue	275.00	80.00

1862 *Rough Perf. 14 to 16*

12	A6	3p blue	140.00	40.00
a.		Imperf., pair		*4,500.*
b.		Imperf. horiz. or vert., pair	*4,750.*	
13	A6	6p gray	250.00	65.00

1862 Wmk. 5

14	A6	1p rose	175.00	82.50

Imperforate copies of the 1p and 3p on paper watermarked small star are proofs.

1864 Wmk. 1 *Perf. 12½*

15	A6	1p carmine red	110.00	50.00
a.		1p brown red	180.00	50.00
b.		1p rose	115.00	45.00
16	A6	6p violet	70.00	35.00
a.		6p dull reddish violet	90.00	22.50

No. 15 imperf is a proof.

1867 Typo. *Perf. 14*

17	A7	1sh green	200.00	40.00

For types A6 and A7 overprinted or surcharged see Nos. 18-50, 61-63, 76, 79.

Stamps of 1860-67 Overprinted: **Postage.**

1869

Overprint 12¾mm

18	A6	1p carmine red (#15)	375.00	82.50
a.		1p rose (#15b)	450.00	95.00
b.		Double overprint	—	*1,700.*
19	A6	3p blue (#12)	575.00	100.00
19A	A6	3p blue (#9)	—	400.00
19B	A6	3p blue (#11)	700.00	260.00
20	A6	6p violet (#16)	525.00	95.00
a.		6p dull reddish violet (#16a)	625.00	85.00
21	A7	1sh green (#17)	*6,750.*	1,175.

Same Overprint 13¾mm

22	A6	1p rose (#15b)	950.00	225.00
a.		1p carmine red (#15)	950.00	225.00
23	A6	3p blue (#12)	1,900.	450.00
a.		Inverted overprint		
23B	A6	3p blue (#9)	—	—
23C	A6	3p blue (#11)	—	900.00
24	A6	6p violet (#16)	1,900.	175.00
a.		6p dull reddish violet (#16a)	2,000.	190.00
25	A7	1sh green (#17)	*11,500.*	*2,300.*

Same Overprint 14½ to 15½mm

26	A6	1p rose (#15b)	750.00	190.00
a.		1p carmine red (#15)	750.00	190.00
27	A6	3p blue (#12)	—	350.00
27A	A6	3p blue (#11)	—	575.00
27B	A6	3p blue (#9)	—	—
28	A6	6p violet (#16)	1,500.	115.00
a.		6p dull reddish violet (#16a)	—	130.00
29	A7	1sh green (#17)	*16,750.*	*2,100.*

Overprinted

30	A6	1p rose (#15b)	125.00	55.00
a.		1p carmine red (#15)	190.00	55.00
b.		Inverted overprint		
31	A6	3p blue (#12)	225.00	55.00
a.		Double overprint		1,275.
31B	A6	3p blue (#11)	200.00	62.50
31C	A6	3p blue (#9)	375.00	95.00
32	A6	6p violet (#16)	175.00	65.00
a.		6p dull reddish violet (#16a)	230.00	77.50
33	A7	1sh green (#17)	250.00	82.50

Overprinted

34	A6	1p rose (#15b)	475.00	100.00
a.		1p carmine red (#15)	425.00	90.00
35	A6	3p blue (#12)	650.00	115.00
35A	A6	3p blue (#11)	825.00	325.00
35B	A6	3p blue (#9)	*2,600.*	*775.00*
36	A6	6p violet (#16)	600.00	100.00
a.		6p dull reddish violet (#16a)	700.00	90.00
b.		Inverted overprint		
37	A7	1sh green (#17)	*9,250.*	*1,550.*

Overprinted in Black or Red

1870-73 Wmk. 1 *Perf. 12½*

38	A6	1p red	100.00	16.00
39	A6	3p ultra (R) ('72)	110.00	16.00
40	A6	6p lilac ('73)	200.00	32.50
		Nos. 38-40 (3)	410.00	64.50

Overprinted in Red, Black or Green

g

1870 *Perf. 14*

41	A7	1sh green (R)	—	*4,500.*
42	A7	1sh green (Bk)	*3,250.*	*1,550.*
a.		Double overprint		*3,250.*
43	A7	1sh green (G)	110.00	12.50

See No. 76.

Type of 1867 Overprinted

1873

44	A7	1sh brown lilac	250.00	27.50

No. 44 without overprint is a revenue.

Type of 1864 Overprinted

1874 *Perf. 12½*

45	A6	1p rose red	325.00	95.00
a.		Double overprint		

Overprinted

1875

46	A6	1p rose red	140.00	82.50
a.		1p carmine	140.00	82.50
b.		Double overprint	625.00	500.00

Overprinted

Overprint 14½mm

1875 *Perf. 12½*

47	A6	1p yellow	90.00	90.00
48	A6	1p rose red	115.00	82.50
a.		Inverted overprint	1,275.	575.00
49	A6	6p violet	77.50	10.00
a.		Inverted overprint	900.00	190.00
b.		Double overprint		775.00

Perf. 14

50	A7	1sh green	115.00	9.00
a.		Double overprint		425.00
		Nos. 47-50 (4)	397.50	191.50

The 1p yellow without overprint is a revenue.

A8

A9

A10

A11

Queen Victoria — A12

1874-78 Typo. Wmk. 1 *Perf. 14*

51	A8	1p rose	32.50	4.25
52	A9	3p ultramarine	140.00	27.50
a.		Perf. 14x12½	2,000.	1,100.
53	A10	4p brown ('78)	150.00	14.00
54	A11	6p violet	70.00	9.00

Perf. 15½x15

55	A12	5sh claret	450.00	115.00

Perf. 14

56	A12	5sh claret ('78)	225.00	62.50
57	A12	5sh carmine	95.00	37.50
		Handstamped "SPECIMEN"	200.00	
a.		5sh rose ('78)	100.00	40.00

Perf. 12½

58	A10	4p brown ('78)	425.00	82.50

See Nos. 65-71. For types A8-A10 surcharged see Nos. 59-60, 72-73, 77, 80.

Surcharged in Black:

n

½

No. 60

o

1877 *Perf. 14*

59	A8(n)	½p on 1p rose	37.50	*82.50*
a.		Double surcharge "1/2"		
60	A8(n)	½p on 1p rose	60.00	*100.00*

The "1/2" only of No. 60 is illustrated. Surcharge "n" exists in 3 or more types each of the large "1/2" (No. 59) and the small "1/2" (No. 60).

"HALF" and "½" were overprinted separately; "½" may be above, below or overlapping.

Perf. 12½

61	A6(o)	½p on 1p yel	110.00	12.50
a.		Double surcharge	325.00	225.00
b.		Inverted surcharge	350.00	240.00
c.		Pair, one without surcharge	2,750.	1,650.
d.		"POTAGE"	300.00	250.00
e.		"POSAGE"	325.00	325.00
f.		"POSTAGE" omitted	2,000.	—
62	A6(o)	1p on 6p vio	65.00	12.50
a.		"POSTAGE" omitted		
b.		"POTAGE"	475.00	190.00
63	A6(o)	1p on 6p rose	125.00	57.50
a.		Inverted surcharge	700.00	375.00
b.		Double surcharge	—	325.00
c.		Dbl. surch., one inverted	325.00	250.00
d.		Triple surch., one invtd.		
e.		Quadruple surcharge	475.00	250.00
f.		"POTAGE"	650.00	375.00
		Nos. 61-63 (3)	300.00	82.50

No. 63 without overprint is a revenue.

A14

1880 Typo. *Perf. 14*

64	A14	½p blue green	17.50	25.00
a.		Vertical pair, imperf. between		

1882-89 Wmk. Crown and CA (2)

65	A14	½p blue green ('84)	115.00	20.00
66	A14	½p gray green ('84)	4.00	1.25
67	A8	1p rose ('84)	4.00	.25
a.		1p carmine	4.75	.35
68	A9	3p ultra ('84)	125.00	21.00
69	A9	3p gray ('89)	5.75	2.50
70	A10	4p brown	7.50	1.60
71	A11	6p violet	7.00	1.90
		Nos. 65-71 (7)	268.25	48.50

Surcharged in Black:

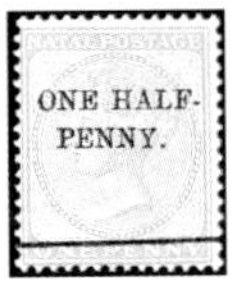

p

q

1885-86

72	A8(p)	½p on 1p rose	20.00	14.00
73	A9(q)	2p on 3p gray ('86)	24.00	7.00

A17

A20

1887

74	A17	2p olive green, die B	4.00	1.75
		Handstamped "SPECIMEN"	75.00	
a.		Die A	45.00	2.75
		Overprinted "SPECIMEN"	95.00	

For explanation of dies A and B see "Dies of British Colonial Stamps" in the catalogue introduction.

Type of 1867 Overprinted Type "g" in Red

1888

76	A7	1sh orange	6.00	1.90
		Handstamped "SPECIMEN"	125.00	
a.		Double overprint		*1,900.*

Surcharged in Black

1891

77	A10	2½p on 4p brown	12.50	16.00
a.		"PENGE"	62.50	*82.50*
b.		"PENN"	325.00	250.00
c.		Double surcharge	350.00	250.00
d.		Inverted surcharge	475.00	375.00

1891, June

78	A20	2½p ultramarine	7.50	1.60
		Handstamped "SPECIMEN"	75.00	

Surcharged in Red or Black:

No. 79

No. 80

1895, Mar. Wmk. 1 *Perf. 12½*

79 A6 ½p on 6p vio (R) 2.50 *5.25*
Handstamped "SPECIMEN" 62.50
a. "Ealf" 25.00 *40.00*
b. "Penny" 22.50 *40.00*
c. Double surcharge, one vertical 325.00
d. Double surcharge 325.00

Stamps with fancy "P," "T" or "A" in surcharge sell for twice as much.

Wmk. 2 *Perf. 14*

80 A8 ½p on 1p rose (Bk) 3.50 2.50
Handstamped "SPECIMEN" 62.50
a. Double surcharge 450.00 450.00
b. Pair, one without surcharge and the other with double surcharge —

A23

King Edward VII — A24

1902-03 Typo. Wmk. 2 *Perf. 14*

81 A23 ½p blue green 3.75 .35
82 A23 1p rose 10.00 .20
83 A23 1½p blk & blue grn 4.25 3.25
84 A23 2p ol grn & scar 3.25 .30
85 A23 2½p ultramarine 1.90 4.00
86 A23 3p gray & red vio 1.60 1.90
87 A23 4p brown & scar 5.75 22.50
88 A23 5p org & black 2.75 3.50
89 A23 6p mar & bl grn 2.75 3.50
90 A23 1sh pale bl & dp rose 3.75 4.00
91 A23 2sh vio & bl grn 62.50 11.50
92 A23 2sh6p red violet 50.00 15.00
93 A23 4sh yel & dp rose 90.00 95.00
Nos. 81-93, ovptd. "SPECIMEN" 225.00

Wmk. 1

94 A24 5sh car lake & dk blue 37.50 14.00
95 A24 10sh brn & dp rose 90.00 32.50
96 A24 £1 ultra & blk 225.00 70.00
97 A24 £1 10sh vio & bl green 500.00 125.00
Overprinted "SPECIMEN" 95.00
Revenue cancel 6.25
98 A24 £5 black & vio *3,500.* *825.00*
Overprinted "SPECIMEN" 150.00
Revenue cancel 14.00
99 A24 £10 org & green *9,500.* *4,000.*
Overprinted "SPECIMEN" 250.00
Revenue cancel 110.00
100 A24 £20 green & car *20,000.* *10,000.*
Overprinted "SPECIMEN" 475.00
Revenue cancel 175.00
Nos. 81-96 (17) 819.75 281.50

1904-08 Wmk. 3

101 A23 ½p blue green 7.50 .20
102 A23 1p rose 7.75 .20
a. Booklet pane of 6
b. Booklet pane of 5 + 1 label 350.00
103 A23 2p ol green & scar 11.50 4.00
104 A23 4p brn & scar 3.50 1.60
105 A23 5p org & blk ('08) 5.50 6.00
106 A23 1sh pale bl & dp rose 100.00 9.00
107 A23 2sh vio & bl grn 70.00 47.50
108 A23 2sh6p red violet 65.00 47.50
109 A24 £1 10sh vio & org brn, chalky paper 1,525. 1,550.
Overprinted "SPECIMEN" 250.00
Revenue cancel
Nos. 101-108 (8) 270.75 116.00

A25

A26

1908-09

110 A25 6p red violet 5.75 3.50
111 A25 1sh blk, *grn* 7.75 3.25
112 A25 2sh bl & vio, *bl* 19.00 3.75
113 A25 2sh6p red & blk, *bl* 32.50 3.75
114 A26 5sh red & grn, *yell* 27.50 32.50
115 A26 10sh red & grn, *grn* 95.00 100.00
116 A26 £1 blk & vio, *red* 350.00 315.00
Nos. 110-115 (6) 187.50 146.75

OFFICIAL STAMPS

Nos. 101-103, 106 and Type A23 Overprinted

1904 Wmk. 3 *Perf. 14*

O1 A23 ½p blue green 3.75 .45
O2 A23 1p rose 5.75 .90
O3 A23 2p ol grn & scar 30.00 15.00
O4 A23 3p gray & red vio 17.50 *5.00*
O5 A23 6p mar & bl grn 60.00 82.50
O6 A23 1sh pale bl & dp rose 190.00 *250.00*
Nos. O1-O6 (6) 307.00 *353.85*

Stamps of Natal were replaced by those of the Union of South Africa.

NAURU

nä-'ü-,rü

LOCATION — An island on the Equator in the west central Pacific Ocean, midway between the Marshall and Solomon Islands.
GOVT. —
AREA — 8½ sq. mi.
POP. — 8,421 (est. 1983)
CAPITAL — None. Parliament House is in Yaren District.

The island, a German possession, was captured by Australian forces in 1914 and, following World War I, was mandated to the British Empire. It was administered jointly by Great Britain, Australia and New Zealand.

See North West Pacific Islands.

12 Pence = 1 Shilling

Great Britain Stamps of 1912-13 Overprinted at Bottom of Stamp

1916-23 Wmk. 33 *Perf. 14½x14*

1 A82 ½p green 2.40 *7.75*
a. Double ovpt, one albino 70.00
2 A83 1p scarlet 1.90 *6.25*
a. 1p carmine red 13.50
b. Double ovpt, one albino 260.00
3 A84 1½p red brn ('23) 57.50 *85.00*
4 A85 2p org (die I) 2.10 *13.00*
a. Double ovpt, one albino 135.00
b. Triple ovpt, two albino
c. 2p deep orange (die II) ('23) 75.00 *110.00*
6 A86 2½p ultra 2.90 *7.25*
a. Double ovpt, one albino 300.00
7 A87 3p violet 2.10 *4.25*
a. Double ovpt, one albino 300.00
8 A88 4p slate green 2.10 *9.00*
a. Double ovpt, one albino 240.00
9 A89 5p yel brown 2.50 *10.00*
a. Double ovpt, one albino 175.00
10 A89 6p dull violet 4.25 *11.00*
a. Double ovpt, one albino 300.00
11 A90 9p black brown 9.00 *24.00*
a. Double ovpt, one albino 300.00
12 A90 1sh bister 8.00 *17.00*
a. Double ovpt, one albino 375.00
Nos. 1-12 (11) 94.75 *194.50*

Overprinted

Nos. of basic British stamps are in parentheses.

Wmk. 34 *Perf. 11x12*

13 A91 2sh6p light brown (#173d) 70.00 *110.00*
a. 2sh6p black brown (#173e) 625.00 *725.00*
b. As "a," double ovpt, one albino 1,500.
c. As "a," triple ovpt, two albino 1,600.
d. 2sh6p pale brown (worn plate) (#173a) 80.00 *100.00*
14 A91 5sh carmine (#174b) 125.00 *160.00*
a. As "a," triple ovpt, two albino 750.00
b. 5sh rose carmine (#174) 2,500. 2,000.
15 A91 10sh light blue (R) (#175a) 300.00 *350.00*
a. Double ovpt, one albino 1,000.
b. Triple ovpt, one black, one red, one albino 2,500.
c. 10sh indigo blue (#175) *8,000.* *5,500.*
d. Double ovpt, one albino 9,250. 8,000.
e. 10sh deep bright blue (#175c) 575.00 *625.00*

Same Ovpt. on Great Britain No. 179a and 179b

1920

16 A91 2sh6p gray brown (#179a) 80.00 *110.00*
a. Double ovpt, one albino 400.00
b. 2sh6p chocolate brown (#179b) 90.00 *140.00*
c. Double ovpt, one albino 425.00
Nos. 13-16 (4) 575.00 *730.00*
Nos. 1-16 (15) 669.75 *924.50*

Overprint Centered

1923

1b A82 ½p 5.50 *42.50*
2c A83 1p 22.50 *35.00*
3a A84 1½p 25.00 *45.00*
a. Double ovpt, one albino 175.00
4d A85 2p As No. 4a 35.00 *65.00*
Nos. 1b-4d (4) 88.00 *187.50*

On Nos. 1-12 "NAURU" is usually 12¾mm wide and at the foot of the stamp. In 1923 four values were overprinted with the word 13½mm wide and across the middle of the stamp.

Forged overprints exist.

Freighter — A1

George VI — A2

1924-48 Unwmk. Engr. *Perf. 11*
Unsurfaced grayish paper '24-'34

17 A1 ½p orange brown 2.00 *2.75*
18 A1 1p green 2.50 2.50
19 A1 1½p red 2.75 *3.75*
20 A1 2p orange 2.75 *10.00*
21 A1 2½p blue 4.25 *21.00*
b. 2½ greenish blue ('34) 5.75 *13.75*
22 A1 3p pale blue 3.00 *12.00*
23 A1 4p olive green 5.25 *16.00*
24 A1 5p dk brown 3.00 *6.00*
25 A1 6p dark violet 3.50 *11.00*
26 A1 9p brown olive 6.75 *17.50*
27 A1 1sh brown red 4.50 *12.00*
28 A1 2sh6p slate green 20.00 *47.50*
29 A1 5sh claret 35.00 *92.50*
30 A1 10sh yellow 92.50 *165.00*
Nos. 17-30 (14) 187.75 *419.50*

Glazed surfaced white paper '37-'48

17a A1 ½p orange brown 4.75 *11.00*
b. Perf. 14 ('47) .85 *8.50*
18a A1 1p green 1.75 *2.75*
19a A1 1½p red 1.00 *1.50*
20a A1 2p orange 1.75 *7.00*
21a A1 2½p blue ('48) 2.25 *3.50*
b. Horiz. pair, imperf between *4,500.* *4,500.*
c. Vert. pair, imperf between *4,500.* *4,500.*
22a A1 3p grnsh gray ('47) 2.75 *10.00*
23a A1 4p olive green 3.25 *12.50*
24a A1 5p dk brown 3.00 *3.50*
25a A1 6p dark violet 3.00 *4.50*
26a A1 9p brown olive 6.00 *18.50*
27a A1 1sh brown red 5.00 2.75
28a A1 2sh6p slate green 20.00 *30.00*
29a A1 5sh claret 27.50 *42.50*
30a A1 10sh yellow 70.00 *115.00*
Nos. 17a-30a (14) 152.00 *265.00*
Set #17a-30a, Never Hinged 185.00

Stamps of Type A1 Overprinted in Black

1935, July 12 *Perf. 11*
Glazed Paper

31 A1 1½p red .80 *.90*
32 A1 2p orange 1.60 *4.50*
33 A1 2½p blue 1.60 *1.60*
34 A1 1sh brown red 5.25 *3.75*
Nos. 31-34 (4) 9.25 *10.75*
Set, never hinged 17.00

25th anniv. of the reign of George V.

1937, May 10 Engr.

35 A2 1½p salmon rose .25 *.50*
36 A2 2p dull orange .25 *1.00*
37 A2 2½p blue .25 *.50*
38 A2 1sh brown violet .40 *.50*
Nos. 35-38 (4) 1.15 *2.50*
Set, never hinged 1.90

Coronation of George VI & Elizabeth.

NEPAL

nə-'pol

LOCATION — In the Himalaya Mountains between India and Tibet
GOVT. — Kingdom
AREA — 56,136 sq. mi.
POP. — 16,100,000 (est. 1982)
CAPITAL — Kathmandu

Nepal stamps were valid only in Nepal and India until April 1959, when they became valid to all parts of the world.

4 Pice = 1 Anna
64 Pice = 16 Annas = 1 Rupee

Nos. 1-24, 29A were issued without gum.

Sripech and Crossed Khukris — A1

Siva's Bow and Two Khukris — A2

1881 Typo. Unwmk. *Pin-perf.*
European Wove Paper

1 A1 1a ultramarine 200.00 *450.00*
2 A1 2a purple 300.00 200.00
a. Tete beche pair
3 A1 4a green 450.00 *550.00*

Imperf

4 A1 1a blue 110.00 90.00
5 A1 2a purple 150.00 *200.00*
a. Tete beche pair
6 A1 4a green 200.00 *450.00*

1886 Native Wove Paper *Imperf.*

7 A1 1a ultramarine 15.00 8.00
a. Tete beche pair *150.00* *175.00*
8 A1 2a violet 17.50 10.00
a. Tete beche pair *200.00* *200.00*
9 A1 4a green 45.00 12.00
a. Tete beche pair *300.00* *250.00*
Nos. 7-9 (3) 77.50 30.00

Used values for Nos. 9-49 are for telegraph cancels.

also have a booth at the show.

Better DANISH WEST INDIES

(Also listed in U.S. Specialized)
Scott Numbers

★ 2,3 c, marginblock, VF $200.
★★ 4, 4 c, VF................ 450.
★★ 4a, 4 c, Imperf/margin ⊞ SUPERB................ 850.
◉ 4, 4 c, F-VF for this #. 325.
★★ 6e, 3 c, SUPERB...... 45.
★ 9,7 c, VF..................... 30.

◉ 11, 12 c, tied to piece addit. St. Thom., VF..................$110.
★ 13, 50 c, F-VF............. 150.
★ 13, 50 c, Fine.............. 100.
★ 13a, 50 c, Fine............ 125.
★★ 14a, 1/7 c, VF .... 175.
★ 14a, 1/7c, Fine .... 50.
★ 15, 10/50 c, VF .... 45.

★★ 19, 5 c, SUPERB...... $60.
★★ 20, 10 c VF............ 110.
★ 20, 10 c F-VF.............. 60.
◉ 25, 8/10c, VF.............. 30.
◉ 30, 8 c, VF.................... 30.
★ 37-39 Ships, VF.......... 95.
★★ same ⊞ VF........... 600.
★★ 40-42, Surch. VF..... 90.

Payment with order, please. (Check or M.O. only) NY residents please add the tax. POSTPAID! Full satisfaction guaranteed or refund within 10 days.

HENRIK POLLAK
303 Fifth Ave., Suite 1209, New York, NY 10016
Phone or FAX 212-545-7630, best after 2 P.M.

SCC

WEEK'S SPEC

Home Phone: ______________________________

Email Address: ______________________________

Please describe what you have for sale: ______________________________

____

____

____

____

____

Approximate Value: $ ______________

Mail to:

Dr. Bob Friedman (Mark your envelope "personal")
2029 West 75th Street · Woodridge IL 60517

ings

We will come to your home and offe

small old collection

1899-1917 *Imperf.*

Native Wove Paper

10	A2	½a black	7.00	.50
a.		Tete beche pair	*100.00*	1.75
11	A2	½a red orange ('17)	*1,350.*	250.00
a.		Tete beche pair		

Pin-perf.

12	A2	½a black	7.00	
a.		Tete beche pair	*50.00*	

No. 11 is known postally used on six covers.

Type of 1881

1898-1904 *Imperf.*

13	A1	1a pale blue	12.50	6.00
a.		1a bluish green	50.00	50.00
b.		Tete beche pair	*150.00*	*150.00*
14	A1	2a gray violet	25.00	10.00
a.		Tete beche pair	*100.00*	*100.00*
15	A1	2a claret ('17)	30.00	12.00
a.		Tete beche pair	*100.00*	*100.00*
16	A1	2a brown ('17)	10.00	
a.		Tete beche pair	25.00	
17	A1	4a dull green	10.00	15.00
a.		Tete beche pair	70.00	*350.00*
b.		Cliche of 1a in plate of 4a ('04)	*350.00*	350.00
		Nos. 13-17 (5)	87.50	43.00

#17b has the recut frame of the 1904 issue. #17b probably was used only on telegraph/telephone forms.

Pin-perf.

18	A1	1a pale blue	17.50	10.00
a.		Tete beche pair	*75.00*	*50.00*
19	A1	2a gray violet	25.00	12.00
a.		Tete beche pair	*75.00*	*75.00*
20	A1	2a claret ('17)	8.75	6.00
a.		Tete beche pair	30.00	30.00
21	A1	2a brown	7.50	
a.		Tete beche pair	30.00	30.00
22	A1	4a dull green	50.00	18.00
a.		Tete beche pair	*100.00*	*100.00*

Frame Recut on All Cliches, Fewer Lines

1903-04 Native Wove Paper *Imperf.*

23	A1	1a bright blue	10.00	
a.		Tete beche pair	50.00	

Pin-perf.

24	A1	1a bright blue	15.00	
a.		Tete beche pair	100.00	

European Wove Paper

23b	A1	1a blue	*650.00*	300.00
23c		Tete beche pair	*1,750.*	

Pin-perf.

24b	A1	1a blue	750.00	
24c		Tete beche pair	*2,750.*	

Siva Mahadeva — A3

A4

1907 **Engr.** *Perf. 13½*

European Wove Paper

26	A3	2p brown	3.25	.50
27	A3	4p green	5.00	.50
28	A3	8p carmine	12.50	.50
29	A3	16p violet	24.00	1.50
		Nos. 26-29 (4)	44.75	3.00

Type A3 has five characters in bottom panel, reading "Gurkha Sirkar." Date divided in lower corners is "1964." Outer side panels carry denomination (also on A5).

1917-18 *Imperf.*

29A	A4	1a bright blue	9.00	3.00
b.		1a indigo	10.00	4.00
c.		Pin-perf.	13.00	11.00

No. 29A may not have been used postally.

In 1917 a telegraph system was started and remainder stocks and further printings of designs A1 and A2 were used to pay telegrams fees. Design A4 was designed for telegraph use but was valid for postal use. After 1929 design A3 was used for telegrams. The usual telegraph cancellation is crescent-shaped.

Type of 1907 Redrawn

A5

Nine characters in bottom panel reading "Nepal Sirkar"

1929 *Perf. 14, 14½*

Size: 24¾x18¾mm

30	A5	2p dark brown	5.00	.30
31	A5	4p green	5.00	.50
32	A5	8p deep red	17.50	1.25
33	A5	16p dark red vio	12.50	1.00
34	A5	24p orange yellow	10.00	2.00
35	A5	32p dark ultra	12.50	2.00

Size: 26x19½mm

36	A5	1r orange red	15.00	4.00

Size: 28x21mm

37	A5	5r brown & black	30.00	*25.00*
		Nos. 30-37 (8)	107.50	*36.05*

On Nos. 30-37 the date divided in lower corners is "1986."

Type of 1929 Redrawn

Date characters in Lower Corners read "1992"

1935 Unwmk. Engr. *Perf. 14*

38	A5	2p dark brown	2.75	.45
39	A5	4p green	3.00	.75
40	A5	8p bright red	75.00	8.00
41	A5	16p dk red violet	4.75	1.25
42	A5	24p orange yellow	4.75	2.00
43	A5	32p dark ultra	10.00	3.25
		Nos. 38-43 (6)	100.25	15.70

NETHERLANDS

'ne-thər-lən,dz

(Holland)

LOCATION — Northwestern Europe, bordering on the North Sea
GOVT. — Kingdom
AREA — 13,203 sq. mi.
POP. — 14,394,589 (1984)
CAPITAL — Amsterdam

100 Cents = 1 Gulden
(Guilder or Florin)

Catalogue values for unused stamps in this country are for Never Hinged items, beginning with Scott 216 in the regular postage section, and Scott B123 in the semi-postal section.

Values for unused stamps are for examples with original gum as defined in the catalogue introduction. Very fine examples of Nos. 4-12 will have perforations touching the frameline on one or more sides due to the narrow spacing of the stamps on the plates. Stamps with perfs clear on all four sides are very scarce and command higher prices.

Watermarks

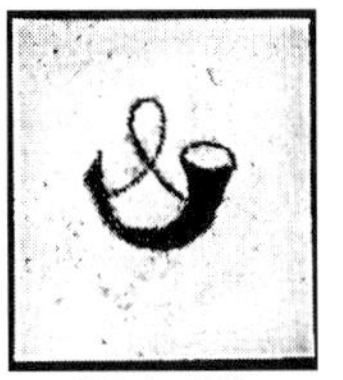

Wmk. 158

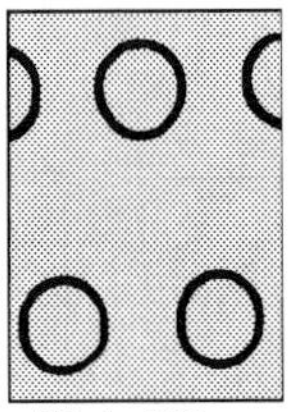

Wmk. 202 — Circles

Syncopated Perforations

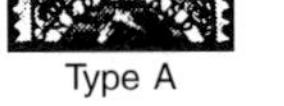

Type A

Type C

Type B

These special "syncopated" or "interrupted" perforations, devised for coil stamps, are found on Nos. 142-156, 158-160, 164-166, 168-185, 187-193 and certain semipostals of 1925-33, between Nos. B9 and B69. There are four types:

A (1st stamp is #142a). On two shorter sides, groups of four holes separated by blank spaces equal in width to two or three holes.

B (1st stamp is #164a). As "A," but on all four sides.

C (1st stamp is #164b). On two shorter sides, end holes are omitted.

D (1st stamp is #174c). Four-hole sequence on horiz. sides, three-hole on vert. sides.

King William III
A1 A2

Wmk. 158

1852, Jan. 1 **Engr.** *Imperf.*

1	A1	5c blue	400.00	32.50
		No gum	200.00	
		On cover, single franking		82.50
		Handstamped "SPECIMEN"	2,000.	
a.		5c light blue	450.00	40.00
b.		5c steel blue (Plates 1-2, '53)	750.00	90.00
c.		5c dark blue	450.00	32.50
d.		5c greenish blue (Plate 5, '62)	—	125.00
e.		Thin paper (Plate 6, '63)	425.00	32.50
f.		Ribbed paper (Plate 2, '54)	—	200.00
2	A1	10c lake	450.00	24.00
		No gum	225.00	
		On cover, single franking		82.50
		Handstamped "SPECIMEN"	2,000.	
a.		10c deep rose red	575.00	47.50
b.		10c brownish red	525.00	24.00
c.		10c car lake (see "f.")	1,550.	40.00
d.		10c dp rose red, thin paper	525.00	25.00
e.		Ribbed paper (Plate 3, '54)	—	—
f.		As "c," horn on forehead	450.00	27.50
3	A1	15c orange yellow	650.00	125.00
		No gum	325.00	
		On cover, single franking		300.00
		Handstamped "SPECIMEN"	2,000.	
a.		15c dark orange yellow	950.00	175.00
b.		15c dark yel org, thin paper	950.00	250.00

Full margins = 1¼mm.

In 1895 the 10c was privately reprinted in several colors on unwatermarked paper by Joh. A. Moesman, whose name appears on the back.

Values for pairs

1	A1	5c blue	975.00	140.00
		On cover, single franking		200.00
2	A1	10c lake	1,000.	140.00
		On cover, single franking		200.00
3	A1	15c orange yellow	1,500.	350.00
		On cover, single franking		500.00

Values for strips of 3

1	A1	5c blue	2,100.	425.00
		On cover		700.00
2	A1	10c lake	2,100.	350.00
		On cover		700.00
3	A1	15c orange yellow	2,500.	775.00
		On cover		1,175.

Values for strips of 4

1	A1	5c blue	*4,000.*	1,325.
2	A1	10c lake	*3,000.*	775.00
3	A1	15c orange yellow	*5,500.*	1,425.

Values for strips of 5

1	A1	5c blue	*5,250.*	3,600.
2	A1	10c lake	*4,500.*	2,750.
3	A1	15c orange yellow	*7,000.*	2,400.

Values for blocks of 4

1	A1	5c blue	*5,250.*	3,100.
2	A1	10c lake	*5,250.*	3,000.
3	A1	15c orange yellow	*6,500.*	*5,750.*

Values for Vert. or Horiz. Gutter Pairs

1	A1	5c blue		*12,500.*
2	A1	10c lake		*24,000.*
3	A1	15c orange yellow		*19,500.*

Gutter = 10mm.

1864 **Unwmk.** *Perf. 12½x12*

4	A2	5c blue	300.00	16.00
		No gum	100.00	
		On cover, single franking		32.50
		Handstamped "SPECIMEN"	1,100.	
5	A2	10c lake	425.00	8.00
		No gum	150.00	
		On cover, single franking		30.00
		Handstamped "SPECIMEN"	1,100.	
6	A2	15c orange	1,050.	100.00
		No gum	350.00	
		On cover, single franking		140.00
		Handstamped "SPECIMEN"	1,100.	
a.		15c yellow ('66)	1,350.	115.00
		No gum	450.00	
		On cover, single franking		200.00

The paper varies considerably in thickness. It is sometimes slightly bluish, also vertically ribbed.

Values for used pairs

4	A2	5c blue	52.50
5	A2	10c lake	25.00
6	A2	15c orange	225.00

Values for used strips of 3

4	A2	5c blue	100.00
5	A2	10c lake	80.00
6	A2	15c orange	375.00

Values for used strips of 4

4	A2	5c blue	200.00
5	A2	10c lake	175.00
6	A2	15c orange	700.00

Values for blocks of 4

4	A2	5c blue	*2,400.*	900.00
5	A2	10c lake	*2,750.*	1,100.
6	A2	15c orange	*5,500.*	*2,750.*

William III — A3

Coat of Arms — A4

1867 *Perf. 12¾x11¾*

7a	A3	5c ultra	97.50	2.50
		No gum	27.50	
		On cover, single franking		8.00
8a	A3	10c lake	200.00	4.75
		No gum	50.00	
		On cover, single franking		8.00
9	A3	15c orange brn	650.00	35.00
		No gum	200.00	
		On cover, single franking		47.50
10	A3	20c dk green	550.00	24.00
		No gum	175.00	
		On cover, single franking		37.50
		Overprinted "SPECIMEN"	4,000.	

11 A3 25c dk violet 2,100. 110.00
No gum 500.00
On cover, single franking 325.00
12 A3 50c gold 2,350. 160.00
No gum 575.00
On cover, single franking 1,125.

The paper of Nos. 7-22 sometimes has an accidental bluish tinge of varying strength. During its manufacture a chemical whitener (bluing agent) was added in varying quantities. No particular printing was made on bluish paper.

Two varieties of numerals in each value, differing chiefly in the thickness.

Oxidized copies of the 50c are worth much less.

Imperforate varieties of Nos. 7-12 are proofs.

Values for blocks of 4

7a A3 5c ultra 500.00 110.00
8a A3 10c lake 800.00 175.00
9 A3 15c orange brn 21,500.
10 A3 20c dk green 7,000. 7,000.
11 A3 25c dk violet 11,500. 1,100.
12 A3 50c gold 12,500. 1,100.

1869-70

Perf. 14

7 A3 5c ultra 97.50 2.75
8 A3 10c lake 200.00 3.50
9a A3 15c org brn 650.00 37.50
10a A3 20c dk grn 1,050. 23.00
11a A3 25c dk vio 3,900.
12a A3 50c gold 10,000.

Perf. 13½

7b A3 5c ultra 1,050. 700.00
d. 5c blue 97.50 2.40
8b A3 10c car lake 160.00 3.25
9b A3 15c org brn 675.00 32.50
10b A3 20c dk grn 950.00 24.00
11b A3 25c dk vio 8,750.

Perf. 10½x10

7c A3 5c ultra 140.00 9.00
8c A3 10c lake 220.00 4.00
9c A3 15c orange brown 2,650. 1,050.
10c A3 20c dark green 1,400. 135.00

Perf. 13¼x14

7e A3 5c ultra 97.50 2.40
8d A3 10c lake 160.00 3.25
9d A3 15c orange brown 650.00 32.50
10d A3 20c dark green 625.00 24.00

1869-71 Typo. *Perf. 13¼, 14*

17 A4 ½c red brown ('71) 23.50 3.75
Never hinged 115.00
No gum 5.75
On cover, single franking 175.00
On cover, two singles 130.00
Overprinted "SPECIMEN" 250.00
c. Perf. 14 2,300. 875.00
18 A4 1c black 200.00 70.00
Never hinged 1,150.
No gum 85.00
On cover, single franking 200.00
On cover, two singles 450.00
Overprinted "SPECIMEN" 250.00
19 A4 1c green 11.50 2.25
Never hinged 115.00
No gum 3.25
On cover, single franking 12.50
On cover, two singles 35.00
Overprinted "SPECIMEN" 250.00
c. Perf. 14 27.50 5.50
20 A4 1½c rose 125.00 77.50
Never hinged 775.00
No gum 72.50
On cover, single franking 875.00
On cover, two singles 700.00
Overprinted "SPECIMEN" 250.00
b. Perf. 14 150.00 97.50
21 A4 2c buff 55.00 14.00
Never hinged 200.00
No gum 13.50
On cover, single franking 125.00
On cover, two singles 250.00
Overprinted "SPECIMEN" 250.00
c. Perf. 14 55.00 14.00
22 A4 2½c violet ('70) 475.00 70.00
Never hinged 1,950.
No gum 120.00
On cover, single franking 160.00
On cover, two singles 175.00
Overprinted "SPECIMEN" 250.00
c. Perf. 14 775.00 425.00

Imperforate varieties are proofs.

Values for blocks of 4

17 A4 ½c red brown ('71) 115.00 57.50
18 A4 1c black 1,125. 700.00
19 A4 1c green 57.50 40.00
20 A4 1½c rose 875.00 475.00
21 A4 2c buff 250.00 115.00
22 A4 2½c violet ('70) 2,300. 575.00

A5

A6

Perf. 12½, 13, 13½, 13x14, 14, 12½x12 and 11½x12

1872-88

23 A5 5c blue 11.50 .30
Never hinged 57.50
No gum 3.00
On cover, single franking 4.00
On cover, two singles 7.00
Overprinted "SPECIMEN" 62.50
a. 5c ultra 14.00 1.25
Never hinged 77.50
No gum 3.50
On cover, single franking 20.00
On cover, two singles 27.50
24 A5 7½c red brn ('88) 35.00 18.00
Never hinged 155.00
No gum 15.00
On cover, single franking —
On cover, two singles 105.00
Overprinted "SPECIMEN" 40.00
25 A5 10c rose 57.50 1.60
Never hinged 195.00
No gum 14.50
On cover, single franking 7.75
On cover, two singles 32.00
Overprinted "SPECIMEN" 100.00
26 A5 12½c gray ('75) 62.50 2.40
Never hinged 195.00
No gum 15.50
On cover, single franking 20.00
On cover, two singles 35.00
Overprinted "SPECIMEN" 92.50
27 A5 15c brn org 350.00 5.25
Never hinged 1,950.
No gum 87.50
On cover, single franking 70.00
On cover, two singles 105.00
Overprinted "SPECIMEN" 92.50
28 A5 20c green 425.00 5.00
Never hinged 2,150.
No gum 105.00
On cover, single franking 70.00
On cover, two singles 105.00
Overprinted "SPECIMEN" 125.00
29 A5 22½c dk grn ('88) 77.50 42.50
Never hinged 400.00
No gum 40.00
On cover, single franking 525.00
On cover, two singles —
Overprinted "SPECIMEN" 80.00
30 A5 25c dull vio 525.00 4.00
Never hinged 2,150.
No gum 130.00
On cover, single franking 105.00
On cover, two singles 195.00
On parcel post receipt card 105.00
Overprinted "SPECIMEN" 125.00
31 A5 50c bister 650.00 11.00
Never hinged 3,275.
No gum 160.00
On cover, single franking 275.00
On cover, two singles —
On parcel post receipt card 125.00
Overprinted "SPECIMEN" 150.00
32 A5 1g gray vio ('88) 475.00 40.00
Never hinged 1,750.
No gum 120.00
On cover, single franking —
On cover, two singles —
Overprinted "SPECIMEN" 110.00
33 A6 2g50c rose & ultra 900.00 105.00
Never hinged 3,850.
No gum 425.00
On cover, single franking —
On cover, two singles —
Overprinted "SPECIMEN" 550.00

Imperforate varieties are proofs.

Values for blocks of 4

23 A5 5c blue 57.50 20.00
a. 5c ultra 75.00 20.00
24 A5 7½c red brown 175.00 350.00
25 A5 10c rose 275.00 65.00
26 A5 12½c gray 325.00 70.00
27 A5 15c brown orange 2,250. 110.00
28 A5 20c green 2,400. 125.00
29 A5 22½c dark green 350.00 325.00
30 A5 25c dull violet 3,000. 75.00
31 A5 50c bister 3,100. 75.00
32 A5 1g gray violet 2,800. 750.00
33 A6 2g50c rose & ultra 4,100. 550.00

Numeral of Value — A7

HALF CENT:
Type I — Fraction bar 8 to 8½mm long.
Type II — Fraction bar 9mm long and thinner.

Perf. 12½, 13½, 14, 12½x12, 11½x12

1876-94

34 A7 ½c rose (II) 11.50 .25
Never hinged 37.50
On cover 47.50
On cover, single franking 70.00
a. ½c rose (I) 14.50 .50
Never hinged 45.00
On cover 77.50
On cover, single franking 60.00
c. Laid paper 60.00
d. Perf. 14 (I) 1,950. 575.00
35 A7 1c emer grn ('94) 2.75 .20
Never hinged 11.50
On cover, single franking 4.00
b. As "c," laid paper 70.00 5.50
c. 1c green 8.00 .20
Never hinged 57.50
On cover, single franking 5.50
36 A7 2c olive yel ('94) 32.50 2.75
Never hinged 110.00
On cover, single franking 55.00
a. 2c yellow 65.00 3.50
Never hinged 290.00
On cover, single franking 55.00
37 A7 2½c violet ('94) 14.00 .25
Never hinged 77.50
On cover, single franking 2.75
b. 2½c dark violet ('94) 17.50 .45
On cover, single franking 3.00
c. 2½c lilac 100.00 .80
Never hinged 500.00
On cover, single franking — 4.00
d. Laid paper — —

Imperforate varieties are proofs.

Values for blocks of 4

34 A7 ½c rose (II) 57.50 62.50
b. ½c red brn 525.00 175.00
35 A7 1c emerald grn 11.00 25.00
c. 1c grn 47.50 27.50
36 A7 2c ol yel 160.00 60.00
a. 2c yel 325.00 62.50
37 A7 2½c vio 70.00 85.00
b. 2½c dk vio 90.00 100.00
c. 2½c lilac 475.00 50.00

Princess Wilhelmina
A8 A9

1891-94 ***Perf. 12½***

40 A8 3c orange ('94) 8.00 2.30
Never hinged 35.00
On cover, single franking 52.50
Overprinted "SPECIMEN" 55.00
a. 3c orange yellow ('92) 11.50 2.75
Never hinged 52.50
On cover, single franking 52.50
41 A8 5c lt ultra ('94) 4.00 .25
Never hinged 24.00
On cover, single franking 2.75
Overprinted "SPECIMEN" 55.00
a. 5c dull blue 5.00 .25
Never hinged 29.00
On cover, single franking 3.00
42 A8 7½c brown ('94) 17.00 6.25
Never hinged 77.50
On postcard 42.50
On cover 50.00
On cover, single franking 190.00
Overprinted "SPECIMEN" 55.00
a. 7½c red brown 27.50 6.25
Never hinged 140.00
On postcard 25.00
On cover 50.00
On cover, single franking 190.00
43 A8 10c brt rose ('94) 23.50 1.50
Never hinged 110.00
On cover, single franking 9.25
Overprinted "SPECIMEN" 55.00
a. 10c brick red 45.00 2.30
Never hinged 175.00
On cover, single franking 14.00
44 A8 12½c bluish gray ('94) 23.50 1.50
Never hinged 110.00
On cover, single franking 9.25
Overprinted "SPECIMEN" 55.00
a. 12½c gray 40.00 1.75
Never hinged 175.00
On cover, single franking 30.00
45 A8 15c yel brn ('94) 55.00 5.00
Never hinged 275.00
On cover, single franking 100.00
Overprinted "SPECIMEN" 55.00
a. 15c orange brown 80.00 5.50
Never hinged 400.00
On cover, single franking 150.00
46 A8 20c green ('94) 62.50 3.00
Never hinged 300.00
On cover, single franking 125.00
Overprinted "SPECIMEN" 55.00
a. 20c yellow green 80.00 3.00
Never hinged 400.00
On cover, single franking 160.00
47 A8 22½c dk grn ('94) 31.00 13.50
Never hinged 140.00
On cover, single franking 175.00
Overprinted "SPECIMEN" 55.00
a. 22½c deep blue green 55.00 13.50
Never hinged 275.00
On cover, single franking 290.00
48 A8 25c dl vio ('94) 110.00 6.00
Never hinged 575.00
On cover, single franking 77.50
Overprinted "SPECIMEN" 77.50
a. 25c dark violet 575.00 6.00
Never hinged 140.00
On cover, single franking 77.50
49 A8 50c yel brn ('94) 550.00 20.00
Never hinged 2,500.
On parcel post receipt card 275.00
On cover, single franking 450.00
Overprinted "SPECIMEN" 150.00
a. 50c bister 575.00 27.50
Never hinged 2,750.
On parcel post receipt card 325.00
On cover, single franking 500.00
50 A8 1g gray vio 625.00 77.50
Never hinged 2,750.
On cover 875.00
On cover, single franking 2,750.
Overprinted "SPECIMEN" 1,250.

The paper used in 1891-93 was white, rough and somewhat opaque. In 1894, a thinner, smooth and sometimes transparent paper was introduced.

The 5c orange was privately produced.

Values for blocks of 4

40 A8 3c org 50.00 14.00
a. 3c org yel 70.00 50.00
41 A8 5c lt ultra 21.00 11.50
a. 5c dull bl 32.50 11.50
42 A8 7½c brn 100.00 72.50
a. 7½c red brn 160.00 77.50
43 A8 10c br rose 150.00 40.00
a. 10c brick red 240.00 50.00
44 A8 12½c bluish gray 150.00 57.50
a. 12½c gray 200.00 70.00
45 A8 15c yel brn 325.00 85.00
a. 15c org brn 500.00 100.00
46 A8 20c green 400.00 57.50
a. 20c yel grn 475.00 77.50
47 A8 22½c dk grn 200.00 160.00
a. 22½c dp bl grn 225.00 160.00
48 A8 25c dull vio 625.00 57.50
a. 25c dk vio 625.00 57.50
49 A8 50c yel brn 2,750. 160.00
a. 50c bister 3,500. 275.00
50 A8 1g gray vio 3,250. 500.00

1893-96 ***Perf. 11½x11***

51 A9 50c emer & yel brn ('96) 70.00 8.50
a. Perf. 11 2,500. 200.00
52 A9 1g brn & ol grn ('96) 200.00 20.00
a. Perf. 11 225.00 60.00
53 A9 2g 50c brt rose & ultra 400.00 125.00
a. 2g 50c lil rose & ultra, perf. 11 475.00 125.00
b. Perf. 11½ 500.00 140.00

Perf. 11

54 A9 5g brnz grn & red brn ('96) 675.00 350.00

Values for blocks of 4

51 A9 50c emer & yel brn 325.00 60.00
52 A9 1g brn & ol grn 850.00 200.00
a. Perf. 11 1,100. 250.00
53 A9 2g 50c brt rose & ultra 1,900. 625.00
a. 2g 50c lil rose & ultra 2,200. 650.00
b. Perf. 11½ 2,250. 750.00
54 A9 5g brnz grn & red brn 3,100. 2,600.

A10

Queen Wilhelmina — A11

Perf. 12½ (#70, 73, 75-77, 81-82), 11½, 11½x11, 11x11½

1898-1924

55 A10 ½c violet .45 .20
Never hinged .80
On cover 2.50
On cover, single franking 50.00
56 A10 1c red .90 .20
Never hinged 2.50
On cover, pair 1.00
On cover, single franking .50
b. Imperf., pair 2,000.
57 A10 1½c ultra ('08) 6.00 .85
Never hinged 11.50
On cover 3.25
On cover, single franking 2.50
58 A10 1½c dp blue ('13) 3.00 .35
Never hinged 7.25
On cover 2.00
On cover, single franking 1.00
59 A10 2c yellow brn 3.75 .20
Never hinged 14.00
On cover 3.25
On cover, single franking 1.75
60 A10 2½c deep green 3.25 .20
Never hinged 8.25
On cover, pair .75
On cover, single franking .50
b. Imperf., pair 6,000.
61 A11 3c orange 16.25 3.25
Never hinged 70.00
On cover 30.00
On cover, single franking 25.00
62 A11 3c pale ol grn ('01) 1.10 .20
Never hinged 2.50
On cover 1.75
On cover, single franking .50
63 A11 4c claret ('21) 1.60 .90
Never hinged 2.50
On cover 8.00
On cover, single franking 32.50
a. 4c lilac 2.50 1.50
64 A11 4½c violet ('19) 3.75 3.75
Never hinged 5.00
On cover 10.00
On cover, single franking 65.00
65 A11 5c car rose 1.60 .20
Never hinged 3.25
On cover 1.00
On cover, single franking .50
a. 5c pale rose 2.50 .20
66 A11 7½c brown .60 .20
Never hinged 1.60
On cover 1.00
On cover, single franking .50
a. Tête bêche pair ('24) 80.00 70.00
Never hinged 110.00
On cover, overfranked 100.00
b. 7½c dark brown 1.40 .25
67 A11 10c gray lilac 6.25 .20
Never hinged 13.00
On cover 6.50
On cover, single franking 1.00
a. 10c dark gray 6.50 .25
68 A11 12½c blue 3.25 .25
Never hinged 10.00
On cover 5.00
On cover, single franking 3.25
69 A11 15c yellow brn 80.00 3.25
Never hinged 400.00
On cover 32.50
On cover, single franking 65.00
70 A11 15c bl & car ('08) 6.25 .20
Never hinged 13.00
On cover 15.00
On cover, single franking 25.00

a. Perf 11½ 7.25 .80
b. Perf 11½x11 75.00 16.00
c. Perf 11x11½ 1,100. 525.00
71 A11 17½c vio ('06) 50.00 11.50
Never hinged 97.50
On cover 40.00
On cover, single franking 150.00
73 A11 17½c ultra & brn ('10) 15.00 .80
Never hinged 40.00
On cover 25.00
On cover, single franking 30.00
a. 17½c ultra & blk brn 15.00 .90
b. Perf 11½ 18.00 3.00
c. Perf 11½x11 18.00 3.00
74 A11 20c yellow green 100.00 .65
Never hinged 725.00
On cover 35.00
On cover, single franking 65.00
75 A11 20c ol grn & gray ('08) 10.00 .45
Never hinged 26.00
On cover 30.00
On cover, single franking 25.00
a. Perf 11½ 12.00 1.40
76 A11 22½c brn & ol grn 9.25 .50
Never hinged 25.00
On cover 25.00
On cover, single franking 30.00
a. Perf 11½ 9.00 1.60
b. Perf 11½x11 9.00 .65
77 A11 25c car & blue 9.00 .35
Never hinged 26.00
On cover 16.50
On cover, single franking 22.50
a. 25c rose & blue 11.50 .40
b. Perf 11½ 10.00 .65
c. Perf 11½x11 10.00 .65
78 A11 30c lil & vio brn ('17) 24.00 .40
Never hinged 65.00
On cover 16.50
On cover, single franking 26.00
79 A11 40c grn & org ('20) 34.00 .80
Never hinged 90.00
On cover 30.00
On cover, single franking 65.00
80 A11 50c brnz grn & red brn 92.50 .90
Never hinged 350.00
On cover 32.50
On cover, single franking 100.00
81 A11 50c gray & vio ('14) 70.00 .80
Never hinged 165.00
On cover 32.50
On cover, single franking 80.00
On parcel post receipt card, multiple 165.00
a. Perf 11½x11 70.00 16.00
On cover, single franking 125.00
b. 50c gray blk & vio 72.50 1.00
82 A11 60c ol grn & grn ('20) 34.00 1.10
Never hinged 90.00
On cover 50.00
On cover, single franking 110.00
a. Perf 11½ 200.00 20.00
b. Perf 11½x11 40.00 1.40
Nos. 55-82 (27) 585.75 32.65
Set, never hinged 2,264.

See Nos. 107-112. For overprints and surcharges see Nos. 102-103, 106, 117-123, 135-136, O1-O8.

Values for blocks of 4

55	A10	½c vio	2.00	5.00
56	A10	1c red	4.50	5.00
57	A10	1½c ultra	30.00	10.00
58	A10	1½c dp bl	13.50	5.00
59	A10	2c yel brn	19.00	5.00
60	A10	2½c dp grn	17.00	5.00
61	A11	3c org	82.50	55.00
62	A11	3c pale ol grn	5.50	3.00
63	A11	4c claret	7.00	5.00
64	A11	4½c vio	18.00	18.00
65	A11	5c car rose	7.00	1.50
66	A11	7½c brn	3.00	1.75
67	A11	10c gray lil	30.00	2.00
68	A11	12½c bl	17.00	5.00
69	A11	15c yel brn	400.00	40.00
70	A11	15c bl & car	30.00	4.00
71	A11	17½c vio	225.00	60.00
73	A11	17½c ultra & brn	75.00	10.00
74	A11	20c yel grn	500.00	32.50
75	A11	20c ol grn & gray	50.00	5.00
76	A11	22½c brn & ol grn	45.00	6.50
77	A11	25c car & bl	45.00	6.00
78	A11	30c lil & vio brn	125.00	9.00
79	A11	40c grn & org	175.00	12.00
80	A11	50c brnz grn & red brn	475.00	18.00
81	A11	50c gray & vio	325.00	11.00
82	A11	60c ol grn & grn	175.00	11.00

A12

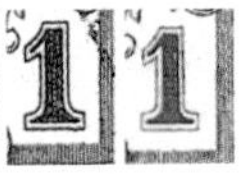
I II

Type I — The figure "1" is 3¾mm high and 2¾mm wide.

Type II — The figure "1" is 3½mm high and 2½mm wide, it is also thinner than in type I.

Perf. 11, 11x11½, 11½, 11½x11

1898-1905 Engr.

83 A12 1g dk grn, II ('99) 52.50 .40
Never hinged 200.00
On parcel post receipt card 65.00
On parcel post receipt card, single franking 225.00
a. Type I ('98) 160.00 90.00
Never hinged 500.00
84 A12 2½g brn lil ('99) 100.00 3.25
Never hinged 250.00
On parcel post receipt card 97.50
On flight cover 50.00
85 A12 5g claret ('99) 225.00 5.00
Never hinged 500.00
On parcel post receipt card 150.00
On flight cover 100.00
86 A12 10g orange ('05) 725.00 625.00
Never hinged 1,500.
On parcel post receipt card —
On flight cover 675.00
Set, never hinged 2,450.

For surcharge see No. 104.

Values for blocks of 4

83	A12	1g dk grn (II)	240.00	5.00
a.		Type I	825.00	600.00
84	A12	2½g brnn lil	450.00	14.50
85	A12	5g claret	1,000.	25.00
86	A12	10g org	3,600.	3,250.

Admiral M. A. de Ruyter and Fleet — A13

King William I — A14

1907, Mar. 23 Typo. *Perf. 12x12½*

87 A13 ½c blue 1.60 1.10
Never hinged 3.25
On cover 16.50
On cover, single franking 57.50
88 A13 1c claret 3.25 2.25
Never hinged 9.75
On cover 16.50
On cover, single franking 25.00
89 A13 2½c vermilion 5.75 2.10
Never hinged 14.00
On cover 22.50
On cover, single franking 32.50
Nos. 87-89 (3) 10.60 5.45
Set, never hinged 27.00

De Ruyter (1607-1676), naval hero. For surcharges see Nos. J29-J41.

Perf. 11½x11, 11½ (#97, 100-101)

1913, Nov. 29 Engr.

Designs: 2½c, 12½c, 1g, King William I. 3c, 20c, 2½g, King William II. 5c, 25c, 5g, King William III. 10c, 50c, 10g, Queen Wilhelmina.

90 A14 2½c green, *grn* .80 .80
Never hinged 1.00
On cover 10.00
On cover, single franking 8.00
91 A14 3c buff, *straw* 1.10 1.10
Never hinged 1.50
On cover 18.00
On cover, single franking 20.00
92 A14 5c rose red, *sal* 1.25 .80
Never hinged 1.75
On cover 10.00
On cover, single franking 6.50
93 A14 10c gray blk 3.75 2.25
Never hinged 5.75
On cover 20.00
On cover, single franking 32.50
94 A14 12½c dp blue, *bl* 3.00 1.90
Never hinged 5.00
On cover 20.00
On cover, single franking 26.00
95 A14 20c orange brn 11.50 9.50
Never hinged 30.00
On cover 57.50
On cover, single franking 65.00
96 A14 25c pale blue 13.50 7.75
Never hinged 30.00
On cover 50.00
On cover, single franking 90.00
97 A14 50c yel grn 30.00 25.00
Never hinged 75.00
On cover 100.00
On cover, single franking 125.00
On parcel post receipt card 160.00
98 A14 1g claret 42.50 17.50
Never hinged 110.00
On cover 100.00
On cover, single franking 160.00
On parcel post receipt card 160.00
99 A14 2½g dull violet 100.00 42.50
Never hinged 275.00
On parcel post receipt card 160.00
100 A14 5g yel, *straw* 225.00 37.50
Never hinged 525.00
On parcel post receipt card 160.00
101 A14 10g red, *straw* 675.00 650.00
Never hinged 1,500.
Nos. 90-101 (12) 1,107. 796.60
Set, never hinged 2,285.

Perf. 11½

90a A14 2½c grn, *grn* .80 .80
91a A14 5c buff, *straw* 1.10 1.10
92a A14 5c rose red, *salmon* 1.10 .80
93a A14 10c gray blk 3.75 2.25
94a A14 12½c dp bl, *bl* 3.00 1.90
95a A14 20c org brn 11.50 9.50
98a A14 1g claret 60.00 17.50
Never hinged 140.00

Centenary of Dutch independence. For surcharge see No. 105.

No. 78 Surcharged in Red or Black

a

b

1919, Dec. 1 *Perf. 12½*

102 A11 (a) 40c on 30c (R) 22.50 3.25
Never hinged 70.00
On cover 65.00
On cover, single franking 100.00
103 A11 (b) 60c on 30c (Bk) 22.50 3.25
Never hinged 70.00
On cover 75.00
On cover, single franking 110.00
Set, never hinged 140.00
Set on overfranked philatelic cover 50.00

Nos. 86 and 101 Surcharged in Black

1920, Aug. 17 *Perf. 11, 11½*

104 A12 2.50g on 10g 140.00 100.00
Never hinged 300.00
On parcel post receipt card, single franking 260.00
On parcel post receipt card, multiple franking 450.00
On overfranked philatelic cover 325.00
105 A14 2.50g on 10g 140.00 85.00
Never hinged 300.00
On parcel post receipt card, single franking 260.00
On parcel post receipt card, multiple franking 325.00
On overfranked philatelic cover 325.00

No. 64 Surcharged in Red

1921, Mar. 1 Typo. *Perf. 12½*

106 A11 4c on 4½c vio 4.00 1.60
Never hinged 8.00
On cover 16.50
On cover, single franking 15.00

A17

1921-22 Typo. *Perf. 12½*

107 A17 5c green ('22) 8.25 .20
Never hinged 32.50
On cover 1.75
On cover, single franking 1.75
108 A17 12½c vermilion ('22) 18.00 1.75
Never hinged 55.00
On cover 9.00
On cover, single franking 8.00
109 A17 20c blue 27.50 .25
Never hinged 82.50
On cover 13.00
On cover, single franking 5.00
Nos. 107-109 (3) 53.75 2.20
Set, never hinged 170.00

Queen Type of 1898-99, 10c Redrawn

1922 *Perf. 12½*

110 A11 10c gray 29.00 .25
Never hinged 75.00

Imperf

111 A11 5c car rose 6.50 6.50
Never hinged 13.50
112 A11 10c gray 7.25 7.25
Never hinged 14.00
Nos. 110-112 (3) 42.75 14.00

In redrawn 10c the horizontal lines behind the Queen's head are wider apart.

Orange Tree and Lion of Brabant
A18

Post Horn and Lion
A19

Numeral of Value — A20

1923, Mar. 9 *Perf. 12½*

113 A18 1c dark violet .55 .60
114 A18 2c orange 6.00 .25
115 A19 2½c bluish green 1.75 .65
116 A20 4c deep blue 1.25 .60
Nos. 113-116 (4) 9.55 2.10
Set, never hinged 16.00

Nos. 56, 58, 62, 65, 68, 73, 76 Surcharged in Various Colors

c

d

1923, July *Perf. 12½*

117 A10(c) 2c on 1c (Bl) .45 .20
118 A10(c) 2c on 1½c (Bk) .45 .25
119 A11(d) 10c on 3c (Br) 4.25 .20
120 A11(d) 10c on 5c (Bk) 8.00 .55
121 A11(d) 10c on 12½c (R) 7.25 .90

Perf. 11½x11

122 A11(d) 10c on 17½c (R) 2.75 3.50
a. Perf. 11½ 1,600. 800.00
b. Perf. 12½ 4.25 4.25
Never hinged 8.00
123 A11(d) 10c on 22½c (R) 2.75 3.50
a. Perf. 11½ 3.00 3.50
b. Perf. 12½ 4.25 4.25
Never hinged 8.00
Nos. 117-123 (7) 25.90 9.10
Set, never hinged 57.50

Queen Wilhelmina
A21 A22

Perf. 11½x12½, 11½x12 (5c)

1923, Oct. Engr.

124 A22 2c myrtle green .25 .20
a. Vert. pair, imperf. between *2,000.*
125 A21 5c green .35 .20
a. Vert. pair, imperf. between *1,800.*
126 A22 7½c carmine .40 .20
127 A22 10c vermilion .40 .20
a. Vert. pair, imperf. between *550.00* *575.00*
128 A22 20c ultra 3.50 .50
129 A22 25c yellow 5.00 .75

Perf. 11½

130 A22 35c orange 5.00 2.00
131 A22 50c black 17.00 .50
132 A21 1g red 27.50 6.50
133 A21 2½g black 200.00 175.00
134 A21 5g dark blue 175.00 150.00
Nos. 124-134 (11) 434.40 336.05
Set, never hinged 900.00

25th anniv. of the assumption as monarch of the Netherlands by Queen Wilhelmina at the age of 18.

Nos. 119, 73 Overprinted in Red "DIENSTZEGEL PORTEN AANTEEKENRECHT; No. 73 with New Value in Blue

1923 Typo. *Perf. 12½*

135	A11	10c on 3c	1.10	1.00
		Never hinged	8.00	
136	A11	1g on 17½c	62.50	15.00
		Never hinged	150.00	
a.		Perf. 11½	85.00	32.50
b.		Perf. 11½x11	72.50	25.00

Stamps with red surcharge were prepared for use as Officials but were not issued.

Queen Wilhelmina — A23

1924, Sept. 6 Photo. *Perf. 12½*

137	A23	10c slate green	30.00	30.00
		Never hinged	52.50	
138	A23	15c gray black	40.00	40.00
		Never hinged	65.00	
139	A23	35c brown orange	30.00	30.00
		Never hinged	52.50	
		Nos. 137-139 (3)	100.00	100.00

These stamps were available solely to visitors to the International Philatelic Exhibition at The Hague and were not obtainable at regular post offices.

See Nos. 147-160, 172-193. For overprints and surcharge see Nos. 194, O11, O13-O15.

Ship in Distress — A23a

Lifeboat — A23b

1924, Sept. 15 Litho. *Perf. 11½*

140	A23a	2c black brn	3.25	2.50
		Never hinged	6.50	
141	A23b	10c orange brn	6.00	2.00
		Never hinged	12.00	

Centenary of Royal Dutch Lifeboat Society.

Type A23 and

Gull — A24

1924-26 *Perf. 12½*

142	A24	1c deep red	.50	.60
143	A24	2c red orange	2.25	.20
144	A24	2½c deep green	2.60	.80
145	A24	3c yel grn ('25)	12.50	1.00
146	A24	4c dp ultra	2.75	.70
		Photo.		
147	A23	5c dull green	3.25	.65
148	A23	6c org brn ('25)	.65	.50
149	A23	7½c orange ('25)	.35	.20
150	A23	9c org red & blk ('26)	1.50	1.25
151	A23	10c red, *shades*	1.25	.20
152	A23	12½c deep rose	1.60	.35
153	A23	15c ultra	6.00	.40
154	A23	20c dp blue ('25)	10.00	.60
155	A23	25c olive bis ('25)	22.50	.85
156	A23	30c violet	13.00	.65
157	A23	35c olive brn ('25)	30.00	6.00
158	A23	40c dp brown	30.00	.65
159	A23	50c blue grn ('25)	60.00	.60
160	A23	60c dk violet ('25)	27.50	.80
		Nos. 142-160 (19)	228.20	17.00
		Set, never hinged	725.00	

See Nos. 164-171, 243A-243Q. For overprints and surcharges see Nos. 226-243, O9-O10.

Syncopated, Type A (2 Sides)

1925-26

142a	A24	1c deep red	.80	.80
143a	A24	2c red orange	2.75	1.90
144a	A24	2½c deep green	2.75	1.25
145a	A24	3c yellow green	18.00	20.00
146a	A24	4c deep ultra	2.75	1.90
147a	A23	5c dull green	5.50	2.50
148a	A23	6c orange brown	110.00	100.00
149a	A23	7½c orange	1.10	1.00
150a	A23	9c org red & blk	1.75	1.25
151a	A23	10c red	11.00	2.75
152a	A23	12½c deep rose	1.75	1.50
153a	A23	15c ultra	67.50	5.50
154a	A23	20c deep blue	10.00	4.00
155a	A23	25c olive bister	42.50	45.00
156a	A23	30c violet	14.50	10.50
158a	A23	40c deep brown	45.00	36.00
159a	A23	50c blue green	55.00	20.00
160a	A23	60c dark violet	27.50	11.00
		Nos. 142a-160a (18)	420.15	266.85
		Set, never hinged	950.00	

A25

1925-30 Engr. *Perf. 11½,*

161	A25	1g ultra	8.00	.30
		Never hinged	25.00	
a.		Perf 12½ ('30)	8.75	.30
		Never hinged	27.50	
162	A25	2½g car ('27)	80.00	3.00
		Never hinged	175.00	
a.		Perf 12½ ('30)	87.50	2.50
		Never hinged	190.00	
163	A25	5g gray blk	160.00	1.75
		Never hinged	275.00	
a.		Perf 12½ ('30)	175.00	1.90
		Never hinged	300.00	
		Nos. 161-163 (3)	248.00	5.05

Types of 1924-26 Issue

Perf. 12½, 13½x12½, 12½x13½

1926-39 Wmk. 202 Litho.

164	A24	½c gray ('28)	.90	1.00
165	A24	1c dp red ('27)	.20	.20
166	A24	1½c red vio ('28)	1.10	.20
c.		"CEN" for "CENT"	160.00	275.00
d.		"GENT" for "CENT"	125.00	110.00
167	A24	1½c gray ('35)	.20	.20
a.		1½c dark gray	.20	.20
168	A24	2c dp org	.20	.20
a.		2c red orange	.20	.20
169	A24	2½c green ('27)	2.75	.25
170	A24	3c yel grn ('27)	.20	.20
171	A24	4c dp ultra ('27)	.20	.20
		Photo.		
172	A23	5c dp green	.20	.20
173	A23	6c org brn ('27)	.20	.20
174	A23	7½c dk vio ('27)	3.25	.20
175	A23	7½c red ('28)	.20	.20
176	A23	9c org red & blk ('28)	11.00	12.00
b.		Value omitted	*14,500.*	
177	A23	10c red	1.25	.20
178	A23	10c dl vio ('29)	2.50	.20
179	A23	12½c dp rose ('27)	42.50	4.50
180	A23	12½c ultra ('28)	.40	.20
181	A23	15c ultra	7.25	.20
182	A23	15c orange ('29)	1.25	.20
183	A23	20c dp blue ('28)	7.25	.20
184	A23	21c ol brn ('31)	25.00	.90
185	A23	22½c ol brn ('27)	7.25	3.00
186	A23	22½c dp org ('39)	15.00	16.00
187	A23	25c ol bis ('27)	4.50	.20
188	A23	27½c gray ('28)	4.50	.75
189	A23	30c violet	5.25	.20
190	A23	35c olive brn	62.50	12.50
191	A23	40c dp brown	10.00	.20
192	A23	50c blue grn	5.25	.20
193	A23	60c black ('29)	27.50	.90
		Nos. 164-193 (30)	249.75	55.80
		Set, never hinged	558.05	

Syncopated, Type A (2 Sides), 12½

1926-27

168b	A24	2c deep orange	.40	.40
170a	A24	3c yellow green	.60	.60
171a	A24	4c deep ultra	.60	.60
172a	A23	5c deep green	.70	.60
173a	A23	6c orange brown	.40	.45
174a	A23	7½c dark violet	4.50	2.00
177a	A23	10c red	1.00	.85
181a	A23	15c ultra	7.00	3.00
185a	A23	22½c olive brown	7.00	2.50
187a	A23	25c olive bister	20.00	18.00
189a	A23	30c violet	19.00	12.00
190a	A23	35c olive brown	77.50	22.50
191a	A23	40c deep brown	50.00	40.00
		Nos. 168b-191a (13)	188.70	103.50
		Set, never hinged	360.00	

1928 *Syncopated, Type B (4 Sides)*

164a	A24	½c gray	.80	.65
165a	A24	1c deep red	.30	.30
166a	A24	1½c red violet	.80	.25
168c	A24	2c deep orange	1.00	.60
169a	A24	2½c green	2.75	.20
170b	A24	3c yellow green	.75	.75
171b	A24	4c deep ultra	.75	.65
172b	A23	5c deep green	1.00	.75
173b	A23	6c orange brown	.75	.50
174b	A23	7½c dark violet	4.25	2.00
175a	A23	7½c red	.25	.25
176a	A23	9c org red & blk	10.00	12.50
178a	A23	10c dull violet	5.25	5.00
179a	A23	12½c deep rose	80.00	80.00
180a	A23	12½c ultra	1.40	.40
181b	A23	15c ultra	9.00	2.00
182a	A23	15c orange	.75	.30
183a	A23	20c deep blue	7.00	3.00
187b	A23	25c olive bister	17.00	10.00
188a	A23	27½c gray	4.50	2.00
189b	A23	30c violet	15.00	8.00
191b	A23	40c deep brown	35.00	22.50
192a	A23	50c blue green	55.00	45.00
193a	A23	60c black	45.00	22.50
		Nos. 164a-193a (24)	298.30	220.10
		Set, never hinged	600.00	

Syncopated, Type C (2 Sides, Corners Only)

1930

164b	A24	½c gray	1.00	.70
165b	A24	1c deep red	1.00	.40
166b	A24	1½c red violet	.90	.25
168d	A24	2c deep orange	.80	.70
169b	A24	2½c green	2.75	.25
170c	A24	3c yellow green	1.10	.50
171c	A24	4c deep ultra	.50	.25
172c	A23	5c deep green	.70	.70
173c	A23	6c orange brown	.70	.70
178b	A23	10c dull violet	8.00	7.00
183b	A23	20c deep blue	7.75	3.75
184a	A23	21c olive brown	25.00	9.00
189c	A23	30c violet	12.00	7.00
192b	A23	50c blue green	45.00	45.00
		Nos. 164b-192b (14)	107.20	76.20
		Set, never hinged	225.00	

1927

Syncopated, Type D (3 Holes Vert., 4 Holes Horiz.)

174c	A23	7½c dark violet	*2,750.*	*2,100.*
		Never hinged	*3,750.*	

No. 185 Surcharged in Red

1929, Nov. 11 *Perf. 12½*

194	A23	21c on 22½c ol brn	20.00	1.00
		Never hinged	40.00	

Queen Wilhelmina — A26

1931, Oct. Photo. *Perf. 12½*

195	A26	70c dk bl & red	27.50	.40
		Never hinged	100.00	
a.		Perf. 14½x13½ ('39)	32.50	7.50
		Never hinged	125.00	

See No. 201.

Arms of the House of Orange — A27

William I — A28

Designs: 5c, William I, Portrait by Goltzius. 6c, Portrait of William I by Van Key. 12½c, Portrait attributed to Moro.

1933, Apr. 1 Unwmk. Engr.

196	A27	1½c black	.50	.20
197	A28	5c dark green	1.60	.35
198	A28	6c dull violet	2.50	.20
199	A28	12½c deep blue	15.00	2.50
		Nos. 196-199 (4)	19.60	3.25
		Set, never hinged	47.50	

400th anniv. of the birth of William I, Count of Nassau and Prince of Orange, frequently referred to as William the Silent.

Star, Dove and Sword — A31

1933, May 18 Photo. Wmk. 202

200	A31	12½c dp ultra	8.00	.30
		Never hinged	24.00	

For overprint see No. O12.

Queen Wilhelmina Design of 1931

Queen Wilhelmina and ships.

Perf. 14½x13½

1933, July 26 Wmk. 202

201	A26	80c Prus bl & red	100.00	2.50
		Never hinged	325.00	

Willemstad Harbor — A33

Van Walbeeck's Ship — A34

Perf. 14x12½

1934, July 2 Engr. Unwmk.

202	A33	6c violet blk	3.00	.20
203	A34	12½c dull blue	19.00	2.00
		Set, never hinged	62.50	

Tercentenary of Curacao.

Minerva — A35

Design: 12½c, Gisbertus Voetius.

Wmk. 202

1936, May 15 Photo. *Perf. 12½*

204	A35	6c brown lake	2.50	.20
205	A35	12½c indigo	3.75	3.25
		Set, never hinged	12.50	

300th anniversary of the founding of the University at Utrecht.

A37

A38

A39

1937, Apr. 1 *Perf. 14½x13½*

206	A37	1½c Boy Scout Emblem	.35	.20
207	A38	6c "Assembly"	1.25	.20
208	A39	12½c Mercury	3.00	1.00
		Nos. 206-208 (3)	4.60	1.40
		Set, never hinged	10.00	

Fifth Boy Scout World Jamboree, Vogelenzang, Netherlands, 7/31-8/13/37.

Wilhelmina A40

St. Willibrord A41

1938, Aug. 27 ***Perf. 12½x12***

209	A40	1½c black	.20	.20
210	A40	5c red orange	.20	.20
211	A40	12½c royal blue	3.25	1.00
		Nos. 209-211 (3)	3.65	1.40
		Set, never hinged	11.00	

Reign of Queen Wilhelmina, 40th anniv.

Perf. 12½x14

1939, June 15 Engr. Unwmk.

Design: 12½c, St. Willibrord as older man.

212	A41	5c dk slate grn	.75	.20
213	A41	12½c slate blue	4.00	2.00
		Set, never hinged	11.00	

12th centenary of the death of St. Willibrord.

Woodburning Engine A43

Queen Wilhelmina A45

Design: 12½c, Streamlined electric car.

Perf. 14½x13½

1939, Sept. 1 Photo. Wmk. 202

214	A43	5c dk slate grn	.75	.20
215	A43	12½c dark blue	8.00	2.75
		Set, never hinged	22.50	

Centenary of Dutch Railroads.

Catalogue values for unused stamps in this section, from this point to the end of the section, are for Never Hinged items.

1940-47 ***Perf. 13½x12½***

216	A45	5c dk green	.20	.20
216B	A45	6c hn brn ('47)	.55	.20
217	A45	7½c brt red	.20	.20
218	A45	10c brt red vio	.20	.20
219	A45	12½c sapphire	.20	.20
220	A45	15c light blue	.20	.20
220B	A45	17½c slate bl ('46)	1.25	.70
221	A45	20c purple	.35	.20
222	A45	22½c olive grn	1.25	.85
223	A45	25c rose brn	.35	.20
224	A45	30c bister	.80	.35
225	A45	40c brt green	1.25	.60
225A	A45	50c orange ('46)	9.50	.60
225B	A45	60c pur brn ('46)	8.50	2.00
		Nos. 216-225B (14)	24.80	6.70

Imperf. copies of Nos. 216, 218-220 were released through philatelic channels during the German occupation, but were never issued at any post office. Value, set, $1.

For overprints see Nos. O16-O24.

Type of 1924-26 Surcharged in Black or Blue

Perf. 12½x13½

1940, Oct. Photo. Wmk. 202

226	A24	2½c on 3c ver	2.00	.20
227	A24	5c on 3c lt grn	.20	.20
228	A24	7½c on 3c ver	.20	.20
a.		Pair, #226, 228	4.00	1.50
229	A24	10c on 3c lt grn	.20	.20
230	A24	12½c on 3c lt bl (Bl)	.30	.20
231	A24	17½c on 3c lt grn	.60	.65
232	A24	20c on 3c lt grn	.40	.20
233	A24	22½c on 3c lt grn	.80	.85
234	A24	25c on 3c lt grn	.50	.20
235	A24	30c on 3c lt grn	.65	.30
236	A24	40c on 3c lt grn	.80	.60
237	A24	50c on 3c lt grn	.70	.40
238	A24	60c on 3c lt grn	1.60	.85
239	A24	70c on 3c lt grn	3.75	1.75
240	A24	80c on 3c lt grn	5.50	4.00
241	A24	1g on 3c lt grn	35.00	32.50
242	A24	2.50g on 3c lt grn	40.00	37.50
243	A24	5g on 3c lt grn	37.50	35.00
		Nos. 226-243 (18)	130.70	115.80
		Set, hinged	70.00	

No. 228a is from coils.

Gull Type of 1924-26

1941

243A	A24	2½c dk green	1.25	.35
b.		Booklet pane of 6	10.00	
243C	A24	5c brt green	.20	.20
243E	A24	7½c henna	.20	.20
r.		Pair, #243A, 243E	1.00	1.00
243G	A24	10c brt violet	.20	.20
243H	A24	12½c ultra	.20	.20
243J	A24	15c lt blue	.20	.20
243K	A24	17½c red org	.20	.20
243L	A24	20c lt violet	.20	.20
243M	A24	22½c dk ol grn	.20	.20
243N	A24	25c lake	.20	.20
243O	A24	30c olive	3.50	.20
243P	A24	40c emerald	.20	.20
243Q	A24	50c orange brn	.20	.20
		Nos. 243A-243Q (13)	6.95	2.75

No. 243r is from coils.

SEMI-POSTAL STAMPS

Design Symbolical of the Four Chief Means for Combating Tuberculosis: Light, Water, Air and Food — SP1

Perf. 12½

1906, Dec. 21 Typo. Unwmk.

B1	SP1	1c (+1c) rose red	15.00	6.50
B2	SP1	3c (+3c) pale ol grn	27.50	17.50
B3	SP1	5c (+5c) gray	27.50	10.00
		Nos. B1-B3 (3)	70.00	*34.00*
		Set, never hinged	475.00	

Surtax aided the Society for the Prevention of Tuberculosis.

Nos. B1-B3 canceled-to-order "AMSTERDAM 31.07 10-12 N," sell at $3 a set.

Symbolical of Charity SP2

SP3

1923, Dec. 15 ***Perf. 11½***

B4	SP2	2c (+5c) vio bl	17.00	14.00
B5	SP3	10c (+5c) org red	17.00	14.00
		Set, never hinged	75.00	

The surtax was for the benefit of charity.

Allegory, Charity Protecting Child — SP6

1924, Dec. 15 Photo. ***Perf. 12½***

B6	SP6	2c (+2c) emer	1.60	1.40
B7	SP6	7½c (+3½c) dk brn	5.00	5.00
B8	SP6	10c (+2½c) vermilion	4.00	1.40
		Nos. B6-B8 (3)	10.60	7.80
		Set, never hinged	24.00	

These stamps were sold at a premium over face value for the benefit of Child Welfare Societies.

Arms of North Brabant SP7

Arms of Gelderland SP8

Arms of South Holland — SP9

Perf. 12½ Syncopated

1925, Dec. 17

B9	SP7	2c (+2c) grn & org	.85	.75
B10	SP8	7½c (+3½c) vio & bl	4.25	4.00
B11	SP9	10c (+2½c) red & org	3.50	.45
		Nos. B9-B11 (3)	8.60	5.20
		Set, never hinged	17.50	

Surtax went to Child Welfare Societies. See note before No. 142a.

Syncopated Perfs., Type A

B9a	SP7	2c (+2c)	12.50	10.00
B10a	SP8	7½c (+3½c)	37.50	30.00
B11a	SP9	10c (+2½c)	65.00	45.00
		Nos. B9a-B11a (3)	115.00	85.00
		Set, never hinged	250.00	

Arms of Utrecht SP10

Arms of Zeeland SP11

Arms of North Holland SP12

Arms of Friesland SP13

1926, Dec. 1 Wmk. 202 ***Perf. 12½***

B12	SP10	2c (+2c) sil & red	.50	.40
B13	SP11	5c (+3c) grn & gray bl	1.40	1.10
B14	SP12	10c (+3c) red & gold	2.10	.25
B15	SP13	15c (+3c) ultra & yel	5.50	4.25
		Nos. B12-B15 (4)	9.50	6.00
		Set, never hinged	25.00	

The surtax on these stamps was devoted to Child Welfare Societies.

Syncopated Perfs., Type A

B12a	SP10	2c (+2c)	4.75	4.75
B13a	SP11	5c (+3c)	7.25	7.25
B14a	SP12	10c (+3c)	13.50	13.50
B15a	SP13	15c (+3c)	14.50	14.50
		Nos. B12a-B15a (4)	40.00	40.00
		Set, never hinged	95.00	

King William III — SP14

Red Cross and Doves — SP18

Designs: 3c, Queen Emma. 5c, Prince Consort Henry. 7½c, Queen Wilhelmina.

Perf. 11½, 11½x12 B

1927, June Photo. Unwmk.

B16	SP14	2c (+2c) scar	2.50	2.25

Engr.

B17	SP14	3c (+2c) dp grn	5.75	*8.00*
B18	SP14	5c (+3c) slate bl	1.00	1.00

Photo.

B19	SP14	7½c (+3½c) ultra	4.50	1.50
B20	SP18	15c (+5c) ultra & red	8.75	8.00
		Nos. B16-B20 (5)	22.50	20.75
		Set, never hinged	52.50	

60th anniversary of the Netherlands Red Cross Society. The surtaxes in parentheses were for the benefit of the Society.

Arms of Drenthe SP19

Arms of Groningen SP20

Arms of Limburg SP21

Arms of Overijssel SP22

1927, Dec. 15 Wmk. 202 ***Perf. 12½***

B21	SP19	2c (+2c) dp rose & vio	.35	.30
B22	SP20	5c (+3c) ol grn & yel	1.50	1.25
B23	SP21	7½c (+3½c) red & blk	3.25	.35
B24	SP22	15c (+3c) ultra & org brn	4.75	4.25
		Nos. B21-B24 (4)	9.85	6.15
		Set, never hinged	26.00	

The surtax on these stamps was for the benefit of Child Welfare Societies.

Syncopated Perfs., Type A

B21a	SP19	2c (+2c)	1.90	1.40
B22a	SP20	5c (+3c)	3.50	1.75
B23a	SP21	7½c (+3½c)	4.25	1.75
B24a	SP22	15c (+3c)	12.50	9.00
		Nos. B21a-B24a (4)	22.15	13.90
		Set, never hinged	57.50	

Rowing — SP23

Fencing — SP24

Soccer SP25

Yachting SP26

Putting the Shot SP27

Running SP28

Riding SP29

Boxing SP30

Perf. 11½, 12, 11½x12, 12x11½

1928, Mar. 27 Litho.

B25	SP23	1½c (+1c) dk grn	1.90	1.40
B26	SP24	2c (+1c) red vio	2.40	1.75
B27	SP25	3c (+1c) green	2.40	2.00
B28	SP26	5c (+1c) lt bl	3.00	1.40
B29	SP27	7½c (+2½c) org	3.00	1.75
B30	SP28	10c (+2c) scarlet	6.75	5.25
B31	SP29	15c (+2c) dk bl	6.75	3.75
B32	SP30	30c (+3c) dk brn	20.00	17.50
		Nos. B25-B32 (8)	46.20	34.80
		Set, never hinged	150.00	

The surtax on these stamps was used to help defray the expenses of the Olympic Games of 1928.

Jean Pierre Minckelers
SP31

Child on Dolphin
SP35

5c, Hermann Boerhaave. 7½c, Hendrik Antoon Lorentz. 12½c, Christian Huygens.

1928, Dec. 10 Photo. *Perf. 12x12½*

B33 SP31 1½c (+1½c) vio .55 .40
B34 SP31 5c (+3c) grn 1.75 .60

Perf. 12

B35 SP31 7½c (+2½c) ver 3.50 .25
a. Perf. 12x12½ 4.75 .70
Never hinged 11.00
B36 SP31 12½c (+3½c) ultra 9.75 7.50
a. Perf. 12x12½ 77.50 7.75
Never hinged 175.00
Nos. B33-B36 (4) 15.55 8.75
Set, never hinged 37.50

The surtax on these stamps was for the benefit of Child Welfare Societies.

1929, Dec. 10 Litho. *Perf. 12½*

B37 SP35 1½c (+1½c) gray 2.10 .45
B38 SP35 5c (+3c) blue grn 3.50 .75
B39 SP35 6c (+4c) scarlet 2.10 .35
B40 SP35 12½c (+3½c) dk bl 13.50 11.00
Nos. B37-B40 (4) 21.20 12.55
Set, never hinged 62.50

Surtax for child welfare.

Syncopated Perfs., Type B

B37a SP35 1½c (+1½c) 3.00 1.25
B38a SP35 5c (+3c) 4.50 1.25
B39a SP35 6c (+4c) 3.25 1.25
B40a SP35 12½c (+3½c) 25.00 14.00
Nos. B37a-B40a (4) 35.75 17.75
Set, never hinged 72.50

Rembrandt and His "Cloth Merchants of Amsterdam"
SP36

"Spring"
SP37

Perf. 11½

1930, Feb. 15 Engr. Unwmk.

B41 SP36 5c (+5c) bl grn 6.75 6.00
B42 SP36 6c (+5c) gray blk 5.25 3.50
B43 SP36 12½c (+5c) dp bl 9.00 8.00
Nos. B41-B43 (3) 21.00 17.50
Set, never hinged 52.50

Surtax for the benefit of the Rembrandt Soc.

1930, Dec. 10 *Perf. 12½*

5c, Summer. 6c, Autumn. 12½c, Winter.

B44 SP37 1½c (+1½c) lt red 1.50 .45
B45 SP37 5c (+3c) gray grn 2.25 .60
B46 SP37 6c (+4c) claret 2.00 .45
B47 SP37 12½c (+3½c) lt ultra 16.00 8.50
Nos. B44-B47 (4) 21.75 10.00
Set, never hinged 52.50

Surtax was for Child Welfare work.

Syncopated Perfs., Type C

B44a SP37 1½c (+1½c) 2.40 1.25
B45a SP37 5c (+3c) 3.50 1.25
B46a SP37 6c (+4c) 2.40 1.25
B47a SP37 12½c (+3½c) 19.00 12.50
Nos. B44a-B47a (4) 27.30 16.25
Set, never hinged 55.00

Stained Glass Window and Detail of Repair Method
SP41

Deaf Mute Learning Lip Reading
SP43

6c, Gouda Church and repair of window frame.

Wmk. 202

1931, Oct. 1 Photo. *Perf. 12½*

B48 SP41 1½c (+1½c) bl grn 17.00 15.00
B49 SP41 6c (+4c) car rose 20.00 17.00
Set, never hinged 75.00

1931, Dec. 10 *Perf. 12½*

Designs: 5c, Imbecile child. 6c, Blind girl learning to read Braille. 12½c, Child victim of malnutrition.

B50 SP43 1½c (+1½c) ver & ultra 1.90 1.25
B51 SP43 5c (+3c) Prus bl & vio 5.25 1.25
B52 SP43 6c (+4c) vio & grn 5.25 1.25
B53 SP43 12½c (+3½c) ultra & dp org 29.00 21.00
Nos. B50-B53 (4) 41.40 24.75
Set, never hinged 95.00

The surtax was for Child Welfare work.

Syncopated Perfs., Type C

B50a SP43 1½c (+1½c) 1.90 1.25
B51a SP43 5c (+3c) 5.25 1.25
B52a SP43 6c (+4c) 5.50 1.25
B53a SP43 12½c (+3½c) 30.00 22.50
Nos. B50a-B53a (4) 42.65 26.25
Set, never hinged 105.00

Drawbridge
SP47

Furze and Boy
SP51

Designs: 2½c, Windmill and Dikes. 6c, Council House, Zierikzee. 12½c, Flower fields.

1932, May 23 *Perf. 12½*

B54 SP47 2½c (+1½c) turq grn & blk 7.00 5.00
B55 SP47 6c (+4c) gray blk & blk 10.50 5.00
B56 SP47 7½c (+3½c) brt red & blk 30.00 12.50
B57 SP47 12½c (+2½c) ultra & blk 32.50 19.00
Nos. B54-B57 (4) 80.00 41.50
Set, never hinged 190.00

The surtax was for the benefit of the National Tourist Association.

1932, Dec. 10 *Perf. 12½*

Designs (Heads of children and flowers typifying the seasons): 5c, Cornflower. 6c, Sunflower. 12½c, Christmas rose.

B58 SP51 1½c (+1½c) brn & yel 2.10 .45
B59 SP51 5c (+3c) red org & ultra 2.75 .75
B60 SP51 6c (+4c) dk grn & ocher 2.10 .35
B61 SP51 12½c (+3½c) ocher & ultra 27.50 18.00
Nos. B58-B61 (4) 34.45 19.55
Set, never hinged 90.00

The surtax aided Child Welfare Societies.

Syncopated Perfs., Type C

B58a SP51 1½c (+1½c) 2.75 1.60
B59a SP51 5c (+3c) 3.50 1.60
B60a SP51 6c (+4c) 3.50 1.60
B61a SP51 12½c (+3½c) 35.00 22.50
Nos. B58a-B61a (4) 44.75 27.30
Set, never hinged 100.00

Monument at Den Helder
SP55

The "Hope," A Church and Hospital Ship
SP56

Lifeboat in a Storm
SP57

Dutch Sailor and Sailors' Home
SP58

1933, June 10 *Perf. 14½x13½*

B62 SP55 1½c (+1½c) dp red 3.50 1.60
B63 SP56 5c (+3c) bl grn & red org 10.50 3.00
B64 SP57 6c (+4c) dp grn 16.00 2.50
B65 SP58 12½c (+3½c) ultra 24.00 17.50
Nos. B62-B65 (4) 54.00 24.60
Set, never hinged 125.00

The surtax was for the aid of Sailors' Homes.

Child Carrying the Star of Hope, Symbolical of Christmas Cheer — SP59

1933, Dec. 11 *Perf. 12½*

B66 SP59 1½c (+1½c) sl & org brn 1.50 .55
B67 SP59 5c (+3c) dk brn & ocher 2.00 .65
B68 SP59 6c (+4c) bl grn & gold 2.50 .55
B69 SP59 12½c (+3½c) dk bl & sil 25.00 18.00
Nos. B66-B69 (4) 31.00 19.75
Set, never hinged 75.00

The surtax aided Child Welfare Societies.

Syncopated Perfs., Type C

B66a SP59 1½c (+1½c) 1.90 .70
B67a SP59 5c (+3c) 2.60 .90
B68a SP59 6c (+4c) 3.25 .90
B69a SP59 12½c (+3½c) 26.00 20.00
Nos. B66a-B69a (4) 33.75 22.50
Set, never hinged 87.50

Queen Wilhelmina
SP60

Princess Juliana
SP61

Perf. 12½

1934, Apr. 28 Engr. Unwmk.

B70 SP60 5c (+4c) dk vio 11.50 3.25
B71 SP61 6c (+5c) blue 10.50 4.25
Set, never hinged 52.50

The surtax was for the benefit of the Anti-Depression Committee.

Dowager Queen Emma — SP62

Poor Child — SP63

1934, Oct. 1 *Perf. 13x14*

B72 SP62 6c (+2c) blue 11.50 1.40
Never hinged 27.50

Surtax for the Fight Tuberculosis Society.

Perf. 13½x13

1934, Dec. 10 Photo. Wmk. 202

B73 SP63 1½c (+1½c) olive 1.40 .45
B74 SP63 5c (+3c) rose red 2.40 1.00
B75 SP63 6c (+4c) bl grn 2.40 .25
B76 SP63 12½c (+3½c) ultra 22.50 16.00
Nos. B73-B76 (4) 28.70 17.70
Set, never hinged 75.00

The surtax aided child welfare.

Henri D. Guyot
SP64

A. J. M. Diepenbrock
SP65

F. C. Donders
SP66

J. P. Sweelinck
SP67

Perf. 12½ x 12, 12

1935, June Engr. Unwmk.

B77 SP64 1½c (+1½c) dk car 1.50 1.25
B78 SP65 5c (+3c) blk brn 4.00 3.50
B79 SP66 6c (+4c) myr grn 4.50 .70
B80 SP67 12½c (+3½c) dp bl 24.00 4.00
Nos. B77-B80 (4) 34.00 9.45
Set, never hinged 87.50

Surtax for social and cultural projects.

Netherlands Map, DC-3 Planes' Shadows
SP68

Girl Picking Apple — SP69

Perf. 14x13

1935, Oct. 16 Photo. Wmk. 202

B81 SP68 6c (+4c) brn 24.00 7.50
Never hinged 60.00

Surtax for Natl. Aviation.

1935, Dec. 4 *Perf. 14½x13½*

B82 SP69 1½c (+1½c) crim .50 .30
B83 SP69 5c (+3c) dk yel grn 1.40 1.10
B84 SP69 6c (+4c) blk brn 1.25 .30
B85 SP69 12½c (+3½c) ultra 20.00 7.00
Nos. B82-B85 (4) 23.15 8.70
Set, never hinged 80.00

The surtax aided child welfare.

H. Kamerlingh Onnes — SP70

Dr. A. S. Talma — SP71

Msgr. Hjam Schaepman SP72

Desiderius Erasmus SP73

Perf. 12½x12

1936, May 1 Engr. Unwmk.

B86 SP70 1½c (+1½c) brn blk .80 .75
B87 SP71 5c (+3c) dl grn .80 *3.25*
B88 SP72 6c (+4c) dk red 3.50 .50
B89 SP73 12½c (+3½c) dl bl 13.00 2.50
Nos. B86-B89 (4) 18.10 7.00
Set, never hinged 60.00

Surtax for social and cultural projects.

Cherub — SP74

Perf. 14½x13½

1936, Dec. 1 Photo. Wmk. 202

B90 SP74 1½c (+1½c) lil gray .50 .30
B91 SP74 5c (+3c) turq grn 2.00 .75
B92 SP74 6c (+4c) dp red brn 1.90 .25
B93 SP74 12½c (+3½c) ind 14.00 4.75
Nos. B90-B93 (4) 18.40 6.05
Set, never hinged 45.00

The surtax aided child welfare.

Jacob Maris — SP75

Franciscus de la Boe Sylvius — SP76

Joost van den Vondel SP77

Anthony van Leeuwenhoek SP78

Perf. 12½x12

1937, June 1 Engr. Unwmk.

B94 SP75 1½c (+1½c) blk brn .50 .40
B95 SP76 5c (+3c) dl grn 4.00 2.75
B96 SP77 6c (+4c) brn vio 1.00 .25
B97 SP78 12½c (+3½c) dl bl 7.00 .85
Nos. B94-B97 (4) 12.50 4.25
Set, never hinged 35.00

Surtax for social and cultural projects.

"The Laughing Child" after Frans Hals — SP79

Perf. 14½x13½

1937, Dec. 1 Photo. Wmk. 202

B98 SP79 1½c (+1½c) blk .20 .20
B99 SP79 3c (+2c) grn 1.50 1.00
B100 SP79 4c (+2c) hn brn .60 .45
B101 SP79 5c (+3c) bl grn .50 .20
B102 SP79 12½c (+3½c) dk bl 7.25 1.40
Nos. B98-B102 (5) 10.05 3.25
Set, never hinged 32.50

The surtax aided child welfare.

Marnix van Sint Aldegonde SP80

Otto Gerhard Heldring SP81

Maria Tesselschade SP82

Hermann Boerhaave SP84

Harmenszoon Rembrandt van Rijn — SP83

Perf. 12½x12

1938, May 16 Engr. Unwmk.

B103 SP80 1½c (+1½c) sep .30 .50
B104 SP81 3c (+2c) dk grn .55 .30
B105 SP82 4c (+2c) rose lake 1.75 1.50
B106 SP83 5c (+3c) dk sl grn 2.25 .30
B107 SP84 12½c (+3½c) dl bl 7.75 1.10
Nos. B103-B107 (5) 12.60 3.70
Set, never hinged 32.50

The surtax was for the benefit of cultural and social relief.

Child with Flowers, Bird and Fish — SP85

Perf. 14½x13½

1938, Dec. 1 Photo. Wmk. 202

B108 SP85 1½c (+1½c) blk .20 .20
B109 SP85 3c (+2c) mar .30 .20
B110 SP85 4c (+2c) dk bl grn .60 .80
B111 SP85 5c (+3c) hn brn .25 .20
B112 SP85 12½c (+3½c) dp bl 9.00 1.75
Nos. B108-B112 (5) 10.35 3.15
Set, never hinged 35.00

The surtax aided child welfare.

Matthijs Maris — SP86

Anton Mauve — SP87

Gerard van Swieten SP88

Nikolaas Beets SP89

Peter Stuyvesant — SP90

Perf. 12½x12

1939, May 1 Engr. Unwmk.

B113 SP86 1½c (+1½c) sepia .60 .60
B114 SP87 2½c (+2½c) gray grn 3.00 2.75
B115 SP88 3c (+3c) ver .80 1.00
B116 SP89 5c (+3c) dk sl grn 2.00 .30
B117 SP90 12½c (+3½c) indigo 5.00 .85
Nos. B113-B117 (5) 11.40 5.50
Set, never hinged 40.00

The surtax was for the benefit of cultural and social relief.

Child Carrying Cornucopia — SP91

Perf. 14½x13½

1939, Dec. 1 Photo. Wmk. 202

B118 SP91 1½c (+1½c) blk .20 .20
B119 SP91 2½c (+2½c) dk ol grn 3.75 2.00
B120 SP91 3c (+3c) hn brn .40 .20
B121 SP91 5c (+3c) dk grn .85 .20
B122 SP91 12½c (+3½c) dk bl 4.00 1.00
Nos. B118-B122 (5) 9.20 3.60
Set, never hinged 40.00

The surtax was used for destitute children.

Catalogue values for unused stamps in this section, from this point to the end of the section, are for Never Hinged items.

Vincent van Gogh SP92

E. J. Potgieter SP93

Petrus Camper SP94

Jan Steen SP95

Joseph Scaliger — SP96

Perf. 12½x12

1940, May 11 Engr. Unwmk.

B123 SP92 1½c +1½c brn blk 1.90 .25
B124 SP93 2½c +2½c dk grn 6.00 1.40
B125 SP94 3c +3c car 3.75 1.10
B126 SP95 5c +3c dp grn 7.75 .25
a. Booklet pane of 4 250.00
B127 SP96 12½c +3½c dp bl 6.75 .80

Surtax for social and cultural projects.

Type of 1940 Surcharged in Black

1940, Sept. 7

B128 SP95 7½c +2½c on 5c +3c dk red .50 .25
Nos. B123-B128 (6) 26.65 4.05

Child with Flowers and Doll — SP97

Perf. 14½x13½

1940, Dec. 2 Photo. Wmk. 202

B129 SP97 1½c +1½c dl bl gray .65 .20
B130 SP97 2½c +2½c dp ol 2.50 .50
B131 SP97 4c +3c royal bl 2.50 .65
B132 SP97 5c +3c dk bl grn 2.50 .20
B133 SP97 7½c +3½c hn .65 .20
Nos. B129-B133 (5) 8.80 1.75

The surtax was used for destitute children.

AIR POST STAMPS

Stylized Seagull — AP1

Perf. 12½

1921, May 1 Unwmk. Typo.

C1 AP1 10c red 1.25 1.50
C2 AP1 15c yellow grn 6.25 2.50
C3 AP1 60c dp blue 19.00 .25
Nos. C1-C3 (3) 26.50 4.25
Set, never hinged 190.00

Nos. C1-C3 were used to pay airmail fee charged by the carrier, KLM.

Lt. G. A. Koppen — AP2

Capt. Jan van der Hoop — AP3

Wmk. Circles (202)

1928, Aug. 20 Litho. *Perf. 12*

C4 AP2 40c orange red .25 .25
C5 AP3 75c blue green .25 .25
Set, never hinged 1.25

Mercury AP4

Queen Wilhelmina AP5

Perf. 11½

1929, July 16 Unwmk. Engr.

C6	AP4	1½g gray	2.50	1.65
C7	AP4	4½g carmine	1.75	3.00
C8	AP4	7½g blue green	24.00	4.50
		Nos. C6-C8 (3)	28.25	9.15
		Set, never hinged	70.00	

Perf. 12½, 14x13

1931, Sept. 24 Photo. Wmk. 202

C9	AP5	36c org red & dk bl	10.00	.60
		Never hinged	70.00	

Fokker Pander AP6

1933, Oct. 9 *Perf. 12½*

C10	AP6	30c dark green	.40	.60
		Never hinged	.80	

Nos. C10-C12 were issued for use on special flights.

Crow in Flight AP7

1938-53 *Perf. 13x14*

C11	AP7	12½c dk blue & gray	.35	.25
C12	AP7	25c dk bl & gray ('53)	1.50	1.50
		Set, never hinged	4.25	

MARINE INSURANCE STAMPS

Floating Safe Attracting Gulls — MI1

Floating Safe with Night Flare — MI2

Fantasy of Floating Safe — MI3

Perf. 11½

1921, Feb. 2 Unwmk. Engr.

GY1	MI1	15c slate grn	4.25	*37.50*
GY2	MI1	60c car rose	4.25	*42.50*
GY3	MI1	75c gray brn	6.50	*52.50*
GY4	MI2	1.50g dk blue	65.00	*425.00*
GY5	MI2	2.25g org brn	110.00	*550.00*
GY6	MI3	4½g black	165.00	*675.00*
GY7	MI3	7½g red	250.00	*925.00*
		Nos. GY1-GY7 (7)	605.00	*2,707.*
		Set, never hinged	1,500.	

POSTAGE DUE STAMPS

Postage due types of Netherlands were also used for Netherlands Antilles, Netherlands Indies and Surinam in different colors.

D1

D2

Perf. 12½x12, 13

1870, May 15 Typo. Unwmk.

J1	D1	5c brown, *org*	72.50	15.00
		No gum	21.50	
		On cover		140.00
		On postcard		80.00
J2	D1	10c violet, *bl*	150.00	20.00
		No gum	47.50	
		On cover		225.00

Type I — 34 loops. "T" of "BETALEN" over center of loop; top branch of "E" of "TE" shorter than lower branch.

Type II — 33 loops. "T" of "BETALEN" between two loops.

Type III — 32 loops. "T" of "BETALEN" slightly to the left of loop; top branch of first "E" of "BETALEN" shorter than lower branch.

Type IV — 37 loops. Letters of "PORT" larger than in the other three types.

Imperforate varieties are proofs.

Perf. 11½x12, 12½x12, 12½, 13½

1881-87

Value in Black

J3	D2	1c lt blue (III)	11.00	11.00
		No gum	4.00	
a.		Type I	15.00	18.00
b.		Type II	20.00	20.00
c.		Type IV	47.50	52.50
J4	D2	1½c lt blue (III)	15.00	15.00
		No gum	4.00	
a.		Type I	18.00	21.00
b.		Type II	24.00	24.00
c.		Type IV	75.00	75.00
J5	D2	2½c lt blue (III)	37.50	5.00
		No gum	8.00	
a.		Type I	45.00	5.50
b.		Type II	55.00	6.00
c.		Type IV	200.00	125.00
J6	D2	5c lt blue (III) ('87)	140.00	3.50
		No gum	20.00	
a.		Type I	165.00	4.50
b.		Type II	190.00	5.25
c.		Type IV	1,750.	325.00
J7	D2	10c lt blue (III) ('87)	140.00	4.00
		No gum	22.50	
a.		Type I	165.00	4.50
b.		Type II	190.00	5.00
c.		Type IV	2,500.	375.00
J8	D2	12½c lt blue (III)	140.00	35.00
		No gum	22.50	
a.		Type I	165.00	40.00
b.		Type II	190.00	45.00
c.		Type IV	475.00	140.00
J9	D2	15c lt blue (III)	125.00	4.00
		No gum	17.00	
a.		Type I	150.00	4.50
b.		Type II	175.00	5.00
c.		Type IV	175.00	25.00
J10	D2	20c lt blue (III)	30.00	4.00
		No gum	7.75	
a.		Type I	47.50	4.25
b.		Type II	50.00	5.50
c.		Type IV	137.50	27.50
J11	D2	25c lt blue (III)	300.00	3.50
		No gum	47.50	
a.		Type I	325.00	3.00
b.		Type II	400.00	4.50
c.		Type IV	600.00	190.00

Value in Red

J12	D2	1g lt blue (III)	110.00	30.00
		No gum	20.00	
a.		Type I	110.00	37.50
b.		Type II	150.00	40.00
c.		Type IV	250.00	75.00

See Nos. J13-J26, J44-J60. For surcharges see Nos. J27-J28, J42-J43, J72-J75.

1896-1910 *Perf. 12½*

Value in Black

J13	D2	½c dk bl (I) ('01)	.20	.20
J14	D2	1c dk blue (I)	1.65	.20
a.		Type III	2.50	3.25
J15	D2	1½c dk blue (I)	.60	.30
a.		Type III	2.50	2.50
J16	D2	2½c dk blue (I)	1.50	.30
a.		Type III	3.25	.40
J17	D2	3c dk bl (I) ('10)	1.65	1.10
J18	D2	4c dk bl (I) ('09)	1.65	2.25
J19	D2	5c dk blue (I)	13.00	.30
a.		Type III	16.00	.30
J20	D2	6½c dk bl (I) ('07)	45.00	45.00
J21	D2	7½c dk bl (I) ('04)	1.65	.55
J22	D2	10c dk blue (I)	35.00	.40
a.		Type III	52.50	1.50
J23	D2	12½c dk blue (I)	30.00	1.00
a.		Type III	45.00	3.50
J24	D2	15c dk blue (I)	35.00	.90
a.		Type III	55.00	1.00
J25	D2	20c dk blue (I)	20.00	8.00
a.		Type III	20.00	8.75
J26	D2	25c dk blue (I)	45.00	.75
a.		Type III	50.00	1.00
		Nos. J13-J26 (14)	231.90	61.25

Surcharged in Black **50 CENT**

1906, Jan. 10 *Perf. 12½*

J27	D2	50c on 1g lt bl (III)	125.00	110.00
a.		50c on 1g light blue (I)	165.00	140.00
b.		50c on 1g light blue (II)	175.00	150.00

Surcharged in Red **6½**

1906, Oct. 6

J28	D2	6½c on 20c dk bl (I)	5.50	5.00

Nos. 87-89 Surcharged

1907, Nov. 1

J29	A13	½c on 1c claret	1.25	1.25
J30	A13	1c on 1c claret	.50	.50
J31	A13	1½c on 1c claret	.50	.50
J32	A13	2½c on 1c claret	1.25	1.25
J33	A13	5c on 2½c ver	1.40	.40
J34	A13	6½c on 2½c ver	3.50	3.50
J35	A13	7½c on ½c blue	2.00	1.25
J36	A13	10c on ½c blue	1.75	.75
J37	A13	12½c on ½c blue	5.00	4.75
J38	A13	15c on 2½c ver	6.00	4.00
J39	A13	25c on ½c blue	9.00	8.50
J40	A13	50c on ½c blue	42.50	40.00
J41	A13	1g on ½c blue	60.00	55.00
		Nos. J29-J41 (13)	134.65	121.65

Two printings of the above surcharges were made. Some values show differences in the setting of the fractions; others are practically impossible to distinguish.

No. J20 Surcharged in Red

1909, June

J42	D2	4c on 6½c dark blue	5.50	5.00
		Never hinged	20.00	

No. J12 Surcharged in Black

1910, July 11

J43	D2	3c on 1g lt bl, type III	30.00	27.50
		Never hinged	100.00	
a.		Type I	37.50	40.00
		Never hinged	110.00	
b.		Type II	40.00	40.00
		Never hinged	125.00	

Type I

1912-21 *Perf. 12½, 13½x13*

Value in Color of Stamp

J44	D2	½c pale ultra	.20	.20
J45	D2	1c pale ultra ('13)	.20	.20
J46	D2	1½c pale ultra ('15)	1.10	.90
J47	D2	2½c pale ultra	.20	.20
J48	D2	3c pale ultra	.40	.40
J49	D2	4c pale ultra ('13)	.20	.20
J50	D2	4½c pale ultra ('16)	5.25	5.00
J51	D2	5c pale ultra	.20	.20
J52	D2	5½c pale ultra ('16)	5.00	5.00
J53	D2	7c pale ultra ('21)	2.25	2.25
J54	D2	7½c pale ultra ('13)	2.50	1.00
J55	D2	10c pale ultra ('13)	.20	.20
J56	D2	12½c pale ultra ('13)	.20	.20
J57	D2	15c pale ultra ('13)	.20	.20
J58	D2	20c pale ultra ('20)	.20	.20
J59	D2	25c pale ultra ('17)	80.00	.60
J60	D2	50c pale ultra ('20)	.40	.20
		Nos. J44-J60 (17)	98.70	17.15
		Set, never hinged	225.00	

D3

1921-38 Typo. *Perf. 12½, 13½x12½*

J61	D3	3c pale ultra ('28)	.20	.20
J62	D3	6c pale ultra ('27)	.20	.20
J63	D3	7c pale ultra ('28)	.20	.20
J64	D3	7½c pale ultra ('26)	.25	.20
J65	D3	8c pale ultra ('38)	.20	.20
J66	D3	9c pale ultra ('30)	.20	.20
J67	D3	11c ultra ('21)	13.00	3.50
J68	D3	12c pale ultra ('28)	.20	.20
J69	D3	25c pale ultra ('25)	.20	.20
J70	D3	30c pale ultra ('35)	.25	.20
J71	D3	1g ver ('21)	.70	.20
		Nos. J61-J71 (11)	15.60	5.50
		Set, never hinged	40.00	

Stamps of 1912-21 Surcharged

1923, Dec. *Perf. 12½*

J72	D2	1c on 3c ultra	.50	.50
J73	D2	2½c on 7c ultra	.50	.45
J74	D2	25c on 1½c ultra	8.00	.40
J75	D2	25c on 7½c ultra	8.00	.35
		Nos. J72-J75 (4)	17.00	1.70
		Set, never hinged	45.00	

Nos. 56, 58, 62, 65 Surcharged

1924, Aug.

J76	A11	4c on 3c olive grn	1.10	1.10
J77	A10	5c on 1c red	.40	.20
a.		Surcharge reading down	550.00	550.00
J78	A10	10c on 1½c blue	.95	.20
a.		Tête bêche pair	8.50	8.50
J79	A11	12½c on 5c carmine	.95	.20
a.		Tête bêche pair	10.00	10.00
		Nos. J76-J79 (4)	3.40	1.70

The 11c on 22½c and 15c on 17½c exist. These were used by the postal service for accounting of parcel post fees.

OFFICIAL STAMPS

Regular Issues of 1898-1908 Overprinted

1913 Typo. Unwmk. *Perf. 12½*

O1	A10	1c red	4.00	2.00
O2	A10	1½c ultra	1.00	1.65
O3	A10	2c yellow brn	7.00	7.00
O4	A10	2½c dp green	16.00	12.00
O5	A11	3c olive grn	4.00	1.00
O6	A11	5c carmine rose	4.00	4.50
O7	A11	10c gray lilac	35.00	37.50
		Nos. O1-O7 (7)	71.00	65.65

Same Overprint in Red on No. 58

1919

O8	A10	1½c deep blue (R)	90.00	110.00

Nos. O1 to O8 were used to defray the postage on matter relating to the Poor Laws. Counterfeit overprints exist.

For the International Court of Justice

Regular Issue of 1926-33 Overprinted in Gold

1934 Wmk. 202 *Perf. 12½*

O9	A24	1½c red violet	.60
O10	A24	2½c deep green	.60
O11	A23	7½c red	1.10
O12	A31	12½c deep ultra	32.50
O13	A23	15c orange	1.25
O14	A23	30c violet	2.00
a.		Perf. 13½x12½	2.00
		Nos. O9-O14 (6)	38.05

Same Overprint on No. 180 in Gold

1937 *Perf. 13½x12½*

O15	A23	12½c ultra	16.00

"Mint" Officials
Nos. O9-O15 were sold to the public only canceled. Uncanceled, they were obtainable only by favor of an official or from UPU specimen copies.

Same on Regular Issue of 1940 Overprinted in Gold

1940 *Perf. 13½x12½*

O16	A45	7½c bright red	16.00	8.75
O17	A45	12½c sapphire	16.00	8.75
O18	A45	15c lt blue	16.00	8.75
O19	A45	30c bister	16.00	8.75
		Nos. O16-O19 (4)	64.00	35.00

NETHERLANDS ANTILLES

ˈne-t͟hər-lən‚dz an-ˈti-lēz

(Curacao)

LOCATION — Two groups of islands about 500 miles apart in the West Indies, north of Venezuela
GOVT. — Dutch Colony
AREA — 383 sq. mi.
POP. — 260,000 (est. 1983)
CAPITAL — Willemstad

100 Cents = 1 Gulden

Values for unused examples of Nos. 1-44 are for stamps without gum.

Watermark

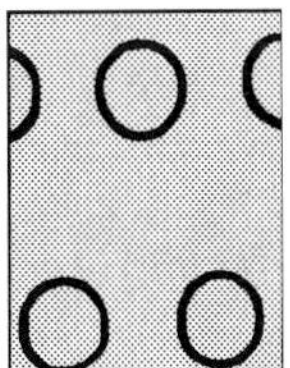

Wmk. 202 — Circles

King William III
A1

Numeral
A2

Regular Perf. 11½, 12½, 11½x12, 12½x12, 13½x13, 14

1873-79 **Typo.** **Unwmk.**

1	A1	2½c green	5.00	8.00
2	A1	3c bister	55.00	*110.00*
3	A1	5c rose	10.00	12.00
4	A1	10c ultra	60.00	17.00
5	A1	25c brown orange	45.00	10.00
6	A1	50c violet	1.75	2.50
7	A1	2.50g bis & pur ('79)	37.50	37.50
		Nos. 1-7 (7)	214.25	*197.00*

See bluish paper note with Netherlands #7-22.

The gulden denominations, Nos. 7 and 12, are of larger size.

See 8-12. For surcharges see #18, 25-26.

Perf. 14, Small Holes

1b	A1	2½c	12.00	15.00
2b	A1	3c	60.00	*140.00*
3b	A1	5c	14.50	21.00
4b	A1	10c	72.50	80.00
5b	A1	25c	65.00	45.00
6b	A1	50c	26.00	30.00
		Nos. 1b-6b (6)	250.00	*331.00*

"Small hole" varieties have the spaces between the holes wider than the diameter of the holes.

1886-89 ***Perf. 11½, 12½, 12½x12***

8	A1	12½c yellow	95.00	52.50
9	A1	15c olive ('89)	27.50	19.00
10	A1	30c pearl gray ('89)	35.00	50.00
11	A1	60c olive bis ('89)	42.50	17.00
12	A1	1.50g lt & dk bl ('89)	100.00	80.00
		Nos. 7-12 (12)	587.50	587.00

Nos. 1-12 were issued without gum until 1890. Imperfs. are proofs.

1889 ***Perf. 12½***

13	A2	1c gray	.85	1.00
14	A2	2c violet	.65	1.25
15	A2	2½c green	4.50	3.00
16	A2	3c bister	5.00	4.50
17	A2	5c rose	21.00	1.75
		Nos. 13-17 (5)	32.00	11.50

King William III
A3

Queen Wilhelmina
A4

Black Surcharge, Handstamped

1891 ***Perf. 12½x12***

Without Gum

18	A3	25c on 30c pearl gray	15.00	14.00

No. 18 exists with dbl. surch., value $225, and with invtd. surch., value $275.

1892-96 ***Perf. 12½***

19	A4	10c ultra ('95)	1.25	1.25
20	A4	12½c green	26.00	6.25
21	A4	15c rose ('93)	2.50	2.50
22	A4	25c brown orange	100.00	5.50
23	A4	30c gray ('96)	2.50	*5.50*
		Nos. 19-23 (5)	132.25	21.00

A5

A6

Magenta Surcharge, Handstamped

1895 ***Perf. 12½, 13½x13***

25	A5	2½c on 10c ultra	13.00	8.00

Perf. 12½x12

Black Surcharge, Handstamped

26	A6	2½c on 30c gray	125.00	6.00

Nos. 25-26 exist with surcharge double or inverted.

No. 26 and No. 25, perf. 13½x13, were issued without gum.

Nos. 27, 29

Queen Wilhelmina — A8

1902, Jan. 1 ***Perf. 12½***

Netherlands Nos. 77, 84, 68 Surcharged in Black

27	A7	25c on 25c car & bl	2.00	2.00

1901, May 1 **Engr.** ***Perf. 11½x11***

28	A8	1.50g on 2.50g brn lil	20.00	21.00

1902, Mar. 1 **Typo.** ***Perf. 12½***

29	A7	12½c on 12½c blue	25.00	7.00

A9

A10

1904-08

30	A9	1c olive green	1.40	.90
31	A9	2c yellow brown	12.00	3.00
32	A9	2½c blue green	4.00	.35
33	A9	3c orange	7.50	4.00
34	A9	5c rose red	7.00	.35
35	A9	7½c gray ('08)	27.50	6.00
36	A10	10c slate	11.00	3.00
37	A10	12½c deep blue	1.25	.50
38	A10	15c brown	14.00	10.00
39	A10	22½c brn & ol ('08)	14.00	8.50
40	A10	25c violet	14.00	1.90
41	A10	30c brown orange	32.50	13.00
42	A10	50c red brown	27.50	8.25
		Nos. 30-42 (13)	173.65	59.75

Queen Wilhelmina — A11

1906, Nov. 1 **Engr.** ***Perf. 11½***

Without Gum

43	A11	1½g red brown	35.00	25.00
44	A11	2½g slate blue	35.00	24.00

A12

A13

Queen Wilhelmina — A14

Perf. 12½, 11, 11½, 11x11½

1915-33 **Typo.**

45	A12	½c lilac ('20)	1.60	1.10
46	A12	1c olive green	.25	.20
47	A12	1½c blue ('20)	.25	.20
48	A12	2c yellow brn	1.25	1.40
49	A12	2½c green	.90	.20
50	A12	3c yellow	2.25	1.50
51	A12	3c green ('26)	2.60	2.50
52	A12	5c rose	2.00	.20
53	A12	5c green ('22)	3.75	2.75
54	A12	5c lilac ('26)	2.00	.20
55	A12	7½c drab	1.10	.30
56	A12	7½c bister ('20)	1.10	.20
57	A12	10c lilac ('22)	5.00	4.50
58	A12	10c rose ('26)	4.25	1.25
59	A13	10c car rose	13.00	3.00
60	A13	12½c blue	2.25	.50
61	A13	12½c red ('22)	2.00	1.60
62	A13	15c olive grn	.65	.65
63	A13	15c lt blue ('26)	4.00	2.50
64	A13	20c blue ('22)	6.50	3.00
65	A13	20c olive grn ('26)	2.50	2.25
66	A13	22½c orange	2.50	2.25
67	A13	25c red violet	3.25	.90
68	A13	30c slate	3.25	.65
69	A13	35c sl & red ('22)	3.25	4.25

Perf. 11½x11, 11½, 12½, 11

Engr.

70	A14	50c green	4.00	.20
71	A14	1½g violet	13.00	11.00
72	A14	2½g carmine	21.00	20.00
a.		Perf. 12½ ('33)	140.00	*300.00*
		Nos. 45-72 (28)	109.45	69.25

Some stamps of 1915 were also issued without gum.

For surcharges see #74, 107-108, C1-C3.

A15

Laid Paper, without Gum

1918, July 16 **Typo.** ***Perf. 12***

73	A15	1c black, *buff*	6.75	3.75

"HAW" are the initials of Postmaster H. A. Willemsen.

No. 60 Surcharged in Black

1918, Sept. 1 ***Perf. 12½***

74	A13	5c on 12½c blue	3.75	2.00
a.		"5" 2¼mm wide	60.00	32.50
b.		Double surcharge		700.00

The "5" of No. 74 is 3mm wide. Illustration shows No. 74a surcharge.

Queen Wilhelmina
A16 A17

1923 **Engr.** ***Perf. 11½, 11x11½***

75	A16	5c green	1.00	2.00
76	A16	7½c olive grn	1.25	1.60
77	A16	10c car rose	1.75	2.00
78	A16	20c indigo	2.50	3.50
a.		Perf. 11x11½	3.25	4.25
79	A16	1g brown vio	30.00	19.00
80	A16	2½g gray black	70.00	*170.00*
81	A16	5g brown	90.00	*200.00*
a.		Perf. 11x11½	625.00	
		Nos. 75-81 (7)	196.50	*398.10*

25th anniv. of the assumption of the government of the Netherlands by Queen Wilhelmina, at the age of 18.

Nos. 80-81 with clear cancel between Aug. 1, 1923 and Apr. 30, 1924, sell for considerably more.

Types of Netherlands Marine Insurance Stamps, Inscribed "CURACAO" Surcharged in Black

1927, Oct. 3

87	MI1	3c on 15c dk green	.25	.30
88	MI1	10c on 60c car rose	.25	.45
89	MI1	12½c on 75c gray brn	.25	.45
90	MI2	15c on 1.50g dk bl	3.00	2.50
a.		Double surcharge	*500.00*	
91	MI2	25c on 2.25g org brn	6.50	6.25
92	MI3	30c on 4½g black	13.00	11.00
93	MI3	50c on 7½g red	7.50	7.25
		Nos. 87-93 (7)	30.75	28.20

Nos. 90, 91 and 92 have "FRANKEER-ZEGEL" in one line of small capitals. Nos. 90 and 91 have a heavy bar across the top of the stamp.

1928-30 **Engr.** ***Perf. 11½, 12½***

95	A17	6c orange red ('30)	1.50	.40
a.		Booklet pane of 6		
96	A17	7½c orange red	.60	.45
97	A17	10c carmine	1.50	.35
98	A17	12½c red brown	1.50	1.00
a.		Booklet pane of 6		
99	A17	15c dark blue	1.50	.35
a.		Booklet pane of 6		
100	A17	20c blue black	5.75	.55
101	A17	21c yellow grn ('30)	9.25	14.00
102	A17	25c brown vio	3.50	1.40
103	A17	27½c black ('30)	12.00	14.00
104	A17	30c deep green	5.75	.55
105	A17	35c brnsh black	2.00	1.75
		Nos. 95-105 (11)	44.85	34.80

No. 96 Surcharged in Black with Bars over Original Value

1929, Nov. 1

106	A17	6c on 7½c org red	1.40	1.00
a.		Inverted surcharge	275.00	260.00

No. 51 Surcharged in Red

1931, Mar. 1 Typo. *Perf. 12½*

107	A12	2½c on 3c green	1.10	1.10

No. 49 Surcharged in Red

1932, Oct. 29

108	A12	1½c on 2½c grn	3.50	3.50

Prince William I, Portrait by Van Key — A18

1933 Photo. *Perf. 12½*

109	A18	6c deep orange	1.75	1.40

400th birth anniv. of Prince William I, Count of Nassau and Prince of Orange, frequently referred to as William the Silent.

Willem Usselinx
A19

Van Walbeeck's Ship
A22

Designs: 2½c, 5c, 6c, Frederik Hendrik. 10c, 12½c, 15c, Jacob Binckes. 27½c, 30c, 50c, Cornelis Evertsen the Younger. 1.50g, 2.50g, Louis Brion.

1934, Jan. 1 Engr. *Perf. 12½*

110	A19	1c black	1.00	1.25
111	A19	1½c dull violet	.75	.30
112	A19	2c orange	1.00	1.25
113	A19	2½c dull green	.85	1.25
114	A19	5c black brn	.85	.85
115	A19	6c violet bl	.75	.25
116	A19	10c lake	2.00	1.00
117	A19	12½c bister brn	6.50	7.00
118	A19	15c blue	1.60	1.00
119	A22	20c black	3.00	2.00
120	A22	21c brown	11.00	13.00
121	A22	25c dull green	11.00	11.00
122	A19	27½c brown vio	14.00	16.00
123	A19	30c scarlet	11.00	5.25
124	A19	50c orange	11.00	8.25
125	A19	1.50g indigo	47.50	50.00
126	A19	2.50g yellow grn	52.50	47.50
		Nos. 110-126 (17)	176.30	167.15

3rd centenary of the founding of the colony.

Numeral
A25

Queen Wilhelmina
A26

1936, Aug. 1 Litho. *Perf. 13½x13*

Size: 18x22mm

127	A25	1c brown black	.20	.20
128	A25	1½c deep ultra	.25	.20
129	A25	2c orange	.25	.25
130	A25	2½c green	.20	.20
131	A25	5c scarlet	.35	.20

Engr.

Perf. 12½

Size: 20¼x30½mm

132	A26	6c brown vio	.45	.20
133	A26	10c orange red	.85	.20
134	A26	12½c dk bl grn	1.50	.95
135	A26	15c dark blue	1.25	.60
136	A26	20c orange yel	1.25	.60
137	A26	21c dk gray	2.25	2.25
138	A26	25c brown lake	1.50	.75
139	A26	27½c violet brn	2.50	2.75
140	A26	30c olive brn	.60	.20

Perf. 13x14

Size: 22x33mm

141	A26	50c dull yel grn	3.00	.20
a.		Perf. 14	50.00	.25
142	A26	1.50g black brn	18.00	13.00
a.		Perf. 14	40.00	20.00
143	A26	2.50g rose lake	16.00	11.00
a.		Perf. 14	16.00	11.00
		Nos. 127-143 (17)	50.40	33.75

See Nos. 147-151. For surcharges see Nos. B1-B3.

Queen Wilhelmina — A27

Perf. 12½x12

1938, Aug. 27 Photo. Wmk. 202

144	A27	1½c dull purple	.20	.25
145	A27	6c red orange	.80	.75
146	A27	15c royal blue	1.50	1.25
		Nos. 144-146 (3)	2.50	2.25

Reign of Queen Wilhelmina, 40th anniv.

AIR POST STAMPS

Regular Issues of 1915-22 Surcharged in Black

Perf. 12½

1929, July 6 Typo. Unwmk.

C1	A13	50c on 12½c red	13.00	13.00
C2	A13	1g on 20c blue	13.00	13.00
C3	A13	2g on 15c ol grn	42.50	47.50
		Nos. C1-C3 (3)	68.50	73.50

Excellent forgeries exist.

Allegory, "Flight" — AP1

1931-39 Engr.

C4	AP1	10c Prus grn ('34)	.20	.20
C5	AP1	15c dull blue ('38)	.25	.20
C6	AP1	20c red	.75	.25
C7	AP1	25c gray ('38)	.75	.60
C8	AP1	30c yellow ('39)	.30	.30
C9	AP1	35c dull blue	.80	.90
C10	AP1	40c green	.60	.40
C11	AP1	45c orange	2.25	2.25
C12	AP1	50c lake ('38)	.75	.50
C13	AP1	60c brown vio	.60	.35
C14	AP1	70c black	6.50	2.50
C15	AP1	1.40g brown	4.25	5.25
C16	AP1	2.80g bister	5.00	5.50
		Nos. C4-C16 (13)	23.00	19.20

No. C6 Surcharged in Black

1934, Aug. 25

C17	AP1	10c on 20c red	19.00	17.00

POSTAGE DUE STAMPS

D1

D2

Type I — 34 loops. "T" of *"BETALEN"* over center of loop, top branch of "E" of *"TE"* shorter than lower branch.
Type II — 33 loops. "T" of *"BETALEN"* over center of two loops.
Type III — 32 loops. "T" of *"BETALEN"* slightly to the left of loop, top of first "E" of *"BETALEN"* shorter than lower branch.

Value in Black

1889 Unwmk. Typo. *Perf. 12½*

Type III

J1	D1	2½c green	3.00	3.25
J2	D1	5c green	2.00	1.75
J3	D1	10c green	32.50	27.50
J4	D1	12½c green	375.00	200.00
J5	D1	15c green	20.00	17.00
J6	D1	20c green	9.00	9.00
J7	D1	25c green	190.00	150.00
J8	D1	30c green	10.00	9.00
J9	D1	40c green	10.00	9.00
J10	D1	50c green	40.00	37.50

Nos. J1-J10 were issued without gum.

Type I

J1a	D1	2½c	3.00	4.00
J2a	D1	5c	40.00	35.00
J3a	D1	10c	35.00	35.00
J4a	D1	12½c	375.00	200.00
J5a	D1	15c	21.00	19.00
J6a	D1	20c	65.00	65.00
J7a	D1	25c	600.00	350.00
J8a	D1	30c	75.00	75.00
J9a	D1	40c	75.00	75.00
J10a	D1	50c	45.00	40.00

Type II

J1b	D1	2½c	5.00	4.75
J2b	D1	5c	200.00	150.00
J3b	D1	10c	40.00	37.50
J4b	D1	12½c	400.00	250.00
J5b	D1	15c	25.00	20.00
J6b	D1	20c	425.00	425.00
J7b	D1	25c	*1,600.*	*1,600.*
J8b	D1	30c	400.00	400.00
J9b	D1	40c	400.00	400.00
10b	D1	50c	47.50	45.00

Value in Black

1892-98 *Perf. 12½*

J11	D2	2½c green (III)	.25	.20
J12	D2	5c green (III)	.60	.45
J13	D2	10c green (III)	1.50	.40
J14	D2	12½c green (III)	1.60	.60
J15	D2	15c green (III) ('95)	2.50	1.10
J17	D2	25c green (III)	1.25	.95
		Nos. J11-J17 (6)	7.70	3.70

Type I

J11a	D2	2½c	.50	.50
J12a	D2	5c	2.50	2.50
J13a	D2	10c	2.75	2.00
J14a	D2	12½c	2.00	1.40
J16	D2	20c green ('95)	3.50	1.40
J17a	D2	25c	1.50	1.50
J18	D2	30c green ('95)	25.00	13.00
J19	D2	40c green ('95)	25.00	15.00
J20	D2	50c green ('95)	30.00	15.00

Type II

J11b	D2	2½c	20.00	20.00
J12b	D2	5c	1.00	1.00
J13b	D2	10c	1.75	1.10
J14b	D2	12½c	9.00	8.00
J17b	D2	25c	*12.50*	*12.50*
		Nos. J11b-J17b (5)	44.25	42.60

Type I
On Yellowish or White Paper
Value in Color of Stamp

1915 *Perf. 12½, 13½x12½*

J21	D2	2½c green	1.00	.95
J22	D2	5c green	1.00	.95
J23	D2	10c green	.90	.80
J24	D2	12½c green	1.25	1.10
J25	D2	15c green	1.90	2.00
J26	D2	20c green	1.00	1.75
J27	D2	25c green	.35	.20
J28	D2	30c green	3.00	3.25
J29	D2	40c green	3.00	3.25
J30	D2	50c green	2.50	3.00
		Nos. J21-J30 (10)	15.90	17.25

1944 *Perf. 11½*

J23a	D2	10c yellow green	20.00	18.00
J24a	D2	12½c yellow green	20.00	10.00
J27a	D2	25c yellow green	40.00	1.00
		Nos. J23a-J27a (3)	80.00	29.00

NETHERLANDS INDIES

'ne-th̲ər-lən͵d͵z 'in-dēs

(Dutch Indies)

LOCATION — East Indies
GOVT. — Dutch colony
AREA — 735,268 sq. mi.
POP. — 76,000,000 (estimated 1949)
CAPITAL — Jakarta (formerly Batavia)

Netherlands Indies consisted of the islands of Sumatra, Java, the Lesser Sundas, Madura, two thirds of Borneo, Celebes, the Moluccas, western New Guinea and many small islands.

100 Cents = 1 Gulden

Values for unused stamps are for examples with original gum as defined in the catalogue introduction. Very fine examples of No. 2 will have perforations touching the frameline on one or more sides due to the narrow spacing of the stamps on the plates. Stamps with perfs clear of the framelines on all four sides are scarce and will command higher prices.

Watermarks

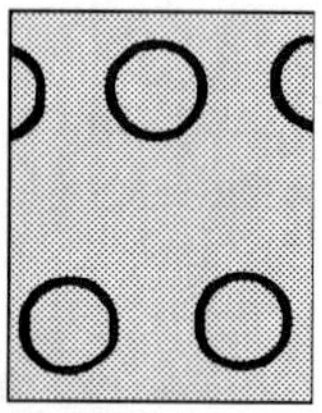

Wmk. 202 — Circles

King William III
A1 A2

Unwmk.

1864, Apr. 1 Engr. *Imperf.*

1	A1	10c lake	250.00	125.00

1868 *Perf. 12½x12*

2	A1	10c lake	800.00	140.00

Privately perforated examples of No. 1 sometimes are mistaken for No. 2.

Perf. 11½x12, 12½, 12½x12, 13x14, 13½, 14, 13½x14

1870-88 Typo.

ONE CENT:
Type I — "CENT" 6mm long.
Type II — "CENT" 7½mm long.

3	A2	1c sl grn, type I	6.00	4.50
a.		Perf. 13x14, small holes	10.00	8.00
4	A2	1c sl grn, type II	2.75	1.75
5	A2	2c red brown	6.00	4.00
a.		2c fawn	6.00	4.00
6	A2	2c violet brn	90.00	80.00
7	A2	2½c orange	35.00	20.00

8	A2	5c pale green	50.00	3.50
a.		Perf. 14, small holes	60.00	4.00
b.		Perf. 13x14, small holes	50.00	5.00
9	A2	10c orange brn	13.00	.20
a.		Perf. 14, small holes	24.00	.80
b.		Perf. 13x14, small holes	35.00	.80
10	A2	12½c gray	3.50	1.50
a.		Perf. 12½x12		1,000.
11	A2	15c bister	17.00	1.50
a.		Perf. 13x14, small holes	27.50	1.75
12	A2	20c ultra	80.00	2.50
a.		Perf. 14, small holes	80.00	2.50
b.		Perf. 13x14, small holes	80.00	2.75
13	A2	25c dk violet	14.00	.55
b.		Perf. 13x14, small holes	25.00	2.50
c.		Perf. 14, large holes	450.00	100.00
14	A2	30c green	27.50	3.25
15	A2	50c carmine	17.00	1.50
a.		Perf. 14, small holes	22.50	1.50
b.		Perf. 13x14, small holes	17.00	1.50
c.		Perf. 14, large holes	25.00	2.50
16	A2	2.50g green & vio	75.00	13.00
b.		Perf. 14, small holes	75.00	13.00
c.		Perf. 14, large holes	85.00	13.00
		Nos. 3-16 (14)	436.75	137.75

Imperforate examples of Nos. 3-16 are proofs. The 1c red brown and 2c yellow are believed to be bogus.

"Small hole" varieties have the spaces between the holes wider than the diameter of the holes.

Numeral of Value
A3

Queen Wilhelmina
A4

1883-90 ***Perf. 12½***

17	A3	1c slate grn ('88)	.75	.20
a.		Perf. 12½x12	1.10	.65
18	A3	2c brown ('84)	.75	.20
a.		Perf. 12½x12	.75	.30
b.		Perf. 11½x12	65.00	22.50
19	A3	2½c yellow	.75	.65
a.		Perf. 12½x12	1.25	.75
b.		Perf. 11½x12	12.00	4.75
20	A3	3c lilac ('90)	.85	.20
21	A3	5c green ('87)	30.00	20.00
22	A3	5c ultra ('90)	9.00	.20
		Nos. 17-22 (6)	42.10	21.45

For surcharges and overprint see Nos. 46-47, O4.

1892-97 ***Perf. 12½***

23	A4	10c orange brn ('95)	3.75	.20
24	A4	12½c gray ('97)	7.50	12.50
25	A4	15c bister ('95)	12.00	1.25
26	A4	20c ultra ('93)	27.50	1.25
27	A4	25c violet	27.50	1.25
28	A4	30c green ('94)	37.50	1.75
29	A4	50c carmine ('93)	25.00	1.25
30	A4	2.50g org brn & ultra	110.00	27.50
		Nos. 23-30 (8)	250.75	46.95

For overprints see Nos. O21-O27.

Netherlands #67-69, 74, 77, 80, 84 Surcharged in Black

1900, July 1

31	A11	10c on 10c gray lil	1.40	.20
32	A11	12½c on 12½c blue	2.25	.55
33	A11	15c on 15c yel brn	2.50	.30
34	A11	20c on 20c yel grn	13.00	.60
35	A11	25c on 25c car & bl	13.00	.70
36	A11	50c on 50c brnz grn & red brn	22.50	.90

1902 ***Perf. 11½x11***

37	A12	2.50g on 2½g brn lil	45.00	11.00
a.		Perf. 11	50.00	12.50
		Nos. 31-37 (7)	99.65	14.25

A6

1902-09 ***Perf. 12½***

38	A6	½c violet	.35	.20
39	A6	1c olive grn	.35	.20
a.		Booklet pane of 6		
40	A6	2c yellow brn	2.75	.20
41	A6	2½c green	1.75	.20
a.		Booklet pane of 6		
42	A6	3c orange	1.75	1.10
43	A6	4c ultra ('09)	11.00	9.00
44	A6	5c rose red	4.25	.20
a.		Booklet pane of 6		
45	A6	7½c gray ('08)	2.25	.30
		Nos. 38-45 (8)	24.45	11.40

For overprints see Nos. 63-69, 81-87, O1-O9.

Nos. 18, 20 Surcharged

1902

46	A3	½c on 2c yel brn	.20	.20
a.		Double surcharge	175.00	150.00
47	A3	2½c on 3c violet	.25	.25

A9

Queen Wilhelmina — A10

1903-08

48	A9	10c slate	1.00	.20
a.		Booklet pane of 6		
49	A9	12½c deep blue ('06)	1.50	.20
a.		Booklet pane of 6		
50	A9	15c chocolate ('06)	7.25	2.00
a.		Ovptd. with 2 horiz. bars	1.50	.75
51	A9	17½c bister ('08)	3.00	.20
52	A9	20c grnsh slate	1.50	1.50
53	A9	20c olive grn ('05)	20.00	.20
54	A9	22½c brn & ol grn ('08)	3.75	.20
55	A9	25c violet ('04)	9.00	.20
56	A9	30c orange brn	25.00	.20
57	A9	50c red brown ('04)	19.00	.20
		Nos. 48-57 (10)	91.00	5.10

For overprints and surcharges see Nos. 58, 70-78, 88-96, 139, O10-O18.

No. 52 Surcharged in Black

1905, July 6

58	A9	10c on 20c grnsh slate	1.90	1.25

1905-12 **Engr.** ***Perf. 11x11½***

59	A10	1g dull lilac ('06)	42.50	.25
a.		Perf. 11½x11	42.50	.40
b.		Perf. 11	52.50	3.50
60	A10	1g dl lil, *bl* ('12)	45.00	6.50
a.		Perf. 11	55.00	57.50
61	A10	2½g slate bl ('05)	52.50	1.50
a.		Perf. 11½	52.50	1.60
b.		Perf. 11½x11	60.00	1.60
c.		Perf. 11	675.00	
62	A10	2½g sl bl, *bl* ('12)	65.00	32.50
a.		Perf. 11	75.00	75.00
		Nos. 59-62 (4)	205.00	40.75

Sheets of Nos. 60 & 62 were soaked in an indigo solution.

For overprints and surcharge see Nos. 79-80, 97-98, 140, O19-O20.

Previous Issues Overprinted

1908, July 1

63	A6	½c violet	.25	.25
64	A6	1c olive grn	.35	.25
65	A6	2c yellow brn	1.50	2.00
66	A6	2½c green	.75	.20
67	A6	3c orange	.65	1.10
68	A6	5c rose red	2.25	.40
69	A6	7½c gray	2.50	2.25
70	A9	10c slate	.55	.20
71	A9	12½c dp blue	8.25	2.00
72	A9	15c choc (#50a)	3.75	2.00
73	A9	17½c bister	1.40	.95
74	A9	20c olive grn	7.50	1.40
75	A9	22½c brn & ol grn	5.75	3.50
76	A9	25c violet	5.75	.30
77	A9	30c orange brn	16.00	1.90
78	A9	50c red brown	7.00	.70
79	A10	1g dull lilac	52.50	3.75
80	A10	2½g slate blue	80.00	57.50
		Nos. 63-80 (18)	196.70	80.65

The above stamps were overprinted for use in the territory outside of Java and Madura, stamps overprinted "Java" being used in these latter places.

The 15c is overprinted, in addition, with two horizontal lines, 2½mm apart.

The overprint also exists on #59a-59b. Same values.

Overprint Reading Down

63a	A6	½c	.55	*3.25*
64a	A6	1c	.55	*2.50*
65a	A6	2c	2.25	*4.50*
66a	A6	2½c	.95	*3.00*
67a	A6	3c	15.00	*40.00*
68a	A6	5c	2.25	*2.50*
70a	A9	10c	.65	*1.90*
71a	A9	12½c	4.50	*8.00*
72a	A9	15c	25.00	*62.50*
74a	A9	20c	7.25	8.00
75a	A9	22½c	*1,400*	*1,400.*
76a	A9	25c	5.50	7.25
77a	A9	30c	11.00	15.00
78a	A9	50c	7.50	9.00
79a	A10	1g	175.00	225.00
80a	A10	2½g	*2,250.*	*2,500.*

Overprinted

1908, July 1

81	A6	½c violet	.20	.20
a.		Inverted overprint	.55	*2.25*
b.		Double overprint	450.00	
82	A6	1c olive grn	.25	.25
a.		Inverted overprint	.45	*2.75*
83	A6	2c yellow brn	1.75	1.75
a.		Inverted overprint	1.50	*6.00*
84	A6	2½c green	.90	.20
a.		Inverted overprint	2.00	*3.25*
85	A6	3c orange	.75	.75
a.		Inverted overprint	17.00	22.50
86	A6	5c rose red	2.25	.20
a.		Inverted overprint	1.50	2.50
87	A6	7½c gray	1.90	1.75
88	A9	10c slate	.55	.20
a.		Inverted overprint	.55	*2.00*
89	A9	12½c deep blue	2.00	.55
a.		Inverted overprint	2.75	5.00
b.		Dbl. ovpt., one inverted	125.00	125.00
90	A9	15c choc (on No. 50a)	3.00	2.50
a.		Inverted overprint	2.75	*9.00*
91	A9	17½c bister	1.50	.65
92	A9	20c olive grn	9.25	.75
a.		Inverted overprint	9.00	10.00
93	A9	22½c brn & ol grn	4.00	2.00
94	A9	25c violet	4.00	.30
a.		Inverted overprint	4.50	*9.00*
95	A9	30c orange brn	24.00	2.00
a.		Inverted overprint	18.00	26.00
96	A9	50c red brown	15.00	.55
a.		Inverted overprint	12.00	19.00
97	A10	1g dull lilac	37.50	2.25
a.		Inverted overprint	150.00	150.00
b.		Perf. 11	47.50	4.00
98	A10	2½g slate blue	57.50	40.00
a.		Inverted overprint	*2,250.*	*2,500.*
		Nos. 81-98 (18)	166.30	56.85

A11

Queen Wilhelmina
A12 A13

Typo., Litho. (#114A)

1912-40 ***Perf. 12½***

101	A11	½c lt vio	.20	.20
102	A11	1c olive grn	.20	.20
103	A11	2c yellow brn	.40	.20
104	A11	2c gray blk ('30)	.40	.20
105	A11	2½c green	1.25	.20
106	A11	2½c lt red ('22)	.25	.20
107	A11	3c yellow	.45	.20
108	A11	3c green ('29)	.70	.20
109	A11	4c ultra	.65	.25
110	A11	4c dp grn ('28)	1.25	.20
111	A11	4c yellow ('30)	8.50	4.00
112	A11	5c rose	1.10	.20
113	A11	5c green ('22)	.90	.20
114	A11	5c chlky bl ('28)	.55	.20
114A	A11	5c ultra ('40)	.85	.20
115	A11	7½c bister	.40	.20
116	A11	10c lilac ('22)	.95	.20
117	A12	10c car rose ('14)	.75	.20
118	A12	12½c dull bl ('14)	.95	.20
119	A12	12½c red ('22)	.95	.20
120	A12	15c blue ('29)	7.50	.20
121	A12	17½c red brn ('15)	.95	.20
122	A12	20c green ('15)	1.75	.20
123	A12	20c blue ('22)	1.75	.20
124	A12	20c orange ('32)	13.00	.20
125	A12	22½c orange ('15)	1.75	.45
126	A12	25c red vio ('15)	1.75	.20
127	A12	30c slate ('15)	1.90	.20
128	A12	32½c vio & red ('22)	1.90	.20
129	A12	35c org brn ('29)	8.50	.60
130	A12	40c green ('22)	1.90	.20

Perf. 11½

Engr.

131	A13	50c green ('13)	4.00	.20
a.		Perf. 11x11½	4.25	.20
b.		Perf. 12½	4.25	.30
132	A13	60c dp blue ('22)	4.75	.20
133	A13	80c orange ('22)	4.00	.20
134	A13	1g brown ('13)	3.00	.20
a.		Perf. 11x11½	3.50	.20
135	A13	1.75g dk vio, p. 12½ ('31)	15.00	1.90
136	A13	2½g carmine ('13)	12.50	.40
a.		Perf. 11x11½	13.00	.65
b.		Perf. 12½	14.00	.60
		Nos. 101-136 (37)	107.55	13.80

For surcharges and overprints see Nos. 137-138, 144-150, 102a-123a, 158, 194-195, B1-B3, C1-C5.

Water Soluble Ink

Some values of types A11 and A12 and late printings of types A6 and A9 are in soluble ink. The design disappears when immersed in water.

Nos. 105, 109, 54, 59 Surcharged

1917-18 **Typo.** ***Perf. 12½***

137	A11	½c on 2½c	.30	.30
138	A11	1c on 4c ('18)	.55	.55
139	A9	17½c on 22½c ('18)	1.25	.55
a.		Inverted surcharge	350.00	425.00

Perf. 11x11½

140	A10	30c on 1g ('18)	7.00	1.60
a.		Perf. 11½x11	110.00	42.50
		Nos. 137-140 (4)	9.10	3.00

Nos. 121, 125, 131, 134 Surcharged in Red or Blue

On A12

On A13

Two types of 32½c on 50c:
I — Surcharge bars spaced as in illustration.
II — Bars more closely spaced.

1922, Jan. ***Perf. 12½***

144	A12	12½c on 17½c (R)	.30	.20
145	A12	12½c on 22½c (R)	.40	.20
146	A12	20c on 22½c (Bl)	.40	.20

Perf. 11½, 11x11½

147	A13	32½c on 50c (Bl) (I, perf. 11½)	1.25	.20
a.		Type II, perf. 11½	10.00	.20
b.		Type I, perf. 11x11½	1,000.	6.00
c.		Type II, perf. 11x11½	19.00	1.00
148	A13	40c on 50c (R)	3.75	.45
149	A13	60c on 1g (Bl)	6.00	.40
150	A13	80c on 1g (R)	6.75	.90
		Nos. 144-150 (7)	18.85	2.55

Stamps of 1912-22 Overprinted in Red, Blue, Green or Black

a

3de N. I. JAARBEURS
BANDOENG 1922
b

1922, Sept. 18 Typo. *Perf. 12½*

102a	A11(a)	1c ol grn (R)	5.75	4.75
103a	A11(a)	2c yel brn (Bl)	5.75	4.75
106a	A11(a)	2½c lt red (G)	47.50	52.50
107a	A11(a)	3c yellow (R)	5.75	5.75
109a	A11(a)	4c ultra (R)	32.50	30.00
113a	A11(a)	5c green (R)	11.00	8.25
115a	A11(a)	7½c drab (Bl)	7.50	4.75
116a	A11(a)	10c lilac (Bk)	57.50	67.50
145a	A12(b)	12½c on 22½c org (Bl)	5.75	5.75
121a	A12(b)	17½c red brn (Bk)	3.75	4.75
123a	A12(b)	20c blue (Bk)	5.75	4.75
		Nos. 102a-123a (11)	188.50	193.50

Issued to publicize the 3rd Netherlands Indies Industrial Fair at Bandoeng, Java. On No. 145a the overprint is vertical.

Nos. 102a-123a were sold at a premium for 3, 4, 5, 6, 8, 9, 10, 12½, 15, 20 and 22½ cents respectively.

Queen Wilhelmina
A15

Prince William I, Portrait by Van Key
A16

1923, Aug. 31 Engr. *Perf. 11½*

151	A15	5c myrtle green	.20	.20
a.		Perf. 11½x11	350.00	110.00
b.		Perf. 11x11½	4.50	.55
152	A15	12½c rose	.20	.20
a.		Perf. 11x11½	1.25	.20
b.		Perf. 11½x11	1.75	.25
153	A15	20c dark blue	.35	.20
a.		Perf. 11½x11	3.25	.40
154	A15	50c red orange	1.40	.60
a.		Perf. 11x11½	6.50	1.25
b.		Perf. 11½x11	2.00	.90
c.		Perf. 11	4.50	.85
155	A15	1g brown vio	2.75	.40
a.		Perf. 11½x11	7.50	.80
156	A15	2½g gray black	22.50	8.75
157	A15	5g orange brown	90.00	87.50
		Nos. 151-157 (7)	117.40	97.85

25th anniversary of the assumption of the government of the Netherlands by Queen Wilhelmina, at the age of 18.

No. 123 Surcharged

1930, Dec. 13 Typo. *Perf. 12½*

158	A12	12½c on 20c bl (R)	.30	.20
a.		Inverted surcharge	375.00	475.00

1933, Apr. 18 Photo.

163	A16	12½c deep orange	1.25	.20

400th anniv. of the birth of Prince William I, Count of Nassau and Prince of Orange, frequently referred to as William the Silent.

Rice Field Scene
A17

Queen Wilhelmina
A18

Queen Wilhelmina
A19

1933-37 Unwmk. *Perf. 11½x12½*

164	A17	1c lilac gray ('34)	.20	.20
165	A17	2c plum ('34)	.20	.20
166	A17	2½c bister ('34)	.20	.20
167	A17	3c yellow grn ('34)	.20	.20
168	A17	3½c dark gray ('37)	.20	.20
169	A17	4c dk olive ('34)	.85	.20
170	A17	5c ultra ('34)	.20	.20
171	A17	7½c violet ('34)	1.25	.20
172	A17	10c ver ('34)	1.75	.20
173	A18	10c ver ('37)	.25	.20
174	A18	12½c dp org ('34)	.25	.20
a.		12½c light orange, perf. 12½ ('33)	6.25	.35
175	A18	15c ultra ('34)	.25	.20
176	A18	20c plum ('34)	.40	.20
177	A18	25c blue grn ('34)	1.75	.20
178	A18	30c lilac gray ('34)	2.75	.20
179	A18	32½c bister ('34)	7.50	6.50
180	A18	35c violet ('34)	4.25	.95
181	A18	40c yel grn ('34)	2.50	.20
182	A18	42½c yellow ('34)	2.50	.20

1934, Jan 16 *Perf. 12½*

183	A19	50c lilac gray	3.25	.20
184	A19	60c ultra	4.00	.45
185	A19	80c vermilion	4.00	.55
186	A19	1g violet	6.25	.40
187	A19	1.75g yellow grn	16.00	11.00
188	A19	2.50g plum	19.00	1.25
		Nos. 164-188 (25)	79.95	24.70

See Nos. 200-225. For overprints and surcharges see Nos. 271-256, B48, B57.

Water Soluble Ink

Nos. 164-188 and the first printing of No. 163 have soluble ink and the design disappears when immersed in water.

Nos. C6-C7, C14, C9-C10 Surcharged in Black:

a

b

1934 Typo. *Perf. 12½x11½, 12½*

189	AP1(a)	2c on 10c	.30	.45
190	AP1(a)	2c on 20c	.20	.20
191	AP3(b)	2c on 30c	.40	.60
192	AP1(a)	42½c on 75c	4.25	.25
193	AP1(a)	42½c on 1.50g	4.25	.40
		Nos. 189-193 (5)	9.40	1.90

Nos. 127-128 Surcharged with New Value in Red or Black

1937, Sept. *Perf. 12½*

194	A12	10c on 30c (R)	2.50	.25
a.		Double surcharge	*675.00*	
195	A12	10c on 32½c (Bk)	2.75	.30

Wilhelmina — A20

Perf. 12½x12

1938, Aug. 30 Photo. Wmk. 202

196	A20	2c dull purple	.20	.20
197	A20	10c car lake	.20	.20
198	A20	15c royal blue	1.25	.75
199	A20	20c red orange	.50	.30
		Nos. 196-199 (4)	2.15	1.45

40th anniv. of the reign of Queen Wilhelmina.

Types of 1933-37

1938-40 Photo. *Perf. 12½x12*

200	A17	1c lilac gray ('39)	.30	*.80*
201	A17	2c plum ('39)	.20	.20
202	A17	2½c bister ('39)	.50	.50
203	A17	3c yellow grn ('39)	1.50	1.25
205	A17	4c gray ol ('39)	1.50	1.25
206	A17	5c ultra ('39)	.20	.20
a.		Perf. 12x12½	1.25	.20
207	A17	7½c violet ('39)	2.50	1.00
208	A18	10c ver ('39)	.20	.20
210	A18	15c ultra ('39)	.20	.20
211	A18	20c plum ('39)	.20	.20
a.		Perf. 12x12½	1.25	.20
212	A18	25c blue grn ('39)	25.00	24.00
213	A18	30c lilac gray ('39)	6.50	.80
215	A18	35c violet ('39)	2.75	.65
216	A18	40c dp yel grn ('40)	5.00	.20

Perf. 12½

218	A19	50c lilac gray ('40)	275.00	
219	A19	60c ultra ('39)	10.50	1.25
220	A19	80c ver ('39)	62.50	26.00
221	A19	1g violet ('39)	27.50	.85
223	A19	2g Prus green	27.50	14.00
225	A19	5g yellow brn	25.00	6.00
		Nos. 200-216,219-225 (19)	199.55	79.55

The note following No. 188 applies also to this issue.

The 50c was sold only at the philatelic window in Amsterdam.

SEMI-POSTAL STAMPS

Regular Issue of 1912-14 Surcharged in Carmine

1915, June 10 Unwmk. *Perf. 12½*

B1	A11	1c + 5c ol grn	4.50	4.50
B2	A11	5c + 5c rose	4.50	4.50
B3	A12	10c + 5c rose	7.25	7.25
		Nos. B1-B3 (3)	16.25	16.25

Surtax for the Red Cross.

Bali Temple
SP1

Watchtower
SP2

Menangkabau Compound — SP3

Borobudur Temple, Java
SP4

Perf. 11½x11, 11x11½

1930, Dec. 1 Photo.

B4	SP1	2c (+ 1c) vio & brn	1.00	.80
B5	SP2	5c (+ 2½c) dk grn & brn	4.75	2.50
B6	SP3	12½c (+ 2½c) dp red & brn	3.25	.50
B7	SP4	15c (+ 5c) ultra & brn	5.75	5.75
		Nos. B4-B7 (4)	14.75	9.55

Surtax for youth care.

Farmer and Carabao
SP5

5c, Fishermen. 12½c, Dancers. 15c, Musicians.

1931, Dec. 1 Engr. *Perf. 12½*

B8	SP5	2c (+ 1c) olive bis	3.00	2.00
B9	SP5	5c (+ 2½c) bl grn	4.25	3.75
B10	SP5	12½c (+ 2½c) dp red	3.25	.55
B11	SP5	15c (+ 5c) dl bl	8.25	7.00
		Nos. B8-B11 (4)	18.75	13.30

The surtax was for the aid of the Leper Colony at Salatiga.

Weaving
SP9

5c, Plaiting rattan. 12½c, Woman batik dyer. 15c, Coppersmith.

1932, Dec. 1 Photo. *Perf. 12½*

B12	SP9	2c (+ 1c) dp vio & bis	.40	.40
B13	SP9	5c (+ 2½c) dp grn & bis	2.50	2.00
B14	SP9	12½c (+ 2½c) brt rose & bis	.85	.30
B15	SP9	15c (+ 5c) bl & bis	3.25	3.00
		Nos. B12-B15 (4)	7.00	5.70

The surtax was donated to the Salvation Army.

Woman and Lotus — SP13

Designs: 5c, "The Light that Shows the Way." 12½c, YMCA emblem. 15c, Jobless man.

1933, Dec. 1 *Perf. 12½*

B16	SP13	2c (+ 1c) red vio & ol bis	.65	.30
B17	SP13	5c (+ 2½c) grn & ol bis	2.25	1.90
B18	SP13	12½c (+ 2½c) ver & ol bis	2.50	.30
B19	SP13	15c (+ 5c) bl & ol bis	2.75	2.00
		Nos. B16-B19 (4)	8.15	4.50

The surtax was for the Amsterdam Young Men's Society for Relief of the Poor in Netherlands Indies.

Dowager Queen Emma — SP17

A Pioneer at Work — SP18

1934, Sept. 15 *Perf. 13x14*

B20	SP17	12½c (+ 2½c) blk brn	1.25	.45

Issued in memory of the late Dowager Queen Emma of Netherlands. The surtax was for the Anti-Tuberculosis Society.

1935 *Perf. 12½*

Designs: 5c, Cavalryman rescuing wounded native. 12½c, Artilleryman under fire. 15c, Bugler.

B21	SP18	2c (+ 1c) plum & ol bis	1.25	1.00
B22	SP18	5c (+ 2½c) grn & ol bis	3.25	2.25
B23	SP18	12½c (+ 2½c) red org & ol bis	3.25	.25
B24	SP18	15c (+ 5c) brt bl & ol bis	4.50	4.50
		Nos. B21-B24 (4)	12.25	8.00

The surtax was for the Indies Committee of the Christian Military Association for the East and West Indies.

Child Welfare Work — SP22

Boy Scouts — SP23

1936, Dec. 1 **Size: 23x20mm**

B25	SP22	2c (+ 1c) plum	1.00	.60

Size: 30x26½mm

B26	SP22	5c (+ 2½c) gray vio	1.25	1.10
B27	SP22	7½c (+ 2½c) dk vio	1.25	1.25
B28	SP22	12½c (+ 2½c) red org	1.25	.30
B29	SP22	15c (+5c) brt bl	2.00	1.75
		Nos. B25-B29 (5)	6.75	5.00

Surtax for Salvation Army.

1937, May 1

B30	SP23	7½c + 2½c dk ol brn	1.25	1.00
B31	SP23	12½c + 2½c rose car	1.25	.50

Fifth Boy Scout World Jamboree, Vogelenzang, Netherlands, July 31-Aug. 13, 1937. Surtax for Netherlands Indies Scout Association.

Sifting Rice — SP24

Designs: 3½c, Mother and children. 7½c, Plowing with carabao team. 10c, Carabao team and cart. 20c, Native couple.

1937, Dec. 1

B32	SP24	2c (+ 1c) dk brn & org	1.10	.80
B33	SP24	3½c (+ 1½c) gray	1.10	.80
B34	SP24	7½c (+ 2½c) Prus grn & org	1.25	.95
B35	SP24	10c (+ 2½c) car & org	1.25	.20
B36	SP24	20c (+ 5c) brt bl	1.25	1.10
		Nos. B32-B36 (5)	5.95	3.85

Surtax for the Public Relief Fund for indigenous poor.

Modern Plane — SP28

Design: 20c, Plane nose facing left.

Wmk. 202

1938, Oct. 15 **Photo.** *Perf. 12½*

B36A	SP28	17½c (+5c) olive brn	.85	.85
B36B	SP28	20c (+5c) slate	.85	.55

10th anniversary of the Dutch East Indies Royal Air Lines (K. N. I. L. M.).

Surtax for the Aviation Fund in the Netherlands Indies.

Nun and Child
SP29 SP30

Designs: 7½c, Nurse examining child's arm. 10c, Nurse bathing baby. 20c, Nun bandaging child's head.

1938, Dec. 1 **Wmk. 202** *Perf. 12½*

B37	SP29	2c (+ 1c) vio	.60	.45

Perf. 11½x12

B38	SP30	3½c (+ 1½c) brt grn	1.00	.90

Perf. 12x11½

B39	SP30	7½c (+ 2½c) cop red	.80	.85
B40	SP30	10c (+ 2½c) ver	.90	.20
B41	SP30	20c (+ 5c) brt ultra	1.00	.95
		Nos. B37-B41 (5)	4.30	3.35

The surtax was for the Central Mission Bureau in Batavia.

Social Workers SP34

Indonesian Nurse Tending Patient SP35

European Nurse Tending Patient — SP36

Perf. 13x11½, 11½x13

1939, Dec. 1 **Photo.**

B42	SP34	2c (+ 1c) purple	.25	.20
B43	SP35	3½c (+ 1½c) bl grn & pale bl grn	.30	.25
B44	SP34	7½c (+ 2½c) cop brn	.25	.20
B45	SP35	10c (+ 2½c) scar & pink	1.40	.80
B46	SP36	10c (+ 2½c) scar	1.40	.80
B47	SP36	20c (+ 5c) dk bl	.40	.35
		Nos. B42-B47 (6)	4.00	2.60

No. B44 shows native social workers.

Nos. B45 and B46 were issued se-tenant vertically and horizontally. The surtax was used for the Bureau of Social Service.

No. 174 Surcharged in Brown

1940, Dec. 2 **Unwmk.** *Perf. 12x12½*

B48	A18	10c + 5c on 12½c dp org	1.10	.40

AIR POST STAMPS

Regular Issues of 1913-1923 Surcharged and New Values in Black or Blue

Perf. 12½, 11½

1928, Sept. 20 **Unwmk.**

C1	A12	10c on 12½c red	1.00	1.00
C2	A12	20c on 25c red vio	2.25	2.25
C3	A13	40c on 80c org	1.90	1.50
C4	A13	75c on 1g brn (Bl)	.90	.55
C5	A13	1½g on 2½g car	6.25	5.50
		Nos. C1-C5 (5)	12.30	10.80

On Nos. C4 and C5 there are stars over the original values and the airplane is of different shape. On No. C3 there are no bars under "OST."

Planes over Temple AP1

1928, Dec. 1 **Litho.** *Perf. 12½x11½*

C6	AP1	10c red violet	.30	.20
C7	AP1	20c brown	.85	.55
C8	AP1	40c rose	1.00	.55
C9	AP1	75c green	2.25	.20
C10	AP1	1.50g orange	4.00	.50
		Nos. C6-C10 (5)	8.40	2.00

For surcharges see Nos. 189-190, 192-193, C11-C12, C17.

No. C8 Surcharged in Black or Green

1930-32

C11	AP1	30c on 40c rose	.90	.20
C12	AP1	30c on 40c rose (G) ('32)	1.25	.20

Pilot at Controls of Plane AP2

1931, Apr. 1 **Photo.** *Perf. 12½*

C13	AP2	1g blue & brown	11.00	11.00

Issued for the first air mail flight from Java to Australia.

Landscape and Garudas AP3

1931, May

C14	AP3	30c red violet	2.25	.20
C15	AP3	4½g bright blue	8.00	3.00
C16	AP3	7½g yellow green	10.00	3.25
		Nos. C14-C16 (3)	20.25	6.45

For surcharge see No. 191.

No. C10 Surcharged in Blue

1932, July 21 *Perf. 12½x11½*

C17	AP1	50c on 1.50g org	2.50	.40
a.		Inverted surcharge	1,800.	2,000.

Airplane AP4

1933, Oct. 18 **Photo.** *Perf. 12½*

C18	AP4	30c deep blue	2.10	1.75

MARINE INSURANCE STAMPS

Floating Safe Attracting Gulls — MI1

Floating Safe with Night Flare — MI2

Artistic Fantasy of Floating Safe — MI3

Perf. 11½

1921, Nov. 1 **Unwmk.** **Engr.**

GY1	MI1	15c slate green	1.90	*30.00*
GY2	MI1	60c rose	3.75	*45.00*
GY3	MI1	75c gray brn	3.75	*50.00*
GY4	MI2	1.50g dark blue	22.50	*225.00*
GY5	MI2	2.25g org brn	30.00	*300.00*
GY6	MI3	4½g black	57.50	*500.00*
GY7	MI3	7½g red	67.50	*575.00*
		Nos. GY1-GY7 (7)	186.90	*1,725.*

POSTAGE DUE STAMPS

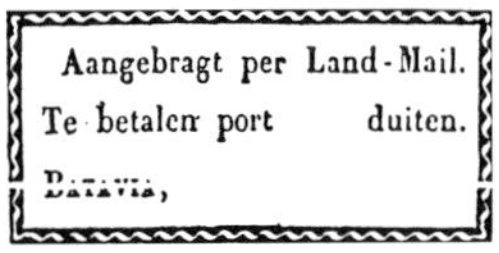

D1

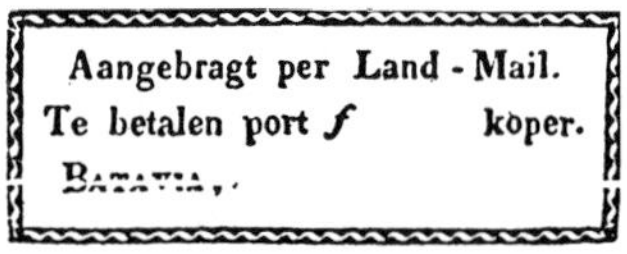

D2

1845-46 **Unwmk.** **Typeset** *Imperf.*

Bluish Paper

J1	D1	black ('46)	*1,400.*
J2	D2	black	*1,400.*
a.		"Maill" instead of "Mail"	*3,200.*

D3

Perf. 12½x12, 13x14, 10½x12

1874 **Typo.**

J3	D3	5c ocher	250.00	225.00
J4	D3	10c green, *yel*	100.00	85.00
J5	D3	15c ocher, *org*	20.00	15.00
a.		Perf. 11½x12	35.00	35.00
J6	D3	20c green, *blue*	30.00	10.00
a.		Perf. 11½x12	65.00	19.00
		Nos. J3-J6 (4)	400.00	335.00

D4

D5

Type I — 34 loops. "T" of "Betalen" over center of loop, top branch of "E" of "Te" shorter than lower branch.

Type II — 33 loops. "T" of "Betalen" over center of two loops.

Type III — 32 loops. "T" of "Betalen" slightly to the left of loop, top branch of first "E" of "Betalen" shorter than lower branch.

Type IV — 37 loops and letters of "PORT" larger than in the other three types.

Value in Black

Perf. 11½x12, 12½, 12½x12, 13½

1882-88

Type III

J7	D4	2½c carmine	.40	1.10
J8	D4	5c carmine	.20	.40
J9	D4	10c carmine	2.50	3.00
J10	D4	15c carmine	3.00	3.00
J11	D4	20c carmine	82.50	.50
J12	D4	30c carmine	1.75	2.50
J13	D4	40c carmine	1.25	2.00
J14	D4	50c deep salmon	.75	.60
J15	D4	75c carmine	.45	.50
		Nos. J7-J15 (9)	92.80	13.60

Type I

J7a	D4	2½c carmine	.40	1.10
J8a	D4	5c carmine	.25	.45
J9a	D4	10c carmine	3.25	4.00
J10a	D4	15c carmine	3.25	3.50
J11a	D4	20c carmine	95.00	.50
J12a	D4	30c carmine	3.25	4.00
J13a	D4	40c carmine	1.40	2.00
J14a	D4	50c deep salmon	.80	.60
J15a	D4	75c carmine	.50	.60
		Nos. J7a-J15a (9)	108.10	16.75

Type II

J7b	D4	2½c carmine	.50	1.40
J8b	D4	5c carmine	.25	.50
J9b	D4	10c carmine	3.50	4.50
J10b	D4	15c carmine	3.75	4.00
J11b	D4	20c carmine	110.00	.65
J12b	D4	30c carmine	7.00	7.50
J13b	D4	40c carmine	1.50	2.50
J14b	D4	50c deep salmon	.85	.75
J15b	D4	75c carmine	.65	.85
		Nos. J7b-J15b (9)	128.00	22.65

Type IV

J7c	D4	2½c carmine	2.25	3.00
J8c	D4	5c carmine	1.00	1.75
J9c	D4	10c carmine	20.00	24.00
J10c	D4	15c carmine	13.00	14.00
J11c	D4	20c carmine	200.00	5.00
J13c	D4	40c carmine	2.50	3.50
J14c	D4	50c deep salmon	9.00	14.00
J15c	D4	75c carmine	1.25	2.50
		Nos. J7c-J15c (8)	249.00	67.75

1892-95 ***Perf. 12½***

Type I

J16	D5	10c carmine	2.25	.30
J17	D5	15c carmine ('95)	12.00	1.75
J18	D5	20c carmine	2.00	.20
		Nos. J16-J18 (3)	16.25	2.25

Type III

J16a	D5	10c dull red	2.75	2.00
J18a	D5	20c dull red	3.75	1.40

Type II

J16b	D5	10c dull red	13.00	13.00
J18b	D5	20c dull red	18.00	6.50

1906-09

Type I

J19	D5	2½c carmine ('08)	.50	.30
J20	D5	5c carmine ('09)	2.25	.20
J21	D5	30c carmine	17.50	5.75
J22	D5	40c carmine ('09)	12.50	1.50
J23	D5	50c carmine ('09)	8.50	.90
J24	D5	75c carmine ('09)	17.00	4.00
		Nos. J19-J24 (6)	58.25	12.65

Value in Color of Stamp

1913-39 ***Perf. 12½***

J25	D5	1c salmon ('39)	.20	*1.25*
J26	D5	2½c salmon	.20	.20
J27	D5	3½c salmon ('39)	.20	*1.25*
J28	D5	5c salmon	.20	.20
J29	D5	7½c salmon ('22)	.20	.20
J30	D5	10c salmon	.20	.20
J31	D5	12½c salmon ('22)	2.75	.20
J32	D5	15c salmon	2.75	.20
J33	D5	20c salmon	.20	.20
J34	D5	25c salmon ('22)	.20	.20
J35	D5	30c salmon	.20	.20
J36	D5	37½c salmon ('30)	18.00	19.00
J37	D5	40c salmon	.20	.20
J38	D5	50c salmon	1.40	.20
J39	D5	75c salmon	2.50	.20
		Nos. J25-J39 (15)	29.40	23.90

Thick White Paper
Invisible Gum
Numerals Slightly Larger

1941 Litho. ***Perf. 12½***

J25a	D5	1c light red	.60	*2.00*
J28a	D5	5c light red	.65	1.00
J30a	D5	10c light red	10.50	10.00
J32a	D5	15c light red	1.00	1.00
J33a	D5	20c light red	.80	.80
J35a	D5	30c light red	1.25	1.00
J37a	D5	40c light red	1.00	.80
		Nos. J25a-J37a (7)	15.80	16.60

No. J36 Surcharged with New Value

1937, Oct. 1 Unwmk. ***Perf. 12½***

J40	D5	20c on 37½c salmon	.25	.30

D6

D7

1939-40

J41	D6	1g salmon	4.50	6.50
J42	D6	1g blue ('40)	.20	*3.00*
a.		1g lt bl, thick paper, invisible gum	.65	.80

OFFICIAL STAMPS

Regular Issues of 1883-1909 Overprinted

Perf. 12½

1911, Oct. 1 Typo. Unwmk.

O1	A6	½c violet	.20	.30
O2	A6	1c olive grn	.20	.20
O3	A6	2c yellow brn	.20	.20
O4	A3	2½c yellow	.75	.75
O5	A6	2½c blue grn	1.40	1.25
O6	A6	3c orange	.40	.40
O7	A6	4c ultra	.20	.20
O8	A6	5c rose red	.80	.80
b.		Double overprint		*325.00*
O9	A6	7½c gray	2.75	2.75
O10	A9	10c slate	.20	.20
O11	A9	12½c deep blue	2.00	2.25
O12	A9	15c chocolate	.65	.65
a.		Overprinted with two bars	32.50	
b.		As "a," "Dienst" inverted	52.50	
O13	A9	17½c bister	2.75	2.50
O14	A9	20c olive grn	.60	.50
O15	A9	22½c brn & ol grn	3.50	3.00
O16	A9	25c violet	2.00	2.00
O17	A9	30c orange brn	.90	.60
O18	A9	50c red brown	12.00	7.00
O19	A10	1g dull lilac	3.00	1.25
O20	A10	2½g slate blue	27.50	30.00
		Nos. O1-O20 (20)	62.00	56.80

The overprint reads diagonally downward on Nos. O1-O3 and O5-O9.

Overprint Inverted

O1a	A6	½c	45.00	*125.00*
O2a	A6	1c	3.00	*19.00*
O3a	A6	2c	3.00	*20.00*
O5a	A6	2½c	9.00	*30.00*
O6a	A6	3c	110.00	*40.00*
O8a	A6	5c	3.00	*20.00*
O10a	A9	10c	3.00	*7.00*
O11a	A9	12½c	32.50	*55.00*
O14a	A9	20c	175.00	70.00
O16a	A9	25c	*1,250.*	*1,000.*
O17a	A9	30c	225.00	140.00
O18a	A9	50c	32.50	32.50
O19a	A10	1g	*525.00*	*850.00*
O20a	A10	2½g	225.00	*625.00*

Regular Issue of 1892-1894 Overprinted

1911, Oct. 1

O21	A4	10c orange brn	1.25	.60
O22	A4	12½c gray	2.75	4.75
O23	A4	15c bister	2.75	2.25
O24	A4	20c blue	2.50	.90
O25	A4	25c lilac	9.00	8.00
O26	A4	50c carmine	2.00	.80
O27	A4	2.50g org brn & bl	45.00	45.00
		Nos. O21-O27 (7)	65.25	62.30

Inverted Overprints

O21a	A4	10c	9.25	*32.50*
O22a	A4	12½c	300.00	300.00
O23a	A4	15c	300.00	300.00
O24a	A4	20c	80.00	90.00
O25a	A4	25c	425.00	425.00
O26a	A4	50c	9.25	*85.00*
O27a	A4	2.50g	500.00	800.00

NEVIS

'nē-vəs

LOCATION — West Indies, southeast of Puerto Rico
GOVT. — Presidency of the Leeward Islands Colony (British)
AREA — 50 sq. mi.
POP. — 9,800 (1990)
CAPITAL — Charlestown

Nevis stamps were discontinued in 1890 and replaced by those of the Leeward Islands. From 1903 to 1956 stamps of St. Kitts-Nevis and Leeward Islands were used concurrently.

See Leeward Islands and St. Kitts-Nevis.

12 Pence = 1 Shilling

PRE-STAMP POSTAL MARKINGS

Crowned Circle handstamp type VI is pictured in the Crowned Circle Handstamps and Great Britain Used Abroad section.

Charlestown

1852

A1	VI	"Nevis" crowned circle handstamp in red, on cover	*4,200.*

The handstamp was used, in black, as a provisional to 1886.

STAMPS OF GREAT BRITAIN USED IN NEVIS

Numeral cancellation type A is pictured in the Crowned Circle Handstamps and Great Britain Used Abroad section.

1858-60

A09 (Charlestown)

A2	A	1p rose red (#20)	500.00
A3	A	2p blue (#29, P7, 8)	1,900.
A4	A	4p rose (#26)	440.00
A5	A	6p lilac (#27)	350.00
A6	A	1sh green (#28)	—

Issued under British Administration

Unused examples of Nos. 1-8 almost always have no original gum, and they are valued without gum. These stamps with original gum are worth more. Other issues are valued with original gum as defined in the catalogue introduction. Very fine examples of Nos. 1-8, will have perforations touching the design on at least one side due to the narrow spacing of the stamps on the plates. Stamps with perfs clear of the design on all four sides are scarce and will command higher prices.

Medicinal Spring
A1 A2

A3 A4

1861 Unwmk. Engr. ***Perf. 13***

Bluish Wove Paper

1	A1	1p lake rose	275.00	140.00
2	A2	4p dull rose	850.00	200.00
3	A3	6p gray	700.00	260.00
4	A4	1sh green	1,050.	225.00

Grayish Wove Paper

5	A1	1p lake rose	82.50	52.50
6	A2	4p dull rose	110.00	62.50
7	A3	6p lilac gray	110.00	57.50
8	A4	1sh green	280.00	80.00

1867 White Wove Paper ***Perf. 15***

9	A1	1p red	47.50	45.00
10	A2	4p orange	110.00	22.50
11	A4	1sh yellow green	950.00	125.00
12	A4	1sh blue green	250.00	32.50

Laid Paper

13	A4	1sh yel green	17,000.	*5,750.*
		Manuscript cancel		1,000.

No. 13 values are for copies with design cut into on one or two sides.

1876 Litho.

Wove Paper

14	A1	1p rose	22.50	17.50
14A	A1	1p red	32.50	27.50
b.		1p vermilion	27.50	27.50
c.		Imperf., pair	775.00	
d.		Half used as ½p on cover		2,250.
15	A2	4p orange	180.00	32.50
a.		Imperf.		
b.		Vert. pair, imperf. between	*5,000.*	
16	A3	6p olive gray	225.00	200.00
17	A4	1sh gray green	95.00	*110.00*
a.		1sh dark green	105.00	*150.00*
b.		Horiz. strip of 3, perf. all around & imperf. btwn.	*6,750.*	

Perf. 11½

18	A1	1p vermilion	50.00	55.00
a.		Horiz. pair, imperf. btwn.		
b.		Half used as ½p on cover		2,250.
c.		Imperf., pair	500.00	
		Nos. 14-18 (6)	605.00	442.50

Queen Victoria — A5

1879-80 Typo. Wmk. 1 ***Perf. 14***

19	A5	1p violet ('80)	80.00	37.50
a.		Diagonal half used as ½p on cover		1,100.
20	A5	2½p red brown	125.00	95.00

1882-90 Wmk. Crown and CA (2)

21	A5	½p green ('83)	5.50	*14.00*
22	A5	1p violet	100.00	32.50
a.		Half used as ½p on cover		800.00
23	A5	1p rose ('84)	10.00	*17.50*
24	A5	2½p red brown	125.00	55.00
25	A5	2½p ultra ('84)	20.00	17.50
26	A5	4p blue	350.00	55.00
27	A5	4p gray ('84)	11.00	4.00
28	A5	6p green ('83)	425.00	400.00
29	A5	6p brown org ('86)	25.00	*67.50*
30	A5	1sh violet ('90)	110.00	*200.00*
		Nos. 21-30 (10)	1,181.	*863.00*

Half of No. 22 Surcharged in Black or Violet

1883

31	A5	½p on half of 1p	*1,150.*	47.50
a.		Double surcharge		350.00
b.		Unsevered pair	*4,000.*	600.00
32	A5	½p on half of 1p (V)	*950.00*	50.00
a.		Double surcharge		350.00

Surcharge reads up or down.

NEW BRITAIN

'nü 'bri-tᵊn

LOCATION — South Pacific Ocean, northeast of New Guinea
GOVT. — Australian military government
AREA — 13,000 sq. mi. (approx.)
POP. — 50,600 (approx.)
CAPITAL — Rabaul

The island Neu-Pommern, a part of former German New Guinea, was captured during World War I by Australian troops and named New Britain. Following the war it was mandated to Australia and designated a part of the Mandated Territory of New Guinea. See German New Guinea, North West Pacific Islands and New Guinea.

12 Pence = 1 Shilling

Kaiser's Yacht "The Hohenzollern"
A3 A4

Stamps of German New Guinea, 1900, Surcharged

First Setting

Surcharge lines spaced 6mm on 1p-8p, 4mm on 1sh-5sh.

Perf. 14, 14½

1914, Oct. 17 **Unwmk.**

1 A3 1p on 3pf brown 425.00 *475.00*
2 A3 1p on 5pf green 50.00 *70.00*
3 A3 2p on 10pf car 55.00 *85.00*
4 A3 2p on 20pf ultra 55.00 *65.00*
a. "2d." dbl., "G.R.I." omitted 2,750.
b. Inverted surcharge 5,750.
5 A3 2½p on 10pf car 70.00 *150.00*
6 A3 2½p on 20pf ultra 80.00 *160.00*
a. Inverted surcharge
7 A3 3p on 25pf org & blk, *yel* 200.00 *290.00*
8 A3 3p on 30pf org & blk, *sal* 275.00 *325.00*
a. Double surcharge *5,250.* *5,000.*
b. Triple surcharge
9 A3 4p on 40pf lake & black 275.00 *350.00*
a. Double surcharge 1,250. *1,750.*
b. Inverted surcharge *5,750.*
c. "4d." omitted
10 A3 5p on 50pf pur & blk, *sal* 500.00 *750.00*
a. Double surcharge *5,750.*
11 A3 8p on 80pf lake & blk, *rose* 700.00 *950.00*
a. No period after "8d" *2,500.*
12 A4 1sh on 1m car 1,750. *2,500.*
13 A4 2sh on 2m blue 1,800. *2,750.*
14 A4 3sh on 3m blk vio 3,500. *4,500.*
15 A4 5sh on 5m slate & car 7,250. *8,750.*
a. No period after "I" — —

"G.R.I." stands for Georgius Rex Imperator.

Second Setting

Surcharge lines spaced 5mm on 1p-8p, 5½mm on 1sh-5sh.

1914, Dec. 16

16 A3 1p on 3pf brown 47.50 *57.500*
a. Double surcharge 500.00 *750.00*
b. "I" for "1" 490.00
c. "1" with straight top serif 85.00 100.00
d. Inverted surcharge 1,350. —
e. "4" for "1" 5,750.
f. Small "1" 225.00
g. Double surcharge, one inverted 2,250.
17 A3 1p on 5pf green 21.00 *35.00*
a. Double surcharge 1,500.
b. "G. I. R." 5,500. *5,750.*
c. "d" inverted 1,150.
d. No periods after "G R I" *3,500.*
e. Small "1" 125.00 190.00
f. "1d" double —
g. No period after "1d"
h. Triple surcharge
18 A3 2p on 10pf car 32.50 *50.00*
a. Double surcharge *6,250.* *6,250.*
b. Dbl. surch., one inverted 4,000.
c. Surcharged "G. I. R., 3d" *5,750.*
d. Surcharged "1d" 4,600. 4,000.
e. Period before "G" *4,000.*
f. No period after "2d" 150.00 210.00
g. Inverted surcharge
h. "2d" double, one inverted
j. Pair, #18, 20 *15,000.*
19 A3 2p on 20pf ultra 32.50 *50.00*
a. Double surcharge 1,150. *1,900.*
b. Double surch., one inverted 1,800. *2,100.*
c. "R" inverted *4,000.*
d. Surcharged "1d" 6,300. 6,300.
f. Inverted surcharge 4,000. *4,600.*
h. Pair, one without surcharge 11,000.
i. Pair, #19, 21 9,750. 11,500.
20 A3 2½p on 10pf car 190.00 290.00
21 A3 2½p on 20pf ultra 1,750. 2,100.
a. Double surcharge, one invtd.
b. "2½" triple
c. Surcharged "3d"
22 A3 3p on 25pf org & blk, *yel* 125.00 *175.00*
a. Double surcharge 4,600. *5,500.*
b. Inverted surcharge 4,600. *5,500.*
c. "G. R. I." only
d. "G. I. R."
e. Pair, one without surcharge *11,000.*
f. Surcharged "G. I. R., 5d"
23 A3 3p on 30pf org & blk, *sal* 100.00 *150.00*
a. Double surcharge 1,400. *2,000.*
b. Double surcharge, one invtd. 1,750. *2,200.*
c. "d" inverted
d. Surcharged "1d" 4,600. 5,750.
e. Triple surcharge
g. Double inverted surcharge 4,600. *5,500.*
h. Pair, one without surcharge *5,750.*
24 A3 4p on 40pf lake & blk 110.00 *175.00*
a. Double surcharge 1,150. —
b. Double surcharge, one invtd. 2,000. —
e. Surcharged "1d" 2,900.
f. "1" on "4"
25 A3 5p on 50pf pur & blk, *sal* 175.00 *210.00*
a. Double surcharge 1,750.
b. Double surcharge, one invtd. 4,000. *5,500.*
c. "5" omitted
d. Inverted surcharge 2,900.
e. Double inverted surcharge 4,600. *5,500.*
f. "G. I. R." 9,200.
26 A3 8p on 80pf lake & blk, *rose* 375.00 *450.00*
a. Double surcharge 3,100. *3,750.*
b. Double surcharge, one invtd. 3,100. *3,750.*
c. Triple surcharge 3,500. *4,000.*
d. No period after "8d"
e. Inverted surcharge 5,100. *5,750.*
f. Surcharged "3d" 9,750.
27 A4 1sh on 1m car 3,100. *4,300.*
28 A4 2sh on 2m bl 3,100. *4,900.*
a. Surcharged "5s"
b. Double surcharge
29 A4 3sh on 3m blk vio 5,500. *8,600.*
a. No periods after "R I"
b. "G.R.I." double *17,250.*
29C A4 5sh on 5m sl & car *25,000.* *30,000.*
d. No periods after "R I"
e. Surcharged "1s"

Nos. 18-19 Surcharged with Large "1"

1915, Jan.

29F A3 1(p) on 2p on 10pf carmine *40,000.* *20,000.*
29G A3 1(p) on 2p on 20pf ultramarine *30,000.* *12,000.*

Same Surcharge on Stamps of Marshall Islands

1914

30 A3 1p on 3pf brown 57.50 97.50
a. Inverted surcharge 3,100.
31 A3 1p on 5pf green 57.50 62.50
a. Double surcharge 1,400. *2,100.*
b. No period after "d"
c. Inverted surcharge 1,600.
32 A3 2p on 10pf car 19.00 30.00
a. Double surcharge 1,250. *2,100.*
b. Double surcharge, one invtd. 1,600. *2,100.*
c. Surcharge sideways 4,900.
d. No period after "2d"
e. No period after "G" 625.00
33 A3 2p on 20 pf ultra 19.00 30.00
a. No period after "d" 55.00 *92.50*
b. Double surcharge 1,600. 2,200.
c. Double surcharge, one invtd. 3,500. 3,750.
d. Inverted surcharge 4,300. 4,300.
e. "I" omitted
34 A3 3p on 25pf org & blk, *yel* 325.00 425.00
a. Double surcharge 1,600. *2,200.*
b. Double surcharge, one invtd. 1,600.
c. No period after "d" 575.00 800.00
d. Inverted surcharge 4,300.
35 A3 3p on 30pf org & blk, *sal* 375.00 450.00
a. No period after "d" 625.00 800.00
b. Inverted surcharge 2,900. 3,500.
c. Double surcharge 2,600.
d. Double surcharge, one invtd.
36 A3 4p on 40pf lake & blk 110.00 150.00
a. No period after "d" 290.00 *450.00*
b. Double surcharge 2,900. *3,500.*
c. "4d" omitted
d. "1d" on "4d"
e. No period after "R"
f. Inverted surcharge 3,750.
g. Surcharged "1d" 7,500.
37 A3 5p on 50pf pur & blk, *sal* 160.00 210.00
a. "d" omitted 1,600.
b. Double surcharge 4,600.
c. "5d" double
38 A3 8p on 80pf lake & blk, *rose* 575.00 425.00
a. Inverted surcharge 4,300.
b. Double surcharge 3,500.
c. Double surcharge, one invtd.
d. Triple surcharge 5,500.
39 A4 1sh on 1m car 2,200. *3,750.*
a. Double surcharge 13,750.
b. Dbl. surch., one with "s1" for "1s" 4,000. 5,500.
c. No period after "I" 4,000. 5,500.
40 A4 2sh on 2m blue 1,400. 2,600.
a. Double surcharge, one invtd. 12,500. *12,500.*
b. Double surcharge 13,750.
c. Large "S"
d. No period after "I" 2,900. *4,300.*
41 A4 3sh on 3m blk vio 4,000. *5,750.*
a. Double surcharge 15,000. 18,500.
b. No period after "I" 5,500.
c. No period after "R I"
d. Inverted surcharge
42 A4 5sh on 5m sl & car *8,000.* *10,250.*
a. Double surcharge, one invtd. *23,000.*

See Nos. 44-45.

A5

Surcharged in Black on Registration Label

1914 ***Perf. 12***

43 A5 3p black & red (Rabaul) 210.00 *225.00*
a. "Friedrich Wilhelmshaven" 200.00 *5250.00*
b. "Herbertshohe" 225.00 *575.00*
c. "Kawieng" 290.00 *550.00*
d. "Kieta" 400.00 *700.00*
e. "Manus" 225.00 *625.00*
f. Double surcharge (Rabaul) 5,750. *5,750.*
g. As "c," double surcharge *2,900.*
h. As "e," double surcharge *3,500.*
i. As "d," pair, one without surcharge *6,250.*
j. "Deulon" *17,500.* —
k. "Stephansort" *4,000.*

Nos. 43a, 43c and 43e exist with town name in letters with serifs. The varieties Deutsch-Neuguinea, Deutsch Neu-Guinea, etc., are known.

1915

44 A3 1(p) on 2p on 10pf 175. 190.
a. "1" double *9,250.*
b. "1" inverted *9,750.* *9,750.*
45 A3 1(p) on 2p on 20pf 3,500. 2,600.
a. "1" inverted *10,500.* *10,500.*

The stamps of Marshall Islands surcharged "G. R. I." and new values in British currency were all used in New Britain and are therefore listed here.

OFFICIAL STAMPS

Nos. 32-33 Surcharged with Large "1" — O1

German New Guinea Nos. 7-8 Surcharged

1915 **Unwmk.** ***Perf. 14***

O1 O1 1p on 3pf brown 30.00 *85.00*
a. Double surcharge 2,600.
O2 O1 1p on 5pf green 200.00 *325.00*

NEW BRUNSWICK

'nü 'brənz-ˌwik

LOCATION — Eastern Canada, bordering on the Bay of Fundy and the Gulf of St. Lawrence.
GOVT. — British Province
AREA — 27,985 sq. mi.
POP. — 285,594 (1871)
CAPITAL — Fredericton

At one time a part of Nova Scotia, New Brunswick became a separate province in 1784. Upon joining the Canadian Confederation in 1867 its postage stamps were superseded by those of Canada.

12 Pence = 1 Shilling
100 Cents = 1 Dollar (1860)

Crown of Great Britain and Heraldic Flowers of the United Kingdom
A1

1851 **Unwmk.** **Engr.** ***Imperf.***

Blue Paper

1 A1 3p red 2,400. 450.
On cover 800.
a. 3p dark red 2,750. 500.
On cover 900.
b. Half used as 1½p on cover *4,000.*
2 A1 6p olive yellow 4,500. 900.
On cover 1,200.
a. 6p orange yellow 4,500. 950.
On cover 1,200.
b. Half used as 3p on cover *3,000.*
c. Quarter used as 1½p on cover *25,000.*
d. 6p mustard yellow 5,750. 1,100.
3 A1 1sh brt red violet 12,500. 4,750.
On cover 9,250.
a. Half used as 6p on cover *20,000.*
b. Quarter used as 3p on cover *20,000.*
4 A1 1sh dull violet 16,000. 5,750.
On cover *13,750.*
a. Half used as 6p on cover *20,000.*
b. Quarter used as 3p on cover *20,000.*

The reprints are on stout white paper. The 3p is printed in orange and the 6p and 1sh in violet black. Value about $275 per set of 3.

Charles Connell — A2

1860 ***Perf. 12***

5 A2 5c brown *10,000.*
Pair, no gum *21,000.*

No. 5 was prepared for use but not issued.

The listed pair is the unique multiple of this issue. The value shown reflects a May, 2000 auction realization.

Most examples of No. 5 have creases or other faults. Value of an average example is about half that shown here.

Locomotive
A3

Victoria
A4

A5

A6

Steam and Sailing Ship — A7

Edward VII as Prince of Wales — A8

1860-63 **White Paper** ***Perf. 12***

6 A3 1c red lilac 32.50 32.50
Never hinged 70.00
On cover 200.00
On circular, single franking 300.00
a. 1c brown violet 57.50 45.00
Never hinged 120.00
On cover 250.00
On circular, single franking 350.00
b. Horiz. pair, imperf. vert. 500.00
Never hinged 850.00
7 A4 2c orange ('63) 12.50 12.50
Never hinged 35.00
On cover 600.00
a. Vertical pair, imperf. horiz. 525.00
Never hinged —
b. 2c deep orange 17.50 17.50
Never hinged 50.00
c. 2c yellow orange 17.50 17.50
Never hinged 50.00
8 A5 5c yellow green 18.00 18.00
Never hinged 40.00
On cover 37.50
a. 5c blue green 18.00 18.00
Never hinged 40.00
On cover 37.50
As "a," "elongated earring" plate flaw (Pos. 60) 100.00 100.00
Never hinged —
On cover 225.00
b. 5c olive green 120.00 30.00
Never hinged 275.00
On cover 37.50
9 A6 10c vermilion 40.00 40.00
Never hinged 75.00
On cover 80.00

a. Half used as 5c on cover — 675.00
b. Double impression 275.00 140.00
On cover —
10 A7 12½c blue 62.50 62.50
Never hinged 110.00
On cover 210.00
11 A8 17c black 40.00 40.00
Never hinged 75.00
On cover 4,500.
Nos. 6-11 (6) 205.50 205.50
Set, never hinged 390.00

NEW CALEDONIA

'nü ˌka-lə-'dō-nyə

LOCATION — Island in the South Pacific Ocean, east of Queensland, Australia
GOVT. — French Overseas Territory
AREA — 7,375 sq. mi.
POP. — 147,200 (est. 1984)
CAPITAL — Noumea

Dependencies of New Caledonia are the Loyalty Islands, Isle of Pines, Huon Islands and Chesterfield Islands.

100 Centimes = 1 Franc

Napoleon III — A1

1859 Unwmk. Litho. *Imperf.*
Without Gum

1 A1 10c black 210.00
On cover 18,000.

Fifty varieties. Counterfeits abound. See No. 315.

Type of French Colonies, 1877 Surcharged in Black:

Nos. 2-5

Nos. 6-7

1881-83

2 A8 5c on 40c red, *straw* ('82) 340.00 340.00
a. Inverted surcharge 1,250. 1,250.
3 A8 05c on 40c red, *straw* ('83) 24.00 24.00
On cover 700.00
4 A8 25c on 35c dp vio, *yel* 250.00 250.00
On cover 700.00
a. Inverted surcharge 700.00 700.00
5 A8 25c on 75c rose car, *rose* ('82) 325.00 325.00
On cover —
a. Inverted surcharge 850.00 850.00

1883-84

6 A8 5c on 40c red, *straw* ('84) 17.50 17.50
On cover 600.00
a. Inverted surcharge 14.00 14.00
7 A8 5c on 75c rose car, *rose* ('83) 35.00 35.00
On cover 600.00
a. Inverted surcharge 29.00 29.00

In type "a" surcharge, the narrower-spaced letters measure 14½mm, and an early printing of No. 4 measures 13½mm. Type "b" letters measure 18mm.

French Colonies No. 59 Surcharged in Black:

No. 8

Nos. 9-10

1886 *Perf. 14x13½*

8 A9 5c on 1fr 17.50 17.50
On cover 475.00
a. Inverted surcharge 26.00 26.00
9 A9 5c on 1fr 17.50 17.50
On cover 475.00

b. Inverted surcharge 40.00 40.00

French Colonies No. 29 Surcharged
Imperf

10 A8 5c on 1fr 8,500. 10,000.
On cover —

Types of French Colonies, 1877-86, Surcharged in Black:

Nos. 11, 13

No. 12

1891-92 *Imperf.*

11 A8 10c on 40c red, *straw* ('92) 27.50 27.50
On cover —
a. Inverted surcharge 27.50 27.50
b. Double surcharge 72.50 72.50
c. No period after "10c" 27.50 27.50

Perf. 14x13½

12 A9 10c on 30c brn, *bis* 18.00 18.00
On cover 300.00
a. Inverted surcharge 18.00 18.00
b. Double surcharge 45.00 45.00
c. Double surcharge, inverted 55.00 55.00
13 A9 10c on 40c red, *straw* ('92) 18.00 18.00
On cover 300.00
a. Inverted surcharge 18.00 18.00
b. No period after "10c" 18.00 18.00
c. Double surcharge 45.00 45.00
Nos. 11-13 (3) 63.50 63.50

Variety "double surcharge, one inverted" exists on Nos. 11-13. Value slightly higher than for "double surcharge."

Types of French Colonies, 1877-86, Handstamped in Black

g

1892 *Imperf.*

16 A8 20c red, *grn* 300.00 325.00
On cover —
17 A8 35c violet, *org* 62.50 62.50
On cover 500.00
18 A8 40c red, *straw* —
On cover —
19 A8 1fr bronz grn, *straw* 250.00 250.00
On cover —

The 1c, 2c, 4c and 75c of type A8 are believed not to have been officially made or actually used.

1892 *Perf. 14x13½*

23 A9 5c green, *grnsh* 14.00 12.50
On cover 300.00
24 A9 10c blk, *lavender* 100.00 57.50
On cover 300.00
25 A9 15c blue 85.00 42.50
On cover 375.00
26 A9 20c red, *grn* 82.50 45.00
On cover —
27 A9 25c yellow, *straw* 21.00 12.50
On cover 250.00
28 A9 25c black, *rose* 85.00 14.00
On cover 250.00
29 A9 30c brown, *bis* 62.50 52.50
On cover —
30 A9 35c violet, *org* 200.00 150.00
On cover —
32 A9 75c carmine, *rose* 175.00 140.00
On cover 375.00
33 A9 1fr bronz grn, *straw* 140.00 125.00
On cover —
Nos. 23-33 (10) 965.00 651.50

The note following No. 19 also applies to the 1c, 2c, 4c and 40c of type A9.

Surcharged in Blue or Black

h

1892-93 *Imperf.*

34 A8 10c on 1fr brnz grn, *straw* (Bl) 4,400. 3,750.
On cover —

Perf. 14x13½

35 A9 5c on 20c red, *grn* (Bk) 20.00 18.00
On cover 300.00
a. Inverted surcharge 100.00 85.00
b. Double surcharge inverted —
36 A9 5c on 75c car, *rose* (Bk) 17.50 12.50
On cover 300.00
a. Inverted surcharge 100.00 85.00
37 A9 5c on 75c car, *rose* (Bl) 14.00 10.00
On cover 300.00
a. Inverted surcharge 100.00 85.00
38 A9 10c on 1fr brnz grn, *straw* (Bk) 15.00 10.00
On cover 300.00
a. Inverted surcharge 500.00 425.00
39 A9 10c on 1fr brnz grn, *straw* (Bl) 17.50 14.00
On cover 300.00
a. Inverted surcharge 100.00 85.00
Nos. 35-39 (5) 84.00 64.50

Navigation and Commerce — A12

1892-1904 Typo. *Perf. 14x13½*
Name of Colony in Blue or Carmine

40 A12 1c black, *blue* .70 .70
On cover or postcard 25.00
41 A12 2c brown, *buff* 1.40 1.10
On cover or postcard 25.00
42 A12 4c claret, *lav* 1.90 1.50
On cover or postcard 25.00
43 A12 5c green, *grnsh* 2.50 1.40
On cover 50.00
44 A12 5c yellow green ('00) 2.00 1.25
On cover 50.00
45 A12 10c blk, *lavender* 7.25 4.00
On cover 50.00
46 A12 10c rose red ('00) 7.75 1.50
On cover 40.00
47 A12 15c bl, quadrille paper 21.00 3.00
On cover 40.00
48 A12 15c gray ('00) 11.50 1.50
On cover 40.00
49 A12 20c red, *grn* 14.00 8.50
On cover —
50 A12 25c black, *rose* 18.00 5.75
On cover —
51 A12 25c blue ('00) 17.00 10.00
On cover 45.00
52 A12 30c brown, *bis* 18.00 10.00
On cover —
53 A12 40c red, *straw* 18.50 10.50
On cover —
54 A12 50c carmine, *rose* 55.00 25.00
On cover 100.00
55 A12 50c brn, *az* (name in car) ('00) 85.00 72.50
On cover —
56 A12 50c brn, *az* (name in bl) ('04) 42.50 36.00
On cover —
57 A12 75c violet, *org* 29.00 21.00
On cover 125.00
58 A12 1fr bronz grn, *straw* 35.00 20.00
On cover —
Nos. 40-58 (19) 388.00 235.20

Perf. 13½x14 stamps are counterfeits.
For overprints and surcharges see Nos. 59-87, 117-121.

Covers: Values for Nos. 40-42 are for covers or postcards with more than one stamp used to make the rate. This also applies to Nos. 66-68, 81-84, 88-90.

Nos. 41-42, 52, 57-58, 53 Surcharged in Black:

j

k

1900-01

59 A12 (h) 5c on 2c ('01) 18.00 14.00
On cover 95.00
a. Double surcharge 125.00 125.00
b. Inverted surcharge 110.00 110.00
60 A12 (h) 5c on 4c 3.50 3.50
On cover 80.00
a. Inverted surcharge 72.50 72.50
b. Double surcharge 80.00 80.00
61 A12 (j) 15c on 30c 4.25 3.50
On cover 80.00
a. Inverted surcharge 57.50 57.50
b. Double surcharge 62.50 62.50
62 A12 (j) 15c on 75c ('01) 17.00 14.00
On cover 80.00
a. Pair, one without surcharge —
b. Inverted surcharge 110.00 110.00
c. Double surcharge 125.00 125.00
63 A12 (j) 15c on 1fr ('01) 21.00 18.00
On cover 95.00
a. Double surcharge 150.00 150.00
b. Inverted surcharge 140.00 140.00
Nos. 59-63 (5) 63.75 53.00

1902

64 A12 (k) 5c on 30c 8.50 7.25
On cover —
a. Inverted surcharge 37.50 35.00
65 A12 (k) 15c on 40c 8.50 7.25
On cover —
a. Inverted surcharge 37.50 35.00

Jubilee Issue

Stamps of 1892-1900 Overprinted in Blue, Red, Black or Gold

1903

66 A12 1c blk, *lil bl* (Bl) 1.75 1.75
On cover or postcard 45.00
a. Inverted overprint 225.00 225.00
67 A12 2c brown, *buff* (Bl) 4.00 3.50
On cover or postcard 45.00
68 A12 4c claret, *lav* (Bl) 5.25 4.00
On cover or postcard 45.00
a. Double overprint 290.00 275.00
69 A12 5c dk grn, *grnsh* (R) 5.25 3.50
On cover 125.00
70 A12 5c yellow green (R) 8.50 6.75
On cover 125.00
71 A12 10c blk, *lav* (R) 14.00 12.00
On cover 125.00
72 A12 10c blk, *lav* (double G & Bk) 8.50 6.75
On cover 125.00
73 A12 15c gray (R) 11.50 6.75
On cover —
74 A12 20c red, *grn* (Bl) 16.00 13.50
On cover —
75 A12 25c blk, *rose* (Bl) 16.00 14.00
On cover 100.00
a. Double overprint 225.00
76 A12 30c brown, *bis* (R) 20.00 19.00
On cover —
77 A12 40c red, *straw* (Bl) 27.50 24.00
On cover —
78 A12 50c car, *rose* (Bl) 45.00 35.00
On cover 250.00
a. Pair, one without overprint
79 A12 75c vio, *org* (Bk) 65.00 57.50
On cover 500.00
a. Dbl. ovpt. in blk and red 400.00
80 A12 1fr brnz grn, *straw* (Bl) 100.00 85.00
On cover —
a. Dbl. ovpt., one in red 400.00 375.00
Nos. 66-80 (15) 348.25 293.00

With Additional Surcharge of New Value in Blue

81 A12 1c on 2c #67 1.25 1.25
On cover or postcard 50.00
a. Numeral double 77.50 77.50
b. Numeral only 290.00
82 A12 2c on 4c #68 2.40 2.40
On cover or postcard 50.00
83 A12 4c on 5c #69 1.75 1.75
On cover or postcard 50.00
a. Small "4" 525.00 525.00
84 A12 4c on 5c #70 2.10 2.10
On cover or postcard 50.00
a. Pair, one without numeral
85 A12 10c on 15c #73 2.10 2.10
On cover 125.00
86 A12 15c on 20c #74 2.90 2.90
On cover 125.00
87 A12 20c on 25c #75 6.00 6.00
On cover —
Nos. 81-87 (7) 18.50 18.50

50 years of French occupation.
Surcharge on Nos. 81-83, 85-86 is horizontal, reading down.
There are three types of numeral on No. 83. The numeral on No. 84 is identical with that of No. 83a except that its position is upright.
Nos. 66-87 are known with "I" of "TENAIRE" missing.

Kagu
A16

Landscape
A17

Ship — A18

1905-28 Typo. *Perf. 14x13½*

88 A16 1c blk, *green* .25 .20
On cover or postcard 20.00
89 A16 2c red brown .25 .20
On cover or postcard 20.00
90 A16 4c bl, *org* .40 .35
On cover or postcard 20.00

91 A16 5c pale green .40 .35
On cover 32.50
92 A16 5c dl bl ('21) .35 .20
On cover 32.50
93 A16 10c carmine 1.25 .90
On cover 32.50
94 A16 10c green ('21) .65 .55
On cover 32.50
95 A16 10c red, *pink* ('25) .70 .55
On cover 32.50
96 A16 15c violet .65 .50
On cover 45.00
97 A17 20c brown .40 .35
On cover 45.00
98 A17 25c blue, *grn* .85 .45
On cover 32.50
99 A17 25c red, *yel* ('21) .50 .50
On cover 32.50
100 A17 30c brn, *org* .95 .65
On cover 45.00
101 A17 30c dp rose ('21) 1.75 1.75
On cover 50.00
102 A17 30c org ('25) .40 .35
On cover 45.00
103 A17 35c blk, *yellow* .55 .50
On cover 45.00
104 A17 40c car, *grn* .95 .85
On cover 50.00
105 A17 45c vio brn, *lav* .55 .55
On cover 45.00
106 A17 50c car, *org* 2.40 2.10
107 A17 50c dk bl ('21) 1.25 1.25
108 A17 50c gray ('25) .70 .70
109 A17 65c dp bl ('28) .55 .55
110 A17 75c ol grn, *straw* .50 .35
111 A17 75c bl, *bluish* ('25) .55 .55
112 A17 75c violet ('27) .80 .80
113 A18 1fr bl, *yel grn* 1.00 .55
114 A18 1fr dp bl ('25) 1.50 1.40
115 A18 2fr car, *bl* 3.00 1.75
116 A18 5fr blk, *straw* 5.75 5.25
Nos. 88-116 (29) 29.80 25.00

See Nos. 311, 317a. For surcharges see Nos. 122-135, B1-B3, Q1-Q3.

Nos. 96, 98, 103, 106, 113 and 115, pasted on cardboard and handstamped "TRESORIER PAYEUR DE LA NOUVELLE CALEDONIE" were used as emergency currency in 1914.

Stamps of 1892-1904 Surcharged in Carmine or Black

1912

Spacing between figures of surcharge 1.5mm (5c), 2mm (10c)

117 A12 5c on 15c gray (C) .70 .70
On cover 60.00
a. Inverted surcharge 160.00 160.00
118 A12 5c on 20c red, *grn* 1.00 1.00
On cover 60.00
119 A12 5c on 30c brn, *bis* (C) 1.00 1.00
On cover 60.00
120 A12 10c on 40c red, *straw* 1.90 1.90
On cover 60.00
121 A12 10c on 50c brn, *az* (C) 1.90 1.90
On cover 60.00
Nos. 117-121 (5) 6.50 6.50

Spacing between figures of surcharge 2.25mm (5c), 2.75mm (10c)

117b A12 5c on 15c gray (C) 140.00 140.00
c. Inverted surcharge 3,900. 3,900.
118a A12 5c on 20c red, *grn* 110.00 110.00
119a A12 5c on 30c brn, *bis* (C) 225.00 225.00
120a A12 10c on 40c red, *straw* 150.00 150.00
121a A12 10c on 50c brn, *az* (C) 190.00 190.00
Nos. 117b-121a (5) 815.00 815.00

No. 96 Surcharged in Brown

1918
122 A16 5c on 15c violet 1.40 1.40
a. Double surcharge 57.50 57.50
b. Inverted surcharge 35.00 35.00

The color of the surcharge on No. 122 varies from red to dark brown.

No. 96 Surcharged

1922
123 A16 5c on 15c vio (R) .60 .60
a. Double surcharge 57.50 57.50

Stamps and Types of 1905-28 Surcharged New Value and Bars in Red or Black

1924-27
124 A16 25c on 15c vio .45 .45
a. Double surcharge 57.50
125 A18 25c on 2fr car, *bl* .55 .55
126 A18 25c on 5fr blk, *straw* .55 .55
a. Double surcharge 90.00 90.00
127 A17 60c on 75c bl grn (R) .50 .50
128 A17 65c on 45c red brn 1.60 1.60
129 A17 85c on 45c red brn 1.60 1.60
130 A17 90c on 75c dp rose .70 .70
131 A18 1.25fr on 1fr dp bl (R) .65 .65
132 A18 1.50fr on 1fr dp bl, *bl* 1.10 1.10
133 A18 3fr on 5fr red vio 1.60 1.60
134 A18 10fr on 5fr ol, *lav* (R) 5.75 5.75
135 A18 20fr on 5fr vio rose, *org* 11.50 11.50
Nos. 124-135 (12) 26.55 26.55

Issue years: Nos. 125-127, 1924. Nos. 124, 128-129, 1925. Nos. 131, 134, 1926. Nos. 130, 132-133, 135, 1927.

Bay of Palétuviers Point A19

Landscape with Chief's House A20

Admiral de Bougainville and Count de La Pérouse — A21

1928-40 **Typo.**
136 A19 1c brn vio & ind .20 .20
137 A19 2c dk brn & yel grn .20 .20
137B A19 3c brn vio & ind .20 .20
138 A19 4c org & Prus grn .20 .20
139 A19 5c Prus bl & dp ol .35 .35
140 A19 10c gray lil & dk brn .20 .20
141 A19 15c yel brn & dp bl .35 .35
142 A19 20c brn red & dk brn .35 .35
143 A19 25c dk grn & dk brn .50 .35
144 A20 30c gray grn & bl grn .35 .35
145 A20 35c blk & brt vio .50 .50
146 A20 40c brt red & olvn .35 .35
147 A20 45c dp bl & red org 1.10 .95
147A A20 45c bl grn & dl grn .80 .80
148 A20 50c vio & brn .50 .50
149 A20 55c vio bl & car 2.75 1.75
150 A20 60c vio bl & car .50 .50
151 A20 65c org brn & bl .95 .80
152 A20 70c dp rose & brn .35 .35
153 A20 75c Prus bl & ol gray 1.10 .70
154 A20 80c red brn & grn .80 .65
155 A20 85c grn & brn 1.40 .80
156 A20 90c dp red & brt red .95 .55
157 A20 90c ol grn & rose red .70 .70
158 A21 1fr dp ol & sal red 5.50 3.50
159 A21 1fr rose red & dk car 1.75 1.25
160 A21 1fr brn red & grn .80 .80
161 A21 1.10fr dp grn & brn 9.75 8.75
162 A21 1.25fr brn red & grn .85 .85
163 A21 1.25fr rose red & dk car .80 .80
164 A21 1.40fr dk bl & red org .95 .95
165 A21 1.50fr dp bl & bl .55 .55
166 A21 1.60fr dp grn & brn 1.10 1.10
167 A21 1.75fr dk bl & red org .65 .65
168 A21 1.75fr violet bl .95 .80
169 A21 2fr red org & brn .55 .50
170 A21 2.25fr vio bl .80 .80
171 A21 2.50fr brn & lt brn 1.25 1.25
172 A21 3fr mag & brn .50 .50
173 A21 5fr dk bl & brn .80 .80
174 A21 10fr vio & brn, *pnksh* 1.00 1.00
175 A21 20fr red & brn, *yel* 2.25 2.25
Nos. 136-175 (42) 46.45 39.75

The 35c in Prussian green and dark green without overprint is listed as Wallis and Futuna No. 53a.

Issue years: 35c, 70c, 85c, #162, 167, 1933; 55c, 80c, #159, 168, 1938; #157, 163, 2.25fr, 1939; 3c, 1.40fr, 1.60fr, 2.50fr, 147A, 160, 1940; others, 1928.

For overprints see #180-207, 217-251, Q4-Q6.

Common Design Types pictured following the introduction.

Colonial Exposition Issue
Common Design Types

1931 **Engr.** ***Perf. 12½***

Country Name Typo. in Black

176 CD70 40c dp green 4.50 4.50
177 CD71 50c violet 4.50 4.50
178 CD72 90c red orange 4.50 4.50
179 CD73 1.50fr dull blue 4.50 4.50
Nos. 176-179 (4) 18.00 18.00

Paris-Nouméa Flight Issue
Regular Issue of 1928 Overprinted:

1932 ***Perf. 14x13½***
180 A20 40c brt red & olvn 400.00 400.00
181 A20 50c vio & brn 400.00 400.00

Arrival on Apr. 5, 1932 at Nouméa, of the French aviators, Verneilh, Dévé and Munch.

Excellent forgeries exist of #180-181.

Types of 1928-33 Overprinted in Black or Red:

1933
182 A19 1c red vio & dl bl 5.00 5.00
183 A19 2c dk brn & yel grn 5.00 5.00
184 A19 4c dl org & Prus bl 5.00 5.00
185 A19 5c Prus grn & ol (R) 5.00 5.00
186 A19 10c gray lil & dk brn (R) 5.00 5.00
187 A19 15c yel brn & dp bl (R) 5.00 5.00
188 A19 20c brn red & dk brn 5.00 5.00
189 A19 25c dk grn & dk brn (R) 5.00 5.00
190 A20 30c gray grn & bl grn (R) 5.00 5.00
191 A20 35c blk & lt vio 5.00 5.00
192 A20 40c brt red & olvn 5.00 5.00
193 A20 45c dp bl & red org 5.00 5.00
194 A20 50c vio & brn 5.00 5.00
195 A20 70c dp rose & brn 6.25 6.25
196 A20 75c Prus bl & ol gray (R) 6.25 6.25
197 A20 85c grn & brn 6.25 6.25
198 A20 90c dp red & brt red 7.00 7.00
199 A21 1fr dp ol & sal red 7.00 7.00
200 A21 1.25fr brn red & grn 7.00 7.00
201 A21 1.50fr dp bl & bl (R) 7.00 7.00
202 A21 1.75fr dk bl & red org 7.00 7.00
203 A21 2fr red org & brn 7.00 7.00
204 A21 3fr mag & brn 7.00 7.00
205 A21 5fr dk bl & brn (R) 7.00 7.00
206 A21 10fr vio & brn, *pnksh* 8.00 8.00
207 A21 20fr red & brn, *yel* 8.00 8.00
Nos. 182-207 (26) 155.75 155.75

1st anniv., Paris-Noumea flight. Plane centered on Nos. 190-207.

Paris International Exposition Issue
Common Design Types

1937 **Engr.** ***Perf. 13***
208 CD74 20c dp vio 1.75 1.75
209 CD75 30c dk grn 1.75 1.75
210 CD76 40c car rose 1.75 1.75
211 CD77 50c dk brn & bl 1.75 1.75
212 CD78 90c red 1.75 1.75
213 CD79 1.50fr ultra 1.75 1.75
Nos. 208-213 (6) 10.50 10.50

Colonial Arts Exhibition Issue
Souvenir Sheet
Common Design Type

1937 ***Imperf.***
214 CD78 3fr sepia 21.00 *25.00*

New York World's Fair Issue
Common Design Type

1939 ***Perf. 12½x12***
215 CD82 1.25fr car lake 1.25 1.25
216 CD82 2.25fr ultra 1.25 1.25

SEMI-POSTAL STAMPS

No. 93 Surcharged

1915 **Unwmk.** ***Perf. 14x13½***
B1 A16 10c + 5c carmine 1.25 1.25
a. Inverted surcharge 57.50 57.50
b. Cross omitted 35.00 35.00

Regular Issue of 1905 Surcharged

1917
B2 A16 10c + 5c rose .80 .80
a. Double surcharge 65.00 45.00
B3 A16 15c + 5c violet .80 .80

Curie Issue
Common Design Type

1938, Oct. 24 ***Perf. 13***
B4 CD80 1.75fr + 50c brt ultra 11.00 11.00

French Revolution Issue
Common Design Type

1939, July 5 **Photo.**

Name and Value Typo. in Black

B5 CD83 45c + 25c green 9.25 9.25
B6 CD83 70c + 30c brown 9.25 9.25
B7 CD83 90c + 35c red org 9.25 9.25
B8 CD83 1.25fr + 1fr rose pink 9.25 9.25
B9 CD83 2.25fr + 2fr blue 9.25 9.25
Nos. B5-B9 (5) 46.25 46.25

AIR POST STAMPS

Seaplane Over Pacific Ocean
AP1

1938-40 Unwmk. Engr. *Perf. 13*

C1	AP1	65c deep violet	.80	.55
a.		"65c" omitted	150.00	
C2	AP1	4.50fr red	1.25	1.10
C3	AP1	7fr dk bl grn ('40)	.80	.55
C4	AP1	9fr ultra	2.50	2.25
C5	AP1	20fr dk orange ('40)	1.75	1.50
C6	AP1	50fr black ('40)	2.90	2.50
		Nos. C1-C6 (6)	10.00	8.45

AIR POST SEMI-POSTAL STAMP

French Revolution Issue
Common Design Type
Unwmk.
1939, July 5 Photo. *Perf. 13*
Name and Value Typo. in Orange

CB1	CD83	4.50fr + 4fr brn blk	25.00	25.00

POSTAGE DUE STAMPS

For a short time in 1894, 5, 10, 15, 20, 25 and 30c postage stamps (Nos. 43, 45, 47, 49, 50 and 52) were overprinted with a "T" in an inverted triangle and used as Postage Due stamps.

French Colonies Postage Due Stamps Overprinted in Carmine, Blue or Silver

1903 Unwmk. *Imperf.*

J1	D1	5c blue (C)	2.25	2.25
J2	D1	10c brown (C)	8.50	6.75
J3	D1	15c yel grn (C)	17.00	6.50
J4	D1	30c carmine (Bl)	13.50	10.50
J5	D1	50c violet (Bl)	50.00	15.00
J6	D1	60c brn, *buff* (Bl)	225.00	60.00
J7	D1	1fr rose, *buff* (S)	27.50	17.50
J8	D1	2fr red brn (Bl)	1,000.	1,000.
		Nos. J1-J8 (8)	1,343.	1,118.

Nos. J1 to J8 are known with the "I" in "TENAIRE" missing.
Fifty years of French occupation.

Men Poling Boat — D2

Malayan Sambar — D3

1906 Typo. *Perf. 13½x14*

J9	D2	5c ultra, *azure*	.50	.50
J10	D2	10c vio brn, *buff*	.50	.50
J11	D2	15c grn, *greenish*	.70	.70
J12	D2	20c blk, *yellow*	.70	.70
J13	D2	30c carmine	1.10	1.10
J14	D2	50c ultra, *buff*	1.75	1.75
J15	D2	60c brn, *azure*	1.25	1.25
J16	D2	1fr dk grn, *straw*	1.90	1.90
		Nos. J9-J16 (8)	8.40	8.40

Type of 1906 Issue Surcharged

1926-27

J17	D2	2fr on 1fr vio	4.50	4.50
J18	D2	3fr on 1fr org brn	4.50	4.50

1928 Typo.

J19	D3	2c sl bl & dp brn	.20	.20
J20	D3	4c brn red & bl grn	.35	.35
J21	D3	5c red org & bl blk	.50	.50
J22	D3	10c mag & Prus bl	.50	.50
J23	D3	15c dl grn & scar	.50	.50
J24	D3	20c mar & ol grn	.75	.75
J25	D3	25c bis brn & sl bl	.55	.55
J26	D3	30c bl grn & ol grn	.75	.75
J27	D3	50c lt brn & dk red	1.00	1.00
J28	D3	60c mag & brt rose	1.00	1.00
J29	D3	1fr dl bl & Prus grn	1.40	1.40
J30	D3	2fr dk red & ol grn	1.60	1.60
J31	D3	3fr violet & brn	2.00	2.00
		Nos. J19-J31 (13)	11.10	11.10

PARCEL POST STAMPS

Type of Regular Issue of 1905-28 Surcharged or Overprinted

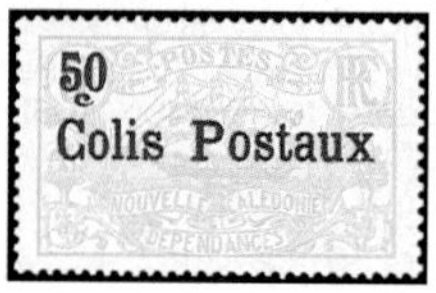

1926 Unwmk. *Perf. 14x13½*

Q1	A18	50c on 5fr olive, *lav*	.90	.90
Q2	A18	1fr deep blue	1.40	1.40
Q3	A18	2fr car, *bluish*	1.60	1.60
		Nos. Q1-Q3 (3)	3.90	3.90

Regular Issue of 1928 Overprinted:

1930

Q4	A20	50c violet & brown	.90	.90
Q5	A21	1fr dp ol & sal red	1.40	1.40
Q6	A21	2fr red org & brn	1.60	1.60
		Nos. Q4-Q6 (3)	3.90	3.90

NEWFOUNDLAND

'nü-fənˌdˌ-lənd

LOCATION — Island in the Atlantic Ocean off the coast of Canada, and Labrador, a part of the mainland
GOVT. — British Dominion
AREA — 42,734 sq. mi.
POP. — 321,177 (1945)
CAPITAL — St. John's

Newfoundland was a self-governing Dominion of the British Empire from 1855 to 1933, when it became a Crown Colony. In 1949 it united with Canada.

12 Pence = 1 Shilling
100 Cents = 1 Dollar (1866)

PRE-STAMP POSTAL MARKINGS

Crowned Circle handstamp type VIII is pictured in the Crowned Circle Handstamps and Great Britain Used Abroad section.

St. John's

1846-57

A1	VIII	"St. John's" crowned circle handstamp in red, on cover	1,050.

Issued under British Administration

Values for unused stamps are for examples with original gum as defined in the catalogue introduction. However, very fine examples of Nos. 2-7, 9, 11, 12, 13 and 15 without gum are often traded at values very close to those for examples with original gum.

Watermark

Wmk. 224 Coat of Arms

Crown of Great Britain and Heraldic Flowers of the United Kingdom — A1

Rose, Thistle and Shamrock — A3

A2

A4

A5

A6

A7

A8

1857 Unwmk. Engr. *Imperf.*
Thick Porous Wove Paper with Mesh

1	A1	1p brown vio	90.00	*150.00*
		Never hinged	150.00	
		On cover		6,000.
a.		Half used as ½p on cover		*12,500.*
2	A2	2p scarlet ver	*12,500.*	4,500.
		On cover		*13,000.*
a.		Vert. half used as 1p on cover		*16,000.*
3	A3	3p green	400.00	400.00
		On cover		4,000.
4	A4	4p scarlet ver	*8,500.*	3,000.
		On cover		7,500.
a.		Half used as 2p on cover		*17,500.*
5	A1	5p brown vio	250.00	*325.00*
		Never hinged	500.00	
		On cover		8,000.
6	A5	6p scarlet ver	*17,500.*	4,000.
		On cover		*24,000.*
7	A6	6½p scarlet ver	3,500.	*3,000.*
		On cover		*10,000.*
8	A7	8p scarlet ver	325.00	*400.00*
		Never hinged	525.00	
		On cover		*17,500.*
a.		Half used as 4p on cover		6,000.
9	A8	1sh scarlet ver	*20,000.*	8,000.
		On cover		*30,000.*
a.		Half used as 6p on cover		*16,000.*

1860
Thin to Thick Wove Paper, No Mesh

11	A2	2p orange	325.00	*400.00*
		On cover		—
11A	A3	3p green	65.00	*100.00*
		Never hinged	110.00	
		On cover		2,000.
12	A4	4p orange	2,500.	1,000.
		On cover		6,000.
b.		Half used as 2p on cover		*12,500.*
12A	A1	5p vio brown	65.00	*125.00*
		Never hinged	110.00	
		On cover		7,000.
13	A5	6p orange	3,250.	800.00
		On cover		*24,000.*
15	A8	1sh orange	*25,000.*	10,000.
		On cover		—
b.		Half used as 6p on cover		*16,000.*

A 6½p orange exists as a souvenir item.
A 1sh exists in orange on horizontally or vertically laid paper. Most authorities consider these to be proofs. Value, $10,500.

1861-62

15A	A1	1p vio brown	140.00	*200.00*
		Never hinged	350.00	
		On cover		—
c.		1p chocolate brown	175.00	*275.00*
		Never hinged	400.00	
		On cover		—
16	A1	1p reddish brown	*8,000.*	
17	A2	2p rose	140.00	*150.00*
		Never hinged	350.00	
		On cover		—
18	A4	4p rose	30.00	*60.00*
		Never hinged	37.50	
		On cover		5,000.
a.		Half used as 2p on cover		—
19	A1	5p reddish brown	55.00	*65.00*
		Never hinged	82.50	
		On cover		*6,000.*
a.		5p orange brown	65.00	*80.00*
		Never hinged	100.00	
		On cover		*6,500.*

b.	5p chocolate brown	80.00	*105.00*
	Never hinged	140.00	
	On cover		*7,000.*
20	A5 6p rose	20.00	*55.00*
	Never hinged	22.50	
	On cover		*9,250.*
a.	Half used as 3p on cover		*8,500.*
21	A6 6½p rose	65.00	*275.00*
	Never hinged	110.00	
	On cover		*7,000.*
22	A7 8p rose	65.00	*275.00*
	Never hinged	110.00	
	On cover		—
23	A8 1sh rose	32.50	*275.00*
	Never hinged	40.00	
	On cover		—
a.	Half used as 6p on cover		*20,000.*

Some sheets of Nos. 11-23 are known with the papermaker's watermark "STACEY WISE 1858" in large capitals. Values unused and used about 25% more than values shown, except about 50% more for unused Nos. 12 and 13.

No. 16 was prepared but not issued.

False cancellations are found on Nos. 1, 3, 5, 8, 11, 11A, 12A and 17-23.

Forgeries exist of most or all of Nos. 1-23.

Codfish — A9

Harp Seal — A10

Prince Albert — A11

Victoria — A12

Fishing Ship — A13

Victoria — A14

1865-94 ***Perf. 12***

White Paper(#24, 27, 28)

Thin Yellowish Paper (#25-26, 29-31)

24	A9 2c green	65.00	25.00
	Never hinged	150.00	
	On cover		375.00
a.	Thin yellowish paper	80.00	32.50
	Never hinged	190.00	
	On cover		500.00
b.	Half used as 1c on cover		*3,750.*
25	A10 5c brown	450.00	300.00
	Never hinged	—	
	On cover		750.00
a.	Half used as 2c on cover		*4,500.*
26	A10 5c black ('68)	250.00	130.00
	Never hinged	575.00	
	On cover		400.00
27	A11 10c black	250.00	50.00
	Never hinged	600.00	
	On cover		300.00
a.	Thin yellowish paper	300.00	95.00
	Never hinged	700.00	
	On cover		275.00
b.	Half used as 5c on cover		*4,000.*
28	A12 12c pale red brn	47.50	40.00
	Never hinged	82.50	
	On cover		120.00
a.	Thin yellowish paper	425.00	160.00
	Never hinged	—	
	On cover		210.00
b.	Half used as 6c on cover		*2,500.*
29	A12 12c brn, *white* ('94)	47.50	40.00
	Never hinged	82.50	
	On cover		110.00
30	A13 13c orange	175.00	100.00
	Never hinged	400.00	
	On cover		350.00
31	A14 24c blue, thin transluscent paper	40.00	25.00
	Never hinged	85.00	
	On cover		450.00
a.	Thicker white paper ('70)	325.00	250.00
	Never hinged	—	
	On cover		—

See Nos. 38, 40.

Edward VII as Prince of Wales A15

Queen Victoria A16

1868-94

32	A15 1c violet	60.00	50.00
	Never hinged	130.00	
	On cover		400.00
32A	A15 1c brown lilac (re-engr. '71)	90.00	65.00
	Never hinged	275.00	
	On cover		375.00
33	A16 3c ver ('70)	325.00	160.00
	Never hinged	—	
	On cover		400.00
34	A16 3c blue ('73)	300.00	60.00
	Never hinged	700.00	
	On cover		190.00
35	A16 6c dull rose ('70)	17.50	12.50
	Never hinged	30.00	
	On cover		50.00
a.	6c bright rose	30.00	18.00
	Never hinged	60.00	
	On cover		70.00
36	A16 6c car lake ('94)	30.00	17.50
	Never hinged	57.50	
	On cover		42.50

In the re-engraved 1c the top of the letters "N" and "F" are about ½mm from the ribbon with "ONE CENT." In No. 32 they are fully 1mm away. There are many small differences in the engraving.

1876-79 ***Rouletted***

37	A15 1c brn lilac ('77)	130.00	45.00
	Never hinged	290.00	
	On cover		250.00
38	A9 2c green ('79)	150.00	45.00
	Never hinged	325.00	
	On cover		225.00
39	A16 3c blue ('77)	325.00	12.50
	Never hinged	700.00	
	On cover		87.50
40	A10 5c blue	200.00	12.50
	Never hinged	360.00	
	On cover		62.50

A17

A19

A18

A20

1880-96 *Perf. 12*

No.	Type	Description	Unused	Used
41	A17	1c violet brown	37.50	10.00
		Never hinged	82.50	
		On cover		45.00
42	A17	1c gray brown	37.50	10.00
		Never hinged	82.50	
		On cover		45.00
43	A17	1c brown ('96)	75.00	45.00
		Never hinged	140.00	
		On cover	75.00	65.00
44	A17	1c deep green ('87)	16.00	3.25
		Never hinged	24.00	
		On cover		17.50
a.		1c gray green	19.00	3.50
		Never hinged	30.00	
		On cover		17.50
45	A17	1c green ('97)	16.00	4.00
		Never hinged	24.00	
		On cover		25.00
a.		1c yellow green	19.00	*6.00*
		Never hinged	27.50	
		On cover		25.00
46	A19	2c yellow green	37.50	12.00
		Never hinged	90.00	
		On cover		40.00
47	A19	2c green ('96)	65.00	22.50
		Never hinged	125.00	
		On cover		45.00
48	A19	2c red org ('87)	25.00	8.00
		Never hinged	40.00	
		On cover		42.50
a.		Imperf., pair	260.00	
		Never hinged	410.00	
b.		2c orange	25.00	8.00
		Never hinged	40.00	
		On cover		42.50
49	A18	3c blue	37.50	5.00
		Never hinged	70.00	
		On cover		14.00
a.		3c pale blue	42.50	5.50
		Never hinged	92.50	
		On cover		15.00
b.		3c deep blue	40.00	5.00
		Never hinged	80.00	
		On cover		15.00
51	A18	3c umber brn ('87)	32.50	4.00
		Never hinged	57.50	
		On cover		10.50
a.		3c brown	35.00	4.25
		Never hinged	65.00	
		On cover		15.00
52	A18	3c vio brown ('96)	95.00	75.00
		Never hinged	175.00	
		On cover		100.00
53	A20	5c pale blue	325.00	8.00
		Never hinged	775.00	
		On cover		35.00
54	A20	5c dark blue ('87)	125.00	6.50
		Never hinged	275.00	
		On cover		30.00
55	A20	5c bright bl ('94)	37.50	6.00
		Never hinged	75.00	
		On cover		17.50

Newfoundland Dog — A21

Schooner — A22

1887-96

No.	Type	Description	Unused	Used
56	A21	½c rose red	8.00	6.00
		Never hinged	12.00	
		On cover		50.00
a.		½c deep rose red	10.00	7.50
		Never hinged	15.00	
		On cover		55.00
57	A21	½c orange red ('96)	60.00	40.00
		Never hinged	100.00	
		On cover		100.00
58	A21	½c black ('94)	8.00	6.00
		Never hinged	12.00	
		On cover		50.00
59	A22	10c black	100.00	65.00
		Never hinged	160.00	
		On cover		140.00

Queen Victoria — A23

1890

No.	Type	Description	Unused	Used
60	A23	3c slate	20.00	1.50
		Never hinged	52.50	
		On cover		6.00
a.		3c gray lilac	24.00	1.50
		Never hinged	60.00	
		On cover		8.00
b.		3c brown lilac	40.00	1.50
		Never hinged	97.50	
		On cover		15.00
c.		3c lilac	24.00	1.50
		Never hinged	60.00	
		On cover		7.50
d.		3c slate violet	60.00	2.50
		Never hinged	140.00	
		On cover		12.00
e.		Vert. pair, imperf. horiz.	625.00	
		Never hinged	1,400.	

Examples of No. 60 on red tinted paper are from a recovered consignment that fell into the sea. Value, used $4.

For surcharges see Nos. 75-77.

Victoria — A24

Cabot (John?) — A25

Cape Bonavista A26

Caribou Hunting A27

Mining — A28

Logging — A29

Fishing — A30

Cabot's Ship "Matthew" A31

Willow Ptarmigan A32

Seals — A33

Salmon Fishing — A34

Colony Seal — A35

Iceberg off St. John's — A36

Henry VII — A37

1897, June 24

No.	Type	Description	Unused	Used
61	A24	1c deep green	1.50	1.50
		Never hinged	2.50	
		On cover		6.50
62	A25	2c carmine lake	1.90	1.10
		Never hinged	3.25	
		On cover		6.00
63	A26	3c ultramarine	3.25	1.25
		Never hinged	6.00	
		On cover		12.50
64	A27	4c olive green	5.00	2.50
		Never hinged	9.50	
		On cover		20.00
65	A28	5c violet	7.50	2.50
		Never hinged	15.00	
		On cover		20.00
66	A29	6c red brown	5.00	3.00
		Never hinged	9.50	
		On cover		22.50
67	A30	8c red orange	16.00	12.50
		Never hinged	27.50	
		On cover		80.00
68	A31	10c black brown	16.00	6.50
		Never hinged	27.50	
		On cover		50.00
69	A32	12c dark blue	20.00	12.50
		Never hinged	35.00	
		On cover		80.00
70	A33	15c scarlet	20.00	11.50
		Never hinged	35.00	
		On cover		80.00
71	A34	24c gray violet	25.00	10.00
		Never hinged	45.00	
		On cover		60.00
72	A35	30c slate	45.00	45.00
		Never hinged	75.00	
		On cover		100.00
73	A36	35c red	100.00	50.00
		Never hinged	220.00	
		On cover		175.00
74	A37	60c black	16.00	10.00
		Never hinged	24.00	
		On cover		55.00
		Nos. 61-74 (14)	282.15	169.85
		Set, never hinged	485.00	

400th anniv. of John Cabot's discovery of Newfoundland; 60th year of Victoria's reign. The ship on the 10c was previously used by the American Bank Note Co. as the "Flagship of Columbus" on US No. 232. The portrait on the 2c, intended to be of John Cabot, is said to be a Holbein painting of his son, Sebastian.

Bisects are known of the 2c, 3c and 6c values but were not authorized. Values, on cover, 2c (1c) $100, 3c (1½c) $140, 6c (3c) $275.

For surcharges and overprints see Nos. 127-130, C2-C4.

No. 60a Surcharged with Bars and

No. 75

No. 76

No. 77

1897, Oct.

No.	Type	Description	Unused	Used
75	A23	1c on 3c gray lilac	50.00	25.00
		Never hinged	90.00	
		On cover		70.00
a.		Dbl. surch., one diagonal	*1,250.*	
b.		Vert. pair, "ONE CENT" and lower bar omitted on bottom stamp	*3,250.*	
76	A23	1c on 3c gray lilac	200.00	175.00
		Never hinged	425.00	
		On cover		250.00
77	A23	1c on 3c gray lilac	650.00	600.00
		Never hinged	1,300.	
		On cover		1,000.
a.		Block of 4, #76-77, 2 #75	1,300.	
		Never hinged	*3,250.*	
		Set, never hinged	1,815.	

Most examples of Nos. 75-77 are poorly centered. Fine copies sell for about 70% of the values given. No. 75b is valued in the grade of fine.

Trial surcharges of Nos. 75-77 exist with red surcharge and with double surcharge, one in red and one in black, but these were not issued.

Edward VIII as a Child — A38

Victoria — A39

Edward VII as Prince of Wales — A40

Queen Alexandra as Princess of Wales — A41

Queen Mary as Duchess of York — A42

George V as Duke of York — A43

1897-1901 *Engr.*

No.	Type	Description	Unused	Used
78	A38	½c olive green	3.00	2.00
		Never hinged	4.00	
		On cover		14.00
79	A39	1c carmine rose	4.00	4.00
		Never hinged	6.00	
		On cover		30.00
80	A39	1c yel grn ('98)	4.25	.25
		Never hinged	6.50	
		On cover		6.00
a.		1c deep green	5.00	.20
		Never hinged	8.00	
		On cover		5.00
b.		Vert. pair, imperf. horiz.	250.00	
		Never hinged	450.00	
81	A40	2c orange	5.25	3.50
		Never hinged	7.00	
		On cover		17.50
82	A40	2c ver ('98)	10.00	.50
		Never hinged	13.00	
		On cover		10.00
b.		Pair, imperf. between	400.00	
		Never hinged	700.00	
83	A41	3c orange ('98)	22.50	.60
		Never hinged	35.00	
		On cover		10.00
a.		Vert. pair, imperf. horiz.	400.00	
		Never hinged	625.00	
c.		3c red orange, *thin bluish* ('98)	20.00	1.50
		Never hinged	40.00	
84	A42	4c violet ('01)	30.00	4.00
		Never hinged	45.00	
		On cover		5.00
85	A43	5c blue ('99)	40.00	2.50
		Never hinged	65.00	
		On cover		35.00
		Nos. 78-85 (8)	119.00	17.35
		Set, never hinged	179.50	

No. 80b is valued in the grade of fine.

Imperf., Pairs

No.	Type	Description	Unused	Used
78a	A38	½c	400.00	
		Never hinged	600.00	
81a	A40	2c		*350.00*
		On cover		*550.00*
82a	A40	2c	250.00	
		Never hinged	375.00	
83b	A41	3c	350.00	
		Never hinged	540.00	
84a	A42	4c	300.00	
		Never hinged	450.00	

Imperf., Pairs

Newfoundland imperforates virtually always are proofs on stamp paper or "postmaster's perquisites." Most part-perforate varieties also are "postmaster's perquisites." These items were not regularly issued, but rather were sold or given to favored persons.

Map of Newfoundland — A44

1908, Sept.

No.	Type	Description	Unused	Used
86	A44	2c rose carmine	37.50	1.50
		Never hinged	62.50	
		On cover		40.00
		On postcard		12.50

Guy Issue

James I — A45

Arms of the London and Bristol Co. — A46

John Guy — A47

Lord Bacon — A50

Guy's Ship, the "Endeavour" A48

View of Cupids — A49

View of Mosquito — A51

Logging Camp — A52

Edward VII — A54

George V — A55

Paper Mills — A53

SIX CENT TYPES
I — "Z" of "COLONIZATION" reversed.
II — "Z" of normal.

1910, Aug. 15 Litho. *Perf. 12*

87	A45	1c deep green, perf. 12x11	2.00	1.00
		Never hinged	3.50	
		On cover		4.00
		"NFW" for "NEW"	50.00	42.50
		Never hinged	80.00	
a.		Perf. 12	4.00	1.75
		Never hinged	6.75	
		On cover		6.00
		"NFW" for "NEW"	50.00	35.00
		Never hinged	80.00	
b.		Perf. 12x14	3.25	2.00
		Never hinged	5.50	
		On cover		6.00
		"NFW" for "NEW"	50.00	35.00
c.		Horiz. pair, imperf. btwn., perf 12x11	300.00	—
		Never hinged	400.00	
		"NFW" for "NEW"	525.00	
		Never hinged	850.00	
d.		Vert. pair, imperf. btwn., perf 12x11	275.00	
		Never hinged	450.00	
e.		Horiz. pair, imperf. btwn., perf 12	350.00	
		Never hinged	600.00	
		"NFW" for "NEW"	400.00	
		Never hinged	675.00	
f.		Vert. pair, imperf. btwn., perf 12	400.00	
		Never hinged	700.00	
g.		Horiz. pair, imperf. btwn., perf 12x14	200.00	—
		Never hinged	325.00	
		"NFW" for "NEW"	350.00	
		Never hinged	550.00	
88	A46	2c carmine	6.00	1.00
		Never hinged	9.50	
		On cover		6.00
a.		Perf. 12x14	5.50	.75
		Never hinged	9.00	
		On cover		6.00
b.		As "a," horiz. pair, imperf. between	250.00	
		Never hinged	425.00	
c.		Perf. 12x11½	400.00	300.00
		Never hinged	525.00	
		On cover		—
89	A47	3c brown olive	12.50	12.50
		Never hinged	21.00	
		On cover		35.00
90	A48	4c dull violet	12.50	10.00
		Never hinged	22.00	
		On cover		26.00
91	A49	5c ultramarine, perf. 14x12	12.50	4.00
		Never hinged	19.00	
		On cover		20.00
a.		Perf. 12	20.00	6.50
		Never hinged	31.00	
		On cover		20.00
92	A50	6c claret, type I	65.00	60.00
		Never hinged	100.00	
		On cover		160.00
92A	A50	6c claret, type II	32.50	32.50
		Never hinged	52.50	
		On cover		37.50
b.		Imperf., pair	300.00	
		Never hinged	450.00	
93	A51	8c pale brown	50.00	45.00
		Never hinged	100.00	
		On cover		75.00
94	A52	9c olive green	50.00	45.00
		Never hinged	100.00	
		On cover		75.00
95	A53	10c vio black	50.00	45.00
		Never hinged	100.00	
		On cover		75.00
96	A54	12c lilac brown	50.00	45.00
		Never hinged	100.00	
		On cover		90.00
a.		Imperf., pair	325.00	
		Never hinged	500.00	
97	A55	15c gray black	65.00	55.00
		Never hinged	130.00	
		On cover		90.00
		Nos. 87-97 (12)	408.00	356.00
		Set, never hinged	760.00	

Tercentenary of the Colonization of Newfoundland.
On No. 87a printing flaw "JANES" exists.

1911 Engr. *Perf. 14*

98	A50	6c brown vio	25.00	20.00
		Never hinged	50.00	
		On cover		50.00
99	A51	8c bister brn	65.00	60.00
		Never hinged	100.00	
		On cover		125.00
100	A52	9c olive grn	50.00	50.00
		Never hinged	85.00	
		On cover		125.00
101	A53	10c violet blk	80.00	80.00
		Never hinged	150.00	
		On cover		200.00
102	A54	12c red brown	65.00	65.00
		Never hinged	125.00	
		On cover		125.00
103	A55	15c slate grn	65.00	65.00
		Never hinged	125.00	
		On cover		500.00
b.		Horiz. pair, imperf. btwn.	325.00	
		Nos. 98-103 (6)	350.00	*340.00*
		Set, never hinged	635.00	

Nos. 100 and 103 are known with papermaker's watermark "E. TOWGOOD FINE."

Imperf., Pairs

98a	A50	6c	250.00
		Never hinged	300.00
99a	A51	8c	250.00
		Never hinged	300.00
100a	A52	9c	250.00
		Never hinged	300.00
101a	A53	10c	250.00
		Never hinged	300.00
102a	A54	12c	250.00
		Never hinged	300.00
103a	A55	15c	250.00
		Never hinged	300.00

Nos. 98a-103a were made with and without gum. Values the same.

Royal Family Issue

Queen Mary — A56

George V — A57

Prince of Wales (Edward VIII) — A58

Prince Albert (George VI) — A59

Princess Mary — A60

Prince Henry — A61

Prince George A62

Prince John A63

Queen Alexandra A64

Duke of Connaught A65

Seal of Colony — A66

1911, June 19 *Perf. 13½x14, 14*

104	A56	1c yellow grn	2.50	.20
		Never hinged	3.75	
		On cover		1.25
b.		1c blue green	3.00	.20
		Never hinged	5.75	
105	A57	2c carmine	2.25	.20
		Never hinged	3.75	
		On cover		1.25
b.		2c rose red (blurred impression)	6.50	.20
		Never hinged	13.00	
		On cover		1.00
106	A58	3c red brown	20.00	16.00
		Never hinged	35.00	
		On cover		200.00
107	A59	4c violet	16.00	12.00
		Never hinged	27.50	
		On cover		16.00
108	A60	5c ultra	6.50	1.25
		Never hinged	11.00	
		On cover		4.00
109	A61	6c black	20.00	20.00
		Never hinged	35.00	
		On cover		25.00
110	A62	8c blue (paper colored through)	65.00	55.00
		Never hinged	110.00	
		On cover		150.00
a.		8c peacock blue	70.00	60.00
		Never hinged	120.00	
		On cover		150.00
111	A63	9c bl violet	20.00	17.50
		Never hinged	35.00	
		On cover		50.00
112	A64	10c dark green	35.00	32.50
		Never hinged	60.00	
		On cover		40.00
113	A65	12c plum	32.50	32.50
		Never hinged	57.50	
		On cover		40.00
114	A66	15c magenta	25.00	*32.50*
		Never hinged	40.00	
		On cover		65.00
		Nos. 104-114 (11)	244.75	219.65
		Set, never hinged	417.50	

Coronation of King George V.

Imperf., Pairs Without Gum

104a	A56	1c	250.00
105a	A57	2c	250.00
108a	A60	5c	250.00
113a	A65	12c	250.00
114a	A66	15c	90.00

Trail of the Caribou Issue

Caribou
A67 A68

1919, Jan. 2 *Perf. 14*

115	A67	1c green	2.00	.30
		Never hinged	3.50	
		On cover		.75
116	A68	2c scarlet	2.25	.40
		Never hinged	3.75	
		On cover		.75
b.		2c carmine red	4.00	.50
		Never hinged	7.00	
		On cover		1.00
117	A67	3c red brown	2.50	.20
		Never hinged	4.25	
		On cover		.75
b.		3c brown	2.50	.20
		Never hinged	4.25	
		On cover		.75
118	A67	4c violet	4.25	1.00
		Never hinged	6.50	
		On cover		2.50
b.		4c mauve	5.25	1.00
		Never hinged	9.00	
		On cover		2.50
119	A68	5c ultramarine	5.00	1.00
		Never hinged	7.50	
		On cover		2.00
120	A67	6c gray	20.00	20.00
		Never hinged	30.00	
		On cover		24.00
121	A68	8c magenta	20.00	16.00
		Never hinged	30.00	
		On cover		21.00
122	A67	10c dark green	10.00	4.50
		Never hinged	15.00	
		On cover		6.50
123	A68	12c orange	60.00	40.00
		Never hinged	95.00	
		On cover		50.00
124	A67	15c dark blue	40.00	37.50
		Never hinged	57.50	
		On cover		47.50
b.		15c Prussian blue	200.00	110.00
		Never hinged	360.00	
		On cover		160.00
125	A67	24c bister	40.00	37.50
		Never hinged	70.00	
		On cover		42.50
126	A67	36c olive green	37.50	32.50
		Never hinged	50.00	
		On cover		42.50
		Nos. 115-126 (12)	243.50	190.90
		Set, never hinged	370.00	

Services of the Newfoundland contingent in WWI.
Each denomination of type A67 is inscribed with the name of a different action in which Newfoundland troops took part.
For overprint and surcharge see Nos. C1, C5.

Imperf., Pairs Without Gum

115a	A67	1c	225.00
116a	A68	2c	225.00
117a	A67	3c red brown	225.00
c.		3c brown	225.00
118a	A67	4c	225.00
119a	A68	5c	225.00
120a	A67	6c	225.00
121a	A68	8c	225.00
122a	A67	10c	225.00
123a	A68	12c	225.00
124a	A67	15c	225.00
125a	A67	24c	225.00
126a	A67	36c	225.00

No. 72 Surcharged in Black

1920 *Perf. 12*

127	A35	2c on 30c slate	5.25	5.00
		Never hinged	8.00	
		On cover		9.00
a.		Inverted surcharge	750.00	
		Never hinged	900.00	

No. 127 with red surcharge is an unissued color trial. 25 examples are known. Value, $1,000.

Nos. 70 and 73 Surcharged in Black

THREE CENTS
Type I — Bars 10½mm apart.
Type II — Bars 13½mm apart.

128	A33	3c on 15c scar (I)	210.00	200.00
		Never hinged	300.00	
		On cover		275.00
a.		Inverted surcharge	*1,750.*	
		Never hinged	*1,650.*	
129	A33	3c on 15c scar (II)	15.00	10.00
		Never hinged	21.00	
		On cover		15.00
130	A36	3c on 35c red	10.00	8.00
		Never hinged	14.00	
		On cover		15.00
a.		Lower bar omitted	110.00	110.00
		Never hinged	140.00	
b.		Inverted surcharge	—	

All copies of the former No. 130c ("THREE" omitted) examined show part of the tops or bottoms of the letters. It is probable that no copies with "THREE" completely omitted exist.

Twin Hills, Tor's Cove — A70

South West Arm, Trinity — A71

War Memorial, St. John's A72

Humber River A73

Coast of Trinity — A74

Upper Steadies, Humber River — A75

Quidi Vidi, near St. John's — A76

Caribou Crossing Lake — A77

Humber River Canyon A78

Shell Bird Island A79

Mt. Moriah, Bay of Islands A80

Humber River near Little Rapids A81

Placentia, from Mt. Pleasant A82

Topsail Falls near St. John's A83

1923-24 Engr. *Perf. 14, 13½x14*

No.		Unused	Used
131	A70 1c gray green	1.60	.25
	Never hinged	2.50	
	On cover		10.00
a.	Booklet pane of 8	400.00	
	Never hinged	525.00	
132	A71 2c carmine	1.60	.20
	Never hinged	2.50	
	On cover		1.00
a.	Booklet pane of 8	250.00	
	Never hinged	350.00	
133	A72 3c brown	1.60	.20
	Never hinged	2.50	
	On cover		1.00
134	A73 4c brn violet	2.00	1.50
	Never hinged	3.50	
	On cover		3.25
135	A74 5c ultramarine	3.25	2.00
	Never hinged	4.75	
	On cover		3.50
136	A75 6c gray black	4.25	4.25
	Never hinged	6.00	
	On cover		5.00
137	A76 8c dull violet	3.25	3.00
	Never hinged	4.75	
	On cover		4.00
138	A77 9c slate green	30.00	24.00
	Never hinged	45.00	
	On cover		45.00
139	A78 10c dark violet	4.00	2.00
	Never hinged	6.00	
	On cover		3.00
b.	10c purple	5.00	2.00
	Never hinged	7.50	
	On cover		3.00
140	A79 11c olive green	5.25	5.25
	Never hinged	8.00	
	On cover		7.00
141	A80 12c lake	6.25	6.25
	Never hinged	10.50	
	On cover		7.00
142	A81 15c deep blue	8.00	7.00
	Never hinged	13.00	
	On cover		8.50
143	A82 20c red brn ('24)	12.00	6.50
	Never hinged	21.00	
	On cover		8.50
144	A83 24c blk brn ('24)	50.00	40.00
	Never hinged	85.00	
	On cover		100.00
	Nos. 131-144 (14)	133.05	102.40
	Set, never hinged	215.00	

For surcharge see No. 160.

Imperf., Pairs

No.		Value
131b	A70 1c	160.00
	Never hinged	200.00
132b	A71 2c	160.00
	Never hinged	200.00
134a	A73 4c	160.00
135a	A74 5c	160.00
136a	A75 6c	160.00
137a	A76 8c	160.00
138a	A77 9c	160.00
139a	A78 10c	160.00
140a	A79 11c	160.00
	Never hinged	200.00
141a	A80 12c	160.00
142a	A81 15c	140.00

Nos. 134a-139a, 141a-142a are without gum. Others are either with or without gum; values about the same.

Map of Newfoundland A84

Steamship "Caribou" A85

Queen Mary, George V — A86

Prince of Wales — A87

Express Train — A88

Newfoundland Hotel, St. John's — A89

Heart's Content — A90

Cabot Tower, St. John's — A91

War Memorial, St. John's — A92

GPO, St. John's — A93

First Nonstop Transatlantic Flight, 1919 — A94

Colonial Building, St. John's — A95

Grand Falls, Labrador — A96

Perf. 14, 13½x13, 13x13½

1928, Jan. 3

No.		Unused	Used
145	A84 1c deep green	1.25	.60
	Never hinged	2.10	
	On cover		.75
146	A85 2c deep carmine	2.00	.55
	Never hinged	3.00	
	On cover		.75
a.	Imperf., pair	250.00	
	Never hinged	*375.00*	
147	A86 3c brown	2.00	.35
	Never hinged	3.25	
	On cover		.75
148	A87 4c lilac rose	2.50	1.60
	Never hinged	4.25	
	On cover		3.00
a.	4c rose purple ('29)	3.75	1.75
	Never hinged	5.00	
149	A88 5c slate green	10.00	3.25
	Never hinged	15.00	
	On cover		4.00
150	A89 6c ultramarine	5.00	2.75
	Never hinged	7.50	
	On cover		4.00
151	A90 8c lt red brown	6.00	3.75
	Never hinged	9.00	
	On cover		5.00
152	A91 9c myrtle green	5.25	4.50
	Never hinged	7.75	
	On cover		6.00
153	A92 10c dark violet	7.50	4.25
	Never hinged	12.00	
	On cover		5.00
154	A93 12c brn carmine	5.25	3.00
	Never hinged	9.50	
	On cover		6.00
155	A91 14c red brown	8.00	4.00
	Never hinged	14.00	
	On cover		7.00
156	A94 15c dark blue	7.50	5.75
	Never hinged	14.00	
	On cover		7.00
157	A95 20c gray black	9.50	4.50
	Never hinged	19.00	
	On cover		6.00
158	A93 28c gray green	25.00	20.00
	Never hinged	42.50	
	On cover		25.00
159	A96 30c olive brown	10.00	5.50
	Never hinged	18.00	
	On cover		7.00
	Nos. 145-159 (15)	106.75	64.35
	Set, never hinged	175.00	

See Nos. 163-182.

No. 136 Surcharged in Red or Black

Type I — 5mm between "CENTS" and bar.
Type II — 3mm between "CENTS" and bar.

1929 ***Perf. 14x13½***

No.		Unused	Used
160	A75 3c on 6c gray black (II) (R)	3.50	3.25
	Never hinged	6.50	
	On cover		4.25
a.	Inverted surcharge (II)	850.00	
	Never hinged	*1,000.*	

The stamps with black surcharge, type I and II, were 1st or trial printings, and were not issued. There were 50 copies of each. Value, each $1,000.

Types of 1928 Issue Re-engraved

1c — On No. 145 the lines of the engraving are thinner and the impression is clearer than on No. 163. On the former "C. BAULD" is above "C. NORMAN." On the latter these words are transposed.

2c — On the 1928 stamp the "D" of "NEWFOUNDLAND" is 1mm from the scroll at the right; the flag at the stern is lower than the top of the boat davit. On the 1929 stamp the "D" is ½mm from the scroll and the flag rises above the davits.

3c — On the 1928 stamp the pearls at the top of the crown, the jewels of the tiara and the pillars flanking the portraits are all unshaded. On the reengraved stamp there are small curved lines inside the pearls, the jewels of the tiara are in solid color, and the pillars have vertical shading lines. On the 1928 stamps the tablets with "THREE" and "CENTS" have a background of crossed lines (vertical and horizontal). On the 1929 stamp the background is of horizontal lines only.

4c — On the 1928 stamp the figures "4" have shading of horizontal and diagonal crossed lines. There are six circles at each side of the portrait.

On the 1929 stamp the "4s" have shading of horizontal lines only. There are five roses at each side of the portrait.

5c — The crossbars of the telegraph pole touch the frame at the left on the 1929 stamp but just clear it on the 1928 stamp. In the 1928 issue the foliate ornaments beside and below the figures "5" end in small scrolls and a small spur. These spurs are omitted on the 1929 stamp.

6c — On the re-engraved stamp the columns at right and left of the picture have heavy wavy outlines on the inner sides. There is no period after "JOHNS." The numerals in the lower corners are 1½mm wide instead of 1¼mm.

8c — The impression of the 1928 stamp is clear, that of 1931 is slightly blurred. The 1928 stamp has three horizontal lines above "EIGHT CENTS" and four berries on the laurel branch at the right side. On the 1931 stamp there are two horizontal lines and three berries.

10c — On the re-engraved stamp there is no period after "ST. JOHN'S." The letters of "TEN CENTS" are slightly larger and the numerals "10" slightly smaller than in 1928. Inside the "0" of "10" at the right there are two vertical lines instead of three. The clouds are fainter in 1929 and the cross upheld by the figure on the monument is more distinct. On the 1928 stamp the torch at the left side terminates in a single tongue of flame. On the 1929-30 stamp it terminates in two tongues.

15c — On the 1928 stamp the "N" of "NEWFOUNDLAND" is 1½mm from the left frame, the "L" of "LEAVING" is under the first "A" of "AIRPLANE" and the apostrophe in "JOHN'S" breaks the first line above it.

On the 1929 stamp the "N" of "NEWFOUNDLAND" is 1mm from the left frame, the "L" of "LEAVING" is below the "T" of "FIRST" and the apostrophe in "JOHN'S" does not touch the line above it.

20c — On the 1928 stamp the points of the "W" of "NEWFOUNDLAND" are truncated. The "O" is wide and nearly round. The columns that form the sides of the frame have a shading of evenly spaced horizontal lines at their inner sides.

On the 1929-31 stamp the points of the "W" form sharp angles. The "O" is narrow and has a small opening. Many lines have been added to the shading on the inner sides of the columns, making it almost solid.

30c — 1928 stamp. Size: 19¼x24½mm. At the outer side of the right column there are three strong and two faint vertical lines. Faint period after "FALLS."

1931 stamp. Size: 19x25mm. At the outer side of the right column there are two strong vertical lines and a fragment of the lower end of a faint one. Clear period after "FALLS." A great many of the small lines of the design have been deepened making the whole stamp appear darker.

1929-31 Unwmk. *Perf. 13½ to 14*

No.		Unused	Used
163	A84 1c green	2.00	.50
	Never hinged	2.75	
	On cover		1.00
a.	Double impression	*275.00*	
	Never hinged	*400.00*	
b.	Vert. pair, imperf. btwn.	175.00	
	Never hinged	*250.00*	
164	A85 2c deep carmine	2.00	.20
	Never hinged	3.00	
	On cover		1.00
165	A86 3c dp red brown	2.25	.20
	Never hinged	3.50	
	On cover		1.00
166	A87 4c magenta	3.25	1.00
	Never hinged	5.75	
	On cover		2.50
167	A88 5c slate green	6.00	1.00
	Never hinged	10.00	
	On cover		2.00
168	A89 6c ultramarine	9.00	7.50
	Never hinged	14.00	
	On cover		10.00
169	A92 10c dark violet	7.50	1.25
	Never hinged	13.00	
	On cover		3.00
170	A94 15c deep blue ('30)	40.00	32.50
	Never hinged	65.00	
	On cover		32.50
171	A95 20c gray blk ('31)	65.00	22.50
	Never hinged	95.00	
	On cover		25.00
	Nos. 163-171 (9)	137.00	66.65
	Set, never hinged	212.00	

Imperf., Pairs

No.		Value
163c	A84 1c	100.00
	Never hinged	135.00
164a	A85 2c pale carmine, *cream*	120.00
	Never hinged	150.00
b.	2c dark carmine	120.00

No.	Description	Unused	Used
165a	A86 3c	100.00	
	Never hinged	135.00	
166a	A87 4c	120.00	
	Never hinged	150.00	

No. 164b is without gum, others with gum.

Types of 1928 Issue

Perf. 13½x14

1931 Re-engraved Wmk. 224

No.	Description	Unused	Used
172	A84 1c green, perf. 13½	2.00	.80
	Never hinged	2.75	
	On cover		1.75
a.	Horiz. pair, imperf. btwn.	375.00	
	Never hinged	*450.00*	
173	A85 2c red	5.00	.90
	Never hinged	7.50	
	On cover		1.25
174	A86 3c red brown	3.25	.75
	Never hinged	5.00	
	On cover		1.00
175	A87 4c rose	4.00	1.25
	Never hinged	5.50	
	On cover		2.00
176	A88 5c grnsh gray	12.50	5.00
	Never hinged	20.00	
	On cover		6.50
177	A89 6c ultramarine	20.00	12.50
	Never hinged	30.00	
	On cover		20.00
178	A90 8c lt red brn	20.00	12.50
	Never hinged	30.00	
	On cover		18.00
179	A92 10c dk violet	14.50	6.00
	Never hinged	21.00	
	On cover		8.00
180	A94 15c deep blue	42.50	25.00
	Never hinged	65.00	
	On cover		30.00
181	A95 20c gray black	52.50	12.50
	Never hinged	82.50	
	On cover		13.00
182	A96 30c olive brown	40.00	22.50
	Never hinged	63.00	
	On cover		25.00
	Nos. 172-182 (11)	216.25	99.70
	Set, never hinged	328.80	

Codfish — A97

George V — A98

Queen Mary — A99

Prince of Wales — A100

Caribou A101

Princess Elizabeth A102

Salmon Leaping Falls — A103

Newfoundland Dog — A104

Harp Seal Pup — A105

Cape Race — A106

Sealing Fleet — A107

Fishing Fleet Leaving for "The Banks" — A108

FIVE CENT
Die I — Antlers even, or equal in height.
Die II — Antler under "T" higher.

1932-37 Engr. *Perf. 13½, 14*

No.	Description	Unused	Used
183	A97 1c green	2.00	.40
	Never hinged	3.00	
	On cover		1.00
a.	Booklet pane of 4, perf. 13	70.00	
	Never hinged	100.00	
c.	Vert. pair, imperf. btwn.	160.00	
	Never hinged	225.00	
184	A97 1c gray black	.30	.20
	Never hinged	.50	
	On cover		.50
a.	Bklt. pane of 4, perf. 13½	50.00	
	Never hinged	70.00	
b.	Booklet pane of 4, perf. 14	65.00	
	Never hinged	80.00	
185	A98 2c rose	2.00	.20
	Never hinged	3.00	
	On cover		.75
a.	Booklet pane of 4, perf. 13½	35.00	
	Never hinged	50.00	
b.	Booklet pane of 4, perf. 13	45.00	
	Never hinged	60.00	
186	A98 2c green	1.00	.20
	Never hinged	1.60	
	On cover		.50
a.	Bklt. pane of 4, perf. 13½	25.00	
	Never hinged	32.50	
b.	Booklet pane of 4, perf. 14	32.50	
	Never hinged	47.50	
d.	Horiz. pair, imperf. btwn.	150.00	
	Never hinged	210.00	
187	A99 3c orange brn	1.00	.20
	Never hinged	1.60	
	On cover		.50
a.	Bklt. pane of 4, perf. 13½	52.50	
	Never hinged	70.00	
b.	Booklet pane of 4, perf. 14	65.00	
	Never hinged	87.50	
c.	Booklet pane of 4, perf. 13	70.00	
	Never hinged	95.00	
e.	Vert. pair, imperf. btwn.	130.00	
	Never hinged	*195.00*	
188	A100 4c deep violet	5.25	1.40
	Never hinged	7.50	
	On cover		1.50
189	A100 4c rose lake	.65	.20
	Never hinged	1.00	
	On cover		1.50
b.	Vert. pair, imperf. btwn.	100.00	
	Never hinged	140.00	
c.	Horiz. pair, imperf. btwn.	100.00	
	Never hinged	140.00	
d.	Perf. 14	5.00	4.00
	Never hinged	7.25	
	On cover		6.00
190	A101 5c vio brn, perf. 13½ (Die I)	8.00	1.00
	Never hinged	12.00	
	On cover		3.00
191	A101 5c dp vio, perf. 13½ (Die II)	1.00	.20
	Never hinged	1.60	
	On cover		.30
a.	5c dp vio, perf. 13½ (Die I)	10.00	.80
	Never hinged	13.50	
	On cover		1.75
c.	Horiz. pair, imperf. btwn. (I)	200.00	
	Never hinged	275.00	
e.	Perf. 14 (Die I)	37.50	17.50
	Never hinged	57.50	
	On cover		60.00
f.	Perf. 14 (Die II)	35.00	14.00
	Never hinged	50.00	
	On cover		60.00
g.	Horiz. pair, imperf. btwn. (II)	200.00	
192	A102 6c dull blue	10.00	10.00
	Never hinged	15.00	
	On cover		22.50
193	A103 10c olive black	1.25	.65
	Never hinged	2.00	
	On cover		1.50
194	A104 14c int black	3.00	2.00
	Never hinged	4.00	
	On cover		3.50
195	A105 15c magenta	2.25	2.00
	Never hinged	3.00	
	On cover		3.50
b.	Perf. 14	12.00	6.00
	Never hinged	16.00	
	On cover		12.50
196	A106 20c gray green	2.25	.80
	Never hinged	3.00	
	On cover		2.50
b.	Perf. 14	47.50	32.50
	Never hinged	67.50	
	On cover		—
197	A107 25c gray	2.50	1.60
	Never hinged	3.50	
	On cover		3.50
b.	Horiz. pair, imperf. btwn.	225.00	
	Never hinged	325.00	
c.	Vert. pair, imperf. btwn.	325.00	
	Never hinged	450.00	
d.	Perf. 14	55.00	40.00
	Never hinged	75.00	
	On cover		—
198	A108 30c ultra	25.00	22.50
	Never hinged	35.00	
	On cover		47.50
b.	Vert. pair, imperf. btwn.	400.00	
	Never hinged	550.00	
c.	Perf. 14	140.00	—
	Never hinged	225.00	
	On cover		—
199	A108 48c red brn ('37)	10.00	4.25
	Never hinged	15.00	
	On cover		13.00
	Nos. 183-199 (17)	77.45	47.80
	Set, never hinged	109.00	

Two dies were used for 2c green, one for 2c rose.

See Nos. 253-266.

Imperf., Pairs

No.	Description	Value
183b	A97 1c	200.00
	Never hinged	290.00
184c	A97 1c	40.00
	Never hinged	50.00
185c	A98 2c	130.00
	Never hinged	180.00
186c	A98 2c	40.00
	Never hinged	50.00
187d	A99 3c	80.00
	Never hinged	95.00
189a	A100 4c	50.00
	Never hinged	62.50
190a	A101 5c	130.00
	Never hinged	160.00
191b	A101 5c (II)	50.00
	Never hinged	65.00
191d	A101 5c (I)	80.00
192a	A102 6c	120.00
	Never hinged	150.00
193a	A103 10c	80.00
	Never hinged	95.00
194a	A103 14c	100.00
	Never hinged	115.00
195a	A103 15c	100.00
	Never hinged	115.00
196a	A106 20c	130.00
	Never hinged	160.00
197a	A107 25c	130.00
	Never hinged	160.00
198a	A108 30c	450.00
	Never hinged	575.00
199a	A108 48c	100.00
	Never hinged	135.00

All with gum. Nos. 186c, 187d, 192a, 193a and 196a also made without gum; values about 10% less.

Queen Elizabeth when Duchess of York — A109

Corner Brook Paper Mills — A110

Loading Iron Ore at Bell Island — A111

1932

No.	Description	Unused	Used
208	A109 7c red brown	1.25	1.00
	Never hinged	1.60	
	On cover		3.50
a.	Imperf., pair	130.00	
	Never hinged	160.00	
b.	Horiz. pair, imperf. between	400.00	
	Never hinged	500.00	
209	A110 8c orange red	1.25	.80
	Never hinged	1.90	
	On cover		3.00
a.	Imperf., pair	100.00	
	Never hinged	125.00	
210	A111 24c light blue	2.50	2.25
	Never hinged	3.50	
	On cover		5.00
a.	Imperf., pair	175.00	
	Never hinged	225.00	
b.	Double impression	1,100.	
	Never hinged	1,400.	
	Nos. 208-210 (3)	5.00	4.05
	Set, never hinged	7.00	

No. 208a was made both with and without gum. Values about the same.

See Nos. 259, 264.

No. C9 Overprinted Bars and

1933, Feb. 9 Wmk. 224 *Perf. 14*

No.	Description	Unused	Used
211	AP6 15c brown	10.00	9.00
	Never hinged	14.00	
	On cover		18.00
a.	Pair, one without overprint	3,750.	
	Never hinged	*3,000.*	
b.	Overprint reading up	3,750.	
	Never hinged	*3,000.*	

"L. & S." stands for "Land and Sea."

Sir Humphrey Gilbert Issue

Sir Humphrey Gilbert — A112

Compton Castle, Home of the Gilbert Family — A113

Gilbert Coat of Arms — A114

Eton College — A115

Token from Queen Elizabeth I — A116

Sir Humphrey Receiving Royal Patents for Colonization A117

Sir Humphrey's Ships Leaving Plymouth, 1583 — A118

The Ships Arriving at St. John's — A119

Annexation of Newfoundland, Aug. 5, 1583 — A120

Coat of Arms of England A121

Sir Humphrey on the Deck of the "Squirrel" A122

Capt. John Mason's Map of Newfoundland, 1626 — A123

Queen Elizabeth I A124

Gilbert Statue at Truro A125

Wmk. 224

1933, Aug. 3 Engr. *Perf. 13½*

212 A112 1c gray black .90 .65
Never hinged 1.40
On cover 1.00
213 A113 2c green 1.00 .65
Never hinged 1.50
On cover 1.00
b. Double impression *500.00*
Never hinged *625.00*
214 A114 3c yellow brn 1.60 .65
Never hinged 2.25
On cover 3.00
215 A115 4c carmine 1.60 .65
Never hinged 2.25
On cover 3.00
216 A116 5c dull violet 2.00 .95
Never hinged 2.75
On cover 2.00
217 A117 7c blue 16.00 11.50
Never hinged 32.50
On cover 20.00
b. Perf. 14 14.00 14.00
Never hinged 27.50
On cover 20.00
218 A118 8c orange red 6.50 6.50
Never hinged 9.25
On cover 20.00
a. 8c brownish red (error), never hinged 450.00
219 A119 9c ultramarine 7.00 7.00
Never hinged 10.00
On cover 20.00
b. Perf. 14 50.00 50.00
Never hinged 75.00
On cover 100.00
220 A120 10c red brown 7.00 5.75
Never hinged 10.00
On cover 14.00
b. Perf. 14 62.50 50.00
Never hinged 90.00
On cover 100.00
221 A121 14c black 14.00 12.50
Never hinged 18.00
On cover 25.00
b. Perf. 14 17.50 16.00
Never hinged 26.00
On cover 22.50
222 A122 15c claret 12.50 12.50
Never hinged 17.00
On cover 25.00
223 A123 20c deep green 12.00 9.00
Never hinged 17.00
On cover 20.00
b. Perf. 14 14.50 11.00
Never hinged 22.00
On cover 20.00
224 A124 24c vio brown 20.00 19.00
Never hinged 29.00
On cover 35.00
b. Perf. 14 21.00 21.00
Never hinged 30.00
On cover 35.00
225 A125 32c gray 20.00 19.00
Never hinged 31.00
On cover 35.00
a. Perf. 14 21.00 21.00
Never hinged 30.00
On cover 30.00
Nos. 212-225 (14) 122.10 106.30
Set, never hinged 180.00

350th anniv. of annexation of Newfoundland to England, Aug. 5, 1583, by authority of Letters Patent issued by Queen Elizabeth I to Sir Humphrey Gilbert.

Imperf., Pairs

212a	A112	1c	40.00
213a	A113	2c	40.00
214a	A114	3c	200.00
215a	A115	4c	42.50
216a	A116	5c	225.00
219a	A119	9c	200.00
220a	A120	10c	200.00
221a	A120	14c	250.00
222a	A120	15c	160.00
224a	A124	24c	130.00

Common Design Types pictured following the introduction.

Silver Jubilee Issue
Common Design Type

1935, May 6 Wmk. 4 *Perf. 11x12*

226 CD301 4c bright rose 1.50 .60
Never hinged 1.75
On cover 1.50
227 CD301 5c violet 1.50 .70
Never hinged 1.75
On cover 1.50
228 CD301 7c dark blue 4.00 3.00
Never hinged 5.00
On cover 7.00
229 CD301 24c olive green 8.00 6.00
Never hinged 12.50
On cover 9.00
a. 24c dark olive 14.00 10.50
Never hinged 20.00
On cover 13.50
Nos. 226-229 (4) 15.00 10.30
Set, never hinged 21.00

Coronation Issue
Common Design Type

1937, May 12 *Perf. 11x11½*

230 CD302 2c deep green 1.50 .60
Never hinged 2.10
On cover 1.40
231 CD302 4c carmine rose 1.50 .60
Never hinged 2.10
On cover 1.40
232 CD302 5c dark violet 3.25 1.25
Never hinged 4.50
On cover 2.75
Nos. 230-232 (3) 6.25 2.45
Nos. 230-232, never hinged 8.70

Codfish A126

Map of Newfoundland — A127

Caribou A128

Corner Brook Paper Mills A129

Salmon A130

Newfoundland Dog — A131

Harp Seal Pup A132

Cape Race A133

Loading Iron Ore at Bell Island A134

Sealing Fleet A135

Fishing Fleet Leaving for "The Banks" A136

Two dies of the 3c
Die I — Fine impression; no lines on bridge of nose.
Die II — Coarse impression; lines on bridge of nose.

Perf. 13½, 14 (#234-235)

1937, May 12 Wmk. 224

233 A126 1c gray black .40 .25
Never hinged .50
On cover .85
"Fish hook" plate flaw (pos. 23) 15.00 9.00
Never hinged 22.50
On cover 12.50
234 A127 3c org brn, die I 2.25 1.00
Never hinged 3.00
On cover 1.50
a. Die II 1.60 .95
Never hinged 2.00
On cover 1.25
b. Vert. pair, imperf. btwn. (I) 450.00
Never hinged 375.00
c. Vert. pair, imperf. btwn. (II) 450.00
Never hinged 475.00
d. Horiz. pair, imperf. btwn. (I) 450.00
Never hinged 375.00
e. Horiz. pair, imperf. btwn. (II) 450.00
Never hinged 475.00
f. Imperf., pair 200.00
Never hinged 300.00
235 A128 7c blue 2.25 2.25
Never hinged 3.25
On cover 1.75
236 A129 8c orange red 2.25 2.25
Never hinged 3.25
On cover 2.00
a. Imperf., pair 225.00
Never hinged 325.00
b. Vert. pair, imperf. between 550.00
Never hinged 825.00
c. Horiz. pair, imperf. between 550.00
Never hinged 825.00
237 A130 10c olive gray 3.25 3.25
Never hinged 4.25
On cover 4.00
a. Double impression *225.00*
Never hinged 450.00
238 A131 14c black 2.50 2.50
Never hinged 3.10
On cover 3.50
a. Imperf., pair 325.00
Never hinged 475.00
239 A132 15c rose lake 3.25 2.50
Never hinged 4.00
On cover 3.50
a. Vert. pair, imperf. between 450.00
Never hinged *675.00*
240 A133 20c green 2.50 1.60
Never hinged 3.10
On cover 3.00
a. Vert. pair, imperf. between 600.00
Never hinged 700.00
241 A134 24c turq blue 3.00 2.75
Never hinged 3.75
On cover 3.50
a. Vert. pair, imperf. between 800.00
Never hinged 1,150.
242 A135 25c gray 3.00 2.75
Never hinged 3.75
On cover 3.50
a. Imperf., pair 160.00
Never hinged 240.00
243 A136 48c dark violet 4.00 3.00
Never hinged 5.50
On cover 4.00
a. Vert. pair, imperf. between 900.00
Never hinged 890.00
b. Imperf., pair 200.00
Never hinged 290.00
Nos. 233-243 (11) 28.65 24.10
Set, never hinged 37.50

Imperfs are with gum. No. 243b also made without gum; value the same.
Two line-perforating machines were used to produce this set, with exact measurements of 13.7 and 14.1 respectively.

Perf. 13¼

233a A126 1c gray black 15.00 18.00
Never hinged 22.50
On cover 30.00
"Fish hook" plate flaw (pos. 23) *175.00* —
Never hinged *225.00*
On cover —
234g A127 3c org brn, die I 1.50 .90
Never hinged 2.25
On cover 1.50
h. Die II 1.90 .90
Never hinged 2.75
On cover 1.60
235a A128 7c blue 200.00 *275.00*
Never hinged 275.00
On cover —
236d A129 8c orange red 2.75 2.75
Never hinged 3.25
On cover 6.00
237b A130 10c olive gray 4.00 *5.00*
Never hinged 7.50
On cover 4.75
238b A131 14c black *20,000.* —
239b A132 15c rose lake 9.25 9.25
Never hinged 13.50
On cover 15.00
240b A133 20c green 2.75 *3.00*
Never hinged 3.25
On cover 4.00
241b A134 24c turq blue 9.25 9.25
Never hinged 13.00
On cover 15.00
242b A135 25c gray 9.00 *12.50*
Never hinged 12.50
On cover 16.00
243c A136 48c dark violet 15.00 *17.50*
Never hinged 20.00
On cover 22.50

This set was produced with a comb perforator with an exact perforation of 13.3x13.2.

Princess Elizabeth — A139

Designs: 2c, King George VI. 3c, Queen Elizabeth. 7c, Queen Mother Mary.

1938, May 12 *Perf. 13½*

245 A139 2c green 1.50 .20
Never hinged 1.80
On cover 1.25
246 A139 3c dark carmine 1.50 .20
Never hinged 1.80
On cover 1.25
b. Perf. 14 175.00 150.00
Never hinged 250.00
On cover 200.00
247 A139 4c light blue 2.00 .20
Never hinged 2.50
On cover 1.25
248 A139 7c dark ultra 1.40 1.10
Never hinged 2.10
On cover 3.50
Nos. 245-248 (4) 6.40 1.70
Set, never hinged 8.00

See Nos. 254-256, 258, 269.

Imperf., Pairs

245a A139 2c 100.00
Never hinged 130.00
246a A139 3c 100.00
Never hinged 130.00
247a A139 4c 100.00
Never hinged 130.00
248a A139 7c 100.00
Never hinged 130.00

George VI and Queen Elizabeth A141

1939, June 17 Unwmk.

249 A141 5c violet blue 1.10 .90
Never hinged 1.40
On cover 1.00

Visit of King George and Queen Elizabeth.

No. 249 Surcharged in Brown or Red

1939, Nov. 20

250 A141 2c on 5c vio blue (Br) 1.10 .80
Never hinged 1.40
On cover 2.00
251 A141 4c on 5c vio blue (R) .90 .60
Never hinged 1.20
On cover 2.00

There are many varieties of broken letters and figures in the settings of the surcharges.

Sir Wilfred Grenfell and "Strathcona II" — A142

1941, Dec. 1 Engr. *Perf. 12*

252 A142 5c dull blue .35 .25
Never hinged .45
On cover 1.10

Grenfell Mission, 50th anniv.

Types of 1931-38

1941-44 Wmk. 224 *Perf. 12½*

253 A97 1c dark gray .30 .20
Never hinged .40
On cover .25
a. Imperf., pair 125.00
Never hinged 175.00
254 A139 2c deep green .30 .20
Never hinged .40
On cover .25
255 A139 3c rose carmine .30 .20
Never hinged .40
On cover .25
256 A139 4c blue .60 .20
Never hinged .70
On cover .25
257 A101 5c violet (Die I) .65 .20
Never hinged .85
On cover .25
a. Imperf., pair 150.00
Never hinged 200.00
b. Horiz. pair, imperf. vert. 400.00
Never hinged 500.00
c. Double impression 300.00
Never hinged 400.00
258 A139 7c vio blue ('42) 1.10 .80
Never hinged 1.25
On cover 1.60
259 A110 8c red .90 .50
Never hinged 1.25
On cover 1.00
260 A103 10c brownish blk .90 .45
Never hinged 1.25
On cover 1.00
261 A104 14c black 1.75 1.50
Never hinged 2.50
On cover 2.00
a. Imperf., pair 200.00
Never hinged 275.00
c. Vert. pair, imperf. horiz. 200.00
Never hinged 275.00
262 A105 15c pale rose vio 1.60 1.25
Never hinged 2.00
On cover 2.00
263 A106 20c green 1.40 1.00
Never hinged 1.75
On cover 1.75
264 A111 24c deep blue 2.00 1.25
Never hinged 2.50
On cover 2.50
265 A107 25c slate 2.00 1.25
Never hinged 2.50
On cover 2.50
266 A108 48c red brown ('44) 2.50 1.40
Never hinged 3.25
On cover 3.00
Nos. 253-266 (14) 16.30 10.40
Set, never hinged 21.50

Nos. 254 and 255 are re-engraved.

Memorial University College A143

Unwmk.

1943, Jan. 2 Engr. *Perf. 12*

267 A143 30c carmine 1.25 .90
Never hinged 1.65
On cover 3.00

No. 267 Surcharged in Black

1946, Mar. 23

268 A143 2c on 30c carmine .25 .25
Never hinged .35
On cover 1.75

Princess Elizabeth — A144

Deck of the Matthew A145

Wmk. 224

1947, Apr. 21 Engr. *Perf. 12½*

269 A144 4c light blue .25 .20
Never hinged .35
On cover .60
a. Imperf., pair 200.00
Never hinged 275.00
b. Horiz. pair, imperf. vert. 250.00
Never hinged 350.00

Princess Elizabeth's 21st birthday.

1947, June 23

270 A145 5c rose violet .25 .20
Never hinged .35
On cover 1.00
a. Horiz. pair, imperf. between 1,000.
Never hinged 1,400.
b. Imperf., pair 200.00
Never hinged 275.00

Cabot's arrival off Cape Bonavista, 450th anniv.

AIR POST STAMPS

No. 117 Overprinted in Black

1919, Apr. 12 Unwmk. *Perf. 14*

C1 A67 3c red brown *20,000. 15,000.*
Never hinged *30,000.*
On cover *18,000.*

No. C1 was issued for the first attempt to cross the Atlantic by air, by Lt. H. G. Hawker (pilot) and Lt. Cdr. K. M. Grieve (navigator). This flight was ended by a controlled crash landing in the ocean after about 13 hours of flying, the crew being rescued. The plane and mail bag were salvaged about five weeks later by an east-bound ship and the envelopes were delivered to England by sea.

Also in April 1919, W. C. Campbell, the Secretary of the Postal Department, prepared stamps for use on the Raynham-Morgan transatlantic flight attempt that took off shortly after the Hawker flight. Campbell is believed to have applied "Aerial Atlantic Mail" to No. 117 in manuscript and J. A. Robinson, the Postmaster, applied his initials "J.A.R.," also in manuscript. This flight lasted only a few hundred yards, as did a second attempt in July. Mail from these attempts was then taken by sea to London and delivered in January 1920. Value, on cover, $16,500.

No. 70 Surcharged in Black

1919, June 9 *Perf. 12*

C2 A33 $1 on 15c scarlet 200.00 200.00
Never hinged 325.00
On cover 1,000.
a. Without comma after "Post" 220.00 *250.00*
Never hinged 300.00
On cover 1,000.
b. As "a," without period after "1919" 375.00 375.00
Never hinged 450.00
On cover 1,200.
c. As "a," "A" of "AIR" under "a" of "Trans" 375.00 375.00
Never hinged 600.00
On cover 1,200.

No. C2 was issued for the June 14, 1919, flight of Capt. J. Alcock and Lt. A. W. Brown. This became the first successful non-stop transatlantic flight. No. C2 also was used on mail of other flights.

No. 73 Overprinted in Black

1921, Nov. 7

C3 A36 35c red, 2½mm between "AIR" and "MAIL" 130.00 *160.00*
Never hinged 220.00
On cover 200.00
a. Inverted overprint 5,000.
Never hinged *6,600.*
b. With period after "1921" 150.00 *180.00*
Never hinged 200.00
On cover 225.00
c. As "b," inverted overprint 5,250.
Never hinged *7,100.*
d. "1" of "1921" below "f" of "Halifax" 400.00 400.00
Never hinged 600.00
On cover 550.00
e. As "d," inverted overprint *12,500.* —
Never hinged
f. 35c red, 1½mm between "AIR" and "MAIL" 300.00 300.00
Never hinged 425.00
On cover 400.00
g. As "f," inverted overprint 7,500.
Never hinged *10,500.*
h. As "f," with period after "1921" 210.00 210.00
Never hinged 300.00
On cover 225.00
i. As "h," inverted overprint 6,500.
Never hinged *9,500.*
j. As "f," "1" of "1921" below "f" of "Halifax" 400.00 400.00
Never hinged 575.00
On cover 500.00
k. As "j," inverted overprint *12,500.* —
Never hinged

No. 74 Overprinted in Red

1927, May 21

C4 A37 60c black *35,000. 15,000.*
Never hinged *48,500.*
On cover *15,000.*
a. Short "7" in "1927" *37,500. 15,500.*
Never hinged *52,500.*
On cover *19,000.*

No. 126 Surcharged in Black

1930, Sept. 25 *Perf. 14*

C5 A67 50c on 36c ol grn *8,000. 8,000.*
Never hinged *12,000.*
On cover *12,000.*

Dog Sled and Airplane — AP6

First Transatlantic Mail Airplane and Packet Ship — AP7

Routes of Historic Transatlantic Flights — AP8

1931, Jan. 2 Engr. Unwmk.

C6 AP6 15c brown 10.00 7.00
Never hinged 15.00
On cover 14.00
a. Horiz. pair, imperf. between 800.00
Never hinged 950.00
b. Vert. pair, imperf. between 800.00
Never hinged 950.00
c. Imperf., pair 525.00
Never hinged 1,250.
C7 AP7 50c green 32.50 22.50
Never hinged 55.00
On cover 30.00
a. Horiz. pair, imperf. between 1,100. 700.00
Never hinged 1,350.
b. Vert. pair, imperf. between 1,100.
Never hinged 1,350.
c. Imperf., pair 600.00
Never hinged 750.00
C8 AP8 $1 blue 65.00 50.00
Never hinged 110.00
On cover 75.00
a. Horiz. pair, imperf. between 800.00
Never hinged 950.00
b. Vert. pair, imperf. between 800.00
Never hinged 950.00
c. Imperf., pair 600.00
Never hinged 750.00
Nos. C6-C8 (3) 107.50 79.50
Set, never hinged 180.00

1931 Wmk. 224

C9 AP6 15c brown 10.00 7.00
Never hinged 15.00
On cover 14.00
a. Horiz. pair, imperf. between 800.00
Never hinged 1,000.
b. Vert. pair, imperf. between 900.00
Never hinged 1,100.
c. Imperf., pair 475.00
Never hinged 575.00
C10 AP7 50c green 42.50 32.50
Never hinged 80.00
On cover 40.00
a. Horiz. pair, imperf. between 800.00
Never hinged 1,000.
b. Vert. pair, imperf. between 800.00
Never hinged 1,000.
c. Horiz. pair, Imperf. vert. 800.00
Never hinged —
C11 AP8 $1 blue 100.00 80.00
Never hinged 165.00
On cover 100.00
a. Vert. pair, imperf. between 850.00
Never hinged 1,050.
c. Horiz. pair, imperf. between 850.00
Never hinged 1,050.
d. Vert. pair, imperf. horiz. 850.00
Never hinged —
e. Imperf., pair 500.00
Never hinged 650.00
Nos. C9-C11 (3) 152.50 119.50
Set, never hinged 260.00

As the watermark 224 does not show on every stamp in the sheet, pairs are found one with and one without watermark.

For overprint and surcharge see Nos. 211, C12.

No. C11 Surcharged in Red

1932, May 19

C12 AP8 $1.50 on $1 blue 275.00 250.00
Never hinged 425.00
On cover 375.00
a. Inverted surcharge *16,000.*
Never hinged *21,000.*

A stamp of this design was produced in the US in 1932 by a private company under contract with Newfoundland authorities. The government canceled the contract and the stamp was not valid for prepayment of postage. Value $25.

"Put to Flight" — AP9

"Land of Heart's Delight" AP10

"Spotting the Herd" AP11

"News from Home" AP12

"Labrador, The Land of Gold" AP13

Perf. 11½ (10, 60c), 14 (5, 30, 75c

1933, June 9 **Engr.**

C13	AP9	5c lt brown	10.00	10.00
		Never hinged	12.50	
		On cover		17.50
b.		Horiz. pair, imperf. between	*1,100.*	
		Never hinged	*1,500.*	
c.		Vert. pair, imperf. between	*1,100.*	
		Never hinged	*1,500.*	
C14	AP10	10c yellow	16.00	15.00
		Never hinged	24.00	
		On cover		20.00
C15	AP11	30c blue	27.50	27.50
		Never hinged	35.00	
		On cover		35.00
C16	AP12	60c green	55.00	52.50
		Never hinged	85.00	
		On cover		65.00
C17	AP13	75c bister	55.00	52.50
		Never hinged	85.00	
		On cover		65.00
b.		Horiz. pair, imperf. between	*1,100.*	
		Never hinged	*1,500.*	
c.		Vert. pair, imperf. between	*1,100.*	
		Never hinged	*1,500.*	
		Nos. C13-C17 (5)	163.50	157.50
		Set, never hinged	240.00	

Beware of clever forgeries of Nos. C13b, C13c, C17b and C17c. Certificates of authenticity are highly recommended.

Imperf., Pairs

C13a	AP9	5c	225.00
		Never hinged	300.00
C14a	AP10	10c	160.00
		Never hinged	240.00
C15a	AP11	30c	500.00
		Never hinged	650.00
C16a	AP12	60c	525.00
		Never hinged	675.00
C17a	AP13	75c	500.00
		Never hinged	625.00
		Set, never hinged	2,500.

No. C17 Surcharged in Black

1933, July 24 ***Perf. 14***

C18	AP13	$4.50 on 75c bister	350.00	325.00
		Never hinged	500.00	
		On cover		825.00
a.		Inverted surcharge	*100,000.*	
		Never hinged	—	

Return flight from Chicago to Rome of the squadron of Italian seaplanes under the command of Gen. Italo Balbo.

No. C18a was not regularly issued. The $4.50 on No. C14, 10c yellow, is a proof.

View of St. John's AP14

1943, June 1 **Unwmk.** ***Perf. 12***

C19	AP14	7c bright ultra	.35	.25
		Never hinged	.45	
		First day cover		2.25

POSTAGE DUE STAMPS

D1

Perf. 10-10½, Compound

1939-49 **Litho.** **Unwmk.**

J1	D1	1c yellow green, perf. 11 ('49)	4.00	5.00
		Never hinged	7.25	
		On cover		400.00
a.		Perf. 10-10½)	6.00	5.00
		Never hinged	7.50	
		On cover		350.00
J2	D1	2c vermilion	6.50	5.00
		Never hinged	9.25	
		On cover		350.00
a.		Perf. 11x9 ('46)	6.50	5.25
		Never hinged	9.25	
		On cover		550.00
J3	D1	3c ultramarine	6.50	5.50
		Never hinged	9.25	
		On cover		450.00
a.		Perf. 11x9 ('49)	7.50	7.50
		Never hinged	10.00	
		On cover		750.00
b.		Perf. 9	*1,200.*	
		Never hinged	525.00	
J4	D1	4c yel org, perf. 11x9 ('49)	8.75	8.75
		Never hinged	14.00	
		On cover		750.00
a.		Perf 10-10½	12.50	12.50
		Never hinged	17.00	
		On cover		450.00
J5	D1	5c pale brown	10.00	4.00
		Never hinged	18.00	
		On cover		600.00
J6	D1	10c dark violet	4.00	3.75
		Never hinged	7.50	
		On cover		550.00
		Nos. J1-J6 (6)	39.75	32.00
		Set, never hinged	65.00	

1949 **Wmk. 224** ***Perf. 11***

J7	D1	10c dark violet	10.00	12.50
		Never hinged	17.50	
		On cover		750.00
		"LUE" instead of "DUE" plate flaw	40.00	40.00
		Never hinged	60.00	
a.		Vert. pair, imperf. between	*650.00*	
		Never hinged	*800.00*	

For used examples of Nos. J1-J7 with dated cancels from 1939-49, triple the values shown.

Covers: Cover values are for proper postage due usages on commercial covers prior to April 1, 1949. Note that multiples and combinations are not additive; therefore, for example, a pair of No. J2 on cover is valued at approximately $355 (cover value plus single used value). Values for philatelic covers range from approximately $55 to $100.

POST OFFICE SEALS

King Edward VII — POS1

1905 **Unwmk.** ***Perf. 12***

OX1	POS1	black, *blue*	650.00	450.00
		Never hinged	1,300.	
		On cover		*2,400.*

No. OX1 used or on cover is valued creased but not torn. Cover value is for presentable cover, with damage to the cover consistent with the application of the seal.

Some copies of No. OX1 show a portion of the papermaker's watermark. Values, unused $925, mint never hinged $1,800, used $550.

NEW GUINEA

'nü 'gi-nē

LOCATION — On an island of the same name in the South Pacific Ocean, north of Australia.

GOVT. — Mandate administered by Australia

AREA — 93,000 sq. mi.

POP. — 675,369 (1940)

CAPITAL — Rabaul

The territory occupies the northeastern part of the island and includes New Britain and other nearby islands. It was formerly a German possession and should not be confused with British New Guinea (Papua) which is in the southeastern part of the same island, nor Netherlands New Guinea. For previous issues see German New Guinea, New Britain, North West Pacific Islands.

12 Pence = 1 Shilling
20 Shillings = 1 Pound

Native Huts — A1

Bird of Paradise — A2

1925-28 **Engr.** ***Perf. 11***

1	A1	½p orange	2.75	*8.00*
2	A1	1p yellow green	2.75	*6.25*
3	A1	1½p vermilion ('26)	3.75	*3.00*
4	A1	2p claret	2.75	*5.00*
5	A1	3p deep blue	5.00	4.50
6	A1	4p olive green	15.00	*24.00*
7	A1	6p yel bister ('28)	5.00	*55.00*
a.		6p light brown	22.50	*55.00*
b.		6p olive bister ('27)	7.00	*55.00*
8	A1	9p deep violet	15.00	*50.00*
9	A1	1sh gray green	17.50	*30.00*
10	A1	2sh red brown	35.00	*55.00*
11	A1	5sh olive bister	55.00	75.00
12	A1	10sh dull rose	110.00	*210.00*
13	A1	£1 grnsh gray	210.00	*350.00*
		Nos. 1-13 (13)	479.50	875.75

For overprints see Nos. C1-C13, O1-O9.

1931, Aug. 2

18	A2	1p light green	4.50	1.75
19	A2	1½p red	5.75	*11.50*
20	A2	2p violet brown	5.75	2.50
21	A2	3p deep blue	5.75	5.50
22	A2	4p olive green	7.50	*22.50*
23	A2	5p slate green	5.75	*22.50*
24	A2	6p bister	8.00	*30.00*
25	A2	9p dull violet	9.00	*21.00*
26	A2	1sh bluish gray	7.00	*17.00*
27	A2	2sh red brown	11.50	*35.00*
28	A2	5sh olive brown	47.50	*62.50*
29	A2	10sh rose red	95.00	*150.00*
30	A2	£1 gray	210.00	*290.00*
		Nos. 18-30 (13)	423.00	*671.75*

10th anniversary of Australian Mandate.

For overprints see #C14-C27, O12-O22.

Type of 1931 without date scrolls

1932-34 ***Perf. 11***

31	A2	1p light green	2.25	.25
32	A2	1½p violet brown	2.25	*12.50*
33	A2	2p red	2.25	.25
34	A2	2½p dp grn ('34)	7.50	*24.00*
35	A2	3p gray blue	2.75	.90
36	A2	3½p magenta ('34)	15.00	*12.50*
37	A2	4p olive green	2.75	*7.00*
38	A2	5p slate green	2.75	.80
39	A2	6p bister	4.50	*3.75*
40	A2	9p dull violet	11.00	*25.00*
41	A2	1sh bluish gray	5.00	*11.50*
42	A2	2sh red brown	4.50	*19.00*
43	A2	5sh olive brown	30.00	*50.00*
44	A2	10sh rose red	55.00	*80.00*
45	A2	£1 gray	110.00	*110.00*
		Nos. 31-45 (15)	257.50	*357.45*

For overprints see #46-47, C28-C43, O23-O35. See footnote following C43.

Silver Jubilee Issue

Stamps of 1932-34 Overprinted

1935, June 27

Glazed Paper

46	A2	1p light green	1.00	.55
47	A2	2p red	2.25	.55
		Set, never hinged	6.00	

King George VI — A3

1937, May 18 **Engr.**

48	A3	2p salmon rose	.20	*.85*
49	A3	3p blue	.20	*1.75*
50	A3	5p green	.35	*1.75*
51	A3	1sh brown violet	.60	*.85*
		Nos. 48-51 (4)	1.35	*5.20*
		Set, never hinged	2.50	

Coronation of George VI and Queen Elizabeth.

AIR POST STAMPS

Regular Issues of 1925-28 Overprinted

1931, June ***Perf. 11***

C1	A1	½p orange	1.75	*7.50*
C2	A1	1p yellow green	1.75	*5.75*
C3	A1	1½p vermilion	1.40	*5.75*
C4	A1	2p claret	1.40	*8.00*
C5	A1	3p deep blue	2.00	*15.00*
C6	A1	4p olive green	1.40	*10.00*
C7	A1	6p light brown	2.00	*16.00*
C8	A1	9p deep violet	3.50	*19.00*
C9	A1	1sh gray green	3.50	*19.00*
C10	A1	2sh red brown	8.00	*47.50*
C11	A1	5sh ol bister	22.50	*75.00*
C12	A1	10sh light red	85.00	*110.00*
C13	A1	£1 grnsh gray	160.00	*290.00*
		Nos. C1-C13 (13)	294.20	*628.50*

Type of Regular Issue of 1931 and Nos. 18-30 Overprinted

1931, Aug.

C14	A2	½p orange	3.75	3.75
C15	A2	1p light green	4.50	*5.50*
C16	A2	1½p red	4.25	*11.50*
C17	A2	2p violet brown	4.25	3.50
C18	A2	3p deep blue	7.00	*7.00*
C19	A2	4p olive green	7.00	7.00
C20	A2	5p slate green	7.00	12.50
C21	A2	6p bister	8.00	*30.00*
C22	A2	9p dull violet	9.00	*17.00*
C23	A2	1sh bluish gray	8.50	*17.00*
C24	A2	2sh red brown	18.00	*55.00*
C25	A2	5sh olive brown	47.50	*80.00*
C26	A2	10sh rose red	70.00	*140.00*
C27	A2	£1 gray	125.00	*290.00*
		Nos. C14-C27 (14)	323.75	*679.75*

10th anniversary of Australian Mandate.

Same Overprint on Type of Regular Issue of 1932-34 and Nos. 31-45

1932-34 **Perf. 11**

C28	A2	½p orange	.65	*1.75*
C29	A2	1p light green	1.40	*1.75*
C30	A2	1½p violet brown	2.00	*8.50*
C31	A2	2p red	2.00	*.35*
C32	A2	2½p dp grn ('34)	7.00	2.75
C33	A2	3p gray blue	3.75	3.50
C34	A2	3½p mag ('34)	5.00	*3.75*
C35	A2	4p olive green	5.00	*11.50*
C36	A2	5p slate green	8.00	*8.50*
C37	A2	6p bister	5.00	*17.00*
C38	A2	9p dull violet	7.00	*10.00*
C39	A2	1sh bluish gray	7.00	*10.00*
C40	A2	2sh red brown	11.50	*55.00*
C41	A2	5sh olive brown	55.00	*62.50*
C42	A2	10sh rose red	92.50	92.50
C43	A2	£1 gray	85.00	62.50
		Nos. C28-C43 (16)	297.80	*351.85*

No. C28 exists without overprint, but is believed not to have been issued in this condition. Value $200.

Plane over Bulolo Goldfield AP1

1935, May 1 **Engr.** **Unwmk.**

C44	AP1	£2 violet	260.00	160.00
C45	AP1	£5 green	625.00	550.00

AP2

1939, Mar. 1

C46	AP2	½p orange	4.25	*8.00*
C47	AP2	1p green	3.75	*5.00*
C48	AP2	1½p vio brown	4.50	*11.00*
C49	AP2	2p red orange	9.00	4.00
C50	AP2	3p dark blue	15.00	*21.00*
C51	AP2	4p ol bister	16.00	9.75
C52	AP2	5p slate grn	13.50	4.25
C53	AP2	6p bister brn	29.00	21.00
C54	AP2	9p dl violet	29.00	27.50
C55	AP2	1sh sage green	29.00	21.00
C56	AP2	2sh car lake	75.00	55.00
C57	AP2	5sh ol brown	150.00	110.00
C58	AP2	10sh rose red	425.00	290.00
C59	AP2	£1 grnsh gray	110.00	*125.00*
		Nos. C46-C59 (14)	913.00	712.50

OFFICIAL STAMPS

Regular Issue of 1925 Overprinted

1925-29 **Unwmk.** ***Perf. 11***

O1	A1	1p yellow green	1.10	*5.00*
O2	A1	1½p vermilion ('29)	6.25	*19.00*
O3	A1	2p claret	2.00	*4.25*
O4	A1	3p deep blue	4.00	*8.50*
O5	A1	4p olive green	5.00	*9.75*
O6	A1	6p yel bister ('29)	8.00	*40.00*
a.		6p olive bister	22.50	*40.00*
O7	A1	9p deep violet	4.50	*40.00*
O8	A1	1sh gray green	6.25	*40.00*
O9	A1	2sh red brown	32.50	*70.00*
		Nos. O1-O9 (9)	69.60	*236.50*

Nos. 18-28 Overprinted

1931, Aug. 2

O12	A2	1p light green	7.00	*15.00*
O13	A2	1½p red	8.00	*13.50*
O14	A2	2p violet brown	11.50	*8.00*
O15	A2	3p deep blue	7.50	*7.00*
O16	A2	4p olive green	7.00	*9.75*
O17	A2	5p slate green	11.50	*13.50*
O18	A2	6p bister	16.00	*19.00*
O19	A2	9p dull violet	18.00	*32.50*
O20	A2	1sh bluish gray	18.00	*32.50*
O21	A2	2sh red brown	45.00	*80.00*
O22	A2	5sh olive brown	110.00	*200.00*
		Nos. O12-O22 (11)	259.50	*430.75*

10th anniversary of Australian Mandate.

Same Overprint on Nos. 31-43

1932-34

O23	A2	1p light green	8.00	*9.00*
O24	A2	1½p violet brown	9.00	*13.50*
O25	A2	2p red	9.00	*3.75*
O26	A2	2½p dp green ('34)	3.75	*7.00*
O27	A2	3p gray blue	9.00	*29.00*
O28	A2	3½p magenta ('34)	3.75	*10.00*
O29	A2	4p olive green	9.00	*21.00*
O30	A2	5p slate green	8.00	*21.00*
O31	A2	6p bister	15.00	*47.50*
O32	A2	9p dull violet	13.50	*47.50*
O33	A2	1sh bluish gray	17.50	*32.50*
O34	A2	2sh red brown	40.00	*85.00*
O35	A2	5sh olive brown	140.00	*190.00*
		Nos. O23-O35 (13)	285.50	*516.75*

NEW HEBRIDES, BRITISH

'nü 'he-brə-ˌdēz

LOCATION — A group of islands in the South Pacific Ocean northeast of New Caledonia

GOVT. — Condominium under the joint administration of Great Britain and France

AREA — 5,790 sq. mi.

POP. — 100,000 (est. 1976)

CAPITAL — Vila (Port-Vila)

See French New Hebrides.

12 Pence = 1 Shilling
100 Centimes = 1 Franc

Catalogue values for unused stamps in this country are for Never Hinged items, beginning with Scott 62 in the regular postage section, Scott J11 in the postage due section.

British Issues

Stamps of Fiji, 1903-06, Overprinted

1908-09 **Wmk. 2** ***Perf. 14***

Colored Bar Covers "FIJI" on #2-6, 9

1	A22	½p gray grn ('09)	60.00	*92.50*
2	A22	2p vio & orange	2.25	*2.50*
3	A22	2½p vio & ultra, *bl*	2.00	*2.50*
4	A22	5p vio & green	3.50	*4.00*
5	A22	6p vio & car rose	3.50	*3.50*
6	A22	1sh grn & car rose	145.00	*290.00*
		Nos. 1-6 (6)	216.25	*395.00*

Wmk. Multiple Crown and CA (3)

7	A22	½p gray green	1.00	*8.00*
8	A22	1p carmine	.60	*1.00*
a.		Pair, one without overprint	10,000.	
9	A22	1sh grn & car rose ('09)	21.00	*4.25*
		Nos. 7-9 (3)	22.60	*13.25*

Nos. 2-6, 9 are on chalk-surfaced paper.

Stamps of Fiji, 1904-11, Overprinted in Black or Red

1910, Dec. 15

10	A22	½p green	4.00	*27.50*
11	A22	1p carmine	11.00	*9.75*
12	A22	2p gray	.80	*3.50*
13	A22	2½p ultra	1.00	*4.75*
14	A22	5p violet & ol grn	1.60	*6.25*
15	A22	6p violet	4.00	*5.75*
16	A22	1sh black, *grn* (R)	6.00	*8.50*
		Nos. 10-16 (7)	28.40	*66.00*

Nos. 14-16 are on chalk-surfaced paper.

Native Idols — A1

1911, July 25 **Engr.** **Wmk. 3**

17	A1	½p pale green	1.00	*2.00*
18	A1	1p red	4.25	*2.25*
19	A1	2p gray	9.25	4.50
20	A1	2½p ultramarine	3.50	*6.25*
21	A1	5p olive green	5.00	*8.00*
22	A1	6p claret	3.50	*5.75*
23	A1	1sh black, *green*	3.00	*15.00*
24	A1	2sh violet, *blue*	25.00	*25.00*
25	A1	5sh green, *yel*	40.00	*55.00*
		Nos. 17-25 (9)	94.50	*123.75*

See Nos. 33-37. For surcharges see Nos. 26-29, 38-39, French Issues No. 36.

Surcharged

1920-21

26	A1	1p on 5p ol green ('21)	10.00	*70.00*
a.		Inverted surcharge	2,250.	
27	A1	1p on 1sh black, *grn*	2.25	*15.00*
28	A1	1p on 2sh violet, *blue*	1.75	*11.50*
29	A1	1p on 5sh green, *yel*	1.75	*11.50*

On French Issue No. 16

30	A2	2p on 40c red, *yel* ('21)	2.00	*21.00*
		Nos. 26-30 (5)	17.75	*129.00*

On French Issue No. 27

Wmk. R F in Sheet

31	A2	2p on 40c red, *yel* ('21)	145.00	*625.00*

The letters "R.F." are the initials of "Republique Francaise." They are large double-lined Roman capitals, about 120mm high. About one-fourth of the stamps in each sheet show portions of the watermark, the other stamps are without watermark.

No. 26a is considered by some to be printers' waste.

Type of 1911 Issue

1921, Oct. **Wmk. 4**

33	A1	1p rose red	2.90	*16.00*
34	A1	2p gray	5.00	*42.50*
37	A1	6p claret	16.00	*85.00*
		Nos. 33-37 (3)	23.90	*143.50*

For surcharge see No. 40.

Stamps of 1911-21 Surcharged with New Values as in 1920-21

1924, May 1 **Wmk. 3**

38	A1	1p on ½p pale green	4.50	*25.00*
39	A1	5p on 2½p ultra	8.50	*24.00*
a.		Inverted surcharge	2,000.	

Wmk. 4

40	A1	3p on 1p rose red	4.50	*12.50*
		Nos. 38-40 (3)	17.50	*61.50*

No. 39a is considered by some to be printers' waste.

A3

The values at the lower right denote the currency and amount for which the stamps were to be sold. The English stamps could be bought at the French post office in French money.

1925 **Engr.**

41	A3	½p (5c) black	1.40	*14.00*
42	A3	1p (10c) green	1.10	*12.50*
43	A3	2p (20c) grnsh gray	2.00	*3.00*
44	A3	2½p (25c) brown	1.10	*15.00*
45	A3	5p (50c) ultra	3.50	*3.00*
46	A3	6p (60c) claret	4.00	*14.00*
47	A3	1sh (1.25fr) black, *grn*	3.75	*21.00*
48	A3	2sh (2.50fr) vio, *bl*	7.00	*25.00*
49	A3	5sh (6.25fr) grn, *yel*	7.00	*29.00*
		Nos. 41-49 (9)	30.85	*136.50*

Beach Scene A5

1938, June 1 **Wmk. 4** ***Perf. 12***

50	A5	5c green	2.90	*4.50*
51	A5	10c dark orange	1.40	*2.25*
52	A5	15c violet	4.00	*4.50*
53	A5	20c rose red	1.90	*3.00*
54	A5	25c brown	1.90	*3.00*
55	A5	30c dark blue	2.50	*2.90*
56	A5	40c olive green	5.00	*7.00*
57	A5	50c brown vio	1.90	*3.00*
58	A5	1fr car, *emerald*	4.50	*9.75*
59	A5	2fr dk blue, *emer*	35.00	19.00
60	A5	5fr red, *yellow*	80.00	55.00
61	A5	10fr violet, *blue*	225.00	85.00
		Nos. 50-61 (12)	366.00	198.90
		Set, never hinged	500.00	

Catalogue values for unused stamps in this section, from this point to the end of the section, are for Never Hinged items.

UPU Issue

Common Design Type

1949, Oct. 10 **Engr.** ***Perf. 13½***

62	CD309	10c red orange	.60	*1.00*
63	CD309	15c violet	.60	*1.00*
64	CD309	30c violet blue	.75	*1.00*
65	CD309	50c rose violet	1.00	*1.25*
		Nos. 62-65 (4)	2.95	*4.25*

Common Design Types pictured following the introduction.

Outrigger Canoes with Sails — A6

Designs: 25c, 30c, 40c and 50c, Native Carving. 1fr, 2fr and 5fr, Island couple.

1953, Apr. 30 ***Perf. 12½***

66	A6	5c green	.75	.20
67	A6	10c red	.75	.20
68	A6	15c yellow	.75	.20
69	A6	20c ultramarine	.75	.30
70	A6	25c olive	.75	.40
71	A6	30c light brown	.75	.50
72	A6	40c black brown	.75	.80
73	A6	50c violet	1.25	.90
74	A6	1fr deep orange	6.25	1.75

75	A6	2fr red violet	6.25	10.00
76	A6	5fr scarlet	11.00	25.00
		Nos. 66-76 (11)	30.00	40.25

POSTAGE DUE STAMPS

British Issues

Type of 1925 Overprinted

1925, June Engr. Wmk. 4 *Perf. 14*

J1	A3	1p (10c) green	37.50	1.25
J2	A3	2p (20c) gray	40.00	1.25
J3	A3	3p (30c) carmine	40.00	3.25
J4	A3	5p (50c) ultra	45.00	5.50
J5	A3	10p (1fr) car, *blue*	52.50	6.50
		Nos. J1-J5 (5)	215.00	17.75

Values for Nos. J1-J5 are for toned copies.

Regular Stamps of 1938 Overprinted in Black

1938, June 1 *Perf. 12*

J6	A5	5c green	20.00	32.50
J7	A5	10c dark orange	20.00	32.50
J8	A5	20c rose red	22.50	50.00
J9	A5	40c olive green	27.50	57.50
J10	A5	1fr car, *emerald*	35.00	67.50
		Nos. J6-J10 (5)	125.00	240.00

Catalogue values for unused stamps in this section, from this point to the end of the section, are for Never Hinged items.

Regular Stamps of 1953 Overprinted in Black

1953, Apr. 30 *Perf. 12½*

J11	A6	5c green	4.75	7.50
J12	A6	10c red	2.25	6.00
J13	A6	20c ultramarine	6.00	11.00
J14	A6	40c black brown	8.50	27.50
J15	A6	1fr deep orange	5.50	32.50
		Nos. J11-J15 (5)	27.00	84.50

NEW HEBRIDES, FRENCH

'nü 'he-brə-ˌdēz

LOCATION — A group of islands in the South Pacific Ocean lying north of New Caledonia

GOVT. — Condominium under the joint administration of Great Britain and France

AREA — 5,790 sq. mi.

POP. — 100,000 (est. 1976)

CAPITAL — Port-Vila (Vila)

Postage stamps are issued by both Great Britain and France. In 1911 a joint issue was made bearing the coats of arms of both countries. The British stamps bore the coat of arms of Great Britain and the value in British currency on the right and the French coat of arms and values at the left. On the French stamps the positions were reversed. This resulted in some confusion when the value of the French franc decreased following World War II but the situation was corrected by arranging that both series of stamps be sold for their value as expressed in French currency. See British New Hebrides.

12 Pence = 1 Shilling
100 Centimes = 1 Franc

Covers
Values are for commercial covers paying correct rates. Philatelic covers sell for less.

French Issues

Stamps of New Caledonia, 1905, Overprinted in Black or Red

Nos. 1-4

No. 5

1908 Unwmk. *Perf. 14x13½*

1	A16	5c green	3.50	3.50
		On cover		—
2	A16	10c rose	4.25	4.25
		On cover		—
3	A17	25c blue, *grnsh* (R)	7.00	7.00
4	A17	50c carmine, *org*	7.75	7.75
		On cover		—
5	A18	1fr bl, *yel grn* (R)	15.00	15.00
		On cover		—
		Nos. 1-5 (5)	37.50	37.50

For overprints and surcharges see #6-10, 33-35.

Stamps of 1908 with Additional Overprint

1910

6	A16	5c green	1.50	1.50
		On cover		—
7	A16	10c rose	1.75	1.75
		On cover		—
8	A17	25c blue, *grnsh* (R)	3.25	3.25
		On cover		200.00
9	A17	50c car, *orange*	4.75	4.75
		On cover		—
10	A18	1fr bl, *yel grn* (R)	13.00	13.00
		On cover		—
		Nos. 6-10 (5)	24.25	24.25

A2

Perf. 14

1911, July 12 Engr. Wmk. 3

11	A2	5c pale green	.55	.55
		On cover		200.00
12	A2	10c red	.55	.55
		On cover		—
13	A2	20c gray	2.00	2.00
		On cover		150.00
14	A2	25c ultramarine	2.50	2.50
		On cover		—
15	A2	30c vio, *yellow*	4.00	4.00
		On cover		—
16	A2	40c red, *yellow*	4.00	4.00
		On cover		—
17	A2	50c olive green	4.00	4.00
		On cover		—
18	A2	75c brn orange	5.25	5.25
		On cover		150.00
19	A2	1fr brn red, *bl*	3.50	3.50
		On cover		—
20	A2	2fr violet	6.75	6.75
		On cover		150.00
21	A2	5fr brn red, *grn*	13.00	13.00
		Nos. 11-21 (11)	46.10	46.10

For surcharges see Nos. 36-37, 43 and British issue No. 30.

1912 Wmk. R F in Sheet

22	A2	5c pale green	1.75	1.75
		On cover		—
23	A2	10c red	1.75	1.75
		On cover		—
24	A2	20c gray	2.10	2.10
		On cover		—
25	A2	25c ultramarine	2.50	2.50
		On cover		—
26	A2	30c vio, *yellow*	2.50	2.50
		On cover		125.00
27	A2	40c red, *yellow*	20.00	20.00
		On cover		150.00
28	A2	50c olive green	8.50	8.50
		On cover		150.00
29	A2	75c brn orange	8.50	8.50
		On cover		150.00
30	A2	1fr brn red, *bl*	4.25	4.25
		On cover		—
31	A2	2fr violet	9.25	9.25
		On cover		—
32	A2	5fr brn red, *grn*	17.00	17.00
		On cover		—
		Nos. 22-32 (11)	78.10	78.10

In the watermark, "R F" (République Française initials) are large double-lined Roman capitals, about 120mm high. About one-fourth of the stamps in each sheet show parts of the watermark. The other stamps are without watermark.

For surcharges see Nos. 38-42 and British issue No. 31.

Nos. 9 and 8 Surcharged

1920 Unwmk. *Perf. 14x13½*

33	A17	5c on 50c red, *org*	2.50	2.50
		On cover		110.00
34	A17	10c on 25c bl, *grnsh*	1.40	1.40
		On cover		—

Same Surcharge on No. 4

35	A17	5c on 50c red, *org*	900.00	1,100.
		On cover		—

British Issue No. 21 and French Issue No. 15 Surcharged

1921 Wmk. 3 *Perf. 14*

36	A1	10c on 5p ol grn	11.50	11.50
		On cover		—
37	A2	20c on 30c vio, *yel*	13.00	11.50
		On cover		—

Nos. 27 and 26 Surcharged

1921 Wmk. R F in Sheet

38	A2	5c on 40c red, *yel*	27.50	27.50
		On cover		120.00
39	A2	20c on 30c vio, *yel*	11.50	11.50
		On cover		—

Stamps of 1910-12 Surcharged with New Values as in 1920-21

1924

40	A2	10c on 5c pale grn	1.75	1.75
		On cover		—
41	A2	30c on 10c red	1.75	1.75
		On cover		—
42	A2	50c on 25c ultra	2.75	2.75
		On cover		100.00

Wmk. 3

43	A2	50c on 25c ultra	14.00	14.00
		On cover		—
		Nos. 40-43 (4)	20.25	20.25

A4

The values at the lower right denote the currency and amount for which the stamps were to be sold. The stamps could be purchased at the French post office and used to pay postage at the English rates.

1925 Engr. Wmk. R F in Sheet

44	A4	5c (½p) black	.90	.90
		On cover		100.00
45	A4	10c (1p) green	.75	.75
		On cover		100.00
46	A4	20c (2p) grnsh gray	.75	.75
		On cover		100.00
47	A4	25c (2½p) brown	.75	.75
		On cover		100.00
48	A4	30c (3p) carmine	.75	.75
		On cover		100.00
49	A4	40c (4p) car, *org*	.90	.90
50	A4	50c (5p) ultra	1.25	1.25
51	A4	75c (7½p) bis brn	1.75	1.75
52	A4	1fr (10p) car, *blue*	3.00	3.00
53	A4	2fr (1sh 8p) gray vio	3.50	3.50
54	A4	5fr (4sh) car, *grnsh*	7.00	7.00
		Nos. 44-54 (11)	21.30	21.30

For overprints see Nos. J1-J5.

Beach Scene
A6

1938 *Perf. 12*

55	A6	5c green	1.00	1.00
56	A6	10c dark orange	1.00	1.00
57	A6	15c violet	.90	.90
58	A6	20c rose red	1.00	1.00
59	A6	25c brown	1.90	1.90
60	A6	30c dark blue	1.90	1.90
61	A6	40c olive grn	1.75	1.75
62	A6	50c brown violet	1.75	1.75
63	A6	1fr dk car, *grn*	2.75	2.75
64	A6	2fr blue, *grn*	8.75	8.75
65	A6	5fr red, *yellow*	25.00	25.00
66	A6	10fr vio, *blue*	50.00	45.00
		Nos. 55-66 (12)	97.70	92.70

For overprints see Nos. 67-78, J6-J15.

POSTAGE DUE STAMPS

French Issues

Nos. 45-46, 48, 50, 52 Overprinted

1925 Wmk. R F in Sheet *Perf. 14*

J1	A4	10c green	50.00	4.75
J2	A4	20c greenish gray	50.00	4.75
J3	A4	30c carmine	50.00	4.75
J4	A4	50c ultramarine	50.00	4.75
J5	A4	1fr carmine, *blue*	50.00	4.75
		Nos. J1-J5 (5)	250.00	23.75

Nos. 55-56, 58, 61, 63 Overprinted

1938 *Perf. 12*

J6	A6	5c green	4.50	4.50
J7	A6	10c dark orange	4.50	4.50
J8	A6	20c rose red	7.00	7.00
J9	A6	40c olive green	12.00	12.00
J10	A6	1fr dark car, *green*	21.00	21.00
		Nos. J6-J10 (5)	49.00	49.00

NEW REPUBLIC

'nü ri-'pə-blik

LOCATION — In South Africa, located in the northern part of the present province of Natal

GOVT. — Republic

CAPITAL — Vryheid

New Republic was created in 1884 by Boer adventurers from Transvaal who proclaimed Dinizulu king of Zululand and claimed as their reward a large tract of country as their own, which they called New Republic. This area was excepted when Great Britain annexed

Zululand in 1887, but New Republic became a part of Transvaal in 1888 and was included in the Union of South Africa.

12 Pence = 1 Shilling
20 Shillings = 1 Pound

New Republic stamps were individually handstamped on gummed and perforated sheets of paper. Naturally many of the impressions are misaligned and touch or intersect the perforations. Values are for stamps with good color and, for Nos. 37-64, sharp embossing. The alignment does not materially alter the value of the stamp.

A1

A2

Handstamped

1886 Unwmk. *Perf. 11½*

1	A1	1p violet, *yel*	12.00	14.00
1A	A1	1p black, *yel*		*3,500.*
2	A1	2p violet, *yel*	10.00	15.00
a.		Without date		
b.		Tête bêche pair		
3	A1	3p violet, *yel*	22.50	30.00
a.		Double impression		
4	A1	4p violet, *yel*	40.00	
a.		Without date		
5	A1	6p violet, *yel*	35.00	37.50
a.		Double impression		
6	A1	9p violet, *yel*	35.00	
7	A1	1sh violet, *yel*	75.00	
a.		"1/S"	550.00	
8	A1	1/6 violet, *yel*	75.00	
a.		Without date		
b.		"1s6d"	475.00	
9	A1	2sh violet, *yel*	45.00	
a.		Tête bêche pair	550.00	
10	A1	2sh6p violet, *yel*	100.00	
a.		Without date		
b.		"2/6"	150.00	
11	A1	4sh violet, *yel*	450.00	
12	A1	5sh violet, *yel*	32.50	35.00
a.		Without date		
13	A1	5/6 violet, *yel*	40.00	
a.		"5s6d"	160.00	
14	A1	7sh6p violet, *yel*	100.00	
a.		"7/6"	190.00	
15	A1	10sh violet, *yel*	100.00	100.00
16	A1	10sh6p violet, *yel*	180.00	
16A	A1	13sh violet, *yel*	425.00	
17	A1	£1 violet, *yel*	125.00	
18	A1	30sh violet, *yel*	110.00	
a.		Tête bêche pair	550.00	

Granite Paper

19	A1	1p violet, *gray*	15.00	16.00
20	A1	2p violet, *gray*	15.00	16.00
a.		Without "ZUID AFRIKA"		
21	A1	3p violet, *gray*	20.00	26.00
a.		Tête bêche pair	350.00	
22	A1	4p violet, *gray*	15.00	17.50
23	A1	6p violet, *gray*	30.00	25.00
24	A1	9p violet, *gray*	27.50	
25	A1	1sh violet, *gray*	32.50	32.50
a.		Tête bêche pair	450.00	
26	A1	1sh6p violet, *gray*	40.00	
a.		Tête bêche pair	525.00	
b.		"1/6"	175.00	
27	A1	2sh violet, *gray*	125.00	
28	A1	2sh6p violet, *gray*	150.00	
a.		"2/6"	200.00	
29	A1	4sh violet, *gray*	210.00	
30	A1	5sh6p violet, *gray*	190.00	
a.		"5/6"	225.00	
31	A1	7/6 violet, *gray*	220.00	
32	A1	10sh violet, *gray*	210.00	225.00
a.		Tête bêche pair	475.00	
32B	A1	10sh 6p vio, *gray*	220.00	
c.		Without date		
33	A1	12sh violet, *gray*	350.00	
34	A1	13sh violet, *gray*	525.00	
35	A1	£1 violet, *gray*	275.00	
36	A1	30sh violet, *gray*	275.00	

Same with Embossed Arms

37	A1	1p violet, *yel*	15.00	16.00
a.		Arms inverted	32.50	32.50
b.		Arms tête bêche, pair	125.00	140.00
38	A1	2p violet, *yel*	15.00	16.00
a.		Arms inverted	32.50	35.00
39	A1	4p violet, *yel*	22.50	25.00
a.		Arms inverted	110.00	80.00
b.		Arms tête bêche, pair	300.00	
40	A1	6p violet, *yel*	50.00	

Granite Paper

41	A1	1p violet, *gray*	16.00	17.50
a.		Imperf. vert., pair		
b.		Arms inverted	40.00	45.00
c.		Arms tête bêche, pair		
42	A1	2p violet, *gray*	16.00	17.50
a.		Imperf. horiz., pair		
b.		Arms inverted	55.00	55.00
c.		Arms tête bêche, pair	550.00	550.00

There were several printings of the above stamps and the date upon them varies from "JAN 86" and "7 JAN 86" to "20 JAN 87."

Nos. 7, 8, 10, 13, 14, 26, 28 and 30 have the denomination expressed in two ways. Example: "1s 6d" or "1/6."

1887 Arms Embossed

43	A2	3p violet, *yel*	15.00	15.00
a.		Arms inverted	24.00	24.00
b.		Tête bêche pair	425.00	450.00
c.		Imperf. vert., pair		
d.		Arms omitted		
e.		Arms tête bêche, pair	260.00	
44	A2	4p violet, *yel*	15.00	15.00
a.		Arms inverted	22.50	22.50
45	A2	6p violet, *yel*	11.00	11.00
a.		Arms inverted	52.50	52.50
b.		Arms omitted	200.00	
c.		Arms tête bêche, pair	350.00	
46	A2	9p violet, *yel*	11.00	11.00
47	A2	1sh violet, *yel*	13.00	13.00
a.		Arms inverted	90.00	
b.		Arms omitted	55.00	
48	A2	1sh6p violet, *yel*	16.00	15.00
49	A2	2sh violet, *yel*	24.00	24.00
a.		Arms inverted	75.00	
b.		Arms omitted	100.00	100.00
50	A2	2sh6p violet, *yel*	21.00	21.00
a.		Arms inverted	24.00	24.00
50B	A2	3sh violet, *yel*	42.50	42.50
c.		Arms inverted	47.50	47.50
51	A2	4sh violet, *yel*	15.00	14.00
a.		Arms omitted		
52	A2	5sh violet, *yel*	16.00	15.00
a.		Imperf. vert., pair		
b.		Arms inverted	—	100.00
53	A2	5sh6p violet, *yel*	14.00	15.00
54	A2	7sh6p violet, *yel*	18.00	18.00
a.		Arms inverted	75.00	
b.		Arms tête bêche, pair		
55	A2	10sh violet, *yel*	15.00	15.00
a.		Arms inverted	22.50	22.50
b.		Arms omitted	90.00	75.00
c.		Imperf. vert., pair		
d.		Arms tête bêche, pair	210.00	
56	A2	10sh6p violet, *yel*	20.00	20.00
a.		Imperf. vert., pair		
b.		Arms inverted		
c.		Arms omitted		
57	A2	£1 violet, *yel*	50.00	50.00
a.		Arms inverted	57.50	
b.		Tête bêche pair	475.00	475.00
58	A2	30sh violet, *yel*	125.00	110.00

Granite Paper

59	A2	1p violet, *gray*	14.00	15.00
a.		Arms omitted	110.00	110.00
b.		Arms inverted	25.00	25.00
c.		Imperf. vert., pair		
d.		Tête bêche pair	400.00	
60	A2	2p violet, *gray*	8.00	8.00
a.		Arms omitted	100.00	100.00
b.		Arms inverted	22.50	22.50
c.		Tête bêche pair	450.00	
61	A2	3p violet, *gray*	12.00	12.00
a.		Arms inverted	65.00	65.00
b.		Tête bêche pair	450.00	
62	A2	4p violet, *gray*	12.00	12.00
a.		Arms inverted	90.00	90.00
b.		Tête bêche pair	450.00	
63	A2	6p violet, *gray*	12.00	12.00
a.		Arms inverted	100.00	100.00
64	A2	1sh6p violet, *gray*	13.00	13.00
a.		Arms inverted	90.00	
		Nos. 59-64 (6)	71.00	72.00

These stamps were valid only in New Republic.

All these stamps may have been valid for postage but bona-fide canceled specimens of any but the 1p and 2p stamps are quite rare.

NEW SOUTH WALES

ˈnü sauth ˈwāəlz

LOCATION — Southeast coast of Australia in the South Pacific Ocean
GOVT. — British Crown Colony
AREA — 309,432 sq. mi.
POP. — 1,500,000 (estimated, 1900)
CAPITAL — Sydney

In 1901 New South Wales united with five other British colonies to form the Commonwealth of Australia. Stamps of Australia are now used.

12 Pence = 1 Shilling
20 Shillings = 1 Pound

Watermarks

Wmk. 12 — Crown and Single-lined A

Wmk. 13 — Large Crown and Double-lined A

Wmk. 49 — Double-lined Numerals Corresponding with the Value

Wmk. 50 — Single-lined Numeral

Wmk. 51 — Single-lined Numeral

Wmk. 52 — Single-lined Numeral

Wmk. 53 — 5/-

Wmk. 54 — Small Crown and NSW

Wmk. 55 — Large Crown and NSW

Wmk. 56 NSW

Wmk. 57 — 5/- NSW in Diamond

Wmk. 58 — 20/- NSW in Circle

Wmk. 70 — V and Crown

Wmk. 199 Crown and A in Circle

Values for unused stamps are for examples with original gum as defined in the catalogue introduction except for Nos. 1-20 which are rarely found with gum and are valued without gum. Very fine examples of Nos. 35-100, F3-F5, J1-J10 and O1-O40 will have perforations touching the framelines or design on one or more sides due to the narrow spacing of the stamps on the plates and imperfect perforation methods. Stamps with perfs clear of the design on all four sides are scarce and will command higher prices.

Seal of the Colony
A1 A2

A1 has no clouds. A2 has clouds added to the design, except in pos. 15.

Unwmk.

1850, Jan. 1 Engr. *Imperf.*

Yellowish Wove Paper

No.	Description	Unused	Used
1	A1 1p red	7,500.	575.00
a.	1p brownish red	8,000.	575.00
c.	1p carmine	7,500.	575.00
d.	1p crimson lake	7,500.	575.00

Bluish Wove Paper

No.	Description	Unused	Used
1b.	A1 1p red	7,500.	575.00
1e.	A1 1p lake	7,500.	575.00

Re-engraved, with Clouds

1850, Aug.

Yellowish Wove Paper

No.	Description	Unused	Used
2	A2 1p red carmine	5,500.	485.00
f.	Hill unshaded (Pos. 2/3)	7,500.	750.00
g.	No clouds (Pos. 3/5	7,500.	750.00
h.	No trees (Pos. 2/2)	7,500.	750.00
2i	A2 1p vermilion	5,500.	675.00

Bluish Wove Paper

No.	Description	Unused	Used
2c	A2 1p carmine red	5,500.	675.00
j.	Hill unshaded	7,500.	650.00
k.	No clouds	7,500.	650.00
l.	No trees	7,500.	650.00
2m	A2 1p brownish lake	3,750.	375.00
2n	A2 1p crimson lake	4,000.	575.00
2o	A2 1p gooseberry red	6,000.	650.00

Laid Paper

No.	Description	Unused	Used
2b	A2 1p carmine red, *yellowish*	9,000.	800.00
p.	Hill unshaded	—	1,200.
q.	No clouds	—	1,200.
r.	No trees	—	1,200.
2e	A2 1p carmine red, *bluish*		
2s	A2 1p vermilion, *bluish*	7,500.	600.00

Printed in panes of 25 (5x5). Twenty-five varieties.

Stamps from early impressions of the plate sell at considerably higher prices.

No. 1 was reproduced by the collotype process in a souvenir sheet distributed at the London International Stamp Exhibition 1950. The paper is white.

Plate I — A3

Plate II — A4

Plate I: Vertically lined background.

Plate I re-touched: Lines above and below "POSTAGE" and "TWO PENCE" deepened. Outlines of circular band around picture also deepened.

Plate II (First re-engraving of Plate I): Horizontally lined background; the bale on the left side is dated and there is a dot in the star in each corner.

Plate II retouched: Dots and dashes added in lower spandrels.

Plate I

1850, Jan. 1

Early Impressions

No.	Description	Unused	Used
3a	A3 2p gray blue, *yelsh wove*	7,500.	725.00
b.	Double line on bale (Pos. 2/7)		950.00
3c	A3 2p deep blue, *yelsh wove*		800.00

Intermediate Impressions

No.	Description	Unused	Used
3d	A3 2p gray blue, *yelsh wove*	11,000.	425.00
3e	A3 2p deep blue, *yelsh wove*	12,000.	550.00

Late (worn plate) Impressions

No.	Description	Unused	Used
3	A3 2p blue, *yelsh wove*	8,000.	225.00
3f	A3 2p deep blue, *yelsh wove*	7,500.	200.00

Printed in panes of 24 (12x2). Twenty-four varieties.

Plate I, Retouched

No.	Description	Unused	Used
4	A3 2p blue, *yelsh wove*	5,750.	375.00
4a	A3 2p gray blue, *yelsh wove*	6,000.	425.00

Twelve varieties.

Plate II

1850, Apr.

Early Impressions

No.	Description	Unused	Used
5h	A3 2p gray blue, *yelsh wove*	5,750.	300.00
j.	"CREVIT" omitted (Pos. 2/1)	—	800.00
k.	Pick & shovel omitted (Pos. 1/10)	—	500.00
l.	No whip (Pos. 1/4, 1/8, 2/8)	—	400.00
5m	A3 2p bright blue, *bluish wove*	5,750.	300.00
5n	A3 2p indigo blue, *yelsh wove*	5,750.	300.00
5o	A3 2p lilac blue, *yelsh wove*		1,600.

Late (worn plate) Impressions

No.	Description	Unused	Used
5	A4 2p blue, *yelsh wove*	4,250.	300.00
5a	A4 2p blue, *bluish wove*	3,000.	250.00
5b	A4 2p blue, *grayish wove*	3,000.	250.00
5p	A4 2p prussian blue, *bluish wove*	5,000.	450.00
c.	"CREVIT" omitted	—	1,000.
d.	Pick and shovel omitted	—	750.00
e.	No whip	6,750.	600.00
h.	Early impressions	6,500.	400.00

Plate II, Retouched

No.	Description	Unused	Used
5F	A4 2p blue, *bluish wove*	5,250.	275.00
g.	No whip	—	425.00
i.	"CREVIT" omitted		575.00
5q	A4 2p prussian blue, *bluish wove*	5,750.	260.00

Eleven varieties.

Plate III
A5

Plate IV
A6

Plate III (Second re-engraving of Plate I): The bale is not dated and, with the exception of Nos. 7, 10 and 12, it is single-lined. There are no dots in the stars.

Plate IV (Third re-engraving of Plate I): The bale is double-lined and there is a circle in the center of each star.

1850-51

Wove Paper

No.	Description	Unused	Used
6	A5 2p bl, *grayish wove*	4,750.	275.00
a.	Fan with 6 segments	—	575.00
b.	Double-lined bale	—	375.00
c.	No whip	—	425.00
6d	A5 2p ultramarine	5,400.	250.00
7	A6 2p blue, *bluish wove* ('51)	4,000.	250.00
7b	A6 2p blue, *grayish wove*	4,500.	300.00
c.	Fan with 6 segments (Pos. 2/8)	—	375.00
d.	No clouds (Pos. 2/10)	—	375.00
e.	Hill not shaded (Pos. 1/12)		500.00
f.	No waves (Pos. 1/9, 2/5)		275.00
7g	A6 2p 2p ultramarine	4,500.	300.00
7h	A6 2p 2p prussian blue	4,000.	250.00

Laid Paper

No.	Description	Unused	Used
7a	A6 2p ultramarine	5,500.	350.00
7i	A6 2p prussian blue	6,000.	375.00
j.	Fan with 6 segments (Pos. 2/8)	—	300.00
k.	No clouds (Pos. 2/10)	—	300.00
l.	Hill not shaded (Pos. 1/12)		300.00
m.	No waves (Pos. 1/9, 2/5)		240.00
n.	"PENOE" (Pos. 1/10, 2/12)		300.00

Twenty-four varieties.

Plate V — A7

A8

Plate V (Fourth re-engraving of Plate I): There is a pearl in the fan-shaped ornament below the central design.

1850-51

Wove Paper

No.	Description	Unused	Used
8	A7 2p blue, *grayish wove* ('51)	4,500.	275.00
b.	Fan with 6 segments (Pos. 2/8)	—	525.00
c.	Pick and shovel omitted (Pos. 2/5)	—	525.00
8d	A7 2p ultramarine	4,500.	275.00

Laid Paper

No.	Description	Unused	Used
8a	A7 2p ultramarine	7,000.	375.00
e.	Fan with 6 segments (Pos. 2/8)	—	650.00
f.	Pick and shovel omitted (Pos. 2/5)	—	490.00

Yellowish Wove Paper

No.	Description	Unused	Used
9a	A8 3p green	5,500.	375.00
9h	A8 3p emerald green	6,750.	400.00
e.	No whip (Pos. 4/3, 4/4)	—	800.00
f.	"SIGIIIUM" for "SIGILLUM" (Pos. 5/3)	—	550.00
9g	A8 3p myrtle green	*17,500.*	*1,600.*

Bluish Wove Paper

No.	Description	Unused	Used
9	A8 3p yellow green	5,000.	375.00
9d	A8 3p emerald green	6,000.	375.00
i.	No whip (Pos. 4/3, 4/4)	—	500.00
j.	"SIGIIIUM" for "SIGILLUM" (Pos. 5/3)	—	625.00

Laid Paper

No.	Description	Unused	Used
9b	A8 3p green, *yellowish laid*	7,750.	750.00
k.	No whip (Pos. 4/3, 4/4)	—	900.00
l.	"SIGIIIUM" for "SIGILLUM" (Pos. 5/3)	—	1,000.
9c	A8 3p green, *bluish laid*	7,750.	750.00
9m	A8 3p bright green, *yellowish laid*	8,250.	800.00

Twenty-four varieties of #8, twenty-five of #9.

Queen Victoria
A9 A10

TWO PENCE
Plate I — Background of wavy lines.
Plate II — Stars in corners.
Plate III (Plate I re-engraved) — Background of crossed lines.

SIX PENCE
Plate I — Background of fine lines.
Plate II (Plate I re-engraved) — Background of coarse lines.

1851 Yellowish Wove Paper

No.	Description	Unused	Used
10	A9 1p carmine	3,500.	375.00
b.	No leaves to right of "SOUTH"	*5,000.*	875.00
c.	Two leaves to right of "SOUTH"	*5,000.*	1,250.
d.	"WALE"	*5,000.*	1,250.
11	A9 2p ultra, Plate I	1,450.	125.00

1852 Bluish Laid Paper

No.	Description	Unused	Used
12	A9 1p orange brown	4,750.	575.00
a.	1p claret	4,750.	975.00
b.	As "a," no leaves to right of "SOUTH"		1,250.
c.	As "a," two leaves to right of "SOUTH"		1,250.
d.	As "a," "WALE"		1,250.

1852-55

Bluish or Grayish Wove Paper

No.	Description	Unused	Used
13	A9 1p red	1,500.	225.00
a.	1p carmine	1,500.	225.00
b.	1p scarlet	1,500.	350.00
c.	1p brick red	1,500.	450.00
d.	As "c," no leaves to right of "SOUTH"		450.00
e.	As "c," two leaves to right of "SOUTH"		350.00
f.	As "c," "WALE"		350.00
14	A9 2p blue, Plate I	475.00	42.50
a.	2p ultramarine	1,250.	47.50
b.	2p slate	1,750.	47.50
c.	2p chalky blue	750.00	35.00
d.	2p prussian blue	750.00	35.00
15	A10 2p blue, Plate II ('53)	1,450.	175.00
a.	"WAEES"	*2,250.*	575.00
b.	2p deep ultramarine	1,600.	140.00
c.	2p prussian blue	1,600.	125.00
d.	As "c," "WAEES"	—	425.00
16	A9 2p blue, Plate III ('55)	750.00	95.00
a.	"WALES" partly covered with wavy lines	—	300.00
b.	2p blue, *white paper* ('55)	750.00	95.00
c.	As "b," "WALES" partly covered with wavy lines	—	300.00
17	A9 3p green	2,100.	225.00
a.	3p emerald	2,750.	350.00
b.	As "a," "WACES"		1,250.
c.	3p deep green	2,750.	325.00
d.	3p yellow green	2,000.	200.00
e.	As "d," "WACES"	—	700.00
f.	3p blue green, *thick paper*	2,000.	350.00
g.	As "f," "WACES"		900.00
18	A9 6p brown, Plate I	2,750.	475.00
a.	"WALLS"	*2,750.*	475.00
b.	6p black brown	4,500.	1,000.
c.	6p yellow brown	3,000.	400.00
d.	6p chocolate brown	2,800.	375.00
e.	6p yellow brown, *white paper*		*1,300.*
f.	As "e," ""WALLS"		*2,400.*
19	A9 6p brown, Plate II	3,250.	475.00
a.	6p bister brown	3,250.	475.00
20	A9 8p yellow ('53)	6,500.	950.00
a.	8p orange	7,000.	1,250.
b.	No leaves to right of "SOUTH"		2,250.
c.	No bow at back of head	—	2,250.
d.	No lines in spandrel	—	1,350.

The plates of the 1, 2, 3 and 8p each contained 50 varieties and those of the 6p 25 varieties.

The 2p, plate II, 6p, plate II, and 8p have been reprinted on grayish blue wove paper. The reprints of the 2p have the spandrels and background much worn. Most of the reprints of the 6p have no floreate ornaments to the right and left of "South." On all the values the wreath has been retouched.

Type of 1851 and:

A11

A12

A13

A14

1854-55 Wmk. 49

No.	Description	Unused	Used
23	A9 1p orange	325.00	40.00
a.	No leaves to right of "SOUTH"	675.00	175.00
b.	Two leaves to right of "SOUTH"	900.00	250.00
c.	"WALE"	925.00	250.00
d.	1d orange vermilion	325.00	40.00
24	A9 2p blue	275.00	20.00
a.	2p ultramarine	275.00	20.00
b.	2p Prussian blue	275.00	20.00
25	A9 3p green	375.00	40.00
a.	"WACES"		225.00
b.	Watermarked "2"	4,750.	2,750.

Value for No. 25b is for copy with the design cut into.

No.	Description	Unused	Used
26	A11 5p green	1,750.	950.00
27	A12 6p sage green	1,100.	90.00
28	A12 6p brown	1,000.	100.00
a.	Watermarked "8"	3,500.	175.00
29	A12 6p gray	875.00	90.00
a.	6p greenish gray	800.00	90.00
b.	6p bluish gray	775.00	150.00
c.	6p deep slate	1,000.	90.00
d.	As "c," wmk sideways		1,200.
e.	6p fawn	925.00	150.00
f.	As "e," watermarked "8"	2,900.	175.00
g.	As "f," wmk sideways		*600.00*
30	A13 8p orange ('55)	7,000.	1,750.
a.	8p yellow	7,500.	1,800.
31	A14 1sh pale red brown	1,750.	150.00
a.	1sh red	1,750.	150.00
b.	1sh rose vermilion	1,750.	150.00
c.	As "b," watermarked "8"	4,000.	275.00

See Nos. 38-42, 56, 58, 65, 67.

Nos. 38-42 exist with wide margins. Copies with perforations trimmed are often offered as Nos. 26, 30, and 30a.

A15

A16

1856

32 A15 1p red 275.00 40.00
a. 1p orange red 275.00 40.00
b. As "a," printed on both sides 2,750. 2,750.
c. Watermarked "2"
d. 1p carmine vermilion 275.00 40.00
33 A15 2p blue 225.00 20.00
a. Watermarked "1" 6,500.
b. Watermarked "5" 750.00 100.00
c. Watermarked "8"
d. 2p dp turquoise blue 225.00 20.00
e. 2p ultramarine 225.00 20.00
f. 2p pale blue 225.00 20.00
34 A15 3p green 1,250. 125.00
a. 3p yellow green 1,200. 125.00
b. Watermarked "2" 4,250.
c. 3p bluish green ('56) 1,250. 125.00
Nos. 32-34 (3) 1,750. 185.00

The two known copies of No. 33c are in museums. Both are used.

The 1p has been reprinted in orange on paper watermarked Small Crown and NSW, and the 2p in deep blue on paper watermarked single lined "2." These reprints are usually overprinted "SPECIMEN."

See Nos. 34C-37, 54, 63, 90.

1859 **Litho.**

34C A15 2p light blue — 925.00
On cover 3,000.

1860-63 Engr. Wmk. 49 *Perf. 13*

35 A15 1p red 125.00 15.00
a. 1p orange 175.00 30.00
b. Perf. 12x13 2,100.
c. Perf. 12 225.00 30.00
36 A15 2p blue, perf. 12 225.00 20.00
a. Watermarked "1" 4,000.
c. Perf. 12x13 3,000. 275.00
37 A15 3p blue green 75.00 20.00
a. 3p yellow green 100.00 18.00
b. 3p deep green 100.00 17.00
c. Watermarked "6" 175.00 25.00
d. Perf. 12 900.00 65.00
38 A11 5p dark green 80.00 25.00
a. 5p yellow green 150.00 60.00
b. Perf. 12 275.00 87.50
39 A12 6p brown, perf. 12 525.00 65.00
a. 6p gray, perf. 12 525.00 80.00
40 A12 6p violet 225.00 10.00
a. 6p aniline lilac 1,400. 200.00
b. Watermarked "5" 600.00 47.50
c. Watermarked "12" 550.00 25.00
e. Perf. 12 525.00 22.50
41 A13 8p yellow 325.00 65.00
a. 8p orange 375.00 65.00
b. Perf. 12 4,500. 1,400.
42 A14 1sh rose 225.00 15.00
a. 1sh carmine 200.00 16.00
b. As "a," perf. 12 950.00 70.00
c. 1sh crimson lake 175.00 18.00
d. 1sh brownish red, perf 12 950.00 70.00
Nos. 35-42 (8) 1,805. 235.00

1864 Wmk. 50 *Perf. 13*

43 A15 1p red 72.50 29.00

1861-80 Wmk. 53 *Perf. 13*

44 A16 5sh dull violet 300.00 50.00
a. 5sh purple 325.00 75.00
b. 5sh dull violet, perf. 12 1,500. 400.00
c. 5sh purple, perf. 12 — 80.00
d. 5sh purple, perf. 10 275.00 80.00
e. 5sh purple, perf. 12x10 425.00 80.00
f. 5sh royal purple, perf 13 ('72) 400.00 65.00
g. 5sh deep rose lilac, perf 13 ('75) 150.00 40.00
h. 5sh rose lilac, perf 10 ('83) 175.00 60.00
i. 5sh purple, perf 10x12 ('85) — 175.00
j. 5sh reddish purple, perf 10 ('86) 175.00 60.00
k. 5sh rose lilac, perf 11 ('88) — 160.00

See No. 101. For overprint see No. O11.

Reprints are perf. 10 and overprinted "REPRINT" in black.

A17

A18

1862-65 Typo. Unwmk. *Perf. 13*

45 A17 1p red ('65) 150.00 42.50
a. Perf. 14 145.00 62.50
b. 1p brick red ('65) 150.00 45.00
46 A18 2p blue 115.00 20.00
a. Perf. 14 125.00 72.50

1863-64 Wmk. 50 *Perf. 13*

47 A17 1p red 40.00 15.00
a. Watermarked "2" 175.00 30.00
b. 1p dark red brown 200.00 25.00
c. 1p brick red 40.00 4.50
d. 1p brick red, shiny surfaced paper ('65) 300.00
e. Horiz. pair, imperf between 1,250.
48 A18 2p blue 25.00 4.25
a. Watermarked "1" 260.00 9.50
b. 2p cobalt blue 25.00 4.25
c. 2p Prussian blue 40.00 6.00

1862 Wmk. 49 *Perf. 13*

49 A18 2p blue 110.00 15.00
a. Watermarked "5" 140.00 19.00
b. Perf. 12x13 675.00 375.00
c. Perf. 12 275.00 60.00

See Nos. 52-53, 61-62, 70-76.

A19

A20

1867, Sept. Wmk. 51, 52 *Perf. 13*

50 A19 4p red brown 75.00 7.50
a. Imperf.
b. 4p pale red brown 75.00 7.50
51 A20 10p lilac 22.50 7.50
a. Imperf. Ovptd. "SPECIMEN" 40.00
b. Horiz. pair, imperf. between 1,750.

See Nos. 55, 64, 91, 97, 117, 129.

A21

A22

A23

Typo.; Engr. (3p, 5p, 8p)

1871-84 Wmk. 54 *Perf. 13*

52 A17 1p red 15.00 1.50
a. Perf. 10 325.00 37.50
b. Perf. 13x10 25.00 .75
c. Horiz. pair imperf. between 1,750.
53 A18 2p blue 18.00 1.25
a. Imperf.
b. Horiz. pair, imperf. vert. 725.00
c. Perf. 10 375.00 30.00
d. Perf. 13x10 20.00 1.25
e. Perf. 12x13
f. Perf. 11x12 325.00 50.00
54 A15 3p green ('74) 37.50 6.75
a. Perf. 11 190.00 125.00
b. Perf. 12 — 275.00
c. Perf. 10x12 190.00 40.00
d. Perf. 11x121 150.00 40.00
e. Perf. 10 125.00 12.50
f. Perf. 13x10 140.00 19.00
55 A19 4p red brown ('77) 90.00 15.00
a. Perf. 10 250.00 75.00
b. Perf. 13x10 125.00 8.75
56 A11 5p dk grn, perf. 10 ('84) 25.00 20.00
a. Imperf.
b. Perf. 12 325.00 150.00
c. Perf. 10x12 175.00 65.00
d. Perf. 10x13
57 A21 6p lilac ('72) 72.50 2.50
a. Imperf.
b. Perf. 13x10 90.00 2.50
c. Perf. 10 275.00 15.00
58 A13 8p yellow ('77) 175.00 25.00
a. Imperf.
b. Perf. 10 450.00 35.00
c. Perf. 13x10 275.00 32.50
59 A22 9p on 10p red brown, perf. 12 (Bk) 22.50 9.50
a. Double surcharge, blk & bl 225.00
b. Perf. 12x10 375.00 275.00
c. Perf. 10 19.00 9.50
d. Perf. 12x11 24.00 8.50
e. Perf. 11x12 — —
f. Perf. 13 47.50 11.00
g. Perf. 11 50.00 11.00
h. Perf. 10x11 75.00 18.00
60 A23 1sh black ('76) 125.00 8.50
a. Imperf. — —
b. Perf. 13x10 300.00 10.00
c. Perf. 10 325.00 25.00
d. Perf. 11 — —
e. Vert. pair, imperf between 1,750.
f. Pair, imperf 1,600.
Nos. 52-60 (9) 580.50 90.00

The surcharge on #59 measures 15mm. See #66, 68. For overprints see #O1-O10.

Typo.; Engr. (3p, 5p, 8p)

1882-91 Wmk. 55 *Perf. 11x12*

61 A17 1p red 9.50 .75
a. Perf. 10 14.50 .80
b. Perf. 10x13 175.00 10.00
c. Perf. 10x12 375.00 95.00
d. Perf. 12x11 175.00
e. Perf. 10x11 775.00 200.00
f. Perf. 11 250.00
g. Perf. 13 1,000. 500.00
62 A18 2p blue 17.50 .75
a. Perf. 10 32.50 .75
b. Perf. 13x10 95.00 4.50
c. Perf. 13 750.00 175.00
d. Perf. 12x10 475.00 125.00
e. Perf. 11 175.00
f. Perf. 12x11 675.00 175.00
g. Perf. 11x10 750.00 225.00
h. Perf. 12 375.00
63 A15 3p green 13.50 3.50
a. Imperf., pair 475.00
b. Vert. pair, imperf. btwn. —
c. Horiz. pair, imperf. vert. 475.00 —
d. Double impression
e. Perf. 10 15.00 3.50
f. Perf. 11 15.00 3.50
g. Perf. 12 17.00 3.75
h. Perf. 12x11 15.00 3.50
i. Perf. 10x12 60.00 5.75
m. Perf. 10x11 30.00 4.00
n. Perf. 12x10 60.00 5.75
64 A19 4p red brown 55.00 3.75
a. Perf. 10 75.00 6.25
b. Perf. 10x12 300.00 90.00
c. Perf. 12 475.00 275.00
65 A11 5p dk blue green 14.50 2.50
a. Imperf., pair 450.00
b. Perf. 11 16.00 2.50
c. Perf. 10 22.50 2.50
d. Perf. 12 30.00 3.00
e. Perf. 10x12 40.00
f. 5p green, perf. 12x11 11.00 1.75
g. 5p green, perf. 11x10 75.00 9.50
h. 5p green, perf. 12x10 175.00 100.00
i. 5p green, perf. 10x11 85.00 7.50
j. 5p green, perf. 11 11.50 1.75
66 A21 6p lilac, perf. 10 72.50 3.75
a. Horiz. pair, imperf. between 1,500.
b. Perf. 10x12 75.00 4.00
c. Perf. 11x12 150.00 18.00
d. Perf. 12 150.00 14.00
e. Perf. 11x10 100.00 4.50
f. Perf. 11 150.00 13.00
g. Perf. 10x13 475.00
67 A13 8p yellow, perf. 10 140.00 22.50
a. Perf. 11 140.00 30.00
b. Perf. 12 250.00 40.00
c. Perf. 10x12 180.00 70.00
68 A23 1sh black 125.00 13.00
a. Perf. 10x13 — —
b. Perf. 10 125.00 10.00
c. Perf. 11 325.00 20.00
d. Perf. 10x12 — 375.00
Nos. 61-68 (8) 447.50 50.50

Nos. 63 and 65 exist with two types of watermark 55 — spacings of 1mm or 2mm between crown and NSW.

See No. 90. For surcharges and overprints see Nos. 92-94, O12-O19.

The 1, 2, 4, 6, 8p and 1sh have been reprinted on paper watermarked Large Crown and NSW. The 1, 2, 4p and 1sh are perforated 11x12, the 6p is perforated 10 and the 8p 11. All are overprinted "REPRINT," the 1sh in red and the others in black.

Perf. 11x12

1886-87 Typo. Wmk. 56

Bluish Revenue Stamp Paper

70 A17 1p scarlet 9.50 4.25
a. Perf. 10 25.00 9.50
71 A18 2p dark blue 22.50 4.25
a. Perf. 10 75.00 11.00

For overprint, see No. O20.

A24

Perf. 12 (#73-75), 12x10 (#72, 75A) and Compound

1885-86

"POSTAGE" in Black

72 A24 5sh green & vio 775.00 350.00
a. Perf. 10 — —
b. Perf. 13 — —
73 A24 10sh rose & vio 1,600. 325.00
a. Perf. 13 — —
74 A24 £1 rose & vio 5,500. —
a. Perf. 13 — 5,250.

"POSTAGE" in Blue

Bluish Paper

75 A24 10sh rose & vio 325.00 100.00
b. Perf. 10 1,200. 350.00
c. Perf. 12x11 — —

White Paper

75A A24 £1 rose & vio 5,500. 3,500.

For overprints, see Nos. O21-O23.

The 5sh with black overprint and the £1 with blue overprint have been reprinted on paper watermarked NSW. They are perforated 12x10 and are overprinted "REPRINT" in black.

1894 White Paper

"POSTAGE" in Blue

76 A24 10sh rose & violet 325.00 75.00
a. Double overprint
b. 10sh mauve & claret, perf 10 550.00 160.00
c. 10sh mauve & violet, perf 11 475.00 110.00
d. 10sh mauve & violet, perf 12x11 325.00 70.00

See No. 108B.

View of Sydney A25

Emu A26

Captain Cook — A27

Victoria and Coat of Arms — A28

Lyrebird A29

Kangaroo A30

1888-89 Wmk. 55 *Perf. 11x12*

77 A25 1p violet 6.50 1.00
a. Perf. 12 10.00 .75
b. Perf. 12x11½ 30.00 1.60
78 A26 2p blue 9.50 1.00
a. Imperf., pair 275.00
b. Perf. 12 18.00 .65
c. Perf. 12x11½ 20.00 .65
79 A27 4p brown 18.00 6.00
a. Perf. 12x11½ 60.00 14.50
b. Perf. 12 50.00 7.00
c. Perf. 11 475.00 150.00
d. Imperf.
80 A28 6p carmine rose 40.00 6.00
a. Perf. 12 35.00 10.50
b. Perf. 12x11½ 40.00 6.00
81 A29 8p red violet 30.00 6.50
a. Perf. 12 30.00 6.50
b. Perf. 12x11½ 52.50 15.00
82 A30 1sh maroon ('89) 35.00 6.25
a. Imperf., pair 1,000.
b. Perf. 12x11½ 40.00 3.00
c. Perf. 12 50.00 3.00
d. 1sh violet brown, perf 11x12 30.00 7.00
e. 1sh violet brown, perf 12x11½ 55.00 8.50
f. 1sh violet brown, perf 12 55.00 7.00
Nos. 77-82 (6) 139.00 26.75
Set, ovptd. "SPECIMEN" 250.00

First British settlement in Australia, cent. For overprints see Nos. O24-O29.

1888 Wmk. 56 *Perf. 11x12*

83 A25 1p violet 22.50 2.50
84 A26 2p blue 75.00 4.00

See #104B-106C, 113-115, 118, 125-127, 130.

Map of Australia — A31

Governors Capt. Arthur Phillip (above) and Lord Carrington — A32

1888-89 Wmk. 53 *Perf. 10*

85 A31 5sh violet ('89) 325.00 75.00
a. 5sh deep purple 325.00 75.00
86 A32 20sh ultra 425.00 200.00

See #88, 120. For overprints see #O30-O31.

1890 Wmk. 57 *Perf. 10*

87 A31 5sh violet 275.00 55.00
a. Perf. 11 325.00 70.00
b. Perf. 10x11 300.00 55.00

c. Perf. 12 475.00 80.00
d. 5sh mauve, perf 10 300.00 55.00
e. 5sh mauve, perf 11 300.00 70.00

Perf. 11x12, 12x11

Wmk. 58

88 A32 20sh ultra 275.00 125.00
a. Perf. 11 375.00 125.00
b. Perf. 12 475.00 200.00
c. 20sh cobalt blue, perf 10 375.00 200.00
d. As "c," perf 11 325.00 85.00
Nos. 87-88, ovptd. "SPECIMEN" 225.00

For overprints see Nos. O32-O33.

"Australia"
A33

Victoria
A37

1890, Dec. 22 Wmk. 55 *Perf. 11x12*
89 A33 2½p ultra 10.00 4.00
a. Perf. 12 20.00 4.00
b. Perf. 12x11½ 75.00 —
Overprinted "SPECIMEN" 25.00

For overprint see No. O35.

Type of 1856

1891 Engr. Wmk. 52 *Perf. 10*
90 A15 3p green 7.75 *25.00*
a. Double impression
b. 3p light green 17.50 *100.00*

Type of 1867

1893 Typo. *Perf. 11*
91 A20 10p lilac 25.00 8.00
a. Perf. 10 30.00 8.75
b. Perf. 11x10 or 10x11 35.00 13.00
c. Perf. 12x11 175.00 25.00

Types of 1862-84 Surcharged in Black:

a

b

1891, Jan. 5 Wmk. 55 *Perf. 11x12*
92 A17(a) ½p on 1p gray 15.00 *10.00*
a. Imperf.
b. Surcharge omitted —
c. Double surcharge *350.00*
93 A21(b) 7½p on 6p brown 15.00 10.00
a. Perf. 10 15.00 10.00
b. Perf. 11 14.00 8.00
c. Perf. 12 17.50 10.00
d. Perf. 10x12 17.00 10.00

Perf. 12x11½

94 A23(b) 12½p on 1sh red 20.00 18.00
a. Perf. 11x12 20.00 16.00
b. Perf. 10 20.00 18.00
c. Perf. 11 21.00 18.00
d. Perf. 12 25.00 18.00
Nos. 92-94 (3) 50.00 38.00
Nos. 92-94 overprinted "SPECIMEN" 80.00

For overprints see Nos. O34, O36-O37.

1892-97 *Perf. 11x12*
95 A37 ½p slate ('97) 4.00 .60
a. Perf. 12x11½ 4.00 .60
b. Perf. 12 4.25 .60
c. Horiz. pair, imperf between *875.00*
d. ½p gray, perf. 10 55.00 3.00
e. As "d," perf. 10x12 100.00 13.50
f. As "d," perf. 11 115.00 9.75
g. As "d," perf. 11x12 4.00 .60
As "g," overprinted "SPECIMEN" 22.50

See #102, 109, 121. For overprint see #O38.

Types of 1867-71

1897 *Perf. 11x12*
96 A22 9p on 10p red brn (Bk) 14.00 12.00
a. 9p on 10p org brn (Bk) 14.00 12.00
b. Surcharge omitted —
c. Double surcharge 325.00 275.00
d. Perf. 11 18.00 17.00
e. Perf. 12 18.00 16.00
97 A20 10p violet 19.00 11.50
a. Perf. 12x11½ 19.00 11.50
b. Perf. 11 35.00 16.00
c. Perf. 12 24.00 12.50
Nos. 96-97, overprinted "SPECIMEN" 75.00

The surcharge on No. 96 measures 13½mm. For overprints see Nos. O39-O40.

Seal
A38

Victoria
A39

A40

ONE PENNY:
Die I — The first pearl in the crown at the left is merged into the arch, the shading under the fleur-de-lis is indistinct, and the "s" of "WALES" is open.
Die II — The first pearl is circular, the vertical shading under the fleur-de-lis is clear, and the "s" of "WALES" not so open.

2½ PENCE:
Die I — There are 12 radiating lines in the star on the Queen's breast.
Die II — There are 16 radiating lines in the star. The eye is nearly full of color.

1897 *Perf. 12*
98 A38 1p rose red, II 3.50 .35
a. Die I, perf. 11x12 4.00 .35
b. Imperf., pair —
c. Imperf. horiz., pair 575.00
d. Die I, perf. 12x11½ 4.25 .35
e. Die I, perf. 12 8.00 1.25
f. Die II, perf. 12x11½ 3.50 .35
g. Die II, perf. 11x12 3.50 .35
99 A39 2p deep blue 9.50 .45
a. Perf. 11x12 6.50 .45
b. Perf. 12x11½ 5.50 .45
100 A40 2½p dp purple, II 14.00 3.00
a. Die I, perf. 12x11 16.00 3.25
b. Die I, perf. 11 18.00 5.50
c. Die I, perf. 11½x12 18.00 3.00
d. Die II, perf. 11x12 15.00 3.00
e. Die II, perf. 11½x12 18.00 3.00
Nos. 98-100 (3) 27.00 3.80
Nos. 98-100 overprinted "SPECIMEN" 70.00

Sixtieth year of Queen Victoria's reign.
See Nos. 103-104, 110-112, 122-124.

Type of 1861

1897 Engr. Wmk. 53 *Perf. 11*
101 A16 5sh red violet 75.00 20.00
a. Horiz. pair, imperf. btwn. *8,000.*
b. Perf. 11x12 or 12x11 95.00 30.00
c. Perf. 12 110.00 37.50

Perf. 12x11½, 11½x12

1899, Oct. Typo. Wmk. 55

HALF PENNY:
Die I — Narrow "H" in "HALF."

102 A37 ½p blue green, I 2.50 .65
a. Imperf., pair 130.00 *225.00*
103 A39 2p ultra 4.00 .65
a. Imperf., pair 225.00
104 A40 2½p dk blue, II 5.75 2.25
a. Imperf., pair 235.00
104B A27 4p org brown 15.00 9.25
c. 4p red brown 21.00 10.50
d. As "c," imperf. pair 475.00
105 A28 6p emerald 92.50 37.50
a. Imperf., pair 425.00
106 A28 6p orange 20.00 4.75
a. 6p yellow 18.00 4.75
b. Imperf., pair 425.00
106C A29 8p magenta 30.00 5.75
Nos. 102-106C (7) 169.75 60.80

Lyrebird
A41

"Australia"
A42

1903 *Perf. 12x11½*
107 A41 2sh6p blue green 60.00 30.00
Overprinted "SPECIMEN" 85.00

See Nos. 119, 131.

1903 Wmk. 70 *Perf. 12½*
108 A42 9p org brn & ultra 20.00 5.00
Overprinted "SPECIMEN" 45.00
a. Perf. 11 2,000. 1,100.

See No. 128.

Type of 1885-86

1904 Wmk. 56 *Perf. 12x11*

"POSTAGE" in Blue

108B A24 10sh brt rose & vio 325.00 110.00
c. Perf. 11 375.00 140.00
d. Perf. 14 275.00 95.00
e. 10sh aniline crimson & violet, perf 12 475.00 140.00
f. As "e," perf 12x11 350.00 90.00
g. 10sh claret & violet, chalky paper, perf 12x11 350.00 125.00

The watermark (NSW) of No. 108B is 20x7mm, with rounded angles in "N" and "W." On No. 75, the watermark is 21x7mm, with sharp angles in the "N" and "W."

HALF PENNY:
Die II — Wide "H" in "HALF."

Perf. 11, 11x12½, 12x11½ and Compound

1905-06 Wmk. 12
109 A37 ½p blue grn, II 4.25 .80
a. ½p blue green, I 4.50 .80
b. Booklet pane of 12 —
110 A38 1p car rose, II 3.50 .35
a. Booklet pane of 6 —
b. Booklet pane of 12 —
111 A39 2p deep ultra 3.50 .35
112 A40 2½p dk blue, II 6.25 3.75
113 A27 4p org brown 15.00 6.00
a. 4p red brown 18.00 6.00
114 A28 6p orange 20.00 4.25
a. 6p yellow 24.00 4.25
b. Perf. 11 375.00
115 A29 8p magenta 36.50 7.75
117 A20 10p violet 23.50 7.00
118 A30 1sh vio brown 40.00 4.00
119 A41 2sh6p blue green 55.00 29.00

Wmk. 199

Perf. 12x11 or 11x12

120 A32 20sh ultra 200.00 75.00
a. Perf 12 260.00 85.00
b. Perf 11 190.00 70.00
Nos. 109-115,117-120 (11) 407.50 138.25

1906-07 Wmk. 13
121 A37 ½p green, I 6.00 2.25
122 A38 1p rose, II 11.75 1.75
123 A39 2p ultra 11.75 1.75
124 A40 2½p blue, II 77.50 *140.00*
125 A27 4p org brown 20.00 18.00
126 A28 6p orange 47.50 27.50
127 A29 8p red violet 30.00 26.00
128 A42 9p org brn & ultra, perf. 12x12½ ('06) 16.00 3.00
a. Perf. 11 125.00 100.00
b. 9p org brn & ultra, perf. 12x12½ 16.00 3.50
129 A20 10p violet 45.00 *60.00*
130 A30 1sh vio brown 65.00 13.50
a. Perf. 11 —
131 A41 2sh6p blue green 90.00 72.50
Nos. 121-131 (11) 420.50 366.25

Portions of some of the sheets on which the above are printed show the watermark "COMMONWEALTH OF AUSTRALIA." Stamps may also be found from portions of the sheet without watermark.

SEMI-POSTAL STAMPS

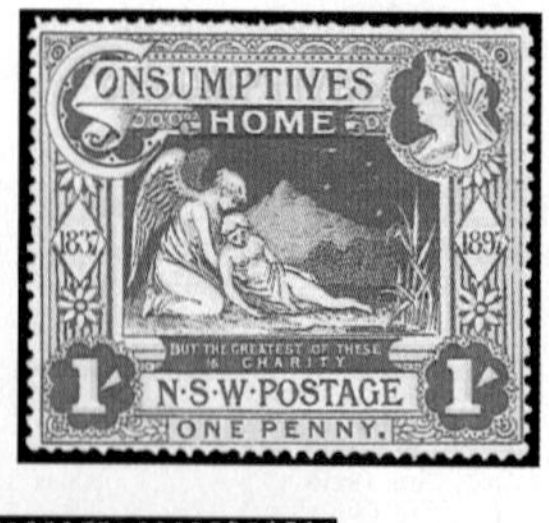
SP1

Allegory of Charity
SP2

Illustrations reduced.

1897, June Wmk. 55 *Perf. 11*
B1 SP1 1p (1sh) grn & brn 47.50 47.50
B2 SP2 2½p (2sh6p) rose, bl & gold 240.00 240.00
Nos. B1-B2 overprinted "SPECIMEN" 275.00

Diamond Jubilee of Queen Victoria.
The difference between the postal and face values of these stamps was donated to a fund for a home for consumptives.

REGISTRATION STAMPS

Queen Victoria — R1

Unwmk.

1856, Jan. 1 Engr. *Imperf.*
F1 R1 (6p) orange & blue 1,375. 325.00
F2 R1 (6p) red & blue 1,375. 300.00
a. Frame printed on back *5,500. 3,500.*

1860 *Perf. 12, 13*
F3 R1 (6p) orange & blue 625.00 135.00
F4 R1 (6p) red & blue 425.00 65.00

Nos. F1 to F4 exist also on paper with papermaker's watermark in sheet.

1863 Wmk. 49
F5 R1 (6p) red & blue 180.00 32.50
a. (6p) red & Prussian blue 240.00 35.00
b. (6p) red & indigo 350.00 47.50
c. Double impression of frame — *725.00*

Fifty varieties.

Nos. F1-F2 were reprinted on thin white wove unwatermarked paper and on thick yellowish wove unwatermarked paper; the former are usually overprinted "SPECIMEN."
No. F4 was reprinted on thin white wove unwatermarked paper; perf. 10 and overprinted "REPRINT" in black.

POSTAGE DUE STAMPS

D1

Perf. 10, 11, 11½, 12 and Compound

1891-92 Typo. Wmk. 55
J1 D1 ½p green, perf 10 7.00 7.00
a. Chalky paper —
J2 D1 1p green 15.00 2.75
a. Perf 12 32.50 6.25
b. Chalky paper 16.50 5.50
J3 D1 2p green 20.00 4.00
a. Perf 12x10 35.00 5.00
b. Chalky paper 20.00 8.00
J4 D1 3p green 35.00 15.00
b. Chalky paper 47.50 32.50
J5 D1 4p green 30.00 8.00
a. Chalky paper 40.00 17.50
J6 D1 6p green, perf 10 40.00 12.00
J7 D1 8p green, perf 10 115.00 30.00
J8 D1 5sh green, perf 10 225.00 75.00
a. Perf 11 500.00 150.00
b. Perf 11x12 — 500.00

Perf. 12x10

J9 D1 10sh green 425.00 225.00
a. Perf. 10 425.00 100.00
J10 D1 20sh green 475.00 275.00
a. Perf. 10 700.00 160.00
b. Perf. 12 750.00
Nos. J1-J10 (10) 1,387. 653.75

Used values for Nos. J8-J10 are for c-t-o copies.

OFFICIAL STAMPS

Regular Issues Overprinted in Black or Red

Perf. 10, 11, 12, 13 and Compound

1879-80 **Wmk. 54**

O1	A17	1p red	25.00	4.00
a.		Perf. 10	250.00	47.50
b.		Perf. 10x13	50.00	6.75
O2	A18	2p blue	35.00	3.75
a.		Perf. 11x12		375.00
b.		Perf. 10	375.00	55.00
O3	A15	3p green (R)	825.00	475.00
O4	A15	3p green	250.00	42.50
a.		Watermarked "6"	—	650.00
b.		Double overprint		
O5	A19	4p red brown	275.00	15.00
a.		Perf. 10x13	325.00	130.00
O6	A11	5p dark green	30.00	24.00
O7	A21	6p lilac	425.00	14.00
a.		Perf. 10	575.00	65.00
b.		Perf. 13x10	300.00	65.00
O8	A13	8p yellow (R)	*1,000.*	375.00
O9	A13	8p yellow	—	37.50
a.		Perf. 10	450.00	120.00
O10	A23	1sh black (R)	425.00	15.00
a.		Perf. 10	—	28.00
b.		Perf. 10x13	—	50.00

1880 **Wmk. 53**

O11	A16	5sh lilac, perf. 11	350.00	120.00
a.		Double overprint	4,250.	*2,500.*
b.		Perf. 10	800.00	275.00
c.		Perf. 12x10	700.00	190.00
d.		Perf. 13	900.00	165.00
e.		Perf. 10x12		—

1881 **Wmk. 55**

O12	A17	1p red	25.00	4.25
a.		Perf. 10x13		175.00
O13	A18	2p blue	15.00	1.75
a.		Perf. 10x13	275.00	150.00
O14	A15	3p green	15.00	6.25
a.		Double overprint		850.00
b.		Perf. 12	225.00	150.00
c.		Perf. 11		
O15	A19	4p red brown	25.00	5.25
a.		Perf. 10x12	325.00	150.00
b.		Perf. 12	325.00	250.00
O16	A11	5p dark green	22.50	*25.00*
a.		Perf. 12	175.00	
b.		Perf. 12x10	—	—
c.		Perf. 12x11 ('85)	65.00	16.00
O17	A21	6p lilac	35.00	8.25
a.		Perf. 12		75.00
b.		Perf. 12x11	—	—
O18	A13	8p yellow	37.50	18.00
a.		Double overprint	—	—
b.		Perf. 12	250.00	47.50
c.		Perf. 11 ('85)	37.50	22.50
d.		Perf. 10x12 or 12x10 ('85)	37.50	16.00
e.		Triple overprint	—	—
O19	A23	1sh black (R)	50.00	*15.00*
a.		Double overprint		375.00
b.		Perf. 10x13		100.00
c.		Perf. 11x12	40.00	15.00
		Nos. O12-O19 (8)	225.00	83.75

Beware of other red overprints on watermark 55 stamps.

1881 **Wmk. 56**

O20	A17	1p red	75.00	12.00

1887-90

O21	A24	10sh on #75	—	*3,250.*
O22	A24	£1 on #75A	*14,500.*	*9,000.*

No. 75 Overprinted

1889

O23	A24	10sh rose & vio	*3,750.*	*1,500.*
		Overprinted "SPECIMEN"	120.00	
a.		Perf. 10	*6,000.*	*3,000.*

Overprinted

1888-89 **Wmk. 55**

O24	A25	1p violet	4.50	1.50
a.		Overprinted "O" only		
O25	A26	2p blue	6.75	1.10
O26	A27	4p red brown	18.00	6.75
O27	A28	6p carmine	13.50	8.75
O28	A29	8p red lilac	35.00	22.50
O29	A30	1sh vio brown	32.50	6.75
a.		Double overprint		
b.		1sh purple brown, perf 12	32.50	6.75
c.		1sh maroon, perf 11x12 ('90)	32.50	6.75
d.		1sh maroon, perf 12	32.50	6.75
		Nos. O24-O29 (6)	110.25	47.35

Wmk. 53

O30	A31	5sh violet (R)	*1,200.*	*775.00*
O31	A32	20sh ultra	*3,000.*	1,250.

1890 **Wmk. 57**

O32	A31	5sh violet	*300.00*	125.00
a.		5sh, dull lilac, perf. 12	825.00	225.00
b.		5sh lilac, perf 10	375.00	140.00

Wmk. 58

O33	A32	20sh ultra	*3,250.*	1,100.
		O32b, O33 ovpted. "SPECIMEN"	350.00	

Centenary of the founding of the Colony (Nos. O24-O33).

1891 **Wmk. 55**

O34	A17(a)	½p on 1p gray & black	85.00	85.00
a.		Double overprint		
O35	A33	2½p ultra	17.50	16.00
O36	A21(b)	7½p on 6p brn & black	50.00	60.00
O37	A23(b)	12½p on 1sh red & black	90.00	*110.00*

1892

O38	A37	½p gray	8.75	*17.50*
a.		Perf 10	8.00	*18.00*
b.		Perf 12	7.50	*12.50*
c.		Perf 12x11½	17.50	15.00
		Overprinted "SPECIMEN"	40.00	

1894 **Wmk. 54**

O39	A22	9p on 10p red brn	1,000.	1,000.
		Overprinted "SPECIMEN"	100.00	

Wmk. 52

O40	A20	10p lilac, perf. 10	275.00	*200.00*
a.		Perf. 11x10 or 10x11	350.00	*325.00*
b.		Perf 10	350.00	
c.		Double overprint, one albino	—	
		Overprinted "SPECIMEN"	65.00	

The official stamps became obsolete on Dec. 31, 1894. In Aug., 1895, sets of 32 varieties of "O.S." stamps, together with some envelopes and postal cards, were placed on sale at the Sydney post office at £2 per set.

These sets contained most of the varieties listed above and a few which are not known in the original issues. An obliteration consisting of the letters G.P.O. or N.S.W. in three concentric ovals was lightly applied to the center of each block of four stamps.

It is understood that the earlier stamps and many of the overprints were reprinted to make up these sets.

NEW ZEALAND

'nü 'zē-lənd

LOCATION — Group of islands in the south Pacific Ocean, southeast of Australia
GOVT. — Self-governing dominion of the British Commonwealth
AREA — 107,241 sq. mi.
POP. — 3,230,000 (est. 1983)
CAPITAL — Wellington

12 Pence = 1 Shilling
20 Shillings = 1 Pound

Catalogue values for unused stamps in this country are for Never Hinged items, beginning with Scott 246 in the regular postage section, Scott B9 in the semi-postal section, Scott J21 in the postage due section, Scott O92 in the officials section, Scott OY29 in the Life Insurance Department section.

Watermarks

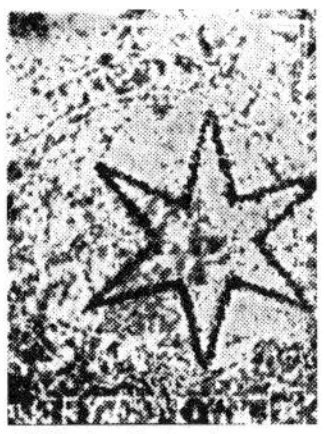

Wmk. 6 — Large Star

Wmk. 59 — N Z

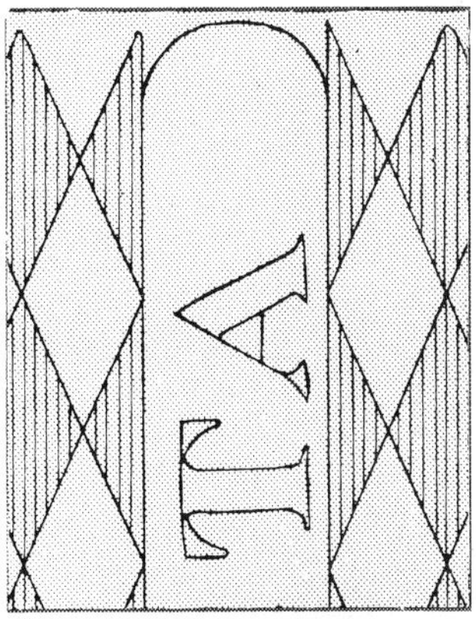

Wmk. 60 — Lozenges

Wmk. 61 — N Z and Star Close Together

Wmk. 62 — N Z and Small Star Wide Apart

Wmk. 63 — Double-lined N Z and Star

Wmk. 64 — Small Star

Wmk. 253 — Multiple N Z and Star

PRE-STAMP POSTAL MARKINGS

Crowned Circle handstamp types I and III are pictured in the Crowned Circle Handstamps and Great Britain Used Abroad section.

Auckland

1846

A1 I "Auckland New Zealand" crowned circle handstamp in red, on cover 300.

Nelson

1846

A2 I "Nelson New Zealand" crowned circle handstamp in red, on cover 1,100.

New Plymouth

1846-54

A3 I "New Plymouth New Zealand" crowned circle handstamp in red, on cover 2,900.
A4 I "New Plymouth New Zealand" crowned circle handstamp in black, on cover 2,900.

Similar to type I, "PAID/AT" straight

A5 "New Plymouth New Zealand" crowned circle handstamp in red, on cover ('54) 3,250.
A6 "New Plymouth New Zealand" crowned circle handstamp in black, on cover ('54) 3,250.

The device used for Nos. A5-A6 was made locally.

Otago

1851

A7 III "Otago New Zealand" crowned circle handstamp in red, on cover 2,000.

Petre

1846

A8 I "Petre New Zealand" crowned circle handstamp in red, on cover 1,400.

Port Victoria

1851
A9 III "Port Victoria New Zealand" crowned circle handstamp in red, on cover 1,200.

Russell

1846
A10 I "Russell New Zealand" crowned circle handstamp in red, on cover 6,500.

Wellington

1846
A11 I "Wellington New Zealand" crowned circle handstamp in red, on cover 350.

Issued under British Administration

Values for unused stamps are for examples with original gum as defined in the catalogue introduction.

Very fine examples of the perforated issues between Nos. 7a-69, AR1-AR30, J1-J11, OY1-OY9 and P1-P4 will have perforations touching the framelines or design on one or more sides due to the narrow spacing of the stamps on the plates and imperfect perforating methods.

The rouletted and serrate rouletted stamps of the same period rarely have complete roulettes and are valued as sound and showing partial roulettes. Stamps with complete roulettes range from very scarce to very rare, are seldom traded, and command great premiums.

Victoria — A1

London Print
Wmk. 6
1855, July 18 Engr. *Imperf.*
White Paper

1 A1 1p dull carmine *60,000.* *12,500.*
On cover —

Blued Paper

2 A1 2p deep blue *32,500.* 625.
On cover, single franking 1,750.
3 A1 1sh yellow green *45,000.* *5,750.*
On cover *45,000.*
a. Half used as 6p on cover *40,000.*

The blueing was caused by chemical action in the printing process.

Auckland Print
1855-58 Blue Paper Unwmk.

4 A1 1p orange red 11,000. 2,000.
On cover *7,500.*
5 Al 2p blue ('56) 3,500. 350.
6 Al 1sh green ('58) *37,500.* 4,250.
On cover *10,000.*
a. Half used as 6p on cover *25,000.*

An imperf, engraved reproduction of No. 1 on unwatermarked paper was produced in 2005 for a sheet that was included in a book commemorating the 150th anniv. of New Zealand stamps.

The blueing of Nos. 2 and 3 was caused by chemical action in the printing process.

1857-61 Unwmk.
Thin Hard or Thick Soft White Paper

7 A1 1p orange ('58) 2,750. 675.
e. 1p org vermilion, Wmk. 6 ('57) *17,500.*
On cover, pair *75,000.*
8 A1 2p blue ('58) 1,100. 210.
e. 2p pale blue ('57) 1,850. 350.
f. 2p deep dull blue 3,000. 275.
g. 2p deep ultra ('58) 2,100. 1,000.
9 A1 6p brown ('59) 2,100. 350.
e. 6p bister brown ('59) 3,200. 575.
f. 6p chestnut ('59) 3,500. 625.
h. 6p pale brown 1,800. 350.
10 A1 1sh blue green ('61) 15,000. 1,750.
e. 1sh emerald 16,000. 1,750.

No. 7e is identical to a shade of No. 11. The only currently known examples are pairs on covers or cover fronts. To qualify as No. 7e, a stamp must have a cancellation prior to 1862.

1859 *Pin Rouletted 9-10*
7a A1 1p dull orange 5,750.
8a A1 2p blue 3,750.
9a A1 6p brown 4,500.
10a A1 1sh greenish blue 6,750.

1859 *Serrate Rouletted 16, 18*
7b A1 1p dull orange 5,000.
8b A1 2p blue 3,750.
9b A1 6p brown 3,500.
g. 6p chestnut 6,750.
10b A1 1sh greenish blue 6,250.

Value for No. 10b is for a damaged stamp.

1859 *Rouletted 7*
7c A1 1p dull orange *7,250.* 5,000.
f. Pair, imperf between —
8c A1 2p blue *7,250.* 3,400.
9c A1 6p brown *6,750.* 2,800.
10c A1 1sh greensh blue — 4,500.

1862 *Perf. 13*
7d A1 1p orange vermilion 5,750.
8d A1 2p blue 4,250. 2,500.
9d A1 6p brown *6,250.*

1862-63 Wmk. 6 *Imperf.*
11 A1 1p orange ver 725.00 250.00
d. 1p carmine vermilion ('63) 475.00 300.00
e. 1p vermilion 550.00 250.00
f. 1p carmine 650.00 400.00
12 A1 2p deep blue 475.00 85.00
d. 2p slate blue 1,850. 210.00
e. Double impression 3,100.
f. 2p milky blue, worn plate — 260.00
g. 2p blue, worn plate 375.00 85.00
13 A1 3p brown lilac ('63) 475.00 160.00
14 A1 6p red brown ('63) 1,250. 100.00
d. 6p black brown 1,900. 110.00
e. 6p brown ('63) 1,300. 100.00
f. 6p pale red brown 900.00 150.00
g. 6p gray brown 950.00 165.00
15 A1 1sh yellow green 1,900. 350.00
d. 1sh deep green 2,100. 375.00
f. 1sh bronze green 1,500. 375.00
g. 1sh olive green 1,600. 375.00

See No. 7e.

1862 *Pin Rouletted 9-10*
12a A1 2p deep blue — 2,800.
14a A1 6p black brown — 4,000.

1862 *Serrate Rouletted 16, 18*
11b A1 1p orange vermilion 8,500. 1,900.
12b A1 2p blue — 1,250.
13b A1 3p brown lilac 4,000. 1,800.
14b A1 6p black brown — 1,900.
15b A1 1sh yellow green 3,750.

1862 *Rouletted 7*
11c A1 1p vermilion 2,800. 900.
12c A1 2p blue 2,250. 625.
13c A1 3p brown lilac 2,800. 800.
14c A1 6p red brown 2,800. 525.
15c A1 1sh green 3,250. 850.

The 1p, 2p, 6p and 1sh come in two or more shades.

1863 *Perf. 13*
16 A1 1p carmine ver 1,750. 350.00
a. 1p orange vermilion 1,400. 350.00
b. 1p vermilion 1,400. 350.00
17 A1 2p blue, no plate wear 500.00 70.00
a. 2p deep blue, no plate wear 425.00 92.50
b. 2p slate blue, slate plate wear — 700.00
c. 2p milky blue, slight plate wear — 575.00
18 A1 3p brown lilac 1,750. 500.00
19 A1 6p red brown 1,200. 100.00
b. 6p black brown 1,150. 210.00
20 A1 1sh green 2,250. 400.00
a. 1sh deep green 1,500. 375.00
b. 1sh yellow green 1,500. 350.00
c. 1sh bluish green 1,500. 350.00
d. 1sh bronze green 1,500. 350.00

This issue was made at Dunedin by perforating stamps of the previous issue. Most of the shades known imperf also are known perf. 13.

1862 Unwmk. *Imperf.*
Pelure Paper

21 A1 1p vermilion 9,250. 2,250.
b. Rouletted 7 5,500.
22 A1 2p pale dull ultra 5,250. 950.00
c. 2p gray blue 4,250. 925.00
23 A1 3p brown lilac *75,000.*
24 A1 6p black brown 2,500. 400.00
b. Rouletted 7 3,750. 700.
c. Serrate perf. 15 — 5,250.
25 A1 1sh deep yel green 11,000. 1,150.
b. 1sh deep green 11,000. 1,150.
c. Rouletted 7 12,000. 1,900.

No. 23 was never placed in use.

1863 *Perf. 13*
21a A1 1p vermilion 15,000. 3,500.
22a A1 2p gray blue 6,500. 800.00
b. 2p pale dull ultramarine 6,500. 800.00
24a A1 6p black brown 5,500. 450.00
25a A1 1sh deep green 12,000. 1,700.

1863 Unwmk. *Perf. 13*
Thick White Paper

26 A1 2p dull dark blue 2,200. 550.00
a. Imperf 3,000. 925.00

Nos. 26 and 26a differ from 8 and 8d by a white patch of wear at right of head.

1864 Wmk. 59 *Imperf.*
27 A1 1p carmine ver 950. 325.
28 A1 2p blue 1,250. 250.
29 A1 6p red brown 4,500. 700.
30 A1 1sh green 1,500. 300.

1864 *Rouletted 7*
27a A1 1p carmine vermilion 6,500. 3,150.
28a A1 2p blue 2,000. 875.
29a A1 6p deep red brown 6,500. 3,150.
30a A1 1sh green 4,500. 1,150.

1864 *Perf. 12½*
27B A1 1p carmine ver 11,000. 5,000.
28B A1 2p blue 375.00 62.50
29B A1 6p red brown 450.00 47.50
30B A1 1sh dp yel green 7,750. 2,500.

1864 *Perf. 13*
27C A1 1p carmine ver 11,000. 5,750.
28C A1 2p blue 1,000. 190.
30C A1 1sh yellow green 1,900. 800.
d. Horiz. pair, imperf. btwn. 14,000.

1864-71 Wmk. 6 *Perf. 12½*
31 A1 1p vermilion 200.00 50.00
a. 1p orange ('71) 500.00 90.00
32 A1 2p blue 175.00 22.50
a. 2p blue, worn plate 225.00 24.00
b. Horiz. pair, imperf. btwn. (#32) *3,750.*
c. Perf. 10x12½ 11,000.
d. Imperf., pair (#32) 1,900. 1,700.
33 A1 3p lilac 150.00 40.00
a. 3p mauve 525.00 80.00
b. Imperf., pair (#33) 3,750. 1,900.
c. As "a", imperf., pair 3,750. 1,900.
d. 3p brown lilac *1,750.* *700.00*
34 A1 4p deep rose ('65) 4,000. 300.00
35 A1 4p yellow ('65) 250.00 110.00
a. 4p orange yellow *2,250.* 1,100.
36 A1 6p red brown 250.00 28.00
a. 6p brown 275.00 42.50
b. Horiz. pair, imperf. btwn. 1,750. 1,900.
37 A1 1sh pale yel green 325.00 100.00
a. 1sh yellow green 400.00 140.00
b. 1sh green 800.00 350.00

The 1p, 2p and 6p come in two or more shades.

The 2p plate used for No. 32 was damaged and retouched in the bottom quarter of the plate. This is found also on all subsequent 2p issues.

Imperforate examples of the 1p pale orange, worn plate; 2p dull blue and 6p dull chocolate brown are reprints. Value, each $100.

1871 Wmk. 6 *Perf. 10*
38 A1 1p deep brown 800.00 125.00

1871 *Perf. 12½*
39 A1 1p brown 175.00 50.00
a. Imperf. 1,000.
40 A1 2p orange 150.00 32.50
a. 2p vermilion 140.00 32.50
b. Imperf., pair
41 A1 6p blue 200.00 77.50
Nos. 39-41 (3) 525.00 160.00

Shades exist.

1871 *Perf. 10x12½*
42 A1 1p brown 250.00 52.50
43 A1 2p orange 210.00 37.50
44 A1 6p blue 1,500. 575.00
Nos. 42-44 (3) 1,960. 665.00

The 6p usually has only one side perf. 10, the 1p and 2p more rarely so.
Shades exist.

1872 Wmk. 59 *Perf. 12½*
45 A1 1p brown 4,600.
46 A1 2p vermilion 800.00 325.00

1872 Unwmk. *Perf. 12½*
47 A1 1p brown 900.00 200.00
48 A1 2p vermilion 140.00 57.50
49 A1 4p yellow orange 160.00 *750.00*

The watermark "T.H. SAUNDERS" in double-line capitals falls on 16 of the 240 stamps in a sheet. The 1p and 2p also are known with script "WT & CO" watermark.

1872 Wmk. 60
50 A1 2p vermilion *3,150.* 575.

A2

A3

A4

A5

A6

A7

Perf. 10x12½, 11½, 12, 12½
1874 Typo. Wmk. 62
51 A2 1p violet 62.50 5.75
a. Bluish paper 105.00 35.00
b. Imperf. 550.00
52 A3 2p rose 62.50 3.75
a. Bluish paper 150.00 35.00
53 A4 3p brown 175.00 62.50
a. Bluish paper 260.00 97.50
54 A5 4p claret 200.00 75.00
a. Bluish paper 500.00 125.00
55 A6 6p blue 240.00 11.50
a. Bluish paper 375.00 57.50
56 A7 1sh green 250.00 32.50
a. Bluish paper 1,150. 225.00
Nos. 51-56 (6) 990.00 191.00

1875 Wmk. 6 *Perf. 12½*
57 A2 1p violet 1,400. 200.00
58 A3 2p rose 500.00 25.00

A8

1878 Wmk. 62 *Perf. 12x11½*
59 A8 2sh deep rose 550.00 450.00
60 A8 5sh gray 550.00 500.00

No. 60 has numeral "5" in each of the four spandrels.

Beware of cleaned fiscally used examples of Nos. 59-60.

A9

A10

A11

A12

A13

A14

A15

Perf. 10, 11, 11½, 12, 12½ and Compound

1882

61 A9 1p rose 7.50 .70
a. Vert. pair, imperf. horiz. *425.00*
b. Perf. 12x11½ 42.50 7.00
c. Perf. 12½ 275.00 150.00
62 A10 2p violet 13.50 .35
a. Vert. pair, imperf. btwn. *525.00*
b. Perf. 12½ 200.00 110.00
63 A11 3p orange 60.00 9.50
a. 3p yellow 62.50 14.00
64 A12 4p blue green 62.50 4.00
a. Perf. 10x11 80.00 13.00
65 A13 6p brown 80.00 8.00
66 A14 8p blue 80.00 52.50
67 A15 1sh red brown 90.00 8.00
Nos. 61-67 (7) 393.50 83.05

See #87. For overprints see #O1-O2, O5, O7-O8.

A15a

A16

A17

1891-95

67A A15a ½p black ('95) 4.25 .25
b. Perf. 12x11½ 35.00 *80.00*
68 A16 2½p ultramarine 57.50 5.00
a. Perf. 12½ 275.00 125.00
69 A17 5p olive gray 55.00 15.00
Nos. 67A-69 (3) 116.75 20.25

In 1893 advertisements were printed on the backs of Nos. 61-67, 68-69.
See #86C. For overprints see #O3-O4, O9.

Mt. Cook — A18

Lake Taupo — A19

Pembroke Peak — A20

Mt. Earnslaw, Lake Wakatipu — A21

Mt. Earnslaw, Lake Wakatipu — A22

Huia, Sacred Birds — A23

White Terrace, Rotomahana A24

Otira Gorge and Mt. Ruapehu A25

Kiwi A26

Maori Canoe A27

Pink Terrace, Rotomahana A28

Kea & Kaka (Hawk-billed Parrots) A29

Milford Sound A30

Mt. Cook — A31

Perf. 12 to 16

1898, Apr. 5 Engr. Unwmk.

70 A18 ½p lilac gray 6.75 1.10
a. Horiz. or vert. pair, imperf. btwn. 1,100. 950.00
71 A19 1p yel brn & bl 5.75 .35
a. Horiz. pair, imperf. btwn. 900.00 900.00
72 A20 2p rose brown 50.00 .30
a. Horiz. pair, imperf. vert. 475.00 475.00
73 A21 2½p bl *(Waki-tipu)* 14.50 *50.00*
74 A22 2½p bl *(Waka-tipu)* 30.00 3.00
75 A23 3p orange brn 40.00 8.00
76 A24 4p rose 22.50 *30.00*
77 A25 5p red brown 60.00 25.00
a. 5p violet brown 90.00 *225.00*
78 A26 6p green 110.00 60.00
79 A27 8p dull blue 60.00 32.50
80 A28 9p lilac 50.00 30.00
81 A29 1sh dull red 100.00 24.00
82 A30 2sh blue green 250.00 125.00
a. Vert. pair, imperf. btwn. 2,800. 2,800.
83 A31 5sh vermilion 400.00 *550.00*
Nos. 70-83 (14) 1,199. *939.25*

The 5sh stamps are often found with revenue cancellations that are embossed or show a crown on the top of a circle. These are worth much less.
See Nos. 84, 88-89, 91-98, 99B, 102, 104, 106-107, 111-112, 114-121, 126-128, 1508-1521. For overprint see No. O10.

A32

A33

A34

1900 Wmk. 63 *Perf. 11*

Thick Soft Wove Paper

84 A18 ½p green 7.00 1.10
85 A32 1p carmine rose 22.50 .65
a. 1p lake 32.50 4.50
86 A33 2p red violet 15.00 1.25
a. Vert. pair, imperf. horiz. 900.00
b. Horiz. pair, imperf. vert.
Nos. 84-86 (3) 44.50 3.00

Nos. 84 and 86 are re-engravings of Nos. 70 and 72 and are slightly smaller.
See No. 110.

1899-1900 Wmk. 63

86C A15a ½p black ('00) 9.50 *12.50*
87 A10 2p violet ('00) 22.50 10.50

Unwmk.

88 A22 2½p blue 15.00 4.00
a. Vert. pair, imperf. horiz. 500.00 —
89 A23 3p org brown 26.00 2.25
a. Horiz. pair, imperf. vert. 500.00
b. Horiz. pair, imperf. btwn. 1,100.
90 A34 4p yel brn & bl ('00) 8.00 4.00
a. Imperf.
b. Double impression of center
91 A25 5p red brown 29.00 4.00
a. 5p violet brown 29.00 4.00
92 A26 6p green 62.50 *70.00*
a. Imperf.
93 A26 6p rose ('00) 45.00 4.75
a. 6p carmine 45.00 4.50
b. Double impression 550.00 *575.00*
c. Imperf., pair
d. Horiz. pair, imperf. vert. 425.00
94 A27 8p dark blue 32.50 13.50
95 A28 9p red lilac 42.50 12.50
96 A29 1sh red 55.00 9.75
97 A30 2sh blue green 100.00 50.00
98 A31 5sh vermilion 225.00 275.00
Revenue cancel 25.00
Nos. 86C-98 (13) 672.50 472.75

See #113. For overprints see #O11-O15.
The 5sh stamps are often found with revenue cancellations that are embossed or show a crown on the top of a circle. These are worth much less.

"Commerce" — A35

1901, Jan. 1 Unwmk. *Perf. 12 to 16*

99 A35 1p carmine 4.00 *4.50*

Universal Penny Postage.
See Nos. 100, 103, 105, 108, 129. For overprint see No. O16. Compare design A35 with A42.

Boer War Contingent A36

Perf. 14, 11x14, 14x11

1901 Wmk. 63

Thick Soft Paper

99B A18 ½p green 15.00 5.50

Perf. 11, 14 and Compound

100 A35 1p carmine 7.00 .20
a. Horiz. pair, imperf. vert. 325.00 325.00
101 A36 1½p brown org 11.00 4.50
a. Vert. pair, imperf. horiz. 850.00
b. Imperf., pair 800.00
Nos. 99B-101 (3) 33.00 10.20

No. 101 was issued to honor the New Zealand forces in the South African War.
See No. 109.

Thin Hard Paper

102 A18 ½p green 29.00 27.50
103 A35 1p carmine 16.00 4.75
a. Horiz. pair, imperf. vert. 300.00

1902 Unwmk.

104 A18 ½p green 14.00 5.75
105 A35 1p carmine 14.00 3.25

1902 *Perf. 11*

Thin White Wove Paper

106 A26 6p rose red 40.00 4.50
a. Watermarked letters 85.00 85.00

The sheets of No. 106 are watermarked with the words "LISBON SUPERFINE" in two lines, covering ten stamps.

Perf. 11, 14, 11x14, 14x13, 14x14½

1902-07 Wmk. 61

107 A18 ½p green 6.25 .80
a. Horiz. pair, imperf. vert. 225.00
108 A35 1p carmine 3.50 .20
a. 1p rose carmine 3.50 .20
b. Imperf., pair
c. Imperf. x serrate perf. 175.00 175.00
d. Imperf. horiz. or vert. pair 200.00 200.00
f. Booklet pane of 6 225.00
109 A36 1½p brown org ('07) 21.00 *62.50*
110 A33 2p dull vio ('03) 7.50 2.00
a. Horiz. pair, imperf. vert. 425.00 *625.00*
b. Vert. pair, imperf. horiz. 450.00
111 A22 2½p blue 17.50 4.25
112 A23 3p org brown 32.50 1.75
113 A34 4p yel brn & bl 10.00 2.75
a. Horiz. pair, imperf. vert. 475.00
114 A25 5p red brown 45.00 12.00
a. 5p violet brown 42.50 8.00
115 A26 6p rose red 40.00 8.50
a. 6p rose 40.00 7.50
b. 6p pink 62.50 11.00
c. 6p brick red 70.00 18.00
d. Horiz. pair, imperf. vert. 575.00
116 A27 8p deep blue 50.00 14.00
117 A28 9p red violet 45.00 9.25
118 A29 1sh scarlet 75.00 11.00
a. 1sh orange red 77.50 8.50
b. 1sh brown red 90.00 15.00
119 A30 2sh blue green 150.00 40.00
120 A31 5sh vermilion 400.00 *350.00*
Nos. 107-120 (14) 903.25 519.00

Wmk. 61 is normally sideways on 3p, 5p, 6p, 8p and 1sh.
The unique example of No. 113 with inverted center is used and is in the New Zealand National Philatelic Collection.
See No. 129. For overprints see Nos. O17-O22.
The 5sh stamps are often found with revenue cancellations that are embossed or show a crown on the top of a circle. These are worth much less.
In 1908 a quantity of the 1p carmine was overprinted "King Edward VII Land" and taken on a Shackleton expedition to the Antarctic. Because of the weather Shackleton landed at Victoria Land instead. The stamp was never sold to the public at face value. See No. 121a.
Similar conditions prevailed for the 1909-12½p green and 1p carmine overprinted "VICTORIA LAND." See Nos. 130d-131d.

1903 Unwmk. *Perf. 11*
Laid Paper
121 A30 2sh blue green 300.00 *225.00*

No. 108a Overprinted in Green: "King Edward VII Land" in Two Lines Reading Up

1908, Jan. 15 *Perf. 14*
121a A35 1p rose carmine 600.00 65.00

See note after No. 120.

Christchurch Exhibition Issue

Arrival of the Maoris A37

Maori Art — A38

Landing of Capt. Cook A39

Annexation of New Zealand A40

Wmk. 61
1906, Nov. Typo. *Perf. 14*
122 A37 ½p emerald 25.00 *32.50*
123 A38 1p vermilion 20.00 22.50
 a. 1p claret *12,000. 15,000.*
124 A39 3p blue & brown 57.50 *90.00*
125 A40 6p gray grn & rose 210.00 *300.00*
 Nos. 122-125 (4) 312.50 445.00

Value for No. 123a is for a fine copy.

Designs of 1902-07 Issue, but smaller

Perf. 14, 14x13, 14x14½
1907-08 Engr.
126 A23 3p orange brown *60.00* 17.50
127 A26 6p carmine rose *62.50* 12.50
128 A29 1sh orange red *200.00* 40.00
 Nos. 126-128 (3) *322.50* 70.00

The small stamps are about 21mm high, those of 1898-1902 about 23mm.

Type of 1902 Redrawn

1908 Typo. *Perf. 14x14½*
129 A35 1p carmine 40.00 1.75

REDRAWN, 1p: The lines of shading in the globe are diagonal and the other lines of the design are generally thicker than on No. 108.

Edward VII A41

"Commerce" A42

1909-12 *Perf. 14x14½*
130 A41 ½p yellow green 8.00 .55
 a. Booklet pane of 6 *225.00*
 b. Booklet pane 5 + label *675.00*
 c. Imperf., pair 225.00
131 A42 1p carmine 2.00 .20
 a. Imperf., pair 350.00
 b. Booklet pane of 6 160.00

Perf. 14x14½, 14x13½, 14
Engr.
Various Frames
132 A41 2p mauve 22.50 7.50
133 A41 3p orange brown 26.00 1.40
134 A41 4p red orange 30.00 *31.00*
135 A41 4p yellow ('12) 20.00 *15.00*
136 A41 5p red brown 19.00 3.50
137 A41 6p carmine rose 45.00 1.40
138 A41 8p deep blue 18.00 2.50
139 A41 1sh vermilion 70.00 7.50
 Nos. 130-139 (10) 260.50 70.55

Nos. 133, 136-138 exist in vert. pairs with perf. 14x13½ on top and perf. 14x14½ on the bottom. These sell for a premium.

See #177. For overprint see Cook Islands #49.

Nos. 130-131 Overprinted in Black: "VICTORIA LAND" in Two Lines

1911-13
130d A41 ½p yellow green *900.00 950.00*
131d A42 1p carmine 60.00 *150.00*

See note after No. 120.
Issue dates: 1p, Feb. 9; ½p, Jan. 18, 1913.

Stamps of 1909 Overprinted in Black: "AUCKLAND EXHIBITION, 1913," in Three Lines

1913
130e A41 ½p yellow green 19.00 *55.00*
131e A42 1p carmine 30.00 *45.00*
133e A41 3p orange brown 225.00 *400.00*
137e A41 6p carmine rose 250.00 *500.00*
 Nos. 130e-137e (4) 524.00 *1,000.*

This issue was valid only within New Zealand and to Australia from Dec. 1, 1913, to Feb. 28, 1914. The Auckland Stamp Collectors Club inspired this issue.

King George V — A43

1915 Typo. *Perf. 14x15*
144 A43 ½p yellow green 2.00 .20
 b. Booklet pane of 6 *125.00*

See Nos. 163-164, 176, 178. For overprints see No. MR1, Cook Islands No. 40.

A44

A45

Perf. 14x14½, 14x13½
1915-22 Engr.
145 A44 1½p gray 3.50 2.00
146 A45 2p purple 12.00 *45.00*
147 A45 2p org yel ('16) 8.00 *35.00*
148 A44 2½p dull blue 7.50 *5.75*
149 A45 3p violet brown 14.00 1.40
150 A45 4p orange yellow 7.75 *57.50*
151 A45 4p purple ('16) 18.00 .55
 c. 4p blackish violet 8.00 .55
 d. Vert. pair, top stamp imperf, bottom stamp perf 3 sides *1,100.*
152 A44 4½p dark green 20.00 26.00
153 A45 5p light blue ('21) 16.00 1.10
 a. Imperf., pair 200.00 200.00
154 A45 6p carmine rose 11.00 .55
 a. Horiz. pair, imperf. vert.
155 A44 7½p red brown 18.00 *26.00*
156 A45 8p blue ('21) 20.00 *50.00*
157 A45 8p red brown ('22) 30.00 4.00
158 A45 9p olive green 25.00 5.00
 a. Imperf., pair *1,150.*
159 A45 1sh vermilion 25.00 .60
 a. Imperf., pair 400.00
 Nos. 145-159 (15) 235.75 260.45

Nos. 145-156, 158-159 exist in vert. pairs with perf 14x13½ on top and perf 14x14½ on the bottom. These sell for a premium. The 5p and No. 151c exist with the perf varieties reversed. These are rare. No. 157 only comes perf 14x13½.

The former Nos. 151a and 151b probably were listed from sheets with No. 151d. They probably do not exist.

For overprints see Cook Islands Nos. 53-60.

A46

A47

1916-19 Typo. *Perf. 14x15, 14*
160 A46 1½p gray black 9.00 1.40
161 A47 1½p gray black 11.00 .60
162 A47 1½p brown orange ('18) 3.50 .60
163 A43 2p yellow 2.60 .20
164 A43 3p chocolate ('19) 12.00 1.50
 Nos. 160-164 (5) 38.10 4.30

The engr. stamps have a background of geometric lathe-work; the typo. stamps have a background of crossed dotted lines.

Type A43 has three diamonds at each side of the crown, type A46 has two, and type A47 has one.

In 1916 the 1½, 2, 3 and 6p of the 1915-16 issue and the 8p of the 1909 issue were printed on paper intended for the long rectangular stamps of the 1902-07 issue. In this paper the watermarks are set wide apart, so that the smaller stamps often show only a small part of the watermark or miss it altogether.

For overprints see Cook Islands #50-52.

Victory Issue

"Peace" and British Lion — A48

Peace and Lion — A49

Maori Chief — A50

British Lion — A51

"Victory" — A52

King George V, Lion and Maori Fern at Sides — A53

1920, Jan. 27 *Perf. 14*
165 A48 ½p yellow green 3.25 2.75
166 A49 1p carmine 2.00 .65
167 A50 1½p brown orange 3.50 .55
168 A51 3p black brown 15.00 *16.00*
169 A52 6p purple 17.00 *19.00*
170 A53 1sh vermilion 25.00 *55.00*
 Nos. 165-170 (6) 65.75 *93.95*

No. 165 Surcharged in Red

1922, Mar.
174 A48 2p on ½p yellow green 6.00 1.50

Map of New Zealand — A54

1923 Typo. *Perf. 14x15*
175 A54 1p carmine rose 3.50 .70

Restoration of Penny Postage. The paper varies from thin to thick.

Types of 1909-15 N Z and Star 'watermark' printed on back, usually in blue

1925 Unwmk. *Perf. 14x14½*
176 A43 ½p yellow green 2.75 *3.50*
177 A42 1p carmine 2.25 .90
178 A43 2p yellow 10.00 *62.50*
 Nos. 176-178 (3) 15.00 *66.90*

Exhibition Buildings A55

1925, Nov. 17 Wmk. 61
Surface Tinted Paper
179 A55 ½p yel green, *grnsh* 3.50 *12.50*
180 A55 1p car rose, *pink* 4.00 *6.25*
181 A55 4p red violet, *lilac* 37.50 *80.00*
 Nos. 179-181 (3) 45.00 *98.75*

Dunedin Exhibition.

George V in Admiral's Uniform A56

In Field Marshal's Uniform A57

1926 *Perf. 14, 14½x14*
182 A56 2sh blue 57.50 35.00
 a. 2sh dark blue 55.00 *62.50*
183 A56 3sh violet 100.00 *160.00*
 a. 3sh deep violet 80.00 *175.00*

Perf. 14, 14x14½
184 A57 1p rose red 1.00 .20
 a. Booklet pane of 6 85.00
 b. Imperf., pair 140.00
 Nos. 182-184 (3) 158.50 195.20

For overprints see Cook Islands Nos. 74-75.

Pied Fantail and Clematis A58

Kiwi and Cabbage Palm A59

Maori Woman Cooking in Boiling Spring A60

Maori Council House (Whare) A61

Mt. Cook and Mountain Lilies — A62

Maori Girl Wearing Tiki — A63

Mitre Peak — A64

Striped Marlin A65

Harvesting — A66

Tuatara Lizard — A67

Maori Panel from Door — A68

Tui or Parson Bird — A69

Capt. Cook Landing at Poverty Bay — A70

Mt. Egmont, North Island A71

Perf. 14x14½, 14x13½, 13½x14, 13½

1935, May 1 Engr. Wmk. 61

185	A58	½p	bright green	1.75	.85
186	A59	1p	copper red	2.00	.70
186A	A59	1p	copper red, re-engraved	6.25	3.50
b.			Booklet pane of 6 + ad labels	*47.50*	
187	A60	1½p	red brown	6.25	7.50
188	A61	2p	red orange	4.00	.20
189	A62	2½p	dk gray & dk brown	6.00	*15.00*
190	A63	3p	chocolate	13.50	2.75
191	A64	4p	blk brn & blk	4.25	2.00
192	A65	5p	violet blue	26.00	20.00
193	A66	6p	red	8.00	5.00
194	A67	8p	dark brown	11.00	*7.50*

Litho.

Size: 18x21½mm

195	A68	9p	black & scarlet	12.50	5.00

Engr.

196	A69	1sh	dk sl green	22.50	10.00
197	A70	2sh	olive green	47.50	30.00
198	A71	3sh	yel brn & brn black	20.00	*45.00*
			Nos. 185-198 (15)	191.50	155.00
			Set, never hinged	325.00	

On No. 186A, the horizontal lines in the sky are much darker.

The 2½p, 5p, 2sh and 3sh are perf. 13½ vertically; perf. 13-14 horizontally on each stamp.

See Nos. 203-216, 244-245.

Silver Jubilee Issue

Queen Mary and King George V A72

1935, May 7 ***Perf. 11x11½***

199	A72	½p	blue green	.75	1.00
200	A72	1p	dark car rose	1.00	.50
201	A72	6p	vermilion	17.50	*27.50*
			Nos. 199-201 (3)	19.25	*29.00*
			Set, never hinged	25.00	

25th anniv. of the reign of King George V.

Types of 1935

Perf. 12½ to 15 and Compound

1936-41 Wmk. 253

203	A58	½p	bright green	1.75	.20
204	A59	1p	copper red	1.50	.20
205	A60	1½p	red brown	7.00	6.00
206	A61	2p	red orange	.20	.20
a.			Perf. 14	15.00	.90
b.			Perf. 14x15	21.00	20.00
c.			Perf. 12½	2.75	.20
207	A62	2½p	dk gray & dk brn	1.50	*6.00*
208	A63	3p	chocolate	20.00	.60
209	A64	4p	black brn & blk	2.00	.20
a.			Perf. 12½	17.50	12.50
210	A65	5p	violet blue	3.00	1.25
a.			Perf. 12½	11.00	3.50
211	A66	6p	red	1.50	.20
a.			Perf. 12½	1.75	3.50
212	A67	8p	dark brown	2.00	.75
a.			Perf. 12½	2.25	1.60

Litho.

Size: 18x21½mm

213	A68	9p	gray & scarlet	25.00	3.50
a.			9p black & scarlet	30.00	3.50

Engr.

214	A69	1sh	dark slate grn	4.00	.60
a.			Perf. 12½	30.00	20.00
215	A70	2sh	olive green	7.00	1.50
a.			Perf. 13½x14	200.00	3.00
b.			Perf. 12½	15.00	8.50
216	A71	3sh	yel brn & blk brn	5.75	2.25
a.			Perf. 12½ ('41)	45.00	50.00
			Nos. 203-216 (14)	82.20	23.45
			Set, never hinged	115.00	

Wool Industry A73

Butter Industry A74

Sheep Farming A75

Apple Industry A76

Shipping A77

1936, Oct. 1 Wmk. 61 ***Perf. 11***

218	A73	½p	deep green	.20	.20
219	A74	1p	red	.20	.20
220	A75	2½p	deep blue	1.65	2.75
221	A76	4p	dark purple	1.25	1.90
222	A77	6p	red brown	2.00	1.65
			Nos. 218-222 (5)	5.30	6.70
			Set, never hinged	6.50	

Congress of the Chambers of Commerce of the British Empire held in New Zealand.

Queen Elizabeth and King George VI A78

Perf. 13½x13

1937, May 13 Wmk. 253

223	A78	1p	rose carmine	.20	.20
224	A78	2½p	dark blue	.20	.50
225	A78	6p	vermilion	.65	.75
			Nos. 223-225 (3)	1.05	1.45
			Set, never hinged	2.25	

Coronation of George VI and Elizabeth.

A79

A80

1938-44 Engr. ***Perf. 13½***

226	A79	½p	emerald	4.50	.20
226B	A79	½p	brown org ('41)	.20	.20
227	A79	1p	rose red	3.75	.20
227A	A79	1p	lt blue grn ('41)	.20	.20
228	A80	1½p	violet brown	19.00	2.25
228B	A80	1½p	red ('44)	.20	.20
228C	A80	3p	blue ('41)	.20	.20
			Nos. 226-228C (7)	28.05	3.45
			Set, never hinged	40.00	

See Nos. 258-264. For surcharges see Nos. 242-243, 279, 285.

Landing of the Maoris in 1350 A81

Captain Cook, His Map of New Zealand, 1769, H.M.S. Endeavour A82

Victoria, Edward VII, George V, Edward VIII and George VI — A83

Abel Tasman, Ship, and Chart of West Coast of New Zealand A84

Treaty of Waitangi, 1840 — A85

Pioneer Settlers Landing on Petone Beach, 1840 A86

The Progress of Transport A87

H.M.S. "Britomart" at Akaroa — A88

Route of Ship Carrying First Shipment of Frozen Mutton to England — A89

Maori Council A90

Gold Mining in 1861 and Modern Gold Dredge A91

Giant Kauri — A92

Perf. 13½x13, 13x13½, 14x13½

1940, Jan. 2 Engr. Wmk. 253

229	A81	½p	dk blue green	.25	.20
230	A82	1p	scarlet & sepia	2.00	.20
231	A83	1½p	brt vio & ultra	.25	.50
232	A84	2p	black brown & Prussian green	1.10	.20
233	A85	2½p	dk bl & myr grn	1.50	.75
234	A86	3p	dp plum & dk vio	2.75	.75
235	A87	4p	dk red vio & vio brn	10.00	1.60
236	A88	5p	brown & lt bl	5.00	4.00
237	A89	6p	vio & brt grn	8.00	2.00
238	A90	7p	org red & black	1.25	*4.50*
239	A90	8p	org red & black	8.00	3.50
240	A91	9p	dp org & olive	5.50	2.25
241	A92	1sh	dk sl grn & ol	10.00	4.25
			Nos. 229-241 (13)	55.60	24.70
			Set, never hinged	95.00	

Centenary of British sovereignty established by the treaty of Waitangi.

Imperfs of #229-241 exist. These probably are plate proofs.

For surcharge see No. 246.

Stamps of 1938 Surcharged with New Values in Black

1941 Wmk. 253 ***Perf. 13½***

242	A79	1p on ½p emerald	.75	.20
243	A80	2p on 1½p violet brn	.75	.20
		Set, never hinged	3.25	

Type of 1935 Redrawn

1941 Typo. Wmk. 61 ***Perf. 14x15***

Size: 17½x20½mm

244	A68	9p int black & scarlet	65.00	30.00

Wmk. 253

245	A68	9p int black & scarlet	4.00	3.50
		Set, never hinged	110.00	

Catalogue values for unused stamps in this section, from this point to the end of the section, are for Never Hinged items.

No 231 Surcharged in Black

1944 *Perf. 13½x13*

246	A83	10p on 1½p brt vio & ultra	.45	.45

Peace Issue

Lake Matheson A93

Parliament House, Wellington — A94

St. Paul's Cathedral, London — A95

The Royal Family — A96

Badge of Royal New Zealand Air Force A97

New Zealand Army Overseas Badge A98

Badge of Royal Navy A99

New Zealand Coat of Arms A100

Knight, Window of Wellington Boys' College A101

Natl. Memorial Campanile, Wellington A103

Southern Alps and Chapel Altar A102

Engr.; Photo. (1½p, 1sh)
Perf. 13x13½, 13½x13

1946, Apr. 1 **Wmk. 253**

247	A93	½p	choc & dk bl grn	.20	.20
248	A94	1p	emerald	.20	.20
249	A95	1½p	scarlet	.20	.20
250	A96	2p	rose violet	.20	.20
251	A97	3p	dk grn & ultra	.20	.20
252	A98	4p	brn org & ol grn	.20	.20
253	A99	5p	ultra & blue grn	.20	.20
254	A100	6p	org red & red brn	.20	.20
255	A101	8p	brown lake & blk	.25	.20
256	A102	9p	black & brt bl	.25	.25
257	A103	1sh	gray black	.35	.30
			Nos. 247-257 (11)	2.45	2.35

Return to peace at the close of WWII.
Imperfs exist from the printer's archives.

George VI Type of 1938 and

King George VI — A104

1947 **Engr.** *Perf. 13½*

258	A80	2p	orange	.20	.20
260	A80	4p	rose lilac	.30	.30
261	A80	5p	gray	.90	.25
262	A80	6p	rose carmine	.90	.20
263	A80	8p	deep violet	1.00	.20
264	A80	9p	chocolate	1.75	.20

Perf. 14

265	A104	1sh	dk car rose & chnt	1.25	.30
266	A104	1sh3p	ultra & chnt	2.00	.35
267	A104	2sh	dk grn & brn org	4.75	.75
268	A104	3sh	gray blk & chnt	8.00	1.25
			Nos. 258-268 (10)	21.05	4.00

Nos. 265-267 have watermark either upright or sideways. On No. 268 watermark is always sideways.

"John Wickliffe" and "Philip Laing" A105

Cromwell, Otago A106

First Church, Dunedin — A107

University of Otago A108

1948, Feb. 23 *Perf. 13½*

269	A105	1p	green & blue	.20	.20
270	A106	2p	brown & green	.20	.20
271	A107	3p	violet	.30	.20
272	A108	6p	lilac rose & gray blk	.30	.20
			Nos. 269-272 (4)	1.00	.80

Otago Province settlement, cent.

A Royal Visit set of four was prepared but not issued. Copies of the 3p have appeared on the stamp market.

A109

Cathedral at Christchurch — A110

"They Passed this Way" A111

Wmk. 253

1950, July 28 **Typo.** *Perf. 14*

Black Surcharge

273	A109	1½p rose red	.30	.30

See No. 367.

1950, Nov. 20 **Engr.** *Perf. 13x13½*

3p, John Robert Godley. 6p, Canterbury University College. 1sh, View of Timaru.

274	A110	1p	blue grn & blue	.30	.30
275	A111	2p	car & red org	.30	.30
276	A110	3p	indigo & blue	.30	.30
277	A111	6p	brown & blue	.40	.40
278	A111	1sh	claret & blue	.55	.55
			Nos. 274-278 (5)	1.85	1.85

Centenary of the founding of Canterbury Provincial District.
Imperfs of #274-278 exist.

No. 227A Surcharged in Black

1952, Dec. *Perf. 13½*

279	A79	3p on 1p lt blue green	.30	.20

POSTAL-FISCAL STAMPS

In 1881 fiscal stamps of New Zealand of denominations over one shilling were made acceptable for postal duty. Values for canceled stamps are for postal cancellations. Denominations above £5 appear to have been used primarily for fiscal purposes.

Queen Victoria
PF1 PF2

Perf. 11, 12, 12½

1882 **Typo.** **Wmk. 62**

AR1	PF1	2sh	blue	90.00	15.00
AR2	PF1	2sh6p	dk brown	95.00	15.00
AR3	PF1	3sh	violet	160.00	16.00
AR4	PF1	4sh	brown vio	200.00	30.00
AR5	PF1	4sh	red brown	160.00	30.00
AR6	PF1	5sh	green	250.00	30.00
AR7	PF1	6sh	rose	350.00	60.00
AR8	PF1	7sh	ultra	350.00	75.00
AR9	PF1	7sh6p	ol gray	1,100.	350.00
AR10	PF1	8sh	dull blue	350.00	70.00
AR11	PF1	9sh	org red	450.00	150.00
AR12	PF1	10sh	red brown	250.00	35.00

1882-90

AR13	PF2	15sh	dk grn	1,100.	300.00
AR15	PF2	£1	rose	500.00	100.00
AR16	PF2	25sh	blue		—
AR17	PF2	30sh	brown		—
AR18	PF2	£1 15sh	yellow		—
AR19	PF2	£2	purple		—

PF3 PF4

AR20	PF3	£2 10sh	red brown		—
AR21	PF3	£3	yel green		—
AR22	PF3	£3 10sh	rose		—
AR23	PF3	£4	ultramarine		—
AR24	PF3	£4 10sh	olive brown		—
AR25	PF3	£5	dark blue		—
AR26	PF4	£6	orange red		—
AR27	PF4	£7	brown red		—
AR28	PF4	£8	green		—
AR29	PF4	£9	rose		—
AR30	PF4	£10	blue		—
AR30A	PF4	£20	yellow	—	—

With "COUNTERPART" at Bottom

1901

AR31	PF1	2sh6p	brown	250.00	225.00

Perf. 11, 14, 14½x14

1903-15 **Wmk. 61**

AR32	PF1	2sh	blue ('07)	65.00	12.00
AR33	PF1	2sh6p	brown	65.00	12.00
AR34	PF1	3sh	violet	130.00	14.00
AR35	PF1	4sh	brown red	150.00	25.00
AR36	PF1	5sh	green ('06)	200.00	25.00
AR37	PF1	6sh	rose	300.00	50.00
AR38	PF1	7sh	dull blue	300.00	60.00
AR39	PF1	7sh6p	ol gray ('06)	900.00	275.00
AR40	PF1	8sh	dark blue	300.00	60.00
AR41	PF1	9sh	dl org ('06)	400.00	125.00
AR42	PF1	10sh	dp claret	225.00	30.00
AR43	PF2	15sh	blue grn	900.00	250.00
AR44	PF2	£1	rose	400.00	80.00

Perf. 14½

AR45	PF2	£2	deep vio ('25)	600.00	100.00
a.			Perf. 14	700.00	100.00
			Nos. AR32-AR45 (14)	4,935.	1,118.

For overprints see Cook Islands Nos. 67-71.

Coat of Arms — PF5

1931-39 **Wmk. 61** *Perf. 14*

Type PF5

AR46	1sh3p	lemon	20.00	4.00
AR47	1sh3p	orange ('32)	8.00	9.00
AR48	2sh6p	brown	16.00	5.25
AR49	4sh	dull red ('32)	17.00	7.50
AR50	5sh	green	21.00	12.50
AR51	6sh	brt rose ('32)	37.50	15.00
AR52	7sh	gray blue	32.50	25.00
AR53	7sh6p	olive gray ('32)	75.00	92.50
AR54	8sh	dark blue	50.00	37.50
AR55	9sh	brn org	52.50	32.50
AR56	10sh	dark car	27.50	10.50
AR57	12sh6p	brn vio ('35)	200.00	160.00
AR58	15sh	ol grn ('32)	70.00	42.50
AR59	£1	pink ('32)	75.00	22.50
AR60	25sh	turq bl ('38)	400.00	450.00
AR61	30sh	dk brn ('36)	300.00	160.00
AR62	35sh	yellow ('37)	4,500.	*6,000.*
AR63	£2	violet ('33)	400.00	70.00

AR64	£2 10sh	dark red ('36)	400.00	*400.00*
AR65	£3	light grn ('32)	400.00	210.00
AR66	£3 10sh	rose ('39)	2,000.	2,000.
AR67	£4	light blue	400.00	175.00
AR68	£4 10sh	dk ol gray ('39)	2,000.	1,500.
AR69	£5	dk blue ('32)	400.00	100.00

For overprints see Cook Islands Nos. 80-83.

No. AR62 Surcharged in Black

1939 ***Perf. 14***

AR70 PF5 35sh on 35sh yel 500.00 250.00

Type PF5 Surcharged in Black

1940

AR71	3sh6p on 3sh6p dl green	28.50	21.00
AR72	5sh6p on 5sh6p rose lilac	60.00	57.50
AR73	11sh on 11sh pale yellow	125.00	150.00
AR74	22sh on 22sh scar	275.00	350.00
	Nos. AR71-AR74 (4)	488.50	578.50

Type of 1931

1940-58 **Wmk. 253** ***Perf. 14***

Type PF5

AR75	1sh3p	orange	5.75	.60
AR76	2sh6p	brown	5.75	.60
AR77	4sh	dull red	6.75	.60
AR78	5sh	green	11.50	.90
AR79	6sh	brt rose	20.00	4.00
AR80	7sh	gray bl	20.00	6.75
AR81	7sh6p	ol gray ('50)	57.50	*45.00*
AR82	8sh	dk blue	35.00	17.00
AR83	9sh	orange ('46)	35.00	22.50
AR84	10sh	dk carmine	20.00	3.25
AR85	15sh	olive ('45)	42.50	20.00
AR86	£1	pink('45)	29.00	8.50
a.	Perf. 14x13½ ('58)		32.50	15.00
AR87	25sh	blue ('46)	225.00	*275.00*
AR88	30sh	choc ('46)	175.00	125.00
AR89	£2	violet ('46)	72.50	40.00
AR90	£2 10sh	dk red ('51)	225.00	*325.00*
AR91	£3	lt grn ('46)	85.00	85.00
AR92	£3 10sh	rose ('48)	2,000.	2,000.
AR93	£4	lt blue ('52)	110.00	100.00
AR94	£5	dk blue ('40)	140.00	100.00

Type PF5 Surcharged in Black

1942-45 **Wmk. 253**

AR95	3sh6p on 3sh6p grn	12.50	8.00
AR96	5sh6p on 5sh6p rose lil ('44)	26.00	8.50
AR97	11sh on 11sh yel	67.50	52.50
AR98	22sh on 22sh car ('45)	250.00	*250.00*
	Nos. AR95-AR98 (4)	356.00	319.00

SEMI-POSTAL STAMPS

Nurse

SP1 SP2

Inscribed: "Help Stamp out Tuberculosis, 1929"

Wmk. 61

1929, Dec. 11 **Typo.** ***Perf. 14***

B1 SP1 1p + 1p scarlet 12.50 *20.00*

Inscribed: "Help Promote Health, 1930"

1930, Oct. 29

B2 SP2 1p + 1p scarlet 30.00 *45.00*

Boy — SP3

Hygeia, Goddess of Health — SP4

1931, Oct. 31 ***Perf. 14½x14***

B3 SP3 1p + 1p scarlet 87.50 87.50
B4 SP3 2p + 1p dark blue 87.50 70.00

1932, Nov. 18 **Engr.** ***Perf. 14***

B5 SP4 1p + 1p carmine 22.50 *30.00*
Never hinged 50.00

Road to Health — SP5

1933, Nov. 8

B6 SP5 1p + 1p carmine 15.00 *20.00*
Never hinged 30.00

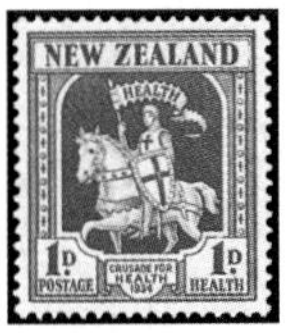

Crusader — SP6

1934, Oct. 25 ***Perf. 14x13½***

B7 SP6 1p + 1p dark carmine 12.50 *20.00*
Never hinged 25.00

Child at Bathing Beach — SP7

Anzac — SP8

1935, Sept. 30 ***Perf. 11***

B8 SP7 1p + 1p scarlet 3.00 3.25
Never hinged 5.00

Catalogue values for unused stamps in this section, from this point to the end of the section, are for Never Hinged items.

1936, Apr. 27

B9 SP8 ½p + ½p green .70 *2.00*
B10 SP8 1p + 1p red .70 *1.60*

21st anniv. of Anzac landing at Gallipoli.

"Health" SP9

1936, Nov. 2

B11 SP9 1p + 1p red 2.00 *4.25*

Boy Hiker — SP10

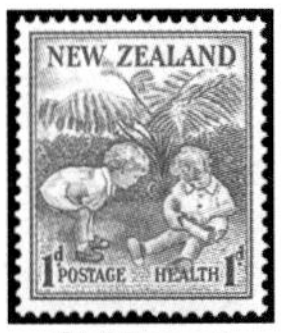

Children at Play — SP11

1937, Oct. 1

B12 SP10 1p + 1p red 3.00 *4.00*

Perf. 14x13½

1938, Oct. 1 **Wmk. 253**

B13 SP11 1p + 1p red 6.25 3.25

Children at Play — SP12

Children in Swing — SP13

1939, Oct. 16 **Wmk. 61** ***Perf. 11½***

Black Surcharge

B14 SP12 1p on ½p + ½p grn 5.00 5.00
B15 SP12 2p on 1p + 1p scar 5.00 5.00

1940, Oct. 1

B16 SP12 1p + ½p green 16.00 17.50
B17 SP12 2p + 1p org brown 16.00 17.50

The surtax was used to help maintain children's health camps.

Semi-Postal Stamps of 1940, Overprinted in Black "1941"

1941, Oct. 4 ***Perf. 11½***

B18 SP12 1p + ½p green .45 *2.50*
B19 SP12 2p + 1p org brown .45 *2.50*

1942, Oct. 1 **Engr.**

B20 SP13 1p + ½p green .35 *1.10*
B21 SP13 2p + 1p dp org brown .35 *1.10*

Imperf plate proofs on card exist for #B22-B27, B32-B33, B38-B39, B46-B48, B59-B60. Imperfs exist for B44-B45, B49-B51. These are from the printer's archives.

Princess Margaret Rose — SP14

Design: 2p+1p, Princess Elizabeth.

1943, Oct. 1 **Wmk. 253** ***Perf. 12***

B22 SP14 1p + ½p dark green .20 *1.40*
a. Vert. pair, imperf. between
B23 SP14 2p + 1p red brown .20 .30
a. Vert. pair, imperf. between

Princesses Margaret Rose and Elizabeth SP16

1944, Oct. 9 ***Perf. 13½***

B24 SP16 1p + ½p blue green .35 .45
B25 SP16 2p + 1p chalky blue .35 .35

Peter Pan Statue, London — SP17

Statue of Eros, London — SP19

Soldier Helping Child over Stile SP18

1945, Oct. 1

B26 SP17 1p + ½p gray green & bister brown .20 .20
B27 SP17 2p + 1p car & olive bis .20 .20

1946, Oct. 24 ***Perf. 13½x13***

B28 SP18 1p + ½p dk grn & org brn .20 .20
B29 SP18 2p + 1p dk brn & org brn .20 .20

1947, Oct. 1 **Engr.** ***Perf. 13x13½***

B30 SP19 1p + ½p deep green .20 .20
B31 SP19 2p + 1p deep carmine .20 .20

Children's Health Camp SP20

1948, Oct. 1 ***Perf. 13½x13***

B32 SP20 1p + ½p blue grn & ultra .20 .20
B33 SP20 2p + 1p red & dk brn .20 .20

Nurse and Child SP21

Princess Elizabeth and Prince Charles SP22

1949, Oct. 3 **Photo.** ***Perf. 14x14½***

B34 SP21 1p + ½p deep green .30 .20
B35 SP21 2p + 1p ultramarine .30 .20

1950, Oct. 2

B36 SP22 1p + ½p green .20 .20
B37 SP22 2p + 1p violet brown .20 .20

Racing Yachts SP23

Perf. 13½x13

1951, Nov. 1 **Engr.** **Wmk. 253**

B38 SP23 1½p + ½p red & yel .20 *1.10*
B39 SP23 2p + 1p dp grn & yel .20 .20

Princess Anne SP24

Prince Charles SP25

Perf. 14x14½

1952, Oct. 1 Wmk. 253 Photo.
B40 SP24 1½p + ½p crimson .20 .35
B41 SP25 2p + 1p brown .20 .20

AIR POST STAMPS

Plane over Lake Manapouri AP1

Perf. 14x14½

1931, Nov. 10 Typo. Wmk. 61
C1 AP1 3p chocolate 27.50 17.50
a. Perf. 14x15 150.00 *500.00*
C2 AP1 4p dark violet 27.50 22.50
C3 AP1 7p orange 30.00 10.50
Nos. C1-C3 (3) 85.00 50.50

Most copies of No. C1a are poorly centered.

Type of 1931 Surcharged in Red

1931, Dec. 18 *Perf. 14x14½*
C4 AP1 5p on 3p yel green 11.50 9.00

Type of 1931 Overprinted in Dark Blue

1934, Jan. 17
C5 AP1 7p bright blue 40.00 45.00

1st official air mail flight between NZ and Australia.

Airplane over Landing Field AP2

1935, May 4 Engr. *Perf. 14*
C6 AP2 1p rose carmine 1.10 .80
C7 AP2 3p dark violet 5.75 3.75
C8 AP2 6p gray blue 11.50 5.75
Nos. C6-C8 (3) 18.35 10.30
Set, never hinged 25.00

SPECIAL DELIVERY STAMPS

SD1

Perf. 14x½,14x15

1903-26 Typo. Wmk. 61
E1 SD1 6p purple & red ('26) 47.50 29.00
a. 6p violet & red, perf. 11 62.50 70.00

Mail Car — SD2

1939, Aug. 16 Engr. *Perf. 14*
E2 SD2 6p violet 1.75 2.10
Never hinged 3.00

POSTAGE DUE STAMPS

D1

D2

Wmk. 62

1899, Dec. 1 Typo. *Perf. 11*
J1 D1 ½p green & red 3.50 *19.00*
a. No period after "D" 75.00 60.00
J2 D1 1p green & red 12.50 2.10
J3 D1 2p green & red 30.00 6.25
J4 D1 3p green & red 15.00 4.00
J5 D1 4p green & red 37.50 10.00
J6 D1 5p green & red 25.00 25.00
J7 D1 6p green & red 32.50 30.00
J8 D1 8p green & red 70.00 *110.00*
J9 D1 10p green & red 80.00 *125.00*
J10 D1 1sh green & red 75.00 97.50
J11 D1 2sh green & red 140.00 *160.00*
Nos. J1-J11 (11) 521.00 588.85

Nos. J1-J11 may be found with N. Z. and D. varying in size.

1902, Feb. 28 Unwmk.
J12 D2 ½p gray grn & red 2.10 7.50

Wmk. 61
J13 D2 ½p gray grn & red 2.10 2.10
J14 D2 1p gray grn & red 10.50 4.00
J15 D2 2p gray grn & red 120.00 120.00

1904-28 *Perf. 14, 14x14½*
J16 D2 ½p green & car 3.75 4.25
J17 D2 1p green & car 4.25 .60
J18 D2 2p green & car 8.00 3.50
J19 D2 3p grn & rose ('28) 25.00 25.00
Nos. J16-J19 (4) 41.00 33.35

N Z and Star printed on the back in Blue

1925 Unwmk. *Perf. 14x14½, 14x15*
J20 D2 ½p green & rose 2.50 *26.00*
J21 D2 2p green & rose 4.00 *25.00*

Catalogue values for unused stamps in this section, from this point to the end of the section, are for Never Hinged items.

D3

1939 Wmk. 61 Typo. *Perf. 15x14*
J22 D3 ½p turquoise green 8.00 *7.50*
J23 D3 1p rose pink 5.00 .60
J24 D3 2p ultramarine 7.00 1.75
J25 D3 3p brown orange 26.00 29.00
Nos. J22-J25 (4) 46.00 38.85

1945-49 Wmk. 253
J27 D3 1p rose pink ('49) 5.00 10.00
J28 D3 2p ultramarine ('47) 5.00 8.00
J29 D3 3p brown orange 15.00 5.75
Nos. J27-J29 (3) 25.00 23.75

The use of postage due stamps was discontinued in Sept., 1951.

WAR TAX STAMP

No. 144 Overprinted in Black

Perf. 14x14½

1915, Sept. 24 Wmk. 61
MR1 A43 ½p green 2.10 .60

OFFICIAL STAMPS

Regular Issues Ovptd. "O. P. S. O." Handstamped on Stamps of 1882-92

1892 Wmk. 62 *Perf as Before*

Rose or Magenta Handstamp
O1 A9 1p rose *250.*
O2 A10 2p violet *425.*
O3 A16 2½p ultramarine *325.*
O4 A17 5p olive gray *500.*
O5 A13 6p brown *700.*

Violet Handstamp
O6 N1 ½p rose *625.*
O7 A9 1p rose *210.*
O8 A10 2p violet

Handstamped on No. 67A in Rose

1899 *Perf. 10, 10x11*
O9 A15a ½p black *250.*

Handstamped on No. 79 in Violet

Unwmk. *Perf. 14, 15*
O10 A27 8p dull blue *575.*

Handstamped on Stamps of 1899-1900 in Violet

1902 *Perf. 11*
O11 A22 2½p blue *425.*
O12 A23 3p org brown *525.*
O13 A25 5p red brown *525.*
O14 A27 8p dark blue *625.*

Green Handstamp
O15 A25 5p red brown *500.*

Handstamped on Stamp of 1901 in Violet

Wmk. 63 *Perf. 11*
O16 A35 1p carmine *275.*

Handstamped on Stamps of 1902-07 in Violet or Magenta

1905-07 Wmk. 61 *Perf. 11, 14*
O17 A18 ½p green *250.*
O18 A35 1p carmine *275.*
O19 A22 2½p blue *350.*
O20 A25 5p red brown
O21 A27 8p deep blue
O22 A30 2sh blue green *1,600.*

The "O. P. S. O." handstamp is usually struck diagonally, reading up, but on No. O19 it also occurs horizontally. The letters stand for "On Public Service Only."

Overprinted in Black

On Stamps of 1902-07

1907 *Perf. 14, 14x13, 14x14½*
O23 A18 ½p green 9.50 .70
O24 A35 1p carmine 8.50 .60
a. Booklet pane of 6 65.00
O25 A33 2p violet 15.00 2.00
O26 A23 3p orange brn 47.50 4.00
O27 A26 6p carmine rose 200.00 27.50
a. Horiz. pair, imperf. vert. *925.00*
O28 A29 1sh brown red 125.00 20.00
O29 A30 2sh blue green 125.00 125.00
a. Horiz. pair, imperf. vert. *1,400.*
O30 A31 5sh vermilion 275.00 250.00
Nos. O23-O30 (8) 805.50 429.80

On No. 127

Perf. 14x13, 14x14½
O31 A26 6p carmine rose 200.00 52.50

On No. 129

1909 *Perf. 14x14½*
O32 A35 1p car (redrawn) 72.50 3.00

On Nos. 130-131, 133, 137, 139

1910 *Perf. 14, 14x13½, 14x14½*
O33 A41 ½p yellow green 5.25 .75
a. Inverted overprint 1,600.
O34 A42 1p carmine 3.75 .20
O35 A41 3p orange brown 16.00 .90
O36 A41 6p carmine rose 30.00 10.00
O37 A41 1sh vermilion 60.00 30.00
Nos. O33-O37 (5) 115.00 41.85

For 3p see note on perf varieties following No. 139.

On Postal-Fiscal Stamps No. AR32, AR36, AR44

1911-14
O38 PF1 2sh blue ('14) 55.00 52.50
O39 PF1 5sh green ('13) 100.00 *150.00*
O40 PF2 £1 rose 800.00 625.00
Nos. O38-O40 (3) 955.00 827.50

On Stamps of 1909-19

Perf. 14x13½, 14x14½

1915-19 Typo.
O41 A43 ½p green 1.60 .20
O42 A46 1½p gray black ('16) 8.00 3.00
O43 A47 1½p gray black ('16) 5.75 1.00
O44 A47 1½p brown org ('19) 5.75 .60
O45 A43 2p yellow ('17) 5.75 .50
O46 A43 3p chocolate ('19) 12.50 1.50

Engr.
O47 A45 3p vio brn ('16) 5.00 1.50
O48 A45 6p car rose ('16) 7.00 1.00
O49 A41 8p dp bl (R) ('16) 12.00 *20.00*
O50 A45 1sh vermilion ('16) 15.00 4.00
a. 1sh orange 15.00 4.00
Nos. O41-O50 (10) 78.35 *33.30*

For 8p see note on perf varieties following No. 139.

On No. 157

1922
O51 A45 8p red brown 100.00 *125.00*

On Nos. 151, 158

1925
O52 A45 4p purple 16.00 4.25
O53 A45 9p olive green 45.00 42.50

On No. 177

1925 *Perf. 14x14½*
O54 A42 1p carmine 5.00 5.00

On Nos. 184, 182

1927-28 Wmk. 61 *Perf. 14, 14½x14*
O55 A57 1p rose red 2.50 .20
O56 A56 2sh blue 100.00 110.00

On No. AR50

1933 *Perf. 14*
O57 PF5 5sh green 300.00 350.00

Nos. 186, 187, 196 Overprinted in Black

1936 *Perf. 14x13½, 13½x14, 14*
O58 A59 1p copper red 2.00 1.40
O59 A60 1½p red brown 14.00 *30.00*
O60 A69 1sh dark slate grn 20.00 *52.50*
Nos. O58-O60 (3) 36.00 83.90
Set, never hinged 80.00

Same Overprint Horizontally in Black or Green on Stamps of 1936

Perf. 12½, 13½, 13x13½, 14x13½, 13½x14, 14

1936-42 Wmk. 253
O61 A58 ½p brt grn ('37) 1.50 5.25
O62 A59 1p copper red 3.00 .60
O63 A60 1½p red brown 4.00 5.25
O64 A61 2p red org ('38) 1.00 .20
a. Perf. 12½ ('42) 110.00 62.50
O65 A62 2½p dk gray & dk brown 8.00 24.00

O66	A63	3p choc ('38)	27.50	4.00
O67	A64	4p blk brn & blk	5.00	1.10
O68	A66	6p red ('37)	5.75	.35
O68B	A67	8p dp brn ('42)	8.50	20.00
O69	A68	9p black & scar (G) ('38)	80.00	45.00
O70	A69	1sh dk slate grn	14.00	1.60
a.		Perf. 12½ ('42)	27.50	1.75

Overprint Vertical

O71	A70	2sh ol grn ('37)	24.00	8.50
a.		Perf. 12½ ('42)	90.00	25.00
		Nos. O61-O71 (12)	182.25	115.85
		Set, never hinged	375.00	

Same Overprint Horizontally in Black on Nos. 226, 227, 228

1938

O72	A79	½p emerald	5.75	1.75
O73	A79	1p rose red	7.25	.30
O74	A80	1½p violet brn	37.50	10.50
		Nos. O72-O74 (3)	50.50	12.55
		Set, never hinged	95.00	

Same Overprint on No. AR50

1938 Wmk. 61 *Perf. 14*

O75	PF5	5sh green	75.00	47.50
		Never hinged	150.00	

Nos. 229-235, 237, 239-241 Overprinted in Red or Black

Perf. 13½x13, 13x13½, 14x13½

1940 Wmk. 253

O76	A81	½p dk bl grn (R)	.60	.75
a.		"ff" joined	29.00	70.00
O77	A82	1p scar & sepia	2.25	.30
a.		"ff" joined	29.00	70.00
O78	A83	1½p brt vio & ultra	1.10	*4.25*
O79	A84	2p black brn & Prus green	2.25	.30
a.		"ff" joined	35.00	70.00
O80	A85	2½p dk bl & myr grn	1.40	4.50
a.		"ff" joined	29.00	77.50
O81	A86	3p deep plum & dark vio (R)	5.75	.95
a.		"ff" joined	24.00	55.00
O82	A87	4p dark red vio & violet brn	14.50	1.60
a.		"ff" joined	70.00	92.50
O83	A89	6p vio & brt grn	14.50	1.60
a.		"ff" joined	40.00	80.00
O84	A90	8p org red & blk	14.50	13.00
a.		"ff" joined	40.00	110.00
O85	A91	9p dp org & olive	5.75	5.75
O86	A92	1sh dk sl grn & ol	35.00	5.25
		Nos. O76-O86 (11)	97.60	38.25
		Set, never hinged	190.00	

Nos. 227A, 228C Overprinted in Black

1941 Wmk. 253 *Perf. 13½*

O88	A79	1p light blue green	.30	.30
O89	A80	3p blue	.75	.30
		Set, never hinged	2.25	

Same Overprint on No. 245

1944 *Perf. 14x15*

Size: 17¼x20¼mm

O90	A68	9p int black & scar	20.00	17.00
		Never Hinged	45.00	

Same Overprint on No. AR78

Perf. 14

O91	PF5	5sh green	12.00	7.00
		Never Hinged	20.00	

Catalogue values for unused stamps in this section, from this point to the end of the section, are for Never Hinged items.

Same Ovpt. on Stamps of 1941-47

1946-51 *Perf. 13½, 14*

O92	A79	½p brn org ('46)	1.75	1.25
O92B	A80	1½p red	5.75	1.25
O93	A80	2p orange	.90	.30
O94	A80	4p rose lilac	4.00	1.25
O95	A80	6p rose carmine	5.75	1.25
O96	A80	8p deep violet	10.00	4.50
O97	A80	9p chocolate	11.50	5.75
O98	A104	1sh dk car rose & chestnut	11.50	1.75
O99	A104	2sh dk green & brown org	26.00	8.50
		Nos. O92-O99 (9)	77.15	25.80

LIFE INSURANCE

Lighthouses
LI1 LI2

Perf. 10, 11, 10x11, 12x11½

1891, Jan. 2 Typo. Wmk. 62

OY1	LI1	½p purple	70.00	7.00
OY2	LI1	1p blue	65.00	2.00
OY3	LI1	2p red brown	110.00	4.25
OY4	LI1	3p chocolate	325.00	22.50
OY5	LI1	6p green	475.00	70.00
OY6	LI1	1sh rose pink	800.00	140.00
		Nos. OY1-OY6 (6)	1,845.	245.75

Stamps from outside rows of the sheets sometimes lack watermark.

1903-04 Wmk. 61 *Perf. 11, 14x11*

OY7	LI1	½p purple	62.50	7.00
OY8	LI1	1p blue	62.50	1.10
OY9	LI1	2p red brown	125.00	10.00
		Nos. OY7-OY9 (3)	250.00	18.10

1905-32 *Perf. 11, 14, 14x14½*

OY10	LI2	½p yel grn ('13)	1.40	.90
OY11	LI2	½p green ('32)	5.75	2.75
OY12	LI2	1p blue ('06)	200.00	29.00
OY13	LI2	1p dp rose ('13)	9.75	1.10
OY14	LI2	1p scarlet ('31)	4.25	2.00
OY15	LI2	1½p gray ('17)	14.00	4.25
OY16	LI2	1½p brn org ('19)	1.75	1.40
OY17	LI2	2p red brown	2,000.	125.00
OY18	LI2	2p violet ('13)	20.00	17.00
OY19	LI2	2p yellow ('21)	6.00	6.00
OY20	LI2	3p ocher ('13)	29.00	20.00
OY21	LI2	3p choc ('31)	11.00	26.00
OY22	LI2	6p carmine rose ('13)	20.00	26.00
OY23	LI2	6p pink ('31)	20.00	45.00
		Nos. OY10-OY23 (14)	2,342.	306.40

#OY15, OY16 have "POSTAGE" at each side.
Stamps from outside rows of the sheets sometimes lack watermark.

1946-47 Wmk. 253 *Perf. 14x15*

OY24	LI2	½p yel grn ('47)	1.90	1.90
OY25	LI2	1p scarlet	1.40	1.25
OY26	LI2	2p yellow	2.25	1.40
OY27	LI2	3p chocolate	10.50	8.50
OY28	LI2	6p pink ('47)	8.50	11.50
		Nos. OY24-OY28 (5)	24.55	24.55
		Set, never hinged	42.50	

Catalogue values for unused stamps in this section, from this point to the end of the section, are for Never Hinged items.

New Zealand Lighthouses

Castlepoint
LI3

Taiaroa — LI4

Cape Palliser
LI5

Cape Campbell
LI6

Eddystone (England)
LI7

Stephens Island
LI8

The Brothers
LI9

Cape Brett — LI10

Perf. 13½x13, 13x13½

1947-65 Engr. Wmk. 253

OY29	LI3	½p dk grn & red orange	1.75	1.70
OY30	LI4	1p dk ol grn & blue	1.75	1.10
OY31	LI5	2p int bl & gray	.90	.90
OY32	LI6	2½p ultra & blk ('63)	11.00	15.00
OY33	LI7	3p red vio & bl	3.50	.75
OY34	LI8	4p dk brn & org	4.50	1.75
a.		Wmkd. sideways ('65)	4.50	16.00
OY35	LI9	6p dk brn & bl	4.25	2.50
OY36	LI10	1sh red brn & bl	4.25	3.50
		Nos. OY29-OY36 (8)	31.90	27.20

Set first issued Aug. 1, 1947.
Exist imperf.

NEWSPAPER STAMPS

Queen Victoria — N1

Wmk. 59

1873, Jan. 1 Typo. *Perf. 10*

P1	N1	½p rose	110.00	47.50
a.		Perf. 12½x10	140.00	75.00
b.		Perf. 12½	210.00	75.00

The "N Z" watermark (illustrated over No. 27) is widely spaced and intended for larger stamps. About a third of the stamps in each sheet are unwatermarked. They are worth a slight premium.
For overprint, see No. O6.

1875, Jan. Wmk. 64 *Perf. 12½*

P3	N1	½p rose	19.00	5.00
a.		Pair, imperf. between	800.00	500.00
b.		Perf. 12	70.00	12.50

1892 Wmk. 62 *Perf. 12½*

P4	N1	½p bright rose	11.00	1.50
a.		Unwatermarked	20.00	10.00

NICARAGUA

ˌni-kə-ˈrä-gwə

LOCATION — Central America, between Honduras and Costa Rica
GOVT. — Republic
AREA — 57,143 sq. mi.
POP. — 2,908,000 (est. 1984)
CAPITAL — Managua

100 Centavos = 1 Peso
100 Centavos = 1 Córdoba (1913)

Watermarks

Wmk. 117 — Liberty Cap

Wmk. 209 — Multiple Ovals

Liberty Cap on Mountain Peak; From Seal of Country — A1

A2

A3

Unwmk.

1862, Dec. 2 Engr. *Perf. 12*

Yellowish Paper

1	A1	2c dark blue	75.00	20.00
		On cover		*25,000.*
2	A1	5c black	150.00	60.00
		On cover		*10,000.*

Values are for copies without gum. Copies with gum sell for more. Nos. 1-2 were canceled only by pen.
There is one reported cover of No. 1, two of No. 2.
See No. C509.

1869-71

White Paper

3	A1	1c bister ('71)	3.00	1.25
		On cover		*7,500.*
4	A1	2c blue	3.00	1.25
		On cover		*7,500.*
5	A1	5c black	55.00	1.00
		On cover		*6,000.*
6	A2	10c vermilion	4.00	1.75
		On cover		*5,000.*
7	A3	25c green	7.50	4.00
		On cover		*7,500.*
		Nos. 3-7 (5)	72.50	9.25

There are two reported covers of No. 5, five of No. 7.

1878-80 *Rouletted 8½*

8	A1	1c brown	2.00	1.25
		On cover		*7,500.*
9	A1	2c blue	2.00	1.25
		On cover		*7,500.*
10	A1	5c black	30.00	1.00
		On cover		*6,000.*
11	A2	10c ver ('80)	2.50	1.50
		On cover		*5,000.*
12	A3	25c green ('79)	2.50	4.00
		On cover		*7,500.*
		Nos. 8-12 (5)	39.00	9.00

Most values exist on thicker soft paper.
Stamps with letter/numeral cancellations other than "3 G," "6 M," "9 C" sell for more.
Nos. 3-12 were reprinted in 1892. The corresponding values of the two series are printed in the same shades which is not usually true of the originals. They are, however, similar to some of the original shades and the only certain test is comparison. Originals have thin white gum; reprints have rather thick yellowish gum. Value 50c each.

Seal of Nicaragua — A4

Locomotive and Telegraph Key — A5

1882 Engr. Perf. 12

13	A4	1c green	.20	.25
14	A4	2c carmine	.20	.25
15	A4	5c blue	.20	.25
16	A4	10c dull violet	.25	.75
17	A4	15c yellow	.60	25.00
18	A4	20c slate gray	.90	5.00
19	A4	50c dull violet	1.25	25.00
		Nos. 13-19 (7)	3.60	56.50

Used Values

of Nos. 13-120 are for stamps with genuine cancellations applied while the stamps were valid. Various counterfeit cancellations exist.

1890 Engr.

20	A5	1c yellow brown	.20	.25
21	A5	2c vermilion	.20	.25
22	A5	5c deep blue	.20	.25
23	A5	10c lilac gray	.20	.25
24	A5	20c red	.20	1.75
25	A5	50c purple	.20	5.00
26	A5	1p brown	.25	8.50
27	A5	2p dark green	.25	9.00
28	A5	5p lake	.25	
29	A5	10p orange	.25	
		Nos. 20-29 (10)	2.20	

The issues of 1890-1899 were printed by the Hamilton Bank Note Co., New York, to the order of N. F. Seebeck who held a contract for stamps with the government of Nicaragua. Reprints were made, for sale to collectors, of the 1896, 1897 and 1898, postage, postage due and official stamps. See notes following those issues.

For overprints see Nos. O1-O10.

Perforation Varieties

Imperfs and part perfs of all the Seebeck issues, Nos. 20-120, exist for all except originals of the 1898 issue, Nos. 99-109M.

Goddess of Plenty — A6

Columbus Sighting Land — A7

1891 Engr.

30	A6	1c yellow brn	.25	.35
31	A6	2c red	.25	.35
32	A6	5c dk blue	.25	.25
33	A6	10c slate	.25	.50
34	A6	20c plum	.25	2.00
35	A6	50c purple	.25	5.00
36	A6	1p black brn	.25	5.00
37	A6	2p green	.25	8.50
38	A6	5p brown red	.25	
39	A6	10p orange	.25	
		Nos. 30-39 (10)	2.50	

For overprints see Nos. O11-O20.

1892 Engr.

40	A7	1c yellow brn	.20	.25
41	A7	2c vermilion	.20	.20
42	A7	5c dk blue	.20	.20
43	A7	10c slate	.20	.25
44	A7	20c plum	.20	2.00
45	A7	50c purple	.20	7.00
46	A7	1p brown	.20	7.00
47	A7	2p blue grn	.20	8.50
48	A7	5p rose lake	.20	
49	A7	10p orange	.20	
		Nos. 40-49 (10)	2.00	

Commemorative of the 400th anniversary of the discovery of America by Columbus.

Stamps of the 1892 design were printed in other colors than those listed and overprinted "Telegrafos". The 1c blue, 10c orange, 20c slate, 50c plum and 2p vermilion are telegraph stamps which did not receive the overprint.

For overprints see Nos. O21-O30.

Arms — A8

"Victory" — A9

1893 Engr.

51	A8	1c yellow brn	.20	.20
52	A8	2c vermilion	.20	.20
53	A8	5c dk blue	.20	.20
54	A8	10c slate	.20	.25
55	A8	20c dull red	.20	1.50
56	A8	50c violet	.20	4.00
57	A8	1p dk brown	.20	7.00
58	A8	2p blue green	.20	8.50
59	A8	5p rose lake	.20	
60	A8	10p orange	.20	
		Nos. 51-60 (10)	2.00	

The 1c blue and 2c dark brown are telegraph stamps which did not receive the "Telegrafos" overprint.

For overprints see Nos. O31-O41.

1894 Engr.

61	A9	1c yellow brn	.20	.30
62	A9	2c vermilion	.20	.40
63	A9	5c dp blue	.20	.30
64	A9	10c slate	.20	.40
65	A9	20c lake	.20	2.00
66	A9	50c purple	.20	5.00
67	A9	1p brown	.20	9.50
68	A9	2p green	.20	17.50
69	A9	5p brown red	.20	22.50
70	A9	10p orange	.20	45.00
		Nos. 61-70 (10)	2.00	

There were three printings of this issue. Only the first is known postally used. Unused values are for the third printing.

Specialists believe the 25c yellow green, type A9, is a telegraph denomination never issued for postal purposes. Stamps in other colors are telegraph stamps without the usual "Telegrafos" overprint.

There was little use of No. 70. Canceled copies are c-t-o or faked cancels.

For overprints see Nos. O42-O51.

Coat of Arms A10

Map of Nicaragua A11

1895 Engr.

71	A10	1c yellow brn	.20	.30
72	A10	2c vermilion	.20	.30
73	A10	5c deep blue	.20	.25
74	A10	10c slate	.20	.25
75	A10	20c claret	.20	.75
76	A10	50c light violet	50.00	5.00
77	A10	1p dark brown	.20	5.00
78	A10	2p deep green	.20	8.00
79	A10	5p brown red	.20	11.00
80	A10	10p orange	.20	
		Nos. 71-80 (10)	51.80	

Frames of Nos. 71-80 differ for each denomination.

A 50c violet blue exists. Its status is questioned. Value 20c.

There was little use of No. 80. Canceled copies are c-t-o or faked cancels.

For overprints see Nos. O52-O71.

1896 Engr.

81	A11	1c violet	.30	1.00
82	A11	2c blue grn	.30	.50
83	A11	5c brt rose	.30	.30
84	A11	10c blue	.50	.50
85	A11	20c bister brn	3.00	4.00
86	A11	50c blue gray	.60	8.00
87	A11	1p black	.75	11.00
88	A11	2p claret	.75	15.00
89	A11	5p deep blue	.75	15.00
		Nos. 81-89 (9)	7.25	55.30

There were two printings of this issue. Only the first is known postally used. Unused values are for the second printing.

See italic note after No. 109M.

For overprints see Nos. O82-O117.

Wmk. 117

89A	A11	1c violet	3.75	.90
89B	A11	2c bl grn	3.75	1.25
89C	A11	5c brt rose	15.00	.30
89D	A11	10c blue	25.00	.90
89E	A11	20c bis brn	22.50	4.25
89F	A11	50c bl gray	42.50	9.00
89G	A11	1p black	37.50	12.50
89H	A11	2p claret		18.00
89I	A11	5p dp bl		40.00

Same, dated 1897

1897 Engr. Unwmk.

90	A11	1c violet	.50	.50
91	A11	2c bl grn	.50	.60
92	A11	5c brt rose	.50	.30
93	A11	10c blue	6.25	.75
94	A11	20c bis brn	2.50	3.75
95	A11	50c bl gray	9.00	9.50
96	A11	1p black	9.00	15.00
97	A11	2p claret	20.00	19.00
98	A11	5p dp bl	20.00	42.50
		Nos. 90-98 (9)	68.25	91.90

See italic note after No. 109M.

Wmk. 117

98A	A11	1c violet	14.00	.50
98B	A11	2c bl grn	14.00	.50
98C	A11	5c brt rose	20.00	.40
98D	A11	10c blue	22.50	.90
98E	A11	20c bis brn	22.50	4.25
98F	A11	50c bl gray	22.50	8.00
98G	A11	1p black	25.00	16.00
98H	A11	2p claret	25.00	25.00
98I	A11	5p dp bl	125.00	50.00
		Nos. 98A-98I (9)	290.50	105.55

Coat of Arms of "Republic of Central America" — A12

1898 Engr. Wmk. 117

99	A12	1c brown	.25	.40
100	A12	2c slate	.25	.40
101	A12	4c red brown	.25	.50
102	A12	5c olive green	40.00	22.50
103	A12	10c violet	15.00	.60
104	A12	15c ultra	.40	1.50
105	A12	20c blue	10.00	2.00
106	A12	50c yellow	10.00	9.50
107	A12	1p violet blue	.40	16.00
108	A12	2p brown	19.00	22.50
109	A12	5p orange	25.00	32.50
		Nos. 99-109 (11)	120.55	108.40

Unwmk.

109A	A12	1c brown	1.25	.30
109B	A12	2c slate	1.25	
109D	A12	4c red brown	2.25	.60
109E	A12	5c olive green	25.00	.20
109G	A12	10c violet	25.00	.60
109H	A12	15c ultra	25.00	
109I	A12	20c blue	25.00	
109J	A12	50c yellow	25.00	
109K	A12	1p deep ultra	25.00	
109L	A12	2p olive brown	25.00	
109M	A12	5p orange	25.00	
		Nos. 109A-109M (11)	204.75	

The paper of Nos. 109A to 109M is slightly thicker and more opaque than that of Nos. 81 to 89 and 90 to 98. The 5c and 10c also exist on very thin, semi-transparent paper.

Many reprints of Nos. 81-98, 98F-98H, 99-109M are on thick, porous paper, with and without watermark. The watermark is sideways. Paper of the originals is thinner for Nos. 81-109 but thicker for Nos. 109A-109M. Value 15 cents each.

In addition, reprints of Nos. 81-89 and 90-98 exist on thin paper, but with shades differing slightly from those of originals.

For overprints see Nos. O118-O128.

"Justice" A13

Mt. Momotombo A14

1899 Litho.

110	A13	1c gray grn	.20	.35
111	A13	2c brown	.20	.25
112	A13	4c dp rose	.35	.40
113	A13	5c dp bl	.20	.25
114	A13	10c buff	.20	.30
115	A13	15c chocolate	.20	.65
116	A13	20c dk grn	.35	.75
117	A13	50c brt rose	.20	3.00
118	A13	1p red	.20	8.50
119	A13	2p violet	.20	20.00
120	A13	5p lt bl	.20	25.00
		Nos. 110-120 (11)	2.50	59.45

Nos. 110-120 exist imperf. and in horizontal pairs imperf. between.

Nos. 110-111, 113 exist perf 6x12 due to defective perforating equipment.

For overprints see Nos. O129-O139.

Imprint: "American Bank Note Co. NY"

1900, Jan. 1 Engr.

121	A14	1c plum	.50	.20
122	A14	2c vermilion	.50	.20
123	A14	3c green	.75	.25
124	A14	4c ol grn	1.00	.25
125	A14	5c dk bl	4.00	.20
126	A14	6c car rose	14.00	5.00
127	A14	10c violet	7.00	.25
128	A14	15c ultra	8.00	.65
129	A14	20c brown	8.00	.65
130	A14	50c lake	7.00	1.10
131	A14	1p yellow	12.00	4.00
132	A14	2p salmon	10.00	2.25
133	A14	5p black	10.00	3.00
		Nos. 121-133 (13)	82.75	18.00

Used values for #123, 126, 130-133 are for canceled to order copies.

See Nos. 159-161. For overprints and surcharges see Nos. 134-136, 144-151, 162-163, 175-178, O150-O154, 1L1-1L13, 1L16-1L19, 1L20, 2L1-2L10, 2L16-2L24, 2L36-2L39.

Nos. 131-133 Surcharged in Black or Red

1901, Mar. 5

134	A14	2c on 1p yel	5.00	3.00
a.		Bar below date	14.00	9.00
b.		Inverted surcharge		35.00
c.		Double surcharge		50.00
135	A14	10c on 5p blk (R)	6.50	4.50
a.		Bar below date	14.00	8.00
136	A14	20c on 2p salmon	7.50	7.50
a.		Bar below date	14.00	10.00
		Nos. 134-136 (3)	19.00	15.00

A 2c surcharge on No. 121, the 1c plum, was not put on sale, nor postally used.

The 2c on 1p yellow without ornaments is a reprint.

Postage Due Stamps of 1900 Overprinted in Black or Gold

1901, Mar.

137	D3	1c plum	4.50	3.50
138	D3	2c vermilion	4.50	3.50
139	D3	5c dk bl	6.00	3.50
140	D3	10c pur (G)	8.50	5.00
a.		Double overprint	14.00	14.00
141	D3	20c org brn	10.00	6.50
142	D3	30c dk grn	10.00	6.50
143	D3	50c lake	8.50	4.00
a.		"1091" for "1901"	35.00	35.00
b.		"Correo"	37.50	
		Nos. 137-143 (7)	52.00	32.50

In 1904 an imitation of this overprint was made to fill a dealer's order. The date is at top and "Correos" at bottom. The overprint is printed in black, sideways on the 1c and 2c and upright on the 5c and 10c. Some copies of the 2c were further surcharged "1 Centavo." None of these stamps was ever regularly used.

Nos. 126, 131-133 Surcharged

Black Surcharge

1901, Oct. 20

144	A14	3c on 6c rose	6.00	5.00
a.		Bar below value	7.00	5.50
b.		Inverted surcharge	8.00	8.00
c.		Double surcharge	8.00	8.00
d.		Double surch., one inverted	25.00	25.00
145	A14	4c on 6c rose	5.00	4.00
a.		Bar below value	5.50	4.50
b.		"1 cent" instead of "4 cent"	8.00	8.00
c.		Double surcharge	20.00	20.00
146	A14	5c on 1p yellow	5.00	4.00
a.		Three bars below value	6.00	4.50
b.		Ornaments at each side of "1901"	6.00	4.50
c.		Double surcharge, one in red	15.00	15.00
147	A14	10c on 2p salmon	5.50	4.00
a.		Inverted surcharge	12.50	12.50
b.		Double surcharge		

Blue Surcharge

148	A14	3c on 6c rose	6.00	4.50
a.		Bar below value	7.00	5.50
b.		Double surcharge	8.00	8.00
149	A14	4c on 6c rose	6.50	5.00
a.		Bar below value	7.50	7.50
b.		"1 cent" instead of "4 cent"	10.00	10.00
c.		Inverted surcharge	20.00	20.00

Red Surcharge

150	A14	5c on 1p yellow	7.50	6.50
a.		Three bars below value	9.00	7.00
b.		Ornaments at each side of "1901"	9.00	7.00
c.		Inverted surcharge	12.00	12.00
d.		Double surcharge, inverted	17.50	17.50

151 A14 20c on 5p black 5.00 3.50
a. Inverted surcharge 16.00 16.00
b. Double surcharge 22.50 22.50
c. Triple surcharge
Nos. 144-151 (8) 46.50 36.50

In 1904 a series was surcharged as above, but with "Centavos" spelled out. About the same time No. 122 was surcharged "1 cent." and "1901," "1902" or "1904." All of these surcharges were made to fill a dealer's order and none of the stamps was regularly issued or used.

Postage Due Stamps of 1900 Overprinted in Black

1901, Oct.
152 D3 1c red violet 1.00 .40
a. Ornaments at each side of the stamp 1.10 .65
b. Ornaments at each side of "1901" 1.10 .65
c. "Correos" in italics 1.50 1.50
d. Double overprint 14.00 14.00
153 D3 2c vermilion .75 .40
a. Double overprint 8.50 5.50
154 D3 5c dark blue 1.00 .60
a. Double overprint, one inverted
b. Double overprint 7.00 7.00
155 D3 10c purple 1.00 .60
b. Double overprint 10.00 10.00
c. Double overprint, one inverted 12.00 12.00
156 D3 20c org brn 1.25 1.25
b. Double overprint 7.00 7.00
157 D3 30c dk grn 1.00 1.10
a. Double overprint 9.00 9.00
b. Inverted overprint 19.00 19.00
158 D3 50c lake 1.00 1.10
a. Triple overprint 25.00 25.00
b. Double overprint 16.00 16.00
Nos. 152-158 (7) 7.00 5.45

One stamp in each group of 25 has the 2nd "o" of "Correos" italic. Value twice normal.

Momotombo Type of 1900 Without Imprint

1902 **Litho.** ***Perf. 14***
159 A14 5c blue .50 .25
a. Imperf., pair 3.75
160 A14 5c carmine .50 .20
a. Imperf., pair 3.75
161 A14 10c violet 1.50 .20
a. Imperf., pair 3.75
Nos. 159-161 (3) 2.50 .65

No. 161 was privately surcharged 6c, 1p and 5p in black in 1903.

Nos. 121 and 122 Surcharged in Black

1902, Oct. ***Perf. 12***
162 A14 15c on 2c ver 2.00 .75
a. Double surcharge 32.50
b. Blue surcharge 90.00
163 A14 30c on 1c plum 1.00 2.25
a. Double surcharge 9.00
b. Inverted surcharge 27.50

Counterfeits of No. 163 exist in slightly smaller type.

President José Santos Zelaya — A15

1903, Jan. **Engr.**
167 A15 1c emer & blk .35 .50
168 A15 2c rose & blk .70 .50
169 A15 5c ultra & blk .35 .50
170 A15 10c yel & blk .35 .85
171 A15 15c lake & blk .60 2.00
172 A15 20c vio & blk .60 2.00
173 A15 50c ol & blk .60 5.00
174 A15 1p red brn & blk .60 6.00
Nos. 167-174 (8) 4.15 17.35

10th anniv. of 1st election of Pres. Zelaya.

The so-called color errors-1c orange yellow and black, 2c ultramarine and black, 5c lake and black and 10c emerald and black-were also delivered to postal authorities. They were intended for official use though not issued as such. Value, $4 each.

Nos. 175-176

No. 177b

No. 161 Surcharged with New Values in Blue

1904-05
175 A14 5c on 10c vio ('05) 1.75 .25
a. Inverted surcharge 2.00 1.40
b. Without ornaments 2.00 .70
c. Character for "cents" inverted 1.75 .40
d. As "b," inverted
e. As "c," inverted 2.75 2.75
f. Double surcharge 8.00 8.00
g. "5" omitted 2.75 2.75
176 A14 15c on 10c vio ('05) .30 .30
a. Inverted surcharge 1.40 1.40
b. Without ornaments 1.40 1.40
c. Character for "cents" inverted 1.10 1.10
d. As "b," inverted
e. As "c," inverted 1.75 1.75
f. Imperf. 6.50
h. As "a," imperf. 9.00 9.00
i. Double surcharge 14.00 14.00
177 A14 15c on 10c vio 4.50 2.75
a. Inverted surcharge 6.00 6.00
b. "Centcvos" 6.00 4.50
c. "5" of "15" omitted 7.50
d. As "b," inverted 8.50 8.50
e. Double surcharge 11.00 11.00
f. Double surcharge, inverted 13.00 13.00
g. Imperf., pair 9.00 9.00
Nos. 175-177 (3) 6.55 3.30

There are two settings of the surcharge on No. 175. In the 1st the character for "cents" and the figure "5" are 2mm apart and in the 2nd 4mm.

The 2c vermilion, No. 122, with surcharge "1 cent. / 1904" was not issued.

No. 161 Surcharged in Black

1905, June
178 A14 5c on 10c violet .60 .35
a. Inverted surcharge 2.75 2.75
b. Double surcharge 4.50 4.50
c. Surcharge in blue 75.00

Coat of Arms — A18

Imprint: "American Bank Note Co. NY"

1905, July 25 **Engr.** ***Perf. 12***
179 A18 1c green .30 .20
180 A18 2c car rose .30 .20
181 A18 3c violet .45 .25
182 A18 4c org red .45 .25
183 A18 5c blue .45 .20
184 A18 6c slate .60 .40
185 A18 10c yel brn .85 .25
186 A18 15c brn olive .75 .35
187 A18 20c lake .60 .40
188 A18 50c orange 3.00 1.50
189 A18 1p black 1.50 1.50
190 A18 2p dk grn 1.50 2.00
191 A18 5p violet 1.75 2.50
Nos. 179-191 (13) 12.50 10.00

See Nos. 202-208, 237-248. For overprints and surcharges see Nos. 193-201, 212-216, 235-236, 249-265, O187-O198, O210-O222, 1L21-1L62, 1L73-1L95, 1LO1-1LO3, 2L26-2L35, 2L42-2L46, 2L48-2L72, 2LO1-2LO4.

Nos. 179-184 and 191 Surcharged in Black or Red Reading Up or Down

1906-08
193 A18 10c on 2c car rose (up) 7.00 4.00
a. Surcharge reading down 13.00 13.00
194 A18 10c on 3c vio (up) .60 .20
a. "¢" normal 2.75 1.35
b. Double surcharge 4.50 4.50
c. Double surch., up and down 7.00 5.00
d. Pair, one without surcharge 9.50
e. Surcharge reading down .30 .20
195 A18 10c on 4c org red (up) ('08) *35.00* *20.00*
a. Surcharge reading down *32.50* *22.50*
196 A18 15c on 1c grn (up) .60 .30
a. Double surcharge 7.50 7.50
b. Dbl. surch., one reading down 11.00 11.00
c. Surcharge reading down .40 .25
197 A18 20c on 2c car rose (down) ('07) .50 .30
a. Double surcharge 13.00 13.00
b. Surcharge reading up 37.50 32.50
c. "V" omitted 10.00 10.00
198 A18 20c on 5c bl (down) .75 .50
a. Surcharge reading up 35.00
199 A18 50c on 6c sl (R) (down) .60 .50
a. Double surcharge
b. Surcharge reading up 30.00 30.00
c. Yellow brown surcharge .60 .40
200 A18 1p on 5p vio (down) ('07) 42.50 25.00
Nos. 193-200 (8) *87.55* *50.80*

There are several settings of these surcharges and many varieties in the shapes of the figures, the spacing, etc.

Surcharged in Red Vertically Reading Up

1908, May
201 A18 35c on 6c slate 3.00 2.25
a. Double surcharge (R) 25.00
b. Double surcharge (R + Bk) 65.00
c. Carmine surcharge 3.00 2.25

Arms Type of 1905

Imprint: "Waterlow & Sons, Ltd."

1907, Feb. ***Perf. 14 to 15***
202 A18 1c green .70 .40
203 A18 2c rose .80 .25
204 A18 4c brn org 2.00 .30
205 A18 10c yel brn 3.00 .25
206 A18 15c brn olive 4.50 .90
207 A18 20c lake 8.00 1.25
208 A18 50c orange 11.00 4.25
Nos. 202-208 (7) 30.00 7.60

Nos. 202-204, 207-208 Surcharged in Black or Blue (Bl) Reading Down

1907-08
212 A18 10c on 2c rose 1.50 .50
a. Double surcharge 10.00
b. "Vale" only 22.50
c. Surcharge reading up 14.00 6.50
213 A18 10c on 4c brn org (up) ('08) 2.25 .85
a. Double surcharge 10.00
b. Surcharge reading down 5.50
214 A18 10c on 20c lake ('08) 3.25 1.40
b. Surcharge reading up 80.00
215 A18 10c on 50c org (Bl) ('08) 2.00 .60
216 A18 15c on 1c grn ('08) 32.50 4.00
Nos. 212-216 (5) 41.50 7.35

Several settings of this surcharge provide varieties of numeral font, spacing, etc.

Revenue Stamps Overprinted "CORREO-1908" — A19

1908, June
217 A19 5c yel & blk .60 .40
a. "CORROE" 2.75 2.75
b. Overprint reading down 7.00
c. Double overprint 13.00
218 A19 10c lt bl & blk .50 .25
a. Double overprint 4.50 4.50
b. Overprint reading down .50 .25
c. Double overprint, up and down 13.00 13.00
219 A19 1p yel brn & blk .50 *2.00*
a. "CORROE" 7.50 7.50
220 A19 2p pearl gray & blk .50 *2.50*
a. "CORROE" 10.00 10.00
Nos. 217-220 (4) 2.10 *5.15*

Remainders of Nos. 219-220 were sold.

Revenue Stamps Surcharged Vertically Reading Up in Red (1c, 15c), Blue(2c), Green (4c) or Orange (35c)

221 A19 1c on 5c yel & blk .40 .25
a. "1008" 1.50 1.50
b. "8908" 1.50 1.50
c. Surcharge reading down 4.00 4.00
d. Double surcharge 4.00 4.00
222 A19 2c on 5c yel & blk .50 .30
b. "ORREO" 1.75 1.75
c. "1008" 1.75 1.75
d. "8908" 1.75 1.75
f. Double surcharge 7.00 7.00
g. Double surcharge, one inverted 7.00 7.00
h. Surcharge reading down 9.00 9.00
223 A19 4c on 5c yel & blk .65 .35
a. "ORREO" 2.50 2.50
b. "1008" 2.00 2.00
c. "8908" 2.00 2.00
224 A19 15c on 50c ol & blk .60 .40
a. "1008" 4.00 4.00
b. "8908" 4.00 4.00
c. Surcharge reading down 10.00 10.00
225 A19 35c on 50c ol & blk 4.00 1.00
a. Double surcharge, one inverted 12.00 12.00
b. Surcharge reading down 12.00 12.00
c. Double surcharge, one in black
Nos. 221-225 (5) 6.15 2.30

For surcharges and overprints see Nos. 225D-225H, 230-234, 266-278, 1L63-1L72A, 1L96-1L106, 2L47.

Revenue Stamps Surcharged Vertically Reading Up in Blue, Black or Orange

1908, Nov.
225D A19 2c on 5c yel & blk (Bl) 20.00 12.50
e. "9c" instead of "2c" 75.00 75.00
225F A19 10c on 50c ol & blk (Bk) *850.00* *325.00*
g. Double surcharge *425.00*
225H A19 35c on 50c ol & blk (O) 17.50 10.00

In this setting there are three types of the character for "cents."

Revenue Stamps Overprinted or Surcharged in Various Colors

No. 226

1908, Dec.

226 2c org (Bk) 3.50 2.00
a. Double overprint 6.00 6.00
b. Overprint reading up 5.00 5.00
227 4c on 2c org (Bk) 1.75 .90
a. Surcharge reading up 5.00 5.00
b. Blue surcharge 80.00 80.00
228 5c on 2c org (Bl) 1.50 .60
a. Surcharge reading up 6.00 6.00
229 10c on 2c org (G) 1.50 .30
a. "1988" for "1908" 4.00 3.00
b. Surcharge reading up 5.00 5.00
c. "¢" inverted 4.00 4.00
d. Double surcharge 7.50
Nos. 226-229 (4) 8.25 3.80

Two printings of No. 229 exist. In the first, the initial of "VALE" is a small capital, and in the second a large capital.

The overprint "Correos-1908." 35mm long, handstamped on 1c blue revenue stamp of type A20, is private and fraudulent.

Revenue Stamps Surcharged in Various Colors

1909, Feb.

Color: Olive & Black

230 A19 1c on 50c (V) 4.00 1.60
231 A19 2c on 50c (Br) 7.00 3.00
232 A19 4c on 50c (G) 7.00 3.00
233 A19 5c on 50c (C) 4.00 1.75
a. Double surcharge 12.50 12.50
234 A19 10c on 50c (Bk) 1.10 .75
Nos. 230-234 (5) 23.10 10.10

Nos. 230 to 234 are found with three types of the character for "cents."

Nos. 190 and 191 Surcharged in Black

1909, Mar. ***Perf. 12***

235 A18 10c on 2p dk grn 20.00 12.00
236 A18 10c on 5p vio *100.00 70.00*

There are three types of the character for "cents."

Arms Type of 1905

Imprint: "American Bank Note Co. NY"

1909, Mar.

237 A18 1c yel grn .35 .20
238 A18 2c vermilion .35 .20
239 A18 3c red org .35 .20
240 A18 4c violet .35 .20
241 A18 5c dp bl .35 .20
242 A18 6c gray brn 3.00 1.50
243 A18 10c lake .85 .20
244 A18 15c black .85 .20
245 A18 20c brn olive .85 .20
246 A18 50c dp grn 1.25 .40
247 A18 1p yellow 1.25 .40
248 A18 2p car rose 1.00 .40
Nos. 237-248 (12) 10.80 4.30

Nos. 239 and 244, Surcharged in Black or Red

1910, July

249 A18 2c on 3c red org 2.75 1.10
250 A18 10c on 15c blk (R) 1.25 .30
a. "VLEA" 3.50 2.00
b. Double surcharge 17.50 17.50

There are two types of the character for "cents."

Nos. 239, 244, 245 Surcharged in Black or Red

1910

252 A18 2c on 3c (Bk) 1.50 1.25
a. Double surcharge 6.00 6.00
b. Pair, one without surcharge
c. "Vale" omitted 10.00 10.00
254 A18 5c on 20c (R) .40 .30
a. Double surcharge (R) 6.00 5.00
b. Inverted surcharge (R) 3.50 2.50
c. Black surcharge 100.00
d. Double surcharge (Bk) 140.00
e. Inverted surcharge (Bk) 110.00
255 A18 10c on 15c (Bk) .90 .30
a. "c" omitted 2.00 1.10
b. "10c" omitted 2.50 1.50
c. Inverted surcharge 4.00 4.00
d. Double surcharge 6.00 6.00
e. Double surch., one inverted 12.00
Nos. 252-255 (3) 2.80 1.85

There are several minor varieties in this setting, such as italic "L" and "E" and fancy "V" in "VALE," small italic "C," and italic "I" for "1" in "10."

Nos. 239, 244, 246 and 247, Surcharged in Black

1910, Dec. 10

256 A18 2c on 3c red org .85 .45
a. Without period 1.00 .75
b. Inverted surcharge 6.00 6.00
c. Double surcharge 6.00 6.00
257 A18 10c on 15c blk 2.00 .75
a. Without period 3.50 1.25
b. Double surcharge 3.50 3.00
c. Inverted surcharge 5.00 5.00
258 A18 10c on 50c dp grn 1.25 .40
a. Without period 1.50 .75
b. Double surcharge 3.00 3.00
c. Inverted surcharge 3.00 3.00
259 A18 10c on 1p yel .90 .40
a. Without period 1.25 .75
b. Double surcharge 3.00 3.00
Nos. 256-259 (4) 5.00 2.00

The 15c on 50c deep green is a telegraph stamp.

Nos. 240, 244-248 Surcharged in Black

Surcharge as on Nos. 256-259 but lines wider apart.

1911, Mar.

260 A18 2c on 4c vio .30 .20
a. Without period .35 .30
b. Double surcharge 3.50 3.00
c. Double surcharge, inverted 4.00 4.00
d. Double surcharge, one invtd. 3.50 3.50
e. Inverted surcharge 7.50 7.50
261 A18 5c on 20c brn ol .30 .20
a. Without period .60 .50
b. Double surcharge 2.50 2.50
c. Inverted surcharge 2.50 2.00
d. Double surcharge, one invtd. 6.00 6.00
262 A18 10c on 15c blk .40 .20
a. Without period 1.00 .50
b. "Yale" 12.00 12.00
c. Double surcharge 3.00 3.00
d. Inverted surcharge 3.00 3.00
e. Double surch., one inverted 5.00 4.00
f. Double surch., both inverted 12.00 12.00
263 A18 10c on 50c dp grn .25 .20
a. Without period 1.00 .50
b. Double surcharge 3.00 2.50
c. Double surcharge, one invtd. 5.00 4.00
d. Inverted surcharge 5.00 5.00
264 A18 10c on 1p yel 1.50 .40
a. Without period 2.00 1.50
b. Double surcharge 4.00 4.00
c. Double surcharge, one invtd. 7.50
265 A18 10c on 2p car rose .60 .50
a. Without period 2.00 1.50
b. Double surcharge 2.50 2.50
c. Double surcharge, one invtd. 6.00 6.00
d. Inverted surcharge 6.00 6.00
Nos. 260-265 (6) 3.35 1.70

Revenue Stamps Surcharged in Black

1911, Apr. 10 ***Perf. 14 to 15***

266 A19 2c on 5p dl bl 1.00 *1.25*
a. Without period 1.25 *1.50*
b. Double surcharge 2.50 2.00
267 A19 2c on 5p ultra .35 *.40*
a. Without period .75 *1.25*
b. Double surcharge *3.50*
268 A19 5c on 10p pink .75 .40
a. Without period 1.50 1.00
b. "cte" for "cts" 1.50 1.00
c. Double surcharge 4.00 4.00
d. Inverted surcharge 2.50 2.50
269 A19 10c on 25c lilac .40 .25
a. Without period 1.00 .75
b. "cte" for "cts" 1.25 1.00
c. Inverted surcharge 4.00 4.00
d. Double surcharge 2.50 2.50
e. Double surcharge, one inverted 4.00 4.00
270 A19 10c on 2p gray .40 .25
a. Without period 1.00 .75
b. "cte" for "cts" 1.25 1.00
c. Double surcharge 5.00 5.00
d. Double surcharge, one inverted 4.00 3.00
271 A19 35c on 1p brown .40 .30
a. Without period 1.00 .75
b. "cte" for "cts" 1.25 1.00
c. "Corre" 1.50 1.50
d. Double surcharge 2.50 2.50
e. Double surcharge, one inverted 2.50 2.50
f. Double surcharge inverted 3.00 3.00
g. Inverted surcharge *5.00*
Nos. 266-271 (6) 3.30 2.85

These surcharges are in settings of twenty-five. One stamp in each setting has a large square period after "cts" and two have no period. One of the 2c has no space between "02" and "cts" and one 5c has a small thin "s" in "Correos."

Surcharged in Black

1911, June

272 A19 5c on 2p gray 1.50 1.00
a. Inverted surcharge 6.00 5.00

In this setting one stamp has a large square period and another has a thick up-right "c" in "cts."

Surcharged in Black

1911, June 12

273 A19 5c on 25c lilac 1.50 1.25
274 A19 5c on 50c ol grn 5.00 5.00
275 A19 5c on 5p blue 7.00 7.00
276 A19 5c on 5p ultra 6.00 6.00
a. Inverted surcharge
277 A19 5c on 50p ver 5.00 5.00
278 A19 10c on 50c ol grn 1.50 .50
Nos. 273-278 (6) 26.00 24.75

This setting has the large square period and the thick "c" in "cts." Many of the stamps have no period after "cts." Owing to broken type and defective impressions letters sometimes appear to be omitted.

A21

Revenue Stamps Surcharged on the Back in Black:

a

b

Railroad coupon tax stamps (1st class red and 2nd class blue) are the basic stamps of Nos. 279-294. They were first surcharged for revenue use in 1903 in two types: I — "Timbre Fiscal" and "ctvs." II — "TIMBRE FISCAL" and "cents" (originally intended for use in Bluefields).

1911, July

279 A21 (a) 2c on 5c on 2 bl .25 .30
a. New value in yellow on face 6.00 6.00
b. New value in black on face 10.00 5.00
c. New value in red on face *100.00*
d. Inverted surcharge .75
e. Double surch., one inverted 7.50 7.50
f. "TIMBRE FISCAL" in black .75 .75
280 A21 (b) 2c on 5c on 2 bl .25 .30
a. New value in yellow on face 3.00 3.00
b. New value in black on face 9.00 4.00
c. New value in red on face *100.00*
d. Inverted surcharge .90 1.00
e. Double surch., one inverted 7.50 7.50
f. "TIMBRE FISCAL" in black 1.00 1.00
281 A21 (a) 5c on 5c on 2 bl .20 .20
a. Inverted surcharge .50 .35
b. "TIMBRE FISCAL" in black 1.00 1.00
c. New value in yellow on face
282 A21 (b) 5c on 5c on 2 bl .25 .20
a. Inverted surcharge .40 .35
b. "TIMBRE FISCAL" in black 1.00 1.00
c. New value in yellow on face
283 A21 (a) 10c on 5c on 2 bl .20 .20
a. Inverted surcharge .75 .50
b. "TIMBRE FISCAL" in black 1.00 1.00
c. New value in yellow on face *100.00*
d. Double surcharge 6.00 6.00
284 A21 (b) 10c on 5c on 2 bl .20 .20
a. Inverted surcharge .75 .50
b. "TIMBRE FISCAL" in black 1.00 1.00
c. Double surcharge 6.00 6.00
d. New value in yellow on face *110.00*
285 A21 (a) 15c on 10c on 1 red .25 .25
a. Inverted surcharge 1.00 1.25
b. "Timbre Fiscal" double 5.00
286 A21 (b) 15c on 10c on 1 red .40 .35
a. Inverted surcharge 1.00 1.00
b. "Timbre Fiscal" double 5.00
Nos. 279-286 (8) 2.00 2.00

These surcharges are in settings of 20. For listing, they are separated into small and large figures, but there are many other varieties due to type and arrangement.

The colored surcharges on the face of the stamps were trial printings. These were then surcharged in black on the reverse. The olive yellow surcharge on the face of the 2c was later applied to prevent use as a 5c revenue stamps. Other colors known on the face are orange and green. Forgeries exist.

For overprints and surcharges see Nos. 287-294, O223-O244, 1L107-1L108.

Surcharged on the Face in Black

1911, Oct.

287 A21 2c on 10c on 1 red 6.50 6.50
a. Inverted surcharge 1.40 1.40
b. Double surcharge 10.00 10.00
288 A21 20c on 10c on 1 red 4.50 4.50
a. Inverted surcharge 5.25 5.00
289 A21 50c on 10c on 1 red 5.25 4.50
a. Inverted surcharge 10.00 10.00
Nos. 287-289 (3) 16.25 15.50

There are two varieties of the figures "2" and "5" in this setting.

Surcharged on the Back in Black

Vale
10 cts.
CORREO DE
1911

1911, Nov.

289B A21 5c on 10c on 1 red 37.50
c. Inverted surcharge 20.00
289D A21 10c on 10c on 1 red 12.50
e. Inverted surcharge 24.00

Surcharged on the Face

1911, Dec.

Dark Blue Postal Surcharge

290 A21 2c on 10c on 1 red .25 .20
a. Inverted surcharge 2.50 2.50
b. Double surcharge 5.00 5.00
291 A21 5c on 10c on 1 red .30 .20
a. Double surcharge 2.50 2.50
b. Inverted surcharge 2.50 2.50
292 A21 10c on 10c on 1 red .35 .20
a. Inverted surcharge 2.50 2.50
b. Double surcharge 2.50 2.50
c. "TIMBRE FISCAL" on back 3.50 3.50

Black Postal Surcharge

293 A21 10c on 10c on 1 red 1.50 1.00
a. Inverted surcharge 7.00 7.00
b. New value surch. on back 12.00 12.00

Red Postal Surcharge

293C A21 5c on 5c on 2 blue 1.40 1.25
d. "TIMBRE FISCAL" in black 2.50 1.75
e. "5" omitted 3.75 3.75
f. Inverted surcharge 4.75 4.75
Nos. 290-293C (5) 3.80 2.85

Bar Overprinted on No. O234 in Dark Blue

294 A21 10c on 10c on 1 red 1.25 1.00
a. Inverted surcharge 2.50 2.50
b. Bar at foot of stamp 5.00 5.00

Nos. 290-294 each have three varieties of the numerals in the surcharge.

"Liberty"
A22

Coat of Arms
A23

1912, Jan. Engr. *Perf. 14, 15*

295 A22 1c yel grn .30 .20
296 A22 2c carmine .40 .20
297 A22 3c yel brn .30 .20
298 A22 4c brn vio .30 .20
299 A22 5c blue & blk .25 .20
300 A22 6c olive bister .30 .80
301 A22 10c red brn .25 .20
302 A22 15c vio .25 .20
303 A22 20c red .25 .20
304 A22 25c blue grn & blk .30 .20
305 A23 35c grn & chnt 2.00 1.50
306 A22 50c lt blue 1.00 .40
307 A22 1p org 1.40 2.00
308 A22 2p dark blue grn 1.50 2.25
309 A22 5p blk 3.50 3.50
Nos. 295-309 (15) 12.30 12.25

For overprints and surcharges see Nos. 310-324, 337A-348, 395-396, O245-O259.

No. 305 Surcharged in Violet

1913, Mar.

310 A23 15c on 35c .40 .25
a. "ats" for "cts" 6.00 6.00

Stamps of 1912 Surcharged in Red or Black

1913-14

311 A22 ½c on 3c yel brn (R) .40 .35
a. "Corooba" 2.50 2.50
b. "do" for "de" 2.50 2.50
c. Inverted surcharge 22.50
312 A22 ½c on 15c vio (R) .25 .20
a. "Corooba" 1.00 1.00
b. "do" for "de" 1.25 1.25
313 A22 ½c on 1p org .25 .20
a. "VALB" 1.50 1.00
b. "ALE" 4.00 3.50
c. "LE" 6.00 5.00
d. "VALE" omitted 3.50 3.50
314 A22 1c on 3c yel brn .75 .60
315 A22 1c on 4c brn vio .25 .20
316 A22 1c on 50c lt blue .25 .20
317 A22 1c on 5p blk .25 .20
318 A22 2c on 4c brn vio .35 .25
a. "do" for "de" 1.25 1.25
319 A22 2c on 20c red 3.50 *4.50*
a. "do" for "de" 17.50 12.50
320 A22 2c on 25c blue grn & blk .35 .20
a. "do" for "de" 3.50 2.50
321 A23 2c on 35c grn & chnt .25 .40
a. "9131" 3.00 2.00
b. "do" for "de" 2.50 2.00
322 A22 2c on 50c lt blue .25 .20
a. "do" for "de" 1.25 1.25
323 A22 2c on 2p dark blue grn .20 .20
a. "VALB" 1.25 .75
b. "ALE" 2.50 1.25
c. "VALE" omitted 6.00
d. "VALE" and "dos" omitted 6.00
324 A22 3c on 6c olive bis .20 .20
a. "VALB" *35.00*
Nos. 311-324 (14) 7.50 7.90

Nos. 311, 312 surcharged in black were not regularly issued.

Surcharged on Zelaya Issue of 1912

325 Z2 ½c on 2c ver .60 .45
a. "Corooba" 1.25 1.25
b. "do" for "de" 1.25 1.25
326 Z2 1c on 3c org brn .50 .20
327 Z2 1c on 4c car .50 .20
328 Z2 1c on 6c red brn .40 .20
329 Z2 1c on 20c dark vio .50 .20
330 Z2 1c on 25c grn & blk .50 .20
331 Z2 2c on 1c yel grn ('14) 6.75 1.25
a. "Centavos" 7.50 1.50
332 Z2 2c on 25c grn & blk 2.25 *3.00*
333 Z2 5c on 35c brn & blk .40 .20
334 Z2 5c on 50c ol grn .40 .20
a. Double surcharge 22.50
335 Z2 6c on 1p org .40 .20
336 Z2 10c on 2p org brn .40 .20
337 Z2 1p on 5p dk bl grn .40 .40
Nos. 325-337 (13) 14.00 6.90

On No. 331 the surcharge has a space of 2½mm between "Vale" and "dos."

Space between "Vale" and "dos" 2½mm instead of 1mm, "de Cordoba" in different type.

1914, Feb.

337A A22 2c on 4c brn vio 27.50 4.00
b. "Ccntavos" 12.00
337C A22 2c on 20c red 13.00 1.25
d. "Ccntavos" 4.00
337E A22 2c on 25c bl grn & blk 6.00
f. "Ccntavos" 12.00
337G A23 2c on 35c grn & chnt 8.50
h. "Ccntavos" 15.00
337I A22 2c on 50c lt bl 22.50 4.00
j. "Ccntavos" 10.00

No. 310 with Additional Surcharge

medio
cvo. Córdoba

1913, Dec.

337K A23 ½c on 15c on 35c *300.00*

The word "Medio" is usually in heavy-faced, shaded letters. It is also in thinner, unshaded letters and in letters from both fonts mixed.

No. 310 Surcharged in Black and Violet

338 A23 ½c on 15c on 35c .20 .20
a. Double surcharge 3.50
b. Inverted surcharge 3.50
c. Surcharged on No. 305 12.00
339 A23 1c on 15c on 35c .25 .20
a. Double surcharge 4.00

Official Stamps of 1912 Surcharged

1914, Feb.

340 A22 1c on 25c lt bl .40 .25
a. Double surcharge 9.00
341 A23 1c on 35c lt bl .40 .25
a. "0.10" for "0.01" 10.00 10.00
341B A22 1c on 50c lt bl *200.00*
342 A22 1c on 1p lt bl .25 .20
342A A22 2c on 20c lt bl *200.00 150.00*
b. "0.12" for "0.02"
343 A22 2c on 50c lt bl .40 .20
a. "0.12" for "0.02" 150.00
344 A22 2c on 2p lt bl .40 .20
345 A22 2c on 5p lt bl *250.00*
346 A22 5c on 5p lt bl .25 .20

Red Surcharge

347 A22 5c on 1p lt bl *75.00*
348 A22 5c on 5p lt bl *500.00*

National Palace, Managua — A24

León Cathedral — A25

Various Frames

1914, May 13 Engr. *Perf. 12*

349 A24 ½c lt blue .85 .20
350 A24 1c dk green .85 .20
351 A25 2c red orange .85 .20
352 A24 3c red brown 1.25 .30
353 A25 4c scarlet 1.25 .40
354 A24 5c gray black .45 .20
355 A25 6c black brn 9.00 5.50
356 A25 10c orange yel .85 .20
357 A24 15c dp violet 5.75 2.00
358 A25 20c slate 11.00 5.50
359 A24 25c orange 1.50 .45
360 A25 50c pale blue 1.40 .40
Nos. 349-360 (12) 35.00 15.55

In 1924 the 5c, 10c, 25c, 50c were issued in slightly larger size, 27x22¾mm. The original set was 26x22½mm.

No. 356 with overprint "Union Panamericana 1890-1940" in green is of private origin.

See Nos. 408-415, 483-495, 513-523, 652-664. For overprints and surcharges see Nos. 361-394, 397-400, 416-419, 427-479, 500, 540-548, 580-586, 600-648, 671-673, 684-685, C1-C3, C9-C13, C49-C66, C92-C105, C121-C134, C147-C149, C155-C163, C174-C185, CO1-CO24, O260-O294, O296-O319, O332-O376, RA1-RA5, RA10-RA11, RA26-RA35, RA39-RA40, RA44, RA47, RA52.

No. 355 Surcharged in Black

1915, Sept.

361 A25 5c on 6c blk brn 1.50 .40
a. Double surcharge 7.00 7.00

Stamps of 1914 Surcharged in Black or Red

New Value in Figures

1918-19

362 A24 1c on 3c red brn 6.50 2.25
a. Double surch., one invtd. 12.50
363 A25 2c on 4c scarlet 32.50 22.50
364 A24 5c on 15c dp vio (R) 7.50 1.50
a. Double surcharge 12.00
364C A24 5c on 15c dp vio 350.00

Surcharged in Black

365 A25 2c on 20c slate 110.00 55.00
a. "ppr" for "por" *125.00*
b. Double surcharge 200.00 100.00
c. "Cordobo" 150.00 110.00
365D A25 5c on 20c slate 325.00 125.00
e. Double surcharge (Bk + R) 250.00
f. "Cordobo" 200.00

The surcharge on No. 365 is in blue black, and that on No. 365D usually has an admixture of red.

Used only at Bluefields and Rama.

Surcharged in Black, Red or Violet

New Value in Words

366 A25 ½c on 6c blk brn 4.00 1.50
a. "Meio" 15.00
b. Double surcharge 12.00
367 A25 ½c on 10c yellow 2.50 .30
a. "Val" for "Vale" 3.00
b. "Codoba" 3.00
c. Inverted surcharge 5.00
d. Double surch., one inverted 10.00
368 A24 ½c on 15c dp vio 2.50 .60
a. Double surcharge 7.50
b. "Codoba" 4.00
c. "Meio" 6.00
369 A24 ½c on 25c orange 5.00 2.00
a. Double surcharge 8.00
b. Double surch., one inverted 6.00
370 A25 ½c on 50c pale bl 2.50 .30
a. "Meio" 6.00
b. Double surcharge 5.00
c. Double surch., one inverted 7.00
371 A25 ½c on 50c pale bl (R) 4.50 1.50
a. Double surcharge 10.00
372 A24 1c on 3c red brown 3.00 .30
a. Double surcharge 3.50
373 A25 1c on 6c blk brn 12.50 3.50
a. Double surcharge 9.00
374 A25 1c on 10c yellow 24.00 8.00
a. "nu" for "un" 22.50
375 A24 1c on 15c dp vio 4.50 .75
a. Double surcharge 10.00
b. "Codoba" 6.00
376 A25 1c on 20c slate 110.00 55.00
a. Black surch. normal and red surch. invtd. 80.00
b. Double surch., red & black 90.00
c. Blue surcharge 110.00
377 A25 1c on 20c sl (V) 110.00 70.00
a. Double surcharge (V + Bk) 90.00
378 A25 1c on 20c sl (R) 2.50 .30
a. Double surch., one inverted
b. "Val" for "Vale" 3.50 3.00
379 A24 1c on 25c orange 4.50 1.00
a. Double surcharge 11.00
380 A25 1c on 50c pale bl 14.00 4.50
a. Double surcharge 17.50
381 A25 2c on 4c scarlet 3.50 .30
a. Double surcharge 10.00
b. "centavo" 5.00
c. "Val" for "Vale"
382 A25 2c on 6c blk brn 24.00 8.00
a. "Centavoss"
b. "Cordobas"
383 A25 2c on 10c yellow 24.00 4.50
a. "centavo"
384 A25 2c on 20c sl (R) 13.00 3.25
a. "pe" for "de" 15.00
b. Double surch., red & blk 27.50
c. "centavo" 12.00
d. Double surcharge (R) 17.50
385 A24 2c on 25c orange 5.50 .40
a. "Vle" for "Vale" 7.50
b. "Codoba" 7.50
c. Inverted surcharge 10.00
386 A25 5c on 6c blk brn 10.00 4.25
a. Double surcharge 13.50
387 A24 5c on 15c dp vio 3.50 .60
a. "cincoun" for "cinco" 15.00
b. "Vle" for "Vale" 12.50
c. "Codoba" 12.50
Nos. 366-387 (22) 389.50 170.85

No. 378 is surcharged in light red and brown red: the latter color is frequently offered as the violet surcharge (No. 377).

Official Stamps of 1915 Surcharged in Black or Blue

1919-21

388 A24 1c on 25c lt blue 1.50 .25
a. Double surcharge 10.00
b. Inverted surcharge 12.00

389 A25 2c on 50c lt blue 1.50 .25
a. "centavo" 4.00 4.00
b. Double surcharge 12.00
390 A25 10c on 20c lt blue 1.40 .40
a. "centovos" 5.00 5.00
b. Double surcharge 8.00
390F A25 10c on 20c lt bl (Bl) 65.00
Nos. 388-390 (3) 4.40 .90

There are numerous varieties of omitted, inverted and italic letters in the foregoing surcharges.

No. 358 Surcharged in Black

VALE
5 Centavos

Types of the numerals:

2 2 2
I II III

2 2 2 2 2
IV V VI VII VIII

5 5 5 5
I II III IV

5 5 5 5
V VI VII VIII

1919, May

391 A25 2c on 20c (I) 160.00 110.00
a. Type II
b. Type III
c. Type IV
d. Type VI
e. Type VIII
392 A25 5c on 20c (I) 110.00 40.00
a. Type II 110.00 45.00
b. Type III 125.00 50.00
c. Type IV 125.00 50.00
d. Type V 140.00 60.00
e. Type VI 140.00 60.00
f. Type VII 400.00 250.00
h. Double surch., one inverted

No. 358 Surcharged in Black

VALE
2 Cents

393 A25 2 Cents on 20c (I) 140.00
a. Type II
b. Type III
c. Type IV
d. Type V
e. Type VI
f. Type VII
393G A25 5 Cents on 20c sl, (VIII) 140.00 55.00

Nos. 391-393G used only at Bluefields and Rama.

No. 351 Surcharged in Black

1920, Jan.

394 A25 1c on 2c red org 1.50 .25
a. Inverted surcharge
b. Double surcharge

Official Stamps of 1912 Overprinted in Carmine

1921, Mar.

395 A22 1c lt blue 1.50 .60
a. "Parricular" 5.00 5.00
b. Inverted overprint 10.00
396 A22 5c lt blue 1.50 .40
a. "Parricular" 5.00 5.00

Official Stamps of 1915 Surcharged in Carmine

1921, May

397 A25 ½c on 2c light blue .50 .20
a. "Mddio" 2.50 2.50
398 A25 ½c on 4c light blue 1.25 .20
a. "Mddio" 2.50 2.50
399 A24 1c on 3c light blue 1.25 .30
Nos. 397-399 (3) 3.00 .70

No. 354 Surcharged in Red

1921, Aug.

400 A24 ½c on 5c gray blk .75 .75

Trial printings of this stamp were surcharged in yellow, black and red, and yellow and red. Some of these were used for postage.

Gen. Manuel José Arce — A26

José Cecilio del Valle — A27

Miguel Larreinaga A28

Gen. Fernando Chamorro A29

Gen. Máximo Jérez — A30

Gen. Pedro Joaquín Chamorro — A31

Rubén Darío — A32

1921, Sept. Engr.

401 A26 ½c lt bl & blk 1.00 1.00
402 A27 1c grn & blk 1.00 1.00
403 A28 2c rose red & blk 1.00 1.00
404 A29 5c ultra & blk 1.00 1.00
405 A30 10c org & blk 1.00 1.00
406 A31 25c yel & blk 1.00 1.00
407 A32 50c vio & blk 1.00 1.00
Nos. 401-407 (7) 7.00 7.00

Centenary of independence.

For overprints and surcharges see Nos. 420-421, RA12-RA16, RA19-RA23.

Types of 1914 Issue Various Frames

1922

408 A24 ½c green .20 .20
409 A24 1c violet .20 .20
410 A25 2c car rose .20 .20
411 A24 3c ol gray .30 .20
411A A25 4c vermilion .35 .25
412 A25 6c red brn .20 .20
413 A24 15c brown .35 .20
414 A25 20c bis brn .50 .20
415 A25 1cor blk brn .90 .50
Nos. 408-415 (9) 3.20 2.15

In 1924 Nos. 408-415 were issued in slightly larger size, 27x22¾mm. The original set was 26x22½mm.

Nos. 408, 410 exist with signature controls. See note before No. 600. Same values.

No. 356 Surcharged in Black

1922, Nov.

416 A25 1c on 10c org yel 1.00 .35
417 A25 2c on 10c org yel 1.00 .25

Nos. 354 and 356 Surcharged in Red

1923, Jan.

418 A24 1c on 5c gray blk 1.25 .20
419 A25 2c on 10c org yel 1.25 .20
a. Inverted surcharge

Nos. 401 and 402 Overprinted in Red

1923

420 A26 ½c lt blue & blk 7.50 7.50
421 A27 1c green & blk 2.50 .85
a. Double overprint 7.50

Francisco Hernández de Córdoba — A33

1924 Engr.

422 A33 1c deep green 1.50 .30
423 A33 2c carmine rose 1.50 .30
424 A33 5c deep blue 1.00 .30
425 A33 10c bister brn 1.00 .60
Nos. 422-425 (4) 5.00 1.50

Founding of León & Granada, 400th anniv.

For overprint & surcharges see #499, 536, O295.

Stamps of 1914-22 Overprinted

Black, Red or Blue Overprint

1927, May 3

427 A24 ½c green (Bk) .25 .20
428 A24 1c violet (R) .20 .20
a. Double overprint 3.00
428B A24 1c violet (Bk) 85.00 55.00
429 A25 2c car rose (Bk) .20 .20
a. Inverted overprint 5.00
b. Double overprint 5.00
430 A24 3c ol gray (Bk) 1.25 1.25
a. Inverted overprint 5.00
b. Double overprint 6.00
c. Double ovpt., one inverted 9.00 7.00
430D A24 3c ol gray (Bl) 8.00 3.25
431 A25 4c ver (Bk) 16.00 13.00
a. Inverted overprint 30.00
432 A24 5c gray blk (R) 1.25 .25
a. Inverted overprint 7.50
432B A24 5c gray blk (Bk) .75 .25
c. Double ovpt., one inverted 8.00
d. Double overprint 8.00
433 A25 6c red brn (Bk) 13.00 11.00
a. Inverted overprint 17.50
b. Double overprint
434 A25 10c yellow (Bl) .65 .40
a. Double overprint 12.50
b. Double ovpt., one inverted 10.00
435 A24 15c brown (Bk) 6.00 2.50
436 A25 20c bis brn (Bk) 6.00 2.50
a. Double overprint 17.50
437 A24 25c orange (Bk) 27.50 5.00
438 A25 50c pale bl (Bk) 7.50 3.00
439 A25 1cor blk brn (Bk) 15.00 9.00
Nos. 427-439 (16) 188.55 107.00

Most stamps of this group exist with tall "1" in "1927." Counterfeits exist of normal stamps and errors of Nos. 427-478.

Violet Overprint

1927, May 19

440 A24 ½c green .20 .20
a. Inverted overprint 2.00 2.00
b. Double overprint 2.00 2.00
441 A24 1c violet .20 .20
a. Double overprint 2.00 2.00
442 A25 2c car rose .20 .20
a. Double overprint 2.00 2.00
b. "1927" double 5.00
d. Double ovpt., one inverted 2.00 2.00
443 A24 3c ol gray .25 .20
a. Inverted overprint 6.00
b. Overprinted "1927" only 12.00
c. Double ovpt., one inverted 9.00
444 A25 4c vermilion 37.50 27.50
a. Inverted overprint 75.00
445 A24 5c gray blk 1.00 .25
a. Double overprint, one inverted 6.00
446 A25 6c red brn 37.50 27.50
a. Inverted overprint 75.00
447 A25 10c yellow .35 .20
a. Double overprint 2.00 2.00
448 A24 15c brown .75 .30
a. Double overprint 5.00
b. Double overprint, one inverted 8.00
449 A25 20c bis brn .35 .20
a. Double overprint
450 A24 25c orange .40 .20
451 A25 50c pale bl .40 .20
a. Double ovpt., one inverted 4.00 4.00
452 A25 1cor blk brn .75 .20
a. Double overprint 3.00
b. "1927" double 5.00
c. Double ovpt., one inverted 6.00
Nos. 440-452 (13) 79.85 57.35

Stamps of 1914-22 Overprinted in Violet

1928, Jan. 3

453 A24 ½c green .25 .20
a. Double overprint 3.00
b. Double overprint, one inverted 4.00
454 A24 1c violet .20 .20
a. Inverted overprint 2.00
b. Double overprint 2.00
c. Double overprint, one inverted 2.00
d. "928" for "1928" 2.50
455 A25 2c car rose .20 .20
a. Inverted overprint 2.00
b. Double overprint 2.00
c. "1928" omitted 5.00
d. "928" for "1928" 2.50
e. As "d," inverted
f. "19" for "1928"
456 A24 3c ol gray .40 .20
457 A25 4c vermilion .20 .20
458 A24 5c gray blk .20 .20
a. Double overprint 5.00
b. Double overprint, one inverted 5.00
459 A25 6c red brn .20 .20
460 A25 10c yellow .25 .20
a. Double overprint 2.50
c. Inverted overprint
461 A24 15c brown .35 .25
462 A25 20c bis brn .50 .25
a. Double overprint
463 A24 25c orange .75 .25
a. Double overprint, one inverted 4.00
464 A25 50c pale bl 1.25 .20
465 A25 1cor blk brn 1.25 .35
Nos. 453-465 (13) 6.00 2.90

Stamps of 1914-22 Overprinted in Violet

1928, June 11

466 A24 ½c green .20 .20
467 A24 1c violet .20 .20
a. "928" omitted
469 A24 3c ol gray .75 .25
a. Double overprint 6.00
470 A25 4c vermilion .35 .20
471 A24 5c gray blk .25 .20
a. Double overprint 4.00
472 A25 6c red brn .40 .20
a. Double overprint 5.00
473 A25 10c yellow .50 .20
474 A24 15c brown 1.75 .20
a. Double overprint
475 A25 20c bis brn 2.00 .20
476 A24 25c orange 2.00 .25
a. Double overprint, one inverted 6.00

477 A25 50c pale bl	2.00	.25
478 A25 1cor blk brn	5.00	2.50
a. Double overprint	10.00	
Nos. 466-478 (12)	15.40	4.85

No. 410 with above overprint in black was not regularly issued.

No. 470 with Additional Surcharge in Violet

1928

479 A25 2c on 4c ver	1.25	.35
a. Double surcharge	9.00	

A34

Inscribed: "Timbre Telegrafico"
Red Surcharge

1928

480 A34 1c on 5c bl & blk	.30	.20
a. Double surcharge	5.00	
b. Double surcharge, one inverted		
481 A34 2c on 5c bl & blk	.30	.20
a. Double surcharge	5.00	
482 A34 3c on 5c bl & blk	.30	.20
Nos. 480-482 (3)	.90	.60

Stamps similar to Nos. 481-482, but with surcharge in black and with basic stamp inscribed "Timbre Fiscal," are of private origin.

See designs A36, A37, A44, PT1, PT4, PT6, PT7.

Types of 1914 Issue
Various Frames

1928

483 A24 ½c org red	.40	.20
484 A24 1c orange	.40	.20
485 A25 2c green	.40	.20
486 A24 3c dp vio	.40	.25
487 A25 4c brown	.40	.25
488 A24 5c yellow	.40	.20
489 A25 6c lt bl	.40	.25
490 A25 10c dk bl	.90	.20
491 A24 15c car rose	1.40	.50
492 A25 20c dk grn	1.40	.50
493 A24 25c blk brn	27.50	6.00
494 A25 50c bis brn	3.25	1.00
495 A25 1cor dl vio	6.25	3.00
Nos. 483-495 (13)	43.50	12.75

No. 425 Overprinted in Violet

1929

499 A33 10c bis brn	.75	.60

No. 408 Overprinted in Red

1929

500 A24 ½c green (R)	.25	.20
a. Inverted overprint	2.50	
b. Double overprint	2.50	
c. Double overprint, one inverted	3.50	

A36

A37

Ovptd. Horiz. in Black "R. de T."
Surcharged Vert. in Red

1929

504 A36 1c on 5c bl & blk (R)	.25	.20
a. Inverted surcharge	3.00	
b. Surcharged "0.10" for "0.01"	3.00	
c. "0.0" instead of "0.01"	5.00	
509 A36 2c on 5c bl & blk (R)	.20	.20
a. Double surcharge	2.50	
b. Double surcharge, one inverted	3.50	
c. Inverted surcharge	5.00	

Overprinted Horizontally in Black "R. de C." Surcharged Vertically in Red

510 A36 2c on 5c bl & blk (R)	22.50	1.25
a. Dbl. surcharge, one inverted	25.00	

Surcharged in Red

511 A37 1c on 10c dk grn & blk (R)	.25	.20
a. Double surcharge		
512 A37 2c on 5c bl & blk (R)	.25	.20
Nos. 504-512 (5)	23.45	2.05

The varieties tall "1" in "0.01" and "O$" for "C$" are found in this surcharge.

Nos. 500, 504, 509-512 and RA38 were surcharged in red and sold in large quantities to the public. Surcharges in various other colors were distributed only to a favored few and not regularly sold at the post offices.

Types of 1914 Issue
Various Frames

1929-31

513 A24 1c ol grn	.20	.20
514 A24 3c lt bl	.30	.20
515 A25 4c dk bl ('31)	.30	.20
516 A24 5c ol brn	.40	.20
517 A25 6c bis brn ('31)	.50	.30
518 A25 10c lt brn ('31)	.60	.20
519 A24 15c org red ('31)	.90	.25
520 A25 20c org ('31)	1.25	.35
521 A24 25c dk vio	.25	.20
522 A25 50c grn ('31)	.50	.20
523 A25 1cor yel ('31)	4.50	1.25
Nos. 513-523 (11)	9.70	3.55

Nos. 513-523 exist with signature controls. See note before No. 600. Same values.

New Post Office at Managua — A38

1930, Sept. 15	**Engr.**	
525 A38 ½c olive gray	1.25	1.25
526 A38 1c carmine	1.25	1.25
527 A38 2c red org	.90	.90
528 A38 3c orange	1.75	1.75
529 A38 4c yellow	1.75	1.75
530 A38 5c ol grn	2.25	2.25
531 A38 6c bl grn	2.25	2.25
532 A38 10c black	2.75	2.75
533 A38 25c dp bl	5.50	5.50
534 A38 50c ultra	9.00	9.00
535 A38 1cor dp vio	25.00	25.00
Nos. 525-535 (11)	53.65	53.65

Opening of the new general post office at Managua. The stamps were on sale on day of issuance and for an emergency in April, 1931.

No. 499 Surcharged in Black and Red

1931, May 29

536 A33 2c on 10c bis brn	.50	1.60
a. Red surcharge omitted	2.50	
b. Red surcharge double	5.00	
c. Red surcharge inverted	3.50	
d. Red surcharge double, one invtd.		

Surcharge exists in brown.

Types of 1914-31 Issue Overprinted

1931, June 11

540 A24 ½c green	.35	.20
a. Double overprint	.80	
b. Double ovpt., one inverted	1.40	
c. Inverted overprint	.80	
541 A24 1c ol grn	.35	.20
a. Double overprint	.80	
b. Double ovpt., one inverted	1.40	
c. Inverted overprint		
542 A25 2c car rose	.35	.20
a. Double overprint	.80	
b. Double ovpt., both inverted	2.50	
c. Inverted overprint	1.40	
543 A24 3c lt bl	.35	.20
a. Double overprint	.80	
b. Double ovpt., one inverted	1.40	
c. Inverted overprint	1.40	
544 A24 5c yellow	3.50	2.25
545 A24 5c ol brn	1.00	.20
a. Double overprint	4.50	
b. Inverted overprint	4.50	
546 A24 15c org red	1.25	.40
a. Double overprint	3.50	
547 A24 25c blk brn	10.00	6.50
a. Double overprint	11.00	7.00
b. Inverted overprint	11.00	7.00
548 A24 25c dk vio	4.00	2.50
a. Double overprint	6.50	
Nos. 540-548 (9)	21.15	12.65

Counterfeits exist of the scarcer values. The 4c brown and 6c light blue with this overprint are bogus.

Managua P.O. Before and After Earthquake A40

1932, Jan. 1 Litho. *Perf. 11½*
Soft porous paper, Without gum

556 A40 ½c emerald	1.50
557 A40 1c yel brn	1.90
558 A40 2c dp car	1.50
559 A40 3c ultra	1.50
560 A40 4c dp ultra	1.50
561 A40 5c yel brn	1.60
562 A40 6c gray brn	1.60
563 A40 10c yel brn	2.50
564 A40 15c dl rose	3.75
565 A40 20c orange	3.50
566 A40 25c dk vio	2.50
567 A40 50c emerald	2.50
568 A40 1cor yellow	6.25
Nos. 556-568 (13)	32.10

Issued in commemoration of the earthquake at Managua, Mar. 31, 1931. The stamps were on sale on Jan. 1, 1932, only. The money received from this sale was for the reconstruction of the Post Office building and for the improvement of the postal service. Many shades exist.

Sheets of 10.

Reprints are on thin hard paper and do not have the faint horiz. ribbing that is on the front or back of the originals. Fake cancels abound. Value 75 cents each.

See Nos. C20-C24. For overprints and surcharges see Nos. C32-C43, C47-C48.

Rivas Railroad Issue

"Fill" at El Nacascolo — A41

1c, Wharf at San Jorge. 5c, Rivas Station. 10c, San Juan del Sur. 15c, Train at Rivas Station.

1932, Dec. 17 Litho. *Perf. 12*
Soft porous paper

570 A41 1c yellow	16.00
a. 1c ocher	18.00
571 A41 2c carmine	16.00
572 A41 5c blk brn	16.00
573 A41 10c chocolate	16.00
574 A41 15c yellow	16.00
a. 15c deep orange	18.00
Nos. 570-574 (5)	80.00

Inauguration of the railroad from San Jorge to San Juan del Sur. On sale only on Dec. 17, 1932.

Sheets of 4, without gum. See #C67-C71.

Reprints exist on thin hard paper and do not have the faint horiz. ribbing that is on the front or back of the originals. Value, $5 each.

Leon-Sauce Railroad Issue

Bridge No. 2 at Santa Lucia — A42

Designs: 1c, Environs of El Sauce. 5c, Santa Lucia. 10c, Works at Km. 64. 15c, Rock cut at Santa Lucia.

1932, Dec. 30 *Perf. 12*
Soft porous paper

575 A42 1c orange	16.00
576 A42 2c carmine	16.00
577 A42 5c blk brn	16.00
578 A42 10c brown	16.00
579 A42 15c orange	16.00
Nos. 575-579 (5)	80.00

Inauguration of the railroad from Leon to El Sauce. On sale only on Dec. 30, 1932.

Sheets of 4, without gum. See #C72-C76.

Reprints exist on thin hard paper and do not have the faint horiz. ribbing that is on the front or back of the originals. Value $5 each.

Nos. 514-515, 543 Surcharged in Red

1932, Dec. 10

580 A24 1c on 3c lt bl (514)	.35	.20
a. Double surcharge	3.50	
581 A24 1c on 3c lt bl (543)	4.00	3.50
582 A25 2c on 4c dk bl (515)	.25	.20
a. Double surcharge	2.50	
Nos. 580-582 (3)	4.60	3.90

Nos. 514, 516, 545 and 518 Surcharged in Black or Red

1933

583 A24 1c on 3c lt bl (Bk) (514)	.20	.20
a. "Censavo"	4.00	2.25
b. Double surcharge, one inverted	4.00	
584 A24 1c on 5c ol brn (R) (516)	.20	.20
a. Inverted surcharge		
b. Double surcharge		
585 A24 1c on 5c ol brn (R) (545)	6.50	5.00
a. Red surcharge double	12.00	
586 A25 2c on 10c lt brn (Bk) (518)	.20	.20
a. Double surcharge	4.00	2.50
b. Inverted surcharge	3.50	3.50
c. Double surcharge, one inverted	4.00	2.50
Nos. 583-586 (4)	7.10	5.60

On No. 586 "Vale Dos" measures 13mm and 14mm.

No. 583 with green surcharge and No. 586 with red surcharge are bogus.

Flag of the Race Issue

Flag with Three Crosses for Three Ships of Columbus A43

1933, Aug. 3 Litho. *Rouletted 9*
Without gum

587 A43 ½c emerald 1.75 1.75
588 A43 1c green 1.50 1.50
589 A43 2c red 1.50 1.50
590 A43 3c dp rose 1.50 1.50
591 A43 4c orange 1.50 1.50
592 A43 5c yellow 1.75 1.75
593 A43 10c dp brn 1.75 1.75
594 A43 15c dk brn 1.75 1.75
595 A43 20c vio bl 1.75 1.75
596 A43 25c dl bl 1.75 1.75
597 A43 30c violet 4.50 4.50
598 A43 50c red vio 4.50 4.50
599 A43 1cor ol brn 4.50 4.50
Nos. 587-599 (13) 30.00 30.00

Commemorating the raising of the symbolical "Flag of the Race"; also the 441st anniversary of the sailing of Columbus for the New World, Aug. 3, 1492. Printed in sheets of 10.
See Nos. C77-C87, O320-O331.

In October, 1933, various postage, airmail and official stamps of current issues were overprinted with facsimile signatures of the Minister of Public Works and the Postmaster-General. These overprints are control marks.

Nos. 410 and 513 Overprinted in Black

1935 *Perf. 12*

600 A24 1c ol grn .20 .20
a. Inverted overprint 1.40 1.60
b. Double overprint 1.40 1.60
c. Double overprint, one inverted 1.60 1.60
601 A25 2c car rose .20 .20
a. Inverted overprint 1.60
b. Double overprint 1.60
c. Double overprint, one inverted 1.60
d. Double overprint, both inverted 2.50 2.25

No. 517 Surcharged in Red as in 1932

1936, June

602 A25 ½c on 6c bis brn .35 .20
a. "Ccentavo" .80 .80
b. Double surcharge 3.50 3.50

Regular Issues of 1929-35 Overprinted in Blue

1935, Dec.

603 A25 ½c on 6c bis brn .65 .20
604 A24 1c ol grn (#600) .80 .20
605 A25 2c car rose (#601) .80 .20
a. Black overprint inverted 6.00
606 A24 3c lt bl .80 .25
607 A24 5c ol brn 1.00 .25
608 A25 10c lt brn 1.60 .80
Nos. 603-608 (6) 5.65 1.90

Nos. 606-608 have signature control overprint. See note before No. 600.

Same Overprint in Red

1936, Jan.

609 A24 ½c dk grn .20 .20
610 A25 ½c on 6c bis brn (602) .20 .20
a. Double surch., one inverted 6.00 6.00
611 A24 1c ol grn (513) .25 .20
612 A24 1c ol grn (600) .25 .20
613 A25 2c car rose (410) .50 .20
614 A25 2c car rose (601) .25 .20
a. Black overprint inverted 2.50 2.50
b. Black ovpt. double, one invtd. 3.50 3.50
615 A24 3c lt bl .25 .20
616 A25 4c dk bl .25 .20
617 A24 5c ol brn .25 .20
618 A25 6c bis brn .25 .20
619 A25 10c lt brn .50 .20
620 A24 15c org red .20 .20
621 A25 20c orange .80 .25
622 A24 25c dk vio .25 .20
623 A25 50c green .35 .20
624 A25 1cor yellow .40 .25
Nos. 609-624 (16) 5.15 3.30

Red or blue "Resello 1935" overprint may be found inverted or double. Red and blue overprints on same stamp are bogus.
Nos. 615-624 have signature control overprint. See note before No. 600.

Regular Issues of 1922-29 Overprinted in Carmine

1936, May

625 A24 ½c green .20 .20
626 A24 1c olive green .20 .20
627 A25 2c carmine rose .50 .20
628 A24 3c light blue .20 .20
Nos. 625-628 (4) 1.10 .80

No. 628 has signature control overprint. See note before No. 600.

Nos. 514, 516 Surcharged in Black

1936, June

629 A24 1c on 3c lt bl .20 .20
a. "1396" for "1936" 1.00 1.00
b. "Un" omitted 1.40 1.40
c. Inverted surcharge 1.60 1.60
d. Double surcharge 1.60 1.60
630 A24 2c on 5c ol brn .20 .20
a. "1396" for "1936" 1.40 1.40
b. Double surcharge 3.50 3.50

Regular Issues of 1929-31 Surcharged in Black or Red

1936

631 A24 ½c on 15c org red (R) .20 .20
a. Double surcharge 4.00
632 A25 1c on 4c dk bl (Bk) .25 .20
633 A24 1c on 5c ol brn (Bk) .25 .20
634 A25 1c on 6c bis brn (Bk) .40 .20
a. "1939" instead of "1936" 2.50 1.60
635 A24 1c on 15c org red (Bk) .25 .20
a. "1939" instead of "1936" 2.50 1.60
636 A25 1c on 20c org (Bk) .20 .20
a. "1939" intead of "1936" 2.50 1.60
b. Double surcharge 4.00
637 A25 1c on 20c org (R) .20 .20
638 A25 2c on 10c lt brn (Bk) .25 .20
639 A24 2c on 15c org red (Bk) 1.00 .80
640 A25 2c on 20c org (Bk) .50 .25
641 A24 2c on 25c dk vio (R) .35 .20
642 A24 2c on 25c dk vio (Bk) .35 .20
a. "1939" instead of "1936" 2.50 1.60
643 A25 2c on 50c grn (Bk) .35 .25
a. "1939" instead of "1936" 2.50 1.60
644 A25 2c on 1 cor yel (Bk) .35 .20
a. "1939" instead of "1936" 2.50 1.60
645 A25 3c on 4c dk bl (Bk) .65 .50
a. "1939" instead of "1936" 2.50 1.60
b. "s" of "Centavos" omitted and "r" of "Tres" inverted 2.50
Nos. 631-645 (15) 5.55 4.00

Nos. 634, 639, 643-644 exist with and without signature controls. Same values, except for No. 639, which is rare without the signature control. Nos. 635-636, 642, 645 do not have signature controls. Others have signature controls only. See note before No. 600.

Regular Issues of 1929-31 Overprinted in Black

1936, Aug.

646 A24 3c lt bl .35 .20
647 A24 5c ol brn .25 .20
648 A25 10c lt brn .50 .35
Nos. 646-648 (3) 1.10 .75

No. 648 bears script control mark.

A44

Surcharged in Red

1936, Oct. 19

649 A44 1c on 5c grn & blk .20 .20
650 A44 2c on 5c grn & blk .20 .20

Types of 1914

1937, Jan. 1 Engr.

652 A24 ½c black .20 .20
653 A24 1c car rose .20 .20
654 A25 2c dp bl .20 .20
655 A24 3c chocolate .20 .20
656 A25 4c yellow .20 .20
657 A24 5c org red .20 .20
658 A25 6c dl vio .20 .20
659 A25 10c ol grn .20 .20
660 A24 15c green .20 .20
661 A25 20c red brn .25 .20
663 A25 50c brown .35 .20
664 A25 1cor ultra .60 .25
Nos. 652-664 (12) 3.00 2.45

See note after No. 360.

Mail Carrier — A45

Designs: 1c, Mule carrying mail. 2c, Mail coach. 3c, Sailboat. 5c, Steamship. 7½c, Plane.

1937, Dec. Litho. *Perf. 11*

665 A45 ½c green .20 .20
666 A45 1c magenta .20 .20
667 A45 2c brown .20 .20
668 A45 3c purple .20 .20
669 A45 5c blue .20 .20
670 A45 7½c red org .55 .35
Nos. 665-670 (6) 1.55 1.35

75th anniv. of the postal service in Nicaragua.
Nos. 665-670 were also issued in sheets of 4, value, set of sheets, $7.
The miniature sheets are ungummed, and also exist imperf. and part-perf.

Nos. 662, 663 and 664 Surcharged in Red

1938 *Perf. 12*

671 A24 3c on 25c org .20 .20
672 A25 5c on 50c brn .25 .20
a. "e" of "Vale" omitted 1.60 1.00
673 A25 6c on 1cor ultra .20 .20
Nos. 671-673 (3) .65 .60

No. 672 has a script signature control and the surcharge is in three lines.

Dario Park A46

1939, Jan. Engr. *Perf. 12½*

674 A46 1½c yel grn .20 .20
675 A46 2c dp rose .20 .20
676 A46 3c brt bl .20 .20
677 A46 6c brn org .20 .20
678 A46 7½c dp grn .20 .20
679 A46 10c blk brn .20 .20
680 A46 15c orange .20 .20
681 A46 25c lt vio .20 .20
682 A46 50c brt yel grn .20 .20
683 A46 1cor yellow .65 .40
Nos. 674-683 (10) 2.45 2.20

Nos. 660 and 661 Surcharged in Red

1939 *Perf. 12*

684 A24 1c on 15c grn .20 .20
a. Inverted surcharge 2.00 2.00
685 A25 1c on 20c red brn .20 .20

AIR POST STAMPS

Counterfeits exist of almost all scarce surcharges among Nos. C1-C66.

Regular Issues of 1914-28 Overprinted in Red

1929, May 15 Unwmk. *Perf. 12*

C1 A24 25c orange 1.75 1.75
a. Double overprint, one inverted 50.00
b. Inverted overprint 50.00
c. Double overprint 50.00
C2 A24 25c blk brn 2.25 2.25
a. Double overprint, one inverted 50.00
b. Double overprint 50.00
c. Inverted overprint 30.00

There are numerous varieties in the setting of the overprint. The most important are: Large "1" in "1929" and large "A" in "Aereo" and "P. A. A."

Similar Overprint on Regular Issue of 1929 in Red

1929, June

C3 A24 25c dk vio 1.25 .75
a. Double overprint 50.00
b. Inverted overprint 50.00
c. Double overprint, one inverted 50.00
Nos. C1-C3 (3) 5.25 4.75

The stamps in the bottom row of the sheet have the letters "P. A. A." larger than usual.
Similar overprints, some including an airplane, have been applied to postage issues of 1914-20, officials of 1926 and Nos. 401-407. These are, at best, essays.

Airplanes over Mt. Momotombo — AP1

1929, Dec. 15 Engr.

C4 AP1 25c olive blk .50 .40
C5 AP1 50c blk brn .75 .75
C6 AP1 1cor org red 1.00 1.00
Nos. C4-C6 (3) 2.25 2.15

See Nos. C18-C19, C164-C168. For surcharges and overprints see Nos. C7-C8, C14-C17, C25-C31, C106-C120, C135-C146, C150-C154, C169-C173, CO25-CO29.

No. C4 Surcharged in Red or Black

1930, May 15

C7 AP1 15c on 25c ol blk (R) .50 .40
a. "$" inverted 3.50
b. Double surcharge (R + Bk) 7.00
c. As "b," red normal, blk invtd. 7.00
d. Double red surch., one inverted 7.00
C8 AP1 20c on 25c ol blk (Bk) .75 .60
a. "$" inverted 7.00
b. Inverted surcharge 15.00

Nos. C1, C2 and C3 Surcharged in Green

1931, June 7

C9	A24 15c on 25c org	50.00	50.00
C10	A24 15c on 25c blk brn	100.00	100.00
C11	A24 15c on 25c dk vio	15.00	15.00
c.	Inverted surcharge	30.00	
C12	A24 20c on 25c dk vio	10.00	10.00
c.	Inverted surcharge	50.00	
d.	Double surcharge	50.00	
C13	A24 20c on 25c blk brn	*375.00*	

No. C13 was not regularly issued.

"1391"

C9a	A24 15c on 25c		
C10a	A24 15c on 25c		
C11a	A24 15c on 25c	60.00	
d.	As "a," inverted	400.00	
C12a	A24 20c on 25c	25.00	
e.	As "a," inverted	400.00	
g.	As "a," double	400.00	
C13a	A24 20c on 25c		

"1921"

C9b	A24 15c on 25c		
C10b	A24 15c on 25c	400.00	
C11b	A24 15c on 25c	60.00	
e.	As "b," inverted	400.00	
C12b	A24 20c on 25c	25.00	
f.	As "b," inverted	400.00	
h.	As "b," double	400.00	
C13b	A24 20c on 25c		

Nos. C8, C4-C6 Surcharged in Blue

1931, June

C14	AP1 15c on 20c on 25c	9.00	9.00
b.	Blue surcharge inverted	25.00	
c.	"$" in blk, surch. invtd.	50.00	
d.	Blue surch. dbl., one invtd.	25.00	
C15	AP1 15c on 25c	5.50	5.50
b.	Blue surcharge inverted	25.00	
c.	Double surch., one invtd.	25.00	
C16	AP1 15c on 50c	40.00	40.00
C17	AP1 15c on 1cor	100.00	100.00
	Nos. C14-C17 (4)	154.50	154.50

"1391"

C14a	AP1 15c on 20c on 25c	50.00	
C15a	AP1 15c on 25c	30.00	
C16a	AP1 15c on 50c	80.00	
C17a	AP1 15c on 1cor	225.00	
	Nos. C14a-C17a (4)	385.00	

Momotombo Type of 1929

1931, July 8

C18	AP1 15c deep violet	.20	.20
C19	AP1 20c deep green	.40	.40

Managua Post Office Before and After Earthquake AP2

Without gum, Soft porous paper

1932, Jan. 1 Litho. *Perf. 11*

C20	AP2 15c lilac	1.50	*1.25*
a.	15c violet	22.50	
b.	Vert. pair, imperf. btwn.	22.50	
C21	AP2 20c emerald	2.00	
b.	Horizontal pair, imperf. between	27.50	
C22	AP2 25c yel brn	6.50	
b.	Vertical pair, imperf. between	60.00	
C23	AP2 50c yel brn	8.00	
C24	AP2 1cor dp car	12.00	
a.	Vert. or horiz. pair, imperf. btwn.	80.00	
	Nos. C20-C24 (5)	30.00	

Sheets of 10. See note after No. 568.

For overprint and surcharges see #C44-C46.

Reprints: see note following No. 568. Value $1 each.

Nos. C5 and C6 Surcharged in Red or Black

1932, July 12 *Perf. 12*

C25	AP1 30c on 50c (Bk)	1.50	1.50
a.	"Valc"	25.00	
b.	Double surcharge	15.00	
c.	Double surch., one inverted	15.00	
d.	Period omitted after "O"	25.00	
e.	As "a," double	300.00	
C26	AP1 35c on 50c (R)	1.50	1.50
a.	"Valc"	30.00	
b.	Double surcharge	12.00	
c.	Double surch., one inverted	12.00	
d.	As "a," double	300.00	
C27	AP1 35c on 50c (Bk)	35.00	35.00
a.	"Valc"	250.00	
C28	AP1 40c on 1cor (Bk)	1.75	1.75
a.	"Valc"	25.00	
b.	Double surcharge	15.00	
c.	Double surch., one inverted	15.00	
d.	Inverted surcharge	15.00	
e.	As "a," inverted	300.00	
f.	As "a," double	300.00	
C29	AP1 55c on 1cor (R)	1.75	1.75
a.	"Valc"	25.00	
b.	Double surcharge	12.00	
c.	Double surch., one inverted	12.00	
d.	Inverted surcharge	12.00	
e.	As "a," inverted	300.00	
f.	As "a," double	300.00	
	Nos. C25-C29 (5)	41.50	41.50

No. C18 Overprinted in Red

Semana Correo Aéreo
Internacional
11-17 Septiembre 1932

1932, Sept. 11

C30	AP1 15c dp vio	70.00	70.00
a.	"Aerreo"	150.00	150.00
b.	Invtd. "m" in "Septiembre"	150.00	

International Air Mail Week.

No. C6 Surcharged

1932, Oct. 12

C31	AP1 8c on 1 cor org red	20.00	20.00
a.	"1232"	30.00	30.00
b.	2nd "u" of "Inauguration" invtd.	30.00	30.00

Inauguration of airmail service to the interior.

Regular Issue of 1932 Overprinted in Red

1932, Oct. 24 *Perf. 11½*

Without Gum

C32	A40 1c yel brn	20.00	20.00
a.	Inverted overprint	125.00	125.00
C33	A40 2c carmine	20.00	20.00
a.	Inverted overprint	125.00	125.00
b.	Double overprint	100.00	100.00
C34	A40 3c ultra	9.50	9.50
a.	Inverted overprint	150.00	150.00
b.	As "a," vert. pair, imperf. btwn.	500.00	
C35	A40 4c dp ultra	9.50	9.50
a.	Inverted overprint	125.00	125.00
b.	Double overprint	100.00	100.00
c.	Vert. or horiz. pair, imperf. btwn.	300.00	
C36	A40 5c yel brn	9.50	9.50
a.	Inverted overprint	125.00	125.00
b.	Vert. pair, imperf. btwn.	75.00	
C37	A40 6c gray brn	9.50	9.50
a.	Inverted overprint	100.00	100.00
C38	A40 50c green	9.00	9.00
a.	Inverted overprint	125.00	125.00
C39	A40 1cor yellow	9.50	9.50
a.	Inverted overprint	125.00	125.00
b.	Horiz. pair, imperf. btwn.	200.00	
	Nos. C32-C39 (8)	96.50	96.50

Nos. 564, C20-C21 exist overprinted as C32-C39. The editors believe they were not regularly issued.

Surcharged in Red

1932, Oct. 24

C40	A40 8c on 10c yel brn	9.00	9.00
a.	Inverted surcharge	125.00	125.00
C41	A40 16c on 20c org	9.00	9.00
a.	Inverted surcharge	125.00	125.00
C42	A40 24c on 25c dp vio	9.00	9.00
a.	Inverted surcharge	125.00	125.00
b.	Horiz. pair, imperf. vert.	300.00	

Surcharged in Red as No. C40 but without the word "Vale"

C43	A40 8c on 10c yel brn	45.00	45.00
a.	Inverted surcharge	125.00	125.00
b.	Horiz. pair, imperf. vert.	300.00	

No. C22 Overprinted in Red

1932, Oct. 24

C44	AP2 25c yel brn	8.00	8.00
a.	Inverted overprint	125.00	125.00

Nos. C23 and C24 Surcharged in Red

Interior—1932

Vale ₡ 0.32

1932, Oct. 24

C45	AP2 32c on 50c yel brn	9.50	9.50
a.	Inverted surcharge	125.00	125.00
b.	"Interior-1932" inverted	150.00	150.00
c.	"Vale $0.32" inverted	150.00	150.00
d.	Horiz. pair, imperf. btwn.	200.00	
C46	AP2 40c on 1cor car	7.00	7.00
a.	Inverted surcharge	125.00	125.00
b.	"Vale $0.40" inverted	200.00	200.00

Nos. 557-558 Overprinted in Black like Nos. C32 to C39

1932, Nov. 16

C47	A40 1c yel brn	25.00	22.50
a.	"1232"	45.00	45.00
b.	Inverted overprint	125.00	125.00
c.	Double ovpt., one invtd.	125.00	125.00
d.	As "a," inverted	500.00	
C48	A40 2c dp car	20.00	17.50
a.	"1232"	45.00	45.00
b.	Inverted overprint	125.00	125.00
c.	As "a," inverted	500.00	

Excellent counterfeits exist of Nos. C27, C30-C48. Forged overprints and surcharges as on Nos. C32-C48 exist on reprints of Nos. C20-C24.

Regular Issue of 1914-32 Surcharged in Black

1932 *Perf. 12*

C49	A25 1c on 2c brt rose	.35	.30
C50	A24 2c on 3c lt bl	.35	.30
C51	A25 3c on 4c dk bl	.35	.30
C52	A24 4c on 5c gray brn	.35	.30
C53	A25 5c on 6c ol brn	.35	.30
C54	A25 6c on 10c lt brn	.35	.30
a.	Double surcharge	25.00	
C55	A24 8c on 15c org red	.35	.30
C56	A25 16c on 20c org	.35	.35
C57	A24 24c on 25c dk vio	1.40	1.00
C58	A24 25c on 25c dk vio	1.40	1.00
a.	Double surcharge	25.00	
C59	A25 32c on 50c grn	1.40	1.25
C60	A25 40vc on 50c grn	1.60	1.40
C61	A25 50c on 1cor yel	2.25	2.25
C62	A25 1cor on 1cor yel	3.00	3.00
	Nos. C49-C62 (14)	13.85	12.35

Nos. C49-C62 exist with inverted surcharge.

In addition to C49 to C62, four other stamps, Type A25, exist with this surcharge:
40c on 50c bister brown, black surcharge.
1cor on 2c bright rose, black surcharge.
1cor on 1cor yellow, red surcharge.
1cor on 1cor dull violet, black surcharge.
The editors believe they were not regularly issued.

Surcharged on Nos. 548, 547

1932

C65	A24 24c on 25c dk vio	45.00	45.00
C66	A24 25c on 25c blk brn	50.00	50.00

Counterfeits of Nos. C65 and C66 are plentiful.

Rivas Railroad Issue

La Chocolata Cut — AP3

El Nacascola — AP4

Designs: 25c, Cuesta cut. 50c, Mole of San Juan del Sur. 1cor, View of El Estero.

1932, Dec. Litho.

Soft porous paper

C67	AP3 15c dk vio	20.00
C68	AP4 20c bl grn	20.00
C69	AP4 25c dk brn	20.00
C70	AP4 50c blk brn	20.00
C71	AP4 1cor rose red	20.00
	Nos. C67-C71 (5)	100.00

Inauguration of the railroad from San Jorge to San Juan del Sur, Dec. 18, 1932. Printed in sheets of 4, without gum.

Reprints: see note following No. 574. Value, $6 each.

Leon-Sauce Railroad Issue

"Fill" at Santa Lucia River AP5

Designs: 15c, Bridge at Santa Lucia. 25c, Malpaicillo Station. 50c, Panoramic view. 1cor, San Andres.

1932, Dec. 30

Soft porous paper

C72	AP5 15c purple	20.00
C73	AP5 20c bl grn	20.00
C74	AP5 25c dk brn	20.00
C75	AP5 50c blk brn	20.00
C76	AP5 1cor rose red	20.00
	Nos. C72-C76 (5)	100.00

Inauguration of the railroad from Leon to El Sauce, 12/30/32. Sheets of 4, without gum.

Reprints: see note following No. 579. Value, $6 each.

Flag of the Race Issue

1933, Aug. 3 Litho. *Rouletted 9*

Without gum

C77 A43 1c dk brn 1.50 1.50
C78 A43 2c red vio 1.50 1.50
C79 A43 4c violet 2.50 2.25
C80 A43 5c dl bl 2.25 2.25
C81 A43 6c vio bl 2.25 2.25
C82 A43 8c dp brn .70 .70
C83 A43 15c ol brn .70 .70
C84 A43 20c yellow 2.25 2.25
a. Horiz. pair, imperf. btwn. 15.00
b. Horiz. pair, imperf. vert. 15.00
C85 A43 25c orange 2.25 2.25
C86 A43 50c rose 2.25 2.25
C87 A43 1cor green 11.00 11.00
Nos. C77-C87 (11) 29.15 28.90

See note after No. 599. Printed in sheets of 10.

Reprints exist, shades differ from postage and official stamps.

Imperf., Pairs

C78a A43 2c 14.00
C79a A43 4c 10.00
C81a A43 6c 10.00
C82a A43 8c 10.00
C83a A43 15c 10.00
C87a A43 1cor 30.00

AP7

1933, Nov. *Perf. 12*

C88 AP7 10c bis brn 1.50 1.50
a. Vert. pair, imperf. between 35.00
C89 AP7 15c violet 1.25 1.25
a. Vert. pair, imperf. between 37.50
C90 AP7 25c red 1.40 1.40
a. Horiz. pair, imperf. between 22.50
C91 AP7 50c dp bl 1.50 1.50
Nos. C88-C91 (4) 5.65 5.65

Intl. Air Post Week, Nov. 6-11, 1933. Printed in sheets of 4. Counterfeits exist.

Stamps and Types of 1928-31 Surcharged in Black

1933, Nov. 3

C92 A25 1c on 2c grn .20 .20
C93 A24 2c on 3c ol gray .20 .20
C94 A25 3c on 4c car rose .20 .20
C95 A24 4c on 5c lt bl .20 .20
C96 A25 5c on 6c dk bl .20 .20
C97 A25 6c on 10c ol brn .20 .20
C98 A24 8c on 15c bis brn .20 .20
C99 A25 16c on 20c brn .20 .20
C100 A24 24c on 25c ver .20 .20
C101 A24 25c on 25c org .25 .20
C102 A25 32c on 50c vio .20 .20
C103 A25 40c on 50c grn .20 .20
C104 A25 50c on 1cor yel .20 .20
C105 A25 1cor on 1cor org red .35 .25
Nos. C92-C105 (14) 3.00 2.85

Nos. C100, C102-C105 exist without script control overprint. Value, each $1.50.

Type of Air Post Stamps of 1929 Surcharged in Black

1933, Oct. 28

C106 AP1 30c on 50c org red .25 .20
C107 AP1 35c on 50c lt bl .25 .20
C108 AP1 40c on 1cor yel .40 .20
C109 AP1 55c on 1cor grn .30 .25
Nos. C106-C109 (4) 1.20 .85

No. C19 Surcharged in Red

1934, Mar. 31

C110 AP1 10c on 20c grn .30 .25
a. Inverted surcharge 15.00
b. Double surcharge, one inverted 15.00
c. "Ceutroamericano" 10.00

No. C110 with black surcharge is believed to be of private origin.

No. C4 Surcharged in Red

1935, Aug.

C111 AP1 10c on 25c ol blk .25 .25
a. Small "v" in "vale" (R) 5.00
b. "centrvos" (R) 5.00
c. Double surcharge (R) 25.00
d. Inverted surcharge (R) 25.00
g. As "a," inverted 400.00
h. As "a," double 400.00

No. C111 with blue surcharge is believed to be private origin.

The editors do not recognize the Nicaraguan air post stamps overprinted in red "VALIDO 1935" in two lines and with or without script control marks as having been issued primarily for postal purposes.

Nos C4-C6, C18-C19 Overprinted Vertically in Blue, Reading Up:

1935-36

C112 AP1 15c dp vio 1.00 1.00
C113 AP1 20c dp grn 1.75 1.75
C114 AP1 25c ol blk 2.25 2.25
C115 AP1 50c blk brn 5.00 5.00
C116 AP1 1cor org red 40.00 40.00
Nos. C112-C116 (5) 50.00 50.00

Same Overprint on Nos. C106-C109 Reading Up or Down

C117 AP1 30c on 50c org red 1.50 1.40
C118 AP1 35c on 50c lt bl 6.50 6.50
C119 AP1 40c on 1cor yel 6.50 6.50
C120 AP1 55c on 1cor grn 6.50 6.50
Nos. C117-C120 (4) 21.00 20.90
Nos. C112-C120 (9) 71.00 70.90

Same Overprint in Red on Nos. C92-C105

1936

C121 A25 1c on 2c grn .20 .20
C122 A24 2c on 3c ol gray .20 .20
C123 A25 3c on 4c car rose .20 .20
C124 A24 4c on 5c lt bl .20 .20
C125 A25 5c on 6c dk bl .20 .20
C126 A25 6c on 10c ol brn .20 .20
C127 A24 8c on 15c bis brn .20 .20
C128 A25 16c on 20c brn .25 .25
C129 A24 24c on 25c ver .35 .30
C130 A24 25c on 25c org .25 .25
C131 A25 32c on 50c vio .20 .20
C132 A25 40c on 50c grn .55 .50
C133 A25 50c on 1cor yel .40 .25
C134 A25 1cor on 1cor org red 1.40 .65
Nos. C121-C134 (14) 4.80 3.80

Nos. C121 to C134 are handstamped with script control mark.

Overprint Reading Down on No. C110

C135 AP1 10c on 20c grn *350.00*

This stamp has been extensively counterfeited.

Overprinted in Red on Nos. C4 to C6, C18 and C19

C136 AP1 15c dp vio .55 .20
C137 AP1 20c dp grn .65 .60
C138 AP1 25c ol blk .65 .55
C139 AP1 50c blk brn .55 .55
C140 AP1 1cor org red 1.10 .55

On Nos. C106 to C109

C141 AP1 30c on 50c org red .65 .60
C142 AP1 35c on 50c lt bl .65 .40
C143 AP1 40c on 1cor yel .65 .55
C144 AP1 55c on 1cor grn .65 .50

Same Overprint in Red or Blue on No. C111 Reading Up or Down

C145 AP1 10c on 25c, down .55 .45
a. "Centrvos" 25.00
C146 AP1 10c on 25c (Bl), up 1.25 1.00
a. "Centrvos" 25.00
Nos. C136-C146 (11) 7.90 5.95

Overprint on No. C145 is at right, on No. C146 in center.

Nos. C92, C93 and C98 Overprinted in Black

Resello
1936

1936

C147 A25 1c on 2c grn .20 .20
C148 A24 2c on 3c ol gray .20 .20
a. "Resello 1936" dbl., one invtd. 2.50
C149 A24 8c on 15c bis brn .25 .25
Nos. C147-C149 (3) .65 .65

With script control handstamp.

Nos. C5 and C6 Surcharged in Red

1936, Nov. 26

C150 AP1 15c on 50c blk brn .20 .20
C151 AP1 15c on 1cor org red .20 .20

Nos. C18 and C19 Overprinted in Carmine

1936, July 2

C152 AP1 15c dp vio .35 .20
C153 AP1 20c dp grn .35 .25

Overprint reading up or down.

No. C4 Surcharged and Overprinted in Red

C154 AP1 10c on 25c olive blk .30 .30
a. Surch. and ovpt. inverted 3.50

Same Overprint in Carmine on Nos. C92 to C99

C155 A25 1c on 2c green .20 .20
C156 A24 2c on 3c olive gray .65 .65
C157 A25 3c on 4c car rose .20 .20
C158 A24 4c on 5c light blue .20 .20
C159 A25 5c on 6c dark blue .20 .20
C160 A25 6c on 10c olive brn .20 .20
C161 A24 8c on 15c bister brn .20 .20
C162 A25 16c on 20c brown .20 .20
Nos. C154-C162 (9) 2.35 2.35

No. 518 Overprinted in Black

C163 A25 10c lt brn .20 .20
a. Overprint inverted 2.25
b. Double overprint 2.25

Two fonts are found in the sheet of #C163.

Momotombo Type of 1929

1937

C164 AP1 15c yel org .20 .20
C165 AP1 20c org red .20 .20
C166 AP1 25c black .20 .20
C167 AP1 50c violet .25 .20
C168 AP1 1cor orange .55 .20
Nos. C164-C168 (5) 1.40 1.00

Surcharged in Black

1937

C169 AP1 30c on 50c car rose .20 .20
C170 AP1 35c on 50c olive grn .20 .20
C171 AP1 40c on 1cor green .25 .20
C172 AP1 55c on 1cor blue .20 .20
Nos. C169-C172 (4) .85 .80

No. C168 Surcharged in Violet

1937 Unwmk. *Perf. 12*

C173 AP1 10c on 1cor org .20 .20
a. "Centauos" 10.00

No. C98 with Additional Overprint "1937"

C174 A24 8c on 15c bis brn .45 .20
a. "1937" double 6.50

Nos. C92-C102 with Additional Overprint in Blue reading "HABILITADO 1937"

C175 A25 1c on 2c grn .20 .20
a. Blue overprint double *2.50*
C176 A24 2c on 3c ol gray .20 .20
a. Double surch., one inverted *2.50*
C177 A25 3c on 4c car rose .20 .20
C178 A24 4c on 5c lt bl .20 .20
C179 A25 5c on 6c dk bl .20 .20
C180 A25 6c on 10c ol brn .20 .20
C181 A24 8c on 15c bis brn .20 .20
a. "Habilitado 1937" double 3.50
C182 A25 16c on 20c brn .20 .20
a. Double surcharge 2.50
C183 A24 24c on 25c ver .20 .20
C184 A24 25c on 25c org .25 .20
C185 A25 32c on 50c vio .25 .25
Nos. C175-C185 (11) 2.30 2.25

Map of Nicaragua AP8

For Foreign Postage

1937, July 30 Engr.

C186 AP8 10c green .20 .20
C187 AP8 15c dp bl .20 .20
C188 AP8 20c yellow .20 .20
C189 AP8 25c bl vio .20 .20
C190 AP8 30c rose car .25 .20
C191 AP8 50c org yel .35 .20
C192 AP8 1cor ol grn .70 .55
Nos. C186-C192 (7) 2.10 1.75

Presidential Palace AP9

For Domestic Postage

C193 AP9 1c rose car .20 .20
C194 AP9 2c dp bl .20 .20
C195 AP9 3c ol grn .20 .20
C196 AP9 4c black .20 .20
C197 AP9 5c dk vio .20 .20
C198 AP9 6c chocolate .20 .20
C199 AP9 8c bl vio .20 .20
C200 AP9 16c org yel .25 .20
C201 AP9 24c yellow .20 .20
C202 AP9 25c yel grn .25 .20
Nos. C193-C202 (10) 2.10 2.00

No. C201 with green overprint "Union Panamericana 1890-1940" is of private origin.

Managua AP10

Designs: 15c, Presidential Palace. 20c, Map of South America. 25c, Map of Central America. 30c, Map of North America. 35c, Lagoon of Tiscapa, Managua. 40c, Road Scene. 45c, Park. 50c, Another park. 55c, Scene in San Juan del Sur. 75c, Tipitapa River. 1cor, Landscape.

Wmk. 209

1937, Sept. 17 Typo. *Perf. 11*

Center in Dark Blue

C203 AP10 10c yel grn 1.60 1.20
C204 AP10 15c orange 1.60 1.40
C205 AP10 20c red 1.00 1.00
C206 AP10 25c vio brn 1.00 1.00
C207 AP10 30c bl grn 1.00 1.00
a. Great Lakes omitted 40.00 40.00
C208 AP10 35c lemon .50 .45
C209 AP10 40c green .40 .40
C210 AP10 45c brt vio .40 .35
C211 AP10 50c rose lil .40 .35
a. Vert. pair, imperf. btwn. 140.00
C212 AP10 55c lt bl .40 .35
C213 AP10 75c gray grn .40 .35

Center in Brown Red

C214 AP10 1cor dk bl 1.00 .50
Nos. C203-C214 (12) 9.70 8.35

150th anniv. of the Constitution of the US.

Diriangen — AP11

Designs: 4c, 10c, Nicarao. 5c, 15c, Bartolomé de Las Casas. 8c, 20c, Columbus.

For Domestic Postage

Without gum

1937, Oct. 12 Unwmk. *Perf. 11*

C215 AP11 1c green .20 .20
C216 AP11 4c brn car .20 .20
C217 AP11 5c dk vio .20 .20
a. Without imprint .40
C218 AP11 8c dp bl .20 .20
a. Without imprint .50

For Foreign Postage

Wmk. 209

With Gum

C219 AP11 10c lt brn .20 .20
C220 AP11 15c pale bl .20 .20
a. Without imprint 1.00
C221 AP11 20c pale rose .20 .20
Nos. C215-C221 (7) 1.40 1.40

Nos. C215-C221 printed in sheets of 4.

Imperf., Pairs

C215a AP11 1c .20 .20
C216a AP11 4c .20 .20
C217b AP11 5c .20 .20
C217c AP11 5c Without imprint
C218b AP11 8c .20
C218c AP11 8c Without imprint
C219a AP11 10c .20 .20
C220b AP11 15c .25 .25
C220c AP11 15c Without imprint
C221a AP11 20c .35 .35

Gen. Tomas Martinez — AP11a

Design: 10c-50c, Gen. Anastasio Somoza.

For Domestic Postage

Without Gum

Perf. 11½, Imperf.

1938, Jan. 18 Typo. Unwmk.

Center in Black

C221B AP11a 1c orange .20 .20
C221C AP11a 5c red vio .20 .20
C221D AP11a 8c dk bl .25 .25
C221E AP11a 16c brown .25 .25
f. Sheet of 4, 1c, 5c, 8c, 16c 1.25 1.25

For Foreign Postage

C221G AP11a 10c green .25 .20
C221H AP11a 15c dk bl .25 .25
C221J AP11a 25c violet .40 .40
C221K AP11a 50c carmine .50 .45
m. Sheet of 4, 10c, 15c, 25c, 50c 2.00 2.00
Nos. C221B-C221K (8) 2.30 2.20

75th anniv. of postal service in Nicaragua. Printed in sheets of four.

Stamps of type AP11a exist in changed colors and with inverted centers, double centers and frames printed on the back. These varieties were private fabrications.

Lake Managua AP12

President Anastasio Somoza — AP13

For Domestic Postage

1939 Unwmk. Engr. *Perf. 12½*

C222 AP12 2c dp bl .20 .20
C223 AP12 3c green .20 .20
C224 AP12 8c pale lil .20 .20
C225 AP12 16c orange .20 .20
C226 AP12 24c yellow .20 .20
C227 AP12 32c dk grn .20 .20
C228 AP12 50c dp rose .20 .20

For Foreign Postage

C229 AP13 10c dk brn .20 .20
C230 AP13 15c dk bl .20 .20
C231 AP13 20c org yel .20 .20
C232 AP13 25c dk pur .20 .20
C233 AP13 30c lake .20 .20
C234 AP13 50c dp org .25 .20
C235 AP13 1cor dk ol grn .35 .40
Nos. C222-C235 (14) 3.00 3.00

For Domestic Postage

Will Rogers and View of Managua AP14

Designs: 2c, Rogers standing beside plane. 3c, Leaving airport office. 4c, Rogers and US Marines. 5c, Managua after earthquake.

1939, Mar. 31 Engr. *Perf. 12*

C236 AP14 1c brt grn .20 .20
C237 AP14 2c org red .20 .20
C238 AP14 3c lt ultra .20 .20
C239 AP14 4c dk bl .20 .20
C240 AP14 5c rose car .20 .20
Nos. C236-C240 (5) 1.00 1.00

Will Rogers' flight to Managua after the earthquake, Mar. 31, 1931.

For surcharges see Nos. 686, 688.

Pres. Anastasio Somoza in US House of Representatives — AP19

President Somoza and US Capitol AP20

President Somoza, Tower of the Sun and Trylon and Perisphere AP21

For Domestic Postage

1940, Feb. 1

C241 AP19 4c red brn .20 .20
C242 AP20 8c blk brn .20 .20
C243 AP19 16c grnsh bl .20 .20
C244 AP20 20c brt plum .50 .30
C245 AP21 32c scarlet .20 .20

For Foreign Postage

C246 AP19 25c dp bl .20 .20
C247 AP19 30c black .20 .20
C248 AP20 50c rose pink .45 .40
C249 AP21 60c green .50 .30
C250 AP19 65c dk vio brn .50 .20
C251 AP19 90c ol grn .65 .30
C252 AP21 1cor violet 1.00 .55
Nos. C241-C252 (12) 4.80 3.25

Visit of Pres. Somoza to US in 1939.

For surcharge see No. C636.

L. S. Rowe, Statue of Liberty, Nicaraguan Coastline, Flags of 21 American Republics, US Shield and Arms of Nicaragua — AP22

1940, Aug. 2 Engr. *Perf. 12½*

C253 AP22 1.25cor multi .65 .60

50th anniversary of Pan American Union.

For overprint see No. C493.

AIR POST OFFICIAL STAMPS

OA1

"Typewritten" Overprint on #O293

1929, Aug. Unwmk. *Perf. 12*

CO1 OA1 25c orange 50.00 45.00

Excellent counterfeits of No. CO1 are plentiful.

Official Stamps of 1926 Overprinted in Dark Blue

1929, Sept. 15

CO2 A24 25c orange .50 .50
a. Inverted overprint 25.00
b. Double overprint 25.00
CO3 A25 50c pale bl .75 .75
a. Inverted overprint 25.00
b. Double overprint 25.00
c. Double overprint, one inverted 25.00

Nos. 519-523 Overprinted in Black

1932, Feb.

CO4 A24 15c org red .40 .40
a. Inverted overprint 25.00
b. Double overprint 25.00
c. Double overprint, one invtd. 25.00
CO5 A25 20c orange .45 .45
a. Double overprint 25.00
CO6 A24 25c dk vio .45 .45
CO7 A25 50c green .55 .55
CO8 A25 1cor yellow 1.00 1.00
Nos. CO4-CO8 (5) 2.85 2.85

Nos. CO4-CO5, CO7-CO8 exist with signature control overprint. Value, each, $2.50.

Overprinted on Stamp No. 547

CO9 A24 25c blk brn 42.50 42.50

The varieties "OFICAL", "OFIAIAL" and "CORROE" occur in the setting and are found on each stamp of the series.

Counterfeits of No. CO9 are plentiful.

Stamp No. CO4 with overprint "1931" in addition is believed to be of private origin.

Type of Regular Issue of 1914 Overprinted Like Nos. CO4-CO8

1933

CO10 A24 25c olive .20 .20
CO11 A25 50c ol grn .25 .25
CO12 A25 1cor org red .40 .40

On Stamps of 1914-28

CO13 A24 15c dp vio .20 .20
CO14 A25 20c dp grn .20 .20
Nos. CO10-CO14 (5) 1.25 1.25

Nos. CO10-CO14 exist without signature control mark. Value, each $2.50.

Air Post Official Stamps of 1932-33 Overprinted in Blue

1935

CO15 A24 15c dp vio 1.00 .80
CO16 A25 20c dp grn 2.00 1.60
CO17 A24 25c olive 3.00 2.50
CO18 A25 50c ol grn 35.00 30.00
CO19 A25 1cor org red 40.00 37.50
Nos. CO15-CO19 (5) 81.00 72.40

Overprinted in Red

CO20 A24 15c dp vio .25 .25
CO21 A25 20c dp grn .25 .25
CO22 A24 25c olive .25 .25
CO23 A25 50c ol grn .80 .80
CO24 A25 1cor org red .80 .80
Nos. CO20-CO24 (5) 2.35 2.35

Nos. CO15 to CO24 are handstamped with script control mark. Counterfeits of blue overprint are plentiful.

The editors do not recognize the Nicaraguan air post Official stamps overprinted in red "VALIDO 1935" in two lines and with or without script control marks as having been issued primarily for postal purposes.

Nos. C164-C168 Overprinted in Black

1937

CO25 AP1 15c yel org .80 .55
CO26 AP1 20c org red .80 .60
CO27 AP1 25c black .80 .70
CO28 AP1 50c violet .80 .70
CO29 AP1 1cor orange .80 .70
Nos. CO25-CO29 (5) 4.00 3.25

Pres. Anastasio Somoza — OA2

1939, Feb. 7 Engr. *Perf. 12½*

CO30	OA2	10c brown	.25	.25
CO31	OA2	15c dk bl	.25	.25
CO32	OA2	20c yellow	.25	.25
CO33	OA2	25c dk pur	.25	.25
CO34	OA2	30c lake	.25	.25
CO35	OA2	50c dp org	.65	.65
CO36	OA2	1cor dk ol grn	1.25	1.25
		Nos. CO30-CO36 (7)	3.15	3.15

POSTAGE DUE STAMPS

D1

D2

1896 Unwmk. Engr. *Perf. 12*

J1	D1	1c orange	.50	*1.25*
J2	D1	2c orange	.50	*1.25*
J3	D1	5c orange	.50	*1.25*
J4	D1	10c orange	.50	*1.25*
J5	D1	20c orange	.50	*1.25*
J6	D1	30c orange	.50	*1.25*
J7	D1	50c orange	.50	*1.50*
		Nos. J1-J7 (7)	3.50	*9.00*

Wmk. 117

J8	D1	1c orange	1.00	*1.50*
J9	D1	2c orange	1.00	*1.50*
J10	D1	5c orange	1.00	*1.50*
J11	D1	10c orange	1.00	*1.50*
J12	D1	20c orange	1.25	*1.50*
J13	D1	30c orange	1.00	*1.50*
J14	D1	50c orange	1.00	*1.50*
		Nos. J8-J14 (7)	7.25	*10.50*

1897 Unwmk.

J15	D1	1c violet	.50	*1.50*
J16	D1	2c violet	.50	*1.50*
J17	D1	5c violet	.50	*1.50*
J18	D1	10c violet	.50	*1.50*
J19	D1	20c violet	1.25	*2.00*
J20	D1	30c violet	.50	*1.50*
J21	D1	50c violet	.50	*1.50*
		Nos. J15-J21 (7)	4.25	*11.00*

Wmk. 117

J22	D1	1c violet	.50	*1.50*
J23	D1	2c violet	.50	*1.50*
J24	D1	5c violet	.50	*1.50*
J25	D1	10c violet	.50	*1.50*
J26	D1	20c violet	1.00	*2.00*
J27	D1	30c violet	.50	*1.50*
J28	D1	50c violet	.50	*1.50*
		Nos. J22-J28 (7)	4.00	*11.00*

Reprints of Nos. J8-J28 are on thick, porous paper. Color of 1896 reprints, reddish orange; or 1897 reprints, reddish violet. On watermarked reprints, liberty cap is sideways. Value 25c each.

1898 Litho. Unwmk.

J29	D2	1c blue green	.20	*2.00*
J30	D2	2c blue green	.20	*2.00*
J31	D2	5c blue green	.20	*2.00*
J32	D2	10c blue green	.20	*2.00*
J33	D2	20c blue green	.20	*2.00*
J34	D2	30c blue green	.20	*2.00*
J35	D2	50c blue green	.20	*2.00*
		Nos. J29-J35 (7)	1.40	*14.00*

1899

J36	D2	1c carmine	.20	*2.00*
J37	D2	2c carmine	.20	*2.00*
J38	D2	5c carmine	.20	*2.00*
J39	D2	10c carmine	.20	*2.00*
J40	D2	20c carmine	.20	*2.00*
J41	D2	50c carmine	.20	*2.00*
		Nos. J36-J41 (6)	1.20	*12.00*

Some denominations are found in se-tenant pairs.

Various counterfeit cancellations exist on #J1-J41.

D3

1900 Engr.

J42	D3	1c plum	.75
J43	D3	2c vermilion	.75
J44	D3	5c dk bl	.75
J45	D3	10c purple	.75
J46	D3	20c org brn	.75
J47	D3	30c dk grn	1.50
J48	D3	50c lake	1.50
		Nos. J42-J48 (7)	6.75

Nos. J42-J48 were not placed in use as postage due stamps. They were only issued with "Postage" overprints. See Nos. 137-143, 152-158, O72-O81, 2L11-2L15, 2L25, 2L40-2L41.

OFFICIAL STAMPS

Types of Postage Stamps Overprinted in Red Diagonally Reading up

1890 Unwmk. Engr. *Perf. 12*

O1	A5	1c ultra	.20	*.30*
O2	A5	2c ultra	.20	*.30*
O3	A5	5c ultra	.20	*.30*
O4	A5	10c ultra	.20	*.40*
O5	A5	20c ultra	.20	*.45*
O6	A5	50c ultra	.20	*.75*
O7	A5	1p ultra	.20	*1.25*
O8	A5	2p ultra	.20	*1.50*
O9	A5	5p ultra	.20	*2.00*
O10	A5	10p ultra	.20	*3.25*
		Nos. O1-O10 (10)	2.00	*10.50*

All values of the 1890 issue are known without overprint and most of them with inverted or double overprint, or without overprint and imperforate. There is no evidence that they were issued in these forms.

Official stamps of 1890-1899 are scarce with genuine cancellations. Forged cancellations are plentiful.

Overprinted Vertically Reading Up

1891 Litho.

O11	A6	1c green	.20	*.30*
O12	A6	2c green	.20	*.30*
O13	A6	5c green	.20	*.30*
O14	A6	10c green	.20	*.30*
O15	A6	20c green	.20	*.50*
O16	A6	50c green	.20	*1.10*
O17	A6	1p green	.20	*1.25*
O18	A6	2p green	.20	*1.25*
O19	A6	5p green	.20	*2.00*
O20	A6	10p green	.20	*3.50*
		Nos. O11-O20 (10)	2.00	*10.80*

All values of this issue except the 2c and 5p exist without overprint and several with double overprint. They are not known to have been issued in this form.

Many of the denominations may be found in se-tenant pairs.

Overprinted in Dark Blue

1892 Engr.

O21	A7	1c yellow brown	.20	*.30*
O22	A7	2c yellow brown	.20	*.30*
O23	A7	5c yellow brown	.20	*.30*
O24	A7	10c yellow brown	.20	*.30*
O25	A7	20c yellow brown	.20	*.50*
O26	A7	50c yellow brown	.20	*1.00*
O27	A7	1p yellow brown	.20	*1.25*
O28	A7	2p yellow brown	.20	*1.50*
O29	A7	5p yellow brown	.20	*2.25*
O30	A7	10p yellow brown	.20	*3.50*
		Nos. O21-O30 (10)	2.00	*11.20*

The 2c and 1p are known without overprint and several values exist with double or inverted overprint. These probably were not regularly issued.

Commemorative of the 400th anniversary of the discovery of America by Christopher Columbus.

Overprinted in Red

1893 Engr.

O31	A8	1c slate	.20	*.30*
O32	A8	2c slate	.20	*.30*
O33	A8	5c slate	.20	*.30*
O34	A8	10c slate	.20	*.30*
O35	A8	20c slate	.20	*.50*
O36	A8	25c slate	.20	*.75*
O37	A8	50c slate	.20	*.85*
O38	A8	1p slate	.20	*1.00*
O39	A8	2p slate	.20	*2.00*
O40	A8	5p slate	.20	*2.50*
O41	A8	10p slate	.20	*5.50*
		Nos. O31-O41 (11)	2.20	*14.30*

The 2, 5, 10, 20, 25, 50c and 5p are known without overprint but probably were not regularly issued. Some values exist with double or inverted overprints.

Overprinted in Black

1894

O42	A9	1c orange	.30	.35
O43	A9	2c orange	.30	.35
O44	A9	5c orange	.30	.35
O45	A9	10c orange	.30	.35
O46	A9	20c orange	.30	*.50*
O47	A9	50c orange	.30	*.75*
O48	A9	1p orange	.30	*1.50*
O49	A9	2p orange	.30	*2.00*
O50	A9	5p orange	2.00	*3.00*
O51	A9	10p orange	2.00	*4.00*
		Nos. O42-O51 (10)	6.40	*13.15*

Reprints are yellow.

1895

Overprinted in Blue

O52	A10	1c green	.20	*.35*
O53	A10	2c green	.20	*.35*
O54	A10	5c green	.20	*.35*
O55	A10	10c green	.20	*.35*
O56	A10	20c green	.20	*.50*
O57	A10	50c green	.20	*1.00*
O58	A10	1p green	.20	*1.50*
O59	A10	2p green	.20	*2.00*
O60	A10	5p green	.20	*3.00*
O61	A10	10p green	.20	*4.00*
		Nos. O52-O61 (10)	2.00	*13.40*

Wmk. 117

O62	A10	1c green
O63	A10	2c green
O64	A10	5c green
O65	A10	10c green
O66	A10	20c green
O67	A10	50c green
O68	A10	1p green
O69	A10	2p green
O70	A10	5p green
O71	A10	10p green

Nos. O62-O71 probably exist only as reprints. Value, each 15 cents.

Postage Due Stamps of Same Date Handstamped in Violet

1896 Unwmk.

O72	D1	1c orange	7.00
O73	D1	2c orange	7.00
O74	D1	5c orange	5.00
O75	D1	10c orange	5.00
O76	D1	20c orange	5.00
		Nos. O72-O76 (5)	29.00

Wmk. 117

O77	D1	1c orange	7.00
O78	D1	2c orange	7.00
O79	D1	5c orange	4.00
O80	D1	10c orange	4.00
O81	D1	20c orange	4.00
		Nos. O77-O81 (5)	26.00

Nos. O72-O81 were handstamped in rows of five. Several handstamps were used, one of which had the variety "Oftcial." Most varieties are known inverted and double.

Forgeries exist.

Types of Postage Stamps Overprinted in Red

1896 Unwmk.

O82	A11	1c red	2.50	3.00
O83	A11	2c red	2.50	3.00
O84	A11	5c red	2.50	3.00
O85	A11	10c red	2.50	3.00
O86	A11	20c red	3.00	3.00
O87	A11	50c red	5.00	*5.00*
O88	A11	1p red	12.00	*12.00*
O89	A11	2p red	12.00	*12.00*
O90	A11	5p red	16.00	*16.00*
		Nos. O82-O90 (9)	58.00	*60.00*

Wmk. 117

O91	A11	1c red	3.00	3.50
O92	A11	2c red	3.00	3.50
O93	A11	5c red	3.00	3.50
O94	A11	10c red	3.00	3.50
O95	A11	20c red	5.00	5.00
O96	A11	50c red	3.00	*5.00*
O97	A11	1p red	14.00	*14.00*
O98	A11	2p red	16.00	*16.00*
O99	A11	5p red	25.00	*25.00*
		Nos. O91-O99 (9)	75.00	*79.00*

Used values for Nos. O88-O90, O97-O99 are for CTO copies. Postally used copies are not known.

Same, Dated 1897

1897 Unwmk.

O100	A11	1c red	3.00	3.00
O101	A11	2c red	3.00	3.00
O102	A11	5c red	3.00	2.50
O103	A11	10c red	3.00	3.00
O104	A11	20c red	3.00	4.00
O105	A11	50c red	5.00	*5.00*
O106	A11	1p red	12.00	*12.00*
O107	A11	2p red	12.00	*12.00*
O108	A11	5p red	16.00	*16.00*
		Nos. O100-O108 (9)	60.00	*60.50*

Wmk. 117

O109	A11	1c red	5.00	5.00
O110	A11	2c red	5.00	5.00
O111	A11	5c red	5.00	5.00
O112	A11	10c red	10.00	10.00
O113	A11	20c red	10.00	10.00
O114	A11	50c red	12.00	*12.00*
O115	A11	1p red	20.00	*20.00*
O116	A11	2p red	20.00	*20.00*
O117	A11	5p red	20.00	*20.00*
		Nos. O109-O117 (9)	107.00	*107.00*

Reprints of Nos. O82-O117 are described in notes after No. 109M. Value 15c each.

Used values for Nos. O106-O108, O115-O117 are for CTO copies. Postally used copies are not known.

Overprinted in Blue

1898 Unwmk.

O118	A12	1c carmine	3.25	3.25
O119	A12	2c carmine	3.25	3.25
O120	A12	4c carmine	3.25	3.25
O121	A12	5c carmine	2.50	2.50
O122	A12	10c carmine	4.00	4.00
O123	A12	15c carmine	6.00	6.00
O124	A12	20c carmine	6.00	6.00
O125	A12	50c carmine	8.50	*8.50*
O126	A12	1p carmine	11.00	*11.00*
O127	A12	2p carmine	11.00	*11.00*
O128	A12	5p carmine	11.00	*11.00*
		Nos. O118-O128 (11)	69.75	*69.75*

Stamps of this set with sideways watermark 117 or with black overprint are reprints. Value 25c each.

Used values for Nos. O126-O128 are for CTO copies. Postally used copies are not known.

Overprinted in Dark Blue

1899

O129 A13 1c gray grn .20 *1.00*
O130 A13 2c bis brn .20 *1.00*
O131 A13 4c lake .20 *1.00*
O132 A13 5c dk bl .20 *.50*
O133 A13 10c buff .20 *1.00*
O134 A13 15c chocolate .20 *2.00*
O135 A13 20c dk grn .20 *3.00*
O136 A13 50c car rose .20 *3.00*
O137 A13 1p red .20 *10.00*
O138 A13 2p violet .20 *10.00*
O139 A13 5p lt bl .20 *15.00*
Nos. O129-O139 (11) 2.20 *47.50*

Counterfeit cancellations on Nos. O129-O139 are plentiful.

"Justice" — O5

1900 **Engr.**

O140 O5 1c plum .60 .60
O141 O5 2c vermilion .50 .50
O142 O5 4c ol grn .60 .60
O143 O5 5c dk bl 1.25 .45
O144 O5 10c purple 1.25 .35
O145 O5 20c brown .90 .35
O146 O5 50c lake 1.25 .50
O147 O5 1p ultra 3.50 2.50
O148 O5 2p brn org 4.00 4.00
O149 O5 5p grnsh blk 5.00 5.00
Nos. O140-O149 (10) 18.85 14.85

For surcharges see Nos. O155-O157.

Nos. 123, 161 Surcharged in Black

1903 ***Perf. 12, 14***

O150 A14 1c on 10c violet .25 .30
a. "Centovo" 1.00
b. "Contavo" 1.00
c. With ornaments .30
d. Inverted surcharge 1.00
e. "1" omitted at upper left 2.00
O151 A14 2c on 3c green .30 .40
a. "Centovos" 1.00
b. "Contavos" 1.00
c. With ornaments .35
d. Inverted surcharge 1.00
O152 A14 4c on 3c green 1.25 1.25
a. "Centovos" 2.50
b. "Contavos" 2.50
c. With ornaments 2.50
d. Inverted surcharge
O153 A14 4c on 10c violet 1.25 1.25
a. "Centovos" 2.50
b. "Contavos" 2.50
c. With ornaments 2.00
d. Inverted surcharge
O154 A14 5c on 3c green .20 .20
a. "Centovos" 1.00
b. "Contavos" 1.00
c. With ornaments .30
d. Double surcharge 2.00
e. Inverted surcharge
Nos. O150-O154 (5) 3.25 3.40

These surcharges are set up to cover 25 stamps. Some of the settings have bars or pieces of fancy border type below "OFICIAL." There are 5 varieties on #O150, 3 on #O151, 1 each on #O152, O153, O154.

In 1904 #O151 was reprinted to fill a dealer's order. This printing lacks the small figure at the upper right. It includes the variety "OFICILA." At the same time the same setting was printed in carmine on official stamps of 1900, 1c on 10c violet and 2c on 1p ultramarine. Also the 1, 2 and 5p official stamps of 1900 were surcharged with new values and the dates 1901 or 1902 in various colors, inverted, etc. It is doubtful if any of these varieties were ever in Nicaragua and certain that none of them ever did legitimate postal duty.

No. O145 Surcharged in Black

1904 ***Perf. 12***

O155 O5 10c on 20c brn .20 .20
a. No period after "Ctvs" 1.00 .75
O156 O5 30c on 20c brn .20 .20
O157 O5 50c on 20c brn .50 .35
a. Lower "50" omitted 2.50 2.50
b. Upper figures omitted 2.50 2.50
c. Top left and lower figures omitted 3.50 3.50
Nos. O155-O157 (3) .90 .75

Coat of Arms — O6

1905, July 25 **Engr.**

O158 O6 1c green .25 .25
O159 O6 2c rose .25 .25
O160 O6 5c blue .25 .25
O161 O6 10c yel brn .25 .25
O162 O6 20c orange .25 .25
O163 O6 50c brn ol .25 .25
O164 O6 1p lake .25 .25
O165 O6 2p violet .25 .25
O166 O6 5p gray blk .25 .25
Nos. O158-O166 (9) 2.25 2.25

Surcharged Vertically Up or Down

1907

O167 O6 10c on 1c grn .75 .75
O168 O6 10c on 2c rose 25.00 22.50
O169 O6 20c on 2c rose 22.50 17.50
O170 O6 50c on 1c grn 1.50 1.50
O171 O6 50c on 2c rose 22.50 12.50

Surcharged

O172 O6 1p on 2c rose 1.50 1.50
O173 O6 2p on 2c rose 1.50 1.50
O174 O6 3p on 2c rose 1.50 1.50
O175 O6 4p on 2c rose
O176 O6 4p on 5c blue 2.25 2.25

The setting for this surcharge includes various letters from wrong fonts, the figure "1" for "l" in "Vale" and an "l" for "1" in "$1.00."

Surcharged

O177 O6 20c on 1c green 1.00 1.00
a. Double surcharge 5.00 5.00
Nos. O167-O174,O176-O177 (10) 80.00 62.50

The preceding surcharges are vertical, reading both up and down.

O7

Revenue Stamps Surcharged

1907 ***Perf. 14 to 15***

O178 O7 10c on 2c org (Bk) .20 .20
O179 O7 35c on 1c bl (R) .20 .20
a. Inverted surcharge 3.00 3.00
O180 O7 70c on 1c bl (V) .20 .20
a. Inverted surcharge 3.00 3.00
O181 O7 70c on 1c bl (O) .20 .20
a. Inverted surcharge 3.00 3.00
O182 O7 1p on 2c org (G) .20 .20
a. Inverted surcharge 2.50 2.50
O183 O7 2p on 2c org (Br) .20 .20
O184 O7 3p on 5c brn (Bl) .20 .20
O185 O7 4p on 5c brn (G) .20 .20
a. Double surcharge 3.00 3.00
O186 O7 5p on 5c brn (G) .20 .20
a. Inverted surcharge 3.50 3.50
Nos. O178-O186 (9) 1.80 1.80

Letters and figures from several fonts were mixed in these surcharges.

See Nos. O199-O209.

No. 202 Surcharged

1907, Nov.

Black or Blue Black Surcharge

O187 A18 10c on 1c grn 15.00 13.00
O188 A18 15c on 1c grn 15.00 13.00
O189 A18 20c on 1c grn 15.00 13.00
O190 A18 50c on 1c grn 15.00 13.00

Red Surcharge

O191 A18 1(un)p on 1c grn 14.00 13.00
O192 A18 2(dos)p on 1c grn 14.00 13.00
Nos. O187-O192 (6) 88.00 78.00

No. 181 Surcharged

1908 **Yellow Surcharge** ***Perf. 12***

O193 A18 10c on 3c vio 15.00 15.00
O194 A18 15c on 3c vio 15.00 15.00
O195 A18 20c on 3c vio 15.00 15.00
O196 A18 35c on 3c vio 15.00 15.00
O197 A18 50c on 3c vio 15.00 15.00
Nos. O193-O197 (5) 75.00 75.00

Black Surcharge

O198 A18 35c on 3c vio *100.00 100.00*

Revenue Stamps Surcharged like 1907 Issue Dated "1908"

1908 ***Perf. 14 to 15***

O199 O7 10c on 1c bl (V) .75 .50
a. Inverted surcharge 3.50 3.50
O200 O7 35c on 1c bl (Bk) .75 .50
a. Inverted surcharge 3.50 3.50
b. Double surcharge 4.00 4.00
O201 O7 50c on 1c bl (R) .75 .50
O202 O7 1p on 1c bl (Br) 37.50 37.50
a. Inverted surcharge 65.00 65.00
O203 O7 2p on 1c bl (G) .90 .75
O204 O7 10c on 2c org (Bk) 1.10 .65
O205 O7 35c on 2c org (R) 1.10 .65
a. Double surcharge 3.50
O206 O7 50c on 2c org (Bk) 1.10 .65
O207 O7 70c on 2c org (Bl) 1.10 .65
O208 O7 1p on 2c org (G) 1.10 .65
O209 O7 2p on 2c org (Br) 1.10 .65
Nos. O199-O209 (11) 47.25 43.65

There are several minor varieties in the figures, etc., in these surcharges.

Nos. 243-248 Overprinted in Black

1909 ***Perf. 12***

O210 A18 10c lake .20 .20
a. Double overprint 2.50 2.50
O211 A18 15c black .60 .50
O212 A18 20c brn ol 1.00 .75
O213 A18 50c dp grn 1.50 1.00
O214 A18 1p yellow 1.75 1.25
O215 A18 2p car rose 2.75 2.00
Nos. O210-O215 (6) 7.80 5.70

Overprinted in Black **OFICIAL**

1910

O216 A18 15c black 1.50 1.25
a. Double overprint 4.00 4.00
O217 A18 20c brn ol 2.50 2.00
O218 A18 50c dp grn 2.50 2.00
O219 A18 1p yellow 2.75 2.50
a. Inverted overprint 7.50 7.50
O220 A18 2p car rose 4.00 3.00
Nos. O216-O220 (5) 13.25 10.75

Nos. 239-240 Surcharged in Black

OFICIAL
Vale 10 *cts.*

1911

O221 A18 5c on 3c red org 6.00 6.00
O222 A18 10c on 4c vio 5.00 5.00
a. Double surcharge 10.00 10.00
b. Pair, one without new value 20.00

Railroad Stamps Surcharged in Black

1911, Nov. ***Perf. 14 to 15***

O223 A21 10c on 1 red 3.00 3.00
a. Inverted surcharge 4.50
b. Double surcharge 4.50
O224 A21 15c on 1 red 3.00 3.00
a. Inverted surcharge 5.00
b. Double surcharge 4.50
O225 A21 20c on 1 red 3.00 3.00
a. Inverted surcharge 5.00
O226 A21 50c on 1 red 3.75 3.75
a. Inverted surcharge 4.50
O227 A21 1p on 1 red 5.00 *7.00*
a. Inverted surcharge 6.00
O228 A21 2p on 1 red 5.50 *10.00*
a. Inverted surcharge 7.50
b. Double surcharge 7.50
Nos. O223-O228 (6) 23.25 29.75

Surcharged in Black

CORREO
OFICIAL
15 centavos

1911, Nov.

O229 A21 10c on 1 red 22.50
O230 A21 15c on 1 red 22.50
O231 A21 20c on 1 red 22.50
O232 A21 50c on 1 red 16.00
Nos. O229-O232 (4) 83.50

Surcharged in Black

Correo oficial
Vale
5 cts.
1911

1911, Dec.

O233 A21 5c on 1 red 4.50 *6.00*
a. Double surcharge 7.50
b. Inverted surcharge 7.50
c. "5" omitted 6.00
O234 A21 10c on 1 red 5.50 *7.00*
O235 A21 15c on 1 red 6.00 *7.50*

O236 A21 20c on 1 red 6.50 *8.50*
O237 A21 50c on 1 red 7.50 *10.00*
Nos. O233-O237 (5) 30.00 39.00

Nos. O233 to O237 have a surcharge on the back like Nos. 285 and 286 with "15 cts" obliterated by a heavy bar.

Surcharged Vertically in Black

1912

O238 A21 5c on 1 red 8.00 8.00
O239 A21 10c on 1 red 8.00 8.00
O240 A21 15c on 1 red 8.00 8.00
O241 A21 20c on 1 red 8.00 8.00
O242 A21 35c on 1 red 8.00 8.00
O243 A21 50c on 1 red 8.00 8.00
O244 A21 1p on 1 red 8.00 8.00
Nos. O238-O244 (7) 56.00 56.00

Nos. O238 to O244 are printed on Nos. 285 and 286 but the surcharge on the back is obliterated by a vertical bar.

Types of Regular Issue of 1912 Overprinted in Black

1912 ***Perf. 12***

O245 A22 1c light blue .20 .20
O246 A22 2c light blue .20 .20
O247 A22 3c light blue .20 .20
O248 A22 4c light blue .20 .20
O249 A22 5c light blue .20 .20
O250 A22 6c light blue .20 .20
O251 A22 10c light blue .20 .20
O252 A22 15c light blue .20 .20
O253 A22 20c light blue .20 .20
O254 A22 25c light blue .20 .20
O255 A22 35c light blue .25 .25
O256 A22 50c light blue 1.50 1.50
O257 A22 1p light blue .30 .30
O258 A22 2p light blue .35 .35
O259 A22 5p light blue .50 .50
Nos. O245-O259 (15) 4.90 4.90

On the 35c the overprint is 15½mm wide, on the other values it is 13mm.

Types of Regular Issue of 1914 Overprinted in Black

1915, May

O260 A24 1c light blue .20 .20
O261 A25 2c light blue .20 .20
O262 A24 3c light blue .20 .20
O263 A25 4c light blue .20 .20
O264 A24 5c light blue .20 .20
O265 A25 6c light blue .20 .20
O266 A25 10c light blue .20 .20
O267 A24 15c light blue .20 .20
O268 A25 20c light blue .20 .20
O269 A24 25c light blue .30 .30
O270 A25 50c light blue .60 .60
Nos. O260-O270 (11) 2.70 2.70

Regular Issues of 1914-22 Overprinted in Red

1925

O271 A24 ½c dp grn .20 .20
a. Double overprint 2.50 2.50
O272 A24 1c violet .20 .20
O273 A25 2c car rose .20 .20
O274 A24 3c ol grn .20 .20
O275 A25 4c vermilion .20 .20
a. Double overprint 2.50 2.50
O276 A24 5c black .20 .20
a. Double overprint 2.50 2.50
O277 A25 6c red brn .25 .25
O278 A25 10c yellow .30 .30
a. Double overprint 3.50 3.50
O279 A24 15c red brn .40 .40
O280 A25 20c bis brn .50 .50
O281 A24 25c orange .60 .60
a. Inverted overprint 4.00 4.00
O282 A25 50c pale bl .75 .75
a. Double overprint 5.00 5.00
Nos. O271-O282 (12) 4.00 4.00

Type II overprint has "f" and "i" separated. Comes on Nos. O272-O274 and O276.

Regular Issues of 1914-22 Overprinted in Black

1926

O283 A24 ½c dk grn .20 .20
O284 A24 1c dp vio .20 .20
O285 A25 2c car rose .20 .20
O286 A24 3c ol gray .20 .20
O287 A25 4c vermilion .20 .20
O288 A24 5c gray blk .20 .20
O289 A25 6c red brn .20 .20
O290 A25 10c yellow .20 .20
O291 A24 15c dp brn .20 .20
O292 A25 20c bis brn .20 .20
O293 A24 25c orange .20 .20
O294 A25 50c pale bl .25 .25
Nos. O283-O294 (12) 2.45 2.45

No. 499 Surcharged in Black

1931

O295 A33 5c on 10c bis brn .20 .20

Nos. 517-518 Overprinted in Red

1931

O296 A25 6c bis brn .20 .20
O297 A25 10c lt brn .20 .20

Nos. 541, 543, 545 With Additional Overprint in Black

O298 A24 1c ol grn .20 .20
O299 A24 3c lt bl .20 .20
a. "OFICIAL" inverted .80 .80
O300 A24 5c gray brn .20 .20
a. "1931" double .80 .80
Nos. O298-O300 (3) .60 .60

Regular Issues of 1914-31 Overprinted in Black

1932, Feb. 6

O301 A24 1c ol grn .20 .20
a. Double overprint 1.40 1.40
O302 A25 2c brt rose .20 .20
a. Double overprint 1.40 1.40
O303 A24 3c lt bl .20 .20
a. Double overprint .50 .50
O304 A25 4c dk bl .20 .20
O305 A24 5c ol brn .20 .20
O306 A25 6c bis brn .20 .20
a. Double overprint 2.00 2.00
O307 A25 10c lt brn .30 .20
O308 A24 15c org red .40 .25
a. Double overprint 2.25 2.25
O309 A25 20c orange .70 .35
O310 A24 25c dk vio 2.00 .50
O311 A25 50c green .20 .20
O312 A25 1cor yellow .20 .20
Nos. O301-O312 (12) 5.00 2.90

With Additional Overprint in Black

1932, Feb. 6

O313 A24 1c ol grn 5.50 5.50
O314 A25 2c brt rose 6.50 6.50
a. Double overprint 8.25 8.25
O315 A24 3c lt bl 5.00 5.00
O316 A24 5c ol brn 5.00 5.00
O317 A24 15c org red .65 .65
O318 A24 25c blk brn .65 .65
O319 A24 25c dk vio 1.50 1.50
Nos. O313-O319 (7) 24.80 24.80

The variety "OFIAIAL" occurs once in each sheet of Nos. O301 to O319 inclusive.

Flag of the Race Issue

1933, Aug. 9 Litho. *Rouletted 9*
Without gum

O320 A43 1c orange 1.00 1.00
O321 A43 2c yellow 1.00 1.00
O322 A43 3c dk brn 1.00 1.00
O323 A43 4c dp brn 1.00 1.00
O324 A43 5c gray brn 1.00 1.00
O325 A43 6c dp ultra 1.25 1.25
O326 A43 10c dp vio 1.25 1.25
O327 A43 15c red vio 1.25 1.25
O328 A43 20c dp grn 1.25 1.25
O329 A43 25c green 2.00 2.00
O330 A43 50c carmine 2.50 2.50
O331 A43 1cor red 4.00 4.00
Nos. O320-O331 (12) 18.50 18.50

See note after No. 599.
Reprints of Nos. O320-O331 exist.
A 25c dull blue exists. Its status is questioned.

Regular Issue of 1914-31 Overprinted in Red

1933, Nov. ***Perf. 12***

O332 A24 1c ol grn .20 .20
O333 A25 2c brt rose .20 .20
O334 A24 3c lt bl .20 .20
O335 A25 4c dk bl .20 .20
O336 A24 5c ol brn .20 .20
O337 A25 6c bis brn .20 .20
O338 A25 10c lt brn .20 .20
O339 A24 15c red org .20 .20
O340 A25 20c orange .20 .20
O341 A24 25c dk vio .20 .20
O342 A25 50c green .20 .20
O343 A25 1cor yellow .35 .20
Nos. O332-O343 (12) 2.55 2.40

Nos. O332-O343 exist with or without signature control overprint. Values are the same.

Official Stamps of 1933 Overprinted as Nos. CO15-CO19 in Blue

1935, Dec.

O344 A24 1c ol grn .65 .40
O345 A25 2c brt rose .65 .50
O346 A24 3c lt bl 1.60 .50
O347 A25 4c dk bl 1.60 1.60
O348 A24 5c ol brn 1.60 1.60
O349 A25 6c bis brn 2.00 2.00
O350 A25 10c lt brn 2.00 2.00
O351 A24 15c org red 27.50 27.50
O352 A25 20c orange 27.50 27.50
O353 A24 25c dk vio 27.50 27.50
O354 A25 50c green 27.50 27.50
O355 A25 1cor yellow 27.50 27.50
Nos. O344-O355 (12) 147.60 146.10

Nos. O344-O355 have signature control overprints. Counterfeits of overprint abound.

Same Overprinted in Red

1936, Jan.

O356 A24 1c ol grn .20 .20
O357 A25 2c brt rose .20 .20
O358 A24 3c lt bl .20 .20
a. Double overprint
O359 A25 4c dk bl .20 .20
O360 A24 5c ol brn .20 .20
O361 A25 6c bis brn .20 .20
O362 A25 10c lt brn .20 .20
O363 A24 15c org red .20 .20
O364 A25 20c orange .20 .20
O365 A24 25c dk vio .20 .20
O366 A25 50c green .20 .20
O367 A25 1cor yellow .35 .35
Nos. O356-O367 (12) 2.55 2.55

Have signature control overprints.

Nos. 653 to 655, 657, 659 660, 662 to 664 Overprinted in Black

1937

O368 A24 1c car rose .20 .20
O369 A25 2c dp bl .20 .20
O370 A24 3c chocolate .25 .25
O371 A24 5c org red .35 .25
O372 A25 10c ol grn .65 .40
O373 A24 15c green .80 .50
O374 A24 25c orange 1.00 .65
O375 A25 50c brown 1.40 .80
O376 A25 1cor ultra 2.50 1.25
Nos. O368-O376 (9) 7.35 4.50

Islands of the Great Lake
O9

1939, Jan. Engr. *Perf. 12½*

O377 O9 2c rose red .20 .20
O378 O9 3c lt bl .20 .20
O379 O9 6c brn org .20 .20
O380 O9 7½c dp grn .20 .20
O381 O9 10c blk brn .20 .20
O382 O9 15c orange .20 .20
O383 O9 25c dk vio .25 .25
O384 O9 50c brt yel grn .45 .45
Nos. O377-O384 (8) 1.90 1.90

POSTAL TAX STAMPS

Official Stamps of 1915 Surcharged in Black

1921, July Unwmk. *Perf. 12*

RA1 A24 1c on 5c lt bl 1.50 .60
RA2 A25 1c on 6c lt bl .65 .20
a. Double surcharge, one inverted
RA3 A25 1c on 10c lt bl 1.00 .25
a. Double surcharge 3.50 3.50
RA4 A24 1c on 15c lt bl 1.50 .25
a. Double surcharge, one inverted 5.00 5.00
Nos. RA1-RA4 (4) 4.65 1.30

"R de C" signifies "Reconstruccion de Comunicaciones." The stamps were intended to provide a fund for rebuilding the General Post Office which was burned in April, 1921. One stamp was required on each letter or parcel, in addition to the regular postage. In the setting of one hundred there are five stamps with antique "C" and twenty-one with "R" and "C" smaller than in the illustration. One or more stamps in the setting have a dotted bar, as illustrated over No. 388, instead of the double bar.

The use of the "R de C" stamps for the payment of regular postage was not permitted.

Official Stamp of 1915 Overprinted in Black

1921, July

RA5 A24 1c light blue 6.00 1.75

This stamp is known with the dotted bar as illustrated over No. 388, instead of the double bar.

Coat of Arms — PT1

PT2

1921, Sept.

Red Surcharge

RA6 PT1 1c on 1c ver & blk .20 .20
RA7 PT1 1c on 2c grn & blk .20 .20
a. Double surcharge 3.00 3.00
b. Double surcharge, one inverted 4.00 4.00
RA8 PT1 1c on 4c org & blk .20 .20
a. Double surcharge 4.00 4.00
RA9 PT1 1c on 15c dk bl & blk .20 .20
a. Double surcharge 3.00 3.00
Nos. RA6-RA9 (4) .80 .80

1922, Feb.

Black Surcharge

RA10 PT2 1c on 10c yellow .20 .20
a. Period after "de" .50 .40
b. Double surcharge 2.00 2.00
c. Double inverted surcharge 3.75 3.75
d. Inverted surcharge 3.00 3.00
e. Without period after "C" 1.00 1.00

No. 409 Overprinted in Black

1922

RA11 A24 1c violet .20 .20
a. Double overprint 2.00 2.00

This stamp with the overprint in red is a trial printing.

Nos. 402, 404-407 Surcharged in Black

1922, June

RA12 A27 1c on 1c grn & blk .75 .75
RA13 A29 1c on 5c ultra & blk .75 .75
RA14 A30 1c on 10c org & blk .75 .40
RA15 A31 1c on 25c yel & blk .75 .30
a. Inverted surcharge 5.00 5.00
RA16 A32 1c on 50c vio & blk .30 .25
a. Double surcharge 4.00 4.00
Nos. RA12-RA16 (5) 3.30 2.45

PT3

Surcharge in Red or Dark Blue

1922, Oct. ***Perf. 11½***

RA17 PT3 1c yellow (R) .20 .20
a. No period after "C" 1.00 1.00
RA18 PT3 1c violet (DBl) .20 .20
a. No period after "C" 1.00 1.00

Surcharge is inverted on 22 out of 50 of No. RA17, 23 out of 50 of No. RA18.

Nos. 403-407 Surcharged in Black

1923 ***Perf. 12***

RA19 A28 1c on 2c rose red & black .50 .45
RA20 A29 1c on 5c ultra & blk .55 .20
RA21 A30 1c on 10c org & blk .25 .20
RA22 A31 1c on 25c yel & blk .35 .30
RA23 A32 1c on 50c vio & blk .25 .20
Nos. RA19-RA23 (5) 1.90 1.35

The variety no period after "R" occurs twice on each sheet.

Red Surcharge

Wmk. Coat of Arms in Sheet

Perf. 11½

RA24 PT3 1c pale blue .20 .20

Unwmk.

Type of 1921 Issue

Without Surcharge of New Value

RA25 PT1 1c ver & blk .20 .20
a. Double overprint, one inverted 3.00 3.00

No. 409 Overprinted in Blue

1924

RA26 A24 1c violet .20 .20
a. Double overprint 8.00 8.00

There are two settings of the overprint on No. RA26, with "1924" 5½mm or 6½mm wide.

No. 409 Overprinted in Blue

1925

RA27 A24 1c violet .20 .20

No. 409 Overprinted in Blue

1926

RA28 A24 1c violet .25 .20

No. RA28 Overprinted in Various Colors

1927

RA29 A24 1c vio (R) .20 .20
a. Double overprint (R) 2.00 2.00
b. Inverted overprint (R) 3.00 3.00
RA30 A24 1c vio (V) .20 .20
a. Double overprint 2.50 2.50
b. Inverted overprint 2.50 2.50
RA31 A24 1c vio (Bl) .20 .20
a. Double overprint 5.00 5.00
RA32 A24 1c vio (Bk) .20 .20
a. Double ovpt., one invtd. 4.25 4.25
b. Double overprint 4.25 4.25

Same Overprint on No. RA27

RA33 A24 1c vio (Bk) 15.00 10.00
Nos. RA29-RA33 (5) 15.80 10.80

No. RA28 Overprinted in Violet

1928

RA34 A24 1c violet .20 .20
a. Double overprint 2.00 2.00
b. "928" 1.00 1.00

Similar to No. RA34 but 8mm space between "Resello" and "1928"

Black Overprint

RA35 A24 1c violet .40 .20
a. "1828" 2.00 2.00

PT4

Inscribed "Timbre Telegrafico"
Horiz. Surch. in Black,
Vert. Surch. in Red

RA36 PT4 1c on 5c bl & blk .60 .20
a. Comma after "R" 1.25 1.25
b. No period after "R" 1.25 1.25
c. No periods after "R" and "C" 1.25 1.25

("CORREOS" at right) — PT5

PT6

1928 **Engr.** ***Perf. 12***

RA37 PT5 1c plum .25 .20

See Nos. RA41-RA43. For overprints see Nos. RA45-RA46, RA48-RA51.

1929

Surcharged in Red

RA38 PT6 1c on 5c bl & blk .20 .20
a. Inverted surcharge 3.00 3.00
b. Double surcharge 2.00 2.00
c. Double surcharge, one inverted 2.00 2.00
d. Period after "de" 1.25 1.25
e. Comma after "R" 1.25 1.25

See note after No. 512.

Regular Issue of 1928 Overprinted in Blue

RA39 A24 1c red orange .20 .20

No. RA39 exists both with and without signature control overprint.

An additional overprint, "1929" in black or blue on No. RA39, is fraudulent.

No. 513 Overprinted in Red

1929

RA40 A24 1c ol grn .20 .20
a. Double overprint .75 .75

No. RA40 is known with overprint in black, and with overprint inverted. These varieties were not regularly issued, but copies have been canceled by favor.

Type of 1928 Issue
Inscribed at right
"COMUNICACIONES"

1930-37

RA41 PT5 1c carmine .20 .20
RA42 PT5 1c orange ('33) .20 .20
RA43 PT5 1c green ('37) .20 .20
Nos. RA41-RA43 (3) .60 .60

No. RA42 has signature control. See note before No. 600.

No. RA39 Overprinted in Black

1931

RA44 A24 1c red orange .20 .20
a. "1931" double overprint .35 .35
b. "1931" double ovpt., one invtd. .40 .40

No. RA44 exists with signature control overprint. See note before No. 600. Value is the same.

No. RA42 Overprinted Vertically, up or down, in Black

1935

RA45 PT5 1c orange .20 .20
a. Double overprint 1.00 1.00
b. Double ovpt., one inverted

No. RA45 and RA45a Overprinted Vertically, Reading Down, in Blue

RA46 PT5 1c orange .50 .20
a. Black overprint double 2.00 2.00

Same Overprint in Red on Nos. RA39, RA42 and RA45

RA47 A24 1c red org (#RA39) *50.00 50.00*
RA48 PT5 1c org (#RA42) .20 .20
RA49 PT5 1c org (#RA45) .20 .20
a. Black overprint double .80 .80

Overprint is horizontal on No. RA47 and vertical, reading down, on Nos. RA48-RA49.

No. RA48 exists with signature control overprint. See note before No. 600. Same values.

No. RA42 Overprinted Vertically, Reading Down, in Carmine

1935 **Unwmk.** ***Perf. 12***

RA50 PT5 1c orange .20 .20

No. RA45 with Additional Overprint "1936", Vertically, Reading Down, in Red

1936

RA51 PT5 1c orange .50 .20

No. RA39 with Additional Overprint "1936" in Red

RA52 A24 1c red orange .50 .20

No. RA52 exists only with script control mark.

PT7

Vertical Surcharge in Red

1936

RA53 PT7 1c on 5c grn & blk .20 .20
a. "Cenavo" 1.40 1.40
b. "Centavos" 1.40 1.40

Horizontal Surcharge in Red

RA54 PT7 1c on 5c grn & blk .20 .20
a. Double surcharge 1.40 1.40

Baseball Player PT8

1937 Typo. ***Perf. 11***

RA55 PT8 1c carmine .35 .20
RA56 PT8 1c yellow .35 .20
RA57 PT8 1c blue .35 .20
RA58 PT8 1c green .35 .20
b. Sheet of 4, #RA55-RA58 3.00 3.00
Nos. RA55-RA58 (4) 1.40 .80

Issued for the benefit of the Central American Caribbean Games of 1937.

Control mark in red is variously placed. See dark oval below "OLIMPICO" in illustration.

Tête bêche Pairs

RA55a PT8 1c .75 .75
RA56a PT8 1c .75 .75
RA57a PT8 1c .75 .75
RA58a PT8 1c .75 .75
Nos. RA55a-RA58a (4) 3.00 3.00

PROVINCE OF ZELAYA

(Bluefields)

A province of Nicaragua lying along the eastern coast. Special postage stamps for this section were made necessary because for a period two currencies, which differed materially in value, were in use in Nicaragua. Silver money was used in Zelaya and Cabo Gracias a Dios while the rest of Nicaragua used paper money. Later the money of the entire country was placed on a gold basis.

Dangerous counterfeits exist of most of the Bluefields overprints.

Regular Issues of 1900-05 Handstamped in Black (4 or more types)

1904-05 Unwmk. ***Perf. 12, 14***

On Engraved Stamps of 1900

1L1 A14 1c plum 1.50 .75
1L2 A14 2c vermilion 1.50 .75
1L3 A14 3c green 1.90 1.50
1L4 A14 4c ol grn 11.00 9.00
1L5 A14 15c ultra 3.00 1.90
1L6 A14 20c brown 3.00 1.90
1L7 A14 50c lake 10.50 9.00
1L8 A14 1p yellow 21.00
1L9 A14 2p salmon 30.00
1L10 A14 5p black 37.50
Nos. 1L1-1L10 (10) 120.90
Nos. 1L1-1L7 (7) 24.80

On Lithographed Stamps of 1902

1L11 A14 5c blue 3.00 .75
1L12 A14 5c carmine 1.90 .90
1L13 A14 10c violet 1.50 .75
Nos. 1L11-1L13 (3) 6.40 2.40

On Postage Due Stamps Overprinted "1901 Correos"

1L14 D3 20c brn (No. 156) 4.50 1.90
1L15 D3 50c lake (No. 158) — —

On Surcharged Stamps of 1904-05

1L16 A16 5c on 10c (#175) 1.50 1.10
1L17 A14 5c on 10c (#178) 3.00 1.50
1L18 A16 15c on 10c vio 1.50 1.50
1L19 A17 15c on 10c vio 14.00 4.50
Nos. 1L16-1L19 (4) 20.00 8.60

On Surcharged Stamp of 1901

1L20 A14 20c on 5p blk 18.00 3.00

On Regular Issue of 1905

1906-07 ***Perf. 12***

1L21 A18 1c green .30 .30
1L22 A18 2c car rose .30 .30
1L23 A18 3c violet .30 .30
1L24 A18 4c org red .45 .45
1L25 A18 5c blue .25 .25
1L26 A18 10c yel brn 3.00 1.50
1L27 A18 15c brn ol 4.50 1.75
1L28 A18 20c lake 9.00 7.50
1L29 A18 50c orange 35.00 30.00
1L30 A18 1p black 30.00 27.50
1L31 A18 2p dk grn 37.50
1L32 A18 5p violet 45.00
Nos. 1L21-1L32 (12) 165.60
Nos. 1L21-1L32 (10) 69.85

On Surcharged Stamps of 1906-08

1L33 A18 10c on 3c vio .40 .40
1L34 A18 15c on 1c grn .50 .50
1L35 A18 20c on 2c rose 3.50 3.50
1L36 A18 20c on 5c bl 1.50 1.50
1L37 A18 50c on 6c sl (R) 1.50 3.00
Nos. 1L33-1L37 (5) 7.40 8.90

B **B**

Dpto. Zelaya **Dto. Zelaya**

Stamps with the above overprints were made to fill dealers' orders but were never regularly issued or used. Stamps with similar overprints handstamped are bogus.

Surcharged Stamps of 1906 Overprinted in Red, Black or Blue

1L38 A18 15c on 1c grn (R) 2.75 2.75
a. Red overprint inverted
1L39 A18 20c on 2c rose (Bk) 1.90 1.90
1L40 A18 20c on 5c bl (R) 3.00 3.00
1L41 A18 50c on 6c sl (Bl) 14.00 14.00
Nos. 1L38-1L41 (4) 21.65 21.65

Stamps of the 1905 issue overprinted as above No. 1L38 or similarly overprinted but with only 2¼mm space between "B" and "Dpto. Zelaya" were made to fill dealers' orders but not placed in use.

No. 205 Handstamped in Black

Perf. 14 to 15

1L42 A18 10c yel brn 24.00 24.00

Stamps of 1907 Overprinted in Red or Black

1L43 A18 15c brn ol (R) 3.00 3.00
1L44 A18 20c lake .90 .90
a. Inverted overprint 11.00 11.00

With Additional Surcharge

1L45 A18 5c brn org .50 .45
a. Inverted surcharge 7.50 7.50

With Additional Surcharge **5 cent.**

1L46 A18 5c on 4c brn org 12.00 12.00

On Provisional Postage Stamps of 1907-08 in Black or Blue

1L47 A18 10c on 2c rose (Bl) 4.50 4.50
1L48 A18 10c on 2c rose *300.00*
1L48A A18 10c on 4c brn org *300.00*
1L49 A18 10c on 20c lake 3.00 3.00
1L50 A18 10c on 50c org (Bl) 3.00 2.25

Arms Type of 1907 Overprinted in Black or Violet

1907

1L51 A18 1c green .30 .22
1L52 A18 2c rose .30 .22
1L53 A18 3c violet .38 .38
1L54 A18 4c brn org .45 .45
1L55 A18 5c blue 4.50 2.25
1L56 A18 10c yel brn .38 .30
1L57 A18 15c brn ol .75 .38
1L58 A18 20c lake .75 .45
1L59 A18 50c orange 2.25 1.50
1L60 A18 1p blk (V) 2.25 1.50
1L61 A18 2p dk grn 2.25 1.90
1L62 A18 5p violet 3.75 2.25
Nos. 1L51-1L62 (12) 18.31 11.80

Nos. 217-225 Overprinted in Green

1908

1L63 A19 1c on 5c yel & blk (R) .45 .40
1L64 A19 2c on 5c yel & blk (Bl) .45 .40
1L65 A19 4c on 5c yel & blk (G) .45 .40
a. Overprint reading down 11.00 11.00
b. Double overprint, reading up and down 18.00 18.00
1L66 A19 5c yel & blk .45 .45
a. "CORROE" 4.50
b. Double overprint 11.00 11.00
c. Double overprint, reading up and down 19.00 19.00
d. "CORREO 1908" double 15.00 15.00
1L67 A19 10c lt bl & blk .45 .45
a. Ovpt. reading down .50 .50
b. "CORREO 1908" triple 37.50
1L68 A19 15c on 50c ol & blk (R) .90 .90
a. "1008" 4.50
b. "8908" 4.50
1L69 A19 35c on 50c ol & blk 1.40 1.40
1L70 A19 1p yel brn & blk 1.90 1.90
a. "CORROE" 12.00 12.00
1L71 A19 2p pearl gray & blk 2.25 2.25
a. "CORROE" 15.00 15.00
Nos. 1L63-1L71 (9) 8.70 8.55

Overprinted Horizontally in Black or Green

1L72 A19 5c yel & blk 9.00 7.50
1L72A A19 2p pearl gray & blk (G) *300.00*

On Nos. 1L72-1L72A, space between "B" and "Dpto. Zelaya" is 13mm.

Nos. 237-248 Overprinted in Black

Imprint: "American Bank Note Co. NY"

1909 ***Perf. 12***

1L73 A18 1c yel grn .25 .25
1L74 A18 2c vermilion .25 .25
a. Inverted overprint
1L75 A18 3c red org .25 .25
1L76 A18 4c violet .25 .25
1L77 A18 5c dp bl .30 .25
a. Inverted overprint 9.00 9.00
b. "B" inverted 7.50 7.50
c. Double overprint 12.00 12.00
1L78 A18 6c gray brn 4.50 3.00
1L79 A18 10c lake .30 .30
a. "B" inverted 9.00 9.00
1L80 A18 15c black .45 .40
a. "B" inverted 11.00 11.00
b. Inverted overprint 12.00 12.00
c. Double overprint 14.00 14.00
1L81 A18 20c brn ol .50 .50
a. "B" inverted 19.00 19.00
1L82 A18 50c dp grn 1.50 1.50
1L83 A18 1p yellow 2.25 2.25
1L84 A18 2p car rose 3.00 3.00
a. Double overprint 27.50 27.50
Nos. 1L73-1L84 (12) 13.80 12.20

One stamp in each sheet has the "o" of "Dpto." sideways.

Overprinted in Black

1910

1L85 A18 3c red org .40 .40
1L86 A18 4c violet .40 .40
a. Inverted overprint 14.00 14.00
1L87 A18 15c black 4.50 2.25
1L88 A18 20c brn ol .25 .30
1L89 A18 50c dp grn .30 .40
1L90 A18 1p yellow .30 .45
a. Inverted overprint 7.50
1L91 A18 2p car rose .40 .75
Nos. 1L85-1L91 (7) 6.55 4.95

Z1

Black Ovpt., Green Surch., Carmine Block-outs

1910

1L92 Z1 5c on 10c lake 3.75 3.00

There are three types of the letter "B." It is stated that this stamp was used exclusively for postal purposes and not for telegrams.

No. 247 Surcharged in Black

1911

1L93 A18 5c on 1p yellow .75 .75
a. Double surcharge 14.00
1L94 A18 10c on 1p yellow 1.50 1.50
1L95 A18 15c on 1p yellow .75 .75
a. Inverted surcharge 9.00
b. Double surcharge 9.00
c. Double surcharge, one invtd. 9.00
Nos. 1L93-1L95 (3) 3.00 3.00

Revenue Stamps Surcharged in Black

Perf. 14 to 15

1L96 A19 5c on 25c lilac .75 1.10
a. Without period 1.50 1.50
b. Inverted surcharge 9.00 9.00
1L97 A19 10c on 1p yel brn 1.10 .75
a. Without period 1.90 1.90
b. "01" for "10" 9.00 7.50
c. Inverted surcharge 13.00 13.00

Surcharged in Black

1L98 A19 5c on 1p yel brn 1.50 1.50
a. Without period 2.25
b. "50" for "05" 14.00 14.00
c. Inverted surcharge 15.00 15.00
1L99 A19 5c on 10p pink 1.50 1.50
a. Without period 2.25 2.25
b. "50" for "05" 11.00 11.00
1L100 A19 10c on 1p yel brn 82.50 82.50
a. Without period 95.00 95.00

1L101	A19	10c on 25p grn	.75	.75
a.		Without period	2.25	2.25
b.		"1" for "10"	7.50	
1L102	A19	10c on 50p ver	11.00	11.00
a.		Without period	16.00	
b.		"1" for "10"	22.50	
		Nos. 1L98-1L102 (5)	97.25	97.25

With Additional Overprint "1904"

1L103	A19	5c on 10p pink	14.00	14.00
a.		Without period	24.00	24.00
b.		"50" for "05"	110.00	110.00
1L104	A19	10c on 2p gray	.75	.75
a.		Without period	1.90	
b.		"1" for "10"	7.50	
1L105	A19	10c on 25p grn	92.50	
a.		Without period	100.00	
1L106	A19	10c on 50p ver	7.50	7.50
a.		Without period	14.00	
b.		"1" for "10"	18.00	
c.		Inverted surcharge		

The surcharges on Nos. 1L96 to 1L106 are in settings of twenty-five. One stamp in each setting has a large square period after "cts" and another has a thick upright "c" in that word. There are two types of "1904".

B

No. 293C Overprinted

Dpto. Zelaya

1911

1L107	A21	5c on 5c on 2c bl (R)	32.50	
a.		"5" omitted	37.50	
b.		Red overprint inverted	40.00	
c.		As "a" and "b"	47.50	

Same Overprint On Nos. 290, 291, 292 and 289D with Lines of Surcharge spaced 2½mm apart Reading Down

1L107D	A21	2c on 10c on 1c red	*250.00*	
e.		Overprint reading up	*250.00*	
1L107F	A21	5c on 10c on 1c red	*92.50*	
1L107G	A21	10c on 10c on 1c red (#292)	*125.00*	
1L108	A21	10c on 10c on 1c red (#289D)	*120.00*	

There is no evidence that Nos. 1L107D-1L108 were issued by the government.

Locomotive — Z2

1912 **Engr.** ***Perf. 14***

1L109	Z2	1c yel grn	.75	.50
1L110	Z2	2c vermilion	.50	.25
1L111	Z2	3c org brn	.75	.45
1L112	Z2	4c carmine	.75	.30
1L113	Z2	5c dp bl	.75	.45
1L114	Z2	6c red brn	4.00	2.50
1L115	Z2	10c slate	.75	.30
1L116	Z2	15c dl lil	.75	.60
1L117	Z2	20c bl vio	.75	.60
1L118	Z2	25c grn & blk	1.00	.80
1L119	Z2	35c brn & blk	1.25	1.00
1L120	Z2	50c ol grn	1.25	1.00
1L121	Z2	1p orange	1.75	1.50
1L122	Z2	2p org brn	4.00	3.00
1L123	Z2	5p dk bl grn	7.00	6.50
		Nos. 1L109-1L123 (15)	26.00	19.75

The stamps of this issue were for use in all places on the Atlantic Coast of Nicaragua where the currency was on a silver basis.

For surcharges see Nos. 325-337.

OFFICIAL STAMPS

Regular Issue of 1909 Overprinted in Black

Oficial

B

1909 **Unwmk.** ***Perf. 12***

1LO1	A18	20c brn ol	15.00	12.00
a.		Double overprint	30.00	

Official Stamp of 1909 Overprinted in Black

B

1LO2	A18	15c black	15.00	10.00

Same Overprint on Official Stamp of 1911

1911

1LO3	A18	5c on 3c red org	22.50	17.50

CABO GRACIAS A DIOS

A cape and seaport town in the extreme northeast of Nicaragua. The name was coined by Spanish explorers who had great difficulty finding a landing place along the Nicaraguan coast and when eventually locating this harbor expressed their relief by designating the point "Cape Thanks to God." Special postage stamps came into use for the same reasons as the Zelaya issues. See Zelaya.

Dangerous counterfeits exist of most of the Cabo Gracias a Dios overprints.

Regular Issues of 1900-04 Handstamped in Violet

On Engraved Stamps of 1900

1904-05 **Unwmk.** ***Perf. 12, 14***

2L1	A14	1c plum	2.25	1.10
2L2	A14	2c vermilion	4.50	1.25
2L3	A14	3c green	6.00	4.50
2L4	A14	4c ol grn	9.75	9.75
2L5	A14	15c ultra	35.00	22.50
2L6	A14	20c brown	3.00	2.25
		Nos. 2L1-2L6 (6)	60.50	41.35

On Lithographed Stamps of 1902

2L7	A14	5c blue	24.00	24.00
2L8	A14	10c violet	24.00	24.00

On Surcharged Stamps of 1904

2L9	A16	5c on 10c vio	22.50	22.50
2L10	A16	15c on 10c vio		

On Postage Due Stamps
Violet Handstamp

2L11	D3	20c org brn (#141)	5.00	1.25
2L12	D3	20c org brn (#156)	3.50	1.25
2L13	D3	30c dk grn (#157)	14.00	14.00
2L14	D3	50c lake (#158)	3.75	.75
		Nos. 2L11-2L14 (4)	26.25	17.25

Black Handstamp

2L15	D3	30c dk grn (#157)	24.00	24.00

Stamps of 1900-05 Handstamped in Violet

On Engraved Stamps of 1900

2L16	A14	1c plum	2.75	2.25
2L17	A14	2c vermilion	27.50	24.00
2L18	A14	3c green	37.50	27.50
2L19	A14	4c ol grn	40.00	37.50
2L20	A14	15c ultra	45.00	45.00
		Nos. 2L16-2L20 (5)	152.75	136.25

On Lithographed Stamps of 1902

2L22	A14	5c dk bl	95.00	50.00
2L23	A14	10c violet	27.50	24.00

On Surcharged Stamp of 1904

2L24	A14	5c on 10c vio		

On Postage Due Stamp

2L25	D3	20c org brn (#141)		

Cabo

The editors have no evidence that stamps with this handstamp were issued. Copies were sent to the UPU and covers are known.

Stamps of 1900-08 Handstamped in Violet

1905

On Stamps of 1905

2L26	A18	1c green	1.10	1.10
2L27	A18	2c car rose	1.50	1.50
2L28	A18	3c violet	1.50	1.50
2L29	A18	4c org red	3.75	3.75
2L30	A18	5c blue	1.50	1.10
2L31	A18	6c slate	3.75	3.75
2L32	A18	10c yel brn	3.00	1.90
2L33	A18	15c brn ol	4.50	4.50
2L34	A18	1p black	20.00	20.00
2L35	A18	2p dk grn	35.00	35.00
		Nos. 2L26-2L35 (10)	75.60	74.10

Magenta Handstamp

2L26a	A18	1c	3.75	3.00
2L27a	A18	2c	3.00	2.75
2L28a	A18	3c	3.75	3.00
2L30a	A18	5c	7.50	6.00
2L33a	A18	15c	13.50	11.00
		Nos. 2L26a-2L33a (5)	31.50	25.75

On Stamps of 1900-04

2L36	A14	5c on 10c vio	14.00	14.00
2L37	A14	10c violet		
2L38	A14	20c brown	12.00	12.00
2L39	A14	20c on 5p blk		95.00

On Postage Due Stamps Overprinted "Correos"

2L40	D3	20c org brn (#141)	9.00	9.00
2L41	D3	20c org brn (#156)	5.00	4.50

On Surcharged Stamps of 1906-08

2L42	A18	10c on 3c vio		*250.00*
2L43	A18	20c on 5c blue	9.00	9.00
2L44	A18	50c on 6c slate	24.00	24.00

On Stamps of 1907
Perf. 14 to 15

2L44A	A18	2c rose		*250.00*
2L45	A18	10c yel brn	*100.00*	*75.00*
2L46	A18	15c brn ol	*90.00*	*75.00*

On Provisional Stamp of 1908 in Magenta

2L47	A19	5c yel & blk	7.50	7.50

Stamps with the above large handstamp in black instead of violet, are bogus. There are also excellent counterfeits in violet.

The foregoing overprints being handstamped are found in various positions, especially the last type.

Stamps of 1907 Type A18, Overprinted in Black or Violet

1907

2L48	A18	1c green	.30	.30
2L49	A18	2c rose	.30	.30
2L50	A18	3c violet	.30	.30
a.		Vert. pair, imperf. btwn.	*350.00*	
2L51	A18	4c brn org	.40	.40
2L52	A18	5c blue	.50	.50
2L53	A18	10c yel brn	.40	.40
2L54	A18	15c brn ol	.75	.75
2L55	A18	20c lake	.75	.75
2L56	A18	50c orange	1.90	1.50
2L57	A18	1p blk (V)	2.25	1.90
2L58	A18	2p dk grn	3.00	2.25
2L59	A18	5p violet	4.50	3.75
		Nos. 2L48-2L59 (12)	15.35	13.10

Nos. 237-248 Overprinted in Black

Imprint: American Bank Note Co.

1909 ***Perf. 12***

2L60	A18	1c yel grn	.35	.40
2L61	A18	2c vermilion	.35	.40
2L62	A18	3c red org	.35	.40
2L63	A18	4c violet	.35	.40
2L64	A18	5c dp bl	.35	.60
2L65	A18	6c gray brn	6.00	6.00
2L66	A18	10c lake	.60	.75
2L67	A18	15c black	.90	.90
2L68	A18	20c brn ol	1.00	1.10
2L69	A18	50c dp grn	2.50	2.50
2L70	A18	1p yellow	4.00	4.00
2L71	A18	2p car rose	5.75	5.75
		Nos. 2L60-2L71 (12)	22.50	23.20

No. 199 Overprinted Vertically

2L72	A18	50c on 6c slate (R)	7.50	7.50

OFFICIAL STAMPS

Official Stamps of 1907 Overprinted in Red or Violet

CABO

1907

2LO1	A18	10c on 1c green		*60.00*
2LO2	A18	15c on 1c green		*75.00*
2LO3	A18	20c on 1c green		*100.00*
2LO4	A18	50c on 1c green		*125.00*

NIGER

'nī-jər

LOCATION — Northern Africa, directly north of Nigeria
GOVT. — Republic
AREA — 458,075 sq. mi.
POP. — 6,265,000 (est. 1984)
CAPITAL — Niamey

The colony, formed in 1922, was originally a military territory.

100 Centimes = 1 Franc

Camel and Rider — A1

Stamps of Upper Senegal and Niger Type of 1914, Overprinted

1921-26 **Unwmk.** ***Perf. 13½x14***

1	A1	1c brn vio & vio	.20	.20
2	A1	2c dk gray & dl vio	.20	.20
3	A1	4c black & blue	.25	.25
4	A1	5c ol brn & dk brn	.25	.25
5	A1	10c yel grn & bl grn	1.10	1.10
6	A1	10c mag, *bluish* ('26)	.45	.45
7	A1	15c red brn & org	.30	.30
8	A1	20c brn vio & blk	.25	.25
9	A1	25c blk & bl grn	.45	.45
10	A1	30c red org & rose	2.00	2.00
11	A1	30c bl grn & red org ('26)	.60	.60
12	A1	35c rose & violet	.75	.75
13	A1	40c gray & rose	.60	.60
14	A1	45c blue & ol brn	.95	.95
15	A1	50c ultra & bl	.60	.60
16	A1	50c dk gray & bl vio ('25)	1.00	1.00
17	A1	60c org red ('26)	.90	.90
18	A1	75c yel & ol brn	1.00	1.00
19	A1	1fr dk brn & dl vio	1.10	1.10
20	A1	2fr green & blue	1.25	1.25
21	A1	5fr violet & blk	2.00	2.00
		Nos. 1-21 (21)	16.20	16.20

Stamps and Type of 1921 Surcharged New Value and Bars in Black or Red

1922-26

22	A1	25c on 15c red brn & org ('25)	.60	.60
a.		Multiple surcharge	125.00	
b.		"25c" inverted	90.00	
23	A1	25c on 2fr grn & bl (R) ('24)	.50	.50
24	A1	25c on 5fr vio & blk (R) ('24)	.60	.60
a.		Double surcharge	125.00	
25	A1	60c on 75c vio,*pnksh*	.50	.50
26	A1	65c on 45c bl & ol brn ('25)	2.00	2.00
27	A1	85c on 75c yel & ol brn ('25)	2.00	2.00
28	A1	1.25fr on 1fr dp bl & lt bl (R) ('26)	.65	.65
a.		Surcharge omitted	200.00	
		Nos. 22-28 (7)	6.85	6.85

Nos. 22-24 are surcharged "25c," No. 28, "1f25." Nos. 25-27 are surcharged like illustration.

Drawing Water from Well — A2

Zinder Fortress — A4

Boat on Niger River — A3

Perf. 13x14, 13½x14, 14x13, 14x13½

1926-40 **Typo.**

29	A2	1c lilac rose & olive	.20	.20
30	A2	2c dk gray & dl red	.20	.20
31	A2	3c red vio & ol gray ('40)	.20	.20
32	A2	4c amber & gray	.20	.20
33	A2	5c ver & yel grn	.20	.20
34	A2	10c dp bl & Prus bl	.20	.20
35	A2	15c gray grn & yel grn	.40	.35
36	A2	15c gray lil & lt red ('28)	.20	.20
37	A3	20c Prus grn & ol brn	.25	.20
38	A3	25c black & dl red	.25	.20
39	A3	30c bl grn & yel grn	.60	.55
40	A3	30c yel & red vio ('40)	.25	.20
41	A3	35c brn org & turq bl, *bluish*	.50	.50
42	A3	35c bl grn & dl grn ('38)	.75	.70
43	A3	40c red brn & slate	.25	.20
44	A3	45c yel & red vio	.95	.95
45	A3	45c bl grn & dl grn ('40)	.25	.20
46	A3	50c scar & grn, *grnsh*	.25	.20
47	A3	55c dk car & brn ('38)	1.40	1.40
48	A3	60c dk car & brn ('40)	.40	.35
49	A3	65c ol grn & rose	.25	.20
50	A3	70c ol grn & rose ('40)	1.25	1.25
51	A3	75c grn & vio, *pink*	1.25	1.25
52	A3	80c cl & ol grn ('38)	1.10	1.10
53	A3	90c brn red & ver	1.00	1.00
54	A3	90c brt rose & yel grn ('39)	1.25	1.25
55	A4	1fr rose & yel grn	6.25	5.00
56	A4	1fr dk red & red org ('38)	1.40	1.40
57	A4	1fr grn & red ('40)	.60	.60
58	A4	1.10fr ol brn & grn	2.75	2.75
59	A4	1.25fr grn & red ('33)	1.25	1.25
60	A4	1.25fr dk red & red org ('39)	.60	.55
61	A4	1.40fr red vio & dk brn ('40)	.60	.55
62	A4	1.50fr dp bl & pale bl	.30	.30
63	A4	1.60fr ol brn & grn ('40)	1.10	1.10
64	A4	1.75fr red vio & dk brn ('33)	2.40	2.25
65	A4	1.75fr dk bl & vio bl ('38)	.95	.95
66	A4	2fr red org & ol brn	.25	.20
67	A4	2.25fr dk bl & vio bl ('39)	.80	.80
68	A4	2.50fr blk brn ('40)	.75	.70
69	A4	3fr dl vio & blk ('27)	.40	.35
70	A4	5fr vio brn & blk, *pink*	.50	.50
71	A4	10fr chlky bl & mag	1.10	1.10
72	A4	20fr yel grn & red org	1.25	1.25
		Nos. 29-72 (44)	37.25	35.05

For surcharges see Nos. B7-B10 in the *Scott Standard Postage Stamp Catalogue*, Vol. 4.

Common Design Types pictured following the introduction.

Colonial Exposition Issue
Common Design Types

1931 **Typo.** ***Perf. 12½***

Name of Country in Black

73	CD70	40c deep green	4.00	4.00
74	CD71	50c violet	4.00	4.00
75	CD72	90c red orange	4.25	4.25
76	CD73	1.50fr dull blue	4.25	4.25
		Nos. 73-76 (4)	16.50	16.50

Paris International Exposition Issue
Common Design Types

1937 ***Perf. 13***

77	CD74	20c deep violet	1.10	1.10
78	CD75	30c dark green	1.10	1.10
79	CD76	40c carmine rose	1.25	1.25
80	CD77	50c dark brown	1.40	1.40
81	CD78	90c red	1.50	1.50
82	CD79	1.50fr ultra	1.50	1.50
		Nos. 77-82 (6)	7.85	7.85

Colonial Arts Exhibition Issue
Souvenir Sheet
Common Design Type

1937 ***Imperf.***

83	CD74	3fr magenta	6.50	*8.00*

Caillie Issue
Common Design Type

1939 ***Perf. 12½x12***

84	CD81	90c org brn & org	.80	.80
85	CD81	2fr brt violet	.80	.80
86	CD81	2.25fr ultra & dk bl	.80	.80
		Nos. 84-86 (3)	2.40	2.40

New York World's Fair Issue
Common Design Type

1939, May 10

87	CD82	1.25fr carmine lake	.85	.70
88	CD82	2.25fr ultra	.95	.80

SEMI-POSTAL STAMPS

Curie Issue
Common Design Type

1938 **Unwmk.** **Engr.** ***Perf. 13***

B1	CD80	1.75fr + 50c brt ultra	14.00	14.00

French Revolution Issue
Common Design Type

1939 **Photo.** ***Perf. 13***

Name and Value Typo. in Black

B2	CD83	45c + 25c grn	9.25	9.25
B3	CD83	70c + 30c brn	9.25	9.25
B4	CD83	90c + 35c red org	9.25	9.25
B5	CD83	1.25fr + 1fr rose pink	9.25	9.25
B6	CD83	2.25fr + 2fr blue	9.25	9.25
		Nos. B2-B6 (5)	46.25	46.25

AIR POST STAMPS

Common Design Type

1940 **Unwmk.** **Engr.** ***Perf. 12½x12***

C1	CD85	1.90fr ultra	.35	.20
C2	CD85	2.90fr dk red	.50	.30
C3	CD85	4.50fr dk gray grn	.80	.60
C4	CD85	4.90fr yel bis	.80	.80
C5	CD85	6.90fr dp org	.80	.80
		Nos. C1-C5 (5)	3.25	2.70

POSTAGE DUE STAMPS

D1

D2

Postage Due Stamps of Upper Senegal and Niger, 1914, Overprinted

1921 **Unwmk.** ***Perf. 14x13½***

J1	D1	5c green	.60	.60
J2	D1	10c rose	.60	.60
J3	D1	15c gray	.70	.70
J4	D1	20c brown	.70	.70
J5	D1	30c blue	.85	.85
J6	D1	50c black	.85	.85
J7	D1	60c orange	1.40	1.40
J8	D1	1fr violet	1.50	1.50
		Nos. J1-J8 (8)	7.20	7.20

1927 **Typo.**

J9	D2	2c dk bl & red	.20	.20
J10	D2	4c ver & blk	.20	.20
J11	D2	5c org & vio	.25	.25
J12	D2	10c red brn & blk vio	.25	.25
J13	D2	15c grn & org	.35	.35
J14	D2	20c cer & ol brn	.50	.50
J15	D2	25c blk & ol brn	.50	.50
J16	D2	30c dl vio & blk	1.10	1.10
J17	D2	50c dp red, *grnsh*	.85	.85
J18	D2	60c gray vio & org, *bluish*	.60	.60
J19	D2	1fr ind & ultra, *bluish*	.85	.85
J20	D2	2fr rose red & vio	.95	.95
J21	D2	3fr org brn & ultra	1.50	1.50
		Nos. J9-J21 (13)	8.10	8.10

NIGER COAST PROTECTORATE

ˈnī-jər ˈkōst prə-ˈtek-tə-ˌrət

(Oil Rivers Protectorate)

LOCATION — West coast of Africa on Gulf of Guinea

GOVT. — British Protectorate

This territory was originally known as the Oil Rivers Protectorate, and its affairs were conducted by the British Royal Niger Company. The Company surrendered its charter to the Crown in 1899. In 1900 all of the territories formerly controlled by the Royal Niger Company were incorporated into the two protectorates of Northern and Southern Nigeria, the latter absorbing the area formerly known as Niger Coast Protectorate. In 1914 Northern and Southern Nigeria joined to form the Crown Colony of Nigeria. (See Nigeria, Northern Nigeria, Southern Nigeria and Lagos.)

12 Pence = 1 Shilling

Stamps of Great Britain, 1881-87, Overprinted in Black

1892 **Wmk. 30** ***Perf. 14***

1	A54	½p vermilion	13.00	9.00
2	A40	1p lilac	8.00	9.00
a.		"OIL RIVERS" at top	*8,000.*	
b.		Half used as ½p on cover		*3,000.*
3	A56	2p green & car	27.50	9.00
a.		Half used as 1p on cover		—
4	A57	2½p violet, *bl*	7.50	2.50
5	A61	5p lilac & blue	11.00	7.25
6	A65	1sh green	62.50	*85.00*
		Nos. 1-6 (6)	129.50	121.75

For surcharges see Nos. 7-36, 50.

Dangerous forgeries exist of all surcharges.

No. 2 Surcharged in Red or Violet

1893

7	A40	½p on half of 1p (R)	175.	160.
c.		Unsevered pair	550.	500.
d.		"½" omitted		
7A	A40	½p on half of 1p (V)	*5,000.*	*4,750.*
b.		Surcharge double	*21,000.*	
c.		Unsevered pair	*13,500.*	*12,500.*

Nos. 3-6 Handstamp Surcharged in Violet, Red, Carmine, Bluish Black, Deep Blue, Green or Black

1893 **Wmk. 30** ***Perf. 14***

8	A56	½p on 2p (V)	*350.*	250.
9	A57	½p on 2½p (V)	3,500.	
10	A57	½p on 2½p (R)	325.	325.
11	A57	½p on 2½p (C)	*9,000.*	*6,500.*
12	A57	½p on 2½p (B)	*10,000.*	*6,500.*
13	A57	½p on 2½p (G)	475.	525.

14	A56	½p on 2p (V)	375.	375.
15	A56	½p on 2p (Bl)	1,700.	800.
16	A57	½p on 2½p (V)	*3,750.*	
17	A57	½p on 2½p (R)	525.	600.
18	A57	½p on 2½p (Bl)	400.	400.
19	A57	½p on 2½p (G)	425.	450.

20	A56	½p on 2p (V)	400.	300.
21	A57	½p on 2½p (R)	350.	350.
22	A57	½p on 2½p (C)	200.	200.
23	A57	½p on 2½p (Bl Bk)	*3,000.*	
24	A57	½p on 2½p (Bl)	325.	400.
25	A57	½p on 2½p (G)	250.	250.
26	A57	½p on 2½p (Bk)	*3,500.*	

HALF
PENNY

27	A57	½p on 2½p (R)	*7,250.*	
28	A57	½p on 2½p (G)	475.	475.

29	A56	1sh on 2p (V)	475.	400.
30	A56	1sh on 2p (R)	675.	*4,250.*
31	A56	1sh on 2p (Bk)	*6,250.*	

32	A56	5sh on 2d (V)	*10,250.*	*11,500.*
33	A61	10sh on 5p (R)	*6,750.*	*9,000.*
34	A65	20sh on 1sh (V)	*77,500.*	
35	A65	20sh on 1sh (R)	*77,500.*	
36	A65	20sh on 1sh (Bk)	*77,500.*	

The handstamped 1893 surcharges are known inverted, vertical, etc.

Queen Victoria
A8 A9

A10

A11

A12

A13

1893 Unwmk. *Perf. 12 to 15*

37	A8	½p vermilion	4.50	4.50
38	A9	1p light blue	6.75	3.75
a.		Half used as ½p on cover		600.00
39	A10	2p green	32.50	27.50
a.		Half used as 1p on cover		*800.00*
b.		Horiz. pair, imperf. between		*9,500.*
40	A11	2½p car lake	9.50	4.00
41	A12	5p gray lilac	19.00	13.50
a.		5p lilac	15.00	20.00
42	A13	1sh black	15.00	13.00
		Nos. 37-42 (6)	87.25	66.25

For surcharge see No. 49.

A15

A16

A17

A18

A19

A20

1894 Engr.

43	A15	½p yel green	5.00	5.00
44	A16	1p vermilion	15.00	9.00
a.		1p orange vermilion	17.50	11.00
b.		Diagonal half, used as ½p on cover		600.00
45	A17	2p car lake	35.00	7.25
a.		Half used as 1p on cover		
46	A18	2½p blue	15.00	4.25
47	A19	5p dp violet	7.25	6.00
48	A20	1sh black	45.00	16.00
		Nos. 43-48 (6)	122.25	47.50

See #55-59, 61. For surcharges see #51-54.

Halves of Nos. 38, 3 and 44 Surcharged in Red, Blue, Violet or Black:

½
No. 49

1
No. 50

½
Nos. 51-53

1894

49	A9	½p on half of 1p (R)	900.	375.
a.		Inverted surcharge	*5,000.*	

Perf. 14

Wmk. 30

50	A56	1p on half of 2p (R)	1,950.	400.
a.		Double surcharge	5,750.	1,350.
b.		Inverted surcharge		1,800.

Perf. 12 to 15

Unwmk.

51	A16	½p on half of 1p (Bl)	2,500.	475.
a.		Double surcharge		
52	A16	½p on half of 1p (V)	3,500.	750.
53	A16	½p on half of 1p (Bk)	*4,500.*	*1,150.*

This surcharge is found on both vertical and diagonal halves of the 1p.

No. 46 Surcharged in Black

1894

54	A18	½p on 2½p blue	425.	250.
a.		Double surcharge	4,500.	1,750.

The surcharge is found in eight types. The "OIE" variety is broken type.

A27

A28

A29

1897-98 Wmk. 2

55	A15	½p yel green	3.75	1.75
56	A16	1p vermilion	5.00	1.60
57	A17	2p car lake	4.50	2.50
58	A18	2½p blue	9.50	2.25
a.		2½p slate blue	8.50	2.25
59	A19	5p dp violet	10.00	*70.00*
60	A27	6p yel brn ('98)	8.00	7.25
61	A20	1sh black	17.50	*32.50*
62	A28	2sh6p olive bister	25.00	*90.00*
63	A29	10sh dp pur ('98)	110.00	*190.00*
a.		10sh bright purple	110.00	*190.00*
		Nos. 55-63 (9)	193.25	*397.85*

The stamps of Niger Coast Protectorate were superseded in Jan. 1900, by those of Northern and Southern Nigeria.

NIGERIA

nī-ˈjir-ē-ə

LOCATION — West coast of Africa, bordering on the Gulf of Guinea
GOVT. — Republic
AREA — 356,669 sq. mi.
POP. — 82,390,000 (est. 1983)
CAPITAL — Lagos

The colony and protectorate were formed in 1914 by the union of Northern and Southern Nigeria. The mandated territory of Cameroons (British) was also attached for administrative purposes. See Niger Coast Protectorate, Lagos, Northern Nigeria and Southern Nigeria.

12 Pence = 1 Shilling
20 Shillings = 1 Pound

Catalogue values for unused stamps in this country are for Never Hinged items, beginning with Scott 71 in the regular postage section.

King George V — A1

Numerals of 3p, 4p, 6p, 5sh and £1 of type A1 are in color on plain tablet.
Dies I and II are described at front of this volume.

Wmk. Multiple Crown and CA (3)

1914-27 Typo. *Perf. 14*

Die I

Ordinary Paper

1	A1	½p green	3.00	.50
a.		Booklet pane of 6		
2	A1	1p carmine	5.25	.20
a.		Booklet pane of 6		
b.		1p scarlet ('16)	7.50	.25
3	A1	2p gray	9.00	2.00
a.		2p slate gray ('18)	10.00	.85
4	A1	2½p ultramarine	7.25	3.25
a.		2½p dull blue ('15)	17.50	5.50

Chalky Paper

5	A1	3p violet, *yel*	1.60	3.00
6	A1	4p black & red, *yel*	1.10	*4.75*
7	A1	6p dull vio & red vio	10.00	11.00
8	A1	1sh black, *green*	1.10	*10.00*
a.		1sh black, *emerald*	1.40	*15.00*
b.		1sh black, *bl grn,* ol back	30.00	30.00
c.		As "a," olive back ('20)	9.00	*42.50*
9	A1	2sh6p blk & red, *bl*	17.50	7.25
10	A1	5sh grn & red, *yel,* white back	15.00	*62.50*
11	A1	10sh grn & red, *grn*	50.00	*95.00*
a.		10sh grn & red, *emer*	40.00	*110.00*
b.		10sh green & red, *blue grn,* olive back	900.00	*1,500.*
c.		As "a," olive back	110.00	160.00
12	A1	£1 vio & blk, *red*	190.00	*225.00*
a.		Die II ('27)	200.00	*325.00*
		Nos. 1-12 (12)	310.80	*424.45*

Surface-colored Paper

13	A1	3p violet, *yel*	3.50	*11.00*
14	A1	4p black & red, *yel*	1.60	*11.50*
15	A1	1sh black, *green*	1.60	*25.00*
a.		1sh black, *emerald*		
16	A1	5sh grn & red, *yel*	15.00	*55.00*
17	A1	10sh grn & red, *grn*	50.00	*150.00*
		Nos. 13-17 (5)	71.70	*252.50*

1921-33 Wmk. 4

Die II

Ordinary Paper

18	A1	½p green	4.00	.90
a.		Die I	1.25	.40
19	A1	1p carmine	1.75	.55
a.		Booklet pane of 6	27.50	
b.		Die I	3.00	.35
c.		Booklet pane of 6, Die I	35.00	
20	A1	1½p orange ('31)	4.50	.20
21	A1	2p gray	8.50	.50
a.		Die I	1.60	*5.50*
b.		Booklet pane of 6, Die I	55.00	
22	A1	2p red brown ('27)	5.00	1.00
a.		Booklet pane of 6	60.00	
23	A1	2p dk brown ('28)	1.40	.20
a.		Booklet pane of 6	27.50	
b.		Die I ('32)	6.00	.50
24	A1	2½p ultra (die I)	1.10	6.75
25	A1	3p dp violet	11.00	1.10
a.		Die I ('24)	5.50	3.50
26	A1	3p ultra ('31)	6.75	1.10

Chalky Paper

27	A1	4p blk & red, *yel*	.70	.60
a.		Die I ('32)	6.25	7.75
28	A1	6p dull vio & red vio	8.00	9.00
a.		Die I	14.00	22.50
29	A1	1sh black, *emerald*	1.40	*2.25*
30	A1	2sh6p blk & red, *bl*	7.25	*29.00*
a.		Die I ('32)	45.00	*72.50*
31	A1	5sh green & red, *yel* ('26)	16.00	*72.50*
a.		Die I ('32)	72.50	*200.00*
32	A1	10sh green & red, *emer*	67.50	*200.00*
a.		Die I ('32)	110.00	*450.00*
		Nos. 18-32 (15)	144.85	325.65

Silver Jubilee Issue

Common Design Type

1935, May 6 Engr. *Perf. 11x12*

34	CD301	1½p black & ultra	.75	*.50*
35	CD301	2p indigo & green	1.50	*.75*
36	CD301	3p ultra & brown	3.25	*7.50*
37	CD301	1sh brown vio & ind	3.25	*17.50*
		Nos. 34-37 (4)	8.75	*26.25*
		Set, never hinged	16.50	

Wharf at Apapa — A2

Picking Cacao Pods — A3

Dredging for Tin — A4

Timber — A5

Fishing Village — A6

Ginning Cotton — A7

Minaret at Habe — A8

Fulani Cattle — A9

Victoria-Buea Road — A10

Oil Palms A11

View of Niger at Jebba
A12

Nigerian Canoe
A13

1936, Feb. 1 *Perf. 11½x13*

38 A2 ½p green .50 .50
39 A3 1p rose car .30 .30
40 A4 1½p brown 1.50 .30
a. Perf. 12½x13½ 60.00 4.50
41 A5 2p black .50 .50
42 A6 3p dark blue 1.75 1.00
a. Perf. 12½x13½ 110.00 25.00
43 A7 4p red brown 2.00 2.00
44 A8 6p dull violet .70 .60
45 A9 1sh olive green 2.25 10.00

Perf. 14

46 A10 2sh6p ultra & blk 5.00 22.50
47 A11 5sh ol grn & blk 14.00 27.50
48 A12 10sh slate & blk 50.00 90.00
49 A13 £1 orange & blk 80.00 160.00
Nos. 38-49 (12) 158.50 315.20
Set, never hinged 325.00

Common Design Types pictured following the introduction.

Coronation Issue
Common Design Type

1937, May 12 *Perf. 11x11½*

50 CD302 1p dark carmine .20 .20
51 CD302 1½p dark brown .55 .25
52 CD302 3p deep ultra .65 .30
Nos. 50-52 (3) 1.40 .75
Set, never hinged 3.50

George VI — A14

Victoria-Buea Road — A15

Niger at Jebba
A16

1938-51 **Wmk. 4** *Perf. 12*

53 A14 ½p deep green .20 .20
a. Perf. 11½ ('50) .20 .20
54 A14 1p dk carmine .20 .20
55 A14 1½p red brown .20 .20
a. Perf. 11½ ('50) .20 .20
56 A14 2p black .30 .20
57 A14 2½p orange ('41) .20 .20
58 A14 3p deep blue .20 .20
59 A14 4p orange 32.50 4.25
60 A14 6p brown violet .20 .20
a. Perf. 11½ ('51) .30 .20
61 A14 1sh olive green .35 .20
a. Perf. 11½ ('50) .35 .20
62 A14 1sh3p turq blue ('40) .50 .20
a. Perf. 11½ ('50) .50 .20
63 A15 2sh6p ultra & blk ('51) 4.50 2.75
a. Perf. 13½ ('42) 1.90 .70
b. Perf. 14 ('42) 1.90 .70
c. Perf. 13x11½ 42.50 9.50
64 A16 5sh org & blk, perf. 13½ ('42) 3.00 1.10
a. Perf. 12 ('49) 5.00 1.10
b. Perf. 14 ('48) 3.00 1.10
c. Perf. 13x11½ 75.00 9.00

1944, Dec. 1 *Perf. 12*

65 A14 1p red violet .20 .20
a. Perf. 11½ ('50) .20 .20
66 A14 2p deep red .20 .20
a. Perf. 11½ ('50) .20 .20
67 A14 3p black .20 .20
68 A14 4p dark blue .20 .20
Nos. 53-68 (16) 43.15 10.70
Set, never hinged 80.00

Issue date: Nos. 65a, 66a, Feb. 15.

Catalogue values for unused stamps in this section, from this point to the end of the section, are for Never Hinged items.

Peace Issue
Common Design Type

1946, Oct. 21 Engr. *Perf. 13½x14*

71 CD303 1½p brown .35 .20
72 CD303 4p deep blue .35 .35

Silver Wedding Issue
Common Design Types

1948, Dec. 20 Photo. *Perf. 14x14½*

73 CD304 1p brt red violet .35 .30

Perf. 11½x11

Engraved; Name Typographed

74 CD305 5sh brown orange 6.75 9.00

UPU Issue
Common Design Types

Engr.; Name Typo. on 3p, 6p
Perf. 13½, 11x11½

1949, Oct. 10 **Wmk. 4**

75 CD306 1p red violet .20 .20
76 CD307 3p indigo .40 .30
77 CD308 6p rose violet .90 .75
78 CD309 1sh olive 1.50 1.25
Nos. 75-78 (4) 3.00 2.50

NIUE

nē-'ü-ˌāˌā

LOCATION — Island in the south Pacific Ocean, northeast of New Zealand
AREA — 100 sq. mi.
POP. — 3,019 (est. 1984)
CAPITAL — Alofi

Niue, also known as Savage Island, was annexed to New Zealand in 1901 with the Cook Islands.

12 Pence = 1 Shilling
20 Shillings = 1 Pound

Catalogue values for unused stamps in this country are for Never Hinged items, beginning with Scott 90 in the regular postage section.

Watermarks

Wmk. 61 — Single-lined NZ and Star Close Together

Wmk. 253 — NZ and Star

New Zealand No. 100 Handstamped in Green **NIUE**

1902 **Wmk. 63** *Perf. 11*
Thick Soft Paper

1 A35 1p carmine 375.00 375.00

Stamps of New Zealand Surcharged in Carmine, Vermilion or Blue:

1/2p

1p

2 1/2p

Perf. 14
Thin Hard Paper

3 A18 ½p green (C) 3.00 4.50
a. Inverted surcharge 300.00 500.00
4 A35 1p carmine (Bl), perf. 11x14 2.00 2.75
a. No period after "PENI" 35.00 50.00
b. Perf. 14 22.50 25.00
c. As "a," perf. 14 300.00 350.00

Perf. 14
Wmk. 61

6 A18 ½p green (V) 1.10 1.10
7 A35 1p carmine (Bl) .85 1.10
a. No period after "PENI" 9.00 16.00
b. Double surcharge 1,400. 1,500.

Perf. 11
Unwmk.

8 A22 2½p blue (C) 4.00 4.50
a. No period after "PENI" 45.00 47.50
9 A22 2½p blue (V) 1.75 2.00
a. No period after "PENI" 20.00 25.00

The surcharge on the ½ & 1p stamps is printed in blocks of 60. Two stamps in each block have a space between the "U" and "E" of "NIUE" and one of the 1p stamps has a broken "E" like an "F."

Blue Surcharge on Stamps of New Zealand, Types of 1898:

e

f

g

NIUE.
Tahae Sileni.
h

1903 **Wmk. 61** *Perf. 11*

10 A23(e) 3p yellow brown 11.00 5.50
11 A26(f) 6p rose 14.00 12.50
13 A29(g) 1sh brown red 40.00 40.00
a. 1sh scarlet 40.00 40.00
b. 1sh orange red 50.00 52.50
c. As "b," surcharge "h" (error) 750.00
Nos. 10-13 (3) 65.00 58.00

Surcharged in Carmine or Blue on Stamps of New Zealand

j

1911-12 *Perf. 14, 14x14½*

14 A41(j) ½p yellow grn (C) .60 .70
15 A41(f) 6p car rose (Bl) 2.50 7.50
16 A41(g) 1sh vermilion (Bl) 8.00 50.00
Nos. 14-16 (3) 11.10 58.20

1915 *Perf. 14*

18 A22(d) 2½p dark blue (C) 17.50 35.00

Surcharged in Brown or Dark Blue on Stamps of New Zealand

1917 *Perf. 14x13½, 14x14½*

19 A42 1p carmine (Br) 12.50 6.25
a. No period after "PENI" 350.00
20 A45(e) 3p violet brn (Bl) 50.00 90.00
a. No period after "Pene" 850.00

New Zealand Stamps of 1909-19 Overprinted in Dark Blue or Red

k

1917-20 **Typo.**

21 A43 ½p yellow grn (R) .80 2.75
22 A42 1p carmine (Bl) 11.00 10.00
23 A47 1½p gray black (R) 1.10 2.50
24 A47 1½p brown org (R) 1.00 4.75
25 A43 3p chocolate (Bl) 1.60 30.00

Engr.

26 A44 2½p dull blue (R) 3.00 8.50
27 A45 3p violet brown (Bl) 1.75 2.25
28 A45 6p car rose (Bl) 7.00 26.00
29 A45 1sh vermilion (Bl) 10.00 27.50
Nos. 21-29 (9) 37.25 114.25

Same Overprint On Postal-Fiscal Stamps of New Zealand, 1906-15

Perf. 14, 14½ and Compound

1918-23

30 PF1 2sh blue (R) 18.00 35.00
31 PF1 2sh6p bn (Bl) ('23) 24.00 55.00
32 PF1 5sh green (R) 29.00 57.50
33 PF1 10sh red brn (Bl) ('23) 110.00 150.00
34 PF2 £1 rose (Bl) ('23) 160.00 210.00
Nos. 30-34 (5) 341.00 507.50

Landing of Captain Cook
A16

Avarua Waterfront
A17

Capt. James Cook — A18

Coconut Palm — A19

Arorangi Village — A20

Avarua Harbor — A21

Unwmk.

1920, Aug. 23 **Engr.** *Perf. 14*

35 A16 ½p yel grn & blk 4.25 4.25
36 A17 1p car & black 2.25 1.40
37 A18 1½p red & black 2.75 9.00
38 A19 3p pale blue & blk 1.00 16.00
39 A20 6p dp grn & red brn 2.00 21.00
a. Center inverted 500.00
40 A21 1sh blk brn & blk 2.00 21.00
Nos. 35-40 (6) 14.25 72.65

See Nos. 41-42. For surcharge see No. 48.

Types of 1920 Issue and

Rarotongan Chief (Te Po) — A22

Avarua Harbor — A23

1925-27 **Wmk. 61**

41	A16	½p yel grn & blk ('26)	1.60	*9.00*
42	A17	1p car & black	2.00	1.00
43	A22	2½p dk blue & blk ('27)	4.50	*12.00*
44	A23	4p dull vio & blk ('27)	8.00	*22.50*
		Nos. 41-44 (4)	16.10	*44.50*

New Zealand No. 182 Overprinted Type "k" in Red

1927

47	A56	2sh blue	18.00	*35.00*
a.		2sh dark blue	17.00	*37.50*

No. 37 Surcharged

1931 **Unwmk.** ***Perf. 14***

48	A18	2p on 1½p red & blk	2.00	1.10

New Zealand Postal-Fiscal Stamps of 1931-32 Overprinted Type "k" in Blue or Red

1931, Nov. 12 **Wmk. 61**

49	PF5	2sh6p deep brown	5.00	13.00
50	PF5	5sh green (R)	40.00	*75.00*
51	PF5	10sh dark car	40.00	*100.00*
52	PF5	£1 pink ('32)	65.00	*150.00*
		Nos. 49-52 (4)	150.00	*338.00*

See Nos. 86-89D, 116-119.

Landing of Captain Cook — A24

Capt. James Cook — A25

Polynesian Migratory Canoe — A26

Islanders Unloading Ship — A27

View of Avarua Harbor — A28

R.M.S. Monowai — A29

King George V — A30

Perf. 13, 14 (4p, 1sh)

1932, Mar. 16 **Engr.** **Unwmk.**

53	A24	½p yel grn & blk	10.00	*25.00*
a.		Perf. 14x13	275.00	
54	A25	1p dp red & blk	1.10	.55
55	A26	2p org brn & blk	2.75	*4.50*
56	A27	2½p indigo & blk	8.50	*80.00*
57	A28	4p Prus blue & blk	16.00	*57.50*
a.		Perf. 13	15.00	*62.50*
58	A29	6p dp org & blk	2.75	2.25
59	A30	1sh dull vio & blk	2.50	*5.50*
		Nos. 53-59 (7)	43.60	*175.30*

For types overprinted see Nos. 67-69.

1933-36 **Wmk. 61** ***Perf. 14***

60	A24	½p yel grn & blk	.50	*3.50*
61	A25	1p deep red & blk	.50	*1.50*
62	A26	2p brown & blk ('36)	.50	*1.50*
63	A27	2½p indigo & blk	.50	*4.75*
64	A28	4p Prus blue & blk	2.00	*4.00*
65	A29	6p org & blk ('36)	.80	*.90*
66	A30	1sh dk vio & blk ('36)	9.00	*25.00*
		Nos. 60-66 (7)	13.80	*41.15*

See Nos. 77-82.

Silver Jubilee Issue

Types of 1932 Overprinted in Black or Red

1935, May 7 ***Perf. 14***

67	A25	1p car & brown red	.80	*2.00*
68	A27	2½p indigo & bl (R)	3.50	*6.00*
a.		Vert. pair, imperf. horiz.	275.00	
69	A29	6p dull org & grn	3.50	*5.00*
		Nos. 67-69 (3)	7.80	*13.00*
		Set, never hinged	14.50	

The vertical spacing of the overprint is wider on No. 69.

No. 68a is from proof sheets.

Coronation Issue

New Zealand Stamps of 1937 Overprinted in Black

Perf. 13½x13

1937, May 13 **Wmk. 253**

70	A78	1p rose carmine	.20	.20
71	A78	2½p dark blue	.20	*1.00*
72	A78	6p vermilion	.30	.30
		Nos. 70-72 (3)	.70	*1.50*
		Set, never hinged	1.25	

George VI — A31

Village Scene — A32

Coastal Scene with Canoe — A33

Mt. Ikurangi behind Avarua — A34

1938, May 2 **Wmk. 61** ***Perf. 14***

73	A31	1sh dp violet & blk	7.50	6.00
74	A32	2sh dk red brown & blk	10.00	*12.00*
75	A33	3sh yel green & blue	27.50	12.00
		Nos. 73-75 (3)	45.00	30.00
		Set, never hinged	65.00	

See Nos. 83-85.

Perf. 13½x14

1940, Sept. 2 **Engr.** **Wmk. 253**

76	A34	3p on 1½p rose vio & blk	.30	.30
		Never hinged	.40	

Examples without surcharge are from printer's archives.

Types of 1932-38

1944-46 **Wmk. 253** ***Perf. 14***

77	A24	½p yel grn & blk	.40	*2.25*
78	A25	1p dp red & blk ('45)	.40	*1.25*
79	A26	2p org brn & blk ('46)	4.00	*6.00*
80	A27	2½p dk bl & blk ('45)	.50	*1.00*
81	A28	4p Prus blue & blk	3.00	.90
82	A29	6p dp orange & blk	1.40	1.40
83	A31	1sh dp vio & blk	.85	1.00
84	A32	2sh brn car & blk ('45)	9.00	3.75
85	A33	3sh yel grn & bl ('45)	12.00	8.50
		Nos. 77-85 (9)	31.55	26.05
		Set, never hinged	40.00	

New Zealand Postal-Fiscal Stamps Overprinted Type "k" (narrow "E") in Blue or Red

1941-45 **Wmk. 61** ***Perf. 14***

86	PF5	2sh6p brown	55.00	*60.00*
87	PF5	5sh green (R)	225.00	150.00
88	PF5	10sh rose	95.00	*150.00*
89	PF5	£1 pink	150.00	*225.00*
		Nos. 86-89 (4)	525.00	*585.00*
		Set, never hinged	725.00	

Wmk. 253

89A	PF5	2sh6p brown	2.50	*10.00*
89B	PF5	5sh green (R)	5.25	*11.00*
e.		5sh light yellow green, wmkd. sideways ('67)	30.00	*80.00*
89C	PF5	10sh rose	37.50	*100.00*
89D	PF5	£1 pink	30.00	*60.00*
		Nos. 89A-89D (4)	75.25	*181.00*
		Set, never hinged	110.00	

No. 89Be exists in both line and comb perf.

Catalogue values for unused stamps in this section, from this point to the end of the section, are for Never Hinged items.

Peace Issue

New Zealand Nos. 248, 250, 254 and 255 Overprinted in Black or Blue:

p

q

1946, June 4 ***Perf. 13x13½, 13½x13***

90	A94 (p)	1p emerald	.20	.20
91	A96 (q)	2p rose violet (Bl)	.20	.20
92	A100 (p)	6p org red & red brn	.20	.20
93	A101 (p)	8p brn lake & blk (Bl)	.25	.25
		Nos. 90-93 (4)	.85	.85

Map of Niue — A35

Thatched Dwelling — A36

Designs: 1p, H.M.S. Resolution. 2p, Alofi landing. 4p, Arch at Hikutavake. 6p, Alofi bay. 9p, Fisherman. 1sh, Cave at Makefu. 2sh, Gathering bananas. 3sh, Matapa Chasm.

Perf. 14x13½, 13½x14

1950, July 3 **Engr.** **Wmk. 253**

94	A35	½p red orange & bl	.20	.20
95	A36	1p green & brown	2.50	2.00
96	A36	2p rose car & blk	1.10	1.00
97	A36	3p blue vio & blue	.25	.20
98	A36	4p brn vio & ol grn	.40	.30
99	A36	6p brn org & bl grn	.70	*1.10*
100	A35	9p dk brn & brn org	.85	*1.00*
101	A36	1sh black & purple	1.00	.85
102	A35	2sh dp grn & brn org	1.35	*3.00*
103	A35	3sh black & dp blue	4.00	3.00
		Nos. 94-103 (10)	12.35	*12.65*

For surcharges see Nos. 106-115.

NORTH BORNEO

'north 'bor-nē-ˌō

LOCATION — Northeast part of island of Borneo, Malay archipelago

AREA — 29,388 sq. mi.

POP. — 470,000 (est. 1962)

CAPITAL — Jesselton

The British North Borneo Company administered North Borneo, under a royal charter granted in 1881.

100 Cents = 1 Dollar

Quantities of most North Borneo stamps through 1912 have been canceled to order with an oval of bars. Values given for used stamps beginning with No. 6 are for those with this form of cancellation. Stamps from No. 6 through Nos. 159 and J31 that do not exist cto have used values in italics. Stamps with dated town cancellations sell for much higher prices.

Catalogue values for unused stamps in this country are for Never Hinged items, beginning with Scott 238.

North Borneo

Coat of Arms — A1

1883-84 **Unwmk.** **Litho.** ***Perf. 12***

1	A1	2c brown	30.00	*60.00*
a.		Horiz. pair, imperf. btwn.		
2	A1	4c rose ('84)	47.50	*55.00*
3	A1	8c green ('84)	90.00	*60.00*
		Nos. 1-3 (3)	167.50	*175.00*

For surcharges see Nos. 4, 19-21.

No. 1 Surcharged in Black **EIGHT CENTS**

4	A1	8c on 2c brown	500.00	*210.00*
a.		Double surcharge		*4,500.*

Coat of Arms with Supporters
A4 A5

Perf. 14

6	A4	50c violet	140.00	27.50
7	A5	$1 red	125.00	12.50

1886 ***Perf. 14***

8	A1	½c magenta	110.00	*200.00*
9	A1	1c orange	*210.00*	*350.00*
a.		Imperf., pair	300.00	
b.		Vert. pair, imperf horiz.	1,100.	
10	A1	2c brown	27.50	25.00
a.		Horiz. pair, imperf. between	675.00	
11	A1	4c rose	20.00	*50.00*
12	A1	8c green	21.00	*50.00*
a.		Horiz. pair, imperf. between	*900.00*	
13	A1	10c blue	32.50	*50.00*
a.		Imperf., pair	375.00	
		Nos. 8-13 (6)	421.00	*725.00*

Nos. 8, 11, 12 and 13 Surcharged or Overprinted in Black:

b

c

d

1886

14	A1 (b)	½c magenta	130.00	*210.00*
15	A1 (c)	3c on 4c rose	75.00	*110.00*
16	A1 (d)	3c on 4c rose	1,500.	
17	A1 (c)	5c on 8c green	82.50	*110.00*
a.		Inverted surcharge	2,000.	
18	A1 (b)	10c blue	190.00	*210.00*

On Nos. 2 and 3

Perf. 12

19	A1 (c)	3c on 4c rose	200.00	*250.00*
20	A1 (d)	3c on 4c rose		*6,000.*
a.		Double surcharge, both types of "3"		
21	A1 (c)	5c on 8c green	225.00	*250.00*

British North Borneo

A9

1886 Unwmk. Litho. *Perf. 12*

22	A9	½c lilac rose	200.00	*400.00*
23	A9	1c orange	160.00	*200.00*

Perf. 14

25	A9	½c rose	3.00	*50.00*
a.		½c lilac rose	*16.00*	45.00
b.		Imperf., pair	40.00	
26	A9	1c orange	2.25	*9.00*
a.		Imperf., pair	35.00	
27	A9	2c brown	2.25	*9.50*
a.		Imperf., pair	35.00	
b.		Horiz. pair, imperf. between	*57.50*	
28	A9	4c rose	3.50	*11.00*
a.		Cliché of 1c in plate of 4c	250.00	*600.00*
b.		Imperf., pair	40.00	
c.		As "a," imperf. in pair with #28	4,500.	
d.		Horiz. pair, imperf vert.	300.00	
29	A9	8c green	12.50	*20.00*
a.		Imperf., pair	37.50	
30	A9	10c blue	8.00	*27.50*
a.		Imperf., pair	35.00	
b.		Vert. pair, imperf btwn.	400.00	
		Nos. 25-30 (6)	31.50	*127.00*

For surcharges see Nos. 54-55.

A10

A11

A12

A13

31	A10	25c slate blue	210.00	14.00
a.		Imperf., pair	325.00	30.00
32	A11	50c violet	300.00	16.00
a.		Imperf., pair	425.00	30.00
33	A12	$1 red	350.00	14.00
a.		Imperf., pair	425.00	30.00
34	A13	$2 sage green	425.00	20.00
a.		Imperf., pair	325.00	35.00
		Nos. 31-34 (4)	1,285.	64.00
		Nos. 22-34 (12)	1,676.	*791.00*

See Nos. 44-47.

A14

1887-92 *Perf. 14*

35	A14	½c rose	1.25	.50
a.		½c magenta	4.00	*3.00*
36	A14	1c orange	2.25	.50
37	A14	2c red brown	9.50	1.00
a.		Horiz. pair imperf. between		*425.00*
38	A14	3c violet	2.75	.40
39	A14	4c rose	6.75	.40
a.		Horiz. pair, imperf. vert.		
40	A14	5c slate	3.00	.40
41	A14	6c lake ('92)	9.00	.40
42	A14	8c green	21.00	.90
a.		Horiz. pair, imperf. between		
43	A14	10c blue	7.25	.40
		Nos. 35-43 (9)	62.75	4.90

Exist imperf. Value $8 each, unused, $4.50 used. Forgeries exist, perf. 11½.

For surcharges see Nos. 52-53, 56-57.

Redrawn

25c. The letters of "BRITISH NORTH BORNEO" are 2mm high instead of 1½mm.

50c. The club of the native at left does not touch the frame. The 0's of "50" are flat at top and bottom instead of being oval.

$1.00. The spear of the native at right does not touch the frame. There are 14 pearls at each side of the frame instead of 13.

$2.00. "BRITISH" is 11mm long instead of 12mm. There are only six oars at the side of the dhow.

1888

44	A10	25c slate blue	65.00	.75
b.		Horiz. pair, imperf. between		
c.		Imperf., pair	225.00	17.50
45	A11	50c violet	95.00	.75
a.		Imperf., pair	325.00	17.50
46	A12	$1 red	30.00	.75
a.		Imperf., pair	225.00	17.50
47	A13	$2 sage green	140.00	1.40
a.		Imperf., pair	400.00	20.00
		Nos. 44-47 (4)	330.00	3.65

For surcharges see Nos. 50-51, 58.

A15

A16

1889

48	A15	$5 red violet	240.00	9.00
a.		Imperf., pair	500.00	40.00
49	A16	$10 brown	300.00	12.50
b.		Imperf., pair	675.00	45.00

e

f

No. 44 Surcharged Type "e" in Red

1890

50	A10	2c on 25c slate blue	75.00	*100.00*
a.		Inverted surcharge	450.00	*450.00*
b.		With additional surcharge "2 cents" in black		
51	A10	8c on 25c slate blue	105.00	*125.00*

Surcharged Type "f" in Black On #42-43

1891-92

52	A14	6c on 8c green	25.00	*11.00*
a.		"c" of "cents" inverted	500.00	*550.00*
b.		"cetns"	500.00	*550.00*
c.		Inverted surcharge	450.00	*500.00*
53	A14	6c on 10c blue	160.00	*27.50*

On Nos. 29 and 30

54	A9	6c on 8c green	9,000.	*4,750.*
55	A9	6c on 10c blue	67.50	*22.50*
a.		Inverted surcharge	275.00	*290.00*
b.		Double surcharge	1,000.	
c.		Triple surcharge	500.00	

Nos. 39, 40 and 44 Surcharged in Red:

8
Cents.

1892

56	A14	1c on 4c rose	25.00	15.00
a.		Double surcharge	1,350.	
b.		Surcharged on face & back		*675.00*
57	A14	1c on 5c slate	8.00	6.50
58	A10	8c on 25c blue	150.00	*175.00*
		Nos. 56-58 (3)	183.00	*196.50*

North Borneo

Dyak Chief — A21

Malayan Sambar — A22

Malay Dhow — A26

Sago Palm — A23

Saltwater Crocodile — A27

Argus Pheasant A24

Mt. Kinabalu A28

Coat of Arms — A25

Coat of Arms with Supporters — A29

A30

A31

A32

A33

A34

A35

Perf. 12 to 15 and Compound

1894 Engr. Unwmk.

59	A21	1c bis brn & blk	1.40	.40
a.		Vert. pair, imperf. btwn.		
60	A22	2c rose & black	4.00	.75
61	A23	3c vio & ol green	4.00	.55
a.		Horiz. pair, imperf. btwn.	—	*725.00*
62	A24	5c org red & blk	3.25	.75
a.		Horiz. pair, imperf. btwn.	625.00	
63	A25	6c brn ol & blk	3.00	.55
64	A26	8c lilac & black	2.50	.75
a.		Vert. pair, imperf. btwn.	475.00	*350.00*
b.		Horiz. pair, imperf. btwn.	*475.00*	
65	A27	12c ultra & black	45.00	3.00
a.		12c blue & black	30.00	2.75
66	A28	18c green & black	30.00	2.00
67	A29	24c claret & blue	25.00	2.00

Litho. *Perf. 14*

68	A30	25c slate blue	10.00	.80
a.		Imperf., pair	40.00	9.00
69	A31	50c violet	25.00	2.00
a.		Imperf., pair		9.00
70	A32	$1 red	12.50	1.25
a.		Perf. 14x11	275.00	
b.		Imperf., pair	37.50	9.50
71	A33	$2 gray green	22.50	2.75
a.		Imperf., pair		14.00
72	A34	$5 red violet	225.00	9.00
a.		Imperf., pair	425.00	45.00
73	A35	$10 brown	250.00	16.00
a.		Imperf., pair	425.00	45.00
		Nos. 59-73 (15)	663.15	42.55

For #68-70 in other colors see Labuan #63a-65a.

For surcharges & overprints see #74-78, 91-94, 97-102, 115-119, 130-135, 115-119, 150-151, 158-159, J1-J8.

No. 70 Surcharged in Black

1895, June

74	A32	4c on $1 red	7.00	1.25
a.		Double surcharge	1,000.	
75	A32	10c on $1 red	21.00	.60
76	A32	20c on $1 red	45.00	.60
77	A32	30c on $1 red	32.50	.75
78	A32	40c on $1 red	32.50	.80
		Nos. 74-78 (5)	138.00	4.00

See No. 99.

A37

A38

A39

A40

A41

A42

A43

"Postal Revenue" — A44

No "Postal Revenue" — A45

Perf. 13 to 16 and Compound

1897-1900 **Engr.**

79	A37	1c bis brn & blk	12.00	.55
a.		Horiz. pair, imperf. btwn.		525.00
80	A38	2c dp rose & blk	25.00	.55
81	A38	2c grn & blk ('00)	50.00	.55
82	A39	3c lilac & ol green	20.00	.55
83	A40	5c orange & black	100.00	.50
84	A41	6c ol brown & blk	30.00	.45
85	A42	8c brn lilac & blk	12.50	.50
86	A43	12c blue & black	100.00	1.50
87	A44	18c green & black	25.00	1.50
a.		Vert. pair, imperf. btwn.		*350.00*
b.		Horiz. pair, imperf. vert.		*95.00*
c.		Imperf, pair		*200.00*
88	A45	24c claret & blue	11.00	.85
		Nos. 79-88 (10)	385.50	7.50

For overprints and surcharges see Nos. 105-107, 109-112, 124-127, J9-J17, J20-J22, J24-J26, J28.

"Postage & Revenue"
A46 A47

1897

89	A46	18c green & black	100.00	1.75
90	A47	24c claret & blue	80.00	2.10

For surcharges & overprints see #95-96, 128-129, 113-114, J18-J19, J30-J31.

Stamps of 1894-97 Surcharged in Black

1899

91	A40	4c on 5c org & blk	27.50	*12.50*
92	A41	4c on 6c ol brn & blk	20.00	*25.00*
93	A42	4c on 8c brn lil & blk	16.00	*13.00*
94	A43	4c on 12c bl & blk	25.00	*15.00*
a.		Horiz. pair, imperf. btwn.	675.00	
b.		Vert. pair, imperf. btwn.		725.00
95	A46	4c on 18c grn & blk	11.00	*18.00*
96	A47	4c on 24c cl & blue	20.00	*20.00*
a.		Perf. 16	55.00	*55.00*
97	A30	4c on 25c sl blue	6.00	*10.00*
98	A31	4c on 50c violet	10.00	*18.00*
99	A32	4c on $1 red	6.25	*14.00*
100	A33	4c on $2 gray grn	6.25	*19.00*

"CENTS" 8½mm below "4"

101	A34	4c on $5 red vio	7.25	*18.00*
a.		Normal spacing	160.00	*250.00*
102	A35	4c on $10 brown	7.25	*18.00*
a.		Normal spacing	125.00	*250.00*
		Nos. 91-102 (12)	162.50	*200.50*

No. 99 differs from No. 74 in the distance between "4" and "cents" which is 4¾mm on No. 99 and 3¾mm on No. 74.

Orangutan — A48

1899-1900 **Engr.**

103	A48	4c green & black	10.00	1.75
104	A48	4c dp rose & blk ('00)	40.00	.75

For overprints see Nos. 108, J23.

Stamps of 1894-1900 Overprinted in Red, Black, Green or Blue

m

1901-05

105	A37	1c bis brn & blk (R)	4.00	.35
106	A38	2c grn & blk (R)	2.75	.35
107	A39	3c lil & ol grn (Bk)	2.00	.35
108	A48	4c dp rose & blk (G)	10.00	.35
109	A40	5c org & blk (G)	16.00	.35
110	A41	6c ol brn & blk (R)	4.50	.75
111	A42	8c brn & blk (Bl)	4.25	.55
a.		Vert. pair, imperf. btwn.		425.00
112	A43	12c blue & blk (R)	57.50	1.50
113	A46	18c grn & blk (R)	12.50	1.40
114	A47	24c red & blue (Bk)	18.00	1.75
115	A30	25c slate blue (R)	3.00	.60
a.		Inverted overprint	550.00	
116	A31	50c violet (R)	7.50	.70
117	A32	$1 red (R)	20.00	3.75
118	A32	$1 red (Bk)	10.00	2.75
a.		Double overprint		425.00
119	A33	$2 gray green (R)	35.00	4.00
a.		Double overprint	1,250.	
		Nos. 105-119 (15)	207.00	19.50

Nos. 110, 111 and 122 are known without period after "PROTECTORATE."
See Nos. 122-123, 150-151.

Bruang (Sun Bear) — A49

Railroad Train — A50

1902 **Engr.**

120	A49	10c slate & dk brn	110.00	3.25
a.		Vertical pair, imperf. between		575.00
121	A50	16c yel brn & grn	150.00	3.75

Overprinted type "m" in Red or Black

122	A49	10c sl & dk brn (R)	62.50	1.10
a.		Double overprint	800.00	350.00
123	A50	16c yel brn & grn (Bk)	150.00	2.50
		Nos. 120-123 (4)	472.50	10.60

For overprints see Nos. J27, J29.

Stamps of 1894-97 Surcharged in Black

1904

124	A40	4c on 5c org & blk	40.00	14.00
125	A41	4c on 6c ol brn & blk	8.00	14.00
a.		Inverted surcharge	350.00	
126	A42	4c on 8c brn lil & blk	15.00	14.00
a.		Inverted surcharge	350.00	
127	A43	4c on 12c blue & blk	30.00	14.00
128	A46	4c on 18c grn & blk	16.00	14.00
129	A47	4c on 24c cl & bl	20.00	14.00
130	A30	4c on 25c sl blue	5.00	14.00
131	A31	4c on 50c violet	5.50	14.00
132	A32	4c on $1 red	7.00	14.00
133	A33	4c on $2 gray grn	10.50	14.00
134	A34	4c on $5 red vio	14.00	14.00
135	A35	4c on $10 brown	14.00	14.00
a.		Inverted surcharge	2,100.	
		Nos. 124-135 (12)	185.00	168.00

Malayan Tapir — A51

Traveler's Palm — A52

Railroad Station — A53

Meeting of the Assembly — A54

Elephant and Mahout
A55

Sumatran Rhinoceros
A56

Natives Plowing — A57

Wild Boar — A58

Palm Cockatoo
A59

Rhinoceros Hornbill
A60

Banteng (Wild Ox)
A61 A62

Cassowary
A63

1909-22 **Unwmk.** **Engr.** ***Perf. 14***
Center in Black

136	A51	1c chocolate	4.25	.20
b.		Perf. 13½		
c.		Perf. 15	17.00	.40
137	A52	2c green	.90	.20
b.		Perf. 15	1.90	.20
138	A53	3c deep rose	2.25	.30
b.		Perf. 15		.40
139	A53	3c green ('22)	6.50	*.40*
140	A54	4c dull red	1.75	.20
b.		Perf. 13½	*11.00*	*10.50*
c.		Perf. 15	7.75	.40
141	A55	5c yellow brn	7.25	.30
b.		Perf. 15		
142	A56	6c olive green	5.50	.30
b.		Perf. 15	42.50	1.00
143	A57	8c rose	2.25	.30
a.		Perf 15		—
144	A58	10c blue	14.00	.30
b.		Perf. 13½		*2.50*
c.		Perf. 15	32.50	*6.50*
145	A59	12c deep blue	20.00	.60
c.		Perf. 15		—
146	A60	16c red brown	16.00	1.25
b.		Perf. 13½	20.00	6.50
147	A61	18c blue green	72.50	1.25
148	A62	20c on 18c bl grn (R)	5.50	.55
b.		Perf. 15	150.00	*75.00*
149	A63	24c violet	22.50	1.50
		Nos. 136-149 (14)	181.15	7.65

Issued: #139, 1922; others, July 1, 1909.
See #167-178. #136a-149a follow #162.
For surcharges and overprints see #160-162, 166, B1-B12, B14-B24, B31-B41, J32-J49.

Nos. 72-73 Overprinted type "m" in Red

1910

150	A34	$5 red violet	100.00	4.50
151	A35	$10 brown	92.50	6.75
a.		Double overprint		
b.		Inverted overprint		

A64

A65

1911 **Engr.** ***Perf. 14***

Center in Black

152	A64	25c yellow green	4.00	1.00
a.		Perf. 15	10.00	
b.		Imperf., pair	50.00	
153	A64	50c slate blue	7.00	1.25
a.		Perf. 15	24.00	*8.50*
b.		Imperf., pair	67.50	
154	A64	$1 brown	14.00	1.50
a.		Perf. 15	32.50	*6.75*
c.		Imperf., pair	67.50	
155	A64	$2 dk violet	32.50	3.25
156	A65	$5 claret	57.50	20.00
a.		Perf. 13½	*82.50*	
b.		Imperf., pair	100.00	
157	A65	$10 vermilion	140.00	40.00
a.		Imperf., pair	100.00	
		Nos. 152-157 (6)	255.00	*67.00*

See #179-184. #152c-153c follow #162.
For overprint and surcharges see Nos. B13, B25-B30, B42-B47.

Nos. 72-73 Overprinted in Red

1912

158	A34	$5 red violet	900.00	9.25
159	A35	$10 brown	1,400.	9.25

Nos. 158 and 159 were prepared for use but not regularly issued.

Nos. 138, 142 and 145 Surcharged in Black or Red

1916 **Center in Black** ***Perf. 14***

160	A53	2c on 3c dp rose	15.00	6.50
a.		Inverted "S"	87.50	87.50
161	A56	4c on 6c ol grn (R)	13.00	6.50
a.		Inverted "S"	100.00	100.00
162	A59	10c on 12c bl (R)	35.00	37.50
a.		Inverted "S"	110.00	110.00
		Nos. 160-162 (3)	63.00	50.50

Stamps and Types of 1909-11 Overprinted in Red or Blue in Three Lines:
"MALAYA-BORNEO EXHIBITION 1922."

1922

Center in Black

136a	A51	1c brown	5.50	*22.50*
137a	A52	2c green	1.90	*13.00*
138a	A53	3c deep rose (B)	4.75	*18.00*
140a	A54	4c dull red (B)	2.50	*13.00*
141a	A55	5c yel brown (B)	5.50	*22.50*
142a	A56	6c olive green	4.75	*27.50*
143a	A57	8c rose (B)	4.75	*27.50*
144a	A58	10c gray blue	5.25	*35.00*
145a	A59	12c deep blue	7.50	*45.00*
146a	A60	16c red brown (B)	7.50	*50.00*
148a	A62	20c on 18c bl grn	13.00	*57.50*
149a	A63	24c violet	11.00	*55.00*
152c	A64	25c yel green	11.00	*40.00*
153c	A64	50c slate blue	9.50	*45.00*
		Nos. 136a-153c (14)	94.40	*471.50*

Industrial fair, Singapore, 3/31-4/15/22.

No. 140 Surcharged in Black

1923

166	A54	3c on 4c dull red & blk	1.50	1.60
a.		Double surcharge		

Types of 1909-22 Issues

1926-28 **Engr.** ***Perf. 12½***

Center in Black

167	A51	1c chocolate	.55	.50
168	A52	2c lake	.40	.40
169	A53	3c green	1.25	.75
170	A54	4c dull red	.40	.25
171	A55	5c yellow brown	3.50	3.50
172	A56	6c yellow green	3.75	.45
173	A57	8c rose	2.25	.30
174	A58	10c bright blue	1.90	.65
175	A59	12c deep blue	5.00	.65
176	A60	16c orange brn	12.50	*22.50*
177	A62	20c on 18c bl grn (R)	3.50	4.00
178	A63	24c dull violet	35.00	*50.00*
179	A64	25c yellow grn	5.50	5.50
180	A64	50c slate blue	8.50	*12.50*
181	A64	$1 brown	30.00	*75.00*
182	A64	$2 dark violet	50.00	*125.00*
183	A65	$5 deep rose	85.00	250.00
184	A65	$10 dull vermilion	200.00	350.00
		Nos. 167-184 (18)	449.00	*901.95*

Murut — A66

Orangutan — A67

Dyak — A68

Mt. Kinabalu A69

Clouded Leopard A70

Arms with Supporters and Motto A72

Coat of Arms — A71

Arms with Supporters — A73

1931, Jan. 1 **Engr.** ***Perf. 12½***

Center in Black

185	A66	3c blue green	.65	*1.50*
186	A67	6c orange red	13.00	4.75
187	A68	10c carmine	2.75	6.25
188	A69	12c ultra	3.25	4.00
189	A70	25c deep violet	30.00	22.50
190	A71	$1 yellow green	18.00	30.00
191	A72	$2 red brown	40.00	37.50
192	A73	$5 red violet	110.00	*225.00*
		Nos. 185-192 (8)	217.65	*331.50*

50th anniv. of the North Borneo Co.

Buffalo Transport A74

Palm Cockatoo — A75

Murut — A76

Proboscis Monkey — A77

Bajaus — A78

Map of North Borneo and Surrounding Lands — A79

Orangutan — A80

Murut with Blowgun — A81

Dyak — A82

River Scene — A83

Proa — A84

Mt. Kinabalu — A85

Coat of Arms — A86

Arms with Supporters A87

1939, Jan. 1 ***Perf. 12½***

193	A74	1c red brn & dk grn	1.90	1.50
194	A75	2c Prus bl & red vio	3.25	1.50
195	A76	3c dk grn & sl blue	2.25	2.00
196	A77	4c rose vio & ol grn	4.00	.50
197	A78	6c dp cl & dk blue	3.75	7.00
198	A79	8c red	6.00	1.50
199	A80	10c olive grn & vio	26.00	6.00
200	A81	12c ultra & grn	17.50	5.50
201	A82	15c bis brn & brt bl grn	15.00	7.50
202	A83	20c ind & rose vio	9.50	3.75
203	A84	25c dk brn & bl grn	12.00	10.00
204	A85	50c purple & brn	13.50	8.00
205	A86	$1 car & brown	50.00	20.00
206	A86	$2 ol grn & pur	75.00	95.00
207	A87	$5 blue & indigo	200.00	200.00
		Nos. 193-207 (15)	439.65	369.75
		Set, never hinged	700.00	

For overprints see #208-237, MR1-MR2, N1-N15, N16-N31.

Nos. 193 to 207 Overprinted in Black

1945, Dec. 17 **Unwmk.** ***Perf. 12½***

208	A74	1c red brn & dk grn	4.25	1.75
209	A75	2c Prus bl & red vio	10.00	1.75
210	A76	3c dk grn & sl bl	.90	1.10
211	A77	4c rose vio & ol grn	11.50	14.00
212	A78	6c dp cl & dk bl	.90	.90
213	A79	8c red	2.10	.65
214	A80	10c ol green & vio	2.10	.35
215	A81	12c ultra & green	4.25	2.50
216	A82	15c bis brn & brt bl grn	1.10	1.10
217	A83	20c ind & rose vio	3.00	.90
218	A84	25c dk brn & bl grn	4.75	1.10
219	A85	50c purple & brn	2.10	1.25
220	A86	$1 carmine & brn	35.00	32.50
221	A86	$2 ol green & pur	32.50	27.50
a.		Double overprint	3,600.	
222	A87	$5 blue & indigo	13.50	12.50
		Nos. 208-222 (15)	127.95	99.85
		Set, never hinged	210.00	

"BMA" stands for British Military Administration.

Nos. 193 to 207 Overprinted in Black or Carmine With Bars

1947

223 A74 1c red brn & dk grn .20 .90
224 A75 2c Prus bl & red vio 1.25 .80
225 A76 3c dk grn & sl bl (C) .20 .80
226 A77 4c rose vio & ol grn .50 .80
227 A78 6c dp cl & dk bl (C) .20 .20
228 A79 8c red .25 .20
229 A80 10c olive grn & vio 1.10 .35
230 A81 12c ultra & grn 1.50 2.50
231 A82 15c bis brn & brt bl grn 1.75 .25
232 A83 20c ind & rose vio 1.75 .75
233 A84 25c dk brn & bl grn 1.90 .45
234 A85 50c purple & brn 1.75 .75
235 A86 $1 carmine & brn 3.50 1.50
236 A86 $2 ol green & pur 9.00 15.00
237 A87 $5 blue & ind (C) 16.00 15.00
Nos. 223-237 (15) 40.85 40.25
Set, never hinged 60.00

The bars obliterate "The State of" and "British Protectorate."

Catalogue values for unused stamps in this section, from this point to the end of the section, are for Never Hinged items.

Silver Wedding Issue
Common Design Types
Perf. 14x14½

1948, Nov. 1 Wmk. 4 Photo.
238 CD304 8c scarlet .30 .50

Engraved; Name Typographed
Perf. 11½x11
239 CD305 $10 purple 20.00 *30.00*

Common Design Types pictured following the introduction.

UPU Issue
Common Design Types
Engr.; Name Typo. on 10c and 30c
1949, Oct. 10 *Perf. 13½, 11x11½*
240 CD306 8c rose carmine .25 .20
241 CD307 10c chocolate .35 .30
242 CD308 30c deep orange 1.10 .85
243 CD309 55c blue 1.75 1.40
Nos. 240-243 (4) 3.45 2.75

Mount Kinabalu — A88

Coconut Grove — A89

Designs: 2c, Musician. 4c, Hemp drying. 5c, Cattle at Kota Belud. 8c, Map. 10c, Logging. 15c, Proa at Sandakan. 20c, Bajau Chief. 30c, Suluk Craft. 50c, Clock tower. $1, Bajau horsemen. $2, Murut with blowgun. $5, Net fishing. $10, Arms.

Perf. 13½x14½, 14½x13½
1950, July 1 Photo.
244 A88 1c red brown .20 .90
245 A88 2c blue .20 .40
246 A89 3c green .20 .20
247 A89 4c red violet .20 .20
248 A89 5c purple .20 .20
249 A88 8c red .75 .75
250 A88 10c violet brn 1.25 .20
251 A88 15c brt ultra 2.00 .55
252 A88 20c dk brown 1.25 .20
253 A89 30c brown 3.50 .20
254 A89 50c cer *(Jessleton)* .85 2.50
255 A89 $1 red orange 3.75 1.75
256 A88 $2 dark green 4.75 11.00
257 A88 $5 emerald 15.00 17.50
258 A88 $10 gray blue 40.00 40.00
Nos. 244-258 (15) 74.10 76.55

Redrawn

1952, May 1 *Perf. 14½x13½*
259 A89 50c cerise *(Jesselton)* 6.50 1.75

SEMI-POSTAL STAMPS

Nos. 136-138, 140-146, 148-149, 152 Overprinted in Carmine or Vermilion

1916 Unwmk. *Perf. 14*
Center in Black
B1 A51 1c chocolate 5.00 *13.00*
B2 A52 2c green 20.00 *30.00*
a. Perf. 15 27.50 *37.50*
B3 A53 3c deep rose 14.00 *22.50*
B4 A54 4c dull red 7.25 *13.50*
a. Perf. 15 *80.00*
B5 A55 5c yellow brown 30.00 *26.00*
B6 A56 6c olive green 22.50 *32.50*
a. Perf. 15
B7 A57 8c rose 14.00 *26.00*
B8 A58 10c brt blue 30.00 *40.00*
B9 A59 12c deep blue 30.00 *42.50*
B10 A60 16c red brown 30.00 *42.50*
B11 A62 20c on 18c bl grn 30.00 *45.00*
B12 A63 24c violet 47.50 *50.00*

Perf. 15
B13 A64 25c yellow green 450.00 *475.00*
Nos. B1-B13 (13) 730.25 *858.50*

All values exist with the vermilion overprint and all but the 4c with the carmine.

Of the total overprinting, a third was given to the National Philatelic War Fund Committee in London to be auctioned for the benefit of the wounded and veterans' survivors. The balance was lost en route from London to Sandakan when a submarine sank the ship. Very few were postally used.

Nos. 136-138, 140-146, 149, 152-157 Surcharged

1918 *Perf. 14*
Center in Black
B14 A51 1c + 2c choc 3.25 *7.00*
B15 A52 2c + 2c green .70 *7.00*
B16 A53 3c + 2c dp rose 5.00 *13.00*
a. Perf. 15 25.00 *60.00*
B17 A54 4c + 2c dull red .50 *4.00*
a. Inverted surcharge 275.00
B18 A55 5c + 2c yel brn 5.50 *21.00*
B19 A56 6c + 2c olive grn 4.50 *15.00*
a. Perf. 15 125.00
B20 A57 8c + 2c rose 4.50 *6.00*
B21 A58 10c + 2c brt blue 5.00 *20.00*
B22 A59 12c + 2c deep bl 12.50 *35.00*
a. Inverted surcharge 550.00
B23 A60 16c + 2c red brn 14.00 *30.00*
B24 A63 24c + 2c violet 15.00 *30.00*
B25 A64 25c + 2c yel grn 12.00 *35.00*
B26 A64 50c + 2c sl blue 14.00 *35.00*
B27 A64 $1 + 2c brown 35.00 *45.00*
B28 A64 $2 + 2c dk vio 50.00 *85.00*
B29 A65 $5 + 2c claret 240.00 *325.00*
B30 A65 $10 + 2c ver 240.00 *325.00*
Nos. B14-B30 (17) 661.45 *1,038.*

On Nos. B14-B24 the surcharge is 15mm high, on Nos. B25-B30 it is 19mm high.

Nos. 136-138, 140-146, 149, 152-157 Surcharged in Red

1918
Center in Black
B31 A51 1c + 4c choc .40 *4.00*
B32 A52 2c + 4c green .60 *6.00*
B33 A53 3c + 4c dp rose .60 *3.00*
B34 A54 4c + 4c dull red .40 *4.00*
B35 A55 5c + 4c yel brn 1.40 *15.00*
B36 A56 6c + 4c olive grn 1.40 *10.00*
a. Vert. pair, imperf. btwn. 900.00
B37 A57 8c + 4c rose 1.00 *8.50*
B38 A58 10c + 4c brt blue 3.25 *10.00*
B39 A59 12c + 4c dp blue 6.00 *10.00*
B40 A60 16c + 4c red brn 4.25 *15.00*
B41 A63 24c + 4c violet 4.25 *17.50*
B42 A64 25c + 4c yel grn 5.00 *40.00*
B43 A64 50c + 4c sl blue 13.00 *40.00*
a. Perf. 15 50.00
B44 A64 $1 + 4c brown 15.00 *50.00*
a. Perf. 15 *60.00*
B45 A64 $2 + 4c dk vio 35.00 *65.00*
B46 A65 $5 + 4c claret 250.00 *400.00*
B47 A65 $10 + 4c ver 250.00 *375.00*
Nos. B31-B47 (17) 591.55 *1,073.*

POSTAGE DUE STAMPS

Regular Issues Overprinted

Reading Up Vert. (V), or Horiz. (H)

1895, Aug. 1 Unwmk. *Perf. 14, 15*
On Nos. 60 to 67
J1 A22 2c rose & blk (V) 15.00 .95
J2 A23 3c vio & ol grn (V) 5.00 .80
J3 A24 5c org red & blk (V) 25.00 1.25
a. Period after "DUE" (V) 45.00
J4 A25 6c ol brn & blk (V) 12.00 1.50
J5 A26 8c lilac & blk (H) 32.50 2.00
a. Double ovpt. (H)
J6 A27 12c blue & blk (H) 60.00 1.50
a. Double overprint (H) *325.00*
J7 A28 18c green & blk (V) 65.00 3.00
a. Ovpt. reading down 400.00 *275.00*
b. Overprinted horizontally 20.00 2.75
c. Same as "b" inverted 300.00 *275.00*
J8 A29 24c claret & bl (H) 60.00 1.60
Nos. J1-J8 (8) 274.50 12.60

On Nos. 80 and 85

1897
J9 A38 2c dp rose & blk (V) 6.00 .45
a. Overprinted horizontally 12.00 *15.00*
J10 A42 8c brn lil & blk (H) 40.00 *40.00*
a. Period after "DUE" 30.00 *60.00*

On Nos. 81-88 and 104 Vertically reading up

1901
J11 A38 2c green & blk 21.00 .55
a. Overprinted horizontally 27.50
J12 A39 3c lilac & ol grn 8.00 .35
a. Period after "DUE" 18.00 *30.00*
J13 A48 4c dp rose & blk 18.00 .45
J14 A40 5c orange & blk 21.00 .55
a. Period after "DUE" 30.00
J15 A41 6c olive brn & blk 3.50 .45
J16 A42 8c brown & blk 7.00 .45
a. Overprinted horizontally 30.00
b. Period after "DUE" (H) 60.00
J17 A43 12c blue & blk 65.00 .90
J18 A46 18c green & blk 35.00 .90
J19 A47 24c red & blue 17.50 .90
Nos. J11-J19 (9) 196.00 5.50

On Nos. 105-114, 122-123 Horizontally

1903-11 *Perf. 14*
J20 A37 1c bis brn & blk, period after "DUE" 13.00 13.00
a. Period omitted
J21 A38 2c green & blk 6.00 .25
a. Ovpt. vert., perf. 16 *150.00*
b. Perf 15 (ovpt. horiz.) 55.00 *55.00*
J22 A39 3c lilac & ol grn 6.00 .35
a. Ovpt. vert. 110.00 *110.00*
b. Perf. 15 (ovpt. horiz.) 95.00 *17.00*
J23 A48 4c dp rose & blk, perf. 15 4.50 .45
a. "Postage Due" double 110.00
b. Perf. 14 4.75 1.00
J24 A40 5c orange & blk 7.00 .45
a. Ovpt. vert., perf. 15 160.00 *110.00*
b. Perf. 13½ (ovpt. horiz.)
c. Perf. 15 (ovpt. horiz.) 13.00 *10.00*
J25 A41 6c olive brn & blk 7.25 .35
a. "Postage Due" double
b. "Postage Due" inverted *110.00*
c. Perf. 16 25.00 *25.00*
J26 A42 8c brown & blk 14.00 .50
a. Overprint vertical 150.00 *125.00*
J27 A49 10c slate & brn 35.00 .90
J28 A43 12c blue & blk 10.50 .75
J29 A50 16c yel brn & grn 18.00 .90
J30 A46 18c green & blk 7.00 .60
a. "Postage Due" double *70.00*
J31 A47 24c claret & blue 15.00 1.25
a. "Postage Due" double *125.00*
b. Overprint vertical *85.00*
Nos. J20-J31 (12) 143.25 19.75

On Nos. 137 and 139-146

1921-31 *Perf. 14, 15*
J32 A52 2c green & blk 11.00 60.00
a. Perf. 13½ 15.00 12.00
J33 A53 3c green & blk 5.25 20.00
J34 A54 4c dull red & blk 1.25 1.25
J35 A55 5c yel brn & blk 5.25 10.00
J36 A56 6c olive grn & blk 13.00 11.00
J37 A57 8c rose & blk 5.25 4.25
J38 A58 10c blue & blk 6.50 12.00
a. Perf. 15 47.50 60.00
J39 A59 12c dp vio & blk 8.50 25.00
J40 A60 16c red brn & blk 24.00 65.00
Nos. J32-J40 (9) 80.00 208.50

On Nos. 168 to 176

1926-28 *Perf. 12½*
J41 A52 2c lake & blk .45 *2.00*
J42 A53 3c green & blk 2.00 *12.50*
J43 A54 4c dull red & blk 3.25 *1.00*
J44 A55 5c yel brown & blk 5.75 *50.00*
J45 A56 6c yel green & blk 8.00 *3.00*
J46 A57 8c rose & black 7.00 8.50
J47 A58 10c brt blue & blk 9.00 *50.00*
J48 A59 12c dp blue & blk 16.00 *85.00*
J49 A60 16c org brn & blk 35.00 *125.00*
Nos. J41-J49 (9) 86.45 *337.00*

Crest of British North Borneo Company — D1

1939, Jan. 1 Engr. *Perf. 12½*
J50 D1 2c brown 4.00 *25.00*
J51 D1 4c carmine 4.00 *32.50*
J52 D1 6c dp rose violet 13.50 *42.50*
J53 D1 8c dk blue green 14.00 *52.50*
J54 D1 10c deep ultra 18.00 *70.00*
Nos. J50-J54 (5) 53.50 *222.50*
Set, never hinged 100.00

WAR TAX STAMPS

Nos. 193-194 Overprinted

No. MR1

No. MR2

1941, Feb. 24 Unwmk. *Perf. 12½*
MR1 A74 1c red brown & dk green .30 .30
MR2 A75 2c Prus blue & red violet .50 .55

For overprints see Nos. N15A-N15B.

OCCUPATION STAMPS

Issued under Japanese Occupation

Nos. 193-207 Handstamped in Violet or Black

On Nos. N1-N15B, the violet overprint is attributed to Jesselton, the black to Sandakan. Nos. N1-N15 are generally found with violet overprint, Nos. N15A-N15B with black.

1942 Unwmk. *Perf. 12½*
N1 A74 1c 125.00 120.00
N2 A75 2c 110.00 125.00
N3 A76 3c 110.00 125.00
N4 A77 4c 65.00 95.00
N5 A78 6c 125.00 125.00
N6 A79 8c 110.00 125.00
N7 A80 10c 110.00 125.00
N8 A81 12c 175.00 190.00
N9 A82 15c 175.00 190.00
N10 A83 20c 275.00 *250.00*
N11 A84 25c 250.00 *250.00*
N12 A85 50c 400.00 *300.00*

N13	A86	$1	300.00	*400.00*
N14	A86	$2	425.00	*550.00*
N15	A87	$5	600.00	*700.00*
		Nos. N1-N15 (15)	3,355.	*3,670.*

For overprints see Nos. N22a, N31a.

Same Overprint on Nos. MR1-MR2 in Black or Violet

1942

N15A	A74	1c	*625.00*	*190.00*
N15B	A75	2c	*1,300.*	*250.00*

Nos. 193 to 207 Overprinted in Black

1944, Sept. 30 Unwmk. *Perf. 12½*

N16	A74	1c	3.50	6.25
N17	A75	2c	6.75	6.25
N18	A76	3c	2.50	3.50
N19	A77	4c	3.50	5.00
N20	A78	6c	3.25	3.50
N21	A79	8c	5.00	*11.00*
N22	A80	10c	6.00	*9.00*
a.		On No. N7	150.00	
N23	A81	12c	4.50	*9.00*
N24	A82	15c	3.50	*9.00*
N25	A83	20c	12.50	*21.00*
N26	A84	25c	12.50	*21.00*
N27	A85	50c	45.00	*57.50*
N28	A86	$1	72.50	*95.00*
		Nos. N16-N28 (13)	181.00	*257.00*

Nos. N1 and 205 Surcharged in Black

No. N30

No. N31

1944, May

N30	A74	$2 on 1c	*4,250.*	*3,250.*
N31	A86	$5 on $1	4,500.	3,800.
a.		On No. N13	2,750.	2,750.

Mt. Kinabalu OS1

Boat and Traveler's Palm OS2

1943, Apr. 29 Litho.

N32	OS1	4c dull rose red	15.00	18.00
N33	OS2	8c dark blue	15.00	18.00

Aviator Saluting and Japanese Flag — A150

Miyajima Torii, Itsukushima Shrine — A96

Stamps of Japan, 1938-43, Overprinted in Black

1s, War factory girl. 2s, Gen. Maresuke Nogi. 3s, Power plant. 4s, Hyuga Monument and Mt. Fuji. 5s, Adm. Heihachiro Togo. 6s, Garambi Lighthouse, Formosa. 8s, Meiji Shrine, Tokyo. 10s, Palms and map of "Greater East Asia." 20s, Mt. Fuji and cherry blossoms. 25s, Horyu Temple, Nara. 50s, Golden Pavilion, Kyoto. 1y, Great Buddha, Kamakura. See Burma, Vol. 1, for illustrations of 2s, 3s, 5s, 8s, 20s and watermark. For others, see Japan.

Wmk. Curved Wavy Lines (257)

1944, Sept. 30 *Perf. 13*

N34	A144	1s	orange brown	5.25	12.00
N35	A84	2s	vermilion	5.25	12.00
N36	A85	3s	green	3.50	12.00
N37	A146	4s	emerald	5.25	12.00
N38	A86	5s	brown lake	6.25	13.00
N39	A88	6s	orange	5.75	13.00
N40	A90	8s	dk purple & pale vio	3.25	13.00
N41	A148	10s	crim & dull rose	4.75	13.00
N42	A150	15s	dull blue	4.75	13.00
N43	A94	20s	ultra	100.00	200.00
N44	A95	25s	brown	65.00	55.00
N45	A96	30s	peacock blue	225.00	125.00
N46	A97	50s	olive	70.00	55.00
N47	A98	1y	lt brown	65.00	100.00
			Nos. N34-N47 (14)	569.00	648.00

The overprint translates "North Borneo."

NORTHERN NIGERIA

'nor-thə̦r̦n nī-'jir-ē-ə

LOCATION — Western Africa
GOVT. — A former British Protectorate
AREA — 281,703 sq. mi.
POP. — 11,866,250
CAPITAL — Zungeru

In 1914 Northern Nigeria united with Southern Nigeria to form the Colony and Protectorate of Nigeria.

12 Pence = 1 Shilling
20 Shillings = 1 Pound

Victoria — A1

Edward VII — A2

Numerals of 5p and 6p, types A1 and A2, are in color on plain tablet.

Wmk. Crown and C A (2)

1900, Mar. Typo. *Perf. 14*

1	A1	½p	lilac & grn	2.75	*10.00*
2	A1	1p	lilac & rose	3.25	3.25
3	A1	2p	lilac & yel	12.50	*35.00*
4	A1	2½p	lilac & blue	9.00	*35.00*
5	A1	5p	lilac & brn	20.00	*37.50*
6	A1	6p	lilac & vio	18.50	*25.00*
7	A1	1sh	green & blk	25.00	*55.00*
8	A1	2sh6p	green & blue	95.00	*400.00*
9	A1	10sh	green & brn	210.00	*575.00*
			Nos. 1-9 (9)	396.00	*1,175.*

1902, July 1

10	A2	½p	violet & green	2.00	1.00
11	A2	1p	vio & car rose	2.50	.75
12	A2	2p	violet & org	2.25	*3.00*
13	A2	2½p	violet & ultra	2.00	*9.00*
14	A2	5p	vio & org brn	2.25	*5.00*
15	A2	6p	violet & pur	9.50	*4.75*
16	A2	1sh	green & black	4.50	*6.00*
17	A2	2sh6p	green & ultra	11.00	*50.00*
18	A2	10sh	green & brown	55.00	*60.00*
			Nos. 10-18 (9)	91.00	*139.50*

1904, Apr. Wmk. 3

18A	A2	£25	green & car	*42,500.*	

No. 18A was available for postage but probably was used only for fiscal purposes.

1905

19	A2	½p	violet & grn	6.75	5.50
20	A2	1p	violet & car rose	6.75	1.00
21	A2	2p	violet & org	15.00	*27.50*
22	A2	2½p	violet & ultra	7.25	8.00
23	A2	5p	violet & org brn	25.00	70.00
24	A2	6p	violet & pur	27.50	42.50
25	A2	1sh	green & black	24.00	*55.00*
26	A2	2sh6p	green & ultra	37.50	55.00
			Nos. 19-26 (8)	149.75	*264.50*

All values exist on ordinary paper and all but the 2½p on chalky paper.

1910-11 Ordinary Paper

28	A2	½p	green	2.25	1.25
29	A2	1p	carmine	2.00	1.25
30	A2	2p	gray	4.75	*2.75*
31	A2	2½p	ultra	2.50	*7.00*

Chalky Paper

32	A2	3p	violet, *yel*	4.50	.75
33	A2	5p	vio & ol grn	5.00	*12.50*
34	A2	6p	vio & red vio ('11)	5.50	*6.00*
a.			6p violet & deep violet	7.50	*17.50*
35	A2	1sh	black, *green*	3.00	.75
36	A2	2sh6p	blk & red, *bl*	12.00	*30.00*
37	A2	5sh	grn & red, *yel*	25.00	*75.00*
38	A2	10sh	grn & red, *grn*	52.50	*50.00*
			Nos. 28-38 (11)	119.00	187.25

George V — A3

For description of dies I and II see back of this section of the Catalogue.

Die I

1912 Ordinary Paper

40	A3	½p	green	1.50	.60
41	A3	1p	carmine	1.25	.60
42	A3	2p	gray	3.00	8.00

Chalky Paper

43	A3	3p	violet, *yel*	2.25	1.25
44	A3	4p	blk & red, *yel*	1.25	*2.25*
45	A3	5p	vio & ol grn	4.00	11.00
46	A3	6p	vio & red vio	4.25	*4.50*
47	A3	9p	violet & scar	2.25	*12.00*
48	A3	1sh	blk, *green*	5.00	2.25
49	A3	2sh6p	blk & red, *bl*	8.75	*45.00*
50	A3	5sh	grn & red, *yel*	25.00	*90.00*
51	A3	10sh	grn & red, *grn*	45.00	*50.00*
52	A3	£1	vio & blk, *red*	200.00	120.00
			Nos. 40-52 (13)	303.50	*347.45*

Numerals of 3p, 4p, 5p and 6p, type A3, are in color on plain tablet.

Stamps of Northern Nigeria were replaced in 1914 by those of Nigeria.

NORTHERN RHODESIA

'nor-thə̦r̦n rō-'dē-zh̦ē-̦ə

LOCATION — In southern Africa, east of Angola and separated from Southern Rhodesia by the Zambezi River.
GOVT. — British Protectorate
AREA — 287,640 sq. mi.
POP. — 2,550,000 (est. 1962)
CAPITAL — Lusaka

Prior to April 1, 1924, Northern Rhodesia was administered by the British South Africa Company. See Rhodesia and Southern Rhodesia.

12 Pence = 1 Shilling
20 Shillings = 1 Pound

Catalogue values for unused stamps in this country are for Never Hinged items, beginning with Scott 46 in the regular postage section.

King George V
A1 A2

1925-29 Engr. Wmk. 4 *Perf. 12½*

1	A1	½p	dk green	1.50	.70
2	A1	1p	dk brown	1.50	.20
3	A1	1½p	carmine	1.50	.25
4	A1	2p	brown org	2.00	.20
5	A1	3p	ultra	2.00	1.30
6	A1	4p	dk violet	4.75	.45
7	A1	6p	gray	4.75	.40
8	A1	8p	rose lilac	4.25	*50.00*
9	A1	10p	olive grn	4.75	*45.00*
10	A2	1sh	black & org	4.00	1.90
11	A2	2sh	ultra & brn	16.00	*25.00*
12	A2	2sh6p	green & blk	15.00	*9.00*
13	A2	3sh	indigo & vio	25.00	20.00
14	A2	5sh	dk vio & gray	35.00	19.00
15	A2	7sh6p	blk & lil rose	110.00	*160.00*
16	A2	10sh	black & green	80.00	*80.00*
17	A2	20sh	rose lil & red	160.00	175.00
			Nos. 1-17 (17)	472.00	*588.40*

High values with revenue cancellations are inexpensive.

Issue dates: 3sh, 1929; others, Apr. 1.

Common Design Types pictured following the introduction.

Silver Jubilee Issue
Common Design Type

1935, May 6 *Perf. 13½x14*

18	CD301	1p	olive grn & ultra	.75	.60
19	CD301	2p	indigo & grn	1.50	1.50
20	CD301	3p	blue & brown	3.50	3.50
21	CD301	6p	brt vio & indigo	4.50	3.75
			Nos. 18-21 (4)	10.25	9.35

Coronation Issue
Common Design Type

1937, May 12 *Perf. 11x11½*

22	CD302	1½p	dark carmine	.25	.25
23	CD302	2p	yellow brown	.50	.50
24	CD302	3p	deep ultra	.75	.75
			Nos. 22-24 (3)	1.50	1.50

King George VI — A3

1938-52 Wmk. 4 *Perf. 12½*

Size: 19x24mm

25	A3	½p	green	.20	.20
26	A3	½p	dk brown ('51)	.75	*1.50*
a.			Perf. 12½x14	1.50	*6.00*
27	A3	1p	dk brown	.25	.25
28	A3	1p	green ('51)	.75	*1.50*
29	A3	1½p	carmine	35.00	.75
a.			Horiz. pair, imperf. between	*14,000.*	
30	A3	1½p	brown org ('41)	.30	.25
31	A3	2p	brown org	45.00	1.75
32	A3	2p	carmine ('41)	.30	.50
33	A3	2p	rose lilac ('51)	.45	1.25
34	A3	3p	ultra	.50	.30
35	A3	3p	red ('51)	.45	2.00
36	A3	4p	dk violet	.30	.40
37	A3	4½p	dp blue ('52)	.75	*5.75*
38	A3	6p	dark gray	.30	.25
39	A3	9p	violet ('52)	.75	4.75

Size: 21½x26¾mm

40	A3	1sh	blk & brn org	1.50	.60
41	A3	2sh6p	green & blk	4.50	4.00
42	A3	3sh	ind & dk vio	8.75	8.50
43	A3	5sh	violet & gray	6.50	9.00
44	A3	10sh	black & green	8.00	*12.00*
45	A3	20sh	rose lil & red	21.00	*40.00*
			Nos. 25-45 (21)	136.30	*95.50*

Catalogue values for unused stamps in this section, from this point to the end of the section, are for Never Hinged items.

Peace Issue
Common Design Type

1946, Nov. 26 Engr. *Perf. 13½x14*

46	CD303	1½p	deep orange	.20	.20
a.			Perf. 13½	12.00	*13.00*
47	CD303	2p	carmine	.25	.25

Silver Wedding Issue
Common Design Types

1948, Dec. 1 Photo. *Perf. 14x14½*

48	CD304	1½p	orange	.30	.20

Engr. *Perf. 11½x11*

49	CD305	20sh	rose brown	57.50	*65.00*

UPU Issue
Common Design Types

Engr.; Name Typo. on 3p, 6p
Perf. 13½, 11x11½

1949, Oct. 10 Wmk. 4

50	CD306	2p	rose carmine	.50	.50
51	CD307	3p	indigo	1.00	1.00
52	CD308	6p	gray	1.50	1.50
53	CD309	1sh	red orange	1.50	1.50
			Nos. 50-53 (4)	4.50	4.50

POSTAGE DUE STAMPS

D1

1929 Typo. Wmk. 4 *Perf. 14*

J1	D1	1p	black	2.75	*2.75*
			On cover		*150.00*
a.			Wmk. 4a (error)	1,750.	
J2	D1	2p	black	3.50	*3.50*
			On cover		*180.00*
a.			Bisected, used as 1d, on cover		*850.00*
J3	D1	3p	black	6.75	*27.50*
			On cover		*350.00*
a.			Crown in watermark missing	200.00	
b.			Wmk. 4a (error)	150.00	
J4	D1	4p	black	9.00	*35.00*
			On cover		*400.00*
			Nos. J1-J4 (4)	22.00	*68.75*

NORTH INGERMANLAND

'north 'iŋ-gər-mən-̦land

LOCATION — In Northern Russia lying between the River Neva and Finland
CAPITAL — Kirjasalo

In 1920 the residents of this territory revolted from Russian rule and set up a provisional government. The new State existed only a short period as the revolution was quickly quelled by Soviet troops.

100 Pennia = 1 Markka

Arms — A1

Perf. 11½

1920, Mar. 21 Unwmk. Litho.

1	A1	5p	green	1.75	*3.50*
2	A1	10p	rose red	1.75	*3.50*
3	A1	25p	bister	1.75	*3.50*
4	A1	50p	dark blue	1.75	*3.50*
5	A1	1m	car & black	26.00	*42.50*
6	A1	5m	lilac & black	125.00	*125.00*
7	A1	10m	brown & blk	210.00	*250.00*
			Nos. 1-7 (7)	368.00	*431.50*

Well centered examples sell for twice the values shown.

Imperf., Pairs

1a	A1	5p	5.25
2a	A1	10p	5.25
3a	A1	25p	5.25
4a	A1	50p	5.25
5a	A1	1m	20.00
6a	A1	5m	125.00
7a	A1	10m	200.00

Arms — A2

Peasant — A3

Plowing — A4

Milking — A5

Planting A6

Ruins of Church A7

Peasants Playing Zithers A8

1920, Aug. 2

8	A2	10p gray grn & ultra	3.00	*7.00*
9	A3	30p buff & gray grn	3.00	*7.00*
10	A4	50p ultra & red brn	3.00	*7.00*
11	A5	80p claret & slate	3.00	*7.00*
12	A6	1m red & slate	21.00	*45.00*
13	A7	5m dk vio & dl rose	9.00	*18.00*
14	A8	10m brn & violet	9.00	*18.00*
a.		Center inverted	1,000.	
		Nos. 8-14 (7)	51.00	*109.00*

Counterfeits abound.

Nos. 8-14 exist imperf. Value for set in pairs, $200.

NORTH WEST PACIFIC ISLANDS

'north 'west pə-'si-fik 'ī-ləndz

LOCATION — Group of islands in the West Pacific Ocean including a part of New Guinea and adjacent islands of the Bismarck Archipelago

GOVT. — Australian military government

AREA — 96,160 sq. mi.

POP. — 636,563

Stamps of Australia were overprinted for use in the former German possessions of Nauru and German New Guinea which Australian troops had captured. Following the League of Nations' decision which placed these territories under mandate to Australia, these provisional issues were discontinued. See German New Guinea, New Britain, Nauru and New Guinea.

12 Pence = 1 Shilling
20 Shillings = 1 Pound

Stamps of Australia Overprinted — a

Type a: "P" of "PACIFIC" above "S" of "ISLANDS.

There are two varieties of the letter "S" in the Type "a" overprint. These occur in three combinations: a, both normal "S"; b, 1st "S" with small head and long bottom stroke, 2nd "S" normal; c, both "S" with small head and long bottom stroke.

DESIGN A1

Die I — The inside frameline has a break at left, even with the top of the letters of the denomination.

Die II — The frameline does not show a break.

Die IV — As Die III, with a break in the top outside frameline above the "ST" of "AUSTRALIA." The upper right inside frameline has an incomplete corner.

Dies are only indicated when there are more than one for any denomination.

1915-16 Wmk. 8 *Perf. 12*

1	A1	2p gray	21.00	*57.50*
2	A1	2½p dark blue	6.00	*18.00*
3	A1	3p ol bis, die I	25.00	*57.50*
a.		Die II	350.00	*450.00*
b.		Pair, #3, 3a	575.00	*800.00*
4	A1	6p ultra	80.00	*85.00*
5	A1	9p violet	55.00	*62.50*
6	A1	1sh blue green	57.50	*62.50*
8	A1	5sh yel & gray ('16)	950.00	*1,400.*
9	A1	10sh pink & gray	125.00	*190.00*
		Revenue cancel		27.50
10	A1	£1 ultra & brown	*500.00*	*750.00*
		Nos. 1-6,8-10 (9)	*1,819.*	*2,683.*

For surcharge see No. 27.

Wmk. Wide Crown and Narrow A (9)
Perf. 12, 14

ONE PENNY

Die I — Normal die, having outside the oval band with "AUSTRALIA" a white line and a heavy colored line.

Die Ia — As die I with a small white spur below the right serif at foot of the "1" in left tablet.

Dies are only indicated when there are more than one for any denomination.

11	A4	½p emerald	3.25	*9.00*
a.		Double overprint		
12	A4	1p car (Die I)	8.00	7.50
a.		1p carmine rose (Die I)	8.00	7.50
b.		1p carmine (Die Ia)	140.00	160.00
13	A1	2p gray	18.00	*22.50*
14	A1	2½p dk bl ('16)	*12,500.*	*12,500.*
16	A4	4p orange	8.00	*17.50*
17	A4	5p org brown	10.00	*18.00*
18	A1	6p ultra	12.00	*14.00*
19	A1	9p violet	18.00	*24.00*
20	A1	1sh blue green	12.50	*27.50*
21	A1	2sh brown	105.00	*125.00*
22	A1	5sh yellow & gray	80.00	*120.00*
		Nos. 11-13,16-22 (10)	274.75	*385.00*

For surcharge see No. 28.

1915-16 Wmk. 10 *Perf. 12*

23	A1	2p gray, die I	7.00	*18.50*
24	A1	3p ol bis, die I	6.50	*12.50*
a.		Die II	90.00	*140.00*
b.		Pair, #24, 24a	450.00	
25	A1	2sh brown ('16)	35.00	*52.50*
26	A1	£1 ultra & brn ('16)	300.00	*450.00*
		Nos. 23-26 (4)	348.50	*533.50*

Nos. 6 and 17 Surcharged

1918, May 23 Wmk. 8 *Perf. 12*

27	A1	1p on 1sh bl grn	105.00	92.50

Wmk. 9 *Perf. 14*

28	A4	1p on 5p org brn	105.00	87.50

Stamps of Australia Overprinted

b

Type "b": "P" of "PACIFIC" above space between "I" and "S" of "ISLANDS."

1918-23 Wmk. 10 *Perf. 12*

29	A1	2p gray	10.00	*22.50*
a.		Die II	12.50	*45.00*
30	A1	2½p dk bl ('19)	8.00	*18.00*
a.		"1" of fraction omitted	*6,300.*	*8,000.*
31	A1	3p ol bis, die I	26.00	*30.00*
a.		Die II	55.00	*70.00*
b.		Pair, #31, 31a	375.00	*450.00*
c.		3p lt olive, die IV	26.00	*37.50*
32	A1	6p ultra ('19)	12.00	*16.00*
a.		6p chalky blue	50.00	*75.00*
33	A1	9p violet ('19)	10.00	*45.00*
34	A1	1sh bl grn ('18)	16.00	*35.00*
35	A1	2sh brown	30.00	*45.00*
36	A1	5sh yel & gray ('19)	70.00	*75.00*
37	A1	10sh pink & gray ('19)	175.00	*225.00*
38	A1	£1 ultra & brn	3,250.	*4,600.*
		Nos. 29-37 (9)	357.00	*511.50*

1919 Wmk. 11

39	A4	½p emerald	5.00	*6.00*

1918-23 Wmk. 9

40	A4	½p emerald	2.50	*4.00*
41	A4	1p car red, die 1	3.00	*2.00*
a.		1p carmine red, die Ia	125.00	55.00
42	A4	1p scar, die I, rough paper	400.00	125.00
a.		1p rose red, die Ia, rough paper	1,100.	400.00
43	A4	1p violet ('22)	4.00	*7.50*
44	A4	2p orange	12.00	*7.00*
45	A4	2p red ('22)	10.50	9.00
46	A4	4p yel org	4.00	*18.00*
47	A4	4p violet ('22)	22.50	*45.00*
48	A4	4p light ultra ('22)	12.50	*70.00*
49	A4	5p brown	9.00	*16.00*
		Nos. 40-41,43-49 (9)	80.00	*178.50*

North West Pacific Islands stamps were largely used in New Britain. Some were used in Nauru. They were intended to serve the Bismarck Archipelago and other places.

NUMBER CHANGES

Old No.	New No.
new	3a, 3b
11	11, 40
12	12, 41, 42
12b	12b, 41a, 42a
16	16, 46
17	17, 49
27	23, 29
new	29a
28, 28a	30, 30a
29	24, 31
new	24a, 24b
new	31a, 31b, 31c
35	25, 35
38	26, 38
39-40	27-28
41	39
42-44	43-45
45-46	47-48

NORWAY

'nor-,wā

LOCATION — Western half of the Scandinavian Peninsula in northern Europe

GOVT. — Kingdom

AREA — 125,051 sq. mi.

POP. — 4,134,353 (1984)

CAPITAL — Oslo

120 Skilling = 1 Specie Daler
100 Ore = 1 Krone (1877)

Watermarks

Wmk. 159 — Lion

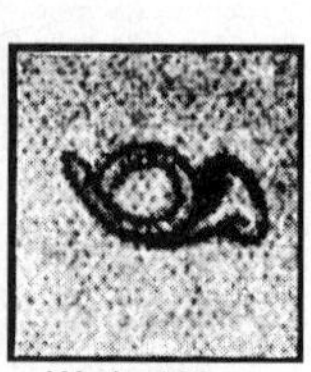

Wmk. 160 — Post Horn

Coat of Arms — A1

King Oscar I — A2

1855 Typo. Wmk. 159 *Imperf.*

1	A1	4s blue	*6,400.*	130.
		On cover		375.
a.		Double foot on right hind leg of lion		2,600.

Full margins = 1¾mm.

Values for multiples

Pair	—	600.
Strip of 3		2,000.
Strip of 4		7,500.
Strip of 5		12,000.
Strip of 6		17,500.
Block of 4		22,500.

Only a few genuine unused copies of No. 1 exist. Copies often offered have had pen-markings removed. The unused catalogue value is for a copy without gum. Copies with original gum sell for much more.

No. 1 was reprinted in 1914 and 1924 unwatermarked. Lowest value reprint, $95.

Rouletted Reprints

1963: No. 1, value $25; Nos. 2-5, 15, value each $15.

1965: Nos. 57, 70a, 100, 152, J1, O1. Value each $10.

1969: Nos. 69, 92, 107, 114, 128, J12. Value each $10.

1856-57 Unwmk. *Perf. 13*

2	A2	2s yellow ('57)	650.00	150.00
		On cover		375.00
a.		2s orange	800.00	200.00
		On cover		600.00
3	A2	3s lilac ('57)	475.00	95.00
		On cover		850.00
4	A2	4s blue	375.00	17.00
		On cover		32.50
a.		Imperf.		*10,000.*
b.		Half used as 2s on cover		—
c.		4s blackish blue	600.00	35.00
		On cover		100.00
d.		4s greenish blue	450.00	17.50
		On cover		40.00
e.		4s pale greenish blue	1,500.	60.00
		On cover		125.00
5	A2	8s dull lake	1,300.	55.00
		On cover		300.00
a.		8s lilac red	1,900.	90.00
		On cover		500.00

Nos. 2-5 were reprinted in 1914 and 1924, perf. 13½. Lowest valued reprint, $50 each.

A3

A4

1863 Litho. *Perf. 14½x13½*

6	A3	2s yellow	1,150.	210.00
		On cover		500.00
7	A3	3s gray lilac	850.00	475.00
		On cover		900.00
8	A3	4s blue	200.00	12.00
		On cover		25.00
a.		4s greenish blue	200.00	24.00
		On cover		35.00
b.		4s dark blue	650.00	75.00
		On cover		—
c.		Half used as 2s on cover		—
9	A3	8s rose	1,000.	65.00
		On cover		250.00
10	A3	24s brown	45.00	125.00
		On cover		1,450.
		On cover, single franking		1,900.
a.		24s dark brown	60.00	150.00
b.		24s reddish brown	72.50	180.00
		Nos. 6-10 (5)	3,245.	887.00

There are four types of the 2, 3, 8 and 24 skilling and eight types of the 4 skilling. See note on used value of No. 10 following No. 21.

1867-68 Typo.

11	A4	1s black, coarse impression ('68)	85.00	55.00
		On cover		140.00
a.		1s dark gray, fine impression ('68)	175.00	120.00
		On cover		—
12	A4	2s orange	30.00	55.00
		On cover		50.00
a.		2s brt yellow orange	90.00	110.00
		On cover		—
b.		Vert. pair, imperf between	*1,750.*	
13	A4	3s dl lil, coarse impression ('68)	525.00	100.00
		On cover		250.00
a.		3s reddish violet, fine impression	1,200.	275.00
		On cover		500.00
14	A4	4s blue, thin paper	125.00	12.00
		On cover		25.00
a.		4s greenish blue, thick paper	210.00	10.00
		On cover		25.00
15	A4	8s car rose	550.00	55.00
		On cover		250.00
a.		8s rose, clear impression	1,600.	450.00
		On cover		1,750.
		Nos. 11-15 (5)	1,315.	277.00

See note on used value of #12 following #21.

For surcharges see Nos. 59-61, 149.

No. 15 was reprinted in 1914 and 1924, perf. 13½. Lowest valued reprint, $50.

Post Horn and Crown — A5

1872-75 Wmk. 160
16 A5 1s yel grn ('75) 11.50 45.00
On cover 35.00
a. 1s deep green ('73) 300.00 65.00
On cover 150.00
b. "E.EN" 25.00 *55.00*
c. 1s blue green, fine impression ('73) 300.00 95.00
On cover 175.00
d. Vert. pair, imperf between —
17 A5 2s ultra ('74) 20.00 70.00
On cover 50.00
a. 2s Prussian blue ('74) *17,000.* *5,000.*
b. 2s gray blue 20.00 *250.00*
On cover 350.00
18 A5 3s rose 85.00 14.00
On cover 17.50
a. 3s carmine 85.00 14.00
On cover 17.50
b. 3s carmine, *bluish* thin paper 350.00 32.50
On cover 42.50
19 A5 4s lilac, thin paper ('73) 19.00 *65.00*
On cover 50.00
a. 4s dark violet, *bluish,* thin paper 625.00 175.00
On cover 350.00
b. 4s brown violet, *bluish,* thin paper ('73) 575.00 210.00
On cover 350.00
c. 4s violet, *white,* thick paper ('73) 140.00 60.00
On cover 200.00
20 A5 6s org brn ('75) 575.00 65.00
On cover 425.00
21 A5 7s red brn ('73) 60.00 *70.00*
On cover 100.00
Nos. 16-21 (6) 770.50 329.00

In this issue there are 12 types each of Nos. 16, 17, 18 and 19; 12 types of No. 20 and 20 types of No. 21. The differences are in the words of value.

Nos. 10, 12, 16, 17, 19 and 21 were re-released in 1888 and used until March 31, 1908. Used values of these stamps are for specimens canceled in this later period, usually with a two-ring cancellation. Examples bearing clear dated cancellations before 1888 are usually worth considerably more.

No. 19 comes on thin and thick paper.

For surcharges see Nos. 62-63.

Post Horn — A6

King Oscar II — A7

"NORGE" in Sans-serif Capitals, Ring of Post Horn Shaded

1877-78
22 A6 1o drab 8.50 *10.00*
On cover 60.00
23 A6 3o orange 100.00 35.00
On cover 50.00
24 A6 5o ultra 37.50 12.50
On cover 42.50
a. 5o dull blue 700.00 125.00
On cover 175.00
b. 5o bright blue 250.00 70.00
On cover 120.00
c. No period after "Postfrim" 57.50 13.00
d. Retouched plate 175.00 20.00
On cover 60.00
e. As "c," retouched plate 200.00 27.50
f. 5o Prussian blue 120.00 24.00
On cover 72.50
g. As "f," retouched plate 150.00 18.00
On cover 75.00
25 A6 10o rose 95.00 3.25
On cover 9.00
a. No period after "Postfrim" — —
b. Retouched plate 85.00 4.00
On cover 9.50
26 A6 12o lt green 125.00 20.00
On cover 90.00
27 A6 20o orange brn 375.00 14.00
On cover 90.00
28 A6 25o lilac 475.00 125.00
On cover 300.00
29 A6 35o bl grn ('78) 25.00 15.00
On cover 60.00
On cover, single franking 300.00
a. Retouched plate 250.00 110.00
b. 35o dark blue green, coarse impression 30.00 18.00
c. 35o pale blue green 2,400. 210.00
30 A6 50o maroon 47.50 10.00
On cover 110.00
On cover, single franking 200.00
31 A6 60o dk bl ('78) 47.50 10.00
On cover 110.00
On cover, single franking 425.00
a. 60o pale steel blue 175.00 60.00
32 A7 1k gray grn & grn ('78) 30.00 8.50
On cover 350.00
33 A7 1.50k ultra & bl ('78) 70.00 32.50
On cover 540.00
34 A7 2k rose & mar ('78) 50.00 22.50
On cover 540.00
Nos. 22-34 (13) 1,486. 318.25

There are 6 types each of Nos. 22, 26 and 28 to 34; 12 types each of Nos. 23, 24, 25 and 27. The differences are in the numerals.

A 2nd plate of the 5o ultramarine has 100 types, the 10o, 200 types.

The retouch on 5o, 10o and 35o shows as a thin white line between crown and post horn.

Philatelic covers exist, especially for Nos. 29-34. They sell for much less.

Post Horn — A8

"NORGE" in Sans-serif Capitals, Ring of Horn Unshaded

1882-93 Wmk. 160 *Perf. 14½x13½*
35 A8 1o black brn ('86) 19.00 *25.00*
On cover 90.00
a. No period after "Postfrim" 60.00 60.00
b. Small "N" in "NORGE" 60.00 60.00
36 A8 1o gray ('93) 11.00 *12.50*
On cover 90.00
37 A8 2o brown ('90) 6.00 *6.50*
On cover 30.00
On cover, single franking 100.00
38 A8 3o yellow ('89) 85.00 12.50
On cover 35.00
a. 3o orange ('83) 200.00 17.50
On cover 55.00
b. Perf. 13½x12½ ('89) 2,500.
39 A8 5o bl grn ('89) 75.00 2.00
On cover 15.00
a. 5o gray green ('86) 100.00 4.50
On cover 27.50
b. 5o emerald ('88) 225.00 10.00
On cover 35.00
c. 5o yellow green ('91) 100.00 3.50
On cover 15.00
d. Perf. 13½x12½ ('92) *1,750.* *950.00*
40 A8 10o rose 70.00 1.25
On cover 7.00
a. 10o rose red ('86) 70.00 1.50
On cover 7.50
b. 10o carmine ('91) 70.00 1.50
On cover 7.50
c. As "b," imperf., pair *3,250.*
41 A8 12o green ('84) 1,450. 425.00
On cover 3,000.
42 A8 12o yellow brn ('84) 35.00 25.00
On cover 1,450.
a. 12o bister brown ('83) 70.00 60.00
43 A8 20o brown 175.00 19.00
On cover 210.00
44 A8 20o blue ('86) 100.00 2.50
On cover 35.00
a. 20o ultramarine ('83) 350.00 22.50
On cover 175.00
b. No period after "Postfrim" ('85) 550.00 20.00
On cover 175.00
c. As "a," imperf., pair *3,250.*
45 A8 25o dull vio ('84) 20.00 15.00
On cover 350.00
On cover, single franking 600.00

Dies vary from 20 to 21mm high. Numerous types exist due to different production methods, including separate handmade dies for value figures. Many shades exist.

Philatelic covers bearing No. 45 sell for less.

No. 42 and 42a Surcharged in Black

1888 *Perf. 14½x13½*
46 A8 2o on 12o yel brn 2.50 3.00
On cover 65.00
On cover, single franking 175.00
a. 2o on 12o bister brown 3.50 3.75

Post Horn — A10

"NORGE" in Roman instead of Sans-serif capitals

Perf. 14½x13½

1893-1908 Wmk. 160

Size: 16x20mm
47 A10 1o gray ('99) 3.25 *3.50*
On cover 7.00
48 A10 2o pale brn ('99) 2.60 2.25
On cover, single franking 27.50
49 A10 3o orange yel 2.00 .40
On cover 2.50
50 A10 5o dp green ('98) 7.00 .20
On cover 1.75
b. Booklet pane of 6
51 A10 10o carmine ('98) 15.00 .20
On cover 1.75
b. Booklet pane of 6
d. 10o rose ('94) 350.00 4.00
52 A10 15o brown ('08) 50.00 11.50
On cover 35.00
53 A10 20o dp ultra 27.50 .40
On cover 3.00
b. Booklet pane of 6
54 A10 25o red vio ('01) 62.50 4.00
On cover 24.00
55 A10 30o sl gray ('07) 50.00 5.00
On cover 30.00
56 A10 35o dk bl grn ('98) 16.00 8.00
On cover 47.50
57 A10 50o maroon ('94) 75.00 2.25
On cover 35.00
58 A10 60o dk blue ('00) 65.00 8.00
On cover 120.00
Nos. 47-58 (12) 375.85 45.70

Two dies exist of 3, 10 and 20o.

See Nos. 74-95, 162-166, 187-191, 193, 307-309, 325-326, 416-419, 606, 709-714, 960-968, 1141-1145.

For overprints and surcharge see Nos. 99, 207-211, 220-224, 226, 329.

Philatelic covers exist, especially for Nos. 54-58. They sell for less than values shown.

1893-98 Wmk. 160 *Perf. 13½x12½*
47a A10 1o gray ('95) 17.50 *35.00*
On cover 42.50
49a A10 3o orange ('95) 40.00 7.00
On cover 17.50
50a A10 5o green 27.50 1.25
On cover 9.00
51a A10 10o carmine ('96) 35.00 1.50
On cover 7.00
c. 10o rose ('95) 100.00 3.25
On cover 7.00
53a A10 20o dull ultra ('95) 95.00 5.50
On cover 30.00
54a A10 25o red violet ('98) 85.00 25.00
On cover 125.00
56a A10 35o dark blue green ('95) 85.00 25.00
On cover 140.00
57a A10 50o maroon ('97) 275.00 22.50
On cover 120.00
Nos. 47a-57a (8) 660.00 122.75

Two dies exist of each except 25 and 35o.

No. 12 Surcharged in Green, Blue or Carmine

1905 Unwmk. *Perf. 14½x13½*
59 A4 1k on 2s org (G) 45.00 37.50
On cover 150.00
60 A4 1.50k on 2s org (Bl) 85.00 75.00
On cover 225.00
61 A4 2k on 2s org (C) 80.00 .65
On cover 175.00
Nos. 59-61 (3) 210.00 113.15

Used values are for copies canceled after 1910. Stamps used before that sell for twice as much.

Philatelic covers sell for less.

Nos. 19 and 21 Surcharged in Black

1906-08 Wmk. 160 *Perf. 14½x13½*
62 A5 15o on 4s lilac ('08) 6.00 6.00
On cover 55.00
a. 15o on 4s violet ('08) 17.50 12.00
On cover 60.00
63 A5 30o on 7s red brown 12.50 8.50
On cover 95.00

Used values are for copies canceled after 1914. Stamps used before that sell for twice as much.

Philatelic covers sell for less.

King Haakon VII — A11

Die A — Background of ruled lines. The coils at the sides are ornamented with fine cross-lines and small dots. Stamps 20¼mm high.

Die B — Background of ruled lines. The coils are ornamented with large white dots and dashes. Stamps 21¼mm high.

Die C — Solid background. The coils are without ornamental marks. Stamps 20¾mm high.

1907 Typo. *Perf. 14½x13½*

Die A
64 A11 1k yellow grn 50.00 30.00
On cover 425.00
65 A11 1.50k ultra 90.00 75.00
On cover 500.00
66 A11 2k rose 150.00 110.00
On cover 600.00
Nos. 64-66 (3) 290.00 215.00

Used values are for copies canceled after 1910. Stamps used before that sell for twice as much.

1909-10

Die B
67 A11 1k green 190.00 110.00
On cover 600.00
68 A11 1.50k ultra 225.00 *300.00*
On cover 1,500.
69 A11 2k rose 175.00 6.00
On cover 300.00
Nos. 67-69 (3) 590.00 *416.00*

Used values are for copies canceled after 1914. Stamps used before that sell for twice as much.

1911-18

Die C
70 A11 1k light green .70 .20
On cover 12.00
a. 1k dark green 75.00 3.00
On cover 50.00
71 A11 1.50k ultra 2.50 .20
On cover 30.00
72 A11 2k rose ('15) 3.00 .20
On cover 47.50
73 A11 5k dk violet ('18) 5.50 2.50
On cover 120.00
Nos. 70-73 (4) 11.70 3.10
Set, never hinged 37.50

See note following No. 180.

Philatelic covers sell for less.

Post Horn Type Redrawn

Original Redrawn

In the redrawn stamps the white ring of the post horn is continuous instead of being broken by a spot of color below the crown. On the 3 and 30 ore the top of the figure "3" in the oval band is rounded instead of flattened.

1910-29 *Perf. 14½x13½*

74	A10	1o pale olive	.40	*.50*
75	A10	2o pale brown	.40	.40
76	A10	3o orange	.40	.40
77	A10	5o green	3.50	.20
a.		Booklet pane of 6	250.00	
		Complete booklet, 4 #77a	2,500.	
78	A10	5o magenta ('22)	.80	.20
79	A10	7o green ('29)	.80	.20
80	A10	10o car rose	4.50	.20
a.		Booklet pane of 6	150.00	
		Complete booklet, 2 #80a	450.00	
81	A10	10o green ('22)	10.00	.20
82	A10	12o purple ('17)	.80	.80
83	A10	15o brown	8.00	.30
a.		Booklet pane of 6	30.00	
		Complete booklet, 2 #83a	70.00	
84	A10	15o indigo ('20)	7.00	.20
85	A10	20o deep ultra	6.50	.20
a.		Booklet pane of 6	500.00	
		Complete booklet, 2 #85a	*3,500.*	
86	A10	20o ol grn ('21)	7.00	.20
87	A10	25o red lilac	40.00	.30
88	A10	25o car rose ('22)	7.00	.80
89	A10	30o slate gray	10.00	.25
90	A10	30o lt blue ('27)	10.00	6.00
91	A10	35o dk olive ('20)	10.00	.30
92	A10	40o ol grn ('17)	4.00	.30
93	A10	40o dp ultra ('22)	27.50	.30
94	A10	50o claret	21.00	.30
95	A10	60o deep blue	27.50	.30
		Nos. 74-95 (22)	207.10	12.85
		Set, never hinged	1,200.	

Constitutional Assembly of 1814 — A12

1914, May 10 **Engr.** *Perf. 13½*

96	A12	5o green	1.00	.50
97	A12	10o car rose	2.50	.50
98	A12	20o deep blue	8.50	7.00
		Nos. 96-98 (3)	12.00	8.00
		Set, never hinged	60.00	

Norway's Constitution of May 17, 1814.

No. 87 Surcharged

1922, Mar. 1 *Perf. 14½x13½*

99	A10	5o on 25o red lilac	1.00	.60
		Never hinged	2.00	

Lion Rampant A13

Polar Bear and Airplane A14

"NORGE" in Roman capitals, Line below "Ore"

1922-24 **Typo.** *Perf. 14½x13½*

100	A13	10o dp grn ('24)	10.00	.30
101	A13	20o dp vio	14.00	.20
102	A13	25o scarlet ('24)	27.50	.60
103	A13	45o blue ('24)	1.50	1.25
		Nos. 100-103 (4)	53.00	2.35
		Set, never hinged	225.00	

For surcharge see No. 129.

1925, Apr. 1

104	A14	2o yellow brn	2.25	*3.00*
105	A14	3o orange	3.25	*5.50*
106	A14	5o magenta	8.25	*16.00*
107	A14	10o yellow grn	11.00	*27.50*
108	A14	15o dark blue	10.00	*25.00*
109	A14	20o plum	16.00	*32.50*
110	A14	25o scarlet	3.25	*7.00*
		Nos. 104-110 (7)	54.00	116.50
		Set, never hinged	160.00	

Issued to help finance Roald Amundsen's attempted flight to the North Pole.

A15

A16

1925, Aug. 19

111	A15	10o yellow green	5.00	*14.00*
112	A15	15o indigo	4.25	*8.00*
113	A15	20o plum	4.75	*2.25*
114	A15	45o dark blue	4.75	*7.50*
		Nos. 111-114 (4)	18.75	31.75
		Set, never hinged	90.00	

Annexation of Spitsbergen (Svalbard). For surcharge see No. 130.

"NORGE" in Sans-serif Capitals, No Line below "Ore"

1926-34 **Wmk. 160**

Size: 16x19½mm

115	A16	10o yel grn	.70	.20
116	A16	14o dp org ('29)	2.25	2.25
117	A16	15o olive gray	.85	.20
118	A16	20o plum	27.50	.20
119	A16	20o scar ('27)	2.00	.20
a.		Booklet pane of 6	110.00	
		Complete booklet, 2 #119a	300.00	
120	A16	25o red	12.00	1.75
121	A16	25o org brn ('27)	1.25	.20
122	A16	30o dull bl ('28)	1.25	.20
123	A16	35o ol brn ('27)	52.50	.20
124	A16	35o red vio ('34)	2.00	.20
125	A16	40o dull blue	3.25	.90
126	A16	40o slate ('27)	2.00	.20
127	A16	50o claret ('27)	2.00	.20
128	A16	60o Prus bl ('27)	2.00	.20
		Nos. 115-128 (14)	111.55	7.10
		Set, never hinged	550.00	

See Nos. 167-176, 192, 194-202A. For overprints and surcharges see Nos. 131, 212-219, 225, 227-234, 237-238, 302-303.

Nos. 103 and 114 Surcharged

1927, June 13

129	A13	30o on 45o blue	11.00	2.50
130	A15	30o on 45o dk blue	5.00	8.00
		Set, never hinged	47.50	

No. 120 Surcharged

1928

131	A16	20o on 25o red	2.50	2.50
		Never hinged	10.00	

See Nos. 302-303.

Henrik Ibsen — A17

Niels Henrik Abel — A18

1928, Mar. 20 **Litho.**

132	A17	10o yellow grn	9.00	4.00
133	A17	15o chnt brown	3.00	*3.25*
134	A17	20o carmine	3.00	.75
135	A17	30o dp ultra	6.00	5.00
		Nos. 132-135 (4)	21.00	13.00
		Set, never hinged	55.00	

Ibsen (1828-1906), dramatist.

Postage Due Stamps of 1889-1923 Overprinted

a

b

1929, Jan.

136	D1	(a)	1o gray	.75	*1.25*
137	D1	(a)	4o lilac rose	.60	.60
138	D1	(a)	10o green	2.25	*4.00*
139	D1	(b)	15o brown	3.00	*6.00*
140	D1	(b)	20o dull vio	1.25	1.00
141	D1	(b)	40o deep ultra	1.90	1.00
142	D1	(b)	50o maroon	8.50	*9.00*
143	D1	(a)	100o orange yel	3.00	*3.50*
144	D1	(b)	200o dk violet	5.00	4.00
			Nos. 136-144 (9)	26.25	30.35
			Set, never hinged	55.00	

1929, Apr. 6 **Litho.** *Perf. 14½x13½*

145	A18	10o green	3.00	1.00
146	A18	15o red brown	2.50	1.60
147	A18	20o rose red	1.25	.35
148	A18	30o deep ultra	3.00	2.50
		Nos. 145-148 (4)	9.75	5.45
		Set, never hinged	40.00	

Abel (1802-1829), mathematician.

No. 12 Surcharged

Perf. 14½x13½

1929, July 1 **Unwmk.**

149	A4	14o on 2s orange	2.25	*6.00*
		Never hinged	5.00	

Saint Olaf A19

Trondheim Cathedral A20

Death of Olaf in Battle of Stiklestad A21

Typo.; Litho. (15o)

Perf. 14½x13½

1930, Apr. 1 **Wmk. 160**

150	A19	10o yellow grn	10.00	.35
151	A20	15o brn & blk	1.75	.45
152	A19	20o scarlet	1.25	.30

Engr.

Perf. 13½

153	A21	30o deep blue	3.50	4.00
		Nos. 150-153 (4)	16.50	5.10
		Set, never hinged	60.00	

King Olaf Haraldsson (995-1030), patron saint of Norway.

Björnson A22

Holberg A23

1932, Dec. 8 *Perf. 14½x13½*

154	A22	10o yellow grn	8.00	.40
155	A22	15o black brn	1.50	1.50
156	A22	20o rose red	1.00	.30
157	A22	30o ultra	2.50	*3.00*
		Nos. 154-157 (4)	13.00	5.20
		Set, never hinged	40.00	

Björnstjerne Björnson (1832-1910), novelist, poet and dramatist.

1934, Nov. 23

158	A23	10o yellow grn	3.00	.75
159	A23	15o brown	.75	.75
160	A23	20o rose red	15.00	.25
161	A23	30o ultra	3.25	3.50
		Nos. 158-161 (4)	22.00	5.25
		Set, never hinged	65.00	

Ludvig Holberg (1684-1754), Danish man of letters.

Types of 1893-1900, 1926-34 Second Redrawing

Perf. 13x13½

1937 **Wmk. 160** **Photo.**

Size: 17x21mm

162	A10	1o olive	.70	1.00
163	A10	2o yellow brn	.70	1.00
164	A10	3o deep orange	1.75	*2.50*
165	A10	5o rose lilac	.55	.20
a.		Booklet pane of 6	55.00	
166	A10	7o brt green	.70	.20
167	A16	10o brt green	.45	.20
a.		Booklet pane of 6	50.00	
		Complete booklet, 2 #167a	550.00	
168	A16	14o dp orange	2.50	4.50
169	A16	15o olive bis	1.50	.20
170	A16	20o scarlet	1.10	.20
a.		Booklet pane of 6	50.00	
		Complete booklet, 2 #170a	1,000.	
		Complete booklet, 1 ea #165a, 167a, 170a	400.00	
171	A16	25o dk org brn	5.50	.25
172	A16	30o ultra	3.00	.25
173	A16	35o brt vio	2.50	.25
174	A16	40o dk slate grn	3.00	.25
175	A16	50o deep claret	3.50	.40
176	A16	60o Prussian bl	2.25	.20
		Nos. 162-176 (15)	29.70	11.60
		Set, never hinged	100.00	

Nos. 162 to 166 have a solid background inside oval. Nos. 74, 75, 76, 78, 79 have background of vertical lines.

King Haakon VII — A24

1937-38

177	A24	1k dark green	.20	.20
178	A24	1.50k sapphire ('38)	1.00	1.00
179	A24	2k rose red ('38)	1.00	1.00
180	A24	5k dl vio ('38)	5.00	5.75
		Nos. 177-180 (4)	7.20	7.95
		Set, never hinged	18.00	

Nos. 70-73, 177-180, 267, B19, B32-B34 and B38-B41 were demonetized from May 15, 1945 until Sept. 1, 1981. Used values are for stamps canceled after this period. Stamps with dated cancellations prior to May 15, 1945 sell for more. False cancellations exist.

Reindeer — A25

Borgund Church — A26

Jolster in Sunnfiord A27

Perf. 13x13½, 13½x13

1938, Apr. 20 **Wmk. 160**

181	A25	15o olive brn	.75	.75
182	A26	20o copper red	4.00	.55
183	A27	30o brt ultra	3.75	2.50
		Nos. 181-183 (3)	8.50	3.80
		Set, never hinged	30.00	

1939 **Unwmk.**

184	A25	15o olive brn	.50	.50
185	A26	20o copper red	.50	.20
186	A27	30o brt ultra	.50	.35
		Nos. 184-186 (3)	1.50	1.05
		Set, never hinged	2.75	

Types of 1937

Perf. 13x13½

1940-49 Unwmk. Photo.

Size: 17x21mm

187 A10 1o olive grn ('41) .20 .20
188 A10 2o yellow brn ('41) .20 .20
189 A10 3o dp orange ('41) .20 .20
190 A10 5o rose lilac ('41) .35 .20
191 A10 7o brt green ('41) .40 .20
192 A16 10o brt green .35 .20
Complete booklet, 2 panes of 6 #192 50.00
193 A10 12o brt vio .80 1.10
194 A16 14o dp org ('41) 1.00 2.00
195 A16 15o olive bister .50 .20
196 A16 20o red .45 .20
Complete booklet, 2 panes of 6 #196 60.00
Complete booklet, pane of 6 ea of #190, 192, 196 150.00
Complete booklet, pane of 10 ea of #190, 192, 196 100.00
197 A16 25o dk org brn 1.25 .20
197A A16 25o scarlet ('46) .40 .20
Complete booklet, pane of 10 ea of #190, 192, 197A 100.00
Complete booklet, pane of 10 ea of #192, 195, 197A 80.00
198 A16 30o brt ultra ('41) 1.25 .20
198A A16 30o gray ('49) 5.75 .20
199 A16 35o brt vio ('41) 1.50 .20
200 A16 40o dk sl grn ('41) 1.00 .20
200A A16 40o dp ultra ('46) 1.50 .20
201 A16 50o dp claret ('41) 1.00 .20
201A A16 55o dp org ('46) 15.00 .20
202 A16 60o Prus bl ('41) 1.00 .20
202A A16 80o dk org brn ('46) 12.50 .20
Nos. 187-202A (21) 46.60 6.90
Set, never hinged 125.00

Lion Rampant — A28

1940 Unwmk. Photo. *Perf. 13x13½*

203 A28 1k brt green 1.00 .20
204 A28 1½k deep blue 1.50 .30
205 A28 2k bright red 2.50 1.25
206 A28 5k dull purple 5.00 *5.50*
Nos. 203-206 (4) 10.00 7.25
Set, never hinged 27.50

For overprints see Nos. 235-238.

SEMI-POSTAL STAMPS

North Cape Issue

North Cape — SP1

Perf. 13½x14

1930, June 28 Wmk. 160 Photo.

Size: 33¼x21½mm

B1 SP1 15o + 25o blk brn 2.00 *5.00*
B2 SP1 20o + 25o car 32.50 *50.00*
B3 SP1 30o + 25o ultra 85.00 *110.00*
Nos. B1-B3 (3) 119.50 *165.00*
Set, never hinged 225.00

The surtax was given to the Tourist Association. See Nos. B9-B10, B28-B30, B54-B56, B59-B61.

Radium Hospital SP2

1931, Apr. 1 *Perf. 14½x13½*

B4 SP2 20o + 10o carmine 12.00 6.00
Never hinged 40.00

The surtax aided the Norwegian Radium Hospital.

Fridtjof Nansen — SP3

Queen Maud — SP4

1935, Dec. 13 *Perf. 13½*

B5 SP3 10o + 10o green 3.25 *6.00*
B6 SP3 15o + 10o red brn 10.00 *12.00*
B7 SP3 20o + 10o crimson 5.00 3.50
B8 SP3 30o + 10o brt ultra 12.00 *15.00*
Nos. B5-B8 (4) 30.25 36.50
Set, never hinged 50.00

The surtax aided the International Nansen Office for Refugees.

North Cape Type of 1930

1938, June 20 *Perf. 13x13½*

Size: 27x21mm

B9 SP1 20o + 25o brn car 3.25 *8.00*
B10 SP1 30o + 25o dp ultra 11.00 21.00
Set, never hinged 25.00

Surtax given to the Tourist Assoc.

Perf. 13x13½

1939, July 24 Photo. Unwmk.

B11 SP4 10o + 5o brt grn .40 10.00
B12 SP4 15o + 5o red brn .40 10.00
B13 SP4 20o + 5o scarlet .40 7.50
B14 SP4 30o + 5o brt ultra .40 12.00
Nos. B11-B14 (4) 1.60 39.50
Set, never hinged 4.00

The surtax was used for charities.

Fridtjof Nansen — SP5

SP6

1940, Oct. 21

B15 SP5 10o + 10o dk grn 2.50 3.50
B16 SP5 15o + 10o henna brn 3.00 4.75
B17 SP5 20o + 10o dark red .50 1.10
B18 SP5 30o + 10o ultra 1.25 2.25
Nos. B15-B18 (4) 7.25 11.60
Set, never hinged 13.00

The surtax was used for war relief work.

AIR POST STAMPS

Airplane over Akershus Castle
AP1 AP2

Perf. 13½x14½

1927-34 Typo. Wmk. 160

C1 AP1 45o lt bl, strong frame line ('34) 5.25 3.00
Never hinged 20.00
a. Faint or broken frame line 20.00 6.00
Never hinged 125.00

1937, Aug. 18 Photo. *Perf. 13*

C2 AP2 45o Prussian blue 1.25 .55
Never hinged 3.00

1941, Nov. 10 Unwmk.

C3 AP2 45o indigo .40 .25
Never hinged 1.25

POSTAGE DUE STAMPS

Numeral of Value — D1

Perf. 14½x13½

1889-1914 Typo. Wmk. 160

Inscribed "at betale"

J1 D1 1o olive green ('15) 1.10 1.25
Never hinged 2.40
a. 1o brown olive ('20) 7.00 18.00
Never hinged 24.00
b. 1o brownish gray ('89) 3.50 3.50
Never hinged 16.00
c. 1o gray ('93) 3.50 3.50
Never hinged 16.00
J2 D1 4o magenta ('11) 1.75 .80
Never hinged 12.00
a. 4o brown lilac ('08) 15.00 6.00
Never hinged 75.00
b. 4o bluish violet ('93) 47.50 11.00
Never hinged 210.00
J3 D1 10o carmine rose ('99) 4.25 .65
Never hinged 15.00
a. 10o rose red ('89) 72.50 16.00
Never hinged 425.00
J4 D1 15o brown ('14) 1.75 .75
Never hinged 13.00
J5 D1 20o ultra ('99) 3.00 .65
Never hinged 15.00
a. Perf. 13½x12½ ('95) 210.00 90.00
Never hinged 1,300.
J6 D1 50o maroon ('89) 6.00 2.50
Never hinged 30.00
Nos. J1-J6 (6) 17.85 6.60

See #J7-J12. For overprint see #136-144.

1922-23

Inscribed "a betale"

J7 D1 4o lilac rose 7.75 10.00
Never hinged 19.00
J8 D1 10o green 2.40 2.00
Never hinged 6.00
J9 D1 20o dull violet 5.50 4.50
Never hinged 12.00
J10 D1 40o deep ultra 8.50 .50
Never hinged 19.00
J11 D1 100o orange yel 30.00 9.00
Never hinged 77.50
J12 D1 200o dark violet 72.50 20.00
Never hinged 110.00
Nos. J7-J12 (6) 126.65 46.00

OFFICIAL STAMPS

Coat of Arms
O1 O2

Perf. 14½x13½

1926 Typo. Wmk. 160

O1 O1 5o rose lilac .75 *1.50*
O2 O1 10o yellow green .35 *.40*
O3 O1 15o indigo 2.00 *3.50*
O4 O1 20o plum .35 .20
O5 O1 30o slate 4.00 *6.00*
O6 O1 40o deep blue 1.25 *2.00*
O7 O1 60o Prussian blue 5.00 *8.00*
Nos. O1-O7 (7) 13.70 *21.60*
Set, never hinged 29.00

Official Stamp of 1926 Surcharged

1929, July 1

O8 O1 2o on 5o magenta .60 *1.25*

Perf. 14½x13½

1933-34 Litho. Wmk. 160

Size: 35x19¼mm

O9 O2 2o ocher .60 *1.50*
O10 O2 5o rose lilac 3.00 *6.50*
O11 O2 7o orange 4.50 *9.00*
O12 O2 10o green 25.00 1.25
O13 O2 15o olive .60 *1.25*
O14 O2 20o vermilion 25.00 .60
O15 O2 25o yellow brn .60 *1.00*
O16 O2 30o ultra .75 *1.00*
O18 O2 40o slate 27.50 1.00
O19 O2 60o blue 14.00 1.50
O20 O2 70o olive brn 1.50 *3.50*
O21 O2 100o violet 2.00 3.00
Nos. O9-O16,O18-O21 (12) 105.05 31.10
Same, never hinged 400.00

On the lithographed stamps, the lion's left leg is shaded.

Typo.

Size: 34x18¾mm

O10a O2 5o rose lilac 1.25 2.50
O11a O2 7o orange 7.50 *20.00*
O12a O2 10o green .70 .60
O13a O2 15o olive 5.00 *14.00*
O14a O2 20o vermilion .70 .25
O17 O2 35o red violet ('34) .85 .75
O18a O2 40o slate .85 .75
O19a O2 60o blue 1.25 .90
Nos. O10a-O14a,O17,O18a-O19a (8) 18.10 *39.75*
Same, never hinged 45.00

Coat of Arms — O3

Norwegian Nazi Party Emblem — O4

1937-38 Photo. *Perf. 13½x13*

O22 O3 5o rose lilac ('38) .65 1.00
O23 O3 7o dp orange .65 2.00
O24 O3 10o brt green .40 .25
O25 O3 15o olive bister .55 .90
O26 O3 20o carmine ('38) .55 2.00
O27 O3 25o red brown ('38) 1.00 .70
O28 O3 30o ultra 1.00 .60
O29 O3 35o red vio ('38) 1.00 .60
O30 O3 40o Prus grn ('38) .85 .40
O31 O3 60o Prus bl ('38) 1.00 .60
O32 O3 100o dk vio ('38) 2.00 1.50
Nos. O22-O32 (11) 9.65 *10.55*
Set, never hinged 23.00

See Nos. O33-O43, O55-O56. For surcharge see No. O57.

1939-47 Unwmk.

O33 O3 5o dp red lil ('41) .40 .20
O34 O3 7o dp orange ('41) .40 *1.00*
O35 O3 10o brt green ('41) .25 .20
O36 O3 15o olive ('45) .40 .25
O37 O3 20o carmine .25 .20
O38 O3 25o red brown 2.00 *6.00*
O38A O3 25o scarlet ('46) .25 .20
O39 O3 30o ultra 2.75 1.50
O39A O3 30o dk gray ('47) .65 .55
O40 O3 35o brt lilac ('41) .55 .25
O41 O3 40o grnsh blk ('41) .55 .25
O41A O3 40o dp ultra ('46) 1.25 .25
O42 O3 60o Prus blue ('41) .65 .25
O43 O3 100o dk violet ('41) .65 .25
Nos. O33-O43 (14) 11.00 *11.35*
Set, never hinged 27.50

NOSSI-BE

ˌno-sē-ˈbā

LOCATION — Island in the Indian Ocean, off the northwest coast of Madagascar
GOVT. — French Protectorate
AREA — 130 sq. mi.
POP. — 9,000 (approx. 1900)
CAPITAL — Hellville

In 1896 the island was placed under the authority of the Governor-General of Madagascar and postage stamps of Madagascar were placed in use.

100 Centimes = 1 Franc

Covers
Values are for commercial covers paying correct rates. Philatelic covers sell for less.

Stamps of French Colonies Surcharged in Blue:

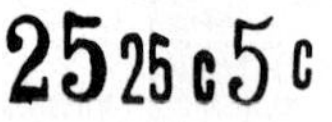

a b c

On the following issues the colors of the French Colonies stamps, type A9, are: 5c, green, *greenish*; 10c, black, *lavender*; 15c, blue; 20c, red, *green*; 30c, brown, *bister*; 40c, vermilion, *straw*; 75c, carmine, *rose*; 1fr, bronze green, *straw*.

1889 Unwmk. *Imperf.*

1 A8(a) 25 on 40c red, *straw* 2,250. 850.
On cover —
a. Double surcharge *1,600.*
2 A8(b) 25c on 40c red, *straw* 2,600. 1,700.
On cover —

Perf. 14x13½

3 A9(b) 5c on 10c 2,750. 775.
On cover —
4 A9(b) 5c on 20c 2,900. 1,950.
On cover —
5 A9(c) 5c on 10c 3,100. 1,150.
On cover —
6 A9(c) 5c on 20c 3,500. 1,300.
On cover —
7 A9(a) 15 on 20c 2,300. 775.
On cover —
a. 15 on 30c (error) *27,500. 24,000.*
8 A9(a) 25 on 30c 2,300. 700.
On cover *2,500.*
9 A9(a) 25 on 40c 2,000. 625.
On cover *2,500.*

d

f

g

Black Surcharge

1890

10 A9(d) 0.25 on 20c 350.00 225.00
On cover 1,200.
11 A9(d) 0.25 on 75c 350.00 225.00
On cover 1,200.
12 A9(d) 0.25 on 1fr 350.00 225.00
On cover 1,200.
a. Without ornament
16 A9(f) 25c on 20c 350.00 225.00
On cover 1,200.
17 A9(f) 25c on 75c 350.00 225.00
On cover 1,200.
18 A9(f) 25c on 1fr 350.00 225.00
On cover 1,200.
19 A9(g) 25 on 20c 775.00 550.00
On cover —
20 A9(g) 25 on 75c 775.00 550.00
On cover —
21 A9(g) 25 on 1fr 775.00 550.00
On cover —

The 25c on 20c with surcharge composed of "25 c." as in "f," "N S B" as in "d," and frame as in "g" is an essay.

Surcharged or Overprinted in Black, Carmine, Vermilion or Blue:

j

k

m

1893

23 A9(j) 25 on 20c (Bk) 37.50 35.00
On cover 500.00
24 A9(j) 50 on 10c (Bk) 50.00 37.50
On cover 600.00
a. Inverted surcharge 300.00 200.00
25 A9(j) 75 on 15c (Bk) 250.00 200.00
On cover —
26 A9(j) 1fr on 5c (Bk) 92.50 85.00
On cover —
a. Inverted surcharge 275.00 225.00
27 A9(k) 10c (C) 19.00 15.00
On cover 500.00
a. Inverted overprint 100.00 85.00
28 A9(k) 10c (V) 19.00 15.00
On cover 500.00
29 A9(k) 15c (Bk) 19.00 15.00
On cover 500.00
a. Inverted overprint 110.00 85.00
30 A9(k) 20c (Bk) 425.00 57.50
On cover 600.00
a. Double overprint
31 A9(m) 20c (Bl) 100.00 55.00
On cover 400.00
a. Inverted overprint 140.00 130.00

Counterfeits exist of surcharges and overprints of Nos. 1-31.

Navigation and Commerce — A14

1894 Typo. *Perf. 14x13½*
Name of Colony in Blue or Carmine

32 A14 1c blk, *lil bl* 1.10 1.10
On cover 150.00
33 A14 2c brn, *buff* 1.50 1.50
On cover 150.00
34 A14 4c claret, *lav* 2.00 1.75
On cover 150.00
35 A14 5c grn, *greenish* 3.00 2.10
On cover 100.00
36 A14 10c blk, *lav* 7.25 5.00
On cover 100.00
37 A14 15c blue, quadrille paper 10.50 5.00
On cover 125.00
38 A14 20c red, *grn* 7.75 5.25
On cover 125.00
39 A14 25c blk, *rose* 11.50 7.75
On cover —
40 A14 30c brn, *bister* 13.00 11.00
On cover —
41 A14 40c red, *straw* 17.00 12.50
On cover 300.00
42 A14 50c carmine, *rose* 17.00 12.50
On cover 300.00
43 A14 75c dp vio, *orange* 29.00 29.00
On cover 500.00
44 A14 1fr brnz grn, *straw* 21.00 21.00
On cover —
Nos. 32-44 (13) 141.60 115.45

Perf. 13½x14 stamps are counterfeits.

POSTAGE DUE STAMPS

Stamps of French Colonies Surcharged in Black:

n

o

1891 Unwmk. *Perf. 14x13½*

J1 A9(n) 20 on 1c blk, *lil bl* 350.00 250.00
On cover —
a. Inverted surcharge 700.00 500.00
b. Surcharged vertically 850.00 925.00
c. Surcharge on back 775.00 700.00
J2 A9(n) 30 on 2c brn, *buff* 350.00 250.00
On cover —
a. Inverted surcharge 700.00 500.00
b. Surcharge on back 775.00 700.00
J3 A9(n) 50 on 30c brn, *bister* 92.50 75.00
On cover *1,500.*
a. Inverted surcharge 700.00 500.00
b. Surcharge on back 775.00 700.00
J4 A9(o) 35 on 4c cl, *lav* 375.00 275.00
On cover —
a. Inverted surcharge 700.00 500.00
b. Surcharge on back 775.00 700.00
c. Pair, one without surcharge
J5 A9(o) 35 on 20c red, *green* 390.00 275.00
On cover —
a. Inverted surcharge 700.00 500.00
J6 A9(o) 1fr on 35c vio, *orange* 390.00 190.00
On cover —
a. Inverted surcharge 700.00 500.00
b. Surcharge on back 775.00 700.00

p

q

r

1891

J7 A9(p) 5c on 20c 190.00 190.00
On cover —
J8 A9(q) 5c on 20c 225.00 225.00
On cover —
J9 A9(r) 0.10c on 5c 23.00 19.00
On cover *850.00*
J10 A9(p) 10c on 15c 190.00 190.00
On cover —
J11 A9(q) 10c on 15c 225.00 225.00
On cover —
J12 A9(p) 15c on 10c 160.00 160.00
On cover —
J13 A9(q) 15c on 10c 170.00 170.00
On cover —
J14 A9(r) 0.15c on 20c 25.00 23.00
On cover *1,200.*
a. 25c on 20c (error) *36,000. 29,000.*
J15 A9(p) 25c on 5c 140.00 140.00
On cover —
J16 A9(q) 25c on 5c 160.00 160.00
On cover —
J17 A9(r) 0.25c on 75c 575.00 500.00
On cover —

Inverted Surcharge

J7a	A9(p)	5c on 20c	350.00	350.00
J8a	A9(q)	5c on 20c	350.00	350.00
J10a	A9(p)	10c on 15c	350.00	350.00
J11a	A9(q)	10c on 15c	350.00	350.00
J12a	A9(p)	15c on 10c	350.00	350.00
J13a	A9(q)	15c on 10c	350.00	350.00
J15a	A9(p)	25c on 5c	300.00	300.00
J16a	A9(q)	25c on 5c	300.00	300.00
J17a	A9(r)	0.25c on 75c	1,400.	1,150.

Stamps of Nossi-Be were superseded by those of Madagascar.
Counterfeits exist of surcharges on #J1-J17.

NOVA SCOTIA

ˌnō-və-ˈskō-shə

LOCATION — Eastern coast of Canada between the Gulf of St. Lawrence and the Atlantic Ocean
GOVT. — British Crown Colony
AREA — 21,428 sq. mi.
POP. — 386,500 (1871)
CAPITAL — Halifax

Nova Scotia joined the Canadian Confederation in 1867 and is now a province of the Dominion. Postage stamps of Canada are used.

12 Pence = 1 Shilling
100 Cents = 1 Dollar (1860)

PRE-STAMP POSTAL MARKINGS

Crowned Circle handstamp type I is pictured in the Crowned Circle Handstamps and Great Britain Used Abroad section.

1845-51

A1 I "Amherst" crowned circle handstamp in red, on cover 1,150.
A2 I "St. Margarets Bay" crowned circle handstamp in red, on cover 11,000.

Values for unused stamps are for examples with original gum as defined in the catalogue introduction except for Nos. 4-7, which are rarely found with any remaining original gum.

Queen Victoria — A1

Crown of Great Britain and Heraldic Flowers of the Empire — A2

1851-57 Unwmk. Engr. *Imperf.*
Blue Paper

1 A1 1p red brown ('53) 2,750. 550.
On cover 2,100.
a. Half used as ½p on cover —
2 A2 3p bright blue 1,100. 200.
On cover 275.
a. Half used as 1½p on cover *3,000.*
b. 3p pale blue ('57) 1,100. 200.
On cover 275.
c. As "b," half used as 1½p on cover *3,000.*
3 A2 3p dark blue 1,250. 250.
On cover 325.
a. Half used as 1½p on cover *3,750.*
4 A2 6p yellow green 4,000. 550.
On cover 1,500.
a. Half used as 3p on cover *3,750.*
5 A2 6p dark green ('57) 7,500. 1,500.
On cover 2,400.
a. Half used as 3p on cover *4,000.*
b. Quarter used as 1½p on cover *40,000.*
6 A2 1sh reddish pur ('57) 20,000. 4,500.
On cover *15,000.*
a. Half used as 6p on cover *30,000.*
b. 1sh deep purple *20,000.* 4,500.
On cover *16,000.*
7 A2 1sh dull violet 20,000. 6,000.
On cover 16,000.
a. Half used as 6p on cover *40,000.*
b. Quarter used as 3p on cover *55,000.*

The 1sh is known with a papermaker's watermark, "T. H. Saunders." Value, $20,000 unused, $6,500 used.

Nos. 2a, 2c, 3a are normally found with a 6p stamp to make up the 7½p rate for a half ounce letter to the United Kingdom.

Reprints are on thin hard white paper. 1p in brown, 3p in blue, 6p dark green, 1sh violet black. Value about $300 per set.

No. 6 was reproduced by the collotype process in a souvenir sheet distributed at the London International Stamp Exhibition 1950.

Queen Victoria — A3

A5

A6

1860-63 ***Perf. 12***

White or Yellowish Paper

8	A3	1c black	9.00	6.00
		Never hinged	12.50	
		On cover		200.00
a.		White paper	9.00	6.00
		Never hinged	12.50	
		On cover		200.00
b.		Half used as ½c on cover		*5,000.*
c.		Horiz. pair, imperf. vert.	240.00	
9	A3	2c lilac	9.00	7.50
		Never hinged	13.00	
		On cover		26.00
a.		Yellowish paper	9.00	7.50
		Never hinged	13.00	
		On cover		26.00
b.		Half used as 1c on cover		*2,500.*
c.		2c grayish purple	12.50	10.50
		Never hinged	17.50	
10	A3	5c blue	325.00	7.00
		Never hinged	*1,050.*	
		On cover		29.00
a.		Yellowish paper	325.00	7.00
		Never hinged	*1,050.*	
		On cover		29.00
b.		Half used as 2½c on cover		—
c.		5c dark blue	350.00	8.50
		Never hinged	*1,100.*	
11	A5	8½c green	9.00	*12.50*
		Never hinged	12.50	
		On cover		*700.00*
a.		White paper	9.00	*10.00*
		Never hinged	12.50	
		On cover		*700.00*
12	A5	10c vermilion	9.00	9.00
		Never hinged	12.50	
		On cover		60.00
a.		Yellowish paper	9.00	9.00
		Never hinged	12.50	
		On cover		60.00
b.		Half used as 5c on cover		*1,000.*
13	A6	12½c black	30.00	30.00
		Never hinged	45.00	
		On cover		225.00
a.		White paper	30.00	30.00
		Never hinged	45.00	
		On cover		225.00
		Nos. 8-13 (6)	391.00	72.00
		Set, never hinged	1,075.	

The stamps of Nova Scotia were replaced by those of Canada.

NYASALAND PROTECTORATE

nī-'a-sə-ˌland prə-'tek-t̩ə-ˌrət

LOCATION — In southern Africa, bordering on Lake Nyasa
GOVT. — British Protectorate
AREA — 49,000 sq. mi.
POP. — 2,950,000 (est. 1962)
CAPITAL — Zomba

For previous issues, see British Central Africa.

12 Pence = 1 Shilling
20 Shillings = 1 Pound

Catalogue values for unused stamps in this country are for Never Hinged items, beginning with Scott 68 in the regular postage section and Scott J1 in the postage due section.

A1

King Edward VII — A2

Wmk. Crown and C A (2)

1908, July 22 Typo. ***Perf. 14***

Chalky Paper

1	A1	1sh black, *green*	3.50	*14.00*

Wmk. Multiple Crown and C A (3)

Ordinary Paper

2	A1	½p green	2.00	2.25
3	A1	1p carmine	4.50	1.10

Chalky Paper

4	A1	3p violet, *yel*	1.75	*4.75*
5	A1	4p scar & blk, *yel*	1.75	*1.75*
6	A1	6p red vio & vio	4.25	*12.50*
7	A2	2sh 6p car & blk, *bl*	55.00	*100.00*
8	A2	4sh black & car	92.50	*140.00*
9	A2	10sh red & grn, *grn*	125.00	*250.00*
10	A2	£1 blk & vio, *red*	500.00	*600.00*
11	A2	£10 ultra & lilac	8,000.	*5,500.*
		Nos. 1-10 (10)	790.25	1,126.

A3

King George V — A4

1913-19

Ordinary Paper

12	A3	½p green	.80	1.00
13	A3	1p scarlet	2.25	.75
a.		1p carmine	1.25	1.00
14	A3	2p gray	3.00	1.00
15	A3	2½p ultra	2.00	*3.00*

Chalky Paper

16	A3	3p violet, *yel*	4.50	4.50
17	A3	4p scar & blk, *yel*	2.00	*2.50*
18	A3	6p red vio & dull vio	3.75	*10.00*
19	A3	1sh black, *green*	1.90	9.00
a.		1sh black, *emerald*	4.00	*6.00*
b.		1sh blk, *bl grn*, olive back	6.00	1.60
20	A4	2sh6p red & blk, *bl* ('18)	12.50	12.50
21	A4	4sh blk & red ('18)	20.00	*50.00*
22	A4	10sh red & grn, *grn*	85.00	*100.00*
23	A4	£1 blk & vio, *red* ('18)	200.00	150.00
24	A4	£10 brt ultra & slate vio ('19)	*3,750.*	*2,000.*
		Revenue cancel		250.00
a.		£10 pale ultra & dull vio ('14)	6,000.	
		Revenue cancel		275.00
		Nos. 12-23 (12)	337.70	*344.25*

Stamps of Nyasaland Protectorate overprinted "N. F." are listed under German East Africa.

1921-30 **Wmk. 4**

Ordinary Paper

25	A3	½p green	1.50	.50
26	A3	1p rose red	2.00	.50
27	A3	1½p orange	7.00	*17.50*
28	A3	2p gray	1.25	.50

Chalky Paper

29	A3	3p violet, *yel*	10.00	3.00
30	A3	4p scar & blk, *yel*	3.25	9.00
31	A3	6p red vio & dl vio	3.50	3.00
32	A3	1sh blk, *grn* ('30)	9.00	4.50
33	A4	2sh ultra & dl vio, *bl*	14.50	*15.00*
34	A4	2sh6p red & blk, *bl* ('24)	22.50	17.50
35	A4	4sh black & car	19.00	*27.50*
36	A4	5sh red & grn, *yel* ('29)	45.00	75.00
37	A4	10sh red & grn, *emer*	97.50	*110.00*
		Nos. 25-37 (13)	236.00	*283.50*

George V and Leopard A5

1934-35 Engr. ***Perf. 12½***

38	A5	½p green	.70	*1.00*
39	A5	1p dark brown	.70	.60
40	A5	1½p rose	.70	*3.50*
41	A5	2p gray	.90	*1.00*
42	A5	3p dark blue	2.25	1.50
43	A5	4p rose lilac ('35)	3.00	4.00
44	A5	6p dk violet	3.50	3.00
45	A5	9p olive bis ('35)	7.00	*10.00*
46	A5	1sh orange & blk	9.00	*15.00*
		Nos. 38-46 (9)	27.75	*39.60*

Common Design Types pictured following the introduction.

Silver Jubilee Issue
Common Design Type

1935, May 6 ***Perf. 11x12***

47	CD301	1p gray blk & ultra	.65	2.00
48	CD301	2p indigo & grn	3.75	2.25
49	CD301	3p ultra & brn	5.50	*12.00*
50	CD301	1sh brown vio & ind	14.00	*40.00*
		Nos. 47-50 (4)	23.90	*56.25*
		Set, never hinged	44.00	

Coronation Issue
Common Design Type

1937, May 12 ***Perf. 11x11½***

51	CD302	½p deep green	.20	.20
52	CD302	1p dark brown	.35	.20
53	CD302	2p gray black	.35	.35
		Nos. 51-53 (3)	.90	.75
		Set, never hinged	1.75	

A6

King George VI — A7

1938-44 Engr. ***Perf. 12½***

54	A6	½p green	.20	*1.50*
54A	A6	½p dk brown ('42)	.20	*2.00*
55	A6	1p dark brown	1.75	*.35*
55A	A6	1p green ('42)	.20	*.90*
56	A6	1½p dark carmine	3.00	*4.50*
56A	A6	1½p gray ('42)	.20	*5.75*
57	A6	2p gray	4.00	1.25
57A	A6	2p dark car ('42)	.20	*2.00*
58	A6	3p blue	.50	*.50*
59	A6	4p rose lilac	1.50	1.25
60	A6	6p dark violet	2.00	1.25
61	A6	9p olive bister	2.00	3.25
62	A6	1sh orange & blk	1.75	*2.00*

Typo.
Perf. 14
Chalky Paper

63	A7	2sh ultra & dl vio, *bl*	7.00	*11.00*
64	A7	2sh6p red & blk, *bl*	8.00	*13.00*
65	A7	5sh red & grn, *yel*	25.00	*22.50*
a.		5sh dk red & dp grn, *yel* ('44)	55.00	80.00
66	A7	10sh red & grn, *grn*	35.00	*45.00*

Wmk. 3

67	A7	£1 blk & vio, *red*	22.50	*32.50*
		Nos. 54-67 (18)	115.00	150.50
		Set, never hinged	200.00	

Catalogue values for unused stamps in this section, from this point to the end of the section, are for Never Hinged items.

Canoe on Lake Nyasa — A8

Soldier of King's African Rifles — A9

Tea Estate, Mlanje Mountain A10

Map and Coat of Arms — A11

Fishing Village, Lake Nyasa — A12

Tobacco Estate — A13

Arms of Nyasaland and George VI A14

1945, Sept. 1 Engr. ***Perf. 12***

68	A8	½p brn vio & blk	.40	.20
69	A9	1p dp green & blk	.20	.20
70	A10	1½p gray grn & blk	.30	.20
71	A11	2p scarlet & blk	.75	.20
72	A12	3p blue & blk	.40	.20
73	A13	4p rose vio & blk	1.25	.50
74	A10	6p violet & blk	1.25	.50
75	A8	9p ol grn & blk	1.25	*2.50*
76	A11	1sh myr grn & ind	1.00	.50
77	A12	2sh dl red brn & grn	3.50	3.50
78	A13	2sh6p ultra & green	8.00	4.00
79	A14	5sh ultra & lt vio	4.75	*5.00*
80	A11	10sh green & lake	15.00	12.00
81	A14	20sh black & scar	20.00	*25.00*
		Nos. 68-81 (14)	58.05	54.50

Peace Issue
Common Design Type
Perf. 13½x14

1946, Dec. 16 **Wmk. 4**

82	CD303	1p bright green	.20	.20
83	CD303	2p red orange	.25	.25

A15

1947, Oct. 20 ***Perf. 12***

84	A15	1p emerald & org brn	.50	.20

Silver Wedding Issue
Common Design Types

1948, Dec. 15 Photo. ***Perf. 14x14½***

85	CD304	1p dark green	.20	.20

Engr.; Name Typo.
Perf. 11½x11

86	CD305	10sh purple	14.00	*22.50*

UPU Issue

Common Design Types

Engr.; Name Typo. on 3p, 6p

Perf. 13½, 11x11½

1949, Nov. 21 **Wmk. 4**

87	CD306	1p blue green	.30	.30
88	CD307	3p Prus blue	2.00	2.00
89	CD308	6p rose violet	.75	.75
90	CD309	1sh violet blue	.30	.30
		Nos. 87-90 (4)	3.35	3.35

Arms of British Central Africa and Nyasaland Protectorate — A16

1951, May 15 **Engr.** ***Perf. 11x12***

Arms in Black

91	A16	2p rose	.90	.75
92	A16	3p blue	.90	.75
93	A16	6p purple	.90	*1.25*
94	A16	5sh deep blue	2.50	*5.25*
		Nos. 91-94 (4)	5.20	*8.00*

60th anniv. of the Protectorate, originally British Central Africa.

POSTAGE DUE STAMPS

Catalogue values for unused stamps in this section are for Never Hinged items.

D1

Perf. 14

1950, July 1 **Wmk. 4** **Typo.**

J1	D1	1p rose red	2.50	*8.00*
		On cover		*300.00*
J2	D1	2p ultramarine	6.00	*16.00*
		On cover		*300.00*
J3	D1	3p green	9.00	*10.00*
		On cover		*300.00*
J4	D1	4p claret	16.00	*35.00*
		On cover		*500.00*
J5	D1	6p ocher	25.00	*65.00*
		On cover		*750.00*
		Nos. J1-J5 (5)	58.50	*134.00*

Covers: Cover values are for properly franked commercial items. Philatelic usages sell for less.

NYASSA

nī-ˈa-sə

LOCATION — In the northern part of Mozambique in southeast Africa
GOVT. — Part of Portuguese East Africa Colony
AREA — 73,292 sq. mi.
POP. — 3,000,000 (estimated)
CAPITAL — Porto Amelia

The district formerly administered by the Nyassa Company is now a part of Mozambique. Postage stamps of Mozambique are used.

1000 Reis = 1 Milreis
100 Centavos = 1 Escudo (1919)

Mozambique Nos. 24-35 Overprinted in Black

1898 **Unwmk.** ***Perf. 11½, 12½***

1	A3	5r yellow	2.00	1.50
2	A3	10r redsh violet	2.00	1.50
3	A3	15r chocolate	2.00	1.50
4	A3	20r gray violet	2.00	1.50
5	A3	25r blue green	2.00	1.50
6	A3	50r light blue	2.00	1.50
a.		Inverted overprint		
b.		Perf. 12½	6.00	3.50
7	A3	75r rose	2.50	2.00
8	A3	80r yellow grn	2.50	2.00
9	A3	100r brown, *buff*	2.50	2.00
10	A3	150r car, *rose*	6.50	4.00
11	A3	200r dk blue, *blue*	4.50	3.00
12	A3	300r dk blue, *salmon*	4.50	3.00
		Nos. 1-12 (12)	35.00	25.00

Reprints of Nos. 1, 5, 8, 9, 10 and 12 have white gum and clean-cut perforation 13½. Value of No. 9, $15; others $3 each.

Same Overprint on Mozambique Issue of 1898

1898 ***Perf. 11½***

13	A4	2½r gray	1.40	.80
14	A4	5r orange	1.40	.80
15	A4	10r light green	1.40	.80
16	A4	15r brown	1.75	1.00
17	A4	20r gray violet	1.75	1.00
18	A4	25r sea green	1.75	1.00
19	A4	50r blue	1.75	1.00
20	A4	75r rose	2.10	1.00
21	A4	80r violet	2.25	.80
22	A4	100r dk bl, *bl*	2.25	.80
23	A4	150r brown, *straw*	2.25	.80
24	A4	200r red lilac, *pnksh*	2.25	1.00
25	A4	300r dk blue, *rose*	3.00	1.00
		Nos. 13-25 (13)	25.30	11.80

Giraffe — A5

Camels — A6

1901 **Engr.** ***Perf. 14***

26	A5	2½r blk & red brn	1.10	.55
27	A5	5r blk & violet	.75	.55
28	A5	10r blk & dp grn	.75	.55
29	A5	15r blk & org brn	1.10	.55
30	A5	20r blk & org red	1.10	.70
31	A5	25r blk & orange	1.10	.70
32	A5	50r blk & dl bl	1.10	.70
33	A6	75r blk & car lake	1.25	.70
34	A6	80r blk & lilac	1.25	.90
35	A6	100r blk & brn bis	1.25	.90
36	A6	150r blk & dp org	1.50	1.00
37	A6	200r blk & grnsh bl	1.50	1.00
38	A6	300r blk & yel grn	1.50	1.00
		Nos. 26-38 (13)	15.25	9.80

Nos. 26 to 38 are known with inverted centers but are believed to be purely speculative and never regularly issued. Value $50 each.

Perf 13½, 14½, 15½ & compound also exist.

For overprints and surcharges see Nos. 39-50, 63-80.

Nos. 34, 36, 38 Surcharged

1903

39	A6	65r on 80r	1.00	.75
40	A6	115r on 150r	1.00	.75
41	A6	130r on 300r	1.00	.75
		Nos. 39-41 (3)	3.00	2.25

Nos. 29, 31 Overprinted

1903

42	A5	15r black & org brn	1.00	.75
43	A5	25r black & orange	1.00	.75

Nos. 34, 36, 38 Surcharged

1903

44	A6	65r on 80r	32.50	25.00
45	A6	115r on 150r	32.50	25.00
46	A6	130r on 300r	32.50	25.00
		Nos. 44-46 (3)	97.50	75.00

Nos. 29, 31 Overprinted

PROVISORIO

1903

47	A5	15r black & org brn	400.00	100.00
48	A5	25r black & orange	150.00	100.00

Forgeries exist of Nos. 44-48.

Nos. 26, 35 Surcharged

1910

49	A5	5r on 2½r	1.00	.75
50	A6	50r on 100r	1.00	.75
a.		"50 REIS" omitted	300.00	

Reprints of Nos. 49-50, made in 1921, have 2mm space between surcharge lines, instead of 1½mm. Value, each 25 cents.

Zebra — A7

Vasco da Gama's Flagship "San Gabriel" — A8

Red Overprint

Designs: Nos. 51-53, Camels. Nos. 57-59, Giraffe and palms.

1911

51	A7	2½r blk & dl vio	1.00	.55
52	A7	5r black	1.00	.55
53	A7	10r blk & gray grn	1.00	.55
54	A7	20r blk & car lake	1.00	.55
55	A7	25r blk & vio brn	1.00	.55
56	A7	50r blk & dp bl	1.00	.55
57	A8	75r blk & brn	1.00	.55
58	A8	100r blk & brn, *grn*	1.00	.55
59	A8	200r blk & dp grn, *sal*	1.10	1.00
60	A8	300r blk, *blue*	2.40	1.60
61	A8	400r blk & dk brn	3.00	2.00
a.		Pair, one without overprint		
62	A8	500r ol & vio brn	4.00	3.00
		Nos. 51-62 (12)	18.50	12.00

Nos. 51-62 exist without overprint but were not issued in that condition. Value $7.50 each.

For surcharges see Nos. 81-105.

Stamps of 1901-03 Surcharged

1918

On Nos. 26-38

63	A5	¼c on 2½r	140.00	95.00
64	A5	½c on 5r	140.00	95.00
65	A5	1c on 10r	140.00	95.00
66	A5	1½c on 15r	2.10	1.10
67	A5	2c on 20r	1.25	1.00
68	A5	3½c on 25r	1.50	1.00
69	A5	5c on 50r	1.25	1.00
70	A6	7½c on 75r	1.25	1.00
71	A6	8c on 80r	1.25	1.00
72	A6	10c on 100r	1.25	1.00
73	A6	15c on 150r	2.10	2.00
74	A6	20c on 200r	2.00	2.00
75	A6	30c on 300r	3.250	2.40
		On Nos. 39-41		
76	A6	40c on 65r on 80r	18.00	16.50
77	A6	50c on 115r on 150r	2.75	2.00
78	A6	1e on 130r on 300r	2.75	2.00
		On Nos. 42-43		
79	A5	1½c on 15r	5.00	3.00
80	A5	3½c on 25r	2.00	1.00
		Nos. 63-80 (18)	469.95	323.00

On Nos. 70-78 there is less space between "REPUBLICA" and the new value than on the other stamps of this issue.

On Nos. 76-78 the 1903 surcharge is canceled by a bar.

The surcharge exists inverted on #64, 66-70, 72, 76, 78-80, and double on #64, 67, 69.

Nos. 51-62 Surcharged in Black or Red

1921

Lisbon Surcharges

Numerals: The "1" (large or small) is thin, sharp-pointed, and has thin serifs. The "2" is italic, with the tail thin and only slightly wavy. The "3" has a flat top. The "4" is open at the top. The "7" has thin strokes.

Centavos: The letters are shaded, i.e., they are thicker in some parts than in others. The "t" has a thin cross bar ending in a downward stroke at the right. The "s" is flat at the bottom and wider than in the next group.

81	A7	¼c on 2½r	3.25	2.75
83	A7	½c on 5r (R)	3.25	2.75
a.		½c on 2½r (R) (error)	275.00	250.00
84	A7	1c on 10r	3.25	2.75
a.		Pair, one without surcharge		
85	A8	1½c on 300r (R)	3.25	2.75
86	A7	2c on 20r	3.25	2.75
87	A7	2½c on 25r	3.25	2.75
88	A8	3c on 400r	3.25	2.75
a.		"Republica" omitted		
89	A7	5c on 50r	3.25	2.75
90	A8	7½c on 75r	3.25	2.75
91	A8	10c on 100r	3.25	2.75
92	A8	12c on 500r	3.25	2.75
93	A8	20c on 200r	3.25	2.75
		Nos. 81-93 (12)	39.00	33.00

The surcharge exists inverted on Nos. 83-85, 87-88 and 92, and double on Nos. 81, 83 and 86.

Forgeries exist of Nos. 81-93.

London Surcharges

Numerals: The "1" has the vertical stroke and serifs thicker than in the Lisbon printing. The "2" is upright and has a strong wave in the tail. The small "2" is heavily shaded. The "3" has a rounded top. The "4" is closed at the top. The "7" has thick strokes.

Centavos: The letters are heavier than in the Lisbon printing and are of even thickness throughout. The "t" has a thick cross bar with scarcely any down stroke at the end. The "s" is rounded at the bottom and narrower than in the Lisbon printing.

94	A7	¼c on 2½r	1.50	1.25
95	A7	½c on 5r (R)	1.50	1.25
96	A7	1c on 10r	1.50	1.25
97	A8	1½c on 300r (R)	1.50	1.25
98	A7	2c on 20r	1.50	1.25
99	A7	2½c on 25r	1.50	1.25
100	A8	3c on 400r	1.50	1.25
101	A7	5c on 50r	1.50	1.25
102	A8	7½c on 75r	1.50	1.25
a.		Inverted surcharge		
103	A8	10c on 100r	1.50	1.25
104	A8	12c on 500r	1.50	1.25
105	A8	20c on 200r	1.50	1.25
		Nos. 94-105 (12)	18.00	15.00

A9

Zebra and Warrior — A10

Designs: 2c-5c, Vasco da Gama. 7½c-20c, "San Gabriel." 2e-5e, Dhow and warrior.

Perf. 12½, 13½-15 & Compound

1921-23 Engr.

106	A9	¼c claret	1.00	.70
107	A9	½c steel blue	1.00	.70
108	A9	1c grn & blk	1.00	.70
109	A9	1½c blk & ocher	1.00	.70
110	A9	2c red & blk	1.00	.70
111	A9	2½c blk & ol grn	1.00	.70
112	A9	4c blk & org	1.00	.70
113	A9	5c ultra & blk	1.00	.70
114	A9	6c blk & vio	1.00	.70
115	A9	7½c blk & blk brn	1.00	.70
116	A9	8c blk & ol grn	1.00	.70
117	A9	10c blk & red brn	1.00	.70
118	A9	15c blk & carmine	1.00	.70
119	A9	20c blk & pale bl	1.00	.70
120	A10	30c blk & bister	1.00	.70
121	A10	40c blk & gray bl	1.00	.70
122	A10	50c blk & green	1.00	.70
123	A10	1e blk & red brn	1.00	.70
124	A10	2e red brn & blk ('23)	3.25	2.50
125	A10	5e ultra & red brn ('23)	3.00	2.25
		Nos. 106-125 (20)	24.25	17.35

POSTAGE DUE STAMPS

Giraffe — D1

½c, 1c, Giraffe. 2c, 3c, Zebra. 5c, 6c, 10c, "San Gabriel." 20c, 50c, Vasco da Gama.

1924 Unwmk. Engr. *Perf. 14*

J1	D1	½c deep green	1.00	1.75
J2	D1	1c gray	1.00	1.75
J3	D1	2c red	1.00	1.75
J4	D1	3c red orange	1.00	1.75
J5	D1	5c dark brown	1.00	1.75
J6	D1	6c orange brown	1.00	1.75
J7	D1	10c brown violet	1.00	1.75
J8	D1	20c carmine	1.00	1.75
J9	D1	50c lilac gray	1.00	1.75
		Nos. J1-J9 (9)	9.00	15.75

Used values are for c-t-o copies.

NEWSPAPER STAMP

Mozambique No. P6 Overprinted Like Nos. 1-25 in Black

1898 Unwmk. *Perf. 13½*

P1	N3	2½r brown	1.75	1.00

Reprints have white gum and clean-cut perf. 13½. Value $1.

POSTAL TAX STAMPS

Pombal Issue

Mozambique Nos. RA1-RA3 Overprinted "NYASSA" in Red

1925 Unwmk. *Perf. 12½*

RA1	CD28	15c brown & blk	5.00	5.00
RA2	CD29	15c brown & blk	5.00	5.00
RA3	CD30	15c brown & blk	5.00	5.00
		Nos. RA1-RA3 (3)	15.00	15.00

POSTAL TAX DUE STAMPS

Pombal Issue

Mozambique Nos. RAJ1-RAJ3 Overprinted "NYASSA" in Red

1925 Unwmk. *Perf. 12½*

RAJ1	CD28	30c brown & blk	12.50	7.75
RAJ2	CD29	30c brown & blk	12.50	7.75
RAJ3	CD30	30c brown & blk	12.50	7.75
		Nos. RAJ1-RAJ3 (3)	37.50	23.25

OBOCK

'ō-ˌbäk

LOCATION — A seaport in eastern Africa on the Gulf of Aden, directly opposite Aden.

Obock was the point of entrance from which French Somaliland was formed. The port was acquired by the French in 1862 but was not actively occupied until 1884 when Sagallo and Tadjoura were ceded to France. In 1888 Djibouti was made into a port and the seat of government moved from Obock to the latter city. In 1902 the name Somali Coast was adopted on the postage stamps of Djibouti, these stamps superseding the individual issues of Obock.

100 Centimes = 1 Franc

Covers

Values are for commercial covers paying correct rates. Philatelic covers sell for less.

Counterfeits exist of Nos. 1-31.

Stamps of French Colonies Handstamped in Black:

#1-11, J1-J4

#12-20, J5-J18

1892 Unwmk. *Perf. 14x13½*

1	A9	1c blk, *lil bl*	28.00	28.00
		On cover		—
2	A9	2c brn, *buff*	28.00	28.00
		On cover		—
3	A9	4c claret, *lav*	325.00	*350.00*
		On cover		—
4	A9	5c grn, *grnsh*	24.50	20.00
		On cover		—
5	A9	10c blk, *lavender*	55.00	28.00
		On cover		*700.00*
6	A9	15c blue	52.50	35.00
		On cover		*700.00*
7	A9	25c blk, *rose*	70.00	55.00
		On cover		*700.00*
8	A9	35c vio, *org*	325.00	325.00
		On cover		—
9	A9	40c red, *straw*	275.00	*300.00*
		On cover		—
10	A9	75c car, *rose*	325.00	*350.00*
		On cover		—
11	A9	1fr brnz grn, *straw*	375.00	375.00
		On cover		—
		Nos. 1-11 (11)	1,883.	1,894.

No. 3 has been reprinted. On the reprints the second "O" of "OBOCK" is 4mm high instead of 3½mm. Value $20.

1892

12	A9	4c claret, *lav*	17.50	14.00
		On cover		—
13	A9	5c grn, *grnsh*	17.50	14.00
		On cover		—
14	A9	10c blk, *lavender*	21.00	17.50
		On cover		*700.00*
15	A9	15c blue	21.00	17.50
		On cover		*700.00*
16	A9	20c red, *grn*	35.00	27.50
		On cover		—
17	A9	25c blk, *rose*	24.00	17.50
		On cover		*700.00*
18	A9	40c red, *straw*	42.50	32.50
		On cover		—
19	A9	75c car, *rose*	240.00	190.00
		On cover		—
20	A9	1fr brnz grn, *straw*	62.50	55.00
		Nos. 12-20 (9)	481.00	385.50
		On cover		—

Exists inverted or double on all denominations.

Nos. 14, 15, 17, 20 with Additional Surcharge Handstamped in Red, Blue or Black:

Nos, 21-30

No. 31

1892

21	A9	1c on 25c blk, *rose*	10.00	10.00
		On cover		—
22	A9	2c on 10c blk, *lav*	47.50	35.00
		On cover		—
23	A9	2c on 15c blue	12.50	12.50
		On cover		—
24	A9	4c on 15c bl (Bk)	14.00	14.00
		On cover		—
25	A9	4c on 25c blk, *rose* (Bk)	14.00	14.00
		On cover		—
26	A9	5c on 25c blk, *rose*	20.00	17.50
		On cover		—
27	A9	20c on 10c blk, *lav*	70.00	70.00
		On cover		—
28	A9	30c on 10c blk, *lav*	82.50	75.00
		On cover		—
29	A9	35c on 25c blk, *rose*	70.00	62.50
		On cover		—
a.		"3" instead of "35"	525.00	500.00
30	A9	75c on 1fr brnz grn, *straw*	75.00	70.00
		On cover		—
b.		"57" instead of "75"	*6,500.*	*6,500.*
c.		"55" instead of "75"	*6,500.*	*6,500.*
31	A9	5fr on 1fr brnz grn, *straw* (Bl)	600.00	550.00
		On cover		—
		Nos. 21-31 (11)	1,015.	930.50

Exists inverted on most denominations.

Navigation and Commerce A4

Camel and Rider A5

1892 Typo. *Perf. 14x13½*

Obock in Red (1c, 5c, 15c, 25c, 75c, 1fr) or Blue

32	A4	1c blk, *lil bl*	2.10	1.75
		On cover		125.00
33	A4	2c brn, *buff*	1.40	1.25
		On cover		125.00
34	A4	4c claret, *lav*	2.10	2.00
		On cover		125.00
35	A4	5c grn, *grnsh*	3.50	2.75
		On cover		90.00
36	A4	10c blk, *lavender*	5.50	3.50
		On cover		90.00
37	A4	15c bl, quadrille paper	14.00	7.00
		On cover		90.00
38	A4	20c red, *grn*	20.00	19.00
		On cover		—
39	A4	25c blk, *rose*	19.00	16.00
		On cover		100.00
40	A4	30c brn, *bis*	18.00	14.00
		On cover		—
41	A4	40c red, *straw*	17.50	14.00
		On cover		150.00
42	A4	50c car, *rose*	20.00	15.00
		On cover		150.00
43	A4	75c vio, *org*	24.50	17.50
		On cover		500.00
a.		Name double	250.00	250.00
b.		Name inverted	*3,100.*	*3,100.*
44	A4	1fr brnz grn, *straw*	35.00	27.50
		On cover		—
		Nos. 32-44 (13)	182.60	141.25

Perf. 13½x14 stamps are counterfeits.

1893 *Imperf.*

Quadrille Lines Printed on Paper

Size: 32mm at base

44A	A5	2fr brnz grn	45.00	42.50

Size: 45mm at base

45	A5	5fr red	100.00	90.00

Somali Warriors A7

A8

1894 *Imperf.*

Quadrille Lines Printed on Paper

46	A7	1c blk & rose	1.75	1.75
		On cover		125.00
47	A7	2c vio brn & grn	1.75	1.75
		On cover		125.00
48	A7	4c brn vio & org	1.75	1.75
		On cover		125.00
49	A7	5c bl grn & brn	2.40	2.40
		On cover		90.00
50	A7	10c blk & grn	6.50	5.50
		On cover		90.00
a.		Half used as 5c on cover ('01)		210.00
51	A7	15c bl & rose	6.50	4.75
		On cover		90.00
52	A7	20c brn org & mar	6.50	5.50
		On cover		*200.00*
a.		Half used as 10c on cover ('01)		210.00
53	A7	25c blk & bl	7.00	5.00
		On cover		90.00
a.		Right half used as 5c on cover ('01)		210.00
b.		Left half used as 2c on cover ('03)		210.00
54	A7	30c bis & yel grn	14.00	10.50
		On cover		*200.00*
a.		Half used as 15c on cover ('01)		1,600.
55	A7	40c red & bl grn	11.50	9.00
		On cover		150.00
56	A7	50c rose & bl	11.00	8.25
		On cover		150.00
a.		Half used as 25c on cover		2,500.
57	A7	75c gray lil & org	12.50	9.00
		On cover		500.00
58	A7	1fr ol grn & mar	11.00	7.00
		On cover		*650.00*

Size: 37mm at base

60	A8	2fr vio & org	82.50	82.50
		On cover		—

Size: 42mm at base

61	A8	5fr rose & bl	70.00	65.00
		On cover		—

Size: 46mm at base

62	A8	10fr org & red vio	110.00	110.00
		On cover		—
63	A8	25fr brn & bl	625.00	600.00
		On cover		—
64	A8	50fr red vio & grn	700.00	700.00
		On cover		—

Counterfeits exist of Nos. 63-64.

Stamps of Obock were replaced in 1901 by those of Somali Coast. The 5c on 75c, 5c on 25fr and 10c on 50fr of 1902 are listed under Somali Coast.

POSTAGE DUE STAMPS

Postage Due Stamps of French Colonies Handstamped Like #1-20

1892 Unwmk. *Imperf.*

J1	D1	5c black	7,500.	
J2	D1	10c black	175.00	200.00
J3	D1	30c black	275.00	350.00
J4	D1	60c black	350.00	400.00
J5	D1	1c black	37.50	37.50
J6	D1	2c black	30.00	30.00
J7	D1	3c black	35.00	35.00
J8	D1	4c black	27.50	27.50
J9	D1	5c black	10.00	10.00
J10	D1	10c black	24.00	24.00
J11	D1	15c black	17.50	17.50
J12	D1	20c black	21.00	21.00
J13	D1	30c black	24.00	24.00
J14	D1	40c black	42.50	42.50
J15	D1	60c black	55.00	55.00
J16	D1	1fr brown	165.00	165.00
J17	D1	2fr brown	180.00	180.00
J18	D1	5fr brown	400.00	400.00
		Nos. J2-J18 (17)	1,869.	2,019.

These handstamped overprints may be found double or inverted on some values. Counterfeits exist of Nos. J1-J18.

No. J1 has been reprinted. The overprint on the original measures 12½x3¾mm and on the reprint 12x3¼mm. Value, $200.

OLTRE GIUBA

ˌōl-trā-ˈjü-bə

(Italian Jubaland)

LOCATION — A strip of land, 50 to 100 miles in width, west of and parallel to the Juba River in East Africa
GOVT. — Italian Protectorate
AREA — 33,000 sq. mi.
POP. — 12,000
CAPITAL — Kismayu

Oltre Giuba was ceded to Italy by Great Britain in 1924 and in 1926 was incorporated with Italian Somaliland. In 1936 it became part of Italian East Africa.

100 Centesimi = 1 Lira

Watermark

Wmk. 140 — Crown

Italian Stamps of 1901-26 Overprinted

On #1-15

On #16-20

1925, July 29 Wmk. 140 *Perf. 14*

1	A42	1c brown	2.50	6.00
a.		Inverted overprint	100.00	
2	A43	2c yel brown	1.90	6.00
3	A48	5c green	1.50	3.00
4	A48	10c claret	1.50	3.00
5	A48	15c slate	1.50	4.50
6	A50	20c brn orange	1.50	4.50
7	A49	25c blue	1.90	4.50
8	A49	30c org brown	2.50	5.00
9	A49	40c brown	3.75	3.75
10	A49	50c violet	3.75	3.75
11	A49	60c carmine	3.75	5.00
12	A46	1 l brn & green	7.50	6.00
13	A46	2 l dk grn & org	50.00	17.00
14	A46	5 l blue & rose	75.00	25.00
15	A51	10 l gray grn & red	9.50	27.50
		Nos. 1-15 (15)	168.05	124.50

1925-26

16	A49	20c green	5.25	4.50
17	A49	30c gray	6.75	4.50
18	A46	75c dk red & rose	32.50	26.00
19	A46	1.25 l bl & ultra	45.00	32.50
20	A46	2.50 l dk grn & org	52.50	42.50
		Nos. 16-20 (5)	142.00	110.00

Issue years: #18-20, 1926; others 1925.

Victor Emmanuel Issue

Italian Stamps of 1925 Overprinted

1925-26 Unwmk. *Perf. 11*

21	A78	60c brown car	.75	4.50
a.		Perf. 13½	5,300.	
22	A78	1 l dark blue	.75	7.50
a.		Perf. 13½	225.00	750.00
23	A78	1.25 l dk bl ('26)	2.25	10.50
a.		Perf. 13½	2.75	11.00
		Nos. 21-23 (3)	3.75	22.50

Saint Francis of Assisi Issue

Italian Stamps and Type of 1926 Overprinted

Overprinted in Red

1926, Apr. 12 Wmk. 140 *Perf. 14*

24	A79	20c gray green	1.90	4.50
25	A80	40c dark violet	1.90	4.50
26	A81	60c red brown	1.90	4.50

Unwmk.

27	A82	1.25 l dk bl, perf. 11	1.90	4.50
28	A83	5 l + 2.50 l ol grn, perf. 13½	4.50	8.25
		Nos. 24-28 (5)	12.10	26.25

Map of Oltre Giuba — A1

1926, Apr. 21 Typo. Wmk. 140

29	A1	5c yellow brown	.25	3.75
30	A1	20c blue green	.25	3.75
31	A1	25c olive brown	.25	3.75
32	A1	40c dull red	.25	3.75
33	A1	60c brown violet	1.25	3.75
34	A1	1 l blue	1.25	3.75
35	A1	2 l dark green	1.25	3.75
		Nos. 29-35 (7)	4.75	26.25

Oltre Giuba was incorporated with Italian Somaliland on July 1, 1926, and stamps inscribed "Oltre Giuba" were discontinued.

SEMI-POSTAL STAMPS

Note preceding Italy semi-postals applies to No. 28.

Colonial Institute Issue

"Peace" Substituting Spade for Sword — SP1

Wmk. 140

1926, June 1 Typo. *Perf. 14*

B1	SP1	5c + 5c brown	.60	3.00
B2	SP1	10c + 5c olive green	.60	3.00
B3	SP1	20c + 5c blue green	.60	3.00
B4	SP1	40c + 5c brown red	.60	3.00
B5	SP1	60c + 5c orange	.60	3.00
B6	SP1	1 l + 5c blue	.60	5.25
		Nos. B1-B6 (6)	3.60	20.25

Surtax for Italian Colonial Institute.

SPECIAL DELIVERY STAMPS

Special Delivery Stamps of Italy Overprinted

1926 Wmk. 140 *Perf. 14*

E1	SD1	70c dull red	19.00	18.00
E2	SD2	2.50 l blue & red	27.50	37.40

POSTAGE DUE STAMPS

Italian Postage Due Stamps of 1870-1903 Overprinted Like Nos. E1-E2

1925, July 29 Wmk. 140 *Perf. 14*

J1	D3	5c buff & magenta	10.50	5.25
J2	D3	10c buff & magenta	10.50	5.25
J3	D3	20c buff & magenta	10.50	9.00
J4	D3	30c buff & magenta	10.50	9.00
J5	D3	40c buff & magenta	10.50	9.75
J6	D3	50c buff & magenta	12.00	13.50
J7	D3	60c buff & brown	12.00	14.50
J8	D3	1 l blue & magenta	17.00	20.00
J9	D3	2 l blue & magenta	80.00	67.50
J10	D3	5 l blue & magenta	100.00	67.50
		Nos. J1-J10 (10)	273.50	221.25

PARCEL POST STAMPS

These stamps were used by affixing them to the waybill so that one half remained on it following the parcel, the other half staying on the receipt given the sender. Most used halves are right halves. Complete stamps were obtainable canceled, probably to order. Both unused and used values are for complete stamps.

Italian Parcel Post Stamps of 1914-22 Overprinted

1925, July 29 Wmk. 140 *Perf. 13½*

Q1	PP2	5c brown	5.25	8.25
Q2	PP2	10c blue	3.00	8.25
Q3	PP2	20c black	3.00	8.25
Q4	PP2	25c red	3.00	8.25
Q5	PP2	50c orange	5.25	8.25
Q6	PP2	1 l violet	4.25	20.00
a.		Double overprint	100.00	
Q7	PP2	2 l green	8.25	20.00
Q8	PP2	3 l bister	22.50	27.50
Q9	PP2	4 l slate	7.25	27.50
Q10	PP2	10 l rose lilac	45.00	42.50
Q11	PP2	12 l red brown	100.00	67.50
Q12	PP2	15 l olive green	82.50	67.50
Q13	PP2	20 l brown violet	82.50	67.50
		Nos. Q1-Q13 (13)	371.75	381.25

Halves Used

Q1, Q10	.45
Q2-Q6	.25
Q7-Q8	.25
Q9	.25
Q11, Q13	1.50
Q12	1.25

OMAN

ˈō-ˌmän

Muscat and Oman

LOCATION — Southeastern corner of the Arabian Peninsula
GOVT. — Sultanate
AREA — 105,000 sq. mi.
POP. — 1,500,000 (est. 1982)
CAPITAL — Muscat

Nos. 16-93, the stamps with 'value only' surcharges, were used not only in Muscat, but also in Dubai (Apr. 1, 1948 - Jan. 6, 1961), Qatar (Aug. 1950 - Mar. 31, 1957), and Abu Dhabi (Mar. 30, 1963 - Mar. 29, 1964). Occasionally they were also used in Bahrain and Kuwait.

12 Pies = 1 Anna
16 Annas = 1 Rupee

Catalogue values for all unused stamps in this country are for Never Hinged items.

Muscat

Stamps of India 1937-43 Overprinted in Black

On #1-13 the overprint is smaller — 13x6mm.

Wmk. Multiple Stars (196)

1944, Nov. 20 *Perf. 13½x14*

1	A83	3p slate	.50	4.50
2	A83	½a rose violet	.50	4.50
3	A83	9p lt green	.50	4.50
4	A83	1a carmine rose	.50	4.50
5	A84	1½a dark purple	.50	4.50
a.		Double overprint	400.00	
6	A84	2a scarlet	.50	4.50
7	A84	3a violet	.80	4.50
8	A84	3½a ultra	.80	4.50
9	A85	4a chocolate	.80	4.50
10	A85	6a pck blue	1.00	4.50
11	A85	8a blue violet	1.00	4.50
12	A85	12a car lake	1.30	4.50
13	A81	14a rose violet	5.00	6.50
14	A82	1r brown & slate	1.40	8.00
15	A82	2r dk brn & dk vio	3.00	14.00
		Nos. 1-15 (15)	18.10	82.50

200th anniv. of Al Busaid Dynasty.

Great Britain, Nos. 258 to 263, 243, 248, 249A Surcharged

Perf. 14½x14

1948, Apr. 1 Wmk. 251

16	A101	½a on ½p green	.20	3.25
17	A101	1a on 1p vermilion	.20	.20
18	A101	1½a on 1½p lt red brn	.40	.35
19	A101	2a on 2p lt org	.45	.45
20	A101	2½a on 2½p ultra	.55	2.75
21	A101	3a on 3p violet	.20	.20
22	A102	6a on 6p rose lilac	.50	.20
23	A103	1r on 1sh brown	2.25	.40

Wmk. 259 *Perf. 14*

24	A104	2r on 2sh6p yel grn	17.50	22.50
		Nos. 16-24 (9)	22.25	30.30

Silver Wedding Issue

Great Britain, Nos. 267 and 268, Surcharged with New Value in Black

Perf. 14½x14, 14x14½

1948, Apr. 26 Wmk. 251

25	A109	2½a on 2½p brt ultra	.20	.20
26	A110	15r on £1 dp chlky bl	30.00	30.00

Three bars obliterate the original denomination on No. 26.

Olympic Games Issue

Great Britain, Nos. 271 to 274, Surcharged with New Value in Black

1948, July 29 ***Perf. 14½x14***

27	A113	2½a on 2½p brt ultra	.30	.75
28	A114	3a on 3p dp violet	.35	.75
29	A115	6a on 6p red violet	.75	.85
30	A116	1r on 1sh dk brown	2.00	2.50
a.		Double surcharge	300.00	
		Nos. 27-30 (4)	3.40	4.85

A square of dots obliterates the original denomination on Nos. 28-30.

UPU Issue

Great Britain Nos. 276 to 279 Surcharged with New Value and Square of Dots in Black

1949, Oct. 10 **Photo.**

31	A117	2½a on 2½p brt ultra	.60	.40
32	A118	3a on 3p brt violet	1.00	.75
33	A119	6a on 6p red violet	1.50	1.10
34	A120	1r on 1sh brown	2.75	2.75
		Nos. 31-34 (4)	5.85	5.00

Great Britain Nos. 280-286 Surcharged with New Value in Black

1951

35	A101	½a on ½p lt org	.35	6.00
36	A101	1a on 1p ultra	.50	3.75
37	A101	1½a on 1½p green	2.00	15.00
38	A101	2a on 2p lt red brn	1.00	5.50
39	A101	2½a on 2½p vermilion	2.25	11.00
40	A102	4a on 4p ultra	2.00	2.00

Perf. 11x12

Wmk. 259

41	A121	2r on 2sh6p green	25.00	5.00
		Nos. 35-41 (7)	33.10	*48.25*

Two types of surcharge on No. 41.

Stamps of Great Britain, 1952-54, Surcharged with New Value in Black and Dark Blue

1952-54 **Wmk. 298** ***Perf. 14½x14***

42	A126	½a on ½p red org ('53)	.20	.75
43	A126	1a on 1p ultra ('53)	.20	.75
44	A126	1½a on 1½p green ('52)	.45	.50
45	A126	2a on 2p red brn ('53)	.25	.20
46	A127	2½a on 2½p scar ('52)	.55	.25
47	A127	3a on 3p dk pur (Dk Bl)	.30	.30
48	A128	4a on 4p ultra ('53)	1.00	1.25
49	A129	6a on 6p lilac rose	.70	.45
50	A132	12a on 1sh3p dk grn ('53)	5.00	1.40
51	A131	1r on 1sh6p dk bl ('53)	5.25	1.60
		Nos. 42-51 (10)	13.90	7.45

OFFICIAL STAMPS

Official Stamps of India 1938-43 Overprinted in Black

Perf. 13½x14

1944, Nov. 20 **Wmk. 196**

O1	O8	3p slate	1.10	*9.00*
O2	O8	½a dk rose violet	1.10	*9.00*
O3	O8	9p green	1.10	*9.00*
O4	O8	1a carmine rose	1.10	*9.00*
O5	O8	1½a dull purple	1.10	*9.00*
O6	O8	2a scarlet	1.60	*9.00*
O7	O8	2½a purple	5.25	*9.00*
O8	O8	4a dark brown	2.25	*9.00*
O9	O8	8a blue violet	4.50	*10.00*
O10	A82	1r brown & slate	5.25	*17.50*
		Nos. O1-O10 (10)	24.35	*99.50*

Al Busaid Dynasty, 200th anniv. On Nos. O1-O9 the overprint is smaller — 13x6mm.

ORANGE RIVER COLONY

'är-inj 'ri-vər 'kä-lə-nē

(Orange Free State)

LOCATION — South Africa, north of the Cape of Good Hope between the Orange and Vaal Rivers
GOVT. — British Crown Colony
AREA — 49,647 sq. mi.
POP. — 528,174 (1911)
CAPITAL — Bloemfontein

Orange Free State was an independent republic, 1854-1900. Orange River Colony existed from May, 1900, to June, 1910, when it united with Cape of Good Hope, Natal and the Transvaal to form the Union of South Africa.

12 Pence = 1 Shilling

Values for unused stamps are for examples with original gum as defined in the catalogue introduction. Very fine examples of Nos. 1-60c will have perforations touching the design on one or more sides due to the narrow spacing of the stamps on the plates. Stamps with perfs clear of the design on all four sides are scarce and will command higher prices.

Een = 1
Twee = 2
Drie = 3
Vier = 4

Issues of the Republic

Orange Tree — A1

1868-1900 **Unwmk.** **Typo.** ***Perf. 14***

1	A1	½p red brown ('83)	3.00	.75
2	A1	½p orange ('97)	2.00	.35
3	A1	1p brown	10.00	.50
4	A1	1p violet ('94)	3.00	.30
5	A1	2p violet ('83)	12.50	.45
6	A1	3p ultra ('83)	2.75	1.75
7	A1	4p ultra ('78)	4.50	2.25
8	A1	6p car rose ('90)	17.50	12.50
a.		6p rose ('68)	50.00	9.00
b.		6p ultramarine ('00)	100.00	
10	A1	1sh orange	35.00	2.00
a.		1sh orange buff	*80.00*	*6.75*
11	A1	1sh brown ('97)	20.00	1.60
12	A1	5sh green ('78)	10.50	*12.50*
		Nos. 1-8,10-12 (11)	120.75	34.95

No. 8b was not placed in use without surcharge.

For surcharges see #13-53, 44j-53c, 57-60.

No. 8a Surcharged:

4 **4** **4** **4**
a *b* *c* *d*

1877

13	(a) 4p on 6p rose	240.00	40.00
a.	Inverted surcharge	*1,250.*	500.00
14	(b) 4p on 6p rose	1,350.	225.00
a.	Inverted surcharge	—	1,250.
b.	Double surcharge, one inverted ("b" and "d")		
15	(c) 4p on 6p rose	200.00	27.50
a.	Inverted surcharge	—	400.00
16	(d) 4p on 6p rose	350.00	60.00
a.	Inverted surcharge	—	600.00
b.	Double surcharge, one inverted ("d" and "c" inverted)		*3,000.*
c.	Double surcharge, one inverted ("d" inverted and "c")	—	*5,000.*

No. 12 Surcharged with Bar and:

1d. **1d.** **1d.** **1d.** **1d.**
f *g* *h* *i* *k*

1881

17	(f) 1p on 5sh green	120.00	20.00
18	(g) 1p on 5sh green	240.00	80.00
a.	Inverted surcharge	—	1,250.
b.	Double surcharge		1,450.
19	(h) 1p on 5sh green	65.00	20.00
a.	Inverted surcharge	—	850.00
b.	Double surcharge	—	1,150.
20	(i) 1p on 5sh green	100.00	20.00
a.	Double surcharge	—	1,000.
b.	Inverted surcharge	1,900.	900.00
21	(k) 1p on 5sh green	600.00	250.00
a.	Inverted surcharge	—	2,250.
b.	Double surcharge		2,250.
	Nos. 17-21 (5)	1,125.	390.00

No. 12 Surcharged:

1882

22	A1	½p on 5sh green	15.00	4.00
a.		Double surcharge	450.00	375.00
b.		Inverted surcharge	*1,350.*	*900.00*

No. 7 Surcharged with Thin Line and:

m

n

o

p

q

1882

23	(m) 3p on 4p ultra	95.00	20.00
a.	Double surcharge		1,400.
24	(n) 3p on 4p ultra	95.00	19.00
a.	Double surcharge		1,400.
25	(o) 3p on 4p ultra	37.50	17.50
a.	Double surcharge		1,400.
26	(p) 3p on 4p ultra	240.00	67.50
a.	Double surcharge		3,500.
27	(q) 3p on 4p ultra	95.00	25.00
a.	Double surcharge		1,500.
	Nos. 23-27 (5)	562.50	149.00

No. 6 Surcharged

1888

28	A1	2p on 3p ultra	32.50	2.25
a.		Wide "2" at top	57.50	10.00
b.		As No. 28, invtd. surch.		350.00
c.		As No. 28a, invtd. surch.		800.00
d.		Curved base on "2"	*1,350.*	*575.00*

Nos. 6 and 7 Surcharged:

r

s

Id
t

1890-91

29	(r) 1p on 3p ultra ('91)	2.00	.75
a.	Double surcharge	77.50	75.00
b.	"1" and "d" wide apart	140.00	100.00
30	(r) 1p on 4p ultra	17.50	4.00
a.	Double surcharge	125.00	100.00
31	(s) 1p on 3p ultra ('91)	11.00	2.75
a.	Double surcharge	200.00	225.00
32	(s) 1p on 4p ultra	75.00	50.00
a.	Double surcharge	350.00	300.00
b.	Triple surcharge		*2,250.*
33	(t) 1p on 4p ultra	*1,300.*	*550.00*

No. 6 Surcharged

1892

34	A1	2½p on 3p ultra	5.00	.80
a.		Without period	60.00	45.00

No. 6 Surcharged:

v

w

x

y

z

1896

35	(v) ½p on 3p ultra	2.50	6.50
a.	Double surcharge "v" and "y"	14.00	12.00
36	(w) ½p on 3p ultra	5.25	2.75
a.	Double surcharge "w" and "y"	15.00	15.00
37	(x) ½p on 3p ultra	5.25	2.75
38	(y) ½p on 3p ultra	3.00	2.50
a.	Double surcharge	12.50	11.00
39	(z) ½p on 3p ultra	4.50	2.75

Surcharged as "v" but "1" with Straight Serif

40	A1	½p on 3p ultra	5.50	5.50
a.		Double surcharge, one type "y"	13.00	13.00

Surcharged as "z" but "1" with Straight Serif

41	A1	½p on 3p ultra	6.00	7.00
a.		Double surcharge, one type "y"	12.50	11.00
		Nos. 35-41 (7)	32.00	29.75

No. 6 Surcharged

1896

42	A1	½p on 3p ultra	.65	.65
a.		No period after "Penny"	10.00	15.00
b.		"Peuny"	8.50	8.50
c.		Inverted surcharge	60.00	60.00
d.		Double surch., one inverted	160.00	160.00
e.		Without bar	5.00	5.00
f.		With additional surcharge as on Nos. 35-41	75.00	75.00

No. 6 Surcharged

1897

43	A1	2½p on 3p ultra	2.00	.75
a.		Roman "I" instead of "1" in "½"	150.00	90.00

Issued under British Occupation

Nos. 2-8, 8a, 10-12 Surcharged or Overprinted

1900, Mar.-Apr. **Unwmk.** ***Perf. 14***

Periods in "V.R.I." Level with Bottoms of Letters

44	A1	½p on ½p org	1.50	1.50
a.		No period after "V"	15.00	15.00
b.		No period after "I"	175.00	175.00
c.		"I" and period after "R" omitted		
f.		"½" omitted	*175.00*	*175.00*
g.		Small "½"	45.00	45.00
h.		Double surcharge	125.00	*125.00*
i.		As "g," double surcharge	300.00	

45	A1	1p on 1p violet	1.60	.75
a.		No period after "V"	10.50	10.50
b.		"I" and period after "R" omitted	160.00	175.00
d.		"1" of "1d" omitted	160.00	175.00
e.		"d" omitted	300.00	300.00
f.		"1d" omitted, "V.R.I." at top	375.00	
45O	A1	1p on 1p brown	*675.00*	*400.00*
y.		No period after "V"	*2,250.*	
46	A1	2p on 2p violet	.35	.60
a.		No period after "V"	10.00	12.00
b.		No period after "R"	250.00	
c.		No period after "I"	250.00	
47	A1	'2½' on 3p ultra	4.50	4.00
a.		No period after "V"	70.00	65.00
b.		Roman "I" in "½"	160.00	275.00
48	A1	3p on 3p ultra	1.50	1.00
a.		No period after "V"	13.00	13.00
b.		Dbl. surch. one diagonal	600.00	
49	A1	4p on 4p ultra	4.50	6.00
a.		No period after "V"	50.00	52.50
50	A1	6p on 6p car rose	35.00	35.00
a.		No period after "V"	250.00	300.00
b.		"6" omitted	300.00	300.00
51	A1	6p on 6p ultra	2.75	3.25
a.		No period after "V"	30.00	30.00
c.		"6" omitted	65.00	65.00
52	A1	1sh on 1sh brown	3.50	3.50
a.		No period after "V"	30.00	30.00
c.		"1" of "1s" omitted	110.00	110.00
52G	A1	1sh on 1sh org	*3,000.*	*2,000.*
53	A1	5sh on 5sh green	18.00	30.00
a.		No period after "V"	175.00	175.00
b.		"5" omitted	950.00	950.00

#47, 47c overprinted "V.R.I." on #43.

No. 45f ("1d" omitted) with "V.R.I." at bottom is a shift which sells for a fifth of the value of the listed item. Varieties such as "V.R.I." omitted, denomination omitted and pair, one without surcharge are also the result of shifts.

For surcharges see Nos. 57, 60.

1900-01

Periods in "V.R.I." Raised Above Bottoms of Letters

44j	A1	½p on ½p orange	.25	.20
k.		Mixed periods	1.75	1.75
l.		Pair, one with level periods	8.00	13.00
m.		No period after "V"	3.00	3.00
n.		No period after "I"	25.00	25.00
o.		"V" omitted	400.00	400.00
p.		Small "½"	12.00	13.00
q.		"1" for "I" in "V.R.I."	9.00	9.00
r.		Thick "V"	.30	.45
45i	A1	1p on 1p violet	.30	.20
j.		Mixed periods	1.50	1.60
k.		Pair, one with level periods	17.00	17.00
l.		No period after "V"	6.00	6.00
m.		No period after "R"	12.00	12.00
n.		No period after "I"	12.00	12.00
p.		Double surcharge	90.00	90.00
q.		Inverted surcharge	200.00	
s.		Small "1" in "1d"	160.00	160.00
t.		"1" for "I" in "V.R.I."	13.00	13.00
u.		Thick "V"	.30	.25
v.		As "u," invtd. "1" for "I" in "V.R.I."	7.25	7.25
w.		As "u," double surcharge	300.00	300.00
z.		As "u," no period after "R"	30.00	30.00
46e	A1	2p on 2p violet	.50	.25
f.		Mixed periods	4.50	4.50
g.		Pair, one with level periods	7.25	7.25
h.		Inverted surcharge	500.00	400.00
i.		Thick "V"	.35	.30
j.		As "i," invtd. "1" for "I" in "V.R.I."	15.00	15.00
47c	A1	'2½' on 3p ultra	190.00	160.00
d.		Thick "V"	350.00	350.00
f.		As "d," Roman "I" on "½"		
48d	A1	3p on 3p ultra	.35	.20
e.		Mixed periods	5.00	5.00
f.		Pair, one with level periods	15.00	15.00
g.		Double surcharge	425.00	
h.		Thick "V"	.90	.90
i.		As "h," invtd. "1" for "I" in "V.R.I."	80.00	80.00
49b	A1	4p on 4p ultra	1.10	2.00
c.		Mixed periods	7.00	7.00
d.		Pair, one with level periods	15.00	18.00
50c	A1	6p on 6p car rose	35.00	47.50
d.		Mixed periods	175.00	175.00
e.		Pair, one with level periods	175.00	
f.		Thick "V"	*450.00*	*450.00*
51d	A1	6p on 6p ultra	.60	.30
e.		Mixed periods	6.00	6.00
f.		Pair, one with level periods	15.00	15.00
g.		Thick "V"	3.00	3.00
52e	A1	1sh on 1sh brown	1.00	.45
f.		Mixed periods	10.00	10.00
h.		Pair, one with level periods	25.00	26.00
i.		Thick "V"	1.75	1.50
52j	A1	1sh on 1sh orange	*1,500.*	*1,500.*
53c	A1	5sh on 5sh green	6.50	9.00
d.		Mixed periods	325.00	325.00
e.		Pair, one with level periods	*1,600.*	*2,500.*
f.		"5" with short flag	60.00	60.00
g.		Thick "V"	18.00	18.00

Stamps with mixed periods have one or two periods level with the bottoms of letters. One stamp in each pane had all periods level. Later settings had several stamps with thick "V." Forgeries of the scarcer varieties exist.

"V.R.I." stands for Victoria Regina Imperatrix. On No. 59, "E.R.I." stands for Edward Rex Imperator.

Cape of Good Hope Stamps of 1893-98 Overprinted

1900 **Wmk. 16**

54	A15	½p green	.40	.20
a.		No period after "COLONY"	8.50	12.00
b.		Double overprint	500.00	600.00
55	A13	2½p ultramarine	.60	.30
a.		No period after "COLONY"	45.00	57.50

Overprinted as in 1900

1902, May

56	A15	1p carmine rose	.60	.30
a.		No period after "COLONY"	10.00	15.00

Nos. 51d, 53c, Surcharged and No. 8b Surcharged like No. 51 but Reading "E.R.I."

Carmine or Vermilion and Black Surcharges

1902 **Unwmk.**

57	A1	4p on 6p on 6p ultra	1.50	.70
a.		Thick "V"	2.00	1.25
b.		As "a," invtd. "1" instead of "I"	4.50	4.50
c.		No period after "R"	30.00	30.00

Black Surcharge

59	A1	6p on 6p ultra	3.00	6.00
a.		Double surcharge, one invtd.	*600.00*	*600.00*

Orange Surcharge

60	A1	1sh on 5sh on 5sh grn	5.00	6.00
a.		Thick "V"	13.00	18.00
b.		"5" with short flag	60.00	60.00
c.		Double surcharge		
		Nos. 57-60 (3)	9.50	12.70

"E.R.I." stands for Edward Rex Imperator.

King Edward VII — A8

1903-04 **Wmk. 2** **Typo.**

61	A8	½p yellow green	8.75	1.25
62	A8	1p carmine	4.50	.20
63	A8	2p chocolate	6.00	.85
64	A8	2½p ultra	1.75	.45
65	A8	3p violet	7.50	.90
66	A8	4p olive grn & car	32.50	2.50
67	A8	6p violet & car	9.00	1.00
68	A8	1sh bister & car	30.00	2.00
69	A8	5sh red brn & bl ('04)	80.00	22.00
		Nos. 61-69 (9)	180.00	31.15

Some of the above stamps are found with the overprint "C. S. A. R." for use by the Central South African Railway.

The "IOSTAGE" variety on the 4p is the result of filled in type.

Issue dates: 1p, Feb. 3. ½p, 2p, 2½p, 3p, 4p, 6p, 1sh, July 6. 5sh, Oct. 31.

1907-08 **Wmk. 3**

70	A8	½p yellow green	7.00	.45
71	A8	1p carmine	7.00	.20
72	A8	4p olive grn & car	4.50	1.75
73	A8	1sh bister & car	42.00	13.50
		Nos. 70-73 (4)	60.50	15.90

The "IOSTAGE" variety on the 4p is the result of filled-in type.

Stamps of Orange River Colony were replaced by those of Union of South Africa.

PAKISTAN

'pa-ki-ˌstan

LOCATION — In southern, central Asia
GOVT. — Republic
AREA — 307,293 sq. mi.
POP. — 88,000,000 (est. 1983)
CAPITAL — Islamabad

Pakistan was formed August 15, 1947, when India was divided into the Dominions of the Union of India and Pakistan, with some princely states remaining independent.

Pakistan had two areas made up of all or part of several predominantly Moslem provinces in the northwest and northeast corners of pre-1947 India. Western Pakistan consists of the entire provinces of Baluchistan, Sind (Scinde) and "Northwest Frontier," and 15 districts of the Punjab. Eastern, consisting of the Sylhet district in Assam and 14 districts in Bengal Province, became independent as Bangladesh in December 1971.

The state of Las Bela was incorporated into Pakistan.

12 Pies = 1 Anna
16 Annas = 1 Rupee

Catalogue values for all unused stamps in this country are for Never Hinged items.

Stamps of India, 1937-43, Overprinted in Black:

Nos. 1-12

Nos. 13-19

Perf. 13½x14

1947, Oct. 1 **Wmk. 196**

1	A83	3p slate	.20	.20
2	A83	½a rose violet	.20	.20
3	A83	9p lt green	.20	.20
4	A83	1a carmine rose	.20	.20
4A	A84	1a3p bister ('49)	4.00	*6.00*
5	A84	1½a dk purple	.20	.20
6	A84	2a scarlet	.20	.35
7	A84	3a violet	.20	.35
8	A84	3½a ultra	1.10	*2.50*
9	A85	4a chocolate	.45	.25
10	A85	6a peacock blue	1.75	1.00
11	A85	8a blue violet	.55	*.70*
12	A85	12a carmine lake	1.75	.35
13	A81	14a rose violet	4.75	3.00
14	A82	1r brn & slate	3.00	1.25
a.		Inverted overprint	175.00	
b.		Pair, one without ovpt.	750.00	
15	A82	2r dk brn & dk vio	5.50	2.25
16	A82	5r dp ultra & dk grn	6.75	4.25
17	A82	10r rose car & dk vio	7.00	3.25
18	A82	15r dk grn & dk brn	50.00	*75.00*
19	A82	25r dk vio & bl vio	72.50	65.00
		Nos. 1-19 (20)	160.50	166.50
		Set, hinged	100.00	

Provisional use of stamps of India with handstamped or printed "PAKISTAN" was authorized in 1947-49. Nos. 4A, 14a 14b exist only as provisional issues.

OFFICIAL STAMPS

Official Stamps of India, 1939-43, Overprinted in Black

1947-49 **Wmk. 196** ***Perf. 13½x14***

O1	O8	3p slate	1.75	.90
O2	O8	½a dk rose vio	.35	.20
O3	O8	9p green	5.50	2.00
O4	O8	1a carmine rose	.35	.20
O4A	O8	1a3p bister ('49)	*7.50*	*10.00*
O5	O8	1½a dull purple	.35	.20
O6	O8	2a scarlet	.35	.20
O7	O8	2½a purple	5.00	*6.00*
O8	O8	4a dk brown	1.60	.65
O9	O8	8a blue violet	2.50	*4.00*
		Nos. O1-O9 (10)	25.25	24.35

India Nos. O100-O103 Overprinted in Black

O10	A82	1r brown & slate	1.00	2.00
O11	A82	2r dk brn & dk vio	5.00	5.00
O12	A82	5r dp ultra & dk grn	40.00	*65.00*
		Telegraph cancel		7.50
O13	A82	10r rose car & dk vio	50.00	*75.00*
		Telegraph cancel		*5.00*
		Set, hinged	62.50	

PALESTINE

'pa-lə-ˌstin

LOCATION — Western Asia bordering on the Mediterranean Sea
GOVT. — British Mandate
AREA — 10,429 sq. mi.
POP. — 1,605,816 (estimated)
CAPITAL — Jerusalem

Formerly a part of Turkey, Palestine was occupied by the Egyptian Expeditionary Forces of the British Army in World War I and was mandated to Great Britain in 1923.

10 Milliemes = 1 Piaster
1000 Milliemes = 1 Egyptian Pound
1000 Mils = 1 Palestine Pound (1928)

Watermark

Wmk. 33

Issued under British Military Occupation

For use in Palestine, Transjordan, Lebanon, Syria and in parts of Cilicia and northeastern Egypt

A1

Wmk. Crown and "GvR" (33)

1918, Feb. 10 **Litho.** ***Rouletted 20***

1	A1	1pi deep blue	175.00	105.00
2	A1	1pi ultra	2.40	2.40

Nos. 2 & 1 Surcharged in Black

1918, Feb. 16

3	A1	5m on 1pi ultra	4.25	3.25
a.		5m on 1pi gray blue	105.00	*550.00*

Nos. 1 and 3a were issued without gum. No. 3a is on paper with a surface sheen.

1918 **Typo.** ***Perf. 15x14***

4	A1	1m dark brown	.35	.45
5	A1	2m blue green	.35	.50
6	A1	3m light brown	.40	.40
7	A1	4m scarlet	.40	.45
8	A1	5m orange	.75	.35
9	A1	1pi indigo	.40	.30
10	A1	2pi olive green	1.40	.75
11	A1	5pi plum	2.00	2.40
12	A1	9pi bister	5.50	5.50

13 A1 10pi ultramarine 4.75 3.75
14 A1 20pi gray 12.50 17.50
Nos. 4-14 (11) 28.80 32.35

Many shades exist.

Nos. 4-11 exist with rough perforation.

Issued: 1m, 2m, 4m, 2pi, 5pi, 7/16; 5m, 9/25; 1pi, 11/9; 3m, 9pi, 10pi, 12/17; 20pi, 12/27.

Nos. 4-11 with overprint "O. P. D. A." (Ottoman Public Debt Administration) or "H.J.Z." (Hejaz-Jemen Railway) are revenue stamps; they exist postally used.

For overprints on stamps and types see #15-62 & Jordan #1-63, 73-90, 92-102, 130-144, J12-J23.

Issued under British Administration

Overprinted at Jerusalem

Stamps and Type of 1918 Overprinted in Black or Silver

1920, Sept. 1 Wmk. 33 *Perf. 15x14*

Arabic Overprint 8mm long

15 A1 1m dark brown 4.50 2.00
16 A1 2m bl grn, perf 14 1.60 1.50
d. Perf 15x14 8.00 4.75
17 A1 3m lt brown 9.25 5.00
d. Perf 14 60.00 57.50
e. Inverted overprint 525.00 *700.00*
18 A1 4m scarlet 2.25 1.40
19 A1 5m org, perf 14 3.50 1.00
e. Perf 15x14 18.50 4.50
20 A1 1pi indigo (S) 4.25 .90
21 A1 2pi olive green 4.00 2.00
22 A1 5pi plum 21.00 *22.50*
23 A1 9pi bister 11.00 *22.50*
24 A1 10pi ultra 11.50 *19.50*
25 A1 20pi gray 30.00 *45.00*
Nos. 15-25 (11) 102.85 123.30

Forgeries exist of No. 17e.

Similar Overprint, with Arabic Line 10mm Long, Arabic "S" and "T" Joined, ".." at Left Extends Above Other Letters

1920-21 *Perf. 15x14*

15a A1 1m dark brown 2.00 1.10
e. Perf. 14 625.00 800.00
g. As "a," invtd. ovpt. 450.00
16a A1 2m blue green 7.50 4.50
e. "PALESTINE" omitted *2,500.* *1,500.*
f. Perf. 14 3.75 4.50
17a A1 3m light brown 3.50 1.10
18a A1 4m scarlet 4.75 1.40
b. Perf. 14 62.50 87.50
19a A1 5m orange 2.50 .90
f. Perf. 14 8.50 1.25
20a A1 1pi indigo, perf. 14 (S) ('21) 57.50 1.40
d. Perf. 15x14 500.00 30.00
21a A1 2pi olive green ('21) 70.00 30.00
22a A1 5pi plum ('21) 45.00 11.00
d. Perf. 14 225.00 *525.00*
Nos. 15a-22a (8) 192.75 51.40

This overprint often looks grayish to grayish black. In the English line the letters are frequently uneven and damaged.

Similar Overprint, with Arabic Line 10mm Long, Arabic "S" and "T" Separated and 6mm Between English and Hebrew Lines

1920, Dec. 6

15b A1 1m dk brn, perf 14 55.00 37.50
17b A1 3m lt brn, perf 15x14 55.00 37.50
19b A1 5m orange, perf 14 400.00 37.50
d. Perf. 15x14 *16,000.* *13,750.*
Nos. 15b-19b (3) 510.00 112.50

Overprinted as Before, 7½mm Between English and Hebrew Lines, ".." at Left Even With Other Letters

1921 *Perf. 15x14*

15c A1 1m dark brown 12.50 4.00
f. 1m dull brown, perf 14 *2,300.*
16c A1 2m blue green 23.00 6.25
17c A1 3m light brown 29.00 6.25
18c A1 4m scarlet 30.00 4.00
19c A1 5m orange 62.50 1.10
20c A1 1pi indigo (S) 21.00 .90
21c A1 2pi olive green 25.00 7.00
22c A1 5pi plum 29.00 9.00
23c A1 9pi bister 57.50 *100.00*
24c A1 10pi ultra 62.50 16.00
25c A1 20pi pale gray 97.50 57.50
d. Perf. 14 *13,750.* *2,900.*
Nos. 15c-25c (11) 449.50 *212.00*

Overprinted at London

Stamps of 1918 Overprinted

1921 *Perf. 15x14*

37 A1 1m dark brown 1.40 .35
38 A1 2m blue green 1.75 .35
39 A1 3m light brown 1.75 .35
40 A1 4m scarlet 2.25 .70
41 A1 5m orange 1.75 .35
42 A1 1pi bright blue 1.75 .40
43 A1 2pi olive green 2.50 .45
44 A1 5pi plum 7.00 5.75
45 A1 9pi bister 16.00 16.00
46 A1 10pi ultra 22.50 *575.00*
47 A1 20pi gray 57.50 *1,400.*
Nos. 37-47 (11) 116.15
Nos. 37-45 (9) 24.70

The 2nd character from left on bottom line that looks like quotation marks consists of long thin lines.

Deformed or damaged letters exist in all three lines of the overprint.

Similar Overprint on Type of 1921

1922 Wmk. 4 *Perf. 14*

48 A1 1m dark brown 1.25 .35
a. Inverted overprint — *13,750.*
b. Double overprint 250.00 500.00
49 A1 2m yellow 1.10 .35
50 A1 3m Prus blue 2.00 .20
51 A1 4m rose 2.00 .20
52 A1 5m orange 2.25 .35
53 A1 6m blue green 2.00 .35
54 A1 7m yellow brown 1.75 .35
55 A1 8m red 1.75 .35
56 A1 1pi gray 2.25 .35
57 A1 13m ultra 2.50 .20
58 A1 2pi olive green 3.00 .40
a. Inverted overprint 350.00 *575.00*
b. 2pi yellow bister *140.00* *7.50*
59 A1 5pi plum 5.50 1.40
a. Perf. 15x14 57.50 4.50

Perf. 15x14

60 A1 9pi bister 10.00 10.00
a. Perf. 14 1,000. 225.00
61 A1 10pi light blue 8.50 3.00
a. Perf. 14 57.50 12.50
62 A1 20pi violet 10.50 6.25
a. Perf. 14 160.00 110.00
Nos. 48-62 (15) 56.35 24.10

The 2nd character from left on bottom line that looks like quotation marks consists of short thick lines.

The "E. F. F." for "E. E. F." on No. 61 is caused by damaged type.

Rachel's Tomb — A3

Mosque of Omar (Dome of the Rock) — A4

Citadel at Jerusalem A5

Tiberias and Sea of Galilee A6

1927-42 Typo. *Perf. 13½x14½*

63 A3 2m Prus blue 1.75 .20
64 A3 3m yellow green 1.10 .20
65 A4 4m rose red 6.00 1.25
66 A4 4m violet brn ('32) 1.50 .20
67 A5 5m brown org 2.75 .20
c. Perf. 14½x14 (coil stamp) ('36) 16.00 *20.00*
68 A4 6m deep green .85 .20
69 A5 7m deep red 7.50 .70
70 A5 7m dk violet ('32) .85 .20
71 A4 8m yellow brown 14.00 6.75
72 A4 8m scarlet ('32) 1.40 .20
73 A3 10m deep gray 1.75 .20
a. Perf. 14½x14 (coil stamp) ('38) 23.50 *26.00*
74 A4 13m ultra 8.75 .40
75 A4 13m olive bister ('32) 1.50 .20
76 A4 15m ultra ('32) 3.75 .50
77 A5 20m olive green 1.75 .20

Perf. 14

78 A6 50m violet brown 1.75 .40
79 A6 90m bister 62.50 *67.50*
80 A6 100m bright blue 2.50 .80
81 A6 200m dk violet 9.00 4.00
82 A6 250m dp brown ('42) 4.75 2.00
83 A6 500m red ('42) 5.00 3.25
84 A6 £1 gray black ('42) 6.75 4.00
Nos. 63-84 (22) 147.45 93.55

Issued: 3m, #74, 6/1; 2m, 5m, 6m, 10m, #65, 69, 71, 77-81, 8/14; #70, 72, 6/1/32; #75, 15m, 8/1/32; #66, 11/1/32; #82-84, 1/15/42.

POSTAGE DUE STAMPS

D1

1923 Unwmk. Typo. *Perf. 11*

J1 D1 1m bister brown 17.50 *27.50*
b. Horiz. pair, imperf. btwn. 1,300.
J2 D1 2m green 13.00 11.50
J3 D1 4m red 11.50 *11.50*
J4 D1 8m violet 8.00 *8.00*
b. Horiz. pair, imperf. btwn. *2,100.*
J5 D1 13m dark blue 7.00 *7.00*
a. Horiz. pair, imperf. btwn. 975.00
Nos. J1-J5 (5) 57.00 *65.50*

Imperfs. of 1m, 2m, 8m, are from proof sheets.

Values for Nos. J1-J5 are for fine centered copies.

D2

D3

1924, Dec. 1 Wmk. 4

J6 D2 1m brown 1.00 2.25
J7 D2 2m yellow 2.50 2.00
J8 D2 4m green 2.25 1.40
J9 D2 8m red 3.50 1.00
J10 D2 13m ultramarine 3.25 2.75
J11 D2 5pi violet 9.75 2.00
Nos. J6-J11 (6) 22.25 11.40

1928-45 *Perf. 14*

J12 D3 1m lt brown 1.10 1.00
a. Perf. 15x14 ('45) 37.50 75.00
J13 D3 2m yellow 1.75 .70
J14 D3 4m green 2.25 1.90
a. 4m bluish grn, perf. 15x14 ('45) 62.50 *90.00*
J15 D3 6m brown org ('33) 17.50 5.75
J16 D3 8m red 2.50 1.00
J17 D3 10m light gray 1.75 .70
J18 D3 13m ultra 3.00 2.00
J19 D3 20m olive green 3.00 1.40
J20 D3 50m violet 3.25 1.40
Nos. J12-J20 (9) 36.10 15.85

The Hebrew word for "mil" appears below the numeral on all values but the 1m.

Issued: 6m, Oct. 1933; others, Feb. 1, 1928.

PANAMA

ˈpa-nə-ˌmä

LOCATION — Central America between Costa Rica and Colombia

GOVT. — Republic

AREA — 30,134 sq. mi.

POP. — 1,970,000 (est. 1983)

CAPITAL — Panama

Formerly a department of the Republic of Colombia, Panama gained its independence in 1903. Dividing the country at its center is the Panama Canal.

100 Centavos = 1 Peso

100 Centesimos = 1 Balboa (1904)

Watermark

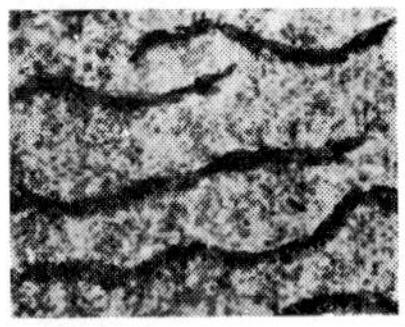

Wmk. 229 — Wavy Lines

Wmk. 233 — "Harrison & Sons, London." in Script

GREAT BRITAIN USED in PANAMA

Stamps of Great Britain cancelled "C35" were used in Panama. Listings appear in the "Stamps of Great Britain Used in Colombia" section, at the beginning of Colombian listings.

Issues of the Sovereign State of Panama Under Colombian Dominion

Valid only for domestic mail.

Coat of Arms
A1 A2

1878 Unwmk. Litho. *Imperf.*

Thin Wove Paper

1 A1 5c gray green 25.00 30.00
a. 5c yellow green 25.00 30.00
2 A1 10c blue 60.00 60.00
3 A1 20c rose red 40.00 32.50
Nos. 1-3 (3) 125.00 122.50

Very Thin Wove Paper

4 A2 50cbuff *1,500.*

All values of this issue are known rouletted unofficially.

Medium Thick Paper

5 A1 5c blue green 25.00 30.00
6 A1 10cblue 65.00 70.00
7 A2 50corange 13.00
Nos. 5-7 (3) 103.00 100.00

Nos. 5-7 were printed before Nos. 1-4, according to Panamanian archives.

Values for used Nos. 1-5 are for handstamped postal cancellations.

These stamps have been reprinted in a number of shades, on thin to moderately thick, white or yellowish paper. They are without gum or with white, crackly gum. All values have been reprinted from new stones made from retouched dies. The marks of retouching are plainly to be seen in the sea and clouds. On the original 10c the shield in the upper left corner has two blank sections; on the reprints the design of this shield is completed. The impression of these reprints is frequently blurred.

Reprints of the 50c are rare. Beware of remainders of the 50c offered as reprints.

Issues of Colombia for use in the Department of Panama

Issued because of the use of different currency.

Map of Panama
A3 A4

1887-88 **Perf. 13½**

8 A3 1c black, *green* .90 .80
9 A3 2c black, *pink* ('88) 1.60 1.25
a. 2c black, *salmon* 1.60
10 A3 5c black, *blue* .90 .35
11 A3 10c black, *yellow* .90 .40
a. Imperf., pair
12 A3 20c black, *lilac* 1.00 .50
13 A3 50c brown ('88) 2.00 1.00
a. Imperf.
Nos. 8-13 (6) 7.30 4.30

See No. 14. For surcharges and overprints see Nos. 24-30, 107-108, 115-116, 137-138.

1892 **Pelure Paper**

14 A3 50c brown 2.50 1.10

The stamps of this issue have been reprinted on papers of slightly different colors from those of the originals.

These are: 1c yellow green, 2c deep rose, 5c bright blue, 10c straw, 20c violet.

The 50c is printed from a very worn stone, in a lighter brown than the originals. The series includes a 10c on lilac paper.

All these stamps are to be found perforated, imperforate, imperforate horizontally or imperforate vertically. At the same time that they were made, impressions were struck upon a variety of glazed and surface-colored papers.

Wove Paper

1892-96 **Engr.** **Perf. 12**

15 A4 1c green .25 .25
16 A4 2c rose .40 .25
17 A4 5c blue 1.50 .50
18 A4 10c orange .35 .25
19 A4 20c violet ('95) .50 .35
20 A4 50c bister brn ('96) .50 .40
21 A4 1p lake ('96) 6.50 4.00
Nos. 15-21 (7) 10.00 6.00

In 1903 Nos. 15-21 were used in Cauca and three other southern Colombia towns. Stamps canceled in these towns are worth much more.

For surcharges and overprints see Nos. 22-23, 51-106, 109-114, 129-136, 139, 151-162, 181-184, F12-F15, H4-H5.

Nos. 16, 12-14 Surcharged:

a

b

c

d

e

f

g

1894 **Black Surcharge**

22 (a) 1c on 2c rose .50 .40
a. Inverted surcharge 2.50 2.50
b. Double surcharge
23 (b) 1c on 2c rose .40 .50
a. "CCNTAVO" 2.50 2.50
b. Inverted surcharge 2.50 2.50
c. Double surcharge

Red Surcharge

24 (c) 5c on 20c black, *lil* 2.50 1.50
a. Inverted surcharge 12.50 12.50
b. Double surcharge
c. Without "HABILITADO"
25 (d) 5c on 20c black, *lil* 3.50 3.00
a. "CCNTAVOS" 7.50 7.50
b. Inverted surcharge 12.50 12.50
c. Double surcharge
d. Without "HABILITADO"
26 (e) 5c on 20c black, *lil* 6.00 5.00
a. Inverted surcharge 12.50 12.50
b. Double surcharge
27 (f) 10c on 50c brown 3.00 3.00
a. "1894" omitted
b. Inverted surcharge
c. "CCNTAVOS" 15.00
28 (g) 10c on 50c brown 12.50 12.50
a. "CCNTAVOS" 32.50
b. Inverted surcharge

Pelure Paper

29 (f) 10c on 50c brown 4.00 3.00
a. "1894" omitted 7.50
b. Inverted surcharge 12.50 12.50
c. Double surcharge
30 (g) 10c on 50c brown 10.00 10.00
a. "CCNTAVOS"
b. Without "HABILITADO"
c. Inverted surcharge 25.00 25.00
d. Double surcharge
Nos. 22-30 (9) 42.40 38.90

There are several settings of these surcharges. Usually the surcharge is about 15½mm high, but in one setting, it is only 13mm. All the types are to be found with a comma after "CENTAVOS." Nos. 24, 25, 26, 29 and 30 exist with the surcharge printed sideways. Nos. 23, 24 and 29 may be found with an inverted "A" instead of "V" in "CENTAVOS." There are also varieties caused by dropped or broken letters.

Issues of the Republic Issued in the City of Panama

Stamps of 1892-96 Overprinted

1903, Nov. 16

Rose Handstamp

51 A4 1c green 2.00 1.50
52 A4 2c rose 5.00 3.00
53 A4 5c blue 2.00 1.25
54 A4 10c yellow 2.00 2.00
55 A4 20c violet 4.00 3.50
56 A4 50c bister brn 10.00 7.00
57 A4 1p lake 50.00 40.00
Nos. 51-57 (7) 75.00 58.25

Blue Black Handstamp

58 A4 1c green 2.00 1.25
59 A4 2c rose 1.00 1.00
60 A4 5c blue 7.00 6.00
61 A4 10c yellow 5.00 3.50
62 A4 20c violet 10.00 7.50
63 A4 50c bister brn 10.00 7.50
64 A4 1p lake 50.00 42.50
Nos. 58-64 (7) 85.00 69.25

The stamps of this issue are to be found with the handstamp placed horizontally, vertically or diagonally; inverted; double; double, one inverted; double, both inverted; in pairs, one without handstamp; etc.

This handstamp is known in brown rose on the 1, 5, 20 and 50c, in purple on the 1, 2, 50c and 1p, and in magenta on the 5, 10, 20 and 50c.

Reprints were made in rose, black and other colors when the handstamp was nearly worn out, so that the "R" of "REPUBLICA" appears to be shorter than usual, and the bottom part of "LI" has been broken off. The "P" of "PANAMA" leans to the left and the tops of "NA" are broken. Many of these varieties are found inverted, double, etc.

Overprinted

1903, Dec. 3

Bar in Similar Color to Stamp

Black Overprint

65 A4 2c rose 2.50 2.50
a. "PANAMA" 15mm long 3.50
b. Violet bar 5.00
66 A4 5c blue 100.00
a. "PANAMA" 15mm long 100.00
67 A4 10c yellow 2.50 2.50
a. "PANAMA" 15mm long 6.00
b. Horizontal overprint 17.50

Gray Black Overprint

68 A4 2c rose 2.00 2.00
a. "PANAMA" 15mm long 2.50

Carmine Overprint

69 A4 5c blue 2.50 2.50
a. "PANAMA" 15mm long 3.50
b. Bar only 75.00 75.00
c. Double overprint
70 A4 20c violet 7.50 6.50
a. "PANAMA" 15mm long 10.00
b. Double overprint, one in black 150.00
Nos. 65,67-70 (5) 17.00 16.00

This overprint was set up to cover fifty stamps. "PANAMA" is normally 13mm long and 1¾mm high but, in two rows in each sheet, it measures 15 to 16mm.

This word may be found with one or more of the letters taller than usual; with one, two or three inverted "V's" instead of "A's"; with an inverted "Y" instead of "A"; an inverted "N"; an "A" with accent; and a fancy "P."

Owing to misplaced impressions, stamps exist with "PANAMA" once only, twice on one side, or three times.

Overprinted in Red

1903, Dec.

71 A4 1c green .75 .60
a. "PANAMA" 15mm long 1.25
b. "PANAMA" reading down 3.00 .75
c. "PANAMA" reading up and down 3.00
d. Double overprint 8.00
72 A4 2c rose .50 .40
a. "PANAMA" 15mm long 1.00
b. "PANAMA" reading down .75 .50
c. "PANAMA" reading up and down 4.00
d. Double overprint 8.00
73 A4 20c violet 1.50 1.00
a. "PANAMA" 15mm long 2.25
b. "PANAMA" reading down
c. "PANAMA" reading up and down 8.00 8.00
d. Double overprint 18.00 18.00
74 A4 50c bister brn 3.00 2.50
a. "PANAMA" 15mm long 5.00
b. "PANAMA" reading up and down 12.00 12.00
c. Double overprint 6.00 6.00
75 A4 1p lake 6.00 4.50
a. "PANAMA" 15mm long 6.25
b. "PANAMA" reading up and down 15.00 15.00
c. Double overprint 15.00
d. Inverted overprint 25.00
Nos. 71-75 (5) 11.75 9.00

This setting appears to be a re-arrangement (or two very similar re-arrangements) of the previous overprint. The overprint covers fifty stamps. "PANAMA" usually reads upward but sheets of the 1, 2 and 20c exist with the word reading upward on one half the sheet and downward on the other half.

In one re-arrangement one stamp in fifty has the word reading in both directions. Nearly all the varieties of the previous overprint are repeated in this setting excepting the inverted "Y" and fancy "P." There are also additional varieties of large letters and "PANAMA" occasionally has an "A" missing or inverted. There are misplaced impressions, as the previous setting.

Overprinted in Red

1904-05

76 A4 1c green .20 .20
a. Both words reading up 1.50
b. Both words reading down 2.75
c. Double overprint
d. Pair, one without overprint 15.00
e. "PANAAM" 20.00
f. Inverted "M" in "PANAMA" 5.00
77 A4 2c rose .20 .20
a. Both words reading up 2.50
b. Both words reading down 2.50
c. Double overprint 10.00
d. Double overprint, one inverted 14.00
e. Inverted "M" in "PANAMA" 5.00
78 A4 5c blue .30 .20
a. Both words reading up 3.00
b. Both words reading down 4.25
c. Inverted overprint 12.50
d. "PANAAM" 25.00
e. "PANANA" 8.00
f. "PAMANA" 5.00
g. Inverted "M" in "PANAMA" 5.00
h. Double overprint 20.00
79 A4 10c yellow .30 .20
a. Both words reading up 5.00
b. Both words reading down 5.00
c. Double overprint 15.00
d. Inverted overprint 6.75
e. "PANAMA" 8.00
f. Inverted "M" in "PANAMA" 15.00
g. Red brown overprint 7.50 3.50
80 A4 20c violet 2.00 1.00
a. Both words reading up 5.00
b. Both words reading down 10.00
81 A4 50c bister brn 2.00 1.60
a. Both words reading up 10.50
b. Both words reading down 10.00
c. Double overprint
82 A4 1p lake 5.00 5.00
a. Both words reading up 12.50
b. Both words reading down 12.50
c. Double overprint
d. Double overprint, one inverted 20.00
e. Inverted "M" in "PANAMA" 45.00
Nos. 76-82 (7) 10.00 8.40

This overprint is also set up to cover fifty stamps. One stamp in each fifty has "PANAMA" reading upward at both sides. Another has the word reading downward at both sides, a third has an inverted "V" in place of the last "A" and a fourth has a small thick "N." In a resetting all these varieties are corrected except the inverted "V." There are misplaced overprints as before.

Later printings show other varieties and have the bar 2½mm instead of 2mm wide. The colors of the various printings of Nos. 76-82 range from carmine to almost pink.

Experts consider the black overprint on the 50c to be speculative.

The 20c violet and 50c bister brown exist with bar 2½mm wide, including the error "PAMANA," but are not known to have been issued. Some copies have been canceled "to oblige."

Issued in Colon

Handstamped in Magenta or Violet

On Stamps of 1892-96

1903-04

101 A4 1c green .75 .75
102 A4 2c rose .75 .75
103 A4 5c blue 1.00 1.00
104 A4 10c yellow 3.50 3.00
105 A4 20c violet 8.00 6.50
106 A4 1p lake 80.00 70.00

On Stamps of 1887-92

Ordinary Wove Paper

107 A3 50c brown 25.00 20.00
Nos. 101-107 (7) 119.00 102.00

Pelure Paper

108 A3 50c brown 70.00

Handstamped in Magenta, Violet or Red

On Stamps of 1892-96

109 A4 1c green 5.50 5.00
110 A4 2c rose 5.50 5.00
111 A4 5c blue 5.50 5.00
112 A4 10c yellow 8.25 7.00
113 A4 20c violet 12.00 9.00
114 A4 1p lake 70.00 60.00

On Stamps of 1887-92

Ordinary Wove Paper

115 A3 50c brown 35.00 25.00
Nos. 109-115 (7) 141.75 116.00

Pelure Paper

116 A3 50c brown 50.00 37.50

The first note after No. 64 applies also to Nos. 101-116.

The handstamps on Nos. 109-116 have been counterfeited.

REPUBLICA DE PANAMA

Stamps with this overprint were a private speculation. They exist on cover. The overprint was to be used on postal cards.

Overprinted g

On Stamps of 1892-96

Carmine Overprint

129	A4 1c green	.40	.40
a.	Inverted overprint	6.00	
b.	Double overprint	2.25	
c.	Double overprint, one inverted	6.00	
130	A4 5c blue	.50	.50

Brown Overprint

131	A4 1c green	12.00	
a.	Double overprint, one inverted		

Black Overprint

132	A4 1c green	60.00	30.00
a.	Vertical overprint	42.50	
b.	Inverted overprint	42.50	
c.	Double overprint, one inverted	42.50	
133	A4 2c rose	.50	.50
a.	Inverted overprint		
134	A4 10c yellow	.50	.50
a.	Inverted overprint	4.00	
b.	Double overprint	16.00	
c.	Double overprint, one inverted	6.00	
135	A4 20c violet	.50	.50
a.	Inverted overprint	4.00	
b.	Double overprint	5.50	
136	A4 1p lake	16.00	14.00

On Stamps of 1887-88

Blue Overprint

Ordinary Wove Paper

137	A3 50c brown	3.00	3.00

Pelure Paper

138	A3 50c brown	3.00	3.00
a.	Double overprint	14.00	

This overprint is set up to cover fifty stamps. In each fifty there are four stamps without accent on the last "a" of "Panama," one with accent on the "a" of "Republica" and one with a thick, upright "i."

Overprinted in Carmine **REPUBLICA DE PANAMA.**

On Stamp of 1892-96

139	A4 20c violet	*200.00*	
a.	Double overprint		

Unknown with genuine cancels.

Issued in Bocas del Toro

Stamps of 1892-96 Overprinted

Handstamped in Violet R DE PANAMA

1903-04

151	A4 1c green	20.00	14.00
152	A4 2c rose	20.00	14.00
153	A4 5c blue	25.00	16.00
154	A4 10c yellow	15.00	8.25
155	A4 20c violet	50.00	30.00
156	A4 50c bister brn	100.00	55.00
157	A4 1p lake	140.00	110.00
	Nos. 151-157 (7)	370.00	247.25

The handstamp is known double and inverted. Counterfeits exist.

Handstamped in Violet Panama

158	A4 1c green	*100.00*	
159	A4 2c rose	*70.00*	
160	A4 5c blue	*80.00*	
161	A4 10c yellow	*100.00*	
	Nos. 158-161 (4)	*350.00*	

This handstamp was applied to these 4 stamps only by favor, experts state. Counterfeits are numerous. The 1p exists only as a counterfeit.

General Issues

A5

1905, Feb. 4 **Engr.** ***Perf. 12***

179	A5 1c green	.60	.40
180	A5 2c rose	.80	.50

Panama's Declaration of Independence from the Colombian Republic, Nov. 3, 1903.

Surcharged in Vermilion on Stamps of 1892-96 Issue:

1906

181	A4 1c on 20c violet	.25	.25
a.	"Panrma"	2.25	2.25
b.	"Pnnama"	2.25	2.25
c.	"Pauama"	2.25	2.25
d.	Inverted surcharge	4.00	4.00
e.	Double surcharge	3.50	3.50
f.	Double surcharge, one inverted		

182	A4 2c on 50c bister brn	.25	.25
a.	3rd "A" of "PANAMA" inverted	2.25	2.25
b.	Both "PANAMA" reading down	4.00	4.00
c.	Double surcharge		
d.	Inverted surcharge	2.50	

The 2c on 20c violet was never issued to the public. All copies are inverted. Value, 75c.

Carmine Surcharge

183	A4 5c on 1p lake	.60	.40
a.	Both "PANAMA" reading down	6.00	6.00
b.	"5" omitted		
c.	Double surcharge		
d.	Inverted surcharge		
e.	3rd "A" of "PANAMA" inverted	5.50	5.50

On Stamp of 1903-04, No. 75

184	A4 5c on 1p lake	.60	.40
a.	"PANAMA" 15mm long		
b.	"PANAMA" reading up and down		
c.	Both "PANAMA" reading down		
d.	Inverted surcharge		
e.	Double surcharge		
f.	3rd "A" of "PANAMA" inverted		
	Nos. 181-184 (4)	1.70	1.30

National Flag — A6

Vasco Núñez de Balboa — A7

Fernández de Córdoba — A8

Coat of Arms — A9

Justo Arosemena A10

Manuel J. Hurtado A11

José de Obaldía — A12

Tomás Herrera — A13

José de Fábrega — A14

1906-07 **Engr.** ***Perf. 11½***

185	A6 ½c orange & multi	.70	.35
186	A7 1c dk green & blk	.70	.35
187	A8 2c scarlet & blk	1.00	.35
188	A9 2½c red orange	1.00	.35
189	A10 5c blue & black	1.75	.35
a.	5c ultramarine & black	2.00	.50
190	A11 8c purple & blk	1.50	.65
191	A12 10c violet & blk	1.50	.50
192	A13 25c brown & blk	3.50	1.10
193	A14 50c black	9.00	3.50
	Nos. 185-193 (9)	20.65	7.50

Inverted centers exist of Nos. 185-187, 189, 189a, 190-193, Value, each $25. Nos. 185-193 exist imperf.

For surcharge see No. F29.

Map — A17

Balboa — A18

Córdoba — A19

Arms — A20

Arosemena A21

Obaldía A23

1909-15 ***Perf. 12***

195	A17 ½c orange ('11)	1.00	.30
a.	Booklet pane of 6		
196	A17 ½c rose ('15)	.70	.60
197	A18 1c dk grn & blk	1.00	.50
a.	Inverted center	7,500.	—
b.	Booklet pane of 6	*160.00*	
198	A19 2c ver & blk	1.00	.30
a.	Booklet pane of 6	*160.00*	
199	A20 2½c red orange	1.50	.30
a.	Booklet pane of 6		
200	A21 5c blue & blk	2.00	.30
a.	Booklet pane of 6	*160.00*	
201	A23 10c violet & blk	3.75	1.10
a.	Booklet pane of 6		
	Nos. 195-201 (7)	10.95	3.40

For overprints and surcharges see #H23, I4-I7.

Balboa Sighting Pacific Ocean, His Dog "Leoncico" at His Feet — A24

1913, Sept.

202	A24 2½c dk grn & yel grn	1.75	.65

400th anniv. of Balboa's discovery of the Pacific Ocean.

Panama-Pacific Exposition Issue

Chorrera Falls — A25

Map of Panama Canal A26

Balboa Taking Possession of the Pacific A27

Ruins of Cathedral of Old Panama A28

Palace of Arts — A29

Gatun Locks — A30

Culebra Cut — A31

Santo Domingo Monastery's Flat Arch — A32

1915-16 ***Perf. 12***

204	A25 ½c ol grn & blk	.40	.30
205	A26 1c dk green & blk	.95	.30
206	A27 2c carmine & blk	.75	.30
a.	2c ver & blk ('16)	.75	.30
208	A28 2½c scarlet & blk	.95	.35
209	A29 3c violet & blk	1.60	.55
210	A30 5c blue & blk	2.10	.35
a.	Center inverted	800.00	650.00
211	A31 10c orange & blk	2.10	.70
212	A32 20c brown & blk	10.50	3.25
a.	Center inverted	300.00	—
	Nos. 204-212 (8)	19.35	6.10

For surcharges and overprints see Nos. 217, 233, E1-E2.

Manuel J. Hurtado — A33

1916

213	A33 8c violet & blk	9.00	4.25

For surcharge see No. F30.

S. S. Panama in Culebra Cut Aug. 11, 1914 A34

S. S. Panama in Culebra Cut Aug. 11, 1914 A35

S. S. Cristobal in Gatun Lock — A36

1918

214	A34	12c purple & blk	15.00	5.75
215	A35	15c brt blue & blk	10.00	3.50
216	A36	24c yellow brn & blk	15.00	3.50
		Nos. 214-216 (3)	40.00	12.75

No. 208 Surcharged in Dark Blue

1919, Aug. 15

217	A28	2c on 2½c scar & blk	.35	.35
a.		Inverted surcharge	11.00	5.00
b.		Double surcharge	15.00	6.00

City of Panama, 400th anniversary.

Dry Dock at Balboa A38

Ship in Pedro Miguel Lock — A39

1920 **Engr.**

218	A38	50c orange & blk	30.00	22.50
219	A39	1b dk violet & blk	40.00	27.50

For overprint and surcharge see Nos. C6, C37.

Arms of Panama City — A40

José Vallarino — A41

"Land Gate" — A42

Simón Bolivar — A43

Statue of Cervantes — A44

Bolívar's Tribute — A45

Carlos de Ycaza — A46

Municipal Building in 1821 and 1921 — A47

Statue of Balboa — A48

Villa de Los Santos Church — A49

Herrera — A50

Fábrega — A51

1921, Nov.

220	A40	½c orange	.80	.25
221	A41	1c green	1.00	.20
222	A42	2c carmine	1.25	.25
223	A43	2½c red	2.75	1.10
224	A44	3c dull violet	2.75	1.10
225	A45	5c blue	2.75	.35
226	A46	8c olive green	10.00	3.50
227	A47	10c violet	6.75	1.50
228	A48	15c lt blue	8.00	2.00
229	A49	20c olive brown	14.50	3.50
230	A50	24c black brown	14.50	4.25
231	A51	50c black	25.00	8.00
		Nos. 220-231 (12)	90.05	26.00

Centenary of independence.

For overprints and surcharges see Nos. 264, 275-276, 299, 304, 308-310, C35.

Hurtado — A52

Arms — A53

1921, Nov. 28

232	A52	2c dark green	.65	.65

Manuel José Hurtado (1821-1887), president and folklore writer.

For overprints see Nos. 258, 301.

No. 208 Surcharged in Black

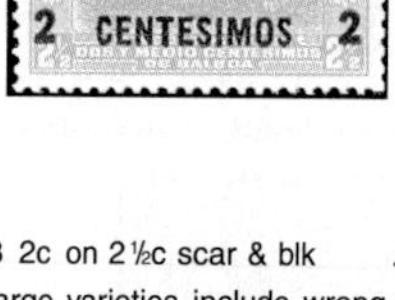

1923

233	A28	2c on 2½c scar & blk	.45	.45

Surcharge varieties include wrong or omitted date, double surcharge and pair, one without surcharge. Value $2.50 each.

Two stamps in each sheet have a bar above "CENTESIMOS."

1924, May **Engr.**

234	A53	½c orange	.20	.20
235	A53	1c dark green	.20	.20
236	A53	2c carmine	.25	.20
237	A53	5c dark blue	.45	.20
238	A53	10c dark violet	.60	.20
239	A53	12c olive green	.75	.40
240	A53	15c ultra	.95	.40
241	A53	24c yellow brown	1.90	.60
242	A53	50c orange	4.50	1.10
243	A53	1b black	6.75	2.50
		Nos. 234-243 (10)	16.55	6.00

For overprints & surcharges see #277, 321A, 331-338, 352, C19-C20, C68, RA5, RA10-RA22.

Bolívar — A54

Statue of Bolívar — A55

Bolívar Hall — A56

1926, June 10 ***Perf. 12½***

244	A54	½c orange	.55	.25
245	A54	1c dark green	.55	.25
246	A54	2c scarlet	.70	.30
247	A54	4c gray	.90	.35
248	A54	5c dark blue	1.40	.50
249	A55	8c lilac	2.25	.80
250	A55	10c dull violet	1.60	.80
251	A55	12c olive green	2.50	1.00
252	A55	15c ultra	3.25	1.25
253	A55	20c brown	6.75	1.60
254	A56	24c black violet	8.00	2.00
255	A56	50c black	13.50	5.00
		Nos. 244-255 (12)	41.95	14.10

Bolivar Congress centennial.

For surcharges and overprints see Nos. 259-263, 266-267, 274, 298, 300, 302-303, 305-307, C33-C34, C36, C38-C39.

Lindbergh's Airplane, "The Spirit of St. Louis" — A57

Lindbergh's Airplane and Map of Panama — A58

1928, Jan. 9 **Typo.** ***Rouletted 7***

256	A57	2c dk red & blk, *salmon*	.40	.25
257	A58	5c dk blue, *grn*	.60	.40

Visit of Colonel Charles A. Lindbergh to Central America by airplane.

No. 256 has black overprint.

No. 232 Overprinted in Red

1928, Nov. 1 ***Perf. 12***

258	A52	2c dark green	.25	.25

25th anniversary of the Republic.

No. 247 Surcharged in Black

1930, Dec. 17 ***Perf. 12½, 13***

259	A54	1c on 4c gray	.25	.20

Centenary of the death of Simón Bolívar, the Liberator.

Nos. 244-246 Overprinted in Red or Blue

1932 ***Perf. 12½***

260	A54	½c orange (R)	.20	.20
261	A54	1c dark green (R)	.35	.20
a.		Double overprint	18.00	
262	A54	2c scarlet (Bl)	.35	.25

No. 252 Surcharged in Red

263	A55	10c on 15c ultra	1.00	.50
a.		Double surcharge	55.00	
		Nos. 260-263 (4)	1.90	1.15

No. 220 Overprinted as in 1932 in Black

1933 ***Perf. 12***

Overprint 19mm Long

264	A40	½c orange	.35	.20
a.		Overprint 17mm long		—

Dr. Manuel Amador Guerrero — A60

1933, July 3 **Engr.** ***Perf. 12½***

265	A60	2c dark red	.50	.20

Centenary of the birth of Dr. Manuel Amador Guerrero, founder of the Republic of Panama and its first President.

No. 251 Surcharged in Red

1933

266	A55	10c on 12c olive grn	1.25	.65

No. 253 Overprinted in Red

267	A55	20c brown	2.25	1.75

José Domingo de Obaldía — A61

Quotation from Emerson — A63

National Institute — A64

Designs: 2c, Eusebio A. Morales. 12c, Justo A. Facio. 15c, Pablo Arosemena.

1934, July Engr. *Perf. 14*

268	A61	1c dark green	1.00	.50
269	A61	2c scarlet	1.00	.45
270	A63	5c dark blue	1.25	.80
271	A64	10c brown	3.25	1.50
272	A61	12c yellow green	6.50	2.00
273	A61	15c Prus blue	8.50	2.50
		Nos. 268-273 (6)	21.50	7.75

25th anniv. of the Natl. Institute.

Nos. 248, 227 Overprinted in Black or Red

1935-36 *Perf. 12½, 12*

274	A54	5c dark blue	.90	.30
275	A47	10c violet (R) ('36)	1.25	.60

No. 225 Surcharged in Red

1936 *Perf. 11½*

276	A45	1c on 5c blue	.40	.40
a.		Lines of surcharge 1½mm btwn.	6.50	

No. 241 Surcharged in Blue

1936, Sept. 24 *Perf. 12*

277	A53	2c on 24c yellow brn	.60	.50
a.		Double surcharge	20.00	

Centenary of the birth of Pablo Arosemena, president of Panama in 1910-12. See Nos. C19-C20.

Ruins of Custom House, Portobelo A67

Designs: 1c, Panama Tree. 2c, "La Pollera." 5c, Simon Bolivar. 10c, Cathedral Tower Ruins. Old Panama. 15c, Francisco Garcia y Santos, 20c, Madden Dam, Panama Canal. 25c, Columbus. 50c, Gaillard Cut. 1b, Panama Cathedral.

1936, Dec. Engr. *Perf. 11½*

278	A67	½c yellow org	.55	.25
279	A67	1c blue green	.55	.20
280	A67	2c carmine rose	.55	.20
281	A67	5c blue	.80	.50
282	A67	10c dk violet	1.75	.75
283	A67	15c turq blue	1.75	.75
284	A67	20c red	2.00	1.50
285	A67	25c black brn	3.50	2.00
286	A67	50c orange	7.75	5.00
287	A67	1b black	18.00	12.00
		Nos. 278-287,C21-C26 (16)	62.70	39.90

4th Postal Congress of the Americas and Spain.

Stamps of 1936 Overprinted in Red or Blue

1937

288	A67	½c yellow org (R)	.35	.30
a.		Inverted overprint	18.00	
289	A67	1c blue green (R)	.45	.20
290	A67	2c car rose (Bl)	.45	.20
291	A67	5c blue (R)	.70	.25
292	A67	10c dk vio (R)	1.10	.35
293	A67	15c turq bl (R)	5.25	3.25
294	A67	20c red (Bl)	2.00	1.25
295	A67	25c black brn (R)	2.75	1.25
296	A67	50c orange (Bl)	9.00	6.00
297	A67	1b black (R)	14.50	10.00
		Nos. 288-297,C27-C32 (16)	84.60	54.05

Stamps of 1921-26 Overprinted in Red or Blue

1937, July *Perf. 12, 12½*

298	A54	½c orange (R)	1.10	.80
a.		Inverted overprint	30.00	
299	A41	1c green (R)	.35	.25
a.		Inverted overprint	30.00	
300	A54	1c dk green (R)	.35	.25
301	A52	2c dk green (R)	.45	.35
302	A54	2c scarlet (Bl)	.55	.35

Stamps of 1921-26 Surcharged in Red

303	A54	2c on 4c gray	.70	.45
304	A46	2c on 8c ol grn	.70	.60
305	A55	2c on 8c lilac	.70	.45
306	A55	2c on 10c dl vio	.70	.50
307	A55	2c on 12c ol grn	.70	.45
308	A48	2c on 15c lt blue	.70	.60
309	A50	2c on 24c blk brn	.70	.75
310	A51	2c on 50c black	.70	.35
		Nos. 298-310 (13)	8.40	6.15

Ricardo Arango A77

Juan A. Guizado A78

La Concordia Fire — A79

Modern Fire Fighting Equipment A80

Firemen's Monument A81

David H. Brandon A82

Perf. 14x14½, 14½x14

1937, Nov. 25 Photo. Wmk. 233

311	A77	½c orange red	2.10	.35
312	A78	1c green	2.10	.35
313	A79	2c red	2.10	.25
314	A80	5c brt blue	4.00	.50
315	A81	10c purple	7.25	1.25
316	A82	12c yellow grn	11.50	2.00
		Nos. 311-316,C40-C42 (9)	44.80	7.05

50th anniversary of the Fire Department.

Old Panama Cathedral Tower and Statue of Liberty Enlightening the World, Flags of Panama and US — A83

Engr. & Litho.

1938, Dec. 7 Unwmk. *Perf. 12½*

Center in Black; Flags in Red and Ultramarine

317	A83	1c deep green	.35	.25
318	A83	2c carmine	.55	.20
319	A83	5c blue	.80	.30
320	A83	12c olive	1.40	.75
321	A83	15c brt ultra	1.75	1.25
		Nos. 317-321,C49-C53 (10)	22.45	15.30

150th anniv. of the US Constitution.

No. 236 Overprinted in Black

1938, June 5 *Perf. 12*

321A	A53	2c carmine	.45	.25
b.		Inverted overprint	22.50	
		Nos. 321A,C53A-C53B (3)	1.25	1.05

Opening of the Normal School at Santiago, Veraguas Province, June 5, 1938.

Gatun Lake — A84

Designs: 1c, Pedro Miguel Locks. 2c, Allegory. 5c, Culebra Cut. 10c, Ferryboat. 12c, Aerial View of Canal. 15c, Gen. William C. Gorgas. 50c, Dr. Manuel A. Guerrero. 1b, Woodrow Wilson.

1939, Aug. 15 Engr. *Perf. 12½*

322	A84	½c yellow	.35	.20
323	A84	1c dp blue grn	.55	.20
324	A84	2c dull rose	.65	.20
325	A84	5c dull blue	1.00	.20
326	A84	10c dk violet	1.10	.35
327	A84	12c olive green	1.10	.50
328	A84	15c ultra	1.10	.80
329	A84	50c orange	2.75	1.60
330	A84	1b dk brown	5.75	3.00
		Nos. 322-330,C54-C61 (17)	34.35	14.05

25th anniversary of the opening of the Panama Canal. For surcharges see Nos. C64, G2.

AIR POST STAMPS

Special Delivery Stamp No. E3 Surcharged in Dark Blue

1929, Feb. 8 Unwmk. *Perf. 12½*

C1	SD1	25c on 10c org	1.00	.80
a.		Inverted surcharge	22.50	22.50

Nos. E3-E4 Overprinted in Blue

1929

C2	SD1	10c orange	.50	.50
a.		Inverted overprint	16.00	14.00
b.		Double overprint	16.00	14.00

Some specialists claim the red overprint is a proof impression.

With Additional Surcharge of New Value

C3	SD1	15c on 10c org	.50	.50
C4	SD1	25c on 20c dk brn	1.10	1.00
a.		Double surcharge	14.00	14.00
		Nos. C2-C4 (3)	2.10	2.00

No. E3 Surcharged in Blue

1930, Jan. 25

C5	SD1	5c on 10c org	.50	.50

No. 219 Overprinted in Red

1930, Feb. 28 *Perf. 12*

C6	A39	1b dk vio & blk	16.00	12.50

AP5

Airplane over Map of Panama — AP6

1930-41 Engr. *Perf. 12*

C6A	AP5	5c blue ('41)	.20	.20
C6B	AP5	7c rose car ('41)	.25	.20
C6C	AP5	8c gray blk ('41)	.25	.20
C7	AP5	15c dp grn	.30	.20
C8	AP5	20c rose	.35	.20
C9	AP5	25c deep blue	.65	.65
		Nos. C6A-C9 (6)	2.00	1.65

See No. C112.

For surcharges and overprints see Nos. 353, C16-C16A, C53B, C69, C82-C83, C109, C122, C124.

1930, Aug. 4 ***Perf. 12½***

C10	AP6 5c ultra	.20	.20
C11	AP6 10c orange	.30	.20
C12	AP6 30c dp vio	5.50	4.00
C13	AP6 50c dp red	1.50	.50
C14	AP6 1b black	5.50	4.00
	Nos. C10-C14 (5)	13.00	8.90

For surcharge and overprints see Nos. C53A, C70-C71, C115.

Amphibian AP7

1931, Nov. 24 **Typo.**

Without Gum

C15	AP7 5c deep blue	.80	1.00
a.	5c gray blue	.80	1.00
b.	Horiz. pair, imperf. btwn.	50.00	

For the start of regular airmail service between Panama City and the western provinces, but valid only on Nov. 28-29 on mail carried by hydroplane "3 Noviembre."

Many sheets have a papermaker's watermark "DOLPHIN BOND" in double-lined capitals.

No. C9 Surcharged in Red 19mm long

1932, Dec. 14 ***Perf. 12***

C16	AP5 20c on 25c dp bl	6.25	.70

Surcharge 17mm long

C16A	AP5 20c on 25c dp bl	200.00	2.50

Special Delivery Stamp No. E4 Overprinted in Red or Black

1934 ***Perf. 12½***

C17	SD1 20c dk brn	1.00	.50
C17A	SD1 20c dk brn (Bk)	100.00	55.00

Surcharged In Black

1935, June

C18	SD1 10c on 20c dk brn	.80	.50

Same Surcharge with Small "10"

C18A	SD1 10c on 20c dk brn	40.00	5.00
b.	Horiz. pair, imperf. vert.	100.00	

Nos. 234 and 242 Surcharged in Blue

1936, Sept. 24

C19	A53 5c on ½c org	400.00	250.00
C20	A53 5c on 50c org	1.00	.80
a.	Double surcharge	60.00	60.00

Centenary of the birth of President Pablo Arosemena.

It is claimed that No. C19 was not regularly issued. Counterfeits of No. C19 exist.

Urracá Monument AP8

Human Genius Uniting the Oceans AP9

20c, Panama City. 30c, Balboa Monument. 50c, Pedro Miguel Locks. 1b, Palace of Justice.

1936, Dec. 1 **Engr.** ***Perf. 12***

C21	AP8 5c blue	.65	.40
C22	AP9 10c yel org	.85	.60
C23	AP9 20c red	3.00	1.50
C24	AP9 30c dk vio	3.50	2.50
C25	AP9 50c car rose	8.00	5.75
C26	AP9 1b black	9.50	6.00
	Nos. C21-C26 (6)	25.50	16.75

4th Postal Congress of the Americas and Spain.

Nos. C21-C26 Overprinted in Red or Blue

1937, Mar. 29

C27	AP8 5c blue (R)	.55	.30
a.	Inverted overprint	35.00	
C28	AP9 10c yel org (Bl)	.75	.45
C29	AP9 20c red (Bl)	1.75	1.00
a.	Double overprint	35.00	
C30	AP8 30c dk vio (R)	4.50	3.25
C31	AP8 50c car rose (Bl)	18.00	13.00
a.	Double overprint	120.00	
C32	AP9 1b black (R)	22.50	13.00
	Nos. C27-C32 (6)	48.05	31.00

Regular Stamps of 1921-26 Surcharged in Red

1937, June 30 ***Perf. 12, 12½***

C33	A55 5c on 15c ultra	.75	.75
C34	A55 5c on 20c brn	.75	.75
C35	A47 10c on 10c vio	1.75	1.50

Regular Stamps of 1920-26 Surcharged in Red

C36	A56 5c on 24c blk vio	.75	.75
C37	A39 5c on 1b dk vio & blk	.75	.50
C38	A56 10c on 50c blk	2.25	2.00
a.	Inverted surcharge	20.00	

No. 248 Overprinted in Red

C39	A54 5c dark blue	.75	.75
a.	Double overprint	18.00	
	Nos. C33-C39 (7)	7.75	7.00

Fire Dept. Badge AP14

Florencio Arosemena AP15

José Gabriel Duque — AP16

Perf. 14x14½

1937, Nov. 25 **Photo.** **Wmk. 233**

C40	AP14 5c blue	3.50	.60
C41	AP15 10c orange	5.00	1.00
C42	AP16 20c crimson	7.25	.75
	Nos. C40-C42 (3)	15.75	2.35

50th anniversary of the Fire Department.

Basketball — AP17

Baseball AP18

1938, Feb. 2 ***Perf. 14x14½, 14½x14***

C43	AP17 1c shown	2.25	.20
C44	AP18 2c shown	2.25	.20
C45	AP18 7c Swimming	3.00	.25
C46	AP18 8c Boxing	3.00	.25
C47	AP17 15c Soccer	5.00	1.25
a.	Souv. sheet of 5, #C43-C47	18.00	18.00
b.	As "a," No. C43 omitted	*2,500.*	
	Nos. C43-C47 (5)	15.50	2.15

4th Central American Caribbean Games.

US Constitution Type

Engr. & Litho.

1938, Dec. 7 **Unwmk.** ***Perf. 12½***

Center in Black, Flags in Red and Ultramarine

C49	A83 7c gray	.35	.25
C50	A83 8c brt ultra	.55	.35
C51	A83 15c red brn	.70	.45
C52	A83 50c orange	8.00	5.75
C53	A83 1b black	8.00	5.75
	Nos. C49-C53 (5)	17.60	12.55

Nos. C12 and C7 Surcharged in Red

1938, June 5 ***Perf. 12½, 12***

C53A	AP6 7c on 30c dp vio	.40	.40
c.	Double surcharge	18.00	
d.	Inverted surcharge	27.50	
C53B	AP5 8c on 15c dp grn	.40	.40
e.	Inverted surcharge	22.50	

Opening of the Normal School at Santiago, Veraguas Province, June 5, 1938. The 8c surcharge has no bars.

Belisario Porras AP23

Designs: 2c, William Howard Taft. 5c, Pedro J. Sosa. 10c, Lucien Bonaparte Wise. 15c, Armando Reclus. 20c, Gen. George W. Goethals. 50c, Ferdinand de Lesseps. 1b, Theodore Roosevelt.

1939, Aug. 15 **Engr.**

C54	AP23 1c dl rose	.40	.20
C55	AP23 2c dp bl grn	.40	.20
C56	AP23 5c indigo	.65	.20
C57	AP23 10c dk vio	.70	.20
C58	AP23 15c ultra	1.60	.35
C59	AP23 20c rose pink	4.00	1.40
C60	AP23 50c dk brn	5.00	.70
C61	AP23 1b black	7.25	3.75
	Nos. C54-C61 (8)	20.00	7.00

Opening of Panama Canal, 25th anniv.

For surcharges see Nos. C63, C65, G1, G3.

Flags of the 21 American Republics AP31

1940, Apr. 15 **Unwmk.**

C62	AP31 15c blue	.40	.35

Pan American Union, 50th anniversary.

For surcharge see No. C66.

Stamps of 1939-40 Surcharged in Black:

a

b

c

d

1940, Aug. 12

C63	AP23 (a) 5c on 15c lt ultra	.25	.25
a.	"7 AEREO 7" on 15c	40.00	40.00
C64	A84 (b) 7c on 15c ultra	.40	.25
C65	AP23 (c) 7c on 20c rose pink	.40	.25
C66	AP31 (d) 8c on 15c blue	.40	.25
	Nos. C63-C66 (4)	1.45	1.00

SPECIAL DELIVERY STAMPS

Nos. 211-212 Overprinted in Red

1926 Unwmk. *Perf. 12*

E1 A31 10c org & blk 7.50 3.25
a. "EXRPESO" 40.00
E2 A32 20c brn & blk 10.00 3.25
a. "EXRPESO" 40.00
b. Double overprint 35.00 35.00

Bicycle Messenger SD1

1929 Engr. *Perf. 12½*

E3 SD1 10c orange 1.25 1.00
E4 SD1 20c dk brn 4.75 2.50

For surcharges and overprints see Nos. C1-C5, C17-C18A, C67.

REGISTRATION STAMPS

Issued under Colombian Dominion

R1

1888 Unwmk. Engr. *Perf. 13½*

F1 R1 10c black, *gray* 8.00 5.25

Imperforate and part-perforate copies without gum and those on surface-colored paper are reprints.

R2

Magenta, Violet or Blue Black Handstamped Overprint

1898 *Perf. 12*

F2 R2 10c yellow 7.00 6.50

The handstamp on No. F2 was also used as a postmark.

R3

1900 Litho. *Perf. 11*

F3 R3 10c blk, *lt bl* 4.00 3.50

1901

F4 R3 10c brown red 30.00 20.00

R4

Blue Black Surcharge

1902

F5 R4 20c on 10c brn red 20.00 16.00

Issues of the Republic Issued in the City of Panama

Registration Stamps of Colombia Handstamped

R9

Handstamped in Blue Black or Rose — REPUBLICA DE PANAMA

1903-04 *Imperf.*

F6 R9 20c red brn, *bl* 45.00 42.50
F7 R9 20c blue, *blue* (R) 45.00 42.50

For surcharges and overprints see Nos. F8-F11, F16-F26.

Reprints exist of Nos. F6 and F7; see note after No. 64.

With Additional Surcharge in Rose

F8 R9 10c on 20c red brn, *bl* 60.00 55.00
b. "10" in blue black 60.00 55.00
F9 R9 10c on 20c bl, *bl* 60.00 45.00

Handstamped in Rose

F10 R9 10c on 20c red brn, *bl* 60.00 55.00
F11 R9 10c on 20c blue, *blue* 45.00 42.50

Issued in Colon

Regular Issues Handstamped "R/COLON" in Circle (as on F2) Together with Other Overprints and Surcharges

Handstamped

1903-04 *Perf. 12*

F12 A4 10c yellow 3.00 2.50

Handstamped PANAMA

F13 A4 10c yellow 22.50

Overprinted in Red

PANAMA PANAMA

F14 A4 10c yellow 3.00 2.50

Overprinted in Black — *República de Panamá*

F15 A4 10c yellow 7.50 5.00

The handstamps on Nos. F12 to F15 are in magenta, violet or red; various combinations of these colors are to be found. They are struck in various positions, including double, inverted, one handstamp omitted, etc.

Colombia No. F13 Handstamped Like No. F12 in Violet

Imperf

F16 R9 20c red brn, *bl* 60.00 55.00

Overprinted Like No. F15 in Black

F17 R9 20c red brn, *bl* 6.00 5.75

No. F17 Surcharged in Manuscript

F18 R9 10c on 20c red brn, *bl* 60.00 55.00

No. F17 Surcharged in Purple **10**

F19 R9 10c on 20c 82.50 80.00

No. F17 Surcharged in Violet **10**

F20 R9 10c on 20c 82.50 80.00

The varieties of the overprint which are described after No. 138 are also to be found on the Registration and Acknowledgment of Receipt stamps. It is probable that Nos. F17 to F20 inclusive owe their existence more to speculation than to postal necessity.

Issued in Bocas del Toro

Colombia Nos. F17 and F13 Handstamped in Violet

R DE PANAMA

1903-04

F21 R9 20c blue, *blue* 125.00 125.00
F22 R9 20c red brn, *bl* 125.00 125.00

No. F21 Surcharged in Manuscript in Violet or Red

F23 R9 10c on 20c bl, *bl* 150.00 140.00

Colombia Nos. F13, F17 Handstamped in Violet

Surcharged in Manuscript (a) "10" (b) "10cs" in Red

F25 R9 10 on 20c red brn, *bl* 70.00 65.00
F26 R9 10cs on 20c bl, *bl* 55.00 50.00
Nos. F21-F26 (5) 525.00 505.00

No. F25 without surcharge is bogus, according to leading experts.

General Issue

R5

1904 Engr. *Perf. 12*

F27 R5 10c green 1.00 .50

Nos. 190 and 213 Surcharged in Red

#F29-F30

#F29b

1916-17

F29 A11 5c on 8c pur & blk 3.00 2.25
a. "5" inverted 55.00
b. Large, round "5" 50.00
c. Inverted surcharge 12.50 11.00
d. Tête bêche surcharge
F30 A33 5c on 8c vio & blk ('17) 3.50 .80
a. Inverted surcharge 10.00 8.25
b. Tête bêche surcharge
c. Double surcharge 40.00

Stamps similar to No. F30, overprinted in green were unauthorized.

ACKNOWLEDGMENT OF RECEIPT STAMPS

Issued under Colombian Dominion

Experts consider this handstamp-"A.R. / COLON / COLOMBIA"-to be a cancellation or a marking intended for a letter to receive special handling. It was applied at Colon to various stamps in 1897-1904 in different colored inks for philatelic sale. It exists on cover, usually with the bottom line removed by masking the handstamp.

Nos. 17-18 Handstamped in Rose

1902

H4 A4 5c blue 5.00 5.00
H5 A4 10c yellow 10.00 10.00

This handstamp was also used as a postmark.

Issues of the Republic Issued in the City of Panama

Colombia No. H3 Handstamped

AR2

Handstamped in Rose — REPUBLICA DE PANAMA

1903-04 Unwmk. *Imperf.*

H9 AR2 10c blue, *blue* 10.00 8.00

Reprints exist of No. H9, see note after No. 64.

No. H9 Surcharged with New Value

H10 AR2 5c on 10c bl, *bl* 5.00 5.00

Colombia No. H3 Handstamped in Rose — Panamá

H11 AR2 10c blue, *blue* 17.50 14.00

Issued in Colon

Handstamped in Magenta or Violet — REPUBLICA DE PANAMA

Imperf

H17 AR2 10c blue, *blue* 15.00 15.00

Handstamped PANAMA

H18 AR2 10c blue, *blue* 82.50 70.00

Overprinted in Black

República de Panamá

H19 AR2 10c blue, *blue* 11.00 8.00

No. H19 Surcharged in Manuscript

H20 AR2 10c on 5c on 10c 100.00 82.50

Issued in Bocas del Toro

Colombia No. H3 Handstamped in Violet and Surcharged in Manuscript in Red Like Nos. F25-F26

1904

H21 AR2 5c on 10c blue, *blue*

No. H21, unused, without surcharge is bogus.

General Issue

AR3

1904 Engr. *Perf. 12*

H22	AR3 5c blue	1.00	.80

No. 199 Overprinted in Violet

1916

H23	A20 2½c red orange	1.00	.80
a.	"R.A." for "A.R."	50.00	
b.	Double overprint	8.00	
c.	Inverted overprint	8.00	

LATE FEE STAMPS

Issues of the Republic Issued in the City of Panama

LF3

Colombia No. I4 Handstamped in Rose or Blue Black

REPUBLICA DE PANAMA

1903-04 Unwmk. *Imperf.*

I1	LF3 5c pur, *rose*	12.50	9.00
I2	LF3 5c pur, *rose* (Bl Blk)	17.50	12.50

Reprints exist of #I1-I2; see note after #64.

General Issue

LF4

1904 Engr. *Perf. 12*

I3	LF4 2½c lake	1.00	.65

No. 199 Overprinted with Typewriter

Retardo

1910, Aug. 12

I4	A20 2½c red orange	125.00	100.00

Used only on Aug. 12-13.
Counterfeits abound.

Handstamped

RETARDO

1910

I5	A20 2½c red orange	60.00	50.00

Counterfeits abound.

No. 195 Surcharged in Green

1917

I6	A17 1c on ½c orange	.80	.80
a.	"UN CENTESIMO" inverted	50.00	
b.	Double surcharge	10.00	
c.	Inverted surcharge	6.50	6.50

Same Surcharge on No. 196

1921

I7	A17 1c on ½c rose	25.00	20.00

POSTAGE DUE STAMPS

San Lorenzo Castle Gate, Mouth of Chagres River
D1

Statue of Columbus
D2

Pedro J. Sosa — D4

D5

Design: 4c, Capitol, Panama City.

1915 Unwmk. Engr. *Perf. 12*

J1	D1 1c olive brown	3.50	.75
J2	D2 2c olive brown	5.25	.65
J3	D1 4c olive brown	7.25	1.25
J4	D4 10c olive brown	5.25	1.75
	Nos. J1-J4 (4)	21.25	4.40

Type D1 was intended to show a gate of San Lorenzo Castle, Chagres, and is so inscribed.

1930 *Perf. 12½*

J5	D5 1c emerald	1.00	.60
J6	D5 2c dark red	1.00	.60
J7	D5 4c dark blue	1.60	.80
J8	D5 10c violet	1.60	.80
	Nos. J5-J8 (4)	5.20	2.80

POSTAL TAX STAMPS

Pierre and Marie Curie — PT1

1939 Unwmk. Engr. *Perf. 12*

RA1	PT1 1c rose carmine	.65	.20
RA2	PT1 1c green	.65	.20
RA3	PT1 1c orange	.65	.20
RA4	PT1 1c blue	.65	.20
	Nos. RA1-RA4 (4)	2.60	.80

See Nos. RA6-RA18, RA24-RA27, RA30.

Stamp of 1924 Overprinted in Black

1940

RA5	A53 1c dark green	1.40	.75

Inscribed 1940

1941

RA6	PT1 1c rose carmine	.65	.20
RA7	PT1 1c green	.65	.20
RA8	PT1 1c orange	.65	.20
RA9	PT1 1c blue	.65	.20
	Nos. RA6-RA9 (4)	2.60	.80

PAPUA

'pa-pyə-wə

LOCATION — The southeastern portion of the island of New Guinea, north of Australia
AREA — 90,540 sq. mi.
POP. — 276,488 (1940)
CAPITAL — Port Moresby

In 1884 a British Protectorate was proclaimed over this part of the island, called "British New Guinea." In 1905 the administration was transferred to Australia and in 1906 the name was changed to Territory of Papua.

12 Pence = 1 Shilling
20 Shillings = 1 Pound

Watermarks

Wmk. 13 — Crown and Double-Lined A

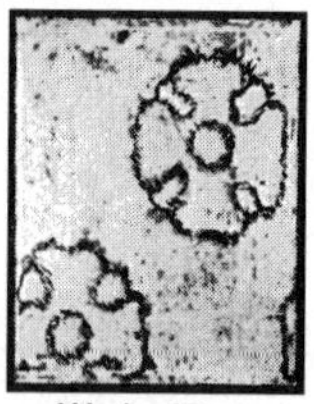
Wmk. 47 — Multiple Rosette

Wmk. 74 — Crown and Single-Lined A Sideways

Wmk. 228 — Small Crown and C of A Multiple

British New Guinea

Lakatoi — A1

Wmk. 47

1901, July 1 Engr. *Perf. 14*

Center in Black

1	A1	½p yellow green	12.00	4.50
2	A1	1p carmine	5.00	4.00
3	A1	2p violet	12.00	7.00
4	A1	2½p ultra	17.50	*20.00*
5	A1	4p black brown	40.00	*40.00*
a.		Deformed "d" at left (pl.3, pos.4 right pane)	275.00	225.00
6	A1	6p dark green	52.50	40.00
7	A1	1sh orange	62.50	*75.00*
8	A1	2sh6p brown ('05)	600.00	*600.00*
		Nos. 1-8 (8)	801.50	*790.50*

The paper varies in thickness and the watermark is found in two positions, with the greater width of the rosette either horizontal or vertical.
For overprints see Nos. 11-26.

Papua

Stamps of British New Guinea, Overprinted

1906, Nov. 8 Wmk. 47 *Perf. 14*

Large Overprint
Center in Black

11	A1	½p yellow green	6.00	*22.50*
12	A1	1p carmine	16.00	*20.00*
13	A1	2p violet	5.75	3.50
14	A1	2½p ultra	4.50	*17.50*
15	A1	4p black brown	200.00	150.00
e.		Deformed "d" at left	225.00	*300.00*
16	A1	6p dark green	45.00	*65.00*
17	A1	1sh orange	23.00	*45.00*
18	A1	2sh6p brown	200.00	*175.00*
		Nos. 11-18 (8)	500.25	*498.50*

Overprinted

Small Overprint

1907 Center in Black

19	A1	½p yellow green	9.25	*11.50*
a.		Double overprint	2,000.	
20	A1	1p carmine	5.50	*7.00*
a.		Vertical overprint, up	2,500.	1,500.
21	A1	2p violet	5.25	3.50
22	A1	2½p ultra	11.00	*22.50*
a.		Double overprint		
b.		2½p dull blue & blk	150.00	*160.00*
23	A1	4p black brown	35.00	*60.00*
a.		Deformed "d" at left	600.00	
24	A1	6p dark green	35.00	*47.50*
a.		Double overprint	3,000.	*5,000.*
25	A1	1sh orange	32.50	*50.00*
a.		Double overprint	*8,000.*	*5,000.*
26	A1	2sh6p brown	50.00	*65.00*
b.		Vert. ovpt., down	*4,600.*	
d.		Double horiz. ovpt.		3,500.
e.		Triple horiz. ovpt.		2,750.
		Nos. 19-26 (8)	183.50	*267.00*

A2

Small "PAPUA"

Perf. 11, 12½

1907-08 Litho. Wmk. 13

Center in Black

28	A2	1p carmine ('08)	5.50	*5.75*
29	A2	2p violet ('08)	10.50	6.00
30	A2	2½p ultra ('08)	7.00	*7.50*
31	A2	4p black brown	6.75	*11.50*
b.		Deformed "d" at left	35.00	*57.50*
32	A2	6p dk green ('08)	12.50	*18.00*
33	A2	1sh orange ('08)	27.50	*24.00*
		Nos. 28-33 (6)	69.75	*72.75*

Perf. 12½

30a	A2	2½p	140.00	*150.00*
31a	A2	4p	9.25	*12.00*
c.		Deformed "d" at left	57.50	57.50
33a	A2	1sh	70.00	*97.50*
		Nos. 30a-33a (3)	219.25	*259.50*

1909-10 Wmk. Sideways

Center in Black

34	A2	½p yellow green	3.50	*6.00*
a.		Perf. 11x12½	*2,600.*	*2,600.*
b.		Perf. 11	2.75	*4.25*
35	A2	1p carmine	8.00	*14.00*
a.		Perf. 11	11.00	9.25
36	A2	2p violet ('10)	6.00	*12.00*
a.		Perf. 11x12½	975.00	
b.		Perf. 11	13.50	*10.50*
37	A2	2½p ultra ('10)	6.00	*22.50*
a.		Perf. 12½	10.50	*45.00*
38	A2	4p black brn ('10)	5.50	*11.00*
a.		Perf. 11x12½	*8,500.*	
b.		As "#38," deformed "d" at left	32.50	*52.50*
39	A2	6p dark green	13.00	21.00
a.		Perf. 12½	3,250.	*4,250.*

40	A2	1sh orange ('10)	17.50	*42.50*
a.		Perf. 11	55.00	*70.00*
		Nos. 34-40 (7)	59.50	*129.00*

One stamp in each sheet has a white line across the upper part of the picture which is termed the "rift in the clouds."

Large "PAPUA"

2sh6p:
Type I — The numerals are thin and irregular. The body of the "6" encloses a large spot of color. The dividing stroke is thick and uneven.
Type II — The numerals are thick and well formed. The "6" encloses a narrow oval of color. The dividing stroke is thin and sharp.

1910 **Wmk. 13**

Center in Black

41	A2	½p yellow green	4.00	*12.50*
42	A2	1p carmine	10.50	9.75
43	A2	2p violet	5.75	*5.75*
44	A2	2½p blue violet	6.50	*20.00*
45	A2	4p black brown	6.50	*11.50*
46	A2	6p dark green	10.00	*8.50*
47	A2	1sh orange	7.50	*22.50*
48	A2	2sh6p brown, type II	45.00	*52.50*
a.		Type I	50.00	*62.50*
		Nos. 41-48 (8)	95.75	*143.00*

Wmk. Sideways

49	A2	2sh6p choc, type I	80.00	*100.00*

1911 **Typo.** **Wmk. 74** ***Perf. 12½***

50	A2	½p yellow green	.60	*2.75*
51	A2	1p lt red	.90	1.00
52	A2	2p lt violet	.90	1.00
53	A2	2½p ultra	6.00	*10.00*
a.		2½p dull ultra	4.00	4.00
54	A2	4p olive green	2.75	*12.50*
55	A2	6p orange brown	4.25	*5.75*
56	A2	1sh yellow	12.00	*45.00*
57	A2	2sh6p rose	37.50	*42.50*
		Nos. 50-57 (8)	64.90	*120.50*

For surcharges see Nos. 74-79.

1915, June ***Perf. 14***

59	A2	1p light red	7.50	2.25

A3

1916-31

60	A3	½p pale yel grn & myr grn ('19)	.95	1.10
61	A3	1p rose red & blk	1.75	.75
62	A3	1½p yel brn & gray bl ('25)	1.75	.95
63	A3	2p red vio & vio brn ('19)	2.25	.85
64	A3	2p red brn & vio brn ('31)	2.50	.85
a.		2p cop red & vio brn ('31)	29.00	2.25
65	A3	2½p ultra & dk grn ('19)	6.00	*16.00*
66	A3	3p emerald & blk	2.25	2.25
a.		3p dp bl grn & blk	5.25	9.25
67	A3	4p org & lt brn ('19)	3.25	5.75
68	A3	5p ol brn & sl ('31)	4.75	*19.00*
69	A3	6p vio & dl vio ('23)	3.75	*11.00*
70	A3	1sh ol grn & dk brn ('19)	4.25	*8.00*
71	A3	2sh6p rose & red brn ('19)	25.00	*47.50*
72	A3	5sh dp grn & blk	55.00	*60.00*
73	A3	10sh gray bl & grn ('25)	160.00	*200.00*
		Nos. 60-73 (14)	273.45	*374.00*

Type A3 is a redrawing of type A2.
The lines of the picture have been strengthened, making it much darker, especially the sky and water.
For surcharges & overprints see #88-91, O1-O10.

Stamps of 1911 Surcharged

1917 ***Perf. 12½***

74	A2	1p on ½p yellow grn	1.10	1.40
75	A2	1p on 2p lt violet	14.00	*17.50*
76	A2	1p on 2½p ultra	1.40	*4.50*
77	A2	1p on 4p olive green	2.00	*5.25*
78	A2	1p on 6p org brn	9.25	*20.00*
79	A2	1p on 2sh6p rose	2.00	*7.00*
		Nos. 74-79 (6)	29.75	*55.65*

No. 62 Surcharged

1931, Jan. 1 ***Perf. 14***

88	A3	2p on 1½p yellow brn & gray blue	1.50	*2.50*

Nos. 70, 71 and 72 Surcharged in Black

1931

89	A3	5p on 1sh #70	2.00	4.00
90	A3	9p on 2sh6p #71	7.00	*10.00*
91	A3	1sh3p on 5sh #72	5.00	*10.50*
		Nos. 89-91 (3)	14.00	*24.50*

Type of 1916 Issue

1932 **Wmk. 228** ***Perf. 11***

92	A3	9p dp violet & gray	7.50	*37.50*
93	A3	1sh3p pale bluish green & grayish violet	12.00	*37.50*

For overprints see Nos. O11-O12.

Motuan Girl — A5

Bird of Paradise and Boar's Tusk — A6

Mother and Child — A7

Papuan Motherhood — A8

Dubu (Ceremonial Platform) — A9

Fire Maker — A10

Designs: 1p, Steve, son of Oala. 1½p, Tree houses. 3p, Papuan dandy. 5p, Masked dancer. 9p, Shooting fish. 1sh3p, Lakatoi. 2sh, Delta art. 2sh6p, Pottery making. 5sh, Sgt.-Major Simoi. £1, Delta house.

Unwmk.

1932, Nov. 14 **Engr.** ***Perf. 11***

94	A5	½p orange & blk	1.75	3.75
a.		½p orange brown & black	14.00	*24.00*
95	A5	1p yel grn & blk	2.00	.70
96	A5	1½p red brn & blk	1.75	*9.25*
97	A6	2p light red	12.50	.35
98	A5	3p blue & blk	3.75	*7.50*
99	A7	4p olive green	7.00	*11.00*
100	A5	5p grnsh sl & blk	3.50	3.50
101	A8	6p bister brown	8.50	6.25
102	A5	9p lilac & blk	11.50	*24.00*
103	A9	1sh bluish gray	4.50	*9.75*
104	A5	1sh3p brown & blk	17.50	*29.00*
105	A5	2sh bluish slate & blk	17.50	*26.00*
106	A5	2sh6p rose lilac & blk	29.00	*42.50*
107	A5	5sh olive & blk	62.50	62.50
108	A10	10sh gray lilac	97.50	97.50
109	A5	£1 lt gray & black	210.00	175.00
		Nos. 94-109 (16)	490.75	*508.55*

For overprints see Nos. 114-117.

Hoisting Union Jack at Port Moresby A21

H. M. S. "Nelson" at Port Moresby A22

1934, Nov. 6

110	A21	1p dull green	1.10	*3.50*
111	A22	2p red brown	2.00	*3.00*
112	A21	3p blue	2.00	*3.00*
113	A22	5p violet brown	12.00	*13.00*
		Nos. 110-113 (4)	17.10	*22.50*
		Set, never hinged	27.50	

Declaration of British Protection, 50th anniv.

Silver Jubilee Issue

Stamps of 1932 Issue Overprinted in Black:

a

b

1935, July 9

Glazed Paper

114	A5(a)	1p yellow grn & blk	.85	*3.25*
115	A6(b)	2p light red	2.25	*3.25*
116	A5(a)	3p lt blue & blk	2.00	*3.25*
117	A5(a)	5p grnsh slate & blk	2.75	*3.25*
		Nos. 114-117 (4)	7.85	*13.00*
		Set, never hinged	14.00	

25th anniv. of the reign of George V.

Coronation Issue

King George VI — A22a

Unwmk.

1937, May 14 **Engr.** ***Perf. 11***

118	A22a	1p green	.45	.20
119	A22a	2p salmon rose	.45	*.60*
120	A22a	3p blue	.45	*.60*
121	A22a	5p brown violet	.45	*1.00*
		Nos. 118-121 (4)	1.80	*2.40*
		Set, never hinged	2.75	

AIR POST STAMPS

Regular Issue of 1916 Overprinted

1929 **Wmk. 74** ***Perf. 14***

C1	A3	3p blue grn & dk gray	2.00	*12.50*
b.		Vert. pair, one without ovpt.	*3,750.*	
c.		Horiz. pair, one without ovpt.	*4,250.*	
d.		3p blue grn & sepia blk	57.50	*75.00*
e.		Overprint on back, vert.	*3,500.*	

No. C1 exists on white and on yellowish paper, No. C1d on yellowish paper only.

Regular Issues of 1916-23 Overprinted in Red

1930, Sept. 15 **Wmk. 74**

C2	A3	3p blue grn & blk	2.00	*7.00*
a.		Yellowish paper	1,850.	*3,250.*
b.		Double overprint	1,400.	
C3	A3	6p violet & dull vio	8.00	*11.50*
a.		Yellowish paper	5.00	*19.00*
C4	A3	1sh ol green & ol brn	6.00	*17.50*
a.		Inverted overprint	*4,000.*	
b.		Yellowish paper	10.00	26.00
		Nos. C2-C4 (3)	16.00	*36.00*

Port Moresby AP1

Unwmk.

1938, Sept. 6 **Engr.** ***Perf. 11***

C5	AP1	2p carmine	2.75	2.50
C6	AP1	3p ultra	2.75	2.50
C7	AP1	5p dark green	2.75	*3.50*
C8	AP1	8p red brown	6.50	*16.50*
C9	AP1	1sh violet	17.50	17.50
		Nos. C5-C9 (5)	32.25	*42.50*
		Set, never hinged	40.00	

Papua as a British possession, 50th anniv.

Papuans Poling Rafts — AP2

1939-41

C10	AP2	2p carmine	2.25	3.50
C11	AP2	3p ultra	2.25	*7.50*
C12	AP2	5p dark green	2.25	1.50
C13	AP2	8p red brown	6.00	2.50
C14	AP2	1sh violet	7.50	7.00
C15	AP2	1sh6p lt olive ('41)	22.50	*32.50*
		Nos. C10-C15 (6)	42.75	*54.50*
		Set, never hinged	60.00	

OFFICIAL STAMPS

Nos. 60-63, 66-71, 92-93 Overprinted

1931 Wmk. 74 *Perf. 14½*

O1	A3	½p #60	2.40	*5.50*
O2	A3	1p #61	4.75	*8.75*
O3	A3	1½p #62	1.90	*14.00*
O4	A3	2p #63	4.50	*10.50*
O5	A3	3p #66	3.00	*25.00*
O6	A3	4p #67	3.00	*21.00*
O7	A3	5p #68	7.00	*42.50*
O8	A3	6p #69	4.75	*9.75*
O9	A3	1sh #70	10.50	*35.00*
O10	A3	2sh6p #71	45.00	*97.50*

1932 Wmk. 228 *Perf. 11½*

O11	A3	9p #92	35.00	*55.00*
O12	A3	1sh3p #93	35.00	*55.00*
		Nos. O1-O12 (12)	156.80	*379.50*

PARAGUAY

ˈpar-ə-ˌgwī

LOCATION — South America, bounded by Bolivia, Brazil and Argentina
GOVT. — Republic
AREA — 157,042 sq. mi.
POP. — 3,477,000 (1983)
CAPITAL — Asuncion

10 Reales = 100 Centavos = 1 Peso

Vigilant Lion Supporting Liberty Cap
A1 A2

A3

1870, Aug. Unwmk. Litho. *Imperf.*

1	A1	1r rose	5.00	*9.*
		On cover		*2,000.*
		On cover, pen canceled		*1,000.*
a.		1r bright rose	4.50	*9.*
		On cover		*2,100.*
		On cover, pen canceled		*1,100.*
2	A2	2r blue	90.00	*100.*
		On cover		*4,000.*
a.		2r dark blue		125.
		On cover		*5,000.*
3	A3	3r black	180.00	*210.*
		On cover		*8,000.*
		On cover, pen canceled		*1,000.*

Counterfeits of 2r in blue and other colors are on thicker paper than originals. They show a colored dot in upper part of "S" of "DOS" in upper right corner.

For surcharges see Nos. 4-9, 19.

Handstamp Surcharged

1878 Black Surcharge

4	A1	5c on 1r rose	80.	*110.*
		On cover (see footnote)		*10,000.*
5	A2	5c on 2r blue	325.	300.
		On cover		*13,000.*
5E	A3	5c on 3r black	450.	450.
		On cover		*15,000.*
		Nos. 4-5E (3)	855.00	860.00

Blue Surcharge

5F	A1	5c on 1r rose	80.	*110.*
		On cover (see footnote)		*10,000.*
5H	A2	5c on 2r blue	*1,000.*	*1,000.*
		On cover		*13,000.*
6	A3	5c on 3r black	425.	425.
		On cover		*15,000.*
		Nos. 5F-6 (3)	*1,505.*	*1,535.*

The surcharge may be found inverted, double, sideways and omitted.

Remainders of Nos. 4 and 5F were placed on sale at Post Offices during 1892. Covers dated 1892 are worth about $7,500.

The originals are surcharged in dull black or dull blue. The reprints are in intense black and bright blue. The reprint surcharges are over-inked and show numerous breaks in the handstamp.

Handstamp Surcharged

Black Surcharge

7	A2	5c on 2r blue	500.00	425.00
		On cover		*13,000.*
8	A3	5c on 3r black	425.00	425.00
		On cover		*15,000.*

Blue Surcharge

9	A3	5c on 3r black	250.00	250.00
		On cover		*15,000.*
a.		Dbl. surch., large & small "5"	—	
		Nos. 7-9 (3)	1,175.	1,100.

The surcharge on Nos. 7, 8 and 9 is usually placed sideways. It may be found double or inverted on Nos. 8 and 9.

Nos. 4 to 9 have been extensively counterfeited.

Two examples recorded of No. 9a, one without gum, the other with full but disturbed original gum.

A4

A4a

1879 Litho. *Perf. 12½*
Thin Paper

10	A4	5r orange	1.25	
11	A4	10r red brown	1.50	
a.		Imperf.		
b.		Horiz. pair, imperf. vert.	40.00	

Nos. 10 and 11 were never placed in use.
For surcharges see Nos. 17-18.

1879-81 Thin Paper

12	A4a	5c orange brown	2.50	2.00
		On cover		500.00
a.		5c reddish brown	2.00	2.00
		On cover		525.00
13	A4a	10c blue grn ('81)	3.50	3.00
		On cover		700.00
a.		Imperf., pair	10.00	*12.00*

Reprints of Nos. 10-13 are imperf., perf. 11½, 12, 12½ or 14. They have yellowish gum and the 10c is deep green.

A5

A6

A7

1881, Aug. Litho. *Perf. 11½-13½*

14	A5	1c blue	.80	.70
		On cover		—
a.		Imperf., pair	—	
b.		Horiz. pair, imperf. btwn.	—	
15	A6	2c rose red	.80	.70
		On cover		*300.00*
a.		2c dull orange red	1.00	.90
		On cover		*300.00*
b.		Imperf., pair	—	
c.		Horiz. pair, imperf. vert.	25.00	25.00
d.		Vert. pair, imperf. horiz.	25.00	25.00
16	A7	4c brown	.80	*.70*
		On cover		*650.00*
a.		Imperf., pair	—	
b.		Horiz. pair, imperf. vert.	25.00	25.00
c.		Vert. pair, imperf. horiz.	25.00	25.00

No. 11 Surcharged

Handstamped in Black or Gray

1881, July *Perf. 12½*

17	A4	1c on 10c blue grn	10.00	9.00
		On cover		400.00
18	A4	2c on 10c blue grn	10.00	9.00
		On cover		450.00

Gray handstamps sell for 10 times more than black as many specialists consider the black to be reprints.

No. 1 Surcharged

1884, May 8 Handstamped *Imperf.*

19	A1	1c on 1r rose	5.00	4.50
		On cover		*1,750.*

The surcharges on Nos. 17-19 exist double, inverted and in pairs with one omitted. Counterfeits exist.

Seal of the Treasury
A11 A12

1884, Aug. 3 Litho. *Perf. 12½*

20	A11	1c green	.70	.65
		On cover		35.00
21	A11	2c rose pink, thin paper	.70	.65
b.		2c rose red, thin paper	.85	.85
c.		2c red, thick paper, perf. 11½	.70	.85

Perf. 11½

22	A11	5c pale blue, yellowish paper	.70	*.65*
b.		5c blue, thin paper, perf. 12½	.65	.65
		On cover		45.00
c.		5c pale blue, thin paper, perf. 12½	.65	.65
d.		5c blue, thin paper	3.75	3.75
e.		5c pale blue, thin paper	2.50	2.50
f.		5c blue, thick paper	11.50	9.00
		Nos. 20-22 (3)	2.10	1.95

There are two types of each value differing mostly in the shape of the numerals. In addition, there are numerous small flaws in the lithographic transfers.

For overprints see Nos. O1, O8, O15.

Imperf., Pairs

20a	A11	1c green	12.50
21a	A11	2c rose red	16.00
d.		2c red, thick paper	10.00
22a	A11	5c blue	16.00
		Nos. 20a-22a (3)	44.50

Perf. 11½, 11½x12, 12½x11½

1887 Typo.

23	A12	1c green	.25	.20
24	A12	2c rose	.25	.20
25	A12	5c blue	.40	.30
26	A12	7c brown	.70	.40
27	A12	10c lilac	.50	.30
28	A12	15c orange	.50	.30
29	A12	20c pink	.50	.30
		Nos. 23-29 (7)	3.10	2.00

See #42-45. For surcharges & overprints see #46, 49-50, 71-72, 167-170A, O20-O41, O49.

Symbols of Liberty from Coat of Arms — A13

1889, Feb. Litho. *Perf. 11½*

30	A13	15c red violet	2.50	2.00
a.		Imperf., pair	10.00	8.00

For overprints see Nos. O16-O19.

Overprint Handstamped in Violet

1892, Oct. 12 *Perf. 12x12½*

31	A15	10c violet blue	7.00	3.50

Discovery of America by Columbus, 400th anniversary. Overprint reads: "1492 / 12 DE OCTUBRE / 1892." Sold only on day of issue.

Cirilo A. Rivarola — A15

Designs: 2c, Salvador Jovellanos. 4c, Juan B. Gil. 5c, Higinio Uriarte. 10c, Cándido Bareiro. 14c, Gen. Bernardino Caballero. 20c, Gen. Patricio Escobar. 30c, Juan G. González.

1892-96 Litho. *Perf. 12x12½*

32	A15	1c gray (centavos)	.20	.20
33	A15	1c gray (centavo) ('96)	.20	.20
34	A15	2c green	.20	.20
a.		Chalky paper ('96)	.20	.20
35	A15	4c carmine	.20	.20
a.		Chalky paper ('96)	.20	.20
36	A15	5c violet ('93)	.20	.20
a.		Chalky paper ('96)	.20	.20
37	A15	10c vio bl (punched) ('93)	.20	.20
		Unpunched ('96)	4.00	
38	A15	10c dull blue ('96)	.20	.20
39	A15	14c yellow brown	.60	.40
40	A15	20c red ('93)	1.00	.40
41	A15	30c light green	1.50	.65
		Nos. 32-41 (10)	4.50	2.85

The 10c violet blue (No. 37) was, until 1896, issued punched with a circular hole in order to prevent it being fraudulently overprinted as No. 31.

Nos. 33 and 38 are on chalky paper.
For surcharge see No. 70.

Seal Type of 1887

1892 Typo.

42	A12	40c slate blue	2.00	.90
43	A12	60c yellow	1.00	.40
44	A12	80c light blue	.90	.40
45	A12	1p olive green	.90	.40
		Nos. 42-45 (4)	4.80	2.10

No. 46

Nos. 47-48

1895, Aug. 1 *Perf. 11½x12*

46	A12	5c on 7c brown, #26	.50	.50

Telegraph Stamps Surcharged

1896, Apr. Engr. *Perf. 11½*

Denomination in Black

47	5c on 2c brown & gray	.60	.40
a.	Inverted surcharge	10.00	10.00
48	5c on 4c yellow & gray	.60	.40
a.	Inverted surcharge	7.50	7.50

Nos. 28, 42 Surcharged

1898-99 Typo.

49 A12 10c on 15c org ('99) .60 .35
a. Inverted surcharge 14.00 14.00
b. Double surcharge 9.00 9.00
50 A12 10c on 40c slate bl .30 .20

Surcharge on No. 49 has small "c."

Telegraph Stamps Surcharged

1900, May 14 Engr. *Perf. 11½*

50A 5c on 30c grn, gray & blk 1.75 1.00
50B 10c on 50c dl vio, gray & blk 4.00 2.50

The basic telegraph stamps are like those used for Nos. 47-48, but the surcharges on Nos. 50A-50B consist of "5 5" and "10 10" above a blackout rectangle covering the engraved denominations.

A 40c red, bluish gray and black telegraph stamp (basic type of A24) was used provisionally in August, 1900, for postage. Value, postally used, $5.

Seal of the Treasury
A25

J. B. Egusquiza
A26

1900, Sept. Engr. *Perf. 11½, 12*

51 A25 2c gray .20 .20
52 A25 3c orange brown .20 .20
53 A25 5c dark green .20 .20
54 A25 8c dark brown .20 .20
55 A25 10c carmine rose .50 .20
56 A25 24c deep blue .60 .20
Nos. 51-56 (6) 1.90 1.20

See Nos. 57-67. For surcharges see Nos. 69, 74, 76, 156-157.

1901, Apr. Litho. *Perf. 11½*

Small Figures

57 A25 2c rose .20 .20
58 A25 5c violet brown .20 .20
59 A25 40c blue .70 .25
Nos. 57-59 (3) 1.10 .65

1901-02

Larger Figures

60 A25 1c gray green ('02) .20 .20
61 A25 2c gray .20 .20
a. Half used as 1c on cover 10.00
62 A25 4c pale blue .20 .20
63 A25 5c violet .20 .20
64 A25 8c gray brown ('02) .20 .20
65 A25 10c rose red ('02) .50 .20
66 A25 28c orange ('02) 1.00 .20
67 A25 40c blue .50 .20
Nos. 60-67 (8) 3.00 1.60

1901, Sept. 24 Typo. *Perf. 12x12½*

Chalky Paper

68 A26 1p slate .30 .20

For surcharge see No. 73.

No. 56 Surcharged

1902, Aug.

Red Surcharge

69 A25 20c on 24c dp blue .25 .20
a. Inverted surcharge 6.25

Counterfeit surcharges exist.

Nos. 39, 43-44 Surcharged

1902, Dec. 22 *Perf. 12x12½*

70 A15 1c on 14c yellow brn .20 .20
a. No period after "cent" .90 .75
b. Comma after "cent" .65 .50
c. Accent over "Un" .65 .50

1903 *Perf. 11½*

71 A12 5c on 60c yellow .25 .20
72 A12 5c on 80c lt blue .20 .20

Nos. 68, 64, 66 Surcharged

#73

#74

#76

1902-03 *Perf. 12*

73 A26 1c on 1p slate ('03) .20 .20
a. No period after "cent" 1.60 1.50

Perf. 11½

74 A25 5c on 8c gray brown .25 .20
a. No period after "cent" .90 .75
b. Double surcharge 3.50 3.00
76 A25 5c on 28c orange .25 .20
a. No period after "cent" .90 .75
b. Comma after "cent" .40 .30
Nos. 73-76 (3) .70 .60

The surcharge on Nos. 73 and 74 is found reading both upward and downward.

Sentinel Lion with Right Paw Ready to Strike for "Peace and Justice"
A32 A33

Perf. 11½

1903, Feb. 28 Litho. Unwmk.

77 A32 1c gray .20 .20
78 A32 2c blue green .30 .20
79 A32 5c blue .40 .20
80 A32 10c orange brown .50 .20
81 A32 20c carmine .50 .20
82 A32 30c deep blue .60 .20
83 A32 60c purple 1.40 .65
Nos. 77-83 (7) 3.90 1.85

For surcharges and overprints see Nos. 139-140, 166, O50-O56.

1903, Sept.

84 A33 1c yellow green .20 .20
85 A33 2c red orange .20 .20
86 A33 5c dark blue .30 .20
87 A33 10c purple .30 .20
88 A33 20c dark green .70 .30
89 A33 30c ultramarine 1.00 .20
90 A33 60c ocher 1.20 .50
Nos. 84-90 (7) 3.90 1.80

Nos. 84-90 exist imperf. Value for pairs, $3 each for 1c-20c, $4 for 30c, $5 for 60c.

The three-line overprint "Gobierno provisorio Ago. 1904" is fraudulent.

Sentinel Lion at Rest
A35 A36

Perf. 11½, 12, 11½x12

1905-10 Engr.

Dated "1904"

91 A35 1c orange .20 .20
92 A35 1c vermilion ('07) .20 .20
93 A35 1c grnsh bl ('07) .20 .20
94 A35 2c vermilion ('06) .20 .20
95 A35 2c olive grn ('07) 40.00
96 A35 2c car rose ('08) .30 .20
97 A35 5c dark blue .20 .20
98 A35 5c slate blue ('06) .20 .20
99 A35 5c yellow ('06) .20 .20
100 A35 10c bister ('06) .20 .20
101 A35 10c emerald ('07) .20 .20
102 A35 10c dp ultra ('08) .20 .20
103 A35 20c violet ('06) .30 .20
104 A35 20c bister ('07) .30 .20
105 A35 20c apple grn ('07) .30 .20
106 A35 30c turq bl ('06) .45 .20
107 A35 30c blue gray ('07) .45 .20
108 A35 30c dull lilac ('08) .60 .20
109 A35 60c chocolate ('07) .40 .20
110 A35 60c org brn ('07) 3.50 1.25
111 A35 60c salmon pink ('10) 3.50 1.25
Nos. 91-94,96-111 (20) 12.10 6.10

All but Nos. 92 and 104 exist imperf. Value for pair, $10 each, except No. 95 at $35.00 and Nos. 109-111 at $15.00 each pair.

For surcharges and overprints see Nos. 129-130, 146-155, 174-190, 266.

1904, Aug. Litho. *Perf. 11½*

112 A36 10c light blue .25 .20
a. Imperf., pair 3.00

No. 112 Surcharged in Black

1904, Dec.

113 A36 30c on 10c light blue .40 .25

Peace between a successful revolutionary party and the government previously in power.

Governmental Palace, Asunción — A37

Dated "1904"

1906-10 Engr. *Perf. 11½, 12*

Center in Black

114 A37 1p bright rose 1.25 .75
115 A37 1p brown org ('07) .50 .25
116 A37 1p ol gray ('07) .50 .25
117 A37 2p turquoise ('07) .25 .20
118 A37 2p lake ('09) .25 .20
119 A37 2p brn org ('10) .30 .20
120 A37 5p red ('07) .75 .50
121 A37 5p ol grn ('10) .75 .50
122 A37 5p dull bl ('10) .75 .50
123 A37 10p brown org ('07) .70 .50
124 A37 10p dp blue ('10) .70 .50
125 A37 10p choc ('10) .75 .50
126 A37 20p olive grn ('07) 1.75 1.60
127 A37 20p violet ('10) 1.75 1.60
128 A37 20p yellow ('10) 1.75 1.60
Nos. 114-128 (15) 12.70 9.65

Nos. 94 and 95 Surcharged

1907

129 A35 5c on 2c vermilion .30 .20
a. "5" omitted 1.00 1.00
b. Inverted surcharge 3.50 3.50
c. Double surcharge
d. Double surcharge, one inverted 1.00 1.00
e. Double surcharge, both invtd. 6.00 6.00
130 A35 5c on 2c olive grn .40 .20
a. "5" omitted 1.00 1.00
b. Inverted surcharge 1.00 1.00
c. Double surcharge 2.00 2.00
d. Bar omitted 2.00 2.00

Official Stamps of 1906-08 Surcharged

1908

131 O17 5c on 10c bister .30 .20
a. Double surcharge 3.00 3.00
132 O17 5c on 10c violet .30 .20
a. Inverted surcharge 2.25 2.25
133 O17 5c on 20c emerald .30 .20
134 O17 5c on 20c violet .30 .20
a. Inverted surcharge 2.25 2.25
135 O17 5c on 30c slate bl 1.00 .65
136 O17 5c on 30c turq bl 1.00 .65
a. Inverted surcharge
b. Double surcharge 6.00 6.00
137 O17 5c on 60c choc .30 .20
a. Double surcharge 6.00 6.00
138 O17 5c on 60c red brown .60 .20
a. Inverted surcharge 1.10 .40
Nos. 131-138 (8) 4.10 2.50

Same Surcharge on Official Stamps of 1903

139 A32 5c on 30c dp blue 1.25 1.10
140 A32 5c on 60c purple .50 .30
a. Double surcharge 2.50 2.50

Official Stamps of 1906-08 Overprinted

141 O17 5c deep blue .20 .20
a. Inverted overprint 1.50 1.50
b. Bar omitted 4.50 4.50
c. Double overprint 2.00 2.00
142 O17 5c slate blue .25 .20
a. Inverted overprint 2.00 2.00
b. Double overprint 1.75 1.75
c. Bar omitted 4.50 4.50
143 O17 5c greenish blue .20 .20
a. Inverted overprint 1.25 1.25
b. Bar omitted 3.75 3.75
144 O18 1p brown org & blk .25 .25
a. Double overprint 1.00 1.00
b. Double overprint, one inverted 1.25 1.25
c. Triple overprint, two inverted 2.25 2.25
145 O18 1p brt rose & blk .45 .35
a. Bar omitted
Nos. 141-145 (5) 1.35 1.20

Regular Issues of 1906-08 Surcharged

1908

146 A35 5c on 1c grnsh bl .20 .20
a. Inverted surcharge 1.00 1.00
b. Double surcharge 1.50 1.50
c. "5" omitted 1.50 1.50
147 A35 5c on 2c car rose .20 .20
a. Inverted surcharge 1.75 1.75
b. "5" omitted 2.00 2.00
c. Double surcharge 3.50 3.50
d. Double surcharge, one invtd.
148 A35 5c on 60c org brn .20 .20
a. Inverted surcharge 2.50 2.50
b. "5" omitted 1.00 1.00
149 A35 5c on 60c sal pink .20 .20
a. Double surcharge .50 .50
b. Double surcharge, one invtd. 3.50 3.50
150 A35 5c on 60c choc .20 .20
a. Inverted surcharge 5.00 5.00
151 A35 20c on 1c grnsh bl .20 .20
a. Inverted surcharge 1.50 1.50
152 A35 20c on 2c ver 6.00 5.00
153 A35 20c on 2c car rose 3.50 3.00
a. Inverted surcharge 12.50
154 A35 20c on 30c dl lil .20 .20
a. Inverted surcharge 1.50 1.50
b. Double surcharge
155 A35 20c on 30c turq bl 1.50 1.50
Nos. 146-155 (10) 12.40 10.90

Same Surcharge on Regular Issue of 1901-02

156 A25 5c on 28c org 1.25 1.10
157 A25 5c on 40c dk bl .40 .30
a. Inverted surcharge 4.00 4.00

Same Surcharge on Official Stamps of 1908

158 O17 5c on 10c emer .20 .20
a. Double surcharge 7.00
159 O17 5c on 10c red lil .20 .20
a. Double surcharge 2.00 2.00
b. "5" omitted 1.50 1.50
160 O17 5c on 20c bis .40 .30
a. Double surcharge 1.25 1.25
161 O17 5c on 20c sal pink .40 .30
a. "5" omitted 1.75 1.75
162 O17 5c on 30c bl gray .20 .20
163 O17 5c on 30c yel .20 .20
a. "5" omitted 1.50 1.50
b. Inverted surcharge 1.25 1.25
164 O17 5c on 60c org brn .20 .20
a. Double surcharge 6.00 6.00
165 O17 5c on 60c dp ultra .20 .20
a. Inverted surcharge 2.50 2.50
b. "5" omitted 1.50
Nos. 158-165 (8) 2.00 1.80

Same Surcharge on No. O52

166 A32 20c on 5c blue 1.25 1.00
a. Inverted surcharge 3.00 3.75

Surcharged

1908

On Stamp of 1887

167	A12	20c on 2c car	2.50	2.00
a.		Inverted surcharge	7.50	

On Official Stamps of 1892

168	A12	5c on 15c org	2.50	1.75
169	A12	5c on 20c pink	40.00	32.50
170	A12	5c on 50c gray	17.50	12.50
170A	A12	20c on 5c blue	1.50	1.25
b.		Inverted surcharge	8.75	8.75
		Nos. 167-170A (5)	64.00	50.00

Nos. 151, 152, 153, 155, 167, 170A, while duly authorized, all appear to have been sold to a single individual, and although they paid postage, it is doubtful whether they can be considered as ever having been placed on sale to the public.

Nos. O82-O84 Surcharged (Date in Red)

1908-09

171	O18	1c on 1p brt rose & blk	.20	.20
172	O18	1c on 1p lake & blk	.20	.20
173	O18	1c on 1p brn org & blk ('09)	.90	.60
		Nos. 171-173 (3)	1.30	1.00

Varieties of surcharge on Nos. 171-173 include: "CETTAVO"; date omitted, double or inverted; third line double or omitted.

Types of 1905-1910 Overprinted

1908, Mar. 5 *Perf. 11½*

174	A35	1c emerald	.20	.20
175	A35	5c yellow	.20	.20
176	A35	10c lilac brown	.20	.20
177	A35	20c yellow orange	.20	.20
178	A35	30c red	.25	.20
179	A35	60c magenta	.20	.20
180	A37	1p light blue	.20	.20
		Nos. 174-180 (7)	1.45	1.40

Overprinted

1909, Sept.

181	A35	1c blue gray	.20	.20
182	A35	1c scarlet	.20	.20
183	A35	5c dark green	.20	.20
184	A35	5c deep orange	.20	.20
185	A35	10c rose	.20	.20
186	A35	10c bister brown	.20	.20
187	A35	20c yellow	.20	.20
188	A35	20c violet	.20	.20
189	A35	30c orange brown	.30	.20
190	A35	30c dull blue	.30	.20
		Nos. 181-190 (10)	2.20	2.00

Counterfeits exist.

Coat of Arms above Numeral of Value A38

"The Republic" A39

1910-21 **Litho.** *Perf. 11½*

191	A38	1c gray black	.20	.20
192	A38	5c bright violet	.20	.20
a.		Pair, imperf. between	1.00	1.00
193	A38	5c blue grn ('19)	.20	.20
194	A38	5c lt blue ('21)	.20	.20
195	A38	10c yellow green	.20	.20
196	A38	10c dp vio ('19)	.20	.20
197	A38	10c red ('21)	.20	.20
198	A38	20c red	.20	.20
199	A38	50c car rose	.30	.20
200	A38	75c deep blue	.20	.20
a.		Diag. half perforated ('11)	.20	.20
		Nos. 191-200 (10)	2.10	2.00

Nos. 191-200 exist imperforate.
No. 200a was authorized for use as 20c.
For surcharges see Nos. 208, 241, 261, 265.

1911 **Engr.**

201	A39	1c olive grn & blk	.20	.20
202	A39	2c dk blue & blk	.30	.20
203	A39	5c carmine & indigo	.30	.20
204	A39	10c dp blue & brn	.30	.20
205	A39	20c olive grn & ind	.40	.20
206	A39	50c lilac & indigo	.50	.20
207	A39	75c ol grn & red lil	.50	.20
		Nos. 201-207 (7)	2.50	1.40

Centenary of National Independence.
The 1c, 2c, 10c and 50c exist imperf. Value for pairs, $1.50 each.

No. 199 Surcharged

1912

208	A38	20c on 50c car rose	.20	.20
a.		Inverted surcharge	1.25	1.25
b.		Double surcharge	1.25	1.25
c.		Bar omitted	1.75	1.75

National Coat of Arms — A40

1913 **Engr.** *Perf. 11½*

209	A40	1c gray	.20	.20
210	A40	2c orange	.20	.20
211	A40	5c lilac	.20	.20
212	A40	10c green	.20	.20
213	A40	20c dull red	.20	.20
214	A40	40c rose	.20	.20
215	A40	75c deep blue	.20	.20
216	A40	80c yellow	.20	.20
217	A40	1p light blue	.30	.20
218	A40	1.25p pale blue	.30	.20
219	A40	3p greenish blue	.30	.20
		Nos. 209-219 (11)	2.50	2.20

For surcharges see Nos. 225, 230-231, 237, 242, 253, 262-263, L3-L4.

Nos. J7-J10 Overprinted

1918

220	D2	5c yellow brown	.20	.20
221	D2	10c yellow brown	.20	.20
222	D2	20c yellow brown	.20	.20
223	D2	40c yellow brown	.20	.20

Nos. J10 and 214 Surcharged

224	D2	5c on 40c yellow brn	.20	.20
225	A40	30c on 40c rose	.20	.20
		Nos. 220-225 (6)	1.20	1.20

Nos. 220-225 exist with surcharge inverted, double and double with one inverted.
The surcharge "Habilitado-1918-5 cents 5" on the 1c gray official stamps of 1914, is bogus.

No. J11 Overprinted

1920

229	D2	1p yellow brown	.20	.20
a.		Inverted overprint	.65	.65
e.		As "g," "AABILITADO"	.75	.75
f.		As "g," "1929" for "1920"	.75	.75
g.		Overprint lines 8mm apart	.20	.20

Nos. 216 and 219 Surcharged

230	A40	50c on 80c yellow	.20	.20
231	A40	1.75p on 3p grnsh bl	.75	.65

Same Surcharge on No. J12

232	D2	1p on 1.50p yel brn	.25	.20
		Nos. 229-232 (4)	1.40	1.25

Nos. 229-232 exist with various surcharge errors, including inverted, double, double inverted and double with one inverted. Those that were issued are listed.

Parliament Building A41

1920 **Litho.** *Perf. 11½*

233	A41	50c red & black	.25	.20
a.		"CORRLOS"	1.50	1.50
234	A41	1p lt blue & blk	.65	.30
235	A41	1.75p dk blue & blk	.20	.20
236	A41	3p orange & blk	1.00	.20
		Nos. 233-236 (4)	2.10	.90

50th anniv. of the Constitution.
All values exist imperforate and Nos. 233, 235 and 236 with center inverted. It is doubtful that any of these varieties were regularly issued.

No. 215 Surcharged

1920

237	A40	50c on 75c deep blue	.30	.20

Nos. 200, 215 Surcharged

1921

241	A38	50c on 75c deep blue	.20	.20
242	A40	50c on 75c deep blue	.20	.20

A42

1922, Feb. 8 **Litho.** *Perf. 11½*

243	A42	50c car & dk blue	.20	.20
a.		Imperf. pair	.50	
b.		Center inverted	10.00	10.00
244	A42	1p dk blue & brn	.20	.20
a.		Imperf. pair	.50	
b.		Center inverted	12.50	12.50

For overprints see Nos. L1-L2.

Rendezvous of Conspirators A43

1922-23

245	A43	1p deep blue	.20	.20
246	A43	1p scar & dk bl ('23)	.20	.20
247	A43	1p red vio & gray ('23)	.20	.20
248	A43	1p org & gray ('23)	.20	.20
249	A43	5p dark violet	.60	.20
250	A43	5p dk bl & org brn ('23)	.60	.20
251	A43	5p dl red & lt bl ('23)	.60	.20
252	A43	5p emer & blk ('23)	.60	.20
		Nos. 245-252 (8)	3.20	1.60

National Independence.

No. 218 Surcharged "Habilitado en $1:-1924" in Red

1924

253	A40	1p on 1.25p pale blue	.20	.20

This stamp was for use in Asunción. Nos. L3 to L5 were for use in the interior, as is indicated by the "C" in the surcharge.

Map of Paraguay — A44

1924 **Litho.** *Perf. 11½*

254	A44	1p dark blue	.20	.20
255	A44	2p carmine rose	.20	.20
256	A44	4p light blue	.20	.20
a.		Perf. 12	.40	.20
		Nos. 254-256 (3)	.60	.60

#254-256 exist imperf. Value $3 each pair.
For surcharges and overprint see Nos. 267, C5, C15-C16, C54-C55, L7.

Gen. José E. Díaz — A45

Columbus — A46

1925-26 *Perf. 11½, 12*

257	A45	50c red	.20	.20
258	A45	1p dark blue	.20	.20
259	A45	1p emerald ('26)	.20	.20
		Nos. 257-259 (3)	.60	.60

#257-258 exist imperf. Value $1 each pair.
For overprints see Nos. L6, L8, L10.

1925 *Perf. 11½*

260	A46	1p blue	.20	.20
a.		Imperf., pair	2.00	

For overprint see No. L9.

Nos. 194, 214-215, J12 Surcharged in Black or Red

1926

261	A38	1c on 5c lt blue	.20	.20
262	A40	7c on 40c rose	.20	.20
263	A40	15c on 75c dp bl (R)	.20	.20
264	D2	1.50p on 1.50p yel brn	.20	.20
		Nos. 261-264 (4)	.80	.80

Nos. 194, 179 and 256 Surcharged "Habilitado" and New Values

1927

265	A38	2c on 5c lt blue	.20	.20
266	A35	50c on 60c magenta	.20	.20
a.		Inverted surcharge	2.00	
267	A44	1.50p on 4p lt blue	.20	.20

Official Stamp of 1914 Surcharged "Habilitado" and New Value

268	O19	50c on 75c dp bl	.20	.20
		Nos. 265-268 (4)	.80	.80

National Emblem — A47

Pedro Juan Caballero — A48

Map of Paraguay — A49

Fulgencio Yegros — A50

Ignacio Iturbe — A51

Oratory of the Virgin, Asunción — A52

Perf. 12, 11, 11½, 11x12

1927-38 **Typo.**

269	A47	1c lt red ('31)	.20	.20
270	A47	2c org red ('30)	.20	.20
271	A47	7c lilac	.20	.20
272	A47	7c emerald ('29)	.20	.20
273	A47	10c gray grn ('28)	.20	.20
a.		10c light green ('31)	.20	.20
274	A47	10c lil rose ('30)	.20	.20
275	A47	10c light bl ('35)	.20	.20
276	A47	20c dull bl ('28)	.20	.20
277	A47	20c lil brn ('30)	.20	.20
278	A47	20c lt vio ('31)	.20	.20
279	A47	20c rose ('35)	.20	.20
280	A47	50c ultramarine	.20	.20
281	A47	50c dl red ('28)	.20	.20
282	A47	50c orange ('30)	.20	.20
283	A47	50c gray ('31)	.20	.20
284	A47	50c brn vio ('34)	.20	.20
285	A47	50c rose ('36)	.20	.20
286	A47	70c ultra ('28)	.20	.20
287	A48	1p emerald	.20	.20
288	A48	1p org red ('30)	.20	.20
289	A48	1p brn org ('34)	.20	.20
290	A49	1.50p brown	.20	.20
291	A49	1.50p lilac ('28)	.20	.20
292	A49	1.50p rose red ('32)	.20	.20
293	A50	2.50p bister	.20	.20
294	A51	3p gray	.20	.20
295	A51	3p rose red ('36)	.20	.20
296	A51	3p brt vio ('36)	.20	.20
297	A52	5p chocolate	.20	.20
298	A52	5p violet ('36)	.20	.20
299	A52	5p pale org ('38)	.20	.20
300	A49	20p red ('29)	1.40	1.10
301	A49	20p emerald ('29)	1.40	1.10
302	A49	20p vio brn ('29)	1.40	1.10
		Nos. 269-302 (34)	10.40	9.50

No. 281 is also known perf. 10½x11½.

Papermaker's watermarks are sometimes found on No. 271 ("GLORIA BOND" in double-lined circle) and No. 280 ("Extra Vencedor Bond" or "ADBANCE/M M C")).

For surcharges and overprints see Nos. 312, C4, C6, C13-C14, C17-C18, C25-C32, C34-C35, L11-L30, O94-O96, O98.

Arms of Juan de Salazar de Espinosa A53

Columbus A54

1928, Aug. 15 ***Perf. 12***

303	A53	10p violet brown	1.75	1.25

Juan de Salazar de Espinosa, founder of Asunción.

A papermaker's watermark ("INDIAN BOND EXTRA STRONG S.&C") is sometimes found on Nos 303, 305-307.

1928 **Litho.**

304	A54	10p ultra	.80	.50
305	A54	10p vermilion	.80	.50
306	A54	10p deep red	.80	.50
		Nos. 304-306 (3)	2.40	1.50

For surcharge and overprint see Nos. C33, L37.

President Rutherford B. Hayes of US and Villa Occidental — A55

1928, Nov. 20 ***Perf. 12***

307	A55	10p gray brown	5.00	2.25
308	A55	10p red brown	5.00	2.25

50th anniv. of the Hayes' Chaco decision.

Portraits of Archbishop Bogarin — A56

1930, Aug. 15

309	A56	1.50p lake	1.00	.75
310	A56	1.50p turq blue	1.00	.75
311	A56	1.50p dull vio	1.00	.75
		Nos. 309-311 (3)	3.00	2.25

Archbishop Juan Sinforiano Bogarin, first archbishop of Paraguay.

For overprints see Nos. 321-322.

No. 272 Surcharged

1930

312	A47	5c on 7c emer	.20	.20

A57

1930-39 **Typo.** ***Perf. 11½, 12***

313	A57	10p brown	.50	.20
314	A57	10p brn red, *bl* ('31)	.50	.20
315	A57	10p dk bl, *pink* ('32)	.50	.20
316	A57	10p gray brn ('36)	.40	.20
317	A57	10p gray ('37)	.40	.20
318	A57	10p blue ('39)	.20	.20
		Nos. 313-318 (6)	2.50	1.20

1st Paraguayan postage stamp, 60th anniv.

For overprint see No. L31.

Gunboat "Humaitá" — A58

1931 ***Perf. 12***

319	A58	1.50p purple	.40	.25
		Nos. 319,C39-C53 (16)	8.70	6.10

Constitution, 60th anniv.

For overprint see No. L33.

View of San Bernardino — A59

1931, Aug.

320	A59	1p light green	.25	.20

Founding of San Bernardino, 50th anniv.

For overprint see No. L32.

Nos. 309-310 Overprinted in Blue or Red

1931, Dec. 31

321	A56	1.50p lake (Bl)	1.00	1.00
322	A56	1.50p turq blue (R)	1.00	1.00

Map of the Gran Chaco — A60

1932-35 **Typo.** ***Perf. 12***

323	A60	1.50p deep violet	.20	.20
324	A60	1.50p rose ('35)	.20	.20

For overprints see Nos. L34-L36, O97.

Nos. C74-C78 Surcharged

1933 **Litho.**

325	AP18	50c on 4p ultra	.25	.20
326	AP18	1p on 8p red	.50	.40
327	AP18	1.50p on 12p bl grn	.50	.40
328	AP18	2p on 16p dk vio	.50	.40
329	AP18	5p on 20p org brn	1.10	.90
		Nos. 325-329 (5)	2.85	2.30

Flag of the Race Issue

Flag with Three Crosses: Caravels of Columbus — A61

1933, Oct. 10 **Litho.** ***Perf. 11***

330	A61	10c multicolored	.30	.20
331	A61	20c multicolored	.30	.20
332	A61	50c multicolored	.30	.20
333	A61	1p multicolored	.30	.20
334	A61	1.50p multicolored	.30	.20
335	A61	2p multicolored	.60	.25
336	A61	5p multicolored	.60	.50
337	A61	10p multicolored	.60	.50
		Nos. 330-337 (8)	3.30	2.25

441st anniv. of the sailing of Christopher Columbus from the port of Palos, Aug. 3, 1492, on his first voyage to the New World.

Nos. 332, 334 and 335 exist with Maltese crosses omitted.

Monstrance A62

Arms of Asunción A63

1937, Aug. **Unwmk.** ***Perf. 11½***

338	A62	1p dk blue, yel & red	.20	.20
339	A62	3p dk blue, yel & red	.20	.20
340	A62	10p dk blue, yel & red	.20	.20
		Nos. 338-340 (3)	.60	.60

1st Natl. Eucharistic Congress, Asuncion.

1937, Aug.

341	A63	50c violet & buff	.30	.20
342	A63	1p bis & lt grn	.30	.20
343	A63	3p red & lt bl	.30	.20
344	A63	10p car rose & buff	.30	.20
345	A63	20p blue & drab	.30	.20
		Nos. 341-345 (5)	1.50	1.00

Founding of Asuncion, 400th anniv.

Oratory of the Virgin, Asunción — A64

Carlos Antonio Lopez — A65

José Eduvigis Diaz — A66

1938-39 Typo. *Perf. 11, 12*

346 A64 5p olive green .30 .20
347 A64 5p pale rose ('39) .30 .20
348 A64 11p violet brown .40 .25
Nos. 346-348 (3) 1.00 .65

Founding of Asuncion, 400th anniv.

1939 *Perf. 12*

349 A65 2p lt ultra & pale brn .30 .20
350 A66 2p lt ultra & brn .30 .20

Reburial of ashes of Pres. Carlos Antonio Lopez (1790-1862) and Gen. José Eduvigis Diaz in the National Pantheon, Asuncion.

Pres. Patricio Escobar and Ramon Zubizarreta A67

Design: 5p, Pres. Bernardino Caballero and Senator José S. Decoud.

1939-40 Litho. *Perf. 11½*
Heads in Black

351 A67 50c dull org ('40) .20 .20
352 A67 1p lt violet ('40) .20 .20
353 A67 2p red brown ('40) .20 .20
354 A67 5p lt ultra .25 .20
Nos. 351-354,C122-C123,O99-O104 (12) 9.40 9.30

Founding of the University of Asuncion, 50th anniv.

Varieties of this issue include inverted heads (50c, 1p, 2p); doubled heads; Caballero and Decoud heads in 50c frame: imperforates and part-perforates. Copies with inverted heads were not officially issued.

Coats of Arms — A69

Pres. Baldomir of Uruguay, Flags of Paraguay, Uruguay A70

Designs: 2p, Pres. Benavides, Peru. 3p, US Eagle and Shield. 5p, Pres. Alessandri, Chile. 6p, Pres. Vargas, Brazil. 10p, Pres. Ortiz, Argentina.

1939 Engr.; Flags Litho. *Perf. 12*
Flags in National Colors

355 A69 50c violet blue .20 .20
356 A70 1p olive .20 .20
357 A70 2p blue green .20 .20
358 A70 3p sepia .25 .25
359 A70 5p orange .20 .20
360 A70 6p dull violet .50 .40
361 A70 10p bister brn .40 .25
Nos. 355-361,C113-C121 (16) 13.45 10.45

First Buenos Aires Peace Conference.
For overprint and surcharge, see Nos. 387, B10.

Coats of Arms of New York and Asunción A76

1939, Nov. 30

362 A76 5p scarlet .20 .20
363 A76 10p deep blue .30 .20
364 A76 11p dk blue grn .40 .30
365 A76 22p olive blk .50 .40
Nos. 362-365,C124-C126 (7) 9.55 8.85

New York World's Fair.

Paraguayan Soldier — A77

Paraguayan Woman — A78

Cowboys — A79

Plowing — A80

View of Paraguay River — A81

Oxcart A82

Pasture A83

Pirareta Falls — A84

1940, Jan. 1 Photo. *Perf. 12½*

366 A77 50c deep orange .20 .20
367 A78 1p brt red violet .20 .20
368 A79 3p bright green .20 .20
369 A80 5p chestnut .20 .20
370 A81 10p magenta .20 .20
371 A82 20p violet .40 .30
372 A83 50p cobalt blue .90 .45
373 A84 100p black 1.90 1.40
Nos. 366-373 (8) 4.20 3.15

Second Buenos Aires Peace Conference.
For surcharge see No. 386.

Map of the Americas — A85

1940, May Engr. *Perf. 12*

374 A85 50c red orange .20 .20
375 A85 1p green .20 .20
376 A85 5p dark blue .30 .20
377 A85 10p brown .75 .50
Nos. 374-377,C127-C130 (8) 4.85 3.75

Pan American Union, 50th anniversary.

Reproduction of Type A1 — A86

Sir Rowland Hill — A87

Designs: 6p, Type A2. 10p, Type A3.

1940, Aug. 15 Photo. *Perf. 13½*

378 A86 1p aqua & brt red vio .50 .25
379 A87 5p dp yel grn & red brn .65 .30
380 A86 6p org brn & ultra 1.50 .65
381 A86 10p ver & black 1.50 1.00
Nos. 378-381 (4) 4.15 2.20

Postage stamp centenary.

Dr. José Francia
A90 A91

1940, Sept. 20 Engr. *Perf. 12*

382 A90 50c carmine rose .20 .20
383 A91 50c plum .20 .20
384 A90 1p bright green .20 .20
385 A91 5p deep blue .20 .20
Nos. 382-385 (4) .80 .80

Centenary of the death of Dr. Jose Francia (1766-1840), dictator of Paraguay, 1814-1840.

No. 366 Surcharged in Black

1940, Sept. 7 *Perf. 12½*

386 A77 5p on 50c dp org .20 .20

In honor of Pres. Jose F. Estigarribia who died in a plane crash Sept. 7, 1940.

SEMI-POSTAL STAMPS

Red Cross Nurse SP1

Unwmk.
1930, July 22 Typo. *Perf. 12*

B1 SP1 1.50p + 50c gray violet 1.25 .75
B2 SP1 1.50p + 50c deep rose 1.25 .75
B3 SP1 1.50p + 50c dark blue 1.25 .75
Nos. B1-B3 (3) 3.75 2.25

The surtax was for the benefit of the Red Cross Society of Paraguay.

College of Agriculture — SP2

1930

B4 SP2 1.50p + 50c blue, *pink* .30 .30

Surtax for the Agricultural Institute.

The sheet of No. B4 has a papermaker's watermark: "Vencedor Bond."

A 1.50p+50c red on yellow was prepared but not regularly issued. Value, 20 cents.

Red Cross Headquarters SP3

1932

B5 SP3 50c + 50c rose .30 .25

AIR POST STAMPS

Official Stamps of 1913 Surcharged

1929, Jan. 1 Unwmk. *Perf. 11½*

C1 O19 2.85p on 5c lilac .90 .65
C2 O19 5.65p on 10c grn .60 .40
C3 O19 11.30p on 50c rose .90 .50
Nos. C1-C3 (3) 2.40 1.55

Counterfeits of surcharge exist.

Regular Issues of 1924-27 Surcharged as in 1929

1929, Feb. 26 *Perf. 12*

C4 A51 3.40p on 3p gray 2.00 1.25
a. Surch. "Correo / en $3.40 / Habilitado / Aereo" 8.75
b. Double surcharge 8.75
c. "Aéro" instead of "Aéreo"
C5 A44 6.80p on 4p lt bl 2.00 1.25
a. Surch. "Correo / Aereo / en $6.80 / Habilitado" 8.75
C6 A52 17p on 5p choc 2.00 1.25
a. Surch. "Correo / Habilitado / Habilitado / en 17p" 4.50
b. Double surcharge 8.75
Nos. C4-C6 (3) 6.00 3.75

Wings AP1

Pigeon with Letter AP2

Airplanes — AP3

1929-31 Typo. *Perf. 12*

C7 AP1 2.85p gray green .65 .50
a. Imperf., pair 37.50

C8	AP1	2.85p turq grn ('31)	.30	.25
C9	AP2	5.65p brown	1.00	.40
C10	AP2	5.65p scar ('31)	.50	.30
C11	AP3	11.30p chocolate	.70	.40
a.		Imperf., pair	37.50	
C12	AP3	11.30p dp blue ('31)	.30	.30
		Nos. C7-C12 (6)	3.45	2.15

Sheets of these stamps sometimes show portions of a papermaker's watermark "Indian Bond C. Extra Strong."

Excellent counterfeits are plentiful.

Regular Issues of 1924-28 Surcharged in Black or Red

1929 *Perf. 11½, 12*

C13	A47	95c on 7c lilac	.25	.20
C14	A47	1.90p on 20c dull bl	.25	.20
C15	A44	3.40p on 4p lt bl (R)	.30	.20
a.		Double surcharge	2.00	
C16	A44	4.75p on 4p lt bl (R)	.60	.50
a.		Double surcharge	2.00	
C17	A51	6.80p on 3p gray	.70	.60
a.		Double surcharge	3.00	
C18	A52	17p on 5p choc	2.00	2.00
a.		Horiz. pair, imperf. between	25.00	
		Nos. C13-C18 (6)	4.10	3.70

Six stamps in the sheet of No. C17 have the "$" and numerals thinner and narrower than the normal type.

Airplane and Arms — AP4

Cathedral of Asunción AP5

Airplane and Globe — AP6

1930 *Perf. 12*

C19	AP4	95c dp red, *pink*	.35	.25
C20	AP4	95c dk bl, *blue*	.35	.25
C21	AP5	1.90p lt red, *pink*	.35	.25
C22	AP5	1.90p violet, *blue*	.35	.25
C23	AP6	6.80p blk, *lt bl*	.35	.25
C24	AP6	6.80p green, *pink*	.35	.30
		Nos. C19-C24 (6)	2.10	1.55

Sheets of Nos. C19-C24 have a papermaker's watermark: "Extra Vencedor Bond."

Counterfeits exist.

Stamps and Types of 1927-28 Overprinted in Red

1930

C25	A47	10c olive green	.30	.20
a.		Double overprint	3.00	
C26	A47	20c dull blue	.30	.20
a.		"CORREO CORREO" instead of "CORREO AEREO"	2.50	
b.		"AEREO AEREO" instead of "CORREO AEREO"	2.50	
C27	A48	1p emerald	.70	.70
C28	A51	3p gray	.70	.70
		Nos. C25-C28 (4)	2.00	1.80

Counterfeits of Nos. C26a and C26b exist.

Nos. 273, 282, 286, 288, 300, 302, 305 Surcharged in Red or Black

#C29-C30, C32

#C31

#C33

#C34-C35

1930

Red or Black Surcharge

C29	A47	5c on 10c gray grn (R)	.20	.20
a.		"AEREO" omitted	15.00	
C30	A47	5c on 70c ultra (R)	.20	.20
a.		Vert. pair, imperf. between	20.00	
C31	A48	20c on 1p org red	.20	.20
a.		"CORREO" double	3.00	3.00
b.		"AEREO" double	3.00	3.00
C32	A47	40c on 50c org (R)	.20	.20
a.		"AEREO" omitted	4.50	4.50
b.		"CORREO" double	3.00	3.00
c.		"AEREO" double	3.00	3.00
C33	A54	6p on 10p red	.85	.70
C34	A49	10p on 20p red	3.25	2.75
C35	A49	10p on 20p vio brn	3.25	2.75
		Nos. C29-C35 (7)	8.15	7.00

Declaration of Independence AP11

1930, May 14 **Typo.**

C36	AP11	2.85p dark blue	.35	.25
C37	AP11	3.40p dark green	.35	.20
C38	AP11	4.75p deep lake	.35	.20
		Nos. C36-C38 (3)	1.05	.65

Natl. Independence Day, May 14, 1811.

Gunboat Type

Gunboat "Paraguay."

1931-39 *Perf. 11½, 12*

C39	A58	1p claret	.20	.20
C40	A58	1p dk blue ('36)	.20	.20
C41	A58	2p orange	.20	.20
C42	A58	2p dk brn ('36)	.20	.20
C43	A58	3p turq green	.25	.25
C44	A58	3p lt ultra ('36)	.30	.25
C45	A58	3p brt rose ('39)	.20	.20
C46	A58	6p dk green	.40	.30
C47	A58	6p violet ('36)	.45	.30
C48	A58	6p dull bl ('39)	.40	.25
C49	A58	10p vermilion	1.00	.60
C50	A58	10p bluish grn ('35)	1.50	1.00
C51	A58	10p yel brn ('36)	1.10	.75
C52	A58	10p dk blue ('36)	.90	.50
C53	A58	10p lt pink ('39)	1.00	.65
		Nos. C39-C53 (15)	8.30	5.85

1st constitution of Paraguay as a Republic and the arrival of the "Paraguay" and "Humaita."

Counterfeits of #C39-C53 are plentiful.

Regular Issue of 1924 Surcharged

1931, Aug. 22

C54	A44	3p on 4p lt bl	10.00	8.00

Overprinted

C55	A44	4p lt blue	9.00	7.00

On Nos. C54-C55 the Zeppelin is handstamped. The rest of the surcharge or overprint is typographed.

War Memorial AP13

Orange Tree and Yerba Mate — AP14

Yerba Mate — AP15

Palms — AP16

Eagle — AP17

1931-36 **Litho.**

C56	AP13	5c lt blue	.20	.20
a.		Horiz. pair, imperf. btwn.	6.25	
C57	AP13	5c dp grn ('33)	.20	.20
C58	AP13	5c lt red ('33)	.30	.20
C59	AP13	5c violet ('35)	.20	.20
C60	AP14	10c dp violet	.20	.20
C61	AP14	10c brn lake ('33)	.20	.20
C62	AP14	10c yel brn ('33)	.20	.20
C63	AP14	10c ultra ('35)	.20	.20
a.		Imperf., pair	5.50	
C64	AP15	20c red	.20	.20
C65	AP15	20c dl blue ('33)	.30	.20
C66	AP15	20c emer ('33)	.25	.20
C67	AP15	20c yel brn ('35)	.20	.20
a.		Imperf., pair	3.75	
C68	AP16	40c dp green	.25	.20
C69	AP16	40c slate bl ('35)	.20	.20
C70	AP16	40c red ('36)	.30	.20
C71	AP17	80c dull blue	.25	.20
C72	AP17	80c dl grn ('33)	.50	.20
C73	AP17	80c scar ('33)	.30	.20
		Nos. C56-C73 (18)	4.45	3.60

Airship "Graf Zeppelin" — AP18

1932, Apr. **Litho.**

C74	AP18	4p ultra	1.50	1.50
a.		Imperf., pair	7.50	
C75	AP18	8p red	2.50	2.00
C76	AP18	12p blue grn	2.00	1.50
C77	AP18	16p dk violet	3.50	2.50
C78	AP18	20p orange brn	3.50	3.00
		Nos. C74-C78 (5)	13.00	10.50

For surcharges see Nos. 325-329.

"Graf Zeppelin" over Brazilian Terrain AP19

"Graf Zeppelin" over Atlantic — AP20

1933, May 5

C79	AP19	4.50p dp blue	2.00	1.50
C80	AP19	9p dp rose	3.50	2.50
a.		Horiz. pair, imperf. between	150.00	
C81	AP19	13.50p blue grn	4.00	3.00
C82	AP20	22.50p bis brn	9.00	7.00
C83	AP20	45p dull vio	12.00	12.00
		Nos. C79-C83 (5)	30.50	26.00

Excellent counterfeits are plentiful.

For overprints see Nos. C88-C97.

Posts and Telegraph Building, Asunción — AP21

1934-37 *Perf. 11½*

C84	AP21	33.75p ultra	2.00	1.75
C85	AP21	33.75p car ('35)	2.00	1.75
a.		33.75p rose ('37)	1.75	1.50
C86	AP21	33.75p emerald ('36)	2.50	2.00
C87	AP21	33.75p bis brn ('36)	.75	.75
		Nos. C84-C87 (4)	7.25	6.25

Excellent counterfeits exist.

For surcharge see No. C107.

Nos. C79-C83 Overprinted in Black

1934, May 26

C88	AP19	4.50p deep bl	2.00	1.50
C89	AP19	9p dp rose	2.50	2.00
C90	AP19	13.50p blue grn	7.00	5.00
C91	AP20	22.50p bis brn	6.00	4.00
C92	AP20	45p dull vio	9.00	7.00
		Nos. C88-C92 (5)	26.50	19.50

Types of 1933 Issue Overprinted in Black

1935

C93	AP19	4.50p	rose red	3.50	2.50
C94	AP19	9p	lt green	4.50	3.00
C95	AP19	13.50p	brown	9.50	7.00
C96	AP20	22.50p	violet	7.50	5.50
C97	AP20	45p	blue	22.50	13.00
			Nos. C93-C97 (5)	47.50	31.00

Tobacco Plant — AP22

1935-39 **Typo.**

C98	AP22	17p	lt brown	2.50	2.50
C99	AP22	17p	carmine	4.25	4.25
C100	AP22	17p	dark blue	3.00	3.00
C101	AP22	17p	pale yel grn ('39)	2.00	2.00
			Nos. C98-C101 (4)	11.75	11.75

Excellent counterfeits are plentiful.

Church of Incarnation AP23

1935-38

C102	AP23	102p	carmine	3.75	2.50
C103	AP23	102p	blue	3.75	2.50
C103A	AP23	102p	indigo ('36)	2.25	2.25
C104	AP23	102p	yellow brn	2.75	2.40
a.			Imperf., pair	15.00	
C105	AP23	102p	violet ('37)	1.25	1.25
C106	AP23	102p	brn org ('38)	1.10	1.10
			Nos. C102-C106 (6)	14.85	12.00

Excellent counterfeits are plentiful.
For surcharges see Nos. C108-C109.

Types of 1934-35 Surcharged in Red

1937, Aug. 1

C107	AP21	24p	on 33.75p sl bl	.50	.35
C108	AP23	65p	on 102p ol bis	1.25	.90
C109	AP23	84p	on 102p bl grn	1.25	.75
			Nos. C107-C109 (3)	3.00	2.00

Plane over Asunción AP24

1939, Aug. 3 **Typo.** ***Perf. 10½, 11½***

C110	AP24	3.40p	yel green	.50	.50
C111	AP24	3.40p	orange brn	.30	.25
C112	AP24	3.40p	indigo	.30	.25
			Nos. C110-C112 (3)	1.10	1.00

Buenos Aires Peace Conference Type and

Map of Paraguay with New Chaco Boundary AP28

Designs: 1p, Flags of Paraguay and Bolivia. 5p, Pres. Ortiz of Argentina, flags of Paraguay, Argentina. 10p, Pres. Vargas, Brazil. 30p, Pres. Alessandri, Chile. 50p, US Eagle and Shield. 100p, Pres. Benavides, Peru. 200p, Pres. Baldomir, Uruguay.

Engr.; Flags Litho.

1939, Nov. ***Perf. 12½***

Flags in National Colors

C113	A69	1p	red brown	.20	.20
C114	A69	3p	dark blue	.20	.20
C115	A70	5p	olive blk	.20	.20
C116	A70	10p	violet	.20	.20
C117	A70	30p	orange	.20	.20
C118	A70	50p	black brn	.25	.20
C119	A70	100p	brt green	.35	.30
C120	A70	200p	green	1.90	1.25
C121	AP28	500p	black	8.00	6.00
			Nos. C113-C121 (9)	11.50	8.75

For overprints see Nos. 388-390.

University of Asuncion Type

Pres. Bernardino Caballero and Senator José S. Decoud.

1939, Sept. **Litho.** ***Perf. 12***

C122	A67	28p	rose & blk	3.25	3.25
C123	A67	90p	yel grn & blk	4.00	4.00

Map with Asunción to New York Air Route — AP35

1939, Nov. 30 **Engr.**

C124	AP35	30p	brown	1.90	1.50
C125	AP35	80p	orange	2.25	2.25
C126	AP35	90p	purple	4.00	4.00
			Nos. C124-C126 (3)	8.15	7.75

New York World's Fair.

Pan American Union Type

1940, May ***Perf. 12***

C127	A85	20p	rose car	.20	.20
C128	A85	70p	violet bl	.45	.20
C129	A85	100p	Prus grn	.50	.50
C130	A85	500p	dk violet	2.25	1.75
			Nos. C127-C130 (4)	3.40	2.65

POSTAGE DUE STAMPS

D1

D2

1904 **Unwmk.** **Litho.** ***Perf. 11½***

J1	D1	2c	green	.20	.20
J2	D1	4c	green	.20	.20
J3	D1	10c	green	.20	.20
J4	D1	20c	green	.20	.20
			Nos. J1-J4 (4)	.80	.80

1913 **Engr.**

J5	D2	1c	yellow brown	.20	.20
J6	D2	2c	yellow brown	.20	.20
J7	D2	5c	yellow brown	.20	.20
J8	D2	10c	yellow brown	.20	.20
J9	D2	20c	yellow brown	.20	.20
J10	D2	40c	yellow brown	.20	.20
J11	D2	1p	yellow brown	.20	.20
J12	D2	1.50p	yellow brown	.20	.20
			Nos. J5-J12 (8)	1.60	1.60

For overprints and surcharges see Nos. 220-224, 229, 232, 264, L5.

INTERIOR OFFICE ISSUES

The "C" signifies "Campana" (rural). These stamps were sold by Postal Agents in country districts, who received a commission on their sales.

These stamps were available for postage in the interior but not in Asunción or abroad.

Nos. 243-244 Overprinted in Red

1922

L1	A42	50c	car & dk bl	.20	.20
L2	A42	1p	dk bl & brn	.20	.20

The overprint on Nos. L2 exists double or inverted. Counterfeits exist. Double or inverted overprints on No. L1 and all overprints in black are counterfeit.

Nos. 215, 218, J12 Surcharged

1924

L3	A40	50c	on 75c deep bl	.20	.20
L4	A40	1p	on 1.25p pale bl	.20	.20
L5	D2	1p	on 1.50p yel brn	.20	.20
			Nos. L3-L5 (3)	.60	.60

Nos. L3-L4 exist imperf.

Nos. 254, 257-260 Overprinted in Black or Red

1924-26

L6	A45	50c	red ('25)	.20	.20
L7	A44	1p	dk blue (R)	.20	.20
L8	A45	1p	dk bl (R) ('25)	.20	.20
L9	A46	1p	blue (R) ('25)	.20	.20
L10	A45	1p	emerald ('26)	.20	.20
			Nos. L6-L10 (5)	1.00	1.00

Nos. L6, L8-L9 exist imperf. Value $2.50 each pair.

Same Overprint on Stamps and Type of 1927-36 in Red or Black

1927-39

L11	A47	50c	ultra (R)	.20	.20
L12	A47	50c	dl red ('28)	.20	.20
L13	A47	50c	orange ('29)	.20	.20
L14	A47	50c	lt bl ('30)	.20	.20
L15	A47	50c	gray (R) ('31)	.20	.20
L16	A47	50c	bluish grn (R) ('33)	.20	.20
L17	A47	50c	vio (R) ('34)	.20	.20
L18	A48	1p	emerald	.20	.20
L19	A48	1p	org red ('29)	.20	.20
L20	A48	1p	lil brn ('31)	.20	.20
L21	A48	1p	dk bl (R) ('33)	.20	.20
L22	A48	1p	brt vio (R) ('35)	.20	.20
L23	A49	1.50p	brown	.20	.20
a.			Double overprint	1.50	
L24	A49	1.50p	lilac ('28)	.20	.20
L25	A49	1.50p	dull bl (R)	.20	.20
L26	A50	2.50p	bister ('28)	.20	.20
L27	A50	2.50p	vio (R) ('36)	.20	.20
L28	A51	3p	gray (R)	.20	.20
L29	A51	3p	rose red ('39)	.20	.20
L30	A52	5p	vio (R) ('36)	.20	.20
L31	A57	10p	gray brn (R) ('36)	.30	.25
			Nos. L11-L31 (21)	4.30	4.25

Types of 1931-35 and No. 305 Overprinted in Black or Red

1931-36

L32	A59	1p	light red	.20	.20
L33	A58	1.50p	dp bl (R)	.20	.20
L34	A60	1.50p	bis brn ('32)	.20	.20
L35	A60	1.50p	grn (R) ('34)	.20	.20
L36	A60	1.50p	bl (R) ('36)	.20	.20
L37	A54	10p	vermilion	1.25	1.25
			Nos. L32-L37 (6)	2.25	2.25

OFFICIAL STAMPS

O1

O2

O3

O4

O5

O6

O7

Unwmk.

1886, Aug. 20 **Litho.** ***Imperf.***

O1	O1	1c	orange	3.00	3.00
O2	O2	2c	violet	3.00	3.00
O3	O3	5c	red	3.00	3.00
O4	O4	7c	green	3.00	3.00
O5	O5	10c	brown	3.00	3.00
O6	O6	15c	slate blue	3.00	3.00
a.			Wavy lines on face of stamp	1.25	
b.			"OFICIAL" omitted		
O7	O7	20c	claret	3.00	3.00
			Nos. O1-O7 (7)	21.00	21.00

Nos. O1 to O7 have the date and various control marks and letters printed on the back of each stamp in blue and black.

The overprint exists inverted on all values.

Nos. O1 to O7 have been reprinted from new stones made from slightly retouched dies.

Types of 1886 With Overprint

1886 ***Perf. 11½***

O8	O1	1c	dark green	.50	.50
O9	O2	2c	scarlet	.50	.50
O10	O3	5c	dull blue	.50	.50
O11	O4	7c	orange	.50	.50
O12	O5	10c	lake	.50	.50
O13	O6	15c	brown	.50	.50
O14	O7	20c	blue	.50	.50
			Nos. O8-O14 (7)	3.50	3.50

The overprint exists inverted on all values. Value, each $1.50.

No. 20 Overprinted

1886, Sept. 1

O15	A11	1c	dark green	1.50	1.50

Types of 1889 Regular Issue Surcharged

Handstamped Surcharge in Black

1889 ***Imperf.***

O16	A13	3c on 15c violet	1.50	1.00
O17	A13	5c on 15c red brn	1.50	1.00

Perf. 11½

O18	A13	1c on 15c maroon	1.50	1.00
O19	A13	2c on 15c maroon	1.50	1.00
		Nos. O16-O19 (4)	6.00	4.00

Counterfeits of Nos. O16-O19 abound.

Regular Issue of 1887 Handstamp Overprinted in Violet

Perf. 11½-12½ & Compounds

1890 **Typo.**

O20	A12	1c green	.20	.20
O21	A12	2c rose red	.20	.20
O22	A12	5c blue	.20	.20
O23	A12	7c brown	3.75	2.50
O24	A12	10c lilac	.20	.20
O25	A12	15c orange	.45	.25
O26	A12	20c pink	.40	.30
		Nos. O20-O26 (7)	5.40	3.85

Nos. O20-O26 exist with double overprint and all but the 20c with inverted overprint.
Nos. O20-O22, O24-O26 exist with blue overprint. The status is questioned. Value, set $15.

Stamps and Type of 1887 Regular Issue Overprinted in Black

1892

O33	A12	1c green	.20	.20
O34	A12	2c rose red	.20	.20
O35	A12	5c blue	.20	.20
O36	A12	7c brown	1.75	1.00
O37	A12	10c lilac	.65	.25
O38	A12	15c orange	.20	.20
O39	A12	20c pink	.25	.20
O40	A12	50c gray	.20	.20
		Nos. O33-O40 (8)	3.65	2.45

No. 26 Overprinted

1893

O41	A12	7c brown	10.00	5.00

Counterfeits of No. O41 exist.

O16

1901, Feb. **Engr.** ***Perf. 11½, 12½***

O42	O16	1c dull blue	.20	.20
O43	O16	2c rose red	.20	.20
O44	O16	4c dark brown	.20	.20
O45	O16	5c dark green	.20	.20
O46	O16	8c orange brn	.20	.20
O47	O16	10c car rose	.20	.20
O48	O16	20c deep blue	.20	.20
		Nos. O42-O48 (7)	1.40	1.40

A 12c deep green, type O16, was prepared but not issued.

No. 45 Overprinted

1902 ***Perf. 12x12½***

O49	A12	1p olive grn	.20	.20
a.		Inverted overprint	10.00	

Counterfeits of No. O49a exist.

Regular Issue of 1903 Overprinted

1903 ***Perf. 11½***

O50	A32	1c gray	.20	.20
O51	A32	2c blue green	.20	.20
O52	A32	5c blue	.20	.20
O53	A32	10c orange brn	.20	.20
O54	A32	20c carmine	.20	.20
O55	A32	30c deep blue	.20	.20
O56	A32	60c purple	.20	.20
		Nos. O50-O56 (7)	1.40	1.40

O17

O18

1905-08 **Engr.** ***Perf. 11½, 12***

O57	O17	1c gray grn	.20	.20
O58	O17	1c ol grn ('05)	.20	.20
O59	O17	1c brn org ('06)	.45	.20
O60	O17	1c ver ('08)	.25	.20
O61	O17	2c brown org	.20	.20
O62	O17	2c gray grn ('05)	.20	.20
O63	O17	2c red ('06)	.75	.25
O64	O17	2c gray ('08)	.40	.20
O65	O17	5c deep bl ('06)	.20	.20
O66	O17	5c gray bl ('08)	1.50	1.00
O67	O17	5c grnsh bl ('08)	.75	.65
O68	O17	10c violet ('06)	.20	.20
O69	O17	20c violet ('08)	.70	.40
		Nos. O57-O69 (13)	6.00	4.10

1908

O70	O17	10c bister	3.50
O71	O17	10c emerald	3.50
O72	O17	10c red lilac	4.50
O73	O17	20c bister	3.00
O74	O17	20c salmon pink	3.50
O75	O17	20c green	3.50
O76	O17	30c turquoise bl	3.50
O77	O17	30c blue gray	3.50
O78	O17	30c yellow	1.50
O79	O17	60c chocolate	4.00
O80	O17	60c orange brn	5.00
O81	O17	60c deep ultra	4.00
O82	O18	1p brt rose & blk	24.00
O83	O18	1p lake & blk	24.00
O84	O18	1p brn org & blk	25.00
		Nos. O70-O84 (15)	116.00

Nos. O70-O84 were not issued, but were surcharged or overprinted for use as regular postage stamps. See Nos. 131-138, 141-145, 158-165, 171-173.

O19

1913 ***Perf. 11½***

O85	O19	1c gray	.20	.20
O86	O19	2c orange	.20	.20
O87	O19	5c lilac	.20	.20
O88	O19	10c green	.20	.20
O89	O19	20c dull red	.20	.20
O90	O19	50c rose	.20	.20
O91	O19	75c deep blue	.20	.20
O92	O19	1p dull blue	.20	.20
O93	O19	2p yellow	.20	.20
		Nos. O85-O93 (9)	1.80	1.80

For surcharges see Nos. 268, C1-C3.

Type of Regular Issue of 1927-38 Overprinted in Red

1935

O94	A47	10c light ultra	.20	.20
O95	A47	50c violet	.20	.20
O96	A48	1p orange	.20	.20
O97	A60	1.50p green	.20	.20
O98	A50	2.50p violet	.20	.20
		Nos. O94-O98 (5)	1.00	1.00

Overprint is diagonal on 1.50p.

University of Asunción Type

1940 **Litho.** ***Perf. 12***

O99	A67	50c red brn & blk	.20	.20
O100	A67	1p rose pink & blk	.20	.20
O101	A67	2p lt bl grn & blk	.20	.20
O102	A67	5p ultra & blk	.20	.20
O103	A67	10p lt vio & blk	.20	.20
O104	A67	50p dp org & blk	.30	.25
		Nos. O99-O104 (6)	1.30	1.25

PENRHYN ISLAND

pen-'rin 'ī-lənd

(Tongareva)

AREA — 3 sq. mi.
POP. — 395 (1926)

Stamps of Cook Islands were used in Penrhyn from 1932 until 1973.

12 Pence = 1 Shilling

Watermarks

Wmk. 61 — N Z and Star Close Together

Wmk. 63 — Double-lined N Z and Star

On watermark 61 the margins of the sheets are watermarked "NEW ZEALAND POSTAGE" and parts of the double-lined letters of these words are frequently found on the stamps. It occasionally happens that a stamp shows no watermark whatever.

Stamps of New Zealand Surcharged in Carmine, Vermilion, Brown or Blue:

½ pence

1 pence

2½ pence

1902 **Wmk. 63** ***Perf. 14***

1	A18	½p green (C)	.90	*8.00*
a.		No period after "ISLAND"	175.00	250.00
2	A35	1p carmine (Br)	3.75	*19.50*
a.		Perf. 11	*1,000.*	*1,000.*
b.		Perf. 11x14	*1,000.*	*1,000.*

Wmk. 61 ***Perf. 14***

5	A18	½p green (V)	2.50	*8.00*
a.		No period after "ISLAND"	150.00	*200.00*
6	A35	1p carmine (Bl)	1.40	*5.00*
a.		No period after "ISLAND"	55.00	*115.00*
b.		Perf. 11x14	*9,000.*	*8,500.*

Unwmk. ***Perf. 11***

8	A22	2½p blue (C)	4.75	*9.00*
a.		"½" and "PENI" 2mm apart	19.00	*35.00*
9	A22	2½p blue (V)	4.75	*9.00*
a.		"½" and "PENI" 2mm apart	19.00	*35.00*
		Nos. 1-9 (6)	18.05	*58.50*

Stamps with compound perfs. also exist perf. 11 or 14 on one or more sides.

d

e

f

1903 **Wmk. 61**

10	A23(d)	3p yel brn (Bl)	11.50	*24.00*
11	A26(e)	6p rose (Bl)	17.50	*40.00*
12	A29(f)	1sh org red (Bl)	62.50	*62.50*
a.		1sh bright red (Bl)	47.50	*47.50*
b.		1sh brown red (Bl)	62.50	*62.50*
		Nos. 10-12 (3)	91.50	*126.50*

1914-15 ***Perf. 14, 14x14½***

13	A41(a)	½p yel grn (C)	.90	*9.25*
a.		No period after "ISLAND"	29.00	*85.00*
b.		No period after "PENI"	100.00	*175.00*
14	A41(a)	½p yel grn (V) ('15)	.90	*9.25*
a.		No period after "ISLAND"	11.50	*52.50*
b.		No period after "PENI"	45.00	*110.00*
15	A41(e)	6p car rose (Bl)	26.00	*80.00*
16	A41(f)	1sh ver (Bl)	47.50	*110.00*
		Nos. 13-16 (4)	75.30	*208.50*

New Zealand Stamps of 1915-19 Overprinted in Red or Dark Blue

Perf. 14x13½, 14x14½

1917-20 **Typo.**

17	A43	½p yel grn (R) ('20)	1.10	*2.25*
18	A47	1½p gray black (R)	7.50	*22.50*
19	A47	1½p brn org (R) ('19)	.70	*22.50*
20	A43	3p choc (Bl) ('19)	4.00	*27.50*

Engr.

21	A44	2½p dull bl (R) ('20)	2.25	7.50
22	A45	3p vio brn (Bl) ('18)	11.00	*80.00*
23	A45	6p car rose (Bl) ('18)	5.75	*21.00*
24	A45	1sh vermilion (Bl)	14.00	*37.50*
		Nos. 17-24 (8)	46.30	*220.75*

Landing of Capt. Cook A10

Avarua Waterfront A11

Capt. James Cook — A12

Coconut Palm — A13

Arorangi Village, Rarotonga — A14

Avarua Harbor — A15

1920 Unwmk. *Perf. 14*

25 A10 ½p emerald & blk 1.10 *19.00*
a. Center inverted 625.00
26 A11 1p red & black 1.75 *17.50*
a. Center inverted 850.00
27 A12 1½p violet & blk 7.50 *22.50*
28 A13 3p red org & blk 3.00 *9.75*
29 A14 6p dk brn & red brn 3.75 *22.50*
30 A15 1sh dull bl & blk 11.50 *30.00*
Nos. 25-30 (6) 28.60 *121.25*

Rarotongan Chief (Te Po) — A16

1927 Engr. Wmk. 61

31 A16 2½p blue & red brn 5.75 *30.00*

Types of 1920 Issue

1928-29

33 A10 ½p yellow grn & blk 6.25 *24.00*
34 A11 1p carmine rose & blk 6.25 *21.00*

PERU

pə-'rü

LOCATION — West coast of South America
GOVT. — Republic
AREA — 496,093 sq. mi.
POP. — 18,300,000 (est. 1982)
CAPITAL — Lima

8 Reales = 1 Peso (1857)
100 Centimos = 8 Dineros = 4 Pesetas = 1 Peso (1858)
100 Centavos = 1 Sol (1874)

Sail and Steamship — A1

Design: 2r, Ship sails eastward.

Unwmk.

1857, Dec. 1 Engr. *Imperf.*

1 A1 1r blue, *blue* 1,250. 1,450.
2 A1 2r brn red, *blue* 1,350. 1,600.

The Pacific Steam Navigation Co. gave a quantity of these stamps to the Peruvian government so that a trial of prepayment of postage by stamps might be made.

Stamps of 1 and 2 reales, printed in various colors on white paper, laid and wove, were prepared for the Pacific Steam Navigation Co. but never put in use. Value $50 each on wove paper, $400 each on laid paper.

Coat of Arms

A2 A3

A4

Wavy Lines in Spandrels

1858, Mar. 1 Litho.

3 A2 1d deep blue 200. 27.50
4 A3 1p rose red 850. 125.
5 A4 ½peso rose red *3,750. 3,000.*
6 A4 ½peso buff *1,600.* 300.
a. ½peso orange yellow *1,600.* 300.

A5 A6

Large Letters

1858, Dec.

Double-lined Frame

7 A5 1d slate blue 250.00 27.50
8 A6 1p red 250.00 37.50

A7 A8

1860-61

Zigzag Lines in Spandrels

9 A7 1d blue 100.00 6.50
a. 1d Prussian blue 100.00 12.00
b. Cornucopia on white ground 225.00 47.50
c. Zigzag lines broken at angles 125.00 14.00
10 A8 1p rose 250.00 25.00
a. 1p brick red 250.00 25.00
b. Cornucopia on white ground 250.00 30.00

Retouched, 10 lines instead of 9 in left label

11 A8 1p rose 125.00 25.00
a. Pelure paper 200.00 25.00
Nos. 9-11 (3) 475.00 56.50

A9 A10

1862-63 Embossed

12 A9 1d red 13.00 3.50
a. Arms embossed sideways 425.00 90.00
b. Thick paper 27.50 8.00
c. Diag. half used on cover 140.00
13 A10 1p brown ('63) 72.50 24.00
a. Diag. half used on cover 1,000.

Counterfeits of Nos. 13 and 15 exist.

A11

1868-72

14 A11 1d green 11.00 2.25
a. Arms embossed inverted *1,250. 750.00*
b. Diag. half used on cover 350.00
15 A10 1p orange ('72) 90.00 32.50
a. Diag. half used on cover —

Nos. 12-15, 19 and 20 were printed in horizontal strips. Stamps may be found printed on two strips of paper where the strips were joined by overlapping.

Llamas — A12

A13

A14

1866-67 Engr. *Perf. 12*

16 A12 5c green 6.00 .60
17 A13 10c vermilion 6.00 1.40
18 A14 20c brown 20.00 4.00
a. Diagonal half used on cover 375.00
Nos. 16-18 (3) 32.00 6.00

See Nos. 109, 111, 113.

Locomotive and Arms — A15

Llama — A16

1871, Apr. Embossed *Imperf.*

19 A15 5c scarlet 75.00 25.00
a. 5c pale red 75.00 25.00

20th anniv. of the first railway in South America, linking Lima and Callao.

The so-called varieties "ALLAO" and "CALLA" are due to over-inking.

1873, Mar. *Rouletted Horiz.*

20 A16 2c dk ultra 30.00 *250.00*

Counterfeits are plentiful.

Sun God of the Incas — A17

Coat of Arms

A18 A19

A20 A21

A22 A23

Embossed with Grill

1874-84 Engr. *Perf. 12*

21 A17 1c orange ('79) .50 .40
22 A18 2c dk violet .65 .50
23 A19 5c blue ('77) .85 .25
24 A19 5c ultra ('79) 8.50 2.00
25 A20 10c green ('76) .25 .20
a. Imperf., pair 25.00
26 A20 10c slate ('84) 2.00 .25
a. Diag. half used as 5c on cover —
27 A21 20c brown red 2.00 .65
28 A22 50c green 9.00 2.50
29 A23 1s rose 1.50 1.50
Nos. 21-29 (9) 25.25 8.25

No. 25a lacks the grill.

No. 26 with overprint "DE OFICIO" is said to have been used to frank mail of Gen. A. A. Caceres during the civil war against Gen. Miguel Iglesias, provisional president. Experts question its status.

1880

30 A17 1c green 2.00
31 A18 2c rose 2.00

Nos. 30 and 31 were prepared for use but not issued without overprint.

See Nos. 104-108, 110, 112, 114-115.

For overprints see Nos. 32-103, 116-128, J32-J33, O2-O22, N11-N23, 1N1-1N9, 3N11-3N20, 5N1, 6N1-6N2, 7N1-7N2, 8N7, 8N10-8N11, 9N1-9N3, 10N3-10N8, 10N10-10N11, 11N1-11N5, 12N1-12N3, 13N1, 14N1-14N16, 15N5-15N8, 15N13-15N18, 16N1-16N22.

Stamps of 1874-80 Overprinted in Red, Blue or Black

Reduced illustration

1880, Jan. 5

32 A17 1c green (R) .50 .40
a. Inverted overprint 10.00 10.00
b. Double overprint 13.50 13.50
33 A18 2c rose (Bl) 1.00 .65
a. Inverted overprint 10.00 10.00
b. Double overprint 14.00 12.00
34 A18 2c rose (Bk) 45.00 35.00
a. Inverted overprint
b. Double overprint
35 A19 5c ultra (R) 2.00 1.00
a. Inverted overprint 10.00 10.00
b. Double overprint 14.00 14.00
36 A22 50c green (R) 27.50 17.50
a. Inverted overprint 45.00 45.00
b. Double overprint 55.00 55.00
37 A23 1s rose (Bl) 70.00 45.00
a. Inverted overprint 110.00 110.00
b. Double overprint 110.00 110.00
Nos. 32-37 (6) 146.00 99.55

Stamps of 1874-80 Overprinted in Red or Blue

Reduced illustration

1881, Jan. 28

38 A17 1c green (R) .75 .60
a. Inverted overprint 8.25 8.25
b. Double overprint 14.00 14.00
39 A18 2c rose (Bl) 14.00 9.00
a. Inverted overprint 17.50 15.00
b. Double overprint 25.00 20.00
40 A19 5c ultra (R) 1.50 .75
a. Inverted overprint 14.00 14.00
b. Double overprint 20.00 20.00
41 A22 50c green (R) 450.00 250.00
a. Inverted overprint 600.00
42 A23 1s rose (Bl) 82.50 55.00
a. Inverted overprint 150.00

Reprints of Nos. 38 to 42 were made in 1884. In the overprint the word "PLATA" is 3mm high instead of 2½mm. The cross bars of the letters "A" of that word are set higher than on the original stamps. The 5c is printed in blue instead of ultramarine.

For stamps of 1874-80 overprinted with Chilean arms or small UPU "horseshoe," see Nos. N11-N23.

Stamps of 1874-79 Handstamped in Black or Blue

1883

65 A17 1c orange (Bk) .85 .65
66 A17 1c orange (Bl) 45.00
68 A19 5c ultra (Bk) 7.50 5.00
69 A20 10c green (Bk) .75 .65
70 A20 10c green (Bl) 5.00 4.00
71 A22 50c green (Bk) 7.00 3.50
73 A23 1s rose (Bk) 10.00 6.00
Nos. 65-73 (7) 76.10 19.80
Nos. 65,68-73 (6) 31.10 19.80

This overprint is found in 11 types.

The 1c green, 2c dark violet and 20c brown red, overprinted with triangle, are fancy varieties made for sale to collectors and never placed in regular use.

Overprinted Triangle and "Union Postal Universal Peru" in Oval

1883

77 A22 50c grn (R & Bk) 125.00 60.00
78 A23 1s rose (Bl & Bk) 140.00 90.00

The 1c green, 2c rose and 5c ultramarine, over printed with triangle and "U. P. U. Peru" oval, were never placed in regular use.

Overprinted Triangle and "Union Postal Universal Lima" in Oval

1883

79 A17 1c grn (R & Bl) 50.00 37.50
80 A17 1c grn (R & Bk) 4.00 4.00
a. Oval overprint inverted
b. Double overprint of oval
81 A18 2c rose (Bl & Bk) 4.00 4.00
82 A19 5c ultra (R & Bk) 6.50 6.00

83	A19	5c ultra (R & Bl)	6.50	6.00
84	A22	50c grn (R & Bk)	140.00	90.00
85	A23	1s rose (Bl & Bk)	150.00	125.00
		Nos. 79-85 (7)	361.00	272.50

Some authorities question the status of No. 79.

Nos. 80, 81, 84, and 85 were reprinted in 1884. They have the second type of oval overprint with "PLATA" 3mm high.

Overprinted Triangle and

86	A17	1c grn (Bk & Bk)	1.00	.80
a.		Horseshoe inverted	10.00	
87	A17	1c grn (Bl & Bk)	5.00	3.50
88	A18	2c ver (Bk & Bk)	1.00	.75
89	A19	5c bl (Bk & Bk)	1.25	1.00
90	A19	5c bl (Bl & Bk)	7.00	6.50
91	A19	5c bl (R & Bk)	*1,500.*	*1,100.*

Overprinted Horseshoe Alone

1883, Oct. 23

95	A17	1c green	1.25	1.25
96	A18	2c vermilion	1.25	*4.00*
a.		Double overprint		
97	A19	5c blue	2.00	2.00
98	A19	5c ultra	20.00	15.00
99	A22	50c rose	57.50	57.50
100	A23	1s ultra	30.00	22.50
		Nos. 95-100 (6)	112.00	102.25

The 2c violet overprinted with the above design in red and triangle in black also the 1c green overprinted with the same combination plus the horseshoe in black, are fancy varieties made for sale to collectors.

No. 23 Overprinted in Black

1884, Apr. 28

103	A19	5c blue	.65	.40
a.		Double overprint	5.00	5.00

Stamps of 1c and 2c with the above overprint, also with the above and "U. P. U. LIMA" oval in blue or "CORREOS LIMA" in a double-lined circle in red, were made to sell to collectors and were never placed in use.

Without Overprint or Grill

1886-95

104	A17	1c dull violet	.50	.20
105	A17	1c vermilion ('95)	.40	.20
106	A18	2c green	.75	.20
107	A18	2c dp ultra ('95)	.35	.20
108	A19	5c orange	.60	.30
109	A12	5c claret ('95)	1.25	.50
110	A20	10c slate	.40	.20
111	A13	10c orange ('95)	.60	.35
112	A21	20c blue	5.00	.65
113	A14	20c dp ultra ('95)	6.00	1.40
114	A22	50c red	1.50	.65
115	A23	1s brown	1.25	.50
		Nos. 104-115 (12)	18.60	5.35

Overprinted Horseshoe in Black and Triangle in Rose Red

1889

116	A17	1c green	.75	.50
a.		Horseshoe inverted	7.50	

Nos. 30 and 25 Overprinted "Union Postal Universal Lima" in Oval in Red

1889, Sept. 1

117	A17	1c green	1.50	1.25
117A	A20	10c green	1.50	1.50

The overprint on Nos. 117 and 117A is of the second type with "PLATA" 3mm high.

Stamps of 1874-80 Overprinted in Black

Pres. Remigio Morales Bermúdez

1894, Oct. 23

118	A17	1c orange	.60	.40
a.		Inverted overprint	7.00	7.00
b.		Double overprint	7.00	7.00
119	A17	1c green	.40	.35
a.		Inverted overprint	3.50	3.50
b.		Dbl. inverted ovpt.	5.00	5.00
120	A18	2c violet	.40	.35
a.		Diagonal half used as 1c		
b.		Inverted overprint	7.00	7.00
c.		Double overprint	7.00	
121	A18	2c rose	.40	.35
a.		Double overprint	7.00	7.00
b.		Inverted overprint	7.00	7.00
122	A19	5c blue	2.50	1.75
122A	A19	5c ultra	4.25	2.00
b.		Inverted overprint	10.00	10.00
123	A20	10c green	.40	.35
a.		Inverted overprint	7.00	7.00
124	A22	50c green	1.40	1.25
a.		Inverted overprint	10.00	10.00
		Nos. 118-124 (8)	10.35	6.80

Same, with Additional Overprint of Horseshoe

125	A18	2c vermilion	.35	.25
a.		Head inverted	2.50	2.50
b.		Head double	5.00	5.00
126	A19	5c blue	1.00	.50
a.		Head inverted	7.00	7.00
127	A22	50c rose	42.50	30.00
a.		Head double	55.00	45.00
b.		Head inverted		
128	A23	1s ultra	100.00	90.00
a.		Both overprints inverted	125.00	110.00
b.		Head double	125.00	110.00
		Nos. 125-128 (4)	143.85	120.75

A23a

1895 *Perf. 11½*

Vermilion Surcharge

129	A23a	5c on 5c grn	10.00	7.50
130	A23a	10c on 10c ver	8.00	6.00
131	A23a	20c on 20c brn	8.50	6.50
132	A23a	50c on 50c ultra	10.00	7.50
133	A23a	1s on 1s red brn	10.00	8.00
		Nos. 129-133 (5)	46.50	35.50

Nos 129-133 were used only in Tumbes. The basic stamps were prepared by revolutionaries in northern Peru.

A23b

"Liberty" A23c

1895, Sept. 8 **Engr.**

134	A23b	1c gray violet	1.75	.95
135	A23b	2c green	1.75	.95
136	A23b	5c yellow	1.75	.95
137	A23b	10c ultra	1.75	.95
138	A23c	20c orange	1.75	1.10
139	A23c	50c dark blue	8.50	6.50
140	A23c	1s car lake	47.50	32.50
		Nos. 134-140 (7)	64.75	43.90

Success of the revolution against the government of General Caceres and of the election of President Pierola.

Manco Capac, Founder of Inca Dynasty — A24

Francisco Pizarro Conqueror of the Inca Empire — A25

General José de La Mar — A26

1896-1900

141	A24	1c ultra	.75	.20
a.		1c blue (error)	65.00	60.00
142	A24	1c yel grn ('98)	.75	.20
143	A24	2c blue	.75	.20
144	A24	2c scar ('99)	.75	.20
145	A25	5c indigo	1.10	.20
146	A25	5c green ('97)	1.10	.20
147	A25	5c grnsh bl ('99)	.75	.20
148	A25	10c yellow	1.50	.35
149	A25	10c gray blk ('00)	1.50	.20
150	A25	20c orange	3.00	.35
151	A26	50c car rose	7.50	1.10
152	A26	1s orange red	11.00	1.50
153	A26	2s claret	3.25	1.10
		Nos. 141-153 (13)	33.70	6.00

The 5c in black is a chemical changeling.

For surcharges and overprints see Nos. 187-188, E1, O23-O26.

Paucartambo Bridge A27

Post and Telegraph Building, Lima — A28

Pres. Nicolás de Piérola — A29

1897, Dec. 31

154	A27	1c dp ultra	1.00	.60
155	A28	2c brown	1.00	.40
156	A29	5c bright rose	1.50	.40
		Nos. 154-156 (3)	3.50	1.40

Opening of new P.O. in Lima.

A30

A31

1897, Nov. 8

157	A30	1c bister	.50	.45
a.		Inverted overprint	2.50	2.50
b.		Double overprint	10.00	10.00

1899

158	A31	5s orange red	2.50	2.50
159	A31	10s blue green	750.00	600.00

For surcharge see No. J36.

Pres. Eduardo de Romaña — A32

Admiral Miguel L. Grau — A33

1900 **Frame Litho., Center Engr.**

160	A32	22c yel grn & blk	12.00	1.40

1901, Jan.

2c, Col. Francisco Bolognes. 5c, Pres. Romaña.

161	A33	1c green & blk	1.50	.75
162	A33	2c red & black	1.50	.75
163	A33	5c dull vio & blk	1.50	.75
		Nos. 161-163 (3)	4.50	2.25

Advent of 20th century.

A34

Municipal Hygiene Institute Lima — A35

1902 **Engr.**

164	A34	22c green	.50	.20

1905

165	A35	12c dp blue & blk	1.50	.50

For surcharges see Nos. 166-167, 186, 189.

Same Surcharged in Red or Violet

1907

166	A35	1c on 12c (R)	.25	.20
a.		Inverted surcharge	8.00	8.00
b.		Double surcharge	8.00	8.00
167	A35	2c on 12c (V)	.50	.35
a.		Double surcharge	8.00	8.00
b.		Inverted surcharge	8.00	8.00

Monument of Bolognesi — A36

Admiral Grau — A37

Llama — A38

Statue of Bolivar — A39

City Hall, Lima, formerly an Exhibition Building — A40

School of Medicine, Lima — A41

Post and Telegraph Building, Lima — A42

Grandstand at Santa Beatrix Race Track — A43

Columbus Monument — A44

1907

168	A36	1c yel grn & blk	.50	.20
169	A37	2c red & violet	.50	.20
170	A38	4c olive green	8.25	1.10
171	A39	5c blue & blk	.90	.20
172	A40	10c red brn & blk	1.50	.35
173	A41	20c dk grn & blk	32.50	.75
174	A42	50c black	32.50	1.50
175	A43	1s purple & grn	175.00	3.75
176	A44	2s dp bl & blk	175.00	150.00
		Nos. 168-176 (9)	426.65	158.05

For surcharges and overprint see #190-195, E2.

Manco Capac A45

Columbus A46

Pizarro A47

San Martin A48

Bolívar A49

La Mar A50

Ramón Castilla A51

Grau A52

Bolognesi — A53

1909

177	A45	1c gray	.20	.20
178	A46	2c green	.20	.20
179	A47	4c vermilion	.40	.20
180	A48	5c violet	.20	.20
181	A49	10c deep blue	.70	.20
182	A50	12c pale blue	1.40	.20
183	A51	20c brown red	1.50	.35
184	A52	50c yellow	7.00	.45
185	A53	1s brn red & blk	14.00	.45
		Nos. 177-185 (9)	25.60	2.45

See types A54, A78-A80, A81-A89.

For surcharges and overprint see Nos. 196-200, 208, E3.

No. 165 Surcharged in Red

1913, Jan.

186	A35	8c on 12c dp bl & blk	.80	.35

Stamps of 1899-1908 Surcharged in Magenta

a

b

c

1915

On Nos. 142, 149

187	A24(a)	1c on 1c	20.00	18.00
a.		Inverted surcharge	22.50	18.00
188	A25(a)	1c on 10c	1.10	1.10

On No. 165

189	A35(c)	2c on 12c	.35	.20
a.		Inverted surcharge		

On Nos. 168-170, 172-174

190	A36(a)	1c on 1c	.95	.95
191	A37(a)	1c on 2c	1.50	1.50
192	A38(b)	1c on 4c	2.40	2.40
a.		Inverted surcharge	6.00	6.00
193	A40(b)	1c on 10c	.50	.45
a.		Inverted surcharge	2.50	2.50
193C	A40(c)	2c on 10c	150.00	110.00
194	A41(c)	2c on 20c	20.00	18.00
195	A42(c)	2c on 50c	3.00	3.00
		Nos. 187-195 (10)	199.80	155.60

Nos. 182-184, 179, 185 Surcharged in Red, Green or Violet

d

e

f

1916

196	A50(d)	1c on 12c (R)	.20	.20
a.		Double surcharge	2.00	2.00
b.		Green surcharge	7.50	7.50
197	A51(d)	1c on 20c (G)	.20	.20
198	A52(d)	1c on 50c (G)	.20	.20
a.		Inverted surcharge	2.00	2.00
199	A47(e)	2c on 4c (V)	.20	.20
200	A53(f)	10c on 1s (G)	1.10	.20
a.		"VALF"	3.50	3.50
		Nos. 196-200 (5)	1.90	1.00

Official Stamps of 1909-14 Overprinted or Surcharged in Green or Red:

g

h

1916

201	O1(g)	1c red (G)	.20	.20
202	O1(h)	2c on 50c ol grn (R)	.20	.20
203	O1(g)	10c bis brn (G)	.20	.20

Postage Due Stamps of 1909 Surcharged in Violet-Black

204	D7	2c on 1c brown	.40	.40
205	D7	2c on 5c brown	.20	.20
206	D7	2c on 10c brown	.20	.20
207	D7	2c on 50c brown	.20	.20
		Nos. 201-207 (7)	1.60	1.60

Many copies of Nos. 187 to 207 have a number of pin holes. It is stated that these holes were made at the time the surcharges were printed.

The varieties which we list of the 1915 and 1916 issues were sold to the public at post offices. Many other varieties which were previously listed are now known to have been delivered to one speculator or to have been privately printed by him from the surcharging plates which he had acquired.

No. 179 Surcharged in Black

1917

208	A47	1c on 4c ver	.50	.20
a.		Double surcharge	7.50	7.50
b.		Inverted surcharge	7.50	7.50

San Martín — A54

Columbus at Salamanca — A62

Funeral of Atahualpa A63

Battle of Arica, "Arica, the Last Cartridge" A64

Designs: 2c, Bolivar. 4c, José Gálvez. 5c, Manuel Pardo. 8c, Grau. 10c, Bolognesi. 12c, Castilla. 20c, General Cáceres.

1918 **Engr.**

Centers in Black

209	A54	1c orange	.20	.20
210	A54	2c green	.20	.20
211	A54	4c lake	.45	.20
212	A54	5c dp ultra	.35	.20
213	A54	8c red brn	1.10	.35
214	A54	10c grnsh bl	.50	.20
215	A54	12c dl vio	1.50	.20
216	A54	20c ol grn	1.75	.20
217	A62	50c vio brn	7.50	.50
218	A63	1s greenish bl	18.00	.75
219	A64	2s deep ultra	32.50	1.00
		Nos. 209-219 (11)	64.05	4.00

For surcharges see Nos. 232-233, 255-256.

Augusto B. Leguía — A65

1919, Dec. **Litho.**

220	A65	5c bl & blk	.20	.20
a.		Imperf.	.35	.35
b.		Center inverted	15.00	15.00
221	A65	5c brn & blk	.20	.20
a.		Imperf.	.35	.35
b.		Center inverted	15.00	15.00

Constitution of 1919.

San Martín — A66

Thomas Cochrane — A70

Oath of Independence — A69

Designs: 2c, Field Marshal Arenales. 4c, Field Marshal Las Heras. 10c, Martin Jorge Guisse. 12c, Vidal. 20c, Leguia. 50c, San Martin monument. 1s, San Martin and Leguia.

1921, July 28 **Engr.; 7c Litho.**

222	A66	1c ol brn & red brn	.45	.20
a.		Center inverted	550.00	525.00
223	A66	2c green	.45	.20
224	A66	4c car rose	1.10	.90
225	A69	5c ol brn	.60	.20
226	A70	7c violet	.95	.35
227	A66	10c ultra	1.10	.60
228	A66	12c blk & slate	3.75	.90
229	A66	20c car & gray blk	3.75	1.10
230	A66	50c vio brn & dl vio	10.50	3.75
231	A69	1s car rose & yel grn	18.00	5.50
		Nos. 222-231 (10)	40.65	13.70

Centenary of Independence.

Nos. 213, 212 Surcharged in Black or Red Brown

1923-24

232	A54	5c on 8c No. 213	.70	.35
233	A54	4c on 5c (RB) ('24)	.50	.20
a.		Inverted surcharge	5.00	5.00
b.		Double surcharge, one inverted	6.00	6.00

A78

A79

Simón Bolívar — A80

Perf. 14, 14x14½, 14½, 13½

1924 Engr.; Photo. (4c, 5c)

234	A78	2c olive grn	.40	.20
235	A79	4c yellow grn	.65	.20
236	A79	5c black	1.25	.20
237	A80	10c carmine	.80	.20
238	A78	20c ultra	1.60	.20
239	A78	50c dull violet	4.75	1.00
240	A78	1s yellow brn	13.00	3.25
241	A78	2s dull blue	27.50	14.00
		Nos. 234-241 (8)	49.95	19.25

Centenary of the Battle of Ayacucho which ended Spanish power in South America.

No. 237 exists imperf.

José Tejada Rivadeneyra A81

Mariano Melgar A82

Iturregui A83

Leguía A84

José de La Mar — A85

Monument of José Olaya — A86

Statue of María Bellido — A87

De Saco — A88

José Leguía — A89

1924-29 Engr. *Perf. 12*

Size: 18½x23mm

242	A81	2c olive gray	.20	.20
243	A82	4c dk grn	.20	.20
244	A83	8c black	3.00	3.00
245	A84	10c org red	.20	.20
245A	A85	15c dp bl ('28)	.90	.20
246	A86	20c blue	1.10	.20
247	A86	20c yel ('29)	2.25	.20
248	A87	50c violet	7.50	.45
249	A88	1s bis brn	13.50	1.10
250	A89	2s ultra	32.50	7.50
		Nos. 242-250 (10)	61.35	13.25

See Nos. 258, 260, 276-282.

For surcharges and overprint see Nos. 251-253, 257-260, 262, 268-271, C1.

No. 246 Surcharged in Red:

DOS
Centavos

1925

a

b

1925

251	A86(a)	2c on 20c blue	500.00	
252	A86(b)	2c on 20c blue	1.50	1.10
a.		Inverted surcharge	35.00	35.00
b.		Double surch., one inverted	50.00	50.00

No. 245 Overprinted

1925

253	A84	10c org red	1.50	1.50
a.		Inverted overprint	17.50	17.50

This stamp was for exclusive use on letters from the plebiscite provinces of Tacna and Arica, and posted on the Peruvian transport "Ucayali" anchored in the port of Arica.

No. 213 Surcharged

a

b

1929

255	A54(a)	2c on 8c	1.10	1.10
256	A54(b)	2c on 8c	1.10	1.10

No. 247 Surcharged

257	A86	15c on 20c yellow	1.10	1.10
a.		Inverted surcharge	12.00	12.00
		Nos. 255-257 (3)	3.30	3.30

Stamps of 1924 Issue
Coil Stamps

1929 *Perf. 14 Horizontally*

258	A81	2c olive gray	60.00	40.00
260	A84	10c orange red	65.00	37.50

Postal Tax Stamp of 1928 Overprinted

1930 *Perf. 12*

261	PT6	2c dark violet	.50	.50
a.		Inverted overprint	2.50	2.50

No. 247 Surcharged

262	A86	2c on 20c yellow	.50	.50

Air Post Stamp of 1928 Surcharged

263	AP1	2c on 50c dk grn	.50	.50
a.		"Habitada"	1.00	1.00

Coat of Arms — A91

Lima Cathedral A92

10c, Children's Hospital. 50c, Madonna & Child.

Perf. 12x11½, 11½x12

1930, July 5 Litho.

264	A91	2c green	1.40	.95
265	A92	5c scarlet	2.50	1.60
266	A92	10c dark blue	1.90	1.25
267	A91	50c bister brown	29.00	15.00
		Nos. 264-267 (4)	34.80	18.80

6th Pan American Congress for Child Welfare. By error the stamps are inscribed "Seventh Congress."

Type of 1924 Overprinted in Black, Green or Blue

1930, Dec. 22 Photo. *Perf. 15x14*

Size: 18¼x22mm

268	A84	10c orange red (Bk)	1.00	.80
a.		Inverted overprint	10.00	10.00
b.		Without overprint	6.50	6.50
c.		Double surcharge	5.00	5.00

Same with Additional Surcharge of Numerals in Each Corner

269	A84	2c on 10c org red (G)	.20	.20
a.		Inverted surcharge	12.00	
270	A84	4c on 10c org red (G)	.20	.20
a.		Double surcharge	8.25	8.25

Engr.

Perf. 12

Size: 19x23½mm

271	A84	15c on 10c org red (Bl)	.30	.20
a.		Inverted surcharge	10.00	10.00
b.		Double surcharge	10.00	10.00
		Nos. 268-271 (4)	1.70	1.40

Bolívar — A95

1930, Dec. 16 Litho.

272	A95	2c buff	.35	.35
273	A95	4c red	.90	.75
274	A95	10c blue green	.35	.25
275	A95	15c slate gray	.90	.90
		Nos. 272-275 (4)	2.50	2.25

Death cent. of General Simón Bolivar.
For surcharges see Nos. RA14-RA16.

Types of 1924-29 Issues
Size: 18x22mm

1931 Photo. *Perf. 15x14*

276	A81	2c olive green	.45	.20
277	A82	4c dark green	.45	.20
279	A85	15c deep blue	1.10	.20
280	A86	20c yellow	1.75	.20
281	A87	50c violet	1.75	.40
282	A88	1s olive brown	3.00	.50
		Nos. 276-282 (6)	8.50	1.70

Pizarro — A96

Old Stone Bridge, Lima — A97

1931, July 28 Litho. *Perf. 11*

283	A96	2c slate blue	1.75	1.50
284	A96	4c deep brown	1.75	1.50
285	A96	15c dark green	1.75	1.50
286	A97	10c rose red	1.75	1.50
287	A97	10c mag & lt grn	1.75	1.50
288	A97	15c yel & bl gray	1.75	1.50
289	A97	15c dk slate & red	1.75	1.50
		Nos. 283-289 (7)	12.25	10.50

1st Peruvian Phil. Exhib., Lima, July, 1931.

Manco Capac A99

Sugar Cane Field A102

Oil Refinery A100

Guano Deposits A104

Picking Cotton A103

Mining A105

Llamas A106

Arms of Piura A107

1931-32 *Perf. 11, 11x11½*

292	A99	2c olive black	.30	.20
293	A100	4c dark green	.65	.20
295	A102	10c red orange	1.25	.20
a.		Vertical pair, imperf. between	30.00	
296	A103	15c turq blue	1.90	.20
297	A104	20c yellow	6.50	.30
298	A105	50c gray lilac	7.75	.30
299	A106	1s brown olive	16.00	1.25
		Nos. 292-299 (7)	34.35	2.65

1932, July 28 *Perf. 11½x12*

300	A107	10c dark blue	7.50	7.00
301	A107	15c deep violet	7.50	7.00
		Nos. 300-301,C3 (3)	39.00	36.50

400th anniv. of the founding of the city of Piura. On sale one day. Counterfeits exist.

Parakas A108

Chimu A109

Inca — A110

1932, Oct. 15 ***Perf. 11½, 12, 11½x12***

302	A108	10c dk vio	.20	.20
303	A109	15c brn red	.60	.20
304	A110	50c dk brn	1.40	.20
		Nos. 302-304 (3)	2.20	.60

4th cent. of the Spanish conquest of Peru.

Arequipa and El Misti — A111

President Luis M. Sánchez Cerro — A112

Monument to Simón Bolívar at Lima — A115

Statue of Liberty — A116

1932-34 **Photo.** ***Perf. 13½***

305	A111	2c black	.20	.20
306	A111	2c blue blk	.20	.20
307	A111	2c grn ('34)	.20	.20
308	A111	4c dk brn	.20	.20
309	A111	4c org ('34)	.20	.20
310	A112	10c vermilion	21.00	15.00
311	A115	15c ultra	.60	.20
312	A115	15c mag ('34)	.60	.20
313	A115	20c red brn	1.25	.20
314	A115	20c vio ('34)	1.25	.20
315	A115	50c dk grn ('33)	1.25	.20
316	A115	1s dp org	10.00	.20
317	A115	1s org brn	12.00	.50
		Nos. 305-317 (13)	48.95	17.70

For overprint see No. RA24.

1934

318	A116	10c rose	.75	.20

Pizarro — A117

The Inca — A119

Coronation of Huascar — A118

1934-35 ***Perf. 13***

319	A117	10c crimson	.40	.20
320	A117	15c ultra	1.10	.20
321	A118	20c deep bl ('35)	2.00	.20
322	A118	50c dp red brn	1.60	.20
323	A119	1s dark vio	4.75	.55
		Nos. 319-323 (5)	9.85	1.35

For surcharges and overprint see Nos. 354-355, J54, O32.

Pizarro and the Thirteen A120

Belle of Lima — A122

Francisco Pizarro — A123

4c, Lima Cathedral. 1s, Veiled woman of Lima.

1935, Jan. 18 ***Perf. 13½***

324	A120	2c brown	.40	.20
325	A120	4c violet	.60	.45
326	A122	10c rose red	.60	.20
327	A123	15c ultra	.95	.70
328	A120	20c slate gray	1.60	.90
329	A122	50c olive grn	2.40	1.75
330	A122	1s Prus bl	5.50	3.50
331	A123	2s org brn	12.50	9.50
		Nos. 324-331,C6-C12 (15)	77.50	54.30

Founding of Lima, 4th cent.

View of Ica — A125

Lake Huacachina, Health Resort — A126

Grapes — A127

Cotton Boll — A128

Zuniga y Velazco and Philip IV — A129

Supreme God of the Nazcas — A130

Engr.; Photo. (10c)

1935, Jan. 17 ***Perf. 12½***

332	A125	4c gray blue	1.25	1.25
333	A126	5c dark car	.45	1.25
334	A127	10c magenta	5.00	2.50
335	A126	20c green	2.00	2.00
336	A128	35c dark car	10.00	4.75
337	A129	50c org & brn	7.00	6.25
338	A130	1s pur & red	20.00	16.00
		Nos. 332-338 (7)	45.70	34.00

Founding of the City of Ica, 300th anniv.

Pizarro and the Thirteen — A131

1935-36 **Photo.** ***Perf. 13½***

339	A131	2c dp claret	.25	.20
340	A131	4c bl grn ('36)	.25	.20

For surcharge and overprints see Nos. 353, J53, RA25-RA26.

"San Cristóbal," First Peruvian Warship — A132

Grand Marshal José de La Mar — A138

Naval College at Punta A133

Independence Square, Callao — A134

Aerial View of Callao A135

Plan of Walls of Callao in 1746 A137

Packetboat "Sacramento" — A139

Viceroy José Antonio Manso de Velasco — A140

Fort Maipú — A141

Plan of Fort Real Felipe A142

Design: 15c, Docks and Custom House.

1936, Aug. 27 **Photo.** ***Perf. 12½***

341	A132	2c black	.65	.30
342	A133	4c bl grn	.65	.30
343	A134	5c yel brn	.65	.30
344	A135	10c bl gray	.65	.30
345	A135	15c green	.65	.30
346	A137	20c dk brn	.70	.30
347	A138	50c purple	1.60	.45
348	A139	1s olive grn	10.00	1.60
		Engr.		
349	A140	2s violet	18.00	8.00
350	A141	5s carmine	24.00	18.00
351	A142	10s red org & brn	60.00	47.50
		Nos. 341-351,C13 (12)	120.55	78.75

Province of Callao founding, cent.

Nos. 340, 321 and 323 Surcharged in Black

1936 ***Perf. 13½, 13***

353	A131	2c on 4c bl grn	.20	.20
a.		"0.20" for "0.02"	3.50	3.50
354	A118	10c on 20c dp bl	.25	.20
a.		Double surcharge	3.50	
b.		Inverted surcharge	3.50	
355	A119	10c on 1s dk vio	.35	.35
		Nos. 353-355 (3)	.80	.75

Many varieties of the surcharge are found on these stamps: no period after "S," no

period after "Cts," period after "2," "S" omitted, various broken letters, etc.
The surcharge on No. 355 is horizontal.

Peruvian Cormorants (Guano Deposits) — A143

Oil Well at Talara — A144

Avenue of the Republic, Lima A146

San Marcos University at Lima A148

Post Office, Lima — A149

Viceroy Manuel de Amat y Junyent — A150

Designs: 10c, "El Chasqui" (Inca Courier). 20c, Municipal Palace and Museum of Natural History. 5s, Joseph A. de Pando y Riva. 10s, Dr. José Dávila Condemarin.

1936-37 Photo. *Perf. 12½*

356	A143	2c lt brn	.70	.20
357	A143	2c grn ('37)	.90	.20
358	A144	4c blk brn	.70	.20
359	A144	4c int blk ('37)	.40	.20
360	A143	10c crimson	.40	.20
361	A143	10c ver ('37)	.20	.20
362	A146	15c ultra	.75	.20
363	A146	15c brt bl ('37)	.40	.20
364	A146	20c black	.75	.20
365	A146	20c blk brn ('37)	.30	.20
366	A148	50c org yel	3.00	.70
367	A148	50c dk gray vio ('37)	.90	.20
368	A149	1s brn vio	6.00	.80
369	A149	1s ultra ('37)	1.60	.20

Engr.

370	A150	2s ultra	12.00	2.50
371	A150	2s dk vio ('37)	3.75	.70
372	A150	5s slate bl	12.00	2.50
373	A150	10s dk vio & brn	62.50	27.50
		Nos. 356-373 (18)	107.25	37.10

No. 370 Surcharged in Black

1937

374	A150	1s on 2s ultra	2.75	2.50

Children's Holiday Center, Ancón — A153

Chavin Pottery — A154

Highway Map of Peru — A155

Archaeological Museum, Lima — A156

Industrial Bank of Peru — A157

Worker's Houses, Lima — A158

Toribio de Luzuriaga A159

Historic Fig Tree A160

Idol from Temple of Chavin — A161

Mt. Huascarán — A162

Imprint: "Waterlow & Sons Limited, Londres"

1938, July 1 Photo. *Perf. 12½, 13*

375	A153	2c emerald	.20	.20
376	A154	4c org brn	.20	.20
377	A155	10c scarlet	.20	.20
378	A156	15c ultra	.40	.20
379	A157	20c magenta	.20	.20
380	A158	50c greenish blue	.50	.20
381	A159	1s dp claret	1.60	.20
382	A160	2s green	4.75	.20

Engr.

383	A161	5s dl vio & brn	11.00	.50
384	A162	10s blk & ultra	19.00	.60
		Nos. 375-384 (10)	38.05	2.70

See Nos. 410-418, 426-433, 438-441.
For surcharges see Nos. 388, 406, 419, 445-446A, 456, 758.

Palace Square A163

Lima Coat of Arms A164

Government Palace — A165

1938, Dec. 9 Photo. *Perf. 12½*

385	A163	10c slate green	.60	.40

Engraved and Lithographed

386	A164	15c blk, gold, red & bl	1.00	.50

Photo.

387	A165	1s olive	2.25	1.50
		Nos. 385-387,C62-C64 (6)	7.35	4.90

8th Pan-American Conf., Lima, Dec. 1938.

No. 377 Surcharged in Black

1940 *Perf. 13*

388 A155	5c on 10c scarlet	.20	.20
a.	Inverted surcharge		

AIR POST STAMPS

No. 248 Overprinted in Black

1927, Dec. 10 Unwmk. *Perf. 12*

C1	A87	50c violet	45.00	25.00

Two types of overprint. Counterfeits exist.

President Augusto Bernardino Leguía — AP1

1928, Jan. 12 Engr.

C2	AP1	50c dark green	1.00	.50

For surcharge see No. 263.

Coat of Arms of Piura Type

1932, July 28 Litho.

C3	A107	50c scarlet	24.00	22.50

Counterfeits exist.

Airplane in Flight — AP3

1934, Feb. Engr. *Perf. 12½*

C4	AP3	2s blue	6.50	.60
C5	AP3	5s brown	13.50	1.25

Funeral of Atahualpa AP4

Palace of Torre-Tagle AP7

Designs: 35c, Mt. San Cristobal. 50c, Avenue of Barefoot Friars. 10s, Pizarro and the Thirteen.

1935, Jan. 18 Photo. *Perf. 13½*

C6	AP4	5c emerald	.30	.20
C7	AP4	35c brown	.40	.35
C8	AP4	50c orange yel	.85	.70
C9	AP4	1s plum	1.50	1.00
C10	AP7	2s red orange	2.40	2.10
C11	AP4	5s dp claret	10.00	6.25
C12	AP4	10s dk blue	37.50	26.50
		Nos. C6-C12 (7)	52.95	37.10

4th centenary of founding of Lima.
Nos. C6-C12 overprinted "Radio Nacional" are revenue stamps.

"La Callao," First Locomotive in South America AP9

1936, Aug. 27 *Perf. 12½*

C13	AP9	35c gray black	3.00	1.40

Founding of the Province of Callao, cent.

Nos. C4-C5 Surcharged "Habilitado" and New Value, like Nos. 353-355

1936, Nov. 4

C14	AP3	5c on 2s blue	.50	.20
C15	AP3	25c on 5s brown	1.00	.50
	a.	Double surcharge	13.50	13.50
	b.	No period btwn. "O" & "25 Cts"	1.40	1.40
	c.	Inverted surcharge	16.50	

There are many broken letters in this setting.

Mines of Peru AP10

Jorge Chávez AP14

Aerial View of Peruvian Coast AP16

View of the "Sierra" — AP17

St. Rosa of Lima — AP22

Designs: 5c, La Mar Park, Lima. 15c, Mail Steamer "Inca" on Lake Titicaca. 20c, Native Queña (flute) Player and Llama. 30c, Ram at Model Farm, Puno. 1s, Train in Mountains. 1.50s, Jorge Chavez Aviation School. 2s, Transport Plane. 5s, Aerial View of Virgin Forests.

1936-37 **Photo.** ***Perf. 12½***

C16	AP10	5c brt green	.20	.20
C17	AP10	5c emer ('37)	.20	.20
C18	AP10	15c lt ultra	.50	.20
C19	AP10	15c blue ('37)	.30	.20
C20	AP10	20c gray blk	1.25	.20
C21	AP10	20c pale ol grn ('37)	.80	.30
C22	AP14	25c mag ('37)	.40	.20
C23	AP10	30c henna brn	4.00	1.10
C24	AP10	30c dk ol brn ('37)	1.10	.20
C25	AP14	35c brown	2.10	2.10
C26	AP10	50c yellow	.40	.30
C27	AP10	50c brn vio ('37)	.60	.20
C28	AP16	70c Prus grn	5.00	5.25
C29	AP16	70c pck grn ('37)	.80	.75
C30	AP17	80c brn blk	6.00	5.25
C31	AP17	80c ol blk ('37)	1.10	.50
C32	AP10	1s ultra	4.00	.40
C33	AP10	1s red brn ('37)	2.10	.20
C34	AP14	1.50s red brn	6.50	6.00
C35	AP14	1.50s org yel ('37)	4.00	.40
		Engr.		
C36	AP10	2s deep blue	12.00	7.75
C37	AP10	2s yel grn ('37)	8.00	.80
C38	AP16	5s green	13.50	3.75
C39	AP22	10s car & brn	115.00	110.00
		Nos. C16-C39 (24)	189.85	146.45

Nos. C23, C25, C28, C30, C36 Surcharged in Black or Red

1936, June 26

C40	AP10	15c on 30c hn brn	.60	.40
C41	AP14	15c on 35c brown	.60	.20
C42	AP16	15c on 70c Prus grn	4.00	3.50
C43	AP17	25c on 80c brn blk (R)	4.00	3.50
C44	AP10	1s on 2s dp bl	6.75	4.75
		Nos. C40-C44 (5)	15.95	12.35

Surcharge on No. C43 is vertical, reading down.

First Flight in Peru, 1911 — AP23

Jorge Chávez — AP24

Airport of Limatambo at Lima — AP25

Map of Aviation Lines from Peru — AP26

Designs: 10c, Juan Bielovucic (1889-?) flying over Lima race course, Jan. 14, 1911. 15c, Jorge Chavez-Dartnell (1887-1910), French-born Peruvian aviator who flew from Brixen to Domodossola in the Alps and died of plane-crash injuries.

1937, Sept. 15 **Engr.** ***Perf. 12***

C45	AP23	10c violet	.55	.20
C46	AP24	15c dk green	.90	.20
C47	AP25	25c gray brn	.55	.20
C48	AP26	1s black	2.50	2.00
		Nos. C45-C48 (4)	4.50	2.60

Inter-American Technical Conference of Aviation, Sept. 1937.

Government Restaurant at Callao — AP27

Monument on the Plains of Junin — AP28

Rear Admiral Manuel Villar — AP29

View of Tarma — AP30

Dam, Ica River — AP31

View of Iquitos AP32

Highway and Railroad Passing AP33

Mountain Road — AP34

Plaza San Martín, Lima — AP35

National Radio of Peru AP36

Stele from Chavin Temple AP37

Ministry of Public Works, Lima — AP38

Crypt of the Heroes, Lima — AP39

Imprint: "Waterlow & Sons Limited, Londres."

1938, July 1 **Photo.** ***Perf. 12½, 13***

C49	AP27	5c violet brn	.20	.20
C50	AP28	15c dk brown	.20	.20
C51	AP29	20c dp magenta	.30	.20
C52	AP30	25c dp green	.20	.20
C53	AP31	30c orange	.20	.20
C54	AP32	50c green	.25	.20
C55	AP33	70c slate bl	.40	.20
C56	AP34	80c olive	1.00	.20
C57	AP35	1s slate grn	8.75	4.00
C58	AP36	1.50s purple	2.00	.20
		Engr.		
C59	AP37	2s ind & org brn	3.00	.80
C60	AP38	5s brown	16.00	1.60
C61	AP39	10s ol grn & ind	62.50	37.50
		Nos. C49-C61 (13)	95.00	45.70

See Nos. C73-C75, C89-C93, C103.
For surcharges see Nos. C65, C76-C77, C82-C88, C108C.

Torre-Tagle Palace — AP40

National Congress Building — AP41

Manuel Ferreyros, José Gregorio Paz Soldán and Antonio Arenas — AP42

1938, Dec. 9 **Photo.** ***Perf. 12½***

C62	AP40	25c brt ultra	.65	.45
C63	AP41	1.50s brown vio	1.75	1.50
C64	AP42	2s black	1.10	.55
		Nos. C62-C64 (3)	3.50	2.50

8th Pan-American Conference at Lima.

SPECIAL DELIVERY STAMPS

No. 149 Overprinted in Black

1908 **Unwmk.** ***Perf. 12***

E1	A25	10c gray black	20.00	15.00

No. 172 Overprinted in Violet

1909

E2	A40	10c red brn & blk	25.00	14.00

No. 1819 Handstamped in Violet

1910

E3	A49	10c deep blue	14.00	12.00

Two handstamps were used to make No. E2. Impressions from them measure 22½x6½mm and 24x6½mm.
Counterfeits exist of Nos. E1-3.

POSTAGE DUE STAMPS

Coat of Arms — D1

Steamship and Llama D2 D3

D4

D5

1874-79 Unwmk. Engr. *Perf. 12*

With Grill

J1	D1 1c bister ('79)	.25	.20
	On cover, postage due usage		1,000.
	On cover, postage usage		500.
J2	D2 5c vermilion	.30	.20
	On cover, postage due usage		350.
	On cover, postage usage		500.
J3	D3 10c orange	.35	.25
	On cover, postage due usage		350.
	On cover, postage usage		500.
J4	D4 20c blue	.60	.35
	On cover, postage due usage		750.
	On cover, postage usage		—
J5	D5 50c brown	9.00	3.50
	On cover, postage due usage		1,000.
	On cover, postage usage		—
	Nos. J1-J5 (5)	10.50	4.50

A 2c green exists, but was not regularly issued.

For overprints and surcharges see Nos. 157, J6-J31, J37-J38, 8N14-8N15, 14N18.

1902-07

Without Grill

J1a	D1 1c bister	.20	
	On cover, postage due usage		250.00
	On cover, postage usage		250.00
J2a	D2 5c vermilion	.20	
	On cover, postage due usage		250.00
	On cover, postage usage		250.00
J3a	D3 10c orange	.20	
	On cover, postage due usage		500.00
	On cover, postage usage		250.00
J4a	D4 20c blue	.35	
	On cover, postage due usage		500.00
	On cover, postage usage		—
	Nos. J1a-J4a (4)	.95	

Nos. J1-J5 Overprinted in Blue or Red

1881

"PLATA" 2½mm High

J6	D1 1c bis (Bl)	3.50	2.50
J7	D2 5c ver (Bl)	6.50	6.00
a.	Double overprint		
b.	Inverted overprint	17.00	17.00
J8	D3 10c org (Bl)	6.50	6.50
a.	Inverted overprint	17.00	17.00
J9	D4 20c bl (R)	25.00	20.00
J10	D5 50c brn (Bl)	55.00	50.00
	Nos. J6-J10 (5)	96.50	85.00

In the reprints of this overprint "PLATA" is 3mm high instead of 2½mm. Besides being struck in the regular colors it was also applied to the 1, 5, 10 and 50c in red and the 20c in blue.

Overprinted in Red

1881

J11	D1 1c bister	5.00	5.00
J12	D2 5c vermilion	6.50	6.00
J13	D3 10c orange	8.00	6.50
J14	D4 20c blue	25.00	20.00
J15	D5 50c brown	80.00	65.00
	Nos. J11-J15 (5)	124.50	102.50

Originals of Nos. J11 to J15 are overprinted in brick-red, oily ink; reprints in thicker, bright red ink. The 5c exists with reprinted overprint in blue.

Overprinted "Union Postal Universal Lima Plata", in Oval in first named color and Triangle in second named color

1883

J16	D1 1c bis (Bl & Bk)	5.00	3.50
J17	D1 1c bis (Bk & Bl)	7.50	7.00
J18	D2 5c ver (Bl & Bk)	7.50	7.00
	On cover, postage due usage		—
	On cover, postage usage		500.00
J19	D3 10c org (Bl & Bk)	7.50	6.00
	On cover, postage due usage		—
	On cover, postage usage		500.00
J20	D4 20c bl (R & Bk)	*450.00*	*450.00*
	On cover, postage due usage		—
	On cover, postage usage		500.00
J21	D5 50c brn (Bl & Bk)	55.00	42.50

Reprints of Nos. J16 to J21 have the oval overprint with "PLATA" 3mm. high. The 1c also exists with the oval overprint in red.

Overprinted in Black

1884

J22	D1 1c bister	.50	.50
	On cover, postage due usage		500.00
	On cover, postage usage		500.00
J23	D2 5c vermilion	.50	.50
	On cover, postage due usage		250.00
	On cover, postage usage		250.00
J24	D3 10c orange	.50	.50
	On cover, postage due usage		250.00
	On cover, postage usage		350.00
J25	D4 20c blue	1.00	.50
	On cover, postage due usage		500.00
	On cover, postage usage		500.00
J26	D5 50c brown	3.00	.90
	On cover, postage due usage		500.00
	On cover, postage usage		—
	Nos. J22-J26 (5)	5.50	2.90

The triangular overprint is found in 11 types.

Overprinted "Lima Correos" in Circle in Red and Triangle in Black

1884

J27	D1 1c bister	12.50	11.00

Reprints of No. J27 have the overprint in bright red. At the time they were made the overprint was also printed on the 5, 10, 20 and 50c Postage Due stamps.

Postage Due stamps overprinted with Sun and "CORREOS LIMA" (as shown above No. 103), alone or in combination with the "U. P. U. LIMA" oval or "LIMA CORREOS" in double-lined circle, are fancy varieties made to sell to collectors and never placed in use.

Overprinted

1896-97

J28	D1 1c bister	.35	.30
	On cover, postage due usage		500.00
	On cover, postage usage		—
a.	Double overprint		
J29	D2 5c vermilion	.45	.25
	On cover, postage due usage		500.00
	On cover, postage usage		150.00
a.	Double overprint		
b.	Inverted overprint		
J30	D3 10c orange	.55	.35
	On cover, postage due usage		500.00
	On cover, postage usage		300.00
a.	Inverted overprint		
J31	D4 20c blue	.65	.50
	On cover, postage due usage		500.00
	On cover, postage usage		300.00
a.	Double overprint		
J32	A22 50c red ('97)	.75	.50
	On cover, postage due usage		750.00
	On cover, postage usage		—
J33	A23 1s brown ('97)	1.00	.65
	On cover, postage due usage		750.00
	On cover, postage usage		—
a.	Double overprint		
b.	Inverted overprint		
	Nos. J28-J33 (6)	3.75	2.55

Liberty — D6

1899 Engr.

J34	D6 5s yel grn	1.00	*5.00*
J35	D6 10s dl vio	900.00	900.00

For surcharge see No. J39.

1902

On No. 159

J36	A31 5c on 10s bl grn	1.00	.80
a.	Double surcharge	12.00	12.00

On No. J4

J37	D4 1c on 20c blue	.50	.40
	On cover, postage due usage		750.00
	On cover, postage usage		—
a.	"DEFICIT" omitted	6.50	2.00
b.	"DEFICIT" double	6.50	2.00
c.	"UN CENTAVO" double	6.00	2.00
d.	"UN CENTAVO" omitted	8.25	6.00

Surcharged Vertically

J38	D4 5c on 20c blue	1.50	1.00

On No. J35

J39	D6 1c on 10s dull vio	.60	.50
	Nos. J36-J39 (4)	3.60	2.70

D7

1909 Engr. *Perf. 12*

J40	D7 1c red brown	.50	.20
	On cover, postage due usage		100.00
	On cover, postage usage		20.00
J41	D7 5c red brown	.50	.20
	On cover, postage due usage		50.00
	On cover, postage usage		10.00
J42	D7 10c red brown	.60	.20
	On cover, postage due usage		50.00
	On cover, postage usage		10.00
J43	D7 50c red brown	.90	.20
	On cover, postage due usage		200.00
	On cover, postage usage		30.00
	Nos. J40-J43 (4)	2.50	.80

1921

Size: 18¼x22mm

J44	D7 1c violet brown	.25	.20
	On cover, postage due usage		100.00
	On cover, postage usage		20.00
J45	D7 2c violet brown	.25	.20
	On cover, postage due usage		50.00
	On cover, postage usage		10.00
J46	D7 5c violet brown	.35	.20
	On cover, postage due usage		50.00
	On cover, postage usage		10.00
J47	D7 10c violet brown	.50	.25
	On cover, postage due usage		50.00
	On cover, postage usage		10.00
J48	D7 50c violet brown	1.60	.75
	On cover, postage due usage		200.00
	On cover, postage usage		30.00
J49	D7 1s violet brown	7.50	3.00
	On cover, postage due usage		—
	On cover, postage usage		30.00
J50	D7 2s violet brown	12.00	3.50
	On cover, postage due usage		—
	On cover, postage usage		30.00
	Nos. J44-J50 (7)	22.45	8.10

Nos. J49 and J50 have the circle at the center replaced by a shield containing "S/.", in addition to the numeral.

In 1929 during a shortage of regular postage stamps, some of the Postage Due stamps of 1921 were used instead.

See Nos. J50A-J52, J55-J56. For surcharges see Nos. 204-207, 757.

Type of 1909-22

Size: 18¾x23mm

J50A	D7 2c violet brown	.75	.20
	On cover, postage due usage		50.00
	On cover, postage usage		10.00
J50B	D7 10c violet brown	.75	.20
	On cover, postage due usage		50.00
	On cover, postage usage		10.00

Type of 1909-22 Issues

1932 Photo. *Perf. 14½x14*

J51	D7 2c violet brown	.75	.25
	On cover, postage due usage		50.00
	On cover, postage usage		10.00
J52	D7 10c violet brown	.75	.25
	On cover, postage due usage		50.00
	On cover, postage usage		10.00

Regular Stamps of 1934-35 Overprinted in Black

1935 *Perf. 13*

J53	A131 2c deep claret	.75	.50
	On cover, postage due usage		100.00
	On cover, postage usage		—
J54	A117 10c crimson	.75	.50
	On cover, postage due usage		100.00
	On cover, postage usage		—

Type of 1909-32

Size: 19x23mm

Imprint: "Waterlow & Sons, Limited, Londres."

1936 Engr. *Perf. 12½*

J55	D7 2c light brown	.20	.20
	On cover, postage due usage		50.00
	On cover, postage usage		100.00
J56	D7 10c gray green	.50	.50
	On cover, postage due usage		50.00
	On cover, postage usage		100.00

OFFICIAL STAMPS

Regular Issue of 1886 Overprinted in Red

1890, Feb. 2

O2	A17 1c dl vio	1.40	1.40
	On cover		150.00
a.	Double overprint	8.25	8.25
O3	A18 2c green	1.40	1.40
	On cover		150.00
a.	Double overprint		
b.	Inverted overprint	8.25	8.25
O4	A19 5c orange	2.00	1.60
	On cover		150.00
a.	Inverted overprint	8.25	8.25
b.	Double overprint	8.25	8.25
O5	A20 10c slate	1.00	.65
	On cover		150.00
a.	Double overprint	8.25	8.25
b.	Inverted overprint	8.25	8.25
O6	A21 20c blue	3.00	2.00
	On cover		200.00
a.	Double overprint	8.25	8.25
b.	Inverted overprint	8.25	8.25
O7	A22 50c red	4.00	2.00
a.	Inverted overprint	12.00	
b.	Double overprint		
O8	A23 1s brown	5.00	4.50
a.	Double overprint	17.00	17.00
b.	Inverted overprint	17.00	17.00
	Nos. O2-O8 (7)	17.80	13.55

Nos. 118-124 (Bermudez Ovpt.) Overprinted Type "a" in Red

1894, Oct.

O9	A17 1c green	1.40	1.40
	On cover		300.00
a.	"Gobierno" and head invtd.	6.50	5.50
b.	Dbl. ovpt. of "Gobierno"		
O10	A17 1c orange	22.50	20.00
	On cover		300.00
O11	A18 2c rose	1.40	1.40
	On cover		300.00
a.	Overprinted head inverted	10.00	10.00
b.	Both overprints inverted		
O12	A18 2c violet	1.40	1.40
	On cover		300.00
a.	"Gobierno" double		
O13	A19 5c ultra	22.50	20.00
	On cover		300.00
a.	Both overprints inverted		
O14	A19 5c blue	10.00	9.00
	On cover		300.00

O15 A20 10c green 3.50 3.50
On cover 300.00
O16 A22 50c green 5.00 5.00
Nos. O9-O16 (8) 67.70 61.70

Nos. 125-126 ("Horseshoe" Ovpt.) Overprinted Type "a" in Red

O17 A18 2c vermilion 2.00 2.00
O18 A19 5c blue 2.00 2.00

Nos. 105, 107, 109, 113 Overprinted Type "a" in Red

1895, May

O19 A17 1c vermilion 8.25 8.25
On cover 300.00
O20 A18 2c dp ultra 8.25 8.25
On cover 300.00
O21 A12 5c claret 6.50 6.50
On cover 300.00
O22 A14 20c dp ultra 6.50 6.50
On cover 300.00
Nos. O19-O22 (4) 29.50 29.50

Nos. O2-O22 have been extensively counterfeited.

Nos. 141, 148, 149, 151 Overprinted in Black

1896-1901

O23 A24 1c ultra .20 .20
On cover 30.00
O24 A25 10c yellow 1.00 .50
On cover 30.00
a. Double overprint
O25 A25 10c gray blk ('01) .20 .20
On cover 30.00
O26 A26 50c brt rose .40 .25
On cover 60.00
Nos. O23-O26 (4) 1.80 1.15

O1

1909-14 Engr. *Perf. 12*
Size: 18½x22mm

O27 O1 1c red .20 .20
On cover 30.00
a. 1c brown red .20 .20
On cover 30.00
O28 O1 1c orange ('14) .50 .35
On cover 30.00
O29 O1 10c bis brn ('14) .20 .20
On cover 30.00
a. 10c violet brown .20 .20
On cover 30.00
O30 O1 50c ol grn ('14) .60 .35
On cover 60.00
a. 50c blue green 1.00 .35
On cover 60.00

Size: 18¾x23½mm

O30B O1 10c vio brn .50 .20
On cover 30.00
Nos. O27-O30B (5) 2.00 1.30

See Nos. O31, O33-O34. For overprints and surcharge see Nos. 201-203, 760.

1933 Photo. *Perf. 15x14*

O31 O1 10c violet brown .50 .20
On cover 40.00

No. 319 Overprinted in Black

1935 Unwmk. *Perf. 13*

O32 A117 10c crimson .20 .20
On cover 40.00

Type of 1909-33
Imprint: "Waterlow & Sons, Limited, Londres."

1936 Engr. *Perf. 12½*
Size: 19x23mm

O33 O1 10c light brown .20 .20
On cover 60.00
O34 O1 50c gray green .35 .35
On cover 60.00

PARCEL POST STAMPS

PP1

PP2

PP3

1897 Typeset Unwmk. *Perf. 12*

Q1 PP1 1c dull lilac 2.25 1.90
Q2 PP2 2c bister 2.50 2.25
a. 2c olive 2.50 2.25
b. 2c yellow 2.50 2.25
c. Laid paper 65.00 65.00
Q3 PP3 5c dk bl 10.00 6.50
a. Tête bêche pair *375.00*
Q4 PP3 10c vio brn 14.00 10.00
Q5 PP3 20c rose red 17.00 14.00
Q6 PP3 50c bl grn 45.00 37.50
Nos. Q1-Q6 (6) 90.75 72.15

Surcharged in Black — UN CENTAVO

1903-04

Q7 PP3 1c on 20c rose red 12.00 10.00
Q8 PP3 1c on 50c bl grn 12.00 10.00
Q9 PP3 5c on 10c vio brn 80.00 65.00
a. Inverted surcharge 125.00 110.00
b. Double surcharge
Nos. Q7-Q9 (3) 104.00 85.00

POSTAL TAX STAMPS

Plebiscite Issues

These stamps were not used in Tacna and Arica (which were under Chilean occupation) but were used in Peru to pay a supplementary tax on letters, etc.

It was intended that the money derived from the sale of these stamps should be used to help defray the expenses of the plebiscite.

Morro Arica — PT1

Adm. Grau and Col. Bolognesi Reviewing Troops — PT2

Bolognesi Monument PT3

1925-26 Unwmk. Litho. *Perf. 12*

RA1 PT1 5c dp bl 1.50 .35
RA2 PT1 5c rose red .80 .25
RA3 PT1 5c yel grn .70 .25
RA4 PT2 10c brown 3.00 .80
RA5 PT3 50c bl grn 19.00 9.00
Nos. RA1-RA5 (5) 25.00 10.65

PT4

1926

RA6 PT4 2c orange .30 .20

PT5

1927-28

RA7 PT5 2c dp org .60 .20
RA8 PT5 2c red brn .60 .20
RA9 PT5 2c dk bl .60 .20
RA10 PT5 2c gray vio .40 .20
RA11 PT5 2c bl grn ('28) .40 .20
RA12 PT5 20c red 2.50 1.00
Nos. RA7-RA12 (6) 5.10 2.00

PT6

1928 Engr.

RA13 PT6 2c dk vio .20 .20

The use of the Plebiscite stamps was discontinued July 26, 1929, after the settlement of the Tacna-Arica controversy with Chile.

For overprint see No. 261.

Unemployment Fund Issues

These stamps were required in addition to the ordinary postage, on every letter or piece of postal matter. The money obtained by their sale was to assist the unemployed.

Nos. 273-275 Surcharged

1931

RA14 A95 2c on 4c red .65 .50
a. Inverted surcharge 3.50 3.50
RA15 A95 2c on 10c bl grn .50 .50
a. Inverted surcharge 3.50 3.50
RA16 A95 2c on 15c sl gray .50 .50
a. Inverted surcharge 3.50 3.50
Nos. RA14-RA16 (3) 1.65 1.50

"Labor" PT7

Blacksmith PT8

Two types of Nos. RA17-RA18:
I — Imprint 15mm.
II — Imprint 13¾mm.

Perf. 12x11½, 11½x12

1931-32 Litho.

RA17 PT7 2c emer (I) .20 .20
a. Type II .20
RA18 PT7 2c rose car (I) ('32) .20 .20
a. Type II .20

1932-34

RA19 PT8 2c dp gray .20 .20
RA20 PT8 2c pur ('34) .20 .20

Monument of 2nd of May — PT9

Perf. 13, 13½, 13x13½

1933-35 Photo.

RA21 PT9 2c bl vio .20 .20
RA22 PT9 2c org ('34) .20 .20
RA23 PT9 2c brn vio ('35) .20 .20
Nos. RA21-RA23 (3) .60 .60

For overprint see No. RA27.

No. 307 Overprinted in Black

1934 *Perf. 13½*

RA24 A111 2c green .20 .20
a. Inverted overprint 2.00 2.00

No. 339 Overprinted in Black

1935

RA25 A131 2c deep claret .20 .20

No. 339 Overprinted Type "a" in Black

1936 Unwmk. *Perf. 13½*

RA26 A131 2c deep claret .20 .20

No. RA23 Overprinted in Black

1936 *Perf. 13x13½*

RA27 PT9 2c brn vio .20 .20
a. Double overprint 1.40
b. Overprint reading down 1.40
c. Overprint double, reading down 1.40

St. Rosa of Lima — PT10

"Protection" by John Q. A. Ward — PT11

1937 **Engr.** ***Perf. 12***

RA28	PT10 2c car rose	.20	.20

Nos. RA27 and RA28 represented a tax to help erect a church.

Imprint: "American Bank Note Company"

1938 **Litho.**

RA29	PT11 2c brown	.20	.20

The tax was to help the unemployed.
See Nos. RA30, RA34, RA40. For surcharges see Nos. 501A, 674-678, 681-682, 709-711, 757.

OCCUPATION STAMPS

Issued under Chilean Occupation

Stamps formerly listed as Nos. N1-N10 are regular issues of Chile canceled in Peru.

Stamps of Peru, 1874-80, Overprinted in Red, Blue or Black

1881-82 ***Perf. 12***

N11	A17 1c org (Bl)	.50	1.00
a.	Inverted overprint		
N12	A18 2c dk vio (Bk)	.50	4.00
a.	Inverted overprint	16.50	
b.	Double overprint	22.50	
N13	A18 2c rose (Bk)	1.60	*18.00*
a.	Inverted overprint		
N14	A19 5c bl (R)	55.00	62.50
a.	Inverted overprint		
N15	A19 5c ultra (R)	90.00	100.00
N16	A20 10c grn (R)	.50	*1.60*
a.	Inverted overprint	6.50	6.50
b.	Double overprint	12.00	12.00
N17	A21 20c brn red (Bl)	80.00	125.00
	Nos. N11-N17 (7)	228.10	312.10

Reprints of No. N17 have the overprint in bright blue; on the originals it is in dull ultramarine. Nos. N11 and N12 exist with reprinted overprint in red or yellow. There are numerous counterfeits with the overprint in both correct and fancy colors.

Same, with Additional Overprint in Black

1882

N19	A17 1c grn (R)	.50	.80
a.	Arms inverted	8.25	10.00
b.	Arms double	5.50	6.50
c.	Horseshoe inverted	12.00	13.50
N20	A19 5c bl (R)	.80	.80
a.	Arms inverted	13.50	15.00
b.	Arms double	13.50	15.00
N21	A22 50c rose (Bk)	1.60	2.00
a.	Arms inverted	10.00	
N22	A22 50c rose (Bl)	1.60	2.75
N23	A23 1s ultra (R)	3.25	4.50
a.	Arms inverted	13.50	
b.	Horseshoe inverted	16.50	
c.	Arms and horseshoe inverted	20.00	
d.	Arms double	13.50	
	Nos. N19-N23 (5)	7.75	10.85

PROVISIONAL ISSUES

Stamps Issued in Various Cities of Peru during the Chilean Occupation of Lima and Callao

During the Chilean-Peruvian War which took place in 1879 to 1882, the Chilean forces occupied the two largest cities in Peru, Lima & Callao. As these cities were the source of supply of postage stamps, Peruvians in other sections of the country were left without stamps and were forced to the expedient of making provisional issues from whatever material was at hand. Many of these were former canceling devices made over for this purpose. Counterfeits exist of many of the overprinted stamps.

ANCACHS

(See Note under "Provisional Issues")

Regular Issue of Peru, Overprinted in Manuscript in Black

1884 **Unwmk.** ***Perf. 12***

1N1	A19 5c blue	57.50	55.00

Regular Issues of Peru, Overprinted in Black

Overprinted **FRANCA**

1N2	A19 5c blue	18.00	16.50

Overprinted

1N3	A19 5c blue	90.00	82.50
1N4	A20 10c green	55.00	40.00
1N5	A20 10c slate	55.00	35.00

Same, with Additional Overprint "FRANCA"

1N6	A20 10c green	82.50	42.50

Overprinted

1N7	A19 5c blue	30.00	25.00
1N8	A20 10c green	30.00	25.00

Same, with Additional Overprint "FRANCA"

1N9	A20 10c green		

A1

Revenue Stamp of Peru, 1878-79, Overprinted in Black "CORREO Y FISCAL" and "FRANCA"

1N10	A1 10c yellow	37.50	37.50

APURIMAC

(See Note under "Provisional Issues")

Provisional Issue of Arequipa Overprinted in Black

ADMON. PRAL. DE
CORREOS DEL DEP^TO^ DE
APURIMAC
==ABANCAY==

Overprint Covers Two Stamps

1885 **Unwmk.** ***Imperf.***

2N1	A6 10c gray	100.00	90.00

Some experts question the status of No. 2N1.

AREQUIPA

(See Note under "Provisional Issues")

Coat of Arms
A1 A2

Overprint ("PROVISIONAL 1881-1882") in Black

1881, Jan. **Unwmk.** ***Imperf.***

3N1	A1 10c blue	2.50	3.50
a.	10c ultramarine	2.50	4.00
b.	Double overprint	12.00	13.50
c.	Overprinted on back of stamp	8.25	10.00
3N2	A2 25c rose	2.50	6.00
a.	"2" in upper left corner invtd.	8.25	
b.	"Cevtavos"	8.25	10.00
c.	Double overprint	12.00	13.50

The overprint also exists on 5s yellow.
The overprints "1883" in large figures or "Habilitado 1883" are fraudulent.
For overprints see Nos. 3N3, 4N1, 8N1, 10N1, 15N1-15N3.

With Additional Overprint Handstamped in Red

1881, Feb.

3N3	A1 10c blue	3.50	3.50
a.	10c ultramarine	13.50	8.25

A4

1883 **Litho.**

3N7	A4 10c dull rose	3.50	5.00
a.	10c vermilion	3.50	5.00

Overprinted in Blue like No. 3N3

3N9	A4 10c vermilion	5.00	4.00
a.	10c dull rose	5.00	4.00

See No. 3N10. For overprints see Nos. 8N2, 8N9, 10N2, 15N4.

Reprints of No. 3N9 are in different colors from the originals, orange, bright red, etc. They are printed in sheets of 20 instead of 25.

Redrawn

3N10	A4 10c brick red (Bl)	160.00	

The redrawn stamp has small triangles without arabesques in the lower spandrels. The palm branch at left of the shield and other parts of the design have been redrawn.

Same Overprint in Black, Violet or Magenta On Regular Issues of Peru

1884 **Embossed with Grill** ***Perf. 12***

3N11	A17 1c org (Bk, V or M)	6.50	6.50
3N12	A18 2c dk vio (Bk)	6.50	6.50
3N13	A19 5c bl (Bk, V or M)	2.00	1.40
a.	5c ultramarine (Bk or M)	8.25	6.50
3N15	A20 10c sl (Bk)	3.50	2.50
3N16	A21 20c brn red (Bk, V or M)	25.00	25.00
3N18	A22 50c grn (Bk or V)	25.00	25.00
3N20	A23 1s rose (Bk or V)	35.00	35.00
	Nos. 3N11-3N20 (7)	103.50	101.90

A5

A6

Rear Admiral M. L. Grau
A7

Col. Francisco Bolognesi
A8

Same Overprint as on Previous Issues

1885 ***Imperf.***

3N22	A5 5c olive (Bk)	5.25	5.25
3N23	A6 10c gray (Bk)	5.25	4.75
3N25	A7 5c blue (Bk)	5.25	4.75
3N26	A8 10c olive (Bk)	5.25	3.25
	Nos. 3N22-3N26 (4)	21.00	18.00

For overprints see Nos. 2N1, 8N5-8N6, 8N12-8N13, 10N9, 10N12, 15N10-15N12.

These stamps have been reprinted without overprint; they exist however with forged overprint. Originals are on thicker paper with distinct mesh, reprints on paper without mesh.

Without Overprint

3N22a	A5 5c olive	5.25	5.25
3N23a	A6 10c gray	4.00	3.25
3N25a	A7 5c blue	4.00	3.25
3N26a	A8 10c olive	4.00	3.25
	Nos. 3N22a-3N26a (4)	17.25	15.00

AYACUCHO

(See Note under "Provisional Issues")

Provisional Issue of Arequipa Overprinted in Black

1881 **Unwmk.** ***Imperf.***

4N1	A1 10c blue	82.50	70.00
a.	10c ultramarine	82.50	70.00

CHACHAPOYAS

(See Note under "Provisional Issues")

Regular Issue of Peru Overprinted in Black

1884 **Unwmk.** ***Perf. 12***

5N1	A19 5c ultra	100.00	90.00

CHALA

(See Note under "Provisional Issues")

Regular Issues of Peru Overprinted in Black

1884 **Unwmk.** ***Perf. 12***

6N1	A19 5c blue	8.25	6.50
6N2	A20 10c slate	10.00	8.25

CHICLAYO

(See Note under "Provisional Issues")

Regular Issue of Peru Overprinted in Black

1884 **Unwmk.** ***Perf. 12***

7N1 A19 5c blue 16.50 10.00

Same, Overprinted

7N2 A19 5c blue 35.00 22.50

CUZCO

(See Note under "Provisional Issues")

Provisional Issues of Arequipa Overprinted in Black

1881-85 **Unwmk.** ***Imperf.***

8N1 A1 10c blue 70.00 60.00
8N2 A4 10c red 70.00 60.00

Overprinted "CUZCO" in an oval of dots

8N5 A5 5c olive 110.00 100.00
8N6 A6 10c gray 80.00 75.00

Regular Issue of Peru Overprinted in Black "CUZCO" in a Circle

Perf. 12

8N7 A19 5c blue 50.00 50.00

Provisional Issues of Arequipa Overprinted in Black

1883 ***Imperf.***

8N9 A4 10c red 10.00 10.00

Same Overprint in Black on Regular Issues of Peru

1884 ***Perf. 12***

8N10 A19 5c blue 16.50 10.00
8N11 A20 10c slate 16.50 10.00

Same Overprint in Black on Provisional Issues of Arequipa

Imperf

8N12 A5 5c olive 27.50 27.50
8N13 A6 10c gray 8.00 8.00

Postage Due Stamps of Peru Surcharged in Black

Perf. 12

8N14 D1 10c on 1c bis 110.00 100.00
8N15 D3 10c on 10c org 110.00 100.00

HUACHO

(See Note under "Provisional Issues")

Regular Issues of Peru Overprinted in Black

1884 **Unwmk.** ***Perf. 12***

9N1 A19 5c blue 8.00 8.00
9N2 A20 10c green 6.00 6.00
9N3 A20 10c slate 16.00 16.00
Nos. 9N1-9N3 (3) 30.00 30.00

MOQUEGUA

(See Note under "Provisional Issues")

Provisional Issues of Arequipa Overprinted in Violet

Overprint 27mm wide (illustration reduced).

1881-83 **Unwmk.** ***Imperf.***

10N1 A1 10c blue 42.50 40.00
10N2 A4 10c red ('83) 42.50 40.00

Same Overprint on Regular Issues of Peru in Violet

1884 ***Perf. 12***

10N3 A17 1c orange 42.50 40.00
10N4 A19 5c blue 37.50 30.00

Red Overprint

10N5 A19 5c blue 30.00 20.00

Same Overprint in Violet on Provisional Issues of Peru of 1880

Perf. 12

10N6 A17 1c grn (R) 8.25 6.50
10N7 A18 2c rose (Bl) 10.00 10.00
10N8 A19 5c bl (R) 20.00 20.00

Same Overprint in Violet on Provisional Issue of Arequipa

1885 ***Imperf.***

10N9 A6 10c gray 57.50 50.00

Regular Issues of Peru Overprinted in Violet

Perf. 12

10N10 A19 5c blue 110.00 65.00
10N11 A20 10c slate 45.00 25.00

Same Overprint in Violet on Provisional Issue of Arequipa

Imperf

10N12 A6 10c gray 70.00 65.00

PAITA

(See Note under "Provisional Issues")

Regular Issues of Peru Overprinted

Black Overprint

1884 **Unwmk.** ***Perf. 12***

11N1 A19 5c blue 22.50 22.50
a. 5c ultramarine
11N2 A20 10c green 15.00 15.00
11N3 A20 10c slate 22.50 22.50

Red Overprint

11N4 A19 5c blue 22.50 22.50

Overprint lacks ornaments on #11N4-11N5.

Violet Overprint. Letters 5½mm High

11N5 A19 5c ultra 22.50 22.50
a. 5c blue

PASCO

(See Note under "Provisional Issues")

Regular Issues of Peru Overprinted in Magenta or Black

1884 **Unwmk.** ***Perf. 12***

1 A19 5c blue (M) 16.00 12.50
a. 5c ultramarine (M) 22.50 22.50
2 A20 10c green (Bk) 35.00 30.00
3 A20 10c slate (Bk) 65.00 57.50
Nos. 12N1-12N3 (3) 116.00 100.00

PISCO

(See Note under "Provisional Issues")

Regular Issue of Peru Overprinted in Black

1884 **Unwmk.** ***Perf. 12***

13N1 A19 5c blue 190.00 160.00

PIURA

(See Note under "Provisional Issues")

Regular Issues of Peru Overprinted in Black

1884 **Unwmk.** ***Perf. 12***

14N1 A19 5c blue 20.00 10.00
a. 5c ultramarine 25.00 13.50
14N2 A21 20c brn red 82.50 82.50
14N3 A22 50c green 200.00 200.00

Same Overprint in Black on Provisional Issues of Peru of 1881

14N4 A17 1c grn (R) 22.50 22.50
14N5 A18 2c rose (Bl) 40.00 40.00
14N6 A19 5c ultra (R) 50.00 50.00

Regular Issues of Peru Overprinted in Violet, Black or Blue

14N7 A19 5c bl (V) 16.00 10.00
a. 5c ultramarine (V) 16.00 10.00
b. 5c ultramarine (Bk) 16.00 10.00
14N8 A21 20c brn red (Bk) 82.50 82.50
14N9 A21 20c brn red (Bl) 82.50 82.50

Same Overprint in Black on Provisional Issues of Peru of 1881

14N10 A17 1c grn (R) 20.00 20.00
14N11 A19 5c bl (R) 22.50 22.50
a. 5c ultramarine (R) 40.00 40.00

Regular Issues of Peru Overprinted in Black

14N13 A19 5c blue 4.00 3.50
14N14 A21 20c brn red 82.50 82.50

Regular Issues of Peru Overprinted in Black

14N15 A19 5c ultra 70.00 65.00
14N16 A21 20c brn red 140.00 125.00

Same Overprint on Postage Due Stamp of Peru

14N18 D3 10c orange 80.00 67.50

PUNO

(See Note under "Provisional Issues")

Provisional Issue of Arequipa Overprinted in Violet or Blue

Diameter of outer circle 20½mm, PUNO 11½mm wide, M 3½mm wide.

Other types of this overprint are fraudulent.

1882-83 **Unwmk.** ***Imperf.***

15N1 A1 10c blue (V) 16.00 16.00
a. 10c ultramarine (V) 20.00 20.00
15N3 A2 25c red (V) 25.00 20.00
15N4 A4 10c dl rose (Bl) 25.00 25.00
a. 10c vermilion (Bl) 25.00 25.00

The overprint also exists on 5s yellow of Arequipa.

Same Overprint in Magenta on Regular Issues of Peru

1884 ***Perf. 12***

15N5 A17 1c orange 12.00 12.00
15N6 A18 2c violet 35.00 35.00
15N7 A19 5c blue 8.25 8.25

Violet Overprint

15N8 A19 5c blue 8.25 8.25
a. 5c ultramarine 12.00 12.00

Same Overprint in Black on Provisional Issues of Arequipa

1885 ***Imperf.***

15N10 A5 5c olive 16.00 13.50
15N11 A6 10c gray 5.50 5.50
15N12 A8 10c olive 10.00 10.00

Regular Issues of Peru Overprinted in Magenta

1884 ***Perf. 12***

15N13 A17 1c orange 10.00 8.25
15N14 A18 2c violet 13.50 12.00
15N15 A19 5c blue 5.50 5.50
a. 5c ultramarine 11.00 11.00
15N16 A20 10c green
15N17 A21 20c brn red 82.50 82.50
15N18 A22 50c green

YCA

(See Note under "Provisional Issues")

Regular Issues of Peru Overprinted in Violet

1884 **Unwmk.** ***Perf. 12***

16N1 A17 1c orange 40.00 40.00
16N3 A19 5c blue 12.00 6.75

Black Overprint

16N5 A19 5c blue 10.00 5.25

Magenta Overprint

16N6 A19 5c blue 10.00 5.25
16N7 A20 10c slate 30.00 30.00

Regular Issues of Peru Overprinted in Black

16N12 A19 5c blue 150.00 140.00
16N13 A21 20c brown 190.00 160.00

Regular Issues of Peru Overprinted in Carmine

16N14 A19 5c blue 150.00 140.00
16N15 A20 10c slate 190.00 160.00

Same, with Additional Overprint

No.	Design	Description	Unused	Used
16N21	A19	5c blue	160.00	150.00
16N22	A21	20c brn red	250.00	225.00

Various other stamps exist with the overprints "YCA" and "YCA VAPOR" but they are not known to have been issued. Some of them were made to fill a dealer's order and others are reprints or merely cancellations.

PHILIPPINES

ˌfi-lə-ˈpēnz

LOCATION — Group of about 7,100 islands and islets in the Malay Archipelago, north of Borneo, in the North Pacific Ocean
AREA — 115,830 sq. mi.
POP. — 53,350,000 (est. 1984)
CAPITAL — Quezon City

The islands were ceded to the United States by Spain in 1898. On November 15, 1935, they were given their independence, subject to a transition period which ended July 4, 1946.

20 Cuartos = 1 Real
100 Centavos de Peso = 1 Peso (1864)
100 Centimos de Escudo = 1 Escudo (1871)
100 Centimos de Peseta = 1 Peseta (1872)
1000 Milesimas de Peso = 100 Centimos or Centavos = 1 Peso (1878)
100 Cents = 1 Dollar (1899)
100 Centavos = 1 Peso (1906)

Watermarks

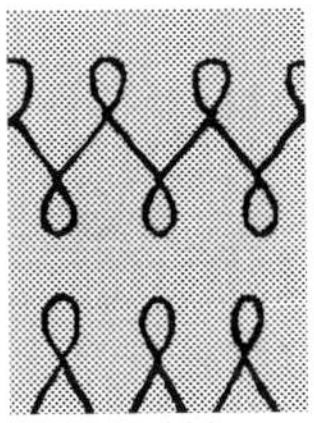

Wmk. 104 — Loops

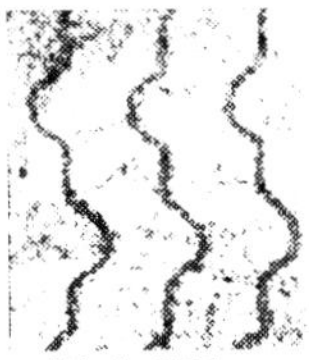

Wmk. 257 — Curved Wavy Lines

Watermark 104: loops from different watermark rows may or may not be directly opposite each other.

Wmk. 190PI — Single-lined PIPS

Wmk. 191PI — Double-lined PIPS

Watermark 191 has double-lined USPS.

Wmk. 233 — "Harrison & Sons, London." in Script

Issued under Spanish Dominion

The stamps of Philippine Islands punched with a round hole were used on telegraph receipts or had been withdrawn from use and punched to indicate that they were no longer available for postage. In this condition they sell for less, as compared to postally used copies.

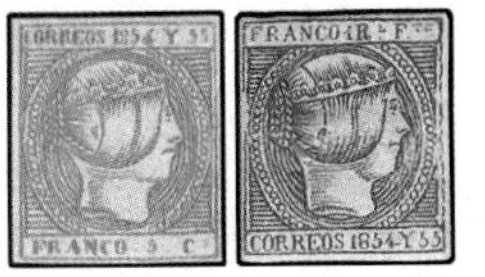

Queen Isabella II
A1 A2

1854 Unwmk. Engr. *Imperf.*

No.	Design	Description	Unused	Used
1	A1	5c orange	2,000.	300.
		On cover		*2,250.*
a.		5c brown orange	2,200.	375.
		On cover		*4,000.*
b.		5c reddish orange	2,200.	375.
		On cover		*4,000.*
2	A1	10c carmine	600.	240.
		On cover		*25,000.*
a.		10c pale rose	875.	375.
		On cover		*30,000.*
b.		10c dark carmine	850.	250.
		On cover		*30,000.*
d.		Half used as 5c on cover		50,000.
4	A2	1r blue	625.	275.
a.		1r slate blue	775.	300.
		On cover		—
b.		1r ultramarine	750.	300.
		On cover	700.	*20,000.*
c.		"CORROS"(#4, pos. 26)	*3,400.*	*2,000.*
d.		"CORROS"(#4a, pos. 26)	*4,250.*	*1,800.*
e.		1r dark bluish green	850.	350.
		On cover		*25,000.*
5	A2	2r green	975.	190.
a.		2r yellow green	850.	425.
		On cover, pair		*50,000.*
b.		2r emerald green	1,100.	225.
c.		2r olive green	950.	300.

Forty varieties of each value.

A 10c black exists. This is a proof or an unissued trial color. Value about $5,000.

For overprints see Nos. 25-25A.

Covers: There are two covers recorded with No. 2; two with No. 2a, four with No. 4a and one with a pair of No. 5a.

Values for pairs

No.	Design	Description	Unused	Used
1	A1	5c orange	4,500.	600.
a.		5c brown orange	4,750.	900.
b.		5c reddish orange	4,750.	900.
2	A1	10c carmine	1,400.	480.
a.		10c pale rose	1,900.	800.
b.		10c dark carmine	1,800.	650.
4	A2	1r blue	1,350.	550.
a.		1r slate blue	1,750.	750.
b.		1r ultramarine	1,750.	750.
c.		"CORROS"(#4, pos. 26)	*6,800.*	*2,500.*
d.		"CORROS"(#4a, pos. 26)	*9,200.*	*3,600.*
e.		1r dark bluish green	2,000.	725.
5	A2	2r green	2,100.	400.
a.		2r yellow green	2,100.	900.
b.		2r emerald green	2,300.	525.
c.		2r olive green	2,000.	700.

Values for blocks of 4

No.	Design	Description	Unused	Used
1	A1	5c orange	15,000.	2,000.
a.		5c brown orange	18,000.	2,800.
b.		5c reddish orange	18,000.	2,800.
2	A1	10c carmine	3,600.	1,400.
a.		10c pale rose	4,500.	2,000.
b.		10c dark carmine	4,100.	1,500.
4	A2	1r blue	3,800.	1,500.
a.		1r slate blue	4,600.	1,900.
b.		1r ultramarine	4,600.	1,900.
c.		"CORROS"(#4, pos. 26)	—	—
d.		"CORROS"(#4a, pos. 26)	—	—
e.		1r dark bluish green	5,100.	2,750.
5	A2	2r green	5,900.	1,400.
a.		2r yellow green	5,900.	1,500.
b.		2r emerald green	6,300.	2,300.
c.		2r olive green	5,700.	1,600.

A3

1855 Litho.

No.	Design	Description	Unused	Used
6	A3	5c pale red	1,500.	425.
		On cover		*8,000.*
a.		5c pale vermilion	1,550.	440.
		On cover		*8,000.*
b.		5c brown red	1,550.	440.
		On cover		*8,000.*

Four varieties.

Redrawn

No.	Design	Description	Unused	Used
7	A3a	5c vermilion	*7,750.*	*900.*
		On cover		*45,000.*

In the redrawn stamp the inner circle is smaller and is not broken by the labels at top and bottom. Only one variety.

Covers: There are five covers recorded with singles of No. 6, two with pairs; two covers with No. 7, plus one with a pair.

Values for pairs

No.	Design	Description	Unused	Used
6	A3	5c red	2,600.	875.
a.		5c pale vermilion	2,750.	950.
b.		5c brown red	2,750.	950.
7	A3	5c vermilion	*14,500.*	*1,800.*

Values for blocks of 4

No.	Design	Description	Unused	Used
6	A3	5c pale red	9,000.	3,750.
a.		5c pale vermilion	9,750.	4,250.
b.		5c brown red	9,750.	4,250.
7	A3	5c vermilion	—	*12,000.*

Queen Isabella II — A4

1856 Typo. Wmk. 104

No.	Design	Description	Unused	Used
8	A4	1r gray green	55.00	80.00
9	A4	2r carmine	325.00	200.00

Nos. 8 and 9 used can be distinguished from Cuba Nos. 2 and 3 only by the cancellations.

For overprints, see Nos. 26-27.

Queen Isabella II — A5

Dot After "CORREOS"

1859, Jan. 1 Litho. Unwmk.

No.	Design	Description	Unused	Used
10	A5	5c vermilion	13.00	6.75
		On cover		800.00
a.		5c scarlet	18.00	9.00
		On cover		805.00
b.		5c orange	26.00	13.00
		On cover		1,000.
11	A5	10c rose	12.50	*20.00*
		On cover		800.00
a.		10c lilac rose	16.50	*21.00*
		On cover		1,000.
b.		10c pale rose	16.50	*21.00*
		On cover		1,000.

Four varieties of each value, repeated in the sheet.

For overprint see No. 28.

Covers: Only one cover recorded bearing No. 11a.

Values for pairs

No.	Design	Description	Unused	Used
10	A5	5c vermilion	30.00	14.00
a.		5c scarlet	35.00	18.00
b.		5c orange	52.50	27.50
11	A5	10c lilac rose	23.00	*40.00*
a.		10c rose	32.50	37.50
b.		10c pale rose	32.50	37.50

Values for blocks of 4

No.	Design	Description	Unused	Used
10	A5	5c vermilion	55.00	27.50
a.		5c scarlet	80.00	40.00
b.		5c orange	115.00	55.00
11	A5	10c lilac rose	52.50	*80.00*
a.		10c rose	72.50	95.00
b.		10c pale rose	72.50	95.00

Covers

Values are for commercial covers paying correct rates. Philatelic covers sell for less.

Dot after CORREOS
A6 A7

1861-62

No.	Design	Description	Unused	Used
12	A6	5c vermilion	30.00	34.00
		On cover		*3,000.*
13	A7	5c dull red ('62)	160.00	75.00
		On cover		*4,000.*
a.		5c brownish red ('62)	190.00	85.00
		On cover		*4,000.*

No. 12, one variety only, repeated in the sheet.

For overprint see No. 29.

Covers: There are about seven covers recorded with No. 12; eight with No. 13.

Values for pairs

No.	Design	Description	Unused	Used
12	A6	5c vermilion	67.50	67.50
13	A7	5c dull red	400.00	225.00
a.		5c brownish red	475.00	300.00

Values for blocks of 4

No.	Design	Description	Unused	Used
12	A6	5c vermilion	180.00	160.00
13	A7	5c dull red	950.00	550.00
a.		5c brownish red	1,100.	450.00

Colon after CORREOS — A8

A8a

A9

A10

1863

No.	Design	Description	Unused	Used
14	A8	5c vermilion	11.00	7.00
		On cover		*3,000.*
a.		10c carmine vermilion	12.50	10.00
		On cover		*3,000.*
b.		10c scarlet vermilion	12.50	10.00
		On cover		*3,000.*
15	A8	10c carmine	30.00	*55.00*
16	A8	1r violet	625.00	350.00
17	A8	2r blue	525.00	300.00
a.		2r dark blue	575.00	325.00
18	A8a	1r gray grn	250.00	125.00
		On cover		*1,250.*
a.		1r deep gray green	310.00	160.00
		On cover		1,700.
20	A9	1r emerald	140.00	40.00
		On cover		800.00
a.		1r green	150.00	45.00
		On cover		900.00
b.		1r yellow green	150.00	45.00
		On cover		*900.00*
c.		1r bluish green	160.00	60.00
		On cover		*1,000.*
		Nos. 14-20 (6)	1,581.	877.00

No. 18 has "CORREOS" 10½mm long, the point of the bust is rounded and is about 1mm from the circle which contains 94 pearls.

No. 20 has "CORREOS" 11mm long, and the bust ends in a sharp point which nearly touches the circle of 76 pearls.

For overprints see Nos. 30-34.

Values for pairs

No.	Design	Description	Unused	Used
14	A8	5c vermilion	29.00	14.50
a.		10c carmine vermilion	35.00	20.00
b.		10c scarlet vermilion	35.00	20.00
15	A8	10c carmine	85.00	*120.00*
16	A8	1r violet	1,400.	1,300.
17	A8	2r blue	1,150.	975.00
a.		2r dark blue	1,250.	1,050.
18	A8a	1r gray grn	525.00	260.00
a.		1r deep gray green	675.00	340.00
20	A9	1r emerald	300.00	125.00
a.		1r green	310.00	130.00
b.		1r yellow green	310.00	130.00
c.		1r bluish green	325.00	160.00

Values for blocks of 4

No.	Design	Description	Unused	Used
14	A8	5c vermilion	65.00	45.00
a.		10c carmine vermilion	75.00	45.00
b.		10c scarlet vermilion	75.00	45.00
15	A8	10c carmine	175.00	*250.00*
16	A8	1r violet	3,100.	2,750.
17	A8	2r blue	2,600.	2,400.
a.		2r dark blue	2,900.	2,650.
18	A8a	1r gray grn	1,200.	675.00
a.		1r deep gray green	1,500.	900.00
20	A9	1r emerald	700.00	300.00
a.		1r green	700.00	325.00
b.		1r yellow green	700.00	325.00
c.		1r bluish green	750.00	400.00

1864 Typo.

No.	Design	Description	Unused	Used
21	A10	3 1/8c blk, *yellow*	3.25	1.60
		On cover		400.00
a.		3 1/8c blk, *buff*	6.25	3.25
		On cover		400.00
22	A10	6 2/8c grn, *rose*	5.75	1.60
		On cover		500.00
23	A10	12 4/8c blue, *sal*	6.00	1.40
		On cover		400.00
a.		12 4/8c blue	26.00	7.50
		On cover		*750.00*
24	A10	25c red, *buff*	8.50	3.00
		On cover		700.00
a.		25c red, *rose*	14.00	5.75
		On cover		*800.00*
		Nos. 21-24 (4)	23.50	7.60

For overprints see Nos. 35-38.

Values for pairs

No.	Design	Description	Unused	Used
21	A10	3 1/8c blk, *yellow*	8.00	5.50
a.		3 1/8c blk, *buff*	16.00	10.00
22	A10	6 2/8c grn, *rose*	12.00	3.25
23	A10	12 4/8c blue, *sal*	16.00	3.00
a.		12 4/8c blue	65.00	24.00
24	A10	25c red, *buff*	19.00	9.00
a.		25c red, *rose*	36.00	17.00

Values for blocks of 4

No.	Design	Description	Unused	Used
21	A10	3 1/8c blk, *yellow*	19.00	14.00
a.		3 1/8c blk, *buff*	37.50	25.00
22	A10	6 2/8c grn, *rose*	24.00	6.50
23	A10	12 4/8c blue, *sal*	36.00	6.25
a.		12 4/8c blue	150.00	55.00
24	A10	25c red, *buff*	45.00	21.00
a.		25c red, *rose*	80.00	40.00

Preceding Issues Handstamped

1868-74

24A	A1 5c orange ('74)	*7,000.*	*1,000.*
25	A2 1r sl bl ('74)	*1,850.*	*800.00*
b.	"CORROS" (pos. 26)		*3,000.*
25A	A2 2r grn ('74)	*3,500.*	*775.00*
26	A4 1r grn, *bl* ('73)	160.00	70.00
27	A4 2r car, *bl* ('73)	300.00	200.00
27A	A5 5c vermilion ('74)	*3,000.*	*2,500.*
28	A5 10c rose ('74)	70.00	40.00
29	A7 5c dull red ('73)	225.00	110.00
30	A8 5c ver ('72)	100.00	30.00
	On cover		*3,500.*
31	A8 1r vio ('72)	650.00	375.00
	On cover		*20,000.*
32	A8 2r bl ('72)	475.00	275.00
33	A8a 1r gray grn ('71)	150.00	40.00
34	A9 1r emer ('71)	45.00	19.00
	On cover		1,000.
a.	1r green	50.00	24.00
35	A10 3 1/8c blk, *yellow*	9.00	4.50
	On cover		500.00
36	A10 6 2/8c grn, *rose*	9.00	4.50
	On cover		500.00
37	A10 12 4/8cbl, *salmon*	30.00	15.00
	On cover		500.00
38	A10 25c red, *buff*	27.50	14.00
	On cover		1,500.

Covers: There is one cover recorded with No. 31.

Reprints exist of #24A-38. These have crisp, sharp letters and a broken first "A" of "HABILITADO."

Imperforates

Imperforates of designs A11-A14 probably are from proof or trial sheets.

"Spain"
A11

King Amadeo
A12

1871 **Typo.** ***Perf. 14***

39	A11 5c blue	57.50	5.50
	On cover		500.00
40	A11 10c deep green	7.75	4.50
	On cover		500.00
41	A11 20c brown	67.50	30.00
	On cover		1,000.
42	A11 40c rose	82.50	37.50
	On cover		800.00
	Nos. 39-42 (4)	215.25	77.50

1872

43	A12 12c rose	12.50	4.00
	On cover		400.00
a.	12c dark rose	20.00	10.00
	On cover		500.00
44	A12 16c blue	120.00	27.50
	On cover		*5,000.*
a.	16c ultramarine	130.00	50.00
	On cover		*1,000.*
45	A12 25c gray lilac	9.25	4.00
	On cover		400.00
a.	25c lilac	13.00	6.50
	On cover		*750.00*
46	A12 62c violet	27.50	7.00
	On cover		500.00
47	A12 1p25c yellow brn	55.00	22.50
	On cover		*3,000.*
	Nos. 43-47 (5)	224.25	65.00

A 12c in deep blue and a 62c in rose exist but were not issued. Value $30 each.

Covers: There are two covers recorded with No. 47.

"Peace"
A13

King Alfonso XII
A14

1874

48	A13 12c gray lilac	18.00	4.25
	On cover		600.00
49	A13 25c ultra	6.50	2.25
	On cover		600.00
50	A13 62c rose	52.50	4.25
	On cover		600.00
51	A13 1p25c brown	275.00	65.00
	On cover		*2,000.*
	Nos. 48-51 (4)	352.00	75.75

1875-77

52	A14 2c rose	3.00	.75
	On cover		300.00
53	A14 2c dk blue ('77)	200.00	80.00
	On cover		*2,500.*
54	A14 6c orange ('77)	11.00	*13.00*
	On cover		800.00
55	A14 10c blue ('77)	4.00	.75
	On cover		400.00
56	A14 12c lilac ('76	4.00	.75
	On cover		300.00
57	A14 20c vio brn ('76	13.00	9.25
	On cover		*3,000.*
58	A14 25c dp green ('76	11.00	2.00
	On cover		*3,000.*
	Nos. 52-58 (7)	246.00	106.50

Imperforates of type A14 are from proof or trial sheets.

Nos. 52, 63 Handstamp Surcharged in Black or Blue

1877-79

59	A14 12c on 2c rose (Bk)	67.50	21.00
	On cover		*3,000.*
a.	Surcharge inverted	*550.00*	*350.00*
b.	Surcharge double	*425.00*	*325.00*
60	A16 12c on 25m blk (Bk) ('79)	80.00	35.00
	On cover		*4,000.*
a.	Surcharge inverted	*800.00*	*600.00*
61	A16 12c on 25m blk (Bl) ('79)	275.00	150.00
	On cover		—
	Nos. 59-61 (3)	422.50	206.00

A16

1878-79 **Typo.**

62	A16 25m black	3.25	.40
	On cover		250.00
63	A16 25m green ('79)	65.00	*60.00*
64	A16 50m dull lilac	32.50	9.75
	On cover		300.00
65	A16 0.0625 (62 1/2m) gray	62.50	14.50
a.	0.0625 (62 1/2m) gray lilac	105.00	30.00
66	A16 100m car ('79)	87.50	35.00
67	A16 100m yel grn ('79)	9.75	2.50
	On cover		350.00
68	A16 125m blue	5.75	.45
	On cover		250.00
69	A16 200m rose ('79)	35.00	5.50
	On cover		400.00
70	A16 200m vio rose ('79)	300.00	*600.00*
71	A16 250m bister ('79)	12.50	2.50
	On cover		400.00
	Nos. 62-71 (10)	613.75	*730.60*

Imperforates of type A16 are from proof or trial sheets.

For surcharges see Nos. 60-61, 72-75.

Covers: There is one cover recorded with No. 70.

Stamps of 1878-79 Surcharged:

a

UNIVERSAL DE
CONVENIO CORREOS
HABILITADO
2 cént de peso
b

1879

72	A16 (a) 2c on 25m grn	42.50	8.25
b.	Inverted surcharge	325.00	180.00
73	A16 (a) 8c on 100m car	37.50	6.75
	On cover		*2,000.*
a.	"COREROS"	115.00	60.00
74	A16 (b) 2c on 25m grn	175.00	42.50
75	A16 (b) 8c on 100m car	175.00	42.50
	Nos. 72-75 (4)	430.00	100.00

Covers: There are four covers recorded with No. 73.

A19

Original state: The medallion is surrounded by a heavy line of color of nearly even thickness, touching the line below "Filipinas"; the opening in the hair above the temple is narrow and pointed.

1st retouch: The line around the medallion is thin, except at the upper right, and does not touch the horizontal line above it; the opening in the hair is slightly wider and rounded; the lock of hair above the forehead is shaped like a broad "V" and ends in a point; there is a faint white line below it, which is not found on the original. The shape of the hair and the width of the white line vary.

2nd retouch: The lock of hair is less pointed; the white line is much broader.

1880-86 **Typo.**

76	A19 2c carmine	.75	*.65*
	On cover		200.00
77	A19 2 1/2c brown	6.50	1.50
	On cover		350.00
78	A19 2 4/8c ultra ('82)	1.00	1.75
	On cover		350.00
79	A19 2 4/8c ultra, 1st retouch ('83)	.75	1.50
	On cover		350.00
80	A19 2 4/8c ultra, 2nd retouch ('86)	8.50	3.50
	On cover		350.00
81	A19 5c gray ('82)	.75	1.50
	On cover		350.00
a.	5c gray blue	1.25	1.75
	On cover		375.00
82	A19 6 2/8c dp grn ('82)	5.75	9.00
	On cover		*1,000.*
83	A19 8c yellow brn	30.00	5.25
	On cover		200.00
84	A19 10c green	375.00	350.00
85	A19 10c brn lil ('82)	3.00	*3.50*
	On cover		350.00
a.	10c brown violet	12.00	5.75
86	A19 12 4/8c brt rose ('82)	1.50	1.50
	On cover		350.00
87	A19 20c bis brn ('82)	3.00	1.50
	On cover		300.00
88	A19 25c dk brn ('82)	3.75	1.50
	On cover		500.00
	Nos. 76-88 (13)	440.25	382.65

See #137-139. For surcharges see #89-108, 110-111.

Surcharges exist double or inverted on many of Nos. 89-136.

Stamps and Type of 1880-86 Handstamp Surcharged in Black, Green Yellow or Red:

c

d

e

f

1881-88

Design A19

Black Surcharge

89	(c) 2c on 2 1/2c	3.75	2.00
91	(f) 10c on 2 4/8c (#80) ('87)	5.50	1.75
92	(d) 20c on 8c brn ('83)	8.50	2.75
93	(d) 1r on 2c ('83)	160.00	*275.00*
94	(d) 2r on 2 4/8c (#78; '83)	5.50	1.75
	On cover		*400.00*
a.	On No. 79	50.00	*85.00*
b.	On No. 80	50.00	*85.00*

Most used copies of No. 93 are hole punched. Postally used copies are rare.

Green or Yellow (#98A) Surcharge

95	(e) 8c on 2c ('83)	6.00	1.90
95A	(d+e) 8c on 1r on 2c ('83)	100.00	*250.00*
96	(d) 10c on 2c ('83)	4.75	1.90
97	(d) 1r on 2c ('83)	110.00	35.00
98	(d) 1r on 5c gray bl ('83)	5.50	2.75
98A	(d) 1r on 5c gray ('83)	105.00	175.00
99	(d) 1r on 8c brn ('83)	8.50	2.75

Red Surcharge

100	(f) 1c on 2 4/8c (#79; '87)	1.00	.75
101	(f) 1c on 2 4/8c (#80; '87)	3.00	1.50
102	(d) 16c on 2 4/8c (#78; '83)	8.50	2.75
103	(d) 1r on 2c ('83)	5.50	2.75
104	(d) 1r on 5c bl gray ('83)	16.00	4.50

Handstamp Surcharged in Magenta

g

h

1887

105	A19 (g) 8c on 2 4/8c (#79)	1.00	.75
	On cover		*400.00*
106	A19 (g) 8c on 2 4/8c (#80)	3.75	2.50
	On cover		*600.00*

1888

107	A19 (h) 2 4/8c on 1c gray grn	1.50	.85
108	A19 (h) 2 4/8c on 5c bl gray	1.70	.75
109	N1 (h) 2 4/8c on 1/8c grn	1.70	1.10
110	A19 (h) 2 4/8c on 50m bis	1.60	.70
111	A19 (h) 2 4/8c on 10c grn	1.50	.55
	Nos. 107-111 (5)	8.00	3.95

No. 109 is surcharged on a newspaper stamp of 1886-89 and has the inscriptions shown on cut N1.

On Revenue Stamps

R1

R2

R3(d)

Handstamp Surcharged in Black, Yellow, Green, Red, Blue or Magenta:

j

k

HABILITADO

PARA

CORREOS

m

1881-88

Black Surcharge

112	R1 (c) 2c on 10c bis	42.50	11.00
113	R1 (j) 2 4/8c on 10c bis	9.00	1.50
114	R1 (j) 2 4/8c on 2r bl	175.00	110.00
	On cover		*500.00*
115	R1 (j) 8c on 10c bis	*360.00*	*350.00*
116	R1 (j) 8c on 2r bl	7.25	1.75
118	R1 (d) 1r on 12 4/8c gray bl ('83)	6.75	3.25
	On cover		*600.00*
119	R1 (d) 1r on 10c bis ('82)	10.00	3.50

Yellow Surcharge

120	R2 (e) 2c on 200m grn ('82)	5.50	2.50
121	R1 (d) 16c on 2r bl ('83)	4.50	2.25

Green Surcharge

122	R1 (d) 1r on 10c bis ('83)	10.00	3.25

Red Surcharge

123	R1(d+e) 2r on 8c on 2r blue	40.00	25.00
a.	On 8c on 2r blue (d+d)	60.00	55.00
124	R1(d) 1r on 12 4/8c gray bl ('83)	14.00	11.00
125	R1(k) 6 2/8c on 12 4/8c gray bl ('85)	5.75	11.00
126	R3(d) 1r on 10p bis ('83)	85.00	20.00
127	R1(m) 1r green	290.00	*360.00*
127A	R1(m) 2r blue	525.00	*625.00*
127B	R1(d) 1r on 1r grn	375.00	360.00
128	R2(d) 1r on 1p grn ('83)	60.00	13.00

129 R2(d) 1r on 200m grn ('83) 70.00 *130.00*
129A R1(d) 2r on 2r blue *250.00 425.00*

The surcharge on No. 129A is pale red.

Blue Surcharge

129B R1(m) 10c bister ('81) *350.00 525.00*

Magenta Surcharge

130 R2(h) 2 4/8c on 200m grn ('88) 3.75 1.50
131 R2(h) 2 4/8c on 20c brn ('88) 11.00 5.00

On Telegraph Stamps

T1

T2

Surcharged in Red, or Black

1883-88

132 T1 (d) 2r on 250m ultra (R) 6.75 3.25
133 T1 (d) 20c on 250m ultra *575.00* 325.00
134 T1 (d) 2r on 250m ultra 8.75 4.00
135 T1 (d) 1r on 20c on 250m ultra (R & Bk) 8.00 4.00

Magenta Surcharge

136 T2 (h) 2 4/8c on 1c bis ('88) .80 .55

Most, if not all, used copies of No. 133 are hole-punched. Used value is for examples with hole punches.

Type of 1880-86 Redrawn

1887-89

137 A19 50m bister .55 *5.00*
On cover *500.00*
138 A19 1c gray grn ('88) .55 *4.00*
On cover *500.00*
a. 1c yellow green ('89) .60 *5.00*
On cover *600.00*
139 A19 6c yellow brn ('88) 8.50 *40.00*
On cover *2,000.*
Nos. 137-139 (3) 9.60 *49.00*

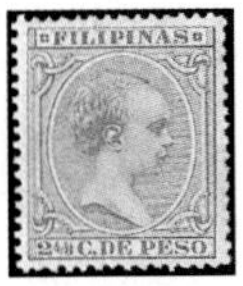
King Alfonso XIII — A36

1890-97 **Typo.**

140 A36 1c violet ('92) .60 *4.00*
On cover *500.00*
141 A36 1c rose ('95) 15.00 11.00
142 A36 1c bl grn ('96) 2.00 *3.25*
On cover *600.00*
143 A36 1c claret ('97) 12.00 *25.00*
144 A36 2c claret ('94) .20 *.20*
On cover *200.00*
145 A36 2c violet ('92) .20 *.20*
On cover *200.00*
146 A36 2c dk brn ('94) .20 *3.00*
On cover *400.00*
147 A36 2c ultra ('96) .30 *.30*
On cover *200.00*
148 A36 2c gray brn ('96) .70 *1.90*
On cover *400.00*
149 A36 2 4/8c dull blue .45 *.25*
On cover *200.00*
150 A36 2 4/8c ol gray ('92) .25 *1.10*
On cover *300.00*
151 A36 5c dark blue .45 *1.10*
On cover *300.00*
152 A36 5c dk ol gray .70 *1.10*
On cover *400.00*
153 A36 5c green ('92) .60 *.50*
On cover *300.00*
155 A36 5c vio brn ('96) 8.00 *11.00*
On cover *400.00*
156 A36 5c blue grn ('96) 5.25 *6.25*
157 A36 6c brown vio ('92) .25 *1.10*
158 A36 6c red orange ('94) .80 1.90
159 A36 6c car rose ('96) 5.25 *6.25*
160 A36 8c yellow grn .25 *.25*
On cover *200.00*
161 A36 8c ultra ('92) .60 *.25*
On cover *200.00*
162 A36 8c red brn ('94) .70 *.25*
On cover *200.00*
163 A36 10c blue grn 1.50 1.00
On cover *400.00*
164 A36 10c pale cl ('91) 1.25 *.35*
On cover *100.00*
165 A36 10c claret ('94) .60 *.25*
On cover *100.00*
166 A36 10c yel brn ('96) .70 *.25*
On cover *200.00*
167 A36 12 4/8c yellow grn .25 *1.10*
On cover *500.00*
168 A36 12 4/8c org ('92) .70 *1.10*
On cover *500.00*
169 A36 15c red brn ('92) .70 *.25*
On cover *300.00*
170 A36 15c rose ('94) 1.75 *.70*
On cover *300.00*
171 A36 15c bl grn ('96) 1.90 *1.75*
On cover *300.00*
172 A36 20c rose 65.00 32.50
173 A36 20c sal ('91) 25.00 16.00
174 A36 20c gray brn ('92) 3.75 *9.00*
On cover *700.00*
175 A36 20c dk vio ('94) 15.00 *16.00*
On cover *600.00*
176 A36 20c org ('96) 4.00 *2.00*
On cover *500.00*
177 A36 25c brown 8.00 *4.00*
On cover *700.00*
178 A36 25c dull bl ('91) 2.00 *3.25*
On cover *600.00*
179 A36 40c dk vio ('97) 14.00 *37.50*
180 A36 80c claret ('97) 30.00 *42.50*

Many of Nos. 140-180 exist imperf and in different colors. These are considered to be proofs.

Stamps of Previous Issues Handstamp Surcharged in Blue, Red, Black or Violet

1897

Blue Surcharge

181 A36 5c on 5c green 3.75 *5.00*
On cover *500.00*
182 A36 15c on 15c red brn 5.50 3.00
On cover *600.00*
183 A36 20c on 20c gray brn 12.00 *12.00*

Red Surcharge

185 A36 5c on 5c green 4.50 4.75
On cover *700.00*

Black Surcharge

187 A36 5c on 5c green 67.50 *175.00*
188 A36 15c on 15c rose 5.50 3.00
On cover *600.00*
189 A36 20c on 20c dk vio 35.00 18.00
190 A36 20c on 25c brown 25.00 *40.00*

Violet Surcharge

191 A36 15c on 15c rose *15.00* *20.00*
On cover *700.00*
Nos. 181-191 (9) 173.75 280.75

Inverted, double and other variations of this surcharge exist.

The 5c on 5c blue gray (#81a) was released during US Administration. The surcharge is a mixture of red and black inks.

Impressions in violet black are believed to be reprints. The following varieties are known: 5c on 2 4/8c olive gray, 5c on 5c blue green, 5c on 25c brown, 15c on 15c rose, 15c on 15c red brown, 15c on 25c brown, 20c on 20c gray brown, 20c on 20c dark violet, 20c on 25c brown. These surcharges are to be found double, inverted, etc.

King Alfonso XIII — A39

1898 **Typo.**

192 A39 1m orange brown .20 1.00
On cover *500.00*
193 A39 2m orange brown .20 *1.25*
On cover *600.00*
194 A39 3m orange brown .20 *1.25*
On cover *600.00*
195 A39 4m orange brown 9.00 *30.00*
196 A39 5m orange brown .20 2.00
On cover *500.00*
197 A39 1c black violet .20 .45
On cover *500.00*
198 A39 2c dk bl grn .20 .45
On cover *400.00*
199 A39 3c dk brown .20 .45
On cover *300.00*
200 A39 4c orange 17.50 *35.00*
201 A39 5c car rose .20 .45
On cover *300.00*
202 A39 6c dk blue .95 *1.25*
203 A39 8c gray brown .40 .25
On cover *200.00*
204 A39 10c vermilion 2.00 1.00
On cover *300.00*
205 A39 15c dull ol grn 1.60 .85
On cover *400.00*
206 A39 20c maroon 1.75 1.10
On cover *400.00*
207 A39 40c violet .95 *1.25*
208 A39 60c black 3.75 3.00
209 A39 80c red brown 6.00 4.00
210 A39 1p yellow green 20.00 *13.00*
211 A39 2p slate blue 27.50 *16.00*
Nos. 192-211 (20) 93.00 *114.00*

One cliche of No. 197 was included in error within the sheet of Puerto Rico No. 140. Pairs showing this error se-tenant are known. See Puerto Rico No. 140b.

Nos. 192-211 exist imperf. Value, set $800.

The Spanish surrendered in May 1898. Some Filipinos continued to fight until 1901. During this period provisional stamps were created in several areas. Some of these stamps may have been totally philatelic. See the Scott Specialized Catalogue of U. S. Stamps for stamps issued by Gen. Aguinaldo's Filipino Revolutionary Government.

Issued under US Administration

Regular Issues of the United States Overprinted in Black

On US No. 260

1899-1900 **Unwmk.** ***Perf. 12***

212 A96 50c orange 350.00 225.00
On cover —

On US Nos. 279, 279B, 279Bd, 279Be, 279Bf, 279Bc, 268, 281, 282C, 283, 284, 275 and 275a

Wmk. 191

213 A87 1c yellow grn 4.25 .60
On cover 10.00
a. Inverted overprint 32,500.
214 A88 2c red, type IV 1.75 .60
On cover 10.00
a. 2c orange red, type IV ('01) 1.75 .60
b. Booklet pane of 6, red, type IV ('00) 250.00 200.00
c. 2c reddish car, type IV 2.50 .90
On cover 12.50
d. 2c rose car, type IV 3.00 1.10
On cover 15.00
215 A89 3c purple 9.00 1.25
On cover 30.00
216 A91 5c blue 9.00 1.00
On cover 20.00
a. Inverted overprint *3,750.*
217 A94 10c brown, type I 35.00 4.00
On cover 60.00
217A A94 10c org brn, type II 135.00 27.50
On cover 160.00
218 A95 15c olive grn 40.00 8.00
On cover 110.00
219 A96 50c orange 125.00 37.50
On cover *400.00*
a. 50c red orange 250.00 55.00
Nos. 213-219 (8) 359.00 80.45

On US Nos. 280b, 282 and 272

1901

220 A90 4c orange brn 30.00 5.00
On cover 50.00
221 A92 6c lake 35.00 7.00
On cover 65.00
222 A93 8c violet brn 37.50 7.50
On cover 50.00

On US Nos. 276, 276A, 277a and 278

Red Overprint

223 A97 $1 blk, type I 450.00 250.00
On cover *800.00*
223A A97 $1 blk, type II 2,400. 750.00
On cover —
224 A98 $2 dk blue 450.00 325.00
On cover 3,250.
225 A99 $5 dk green 800.00 900.00
On cover *12,500.*

On US Nos. 300-313 and shades

1903-04

226 A115 1c blue green 7.00 .40
On cover 8.25
227 A116 2c carmine 9.00 1.10
On cover 10.00
228 A117 3c brt violet 67.50 12.50
On cover 55.00
229 A118 4c brown ('04) 75.00 22.50
On cover 40.00
a. 4c orange brown 80.00 20.00
230 A119 5c blue 17.50 1.00
On cover 22.50
231 A120 6c brnsh lake ('04) 85.00 22.50
On cover 65.00
232 A121 8c vio blk ('04) 50.00 15.00
On cover 300.00
233 A122 10c pale red brn ('04) 35.00 2.25
On cover 27.50
a. 10c red brown 30.00 3.00
b. Pair, one without ovpt. *1,500.*
234 A123 13c purple blk 35.00 17.50
a. 13c brown violet 35.00 17.50
On cover 55.00
235 A124 15c olive grn 60.00 15.00
On cover 100.00
236 A125 50c orange 125.00 35.00
On cover 300.00
Nos. 226-236 (11) 566.00 144.75

Red Overprint

237 A126 $1 black 450.00 250.00
On cover 750.00
238 A127 $2 dk blue ('04) 750.00 800.00
239 A128 $5 dk green ('04) 1,000. *5,000.*

On US Nos. 319, 319c in Black

1904

240 A129 2c carmine 7.00 2.25
a. Booklet pane of 6 *1,100.*
b. 2c scarlet 7.50 2.75
c. As "b," booklet pane of 6 —

José Rizal — A40

Arms of Manila — A41

4c, McKinley. 6c, Magellan. 8c, Miguel Lopez de Legaspi. 10c, Gen. Henry W. Lawton. 12c, Lincoln. 16c, Adm. William T. Sampson. 20c, Washington. 26c, Francisco Carriedo. 30c, Franklin.

Each Inscribed "Philippine Islands / United States of America"

1906, Sept. 8 **Engr.** **Wmk. 191PI**

241 A40 2c dp green .40 .20
a. 2c yellow green ('10) .60 .20
b. Booklet pane of 6 750.00
242 A40 4c carmine .50 .20
a. 4c carmine lake ('10) 1.00 .20
b. Booklet pane of 6 650.00
243 A40 6c violet 2.50 .20
244 A40 8c brown 4.50 .90
245 A40 10c blue 3.50 .30
246 A40 12c brown lake 9.00 2.50
247 A40 16c violet blk 6.00 .35
248 A40 20c orange brn 7.00 .35
249 A40 26c violet brn 11.00 3.00
250 A40 30c olive grn 6.50 1.75
251 A41 1p orange 45.00 7.50
252 A41 2p black 55.00 1.75
253 A41 4p dk blue 160.00 20.00
254 A41 10p dk green 275.00 80.00
Nos. 241-254 (14) 585.90 119.00

See Nos. 255-304, 326-353. For surcharges see Nos. 368-369, 450. For overprints see Nos. C1-C28, C36-C46, C54-C57, O5-O14.

Change of Colors

1909-13 ***Perf. 12***

255 A40 12c red orange 11.00 3.00
256 A40 16c olive green 6.00 .75
257 A40 20c yellow 9.00 1.25
258 A40 26c blue green 3.50 .75
259 A40 30c ultra 13.00 3.50
260 A41 1p pale violet 45.00 5.00
260A A41 2p vio brn ('13) 100.00 4.00
Nos. 255-260A (7) 187.50 18.25

1911 **Wmk. 190PI** ***Perf. 12***

261 A40 2c green .75 .20
a. Booklet pane of 6 800.00
262 A40 4c car lake 3.00 .20
a. 4c carmine — —
b. Booklet pane of 6 600.00
263 A40 6c dp violet 3.00 .20
264 A40 8c brown 9.50 .50
265 A40 10c blue 4.00 .20
266 A40 12c orange 4.00 .45
267 A40 16c olive grn 4.50 .40
a. 16c pale olive green 4.50 .50
268 A40 20c yellow 3.50 .20
a. 20c orange 4.00 .30
269 A40 26c blue green 6.00 .30
270 A40 30c ultra 6.00 .50
271 A41 1p pale violet 27.50 .60
272 A41 2p violet brn 45.00 1.00
273 A41 4p dp blue 700.00 110.00
274 A41 10p dp green 250.00 32.50
Nos. 261-274 (14) 1,066. 147.25

1914

275 A40 30c gray 12.00 .50

1914-23 ***Perf. 10***

276 A40 2c green 2.00 .20
a. Booklet pane of 6 *750.00*
277 A40 4c carmine 3.50 .30
a. Booklet pane of 6 *750.00*
278 A40 6c lt violet 45.00 9.50
a. 6c deep violet 50.00 6.25
279 A40 8c brown 50.00 10.50
280 A40 10c dk blue 30.00 .20
281 A40 16c olive grn 100.00 5.00
282 A40 20c orange 32.50 1.00
283 A40 30c gray 70.00 4.50
284 A41 1p pale vio 140.00 3.75
Nos. 276-284 (9) 473.00 34.95

1918-26 *Perf. 11*

285	A40	2c green	21.00	4.25
a.		Booklet pane of 6	*750.00*	
286	A40	4c carmine	26.00	2.50
a.		Booklet pane of 6	*1,350.*	
287	A40	6c dp violet	40.00	1.75
287A	A40	8c lt brown	220.00	25.00
288	A40	10c dk blue	60.00	1.50
289	A40	16c olive grn	110.00	7.50
289A	A40	20c orange	85.00	8.00
289C	A40	30c gray	95.00	13.00
289D	A41	1p pale violet	100.00	17.50
		Nos. 285-289D (9)	757.00	81.00

1917-25 Unwmk. *Perf. 11*

290	A40	2c yellow grn	.25	.20
a.		2c dark green	.30	.20
b.		Vert. pair, imperf. horiz.	*1,500.*	
c.		Horiz. pair, imperf. btwn.	*1,500.*	—
d.		Vert. pair, imperf. btwn.	*1,750.*	*1,000.*
e.		Booklet pane of 6	*27.50*	
291	A40	4c carmine	.30	.20
a.		4c light rose	.30	.20
b.		Booklet pane of 6	20.00	—
292	A40	6c deep violet	.35	.20
a.		6c lilac	.40	.20
b.		6c red violet	.40	.20
c.		Booklet pane of 6	*550.00*	—
293	A40	8c yellow brown	.35	.20
a.		8c orange brown	.35	.20
294	A40	10c deep blue	.30	.20
295	A40	12c red orange	.35	.20
296	A40	16c lt ol grn	65.00	.25
a.		16c olive bister	65.00	.50
297	A40	20c orange yel	.35	.20
298	A40	26c green	.50	.45
a.		26c blue green	.60	.25
299	A40	30c gray	.55	.20
300	A41	1p pale violet	40.00	1.00
a.		1p red lilac	40.00	1.00
b.		1p pale rose lilac	40.00	1.10
301	A41	2p violet brn	35.00	1.00
302	A41	4p blue	32.50	.50
a.		4p dark blue	35.00	.55
		Nos. 290-302 (13)	175.80	4.80

1923-26

Design: 16c, Adm. George Dewey.

303	A40	16c olive bister	1.00	.20
a.		16c olive green	1.25	.20
304	A41	10p deep green ('26)	50.00	6.00

Legislative Palace A42

1926, Dec. 20 Unwmk. *Perf. 12*

319	A42	2c green & blk	.50	.25
a.		Horiz. pair, imperf. btwn.	*300.00*	
b.		Vert. pair, imperf. btwn.	*575.00*	
320	A42	4c carmine & blk	.55	.40
a.		Horiz. pair, imperf. btwn.	*325.00*	
b.		Vert. pair, imperf. btwn.	*600.00*	
321	A42	16c ol grn & blk	1.00	.65
a.		Horiz. pair, imperf. btwn.	*350.00*	
b.		Vert. pair, imperf. btwn.	*625.00*	
c.		Double impression of center	*675.00*	
322	A42	18c lt brown & blk	1.10	.50
a.		Double impression of center	*1,250.*	
b.		Vert. pair, imperf. btwn.	*675.00*	
323	A42	20c orange & blk	2.00	1.00
a.		20c orange & brown	*600.00*	—
b.		Imperf., pair	*575.00*	*575.00*
c.		As "a," imperf., pair	*1,750.*	
d.		Vert. pair, imperf. btwn.	*700.00*	
324	A42	24c gray & blk	1.00	.55
a.		Vert. pair, imperf. btwn.	*700.00*	
325	A42	1p rose lil & blk	47.50	32.50
a.		Vert. pair, imperf. btwn.	*700.00*	
		Nos. 319-325 (7)	53.65	35.85

Opening of the Legislative Palace.

For overprints see Nos. O1-O4.

Coil Stamp

Rizal Type of 1906

1928 *Perf. 11 Vertically*

326	A40	2c green	8.00	*16.00*

Types of 1906-23

1925-31 Unwmk. *Imperf.*

340	A40	2c yel grn ('31)	.40	.40
a.		2c green ('25)	.80	.50
341	A40	4c car rose ('31)	.45	.40
a.		4c carmine ('25)	1.20	.60
342	A40	6c violet ('31)	2.00	1.75
a.		6c deep violet('25)	12.00	6.00
343	A40	8c brown ('31)	2.00	2.00
a.		8c yellow brown ('25)	12.00	6.00
344	A40	10c blue ('31)	3.75	3.00
a.		10c deep blue ('25)	45.00	16.00
345	A40	12c dp org ('31)	5.00	4.00
a.		12c red orange('25)	55.00	30.00
346	A40	16c ol grn *(Dewey)* ('31)	3.50	3.00
a.		16c bister green ('25)	40.00	12.50
347	A40	20c dp yel org ('31)	4.00	3.00
a.		20c yellow orange ('25)	42.50	15.00
348	A40	26c green ('31)	4.00	3.00
a.		26c blue green ('25)	45.00	16.00
349	A40	30c lt gray ('31)	5.00	4.00
a.		30c gray ('25)	45.00	16.00
350	A41	1p lt violet ('31)	7.50	7.00
a.		1p violet ('25)	175.00	85.00
351	A41	2p brown vio ('31)	18.00	15.00
a.		2p violet brown ('25)	375.00	200.00
352	A41	4p blue ('31)	65.00	55.00
a.		4p deep blue ('25)	2,000.	875.00
353	A41	10p green ('31)	135.00	130.00
a.		10p deep green ('25)	2,875.	1,550.
		Nos. 340-353 (14)	255.60	231.55
		Nos. 340a-353a (14)	5,723.	2,828.

Mount Mayon, Luzon A43

Post Office, Manila A44

Pier No. 7, Manila Bay — A45

(See footnote) — A46

Rice Planting A47

Rice Terraces A48

Baguio Zigzag A49

1932, May 3 *Perf. 11*

354	A43	2c yellow green	.60	.30
355	A44	4c rose carmine	.60	.30
356	A45	12c orange	.75	.60
357	A46	18c red orange	30.00	10.00
358	A47	20c yellow	1.00	.65
359	A48	24c deep violet	1.50	.80
360	A49	32c olive brown	1.40	.80
		Nos. 354-360 (7)	35.85	13.45

The 18c vignette was intended to show Pagsanjan Falls in Laguna, central Luzon, and is so labeled. Through error the stamp pictures Vernal Falls in Yosemite National Park, California.

For overprints see #C29-C35, C47-C51, C63.

Nos. 302, 302a Surcharged in Orange or Red

1932

368	A41	1p on 4p blue (O)	5.00	.75
a.		1p on 4p dark blue (O)	5.00	1.50
369	A41	2p on 4p dk bl (R)	7.50	1.00
a.		2p on 4p blue (R)	7.50	1.00

Baseball Players A50

Tennis Player — A51

Basketball Players — A52

1934, Apr. 14 Typo. *Perf. 11½*

380	A50	2c yellow brn	*1.75*	*.90*
381	A51	6c ultra	.25	.20
a.		Vert. pair, imperf. btwn.	*1,250.*	
382	A52	16c violet brown	.50	.50
a.		Vert. pair, imperf. horiz.	*1,750.*	
		Nos. 380-382 (3)	2.50	1.60

Tenth Far Eastern Championship Games.

José Rizal — A53

Woman and Carabao A54

La Filipina — A55

Pearl Fishing A56

Fort Santiago A57

Salt Spring — A58

Magellan's Landing, 1521 — A59

"Juan de la Cruz" — A60

Rice Terraces A61

"Blood Compact," 1565 — A62

Barasoain Church, Malolos A63

Battle of Manila Bay, 1898 A64

Montalban Gorge A65

George Washington A66

1935, Feb. 15 Engr. *Perf. 11*

383	A53	2c rose	.20	.20
384	A54	4c yellow grn	.20	.20
385	A55	6c dk brown	.25	.20
386	A56	8c violet	.25	.20
387	A57	10c rose car	.30	.20
388	A58	12c black	.35	.20
389	A59	16c dk blue	.35	.30
390	A60	20c lt ol grn	.35	.20
391	A61	26c indigo	.40	.40
392	A62	30c orange red	.40	.25
393	A63	1p red org & blk	2.00	1.25
394	A64	2p bister brn & blk	5.50	1.25
395	A65	4p blue & blk	7.00	3.50
396	A66	5p green & blk	16.50	3.50
		Nos. 383-396 (14)	34.05	11.85

For overprints see Nos. 411-424, 433-446, 463-466, 468, 472-474, 478-484, 485-494, C52-C53, O15-O36, O38, O40-O43, N2-N3, NO6. For surcharges see Nos. 449, N4-N9, N28, NO2-NO5.

Commonwealth Issues

The Temples of Human Progress — A67

1935, Nov. 15

397 A67 2c carmine rose .25 .20
398 A67 6c dp violet .25 .20
399 A67 16c blue .25 .20
400 A67 36c yellow grn .40 .30
401 A67 50c brown .60 .55
Nos. 397-401 (5) 1.75 1.45

Inauguration of the Philippine Commonwealth, Nov. 15, 1935.

Jose Rizal — A68

President Manuel L. Quezon — A69

1936, June 19 ***Perf. 12***

402 A68 2c yellow brown .20 .20
403 A68 6c slate blue .20 .20
a. Horiz. pair, imperf. vert. *1,350.*
404 A68 36c red brown .50 .45
Nos. 402-404 (3) .90 .85

75th anniv. of the birth of José Rizal.

1936, Nov. 15 ***Perf. 11***

408 A69 2c orange brown .20 .20
409 A69 6c yellow green .20 .20
410 A69 12c ultra .20 .20
Nos. 408-410 (3) .60 .60

1st anniversary of the Commonwealth.
For overprints see Nos. 467, 475.

Stamps of 1935 Overprinted in Black

a

b

1936-37 ***Perf. 11***

411 A53 (a) 2c rose .20 .20
a. Booklet pane of 6 3.00 *4.00*
412 A54 (b) 4c yel grn ('37) *.50* 4.00
413 A55 (a) 6c dark brown .20 .20
414 A56 (b) 8c violet ('37) .25 .20
415 A57 (b) 10c rose carmine .20 .20
a. "Commonwealt" 20.00 —
416 A58 (b) 12c black ('37) .20 .20
417 A59 (b) 16c dk blue .30 .20
418 A60 (a) 20c lt ol grn ('37) 1.00 .40
419 A61 (b) 26c indigo ('37) .90 .35
420 A62 (b) 30c orange red .50 .20
421 A63 (b) 1p red org & blk 1.00 .25
422 A64 (b) 2p bis brn & blk ('37) 7.50 3.00
423 A65 (b) 4p bl & blk ('37) 32.50 6.50
424 A66 (b) 5p grn & blk ('37) 8.00 2.50
Nos. 411-424 (14) 53.25 18.40
Nos. 411,413-424 (13) 14.40

Map of Philippines A70

Arms of Manila A71

1937, Feb. 3

425 A70 2c yellow green .20 .20
426 A70 6c lt brown .20 .20
427 A70 12c sapphire .20 .20
428 A70 20c dp orange .30 .20
429 A70 36c dp violet .55 .40
430 A70 50c carmine .70 .35
Nos. 425-430 (6) 2.15 1.55

33rd Eucharistic Congress.

1937, Aug. 27 ***Perf. 11***

431 A71 10p gray 5.00 2.00
432 A71 20p henna brown 3.00 1.40

For overprints see Nos. 495-496. For surcharges see Nos. 451, C58.

Stamps of 1935 Overprinted in Black

a

b

1938-40 ***Perf. 11***

433 A53 (a) 2c rose ('39) .20 .20
a. Booklet pane of 6 3.50 2.50
b. As "a," lower left-hand stamp overprinted "WEALTH COMMON-" 4,000.
c. Hyphen omitted — —
434 A54 (b) 4c yel grn ('40) 3.00 *30.00*
435 A55 (a) 6c dk brn ('39) .25 .20
a. 6c golden brown .25 .20
436 A56 (b) 8c violet ('39) .25 .20
a. "Commonwealt" 90.00
437 A57 (b) 10c rose car ('39) .20 .20
a. "Commonwealt" 65.00 —
438 A58 (b) 12c black ('40) .20 .20
439 A59 (b) 16c dk blue .20 .20
440 A60 (a) 20c lt ol grn ('39) .20 .20
441 A61 (b) 26c indigo ('40) .30 .20
442 A62 (b) 30c org red ('39) 1.50 .70
443 A63 (b) 1p red org & blk .50 .20
444 A64 (b) 2p bis brn & blk 5.00 .75
445 A65 (b) 4p bl & blk ('40) 300.00 300.00
446 A66 (b) 5p grn & blk ('40) 12.50 4.00
Nos. 433-446 (14) 324.30 *337.25*

Overprint "b" measures 18½x1¾mm. No. 433b occurs in booklet pane, No. 433a, position 5; all copies are straight-edged, left and bottom.

Stamps of 1917-37 Surcharged in Red, Violet or Black

a

b

c

1939, July 5

449 A54 2c on 4c yel grn (R) .20 .20
450 A40 6c on 26c bl grn (V) .20 .20
a. 6c on 26c green 1.00 .30
451 A71 50c on 20p hn brn (Bk) 1.25 1.00
Nos. 449-451 (3) 1.65 1.40

Foreign Trade Week.

Triumphal Arch — A72

Malacañan Palace A73

1939, Nov. 15 ***Perf. 11***

452 A72 2c yellow green .20 .20
453 A72 6c carmine .20 .20
454 A72 12c bright blue .20 .20
Nos. 452-454 (3) .60 .60

For overprints see Nos. 469, 476.

1939, Nov. 15

455 A73 2c green .20 .20
456 A73 6c orange .20 .20
457 A73 12c carmine .20 .20
Nos. 455-457 (3) .60 .60

Nos. 452-457 commemorate the 4th anniv. of the Commonwealth.
For overprint see No. 470.

Pres. Quezon Taking Oath of Office — A74

1940, Feb. 8

458 A74 2c dk orange .20 .20
459 A74 6c dk green .20 .20
460 A74 12c purple .25 .20
Nos. 458-460 (3) .65 .60

4th anniversary of Commonwealth.
For overprints see Nos. 471, 477.

AIR POST STAMPS

Madrid-Manila Flight Issue

Regular Issue of 1917-26 Overprinted in Red or Violet

1926, May 13 **Unwmk.** ***Perf. 11***

C1 A40 2c green (R) 18.00 15.00
C2 A40 4c carmine 20.00 17.50
a. Inverted overprint *3,750.* —
C3 A40 6c lilac (R) 55.00 55.00
C4 A40 8c orange brn 57.50 50.00
C5 A40 10c dp blue (R) 57.50 50.00
C6 A40 12c red orange 65.00 50.00
C7 A40 16c lt ol grn (Sampson) *3,250.* *1,600.*
C8 A40 16c ol bis (Sampson) (R) *5,000.* *3,000.*
C9 A40 16c ol grn (Dewey) 70.00 50.00
C10 A40 20c orange yel 70.00 65.00
C11 A40 26c blue green 70.00 65.00
C12 A40 30c gray 70.00 65.00
C13 A41 2p vio brn (R) 650.00 300.00
C14 A41 4p dk blue (R) 750.00 500.00
C15 A41 10p dp green 1,350. 700.00

Same Overprint on No. 269

Perf. 12

Wmk. 190PI

C16 A40 26c blue green *6,250.*

Same Overprint on No. 284

Perf. 10

C17 A41 1p pale violet 225.00 175.00

Flight of Spanish aviators Gallarza and Loriga from Madrid to Manila.

London-Orient Flight Issue

Regular Issue of 1917-25 Overprinted in Red

1928, Nov. 9 **Unwmk.** ***Perf. 11***

C18 A40 2c green 1.00 .50
C19 A40 4c carmine 1.10 .75
C20 A40 6c violet 3.50 2.25
C21 A40 8c orange brn 4.00 2.50
C22 A40 10c dp blue 4.00 2.50
C23 A40 12c red orange 5.00 3.25
C24 A40 16c ol grn *(Dewey)* 4.50 2.50
C25 A40 20c orange yel 6.00 3.25
C26 A40 26c blue green 16.00 7.25
C27 A40 30c gray 16.00 7.25

Same Overprint on No. 271

Perf. 12

Wmk. 190PI

C28 A41 1p pale violet 90.00 30.00
Nos. C18-C28 (11) 151.10 62.00

Commemorating an airplane flight from London to Manila.

Nos. 354-360 Overprinted

1932, Sept. 27 **Unwmk.** ***Perf. 11***

C29 A43 2c yellow green .90 .35
C30 A44 4c rose carmine 1.00 .40
C31 A45 12c orange 1.25 .65
C32 A46 18c red orange 5.00 3.25
C33 A47 20c yellow 4.00 2.00
C34 A48 24c deep violet 4.00 2.00
C35 A49 32c olive brown 3.50 2.25
Nos. C29-C35 (7) 19.65 10.90

Visit of Capt. Wolfgang von Gronan on his round-the-world flight.

Regular Issue of 1917-25 Overprinted

1933, Apr. 11

C36 A40 2c green .75 .45
C37 A40 4c carmine .90 .45
C38 A40 6c deep violet 1.10 .80
C39 A40 8c orange brn 3.75 1.75
C40 A40 10c dk blue 3.75 1.25
C41 A40 12c orange 3.75 1.25
C42 A40 16c ol grn *(Dewey)* 3.50 1.25
C43 A40 20c yellow 3.75 1.25
C44 A40 26c green 3.75 1.75
a. 26c blue green 4.00 2.00
C45 A40 30c gray 4.00 2.00
Nos. C36-C45 (10) 29.00 12.20

Commemorating the flight from Madrid to Manila of aviator Fernando Rein y Loring.

No. 290a Overprinted

1933, May 26 **Unwmk.** ***Perf. 11***

C46 A40 2c green .65 .40

Regular Issue of 1932 Overprinted

C47 A44 4c rose carmine .30 .20
C48 A45 12c orange .60 .20
C49 A47 20c yellow .60 .20
C50 A48 24c deep violet .65 .25
C51 A49 32c olive brown .85 .35
Nos. C46-C51 (6) 3.65 1.60

Nos. 387, 392 Overprinted in Gold

1935, Dec. 2
C52 A57 10c rose carmine .40 .30
C53 A62 30c orange red .60 .50

China Clipper flight from Manila to San Francisco, December 2-5, 1935.

Regular Issue of 1917-25 Surcharged in Various Colors

1936, Sept. 6 ***Perf. 11***
C54 A40 2c on 4c car (Bl) .20 .20
C55 A40 6c on 12c red org (V) .20 .20
C56 A40 16c on 26c bl grn (Bk) .25 .20
a. 16c on 26c green 2.00 .70
Nos. C54-C56 (3) .65 .60

Manila-Madrid flight by aviators Antonio Arnaiz and Juan Calvo.

Regular Issue of 1917-37 Surcharged in Black or Red

1939, Feb. 17
C57 A40 8c on 26c bl grn (Bk) 1.00 .40
a. 8c on 26c green (Bk) 3.75 .80
C58 A71 1p on 10p gray (R) 3.25 2.25

1st Air Mail Exhibition, held 2/17-19/39.

SPECIAL DELIVERY STAMPS

United States No. E5 Overprinted in Red

1901, Oct. 15 **Wmk. 191** ***Perf. 12***
E1 SD3 10c dark blue 100.00 75.00

Special Delivery Messenger SD2

1906 **Engr.** **Wmk. 191PI**
E2 SD2 20c ultra 45.00 8.00
b. 20c pale ultra 35.00 8.00

See Nos. E3-E6. For overprints see Nos. E7-E10, EO1.

Special Printing

Overprinted in Red as No. E1 on United States No. E6

1907
E2A SD4 10c ultra *2,750.*

Type of 1906

1911 **Wmk. 190PI**
E3 SD2 20c dp ultra 21.00 1.90

1916 ***Perf. 10***
E4 SD2 20c dp ultra 175.00 75.00

1919 **Unwmk.** ***Perf. 11***
E5 SD2 20c ultra .60 .20
a. 20c pale blue .75 .20
b. 20c dull violet .60 .20

1925-31 ***Imperf.***
E6 SD2 20c dull vio ('31) 30.00 *75.00*
a. 20c violet blue ('25) 42.50 30.00

Type of 1919 Overprinted in Black

1939 ***Perf. 11***
E7 SD2 20c blue violet .25 .20

SPECIAL DELIVERY OFFICIAL STAMP

Type of 1906 Issue Overprinted

1931 **Unwmk.** ***Perf. 11***
EO1 SD2 20c dull violet 3.00 *80.00*
a. No period after "B" 40.00 —
b. Double overprint —

It is strongly recommended that expert opinion be acquired for No. EO1 used.

POSTAGE DUE STAMPS

Postage Due Stamps of the United States Nos. J38 to J44 Overprinted in Black

1899, Aug. 16 **Wmk. 191** ***Perf. 12***
J1 D2 1c deep claret 7.50 2.50
On cover 27.50
J2 D2 2c deep claret 7.50 2.50
On cover 35.00
J3 D2 5c deep claret 15.00 2.50
On cover *65.00*
J4 D2 10c deep claret 19.00 5.50
On cover 90.00
J5 D2 50c deep claret 200.00 100.00
On cover —

1901, Aug. 31
J6 D2 3c deep claret 17.50 7.00
On cover 60.00
J7 D2 30c deep claret 250.00 110.00
On cover —
Nos. J1-J7 (7) 516.50 230.00

No. J1 was used to pay regular postage September 5-19, 1902.

Post Office Clerk — D3

Unwmk.

1928, Aug. 21 **Engr.** ***Perf. 11***
J8 D3 4c brown red .25 .20
J9 D3 6c brown red .30 .20
J10 D3 8c brown red .25 .20
J11 D3 10c brown red .30 .20
J12 D3 12c brown red .25 .20
J13 D3 16c brown red .30 .20
J14 D3 20c brown red .30 .20
Nos. J8-J14 (7) 1.95 1.40

For overprints see Nos. O16-O22, NJ1. For surcharge see No. J15.

No. J8 Surcharged in Blue

1937
J15 D3 3c on 4c brown red .25 .20

OFFICIAL STAMPS

Official Handstamped Overprints

"Officers purchasing stamps for government business may, if they so desire, overprint them with the letters 'O.B.' either in writing with black ink or by rubber stamps but in such a manner as not to obliterate the stamp that postmasters will be unable to determine whether the stamps have been previously used." C. M. Cotterman, Director of Posts, Dec. 26, 1905. Beginning with Jan. 1, 1906, all branches of the Insular Government used postage stamps to prepay postage instead of franking them as before. Some officials used manuscript, some utilized typewriters, some made press-printed overprints, but by far the larger number used rubber stamps. The majority of these read "O.B." but other forms were: "OFFICIAL BUSINESS" or "OFFICIAL MAIL" in two lines, with variations on many of these. These "O.B." overprints are known on US 1899-1901 stamps; on 1903-06 stamps in red and blue; on 1906 stamps in red, blue, black, yellow and green. "O.B." overprints were also made on the centavo and peso stamps of the Philippines, per order of May 25, 1907. Beginning in 1926 the stamps were overprinted and issued by the Post Office, but some government offices continued to handstamp "O.B."

Regular Issue of 1926 Overprinted in Red

1926, Dec. 20 **Unwmk.** ***Perf. 12***
O1 A42 2c green & blk 3.00 1.00
O2 A42 4c carmine & blk 3.00 1.25
a. Vert. pair, imperf. btwn. *750.00*
O3 A42 18c lt brn & blk 8.00 4.00
O4 A42 20c orange & blk 7.75 1.75
Nos. O1-O4 (4) 21.75 8.00

Opening of the Legislative Palace.

Regular Issue of 1917-26 Overprinted

1931 ***Perf. 11***
O5 A40 2c green .40 .20
a. No period after "B" 17.50 5.00
b. No period after "O" —
O6 A40 4c carmine .45 .20
a. No period after "B" 20.00 5.00
O7 A40 6c dp violet .75 .20
O8 A40 8c yellow brn .75 .20
O9 A40 10c deep blue 1.20 .20
O10 A40 12c red orange 2.00 .20
a. No period after "B" 65.00
O11 A40 16c lt ol grn *(Dewey)* 1.00 .20
a. 16c olive bister 2.00 .20
O12 A40 20c orange yel 1.25 .20
a. No period after "B" 50.00 15.00
O13 A40 26c green 2.00 .30
a. 26c blue green 2.50 .65
O14 A40 30c gray 2.00 .25
Nos. O5-O14 (10) 11.80 2.15

Same Overprint on Nos. 383-392

1935
O15 A53 2c rose .20 .20
a. No period after "B" 15.00 5.00
O16 A54 4c yellow green .20 .20
a. No period after "B" 15.00 8.50
O17 A55 6c dk brown .25 .20
a. No period after "B" 35.00 17.50
O18 A56 8c violet .30 .20
O19 A57 10c rose carmine .30 .20
O20 A58 12c black .75 .20
O21 A59 16c dark blue .55 .20
O22 A60 20c lt olive grn .60 .20
O23 A61 26c indigo .90 .25
O24 A62 30c orange red .80 .20
Nos. O15-O24 (10) 4.85 2.05

Same Overprint on Nos. 411, 418

1937-38 ***Perf. 11***
O25 A53 2c rose .20 .20
a. No period after "B" 15.00 2.25
b. Period after "B" raised (UL4) 150.00
O26 A60 20c lt ol grn ('38) .70 .50

Nos. 383-392 Overprinted in Black:

a

b

1938-40 ***Perf. 11***
O27 A53(a) 2c rose .20 .20
a. Hyphen omitted 20.00 20.00
b. No period after "B" 25.00 25.00
O28 A54(b) 4c yellow grn .75 .25
O29 A55(a) 6c dk brown .30 .20
O30 A56(b) 8c violet .75 .25
O31 A57(b) 10c rose car .20 .20
a. No period after "O" 40.00 30.00
O32 A58(b) 12c black .30 .20
O33 A59(b) 16c dark blue .30 .20
O34 A60(a) 20c lt ol grn ('40) .55 .25
O35 A61(b) 26c indigo .75 .30
O36 A62(b) 30c orange red .75 .25
Nos. O27-O36 (10) 4.85 2.30

NEWSPAPER STAMPS

N1

N2

1886-89 **Unwmk.** **Typo.** ***Perf. 14***
P1 N1 ⅛c yellow green .30 *3.25*
On cover or wrapper *200.00*
P2 N1 1m rose ('89) .30 *21.00*
On cover or wrapper *800.00*
P3 N1 2m blue ('89) .30 *21.00*
On cover or wrapper *800.00*
P4 N1 5m dk brown ('89) .30 *21.00*
On cover or wrapper *1,000.*
Nos. P1-P4 (4) 1.20 *66.25*

1890-96
P5 N2 ⅛c dark violet .25 .20
On cover or wrapper *400.00*
P6 N2 ⅛c green ('92) 8.00 *10.00*
On cover or wrapper *600.00*
P7 N2 ⅛c orange brn ('94) .25 .20
On cover or wrapper *200.00*
P8 N2 ⅛c dull blue ('96) .85 .60
On cover or wrapper *200.00*
P9 N2 1m dark violet .25 .20
On cover or wrapper *200.00*
P10 N2 1m green ('92) 2.25 *5.50*
On cover or wrapper *400.00*
P11 N2 1m olive gray ('94) .25 .45
On cover or wrapper *200.00*
P12 N2 1m ultra ('96) .35 .20
On cover or wrapper *200.00*
P13 N2 2m dark violet .25 .45
On cover or wrapper *200.00*
P14 N2 2m green ('92) 2.50 *13.00*
On cover or wrapper *500.00*

P15 N2 2m olive gray ('94) .25 .45
On cover or wrapper *200.00*
P16 N2 2m brown ('96) .30 .20
On cover or wrapper *200.00*
P17 N2 5m dark violet .25 *1.10*
On cover or wrapper *500.00*
P18 N2 5m green ('92) 200.00 55.00
P19 N2 5m olive gray ('94) .25 .45
On cover or wrapper *500.00*
P20 N2 5m dp blue grn ('96) 2.50 1.40
On cover or wrapper *600.00*
Nos. P5-P20 (16) 218.75 *89.40*

Imperfs. exist of Nos. P8, P9, P11, P12, P16, P17 and P20.

FILIPINO REVOLUTIONARY GOVERNMENT

The Filipino Republic was instituted by Gen. Emilio Aguinaldo on June 23, 1899. At the same time he assumed the office of President. Aguinaldo dominated the greater part of the island of Luzon and some of the smaller islands until late in 1899. He was taken prisoner by United States troops on March 23, 1901.

The devices composing the National Arms, adopted by the Filipino Revolutionary Government, are emblems of the Katipunan political secret society or of Katipunan origin. The letters "K K K" on these stamps are the initials of this society whose complete name is "Kataas-taasang, Kagalang-galang Katipunan nang Mañga Anak nang Bayan," meaning "Sovereign Worshipful Association of the Sons of the Country."

The regular postage and telegraph stamps were in use on Luzon as early as Nov. 10, 1898. Owing to the fact that stamps for the different purposes were not always available together with a lack of proper instructions, any of the adhesives were permitted to be used in the place of the other. Hence telegraph and revenue stamps were accepted for postage and postage stamps for revenue or telegraph charges. In addition to the regular postal emission, there are a number of provisional stamps, issues of local governments of islands and towns.

POSTAGE ISSUES

A1

A2

Coat of Arms — A3

1898-99 **Unwmk.** ***Perf. 11½***

Y1 A1 2c red 200.00 150.00
a. Double impression *225.00*
Y2 A2 2c red .20 2.00
On cover 450.00
b. Double impression —
d. Horiz. pair, imperf. between —
e. Vert. pair, imperf. between *200.00*
Y3 A3 2c red 175.00 *250.00*

Imperf pairs and pairs, imperf horizontally, have been created from No. Y2e.

RS1

N1

REGISTRATION STAMP

YF1 RS1 8c green 3.50 *10.00*
On cover with #Y2 *3,500.*
a. Imperf., pair 400.00
b. Imperf. vertically, pair —

NEWSPAPER STAMP

YP1 N1 1m black 2.00
a. Imperf., pair 2.00

PITCAIRN ISLANDS

'pit-ˌkarn 'ī-ləndz

LOCATION — South Pacific Ocean, nearly equidistant from Australia and South America
GOVT. — British colony under the British High Commissioner in New Zealand
AREA — 1.75 sq. mi.
POP. — 57 (1984)

The district of Pitcairn also includes the uninhabited islands of Ducie, Henderson and Oeno.

Postal affairs are administered by Fiji.

12 Pence = 1 Shilling

Catalogue values for all unused stamps in this country are for Never Hinged items.

Cluster of Oranges A1

Fletcher Christian with Crew and View of Pitcairn Island — A2

John Adams and His House A3

William Bligh and H. M. Armed Vessel "Bounty" A4

Map of Pitcairn and Pacific Ocean — A5

Bounty Bible — A6

H.M. Armed Vessel "Bounty" A7

Pitcairn School, 1949 — A8

Fletcher Christian and View of Pitcairn Island — A9

Fletcher Christian with Crew and Coast of Pitcairn A10

Perf. 12½, 11½x11

1940-51 Engr. Wmk. 4

1	A1	½p blue grn & org	.50	*.65*
2	A2	1p red lil & rose vio	.65	*.90*
3	A3	1½p rose car & blk	.65	.55
4	A4	2p dk brn & brt grn	2.25	1.50
5	A5	3p dk blue & yel grn	1.50	*1.50*
5A	A6	4p dk blue grn & blk	18.50	12.00
6	A7	6p sl grn & dp brn	5.75	1.75
6A	A8	8p lil rose & grn	19.50	8.00
7	A9	1sh slate & vio	4.00	2.50
8	A10	2sh6p dk brn & brt grn	9.50	4.00
		Nos. 1-8 (10)	62.80	33.35

Nos. 1-5, 6 and 7-8 exist in a booklet of eight panes of one. Value $2,000.

Issued: 4p, 8p, 9/1/51; others, 10/15/40.

Common Design Types pictured following the introduction.

Peace Issue

Common Design Type

1946, Dec. 2 ***Perf. 13½x14***

9	CD303	2p brown	.50	.50
10	CD303	3p deep blue	.65	.65

Silver Wedding Issue

Common Design Types

1949, Aug. 1 Photo. ***Perf. 14x14½***

11	CD304	1½p scarlet	1.50	.75

Engraved; Name Typographed
Perf. 11½x11

12	CD305	10sh purple	72.50	*80.00*

UPU Issue

Common Design Types

Engr.; Name Typo. on 3p & 6p

1949, Oct. 10 ***Perf. 13½, 11x11½***

13	CD306	2½p red brown	5.50	4.00
14	CD307	3p indigo	8.50	4.00
15	CD308	6p green	12.00	4.00
16	CD309	1sh rose violet	18.00	8.00
		Nos. 13-16 (4)	44.00	20.00

POLAND

'pō-lənd

LOCATION — Europe between Russia and Germany
GOVT. — Republic
AREA — 120,628 sq. mi.
POP. — 36,399,000 (est. 1983)
CAPITAL — Warsaw

100 Kopecks = 1 Ruble
100 Fenigi = 1 Marka (1918)
100 Halerzy = 1 Korona (1918)
100 Groszy = 1 Zloty (1924)

Watermarks

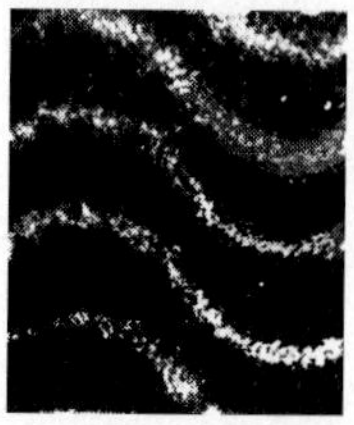
Wmk. 145 — Wavy Lines

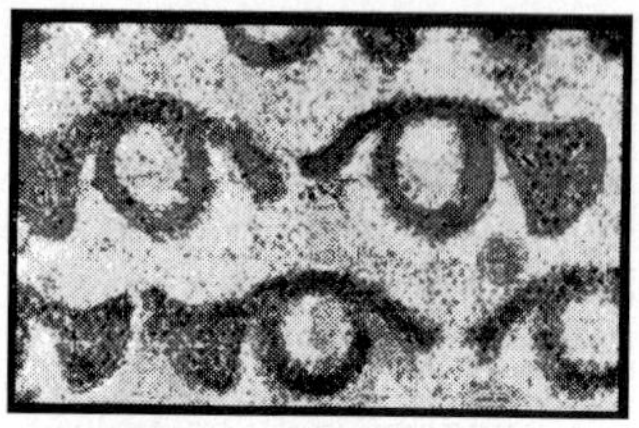
Wmk. 234 — Multiple Post Horns

Issued under Russian Dominion

Coat of Arms — A1

Perf. 11½ to 12½

1860 Typo. Unwmk.

1	A1	10k blue & rose	800.	200.
		On cover		1,000.
a.		10k blue & carmine	950.	275.
b.		10k dark blue & rose	950.	275.
c.		Added blue frame for inner oval	1,400.	475.
d.		Imperf.		

Used for letters within the Polish territory and to Russia. Postage on all foreign letters was paid in cash.

These stamps were superseded by those of Russia in 1865.

Counterfeits exist.

Issues of the Republic

Local issues were made in various Polish cities during the German occupation.

In the early months of the Republic many issues were made by overprinting the German occupation stamps with the words "Poczta Polska" and an eagle or bars often with the name of the city.

These issues were not authorized by the Government but were made by the local authorities and restricted to local use. In 1914 two stamps were issued for the Polish Legion and in 1918 the Polish Expeditionary Force used surcharged Russian stamps. The regularity of these issues is questioned.

Numerous counterfeits of these issues abound.

Warsaw Issues

Statue of Sigismund III — A2

Coat of Arms of Warsaw — A3

Polish Eagle A4

Sobieski Monument A5

Stamps of the Warsaw Local Post Surcharged

1918, Nov. 17 Wmk. 145 ***Perf. 11½***

11	A2	5f on 2gr brn & buff	.60	.35
a.		Inverted surcharge	37.50	32.50
12	A3	10f on 6gr grn & buff	.40	.35
a.		Inverted surcharge	4.50	4.00
13	A4	25f on 10gr rose & buff	4.75	1.75
a.		Inverted surcharge	9.00	8.00
14	A5	50f on 20gr bl & buff	4.25	4.25
a.		Inverted surcharge	125.00	100.00
		Nos. 11-14 (4)	10.00	6.70

Counterfeits exist.

Occupation Stamps Nos. N6-N16 Overprinted or Surcharged:

a

b

1918-19 Wmk. 125 ***Perf. 14, 14½***

15	A16	3pf brown ('19)	19.00	12.00
16	A22	5pf on 2½pf gray	.30	.30
17	A16	5pf on 3pf brown	3.50	2.25
18	A16	5pf green	.65	.50
19	A16	10pf carmine	.20	.20
20	A22	15pf dark violet	.20	.20
21	A16	20pf blue	.20	.20
a.		20pf ultramarine	*750.00*	*1,500.*
23	A22	25pf on 7½pf org	.30	.20
24	A16	30pf org & blk, *buff*	.20	.20
25	A16	40pf lake & black	.45	.45
26	A16	60pf magenta	.65	.65
		Nos. 15-26 (11)	25.65	17.15

There are two settings of this overprint. The first printing, issued Dec. 5, 1918, has space of 3½mm between the middle two bars. The second printing, issued Jan. 15, 1919, has space of 4mm. No. 15 comes only in the second setting; all others in both. The German overprint on No. 21a is very glossy.

Varieties of this overprint and surcharge are numerous: double; inverted; misspellings (Pocata, Poczto, Pelska); letters omitted, inverted or wrong font; 3 bars instead of 4, etc.

No. 21a requires competent expertization. A number of shades of the blue No. 21 exist.

Counterfeits exist.

Lublin Issue

Austrian Military Semi-Postal Stamps of 1918 Overprinted

1918, Dec. 5 Unwmk. ***Perf. 12½x13***

27	MSP7	10h gray green	7.50	5.50
a.		Inverted overprint	19.00	19.00
28	MSP8	20h magenta	6.25	5.50
a.		Inverted overprint	19.00	19.00
29	MSP7	45h blue	5.50	5.50
a.		Inverted overprint	19.00	19.00
		Nos. 27-29 (3)	19.25	16.50

Austrian Military Stamps of 1917 Surcharged

1918-19 ***Perf. 12½***

30	M3	3hal on 3h ol gray	17.50	13.00
a.		Inverted surcharge	225.00	225.00
b.		Perf. 11½	17.50	13.00
c.		Perf. 11½x12½	24.00	22.50
31	M3	3hal on 15h brt rose	3.00	2.50
a.		Inverted surcharge	20.00	20.00

Surcharged in Black

32	M3	10hal on 30h sl grn	3.00	2.50
a.		Inverted surcharge	20.00	20.00
b.		Brown surcharge (error)	60.00	50.00
34	M3	25hal on 40h ol bis	6.25	5.25
a.		Inverted surcharge	30.00	30.00
b.		Perf. 11½	10.00	7.75
35	M3	45hal on 60h rose	3.00	2.50
a.		Inverted surcharge	20.00	20.00
36	M3	45hal on 80h dl blue	4.25	3.25
a.		Inverted surcharge	30.00	30.00
37	M3	50hal on 60h rose	6.25	6.25
a.		Inverted surcharge	20.00	20.00

Similar surcharge with bars instead of stars over original value

38	M3	45hal on 80h dl blue	5.00	3.50
a.		Inverted surcharge	20.00	20.00

Overprinted

39 M3 50h deep green 15.00 13.00
a. Inverted overprint 80.00 80.00
40 M3 90h dark violet 4.25 2.50
a. Inverted overprint 20.00 20.00
Nos. 30-40 (10) 67.50 54.25

Counterfeits

All Cracow issues, Nos. 41-60, J1-J12 and P1-P5, have been extensively counterfeited. Competent expertization is necessary. Prices apply only for authenticated stamps with identified plating position. Cost of certificate is not included in the catalogue value.

Cracow Issues

Austrian Stamps of 1916-18 Overprinted

1919, Jan. 17 **Typo.**

41 A37 3h brt violet 190.00 200.00
42 A37 5h lt green 190.00 210.00
43 A37 6h deep orange 25.00 19.50
a. Inverted overprint *6,000.*
44 A37 10h magenta 190.00 190.00
45 A37 12h lt blue 35.00 35.00
46 A39 40h olive green 13.00 13.00
a. Inverted overprint 100.00 100.00
b. Double overprint 400.00
47 A39 50h blue green 7.00 7.00
a. Inverted overprint *8,000.*
48 A39 60h deep blue 4.00 4.00
a. Inverted overprint 100.00 75.00
49 A39 80h orange brown 4.00 4.50
a. Inverted overprint. 100.00 100.00
b. Double overprint *125.00 125.00*
50 A39 90h red violet 625.00 725.00
51 A39 1k carmine, *yel* 7.00 6.00

Engr.

52 A40 2k blue 4.00 4.50
53 A40 3k carmine rose 75.00 60.00
54 A40 4k yellow green 125.00 100.00
55 A40 10k deep violet *4,000. 5,000.*

The 3k is on granite paper.
The overprint on Nos. 52-55 is litho. and slightly larger than illustration with different ornament between lines of type.

Same Overprint on Nos. 168-171

1919 **Typo.**

56 A42 15h dull red 25.00 6.50
57 A42 20h dark green 125.00 125.00
58 A42 25h blue 1,250. 850.00
59 A42 30h dull violet 225.00 190.00

Austria No. 157 Surcharged

1919, Jan. 24

60 A39 25h on 80h org brn 2.75 2.75
a. Inverted surcharge 100.00 60.00

Excellent counterfeits of Nos. 27 to 60 exist.

Polish Eagle — A9

1919, Feb. 25 **Litho.** ***Imperf.***

Without gum

Yellowish Paper

61 A9 2h gray .30 .35
62 A9 3h dull violet .30 .35
63 A9 5h green .20 .20
64 A9 6h orange 13.00 19.00
65 A9 10h lake .20 .20
66 A9 15h brown .20 .20
67 A9 20h olive green .30 .35

Bluish Paper

68 A9 25h carmine .20 .20
69 A9 50h indigo .20 .20
70 A9 70h deep blue .30 .35
71 A9 1k ol gray & car .55 .95
Nos. 61-71 (11) 15.75 22.35

Nos. 61-71 exist with privately applied perforations.
Counterfeits exist.
For surcharges see Nos. J35-J39.

Posen (Poznan) Issue

Germany Nos. 84-85, 87, 96, 98 Overprinted in Black

Perf. 14, 14½

1919, Aug. 5 **Wmk. 125**

72 A22 5pf on 2pf gray 18.00 15.00
73 A22 5pf on 7½pf org 1.90 1.25
a. Inverted surcharge 100.00
74 A16 5pf on 20pf bl vio 1.50 1.10
75 A16 10pf on 25pf org & blk, *yel* 3.75 3.00
76 A16 10pf on 40pf lake & blk 2.00 1.25
Nos. 72-76 (5) 27.15 21.60

Counterfeits exist.

Germany Nos. 96 and 98 Surcharged in Red or Green

5 **10**

a b

1919, Sept. 15

77 A22 5pf on 2pf (R) 250.00 150.00
a. Inverted surcharge *4,250.*
78 A22 10pf on 7½pf (G) 150.00 110.00

Nos. 77-78 are a provisional issue for use in Gniezno. Counterfeit surcharges abound.

Eagle and Fasces, Symbolical of United Poland
A10 A11

"Agriculture" A12

"Peace" — A13

Polish Cavalryman A14

For Northern Poland

Denominations as "F" or "M"

1919, Jan. 27 ***Imperf.***

Wove or Ribbed Paper

81 A10 3f bister brn .20 .20
82 A10 5f green .20 .20
83 A10 10f red violet .20 .20
84 A10 15f deep rose .20 .20
85 A11 20f deep blue .20 .20
86 A11 25f olive green .25 .20
87 A11 50f blue green .25 .20
88 A12 1m violet 2.50 2.00
89 A12 1.50m deep green 4.50 2.50
90 A12 2m dark brown 3.75 2.50
91 A13 2.50m orange brn 16.00 11.00
92 A14 5m red violet 20.00 11.00
Nos. 81-92 (12) 48.25 30.40

Perf. 10, 11, 11½, 10x11½, 11½x10

1919-20

93 A10 3f bister brn .20 .20
94 A10 5f green .20 .20
95 A10 10f red violet .20 .20
96 A10 10f brown ('20) .20 .20
97 A10 15f deep rose .20 .20
98 A10 15f vermilion ('20) .20 .20
99 A11 20f deep blue .20 .20
100 A11 25f olive green .20 .20
101 A11 40f brt violet ('20) .20 .20
102 A11 50f blue green .20 .20
103 A12 1m violet .45 .20
105 A12 1.50m deep green .75 .40
106 A12 2m dark brown .75 .40
107 A13 2.50m orange brn 1.25 1.00
108 A14 5m red violet 2.00 1.00
Nos. 93-108 (15) 7.20 5.00

Several denominations among Nos. 81-132 are found with double impression or in pairs imperf. between.
See #109-132, 140-152C, 170-175. For surcharges & overprints see #153, 199-200, B1-B14, 2K1-2K10, Eastern Silesia 41-50.

For Southern Poland

Denominations as "H" or "K"

1919, Jan. 27 ***Imperf.***

109 A10 3h red brown .30 .20
110 A10 5h emerald .20 .20
111 A10 10h orange .20 .20
112 A10 15h vermilion .20 .20
113 A11 20h gray brown .20 .20
114 A11 25h light blue .20 .20
115 A11 50h orange brn .30 .20
116 A12 1k dark green .50 .20
117 A12 1.50k red brown 2.50 4.00
118 A12 2k dark blue 2.50 2.25
119 A13 2.50k dark violet 8.50 6.50
120 A14 5k slate blue 24.00 8.25
Nos. 109-120 (12) 39.60 22.60

Perf. 10, 11½, 10x11½, 11½x10

121 A10 3h red brown .20 .20
122 A10 5h emerald .20 .20
123 A10 10h orange .20 .20
124 A10 15h vermilion .20 .20
125 A11 20h gray brown .20 .20
126 A11 25h light blue .20 .20
127 A11 50h orange brn .20 .20
128 A12 1k dark green .50 .35
129 A12 1.50k red brown 1.10 .50
130 A12 2k dark blue 1.10 .50
131 A13 2.50k dark violet 1.25 .65
132 A14 5k slate blue 2.00 1.10
Nos. 121-132 (12) 7.35 4.50

National Assembly Issue

A20

Ignacy Jan Paderewski — A21

Adalbert Trampczynski — A22

Eagle Watching Ship — A24

25f, Gen. Josef Pilsudski. 1m, Griffin.

1919-20 ***Perf. 11½***

Wove or Ribbed Paper

133 A20 10f red violet .20 .20
134 A21 15f brown red .40 .25
a. Imperf., pair 25.00
135 A22 20f dp brown (21x25mm) .30 .25
136 A22 20f dp brown (17x20mm) ('20) .60 .80
137 A21 25f olive green .20 .20
138 A24 50f Prus blue .25 .20
139 A24 1m purple .30 .25
Nos. 133-139 (7) 2.25 2.15

First National Assembly of Poland.

General Issue

1919 ***Perf. 9 to 14½ and Compound***

Thin Laid Paper

140 A11 25f olive green .20 .20
141 A11 50f blue green .20 .20
142 A12 1m dark gray .35 .20
143 A12 2m bister brn 1.10 .20
144 A13 3m red brown .50 .20
a. Pair, imperf. vert. 5.00 5.75
145 A14 5m red violet .20 .20
146 A14 6m deep rose .20 .20
a. Pair, imperf. vert. 6.50 6.50
147 A14 10m brown red .35 .25
a. Horizontal pair, imperf. 6.50 6.50
148 A14 20m gray green .75 .40
Nos. 140-148 (9) 3.85 2.05

Type of 1919 Redrawn

Perf. 9 to 14½ and Compound

1920-22

Thin Laid or Wove Paper

149 A10 1m red .20 .20
150 A10 2m gray green .20 .20
151 A10 3m light blue .20 .20
152 A10 4m rose red .20 .20
152A A10 5m dark violet .20 .20
b. Horiz. pair, imperf. vert. 5.25 5.25
152C A10 8m gray brown ('22) .35 .25
Nos. 149-152C (6) 1.35 1.25

The word "POCZTA" is in smaller letters and the numerals have been enlarged.
The color of No. 152A varies from dark violet to red brown.

No. 101 Surcharged

Perf. 10, 11½, 10x11½, 11½x10

1921, Jan. 25

Thick Wove Paper

153 A11 3m on 40f brt vio .20 .20
a. Double surcharge 20.00 20.00
b. Inverted surcharge 20.00 20.00

Sower and Rainbow of Hope — A27

Perf. 9 to 14½ and Compound

1921 **Litho.**

Thin Laid or Wove Paper

Size: 28x22mm

154 A27 10m slate blue .20 .20
155 A27 15m light brown .40 .20
155A A27 20m red .20 .20
Nos. 154-155A (3) .80 .60

Signing of peace treaty with Russia.
See No. 191. For surcharges see Nos. 196-198.

Sun (Peace) Breaking into Darkness (Despair) — A28

"Peace" and "Agriculture"
A29

"Peace"
A30

Perf. 11, 11½, 12, 12½, 13 and Compound

1921, May 2

156	A28	2m green	1.40	.60
157	A28	3m blue	1.40	.60
158	A28	4m red	.90	.60
a.		4m carmine rose (error)	300.00	
159	A29	6m carmine rose	1.40	.65
160	A29	10m slate blue	1.00	.80
161	A30	25m dk violet	2.50	1.90
162	A30	50m slate bl & buff	1.50	1.10
		Nos. 156-162 (7)	10.10	6.25

Issued to commemorate the Constitution.

Polish Eagle — A31

Perf. 9 to 14½ and Compound

1921-23

163	A31	25m violet & buff	.20	.20
164	A31	50m carmine & buff	.20	.20
a.		Vert. pair, imperf. horiz.		
165	A31	100m blk brn & org	.20	.20
166	A31	200m black & rose ('23)	.35	.20
167	A31	300m olive grn ('23)	.35	.20
168	A31	400m brown ('23)	.35	.20
169	A31	500m brn vio ('23)	.35	.20
169A	A31	1000m orange ('23)	.35	.20
169B	A31	2000m dull blue ('23)	.35	.20
		Nos. 163-169B (9)	2.70	1.80

For surcharge see No. 195.

Type of 1919 and

Miner — A32

Perf. 9 to 14½ and Compound

1922-23

170	A10	5f blue	.20	.25
171	A10	10f lt violet	.20	.25
172	A11	20f pale red	.20	.50
173	A11	40f violet brn	.20	.25
174	A11	50f orange	.20	1.00
175	A11	75f blue green	.20	.50
176	A32	1m black	.20	.25
177	A32	1.25m dark green	.20	.25
178	A32	2m deep rose	.20	.25
179	A32	3m emerald	.20	.25
180	A32	4m deep ultra	.20	.25
181	A32	5m yellow brn	.20	.25
182	A32	6m red orange	.20	.50
183	A32	10m lilac brn	.20	.25
184	A32	20m deep violet	.20	1.00
185	A32	50m olive green	.20	1.00
187	A32	80m vermilion ('23)	.40	3.00
188	A32	100m violet ('23)	.40	3.50
189	A32	200m orange ('23)	1.50	4.50
190	A32	300m pale blue ('23)	4.50	5.00
		Nos. 170-190 (20)	10.00	23.00

Union of Upper Silesia with Poland.

There were 2 printings of Nos. 176 to 190, the 1st being from flat plates, the 2nd from rotary press on thin paper, perf. 12½.

Nos. 173 and 175 are printed from new plates showing larger value numerals and a single "f."

Sower Type Redrawn
Size: 25x21mm

1922 **Thick or Thin Wove Paper**

191 A27 20m carmine .30 .20

In this stamp the design has been strengthened and made more distinct, especially the ground and the numerals in the upper corners.

Nicolaus Copernicus
A33

Father Stanislaus Konarski — A34

1923 ***Perf. 10 to 12½***

192	A33	1000m indigo	.80	.30
193	A34	3000m brown	.45	.30
a.		"Konapski"	15.00	15.00
194	A33	5000m rose	.80	.30
		Nos. 192-194 (3)	2.05	.90

Nicolaus Copernicus (1473-1543), astronomer (Nos. 192, 194); Stanislaus Konarski (1700-1773), educator, and the creation by the Polish Parliament of the Commission of Public Instruction (No. 193).

No. 163 Surcharged

1923 ***Perf. 9 to 14½ and Compound***

195	A31	10000m on 25m	.30	.20
a.		Double surcharge	5.00	
b.		Inverted surcharge	7.50	

Stamps of 1921 Surcharged

196	A27	25000m on 20m red	.60	.20
a.		Double surcharge	5.00	5.00
b.		Inverted surcharge	10.00	
197	A27	50000m on 10m grnsh bl	.30	.20
a.		Double surcharge	5.00	5.00
b.		Inverted surcharge	7.50	7.50

No. 191 Surcharged

198	A27	25000m on 20m car	.50	.20
a.		Double surcharge	5.00	5.00
b.		Inverted surcharge	7.50	

No. 150 Surcharged with New Value

1924

199	A10	20000m on 2m gray grn	.70	.20
a.		Inverted surcharge	7.50	7.50
b.		Double surcharge	5.00	5.00

Type of 1919 Issue Surcharged with New Value

200	A10	100000m on 5m red brn	.30	.20
a.		Double surcharge	5.00	5.00
b.		Inverted surcharge	7.50	7.50
		Nos. 195-200 (6)	2.70	1.20

Arms of Poland — A35

Perf. 10 to 14½ and Compound

1924 **Litho.**

Thin Paper

205	A35	10,000m lilac brn	.30	.25
206	A35	20,000m ol grn	.30	.20
207	A35	30,000m scarlet	1.10	.35
208	A35	50,000m apple grn	2.25	.35
209	A35	100,000m brn org	.60	.30
210	A35	200,000m lt blue	.30	.20
211	A35	300,000m red vio	.60	.35
212	A35	500,000m brn	.60	.65
213	A35	1,000,000m ple rose	.60	8.00
214	A35	2,000,000m dk grn	1.10	100.00
		Nos. 205-214 (10)	7.75	110.65
		Set, never hinged	20.00	

Arms of Poland
A36

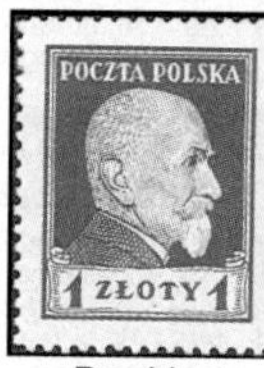
President Stanislaus Wojciechowski
A37

Perf. 10 to 13½ and Compound

1924

215	A36	1g orange brown	.35	.20
216	A36	2g dark brown	.35	.20
217	A36	3g orange	.40	.20
218	A36	5g olive green	.90	.20
219	A36	10g blue green	1.10	.20
220	A36	15g red	1.10	.20
221	A36	20g blue	2.25	.20
222	A36	25g red brown	3.00	.35
a.		25g indigo	3,000.	4,250.
223	A36	30g deep violet	21.00	.25
a.		30g gray blue	250.00	
224	A36	40g indigo	4.00	.35
225	A36	50g magenta	3.75	.30

Perf. 11½, 12

226	A37	1z scarlet	22.50	1.25
		Nos. 215-226 (12)	60.70	3.90
		Set, never hinged	125.00	

For overprints see Nos. 1K1-1K11.

Holy Gate of Wilno (Vilnius) — A38

Poznan Town Hall — A39

Sigismund Monument, Warsaw — A40

Wawel Castle at Cracow — A41

Sobieski Statue at Lwow — A42

Ship of State — A43

1925-27 ***Perf. 10 to 13***

227	A38	1g bister brown	.40	.20
228	A42	2g brown olive	.45	.25
229	A40	3g blue	1.75	.20
230	A39	5g yellow green	1.75	.20
231	A40	10g violet	1.75	.20
232	A41	15g rose red	1.65	.20
233	A43	20g dull red	1.90	.20
234	A38	24g gray blue	7.50	1.10
235	A42	30g dark blue	3.00	.20
236	A41	40g lt blue ('27)	3.50	.20
237	A43	45g dark violet	7.50	.20
		Nos. 227-237 (11)	31.15	3.15
		Set, never hinged	42.50	

For overprints see Nos. 1K11A-1K17.

1926-27 **Redrawn**

238	A40	3g blue	2.75	.45
239	A39	5g yellow green	3.25	.20
240	A40	10g violet	4.75	.20
241	A41	15g rose red	4.75	.20
		Nos. 238-241 (4)	15.50	1.05
		Set, never hinged	22.50	

On Nos. 229-232 the lines representing clouds touch the numerals. On the redrawn stamps the numerals have white outlines, separating them from the cloud lines.

Marshal Pilsudski — A44

Frederic Chopin — A45

1927 **Typo.** ***Perf. 12½, 11½***

242	A44	20g red brown	3.25	.50
243	A45	40g deep ultra	16.00	1.75
		Set, never hinged	27.50	

See No. 250. For overprint see No. 1K18.

President Ignacy Moscicki — A46

1927, May 4 ***Perf. 11½***

245	A46	20g red	5.50	.45
		Never hinged	7.00	

Dr. Karol Kaczkowski
A47

Juliusz Slowacki
A48

1927, May 27 ***Perf. 11½, 12½***

246	A47	10g gray green	2.75	2.25
247	A47	25g carmine	6.50	3.00
248	A47	40g dark blue	8.75	3.00
		Nos. 246-248 (3)	18.00	8.25
		Set, never hinged	40.00	

4th Intl. Congress of Millitary Medicine and Pharmacy, Warsaw, May 30-June 4.

1927, June 28 ***Perf. 12½***

249	A48	20g rose	6.00	.50
		Never hinged	8.00	

Transfer from Paris to Cracow of the remains of Julius Slowacki, poet.

Pilsudski Type of 1927
Design Redrawn

1928 ***Perf. 11½, 12x11½, 12½x13***

250	A44	25g yellow brown	2.75	.25
		Never hinged	6.00	

Souvenir Sheet

A49

1928, May 3 Engr. *Perf. 12½*
251 A49 Sheet of 2 250.00 325.00
Never hinged 375.00
a. 50g black brown 110.00 140.00
b. 1z black brown 110.00 140.00

1st Natl. Phil. Exhib., Warsaw, May 3-13. Sold to each purchaser of a 1.50z ticket to the Warsaw Philatelic Exhibition.
Counterfeits exist.

Marshal Pilsudski A49a

Pres. Moscicki A50

Perf. 10½ to 14 and Compound
1928-31
Wove Paper
253 A49a 50g bluish slate 4.00 .20
254 A49a 50g blue grn ('31) 12.50 .20
Set, never hinged 22.50

See No. 315.

Perf. 12x12½, 11½ to 13½ and Compound
1928
Laid Paper
255 A50 1z black, *cream* 11.00 .20
Never hinged 17.00
a. Horizontally laid paper ('30) 70.00 2.50
Never hinged 90.00

See Nos. 305, 316. For surcharges and overprints see Nos. J92-J94, 1K19, 1K24.

General Josef Bem A51

Henryk Sienkiewicz A52

1928, May Typo. *Perf. 12½*
Wove Paper
256 A51 25g rose red 4.00 .25
Never hinged 5.25

Return from Syria to Poland of the ashes of General Josef Bem.

1928, Oct.
257 A52 15g ultra 2.00 .20
Never hinged 3.25

For overprint see No. 1K23.

Eagle Arms — A53

"Swiatowid," Ancient Slav God — A54

1928-29 *Perf. 12x12½*
258 A53 5g dark violet .35 .20
259 A53 10g green 1.00 .20
260 A53 25g red brown .55 .20
Nos. 258-260 (3) 1.90 .60
Set, never hinged 3.75

See design A58. For overprints see Nos. 1K20-1K22.

1928, Dec. 15 *Perf. 12½x12*
261 A54 25g brown 2.50 .20
Never hinged 3.25

Poznan Agricultural Exhibition.

King John III Sobieski A55

Stylized Soldiers A56

1930, July *Perf. 12x12½*
262 A55 75g claret 5.75 .25
Never hinged 7.50

1930, Nov. 1 *Perf. 12½*
263 A56 5g violet brown .35 .20
264 A56 15g dark blue 2.25 .35
265 A56 25g red brown 1.25 .20
266 A56 30g dull red 6.25 3.75
Nos. 263-266 (4) 10.10 4.50
Set, never hinged 25.00

Centenary of insurrection of 1830.

Kosciuszko, Washington, Pulaski — A57

1932, May 3 *Perf. 11½*
Laid Paper
267 A57 30g brown 2.75 .30
Never hinged 3.50

200th birth anniv. of George Washington.

A58

Torun City Hall — A59

Perf. 12x12½
1932-33 Typo. Wmk. 234
268 A58 5g dull vio ('33) .35 .20
269 A58 10g green .35 .20
270 A58 15g red brown ('33) .35 .20
271 A58 20g gray .75 .20
272 A58 25g buff .95 .20
273 A58 30g deep rose 3.25 .20
274 A58 60g blue 19.00 .35
Nos. 268-274 (7) 25.00 1.55
Set, never hinged 32.50

For overprints and surcharge see Nos. 280-281, 284, 292, 1K25-1K27.

1933, Jan. 2 Engr. *Perf. 11½*
275 A59 60g blue 37.50 .75
Never hinged 80.00

700th anniversary of the founding of the City of Torun by the Grand Master of the Knights of the Teutonic Order.
See No. B28.

Altar Panel of St. Mary's Church, Cracow — A60

Perf. 11½-12½ & Compound
1933, July 10 Unwmk.
Laid Paper
277 A60 80g red brown 15.00 1.50
Never hinged 21.00

400th death anniv. of Veit Stoss, sculptor and woodcarver.
For surcharge see No. 285.

John III Sobieski and Allies before Vienna, painted by Jan Matejko — A61

1933, Sept. 12 Laid Paper
278 A61 1.20z indigo 37.50 6.00
Never hinged 60.00

250th anniv. of the deliverance of Vienna by the Polish and allied forces under command of John III Sobieski, King of Poland, when besieged by the Turks in 1683.
For surcharge see No. 286.

Cross of Independence A62

Josef Pilsudski A63

Wmk. 234
1933, Nov. 11 Typo. *Perf. 12½*
279 A62 30g scarlet 7.50 .40
Never hinged 8.75

15th anniversary of independence.

Type of 1932 Overprinted in Red or Black

1934, May 5 *Perf. 12*
280 A58 20g gray (R) 30.00 24.00
281 A58 30g deep rose 30.00 24.00
Set, never hinged 100.00

Katowice Philatelic Exhibition. Counterfeits exist.

Perf. 11½ to 12½ and Compound
1934, Aug. 6 Engr. Unwmk.
282 A63 25g gray blue 1.25 .25
283 A63 30g black brown 3.00 .40
Set, never hinged 5.25

Polish Legion, 20th anniversary.
For overprint see No. 293.

Nos. 274, 277-278 Surcharged in Black or Red

1934 Wmk. 234 *Perf. 12x12½*
284 A58 55g on 60g blue 6.00 .50
Perf. 11½-12½ & Compound
Unwmk.
285 A60 25g on 80g red brn 6.50 .65
286 A61 1z on 1.20z ind (R) 16.00 2.50
a. Figure "1" in surcharge 5mm high instead of 4½mm 18.00 2.50
Never hinged 21.00
Nos. 284-286 (3) 28.50 3.65
Set, never hinged 48.00

Surcharge of No. 286 includes bars.

Marshal Pilsudski — A64

1935 *Perf. 11 to 13 and Compound*
287 A64 5g black .40 .20
288 A64 15g black .40 .20
289 A64 25g black 1.65 .20
290 A64 45g black 6.75 2.40
291 A64 1z black 10.75 5.00
Nos. 287-291 (5) 19.95 8.00
Set, never hinged 24.00

Pilsudski mourning issue.
Nos. 287-288 are typo., Nos. 290-291 litho. No. 289 exists both typo. and litho.
See No. B35b.

Nos. 270, 282 Overprinted in Blue or Red

1935 Wmk. 234 *Perf. 12x12½*
292 A58 15g red brown 1.00 .45
Perf. 11½, 11½x12½
Unwmk.
293 A63 25g gray blue (R) 3.25 1.50
Set, never hinged 5.75

Issued in connection with the proposed memorial to Marshal Pilsudski, the stamps were sold at Cracow exclusively.

"The Dog Cliff" — A65

President Ignacy Moscicki — A75

Designs: 10g, "Eye of the Sea." 15g, M. S. "Pilsudski." 20g, View of Pieniny. 25g, Belvedere Palace. 30g, Castle in Mira. 45g, Castle at Podhorce. 50g, Cloth Hall, Cracow. 55g, Raczynski Library, Poznan. 1z, Cathedral, Wilno.

1935-36 Typo. *Perf. 12½x13*
294 A65 5g violet blue .60 .20
295 A65 10g yellow green .60 .20
296 A65 15g Prus green 1.90 .20
297 A65 20g violet black .95 .20
Engr.
298 A65 25g myrtle green .80 .20
299 A65 30g rose red 2.00 .30
300 A65 45g plum ('36) 1.00 .30
301 A65 50g black ('36) 1.00 .30
302 A65 55g blue ('36) 9.50 .60
303 A65 1z brown ('36) 3.75 1.65
304 A75 3z black brown 2.25 2.50
Nos. 294-304 (11) 24.35 6.65
Set, never hinged 32.50

See Nos. 308-311. For overprints see Nos. 306-307, 1K28-1K32.

Type of 1928 inscribed "1926. 3. VI. 1936" on Bottom Margin

1936, June 3
305 A50 1z ultra 7.50 6.00
Never hinged 9.50

Presidency of Ignacy Moscicki, 10th anniv.

Nos. 299, 302 Overprinted in Blue or Red

1936, Aug. 15
306 A65 30g rose red 12.00 6.00
307 A65 55g blue (R) 12.00 6.00
Set, never hinged 30.00

Gordon-Bennett Intl. Balloon Race. Counterfeits exist.

Scenic Type of 1935-36

Designs: 5g, Church at Czestochowa. 10g, Maritime Terminal, Gdynia. 15g, University, Lwow. 20g, Municipal Building, Katowice.

1937 Engr. *Perf. 12½*

308 A65 5g violet blue .20 .20
309 A65 10g green .55 .20
310 A65 15g red brown .40 .20
311 A65 20g orange brown .55 .20
Nos. 308-311 (4) 1.70 .80
Set, never hinged 3.00

For overprints see Nos. 1K31-1K32.

Marshal Smigly-Rydz
A80

President Moscicki
A81

1937 *Perf. 12½x13*

312 A80 25g slate green .25 .20
313 A80 55g blue .60 .20
Set, never hinged 1.50

For surcharges see Nos. N30, N32.

Types of 1928-37
Souvenir Sheets

1937

314 Sheet of 4 25.00 25.00
a. A80 25g, dark brown 2.75 2.75
315 Sheet of 4 25.00 25.00
a. A49a 50g, deep blue 2.75 2.75
316 Sheet of 4 25.00 25.00
a. A50 1z, gray black 2.75 2.75
Set, never hinged 110.00

Visit of King Carol of Romania to Poland, June 26-July 1.
See No. B35c.

1938, Feb. 1 *Perf. 12½*

317 A81 15g slate green .20 .20
318 A81 30g rose violet .60 .20
Set, never hinged 1.10

71st birthday of President Moscicki.
For surcharge see No. N31.

Kosciuszko, Paine and Washington and View of New York City — A82

1938, Mar. 17 *Perf. 12x12½*

319 A82 1z gray blue 1.25 1.75
Never hinged 2.00

150th anniv. of the US Constitution.

Boleslaus I and Emperor Otto III at Gnesen — A83

Marshal Pilsudski — A95

Designs: 10g, King Casimir III. 15g, King Ladislas II Jagello and Queen Hedwig. 20g, King Casimir IV. 25g, Treaty of Lublin. 30g, King Stephen Bathory commending Wielock, the peasant. 45g, Stanislas Zolkiewski and Jan Chodkiewicz. 50g, John III Sobieski entering Vienna. 55g, Union of nobles, commoners and peasants. 75g, Dabrowski, Kosciuszko and Poniatowski. 1z, Polish soldiers. 2z, Romuald Traugutt.

1938, Nov. 11 Engr. *Perf. 12½*

320 A83 5g red orange .20 .20
321 A83 10g green .20 .20
322 A83 15g fawn .30 .20
323 A83 20g peacock blue .40 .20
324 A83 25g dull violet .20 .20
325 A83 30g rose red .65 .20
326 A83 45g black .40 .20
327 A83 50g brt red vio 2.75 .20
328 A83 55g ultra .85 .20
329 A83 75g dull green 2.00 1.50
330 A83 1z orange 1.60 1.40
331 A83 2z carmine rose 11.00 8.00
332 A95 3z gray black 9.00 14.00
Nos. 320-332 (13) 29.55 26.70
Set, never hinged 37.50

20th anniv. of Poland's independence. See No. 339. For surcharges see Nos. N33-N47.

Souvenir Sheet

Marshal Pilsudski, Gabriel Narutowicz, President Moscicki, Marshal Smigly-Rydz — A96

1938, Nov. 11 *Perf. 12½*

333 A96 Sheet of 4 16.00 18.00
Never hinged 21.00
a. 25g dull violet (Pilsudski) 1.60 1.75
b. 25g dull violet (Narutowicz) 1.60 1.75
c. 25g dull violet (Moscicki) 1.60 1.75
d. 25g dull violet (Smigly-Rydz) 1.60 1.75

20th anniv. of Poland's independence.

Poland Welcoming Teschen People — A97

Skier — A98

1938, Nov. 11

334 A97 25g dull violet 1.50 .45
Never hinged 2.00

Restoration of the Teschen territory ceded by Czechoslovakia.

1939, Feb. 6

335 A98 15g orange brown 1.00 *1.10*
336 A98 25g dull violet 1.75 .50
337 A98 30g rose red 2.25 1.10
338 A98 55g brt ultra 10.00 4.00
Nos. 335-338 (4) 15.00 6.70
Set, never hinged 25.00

Intl. Ski Meet, Zakopane, Feb. 11-19.

Type of 1938

15g, King Ladislas II Jagello, Queen Hedwig.

Re-engraved

1939, Mar. 2 *Perf. 12½*

339 A83 15g redsh brown .25 .20
Never hinged .55

No. 322 with crossed swords and helmet at lower left. No. 339, swords and helmet have been removed.

Marshal Pilsudski Reviewing Troops — A99

1939, Aug. 1 Engr.

340 A99 25g dull rose violet .60 .50
Never hinged .80

Polish Legion, 25th anniv. See No. B35a.

SEMI-POSTAL STAMPS

Regular Issue of 1919 Surcharged in Violet

a

b

1919, May 3 Unwmk. *Imperf.*

B1 A10(a) 5f + 5f grn .20 .20
B2 A10(a) 10f + 5f red vio 2.00 1.40
B3 A10(a) 15f + 5f dp red .40 .20
B4 A11(b) 25f + 5f ol grn .40 .20
B5 A11(b) 50f + 5f bl grn .60 .30

Perf. 11½

B6 A10(a) 5f + 5f grn .25 .20
B7 A10(a) 10f + 5f red vio .50 .20
B8 A10(a) 15f + 5f dp red .25 .20
B9 A11(b) 25f + 5f ol grn .30 .20
B10 A11(b) 50f + 5f bl grn 1.00 .40
Nos. B1-B10 (10) 5.90 3.50

First Polish Philatelic Exhibition. The surtax benefited the Polish White Cross Society.

Regular Issue of 1920 Surcharged in Carmine

1921, Mar. 5 *Perf. 9*

Thin Laid Paper

B11 A14 5m + 30m red vio 5.00 7.00
B12 A14 6m + 30m dp rose 5.00 7.00
B13 A14 10m + 30m lt red 12.00 *19.00*
B14 A14 20m + 30m gray grn 37.50 *65.00*
Nos. B11-B14 (4) 59.50 98.00

Counterfeits, differently perforated, exist of Nos. B11-B14.

SP1

Light of Knowledge — SP2

1925, Jan. 1 Typo. *Perf. 12½*

B15 SP1 1g orange brn 12.00 14.00
B16 SP1 2g dk brown 12.00 14.00
B17 SP1 3g orange 12.00 14.00
B18 SP1 5g olive grn 12.00 14.00
B19 SP1 10g blue grn 12.00 14.00
B20 SP1 15g red 12.00 14.00
B21 SP1 20g blue 12.00 14.00
B22 SP1 25g red brown 12.00 14.00
B23 SP1 30g dp violet 12.00 14.00
B24 SP1 40g indigo 35.00 14.00
B25 SP1 50g magenta 12.00 14.00
Nos. B15-B25 (11) 155.00 154.00
Set, never hinged 200.00

"Na Skarb" means "National Funds." These stamps were sold at a premium of 50 groszy each, for charity.

1927, May 3 *Perf. 11½*

B26 SP2 10g + 5g choc & grn 7.00 4.50
B27 SP2 20g + 5g dk bl & buff 7.00 4.50
Set, never hinged 24.00

"NA OSWIATE" means "For Public Instruction." The surtax aided an Association of Educational Societies.

Torun Type of 1933

1933, May 21 Engr.

B28 A59 60g (+40g) red brn, *buff* 16.00 12.00
Never hinged 21.00

Philatelic Exhibition at Torun, May 21-28, 1933, and sold at a premium of 40g to aid the exhibition funds.

Souvenir Sheet

Stagecoach and Wayside Inn — SP3

1938, May 3 Engr. *Perf. 12, Imperf.*

B29 SP3 Sheet of 4 72.50 65.00
Never hinged 90.00
a. 45g green 7.50 7.50
b. 55g blue 7.50 7.50

5th Phil. Exhib., Warsaw, May 3-8. The sheet contains two 45g and two 55g stamps. Sold for 3z.

Souvenir Sheet

Stratosphere Balloon over Mountains — SP4

1938, Sept. 15 *Perf. 12½*

B31 SP4 75g dp vio, sheet 55.00 60.00
Never hinged 75.00

Issued in advance of a proposed Polish stratosphere flight. Sold for 2z.

Winterhelp Issue

SP5

1938-39

B32 SP5 5g + 5g red org .55 .95
B33 SP5 25g + 10g dk vio ('39) .90 1.40
B34 SP5 55g + 15g brt ultra ('39) 1.75 2.25
Nos. B32-B34 (3) 3.20 4.60
Set, never hinged 5.00

For surcharges see Nos. N48-N50.

Souvenir Sheet

SP6

1939, Aug. 1

B35	SP6	Sheet of 3, dark blue gray	27.50	20.00
		Never hinged	32.50	
a.		25g Marshal Pilsudski Reviewing Troops	4.75	3.50
b.		25g Marshal Pilsudski	4.75	3.50
c.		25g Marshal Smigly-Rydz	4.75	3.50

25th anniv. of the founding of the Polish Legion. The sheets sold for 1.75z, the surtax going to the National Defense fund.

See types A64, A80, A99.

AIR POST STAMPS

Biplane — AP1

Perf. 12½

1925, Sept. 10 Typo. Unwmk.

C1	AP1	1g	lt blue	.65	2.25
C2	AP1	2g	orange	.65	2.25
C3	AP1	3g	yellow brn	.65	2.25
C4	AP1	5g	dk brown	.65	.85
C5	AP1	10g	dk green	1.65	.75
C6	AP1	15g	red violet	2.50	.85
C7	AP1	20g	olive grn	10.50	4.25
C8	AP1	30g	dull rose	6.75	1.50
C9	AP1	45g	dk violet	8.50	4.25
			Nos. C1-C9 (9)	32.50	19.20
			Set, never hinged	45.00	

Counterfeits exist.

For overprint see No. C11.

Capt. Franciszek Zwirko and Stanislaus Wigura — AP2

Perf. 11½ to 12½ and Compound

1933, Apr. 15 Engr. Wmk. 234

C10	AP2	30g gray green	14.00	1.00
		Never hinged	20.00	

Winning of the circuit of Europe flight by two Polish aviators in 1932. The stamp was available for both air mail and ordinary postage.

For overprint see No. C12.

Nos. C7 and C10 Overprinted in Red

1934, Aug. 28 Unwmk. *Perf. 12½*

C11	AP1	20g olive green	12.50	6.75

Wmk. 234

Perf. 11½

C12	AP2	30g gray green	7.00	2.25
		Set, never hinged	26.00	

POSTAGE DUE STAMPS

Cracow Issues

Postage Due Stamps of Austria, 1916, Overprinted in Black or Red

1919, Jan. 10 Unwmk. *Perf. 12½*

J1	D4	5h	rose red	7.00	6.00
J2	D4	10h	rose red	*2,500.*	*1,750.*
J3	D4	15h	rose red	3.75	*6.00*
a.			Inverted overprint	150.00	
J4	D4	20h	rose red	*275.00*	*350.00*
J5	D4	25h	rose red	*17.50*	*25.00*
J6	D4	30h	rose red	*800.00*	*750.00*
J7	D4	40h	rose red	*700.00*	*600.00*
J8	D5	1k	ultra (R)	*2,400.*	*2,400.*
J9	D5	5k	ultra (R)	*2,400.*	*2,400.*
J10	D5	10k	ultra (R)	*10,000.*	*9,000.*
a.			Black overprint	*42,500.*	—

Overprint on Nos. J1-J7, J10a is type. Overprint on Nos. J8-J10 is slightly larger than illustration, has a different ornament between lines of type and is litho.

D6

Type of Austria, 1916-18, Surcharged in Black

1919, Jan. 10

J11	D6	15h on 36h vio	300.00	200.00
J12	D6	50h on 42h choc	30.00	*50.00*
a.		Double surcharge	—	*8,000.*

See note above No. 41.
Counterfeits exist of Nos. J1-J12.

Regular Issues

Numerals of Value
D7 D8

1919 Typo. *Perf. 11½*

For Northern Poland

J13	D7	2f	red orange	.40	.30
J14	D7	4f	red orange	.20	.20
J15	D7	5f	red orange	.20	.20
J16	D7	10f	red orange	.20	.20
J17	D7	20f	red orange	.20	.20
J18	D7	30f	red orange	.20	.20
J19	D7	50f	red orange	.20	.20
J20	D7	100f	red orange	.75	.45
J21	D7	500f	red orange	1.75	1.25

For Southern Poland

J22	D7	2h	dark blue	.20	.20
J23	D7	4h	dark blue	.20	.20
J24	D7	5h	dark blue	.20	.20
J25	D7	10h	dark blue	.20	.20
J26	D7	20h	dark blue	.20	.20
J27	D7	30h	dark blue	.20	.20
J28	D7	50h	dark blue	.20	.20
J29	D7	100h	dark blue	.30	.25
J30	D7	500h	dark blue	1.40	1.10
			Nos. J13-J30 (18)	7.20	5.95

Counterfeits exist.

1920 *Perf. 9, 10, 11½*

Thin Laid Paper

J31	D7	20f	dark blue	.70	.50
J32	D7	100f	dark blue	.35	.25
J33	D7	200f	dark blue	.60	.50
J34	D7	500f	dark blue	.35	.25
			Nos. J31-J34 (4)	2.00	1.50

Regular Issue of 1919 Surcharged

1921, Jan. 25 *Imperf.*

Wove Paper

J35	A9	6m on 15h brown	.75	.40
J36	A9	6m on 25h car	.75	.40
J37	A9	20m on 10h lake	1.50	1.10
J38	A9	20m on 50h indigo	2.00	1.40
J39	A9	35m on 70h dp bl	12.00	12.00
		Nos. J35-J39 (5)	17.00	15.30

Counterfeits exist.

Perf. 9 to 14½ and Compound

1921-22 Typo.

Thin Laid or Wove Paper

Size: 17x22mm

J40	D8	1m	indigo	.30	.20
J41	D8	2m	indigo	.30	.20
J42	D8	4m	indigo	.30	.20
J43	D8	6m	indigo	.30	.20
J44	D8	8m	indigo	.30	.20
J45	D8	20m	indigo	.30	.20
J46	D8	50m	indigo	.30	.20
J47	D8	100m	indigo	.60	.20
			Nos. J40-J47 (8)	2.70	1.60

Nos. J44-J45, J41 Surcharged

Perf. 9 to 14½ and Compound

1923, Nov.

J48	D8	10,000(m) on 8m indigo	1.50	.20
J49	D8	20,000(m) on 20m indigo	1.50	.20
J50	D8	50,000(m) on 2m indigo	7.00	.70
		Nos. J48-J50 (3)	10.00	1.10

Type of 1921-22 Issue

1923 Typo. *Perf. 12½*

Size: 19x24mm

J51	D8	50m	indigo	.20	.20
J52	D8	100m	indigo	.20	.20
J53	D8	200m	indigo	.20	.20
J54	D8	500m	indigo	.20	.20
J55	D8	1000m	indigo	.20	.20
J56	D8	2000m	indigo	.20	.20
J57	D8	10,000m	indigo	.20	.20
J58	D8	20,000m	indigo	.20	.20
J59	D8	30,000m	indigo	.20	.20
J60	D8	50,000m	indigo	.40	.20
J61	D8	100,000m	indigo	.40	.20
J62	D8	200,000m	indigo	.45	.20
J63	D8	300,000m	indigo	.45	.30
J64	D8	500,000m	indigo	.65	.20
J65	D8	1,000,000m	indigo	1.50	.60
J66	D8	2,000,000m	indigo	2.75	.60
J67	D8	3,000,000m	indigo	3.00	.85
			Nos. J51-J67 (17)	11.40	4.95

D9 D10

Perf. 10 to 13½ and Compound

1924

Size: 20x25½mm

J68	D9	1g	brown	.30	.25
J69	D9	2g	brown	.30	.25
J70	D9	4g	brown	.30	.25
J71	D9	6g	brown	.55	.25
J72	D9	10g	brown	3.25	.25
J73	D9	15g	brown	2.50	.40
J74	D9	20g	brown	6.00	.40
J75	D9	25g	brown	5.00	.40
J76	D9	30g	brown	1.10	.40
J77	D9	40g	brown	1.10	.40
J78	D9	50g	brown	1.10	.40
J79	D9	1z	brown	1.00	.55
J80	D9	2z	brown	1.00	.55
J81	D9	3z	brown	1.90	2.25
J82	D9	5z	brown	1.90	.85
			Nos. J68-J82 (15)	27.30	7.85

Nos. J68-J69 and J72-J75 exist measuring 19½x24½mm.

For surcharges see Nos. J84-J91.

1930, July *Perf. 12½*

J83	D10	5g olive brown	.70	.20
		Never hinged	1.00	

Postage Due Stamps of 1924 Surcharged

Perf. 10 to 13½ and Compound

1934-38

J84	D9	10g on 2z brown ('38)	.40	.30
J85	D9	15g on 2z brown	.40	.30
J86	D9	20g on 1z brown	.40	.30
J87	D9	20g on 5z brown	2.00	.55
J88	D9	25g on 40g brown	1.25	.55
J89	D9	30g on 40g brown	.85	.55
J90	D9	50g on 40g brown	.85	.70
J91	D9	50g on 3z brown ('35)	1.75	1.00
		Nos. J84-J91 (8)	7.90	4.25
		Set, never hinged	18.00	

No. 255a Surcharged in Red or Indigo

1934-36 Laid Paper

J92	A50	10g on 1z (R) ('36)	.80	.20
a.		Vertically laid paper (No. 255)	25.00	18.00
J93	A50	20g on 1z (R) ('36)	2.50	.80
J94	A50	25g on 1z (I)	.80	.30
a.		Vertically laid paper (No. 255)	30.00	18.00
		Nos. J92-J94 (3)	4.10	1.30
		Set, never hinged	8.00	

D11

1938-39 Typo. *Perf. 12½x12*

J95	D11	5g	dark blue green	.20	.20
J96	D11	10g	dark blue green	.20	.20
J97	D11	15g	dark blue green	.20	.20
J98	D11	20g	dark blue green	.60	.20
J99	D11	25g	dark blue green	.20	.20
J100	D11	30g	dark blue green	.40	.20
J101	D11	50g	dark blue green	.80	1.25
J102	D11	1z	dark blue green	2.50	1.65
			Nos. J95-J102 (8)	5.10	4.10
			Set, never hinged	12.00	

For surcharges see Nos. N51-N55.

OFFICIAL STAMPS

O1

Perf. 10, 11½, 10x11½, 11½x10

1920, Feb. 1 Litho. Unwmk.

O1	O1	3f	vermilion	.35	*.45*
O2	O1	5f	vermilion	.35	*.45*
O3	O1	10f	vermilion	.35	*.45*
O4	O1	15f	vermilion	.35	*.45*
O5	O1	25f	vermilion	.35	*.45*
O6	O1	50f	vermilion	.35	*.45*
O7	O1	100f	vermilion	.35	*.45*
O8	O1	150f	vermilion	.65	.45
O9	O1	200f	vermilion	.65	.45
O10	O1	300f	vermilion	.50	.45
O11	O1	600f	vermilion	.75	.45
			Nos. O1-O11 (11)	5.00	4.95

The stars on either side of the denomination do not appear on Nos. O7-O11.

Numerals Larger
Stars inclined outward

1920, Nov. 20 *Perf. 11½*

Thin Laid Paper

O12	O1	5f	red	.25	*.40*
O13	O1	10f	red	.75	.70
O14	O1	15f	red	.50	*.95*
O15	O1	25f	red	1.10	.95
O16	O1	50f	red	1.40	1.00
			Nos. O12-O16 (5)	4.00	4.00

Polish Eagle
O3 O4

Perf. 12x12½

1933, Aug. 1 Typo. Wmk. 234

O17	O3	(30g) vio (Zwyczajna)	.95	.20
O18	O3	(80g) red (Polecona)	2.25	.30
		Set, never hinged	4.00	

1935, Apr. 1

O19	O4	(25g) bl vio (Zwyczajna)	.20	.20
O20	O4	(55g) car (Polecona)	.30	.20
		Set, never hinged	.75	

Stamps inscribed "Zwyczajna" or "Zwykla" were for ordinary official mail. Those with "Polecona" were for registered official mail.

NEWSPAPER STAMPS

Austrian Newspaper Stamps of 1916 Overprinted

1919, Jan. 10 Unwmk. *Imperf.*

P1	N9	2h brown	9.50	*15.75*
P2	N9	4h green	2.75	*5.25*
P3	N9	6h dark blue	2.75	*5.25*
P4	N9	10h orange	67.50	62.50
P5	N9	30h claret	7.50	11.25
		Nos. P1-P5 (5)	90.00	100.00

See note above No. 41.
Counterfeits exist of Nos. P1-P5.

OCCUPATION STAMPS

Issued under German Occupation

German Stamps of 1905 Overprinted

Perf. 14, 14½

1915, May 12 Wmk. 125

N1	A16	3pf brown	.60	.50
N2	A16	5pf green	1.25	.50
N3	A16	10pf carmine	1.25	.50
N4	A16	20pf ultra	2.50	.75
N5	A16	40pf lake & blk	7.50	3.75
		Nos. N1-N5 (5)	13.10	6.00

German Stamps of 1905-17 Overprinted

1916-17

N6	A22	2½pf gray	1.25	*2.50*
N7	A16	3pf brown	1.25	*2.50*
N8	A16	5pf green	1.25	*2.50*
N9	A22	7½pf orange	1.25	*2.50*
N10	A16	10pf carmine	1.25	*2.50*
N11	A22	15pf yel brn	3.50	3.50
N12	A22	15pf dk vio ('17)	1.25	*2.50*
N13	A16	20pf ultra	1.75	*2.50*
N14	A16	30pf org & blk, *buff*	7.00	*15.00*
N15	A16	40pf lake & blk	2.50	2.50
N16	A16	60pf magenta	3.00	*3.50*
		Nos. N6-N16 (11)	25.25	42.00

For overprints and surcharges see #15-26.

German Stamps of 1934 Surcharged in Black

1939, Dec. 1 Wmk. 237 *Perf. 14*

N17	A64	6g on 3pf bister	.20	*.40*
N18	A64	8g on 4pf dl bl	.20	*.40*
N19	A64	12g on 6pf dk grn	.20	*.40*
N20	A64	16g on 8pf vermilion	.40	1.00
N21	A64	20g on 10pf choc	.20	.40
N22	A64	24g on 12pf dp car	.20	.20
N23	A64	30g on 15pf maroon	.50	.90
N24	A64	40g on 20pf brt bl	.40	.40
N25	A64	50g on 25pf ultra	.40	.75
N26	A64	60g on 30pf ol grn	.40	.40
N27	A64	80g on 40pf red vio	.50	.80
N28	A64	1z on 50pf dk grn & blk	1.00	1.25
N29	A64	2z on 100(pf) org & blk	2.00	*3.50*
		Nos. N17-N29 (13)	6.60	10.80
		Set, never hinged	17.50	

Stamps of Poland 1937, Surcharged in Black or Brown

1940 Unwmk. *Perf. 12½, 12½x13*

N30	A80	24g on 25g sl grn	1.25	*3.25*
N31	A81	40g on 30g rose vio	.40	1.25
N32	A80	50g on 55g blue	.25	*.65*

Similar Surcharge on Stamps of 1938-39

N33	A83	2g on 5g red org	.20	*.40*
N34	A83	4(g) on 5g red org	.20	*.40*
N35	A83	6(g) on 10g grn	.20	*.40*
N36	A83	8(g) on 10g grn (Br)	.20	*.40*
N37	A83	10(g) on 10g grn	.20	*.40*
N38	A83	12(g) on 15g redsh brn (#339)	.20	*.40*
N39	A83	16(g) on 15g redsh brn (#339)	.20	*.40*
N40	A83	24g on 25g dl vio	.20	*.40*
N41	A83	30(g) on 30g rose red	.20	*.40*
N42	A83	50(g) on 50g brt red vio	.25	*.65*
N43	A83	60(g) on 55g ultra	6.00	*17.00*
N44	A83	80(g) on 75g dl grn	6.00	*17.00*
N45	A83	1z on 1z org	6.00	*17.00*
N46	A83	2z on 2z car rose	3.00	*7.50*
N47	A95	3z on 3z gray blk	4.00	*10.00*

Similar Surcharge on Nos. B32-B34

N48	SP5	30g on 5g+5g	.25	.65
N49	SP5	40g on 25g+10g	.25	.65
N50	SP5	1z on 55g+15g	4.00	*10.00*

Similar Surcharge on Nos. J98-J102

Perf. 12½x12

N51	D11	50(g) on 20g	1.25	*3.25*
N52	D11	50(g) on 25g	6.00	*17.50*
N53	D11	50(g) on 30g	14.00	*37.50*
N54	D11	50(g) on 50g	.75	*2.40*
N55	D11	50(g) on 1z	1.75	*4.75*
		Nos. N30-N55 (26)	57.20	154.60
		Set, never hinged	140.00	

The surcharge on Nos. N30 to N55 is arranged to fit the shape of the stamp and obliterate the original denomination. On some values, "General Gouvernement" appears at the bottom. Counterfeits exist.

St. Florian's Gate, Cracow — OS1

Palace, Warsaw — OS13

Designs: 8g, Watch Tower, Cracow. 10g, Cracow Gate, Lublin. 12g, Courtyard and statue of Copernicus. 20g, Dominican Church, Cracow. 24g, Wawel Castle, Cracow. 30g, Church, Lublin. 40g, Arcade, Cloth Hall, Cracow. 48g, City Hall, Sandomierz. 50g, Court House, Cracow. 60g, Courtyard, Cracow. 80g, St. Mary's Church, Cracow.

1940-41 Unwmk. Photo. *Perf. 14*

N56	OS1	6g brown	.20	*.75*
N57	OS1	8g brn org	.20	*.75*
N58	OS1	8g bl blk ('41)	.20	*.50*
N59	OS1	10g emerald	.20	*.25*
N60	OS1	12g dk grn	1.75	.70
N61	OS1	12g dp vio ('41)	.20	*.25*
N62	OS1	20g dk ol brn	.20	.20
N63	OS1	24g henna brn	.20	.20
N64	OS1	30g purple	.20	.20
N65	OS1	30g vio brn ('41)	.20	*.25*
N66	OS1	40g slate blk	.20	.20
N67	OS1	48g chnt brn ('41)	.50	*1.50*
N68	OS1	50g brt bl	.20	.20
N69	OS1	60g slate grn	.20	*.25*
N70	OS1	80g dull pur	.20	*.50*
N71	OS13	1z rose lake	1.25	1.25
N72	OS13	1z Prus grn ('41)	.55	*1.00*
		Nos. N56-N72 (17)	6.65	8.95
		Set, never hinged	14.50	

For surcharges see Nos. NB1-NB4.

OCCUPATION SEMI-POSTAL STAMPS

Issued under German Occupation

Types of 1940 Occupation Postage Stamps Surcharged in Red

1940, Aug. 17 Unwmk. Photo. *Perf. 14*

NB1	OS1	12g + 8g olive gray	1.25	3.50
NB2	OS1	24g + 16g olive gray	1.25	3.50
NB3	OS1	50g + 50g olive gray	1.50	4.00
NB4	OS1	80g + 80g olive gray	1.50	4.00
		Nos. NB1-NB4 (4)	5.50	15.00
		Set, never hinged	15.00	

German Peasant Girl in Poland
OSP1

Designs: 24g+26g, Woman wearing scarf. 30g+20g, Similar to type OSP4.

1940, Oct. 26 Engr. *Perf. 14½*
Thick Paper

NB5	OSP1	12g + 38g dk sl grn	.85	2.75
NB6	OSP1	24g + 26g cop red	.85	2.75
NB7	OSP1	30g + 20g dk pur	1.50	*5.00*
		Nos. NB5-NB7 (3)	3.20	10.50
		Nos. NB5-NB7 (3)	3.20	10.50
		Set, never hinged	8.50	

1st anniversary of the General Government.

German Peasant
OSP4

1940, Dec. 1 *Perf. 12*

NB8	OSP4	12g + 8g dk grn	.35	*.90*
NB9	OSP4	24g + 16g rose red	.40	*1.75*
NB10	OSP4	30g + 30g vio brn	1.00	*2.50*
NB11	OSP4	50g + 50g ultra	1.00	*3.00*
		Nos. NB8-NB11 (4)	2.75	8.15
		Set, never hinged	7.00	

The surtax was for war relief.

OCCUPATION RURAL DELIVERY STAMPS

Issued under German Occupation

OSD1

Perf. 13½

1940, Dec. 1 Photo. Unwmk.

NL1	OSD1	10g red orange	.45	*1.00*
NL2	OSD1	20g red orange	.45	*1.25*
NL3	OSD1	30g red orange	.45	*1.25*
NL4	OSD1	50g red orange	1.10	*3.00*
		Nos. NL1-NL4 (4)	2.45	*6.50*
		Set, never hinged	4.00	

OCCUPATION OFFICIAL STAMPS

Issued under German Occupation

Eagle and Swastika
OOS1

Perf. 12, 13½x14

1940, Apr. Photo. Unwmk.

Size: 31x23mm

NO1	OOS1	6g lt brown	.50	*2.00*
NO2	OOS1	8g gray	.50	*2.00*
NO3	OOS1	10g green	.50	*2.00*
NO4	OOS1	12g dk green	.50	*1.75*
NO5	OOS1	20g dk brown	.50	*2.50*
NO6	OOS1	24g henna brn	8.00	1.75
NO7	OOS1	30g rose lake	.60	*2.75*
NO8	OOS1	40g dl violet	.60	*5.00*
NO9	OOS1	48g dl olive	6.50	*5.00*
NO10	OOS1	50g royal bl	.50	2.75
NO11	OOS1	60g dk ol grn	.50	*2.00*
NO12	OOS1	80g rose vio	.50	*2.00*

Size: 35x26mm

NO13	OOS1	1z gray blk & brn vio	1.25	*4.75*
NO14	OOS1	3z gray blk & chnt	1.25	*4.75*
NO15	OOS1	5z gray blk & org brn	2.00	*5.50*
		Nos. NO1-NO15 (15)	24.20	46.50
		Set, never hinged	65.00	

1940 *Perf. 12*

Size: 21¼x16¼mm

NO16	OOS1	6g brown	.35	1.10
NO17	OOS1	8g slate	.50	1.75
NO18	OOS1	10g dp grn	.85	2.00
NO19	OOS1	12g slate grn	.85	2.00
NO20	OOS1	20g blk brn	.50	1.10
NO21	OOS1	24g cop brn	.35	1.10
NO22	OOS1	30g rose lake	.50	1.75
NO23	OOS1	40g dl pur	.85	2.00
NO24	OOS1	50g royal blue	.85	2.00
		Nos. NO16-NO24 (9)	5.60	14.80
		Set, never hinged	16.00	

POLISH OFFICES ABROAD

OFFICES IN DANZIG

Poland Nos. 215-225 Overprinted

1925, Jan. 5 Unwmk. *Perf. 11½x12*

1K1	A36	1g orange brn	.45	1.10
1K2	A36	2g dk brown	.60	3.25
1K3	A36	3g orange	.60	1.10
1K4	A36	5g olive grn	15.00	7.50
1K5	A36	10g blue grn	5.00	2.25
1K6	A36	15g red	30.00	5.75
1K7	A36	20g blue	1.75	1.10
1K8	A36	25g red brown	1.75	1.10
1K9	A36	30g dp violet	2.00	1.10

1K10	A36	40g indigo	2.00	1.10
1K11	A36	50g magenta	5.50	1.65
		Nos. 1K1-1K11 (11)	64.65	27.00

Same Ovpt. on Poland Nos. 230-231

1926 ***Perf. 11½, 12***

1K11A	A39	5g yellow grn	52.50	37.50
1K12	A40	10g violet	12.50	15.00

Counterfeit overprints are known on Nos. 1K1-1K32.

No. 232 Overprinted

1926-27

1K13	A41	15g rose red	45.00	40.00

Same Overprint on Redrawn Stamps of 1926-27

Perf. 13

1K14	A39	5g yellow grn	2.00	1.75
1K15	A40	10g violet	2.00	1.75
1K16	A41	15g rose red	4.00	3.75
1K17	A43	20g dull red	3.25	2.25
		Nos. 1K14-1K17 (4)	11.25	9.50

Same Ovpt. on Poland Nos. 250, 255a

1928-30 ***Perf. 12½***

1K18	A44	25g yellow brn	4.75	1.50

Laid Paper

Perf. 11½x12, 12½x11½

1K19	A50	1z blk, *cr* ('30)	30.00	30.00
		Set, never hinged	47.50	

Poland Nos. 258-260 Overprinted

1929-30 ***Perf. 12x12½***

1K20	A53	5g dk violet	1.65	1.40
1K21	A53	10g green ('30)	1.65	1.40
1K22	A53	25g red brown	2.75	1.40
		Nos. 1K20-1K22 (3)	6.05	4.20
		Set, never hinged	8.00	

Same Overprint on Poland No. 257

1931, Jan. 5 ***Perf. 12½***

1K23	A52	15g ultra	3.50	4.00
		Never hinged	5.00	

Poland No. 255 Overprinted in Dark Blue

1933, July 1 ***Perf. 11½***

Laid Paper

1K24	A50	1z black, *cream*	82.50	100.00
		Never hinged	110.00	

Poland Nos. 268-270 Overprinted in Black

1934-36 **Wmk. 234** ***Perf. 12x12½***

1K25	A58	5g dl violet	3.25	3.75
1K26	A58	10g green ('36)	35.00	*72.50*
1K27	A58	15g red brown	3.25	3.75
		Nos. 1K25-1K27 (3)	41.50	*80.00*
		Set, never hinged	60.00	

Poland Nos. 294, 296, 298 Overprinted in Black in one or two lines

1935-36 **Unwmk.** ***Perf. 12½x13***

1K28	A65	5g violet blue	3.50	3.00
1K29	A65	15g Prus green	3.50	4.75
1K30	A65	25g myrtle green	3.50	2.00
		Nos. 1K28-1K30 (3)	10.50	9.75
		Set, never hinged	14.00	

Same Overprint in Black on Poland Nos. 308, 310

1937, June 5

1K31	A65	5g violet blue	1.10	1.75
1K32	A65	15g red brown	1.10	1.75
		Set, never hinged	3.25	

Polish Merchants Selling Wheat in Danzig, 16th Century — A2

1938, Nov. 11 **Engr.** ***Perf. 12½***

1K33	A2	5g red orange	.65	.95
1K34	A2	15g red brown	.65	.95
1K35	A2	25g dull violet	.65	1.65
1K36	A2	55g brt ultra	1.65	3.00
		Nos. 1K33-1K36 (4)	3.60	6.55
		Set, never hinged	5.25	

OFFICES IN THE TURKISH EMPIRE

Stamps of Poland 1919, Overprinted in Carmine

1919, May **Unwmk.** ***Perf. 11½***

Wove Paper

2K1	A10	3f bister brn	42.50	75.00
2K2	A10	5f green	42.50	75.00
2K3	A10	10f red vio	42.50	75.00
2K4	A10	15f red	42.50	75.00
2K5	A11	20f dp blue	42.50	75.00
2K6	A11	25f olive grn	42.50	75.00
2K7	A11	50f blue grn	42.50	75.00

Overprinted

2K8	A12	1m violet	42.50	75.00
2K9	A12	1.50m dp green	42.50	75.00
2K10	A12	2m dk brown	42.50	75.00
2K11	A13	2.50m orange brn	42.50	75.00
2K12	A14	5m red violet	42.50	75.00
		Nos. 2K1-2K12 (12)	510.00	900.00

Counterfeit cancellations are plentiful. Counterfeits exist of Nos. 2K1-2K12.

Reissues are lighter, shiny red ink. Value, set $17.50.

Polish stamps with "P.P.C." overprint (Poste Polonaise Constantinople) were used on consular mail for a time.

Seven stamps with these overprints were not issued. Value, set $20.

PONTA DELGADA

ˌpän-tə del-ˈgä-də

LOCATION — Administrative district of the Azores comprising the islands of Sao Miguel and Santa Maria

GOVT. — A district of Portugal
AREA — 342 sq. mi.
POP. — 124,000 (approx.)
CAPITAL — Ponta Delgada

1000 Reis = 1 Milreis

STAMPS OF PORTUGAL USED IN PONTA DELGADA

Barred Numeral "50"

1853 **Queen Maria II**

A1	5r org brn (#1)	1,300.
A2	25r blue (#2)	75.
A3	50r dp yel grn (#3)	1,350.
a.	50r blue grn (#3a)	2,000.
A4	100r lilac (#4)	2,750.

1855 **King Pedro V (Straight Hair)**

A5	5r red brn (#5)	1,400.
A6	25r blue, type II (#6)	70.00
a.	Type I (#6a)	70.00
A7	50r green (#7)	110.00
A8	100r lilac (#8)	140.00

1856-58

King Pedro V (Curled Hair)

A9	5r red brn (#9)	150.00
A10	25r blue, type II (#10)	110.00
a.	Type I (#10a)	80.00
A11	25r rose, type II (#11; '58)	24.00

1862-64 **King Luiz**

A12	5r brown (#12)	77.50
A13	10r orange (#13)	85.00
A14	25r rose (#14)	15.00
A15	50r yel green (#15)	110.00
A16	100r lilac (#16; '64)	125.00

1866-67 **King Luiz**

Imperf.

A17	5r black (#17)	75.00
A18	10r yellow (#18)	160.00
A19	20r bister (#19)	150.00
A20	25r rose (#20)	50.00
A21	50r green (#21)	150.00
A22	80r orange (#22)	150.00
A23	100r dk lilac (#23; '67)	190.00
A24	120r blue (#24)	140.00

Perf. 12½

A28	25r rose (#28)	130.00

Issued under Portuguese Administration

King Carlos
A1 A2

1892-93 **Typo.** **Unwmk.**

Enamel Surfaced Paper

Perf. 12½

1	A1	5r yellow	2.75	1.60
		Never hinged	3.75	
c.		Diagonal half used as 2½r on piece		17.50
2	A1	10r reddish vio	2.75	1.60
		Never hinged	3.75	
3	A1	15r chocolate	3.50	2.25
		Never hinged	4.75	
4	A1	20r lavender	3.50	2.25
		Never hinged	4.75	
5a	A1	25r deep green	7.50	1.60
		Never hinged	11.00	
6	A1	50r ultra	7.50	3.25
		Never hinged	11.00	
7a	A1	75r carmine	7.75	5.25
		Never hinged	11.00	
8	A1	80r yellow grn	11.00	9.00
		Never hinged	15.00	
9	A1	100r brn, *yel*	11.00	5.50
		Never hinged	15.00	
11	A1	200r dk bl, *bl*	62.50	45.00
		Never hinged	80.00	
12	A1	300r dk bl, *salmon*	62.50	47.50
		Never hinged	80.00	

Perf. 13½

1a	A1	5r yellow	3.00	1.60
		Never hinged	4.00	
2a	A1	10r reddish vio	4.00	2.25
		Never hinged	5.25	
3a	A1	15r chocolate	3.75	2.25
		Never hinged	5.25	
4a	A1	20r lavender	5.25	2.00
		Never hinged	6.75	
6a	A1	50r blue	11.00	5.50
		Never hinged	16.50	
7	A1	75r carmine	7.75	5.50
		Never hinged	11.00	
8a	A1	80r yellow grn	15.50	8.75
		Never hinged	22.50	
9a	A1	100r brn, *yel*	15.50	7.50
		Never hinged	22.50	
10	A1	150r car, *rose*	70.00	32.50
		Never hinged	87.50	

Perf. 11½

1b	A1	5r yellow	8.50	5.50
		Never hinged	14.50	
5	A1	25r green	7.50	1.60
		Never hinged	12.00	
6b	A1	50r blue	10.50	3.00
		Never hinged	17.50	

Chalky Paper

Perf. 11½

1d	A1	5r yellow	5.00	1.50
		Never hinged	6.75	
5b	A1	25r green	12.50	3.25
		Never hinged	17.50	

Perf. 12½

5c	A1	25r green	10.00	4.75
		Never hinged	13.00	

Perf. 13½

1e	A1	5r yellow	3.00	.80
		Never hinged	4.00	
5d	A1	25r green	7.50	1.10
		Never hinged	11.00	

The 5r and 25r values were issued on two types of paper: enamel surfaced, which is white, with a uniform low gloss; and chalky, which bears a low-gloss application in a pattern of tiny lozenges, producing a somewhat duller appearance.

Nos. 1, 4 and 9-12 were reprinted in 1900 (perf. 11½). Value, each $50. All values were reprinted in 1905 (perf. 13½). Value, each $25. The reprints are on paper slightly thinner than that of the originals, and unsurfaced. They have white gum and clean-cut perfs.

1897-1905 ***Perf. 11½***

Name and Value in Black except Nos. 25 and 34

13	A2	2½r gray	.60	.35
		Never hinged	.95	
14	A2	5r orange	.60	.35
		Never hinged	.95	
15	A2	10r lt green	.60	.35
		Never hinged	.95	
16	A2	15r brown	6.50	4.50
		Never hinged	10.50	
17	A2	15r gray grn ('99)	2.25	1.10
		Never hinged	2.75	
18	A2	20r dull violet	2.25	1.25
		Never hinged	2.75	
19	A2	25r sea green	3.00	1.25
		Never hinged	3.75	
20	A2	25r rose red ('99)	2.25	.40
		Never hinged	2.75	
21	A2	50r blue	3.00	1.25
		Never hinged	3.75	
22	A2	50r ultra ('05)	18.50	11.00
		Never hinged	22.50	
23	A2	65r slate blue ('98)	1.40	.45
		Never hinged	1.75	
24	A2	75r rose	7.00	1.25
		Never hinged	8.75	
25	A2	75r brn & car, *yel* ('05)	15.00	8.75
		Never hinged	17.50	
26	A2	80r violet	1.90	1.25
		Never hinged	2.25	
27	A2	100r dk bl, *bl*	4.25	1.25
		Never hinged	5.25	
28	A2	115r org brn, *rose* ('98)	3.25	1.60
		Never hinged	3.75	
29	A2	130r gray brn, *buff* ('98)	3.75	1.60
		Never hinged	4.50	
30	A2	150r lt brn, *buff*	3.75	2.25
		Never hinged	4.50	
31	A2	180r sl, *pnksh* ('98)	3.75	2.25
		Never hinged	4.50	
32	A2	200r red vio, *pnksh*	7.75	5.50
		Never hinged	9.25	
33	A2	300r blue, *rose*	9.00	5.50
		Never hinged	9.25	
a.		Perf. 12½	45.00	30.00
		Never hinged	55.00	
34	A2	500r blk & red, *bl*	18.00	10.00
		Never hinged	19.00	
a.		Perf. 12½	22.50	13.00
		Never hinged	27.50	
		Nos. 13-34 (22)	118.35	63.45

Yellowish Paper

14a	A2	5r orange	.55	.30
		Never hinged	.75	
15a	A2	10r lt green	.55	.30
		Never hinged	.75	
23a	A2	65r slate blue ('98)	1.25	.45
		Never hinged	1.60	

Imperfs are proofs.

The stamps of Ponta Delgada were superseded by those of the Azores, which in 1931 were replaced by those of Portugal.

PORTUGAL

'pōr-chi-gəl

LOCATION — Southern Europe, on the western coast of the Iberian Peninsula
GOVT. — Republic
AREA — 35,516 sq. mi.
POP. — 9,930,000 (est. 1983)
CAPITAL — Lisbon

Figures for area and population include the Azores and Madeira, which are integral parts of the republic. The republic was established in 1910. See Azores, Funchal, Madeira.

1000 Reis = 1 Milreis
10 Reis = 1 Centimo
100 Centavos = 1 Escudo (1912)

Queen Maria II
A1 A2

A3 A4

Typo. & Embossed

1853 Unwmk. *Imperf.*

1	A1 5r reddish brown	2,850.	850.00
	On newspaper or wrapper		3,500.
a.	5r orange brown	3,250.	1,000.
	On newspaper or wrapper		3,900.
b.	Double impression		*4,250.*
	On cover		*24,000.*
2	A2 25r blue	925.	19.00
	On cover		75.00
a.	25r greenish blue	1,600.	32.50
	On cover		125.00
b.	Double impression	*4,750.*	*1,500.*
	On cover		*6,200.*
3	A3 50r dp yellow grn	3,400.	875.00
	On cover		3,500.
a.	50r blue green	6,750.	1,650.
	On cover		6,500.
b.	50r green	3,400.	875.00
	On cover		3,500.
c.	Double impression	*14,000.*	*6,000.*
	On cover		*24,000.*
4	A4 100r lilac	31,000.	1,900.
	On cover		*9,000.*

Full margins = 2mm.

Values for pairs

1	A1	5r reddish brown	2,600.
1a	A1	5r orange brown	2,900.
2	A2	25r blue	57.50
2a	A2	25r greenish blue	100.00
3	A3	50r deep yellow green	2,650.
3a	A3	50r blue green	4,800.
3b	A3	50r green	2,650.
4	A4	100r lilac	*5,750.*

Values for blocks of 4

1	A1	5r reddish brown	*6,900.*
1a	A1	5r orange brown	*7,750.*
2	A2	25r blue	150.00
2a	A2	25r greenish blue	275.00
3	A3	50r deep yellow green	*7,000.*
3a	A3	50r blue green	*13,000.*
3b	A3	50r green	*7,000.*
4	A4	100r lilac	*15,000.*

The stamps of the 1853 issue were reprinted in 1864, 1885, 1905 and 1953. Many stamps of subsequent issues were reprinted in 1885 and 1905. The reprints of 1864 are on thin white paper with white gum. The originals have brownish gum which often stains the paper. The reprints of 1885 are on a stout, very white paper. They are usually ungummed, but occasionally have a white gum with yellowish spots. The reprints of 1905 are on creamy white paper of ordinary quality with shiny white gum.

When perforated the reprints of 1885 have a rather rough perforation 13½ with small holes; those of 1905 have a clean-cut perforation 13½ with large holes making sharp pointed teeth.

The colors of the reprints usually differ from those of the originals, but actual comparison is necessary.

The reprints are often from new dies which differ slightly from those used for the originals.

5 reis: There is a defect in the neck which makes the Adam's apple appear very large in the first reprint. The later ones can be distinguished by the paper and the shades and by the absence of the pendant curl.

25 reis: The burelage of the ground work in the original is sharp and clear, while in the 1864 reprints it is blurred in several places; the upper and lower right hand corners are very thick and blurred. The central oval is less than ½mm from the frame at the sides in the originals and fully ¾mm in the 1885 and 1905 reprints.

50 reis: In the reprints of 1864 and 1885 there is a small break in the upper right hand diagonal line of the frame, and the initials of the engraver (F. B. F.), which in the originals are plainly discernible in the lower part of the bust, do not show. The reprints of 1905 have not the break in the frame and the initials are distinct.

100 reis: The small vertical lines at top and bottom at each side of the frame are heavier in the reprints of 1864 than in the originals. The reprints of 1885 and 1905 can be distinguished only by the paper, gum and shades.

Reprints of 1953 have thick paper, no gum and dates "1853/1953" on back. Value $55 each.

Values of lowest-cost earlier reprints (1905) of Nos. 1, $100; No. 2, $120; Nos. 3, 4, $150.

King Pedro V
A5 A6

A7 A8

1855 With Straight Hair

TWENTY-FIVE REIS:
Type I — Pearls mostly touch each other and oval outer line.
Type II — Pearls are separate from each other and oval outer line.

5	A5 5r red brown	8,250.	900.00
	On newspaper or wrapper		3,500.
6	A6 25r blue, type II	950.00	25.00
	On cover		100.00
a.	25r blue, type I	1,150.	30.00
	On cover		125.00
7	A7 50r green	500.00	70.00
	On cover		275.00
a.	50r blue green	825.00	100.00
	On cover		400.00
b.	Double impression	1,900.	725.00
	On cover		—
8	A8 100r lilac	750.00	90.00
	On cover		375.00
	On cover, single franking		600.00

Full margins = 2mm.

Values for pairs

5	A5	5r red brown	*2,650.*
6	A6	25r blue, type II	72.50
6a	A6	25r blue, type I	87.50
7	A7	50r green	210.00
7a	A7	50r blue green	300.00
8	A8	100r lilac	275.00

Values for blocks of 4

5	A5	5r red brown	*7,000.*
6	A6	25r blue, type II	200.00
6a	A6	25r blue, type I	250.00
7	A7	50r green	550.00
7a	A7	50r ble green	800.00
8	A8	100r lilac	725.00

Several types of No. 5 exist, differing in number of pearls encircling head (74 to 89) and other details.

All values were reprinted in 1885 and 1905. Value for lowest-cost, $60 each.
See note after No. 4.

1856 With Curled Hair

TWENTY-FIVE REIS:
Type I — The network is fine (single lines).
Type II — The network is coarse (double lines).

9	A5 5r brown	375.00	70.00
	On cover		275.00
	On newspaper or wrapper		550.00
a.	5r yellow brown	525.00	140.00
	On cover		575.00
b.	5r red brown	475.00	92.50
	On cover		375.00
c.	5r rose brown	475.00	92.50
	On cover		375.00
d.	5r bister brown	475.00	92.50
	On cover		375.00
e.	5r gray brown	475.00	92.50
	On cover		375.00
f.	5r dark brown	475.00	92.50
	On cover		375.00
g.	Double impression	1,400.	375.00
	On cover		*1,500.*
10	A6 25r blue, type II	375.00	13.50
	On cover		52.50
a.	25r blue, type I	*9,500.*	55.00
	On cover		225.00

Full margins = 2mm.

Values for pairs

9	A5	5r brown	400.00
9a	A5	5r yellow brown	275.00
9b	A5	5r red brown	275.00
9c	A5	5r rose brown	275.00
9d	A5	5r bister brown	275.00
9e	A5	5r gray brown	275.00
9f	A5	5r dark brown	275.00
10	A6	25r blue, type II	40.00
10a	A6	25r blue, type I	175.00

Values for blocks of 4

9	A5	5r brown	1,100.
9a	A5	5r yellow brown	750.00
9b	A5	5r red brown	750.00
9c	A5	5r rose brown	750.00
9d	A5	5r bister brown	750.00
9e	A5	5r gray brown	750.00
9f	A5	5r dark brown	750.00
10	A6	25r blue, type II	100.00
10a	A6	25r blue, type I	450.00

1858

11	A6 25r rose, type II	275.00	6.50
	On cover		19.00
	Pair		13.50
	Block of 4		42.50
a.	Double impression	525.00	*275.00*
	On cover		*1,100.*

Full margins = 2mm.

The 5r dark brown, formerly listed and sold at about $1, is now believed by the best authorities to be a reprint made before 1866. It is printed on thin yellowish white paper with yellowish white gum and is known only unused. The same remarks will apply to a 25r blue which is common unused but not known used. It is printed from a die which was not used for the issued stamps but the differences are slight and can only be told by expert comparison.

Nos. 9 and 10, also 10a in rose, were reprinted in 1885 and Nos. 9, 10, 10a and 11 in 1905. Value of lowest-cost reprints, $40 each.
See note after No. 4.

King Luiz
A9 A10

A11 A12

A13

1862-64

FIVE REIS:
Type I — The distance between "5" and "reis" is 3mm.
Type II — The distance between "5" and "reis" is 2mm.

12	A9 5r brown, type I	125.00	10.00
	On cover		40.00
	On newspaper or wrapper		325.00
a.	5r brown, type II	160.00	25.00
	On cover		110.00
	On newspaper or wrapper		410.00
b.	Double impression, type II	650.00	350.00
	On cover		1,300.
c.	5r reddish brown	—	125.00
	On cover		500.00
d.	Double embossing, type I	—	275.00
	On cover		1,100.
13	A10 10r orange	140.00	47.50
	On cover		275.00
14	A11 25r rose	100.00	4.75
	On cover		17.50
a.	Double impression	1,350.	375.00
	On cover		1,400.
b.	Double embossing, type I	1,350.	375.00
	On cover		1,400.
15	A12 50r yellow green	725.00	77.50
	On cover		360.00
a.	50r blue green	850.00	100.00
	On cover		450.00
16	A13 100r lilac ('64)	825.00	90.00
	On cover		400.00
	Nos. 12-16 (5)	1,915.	229.75

Full margins = 2mm.

Values for pairs

12	A9	5r brown, type I	30.00
12a	A9	5r brown, type II	75.00
12c	A9	5r reddish brown	375.00
13	A10	10r orange	140.00
14	A11	25r rose	14.00
15	A12	50r yellow green	225.00
15a	A12	50r blue green	300.00
16	A13	100r lilac ('64)	275.00

Values for blocks of 4

12	A9	5r brown, type I	80.00
12a	A9	5r brown, type II	210.00
12c	A9	5r reddish brown	1,000.
13	A10	10r orange	375.00
14	A11	25r rose	37.50
15	A12	50r yellow green	600.00
15a	A12	50r blue green	800.00
16	A13	100r lilac ('64)	700.00

All values were reprinted in 1885 and all except the 25r in 1905. Value of lowest-cost reprints, $10 each.
See note after No. 4.

King Luiz
A14 A15

1866-67 *Imperf.*

17	A14 5r black	110.00	10.00
	On cover		40.00
a.	Double impression	275.00	190.00
	On cover		750.00
18	A14 10r yellow	225.00	140.00
	On cover		575.00
19	A14 20r bister	190.00	67.50
	On cover		260.00
	On cover, single franking		550.00
20	A14 25r rose ('67)	225.00	8.00
	On cover		32.50
a.	Double impression		225.00
	On cover		800.00
21	A14 50r green	250.00	67.50
	On cover		260.00
	On cover, single franking		550.00
22	A14 80r orange	250.00	67.50
	On cover		260.00
23	A14 100r dk lilac ('67)	300.00	97.50
	On cover		500.00
24	A14 120r blue	325.00	70.00
	On cover		275.00
a.	Double impression	725.00	450.00
	On cover		1,800.
	Nos. 17-24 (8)	1,875.	528.00

Full margins = 1¾mm.

Some values with unofficial percé en croix (diamond) perforation were used in Madeira.

All values were reprinted in 1885 and 1905. Value: Nos. 17-23, each $30-$40; No. 24, $100.
See note after No. 4.

Typographed & Embossed

1867-70 *Perf. 12½*

25	A14 5r black	125.00	42.50
	On cover		225.00
a.	Double impression	225.00	110.00
	On cover		425.00
26	A14 10r yellow	250.00	110.00
	On cover		425.00
27	A14 20r bister ('69)	300.00	110.00
	On cover		425.00
28	A14 25r rose	65.00	6.75
	On cover		25.00
a.	Double impression	550.00	200.00
	On cover		800.00
29	A14 50r green ('68)	250.00	110.00
	On cover		425.00
30	A14 80r orange ('69)	350.00	110.00
	On cover		425.00
31	A14 100r lilac ('69)	250.00	110.00
	On cover		425.00
32	A14 120r blue	300.00	67.50
	On cover		260.00
a.	Double impression	625.00	160.00
	On cover		650.00
33	A14 240r pale violet ('70)	1,000.	475.00
	On cover		1,900.
	Nos. 25-33 (9)	2,890.	1,141.

Nos. 25-33 frequently were separated with scissors. Slightly blunted perfs on one or two sides are to be expected for stamps of this issue.

Two types each of 5r and 100r differ in the position of the "5" at upper right and the "100" at lower right in relation to the end of the label.

Nos. 25-33 were reprinted in 1885 and 1905. Some of the 1885 reprints were perforated 12½ as well as 13½. Value of the lowest-cost reprints, $40 each.
See note after No. 4.

Typographed & Embossed

1870-84

Plain Paper

Perf. 12½

34 A15 5r black 55.00 5.25
On newspaper or wrapper 55.00
f. Double impression 275.00 67.50
On cover 260.00
35 A15 10r yellow ('71) 77.50 27.50
On cover 150.00
f. Double impression 300.00 125.00
On cover 500.00
36 A15 10r blue grn ('79) 375.00 175.00
On cover 1,000.
37 A15 10r yellow grn ('80) 110.00 24.00
On newspaper or wrapper 125.00
On post card 160.00
d. Double impression 250.00 130.00
On cover 575.00
38 A15 15r lilac brn ('75) 100.00 29.00
On cover 110.00
39 A15 20r bister 72.50 25.00
On cover 150.00
g. Double impression — 175.00
On cover
40 A15 20r rose ('84) 325.00 55.00
On cover 400.00
41 A15 25r rose 30.00 3.75
On cover 15.00
f. Double impression 240.00 30.00
On cover 120.00
42 A15 50r pale green 140.00 40.00
On cover 150.00
43 A15 50r blue ('79) 350.00 50.00
On cover 210.00
44 A15 80r orange 140.00 30.00
On cover 120.00
45 A15 100r pale lilac ('71) 110.00 21.00
On cover 85.00
46 A15 120r blue ('71) 300.00 62.50
On cover 275.00
47 A15 150r pale bl ('76) 375.00 110.00
On cover 460.00
d. Double impression 1,050. 390.00
On cover 1,550.
48 A15 150r yellow ('80) 140.00 15.00
On cover 500.00
49 A15 240r pale violet ('73) 1,700. 1,050.
On cover *4,100.*
50 A15 300r dull violet ('76) 110.00 27.50
On cover 550.00
51 A15 1000r black ('84) 275.00 77.50
On cover 410.00
On cover, single franking 1,100.

Perf. 13½

34d A15 5r black 65.00 8.25
On newspaper or wrapper 32.50
35d A15 10r yellow 95.00 35.00
On cover 150.00
36a A15 10r blue green 675.00 300.00
On cover 1,250.
37a A15 10r yellow grn ('80) 125.00 27.50
On newspaper or wrapper 110.00
On post card 165.00
38a A15 15r lilac brown 140.00 57.50
On cover 225.00
39c A15 20r bister 110.00 27.50
On cover 160.00
40a A15 20r rose ('84) 350.00 85.00
On cover 425.00
b. Double impression — *1,050.*
On cover —
41d A15 25r rose 30.00 4.00
On cover 16.00
g. Double impression — *32.50*
On cover —
42a A15 50r pale green 160.00 40.00
On cover 160.00
43a A15 50r blue ('79) 325.00 52.50
On cover 210.00
44c A15 80r orange 165.00 40.00
On cover 160.00
45b A15 100r pale lilac 165.00 50.00
On cover 200.00
46a A15 120r blue 3,500.
On cover —
47b A15 150r blue 750.00 300.00
On cover 1,200.
48a A15 150r yellow ('80) 175.00 77.50
On cover 300.00
50a A15 300r dull violet ('76) 110.00 27.50
On cover 360.00
51a A15 1000r black ('84) 275.00 77.50
On cover 325.00
On cover, single franking *1,350.*

Perf. 11

34b A15 5r black *550.00*
On newspaper or wrapper —
35b A15 10r yellow *550.00*
On cover —
39b A15 20r bister *550.00*
On cover —
41b A15 25r rose *3,500.*
On cover —
42b A15 50r pale green *550.00*
On cover —
44b A15 80r orange *550.00*
On cover —
49b A15 240r pale violet — —
On cover —

Perf. 14¼

34c A15 5r black 225.00 *125.00*
On newspaper or wrapper 600.00
35c A15 10r yellow 425.00 *275.00*
On cover 1,600.
41c A15 25r rose 425.00 25.00
On cover 110.00
44c A15 80r orange 1,050. 800.00
On cover *3,200.*
45a A15 100r pale lilac 1,300. 800.00
On cover *3,200.*

Imperforate

34a A15 5r black *550.00*
35a A15 10r yellow. *550.00*
39a A15 20r bister *550.00*
41a A15 25r rose *550.00*

Ribbed Paper

Perf. 12½

34e A15 5r black 150.00 22.50
On cover 92.50
35e A15 10r yellow 210.00 110.00
On cover 450.00
39d A15 20r bister 300.00 100.00
On cover 400.00
41e A15 25r rose 125.00 21.00
On cover 85.00
42c A15 50r pale green 400.00 90.00
On cover 350.00
44d A15 80r orange 400.00 100.00
On cover 425.00
45c A15 100r pale lilac 400.00 100.00
On cover 400.00
46b A15 120r blue 950.00 225.00
On cover 950.00
49c A15 240r pale violet 3,250. 2,100.
On cover *8,750.*

Enamel Surfaced Paper

Perf. 12½

37b A15 10r yellow grn ('80) 110.00 24.00
On newspaper or wrapper 125.00
On post card 175.00
38b A15 15r lilac brown 110.00 30.00
On cover 125.00
d. Double impression 500.00 260.00
On cover 1,050.
39e A15 20r bister 100.00 25.00
On cover 110.00
44e A15 80r orange 125.00 19.00
On cover 75.00
45e A15 100r pale lilac 65.00 12.00
On cover 75.00
48b A15 150r yellow ('80) 125.00 13.50
On cover 55.00
50a A15 300r dull violet ('76) 110.00 30.00
On cover 225.00

Perf. 13½

37c A15 10r yellow grn ('80) 140.00 45.00
On newspaper or wrapper 175.00
On post card 190.00
38c A15 15r lilac brown 110.00 30.00
On cover 125.00
39f A15 20r bister 140.00 30.00
On cover 125.00
44f A15 80r orange 140.00 30.00
On cover 120.00
45e A15 100r pale lilac 160.00 42.50
On cover 175.00
48c A15 150r yellow ('80) 150.00 35.00
On cover 250.00
50c A15 300r dull violet ('76) 150.00 40.00
On cover 250.00

Two types each of 15r, 20r and 80r differ in the distance between the figures of value.
Imperfs probably are proofs.
For overprints and surcharges see Nos. 86-87, 94-96.
All values of the issues of 1870-84 were reprinted in 1885 and 1905. Value of the lowest-cost reprints, $30 each.
See note after No. 4.

King Luiz
A16 A17

A18 A19

1880-81 Typo. *Perf. 12½, 13½*

52 A16 5r black 27.50 4.00
On newspaper or wrapper 32.50
a. Enamel surfaced paper, perf 12½ *150.00 50.00*
On cover *200.00*
b. Enamel surfaced paper, perf 13½ *140.00 50.00*
On cover *200.00*
53 A17 25r bluish gray 300.00 29.00
On cover 110.00
54 A18 25r gray 30.00 3.50
On cover 15.00
55 A18 25r brown vio ('81) 30.00 3.50
On cover 15.00
56 A19 50r blue ('81) 300.00 15.00
On cover 75.00
Nos. 52-56 (5) 687.50 55.00

All values were reprinted in 1885 and 1905. Value of the lowest-cost reprints, $15 each.
See note after No. 4.

A20 A21

King Luiz
A22 A23

A24 A24a

1882-87

Plain Paper

Perf. 12½

57 A20 2r black ('84) 24.00 17.50
On cover 110.00
60a A23 25r brown 42.50 3.00
On cover 13.50
61a A23 50r blue 52.50 3.00
On cover 25.00
62 A24a 500r black ('84) 500.00 300.00
On cover *1,200.*
63 A24a 500r violet ('87) 275.00 52.50
On cover 500.00

Perf. 13½

57a A20 2r black ('84) 25.00 16.00
On cover 110.00
60b A23 25r brown 37.50 3.60
On cover 15.00
61b A23 50r blue 52.50 4.00
On cover 27.50
62a A24a 500r black ('84) 900.00 725.00
On cover *2,900.*
63a A24a 500r violet ('87) 825.00 275.00
On cover *1,800.*

Perf. 11½

57b A20 2r black ('84) — —
On cover —
58c A21 5r black ('84) 32.50 3.25
On newspaper or wrapper 27.50
60 A23 25r brown 27.50 2.25
On cover 10.00

Enamel Surfaced Paper

Perf. 12½

58a A21 5r black ('84) 30.00 3.00
On newspaper or wrapper 22.50
58d A21 5r gray ('83) 32.50 3.50
On newspaper or wrapper 27.50
59a A22 10r green ('84) 50.00 4.00
On newspaper or wrapper 55.00
60c A23 25r brown 32.50 2.60
On cover 10.00
61c A23 50r blue 52.50 3.25
On cover 25.00

Perf. 13½

58b A21 5r black ('84) 35.00 7.25
On newspaper or wrapper 45.00
58e A21 5r gray ('83) 37.50 7.25
On newspaper or wrapper 45.00
59b A22 10r green ('84) 62.50 7.25
On newspaper or wrapper 100.00
60d A23 25r brown 37.50 3.50
On cover 13.50
61d A23 50r blue 50.00 10.00
On cover 42.50

Perf. 11½

58 A21 5r black ('84) 32.50 3.50
On newspaper or wrapper 11.00
58f A21 5r gray ('83) 50.00 11.00
On newspaper or wrapper 55.00
59 A22 10r green ('84) 35.00 4.00
On newspaper or wrapper 55.00
60e A23 25r brown 32.50 2.25
On cover 10.00
61 A24 50r blue 45.00 3.00
On cover 22.50

For overprints see Nos. 79-82, 85, 88-89, 93.
The stamps of the 1882-87 issues were reprinted in 1885, 1893 and 1905. Value of the lowest-cost reprints, $20 each.
See note after No. 4.
Covers: The values for Nos. 57, 57a and 57b are for philatelic covers or post cards.

A25 A26

1887 *Perf. 11½*

64 A25 20r rose 42.50 17.00
On cover 65.00
65 A26 25r violet 27.50 3.00
On cover 12.00
66 A26 25r lilac rose 27.50 3.00
On cover 11.00
Nos. 64-66 (3) 97.50 23.00

For overprints see Nos. 83-84, 90-92.
Nos. 64-66 were reprinted in 1905. Value $22.50 each. See note after No. 4.

King Carlos — A27

1892-93

Enamel Surfaced Paper

Perf. 12½

68 A27 10r redsh violet 30.00 5.25
On cover 55.00
69 A27 15r chocolate 27.50 6.00
On cover 55.00

70 A27 20r lavender 35.00 9.25
On cover 55.00
72 A27 50r blue 35.00 9.25
On cover 65.00
73 A27 75r carmine ('93) 67.50 8.00
On cover 82.50
74 A27 80r yellow grn 100.00 52.50
On cover 325.00
75 A27 100r brn, *buff* ('93) 65.00 6.25
On cover 110.00
76a A27 150r car, *rose* ('93) 250.00 100.00
On cover *400.00*
77 A27 200r dk bl, *bl* ('93) 160.00 35.00
On cover 550.00
78 A27 300r dk bl, *sal* ('93) 175.00 57.50
On cover 550.00

Perf. 13½

68b A27 10r reddish violet 30.00 6.50
On cover 65.00
69a A27 15r chocolate 32.50 8.50
On cover 70.00
70a A27 20r lavender 50.00 11.50
On cover 65.00
72b A27 50r blue 100.00 12.00
On cover 72.50
73a A27 75r carmine ('93) 175.00 30.00
On cover *225.00*
74a A27 80r yellow green 85.00 42.50
On cover 325.00
75b A27 100r brown, *buff* ('93) 100.00 12.50
On cover *175.00*
76 A27 150r car, *rose* ('93) 160.00 42.50
On cover 225.00
77a A27 200r dk blue, *blue* ('93) 175.00 65.00
On cover *650.00*

Perf. 11½

67 A27 5r orange 11.00 2.00
On newspaper or wrapper *11.00*
68a A27 10r reddish violet 1,700. 45.00
On cover 275.00
71 A27 25r dark green 37.50 2.50
On cover 10.00
72a A27 50r blue 52.50 6.00
On cover 55.00
73b A27 75r carmine ('93) 350.00 13.00
On cover 110.00
75a A27 100r brown, *buff* ('93) 400.00 16.00
On cover *200.00*

Chalky Paper

Perf. 12½

68d A27 10r reddish violet 275.00 42.50
On cover *325.00*
70b A27 20r lavender 1,100. 550.00
On cover *2,250.*
73c A27 75r carmine ('93) 225.00 37.50
On cover *275.00*

Perf. 13½

68e A27 10r reddish violet 37.50 8.00
On cover 65.00
69b A27 15r chocolate 27.50 6.00
On cover 55.00
73d A27 75r carmine ('93) 225.00 18.00
On cover 140.00

Perf. 11½

67a A27 5r orange 13.00 2.00
On newspaper or wrapper 11.00
68c A27 10r reddish violet 35.00 2.00
On cover 55.00
71a A27 25r dark green 27.50 2.00
On cover 8.25

Nos. 67-78 were issued on two types of paper: enamel surfaced, which is white, with a uniform low gloss; and chalky, which bears a low-gloss application in a pattern of tiny lozenges, producing a somewhat duller appearance.

Nos. 76-78 were reprinted in 1900 (perf. 11½). Value, each $100. All values were reprinted in 1905 (perf. 13½). Value, each $50.

See note after No. 4.

Stamps and Types of Previous Issues Overprinted in Black or Red:

a

b

c

1892

79 A21 (a) 5r gray blk 16.00 8.75
On newspaper or wrapper 45.00
a. Double overprint 650.00 450.00
80 A22 (b) 10r green 16.00 8.75
On newspaper or wrapper 110.00
a. Inverted overprint — —
b. Double overprint 650.00 450.00

1892-93

81 A21 (c) 5r gray blk (R) 13.50 6.75
On newspaper or wrapper 55.00
82 A22 (c) 10r green (R) 16.00 9.25
On newspaper or wrapper 110.00
a. Inverted overprint 160.00 160.00
83 A25 (c) 20r rose 42.50 22.50
On cover 160.00
a. Inverted overprint 225.00 225.00
84 A26 (c) 25r rose lilac, perf. 11½ 14.50 5.25
On cover 160.00
a. Perf. 12½ 475.00 70.00
On cover 275.00
85 A24 (c) 50r blue (R) ('93) 77.50 62.50
On cover 375.00
Nos. 81-85 (5) 164.00 106.25

1893

86 A15 (c) 15r bister brn, plain paper, perf 12½ (R) 20.00 12.00
On cover *120.00*
a. Perf 13½ 550.00 310.00
On cover *1,250.*
b. Surfaced paper, perf 12½ 20.00 11.50
On cover 110.00
c. Surfaced paper, perf 13½ 27.50 22.50
On cover *175.00*
87 A15 (c) 80r yellow 110.00 87.50
On cover *275.00*

Nos. 86-87 are found in two types each. See note below No. 51.

Some of Nos. 79-87 were reprinted in 1900 and all values in 1905. Value of lowest-cost reprint, $10.

See note after No. 4.

Stamps and Types of Previous Issues Overprinted or Surcharged in Black or Red:

d

e

1893 ***Perf. 11½, 12½***

88 A21 (d) 5r gray blk (R) 26.00 22.50
On cover 160.00
89 A22 (d) 10r green, perf. 11½ (R) 24.00 20.00
On cover 160.00
a. "1938" 300.00 300.00
On cover *3,250.*
b. "1863" 300.00 300.00
On cover *3,250.*
c. "1838" 300.00 300.00
On cover *3,250.*
d. Perf. 12½ 1,650. 1,100.
On cover —
90 A25 (d) 20r rose 40.00 32.50
On cover 160.00
a. Inverted overprint 125.00 100.00
b. "1938" 300.00 300.00
On cover *3,250.*
91 A26 (e) 20r on 25r lil rose 52.50 47.50
On cover 190.00
92 A26 (d) 25r lilac rose 110.00 100.00
On cover 350.00
a. Inverted overprint 275.00 275.00
93 A24 (d) 50r blue (R) 110.00 110.00
On cover 450.00

Perf. 12½

94 A15 (e) 50r on 80r yel 125.00 100.00
On cover 275.00
95 A15 (e) 75r on 80r yel 75.00 72.50
On cover 375.00
a. "1893" and "50rs" double 350.00 200.00
On cover —
96 A15 (d) 80r yellow 110.00 95.00
On cover 375.00
a. "1893" double 450.00 450.00
On cover —
Nos. 88-96 (9) 672.50 600.00

Nos. 94-96 are found in two types each. See note below No. 51.

Some of Nos. 88-96 were reprinted in 1900 and all values in 1905. Value of lowest-cost reprint, $45 each.

See note after No. 4.

Covers: Values for Nos. 89a and 89b are for philatelic covers.

Prince Henry on his Ship — A46

Prince Henry Directing Fleet Maneuvers A47

Symbolic of Prince Henry's Studies — A48

1894 **Litho.** ***Perf. 14***

97 A46 5r orange 3.75 .65
Never hinged 15.00
On cover or post card 82.50
98 A46 10r magenta 3.75 .65
Never hinged 15.00
On cover or post card 82.50
99 A46 15r red brown 11.00 3.25
Never hinged 45.00
On cover 225.00
100 A46 20r dull violet 11.00 4.00
Never hinged 45.00
On cover 225.00
101 A47 25r gray green 9.75 1.40
Never hinged —
On cover 110.00
102 A47 50r blue 27.50 6.00
Never hinged —
On cover 110.00
103 A47 75r car rose 52.50 11.50
Never hinged —
On cover 225.00
104 A47 80r yellow grn 52.50 14.00
Never hinged —
On cover 225.00
105 A47 100r lt brn, *pale buff* 40.00 10.00
Never hinged —
On cover 110.00

Engr.

106 A48 150r lt car, *pale rose* 125.00 32.50
Never hinged —
On cover 225.00
107 A48 300r dk bl, *sal buff* 140.00 37.50
Never hinged —
On cover 225.00
108 A48 500r dp vio, *pale lil* 325.00 77.50
Never hinged —
On cover 300.00
109 A48 1000r gray blk, *grysh* 550.00 110.00
Never hinged —
On cover 300.00
Nos. 97-109 (13) 1,351. 308.95

5th centenary of the birth of Prince Henry the Navigator.

Covers: Values for Nos. 99-100, 103-104, 106-109 are for overfranked covers, usually philatelic.

King Carlos — A49

1895-1905 **Typo.** ***Perf. 11½***

Value in Black or Red (#122, 500r)

110 A49 2½r gray .25 .20
Never hinged .50
On newspaper or wrapper 5.50
111 A49 5r orange .25 .20
Never hinged .80
On newspaper or wrapper 5.50
112 A49 10r lt green .50 .25
Never hinged 1.10
On postcard 5.50
113 A49 15r brown 90.00 3.50
Never hinged 160.00
On cover 110.00
114 A49 15r gray grn ('99) 47.50 2.40
Never hinged 85.00
On cover 11.00
115 A49 20r gray violet .85 .35
Never hinged 1.40
On cover or postcard 5.50
116 A49 25r sea green 65.00 .25
Never hinged 120.00
On cover 5.50
117 A49 25r car rose ('99) .40 .20
Never hinged .70
On cover 4.50
118 A49 50r blue 82.50 .40
Never hinged 150.00
On cover 22.50
119 A49 50r ultra ('05) .55 .25
Never hinged 1.10
On cover 11.00
120 A49 65r slate bl ('98) .55 .25
Never hinged 1.10
On cover 11.00
121 A49 75r rose 110.00 4.50
Never hinged 225.00
On cover 110.00
122 A49 75r brn, *yel* ('05) 1.75 .65
Never hinged 3.00
On cover 55.00
123 A49 80r violet 2.10 1.25
Never hinged 4.50
On cover 110.00
124 A49 100r dk bl, *bl* 1.00 .40
Never hinged 2.00
On cover 55.00
125 A49 115r org brn, *pink* ('98) 4.75 2.75
Never hinged 9.50
On cover 110.00
126 A49 130r gray brn, *straw* ('98) 3.75 1.40
Never hinged 7.25
On cover 160.00
127 A49 150r lt brn, *straw* 140.00 22.50
Never hinged 275.00
On cover 325.00
128 A49 180r sl, *pnksh* ('98) 15.00 9.00
Never hinged 30.00
On cover 225.00
129 A49 200r red lil, *pnksh* 5.00 1.25
Never hinged 10.00
On cover 110.00
a. 200r brown violet, *rose* 16.00 2.25
Never hinged 32.50
On cover *190.00*
130 A49 300r blue, *rose* 3.75 2.00
Never hinged 7.50
On cover 275.00
131 A49 500r blk, *bl* ('96) 9.75 4.50
Never hinged 19.00
On cover 275.00
a. Perf. 12½ 110.00 26.00
Never hinged 225.00
On cover —
Nos. 110-131 (22) 585.20 58.45

Several values of the above type exist without figures of value, also with figures inverted or otherwise misplaced but they were not regularly issued.

St. Anthony and his Vision — A50

St. Anthony Ascends to Heaven — A52

St. Anthony Preaching to Fishes — A51

St. Anthony, from Portrait — A53

Perf. 11½, 12½ and Compound

1895 **Typo.**

132 A50 2½r black 4.00 1.10
Never hinged 16.00
On newspaper or wrapper 225.00

Litho.

133 A51 5r brown org 4.00 1.10
Never hinged 16.00
On newspaper or wrapper 160.00
134 A51 10r red lilac 13.50 8.25
Never hinged 55.00
On newspaper or wrapper 160.00
135 A51 15r chocolate 14.50 8.25
Never hinged 60.00
On cover 225.00
136 A51 20r gray violet 14.50 8.25
Never hinged 60.00
On cover 225.00
137 A51 25r green & vio 13.00 1.00
Never hinged 52.50
On cover 225.00
138 A52 50r blue & brn 32.50 22.50
Never hinged 125.00
On cover 225.00
139 A52 75r rose & brn 50.00 40.00
Never hinged 200.00
On cover 225.00
140 A52 80r lt grn & brn 62.50 60.00
Never hinged —
On cover 225.00
141 A52 100r choc & blk 55.00 30.00
Never hinged —
On cover 225.00
142 A53 150r carmine & bis 160.00 100.00
Never hinged —
On cover 225.00
143 A53 200r blue & bis 150.00 125.00
Never hinged —
On cover 450.00

144 A53 300r slate & bis 210.00 140.00
Never hinged —
On cover 550.00
145 A53 500r vio brn & grn 375.00 300.00
Never hinged —
On cover 1,100.
146 A53 1000r violet & grn 625.00 375.00
Never hinged —
On cover *1,300.*
Nos. 132-146 (15) 1,783. 1,220.

7th centenary of the birth of Saint Anthony of Padua. Stamps have eulogy in Latin printed on the back.

Covers: Values for Nos. 135-136, 139-140, 142 are for overfranked covers, usually philatelic.

Vasco da Gama Issue
Common Design Types

1898 Engr. *Perf. 12½ to 16*
147 CD20 2½r blue green 1.40 .35
On newspaper or wrapper 55.00
148 CD21 5r red 1.40 .35
On cover 55.00
149 CD22 10r red violet 8.50 1.50
On cover or postcard 55.00
150 CD23 25r yellow green 5.00 .50
On cover 55.00
151 CD24 50r dark blue 10.50 3.00
On cover 110.00
152 CD25 75r violet brown 45.00 10.50
On cover 82.50
153 CD26 100r bister brown 30.00 10.50
On cover 110.00
154 CD27 150r bister 67.50 27.50
On cover 160.00
Nos. 147-154 (8) 169.30 54.20

For overprints and surcharges see Nos. 185-192, 199-206.

King Manuel II
A62 A63

1910 Typo. *Perf. 14½x15*
156 A62 2½r violet .20 .20
157 A62 5r black .20 .20
158 A62 10r gray green .25 .20
159 A62 15r lilac brown 2.75 1.40
160 A62 20r carmine .80 .65
161 A62 25r violet brn .60 .20
162 A62 50r dark blue 1.50 .65
163 A62 75r bister brn 9.25 5.00
164 A62 80r slate 2.50 2.25
165 A62 100r brn, *lt grn* 10.00 3.00
166 A62 200r dk grn, *sal* 6.00 4.25
167 A62 300r blk, *azure* 6.75 5.00
168 A63 500r ol grn & vio brn 13.50 11.50
169 A63 1000r dk bl & blk 30.00 24.00
Nos. 156-169 (14) 84.30 58.50

For overprint see No. RA1.

Preceding Issue Overprinted in Carmine or Green

1910
170 A62 2½r violet .25 .20
171 A62 5r black .25 .20
172 A62 10r gray green 3.50 1.25
173 A62 15r lilac brn 1.25 .85
174 A62 20r carmine (G) 4.25 1.50
175 A62 25r violet brn .80 .25
176 A62 50r dk blue 6.00 2.00
177 A62 75r bister brn 9.00 3.75
178 A62 80r slate 3.25 2.40
179 A62 100r brn, *lt grn* 2.00 .75
180 A62 200r dk grn, *sal* 2.50 1.60
181 A62 300r blk, *azure* 3.75 2.75
182 A63 500r ol grn & vio brn 9.50 8.25
183 A63 1000r dk bl & blk 24.00 20.00
Nos. 170-183 (14) 70.30 45.75

The numerous inverted and double overprints on this issue were unofficially and fraudulently made.

The 50r with blue overprint is a fraud.

Vasco da Gama Issue Overprinted or Surcharged:

a

b

c

1911 *Perf. 12½ to 16*
185 CD20(a) 2½r blue green .45 .20
a. Inverted overprint 14.00 12.00
186 CD21(b) 15r on 5r red .80 .35
a. Inverted surcharge 10.50 9.00
187 CD23(a) 25r yellow grn .45 .20
188 CD24(a) 50r dark blue 3.25 1.60
a. Inverted overprint
189 CD25(a) 75r violet brn 42.50 32.50
190 CD27(b) 80r on 150r bis 6.75 4.75
191 CD26(a) 100r bister brn 6.75 3.00
a. Inverted overprint 29.00 24.00
192 CD22(c) 1000r on 10r red vio 62.50 37.50
Nos. 185-192 (8) 123.45 80.10

Postage Due Stamps of 1898 Overprinted or Surcharged for Regular Postage:

d

e

1911 *Perf. 12*
193 D1(d) 5r black .85 .35
a. Double ovpt., one inverted 14.00 11.00
194 D1(d) 10r magenta 1.50 .65
195 D1(d) 20r orange 5.75 3.00
196 D1(d) 200r brn, *buff* 125.00 67.50
197 D1(e) 300r on 50r slate 90.00 42.50
198 D1(e) 500r on 100r car, *pink* 47.50 24.00
a. Inverted surcharge 125.00 87.50
Nos. 193-198 (6) 270.60 138.00

Vasco da Gama Issue of Madeira Overprinted or Surcharged Types "a," "b" and "c"

1911 *Perf. 12½ to 16*
199 CD20(a) 2½r blue grn 11.50 8.25
a. Double overprint
200 CD21(b) 15r on 5r red 2.50 2.00
a. Inverted surcharge 12.50 11.00
201 CD23(a) 25r yellow grn 5.75 4.75
202 CD24(a) 50r dk blue 11.00 8.25
a. Inverted overprint
203 CD25(a) 75r violet brn 11.00 5.50
a. Inverted overprint 35.00 30.00
204 CD27(b) 80r on 150r bis 12.50 11.00
a. Inverted surcharge 47.50 40.00
205 CD26(a) 100r bister brn 37.50 8.25
a. Inverted overprint 125.00 100.00
206 CD22(c) 1000r on 10r red vio 37.50 50.00
Nos. 199-206 (8) 129.25 98.00

Ceres — A64

With Imprint

1912-31 Typo. *Perf. 15x14, 12x11½*
207 A64 ¼c dark olive .40 .25
208 A64 ½c black .40 .25
209 A64 1c deep green .65 .20
210 A64 1c choc ('18) .20 .20
211 A64 1½c chocolate 5.50 2.50
212 A64 1½c dp grn ('18) .20 .20
213 A64 2c carmine 5.50 2.50
214 A64 2c org ('18) .20 .20
215 A64 2c yellow ('24) .55 .25
216 A64 2c choc ('26) 1.40 1.40
217 A64 2½c violet .20 .20
218 A64 3c car rose ('17) .20 .20
219 A64 3c ultra ('21) .50 .25
220 A64 3½c lt grn ('18) .20 .20
221 A64 4c lt grn ('19) .20 .20
222 A64 4c orange ('26) 1.40 1.60
223 A64 5c dp blue 5.50 .55
224 A64 5c yell brn ('18) 1.00 .40
225 A64 5c ol brn ('23) .25 .25
226 A64 5c blk brn ('31) .20 .20
227 A64 6c ple rose ('20) .20 .20
228 A64 6c brown ('24) .55 .25
229 A64 6c red brn ('30) .20 .20
230 A64 7½c yellow brn 12.00 2.50
231 A64 7½c dp blue ('18) .20 .20
232 A64 8c slate .20 .20
233 A64 8c bl grn ('22) .45 .25
234 A64 8c org ('24) .45 .45
235 A64 10c org brn .45 .25
236 A64 10c red ('31) .45 .25
237 A64 12c bl gray ('20) 1.25 .65
238 A64 12c dp grn ('21) .45 .40
239 A64 13½c chlky bl ('20) 1.40 .45
240 A64 14c dk bl, *yel* ('20) 3.25 1.25
241 A64 14c brt vio ('21) 1.10 .55
242 A64 15c plum 3.25 .85
243 A64 15c black ('23) .40 .25
244 A64 16c brt ultra ('24) .90 .65
245 A64 20c vio brn, *grn* 13.00 1.50
246 A64 20c brn, *buff* ('20) 15.00 3.50
247 A64 20c dk brn ('21) .50 .25
248 A64 20c dp grn ('23) .45 .25
249 A64 20c gray ('24) .20 .20
250 A64 24c grnsh bl ('21) .45 .25
251 A64 25c salmon pink ('23) .45 .25
252 A64 25c lt gray ('26) .45 .25
253 A64 25c blue grn ('30) .90 .25
254 A64 30c brn, *pink* 100.00 9.50
255 A64 30c lt brn, *yel* ('17) 8.75 1.60
256 A64 30c gray brn ('21) .50 .25
257 A64 30c dk brn ('24) 6.50 1.60
258 A64 32c dp grn ('24) 1.10 .40
259 A64 36c red ('21) 1.75 .45
260 A64 40c dk bl ('23) .90 .55
261 A64 40c choc ('24) .45 .45
262 A64 40c green ('26) .20 .20
263 A64 48c rose ('24) 5.50 3.25
264 A64 50c org, *sal* 12.00 1.10
265 A64 50c yellow ('21) 1.90 .70
266 A64 50c bister ('30) 2.25 1.40
267 A64 50c red brn ('30) 2.25 1.40
268 A64 60c blue ('21) 1.40 .60
269 A64 64c pale ultra ('24) 6.50 4.50
270 A64 75c dull rose ('23) 12.00 5.50
271 A64 75c car rose ('30) 2.25 1.10
272 A64 80c brn rose ('21) 1.40 1.10
273 A64 80c violet ('24) 1.00 .55
274 A64 80c dk grn ('30) 2.25 1.10
275 A64 90c chalky bl ('21) 1.60 .85
276 A64 96c dp rose ('26) 27.50 25.00
277 A64 1e dp grn, *bl* 19.00 1.40
278 A64 1e violet ('21) 4.50 1.90
a. Perf. 15x14 140.00 77.50
279 A64 1e dk blue ('23) 5.00 2.25
280 A64 1e gray vio ('24) 1.50 1.10
281 A64 1e brn lake ('30) 6.50 1.10
282 A64 1.10e yel brn ('21) 4.50 1.60
283 A64 1.20e yel grn ('21) 2.50 1.40
284 A64 1.20e buff ('24) 50.00 32.50
285 A64 1.20e pur brn ('31) 4.50 1.10
286 A64 1.25e dk bl ('31) 4.50 1.10
287 A64 1.50e blk vio ('23) 13.00 3.25
288 A64 1.50e lilac ('24) 30.00 5.00
289 A64 1.60e dp bl ('24) 19.00 5.00
290 A64 2e sl grn ('21) 37.50 5.50
291 A64 2e red vio ('31) 19.00 6.50
292 A64 2.40e ap grn ('26) 160.00 110.00
293 A64 3e pink ('26) 160.00 100.00
294 A64 3.20e gray grn ('24) 32.50 12.00
295 A64 4.50e org ('31) 65.00 45.00
296 A64 5e emer ('24) 35.00 9.00
297 A64 10e pink ('24) 140.00 50.00
298 A64 20e pale turq ('24) 275.00 160.00
Nos. 207-298 (92) 1,371. 648.35

See design A85. For surcharges & overprints see #453-495, RA2.

Presidents of Portugal and Brazil and Aviators Cabral and Coutinho
A65

1923 Litho. *Perf. 14*
299 A65 1c brown .20 *.65*
300 A65 2c orange .20 *.65*
301 A65 3c ultra .20 *.65*
302 A65 4c yellow grn .20 *.65*
303 A65 5c bister brn .20 *.65*
304 A65 10c brown org .20 *.65*
305 A65 15c black .20 *.65*
306 A65 20c blue grn .20 *.65*
307 A65 25c rose .20 *.65*
308 A65 30c olive brn .60 *1.90*
309 A65 40c chocolate .20 *.65*
310 A65 50c yellow .35 *.85*
311 A65 75c violet .35 *1.00*
312 A65 1e dp blue .35 *2.00*
313 A65 1.50e olive grn .65 *2.50*
314 A65 2e myrtle grn .65 *6.00*
Nos. 299-314 (16) 4.95 *20.75*

Flight of Sacadura Cabral and Gago Coutinho from Portugal to Brazil.

Camoens at Ceuta
A66

Camoens Saving the Lusiads — A67
Luis de Camoens — A68

First Edition of the Lusiads — A69

Monument to Camoens — A72

Camoens Dying — A70

Tomb of Camoens A71

Engr.; Values Typo. in Black

1924, Nov. 11 ***Perf. 14, 14½***

315	A66	2c lt blue	.20	.20
316	A66	3c orange	.20	.20
317	A66	4c dk gray	.20	.20
318	A66	5c yellow grn	.20	.20
319	A66	6c lake	.20	.20
320	A67	8c orange brn	.20	.20
321	A67	10c gray vio	.20	.20
322	A67	15c olive grn	.20	.20
323	A67	16c violet brn	.20	.20
324	A67	20c dp orange	.30	.20
325	A68	25c lilac	.30	.20
326	A68	30c dk brown	.30	.20
327	A68	32c dk green	.90	1.00
328	A68	40c ultra	.30	.25
329	A68	48c red brown	1.25	1.25
330	A69	50c red orange	1.40	.90
331	A69	64c green	1.40	.90
332	A69	75c dk violet	1.40	.90
333	A69	80c bister	1.10	.90
334	A69	96c lake	1.10	.90
335	A70	1e slate	1.10	.80
336	A70	1.20e lt brown	5.25	4.75
337	A70	1.50e red	1.25	.90
338	A70	1.60e dk blue	1.25	.90
339	A70	2e apple grn	5.25	4.75
340	A71	2.40e green, *grn*	3.75	2.75
341	A71	3e dk bl, *bl*	1.60	1.00
a.		Value double	125.00	125.00
b.		Value omitted		
342	A71	3.20e blk, *green*	1.60	1.00
343	A71	4.50e blk, *orange*	4.25	2.75
344	A71	10e dk brn, *pnksh*	9.25	8.00
345	A72	20e dk vio, *lil*	9.25	7.00
		Nos. 315-345 (31)	55.35	44.00

Birth of Luis de Camoens, poet, 400th anniv.
For overprints see Nos. 1S6-1S71.

Castello-Branco's House at Sao Miguel de Seide — A73

Castello-Branco's Study — A74

Camillo Castello-Branco A75

Teresa de Albuquerque A76

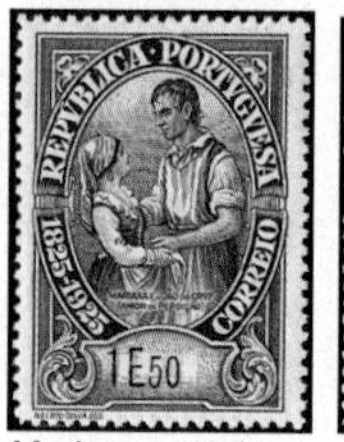

Mariana and Joao de Cruz — A77

Simao de Botelho — A78

1925, Mar. 26 ***Perf. 12½***

346	A73	2c orange	.20	.20
347	A73	3c green	.20	.20
348	A73	4c ultra	.20	.20
349	A73	5c scarlet	.20	.20
350	A73	6c brown vio	.20	.20
a.		"6" and "C" omitted		
351	A73	8c black brn	.20	.20
352	A74	10c pale blue	.20	.20
353	A75	15c olive grn	.20	.20
354	A74	16c red orange	.30	.30
355	A74	20c dk violet	.30	.30
356	A75	25c car rose	.30	.30
357	A74	30c bister brn	.30	.30
358	A74	32c green	1.10	1.00
359	A75	40c green & blk	.65	.65
360	A74	48c red brn	3.00	3.00
361	A76	50c blue green	.65	.65
362	A76	64c orange brn	3.00	3.00
363	A76	75c gray blk	.60	.60
364	A75	80c brown	.60	.60
365	A76	96c car rose	1.50	1.50
366	A76	1e gray vio	1.50	1.50
367	A76	1.20e yellow grn	1.50	1.50
368	A77	1.50e dk bl, *bl*	25.00	13.50
369	A75	1.60e indigo	4.75	3.75
370	A77	2e dk grn, *grn*	6.25	4.25
371	A77	2.40e red, *org*	52.50	32.50
372	A77	3e lake, *bl*	67.50	40.00
373	A77	3.20e *green*	32.50	32.50
374	A75	4.50e red & blk	12.50	3.00
375	A77	10e brn, *yel*	13.00	3.00
376	A78	20e *orange*	13.50	3.00
		Nos. 346-376 (31)	244.40	152.30
		Set, never hinged	375.00	

Centenary of the birth of Camillo Castello-Branco, novelist.

First Independence Issue

Alfonso the Conqueror, First King of Portugal — A79

Batalha Monastery and King John I — A80

Battle of Aljubarrota A81

Filipa de Vilhena Arming her Sons A82

King John IV (The Duke of Braganza) A83

Independence Monument, Lisbon — A84

1926, Aug. 13 ***Perf. 14, 14½***

Center in Black

377	A79	2c orange	.20	.20
378	A80	3c ultra	.20	.20
379	A79	4c yellow grn	.20	.20
380	A80	5c black brn	.20	.20
381	A79	6c ocher	.20	.20
382	A80	15c dk green	.20	.20
383	A79	16c dp blue	.70	.65
384	A81	20c dull violet	.70	.65
385	A82	25c scarlet	.70	.65
386	A81	32c dp green	.90	.90
387	A82	40c yellow brn	.55	.55
388	A80	46c carmine	3.25	3.25
389	A82	50c olive bis	3.25	3.25
390	A83	64c blue green	4.50	4.50
391	A82	75c red brown	4.50	4.50
392	A84	96c dull red	6.75	6.75
393	A83	1e black vio	7.00	7.00
394	A81	1.60e myrtle grn	9.25	9.25
395	A84	3e plum	27.50	27.50
396	A84	4.50e olive grn	35.00	35.00
397	A81	10e carmine	55.00	55.00
		Nos. 377-397 (21)	160.75	160.60
		Set, never hinged	240.00	

The use of these stamps instead of the regular issue was obligatory on Aug. 13th and 14th, Nov. 30th and Dec. 1st, 1926.

Surcharged with Bars and

1926

Center in Black

397A	A80	2c on 5c blk brn	1.10	1.10
397B	A80	2c on 46c car	1.10	1.10
397C	A83	2c on 64c bl grn	1.50	1.50
397D	A82	3c on 75c red brn	1.50	1.50
397E	A84	3c on 96c dull red	2.00	2.00
397F	A83	3c on 1e blk vio	1.60	1.60
397G	A81	4c on 1.60e myr grn	11.50	11.50
397H	A84	4c on 3e plum	4.00	4.00
397J	A84	6c on 4.50e ol grn	4.00	4.00
397K	A81	6c on 10e carmine	4.00	4.00
		Nos. 397A-397K (10)	32.30	32.30
		Set, never hinged	47.50	

There are two styles of the ornaments in these surcharges.

Ceres — A85

Without Imprint

1926, Dec. 2 **Typo.** ***Perf. 13½x14***

398	A85	2c chocolate	.20	.20
399	A85	3c brt blue	.20	.20
400	A85	4c dp orange	.20	.20
401	A85	5c dp brown	.20	.20
402	A85	6c orange brn	.20	.20
403	A85	10c orange red	.20	.20
404	A85	15c black	.25	.20
405	A85	16c ultra	.25	.20
406	A85	25c gray	.25	.20
407	A85	32c dp green	.55	.35
408	A85	40c blue green	.35	.20
409	A85	48c rose	1.10	.90
410	A85	50c ocher	2.00	1.60
411	A85	64c deep blue	2.00	1.60
412	A85	80c violet	3.75	.55
413	A85	96c car rose	2.10	1.10
414	A85	1e red brown	10.00	1.00
415	A85	1.20e yellow brn	10.00	1.00
416	A85	1.60e dark blue	2.40	.55
417	A85	2e green	14.50	1.00
418	A85	3.20e olive grn	5.50	1.00
419	A85	4.50e yellow	5.50	1.00
420	A85	5e brown olive	77.50	3.75
421	A85	10e red	8.75	2.00
		Nos. 398-421 (24)	147.95	19.40
		Set, never hinged	275.00	

See design A64.

Second Independence Issue

Gonçalo Mendes da Maia — A86

Dr. Joao das Regras — A88

Guimaraes Castle — A87

Battle of Montijo — A89

Brites de Almeida — A90

Joao Pinto Ribeiro — A91

1927, Nov. 29 **Engr.** ***Perf. 14***

Center in Black

422	A86	2c brown	.20	.20
423	A87	3c ultra	.20	.20
424	A86	4c orange	.20	.20
425	A88	5c olive brn	.20	.20
426	A89	6c orange brn	.20	.20
427	A87	15c black brn	.45	.35
428	A88	16c deep blue	1.00	.35
429	A86	25c gray	1.25	1.10
430	A89	32c blue grn	2.50	1.60
431	A90	40c yellow grn	.65	.50
432	A86	48c brown red	11.50	10.00
433	A87	80c dk violet	8.25	7.00
434	A90	96c dull red	14.50	13.50
435	A88	1.60e myrtle grn	15.00	14.50
436	A91	4.50e bister	22.50	22.50
		Nos. 422-436 (15)	78.60	72.40
		Set, never hinged	125.00	

The use of these stamps instead of the regular issue was compulsory on Nov. 29-30, Dec. 1-2, 1927. The money derived from their sale was used for the purchase of a palace for a war museum, the organization of an international exposition in Lisbon, in 1940, and for fêtes to be held in that year in commemoration of the 8th cent. of the founding of Portugal and the 3rd cent. of its restoration.

Third Independence Issue

Gualdim Paes — A93

The Siege of Santarem — A94

Battle of Rolica — A95

Battle of Atoleiros A96

Joana de Gouveia A97

Matias de Albuquerque A98

1928, Nov. 28

Center in Black

437	A93	2c lt blue	.20	.20
438	A94	3c lt green	.20	.20
439	A95	4c lake	.20	.20
440	A96	5c olive grn	.20	.20
441	A97	6c orange brn	.20	.20

442	A94	15c slate	.75	.75
443	A95	16c dk violet	.75	.75
444	A93	25c ultra	.75	.75
445	A97	32c dk green	3.75	3.75
446	A96	40c olive brn	.75	.75
447	A95	50c red orange	9.25	5.75
448	A94	80c lt gray	9.75	7.00
449	A97	96c carmine	17.50	15.00
450	A96	1e claret	27.50	27.50
451	A93	1.60e dk blue	13.00	11.50
452	A98	4.50e yellow	14.00	13.50
		Nos. 437-452 (16)	98.75	88.00
		Set, never hinged	150.00	

Obligatory Nov. 27-30. See note after No. 436.

Type and Stamps of 1912-28 Surcharged in Black

1928-29 ***Perf. 12x11½, 15x14***

453	A64	4c on 8c orange	.40	.35
454	A64	4c on 30c dk brn	.40	.35
455	A64	10c on ¼c dk ol	.40	.35
a.		Inverted surcharge	110.00	100.00
456	A64	10c on ½c blk (R)	.60	.45
a.		Perf. 15x14	17.50	12.50
457	A64	10c on 1c choc	.60	.45
a.		Perf. 15x14	*75.00*	*55.00*
458	A64	10c on 4c grn	.45	.35
a.		Perf. 15x14	*87.50*	*67.50*
459	A64	10c on 4c orange	.45	.35
460	A64	10c on 5c ol brn	.45	.35
461	A64	15c on 16c blue	1.10	.80
462	A64	15c on 16c ultra	1.10	.80
463	A64	15c on 20c brown	32.50	32.50
464	A64	15c on 20c gray	.45	.35
465	A64	15c on 24c grnsh bl	2.10	1.60
466	A64	15c on 25c gray	.45	.35
467	A64	15c on 25c sal pink	.45	.35
468	A64	16c on 32c dp grn	.90	.80
469	A64	40c on 2c orange	.45	.35
470	A64	40c on 2c yellow	4.50	3.25
471	A64	40c on 2c choc	.40	.35
472	A64	40c on 3c ultra	.45	.35
473	A64	40c on 50c yellow	.40	.25
474	A64	40c on 60c dull bl	.90	.65
a.		Perf. 15x14	10.00	8.00
475	A64	40c on 64c pale ultra	.90	.80
476	A64	40c on 75c dl rose	.90	.90
477	A64	40c on 80c violet	.65	.55
478	A64	40c on 90c chlky bl	4.50	3.25
a.		Perf. 15x14	11.50	8.75
479	A64	40c on 1e gray vio	.85	.85
480	A64	40c on 1.10e yel brn	.90	.80
481	A64	80c on 6c pale rose	.85	.70
482	A64	80c on 6c choc	.85	.70
483	A64	80c on 48c rose	1.25	1.10
484	A64	80c on 1.50e lilac	3.00	1.25
485	A64	96c on 1.20e yel grn	3.50	2.40
486	A64	96c on 1.20e buff	3.50	2.75
487	A64	1.60e on 2e slate grn	35.00	27.50
488	A64	1.60e on 3.20e gray grn	10.00	7.25
489	A64	1.60e on 20e pale turq	14.00	10.00
		Nos. 453-489 (37)	130.55	106.55
		Set, never hinged	275.00	

Stamps of 1912-26 Overprinted in Black or Red

1929 ***Perf. 12x11½***

490	A64	10c orange brn	.45	.35
a.		Perf. 15x14	275.00	275.00
		Never hinged	425.00	
491	A64	15c black (R)	.40	.35
492	A64	40c lt green	.65	.55
493	A64	40c chocolate	.55	.45
494	A64	96c dp rose	5.50	4.50
495	A64	1.60e brt blue	22.50	17.50
a.		Double overprint	110.00	100.00
		Never hinged	160.00	
		Nos. 490-495 (6)	30.05	23.70
		Set, never hinged	45.00	

Liberty
A100

"Portugal" Holding Volume of "Lusiads"
A101

1929, May ***Perf. 12x11½***

496	A100	1.60e on 5c red brn	11.50	7.00

1931-38 **Typo.** ***Perf. 14***

497	A101	4c bister brn	.25	.20
498	A101	5c olive gray	.25	.20
499	A101	6c lt gray	.25	.20
500	A101	10c dk violet	.25	.20
501	A101	15c gray blk	.25	.20
502	A101	16c brt blue	1.25	.65
503	A101	25c deep green	3.00	.35
504	A101	25c brt bl ('33)	3.50	.40
505	A101	30c dk grn ('33)	1.90	.40
506	A101	40c orange red	6.25	.20
507	A101	48c fawn	1.25	.95
508	A101	50c lt brown	.30	.20
509	A101	75c car rose	5.00	1.10
510	A101	80c emerald	.40	.20
511	A101	95c car rose ('33)	16.00	6.75
512	A101	1e claret	30.00	.20
513	A101	1.20e olive grn	2.10	.95
514	A101	1.25e dk blue	1.90	.20
515	A101	1.60e dk blue ('33)	32.50	4.25
516	A101	1.75e dk blue ('38)	.65	.25
517	A101	2e dull violet	.75	.25
518	A101	4.50e orange	1.50	.25
519	A101	5e yellow grn	1.50	.25
		Nos. 497-519 (23)	111.00	18.80
		Set, never hinged	175.00	

Birthplace of St. Anthony
A102

Font where St. Anthony was Baptized
A103

Lisbon Cathedral
A104

St. Anthony with Infant Jesus
A105

Santa Cruz Cathedral
A106

St. Anthony's Tomb at Padua
A107

1931, June **Typo.** ***Perf. 12***

528	A102	15c plum	.65	.25

Litho.

529	A103	25c gray & pale grn	1.00	.25
530	A104	40c gray brn & buff	.65	.25
531	A105	75c dl rose & pale rose	22.50	14.00
532	A106	1.25e gray & pale bl	52.50	30.00
533	A107	4.50e gray vio & lil	25.00	3.50
		Nos. 528-533 (6)	102.30	48.25
		Set, never hinged	190.00	

7th centenary of the death of St. Anthony of Padua and Lisbon.

For surcharges see Nos. 543-548.

Nuno Alvares Pereira (1360-1431), Portuguese Warrior and Statesman — A108

1931, Nov. 1 **Typo.** ***Perf. 12x11½***

534	A108	15c black	1.00	1.10
535	A108	25c gray grn & blk	10.50	1.10
536	A108	40c orange	2.75	.50
a.		Value omitted	150.00	150.00
537	A108	75c car rose	21.00	21.00
538	A108	1.25e dk bl & pale bl	26.00	20.00
539	A108	4.50e choc & lt grn	125.00	52.50
a.		Value omitted	350.00	350.00
		Nos. 534-539 (6)	186.25	96.20
		Set, never hinged	325.00	

For surcharges see Nos. 549-554.

Nos. 528-533 Surcharged

1933 ***Perf. 12***

543	A104	15c on 40c	.80	.35
544	A102	40c on 15c	2.40	1.25
545	A103	40c on 25c	1.90	.35
546	A105	40c on 75c	8.00	5.25
547	A106	40c on 1.25e	8.00	5.25
548	A107	40c on 4.50e	8.00	5.25
		Nos. 543-548 (6)	29.10	17.70
		Set, never hinged	40.00	

Nos. 534-539 Surcharged

1933 ***Perf. 12x11½***

549	A108	15c on 40c	.65	.35
550	A108	40c on 15c	3.75	2.40
551	A108	40c on 25c	1.00	.80
552	A108	40c on 75c	8.00	4.00
553	A108	40c on 1.25e	8.00	4.00
554	A108	40c on 4.50e	8.00	4.00
		Nos. 549-554 (6)	29.40	15.55
		Set, never hinged	40.00	

President Carmona
A109

Head of a Colonial
A110

1934, May 28 **Typo.** ***Perf. 11½***

556	A109	40c brt violet	18.00	.35
		Never hinged	29.00	

1934, July ***Perf. 11½x12***

558	A110	25c dk brown	3.00	1.60
559	A110	40c scarlet	19.00	.40
560	A110	1.60e dk blue	29.00	5.00
		Nos. 558-560 (3)	51.00	7.00
		Set, never hinged	110.00	

Colonial Exposition.

Roman Temple, Evora
A111

Prince Henry the Navigator
A112

"All for the Nation"
A113

Coimbra Cathedral
A114

1935-41 ***Perf. 11½x12***

561	A111	4c black	.45	.20
562	A111	5c blue	.50	.20
563	A111	6c choc ('36)	.75	.35

Perf. 11½, 12x11½ (1.75e)

564	A112	10c turq grn	.65	.20
565	A112	15c red brown	.35	.20
a.		Booklet pane of 4		
566	A113	25c dp blue	6.00	.45
a.		Booklet pane of 4		
567	A113	40c brown	2.00	.20
a.		Booklet pane of 4		
568	A113	1e rose red	9.25	.50
568A	A114	1.75e blue	75.00	1.25
568B	A113	10e gray blk ('41)	30.00	2.50
569	A113	20e turq grn ('41)	40.00	2.10
		Nos. 561-569 (11)	164.95	8.15
		Set, never hinged	250.00	

For overprint see No. O1.

Queen Maria
A115

Rod and Bowl of Aesculapius
A116

Typographed, Head Embossed

1935, June 1 ***Perf. 11½***

570	A115	40c scarlet	1.40	.25
		Never hinged	1.90	

First Portuguese Philatelic Exhibition.

1937, July 24 **Typo.** ***Perf. 11½x12***

571	A116	25c blue	10.50	.85
		Never hinged	15.00	

Centenary of the establishment of the School of Medicine in Lisbon and Oporto.

Gil Vicente
A117

Grapes
A118

1937

572	A117	40c dark brown	19.00	.20
573	A117	1e rose red	2.50	.20
		Set, never hinged	32.50	

400th anniversary of the death of Gil Vicente (1465-1536), Portuguese playwright. Design shows him in cowherd role in his play, "Auto do Vaqueiro."

1938 *Perf. 11½*

575	A118	15c brt purple	1.40	.55
576	A118	25c brown	3.00	1.60
577	A118	40c dp red lilac	10.00	.35
578	A118	1.75e dp blue	30.00	8.00
		Nos. 575-578 (4)	44.40	10.50
		Set, never hinged	65.00	

International Vineyard and Wine Congress.

Emblem of Portuguese Legion — A119

1940, Jan. 27 **Unwmk.** *Perf. 11½*

579	A119	5c dull yellow	.35	.20
580	A119	10c violet	.35	.20
581	A119	15c brt blue	.35	.20
582	A119	25c brown	22.50	1.10
583	A119	40c dk green	37.50	.40
584	A119	80c yellow grn	2.40	.55
585	A119	1e brt red	57.50	3.50
586	A119	1.75e dark blue	8.00	2.75
a.		Souv. sheet of 8, #579-586	300.00	350.00
		Never hinged	600.00	
		Nos. 579-586 (8)	128.95	8.90
		Set, never hinged	190.00	

Issued in honor of the Portuguese Legion.
No. 586a sold for 5.50e, the proceeds going to various charities.

Portuguese World Exhibition A120

King John IV — A121

Discoveries Monument, Belém — A122

King Alfonso I — A123

1940 **Engr.** *Perf. 12x11½, 11½x12*

587	A120	10c brown violet	.25	.20
588	A121	15c dk grnsh bl	.25	.20
589	A122	25c dk slate grn	1.40	.20
590	A121	35c yellow green	1.10	.35
591	A123	40c olive bister	2.75	.20
592	A120	80c dk violet	5.25	.35
593	A122	1e dark red	12.00	1.60
594	A123	1.75e ultra	7.00	2.75
a.		Souv. sheet of 8, #587-594 ('41)	140.00	110.00
		Never hinged	275.00	
		Nos. 587-594 (8)	30.00	5.85
		Set, never hinged	47.50	

Portuguese Intl. Exhibition, Lisbon (10c, 80c); restoration of the monarchy, 300th anniv (15c, 35c); Portuguese independence, 800th anniv (40c, 1.75e).
No. 594a sold for 10e.

Sir Rowland Hill — A124

1940, Aug. 12 **Typo.** *Perf. 11½x12*

595	A124	15c dk violet brn	.25	.20
596	A124	25c dp org brn	.30	.20
597	A124	35c green	.30	.20
598	A124	40c brown violet	.50	.20
599	A124	50c turq green	18.00	4.25
600	A124	80c lt blue	2.10	1.10
601	A124	1e crimson	21.00	3.50
602	A124	1.75e dk blue	6.75	3.50
a.		Souv. sheet of 8, #595-602 ('41)	75.00	75.00
		Never hinged	125.00	
		Nos. 595-602 (8)	49.20	13.15
		Set, never hinged	75.00	

Postage stamp centenary.
No. 602a sold for 10e.

AIR POST STAMPS

Symbol of Aviation AP1

Perf. 12x11½

1936-41 **Unwmk.** **Typo.**

C1	AP1	1.50e dark blue	.45	.30
C2	AP1	1.75e red orange	.75	.35
C3	AP1	2.50e rose red	.85	.35
C4	AP1	3e brt blue ('41)	14.00	12.00
C5	AP1	4e dp yel grn ('41)	18.00	18.00
C6	AP1	5e car lake	1.75	1.25
C7	AP1	10e brown lake	3.00	1.25
C8	AP1	15e orange ('41)	11.50	7.00
C9	AP1	20e black brn	9.00	2.75
C10	AP1	50e brn vio ('41)	160.00	75.00
		Nos. C1-C10 (10)	219.30	118.25
		Never hinged	390.00	

Nos. C1-C10 exist imperf.

POSTAGE DUE STAMPS

Vasco da Gama Issue

The Zamorin of Calicut Receiving Vasco da Gama — D1

Unwmk.

1898, May 1 **Typo.** *Perf. 12*

Denomination in Black

J1	D1	5r black	2.40	1.25
		On cover		—
a.		Value and "Continente" omitted	10.00	5.00
J2	D1	10r lilac & blk	4.00	1.75
		On cover		1,100.
J3	D1	20r orange & blk	6.50	2.50
		On cover		550.00
J4	D1	50r slate & blk	50.00	11.00
		On cover		1,100.
J5	D1	100r car & blk, *pink*	87.50	40.00
		On cover		1,100.
J6	D1	200r brn & blk, *buff*	92.50	60.00
		On cover		—

For overprints and surcharges see Nos. 193-198.

D2

D3

1904 *Perf. 11½x12*

J7	D2	5r brown	.45	.40
J8	D2	10r orange	2.75	.90
a.		Imperf.	—	
J9	D2	20r lilac	8.00	3.75
J10	D2	30r gray green	5.75	2.75
J11	D2	40r gray violet	7.00	2.75
J12	D2	50r carmine	52.50	4.50
a.		Imperf.		
J13	D2	100r dull blue	8.75	6.50
a.		Imperf.		
		Nos. J7-J13 (7)	85.20	21.55

Preceding Issue Overprinted in Carmine or Green

1910

J14	D2	5r brown	.40	.25
J15	D2	10r orange	.40	.25
J16	D2	20r lilac	1.40	1.00
J17	D2	30r gray green	1.25	.25
J18	D2	40r gray violet	1.40	.25
J19	D2	50r carmine (G)	6.00	4.50
J20	D2	100r dull blue	6.50	5.25
		Nos. J14-J20 (7)	17.35	11.75

See note after No. 183.

1915, Mar. 18 **Typo.**

J21	D3	½c brown	.60	.60
J22	D3	1c orange	.60	.60
J23	D3	2c claret	.60	.60
J24	D3	3c green	.60	.60
J25	D3	4c gray violet	.60	.60
J26	D3	5c carmine	.60	.60
J27	D3	10c dark blue	.60	.60
		Nos. J21-J27 (7)	4.20	4.20

1921-27

J28	D3	½c gray green ('22)	.35	.35
J29	D3	4c gray green ('27)	.35	.35
J30	D3	8c gray green ('23)	.35	.35
J31	D3	10c gray green ('22)	.35	.35
J32	D3	12c gray green	.50	.50
J33	D3	16c gray green ('23)	.50	.50
J34	D3	20c gray green	.50	.50
J35	D3	24c gray green	.50	.50
J36	D3	32c gray green ('23)	.50	.50
J37	D3	36c gray green	1.50	.75
J38	D3	40c gray green ('23)	1.50	.75
J39	D3	48c gray green ('23)	.65	.65
J40	D3	50c gray green	.65	.65
J41	D3	60c gray green	.65	.65
J42	D3	72c gray green	.65	.65
J43	D3	80c gray green ('23)	7.50	7.50
J44	D3	1.20e gray green	3.00	3.00
		Nos. J28-J44 (17)	20.00	18.50

D4

D5

1932-33

J45	D4	5c buff	.50	.45
J46	D4	10c lt blue	.50	.45
J47	D4	20c pink	1.25	1.00
J48	D4	30c blue green	1.50	1.00
J49	D4	40c lt green	1.50	1.00
J50	D4	50c gray	1.60	1.00
J51	D4	60c rose	4.25	2.00
J52	D4	80c violet brn	8.00	4.00
J53	D4	1.20e gray ol ('33)	13.00	12.00
		Nos. J45-J53 (9)	32.10	22.90

1940, Feb. 1 **Unwmk.** *Perf. 12½*

J54	D5	5c bister, perf. 14	.50	.35
J55	D5	10c rose lilac	.30	.20
J56	D5	20c dk car rose	.30	.20
J57	D5	30c purple	.30	.20
J58	D5	40c cerise	.30	.20
J59	D5	50c brt blue	.30	.20
J60	D5	60c yellow grn	.30	.20
J61	D5	80c scarlet	.30	.20
J62	D5	1e brown	.30	.20
J63	D5	2e dk rose vio	.55	.45
J64	D5	5e org yel, perf. 14	11.00	9.00
a.		Perf. 12½	175.00	125.00
		Nos. J54-J64 (11)	14.45	11.40

Nos. J54-J64 were first issued perf. 14. In 1955 all but the 5c were reissued in perf. 12½.

OFFICIAL STAMPS

No. 567 Overprinted in Black

1938 **Unwmk.** *Perf. 11½*

O1	A113	40c brown	.45	.20

NEWSPAPER STAMPS

N1

Perf. 11½, 12½, 13½

1876 **Typo.** **Unwmk.**

P1	N1	2½r bister	14.00	1.40
		On newspaper or wrapper		5.00
a.		2½r olive green	14.00	1.40
		On newspaper or wrapper		5.00

Various shades.

PARCEL POST STAMPS

Mercury and Commerce PP1

1920-22 **Unwmk.** **Typo.** *Perf. 12*

Q1	PP1	1c lilac brown	.20	.20
Q2	PP1	2c orange	.20	.20
Q3	PP1	5c lt brown	.20	.20
Q4	PP1	10c red brown	.20	.20
Q5	PP1	20c gray blue	.30	.25
Q6	PP1	40c carmine rose	.35	.25
Q7	PP1	50c black	.50	.45
Q8	PP1	60c dk blue ('21)	.50	.45
Q9	PP1	70c gray brn ('21)	3.00	2.00
Q10	PP1	80c ultra ('21)	3.50	3.25
Q11	PP1	90c lt vio ('21)	3.50	2.25
Q12	PP1	1e lt green	4.00	2.25
Q13	PP1	2e pale lilac ('22)	11.00	3.50
Q14	PP1	3e olive ('22)	21.00	4.00
Q15	PP1	4e ultra ('22)	42.50	7.00
Q16	PP1	5e gray ('22)	55.00	4.75
Q17	PP1	10e chocolate ('22)	82.50	9.25
		Nos. Q1-Q17 (17)	228.45	40.45

Parcel Post Package PP2

1936 *Perf. 11½*

Q18	PP2	50c olive brown	.65	.50
Q19	PP2	1e bister brown	.65	.50
Q20	PP2	1.50e purple	.65	.50
Q21	PP2	2e carmine lake	2.75	.60
Q22	PP2	2.50e olive green	2.75	.60
Q23	PP2	4.50e brown lake	5.75	.65
Q24	PP2	5e violet	9.00	.75
Q25	PP2	10e orange	12.00	1.75
		Nos. Q18-Q25 (8)	34.20	5.85

POSTAL TAX STAMPS

These stamps represent a special fee for the delivery of postal matter on certain days in each year. The money derived from their sale is applied to works of public charity.

Regular Issues Overprinted in Carmine

1911, Oct. 4 Unwmk. *Perf. 14½x15*

RA1	A62	10r gray green	8.50	2.25

The 20r carmine of this type was for use on telegrams.

1912, Oct. 4 *Perf. 15x14½*

RA2	A64	1c deep green	6.00	1.75

The 2c carmine of this type was for use on telegrams.

"Lisbon" — PT1

"Charity" — PT2

1913, June 8 Litho. *Perf. 12x11½*

RA3	PT1	1c dark green	.95	.70

The 2c dark brown of this type was for use on telegrams.

1915, Oct. 4 Typo.

RA4	PT2	1c carmine	.35	.30

The 2c plum of this type was for use on telegrams.

See No. RA6.

No. RA4 Surcharged

1924, Oct. 4

RA5	PT2	15c on 1c dull red	1.25	.70

The 30c on 2c claret of this type was for use on telegrams.

Charity Type of 1915 Issue

1925, Oct. 4 *Perf. 12½*

RA6	PT2	15c carmine	.35	.35

The 30c brown violet of this type was for use on telegrams.

Comrades of the Great War Issue

Muse of History with Tablet — PT3

1925, Apr. 8 Litho. *Perf. 11*

RA7	PT3	10c brown	1.10	1.10
RA8	PT3	10c green	1.10	1.10
RA9	PT3	10c rose	1.10	1.10
RA10	PT3	10c ultra	1.10	1.10
		Nos. RA7-RA10 (4)	4.40	4.40

The use of these stamps, in addition to the regular postage, was obligatory on certain days of the year. If the tax represented by these stamps was not prepaid, it was collected by means of Postal Tax Due Stamp No. RAJ1.

Pombal Issue

Common Design Types

Engraved; Value and "Continente" Typographed in Black

1925, May 8 *Perf. 12½*

RA11	CD28	15c ultra	.50	.40
RA12	CD29	15c ultra	1.00	.75
RA13	CD30	15c ultra	1.00	.75
		Nos. RA11-RA13 (3)	2.50	1.90

Olympic Games Issue

Hurdler — PT7

1928 Litho. *Perf. 12*

RA14	PT7	15c dull red & blk	4.00	*2.75*

The use of this stamp, in addition to the regular postage, was obligatory on May 22-24, 1928. 10% of the money thus obtained was retained by the Postal Administration; the balance was given to a Committee in charge of Portuguese participation in the Olympic games at Amsterdam.

POSTAL TAX DUE STAMPS

PTD1

PTD2

Comrades of the Great War Issue

1925 Unwmk. Typo. *Perf. 11x11½*

RAJ1	PTD1	20c brown orange	.55	.45

See Note after No. RA10.

Pombal Issue

Common Design Types

1925 *Perf. 12½*

RAJ2	CD28	30c ultra	1.10	1.10
RAJ3	CD29	30c ultra	1.10	1.10
RAJ4	CD30	30c ultra	1.10	1.10
		Nos. RAJ2-RAJ4 (3)	3.30	3.30

When the compulsory tax was not paid by the use of stamps #RA11-RA13, double the amount was collected by means of #RAJ2-RAJ4.

Olympic Games Issue

1928 Litho. *Perf. 11½*

RAJ5	PTD2	30c lt red & blk	1.75	1.75

FRANCHISE STAMPS

These stamps are supplied by the Government to various charitable, scientific and military organizations for franking their correspondence. This franking privilege was withdrawn in 1938.

FOR THE RED CROSS SOCIETY

F1

Perf. 11½

1889-1915 Unwmk. Typo.

1	F1	rose & blk ('15)	.45	.40
		On cover or postcard		82.50
a.		Vermilion & black ('08)	5.75	1.25
		On cover or postcard		82.50
b.		Red & black, perf. 12½	65.00	6.25
		On cover or postcard		*190.00*

No. 1S1 Overprinted in Green

1917

3	F1	rose & black	80.00	77.50
a.		Inverted overprint	150.00	150.00

"Charity" Extending Hope to Invalid — F1a

1926 Litho. *Perf. 14*

Inscribed "LISBOA"

4	F1a	black & red	7.00	7.00

Inscribed "DELEGACOES"

5	F1a	black & red	7.00	7.00

No. 1S4 was for use in Lisbon. No. 1S5 was for the Red Cross chapters outside Lisbon.

For overprints see Nos. 1S72-1S73.

Camoens Issue of 1924 Overprinted in Black or Red

1927

6	A68	40c ultra	1.10	1.00
7	A68	48c red brown	1.10	1.00
8	A69	64c green	1.10	1.00
9	A69	75c dk violet	1.10	1.00
10	A71	4.50e blk, *org* (R)	1.10	1.00
11	A71	10e dk brn, *pnksh*	1.10	1.00
		Nos. 1S6-1S11 (6)	6.60	6.00

Camoens Issue of 1924 Overprinted in Red

1928

12	A67	15c olive grn	1.10	1.00
13	A67	16c violet brn	1.10	1.00
14	A68	25c lilac	1.10	1.00
15	A68	40c ultra	1.10	1.00
16	A70	1.20e lt brown	1.10	1.00
17	A70	2e apple green	1.10	1.00
		Nos. 1S12-1S17 (6)	6.60	6.00

Camoens Issue of 1924 Overprinted in Red

1929

18	A68	30c dk brown	1.10	1.00
19	A68	40c ultra	1.10	1.00
20	A69	80c bister	1.10	1.00
21	A70	1.50e red	1.10	1.00
22	A70	1.60e dark blue	1.10	1.00
23	A71	2.40e green, *grn*	1.10	1.00
		Nos. 1S18-1S23 (6)	6.60	6.00

Same Overprint Dated "1930"

1930

24	A68	40c ultra	1.10	1.00
25	A69	50c red orange	1.10	1.00
26	A69	96c lake	1.10	1.00
27	A70	1.60e dk blue	1.10	1.00
28	A71	3e dk blue, *bl*	1.10	1.00
29	A72	20e dk violet, *lil*	1.10	1.00
		Nos. 1S24-1S29 (6)	6.60	6.00

Camoens Issue of 1924 Overprinted in Red

1931

30	A68	25c lilac	1.25	1.10
31	A68	32c dk green	1.25	1.10
32	A68	40c ultra	1.25	1.10
33	A69	96c lake	1.25	1.10
34	A70	1.60e dark blue	1.25	1.10
35	A71	3.20e black, *green*	1.25	1.10
		Nos. 1S30-1S35 (6)	7.50	6.60

Same Overprint Dated "1932"

1931

36	A67	20c dp orange	1.75	1.75
37	A68	40c ultra	1.75	1.75
38	A68	48c red brown	1.75	1.75
39	A69	64c green	1.75	1.75
40	A70	1.60e dark blue	1.75	1.75
41	A71	10e dk brown, *pnksh*	1.75	1.75
		Nos. 1S36-1S41 (6)	10.50	10.50

Nos. 1S6-1S11 Overprinted in Red

1932

42	A68	40c ultra	1.75	1.75
43	A68	48c red brown	1.75	1.75
44	A69	64c green	1.75	1.75
45	A69	75c dk violet	1.75	1.75
46	A71	4.50e blk, *orange*	1.75	1.75
47	A71	10e dk brn, *pnksh*	1.75	1.75
		Nos. 1S42-1S47 (6)	10.50	10.50

Dated "1934"

1933

48	A68	40c ultra	2.25	2.25
49	A68	48c red brown	2.25	2.25
50	A69	64c green	2.25	2.25
51	A69	75c dark violet	2.25	2.25
52	A71	4.50e blk, *orange*	2.25	2.25
53	A71	10e dk brown, *pnksh*	2.25	2.25
		Nos. 1S48-1S53 (6)	13.50	13.50

Dated "1935"

1935

54	A68	40c ultra	2.60	2.60
55	A68	48c red brown	2.60	2.60
56	A69	64c green	2.60	2.60
57	A69	75c dk violet	2.60	2.60
58	A71	4.50e black, *orange*	2.60	2.60
59	A71	10e dk brn, *pnksh*	2.60	2.60
		Nos. 1S54-1S59 (6)	15.60	15.60

Camoens Issue of 1924 Overprinted in Black or Red

1935

60	A68 25c lilac		1.10	1.00
61	A68 40c ultra (R)		1.10	1.00
62	A69 50c red orange		1.10	1.00
63	A70 1e slate		1.10	1.00
64	A70 2e apple green		1.10	1.00
65	A72 20e dk violet, *lilac*		1.10	1.00
	Nos. 1S60-1S65 (6)		6.60	6.00

Camoens Issue of 1924 Overprinted in Red

1936

66	A68 30c dk brown	1.10	1.10
67	A68 32c dk green	1.10	1.10
68	A69 80c bister	1.10	1.10
69	A70 1.20e lt brown	1.10	1.10
70	A71 3e dk blue, *bl*	1.10	1.10
71	A71 4.50e black, *yel*	1.10	1.10
	Nos. 1S66-1S71 (6)	6.60	6.60

No. 1S4 Overprinted "1935"

1936 Unwmk. *Perf. 14*

72	F1a black & red	8.25	8.25

Same Stamp with Additional Overprint "Delegacoes"

73	F1a black & red	8.25	8.25

After the government withdrew the franking privilege in 1938, the Portuguese Red Cross Society distributed charity labels which lacked postal validity.

FOR CIVILIAN RIFLE CLUBS

Rifle Club Emblem — F2

Perf. 11½x12

1899-1910 Typo. Unwmk.

2S1	F2 bl grn & car ('99)	10.00	10.00
2S2	F2 brn & yel grn ('00)	10.00	10.00
2S3	F2 car & buff ('01)	1.00	1.00
2S4	F2 bl & org ('02)	1.00	1.00
2S5	F2 grn & org ('03)	1.00	1.00
2S6	F2 lt brn & car ('04)	1.60	1.60
2S7	F2 mar & ultra ('05)	4.25	4.25
2S8	F2 ultra & buff ('06)	1.00	1.00
2S9	F2 choc & yel ('07)	1.00	1.00
2S10	F2 car & ultra ('08)	1.60	1.60
2S11	F2 bl & yel grn ('09)	1.00	1.00
2S12	F2 bl grn & brn, *pink* ('10)	4.00	4.00
	Nos. 2S1-2S12 (12)	37.45	37.45

FOR THE GEOGRAPHICAL SOCIETY OF LISBON

Coat of Arms

F3 F4

1903-34 Unwmk. Litho. *Perf. 11½*

3S1	F3 blk, rose, bl & red	9.00	5.00
3S2	F3 bl, yel, red & grn ('09)	12.00	5.00
3S3	F4 blk, org, bl & red ('11)	5.50	4.00
3S4	F4 blk & brn org ('22)	6.75	4.75
3S5	F4 blk & bl ('24)	15.00	8.50
3S6	F4 blk & rose ('26)	6.75	4.75
3S7	F4 blk & grn ('27)	6.75	4.75
3S8	F4 bl, yel & red ('29)	4.75	3.50
3S9	F4 bl, red & vio ('30)	4.75	3.50
3S10	F4 dp bl, lil & red ('31)	4.75	3.50
3S11	F4 bis brn & red ('32)	4.75	3.50
3S12	F4 lt grn & red ('33)	4.75	3.50
3S13	F4 blue & red ('34)	4.75	3.50
	Nos. 3S1-3S13 (13)	90.25	57.75

No. 3S12 with three-line overprint, "C.I.C.I. Portugal 1933," was not valid for postage and was sold only to collectors.

No. 3S2 was reprinted in 1933. Green vertical lines behind "Porte Franco" omitted. Value $7.50.

F5

1934 Litho. *Perf. 11½*

3S15	F5 blue & red	5.00	3.50

1935-38 *Perf. 11*

3S16	F5 blue	6.50	5.25
3S17	F5 dk bl & red ('36)	4.75	4.25
3S18	F5 lil & red ('37)	3.50	2.75
3S19	F5 blk, grn & car ('38)	3.50	2.75
	Nos. 3S16-3S19 (4)	18.25	15.00

The inscription in the inner circle is omitted on No. 3S16.

FOR THE NATIONAL AID SOCIETY FOR CONSUMPTIVES

F10

Perf. 11½x12

1904, July Typo. Unwmk.

4S1	F10 brown & green	5.00	5.00
4S2	F10 carmine & yellow	5.00	5.00

PORTUGUESE AFRICA

'pōr-chə-,gēz 'a-fri-kə

For use in any of the Portuguese possessions in Africa.

1000 Reis = 1 Milreis
100 Centavos = 1 Escudo

Common Design Types pictured following the introduction.

Vasco da Gama Issue
Common Design Types
Inscribed "Africa - Correios"

Perf. 13½ to 15½

1898, Apr. 1 Engr. Unwmk.

1	CD20 2½r blue green	.90	.90
	Never hinged	1.15	
2	CD21 5r red	.90	.90
	Never hinged	1.15	
3	CD22 10r red violet	.90	.90
	Never hinged	1.15	
4	CD23 25r yellow green	.90	.90
	Never hinged	1.15	
5	CD24 50r dark blue	1.10	1.10
	Never hinged	1.30	
6	CD25 75r violet brown	6.25	6.25
	Never hinged	7.50	
7	CD26 100r bister brown	5.00	4.50
	Never hinged	7.00	
8	CD27 150r bister	8.00	6.25
	Never hinged	10.50	
	Nos. 1-8 (8)	23.95	21.70
	Set, never hinged	32.50	

Vasco da Gama's voyage to India.

WAR TAX STAMPS

Liberty WT1

Perf. 12x11½, 15x14

1919 Typo. Unwmk.

Overprinted in Black, Orange or Carmine

MR1	WT1 1c green (Bk)	.75	.75
a.	Figures of value omitted	25.00	
MR2	WT1 4c green (O)	1.00	
MR3	WT1 5c green (C)	.75	.75
	Nos. MR1-MR3 (3)	2.50	

Values the same for either perf.

No. MR2 used is known only with fiscal cancelation. Some authorities consider No. MR2 a revenue stamp.

PORTUGUESE CONGO

'pōr-chi-gēz 'käŋ-,gō

LOCATION — The northernmost district of the Portuguese Angola Colony on the southwest coast of Africa
CAPITAL — Cabinda

Stamps of Angola replaced those of Portuguese Congo.

1000 Reis = 1 Milreis
100 Centavos = 1 Escudo (1913)

King Carlos
A1 A2

Perf. 12½

1894, Aug. 5 Typo. Unwmk.

1	A1 5r yellow	.90	.75
a.	5r orange yellow	.90	.75
b.	As "a," Perf. 13½	17.00	12.50
2	A1 10r redsh violet	1.60	.80
a.	Perf. 13½	17.50	12.50
3	A1 15r chocolate	2.75	2.00
a.	Perf. 11½	5.00	2.10
4	A1 20r lavender, ordinary paper	2.50	2.00
a.	Paper with enamel lozenges	2.50	1.75
b	Perf. 11½	5.00	2.10
5	A1 25r green	1.50	.80
a.	Paper with enamel lozenges	3.50	.85
b.	Perf. 11½	3.25	.85

Perf. 13½

6	A1 50r light blue	2.75	2.00
a	Perf. 11½	13.00	4.50

Perf. 11½

7	A1 75r rose	5.00	3.75
a.	Perf. 12½	20.00	15.00
8	A1 80r yellow green	7.00	6.00
a.	Perf. 12½	60.00	37.50
9	A1 100r brown, *yel*	5.50	3.75
a.	Perf. 13½	32.50	19.00

Perf. 12½

10	A1 150r carmine, *rose*	10.50	9.00
11	A1 200r dk blue, *bl*	10.50	9.00
12	A1 300r dk blue, *salmon*	13.00	11.00
	Nos. 1-12 (12)	63.50	50.85

For surcharges and overprints see Nos. 36-47, 127-131.

1898-1903 *Perf. 11½*

Name & Value in Black except 500r

13	A2 2½r gray	.35	.30
14	A2 5r orange	.35	.30
15	A2 10r lt green	.55	.30
16	A2 15r brown	1.50	1.25
17	A2 15r gray grn ('03)	1.00	.55
18	A2 20r gray violet	1.00	.70
19	A2 25r sea green	1.40	.90
20	A2 25r car rose ('03)	.90	.45
21	A2 50r deep blue	1.60	1.25
22	A2 50r brown ('03)	2.75	1.75
23	A2 65r dull blue ('03)	7.50	6.50
24	A2 75r rose	4.00	2.25
25	A2 75r red lilac ('03)	2.75	2.25
26	A2 80r violet	3.00	2.50
27	A2 100r dk bl, *bl*	2.40	1.75
28	A2 115r org brn, *pink* ('03)	6.50	5.00
29	A2 130r brn, *straw* ('03)	17.00	11.00
30	A2 150r brown, *buff*	4.00	2.50
31	A2 200r red lilac, *pnksh*	5.00	3.00
32	A2 300r dk blue, *rose*	6.00	3.25
33	A2 400r dl bl, *straw* ('03)	11.00	9.50
34	A2 500r blk & red, *bl* ('01)	15.00	9.00
35	A2 700r vio, *yelsh* ('01)	25.00	17.50
	Nos. 13-35 (23)	120.55	83.75

For overprints and surcharges see Nos. 49-53, 60-74, 117-126, 136-138.

Surcharged in Black

Perf. 12½, 11½ (#41, 43), 13½ (#44)

1902

On Issue of 1894

36	A1 65r on 15r choc	3.50	3.00
a.	Perf. 11½	17.00	9.00
37	A1 65r on 20r lav (#4)	4.00	3.00
a.	Lozenge paper (#4a)	13.50	11.00
38	A1 65r on 25r green (#5)	4.00	3.00
a.	Perf. 11½	17.00	12.50
b.	Lozenge paper (#5a)	4.75	4.50
39	A1 65r on 300r bl, *sal*	4.75	4.50
40	A1 115r on 10r red vio	4.00	3.00
41	A1 115r on 50r lt bl	3.75	2.50
a.	Perf. 13½	4.00	2.75
42	A1 130r on 5r yellow	4.00	2.75
a.	Inverted surcharge	27.50	27.50
b.	Perf. 13½	4.00	2.75
43	A1 130r on 75r rose	3.50	3.00
a.	Perf. 12½	7.00	6.00
44	A1 130r on 100r brn, *yel*	3.75	3.75
a.	Inverted surcharge	40.00	35.00
b.	Perf. 11½	20.00	12.50
45	A1 400r on 80r yel grn	1.75	1.25
a.	Perf. 12½	5.00	3.50
46	A1 400r on 150r car, *rose*	2.25	1.90
47	A1 400r on 200r bl, *bl*	2.25	1.90

On Newspaper Stamps of 1894

48	N1 115r on 2½r brn	3.75	2.50
a.	Inverted surcharge	25.00	25.00
b.	Perf. 13½	3.75	3.25
	Nos. 36-48 (13)	45.25	36.05

Nos. 16, 19, 21 and 24 Overprinted in Black

1902 *Perf. 11½*

49	A2 15r brown	2.00	1.25
50	A2 25r sea green	2.00	1.40
51	A2 50r blue	2.00	1.40
a.	Double overprint	20.00	18.00
52	A2 75r rose	4.00	2.75
a.	Double ovpt, one albino	10.00	6.00
	Nos. 49-52 (4)	10.00	6.80

No. 23 Surcharged

1905

53	A2 50r on 65r dull blue	4.00	2.50

Angola Stamps of 1898-1903 (Port. Congo type A2) Overprinted or Surcharged:

a b

1911

54 (a) 2½r gray 1.10 .90
55 (a) 5r orange 1.60 1.25
56 (a) 10r lt green 1.60 1.25
a. "REPUBLICA" inverted 17.50 17.50
57 (a) 15r gray green 1.60 1.25
a. "REPUBLICA" inverted 17.50 17.50
58 (b) 25r on 200r red vio, *pnksh* 2.50 2.00
a. "REPUBLICA" inverted 17.50 17.50
b. "CONGO" double 17.50 17.50

Thin Bar and "CONGO" as Type "b"

59 (a) 2½r gray 1.10 .90
Nos. 54-59 (6) 9.50 7.55

Issue of 1898-1903 Overprinted in Carmine or Green — c

1911

60 A2 2½r gray .20 .20
61 A2 5r orange .25 .20
62 A2 10r lt green .25 .20
63 A2 15r gray grn .25 .25
64 A2 20r gray vio .45 .25
65 A2 25r car rose (G) .55 .25
66 A2 50r brown .65 .35
67 A2 75r red lilac 1.10 .55
68 A2 100r dk bl, *bl* .80 .60
69 A2 115r org brn, *pink* 2.10 1.40
70 A2 130r brown, *straw* 2.10 1.40
71 A2 200r red vio, *pnksh* 3.00 1.90
72 A2 400r dull bl, *straw* 3.00 2.50
73 A2 500r blk & red, *bl* 4.25 2.25
74 A2 700r violet, *yelsh* 4.25 2.25
Nos. 60-74 (15) 23.20 14.55

Numerous inverts and doubles exist. These are printer's waste or made to order.

Common Design Types pictured following the introduction.

Vasco da Gama Issue of Various Portuguese Colonies Surcharged

1913

On Stamps of Macao

75 CD20 ¼c on ½a bl grn 1.25 1.25
76 CD21 ½c on 1a red 1.25 1.25
77 CD22 1c on 2a red vio 1.25 1.25
78 CD23 2½c on 4a yel grn 1.25 1.25
79 CD24 5c on 8a dk blue 1.25 1.25
80 CD25 7½c on 12a vio brn 2.50 2.50
81 CD26 10c on 16a bis brn 1.75 1.75
82 CD27 15c on 24a bister 1.75 1.75
Nos. 75-82 (8) 12.25 12.25

On Stamps of Portuguese Africa

83 CD20 ¼c on 2½r bl grn .80 .80
84 CD21 ½c on 5r red .80 .80
85 CD22 1c on 10r red vio .80 .80
86 CD23 2½c on 25r yel grn .80 .80
87 CD24 5c on 50r dk bl 1.10 1.10
88 CD25 7½c on 75r vio brn 1.90 1.90
89 CD26 10c on 100r bis brn 1.25 1.25
a. Inverted surcharge 25.00 25.00
90 CD27 15c on 150r bister 1.50 1.50
Nos. 83-90 (8) 8.95 8.95

On Stamps of Timor

91 CD20 ¼c on ½a bl grn 1.25 1.25
92 CD21 ½c on 1a red 1.25 1.25
93 CD22 1c on 2a red vio 1.25 1.25
94 CD23 2½c on 4a yel grn 1.25 1.25
95 CD24 5c on 8a dk blue 1.25 1.25
a. Double surcharge 25.00 25.00
96 CD25 7½c on 12a vio brn 2.50 2.50
97 CD26 10c on 16a bis brn 2.25 2.25
98 CD27 15c on 24a bister 2.25 2.25
Nos. 91-98 (8) 13.25 13.25
Nos. 75-98 (24) 34.45 34.45

Ceres — A3

1914 Typo. *Perf. 15x14*

Name and Value in Black

99 A3 ¼c olive brn .35 *.50*
a. Inscriptions inverted

100 A3 ½c black .65 *1.00*
101 A3 1c blue grn 3.00 *4.25*
102 A3 1½c lilac brn 1.25 *1.40*
103 A3 2c carmine 1.25 *1.40*
104 A3 2½c lt violet .40 *.90*
105 A3 5c dp blue .70 *1.40*
106 A3 7½c yellow brn 1.00 *1.40*
107 A3 8c slate 1.60 *3.25*
108 A3 10c orange brn 1.60 *3.25*
109 A3 15c plum 1.90 *3.25*
110 A3 20c yellow grn 2.25 *3.25*
111 A3 30c brown, *grn* 2.75 *5.00*
112 A3 40c brown, *pink* 4.50 *6.50*
113 A3 50c orange, *salmon* 4.50 *6.50*
114 A3 1e green, *blue* 5.50 *8.75*
Nos. 99-114 (16) 33.20 *52.00*

Issue of 1898-1903 Overprinted Locally in Green or Red

1914-18 *Perf. 11½*

117 A2 50r brown (G) .95 .65
118 A2 75r rose (G) *450.00*
119 A2 75r red lilac (G) 2.25 1.50
120 A2 100r blue, *bl* (R) .95 .80
121 A2 200r red vio, *pink* (G) 1.90 1.25
122 A2 400r dl bl, *straw* (R) ('18) 80.00 55.00
123 A2 500r blk & red, *bl* (R) 65.00 42.50

Same on Nos. 51-52

124 A2 50r blue (R) .95 .70
125 A2 75r rose (G) 1.50 1.10

Same on No. 53

126 A2 50r on 65r dl bl (R) 1.25 1.10
Nos. 117,119-126 (9) 154.75 104.60

No. 118 was not regularly issued.

Provisional Issue of 1902 Overprinted Type "c" in Red

1915 *Perf. 11½, 12½, 13½*

127 A1 115r on 10r red vio .25 .20
a. Perf. 13½ 17.00 14.00
128 A1 115r on 50r lt bl .25 .20
a. Perf. 11½ 1.90 .65
129 A1 130r on 5r yellow .35 .25
130 A1 130r on 75r rose 1.50 .65
131 A1 130r on 100r brn, *buff* .45 .40
135 N1 115r on 2½r brn .45 .40

Nos. 49, 51 Overprinted Type "c"

136 A2 15r brown .65 .55
137 A2 50r blue .45 .40

No. 53 Overprinted Type "c"

138 A2 50r on 65r dull blue .55 .40
Nos. 127-138 (9) 4.90 3.45

NEWSPAPER STAMP

N1

Perf. 12½

1894, Aug. 5 Typo. Unwmk.

P1 N1 2½r brown 1.00 .60
a. Perf. 13½ 1.00 .60

For surcharge and overprint see Nos. 48, 135.

PORTUGUESE GUINEA

'pōr-chi-gēz 'gi-nē

LOCATION — On the west coast of Africa between Senegal and Guinea
GOVT. — Portuguese Overseas Territory
AREA — 13,944 sq. mi.
POP. — 560,000 (est. 1970)
CAPITAL — Bissau

1000 Reis = 1 Milreis
100 Centavos = 1 Escudo (1913)

STAMPS OF CAPE VERDE USED IN PORTUGUESE GUINEA

Before Mar. 19, 1879, Portuguese Guinea was an administrative dependency of Cape Verde. Cape Verde stamps Nos. 1-4, 4a, 5-7 and 14 were used in Portuguese Guinea in 1877-1881, overlapping slightly with the issues of Portuguese Guinea.

Use in Portuguese Guinea can be distinguished by the cancellations composed of several concentric rings, with or without a heavy dot at the center. There are several types of these canceling devices, and some similar ones were also at Cape Verde. Identification of the cancellations by experts is advised.

1877-81

A1 A1 5r black (#1)
A2 A1 10r yellow (#2)
A3 A1 20r bister (#3)
A4 A1 25r rose, perf 12½ (#4)
A1 25r rose, perf 13½ (#4a)
A5 A1 40r blue, perf 12½ (#5)
A6 A1 50r green (#6)
A7 A1 50r blue (#14)
A8 A1 100r lilac (#7)

Issued under Portuguese Administration

Nos. 1-7 are valued with small faults such as short perfs or small thins. Completely fault-free examples of any of these stamps are very scarce and are worth more than the values given.

Stamps of Cape Verde, 1877-85 Overprinted in Black

1881 Unwmk. *Perf. 12½*

Without Gum (Nos. 1-7)

1 A1 5r black *1,000.* *800.*
1A A1 10r yellow *1,750.* *800.*
2 A1 20r bister *475.* *250.*
3 A1 25r rose *1,400.* *775.*
4 A1 40r blue *1,250.* *800.*
a. Cliché of Mozambique in Cape Verde plate *16,500.* *15,250.*
4B A1 50r green *2,000.* *725.*
5 A1 100r lilac 275. 175.
6 A1 200r orange *575.* *475.*
7 A1 300r brown *575.* *475.*

Excellent forgeries exist of Nos. 1-7.

Overprinted in Red or Black

1881-85 *Perf. 12½*

8 A1 5r black (R) 4.00 2.75
10 A1 10r green ('85) 6.00 5.50
11 A1 20r bister 3.00 2.25
12 A1 20r rose ('85) 6.75 5.00
a. Double overprint
13 A1 25r carmine 2.40 1.75
14 A1 25r violet ('85) 3.00 1.90
a. Double overprint
15b A1 40r blue 180.00 115.00
c. Cliché of Mozambique in Cape Verde plate *1,350.* *900.00*
16 A1 40r yellow ('85) 1.90 1.60
a. Cliché of Mozambique in Cape Verde plate 50.00 45.00
b. Imperf.
c. As "a," imperf.
17a A1 50r green 180.00 115.00
18 A1 50r blue ('85) 5.75 2.75
a. Imperf.
b. Double overprint
19 A1 100r lilac 7.75 6.00
a. Inverted overprint 7.75 6.00
b. 100r lilac 11.00 6.00
20 A1 200r orange 11.50 8.00
21 A1 300r yellow brn 14.00 11.00
a. 300r lake brown 16.00 12.50

Perf. 13½

8a A1 5r black (R) 4.00 3.00
9 A1 10r yellow 160.00 160.00
10a A1 10r green ('85) 6.75 5.00
11a A1 20r bister 3.25 2.25
12b A1 20r rose ('85) 6.75 5.50
13a A1 25r rose 67.50 37.50
15 A1 40r blue 175.00 110.00
a. Cliché of Mozambique in Cape Verde plate *1,250.* *875.00*
16d A1 40r yellow ('85) 4.00 3.00
e. Cliché of Mozambique in Cape Verde plate 50.00 45.00
f. Imperf.
17 A1 50r green 175.00 110.00
18c A1 50r blue ('85) 10.50 4.00
19c A1 100r pale lilac 9.00 5.50
d. 100r gray lilac 9.00 5.50

Varieties of this overprint may be found without accent on "E" of "GUINE," or with grave instead of acute accent.

Stamps of the 1881-85 issues were reprinted on a smooth white chalky paper, ungummed, and on thin white paper with shiny white gum and clean-cut perforation 13½.

King Luiz — A3

1886 Typo. *Perf. 12½, 13½*

22 A3 5r gray black 6.00 5.50
a. Imperf.
23 A3 10r green 7.25 4.00
a. Perf. 13½ 8.25 6.75
b. Imperf.
24 A3 20r carmine 10.50 4.00
25 A3 25r red lilac 10.50 6.25
a. Imperf.
26 A3 40r chocolate 8.50 6.25
a. Perf. 12½ 82.50 60.00
27 A3 50r blue 17.00 6.25
a. Imperf.
28 A3 80r gray 16.00 11.00
a. Perf. 12½ 82.50 60.00
29 A3 100r brown 16.00 11.00
a. Perf. 12½ 37.50 22.50
30 A3 200r gray lilac 37.50 22.50
31 A3 300r orange 47.50 35.00
a. Perf. 13½ 210.00 210.00
Nos. 22-31 (10) 176.75 111.75

For surcharges and overprints see Nos. 67-76, 180-183.

Reprinted in 1905 on thin white paper with shiny white gum and clean-cut perforation 13½.

King Carlos
A4 A5

1893-94 *Perf. 11½*

32 A4 5r yellow 1.90 1.10
a. Perf. 12½ 2.00 1.25
33 A4 10r red violet 1.90 1.10
34 A4 15r chocolate 2.40 1.60
35 A4 20r lavender 2.40 1.60
36 A4 25r blue green 2.40 1.60
37 A4 50r lt blue 4.25 3.75
a. Perf. 12½ 17.00 12.50
b. Perf. 11½, lozenge paper 175.00 125.00
38 A4 75r rose 11.50 7.50
39 A4 80r lt green 11.50 7.50
40 A4 100r brn, *buff* 11.50 7.50
41 A4 150r car, *rose* 11.50 8.00
42 A4 200r dk bl, *bl* 19.00 15.00
43 A4 300r dk bl, *sal* 18.00 15.00
Nos. 32-43 (12) 98.25 71.25

Almost all of Nos. 32-43 were issued without gum.

For surcharges and overprints see #77-88, 184-188, 203-205.

1898-1903 *Perf. 11½*

Name & Value in Black except 500r

44 A5 2½r gray .40 .35
45 A5 5r orange .40 .35
46 A5 10r lt green .40 .35
47 A5 15r brown 3.25 2.25
48 A5 15r gray grn ('03) 1.75 1.25
49 A5 20r gray violet 1.40 1.10
50 A5 25r sea green 1.75 .90
51 A5 25r carmine ('03) 1.00 .55
52 A5 50r dark blue 2.75 1.40
53 A5 50r brown ('03) 3.25 2.25
54 A5 65r dl blue ('03) 11.00 8.75
55 A5 75r rose 17.00 8.00
56 A5 75r lilac ('03) 4.00 2.25
57 A5 80r brt violet 3.00 1.90
58 A5 100r dk bl, *bl* 2.75 1.90
a. Perf. 12½ 52.50 22.50
59 A5 115r org brn, *pink* ('03) 8.50 6.00
a. 115r orange brown, *yellowish* 8.25 5.00
60 A5 130r brn, *straw* ('03) 10.00 7.50
61 A5 150r lt brn, *buff* 11.00 3.25
62 A5 200r red lilac, *pnksh* 10.00 3.25
63 A5 300r blue, *rose* 11.00 4.25

64	A5	400r dl bl, *straw* ('03)	13.00	10.00
65	A5	500r blk & red, *bl* ('01)	14.50	7.75
66	A5	700r vio, *yelsh* ('01)	17.00	10.00
		Nos. 44-66 (23)	149.10	85.55

Stamps issued in 1903 were without gum.

For overprints and surcharges see Nos. 90-115, 190-194, 197.

Issue of 1886 Surcharged in Black or Red

1902, Oct. 20 ***Perf. 12½***

67	A3	65r on 10r green	6.50	5.50
a.		Inverted surcharge	30.00	25.00
68	A3	65r on 20r car	6.50	5.00
69	A3	65r on 25r red lilac	6.50	5.00
70	A3	115r on 40r choc	5.75	4.50
a.		Perf. 13½	13.00	9.50
71	A3	115r on 50r blue	5.75	4.50
a.		Inverted surcharge	30.00	25.00
72	A3	115r on 300r orange	7.25	5.75
73	A3	130r on 80r gray	7.25	5.00
a.		Perf. 13½	14.00	5.75
74	A3	130r on 100r brown	7.75	5.75
a.		Perf. 13½	20.00	14.00
75	A3	400r on 200r gray lil	13.00	8.75
76	A3	400r on 5r gray blk (R)	32.50	24.00
		Nos. 67-76 (10)	98.75	73.75

Reprints of No. 76 are in black and have clean-cut perforation 13½.

Same Surcharge on Issue of 1893-94

Perf. 11½, 12½ (#80)

77	A4	65r on 10r red vio	5.75	3.50
78	A4	65r on 15r choc	5.75	3.50
79	A4	65r on 20r lav	5.75	3.50
80	A4	65r on 50r lt bl	3.00	2.25
a.		Perf. 13½	3.25	2.50
81	A4	115r on 5r yel	5.50	3.00
a.		Inverted surcharge	45.00	45.00
b.		Perf. 12½	55.00	40.00
82	A4	115r on 25r bl grn	6.00	3.25
83	A4	130r on 150r car, *rose*	6.00	3.25
84	A4	130r on 200r dk bl, *bl*	6.50	4.50
85	A4	130r on 300r dk bl, *sal*	6.50	4.50
86	A4	400r on 75r rose	4.50	3.00
87	A4	400r on 80r lt grn	3.00	1.60
88	A4	400r on 100r brn, *buff*	4.00	1.60

Same Surcharge on No. P1

Perf. 13½

89	N1	115r on 2½r brn	4.50	3.25
a.		Inverted surcharge	30.00	25.00
b.		Perf. 12½	4.75	3.50
c.		As "b," inverted surcharge	30.00	25.00
		Nos. 77-89 (13)	66.75	40.70

Issue of 1898 Overprinted in Black

1902, Oct. 20 ***Perf. 11½***

90	A5	15r brown	2.50	1.25
91	A5	25r sea green	2.50	1.60
92	A5	50r dark blue	3.00	1.60
93	A5	75r rose	5.75	4.00
		Nos. 90-93 (4)	13.75	8.45

No. 54 Surcharged in Black

1905

94	A5	50r on 65r dull blue	4.50	2.50

Issue of 1898-1903 Overprinted in Carmine or Green

1911 ***Perf. 11½***

95	A5	2½r gray	.40	.35
a.		Inverted overprint	19.00	19.00
96	A5	5r orange	.40	.35
97	A5	10r lt green	.70	.50
98	A5	15r gray green	.70	.50
99	A5	20r gray violet	.70	.50
100	A5	25r carmine (G)	.70	.50
a.		Double overprint	15.00	15.00
101	A5	50r brown	.45	.40
102	A5	75c lilac	.45	.40
103	A5	100r dk bl, *bl*	1.50	.75
104	A5	115r org brn, *pink*	1.50	1.00
105	A5	130r brn, *straw*	1.50	1.00
106	A5	200r red lil, *pink*	6.50	3.25
107	A5	400r dl bl, *straw*	2.50	1.50
108	A5	500r blk & red, *bl*	2.75	1.50
109	A5	700r vio, *yelsh*	4.25	2.25
		Nos. 95-109 (15)	25.00	14.75

Issued without gum: #101-102, 104-105, 107.

Issue of 1898-1903 Overprinted in Red

1913 ***Perf. 11½***

Without Gum (Nos. 110-115)

110	A5	15r gray grn	10.00	6.50
111	A5	75r lilac	10.00	6.50
a.		Inverted overprint	35.00	35.00
112	A5	100r bl, *bl*	6.00	4.50
a.		Inverted overprint	35.00	35.00
113	A5	200r red lil, *pnksh*	30.00	25.00
a.		Inverted overprint	82.50	82.50

Same Overprint on Nos. 90, 93 in Red

114	A5	15r brown	10.00	7.25
a.		"REPUBLICA" double	*35.00*	*35.00*
b.		"REPUBLICA" inverted	*30.00*	*30.00*
115	A5	75r rose	10.00	7.25
a.		"REPUBLICA" inverted	35.00	35.00
		Nos. 110-115 (6)	76.00	57.00

Vasco da Gama Issue of Various Portuguese Colonies Surcharged

1913

On Stamps of Macao

116	CD20	¼c on ½a bl grn	1.60	1.60
117	CD21	½c on 1a red	1.60	1.60
118	CD22	1c on 2a red vio	1.60	1.60
119	CD23	2½c on 4a yel grn	1.60	1.60
120	CD24	5c on 8a dk bl	1.60	1.60
121	CD25	7½c on 12a vio brn	3.25	3.25
122	CD26	10c on 16a bis brn	1.60	1.60
a.		Inverted surcharge	30.00	30.00
123	CD27	15c on 24a bis	2.75	2.75
		Nos. 116-123 (8)	15.60	15.60

On Stamps of Portuguese Africa

124	CD20	¼c on 2½c bl grn	1.40	1.40
125	CD21	½c on 5r red	1.40	1.40
126	CD22	1c on 10r red vio	1.40	1.40
127	CD23	2½c on 25r yel grn	1.40	1.40
128	CD24	5c on 50r dk bl	1.40	1.40
129	CD25	7½c on 75r vio brn	3.00	3.00
130	CD26	10c on 100r bis brn	1.40	1.40
131	CD27	15c on 150r bis	4.00	4.00
		Nos. 124-131 (8)	15.40	15.40

On Stamps of Timor

132	CD20	¼c on ½a bl grn	1.60	1.60
133	CD21	½c on 1a red	1.60	1.60
134	CD22	1c on 2a red vio	1.60	1.60
135	CD23	2½c on 4a yel grn	1.60	1.60
136	CD24	5c on 8a dk blue	1.60	1.60
137	CD25	7½c on 12a vio brn	3.00	3.00
138	CD26	10c on 16a bis brn	1.60	1.60
139	CD27	15c on 24a bister	3.00	3.00
		Nos. 132-139 (8)	15.60	15.60
		Nos. 116-139 (24)	46.60	46.60

Ceres — A6

1914-26 ***Perf. 15x14, 12x11½***

Name and Value in Black

140	A6	¼c olive brown	.20	.20
141	A6	½c black	.20	.20
142	A6	1c blue green	1.40	1.40
143	A6	1c yel grn ('22)	.20	.20
144	A6	1½c lilac brn	.20	.20
145	A6	2c carmine	.20	.20
146	A6	2c gray ('25)	.20	*1.60*
147	A6	2½c lt violet	.20	.20
148	A6	3c orange ('22)	.20	*1.60*
149	A6	4c deep red ('22)	.20	*1.60*
150	A6	4½c gray ('22)	.20	*1.60*
151	A6	5c deep blue	.65	.55
152	A6	5c brt blue ('22)	.20	.20
153	A6	6c lilac ('22)	.20	*1.60*
154	A6	7c ultra ('22)	.30	*1.60*
155	A6	7½c yellow brn	.20	.20
156	A6	8c slate	.20	.20
157	A6	10c orange brn	.20	.20
158	A6	12c blue grn ('22)	.65	.50
159	A6	15c plum	8.25	7.25
160	A6	15c brn rose ('22)	.50	.35
161	A6	20c yellow grn	.20	.20
162	A6	24c ultra ('25)	1.90	1.60
163	A6	25c brown ('25)	2.50	2.25
164	A6	30c brown, *grn*	7.00	6.00
165	A6	30c gray grn ('22)	.90	.25
166	A6	40c brown, *pink*	3.50	3.25
167	A6	40c turq bl ('22)	.90	.40
168	A6	50c orange, *salmon*	3.50	3.25
169	A6	50c violet ('25)	1.90	.90
170	A6	60c dk blue ('22)	1.90	.95
171	A6	60c dp rose ('26)	2.50	1.75
172	A6	80c brt rose ('22)	1.60	1.00
173	A6	1e green, *blue*	4.00	3.50
174	A6	1e pale rose ('22)	2.75	1.50
175	A6	1e indigo ('26)	3.50	2.75
176	A6	2e dk violet ('22)	3.00	1.50
177	A6	5e buff ('25)	13.00	10.50
178	A6	10e pink ('25)	27.50	17.50
179	A6	20e pale turq ('25)	60.00	35.00
		Nos. 140-179 (40)	156.80	115.70

For surcharges see Nos. 195-196, 211-213.

Provisional Issue of 1902 Overprinted in Carmine

1915 ***Perf. 11½, 12½, 13½***

180	A3	115r on 40r choc	1.10	.65
a.		Perf. 13½	13.00	8.50
181	A3	115r on 50r blue	1.40	.75
182	A3	130r on 80r gray	4.50	1.90
a.		Perf. 12½	27.50	22.50
183	A3	130r on 100r brn	3.50	1.90
a.		Perf. 13½	14.50	11.00
184	A4	115r on 5r yellow	.80	.65
a.		Perf. 11½	5.00	4.50
185	A4	115r on 25r bl grn	.75	.65
186	A4	130r on 150r car, *rose*	1.25	.80
187	A4	130r on 200r bl, *bl*	.80	.70
188	A4	130r on 300r dk bl, *sal*	1.10	.80
189	N1	115r on 2½r brn	1.25	.90
a.		Perf. 13½	13.00	11.00
b.		Inverted overprint	22.50	22.50

On Nos. 90, 92, 94

Perf. 11½

190	A5	15r brown	.80	.70
191	A5	50r dark blue	.80	.70
192	A5	50r on 65r dl bl	.80	.70
		Nos. 180-192 (13)	18.85	11.80

Nos. 64, 66 Overprinted

1919 **Without Gum** ***Perf. 11½***

193	A5	400r dl bl, *straw*	50.00	21.00
194	A5	700r vio, *yelsh*	11.00	6.25

Nos. 140, 141 and 59 Surcharged:

a

b

1920, Sept. ***Perf. 15x14, 11½***

Without Gum

195	A6(a)	4c on ¼c	3.25	2.75
196	A6(a)	6c on ½c	4.00	2.75
197	A5(b)	12c on 115r	5.50	4.50
		Nos. 195-197 (3)	12.75	10.00

Nos. 86-88 Surcharged

1925 ***Perf. 11½***

203	A4	40c on 400r on 75r	.95	.75
204	A4	40c on 400r on 80r	.70	.55
205	A4	40c on 400r on 100r	.70	.55
		Nos. 203-205 (3)	2.35	1.85

Nos. 171-172, 176 Surcharged

1931 ***Perf. 12x11½***

211	A6	50c on 60c dp rose	3.25	1.60
212	A6	70c on 80c pink	3.25	1.90
213	A6	1.40e on 2e dk vio	6.50	4.00
		Nos. 211-213 (3)	13.00	7.50

Ceres — A7

1933 **Wmk. 232** ***Perf. 12 x 11½***

214	A7	1c bister	.20	.20
215	A7	5c olive brn	.20	.20
216	A7	10c violet	.20	.20
217	A7	15c black	.20	.20
218	A7	20c gray	.20	.20
219	A7	30c dk green	.25	.20
220	A7	40c red orange	.45	.20
221	A7	45c lt blue	1.10	.80
222	A7	50c lt brown	1.10	.55
223	A7	60c olive grn	1.40	.55
224	A7	70c orange brn	2.75	.65
225	A7	80c emerald	1.50	.80
226	A7	85c deep rose	3.00	1.40
227	A7	1e red brown	1.40	.90
228	A7	1.40e dk blue	6.50	2.25
229	A7	2e red violet	4.50	1.90
230	A7	5e apple green	10.00	5.75
231	A7	10e olive bister	17.50	9.50
232	A7	20e orange	55.00	25.00
		Nos. 214-232 (19)	107.45	51.45

Common Design Types pictured following the introduction.

Common Design Types

Engr.; Name & Value Typo. in Black

1938 **Unwmk.** ***Perf. 13½x13***

233	CD34	1c gray grn	.20	.20
234	CD34	5c orange brn	.20	.20
235	CD34	10c dk carmine	.20	.20
236	CD34	15c dk vio brn	.20	.20
237	CD34	20c slate	.40	.20
238	CD35	30c rose violet	.60	.25
239	CD35	35c brt green	.65	.35
240	CD35	40c brown	1.10	.35
241	CD35	50c brt red vio	1.10	.35
242	CD36	60c gray black	1.60	.35
243	CD36	70c brown vio	1.60	.35
244	CD36	80c orange	1.90	.70
245	CD36	1e red	1.50	.50
246	CD37	1.75e blue	2.10	1.00
247	CD37	2e brown car	5.00	1.40
248	CD37	5e olive grn	5.50	2.25
249	CD38	10e blue vio	7.50	2.75
250	CD38	20e red brown	22.50	4.50
		Nos. 233-250 (18)	53.85	16.10

AIR POST STAMPS

Common Design Type

Perf. 13½x13

1938, Sept. 19 **Engr.** **Unwmk.**

Name and Value in Black

C1	CD39	10c red orange	.45	.35
C2	CD39	20c purple	.50	.35
C3	CD39	50c orange	.50	.35
C4	CD39	1e ultra	.60	.45
C5	CD39	2e lilac brown	5.25	3.50
C6	CD39	3e dark green	1.40	.95
C7	CD39	5e red brown	4.00	1.00
C8	CD39	9e rose carmine	4.00	2.25
C9	CD39	10e magenta	9.25	3.00
		Nos. C1-C9 (9)	25.95	12.20

No. C7 exists with overprint "Exposicao Internacional de Nova York, 1939-1940" and Trylon and Perisphere.

POSTAGE DUE STAMPS

D1

D2

1904 Unwmk. Typo. ***Perf. 12***
Without Gum

J1	D1	5r yellow green	.60	.45
J2	D1	10r slate	.60	.45
J3	D1	20r yellow brown	.65	.55
J4	D1	30r red orange	1.90	1.60
J5	D1	50r gray brown	1.90	1.60
J6	D1	60r red brown	4.25	2.75
J7	D1	100r lilac	4.25	2.75
J8	D1	130r dull blue	3.25	2.10
J9	D1	200r carmine	6.50	5.25
J10	D1	500r violet	11.00	6.00
		Nos. J1-J10 (10)	34.90	23.50

Same Overprinted in Carmine or Green

1911
Without Gum

J11	D1	5r yellow green	.25	.20
J12	D1	10r slate	.25	.20
J13	D1	20r yellow brown	.35	.35
J14	D1	30r red orange	.35	.35
J15	D1	50r gray brown	.35	.35
J16	D1	60r red brown	1.00	.80
J17	D1	100r lilac	1.90	1.40
J18	D1	130r dull blue	1.90	1.00
J19	D1	200r carmine (G)	1.90	1.50
J20	D1	500r violet	1.10	1.00
		Nos. J11-J20 (10)	9.35	7.15

Nos. J2-J10 Overprinted

1919
Without Gum

J21	D1	10r slate	8.25	8.25
J22	D1	20r yellow brown	9.00	9.00
J23	D1	30r red orange	6.50	5.75
J24	D1	50r gray brown	2.50	2.10
J25	D1	60r red brown	550.00	450.00
J26	D1	100r lilac	2.25	1.90
J27	D1	130r dull blue	22.50	19.00
J28	D1	200r carmine	2.75	2.50
J29	D1	500r violet	24.00	20.00
		Nos. J21-J24,J26-J29 (8)	77.75	68.50

No. J25 was not regularly issued but exists on genuine covers.

1921

J30	D2	½c yellow green	.20	.20
J31	D2	1c slate	.20	.20
J32	D2	2c orange brown	.20	.20
J33	D2	3c orange	.20	.20
J34	D2	5c gray brown	.20	.20
J35	D2	6c light brown	.20	.20
J36	D2	10c red violet	.25	.25
J37	D2	13c dull blue	.25	.25
J38	D2	20c carmine	.35	.35
J39	D2	50c gray	.35	.35
		Nos. J30-J39 (10)	2.40	2.40

WAR TAX STAMPS

WT1

Perf. 11½x12
1919, May 20 Typo. Unwmk.

MR1	WT1	10r brn, buff & blk	45.00	27.50
MR2	WT1	40r brn, buff & blk	40.00	22.50
MR3	WT1	50r brn, buff & blk	42.50	25.00
		Nos. MR1-MR3 (3)	127.50	75.00

The 40r is not overprinted "REPUBLICA."
Some authorities consider Nos. MR2-MR3 to be revenue stamps.

NEWSPAPER STAMP

N1

1893 Typo. Unwmk. ***Perf. 12½***

P1	N1	2½r brown	1.25	.75
a.		Perf. 13½	1.25	.90

For surcharge and overprint see Nos. 89, 189.

POSTAL TAX STAMPS

Pombal Issue
Common Design Types

1925 Unwmk. Engr. ***Perf. 12½***

RA1	CD28	15c red & black	.55	.45
RA2	CD29	15c red & black	.55	.45
RA3	CD30	15c red & black	.55	.45
		Nos. RA1-RA3 (3)	1.65	1.35

Coat of Arms — PT7

1934, Apr. 1 Typo. ***Perf. 11½***
Without Gum

RA4	PT7	50c red brn & grn	6.25	4.00
a.		Tête beche pair		450.00

Coat of Arms
PT8 PT9

1938-40
Without Gum

RA5	PT8	50c ol bis & citron	6.00	3.25
RA6	PT8	50c lt grn & ol brn ('40)	6.00	3.25

POSTAL TAX DUE STAMPS

Pombal Issue
Common Design Types

1925 Unwmk. ***Perf. 12½***

RAJ1	CD28	30c red & black	.55	.45
RAJ2	CD29	30c red & black	.55	.45
RAJ3	CD30	30c red & black	.55	.45
		Nos. RAJ1-RAJ3 (3)	1.65	1.35

PORTUGUESE INDIA

'pōr-chi-gēz 'in-dē-ə

LOCATION — West coast of the Indian peninsula
GOVT. — Portuguese colony
AREA — 1,537 sq. mi.
POP. — 649,000 (1958)
CAPITAL — Panjim (Nova-Goa)

1000 Reis = 1 Milreis
12 Reis = 1 Tanga (1881-82)
(Real = singular of Reis)
16 Tangas = 1 Rupia

Expect Nos. 1-55, 70-112 to have rough perforations. Stamps frequently were cut apart because of the irregular and missing perforations. Scissor separations that do not remove perfs do not negatively affect value.

Numeral of Value
A1 A2

A1: Large figures of value.
"REIS" in Roman capitals. "S" and "R" of "SERVICO" smaller and "E" larger than the other letters. 33 lines in background. Side ornaments of four dashes.
A2: Large figures of value.
"REIS" in block capitals. "S," "E" and "R" same size as other letters of "SERVICO." 44 lines in background. Side ornaments of five dots.

Handstamped from a Single Die
Perf. 13 to 18 & Compound
1871, Oct. 1 Unwmk.
Thin Transparent Brittle Paper

1	A1	10r black	625.00	325.00
2	A1	20r dk carmine	1,350	300.00
a.		20r orange vermilion	1,350.	300.00
3	A1	40r Prus blue	475.00	325.00
4	A1	100r yellow grn	550.00	375.00
5	A1	200r ocher yel	850.00	450.00

1872
Thick Soft Wove Paper

5A	A1	10r black	*1,500.*	350.00
6	A1	20r dk carmine	*1,650.*	400.00
7	A1	20r orange ver	*1,800.*	400.00
7A	A1	100r yellow grn		—
8	A1	200r ocher yel	*1,700.*	1,000.
9	A1	300r dp red violet		*2,250.*

The 600r and 900r of type A1 are bogus.
See Nos. 24-28. For surcharges see Nos. 70-71, 73, 83, 94, 99, 104, 108.

Perf. 12½ to 14½ & Compound
1872

10	A2	10r black	260.00	100.00
11	A2	20r vermilion	225.00	85.00
a.		"20" omitted		*1,000.*
12	A2	40r blue	70.00	60.00
a.		Tête bêche pair	*5,750.*	*5,750.*
b.		40r dark blue	85.00	60.00
13	A2	100r deep green	70.00	60.00
14	A2	200r yellow	275.00	250.00
15	A2	300r red violet	275.00	225.00
a.		Imperf.		
16	A2	600r red violet	175.00	140.00
a.		"600" double	*700.00*	
17	A2	900r red violet	200.00	175.00
		Nos. 10-17 (8)	1,550.	1,095.

An unused 100r blue green exists with watermark of lozenges and gray burelage on back. Experts believe it to be a proof.

White Laid Paper

18	A2	10r black	37.50	32.50
a.		Tête bêche pair	*14,000.*	*8,500.*
b.		10r brownish black	37.50	30.00
19	A2	20r vermilion	35.00	27.50
20	A2	40r blue	70.00	57.50
a.		"40" double	—	
b.		Tête bêche pair	—	—
21	A2	100r green	62.50	45.00
a.		"100" double	*450.00*	
22	A2	200r yellow	175.00	175.00
		Nos. 18-22 (5)	380.00	337.50

See No. 23. For surcharges see Nos. 72, 82, 95-96, 100-101, 105-106, 109-110.

1873
Re-issues
Thin Bluish Toned Paper

23	A2	20r vermilion	200.00	160.00
24	A1	10r black	14.00	8.50
a.		"1" inverted	125.00	100.00
b.		"10" double	400.00	
25	A1	20r vermilion	17.00	11.50
a.		"20" double	400.00	
b.		"20" inverted		
26	A1	300r dp violet	110.00	85.00
a.		"300" double	475.00	
27	A1	600r dp violet	140.00	100.00
a.		"600" double	575.00	
b.		"600" inverted	575.00	
28	A1	900r dp violet	140.00	100.00
a.		"900" double	675.00	
b.		"900" triple	1,000.	
		Nos. 23-28 (6)	621.00	465.00

Nos. 23 to 26 are re-issues of Nos. 11, 5A, 7, and 9. The paper is thinner and harder than that of the 1871-72 stamps and slightly transparent. It was originally bluish white but is frequently stained yellow by the gum.
Nos. 23 to 26 may be found with part of the papermaker's watermark "ORIGINAL TURKISH MILL KENT."

A3 A4

A3: Same as A1 with small figures.
A4: Same as A2 with small figures.

1874
Thin Bluish Toned Paper

29	A3	10r black	35.00	27.50
a.		"10" and "20" superimposed	475.00	*450.00*
30	A3	20r vermilion	550.00	350.00
a.		"20" double		*625.00*

For surcharge see No. 84.
Nos. 29 and 30 may be found with part of the papermaker's watermark "ORIGINAL TURKISH MILL KENT."

1875

31	A4	10r black	37.50	22.50
a.		Value sideways		550.00
32	A4	15r rose	12.50	9.00
a.		"15" inverted	475.00	
b.		"15" double		
c.		Value omitted	1,150.	
33	A4	20r vermilion	70.00	42.50
a.		"0" missing	850.00	575.00
b.		"20" sideways	*850.00*	
c.		"20" double		
		Nos. 31-33 (3)	120.00	74.00

Nos. 31 to 33 may be found with part of the papermaker's watermark "HODGKINSON & CO."
For surcharges see Nos. 74, 78, 85.

A5 A6

A5: Re-cutting of A1.
Small figures. "REIS" in Roman capitals. Letters larger. "V" of "SERVICO" barred. 33 lines in background. Side ornaments of five dots.
A6: First re-cutting of A2.
Small figures. "REIS" in block capitals. Letters re-cut. "V" of "SERVICO" barred. 41 lines above and 43 below "REIS." Side ornaments of five dots.

Perf. 12½ to 13½ & Compound
1876

34	A5	10r black	20.00	14.00
35	A5	20r vermilion	16.00	11.50
a.		"20" double	—	
36	A6	10r black	6.25	4.25
a.		Double impression	525.00	
b.		"10" double	525.00	
37	A6	15r rose	425.00	325.00
a.		"15" omitted	—	*1,000.*
38	A6	20r vermilion	22.50	17.00
39	A6	40r blue	110.00	85.00
40	A6	100r green	160.00	150.00
a.		Imperf.		
41	A6	200r yellow	950.00	675.00
42	A6	300r violet	550.00	450.00
a.		"300" omitted		
43	A6	600r violet	*800.00*	*675.00*
44	A6	900r violet	*1,000.*	*750.00*
a.		"900" omitted		

For surcharges see Nos. 75-76, 78C-80, 86-87, 91-92, 98, 102, 107, 111.

Nos. 34 to 44 may be found with part of the papermaker's watermark "SPICER BROTHERS."

A7

A8

A9

A7: Same as A5 with addition of a star above and a bar below the value.

A8: Second re-cutting of A2. Same as A6 but 41 lines both above and below "REIS." Star above and bar below value.

A9: Third re-cutting of A2. 41 lines above and 38 below "REIS." Star above and bar below value. White line around central oval.

1877

45 A7 10r black 30.00 25.00
46 A8 10r black 42.50 37.50
47 A9 10r black 29.00 25.00
a. "10" omitted
48 A9 15r rose 32.50 27.50
49 A9 20r vermilion 8.50 8.00
50 A9 40r blue 17.00 16.00
a. "40" omitted 42.50 35.00
51 A9 100r green 70.00 60.00
a. "100" omitted
52 A9 200r yellow 75.00 70.00
53 A9 300r violet 100.00 85.00
54 A9 600r violet 100.00 85.00
55 A9 900r violet 100.00 85.00
Nos. 45-55 (11) 604.50 524.00

No. 47, 20r, 40r and 200r exist imperf.

Nos. 45 to 55 may be found with part of the papermaker's watermark "SPICER BROTHERS."

For surcharges see Nos. 77, 81, 88-90, 93, 112.

Portuguese Crown — A10

1877, July 15 **Typo.**

Perf 12½, Thin paper

56 A10 5r black 5.00 3.50
57 A10 10r yellow 9.00 7.25
a. Imperf.
58 A10 20r bister 9.50 7.00
59 A10 25r rose 10.00 8.00
60a A10 40r blue 175.00 140.00
61 A10 50r yellow grn 32.50 20.00
62 A10 100r lilac 16.00 11.50
63 A10 200r orange 22.50 17.00

Perf 13½, Thin paper

56a A10 5r black 5.00 3.50
57b A10 10r yellow 10.00 8.50
58a A10 20r bister 9.50 6.00
59a A10 25r rose 10.00 8.00
60 A10 40r blue 14.00 11.00
61a A10 50r yellow grn 32.50 20.00
62a A10 100r lilac 15.00 11.50
64 A10 300r yel brn 29.00 25.00

Perf 13½, Medium paper

56b A10 5r black 5.00 3.50
57c A10 10r yellow 9.00 7.25
58b A10 20r bister 9.50 6.00
59b A10 25r rose 10.00 8.00
60a A10 40r blue 13.50 11.00
63a A10 200r orange 22.50 17.00
63b A10 200r pale orange 22.50 17.00
64a A10 300r yel brn 29.00 25.00

1880-81

Perf 12½, Thin Paper

65 A10 10r green 17.00 13.50
66a A10 25r slate 72.50 55.00
67 A10 25r violet 37.50 25.00
68 A10 40r yellow 37.50 25.00
69 A10 50r dk blue 37.50 25.00

Perf 13½, Thin Paper

65a A10 10r green 10.00 8.50
66 A10 25r slate 37.50 27.50
67a A10 25r violet 27.50 20.00
68a A10 40r yellow 32.50 25.00
69a A10 50r dk blue 17.00 15.00

Perf 13½, Medium Paper

65b A10 10r green 10.00 8.50
66b A10 25r slate 37.50 27.50
67b A10 25r violet 27.50 20.00
68b A10 40r yellow 32.50 25.00
69b A10 50r blue 17.50 15.00
c. 50c dark blue 19.00 16.00

For surcharges see Nos. 113-161.

The stamps of the 1877-81 issues were reprinted in 1885, on stout very white paper, ungummed and with rough perforation 13½. They were again reprinted in 1905 on thin white paper with shiny white gum and clean-cut perforation 13½ with large holes. Value of the lowest-cost reprint, $3 each.

Stamps of 1871-77 Surcharged with New Values Black Surcharge

1881

70 A1 1½r on 20r (#2) *1,000.*
71 A1 1½r on 20r (#7) *900.00*
72 A2 1½r on 20r (#11) *600.00*
73 A1 1½r on 20r (#25) 225.00 200.00
74 A4 1½r on 20r (#33) 140.00 125.00
a. Inverted surcharge 250.00
75 A5 1½r on 20r (#35) 110.00 85.00
76 A6 1½r on 20r (#38) 125.00 110.00
77 A9 1½r on 20r (#49) 200.00 140.00
78 A4 5r on 15r (#32) 2.50 2.50
a. Double surcharge 10.00
b. Inverted surcharge 10.00
78C A6 5r on 15r (#37) 2.50 2.50
79 A5 5r on 20r (#35) 2.50
a. Double surcharge 14.00
b. Inverted surcharge —
80 A6 5r on 20r (#38) 2.75 2.50
a. Double surcharge —
b. Inverted surcharge —
81 A9 5r on 20r (#49) 5.00 4.00
a. Double surcharge —
b. Invtd. surcharge —

Red Surcharge

82 A2 5r on 10r (#18) *475.00* *350.00*
83 A1 5r on 10r (#24) *525.00* *300.00*
84 A3 5r on 10r (#29) *1,750.*
85 A4 5r on 10r (#31) *125.00* *125.00*
86 A5 5r on 10r (#34) 6.00 6.00
a. Double surcharge 17.00
87 A6 5r on 10r (#36) 9.50 7.75
a. Inverted surcharge
88 A7 5r on 10r (#45) 90.00 50.00
a. Inverted surcharge 175.00
89 A8 5r on 10r (#46) 190.00 82.50
90 A9 5r on 10r (#47) 40.00 35.00
a. Inverted surcharge 82.50
b. Double surcharge 82.50

Similar Surcharge, Handstamped Black Surcharge

1883

91 A5 1½r on 10r (#34) 1,650. *825.00*
92 A6 1½r on 10r (#36) 1,100. *825.00*
93 A9 1½r on 10r (#47) *825.00* *600.00*
94 A1 4½r on 40r (#3) 2,200. *775.00*
95 A2 4½r on 40r (#12) 35.00 35.00
96 A2 4½r on 40r (#20) 35.00 35.00
98 A6 4½r on 40r (#39) 35.00 35.00
99 A1 4½r on 100r (#4) 2,200. *775.00*
100 A2 4½r on 100r (#13) 45.00 42.50
101 A2 4½r on 100r (#21) 45.00 42.50
102 A6 4½r on 100r (#40) 40.00 42.50
104 A1 6r on 100r (#4) 2,200. *1,200.*
105 A2 6r on 100r (#13) 375.00 *275.00*
106 A2 6r on 100r (#21) *275.00* *225.00*
107 A6 6r on 100r (#40) *350.00* *275.00*
108 A1 6r on 200r (#5) *825.00* *600.00*
109 A2 6r on 200r (#14) *275.00*
110 A2 6r on 200r (#22) *275.00* *275.00*
111 A6 6r on 200r (#41) *450.00*
112 A9 6r on 200r (#52) *550.00* *500.00*

Stamps of 1877-81 Surcharged in Black

1881-82

113 A10 1½r on 5r blk 1.40 1.10
a. With additional surcharge "4½" in blue 125.00 110.00
114 A10 1½r on 10r grn 1.40 1.10
a. With additional surch. "6" 160.00 110.00
115 A10 1½r on 20r bis 11.50 8.75
a. Inverted surcharge 27.50
b. Double surcharge 27.50
c. Pair, one without surcharge —
116 A10 1½r on 25r slate 40.00 35.00
117 A10 1½r on 100r lil 60.00 47.50
118 A10 4½r on 10r grn 190.00 160.00
119 A10 4½r on 20r bis 4.00 2.75
a. Inverted surcharge 82.50 65.00
120 A10 4½r on 25r vio 11.50 11.00
121 A10 4½r on 100r lil 225.00 160.00
122 A10 6r on 10r yel 47.50 45.00
123 A10 6r on 10r grn 10.00 8.00
124 A10 6r on 20r bis 17.00 15.00
125 A10 6r on 25r slate 35.00 27.50
126 A10 6r on 25r vio 2.25 1.75
127 A10 6r on 40r blue 82.50 70.00
128 A10 6r on 40r yel 42.50 35.00
129 A10 6r on 50r grn 47.50 38.50
130 A10 6r on 50r blue 110.00 90.00
Nos. 113-130 (18) 939.05 757.95

Surcharged in Black

131 A10 1t on 10r grn 450.00 325.00
a. With additional surch. "6" 875.00 775.00
132 A10 1t on 20r bis 47.50 42.50
133 A10 1t on 25r slate 35.00 30.00
134 A10 1t on 25r vio 13.00 9.00
135 A10 1t on 40r blue 19.00 17.50
136 A10 1t on 50r grn 55.00 47.50
137 A10 1t on 50r blue 25.00 19.00
138 A10 1t on 100r lil 24.00 13.00
139 A10 1t on 200r org 47.50 42.50
140 A10 2t on 25r slate 35.00 35.00
a. Small "T" 55.00 40.00
141 A10 2t on 25r vio 14.00 11.50
142 A10 2t on 40r blue 42.50 35.00
143 A10 2t on 40r yel 52.50 42.50
144 A10 2t on 50r grn 15.00 13.00
a. Inverted surcharge 110.00 100.00
145 A10 2t on 50r blue 90.00 75.00
146 A10 2t on 100r lil 11.50 9.25
147 A10 2t on 200r org 40.00 35.00
148 A10 2t on 300r brn 35.00 30.00
149 A10 4t on 10r grn 14.00 11.50
a. Inverted surcharge 45.00 45.00
150 A10 4t on 50r grn 13.00 10.00
a. With additional surch. "2" 160.00 110.00
151 A10 4t on 200r org 40.00 35.00
152 A10 8t on 20r bis 35.00 24.00
153 A10 8t on 25r rose 190.00 160.00
154 A10 8t on 40r blue 47.50 40.00
155 A10 8t on 100r lil 40.00 35.00
156 A10 8t on 200r org 35.00 30.00
157 A10 8t on 300r brn 47.50 40.00
Nos. 131-157 (27) 1,513. 1,217.

1882

Blue Surcharge

158 A10 4½r on 5r black 12.00 10.50

Similar Surcharge, Handstamped

1883

159 A10 1½r on 5r black 55.00 35.00
160 A10 1½r on 10r grn 82.50 45.00
161 A10 4½r on 100r lil *400.00* *325.00*

The "2" in "½" is 3mm high, instead of 2mm as on Nos. 113, 114 and 121.

The handstamp is known double on #159-161.

A12

1882-83 **Typo.**

With or Without Accent on "E" of "REIS"

162 A12 1½r black .55 .45
a. "½" for "1½"
163 A12 4½r olive bister .95 .45
164 A12 6r green .80 .45
165 A12 1t rose .80 .45
166 A12 2t blue .80 .45
167 A12 4t lilac 3.25 2.75
168 A12 8t orange 3.25 2.75
Nos. 162-168 (7) 10.40 7.75

There were three printings of the 1882-83 issue. The first had "REIS" in thick letters with acute accent on the "E." The second had "REIS" in thin letters with accent on the "E." The third had the "E" without accent. In the first printing the "E" sometimes had a grave or circumflex accent.

The third printing may be divided into two sets, with or without a small circle in the cross of the crown.

Stamps doubly printed or with value omitted, double, inverted or misplaced are printer's waste.

Nos. 162-168 were reprinted on thin white paper, with shiny white gum and clean-cut perforation 13½. Value of lowest-cost reprint, $1 each.

"REIS" no serifs — A13

"REIS" with serifs — A14

1883 **Litho.** ***Imperf.***

169 A13 1½r black 1.40 1.10
a. Tête bêche pair
b. "1½" double *425.00* *325.00*
170 A13 4½r olive grn 14.00 11.00
a. "4½" omitted 350.00 275.00
171 A13 6r green 14.00 11.00
a. Tête bêche pair 1,200.
b. "6" omitted 400.00 300.00
172 A14 1½r black 95.00 55.00
a. "1½" omitted 350.00 325.00
173 A14 6r green 62.50 47.50
a. "6" omitted 425.00 350.00
Nos. 169-173 (5) 186.90 125.60

Nos. 169-171 exist with unofficial perf. 12.

King Luiz — A15

King Carlos — A16

Perf. 12½, 13½

1886, Apr. 29 **Embossed**

174 A15 1½r black 2.50 1.40
a. Perf. 13½ 110.00 70.00
175 A15 4½r bister 3.25 1.50
a. Perf. 13½ 30.00 14.00
176 A15 6r dp green 4.50 1.75
a. Perf. 13½ 35.00 15.00
177 A15 1t brt rose 6.50 3.00
178 A15 2t deep blue 8.75 4.50
179 A15 4t gray vio 11.00 4.50
180 A15 8t orange 10.00 4.75
Nos. 174-180 (7) 46.50 21.40

For surcharges and overprints see Nos. 224-230, 277-278, 282, 317-323, 354, 397.

Nos. 178-179 were reprinted. Originals have yellow gum. Reprints have white gum and clean-cut perforation 13½. Value, $4 each.

1895-96 **Typo.** ***Perf. 11½, 12½, 13½***

181 A16 1½r black 1.40 .65
182 A16 4½r pale orange 1.40 .65
a. Perf. 13½ 8.00 1.60
183 A16 6r green 1.40 .65
a. Perf. 12½ 3.00 1.10
184 A16 9r gray lilac 4.25 3.00
185 A16 1t lt blue 1.40 .55
a. Perf. 12½ 5.50 2.50
186 A16 2t rose 1.00 .65
a. Perf. 12½ 4.25 2.25
187 A16 4t dk blue 1.60 .80
a. Perf. 12½ 5.25 3.25
188 A16 8t brt violet 3.25 2.75
Nos. 181-188 (8) 15.70 9.70

For surcharges and overprints see Nos. 231-238, 275-276, 279-281, 324-331, 352.

No. 184 was reprinted. Reprints have white gum, and clean-cut perforation 13½. Value $10.

Common Design Types pictured following the introduction.

Vasco da Gama Issue

Common Design Types

1898, May 1 **Engr.** ***Perf. 14 to 15***

189 CD20 1½r blue green 1.00 .90
190 CD21 4½r red 1.00 .90
191 CD22 6r red violet 1.00 .75
192 CD23 9r yellow green 1.00 1.00
193 CD24 1t dk blue 1.60 1.60
194 CD25 2t violet brn 2.25 1.90
195 CD26 4t bister brn 2.25 1.90
196 CD27 8t bister 4.50 4.00
Nos. 189-196 (8) 14.60 12.95

For overprints and surcharges see Nos. 290-297, 384-389.

King Carlos — A17

1898-1903 Typo. *Perf. 11½*

Name and Value in Black except No. 219

197 A17 1r gray ('02) .35 .20
198 A17 1½r orange .35 .25
199 A17 1½r slate ('02) .45 .25
200 A17 2r orange ('02) .35 .25
201 A17 2½r yel brn ('02) .45 .25
202 A17 3r dp blue ('02) .45 .25
203 A17 4½r lt green .70 .55
204 A17 6r brown .70 .55
205 A17 6r gray grn ('02) .45 .25
206 A17 9r dull vio .80 .55
a. 9r gray lilac 1.75 1.75
208 A17 1t sea green .80 .50
209 A17 1t car rose ('02) .60 .25
210 A17 2t blue 1.40 .55
a. Perf. 13½ 30.00 7.75
211 A17 2t brown ('02) 3.25 2.10
212 A17 2½t dull bl ('02) 11.00 6.50
213 A17 4t blue, *blue* 3.25 2.25
214 A17 5t brn, *straw* ('02) 4.50 2.10
215 A17 8t red lil, *pnksh* 5.50 1.40
216 A17 8t red vio, *pink* ('02) 5.00 3.00
217 A17 12t blue, *pink* 6.50 2.25
218 A17 12t grn, *pink* ('02) 5.00 3.25
219 A17 1rp blk & red, *bl* 10.00 6.50
220 A17 1rp dl bl, *straw* ('02) 11.00 7.25
221 A17 2rp vio, *yelsh* 14.50 8.25
222 A17 2rp gray blk, *straw* ('03) 17.00 12.00
Nos. 197-222 (25) 104.35 61.50

Several stamps of this issue exist without value or with value inverted but they are not known to have been issued in this condition. The 1r and 6r in carmine rose are believed to be color trials.

For surcharges and overprints see Nos. 223, 239-259, 260C-274, 283-289, 300-316, 334-350, 376-383, 390-396, 398-399.

No. 210 Surcharged in Black

1900

223 A17 1½r on 2t blue 4.50 1.10
a. Inverted surcharge
b. Perf. 13½ 35.00 22.50

Stamps of 1885-96 Surcharged in Black or Red

On Stamps of 1886

1902 *Perf. 12½, 13½*

224 A15 1r on 2t blue 1.10 .50
225 A15 2r on 4½r bis .65 .50
a. Inverted surcharge *22.50 22.50*
b. Double surcharge
226 A15 2½r on 6r green .55 .25
227 A15 3r on 1t rose .55 .25
228 A15 2½t on 1½r blk (R) 2.25 1.40
229 A15 2½t on 4t gray vio 3.25 1.40
230 A15 5t on 8t orange 2.25 .65
a. Perf. 12½ 27.50 17.00

On Stamps of 1895-96

Perf. 11½, 12½, 13½

231 A16 1r on 6r green .50 .25
232 A16 2r on 8t brt vio .35 .25
233 A16 2½r on 9r gray vio .35 .35
234 A16 3r on 4½r yel 1.75 1.00
a. Inverted surcharge 24.00 24.00
235 A16 3r on 1t lt bl 1.40 .90
236 A16 2½t on 1½r blk (R) 2.25 .80
237 A16 5t on 2t rose 2.25 .80
a. Perf. 12½ 35.00 22.50
238 A16 5t on 4t dk bl 2.25 .80
a. Perf. 12½ 35.00 22.50
Nos. 224-238 (15) 21.70 10.10

Nos. 224, 229, 231, 233, 234, 235 and 238 were reprinted in 1905. They have whiter gum than the originals and very clean-cut perf. 13½. Value $2.50 each.

Nos. 204, 208, 210 Overprinted

1902 *Perf. 11½*

239 A17 6r brown 2.25 1.40
a. Inverted overprint
240 A17 1t sea green 3.25 1.40
241 A17 2t blue 2.75 1.40
a. Perf. 13½ 150.00 100.00
Nos. 239-241 (3) 8.25 4.20

No. 212 Surcharged in Black

1905

243 A17 2t on 2½t dull blue 2.25 1.60

Stamps of 1898-1903 Overprinted in Lisbon in Carmine or Green

1911

244 A17 1r gray .20 .20
a. Inverted overprint 11.00 11.00
245 A17 1½r slate .20 .20
a. Double overprint 11.00 11.00
246 A17 2r orange .25 .20
a. Double overprint 15.00 15.00
b. Inverted overprint 11.00 11.00
247 A17 2½r yellow brn .25 .20
248 A17 3r deep blue .25 .20
249 A17 4½r light green .35 .20
250 A17 6r gray green .20 .20
251 A17 9r gray lilac .35 .20
252 A17 1t car rose (G) .35 .20
253 A17 2t brown .35 .20
254 A17 4t blue, *blue* 1.40 1.00
255 A17 5t brn, *straw* 1.40 1.00
256 A17 8t vio, *pink* 4.25 2.50
257 A17 12t grn, *pink* 4.50 2.50
258 A17 1rp dl bl, *straw* 5.75 4.75
259 A17 2rp gray blk, *straw* 8.75 7.50
Nos. 244-259 (16) 28.80 21.25

A18

Values are for pairs, both halves.

1911 Perforated Diagonally

260 A18 1r on 2r orange .80 .70
a. Without diagonal perf. 4.50 4.00
b. Cut diagonally instead of perf. 3.50 3.25

Stamps of Preceding Issues Perforated Vertically through the Middle and Each Half Surcharged with New Value:

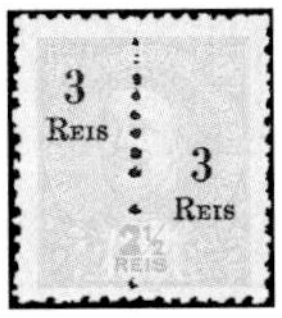

a

b

Values are for pairs, both halves of the stamp.

1912-13

On Issue of 1898-1903

260C A17(a) 1r on 2r org .25 .20
261 A17(a) 1r on 1t car .25 .20
262 A17(a) 1r on 5t brn, *straw* 275.00 225.00
263 A17(b) 1r on 5t brn, *straw* 7.75 6.00
264 A17(a) 1½r on 2½r yel brn .75 .65
264C A17(a) 1½r on 4½r lt grn 12.00 7.75
265 A17(a) 1½r on 9r gray lil .55 .45
266 A17(a) 1½r on 4t bl, *bl* .55 .45
267 A17(a) 2r on 2½r yel brn .70 .45
268 A17(a) 2r on 4t bl, *bl* 1.00 .70
269 A17(a) 3r on 2½r yel brn .70 .45
270 A17(a) 3r on 2t brown .70 .50
271 A17(a) 6r on 4½r lt grn .70 .60
272 A17(a) 6r on 9r gray lil .70 .55
273 A17(a) 6r on 9r dull vio 4.50 3.50
274 A17(b) 6r on 8t red vio, *pink* 1.60 1.00

On Nos. 237-238, 230, 226, 233

275 A16(b) 1r on 5t on 2t 20.00 17.00
276 A16(b) 1r on 5t on 4t 10.00 9.25
277 A15(b) 1r on 5t on 8t 5.00 3.25
278 A15(a) 2r on 2½r on 6r 4.25 3.25
279 A16(a) 2r on 2½r on 9r 25.00 24.00
280 A16(b) 3r on 5t on 2t 7.75 6.25
281 A16(b) 3r on 5t on 4t 7.75 6.25
282 A15(b) 3r on 5t on 8t 2.50 1.60

On Issue of 1911

283 A17(a) 1r on 1r gray .25 .25
283B A17(a) 1r on 2r org .25 .25
284 A17(a) 1r on 1t car .35 .25
285 A17(a) 1r on 5t brn, *straw* .35 .25
285A A17(b) 1r on 5t brn, *straw* 825.00 550.00
285B A17(a) 1½r on 4½r lt grn .65 .50
286 A17(a) 3r on 2t brn 11.50 8.50
289 A17(a) 6r on 9r gray lil .55 .45

There are several settings of these surcharges and many minor varieties of the letters and figures, notably a small "6." Nos. 260-289 were issued mostly without gum.

More than half of Nos. 260C-289 exist with inverted or double surcharge, or with bisecting perforation omitted. The legitimacy of these varieties is questioned. Price of inverted surcharges, $3-$15; double surcharges, $1-$4; perf. omitted, $1.50-$15.

Similar surcharges made without official authorization on stamps of type A17 are: 2r on 2½r, 3r on 2½r, 3r on 5t, and 6r on 4½r.

Vasco da Gama Issue Overprinted

1913

290 CD20 1½r blue green .35 .25
291 CD21 4½r red .35 .25
a. Double overprint 22.50
292 CD22 6r red violet .45 .40
a. Double overprint 22.50
293 CD23 9r yellow grn .45 .40
294 CD24 1t dark blue 1.00 .55
295 CD25 2t violet brown 2.25 1.25
296 CD26 4t orange brn 1.25 1.00
297 CD27 8t bister 2.25 1.40
Nos. 290-297 (8) 8.35 5.50

Issues of 1898-1913 Overprinted Locally in Red

1913-15

On Issues of 1898-1903

300 A17 2r orange 10.00 10.00
301 A17 2½r yellow brn .95 .80
302 A17 3r dp blue 19.00 17.00
303 A17 4½r lt green 1.90 1.60
304 A17 6r gray grn 25.00 20.00
305 A17 9r gray lilac 1.90 1.40
306 A17 1t sea green 45.00 35.00
307 A17 2t blue 50.00 35.00
309 A17 4t blue, *blue* 40.00 27.50
310 A17 5t brn, *straw* 55.00 35.00
311 A17 8t red vio, *pink* 65.00 45.00
312 A17 12t grn, *pink* 3.50 2.50
313 A17 1rp blk & red, *bl* 100.00 82.50
314 A17 1rp dl bl, *straw* 65.00 45.00
315 A17 2rp gray blk, *straw* 82.50 55.00
316 A17 2rp vio, *yelsh* 77.50 45.00
Nos. 300-316 (16) 642.25 458.30

Inverted or double overprints exist on 2½r, 4½r, 9r, 1rp and 2rp.

Nos. 300-316 were issued without gum except 4½r and 9r.

Nos. 302, 304, 306, 307, 310, 311 and 313 were not regularly issued. Nor were the 1½r, 2t brown and 12t blue on pink with preceding overprint.

Same Overprint in Red or Green On Provisional Issue of 1902

317 A15 1r on 2t blue 45.00 27.50
a. "REPUBLICA" inverted 140.00
318 A15 2r on 4½r bis 45.00 27.50
a. "REPUBLICA" inverted 140.00
319 A15 2½r on 6r grn .75 .65
a. "REPUBLICA" inverted 19.00 19.00
320 A15 3r on 1t rose (R) 11.00 8.75
321 A15 2½t on 4t gray vio 110.00 45.00
323 A15 5t on 8t org (G) 11.00 8.25
a. Red overprint 27.50 22.50
324 A16 1r on 6r grn 35.00 22.50
325 A16 2r on 8t vio 35.00 22.50
a. Inverted surcharge 110.00
327 A16 3r on 4½r yel 82.50 55.00
328 A16 3r on 1t lt bl 82.50 55.00
329 A16 5t on 2t rose (G) 7.75 3.00
330 A16 5t on 4t bl (G) 7.75 3.00
331 A16 5t on 4t bl (R) 7.75 4.25
a. "REPUBLICA" inverted 55.00
b. "REPUBLICA" double 55.00
Nos. 317-331 (13) 481.00 282.90

The 2½r on 1½r of types A15 and A16, the 3r on 1t (A15) and 2½r on 9r (A16) were clandestinely printed.

Some authorities question the status of No. 317-318, 320-321, 324, 327-328.

Same Overprint on Nos. 240-241

1913-15

334 A17 1t sea green 15.00 5.00
335 A17 2t blue 15.00 6.00

This overprint was applied to No. 239 without official authorization.

On Issue of 1912-13 Perforated through the Middle

Values are for pairs, both halves of the stamp.

336 A17(a) 1r on 2r org 17.00 11.00
340 A17(a) 1½r on 4½r lt grn 17.00 11.00
341 A17(a) 1½r on 9r gray lil 20.00
342 A17(a) 1½r on 4t bl, *bl* 27.50
343 A17(a) 2r on 2½r yel brn 20.00
344 A17(a) 2r on 4t bl, *bl* 27.50 7.25
345 A17(a) 3r on 2½r yel brn 22.50
346 A17(a) 3r on 2t brn 17.00 5.25
347 A17(a) 6r on 4½r lt grn 1.10 .90
348 A17(a) 6r on 9r gray lil 1.60 1.60
350 A17(b) 6r on 8t red vio, *pink* 1.60 1.60
352 A16(b) 1r on 5t on 4t bl 110.00
354 A15(a) 2r on 2½r on 6r grn 13.00
Nos. 334-354 (15) 325.80

The 1r on 5t (A15), 1r on 1t (A17), 1½r on 2½r (A17), 3r on 5t on 8t (A15), and 6r on 9r (A17) were clandestinely printed.

Nos. 336, 347 exist with inverted surcharge.

Some authorities question the status of Nos. 341-345, 352 and 354.

Ceres — A21

1913-21 Typo. *Perf. 12x11½, 15x14*

Name and Value in Black

357 A21 1r olive brn .35 .25
358 A21 1½r yellow grn .35 .25
a. Imperf.
359 A21 2r black .40 .35
360 A21 2½r olive grn .40 .45
361 A21 3r lilac .40 .20
362 A21 4½r orange brn .40 .20
363 A21 5r blue green .70 .50
364 A21 6r lilac brown .40 .20
365 A21 9r ultra .60 .25
366 A21 10r carmine .95 .55
367 A21 1t lt violet .45 .25
368 A21 2t deep blue .95 .35
369 A21 3t yellow brown 1.90 .95
370 A21 4t slate 2.25 1.25
371 A21 8t plum 4.50 4.00
372 A21 12t brown, *green* 4.00 3.25
373 A21 1rp brown, *pink* 24.00 17.50
374 A21 2rp org, *salmon* 15.00 12.00
375 A21 3rp green, *blue* 22.50 17.00
Nos. 357-375 (19) 80.50 59.75

The 1, 2, 2½, 3, 4½r, 1, 2, and 4t exist with the black inscriptions inverted and the 2½r with them double, one inverted, but it is not known that any of these were regularly issued.

See Nos. 401-410. For surcharges see Nos. 400, 420, 423.

Nos. 249, 251-253, 256-259 Surcharged in Black

1914

376	A17	1½r on 4½r grn	.35	.25
377	A17	1½r on 9r gray lil	.45	.35
378	A17	1½r on 12t grn, *pink*	.55	.50
379	A17	3r on 1t car rose	.45	.40
380	A17	3r on 2t brn	3.25	2.75
381	A17	3r on 8t red vio, *pink*	2.50	2.25
382	A17	3r on 1rp dl bl, *straw*	1.00	.60
383	A17	3r on 2rp gray blk, *straw*	1.10	.80

There are 3 varieties of the "2" in "1½."
Nos. 376-377 exist with inverted surcharge.

Vasco da Gama Issue Surcharged in Black

384	CD21	1½r on 4½r red	.40	.35
385	CD23	1½r on 9r yel grn	.50	.35
386	CD24	3r on 1t dk bl	.40	.35
387	CD25	3r on 2t vio brn	.60	.50
388	CD26	3r on 4t org brn	.35	.25
389	CD27	3r on 8t bister	1.40	1.25
		Nos. 376-389 (14)	13.30	10.95

Double, inverted and other surcharge varieties exist on Nos. 384-386, 389.

Stamps of 1898-1903 Surcharged in Red

1915

390	A17	1½r on 4½r grn	45.00	22.50
a.		"REPUBLICA" omitted	*77.50*	*47.50*
b.		"REPUBLICA" inverted	82.50	
391	A17	1½r on 9r gray lil	14.00	8.25
a.		"REPUBLICA" omitted	35.00	
392	A17	1½r on 12t grn, *pink*	1.40	1.10
396	A17	3r on 2rp gray blk, *straw*	55.00	22.50
		Nos. 390-396 (4)	115.40	54.35

Nos. 390, 390a, 390b, 391, and 391a were not regularly issued. The 3r on 2½r (A17) was surcharged without official authorization.

Preceding Issues Overprinted in Carmine

1915

On No. 230

397	A15	5t on 8t org	2.75	1.50

On Nos. 241, 243

398	A17	2t blue	2.25	1.40
399	A17	2t on 2½t dl bl	2.75	1.40
		Nos. 397-399 (3)	7.75	4.30

No. 359 Surcharged in Carmine

1922

400	A21	1½r on 2r black	.50	.40

Ceres Type of 1913-21

1922-25 Typo. *Perf. 12x11½*

Name and Value in Black

401	A21	4r blue	1.40	1.25
402	A21	1½t gray green	1.40	.95
403	A21	2½t turq blue	1.50	1.25
404	A21	3t yellow brn 4r	5.50	4.50
405	A21	4t gray ('25)	2.25	1.25
406	A21	8t dull rose	7.75	5.50
407	A21	1rp gray brn	17.50	17.00
408	A21	2rp yellow	25.00	*45.00*
409	A21	3rp bluish grn	35.00	*65.00*
410	A21	5rp carmine rose	40.00	*110.00*
		Nos. 401-410 (10)	137.30	251.70

Vasco da Gama and Flagship A22

1925, Jan. 30 Litho.

Without Gum

411	A22	6r brown	5.00	3.25
412	A22	1t red violet	7.00	5.00

400th anniv. of the death of Vasco da Gama (1469?-1524), Portuguese navigator.

Monument to St. Francis — A23

Image of St. Francis — A25

Autograph of St. Francis A24

Image of St. Francis — A26

Tomb of St. Francis — A28

Church of Bom Jesus at Goa — A27

1931, Dec. 3 *Perf. 14*

414	A23	1r gray green	.55	.50
415	A24	2r brown	.55	.50
416	A25	6r red violet	1.60	.55
417	A26	1½t yellow brn	5.75	3.50
418	A27	2t deep blue	7.00	4.25
419	A28	2½t light red	11.50	4.25
		Nos. 414-419 (6)	26.95	13.55

Exposition of St. Francis Xavier at Goa, in December, 1931.

Nos. 371 and 404 Surcharged

1931-32 *Perf. 15x14, 12x11½*

420	A21	1½r on 8t plum ('32)	1.50	1.10
423	A21	2½t on 3t4r yel brn	65.00	50.00

"Portugal" and Vasco da Gama's Flagship "San Gabriel" — A29

Perf. 11½x12

1933 Typo. Wmk. 232

424	A29	1r bister	.20	.20
425	A29	2r olive brn	.20	.20
426	A29	4r violet	.20	.20
427	A29	6r dk green	.20	.20
428	A29	8r black	.20	.20
429	A29	1t gray	.25	.20
430	A29	1½t dp rose	.35	.20
431	A29	2t brown	.40	.20
432	A29	2½t dk blue	2.25	.45
433	A29	3t brt blue	2.50	.45
434	A29	5t red orange	2.50	.45
435	A29	1rp olive grn	11.00	3.25
436	A29	2rp maroon	27.50	7.50
437	A29	3rp orange	40.00	8.75
438	A29	5rp apple grn	55.00	25.00
		Nos. 424-438 (15)	142.75	47.45

For surcharges see Nos. 454-463, 472-474, J34-J36.

Common Design Types

Perf. 13½x13

1938, Sept. 1 Engr. Unwmk.

Name and Value in Black

439	CD34	1r gray grn	.20	.20
440	CD34	2r orange brn	.20	.20
441	CD34	3r dk vio brn	.20	.20
442	CD34	6r brt green	.20	.20
443	CD35	10r dk carmine	.35	.25
444	CD35	1t brt red vio	.55	.25
445	CD35	1½t red	.90	.25
446	CD37	2t orange	.90	.25
447	CD37	2½t blue	.90	.25
448	CD37	3t slate	1.75	.35
449	CD36	5t rose vio	2.75	.50
450	CD36	1rp brown car	4.50	.90
451	CD36	2rp olive grn	7.75	2.75
452	CD38	3rp blue vio	13.00	6.50
453	CD38	5rp red brown	22.50	3.50
		Nos. 439-453 (15)	56.65	16.55

For surcharges see Nos. 492-495, 504-505.

AIR POST STAMPS

Common Design Type

Perf. 13½x13

1938, Sept. 1 Engr. Unwmk.

Name and Value in Black

C1	CD39	1t red orange	.55	.25
C2	CD39	2½t purple	.65	.25
C3	CD39	3½t orange	.65	.25
C4	CD39	4½t ultra	1.60	.45
C5	CD39	7t lilac brown	1.75	.55
C6	CD39	7½t dark green	2.50	.80
C7	CD39	9t red brown	4.50	1.25
C8	CD39	11t magenta	5.00	1.25
		Nos. C1-C8 (8)	17.20	5.05

No. C4 exists with overprint "Exposicao Internacional de Nova York, 1939-1940" and Trylon and Perisphere. Value, unused $90, never hinged $125.

POSTAGE DUE STAMPS

D1

1904 Unwmk. Typo. *Perf. 11½*

Name and Value in Black

J1	D1	2r gray green	.50	.35
J2	D1	3r yellow grn	.50	.35
J3	D1	4r orange	.50	.45
J4	D1	5r slate	.50	.50
J5	D1	6r gray	.50	.50
J6	D1	9r yellow brn	.60	.60
J7	D1	1t red orange	2.25	.80
J8	D1	2t gray brown	3.25	1.60
J9	D1	5t dull blue	4.50	3.00
J10	D1	10t carmine	7.75	3.50
J11	D1	1rp dull vio	13.00	7.50
		Nos. J1-J11 (11)	33.85	19.15

Nos. J1-J11 Overprinted in Carmine or Green

1911

J12	D1	2r gray grn	.20	.20
J13	D1	3r yellow grn	.20	.20
J14	D1	4r orange	.20	.20
J15	D1	5r slate	.20	.20
J16	D1	6r gray	.45	.20
J17	D1	9r yellow brn	.55	.35
J18	D1	1t red org	.65	.35
J19	D1	2t gray brn	.90	.55
J20	D1	5t dull blue	2.25	1.40
J21	D1	10t carmine (G)	3.25	1.90
J22	D1	1rp dull violet	7.75	3.25
		Nos. J12-J22 (11)	16.60	8.80

Nos. J1-J11 Overprinted

1914

J23	D1	2r gray grn	1.10	1.10
J24	D1	3r yellow grn	1.10	1.10
J25	D1	4r orange	1.10	1.10
J26	D1	5r slate	1.10	1.10
J27	D1	6r gray	1.40	1.10
J28	D1	9r yellow brn	1.40	1.10
J29	D1	1t red org	3.25	1.10
J30	D1	2t gray brn	11.00	3.25
J31	D1	5t dull blue	17.00	4.50
J32	D1	10t carmine	22.50	6.50
J33	D1	1rp dull violet	35.00	8.75
		Nos. J23-J33 (11)	95.95	30.70

WAR TAX STAMPS

WT1

Overprinted in Black or Carmine

Perf. 15x14

1919, Apr. 15 Typo. Unwmk.

Denomination in Black

MR1	WT1	0:00:05,48rp grn	1.50	1.25
MR2	WT1	0:01:09,94rp grn	4.50	3.00
MR3	WT1	0:02:03,43rp grn (C)	4.50	3.00
		Nos. MR1-MR3 (3)	10.50	7.25

Some authorities consider No. MR2 a revenue stamp.

POSTAL TAX STAMPS

Pombal Issue

Common Design Types

1925 Unwmk. *Perf. 12½*

RA1	CD28	6r rose & black	.50	.50
RA2	CD29	6r rose & black	.50	.50
RA3	CD30	6r rose & black	.50	.50
		Nos. RA1-RA3 (3)	1.50	1.50

POSTAL TAX DUE STAMPS

Pombal Issue

Common Design Types

1925 Unwmk. *Perf. 12½*

RAJ1	CD28	1t rose & black	.65	.65
RAJ2	CD29	1t rose & black	.65	.65
RAJ3	CD30	1t rose & black	.65	.65
		Nos. RAJ1-RAJ3 (3)	1.95	1.95

See note after Portugal No. RAJ4.

PRINCE EDWARD ISLAND

'prin(t)s 'ed-wərd 'ī-lənds

LOCATION — In the Gulf of St. Lawrence, opposite the provinces of New Brunswick and Nova Scotia
GOVT. — British Crown Colony
AREA — 2,184 sq. mi.
POP. — 92,000 (estimated)
CAPITAL — Charlottetown

Originally annexed to Nova Scotia, Prince Edward Island was a separate colony from 1769 to 1873, when it became a part of the Canadian Confederation. Postage stamps of Canada are now used.

12 Pence = 1 Shilling
100 Cents = 1 Dollar (1872)

Values for covers are for examples in fine condition. Very fine covers are extremely scarce and command substantial premiums.

A1

A2

Queen Victoria — A3

1861, Jan. 1 Unwmk. Typo. *Perf. 9*

1	A1 2p dull rose	500.	250.
	Never hinged	*1,200.*	
	On cover		375.
a.	2p deep rose	600.	300.
	Never hinged	*1,600.*	
	On cover		400.
b.	Rouletted		*20,000.*
	Never hinged	*6,000.*	
c.	Horiz. pair, imperf. between	*5,000.*	
d.	Diagonal half used as 1p on cover		*1,600.*
2	A2 3p blue	1,000.	500.
	Never hinged	*2,500.*	
	On cover		1,100.
a.	Diagonal half used as 1½p on cover		*1,750.*
b.	Double impression	2,000.	
3	A3 6p yellow green	1,600.	1,000.
	Never hinged	*3,750.*	
	On cover		1,900.

A4

A5

1862-65 *Perf. 11½-12*

White or Yellowish Paper

4	A4 1p yellow orange	25.00	25.00
	Never hinged	40.00	
	On cover		350.00
a.	1p brown orange, perf. 11	25.00	25.00
	Never hinged	40.00	
	On cover		375.00
b.	Imperf., pair	200.00	
	Never hinged	300.00	
c.	Half used as ½p on cover		*1,250.*
d.	Perf. 11x11½-12	50.00	25.00
	Never hinged	100.00	
	On cover		—
5	A1 2p rose	6.50	6.50
	Never hinged	9.50	
	On cover		90.00
a.	Yellowish paper	6.50	6.50
	Never hinged	9.00	
	On cover		90.00
b.	Imperf., pair	65.00	
	Never hinged	100.00	
c.	Horiz. pair, imperf. vert.	250.00	
	Never hinged	375.00	
d.	Vert. pair, imperf. horiz.	300.00	
	Never hinged	250.00	
e.	Diagonal half used as 1p on cover		*1,600.*
f.	"TWC" for "TWO"	50.00	25.00
	Never hinged	75.00	
	On cover		175.00
g.	Perf. 11x11½-12	8.00	8.00
	Never hinged	12.50	
	On cover		225.00
6	A2 3p blue	9.00	*12.50*
	Never hinged	13.50	
	On cover		30.00
a.	Yellowish paper	12.50	12.50
	Never hinged	18.00	
	On cover		30.00
b.	Imperf., pair	80.00	
	Never hinged	120.00	
c.	Vert. pair, imperf. horiz.	200.00	
	Never hinged	325.00	
d.	Horiz. pair, imperf. vert.	200.00	
	Never hinged	325.00	
e.	Diagonal half used as 1½p on cover		200.00
f.	Perf. 11x11½-12	12.50	10.00
	Never hinged	22.50	
	On cover		65.00
7	A3 6p yellow green	90.00	80.00
	Never hinged	160.00	
	On cover		400.00
a.	6p blue green	90.00	80.00
	Never hinged	160.00	
	On cover		400.00
b.	Imperf.	—	
c.	Diagonal half used as 3p on cover		*2,500.*
d.	Perf. 11x11½-12	75.00	75.00
	Never hinged	150.00	
	On cover		—
8	A5 9p violet	80.00	70.00
	Never hinged	125.00	
	On cover		550.00
a.	Imperf., pair	250.00	
	Never hinged	400.00	
b.	Horiz. pair, imperf. vert.	300.00	
	Never hinged	475.00	
c.	Diagonal half used as 4½p on cover		*1,750.*
d.	Perf. 11	80.00	70.00
	Never hinged	*200.00*	
	On cover		875.00

Queen Victoria
A6 A7

1868

9	A6 4p black	8.00	17.50
	Never hinged	9.50	
	On cover		175.00
a.	Yellowish paper	12.50	20.00
	Never hinged	18.00	
	On cover		175.00
b.	Horiz. pair, imperf. vert.	150.00	
	Never hinged	175.00	
c.	Diagonal half used as 2p on cover		*1,250.*
d.	Imperf., pair	90.00	
	Never hinged	120.00	
e.	Horiz. pair, imperf. between	125.00	
	Never hinged	175.00	
f.	Perf. 11x11½-12	40.00	40.00
	Never hinged	70.00	
	On cover		275.00

1870, June 1 Engr. *Perf. 12*

10	A7 4½p brown	55.00	55.00
	Never hinged	110.00	
	On cover		*2,000.*
	Without gum	42.50	
	Block of 4 with horiz. gutter btwn.	375.00	
	Never hinged	*800.00*	
	Without gum	275.00	

A8

A9

A10

A11

A12

A13

1872, Jan. 1 Typo. *Perf. 12, 12½*

11	A8 1c brown orange	4.75	*6.50*
	Never hinged	7.00	
	On cover		140.00
a.	Imperf., pair	200.00	
	Never hinged	375.00	
b.	Perf. 12½	5.50	*7.50*
	Never hinged	8.00	
	On cover		140.00
c.	1c orange, perf. 12x12½	10.00	*12.50*
	Never hinged	15.00	
	On cover		140.00
12	A9 2c ultra	20.00	*25.00*
	Never hinged	30.00	
	On cover		650.00
a.	Imperf., pair	250.00	
	Never hinged	450.00	
b.	Diagonal half used as 1c on cover		—
13	A10 3c rose	20.00	20.00
	Never hinged	32.50	
	On cover		55.00
a.	Imperf., pair	200.00	
	Never hinged	375.00	
b.	Diagonal half used as 1½c on cover		—
c.	Horiz. or vert. pair, imperf. between	200.00	
	Never hinged	350.00	
d.	Perf. 12½	20.00	20.00
	Never hinged	32.50	
	On cover		50.00
e.	Perf. 12x12½	20.00	20.00
	Never hinged	32.50	
	On cover		50.00
14	A11 4c green	5.00	*11.50*
	Never hinged	7.50	
	On cover		150.00
a.	Imperf., pair	200.00	
	Never hinged	375.00	
b.	Diagonal half used as 2c on cover		1,000.
15	A12 6c black	5.00	*11.50*
	Never hinged	7.50	
	On cover		150.00
a.	Horiz. pair, imperf. btwn.	200.00	
	Never hinged	375.00	
b.	Half used as 3c on cover		*700.00*
c.	Perf. 12½	65.00	*125.00*
	Never hinged	125.00	
	On cover		*375.00*
16	A13 12c violet	6.50	*25.00*
	Never hinged	10.00	
	On cover		*1,750.*
a.	Imperf., pair	200.00	
	Never hinged	375.00	
b.	Half used as 6c on cover		—
	Nos. 11-16 (6)	61.25	*99.50*

PUERTO RICO

ˌpwer-tə-ˈrē-(ˌ)kō

(Porto Rico)

LOCATION — A large island in the West Indies, east of Hispaniola
GOVT. — Former Spanish Colony
AREA — 3,435 sq. mi.
POP. — 953,243 (1899)
CAPITAL — San Juan

The island was ceded to the United States by the Treaty of 1898.

100 Centimes = 1 Peseta
1000 Milesimas = 100 Centavos = 1 Peso (1881)
100 Cents = 1 Dollar (1898)

Values for unused stamps are for examples with original gum as defined in the catalogue introduction. Very fine examples of Nos. 1-170, MR1-MR13 will have perforations clear of the design but will be noticeably poorly centered. Extremely fine examples will be well centered; these are scarce and command substantial premiums.

Issued under Spanish Dominion

Puerto Rican stamps of 1855-73, a part of the Spanish colonial period, were also used in Cuba. They are listed as Cuba Nos. 1-4, 9-14, 18-21, 31-34, 39-41, 47-49, 51-53, 55-57.

Stamps of Cuba Overprinted in Black:

a

b

c

d

1873 Unwmk. *Perf. 14*

1	A10 (a) 25c gray	45.00	1.90
	On cover		50.00
a.	25c lilac	62.50	3.00
	On cover		75.00
2	A10 (a) 50c brown	115.00	5.75
	On cover		200.00
3	A10 (a) 1p red brown	300.00	19.00
	On cover		500.00
	Nos. 1-3 (3)	460.00	26.65

1874

4	A11 (b) 25c ultra	37.50	2.50
	On cover		50.00
a.	Double overprint	210.00	
b.	Inverted overprint	210.00	

1875

5	A12 (b) 25c ultra	27.50	2.75
	On cover		50.00
a.	Inverted overprint	75.00	45.00
6	A12 (b) 50c green	35.00	3.00
	On cover		200.00
a.	Inverted overprint	*175.00*	*87.50*
7	A12 (b) 1p brown	140.00	14.50
	On cover		500.00
	Nos. 5-7 (3)	202.50	20.25

1876

8	A13 (c) 25c pale violet	4.25	1.90
	On cover		50.00
a.	25c bluish gray	5.50	2.75
	On cover		60.00
9	A13 (c) 50c ultra	10.50	3.25
	On cover		200.00
10	A13 (c) 1p black	42.50	12.00
	On cover		700.00
11	A13 (d) 25c pale violet	35.00	1.40
	On cover		100.00
12	A13 (d) 1p black	75.00	11.00
	On cover		500.00
	Nos. 8-12 (5)	167.25	29.55

Varieties of overprint on Nos. 8-11 include: inverted, double, partly omitted and sideways. Counterfeit overprints exist.

King Alfonso XII
A5 A6

1877 Typo.

13	A5 5c yellow brown	7.25	2.60
	On cover		100.00
a.	5c carmine (error)	225.00	—
14	A5 10c carmine	24.00	6.75
	On cover		100.00
a.	10c brown (error)	225.00	—
15	A5 15c deep green	35.00	14.00
	On cover		200.00
16	A5 25c ultra	15.00	2.40
	On cover		50.00
17	A5 50c bister	24.00	6.00
	On cover		300.00
	Nos. 13-17 (5)	105.25	31.75

Dated "1878"

1878

18	A5 5c ol bister	15.00	15.00
	On cover		300.00
19	A5 10c red brown	250.00	85.00
	On cover		500.00
20	A5 25c deep green	1.90	1.20
	On cover		50.00
21	A5 50c ultra	6.75	2.60
	On cover		200.00
22	A5 1p bister	12.50	5.75
	On cover		500.00
	Nos. 18-22 (5)	286.15	109.55

Dated "1879"

1879

23	A5 5c lake	12.00	5.50
	On cover		200.00
24	A5 10c dark brown	12.00	5.50
	On cover		300.00
25	A5 15c dk olive grn	12.00	5.50
	On cover		300.00
26	A5 25c blue	4.00	1.75
	On cover		50.00
27	A5 50c dark green	12.00	5.50
	On cover		200.00
28	A5 1p gray	57.50	25.00
	On cover		500.00
	Nos. 23-28 (6)	109.50	48.75

Imperforates of type A5 are from proof or trial sheets.

1880

29	A6 ¼c deep green	27.50	20.00
	On cover		400.00
30	A6 ½c brt rose	6.75	2.50
	On cover		300.00
31	A6 1c brown lilac	12.00	10.00
	On cover		300.00
32	A6 2c gray lilac	6.25	4.25
	On cover		300.00
33	A6 3c buff	7.00	4.75
	On cover		300.00
34	A6 4c black	7.00	4.75
	On cover		300.00

35 A6 5c gray green 3.50 1.90
On cover 200.00
36 A6 10c rose 4.00 2.30
On cover 200.00
37 A6 15c yellow brn 7.00 3.50
On cover 200.00
38 A6 25c gray blue 3.50 1.60
On cover 50.00
39 A6 40c gray 14.00 1.75
On cover 100.00
40 A6 50c dark brown 29.00 15.50
On cover 400.00
41 A6 1p olive bister 97.50 21.00
On cover 700.00
Nos. 29-41 (13) 225.00 93.80

Dated "1881"

1881

42 A6 ½m lake .40 .40
On cover 300.00
a. ½m carmine rose .50 .45
On cover 300.00
43 A6 1m violet .40 .20
On cover 200.00
a. 1m reddish violet .65 .35
On cover 200.00
44 A6 2m pale rose .60 .40
On cover 200.00
a. 2m deep rose .65 .40
On cover 200.00
45 A6 4m brt yellowish green 1.00 .20
On cover 200.00
a. 4m emerald green 3.25 1.25
On cover 200.00
46 A6 6m brown lilac 1.00 .60
On cover 200.00
a. 6m pale lilac 3.25 1.25
On cover 200.00
47 A6 8m ultra 2.50 1.40
On cover 200.00
a. 8m steel blue 5.00 1.90
On cover 200.00
48 A6 1c gray green 3.25 1.20
On cover 100.00
49 A6 2c lake 4.50 3.75
On cover 75.00
50 A6 3c dark brown 10.00 6.25
On cover 100.00
a. 3c chestnut brown 13.00 7.00
On cover 100.00
b. Double impression of top inscriptions 30.00 15.00
51 A6 5c grayish ultra 3.50 .45
On cover 50.00
a. 5c blue 6.50 2.25
On cover 60.00
52 A6 8c brown 3.50 1.80
On cover 100.00
53 A6 10c slate 32.50 9.50
On cover 400.00
54 A6 20c olive bister 37.50 17.50
On cover 700.00
Nos. 42-54 (13) 100.65 43.65

Alfonso XII
A7

Alfonso XIII
A8

1882-86

55 A7 ½m rose .30 .20
On cover 200.00
a. ½m salmon rose .55 .35
On cover 200.00
56 A7 ½m lake ('84) .55 .40
On cover 200.00
57 A7 1m pale lake .85 1.10
On cover 200.00
58 A7 1m brt rose ('84) .30 .20
On cover 200.00
59 A7 2m violet .30 .20
On cover 200.00
60 A7 4m brown lilac .30 .20
On cover 150.00
61 A7 6m brown .45 .20
On cover 150.00
62 A7 8m yellow green .45 .20
On cover 300.00
63 A7 1c gray green .30 .20
On cover 100.00
64 A7 2c rose 1.10 .20
On cover 100.00
65 A7 3c yellow 4.00 2.10
On cover 100.00
a. Cliché of 8c in plate of 3c 120.00
66 A7 3c yellow brn ('84) 4.00 .85
On cover 100.00
a. Cliché of 8c in plate of 3c 25.00
67 A7 5c gray blue 14.50 1.20
On cover 50.00
68 A7 5c gray bl, 1st retouch ('84) 14.50 2.75
On cover *75.00*
69 A7 5c gray bl, 2nd retouch ('86) 110.00 5.50
On cover *75.00*
70 A7 8c gray brown 3.50 .20
On cover 75.00
71 A7 10c dark green 3.50 .30
On cover 200.00
72 A7 20c gray lilac 5.25 .30
On cover 500.00
a. 20c olive brown (error) *110.00*
73 A7 40c blue 40.00 14.50
On cover —
74 A7 80c olive bister 55.00 20.00
On cover —
Nos. 55-74 (20) 259.15 50.80

For differences between the original and the retouched stamps see note on the 1883-86 issue of Cuba.

1890-97

75 A8 ½m black .30 .20
On cover 150.00
a. ½m jet black .25 .25
On cover 150.00
76 A8 ½m olive gray ('92) .20 .20
On cover 150.00
a. ½m bronze green .25 .25
On cover 150.00
77 A8 ½m red brn ('94) .20 .20
On cover 150.00
78 A8 ½m dull vio ('96) .20 .20
On cover 150.00
79 A8 1m emerald .25 .20
On cover 150.00
80 A8 1m dk violet ('92) .20 .20
On cover 150.00
81 A8 1m ultra ('94) .20 .20
On cover 100.00
82 A8 1m dp brown ('96) .20 .20
On cover 100.00
83 A8 2m lilac rose .20 .20
On cover 100.00
84 A8 2m violet brn ('92) .20 .20
On cover 100.00
85 A8 2m red orange ('94) .20 .20
On cover 100.00
86 A8 2m yellow grn ('96) .20 .20
On cover 100.00
87 A8 4m dk olive grn 11.00 5.50
On cover 200.00
88 A8 4m ultra ('92) .20 .20
On cover 150.00
89 A8 4m yellow brn ('94) .20 .20
On cover 100.00
90 A8 4m blue grn ('96) 1.00 .35
On cover 100.00
91 A8 6m dk brown 35.00 14.00
On cover 200.00
92 A8 6m pale rose ('92) .20 .20
On cover 150.00
93 A8 8m olive bister 27.50 21.00
On cover 200.00
94 A8 8m yellow grn ('92) .20 .20
On cover 150.00
95 A8 1c yellow brown .30 .20
On cover 100.00
96 A8 1c blue grn ('91) .55 .20
On cover 100.00
97 A8 1c violet brn ('94) 5.75 .45
On cover 100.00
98 A8 1c claret ('96) .65 .20
On cover 100.00
99 A8 2c brownish violet 1.00 .85
On cover 150.00
a. 2c blackish violet 1.40 1.10
On cover 150.00
100 A8 2c red brown ('92) .95 .20
On cover 100.00
101 A8 2c lilac ('94) 2.25 .45
On cover 75.00
102 A8 2c orange brn ('96) .65 .20
On cover 50.00
103 A8 3c slate blue 7.25 1.00
On cover 150.00
104 A8 3c orange ('92) .90 .20
On cover 100.00
105 A8 3c ol gray ('94) 5.75 .45
On cover 100.00
106 A8 3c blue ('96) 21.00 .35
On cover 100.00
107 A8 3c claret brn ('97) .30 .20
On cover 100.00
108 A8 4c slate bl ('94) 1.40 .45
On cover 75.00
109 A8 4c gray brn ('96) .70 .20
On cover 75.00
110 A8 5c brown violet 12.50 .45
On cover 50.00
111 A8 5c yellow grn ('94) 5.50 1.10
On cover 50.00
112 A8 5c blue green ('92) .90 .20
On cover 50.00
113 A8 5c blue ('96) .30 .20
On cover 50.00
114 A8 6c orange ('94) .45 .20
On cover 100.00
115 A8 6c violet ('96) .35 .20
On cover 100.00
116 A8 8c ultra 15.00 1.60
On cover 150.00
117 A8 8c gray brown ('92) .20 .20
On cover 100.00
118 A8 8c dull vio ('94) 12.00 4.75
On cover 75.00
119 A8 8c car rose ('96) 2.75 1.40
On cover 75.00
120 A8 10c rose 4.50 1.10
On cover 150.00
a. 10c salmon rose 11.00 2.50
On cover 150.00
b. 10c carmine rose 5.75 1.10
On cover 150.00
121 A8 10c lilac rose ('92) 1.40 .35
On cover 150.00
122 A8 20c red orange 5.00 4.50
On cover 400.00
123 A8 20c lilac ('92) 2.25 .55
On cover 400.00
a. 20c violet 2.25 .55
On cover 400.00
124 A8 20c car rose ('94) 1.50 .45
On cover 400.00
125 A8 20c olive gray ('96) 6.50 1.40
On cover 300.00
126 A8 40c orange 160.00 47.50
On cover —
127 A8 40c slate blue ('92) 5.50 3.75
On cover —
128 A8 40c claret ('94) 7.25 12.50
On cover 800.00
129 A8 40c salmon ('96) 6.75 1.60
On cover 500.00
130 A8 80c yellow green 600.00 200.00
On cover 5,000.
131 A8 80c orange ('92) 14.00 11.00
On cover —
132 A8 80c black ('97) 26.00 22.50
On cover —

Imperforates of type A8 were not issued and are variously considered to be proofs or printer's waste.

For overprints see Nos. 154A-170, MR1-MR13.

Landing of Columbus on Puerto Rico — A9

1893 Litho. *Perf. 12*

133 A9 3c dark green 200.00 50.00
On cover, philatelic 200.00
On cover, commercial 500.00

400th anniversary, landing of Columbus on Puerto Rico. Counterfeits exist.

Alfonso XIII — A10

1898 Typo.

135 A10 1m orange brown .20 .20
On cover 100.00
136 A10 2m orange brown .20 .20
On cover 100.00
137 A10 3m orange brown .20 .20
On cover 150.00
138 A10 4m orange brown 1.60 .65
On cover 150.00
139 A10 5m orange brown .20 .20
On cover 150.00
140 A10 1c black violet .20 .20
On cover 100.00
a. Tête bêche pair *1,500.*
b. Pair, #140 & Philippines #197 (cliche error) *1,500.*
141 A10 2c dk blue green .20 .20
On cover 100.00
142 A10 3c dk brown .20 .20
On cover 75.00
143 A10 4c orange 1.60 1.30
On cover 100.00
144 A10 5c brt rose .20 .20
On cover 75.00
145 A10 6c dark blue .65 .20
On cover 100.00
146 A10 8c gray brown .20 .20
On cover 100.00
147 A10 10c vermilion .20 .20
On cover 150.00
148 A10 15c dull olive grn .20 .20
On cover 200.00
149 A10 20c maroon 1.90 .60
On cover 200.00
150 A10 40c violet 1.50 1.60
On cover 500.00
151 A10 60c black 1.50 1.60
On cover —
152 A10 80c red brown 5.50 6.00
On cover —
153 A10 1p yellow green 12.00 12.00
On cover —
154 A10 2p slate blue 27.50 17.50
On cover —
Nos. 135-154 (20) 55.95 43.65

Nos. 135-154 exist imperf. Value, set $900.

Stamps of 1890-97 Handstamped in Rose or Violet

1898

154A A8 ½m dull violet 16.00 9.00
On cover 300.00
155 A8 1m deep brown 1.40 1.40
On cover 300.00
156 A8 2m yellow green .40 .40
On cover 200.00
157 A8 4m blue green .40 .40
On cover 300.00
158 A8 1c claret 4.00 4.00
On cover 300.00
159 A8 2c orange brown .55 .80
On cover 300.00
160 A8 3c blue 35.00 15.00
On cover —
161 A8 3c claret brn 2.75 2.75
On cover 300.00
162 A8 4c gray brn .65 .65
On cover 300.00
163 A8 4c slate blue 19.00 13.50
On cover —
164 A8 5c yellow grn 9.00 7.00
On cover —
165 A8 5c blue .65 .65
On cover 300.00
166 A8 6c violet .65 .45
On cover 300.00
a. Inverted Ovpt., on cover —
167 A8 8c car rose (V) 1.10 .80
On cover 200.00
a. Rose overprint 17.50 17.50
On cover 1,000.
168 A8 20c olive gray 1.10 1.10
On cover —
169 A8 40c salmon 2.75 2.75
On cover —
170 A8 80c black 35.00 22.50
On cover —
Nos. 154A-170 (17) 130.40 83.15

As usual with handstamps there are many inverted, double and similar varieties. Counterfeits of Nos. 154A-170 abound.

Issued under U.S. Administration

A11

Ponce Issue

1898 Unwmk. *Imperf.*

200 A11 5c vio, *yelsh* *7,500.*

The only way No. 200 is known used is handstamped on envelopes. Uses on 2c U.S. stamps on cover were strictly as a cancellation, not as provisional postage Both unused stamps and used envelopes have a violet control mark. Counterfeits exist of Nos. 200-201.

A12

Coamo Issue

1898 Unwmk. *Imperf.*

201 A12 5c black 650. 1,050.
On cover *32,500.*

There are ten varieties in the setting (See the Scott United States Specialized Catalogue). The stamps bear the control mark "F. Santiago" in violet.

United States Nos. 279, 279Bf, 281, 272 and 282C Overprinted in Black at 36 degree angle

1899 Wmk. 191 *Perf. 12*

210 A87 1c yellow green 5.00 1.40
On cover 50.00
a. Ovpt. at 25 degree angle 7.50 2.25
211 A88 2c reddish car, type IV 4.25 1.25
On cover 50.00
a. Ovpt. at 25 degree angle 5.50 2.25
On cover 50.00
212 A91 5c blue 12.50 2.50
On cover 50.00
213 A93 8c violet brown 35.00 17.50
On cover 125.00
a. Ovpt. at 25 degree angle 40.00 19.00
c. "PORTO RIC" 150.00 110.00
214 A94 10c brown, type I 25.00 6.00
On cover 120.00
Nos. 210-214 (5) 81.75 28.65

Misspellings of the overprint, actually broken letters (PORTO RICU, PORTU RICO, FORTO RICO, PURTO RICO, FURTO RICO), are found on 1c, 2c, 8c and 10c.

United States Nos. 279 and 279B Overprinted Diagonally in Black

1900

215 A87 1c yellow green 6.50 1.40
On cover 50.00

216	A88 2c red, type IV	4.75	2.00
	On cover		50.00
b.	Inverted overprint		*8,250.*

Stamps of Puerto Rico were replaced by those of the United States.

POSTAGE DUE STAMPS

United States Nos. J38, J39 and J42 Overprinted in Black at 36 degree angle

1899 Wmk. 191 *Perf. 12*

J1	D2 1c deep claret	25.00	6.00
	On cover		500.00
a.	Overprint at 25 degree angle	25.00	8.25
J2	D2 2c deep claret	22.50	6.50
	On cover		800.00
a.	Overprint at 25 degree angle	22.50	7.75
J3	D2 10c deep claret	200.00	65.00
	On cover		—
a.	Overprint at 25 degree angle	190.00	90.00
	Nos. J1-J3 (3)	247.50	77.50

WAR TAX STAMPS

Stamps of 1890-94 Overprinted or Surcharged by Handstamp

1898 Unwmk. *Perf. 14*

Purple Overprint or Surcharge

MR1	A8 1c yellow brn	6.00	*4.50*
	On cover		—
MR2	A8 2c on 2m orange	2.75	2.25
	On cover		—
MR3	A8 2c on 5c blue grn	3.60	2.75
	On cover		—
MR4	A8 2c dark violet	.70	.70
	On cover		300.00
MR5	A8 2c lilac	.65	.65
	On cover		300.00
MR6	A8 2c red brown	.35	.20
	On cover		200.00
MR7	A8 5c blue green	1.40	1.40
	On cover		300.00
MR8	A8 5c on 5c bl grn	6.50	4.50
	On cover		300.00

Rose Surcharge

MR9	A8 2c on 2m orange	1.40	1.40
	On cover		300.00
MR10	A8 5c on 1m dk vio	.20	.20
	On cover		300.00
MR11	A8 5c on 1m dl bl	.60	.60
	On cover		300.00

Magenta Surcharge

MR12	A8 5c on 1m dk vio	.35	.20
	On cover		300.00
MR13	A8 5c on 1m dl bl	2.25	2.25
	On cover		300.00
	Nos. MR1-MR13 (13)	26.75	21.60

Nos. MR2-MR13 were issued as War Tax Stamps (2c on letters or sealed mail; 5c on telegrams) but, during the early days of the American occupation, they were accepted for ordinary postage.

Double, inverted and similar varieties of overprints are numerous in this issue.

Counterfeit overprints exist.

QUEENSLAND

ˈkwēnz-ˌland

LOCATION — Northeastern part of Australia
GOVT. — British Crown Colony
AREA — 670,500 sq. mi.
POP. — 498,129 (1901)
CAPITAL — Brisbane

Originally a part of New South Wales, Queensland was constituted a separate colony in 1859. It was one of the six British Colonies that united in 1901 to form the Commonwealth of Australia.

12 Pence = 1 Shilling
20 Shillings = 1 Pound

MORETON BAY

Until 1860, Queensland, then known as Moreton Bay, utilized the postal service of New South Wales, and stamps of New South Wales were used until November 1, 1860. The New South Wales post offices in Queensland, with their opening dates and assigned canceler numbers, were:

Post Office	Opened
Brisbane	1834 (#95)
Burnett's Inn (became Goodes Inn)	1850 (#108)
Callandoon	1850 (#74)
Condamine	1856 (#151)
Dalby	1854 (#133)
Drayton	1846 (#85)
Gayndah	1850 (#86)
Gladstone	1854 (#131)
Goodes Inn	1858 (#108)
Ipswich	1846 (#87)
Maryborough	1849 (#96)
Rockhampton	1858 (#201)
Surat	1852 (#110)
Taroom	1856 (#152)
Toowoombs	1858 (#214)
Warwick	1848 (#81)

Values for unused stamps are for examples with original gum as defined in the catalogue introduction. Very fine examples of Nos. 4-73, 84-125, 128-140, and F1-F3b will have perforations touching the design on at least one or more sides due to the narrow spacing of the stamps on the plates. Stamps with perfs clear of the design on all four sides are scarce and will command higher prices.

Watermarks

Wmk. 5 — Small Star

Wmk. 6 — Large Star

Wmk. 12 — Crown and Single-lined A

Wmk. 13 — Crown and Double-lined A

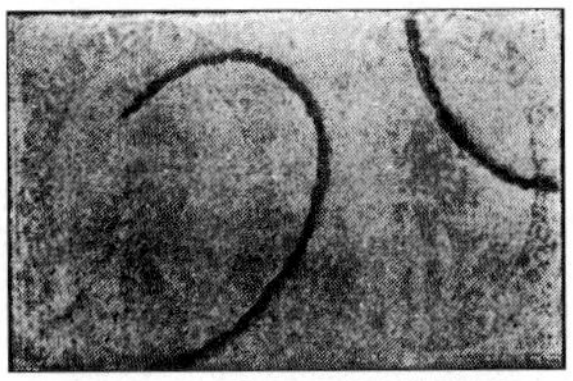

Wmk. 65 — "Queensland Postage Stamps" in Sheet in Script Capitals

Wmk. 66

Wmks. 66 & 67 — "Queensland" in Large Single-lined Roman Capitals in the Sheet and Short-pointed Star to Each Stamp (Stars Vary Slightly in Size and Shape)

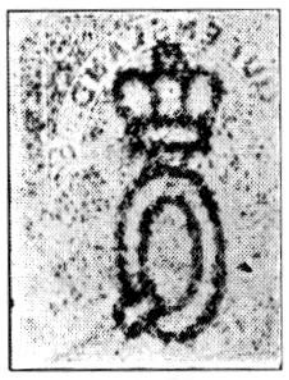

Wmk. 68 — Crown and Q

Wmk. 69 — Large Crown and Q

There are two varieties of the watermark 68, differing slightly in the position and shape of the crown and the tongue of the "Q."

Wmk. 70 — V and Crown

Queen Victoria — A1

Wmk. 6

1860, Nov. 1 Engr. *Imperf.*

1	A1 1p deep rose	3,750.	1,000.
2	A1 2p deep blue	8,750.	2,250.
3	A1 6p deep green	5,750.	1,000.

Clean-Cut Perf. 14 to 16

4	A1 1p deep rose	1,900.	375.
5	A1 2p deep blue	750.	140.
a.	Horiz. pair, imperf between	—	—
6	A1 6p deep green	800.	95.00

Clean-Cut Perf. 14 to 16

1860-61 Wmk. 5

6A	A1 2p blue	675.00	140.00
b.	Horiz. pair, imperf. vert		2,200.
6D	A1 3p brown ('61)	425.00	90.00
6E	A1 6p deep green	800.00	95.00
6F	A1 1sh gray violet	775.00	125.00

Regular Perf. 14

6H	A1 1p rose	185.00	55.00
6I	A1 2p deep blue	500.00	75.00

Rough Perf. 14 to 16

7	A1 1p deep rose	100.00	39.00
8	A1 2p blue	160.00	37.50
a.	Horiz. pair, imperf between	3,500.	
9	A1 3p brown ('61)	72.50	42.50
a.	Horiz. pair, imperf. vert.	3,500.	
10	A1 6p deep green	210.00	37.50
a.	6p yellow green	325.00	37.50
11	A1 1sh dull violet	575.00	110.00

Thick Yellowish Paper

Square Perf. 12½ to 13

1862-67 Unwmk.

12	A1 1p Indian red	425.00	80.00
13	A1 1p orange ('63)	110.00	16.00
a.	Perf. 13, round holes ('67)	115.00	30.00
b.	Horiz. pair, imperf. between		—
c.	Imperf., pair	—	1,200.
14	A1 2p deep blue	70.00	13.50
a.	2p pale blue	140.00	42.50
b.	Perf. 13, round holes ('67)	70.00	12.00
c.	Imperf., pair	—	1,200.
e.	Horiz. pair, imperf. between		*1,800.*
f.	Vert. pair, imperf. between	*3,250.*	
15	A1 3p brown ('63)	92.50	45.00
a.	Imperf.		
b.	Perf. 13, round holes ('67)	92.50	45.00
16	A1 6p yellow grn ('63)	150.00	22.50
a.	6p green	210.00	40.00
b.	Perf. 13, round holes ('67)	160.00	22.50
c.	Imperf., pair	—	1,250.
d.	Horiz. pair, imperf. between	—	2,100.
e.	6p apple green ('63)	165.00	27.50
17	A1 1sh gray ('63)	375.00	35.00
b.	Imperf. horizontally		
c.	Horiz. pair, imperf. between	—	2,100.
d.	Perf. 13, round holes ('67)		
e.	Vert. pair, imperf between	—	

White Wove Paper

1865 Wmk. 5 *Rough Perf. 13*

18	A1 1p orange	90.00	35.00
a.	Horiz. pair, imperf. vert.	975.00	
19	A1 2p light blue	90.00	21.00
a.	Vert. pair, imperf. horiz.	1,850.	
b.	Half used as 1p on cover		*3,600.*
20	A1 6p yellow green	160.00	32.50
	Nos. 18-20 (3)	340.00	88.50

1865 *Perf. 12½x13*

18B	A1 1p orange vermilion	125.00	60.00
19C	A1 2p blue	150.00	60.00

Perf. 13, Round Holes

1866 Wmk. 65

21	A1 1p orange vermilion	185.00	37.50
22	A1 2p blue	72.50	22.50
b.	Diagonal half used as 1p on cover		—

1865 *Perf. 12½x13*

21A	A1 1p orange vermilion	225.00	65.00
22C	A1 2p blue	225.00	65.00

1866 Unwmk. Litho. *Perf. 13*

23	A1 4p lilac	210.00	30.00
a.	4p slate	210.00	30.00
	Handstamped "SPECIMEN"	57.50	
24	A1 5sh pink	750.00	225.00
a.	5sh bright rose	350.00	92.50
	Handstamped "SPECIMEN"	62.50	
b.	Vert. pair, imperf between		*2,250.*

Wmk. 66, 67

1868-74 Engr. *Perf. 13*

25	A1 1p orange ('71)	60.00	6.00
26	A1 2p blue	55.00	4.00
a.	2p pale blue	52.50	4.50
b.	2p bright blue	57.50	3.50
c.	2p greenish blue	130.00	3.00
d.	2p dark blue	52.50	3.00
27	A1 3p grnsh brn ('71)	115.00	9.00
a.	3p brown	100.00	8.00
b.	3p olive brown	130.00	8.00
28	A1 6p yel green ('71)	185.00	10.00
a.	6p deep green	225.00	25.00
b.	6p green	175.00	14.00
30	A1 1sh grnsh gray ('72)	525.00	125.00
31	A1 1sh violet ('74)	325.00	30.00
a.	1sh brownish gray	525.00	125.00

Perf. 12

32	A1 1p orange	425.00	35.00
33	A1 2p blue	1,000.	60.00
34	A1 3p brown	600.00	225.00
a.	3p greenish gray	—	225.00
35	A1 6p deep green	1,600.	55.00
36	A1 1sh violet	625.00	60.00

Perf. 13x12

36A	A1 1p orange		225.00
37	A1 2p blue	*1,350.*	50.00
37A	A1 3p brown		*500.00*

The reprints are perforated 13 and the colors differ slightly from those of the originals.

1868-75 Wmk. 68 *Perf. 13*

38	A1 1p orange	80.00	6.00
a.	Imperf pair	375.00	
39	A1 1p rose ('74)	75.00	11.00
a.	1p deep rose red	125.00	11.50
40	A1 2p blue	55.00	2.75
b.	Imperf., pair	500.00	
c.	2p pale blue ('74)	65.00	7.00
41	A1 3p brown ('75)	110.00	15.00
42	A1 6p yel green ('69)	130.00	10.00
a.	6p apple green	170.00	12.00
b.	6p deep green	160.00	12.00
c.	As "a," imperf pair	475.00	
43	A1 1sh violet ('75)	*260.00*	60.00
	Nos. 38-43 (6)	*710.00*	104.75

No. 40 exists in vert. pair, imperf. btwn.

1876-78 *Perf. 12*

44	A1 1p orange	50.00	6.75
a.	Imperf.	*500.00*	
b.	1p pale org vermilion	62.50	6.75
45	A1 1p rose	62.50	14.00
a.	1p salmon	85.00	14.00
46	A1 2p blue	45.00	1.75
a.	2p pale blue	110.00	20.00
b.	2p deep blue	50.00	2.50

47 A1 3p brown 92.50 12.00
48 A1 6p yellow green 185.00 6.75
a. 6p apple green 200.00 11.00
b. 6p deep green 180.00 11.50
c. 6p green 200.00 6.50
49 A1 1sh violet 65.00 12.50
m. Vert. pair, imperf between —
n. 1sh purple 175.00 7.00
Nos. 44-49 (6) 500.00 53.75

#44, 49 exist in vertical pairs, imperf. between.

Perf. 13x12

49B A1 1p orange 200.00
49C A1 2p blue *1,450.* 325.00
49D A1 4p yellow 400.00
49E A1 6p deep green 400.00

Perf. 12½x13

49G A1 1p orange vermilion 475.00
49H A1 2p deep blue 475.00

The reprints are perforated 12 and are in paler colors than the originals.

1879 Unwmk. *Perf. 12*

50 A1 6p pale emerald 300.00 35.00
a. Horiz. pair, imperf. vert. 1,450.

A2

A3

1875-81 Litho. Wmk. 68 *Perf. 13*

50B A1 4p yellow ('75) 1,100. 75.00
a. Handstamped "SPECIMEN" 90.00

Perf. 12

51 A1 4p buff ('76) 925.00 32.50
a. 4p yellow 925.00 35.00
52 A1 2sh pale blue ('81) 135.00 37.50
Fiscal cancellation 5.00
a. 2sh deep blue 135.00 37.50
b. Imperf.
c. 2sh blue 135.00 37.50
53 A2 2sh6p lt red ('81) 225.00 125.00
Fiscal cancellation 5.00
a. 2sh6p bright scarlet 260.00 125.00
54 A1 5sh orange brn ('81) 300.00 150.00
Fiscal cancellation 6.00
a. 5sh fawn 300.00 150.00
55 A1 10sh brown ('81) 600.00 275.00
Fiscal cancellation 6.00
a. Imperf., pair *1,300.*
b. 10sh bister brown 600.00 275.00
56 A1 20sh rose ('81) 2,000. 450.00
Fiscal cancellation 8.00
Nos. 50B-56 (7) 5,285. 1,145.

Nos. 53-56, 62-64, 74-83 with pen (revenue) cancellations removed are often offered as unused.

1879-81 Typo. Wmk. 68 *Perf. 12*

57 A3 1p rose red 45.00 10.00
a. 1p red orange 60.00 15.00
b. 1p brown orange 80.00 20.00
c. "QOEENSLAND" 110.00 30.00
d. Imperf.
e. Vert. pair, imperf. horiz. *725.00*
58 A3 2p gray blue 80.00 5.00
a. 2p deep ultra 85.00 5.00
b. Imperf.
c. "PENGE" 225.00 60.00
d. "TW" joined 60.00 5.00
e. Vert. pair, imperf. horiz. 1,100.
59 A3 4p orange yellow 250.00 30.00
a. Imperf.
60 A3 6p yellow green 80.00 8.00
a. Imperf.
61 A3 1sh pale violet ('81) 90.00 12.00
a. 1sh deep violet 110.00 10.00
Nos. 57-61 (5) 545.00 65.00

The stamps of type A3 were electrotyped from plates made up of groups of four types, differing in minor details. Two dies were used for the 1p and 2p, giving eight varieties for each of those values.
Nos. 59-60 exist imperf. vertically.
For surcharge see No. 65.

Moire on Back

1878-79 Unwmk.

62 A3 1p brown org ('79) 500.00 65.00
a. "QOEENSLAND" 2,000.
63 A3 2p deep ultra ('79) 575.00 40.00
a. "PENGE" *4,750.* 875.00
64 A1 1sh red violet 175.00 75.00
Nos. 62-64 (3) 1,250. 180.00

No. 57b Surcharged Vertically in Black

1880 Wmk. 68

65 A3 ½p on 1p brn org 425.00 250.00
a. "QOEENSLAND" 2,000. 1,300.

On No. 65, the surcharge reads from bottom to top. Stamps with surcharges reading downward are fakes.

A4

A5

1882-83 Typo. *Perf. 12*

66 A4 1p pale red 5.25 .60
a. 1p rose 6.25 .80
b. Imperf. pair —
c. 1p deep vermilion 6.00 .80
67 A4 2p gray blue 9.00 .80
a. 2p deep ultra 9.00 .80
b. Imperf. —
68 A4 4p yellow ('83) 25.00 3.25
a. "PENGE" 210.00 60.00
b. Imperf., pair —
69 A4 6p yellow green 16.00 2.25
70 A4 1sh violet ('83) 25.00 3.25
a. 1sh lilac 12.50 3.25
b. 1sh deep purple 25.00 5.00
c. 1sh pale mauve 14.00 3.00
Nos. 66-70 (5) 80.25 10.15

There are eight minor varieties of the 1p, twelve of the 2p and four each of the other values. On the 1p there is a period after "PENNY." On all values the lines of shading on the neck extend from side to side.
Compare design A4 with A6, A10, A11, A15, A16.

1883 *Perf. 9½x12*

71 A4 1p rose 170.00 50.00
72 A4 2p gray blue 575.00 80.00
73 A4 1sh pale violet 300.00 62.50
Nos. 71-73 (3) 1,045. 192.50

Beware of faked perfs.
See Nos. 94, 95, 100.

Wmk. 68 Twice Sideways

1882-85 Engr. *Perf. 12*

Thin Paper

74 A5 2sh ultra 150.00 40.00
75 A5 2sh6p vermilion 110.00 27.50
76 A5 5sh car rose ('85) 110.00 30.00
77 A5 10sh brown 200.00 55.00
78 A5 £1 dk grn ('83) 400.00 185.00
Nos. 74-78 (5) 970.00 337.50

The 2sh, 5sh and £1 exist imperf.
There are two varieties of the watermark on Nos. 74-78, as in the 1879-81 issue.
Copies with revenue cancels sell for $3.25-6.50.

1886 Wmk. 69 *Perf. 12*

Thick Paper

79 A5 2sh ultra 175.00 45.00
80 A5 2sh6p vermilion 60.00 30.00
81 A5 5sh car rose 57.50 45.00
82 A5 10sh dark brown 130.00 60.00
83 A5 £1 dark green 300.00 85.00
Nos. 79-83 (5) 722.50 265.00

High value stamps with cancellations removed are offered as unused.
Copies with revenue cancels sell for $3.25-6.50.
See Nos. 126-127, 141-144.

A6

Redrawn

1887-89 Typo. Wmk. 68 *Perf. 12*

84 A6 1p orange 6.00 1.00
85 A6 2p gray blue 10.00 1.00
a. 2p deep ultra 13.00 1.25
86 A6 2sh red brown ('89) 95.00 50.00

Perf. 9½x12

88 A6 2p deep ultra *550.00* 90.00
Nos. 84-88 (4) *661.00* 142.00

The 1p has no period after the value.
In the redrawn stamps the shading lines on the neck are not completed at the left, leaving an irregular white line along that side.
Variety "LA" joined exists on Nos. 84-86, 88, 90, 91, 93, 97, 98, 102.
On No. 88 beware of faked perfs.

A7

A8

1890-92 *Perf. 12½, 13*

89 A7 ½p green 6.00 2.25
a. ½p pale green 7.00 2.25
b. ½p deep blue green 6.00 2.25
90 A6 1p orange red 4.50 .75
a. Imperf, pair 210.00 210.00
91 A6 2p gray blue 8.00 .50
a. 2p pale blue 8.00 .50
92 A8 2½p rose carmine 17.50 5.00
93 A6 3p brown ('92) 12.50 4.00
94 A4 4p orange 35.00 8.00
a. 4p yellow 30.00 8.00
b. "PENGE" 85.00 30.00
c. 4p lemon yellow 20.00 2.25
95 A4 6p green 15.00 2.25
96 A6 2sh red brown 75.00 40.00
a. 2sh pale brown 85.00 45.00
Nos. 89-96 (8) 173.50 62.75

The ½p and 3p exist imperf.

1895 Wmk. 69 *Perf. 12½, 13*

Thick Paper

98 A6 1p orange 6.00 .65
a. 1p reddish vermilion 6.50 .65
99 A6 2p gray blue 3.75 .45

Perf. 12

100 A4 1sh pale violet 17.50 6.50
Nos. 98-100 (3) 27.25 7.60

A9

A10

Moiré on Back

1895 Unwmk. *Perf. 12½, 13*

101 A9 ½p green 6.00 3.25
a. Without moire 57.50
b. ½p deep green 6.00
102 A6 1p orange 3.50 1.00
a. "PE" missing 240.00 240.00
b. 1p reddish vermilion 3.50 .80

Wmk. 68

103 A9 ½p green 3.00 1.50
a. ½p deep green 3.00 1.50
b. Printed on both sides 150.00
104 A10 1p orange 3.50 .50
a. 1p pale red 4.50 .50
105 A10 2p gray blue 10.00 1.00

Wmk. 69

Thick Paper

106 A9 ½p green, perf 12½ 4.25 2.75
a. Perf 13 5.25 2.90
b. Perf 12 25.00
c. 1p deep green, perf 12 25.00

1895-96 Unwmk. Thin Paper

Crown and Q Faintly Impressed

107 A9 ½p green 3.00 3.00
108 A10 1p orange 4.75 2.75
108A A6 2p gray blue 16.00 *200.00*

A11

A12

A13

1895-96 Wmk. 68

109 A11 1p red 8.00 .75
110 A12 2½p rose 20.00 6.50
a. 2½p carmine 20.00 6.50
111 A13 5p violet brown 25.00 6.50
111A A11 6p yellow green *25,000.*

A14

A15

A16

A17

A18

A19

TWO PENCE:
Type I — Point of bust does not touch frame.
Type II — First redrawing. The top of the crown, the chignon and the point of the bust touch the frame. The forehead is completely shaded.
Type III — Second redrawing. The top of crown does not touch the frame, though the chignon and the point of the bust do. The forehead and the bridge of the nose are not shaded.

1897-1900 *Perf. 12½, 13*

112 A14 ½p deep green 7.00 7.00
a. Perf. 12 175.00
113 A15 1p red 3.50 .40
a. Perf. 12 11.00 4.00
114 A16 2p gray blue (I) 4.50 .40
a. Perf. 12 1,300. 10.00
115 A17 2½p rose 35.00 27.50
116 A17 2½p violet, *blue* 13.00 3.00
117 A15 3p brown 14.50 3.00
118 A15 4p bright yellow 14.50 3.00
119 A18 5p violet brown 12.50 3.00
120 A15 6p yellow green 12.50 3.00
121 A19 1sh lilac 19.00 3.50
a. 1sh light violet 22.50 5.00
122 A19 2sh turq blue 47.50 32.50
Nos. 112-122 (11) 183.50 86.30

1898 *Serrated Roulette 13*

123 A15 1p scarlet 8.50 5.50
a. Serrated and perf. 13 11.50 8.00
b. Serrated in black 17.50 12.50
c. Serrated without color and in black 17.50 *25.00*
d. Same as "b," and perf. 13 90.00 *125.00*
e. Same as "c," and perf. 13 125.00 125.00

Victoria
A20

"Australia"
A21

1899 Typo. *Perf. 12, 12½, 13*

124 A20 ½p blue green 3.75 2.25
a. ½p green, perf 12 125.00 60.00
b. ½p pale green 3.75 2.25

Unwatermarked stamps are proofs.

1903 Wmk. 70 *Perf. 12½*

NINE PENCE:
Type I — "QUEENSLAND" 18x1½mm.
Type II — "QUEENSLAND" 17½x1¼mm.

125 A21 9p org brn & ultra, II 30.00 5.50
a. Type I 30.00 5.50

See No. 128.

Type of 1882

Perf. 12, 12½, 13

1906 Litho. Wmk. 68

126 A5 5sh rose 140.00 100.00
127 A5 £1 dark green 500.00 150.00

1907 Typo. Wmk. 13 *Perf. 12½*

128 A21 9p yel brn & ultra, I 17.50 5.50
a. Type II 17.50 5.00
b. Perf. 11, type II 6,000. 725.00

1907 Wmk. 68 *Perf. 12½, 13*

129 A16 2p ultra, type II 12.50 5.00
129A A18 5p dark brown 12.50 4.50
b. 5p olive brown 11.00 3.50

1907-09 Wmk. 12

130 A20 ½p deep green 2.50 *4.00*
131 A15 1p red 4.00 .60
a. Imperf., pair 325.00
132 A16 2p ultra, II 10.00 1.75
133 A16 2p ultra, III 5.00 .55
134 A15 3p pale brown 17.50 3.00
135 A15 4p bright yellow 15.00 4.00
136 A15 4p gray black ('09) 22.50 6.25
137 A18 5p brown 14.00 8.00
a. 5p olive brown 19.00 9.00
138 A15 6p yellow green 15.00 5.50
139 A19 1sh violet 16.00 4.25
140 A19 2sh turquoise bl 47.50 30.00

Wmk. 12 Sideways
Litho.

141 A5 2sh6p deep orange 55.00 52.50
a. 2sh6p dull orange ('10) 90.00 85.00
b. 2sh6p reddish orange ('12) 225.00 *260.00*
142 A5 5sh rose 85.00 55.00
a. 5sh deep rose ('10) 100.00 80.00
b. 5sh carmine red ('12) 240.00 *300.00*
143 A5 10sh dark brown 160.00 95.00
a. 10sh sepia ('12) 500.00 400.00
144 A5 £1 blue green 350.00 150.00
a. £1 dp blue green ('10) 625.00 400.00
b. £1 yellow green ('12) 2,250. 1,350.
Nos. 130-144 (15) 819.00 420.40

FISCAL STAMPS

Authorized for postal use from Jan. 1, 1880. Authorization withdrawn July 1, 1892.

Used values are for examples with postal cancellations used from Jan. 1, 1880 through June 30, 1892.

Beware of copies with a pen cancellation removed and a fake postmark added.

Queen Victoria
PF1 PF2

1866-74 Engr. Unwmk. *Perf. 13*

AR1 PF1 1p blue 75.00 35.00
AR2 PF1 6p violet 175.00 125.00
AR3 PF1 1sh green 175.00 100.00
AR4 PF1 2sh brown 175.00 125.00
AR5 PF1 2sh 6p red 350.00 200.00
AR6 PF1 5sh yellow 650.00 275.00
AR7 PF1 6sh yellow *850.00*
AR8 PF1 10sh yellow green 750.00 275.00
AR9 PF1 20sh rose 1,200. *500.00*

Wmk. 68

AR10 PF1 1p blue 35.00 *40.00*
AR11 PF1 6p violet 75.00 *75.00*
AR12 PF1 6p blue 300.00 225.00
AR13 PF1 1sh green 85.00 60.00
AR14 PF1 2sh brown 175.00 90.00
AR15 PF1 5sh yellow 425.00 140.00
AR16 PF1 10sh yellow green 625.00 *240.00*
AR17 PF1 20sh rose 1,000. *400.00*

1872-73 Wmk. 69 *Perf. 13*

AR18 PF2 1p lilac 30.00 20.00
AR19 PF2 6p brown 125.00 60.00
AR20 PF2 1sh green 150.00 75.00
AR21 PF2 2sh blue 225.00 100.00
AR22 PF2 2sh 6p vermilion 275.00 150.00
AR23 PF2 5sh orange brown 425.00 200.00
AR24 PF2 10sh brown 700.00 *325.00*
AR25 PF2 20sh rose 850.00 *350.00*

Perf. 12

AR26 PF2 1p lilac 30.00 20.00
AR27 PF2 6p brown 125.00 60.00
AR28 PF2 2sh blue 225.00 100.00
AR29 PF2 2sh 6p vermilion 275.00 150.00
AR30 PF2 5sh orange brown 425.00 200.00
AR31 PF2 10sh brown 700.00 *325.00*
AR32 PF2 20sh rose 850.00 *350.00*

Unwmk.
Perf. 13

AR33 PF2 1p lilac 35.00 16.00
AR34 PF2 6p lilac 140.00 70.00
AR35 PF2 6p brown 62.50 32.50
AR36 PF2 1sh green 75.00 32.50
AR37 PF2 2sh blue 125.00 *100.00*
AR38 PF2 2sh 6p vermilion 200.00 90.00
AR39 PF2 5sh orange brown 260.00 110.00
AR40 PF2 10sh brown 525.00 200.00
AR41 PF2 20sh rose 800.00 300.00

Perf. 12

AR42 PF2 1p lilac 35.00 16.00
AR43 PF2 6p lilac 140.00 70.00
AR44 PF2 6p brown 62.50 32.50
AR45 PF2 1sh green 75.00 32.50
AR46 PF2 2sh blue 125.00 100.00
AR47 PF2 2sh 6p vermilion 200.00 90.00
AR48 PF2 5sh orange brown 260.00 110.00
AR49 PF2 10sh brown 525.00 200.00
AR50 PF2 20sh rose 800.00 300.00

Queen Victoria — PF3

1878-79 Engr. Unwmk. *Perf. 12*

AR51 PF3 1p violet 200.00 100.00

Wmk. 68

AR52 PF3 1p violet 125.00 75.00

SEMI-POSTAL STAMPS

Queen Victoria, Colors and Bearers — SP1

SP2

Perf. 12, 12½

1900, June 19 Wmk. 68

B1 SP1 1p red lilac 160.00 150.00
On cover 500.00
B2 SP2 2p deep violet 425.00 375.00
On cover 600.00
Nos. B1-B2 on one cover 1,000.

These stamps were sold at 1sh and 2sh respectively. The difference was applied to a patriotic fund in connection with the Boer War.

REGISTRATION STAMPS

R1

Clean-Cut Perf. 14 to 16

1861 Wmk. 5 Engr.

F1 R1 (6p) olive yellow 550.00 110.00
a. Horiz. pair, imperf. vert. *5,250.*

Rough Perf. 14 to 16

F2 R1 (6p) dull yellow 95.00 50.00

1864 *Perf. 12½ to 13*

F3 R1 (6p) golden yellow 135.00 75.00
a. Imperf.
b. Double impression 1,200.

The reprints are watermarked with a small truncated star and perforated 12.

QUELIMANE

ˌkel-ə-ˈmän-ə

LOCATION — A district of the Mozambique Province in Portuguese East Africa
GOVT. — Part of the Portuguese East Africa Colony
AREA — 39,800 sq. mi.
POP. — 877,000 (approx.)
CAPITAL — Quelimane

This district was formerly a part of Zambezia. Quelimane stamps were replaced by those of Mozambique.

100 Centavos = 1 Escudo

Vasco da Gama Issue of Various Portuguese Colonies Surcharged as

1913 Unwmk. *Perf. 12½ to 16*
On Stamps of Macao

1 CD20 ¼c on ½a bl grn 6.00 6.00
2 CD21 ½c on 1a red 3.00 3.00
3 CD22 1c on 2a red vio 3.00 3.00
4 CD23 2½c on 4a yel grn 3.00 3.00
5 CD24 5c on 8a dk bl 3.00 3.00
6 CD25 7½c on 12a vio brn 4.00 *5.00*
7 CD26 10c on 16a bis brn 3.00 3.00
a. Inverted surcharge 45.00
8 CD27 15c on 24a bister 3.00 3.00
Nos. 1-8 (8) 28.00 29.00

On Stamps of Portuguese Africa

9 CD20 ¼c on 2½r bl grn 2.00 *3.00*
10 CD21 ½c on 5r red 2.00 *3.00*
11 CD22 1c on 10r red vio 2.00 *3.00*
12 CD23 2½c on 25r yel grn 2.00 *3.00*
13 CD24 5c on 50r dk bl 2.00 *3.00*
14 CD25 7½c on 75r vio brn 2.50 *4.50*
15 CD26 10c on 100r bister 2.00 *3.00*
16 CD27 15c on 150r bister 2.00 *3.00*
Nos. 9-16 (8) 16.50 25.50

On Stamps of Timor

17 CD20 ¼c on ½a bl grn 2.50 *3.00*
18 CD21 ½c on 1a red 2.50 *3.00*
19 CD22 1c on 2a red vio 2.50 *3.00*
20 CD23 2½c on 4a yel grn 2.50 *3.00*
21 CD24 5c on 8a dk bl 2.50 *3.00*
22 CD25 7½c on 12a vio brn 4.00 *4.50*
23 CD26 10c on 16a bis brn 2.50 *3.00*
24 CD27 15c on 24a bister 2.50 *3.00*
Nos. 17-24 (8) 21.50 25.50
Nos. 1-24 (24) 66.00 80.00

Ceres — A1

1914 Typo. *Perf. 15x14*
Name and Value in Black

25 A1 ¼c olive brown .80 *3.00*
26 A1 ½c black 1.25 *3.00*
27 A1 1c blue green 1.10 *3.00*
a. Imperf.
28 A1 1½c lilac brown 1.60 *3.00*
29 A1 2c carmine 1.75 *3.00*
30 A1 2½c light violet .50 *1.50*
31 A1 5c deep blue 1.25 *3.00*
32 A1 7½c yellow brown 1.25 *3.00*
33 A1 8c slate 2.00 *3.00*
34 A1 10c orange brown 1.75 *3.00*
35 A1 15c plum 3.00 *5.00*
36 A1 20c yellow green 2.50 *2.50*
37 A1 30c brown, *green* 5.00 *8.50*
38 A1 40c brown, *pink* 6.00 *9.00*
39 A1 50c orange, *salmon* 10.00 *10.00*
40 A1 1e green, *blue* 14.00 *12.00*
Nos. 25-40 (16) 53.75 *75.50*

REUNION

LOCATION — An island in the Indian Ocean about 400 miles east of Madagascar
GOVT. — French Colony
AREA — 970 sq. mi.
POP. — 490,000 (est. 1974)
CAPITAL — St. Denis

100 Centimes = 1 Franc

A1

A2

1852 Unwmk. Typo. *Imperf.*

1 A1 15c black, *blue* *32,000.* *17,500.*
On cover *37,500.*
2 A2 30c black, *blue* *30,000.* *17,500.*
On cover *30,000.*

Four varieties of each value.

The reprints are printed on a more bluish paper than the originals. They have a frame of a thick and a thin line, instead of one thick and two thin lines. Value, $45 each.

Stamps of French Colonies Surcharged or Overprinted in Black:

a

b

1885

3 A1(a) 5c on 40c org, *yelsh* 325.00 300.00
On cover 1,200.
a. Inverted surcharge 1,050. 1,050.
4 A1(a) 25c on 40c org, *yelsh* 42.50 35.00
On cover 950.00
a. Inverted surcharge 500.00 500.00
b. Double surcharge 500.00 500.00
5 A5(a) 5c on 30c brn, *yelsh* 42.50 35.00
On cover 950.00
a. "5" inverted 2,100. 2,100.
b. Double surcharge 500.00 500.00
6 A4(a) 5c on 40c org, *yelsh* (I) 35.00 29.00
On cover 950.00
a. 5c on 40c org, *yelsh* (II) 1,850. 1,850.
b. Inverted surcharge (I) 500.00 500.00
c. Double surcharge (I) 500.00 500.00
7 A8(a) 5c on 30c brn, *yelsh* 11.00 10.50
On cover 950.00
8 A8(a) 5c on 40c ver, *straw* 92.50 77.50
On cover 950.00
a. Inverted surcharge 500.00 500.00
b. Double surcharge 500.00 500.00
9 A8(a) 10c on 40c ver, *straw* 13.00 11.00
On cover 950.00
a. Inverted surcharge 500.00 500.00
b. Double surcharge 525.00 525.00
10 A8(a) 20c on 30c brn, *yelsh* 57.50 50.00
On cover 1,050.

Overprint Type "b"
With or Without Accent on "E"

1891

11 A4 40c org, *yelsh* (I) 425.00 400.00
On cover *1,750.*
a. 40c orange, *yelsh* (II) *5,000.* *5,000.*
b. Double overprint 350.00 350.00
12 A7 80c car, *pnksh* 57.50 45.00
13 A8 30c brn, *yelsh* 32.50 32.50
14 A8 40c ver, *straw* 25.00 25.00
On cover 825.00
a. With accent on "E" 175.00 130.00
15 A8 75c car, *rose* 325.00 325.00
a. With accent on "E" 925.00 925.00
16 A8 1fr brnz grn, *straw* 35.00 32.50
a. With accent on "E" 300.00 300.00

Perf. 14x13½

17 A9 1c blk, *lil bl* 3.50 2.75
On cover 475.00
a. Inverted overprint 25.00 25.00
b. Double overprint 42.50 42.50
18 A9 2c brn, *buff* 4.25 3.50
On cover 475.00
a. Inverted overprint 25.00 25.00
19 A9 4c claret, *lav* 7.50 5.75
On cover 475.00
a. Inverted overprint 65.00 60.00
20 A9 5c grn, *grnsh* 7.50 5.75
On cover 300.00
a. Inverted overprint 40.00 40.00
b. Double overprint 40.00 40.00

21 A9 10c blk, *lav* 27.00 5.75
On cover 300.00
a. Inverted overprint 50.00 50.00
b. Double overprint 55.00 47.50
22 A9 15c blue 42.50 5.75
On cover 300.00
a. Inverted overprint 85.00 77.50
23 A9 20c red, *grn* 30.00 22.50
On cover —
a. Inverted overprint 95.00 90.00
b. Double overprint 90.00 85.00
24 A9 25c blk, *rose* 30.00 5.50
On cover 240.00
a. Inverted overprint 95.00 90.00
25 A9 35c dp vio, *yel* 25.00 18.00
On cover —
b. Inverted overprint 125.00 125.00
26 A9 40c red, *straw* 60.00 47.50
On cover 475.00
a. Inverted overprint 150.00 150.00
27 A9 75c car, *rose* 600.00 500.00
On cover 600.00
a. Inverted overprint 950.00 950.00
28 A9 1fr brnz grn, *straw* 475.00 400.00
On cover —
a. Inverted overprint 1,250. 1,250.
b. Double overprint 1,000. 1,000.

Overprinted "RUNION"

17c A9 1c blk, *lil bl* 19.00 19.00
18c A9 2c brn, *buff* 23.00 23.00
19c A9 4c claret, *lav* 27.00 27.00
20c A9 5c grn, *grnsh* 27.00 25.00
21c A9 10c blk, *lav* 52.50 52.50
22c A9 15c blue 70.00 70.00
23c A9 20c red, *grn* 85.00 85.00
24c A9 25c blk, *rose* 57.50 57.50
25c A9 35c dp vio, *yel* 57.50 57.50
26c A9 40c red, *straw* 150.00 150.00
27c A9 75c car, *rose* 1,250. 1,150.
28c A9 1fr brnz grn, *straw* 1,250. 1,150.

Overprinted "REUNIONR"

13d A8 30c brn, *yelsh* 425.00 425.00
14d A8 40c ver, *straw* 375.00 375.00
15d A8 75c car, *rose* *1,150. 1,150.*
16d A8 1fr brnz grn, *straw* *850.00 850.00*
17d A9 1c blk, *lil bl* 19.00 19.00
18d A9 2c brn, *buff* 23.00 23.00
19d A9 4c claret, *lav* 27.00 27.00
20d A9 5c grn, *grnsh* 27.00 25.00
21d A9 10c blk, *lav* 52.50 52.50
22d A9 15c blue 70.00 70.00
23d A9 20c red, *grn* 85.00 85.00
24d A9 25c blk, *rose* 57.50 50.00
25d A9 35c dp vio, *yel* 57.50 57.50
26d A9 40c red, *straw* 150.00 150.00
27d A9 75c car, *rose* *1,250. 1,150.*
28d A9 1fr brnz grn, *straw* *1,250. 1,150.*

Overprinted "REUNIOU"

17e A9 1c blk, *lil bl* 27.00 27.00
20e A9 5c grn, *grnsh* 27.00 27.00
24e A9 25c blk, *rose* 70.00 70.00
27e A9 75c car, *rose* *1,250. 1,150.*
28e A9 1fr brnz grn, *straw* *1,250. 1,150.*

Overprinted "REUNOIN"

17f A9 1c blk, *lil bl* 23.00 23.00
18f A9 2c brn, *buff* 23.00 23.00
19f A9 4c claret, *lav* 23.00 23.00
20f A9 5c grn, *grnsh* 30.00 27.00
21f A9 10c blk, *lav* 52.50 50.00
22f A9 15c blue 65.00 52.50
23f A9 20c red, *grn* 75.00 75.00
24f A9 25c blk, *rose* 70.00 70.00
25f A9 35c dp vio, *yel* 70.00 70.00
26f A9 40c red, *straw* 160.00 160.00
27f A9 75c car, *rose* *1,250. 1,150.*
28f A9 1fr brnz grn, *straw* *1,250. 1,150.*

Overprinted "RUENION"

15g A8 75c car, *rose* *1,250. 1,250.*
17g A9 1c blk, *lil bl* 19.00 19.00
18g A9 2c brn, *buff* 30.00 30.00
19g A9 4c claret, *lav* 30.00 30.00
20g A9 5c grn, *grnsh* 57.50 57.50
21g A9 10c blk, *lav* 57.50 57.50
22g A9 15c blue 85.00 75.00
26g A9 40c red, *straw* 150.00 150.00

Overprinted "EUNION"

11h A4 40c org, *yelsh* (I) *3,500. 3,500.*
12h A7 80c car, *pnksh* *500.00 500.00*
14h A8 40c ver, *straw* 140.00 140.00
15h A8 75c car, *rose* *1,250. 1,250.*
17h A9 1c blk, *lil bl* 19.00 19.00
18h A9 2c brn, *buff* 21.00 21.00
19h A9 4c claret, *lav* 37.50 37.50
20h A9 5c grn, *grnsh* 42.50 37.50
21h A9 10c blk, *lav* 57.50 57.50
22h A9 15c blue 60.00 52.50
23h A9 20c red, *grn* 70.00 70.00
24h A9 25c blk, *rose* 85.00 85.00
25h A9 35c dp vio, *yel* 57.50 57.50
26h A9 40c red, *straw* 150.00 150.00
27h A9 75c car, *rose* 1,250. 1,150.
28h A9 1fr brnz grn, *straw* 1,250. 1,150.

Overprinted "ERUNION"

17i A9 1c blk, *lil bl* 19.00 19.00
18i A9 2c brn, *buff* 23.00 23.00
19i A9 4c claret, *lav* 37.50 37.50
20i A9 5c grn, *grnsh* 42.50 35.00
21i A9 10c blk, *lav* 57.50 52.50
22i A9 15c blue 60.00 52.50
23i A9 20c red, *grn* 85.00 75.00
24i A9 25c blk, *rose* 75.00 60.00
25i A9 35c dp vio, *yel* 65.00 65.00
26i A9 40c red, *straw* 150.00 150.00
27i A9 75c car, *rose* 1,250. 1,150.
28i A9 1fr brnz grn, *straw* 1,250. 1,150.

Overprinted "REUNIN"

18j A9 2c brn, *buff* 23.00 23.00
23j A9 20c red, *grn* 65.00 60.00

For surcharges see Nos. 29-33, 53-55.

No. 23 with Additional Surcharge in Black:

c

d

e

f

1891

29 A9(c) 02c on 20c red, *grn* 9.25 9.25
On cover 300.00
a. Inverted surcharge 40.00 40.00
b. No "c" after "02" 30.00 30.00
c. Overprinted "RUNION" 60.00 60.00
30 A9(c) 15c on 20c red, *grn* 11.50 11.50
On cover 300.00
a. Inverted surcharge 40.00 40.00
b. No "c" after "15" 39.00 39.00
c. Overprinted "RUNION" 100.00 100.00
31 A9(d) 2c on 20c red, *grn* 3.50 3.50
On cover 300.000
32 A9(e) 2c on 20c red, *grn* 2.50 2.50
On cover 300.00
a. Overprinted "RUENION" 23.00 23.00
b. Overprinted "RUNOIN" 23.00 23.00
33 A9(f) 2c on 20c red, *grn* 5.50 5.50
On cover 300.00
Nos. 29-33 (5) 32.25 32.25

Navigation and Commerce — A14

1892-1905 Typo. *Perf. 14x13½*
Name of Colony in Blue or Carmine

34 A14 1c blk, *lil bl* 1.40 .95
On cover 35.00
35 A14 2c brn, *buff* 1.40 .95
On cover 35.00
36 A14 4c claret, *lav* 2.00 1.60
On cover 35.00
37 A14 5c grn, *grnsh* 5.00 1.60
On cover 19.00
38 A14 5c yel grn ('00) 1.10 1.00
On cover 18.00
39 A14 10c blk, *lav* 8.00 2.00
On cover 18.00
40 A14 10c red ('00) 2.50 2.00
On cover 18.00
41 A14 15c bl, quadrille paper 24.00 2.40
On cover 25.00
42 A14 15c gray ('00) 5.75 2.00
On cover 25.00
43 A14 20c red, *grn* 14.50 6.50
On cover —
44 A14 25c blk, *rose* 16.00 2.50
On cover 25.00
a. "Reunion" double 300.00 300.00
45 A14 25c blue ('00) 18.00 18.00
On cover 40.00
46 A14 30c brn, *bis* 17.00 8.50
On cover 70.00
47 A14 40c red, *straw* 22.50 16.00
On cover 70.00
48 A14 50c car, *rose* 62.50 30.00
On cover 90.00
a. "Reunion" in red and blue 350.00 350.00
49 A14 50c brn, *az* ("Reunion" in car) ('00) 42.50 37.50
On cover 120.00
50 A14 50c brn, *az* ("Reunion" in bl) ('05) 42.50 37.50
On cover 120.00
51 A14 75c dp vio, *org* 55.00 32.50
On cover 125.00
a. "Reunion" double 325.00 325.00
52 A14 1fr brnz grn, *straw* 42.50 27.50
On cover 150.00
a. "Reunion" double 300.00 300.00
Nos. 34-52 (19) 384.15 231.00

Perf. 13½x14 stamps are counterfeits.
For surcharges and overprint see Nos. 56-59, 99-106, Q1.

French Colonies No. 52 Surcharged in Black:

g

h

j

1893

53 A9(g) 2c on 20c red, *grn* 2.10 2.10
On cover 250.00
54 A9(h) 2c on 20c red, *grn* 3.50 3.50
On cover 250.00
55 A9(j) 2c on 20c red, *grn* 16.00 16.00
On cover 250.00
Nos. 53-55 (3) 21.60 21.60

Reunion Nos. 47-48, 51-52 Surcharged in Black

1901

56 A14 5c on 40c red, *straw* 4.25 4.25
On cover 60.00
a. Inverted surcharge 29.00 29.00
b. No bar 140.00 140.00
c. Thin "5" — —
d. "5" inverted 450.00 450.00
57 A14 5c on 50c car, *rose* 5.00 5.00
On cover 60.00
a. Inverted surcharge 29.00 29.00
b. No bar 140.00 140.00
c. Thin "5" —
58 A14 15c on 75c vio, *org* 14.50 14.50
On cover 90.00
a. Inverted surcharge 35.00 35.00
b. No bar 140.00 140.00
c. Thin "5" and small "1" 27.50 27.50
d. As "c," inverted — —
59 A14 15c on 1fr brnz grn, *straw* 12.50 12.50
On cover 90.00
a. Inverted surcharge 35.00 35.00
b. No bar 140.00 140.00
c. Thin "5" and small "1" 27.50 27.50
d. As "c," inverted —
Nos. 56-59 (4) 36.25 36.25

Map of Réunion A19

Coat of Arms and View of St. Denis A20

View of St. Pierre — A21

1907-30 Typo.

60 A19 1c vio & car rose .20 .20
61 A19 2c brn & ultra .25 .25
62 A19 4c ol grn & red .25 .25
63 A19 5c grn & red .85 .25
64 A19 5c org & vio ('22) .25 .25
65 A19 10c car & grn 2.00 .25
66 A19 10c grn ('22) .25 .25
67 A19 10c brn red & org red, *bluish* ('26) .50 .50
68 A19 15c blk & ultra .30 .30
69 A19 15c gray grn & bl grn ('26) .30 .30
70 A19 15c bl & lt red ('28) .30 .30
71 A20 20c gray grn & bl grn .30 .30
72 A20 25c dp bl & vio brn 4.75 2.50
73 A20 25c lt brn & bl ('22) .30 .30
74 A20 30c yel brn & grn 1.00 .55
75 A20 30c rose & pale rose ('22) 1.10 1.00
76 A20 30c gray & car rose ('26) .40 .40
77 A20 30c dp grn & yel grn ('28) .90 .90
78 A20 35c ol grn & bl 1.25 .75
79 A20 40c gray grn & brn ('25) .50 .50
80 A20 45c vio & car rose 1.40 .75
81 A20 45c red brn & ver ('26) .65 .65
82 A20 45c vio & red org ('28) 2.00 2.00
83 A20 50c red brn & ultra 3.25 1.10
84 A20 50c bl & ultra ('22) 1.00 1.00
85 A20 50c yel & vio ('26) .80 .80
86 A20 60c dk bl & yel brn ('26) .80 .80
87 A20 65c vio & lt bl ('28) 1.25 1.25
88 A20 75c red & car rose .65 .55
89 A20 75c ol brn & red vio ('28) 1.75 1.75
90 A20 90c brn red & brt red ('30) 5.75 5.50
91 A21 1fr ol grn & bl 1.10 1.10
92 A21 1fr blue ('26) .65 .65
93 A21 1fr yel brn & lav ('28) 1.10 .60
94 A21 1.10fr org brn & rose lil ('28) 1.00 .75
95 A21 1.50fr dk bl & ultra ('30) 9.75 9.75
96 A21 2fr red & grn 3.75 2.40
97 A21 3fr red vio ('30) 9.50 6.50
98 A21 5fr car & vio brn 6.75 4.50
Nos. 60-98 (39) 68.85 52.70

For surcharges see #107-121, 178-180, B1-B3.

Stamps of 1892-1900 Surcharged in Black or Carmine

1912
Spacing between figures of surcharge 1.5mm (5c), 2mm (10c)

99 A14 5c on 2c brn, *buff* 1.10 1.10
100 A14 5c on 15c gray (C) 1.00 1.00
a. Inverted surcharge 125.00 125.00
101 A14 5c on 20c red, *grn* 1.50 1.50
102 A14 5c on 25c blk, *rose* (C) 1.00 1.00
103 A14 5c on 30c brn, *bis* (C) .80 .80
104 A14 10c on 40c red, *straw* .95 .95
105 A14 10c on 50c brn, *az* (C) 4.00 4.00
106 A14 10c on 75c dp vio, *org* 7.25 7.25
Nos. 99-106 (8) 17.60 17.60

Spacing between figures of surcharge 2.25mm (5c), 2.75mm (10c)

99a A14 5c on 2c brn, *buff* 25.00 25.00
100b A14 5c on 15c gray (C) 25.00 25.00
101a A14 5c on 20c red, *grn* 275.00 275.00
102a A14 5c on 25c blk, *rose* (C) 77.50 77.50
103a A14 5c on 30c brn, *bis* (C) 77.50 77.50
104a A14 10c on 40c red, *straw* 45.00 45.00
105a A14 10c on 50c brn, *az* (C) 77.50 77.50
106a A14 10c on 75c dp vio, *org* 210.00 210.00
Nos. 99a-106a (8) 812.50 812.50

No. 62 Surcharged

1917

107 A19 1c on 4c ol grn & red 1.25 1.25
a. Inverted surcharge 40.00 40.00
b. Double surcharge 60.00 60.00

Stamps and Types of 1907-30 Surcharged in Black or Red

1922-33

108	A20	40c on 20c grn & yel	.50	.50
109	A20	50c on 45c red brn & ver ('33)	.85	.75
109A	A20	50c on 45c vio & red org ('33)	210.00	200.00
b.		Double surcharge	1,000.	
110	A20	50c on 65c vio & lt bl ('33)	.85	.75
111	A20	60c on 75c red & rose	.65	.65
112	A19	65c on 15c blk & ultra (R) ('25)	1.50	1.50
113	A19	85c on 15c blk & ultra (R) ('25)	1.50	1.50
114	A20	85c on 75c red & cer ('25)	1.60	1.60
115	A20	90c on 75 brn red & rose red ('27)	1.60	1.60
		Nos. 108-109,110-115 (8)	9.05	8.85

Stamps and Type of 1907-30 Surcharged with New Value and Bars in Black or Red

1924-27

116	A21	25c on 5fr car & brn	.80	.80
a.		Double surcharge	72.50	
117	A21	1.25fr on 1fr bl (R) ('26)	.75	.50
a.		Double surcharge	85.00	
118	A21	1.50fr on 1fr ind & ultra, *bluish* ('27)	1.00	.90
a.		Double surcharge	100.00	
119	A21	3fr on 5fr dl red & lt bl ('27)	2.50	2.10
120	A21	10fr on 5fr bl grn & brn red ('27)	14.00	11.50
121	A21	20fr on 5fr blk brn & rose ('27)	17.50	13.00
		Nos. 116-121 (6)	36.55	28.80

Colonial Exposition Issue
Common Design Types

1931 Engr. *Perf. 12½*
Name of Country Typo. in Black

122	CD70	40c dp green	4.00	4.00
123	CD71	50c violet	4.00	4.00
124	CD72	90c red orange	4.00	4.00
125	CD73	1.50fr dull blue	4.00	4.00
		Nos. 122-125 (4)	16.00	16.00

Cascade of Salazie — A22

Waterfowl Lake and Anchain Peak — A23

Léon Dierx Museum, St. Denis — A24

Perf. 12, 12½ and Compound
1933-40 Engr.

126	A22	1c violet	.20	.20
127	A22	2c dark brown	.20	.20
128	A22	3c rose vio ('40)	.20	.20
129	A22	4c olive green	.20	.20
130	A22	5c red orange	.20	.20
131	A22	10c ultramarine	.20	.20
132	A22	15c black	.20	.20
133	A22	20c indigo	.25	.25
134	A22	25c red brown	.25	.25
135	A22	30c dark green	.25	.25
136	A23	35c green ('38)	.40	.40
137	A23	40c ultramarine	.40	.40
138	A23	40c brn blk ('40)	.30	.30
139	A23	45c red violet	.60	.60
140	A23	45c green ('40)	.30	.30
141	A23	50c red	.25	.25
142	A23	55c brn org ('38)	.95	.65
143	A23	60c dull bl ('40)	.30	.30
144	A23	65c olive green	.75	.60
145	A23	70c ol grn ('40)	.45	.45
146	A23	75c dark brown	3.50	2.75
147	A23	80c black ('38)	.60	.55
148	A23	90c carmine	1.75	1.50
149	A23	90c dl rose vio ('39)	.65	.65
150	A23	1fr green	1.40	.40
151	A23	1fr dk car ('38)	1.75	.40
152	A23	1fr black ('40)	.50	.50
153	A24	1.25fr orange brown	.50	.40
154	A24	1.25fr brt car rose ('39)	.65	.65
155	A22	1.40fr pck bl ('40)	.65	.65
156	A24	1.50fr ultramarine	.25	.25
157	A22	1.60fr dk car rose ('40)	1.00	1.00
158	A24	1.75fr olive green	.60	.35
159	A22	1.75fr dk bl ('38)	1.25	.45
160	A24	2fr vermilion	.40	.40
161	A22	2.25fr brt ultra ('39)	1.25	1.25
162	A22	2.50fr chnt ('40)	.95	.95
163	A24	3fr purple	.40	.40
164	A24	5fr magenta	.40	.40
165	A24	10fr dark blue	.75	.65
166	A24	20fr red brown	1.10	1.10
		Set value	9.85	8.00

For overprints and surcharges see Nos. 177A, 181-220, 223, C1.

Paris International Exposition Issue
Common Design Types

1937 *Perf. 13*

167	CD74	20c dp vio	1.75	1.75
168	CD75	30c dk grn	1.75	1.75
169	CD76	40c car rose	1.75	1.75
170	CD77	50c dk brn & blk	1.90	1.90
171	CD78	90c red	1.90	1.90
172	CD79	1.50fr ultra	1.90	1.90
		Nos. 167-172 (6)	10.95	10.95

Colonial Arts Exhibition Issue
Souvenir Sheet
Common Design Type

1937 *Imperf.*

173	CD74	3fr ultra	7.00	*8.50*

New York World's Fair Issue
Common Design Type

1939 Engr. *Perf. 12½x12*

174	CD82	1.25fr car lake	1.00	1.00
175	CD82	2.25fr ultra	1.00	1.00

For overprints see Nos. 221-222.

SEMI-POSTAL STAMPS

No. 65 Surcharged in Black or Red

1915 Unwmk. *Perf. 14x13½*

B1	A19	10c + 5c (Bk)	110.00	80.00
a.		Inverted surcharge	275.00	210.00
B2	A19	10c + 5c (R)	1.10	1.10
a.		Inverted surcharge	57.50	57.50

No. 65 Surcharged in Red

1916

B3	A19	10c + 5c	1.25	1.25

Curie Issue
Common Design Type

1938 *Perf. 13*

B4	CD80	1.75fr + 50c brt ultra	11.00	11.00

French Revolution Issue
Common Design Type

1939 Photo. Unwmk.
Name and Value Typo. in Black

B5	CD83	45c + 25c grn	10.00	10.00
B6	CD83	70c + 30c brn	10.00	10.00
B7	CD83	90c + 35c red org	10.00	10.00
B8	CD83	1.25fr + 1fr rose pink	10.00	10.00
B9	CD83	2.25fr + 2fr blue	10.00	10.00
		Nos. B5-B9 (5)	50.00	50.00

AIR POST STAMPS

No. 141 Overprinted in Blue

1937, Jan. 23 Unwmk. *Perf. 12½*

C1	A23	50c red	225.00	200.00
a.		Vert. pair, one without overprint	1,300.	1,300.
b.		Inverted overprint	3,500.	

Flight of the "Roland Garros" from Reunion to France by aviators Laurent, Lenier and Touge in Jan.-Feb., 1937.

Airplane and Landscape — AP2

1938, Mar. 1 Engr. *Perf. 12½*

C2	AP2	3.65fr slate blue & car	.75	.60
C3	AP2	6.65fr brown & org red	.75	.60
C4	AP2	9.65fr car & ultra	.75	.60
C5	AP2	12.65fr brown & green	1.50	1.25
		Nos. C2-C5 (4)	3.75	3.05

For overprints see Nos. C14-C17.

AIR POST SEMI-POSTAL STAMP

French Revolution Issue
Common Design Type

1939 Unwmk. *Perf. 13*
Name and Value Typo. in Orange

CB1	CD83	3.65fr + 4fr brn blk	18.00	18.00

POSTAGE DUE STAMPS

D1

D2

1889-92 Unwmk. Type-set *Imperf.*
Without Gum

J1	D1	5c black	19.00	9.25
		On cover		*800.00*
a.		Missing "ti" of "Centimes" and "à"	150.00	150.00
b.		Double impression	125.00	125.00
J2	D1	10c black	24.00	9.25
		On cover		700.00
a.		Double impression	125.00	125.00
J3	D1	15c black ('92)	46.50	29.00
a.		Missing "ti" of "Centimes" and "à"	200.00	200.00
b.		Double impression	190.00	190.00
J4	D1	20c black	32.50	18.00
a.		Double impression	190.00	190.00
J5	D1	30c black	30.00	18.00
a.		Double impression	125.00	125.00
		Nos. J1-J5 (5)	152.00	83.50

Ten varieties of each value.

Nos. J1-J2, J4-J5 issued on yellowish paper in 1889; Nos. J1-J3, J5 on bluish white paper in 1892.

Many small printing varieties exist, as well as intermediate stages of the plate deterioration that resulted in Nos. J1a and J3a, Which appear in one position in the second printing of the 5c and 15c values.

1907 Typo. *Perf. 14x13½*

J6	D2	5c carmine, *yel*	.60	.60
		On cover		150.00
J7	D2	10c blue, *bl*	.60	.60
		On cover		150.00
J8	D2	15c black, *bluish*	.95	.95
		On cover		150.00
J9	D2	20c carmine	.95	.95
		On cover		150.00
J10	D2	30c green, *grnsh*	1.50	1.50
		On cover		*175.00*
J11	D2	50c red, *green*	1.75	1.75
		On cover		*210.00*
J12	D2	60c carmine, *bl*	1.75	1.75
		On cover		*210.00*
J13	D2	1fr violet	2.00	2.00
		On cover		*300.00*
		Nos. J6-J13 (8)	10.10	10.10

Type of 1907 Issue Surcharged

1927

J14	D2	2fr on 1fr org red	9.00	9.00
J15	D2	3fr on 1fr org brn	9.00	9.00

Arms of Réunion D3

Numeral D4

1933 Engr. *Perf. 13x13½*

J16	D3	5c deep violet	.20	.20
J17	D3	10c dark green	.20	.20
J18	D3	15c orange brown	.20	.20
J19	D3	20c light red	.25	.25
J20	D3	30c olive green	.25	.25
J21	D3	50c ultramarine	.60	.60
J22	D3	60c black brown	.60	.60
J23	D3	1fr light violet	.60	.60
J24	D3	2fr deep blue	.60	.60
J25	D3	3fr carmine	.80	.80
		Nos. J16-J25 (10)	4.30	4.30

PARCEL POST STAMP

No. 40 Overprinted

1906 Unwmk. *Perf. 14x13½*

Q1	A14	10c red	14.50	14.50

RHODESIA

rō-'dē-zh‿ē-‿ə

(British South Africa)

LOCATION — Southeastern Africa
GOVT. — Administered by the British South Africa Company
AREA — 440,653 sq. mi.
POP. — 1,738,000 (estimated 1921)
CAPITAL — Salisbury

In 1923 the area was divided and the portion south of the Zambezi River became the British Crown Colony of Southern Rhodesia. In the following year the remaining territory was formed into the Protectorate of Northern Rhodesia.

12 Pence = 1 Shilling
20 Shillings = 1 Pound

A1

A2

Coat of Arms — A3

Thin Paper

Engr. (A1, A3); Engr., Typo. (A2)

1890-94 Unwmk. *Perf. 14, 14½*

1	A2	½p blue & ver ('91)	2.50	3.25
a.		½p dp blue & ver ('93)	3.00	*5.00*
2	A1	1p black	11.00	3.00
3	A2	2p gray grn & ver ('91)	20.00	2.75
4	A2	3p gray & grn ('91)	11.50	4.00
5	A2	4p red brn & blk ('91)	22.50	2.50
6	A1	6p ultra	60.00	25.00
7	A1	6p deep blue	27.50	3.75
8	A2	8p rose & bl ('91)	11.50	11.50
a.		8p red & ultramarine ('92)	10.50	11.50
9	A1	1sh gray brown	42.50	10.00
10	A1	2sh vermilion	45.00	27.50
11	A1	2sh6p dull lilac	36.00	40.00
		Revenue cancellation		.75
a.		2sh6p lilac ('93)	55.00	47.50
		Revenue cancellation		.85
12	A2	3sh brn & grn ('94)	150.00	77.50
		Revenue cancellation		2.25
13	A2	4sh gray & ver ('93)	42.50	60.00
		Revenue cancellation		1.00
14	A1	5sh yellow	67.50	52.50
		Revenue cancellation		1.25
15	A1	10sh deep green	82.50	*100.00*
		Revenue cancellation		1.25
16	A3	£1 dark blue	*190.00*	*140.00*
		Revenue cancellation		6.75
17	A3	£2 rose	*400.00*	*160.00*
		Revenue cancellation		22.50
18	A3	£5 yellow grn	*1,650.*	*450.00*
		Revenue cancellation		50.00
19	A3	£10 orange brn	*2,850.*	*800.00*
		Revenue cancellation		75.00
		Nos. 1-16 (16)	822.50	*563.25*

The paper of the 1891 issue has the trademark and initials of the makers in a monogram watermarked in each sheet. Some of the lower values were also printed on a slightly thicker paper without watermark.

Copies of #16-19 with cancellations removed are frequently offered as unused specimens.

See #24-25, 58.

For surcharges see #20-23, 40-42. For overprints see British Central Africa #1-20.

Nos. 6 and 9 Surcharged in Black

1891, Mar.

20	A1	½p on 6p ultra	110.00	*450.00*
21	A1	2p on 6p ultra	110.00	*475.00*
22	A1	4p on 6p ultra	150.00	*675.00*
23	A1	8p on 1sh brown	150.00	*800.00*
		Nos. 20-23 (4)	520.00	*2,400.*

Beware of forged surcharges.

Thick Soft Paper

1895 *Perf. 12½*

24	A2	2p green & red	25.00	11.50
25	A2	4p ocher & black	25.00	*14.00*
a.		Imperf., pair	2,000.	

A4

Die I — Small dot at the right of the tail of the supporter at the right of the shield, and the body of the lion is not fully shaded.

Die II — No dot and the lion is heavily shaded.

1896 Engraved, Typo. *Perf. 14*

26	A4	½p slate & violet	3.00	*3.75*
27	A4	1p scar & emer	4.50	4.25
a.		1p scarlet & emerald (I)	17.50	5.00
b.		1p car red & emerald green (I)		—
28	A4	2p brown & rose lil (II)	19.00	4.50
a.		2p brown & rose lilac (I)	27.50	2.50
29	A4	3p red brn & ultra	4.25	2.00
30	A4	4p blue & red lil	9.25	.60
a.		4p ultra & red lilac (II)	85.00	13.00
b.		4p blue & red lilac (I)	30.00	19.00
c.		4p ultra & red lilac (I)	62.50	
d.		Horiz. pair, imperf. btwn. (I)		
31	A4	6p vio & pale rose (II)	7.25	.85
a.		6p violet & pink (I)	90.00	21.00
32	A4	8p dp grn & vio, *buff* (I)	5.25	.70
a.		Imperf. pair	2,750.	
b.		Horiz. pair, imperf. btwn.		
33	A4	1sh brt grn & ultra	17.50	4.00
34	A4	2sh dk bl & grn, *buff*	25.00	9.75
35	A4	2sh6p brn & vio, *yel*	80.00	55.00
36	A4	3sh grn & red vio, *bl*	75.00	37.50
a.		Imperf. pair	7,000.	
37	A4	4sh red & bl, *grn*	60.00	4.00
38	A4	5sh org red & grn	52.50	10.50
39	A4	10sh sl & car, *rose*	100.00	70.00
		Nos. 26-39 (14)	462.50	207.40

See type A7.

Nos. 4, 13-14 Surcharged in Black

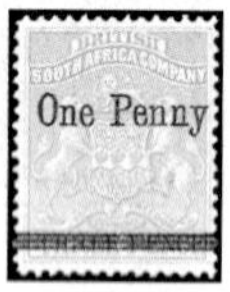

1896, Apr. *Perf. 14*

40	A2	1p on 3p	525.00	625.00
a.		"P" of "Penny" inverted	26,500.	
b.		"y" of "Penny" inverted		—
c.		Double surcharge		—
41	A2	1p on 4sh	300.00	325.00
a.		"P" of "Penny" inverted	22,000.	
b.		Single bar in surch.	1,150.	1,400.
c.		"y" of "Penny" inverted	22,000.	
42	A1	3p on 5s yellow	200.00	*250.00*
a.		"T" of "THREE" inverted	26,500.	
b.		"R" of "THREE" inverted	23,000.	
		Nos. 40-42 (3)	1,025.	1,200.

Cape of Good Hope Stamps Overprinted in Black

1896, May 22 Wmk. 16

43	A6	½p slate	11.50	*18.00*
44	A15	1p carmine	14.00	*20.00*
45	A6	2p bister brown	17.50	10.50
46	A6	4p deep blue	20.00	20.00
a.		"COMPANY" omitted	9,250.	
47	A3	6p violet	57.50	*75.00*
48	A6	1sh yellow buff	160.00	*160.00*

Wmk. 2

49	A6	3p claret	57.50	*80.00*
		Nos. 43-49 (7)	338.00	*383.50*

Nos. 42-49 were used at Bulawayo during the Matabele Rebellion.

Forgeries are known.

Remainders

Rhodesian authorities made available remainders in large quantities of all stamps in 1897, 1898-1908, 1905, 1909 and 1910 issues, CTO. Some varieties exist only as remainders. See notes following Nos. 100 and 118.

A7

Type A7 differs from type A4 in having the ends of the scroll which is below the shield curved between the hind legs of the supporters instead of passing behind one leg of each. There are other minor differences.

Perf. 13½ to 16

1897 Unwmk. Engr.

50	A7	½p slate & violet	2.75	*5.25*
51	A7	1p ver & gray grn	3.50	*4.75*
52	A7	2p brown & lil rose	7.25	1.75
53	A7	3p red brn & gray bl	3.00	.45
a.		Vert. pair, imperf. btwn.	2,850.	
54	A7	4p ultra & red lilac	10.50	1.75
a.		Horiz. pair, imperf. btwn.	10,500.	10,500.
55	A7	6p violet & salmon	9.00	4.50
56	A7	8p dk grn & vio, *buff*	12.50	.45
a.		Vert. pair, imperf. btwn.	—	2,600.
57	A7	£1 black & red, *grn*	400.00	250.00
		Revenue cancellation		12.00
		Nos. 50-56 (7)	48.50	*18.90*

Thick Paper

Perf. 15

58	A3	£2 bright red	*1,775.*	450.00
		Revenue cancellation		60.00

See note on remainders following No. 49.

A8

A9

A10

1898-1908 *Perf. 13½ to 16*

59	A8	½p yellow green	2.50	1.00
a.		Imperf. pair	800.00	
b.		Horiz. pair, imperf. vert.	750.00	
60	A8	1p rose	3.75	.60
a.		1p red	4.75	.60
b.		Horiz. or vert. pair, imperf. btwn.	575.00	
d.		Imperf. pair	600.00	625.00
61	A8	2p brown	3.25	.70
62	A8	2½p cobalt bl ('03)	5.25	1.00
a.		Horiz. pair, imperf. between	925.00	1,050.
63	A8	3p claret ('08)	4.75	.90
a.		Vert. pair, imperf. between	800.00	
64	A8	4p olive green	5.00	.35
a.		Vert. pair, imperf. between	800.00	
65	A8	6p lilac	11.50	1.00
66	A9	1sh olive bister	16.00	2.50
a.		Imperf., pair	2,900.	
b.		Horiz. or vert. pair, imperf. btwn.	3,150.	
67	A9	2sh6p bluish gray ('06)	52.50	.85
a.		Vert. pair, imperf. between	1,150.	575.00
68	A9	3sh purple ('02)	15.00	1.90
69	A9	5sh orange ('01)	42.50	11.00
70	A9	7sh6p black ('01)	75.00	19.00
71	A9	10sh bluish grn ('08)	25.00	1.10
72	A10	£1 gray vio ('01)	250.00	92.50
		Revenue cancellation		10.00
73	A10	£2 red brown ('08)	85.00	7.50
74	A10	£5 dk blue ('01)	*3,500.*	2,350.
		Revenue cancellation		27.50
75	A10	£10 blue lil ('01)	*3,750.*	2,600.
		Revenue cancellation		75.00
75A	A10	£20 bister ('01?)	*19,000.*	
		Revenue cancellation		150.00
		Nos. 59-73 (15)	597.00	141.90

For overprints and surcharges see #82-100.

See note on remainders following #49.

A £100 in cherry red, perf 13½ was produced in June 1901 and is known unused and with revenue cancellations. Value for example with revenue cancellation $1,000.

Victoria Falls — A11

1905, July 13 *Perf. 13½ to 15*

76	A11	1p rose red	3.75	5.00
77	A11	2½p ultra	9.25	6.25
78	A11	5p magenta	25.00	55.00
79	A11	1sh blue green	26.00	40.00
a.		Imperf., pair	*21,000.*	
b.		Horiz. pair, imperf. vert.	*27,500.*	
c.		Horiz. pair, imperf. btwn.	*27,500.*	
d.		Vert. pair, imperf. btn.	*22,000.*	
80	A11	2sh6p black	110.00	*175.00*
81	A11	5sh violet	97.50	45.00
		Nos. 76-81 (6)	271.50	*326.25*

Opening of the Victoria Falls bridge across the Zambezi River.

See note on remainders following No. 49.

Stamps of 1898-1908 Overprinted or Surcharged:

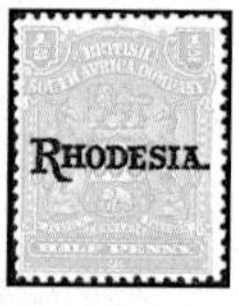

1909 *Perf. 14, 15*

82	A8	½p yellow green	2.00	1.40
83	A8	1p red	2.75	.85
a.		Horiz. pair, imperf., vert.	475.00	
84	A8	2p brown	1.90	*3.75*
85	A8	2½p cobalt blue	1.40	.80
86	A8	3p claret	1.90	.60
87	A8	4p olive green	3.25	1.10
88	A8	5p on 6p lilac	7.50	*14.00*
89	A8	6p lilac	5.75	4.25
90	A9	7½p on 2sh6p	4.00	4.25
91	A9	10p on 3sh pur	15.00	*18.00*
92	A9	1sh olive bis	9.75	3.50
93	A9	2sh on 5sh org	14.00	8.50
94	A9	2sh6p bluish gray	20.00	9.75
95	A9	3sh purple	17.50	9.75
96	A9	5sh orange	29.00	*35.00*
97	A9	7sh6p black	97.50	20.00
98	A9	10sh bluish grn	37.50	12.50
99	A10	£1 gray violet	160.00	85.00
a.		Pair, one without overprint	*28,750.*	
b.		Violet overprint	400.00	210.00
100	A10	£2 red brown	*3,750.*	325.00
		Nos. 82-99 (18)	430.70	233.00

See note on remainders following No. 49. The remainders included inverted overprints of the 3p ($35), 4p ($15) and 2s6p ($27.50).

Nos. 82-87, 89, 92, 94, 96 and 98 exist without period after "Rhodesia."

Queen Mary and King George V
A12 A13

1910 Engr. *Perf. 14, 15x14, 14x15*

101	A12	½p green	11.00	2.00
a.		½p olive green	30.00	3.00
b.		Perf. 15	325.00	13.00
c.		Imperf., pair	*12,500.*	*5,250.*
d.		Perf. 13½	325.00	45.00
102	A12	1p rose car	18.00	2.00
a.		Vertical pair, imperf. btwn.	*17,500.*	*11,500.*
b.		Perf. 15	325.00	9.75
c.		Perf. 13½	*2,050.*	55.00
103	A12	2p gray & blk	55.00	6.25
b.		Perf. 15	975.00	35.00

104 A12 2½p ultramarine 22.50 6.25
a. 2½p light blue 22.50 15.00
b. Perf. 15 80.00 40.00
c. Perf. 13½ 40.00 70.00
105 A12 3p ol yel & vio 30.00 12.50
a. Perf. 15 2,900. 57.50
106 A12 4p org & blk 37.50 12.50
a. 4p orange & violet black 75.00 57.50
b. Perf. 15x14 475.00
c. Perf. 15 47.50 70.00
107 A12 5p ol grn & brn 27.50 45.00
a. 5p olive yel & brn (error) 625.00 175.00
b. Perf. 15 800.00 85.00
108 A12 6p claret & brn 32.50 14.00
a. Perf. 15 950.00 70.00
109 A12 8p brn vio & gray blk 150.00 100.00
a. Perf. 13½ 70.00 *275.00*
110 A12 10p plum & rose red 35.00 55.00
111 A12 1sh turq grn & black 40.00 19.00
b. Perf. 15 1,100. 62.50
112 A12 2sh gray bl & black 85.00 57.50
a. Perf. 15 2,100 375.00
113 A12 2sh6p car rose & blk 350.00 325.00
114 A12 3sh vio & bl grn 175.00 175.00
115 A12 5sh yel grn & brn red 250.00 225.00
116 A12 7sh6p brt bl & car 700.00 475.00
117 A12 10sh red org & bl grn 425.00 425.00
a. 10sh red org & myrtle grn 700.00 275.00
118 A12 £1 bluish sl & car 1,150. 550.00
a. £1 black & red 1,250. 400.00
c. Perf. 15 *17,500.* *3,500.*
Nos. 101-118 (18) 3,594. 2,507.

See note on remainders following No. 49. The £1 in plum and red is from the remainders.

1913-19 ***Perf. 14***
119 A13 ½p green 5.00 1.75
a. Horiz. pair, imperf. vert. *800.00* *750.00*
b. Perf. 15 12.00 15.00
c. Perf. 14x15 *5,750.* 200.00
d. Perf. 15x14 *5,750.* 375.00
120 A13 1p brown rose 4.25 1.40
a. 1p bright rose 5.25 1.40
b. As "a," horiz. pair, imperf btwn. 800.00 575.00
c. Perf. 15, brown rose 3.25 5.50
d. Perf. 15, rose red 625.00 25.00
e. As "d," horiz. pair, imperf btwn. *12,500.*
121 A13 1½p bister 3.75 1.40
a. Perf. 15 29.00 6.00
b. Perf. 15x14
c. Vert. pair, imperf. btwn. *1,850.*
d. Horiz. pair, imperf. btwn. *625.00*
122 A13 2p vio blk & blk 7.50 2.75
a. 2p gray & black 9.25 3.75
b. Perf. 15 7.50 7.50
c. Horiz. pair, imperf. btwn. *5,200.*
123 A13 2½p ultra 4.50 *26.00*
a. Perf. 15 18.00 *40.00*
124 A13 3p org yel & blk 9.00 2.00
a. 3p yellow & black 9.00 2.00
b. Perf. 15 5.50 *19.00*
125 A13 4p org red & blk 11.00 7.50
a. Perf. 15 150.00 18.00
126 A13 5p yel grn & blk 4.25 *11.50*
127 A13 6p lilac & blk 5.50 3.25
a. Perf. 15 5.50 *6.25*
128 A13 8p gray grn & violet 11.50 *55.00*
a. Perf. 15 210.00 175.00
129 A13 10p car rose & bl, perf. 15 7.50 *30.00*
a. Perf. 14 14.00 *50.00*
130 A13 1sh turq bl & blk 7.50 6.50
a. Perf. 15 55.00 11.00
131 A13 1sh lt grn & blk ('19) 80.00 30.00
132 A13 2sh brn & blk, perf. 14 14.00 *17.00*
a. Perf. 15 11.00 *35.00*
133 A13 2sh6p ol gray & vio bl 35.00 *60.00*
a. 2sh6p gray & blue 50.00 32.50
b. Perf. 15 11.50 35.00
134 A13 3sh brt blue & red brown 85.00 *110.00*
a. Perf. 15 700.00 *290.00*
135 A13 5sh grn & bl 55.00 *62.50*
a. Perf. 15 125.00 *140.00*
136 A13 7sh6p black & vio, perf. 15 125.00 *175.00*
a. Perf. 14 260.00 *290.00*
137 A13 10sh yel grn & car 200.00 *310.00*
a. Perf. 15 200.00 *425.00*
138 A13 £1 violet & blk 400.00 *625.00*
a. £1 magenta & black 475.00 *675.00*
b. Perf. 15 1,400. *1,500.*
c. Perf. 15, black & purple 1,250. 1,200.
Nos. 119-138 (20) 1,075. *1,538.*

Three dies were used for the stamps of this issue: 1) Outline at top of cap absent or very faint and broken. Left ear not shaded or outlined and appears white; 2) Outline at top of cap faint and broken. Ear shaded all over, with no outline; 3) Outline at top of cap continuous. Ear shaded all over, with continuous outline.

The existence of #121b has been questioned.

No. 120 Surcharged in Dark Violet:

No. 139

No. 140

1917
139 A13 ½p on 1p 3.00 8.00
a. Inverted surcharge *1,600.* *1,700.*
140 A13 ½p on 1p 2.00 7.50

RIO DE ORO

ˌrē-ō dē ˈōr-ˌō

LOCATION — On the northwest coast of Africa, bordering on the Atlantic Ocean
GOVT. — Spanish Colony
AREA — 71,600 sq. mi.
POP. — 24,000
CAPITAL — Villa Cisneros

Rio de Oro became part of Spanish Sahara.

100 Centimos = 1 Peseta

King Alfonso XIII
A1 A2

Control Numbers on Back in Blue

1905 **Unwmk.** **Typo.** ***Perf. 14***
1 A1 1c blue green 3.75 2.75
2 A1 2c claret 4.50 2.75
3 A1 3c bronze green 4.50 2.75
4 A1 4c dark brown 4.50 2.75
5 A1 5c orange red 4.50 2.75
6 A1 10c dk gray brown 4.50 2.75
7 A1 15c red brown 4.50 2.75
8 A1 25c dark blue 85.00 30.00
9 A1 50c dark green 40.00 12.00
10 A1 75c dark violet 40.00 17.50
11 A1 1p orange brown 30.00 7.25
12 A1 2p buff 90.00 47.50
13 A1 3p dull violet 70.00 16.00
14 A1 4p blue green 70.00 16.00
15 A1 5p dull blue 110.00 35.00
16 A1 10p pale red 275.00 110.00
Nos. 1-16 (16) 840.75 310.50
Set, never hinged 1,300.

For surcharges see Nos. 17, 34-36, 60-66.

No. 8 Handstamp Surcharged in Rose

a

1907
17 A1 15c on 25c dk blue 220.00 60.00
Never hinged 350.00

The surcharge exists inverted, double and in violet, normally positioned. Value for each, $450.

Control Numbers on Back in Blue

1907 **Typo.**
18 A2 1c claret 2.25 2.00
19 A2 2c black 2.75 2.00
20 A2 3c dark brown 2.75 2.00
21 A2 4c red 2.75 2.00
22 A2 5c black brown 2.75 2.00
23 A2 10c chocolate 2.75 2.00
24 A2 15c dark blue 2.75 2.00
25 A2 25c deep green 7.25 2.00
26 A2 50c black violet 7.25 2.00
27 A2 75c orange brown 7.25 2.00
28 A2 1p orange 12.50 2.00
29 A2 2p dull violet 4.00 2.00
30 A2 3p blue green 4.00 2.00
a. Cliché of 4p in plate of 3p 300.00 200.00
31 A2 4p dark blue 6.75 3.50
32 A2 5p red 6.75 3.75
33 A2 10p deep green 6.75 9.00
Nos. 18-33 (16) 81.25 42.25
Set, never hinged 160.00

For surcharges see Nos. 38-43, 67-70.

Nos. 9-10 Handstamp Surcharged in Red

1907
34 A1 10c on 50c dk green 80.00 24.00
Never hinged 140.00
a. "10" omitted 140.00 75.00
Never hinged 190.00
35 A1 10c on 75c dk violet 57.50 24.00
Never hinged 95.00

No. 12 Handstamp Surcharged in Violet

1908
36 A1 2c on 2p buff 52.50 24.00
Never hinged 77.50

No. 36 is found with "1908" measuring 11mm and 12mm.

Same Surcharge in Red on No. 26
38 A2 10c on 50c blk vio 22.50 3.75
Never hinged 35.00

A 5c on 10c (No. 23) was not officially issued.

Nos. 25, 27-28 Handstamp Surcharged Type "a" in Red, Violet or Green

1908
39 A2 15c on 25c dp grn (R) 30.00 3.75
40 A2 15c on 75c org brn (V) 45.00 17.50
a. Green surcharge 50.00 6.75
Never hinged 70.00
41 A2 15c on 1p org (V) 40.00 15.00
42 A2 15c on 1p org (R) 37.50 15.00
43 A2 15c on 1p org (G) 26.00 6.75
Nos. 39-43 (5) 178.50 58.00
Set, never hinged 300.00

As this surcharge is handstamped, it exists in several varieties: double, inverted, in pairs with one surcharge omitted, etc.

A3

Revenue stamps overprinted and surcharged

1908 ***Imperf.***
44 A3 5c on 50c green (C) 75.00 25.00
Never hinged 120.00
45 A3 5c on 50c green (V) 110.00 42.50
Never hinged 175.00

The surcharge, which is handstamped, exists in many variations.

Nos. 44-45 are found with and without control numbers on back. Stamps with control numbers sell at about double the above values.

King Alfonso XIII — A4

Control Numbers on Back in Blue

1909 **Typo.** ***Perf. 14½***
46 A4 1c red .70 .45
47 A4 2c orange .70 .45
48 A4 5c dark green .70 .45
49 A4 10c orange red .70 .45
50 A4 15c blue green .70 .45
51 A4 20c dark violet 1.75 .65
52 A4 25c deep blue 1.75 .65
53 A4 30c claret 1.75 .65
54 A4 40c chocolate 1.75 .65
55 A4 50c red violet 3.25 .65
56 A4 1p dark brown 4.50 3.00
57 A4 4p carmine rose 5.50 4.25
58 A4 10p claret 12.00 7.00
Nos. 46-58 (13) 35.75 19.75
Set, never hinged 60.00

Stamps of 1905 Handstamped in Black

1910
10
Céntimos

1910
60 A1 10c on 5p dull bl 15.00 6.25
a. Red surcharge 67.50 40.00
Never hinged 110.00
62 A1 10c on 10p pale red 15.00 6.25
a. Violet surcharge 110.00 47.50
Never hinged 160.00
b. Green surcharge 110.00 47.50
Never hinged 160.00
65 A1 15c on 3p dull vio 15.00 6.25
a. Imperf. 82.50
Never hinged 140.00
66 A1 15c on 4p blue grn 15.00 6.25
a. 10c on 4p bl grn 700.00 210.00
Never hinged 1,000.
Nos. 60-66 (4) 60.00 25.00
Set, never hinged 90.00

See note after No. 43.

Nos. 31 and 33 Surcharged in Red or Violet

1911-13
67 A2 2c on 4p dk blue (R) 9.00 6.50
68 A2 5c on 10p dp grn (V) 27.50 6.50

Nos. 29-30 Surcharged in Black

10
Céntimos

69 A2 10c on 2p dull vio 15.00 6.50
69A A2 10c on 3p bl grn ('13) 175.00 40.00

Nos. 30, 32 Handstamped Type "a"
69B A2 15c on 3p bl grn ('13) 160.00 19.00
70 A2 15c on 5p red 11.00 7.25
Nos. 67-70 (6) 397.50 85.75
Set, never hinged 525.00

King Alfonso XIII
A5 A6

Control Numbers on Back in Blue

1912 **Typo.** ***Perf. 13½***
71 A5 1c carmine rose .30 .25
72 A5 2c lilac .30 .25
73 A5 5c deep green .30 .25
74 A5 10c red .30 .25
75 A5 15c brown orange .30 .25
76 A5 20c brown .30 .25
77 A5 25c dull blue .30 .25
78 A5 30c dark violet .30 .25
79 A5 40c blue green .30 .25
80 A5 50c lake .30 .25
81 A5 1p red 3.00 .65
82 A5 4p claret 6.00 3.00
83 A5 10p dark brown 8.50 4.75
Nos. 71-83 (13) 20.50 10.90
Set, never hinged 30.00

For overprints see Nos. 97-109.

Control Numbers on Back in Blue

1914 ***Perf. 13***
84 A6 1c olive black .30 .25
85 A6 2c maroon .30 .25
86 A6 5c deep green .30 .25

87	A6	10c	orange red	.30	.25
88	A6	15c	orange red	.30	.25
89	A6	20c	deep claret	.30	.25
90	A6	25c	dark blue	.30	.25
91	A6	30c	blue green	.30	.25
92	A6	40c	brown orange	.30	.25
93	A6	50c	dark brown	.30	.25
94	A6	1p	dull lilac	2.50	1.90
95	A6	4p	carmine rose	6.00	5.25
96	A6	10p	dull violet	8.00	5.25
			Nos. 84-96 (13)	19.50	14.90
			Set, never hinged	30.00	

Nos. 71-83 Overprinted in Black

1917 ***Perf. 13½***

97	A5	1c	carmine rose	8.25	1.10
98	A5	2c	lilac	8.25	1.10
99	A5	5c	deep green	2.40	1.10
100	A5	10c	red	2.40	1.10
101	A5	15c	orange brn	2.40	1.10
102	A5	20c	brown	2.40	1.10
103	A5	25c	dull blue	2.40	1.10
104	A5	30c	dark violet	2.40	1.10
105	A5	40c	blue green	2.40	1.10
106	A5	50c	lake	2.40	1.10
107	A5	1p	red	11.50	3.75
108	A5	4p	claret	20.00	5.25
109	A5	10p	dark brown	32.50	7.75
			Nos. 97-109 (13)	99.70	27.75
			Set, never hinged	150.00	

Nos. 97-109 exist with overprint inverted or double (value 50 percent over normal) and in dark blue (value twice normal).

King Alfonso XIII — A7

Control Numbers on Back in Blue

1919 **Typo.** ***Perf. 13***

114	A7	1c	brown	.75	.40
115	A7	2c	claret	.75	.40
116	A7	5c	light green	.75	.40
117	A7	10c	carmine	.75	.40
118	A7	15c	orange	.75	.40
119	A7	20c	orange	.75	.40
120	A7	25c	blue	.75	.45
121	A7	30c	green	.75	.45
122	A7	40c	vermilion	.75	.45
123	A7	50c	brown	.75	.45
124	A7	1p	lilac	6.00	3.00
125	A7	4p	rose	10.50	5.25
126	A7	10p	violet	18.00	7.50
			Nos. 114-126 (13)	42.00	19.95
			Set, never hinged	62.50	

A8

A9

Control Numbers on Back in Blue

1920 ***Perf. 13***

127	A8	1c	gray lilac	.70	.40
128	A8	2c	rose	.70	.40
129	A8	5c	light red	.70	.40
130	A8	10c	lilac	.70	.40
131	A8	15c	light brown	.70	.40
132	A8	20c	greenish blue	.70	.40
133	A8	25c	yellow	.70	.45
134	A8	30c	dull blue	4.25	3.50
135	A8	40c	orange	2.50	1.50
136	A8	50c	dull rose	2.50	1.50
137	A8	1p	gray green	2.50	1.50
138	A8	4p	lilac rose	4.50	3.25
139	A8	10p	brown	11.00	7.50
			Nos. 127-139 (13)	32.15	21.60
			Set, never hinged	60.00	

Control Numbers on Back in Blue

1922

140	A9	1c	yellow	.70	.55
141	A9	2c	red brown	.70	.55
142	A9	5c	blue green	.70	.55
143	A9	10c	pale red	.70	.55
144	A9	15c	myrtle green	.70	.55
145	A9	20c	turq blue	.70	.60
146	A9	25c	deep blue	.70	.60
147	A9	30c	deep rose	1.50	1.10
148	A9	40c	violet	1.50	1.10
149	A9	50c	orange	1.50	1.10
150	A9	1p	lilac	4.00	1.60
151	A9	4p	claret	6.50	3.50
152	A9	10p	dark brown	9.50	7.50
			Nos. 140-152 (13)	29.40	19.85
			Set, never hinged	65.00	

For subsequent issues see Spanish Sahara.

ROMANIA

rō-ˈmā-nēə

(Rumania, Roumania)

LOCATION — Southeastern Europe, bordering on the Black Sea
GOVT. — Kingdom
AREA — 91,699 sq. mi.
POP. — 22,600,000 (est. 1984)
CAPITAL — Bucharest

Romania was formed in 1861 from the union of the principalities of Moldavia and Walachia in 1859. It became a kingdom in 1881. Following World War I, the original territory was considerably enlarged by the addition of Bessarabia, Bukovina, Transylvania, Crisana, Maramures and Banat.

40 Parale = 1 Piaster
100 Bani = 1 Leu (plural "Lei") (1868)

Catalogue values for unused stamps in this country are for Never Hinged items, beginning with Scott 475 in the regular postage section, Scott B82 in the semi-postal section, Scott CB1 in the airpost semi-postal section, Scott J82 in the postage due section, Scott O1 in the official section, Scott RA16 in the postal tax section, and Scott RAJ1 in the postal tax postage due section.

Watermarks

Wmk. 95 — Wavy Lines

Wmk. 163 — Coat of Arms

No. 163 is not a true watermark, having been impressed after the paper was manufactured.

Wmk. 164 — PR

Wmk. 165 — PR Interlaced

Wmk. 167 — Coat of Arms Covering 25 Stamps

Reduced illustration.

Wmk. 200 — PR

Wmk. 225 — Crown over PTT, Multiple

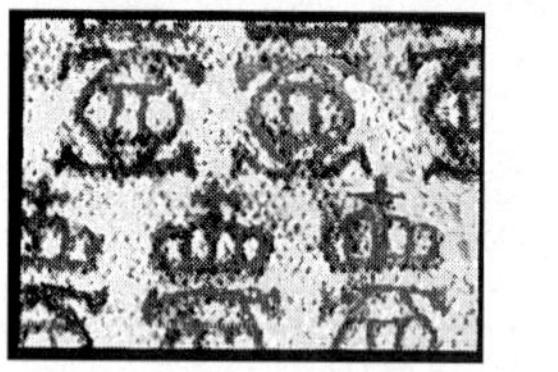

Wmk. 230 — Crowns and Monograms

Values for unused stamps are for examples with original gum as defined in the catalogue introduction except for Nos. 1-4 which are valued without gum.

Moldavia

Coat of Arms
A1 A2

Handstamped

1858, July **Unwmk.** ***Imperf.***

Laid Paper

1	A1	27pa	blk, *rose*	*60,000*	*25,000.*
a.			Tête bêche pair		
2	A1	54pa	blue, *grn*	*15,500.*	*8,000.*
3	A1	108pa	blue, *rose*	*35,000.*	*12,000.*

Wove Paper

4	A1	81pa	blue, *bl*	*50,000.*	*55,000.*

Full margins = 3mm.

Cut to shape or octagonally, Nos. 1-4 sell for one-fourth to one-third of these prices.

1858

Bluish Wove Paper

5	A2	5pa	black	*12,000.*	*4,750.*
a.			Tête bêche pair		
6	A2	40pa	blue	175.	125.
a.			Tête bêche pair	*750.*	*2,000.*
7	A2	80pa	red	*6,750.*	*400.*
a.			Tête bêche pair		

Full margins = 3mm.

1859

White Wove Paper

8	A2	5pa	black	*9,000.*	*5,000.*
a.			Tête bêche pair		
b.			Frame broken at bottom	100.	
c.			As "b," tête bêche pair	325.	
9	A2	40pa	blue	110.	100.
b.			Tête bêche pair	375.	*1,150.*
10	A2	80pa	red	300.	160.
b.			Tête bêche pair	*1,050.*	*3,100.*

Full margins = 3mm.

No. 8b has a break in the frame at bottom below "A." It was never placed in use.

Moldavia-Walachia

Coat of Arms — A3

Printed by Hand from Single Dies

1862

White Laid Paper

11	A3	3pa	orange	200.00	*2,250.*
a.			3pa yellow	210.00	*2,250.*
12	A3	6pa	carmine	190.00	250.00
13	A3	6pa	red	190.00	250.00
14	A3	30pa	blue	55.00	75.00
			Nos. 11-14 (4)	635.00	2,825.

White Wove Paper

15	A3	3pa	orange yel	55.00	*160.00*
a.			3pa lemon	60.00	*160.00*
16	A3	6pa	carmine	55.00	*110.00*
17	A3	6pa	vermilion	35.00	*90.00*
18	A3	30pa	blue	50.00	30.00
			Nos. 15-18 (4)	195.00	390.00

Tête bêche pairs

11b	A3	3pa	orange	1,000.	
12a	A3	6pa	carmine	1,000.	1,250.
14a	A3	30pa	blue	150.00	1,000.
15b	A3	3pa	orange yellow	140.00	*1,000.*
16a	A3	6pa	carmine	150.00	1,000.
17a	A3	6pa	vermilion	100.00	1,000.
18a	A3	30pa	blue	140.00	1,000.

Full margins = 2mm.

Nos. 11-18 were printed with a hand press, one at a time, from single dies. The impressions were very irregularly placed and occasionally overlapped. Sheets of 32 (4x8). The 3rd and 4th rows were printed inverted, making the second and third rows tête bêche. All values come in distinct shades, frequently even on the same sheet. The paper of this and the following issues through No. 52 often shows a bluish, grayish or yellowish tint.

1864 **Typographed from Plates**

White Wove Paper

19	A3	3pa	yellow	32.50	*1,250.*
a.			Tête bêche pair	200.00	
b.			Pair, one sideways	100.00	
20	A3	6pa	deep rose	4.50	
a.			Tête bêche pair	27.50	
b.			Pair, one sideways	11.00	
21	A3	30pa	deep blue	5.25	*60.00*
a.			Tête bêche pair	32.50	
b.			Pair, one sideways	12.00	
c.			Bluish wove paper	*125.00*	
			Nos. 19-21 (3)	42.25	

Full margins = 1¼mm.

Stamps of 1862 issue range from very clear to blurred impressions but rarely have broken or deformed characteristics. The 1864 issue, though rarely blurred, usually have various imperfections in the letters and numbers. These include breaks, malformations, occasional dots at left of the crown or above the "R" of "PAR," a doton the middle stroke of the "F," and many other bulges, breaks and spots of color.

The 1864 issue were printed in sheets of 40 (5x8). The first and second rows were inverted. Clichés in the third row were placed sideways, 4 with head to right and 4 with head to left, making one tête bêche pair. The fourth and fifth rows were normally placed.

No. 20 was never placed in use.

All values exist in shades, light to dark.

Counterfeit cancellations exist on #11-21.

Three stamps in this design — 2pa, 5pa, 20pa — were printed on white wove paper in 1864, but never placed in use. Value, set $9.

Romania

Prince Alexandru Ioan Cuza — A4

TWENTY PARALES:

Type I — The central oval does not touch the inner frame. The "I" of "DECI" extends above and below the other letters.

Type II — The central oval touches the frame at the bottom. The "I" of the "DECI" is the same height as the other letters.

1865, Jan. **Unwmk.** **Litho.** ***Imperf.***

22	A4	2pa	orange	30.00	*125.00*
a.			2pa yellow	42.50	*150.00*
b.			2pa ocher	90.00	*175.00*

23	A4	5pa blue	20.00	*150.00*
24	A4	20pa red, type I	7.50	10.00
a.		Bluish paper	175.00	
25	A4	20pa red, type II	7.50	10.00
a.		Bluish paper	175.00	
		Nos. 22-25 (4)	65.00	295.00

Full margins = 1¼mm.

The 20pa types are found se-tenant.

White Laid Paper

26	A4	2pa orange	37.50	*125.00*
a.		2pa ocher	75.00	
27	A4	5pa blue	60.00	*275.00*

Full margins = 1¼mm.

Prince Carol — A5

Type I — A6

Type II — A7

TWENTY PARALES:
Type I — A6. The Greek border at the upper right goes from right to left.
Type II — A7. The Greek border at the upper right goes from left to right.

1866-67

Thin Wove Paper

29	A5	2pa blk, *yellow*	8.00	*45.00*
a.		Thick paper	45.00	*200.00*
30	A5	5pa blk, *dk bl*	35.00	*275.00*
a.		5pa black, *indigo*	75.00	—
b.		Thick paper	45.00	*275.00*
31	A6	20pa blk, *rose*, (I)	9.00	9.00
a.		Dot in Greek border, thin paper	350.00	125.00
b.		Thick paper	95.00	45.00
c.		Dot in Greek border, thick paper	125.00	72.50
32	A7	20pa blk, *rose*, (II)	9.00	9.00
a.		Thick paper	100.00	50.00
		Nos. 29-32 (4)	61.00	338.00

Full margins = 1¼mm.

The 20pa types are found se-tenant.
Faked cancellations are known on Nos. 22-27, 29-32.
The white dot of Nos. 31a and 31c occurs in extreme upper right border.
Thick paper was used in 1866, thin in 1867.

Prince Carol
A8 A9

1868-70

33	A8	2b orange	22.50	12.50
a.		2b yellow	30.00	27.50
34	A8	3b violet ('70)	22.50	20.00
35	A8	4b dk blue	45.00	25.00
36	A8	18b scarlet	175.00	9.00
a.		18b rose	175.00	9.00
		Nos. 33-36 (4)	265.00	66.50

Full margins = 1¼mm.

1869

37	A9	5b orange yel	52.50	20.00
a.		5b deep orange	55.00	*50.00*
38	A9	10b blue	25.00	12.50
a.		10b ultramarine	55.00	17.50
b.		10b indigo	65.00	27.50
40	A9	15b vermilion	25.00	12.50
41	A9	25b orange & blue	25.00	12.50
42	A9	50b blue & red	140.00	17.50
a.		50b indigo & red	150.00	20.00
		Nos. 37-42 (5)	267.50	75.00

Full margins = 1mm.

No. 40 on vertically laid paper was not issued. Value $1,250.

Prince Carol
A10 A11

1871-72 ***Imperf.***

43	A10	5b rose	32.50	11.00
a.		5b vermilion	35.00	12.50
44	A10	10b orange yel	47.50	17.50
a.		Vertically laid paper	*450.00*	*450.00*
45	A10	10b blue	125.00	30.00
46	A10	15b red	125.00	65.00
47	A10	25b olive brown	30.00	21.00
		Nos. 43-47 (5)	360.00	144.50

Full margins = 1mm.

1872

48	A10	10b ultra	20.00	26.00
a.		Vertically laid paper	100.00	150.00
b.		10b greenish blue	110.00	125.00
49	A10	50b blue & red	150.00	165.00

Full margins = 1mm.

No. 48 is a provisional issue printed from a new plate in which the head is placed further right.
Faked cancellations are found on No. 49.

1872 ***Perf. 12½***

Wove Paper

50	A10	5b rose	40.00	20.00
a.		5b vermilion	*1,000.*	*500.00*
51	A10	10b blue	47.50	20.00
a.		10b ultramarine	50.00	25.00
52	A10	25b dark brown	22.50	22.50
		Nos. 50-52 (3)	110.00	62.50

No. 43a with faked perforation is frequently offered as No. 50a.

Paris Print, Fine Impression

1872 **Typo.** ***Perf. 14x13½***

Tinted Paper

53	A11	1½b brnz grn, *bluish*	7.50	.75
54	A11	3b green, *bluish*	12.50	1.25
55	A11	5b bis, *pale buff*	9.00	1.00
56	A11	10b blue	8.50	1.10
57	A11	15b red brn, *pale buff*	75.00	7.50
58	A11	25b org, *pale buff*	77.50	8.00
59	A11	50b rose, *pale rose*	100.00	12.50
		Nos. 53-59 (7)	290.00	32.10

Nos. 53-59 exist imperf.

Bucharest Print, Rough Impression

Perf. 11, 11½, 13½, and Compound

1876-79

60	A11	1½b brnz grn, *bluish*	5.00	.50
61	A11	5b bis, *yelsh*	13.00	.55
b.		Printed on both sides		*75.00*
62	A11	10b bl, *yelsh* ('77)	14.00	.75
a.		10b pale bl, *yelsh*	12.00	.75
b.		10b dark blue, *yelsh*	22.50	1.25
d.		Cliché of 5b in plate of 10b ('79)	190.00	80.00
63	A11	10b ultra, *yelsh* ('77)	25.00	1.25
64	A11	15b red brn, *yelsh*	27.50	1.25
a.		Printed on both sides		*100.00*
65	A11	30b org red, *yelsh* ('78)	125.00	10.00
a.		Printed on both sides		*210.00*
		Nos. 60-65 (6)	209.50	14.30

#60-65 are valued in the grade of fine.
#62d has been reprinted in dark blue. The originals are in dull blue. Value of reprint, $35.

Perf. 11, 11½, 13½ and Compound

1879

66	A11	1½b blk, *yelsh*	2.50	.35
b.		Imperf.		*12.00*
67	A11	3b ol grn, *bluish*	7.00	1.00
a.		Diagonal half used as 1½b on cover		
68	A11	5b green, *bluish*	2.50	.35
69	A11	10b rose, *yelsh*	9.00	.40
b.		Cliché of 5b in plate of 10b	100.00	*475.00*
70	A11	15b rose red, *yelsh*	35.00	5.00
71	A11	25b blue, *yelsh*	75.00	4.50
72	A11	50b bister, *yelsh*	55.00	6.50
		Nos. 66-72 (7)	186.00	18.10

#66-72 are valued in the grade of fine.
There are two varieties of the numerals on the 15b and 50b.
No. 69b has been reprinted in dark rose. Originals are in pale rose. Value of reprint, $40.

King Carol I
A12 A13

1880

White Paper

73	A12	15b brown	7.50	.40
74	A12	25b blue	14.00	.60

#73-74 are valued in the grade of fine.
No. 74 exists imperf.

Perf. 13½, 11½ & Compound

1885-89

75	A13	1½b black	2.00	.50
a.		Printed on both sides		
76	A13	3b violet	5.00	.60
a.		Half used as 1½b on cover		
77	A13	5b green	52.50	6.00
78	A13	15b red brown	10.00	.85
79	A13	25b blue	11.00	1.00
		Nos. 75-79 (5)	80.50	8.95

Tinted Paper

80	A13	1½b blk, *bluish*	3.50	.65
81	A13	3b vio, *bluish*	3.50	.75
82	A13	3b ol grn, *bluish*	4.25	.65
83	A13	5b bl grn, *bluish*	4.25	.60
84	A13	10b rose, *pale buff*	4.25	.65
85	A13	15b red brn, *pale buff*	15.00	.75
86	A13	25b bl, *pale buff*	15.00	1.00
87	A13	50b bis, *pale buff*	55.00	6.00
		Nos. 80-87 (8)	104.75	11.05

1889 **Wmk. 163**

Thin Pale Yellowish Paper

88	A13	1½b black	22.50	3.00
89	A13	3b violet	17.50	3.00
90	A13	5b green	17.50	3.00
91	A13	10b rose	17.50	3.25
92	A13	15b red brown	50.00	5.50
93	A13	25b dark blue	40.00	5.00
		Nos. 88-93 (6)	165.00	22.75

King Carol I
A14 A15

1890 ***Perf. 13½, 11½ & Compound***

94	A14	1½b maroon	4.25	.80
95	A14	3b violet	22.50	1.10
96	A14	5b emerald	9.50	1.10
97	A14	10b red	11.00	2.00
a.		10b rose	15.00	3.50
98	A14	15b dk brown	17.50	2.00
99	A14	25b gray blue	13.00	1.60
100	A14	50b orange	65.00	13.50
		Nos. 94-100 (7)	142.75	22.10

1891 **Unwmk.**

101	A14	1½b lilac rose	1.40	.30
b.		Printed on both sides		*65.00*
102	A14	3b lilac	1.10	.40
a.		3b violet	2.00	.50
b.		Printed on both sides		
c.		Impressions of 5b on back	*100.00*	*75.00*
103	A14	5b emerald	2.10	.50
104	A14	10b pale red	7.75	.60
a.		Printed on both sides	*140.00*	*110.00*
105	A14	15b gray brown	9.50	.40
106	A14	25b gray blue	5.50	.70
107	A14	50b orange	57.50	6.00
		Nos. 101-107 (7)	84.85	8.90

Nos. 101-107 exist imperf.

1891

108	A15	1½b claret	2.00	1.25
109	A15	3b lilac	2.00	1.25
110	A15	5b emerald	2.50	2.25
111	A15	10b red	2.75	2.25
112	A15	15b gray brown	2.25	2.00
		Nos. 108-112 (5)	11.50	9.00

25th year of the reign of King Carol I.

1894 **Wmk. 164**

113	A14	3b lilac	6.50	2.50
114	A14	5b pale green	6.50	2.50
115	A14	25b gray blue	10.00	4.50
116	A14	50b orange	20.00	10.00
		Nos. 113-116 (4)	43.00	19.50

King Carol I
A17 A18

A19

A20

A21

A23

1893-98 **Wmk. 164 & 200**

117	A17	1b pale brown	.80	.20
118	A17	1½b black	.60	.20
119	A18	3b chocolate	.80	.20
120	A19	5b blue	1.10	.20
a.		Cliché of the 25b in the plate of 5b	47.50	*60.00*
121	A19	5b yel grn ('98)	3.25	.35
a.		5b emerald	4.00	.35
122	A20	10b emerald	1.60	.20
123	A20	10b rose ('98)	3.25	.30
124	A21	15b rose	1.60	.20
125	A21	15b black ('98)	3.25	.30
126	A19	25b violet	2.50	.20
127	A19	25b indigo ('98)	5.75	.45
128	A19	40b gray grn	13.50	.50
129	A19	50b orange	6.50	.25
130	A23	1 l bis & rose	13.50	.35
131	A23	2 l orange & brn	17.00	.55
		Nos. 117-131 (15)	75.00	4.45

This watermark may be found in four versions (Wmks. 164, 200 and variations). The paper also varies in thickness.
A 3b orange of type A18; 10b brown, type A20; 15b rose, type A21, and 25b bright green with similar but different border, all watermarked "P R," were prepared but never issued. Value, each $15.
See Nos. 132-157, 224-229. For overprints and surcharges see Romanian Post Offices in the Turkish Empire Nos. 1-6, 10-11.

King Carol I — A24

Perf. 11½, 13½ and Compound

1900-03 **Unwmk.**

Thin Paper, Tinted Rose on Back

132	A17	1b pale brown	.75	.25
133	A24	1b brown ('01)	.75	.25
134	A24	1b black ('03)	.75	.25
135	A18	3b red brown	1.00	.20
136	A19	5b emerald	1.40	.20
137	A20	10b rose	1.75	.20
138	A21	15b black	1.40	.20
139	A21	15b lil gray ('01)	1.40	.20
140	A21	15b dk vio ('03)	1.40	.25
141	A19	25b blue	2.50	.25
142	A19	40b gray grn	5.00	.30
143	A19	50b orange	9.50	.40
144	A23	1 l bis & rose ('01)	20.00	.65
145	A23	1 l grn & blk ('03)	14.00	.90
146	A23	2 l org & brn ('01)	14.00	.90
147	A23	2 l red brn & blk ('03)	12.00	1.00
		Nos. 132-147 (16)	87.60	6.40

#132 inscribed BANI; #133-134 BAN.

1900, July **Wmk. 167**

148	A17	1b pale brown	5.50	2.00
149	A18	3b red brown	4.75	2.00
150	A19	5b emerald	5.50	2.00
151	A20	10b rose	5.50	2.00
152	A21	15b black	7.00	3.25
153	A19	25b blue	8.00	3.75
154	A19	40b gray grn	14.00	4.25
155	A19	50b orange	14.00	4.25

156 A23 1 l bis & rose 16.00 5.25
157 A23 2 l orange & brn 21.00 6.50
Nos. 148-157 (10) 101.25 35.25

Mail Coach Leaving PO — A25

King Carol I and Façade of New Post Office — A26

1903 Unwmk. *Perf. 14x13½*
Thin Paper, Tinted Rose on Face

158 A25 1b gray brown *1.00* .40
159 A25 3b brown violet *1.75* .75
160 A25 5b pale green *4.00* 1.60
161 A25 10b rose *3.50* 1.60
162 A25 15b black *3.50* 1.60
163 A25 25b blue *15.00* 6.50
164 A25 40b dull green *20.00* 8.50
165 A25 50b orange *27.50* 11.00
Nos. 158-165 (8) *76.25* 31.95

Counterfeits are plentiful. See note after No. 172. See No. 428.

1903 Engr. *Perf. 13½x14*
Thick Toned Paper

166 A26 15b black 2.00 .80
167 A26 25b blue 6.00 2.00
168 A26 40b gray grn 8.00 3.25
169 A26 50b orange 8.00 3.50
170 A26 1 l dk brown 8.00 3.50
171 A26 2 l dull red 75.00 30.00
a. 2 l orange (error) 87.50 75.00
172 A26 5 l dull violet 67.50 30.00
a. 5 l red violet 75.00 30.00
Nos. 166-172 (7) 174.50 73.05

Opening of the new PO in Bucharest (Nos. 158-172).
Counterfeits exist.

Prince Carol Taking Oath of Allegiance, 1866 — A27

Prince in Royal Carriage A28

Prince Carol at Calafat in 1877 — A29

Prince Carol Shaking Hands with His Captive, Osman Pasha — A30

Carol I as Prince in 1866 and King in 1906 — A31

Romanian Army Crossing Danube A32

Romanian Troops Return to Bucharest in 1878 — A33

Prince Carol at Head of His Command in 1877 — A34

King Carol I at the Cathedral in 1896 — A35

King Carol I at Shrine of St. Nicholas, 1904 — A36

1906 Engr. *Perf. 12*

176 A27 1b bister & blk .50 .25
177 A28 3b red brn & blk 1.25 .25
178 A29 5b dp grn & blk 1.50 .25
179 A30 10b carmine & blk .75 .25
180 A31 15b dull vio & blk .75 .25
181 A32 25b ultra & blk 5.50 4.50
a. 25b olive green & black 8.75 5.00
182 A33 40b dk brn & blk 1.50 1.50
183 A34 50b bis brn & blk 1.60 1.50
184 A35 1 l vermilion & blk 1.75 1.75
185 A36 2 l orange & blk 2.00 1.90
Nos. 176-185 (10) 17.10 12.40

40 years' rule of Carol I as Prince & King.
No. 181a was never placed in use. Cancellations were by favor.

King Carol I — A37

1906

186 A37 1b bister & blk 1.00 .45
187 A37 3b red brn & blk 1.75 .85
188 A37 5b dp grn & blk 1.50 .75
189 A37 10b carmine & blk 1.50 .75
190 A37 15b dl vio & blk 1.50 .75
191 A37 25b ultra & blk 12.00 6.75
192 A37 40b dk brn & blk 3.50 1.50
193 A37 50b bis brn & blk 3.50 1.50
194 A37 1 l red & blk 3.50 1.50
195 A37 2 l orange & blk 3.50 1.50
Nos. 186-195 (10) 33.25 16.30

25th anniversary of the Kingdom.

Plowman and Angel — A38

Exposition Building — A39

Exposition Buildings
A40 A41

King Carol I — A42

Queen Elizabeth (Carmen Sylva) — A43

1906 Typo. *Perf. 11½, 13½*

196 A38 5b yel grn & blk 1.10 .55
197 A38 10b carmine & blk 1.75 .80
198 A39 15b violet & blk 4.50 1.10
199 A39 25b blue & blk 4.75 1.40
200 A40 30b red & blk brn 5.75 1.40
201 A40 40b green & blk brn 7.00 1.60
202 A41 50b orange & blk 5.75 2.00
203 A41 75b lt brn & dk brn 5.75 2.00
204 A42 1.50 l red lil & blk brn 65.00 35.00
a. Center inverted
205 A42 2.50 l yellow & brn 24.00 18.00
a. Center inverted
206 A43 3 l brn org & brn 18.00 17.00
Nos. 196-206 (11) 143.35 80.85

General Exposition. They were sold at post offices July 29-31, 1906, and were valid only for those three days. Those sold at the exposition are overprinted "S E" in black. Remainders were sold privately, both unused and canceled to order, by the Exposition promoters. Value, unused or used, $275.

A44

A45

King Carol I — A46

Perf. 11½, 13½ & Compound
1908-18 Engr.

207 A44 5b pale yel grn 2.00 .20
208 A44 10b carmine .70 .20
209 A45 15b purple 11.50 2.25
210 A44 25b deep blue 1.25 .20
211 A44 40b brt green .85 .20
212 A44 40b dk brn ('18) 5.25 2.25
213 A44 50b orange .65 .20
214 A44 50b lt red ('18) 2.00 .70
215 A44 1 l brown 1.75 .35
216 A44 2 l red 10.00 2.25
Nos. 207-216 (10) 35.95 8.80

Perf. 13½x14, 11½, 13½ & Compound
1909-18 Typo.

217 A46 1b black .60 .20
218 A46 3b red brown 1.25 .20
219 A46 5b yellow grn .60 .20
220 A46 10b rose 1.25 .20
221 A46 15b dull violet 17.50 11.00
222 A46 15b olive green 1.25 .20
223 A46 15b red brn ('18) 1.10 .65
Nos. 217-223 (7) 23.55 12.65

Nos. 217-219, 222 exist imperf.
No. 219 in black is a chemical changeling.
For surcharge and overprints see Nos. 240-242, 245-247, J50-J51, RA1-RA2, RA11-RA12, Romanian Post Offices in the Turkish Empire 7-9.

Types of 1893-99
1911-19 White Paper Unwmk.

224 A17 1½b straw 1.75 .45
225 A19 25b deep blue ('18) .55 .20
226 A19 40b gray brn ('19) 1.00 .20
227 A19 50b dull red ('19) 1.00 .20
228 A23 1 l gray grn ('18) 1.75 .20
229 A23 2 l orange ('18) 2.00 .20
Nos. 224-229 (6) 8.05 1.45

For overprints see Romanian Post Offices in the Turkish Empire Nos. 10-11.

Romania Holding Flag — A47

Romanian Crown and Old Fort on Danube — A48

Troops Crossing Danube — A49

View of Turtucaia — A50

Mircea the Great and Carol I — A51

View of Silistra — A52

Perf. 11½x13½, 13½x11½
1913, Dec. 25

230 A47 1b black .55 .20
231 A48 3b ol gray & choc 1.75 .40
232 A49 5b yel grn & blk brn 1.10 .20
233 A50 10b org & gray .55 .20
234 A51 15b bister & vio 1.75 .40
235 A52 25b blue & choc 2.25 .65
236 A49 40b bis & red vio 3.50 1.40
237 A48 50b yellow & bl 4.25 3.25
238 A48 1 l bl & ol bis 11.50 7.50
239 A48 2 l org red & rose 16.50 8.75
Nos. 230-239 (10) 43.70 22.95

Romania's annexation of Silistra.

No. 217 Handstamped in Red

Perf. 13½x14, 11½, 13½ & Compound

1918, May 1

No.	Design	Description	Unused	Used
240	A46	25b on 1b black	2.25	2.25

This handstamp is found inverted.

No. 219 and 220 Overprinted in Black

1918

No.	Design	Description	Unused	Used
241	A46	5b yellow green	.45	.40
a.		Inverted overprint	3.25	3.25
b.		Double overprint	3.25	3.25
242	A46	10b rose	.50	.40
a.		Inverted overprint	3.25	3.25
b.		Double overprint	3.25	3.25

Nos. 217, 219 and 220 Overprinted in Red or Black

1919, Nov. 8

No.	Design	Description	Unused	Used
245	A46	1b black (R)	.40	.20
a.		Inverted overprint	6.75	
b.		Double overprint	10.00	2.25
246	A46	5b yel grn (Bk)	.40	.20
a.		Double overprint	10.00	3.25
b.		Inverted overprint	6.75	2.00
247	A46	10b rose (Bk)	.40	.20
a.		Inverted overprint	6.75	2.00
b.		Double overprint	10.00	3.00
		Nos. 245-247 (3)	1.20	.60

Recovery of Transylvania and the return of the King to Bucharest.

King Ferdinand
A53 A54

1920-22 **Typo.**

No.	Design	Description	Unused	Used
248	A53	1b black	.20	.20
249	A53	5b yellow grn	.20	.20
250	A53	10b rose	.20	.20
251	A53	15b red brown	.75	.25
252	A53	25b deep blue	1.50	.40
253	A53	25b brown	.75	.25
254	A53	40b gray brown	1.25	.35
255	A53	50b salmon	.35	.20
256	A53	1 l gray grn	1.25	.20
257	A53	1 l rose	.75	.25
258	A53	2 l orange	1.25	.25
259	A53	2 l dp blue	1.25	.25
260	A53	2 l rose ('22)	3.00	1.75
		Nos. 248-260 (13)	12.70	4.75

Nos. 248-260 are printed on two papers: coarse, grayish paper with bits of colored fiber, and thinner white paper of better quality.

Nos. 248-251, 253 exist imperf.

I II III

I II I II

TWO LEI:

Type I — The "2" is thin, with tail 2½mm wide. Top of "2" forms a hook.

Type II — The "2" is thick, with tail 3mm wide. Top of "2" forms a ball.

Type III — The "2" is similar to type II. The "E" of "LEI" is larger and about 2mm wide.

THREE LEI:

Type I — Top of "3" begins in a point. Top and middle bars of "E" of "LEI" are without serifs.

Type II — Top of "3" begins in a ball. Top and middle bars of "E" of "LEI" have serifs.

FIVE LEI:

Type I — The "5" is 2½mm wide. The end of the final stroke of the "L" of "LEI" almost touches the vertical stroke.

Type II — The "5" is 3mm wide and the lines are broader than in type I. The end of the final stroke of the "L" of "LEI" is separated from the vertical by a narrow space.

Perf. 13½x14, 11½, 13½ & Compound

1920-26

No.	Design	Description	Unused	Used
261	A54	3b black	.20	.20
262	A54	5b black	.20	.20
263	A54	10b yel grn ('25)	.20	.20
a.		10b olive green ('25)	.40	
264	A54	25b bister brn	.20	.20
265	A54	25b salmon	.20	.20
266	A54	30b violet	.20	.20
267	A54	50b orange	.20	.20
268	A54	60b gray grn	1.00	.45
269	A54	1 l violet	.20	.20
270	A54	2 l rose (I)	1.25	.25
a.		2 l claret (I)	25.00	
271	A54	2 l lt green (II)	.70	.20
a.		2 l light green (I)	.95	.20
b.		2 l light green (III)	.80	.20
272	A54	3 l blue (I)	2.60	.35
273	A54	3 l buff (II)	2.60	.25
a.		3 l buff (I)	11.00	.65
274	A54	3 l salmon (II)	.20	.20
a.		3 l salmon (I)	1.60	1.00
275	A54	3 l car rose (II)	.65	.20
276	A54	5 l emer (I)	2.10	.25
277	A54	5 l lt brn (II)	.45	.20
a.		5 l light brown (I)	1.60	.55
278	A54	6 l blue	2.60	.85
279	A54	6 l carmine	5.75	1.40
280	A54	6 l ol grn ('26)	2.50	.45
281	A54	7½ l pale bl	2.10	.25
282	A54	10 l deep blue	2.10	.25
		Nos. 261-282 (22)	28.20	7.15

#273 and 273a, 274 and 274a, exist se-tenant. The 50b exists in three types.

For surcharge see No. Q7.

Alba Iulia Cathedral
A55

King Ferdinand
A56

Coat of Arms — A57

Queen Marie as Nurse — A58

Michael the Brave and King Ferdinand
A59

King Ferdinand
A60

Queen Marie — A61

Perf. 13½x14, 13½, 1½ & Compound

1922, Oct. 15 **Photo.** **Wmk. 95**

No.	Design	Description	Unused	Used
283	A55	5b black	.20	.25
a.		Engraver's name omitted	7.50	.90
284	A56	25b chocolate	.65	.25
285	A57	50b dp green	.75	.30
286	A58	1 l olive grn	1.00	.60
287	A59	2 l carmine	1.10	.60
288	A60	3 l blue	2.10	1.00
289	A61	6 l violet	8.50	6.00
		Nos. 283-289 (7)	14.30	9.00

Coronation of King Ferdinand I and Queen Marie on Oct. 15, 1922, at Alba Iulia. All values exist imperforate. Value $90, unused or used.

King Ferdinand
A62 A63

1926, July 1 **Unwmk.** ***Perf. 11***

No.	Design	Description	Unused	Used
291	A62	10b yellow grn	.40	.30
292	A62	25b orange	.40	.30
293	A62	50b orange brn	.40	.30
294	A63	1 l dk violet	.40	.30
295	A63	2 l dk green	.40	.30
296	A63	3 l brown car	.40	.30
297	A63	5 l black brn	.40	.30
298	A63	6 l dk olive	.40	.30
a.		6 l bright blue (error)	65.00	65.00
300	A63	9 l slate	.40	.30
301	A63	10 l brt blue	.40	.30
b.		10 l brown carmine (error)	65.00	65.00
		Nos. 291-301 (10)	4.00	3.00

60th birthday of King Ferdinand.

Exist imperf. Value $35, unused or used. Imperf. examples with watermark 95 are proofs.

King Carol I and King Ferdinand
A69

King Ferdinand
A70

A71

1927, Aug. 1 ***Perf. 13½***

No.	Design	Description	Unused	Used
308	A69	25b brown vio	.25	.20
309	A70	30b gray blk	.20	.20
310	A71	50b dk green	.25	.20
311	A69	1 l bluish slate	.25	.20
312	A70	2 l dp green	.25	.25
313	A70	3 l violet	.35	.35
314	A71	4 l dk brown	.50	.40
315	A71	4.50 l henna brn	1.50	1.00
316	A70	5 l red brown	.35	.35
317	A71	6 l carmine	.85	.45
318	A69	7.50 l grnsh bl	.45	.35
319	A69	10 l brt blue	1.50	.45
		Nos. 308-319 (12)	6.70	4.40

50th anniversary of Romania's independence from Turkish suzerainty.

Some values exist imperf. All exist imperf. and with value numerals omitted.

King Michael
A72 A73

Perf. 13½x14 (25b, 50b); 13½

1928-29 **Typo.** **Unwmk.**

Size: 19x25mm

No.	Design	Description	Unused	Used
320	A72	25b black	.25	.20
321	A72	30b fawn ('29)	.40	.20
322	A72	50b olive grn	.25	.20

Photo.

Size: 18½x24½mm

No.	Design	Description	Unused	Used
323	A73	1 l violet	.45	.20
324	A73	2 l dp green	.45	.20
325	A73	3 l brt rose	.90	.20
326	A73	5 l red brown	1.40	.20
327	A73	7.50 l ultra	6.25	.45
328	A73	10 l blue	5.25	.20
		Nos. 320-328 (9)	15.60	2.05

See Nos. 343-345, 353-357. For overprints see Nos. 359-368A.

Parliament House, Bessarabia — A74

Designs: 1 l, 2 l, Parliament House, Bessarabia. 3 l, 5 l, 20 l, Hotin Fortress. 7.50 l, 10 l, Fortress Cetatea Alba.

1928, Apr. 29 **Wmk. 95** ***Perf. 13½***

No.	Design	Description	Unused	Used
329	A74	1 l deep green	1.75	.75
330	A74	2 l deep brown	1.75	.75
331	A74	3 l black brown	2.00	.75
332	A74	5 l carmine lake	2.25	.75
333	A74	7.50 l ultra	2.25	.95
334	A74	10 l Prus blue	5.50	2.25
335	A74	20 l black vio	7.00	3.25
		Nos. 329-335 (7)	22.50	9.45

Reunion of Bessarabia with Romania, 10th anniv.

King Carol I and King Michael
A77

View of Constanta Harbor
A78

Trajan's Monument at Adam Clisi
A79

Cernavoda Bridge — A80

1928, Oct. 25

No.	Design	Description	Unused	Used
336	A77	1 l blue green	1.10	.40
337	A78	2 l red brown	1.10	.45
338	A77	3 l gray black	1.40	.50
339	A79	5 l dull lilac	1.75	.60
340	A79	7.50 l ultra	2.10	.80
341	A80	10 l blue	3.25	1.90
342	A80	20 l carmine rose	5.50	3.25
		Nos. 336-342 (7)	16.20	7.90

Union of Dobruja with Romania, 50th anniv.

Michael Types of 1928-29

Perf. 13½x14

1928, Sept. 1 **Typo.** **Wmk. 95**

No.	Design	Description	Unused	Used
343	A72	25b black	.55	.20

Photo.

No.	Design	Description	Unused	Used
344	A73	7.50 l ultra	1.75	.60
345	A73	10 l blue	3.75	.35
		Nos. 343-345 (3)	6.05	1.15

Ferdinand I; Stephen the Great; Michael the Brave; Corvin and Constantine Brancoveanu — A81

Union with Transylvania A82

Avram Jancu — A83

Prince Michael the Brave — A84

Castle Bran — A85

King Ferdinand I — A86

1929, May 10 Photo. Wmk. 95

347	A81	1 l	dark violet	1.75	.75
348	A82	2 l	olive green	1.75	.85
349	A83	3 l	violet brown	2.10	.85
350	A84	4 l	cerise	2.25	1.25
351	A85	5 l	orange	3.75	1.25
352	A86	10 l	brt blue	6.50	3.75
			Nos. 347-352 (6)	18.10	8.70

Union of Transylvania and Romania.

Michael Type of 1928

1930 Unwmk. *Perf. 14½x14*

Size: 18x23mm

353	A73	1 l	deep violet	.70	.20
354	A73	2 l	deep green	1.00	.20
355	A73	3 l	carmine rose	1.90	.20
356	A73	7.50 l	ultra	4.25	.20
357	A73	10 l	deep blue	12.50	4.25
			Nos. 353-357 (5)	20.35	5.05

Stamps of 1928-30 Overprinted

On Nos. 320-322, 326, 328

Perf. 13½x14, 13½

1930, June 8 Typo.

359	A72	25b	black	.20	.20
360	A72	30b	fawn	.65	.20
361	A72	50b	olive green	.65	.20

Photo.

Size: 18½x24½mm

362	A73	5 l	red brown	1.10	.20
362A	A73	10 l	brt blue	4.75	.85

On Nos. 353-357

Perf. 14½x14

Size: 18x23mm

363	A73	1 l	deep violet	.40	.20
364	A73	2 l	deep green	.45	.20
365	A73	3 l	carmine rose	.85	.20
366	A73	7.50 l	ultra	2.25	.30
367	A73	10 l	deep blue	2.10	.45

On Nos. 343-344

Perf. 13½x14, 13½

Typo. Wmk. 95

368	A72	25b	black	.65	.20

Photo.

Size: 18½x24½mm

368A	A73	7.50 l	ultra	3.25	.85
			Nos. 359-368A (12)	17.30	4.05

Accession to the throne by King Carol II. This overprint exists on Nos. 323, 345.

A87

A88

King Carol II — A89

Perf. 13½, 14, 14x13½

1930 Wmk. 225

369	A87	25b	black	1.10	.20
370	A87	50b	chocolate	3.25	.25
371	A87	1 l	dk violet	2.25	.20
372	A87	2 l	gray green	2.75	.20
373	A88	3 l	carmine rose	2.25	.20
374	A88	4 l	orange red	3.25	.20
375	A88	6 l	carmine brn	4.25	.20
376	A88	7.50 l	ultra	4.25	.30
377	A89	10 l	deep blue	2.25	.20
378	A89	16 l	peacock grn	4.75	.20
379	A89	20 l	orange	1.40	.35
			Nos. 369-379 (11)	31.75	2.50

Exist imperf. Value, unused or used, $125.
See Nos. 405-414.

A90

A91

1930, Dec. 24 Unwmk. *Perf. 13½*

380	A90	1 l	dull violet	1.25	.20
381	A91	2 l	green	2.25	.30
382	A91	4 l	vermilion	2.50	.20
383	A91	6 l	brown carmine	6.50	.30
			Nos. 380-383 (4)	12.50	1.00

First census in Romania.

King Carol II — A92

King Carol I — A93

King Ferdinand — A96

King Carol II — A94

King Carol II, King Ferdinand and King Carol I — A95

1931, May 10 Photo. Wmk. 225

384	A92	1 l	gray violet	2.00	.95
385	A93	2 l	green	4.00	1.00
386	A94	6 l	red brown	9.75	1.75
387	A95	10 l	blue	14.00	2.50
388	A96	20 l	orange	20.00	4.00
			Nos. 384-388 (5)	49.75	10.20

50th anniversary of Romanian Kingdom.

Using Bayonet — A97

Romanian Infantryman 1870 — A98

Romanian Infantry 1830 — A99

King Carol I A100

Infantry Advance A101

King Ferdinand A102

King Carol II A103

1931, May 10

389	A97	25b	gray black	1.40	.50
390	A98	50b	dk red brn	2.10	.80
391	A99	1 l	gray violet	2.75	.80
392	A100	2 l	deep green	4.25	1.10
393	A101	3 l	carmine rose	10.00	2.75
394	A102	7.50 l	ultra	13.00	7.00
395	A103	16 l	blue green	16.00	3.25
			Nos. 389-395 (7)	49.50	16.20

Centenary of the Romanian Army.

Naval Cadet Ship "Mircea" A104

King Carol II — A108

10 l, Ironclad. 16 l, Light cruiser. 20 l, Destroyer.

1931, May 10

396	A104	6 l	red brown	7.00	3.75
397	A104	10 l	blue	9.50	4.00
398	A104	16 l	blue green	40.00	5.00
399	A104	20 l	orange	17.50	9.00
			Nos. 396-399 (4)	74.00	21.75

50th anniversary of the Romanian Navy.

1931 Unwmk. Engr. *Perf. 12*

400	A108	30 l	ol bis & dk bl	1.00	.30
401	A108	50 l	red & dk bl	2.00	.45
402	A108	100 l	dk grn & dk bl	5.00	1.00
			Nos. 400-402 (3)	8.00	1.75

Exist imperf. Value, unused or used, $150.

Carol II, Ferdinand, Carol I — A109

Wmk. 230

1931, Nov. 1 Photo. *Perf. 13½*

403	A109	16 l	Prus green	11.00	.40

Exists imperf. Value, unused or used, $200.

Carol II Types of 1930-31

Perf. 13½, 14, 14½ and Compound

1932 Wmk. 230

405	A87	25b	black	.50	.20
406	A87	50b	dark brown	1.00	.20
407	A87	1 l	dark violet	1.40	.20
408	A87	2 l	gray green	1.75	.20
409	A88	3 l	carmine rose	2.25	.20
410	A88	4 l	orange red	5.25	.20
411	A88	6 l	carmine brn	12.50	.20
412	A88	7.50 l	ultra	21.50	.25
413	A89	10 l	deep blue	125.00	.25
414	A89	20 l	orange	110.00	4.50
			Nos. 405-414 (10)	281.15	6.40

Alexander the Good — A110

King Carol II — A111

1932, May *Perf. 13½*

415	A110	6 l	carmine brown	12.00	5.00

500th death anniv. of Alexander the Good, Prince of Moldavia, 1400-1432.

1932, June

416	A111	10 l	brt blue	12.00	.35

Exists imperf. Value, unused or used, $150.

Cantacuzino and Gregory Ghika, Founders of Coltea and Pantelimon Hospitals — A112

Session of the Congress A113

Aesculapius and Hygeia — A114

1932, Sept. *Perf. 13½*

417	A112	1 l carmine rose	7.25	3.75
418	A113	6 l deep orange	19.00	5.50
419	A114	10 l brt blue	32.50	10.50
		Nos. 417-419 (3)	58.75	19.75

9th Intl. History of Medicine Congress, Bucharest.

Bull's Head and Post Horn A116

Lion Rampant and Bridge A117

Dolphins A118

Eagle and Castles A119

Coat of Arms — A120

Eagle and Post Horn — A121

Bull's Head and Post Horn — A122

1932, Nov. 20 **Typo.** ***Imperf.***

421	A116	25b black	.85	.20
422	A117	1 l violet	2.00	.30
423	A118	2 l green	2.50	.70
424	A119	3 l car rose	2.80	.80
425	A120	6 l red brown	3.50	1.00
426	A121	7.50 l lt blue	4.25	1.50
427	A122	10 l dk blue	8.00	2.25
		Nos. 421-427 (7)	23.90	6.75

75th anniv. of the first Moldavian stamps.

Mail Coach Type of 1903

1932, Nov. 20 *Perf. 13½*

428	A25	16 l blue green	11.00	3.25

30th anniv. of the opening of the new post office, Bucharest, in 1903.

Arms of City of Turnu-Severin, Ruins of Tower of Emperor Severus — A123

Inauguration of Trajan's Bridge — A124

Prince Carol Landing at Turnu-Severin — A125

Bridge over the Danube A126

1933, June 2 **Photo.** ***Perf. 14½x14***

429	A123	25b gray green	.75	.20
430	A124	50b dull blue	1.10	.25
431	A125	1 l black brn	1.75	.65
432	A126	2 l olive blk	3.25	.90
		Nos. 429-432 (4)	6.85	2.00

Centenary of the incorporation in Walachia of the old Roman City of Turnu-Severin. Exist imperf. Value, unused or used, $150.

Queen Elizabeth and King Carol I — A127

Profiles of Kings Carol I, Ferdinand and Carol II — A128

Castle Peles, Sinaia A129

1933, Aug.

433	A127	1 l dark violet	2.00	.80
434	A128	3 l olive brown	2.25	.80
435	A129	6 l vermilion	3.75	1.50
		Nos. 433-435 (3)	8.00	3.10

50th anniversary of the erection of Castle Peles, the royal summer residence at Sinaia. Exist imperf. Value, unused or used, $125.

A130

A131

King Carol II — A132

1934, Aug. *Perf. 13½*

436	A130	50b brown	1.00	.20
437	A131	2 l gray green	2.00	.20
438	A131	4 l red	3.50	.25
439	A132	6 l deep claret	8.00	.20
		Nos. 436-439 (4)	14.50	.85

See Nos. 446-460 for stamps inscribed "Posta." Nos. 436, 439 exist imperf. Value for both, unused or used, $100.

Child and Grapes — A133

Woman and Fruit — A134

1934, Sept. 14

440	A133	1 l dull green	5.00	1.60
441	A134	2 l violet brown	5.00	1.60

Natl. Fruit Week, Sept. 14-21. Exist imperf. Value, unused or used, $125.

Crisan, Horia and Closca A135

1935, Feb. 28

442	A135	1 l shown	.65	.25
443	A135	2 l Crisan	.90	.30
444	A135	6 l Closca	2.25	.55
445	A135	10 l Horia	5.00	1.25
		Nos. 442-445 (4)	8.80	2.35

150th anniversary of the death of three Romanian martyrs. Exist imperf. Value, unused or used, $110.

A139

A140

A141

A142

King Carol II — A143

Wmk. 230

1935-40 **Photo.** ***Perf. 13½***

446	A139	25b black brn	.20	.20
447	A142	50b brown	.20	.20
448	A140	1 l purple	.25	.20
449	A141	2 l green	.45	.20
449A	A141	2 l dk bl grn ('40)	.65	.25
450	A142	3 l deep rose	.70	.20
450A	A142	3 l grnsh bl ('40)	.85	.30
451	A141	4 l vermilion	1.25	.20
452	A140	5 l rose car ('40)	1.25	.80
453	A143	6 l maroon	1.60	.20
454	A140	7.50 l ultra	1.90	.30
454A	A142	8 l magenta ('40)	1.90	.70
455	A141	9 l brt ultra ('40)	2.50	.80
456	A142	10 l brt blue	1.00	.20
456A	A143	12 l slate bl ('40)	1.60	1.25
457	A139	15 l dk brn ('40)	1.60	.95
458	A143	16 l Prus blue	2.10	.25
459	A143	20 l orange	1.25	.35
460	A143	24 l dk car ('40)	2.10	.95
		Nos. 446-460 (19)	23.35	8.50

Exist imperf. Value, unused or used, $240.

Nos. 454, 456 Overprinted in Red

1936, Dec. 5

461	A140	7.50 l ultra	3.75	2.25
462	A142	10 l brt blue	3.75	2.25

16th anniversary of the Little Entente. Overprints in silver or gold are fraudulent.

Birthplace of Ion Creanga A144

Ion Creanga A145

1937, May 15

463	A144	2 l green	1.10	.25
464	A145	3 l carmine rose	1.60	.40
465	A144	4 l dp violet	1.75	.45
466	A145	6 l red brown	4.50	1.10
		Nos. 463-466 (4)	8.95	2.20

Creanga (1837-89), writer. Exist imperf. Value, unused or used, $125.

Cathedral at Curtea de Arges — A146

1937, July 1

467	A146	7.50 l ultra	1.25	.50
468	A146	10 l blue	2.25	.40

The Little Entente (Romania, Czechoslovakia, Yugoslavia). Exist imperf. Value, unused or used, $125.

Souvenir Sheet

A146a

Surcharged in Black with New Values

1937, Oct. 25 **Unwmk.** ***Perf. 13½***

469	A146a	Sheet of 4	9.00	9.00
a.		2 l on 20 l orange	.35	.35
b.		6 l on 10 l bright blue	.35	.35
c.		10 l on 6 l maroon	.45	.45
d.		20 l on 2 l green	1.00	1.00

Promotion of the Crown Prince Michael to the rank of Lieutenant on his 17th birthday.

Arms of Romania, Greece, Turkey and Yugoslavia A147

Perf. 13x13½

1938, Feb. 10 **Wmk. 230**

470	A147	7.50 l	ultra	1.50	.60
471	A147	10 l	blue	2.00	.50

The Balkan Entente.
Exist imperf. Value, unused or used, $100.

A148

King Carol II

A149 A150

1938, May 10 *Perf. 13½*

472	A148	3 l	dk carmine	.75	.25
473	A149	6 l	violet brn	1.25	.25
474	A150	10 l	blue	2.00	.40
			Nos. 472-474 (3)	4.00	.90

New Constitution of Feb. 27, 1938.
Exist imperf. Value, unused or used, $100.

Catalogue values for unused stamps in this section, from this point to the end of the section, are for Never Hinged items.

Prince Carol at Calatorie, 1866 A151

Examining Plans for a Monastery A153

Prince Carol and Carmen Sylva (Queen Elizabeth) A155

Sigmaringen and Peles Castles — A154

Prince Carol, Age 6 — A156

Equestrian Statue — A159

Battle of Plevna — A160

On Horseback A161

Cathedral of Curtea de Arges A164

King Carol I and Queen Elizabeth A163

Designs: 50b, At Calafat. 4 l, In 1866. 5 l, In 1877. 12 l, in 1914.

Perf. 14, 13½

1939, Apr. 10 **Wmk. 230**

475	A151	25b	olive blk	.20	.20
476	A151	50b	violet brn	.20	.20
477	A153	1 l	dk purple	.25	.20
478	A154	1.50 l	green	.20	.20
479	A155	2 l	myrtle grn	.20	.20
480	A156	3 l	red orange	.20	.20
481	A156	4 l	rose lake	.20	.20
482	A156	5 l	black	.20	.20
483	A159	7 l	olive blk	.20	.20
484	A160	8 l	dark blue	.25	.20
485	A161	10 l	deep mag	.25	.20
486	A161	12 l	dull blue	.30	.20
487	A163	15 l	ultra	.35	.20
488	A164	16 l	Prus green	.75	.40
			Nos. 475-488 (14)	3.75	3.00

Centenary of the birth of King Carol I.
Nos 475-488 exist imperf. Value, unused or used, $150.

Souvenir Sheets

1939 *Perf. 14x13½*

488A	Sheet of 3, #475-476, 478	1.50	1.50
d.	Imperf. ('40)	3.50	3.50

Perf. 14x15½

488B	Sheet of 4, #480-482, 486	1.50	1.50
e.	Imperf. ('40)	3.50	3.50
488C	Sheet of 4, #479, 483-485	1.50	1.50
f.	Imperf. ('40)	3.50	3.50

No. 488A sold for 20 l, Nos. 488B-488C for 50 l, the surtax for national defense.

Nos. 488A-488C and 488Ad-488Cf were overprinted "PRO-PATRIA 1940" to aid the armament fund. Value, set of 6, $100.

Nos. 488A-488C exist with overprint of "ROMA BERLIN 1940" and bars, but these are not recognized as having been officially issued.

Romanian Pavilion A165

Romanian Pavilion A166

1939, May 8 *Perf. 14x13½, 13½*

489	A165	6 l	brown carmine	.55	.40
490	A166	12 l	brt blue	.55	.40

New York World's Fair.
Nos 489-490 exist imperf. Value, unused or used, $250.

Mihail Eminescu

A167 A168

1939, May 22 *Perf. 13½*

491	A167	5 l	olive gray	.55	.40
492	A168	7 l	brown carmine	.55	.40

Mihail Eminescu, poet, 50th death anniv.
Nos 491-492 exist imperf. Value, unused or used, $250.

Three Types of Locomotives — A169

Modern Train A170

Wood-burning Locomotive A171

Streamlined Locomotive A172

Railroad Terminal A173

1939, June 10 **Typo.** *Perf. 14*

493	A169	1 l	red violet	.95	.30
494	A170	4 l	deep rose	.95	.30
495	A171	5 l	gray lilac	.95	.30
496	A171	7 l	claret	.95	.40
497	A172	12 l	blue	2.00	1.10
498	A173	15 l	green	2.00	1.50
			Nos. 493-498 (6)	7.80	3.90

Romanian Railways, 70th anniversary.
Nos 493-498 exist imperf. Value, unused or used, $150.

Arms of Romania, Greece, Turkey and Yugoslavia — A174

Wmk. 230

1940, May 27 **Photo.** *Perf. 13½*

504	A174	12 l	lt ultra	1.00	.65
505	A174	16 l	dull blue	1.00	.65

The Balkan Entente.
Nos 504-505 exist imperf. Value, unused or used, $125.

King Michael — A175

1940-42 **Wmk. 230** *Perf. 14*

506	A175	25b	Prus green	.20	.20
506A	A175	50b	dk grn ('42)	.20	.20
507	A175	1 l	purple	.20	.20
508	A175	2 l	red orange	.20	.20
508A	A175	4 l	slate ('42)	.20	.20
509	A175	5 l	rose pink	.20	.20
509A	A175	7 l	dp blue ('42)	.20	.20
510	A175	10 l	dp magenta	.25	.20
511	A175	12 l	dull blue	.20	.20
511A	A175	13 l	dk vio ('42)	.20	.20
512	A175	16 l	Prus blue	.30	.20
513	A175	20 l	brown	1.10	.20
514	A175	30 l	yellow grn	.20	.20
515	A175	50 l	olive brn	.20	.20
516	A175	100 l	rose brown	.35	.20
			Nos. 506-516 (15)	4.20	3.00

See Nos. 535A-553.

SEMI-POSTAL STAMPS

Queen Elizabeth Spinning — SP1

The Queen Weaving — SP2

Queen as War Nurse SP3

Perf. 11½, 11½x13½

1906, Jan. 14 **Typo.** **Unwmk.**

B1	SP1	3b (+ 7b)	brown	3.00	2.00
B2	SP1	5b (+ 10b)	lt grn	3.00	2.00
B3	SP1	10b (+ 10b)	rose red	14.00	6.50
B4	SP1	15b (+ 10b)	violet	10.00	4.50
			Nos. B1-B4 (4)	30.00	15.00

1906, Mar. 18

B5	SP2	3b (+ 7b)	org brn	3.00	2.00
B6	SP2	5b (+ 10b)	bl grn	3.00	2.00
B7	SP2	10b (+ 10b)	car	16.50	6.50
B8	SP2	15b (+ 10b)	red vio	10.00	4.50
			Nos. B5-B8 (4)	32.50	15.00

1906, Mar. 23 *Perf. 11½, 13½x11½*

B9	SP3	3b (+ 7b)	org brn	3.00	2.00
B10	SP3	5b (+ 10b)	bl grn	3.00	2.00
B11	SP3	10b (+ 10b)	car	16.50	6.50
B12	SP3	15b (+ 10b)	red vio	10.00	4.50
			Nos. B9-B12 (4)	32.50	15.00
			Nos. B1-B12 (12)	95.00	45.00

Booklet panes of 4 exist of Nos. B1-B3, B5-B7, B9-B12.

Counterfeits of Nos. B1-B12 are plentiful. Copies of Nos. B1-B12 with smooth, even gum are counterfeits.

SP4

1906, Aug. 4 *Perf. 12*

B13 SP4	3b (+ 7b) ol brn, buff & bl	1.50	1.00
B14 SP4	5b (+ 10b) grn, rose & buff	1.50	1.00
B15 SP4	10b (+ 10b) rose red, buff & bl	3.00	2.00
B16 SP4	15b (+ 10b) vio, buff & bl	6.50	3.00
	Nos. B13-B16 (4)	12.50	7.00

Guardian Angel Bringing Poor to Crown Princess Marie SP5

1907, Feb. **Engr.** *Perf. 11*
Center in Brown

B17 SP5	3b (+ 7b) org brn	3.25	1.90
B18 SP5	5b (+ 10b) dk grn	2.25	1.00
B19 SP5	10b (+ 10b) dk car	2.25	1.00
B20 SP5	15b (+ 10b) dl vio	2.25	1.10
	Nos. B17-B20 (4)	10.00	5.00

Nos. B1-B20 were sold for more than face value. The surtax, shown in parenthesis, was for charitable purposes.

Map of Romania SP9

Stephen the Great SP10

Michael the Brave SP11

Kings Carol I and Ferdinand SP12

Adam Clisi Monument — SP13

1927, Mar. 15 **Typo.** *Perf. 13½*

B21 SP9	1 l + 9 l lt vio	.80	.45
B22 SP10	2 l + 8 l Prus grn	.80	.45
B23 SP11	3 l + 7 l dp rose	.80	.45
B24 SP12	5 l + 5 l dp bl	.80	.45
B25 SP13	6 l + 4 l ol grn	2.25	.45
	Nos. B21-B25 (5)	5.45	2.25

50th anniv. of the Royal Geographical Society. The surtax was for the benefit of that society. The stamps were valid for postage only from 3/15-4/14.

Boy Scouts in Camp — SP15

The Rescue — SP16

Designs: 3 l+3 l, Swearing in a Tenderfoot. 4 l+4 l, Prince Nicholas Chief Scout. 6 l+6 l, King Carol II in Scout's Uniform.

1931, July 15 **Photo.** **Wmk. 225**

B26 SP15	1 l + 1 l car rose	1.25	1.00
B27 SP16	2 l + 2 l dp grn	1.60	1.25
B28 SP15	3 l + 3 l ultra	2.00	1.50
B29 SP16	4 l + 4 l ol gray	2.40	2.00
B30 SP16	6 l + 6 l red brn	3.25	2.00
	Nos. B26-B30 (5)	10.50	7.75

The surtax was for the benefit of the Boy Scout organization.

Boy Scout Jamboree Issue

Scouts in Camp SP20

Semaphore Signaling SP21

Trailing — SP22

Camp Fire — SP23

King Carol II — SP24

King Carol II and Prince Michael — SP25

1932, June 8 **Wmk. 230**

B31 SP20	25b + 25b pck grn	3.00	1.10
B32 SP21	50b + 50b brt bl	4.00	2.25
B33 SP22	1 l + 1 l ol grn	4.50	3.25
B34 SP23	2 l + 2 l org red	7.50	4.50
B35 SP24	3 l + 3 l Prus bl	14.00	9.00
B36 SP25	6 l + 6 l blk brn	16.00	11.50
	Nos. B31-B36 (6)	49.00	31.60

For overprints see Nos. B44-B49.

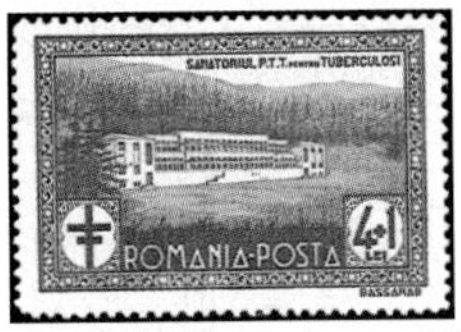
Tuberculosis Sanatorium — SP26

Memorial Tablet to Postal Employees Who Died in World War I — SP27

Carmen Sylva Convalescent Home — SP28

1932, Nov. 1

B37 SP26	4 l + 1 l dk grn	2.50	2.00
B38 SP27	6 l + 1 l chocolate	2.50	2.25
B39 SP28	10 l + 1 l dp bl	5.00	3.75
	Nos. B37-B39 (3)	10.00	8.00

The surtax was given to a fund for the employees of the postal and telegraph services.

Philatelic Exhibition Issue

Souvenir Sheet

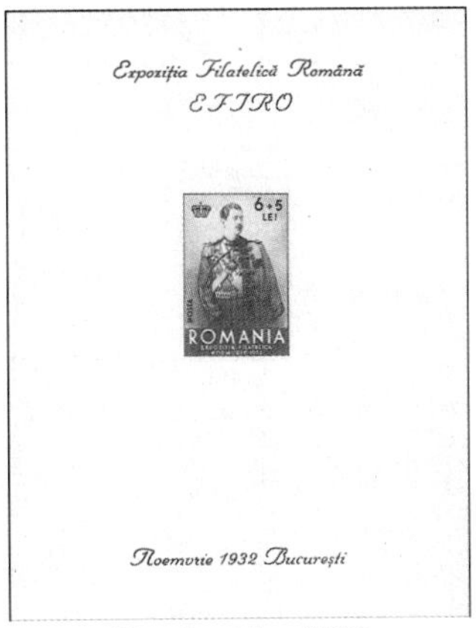
King Carol II — SP29

1932, Nov. 20 **Unwmk.** *Imperf.*

B40 SP29	6 l + 5 l dk ol grn	50.00	50.00

Intl. Phil. Exhib. at Bucharest, Nov. 20-24, 1932. Each holder of a ticket of admission to the exhibition could buy a copy of the stamp. The ticket cost 20 lei.

Roadside Shrine — SP31

Woman Spinning — SP33

Woman Weaving SP32

1934, Apr. 16 **Wmk. 230** *Perf. 13½*

B41 SP31	1 l + 1 l dk brn	.85	.75
B42 SP32	2 l + 1 l blue	1.10	1.00
B43 SP33	3 l + 1 l slate grn	1.40	1.25
	Nos. B41-B43 (3)	3.35	3.00

Weaving Exposition.

Boy Scout Mamaia Jamboree Issue

Semi-Postal Stamps of 1932 Overprinted in Black or Gold

1934, July 8

B44 SP20	25b + 25b pck grn	2.00	2.00
B45 SP21	50b + 50b brt bl (G)	3.25	2.50
B46 SP22	1 l + 1 l ol grn	4.00	4.00
B47 SP23	2 l + 2 l org red	4.50	4.50
B48 SP24	3 l + 3 l Prus bl (G)	8.75	8.00
B49 SP25	6 l + 6 l blk brn (G)	14.00	11.00
	Nos. B44-B49 (6)	36.50	32.00

Sea Scout Saluting SP34

Scout Bugler SP35

Sea and Land Scouts SP36

King Carol II — SP37

Sea, Land and Girl Scouts — SP38

1935, June 8

B50 SP34	25b ol blk	1.00	.75
B51 SP35	1 l violet	2.25	2.00
B52 SP36	2 l green	2.75	2.50
B53 SP37	6 l + 1 l red brn	4.25	3.75
B54 SP38	10 l + 2 l dk ultra	12.00	11.00
	Nos. B50-B54 (5)	22.25	20.00

Fifth anniversary of accession of King Carol II, and a national sports meeting held June 8. Surtax aided the Boy Scouts.

Nos. B50-B54 exist imperf.

King Carol II — SP39

1936, May

B55 SP39	6 l + 1 l rose car	.55	.40

Bucharest Exhibition and 70th anniversary of the dynasty. Exists imperf.

Girl of Oltenia — SP40

Girl of Saliste — SP42

Youth from Gorj — SP44

Designs: 1 l+1 l, Girl of Banat. 3 l+1 l, Girl of Hateg. 6 l+3 l, Girl of Neamt. 10 l+5 l, Youth and girl of Bucovina.

1936, June 8

B56	SP40	50b + 50b brown	.45	.30
B57	SP40	1 l + 1 l violet	.45	.30
B58	SP42	2 l + 1 l Prus grn	.45	.30
B59	SP42	3 l + 1 l car rose	.45	.30
B60	SP44	4 l + 2 l red org	.80	.65
B61	SP40	6 l + 3 l ol gray	.80	.75
B62	SP42	10 l + 5 l brt bl	1.60	1.40
		Nos. B56-B62 (7)	5.00	4.00

6th anniv. of accession of King Carol II. The surtax was for child welfare. Exist imperf.

Insignia of Boy Scouts
SP47 SP48

Jamboree Emblem — SP49

Submarine "Delfinul" SP50

1936, Aug. 20

B63	SP47	1 l + 1 l brt bl	5.75	4.75
B64	SP48	3 l + 3 l ol gray	9.75	5.25
B65	SP49	6 l + 6 l car rose	13.00	5.75
		Nos. B63-B65 (3)	28.50	15.75

Boy Scout Jamboree at Brasov (Kronstadt).

1936, Oct.

Designs: 3 l+2 l, Training ship "Mircea." 6 l+3 l, Steamship "S.M.R."

B66	SP50	1 l + 1 l pur	2.10	2.00
B67	SP50	3 l + 2 l ultra	2.00	1.75
B68	SP50	6 l + 3 l car rose	2.75	1.75
		Nos. B66-B68 (3)	6.85	5.50

Marine Exhibition at Bucharest. Exist imperf.

Soccer SP53

Swimming SP54

Throwing the Javelin — SP55

Skiing — SP56

King Carol II Hunting — SP57

Rowing SP58

Horsemanship SP59

Founding of the U.F.S.R. SP60

1937, June 8 Wmk. 230 *Perf. 13½*

B69	SP53	25b + 25b ol blk	.25	.20
B70	SP54	50b + 50b brown	.25	.25
B71	SP55	1 l + 50b violet	.30	.30
B72	SP56	2 l + 1 l slate grn	.35	.35
B73	SP57	3 l + 1 l rose lake	.50	.45
B74	SP58	4 l + 1 l red org	.80	.60
B75	SP59	6 l + 2 l dp claret	1.00	1.00
B76	SP60	10 l + 4 l brt blue	1.25	1.25
		Nos. B69-B76 (8)	4.70	4.40

25th anniversary of the Federation of Romanian Sports Clubs (U.F.S.R.); 7th anniversary of the accession of King Carol II. Exist imperf.

Start of Race — SP61

Javelin Thrower — SP62

Designs: 4 l+1 l, Hurdling. 6 l+1 l, Finish of race. 10 l+1 l, High jump.

1937, Sept. 1 Wmk. 230 *Perf. 13½*

B77	SP61	1 l + 1 l purple	.40	.40
B78	SP62	2 l + 1 l green	.50	.50
B79	SP61	4 l + 1 l vermilion	.60	.60
B80	SP62	6 l + 1 l maroon	1.00	1.00
B81	SP61	10 l + 1 l brt bl	2.50	2.50
		Nos. B77-B81 (5)	5.00	5.00

8th Balkan Games, Bucharest. Exist imperf.

Catalogue values for unused stamps in this section, from this point to the end of the section, are for Never Hinged items.

King Carol II — SP66

1938, May 24

B82	SP66	6 l + 1 l deep magenta	.90	.20

Bucharest Exhibition (for local products), May 19-June 19, celebrating 20th anniversary of the union of Rumanian provinces. Exists imperf.

Dimitrie Cantemir — SP67

Maria Doamna — SP68

Mircea the Great SP69

Constantine Brancoveanu SP70

Stephen the Great — SP71

Prince Cuza — SP72

Michael the Brave — SP73

Queen Elizabeth — SP74

King Carol II — SP75

King Ferdinand I — SP76

King Carol I — SP77

1938, June 8 *Perf. 13½*

B83	SP67	25b + 25b ol blk	.80	.50
B84	SP68	50b + 50b brn	1.25	.50
B85	SP69	1 l + 1 l blk vio	1.25	.50
B86	SP70	2 l + 2 l dk yel grn	1.40	.50
B87	SP71	3 l + 2 l dp mag	1.40	.50
B88	SP72	4 l + 2 l scarlet	1.40	.50
B89	SP73	6 l + 2 l vio brn	1.50	.80
B90	SP74	7.50 l gray bl	1.75	.80
B91	SP75	10 l brt bl	2.25	1.00
B92	SP76	16 l dk slate grn	3.50	2.00
B93	SP77	20 l vermilion	4.75	2.50
		Nos. B83-B93 (11)	21.25	10.10

8th anniv. of accession of King Carol II. Surtax was for Straja Tarii, a natl. org. for boys. Exist imperf.

"The Spring" — SP78

"Escorting Prisoners" SP79

"Rodica, the Water Carrier" SP81

Nicolae Grigorescu SP82

Design: 4 l+1 l, "Returning from Market."

1938, June 23 *Perf. 13½*

B94	SP78	1 l + 1 l brt bl	1.00	.40
B95	SP79	2 l + 1 l yel grn	1.25	.65
B96	SP79	4 l + 1 l vermilion	1.25	.70
B97	SP81	6 l + 1 l lake	1.75	1.00
B98	SP82	10 l + 1 l brt bl	2.50	1.25
		Nos. B94-B98 (5)	7.75	4.00

Birth centenary of Nicolae Grigorescu, Romanian painter. Exist imperf.

St. George and the Dragon — SP83

1939, June 8 Photo.

B99	SP83	25b + 25b ol gray	.45	.30
B100	SP83	50b + 50b brn	.45	.30
B101	SP83	1 l + 1 l pale vio	.45	.30
B102	SP83	2 l + 2 l lt grn	.45	.30
B103	SP83	3 l + 2 l red vio	.70	.30
B104	SP83	4 l + 2 l red org	.90	.35
B105	SP83	6 l + 2 l car rose	1.00	.35
B106	SP83	8 l gray vio	1.10	.45
B107	SP83	10 l brt bl	1.40	.55
B108	SP83	12 l brt ultra	1.60	1.10
B109	SP83	16 l bl grn	2.00	1.40
		Nos. B99-B109 (11)	10.50	5.70

9th anniv. of accession of King Carol II. Exist imperf.

King Carol II
SP87 SP88

SP89

SP90

SP91

Wmk. 230

1940, June 8 Photo. *Perf. 13½*

B113	SP87	1 l + 50b dl pur	.65	.20
B114	SP88	4 l + 1 l fawn	.65	.35
B115	SP89	6 l + 1 l blue	.65	.45
B116	SP90	8 l rose brn	.90	.55
B117	SP89	16 l ultra	1.10	.70
B118	SP91	32 l dk vio brn	1.60	1.10
		Nos. B113-B118 (6)	5.55	3.35

10th anniv. of accession of King Carol II. Exist imperf.

King Carol II
SP92 SP93

1940, June 1

B119	SP92	1 l + 50b dk grn	.20	.20
B120	SP92	2.50 l + 50b Prus grn	.25	.20
B121	SP93	3 l + 1 l rose car	.35	.25
B122	SP92	3.50 l + 50b choc	.35	.35
B123	SP93	4 l + 1 l org brn	.50	.35
B124	SP93	6 l + 1 l sapphire	.75	.20
B125	SP93	9 l + 1 l brt bl	.85	.70
B126	SP93	14 l + 1 l dk bl grn	1.10	.90
		Nos. B119-B126 (8)	4.35	3.15

Surtax was for Romania's air force. Exist imperf.

View of Danube SP94

Greco-Roman Ruins — SP95

Designs: 3 l+1 l, Hotin Castle. 4 l+1 l, Hurez Monastery. 5 l+1 l, Church in Bucovina. 8 l+1 l, Tower. 12 l+2 l, Village church, Transylvania. 16 l+2 l, Arch in Bucharest.

1940, June 8 *Perf. 14½x14, 14x14½*
Inscribed: "Straja Tarii 8 Junie 1940"

B127	SP94	1 l + 1 l dp vio	.40	.20
B128	SP95	2 l + 1 l red brn	.45	.30
B129	SP94	3 l + 1 l yel grn	.50	.35
B130	SP94	4 l + 1 l grnsh blk	.55	.40
B131	SP95	5 l + 1 l org ver	.60	.45
B132	SP95	8 l + 1 l brn car	.85	.60
B133	SP95	12 l + 2 l ultra	1.00	.90
B134	SP95	16 l + 2 l dk bl gray	1.75	1.40
		Nos. B127-B134 (8)	6.10	4.60

Issued to honor Straja Tarii, a national organization for boys. Exist imperf.

King Michael SP102

Corneliu Codreanu SP103

1940-42 Photo. Wmk. 230

B138	SP102	1 l + 50b yel grn	.20	.20
B138A	SP102	2 l + 50b yel grn	.20	.20
B139	SP102	2.50 l + 50b dk bl grn	.20	.20
B140	SP102	3 l + 1 l pur	.20	.20
B141	SP102	3.50 l + 50b rose pink	.20	.20
B141A	SP102	4 l + 50b org ver	.20	.20
B142	SP102	4 l + 1 l brn	.20	.20
B142A	SP102	5 l + 1 l dp plum	.45	.35
B143	SP102	6 l + 1 l lt ultra	.20	.20
B143A	SP102	7 l + 1 l sl grn	.30	.20
B143B	SP102	8 l + 1 l dp vio	.20	.20
B143C	SP102	12 l + 1 l brn vio	.30	.20
B144	SP102	14 l + 1 l brt bl	.30	.20
B144A	SP102	19 l + 1 l lil rose	.40	.35
		Nos. B138-B144A (14)	3.55	3.10

Issue years: #B138A, B141A, B142A, B143A, B143B, B143C, B144A, 1942; others, 1940.

1940, Nov. 8 Unwmk. *Perf. 13½*

B145	SP103	7 l + 30 l dk grn	4.25	3.50

13th anniv. of the founding of the Iron Guard by Corneliu Codreanu.

AIR POST STAMPS

Capt. C. G. Craiu's Airplane AP1

Wmk. 95 Vertical

1928 Photo. *Perf. 13½*

C1	AP1	1 l red brown	2.50	2.00
C2	AP1	2 l brt blue	2.50	2.00
C3	AP1	5 l carmine rose	2.50	2.00

Wmk. 95 Horizontal

C4	AP1	1 l red brown	3.50	2.75
C5	AP1	2 l brt blue	3.50	2.75
C6	AP1	5 l carmine rose	3.50	2.75
		Nos. C1-C6 (6)	18.00	14.25

Nos. C4-C6 also come with white gum.

Nos. C4-C6 Overprinted

1930

C7	AP1	1 l red brown	5.25	4.50
C8	AP1	2 l brt blue	5.25	4.50
a.		Vert. pair, imperf. btwn.	*175.00*	
C9	AP1	5 l carmine rose	5.25	4.50
		Nos. C7-C9 (3)	15.75	13.50

Same Overprint on Nos. C1-C3
Wmk. 95 Vertical

C10	AP1	1 l red brown	37.50	37.50
C11	AP1	2 l brt blue	37.50	37.50
C12	AP1	5 l carmine rose	37.50	37.50
		Nos. C10-C12 (3)	112.50	112.50
		Nos. C7-C12 (6)	128.25	126.00

#C7-C12 for the accession of King Carol II. Excellent connterfeits are known of #C10-C12.

King Carol II — AP2

1930, Oct. 4 Unwmk.
Bluish Paper

C13	AP2	1 l dk violet	2.00	2.25
C14	AP2	2 l gray green	2.50	2.50
C15	AP2	5 l red brown	5.00	3.00
C16	AP2	10 l brt blue	9.00	7.00
		Nos. C13-C16 (4)	18.50	14.75
		Never hinged	36.50	

Junkers Monoplane AP3

Monoplanes AP7

Designs: 3 l, Monoplane with biplane behind. 5 l, Biplane. 10 l, Monoplane flying leftward.

1931, Nov. 4 Wmk. 230

C17	AP3	2 l dull green	.50	.35
C18	AP3	3 l carmine	.60	.45
C19	AP3	5 l red brown	.90	.60
C20	AP3	10 l blue	2.00	1.25
C21	AP7	20 l dk violet	3.75	1.75
		Nos. C17-C21 (5)	7.75	4.40
		Never hinged	17.50	

Exist imperforate.

AIR POST SEMI-POSTAL STAMPS

Catalogue values for unused stamps in this section are for Never Hinged items.

Corneliu Codreanu SPAP1

Unwmk.
1940, Dec. 1 Photo. *Perf. 14*

CB1	SPAP1	20 l + 5 l Prus grn	2.00	1.10

Propaganda for the Rome-Berlin Axis.
No. CB1 exists with overprint "1 Mai 1941 Jamboreea Nationala."

POSTAGE DUE STAMPS

D1

Perf. 11, 11½, 13½ and Compound

1881 Typo. Unwmk.

J1	D1	2b brown	4.00	1.25
J2	D1	5b brown	22.50	2.00
a.		Tête bêche pair	*190.00*	*75.00*
J3	D1	10b brown	30.00	1.25
J4	D1	30b brown	32.50	1.25
J5	D1	50b brown	26.00	2.50
J6	D1	60b brown	21.00	3.00
		Nos. J1-J6 (6)	136.00	11.25

1885

J7	D1	10b pale red brown	8.00	.50
J8	D1	30b pale red brown	8.00	.50

1887-90

J9	D1	2b gray green	4.00	.75
J10	D1	5b gray green	8.00	3.00
J11	D1	10b gray green	8.00	3.00
J12	D1	30b gray green	8.00	.75
		Nos. J9-J12 (4)	28.00	7.50

1888

J14	D1	2b green, *yellowish*	.90	.75
J15	D1	5b green, *yellowish*	2.25	2.25
J16	D1	10b green, *yellowish*	32.50	2.75
J17	D1	30b green, *yellowish*	17.50	1.25
		Nos. J14-J17 (4)	53.15	7.00

1890-96 Wmk. 163

J18	D1	2b emerald	1.60	.45
J19	D1	5b emerald	.80	.45
J20	D1	10b emerald	1.25	.45
J21	D1	30b emerald	2.00	.45
J22	D1	50b emerald	6.50	.95
J23	D1	60b emerald	8.75	3.25
		Nos. J18-J23 (6)	20.90	6.00

1898 Wmk. 200

J24	D1	2b blue green	.70	.45
J25	D1	5b blue green	.90	.30
J26	D1	10b blue green	1.40	.30
J27	D1	30b blue green	1.90	.30
J28	D1	50b blue green	4.75	.90
J29	D1	60b blue green	5.50	1.75
		Nos. J24-J29 (6)	15.15	4.00

1902-10 Unwmk.
Thin Paper, Tinted Rose on Back

J30	D1	2b green	.85	.25
J31	D1	5b green	.50	.20
J32	D1	10b green	.40	.20
J33	D1	30b green	.50	.20
J34	D1	50b green	2.50	.90
J35	D1	60b green	5.25	2.25
		Nos. J30-J35 (6)	10.00	4.00

1908-11
White Paper

J36	D1	2b green	.80	.50
J37	D1	5b green	.60	.50
a.		Tête bêche pair	12.00	12.00
J38	D1	10b green	.40	.30
a.		Tête bêche pair	12.00	12.00
J39	D1	30b green	.50	.30
a.		Tête bêche pair	12.00	12.00
J40	D1	50b green	2.00	1.25
		Nos. J36-J40 (5)	4.30	2.85

D2

1911 Wmk. 165

J41	D2	2b dark blue, *green*	.20	.20
J42	D2	5b dark blue, *green*	.20	.20
J43	D2	10b dark blue, *green*	.20	.20
J44	D2	15b dark blue, *green*	.20	.20
J45	D2	20b dark blue, *green*	.20	.20
J46	D2	30b dark blue, *green*	.25	.25
J47	D2	50b dark blue, *green*	.30	.30
J48	D2	60b dark blue, *green*	.40	.40
J49	D2	2 l dark blue, *green*	.80	.80
		Nos. J41-J49 (9)	2.75	2.75

The letters "P.R." appear to be embossed instead of watermarked. They are often faint or entirely invisible.

The 20b, type D2, has two types, differing in the width of the head of the "2." This affects Nos. J45, J54, J58, and J63.

See Nos. J52-J77, J82, J87-J88. For overprints see Nos. J78-J81, RAJ1-RAJ2, RAJ20-RAJ21, 3NJ1-3NJ7.

Regular Issue of 1908 Overprinted

1918 Unwmk.

J50	A46	5b yellow green	.75	.25
a.		Inverted overprint	5.00	5.00
J51	A46	10b rose	.75	.25
a.		Inverted overprint	3.75	3.75

Postage Due Type of 1911

1920 Wmk. 165

J52	D2	5b black, *green*	.20	.20
J53	D2	10b black, *green*	.20	.20
J54	D2	20b black, *green*	4.00	.60
J55	D2	30b black, *green*	1.10	.40
J55A	D2	50b black, *green*	3.00	.90
		Nos. J52-J55A (5)	8.50	2.30

Perf. 11½, 13½ and Compound

1919 **Unwmk.**

J56 D2 5b black, *green* .30 .20
J57 D2 10b black, *green* .30 .20
J58 D2 20b black, *green* 1.00 .20
J59 D2 30b black, *green* .90 .20
J60 D2 50b black, *green* 2.25 .40
Nos. J56-J60 (5) 4.75 1.20

1920-26

White Paper

J61 D2 5b black .20 .20
J62 D2 10b black .20 .20
J63 D2 20b black .20 .20
J64 D2 30b black .25 .25
J65 D2 50b black .40 .40
J66 D2 60b black .20 .20
J67 D2 1 l black .30 .30
J68 D2 2 l black .20 .20
J69 D2 3 l black ('26) .20 .20
J70 D2 6 l black ('26) .30 .30
Nos. J61-J70 (10) 2.45 2.45

1923-24

J74 D2 1 l black, *pale green* .25 .20
J75 D2 2 l black, *pale green* .45 .25
J76 D2 3 l black, *pale green* ('24) 1.10 .55
J77 D2 6 l blk, *pale green* ('24) 1.40 .55
Nos. J74-J77 (4) 3.20 1.55

Postage Due Stamps of 1920-26 Overprinted

1930 ***Perf. 13½***

J78 D2 1 l black .20 .20
J79 D2 2 l black .20 .20
J80 D2 3 l black .30 .20
J81 D2 6 l black .45 .25
Nos. J78-J81 (4) 1.15 .85

Accession of King Carol II.

Catalogue values for unused stamps in this section, from this point to the end of the section, are for Never Hinged items.

Type of 1911 Issue

1931 **Wmk. 225**

J82 D2 2 l black .70 .35

D3

1932-37 **Wmk. 230**

J83 D3 1 l black .20 .20
J84 D3 2 l black .20 .20
J85 D3 3 l black ('37) .20 .20
J86 D3 6 l black ('37) .20 .20
Nos. J83-J86 (4) .80 .80

See Nos. J89-J98.

OFFICIAL STAMPS

Catalogue values for unused stamps in this section are for Never Hinged items.

Eagle Carrying National Emblem
O1

Coat of Arms
O2

1929 **Photo.** **Wmk. 95** ***Perf. 13½***

O1 O1 25b red orange .25 .20
O2 O1 50b dk brown .25 .20
O3 O1 1 l dk violet .30 .20
O4 O1 2 l olive grn .30 .20
O5 O1 3 l rose car .45 .20
O6 O1 4 l dk olive .45 .20
O7 O1 6 l Prus blue 2.50 .20
O8 O1 10 l deep blue .80 .20
O9 O1 25 l carmine brn 1.60 1.25
O10 O1 50 l purple 4.75 3.50
Nos. O1-O10 (10) 11.65 6.35

Type of Official Stamps of 1929 Overprinted

1930 **Unwmk.**

O11 O1 25b red orange .20 .20
O12 O1 50b dk brown .20 .20
O13 O1 1 l dk violet .35 .20
O14 O1 3 l rose carmine .50 .20
Nos. O11-O14 (4) 1.25 .80

Nos. O11-O14 were not placed in use without overprint.

Same Overprint on Nos. O1-O10

Wmk. 95

O15 O1 25b red orange .25 .20
O16 O1 50b dk brown .25 .20
O17 O1 1 l dk violet .25 .20
O18 O1 2 l dp green .25 .20
O19 O1 3 l rose carmine .60 .20
O20 O1 4 l olive black .75 .20
O21 O1 6 l Prus blue 2.00 .20
O22 O1 10 l deep blue .80 .20
O23 O1 25 l carmine brown 3.00 2.50
O24 O1 50 l purple 4.00 3.50
Nos. O15-O24 (10) 12.15 7.60

Accession of King Carol II to the throne of Romania (Nos O11-O24).

Perf. 13½, 13½x14½

1931-32 **Typo.** **Wmk. 225**

O25 O2 25b black .30 .20
O26 O2 1 l lilac .30 .20
O27 O2 2 l emerald .60 .40
O28 O2 3 l rose 1.00 .70
Nos. O25-O28 (4) 2.20 1.50

1932 **Wmk. 230** ***Perf. 13½***

O29 O2 25b black .30 .25
O30 O2 1 l violet .40 .35
O31 O2 2 l emerald .65 .55
O32 O2 3 l rose .80 .65
O33 O2 6 l red brown 1.25 1.00
Nos. O29-O33 (5) 3.40 2.80

PARCEL POST STAMPS

PP1

Perf. 11½, 13½ and Compound

1895 **Wmk. 163** **Typo.**

Q1 PP1 25b brown red 12.50 2.25

1896

Q2 PP1 25b vermilion 10.00 1.25

Perf. 13½ and 11½x13½

1898 **Wmk. 200**

Q3 PP1 25b brown red 7.00 1.25
a. Tête bêche pair
Q4 PP1 25b vermilion 7.00 .90

Thin Paper
Tinted Rose on Back

1905 **Unwmk.** ***Perf. 11½***

Q5 PP1 25b vermilion 6.00 1.25

1911 **White Paper**

Q6 PP1 25b pale red 6.00 1.25

No. 263 Surcharged in Carmine

1928 ***Perf. 13½***

Q7 A54 5 l on 10b yellow green .90 .20

POSTAL TAX STAMPS

Regular Issue of 1908 Overprinted

Perf. 11½, 13½, 11½x13½

1915 **Unwmk.**

RA1 A46 5b green .20 .20
RA2 A46 10b rose .30 .20

The "Timbru de Ajutor" stamps represent a tax on postal matter. The money obtained from their sale was turned into a fund for the assistance of soldiers' families.

Until 1923 the only "Timbru de Ajutor" stamps used for postal purposes were the 5b and 10b. Stamps of higher values with this inscription were used to pay the taxes on railway and theater tickets and other fiscal taxes. In 1923 the postal rate was advanced to 25b.

The Queen Weaving — PT1

1916-18 **Typo.**

RA3 PT1 5b gray blk .20 .20
RA4 PT1 5b green ('18) .45 .20
RA5 PT1 10b brown .30 .20
RA6 PT1 10b gray blk ('18) .45 .20
Nos. RA3-RA6 (4) 1.40 .80

For overprints see Nos. RA7-RA8, RAJ7-RAJ9, 3NRA1-3NRA8.

Stamps of 1916 Overprinted in Red or Black

1918 ***Perf. 13½***

RA7 PT1 5b gray blk (R) .40 .25
a. Double overprint 5.00
c. Black overprint 5.00
RA8 PT1 10b brn (Bk) .45 .25
a. Double overprint 5.00
b. Double overprint, one inverted 5.00
c. Inverted overprint 5.00

Same Overprint on RA1 and RA2

1919

RA11 A46 5b yel grn (R) *19.00 12.50*
RA12 A46 10b rose (Bk) *19.00 12.50*

Charity — PT3

Perf. 13½, 11½, 13½x11½

1921-24 **Typo.** **Unwmk.**

RA13 PT3 10b green .20 .20
RA14 PT3 25b blk ('24) .20 .20

Type of 1921-24 Issue

1928 **Wmk. 95**

RA15 PT3 25b black .75 .25

Nos. RA13, RA14 and RA15 are the only stamps of type PT3 issued for postal purposes. Other denominations were used fiscally.

Catalogue values for unused stamps in this section, from this point to the end of the section, are for Never Hinged items.

Airplane
PT4

Head of Aviator
PT5

1931 **Photo.** **Unwmk.**

RA16 PT4 50b Prus bl .30 .20
a. Double impression 15.00
RA17 PT4 1 l dk red brn .30 .20
RA18 PT4 2 l ultra .60 .20
Nos. RA16-RA18 (3) 1.20 .60

The use of these stamps, in addition to the regular postage, was obligatory on all postal matter for the interior of the country. The money thus obtained was to augment the National Fund for Aviation. When the stamps were not used to prepay the special tax, it was collected by means of Postal Tax Due stamps Nos. RAJ20 and RAJ21.

Nos. RA17 and RA18 were also used for other than postal tax.

1932 **Wmk. 230** ***Perf. 14 x 13½***

RA19 PT5 50b Prus bl .20 .20
RA20 PT5 1 l red brn .35 .20
RA21 PT5 2 l ultra .45 .20
Nos. RA19-RA21 (3) 1.00 .60

See notes after No. RA18.

After 1937 use of Nos. RA20-RA21 was limited to other than postal matter.

Nos. RA19-RA21 exist imperf.

Two stamps similar to type PT5, but inscribed "Fondul Aviatiei," were issued in 1936: 10b sepia and 20b violet.

Aviator
PT6

King Michael
PT7

1937 ***Perf. 13½***

RA22 PT6 50b Prus grn .20 .20
RA23 PT6 1 l red brn .35 .20
RA24 PT6 2 l ultra .45 .20
Nos. RA22-RA24 (3) 1.00 .60

Stamps overprinted or inscribed "Fondul Aviatiei" other than Nos. RA22, RA23 or RA24 were used to pay taxes on other than postal matters.

POSTAL TAX DUE STAMPS

Catalogue values for unused stamps in this section are for Never Hinged items.

Postage Due Stamps of 1911 Overprinted

Perf. 11½, 13½, 11½x13½

1915 **Unwmk.**

RAJ1 D2 5b dk bl, *grn* .75 .20
RAJ2 D2 10b dk bl, *grn* .75 .20
a. Wmk. 165 10.00 1.00

PTD1

PTD2

1916 Typo. Unwmk.

RAJ3 PTD1 5b brn, *grn* .40 .20
RAJ4 PTD1 10b red, *grn* .40 .20

See Nos. RAJ5-RAJ6, RAJ10-RAJ11. For overprint see No. 3NRAJ1.

1918

RAJ5 PTD1 5b red, *grn* .25 .20
a. Wmk. 165 1.00 .25
RAJ6 PTD1 10b brn, *grn* .25 .20
a. Wmk. 165 1.75 .25

Postal Tax Stamps of 1916, Overprinted in Red, Black or Blue

RAJ7 PT1 5b gray blk (R) .40 .20
a. Inverted overprint 7.50
RAJ8 PT1 10b brn (Bk) .80 .20
a. Inverted overprint 7.50
RAJ9 PT1 10b brn (Bl) *5.00 5.00*
a. Vertical overprint *20.00 15.00*
Nos. RAJ7-RAJ9 (3) 6.20 5.40

Type of 1916

1921

RAJ10 PTD1 5b red .50 .20
RAJ11 PTD1 10b brown .50 .20

1922-25 Typo.

Greenish Paper

RAJ12 PTD2 10b brown .20 .20
RAJ13 PTD2 20b brown .20 .20
RAJ14 PTD2 25b brown .20 .20
RAJ15 PTD2 50b brown .20 .20
Nos. RAJ12-RAJ15 (4) .80 .80

1923-26

RAJ16 PTD2 10b lt brn .20 .20
RAJ17 PTD2 20b lt brn .20 .20
RAJ18 PTD2 25b brown ('26) .20 .20
RAJ19 PTD2 50b brown ('26) .20 .20
Nos. RAJ16-RAJ19 (4) .80 .80

J82 and Type of 1911 Postage Due Stamps Overprinted in Red

1931 Wmk. 225 *Perf. 13½*

RAJ20 D2 1 l black .20 .20
RAJ21 D2 2 l black .20 .20

When the Postal Tax stamps for the Aviation Fund issue (Nos. RA16 to RA18) were not used to prepay the obligatory tax on letters, etc., it was collected by affixing Nos. RAJ20 and RAJ21.

OCCUPATION STAMPS

ISSUED UNDER AUSTRIAN OCCUPATION

Emperor Karl of Austria
OS1 OS2

1917 Unwmk. Engr. *Perf. 12½*

1N1 OS1 3b ol gray 1.10 .75
1N2 OS1 5b ol grn .80 .50
1N3 OS1 6b violet .80 .50
1N4 OS1 10b org brn .20 .20
1N5 OS1 12b dp bl 1.00 .60
1N6 OS1 15b brt rose .80 .50
1N7 OS1 20b red brn .20 .20
1N8 OS1 25b ultra .20 .20
1N9 OS1 30b slate .30 .25
1N10 OS1 40b olive bis .30 .25
a. Perf. 11½ 40.00 19.00
b. Perf. 11½x12½ 45.00 20.00
1N11 OS1 50b dp grn .30 .25
1N12 OS1 60b rose .30 .25
1N13 OS1 80b dl bl .20 .20
1N14 OS1 90b dk vio .30 .25
1N15 OS2 2 l rose, *straw* .45 .30
1N16 OS2 3 l grn, *bl* .75 .40
1N17 OS2 4 l rose, *grn* .75 .40
Nos. 1N1-1N17 (17) 8.75 6.00

Nos. 1N1-1N14 have "BANI" surcharged in red.

Nos. 1N1-1N17 also exist imperforate. Value, set $20.

For overprints see Austria Nos. M51-M64 with "BANI" in red; Nos. M65-M67 for "LEI" in black.

OS3

OS4

1918

1N18 OS3 3b ol gray .20 .20
1N19 OS3 5b ol grn .20 .20
1N20 OS3 6b violet .25 .25
1N21 OS3 10b org brn .25 .25
1N22 OS3 12b dp bl .20 .20
1N23 OS3 15b brt rose .20 .20
1N24 OS3 20b red brn .20 .20
1N25 OS3 25b ultra .20 .20
1N26 OS3 30b slate .20 .20
1N27 OS3 40b ol bis .20 .20
1N28 OS3 50b dp grn .25 .25
1N29 OS3 60b rose .25 .25
1N30 OS3 80b dl bl .20 .20
1N31 OS3 90b dk vio .20 .20
1N32 OS4 2 l rose, *straw* .25 .25
1N33 OS4 3 l grn, *bl* .30 .30
1N34 OS4 4 l rose, *grn* .30 .30
Nos. 1N18-1N34 (17) 3.85 3.85

Exist. imperf. Value, set $17.50.

The complete series exists with "BANI" or "LEI" inverted, also with those words and the numerals of value inverted. Neither of these sets was regularly issued.

A set of 13 stamps similar to Austria Nos. M69-M81 was prepared for use in Romania in 1918, but not placed in use there. Denominations are in bani. It is reported that they were on sale after the armistice at the Vienna post office for a few days. Value $850.

ISSUED UNDER BULGARIAN OCCUPATION

Dobruja District

Bulgarian Stamps of 1915-16 Overprinted in Red or Blue

1916 Unwmk. *Perf. 11½, 14*

2N1 A20 1s dk blue grn (R) .20 .20
2N2 A23 5s grn & vio brn (R) 1.75 .40
2N3 A24 10s brn & brnsh blk (Bl) .25 .20
2N4 A26 25s indigo & blk (Bl) .25 .20
Nos. 2N1-2N4 (4) 2.45 1.00

Many varieties of overprint exist.

ISSUED UNDER GERMAN OCCUPATION

German Stamps of 1905-17 Surcharged

1917 Wmk. 125 *Perf. 14*

3N1 A22 15b on 15pf dk vio (R) 1.00 1.00
3N2 A16 25b on 20pf ultra (Bk) 1.00 1.00
3N3 A16 40b on 30pf org & blk, *buff* (R) 17.50 17.50
Nos. 3N1-3N3 (3) 19.50 19.50

"M.V.iR." are the initials of "Militär Verwaltung in Rumänien" (Military Administration of Romania).

German Stamps of 1905-17 Surcharged

1917-18

3N4 A16 10b on 10pf car .85 .60
3N5 A22 15b on 15pf dk vio 4.50 4.50
3N6 A16 25b on 20pf ultra .75 *1.50*
3N7 A16 40b on 30pf org & blk, *buff* 1.00 1.00
a. "40" omitted 50.00 67.50
Nos. 3N4-3N7 (4) 7.10 7.60

German Stamps of 1905-17 Surcharged

1918

3N8 A16 5b on 5pf grn .20 .80
3N9 A16 10b on 10pf car .20 .75
3N10 A22 15b on 15pf dk vio .20 .20
3N11 A16 25b on 20pf bl vio .20 .75
a. 25b on 20pf blue 1.50 4.00
3N12 A16 40b on 30pf org & blk, *buff* .30 .30
Nos. 3N8-3N12 (5) 1.10 2.80

German Stamps of 1905-17 Overprinted

1918

3N13 A16 10pf carmine 7.50 *10.00*
3N14 A22 15pf dk vio 12.50 *15.00*
3N15 A16 20pf blue 1.25 *1.50*
3N16 A16 30pf org & blk, *buff* 10.00 *12.50*
Nos. 3N13-3N16 (4) 31.25 *39.00*

POSTAGE DUE STAMPS ISSUED UNDER GERMAN OCCUPATION

Postage Due Stamps and Type of Romania Overprinted in Red

Perf. 11½, 13½ and Compound

1918 Wmk. 165

3NJ1 D2 5b dk bl, *grn* 19.00 24.00
3NJ2 D2 10b dk bl, *grn* 26.00 30.00

The 20b, 30b and 50b with this overprint are fraudulent.

Unwmk.

3NJ3 D2 5b dk bl, *grn* 2.50 2.25
3NJ4 D2 10b dk bl, *grn* 2.50 2.25
3NJ5 D2 20b dk bl, *grn* 2.50 2.25
3NJ6 D2 30b dk bl, *grn* 2.50 2.25
3NJ7 D2 50b dk bl, *grn* 2.50 2.25
Nos. 3NJ1-3NJ7 (7) 57.50 65.25

POSTAL TAX STAMPS ISSUED UNDER GERMAN OCCUPATION

Romanian Postal Tax Stamps and Type of 1916

Overprinted in Red or Black

Perf. 11½, 13½ and Compound

1917 Unwmk.

3NRA1 PT1 5b gray blk (R) .20 .20
3NRA2 PT1 10b brown (Bk) .20 .20

Same, Overprinted

1917-18

3NRA3 PT1 5b gray blk (R) .40 .20
a. Black overprint 5.00 5.00
3NRA4 PT1 10b brown (Bk) .40 .20
3NRA5 PT1 10b violet (Bk) .35 .20
Nos. 3NRA3-3NRA5 (3) 1.15 .60

Same, Overprinted in Red or Black

1918

3NRA6 PT1 5b gray blk (R) *20.00*
3NRA7 PT1 10b brown (Bk) *20.00*

Same, Overprinted

1918

3NRA8 PT1 10b violet (Bk) .20 .20

POSTAL TAX DUE STAMP ISSUED UNDER GERMAN OCCUPATION

Type of Romanian Postal Tax Due Stamp of 1916 Overprinted

Perf. 11½, 13½, and Compound

1918 Wmk. 165

3NRAJ1 PTD1 10b red, *green* 2.00 2.50

ROMANIAN POST OFFICES IN THE TURKISH EMPIRE

40 Paras = 1 Piaster

King Carol I
A1 A2

Perf. 11½, 13½ and Compound

1896 Wmk. 200

Black Surcharge

1	A1	10pa on 5b blue	32.50	30.00
2	A2	20pa on 10b emer	24.00	22.50
3	A1	1pia on 25b violet	24.00	22.50
		Nos. 1-3 (3)	80.50	75.00

Violet Surcharge

4	A1	10pa on 5b blue	17.00	15.00
5	A2	20pa on 10b emer	17.00	15.00
6	A1	1pia on 25b violet	17.00	15.00
		Nos. 4-6 (3)	51.00	45.00

Romanian Stamps of 1908-18 Overprinted in Black or Red

1919 Typo. Unwmk.

7	A46	5b yellow grn	.40	.40
8	A46	10b rose	.55	.55
9	A46	15b red brown	.55	.55
10	A19	25b dp blue (R)	.70	.70
11	A19	40b gray brn (R)	1.40	1.40
		Nos. 7-11 (5)	3.60	3.60

All values exist with inverted overprint.

ROMANIAN POST OFFICES IN THE TURKISH EMPIRE POSTAL TAX STAMP

Romanian Postal Tax Stamp of 1918 Overprinted

1919 Unwmk. *Perf. 11½, 11½x13½*

RA1 PT1 5b green 1.25 1.25

ROUAD, ILE

ēl-ru-ad

(Arwad)

LOCATION — An island in the Mediterranean, off the coast of Latakia, Syria

GOVT. — French Mandate

In 1916, while a French post office was maintained on Ile Rouad, stamps were issued by France.

25 Centimes = 1 Piaster

Stamps of French Offices in the Levant, 1902-06, Overprinted

Perf. 14x13½

1916, Jan. 12 Unwmk.

1	A2	5c green	400.00	200.00
2	A3	10c rose red	400.00	200.00
3	A5	1pi on 25c blue	400.00	200.00

Dangerous counterfeits exist.

Stamps of French Offices in the Levant, 1902-06, Overprinted Horizontally

1916, Dec.

4	A2	1c gray	1.00	1.00
5	A2	2c violet brown	1.00	1.00
6	A2	3c red orange	1.00	1.00
a.		Double overprint	120.00	
7	A2	5c green	1.40	1.40
8	A3	10c rose	1.60	1.60
9	A3	15c pale red	1.60	1.60
10	A3	20c brown violet	2.50	2.50
11	A5	1pi on 25c blue	2.00	2.00
12	A3	30c violet	2.00	2.00
13	A4	40c red & pale bl	3.75	3.75
14	A6	2pi on 50c bis brn & lavender	6.00	6.00
15	A6	4pi on 1fr cl & ol grn	11.50	11.50
16	A6	20pi on 5fr dk bl & buff	27.50	27.50
		Nos. 4-16 (13)	62.85	62.85

There is a wide space between the two words of the overprint on Nos. 13 to 16 inclusive. Nos. 4, 5 and 6 are on white and coarse, grayish (G. C.) papers.

(Note on G. C. paper follows France No. 184.)

RUANDA-URUNDI

rü-ˌän-də ü'rün-dē

(Belgian East Africa)

LOCATION — In central Africa, bounded by Congo, Uganda and Tanganyika

AREA — 20,540 sq. mi.

POP. — 4,700,000 (est. 1958)

CAPITAL — Usumbura

See German East Africa for stamps issued under Belgian occupation.

100 Centimes = 1 Franc

Stamps of Belgian Congo, 1923-26, Overprinted

1924-26 *Perf. 12*

6	A32	5c orange yel	.20	.20
7	A32	10c green	.20	.20
a.		Double overprint	—	—
8	A32	15c olive brn	.20	.20
9	A32	20c olive grn	.20	.20
10	A44	20c green ('26)	.20	.20
11	A44	25c red brown	.35	.20
12	A44	30c rose red	.20	.20
13	A44	30c olive grn ('25)	.20	.20
14	A32	40c violet ('25)	.20	.20
a.		Inverted overprint	—	—
15	A44	50c gray blue	.20	.20
16	A44	50c buff ('25)	.25	.20
17	A44	75c red org	.25	.25
18	A44	75c gray blue ('25)	.35	.20
19	A44	1fr bister brown	.40	.35
20	A44	1fr dull blue ('26)	.70	.40
21	A44	3fr gray brown	5.50	2.00
22	A44	5fr gray	10.00	7.00
23	A44	10fr gray black	20.00	15.00
		Nos. 6-23 (18)	39.60	27.40

Belgian Congo Nos. 112-113 Overprinted in Red or Black

1925-27 *Perf. 12½*

24	A44	45c dk vio (R) ('27)	.20	.20
25	A44	60c car rose (Bk)	.40	.30

Stamps of Belgian Congo, 1923-1927, Overprinted

1927-29

26	A32	10c green ('29)	.20	.20
27	A32	15c ol brn ('29)	.80	.60
28	A44	35c green	.20	.20
29	A44	75c salmon red	.25	.25
30	A44	1fr rose red	.40	.30
31	A32	1.25fr dull blue	.50	.35
32	A32	1.50fr dull blue	.45	.35
33	A32	1.75fr dull blue	1.40	.65

No. 32 Surcharged

34	A32	1.75fr on 1.50fr dl bl	.45	.40
		Nos. 26-34 (9)	4.65	3.30

Nos. 30 and 33 Surcharged

1931

35	A44	1.25fr on 1fr rose red	2.25	1.25
36	A32	2fr on 1.75fr dl bl	3.00	1.75

Porter — A1

Mountain Scene — A2

Designs: 5c, 60c, Porter. 15c, Warrior. 25c, Kraal. 40c, Cattle herders. 50c, Cape buffalo. 75c, Bahutu greeting. 1fr, Barundi women. 1.25fr, Bahutu mother. 1.50fr, 2fr, Making wooden vessel. 2.50fr, 3.25fr, Preparing hides. 4fr, Watuba potter. 5fr, Mututsi dancer. 10fr, Watusi warriors. 20fr, Urundi prince.

1931-38 Engr. *Perf. 11½*

37	A1	5c dp lil rose ('38)	.20	.20
38	A2	10c gray	.20	.20
39	A2	15c pale red	.20	.20
40	A2	25c brown vio	.20	.20
41	A1	40c green	.25	.25
42	A2	50c gray lilac	.20	.20
43	A1	60c lilac rose	.20	.20
44	A1	75c gray black	.20	.20
45	A2	1fr rose red	.20	.20
46	A1	1.25fr red brown	.20	.20
47	A2	1.50fr brown vio ('37)	.20	.20
48	A2	2fr deep blue	.25	.25
49	A2	2.50fr dp blue ('37)	.25	.25
50	A2	3.25fr brown vio	.25	.25
51	A2	4fr rose	.25	.25
52	A1	5fr gray	.30	.30
53	A1	10fr brown violet	.50	.40
54	A1	20fr brown	1.75	1.75
		Nos. 37-54 (18)	5.80	5.70
		Set, never hinged	13.00	

King Albert Memorial Issue

King Albert — A16

1934 Photo.

55	A16	1.50fr black	.35	.35
		Never hinged	1.25	

SEMI-POSTAL STAMPS

Belgian Congo Nos. B10-B11 Overprinted

1925 Unwmk. *Perf. 12½*

B1	SP1	25c + 25c car & blk	.20	.25
B2	SP1	25c + 25c car & blk	.20	.25
		Set, never hinged	1.50	

No. B2 inscribed "BELGISCH CONGO."

Commemorative of the Colonial Campaigns in 1914-1918. Nos. B1 and B2 alternate in the sheet.

Belgian Congo Nos. B12-B20 Overprinted in Blue or Red

1930 *Perf. 11½*

B3	SP3	10c + 5c ver	.35	.35
B4	SP3	20c + 10c dk brn	.70	.70
B5	SP5	35c + 15c dp grn	1.40	1.40
B6	SP5	60c + 30c dl vio	1.60	1.60
B7	SP3	1fr + 50c dk car	2.50	2.50
B8	SP5	1.75fr + 75c dp bl (R)	2.75	2.75
B9	SP5	3.50fr + 1.50fr rose lake	5.75	5.75
B10	SP5	5fr + 2.50fr red brn	4.50	4.50
B11	SP5	10fr + 5fr gray blk	5.00	5.00
		Nos. B3-B11 (9)	24.55	24.55
		Set, never hinged	80.00	

On Nos. B3, B4 and B7 there is a space of 26mm between the two words of the overprint. The surtax was for native welfare.

Queen Astrid with Native Children — SP1

1936 Photo.

B12	SP1	1.25fr + 5c dk brn	.45	.45
B13	SP1	1.50fr + 10c dl rose	.45	.45
B14	SP1	2.50fr + 25c dk bl	.55	.55
		Nos. B12-B14 (3)	1.45	1.45
		Set, never hinged	4.00	

Issued in memory of Queen Astrid. The surtax was for the National League for Protection of Native Children.

POSTAGE DUE STAMPS

Belgian Congo Nos. J1-J7 Overprinted

1924-27 Unwmk. *Perf. 14*

J1	D1	5c black brn	.20	.20
J2	D1	10c deep rose	.20	.20
J3	D1	15c violet	.20	.20
J4	D1	30c green	.25	.25
J5	D1	50c ultra	.30	.30
J6	D1	50c brt blue ('27)	.30	.30
J7	D1	1fr gray	.40	.40
		Nos. J1-J7 (7)	1.85	1.85
		Set, never hinged	3.50	

RUSSIA

'rəsh-ə

(Union of Soviet Socialist Republics)

LOCATION — Eastern Europe and Northern Asia
GOVT. — Republic
AREA — 8,650,000 sq. mi.
POP. — 276,300,000 (est. 1985)
CAPITAL — Moscow

An empire until 1917, the government was overthrown in that year and a socialist union of republics was formed under the name of the Union of Soviet Socialist Republics. The USSR includes the following autonomous republics which have issued their own stamps: Armenia, Azerbaijan, Georgia and Ukraine.

100 Kopecks = 1 Ruble

Watermarks

Wmk. 166 — Colorless Numerals ("1" for Nos. 1-2, "2" for No. 3, "3" for No. 4)

Wmk. 168 — Cyrillic EZGB & Wavy Lines

Initials are those of the State Printing Plant.

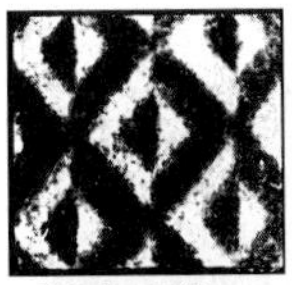

Wmk. 169 — Lozenges

Wmk. 171 — Diamonds

Wmk. 170 — Greek Border and Rosettes

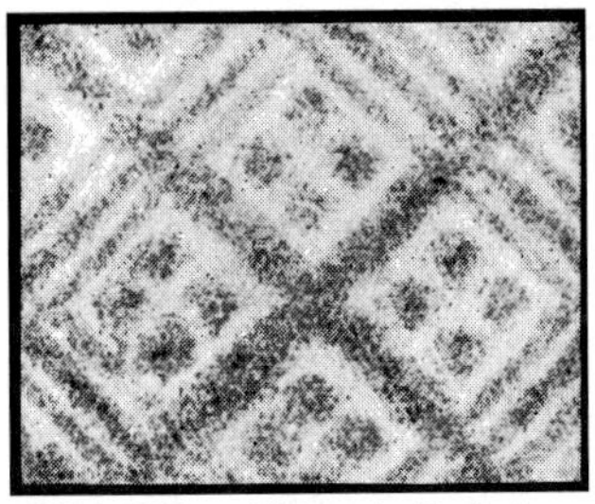

Wmk. 226 — Diamonds Enclosing Four Dots

Empire

A1

A2

Coat of Arms — A3

Wmk. 166

1857, Dec. 10 Typo. *Imperf.*

1 A1 10k brown & blue 12,500. 800.
Pen cancellation 675.
Penmark & postmark 700.
Pair 2,500.
On cover, postal cancellation only *3,500.*
On cover, pen cancellation *1,750.*
On cover, pen & postal cancellations *3,000.*

Full margins = ¾mm.

Genuine unused copies of No. 1 are exceedingly rare. Most of those offered are used with pen cancellation removed. The unused value is for an example without gum. The very few known stamps with original gum sell for much more.

See Poland for similar stamp inscribed "ZALOT KOP. 10."

1858, Jan. 10 *Perf. 14½, 15*

2 A1 10k brown & blue 4,250. 125.
On cover 350.
3 A1 20k blue & orange 5,750. 850.
On cover *3,250.*
4 A1 30k carmine & green 6,250. 1,750.
On cover *7,250.*

No. 3 exists in green & violet. It is an essay, value about $1,000 without watermark, about $750 with watermark.

1858-64 Unwmk. *Perf. 12½*
Wove Paper

5 A2 1k black & yel ('64) 67.50 42.50
On cover 100.00
On cover, single franking 425.00
a. 1k black & orange 100.00 42.50
On cover 100.00
On cover, single franking 425.00
6 A2 3k black & green ('64) 425.00 80.00
On cover 160.00
7 A2 5k black & lilac ('64) 300.00 90.00
On cover 300.00
8 A1 10k brown & blue 275.00 10.00
On cover 70.00
9 A1 20k blue & orange 625.00 90.00
On cover 400.00
a. Half used as 10k on cover —
10 A1 30k carmine & green 850.00 100.00
On cover 700.00
Nos. 5-10 (6) 2,542. 412.50

1863

11 A3 5k black & blue 25.00 *150.00*
On cover, local use, dated 1863-July 1864 *4,500.*
On cover, dated after July 1864 *1,250.*

No. 11 was issued to pay local postage in St. Petersburg and Moscow. It is known to have been used in other cities. In Aug. 1864 it was authorized for use on mail addressed to other destinations. No. 11 was withdrawn from use 12/21/84.

1865, June 2 *Perf. 14½, 15*

12 A2 1k black & yellow 100.00 20.00
On cover 35.00
On cover, single franking 110.00
a. 1k black & orange 110.00 30.00
On cover 45.00
On cover, single franking 135.00
13 A2 3k black & green 110.00 10.00
On cover 30.00
14 A2 5k black & lilac 125.00 20.00
On cover 40.00
15 A1 10k brown & blue 100.00 3.00
On cover 15.00
a. Thick paper 125.00 7.50
On cover 35.00
17 A1 20k blue & orange 400.00 40.00
On cover 90.00
18 A1 30k carmine & green 500.00 50.00
On cover 175.00
Nos. 12-18 (6) 1,335. 143.00

1866-70 Wmk. 168
Horizontally Laid Paper

19 A2 1k black & yellow 6.50 .75
On cover 2.50
On cover, single franking 27.50
a. 1k black & orange 6.50 1.25
On cover 3.00
On cover, single franking 30.00
b. Imperf. *3,250.*
c. Vertically laid 225.00 50.00
On cover 100.00
On cover, single franking 200.00
d. Groundwork inverted *6,250.* *2,250.*
e. Thick paper 75.00 60.00
f. As "c," imperf. 8,500. 8,000.
g. As "b," "c" & "d" *10,000.* *10,000.*
h. 1k blk & org, vert. laid paper 275.00 40.00
On cover 100.00
On cover, single franking 200.00
20 A2 3k black & dp green 6.50 1.00
On cover 3.00
a. 3k black & yellow green 6.50 1.00
On cover 3.00
b. Imperf. *2,500.*
c. Vertically laid 375.00 55.00
On cover 100.00
d. V's in groundwork (error) ('70) 1,000. 80.00
On cover 450.00
e. 3k black & blue green 5.00 .60
On cover 3.00
22 A2 5k black & lilac 7.50 2.00
On cover 3.00
a. 5k black & gray 125.00 20.00
On cover 175.00
b. Imperf. 3,500. 2,000.
c. Vertically laid 1,050. 175.00
On cover 275.00
d. As "c," imperf. *4,000.*
23 A1 10k brown & blue 45.00 1.50
On cover 2.50
a. Vertically laid 250.00 11.00
On cover 60.00
b. Center inverted *60,000.*
c. Imperf. *5,000.*
24 A1 20k blue & orange 100.00 15.00
On cover 30.00
a. Vertically laid 2,000. 150.00
On cover 175.00
25 A1 30k carmine & green 110.00 35.00
On cover 225.00
On cover, single franking 450.00
a. Vertically laid 750.00 52.50
On cover 225.00
On cover, single franking 525.00
Nos. 19-25 (6) 275.50 55.25

Arms — A4

1875-82
Horizontally Laid Paper

26 A2 2k black & red 9.50 .75
On cover 4.00
On cover, single franking 37.50
a. Vertically laid 3,750. 125.00
On cover 275.00
On cover, single franking 2,250.
b. Groundwork inverted *45,000.*
27 A4 7k gray & rose ('79) 6.00 .50
On cover 2.00
a. Imperf. *25,000.*
b. Vertically laid 1,750. 65.00
On cover 300.00
c. Wmkd. hexagons ('79) *110,000.*
d. Center inverted *50,000.*
e. Center omitted *3,000.* *3,000.*
f. 7k black & carmine ('80) 5.75 .60
On cover 3.50
g. 7k pale gray & carmine ('82) 6.25 .60
On cover 2.50
28 A4 8k gray & rose 7.50 .85
On cover 2.25
a. Vertically laid 1,500. 70.00
On cover 475.00
b. Imperf. *25,000.*
c. "C" instead of "B" in "Bocem" 200.00 75.00

29 A4 10k brown & blue 50.00 6.50
On cover 20.00
a. Center inverted 65,000.
30 A4 20k blue & orange 70.00 11.00
On cover 20.00
a. Cross-shaped "T" in bottom word 125.00 30.00
b. Center inverted 85,000.
Nos. 26-30 (5) 143.00 19.60

The hexagon watermark of No. 27c is that of revenue stamps. Four examples of No. 27c are recorded, all used at Perm. One example of No. 27d is recorded.

See Finland for stamps similar to designs A4-A15, which have "dot in circle" devices or are inscribed "Markka," "Markkaa," "Pen.," or "Pennia."

Imperial Eagle and Post Horns
A5 A6

Perf. 14 to 15 and Compound

1883-88 Wmk. 168

Horizontally Laid Paper

31 A5 1k orange 4.00 .50
a. Imperf. 700.00 700.00
b. Groundwork inverted 4,000. 4,000.
c. 1k yellow 3.00 .55
32 A5 2k dark green 4.75 .65
a. 2k yellow green ('88) 3.75 .55
b. Imperf. 700.00 700.00
c. Wove paper 700.00 500.00
d. Groundwork inverted 4,000.
33 A5 3k carmine 6.25 .45
a. Imperf. 3,000. 3,000.
b. Groundwork inverted 6,000.
c. Wove paper 500.00 425.00
34 A5 5k red violet 7.25 .45
a. Groundwork inverted 4,000.
35 A5 7k blue 6.25 .45
a. Imperf. 750.00 500.00
b. Groundwork inverted 1,600. 1,600.
c. Double impression of frame and center 5,000.
36 A6 14k blue & rose 15.00 .75
a. Imperf. 800.00 800.00
b. Center inverted 7,000. 6,000.
c. Diagonal half surcharge "7" in red, on cover ('84) 10,000.
37 A6 35k violet & green 50.00 6.00
38 A6 70k brown & orange 60.00 7.00
Nos. 31-38 (8) 153.50 16.25

Before 1882 the 1, 2, 3 and 5 kopecks had small numerals in the background; beginning with No. 31 these denominations have a background of network, like the higher values.

No. 36c is handstamped. It is known with cancellations of Tiflis and Kutais, both in Georgia. It is believed to be of philatelic origin.

A7

1884 ***Perf. 13½, 13½x11½***

Vertically Laid Paper

39 A7 3.50r black & gray 700. 700.
a. Horiz. laid 100,000. 15,000.
40 A7 7r black & orange 750. 750.

Forgeries exist, especially with forged postmarks.

A8

Imperial Eagle and Post Horns with Thunderbolts — A9

With Thunderbolts Across Post Horns

Perf. 14 to 15 and Compound

1889, May 14

Horizontally Laid Paper

41 A8 4k rose .75 .30
a. Groundwork inverted 3,250.
42 A8 10k dark blue .85 .25
43 A8 20k blue & carmine 2.50 .75
44 A8 50k violet & green 6.50 1.00

Perf. 13½

45 A9 1r lt brn, brn & org 20.00 3.00
a. Pair, imperf. between 750.00 750.00
b. Center omitted 500.00 500.00
Nos. 41-45 (5) 30.60 5.30

See #57C, 60, 63, 66, 68, 82, 85, 87, 126, 129, 131. For surcharges see #216, 219, 223, 226.

A10 A11

A12 A13

With Thunderbolts Across Post Horns

1889-92 ***Perf. 14½x15***

Horizontally Laid Paper

46 A10 1k orange 1.50 .40
a. Imperf. 500.00 500.00
47 A10 2k green 1.50 .40
a. Imperf. 350.00 350.00
b. Groundwork inverted
48 A10 3k carmine 1.50 .40
a. Imperf. 350.00 350.00
49 A10 5k red violet 2.00 .50
b. Groundwork omitted 725.00 725.00
50 A10 7k dark blue 1.50 .40
a. Imperf. 500.00 500.00
b. Groundwork inverted 6,000. 6,000.
c. Groundwork omitted 200.00 200.00
51 A11 14k blue & rose 5.00 .40
a. Center inverted 4,500. 4,000.
52 A11 35k violet & green 12.00 1.50

Perf. 13½

53 A12 3.50r black & gray 25.00 9.00
54 A12 7r black & yellow 75.00 12.00
a. Dbl. impression of black 28,000.
Nos. 46-54 (9) 125.00 25.00

Perf. 14 to 15 and Compound

1902-05

Vertically Laid Paper

55 A10 1k orange 3.00 .35
a. Imperf. 1,100. 1,100.
b. Groundwork inverted 850.00 850.00
c. Groundwork omitted 200.00 200.00
56 A10 2k yellow green 3.00 .35
a. 2k deep green 9.00 .70
b. Groundwork omitted 600.00 300.00
c. Groundwork inverted 850.00 850.00
d. Groundwork double 425.00 425.00
57 A10 3k rose red 3.00 .35
a. Groundwork omitted 350.00 175.00
b. Double impression 200.00 165.00
d. Imperf. 500.00 500.00
e. Groundwork inverted 210.00 210.00
57C A8 4k rose red ('04) 3.00 .50
f. Double impression 200.00 200.00
g. Groundwork inverted 4,000. 4,000.
58 A10 5k red violet 5.00 .60
a. 5k dull violet 7.00 2.50
b. Groundwork inverted 850.00 850.00
c. Imperf. 250.00 250.00
d. Groundwork omitted 250.00 165.00
59 A10 7k dark blue 3.00 .35
a. Groundwork omitted 350.00 300.00
b. Imperf. 375.00 375.00
c. Groundwork inverted 800.00 800.00

60 A8 10k dark blue ('04) 3.00 .35
a. Groundwork inverted 12.50 5.00
b. Groundwork omitted 165.00 35.00
c. Groundwork double 165.00 35.00
61 A11 14k blue & rose 7.50 .35
a. Center inverted 5,000. 3,750.
b. Center omitted 1,100. 700.00
62 A11 15k brown vio & blue ('05) 10.00 1.25
a. Center omitted
b. Center inverted 4,000. 3,500.
63 A8 20k blue & car ('04) 9.00 .75
64 A11 25k dull grn & lil ('05) 10.00 1.25
a. Center inverted 4,000. 3,750.
b. Center omitted 1,500. 1,500.
65 A11 35k dk vio & grn 18.00 2.00
a. Center inverted 5,500.
b. Center omitted 1,500.
66 A8 50k vio & grn ('05) 22.50 1.00
67 A11 70k brown & org 27.50 1.25

Perf. 13½

68 A9 1r lt brown, brn & orange 20.00 1.00
a. Perf. 11½ 500.00 50.00
b. Perf. 13½x11½, 11½x13½ 675.00 575.00
c. Imperf. 600.00
d. Center inverted 250.00 250.00
e. Center omitted 250.00 150.00
f. Pair, imperf. btwn. 1,200. 250.00
69 A12 3.50r black & gray 10.00 3.00
a. Center inverted 10,500.
b. Imperf., pair 2,000. 2,000.
70 A12 7r black & yel 10.00 4.00
a. Center inverted 7,500. 7,500.
b. Horiz. pair, imperf. btwn. 1,600. 1,600.
c. Imperf., pair 5,000. 5,000.

1906 ***Perf. 13½***

71 A13 5r dk blue, grn & pale blue 25.00 5.00
a. Perf. 11½ 250.00 275.00
72 A13 10r car rose, yel & gray 100.00 11.50
Nos. 55-72 (19) 292.50 35.20

The design of No. 72 differs in many details from the illustration. Nos. 71-72 were printed in sheets of 25.

See Nos. 80-81, 83-84, 86, 108-109, 125, 127-128, 130, 132-135, 137-138. For surcharges see Nos. 217-218, 220-222, 224-225, 227-229.

A14 A15

Vertical Lozenges of Varnish on Face

1909-12 Unwmk. ***Perf. 14x14½***

Wove Paper

73 A14 1k dull orange yellow .25 .20
a. 1k orange yellow ('09) .25 .20
c. Double impression 100.00 100.00
74 A14 2k dull green .25 .20
a. 2k green ('09) .25 .20
b. Double impression 100.00 100.00
75 A14 3k carmine .25 .20
a. 3k rose red ('09) .25 .20
76 A15 4k carmine .25 .20
a. 4k carmine rose ('09) .25 .20
77 A14 5k claret .25 .20
a. 5k lilac ('12) .75 .65
b. Double impressions 100.00 100.00
78 A14 7k blue .25 .20
a. 7k light blue ('09) 1.75 .65
b. Imperf. 1,000. 250.00
79 A15 10k dark blue .25 .20
a. 10k light blue ('09) 500.00 85.00
b. 10k pale blue 6.50 1.00
80 A11 14k dk blue & car .25 .20
a. 14k blue & rose ('09) .25 .20
81 A11 15k red brown & dp blue .25 .20
a. 15k dull violet & blue ('09) .95 .40
c. Center omitted 115.00 85.00
d. Center double 50.00 50.00
82 A8 20k dull bl & dk car .25 .20
a. 20k blue & carmine ('10) .95 .55
b. Groundwork omitted 20.00 13.00
c. Center double 30.00 30.00
d. Center and value omitted 85.00 85.00
83 A11 25k dl grn & dk vio .25 .20
a. 25k green & violet ('09) .35 .30
b. Center omitted 115.00 115.00
c. Center double 25.00 25.00
84 A11 35k red brn & grn .25 .20
a. 35k brown vio & yel green .60 .40
b. 35k violet & green ('09) .60 .40
c. Center double 25.00 25.00
85 A8 50k red brn & grn .25 .20
a. 50k violet & green ('09) .60 .40
b. Groundwork omitted 20.00 20.00

c. Center double 32.50 32.50
d. Center and value omitted 115.00 115.00
86 A11 70k brn & red org .25 .20
a. 70k lt brown & orange ('09) .35 .25
b. Center double 40.00 40.00
c. Center omitted 115.00 115.00

Perf. 13½

87 A9 1r pale brown, dk brn & orange .25 .25
a. 1r pale brn, brn & org ('10) .30 .20
b. Perf. 12½ .30 .20
c. Groundwork inverted 20.00 20.00
d. Pair, imperf. between 22.50 22.50
e. Center inverted 25.00 25.00
f. Center double 16.00 16.00
Nos. 73-87 (15) 3.75 3.05

See Nos. 119-124. For surcharges see Nos. 117-118, B24-B29.

No. 87a was issued in sheets of 40 stamps, while Nos. 87 and 87b came in sheets of 50. Nos. 87g-87k are listed below No. 138a.

Nearly all values of this issue are known without the lines of varnish.

The 7k has two types:

I — The scroll bearing the top inscription ends at left with three short lines of shading beside the first letter. Four pearls extend at lower left between the leaves and denomination panel.

II — Inner lines of scroll at top left end in two curls; three pearls at lower left.

Three clichés of type II (an essay) were included by mistake in the plate used for the first printing. Value of pair, type I with type II, unused $2,500.

SURCHARGES

Russian stamps of types A6-A15 with various surcharges may be found listed under Armenia, Batum, Far Eastern Republic, Georgia, Latvia, Siberia, South Russia, Transcaucasian Federated Republics, Ukraine, Russian Offices in China, Russian Offices in the Turkish Empire and Army of the Northwest.

Peter I — A16

Alexander II — A17

Alexander III — A18

Peter I — A19

Nicholas II
A20 A21

Catherine II — A22

Nicholas I — A23

Alexander I — A24

Alexis Mikhailovich A25

Paul I A26

Elizabeth Petrovna A27

Michael Feodorovich A28

The Kremlin — A29

Winter Palace — A30

Romanov Castle — A31

Nicholas II — A32

Without Lozenges of Varnish

1913, Jan. 2 Typo. *Perf. 13½*

88	A16	1k brown orange	.35	.20
89	A17	2k yellow green	.40	.20
90	A18	3k rose red	.50	.20
b.		Double impression	700.00	
91	A19	4k dull red	.60	.20
92	A20	7k brown	.80	.25
b.		Double impression	900.00	350.00
93	A21	10k deep blue	1.00	.30
94	A22	14k blue green	1.50	.40
95	A23	15k yellow brown	2.50	.60
96	A24	20k olive green	3.50	.70
97	A25	25k red violet	3.00	1.10
98	A26	35k gray vio & dk grn	2.75	.75
99	A27	50k brown & slate	3.00	1.10
100	A28	70k yel grn & brn	3.25	1.50

Engr.

101	A29	1r deep green	18.00	5.00
102	A30	2r red brown	22.50	8.00
103	A31	3r dark violet	27.50	15.00
104	A32	5r black brown	22.50	20.00
		Nos. 88-104 (17)	113.65	55.50

Imperf

88a	A16	1k brown orange	*775.00*
90a	A18	3k rose red	*775.00*
92a	A20	7k brown	*775.00*
93a	A21	10k deep blue	*775.00*
102a	A30	2r red brown	*775.00*
103b	A31	3r dark violet	*775.00*

Tercentenary of the founding of the Romanov dynasty.

See #105-107, 112-116, 139-141. For surcharges see #110-111, Russian Offices in the Turkish Empire 213-227.

Arms and 5-line Inscription on Back

1915, Oct. Typo. *Perf. 13½*

Thin Cardboard

Without Gum

105	A21	10k blue	1.00	*4.25*
106	A23	15k brown	1.00	*4.25*
107	A24	20k olive green	1.00	*4.25*
		Nos. 105-107 (3)	3.00	*12.75*

Imperf

105a	A21	10k	75.00	
106a	A23	15k	75.00	50.00
107a	A24	20k	75.00	

Nos. 105-107, 112-116 and 139-141 were issued for use as paper money, but contrary to regulations were often used for postal purposes. Back inscription means: "Having circulation on par with silver subsidiary coins."

Types of 1906 Issue

Vertical Lozenges of Varnish on Face

1915 *Perf. 13½, 13½x13*

108	A13	5r ind, grn & lt blue	.50	.45
a.		5r dk bl, grn & pale bl ('15)	2.50	.70
b.		Perf. 12½	3.25	1.00
c.		Center double	50.00	
d.		Pair, imperf. between	200.00	
109	A13	10r car lake, yel & gray	.50	.45
a.		10r carmine, yel & light gray	.65	.50
b.		10r rose red, yel & gray ('15)	1.10	.65
c.		10r car, yel & gray blue (error)	3,000.	
d.		Groundwork inverted	375.00	
e.		Center double	50.00	50.00

Nos. 108a and 109b were issued in sheets of 25. Nos. 108, 108b, 109 and 109a came in sheets of 50. Chemical forgeries of No. 109c exist. Genuine copies usually are centered to upper right.

Nos. 92, 94 Surcharged

1916

110	A20	10k on 7k brown	.50	.45
a.		Inverted surcharge	70.00	70.00
111	A22	20k on 14k bl grn	.50	.45

Types of 1913 Issue

Arms, Value & 4-line inscription on Back

Surcharged Large Numerals on Nos. 112-113

1916-17

Thin Cardboard

Without Gum

112	A16	1 on 1k brn org ('17)	2.50	*5.00*
113	A17	2 on 2k yel green ('17)	2.50	*5.00*

Without Surcharge

114	A16	1k brown orange	25.00	*32.50*
115	A17	2k yellow green	35.00	*55.00*
116	A18	3k rose red	.75	*4.50*

See note after No. 107.

Nos. 78a, 80a Surcharged:

a

b

1917 *Perf. 14x14½*

117	A14	10k on 7k lt blue	.50	.25
a.		Inverted surcharge	50.00	*60.00*
b.		Double surcharge	60.00	
118	A11	20k on 14k bl & rose	.50	.25
a.		Inverted surcharge	50.00	50.00

Provisional Government

Civil War

Type of 1889-1912 Issues

Vertical Lozenges of Varnish on Face

Two types of 7r:
Type I — Single outer frame line.
Type II — Double outer frame line.

1917 Typo. *Imperf.*

Wove Paper

119	A14	1k orange	.20	.20
120	A14	2k gray green	.20	.20
121	A14	3k red	.20	.20
122	A15	4k carmine	.20	.20
123	A14	5k claret	.20	.20
124	A15	10k dark blue	18.00	18.00
125	A11	15k red brn & dp blue	.20	.20
a.		Center omitted	65.00	
126	A8	20k blue & car	.20	.35
a.		Groundwork omitted	25.00	25.00
127	A11	25k grn & gray vio	.75	1.00
128	A11	35k red brn & grn	.20	.35
129	A8	50k brn vio & grn	.20	.25
a.		Groundwork omitted	25.00	25.00
130	A11	70k brn & orange	.20	.40
a.		Center omitted	115.00	
131	A9	1r pale brn, brn & red org	.20	.20
a.		Center inverted	20.00	20.00
b.		Center omitted	20.00	20.00
c.		Center double	20.00	20.00
d.		Groundwork double	14.00	14.00
e.		Groundwork inverted	20.00	20.00
f.		Groundwork omitted	22.50	22.50
g.		Frame double	16.00	16.00
132	A12	3.50r mar & lt green	.20	.25
133	A13	5r dk blue, grn & pale blue	.30	.35
a.		5r dk bl, grn & yel (error)	1,000.	
b.		Groundwork inverted	400.00	
134	A12	7r dk green & pink (I)	.75	1.00
a.		Center inverted		*5,000.*
135	A13	10r scarlet, yel & gray	40.00	*40.00*
a.		10r scarlet, green & gray (error)	1,250.	
		Nos. 119-135 (17)	62.20	63.35

Beware of trimmed copies of No. 109 offered as No. 135.

Vertical Lozenges of Varnish on Face

1917 *Perf. 13½, 13½x13*

137	A12	3.50r mar & lt grn	.20	.20
138	A12	7r dark green & pink (II)	.20	.20
d.		Type I	2.00	2.00

Perf. 12½

137a	A12	3.50r maroon & lt grn	.20	.20
138a	A12	7r dk grn & pink (II)	1.00	1.00

Horizontal Lozenges of Varnish on Face

Perf. 13½x13

87g	A9	1r pale brown, brn & red orange	.20	.20
h.		Imperf.	12.50	
i.		As "h," center omitted	25.00	
j.		As "h," center inverted	25.00	
k.		As "h," center double	25.00	
137b	A12	3.50r mar & lt green	.65	.20
d.		Imperf.	250.00	
138b	A12	7r dk grn & pink (II)	.65	.20
c.		Imperf.	250.00	

Nos. 87g, 137b and 138b often show the eagle with little or no embossing.

Types of 1913 Issue

Surcharge & 4-line Inscription on Back

Surcharged Large Numerals

1917

Thin Cardboard, Without Gum

139	A16	1 on 1k brown org	1.50	*6.00*
a.		Imperf.	30.00	30.00
140	A17	2 on 2k yel green	1.50	*6.00*
a.		Imperf.	30.00	30.00
b.		Surch. omitted, imperf.	45.00	45.00

Without Surcharge

141	A18	3k rose red	2.00	*6.00*
a.		Imperf.		
		Nos. 139-141 (3)	5.00	*18.00*

See note after No. 107.

Stamps overprinted with a Liberty Cap on Crossed Swords or with reduced facsimiles of pages of newspapers were a private speculation and without official sanction.

RUSSIAN TURKESTAN

Russian stamps of 1917-18 surcharged as above are frauds.

Russian Soviet Federated Socialist Republic

Severing Chain of Bondage — A33

1918 Typo. *Perf. 13½*

149	A33	35k blue	.25	*5.00*
a.		Imperf., pair	225.00	
150	A33	70k brown	.25	*5.00*
a.		Imperf., pair	750.00	

In 1918-1922 various revenue stamps were permitted to be used for postal duty, sometimes surcharged with new values, more often not.

For surcharges see Nos. B18-B23, J1-J9 and note following No. B17.

Symbols of Agriculture — A40

Symbols of Industry — A41

Soviet Symbols of Agriculture and Industry — A42

Science and Arts — A43

1921 Unwmk. Litho. *Imperf.*

177	A40	1r orange	1.75	*1.75*
178	A40	2r lt brown	1.25	*1.25*
179	A41	5r dull ultra	1.50	.45
180	A42	20r blue	1.50	*3.00*
a.		Pelure paper	3.25	2.75
b.		Double impression	35.00	
181	A40	100r orange	.20	.20
a.		Pelure paper	.20	.20
182	A40	200r lt brown	.20	.25
a.		200r olive brown	15.00	15.00
183	A43	250r dull violet	.20	.20
a.		Pelure paper	.20	.20
b.		Chalk surfaced paper	.20	.20
c.		Tête bêche pair	20.00	20.00
d.		Double impression	35.00	
184	A40	300r green	.20	.25
a.		Pelure paper	20.00	20.00
185	A41	500r blue	.20	.35
186	A41	1000r carmine	.20	.30
a.		Chalk surfaced paper	.20	.20
b.		Thick paper	.20	.20
c.		Pelure paper	.20	.20
		Nos. 177-186 (10)	7.20	8.00

See #203, 205. For surcharges see #191-194, 196-199, 201, 210, B40, B43-B47, J10.

New Russia Triumphant A44

Type I — 37½mm by 23½mm.
Type II — 38½mm by 23¼mm.

1921, Aug. 10 Wmk. 169 Engr.

187	A44	40r slate, type II	.60	1.00
a.		Type I	2.00	1.25

The types are caused by paper shrinkage. One type has the watermark sideways in relation to the other.

For surcharges see Nos. 195, 200.

Initials Stand for Russian Soviet Federated Socialist Republic — A45

1921 Litho. Unwmk.

188	A45	100r orange	.50	.55
189	A45	250r violet	.50	.55
190	A45	1000r carmine rose	1.00	1.40
		Nos. 188-190 (3)	2.00	2.50

4th anniversary of Soviet Government.

A 200r was not regularly issued. Value $45.

Nos. 177-179 Surcharged in Black

1922

191	A40	5000r on 1r orange	1.50	.80
a.		Inverted surcharge	100.00	22.50
b.		Double surch., red & blk	100.00	22.50
c.		Pair, one without surcharge	125.00	
192	A40	5000r on 2r lt brown	1.25	1.25
a.		Inverted surcharge	75.00	15.00
b.		Double surcharge	70.00	
193	A41	5000r on 5r ultra	2.00	2.00
a.		Inverted surcharge	75.00	30.00
b.		Double surcharge	75.00	

Beware of digitally created forgeries of the errors of Nos. 191-193 and 196-199.

No. 180 Surcharged

194	A42	5000r on 20r blue	2.00	2.50
a.		Pelure paper	2.00	2.25
b.		Pair, one without surcharge	100.00	

Nos. 177-180, 187-187a Surcharged in Black or Red

Wmk. Lozenges (169)

195	A44	10,000r on 40r, type I	5.00	*3.25*
a.		Inverted surcharge	65.00	15.00
b.		Type II	6.00	2.50
c.		"1.0000" instead of "10.000"	200.00	
d.		Double surcharge	85.00	

Red Surcharge

Unwmk.

196	A40	5000r on 1r org	2.50	2.00
a.		Inverted surcharge	75.00	15.00
197	A40	5000r on 2r lt brn	2.25	2.00
a.		Inverted surcharge	100.00	100.00
198	A41	5000r on 5r ultra	2.25	2.00
199	A42	5000r on 20r blue	2.25	2.25
a.		Inverted surcharge	100.00	100.00
b.		Pelure paper	5.00	5.00

Wmk. Lozenges (169)

200	A44	10,000r on 40r, type I (R)	2.00	1.50
a.		Inverted surcharge	100.00	18.00
b.		Double surcharge	100.00	18.00
c.		With periods after Russian letters	300.00	35.00
d.		Type II	.75	.75
e.		As "a," type II	100.00	30.00
f.		As "c," type II	225.00	45.00

No. 183 Surcharged in Black or Blue Black

1922, Mar. Unwmk.

201	A43	7500r on 250r (Bk)	.20	.20
a.		Pelure paper	.20	.20
b.		Chalk surfaced paper	.20	.25
c.		Blue black surcharge	.20	.20
		Nos. 191-201 (11)	23.20	19.75

Nos. 201, 201a and 201b exist with surcharge inverted (value about $20 each), and double (value about $25 each).

The horizontal surcharge was prepared but not issued.

Type of 1921 and

"Workers of the World Unite" A46

1922 Litho. Wmk. 171

202	A46	5000r dark violet	.75	3.25
203	A42	7500r blue	.25	.35
204	A46	10,000r blue	25.00	18.00

Unwmk.

205	A42	7500r blue, *buff*	.25	.40
a.		Double impression	100.00	
206	A46	22,500r dk violet, *buff*	.50	.60
		Nos. 202-206 (5)	26.75	22.60

For surcharges see Nos. B41-B42.

No. 183 Surcharged Diagonally

1922 Unwmk. *Imperf.*

210	A43	100,000r on 250r	.50	.50
a.		Inverted surcharge	60.00	60.00
b.		Pelure paper	.70	.70
c.		Chalk surfaced paper	.50	.50
d.		As "b," inverted surcharge	100.00	100.00

Marking 5th Anniversary of October Revolution — A48

1922 Typo.

211	A48	5r ocher & black	.20	.25
212	A48	10r brown & black	.20	.25
213	A48	25r violet & black	.50	.60
214	A48	27r rose & black	1.25	1.00
215	A48	45r blue & black	.90	.75
		Nos. 211-215 (5)	3.05	2.85

Pelure Paper

213a	A48	25r violet & black	60.00
214a	A48	27r rose & black	60.00
215a	A48	45r blue & black	65.00

5th anniv. of the October Revolution. Sold in the currency of 1922 which was valued at 10,000 times that of the preceding years.

For surcharges see Nos. B38-B39.

Nos. 81, 82a, 85-86, 125-126, 129-130 Surcharged

1922-23 *Perf. 14½x15*

216	A8	5r on 20k	.90	2.00
a.		Inverted surcharge	30.00	30.00
b.		Double surcharge	35.00	35.00
217	A11	20r on 15k	1.50	2.00
a.		Inverted surcharge	45.00	45.00
218	A11	20r on 70k	.90	.35
a.		Inverted surcharge	25.00	17.00
b.		Double surcharge	20.00	20.00
219	A8	30r on 50k	1.50	.50
a.		Inverted surcharge	25.00	25.00
c.		Groundwork omitted	50.00	50.00
d.		Double surcharge	16.00	16.00
220	A11	40r on 15k	.95	.35
a.		Inverted surcharge	25.00	25.00
b.		Double surcharge	30.00	30.00
221	A11	100r on 15k	.95	.35
a.		Inverted surcharge	22.50	22.50
b.		Double surcharge	30.00	30.00
222	A11	200r on 15k	.95	.35
a.		Inverted surcharge	30.00	30.00
b.		Double surcharge	20.00	20.00

Nos. 218-220, 222 exist in pairs, one without surcharge; Nos. 221-222 with triple surcharge; No. 221 with double surcharge, one inverted. Value, each $100.

Imperf

223	A8	5r on 20k	10.00	15.00
224	A11	20r on 15k	*1,500.*	
225	A11	20r on 70k	1.00	1.00
a.		Inverted surcharge	17.50	17.50
226	A8	30r on 50k brn vio & green	5.00	4.50
227	A11	40r on 15k	.30	.30
a.		Inverted surcharge	35.00	35.00
b.		Double surcharge	27.50	27.50
228	A11	100r on 15k	2.25	1.10
a.		Inverted surcharge	50.00	50.00
229	A11	200r on 15k	2.25	1.00
a.		Inverted surcharge	50.00	50.00
b.		Double surcharge	35.00	35.00
		Nos. 216-223,225-229 (13)	28.45	28.80

Forgeries of No. 223-229 exist, including a dangerous digital forgery of No. 224.

Worker A49

Soldier A50

1922-23 Typo. *Imperf.*

230	A49	10r blue	.25	.25
231	A50	50r brown	.25	.25
232	A50	70r brown violet	.25	.25
233	A50	100r red	.25	.30
		Nos. 230-233 (4)	1.00	1.05

1923 *Perf. 14x14½*

234	A49	10r dp bl, perf. 13½	.30	.25
a.		Perf. 14	15.00	16.00
b.		Perf. 12½	1.00	.85
235	A50	50r brown	.30	.25
a.		Perf. 12½	7.50	6.00
b.		Perf. 13½	1.50	2.00
236	A50	70r brown violet	.30	.25
a.		Perf. 12½	2.00	2.00
237	A50	100r red	.30	.40
a.		Cliché of 70r in plate of 100r	40.00	35.00
b.		Corrected cliché	150.00	175.00
		Nos. 234-237 (4)	1.20	1.15

No. 237b has extra broken line at right.

Soldier — Worker — Peasant
A51 A52 A53

1923 *Perf. 14½x15*

238	A51	3r rose	.20	.25
239	A52	4r brown	.20	.25
240	A53	5r light blue	.20	.25
a.		Double impression	*50.00*	*50.00*
241	A51	10r gray	.20	.25
e.		Double impression	75.00	
241A	A51	20r brown violet	.20	.75
b.		Double impression	*75.00*	*75.00*
		Nos. 238-241A (5)	1.00	1.75

Imperf

238a	A51	3r rose	15.00	*20.00*
239a	A52	4r brown	25.00	*25.00*
b.		As "a," double impression	*75.00*	
240b	A53	5r light blue	8.00	*10.00*
241d	A51	10r gray	10.00	*10.00*
f.		As "d," double impression	75.00	
241c	A51	20r brown violet	225.00	75.00

Stamps of 1r buff, type A52, and 2r green, type A53, perf. 12 and imperf. were prepared but not put in use. Value $1 each.

The imperfs of Nos. 238-241A were sold only by the philatelic bureau in Moscow.

Stamps of 20r, type A51, printed in gray black or dull violet are essays. Value, $75 each.

The stamps of this and the following issues were sold for the currency of 1923, one ruble of which was equal to 100 rubles of 1922 and 1,000,000 rubles of 1921.

Union of Soviet Socialist Republics

Reaping — A54

Sowing — A55

Fordson Tractor A56

Symbolical of the Exhibition — A57

1923, Aug. 19 Litho. *Imperf.*

242	A54	1r brown & orange	1.50	*3.00*
243	A55	2r dp grn & pale grn	1.50	*3.00*
244	A56	5r dp bl & pale blue	1.50	*4.00*
245	A57	7r rose & pink	1.50	*5.00*

Perf. 12½, 13½

246	A54	1r brown & orange	3.00	*3.50*
a.		Perf. 12½	35.00	*45.00*
247	A55	2r dp grn & pale grn, perf. 12½	3.00	2.50
248	A56	5r dp bl & pale bl, perf. 12½	3.00	*4.25*
a.		Perf. 13½	16.00	16.00
249	A57	7r rose & pink	4.00	*5.00*
a.		Perf. 12½	16.00	*25.00*
		Nos. 242-249 (8)	19.00	30.25

1st Agriculture and Craftsmanship Exhibition, Moscow.

Worker — Soldier — Peasant
A58 A59 A60

1923 Unwmk. Litho. *Imperf.*

250	A58	1k orange	.60	.25
251	A60	2k green	.90	.40
252	A59	3k red brown	.80	.40
253	A58	4k deep rose	1.75	.65
254	A58	5k lilac	.90	.65
255	A60	6k light blue	1.50	.30
256	A59	10k dark blue	1.50	.30
257	A58	20k yellow green	2.75	.55
258	A60	50k dark brown	4.00	1.90
259	A59	1r red & brown	8.00	5.00
		Nos. 250-259 (10)	22.70	10.40

1924 *Perf. 14½x15*

261	A58	4k deep rose	100.00	*150.00*
262	A59	10k dark blue	100.00	*100.00*
263	A60	30k violet	25.00	8.00
264	A59	40k slate gray	25.00	8.00
		Nos. 261-264 (4)	250.00	266.00

See Nos. 273-290, 304-321. For surcharges see Nos. 349-350.

Vladimir Ilyich Ulyanov (Lenin) A61

Worker A62

1924 *Imperf.*

265	A61	3k red & black	3.00	1.50
266	A61	6k red & black	3.00	1.50
267	A61	12k red & black	3.00	1.50
268	A61	20k red & black	3.00	1.50
		Nos. 265-268 (4)	12.00	6.00

Three printings of Nos. 265-268 differ in size of red frame.

Perf. 13½

269	A61	3k red & black	2.75	2.00
270	A61	6k red & black	2.75	2.00
271	A61	12k red & black	2.75	2.75
272	A61	20k red & black	4.00	3.25
		Nos. 269-272 (4)	12.25	10.00
		Nos. 265-272 (8)	24.25	16.00

Death of Lenin (1870-1924).
Forgeries of Nos. 265-272 exist.

Types of 1923

There are small differences between the lithographed stamps of 1923 and the typographed of 1924-25. On a few values this may be seen in the numerals.

Type A58: Lithographed. The two white lines forming the outline of the ear are continued across the cheek. Typographed. The outer lines of the ear are broken where they touch the cheek.

Type A59: Lithographed. At the top of the right shoulder a white line touches the frame at the left. Counting from the edge of the visor of the cap, lines 5, 6 and sometimes 7 touch at their upper ends. Typographed. The top line of the shoulder does not reach the frame. On the cap lines 5, 6 and 7 run together and form a white spot.

Type A60: In the angle above the first letter "C" there is a fan-shaped ornament enclosing four white dashes. On the lithographed stamps these dashes reach nearly to the point of the angle. On the typographed stamps the dashes are shorter and often only three are visible.

On unused copies of the typographed stamps the raised outlines of the designs can be seen on the backs of the stamps.

1924-25 Typo. *Imperf.*

273	A59	3k red brown	2.00	1.25
274	A58	4k deep rose	2.00	1.25
275	A59	10k dark blue	3.25	1.25
275A	A60	50k brown	850.00	25.00

Other typographed and imperf. values include: 2k green, 5k lilac, 6k light blue, 20k green and 1r red and brown. Value, unused: $150, $100, $37.50, $150, and $,000, respectively.

Nos. 273-275A were regularly issued. The 7k, 8k, 9k, 30k, 40k, 2r, 3r, and 5r also exist imperf. Value, set of 8, $75.

Perf. 14½x15

Typo.

276	A58	1k orange	65.00	5.50
277	A60	2k green	2.00	.30
278	A59	3k red brown	2.25	.40
279	A58	4k deep rose	2.00	.40
280	A58	5k lilac	10.00	2.50
281	A60	6k lt blue	2.00	.50
282	A59	7k chocolate	2.00	.50
283	A58	8k brown olive	2.25	.70
284	A60	9k orange red	2.25	1.10
285	A59	10k dark blue	2.50	.55
286	A58	14k slate blue	45.00	5.00
287	A60	15k yellow	*6,000.*	*150.00*
288	A58	20k gray green	5.00	.80
288A	A60	30k violet	200.00	8.00
288B	A59	40k slate gray	300.00	8.00
289	A60	50k brown	75.00	15.00
290	A59	1r red & brown	12.00	2.00
291	A62	2r green & rose	15.00	4.00
		Nos. 276-286,288-291 (17)	744.25	55.25

See No. 323. Forgeries of No. 287 exist.

1925 *Perf. 12*

276a	A58	1k orange	1.50	.25
277a	A60	2k green	8.00	.95
278a	A59	3k red brown	2.75	.70
279a	A58	4k deep rose	55.00	3.25
280a	A58	5k lilac	4.00	.80
282a	A59	7k chocolate	2.75	.20
283a	A58	8k brown olive	80.00	12.50
284a	A60	9k orange red	13.00	7.50
285a	A59	10k dark blue	3.25	.25
286a	A58	14k slate blue	3.50	.40
287a	A60	15k yellow	4.50	1.00
288c	A58	20k gray green	18.00	.45
288d	A60	30k violet	25.00	2.50
288e	A59	40k slate gray	20.00	2.75
289a	A60	50k brown	8.00	1.10
290a	A59	1r red & brown	750.00	150.00
		Nos. 276a-290a (16)	999.25	184.60

Soldier — A63

Worker — A64

1924-25 *Perf. 13½*

292	A63	3r blk brn & grn	15.00	4.75
a.		Perf. 10	500.00	50.00
b.		Perf. 13½x10	*1,000.*	325.00
293	A64	5r dk bl & gray brn	35.00	9.25
a.		Perf. 10½	50.00	65.00

See Nos. 324-325.

Lenin Mausoleum, Moscow — A65

Wmk. 170

1925, Jan. Photo. *Imperf.*

294	A65	7k deep blue	4.00	3.25
295	A65	14k dark green	15.00	4.50
296	A65	20k carmine rose	9.00	3.50
297	A65	40k red brown	11.00	4.00
		Nos. 294-297 (4)	39.00	15.25

Perf. 13½x14

298	A65	7k deep blue	5.00	3.00
299	A65	14k dark green	17.00	4.50
300	A65	20k carmine rose	10.00	3.50
301	A65	40k red brown	12.00	4.25
		Nos. 298-301 (4)	44.00	15.25
		Nos. 294-301 (8)	83.00	30.50

First anniversary of Lenin's death.

Nos. 294-301 are found on both ordinary and thick paper. Those on thick paper sell for twice as much, except for No. 301, which is scarcer on ordinary paper.

Lenin — A66

Wmk. 170

1925, July Engr. *Perf. 13½*

302	A66	5r red brown	35.00	6.00
a.		Perf. 12½	40.00	11.00
b.		Perf. 10½ ('26)	37.50	8.00
303	A66	10r indigo	35.00	11.00
a.		Perf. 12½	190.00	90.00
b.		Perf. 10½ ('26)	27.50	11.00

Imperfs. exist. Value, set $75.
See Nos. 407-408, 621-622

Types of 1923 Issue

1925-27 Wmk. 170 Typo. *Perf. 12*

304	A58	1k orange	.50	.35
305	A60	2k green	.45	.20
306	A59	3k red brown	.50	.35
307	A58	4k deep rose	.30	.25
308	A58	5k lilac	.40	.25
309	A60	6k lt blue	.60	.25
310	A59	7k chocolate	.45	.20
311	A58	8k brown olive	.95	.20
a.		Perf. 14½x15	100.00	50.00
312	A60	9k red	.70	.40
313	A59	10k dark blue	.70	.30
a.		10k pale blue ('27)	1.25	1.00
314	A58	14k slate blue	1.50	.35
315	A60	15k yellow	2.25	1.25
316	A59	18k violet	1.50	.25
317	A58	20k gray green	1.25	.25
318	A60	30k violet	1.50	.25
319	A59	40k slate gray	2.00	.35
320	A60	50k brown	3.25	.35
321	A59	1r red & brown	3.75	.50
a.		Perf. 14½x15	100.00	40.00
323	A62	2r green & rose red	27.50	6.00
a.		Perf. 14½x15	14.00	3.25

Perf. 13½

324	A63	3r blk brn & green	10.00	5.00
a.		Perf. 12½	40.00	14.00
325	A64	5r dark blue & gray brown	15.00	5.00
		Nos. 304-325 (21)	75.05	22.30

Nos. 304-315, 317-325 exist imperf. Value, set $100.

Mikhail V. Lomonosov and Academy of Sciences — A67

1925, Sept. Photo. *Perf. 12½, 13½*

326	A67	3k orange brown	5.00	3.00
a.		Perf. 12½x12	11.00	7.50
b.		Perf. 13½x12½	*700.00*	*850.00*
c.		Perf. 13½	20.00	10.00
327	A67	15k dk olive green	5.00	3.00
a.		Perf. 12½	20.00	7.50

Russian Academy of Sciences, 200th anniv. Exist unwatermarked, on thick paper with yellow gum, perf. 13½. These are essays, later perforated and gummed. Value, each $50.

Prof. Aleksandr S. Popov (1859-1905), Radio Pioneer — A68

1925, Oct. *Perf. 13½*

328	A68	7k deep blue	2.00	1.50
329	A68	14k green	3.25	1.90

For surcharge see No. 353.

Decembrist Exiles — A69

Street Rioting in St. Petersburg — A70

Revolutionist Leaders — A71

1925, Dec. 28 *Imperf.*

330 A69 3k olive green 4.00 *3.00*
331 A70 7k brown 4.00 *2.50*
332 A71 14k carmine lake 6.00 *3.75*

Perf. 13½

333 A69 3k olive green 2.50 2.25
a. Perf. 12½ 60.00 50.00
334 A70 7k brown 2.00 *2.25*
335 A71 14k carmine lake 3.00 2.50
Nos. 330-335 (6) 21.50 16.25

Centenary of Decembrist revolution.
For surcharges see Nos. 354, 357.

Revolters Parading — A72

Speaker Haranguing Mob — A73

Street Barricade, Moscow — A74

1925, Dec. 20 *Imperf.*

336 A72 3k olive green 5.75 1.50
337 A73 7k brown 6.25 1.60
338 A74 14k carmine lake 8.00 2.00

Perf. 12½, 12x12½

339 A72 3k olive green 1.50 1.25
a. Perf. 13½ 4.50 4.25
340 A73 7k brown 3.50 3.00
a. Perf. 13½ 15.00 10.50
b. Horiz. pair, imperf. btwn. 55.00 50.00
341 A74 14k carmine lake 2.50 2.00
a. Perf. 13½ 22.50 12.00
Nos. 336-341 (6) 27.50 11.35

20th anniversary of Revolution of 1905.
For surcharges see Nos. 355, 358.

Lenin — A75

Liberty Monument, Moscow — A76

1926 Wmk. 170 Engr. *Perf. 10½*

342 A75 1r dark brown 7.50 2.50
343 A75 2r black violet 10.00 4.50
a. Perf. 12½ 100.00 50.00
344 A75 3r dark green 14.00 4.50
Nos. 342-344 (3) 31.50 11.50

Nos. 342-343 exist imperf.
See Nos. 406, 620.

1926, July Litho. *Perf. 12x12½*

347 A76 7k blue green & red 2.25 1.50
348 A76 14k blue green & violet 2.75 1.50

6th International Esperanto Congress at Leningrad. Exist perf. 11½. Value, set $1,500.
For surcharge see No. 356.

Nos. 282, 282a and 310 Surcharged in Black

1927, June Unwmk. *Perf. 14½x15*

349 A59 8k on 7k chocolate 5.50 1.50
a. Perf. 12 9.00 7.50
b. Inverted surcharge 125.00 110.00

Perf. 12

Wmk. 170

350 A59 8k on 7k chocolate 3.50 1.50
a. Inverted surcharge 100.00 35.00

The surcharge on Nos. 349-350 comes in two types: With space of 2mm between lines, and with space of ¾mm. The latter is much scarcer.

Same Surcharge on Stamps of 1925-26 in Black or Red

Perf. 13½, 12½, 12x12½

353 A68 8k on 7k dp bl (R) 2.75 *4.50*
a. Inverted "8" 75.00 *100.00*
354 A70 8k on 7k brown 8.00 *9.25*
355 A73 8k on 7k brown 10.50 *12.25*
356 A76 8k on 7k blue green & red 8.75 *11.00*

Imperf

357 A70 8k on 7k brown 3.50 *5.25*
358 A73 8k on 7k brown 3.50 *5.25*
Nos. 349-350,353-358 (8) 46.00 50.50

Postage Due Stamps of 1925 Surcharged

Two settings: A's aligned (shown), bottom A to left.

Lithographed or Typographed

1927, June Unwmk. *Perf. 12*

359 D1 8k on 1k red, typo. 3.00 4.00
a. Litho. *750.00* 100.00
360 D1 8k on 2k violet 4.00 4.00

Perf. 12, 14½x14

361 D1 8k on 3k lt blue 4.25 3.00
362 D1 8k on 7k orange 4.75 2.50
363 D1 8k on 8k green 3.75 4.00
364 D1 8k on 10k dk blue 4.50 2.50
365 D1 8k on 14k brown 3.75 4.00
Nos. 359-365 (7) 28.00 24.00

Exist with inverted surcharge. Value each, $100.

Wmk. 170

1927, June Typo. *Perf. 12*

366 D1 8k on 1k red 1.50 *1.90*
367 D1 8k on 2k violet 1.50 *1.90*
368 D1 8k on 3k lt blue 3.00 2.25
369 D1 8k on 7k orange 3.00 2.25
370 D1 8k on 8k green 1.50 *1.90*
371 D1 8k on 10k dk blue 1.50 *1.90*
372 D1 8k on 14k brown 2.25 *1.90*
Nos. 366-372 (7) 14.25 14.00

Nos. 366, 368-372 exist with inverted surcharge. Value each, $100.

Dr. L. L. Zamenhof A77

1927 Photo. *Perf. 10½*

373 A77 14k yel green & brown 2.50 3.00

Unwmk.

374 A77 14k yel green & brown 2.50 3.00

40th anniversary of creation of Esperanto.
No. 374 exists perf. 10, 10x10½ and imperf. Value, imperf. pair $500.

Worker, Soldier, Peasant — A78

Worker and Sailor — A81

Lenin in Car Guarded by Soldiers A79

Smolny Institute, Leningrad A80

Map of the USSR A82

Men of Various Soviet Republics — A83

Workers of Different Races; Kremlin in Background — A84

Typo. (3k, 8k, 18k), Engr. (7k), Litho. (14k), Photo. (5k, 28k)

Perf. 13½, 12½x12, 11

1927, Oct. Unwmk.

375 A78 3k bright rose 2.00 .80
a. Imperf., pair 500.00
376 A79 5k deep brown 4.00 2.25
a. Imperf. 500.00 175.00
b. Perf. 12½ 25.00 27.50
c. Perf. 12½x10½ 50.00 30.00
377 A80 7k myrtle green 5.00 2.75
a. Perf. 11½ 50.00 30.00
b. Imperf., pair 500.00
378 A81 8k brown & black 2.75 .95
a. Perf. 10½x12½ *32.50* *27.50*
379 A82 14k dull blue & red 6.00 1.65
380 A83 18k blue 4.00 1.65
a. Imperf. 1,000.
381 A84 28k olive brown 15.00 5.75
a. Perf. 10 40.00 35.00
Nos. 375-381 (7) 38.75 15.80

10th anniversary of October Revolution.
The paper of No. 375 has an overprint of pale yellow wavy lines.
No. 377b exists with watermark 170. Value, $1,000.

Worker — A85

Peasant — A86

Lenin — A87

1927-28 Typo. *Perf. 13½*

Chalk Surfaced Paper

382 A85 1k orange .75 .45
383 A86 2k apple green .75 .30
385 A85 4k bright blue .75 .30
386 A86 5k brown .75 .30
388 A86 7k dark red ('28) 3.50 .85
389 A85 8k green 2.00 .40
391 A85 10k light brown 1.75 .40
392 A87 14k dark green ('28) 2.00 .50
393 A87 18k olive green 3.50 .85
394 A87 18k dark blue ('28) 3.25 1.00
395 A86 20k dark gray green 2.25 .60
396 A85 40k rose red 8.00 3.00
397 A86 50k bright blue 4.25 1.00
399 A85 70k gray green 8.00 1.75
400 A86 80k orange 13.50 2.50
Nos. 382-400 (15) 55.00 14.20

The 1k, 2k and 10k exist imperf. Value, each $750.

Soldier and Kremlin — A88

Sailor and Flag — A89

Cavalryman A90

Aviator A91

1928, Feb. 6

Chalk Surfaced Paper

402 A88 8k light brown 2.00 .35
a. Imperf. 250.00 200.00
403 A89 14k deep blue 2.50 .90
404 A90 18k carmine rose 2.50 1.75
a. Imperf. 750.00
405 A91 28k yellow green 3.50 2.00
Nos. 402-405 (4) 10.50 5.00

10th anniversary of the Soviet Army.

Lenin Types of 1925-26

Perf. 10, 10½

1928-29 Engr. Wmk. 169

406 A75 3r dark green ('29) 7.00 2.00
407 A66 5r red brown 8.00 2.50
408 A66 10r indigo 15.00 4.50
Nos. 406-408 (3) 30.00 9.00

No. 406 exists imperf. Value, $500.

Bugler Sounding Assembly
A92 A93

Perf. 12½x12

1929, Aug. 18 Photo. Wmk. 170

411 A92 10k olive brown 10.00 5.00
a. Perf. 10½ 35.00 25.00
b. Perf. 12½x12x10½x12 45.00 21.00
412 A93 14k slate 6.50 2.00
a. Perf. 12½x12x10½x12 75.00 45.00

First All-Soviet Assembly of Pioneers.

Factory Worker A95

Peasant A96

Farm Worker A97

Soldier A98

Worker, Soldier, Peasant A100

Worker A103

Lenin A104

Peasant A107

Factory Worker A109

Farm Worker A111

Perf. 12x12½

1929-31 Typo. Wmk. 170

413	A103	1k orange	.40	.20
a.		Perf. 10½	30.00	13.00
b.		Perf. 14x14½	50.00	35.00
414	A95	2k yellow green	.50	.20
415	A96	3k blue	.65	.20
a.		Perf. 14x14½	50.00	35.00
416	A97	4k claret	.85	.20
417	A98	5k orange brown	1.00	.20
a.		Perf. 10½	75.00	75.00
418	A100	7k scarlet	1.25	.90
419	A103	10k olive green	1.60	.20
a.		Perf. 10½	40.00	22.50

Unwmk.

420	A104	14k indigo	1.10	1.00
a.		Perf. 10½	7.50	3.25

Wmk. 170

421	A100	15k dk ol grn ('30)	1.75	.25
422	A107	20k green	1.75	.25
a.		Perf. 10½	*200.00*	*100.00*
423	A109	30k dk violet	2.75	.85
424	A111	50k dp brown	3.50	1.75
425	A98	70k dk red ('30)	4.25	1.90
426	A107	80k red brown ('31)	5.50	1.90
		Nos. 413-426 (14)	26.85	10.00

Nos. 422, 423, 424 and 426 have a background of fine wavy lines in pale shades of the colors of the stamps.

See Nos. 456-466, 613A-619A. For surcharge see No. 743.

Symbolical of Industry A112

Tractors Issuing from Assembly Line — A113

Iron Furnace (Inscription reads, "More Metal More Machines") A114

Blast Furnace and Chart of Anticipated Iron Production A115

1929-30 *Perf. 12x12½*

427	A112	5k orange brown	1.75	1.50
428	A113	10k olive green	1.75	2.00

Perf. 12½x12

429	A114	20k dull green	4.00	3.50
430	A115	28k violet black	2.50	2.25
		Nos. 427-430 (4)	10.00	9.25

Publicity for greater industrial production.
No. 429 exists perf. 10½. Value *$800.*

Red Cavalry in Polish Town after Battle A116

Cavalry Charge A117

Staff Officers of 1st Cavalry Army A118

Plan of Action for 1st Cavalry Army — A119

1930, Feb. *Perf. 12x12½*

431	A116	2k yellow green	2.00	1.75
432	A117	5k light brown	2.00	1.75
433	A118	10k olive gray	3.75	2.75
434	A119	14k indigo & red	2.75	1.75
		Nos. 431-434 (4)	10.50	8.00

1st Red Cavalry Army, 10th anniversary.

Students Preparing a Poster Newspaper A120

1930, Aug. 15

435	A120	10k olive green	2.50	1.50

Educational Exhibition, Leningrad, 7/1-8/15/30.

Telegraph Office, Moscow A121

Lenin Hydroelectric Power Station on Volkhov River A122

1930 Photo. Wmk. 169 *Perf. 10½*

436	A121	1r deep blue	10.00	5.00

Wmk. 170

437	A122	3r yel green & blk brn	11.50	6.00

See Nos. 467, 469.

Battleship Potemkin A123

Inside Presnya Barricade A124

Moscow Barricades in 1905 — A125

1930 Typo. *Perf. 12x12½, 12½x12*

438	A123	3k red	1.40	.55
439	A124	5k blue	1.40	.70
440	A125	10k dk green & red	2.50	1.00
		Nos. 438-440 (3)	5.30	2.25

1931 *Imperf.*

452	A123	3k red	5.00	5.00
453	A124	5k deep blue	7.00	7.00
454	A125	10k dk green & red	10.00	10.00
		Nos. 452-454 (3)	22.00	22.00
		Nos. 438-454 (6)	27.30	24.25

Revolution of 1905, 25th anniversary.

Types of 1929-31 Regular Issue

1931-32 *Imperf.*

456	A103	1k orange	1.00	1.00
457	A95	2k yellow green	1.00	1.25
458	A96	3k blue	1.00	1.25
459	A97	4k claret	30.00	12.50
460	A98	5k orange brown	3.00	3.00
462	A103	10k olive green	50.00	25.00
464	A100	15k dk olive green	45.00	35.00
466	A109	30k dull violet	70.00	50.00
467	A121	1r dark blue	75.00	75.00
		Nos. 456-467 (9)	276.00	204.00

Nos. 459, 462-467 were sold only by the philatelic bureau.

Type of 1930 Issue

1931 Wmk. 170 *Perf. 12x12½*

469	A121	1r dark blue	2.00	1.00
		Never hinged	3.50	

Maxim Gorki — A133

1932-33 Photo.

470	A133	15k dark brown	6.00	3.50
a.		Imperf.	125.00	125.00
471	A133	35k dp ultra ('33)	15.00	11.00
		Set, never hinged	50.00	

40th anniversary of Gorki's literary activity.

Lenin Addressing the People A134

Revolution in Petrograd (Leningrad) A135

Dnieper Hydroelectric Power Station A136

Asiatics Saluting the Soviet Flag — A139

Breaking Prison Bars — A140

Designs (dated 1917 1932): 15k, Collective farm. 20k, Magnitogorsk metallurgical plant in Urals. 30k, Radio tower and heads of 4 men.

1932-33 *Perf. 12½x12; 12½ (30k)*

472	A134	3k dark violet	1.40	.75
473	A135	5k dark brown	1.40	.75
474	A136	10k ultra	3.25	1.40
475	A136	15k dark green	2.00	.85
476	A136	20k lake ('33)	2.50	1.10
477	A136	30k dark gray ('33)	50.00	15.00
478	A139	35k gray black	75.00	57.50
		Nos. 472-478 (7)	135.55	77.35
		Set, never hinged	200.00	

October Revolution, 15th anniversary.

1932, Nov. Litho. *Perf. 12½x12*

479	A140	50k dark red	12.50	8.00
		Never hinged	25.00	

Intl. Revolutionaries' Aid Assoc., 10th anniv.

Trier, Birthplace of Marx — A141

Grave, Highgate Cemetery, London — A142

35k, Portrait & signature of Karl Marx (1818-83).

Perf. 12x12½, 12½x12

1933, Mar. Photo.

480	A141	3k dull green	5.00	1.25
481	A142	10k black brown	7.50	2.50
482	A142	35k brown violet	18.00	10.00
		Nos. 480-482 (3)	30.50	13.75
		Set, never hinged	75.00	

Fine Arts Museum, Moscow — A145

1932, Dec. *Perf. 12½*

485	A145	15k black brown	17.50	13.00
486	A145	35k ultra	40.00	45.00
a.		Perf. 10½	60.00	40.00
		Set, never hinged	150.00	

Moscow Philatelic Exhibition, 1932.

Nos. 485 and 486 were also issued in imperf. sheets of 4 containing 2 of each value, on thick paper for presentation purposes. They were not valid for postage. Replicas of the sheet were made for Moscow 97 by the Canadian Society of Russian Philately.

Nos. 485 and 486a Surcharged

1933, Mar. *Perf. 12½*

487 A145 30k on 15k black brn	35.00	25.00
Perf. 10½		
488 A145 70k on 35k ultra	125.00	75.00
Set, never hinged	300.00	

Leningrad Philatelic Exhibition, 1933.

Peoples of the Soviet Union

Kazaks A146

Lezghians A147

Tungus A150

Crimean Tartars A148

Jews, Birobidzhan A149

Buryats — A151

Yakuts — A156

Chechens A152

Abkhas A153

Georgians A154

Nientzians A155

Great Russians — A157

Tadzhiks — A158

Transcaucasians — A159

Turkmen — A160

Ukrainians — A161

Uzbeks — A162

Byelorussians — A163

Koryaks A164

Bashkirs A165

Chuvashes A166

Perf. 12, 12x12½, 12½x12, 11x12, 12x11

1933, Apr. **Photo.**

489 A146 1k black brown	3.50	1.25
490 A147 2k ultra	3.00	1.25
491 A148 3k gray green	4.00	2.50
492 A149 4k gray black	3.25	1.25
493 A150 5k brown violet	3.50	1.00
494 A151 6k indigo	6.00	1.75
495 A152 7k black brown	6.00	1.75
496 A153 8k rose red	6.00	1.75
497 A154 9k ultra	7.00	2.00
498 A155 10k black brown	4.50	3.00
499 A156 14k olive green	3.75	1.25
500 A157 15k orange	4.25	1.25
501 A158 15k ultra	4.00	1.00
502 A159 15k dark brown	4.00	1.00
503 A160 15k rose red	5.50	2.75
504 A161 15k violet brown	5.25	1.25
505 A162 15k gray black	5.25	1.25
506 A163 15k dull green	5.50	1.25
507 A164 20k dull blue	13.00	3.00
508 A165 30k brown violet	15.00	3.00
509 A166 35k black	27.50	5.00
Nos. 489-509 (21)	139.75	39.50
Set, never hinged	500.00	

V. V. Vorovsky A169

3k, V. M. Volodarsky. 5k, M. S. Uritzky.

1933, Oct. *Perf. 12x12½*

514 A169 1k dull green	.90	.55
515 A169 3k blue black	1.50	.75
516 A169 5k olive brown	3.25	.90
Nos. 514-516 (3)	5.65	2.20
Set, never hinged	30.00	

10th anniv, of the murder of Soviet Representative Vorovsky; 15th anniv. of the murder of the Revolutionists Volodarsky and Uritzky. See Nos. 531-532, 580-582.

Order of the Red Banner, 15th Anniv. — A173

1933, Nov. 17 **Unwmk.** *Perf. 14*

518 A173 20k black, red & yellow	3.00	2.00
Never hinged	10.00	

No. 518, perf. 9½, is a proof. Value $950.

Commissar Schaumyan A174

Commissar Prokofii A. Dzhaparidze A175

Commissars Awaiting Execution — A176

Designs: 35k, Monument to the 26 Commissars. 40k, Worker, peasant and soldier dipping flags in salute.

1933, Dec. 1

519 A174 4k brown	12.00	2.00
520 A175 5k dark gray	12.00	2.00
521 A176 20k purple	8.00	2.00
522 A176 35k ultra	35.00	7.75
523 A176 40k carmine	22.50	9.50
Nos. 519-523 (5)	89.50	23.25
Set, never hinged	185.00	

15th anniv. of the execution of 26 commissars at Baku. No. 521 exists imperf.

Lenin's Mausoleum A179

1934, Feb. 7 **Engr.** *Perf. 14*

524 A179 5k brown	6.00	1.00
a. Imperf.	160.00	140.00
525 A179 10k slate blue	17.00	3.50
a. Imperf.	160.00	140.00
526 A179 15k dk carmine	11.00	1.75
527 A179 20k green	9.00	1.75
528 A179 35k dark brown	15.00	3.00
Nos. 524-528 (5)	58.00	11.00
Set, never hinged	160.00	

10th anniversary of Lenin's death.

Ivan Fedorov A180

1934, Mar. 5

529 A180 20k carmine rose	27.50	5.00
a. Imperf.	250.00	250.00
530 A180 40k indigo	12.50	5.00
a. Imperf.	250.00	250.00
Set, never hinged	100.00	

350th anniv. of the death of Ivan Fedorov, founder of printing in Russia.

Portrait Type of 1933

Designs: 10k, Yakov M. Sverdlov. 15k, Victor Pavlovich Nogin.

1934, Mar. **Photo.** **Wmk. 170**

531 A169 10k ultra	35.00	7.50
532 A169 15k red	50.00	17.50
Set, never hinged	150.00	

Deaths of Yakov M. Sverdlov, chairman of the All-Russian Central Executive Committee of the Soviets, 15th anniv., Victor Pavlovich Nogin, chairman Russian State Textile Syndicate, 10th anniv.

A184

Dmitri Ivanovich Mendeleev A185

1934, Sept. 15 **Wmk. 170** *Perf. 14*

536 A184 5k emerald	9.00	2.00
537 A185 10k black brown	21.00	6.00
538 A185 15k vermilion	18.00	5.00
539 A184 20k ultra	14.00	3.50
Nos. 536-539 (4)	62.00	16.50
Set, never hinged	150.00	

Prof. D. I. Mendeleev (1834-1907), chemist who discovered the Periodic Law of Classification of the Elements.

Imperfs. exist of 5k (value $400) and 15k (value $400).

Lenin as Child and Youth
A186 A187

Demonstration before Lenin Mausoleum — A190

Designs: 5k, Lenin in middle age. 10k, Lenin the orator. 30k, Lenin and Stalin.

1934, Nov. 23 Unwmk. *Perf. 14*

540	A186	1k indigo & black	5.00	1.50
541	A187	3k indigo & black	5.00	1.75
542	A187	5k indigo & black	9.50	2.50
543	A187	10k indigo & black	7.50	2.50
544	A190	20k brn org & ultra	17.50	5.00
545	A190	30k brn org & car	55.00	10.00
		Nos. 540-545 (6)	99.50	23.25
		Set, never hinged	200.00	

First decade without Lenin.
See Nos. 931-935, 937.

Bombs Falling on City
A192

"Before War and Afterwards"
A194

Designs: 10k, Refugees from burning town. 20k, "Plowing with the sword." 35k, "Comradeship."

1935, Jan. 1 Wmk. 170 *Perf. 14*

546	A192	5k violet black	10.00	5.00
547	A192	10k ultra	20.00	8.00
548	A194	15k green	40.00	12.00
549	A194	20k dark brown	15.00	7.50
550	A194	35k carmine	75.00	25.00
		Nos. 546-550 (5)	160.00	57.50
		Set, never hinged	375.00	

Ati-war propaganda, the designs symbolize the horrors of modern warfare.

Subway Tunnel
A197

Subway Station Cross Section
A198

Subway Station
A199

Train in Station — A200

1935, Feb. 25 Wmk. 170 *Perf. 14*

551	A197	5k orange	22.50	2.00
552	A198	10k dark ultra	14.00	3.25
553	A199	15k rose carmine	75.00	20.00
554	A200	20k emerald	30.00	12.00
		Nos. 551-554 (4)	141.50	37.25
		Set, never hinged	250.00	

Completion of Moscow subway.

Friedrich Engels (1820-1895), German Socialist and Collaborator of Marx — A201

1935, May Wmk. 170 *Perf. 14*

555	A201	5k carmine	15.00	1.50
556	A201	10k dark green	8.00	2.25
557	A201	15k dark blue	15.00	4.00
558	A201	20k brown black	12.00	3.50
		Nos. 555-558 (4)	50.00	11.25
		Set, never hinged	125.00	

Running — A202

Designs: 2k, Diving. 3k, Rowing. 4k, Soccer. 5k, Skiing. 10k, Bicycling. 15k, Tennis. 20k, Skating. 35k, Hurdling. 40k, Parade of athletes.

1935, Apr. 22 Unwmk. *Perf. 14*

559	A202	1k orange & ultra	2.75	1.25
560	A202	2k black & ultra	3.50	1.25
561	A202	3k grn & blk brn	5.50	3.75
562	A202	4k rose red & ultra	3.25	1.25
563	A202	5k pur & blk brn	3.25	1.25
564	A202	10k rose red & vio	6.00	3.00
565	A202	15k black & blk brn	40.00	16.00
566	A202	20k blk brn & ultra	10.00	5.50
567	A202	35k ultra & blk brn	35.00	10.00
568	A202	40k black brn & car	25.00	7.50
		Nos. 559-568 (10)	134.25	50.75
		Set, never hinged	400.00	

International Spartacist Games, Moscow. The games never took place.

Silver Plate of Sassanian Dynasty
A212

1935, Sept. 10 Wmk. 170

569	A212	5k orange red	10.00	1.50
570	A212	10k dk yellow green	10.00	2.50
571	A212	15k dark violet	11.00	3.75
572	A212	35k black brown	19.00	6.50
		Nos. 569-572 (4)	50.00	14.25
		Set, never hinged	150.00	

3rd International Exposition of Persian Art, Leningrad, Sept. 12-18, 1935.

Kalinin, the Worker — A213

Mikhail Kalinin — A216

Kalinin as: 5k, farmer. 10k, orator.

1935, Nov. 20 Unwmk. *Perf. 14*

573	A213	3k rose lilac	1.25	.55
574	A213	5k green	1.50	.55
575	A213	10k blue slate	2.00	.85
576	A216	20k brown black	4.50	1.50
		Nos. 573-576 (4)	9.25	3.45
		Set, never hinged	30.00	

60th birthday of Mikhail Kalinin, chairman of the Central Executive Committee of the USSR.
The 20k exists imperf. Value $150.

A217

Leo Tolstoy — A218

Design: 20k, Statue of Tolstoy.

1935, Dec. 4 *Perf. 14*

577	A217	3k ol black & vio	1.00	.75
578	A218	10k vio blk & blk brn	2.25	1.25
579	A217	20k dk grn & blk brn	6.50	3.00
		Nos. 577-579 (3)	9.75	5.00
		Set, never hinged	25.00	

Perf. 11

577a	A217	3k	2.50	.75
578a	A218	10k	4.50	1.75
579a	A217	20k	10.00	2.50
		Nos. 577a-579a (3)	17.00	5.00
		Set, never hinged	30.00	

25th anniv. of the death of Count Leo N. Tolstoy (1828-1910).

Portrait Type of 1933

Designs: 2k, Mikhail V. Frunze. 4k, N. E. Bauman. 40k, Sergei M. Kirov.

1935, Nov. Wmk. 170 *Perf. 11*

580	A169	2k purple	3.00	*2.75*
581	A169	4k brown violet	4.00	*6.00*
582	A169	40k black brown	8.00	*10.00*
		Nos. 580-582 (3)	15.00	18.75
		Set, never hinged	50.00	

Perf. 14

580a	A169	2k	8.50	1.00
581a	A169	4k	12.50	2.00
582a	A169	40k	29.00	3.00
		Nos. 580a-582a (3)	50.00	6.00
		Set, never hinged	75.00	

Death of three revolutionary heroes.
Nos. 580-582 exist imperf. but were not regularly issued. Value, set $1,000.

Pioneers Preventing Theft from Mailbox
A223

Designs: 3k, 5k, Pioneers preventing destruction of property. 10k, Helping recover kite. 15k, Girl Pioneer saluting.

1936, Apr. Unwmk. *Perf. 14*

583	A223	1k yellow green	1.50	.35
584	A223	2k copper red	2.25	.45
585	A223	3k slate blue	3.50	1.00
586	A223	5k rose lake	4.25	1.00
587	A223	10k gray blue	9.00	3.25
588	A223	15k brown olive	12.00	6.00
		Nos. 583-588 (6)	32.50	12.05
		Set, never hinged	70.00	

Perf. 11

583a	A223	1k	1.25	.55
584a	A223	2k	2.50	.60
585a	A223	3k	4.00	1.25
586a	A223	5k	6.50	1.50
587a	A223	10k	22.00	4.00
588a	A223	15k	12.00	2.25
		Nos. 583a-588a (6)	48.25	10.15
		Set, never hinged	125.00	

Nikolai A. Dobrolyubov, Writer and Critic, Birth Cent. — A227

1936, Aug. 13 Typo. *Perf. 11½*

589	A227	10k rose lake	4.00	2.00
		Never hinged	10.00	
a.		Perf. 14	5.00	2.50
		Never hinged	11.00	

Aleksander Sergeyevich Pushkin — A228

Statue of Pushkin, Moscow — A229

Perf. 11 to 14 and Compound

1937, Feb. 1

Chalky or Ordinary Paper

590	A228	10k yellow brown	.75	.35
591	A228	20k Prus green	1.00	.40
592	A228	40k rose lake	1.75	.45
593	A229	50k blue	2.75	.55
594	A229	80k carmine rose	3.00	.75
595	A229	1r green	12.00	1.50
		Nos. 590-595 (6)	21.25	4.00
		Set, never hinged	50.00	

Souvenir Sheet

Imperf

596		Sheet of 2	12.00	*150.00*
		Never hinged	25.00	
a.		A228 10k brown	3.00	*20.00*
b.		A229 50k brown	3.00	*27.50*

Pushkin (1799-1837), writer and poet.

Tchaikovsky Concert Hall — A230

Designs: 5k, 15k, Telegraph Agency House. 10k, Tchaikovsky Concert Hall. 20k, 50k, Red Army Theater. 30k, Hotel Moscow. 40k, Palace of the Soviets.

Unwmk.

1937, June Photo. *Perf. 12*

597	A230	3k	brown violet	2.25	.40
598	A230	5k	henna brown	2.50	.40
599	A230	10k	dark brown	3.50	.40
600	A230	15k	black	9.00	.40
601	A230	20k	olive green	2.50	.90
602	A230	30k	gray black	3.00	.90
a.			Perf. 11	50.00	32.50
603	A230	40k	violet	3.25	1.25
a.			Souv. sheet of 4, imperf.	12.50	*50.00*
604	A230	50k	dark brown	5.00	1.25
			Nos. 597-604 (8)	31.00	5.90
			Set, never hinged	55.00	

First Congress of Soviet Architects. The 30k is watermarked Greek Border and Rosettes (170).

Nos. 597-601, 603-604 exist imperf. Value, each $300.

Feliks E. Dzerzhinski A235

Shota Rustaveli A236

1937, July 27 Typo. *Perf. 12*

606	A235	10k	yellow brown	.75	.35
607	A235	20k	Prus green	1.25	.75
608	A235	40k	rose lake	3.00	1.10
609	A235	80k	carmine	5.00	1.75
			Nos. 606-609 (4)	10.00	3.95
			Set, never hinged	25.00	

Dzerzhinski, organizer of Soviet secret police, 10th death anniv. Exist imperf. Value, each $500.

Unwmk.

1938, Feb. Photo. *Perf. 12*

610	A236	20k	deep green	2.00	1.00
			Never hinged	6.00	

750th anniversary of the publication of the poem "Knight in the Tiger Skin," by Shota Rustaveli, Georgian poet.

Exists imperf. Value $500.

Statue Surmounting Pavilion A237

Soviet Pavilion at Paris Exposition A238

1938 Typo.

611	A237	5k	red	.70	.20
a.			Imperf.	200.00	
612	A238	20k	rose	1.50	.25
613	A237	50k	dark blue	2.75	.55
			Nos. 611-613 (3)	4.95	1.00
			Set, never hinged	20.00	

USSR participation in the 1937 International Exposition at Paris.

Types of 1929-32 and Lenin Types of 1925-26

1937-52 Unwmk. *Perf. 11½x12, 12*

613A	A103	1k	dull org ('40)	15.00	5.00
614	A95	2k	yel grn ('39)	6.00	2.00
615	A97	4k	claret ('40)	15.00	2.00
615A	A98	5k	org brn ('46)	100.00	15.00
616	A109	10k	blue ('38)	1.00	.75
616A	A103	10k	olive ('40)	100.00	25.00
616B	A109	10k	black ('52)	.50	.50
617	A97	20k	dull green	1.00	.35
617A	A107	20k	green ('39)	100.00	12.50
618	A109	30k	claret ('39)	15.00	4.50
619	A104	40k	indigo ('38)	2.00	1.00
619A	A111	50k	dp brn ('40)	.85	.50

Engr.

620	A75	3r	dk grn ('39)	1.50	1.00
621	A66	5r	red brn ('39)	3.00	3.00
622	A66	10r	indigo ('39)	3.50	2.75
			Nos. 613A-622 (15)	364.35	75.85
			Set, never hinged	550.00	

#615-619 exist imperf but were not regularly issued.

No. 616B was re-issued in 1954-56 in slightly smaller format, 14½x21mm, and in gray black. See note after No. 738.

Airplane Route from Moscow to North Pole — A239

Soviet Flag and Airplanes at North Pole — A240

1938, Feb. 25 Litho. *Perf. 12*

625	A239	10k	drab & black	1.50	.45
626	A239	20k	blue gray & blk	1.60	.65

Typo.

627	A240	40k	dull green & car	5.00	2.50
a.			Imperf.	200.00	
628	A240	80k	rose car & car	1.90	1.75
a.			Imperf.	90.00	
			Nos. 625-628 (4)	10.00	5.35
			Set, never hinged	25.00	

Soviet flight to the North Pole.

Infantryman A241

Soldier A242

Stalin Reviewing Cavalry A246

Chapayev and Boy — A247

Designs: 30k, Sailor, 40k, Aviator. 50k, Antiaircraft soldier.

Unwmk.

1938, Mar. Photo. *Perf. 12*

629	A241	10k	gray blk & dk red	1.00	.50
630	A242	20k	gray blk & dk red	1.50	.80
631	A242	30k	gray blk & dk red	2.75	1.00
632	A242	40k	gray blk & dk red	4.25	1.75
633	A242	50k	gray blk & dk red	5.25	1.50
634	A246	80k	gray blk & dk red	7.50	1.75

Typo.

Perf. 12x12½

635	A247	1r	black & carmine	4.50	2.00
			Nos. 629-635 (7)	26.75	9.30
			Set, never hinged	60.00	

Workers' & Peasants' Red Army, 20th anniv. No. 635 exists imperf. Value $500.

Aviators Chkalov, Baidukov, Beliakov and Flight Route — A248

Aviators Gromov, Danilin, Yumashev and Flight Route — A249

1938, Apr. 10 Photo.

636	A248	10k	black & red	1.75	.60
637	A248	20k	brn blk & red	2.50	.90
638	A248	40k	brown & red	3.00	2.00
639	A248	50k	brown vio & red	5.75	2.00
			Nos. 636-639 (4)	13.00	5.50
			Set, never hinged	35.00	

First Trans-Polar flight, June 18-20, 1937, from Moscow to Vancouver, Wash. Nos. 636-639 exist imperf. Value $250 each.

1938, Apr. 13

640	A249	10k	claret	2.25	.75
641	A249	20k	brown black	3.50	1.75
642	A249	50k	dull violet	4.25	2.50
			Nos. 640-642 (3)	10.00	5.00
			Set, never hinged	35.00	

First Trans-Polar flight, July 12-14, 1937, from Moscow to San Jacinto, Calif. Nos. 640-642 exist imperf. Value, each $500.

Arrival of the Rescuing Ice-breakers Taimyr and Murmansk A250

Ivan Papanin and His Men Aboard Ice-breaker Yermak — A251

1938, June 21 Typo. *Perf. 12, 12½*

643	A250	10k	violet brown	2.25	1.25
644	A250	20k	dark blue	2.25	1.50

Photo.

645	A251	30k	olive brown	6.00	3.00
646	A251	50k	ultra	6.00	4.00
a.			Imperf.	300.00	
			Nos. 643-646 (4)	16.50	9.75
			Set, never hinged	50.00	

Rescue of Papanin's North Pole Expedition.

Arms of Uzbek — A252

Arms of USSR A253

#650

#651

#654

#655

#656

Designs: Different arms on each stamp.

Perf. 12, 12½

1937-38 Unwmk. Typo.

647	A252	20k	dp bl (Armenia)	2.50	1.25
648	A252	20k	dull violet (Azerbaijan)	2.50	1.25
649	A252	20k	brown orange (Byelorussia)	*2.50*	*1.25*
650	A252	20k	carmine rose (Georgia)	2.50	1.25
651	A252	20k	bl grn (Kazakh)	2.50	1.25
652	A252	20k	emer (Kirghiz)	2.50	1.25
653	A252	20k	yel org (Uzbek)	2.50	1.25
654	A252	20k	bl (R.S.F.S.R.)	2.50	1.25
655	A252	20k	claret (Tadzhik)	2.50	1.25
656	A252	20k	car (Turkmen)	2.50	1.25
657	A252	20k	red (Ukraine)	3.25	1.25

Engr.

658	A253	40k	brown red	3.50	3.50
			Nos. 647-658 (12)	31.75	17.25
			Set, never hinged	100.00	

Constitution of USSR. No. 649 has inscriptions in Yiddish, Polish, Byelorussian and Russian.

Issue dates: 40k, 1937. Others, 1938. See Nos. 841-842.

Nurse Weighing Child — A264

Children at Lenin's Statue — A265

Biology Lesson A266

Health Camp A267

Young Model Builders A268

1938, Sept. 15 Unwmk. *Perf. 12*

659	A264	10k	dk blue green	2.50	.90
660	A265	15k	dk blue green	2.50	1.00
661	A266	20k	violet brown	3.50	1.25
662	A267	30k	claret	4.50	2.00
663	A266	40k	light brown	5.00	2.25
664	A268	50k	deep blue	12.00	4.00
665	A268	80k	light green	9.00	3.50
			Nos. 659-665 (7)	39.00	14.90
			Set, never hinged	100.00	

Child welfare.

View of Yalta A269

Crimean Shoreline — A272

Designs: No. 667, View along Crimean shore. No. 668, Georgian military highway. No, 670, View near Yalta. No. 671, "Swallows' Nest" Castle. 20k, Dzerzhinski Rest House for workers. 30k, Sunset in Crimea. 40k, Alupka. 50k, Gursuf. 80k, Crimean Gardens. 1r, "Swallows' Nest" Castle, horiz.

Unwmk.

1938, Sept. 21 Photo. *Perf. 12*

666 A269 5k brown 1.75 1.25
667 A269 5k black brown 1.75 1.25
668 A269 10k slate green 2.50 1.25
669 A272 10k brown 2.50 1.25
670 A269 15k black brown 5.00 1.25
671 A272 15k black brown 5.00 1.25
672 A269 20k dark brown 5.75 1.25
673 A272 30k black brown 6.25 1.75
674 A269 40k brown 6.50 1.75
675 A272 50k slate green 8.00 3.50
676 A269 80k brown 10.00 3.50
677 A269 1r slate green 17.50 5.50
Nos. 666-677 (12) 72.50 24.75
Set, never hinged 150.00

Children Flying Model Plane A281

Glider A282

Captive Balloon — A283

Dirigible over Kremlin — A284

Parachute Jumpers — A285

Hydroplane A286

Balloon in Flight — A287

Balloon Ascent — A288

Four-motor Plane A289

Unwmk.

1938, Oct. 7 Typo. *Perf. 12*

678 A281 5k violet brown 2.00 .85
679 A282 10k olive gray 2.00 .85
680 A283 15k pink 3.00 1.00
681 A284 20k deep blue 4.50 1.00
682 A285 30k claret 5.00 2.00
683 A286 40k deep blue 6.00 2.00
684 A287 50k blue green 11.00 2.50
685 A288 80k brown 11.00 2.75
686 A289 1r blue green 18.00 3.00
Nos. 678-686 (9) 62.50 15.95
Set, never hinged 150.00

For overprints see Nos. C76-C76D.

Mayakovsky Station, Moscow Subway — A290

Sokol Terminal — A291

Kiev Station — A292

Dynamo Station A293

Train in Tunnel A294

Revolution Square Station A295

Unwmk.

1938, Nov. 7 Photo. *Perf. 12*

687 A290 10k deep red violet 2.00 .90
688 A291 15k dark brown 3.00 1.00
689 A292 20k black brown 4.25 1.50
690 A293 30k dark red violet 5.00 2.00
691 A294 40k black brown 6.00 3.00
692 A295 50k dark brown 9.00 4.00
Nos. 687-692 (6) 29.25 12.40
Set, never hinged 75.00

Second line of the Moscow subway opening.

Girl with Parachute A296

Young Miner A297

Harvesting A298

Designs: 50k, Students returning from school. 80k, Aviator and sailor.

1938, Dec. 7 Typo. *Perf. 12*

693 A296 20k deep blue 2.50 .60
694 A297 30k deep claret 3.50 .60
695 A298 40k violet brown 4.00 .60
696 A296 50k deep rose 5.00 1.25
697 A298 80k deep blue 10.00 2.10
Nos. 693-697 (5) 25.00 5.15
Set, never hinged 55.00

20th anniv. of the Young Communist League (Komsomol).

Diving — A301

Discus Thrower — A302

Designs: 15k, Tennis. 20k, Acrobatic motorcyclists. 30k, Skier. 40k, Runners. 50k, Soccer. 80k, Physical culture.

Unwmk.

1938, Dec. 28 Photo. *Perf. 12*

698 A301 5k scarlet 1.75 .55
699 A302 10k black 2.25 .60
700 A302 15k brown 3.75 .80
701 A302 20k green 4.25 1.10
702 A302 30k dull violet 7.00 1.75
703 A302 40k deep green 8.00 2.00
704 A302 50k blue 12.00 2.50
705 A302 80k deep blue 16.00 3.00
Nos. 698-705 (8) 55.00 12.30
Set, never hinged 150.00

Gorki Street, Moscow — A309

Dynamo Subway Station A315

Foundryman A316

Moscow scenes: 20k, Council House & Hotel Moscow. 30k, Lenin Library. 40k, Crimea Bridge. 50k, Bridge over Moscow River. 80k, Khimki Station.

Paper with network as in parenthesis

1939, Mar. Typo. *Perf. 12*

706 A309 10k brn *(red brown)* 1.25 .50
707 A309 20k dk sl grn *(lt blue)* 2.25 1.00
708 A309 30k brn vio *(red brn)* 3.00 1.50
709 A309 40k blue *(lt blue)* 3.75 1.75
710 A309 50k rose lake *(red brn)* 5.75 2.25
711 A309 80k gray ol *(lt blue)* 8.50 3.00
712 A315 1r dk blue *(lt blue)* 10.00 3.75
Nos. 706-712 (7) 34.50 13.75
Set, never hinged 100.00

"New Moscow." On 30k, denomination is at upper right.

1939, Mar.

713 A316 15k dark blue 1.50 .90
Never hinged 5.00
a. Imperf. 300.00
Never hinged 500.00

Statue on USSR Pavilion — A317

USSR Pavilion A318

1939, May Photo.

714 A317 30k indigo & red 1.75 .35
a. Imperf. ('40) 2.75 .80
715 A318 50k blue & bister brn 1.75 .60
a. Imperf. ('40) 2.75 .90
Set, never hinged 5.00
Set, imperf., never hinged 9.00

Russia's participation in the NY World's Fair.

Paulina Osipenko A318a

Marina Raskova A318b

Design: 60k, Valentina Grizodubova.

1939, Mar.

718 A318a 15k green 1.50 .75
719 A318b 30k brown violet 3.00 1.00
720 A318b 60k red 5.00 2.00
Nos. 718-720 (3) 9.50 3.75
Set, never hinged 50.00

Non-stop record flight from Moscow to the Far East.

Exist imperf. Value, each $350.

Shevchenko, Early Portrait — A319

Monument at Kharkov — A321

30k, Shevchenko portrait in later years.

1939, Mar. 9

721	A319	15k black brn & blk	3.00	.75
722	A319	30k dark red & blk	4.00	1.25
723	A321	60k green & dk brn	7.50	2.75
		Nos. 721-723 (3)	14.50	4.75
		Set, never hinged	45.00	

Taras G. Shevchenko (1814-1861), Ukrainian poet and painter.

Milkmaid with Prize Cow — A322

Tractor-plow at Work on Abundant Harvest A323

Designs: 20k, Shepherd tending sheep. No. 727, Fair pavilion. No. 728, Fair emblem. 45k, Turkmen picking cotton. 50k, Drove of horses. 60k, Symbolizing agricultural wealth. 80k, Kolkhoz girl with sugar beets. 1r, Hunter with Polar foxes.

1939, Aug.

724	A322	10k rose pink	.80	.25
725	A323	15k red brown	.80	.25
726	A323	20k slate black	2.00	1.00
727	A323	30k purple	1.25	.75
728	A322	30k red orange	1.25	.75
729	A322	45k dark green	2.00	1.00
730	A322	50k copper red	2.00	1.00
731	A322	60k bright purple	3.00	1.25
732	A322	80k dark violet	2.50	1.25
733	A322	1r dark blue	5.00	1.50
		Nos. 724-733 (10)	20.60	9.00
		Set, never hinged	75.00	

Soviet Agricultural Fair.

A331

A332

Worker -Soldier - Aviator — A333

Arms of USSR
A334 A335

1939-43 Unwmk. Typo. *Perf. 12*

734	A331	5k red	.20	.20
735	A332	15k dark green	.25	.25
736	A333	30k deep blue	.25	.25
737	A334	60k fawn ('43)	.60	.25

Photo.

738	A335	60k rose carmine	.50	.35
		Nos. 734-738 (5)	1.80	1.30
		Set, never hinged	3.00	

No. 734 was re-issued in 1954-56 in slightly smaller format: 14x21½mm, instead of 14¾x22¼mm. Other values reissued in smaller format: 10k, 15k, 20k, 25k, 30k, 40k and 1r. (See notes following Nos. 622, 1260, 1347 and 1689.)

No. 416 Surcharged with New Value in Black

1939 Wmk. 170

743	A97	30k on 4k claret	15.00	8.00
		Never hinged	35.00	
a.		Unwmkd.	100.00	40.00

M.E. Saltykov (N. Shchedrin)
A336 A337

1939, Sept. Typo. Unwmk.

745	A336	15k claret	1.00	.35
746	A337	30k dark green	1.50	.75
747	A336	45k olive gray	2.50	1.00
748	A337	60k dark blue	3.50	1.25
		Nos. 745-748 (4)	8.50	3.35
		Set, never hinged	25.00	

Mikhail E. Saltykov (1826-89), writer & satirist who used pen name of N. Shchedrin.

Sanatorium of the State Bank — A338

Designs: 10k, 15k, Soviet Army sanatorium. 20k, Rest home, New Afyon. 30k, Clinical Institute. 50k, 80k, Sanatorium for workers in heavy industry. 60k, Rest home, Sukhumi.

1939, Nov. Photo. *Perf. 12*

749	A338	5k dull brown	1.10	.20
750	A338	10k carmine	1.10	.25
751	A338	15k yellow green	1.10	.30
752	A338	20k dk slate green	1.10	.35
753	A338	30k bluish black	1.50	.45
754	A338	50k gray black	2.50	.65
755	A338	60k brown violet	3.50	.85
756	A338	80k orange red	4.50	1.25
		Nos. 749-756 (8)	16.40	4.30
		Set, never hinged	45.00	

Mikhail Y. Lermontov (1814-1841), Poet and Novelist, in 1837 — A346

Portrait in 1838 — A347

Portrait in 1841 — A348

1939, Dec.

757	A346	15k indigo & sepia	2.75	.75
758	A347	30k dk grn & dull blk	6.00	1.25
759	A348	45k brick red & indigo	5.25	2.75
		Nos. 757-759 (3)	14.00	4.75
		Set, never hinged	35.00	

Nikolai Chernyshevski A349

Anton Chekhov A350

1939, Dec. Photo.

760	A349	15k dark green	1.25	.50
761	A349	30k dull violet	1.75	.75
762	A349	60k Prus green	2.50	1.00
		Nos. 760-762 (3)	5.50	2.25
		Set, never hinged	15.00	

50th anniversary of the death of Nikolai Chernyshevski, scientist and critic.

1940, Feb. Unwmk. *Perf. 12*

Design: 20k, 30k, Portrait with hat.

763	A350	10k dark yellow green	1.00	.25
764	A350	15k ultra	1.00	.30
765	A350	20k violet	2.00	.50
766	A350	30k copper brown	3.00	1.00
		Nos. 763-766 (4)	7.00	2.05
		Set, never hinged	20.00	

Chekhov (1860-1904), playwright.

Welcome to Red Army by Western Ukraine and Western Byelorussia A352

Designs: 30k, Villagers welcoming tank crew. 50k, 60k, Soldier giving newspapers to crowd. 1r, Crowd waving to tank column.

1940, Apr.

767	A352	10k deep rose	1.25	.75
768	A352	30k myrtle green	1.75	.85
769	A352	50k gray black	2.50	1.75
770	A352	60k indigo	3.50	2.00
771	A352	1r red	5.75	3.50
		Nos. 767-771 (5)	14.75	8.85
		Set, never hinged	35.00	

Liberation of the people of Western Ukraine and Western Byelorussia.

Ice-breaker "Josef Stalin," Captain Beloussov and Chief Ivan Papanin A356

Vadygin and Papanin A358

Map of the Drift of the Sedov and Crew Members — A359

Design: 30k, Icebreaker Georgi Sedov, Captain Vadygin and First Mate Trofimov.

1940, Apr.

772	A356	15k dull yel green	2.00	.55
773	A356	30k dull purple	4.00	.65
774	A358	50k copper brown	4.50	.90
775	A359	1r dark ultra	5.75	2.25
		Nos. 772-775 (4)	16.25	4.35
		Set, never hinged	55.00	

Heroism of the Sedov crew which drifted in the Polar Basin for 812 days.

A360

Vladimir V. Mayakovsky — A361

1940, June

776	A360	15k deep red	.75	.20
777	A360	30k copper brown	1.25	.30
778	A361	60k dark gray blue	2.25	.60
779	A361	80k bright ultra	3.75	.90
		Nos. 776-779 (4)	8.00	2.00
		Set, never hinged	22.50	

Mayakovsky, poet (1893-1930).

K.A. Timiryazev and Academy of Agricultural Sciences A362

In the Laboratory of Moscow University A363

Last Portrait A364

Monument in Moscow — A365

1940, June

780	A362	10k indigo	.75	.25
781	A363	15k purple	1.00	.50
782	A364	30k dk violet brown	2.25	1.25
783	A365	60k dark green	4.25	2.00
		Nos. 780-783 (4)	8.25	4.00
		Set, never hinged	25.00	

20th anniversary of the death of K. A. Timiryasev, scientist and professor of agricultural and biological sciences.

Relay Race — A366

Sportswomen Marching A367

Children's Sport Badge — A368

Skier
A369

Throwing the Grenade
A370

1940, July 21

784	A366	15k carmine rose	1.50	.30
785	A367	30k sepia	2.50	.30
786	A368	50k dk violet blue	3.75	.60
787	A369	60k dk violet blue	4.75	.60
788	A370	1r grayish green	7.50	2.00
		Nos. 784-788 (5)	20.00	3.80
		Set, never hinged	55.00	

2nd All-Union Physical Culture Day.

Tchaikovsky Museum at Klin
A371

Tchaikovsky & Passage from his Fourth Symphony
A372

Peter Ilich Tchaikovsky and Excerpt from Eugene Onegin — A373

1940, Aug. Unwmk. Typo. *Perf. 12*

789	A371	15k Prus green	1.90	.75
790	A372	20k brown	2.00	.75
791	A372	30k dark blue	2.25	.75
792	A371	50k rose lake	3.75	1.00
793	A373	60k red	5.00	1.75
		Nos. 789-793 (5)	14.90	5.00
		Set, never hinged	50.00	

Tchaikovsky (1840-1893), composer.

Volga Provinces Pavilion
A374

Northeast Provinces Pavilion — A376

ПАВИЛЬОН МОСКОВСКОЙ, РЯЗАНСКОЙ И ТУЛЬСКОЙ ОБЛ.
#797

ПАВИЛЬОН УКРАИНСКОЙ ССР
#798

ПАВИЛЬОН БЕЛОРУССКОЙ ССР
#799

ПАВИЛЬОН АЗЕРБАЙДЖАНСКОЙ ССР
#800

ПАВИЛЬОН ГРУЗИНСКОЙ ССР
#801

ПАВИЛЬОН АРМЯНСКОЙ ССР
#802

„У ВХОДА В ПАВИЛЬОН УЗБЕКСКОЙ ССР"
#803

ПАВИЛЬОН ТУРКМЕНСКОЙ ССР
#804

ПАВИЛЬОН ТАДЖИКСКОЙ ССР
#805

ПАВИЛЬОН КИРГИЗСКОЙ ССР
#806

ПАВИЛЬОН КАЗАХСКОЙ ССР
#807

ПАВИЛЬОН КАРЕЛО-ФИНСКОЙ ССР
#808

1940, Oct. Photo.

794	A374	10k shown	2.00	.50
795	A374	15k Far East Provinces	2.50	.50
796	A376	30k shown	2.75	.70
797	A376	30k Central Regions	2.75	.70
798	A376	30k Ukrainian	2.75	.70
799	A376	30k Byelorussian	2.75	.70
800	A376	30k Azerbaijan	2.75	.70
801	A374	30k Georgian	2.75	.70
802	A376	30k Armenian	2.75	.70
803	A376	30k Uzbek	2.75	.70
804	A374	30k Turkmen	2.75	.70
805	A376	30k Tadzhik	2.75	.70
806	A376	30k Kirghiz	2.75	1.40
807	A376	30k Kazakh	2.75	1.40
808	A376	30k Karelian Finnish	2.75	1.40
809	A376	50k Main building	6.00	1.40
810	A376	60k Mechanizaton Pavilion, Stalin statue	8.00	1.40
		Nos. 794-810 (17)	54.25	15.00
		Set, never hinged	125.00	

All-Union Agricultural Fair.

Nos. 796-808 printed in three sheet formats with various vertical and horizontal se-tenant combinations.

Monument to Red Army Heroes — A391

Map of War Operations and M. V. Frunze — A393

Heroic Crossing of the Sivash
A394

Designs: 15k, Grenade thrower. 60k, Frunze's headquarters, Stroganovka. 1r, Victorious soldier.

1940 *Imperf.*

811	A391	10k dark green	.75	.30
812	A391	15k orange ver	.75	.30
813	A393	30k dull brown & car	.75	.30
814	A394	50k violet brn	.75	.50
815	A394	60k indigo	.75	.75
816	A391	1r gray black	1.25	.75
		Nos. 811-816 (6)	5.00	2.90
		Set, never hinged	10.00	

20th anniversary of battle of Perekop.

Also issued perf. 12. Set price about 25% more.

SEMI-POSTAL STAMPS

Empire

Admiral Kornilov Monument, Sevastopol
SP1

Pozharski and Minin Monument, Moscow
SP2

Statue of Peter the Great, Leningrad
SP3

Alexander II Memorial and Kremlin, Moscow
SP4

Perf. 11½ to 13½ and Compound

1905 Typo. Unwmk.

B1	SP1	3k red, brn & grn	4.50	3.50
a.		Perf. 13½x 11½	300.00	225.00
b.		Perf. 13½	40.00	40.00
c.		Perf. 11½x13½	300.00	225.00
B2	SP2	5k lilac, vio & straw	3.50	2.50
B3	SP3	7k lt bl, dk bl & pink	5.25	3.50
a.		Perf. 13½	65.00	65.00
B4	SP4	10k lt blue, dk bl & yel	9.00	5.00
		Nos. B1-B4 (4)	22.25	14.50

These stamps were sold for 3 kopecks over face value. The surtax was donated to a fund for the orphans of soldiers killed in the Russo-Japanese war.

Ilya Murometz Legendary Russian Hero — SP5

Designs: 3k, Don Cossack Bidding Farewell to His Sweetheart. 7k, Symbolical of Charity. 10k, St. George Slaying the Dragon.

1914 *Perf. 11½, 12½*

B5	SP5	1k red brn & dk grn, *straw*	.60	.65
B6	SP5	3k mar & gray grn, *pink*	.60	.65
B7	SP5	7k dk brn & dk grn, *buff*	.60	.65
B8	SP5	10k dk blue & brn, *blue*	2.75	3.25
		Nos. B5-B8 (4)	4.55	5.20

Perf. 13½

B5a	SP5	1k	.40	.60
B6a	SP5	3k	50.00	50.00
B7a	SP5	7k	.30	.60
B8a	SP5	10k	7.00	9.00
		Nos. B5a-B8a (4)	57.70	60.20

1915 White Paper

B9	SP5	1k orange brn & gray	.30	.40
B10	SP5	3k car & gray black	.40	.50
a.		Horiz. pair, imperf btwn.	150.00	
B12	SP5	7k dk brn & dk grn	6.50	
B13	SP5	10k dk blue & brown	.25	.40
		Nos. B9-B13 (4)	7.45	

These stamps were sold for 1 kopeck over face value. The surtax was donated to charities connected with the war of 1914-17.

No. B12 not regularly issued.

Nos. B5-B13 exist imperf. Value each, $150 unused, $250 canceled.

Russian Soviet Federated Socialist Republic

Volga Famine Relief Issue

Relief Work on Volga River — SP9

Administering Aid to Famine Victim — SP10

1921 Litho. *Imperf.*

B14	SP9	2250r green	3.75	10.00
a.		Pelure paper	125.00	85.00
B15	SP9	2250r deep red	3.25	6.50
a.		Pelure paper	19.00	18.00
B16	SP9	2250r brown	3.25	16.00
B17	SP10	2250r dark blue	7.75	21.00
		Nos. B14-B17 (4)	18.00	53.50

Forged cancels and counterfeits of Nos. B14-B17 are plentiful.

Stamps of type A33 with this overprint were not charity stamps nor did they pay postage in any form.

They represent taxes paid on stamps exported from or imported into Russia. In 1925 the semi-postal stamps of 1914-15 were surcharged for the same purpose. Stamps of the regular issues 1918 and 1921 have also been surcharged with inscriptions and new values, to pay the importation and exportation taxes.

Nos. 149-150 Surcharged in Black, Red, Blue or Orange

1922, Feb. *Perf. 13½*

B18	A33	100r + 100r on 70k	.75	2.50
a.		"100 p. + p. 100"	140.00	140.00
B19	A33	100r + 100r on 70k (R)	.75	2.50
B20	A33	100r + 100r on 70k (Bl)	.40	1.25
B21	A33	250r + 250r on 35k	.40	1.25
B22	A33	250r + 250r on 35k (R)	.75	2.50
B23	A33	250r + 250r on 35k (O)	1.40	5.00
		Nos. B18-B23 (6)	4.45	15.00

Issued to raise funds for Volga famine relief.

Nos. B18-B22 exist with surcharge inverted. Values $20 to $40.

Regular Issues of 1909-18 Overprinted

1922, Aug. 19 *Perf. 14*

B24 A14	1k orange	300.00	260.00
B25 A14	2k green	22.50	*37.50*
B26 A14	3k red	18.00	*37.50*
B27 A14	5k claret	22.50	*37.50*
B28 A15	10k dark blue	22.50	*37.50*

Imperf

B29 A14	1k orange	300.00	300.00
	Nos. B24-B29 (6)	685.50	710.00

The overprint means "Philately for the Children". The stamps were sold at five million times their face values and 80% of the amount was devoted to child welfare. The stamps were sold only at Moscow and for one day.

Exist with overprint reading up. Counterfeits exist including those with overprint reading up. Reprints exist.

Worker and Peasant (Industry and Agriculture) — SP11

Allegory: Agriculture Will Help End Distress SP12

Star of Hope, Wheat and Worker-Peasant Handclasp — SP13

Sower — SP14

1922 **Litho.** *Imperf.*

Without Gum

B30 SP11	2t (2000r) green	30.00	*250.00*
B31 SP12	2t (2000r) rose	40.00	*250.00*
B32 SP13	4t (4000r) rose	40.00	*250.00*
B33 SP14	6t (6000r) green	40.00	*250.00*
	Nos. B30-B33 (4)	150.00	1,000.

Nos. B30-B33 exist with double impression.

Counterfeits of Nos. B30-B33 exist; beware also of forged cancellations.

Miniature copies of Nos. B30-B33 exist, taken from the 1933 Soviet catalogue.

Automobile SP15

Steamship SP16

Railroad Train SP17

Airplane SP18

1922 *Imperf.*

B34 SP15	(20r+5r) light violet	.25	.25
B35 SP16	(20r+5r) violet	.25	.25
B36 SP17	(20r+5r) gray blue	.25	.25
B37 SP18	(20r+5r) blue gray	3.75	*6.75*
	Nos. B34-B37 (4)	4.50	*7.50*

Inscribed "For the Hungry." Each stamp was sold for 200,000r postage and 50,000r charity.

Counterfeits of Nos. B34-B37 exist.

Nos. 212, 183, 202 Surcharged in Bronze, Gold or Silver

1923 *Imperf.*

B38 A48	1r +1r on 10r	225.00	225.00
a.	Inverted surcharge	350.00	350.00
B39 A48	1r +1r on 10r (G)	30.00	45.00
a.	Inverted surcharge	350.00	350.00
B40 A43	2r +2r on 250r	30.00	37.50
a.	Pelure paper	30.30	30.00
b.	Inverted surcharge	300.00	300.00
c.	Double surcharge		

Wmk. 171

B41 A46	4r +4r on 5000r	30.00	30.00
a.	Date spaced "1 923"	250.00	250.00
b.	Inverted surcharge	400.00	400.00
B42 A46	4r +4r on 5000r (S)	675.00	600.00
a.	Inverted surcharge	1,500.	1,250.
b.	Date spaced "1 923"	1,500.	1,250.
c.	As "b," inverted surch.	*5,000.*	
	Nos. B38-B42 (5)	990.00	937.50

The inscriptions mean "Philately's Contribution to Labor." The stamps were on sale only at Moscow and for one day. The surtax was for charitable purposes.

Counterfeits of No. B42 exist.

Leningrad Flood Issue

Nos. 181-182, 184-186 Surcharged

1924 **Unwmk.** *Imperf.*

B43 A40	3k + 10k on 100r	1.50	1.50
a.	Pelure paper	6.00	8.00
b.	Inverted surcharge	500.00	250.00
B44 A40	7k + 20k on 200r	1.50	1.50
a.	Inverted surcharge	500.00	250.00
B45 A40	14k + 30k on 300r	1.75	1.75
a.	Pelure paper	500.00	400.00

Similar Surcharge in Red or Black

B46 A41	12k + 40k on 500r (R)	3.25	3.25
a.	Double surcharge	500.00	500.00
b.	Inverted surcharge	500.00	500.00
B47 A41	20k + 50k on 1000r	2.25	2.25
a.	Thick paper	22.50	22.50
b.	Pelure paper	40.00	40.00
c.	Chalk surface paper	20.00	20.00
	Nos. B43-B47 (5)	10.25	10.25

The surcharge on Nos. B43 to B45 reads: "S.S.S.R. For the sufferers by the inundation at Leningrad." That on Nos. B46 and B47 reads: "S.S.S.R. For the Leningrad Proletariat, 23, IX, 1924."

No. B46 is surcharged vertically, reading down, with the value as the top line.

Orphans SP19

Lenin as a Child SP20

1926 **Typo.** *Perf. 13½*

B48 SP19	10k brown	*12.00*	*17.50*
B49 SP20	20k deep blue	*13.00*	*22.50*

Wmk. 170

B50 SP19	10k brown	1.00	.90
B51 SP20	20k deep blue	2.50	1.65
	Nos. B48-B51 (4)	*28.50*	*42.55*

Two kopecks of the price of each of these stamps was donated to organizations for the care of indigent children.

Types of 1926 Issue

1927

B52 SP19	8k + 2k yel green	4.00	1.00
B53 SP20	18k + 2k deep rose	7.50	2.00

Surtax was for child welfare.

Industrial Training SP21

Agricultural Training SP22

Perf. 10, 10½, 12½

1929-30 **Photo.** **Unwmk.**

B54 SP21	10k +2k ol brn & org brn	5.00	2.50
a.	Perf. 10½	200.00	110.00
B55 SP21	10k +2k ol grn ('30)	2.50	2.00
B56 SP22	20k +2k blk brn & bl, perf. 10½	5.00	4.00
a.	Perf. 12½	60.00	50.00
b.	Perf. 10	10.00	10.00
B57 SP22	20k +2k bl grn ('30)	3.00	4.50
	Nos. B54-B57 (4)	15.50	13.00

Surtax was for child welfare.

AIR POST STAMPS

AP1

Fokker F-111 — AP2

Plane Overprint in Red

1922 **Unwmk.** *Imperf.*

C1 AP1	45r green & black	15.00	*50.00*

5th anniversary of October Revolution.

No. C1 was on sale only at the Moscow General Post Office. Counterfeits exist.

1923 **Photo.**

C2 AP2	1r red brown	4.50	
C3 AP2	3r deep blue	6.00	
C4 AP2	5r green	5.50	
a.	Wide "5"	*5,000.*	
C5 AP2	10r carmine	4.00	
	Nos. C2-C5 (4)	20.00	

Nos. C2-C5 were not placed in use.

Nos. C2-C5 Surcharged

1924

C6 AP2	5k on 3r dp blue	4.00	2.00
C7 AP2	10k on 5r green	4.00	2.00
a.	Wide "5"	*250.00*	*250.00*
b.	Inverted surcharge	*900.00*	*450.00*
C8 AP2	15k on 1r red brown	4.00	2.00
a.	Inverted surcharge	*1,000.*	*500.00*
C9 AP2	20k on 10r car	4.00	2.00
a.	Inverted surcharge	*1,000.*	*500.00*
	Nos. C6-C9 (4)	16.00	8.00

Airplane over Map of World AP3

1927, Sept. 1 **Litho.** *Perf. 13x12*

C10 AP3	10k dk bl & yel brn	10.00	5.00
C11 AP3	15k dp red & ol grn	12.50	10.00

1st Intl. Air Post Cong. at The Hague, initiated by the USSR.

Graf Zeppelin and "Call to Complete 5-Year Plan in 4 Years" — AP4

1930 **Photo.** **Wmk. 226** *Perf. 12½*

C12 AP4	40k dk & dl blue	27.50	12.50
a.	Perf. 10½	27.50	12.50
b.	Imperf.	*1,000.*	*700.00*
C13 AP4	80k dk car & rose	32.50	17.50
a.	Perf. 10½	32.50	17.50
b.	Imperf.	*1,000.*	*700.00*

Flight of the Graf Zeppelin from Friedrichshafen to Moscow and return.

Symbolical of Airship Communication from the Tundra to the Steppes — AP5

Airship over Dneprostroi Dam — AP6

Airship over Lenin Mausoleum — AP7

Airship Exploring Arctic Regions — AP8

Constructing an Airship AP9

1931-32 Wmk. 170 Photo. *Imperf.*

C15	AP5	10k dark violet	25.00	25.00
		Litho.		
C16	AP6	15k gray blue	25.00	25.00
		Typo.		
C17	AP7	20k dk carmine	25.00	25.00
		Photo.		
C18	AP8	50k black brown	25.00	25.00
C19	AP9	1r dark green	25.00	25.00
		Nos. C15-C19 (5)	125.00	125.00

Perf. 10½, 12, 12½ and Compound

C20	AP5	10k dark violet	7.00	3.50
		Litho.		
C21	AP6	15k gray blue	13.50	5.50
		Typo.		
C22	AP7	20k dk carmine	9.50	3.00
a.		20k light red	11.00	4.50
		Photo.		
C23	AP8	50k black brown	7.00	3.00
a.		50k gray blue (error)	300.00	300.00
C24	AP9	1r dark green	8.00	3.00

Perf. 12½

Unwmk.

Engr.

C25	AP6	15k gray blk ('32)	1.50	.75
a.		Perf. 10½	*600.00*	200.00
b.		Perf. 14	60.00	45.00
c.		Imperf.	750.00	
		Nos. C20-C25 (6)	46.50	18.75

The 11½ perforation on Nos. C20-C25 is of private origin; beware also of bogus perforation "errors."

North Pole Issue

Graf Zeppelin and Icebreaker "Malygin" Transferring Mail — AP10

1931 Wmk. 170 *Imperf.*

C26	AP10	30k dark violet	17.50	*25.00*
C27	AP10	35k dark green	17.50	*20.00*
C28	AP10	1r gray black	17.50	*27.50*
C29	AP10	2r deep ultra	29.00	29.00
		Nos. C26-C29 (4)	81.50	101.50

Perf. 12x12½

C30	AP10	30k dark violet	32.50	40.00
C31	AP10	35k dark green	32.50	40.00
C32	AP10	1r gray black	32.50	40.00
C33	AP10	2r deep ultra	32.50	40.00
		Nos. C30-C33 (4)	130.00	160.00

Map of Polar Region, Airplane and Icebreaker "Sibiryakov" — AP11

Perf. 12, 10½

1932, Aug. 26 Wmk. 170

C34	AP11	50k carmine rose	50.00	20.00
a.		Perf. 10½	*2,750.*	*2,750.*
b.		Perf. 10½x12		*3,000.*
C35	AP11	1r green	50.00	20.00
a.		Perf. 12	125.00	40.00

2nd International Polar Year in connection with proposed flight from Franz-Josef Land to Archangel which, being impossible, actually went from Archangel to Moscar to destinations.

Stratostat "U.S.S.R." — AP12

1933 Photo. *Perf. 14*

C37	AP12	5k ultra	70.00	10.00
a.		Vert. pair, imperf. btwn.		*1,200.*
C38	AP12	10k carmine	35.00	10.00
a.		Horiz. pair, imperf. btwn.		*2,250.*
C39	AP12	20k violet	35.00	10.00
		Nos. C37-C39 (3)	140.00	30.00

Ascent into the stratosphere by Soviet aeronauts, Sept. 30th, 1933.

Furnaces of Kuznetsk AP13

Designs: 10k, Oil wells. 20k, Collective farm. 50k, Map of Moscow-Volga Canal project. 80k, Arctic cargo ship.

1933 Wmk. 170 *Perf. 14*

C40	AP13	5k ultra	20.00	5.00
C41	AP13	10k green	20.00	5.00
C42	AP13	20k carmine	42.50	10.00
C43	AP13	50k dull blue	55.00	10.00
C44	AP13	80k purple	42.50	10.00
		Nos. C40-C44 (5)	180.00	40.00
		Unwmk.		
C45	AP13	5k ultra	19.00	5.00
C46	AP13	10k green	19.00	5.00
a.		Horiz. pair, imperf. btwn.	900.00	350.00
C47	AP13	20k carmine	26.00	9.00
C48	AP13	50k dull blue	72.50	17.50
C49	AP13	80k purple	40.00	9.00
		Nos. C45-C49 (5)	176.50	45.50

10th anniversary of Soviet civil aviation and airmail service. Counterfeits exist, perf 11½.

I. D. Usyskin AP18

10k, A. B. Vasenko. 20k, P. F. Fedoseinko.

1934 Wmk. 170 *Perf. 11*

C50	AP18	5k vio brown	29.00	5.00
C51	AP18	10k brown	55.00	5.00
C52	AP18	20k ultra	29.00	5.00
		Nos. C50-C52 (3)	113.00	15.00
		Perf. 14		
C50a	AP18	5k	110.00	*225.00*
C51a	AP18	10k	1,100.	*2,000.*
C52a	AP18	20k	1,350.	*2,000.*
		Nos. C50a-C52a (3)	2,560.	4,225.

Honoring victims of the stratosphere disaster. See Nos. C77-C79.

Beware of copies of Nos. C50-C52 reperforated to resemble Nos. C50a-C52a.

Airship "Pravda" — AP19

Airship Landing — AP20

Airship "Voroshilov" — AP21

Sideview of Airship — AP22

Airship "Lenin" — AP23

1934 *Perf. 14*

C53	AP19	5k red orange	22.50	4.75
C54	AP20	10k claret	22.50	7.25
C55	AP21	15k brown	20.00	10.00
C56	AP22	20k black	45.00	15.00
C57	AP23	30k ultra	80.00	15.00
		Nos. C53-C57 (5)	190.00	52.00

Capt. V. Voronin and "Chelyuskin" — AP24

Prof. Otto Y. Schmidt — AP25

A. V. Lapidevsky AP26

S. A. Levanevsky AP27

"Schmidt Camp" — AP28

Designs: 15k, M. G. Slepnev. 20k, I. V. Doronin. 25k, M. V. Vodopianov. 30k, V. S. Molokov. 40k, N. P. Kamanin.

1935 *Perf. 14*

C58	AP24	1k red orange	12.50	3.50
C59	AP25	3k rose carmine	15.00	3.50
C60	AP26	5k emerald	12.50	3.50
C61	AP27	10k dark brown	15.00	3.50
C62	AP27	15k black	18.00	3.50
C63	AP27	20k deep claret	25.00	6.50
C64	AP27	25k indigo	62.50	13.00
C65	AP27	30k dull green	90.00	15.00
C66	AP27	40k purple	62.50	10.00
C67	AP28	50k dark ultra	62.50	13.00
		Nos. C58-C67 (10)	375.50	75.00

Aerial rescue of ice-breaker Chelyuskin crew and scientific expedition.

No. C61 Surcharged in Red

1935, Aug.

C68	AP27 1r on 10k dk brn	375.00	375.00
	Never hinged	800.00	
a.	Inverted surcharge	*7,000.*	*7,000.*
b.	Small Cyrillic "f"	800.00	1,100.
c.	As "b," inverted surcharge	*30,000.*	

Moscow-San Francisco flight. Counterfeits exist.

Single-Engined Monoplane — AP34

Five-Engined Transport — AP35

20k, Twin-engined cabin plane. 30k, 4r-motored transport. 40k, Single-engined amphibian. 50k, Twin-motored transport. 80k, 8-motored transport.

1937 Unwmk. *Perf. 12*

C69	AP34 10k yel brn & blk	2.50	1.00
a.	Imperf.		250.00
C70	AP34 20k gray grn & blk	2.50	1.00
C71	AP34 30k red brn & blk	3.00	1.00
C72	AP34 40k vio brn & blk	4.50	1.25
C73	AP34 50k dk vio & blk	7.00	2.00
C74	AP35 80k bl vio & brn	6.50	2.00
C75	AP35 1r black, brown & buff	19.00	4.00
a.	Sheet of 4, imperf.	125.00	150.00
	Nos. C69-C75 (7)	45.00	12.25
	Set, never hinged	150.00	

Jubilee Aviation Exhib., Moscow, Nov. 15-20.
Vertical pairs, imperf. between, exist for No. C71, value $500; No. C73, value $350.

Types of 1938 Regular Issue Overprinted in Various Colors

1939 Typo.

C76	A282 10k red (C)	1.75	.70
C76A	A285 30k blue (R)	1.75	.70
C76B	A286 40k dull green (Br)	1.75	.70
C76C	A287 50k dull violet (R)	2.75	.95
C76D	A289 1r brown (Bl)	3.75	3.00
a.	Double overprint		1,000.
	Nos. C76-C76D (5)	11.75	6.05
	Set, never hinged	30.00	

Soviet Aviation Day, Aug. 18, 1939.

AIR POST OFFICIAL STAMPS

Used on mail from Russian embassy in Berlin to Moscow. Surcharged on Consular Fee stamps. Currency: the German mark.

OA1

Surcharge in Carmine

1922, July Litho. *Perf. 13½*

Bicolored Burelage

CO1	OA1 12m on 2.25r	100.00	150.00
CO2	OA1 24m on 3r	100.00	225.00
CO3	OA1 120m on 2.25r	120.00	
CO4	OA1 600m on 3r	190.00	
CO5	OA1 1200m on 10k	525.00	
CO6	OA1 1200m on 50k	*16,000.*	
CO7	OA1 1200m on 2.25r	1,300.	
CO8	OA1 1200m on 3r	1,500.	

Three types of each denomination, distinguished by shape of "C" in surcharge and length of second line of surcharge. Used copies have pen or crayon cancel. Forgeries exist.

SPECIAL DELIVERY STAMPS

Motorcycle Courier — SD1

Express Truck — SD2

Design: 80k, Locomotive.

Perf. 12½x12, 12x12½

1932 Photo. Wmk. 170

E1	SD1 5k dull brown	7.50	6.25
E2	SD2 10k violet brown	9.75	6.25
E3	SD2 80k dull green	40.00	12.50
	Nos. E1-E3 (3)	57.25	25.00
	Set, never hinged	100.00	

Used values are for c-t-o.

POSTAGE DUE STAMPS

Regular Issue of 1918 Surcharged in Red or Carmine

1924-25 Unwmk. *Perf. 13½*

J1	A33 1k on 35k blue	.25	*.90*
J2	A33 3k on 35k blue	.25	*.90*
J3	A33 5k on 35k blue	.25	*.90*
a.	Imperf.	60.00	
J4	A33 8k on 35k blue ('25)	.50	*.90*
a.	Imperf.	40.00	
J5	A33 10k on 35k blue	.50	*1.40*
a.	Pair, one without surcharge	40.00	
J6	A33 12k on 70k brown	.30	*1.10*
J7	A33 14k on 35k blue ('25)	.30	*1.10*
a.	Imperf.	65.00	
J8	A33 32k on 35k blue	.35	*3.00*
J9	A33 40k on 35k blue	.35	*3.00*
a.	Imperf.	60.00	
	Nos. J1-J9 (9)	3.05	*13.20*

Surcharge is found inverted on Nos. J1-J2, J4, J6-J9, value $25-$50. Double on Nos. J2, J4-J6; value, $40-$50.

Regular Issue of 1921 Surcharged in Violet

1924 *Imperf.*

J10	A40 1k on 100r orange	6.00	*15.00*
a.	1k on 100r yellow	7.00	*20.00*
b.	Pelure paper	7.00	*20.00*
c.	Inverted surcharge	*100.00*	

D1

Lithographed or Typographed

1925 *Perf. 12*

J11	D1 1k red	2.00	1.50
J12	D1 2k violet	1.00	2.25
J13	D1 3k light blue	1.00	2.25
J14	D1 7k orange	1.00	2.25
J15	D1 8k green	1.00	3.00
J16	D1 10k dark blue	1.65	4.50
J17	D1 14k brown	2.00	4.50
	Nos. J11-J17 (7)	9.65	20.25

Perf. 14½x14

J13a	D1 3k	4.00	6.00
J14a	D1 7k	8.25	12.50
J16a	D1 10k	—	40.00
J17a	D1 14k	2.25	3.50
	Nos. J13a-J17a (4)	14.50	62.00

1925 Wmk. 170 Typo. *Perf. 12*

J18	D1 1k red	.85	.85
J19	D1 2k violet	.85	.85
J20	D1 3k light blue	1.10	1.10
J21	D1 7k orange	1.20	1.10
J22	D1 8k green	1.20	1.10
J23	D1 10k dark blue	1.60	2.00
J24	D1 14k brown	2.50	2.50
	Nos. J18-J24 (7)	9.30	9.50

For surcharges see Nos. 359-372.

WENDEN (LIVONIA)

A former district of Livonia, a province of the Russian Empire, which became part of Latvia, under the name of Vidzeme.

Used values for Nos. L2-L12 are for pen-canceled copies. Postmarked specimens sell for considerably more.

A1

1862 Unwmk. *Imperf.*

L1	A1 (2k) blue	30.00	
a.	Tête bêche pair	*350.00*	

No. L1 may have been used for a short period of time but withdrawn because of small size. Some consider it an essay.

A2

A3

1863

L2	A2 (2k) rose & black	240.00	240.00
a.	Background inverted	600.00	600.00
L3	A3 (4k) blue grn & blk	175.00	175.00
a.	(4k) yellow green & black	300.00	300.00
b.	Half used as 2k on cover		*2,500.*
c.	Background inverted	300.00	300.00
d.	As "a," background inverted	350.00	350.00

The official imitations of Nos. L2 and L3 have a single instead of a double hyphen after "WENDEN."

Coat of Arms

A4 A5 A6

1863-71

L4	A4 (2k) rose & green	90.00	90.00
a.	Yellowish paper		
b.	Green frame around central oval	95.00	60.00
c.	Tête bêche pair	*2,500.*	
L5	A5 (2k) rose & grn ('64)	60.00	60.00
L6	A6 (2k) rose & green	35.00	35.00
	Nos. L4-L6 (3)	185.00	185.00

Official imitations of Nos. L4b and L5 have a rose instead of a green line around the central oval. The first official imitation of No. L6 has the central oval 5½mm instead of 6¼mm wide; the second imitation is less clearly printed than the original and the top of the "f" of "Briefmarke" is too much hooked.

Coat of Arms

A7 A8

1872-75 *Perf. 12½*

L7	A7 (2k) red & green	60.00	*70.00*
L8	A8 2k yel grn & red ('75)	8.50	*11.00*
a.	Numeral in upper right corner resembles an inverted "3"	30.00	*30.00*

Reprints of No. L8 have no horizontal lines in the background. Those of No. L8a have the impression blurred and only traces of the horizontal lines.

A9

Wenden Castle — A10

1878-80

L9	A9 2k green & red	8.50	*10.00*
a.	Imperf.		
L10	A9 2k blk, grn & red ('80)	10.00	10.00
a.	Imperf., pair	35.00	

No. L9 has been reprinted in blue green and yellow green with perforation 11½ and in gray green with perforation 12½ or imperforate.

1884 *Perf. 11½*

L11	A9 2k black, green & red	10.00	3.00
a.	Green arm omitted	21.00	
b.	Arm inverted	21.00	
c.	Arm double	27.50	
d.	Imperf., pair	21.00	

1901 Litho.

L12	A10 2k dk green & brown	12.00	7.50
a.	Tête bêche pair	45.00	
b.	Imperf., pair	120.00	

OCCUPATION STAMPS

Issued under Finnish Occupation

Finnish Stamps of 1917-18 Overprinted

1919 Unwmk. *Perf. 14*

N1	A19 5p green	12.50	12.50
N2	A19 10p rose	12.50	12.50
N3	A19 20p buff	12.50	12.50
N4	A19 40p red violet	12.50	12.50
N5	A19 50p orange brn	150.00	150.00
N6	A19 1m dl rose & blk	140.00	140.00
N7	A19 5m violet & blk	425.00	425.00
N8	A19 10m brown & blk	725.00	725.00
	Nos. N1-N8 (8)	1,490.	1,490.

"Aunus" is the Finnish name for Olonets, a town of Russia.

Counterfeits overprints exist.

ARMY OF THE NORTHWEST

(Gen. Nicolai N. Yudenich)

Russian Stamps of 1909-18 Overprinted in Black or Red

On Stamps of 1909-12

Perf. 14 to 15 and Compound

1919, Aug. 1

1 A14 2k green 3.50 *7.25*
2 A14 5k claret 3.50 *7.25*
3 A15 10k dk blue (R) 3.50 *7.25*
4 A11 15k red brn & bl 3.50 *6.00*
5 A8 20k blue & car 6.00 *12.00*
6 A11 25k grn & gray violet 10.00 *18.00*
7 A8 50k brn vio & grn 6.00 *12.00*

Perf. 13½

8 A9 1r pale brn, dk brn & org 12.00 *30.00*
9 A13 10r scar, yel & gray 60.00 *100.00*

On Stamps of 1917

Imperf

10 A14 3k red 2.40 *6.00*
11 A12 3.50r mar & lt grn 17.50 *35.00*
12 A13 5r dk blue, grn & pale bl 17.50 *30.00*
13 A12 7r dk green & pink 150.00 *200.00*

No. 2 Surcharged

Perf. 14, 14½x15

14 A14 10k on 5k claret 12.00 *24.00*
Nos. 1-14 (14) 307.40 *494.75*

Nos. 1-14 exist with inverted overprint or surcharge. The 1, 3½, 5, 7 and 10 rubles with red overprint are trial printings (value $150 each). The 20k on 14k, perforated, and the 1, 2, 5, 15, 70k and 1r imperforate were overprinted but never placed in use. Value: $300, $30, $45, $45, $45 and $65.

These stamps were in use from Aug. 1 to Oct. 15, 1919.

Counterfeits of Nos. 1-14 abound.

ARMY OF THE NORTH

A1

A2

A3

A4

A5

1919, Sept. Typo. *Imperf.*

1 A1 5k brown violet .40 *.70*
2 A2 10k blue .40 *.70*
3 A3 15k yellow .40 *.70*
4 A4 20k rose .40 *.70*
5 A5 50k green .40 *.70*
Nos. 1-5 (5) 2.00 *3.50*

The letters OKCA are the initials of Russian words meaning "Special Corps, Army of the North." The stamps were in use from about the end of September to the end of December, 1919.

Used values are for c-t-o stamps.

(General Miller)

A set of seven stamps of this design was prepared in 1919, but not issued. Value, set $35. Counterfeits exist.

RUSSIAN OFFICES ABROAD

For various reasons the Russian Empire maintained Post Offices to handle its correspondence in several foreign countries. These were similar to the Post Offices in foreign countries maintained by other world powers.

OFFICES IN CHINA

100 Kopecks = 1 Ruble
100 Cents = 1 Dollar (1917)

Russian Stamps Overprinted in Blue or Red

On Issues of 1889-92
Horizontally Laid Paper

1899-1904 Wmk. 168 *Perf. 14½x15*

1 A10 1k orange (Bl) .75 *1.00*
2 A10 2k yel green (R) .75 *1.00*
3 A10 3k carmine (Bl) .75 *1.00*
4 A10 5k red violet (Bl) .75 *1.00*
5 A10 7k dk blue (R) 1.50 *2.50*
a. Inverted overprint 500.00
6 A8 10k dk blue (R) 1.50 *2.50*
7 A8 50k vio & grn (Bl) ('04) 12.00 *8.50*

Perf. 13½

8 A9 1r lt brn, brn & org (Bl) ('04) 60.00 60.00
Nos. 1-8 (8) 78.00 77.50

On Issues of 1902-05
Vertically Laid Paper

Perf. 14½ to 15 and Compound

1904-08

Overprinted in Black, Red or Blue

9 A8 4k rose red (Bl) 6.00 *3.50*
10 A10 7k dk blue (R) 12.00 12.00
11 A8 10k dk blue (R) 1,450. 1,300.
a. Groundwork inverted 3,500.
12 A11 14k bl & rose (R) 6.00 6.00
13 A11 15k brn vio & blue (Bl) ('08) 12.00 *4.50*
14 A8 20k blue & car (Bl) 5.00 2.50
15 A11 25k dull grn & lil (R) ('08) 18.00 14.00
16 A11 35k dk vio & grn (R) 8.50 8.50
17 A8 50k vio & grn (Bl) 150.00 120.00
18 A11 70k brn & org (Bl) 20.00 15.00

Perf. 13½

19 A9 1r lt brn, brn & org (Bl) 18.00 18.00
20 A12 3.50r blk & gray (R) 10.00 *13.00*
21 A13 5r dk bl, grn & pale bl (R) ('07) 8.50 *12.00*
a. Inverted overprint 375.00
22 A12 7r blk & yel (Bl) 15.00 12.00
23 A13 10r scar, yel & gray (Bl) ('07) 50.00 *60.00*
Nos. 9-10,12-23 (14) 339.00 301.00

On Issues of 1909-12
Wove Paper
Lozenges of Varnish on Face

1910-16 Unwmk. *Perf. 14x14½*

24 A14 1k orange yel (Bl) .50 .50
25 A14 1k org yel (Bl Bk) 6.00 5.00
26 A14 2k green (Bk) .60 .60
27 A14 2k green (Bl) 7.25 *12.00*
a. Double ovpt. (Bk and Bl)
28 A14 3k rose red (Bl) .30 *.50*
29 A14 3k rose red (Bk) 12.00 12.00
30 A15 4k carmine (Bl) .60 .60
31 A15 4k carmine (Bk) 8.50 8.50
32 A14 7k lt blue (Bk) .60 *1.25*
33 A15 10k blue (Bk) .60 .60
34 A11 14k blue & rose (Bk) *.65* *.65*
35 A11 14k blue & rose (Bl)
36 A11 15k dl vio & bl (Bk) .60 *1.25*
37 A8 20k blue & car (Bk) *.40* *.65*
38 A11 25k green & vio (Bl) 3.50 *6.00*
39 A11 25k grn & vio (Bk) .60 *1.60*
40 A11 35k vio & grn (Bk) .60 .60
42 A8 50k vio & grn (Bl) .60 *.60*
43 A8 50k brn vio & grn (Bk) 18.00 *20.00*
44 A11 70k lt brn & org (Bl) .30 *.60*

Perf. 13½

45 A9 1r pale brn, brn & org (Bl) 1.25 *2.40*
47 A13 5r dk bl, grn & pale bl (R) 25.00 15.00
Nos. 24-34,36-47 (21) 88.45 90.90

The existence of #35 is questioned.

Russian Stamps of 1902-12 Surcharged:

a

b

c

On Stamps of 1909-12

1917 *Perf. 11½, 13½, 14, 14½x15*

50 A14(a) 1c on 1k dl org yel .60 *5.50*
51 A14(a) 2c on 2k dull grn .60 *5.50*
52 A14(a) 3c on 3k car .60 *5.50*
a. Inverted surcharge 65.00
b. Double surcharge 150.00
53 A15(a) 4c on 4k car 1.25 *4.25*
54 A14(a) 5c on 5k claret 1.25 *15.00*
55 A15(b) 10c on 10k dk blue 1.25 *15.00*
a. Inverted surcharge 85.00 85.00
b. Double surcharge 115.00
56 A11(b) 14c on 14k dk blue & carmine 1.25 *10.00*
a. Imperf. 6.00
b. Inverted surcharge 100.00
57 A11(a) 15c on 15k brn lilac & dp blue 1.25 *15.00*
58 A8(b) 20c on 20k bl & car 1.25 *15.00*
59 A11(a) 25c on 25k grn & violet 1.25 *15.00*
60 A11(a) 35c on 35k brn vio & green 1.50 *15.00*
a. Inverted surcharge 27.50
61 A8(a) 50c on 50k brn vio & green 1.25 *15.00*
62 A11(a) 70c on 70k brn & red orange 1.25 *15.00*
63 A9(c) $1 on 1r pale brn, brn & org 1.25 *15.00*
Nos. 50-63 (14) 15.80

On Stamps of 1902-05
Vertically Laid Paper

Perf. 11½, 13, 13½, 13½x11½

Wmk. Wavy Lines (168)

64 A12 $3.50 on 3.50r blk & gray 9.00 *32.50*
65 A13 $5 on 5r dk bl, grn & pale blue 9.00 *32.50*
66 A12 $7 on 7r blk & yel 8.50 *32.50*

On Stamps of 1915

Unwmk. *Perf. 13½*

Wove Paper

68 A13 $5 on 5r ind, grn & lt blue 25.00 *50.00*
a. Inverted surcharge 250.00
70 A13 $10 on 10r car lake, yel & gray 18.00 *100.00*
Nos. 64-70 (5) 69.50 247.50

The surcharge on Nos. 64-70 is in larger type than on the $1.

Russian Stamps of 1909-18 Surcharged in Black or Red

On Stamps of 1909-12

1920 *Perf. 14, 14½x15*

72 A14 1c on 1k dull org yellow 75.00 *90.00*
73 A14 2c on 2k dull grn (R) 16.00 *18.00*
74 A14 3c on 3k car 16.00 *24.00*
75 A15 4c on 4k car 18.00 15.00
a. Inverted surcharge 130.00
76 A14 5c on 5k claret 60.00 60.00
77 A15 10c on 10k dk bl (R) 125.00 125.00
78 A14 10c on 10k on 7k blue (R) 125.00 125.00

On Stamps of 1917-18

Imperf

79 A14 1c on 1k orange 42.50 25.00
a. Inverted surcharge 125.00 *150.00*
80 A14 5c on 5k claret 35.00 35.00
a. Inverted surcharge 140.00
b. Double surcharge 240.00
c. Surcharged "Cent" only 95.00
Nos. 72-80 (9) 512.50 517.00

OFFICES IN THE TURKISH EMPIRE

Various powers maintained post offices in the Turkish Empire before World War I by authority of treaties which ended with the signing of the Treaty of Lausanne in 1923. The foreign post offices were closed Oct. 27, 1923.

100 Kopecks = 1 Ruble
40 Paras = 1 Piaster (1900)

Coat of Arms
A1

1863 Unwmk. Typo. *Imperf.*

1 A1 6k blue 275.00 *1,000.*
a. 6k light blue, thin paper 350.00 *1,350.*
b. 6k light blue, medium paper 325.00 *1,350.*
c. 6k dark blue, chalky paper 200.00

Forgeries exist.

A2

A3

1865 Litho.

2 A2 (2k) brown & blue 700.00 625.00
3 A3 (20k) blue & red 900.00 850.00

Twenty-eight varieties of each.

A4

A5

A6

1866 Horizontal Network

4 A4 (2k) rose & pale bl 35.00 *52.50*
a. (2k) pale rose & blue 50.00 *75.00*
5 A5 (20k) deep blue & rose 55.00 *57.50*
a. (20k) pale blue & rose 67.50 *70.00*

1867 Vertical Network

6 A4 (2k) rose & pale bl 72.50 *90.00*
a. (2k) pale rose & deep blue 80.00 *95.00*
7 A5 (20k) dp blue & rose 100.00 *150.00*

The initials inscribed on Nos. 2 to 7 are those of the Russian Company of Navigation and Trade.

The official imitations of Nos. 2 to 7 are on yellowish white paper. The colors are usually paler than those of the originals and there are minor differences in the designs.

Horizontally Laid Paper

1868 Typo. Wmk. 168 *Perf. 11½*

8 A6 1k brown 42.50 25.00
9 A6 3k green 42.50 25.00
10 A6 5k blue 42.50 25.00
11 A6 10k car & green 42.50 25.00
Nos. 8-11 (4) 170.00 100.00

Colors of Nos. 8-11 dissolve in water.

1872-90 *Perf. 14½x15*

12 A6 1k brown 8.50 3.00
13 A6 3k green 30.00 3.50
14 A6 5k blue 4.75 1.25
15 A6 10k pale red & grn ('90) 1.25 .60
b. 10k carmine & green 24.00 3.75
Nos. 12-15 (4) 44.50 8.35

Vertically Laid Paper

12a A6 1k 42.50 18.00
13a A6 3k 42.50 18.00
14a A6 5k 42.50 18.00
15a A6 10k 190.00 47.50
Nos. 12a-15a (4) 317.50 101.50

Nos. 12-15 exist imperf.

No. 15 Surcharged in Black or Blue:

a

b

c

1876

16 A6(a) 8k on 10k (Bk) 90.00 55.00
a. Vertically laid
b. Inverted surcharge 400.00
17 A6(a) 8k on 10k (Bl) 90.00 77.50
a. Vertically laid
b. Inverted surcharge

1879

18 A6(b) 7k on 10k (Bk) 95.00 77.50
a. Vertically laid 750.00 750.00
b. Inverted surcharge
19 A6(b) 7k on 10k (Bl) 100.00 85.00
a. Vertically laid 1,000. 1,000.
b. Inverted surcharge 500.00
19C A6(c) 7k on 10k (Bl) 900.00 900.00
19D A6(c) 7k on 10k (Bk) 900.00 900.00

Nos. 16-19D have been extensively counterfeited.

1879 *Perf. 14½x15*

20 A6 1k black & yellow 3.00 1.50
a. Vertically laid 9.00 7.50
21 A6 2k black & rose 4.50 4.25
a. Vertically laid 10.00 6.00
22 A6 7k carmine & gray 6.50 1.75
a. Vertically laid 42.50 15.00
Nos. 20-22 (3) 14.00 7.50

1884

23 A6 1k orange .50 .35
24 A6 2k green .80 .50
25 A6 5k pale red violet 3.00 1.10
26 A6 7k blue 1.60 .50
Nos. 23-26 (4) 5.90 2.45

Nos. 23-26 imperforate are believed to be proofs.

No. 23 surcharged "40 PARAS" is bogus, though some copies were postally used.

Russian Company of Navigation and Trade

Р.О.П.иТ.

This overprint, in two sizes, was privately applied in various colors to Russian Offices in the Turkish Empire stamps of 1900-1910.

A7

A8

A9

A10

A11

Surcharged in Blue, Black or Red

1900

Horizontally Laid Paper

27 A7 4pa on 1k orange (Bl) 1.25 1.25
a. Inverted surcharge 30.00 30.00
28 A7 4pa on 1k orange (Bk) 1.25 1.25
a. Inverted surcharge 30.00 30.00
29 A7 10pa on 2k green .25 .25
a. Inverted surcharge
30 A8 1pi on 10k dk blue .50 .60
a. Inverted surcharge
Nos. 27-30 (4) 3.25 3.35

1903-05

Vertically Laid Paper

31 A7 10pa on 2k yel green .30 .50
a. Inverted surcharge 90.00
32 A8 20pa on 4k rose red (Bl) .30 .50
a. Inverted surcharge 60.00
33 A8 1pi on 10k dk blue .30 .50
a. Groundwork inverted 60.00 17.50
34 A8 2pi on 20k blue & car (Bk) .70 1.00
35 A8 5pi on 50k brn vio & grn 1.75 2.00
36 A9 7pi on 70k brn & org (Bl) 2.00 3.00

Perf. 13½

37 A10 10pi on 1r lt brn, brn & org (Bl) 3.25 4.75
38 A11 35pi on 3.50r blk & gray 9.75 13.00
39 A11 70pi on 7r blk & yel 12.00 15.00
Nos. 31-39 (9) 30.35 40.25

A12

A13

A14

Wove Paper
Lozenges of Varnish on Face

1909 **Unwmk.** *Perf. 14½x15*

40 A12 5pa on 1k orange .30 .40
41 A12 10pa on 2k green .35 .65
a. Inverted surcharge 30.00 30.00
42 A12 20pa on 4k carmine .70 1.00
43 A12 1pi on 10k blue .75 1.20
44 A12 5pi on 50k vio & grn 1.60 2.00
45 A12 7pi on 70k brn & org 2.40 3.25

Perf. 13½

46 A13 10pi on 1r brn & org 3.50 6.00
47 A14 35pi on 3.50r mar & lt grn 14.50 16.50
48 A14 70pi on 7r dk grn & pink 24.00 30.00
Nos. 40-48 (9) 48.10 61.00

50th anniv. of the establishing of the Russian Post Offices in the Levant.

Nos. 40-48 Overprinted with Names of Various Cities
Overprinted "Constantinople"
Black Overprint

1909-10 *Perf. 14½x15*

61 A12 5pa on 1k .20 .30
62 A12 10pa on 2k .20 .30
63 A12 20pa on 4k .35 .45
64 A12 1pi on 10k .35 .55
65 A12 5pi on 50k .65 .90
66 A12 7pi on 70k 1.50 2.00

Perf. 13½

67 A13 10pi on 1r 6.25 8.75
a. "Constantnople" 90.00 90.00
68 A14 35pi on 3.50r 17.50 27.50
69 A14 70pi on 7r 32.50 42.50

Blue Overprint

Perf. 14½x15

70 A12 5pa on 1k 3.00 3.50
Nos. 61-70 (10) 62.50 86.75

"Consnantinople"

61a A12 5pa on 1k 10.00
62a A12 10pa on 2k 10.00
63a A12 20pa on 4k 10.00
64a A12 1pi on 10k 10.00
65a A12 5pi on 50k 10.00
66a A12 7pi on 70k 12.00
68a A14 35pi on 3.50r 50.00
69a A14 70pi on 7r 90.00
70a A12 5pa on 1k 10.00
Nos. 61a-70a (9) 212.00

"Constantinopie"

61b A12 5pa on 1k 12.00
62b A12 10pa on 2k 12.00
63b A12 20pa on 4k 30.00
64b A12 1pi on 10k 30.00
65b A12 5pi on 50k 30.00
66b A12 7pi on 70k 30.00
68b A14 35pi on 3.50r 60.00
69b A14 70pi on 7r 90.00
Nos. 61b-69b (8) 294.00

Overprinted "Jaffa"

Black Overprint

71 A12 5pa on 1k 2.10 3.75
a. Inverted overprint 20.00
72 A12 10pa on 2k 2.50 4.00
a. Inverted overprint 20.00
73 A12 20pa on 4k 3.00 5.25
a. Inverted overprint 30.00
74 A12 1pi on 10k 3.75 5.25
a. Double overprint 35.00
75 A12 5pi on 50k 9.00 10.50
76 A12 7pi on 70k 11.00 14.00

Perf. 13½

77 A13 10pi on 1r 35.00 42.50
78 A14 35pi on 3.50r 90.00 100.00
79 A14 70pi on 7r 125.00 150.00

Blue Overprint

Perf. 14½x15

80 A12 5pa on 1k 12.00 12.00
Nos. 71-80 (10) 293.35 347.25

Overprinted "Ierusalem"

Black Overprint

81 A12 5pa on 1k 1.75 2.40
a. Inverted overprint 60.00
b. "erusalem" 17.50
82 A12 10pa on 2k 2.40 3.50
a. Inverted overprint 30.00
b. "erusalem" 17.50
83 A12 20pa on 4k 3.50 4.75
a. Inverted overprint 30.00
b. "erusalem" 17.50
84 A12 1pi on 10k 3.50 4.75
a. "erusalem" 30.00
85 A12 5pi on 50k 6.00 9.50
a. "erusalem" 35.00
86 A12 7pi on 70k 12.00 15.00
a. "erusalem" 35.00

Perf. 13½

87 A13 10pi on 1r 42.50 60.00
88 A14 35pi on 3.50r 100.00 120.00
89 A14 70pi on 7r 120.00 180.00

Blue Overprint

Perf. 14½x15

90 A12 5pa on 1k 12.00 12.00
Nos. 81-90 (10) 303.65 411.90

Overprinted "Kerassunde"

Black Overprint

91 A12 5pa on 1k .30 .45
a. Inverted overprint 25..00
92 A12 10pa on 2k .30 .45
a. Inverted overprint 15.00
93 A12 20pa on 4k .45 .60
a. Inverted overprint 20.00
94 A12 1pi on 10k .55 .70
95 A12 5pi on 50k 1.00 1.25
96 A12 7pi on 70k 1.50 2.00

Perf. 13½

97 A13 10pi on 1r 6.00 7.75
98 A14 35pi on 3.50r 19.00 21.00
99 A14 70pi on 7r 27.50 30.00

Blue Overprint

Perf. 14½x15

100 A12 5pa on 1k 4.00 5.50
Nos. 91-100 (10) 60.60 69.70

Overprinted "Mont Athos"

Black Overprint

101 A12 5pa on 1k .45 .75
b. Inverted overprint 35.00
102 A12 10pa on 2k .45 .75
b. Inverted overprint 35.00
103 A12 20pa on 4k .50 .80
b. Inverted overprint 35.00
104 A12 1pi on 10k .90 1.20
b. Double overprint 40.00
105 A12 5pi on 50k 2.90 3.25
106 A12 7pi on 70k 4.50 5.50
b. Pair, one without "Mont Athos" 35.00

Perf. 13½

107 A13 10pi on 1r 15.00 16.00
108 A14 35pi on 3.50r 32.50 35.00
109 A14 70pi on 7r 60.00 70.00

Blue Overprint

Perf. 14½x15

110 A12 5pa on 1k 5.00 8.00
Nos. 101-110 (10) 122.20 141.25

"Mont Atho"

101a A12 5pa on 1k 20.00
102a A12 10pa on 2k 20.00
103a A12 20pa on 4k 20.00
104a A12 1pi on 10k 30.00
c. As "a," double overprint 100.00
105a A12 5pi on 50k 40.00
106a A12 7pi on 70k 60.00
110a A12 5pa on 1k 17.50

Overprinted

111 A12 5pa on 1k .45 .70
112 A12 10pa on 2k .45 .70
113 A12 20pa on 4k .65 1.10
114 A12 1pi on 10k 1.25 2.25
115 A12 5pi on 50k 2.40 3.50
116 A12 7pi on 70k 4.25 6.50

Perf. 13½

117 A13 10pi on 1r 26.00 32.50
Nos. 111-117 (7) 35.45 47.25

The overprint is larger on No. 117.

Overprinted "Salonique"

Black Overprint

Perf. 14½x15

131 A12 5pa on 1k .30 .60
a. Inverted overprint 30.00
b. Pair, one without overprint 125.00
132 A12 10pa on 2k .45 .90
a. Inverted overprint 30.00
133 A12 20pa on 4k .60 .90
a. Inverted overprint 30.00
134 A12 1pi on 10k .60 .90
135 A12 5pi on 50k 1.25 1.75
136 A12 7pi on 70k 2.75 3.00

Perf. 13½

137 A13 10pi on 1r 16.00 15.00
138 A14 35pi on 3.50r 30.00 32.50
139 A14 70pi on 7r 52.50 50.00

Blue Overprint

Perf. 14½x15

140 A12 5pa on 1k 7.50 8.00
Nos. 131-140 (10) 111.95 113.55

Overprinted "Smyrne"

Black Overprint

141 A12 5pa on 1k .60 1.25
a. Double overprint
b. Inverted overprint 10.00
142 A12 10pa on 2k .60 1.25
a. Inverted overprint 13.00
143 A12 20pa on 4k 1.25 1.60
a. Inverted overprint 17.50
144 A12 1pi on 10k 1.25 1.75
145 A12 5pi on 50k 2.75 3.00
146 A12 7pi on 70k 4.00 6.00

Perf. 13½

147 A13 10pi on 1r 17.00 22.50
148 A14 35pi on 3.50r 30.00 40.00
149 A14 70pi on 7r 47.50 62.50

Blue Overprint

Perf. 14½x15

150 A12 5pa on 1k 6.25 9.25
Nos. 141-150 (10) 111.20 149.10

"Smyrn"

141c A12 5pa on 1k 18.00 20.00
142b A12 10pa on 2k 18.00 20.00
143b A12 20pa on 4k 18.00 20.00
144a A12 1pi on 10k 20.00 25.00
145a A12 5pi on 50k 20.00 25.00
146a A12 7pi on 70k 20.00 25.00
Nos. 141c-146a (6) 114.00 135.00

Overprinted "Trebizonde"

Black Overprint

151 A12 5pa on 1k .50 .75
a. Inverted overprint 24.00
152 A12 10pa on 2k .50 .75
a. Inverted overprint 12.00
b. Pair, one without "Trebizonde" 60.00
153 A12 20pa on 4k .60 .60
a. Inverted overprint 24.00
154 A12 1pi on 10k .60 .95
a. Pair, one without "Trebizonde" 35.00
155 A12 5pi on 50k 1.50 1.90
156 A12 7pi on 70k 2.75 3.75

Perf. 13½

157 A13 10pi on 1r 12.50 13.00
158 A14 35pi on 3.50r 25.00 26.00
159 A14 70pi on 7r 37.50 40.00

Blue Overprint

Perf. 14½x15

160 A12 5pa on 1k 4.75 6.00
Nos. 151-160 (10) 86.20 93.70

On Nos. 158 and 159 the overprint is spelled "Trebisonde".

Overprinted "Beyrouth"

Black Overprint

1910

161 A12 5pa on 1k .30 .50
162 A12 10pa on 2k .30 .50
a. Inverted overprint 24.00
163 A12 20pa on 4k .45 .65
164 A12 1pi on 10k .45 .80
165 A12 5pi on 50k 1.10 1.60
166 A12 7pi on 70k 2.25 3.25

Perf. 13½

167	A13	10pi on 1r	11.00	*12.00*
168	A14	35pi on 3.50r	22.50	*24.00*
169	A14	70pi on 7r	32.50	*35.00*
		Nos. 161-169 (9)	70.85	78.30

Overprinted "Dardanelles"

Perf. 14½x15

171	A12	5pa on 1k	.35	*.70*
172	A12	10pa on 2k	.35	*.70*
a.		Pair, one without overprint		
173	A12	20pa on 4k	.90	.90
a.		Inverted overprint	12.00	
174	A12	1pi on 10k	.90	*1.00*
175	A12	5pi on 50k	1.75	*2.00*
176	A12	7pi on 70k	3.75	3.75

Perf. 13½

177	A13	10pi on 1r	11.50	*12.00*
178	A14	35pi on 3.50r	22.50	*24.00*
a.		Center and ovpt. inverted		
179	A14	70pi on 7r	35.00	*37.50*
		Nos. 171-179 (9)	77.00	82.55

Overprinted "Metelin"

Perf. 14½x15

181	A12	5pa on 1k	.60	*.95*
a.		Inverted overprint	30.00	
182	A12	10pa on 2k	.60	*.95*
a.		Inverted overprint	30.00	
183	A12	20pa on 4k	1.40	*1.60*
a.		Inverted overprint	18.00	
184	A12	1pi on 10k	1.40	*1.60*
185	A12	5pi on 50k	3.50	3.50
186	A12	7pi on 70k	4.25	4.25

Perf. 13½

187	A13	10pi on 1r	22.50	22.50
188	A14	35pi on 3.50r	50.00	50.00
189	A14	70pi on 7r	67.50	67.50
		Nos. 181-189 (9)	151.75	*152.85*

Overprinted "Rizeh"

Perf. 14½x15

191	A12	5pa on 1k	.60	*.90*
a.		Inverted overprint	30.00	
192	A12	10pa on 2k	.60	*.90*
a.		Inverted overprint	30.00	
193	A12	20pa on 4k	1.00	*1.25*
a.		Inverted overprint	30.00	
194	A12	1pi on 10k	1.00	*1.25*
195	A12	5pi on 50k	1.60	*3.50*
196	A12	7pi on 70k	3.00	*5.50*

Perf. 13½

197	A13	10pi on 1r	16.00	*19.00*
198	A14	35pi on 3.50r	26.00	*30.00*
199	A14	70pi on 7r	40.00	*47.50*
		Nos. 191-199 (9)	89.80	109.80

Nos. 61-199 for the establishing of Russian Post Offices in the Levant, 50th anniv.

A15

A16

A17

Vertically Laid Paper

1910 **Wmk. 168** ***Perf. 14½x15***

200	A15	20pa on 5k red violet (Bl)	.60	.60

Wove Paper

Vertical Lozenges of Varnish on Face

1910 **Unwmk.** ***Perf. 14x14½***

201	A16	5pa on 1k org yel (Bl)	.20	*.25*
202	A16	10pa on 2k green (R)	.20	*.25*
203	A17	20pa on 4k car rose (Bl)	.20	*.25*
204	A17	1pi on 10k blue (R)	.20	*.25*
205	A8	5pi on 50k vio & grn (Bl)	.40	*.60*
206	A9	7pi on 70k lt brn & org (Bl)	.50	*.65*

Perf. 13½

207	A10	10pi on 1r pale brn, brn & org (Bl)	.70	*.75*
		Nos. 201-207 (7)	2.40	*3.00*

Russian Stamps of 1909-12 Surcharged in Black:

No. 208

Nos. 209-212

1912 ***Perf. 14x14½***

208	A14	20pa on 5k claret	.20	.20
209	A11	1½pi on 15k dl vio & blue	.20	*.25*
210	A8	2pi on 20k bl & car	.20	*.30*
211	A11	2½pi on 25k grn & vio	.25	*.45*
a.		Double surcharge	60.00	60.00
212	A11	3½pi on 35k vio & grn	.40	*.55*
		Nos. 208-212 (5)	1.25	1.75

Russia Nos. 88-91, 93, 95-104 Surcharged:

c

d

e

f

g

1913 ***Perf. 13½***

213	A16(c)	5pa on 1k	.20	.20
214	A17(d)	10pa on 2k	.20	.20
215	A18(c)	15pa on 3k	.20	.20
216	A19(c)	20pa on 4k	.20	.20
217	A21(e)	1pi on 10k	.20	.20
218	A23(f)	1½pi on 15k	.45	*.50*
219	A24(f)	2pi on 20k	.45	*.50*
220	A25(f)	2½pi on 25k	.60	*.70*
221	A26(f)	3½pi on 35k	1.50	1.40
222	A27(e)	5pi on 50k	1.75	1.75
223	A28(f)	7pi on 70k	7.00	7.00
224	A29(e)	10pi on 1r	7.00	7.00
225	A30(e)	20pi on 2r	1.50	1.40
226	A31(g)	30pi on 3r	2.25	2.00
227	A32(e)	50pi on 5r	75.00	75.00
		Nos. 213-227 (15)	98.50	98.25

Romanov dynasty tercentenary.
Forgeries exist of overprint on No. 227.

Russia Nos. 75, 71, 72 Surcharged:

h

i

Perf. 14x14½

Wove Paper

228	A14(h)	15pa on 3k	.20	.20

Perf. 13, 13½

230	A13(i)	50pi on 5r	5.00	*10.00*

Vertically Laid Paper

Wmk. Wavy Lines (168)

231	A13(i)	100pi on 10r	10.00	*20.00*
a.		Double surcharge	600.00	*125.00*
		Nos. 228-231 (3)	15.20	30.20

No. 228 has lozenges of varnish on face but No. 230 has not.

Wrangel Issues

For the Posts of Gen. Peter Wrangel's army and civilian refugees from South Russia, interned in Turkey, Serbia, etc.

Very few of the Wrangel overprints were actually sold to the public, and many of the covers were made up later with the original cancels. Reprints abound. Values probably are based on sales of reprints in most cases.

Russian Stamps of 1902-18 Surcharged in Blue, Red or Black

On Russia Nos. 69-70

Vertically Laid Paper

1921 **Wmk. 168** ***Perf. 13½***

232	A12	10,000r on 3.50r	60.00	60.00
233	A12	10,000r on 7r	60.00	60.00
234	A12	20,000r on 3.50r	60.00	60.00
235	A12	20,000r on 7r	60.00	60.00
		Nos. 232-235 (4)	240.00	240.00

On Russia Nos. 71-86, 87a, 117-118, 137-138

Wove Paper

Perf. 14x14½, 13½

Unwmk.

236	A14	1000r on 1k	.75	.75
237	A14	1000r on 2k (R)	.75	.75
237A	A14	1000r on 2k (Bk)	11.00	11.00
238	A14	1000r on 3k	.25	.25
a.		Inverted surcharge	12.00	12.00
239	A15	1000r on 4k	.25	.25
a.		Inverted surcharge	12.00	12.00
240	A14	1000r on 5k	.25	.25
a.		Inverted surcharge	12.00	12.00
241	A14	1000r on 7k	.25	.25
a.		Inverted surcharge	12.00	12.00
242	A15	1000r on 10k	.25	.25
a.		Inverted surcharge	12.00	12.00
243	A14	1000r on 10k on 7k	.25	.25
244	A14	5000r on 3k	.25	.25
245	A11	5000r on 14k	2.50	2.50
246	A11	5000r on 15k	.25	.25
a.		"PYCCKIN"	12.00	12.00
247	A8	5000r on 20k	.80	.80
a.		"PYCCKIN"	12.00	12.00
248	A11	5000r on 20k on 14k	.80	.80
249	A11	5000r on 25k	.25	.25
250	A11	5000r on 35k	.25	.25
a.		Inverted surcharge	12.00	12.00
b.		New value omitted		
251	A8	5000r on 50k	.25	.25
a.		Inverted surcharge	12.00	12.00
252	A11	5000r on 70k	.25	.25
a.		Inverted surcharge	12.00	12.00
253	A9	10,000r on 1r (Bl)	.25	.25
254	A9	10,000r on 1r (Bk)	1.90	1.90
255	A12	10,000r on 3.50r	.80	.80
256	A13	10,000r on 5r	11.00	11.00
257	A13	10,000r on 10r	1.00	1.00
258	A9	20,000r on 1r	.55	.55
259	A12	20,000r on 3.50r	.55	.55
a.		Inverted surcharge	12.00	12.00
b.		New value omitted	60.00	60.00
260	A12	20,000r on 7r	22.00	22.00
261	A13	20,000r on 10r	.55	.55
		Nos. 236-261 (27)	58.20	58.20

On Russia No. 104

261A	A32	20,000r on 5r	300.00	

On Russia Nos. 119-123, 125-135

Imperf

262	A14	1000r on 1k	.40	.40
263	A14	1000r on 2k (R)	.40	.40
263A	A14	1000r on 2k (Bk)	.50	.50
264	A14	1000r on 3k	.40	.40
265	A15	1000r on 4k	13.00	13.00
266	A14	1000r on 5k	.50	.50
267	A14	5000r on 3k	.40	.40
268	A11	5000r on 15k	.50	.50
268A	A8	5000r on 20k	20.00	
268B	A11	5000r on 25k	20.00	
269	A11	5000r on 35k	1.00	1.00
270	A8	5000r on 50k	1.00	1.00
271	A11	5000r on 70k	.40	.40
272	A9	10,000r on 1r (Bl)	.40	.40
a.		Inverted surcharge	12.00	12.00
273	A9	10,000r on 1r (Bk)	.40	.40
274	A12	10,000r on 3.50r	.40	.40
275	A13	10,000r on 5r	3.50	3.50
276	A12	10,000r on 7r	20.00	20.00
276A	A13	10,000r on 10r	*65.00*	
277	A9	20,000r on 1r (Bl)	.40	.40
a.		Inverted surcharge	12.00	12.00
278	A9	20,000r on 1r (Bk)	.40	.40
279	A12	20,000r on 3.50r	3.50	3.50
280	A13	20,000r on 5r	.40	.40
281	A12	20,000r on 7r	16.00	16.00
281A	A13	20,000r on 10r	*90.00*	
		Nos. 262-268,269-276,277-281 (21)	63.90	63.90

A18

A19

On Postal Savings Stamps

Perf. 14½x15

Wmk. 171

282	A18	10,000r on 1k red, *buff*	.40	.40
283	A19	10,000r on 5k grn, *buff*	.40	.40
a.		Inverted surcharge	12.00	
284	A19	10,000r on 10k brn, *buff*	.40	.40
a.		Inverted surcharge	12.00	
		Nos. 282-284 (3)	1.20	1.20

On Stamps of Russian Offices in Turkey

On No. 38-39

Vertically Laid Paper

Wmk. Wavy Lines (168)

284B	A11	20,000r on 35pi on 3.50r	300.00	
284C	A11	20,000r on 70pi on 7r	300.00	

On Nos. 200-207

Vertically Laid Paper

284D	A15	1000r on 20pa on 5k	3.00	3.00

Wove Paper

Unwmk.

285	A16	1000r on 5pa on 1k	1.00	1.00
286	A16	1000r on 10pa on 2k	1.00	1.00
287	A17	1000r on 20pa on 4k	1.00	1.00
288	A17	1000r on 1pi on 10k	1.00	1.00
289	A8	5000r on 5pi on 50k	1.00	1.00
290	A9	5000r on 7pi on 70k	1.00	1.00
291	A10	10,000r on 10pi on 1r	5.00	5.00
a.		Inverted surcharge	12.00	12.00
b.		Pair, one without surcharge	12.00	12.00
292	A10	20,000r on 10pi on 1r	1.00	1.00
a.		Inverted surcharge	12.00	12.00
b.		Pair, one without surcharge	12.00	12.00
		Nos. 284D-292 (9)	15.00	15.00

On Nos. 208-212

293	A14	1000r on 20pa on 5k	1.25	1.25
294	A11	5000r on 1½pi on 15k	1.25	1.25
295	A8	5000r on 2pi on 20k	1.25	1.25
296	A11	5000r on 2½pi on 25k	1.25	1.25
297	A11	5000r on 3½pi on 35k	1.25	1.25
		Nos. 293-297 (5)	6.25	6.25

On Nos. 228, 230-231

298	A14	1000r on 15pa on 3k	.40	.40
299	A13	10,000r on 50pi on 5r	22.50	22.50
300	A13	10,000r on 100pi on 10r	32.50	32.50
301	A13	20,000r on 50pi on 5r	.40	.40
302	A13	20,000r on 100pi on 10r	32.50	32.50
		Nos. 298-302 (5)	88.30	88.30

On Stamps of South Russia

Denikin Issue

Imperf

303	A5	5000r on 5k org	.25	.25
a.		Inverted surcharge	30.00	
304	A5	5000r on 10k green	.25	.25
305	A5	5000r on 15k red	.25	.25
306	A5	5000r on 35k lt bl	.25	.25
307	A5	5000r on 70k dk blue	.25	.25
307A	A5	10,000r on 70k dk blue	12.00	12.00
308	A6	10,000r on 1r brn & red	.25	.25
309	A6	10,000r on 2r gray vio & yel	.30	.30
a.		Inverted surcharge	30.00	30.00
310	A6	10,000r on 3r dull rose & grn	.90	.90
311	A6	10,000r on 5r slate & vio	.60	.60
312	A6	10,000r on 7r gray grn & rose	24.00	24.00
313	A6	10,000r on 10r red & gray	.50	.50
314	A6	20,000r on 1r brn & red	.25	.25
315	A6	20,000r on 2r gray vio & yel (Bl)	9.00	9.00
a.		Inverted surcharge	30.00	30.00
315B	A6	20,000r on 2r gray vio & yel (Bk)	.25	.25
316	A6	20,000r on 3r dull rose & grn (Bl)	12.00	12.00

316A A6 20,000r on 3r dull rose & grn (Bk) 7.25 7.25
317 A6 20,000r on 5r slate & vio .25 .25
318 A6 20,000r on 7r gray grn & rose 15.00 15.00
319 A6 20,000r on 10r red & gray .25 .25
Nos. 303-319 (20) 84.05 84.05

Trident Stamps of Ukraine Surcharged in Blue, Red, Black or Brown

1921 ***Perf. 14, 14½x15***

320 A14 10,000r on 1k org .30 .30
321 A14 10,000r on 2k grn 3.50 3.50
322 A14 10,000r on 3k red .30 .30
a. Inverted surcharge 30.00 30.00
323 A15 10,000r on 4k car .30 .30
324 A14 10,000r on 5k cl .30 .30
325 A14 10,000r on 7k lt bl .30 .30
a. Inverted surcharge 30.00 30.00
326 A15 10,000r on 10k dk bl .30 .30
a. Inverted surcharge 30.00 30.00
327 A14 10,000r on 10k on 7k lt bl .30 .30
a. Inverted surcharge 30.00 30.00
328 A8 20,000r on 20k bl & car (Br) .30 .30
a. Inverted surcharge 12.00 12.00
329 A8 20,000r on 20k bl & car (Bk) .30 .30
a. Inverted surcharge 12.00 12.00
330 A11 20,000r on 20k on 14k bl & rose .30 .30
331 A11 20,000r on 35k red brn & grn 50.00 50.00
332 A8 20,000r on 50k brn vio & grn .30 .30
a. Inverted surcharge 12.00 12.00
Nos. 320-332 (13) 56.80 56.80

Imperf

333 A14 10,000r on 1k org .25 .25
a. Inverted surcharge 12.00
334 A14 10,000r on 2k grn 1.00 1.00
335 A14 10,000r on 3k red .25 .25
336 A8 20,000r on 20k bl & car .25 .25
337 A11 20,000r on 35k red brn & grn 26.00 26.00
338 A8 20,000r on 50k brn vio & grn 1.25 1.25
Nos. 333-338 (6) 29.00 29.00

There are several varieties of the trident surcharge on Nos. 320 to 338.

Same Surcharge on Russian Stamps

On Stamps of 1909-18

Perf. 14x14½

338A A14 10,000r on 1k dl org yel 1.75 1.75
339 A14 10,000r on 2k dl grn 1.75 1.75
340 A14 10,000r on 3k car .35 .35
341 A15 10,000r on 4k car .35 .35
342 A14 10,000r on 5k dk cl .35 .35
343 A14 10,000r on 7k blue .35 .35
344 A15 10,000r on 10k dk bl 1.75 1.75
344A A14 10,000r on 10k on 7k bl 2.50 2.50
344B A11 20,000r on 14k dk bl & car 26.00 26.00
345 A11 20,000r on 15k red brn & dp bl .35 .35
346 A8 20,000r on 20k dl bl & dk car .35 .35
347 A11 20,000r on 20k on 14k dk bl & car 2.50 2.50
348 A11 20,000r on 35k red brn & grn 1.40 1.40
349 A8 20,000r on 50k brn vio & grn .35 .35
349A A11 20,000r on 70k brn & red org 1.75 1.75
Nos. 338A-349A (15) 41.85 41.85

On Stamps of 1917-18

Imperf

350 A14 10,000r on 1k org .50 .50
351 A14 10,000r on 2k gray grn .50 .50
352 A14 10,000r on 3k red .50 .50
353 A15 10,000r on 4k car 30.00 30.00
354 A14 10,000r on 5k claret .50 .50
355 A11 20,000r on 15k red brn & dp bl .50 .50
356 A8 20,000r on 50k brn vio & grn 1.40 1.40
357 A11 20,000r on 70k brn & org .50 .50
Nos. 350-357 (8) 34.40 34.40

Same Surcharge on Stamps of Russian Offices in Turkey

On Nos. 40-45

Perf. 14½x15

358 A12 10,000r on 5pa on 1k 3.50 3.50
359 A12 10,000r on 10pa on 2k 3.50 3.50
360 A12 10,000r on 20pa on 4k 3.50 3.50
361 A12 10,000r on 1pi on 10k 3.50 3.50
362 A12 20,000r on 5pi on 50k 3.50 3.50
363 A12 20,000r on 7pi on 70k 3.50 3.50
Nos. 358-363 (6) 21.00 21.00

On Nos. 201-206

364 A16 10,000r on 5pa on 1k 4.00 4.00
365 A16 10,000r on 10pa on 2k 4.00 4.00
366 A17 10,000r on 20pa on 4k 4.00 4.00
367 A17 10,000r on 1pi on 10k 4.00 4.00
368 A8 20,000r on 5pi on 50k 4.00 4.00
369 A9 20,000r on 7pi on 70k 4.00 4.00
Nos. 364-369 (6) 24.00 24.00

On Nos. 228, 208-212, Stamps of 1912-13

370 A14 10,000r on 15pa on 3k 4.00 4.00
371 A14 10,000r on 20pa on 5k 4.00 4.00
372 A11 20,000r on 1½pi on 15k 4.00 4.00
373 A8 20,000r on 2pi on 20k 4.00
374 A11 20,000r on 2½pi on 25k 4.00
375 A11 20,000r on 3½pi on 35k 4.00

Same Surcharge on Stamp of South Russia, Crimea Issue

376 A8 20,000r on 5r on 20k bl & car 20.00
Nos. 370-376 (7) 44.00

SAAR

'sär

LOCATION — On the Franco-German border southeast of Luxembourg
GOVT. — A German state
POP. — 1,400,000 (1959)
AREA — 991 sq. mi.
CAPITAL — Saarbrücken

A former German territory, the Saar was administered by the League of Nations 1920-35. After a January 12, 1935, plebiscite, it returned to Germany, and the use of German stamps was resumed.

100 Pfennig = 1 Mark
100 Centimes = 1 Franc (1921)

German Stamps of 1906-19 Overprinted

Nos. 1-16 exist in three types. Type I: larger letters, "Sarre" 10.7mm wide, no control mark below bar. Type II: as Type I, control mark (a short, thin line) below bar. Type III: smaller letters, "Sarre" 10.5mm wide, control mark below bar.

Type I

Perf. 14, 14½

1920, Jan. 30 **Wmk. 125**

1 A22 2pf gray 1.10 *3.75*
Never hinged 2.50
On cover 7.50
c. Inverted overprint 300.00 *525.00*
Never hinged 475.00
On cover 675.00
2 A22 2½pf gray 8.75 *25.00*
Never hinged 22.50
On cover 32.50
c. Inverted overprint 325.00 *600.00*
Never hinged 550.00
On cover 750.00
d. 2½pf deep greenish gray or bronze 90.00 *225.00*
Never hinged 180.00
On cover 300.00
3 A16 3pf brown .90 *2.00*
Never hinged 2.00
On cover 3.75
c. Inverted overprint 300.00 *525.00*
Never hinged 475.00
On cover 675.00
4 A16 5pf deep green .40 *.90*
Never hinged .75
On cover 1.50
c. Inverted overprint 550.00 *1,050.*
Never hinged 900.00
d. 5pf dark bluish green 1.20 *3.25*
Never hinged 2.40
On cover 4.50
5 A22 7½pf orange .55 *1.25*
Never hinged .95
On cover 2.60
c. Inverted overprint — 750.00
Never hinged —
d. 7½pf red orange 3.00 *9.75*
Never hinged 6.00
On cover 19.00
e. 7½pf pale reddish orange 1.50 *5.50*
Never hinged 3.00
On cover 12.50
6 A16 10pf carmine .50 *1.25*
Never hinged .95
On cover 1.50
c. Inverted overprint 525.00 *975.00*
Never hinged 900.00
d. Double overprint 675.00 *1,100.*
Never hinged 1,100.
On cover 1,350.
e. 10pf rose red 1.75 *4.00*
Never hinged 3.25
On cover 6.00
f. As "e," double overprint 675.00 *1,100.*
Never hinged 1,100.
On cover 1,350.
g. 10pf scarlet red 125.00 *210.00*
Never hinged 225.00
On cover 260.00
7 A22 15pf dk violet .40 *.90*
Never hinged .95
On cover 1.50
c. Double overprint 750.00 *1,350.*
Never hinged 1,250.
d. 15pf blackish violet 6.25 *15.00*
Never hinged 13.50
On cover 26.00
e. 15pf bluish violet 19.00 *97.50*
Never hinged 37.50
On cover 150.00
8 A16 20pf blue violet .50 *.85*
Never hinged .95
On cover 1.50
c. Double overprint 550.00 *900.00*
Never hinged 900.00
On cover 1,100.
9 A16 25pf red org & blk, *yellow* 10.50 17.50
Never hinged 22.50
On cover 27.50
c. Inverted overprint 750.00 *2,250.*
Never hinged 1,250.
d. 25pf yel org & blk, *yellow* 26.00 *97.50*
Never hinged 52.50
On cover 125.00
10 A16 30pf org & blk, *yel buff* 17.50 *27.50*
Never hinged 32.50
On cover 52.50
d. 30pf org & blk, *org buff* 210.00 *450.00*
Never hinged 375.00
On cover 675.00
11 A22 35pf red brown .50 *.85*
Never hinged .95
On cover 1.50
c. Inverted overprint 450.00 *975.00*
Never hinged 825.00
On cover 1,100.
12 A16 40pf dp lake & blk .60 *.90*
Never hinged .95
On cover 1.50
c. Inverted overprint 450.00 *975.00*
Never hinged 825.00
On cover 1,100.
d. 40pf reddish lake & blk 5.25 *7.50*
Never hinged 9.00
On cover 13.00
13 A16 50pf pur & blk, *yel buff* .50 *.85*
Never hinged .95
On cover 1.50
c. Inverted overprint 375.00 *675.00*
Never hinged 675.00
On cover 750.00
d. 50pf pur & blk, *org buff* 19.00 *67.50*
Never hinged 45.00
On cover 105.00
14 A16 60pf dp gray lilac .50 *1.10*
Never hinged .95
On cover 1.90
c. 60pf red lilac 275.00 *675.00*
Never hinged 550.00
On cover 1,250.
15 A16 75pf green & blk .50 .90
Never hinged .90
On cover 2.25
c. Inverted overprint 225.00 *375.00*
Never hinged 375.00
On cover 450.00
16 A16 80pf lake & blk, *rose* 190.00 *240.00*
Never hinged 400.00
On cover 900.00

Type II

1a A22 2pf gray 150.00 *400.00*
Never hinged 325.00
On cover 550.00
2a A22 2½pf olive gray 475.00 *900.00*
Never hinged 900.00
On cover 2,250.
2e A22 2½pf dp grnsh gray or bronze 1,500. *3,100.*
Never hinged 3,100.
On cover —
3a A16 3pf brown 160.00 *375.00*
Never hinged 300.00
On cover 550.00
4a A16 5pf deep green 10.00 *60.00*
Never hinged 18.00
On cover 90.00
4e A16 5pf dark bluish green 52.50 *140.00*
Never hinged 105.00
On cover 180.00
5a A22 7½pf yellow orange 45.00 *160.00*
Never hinged 90.00
On cover 240.00
5f A22 7½pf red orange 1,500. *3,100.*
Never hinged 3,100.
On cover —
12a A16 40pf deep lake & blk 1.60 *5.50*
Never hinged 3.75
On cover 10.00
13a A16 50pf pur & blk, *yel buff* 1.50 *5.75*
Never hinged 3.25
On cover 10.00

Type III

1b A22 2pf gray 4.50 *19.00*
Never hinged 10.50
On cover 32.50
d. Double overprint 1,900. *2,400.*
Never hinged 3,100.
2b A22 2½pf olive gray 1.50 *5.25*
Never hinged 3.00
On cover 7.50
2f A22 2½pf dp grnsh gray or bronze 47.50 *105.00*
Never hinged 82.50
On cover 140.00
3b A16 3pf brown 1.20 *4.00*
Never hinged 2.40
On cover 6.50
4b A16 5pf deep green .45 *.75*
Never hinged .75
On cover 1.40
f. Double overprint 750.00 *1,350.*
Never hinged 1,350.
4g A16 5pf dk bluish green 1.10 *3.50*
Never hinged 2.00
On cover 5.50
h. Double overprint 900.00 *1,350.*
Never hinged 1,600.
5b A22 7½pf yellow orange 4.50 *22.50*
Never hinged 9.00
On cover 37.50
5g A22 7½pf red orange 22.50 *60.00*
Never hinged 45.00
On cover 90.00
5h A22 7½pf pale reddish org 15.00 *1,050.*
Never hinged 30.00
On cover 1,200.
6b A16 10pf carmine .45 *.90*
Never hinged .90
On cover 1.25
6h A16 10pf rose red 1.60 *5.50*
Never hinged 3.00
On cover 8.25
6i A16 10pf scarlet red 55.00 *110.00*
Never hinged 110.00
On cover 190.00
7b A22 15pf dk violet .45 *.95*
Never hinged .95
On cover 1.40
7f A22 15pf blackish violet 1.40 *4.50*
Never hinged 2.60
On cover 10.00
8b A16 20pf blue violet .45 *1.10*
Never hinged .75
On cover 1.90
9b A16 25pf red org & blk, *yellow* 105.00 310.00
Never hinged 240.00
On cover 525.00
9e A16 25pf yel org & blk, *yel* 55.00 *110.00*
Never hinged 110.00
On cover 160.00
10b A16 30pf org & blk, *yel buff* 40.00 *90.00*
Never hinged 82.50
On cover 140.00
10c A16 30pf org & blk, *org buff* 210.00 *450.00*
Never hinged 350.00
On cover 700.00
11b A22 35pf red brown 4.75 *40.00*
Never hinged 11.00
On cover 52.50
12b A16 40pf deep lake & blk 2.25 *7.50*
Never hinged 4.10
On cover 11.00
e. Inverted overprint 525.00 *900.00*
Never hinged 900.00
On cover 1,200.
13b A16 50pf pur & blk, *yel buff* .45 *.95*
Never hinged .95
On cover 1.90
14b A16 60pf dp gray lilac .45 *.95*
Never hinged .75
On cover 1.60
15b A16 75pf green & blk .45 *.95*
Never hinged .90
On cover 1.60
d. Double overprint 1,900.
Never hinged 3,100.
16b A16 80pf lake & blk, *rose* 190.00 *260.00*
Never hinged 450.00
On cover 900.00

Overprinted

17 A17 1m carmine rose (25x17 holes) 30.00 *38.50*
Never hinged 52.50
On cover 105.00
a. Inverted overprint 675.00 *1,350.*
Never hinged 1,100.
On cover 1,650.
b. Double overprint 750.00 *1,350.*
Never hinged 1,250.
On cover 1,650.
c. 1m carmine rose (26x17 holes) 975.00 *1,400.*
Never hinged 2,600.
On cover 3,000.
d. As "c," double overprint *7,500.* *13,500.*
Never hinged *13,500.*
Nos. 1-17 (52) 4,925. 11,273.

Three types of overprint exist on Nos. 1-5, 12, 13; two types on Nos. 6-11, 14-16.

The 3m type A19 exists overprinted like No. 17, but was not issued. Value, $15,000 unused, $31,500 never hinged.

Overprint forgeries exist.

Bavarian Stamps of 1914-16 Overprinted

Perf. 14x14½

1920, Mar. 1 **Wmk. 95**

19 A10 2pf gray 1,000. *4,250.*
Never hinged 1,900.
On cover *6,000.*
20 A10 3pf brown 90.00 *575.00*
Never hinged 210.00
On cover 900.00
21 A10 5pf yellow grn .85 *1.40*
Never hinged 1.50
On cover 4.50
a. Double overprint 700.00
b. Pair, one stamp without ovpt. — —
22 A10 7½pf green 32.50 *250.00*
Never hinged 62.50
On cover 410.00
23 A10 10pf carmine rose .80 *1.40*
Never hinged 1.50
On cover 3.75
a. Double overprint 275.00 *575.00*
Never hinged 450.00
b. Pair, one stamp without ovpt. —
Never hinged —
24 A10 15pf vermilion 1.00 *1.75*
Never hinged 1.50
On cover 4.50
a. Double overprint 350.00 *700.00*
Never hinged 525.00
25 A10 15pf carmine 7.00 *12.50*
Never hinged 13.50
On cover 22.50
26 A10 20pf blue .80 *1.40*
Never hinged 1.50
On cover 3.75
a. Double overprint 275.00 *575.00*
Never hinged 450.00
27 A10 25pf gray 10.00 *16.00*
Never hinged 21.00
On cover 30.00
28 A10 30pf orange 7.50 *11.00*
Never hinged 13.50
On cover 22.50
30 A10 40pf olive green 10.00 *15.00*
Never hinged 19.00
On cover 30.00
31 A10 50pf red brown 1.50 *2.25*
Never hinged 2.40
On cover 3.75
a. Double overprint 325.00 *575.00*
Never hinged 525.00
32 A10 60pf dark green 3.00 *8.50*
Never hinged 6.25
On cover 25.00
a. 60pf blackish green on thick paper 3.00 *9.00*
Never hinged 6.75
On cover 26.00

Overprinted

Perf. 11½

35 A11 1m brown 20.00 *35.00*
Never hinged 45.00
On cover 120.00
a. 1m dark brown 15.00 *30.00*
Never hinged 37.50
On cover 110.00
36 A11 2m dk gray violet 55.00 *130.00*
Never hinged 120.00
On cover 340.00
a. 2m dk purple violet 1,650. 2,500.
Never hinged 3,100.
On cover 3,000.
37 A11 3m scarlet 95.00 *150.00*
Never hinged 240.00
On cover 1,100.
Nos. 35-37 (3) 170.00 *315.00*

Overprinted

38 A12 5m deep blue 650.00 *800.00*
Never hinged 1,900.
On cover 3,000.
39 A12 10m yellow green 115.00 *225.00*
Never hinged 300.00
On cover 900.00
a. Double overprint *3,000.* *7,500.*
Never hinged *5,600.*

Nos. 19, 20 and 22 were not officially issued, but were available for postage. Examples are known legitimately used on cover. The 20m type A12 was also overprinted in small quantity. Value, $120,000.

Overprint forgeries exist.

German Stamps of 1906-20 Overprinted

Perf. 14, 14½

1920, Mar. 26 **Wmk. 125**

41 A16 5pf green .25 *.50*
Never hinged .45
On cover 2.60
42 A16 5pf red brown .45 .75
Never hinged .95
On cover 2.25
b. 5pf brown 3.00 *10.50*
Never hinged 8.25
On cover 15.00
43 A16 10pf carmine .25 *.50*
Never hinged .45
On cover 2.60
44 A16 10pf orange .35 .50
Never hinged .75
On cover 2.25
b. Double ovpt., never hinged 75.00
45 A22 15pf dk violet .25 *.50*
Never hinged .45
On cover 2.60
46 A16 20pf blue violet .25 *.50*
Never hinged .45
On cover 2.60
47 A16 20pf green .50 .50
Never hinged 1.00
On cover 2.25
a. Double overprint, never hinged 75.00
48 A16 30pf org & blk, *buff* .30 *.50*
Never hinged .75
On cover 2.60
a. Double overprint 65.00
Never hinged 110.00
49 A16 30pf dull blue .55 *.75*
Never hinged 1.25
On cover 3.00
50 A16 40pf lake & blk .25 *.50*
Never hinged .45
On cover 2.60
51 A16 40pf car rose 1.00 .75
Never hinged 1.90
On cover 3.00
52 A16 50pf pur & blk, *buff* .25 *.50*
Never hinged .75
On cover 2.60
a. Double overprint 65.00 *375.00*
Never hinged 110.00
c. 50pf pur & blk, *orange buff* 3.00 *21.00*
Never hinged 6.00
On cover 30.00
53 A16 60pf red violet .50 .50
Never hinged .95
On cover 3.00
54 A16 75pf green & blk .70 .50
Never hinged 1.50
On cover 3.00
a. Double overprint 100.00 *375.00*
Never hinged 190.00
55 A17 1.25m green 1.25 1.25
Never hinged 2.50
On cover 6.75
56 A17 1.50m yellow brn 1.25 1.25
Never hinged 2.50
On cover 6.75
57 A21 2.50m lilac red 3.50 *12.00*
Never hinged 7.50
On cover 22.50
a. 2.50m lilac rose 11.00 *55.00*
Never hinged 24.00
On cover 75.00
b. 2.50m lilac 90.00 *825.00*
Never hinged 190.00
On cover *975.00*
c. 2.50m brown lilac 9.00 *47.50*
Never hinged 19.00
On cover 75.00
58 A16 4m black & rose 7.50 *20.00*
Never hinged 18.00
On cover 67.50
a. Double overprint, never hinged 75.00
Nos. 41-58 (18) 19.35 *42.25*

On No. 57 the overprint is placed vertically at each side of the stamp.
Counterfeit overprints exist.

Inverted Overprint

41a A16 5pf green 20.00 *140.00*
Never hinged 26.00
On cover 225.00
43a A16 10pf carmine 45.00 *300.00*
Never hinged 75.00
On cover 450.00
44a A16 10pf orange 17.50 30.00
Never hinged 26.00
45a A22 15pf dark violet 25.00 *210.00*
Never hinged 47.50
On cover 300.00
46a A16 20pf blue violet 25.00 100.00
Never hinged 60.00
48b A16 30pf org & blk, *buff* —
Never hinged —
50a A16 40pf lake & blk —
Never hinged —
52b A16 50pf pur & blk, *buff* —
Never hinged —
53a A16 60pf red violet 70.00 *225.00*
Never hinged 150.00
On cover 450.00
54b A16 75pf green & black 110.00
Never hinged 210.00
55a A17 1.25m green 115.00 750.00
Never hinged 190.00
56a A17 1.50m yellow brown 100.00 700.00
Never hinged 190.00

Germany No. 90 Surcharged in Black

1921, Feb.

65 A16 20pf on 75pf grn & blk .35 *1.25*
Never hinged .90
On cover 3.75
a. Inverted surcharge 25.00 *45.00*
Never hinged 45.00
On cover 97.50
b. Double surcharge 65.00 *95.00*
Never hinged 90.00
On cover 150.00

Germany No. 120 Surcharged

66 A22 5m on 15pf vio brn 5.50 *14.00*
Never hinged 12.00
On cover 75.00
67 A22 10m on 15pf vio brn 6.50 *18.00*
Never hinged 13.50
On cover 90.00
Nos. 65-67 (3) 12.35 *33.25*

Forgeries exist of Nos. 66-67.

Old Mill near Mettlach — A3

Miner at Work — A4

Entrance to Reden Mine — A5

Saar River Traffic — A6

Saar River near Mettlach — A7

Slag Pile at Völklingen — A8

Signal Bridge, Saarbrücken — A9

Church at Mettlach — A10

"Old Bridge," Saarbrücken A11

Cable Railway at Ferne — A12

Colliery Shafthead — A13

Saarbrücken City Hall — A14

Pottery at Mettlach — A15

St. Ludwig's Cathedral — A16

Presidential Residence, Saarbrücken A17

Burbach Steelworks, Dillingen A18

1921 **Unwmk.** **Typo.** ***Perf. 12½***

68 A3 5pf ol grn & vio .30 *.50*
Never hinged .55
On cover 4.50
a. Tête bêche pair 3.50 *6.75*
Never hinged 6.75
On cover 60.00
c. Center inverted 100.00 *300.00*
Never hinged 190.00
d. Center printed in green 75.00 260.00
Never hinged 160.00
On cover 450.00
69 A4 10pf org & ultra .30 *.50*
Never hinged .55
On cover 4.50
70 A5 20pf grn & slate .40 *.80*
Never hinged .55
On cover 10.50
a. Tête bêche pair 6.00 *37.50*
Never hinged 11.50
On cover 110.00
c. Perf. 10½ 20.00 *190.00*
Never hinged 37.50
On cover 260.00
d. As "c," tête bêche pair 100.00 *550.00*
Never hinged 190.00
On cover 1,100.
71 A6 25pf brn & dk bl .35 *.80*
Never hinged .75
On cover 10.50
a. Tête bêche pair 7.50 *40.00*
Never hinged 14.00
On cover 110.00
72 A7 30pf gray grn & brn .45 *.70*
Never hinged .75
On cover 10.50
a. Tête bêche pair 12.00 *67.50*
Never hinged 22.50
On cover 210.00
c. 30pf ol grn & blk 3.00 *17.50*
Never hinged 4.50
On cover 55.00
d. As "c," tête bêche pair 11.00 *55.00*
Never hinged 21.00
On cover 180.00
e. As "c," imperf., pair 140.00
Never hinged 210.00
73 A8 40pf vermilion .45 .45
Never hinged .75
On cover 4.50
a. Tête bêche pair 18.00 *75.00*
Never hinged 37.50
On cover 225.00

74 A9 50pf gray & blk .90 *3.75*
Never hinged 1.90
On cover 11.00
75 A10 60pf red & dk brn 1.50 *3.00*
Never hinged 3.25
On cover 19.00
76 A11 80pf deep blue .80 *1.10*
Never hinged 1.25
On cover 11.00
a. Tête bêche pair 20.00 *100.00*
Never hinged 37.50
On cover 190.00
77 A12 1m lt red & blk .85 *1.50*
Never hinged 1.50
On cover 11.00
a. 1m grn & blk *400.00*
Never hinged 1,200.
78 A13 1.25m lt brn & dk grn 1.10 *1.90*
Never hinged 2.10
On cover 18.00
79 A14 2m red & black 2.25 *3.50*
Never hinged 5.50
On cover 19.00
80 A15 3m brn & dk ol 3.00 *7.75*
Never hinged 7.50
On cover 26.00
a. Center inverted 110.00
Never hinged 260.00
b. 3m orange brown & black 24.00 *75.00*
Never hinged 47.50
On cover 110.00
81 A16 5m yellow & vio 8.75 *21.00*
Never hinged 19.00
On cover 82.50
82 A17 10m grn & red brn 11.00 *21.00*
Never hinged 22.50
On cover 100.00
83 A18 25m ultra, red & blk 32.50 *65.00*
Never hinged 75.00
On cover 300.00
a. 25m deep gray blue, deep cinnamon & black *2,400.* *3,750.*
Never hinged *3,750.*
On cover
Nos. 68-83 (16) 64.90 *133.25*

Values for tête bêche pairs are for vertical pairs. Horizontal pairs sell for about twice as much.

The ultramarine ink on No. 69 appears to be brown where it overlays the orange.

Exist imperf but were not regularly issued.

Nos. 70-83 Surcharged in Red, Blue or Black

a 

b 

c 

1921, May 1

85 A5(a) 3c on 20pf (R) .35 *.40*
Never hinged .65
On cover 1.90
a. Tête bêche pair 4.50 *30.00*
Never hinged 9.00
On cover 90.00
b. Inverted surcharge 125.00
Never hinged 165.00
d. Perf. 10½ 4.50 *150.00*
Never hinged 11.00
On cover 210.00
e. As "d," tête bêche pair 20.00 *60.00*
Never hinged 37.50
86 A6(a) 5c on 25pf (R) .35 .35
Never hinged .75
On cover .75
a. Tête bêche pair 90.00 *375.00*
Never hinged 150.00
On cover 1,100.
87 A7(a) 10c on 30pf (Bl) .40 .40
Never hinged .75
On cover 1.50
a. Tête bêche pair 4.50 *24.00*
Never hinged 8.25
On cover 67.50
b. Inverted surcharge 110.00 *450.00*
Never hinged 160.00
c. Double surcharge 100.00 *450.00*
Never hinged 160.00
On cover *1,000.*
88 A8(a) 15c on 40pf (Bk) .50 .40
Never hinged 1.00
On cover 1.50
a. Tête bêche pair 90.00 *375.00*
Never hinged 150.00
On cover 1,100.
b. Inverted surcharge 110.00 *450.00*
Never hinged 160.00
89 A9(a) 20c on 50pf (R) .35 .35
Never hinged .75
On cover 1.10
90 A10(a) 25c on 60pf (Bl) .45 .40
Never hinged .95
On cover 1.10
91 A11(a) 30c on 80pf (Bk) 1.50 .90
Never hinged 3.75
On cover 1.90
a. Tête bêche pair 12.00 *55.00*
Never hinged 22.50
On cover 210.00
c. Inverted surcharge 140.00 *525.00*
Never hinged 225.00
d. Double surcharge *150.00* *525.00*
Never hinged 225.00
92 A12(a) 40c on 1m (Bl) 2.00 .50
Never hinged 5.25
On cover 1.90
a. Inverted surcharge 100.00 *450.00*
Never hinged 160.00
On cover —
b. Double surcharge 150.00 *525.00*
Never hinged 225.00
93 A13(a) 50c on 1.25m (Bk) 3.00 1.00
Never hinged 9.00
On cover 2.50
a. Double surcharge 275.00 *900.00*
Never hinged 450.00
b. Perf. 10½ 72.50 *125.00*
Never hinged 140.00
On cover 300.00
94 A14(a) 75c on 2m (Bl) 2.75 1.25
Never hinged 15.00
On cover 6.00
a. Inverted surcharge 125.00
Never hinged 190.00
95 A15(b) 1fr on 3m (Bl) 3.75 2.25
Never hinged 16.00
On cover 5.00
a. On No. 80b 22.50 *25.00*
Never hinged 45.00
On cover 40.00
96 A16(b) 2fr on 5m (Bl) 12.50 5.50
Never hinged 37.50
On cover 15.00
97 A17(b) 3fr on 10m (Bk) 15.00 *22.50*
Never hinged 35.00
On cover 67.50
b. Double surcharge 190.00 *700.00*
Never hinged 300.00
98 A18(c) 5fr on 25m (Bl) 21.00 *32.50*
Never hinged 52.50
On cover 225.00
Nos. 85-98 (14) 63.90 *68.70*

In these surcharges the period is occasionally missing and there are various wrong font and defective letters.

Values for tête bêche pairs are for vertical pairs. Horizontal pairs sell for about twice as much.

Nos. 85-89, 91, 93, 97-98 exist imperforate but were not regularly issued.

Cable Railway, Ferne — A19

Miner at Work — A20

"Old Bridge," Saarbrücken A21

Saarbrücken City Hall — A22

Slag Pile at Völklingen A23

Pottery at Mettlach — A24

Saar River Traffic — A25

St. Ludwig's Cathedral A26

Colliery Shafthead A27

Mettlach Church — A28

Burbach Steelworks, Dillingen A29

Perf. 12½x13½, 13½x12½

1922-23 **Typo.**

99 A19 3c ol grn & straw .40 *.55*
Never hinged .65
On cover 2.25
100 A20 5c orange & blk .40 .35
Never hinged .65
On cover 1.10
101 A21 10c blue green .40 .35
Never hinged .65
On cover 1.10
102 A19 15c deep brown 1.10 .35
Never hinged 2.50
On cover 1.50
103 A19 15c orange ('23) 2.25 .35
Never hinged 6.25
On cover 2.25
104 A22 20c dk bl & lem 10.50 .35
Never hinged 37.50
On cover 2.25
105 A22 20c brt bl & straw ('23) 3.50 .35
Never hinged 9.00
On cover 2.25
106 A22 25c red & yellow 4.00 2.00
Never hinged 9.75
On cover 6.75
107 A22 25c mag & straw ('23) 2.10 .35
Never hinged 6.25
On cover 1.10
108 A23 30c carmine & yel 1.90 2.00
Never hinged 4.75
On cover 3.00
109 A24 40c brown & yel 1.00 .35
Never hinged 2.10
On cover 1.50
110 A25 50c dk bl & straw 1.00 .35
Never hinged 2.10
On cover 1.50
111 A24 75c dp grn & straw 11.00 *19.00*
Never hinged 37.50
On cover 60.00
112 A24 75c blk & straw ('23) 27.50 2.75
Never hinged 72.50
On cover 6.75
113 A26 1fr brown red 2.10 .70
Never hinged 9.00
On cover 2.25
114 A27 2fr deep violet 3.50 2.50
Never hinged 10.50
On cover 4.50
115 A28 3fr org & dk grn 14.50 5.50
Never hinged 52.50
On cover 7.50
116 A29 5fr brn & red brn 17.50 *40.00*
Never hinged 52.50
On cover 90.00
Nos. 99-116 (18) 104.65 *78.15*

Nos. 99-116 exist imperforate but were not regularly issued.

For overprints see Nos. O1-O15.

Madonna of Blieskastel — A30

1925, Apr. 9 Photo. ***Perf. 13½x12½***

Size: 23x27mm

118 A30 45c lake brown 3.00 *3.50*
Never hinged 6.25
On cover 19.00

Size: 31½x36mm

Perf. 12

119 A30 10fr black brown 14.00 *27.50*
Never hinged 29.00
On cover 82.50

Nos. 118-119 exist imperforate but were not regularly issued.

For overprint see No. 154.

Market Fountain, St. Johann — A31

View of Saar Valley A32

Colliery Shafthead A35

Burbach Steelworks A36

Designs: 15c, 75c, View of Saar Valley. 20c, 40c, 90c, Scene from Saarlouis fortifications. 25c, 50c, Tholey Abbey.

1927-32 ***Perf. 13½***

120 A31 10c deep brown .65 .30
Never hinged 1.25
On cover 1.50
121 A32 15c olive black .40 *.90*
Never hinged .95
On cover 3.00
122 A32 20c brown orange .40 .30
Never hinged .95
On cover 1.50
123 A32 25c bluish slate .65 .30
Never hinged 1.10
On cover 3.00
124 A31 30c olive green .85 .30
Never hinged 1.50
On cover 1.50
125 A32 40c olive brown .65 .30
Never hinged 1.20
On cover 3.00
126 A32 50c magenta .85 .30
Never hinged 1.90
On cover 1.50
127 A35 60c red org ('30) 3.00 .50
Never hinged 9.00
On cover 3.00
128 A32 75c brown violet .65 .30
Never hinged 1.20
On cover 2.25
129 A35 80c red orange 2.75 *8.25*
Never hinged 6.50
On cover 19.00
130 A32 90c deep red ('32) 8.00 *17.00*
Never hinged 30.00
On cover 52.50
131 A35 1fr violet 2.40 .30
Never hinged 5.25
On cover 2.25

132 A36 1.50fr sapphire 4.25 .35
Never hinged 10.50
On cover 2.25
133 A36 2fr brown red 5.00 .35
Never hinged 12.00
On cover 3.00
134 A36 3fr dk olive grn 10.00 1.10
Never hinged 22.50
On cover 4.50
135 A36 5fr deep brown 11.50 7.00
Never hinged 24.00
On cover 19.00
Nos. 120-135 (16) 52.00 *37.85*

For surcharges and overprints see Nos. 136-153, O16-O26.

Nos. 126 and 129 Surcharged

1930-34
136 A32 40c on 50c mag ('34) 1.25 *1.40*
Never hinged 3.25
On cover 9.00
137 A35 60c on 80c red orange 1.75 *2.25*
Never hinged 4.50
On cover 7.50

Plebiscite Issue

Stamps of 1925-32 Overprinted in Various Colors

Perf. 13½, 13½x13, 13x13½

1934, Nov. 1
139 A31 10c brown (Br) .40 *.45*
Never hinged 1.10
On cover 1.90
140 A32 15c black grn (G) .40 *.45*
Never hinged 1.10
On cover 1.90
141 A32 20c brown org (O) .60 *1.25*
Never hinged 1.50
On cover 2.50
142 A32 25c bluish sl (Bl) .60 *1.25*
Never hinged 1.50
On cover 2.50
143 A31 30c olive grn (G) .40 .45
Never hinged .75
On cover 1.10
144 A32 40c olive brn (Br) .40 *.65*
Never hinged .95
On cover 1.75
145 A32 50c magenta (R) .75 *1.10*
Never hinged 1.90
On cover 2.50
146 A35 60c red orge (O) .65 *.45*
Never hinged .95
On cover 1.50
147 A32 75c brown vio (V) .75 *1.25*
Never hinged 1.90
On cover 3.75
148 A32 90c deep red (R) .75 *1.25*
Never hinged 1.90
On cover 3.75
149 A35 1fr violet (V) .75 *1.40*
Never hinged 1.90
On cover 3.75
150 A36 1.50fr sapphire (Bl) 1.25 *2.75*
Never hinged 3.75
On cover 9.00
151 A36 2fr brown red (R) 1.50 *3.75*
Never hinged 5.25
On cover 13.50
152 A36 3fr dk ol grn (G) 2.75 *8.00*
Never hinged 7.50
On cover 22.50
153 A36 5fr dp brown (Br) 17.50 *30.00*
Never hinged 47.50
On cover 75.00

Size: 31½x36mm

Perf. 12

154 A30 10fr black brn (Br) 24.00 *57.50*
Never hinged 47.50
On cover 190.00
Nos. 139-154 (16) 53.45 *111.95*

SEMI-POSTAL STAMPS

Red Cross Dog Leading Blind Man — SP1

Maternity Nurse with Child — SP4

Designs: #B2, Nurse and invalid. #B3, Children getting drink at spring.

Perf. 13½

1926, Oct. 25 Photo. Unwmk.
B1 SP1 20c + 20c dk ol grn 7.50 *15.00*
Never hinged 19.00
On cover 60.00
B2 SP1 40c + 40c dk brn 7.50 *15.00*
Never hinged 19.00
On cover 60.00
B3 SP1 50c + 50c red org 7.50 *14.00*
Never hinged 19.00
On cover 52.50
B4 SP4 1.50fr + 1.50fr brt bl 18.00 *45.00*
Never hinged 40.00
On cover 150.00
Nos. B1-B4 (4) 40.50 *89.00*

Nos. B1-B4 Overprinted

1927, Oct. 1
B5 SP1 20c + 20c dk ol grn 11.00 *25.00*
Never hinged 30.00
On cover 97.50
B6 SP1 40c + 40c dk brn 11.00 *25.00*
Never hinged 30.00
On cover 140.00
B7 SP1 50c + 50c red org 9.00 *17.50*
Never hinged 22.50
On cover 97.50
B8 SP4 1.50fr + 1.50fr brt bl 17.00 *55.00*
Never hinged 37.50
On cover 260.00
Nos. B5-B8 (4) 48.00 *122.50*

"The Blind Beggar" by Dyckmans SP5

"Almsgiving" by Schiestl SP6

"Charity" by Raphael — SP7

1928, Dec. 23 Photo.
B9 SP5 40c (+40c) blk brn 11.00 *65.00*
Never hinged 29.00
On cover 90.00
B10 SP5 50c (+50c) brn rose 11.00 *65.00*
Never hinged 29.00
On cover 90.00
B11 SP5 1fr (+1fr) dl vio 11.00 *65.00*
Never hinged 29.00
On cover 110.00
B12 SP6 1.50fr (+1.50fr) cob bl 11.00 *65.00*
Never hinged 29.00
On cover 120.00
B13 SP6 2fr (+2fr) red brn 14.00 *92.50*
Never hinged 30.00
On cover 180.00
B14 SP6 3fr (+3fr) dk ol grn 14.00 *125.00*
Never hinged 30.00
On cover 325.00
B15 SP7 10fr (+10fr) dk brn 350.00 *3,600.*
Never hinged 675.00
On cover *5,600.*
Nos. B9-B15 (7) 422.00 4,077.
Set on first day cover *7,500.*
Nos. B9-B12 on first day cover 550.00

"Orphaned" by Kaulbach SP8

"St. Ottilia" by Feuerstein SP9

"Madonna" by Ferruzzio — SP10

1929, Dec. 22
B16 SP8 40c (+15c) ol grn 2.00 *5.00*
Never hinged 3.75
On cover 26.00
B17 SP8 50c (+20c) cop red 4.25 *8.50*
Never hinged 9.00
On cover 40.00
B18 SP8 1fr (+50c) vio brn 4.25 *10.00*
Never hinged 9.00
On cover 62.50
B19 SP9 1.50fr (+75c) Prus bl 4.25 *10.00*
Never hinged 9.00
On cover 82.50
B20 SP9 2fr (+1fr) brn car 4.25 *10.00*
Never hinged 9.00
On cover 97.50
B21 SP9 3fr (+2fr) sl grn 7.50 *22.50*
Never hinged 15.00
On cover 140.00
B22 SP10 10fr (+8fr) blk brn 45.00 *125.00*
Never hinged 97.50
On cover 525.00
Nos. B16-B22 (7) 71.50 *191.00*

"The Safety-Man" SP11

"The Good Samaritan" SP12

"In the Window" — SP13

1931, Jan. 20
B23 SP11 40c (+15c) 7.50 *22.50*
Never hinged 19.00
On cover 60.00
B24 SP11 60c (+20c) 7.50 *22.50*
Never hinged 18.00
On cover 60.00
B25 SP12 1fr (+50c) 7.50 *42.50*
Never hinged 18.00
On cover 140.00
B26 SP11 1.50fr (+75c) 11.00 *42.50*
Never hinged 26.00
On cover 190.00
B27 SP12 2fr (+1fr) 11.00 *42.50*
Never hinged 26.00
On cover 210.00
B28 SP12 3fr (+2fr) 18.50 *42.50*
Never hinged 37.50
On cover 260.00
B29 SP13 10fr (+10fr) 90.00 *250.00*
Never hinged 190.00
On cover 750.00
Nos. B23-B29 (7) 153.00 *465.00*
Set on first day cover 1,100.

St. Martin of Tours — SP14

#B33-B35, Charity. #B36, The Widow's Mite.

1931, Dec. 23
B30 SP14 40c (+15c) 12.00 *32.50*
Never hinged 32.50
On cover 60.00
B31 SP14 60c (+20c) 12.00 *32.50*
Never hinged 32.50
On cover 60.00
B32 SP14 1fr (+50c) 15.00 *50.00*
Never hinged 37.50
On cover 120.00
B33 SP14 1.50fr (+75c) 18.00 *50.00*
Never hinged 40.00
On cover 195.00
B34 SP14 2fr (+1fr) 21.00 *50.00*
Never hinged 52.50
On cover 210.00
B35 SP14 3fr (+2fr) 26.00 *85.00*
Never hinged 67.50
On cover 325.00
B36 SP14 5fr (+5fr) 90.00 *300.00*
Never hinged 240.00
On cover 1,100.
Nos. B30-B36 (7) 194.00 *600.00*
Set on first day cover 1,800.

Ruins at Kirkel — SP17

Illingen Castle, Kerpen SP23

Designs: 60c, Church at Blie. 1fr, Castle Ottweiler. 1.50fr, Church of St. Michael, Saarbrucken. 2fr, Statue of St. Wendel. 3fr, Church of St. John, Saarbrucken.

1932, Dec. 20
B37 SP17 40c (+15c) 9.00 *20.00*
Never hinged 22.50
On cover 75.00
B38 SP17 60c (+20c) 9.00 *20.00*
Never hinged 22.50
On cover 90.00
B39 SP17 1fr (+50c) 14.00 *35.00*
Never hinged 35.00
On cover 120.00
B40 SP17 1.50fr (+75c) 18.50 *42.50*
Never hinged 45.00
On cover 150.00
B41 SP17 2fr (+1fr) 18.50 *50.00*
Never hinged 45.00
On cover 160.00
B42 SP17 3fr (+2fr) 55.00 *160.00*
Never hinged 120.00
On cover 525.00
B43 SP23 5fr (+5fr) 120.00 *250.00*
Never hinged 240.00
On cover 900.00
Nos. B37-B43 (7) 244.00 *577.50*
Set on first day cover 1,500.

Scene of Neunkirchen Disaster — SP24

1933, June 1

B44 SP24 60c (+ 60c) org red 15.00 17.50
Never hinged 37.50
On cover 47.50
B45 SP24 3fr (+ 3fr) ol grn 35.00 *65.00*
Never hinged 82.50
On cover 125.00
B46 SP24 5fr (+ 5fr) org brn 35.00 *65.00*
Never hinged 82.50
On cover 225.00
Nos. B44-B46 (3) 85.00 *147.50*
Set on first day cover 525.00

The surtax was for the aid of victims of the explosion at Neunkirchen, Feb. 10.

"Love" — SP25

Designs: 60c, "Anxiety." 1fr, "Peace." 1.50fr, "Solace." 2fr, "Welfare." 3fr, "Truth." 5fr, Figure on Tomb of Duchess Elizabeth of Lorraine

1934, Mar. 15 Photo.

B47 SP25 40c (+15c) blk brn 4.75 *14.00*
Never hinged 12.00
On cover 37.50
B48 SP25 60c (+20c) red org 4.75 *14.00*
Never hinged 12.00
On cover 37.50
B49 SP25 1fr (+50c) dl vio 6.75 *17.50*
Never hinged 18.00
On cover 52.50
B50 SP25 1.50fr (+75c) blue 12.00 *32.50*
Never hinged 32.50
On cover 110.00
B51 SP25 2fr (+1fr) car rose 11.00 *32.50*
Never hinged 30.00
On cover 105.00
B52 SP25 3fr (+2fr) ol grn 12.00 *32.50*
Never hinged 32.50
On cover 120.00
B53 SP25 5fr (+5fr) red brn 30.00 *77.50*
Never hinged 75.00
On cover 310.00
Nos. B47-B53 (7) 81.25 *220.50*
Set on first day cover 750.00

Nos. B47-B53 Overprinted like Nos. 139-154 in Various Colors Reading up

1934, Dec. 1 *Perf. 13x13½*

B54 SP25 40c (+15c) (Br) 3.50 *13.00*
Never hinged 7.50
On cover 37.50
B55 SP25 60c (+20c) (R) 3.50 *14.00*
Never hinged 7.50
On cover 37.50
B56 SP25 1fr (+50c) (V) 11.00 *25.00*
Never hinged 20.00
On cover 67.50
B57 SP25 1.50fr (+75c) (Bl) 6.75 *25.00*
Never hinged 16.50
On cover 75.00
B58 SP25 2fr (+1fr) (R) 11.00 *35.00*
Never hinged 24.00
On cover 82.50
B59 SP25 3fr (+2fr) (G) 9.50 *30.00*
Never hinged 22.50
On cover 90.00
B60 SP25 5fr (+5fr) (Br) 14.00 *35.00*
Never hinged 35.00
On cover 120.00
Nos. B54-B60 (7) 59.25 *177.00*

AIR POST STAMPS

Airplane over Saarbrücken — AP1

Perf. 13½

1928, Sept. 19 Unwmk. Photo.

C1 AP1 50c brown red 3.75 3.25
Never hinged 9.00
On cover 13.50
On first day cover 110.00
C2 AP1 1fr dark violet 6.00 3.75
Never hinged 13.50
On cover 22.50
On first day cover 150.00

For overprints see Nos. C5, C7.

Saarbrücken Airport and Church of St. Arnual — AP2

1932, Apr. 30

C3 AP2 60c orange red 6.00 4.25
Never hinged 15.00
On cover 19.00
On first day cover 55.00
C4 AP2 5fr dark brown 42.50 *85.00*
Never hinged 120.00
On cover 180.00
On first day cover 225.00

For overprints see Nos. C6, C8.

Nos. C1-C4 Overprinted like Nos. 139-154 in Various Colors

1934, Nov. 1 *Perf. 13½, 13½x13*

C5 AP1 50c brn red (R) 3.75 *6.50*
Never hinged 9.00
On cover 19.00
On first day cover 37.50
C6 AP2 60c org red (O) 3.25 *2.50*
Never hinged 6.75
On cover 7.50
On first day cover 37.50
C7 AP1 1fr dk vio (V) 5.25 *8.50*
Never hinged 15.00
On cover 30.00
On first day cover 75.00
C8 AP2 5fr dk brn (Br) 6.25 *11.50*
Never hinged 19.00
On cover 60.00
On first day cover 90.00
Nos. C5-C8 (4) 18.50 *29.00*
Set on first day cover 225.00

OFFICIAL STAMPS

Regular Issue of 1922-1923 Overprinted Diagonally in Red or Blue

Perf. 12½x13½, 13½x12½

1922-23 Unwmk.

Nos. O1-O15 have two types of overprint: Type I, center bar of "E" slightly above center, "S" has rounded bottom, "A" symetrical; Type 2, center bar of "E" centered, "S" has flat bottom, "A" slightly inclined to right. Overprints are Type I unless noted.

O1 A19 3c ol grn & straw (R) .70 *27.50*
Never hinged 2.25
On cover 110.00
O2 A20 5c org & blk (R) .35 *.35*
Never hinged .75
On cover 6.00
a. Pair, one without overprint 250.00
Never hinged 525.00
O3 A21 10c bl grn (R) .35 .30
Never hinged .95
On cover 6.00
a. Inverted overprint 30.00
Never hinged 75.00
O4 A19 15c dp brn (Bl) .35 .30
Never hinged .95
On cover 6.00
a. Pair, one without overprint 275.00
Never hinged 560.00
b. Double overprint 60.00
Never hinged 150.00
O5 A19 15c org (Bl) ('23) 2.10 .45
Never hinged 4.50
On cover 9.00
O6 A22 20c dk bl & lem (R) .35 .30
Never hinged .95
On cover 6.00
a. Inverted overprint 30.00
Never hinged 75.00
b. Double overprint 60.00
Never hinged 150.00
O7 A22 20c brt bl & straw (R) ('23) 2.10 .45
Never hinged 4.50
On cover 9.00
O8 A22 25c red & yel (Bl) 3.00 1.00
Never hinged 9.00
On cover 19.00
O9 A22 25c mag & straw (Bl) ('23) 2.10 .45
Never hinged 4.50
On cover 9.00
a. Overprint Type II ('24) 15.00 2.25
Never hinged 37.50
On cover 45.00
O10 A23 30c car & yel (Bl) .35 .30
Never hinged 1.00
On cover 7.50
a. Inverted overprint 47.50
Never hinged 110.00
O11 A24 40c brn & yel (Bl) .45 .30
Never hinged 1.50
On cover 7.50
O12 A25 50c dk bl & straw (R) .45 .30
Never hinged 1.50
On cover 6.00
a. Inverted overprint 30.00
Never hinged 75.00
O13 A24 75c dp grn & straw (R) 16.00 25.00
Never hinged 52.50
On cover 135.00
O14 A24 75c blk & straw (R) ('23) 4.25 2.25
Never hinged 9.00
On cover 19.00
O15 A26 1fr brn red (Bl) 27.50 15.00
Never hinged 75.00
On cover 90.00
a. Inverted overprint 140.00
Never hinged 300.00
b. Double overprint 140.00
Never hinged 300.00
c. Overprint Type II ('24) 8.50 2.25
Never hinged 24.00
On cover 30.00
Nos. O1-O15 (15) 60.40 *74.25*

Regular Issue of 1927-30 Overprinted in Various Colors

1927-34 *Perf. 13½*

Two types of overprint: Type I, overprint at 32 degree angle ('27-'32); Type II, overprint at 23 to 25 degree angle ('29-'34).

O16 A31 10c dp brn (Bl) (II) ('34) 1.75 2.10
Never hinged 6.00
On cover 15.00
O17 A32 15c ol blk (Bl) (II) ('34) 1.75 *6.00*
Never hinged 6.00
On cover 45.00
O18 A32 20c brn org (Bk) (II) ('31) 1.75 1.40
Never hinged 6.00
On cover 15.00
O19 A32 25c bluish sl (Bl) (II) 2.10 *5.75*
Never hinged 7.50
On cover 15.00
O20 A31 30c ol grn (C) (I) 3.50 .35
Never hinged 11.00
On cover 6.00
a. orange red ovpt. (II) 1.90 .35
Never hinged 6.00
On cover 6.00
b. olive green, carmine ovpt. (II) 3.75 1.90
Never hinged 11.00
On cover 11.00
O21 A32 40c ol brn (C) (I) 3.75 .35
Never hinged 11.00
On cover 6.00
a. Double overprint 75.00
b. 40c olive brown (C)(II) 1.75 .30
Never hinged 6.00
On cover 6.00
c. As "b," double overprint 95.00
Never hinged 150.00
O22 A32 50c mag (Bl) (I) 12.00 .60
Never hinged 45.00
On cover 6.00
a. Double overprint 75.00
b. 50c magenta (Bl) (II) 3.50 .35
Never hinged 12.50
On cover 6.00
c. As "b," double overprint 52.50
Never hinged 90.00
O23 A35 60c red org (Bk) (II) ('30) 1.10 .30
Never hinged 3.75
On cover 6.00
a. Double overprint 52.50
Never hinged 90.00
O24 A32 75c brn vio (C) (I) 4.50 .75
Never hinged 12.50
On cover 9.00
a. Double overprint 75.00
b. 75c brown violet (C) (II) 2.10 .70
Never hinged 7.50
On cover 15.00
O25 A35 1fr vio (RO) (I) 3.75 .75
Never hinged 11.00
On cover 3.75
a. Double overprint 75.00
b. 1fr violet (RO) (II) 2.10 .35
Never hinged 7.50
On cover 7.50
c. As "b," double overprint 85.00
Never hinged 150.00
O26 A36 2fr brn red (Bl) (I) 9.00 1.00
Never hinged 30.00
On cover 11.00
a. Double overprint 75.00
b. 1fr brown red (Bl) (II) 2.10 .35
Never hinged 7.50
On cover 7.50
c. As "b," double overprint 65.00
Never hinged 110.00
Nos. O16-O26 (11) 44.95 *19.35*

The overprint on Nos. O16 and O20 is known only inverted.

ST. CHRISTOPHER

sānt ˈkris-tə-fər

LOCATION — Island in the West Indies, southeast of Puerto Rico
GOVT. — A Presidency of the Leeward Islands Colony
AREA — 68 sq. mi.
POP. — 18,578 (estimated)
CAPITAL — Basseterre

Stamps of St. Christopher were discontinued in 1890 and replaced by those of Leeward Islands. For later issues see St. Kitts-Nevis.

12 Pence = 1 Shilling

STAMPS OF GREAT BRITAIN USED IN ST. CHRISTOPHER

Numeral cancellation type A is pictured in the Crowned Circle Handstamps and Great Britain Used Abroad section.

1858-60

A12 (Basseterre)

A1 A 1p rose red (#20) 700.00
A2 A 2p blue (#29, P7) 1,050.
A3 A 4p rose (#26) 375.00
A4 A 6p lilac (#27) 225.00
A5 A 1sh green (#28) 1,650.

See footnote after No. 23.

Issued under British Administration

Queen Victoria — A1

Wmk. Crown and C C (1)

1870, Apr. 1 Typo. *Perf. 12½*

1 A1 1p dull rose 95.00 52.50
2 A1 1p lilac rose 77.50 35.00
3 A1 6p green ('71) 140.00 8.75
a. 6p yellow green ('70) 140.00 21.00
Nos. 1-3 (3) 312.50 96.25

1875-79 *Perf. 14*

4 A1 1p lilac rose 75.00 8.00
b. Half used as ½p on cover (2½p rate) *2,250.*
c. Half used as ½p on newsprint (½p rate) *2,100.*
5 A1 2½p red brown ('79) 200.00 *275.00*
6 A1 4p blue ('79) 225.00 16.00
7 A1 6p green 60.00 6.00
a. Horiz. pair, imperf. vert. —
Nos. 4-7 (4) 560.00 305.00

The value for No. 4b is for covers dated between March and June, 1882.

For surcharges see Nos. 18-20.

1882-90 Wmk. Crown and C A (2)

8 A1 ½p green 2.50 2.10
9 A1 1p rose 2.00 2.50
a. Half used as ½p on cover —
10 A1 1p lilac rose 600.00 77.50
a. Diagonal half used as ½p on cover —
11 A1 2½p red brown 200.00 67.50
a. 2½p deep red brown 210.00 72.50
12 A1 2½p ultra ('84) 2.75 2.00
13 A1 4p blue 525.00 27.50
14 A1 4p gray ('84) 1.60 1.10
15 A1 6p olive brn ('90) 95.00 *425.00*
16 A1 1sh violet ('87) 105.00 75.00
a. 1sh bright mauve ('90) 95.00 175.00
Nos. 8-16 (9) 1,533. 680.20

For surcharges see Nos. 17, 21-23.

No. 9 Bisected and Handstamp Surcharged in Black

1885, Mar.

17 A1 ½p on half of 1p 27.50 45.00
- *b.* Inverted surcharge 250.00 125.00
- *c.* Unsevered pair 125.00 *125.00*
- *d.* As "c," one surcharge inverted *450.00* *325.00*
- *e.* Double surcharge — —

No. 7 Surcharged in Black:

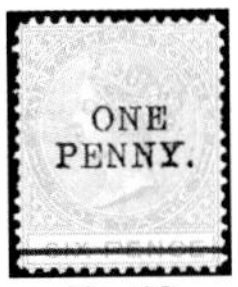

No. 18

No. 19

No. 20

1884-86 **Wmk. 1**

18 A1 1p on 6p green ('86) 22.50 35.00
- *a.* Inverted surcharge 9,000.
- *b.* Double surcharge 1,650.

19 A1 4p on 6p green 75.00 57.50
- *a.* Period after "PENCE" 75.00 57.50
- *b.* Double surcharge — 3,000.

20 A1 4p on 6p green ('86) 60.00 105.00
- *a.* Without period after "d" 250.00 325.00
- *b.* Double surcharge *2,750.* *3,000.*

Nos. 18-20 (3) 157.50 197.50

The line through original value on Nos. 18 and 20 was added by hand. Value for No. 18b is for stamp with pen cancellation or with violet handstamp (revenue cancels).

Nos. 8 and 12 Surcharged in Black Like No. 18 or:

No. 21

ONE PENNY.

No. 22

No. 23

1887-88 **Wmk. 2**

21 A1 1p on ½p green 45.00 50.00

22 A1 1p on 2½p ('88) 72.50 72.50
- *a.* Inverted surcharge *16,500.* *9,500.*

23 A1 1p on 2½p ('88) *20,000.* *13,250.*

Nos. 18, 21 and 23 all have the same type of One Penny surcharge. The line through the original value on Nos. 21 and 22 were added by hand. No. 23 probably is a sheet that was missed when the bars were added.

Antigua No. 18 was used in St. Christopher in 1890. It is canceled "A12" instead of "A02." Values: used $140, on cover $850.

POSTAL FISCAL ISSUES

St. Kitts Nos. 22 and 28 Overprinted "REVENUE" Horizontally and "Saint Christopher" Diagonally

1883

AR1 A5 1p violet 425.00

AR2 A5 6p green 95.00 *150.00*

Stamps of St. Christopher Ovptd. "SAINT KITTS / NEVIS / REVENUE" in 3 Lines

1885

AR3 A1 1p rose 3.00 *17.50*

AR4 A1 3p violet 17.50 *72.50*

AR5 A1 6p orange brown 11.00 *55.00*

AR6 A1 1sh olive 3.25 *47.50*

Other values exist with the above overprints but were not available for postal purposes.

ST. HELENA

sānt 'he-lə-nə

LOCATION — Island in the Atlantic Ocean, 1,200 miles west of Angola
GOVT. — British Crown Colony
AREA — 47 sq. mi.
POP. — 5,499 (1982)
CAPITAL — Jamestown

12 Pence = 1 Shilling
20 Shillings = 1 Pound

Catalogue values for unused stamps in this country are for Never Hinged items, beginning with Scott 128 in the regular postage section.

Values for unused stamps are for examples with original gum as defined in the catalogue introduction. Very fine examples of Nos. 2-7, 11-39a and 47-47b will have perforations touching the design on one or more sides due to the narrow spacing of the stamps on the plates. Stamps with perfs clear of the design on all four sides are scarce and will command higher prices.

Watermark

Wmk. 6 — Star

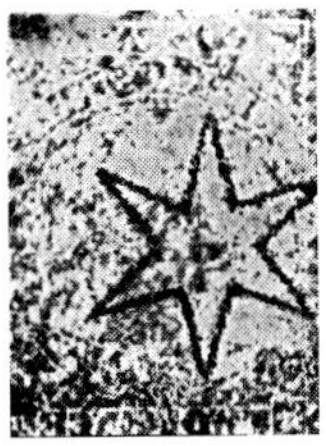

Queen Victoria — A1

1856, Jan. **Wmk. 6** **Engr.** ***Imperf.***

1 A1 6p blue 600.00 210.00

For types surcharged see Nos. 8-39, 47.

1861 ***Clean-Cut Perf. 14 to 15½***

2 A1 6p blue 2,100. 325.00

1863 ***Rough Perf. 14 to 15½***

2B A1 6p blue 525.00 160.00

1871-74 **Wmk. 1** ***Perf. 12½***

3 A1 6p dull blue 850.00 115.00

4 A1 6p ultra ('74) 475.00 97.50

1879 ***Perf. 14x12½***

5 A1 6p gray blue 450.00 60.00

1889 ***Perf. 14***

6 A1 6p gray blue 450.00 60.00

1889 **Wmk. Crown and C A (2)**

7 A1 6p gray 26.50 6.00

Type of 1856 Surcharged

a

b

1863 **Wmk. 1** ***Imperf.***

Long Bar, 16, 17, 18 or 19mm

8 A1(a) 1p on 6p brown red (surch. 17mm) 125.00 *190.00*
- *a.* Double surcharge 6,750. 4,000.
- *b.* Surcharge omitted *21,500.*

9 A1(a) 1p on 6p brown red (surch. 19mm) 150.00 *200.00*
- *a.* Vertical pair, #8, 9 *11,000.*

10 A1(b) 4p on 6p carmine 600.00 300.00
- *b.* Double surcharge *16,000.* *11,000.*

The status of No. 10a has been questioned. The editors would like to see proof of its existence.

1864-73 ***Perf. 12½***

11 A1(a) 1p on 6p brn red 60.00 32.50
- *a.* Double surcharge *10,500.*

12 A1(b) 1p on 6p brn red ('71) 115.00 21.00
- *a.* Blue black surcharge *1,200.* *675.00*

13 A1(b) 2p on 6p yel ('73) 115.00 50.00
- *a.* Blue black surcharge *4,800.* *2,700.*

14 A1(b) 3p on 6p dk vio ('73) 115.00 72.50

15 A1(b) 4p on 6p car 160.00 60.00
- *a.* Double surcharge *6,750.*

16 A1(b) 1sh on 6p grn (bar 16 to 17mm) 360.00 35.00
- *a.* Double surcharge *24,000.*

17 A1(b) 1sh on 6p dp grn (bar 18mm) ('73) 575.00 20.00
- *a.* Blue black surcharge —

1868

Short Bar, 14 or 15mm

18 A1(a) 1p on 6p brn red 200.00 67.50
- *a.* Imperf., pair *5,500.*
- *b.* Double surcharge —

19 A1(b) 2p on 6p yellow 200.00 72.50
- *a.* Imperf 12,000.

20 A1(b) 3p on 6p dk vio 100.00 60.00
- *a.* Double surcharge 7,250.
- *b.* Imperf., pair *2,000.*
- *c.* 3p on 6p pale purple 3,300. 900.00

21 A1(b) 4p on 6p car (words 18mm) 115.00 67.50
- *a.* Double surcharge *6,000.*
- *b.* Imperf, single 13,500.

22 A1(b) 4p on 6p car (words 19mm) 240.00 150.00
- *a.* Words double, 18mm and 19mm *25,000.* *11,000.*
- *b.* Imperf. —
- *c.* Surcharge omitted —

23 A1(a) 1sh on 6p yel grn 725.00 150.00
- *a.* Double surcharge *18,000.*
- *b.* Pair, one without surcharge *18,000.*
- *c.* Imperf *15,750.*

24 A1(a) 5sh on 6p org 60.00 72.50
- *a.* 5sh on 6p yellow 550.00 450.00

1882 ***Perf. 14x12½***

25 A1(a) 1p on 6p brown red 90.00 18.00

26 A1(b) 2p on 6p yellow 115.00 60.00

27 A1(b) 3p on 6p violet 240.00 85.00

28 A1(b) 4p on 6p carmine (words 16mm) 125.00 72.50

1883 ***Perf. 14***

29 A1(a) 1p on 6p brown red 110.00 21.00

30 A1(b) 2p on 6p yellow 125.00 37.50

31 A1(a) 1sh on 6p yel grn 25.00 15.00

1882 ***Perf. 14x12½***

Long Bar, 18mm

32 A1(b) 1sh on 6p dp green 800.00 30.00

1884-94 **Wmk. 2** ***Perf. 14***

Short Bar, 14 or 14½mm

33 A1(b) ½p on 6p grn (words 17mm) 11.50 20.00
- *a.* ½p on 6p emer, blurred print (words 17mm) ('84) 14.50 20.00
- *b.* Double surcharge 1,450. 1,575.
- *c.* "N" and "Y" spaced .8mm (#33) 550.00 *800.00*
- *d.* "N" and "Y" spaced .8mm (#33a) 1,300.
- *e.* As "d," double surcharge 13,500.

34 A1(b) ½p on 6p grn (words 15mm) ('94) 3.00 3.50
- *a.* "N" and "Y" spaced .8mm 1,800.

35 A1(a) 1p on 6p red ('87) 5.75 4.50
- *a.* 1p on 6p pale red 7.25 3.75

36 A1(b) 2p on 6p yel ('94) 3.00 9.50

37 A1(b) 3p on 6p dp vio ('87) 9.00 13.50
- *a.* 3p on 6p red violet 6.00 6.00
- *b.* Double surcharge,#37a *11,500.* *7,250.*
- *c.* Double surcharge, #37 *11,000.*

38 A1(b) 4p on 6p pale brn (words 16½mm; '90) 27.50 *29.00*
- *a.* 4p on 6p dk brn (words 17mm; '94) 30.00 21.00
- *b.* With thin bar below thick one 800.00

The spacing between "N" and "Y" in surcharges on Nos. 33 and 34 is normally .5mm. Examples with .8mm spacing are from one position within the pane.

1894

Long Bar, 18mm

39 A1(b) 1sh on 6p yel grn 50.00 25.00
- *a.* Double surcharge *4,750.*

See note after No. 47.

Queen Victoria — A3

1890-97 **Typo.** ***Perf. 14***

40 A3 ½p green ('97) 3.25 7.75

41 A3 1p rose ('96) 20.00 2.40

42 A3 1½p red brn & grn 5.50 9.75

43 A3 2p yellow ('96) 6.00 14.50

44 A3 2½p ultra ('96) 17.00 14.50

45 A3 5p violet ('96) 13.25 36.00

46 A3 10p brown ('96) 29.00 *72.50*

Nos. 40-46 (7) 94.00 *157.40*

Set, ovptd. "SPECIMEN" 360.00

Type of 1856 Surcharged

1893 **Engr.** **Wmk. 2**

47 A1 2½p on 6p blue 3.50 6.75
- *a.* Double surcharge *22,000.*
- *b.* Double impression *11,500.*

In 1905 remainders of Nos. 34-47 were sold by the postal officials. They are canceled with bars, arranged in the shape of diamonds, in purple ink. No such cancellation was ever used on the island and the stamps so canceled are of slight value. With this cancellation removed, these remainders are sometimes offered as unused. Some have been recanceled with a false dated postmark.

King Edward VII — A5

1902 **Typo.** **Wmk. 2**

48 A5 ½p green 1.75 *3.00*

49 A5 1p carmine rose 9.75 .85

Nos. 48, 49, ovptd. "SPECIMEN" 90.00

Government House — A6

"The Wharf" — A7

1903, June **Wmk. 1**

50 A6 ½p gray grn & brn 2.40 4.00

51 A7 1p carmine & blk 1.75 .50

52 A6 2p ol grn & blk 8.00 1.50

53 A7 8p brown & blk 26.50 *37.50*

54	A6	1sh org buff & brn	27.50	*47.50*
55	A7	2sh violet & blk	57.50	*100.00*
		Nos. 50-55 (6)	123.65	*191.00*
		Set, ovptd. "SPECIMEN"	275.00	

A8

1908, May **Wmk. 3**

Ordinary Paper

56	A8	2½p ultra	1.75	*1.75*
57	A8	4p black & red, *yel* ('11)	3.75	*21.00*
a.		Chalky paper	10.00	*22.50*
58	A8	6p dull violet ('11)	6.75	*16.00*
a.		Chalky paper	17.00	*36.00*
		Nos. 56-58 (3)	12.25	*38.75*

Wmk. 2

Chalky Paper

60	A8	10sh grn & red, *grn*	240.00	*300.00*
		Set, ovptd. "SPECIMEN"	300.00	

Government House — A9

"The Wharf" — A10

1912-16 **Ordinary Paper** **Wmk. 3**

61	A9	½p green & blk	3.25	12.00
62	A10	1p carmine & blk	5.75	2.00
a.		1p scarlet & black ('16)	14.50	*24.00*
63	A10	1½p orange & blk	4.25	7.75
64	A9	2p gray & black	5.50	2.00
65	A10	2½p ultra & blk	4.25	6.75
66	A9	3p vio & blk, *yel*	4.25	6.00
67	A10	8p dull vio & blk	8.50	60.00
68	A9	1sh black, *green*	11.00	42.50
69	A10	2sh ultra & blk, *bl*	47.50	*95.00*
70	A10	3sh violet & blk	67.50	*150.00*
		Nos. 61-70 (10)	161.75	*384.00*
		Set, ovptd. "SPECIMEN"	360.00	

See Nos. 75-77.

A11

A12

Die I

For description of dies I and II see front section of the Catalogue.

1912

Chalky Paper

71	A11	4p black & red, *yel*	14.50	*30.00*
72	A11	6p dull vio & red vio	4.75	*6.00*
		Set, ovptd. "SPECIMEN"	110.00	

1913

Ordinary Paper

73	A12	4p black & red, *yel*	12.00	3.25
74	A12	6p dull vio & red vio	16.00	*32.50*
		Set, ovptd. "SPECIMEN"	110.00	

1922 **Wmk. 4**

75	A10	1p green	2.10	*35.00*
76	A10	1½p rose red	12.00	*35.00*
77	A9	3p ultra	22.50	*72.50*
		Nos. 75-77 (3)	36.60	*142.50*
		Set, ovptd. "SPECIMEN"	140.00	

Badge of the Colony — A13

1922-27 **Wmk. 4**

Chalky Paper

79	A13	½p black & gray	2.75	3.00
80	A13	1p grn & blk	3.00	2.00
81	A13	1½p rose red	3.25	*15.00*
82	A13	2p pale gray & gray	4.50	2.40
83	A13	3p ultra	2.40	*4.75*
84	A13	5p red & grn, *emer*	3.50	*6.75*
85	A13	6p red vio & blk	5.50	*9.75*
86	A13	8p violet & blk	4.50	*8.50*
87	A13	1sh dk brn & blk	7.75	*11.00*
88	A13	1sh6p grn & blk, *emer*	18.00	*55.00*
89	A13	2sh ultra & vio, *bl*	21.00	*50.00*
90	A13	2sh6p car & blk, *yel*	17.00	*72.50*
91	A13	5sh grn & blk, *yel*	45.00	*90.00*
92	A13	7sh6p orange & blk	105.00	*150.00*
93	A13	10sh ol grn & blk	140.00	*200.00*
94	A13	15sh vio & blk, *bl*	1,025.	*1,800.*
		Nos. 79-93 (15)	383.15	*680.65*
		Set, ovptd. "SPECIMEN"	1,200.	

Nos. 88, 90, and 91 are on ordinary paper.

Wmk. 3

Chalky Paper

95	A13	4p black, *yel*	13.00	*7.25*
96	A13	1sh6p bl grn & blk, *grn*	26.50	*67.50*
97	A13	2sh6p car & blk, *yel*	30.00	*72.50*
98	A13	5sh grn & blk, *yel*	45.00	*105.00*
99	A13	£1 red vio & blk, *red*	475.00	*575.00*
		Nos. 95-99 (5)	589.50	*827.25*
		Set, ovptd. "SPECIMEN"	600.00	

Issue dates: ½p, 1½p, 2p, 3p, 4p, 8p, February, 1923; 5p, Nos. 88-91, 1927; others, June 1922.

Centenary Issue

Lot and Lot's Wife — A14

Plantation; Queen Victoria and Kings William IV, Edward VII, George V A15

Map of the Colony A16

Quay, Jamestown A17

View of James Valley — A18

View of Jamestown A19

View of Mundens A20

St. Helena — A21

View of High Knoll — A22

Badge of the Colony A23

Perf. 12

1934, Apr. 23 **Engr.** **Wmk. 4**

101	A14	½p dk vio & blk	1.25	*10.00*
102	A15	1p green & blk	.80	*1.00*
103	A16	1½p red & blk	3.00	*4.00*
104	A17	2p orange & blk	2.75	*1.50*
105	A18	3p blue & blk	1.75	*5.50*
106	A19	6p lt blue & blk	4.00	*3.75*
107	A20	1sh dk brn & blk	8.00	*22.50*
108	A21	2sh6p car & blk	42.50	*57.50*
109	A22	5sh choc & blk	92.50	*95.00*
110	A23	10sh red vio & black	275.00	*300.00*
		Nos. 101-110 (10)	431.55	*500.75*
		Set, never hinged	675.00	
		Set, ovptd. "SPECIMEN"	450.00	

Common Design Types

For description of dies I and II see "Dies of British Colonial Stamps" in Table of Contents.

Silver Jubilee Issue

Common Design Type

1935, May 6 ***Perf. 13½x14***

111	CD301	1½p car & dk blue	.75	*5.75*
112	CD301	2p gray blk & ultra	1.50	1.00
113	CD301	6p indigo & grn	7.00	3.50
114	CD301	1sh brt vio & ind	10.00	*15.00*
		Nos. 111-114 (4)	19.25	*25.25*
		Set, never hinged	37.50	

Coronation Issue

Common Design Type

1937, May 19

115	CD302	1p deep green	.40	.75
116	CD302	2p deep orange	.35	.50
117	CD302	3p bright ultra	.50	.50
		Nos. 115-117 (3)	1.25	1.75
		Set, never hinged	2.00	

Badge of the Colony — A24

1938-40 ***Perf. 12½***

118	A24	½p purple	.20	.75
119	A24	1p dp green	5.00	2.40
119A	A24	1p org yel ('40)	.20	.30
120	A24	1½p carmine	.20	.40
121	A24	2p orange	.20	.20
122	A24	3p ultra	45.00	20.00
122A	A24	3p gray ('40)	.20	.30
122B	A24	4p ultra ('40)	1.10	.85
123	A24	6p gray blue	1.10	1.25
123A	A24	8p olive ('40)	1.75	1.00
124	A24	1sh sepia	1.10	.35
125	A24	2sh6p deep claret	9.00	6.75
126	A24	5sh brown	10.00	12.50
127	A24	10sh violet	10.00	*18.00*
		Nos. 118-127 (14)	85.05	65.05
		Set, never hinged	160.00	

Issue dates: May 12, 1938, July 8, 1940.

See Nos. 136-138.

Catalogue values for unused stamps in this section, from this point to the end of the section, are for Never Hinged items.

Peace Issue

Common Design Type

Perf. 13½x14

1946, Oct. 21 **Wmk. 4** **Engr.**

128	CD303	2p deep orange	.30	.30
129	CD303	4p deep blue	.40	.30

Silver Wedding Issue

Common Design Types

1948, Oct. 20 **Photo.** ***Perf. 14x14½***

130	CD304	3p black	.30	.30

Engr.; Name Typo.

Perf. 11½x11

131	CD305	10sh blue violet	26.00	*37.50*

UPU Issue

Common Design Types

Engr.; Name Typo. on 4p, 6p

1949, Oct. 10 ***Perf. 13½, 11x11½***

132	CD306	3p rose carmine	.25	1.00
133	CD307	4p indigo	3.25	1.50
134	CD308	6p olive	.50	*1.75*
135	CD309	1sh slate	.40	*1.25*
		Nos. 132-135 (4)	4.40	5.50

George VI Type of 1938

1949, Nov. 1 **Engr.** ***Perf. 12½***

Center in Black

136	A24	1p blue green	1.00	1.50
137	A24	1½p carmine rose	1.00	1.50
138	A24	2p carmine	1.00	1.50
		Nos. 136-138 (3)	3.00	4.50

WAR TAX STAMPS

No. 62a Surcharged

1916 **Wmk. 3** ***Perf. 14***

MR1	A10	1p + 1p scarlet & blk	1.75	3.50
a.		Double surcharge		*8,500.*

No. 62 Surcharged

1919

MR2	A10	1p + 1p carmine & blk	1.50	4.75

ST. KITTS-NEVIS

sānt 'kits-'nē-vəs

LOCATION — West Indies southeast of Puerto Rico
GOVT. — Associated State in British Commonwealth
AREA — 153 sq. mi.
POP. — 48,000, excluding Anguilla (est. 1976)
CAPITAL — Basseterre, St. Kitts

A presidency of the Leeward Islands colony.

See "St. Christopher" for stamps used in St. Kitts before 1890. From 1890 until 1903, stamps of the Leeward Islands were used. From 1903 until 1956, stamps of St. Kitts-Nevis and Leeward Islands were used concurrently.

12 Pence = 1 Shilling
20 Shillings = 1 Pound
100 Cents = 1 Dollar (1951)

Catalogue values for unused stamps in this country are for Never Hinged items, beginning with Scott 91 in the regular postage section.

Columbus Looking for Land — A1

Medicinal Spring — A2

Wmk. Crown and C A (2)

1903 Typo. Perf. 14

1	A1	½p grn & vio	2.00	.80
2	A2	1p car & black	5.25	.25
3	A1	2p brn & vio	2.75	12.00
4	A1	2½p ultra & black	19.00	4.75
5	A2	3p org & green	16.50	32.50
6	A1	6p red vio & blk	5.25	42.50
7	A1	1sh org & grn	7.25	12.00
8	A2	2sh blk & grn	13.50	22.50
9	A1	2sh6p violet & blk	20.00	47.50
10	A2	5sh ol grn & gray vio	60.00	60.00
		Nos. 1-10 (10)	151.50	234.80
		Set, ovptd. "SPECIMEN"	140.00	

1905-18 Wmk. 3

11	A1	½p green & violet	8.25	6.00
12	A1	½p green ('07)	1.10	.65
a.		½p dull blue green ('16)	.55	2.00
13	A2	1p carmine & blk	2.50	.30
14	A2	1p carmine ('07)	2.40	.25
a.		1p scarlet ('16)	.90	.25
15	A1	2p brn & vio, ordinary paper	11.00	9.00
a.		Chalky paper	7.25	9.00
16	A1	2½p ultra & blk	16.00	3.50
17	A1	2½p ultra	2.75	.60
18	A2	3p org & grn, chalky paper	3.00	3.00
a.		Ordinary paper	11.00	10.00
19	A1	6p red violet & gray blk ('16)	6.75	27.50
a.		6p purple & gray, chalky paper ('08)	19.00	27.50
b.		6p dp vio & gray blk, ordinary paper	25.00	52.50
20	A1	1sh org & grn, chalky paper ('09)	4.00	32.50
a.		Ordinary paper ('09)	27.50	47.50
21	A2	5sh ol grn & gray vio ('18)	35.00	90.00
		Nos. 11-21 (11)	92.75	173.30

Nos. 13, 19a and 21 are on chalky paper only and Nos. 15, 18 and 20 are on both ordinary and chalky paper.

For stamp and type overprinted see #MR1-MR2.

King George V — A3

A4

1920-22

Ordinary Paper

24	A3	½p green	4.25	6.00
25	A4	1p carmine	2.50	6.50
26	A3	1½p orange	1.40	2.00
27	A4	2p gray	3.25	4.25
28	A3	2½p ultramarine	2.50	10.00
a.		"A" missing from watermark	450.00	

Chalky Paper

29	A4	3p vio & dull vio, yel	2.00	12.00
30	A3	6p red vio & dull vio	4.00	12.00
31	A4	1sh blk, gray grn	4.00	4.50
32	A3	2sh ultra & dull vio, bl	16.00	27.50
33	A4	2sh 6p red & blk, bl	5.50	35.00
34	A3	5sh red & grn, yel	5.50	45.00
35	A4	10sh red & grn, grn	13.50	52.50
36	A3	£1 blk & vio, red ('22)	250.00	325.00
		Nos. 24-36 (13)	314.40	542.25
		Set, ovptd. "SPECIMEN"	360.00	

1921-29 Wmk. 4

Ordinary Paper

37	A3	½p yel green	1.60	.90
a.		½p blue green	2.50	1.60
38	A4	1p rose red	.75	.25
39	A4	1p dp violet ('22)	5.50	1.10
a.		1p pale violet ('29)	7.75	1.75
40	A3	1½p rose red ('25)	3.00	3.00
41	A3	1½p fawn ('28)	1.10	.35
42	A4	2p gray	.65	.65
43	A3	2½p pale bright blue ('22)	3.25	2.50
44	A3	2½p brown ('22)	2.50	10.00

Chalky Paper

43a	A3	2½p ultra ('27)	1.75	2.00
45	A4	3p ultra ('22)	1.10	4.75
46	A4	3p vio & dull vio, yel	.85	5.00
47	A3	6p red vio & dull vio ('24)	5.50	6.75
48	A4	1sh black, grn ('29)	4.25	7.25
49	A3	2sh ultra & vio, bl ('22)	8.75	25.00
50	A4	2sh6p red & blk, bl ('27)	17.00	32.50
51	A3	5sh red & grn, yel ('29)	45.00	77.50
		Nos. 37-51 (16)	102.55	179.50

No. 43 exists on ordinary and chalky paper.

Caravel in Old Road Bay — A5

1923 Wmk. 4

52	A5	½p green & blk	2.50	7.75
53	A5	1p violet & blk	5.00	1.60
54	A5	1½p carmine & blk	5.00	11.00
55	A5	2p dk gray & blk	4.25	1.60
56	A5	2½p brown & blk	6.50	35.00
57	A5	3p ultra & blk	4.00	16.00
58	A5	6p red vio & blk	10.50	35.00
59	A5	1sh ol grn & blk	15.00	35.00
60	A5	2sh ultra & blk, bl	50.00	72.50
61	A5	2sh6p red & blk, blue	52.50	87.50
62	A5	10sh red & blk, emer	300.00	475.00

Wmk. 3

63	A5	5sh red & blk, yel	87.50	200.00
64	A5	£1 vio & blk, red	850.00	1,650.
		Nos. 52-63 (12)	542.75	977.95
		Set, ovptd. "SPECIMEN"	775.00	

Tercentenary of the founding of the colony of St. Kitts (or St. Christopher).

Common Design Types pictured following the introduction.

Silver Jubilee Issue
Common Design Type
Inscribed "St. Christopher and Nevis"

Perf. 11x12

1935, May 6 Engr. Wmk. 4

72	CD301	1p car & dk blue	1.10	.75
73	CD301	1½p gray blk & ultra	.85	.85
74	CD301	2½p ultra & brown	1.10	.90
75	CD301	1sh brn vio & ind	6.00	16.00
		Nos. 72-75 (4)	9.05	18.50
		Set, never hinged	18.50	
		Set, ovptd. "SPECIMEN"	105.00	

Coronation Issue
Common Design Type
Inscribed "St. Christopher and Nevis"

1937, May 12 Perf. 13½x14

76	CD302	1p carmine	.35	.30
77	CD302	1½p brown	.45	.20
78	CD302	2½p bright ultra	.65	1.10
		Nos. 76-78 (3)	1.45	1.60
		Set, never hinged	2.50	
		Set, ovptd. "SPECIMEN"	82.50	

George VI A6

Medicinal Spring A7

Columbus Looking for Land — A8

Map Showing Anguilla A9

Perf. 13½x14 (A6, A9), 14 (A7, A8)

1938-48 Typo.

79	A6	½p green	.20	.20
80	A6	1p carmine	1.00	.55
81	A6	1½p orange	.20	.30
82	A7	2p gray & car	1.00	1.40
83	A6	2½p ultra	.75	.35
84	A7	3p car & pale lilac	20.00	4.25
85	A8	6p rose lil & dull grn	3.00	1.60
86	A7	1sh green & gray blk	2.75	1.00
87	A7	2sh6p car & gray blk	7.50	4.25
88	A8	5sh car & dull grn	14.50	13.00

Typo., Center Litho.

Chalky Paper

89	A9	10sh brt ultra & blk	13.50	21.00
90	A9	£1 brown & blk	13.50	25.00
		Nos. 79-90 (12)	77.90	72.90
		Set, never hinged	120.00	
		Set, ovptd. "SPECIMEN"	225.00	

Issued: ½, 1, 1½, 2½p, 8/15/38; 2p, 1941; 3, 6p, 2sh6p, 5sh, 1942; 1sh, 1943; 10sh, £1, 9/1/48.

For types overprinted see Nos. 99-104.

1938, Aug. 15 Perf. 13x11½

82a	A7	2p	13.50	3.00
84a	A7	3p	11.00	4.50
85a	A8	6p	3.75	2.50
86a	A7	1sh	7.50	1.75
87a	A7	2sh6p	20.00	10.00
88a	A8	5sh	37.50	20.00
		Nos. 82a-88a (6)	93.25	41.75

Catalogue values for unused stamps in this section, from this point to the end of the section, are for Never Hinged items.

Peace Issue
Common Design Type
Inscribed "St. Kitts-Nevis"

1946, Nov. 1 Engr. Perf. 13½x14

91	CD303	1½p deep orange	.20	.20
92	CD303	3p carmine	.20	.20
		Set, perf "SPECIMEN"	82.50	

Silver Wedding Issue
Common Design Types
Inscribed: "St. Kitts-Nevis"

1949, Jan. 3 Photo. Perf. 14x14½

93	CD304	2½p bright ultra	.20	.50

Engraved; Name Typographed

Perf. 11½x11

94	CD305	5sh rose carmine	7.25	4.75

UPU Issue
Common Design Types
Inscribed: "St. Kitt's-Nevis"

Engr.; Name Typo. on 3p, 6p

1949, Oct. 10 Perf. 13½, 11x11½

95	CD306	2½p ultra	.20	.35
96	CD307	3p deep carmine	1.60	2.00
97	CD308	6p red lilac	.20	1.10
98	CD309	1sh blue green	.20	.45
		Nos. 95-98 (4)	2.20	3.90

Types of 1938 Overprinted in Black or Carmine:

On A6

On A7-A8

Perf. 13½x14, 13x12½

1950, Nov. 10 Wmk. 4

99	A6	1p carmine	.20	.20
100	A6	1½p orange	.20	.55
a.		Wmk. 4a (error)	1,100.	
101	A6	2½p ultra	.20	.20
102	A7	3p car & pale lilac	.20	.85
103	A8	6p rose lil & dl grn	.20	.20
104	A7	1sh grn & gray blk (C)	.75	.30
		Nos. 99-104 (6)	1.75	2.30

300th anniv. of the settlement of Anguilla.

University Issue
Common Design Types
Inscribed: "St. Kitts-Nevis"

Perf. 14x14½

1951, Feb. 16 Engr. Wmk. 4

105	CD310	3c org yel & gray blk	.30	.20
106	CD311	12c red violet & aqua	.30	1.25

St. Christopher-Nevis-Anguilla

Bath House and Spa, Nevis — A10

Map — A11

Designs: 2c, Warner Park, St. Kitts. 4c, Brimstone Hill, St. Kitts. 5c, Nevis. 6c, Pinney's Beach, Nevis. 12c, Sir Thomas Warner's Tomb. 24c, Old Road Bay, St. Kitts. 48c, Picking Cotton. 60c, Treasury, St. Kitts. $1.20, Salt Pond, Anguilla. $4.80, Sugar Mill, St. Kitts.

1952, June 14 Perf. 12½

107	A10	1c ocher & dp grn	.20	1.25
108	A10	2c emerald	1.10	1.00
109	A11	3c purple & red	.30	1.25
110	A10	4c red	.20	.20
111	A10	5c gray & ultra	.30	.20
112	A10	6c deep ultra	.30	.20
113	A11	12c redsh brn & dp blue	1.25	.20
114	A10	24c car & gray blk	.30	.20

No.	Type	Description	Unused	Used
115	A10	48c vio brn & ol bister	2.25	2.75
116	A10	60c dp grn & och	2.10	3.00
117	A10	$1.20 dp ultra & dp green	7.25	3.00
118	A10	$4.80 car & emer	13.25	20.00
		Nos. 107-118 (12)	28.80	33.25

WAR TAX STAMPS

No. 12 Overprinted

1916 Wmk. 3 *Perf. 14*

No.	Type	Description	Unused	Used
MR1	A1	½p green	1.10	.55
		Overprinted "SPECIMEN"	45.00	

Type of 1905-18 Issue Overprinted

1918

No.	Type	Description	Unused	Used
MR2	A1	1½p orange	.90	.90
		Overprinted "SPECIMEN"	50.00	

ST. LUCIA

sānt 'lü-shə

LOCATION — Island in the West Indies, one of the Windward group
GOVT. — British Colony
AREA — 240 sq. mi.
POP. — 126,800 (est. 1984)
CAPITAL — Castries

12 Pence = 1 Shilling
100 Cents = 1 Dollar (1949)

Catalogue values for unused stamps in this country are for Never Hinged items, beginning with Scott 127 in the regular postage section, Scott J3 in the postage due section.

Watermark

Wmk. 5 — Small Star

PRE-STAMP POSTAL MARKINGS

Crowned Circle handstamp type I is pictured in the Crowned Circle Handstamps and Great Britain Used Abroad section.

Castries

1844

No.	Type	Description	Value
A1	I	"St. Lucia" crowned circle handstamp in red, on cover	1,000.

The handstamp was used, in black, as a provisional in 1904, due to a stamp shortage.

STAMPS OF GREAT BRITAIN USED IN ST. LUCIA

Numeral cancellation type A is pictured in the Crowned Circle Handstamps and Great Britain Used Abroad section.

1858-60

A11 (Castries)

No.	Type	Description	Value
A2	A	1p rose red (#20)	1,100.
A3	A	2p blue (#29, P7, 8)	—
A4	A	4p rose (#26)	475.00
A5	A	6p lilac (#27)	250.00
A6	A	1sh green (#28)	1,550.

Issued under British Administration

Values for unused stamps are for examples with original gum as defined in the catalogue introduction. Very fine examples of Nos. 1-26 will have perforations touching the design on at least one side due to the narrow spacing of the stamps on the plates. Stamps with perfs clear of the framelines on all four sides are very scarce and will command higher prices.

Queen Victoria — A1

Perf. 14 to 16

1860, Dec. 18 Engr. Wmk. 5

No.	Type	Description	Unused	Used
1	A1	(1p) rose red	110.00	75.00
a.		Double impression	2,200.	
b.		Horiz. pair, imperf vert.	—	
2	A1	(4p) deep blue	250.00	175.00
a.		Horiz. pair, imperf vert.	—	
b.		4p deep blue	—	—
3	A1	(6p) green	325.00	225.00
a.		Horiz. pair, imperf vert.	—	
b.		6p deep green	400.00	275.00
		Nos. 1-3 (3)	685.00	475.00

For types overprinted see #15, 17, 19-26.

1863 Wmk. 1 *Perf. 12½*

No.	Type	Description	Unused	Used
4	A1	(1p) lake	82.50	100.00
a.		(1p) brownish lake	100.00	100.00
5	A1	(4p) slate blue	125.00	140.00
6	A1	(6p) emerald	190.00	190.00
a.		Watermark inverted	—	
		Nos. 4-6 (3)	397.50	430.00

Nos. 4-6 exist imperforate on stamp paper, from proof sheets.

1864

No.	Type	Description	Unused	Used
7	A1	(1p) black	25.00	14.00
a.		(1p) deep black	23.00	12.00
8	A1	(4p) yellow	190.00	42.50
a.		(4p) olive yellow	425.00	100.00
b.		(4p) lemon yellow	1,750.	
c.		(4p) chrome yellow	225.00	42.50
d.		Watermark inverted	250.00	50.00
9	A1	(6p) violet	125.00	35.00
a.		(6p) lilac	210.00	32.50
b.		(6p) deep lilac	160.00	37.50
10	A1	(1sh) red orange	250.00	30.00
a.		(1sh) orange	275.00	32.50
b.		(1sh) brown orange	360.00	32.50
c.		Horiz. pair, imperf between	—	
		Nos. 7-10 (4)	590.00	121.50

Nos. 7-10 exist imperforate on stamp paper, from proof sheets.

Perf. 14

No.	Type	Description	Unused	Used
11	A1	(1p) deep black	30.00	20.00
a.		Horiz. pair, imperf between	—	
12	A1	(4p) yellow	125.00	22.50
a.		(4p) olive yellow	325.00	105.00
13	A1	(6p) pale lilac	115.00	22.50
a.		(6p) deep lilac	125.00	42.50
b.		(6p) violet	275.00	77.50
14	A1	(1sh) deep orange	160.00	19.00
a.		(1sh) orange	250.00	25.00
		Nos. 11-14 (4)	430.00	84.00

Type of 1860 Surcharged in Black or Red:

a

b

1881

No.	Type	Description	Unused	Used
15	A1(a)	½p green	77.50	100.00
17	A1(b)	2½p scarlet	37.50	25.00

1883-84 **Wmk. Crown and CA (2)**

No.	Type	Description	Unused	Used
19	A1(a)	½p green	22.50	32.50
20	A1(a)	1p black (R)	30.00	12.00
a.		Half used as ½p on cover		—
21	A1(a)	4p yellow	325.00	22.50
22	A1(a)	6p violet	32.50	32.50
23	A1(a)	1sh orange	310.00	190.00
		Nos. 19-23 (5)	720.00	289.50

1884 *Perf. 12*

No.	Type	Description	Unused	Used
24	A1(a)	4p yellow	300.00	32.50

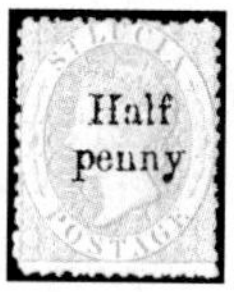

1885 Wmk. 1 *Perf. 12½*

No.	Type	Description	Unused	Used
25	A1	½p emerald	77.50	
26	A1	6p slate blue	1,250.	

Nos. 25 and 26 were prepared for use but not issued.

A5

Die A

For explanation of dies A and B see "Dies of British Colonial Stamps..." in the catalogue Table of Contents.

1883-98 Typo. Wmk. 2 *Perf. 14*

No.	Type	Description	Unused	Used
27a	A5	½p green	10.00	5.50
28	A5	1p rose	47.50	13.00
29a	A5	1p lilac ('86)	9.00	7.25
b.		Imperf., pair	900.00	
31a	A5	2½p ultra	50.00	2.40
32a	A5	3p lilac & grn ('86)	140.00	20.00
33a	A5	4p brown ('85)	37.50	1.50
b.		Imperf., pair	1,050.	
34	A5	6p violet ('86)	300.00	240.00
a.		Imperf., pair	2,000.	
35	A5	6p lilac & blue ('87)	5.00	12.00
36	A5	1sh brn org ('85)	450.00	175.00
37a	A5	1sh lil & red ('87)	125.00	32.50
		Nos. 27a-37a (10)	1,174.	509.15

Die B

No.	Type	Description	Unused	Used
27	A5	½p green ('91)	3.00	1.10
29	A5	1p lilac ('91)	4.75	.35
30	A5	2p ultra & brn org ('98)	4.50	1.25
31	A5	2½p ultra ('91)	6.00	1.25
32	A5	3p lilac & grn ('91)	5.75	6.50
33	A5	4p brown ('93)	3.50	2.75
35a	A5	6p lilac & blue ('91)	29.00	29.00
37	A5	1sh lil & red ('91)	8.50	6.00
38	A5	5sh lil & org ('91)	60.00	150.00
39	A5	10sh lil & blk ('91)	110.00	160.00
		Nos. 27-39 (10)	235.00	358.20

Nos. 32, 32a, 35a and 33a Surcharged in Black:

No. 40

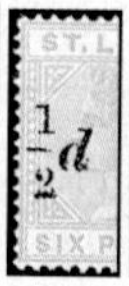

No. 41

No. 42

Die A

1892

No.	Type	Description	Unused	Used
40a	A5	½p on 3p lil & grn	425.00	180.00
e.		Small "A" in "HALF"	425.00	180.00
f.		Small "O" in "ONE"	425.00	180.00
41	A5	½p on half of 6p lilac & blue	29.00	4.00
a.		Slanting serif	240.00	150.00
c.		Without the bar of "½"	300.00	160.00
d.		"2" of "½" omitted	575.00	600.00
e.		Surcharged sideways	1,550.	
f.		Double surcharge	725.00	725.00
g.		Triple surcharge	1,325.	
h.		Figure "1" used as fraction bar	575.00	325.00
42	A5	1p on 4p brown	6.00	4.25
b.		Double surcharge	275.00	
c.		Inverted surcharge	975.00	850.00
d.		Thick diagonal stroke in first "N"	27.50	24.00
e.		Thick diagonal stroke in second "N"	27.50	24.00

Die B

No.	Type	Description	Unused	Used
40	A5	½p on 3p lil & grn	95.00	29.00
b.		Double surcharge	950.00	725.00
c.		Inverted surcharge	2,100.	725.00
d.		Triple surcharge, one on back		1,500.
g.		Small "O" in "ONE"	225.00	110.00
h.		Small "A" in "HALF"	210.00	110.00
i.		"O" over "H" shift	210.00	110.00

Edward VII
A9

The Pitons
A10

Numerals of 3p, 6p, 1sh and 5sh of type A9 are in color on plain tablet.

1902-03 **Typo.**

No.	Type	Description	Unused	Used
43	A9	½p violet & green	3.25	1.75
44	A9	1p violet & car rose	6.00	.90
46	A9	2½p violet & ultra	29.00	6.50
47	A9	3p violet & yellow	7.25	10.00
48	A9	1sh green & black	12.00	35.00
		Nos. 43-48 (5)	57.50	54.15
		Set, ovptd. "SPECIMEN"	120.00	

Wmk. 1 sideways

1902, Dec. 16 **Engr.**

No.	Type	Description	Unused	Used
49	A10	2p brown & green	10.50	2.50
		Overprinted "SPECIMEN"	67.50	

Fourth centenary of the discovery of the island by Columbus.

1904-05 Typo. Wmk. 3

No.	Type	Description	Unused	Used
50	A9	½p violet & green	5.00	.65
51	A9	1p violet & car rose	6.75	1.40
52	A9	2½p violet & ultra	20.00	1.40
53	A9	3p violet & yellow	8.25	3.25
54	A9	6p vio & dp vio ('05)	18.00	21.00
55	A9	1sh green & blk ('05)	35.00	29.00
56	A9	5sh green & car ('05)	77.50	175.00
		Nos. 50-56 (7)	170.50	231.70

#50, 51, 52, 54 are on both ordinary and chalky paper. #55 is on chalky paper only.

1907-10

No.	Type	Description	Unused	Used
57	A9	½p green	2.00	1.10
58	A9	1p carmine	4.75	.35
59	A9	2½p ultra	4.25	2.00

Chalky Paper

No.	Type	Description	Unused	Used
60	A9	3p violet, *yel* ('09)	3.25	14.50
61	A9	6p violet & red violet	9.25	30.00
a.		6p violet & dull vio ('10)	65.00	82.50
62	A9	1sh black, *grn* ('09)	5.25	8.75
63	A9	5sh green & red, *yel*	65.00	77.50
		Nos. 57-63 (7)	93.75	134.20
		Set, ovptd. "SPECIMEN"	275.00	

King George V
A11 A12

Numerals of 3p, 6p, 1sh and 5sh of type A11 are in color on plain tablet.

For description of dies I and II see "Dies of British Colonial Stamps" in Table of Contents.

Die I

1912-19

Ordinary Paper

No.	Type	Description	Unused	Used
64	A11	½p deep green	.75	.50
65	A11	1p scarlet	3.75	.20
a.		1p carmine	2.00	.20
66	A12	2p gray ('13)	1.60	4.50
67	A11	2½p ultra	2.50	3.00

Chalky Paper

Numeral on White Tablet

No.	Type	Description	Unused	Used
68	A11	3p violet, *yel*	1.40	2.50
a.		Die II	11.00	42.50
69	A11	6p vio & red vio	2.25	12.00
70	A11	1sh black, *green*	3.50	5.25
a.		1sh black, *bl grn, ol back*	8.25	8.75
71	A11	1sh fawn	10.50	47.50
72	A11	5sh green & red, *yel*	25.00	77.50
		Nos. 64-72 (9)	51.25	152.95

A13

A14

1913-14

Chalky Paper

73 A13 4p scar & blk, *yel* 1.00 *2.25*
74 A14 2sh6p black & red, *bl* 24.00 *40.00*
#62-74, ovptd. "SPECIMEN" 210.00

Surface-colored Paper

75 A13 4p scarlet & blk, *yel* .75 *1.60*
Overprinted "SPECIMEN" 28.00

Die II

1921-24 **Wmk. 4**

Ordinary Paper

76 A11 ½p green .80 .50
77 A11 1p carmine 9.75 *15.00*
78 A11 1p dk brn ('22) 1.50 .20
79 A13 1½p rose red ('22) .75 *2.75*
80 A12 2p gray .75 .20
81 A11 2½p ultra 4.00 *2.75*
82 A11 2½p orange ('24) 11.50 *52.50*
83 A11 3p dull blue ('24) 2.75 *11.50*
a. 3p bright blue ('22) 15.25 16.50

Chalky Paper

84 A11 3p violet, *yel* 1.25 *12.50*
85 A13 4p scar & blk, *yel* ('24) 1.25 *2.75*
86 A11 6p vio & red vio 2.00 *5.00*
87 A11 1sh fawn 2.50 *3.50*
88 A14 2sh6p blk & red, *bl* ('24) 19.00 *27.50*
89 A11 5sh grn & red, *yel* 50.00 *77.50*
Nos. 76-89 (14) 107.80 *214.15*

Common Design Types
For description of dies I and II see "Dies of British Colonial Stamps" in Table of Contents.

Silver Jubilee Issue

Common Design Type

1935, May 6 Engr. *Perf. 13½x14*

91 CD301 ½p green & blk .20 1.00
92 CD301 2p gray blk & ultra .50 1.00
93 CD301 2½p blue & brn 1.00 1.25
94 CD301 1sh brt vio & ind 7.75 *9.25*
Nos. 91-94 (4) 9.45 *12.50*
Set, never hinged 19.00
Set, perforated "SPECIMEN" 90.00

Port Castries A15

Columbus Square, Castries A16

Ventine Falls A17

Soldiers' Monument A19

Fort Rodney, Pigeon Island A18

Government House A20

Seal of the Colony A21

1936, Mar. 1 ***Perf. 14***

Center in Black

95 A15 ½p light green .30 .50
a. Perf. 13x12 2.50 *13.50*
96 A16 1p dark brown .40 .20
a. Perf. 13x12 3.00 2.75
97 A17 1½p carmine .60 .30
a. Perf. 12x13 7.75 2.50
98 A15 2p gray .55 .20
99 A16 2½p blue .55 .20
100 A17 3p dull green 1.40 .75
101 A15 4p brown .55 *1.00*
102 A16 6p orange 1.00 1.00
103 A18 1sh light blue, perf. 13x12 1.25 *2.50*
104 A19 2sh6p ultra 9.50 *14.50*
105 A20 5sh violet 10.00 *21.00*
106 A21 10sh car rose, perf. 13x12 52.50 *72.50*
Nos. 95-106 (12) 78.60 *114.65*
Set, never hinged 145.00
Set, perforated "SPECIMEN" 190.00

Nos. 95a, 96a and 97a are coils.
Issue date: Nos. 95a, 96a, Apr. 8.

Coronation Issue

Common Design Type

1937, May 12 ***Perf. 11x11½***

107 CD302 1p dark purple .30 .35
108 CD302 1½p dark carmine .55 .20
109 CD302 2½p deep ultra .55 1.25
Nos. 107-109 (3) 1.40 1.80
Set, never hinged 2.50
Set, perforated "SPECIMEN" 75.00

King George VI — A22

Columbus Square, Castries A23

Government House A24

The Pitons A25

Loading Bananas A26

Arms of the Colony — A27

Perf. 12½ (#110-111, 1½p-3½p, 8p, 3sh, 5sh, £1), 12 (6p, 1sh, 2sh, 10sh)

1938-48

110 A22 ½p green ('43) .20 .20
a. Perf. 14½x14 1.40 .20
111 A22 1p deep violet .20 .20
a. Perf. 14½x14 1.60 .75
112 A22 1p red, Perf. 14½x14 ('47) .20 .20
a. Perf. 12½ .40 .20
113 A22 1½p carmine ('43) .70 1.00
a. Perf. 14½x14 1.25 .40
114 A22 2p gray ('43) .20 .20
a. Perf. 14½x14 2.00 *1.50*
115 A22 2½p ultra ('43) .20 .20
a. Perf. 14½x14 3.00 .20
116 A22 2½p violet ('47) .65 .20
117 A22 3p red org ('43) .20 .20
a. Perf. 14½x14 .80 .20
118 A22 3½p brt ultra ('47) .60 .20
119 A23 6p magenta ('48) 7.00 1.75
a. Perf. 13½ 2.00 .35
120 A22 8p choc ('46) 2.50 .30
121 A24 1sh lt brn ('48) .50 .20
a. Perf. 13½ .40 .30
122 A25 2sh red vio & sl bl 2.25 1.25
123 A22 3sh brt red vio ('46) 5.75 1.75
124 A26 5sh rose vio & blk 8.50 8.25
125 A27 10sh black, *yel* 5.75 *9.25*
126 A22 £1 sepia ('46) 7.50 8.25
Nos. 110-126 (17) 42.90 33.60
Set, never hinged 57.50
Set, perforated "SPECIMEN" 375.00

See Nos. 135-148.

Catalogue values for unused stamps in this section, from this point to the end of the section, are for Never Hinged items.

Peace Issue

Common Design Type

Perf. 13½x14

1946, Oct. 8 Wmk. 4 Engr.

127 CD303 1p lilac .20 .20
128 CD303 3½p deep blue .20 .20
Set, perforated "SPECIMEN" 70.00

Silver Wedding Issue

Common Design Types

1948, Nov. 26 Photo. *Perf. 14x14½*

129 CD304 1p scarlet .20 .20

Engraved; Name Typographed

Perf. 11½x11

130 CD305 £1 violet brown 15.00 35.00

UPU Issue

Common Design Types

Engr.; Name Typo. on 6c, 12c.

Perf. 13½, 11x11½

1949, Oct. 10 Wmk. 4

131 CD306 5c violet .20 .60
132 CD307 6c deep orange 1.60 2.00
133 CD308 12c red lilac .20 .20
134 CD309 24c blue green .30 .20
Nos. 131-134 (4) 2.30 3.00

Types of 1938

Values in Cents and Dollars

1949, Oct. 1 Engr. *Perf. 12½*

135 A22 1c green .25 .20
a. Perf. 14 2.50 .40
136 A22 2c rose lilac 1.00 .20
a. Perf. 14½x14 2.50 1.00
137 A22 3c red 1.00 *1.75*
138 A22 4c gray .75 .20
a. Perf. 14½x14 *8,250.*
139 A22 5c violet 1.00 .20
140 A22 6c red orange .75 *2.75*
141 A22 7c ultra 3.00 3.75
142 A22 12c rose lake 5.75 2.75
a. Perf. 14½x14 ('50) 525.00 410.00
143 A22 16c brown 3.50 .50

Perf. 11½

144 A27 24c Prus blue .50 .20
145 A27 48c olive green 1.60 1.25
146 A27 $1.20 purple 2.40 *8.25*
147 A27 $2.40 blue green 3.50 *17.50*
148 A27 $4.80 dark car rose 9.25 18.00
Nos. 135-148 (14) 34.25 *57.50*

Nos. 144 to 148 are of a type similar to A27, but with the denomination in the top corners and "St. Lucia" at the bottom.

For overprints see Nos. 152-155.

University Issue

Common Design Types

Perf. 14x14½

1951, Feb. 16 Wmk. 4

149 CD310 3c red & gray black .45 .50
150 CD311 12c brown carmine & blk .65 .50

Phoenix Rising from Burning Buildings — A28

Engr. & Typo.

1951, June 19 ***Perf. 13½x13***

151 A28 12c deep blue & carmine .25 1.00

Reconstruction of Castries.

Nos. 136, 138, 139 and 142 Overprinted in Black

1951, Sept. 25 ***Perf. 12½***

152 A22 2c rose lilac .20 .85
153 A22 4c gray .20 .60
154 A22 5c violet .20 .85
155 A22 12c rose lilac .75 .60
Nos. 152-155 (4) 1.35 2.90

Adoption of a new constitution for the Windward Islands, 1951.

POSTAGE DUE STAMPS

D1

D2

Type I — "No." 3mm wide (shown).
Type II — "No." 4mm wide.

Rough Perf. 12

1931 Unwmk. Typeset

J1 D1 1p blk, *gray bl*, type I 5.00 *15.00*
a. Type II 17.50 *40.00*
J2 D1 2p blk, *yel*, type I 12.50 *42.50*
a. Type II 35.00 *95.00*
b. Vertical pair, imperf. btwn. *5,250.*

The serial numbers are handstamped. Type II has round "o" and period. Type I has tall "o" and square period.

Catalogue values for unused stamps in this section, from this point to the end of the section, are for Never Hinged items.

1933-47 Typo. Wmk. 4 *Perf. 14*

J3 D2 1p black 5.00 *6.25*
J4 D2 2p black 20.00 *8.25*
J5 D2 4p black ('47) 5.75 *42.50*
J6 D2 8p black ('47) 5.75 *52.50*
Nos. J3-J6 (4) 36.50 *109.50*
Set, perforated "SPECIMEN" 140.00

Issue date: June 28, 1947.

Values in Cents

1949, Oct. 1

J7 D2	2c black	.20	*8.75*
J8 D2	4c black	.50	*11.00*
J9 D2	8c black	3.00	*40.00*
J10 D2	16c black	4.75	*52.50*
	Nos. J7-J10 (4)	8.45	*112.25*

Values are for examples on chalky paper, which were issued in 1952. Regular paper examples are worth more.

Wmk. 4a (error)

J7a	D2	2c	32.50
J8a	D2	4c	47.50
J9a	D2	8c	350.00
J10a	D2	16c	475.00
		Nos. J7a-J10a (4)	905.00

WAR TAX STAMPS

No. 65 Overprinted

1916 Wmk. 3 *Perf. 14*

MR1 A11 1p scarlet		10.50	10.50
a.	Double overprint	450.00	*450.00*
b.	1p carmine	60.00	37.50

Overprinted

MR2 A11 1p scarlet		1.25	.35
a.	Overprinted "SPECIMEN"	42.50	

STE.-MARIE DE MADAGASCAR

sānt-mə-rē-də-ˌmad-ə-ˈgas-kər

LOCATION — An island off the east coast of Madagascar
GOVT. — French Possession
AREA — 64 sq. mi.
POP. — 8,000 (approx.)

In 1896 Ste.-Marie de Madagascar was attached to the colony of Madagascar for administrative purposes.

100 Centimes = 1 Franc

Navigation and Commerce — A1

1894 Unwmk. Typo. *Perf. 14x13½*
Name of Colony in Blue or Carmine

1 A1 1c black, *lil bl*		1.25	1.25
	Never hinged	2.00	
	On cover		125.00
2 A1 2c brown, *buff*		2.00	2.00
	Never hinged	3.25	
	On cover		125.00
3 A1 4c claret, *lavender*		4.00	4.00
	Never hinged	7.75	
	On cover		125.00
4 A1 5c green, *grnsh*		11.00	9.75
	Never hinged	21.00	
	On cover		70.00
5 A1 10c black, *lavender*		13.00	9.00
	Never hinged	24.00	
	On cover		70.00
6 A1 15c blue		35.00	30.00
	Never hinged	72.50	
	On cover		100.00
7 A1 20c red, *green*		27.50	21.00
	Never hinged	57.50	
	On cover		95.00
	On cover, single franking		160.00
8 A1 25c black, *rose*		21.00	18.00
	Never hinged	45.00	
	On cover		80.00
	On cover, single franking		140.00
9 A1 30c brown, *bister*		13.50	13.50
	Never hinged	27.50	
	On cover		80.00
	On cover, single franking		115.00
10 A1 40c red, *straw*		13.50	13.50
	Never hinged	27.50	
	On cover		90.00
	On cover, single franking		250.00
11 A1 50c carmine, *rose*		47.50	40.00
	Never hinged	100.00	
	On cover		250.00
	On cover, single franking		350.00
12 A1 75c violet, *org*		90.00	52.50
	Never hinged	180.00	
	On cover		250.00
	On cover, single franking		400.00
13 A1 1fr brnz grn, *straw*		47.50	35.00
	Never hinged	100.00	
	On cover		325.00
	On cover, single franking		525.00
	Nos. 1-13 (13)	326.75	249.50

Perf. 13½x14 stamps are counterfeits.

Covers: Values are for usages on Ste. Marie de Madagascar. These stamps were also used on Madagascar.

Values are for commercial covers paying correct rates. Philatelic covers sell for less.

These stamps were replaced by those of Madagascar.

ST. PIERRE & MIQUELON

sānt-ˈpiˌəˌr and ˈmik-ə-ˌlän

LOCATION — Two small groups of islands off the southern coast of Newfoundland
GOVT. — French Colony
AREA — 93 sq. mi.
POP. — 6,051 (est. 1984)
CAPITAL — St. Pierre

100 Centimes = 1 Franc

STAMPS OF FRENCH COLONIES GENERAL ISSUES USED IN ST. PIERRE & MIQUELON

Canceled SPM in Lozenze of Dots

On Eagle & Crown Type, #1-6

1859-65

A1 A1 1c ol grn, *pale bl* ('62)	400.00
On cover	—
A2 A1 5c yel grn, *grnsh* ('62)	390.00
On cover	—
A3 A1 10c bister, *yel*	175.00
On cover	1,750.
A4 A1 20c bl, *bluish* ('65)	190.00
On cover	2,050.
A5 A1 40c org, *yelsh*	140.00
On cover	1,750.
A6 A1 80c car rose, *pnksh* ('65)	100.00
On cover	450.00

On Ceres and Napoleon III Types, #7//15

1871-72

A7 A2 1c ol grn, *pale bl* ('72)	300.00
On cover	—
A10 A4 15c bis, *yelsh* ('72)	900.00
On cover	—
A12 A4 25c bl, *bluish* ('72)	575.00
On cover	*6,250.*
a. With circular date stamp	*625.00*
On cover	—
A13 A5 30c brn, *yelsh*	325.00
On cover	*5,250.*
A14 A4 40c org, *yelsh* (I)	100.00
On cover	950.00
a. With circular date stamp	*140.00*
On cover	—
A15 A5 80c rose, *pnksh*	325.00
On cover	*6,000.*

On Ceres Type, #16//23

1872-77

A16 A6 1c ol grn, *pale bl* ('73)	325.00
On cover	—
A19 A6 5c grn, *pale bl*	150.00
On cover	—
a. With circular date stamp	160.00
On cover	—
A20 A7 10c bis, *rose* ('76)	82.50
On cover	600.00
a. With circular date stamp	100.00
On cover	725.00
A22 A7 30c brn, *yelsh*	225.00
On cover	—
a. With circular date stamp	250.00
On cover	—
A23 A7 80c rose, *pnksh* ('73)	140.00
On cover	1,100.
a. With circular date stamp	150.00
On cover	—

Cancelled with Circular Date Stamps

On Peace & Commerce Types, #24//59

1877-78

Type I

A24 A8 1c grn, *grnsh*	400.00
On cover	—
A25 A8 4c grn, *grnsh*	400.00
On cover	—
A26 A8 30c brn, *yelsh* ('78)	225.00
On cover	—
A27 A8 40c ver, *straw*	125.00
On cover	—
A28 A8 75c rose, *rose* ('78)	300.00
On cover	—
A29 A8 1fr brnz grn, *straw*	300.00
On cover	—

Type II

A30 A8 2c grn, *grnsh*	375.00
On cover	—
A31 A8 5c grn, *grnsh*	125.00
On cover	—
A32 A8 10c grn, *grnsh*	160.00
On cover	—
A33 A8 15c gray, *grnsh*	190.00
On cover	290.00
A34 A8 20c red brn, *straw*	150.00
On cover	—
A35 A8 25c ultra *bluish*	250.00
On cover	—
A36 A8 35c vio blk, *org* ('78)	95.00
On cover	—

On Peace & Commerce Type, #38//45

1878-80

Type II

A38 A8 1c blk, *lil bl*	290.00
On cover	—
A40 A8 4c claret, *lav*	290.00
On cover	—
A41 A8 10c blk, *lav* ('79)	250.00
On cover	—
A42 A8 15c blue ('79)	82.50
On cover	—
A43 A8 20c red, *grn* ('79)	225.00
On cover	—
A45 A8 25c yel, *straw* ('80)	62.50
On cover	*500.00*

On Commerce Type, #46-59

1881-86

A46 A9 1c blk, *lil bl*	265.00
On cover	—
A47 A9 2c brn, *buff*	265.00
On cover	—
A48 A9 4c claret, *lav*	225.00
On cover	—
A49 A9 5c grn, *grnsh*	82.50
On cover	650.00
A50 A9 10c blk, *lavender*	100.00
On cover	825.00
A51 A9 15c blue	100.00
On cover	—
A52 A9 20c red, *yel grn*	150.00
On cover	1,350.
A53 A9 25c yel, *straw*	40.00
On cover	—
A54 A9 25c blk, *rose* ('86)	32.50
On cover	475.00
A55 A9 30c brn, *bis*	82.50
On cover	—
A56 A9 35c vio blk, *yel org*	140.00
On cover	—
a. 35c violet black, *yellow*	200.00
On cover	—
A57 A9 40c ver, *straw*	200.00
On cover	—
A58 A9 75c car, *rose*	100.00
On cover	—
A59 A9 1fr brnz grn, *straw*	160.00
On cover	—

Covers

Values are for commercial covers bearing correct frankings. Philatelic covers generally sell for less.

REGULAR ISSUES

Stamps of French Colonies Handstamp Surcharged in Black

1885 Unwmk. *Imperf.*

1 A8 05c on 40c ver, *straw*		125.00	55.00
	On cover		1,000.
a.	Surcharge "05" missing		200.00
b.	Surcharge "05" double	325.00	290.00
2 A8 10c on 40c ver, *straw*		32.50	27.50
	On cover		850.00
a.	"M" inverted	375.00	350.00
b.	Surcharge "10" double	160.00	140.00
c.	As "b," one inverted	750.00	
3 A8 15c on 40c ver, *straw*		37.50	27.50
	On cover		850.00
a.	Double surcharge	525.00	500.00
	Nos. 1-3 (3)	195.00	110.00

Nos. 2 and 3 exist with "SPM" 17mm wide instead of 15½mm.

Nos. 1-3 exist with surcharge inverted and with it doubled.

Handstamp Surcharged in Black

b

c

d

1885

4 A8 (b) 05c on 35c blk, *yel*		125.00	100.00
	On cover		950.00
a.	Double surcharge	625.00	
5 A8 (b) 05c on 75c car, *rose*		350.00	260.00
	On cover		1,100.
a.	Double surcharge	1,100.	
6 A8 (b) 05c on 1fr brnz grn, *straw*		27.50	27.50
	On cover		850.00
a.	Double surcharge	300.00	265.00
b.	"SPM" omitted		200.00
7 A8 (c) 25c on 1fr brnz grn, *straw*		*13,000.*	*2,750.*
	On cover		—
a.	"25" sideways		*3,750.*
b.	"25" reversed		*5,000.*
c.	Surcharge reversed		*4,500.*
8 A8 (d) 25c on 1fr brnz grn, *straw*		*2,500.*	*1,850.*
	On cover		—
a.	Surcharge sideways	*3,750.*	*2,500.*
b.	"SPM" reversed	4,500.	

Nos. 7 and 8 exist with surcharge inverted, and with it vertical. No. 7 exists with "S P M" above "25" (the handstamping was done in two steps).

1885 *Perf. 14x13½*

9 A9 (c) 5c on 2c brn, *buff*		*6,500.*	*2,400.*
	On cover		—
a.	Surcharge upright	*16,500.*	
10 A9 (d) 5c on 4c cl, *lav*		500.00	325.00
	On cover		—
a.	Surcharge inverted	1,100.	950.00
b.	"SPM" double	1,100.	950.00
11 A9 (b) 05c on 20c red, *grn*		37.50	37.50
	On cover		850.00
a.	Double surcharge	300.00	265.00
b.	"SPM" in larger letters	200.00	165.00

1886, Feb. Typo. *Imperf.*
Without Gum

12 A15 5c black	1,275.
On cover	*2,750.*
13 A15 10c black	1,300.
On cover	*2,850.*
14 A15 15c black	1,250.
On cover	*2,650.*
Nos. 12-14 (3)	3,825.

Used values for Nos. 12-14 are for examples canceled with c.d.s. "St. Pierre et Miquelon." Stamps canceled at Langlade, Miquelon or Ile des Chiens sell for about double these values.

"P D" are the initials for "Payé a destination." Excellent forgeries exist.

Stamps of French Colonies Surcharged in Black

e

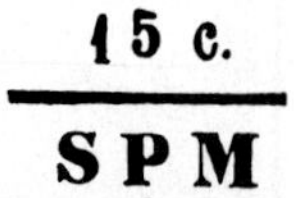

f

1891 *Perf. 14x13½*

15 A9 (e) 15c on 30c brn, *bis* 40.00 32.50
On cover 700.00
a. Inverted surcharge *250.00* *200.00*
b. Double surcharge 200.00 160.00
16 A9 (e) 15c on 35c blk, *org* 675.00 550.00
On cover *950.00*
a. Inverted surcharge *700.00* *625.00*
17 A9 (f) 15c on 35c blk, *org* 2,000. 1,650.
On cover —
a. Inverted surcharge *2,000.*
18 A9 (e) 15c on 40c red, *straw* 110.00 90.00
On cover 700.00
a. Inverted surcharge *250.00* *225.00*

Stamps of French Colonies Overprinted in Black or Red

1891, Oct. 15

19 A9 1c blk, *lil bl* 14.50 12.00
Never hinged 29.00
On cover 450.00
a. Inverted overprint 32.50 32.50
20 A9 1c blk, *lil bl* (R) 14.50 13.00
Never hinged 29.00
On cover 450.00
a. Inverted overprint 32.50 32.50
21 A9 2c brn, *buff* 14.50 12.00
Never hinged 29.00
On cover 450.00
a. Inverted overprint 25.00 25.00
22 A9 2c brn, *buff* (R) 29.00 26.00
Never hinged 57.50
On cover 450.00
a. Inverted overprint 57.50 57.50
23 A9 4c claret, *lav* 14.50 12.00
Never hinged 29.00
On cover 450.00
a. Inverted overprint 27.50 27.50
24 A9 4c claret, *lav* (R) 29.00 26.00
Never hinged 57.50
On cover 450.00
a. Inverted overprint 42.50 42.50
25 A9 5c grn, *grnsh* 24.50 16.00
Never hinged 45.00
On cover 400.00
a. Double surcharge 95.00
26 A9 10c blk, *lav* 45.00 35.00
Never hinged 72.50
On cover 400.00
a. Inverted overprint 65.00 *65.00*
27 A9 10c blk, *lav* (R) 32.50 27.50
Never hinged 60.00
On cover 400.00
a. Inverted overprint 42.50 *42.50*
28 A9 15c blue 40.00 27.50
Never hinged 65.00
On cover 300.00
29 A9 20c red, *grn* 90.00 80.00
Never hinged —
On cover *400.00*
30 A9 25c blk, *rose* 40.00 27.50
Never hinged 65.00
On cover 250.00
31 A9 30c brn, *bis* 140.00 115.00
Never hinged —
On cover *450.00*
32 A9 35c vio, *org* 400.00
Never hinged *525.00*
On cover —
33 A9 40c red, *straw* 90.00 72.50
Never hinged —
On cover 450.00
a. Double surcharge 175.00
34 A9 75c car, *rose* 115.00 100.00
Never hinged —
On cover 475.00
a. Inverted overprint 215.00 210.00
35 A9 1fr brnz grn, *straw* 95.00 90.00
Never hinged —
On cover *525.00*
a. Inverted overprint 200.00 200.00
Nos. 19-35 (17) 1,228. 692.00

Numerous varieties of mislettering occur in the preceding overprint: "S," "ST," "P," "M," "ON," or "-" missing; "-" instead of "ON"; "=" instead of "-" These varieties command values double or triple those of normal stamps.

Surcharged in Black

1891-92

36 A9 1c on 5c grn, *grnsh* 10.50 10.00
Never hinged 16.00
On cover *450.00*
37 A9 1c on 10c blk, *lav* 14.50 13.00
Never hinged 20.00
On cover *450.00*
38 A9 1c on 25c blk, *rose* ('92) 10.00 9.00
Never hinged 16.00
On cover *450.00*
39 A9 2c on 10c blk, *lav* 10.50 10.00
Never hinged 16.00
On cover *450.00*
a. Double surcharge 140.00 140.00
40 A9 2c on 15c bl 12.00 10.50
Never hinged 18.00
On cover *450.00*
41 A9 2c on 25c blk, *rose* ('92) 10.00 9.00
Never hinged 16.00
On cover *450.00*
42 A9 4c on 20c red, *grn* 10.50 10.00
Never hinged 16.00
On cover *450.00*
43 A9 4c on 25c blk, *rose* ('92) 10.00 9.00
Never hinged 16.00
On cover *450.00*
a. Double surcharge *140.00* 140.00
44 A9 4c on 30c brn, *bis* 24.50 19.00
Never hinged 40.00
On cover *450.00*
45 A9 4c on 40c red, *straw* 30.00 22.50
Never hinged 50.00
On cover *450.00*
Nos. 36-45 (10) 142.50 122.00

See note after No. 35.

Surcharged

j

k

1892, Nov. 4

46 A9 (j) 1c on 5c grn, *grnsh* 13.00 11.50
Never hinged 20.00
On cover *450.00*
47 A9 (j) 2c on 5c grn, *grnsh* 13.00 11.50
Never hinged 20.00
On cover *450.00*
48 A9 (j) 4c on 5c grn, *grnsh* 13.00 11.50
Never hinged 20.00
On cover *450.00*
49 A9 (k) 1c on 25c blk, *rose* 10.00 9.00
Never hinged 16.00
On cover *450.00*
50 A9 (k) 2c on 25c blk, *rose* 10.00 9.00
Never hinged 16.00
On cover *450.00*
51 A9 (k) 4c on 25c blk, *rose* 10.00 9.00
Never hinged 16.00
On cover *450.00*
Nos. 46-51 (6) 69.00 61.50

See note after No. 35.

Postage Due Stamps of French Colonies Overprinted in Red

1892, Dec. 1 *Imperf.*

52 D1 10c black 40.00 40.00
Never hinged 70.00
On cover *450.00*
53 D1 20c black 35.00 35.00
Never hinged 57.50
On cover *450.00*
54 D1 30c black 30.00 30.00
Never hinged 50.00
On cover *500.00*
55 D1 40c black 27.50 27.50
Never hinged 45.00
On cover *500.00*
56 D1 60c black 125.00 125.00
Never hinged —
On cover —

Black Overprint

57 D1 1fr brown 175.00 175.00
Never hinged —
On cover —
58 D1 2fr brown 315.00 315.00
Never hinged —
On cover —
59 D1 5fr brown 460.00 475.00
Never hinged —
On cover —
Nos. 52-59 (8) 1,207. 1,222.

See note after No. 35. "T P" stands for "Timbre Poste."

Navigation and Commerce — A16

1892-1908 Typo. *Perf. 14x13½*

60 A16 1c blk, *lil bl* .85 .85
On cover 250.00
61 A16 2c brown, *buff* .95 .95
On cover 250.00
62 A16 4c claret, *lav* 1.75 1.75
On cover 250.00
63 A16 5c green, *grnsh* 3.25 2.25
On cover 50.00
64 A16 5c yel grn ('08) 3.50 2.25
On cover 50.00
65 A16 10c black, *lav* 5.75 4.50
On cover 30.00
66 A16 10c red ('00) 4.25 2.25
On cover 25.00
67 A16 15c bl, quadrille paper 12.00 4.00
On cover 35.00
68 A16 15c gray, *lt gray* ('00) 85.00 47.50
On cover 100.00
69 A16 20c red, *grn* 21.00 17.50
On cover —
70 A16 25c black, *rose* 10.00 2.25
On cover 35.00
71 A16 25c blue ('00) 15.00 10.50
On cover 45.00
72 A16 30c brown, *bis* 9.25 5.25
On cover —
73 A16 35c blk, *yel* ('06) 5.75 5.25
On cover 250.00
74 A16 40c red, *straw* 6.00 5.75
On cover 200.00
75 A16 50c car, *rose* 37.50 35.00
On cover 150.00
76 A16 50c brown, *az* ('00) 30.00 29.00
On cover 150.00
77 A16 75c violet, *org* 24.00 21.00
On cover 250.00
78 A16 1fr brnz grn, *straw* 24.00 16.00
On cover —
Nos. 60-78 (19) 299.80 213.80

Perf. 13½x14 stamps are counterfeits.
For surcharges and overprints see Nos. 110-120, Q1-Q2.

Fisherman A17

Fulmar Petrel A18

Fishing Schooner A19

1909-30

79 A17 1c orange red & ol .20 .20
80 A17 2c olive & dp bl .20 .20
81 A17 4c violet & ol .35 .20
82 A17 5c bl grn & ol grn .80 .20
83 A17 5c blue & blk ('22) .35 .35
84 A17 10c car rose & red .80 .55
85 A17 10c bl grn & ol grn ('22) .40 .40
86 A17 10c bister & mag ('25) .35 .35
86A A17 15c dl vio & rose ('17) .55 .20
87 A17 20c bis brn & vio brn .95 .80
88 A18 25c dp blue & blue 3.25 1.60
89 A18 25c ol brn & bl grn ('22) .95 .95
90 A18 30c orange & vio brn 1.75 1.40
91 A18 30c rose & dull red ('22) 1.25 1.25
92 A18 30c red brn & bl ('25) .70 .70
93 A18 30c gray grn & bl grn ('26) .95 .95
94 A18 35c ol grn & vio brn .55 .35
95 A18 40c vio brn & ol grn 2.90 1.60
96 A18 45c violet & ol grn .70 .55
97 A18 50c olive & ol grn 1.40 1.10
98 A18 50c bl & pale bl ('22) 1.10 1.10
99 A18 50c yel brn & mag ('25) .95 .95
100 A18 60c dk bl & ver ('25) .95 .95
101 A18 65c vio & org brn ('28) 1.60 1.60
102 A18 75c brown & olive 1.40 1.10
103 A18 90c brn red & org red ('30) 27.50 27.50
104 A19 1fr ol grn & dp bl 4.00 2.10
105 A19 1.10fr bl grn & org red ('28) 4.00 4.00
106 A19 1.50fr bl & dp bl ('30) 11.50 11.50
107 A19 2fr violet & brn 4.00 2.50
108 A19 3fr red violet ('30) 13.00 13.00
109 A19 5fr vio brn & ol grn 10.00 8.00
Nos. 79-109 (32) 99.35 88.20

For overprints and surcharges see Nos. 121-131, 206C-206D, B1-B2, Q3-Q5.

Stamps of 1892-1906 Surcharged in Carmine or Black

1912

Spacing between figures of surcharge 1.5mm (5c), 2mm (10c)

110 A16 5c on 2c brn, *buff* 2.25 2.25
111 A16 5c on 4c claret, *lav* (C) .65 .65
112 A16 5c on 15c blue (C) .65 .65
113 A16 5c on 20c red, *grn* .55 .55
114 A16 5c on 25c blk, *rose* (C) .55 .55
115 A16 5c on 30c brn, *bis* (C) .55 .55
116 A16 5c on 35c blk, *yel* (C) 1.25 1.25
117 A16 10c on 40c red, *straw* .85 .85
b. Pair, one stamp without surcharge 450.00
118 A16 10c on 50c car, *rose* .85 .85
119 A16 10c on 75c dp vio, *org* 2.40 2.40
120 A16 10c on 1fr brnz grn, *straw* 3.50 3.50
Nos. 110-120 (11) 14.05 14.05

Spacing between figures of surcharge 2.25mm (5c), 2.75mm (10c)

110a A16 5c on 2c brn, *buff* 350.00 350.00
111a A16 5c on 4c claret, *lav* (C) 27.00 27.00
112a A16 5c on 15c blue (C) 45.00 45.00
113a A16 5c on 20c red, *grn* 17.00 17.00
114a A16 5c on 25c blk, *rose* (C) 19.00 19.00
115a A16 5c on 30c brn, *bis* (C) 42.50 42.50
116a A16 5c on 35c blk, *yel* (C) 17.00 17.00
117a A16 10c on 40c red, *straw* 19.00 19.00
118a A16 10c on 50c car, *rose* 25.00 25.00
119a A16 10c on 75c dp vio, *org* 60.00 60.00
120a A16 10c on 1fr brnz grn, *straw* 70.00 70.00
Nos. 110a-120a (11) 691.50 691.50

Stamps and Types of 1909-17 Surcharged with New Value and Bars in Black, Blue (Bl) or Red

1924-27

121 A17 25c on 15c dl vio & rose ('25) .35 .35
a. Double surcharge 140.00
b. Triple surcharge 140.00
122 A19 25c on 2fr vio & lt brn (Bl) .50 .50
123 A19 25c on 5fr brn & ol grn (Bl) .55 .55
a. Triple surcharge 140.00
124 A18 65c on 45c vio & ol grn ('25) 1.60 1.60
125 A18 85c on 75c brn & ol ('25) 1.60 1.60
126 A18 90c on 75c brn red & dp org ('27) 2.25 2.25
127 A19 1.25fr on 1fr dk bl & ultra (R) ('26) 2.25 2.25

128 A19 1.50fr on 1fr ultra & dk bl ('27) 2.90 2.90
129 A19 3fr on 5fr ol brn & red vio ('27) 4.00 4.00
130 A19 10fr on 5fr ver & ol grn ('27) 19.00 19.00
131 A19 20fr on 5fr vio & ver ('27) 24.00 24.00
Nos. 121-131 (11) 59.00 59.00

Common Design Types pictured following the introduction.

Colonial Exposition Issue
Common Design Types

1931, Apr. 13 Engr. *Perf. 12½*

Name of Country in Black

132 CD70 40c deep green 4.50 4.50
133 CD71 50c violet 4.50 4.50
134 CD72 90c red orange 4.50 4.50
135 CD73 1.50fr dull blue 4.50 4.50
Nos. 132-135 (4) 18.00 18.00

Map and Fishermen — A20

Lighthouse and Fish — A21

Fishing Steamer and Sea Gulls A22

Perf. 13½x14, 14x13½

1932-33 Typo.

136 A20 1c red brn & ultra .20 .20
137 A21 2c blk & dk grn .20 .20
138 A22 4c mag & ol brn .20 .20
139 A22 5c vio & dk brn .55 .55
140 A21 10c red brn & blk .55 .55
141 A21 15c dk blue & vio 1.10 1.10
142 A20 20c blk & red org 1.40 1.40
143 A20 25c lt vio & lt grn 1.40 1.40
144 A22 30c ol grn & bl grn 1.40 1.40
145 A22 40c dp bl & dk brn 1.40 1.40
146 A21 45c ver & dp grn 1.40 1.40
147 A21 50c dk brn & dk grn 1.40 1.40
148 A22 65c ol brn & org 1.75 1.75
149 A20 75c grn & red org 1.90 1.90
150 A20 90c dull red & red 2.25 2.25
151 A22 1fr org brn & org red 2.10 2.10
152 A20 1.25fr dp bl & lake ('33) 2.10 2.10
153 A20 1.50fr dp blue & blue 2.10 2.10
154 A22 1.75fr blk & dk brn ('33) 2.40 2.40
155 A22 2fr bl blk & Prus bl 9.25 9.25
156 A21 3fr dp grn & dk brn 10.00 10.00
157 A21 5fr brn red & dk brn 22.50 22.50
158 A22 10fr dk grn & vio 60.00 60.00
159 A20 20fr ver & dp grn 65.00 65.00
Nos. 136-159 (24) 192.55 192.55

For overprints and surcharges see Nos. 160-164, 207-221.

Nos. 147, 149, 153-154, 157 Overprinted in Black, Red or Blue

p

q

1934, Oct. 18

160 A21(p) 50c (Bk) 3.50 3.50
161 A20(q) 75c (Bk) 4.00 4.00
162 A20(q) 1.50fr (Bk) 4.50 4.50
163 A22(p) 1.75fr (R) 5.75 5.75
164 A21(p) 5fr (Bl) 27.50 27.50
Nos. 160-164 (5) 45.25 45.25

400th anniv. of the landing of Jacques Cartier.

Paris International Exposition Issue
Common Design Types

1937 *Perf. 13*

165 CD74 20c deep violet 1.90 1.90
166 CD75 30c dark green 1.90 1.90
167 CD76 40c carmine rose 1.90 1.90
168 CD77 50c dk brown & blue 1.90 1.90
169 CD78 90c red 1.90 1.90
170 CD79 1.50fr ultra 1.90 1.90
Nos. 165-170 (6) 11.40 11.40

Colonial Arts Exhibition Issue
Souvenir Sheet
Common Design Type

1937 *Imperf.*

171 CD78 3fr dark ultra 27.50 *35.00*

Dog Team A23

Port St. Pierre A24

Tortue Lighthouse A25

Soldiers' Bay at Langlade A26

1938-40 Photo. *Perf. 13½x13*

172 A23 2c dk blue green .20 .20
173 A23 3c brown violet .20 .20
174 A23 4c dk red violet .20 .20
175 A23 5c carmine lake .20 .20
176 A23 10c bister brown .20 .20
177 A23 15c red violet .50 .50
178 A23 20c blue violet .70 .70
179 A23 25c Prus blue 2.10 2.10
180 A24 30c dk red violet .50 .50
181 A24 35c deep green .70 .70
182 A24 40c slate blue ('40) .20 .20
183 A24 45c dp grn ('40) .35 .35
a. Value omitted *77.50*
184 A24 50c carmine rose .70 .70
185 A24 55c Prus blue 3.25 3.25
186 A24 60c violet ('39) .50 .50
187 A24 65c brown 5.00 5.00
188 A24 70c org yel ('39) .55 .55
189 A25 80c violet 1.25 1.25
190 A25 90c ultra ('39) .70 .70
191 A25 1fr brt pink 10.50 10.50
192 A25 1fr pale ol grn ('40) .80 .80
193 A25 1.25fr brt rose ('39) 1.75 1.75
194 A25 1.40fr dk brown ('40) .95 .95
195 A25 1.50fr blue green .95 .95
196 A25 1.60fr rose violet ('40) .95 .95
197 A25 1.75fr deep blue 2.90 2.90
198 A26 2fr rose violet .70 .70
199 A26 2.25fr brt blue ('39) .95 .95
200 A26 2.50fr org yel ('40) .95 .95
201 A26 3fr gray brown .85 .85
202 A26 5fr henna brown .95 .95
203 A26 10fr dk bl, *bluish* 1.40 1.40
204 A26 20fr slate green 1.75 1.75
Nos. 172-204 (33) 44.35 44.35

For overprints and surcharges see Nos. 222-255, 260-299, B9-B10.

New York World's Fair Issue
Common Design Type

1939, May 10 Engr. *Perf. 12½x12*

205 CD82 1.25fr carmine lake 1.90 1.60
206 CD82 2.25fr ultra 2.00 1.60

For overprints and surcharges see Nos. 256-259.

SEMI-POSTAL STAMPS

Regular Issue of 1909-17 Surcharged in Red

1915-17 Unwmk. *Perf. 14x13½*

B1 A17 10c + 5c car rose & red 1.75 1.75
B2 A17 15c + 5c dl vio & rose ('17) 1.75 1.75

Curie Issue
Common Design Type

1938, Oct. 24 Engr. *Perf. 13*

B3 CD80 1.75fr + 50c brt ultra 15.00 15.00

French Revolution Issue
Common Design Type

1939, July 5 Photo.

Name and Value Typo. in Black

B4 CD83 45c + 25c green 12.00 3.00
B5 CD83 70c + 30c brown 12.00 3.00
B6 CD83 90c + 35c red org 12.00 3.00
B7 CD83 1.25fr + 1fr rose pink 12.00 3.00
B8 CD83 2.25fr + 2fr blue 12.00 3.00
Nos. B4-B8 (5) 60.00 15.00

POSTAGE DUE STAMPS

Postage Due Stamps of French Colonies Overprinted in Red

ST · PIERRE M · on

1892 Unwmk. *Imperf.*

J1 D1 5c black 57.50 57.50
On cover —
J2 D1 10c black 17.50 17.50
On cover *1,000.*
J3 D1 15c black 17.50 17.50
On cover *1,000.*
J4 D1 20c black 17.50 17.50
On cover *1,000.*
J5 D1 30c black 17.50 17.50
On cover *1,000.*
J6 D1 40c black 17.50 17.50
On cover —
J7 D1 60c black 60.00 60.00
On cover —

Black Overprint

J8 D1 1fr brown 150.00 150.00
On cover —
J9 D1 2fr brown 150.00 150.00
On cover —
Nos. J1-J9 (9) 505.00 505.00

These stamps exist with and without hyphen. See note after No. 59.

Postage Due Stamps of France, 1893-1924, Overprinted

1925-27 *Perf. 14x13½*

J10 D2 5c blue .35 .35
J11 D2 10c dark brown .35 .35
J12 D2 20c olive green .55 .55
J13 D2 25c rose .55 .55
J14 D2 30c red 1.25 1.25
J15 D2 45c blue green 1.25 1.25
J16 D2 50c brown vio 1.90 1.90
J17 D2 1fr red brn, *straw* 2.25 2.25
J18 D2 3fr magenta ('27) 9.25 9.25

Surcharged

J19 D2 60c on 50c buff 2.10 2.10
J20 D2 2fr on 1fr red 3.50 3.50
Nos. J10-J20 (11) 23.30 23.30

Newfoundland Dog — D3

1932, Dec. 5 Typo.

J21 D3 5c dk blue & blk 1.10 1.10
J22 D3 10c green & blk 1.10 1.10
J23 D3 20c red & blk 1.40 1.40
J24 D3 25c red vio & blk 1.40 1.40
J25 D3 30c orange & blk 2.75 2.75
J26 D3 45c lt blue & blk 4.50 4.50
J27 D3 50c blue grn & blk 6.75 6.75
J28 D3 60c brt rose & blk 10.00 10.00
J29 D3 1fr yellow brn & blk 18.00 18.00
J30 D3 2fr dp violet & blk 27.50 27.50
J31 D3 3fr dk brown & blk 35.00 35.00
Nos. J21-J31 (11) 109.50 109.50

For overprints and surcharge see Nos. J42-J46.

Codfish — D4

1938, Nov. 17 Photo. *Perf. 13*

J32 D4 5c gray black .20 .20
J33 D4 10c dk red violet .20 .20
J34 D4 15c slate green .20 .20
J35 D4 20c deep blue .20 .20
J36 D4 30c rose carmine .35 .35
J37 D4 50c dk blue green .50 .50
J38 D4 60c dk blue .80 .80
J39 D4 1fr henna brown 1.40 1.40
J40 D4 2fr gray brown 2.50 2.50
J41 D4 3fr dull violet 4.00 4.00
Nos. J32-J41 (10) 10.35 10.35

For overprints see Nos. J48-J67.

PARCEL POST STAMPS

No. 65 Overprinted

COLIS
POSTAUX

1901 Unwmk. *Perf. 14x13½*

Q1 A16 10c black, *lavender* 87.50 87.50
a. Inverted overprint

No. 66 Overprinted

Q2 A16 10c red 18.00 18.00

Nos. 84 and 87 Overprinted

1917-25

Q3 A17 10c 2.75 2.75
a. Double overprint 160.00
Q4 A17 20c ('25) 2.10 2.10
a. Double overprint 125.00

ST. THOMAS AND PRINCE ISLANDS

sănt-'tăm-əs and 'prin,t,s 'ī-lənd

LOCATION — Two islands in the Gulf of Guinea, 125 miles off the west coast of Africa
GOVT. — Portuguese Colony
AREA — 372 sq. mi.
POP. — 102,000 (est. 1984)
CAPITAL — Sao Tome

1000 Reis = 1 Milreis
100 Centavos = 1 Escudo (1913)

Portuguese Crown — A1

King Luiz — A2

5, 25, 50 REIS:
Type I — "5" is upright.
Type II — "5" is slanting.

10 REIS:
Type I — "1" has short serif at top.
Type II — "1" has long serif at top.

40 REIS:
Type I — "4" is broad.
Type II — "4" is narrow.

Perf. 12½, 13½

1869-75 Unwmk. Typo.

1 A1 5r black, I 2.00 1.90
a. Type II 2.00 1.90
2 A1 10r yellow, I 14.00 8.50
a. Type II 17.50 10.50
3 A1 20r bister 3.50 2.75
4 A1 25r rose, I 1.25 1.10
a. 25r red 4.50 1.50
5 A1 40r blue ('75), I 4.75 3.50
a. Type II 5.50 4.50
6 A1 50r gray grn, II 9.00 7.00
a. Type I 15.00 14.00
7 A1 100r gray lilac 6.00 5.50
8 A1 200r red orange ('75) 8.25 6.25
9 A1 300r chocolate ('75) 8.25 7.00
Nos. 1-9 (9) 57.00 43.50

1881-85

10 A1 10r gray grn, I 8.00 6.75
a. Type II 9.50 6.00
b. Perf. 13½, I 11.00 8.00
11 A1 20r car rose ('85) 3.50 3.00
12 A1 25r vio ('85), II 2.25 1.75
13 A1 40r yel buff, II 5.00 4.00
a. Perf. 13½ 6.00 4.50
14 A1 50r dk blue, I 2.50 2.25
a. Type II 2.50 2.25
Nos. 10-14 (5) 21.25 17.75

For surcharges and overprints see Nos. 63-64, 129-129B, 154.

Nos. 1-14 have been reprinted on stout white paper, ungummed, with rough perforation 13½, also on ordinary paper with shiny white gum and clean-cut perforation 13½ with large holes.

Typo., Head Embossed

1887 ***Perf. 12½, 13½***

15 A2 5r black 3.75 2.50
16 A2 10r green 4.25 2.50
17 A2 20r brt rose 4.25 3.00
a. Perf. 12½ 55.00 55.00
18 A2 25r violet 4.25 1.60
19 A2 40r brown 4.25 2.25
20 A2 50r blue 4.25 2.50
21 A2 100r yellow brn 4.25 2.00
22 A2 200r gray lilac 15.00 10.50
23 A2 300r orange 15.00 10.50
Nos. 15-23 (9) 59.25 37.35

For surcharges and overprints see Nos. 24-26, 62, 65-72, 130-131, 155-158, 234-237.

Nos. 15, 16, 19, 21, 22, and 23 have been reprinted in paler colors than the originals, with white gum and cleancut perforation 13½. Value $1.50 each.

Nos. 16-17, 19 Surcharged:

5
rèis
a

b

c

1889-91 **Without Gum**

24 A2(a) 5r on 10r 35.00 20.00
25 A2(b) 5r on 20r 25.00 20.00
26 A2(c) 50r on 40r ('91) 225.00 50.00
Nos. 24-26 (3) 285.00 90.00

Varieties of Nos. 24-26, including inverted and double surcharges, "5" inverted, "Cinoc" and "Cinco," were deliberately made and unofficially issued.

King Carlos
A6 A7

1895 Typo. ***Perf. 11½, 12½***

27 A6 5r yellow .80 .60
28 A6 10r red lilac 1.25 1.00
29 A6 15r red brown 1.40 1.10
30 A6 20r lavender 1.50 1.10
31 A6 25r green 1.50 .75
32 A6 50r light blue 1.60 .70
a. Perf. 13½ 2.00 1.50
33 A6 75r rose 3.75 3.25
34 A6 80r yellow grn 8.00 6.25
35 A6 100r brn, *yel* 3.50 3.00
36 A6 150r car, *rose* 6.00 5.00
37 A6 200r dk bl, *bl* 7.75 6.50
38 A6 300r dk bl, *sal* 8.50 7.75
Nos. 27-38 (12) 45.55 37.00

For surcharges and overprints see Nos. 73-84, 132-137, 159-165, 238-243, 262-264, 268-274.

1898-1903 ***Perf. 11½***

Name and Value in Black except 500r

39 A7 2½r gray .30 .25
40 A7 5r orange .30 .25
41 A7 10r lt green .40 .30
42 A7 15r brown 2.00 1.75
43 A7 15r gray grn ('03) 1.10 1.10
44 A7 20r gray violet .90 .50
45 A7 25r sea green .70 .25
46 A7 25r carmine ('03) 1.10 .30
47 A7 50r blue 1.00 .50
48 A7 50r brown ('03) 4.50 4.50
49 A7 65r dull blue ('03) 11.00 9.00
50 A7 75r rose 10.00 6.50
51 A7 75r red lilac ('03) 2.50 1.40
52 A7 80r brt violet 5.00 5.00
53 A7 100r dk blue, *bl* 3.00 2.00
54 A7 115r org brn, *pink* ('03) 10.00 8.00
55 A7 130r brn, *straw* ('03) 10.00 6.00
56 A7 150r brn, *buff* 5.00 2.25
57 A7 200r red lil, *pnksh* 6.00 2.75
58 A7 300r dk blue, *rose* 8.00 5.00
59 A7 400r dull bl, *straw* ('03) 13.00 8.50
60 A7 500r blk & red, *bl* ('01) 10.00 5.00
61 A7 700r vio, *yelsh* ('01) 16.00 12.00
Nos. 39-61 (23) 121.80 83.10

For overprints and surcharges see Nos. 86-105, 116-128, 138-153, 167-169, 244-249, 255-261, 265-267.

Stamps of 1869-95 Surcharged in Red or Black

1902

On Stamp of 1887

62 A2 130r on 5r blk (R) 6.00 5.00
a. Perf. 13½ 32.50 32.50

On Stamps of 1869

63 A1 115r on 50r grn 10.00 7.50
64 A1 400r on 10r yel 25.00 12.00
a. Double surcharge 75.00 50.00

On Stamps of 1887

65 A2 65r on 20r rose 6.25 4.50
a. Perf. 13½ 8.50 7.00
66 A2 65r on 25r violet 4.50 4.00
a. Inverted surcharge 35.00 25.00
67 A2 65r on 100r yel brn 4.50 4.75
68 A2 115r on 10r blue grn 4.50 4.00
69 A2 115r on 300r orange 4.50 4.00
70 A2 130r on 200r gray lil 6.00 5.00
71 A2 400r on 40r brown 8.00 7.00
72 A2 400r on 50r blue 14.00 12.00
a. Perf. 13½ 110.00 90.00

On Stamps of 1895

73 A6 65r on 5r yellow 5.00 3.00
74 A6 65r on 10r red vio 5.00 3.00
75 A6 65r on 15r choc 5.00 3.00
76 A6 65r on 20r lav 5.00 3.00
77 A6 115r on 25r grn 5.00 3.00
78 A6 115r on 150r car, *rose* 5.00 3.00
79 A6 115r on 200r bl, *bl* 5.00 3.00
80 A6 130r on 75r rose 5.00 3.00
81 A6 130r on 100r brn, *yel* 5.00 3.50
a. Double surcharge 30.00 20.00
82 A6 130r on 300r bl, *sal* 5.00 3.00
83 A6 400r on 50r lt blue 1.10 .95
a. Perf. 13½ 2.00 1.60
84 A6 400r on 80r yel grn 2.00 1.50

On Newspaper Stamp No. P12

85 N3 400r on 2½r brown 1.10 .95
a. Double surcharge
Nos. 62-85 (24) 147.45 103.65

Reprints of Nos. 63, 64, 67, 71, and 72 have shiny white gum and clean-cut perf. 13½.

Stamps of 1898 Overprinted

1902

86 A7 15r brown 2.00 1.50
87 A7 25r sea green 2.00 1.25
88 A7 50r blue 2.25 1.25
89 A7 75r rose 5.00 3.50
Nos. 86-89 (4) 11.25 7.50

No. 49 Surcharged in Black

1905

90 A7 50r on 65r dull blue 3.25 2.75

Stamps of 1898-1903 Overprinted in Carmine or Green

1911

91 A7 2½r gray .25 .20
a. Inverted overprint 15.00 11.00
92 A7 5r orange .25 .20
93 A7 10r lt green .25 .20
a. Inverted overprint 15.00 12.00
94 A7 15r gray green .25 .20
95 A7 20r gray violet .25 .20
96 A7 25r carmine (G) .60 .20
97 A7 50r brown .30 .20
a. Inverted overprint 15.00 12.00
98 A7 75r red lilac .40 .20
99 A7 100r dk bl, *bl* .75 .50
a. Inverted overprint 17.50 14.00
100 A7 115r org brn, *pink* 1.50 .95
101 A7 130r brown, *straw* 1.50 .95
102 A7 200r red lil, *pnksh* 6.00 4.25
103 A7 400r dull blue, *straw* 2.00 1.00
104 A7 500r blk & red, *bl* 2.00 1.00
105 A7 700r violet, *yelsh* 2.00 1.00
Nos. 91-105 (15) 18.30 11.25

King Manuel II — A8

Overprinted in Carmine or Green

1912 ***Perf. 11½, 12***

106 A8 2½r violet .20 .20
a. Double overprint 16.00 16.00
b. Double overprint, one inverted 25.00
107 A8 5r black .20 .20
108 A8 10r gray green .20 .20
a. Double overprint 14.00 14.00
109 A8 20r carmine (G) 1.00 .75
110 A8 25r violet brn .60 .45
111 A8 50r dk blue .60 .55
112 A8 75r bister brn .90 .55
113 A8 100r brn, *lt grn* 1.10 .50
114 A8 200r dk grn, *sal* 2.00 1.40
115 A8 300r black, *azure* 2.00 2.00
Nos. 106-115 (10) 8.80 6.80

Stamps of 1898-1905 Overprinted in Black

1913

On Stamps of 1898-1903

116 A7 2½r gray 1.00 1.00
a. Inverted overprint 15.00 15.00
b. Double overprint 12.00 12.00
117 A7 5r orange 1.40 1.00
118 A7 15r gray green 22.50 17.50
a. Inverted overprint 75.00
119 A7 20r gray violet 1.50 1.50
a. Inverted overprint 15.00
120 A7 25r carmine 8.00 4.50
a. Inverted overprint 30.00
b. Double overprint 30.00
121 A7 75r red lilac 5.00 5.00
122 A7 100r bl, *bluish* 8.50 7.50
123 A7 115r org brn, *pink* 37.50 35.00
a. Double overprint 75.00 60.00
124 A7 130r brn, *straw* 13.00 13.00
125 A7 200r red lil, *pnksh* 20.00 13.00
126 A7 400r dl bl, *straw* 14.00 12.50
127 A7 500r blk & red, *gray* 35.00 42.50
128 A7 700r vio, *yelsh* 47.50 40.00
Nos. 116-128 (13) 214.90 194.00

On Provisional Issue of 1902

129 A1 115r on 50r grn 110.00 85.00
a. Inverted overprint
129B A1 400r on 10r yel 600.00 500.00
130 A2 115r on 10r blue grn 2.75 2.50
a. Inverted overprint 25.00
131 A2 400r on 50r blue 75.00 75.00
132 A6 115r on 25r grn 2.00 1.75
a. Inverted overprint 20.00
133 A6 115r on 150r car, *rose* 42.50 40.00
a. Inverted overprint 20.00
134 A6 115r on 200r bl, *bl* 2.50 2.00
135 A6 130r on 75r rose 2.25 2.00
a. Inverted overprint 25.00
136 A6 400r on 50r lt bl 4.00 4.00
a. Perf. 13½ 20.00 10.00
137 A6 400r on 80r yel grn 5.00 4.25

Same Overprint on Nos. 86, 88, 90

138 A7 15r brown 2.00 1.75
139 A7 50r blue 2.25 2.00
140 A7 50r on 65r dl bl 16.00 12.00
Nos. 138-140 (3) 20.25 15.75

No. 123-125, 130-131 and 137 were issued without gum.

Stamps of 1898-1905 Overprinted in Black

On Stamps of 1898-1903

141 A7 2½r gray .60 .50
a. Inverted overprint 9.00
b. Double overprint 11.00 11.00
c. Double overprint inverted 30.00
142 A7 5r orange 27.50 22.50
143 A7 15r gray green 1.75 1.50
a. Inverted overprint 25.00
144 A7 20r gray violet 250.00 200.00
a. Inverted overprint 500.00
145 A7 25r carmine 37.50 27.50
a. Inverted overprint 75.00
146 A7 75r red lilac 2.75 2.25
a. Inverted overprint 5.00

147 A7 100r blue, *bl* 2.25 1.75
148 A7 115r org brn, *pink* 10.00 8.00
a. Inverted overprint 25.00
149 A7 130r brown, *straw* 8.00 7.00
a. Inverted overprint 25.00
150 A7 200r red lil, *pnksh* 2.50 1.75
a. Inverted overprint 10.00
151 A7 400r dull bl, *straw* 10.00 8.00
152 A7 500r blk & red, *gray* 9.00 8.50
153 A7 700r violet, *yelsh* 9.00 8.50

On Provisional Issue of 1902

154 A1 115r on 50r green 200.00 150.00
155 A2 115r on 10r bl grn 2.50 2.25
156 A2 115r on 300r org 250.00 125.00
157 A2 130r on 5r black 300.00 125.00
158 A2 400r on 50r blue 200.00 90.00
159 A6 115r on 25r green 2.00 1.75
160 A6 115r on 150r car, *rose* 2.50 2.25
a. "REPUBLICA" inverted 20.00
161 A6 115r on 200r bl, *bl* 2.50 2.25
162 A6 130r on 75r rose 2.25 2.00
a. Inverted surcharge 20.00
163 A6 130r on 100r brn, *yel* 600.00 500.00
164 A6 400r on 50r lt bl 3.50 3.00
a. Perf. 13½ 17.50 6.00
165 A6 400r on 80r yel grn 2.50 2.25
166 N3 400r on 2½r brn 2.00 1.75

Same Overprint on Nos. 86, 88, 90

167 A7 15r brown 1.50 1.25
a. Inverted overprint 20.00
168 A7 50r blue 1.50 1.25
a. Inverted overprint 20.00
169 A7 50r on 65r dull bl 2.25 1.50
Nos. 167-169 (3) 5.25 4.00

Most of Nos. 141-169 were issued without gum.

Common Design Types pictured following the introduction.

Vasco da Gama Issue of Various Portuguese Colonies Surcharged as

On Stamps of Macao

170 CD20 ¼c on ½a bl grn 1.60 1.40
171 CD21 ½c on 1a red 1.60 1.40
172 CD22 1c on 2a red vio 1.60 1.40
173 CD23 2½c on 4a yel grn 1.60 1.40
174 CD24 5c on 8a dk bl 1.90 1.60
175 CD25 7½c on 12a vio brn 3.00 3.00
176 CD26 10c on 16a bis brn 1.90 1.60
177 CD27 15c on 24a bister 1.90 1.60
Nos. 170-177 (8) 15.10 13.40

On Stamps of Portuguese Africa

178 CD20 ¼c on 2½r bl grn 1.10 1.00
179 CD21 ½c on 5r red 1.10 1.00
180 CD22 1c on 10r red vio 1.10 1.00
181 CD23 2½c on 25r yel grn 1.10 1.00
182 CD24 5c on 50r dk bl 1.10 1.00
183 CD25 7½c on 75r vio brn 2.10 2.00
184 CD26 10c on 100r bis brn 1.10 1.00
185 CD27 15c on 150r bister 1.40 1.00
Nos. 178-185 (8) 10.10 9.00

On Stamps of Timor

186 CD20 ¼c on ½a bl grn 1.40 1.25
187 CD21 ½c on 1a red 1.40 1.25
188 CD22 1c on 2a red vio 1.40 1.25
a. Double surcharge 30.00
189 CD23 2½c on 4a yel grn 1.40 1.25
190 CD24 5c on 8a dk bl 1.75 1.60
191 CD25 7½c on 12a vio brn 2.50 2.50
192 CD26 10c on 16a bis brn 1.40 1.40
193 CD27 15c on 24a bister 1.40 1.40
Nos. 186-193 (8) 12.65 11.90
Nos. 170-193 (24) 37.85 34.30

Ceres — A9

1914-26 Typo. *Perf. 12x11½, 15x14*

Name and Value in Black

194 A9 ¼c olive brown .20 .20
195 A9 ½c black .20 .20
196 A9 1c blue green .50 .40
197 A9 1c yellow grn ('22) .20 .20
198 A9 1½c lilac brn .30 .20
199 A9 2c carmine .20 .20
200 A9 2c gray ('26) .20 .20
201 A9 2½c lt violet .20 .20
202 A9 3c orange ('22) .20 .20
203 A9 4c rose ('22) .20 .20
204 A9 4½c gray ('22) .20 .20
205 A9 5c deep blue .45 .35
206 A9 5c brt blue ('22) .20 .20
207 A9 6c lilac ('22) .20 .20
208 A9 7c ultra ('22) .20 .20
209 A9 7½c yellow brn .25 .20
210 A9 8c slate .25 .20
211 A9 10c orange brn .30 .25
212 A9 12c blue green ('22) .40 .40
213 A9 15c plum 1.50 1.25
214 A9 15c brn rose ('22) .25 .20
215 A9 20c yellow green 1.25 .75
216 A9 24c ultra ('26) 3.00 2.00
217 A9 25c choc ('26) 3.00 2.00
218 A9 30c brown, *grn* 1.75 1.40
219 A9 30c gray grn ('22) .40 .30
220 A9 40c brown, *pink* 1.75 1.40
221 A9 40c turq bl ('22) .40 .30
222 A9 50c orange, *sal* 4.00 3.00
223 A9 50c lt violet ('26) .40 .30
224 A9 60c dk blue ('22) .40 .30
225 A9 60c rose ('26) 1.50 .75
226 A9 80c brt rose ('22) 1.60 .50
227 A9 1e green, *blue* 4.00 3.00
228 A9 1e pale rose ('22) 2.50 1.40
229 A9 1e blue ('26) 2.00 1.00
230 A9 2e dk violet ('22) 2.75 1.50
231 A9 5e buff ('26) 11.50 7.50
232 A9 10e pink ('26) 19.00 14.00
233 A9 20e pale turq ('26) 60.00 40.00
Nos. 194-233 (40) 127.80 87.25

Perforation and paper variations command a premium for some of Nos. 194-233.
For surcharges see Nos. 250-253, 281-282.

Preceding Issues Overprinted in Carmine

1915

On Provisional Issue of 1902

234 A2 115r on 10r green 1.75 1.60
235 A2 115r on 300r org 1.75 1.75
236 A2 130r on 5r black 4.00 2.75
237 A2 130r on 200r gray lil 1.40 1.25
238 A6 115r on 25r green .60 .40
239 A6 115r on 150r car, *rose* .60 .40
240 A6 115r on 200r bl, *bl* .60 .40
241 A6 130r on 75r rose .60 .40
242 A6 130r on 100r brn, *yel* 1.10 1.25
243 A6 130r on 300r bl, *sal* 1.00 .75

Same Overprint on Nos. 88 and 90

244 A7 50r blue .70 .55
245 A7 50r on 65r dull bl .70 .55
Nos. 234-245 (12) 14.80 12.05

No. 86 Overprinted in Blue and Surcharged in Black

1919

246 A7 2½c on 15r brown .60 .55

No. 91 Surcharged in Black

247 A7 ½c on 2½r gray 3.00 2.75
248 A7 1c on 2½r gray 2.25 2.00
249 A7 2½c on 2½r gray 1.10 .65

No. 194 Surcharged in Blue

250 A9 ½c on ¼c ol brn 2.00 1.75
251 A9 2c on ¼c ol brn 2.25 1.90
252 A9 2½c on ¼c ol brn 6.00 5.00

No. 201 Surcharged in Black

253 A9 4c on 2½c lt vio .90 .75
Nos. 246-253 (8) 18.10 15.35

Nos. 246-253 were issued without gum.

Stamps of 1898-1905 Overprinted in Green or Red

1920

On Stamps of 1898-1903

255 A7 75r red lilac (G) .55 .50
256 A7 100r blue, *blue* (R) .80 .75
257 A7 115r org brn, *pink* (G) 2.00 1.40
258 A7 130r brn, *straw* (G) 80.00 50.00
259 A7 200r red lil, *pnksh* (G) 2.00 1.00
260 A7 500r blk, & red, *gray* (G) 1.50 1.00
261 A7 700r vio, *yelsh* (G) 2.00 1.25

On Stamps of 1902

262 A6 115r on 25r grn (R) 1.00 .60
263 A6 115r on 200r bl, *bl* (R) 1.50 1.00
264 A6 130r on 75r rose (G) 2.00 1.50

On Nos. 88-89

265 A7 50r blue (R) 1.50 1.10
266 A7 75r rose (G) 10.00 7.00

On No. 90

267 A7 50r on 65r dl bl (R) 12.00 7.00
Nos. 255-257,259-267 (12) 36.85 24.10

Nos. 238-243 Surcharged in Blue or Red

1923 Without Gum

268 A6 10c on 115r on 25r (Bl) .70 .50
269 A6 10c on 115r on 150r (Bl) .70 .50
270 A6 10c on 115r on 200r (R) .70 .50
271 A6 10c on 130r on 75r (Bl) .70 .50
272 A6 10c on 130r on 100r (Bl) .70 .50
273 A6 10c on 130r on 300r (R) .70 .50
Nos. 268-273 (6) 4.20 3.00

Nos. 268-273 are usually stained and discolored.

Nos. 84-85 Surcharged

1925

274 A6 40c on 400r on 80r yel grn .90 .45
275 N3 40c on 400r on 2½r brn .90 .45

Nos. 228 and 230 Surcharged

1931

281 A9 70c on 1e pale rose 2.00 1.25
282 A9 1.40e on 2e dk vio 2.75 2.50

Ceres — A11

Perf. 12x11½

1934 Typo. Wmk. 232

283 A11 1c bister .20 .20
284 A11 5c olive brown .20 .20
285 A11 10c violet .20 .20
286 A11 15c black .20 .20
287 A11 20c gray .20 .20
288 A11 30c dk green .20 .20
289 A11 40c red orange .20 .20
290 A11 45c brt blue .50 .50
291 A11 50c brown .20 .20
292 A11 60c olive grn .50 .50
293 A11 70c brown org .50 .50
294 A11 80c emerald .50 .50
295 A11 85c deep rose 2.25 1.60
296 A11 1e maroon .95 .65
297 A11 1.40e dk blue 2.50 2.10
298 A11 2e dk violet 2.50 1.75
299 A11 5e apple green 8.25 3.75
300 A11 10e olive bister 14.00 6.00
301 A11 20e orange 50.00 18.00
Nos. 283-301 (19) 84.05 37.45

Common Design Types Inscribed "S. Tomé"

1938 Unwmk. *Perf. 13½x13*

Name and Value in Black

302 CD34 1c gray green .20 .20
303 CD34 5c orange brown .20 .20
304 CD34 10c dk carmine .20 .20
305 CD34 15c dk violet brn .20 .20
306 CD34 20c slate .20 .20
307 CD35 30c rose violet .20 .20
308 CD35 35c brt green .20 .20
309 CD35 40c brown .20 .20
310 CD35 50c brt red vio .20 .20
311 CD36 60c gray black .20 .20
312 CD36 70c brown violet .20 .20
313 CD36 80c orange .45 .20
314 CD36 1e red 2.25 1.10
315 CD37 1.75e blue 2.00 1.50
316 CD37 2e brown car 15.00 5.00
317 CD37 5e olive green 15.00 5.50
318 CD38 10e blue violet 17.00 7.50
319 CD38 20e red brown 30.00 9.50
Nos. 302-319 (18) 83.90 32.50

Marble Column and Portuguese Arms with Cross — A12

1938 *Perf. 12½*

320 A12 80c blue green 2.75 1.40
321 A12 1.75e deep blue 10.50 4.00
322 A12 20e brown 40.00 17.50
Nos. 320-322 (3) 53.25 22.90

Visit of the President of Portugal in 1938.

Common Design Types Inscribed "S. Tomé e Principe"

1939 *Perf. 13½x13*

Name and Value in Black

323 CD34 1c gray grn .20 .20
324 CD34 5c orange brn .20 .20
325 CD34 10c dk carmine .20 .20
326 CD34 15c dk vio brn .20 .20
327 CD34 20c slate .45 .20
328 CD35 30c rose violet .20 .20
329 CD35 35c brt green .20 .20
330 CD35 40c brown .45 .20
331 CD35 50c brt red vio .45 .20
332 CD36 60c gray black .45 .20
333 CD36 70c brown violet .45 .20
334 CD36 80c orange .45 .20
335 CD36 1e red .90 .60
336 CD37 1.75e blue 1.50 .60
337 CD37 2e brown car 2.40 1.50
338 CD37 5e olive green 6.25 2.75
339 CD38 10e blue violet 9.00 4.00
340 CD38 20e red brown 15.00 5.50
Nos. 323-340 (18) 38.95 17.35

AIR POST STAMPS

Common Design Type Inscribed "S. Tomé"

1938 *Perf. 13½x13*

Name and Value in Black

C1 CD39 10c red orange 62.50 45.00
C2 CD39 20c purple 30.00 22.50
C3 CD39 50c orange 3.00 2.50
C4 CD39 1e ultra 5.25 4.00
C5 CD39 2e lilac brown 7.75 6.25
C6 CD39 3e dark green 12.00 8.00
C7 CD39 5e red brown 15.00 13.00
C8 CD39 9e rose carmine 17.50 13.00
C9 CD39 10e magenta 19.00 13.00
Nos. C1-C9 (9) 172.00 127.25

Common Design Type
Inscribed "S. Tomé e Principe"

1939 Engr. Unwmk.
Name and Value Typo. in Black

C10	CD39	10c scarlet	.60	.30
C11	CD39	20c purple	.60	.30
C12	CD39	50c orange	.60	.30
C13	CD39	1e deep ultra	.60	.30
C14	CD39	2e lilac brown	1.75	1.25
C15	CD39	3e dark green	2.40	1.50
C16	CD39	5e red brown	3.50	2.10
C17	CD39	9e rose carmine	6.25	3.00
C18	CD39	10e magenta	7.25	3.00
		Nos. C10-C18 (9)	23.55	12.05

No. C16 exists with overprint "Exposicao Internacional de Nova York, 1939-1940" and Trylon and Perisphere.

POSTAGE DUE STAMPS

"S. Thomé" — D1

1904 Unwmk. Typo. *Perf. 12*

J1	D1	5r yellow green	.55	.55
J2	D1	10r slate	.65	.65
J3	D1	20r yellow brown	.65	.65
J4	D1	30r orange	1.00	.65
J5	D1	50r gray brown	1.75	1.40
J6	D1	60r red brown	2.50	1.60
J7	D1	100r red lilac	3.00	1.75
J8	D1	130r dull blue	4.00	3.25
J9	D1	200r carmine	4.50	3.50
J10	D1	500r gray violet	8.00	5.00
		Nos. J1-J10 (10)	26.60	19.00

Overprinted in Carmine or Green

1911

J11	D1	5r yellow green	.30	.30
J12	D1	10r slate	.30	.30
J13	D1	20r yellow brown	.30	.30
J14	D1	30r orange	.30	.30
J15	D1	50r gray brown	.30	.30
J16	D1	60r red brown	.65	.65
J17	D1	100r red lilac	.80	.80
J18	D1	130r dull blue	.80	.80
J19	D1	200r carmine (G)	.80	.80
J20	D1	500r gray violet	1.25	1.25
		Nos. J11-J20 (10)	5.80	5.80

Nos. J1-J10 Overprinted in Black

1913 Without Gum

J21	D1	5r yellow green	3.75	3.75
J22	D1	10r slate	5.00	4.50
J23	D1	20r yellow brown	2.50	2.50
J24	D1	30r orange	2.50	2.50
J25	D1	50r gray brown	2.50	2.50
J26	D1	60r red brown	3.00	3.00
J27	D1	100r red lilac	5.00	4.00
J28	D1	130r dull blue	35.00	35.00
a.		Inverted overprint	70.00	70.00
J29	D1	200r carmine	50.00	50.00
J30	D1	500r gray violet	75.00	40.00
		Nos. J21-J30 (10)	184.25	147.75

Nos. J1-J10 Overprinted in Black

1913 Without Gum

J31	D1	5r yellow green	3.00	3.00
a.		Inverted overprint	40.00	40.00
J32	D1	10r slate	4.00	4.00
J33	D1	20r yellow brown	3.00	3.00
J34	D1	30r orange	3.00	3.00
a.		Inverted overprint	40.00	
J35	D1	50r gray brown	3.00	3.00
J36	D1	60r red brown	4.00	4.00
J37	D1	100r red lilac	4.00	4.00
J38	D1	130r dull blue	4.00	4.00
J39	D1	200r carmine	7.00	6.00
J40	D1	500r gray violet	17.00	15.00
		Nos. J31-J40 (10)	52.00	49.00

No. J5 Overprinted "Republica" in Italic Capitals like Regular Issue in Green

1920 Without Gum

J41	D1	50r gray brn	40.00	35.00

"S. Tomé" — D2

1921 Typo. *Perf. 11½*

J42	D2	½c yellow green	.20	.20
J43	D2	1c slate	.20	.20
J44	D2	2c orange brown	.20	.20
J45	D2	3c orange	.20	.20
J46	D2	5c gray brown	.20	.20
J47	D2	6c lt brown	.20	.20
J48	D2	10c red violet	.20	.20
J49	D2	13c dull blue	.25	.20
J50	D2	20c carmine	.25	.20
J51	D2	50c gray	.35	.40
		Nos. J42-J51 (10)	2.25	2.20

In each sheet one stamp is inscribed "S. Thomé" instead of "S. Tomé." Value, set of 10, $60.

NEWSPAPER STAMPS

N1

N2

Perf. 11½, 12½ and 13½
1892 Without Gum Unwmk.
Black Surcharge

P1	N1	2½r on 10r green	95.00	55.00
P2	N1	2½r on 20r rose	125.00	57.50
P3	N2	2½r on 10r green	125.00	57.50
P4	N2	2½r on 20r rose	125.00	57.50
		Nos. P1-P4 (4)	470.00	227.50

Green Surcharge

P5	N1	2½r on 5r black	67.50	30.00
P6	N1	2½r on 20r rose	125.00	57.50
P8	N2	2½r on 5r black	125.00	60.00
P9	N2	2½r on 10r green	125.00	62.50
P10	N2	2½r on 20r rose	125.00	77.50
		Nos. P5-P10 (5)	567.50	287.50

Both surcharges exist on No. 18 in green.

N3

d

1893 Typo. *Perf. 11½, 13½*

P12	N3	2½r brown	.45	.40

For surcharges and overprints see Nos. 85, 166, 275, P13.

No. P12 Overprinted Type "d" in Blue

1899
Without Gum

P13	N3	2½r brown	25.00	16.00

POSTAL TAX STAMPS

Pombal Issue
Common Design Types

1925 Unwmk. *Perf. 12½*

RA1	CD28	15c orange & black	.45	.45
RA2	CD29	15c orange & black	.45	.45
RA3	CD30	15c orange & black	.45	.45
		Nos. RA1-RA3 (3)	1.35	1.35

Certain revenue stamps (5e, 6e, 7e, 8e and other denominations) were surcharged in 1946 "Assistencia," 2 bars and new values (1e or 1.50e) and used as postal tax stamps.

POSTAL TAX DUE STAMPS

Pombal Issue
Common Design Types

1925 Unwmk. *Perf. 12½*

RAJ1	CD28	30c orange & black	.75	.75
RAJ2	CD29	30c orange & black	.75	.75
RAJ3	CD30	30c orange & black	.75	.75
		Nos. RAJ1-RAJ3 (3)	2.25	2.25

ST. VINCENT

sānt 'vin,t-sənt

LOCATION — Island in the West Indies
GOVT. — British Colony
AREA — 150 sq. mi.
POP. — 123,000 (est. 1984)
CAPITAL — Kingstown

12 Pence = 1 Shilling
20 Shillings = 1 Pound
100 Cents = 1 Dollar (1949)

Catalogue values for unused stamps in this country are for Never Hinged items, beginning with Scott 152 in the regular postage section.

PRE-STAMP POSTAL MARKINGS

Crowned Circle handstamp type I is pictured in the Crowned Circle Handstamps and Great Britain Used Abroad section.

1852

A1	I	"St. Vincent" crowned circle handstamp in red, on cover	1,050.

STAMPS OF GREAT BRITAIN USED IN ST. VINCENT

Numeral cancellation type A is pictured in the Crowned Circle Handstamps and Great Britain Used Abroad section.

1858-60
A10

A2	A	1p rose red (#20)	775.
A3	A	2p blue (#29, p7, 8)	—
A4	A	4p rose (#26)	475.
A5	A	6p lilac (#27)	360.
A6	A	1sh green (#28)	1,900.

Issued under British Administration

Values for unused stamps are for examples with original gum as defined in the catalogue introduction. Early stamps were spaced extremely narrowly on the plates, and the perforations were applied irregularly.

Therefore, very fine examples of Nos. 1-28, 30-39 will have perforations that cut into the design slightly on one or more sides. Also, very fine examples of Nos. 40-53, 55-60 will have perforations touching the design on at least one side. These stamps with perfs clear of the design on all four sides, especially Nos. 1-28, 30-39, are extremely scarce and command substantially higher prices.

Watermark

Wmk. 5 — Small Star

Queen Victoria — A1

1861 Engr. Unwmk. *Perf. 14 to 16*

1	A1	1p rose	*57.50*	16.00
a.		Imperf., pair	325.00	
c.		Horiz. pair, imperf. vert.	425.00	
1B	A1	6p yellow green	*9,000.*	250.00

Perfs on Nos. 1-1B are not clean cut. See Nos. 2-3 for rough perfs.

1862-66 *Rough Perf. 14 to 16*

2	A1	1p rose	57.50	16.00
a.		Horiz. pair, imperf. vert.	425.00	
3	A1	6p dark green	65.00	22.50
a.		Imperf., pair	1,200.	
b.		Horiz. pair, imperf. between	*12,000.*	*13,250.*
4	A1	1sh slate ('66)	425.00	160.00
		Nos. 2-4 (3)	547.50	198.50

1863-69 ***Perf. 11 to 13***
5 A1 1p rose 47.50 19.00
6 A1 4p blue ('66) 325.00 125.00
a. Horiz. pair, imperf. vert.
7 A1 4p orange ('69) 425.00 190.00
8 A1 6p deep green 275.00 90.00
8A A1 1sh slate ('66) *3,000.* 1,100.
9 A1 1sh indigo ('69) 450.00 110.00
10 A1 1sh brown ('69) 600.00 190.00

Perf. 11 to 13x14 to 16
11 A1 1p rose *6,500.* 1,325.
12 A1 1sh slate 325.00 140.00

Rough Perf. 14 to 16
1871-78 **Wmk. 5**
13 A1 1p black 65.00 14.50
a. Vert. pair, imperf. btwn. *16,500.*
14 A1 6p dk blue green 400.00 85.00
a. Watermark sideways 90.00

Clean-Cut Perf. 14 to 16
14A A1 1p black 60.00 12.00
14B A1 6p dp bl grn 1,800. 57.50
c. 6p dull blue green 2,400. 60.00
15 A1 6p pale yel green ('78) 850.00 30.00
15A A1 1sh vermilion ('77) *48,000.*

For surcharge see No. 30.

Perf. 11 to 13
16 A1 4p dk bl ('77) 600.00 110.00
17 A1 1sh deep rose ('72) 900.00 160.00
18 A1 1sh claret ('75) 650.00 275.00

Perf. 11 to 13x14 to 16
20 A1 1p black 95.00 12.00
a. Horiz. pair, imperf. btwn. *24,000.*
21 A1 6p pale yel grn ('77) 775.00 60.00
22 A1 1sh lilac rose ('72) *6,500.* 425.00
23 A1 1sh vermilion ('77) 1,150. 100.00
a. Horiz. pair, imperf. vert. —

See Nos. 25-28A, 36-39, 42-53. For surcharges see Nos. 30, 32-33, 40, 55-60.

Victoria
A2

Seal of Colony
A3

1880-81 ***Perf. 11 to 13***
24 A2 ½p orange ('81) 8.00 4.50
25 A1 1p gray green 150.00 4.50
26 A1 1p drab ('81) 650.00 9.50
27 A1 4p ultra ('81) 1,350. 125.00
a. Horiz. pair, imperf. btwn.
28 A1 6p yellow green 425.00 77.50
a. Horiz. pair, imperf. btwn. *10,000.*
28A A1 1sh vermilion 725.00 60.00
29 A3 5sh rose 1,250. *1,450.*
a. Imperf *4,500.*

No. 29 is valued well centered with design well clear of the perfs.
See #35, 41, 54, 598. For surcharges see #31-33.

No. 14B Bisected and Surcharged in Red

1880, May ***Perf. 14 to 16***
30 A1 1p on half of 6p 475.00 350.00
a. Unsevered pair *1,250.* *900.00*

No. 28 Bisected and Surcharged in Red

1881, Sept. 1
31 A1 ½p on half of 6p yel grn ('81) 190. 200.
a. Unsevered pair 550. 575.
b. "1" with straight top 1,000.
c. Without fraction bar, pair, #31, 31c 5,000. *6,000.*

Nos. 28 and 28A Surcharged in Black:

c

d

1881, Nov. ***Perf. 11 to 13***
32 A1(c) 1p on 6p yel green 550. 425.
33 A1(d) 4p on 1sh ver 1,900. 950.

1883-84 **Wmk. 2** ***Perf. 12***
35 A2 ½p green ('84) 95.00 30.00
36 A1 4p ultra 900.00 47.50
37 A1 4p dull blue ('84) 2,400. 300.00
38 A1 6p yellow grn 175.00 360.00
39 A1 1sh orange ver 150.00 72.50
a. Imperf., pair

The ½p orange, 1p rose red, 1p milky blue and 5sh carmine lake were never placed in use. Some authorities believe them to be color trials.

Nos. 35-60 may be found watermarked with single straight line. This is from the frame which encloses each group of 60 watermark designs.

Type of A1 Surcharged in Black

e

1883 ***Perf. 14***
40 A1 2½p on 1p lake 17.50 1.75

1883-97
41 A2 ½p green ('85) 1.15 .70
a. ½p deep green 3.00 .70
42 A1 1p drab 65.00 3.00
43 A1 1p rose red ('85) 2.00 1.00
44 A1 1p pink ('86) 5.75 2.10
a. 1p carmine red ('89) 29.00 4.50
45 A1 2½p brt blue ('97) 6.00 2.10
46 A1 4p ultra 775.00 90.00
a. 4p dull ultramarine 1,200. 425.00
47 A1 4p red brown ('85) 1,150. 26.00
48 A1 4p lake brn ('86) 85.00 1.60
a. 4p purple brown ('86) 85.00 1.60
49 A1 4p yellow ('93) 2.00 *10.00*
a. 4p olive yellow *350.00* *350.00*
50 A1 5p gray brn ('97) 6.50 *27.50*
a. 5p black brown 6.50 *25.00*
51 A1 6p violet ('88) 175.00 *200.00*
52 A1 6p red violet ('91) 2.75 *18.00*
53 A1 1sh org ver ('91) 6.50 13.00
a. 1sh red orange 13.00 *20.00*
54 A3 5sh car lake ('88) 32.50 *60.00*
a. 5sh brown lake 35.00 *60.00*
b. Printed on both sides *7,250.*

Grading footnote after No. 29 applies equally to Nos. 54-54a.

No. 40 Resurcharged in Black

1885, Mar.
55 A1 1p on 2½p on 1p lake 26.00 21.00

Copies with 3-bar cancel are proofs.

Stamps of Type A1 Surcharged in Black or Violet:

g

h

j

1890-91
56 A1(e) 2½p on 1p brt blue 1.75 .40
a. 2½p on 1p milky blue 27.50 6.50
b. 2½p on 1p gray blue 24.00 .75
57 A1(g) 2½p on 4p vio brn ('90) 95.00 *125.00*
a. Without fraction bar 475.00 *575.00*

1892-93
58 A1(h) 5p on 4p lake brn (V) 26.00 *42.50*
59 A1(j) 5p on 6p dp lake ('93) 1.15 *2.10*
a. 5p on 6p carmine lake 24.00 *35.00*
b. Double surcharge *6,500.* *4,250.*

1897
60 A1(j) 3p on 1p lilac 6.00 *21.00*
a. 3p on 1p reddish lilac 12.00 *36.00*
Ovptd. "SPECIMEN" 47.50

Victoria
A13

Edward VII
A14

Numerals of 1sh and 5sh, type A13, and of 2p, 1sh, 5sh and £1, type A14, are in color on plain tablet.

1898 **Typo.** ***Perf. 14***
62 A13 ½p lilac & grn 3.25 3.00
63 A13 1p lil & car rose 5.25 1.50
64 A13 2½p lilac & ultra 4.75 2.40
65 A13 3p lilac & ol grn 4.75 *15.00*
66 A13 4p lilac & org 4.75 *20.00*
67 A13 5p lilac & blk 8.25 *15.00*
68 A13 6p lilac & brn 15.00 *45.00*
69 A13 1sh grn & car rose 15.00 *57.50*
70 A13 5sh green & ultra 95.00 *160.00*
Nos. 62-70 (9) 156.00 *319.40*
Set, ovptd. "SPECIMEN" 200.00

1902
71 A14 ½p violet & green 4.25 .85
72 A14 1p vio & car rose 5.00 .35
73 A14 2p violet & black 4.00 3.25
74 A14 2½p violet & ultra 6.00 4.25
75 A14 3p violet & ol grn 6.00 4.50
76 A14 6p violet & brn 13.00 *35.00*
77 A14 1sh grn & car rose 29.00 *65.00*
78 A14 2sh green & violet 30.00 *65.00*
79 A14 5sh green & ultra 85.00 *140.00*
Nos. 71-79 (9) 182.25 *318.20*
Set, ovptd. "SPECIMEN" 145.00

1904-11 **Wmk. 3**
Chalky Paper
82 A14 ½p vio & grn 1.50 1.50
a. Ordinary paper 9.00 4.75
83 A14 1p vio & car rose 25.00 1.75
a. Ordinary paper 29.00 1.90
84 A14 2½p vio & ultra 19.00 *50.00*
85 A14 6p vio & brn 19.00 *50.00*
86 A14 1sh grn & car rose 13.00 *65.00*
a. Ordinary paper 22.50 *57.50*
87 A14 2sh vio & bl, *bl* 27.50 *50.00*
88 A14 5sh grn & red, *yel* 20.00 *60.00*
89 A14 £1 vio & blk, *red* 325.00 *400.00*
Nos. 82-88 (7) 125.00 *278.25*
Nos. 87-89, ovptd. "SPECIMEN" 225.00

Issued: 1p, 1904, ½p, 6p, 1905; 2½p, 1906; 1sh, 1908; 2sh, 5sh, 1909; £1, July 22, 1911.

"Peace and Justice"
A15 A16

1907 **Engr.**
Ordinary Paper
90 A15 ½p yellow green 4.00 2.75
91 A15 1p carmine 4.25 .20
92 A15 2p orange 1.75 *7.75*
93 A15 2½p ultra 32.50 10.00
94 A15 3p dark violet 9.50 *18.00*
Nos. 90-94 (5) 52.00 *38.70*
Set, ovptd. "SPECIMEN" 130.00

1909
Without Dot under "d"
95 A16 1p carmine 1.50 .35
96 A16 6p red violet 6.50 *37.50*
97 A16 1sh black, *green* 5.00 *10.00*
Nos. 95-97 (3) 13.00 *47.85*
Set, ovptd. "SPECIMEN" 85.00

1909-11
With Dot under "d"
98 A16 ½p yellow grn ('10) 1.75 .70
99 A16 1p carmine 1.75 .25
100 A16 2p gray ('11) 4.75 10.00
101 A16 2½p ultra 9.50 4.25
102 A16 3p violet, *yel* 3.00 *9.50*
103 A16 6p red violet 12.00 6.00
Nos. 98-103 (6) 32.75 *30.70*

King George V — A17

1913-17 ***Perf. 14***
104 A17 ½p gray green .90 .25
105 A17 1p carmine 1.00 .90
a. 1p rose red 1.10 .85
b. 1p scarlet 16.50 6.00
106 A17 2p slate 3.50 *35.00*
a. 2p gray 8.50 *36.00*
107 A17 2½p ultra .60 .90
108 A17 3p violet, *yellow* 1.00 *14.00*
a. 3p violet, *lemon* 3.25 *14.00*
b. 3p violet, *pale yellow* 2.75 *10.00*
109 A17 4p red, *yellow* 1.00 *2.40*
110 A17 5p olive green 16.00 *16.00*
111 A17 6p claret 2.50 *5.50*
112 A17 1sh black, *green* 1.75 *4.50*
113 A17 1sh bister ('14) 4.75 *29.00*
114 A16 2sh vio & ultra 5.75 *32.50*
115 A16 5sh dk grn & car 15.00 *60.00*
116 A16 £1 black & vio 100.00 *190.00*
Nos. 104-116 (13) 153.75 *390.95*
Set, ovptd. "SPECIMEN" 300.00

Issued: 5p, 11/7; #113, 5/1/14; others, 1/1/13.
For overprints see Nos. MR1-MR2.

No. 112 Surcharged in Carmine

1915
117 A17 1p on 1sh black, *grn* 9.00 *32.50*
a. "PENNY" & bar double 775.00 775.00
b. Without period 15.00
c. "ONE" omitted 1,200. 1,000.
d. "ONE" double 775.00

Space between surcharge lines varies from 8 to 10mm.

1921-32 **Wmk. 4**
118 A17 ½p green 2.10 .35
119 A17 1p carmine ('21) 1.15 1.00
a. 1p red 2.75 .20
120 A17 1½p yel brn ('32) 4.00 .20
121 A17 2p gray 3.00 1.00
122 A17 2½p ultra ('26) 1.50 1.75
123 A17 3p ultra 1.15 *7.25*
124 A17 3p vio, *yel* ('27) 1.15 *1.75*
125 A17 4p red, *yel* ('30) 2.10 *7.25*
126 A17 5p olive green 1.15 *7.75*
127 A17 6p claret ('27) 1.75 *4.25*
128 A17 1sh ocher ('27) 4.00 *20.00*
a. 1sh bistre 6.75 *27.50*
129 A16 2sh brn vio & ultra 9.00 *15.00*
130 A16 5sh dk grn & car 21.00 *37.50*
131 A16 £1 blk & vio ('28) 110.00 *150.00*
Nos. 118-131 (14) 163.05 *255.05*
Set, ovptd. or perf "SPECIMEN" 360.00

Common Design Types pictured following the introduction.

Silver Jubilee Issue
Common Design Type

1935, May 6 ***Perf. 11x12***
134 CD301 1p car & dk blue .55 *2.50*
135 CD301 1½p gray blk & ultra 1.40 *4.00*

136	CD301	2½p ultra & brn	2.50	*4.00*
137	CD301	1sh brn vio & ind	2.75	4.00
		Nos. 134-137 (4)	7.20	*14.50*
		Set, never hinged	13.50	
		Set, perforated "SPECIMEN"	100.00	

Coronation Issue

Common Design Type

1937, May 12 *Perf. 11x11½*

138	CD302	1p dark purple	.20	*.40*
139	CD302	1½p dark carmine	.25	*.40*
140	CD302	2½p deep ultra	.30	*1.25*
		Nos. 138-140 (3)	.75	*2.05*
		Set, never hinged	1.25	
		Set, perforated "SPECIMEN"	80.00	

Seal of the Colony — A18

Young's Island and Fort Duvernette — A19

Kingstown and Fort Charlotte — A20

Villa Beach — A21

Victoria Park, Kingstown — A22

1938-47 **Wmk. 4** *Perf. 12*

141	A18	½p grn & brt bl	.20	.20
142	A19	1p claret & blue	.20	.20
143	A20	1½p scar & lt grn	.20	.20
144	A18	2p black & green	.30	.20
145	A21	2½p pck bl & ind	.20	.20
145A	A22	2½p choc & grn ('47)	.20	.20
146	A18	3p dk vio & org	.20	.20
146A	A21	3½p dp bl grn & ind ('47)	.35	*1.50*
147	A18	6p claret & blk	.60	.25
148	A22	1sh green & vio	.60	.45
149	A18	2sh dk vio & brt blue	4.50	.85
149A	A18	2sh6p dp bl & org brn ('47)	.80	*3.75*
150	A18	5sh dk grn & car	7.50	2.75
150A	A18	10sh choc & dp vio ('47)	3.00	*10.00*
151	A18	£1 black & vio	11.00	*16.00*
		Nos. 141-151 (15)	29.85	*36.95*
		Set, never hinged	50.00	

Issue date: Mar. 11, 1938.
See Nos. 156-169, 180-184.

Catalogue values for unused stamps in this section, from this point to the end of the section, are for Never Hinged items.

Peace Issue

Common Design Type

1946, Oct. 15 **Engr.** *Perf. 13½x14*

152	CD303	1½p carmine	.20	.20
153	CD303	3½p deep blue	.20	.20

Silver Wedding Issue

Common Design Types

1948, Nov. 30 **Photo.** *Perf. 14x14½*

154	CD304	1½p scarlet	.20	.20

Engraved; Name Typographed
Perf. 11½x11

155	CD305	£1 red violet	25.00	25.00

Types of 1938

1949, Mar. 26 **Engr.** *Perf. 12*

156	A18	1c grn & brt bl	.20	*1.75*
157	A19	2c claret & bl	.20	*.50*
158	A20	3c scar & lt grn	.55	*.95*
159	A18	4c gray blk & grn	.40	.20
160	A22	5c choc & grn	.20	.20
161	A18	6c dk vio & org	.55	*1.20*
162	A21	7c pck blue & ind	5.25	1.40
163	A18	12c claret & blk	.50	.20
164	A22	24c green & vio	.50	.55
165	A18	48c dk vio & brt bl	2.75	2.75
166	A18	60c dp bl & org brn	2.00	*3.75*
167	A18	$1.20 dk grn & car	4.75	4.75
168	A18	$2.40 choc & dp vio	6.75	*9.25*
169	A18	$4.80 gray blk & vio	12.50	*19.00*
		Nos. 156-169 (14)	37.10	*46.45*

For overprints see Nos. 176-179.

UPU Issue

Common Design Types

Engr.; Name Typo. on 6c, 12c
Perf. 13½, 11x11½

1949, Oct. 10 **Wmk. 4**

170	CD306	5c blue	.20	.20
171	CD307	6c dp rose violet	.45	.90
172	CD308	12c red lilac	.25	.90
173	CD309	24c blue green	1.00	.25
		Nos. 170-173 (4)	1.90	*2.25*

University Issue

Common Design Types

1951, Feb. 16 **Engr.** *Perf. 14x14½*

174	CD310	3c red & blue green	.60	.60
175	CD311	12c rose lilac & blk	.60	*1.10*

Nos. 158-160 and 163 Overprinted in Black

1951, Sept. 21 *Perf. 12*

176	A20	3c scarlet & lt grn	.20	*1.25*
177	A18	4c gray blk & grn	.20	.30
178	A22	5c chocolate & grn	.20	.30
179	A18	12c claret & blk	.60	*.60*
		Nos. 176-179 (4)	1.20	*2.45*

Adoption of a new constitution for the Windward Islands, 1951.

Type of 1938-47

1952

180	A18	1c gray black & green	.20	.20
181	A18	3c dk violet & orange	.20	.20
182	A18	4c green & brt blue	.20	.20
183	A20	6c scarlet & dp green	.20	.20
184	A21	10c peacock blue & ind	.35	.35
		Nos. 180-184 (5)	1.15	1.15

WAR TAX STAMPS

No. 105 Overprinted

Type I — Words 2 to 2½mm apart.
Type II — Words 1½mm apart.
Type III — Words 3½mm apart.

1916 **Wmk. 3** *Perf. 14*

MR1	A17	1p car, type III	3.25	*13.50*
	a.	Double ovpt., type III	250.00	250.00
	b.	1p carmine, type I	5.50	*9.25*
	c.	Comma after "STAMP", type I	8.75	*17.50*
	d.	Double overprint, type I	175.00	175.00
	e.	1p carmine, type II	87.50	87.50

Overprinted

MR2	A17	1p carmine	.35	*.90*

SALVADOR, EL

'el 'sal-və-ˌdor

LOCATION — On the Pacific coast of Central America, between Guatemala, Honduras and the Gulf of Fonseca
GOVT. — Republic
AREA — 8,236 sq. mi.
POP. — 5,300,000 (est. 1984)
CAPITAL — San Salvador

8 Reales = 100 Centavos = 1 Peso
100 Centavos = 1 Colón

Watermarks

Wmk. 117 — Liberty Cap

Position of wmk. on reprints

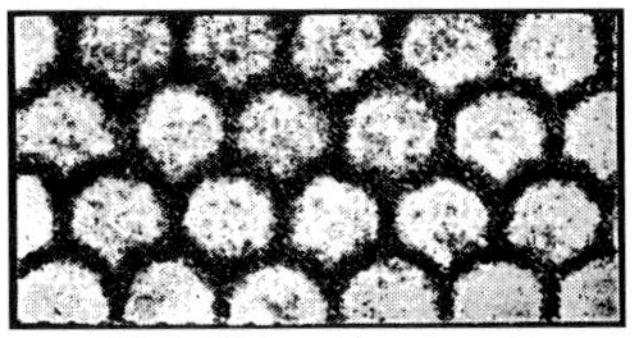

Wmk. 172 — Honeycomb

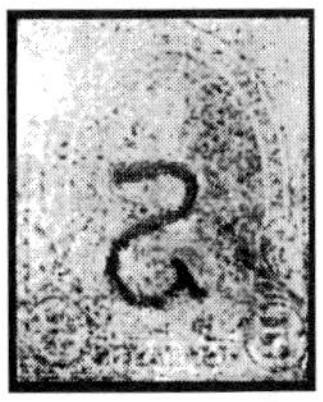

Wmk. 173 — S

Wmk. 240 — REPUBLICA DE EL SALVADOR in Sheet

Volcano San Miguel — A1

1867 **Unwmk.** **Engr.** *Perf. 12*

1	A1	½r blue	.55	*.70*
2	A1	1r red	.55	.55
3	A1	2r green	2.40	*2.75*
4	A1	4r bister	4.50	3.50
		Nos. 1-4 (4)	8.00	7.50

Nos. 1-4 when overprinted "Contra Sello" and shield with 14 stars, are telegraph stamps. For similar overprint see Nos. 5-12.
Counterfeits exist.

Nos. 1-4 Handstamped

1874

5	A1	½r blue	6.50	3.50
6	A1	1r red	6.50	3.50
7	A1	2r green	6.50	3.50
8	A1	4r bister	19.00	17.50
		Nos. 5-8 (4)	38.50	28.00

Nos. 1-4 Handstamped

9	A1	½r blue	3.75	2.00
10	A1	1r red	3.75	2.00
11	A1	2r green	3.75	2.00
12	A1	4r bister	7.50	5.00
		Nos. 9-12 (4)	18.75	11.00

The overprints on Nos. 5-12 exist double.
Counterfeits are plentiful.

Coat of Arms
A2 A3

A4

A5

A6

1879 **Litho.** *Perf. 12½*

13	A2	1c green	2.00	.90
	a.	Invtd. "V" for 2nd "A" in "SALVADOR"	4.00	2.00
	b.	Invtd. "V" for "A" in "REPUBLICA"	4.00	2.00
	c.	Invtd. "V" for "A" in "UNIVERSAL"	4.00	2.00
14	A3	2c rose	2.75	1.50
	a.	Invtd. scroll in upper left corner	8.00	5.00
15	A4	5c blue	5.00	1.25
	a.	5c ultra	8.00	4.00
16	A5	10c black	10.00	3.50
17	A6	20c violet	16.00	10.00
		Nos. 13-17 (5)	35.75	17.15

There are fifteen varieties of the 1c and 2c, twenty-five of the 5c and five each of the 10 and 20c.

In 1881 the 1c, 2c and 5c were redrawn, the 1c in fifteen varieties and the 2c and 5c in five varieties each.

No. 15 comes in a number of shades from light to dark blue.

These stamps, when overprinted "Contra sello" and arms, are telegraph stamps.

Counterfeits of No. 14 exist.

For overprints see Nos. 25D-25E, 28A-28C.

Allegorical Figure of El Salvador — A7

Volcano — A8

1887 **Engr.** *Perf. 12*

18	A7	3c brown	.40	.20
	a.	Imperf., pair	2.50	2.50
19	A8	10c orange	3.00	.90

For surcharges and overprints see Nos. 25, 26C-28, 30-32.

A9

A10

1888 *Rouletted*

20	A9	5c deep blue	.40	.35

For overprints see Nos. 35-36.

1889 *Perf. 12*

21	A10	1c green	.20	
22	A10	2c scarlet	.20	

Same Overprinted with Heavy Bar Obliterating "UNION POSTAL DEL"

23	A10	1c green	.30	.25
24	A10	2c scarlet	.30	

Nos. 21, 22 and 24 were never placed in use.

For overprints see Nos. 26, 29.

No. 18 Surcharged

Type I — thick numerals, heavy serifs.
Type II — thin numerals, straight serifs.

25	A7	1c on 3c brn, type II	.65	.50
a.		Double surcharge	1.50	
b.		Triple surcharge	3.50	
c.		Type I	.65	

The 1c on 2c scarlet is bogus.

Handstamped

1889

Violet Handstamp

25D	A2	1c green	12.50	12.50
25E	A6	20c violet	30.00	30.00
26	A10	1c green, #23	1.00	.90
26C	A7	1c on 3c, #27	20.00	20.00
27	A7	3c brown	1.00	.90
28	A8	10c orange	5.00	4.00

Black Handstamp

28A	A2	1c green	15.00	14.00
28B	A3	2c rose	17.50	17.50
28C	A6	20c violet	30.00	30.00
29	A10	1c green, #23	1.25	1.00
30	A7	3c brown	1.25	1.00
31	A7	1c on 3c, #27	17.50	17.50
32	A8	10c orange	4.50	3.50

Rouletted

Black Handstamp

35	A9	5c deep blue	1.25	.75

Violet Handstamp

36	A9	5c deep blue	1.25	.75

The 1889 handstamps as usual, are found double, inverted, etc. Counterfeits are plentiful.

A13

A14

1890 **Engr.** *Perf. 12*

38	A13	1c green	.20	.20
39	A13	2c bister brown	.20	.20
40	A13	3c yellow	.20	.20
41	A13	5c blue	.20	.20
42	A13	10c violet	.20	.20
43	A13	20c orange	.25	.20
44	A13	25c red	.90	*1.00*
45	A13	50c claret	.50	*.65*
46	A13	1p carmine	.75	*1.50*
		Nos. 38-46 (9)	3.40	*4.35*

The issues of 1890 to 1899 inclusive were printed by the Hamilton Bank Note Co., New York, to the order of N. F. Seebeck, who held a contract for stamps with the government of El Salvador. This contract gave the right to make reprints of the stamps and such were subsequently made in some instances, as will be found noted in italic type.

Used values of 1890-1899 issues are for stamps with genuine cancellations applied while the stamps were valid. Various counterfeit cancellations exist.

1891

47	A14	1c vermilion	.20	.20
48	A14	2c yellow green	.20	.20
49	A14	3c violet	.20	.20
50	A14	5c carmine lake	1.00	*2.00*
51	A14	10c blue	.20	.20
52	A14	11c violet	.20	.20
53	A14	20c green	.20	*.30*
54	A14	25c yellow brown	.20	*.40*
55	A14	50c dark blue	.20	*.90*
56	A14	1p dark brown	.20	*1.50*
		Nos. 47-56 (10)	2.80	*6.10*

For surcharges see Nos. 57-59.

Nos. 47 and 56 have been reprinted in thick toned paper with dark gum.

A15

Nos. 48, 49 Surcharged in Black or Violet:

b

c

1891

57	A15	1c on 2c yellow grn	2.25	2.00
a.		Inverted surcharge	4.00	
58	A14 (b)	1c on 2c yellow grn	1.60	1.40
59	A14 (c)	5c on 3c violet	4.00	3.25
		Nos. 57-59 (3)	7.85	6.65

Landing of Columbus — A18

1892 **Engr.**

60	A18	1c blue green	.35	.20
61	A18	2c orange brown	.35	.20
62	A18	3c ultra	.35	.20
63	A18	5c gray	.35	.20
64	A18	10c vermilion	.35	.20
65	A18	11c brown	.35	.35
66	A18	20c orange	.35	.35
67	A18	25c maroon	.35	*.55*
68	A18	50c yellow	.35	*1.10*
69	A18	1p carmine lake	.35	*1.90*
		Nos. 60-69 (10)	3.50	*5.25*

400th anniversary of the discovery of America by Columbus.

Nos. 63, 66-67 Surcharged

Nos. 70, 72

Nos. 73-75

Surcharged in Black, Red or Yellow

1892

70	A18	1c on 5c gray (Bk) (down)	1.00	.65
a.		Surcharge reading up	1.75	1.10
72	A18	1c on 5c gray (R) (up)	1.00	.80
a.		Surcharge reading down		
73	A18	1c on 20c org (Bk)	1.50	.75
a.		Inverted surcharge	3.50	2.50
b.		"V" of "CENTAVO" inverted	3.50	2.50
		Nos. 70-73 (3)	3.50	2.20

Similar Surcharge in Yellow or Blue, "centavo" in lower case letters

74	A18	1c on 25c mar (Y)	1.50	1.25
a.		Inverted surcharge	2.50	2.50
75	A18	1c on 25c mar (Bl)	*200.00*	*200.00*
a.		Double surcharge (Bl + Bk)	*225.00*	*225.00*

Counterfeits exist of Nos. 75 and 75a. Nos. 75, 75a have been questioned.

Pres. Carlos Ezeta — A21

1893 **Engr.**

76	A21	1c blue	.20	.20
77	A21	2c brown red	.20	.20
78	A21	3c purple	.20	.20
79	A21	5c deep brown	.20	.20
80	A21	10c orange brown	.20	.20
81	A21	11c vermilion	.25	*.25*
82	A21	20c green	.25	*.30*
83	A21	25c dk olive gray	.25	*.40*
84	A21	50c red orange	.25	*.50*
85	A21	1p black	.30	*.75*
		Nos. 76-85 (10)	2.30	*3.20*

For surcharge see No. 89.

Founding City of Isabela — A22

Columbus Statue, Genoa — A23

Departure from Palos — A24

1893

86	A22	2p green	.75	—
87	A23	5p violet	.75	
88	A24	10p orange	.75	
		Nos. 86-88 (3)	2.25	

Discoveries by Columbus. No. 86 is known on cover, but experts are not positive that Nos. 87 and 88 were postally used.

No. 77 Surcharged "UN CENTAVO"

1893

89	A21	1c on 2c brown red	.50	.40
a.		"CENTNVO"	3.00	2.50

Liberty — A26

Columbus before Council of Salamanca A27

Columbus Protecting Indian Hostages A28

Columbus Received by Ferdinand and Isabella A29

1894, Jan.

91	A26	1c brown	.20	.20
92	A26	2c blue	.20	.20
93	A26	3c maroon	.20	.20
94	A26	5c orange brn	.20	.20
95	A26	10c violet	.20	.20
96	A26	11c vermilion	.20	*.25*
97	A26	20c dark blue	.20	*.30*
98	A26	25c orange	.20	*.40*
99	A26	50c black	.20	*.65*
100	A26	1p slate blue	.20	*.90*
101	A27	2p deep blue	.75	
102	A28	5p carmine lake	.75	
103	A29	10p deep brown	.75	
		Nos. 91-103 (13)	4.25	
		Nos. 91-100 (10)		*3.50*

Nos. 101-103 for the discoveries by Columbus. Experts are not positive that these were postally used.

No. 96 Surcharged

1894, Dec.

104	A26	1c on 11c vermilion	1.50	.65
a.		"Ccntavo"	*40.00*	*40.00*
b.		Double surcharge		

Coat of Arms
A31 A32

Arms Overprint in Second Color
Various Frames

1895, Jan. 1

105	A31	1c olive & green	.20	.20
106	A31	2c dk green & bl	.20	.20
a.		2c dark green & green	1.00	.85
107	A31	3c brown & brown	.20	.20
108	A31	5c blue & brown	.20	.20
109	A31	10c orange & brn	.20	*.25*
110	A31	12c magenta & brn	.20	*.30*
111	A31	15c ver & ver	.20	*.35*
112	A31	20c yellow & brn	.20	*.40*
a.		Inverted overprint	2.00	
113	A31	24c violet & brn	.20	*.45*
114	A31	30c dp blue & blue	.20	*.50*

115	A31	50c carmine & brn	.20	*.65*
116	A31	1p black & brn	.20	*.90*
		Nos. 105-116 (12)	2.40	*4.60*

As printed, Nos. 105-116 portrayed Gen. Antonio Ezeta, brother of Pres. Carlos Ezeta. Before issuance, Ezeta's overthrow caused the government to obliterate his features with the national arms overprint. The 3c, 10c, 30c exist without overprint. Value $1 each.

Reprints of 2c are in dark yellow green on thick paper. Value 20 cents.

1895 Engr. *Perf. 12*

117	A32	1c olive	.55	.50
118	A32	2c dk blue grn	.20	.20
119	A32	3c brown	.20	.20
120	A32	5c blue	.20	.20
121	A32	10c orange	.65	.30
122	A32	12c claret	.65	.30
123	A32	15c vermilion	.20	*.30*
124	A32	20c deep green	.20	*.50*
125	A32	24c violet	.20	*.50*
126	A32	30c deep blue	.20	*.45*
127	A32	50c carmine lake	1.25	1.25
128	A32	1p gray black	1.50	*1.75*
		Nos. 117-128 (12)	6.00	*6.45*

The reprints are on thicker paper than the originals, and many of the shades differ. Value 15c each.

Nos. 122, 124-126 Surcharged in Black or Red:

1895

129	A32	1c on 12c claret (Bk)	1.00	.90
130	A32	1c on 24c violet	1.00	.90
131	A32	1c on 30c dp blue	1.00	.90
132	A32	2c on 20c dp green	1.00	.90
133	A32	3c on 30c dp blue	1.25	1.10
a.		Double surcharge	4.50	
		Nos. 129-133 (5)	5.25	4.70

"Peace" — A45

1896, Jan. 1 Engr. Unwmk.

134	A45	1c blue	.20	.20
135	A45	2c dark brown	.20	.20
136	A45	3c blue green	.20	.20
137	A45	5c brown olive	.20	.20
138	A45	10c yellow	.20	.20
139	A45	12c dark blue	.75	.90
140	A45	15c brt ultra	.20	*.20*
a.		15c light violet	1.10	*2.00*
141	A45	20c magenta	.65	.50
142	A45	24c vermilion	.20	*.25*
143	A45	30c orange	.20	*.40*
144	A45	50c black brn	.20	*.50*
145	A45	1p rose lake	.20	*.90*
		Nos. 134-145 (12)	3.40	*4.65*

The frames of Nos. 134-145 differ slightly on each denomination.

For overprints see Nos. O1-O12, O37-O48.

Wmk. 117

145B	A45	2c dark brown	.20	.20

The 1c, 2c, 12c, 20c, 30c, 50c and 1p on unwatermarked paper and the 2c on watermarked have been reprinted. The paper is thicker than that of the originals and the shades are different. The watermark is always upright on original stamps of Salvador, sideways on the reprints. Value 15c each.

Coat of Arms — A46

"White House" — A47

Locomotive A48

Mt. San Miguel A49

Ocean Steamship A50 A51

Post Office A52

Lake Ilopango A53

Atehausillas Waterfall A54

Coat of Arms A55

Coat of Arms A56

Columbus A57

1896

146	A46	1c emerald	.20	.20
147	A47	2c lake	.20	.20
148	A48	3c yellow brn	.20	.20
149	A49	5c deep blue	.20	.20
150	A50	10c brown	.20	.20
151	A51	12c slate	.20	*.20*
152	A52	15c blue green	.20	*.25*
153	A53	20c carmine rose	.20	*.30*
154	A54	24c violet	.20	*.40*
155	A55	30c deep green	.20	.40
156	A56	50c orange	.20	*.40*
157	A57	100c dark blue	.20	*.90*
		Nos. 146-157 (12)	2.40	*3.85*

Nos. 146-157 exist imperf.

Unwmk.

157B	A46	1c emerald	.20	.20
157C	A47	2c lake	.20	.20
157D	A48	3c yellow brn	.20	.20
157E	A49	5c deep blue	.20	.20
157F	A50	10c brown	.20	.20
157G	A51	12c slate	.20	.20
157I	A52	15c blue green	.25	.20
157J	A53	20c carmine rose	.20	*.45*
157K	A54	24c violet	.50	*.80*
157M	A55	30c deep green	.20	*.55*
157N	A56	50c orange	.20	*.55*
157O	A57	100c dark blue	.20	*1.00*
		Nos. 157B-157O (12)	2.75	*4.75*

See Nos. 159-170L. For surcharges and overprints see Nos. 158, 158D, 171-174C, O13-O36, O49-O72, O79-O126.

The 15c, 30c, 50c and 100c have been reprinted on watermarked and the 1c, 2c, 3c, 5c, 12c, 20c, 24c and 100c on unwatermarked paper. The papers of the reprints are thicker than those of the originals and the shades are different. Value, set of 12, $1.20.

Black Surcharge on Nos. 154, 157K

1896 Wmk. 117

158	A54	15c on 24c violet	4.00	4.00
a.		Double surcharge		
b.		Inverted surcharge	8.50	

Unwmk.

158D	A54	15c on 24c violet	4.00	3.00

Exist spelled "Qnince."

Types of 1896

1897 Engr. Wmk. 117

159	A46	1c scarlet	*.20*	*.20*
160	A47	2c yellow grn	.20	.20
161	A48	3c bister brn	.20	.20
162	A49	5c orange	.20	.20
163	A50	10c blue grn	.20	.20
164	A51	12c blue	.40	.30
165	A52	15c black	2.50	2.00
166	A53	20c slate	.20	.20
167	A54	24c yellow	.20	.25
168	A55	30c rose	.20	.20
169	A56	50c violet	.20	.50
170	A57	100c brown lake	2.50	2.00
		Nos. 159-170 (12)	7.20	6.45

Unwmk.

170A	A46	1c scarlet	.20	.20
170B	A47	2c yellow grn	.20	.20
170C	A48	3c bister brn	.20	.20
170D	A49	5c orange	.20	.20
170E	A50	10c blue grn	.75	.50
170F	A51	12c blue	.75	.75
170G	A52	15c black	2.00	2.00
170H	A53	20c slate	.20	*.25*
170I	A54	24c yellow	.20	*.50*
170J	A55	30c rose	1.90	1.25
170K	A56	50c violet	.90	.90
170L	A57	100c brown lake	6.25	6.25
		Nos. 170A-170L (12)	13.75	13.20

The 1c, 2c, 3c, 5c, 12c, 15c, 50c and 100c have been reprinted on watermarked and the entire issue on unwatermarked paper. The papers of the reprints are thicker than those of the originals. Value, set of 20, $2.

Surcharged in Red or Black

1897 Wmk. 117

171	A54	13c on 24c yel (R)	2.50	2.50
172	A55	13c on 30c rose (Bk)	2.50	2.50
173	A56	13c on 50c vio (Bk)	2.50	2.50
174	A57	13c on 100c brn lake (Bk)	2.50	2.50

Unwmk.

174A	A54	13c on 24c yel (R)	2.50	2.50
174B	A55	13c on 30c rose (Bk)	2.50	2.50
174C	A56	13c on 50c vio (Bk)	2.50	2.50
		Nos. 171-174C (7)	17.50	17.50

Coat of Arms of "Republic of Central America" — A59

ONE CENTAVO:

Originals: The mountains are outlined in red and blue. The sea is represented by short red and dark blue lines on a light blue background.

Reprints: The mountains are outlined in red only. The sea is printed in green and dark blue, much blurred.

FIVE CENTAVOS:

Originals: The sea is represented by horizontal and diagonal lines of dark blue on a light blue background.

Reprints: The sea is printed in green and dark blue, much blurred. The inscription in gold is in thicker letters.

1897 Litho.

175	A59	1c bl, gold, rose & grn	.50	*1.50*
176	A59	5c rose, gold, bl & grn	.50	*1.50*

Forming of the "Republic of Central America."

For overprints see Nos. O73-O76.

Stamps of type A59 formerly listed as "Type II" are now known to be reprints.

Allegory of Central American Union — A60

1898 Engr. Wmk. 117

177	A60	1c orange ver	.20	.20
178	A60	2c rose	.20	.20
179	A60	3c pale yel grn	.20	.20
180	A60	5c blue green	.20	.20
181	A60	10c gray blue	.20	.20
182	A60	12c violet	.20	.25
183	A60	13c brown lake	.20	.20
184	A60	20c deep blue	.20	*.30*
185	A60	24c deep ultra	.20	*.35*
186	A60	26c bister brn	.20	*.40*
187	A60	50c orange	.20	*.75*
188	A60	1p yellow	.20	*1.00*
		Nos. 177-188 (12)	2.40	*4.25*

For overprints and surcharges see Nos. 189-198A, 224-241, 269A-269B, O129-O142.

The entire set has been reprinted on unwatermarked paper and all but the 12c and 20c on watermarked paper. The shades of the reprints are not the same as those of the originals, and the paper is thicker. Value, set of 22, $2.25.

No. 180 Overprinted Vertically, up or down in Black, Violet, Red, Magenta and Yellow

1899

189	A60	5c blue grn (Bk)	7.50	6.25
a.		Italic 3rd "r" in "Territorial"	12.50	12.50
b.		Double ovpt. (Bk + Y)	37.50	37.50
190	A60	5c blue grn (V)	*82.50*	*82.50*
191	A60	5c blue grn (R)	*70.00*	*70.00*
191A	A60	5c blue grn (M)	*70.00*	*70.00*
191B	A60	5c blue grn (Y)	*75.00*	*75.00*
		Nos. 189-191B (5)	*305.00*	*303.75*

Counterfeits exist.

Nos. 177-184 Overprinted in Black

1899

192	A60	1c orange ver	1.00	.50
193	A60	2c rose	1.25	1.00
194	A60	3c pale yel grn	1.25	.50
195	A60	5c blue green	1.25	.50
196	A60	10c gray blue	2.00	1.25
197	A60	12c violet	3.25	2.50
198	A60	13c brown lake	3.25	2.00
198A	A60	20c deep blue	—	—
		Nos. 192-198 (7)	13.25	8.25

Counterfeits exist of the "wheel" overprint used in 1899-1900.

Ceres ("Estado") — A61

Inscribed: "Estado de El Salvador"

1899 Unwmk. Litho. *Perf. 12*

199	A61	1c brown	.20
200	A61	2c gray green	.20
201	A61	3c blue	.20
202	A61	5c brown org	.20
203	A61	10c chocolate	.20
204	A61	12c dark green	.20
205	A61	13c deep rose	.20
206	A61	24c light blue	.20
207	A61	26c carmine rose	.20
208	A61	50c orange red	.20
209	A61	100c violet	.20
		Nos. 199-209 (11)	2.20

#208-209 were probably not placed in use.

For overprints and surcharges see Nos. 210-223, 242-252D, O143-O185.

Same, Overprinted

Red Overprint

210 A61 1c brown 50.00 32.50

Blue Overprint

211 A61 1c brown .50 .20
212 A61 5c brown org .50 .20
212A A61 10c chocolate 5.00 3.50

Black Overprint

213 A61 1c brown .50 .20
214 A61 2c gray grn .75 .20
215 A61 3c blue .75 .25
216 A61 5c brown org .35 .20
217 A61 10c chocolate .50 .20
218 A61 12c dark green 1.25 .50
219 A61 13c deep rose 1.10 .65
220 A61 24c light blue 12.50 10.00
221 A61 26c car rose 3.25 2.00
222 A61 50c orange red 3.25 2.75
223 A61 100c violet 3.25 3.25
Nos. 213-223 (11) 27.45 20.20

"Wheel" overprint exists double and triple.

No. 177 Handstamped

1900 Wmk. 117

224 A60 1c orange ver 1.00 1.00

No. 177 Overprinted **1900**

225 A60 1c orange ver 15.00 15.00

1900

Stamps of 1898 Surcharged in Black

1 centavo

1900

226 A60 1c on 10c gray blue 5.00 4.25
a. Inverted surcharge 7.50 6.50
227 A60 1c on 13c brn lake *275.00*
228 A60 2c on 12c vio 17.50 12.50
a. "eentavo"
b. Inverted surcharge
c. "centavos" 30.00
d. As "c," double surcharge
e. Vertical surcharge
229 A60 2c on 13c brn lake 2.00 1.75
a. "eentavo" 3.25 2.75
b. Inverted surcharge 5.00 4.00
c. "1900" omitted
230 A60 2c on 20c dp blue 2.00 2.00
a. Inverted surcharge 3.25 3.25
230B A60 2c on 26c bis brn *175.00 175.00*
231 A60 3c on 12c vio *37.50 37.50*
a. "eentavo"
b. Inverted surcharge *35.00 35.00*
c. Double surcharge
232 A60 3c on 50c org 10.00 10.00
a. Inverted surcharge 10.00 10.00
233 A60 5c on 12c vio
234 A60 5c on 24c ultra 11.00 11.00
a. "eentavo"
b. "centavos" 11.00
235 A60 5c on 26c bis brn *37.50 37.50*
a. Inverted surcharge *35.00 35.00*
236 A60 5c on 1p yel 15.00 15.00
a. Inverted surcharge 15.00 15.00

With Additional Overprint in Black

237 A60 2c on 12c vio 2.50 2.50
a. Inverted surcharge 2.50 2.50
b. "eentavo" 8.00
c. "centavos" (plural) 75.00
d. "1900" omitted
237H A60 2c on 13c brn lake
238 A60 3c on 12c vio 42.50 42.50
a. "eentavo" 35.00 35.00
239 A60 5c on 26c bis brn 67.50 67.50
a. Inverted surcharge

Vertical Surcharge "Centavos" in the Plural

240 A60 2c on 12c vio 95.00 95.00
b. Without wheel
240A A60 5c on 24c dp ultra 95.00 95.00

With Additional Overprint in Black

241 A60 5c on 12c vio 17.50 17.50
a. Surcharge reading downward

Counterfeits exist of the surcharges on Nos. 226-241 and the "wheel" overprint on Nos. 237-239, 241.

Same Surcharge on Stamps of 1899 Without Wheel

1900 Unwmk.

242 A61 1c on 13c dp rose .40 .40
a. Inverted surcharge 1.00 .75
b. "eentavo" 1.00 .75
c. "ecntavo" 1.50 .75
d. "1 centavo 1" 4.50 3.00
e. Double surcharge
243 A61 2c on 12c dk grn 1.75 1.25
a. Inverted surcharge 3.00 2.50
b. "eentavo"
244 A61 2c on 13c dp rose 1.00 .75
a. "eentavo" 1.00 1.25
b. "ecntavo" 2.00 1.40
c. Inverted surcharge 3.00
245 A61 3c on 12c dk grn 1.00 .85
a. Inverted surcharge 3.00 1.50
b. "eentavo" 4.00 4.00
c. Double surcharge 3.00
Nos. 242-245 (4) 4.15 3.25

With Additional Overprint in Black

246 A61 1c on 2c gray grn .25 .20
a. "eentavo" .90 .65
b. Inverted surcharge 4.00 3.00
247 A61 1c on 13c dp rose 1.00 .85
a. "eentavo" 4.00
b. "1 centavo 1"
248 A61 2c on 12c dk grn 1.40 1.00
a. "eentavo" 4.00
b. Inverted surcharge 1.25 1.25
c. Double surcharge 2.00
249 A61 2c on 13c dp rose 42.50
a. "eentavo"
b. Double surcharge 75.00 75.00
250 A61 3c on 12c dk grn 1.40 .90
a. Inverted surcharge 1.50 1.25
b. "eentavo" 2.50 2.25
c. Date double 4.00
251 A61 5c on 24c lt bl 2.50 1.25
a. "eentavo" 4.00 4.00
252 A61 5c on 26c car rose 1.10 1.00
a. Inverted surcharge 4.00 2.50
b. "eentavo" 1.75 1.50
252D A61 5c on 1c on 26c car rose
Nos. 246-248,250-252 (6) 7.65 5.20

Counterfeits exist of the surcharges on Nos. 242-252D and the "wheel" overprint on Nos. 246-252D.

Ceres ("Republica") — A63

There are two varieties of the 1c, type A63, one with the word "centavo" in the middle of the label (#253, 263, 270, 299, 305, 326), the other with "centavo" nearer the left end than the right (#270, 299, 305, 326).

The stamps of type A63 are found in a great variety of shades. Stamps of type A63 without handstamp were not regularly issued.

Handstamped in Violet or Black

Inscribed: "Republica de El Salvador"

1900

253 A63 1c blue green .20 .20
a. 1c yellow green .20 .20
254 A63 2c rose .30 .20
255 A63 3c gray black .20 .20
256 A63 5c pale blue .50 .35
a. 5c deep blue .50 .35
257 A63 10c deep blue .60 .45
258 A63 12c yel green .60 .45
259 A63 13c yel brown .50 .45
260 A63 24c gray 4.00 4.00
261 A63 26c yel brown 1.75 1.75
262 A63 50c rose red 1.75 1.50
Nos. 253-262 (10) 10.40 9.55

For overprints and surcharges see Nos. 263-269, 270-282, 293A-311B, 317, 326-335, O223-O242, O258-O262, O305-O312.

Handstamped in Violet or Black

263 A63 1c lt green 1.75 1.75
264 A63 2c pale rose 1.75 1.75
265 A63 3c gray black 1.75 .75
266 A63 5c slate blue 1.75 .50
267 A63 10c deep blue — —
268 A63 13c yellow brn 12.50 8.75
269 A63 50c dull rose 1.75 1.75
Nos. 263-266,268-269 (6) 21.25 15.25

Handstamped on 1898 Stamps

Wmk. 117

269A A60 2c rose 30.00 30.00
269B A60 10c gray blue 30.00 30.00

The overprints on Nos. 253 to 269B are handstamped and, as usual with that style of overprint, are to be found double, inverted, omitted, etc.

Specialists have questioned the existence of No. 267. The editors would like to see authenticated evidence of the existence of a genuine example.

Stamps of Type A63 Overprinted in Black

1900 Unwmk.

270 A63 1c light green .20 .20
271 A63 2c rose .20 .20
272 A63 3c gray black .20 .20
273 A63 5c pale blue .20 .20
a. 5c dark blue .20 .20
274 A63 10c deep blue .40 .20
a. 10c pale blue .30 .20
275 A63 12c light green .40 .30
276 A63 13c yellow brown .20 .20
277 A63 24c gray .40 .40
278 A63 26c yellow brown .50 .50
Nos. 270-278 (9) 2.70 2.40

This overprint is known double, inverted, etc.

Nos. 271-273 Surcharged in Black

1902

280 A63 1c on 2c rose 2.75 2.25
281 A63 1c on 3c black 2.00 1.40
282 A63 1c on 5c blue 1.25 1.00
Nos. 280-282 (3) 6.00 4.65

Morazán Monument — A64

Perf. 14, 14½

1903 Engr. Wmk. 173

283 A64 1c green .35 .20
284 A64 2c carmine .35 .20
285 A64 3c orange .80 .50
286 A64 5c dark blue .35 .20
287 A64 10c dull violet .35 .20
288 A64 12c slate .40 .20
289 A64 13c red brown .40 .20
290 A64 24c scarlet 2.50 1.25
291 A64 26c yellow brn 2.50 1.25
292 A64 50c bister 1.25 .75
293 A64 100c grnsh blue 3.75 2.50
Nos. 283-293 (11) 13.00 7.45

For surcharges and overprint see Nos. 312-316, 318-325, O253.

Stamps of 1900 with Shield in Black Overprinted:

1905 (5¾x13½mm) — a

1905 (5x14¾mm) — b

(4½x16mm) — c **1905**

(4½x13½mm) — d **1905**

(5x14½mm) — e **1905**

1905-06 Unwmk. *Perf. 12*

Blue Overprint

293A A63 (a) 2c rose
294 A63 (a) 3c gray blk 4.00 3.00
a. Without shield
295 A63 (a) 5c blue 4.50 3.00

Purple Overprint

296 A63 (b) 3c gray blk (Shield in pur) 4.50 4.00
296A A63 (b) 5c bl (Shield in pue) 3.25 3.00
297 A63 (b) 3c gray blk 6.00 4.50
298 A63 (b) 5c blue 4.00 3.00

Black Overprint

298A A63 (b) 5c blue

Blue Overprint

299 A63 (c) 1c green 6.50 3.00
299B A63 (c) 2c rose .40 .35
c. "1905" vert. .80
300 A63 (c) 5c blue 1.25 .60
301 A63 (c) 10c deep blue .75 .60

Black Overprint

302 A63 (c) 2c rose 3.00 1.50
303 A63 (c) 5c blue 12.50 12.50
304 A63 (c) 10c deep blue 6.00 3.50

Blue Overprint

305 A63 (d) 1c green 7.00 6.50
306 A63 (d) 2c rose, ovpt. vert. 6.00 1.50
a. Overprint horiz.
306B A63 (d) 3c gray black 7.00 1.75
307 A63 (d) 5c blue 2.50 1.00

Blue Overprint

311 A63 (e) 2c rose 4.00 2.00
a. Without shield 6.50 3.00

Black Overprint

311B A63 (e) 5c blue 20.00 19.00
Nos. 293-311B (20) 106.90 76.80

These overprints are found double, inverted, omitted, etc. Counterfeits exist.

Regular Issue of 1903 Surcharged with New Values:

f

g

h

1905-06 Wmk. 173 *Perf. 14, 14½*

Black Surcharge

312 A64 (f) 1c on 2c car .40 .25
a. Double surcharge 3.00 3.00

Red Surcharge

312B A64 (g) 5c on 12c slate .75 .50
c. Double surcharge
d. Black surcharge 3.50 3.50
e. As "d," double surcharge

Blue Handstamped Surcharge

313 A64 (h) 1c on 2c car .25 .20
314 A64 (h) 1c on 10c vio .20 .20
315 A64 (h) 1c on 12c sl ('06) 1.00 .50
316 A64 (h) 1c on 13c red brn 4.00 3.25

No. 271 with Handstamped Surcharge in Blue

Unwmk.

317 A63 (h) 1c on 2c rose 42.50 37.50
Nos. 312-317 (7) 49.10 42.40

The "h" is handstamped in strips of four stamps each differing from the others in the size of the upper figures of value and in the letters of the word "CENTAVO," particularly in the size of the "N" and the "O" of that word. The surcharge is known inverted, double, etc.

Regular Issue of 1903 with Handstamped Surcharge:

i **5 5**

5 5 5 5

5 5 5 5

j k

Wmk. 173

Red Handstamped Surcharge

318 A64 (i) 5c on 12c slate 3.00 1.50
319 A64 (j) 5c on 12c slate 3.00 1.75
a. Blue surcharge

Blue Handstamped Surcharge

320 A64 (k) 5c on 12c slate 2.50 1.75
Nos. 318-320 (3) 8.50 5.00

One or more of the numerals in the handstamped surcharges on Nos. 318, 319 and 320 are frequently omitted, inverted, etc.

Surcharged:

6 6

6CENTAVOS6

l m

Blue Handstamped Surcharge

321 A64 (l) 6c on 12c slate .50 .30
322 A64 (l) 6c on 13c red brn 1.00 .40

Red Handstamped Surcharge

323 A64 (l) 6c on 12c slate 17.50 12.00

Type "l" is handstamped in strips of four varieties, differing in the size of the numerals and letters. The surcharge is known double and inverted.

Black Surcharge

324 A64 (m) 1c on 13c red brn 1.50 1.00
a. Double surcharge 4.00 3.00
b. Right "1" & dot omitted
c. Both numerals omitted
325 A64 (m) 3c on 13c red brn .50 .40

Stamps of 1900, with Shield in Black, Overprinted — n

1905 Unwmk. *Perf. 12*

Blue Overprint

326 A63 (n) 1c green 7.00 3.25
a. Inverted overprint
327 A63 (n) 2c rose 3.25 3.25
a. Vertical overprint 9.00 5.00
327B A63 (n) 3c black 30.00 27.50
327C A63 (n) 5c blue 12.50 10.00
328 A63 (n) 10c deep blue 6.00 4.50

Black Overprint

328A A63 (n) 10c deep blue 7.50 4.50
Nos. 326-328A (6) 66.25 53.00

Counterfeits of Nos. 326-335 abound.

Stamps of 1900, with Shield in Black Surcharged or Overprinted:

1906

2 2 1906

o p

1906 q

1906

Blue and Black Surcharge

329 A63 (o) 2c on 26c brn org .50 .40
a. "2" & dot double 7.50 7.50
330 A63 (o) 3c on 26c brn org 4.00 3.25
a. "3" & dot double

Black Surcharge or Overprint

331 A63 (o) 3c on 26c brn org 3.00 2.50
a. Disks & numerals omitted
b. "3" and disks double
c. "1906" omitted
333 A63 (p) 10c deep blue 4.00 3.75
334 A63 (q) 10c deep blue 3.50 3.50
334A A63 (q) 26c brown org 22.50 20.00
b. "1906" in blue

No. 257 Overprinted in Black

335 A63 (q) 10c dp bl (Shield in violet) 17.50 15.00
a. Overprint type "p"
Nos. 329-335 (7) 55.00 48.40

There are numerous varieties of these surcharges and overprints.

Pres. Pedro José Escalón — A65

1906 Engr. *Perf. 11½*

Glazed Paper

336 A65 1c green & blk .20 .20
a. Thin paper .75 .20
337 A65 2c red & blk .20 .20
338 A65 3c yellow & blk .20 .20
339 A65 5c ultra & blk .20 .20
a. 5c dark blue & black .20 .20
340 A65 6c carmine & blk .20 .20
341 A65 10c violet & blk .20 .20
342 A65 12c violet & blk .20 .20
343 A65 13c dk brn & blk .20 .20
345 A65 24c carmine & blk .35 .35
346 A65 26c choc & blk .35 .35
347 A65 50c yellow & blk .35 .45
348 A65 100c blue & blk *3.00 3.00*
Nos. 336-348 (12) *5.65 5.75*

All values of this set are known imperforate but are not believed to have been issued in this condition.

See Nos. O263-O272. For overprints and surcharges see Nos. 349-354.

The entire set has been reprinted. The shades of the reprints differ from those of the originals, the paper is thicker and the perforation 12. Value, set of 12, $1.20.

Nos. 336-338 Overprinted in Black

1907

349 A65 1c green & blk .25 .20
a. Shield in red 3.50
350 A65 2c red & blk .25 .20
a. Shield in red 3.50
351 A65 3c yellow & blk .25 .20
Nos. 349-351 (3) .75 .60

Reprints of Nos. 349 to 351 have the same characteristics as the reprints of the preceding issue. Value, set of 3, 15c.

Stamps of 1906 Surcharged with Shield and

352 A65 1c on 5c ultra & blk .20 .20
a. 1c on 5c dark blue & black .20 .20
b. Inverted surcharge .35 .35
c. Double surcharge .45 .45
352D A65 1c on 6c rose & blk .20 .20
e. Double surcharge 1.25 1.25
353 A65 2c on 6c rose & blk 2.00 1.00
354 A65 10c on 6c rose & blk .50 .35
Nos. 352-354 (4) 2.90 1.75

The above surcharges are frequently found with the shield double, inverted, or otherwise misplaced.

National Palace — A66

Overprinted with Shield in Black

1907 Engr. Unwmk.

Paper with or without colored dots

355 A66 1c green & blk .20 .20
356 A66 2c red & blk .20 .20
357 A66 3c yellow & blk .20 .20
358 A66 5c blue & blk .20 .20
a. 5c ultramarine & black .20 .20
359 A66 6c ver & blk .20 .20
a. Shield in red 3.25
360 A66 10c violet & blk .20 .20
361 A66 12c violet & blk .20 .20
362 A66 13c sepia & blk .20 .20
363 A66 24c rose & blk .20 .20
364 A66 26c yel brn & blk .30 .20
365 A66 50c orange & blk .50 .35
a. 50c yellow & black 3.50
366 A66 100c turq bl & blk 1.00 .50
Nos. 355-366 (12) 3.60 2.85

Most values exist without shield, also with shield inverted, double, and otherwise misprinted. Many of these were never sold to the public.

See 2nd footnote following No. 421.

See Nos. 369-373, 397-401. For surcharges and overprints see Nos. 367-368A, 374-77, 414-421, 443-444, J71-J74, J76-J80, O329-O331.

No. 356 With Additional Surcharge in Black

1908

367 A66 1c on 2c red & blk .25 .25
a. Double surcharge 1.00 1.00
b. Inverted surcharge .50 .50
c. Double surcharge, one inverted .50 .50
d. Red surcharge

Same Surcharged in Black or Red

UN CENTAVO

368 A66 1c on 2c *19.00 17.50*
368A A66 1c on 2c (R) *27.50 25.00*

Counterfeits exist of the surcharges on Nos. 368-368A.

Type of 1907

1909 Engr. Wmk. 172

369 A66 1c green & blk .20 .20
370 A66 2c rose & blk .20 .20
371 A66 3c yellow & blk .25 .20
372 A66 5c blue & blk .25 .20
373 A66 10c violet & blk .30 .20
Nos. 369-373 (5) 1.20 1.00

The note after No. 366 will apply here also.

Nos. 355, 369 Overprinted in Red

1909, Sept. Unwmk.

374 A66 1c green & blk 2.25 1.10
a. Inverted overprint 10.00

Wmk. 172

375 A66 1c green & blk 1.75 1.40
a. Inverted overprint

88th anniv. of El Salvador's independence.

Nos. 362, 364 Surcharged

1909 Unwmk.

376 A66 2c on 13c sep & blk 1.50 1.25
a. Inverted surcharge
377 A66 3c on 26c yel brn & blk 1.75 1.40
a. Inverted surcharge

A67

A68

Design: Pres. Fernando Figueroa.

1910 Engr. Wmk. 172

378 A67 1c sepia & blk .20 .20
379 A67 2c dk grn & blk .20 .20
380 A67 3c orange & blk .20 .20
381 A67 4c carmine & blk .20 .20
a. 4c scarlet & black .20 .20
382 A67 5c purple & blk .20 .20
383 A67 6c scarlet & blk .20 .20
384 A67 10c purple & blk .20 .20
385 A67 12c dp bl & blk .20 .20
386 A67 17c ol grn & blk .20 .20
387 A67 19c brn red & blk .20 .20
388 A67 29c choc & blk .20 .20
389 A67 50c yellow & blk .20 .20
390 A67 100c turq bl & blk .20 .20
Nos. 378-390 (13) 2.60 2.60

1911 Unwmk.

5c, José Matías Delgado. 6c, Manuel José Arce. 12c, Centenary Monument.

Paper with colored dots

391 A68 5c dp blue & brn .20 .20
392 A68 6c orange & brn .20 .20
393 A68 12c violet & brn .20 .20

Wmk. 172

394 A68 5c dp blue & brn .20 .20
395 A68 6c orange & brn .20 .20
396 A68 12c violet & brn .20 .20
Nos. 391-396 (6) 1.20 1.20

Centenary of the insurrection of 1811.

Palace Type of 1907 without Shield

1911

Paper without colored dots

397 A66 1c scarlet .20 .20
398 A66 2c chocolate .30 .30
a. Paper with brown dots
399 A66 13c deep green .20 .20
400 A66 24c yellow .20 .20
401 A66 50c dark brown .20 .20
Nos. 397-401 (5) 1.10 1.10

José Matías Delgado — A71

Manuel José Arce — A72

Francisco Morazán A73

Rafael Campo A74

Trinidad Cabañas A75

Monument of Gerardo Barrios A76

Centenary Monument A77

National Palace A78

Rosales Hospital — A79

Coat of Arms — A80

1912 **Unwmk.** ***Perf. 12***

402 A71 1c dp bl & blk .20 .20
403 A72 2c bis brn & blk .25 .20
404 A73 5c scarlet & blk .25 .20
405 A74 6c dk grn & blk .20 .20
406 A75 12c ol grn & blk 1.00 .20
407 A76 17c violet & slate .60 .20
408 A77 19c scar & slate 1.25 .30
409 A78 29c org & slate 1.50 .30
410 A79 50c blue & slate 1.75 .45
411 A80 1col black & slate 2.50 1.00
Nos. 402-411 (10) 9.50 3.25

Juan Manuel Rodríguez A81

Pres. Manuel E. Araujo A82

1914 ***Perf. 11½***

412 A81 10c orange & brn 2.50 .75
413 A82 25c purple & brn 2.50 .75

Type of 1907 without Shield Overprinted in Black

1915

Paper overlaid with colored dots

414 A66 1c gray green .20 .20
415 A66 2c red .20 .20
416 A66 5c ultra .20 .20
417 A66 6c pale blue .20 .20
418 A66 10c yellow .60 .30
419 A66 12c brown .50 .20
420 A66 50c violet .20 .20
421 A66 100c black brn 1.40 1.40
Nos. 414-421 (8) 3.50 2.90

Varieties such as center omitted, center double, center inverted, imperforate exist with or without date, date inverted, date double, etc., but are believed to be entirely unofficial.

Preceding the stamps with the "1915" overprint a quantity of stamps of this type was overprinted with the letter "S." Evidence is lacking that they were ever placed in use. The issue was demonetized in 1916.

National Theater — A83

Various frames.

1916 **Engr.** ***Perf. 12***

431 A83 1c deep green .20 .20
432 A83 2c vermilion .20 .20
433 A83 5c deep blue .20 .20
434 A83 6c gray violet .25 .20
435 A83 10c black brn .25 .20
436 A83 12c violet 2.50 .50
437 A83 17c orange .35 .20
438 A83 25c dk brown .80 .20
439 A83 29c black 5.00 .75
440 A83 50c slate 2.50 1.50
Nos. 431-440 (10) 12.25 4.15

Watermarked letters which occasionally appear are from the papermaker's name.

For surcharges and overprints see Nos. 450-455, 457-466, O332-O341.

Nos. O324-O325 with "OFICIAL" Barred out in Black

1917

441 O3 2c red .45 .45
a. Double bar
442 O3 5c ultramarine .50 .35
a. Double bar

Regular Issue of 1915 Overprinted "OFICIAL" and Re-overprinted In Red

443 A66 6c pale blue .65 .50
a. Double bar
444 A66 12c brown .85 .65
a. Double bar
b. "CORRIENTE" inverted

Same Overprint in Red On Nos. O323-O327

445 O3 1c gray green 1.75 1.25
a. "CORRIENTE" inverted
b. Double bar
c. "CORRIENTE" omitted
446 O3 2c red 1.75 1.25
a. Double bar
447 O3 5c ultra 9.00 6.00
a. Double bar, both in black
448 O3 10c yellow 1.00 .50
a. Double bar
b. "OFICIAL" and bar omitted
449 O3 50c violet .50 .50
a. Double bar
Nos. 443-449 (7) 15.50 10.65

Nos. O334-O335 Overprinted or Surcharged in Red:

a

b

450 A83 (a) 5c deep blue 1.50 1.00
a. "CORRIENTE" double
451 A83 (b) 1c on 6c gray vio 1.00 .75
a. "CORRIERTE"
b. "CORRIENRE" 5.00
c. "CORRIENTE" double

No. 434 Surcharged in Black

1918

452 A83 1c on 6c gray vio 1.75 1.00
a. Double surcharge
b. Inverted surcharge

No. 434 Surcharged in Black

1918

453 A83 1c on 6c gray vio 1.50 .75
a. "Centado" 2.25 1.50
b. Double surcharge 2.50 1.75
c. Inverted surcharge

No. 434 Surcharged in Black or Red

454 A83 1c on 6c gray vio 4.00 3.25
a. Double surcharge
b. Inverted surcharge 5.00 5.00
455 A83 1c on 6c gray vio (R) 4.00 3.25
a. Double surcharge
b. Inverted surcharge 5.00 5.00
Nos. 454-455 (2) 8.00 6.50

Counterfeits exist of Nos. 454-455.

Pres. Carlos Meléndez — A85

1919 **Engr.**

456 A85 1col dk blue & blk .50 .50

For surcharge see No. 467.

No. 437 Surcharged in Black

1919

457 A83 1c on 17c orange .25 .25
a. Inverted surcharge 1.00 1.00
b. Double surcharge 1.00 1.00

Nos. 435-436, 438, 440 Surcharged in Black or Blue

1920-21

458 A83 1c on 12c violet .20 .20
a. Double surcharge 1.00 1.00
459 A83 2c on 10c dk brn .25 .20
460 A83 5c on 50c slate ('21) .40 .20
461 A83 6c on 25c dk brn (Bl) ('21) .40 .20

Same Surch. in Black on No. O337

462 A83 1c on 12c violet 1.00 1.00
a. Double surcharge
Nos. 458-462 (5) 2.25 1.80

No. 460 surcharged in yellow and 461 surcharged in red are essays.

No. 462 is due to some sheets of Official Stamps being mixed with the ordinary 12c stamps at the time of surcharging. The error stamps were sold to the public and used for ordinary postage.

Surcharged in Red, Blue or Black:

15c Types:

15	15	15	15
I	II	III	IV

463 A83 15c on 29c blk (III) ('21) 1.00 .40
a. Double surcharge 2.00
b. Type I 1.50 1.00
c. Type II 1.00 .75
d. Type IV 2.50
464 A83 26c on 29c blk (Bl) 1.00 .60
a. Double surcharge
466 A83 35c on 50c slate (Bk) 1.00 .60
467 A85 60c on 1col dk bl & blk (R) .30 .25
Nos. 463-467 (4) 3.30 1.85

Surcharge on No. 464 differs from 15c illustration in that bar at bottom extends across stamp and denomination includes "cts." One stamp in each row of ten of No. 464 has the "t" of "cts" inverted and one stamp in each row of No. 466 has the letters "c" in "cinco" larger than the normal.

Setting for No. 467 includes three types of numerals and "CENTAVOS" measuring from 16mm to 20mm wide.

No. 464 surcharged in green or yellow and the 35c on 29c black are essays.

A93

1921

468 A93 1c on 1c ol grn .20 .20
a. Double surcharge .75
469 A93 1c on 5c yellow .20 .20
a. Inverted surcharge
b. Double surcharge
470 A93 1c on 10c blue .20 .20
a. Double surcharge .50
471 A93 1c on 25c green .20 .20
a. Double surcharge
472 A93 1c on 50c olive .20 .20
a. Double surcharge
473 A93 1c on 1p gray blk .20 .20
a. Double surcharge
Nos. 468-473 (6) 1.20 1.20

The frame of No. 473 differs slightly from the illustration.

Setting includes many wrong font letters and numerals.

Francisco Menéndez A94

Manuel José Arce A95

Confederation Coin — A96

Delgado Addressing Crowd — A97

Coat of Arms of Confedera-tion A98

Francisco Morazán A99

Independence Monument A100

Columbus A101

1921 **Engr.** ***Perf. 12***

474 A94 1c green .25 .20
475 A95 2c black .25 .20
476 A96 5c orange 1.00 .20
477 A97 6c carmine rose .50 .20
478 A98 10c deep blue .50 .20
479 A99 25c olive grn 2.50 .20
480 A100 60c violet 6.00 .50
481 A101 1col black brn 10.00 .75
Nos. 474-481 (8) 21.00 2.45

For overprints and surcharges see Nos. 481A-485, 487-494, 506, O342-O349.

Nos. 474-477 Overprinted in Red, Black or Blue

a

b

1921

481A A94 (a) 1c green (R) 5.00 4.00
481B A95 (a) 2c black (R) 5.00 4.00
481C A96 (b) 5c orange (Bk) 5.00 4.00
481D A97 (b) 6c car rose (Bl) 5.00 4.00
Nos. 481A-481D (4) 20.00 16.00

Centenary of independence.

No. 477 Surcharged:

a

b

1923

482 A97 (a) 5c on 6c .35 .20
483 A97 (b) 5c on 6c .30 .20
484 A97 (b) 20c on 6c .35 .25
Nos. 482-484 (3) 1.00 .65

Nos. 482-484 exist with double surcharge.

No. 475 Surcharged in Red

1923

485 A95 10c on 2c black .50 .20

José Simeón Cañas y Villacorta — A102

1923 **Engr.** ***Perf. 11½***

486 A102 5c blue .50 .30

Centenary of abolition of slavery. For surcharge see No. 571.

Nos. 479, 481 Surcharged in Red or Black

1924 ***Perf. 12***

487 A99 1c on 25c ol grn (R) .20 .20
a. Numeral at right inverted
b. Double surcharge
488 A99 6c on 25c ol grn (R) .20 .20
489 A99 20c on 25c ol grn (R) .50 .25
490 A101 20c on 1col blk brn (Bk) .65 .35
Nos. 487-490 (4) 1.55 1.00

Nos. 476, 478 Surcharged:

1924

491 A96 1c on 5c orange (Bk) .35 .20
492 A98 6c on 10c dp bl (R) .35 .20

Nos. 491-492 exist with double surcharge. A stamp similar to No. 492 but with surcharge "6 centavos 6" is an essay.

No. 476 Surcharged

2
Dos centavos

493 A96 2c on 5c orange .40 .35
a. Top ornament omitted 2.00 2.00
Nos. 491-493 (3) 1.10 .75

No. 480 Surcharged:

1924

Red Surcharge

494 A100 5c on 60c violet 4.25 3.75
a. "1781" for "1874" 10.00 8.75
b. "1934" for "1924" 10.00 8.75

Universal Postal Union, 50th anniversary. This stamp with black surcharge is an essay. Copies have been passed through the post.

Daniel Hernández Monument A106

National Gymnasium A107

Atlacatl — A108

Conspiracy of 1811 — A109

Bridge over Lempa River — A110

Map of Central America — A111

Balsam Tree — A112

Tulla Serra — A114

Columbus at La Rábida — A115

Coat of Arms — A116

Photogravure; Engraved (35c, 1col)

1924-25 ***Perf. 12½; 14 (35c, 1col)***

495 A106 1c red violet .20 .20
496 A107 2c dark red .25 .20
497 A108 3c chocolate .20 .20
498 A109 5c olive blk .20 .20
499 A110 6c grnsh blue .25 .20
500 A111 10c orange .60 .20
a. "ATLANT CO" 5.50 5.50
501 A112 20c deep green 1.00 .25
502 A114 35c scar & grn 2.50 .35
503 A115 50c orange brown 2.00 .30
504 A116 1col grn & vio ('25) 3.00 .30
Nos. 495-504 (10) 10.20 2.40

For overprints and surcharges see Nos. 510-511, 520-534, 585, C1-C10, C19, O350-O361, RA1-RA4.

No. 480 Surcharged in Red

1925, Aug. ***Perf. 12***

506 A100 2c on 60c violet 1.25 1.25

City of San Salvador, 400th anniv. The variety with dates in black is an essay.

View of San Salvador — A118

1925 **Photo.** ***Perf. 12½***

507 A118 1c blue .65 .65
508 A118 2c deep green .65 .65
509 A118 3c Mahogany red .65 .65
Nos. 507-509 (3) 1.95 1.95

#506-509 for the 4th centenary of the founding of the City of San Salvador.

Black Surcharge

1928, July 17

510 A111 3c on 10c orange .75 .50
a. "ATLANT CO" 12.50 12.50

Industrial Exhibition, Santa Ana, July 1928.

Red Surcharge

1928

511 A109 1c on 5c olive black .25 .20
a. Bar instead of top left "1" .40 .25

Pres. Pío Romero Bosque, Salvador, and Pres. Lázaro Chacón, Guatemala A121

1929 **Litho.** ***Perf. 11½***

Portraits in Dark Brown

512 A121 1c dull violet .35 .25
a. Center inverted 11.50 11.50
513 A121 3c bister brn .35 .25
a. Center inverted 35.00 35.00
514 A121 5c gray grn .35 .25
515 A121 10c orange .35 .25
Nos. 512-515 (4) 1.40 1.00

Opening of the international railroad connecting El Salvador and Guatemala.

Nos. 512-515 exist imperforate. No. 512 in the colors of No. 515.

Tomb of Menéndez A122

1930, Dec. 3

516 A122 1c violet 3.00 2.50
517 A122 3c brown 3.00 2.50
518 A122 5c dark green 3.00 2.50
519 A122 10c yellow brn 3.00 2.50
Nos. 516-519 (4) 12.00 10.00

Centenary of the birth of General Francisco Menéndez.

Stamps of 1924-25 Issue Overprinted

1932 ***Perf. 12½, 14***
520 A106 1c deep violet .20 .20
521 A107 2c dark red .20 .20
522 A108 3c chocolate .30 .20
523 A109 5c olive blk .30 .20
524 A110 6c deep blue .35 .20
525 A111 10c orange 1.00 .20
a. "ATLANT CO" 7.50 6.25
526 A112 20c deep green 1.50 .45
527 A114 35c scar & grn 2.25 .75
528 A115 50c orange brown 3.00 1.00
529 A116 1col green & vio 5.00 2.25
Nos. 520-529 (10) 14.10 5.65

Values are for the overprint measuring 7½x3mm. It is found in two other sizes: 7½x3¼mm and 8x3mm.

Types of 1924-25 Surcharged with New Values in Red or Black

1934 ***Perf. 12½***
530 A109 2(c) on 5c grnsh blk .20 .20
a. Double surcharge
531 A111 3(c) on 10c org (Bk) .25 .20
a. "ATLANT CO" 4.00 4.00

Nos. 503, 504, 502 Surcharged with New Values in Black

Perf. 12½, 14½
532 A115 2(c) on 50c .30 .20
a. Double surcharge 3.00
533 A116 8(c) on 1col .20 .20
534 A114 15(c) on 35c .30 .20
Nos. 530-534 (5) 1.25 1.00

Police Barracks — A123

Two types of the 2c:
Type I — The clouds have heavy lines of shading.
Type II — The lines of shading have been removed from the clouds.

Wmk. 240
1934-35 **Litho.** ***Perf. 12½***
535 A123 2c gray brn, type I .20 .20
a. 2c brown, type II .20 .20
536 A123 5c car, type II .20 .20
537 A123 8c lt ultra, type II .20 .20
Nos. 535-537,C33-C35 (6) 3.10 2.10

Discus Thrower A124

1935, Mar. 16 **Engr.** **Unwmk.**
538 A124 5c carmine 2.00 1.65
539 A124 8c blue 2.25 1.90
540 A124 10c orange yel 2.75 2.00
541 A124 15c bister 3.25 2.25
542 A124 37c green 4.00 3.25
Nos. 538-542,C36-C40 (10) 50.50 39.30

3rd Central American Games.

Same Overprinted in Black

1935, June 27
543 A124 5c carmine 3.50 2.00
544 A124 8c blue 5.00 2.00
545 A124 10c orange yel 5.00 2.50
546 A124 15c bister 5.00 2.50
547 A124 37c green 8.00 4.00
Nos. 543-547,C41-C45 (10) 68.00 43.25

Flag of El Salvador A125

Tree of San Vicente A126

1935, Oct. 26 **Litho.** **Wmk. 240**
548 A125 1c gray blue .20 .20
549 A125 2c black brn .20 .20
550 A125 3c plum .20 .20
551 A125 5c rose carmine .25 .20
552 A125 8c ultra .30 .20
553 A125 15c fawn .40 .25
Nos. 548-553,C46 (7) 2.05 1.50

1935, Dec. 26
Numerals in Black, Tree in Yellow Green
554 A126 2c black brn .50 .25
555 A126 3c dk blue grn .50 .30
556 A126 5c rose red .50 .35
557 A126 8c dark blue .50 .40
558 A126 15c brown .50 .50
Nos. 554-558,C47-C51 (10) 6.50 5.30

Tercentenary of San Vicente.

Volcano of Izalco — A127

Wharf at Cutuco — A128

Doroteo Vasconcelos A129

Parade Ground A130

Dr. Tomás G. Palomo — A131

Sugar Mill — A132

Coffee at Pier — A133

Gathering Balsam — A134

Pres. Manuel E. Araujo — A135

1935, Dec. **Engr.** **Unwmk.**
559 A127 1c deep violet .20 .20
560 A128 2c chestnut .20 .20
561 A129 3c green .20 .20
562 A130 5c carmine .40 .20
563 A131 8c dull blue .20 .20
564 A132 10c orange .25 .20
565 A133 15c dk olive bis .40 .20
566 A134 50c indigo 2.00 1.25
567 A135 1col black 5.00 3.00
Nos. 559-567 (9) 8.85 5.65

Paper has faint imprint "El Salvador" on face.
For surcharges and overprint see Nos. 568-570, 573, 583-584, C52.

Stamps of 1935 Surcharged with New Value in Black

1938 ***Perf. 12½***
568 A130 1c on 5c carmine .20 .20
569 A132 3c on 10c orange .20 .20
570 A133 8c on 15c dk ol bis .20 .20
Nos. 568-570 (3) .60 .60

No. 486 Surcharged with New Value in Red

1938 ***Perf. 11½***
571 A102 3c on 5c blue .25 .25

Centenary of the death of José Simeón Cañas, liberator of slaves in Latin America.

Map of Flags of US and El Salvador — A136

Engraved and Lithographed
1938, Apr. 21 ***Perf. 12***
572 A136 8c multicolored .65 .50

US Constitution, 150th anniv. See #C61.

No. 560 Surcharged with New Value in Black

1938 ***Perf. 12½***
573 A128 1c on 2c chestnut .20 .20

Indian Sugar Mill — A137

Designs: 2c, Indian women washing. 3c, Indian girl at spring. 5c, Indian plowing. 8c, Izote flower. 10c, Champion cow. 20c, Extracting balsam. 50c, Maquilishuat in bloom. 1col, Post Office, San Salvador.

1938-39 **Engr.** ***Perf. 12***
574 A137 1c dark violet .20 .20
575 A137 2c dark green .20 .20
576 A137 3c dark brown .25 .20
577 A137 5c scarlet .25 .20
578 A137 8c dark blue 1.25 .20
579 A137 10c yel org ('39) 2.00 .20
580 A137 20c bis brn ('39) 1.75 .20
581 A137 50c dull blk ('39) 2.25 .45
582 A137 1col black ('39) 2.00 .75
Nos. 574-582 (9) 10.15 2.60

For surcharges & overprints see #591-592, C96.

Nos. 566-567, 504 Surcharged in Red

1939, Sept. 25 ***Perf. 12½, 14***
583 A134 8c on 50c indigo .30 .20
584 A135 10c on 1col blk .45 .20
585 A116 50c on 1col grn & vio 2.75 2.10
Nos. 583-585 (3) 3.50 2.50

Battle of San Pedro Perulapán, 100th anniv.

Sir Rowland Hill — A146

1940, Mar. 1 ***Perf. 12½***
586 A146 8c dk bl, lt bl & blk 5.50 1.75
Nos. 586,C69-C70 (3) 24.00 14.00

Postage stamp centenary.

AIR POST STAMPS

Regular Issue of 1924-25 Overprinted in Black or Red

First Printing.
15c on 10c: "15 QUINCE 15" measures 22½mm.
20c: Shows on the back of the stamp an albino impression of the 50c surcharge.
25c on 35c: Original value canceled by a long and short bar.
40c on 50c: Only one printing.
50c on 1col: Surcharge in dull orange red.

Perf. 12½, 14
1929, Dec. 28 **Unwmk.**
C1 A112 20c dp green (Bk) 3.25 3.25
a. Red overprint 600.00 600.00

Counterfeits exist of No. C1a.

With Additional Surcharge of New Values and Bars in Black or Red
C3 A111 15c on 10c orange .50 .50
a. "ALTANT CO" 14.00 14.00
C4 A114 25c on 35c scar & grn 1.25 1.25
a. Bars inverted 7.50 7.50
C5 A115 40c on 50c org brn .50 .35
C6 A116 50c on 1col grn & vio (R) 8.00 6.50
Nos. C1-C6 (5) 13.50 11.85

Second Printing.
15c on 10d: "15 QUINCE 15" measures 20½mm.
20c: Has not the albino impression on the back of the stamp.
25c on 35c: Original value cancelled by two bars of equal length.
50c on 1col: Surcharge in carmine rose.

1930, Jan. 10
C7 A112 20c deep green .45 .45
C8 A111 15c on 10c org .45 .45
a. "ATLANT CO" 17.50
b. Double surcharge 10.00
c. As "a," double surcharge 75.00
d. Pair, one without surcharge *175.00*
C9 A114 25c on 35c scar & grn .40 .40
C10 A116 50c on 1col grn & vio (C) .90 .90
a. Without bars over "UN COLON" 2.50
b. As "a," without block over "1" 2.50
Nos. C7-C10 (4) 2.20 2.20

Numerous wrong font and defective letters exist in both printings of the surcharges.
No. C10 with black surcharge is bogus.

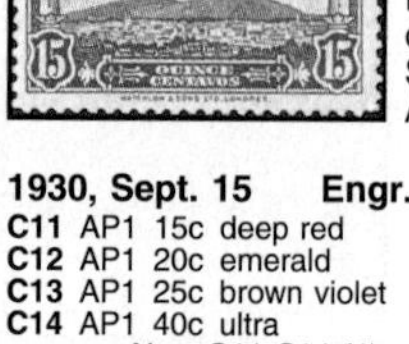

Mail Plane over San Salvador AP1

1930, Sept. 15 **Engr.** ***Perf. 12½***
C11 AP1 15c deep red .20 .20
C12 AP1 20c emerald .20 .20
C13 AP1 25c brown violet .20 .20
C14 AP1 40c ultra .30 .20
Nos. C11-C14 (4) .90 .80

Simón Bolivar — AP2

1930, Dec. 17 Litho. *Perf. 11½*

C15 AP2 15c deep red 4.00 3.50
a. "15" double 82.50
C16 AP2 20c emerald 4.00 3.50
C17 AP2 25c brown violet 4.00 3.50
a. Vert. pair, imperf. btwn. 110.00
b. Imperf., pair
C18 AP2 40c dp ultra 4.00 3.50
Nos. C15-C18 (4) 16.00 14.00

Centenary of death of Simón Bolivar. Counterfeits of Nos. C15-C18 exist.

No. 504 Overprinted in Red

1931, June 29 Engr. *Perf. 14*

C19 A116 1col green & vio 3.25 2.00

Tower of La Merced Church — AP3

1931, Nov. 5 Litho. *Perf. 11½*

C20 AP3 15c dark red 3.00 2.25
a. Imperf., pair 50.00
C21 AP3 20c blue green 3.00 2.25
C22 AP3 25c dull violet 3.00 2.25
a. Vert. pair, imperf. btwn. 110.00
C23 AP3 40c ultra 3.00 2.25
a. Imperf., pair 60.00
Nos. C20-C23 (4) 12.00 9.00

120th anniv. of the 1st movement toward the political independence of El Salvador. In the tower of La Merced Church (AP3) hangs the bell which José Matias Delgado-called the Father of his Country-rang to initiate the movement for liberty.

José Matias Delgado AP4

Airplane and Caravels of Columbus AP5

1932, Nov. 12 Wmk. 271 *Perf. 12½*

C24 AP4 15c dull red & vio .75 .75
C25 AP4 20c blue grn & bl 1.00 1.00
C26 AP4 25c dull vio & brn 1.00 1.00
C27 AP4 40c ultra & grn 1.25 1.25
Nos. C24-C27 (4) 4.00 4.00

1st centenary of the death of Father José Matías Delgado, who is known as the Father of El Salvadoran Political Emancipation.

Nos. C24-C27 show cheek without shading in the 72nd stamp of each sheet.

1933, Oct. 12 Wmk. 240 *Perf. 13*

C28 AP5 15c red orange 1.25 1.00
C29 AP5 20c blue green 2.00 1.40
C30 AP5 25c lilac 2.00 1.40
C31 AP5 40c ultra 2.00 1.40
C32 AP5 1col black 2.00 1.40
Nos. C28-C32 (5) 9.25 6.60

Saling of Chistopher Columbus from Palos, Spain, for the New World, 441st anniv

Police Barracks Type

1934, Dec. 16 *Perf. 12½*

C33 A123 25c lilac .40 .25
C34 A123 30c brown .60 .40
a. Imperf., pair 42.50
C35 A123 1col black 1.50 .85
Nos. C33-C35 (3) 2.50 1.50

Runner AP7

1935, Mar. 16 Engr. Unwmk.

C36 AP7 15c carmine 3.25 3.00
C37 AP7 25c violet 3.25 3.00
C38 AP7 30c brown 2.75 2.25
C39 AP7 55c blue 16.00 11.00
C40 AP7 1col black 11.00 9.00
Nos. C36-C40 (5) 36.25 28.25

Third Central American Games.

For overprints and surcharge see Nos. C41-C45, C53.

Same Overprinted in Black

1935, June 27

C41 AP7 15c carmine 3.00 1.75
C42 AP7 25c violet 3.00 1.75
C43 AP7 30c brown 3.00 1.75
C44 AP7 55c blue 22.50 17.50
C45 AP7 1col black 10.00 7.50
Nos. C41-C45 (5) 41.50 30.25

Flag of El Salvador Type

1935, Oct. 26 Litho. Wmk. 240

C46 A125 30c black brown .50 .25

Tree of San Vicente Type

1935, Dec. 26 *Perf. 12½*

Numerals in Black, Tree in Yellow Green

C47 A126 10c orange .80 .70
C48 A126 15c brown .80 .70
C49 A126 20c dk blue grn .80 .70
C50 A126 25c dark purple .80 .70
C51 A126 30c black brown .80 .70
Nos. C47-C51 (5) 4.00 3.50

Tercentenary of San Vicente.

No. 565 Overprinted in Red

1937 Engr. Unwmk.

C52 A133 15c dk olive bis .35 .25
a. Double overprint 25.00

No. C44 Surcharged in Red

C53 AP7 30c on 55c blue 2.00 .75

Panchimalco Church — AP10

1937, Dec. 3 Engr. *Perf. 12*

C54 AP10 15c orange yel .25 .20
C55 AP10 20c green .25 .20
C56 AP10 25c violet .25 .20
C57 AP10 30c brown .25 .20
C58 AP10 40c blue .25 .25
C59 AP10 1col black .90 .25
C60 AP10 5col rose carmine 3.25 2.25
Nos. C54-C60 (7) 5.40 3.55

US Constitution Type of Regular Issue

1938, Apr. 22 Engr. & Litho.

C61 A136 30c multicolored .60 .50

José Simeón Cañas y Villacorta — AP12

1938, Aug. 18 Engr.

C62 AP12 15c orange .90 .85
C63 AP12 20c brt green 1.10 .85
C64 AP12 30c redsh brown 1.10 .85
C65 AP12 1col black 3.75 2.75
Nos. C62-C65 (4) 6.85 5.30

José Simeón Cañas y Villacorta (1767-1838), liberator of slaves in Central America.

Golden Gate Bridge, San Francisco Bay — AP13

1939, Apr. 14 *Perf. 12½*

C66 AP13 15c dull yel & blk .25 .20
C67 AP13 30c dk brown & blk .30 .20
C68 AP13 40c dk blue & blk .40 .25
Nos. C66-C68 (3) .95 .65

Golden Gate Intl. Exposition, San Francisco.

For surcharges see Nos. C86-C91.

Sir Rowland Hill Type

1940, Mar. 1 Engr.

C69 A146 30c dk brn, buff & blk 5.00 1.75
C70 A146 80c org red & blk 13.50 10.50

Centenary of the postage stamp. Covers postmarked Feb. 29 were predated. Actual first day was Mar. 1.

Map of the Americas, Figure of Peace, Plane — AP15

1940, May 22 *Perf. 12*

C71 AP15 30c brown & blue .25 .20
C72 AP15 80c dk rose & blk .50 .40

Pan American Union, 50th anniversary.

Coffee Tree in Bloom — AP16

Coffee Tree with Ripe Berries — AP17

1940, Nov. 27

C73 AP16 15c yellow orange 1.00 .20
C74 AP16 20c deep green 1.25 .20
C75 AP16 25c dark violet 1.50 .40
C76 AP17 30c copper brown 2.00 .20
C77 AP17 1col black 6.00 .45
Nos. C73-C77 (5) 11.75 1.45

REGISTRATION STAMPS

Gen. Rafael Antonio Gutiérrez — R1

1897 Engr. Wmk. 117 *Perf. 12*

F1 R1 10c dark blue *125.00*
F2 R1 10c brown lake .20

Unwmk.

F3 R1 10c dark blue .20
F4 R1 10c brown lake .20

Nos. F1 and F3 were probably not placed in use without the overprint "FRANQUEO OFICIAL" (Nos. O127-O128).

The reprints are on thick unwatermarked paper. Value, set of 2, 16c.

ACKNOWLEDGMENT OF RECEIPT STAMPS

AR1

1897 Engr. Wmk. 117 *Perf. 12*

H1 AR1 5c dark green .20

Unwmk.

H2 AR1 5c dark green .20

No. H2 has been reprinted on thick paper. Value 15c.

POSTAGE DUE STAMPS

D1

1895 Unwmk. Engr. *Perf. 12*

J1 D1 1c olive green .20 .20
J2 D1 2c olive green .20 .20
J3 D1 3c olive green .20 .20
J4 D1 5c olive green .20 .20
J5 D1 10c olive green .20 .20
J6 D1 15c olive green .20 .20
J7 D1 25c olive green .20 .20
J8 D1 50c olive green .20 .25
Nos. J1-J8 (8) 1.60 1.65

See Nos. J9-J56. For overprints see Nos. J57-J64, O186-O214.

1896 Wmk. 117

J9 D1 1c red .20 .20
J10 D1 2c red .20 .20
J11 D1 3c red .20 .25
J12 D1 5c red .20 .25
J13 D1 10c red .20 .25
J14 D1 15c red .20 .30

J15 D1 25c red .20 .30
J16 D1 50c red .20 .35
Nos. J9-J16 (8) 1.60 2.10

Unwmk.

J17 D1 1c red .20 .20
J18 D1 2c red .20 .20
J19 D1 3c red .20 .20
J20 D1 5c red .20 .20
J21 D1 10c red .20 .20
J22 D1 15c red .20 .20
J23 D1 25c red .20 .20
J24 D1 50c red .20 .20
Nos. J17-J24 (8) 1.60 1.60

Nos. J17-J24 exist imperforate.

1897

J25 D1 1c deep blue .20 .20
J26 D1 2c deep blue .20 .20
J27 D1 3c deep blue .20 .20
J28 D1 5c deep blue .20 .20
J29 D1 10c deep blue .20 .20
J30 D1 15c deep blue .20 .20
J31 D1 25c deep blue .20 .20
J32 D1 50c deep blue .20 .20
Nos. J25-J32 (8) 1.60 1.60

1898

J33 D1 1c violet .20
J34 D1 2c violet .20
J35 D1 3c violet .20
J36 D1 2c violet .20
J37 D1 10c violet .20
J38 D1 15c violet .20
J39 D1 25c violet .20
J40 D1 50c violet .20
Nos. J33-J40 (8) 1.60

Reprints of Nos. J1 to J40 are on thick paper, often in the wrong shades and usually with the impression somewhat blurred. Value, set of 40, $2, watermarked or unwatermarked.

1899 Wmk. 117 Sideways

J41 D1 1c orange .20
J42 D1 2c orange .20
J43 D1 3c orange .20
J44 D1 5c orange .20
J45 D1 10c orange .20
J46 D1 15c orange .20
J47 D1 25c orange .20
J48 D1 50c orange .20
Nos. J41-J48 (8) 1.60

Unwmk.

Thick Porous Paper

J49 D1 1c orange .20
J50 D1 2c orange .20
J51 D1 3c orange .20
J52 D1 5c orange .20
J53 D1 10c orange .20
J54 D1 15c orange .20
J55 D1 25c orange .20
J56 D1 50c orange .20
Nos. J49-J56 (8) 1.60

Nos. J41-J56 were probably not put in use without the wheel overprint.

Nos. J49-J56 Overprinted in Black

1900

J57 D1 1c orange .50
J58 D1 2c orange .50
J59 D1 3c orange .50
J60 D1 5c orange .75
J61 D1 10c orange 1.00
J62 D1 15c orange 1.00
J63 D1 25c orange 1.25
J64 D1 50c orange 1.50
Nos. J57-J64 (8) 7.00

See note after No. 198A.

Morazán Monument — D2

Perf. 14, 14½

1903 Engr. Wmk. 173

J65 D2 1c yellow green 1.75 1.00
J66 D2 2c carmine 2.75 1.50
J67 D2 3c orange 2.75 1.50
J68 D2 5c dark blue 2.75 1.50
J69 D2 10c dull violet 2.75 1.50
J70 D2 25c blue green 2.75 1.50
Nos. J65-J70 (6) 15.50 8.50

Nos. 355, 356, 358 and 360 Overprinted

1908 Unwmk. *Perf. 11½*

J71 A66 1c green & blk .40 .35
J72 A66 2c red & blk .30 .25
J73 A66 5c blue & blk .75 .50
J74 A66 10c violet & blk 1.10 1.00

Same Overprint on No. O275

J75 O3 3c yellow & blk .75 .65
Nos. J71-J75 (5) 3.30 2.75

Nos. 355-358, 360 Overprinted

J76 A66 1c green & blk .25 .25
J77 A66 2c red & blk .30 .30
J78 A66 3c yellow & blk .35 .35
J79 A66 5c blue & blk .50 .50
J80 A66 10c violet & blk 1.00 1.00
Nos. J76-J80 (5) 2.40 2.40

It is now believed that stamps of type A66, on paper with Honeycomb watermark, do not exist with genuine overprints of the types used for Nos. J71-J80.

Pres. Fernando Figueroa — D3

1910 Engr. Wmk. 172

J81 D3 1c sepia & blk .20 .20
J82 D3 2c dk grn & blk .20 .20
J83 D3 3c orange & blk .20 .20
J84 D3 4c scarlet & blk .20 .20
J85 D3 5c purple & blk .20 .20
J86 D3 12c deep blue & blk .20 .20
J87 D3 24c brown red & blk .20 .20
Nos. J81-J87 (7) 1.40 1.40

OFFICIAL STAMPS

Overprint Types

a

Nos. 134-157O Overprinted Type a

1896 Unwmk. *Perf. 12*

O1 A45 1c blue .20
O2 A45 2c dk brown .20
a. Double overprint
O3 A45 3c blue grn .30
O4 A45 5c brown ol .20
O5 A45 10c yellow .20
O6 A45 12c dk blue .20
O7 A45 15c blue vio .20
O8 A45 20c magenta .30
O9 A45 24c vermilion .20
O10 A45 30c orange .30
O11 A45 50c black brn .20
O12 A45 1p rose lake .20
Nos. O1-O12 (12) 2.70

The 1c has been reprinted on thick unwatermarked paper. Value 15c.

Wmk. 117

O13 A46 1c emerald .20
O14 A47 2c lake .20
O15 A48 3c yellow brn .20
a. Inverted overprint 1.00
O16 A49 5c dp blue .20
O17 A50 10c brown .20
a. Inverted overprint 1.25
O18 A51 12c slate .20
O19 A52 15c blue grn .20
O20 A53 20c car rose .20
a. Inverted overprint
O21 A54 24c violet .20
O22 A55 30c dp green .20
O23 A56 50c orange .20
O24 A57 100c dk blue .20
Nos. O13-O24 (12) 2.40

Unwmk.

O25 A46 1c emerald .20
a. Double overprint
O26 A47 2c lake .20
O27 A48 3c yellow brn .20
O28 A49 5c dp blue .85
O29 A50 10c brown .20
a. Inverted overprint
O30 A51 12c slate .20
O31 A52 15c blue grn .20
O32 A53 20c car rose .20
a. Inverted overprint
O33 A54 24c violet .40
O34 A55 30c dp green .20
O35 A56 50c orange .85
O36 A57 100c dk blue 1.10
Nos. O25-O36 (12) 4.80

The 3, 5, 10, 12, 15, 20, 24, 30 and 100c have been reprinted on thick unwatermarked paper and the 15c, 50c and 100c on thick watermarked paper. Value, set of 12, $1.20.

Nos. 134-145 Handstamped Type b in Black or Violet

b

1896

O37 A45 1c blue 7.50
O38 A45 2c dk brown 7.50
O39 A45 3c blue green 7.50
O40 A45 5c brown olive 7.50
O41 A45 10c yellow 8.75
O42 A45 12c dk blue 11.50
O43 A45 15c blue violet 11.50
O44 A45 20c magenta 11.50
O45 A45 24c vermilion 11.50
O46 A45 30c orange 11.50
O47 A45 50c black brown 15.00
O48 A45 1p rose lake 15.00
Nos. O37-O48 (12) 126.25

Reprints of the 1c and 2c on thick paper exist with this handstamp. Value, set of 2, 20c.

Forged overprints exist of Nos. O37-O78, O103-O126 and of the higher valued stamps of O141-O214.

Nos. 146-157F, 157I-157O, 158D Handstamped Type b in Black or Violet

1896 Wmk. 117

O49 A46 1c emerald 6.25
O50 A47 2c lake 6.25
O51 A48 3c yellow brn 6.25
O52 A49 5c deep blue 6.25
O53 A50 10c brown 6.25
O54 A51 12c slate 10.00
O55 A52 15c blue green 11.50
O56 A53 20c carmine rose 11.50
O57 A54 24c violet 11.50
O58 A55 30c deep green 11.50
O59 A56 50c orange 11.50
O60 A57 100c dark blue 11.50
Nos. O49-O60 (12) 110.25

Unwmk.

O61 A46 1c emerald 6.25
O62 A47 2c lake 6.25
O63 A48 3c yellow brn 6.25
O64 A49 5c deep blue 6.25
O65 A50 10c brown 8.75
O66 A52 15c blue green 11.50
O67 A58 15c on 24c vio 11.50
O68 A53 20c carmine rose 11.50
O69 A54 24c violet 11.50
O70 A55 30c deep green 11.50
O71 A56 50c orange 12.50
O72 A57 100c dark blue 12.50
Nos. O61-O72 (12) 116.25

Nos. 175-176 Overprinted Type a in Black

1897

O73 A59 1c bl, gold, rose & grn .25
O74 A59 5c rose, gold, bl & grn .25

These stamps were probably not officially issued.

Nos. 175-176 Handstamped Type b in Black or Violet

1900

O75 A59 1c bl, gold, rose & grn 17.50
O76 A59 5c rose, gold, bl & grn 17.50

Nos. 159-170L Overprinted Type a in Black

1897 Wmk. 117

O79 A46 1c scarlet .20
O80 A47 2c yellow green 1.25
O81 A48 3c bister brown .50
O82 A49 5c orange .20 .20
O83 A50 10c blue green .20
O84 A51 12c blue .25
O85 A52 15c black .25 .50
O86 A53 20c slate .20
O87 A54 24c yellow .20
a. Inverted overprint
O88 A55 30c rose .50
O89 A56 50c violet 1.25 1.00
O90 A57 100c brown lake 1.75
Nos. O79-O90 (12) 6.75

Unwmk.

O91 A46 1c scarlet .20
O92 A47 2c yellow green .30
O93 A48 3c bister brown .20
O94 A49 5c orange .20 .20
O95 A50 10c blue green .65
O96 A51 12c blue .65
O97 A52 15c black .75
O98 A53 20c slate .20 .35
O99 A54 24c yellow .20 .35
O100 A55 30c rose .20 .35
O101 A56 50c violet .65
O102 A57 100c brown lake .40 1.00
Nos. O91-O102 (12) 4.60

All values have been reprinted on thick paper without watermark and the 1c, 12c, 15c and 100c on thick paper with watermark. Value, set of 16, $1.60.

Nos. 159-170L Handstamped Type b in Violet or Black

1897 Wmk. 117

O103 A46 1c scarlet 7.50
O104 A47 2c yellow green 7.50
O105 A48 3c bister brown 7.50
O106 A49 5c orange 7.50
O107 A50 10c blue green 8.75
O108 A51 12c blue
O109 A52 15c black
O110 A53 20c slate 15.00
O111 A54 24c yellow 17.50
O112 A55 30c rose
O113 A56 50c violet
O114 A57 100c brown lake

Unwmk.

O115 A46 1c scarlet 7.50
O116 A47 2c yellow grn 7.50
O117 A48 3c bister brn 7.50
O118 A49 5c orange 7.50
O119 A50 10c blue green 7.50
O120 A51 12c blue
O121 A52 15c black
O122 A53 20c slate
O123 A54 24c yellow
O124 A55 30c rose 15.00
O125 A56 50c violet
O126 A57 100c brown lake 17.50

Reprints of the 1 and 15c on thick watermarked paper and the 12, 30, 50 and 100c on thick unwatermarked paper are known with this overprint. Value, set of 6, 60c.

Nos. F1, F3 Overprinted Type a in Red

Wmk. 117

O127 R1 10c dark blue .20

Unwmk.

O128 R1 10c dark blue .20

The reprints are on thick paper. Value 15c.
Originals of the 10c brown lake Registration Stamp and the 5c Acknowledgment of Receipt stamp are believed not to have been issued with the "FRANQUEO OFICIAL" overprint. They are believed to exist only as reprints.

Nos. 177-188 Overprinted Type a

1898 Wmk. 117

O129 A60 1c orange ver .20
O130 A60 2c rose .20
O131 A60 3c pale yel grn 1.40
O132 A60 5c blue green .20
O133 A60 10c gray blue .20
O134 A60 12c violet 1.40
O135 A60 13c brown lake .20
O136 A60 20c deep blue .20
O137 A60 24c ultra .20
O138 A60 26c bister brn .20

O139 A60 50c orange .20
O140 A60 1p yellow .20
Nos. O129-O140 (12) 4.80

Reprints of the above set are on thick paper. Value, set of 12, $1.20, with or without watermark.

No. 177 Handstamped Type b in Violet

O141 A60 1c orange ver 30.00

No. O141 with Additional Overprint Type c in Black

c

Type "c" is called the "wheel" overprint.

O142 A60 1c orange ver

Counterfeits exist of the "wheel" overprint.

Nos. 204-205, 207 and 209 Overprinted Type a

1899 **Unwmk.**

O143 A61 12c dark green
O144 A61 13c deep rose
O145 A61 26c carmine rose
O146 A61 100c violet

Nos. O143-O144 Punched With Twelve Small Holes

O147 A61 12c dark green
O148 A61 13c deep rose

Official stamps punched with twelve small holes were issued and used for ordinary postage.

Nos. 199-209 Overprinted

d

1899

Blue Overprint

O149 A61 1c brown .20
O150 A61 2c gray green .20
O151 A61 3c blue .20
O152 A61 5c brown orange .20
O153 A61 10c chocolate .20
O154 A61 13c deep rose .20
O155 A61 26c carmine rose .20
O156 A61 50c orange red .20
O157 A61 100c violet .20

Black Overprint

O158 A61 3c blue .20
O159 A61 12c dark green .20
O160 A61 24c lt blue .20
Nos. O149-O160 (12) 2.40

#O149-O160 were probably not placed in use.

With Additional Overprint Type c in Black

O161 A61 1c brown .40 .35
O162 A61 2c gray green .60 .50
O163 A61 3c blue .40 .35
O164 A61 5c brown org .40 .35
O165 A61 10c chocolate .50 .40
O166 A61 12c dark green
O167 A61 13c deep rose 1.00 .85
O168 A61 24c lt blue 15.00 15.00
O169 A61 26c carmine rose 1.00 .60
O170 A61 50c orange red 1.00 .85
O171 A61 100c violet 1.25 .85
Nos. O161-O165,O167-O171 (10) 21.55 20.10

Nos. O149-O155, O159-O160 Punched With Twelve Small Holes

Blue Overprint

O172 A61 1c brown 2.75 1.00
O173 A61 2c gray green 3.25 1.00
O174 A61 3c blue 4.50 3.75
O175 A61 5c brown org 6.00 3.00
O176 A61 10c chocolate 7.50 5.00
O177 A61 13c deep rose 7.50 3.75
O177A A61 24c lt blue
O178 A61 26c carmine rose 75.00 35.00

Black Overprint

O179 A61 12c dark green 6.00 4.50
Nos. O172-O177,O178-O179 (8) 112.50 57.00

It is stated that Nos. O172-O214 inclusive were issued for ordinary postage and not for use as official stamps.

Nos. O161-O167, O169 Overprinted Type c in Black

O180 A61 1c brown 1.25 1.10
O180A A61 2c gray green
O181 A61 3c blue
O182 A61 5c brown orange 1.25
O182A A61 10c chocolate
O182B A61 12c dark green
O183 A61 13c deep rose 4.00 2.00
O184 A61 26c carmine rose

Overprinted Types a and e in Black

e

O185 A61 100c violet

Nos. J49-J56 Overprinted Type a in Black

1900

O186 D1 1c orange 22.50
O187 D1 2c orange 22.50
O188 D1 3c orange 22.50
O189 D1 5c orange 22.50
O190 D1 10c orange 22.50
O191 D1 15c orange 50.00
O192 D1 25c orange 50.00
O193 D1 50c orange 50.00
Nos. O186-O193 (8) 262.50

Nos. O186-O189, O191-O193 Overprinted Type c in Black

O194 D1 1c orange
O195 D1 2c orange 12.50
O196 D1 3c orange
O197 D1 5c orange
O198 D1 15c orange 12.50
O199 D1 25c orange 15.00
O200 D1 50c orange 140.00

Nos. O186-O189 Punched With Twelve Small Holes

O201 D1 1c orange 35.00
O202 D1 2c orange 35.00
O203 D1 3c orange 35.00
O204 D1 5c orange 35.00
Nos. O201-O204 (4) 140.00

Nos. O201-O204 Overprinted Type c in Black

O205 D1 1c orange 9.00 6.50
O206 D1 2c orange 6.50
O207 D1 3c orange 6.50
O208 D1 5c orange 9.00 6.50

Overprinted Type a in Violet and Type c in Black

O209 D1 2c orange 12.50
a. Inverted overprint
O210 D1 3c orange
O211 D1 10c orange 3.00

Nos. O186-O188 Handstamped Type e in Violet

O212 D1 1c orange 9.00 7.50
O213 D1 2c orange 9.00 7.50
O214 D1 3c orange 9.00 9.00
Nos. O212-O214 (3) 27.00 24.00

See note after No. O48.

Type of Regular Issue of 1900 Overprinted Type a in Black

O223 A63 1c lt green 22.50 —
a. Inverted overprint
O224 A63 2c rose 27.50 —
a. Inverted overprint
O225 A63 3c gray black 17.50 —
a. Overprint vertical
O226 A63 5c blue 17.50 —
O227 A63 10c blue 45.00 —
a. Inverted overprint
O228 A63 12c yellow grn 45.00 —
O229 A63 13c yellow brn 45.00 —
O230 A63 24c gray black 32.50 —
O231 A63 26c yellow brn 30.00 —
a. Inverted overprint
O232 A63 50c dull rose
a. Inverted overprint
Nos. O223-O231 (9) 282.50 .00

Nos. O223-O224, O231-O232 Overprinted in Violet

f

O233 A63 1c lt green 4.75 4.00
O234 A63 2c rose 25.00
a. "FRANQUEO OFICIAL" invtd.
O235 A63 26c yellow brown .50 .50
O236 A63 50c dull rose .75 .55

Nos. O223, O225-O228, O232 Overprinted in Black

g

O237 A63 1c lt green 5.00 5.00
O238 A63 3c gray black
O239 A63 5c blue 40.00
O240 A63 10c blue
O241 A63 12c yellow green

Violet Overprint

O242 A63 50c dull rose 10.00

The shield overprinted on No. O242 is of the type on No. O212.

O1

1903 **Wmk. 173** ***Perf. 14, 14½***

O243 O1 1c yellow green .45 .25
O244 O1 2c carmine .45 .20
O245 O1 3c orange 1.40 .85
O246 O1 5c dark blue .45 .20
O247 O1 10c dull violet .70 .35
O248 O1 13c red brown .70 .35
O249 O1 15c yellow brown 5.00 1.75
O250 O1 24c scarlet .45 .35
O251 O1 50c bister .70 .35
O252 O1 100c grnsh blue .70 .75
Nos. O243-O252 (10) 11.00 5.40

For surcharges see Nos. O254-O257.

No. 285 Handstamped Type b in Black

1904

O253 A64 3c orange 35.00

Nos. O246-O248 Surcharged in Black

1905

O254 O1 2c on 5c dark blue 3.25 2.75
O255 O1 3c on 5c dark blue
a. Double surcharge
O256 O1 3c on 10c dl vio 9.00 6.00
O257 O1 3c on 13c red brn .85 .70

A 2c surcharge of this type exists on No. O247.

No. O225 Overprinted in Blue

a

1905

b

1905 **Unwmk.**

O258 A63(a) 3c gray black 2.00 1.75
O259 A63(b) 3c gray black 1.75 1.50

Nos. O224-O225 Overprinted in Blue

1906

c

d

1906

O260 A63(c) 2c rose 11.25 10.00
O261 A63(c) 3c gray black 1.25 1.00
a. Overprint "1906" in blk
O262 A63(d) 3c gray black 1.40 1.25
Nos. O260-O262 (3) 13.90 12.25

Escalón — O2

National Palace — O3

1906 **Engr.** ***Perf. 11½***

O263 O2 1c green & blk .20 .20
O264 O2 2c carmine & blk .20 .20
O265 O2 3c yellow & blk .20 .20
O266 O2 5c blue & blk .20 .30
O267 O2 10c violet & blk .20 .20
O268 O2 13c dk brown & blk .20 .20
O269 O2 15c red org & blk .20 .20
O270 O2 24c carmine & blk .25 .20
O271 O2 50c orange & blk .25 *.65*
O272 O2 100c dk blue & blk .25 *2.00*
Nos. O263-O272 (10) 2.15 *4.35*

The centers of these stamps are also found in blue black.

Nos. O263 to O272 have been reprinted. The shades differ, the paper is thicker and the perforation 12. Value, set of 10, 50c.

1908

O273 O3 1c green & blk .20 .20
O274 O3 2c red & blk .20 .20
O275 O3 3c yellow & blk .20 .20
O276 O3 5c blue & blk .20 .20
O277 O3 10c violet & blk .20 .20
O278 O3 13c violet & blk .20 .20
O279 O3 15c pale brn & blk .20 .20
O280 O3 24c rose & blk .20 .20
O281 O3 50c yellow & blk .20 .20
O282 O3 100c turq blue & blk .20 .20
Nos. O273-O282 (10) 2.00 2.00

For overprints see Nos. 441-442, 445-449, J75, O283-O292, O323-O328.

Nos. O273-O282 Overprinted Type g in Black

O283 O3 1c green & blk .85
O284 O3 2c red & blk 1.00
O285 O3 3c yellow & blk 1.00
O286 O3 5c blue & blk 1.25
O287 O3 10c violet & blk 1.25
O288 O3 13c violet & blk 1.50
O289 O3 15c pale brn & blk 1.50
O290 O3 24c rose & blk 2.00
O291 O3 50c yellow & blk 2.50
O292 O3 100c turq & blk 3.00
Nos. O283-O292 (10) 15.85

Pres. Figueroa — O4

1910 **Engr.** **Wmk. 172**

O293 O4 2c dk green & blk .20 .20
O294 O4 3c orange & blk .20 .20
O295 O4 4c scarlet & blk .20 .20
a. 4c carmine & black
O296 O4 5c purple & blk .20 .20
O297 O4 6c scarlet & blk .20 .20
O298 O4 10c purple & blk .20 .20
O299 O4 12c dp blue & blk .20 .20
O300 O4 17c olive grn & blk .20 .20
O301 O4 19c brn red & blk .20 .20
O302 O4 29c choc & blk .20 .20
O303 O4 50c yellow & blk .20 .20
O304 O4 100c turq & blk .20 .20
Nos. O293-O304 (12) 2.40 2.40

Regular Issue, Type A63, Overprinted or Surcharged:

a

b

c

1911 **Unwmk.**

O305	A63(a)	1c lt green	.20	.20
O306	A63(b)	3c on 13c yel brn	.20	.20
O307	A63(b)	5c on 10c dp bl	.20	.20
O308	A63(a)	10c deep blue	.20	.20
O309	A63(a)	12c lt green	.20	.20
O310	A63(a)	13c yellow brn	.20	.20
O311	A63(b)	50c on 10c dp bl	.20	.20
O312	A63(c)	1col on 13c yel brn	.20	.20
		Nos. O305-O312 (8)	1.60	1.60

O5

O6

1914 Typo. *Perf. 12*

Background in Green, Shield and "Provisional" in Black

O313	O5	2c yellow brn	.20	.20
O314	O5	3c yellow	.20	.20
O315	O5	5c dark blue	.20	.20
O316	O5	10c red	.20	.20
O317	O5	12c green	.20	.20
O318	O5	17c violet	.20	.20
O319	O5	50c brown	.20	.20
O320	O5	100c dull rose	.20	.20
		Nos. O313-O320 (8)	1.60	1.60

Stamps of this issue are known imperforate or with parts of the design omitted or misplaced. These varieties were not regularly issued.

1914 **Typo.**

O321	O6	2c blue green	.20	.20
O322	O6	3c orange	.20	.20

Type of Official Stamps of 1908 With Two Overprints

1915

O323	O3	1c gray green	.30	.25
a.		"1915" double		
b.		"OFICIAL" inverted		
O324	O3	2c red	.30	.25
O325	O3	5c ultra	.30	.25
O326	O3	10c yellow	.30	.25
a.		Date omitted		
O327	O3	50c violet	.55	.50
O328	O3	100c black brown	1.25	1.00
		Nos. O323-O328 (6)	3.00	2.50

Same Overprint on #414, 417, 429

O329	A66	1c gray green	1.60	1.60
O330	A66	6c pale blue	.50	.40
a.		6c ultramarine		
O331	A66	12c brown	.60	.60
		Nos. O329-O330 (2)	2.10	2.00

\# O323-O327, O329-O331 exist imperf.
Nos. O329-O331 exist with "OFICIAL" inverted and double. See note after No. 421.

Nos. 431-440 Overprinted in Blue or Red

1916

O332	A83	1c deep green	.20	.20
O333	A83	2c vermilion	.35	.20
O334	A83	5c dp blue (R)	.25	.20
O335	A83	6c gray vio (R)	.20	.20
O336	A83	10c black brown	.20	.20
O337	A83	12c violet	.40	.25
O338	A83	17c orange	.20	.20
O339	A83	25c dark brown	.20	.20
O340	A83	29c black (R)	.20	.20
O341	A83	50c slate (R)	.20	.20
		Nos. O332-O341 (10)	2.40	2.05

Nos. 474-481 Overprinted

a

b

1921

O342	A94(a)	1c green	.20	.20
O343	A95(a)	2c black	.20	.20
a.		Inverted overprint		
O344	A96(b)	5c orange	.20	.20
O345	A97(a)	6c carmine rose	.20	.20
O346	A98(a)	10c deep blue	.20	.20
O347	A99(a)	25c olive green	.50	.25
O348	A100(a)	60c violet	.60	.50
O349	A101(a)	1col black brown	.65	.65
		Nos. O342-O349 (8)	2.75	2.40

Nos. 498 and 500 Overprinted in Black or Red

1925

O350	A109	5c olive black	.35	.20
O351	A111	10c orange (R)	.50	.20
a.		"ATLANT CO"	7.50	6.25

Inverted overprints exist.

Regular Issue of 1924-25 Overprinted in Black or Red

1927

O352	A106	1c red violet	.20	.20
O353	A107	2c dark red	.40	.25
O354	A109	5c olive blk (R)	.40	.25
O355	A110	6c dp blue (R)	3.00	2.50
O356	A111	10c orange	.50	.30
a.		"ATLANT CO"	12.50	11.50
O357	A116	1col grn & vio (R)	1.50	1.00
		Nos. O352-O357 (6)	6.00	4.50

Inverted overprints exist on 1c, 2c, 5c, 10c.

Regular Issue of 1924-25 Overprinted in Black

1932 ***Perf. 12½***

O358	A106	1c deep violet	.20	.20
O359	A107	2c dark red	.40	.20
O360	A109	5c olive black	.20	.20
O361	A111	10c orange	.70	.30
a.		"ATLANT CO"	14.00	12.50
		Nos. O358-O361 (4)	1.50	.90

PARCEL POST STAMPS

Mercury PP1

1895 Unwmk. Engr. *Perf. 12*

Q1	PP1	5c brown orange	.25
Q2	PP1	10c dark blue	.25
Q3	PP1	15c red	.25
Q4	PP1	20c orange	.25
Q5	PP1	50c blue green	.25
		Nos. Q1-Q5 (5)	1.25

POSTAL TAX STAMPS

Nos. 503, 501 Surcharged

1931 Unwmk. *Perf. 12½*

RA1	A115	1c on 50c org brn	.20	.20
a.		Double surcharge	2.00	2.00
RA2	A112	2c on 20c dp grn	.20	.20

Nos. 501, 503 Surcharged

RA3	A112	1c on 20c dp grn	.20	.20
RA4	A115	2c on 50c org brn	.20	.20
a.		Without period in "0.02"	1.25	

The use of these stamps was obligatory, in addition to the regular postage, on letters and other postal matter. The money obtained from their sale was to be used to erect a new post office in San Salvador.

SAMOA

LOCATION — An archipelago in the South Pacific Ocean, east of Fiji
GOVT. — Monarchy and (partially) German possession
AREA — 1,130 sq. mi.
POP. — 39,000 (est. 1910)
CAPITAL — Apia

In 1861-99, Samoa was an independent kingdom under the influence of the US, to which the harbor of Pago Pago had been ceded, and that of Great Britain and Germany. In 1898 a disturbance arose, resulting in the withdrawal of Great Britain, and the partitioning of the islands between Germany and the US. Early in World War I the islands under German domination were occupied by New Zealand troops and in 1920 the League of Nations declared them a mandate to New Zealand.

12 Pence = 1 Shilling
20 Shillings = 1 Pound
100 Pfennig = 1 Mark (1900)

Catalogue values for unused stamps in this country are for Never Hinged items, beginning with Scott 191 in the regular postage section.

Watermark

Wmk. 61 — N Z and Star Close Together

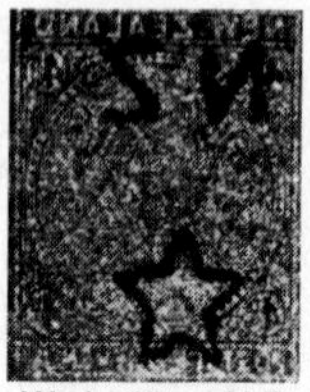
Wmk. 62 — N Z and Star Wide Apart

On watermark 61 the margins of the sheets are watermarked "NEW ZEALAND POSTAGE" and parts of the double-lined letters of these words are frequently found on the stamps. It occasionally happens that a stamp shows no watermark whatever.

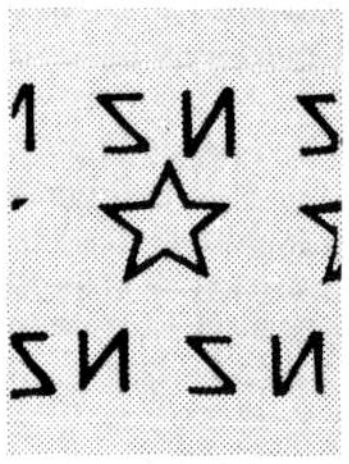
Wmk. 253 — Multiple N Z and Star

Issues of the Kingdom

A1

Perf. 11¾, 12½

1877-82 Litho. Unwmk.

Type I

Line above "X" is usually unbroken. Dots over "SAMOA" are uniform and evenly spaced. Upper right serif of "M" is horizontal.

Printed in sheets of 20 (5x4), imperf on outer edges. Only six stamps may be perforated all around. Eight stamps in each pane of the 1p have a stop after "PENNY."

1877 ***Perf. 12½***

1c	A1	1p sky blue	300.00	*400.00*
3c	A1	3p vermilion	300.00	*350.00*
4b	A1	6p bright violet	300.00	*350.00*
4c	A1	6p pale lilac	400.00	350.00

No. 6a shows the line above "X" unbroken, but has the dot between "M" and "O" characteristic of type I.

Stamps were pen cancelled from October 1877 to March 1878, when the circular date stamp arrived.

Type II

Line above "X" is usually broken. Small dot near upper right serif of letter "M." Printed in sheets of 10 (5x2), imperf on outer edges, so that all stamps have at least one straight edge.

1878-79 ***Perf. 12½***

1b	A1	1p sky blue	150.00	*250.00*
3b	A1	3p vermilion	400.00	*750.00*
4a	A1	6p violet	900.00	*1,000.*
6	A1	1sh orange yellow	125.00	125.00
6a	A1	1sh dull yellow	400.00	100.00
6b	A1	1sh lemon yellow	400.00	100.00
6c	A1	1sh golden yellow, Perf 11¾ ('79)	75.00	*400.00*
7a	A1	2sh red brown	450.00	*750.00*
7b	A1	2sh chocolate	450.00	*750.00*
8b	A1	5sh gray green	4,000.	1,500.

Type III

Line above "X" roughly retouched. Upper right serif of letter "M" bends down (joined to dot).

Printed in sheets of 10 (5x2), except the 1p, which was printed in sheets of 20 (5x4).

1879 ***Perf. 12½***

1a	A1	1p sky blue	350.00	140.00
3	A1	3p vermilion	550.00	300.00
4	A1	6p lilac	600.00	200.00

7 A1 2sh deep brown 450.00 *500.00*
7c A1 2sh chocolate 450.00 *500.00*
8 A1 5sh emerald green 2,500. 1,000.
8c A1 5sh line above "X" not repaired (pos. 2/3) —

1879-82 ***Perf. 11¾***

1 A1 1p blue 32.50
1d A1 1p ultramarine 75.00
1e A1 1p deep blue 35.00
3a A1 3p scarlet vermilion, clean-cut perfs 120.00
3d A1 3p vermilion, rough perfs 65.00
4c A1 6p dull lilac 55.00 *100.00*
4d A1 6p bright violet 40.00 *800.00*
7d A1 2sh deep brown 200.00
8a A1 5sh yellow green 550.00
8d A1 5sh deep green 1,000.
8e A1 5sh line above "X" not repaired (pos. 2/3) —

Nos. 1-8e are found with either clean-cut or rough-cut perforations.

Only the 6p and 1sh denominations of the type III, perf 11¾ issue are known used.

Type IV

Speck of color on curved line below center of "M."

1880-82 ***Perf. 11¾***

2 A1 2p lilac rose ('82) 25.00
5 A1 9p pale chestnut 80.00 *160.00*
5a A1 9p pale org brown 100.00 *800.00*

The 2p was never placed in use since the Samoa Express service was discontinued late in 1881.

Some examples of Nos. 1-8 appear with portions of the papermaker's watermark.

Imperforates of this issue are proofs.

Reprints are of type IV and nearly always perforated on all sides. They have a spot of color at the edge of the panel below the "M." This spot is not on any originals except the 2p, which may be distinguished by its color, and the 9p which may be distinguished by having a rough blind perf. 12.

Forgeries abound

Covers: Covers with Nos. 1-8 are rare. Last known date is Sept. 24, 1881, although the service officially ended Aug. 31st.

Palms
A2

King Malietoa Laupepa
A3

1886-1900 Typo. Wmk. 62

Three forms of watermark 62 are found on stamps of type A2:

1 — Wide "N Z" and wide star, 6mm apart (used 1886-87).

2 — Wide "N Z" and narrow star, 4mm apart (1890).

3 — Narrow "NZ" and narrow star, 7mm apart (1890-1900).

Wmk. 62, Type 1 (6mm spacing)

1886 ***Perf. 12½***

9 A2 ½p purple brown 40.00 40.00
11 A2 1p yellow green 20.00 20.00
13 A2 2p brown orange 20.00 20.00
16 A2 4p blue 20.00 20.00
18 A2 1sh rose carmine 20.00 10.00
a. Diagonal half canceled in blue, on cover (Apr-June '95) 300.00
19 A2 2sh6p violet 50.00 *40.00*

No. 18e was authorized for use between April 24 and June, 1895, after stocks of other values were destroyed in a fire, and was canceled in blue. No. 18a was used to pay various rates, most commonly 2½p. Value is for examples paying this rate.

No. 18 was later bisected for sale to collectors. These copies were canceled in black, and most were bisected vertically. Value on piece $7.50.

Wmk. 62, Type 1 (6mm spacing)

1887 ***Perf. 12x11½***

9a A2 ½p purple brown 40.00 *100.00*
11a A2 1p yellow green 100.00 40.00
13a A2 2p yellow 40.00 *100.00*
16a A2 4p blue 100.00 100.00
17 A2 6p brown lake 20.00 20.00
18b A2 1sh rose carmine 100.00
19a A2 2sh6p violet 2,000.

Wmk. 62, Type 2 (4 mm spacing)

May, 1890 ***Perf. 12x11½***

9b A2 ½p dp pur brown 100.00 40.00
11b A2 1p yellow green 20.00 20.00
13b A2 2p orange brown 40.00 10.00
16b A2 4p deep blue 100.00 10.00
17a A2 6p maroon 40.00 10.00
18c A2 1sh rose 200.00 20.00
19b A2 2sh6p bright violet 100.00 10.00

Wmk. 62, Type 3 (7 mm spacing)

1890-92 ***Perf. 12x11½***

9c A2 ½p purple brown 10.00 10.00
11c A2 1p green ('91) 20.00 10.00
d. 1p blue green 20.00 10.00
13c A2 2p orange 10.00 10.00
14 A3 2½p rose ('92) 100.00 10.00
16c A2 4p blue 100.00 20.00
17b A2 6p brown lake 40.00 10.00
18d A2 1sh rose 100.00 10.00
19c A2 2sh6p violet 100.00 10.00

Wmk. 62, Type 3 (7 mm spacing)

1891-92 ***Perf. 12½***

13d A2 2p orange yellow 750.00
14a A3 2½p rose ('92) 10.00 *20.00*
16d A2 4p blue 750.00
17c A2 6p brown lake 3,000. 1,250.
18e A2 1sh rose 2,500. 1,500.
19d A2 2sh6p violet *2,500.*

1/2p and 1p values, perf 12½ with watermark 62 type 3, may exist. The editors would like to examine any documentation of certified examples.

Wmk. 62, Type 3 (7 mm spacing)

1895, May-1900 ***Perf. 11***

9d A2 ½p purple brown 2.00 *10.00*
e. ½p deep purple brown ('00) 2.00 *100.00*
10 A2 ½p dull bl grn ('99) 2.00 *40.00*
11e A2 1p green 10.00 *20.00*
f. 1p bluish green ('97) 2.00 *10.00*
g. 1p deep green ('00) 2.00 *100.00*
12 A2 1p red brown 2.00 *20.00*
13e A2 2p yellow 40.00 40.00
f. 2p orange yellow ('96) 20.00 20.00
g. 2p bright yellow ('97) 2.00 *20.00*
h. 2p pale ocher ('97) 2.00 *20.00*
i. 2p brown ocher ('00) 2.00
14b A3 2½p rose 2.00 *40.00*
c. 2½p dp rose carmine ('00) 2.00 *100.00*
15 A3 2½p black, perf 10x11 ('96) 1.50 *3.50*
a. Perf 11 ('96) 150.00 100.00
b. Mixed perfs, 10 and 11 100.00 —
16e A2 4p blue 40.00 20.00
f. 4p deep blue ('00) 2.00 *100.00*
17d A2 6p brown lake 20.00 20.00
e. 6p maroon ('00) 2.00 *100.00*
18f A2 1sh rose 10.00 *20.00*
g. 1sh carmine ('00) 2.00 —
19e A2 2sh6p reddish lilac 10.00 20.00
f. 2sh6p purple ('97) 10.00 *20.00*
g. 2sh6p purple ('97) 40.00 —
h. 2sh6p deep purple ('98) 5.00 *20.00*
i. As "h," vert. pair, imperf btw. 500.00

Watermark is inverted on No. 19d and reversed on No. 19g.

The 1900 printings are on a coarse paper.

For surcharges or overprints on stamps or types of design A2 see Nos. 20-22, 24-38.

Nos. 16b and 16c Handstamp Surcharged in Black or Red:

a

b

c

1893 ***Perf. 12x11½***

20 A2(a) 5p on 4p blue (#16c) 40.00 —
a. On 4p deep blue (#16b) 100.00 100.00
21 A2(b) 5p on 4p blue (#16c) 40.00 *100.00*
a. On 4p deep blue (#16b) 100.00 100.00
22 A2(c) 5p on 4p blue (#16c) (R) 10.00 *20.00*
a. On 4p deep blue (#16b) 10.00 *40.00*

As the surcharges on Nos. 20-21 were handstamped in two steps, with bars of differing lengths, and on No. 22 in three steps. Various varieties exist.

Flag Design — A7

1894-95 Typo. ***Perf. 11½x12***

23 A7 5p vermilion 20.00 10.00
a. Perf. 11 ('95) 100.00 20.00

Types of 1887-1895 Surcharged in Blue, Black, Red or Green:

1½p, 2½p

3p

Handstamped Surcharges

1895 ***Perf. 11***

24 A2 1½p on 2p orange (Bl) 20.00 *10.00*
a. 1½p on 2p brn org, perf 12x11½ (Bl) 40.00 20.00
b. 1½p on 2p yellow, "2" ends with vertical stroke 5.00 *20.00*
25 A2 3p on 2p orange (Bk) 5.00 5.00
a. 3p on 2p brn org, perf. 12x11½ (Bk) 40.00 40.00
b. 3p on 2p org yellow (Bk) 2.00 40.00
c. Vert. pair, imperf. btwn. 500.00

Typographed Surcharges (#26 Handstamped)

1898-1900 ***Perf. 11***

26 A2 2½p on 1sh rose (Bk), handstamped surcharge 10.00 *20.00*
a. As #26, double surcharge 100.00 100.00
b. 2½p, typo surcharge 5.00 *40.00*
27 A2 2½p on 2sh6p vio (Bk) 5.00 *40.00*
28 A2 2½p on 1p bl grn (R) 2.00 *40.00*
a. Inverted surcharge 200.00 *200.00*
29 A2 2½p on 1sh rose car (R) 5.00 *40.00*
30 A2 3p on 2p dp red org (G) 10.00 20.00
Nos. 26-30 (5) 32.00 160.00

No. 30 was a reissue, available for postage. The surcharge is not as tall as the 3p surcharge illustrated, which is the surcharge on No. 25.

Stamps of 1886-99 Overprinted in Red or Blue

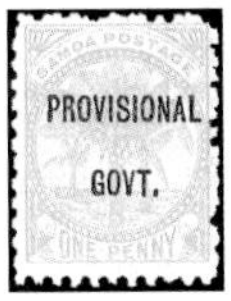

1899

31 A2 ½p dull bl green (R) 2.00 *20.00*
32 A2 1p red brown (Bl) 2.00 *20.00*
33 A2 2p br orange (R) 2.00 *20.00*
a. 2p deep ocher 2.00 *40.00*
34 A2 4p blue (R) 2.00 *40.00*
35 A7 5p dp scarlet (Bl) 2.00 *20.00*
36 A2 6p maroon (Bl) 2.00 *20.00*
37 A2 1sh rose car (Bl) 2.00 *40.00*
38 A2 2sh6p mauve (R) 2.00 *40.00*
Nos. 31-38 (8) 16.00 *220.00*

In 1900 the Samoan islands were partitioned between the US and Germany. The part which became American has since used US stamps.

Issued under German Dominion

Stamps of Germany Overprinted

1900 Unwmk. ***Perf. 13½x14½***

51 A9 3pf dark brown 8.50 *11.50*
Never hinged 26.00
On cover 75.00
52 A9 5pf green 10.50 *15.00*
Never hinged 37.50
On cover 75.00
53 A10 10pf carmine 8.50 *15.00*
Never hinged 21.00
On cover 60.00
54 A10 20pf ultra 17.50 *26.00*
Never hinged 50.00
On cover 115.00
55 A10 25pf orange 35.00 *70.00*
Never hinged 100.00
On cover 375.00
56 A10 50pf red brown 35.00 *65.00*
Never hinged 110.00
On cover 110.00
Nos. 51-56 (6) 115.00 *202.50*

Covers: Value for No. 56 on cover is for overfranked complete covers, usually philatelic.

Kaiser's Yacht "Hohenzollern"
A12 A13

1900 Typo. ***Perf. 14***

57 A12 3pf brown .90 *1.00*
Never hinged 1.80
On cover 55.00
58 A12 5pf green .90 *1.00*
Never hinged 1.80
On cover 23.00
59 A12 10pf carmine .90 *1.00*
Never hinged 1.80
On cover 27.00
60 A12 20pf ultra .90 *1.90*
Never hinged 1.75
On cover 50.00
61 A12 25pf org & blk, *yel* 1.00 *10.50*
Never hinged 2.10
On cover 85.00
62 A12 30pf org & blk, *sal* 1.25 *9.25*
Never hinged 2.75
On cover 85.00
63 A12 40pf lake & blk 1.25 *10.50*
Never hinged 2.75
On cover 85.00
64 A12 50pf pur & blk, *sal* 1.25 *11.50*
Never hinged 2.75
On cover 35.00
65 A12 80pf lake & blk, *rose* 2.40 *27.50*
Never hinged 5.00
On cover 65.00

Perf. 14½x14

Engr.

66 A13 1m carmine 3.00 *52.50*
Never hinged 14.00
On cover 100.00
67 A13 2m blue 4.25 *92.50*
Never hinged 23.00
On cover 160.00
68 A13 3m black vio 6.00 *125.00*
Never hinged 30.00
On cover 275.00
69 A13 5m slate & car 125.00 *450.00*
Never hinged 450.00
On cover 875.00
Nos. 57-69 (13) 149.00

Covers: Values for Nos. 64-69 on cover are for overfranked complete covers, usually philatelic.

1915 Wmk. 125 Typo. ***Perf. 14***

70 A12 3pf brown .90
Never hinged 2.25
71 A12 5pf green 1.10
Never hinged 2.75
72 A12 10pf carmine 1.10
Never hinged 2.90

Perf. 14½x14

Engr.

73 A13 5m slate & car, 25x17 holes ('19) 27.50
Never hinged 92.50
a. 26x17 holes ('15) 37.50
Never hinged 150.00

Nos. 70-73 were never put in use.

Issued under British Dominion

#57-69 Surcharged:

On A12

On A13

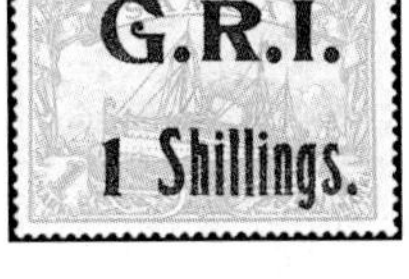

1914 Unwmk. *Perf. 14*

101 A12 ½p on 3pf brn 22.50 9.00
a. Double surcharge 600.00 450.00
b. Fraction bar omitted 50.00 30.00
c. Comma after "I" 550.00 375.00
102 A12 ½p on 5pf grn 45.00 10.00
a. Double surcharge 600.00 450.00
b. Fraction bar omitted 110.00 55.00
d. Comma after "I" 325.00 225.00
103 A12 1p on 10pf car 90.00 40.00
a. Double surcharge 600.00 450.00
104 A12 2½p on 20pf ultra 35.00 10.00
a. Fraction bar omitted 70.00 37.50
b. Inverted surcharge 725.00 650.00
c. Double surcharge 600.00 500.00
d. Commas after "I" 375.00 310.00
105 A12 3p on 25pf org & blk, *yel* 50.00 40.00
a. Double surcharge 700.00 550.00
b. Comma after "I" 4,000. 800.00
106 A12 4p on 30pf org & blk, *sal* 100.00 62.50
107 A12 5p on 40pf lake & blk 100.00 70.00
108 A12 6p on 50pf pur & blk, *sal* 60.00 35.00
a. Inverted "9" for "6" 165.00 110.00
b. Double surcharge 750.00 700.00
109 A12 9p on 80pf lake & blk, *rose* 200.00 100.00

Perf. 14½x14

110 A13 1sh on 1m car ("1 Shillings") 3,000. *3,500.*
a. "1 Shilling." *9,500.* *7,000.*
111 A13 2sh on 2m blue 3,000. 2,750.
112 A13 3sh on 3m blk vio 1,200. 1,000.
a. Double surcharge *7,500.* *8,500.*
113 A13 5sh on 5m slate & car 1,000. 900.00

G.R.I. stands for Georgius Rex Imperator.

The 3d on 30pf and 4d on 40pf were produced at a later time.

Stamps of New Zealand Overprinted in Red or Blue:

k

m

Perf. 14, 14x13½, 14x14½

1914, Sept. 29 Wmk. 61

114 A41(k) ½p yel grn (R) .60 .25
115 A42(k) 1p carmine .60 .20
116 A41(k) 2p mauve (R) .75 *.80*
117 A22(m) 2½p blue (R) 1.40 *1.50*
118 A41(k) 6p car rose, perf. 14x14½ 1.40 *1.50*
a. Perf. 14x13½ 17.00 20.00
119 A41(k) 1sh vermilion 4.25 *13.50*
Nos. 114-119 (6) 9.00 *17.75*

Overprinted Type "m"

1914-25 *Perf. 14, 14½x14*

120 PF1 2sh blue (R) 6.00 *7.00*
121 PF1 2sh6p brown (Bl) 6.00 *9.50*
122 PF1 3sh vio (R) ('22) 17.50 *52.50*
123 PF1 5sh green (R) 14.00 *12.00*
124 PF1 10sh red brn (Bl) 30.00 *32.50*
125 PF2 £1 rose (Bl) 75.00 *50.00*
126 PF2 £2 vio (R) ('25) 400.00
Nos. 120-126 (7) 548.50
Nos. 120-125 (6) *163.50*

Postal use of the £2 is questioned.

Overprinted Type "k"

Perf. 14x13½, 14x14½

1916-19 Typo.

127 A43 ½p yellow grn (R) .50 *.60*
128 A47 1½p gray blk (R) ('17) .40 .20
129 A47 1½p brn org (R) ('19) .30 .25
130 A43 2p yellow (R) ('18) 1.25 .20
131 A43 3p chocolate (Bl) 1.25 *9.50*

Engr.

132 A44 2½p dull blue (R) .55 .25
133 A45 3p violet brn (Bl) .50 *.75*
134 A45 6p carmine rose (Bl) 1.50 *2.25*
135 A45 1sh vermilion (Bl) 1.75 1.00
Nos. 127-135 (9) 8.00 15.00

Overprinted Type "k"

On New Zealand Victory Issue of 1919

1920, June *Perf. 14*

136 A48 ½p yellow grn (R) 2.75 *10.00*
137 A49 1p carmine (Bl) 2.25 *10.00*
138 A50 1½p brown org (R) 1.25 *9.25*
139 A51 3p black brn (Bl) 6.75 *9.00*
140 A52 6p purple (R) 3.50 *7.50*
141 A53 1sh vermilion (Bl) 11.50 11.00
Nos. 136-141 (6) 28.00 56.75

British Flag and Samoan House — A22

1921, Dec. 23 Engr. *Perf. 14x13½*

142 A22 ½p green 5.00 *2.00*
a. Perf. 14x14½ 1.75 *5.00*
143 A22 1p lake 5.00 .50
a. Perf. 14x14½ 2.75 2.00
144 A22 1½p orange brn, perf. 14x14½ 9.50 *8.25*
a. Perf. 14x13½ 4.00 *8.00*
145 A22 2p yel, perf. 14x14½ 1.90 2.00
a. Perf. 14x13½ 5.00 *7.00*
146 A22 2½p dull blue 2.00 *6.75*
147 A22 3p dark brown 2.00 *5.00*
148 A22 4p violet 2.00 *4.00*
149 A22 5p brt blue 2.00 *7.00*
150 A22 6p carmine rose 2.00 *6.50*
151 A22 8p red brown 2.25 *10.00*
152 A22 9p olive green 2.50 *27.00*
153 A22 1sh vermilion 2.25 *24.00*
Nos. 142-153 (12) 38.40 *103.00*

For overprints see Nos. 163-165.

New Zealand Nos. 182-183 Overprinted Type "m" in Red

1926-27 *Perf. 14½x14*

154 A56 2sh dark blue 5.00 *12.00*
a. 2sh blue ('27) 10.00 *35.00*
155 A56 3sh deep violet 11.00 *30.00*
a. 3sh violet ('27) 45.00 *75.00*

Issued: 2sh, Nov.; 3sh, Oct.; #154a, 155a, 11/10.

New Zealand Postal-Fiscal Stamps, Overprinted Type "m" in Blue or Red

1932, Aug. *Perf. 14*

156 PF5 2sh6p brown 15.00 *35.00*
157 PF5 5sh green (R) 22.50 *37.50*
158 PF5 10sh lake 45.00 *80.00*
159 PF5 £1 pink 55.00 *100.00*
160 PF5 £2 violet (R) *650.00*
161 PF5 £5 dk bl (R) *1,600.*
Nos. 156-159 (4) 137.50 *252.50*

See Nos. 175-180, 195-202, 216-219.

Silver Jubilee Issue

Stamps of 1921 Overprinted in Black

1935, May 7 *Perf. 14x13½*

163 A22 1p lake .40 *.50*
a. Perf. 14x14½ *80.00* *140.00*
164 A22 2½p dull blue .75 *1.00*
165 A22 6p carmine rose 3.25 *3.50*
Nos. 163-165 (3) 4.40 5.00
Set, never hinged 8.50

25th anniv. of the reign of George V.

Western Samoa

Samoan Girl and Kava Bowl — A23

View of Apia — A24

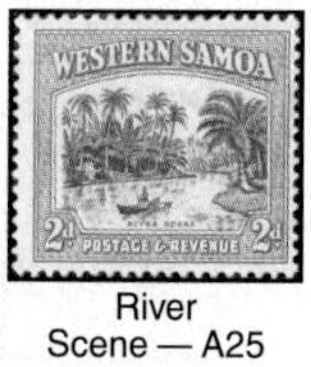

River Scene — A25

Samoan Chief and Wife — A26

Samoan Canoe and House — A27

"Vailima," Stevenson's Home — A28

Stevenson's Tomb — A29

Lake Lanuto'o — A30

Falefa Falls — A31

Perf. 14x13½, 13½x14

1935, Aug. 7 Engr. Wmk. 61

166 A23 ½p yellow grn .20 .40
167 A24 1p car lake & blk 2.75 2.50
168 A25 2p red org & blk, perf. 14 4.25 2.50
a. Perf. 13½x14 5.00 *4.00*
169 A26 2½p dp blue & blk .25 .25
170 A27 4p blk brn & dk gray .50 .50
171 A28 6p plum .70 .50
172 A29 1sh brown & violet .50 .80
173 A30 2sh red brn & yel grn 1.10 1.25
174 A31 3sh org brn & brt bl 2.00 *3.50*
Nos. 166-174 (9) 12.25 *12.20*
Set, never hinged 16.00

See Nos. 186-188.

Postal-Fiscal Stamps of New Zealand Overprinted in Blue or Carmine

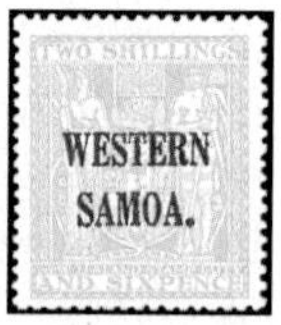

1935 *Perf. 14*

175 PF5 2sh6p brown 11.00 *18.00*
176 PF5 5sh green 18.50 *25.00*
177 PF5 10sh dp carmine 62.50 *85.00*
178 PF5 £1 pink 62.50 *110.00*
179 PF5 £2 violet (C) 180.00 *400.00*
180 PF5 £5 dk bl (C) 260.00 *525.00*
Nos. 175-180 (6) 594.50 *1,163.*

See Nos. 195-202, 216-219.

Samoan Coastal Village — A32

Map of Western Samoa — A33

Samoan Dancing Party A34

Robert Louis Stevenson A35

Perf. 13½x14

1939, Aug. 29 Engr. Wmk. 253

181 A32 1p scar & olive .60 .35
182 A33 1½p copper brn & bl 1.00 .90
183 A34 2½p dk blue & brn 1.00 1.00

Perf. 14x13½

184 A35 7p dp sl grn & vio 3.50 3.00
Nos. 181-184 (4) 6.10 5.25
Set, never hinged 11.00

25th anniv. of New Zealand's control of the mandated territory of Western Samoa.

Samoan Chief — A36

1940, Sept. 2 *Perf. 14x13½*

185 A36 3p on 1½p brown .50 .35
Never hinged .75

Issued only with surcharge. Examples without surcharge are from printer's archives.

Types of 1935 and A37

Apia Post Office — A37

1944-49 Wmk. 253 *Perf. 14*

186 A23 ½p yellow green .30 *16.50*
187 A25 2p red orange & blk 1.50 *5.00*
188 A26 2½p dp blue & blk ('48) 2.50 *27.50*

Perf. 13½x14

189 A37 5p dp ultra & ol brn ('49) 1.00 .75
Nos. 186-189 (4) 5.30 *49.75*
Set, never hinged 11.00

Issue date: 5p, June 8.

Catalogue values for unused stamps in this section, from this point to the end of the section, are for Never Hinged items.

Peace Issue

New Zealand Nos. 248, 250, 254, and 255 Overprinted in Black or Blue

p

q

1946, June 1 *Perf. 13x13½, 13½x13*

191 A94(p) 1p emerald .25 .20
192 A96(q) 2p rose violet (Bl) .25 .20
193 A100(p) 6p org red & red brn .30 .20
194 A101(p) 8p brn lake & blk (Bl) .30 .20
Nos. 191-194 (4) 1.10 .80

Stamps and Type of New Zealand, 1931-50 Overprinted Like Nos. 175-180 in Blue or Carmine

1945-50 Wmk. 253 *Perf. 14*

195 PF5 2sh6p brown 4.00 *10.00*
196 PF5 5sh green 6.50 *12.00*
197 PF5 10sh car ('48) 19.00 17.00
198 PF5 £1 pink ('48) 75.00 *125.00*
199 PF5 30sh choc ('48) 185.00 *200.00*
200 PF5 £2 violet (C) 140.00 *225.00*
201 PF5 £3 lt grn ('50) 225.00 *300.00*
202 PF5 £5 dk bl (C) ('50) 300.00 *400.00*

Making Siapo Cloth — A38

Thatching Hut — A40

Western Samoa and New Zealand Flags, Village A39

Samoan Chieftainess — A41

Designs: 2p, Western Samoa seal. 3p, Aleisa Falls (actually Malifa Falls). 5p, Manumea (tooth-billed pigeon). 6p, Fishing canoe. 8p, Harvesting cacao. 2sh, Preparing copra.

Perf. 13, 13½x13

1952, Mar. 10 Engr. Wmk. 253

203	A38	½p	org brn & claret	.20	*1.60*
204	A39	1p	green & olive	.20	.20
205	A38	2p	deep carmine	.20	.20
206	A39	3p	indigo & blue	.45	.25
207	A38	5p	dk grn & org brn	6.50	.75
208	A39	6p	dp rose pink & bl	.80	.25
209	A39	8p	rose carmine	.35	.30
210	A40	1sh	blue & brown	.20	.25
211	A39	2sh	yellow brown	1.10	.50
212	A41	3sh	ol gray & vio brn	2.75	*3.25*
			Nos. 203-212 (10)	12.75	7.55

SAN MARINO

LOCATION — Eastern Italy, about 20 miles inland from the Adriatic Sea
GOVT. — Republic
AREA — 24.1 sq. mi.
POP. — 21,622 (1981)
CAPITAL — San Marino

100 Centesimi = 1 Lira

Watermarks

Wmk. 140 — Crown

Wmk. 174 — Coat of Arms

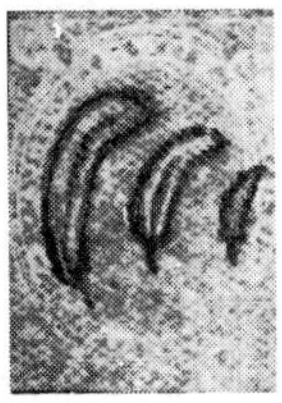

Wmk. 217 — Three Plumes

Nos. 1-28 were spaced very narrowly on the plates, so that perforations often cut into the design on one or two sides. Values are for very fine stamps, with perforations clear of the design. Examples with perfs cutting in the design sell for less, while examples with four clear, full margins sell for substantially more than the values shown. Never hinged premiums do not apply to stamps with perforations cutting the design.

A1 Numeral

A2 Coat of Arms

1877-99 Typo. Wmk. 140 *Perf. 14*

1	A1 2c green		30.00	11.00
	Never hinged		75.00	
	No gum		6.00	
	On cover			165.00
2	A1 2c blue ('94)		15.00	11.00
	Never hinged		37.50	
	No gum		3.00	
	On cover			55.00
3	A1 2c claret ('95)		13.50	13.50
	Never hinged		32.50	
	No gum		2.50	
	On cover			67.50
4	A2 5c orange ('90)		160.00	30.00
	Never hinged		400.00	
	No gum		32.50	
	On cover			200.00
5	A2 5c olive grn ('92)		9.00	6.00
	Never hinged		22.50	
	No gum		1.90	
	On cover			60.00
6	A2 5c green ('99)		9.00	9.00
	Never hinged		22.50	
	No gum		1.90	
	On cover			45.00
7	A2 10c ultra		300.00	55.00
	Never hinged		750.00	
	No gum		60.00	
	On cover			275.00
	a. 10c blue ('90)		825.00	190.00
	Never hinged		2,000.	
	No gum		160.00	
	On cover			1,500.
8	A2 10c dk green ('92)		9.00	7.50
	Never hinged		22.50	
	No gum		1.90	
	On cover			50.00
9	A2 10c claret ('99)		9.00	9.00
	Never hinged		22.50	
	No gum		1.90	
	On cover			45.00
10	A2 15c claret ('94)		160.00	90.00
	Never hinged		400.00	
	No gum		40.00	
	On cover			600.00
11	A2 20c vermilion		40.00	11.00
	Never hinged		92.50	
	No gum		7.50	
	On cover			140.00
12	A2 20c lilac ('95)		9.00	10.00
	Never hinged		22.50	
	No gum		1.90	
	On cover			45.00
13	A2 25c maroon ('90)		150.00	55.00
	Never hinged		375.00	
	No gum		30.00	
	On cover			275.00
14	A2 25c blue ('99)		9.00	10.00
	Never hinged		22.50	
	No gum		1.90	
	On cover			55.00
15	A2 30c brown		900.00	100.00
	Never hinged		2,600.	
	No gum		190.00	
	On cover			925.00
16	A2 30c org yel ('92)		9.00	11.00
	Never hinged		22.50	
	No gum		1.90	
	On cover			55.00
	a. 30c yellow ochre		10.00	13.50
	On cover			67.50
17	A2 40c violet		900.00	100.00
	Never hinged		2,600.	
	No gum		190.00	
	On cover			1,200.
18	A2 40c dk brown ('92)		9.00	11.00
	Never hinged		22.50	
	No gum		1.90	
	On cover			55.00
19	A2 45c gray grn ('92)		9.00	11.00
	Never hinged		22.50	
	No gum		1.90	
	On cover			55.00
	a. 45c deep olive green		7.50	8.00
	On cover			45.00
20	A2 65c red brown ('92)		9.00	11.00
	Never hinged		22.50	
	No gum		1.90	
	On cover			55.00
21	A2 1 l car & yel ('92)		1,800.	675.00
	Never hinged		4,500.	
	No gum		625.00	
	On cover			2,600.
22	A2 1 l lt blue ('95)		1,650.	525.00
	Never hinged		4,000.	
	No gum		550.00	
	On cover			2,600.
23	A2 2 l brn & yel ('94)		90.00	90.00
	Never hinged		225.00	
	No gum		22.50	
	On cover			600.00
24	A2 5 l vio & grn ('94)		225.00	250.00
	Never hinged		550.00	
	No gum		55.00	
	On cover			2,600.

Values for Blocks of 4
(2 stamps never hinged)

1	A1	2c	green	225.00	55.00
2	A1	2c	blue ('94)	110.00	90.00
3	A1	2c	claret ('95)	100.00	90.00
4	A2	5c	orange ('90)	1,300.	*450.00*
5	A2	5c	olive grn ('92)	67.50	60.00
6	A2	5c	green ('99)	67.50	60.00
7	A2	10c	ultra	2,250.	*675.00*
a.			10c blue ('90)	6,250.	*2,200.*
8	A2	10c	dk green ('92)	67.50	60.00
9	A2	10c	claret ('99)	67.50	67.50
10	A2	15c	claret ('94)	1,150.	*675.00*
11	A2	20c	vermilion	275.00	75.00
12	A2	20c	lilac ('95)	67.50	90.00
13	A2	25c	maroon ('90)	1,100.	*900.00*
14	A2	25c	blue ('99)	67.50	90.00
15	A2	30c	brown	8,250.	*2,600.*
16	A2	30c	org yel ('92)	67.50	90.00
17	A2	40c	violet	8,250.	*2,500.*
18	A2	40c	dk brown ('92)	67.50	90.00
19	A2	45c	gray grn ('92)	67.50	90.00
20	A2	65c	red brown ('92)	67.50	90.00
21	A2	1 l	car & yel ('92)	*15,000.*	*13,500.*
22	A2	1 l	lt blue ('95)	*13,500.*	*10,000.*
23	A2	2 l	brn & yel ('94)	700.00	*675.00*
24	A2	5 l	vio & grn ('94)	1,750.	*1,400.*

See Nos. 911-915.

Nos. 7a, 15, 11 Surcharged in Black

1892

25	A2 5c on 10c blue	90.00	25.00
	Never hinged	225.00	
	No gum	22.50	
	On cover		200.00
a.	Inverted surcharge	100.00	32.50
	Never hinged	260.00	
	On cover		250.00
b.	5c on 10c ultramarine	*40,000.*	*7,500.*
	Never hinged	*50,000.*	
	No gum	*10,000.*	
c.	As "b," inverted surch.	—	—
d.	Double surcharge, one inverted	—	
	On cover		—
e.	Pair, one without surcharge	1,850.	
	Never hinged	*3,750.*	
f.	Pair, one without surcharge, surcharge inverted	1,850.	
	Never hinged	*3,750.*	
26	A2 5c on 30c brown	300.00	95.00
	Never hinged	750.00	
	No gum	75.00	
	On cover		*1,200.*
a.	Inverted surcharge	375.00	120.00
	Never hinged	925.00	
	On cover		1,500.
b.	Double surch., one inverted	375.00	150.00
	Never hinged	925.00	
c.	Double invtd. surcharge	375.00	150.00
	Never hinged	925.00	
27	A2 10c on 20c ver	67.50	15.00
	Never hinged	160.00	
	No gum	16.50	
	On cover		90.00
a.	Inverted surcharge	75.00	22.50
	Never hinged	190.00	
	On cover		150.00
b.	Double surch., one inverted	82.50	30.00
	Never hinged	200.00	
	On cover		180.00
c.	Double surcharge	82.50	30.00
	Never hinged	200.00	
	On cover		180.00

Ten to twelve varieties of each surcharge.

No. 11 Surcharged

28	A2 10c on 20c ver	300.00	18.50
	Never hinged	750.00	
	No gum	75.00	
	On cover		125.00
a.	Only one "10" in surcharge	600.00	
	Never hinged	1,500.	

Values for Blocks of 4
(2 stamps never hinged)

25	A2	5c	on 10c blue	675.00	120.00
b.			5c on 10c ultramarine		*35,000.*
26	A2	5c	on 30c brown	2,250.	450.00
27	A2	10c	on 20c ver	525.00	67.50
28	A2	10c	on 20c ver	2,250.	82.50

Government Palace and Portraits of Regents, Tonnini and Marcucci
A6 A7

Portraits of Regents and View of Interior of Palace — A8

Wmk. 174

1894, Sept. 30 Litho. *Perf. 15½*

29	A6 25c blue & dk brn	7.50	3.00
	Never hinged	52.50	
	On cover		60.00
30	A7 50c dull red & dk brn	45.00	7.50
	Never hinged	300.00	
	On cover		190.00
31	A8 1 l green & dk brown	32.50	9.00
	Never hinged	225.00	
	On cover		225.00

Opening of the new Government Palace and the installation of the new Regents.

Statue of Liberty — A9

Wmk. 140

1899-1922 Typo. *Perf. 14*

32	A9 2c brown	3.75	1.85
	Never hinged	9.00	
	On cover		40.00
33	A9 2c claret ('22)	.75	.75
	Never hinged	1.90	
34	A9 5c brown org	7.50	4.50
	Never hinged	18.00	
	On cover		45.00
35	A9 5c olive grn ('22)	.75	.75
	Never hinged	1.90	
36	A9 10c brown org ('22)	.75	.75
	Never hinged	1.90	
37	A9 20c dp brown ('22)	.75	.75
	Never hinged	1.90	
38	A9 25c ultra ('22)	1.50	1.50
	Never hinged	3.75	
39	A9 45c red brown ('22)	3.00	3.00
	Never hinged	7.50	
	Nos. 32-39 (8)	18.75	13.85

Numeral of Value — A10

Mt. Titano — A11

1903-25 ***Perf. 14, 14½x14***

No.	Type	Description	Unused	Used
40	A10	2c violet	22.00	12.00
		Never hinged	55.00	
		On cover		75.00
41	A10	2c orange brn ('21)	1.50	1.10
		Never hinged	3.75	
		On cover		30.00
42	A11	5c blue grn	11.00	7.50
		Never hinged	27.50	
		On cover		22.50
43	A11	5c olive grn ('21)	1.50	1.10
		Never hinged	3.75	
		On cover		18.00
44	A11	5c red brn ('25)	.75	.75
		Never hinged	1.90	
		On cover		7.50
45	A11	10c claret	11.00	7.50
		Never hinged	27.50	
		On cover		22.50
46	A11	10c brown org ('21)	1.50	1.10
		Never hinged	3.75	
		On cover		18.00
47	A11	10c olive grn ('25)	.75	.75
		Never hinged	1.90	
		On cover		7.50
48	A11	15c blue grn ('22)	1.50	1.10
		Never hinged	3.75	
		On cover		18.00
49	A11	15c brown vio ('25)	.75	.75
		Never hinged	1.90	
		On cover		7.50
50	A11	20c brown orange	150.00	60.00
		Never hinged	375.00	
		On cover		550.00
51	A11	20c brown ('21)	1.50	1.10
		Never hinged	3.75	
		On cover		26.00
52	A11	20c blue grn ('25)	.75	.75
		Never hinged	1.90	
		On cover		11.00
53	A11	25c blue	26.00	12.00
		Never hinged	67.50	
		On cover		37.50
54	A11	25c gray ('21)	1.50	1.10
		Never hinged	3.75	
		On cover		26.00
55	A11	25c violet ('25)	.75	.75
		Never hinged	1.90	
		On cover		7.50
56	A11	30c brown red	12.00	*17.50*
		Never hinged	30.00	
		On cover		80.00
57	A11	30c claret ('21)	1.50	1.10
		Never hinged	3.75	
		On cover		75.00
58	A11	30c orange ('25)	22.00	3.75
		Never hinged	55.00	
		On cover		45.00
59	A11	40c orange red	22.00	17.50
		Never hinged	55.00	
		On cover		67.50
60	A11	40c dp rose ('21)	1.50	1.10
		Never hinged	3.75	
		On cover		26.00
61	A11	40c brown ('25)	.75	.75
		Never hinged	1.90	
		On cover		10.00
62	A11	45c yellow	16.50	17.50
		Never hinged	40.00	
		On cover		67.50
63	A11	50c brown vio ('23)	3.00	3.00
		Never hinged	7.50	
		On cover		67.50
64	A11	50c gray blk ('25)	.75	.75
		Never hinged	1.90	
		On cover		7.50
65	A11	60c brown red ('25)	1.50	.75
		Never hinged	3.75	
		On cover		45.00
66	A11	65c chocolate	16.50	17.50
		Never hinged	40.00	
		On cover		67.50
67	A11	80c blue ('21)	6.00	6.00
		Never hinged	15.00	
		On cover		67.50
68	A11	90c brown ('23)	6.00	6.00
		Never hinged	15.00	
		On cover		67.50
69	A11	1 l olive green	60.00	30.00
		Never hinged	150.00	
		On cover		600.00
70	A11	1 l ultra ('21)	6.00	6.00
		Never hinged	15.00	
		On cover		67.50
71	A11	1 l lt blue ('25)	1.50	.75
		Never hinged	3.75	
		On cover		45.00
72	A11	2 l violet	1,000.	340.00
		Never hinged	2,000.	
		On cover		2,600.
73	A11	2 l orange ('21)	22.00	26.00
		Never hinged	55.00	
		On cover		300.00
74	A11	2 l lt green ('25)	7.50	7.50
		Never hinged	18.00	
		On cover		325.00
75	A11	5 l slate	265.00	225.00
		Never hinged	675.00	
		On cover		1,250.
76	A11	5 l ultra ('25)	16.50	18.50
		Never hinged	40.00	
		On cover		400.00
		Nos. 40-76 (37)	1,721.	856.30

For overprints and surcharges see Nos. 77, 93-96, 103, 107, 188-189, B1-B2, E2, E4.

No. 50 Surcharged

1905, Sept. 1

No.	Type	Description	Unused	Used
77	A11	15c on 20c brown org	11.00	3.75
		Never hinged	37.50	
		On cover		52.50
a.		Large 5 in 1905 on level with 9	90.00	45.00

Coat of Arms
A12 A13

Two types:
I — Width 18½mm.
II — Width 19mm.

1907-10 Unwmk. Engr. ***Perf. 12***

No.	Type	Description	Unused	Used
78	A12	1c brown, II ('10)	3.75	.70
a.		Type I	6.25	1.00
79	A13	15c gray, I	17.50	3.00
a.		Type II ('10)	190.00	19.00

No. 79a Surcharged in Brown

1918, Mar. 15

No.	Type	Description	Unused	Used
80	A13	20c on 15c gray	3.75	1.90

St. Marinus — A14

Perf. 14½x14, 14x14½

1923, Aug. 11 Typo. Wmk. 140

No.	Type	Description	Unused	Used
81	A14	30c dark brown	.75	.75

San Marino Intl. Exhib. of 1923. Proceeds from the sale of this stamp went to a mutual aid society.

Italian Flag and Views of Arbe and Mt. Titano A15

1923, Aug. 6

No.	Type	Description	Unused	Used
82	A15	50c olive green	.75	.75

Presentation to San Marino of the Italian flag which had flown over the island of Arbe, the birthplace of the founder of San Marino. Inscribed on back: "V. Moraldi dis. Blasi inc. Petiti impr.-Roma."

Mt. Titano and Sword — A16

1923, Sept. 29 ***Perf. 14x14½***

No.	Type	Description	Unused	Used
83	A16	1 l dark brown	15.00	15.00

In honor of the San Marino Volunteers who were killed or wounded in WWI.

Giuseppe Garibaldi A17

Allegory-San Marino Sheltering Garibaldi A18

1924, Sept. 25 ***Perf. 14***

No.	Type	Description	Unused	Used
84	A17	30c dark violet	2.50	2.50
85	A17	50c olive brown	2.60	2.60
86	A17	60c dull red	3.00	3.00
87	A18	1 l deep blue	5.25	5.25
88	A18	2 l gray green	6.50	6.50
		Nos. 84-88 (5)	19.85	19.85

75th anniv. of Garibaldi's taking refuge in San Marino.

Semi-Postal Stamps of 1918 Surcharged with New Values and Bars

1924, Oct. 9

No.	Type	Description	Unused	Used
89	SP1	30c on 45c yel brn & blk	.90	.90

Surcharged

No.	Type	Description	Unused	Used
90	SP2	60c on 1 l bl grn & blk	6.75	6.75
91	SP2	1 l on 2 l vio & blk	17.50	17.50
92	SP2	2 l on 3 l red brn & blk	13.50	13.50
		Nos. 89-92 (4)	38.65	38.65

Nos. 67 and 68 Surcharged in Black or Red

1926, July 1

No.	Type	Description	Unused	Used
93	A11	75c on 80c blue	1.25	1.25
94	A11	1.20 l on 90c brown	1.25	1.25
95	A11	1.25 l on 90c brn (R)	2.75	2.75
96	A11	2.50 l on 80c blue (R)	6.00	6.00
		Nos. 93-96 (4)	11.25	11.25

Antonio Onofri — A19

A20

Unwmk.

1926, July 29 Engr. ***Perf. 11***

No.	Type	Description	Unused	Used
97	A19	10c dk blue & blk	.20	.20
98	A19	20c olive grn & blk	.45	.45
99	A19	45c dk vio & blk	.30	.30
100	A19	65c green & blk	.30	.30
101	A19	1 l orange & blk	3.50	3.50
102	A19	2 l red vio & blk	3.50	3.50
		Nos. 97-102 (6)	8.25	8.25

For surcharges see Nos. 104-106, 181-182.

Special Delivery Stamp No. E2 surcharged with New Value and Bars

Perf. 14½x14

1926, Nov. 25 Wmk. 140

No.	Type	Description	Unused	Used
103	A20	1.85 l on 60c violet	.50	.50

Nos. 101 and 102 Surcharged

1927, Mar. 10 Unwmk. ***Perf. 11***

No.	Type	Description	Unused	Used
104	A19	1.25 l on 1 l	4.25	4.25
105	A19	2.50 l on 2 l	8.00	8.00
106	A19	5 l on 2 l	37.50	37.50
		Nos. 104-106 (3)	49.75	49.75

Type of Special Delivery Stamp of 1923 Surcharged

1927, Sept. 15 Wmk. 140 ***Perf. 14***

No.	Type	Description	Unused	Used
107	A11	1.75 l on 50c on 25c vio	1.10	1.10

The 50c on 25c violet was not issued without 1.75-lire surcharge.

War Memorial A21

Unwmk.

1927, Sept. 28 Engr. ***Perf. 12***

No.	Type	Description	Unused	Used
108	A21	50c brown violet	1.60	1.60
109	A21	1.25 l blue	2.25	2.25
110	A21	10 l gray	22.00	22.00
		Nos. 108-110 (3)	25.85	25.85

Erection of a cenotaph in memory of the San Marino volunteers in WWI.

Capuchin Church and Convent A22

Design: 2.50 l, 5 l, Death of St. Francis.

1928, Jan. 2

No.	Type	Description	Unused	Used
111	A22	50c red	18.00	4.25
112	A22	1.25 l dp blue	7.25	6.50
113	A22	2.50 l dk brown	7.25	6.50
114	A22	5 l dull violet	24.00	19.00
		Nos. 111-114 (4)	56.50	36.25

7th centenary of the death of St. Francis of Assisi.

For surcharges see Nos. 183-184.

The Rocca (State Prison) A24

Government Palace A25

Statue of Liberty — A26

1929-35 **Wmk. 217**

115	A24	5c vio brn & ultra	1.50	.60
116	A24	10c bl gray & red vio	1.90	.90
117	A24	15c dp org & emer	1.50	.60
118	A24	20c dk bl & org red	1.50	.60
119	A24	25c grn & gray blk	1.50	.60
120	A24	30c gray brn & red	1.50	.60
121	A24	50c red vio & ol gray	1.50	.60
122	A24	75c dp red & gray blk	1.50	.60
123	A25	1 l dk brn & emer	1.50	.60
124	A25	1.25 l dk blue & blk	1.50	.60
125	A25	1.75 l green & org	3.50	1.50
126	A25	2 l bl gray & red	1.90	.90
127	A25	2.50 l car rose & ultra	1.90	.90
128	A25	3 l dp org & bl	1.90	.90
129	A25	3.70 l ol blk & red brn ('35)	1.90	.90
130	A26	5 l dk vio & dk grn	2.75	2.00
131	A26	10 l bis brn & dk bl	7.75	6.50
132	A26	15 l green & red vio	57.50	45.00
133	A26	20 l dk bl & red	275.00	230.00
		Nos. 115-133 (19)	369.50	294.90

General Post Office — A27

San Marino-Rimini Electric Railway — A28

1932, Feb. 4

134	A27	20c blue green	9.00	5.50
135	A27	50c dark red	14.00	9.50
136	A27	1.25 l dark blue	225.00	100.00
137	A27	1.75 l dark brown	100.00	50.00
138	A27	2.75 l dark violet	40.00	22.50
		Nos. 134-138 (5)	388.00	187.50

Opening of new General Post Office.
For surcharges see Nos. 151-160.

1932, June 11

139	A28	20c deep green	1.90	1.90
140	A28	50c dark red	2.50	2.50
141	A28	1.25 l dark blue	7.75	7.75
142	A28	5 l deep brown	62.50	55.00
		Nos. 139-142 (4)	74.65	67.15

Opening of the new electric railway between San Marino and Rimini.

Giuseppe Garibaldi — A29

Garibaldi's Arrival at San Marino — A30

1932, July 30

143	A29	10c violet brown	2.50	.85
144	A29	20c violet	2.50	.85
145	A29	25c green	2.50	.85
146	A29	50c yellow brn	5.25	2.60
147	A30	75c dark red	6.75	5.00
148	A30	1.25 l dark blue	12.50	10.50
149	A30	2.75 l brown org	37.50	26.00
150	A30	5 l olive green	240.00	240.00
		Nos. 143-150 (8)	309.50	286.65

Garibaldi (1807-1882), Italian patriot.

Nos. 138 and 137 Surcharged

1933, May 27

151	A27	25c on 2.75 l	5.25	5.25
152	A27	50c on 1.75 l	10.50	10.50
153	A27	75c on 2.75 l	22.50	22.50
154	A27	1.25 l on 1.75 l	275.00	275.00
		Nos. 151-154 (4)	313.25	313.25

Convention of philatelists, San Marino, May 28.

Nos. 134-137 Surcharged in Black

1934, Apr. 12

155	A27	25c on 1.25 l	1.60	1.60
156	A27	50c on 1.75 l	3.25	3.25
157	A27	75c on 50c	7.00	7.00
158	A27	1.25 l on 20c	26.00	26.00
		Nos. 155-158 (4)	37.85	37.85

San Marino's participation (with a philatelic pavilion) in the 15th annual Trade Fair at Milan, Apr. 12-27.

Nos. 136 and 138 Surcharged Wheel and New Value

1934, Apr. 12

159	A27	3.70 l on 1.25 l	55.00	55.00
160	A27	3.70 l on 2.75 l	67.50	67.50

Ascent to Mt. Titano A31

Unwmk.

1935, Feb. 7 **Engr.** ***Perf. 14***

161	A31	5c choc & blk	.40	.40
162	A31	10c dk vio & blk	.40	.40
163	A31	20c orange & blk	.40	.40
164	A31	25c green & blk	.40	.40
165	A31	50c olive bis & blk	.40	.40
166	A31	75c brown red & blk	3.50	3.50
167	A31	1.25 l blue & blk	7.00	7.00
		Nos. 161-167 (7)	12.50	12.50

12th anniv. of the founding of the Fascist Movement.

Melchiorre Delfico — A32

Statue of Delfico — A33

1935, Apr. 15 **Wmk. 217** ***Perf. 12***

Center in Black

169	A32	5c brown lake	.85	.65
170	A32	7½c lt brown	.85	.65
171	A32	10c dk blue grn	.85	.65
172	A32	15c rose carmine	11.00	3.50
173	A32	20c orange	1.90	1.40
174	A32	25c green	1.90	1.40
175	A33	30c dull violet	1.90	1.40
176	A33	50c olive green	3.50	3.50
177	A33	75c red	10.50	8.00
178	A33	1.25 l dark blue	3.00	2.50
179	A33	1.50 l dk brown	47.50	37.50
180	A33	1.75 l brown org	67.50	60.00
		Nos. 169-180 (12)	151.25	121.15

Melchiorre Delfico (1744-1835), historian.
For surcharges see Nos. 202, 277.

Nos. 99-100 Surcharged in Black  80

Nos. 112-113 Surcharged in Black

1936 **Unwmk.** ***Perf. 11***

181	A19	80c on 45c dk vio & blk	2.50	2.50
182	A19	80c on 65c grn & blk	2.50	2.50

Perf. 12

183	A22	2.05 l on 1.25 l	7.50	7.50
184	A22	2.75 l on 2.50 l	24.00	24.00
		Nos. 181-184 (4)	36.50	36.50

Issued: #181-182, 4/14; #183-184, 8/23.

Souvenir Sheet

Design from Base of Roman Column — A34

1937, Aug. 23 **Engr.** **Wmk. 217**

185	A34	5 l steel blue	10.00	10.00

Unveiling of the Roman Column at San Marino. The date "1636 d. F. R." means the 1,636th year since the founding of the republic.

No. 185 was privately surcharged "+ 10 L 1941."

Souvenir Sheets

Abraham Lincoln — A35

1938, Apr. 7 **Wmk. 217** ***Perf. 13***

186	A35	3 l dark blue	1.25	1.25
187	A35	5 l rose red	15.00	15.00

Dedication of a Lincoln bust, Sept. 3, 1937.

SEMI-POSTAL STAMPS

Regular Issue of 1903 Surcharged:

a

b

1917, Dec. 15 **Wmk. 140** ***Perf. 14***

B1	A10(a)	25c on 2c violet	5.00	4.00
B2	A11(b)	50c on 2 l violet	25.00	20.00

Statue of Liberty — SP1

View of San Marino SP2

1918, June 1 **Typo.**

B3	SP1	2c dl vio & blk	.70	.70
B4	SP1	5c bl grn & blk	.70	.70
B5	SP1	10c lake & blk	.70	.70
B6	SP1	20c brn org & blk	.70	.70
B7	SP1	25c ultra & blk	.70	.70
B8	SP1	45c yel brn & blk	.70	.70
B9	SP2	1 l bl grn & blk	8.25	8.25
B10	SP2	2 l vio & blk	7.75	7.75
B11	SP2	3 l claret & blk	7.75	7.75
		Nos. B3-B11 (9)	27.95	27.95

These stamps were sold at an advance of 5c each over face value, the receipts from that source being devoted to the support of a hospital for Italian soldiers.
For surcharges see Nos. 89-92.

Nos. B6-B8 Overprinted

1918, Dec. 12

B12	SP1	20c brn org & blk	1.40	1.25
B13	SP1	25c ultra & blk	1.40	1.25
B14	SP1	45c yel brn & blk	1.40	1.25

Overprinted

B15 SP2 1 l blue grn & blk 3.25 3.25
B16 SP2 2 l violet & blk 7.00 6.50
B17 SP2 3 l claret & blk 7.00 6.50
Nos. B12-B17 (6) 21.45 20.00

Celebration of Italian Victory over Austria. Inverted overprints were privately produced.

Coat of Arms SP3

Liberty SP4

1923, Sept. 20 **Engr.**

B18 SP3 5c + 5c olive grn .30 .20
B19 SP3 10c + 5c orange .30 .20
B20 SP3 15c + 5c dk green .30 .20
B21 SP3 25c + 5c brn lake .30 .25
B22 SP3 40c + 5c vio brn 2.25 2.25
B23 SP3 50c + 5c gray 1.25 .20
B24 SP4 1 l + 5c blk & bl 5.00 5.00
Nos. B18-B24 (7) 9.70 8.30

AIR POST STAMPS

View of San Marino AP1

Wmk. 217

1931, June 11 **Engr.** ***Perf. 12***

C1 AP1 50c blue grn 5.00 5.00
C2 AP1 80c red 5.00 5.00
C3 AP1 1 l bister brn 1.75 1.75
C4 AP1 2 l brt violet 1.75 1.75
C5 AP1 2.60 l Prus bl 21.00 21.00
C6 AP1 3 l dk gray 21.00 21.00
C7 AP1 5 l olive grn 1.75 1.75
C8 AP1 7.70 l dk brown 5.00 5.00
C9 AP1 9 l dp orange 5.00 5.00
C10 AP1 10 l dk blue 225.00 225.00
Nos. C1-C10 (10) 292.25 292.25

Exist imperf.

Graf Zeppelin Issue

Stamps of Type AP1 Surcharged in Blue or Black

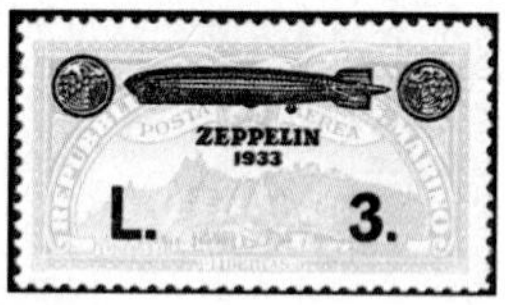

1933, Apr. 28

C11 AP1 3 l on 50c org 1.60 *45.00*
C12 AP1 5 l on 80c ol grn 30.00 *45.00*
C13 AP1 10 l on 1 l dk bl (Bk) 30.00 *55.00*
C14 AP1 12 l on 2 l yel brn 30.00 *67.50*
C15 AP1 15 l on 2.60 l dl red (Bk) 30.00 *75.00*
C16 AP1 20 l on 3 l bl grn (Bk) 30.00 *87.50*
Nos. C11-C16 (6) 151.60 *375.00*

Exist imperf.

Nos. C1 and C2 Surcharged

1936, Apr. 14

C17 AP1 75c on 50c blue grn 1.25 1.25
C18 AP1 75c on 80c red 6.00 6.00

SPECIAL DELIVERY STAMPS

SD1

Unwmk.

1907, Apr. 25 **Engr.** ***Perf. 12***

E1 SD1 25c carmine 15.00 7.50

For surcharges see Nos. E3, E5.

Type of Regular Issue of 1903 Overprinted

Perf. 14½x14

1923, May 30 **Wmk. 140**

E2 A11 60c violet .50 .50

For surcharge see No. 103.

Type of 1907 Issue Surcharged

1923, July 26 ***Perf. 14***

E3 SD1 60c on 25c carmine .50 .50
a. Vert. pair, imperf. between 125.00

No. E2 Surcharged

1926, Nov. 25 ***Perf. 14½x14***

E4 A11 1.25 l on 60c violet 1.00 1.00

No. E3 Surcharged

1927, Sept. 15

E5 SD1 1.25 l on 60c on 25c .50 .50
a. Inverted surcharge 72.50
b. Vert. pair, imperf. between 300.00
c. Double surcharge 85.00

Statue of Liberty and View of San Marino — SD2

Wmk. 217

1929, Aug. 29 **Engr.** ***Perf. 12***

E6 SD2 1.25 l green .20 .20

Overprinted in Red UNION POSTALE UNIVERSELLE

E7 SD2 2.50 l deep blue .60 .60

SEMI-POSTAL SPECIAL DELIVERY STAMP

SPSD1

Wmk. 140

1923, Sept. 20 **Engr.** ***Perf. 14***

EB1 SPSD1 60c + 5c brown red .75 .75

POSTAGE DUE STAMPS

D1

Wmk. 140

1897-1920 **Typo.** ***Perf. 14***

J1 D1 5c bl grn & dk brn 1.50 1.50
Never hinged 3.00
On cover 11.00
J2 D1 10c bl grn & dk brn 1.50 1.50
Never hinged 3.00
On cover 11.00
a. Numerals inverted 300.00 —
J3 D1 30c bl grn & dk brn 3.00 3.00
Never hinged 6.00
On cover 11.00
J4 D1 50c bl grn & dk brn 3.75 3.75
Never hinged 7.50
On cover 25.00
a. Numerals inverted 300.00 —
J5 D1 60c bl grn & dk brn 45.00 18.50
Never hinged 90.00
On cover 55.00
J6 D1 1 l claret & dk brn 9.00 9.00
Never hinged 18.00
On cover 25.00
J7 D1 3 l claret & brn ('20) 30.00 30.00
Never hinged 60.00
On cover 120.00
J8 D1 5 l claret & dk brn 90.00 67.50
Never hinged 180.00
On cover 100.00
J9 D1 10 l claret & dk brn 37.50 40.00
Never hinged 150.00
On cover 150.00
Nos. J1-J9 (9) 221.25 174.75

See Nos. J10-J36. For surcharges see Nos. J37-J60, J64.

1924

J10 D1 5c rose & brown 2.25 2.25
Never hinged 4.50
On cover 22.00
J11 D1 10c rose & brown 2.25 2.25
Never hinged 4.50
On cover 15.00
J12 D1 30c rose & brown 3.75 3.75
Never hinged 7.50
On cover 22.00
J13 D1 50c rose & brown 4.50 4.50
Never hinged 9.00
On cover 26.00
J14 D1 60c rose & brown 15.00 15.00
Never hinged 30.00
On cover 75.00
J15 D1 1 l green & brown 22.50 22.00
Never hinged 45.00
On cover 75.00
J16 D1 3 l green & brown 60.00 60.00
Never hinged 120.00
On cover 325.00
J17 D1 5 l green & brown 75.00 75.00
Never hinged 150.00
On cover 400.00
J18 D1 10 l green & brown 325.00 325.00
Never hinged 650.00
On cover —
Nos. J10-J18 (9) 510.25 509.75

1925-39 ***Perf. 14***

J19 D1 5c blue & brn .35 .20
a. Numerals inverted 125.00 —
J20 D1 10c blue & brn .35 .20
a. Numerals inverted 125.00 —
J21 D1 15c blue & brn ('39) .20 .20
J22 D1 20c blue & brn ('39) .20 .20
J23 D1 25c blue & brn ('39) .25 .25
J24 D1 30c blue & brn .35 .20
J25 D1 40c blue & brn ('39) 2.50 2.50
J26 D1 50c blue & brn .75 .25
a. Numerals inverted 125.00 —
J27 D1 60c blue & brn 1.50 .60
J28 D1 1 l buff & brn 3.00 .50
J29 D1 2 l buff & brn ('39) 1.50 1.50
J30 D1 3 l buff & brn 50.00 22.50
J31 D1 5 l buff & brn 13.50 3.75
J32 D1 10 l buff & brn 18.00 9.75
J33 D1 15 l buff & brn ('28) 1.50 .85
J34 D1 25 l buff & brn ('28) 27.50 16.00
J35 D1 30 l buff & brn ('28) 6.00 6.00
J36 D1 50 l buff & brn ('28) 7.25 6.75
Nos. J19-J36 (18) 134.70 72.20

Postage Due Stamps of 1925 Surcharged in Black and Silver

1931, May 18

J37 D1 15c on 5c bl & brn .60 .20
J38 D1 15c on 10c bl & brn .60 .20
J39 D1 15c on 30c bl & brn .60 .20
J40 D1 20c on 5c bl & brn .60 .20
J41 D1 20c on 10c bl & brn .60 .20
J42 D1 20c on 30c bl & brn .60 .20
J43 D1 25c on 5c bl & brn 1.75 .75
J44 D1 25c on 10c bl & brn 1.90 .75
J45 D1 25c on 30c bl & brn 11.00 7.50
J46 D1 40c on 5c bl & brn 1.90 .20
J47 D1 40c on 10c bl & brn 2.40 .25
J48 D1 40c on 30c bl & brn 2.50 .25
J49 D1 2 l on 5c bl & brn 45.00 30.00
J50 D1 2 l on 10c bl & brn 92.50 55.00
J51 D1 2 l on 30c bl & brn 60.00 45.00
Nos. J37-J51 (15) 222.55 140.90

Nos. J19, J24-J25, J30, J34, J33, J22 Surcharged in Black

Perf. 14, 14½x14

1936-40 **Wmk. 140**

J52 D1 10c on 5c ('38) .65 .50
J53 D1 25c on 30c ('38) 9.00 7.25
J54 D1 50c on 5c ('37) 9.25 7.25
J55 D1 1 l on 30c 35.00 5.50
J56 D1 1 l on 40c ('40) 6.25 3.75
J57 D1 1 l on 3 l ('37) 35.00 1.90
J58 D1 1 l on 25 l ('39) 70.00 12.00
J59 D1 2 l on 15 l ('38) 35.00 14.50
J60 D1 3 l on 20c ('40) 26.00 14.00
Nos. J52-J60 (9) 226.15 66.65

Coat of Arms — D6

1939 **Typo.** ***Perf. 14***

J61 D6 5c blue & brown .20 .20

Nos. J61 and J36 Surcharged with New Values and Bars

1940-43

J62 D6 10c on 5c .25 .20
J63 D6 50c on 5c 2.00 .60
J64 D1 25 l on 50 l ('43) 2.75 1.75
Nos. J62-J64 (3) 5.00 2.55

PARCEL POST STAMPS

These stamps were used by affixing them to the way bill so that one half remained on it following the parcel, the other half staying on the receipt given the sender. Most used halves are right halves. Complete stamps were and are obtainable canceled, probably to order. Both unused and used values are for complete stamps.

PP1

Engraved, Typographed

1928, Nov. 22 Unwmk. *Perf. 12*

Pairs are imperforate between

Q1	PP1	5c blk brn & bl	.20	.20
a.		Imperf.	40.00	
Q2	PP1	10c dk bl & bl	.20	.20
Q3	PP1	20c gray blk & bl	.20	.20
a.		Imperf.	40.00	
Q4	PP1	25c car & blue	.20	.20
Q5	PP1	30c ultra & blue	.20	.20
Q6	PP1	50c orange & bl	.20	.20
Q7	PP1	60c rose & blue	.20	.20
Q8	PP1	1 l violet & brn	.20	.20
a.		Imperf.	40.00	
Q9	PP1	2 l green & brn	.60	.60
Q10	PP1	3 l bister & brn	.75	.75
Q11	PP1	4 l gray & brn	1.00	1.00
Q12	PP1	10 l rose lilac & brn	2.40	2.40
Q13	PP1	12 l red brn & brn	8.50	8.50
Q14	PP1	15 l olive grn & brn	13.50	13.50
a.		Imperf.	40.00	
Q15	PP1	20 l brn vio & brn	21.00	21.00
		Nos. Q1-Q15 (15)	49.35	49.35

Halves Used

Q1-Q8	.20
Q9-Q10	.20
Q11	.20
Q12	.35
Q13	.65
Q14	2.75
Q15	3.00

SARAWAK

LOCATION — Northwestern part of the island of Borneo, bordering on the South China Sea
GOVT. — British Crown Colony
AREA — 48,250 sq. mi. (approx.)
POP. — 975,918 (1970)
CAPITAL — Kuching

The last ruling Raja, who retired in 1946 when he ceded Sarawak to the British Crown, was Sir Charles Vyner Brooke, an Englishman. He inherited the title from his father, Sir Charles Johnson Brooke, who in turn received it from his uncle, Sir James Brooke. The title of Raja was conferred on Sir James by Raja Muda Hassim after Sir James had aided him in subduing a rebellion. The title and right of succession were duly recognized by the Sultan of Brunei and by Great Britain.

100 Cents = 1 Dollar

Catalogue values for unused stamps in this country are for Never Hinged items, beginning with Scott 155.

Watermarks

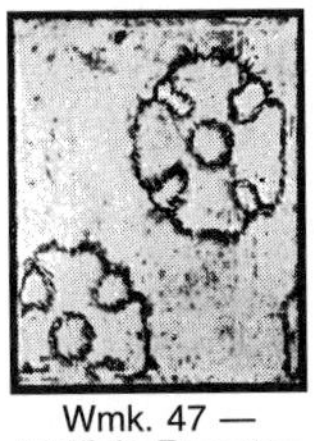

Wmk. 47 — Multiple Rosettes

Wmk. 71 — Rosette

Wmk. 231 — Oriental Crown

Unused examples of Nos. 1-7, 25 and 32-35 are valued without gum. Stamps with original gum are worth more.

Sir James Brooke — A1

Sir Charles Johnson Brooke — A2

Unwmk.

1869, Mar. 1 Litho. *Perf. 11*

1	A1	3c brown, *yellow*	55.00	*240.00*
		On cover		—

Covers: Only one authenticated cover is recorded with No. 1.

1871, Jan.

2	A2	3c brown, *yellow*	2.00	*4.00*
		On cover		—
a.		Vertical pair, imperf between	*575.00*	
b.		Horizontal pair, imperf between	*900.00*	
c.		Period after "THREE"	52.50	*62.50*

No. 2 surcharged "TWO CENTS" is believed to be bogus.

There are a number of lithographic flaws, including narrow A, "period" after THREE, etc.

Imperfs. of Nos. 1, 2 are proofs.

A papermaker's watermark, "LNL," usually appears once or twice in each pane.

For surcharges see Nos. 25, 32.

Covers: Only one authenticated cover is recorded with No. 2.

1875, Jan. 1 *Perf. 12*

3	A2	2c gray lilac, *lilac*	6.50	*21.00*
4	A2	4c brown, *yellow*	4.50	4.00
b.		Vertical pair, imperf between	*825.00*	
5	A2	6c green, *green*	6.00	*6.25*
6	A2	8c blue, *blue*	6.00	*6.25*
7	A2	12c red, *rose*	9.00	*9.00*
		Nos. 3-7 (5)	32.00	*46.50*

Nos. 3-7 have each five varieties of the words of value.

Imperfs are proofs.

A papermaker's watermark usually appears once or twice in each pane of Nos. 3-7, "LNT" on No. 5, "LNL" on others.

Some examples of No. 7 have the appearance of being on laid paper, but the lines are accidental and not constant within the sheets.

For surcharges see Nos. 33-35.

Sir Charles Johnson Brooke — A4

1888-97 Typo. *Perf. 14*

8	A4	1c lilac & blk ('92)	2.00	.55
9	A4	2c lilac & carmine	3.00	1.40
a.		2c pur & rose ('97)	10.00	4.50
10	A4	3c lilac & blue	4.00	*4.25*
11	A4	4c lilac & yellow	21.00	*57.50*
12	A4	5c lilac & grn ('91)	14.00	2.50
13	A4	6c lilac & brown	18.00	*62.50*
14	A4	8c green & car	12.00	3.00
a.		8c green & rose ('97)	24.00	17.00
15	A4	10c grn & vio ('91)	42.50	16.00
16	A4	12c green & blue	11.00	*11.00*
17	A4	16c gray grn & org ('97)	50.00	*80.00*
18	A4	25c green & brown	47.50	*40.00*
19	A4	32c gray grn & blk ('97)	35.00	*57.50*
20	A4	50c gray green ('97)	47.50	*95.00*
21	A4	$1 gray grn & blk ('97)	82.50	*85.00*
		Nos. 8-21 (14)	390.00	*516.20*

No. 21 shows the numeral on white tablet.

Three higher values —$2, $5, $10— were prepared but not issued. Value $750 each.

For surcharges see Nos. 22-24, 26-27.

Nos. 14 and 16 Surcharged in Black:

No. 22

No. 23

5c. No. 24

1889-91

22	A4	2c on 8c	3.50	*5.75*
a.		Double surcharge	450.00	
b.		Pair, one without surcharge	4,500.	
c.		Inverted surcharge	2,600.	
23	A4	5c on 12c ('91)	27.50	*50.00*
a.		Double surcharge	1,100.	
b.		Pair, one without surcharge	*8,000.*	
c.		No period after "C"	29.00	*50.00*
d.		Without "C"	425.00	425.00
e.		Double surch., one vert.	2,750.	
24	A4	5c on 12c ('91)	135.00	*175.00*
a.		No period after "C"	100.00	*110.00*
b.		Double surcharge	1,400.	
c.		"C" omitted	675.00	725.00

No. 2 Surcharged in Black

1892, May 23 *Perf. 11*

25	A2	1c on 3c brown, *yel*	2.00	*3.00*
b.		Without bar	275.00	
c.		Period after "THREE"	50.00	52.50
d.		Double surcharge	475.00	500.00
e.		Vertical pair, imperf between	*750.00*	
f.		Vertical pair, imperf horiz.	*700.00*	

Examples of No. 25b must be from the first printing, wherein the bar was applied after the surcharge. Examples of No. 25 with parts of the surcharge and/or bar omitted are stamps that had gum on the face prior to the surcharging operation. The ink was removed when the gum was washed off.

No. 10 Surcharged in Black:

e

f

1892 *Perf. 14*

26	A4(e)	1c on 3c lil & bl	4.00	*4.00*
a.		No period after "cent"	175.00	*225.00*
27	A4(f)	1c on 3c lil & bl	52.50	32.50
b.		Double surcharge	725.00	600.00

Issued: #26, Feb.; #27, Jan. 12.

Sir Charles Johnson Brooke
A11 A12

A13 A14

1895, Jan. 1 Engr. *Perf. 11½, 12*

28	A11	2c red brn	10.00	*11.00*
a.		Perf. 12½	13.00	6.00
b.		Vertical pair, imperf between	*475.00*	
c.		Horizontal pair, imperf between	*400.00*	
d.		As "a," horiz. pair, imperf between	*500.00*	
29	A12	4c black	10.00	4.00
a.		Horizontal pair, imperf between	*650.00*	
30	A13	6c violet	11.50	*11.50*
31	A14	8c deep green	30.00	7.00
		Nos. 28-31 (4)	61.50	33.50

The 2c and 8c imperf are proofs. Perforated stamps of these designs in other colors are color trials, which exist surcharged with new values in pence. These surcharged varieties were used in trial printings of a British South African issue.

Stamps of 1871-75 Surcharged in Black or Red

1899 *Perf. 11*

32	A2	2c on 3c brown, *yel*	2.00	*2.00*
a.		Period after "THREE"	57.50	*62.50*
b.		Vertical pair, imperf between	*1,000.*	

Perf. 12

33	A2	2c on 12c red, *rose*	3.50	*3.50*
a.		Inverted surcharge	900.00	*1,400.*
34	A2	4c on 6c green, *grn* (R)	32.50	*70.00*
35	A2	4c on 8c blue, *bl* (R)	5.00	*8.50*
		Nos. 32-35 (4)	43.00	*84.00*

Sir Charles J. Brooke A16

Sir Charles Vyner Brooke A17

1899-1908 Typo. *Perf. 14*

36	A16	1c blue & car ('01)	1.40	*1.40*
a.		1c ultra & pink	5.00	2.00
37	A16	2c gray green	2.25	1.00
38	A16	3c dull violet ('08)	11.00	.75
39	A16	4c analine carmine	2.75	2.75
a.		4c rose ('99)	5.00	2.00
40	A16	8c yellow & black	2.50	.90
41	A16	10c ultra	3.00	1.10
42	A16	12c light violet ('99)	5.00	5.00
a.		12c bright purple ('05)	13.50	7.00
43	A16	16c org brn & grn	4.25	2.00
44	A16	20c brn ol & vio ('00)	6.25	4.00
45	A16	25c brown & ultra	6.50	*5.75*
46	A16	50c ol grn & rose	25.00	*27.50*

47	A16	$1 rose & green	60.00	*125.00*
a.		$1 pink & pale green	50.00	*80.00*
		Nos. 36-47 (12)	129.90	*177.15*

A 5c was prepared but not issued. Value $13.50.

1901 **Wmk. 71**

48	A16	2c gray green	29.00	16.00

1918-23 **Unwmk.**

50	A17	1c slate bl & rose	2.50	*2.75*
51	A17	2c deep green	2.90	1.75
52	A17	2c violet ('23)	2.25	*3.00*
53	A17	3c violet brown	3.75	3.00
54	A17	3c dp grn ('22)	1.75	*1.40*
55	A17	4c carmine rose	4.50	3.50
56	A17	4c purple brn ('23)	1.75	.95
57	A17	5c orange ('23)	2.00	1.00
58	A17	6c lake brown ('22)	1.75	*1.60*
59	A17	8c yellow & blk	14.00	*70.00*
60	A17	8c car rose ('22)	5.00	*35.00*
61	A17	10c ultra	3.50	3.50
a.		10c blue	3.50	3.50
62	A17	10c black ('23)	2.25	*4.50*
63	A17	12c violet	12.50	*30.00*
64	A17	12c ultra ('22)	11.00	*21.00*
65	A17	16c brn & blue grn	6.25	*8.50*
66	A17	20c olive bis & vio	8.00	*7.50*
a.		20c olive green & violet	8.00	*7.50*
67	A17	25c brown & blue	4.50	*14.00*
68	A17	30c bis & gray ('22)	4.25	*4.75*
69	A17	50c olive grn & rose	11.50	*17.00*
70	A17	$1 car rose & grn	19.00	*32.50*
		Nos. 50-70 (21)	124.90	*267.20*

In 1918 a supply of the 1c (No. 50) had the value tablet printed, by error, in slate blue instead of rose. It is officially stated that this stamp was never issued and had no franking power. Value $10.

The $1 denomination shows numeral of value in color on white tablet.

Nos. 61 and 63 Surcharged

1st Printing — bars 1 ¼mm apart.
2nd Printing — Bars ¾mm apart.

1923, Jan.

77	A17	1c on 10c ultra	11.00	*62.50*
a.		"cnet"	400.00	*900.00*
b.		Bars ¾mm apart	140.00	*400.00*
78	A17	2c on 12c violet	7.50	*47.50*
a.		Bars ¾mm apart	80.00	*225.00*

Type of 1918 Issue

1928-29 **Typo.** **Wmk. 47**

79	A17	1c slate blue & rose	1.60	.40
80	A17	2c dull violet	2.00	1.40
81	A17	3c deep green	2.00	*5.75*
82	A17	4c purple brown	1.75	.20
83	A17	5c orange ('29)	2.50	5.75
84	A17	6c brown lake	1.75	.35
85	A17	8c carmine	3.75	*17.50*
86	A17	10c black	2.00	1.40
87	A17	12c ultra	3.75	*25.00*
88	A17	16c dp brn & bl grn	3.75	*4.50*
89	A17	20c dp olive & vio	3.75	*6.25*
90	A17	25c dk brown & ultra	6.25	*9.75*
91	A17	30c olive bis & gray	5.25	*11.50*
92	A17	50c olive grn & rose	7.00	*15.00*
93	A17	$1 car rose & grn	20.00	*27.50*
		Nos. 79-93 (15)	67.10	*132.25*

Sir Charles Vyner Brooke
A18 A19

Wmk. 231

1932, Jan. 1 **Engr.** ***Perf. 12½***

94	A18	1c indigo	.90	1.10
95	A18	2c dark green	1.10	*1.75*
96	A18	3c deep violet	4.00	1.10
97	A18	4c deep orange	3.00	.85
98	A18	5c brown lake	8.50	1.40
99	A18	6c deep red	9.75	*11.00*
100	A18	8c orange yel	7.50	*9.75*
101	A18	10c black	2.50	*3.75*
102	A18	12c violet blue	4.50	*11.00*
103	A18	15c orange brown	8.00	*9.75*
104	A18	20c violet & org	6.25	*9.00*
105	A18	25c org brn & yel	15.00	*25.00*
106	A18	30c org red & ol brn	11.00	*25.00*
107	A18	50c olive grn & red	14.00	*15.00*
108	A18	$1 car & green	25.00	*40.00*
		Nos. 94-108 (15)	121.00	*165.45*

1934-41 **Unwmk.** ***Perf. 12***

109	A19	1c brown violet	1.25	.20
110	A19	2c blue green	1.50	.20
111	A19	2c black ('41)	3.50	*1.75*
112	A19	3c black	1.25	.20
113	A19	3c blue grn ('41)	7.00	*5.00*
114	A19	4c magenta	1.50	.20
115	A19	5c violet	1.75	.20
116	A19	6c deep rose	2.50	.70
117	A19	6c red brn ('41)	7.00	*9.00*
118	A19	8c red brown	2.25	.20
119	A19	8c dp rose ('41)	7.75	.20
120	A19	10c red	2.50	.45
121	A19	12c deep ultra	3.00	.30
122	A19	12c orange ('41)	5.50	*6.25*
123	A19	15c orange	4.00	*12.00*
124	A19	15c deep blue ('41)	8.25	*20.00*
125	A19	20c dp rose & olive	4.00	1.10
126	A19	25c orange & vio	4.00	*2.00*
127	A19	30c violet & red brn	4.00	*3.25*
128	A19	50c red & violet	4.50	1.00
129	A19	$1 dk brn & red	1.75	1.00
130	A19	$2 violet & mag	15.00	10.00
131	A19	$3 bl grn & rose	29.00	*32.50*
132	A19	$4 red & ultra	29.00	*50.00*
133	A19	$5 red brn & red	32.50	*50.00*
134	A19	$10 orange & blk	22.50	*57.50*
		Nos. 109-134 (26)	206.75	*265.20*

Issue dates: May 1, 1934, Mar. 1, 1941.
For overprints see #135-154, 159-173, N1-N22.

Stamps of 1934-41 Overprinted in Black or Red

1945, Dec. 17

135	A19	1c brown violet	.75	*.45*
136	A19	2c black (R)	.75	*1.00*
137	A19	3c blue green	.75	*1.10*
138	A19	4c magenta	.75	.35
139	A19	5c violet (R)	1.40	1.00
140	A19	6c red brown	1.75	.90
141	A19	8c deep rose	9.50	*13.50*
142	A19	10c red	.90	.80
143	A19	12c orange	1.25	*4.25*
144	A19	15c deep blue	2.25	.45
145	A19	20c dp rose & ol	1.75	*2.50*
146	A19	25c org & vio (R)	2.00	*3.00*
147	A19	30c vio & red brn	4.50	*3.00*
148	A19	50c red & violet	.90	.40
149	A19	$1 dk brn & red	1.75	1.40
150	A19	$2 violet & mag	6.50	*11.00*
151	A19	$3 bl grn & rose	12.50	*55.00*
152	A19	$4 red & ultra	25.00	*45.00*
153	A19	$5 red brn & red	140.00	*210.00*
154	A19	$10 org & blk (R)	125.00	*225.00*
		Nos. 135-154 (20)	339.95	*580.10*
		Set, never hinged	550.00	

Catalogue values for unused stamps in this section, from this point to the end of the section, are for Never Hinged items.

Sir James Brooke, Sir Charles V. Brooke and Sir Charles J. Brooke
A20

1946, May 18

155	A20	8c dark carmine	1.75	1.00
156	A20	15c dark blue	1.75	*2.25*
157	A20	50c red & black	2.50	*2.75*
158	A20	$1 sepia & black	3.25	*18.00*
		Nos. 155-158 (4)	9.25	*24.00*

Type of 1934-41 Overprinted in Blue or Red

1947, Apr. 16 **Wmk. 4** ***Perf. 12***

159	A19	1c brown violet	.20	.30
160	A19	2c black (R)	.20	.20
161	A19	3c blue green (R)	.20	.20
162	A19	4c magenta	.20	.20
163	A19	6c red brown	.30	*1.00*
164	A19	8c deep rose	.85	.20
165	A19	10c red	.30	.20
166	A19	12c orange	.30	*1.10*
167	A19	15c deep blue (R)	.30	*.55*
168	A19	20c dp rose & ol (R)	2.25	.65
169	A19	25c orange & vio (R)	.60	.55
170	A19	50c red & violet (R)	.60	.75
171	A19	$1 dk brown & red	1.10	*1.50*
172	A19	$2 violet & magenta	2.00	*4.00*
173	A19	$5 red brown & red	4.50	4.00
		Nos. 159-173 (15)	13.90	15.40

Common Design Types pictured following the introduction.

Silver Wedding Issue
Common Design Types

1948, Oct. 25 **Photo.** ***Perf. 14x14½***

174	CD304	8c scarlet	.40	.40

Engraved; Name Typographed
Perf. 11½x11

175	CD305	$5 light brown	40.00	*45.00*

UPU Issue
Common Design Types
Engr.; Name Typo. on 15c, 25c
Perf. 13½, 11x11½

1949, Oct. 10 **Wmk. 4**

176	CD306	8c rose carmine	1.50	.60
177	CD307	15c indigo	3.00	2.25
178	CD308	25c green	2.10	1.50
179	CD309	50c violet	2.10	*4.50*
		Nos. 176-179 (4)	8.70	8.85

Troides Brookiana A21

Western Tarsier — A22

Designs: 3c, Kayan tomb. 4c, Kayan girl and boy. 6c, Bead work. 8c, Dyak dancer. 10c, Scaly anteater. 12c, Kenyah boys. 15c, Fire making. 20c, Kelemantan rice barn. 25c, Pepper vines. 50c, Iban woman. $1, Kelabit smithy. $2, Map of Sarawak. $5, Arms of Sarawak.

Perf. 11½x11, 11x11½

1950, Jan. 3 **Engr.**

180	A21	1c black	.45	.30
181	A22	2c orange red	.20	*.40*
182	A22	3c green	.25	*.60*
183	A22	4c brown	.25	.20
184	A22	6c aquamarine	.30	.20
185	A21	8c red	.25	.30
186	A21	10c orange	1.25	*4.00*
187	A21	12c purple	3.75	1.50
188	A21	15c deep blue	2.50	.25
189	A21	20c red org & brn	2.00	.50
190	A22	25c carmine & grn	3.00	.60
191	A22	50c purple & brn	4.00	.20
192	A21	$1 dk brn & bl grn	22.50	4.00
193	A21	$2 rose car & blue	30.00	15.00

Engr. and Typo.

194	A21	$5 dp vio, blk, red & yel	20.00	15.00
		Nos. 180-194 (15)	90.70	43.05

1952, Feb. 1

195	A21	10c orange *(Map)*	1.75	.55

OCCUPATION STAMPS

Issued under Japanese Occupation

Stamps of 1934-41 Handstamped in Violet

1942 **Unwmk.** ***Perf. 12***

N1	A19	1c brown violet	45.00	*60.00*
N2	A19	2c blue green	110.00	*175.00*
N3	A19	2c black	100.00	*90.00*
N3A	A19	3c black	*275.00*	*275.00*
N4	A19	3c blue green	60.00	*72.50*
N5	A19	4c magenta	65.00	*80.00*
N6	A19	5c violet	80.00	*72.50*
N7	A19	6c deep rose	140.00	125.00
N8	A19	6c red brown	90.00	*90.00*
N8A	A19	8c red brown	*300.00*	*325.00*
N9	A19	8c deep rose	110.00	*110.00*
N10	A19	10c red	75.00	*75.00*
N11	A19	12c deep ultra	165.00	140.00
N12	A19	12c orange	165.00	150.00
N12A	A19	15c orange	*300.00*	*300.00*
N13	A19	15c deep blue	110.00	100.00
N14	A19	20c dp rose & ol	60.00	*80.00*
N15	A19	25c orange & vio	100.00	*80.00*
N16	A19	30c violet & red brn	65.00	*80.00*
N17	A19	50c red & violet	80.00	*80.00*
N18	A19	$1 dk brown & red	100.00	*100.00*
N19	A19	$2 violet & mag	200.00	*200.00*
N19A	A19	$3 blue grn & rose	*1,250.*	*1,300.*
N20	A19	$4 red & ultra	225.00	*260.00*
N21	A19	$5 red brown & red	240.00	*300.00*
N22	A19	$10 orange & blk	240.00	*300.00*
		Nos. N1-N22 (26)	*4,750.*	*5,020.*

Stamps overprinted with Japanese characters in oval frame or between 2 vertical black lines were not for paying postage.

SASENO

LOCATION — An island in the Adriatic Sea, lying at the entrance of Valona Bay, Albania
GOVT. — Italian possession
AREA — 2 sq. mi.

Italy occupied this Albanian islet in 1914, and returned it to Albania in 1947.

100 Centesimi = 1 Lira

Used values in italics are for postally used stamps. CTO's sell for about the same as unused, hinged stamps.

Italian Stamps of 1901-22 Overprinted

1923 **Wmk. 140** ***Perf. 14***

1	A48	10c claret	13.00	*22.50*
2	A48	15c slate	13.00	*22.50*
3	A50	20c brown orange	13.00	*22.50*
4	A49	25c blue	13.00	*22.50*
5	A49	30c yellow brown	13.00	*22.50*
6	A49	50c violet	13.00	*22.50*
7	A49	60c carmine	13.00	*22.50*
8	A46	1 l brown & green	13.00	*22.50*
a.		Double overprint	190.00	
		Nos. 1-8 (8)	104.00	*180.00*
		Set, never hinged	250.00	

Superseded by postage stamps of Italy.

SAUDI ARABIA

LOCATION — Southwestern Asia, on the Arabian Peninsula between the Red Sea and the Persian Gulf
GOVT. — Kingdom
AREA — 927,000 sq. mi.
POP. — 8,400,000 (est. 1984)
CAPITAL — Riyadh

In 1916 the Grand Sherif of Mecca declared the Sanjak of Hejaz independent of Turkish rule. In 1925, Ibn Saud, then Sultan of the Nejd, captured the Hejaz after a prolonged siege of Jedda, the last Hejaz stronghold.

The resulting Kingdom of the Hejaz and Nejd was renamed Saudi Arabia in 1932.

40 Paras = 1 Piaster = 1 Guerche (Garch, Qirsh)
11 Guerche = 1 Riyal (1928)
110 Guerche = 1 Sovereign (1931)

HEJAZ

Sherifate of Mecca

Adapted from Carved Door Panels of Mosque El Salih Talay, Cairo — A1

Taken from Page of Koran in Mosque of El Sultan Barquq, Cairo — A2

Taken from Details of an Ancient Prayer Niche in the Mosque of El Amri at Qus in Upper Egypt — A3

Perf. 10, 12

1916, Oct. Unwmk. Typo.

L1	A1	¼pi green	45.00	32.50
L2	A2	½pi red	45.00	30.00
a.		Perf. 10	200.00	90.00
L3	A3	1pi blue	17.50	11.00
a.		Perf. 12	140.00	140.00
b.		Perf. 10x12		1,000.
		Nos. L1-L3 (3)	107.50	73.50

Exist imperf. Forged perf. exist.

See Nos. L5-L7, L10-L12. For overprints see Nos. L16-L18, L26-L28, L52-L54, L57-L59, L61-L66, L67, L70-L72, L77-L81, 37.

Central Design Adapted from a Koran Design for a Tomb. Background is from Stone Carving on Entrance Arch to the Ministry of Wakfs — A4

1916-17 ***Roulette 20***

L4	A4	⅛pi orange ('17)	4.00	1.40
L5	A1	¼pi green	5.00	1.40
L6	A2	½pi red	8.00	1.40
L7	A3	1pi blue	8.50	1.40
		Nos. L4-L7 (4)	25.50	5.60

See #L9. For overprints & surcharge see #L15a, L16c, L17b, L18d, L25, L51, L56, L69, 33.

Adapted from Stucco Work above Entrance to Cairo R. R. Station
A5

Adapted from First Page of the Koran of Sultan Farag — A6

1917 ***Serrate Roulette 13***

L8	A5	1pa lilac brown	3.25	1.40
L9	A4	⅛pi orange	3.75	1.40
L10	A1	¼pi green	4.25	1.40
L11	A2	½pi red	4.75	1.40
L12	A3	1pi blue	5.00	1.40
L13	A6	2pi magenta	20.00	9.00
		Nos. L8-L13 (6)	41.00	16.00

Designs A1-A6 are inscribed "Hejaz Postage."

For overprints and surcharge see #L14-L31, L55-60, L62, L65--L75, L79a-81.

Kingdom of the Hejaz

Stamps of 1917-18 Overprinted in Black, Red or Brown:

1921, Dec. 21 ***Serrate Roulette 13***

L14	A5	1pa lilac brown	30.00	14.00
L15	A4	⅛pi orange	57.50	16.00
a.		Inverted overprint	90.00	
b.		Double overprint	175.00	
c.		Roulette 20	650.00	
d.		As "c," invtd. overprint	1,500.	*1,400.*
e.		Double overprint, one inverted	425.00	
f.		Double overprint, both inverted	425.00	
L16	A1	¼pi green	12.50	5.50
a.		Inverted overprint	90.00	
b.		Double overprint	175.00	
c.		Roulette 20	650.00	
d.		As "c," invtd. overprint	1,500.	
e.		Double overprint, one inverted	550.00	
f.		Double overprint, both inverted	150.00	
L17	A2	½pi red	15.00	6.75
a.		Inverted overprint	140.00	77.50
b.		Roulette 20	550.00	
c.		Double overprint	425.00	
d		Double overprint, both inverted	425.00	
L18	A3	1pi blue (R)	12.50	6.25
a.		Brown overprint	25.00	18.00
b.		Black overprint	32.50	27.50
c.		As "b," invtd. overprint	350.00	
d.		Roulette 20	625.00	
L19	A6	2pi magenta	17.50	9.00
a.		Double overprint	*2,500.*	
		Nos. L14-L19 (6)	145.00	57.50

Nos. L15-L17, L18b and L19 exist with date (1340) omitted at left or right side.

Some values exist with gold overprint.

Forgeries of Nos. L14-L23 abound.

No. L14 With Additional Surcharge:

a

b

L22	A5(a)	½pi on 1pa	325.00	125.00
L23	A5(b)	1pi on 1pa	325.00	125.00

Stamps of 1917-18 Overprinted in Black

1922, Jan. 7

L24	A5	1pa lilac brown	4.00	2.75
a.		Inverted overprint	140.00	
b.		Double overprint	90.00	
c.		Double ovpt., one inverted	175.00	
L25	A4	⅛pi orange	10.00	6.25
a.		Inverted overprint	90.00	
b.		Double ovpt., one inverted	175.00	
L26	A1	¼pi green	4.50	2.75
a.		Inverted overprint	90.00	
b.		Double ovpt., one inverted	175.00	
L27	A2	½pi red	3.00	1.75
a.		Inverted overprint	90.00	
b.		Double ovpt., one inverted	175.00	
L28	A3	1pi blue	3.25	.80
a.		Double overprint	80.00	
b.		Inverted overprint	140.00	
L29	A6	2pi magenta	7.50	5.50
a.		Double overprint	140.00	

With Additional Surcharge of New Value

L30	A5(a)	½pi on 1pa lil brn	22.50	14.00
L31	A5(b)	1pi on 1pa lil brn	3.00	.90
a.		Inverted surcharge	90.00	
b.		Double surcharge	80.00	
c.		Dbl. surch., one invtd., ovpt. invtd.	250.00	
d.		Inverted overprint	100.00	
e.		Inverted overprint and surcharge	210.00	
f.		Inverted overprint, double surcharge	210.00	
g.		Words of surcharge transposed	200.00	
h.		Overprint and surcharge inverted, words of surcharge transposed	400.00	
i.		Right hand character of surcharge inverted	75.00	
		Nos. L24-L31 (8)	57.75	34.70

The 1921 and 1922 overprints read: "The Government of Hashemite Arabia, 1340."

The overprint on No. L28 in red is bogus.

Forgeries abound.

Types A7 and A8

Very fine examples will be somewhat off center but perforations will be clear of the framelines.

Arms of Sherif of Mecca — A7

1922, Feb. Typo. ***Perf. 11½***

L32	A7	⅛pi red brown	2.25	.45
L34	A7	½pi red	2.50	.45
L35	A7	1pi dark blue	2.75	.45
L36	A7	1½pi violet	3.00	.45
L37	A7	2pi orange	4.00	.45
L38	A7	3pi olive brown	3.25	.45
L39	A7	5pi olive green	3.50	.55
		Nos. L32-L39 (7)	21.25	3.25

Numerous shades exist. Some values were printed in other colors in 1925 for handstamping by the Nejdi authorities in Mecca. These exist without handstamps.

Exist imperf.

Forgeries exist, usually perf. 11.

Reprints of Nos. L32, L35 exist; paper and shades differ.

See Nos. L48A-L49. For surcharges and overprints see Nos. L40-L48, L76, L82-L159, 7-20, 38A-48, 55A-58A, LJ11-LJ16, LJ26-LJ39, J1-J8, J10-J11, P1-P3, Jordan 64-72, 91, 103-120, J1-J17, O1.

Stamps of 1922 Surcharged with New Values in Arabic:

c

d

1923

L40	A7(c)	¼pi on ⅛pi org brn	35.00	32.50
a.		Double surcharge	125.00	
b.		Double inverted surcharge	325.00	
c.		Double surch., one invtd.	325.00	
L41	A7(d)	10pi on 5pi ol grn	30.00	27.50
a.		Double surch., one invtd.	150.00	
b.		Inverted surcharge	125.00	

Forgeries exist.

Caliphate Issue

Stamps of 1922 Overprinted in Gold

1924

L42	A7	⅛pi orange brown	4.75
L43	A7	½pi red	3.50
L44	A7	1pi dark blue	5.00
a.		Inverted overprint	200.00
L45	A7	1½pi violet	4.75
L46	A7	2pi orange	4.50
a.		Inverted overprint	200.00
L47	A7	3pi olive brown	5.00
L48	A7	5pi olive green	5.50
a.		Inverted overprint	200.00
		Nos. L42-L48 (7)	33.00

Assumption of the Caliphate by King Hussein in Mar., 1924. The overprint reads "In commemoration of the Caliphate, Shaaban, 1342."

The overprint was typographed in black and dusted with "gold" powder while wet. Inverted overprints on other values are forgeries. So-called black overprints are either forgeries or gold overprints with the gold rubbed off. No genuine black overprints are known.

The overprint is 18-20mm wide. The 1st setting of the ½p is 16mm.

Forgeries exist.

Nos. L43-L44, L46 exist with postage due overprint as on Nos. LJ11-LJ13.

Type of 1922 and

Arms of Sherif of Mecca — A8

1924 ***Perf. 11½***

L48A	A7	¼pi yellow green	4.50	*5.75*
b.		Tête bêche pair	*27.50*	
L49	A7	3pi brown red	10.00	*9.00*
a.		3pi dull red	3.00	*4.50*
L50	A8	10pi vio & dk brn	5.00	*4.50*
a.		Center inverted	*55.00*	55.00
b.		Center omitted	67.50	
c.		10pi purple & sepia	3.00	*4.50*
		Nos. L48A-L50 (3)	19.50	19.25

Nos. L48A, L50, L50a exist imperf.

Several printings of Nos. L48A-L50 exist; paper and shades differ.

Forgeries exist, usually perf. 11.

For overprint see Nos. L76A, Jordan 121.

Jedda Issues

Stamps of 1916-17 Overprinted

The control overprints on Nos. L51-L159 read: "Hukumat al Hejaziyeh, 5 Rabi al'awwal 1343"

(The Hejaz Government, October 4, 1924). This is the date of the accession of King Ali.

Counterfeits exist of all Jedda overprints.

Jedda issues were also used in Medina and Yambo.

Used values for #L51-L186 and LJ17-LJ39 are for genuine cancels. Privately applied cancels exist for "Mekke" (Mecca, bilingual or all Arabic), Khartoum, Cairo, as well as for Jeddah. Many private cancels have wrong dates, some as early as 1916. These are worth half the used values.

Red Overprint

1925, Jan. *Roulette 20*

L51 A4 ⅛pi orange 17.50 *14.00*
 a. Inverted overprint 90.00
 b. Ovptd. on face and back 175.00
 c. Normal ovpt. on face, double ovpt. on back 225.00
L52 A1 ¼pi green 17.50 *14.00*
 a. Inverted overprint 60.00
 b. Double overprint 55.00
 c. Double overprint, one invtd. 140.00
L53 A2 ½pi red 70.00 *67.50*
 a. Inverted overprint 150.00
L54 A3 1pi blue 35.00 *32.50*
 a. Inverted overprint *140.00*
 b. Double ovpt., one invtd. 125.00
 Nos. L51-L53 (3) 105.00 *95.50*

Serrate Roulette 13

L55 A5 1pa lilac brown 15.00 *12.50*
 a. Inverted overprint 67.50
 b. Double overprint 60.00
 c. Ovptd. on face and back *175.00*
 d. Normal ovpt. on face, double ovpt. on back 125.00
L56 A4 ⅛pi orange 37.50 *35.00*
 a. Inverted overprint 80.00
L57 A1 ¼pi green 22.50 *20.00*
 a. Pair, one without overprint *1,600.*
 b. Inverted overprint 45.00
 c. Double ovpt., one inverted 275.00
L58 A2 ½pi red 30.00 *27.50*
 a. Inverted overprint *140.00*
L59 A3 1pi blue 35.00 *32.50*
 a. Inverted overprint *100.00*
L60 A6 2pi magenta 40.00 *35.00*
 a. Inverted overprint *140.00*
 Nos. L55-L60 (6) 180.00 *162.50*

Gold Overprint

Roulette 20

L61 A1 ¼pi green, gold on red ovpt. *3,000.*
 a. Gold on blue ovpt. 3,750. *7,000.*

Serrate Roulette 13

L62 A1 ¼pi green, gold on red ovpt. 25.00 *22.50*
 a. Inverted overprint *125.00*

The overprint on No. L61 was typographed in red or blue (No. L62 only in red) and dusted with "gold" powder while wet.

Blue Overprint

Roulette 20

L63 A1 ¼pi green 80.00 *22.50*
 a. Inverted overprint 150.00
 b. Ovptd. on face and back 175.00
L64 A2 ½pi red, invtd. ovpt. 90.00 *80.00*
 a. Upright overprint 140.00

Serrate Roulette 13

L65 A1 ¼pi green 17.50 *16.00*
 a. Inverted overprint 67.50
 b. Vertical overprint 900.00
L66 A2 ½pi red 30.00 *27.50*
 a. Inverted overprint *90.00*
L66B A6 2pi mag, invtd. ovpt. *1,500.*

Blue overprint on Nos. L4, L8, L9 are bogus.

Same Overprint in Blue on Provisional Stamps of 1922

Overprinted on No. L17

L67 A2 ½pi red *2,500.*

Overprinted on Nos. L24-L29

L68 A5 1pa lilac brn 175.00 *160.00*
L69 A4 ⅛pi orange *2,500.* *1,800.*
 a. Inverted overprint 4,000.
L70 A1 ¼pi green 70.00 *65.00*
 a. Inverted overprint 725.00
L71 A2 ½pi red 90.00 *85.00*
 a. Inverted overprint 800.00
L72 A3 1pi blue 110.00 *110.00*
L73 A6 2pi magenta 160.00 *160.00*
 a. Inverted overprint 1,400.

Same Overprint on Nos. L30 and L31

L74 A5(a) ½pi on 1pa 95.00 *90.00*
L75 A5(b) 1pi on 1pa 80.00 *75.00*
 a. Inverted overprint 600.00

Same Overprint in Blue Vertically, Reading Up or Down, on Stamps of 1922-24

Perf. 11½

L76 A7 ½pi red 900.00 *900.00*
L76A A8 10pi vio & dk brn *1,800.* *1,800.*

Nos. L5, L10 Overprinted Reading Up in Blue or Red (Overprint reads up in illustration)

Roulette 20

L77a A1 ¼pi green (Bl) 500.00 *500.00*
L78 A1 ¼pi green (R) *450.00* *450.00*

Serrate Roulette 13

L79a A1 ¼pi green (Bl) 300.00 *300.00*
L80 A1 ¼pi green (R) 60.00 *60.00*

Overprint Reading Down

Roulette 20

L77 A1 ¼pi green (Bl) *175.00* *175.00*

Serrate Roulette 13

L79 A1 ¼pi green (Bl) 90.00 *90.00*
L80a A1 ¼pi green (R) 200.00 *200.00*

Nos. L10, L32-L39, L48A, L49a, L50 Overprinted

Serrate Roulette 13

Red Overprint (vertical, reading up)

L81 A1 ¼pi green *1,200.*

Overprint on No. L81 also exists horizontal and inverted.

Perf. 11½

Blue Overprint

L82 A7 ⅛pi red brown 7.00 *5.50*
 a. Inverted overprint 45.00
L83 A7 ½pi red 8.50 *7.25*
 a. Double overprint 67.50
 b. Inverted overprint 45.00 *45.00*
 c. Double ovpt., one invtd. 67.50
 d. Overprint reading up 85.00
L84 A7 1pi dark blue *350.00*
 a. Inverted overprint *350.00*
L85 A7 1½pi violet 12.50 *11.00*
 a. Inverted overprint 45.00 *45.00*
L86 A7 2pi orange 12.50 *11.00*
 a. Double ovpt., one invtd. 67.50
 b. Inverted overprint 45.00
 c. Double overprint 67.50
L87 A7 3pi olive brown 10.00 *9.00*
 a. Inverted overprint 45.00
 b. Double ovpt., one invtd. 67.50
 c. Overprint reading up 160.00
 d. Dbl. ovpt., both invtd. 90.00
L88 A7 3pi dull red 12.50 *11.00*
 a. Inverted overprint 45.00
 b. Double ovpt., one invtd. 67.50
L89 A7 5pi olive green 13.00 *11.00*
 a. Inverted overprint 45.00

Some values exist in pairs, one without overprint.

Black Overprint

L90 A7 ⅛pi red brown *50.00*
 a. Inverted overprint *140.00*
L91 A7 ½pi red 6.00 *4.50*
 a. Inverted overprint 60.00
L92 A7 1pi dark blue *350.00*
 a. Inverted overprint *350.00*
L93 A7 1½pi violet 15.00 *12.00*
 a. Inverted overprint 67.50
L94 A7 2pi orange 9.00 *7.25*
 a. Inverted overprint 45.00
L95 A7 3pi olive brown 7.00 *5.50*
 a. Inverted overprint 67.50 *67.50*
L96 A7 3pi dull red 9.00 *7.25*
 a. Inverted overprint 45.00
L97 A7 5pi olive green 11.00 *9.00*
 a. Inverted overprint 45.00

Red Overprint

L98 A7 ⅛pi red brn, invtd. *725.00*
L99 A7 ¼pi yellow grn 20.00 *16.00*
 a. Tête bêche pair 62.50
 b. Inverted overprint 45.00
 c. Tête bêche pair, one with inverted overprint 75.00
L100 A7 ½pi red *1,000.* *500.00*
 a. Inverted overprint *1,000.* *500.00*
L101 A7 1pi dark blue 10.00 *8.00*
 a. Inverted overprint 45.00
 b. Double ovpt., one invtd. 32.50
L102 A7 1½pi violet 6.00 *4.50*
 a. Inverted overprint 45.00
L103 A7 2pi orange 15.00 *12.00*
 a. Inverted overprint 45.00
 b. Overprint reading up 160.00
L104 A7 3pi olive brown 15.00 *12.00*
 a. Inverted overprint 45.00
L105 A7 3pi dull red, invtd. *1,500.*
L106 A7 5pi olive green 10.00 *7.25*
 a. Inverted overprint 45.00
 b. Overprint reading up 125.00
 c. Overprint reading down 125.00
L107 A8 10pi vio & dk brn 20.00 *16.00*
 a. Inverted overprint 45.00
 b. Center inverted 90.00
 c. As "b," invtd. ovpt. *140.00*

Nos. L98, L105 with normal overprint are fakes.

Gold Overprint

L108 A7 ⅛pi red brown 30.00 *27.50*
L109 A7 ½pi red 30.00 *27.50*
L110 A7 1pi dark blue 35.00 *27.50*
L111 A7 1½pi violet 110.00 *110.00*
L112 A7 2pi orange 100.00 *90.00*
L113 A7 3pi olive brown 40.00 *35.00*
L114 A7 3pi dull red 120.00 *100.00*
L115 A7 5pi olive green 95.00 *85.00*
 Nos. L108-L115 (8) 560.00 *502.50*

Inverted overprints are forgeries.

Same Overprint on Nos. L42-L48

Blue Overprint

L116 A7 ⅛pi red brown 45.00 *42.50*
 a. Double ovpt., one invtd. *275.00*
L117 A7 ½pi red 85.00 *80.00*
L118 A7 1pi dark blue 70.00 *55.00*
L119 A7 1½pi violet 75.00 *65.00*
L120 A7 2pi orange 275.00 *275.00*
 a. Inverted overprint *425.00*
L121 A7 3pi olive brown 110.00 *110.00*
 a. Inverted overprint *175.00*
L122 A7 5pi olive green 40.00 *37.50*
 a. Inverted overprint *200.00*
 Nos. L116-L122 (7) 700.00 *665.00*

Black Overprint

L123 A7 ⅛pi red brown 45.00 *42.50*
 a. Inverted overprint *225.00*
L125 A7 1½pi violet 140.00 *140.00*
 a. Inverted overprint *225.00*
L127 A7 3pi olive brown 110.00 *110.00*
 a. Inverted overprint *225.00*
L128 A7 5pi olive green 140.00 *140.00*
 a. Inverted overprint *225.00*
 Nos. L123-L128 (4) 435.00 *432.50*

Red Overprint

L129 A7 1pi dark blue 100.00 *90.00*
L130 A7 1½pi violet 110.00 *110.00*
L131 A7 2pi orange 110.00 *90.00*
 Nos. L129-L131 (3) 320.00 *290.00*

Overprints on stamps or in colors other than those listed are forgeries.

Stamps of 1922-24 Surcharged

a

and Handstamp Surcharged

b — 1/4pi

b — 1pi

b — 10pi

1925 **Litho.** *Perf. 11½*

L135 A7 ¼pi on ⅛pi red brn 50.00 *47.50*
 b. 1pi on ¼pi on ⅛pi red brown 110.00
L136 A7 ¼pi on ¼pi on ½pi red 35.00 *30.00*
 c. 1pi on ¼pi on ½pi 55.00 *55.00*
L138 A7 1pi on 1pi on 2pi orange 35.00 *30.00*
 a. ¼pi on ¼pi on 2pi org 105.00
 b. 10pi on 1pi on 2pi org 90.00
 c. ¼pi on 1pi on 2pi org 45.00
 d. 1pi on ¼pi on 2pi org *90.00*
L139 A7 1pi on 1pi on 3pi ol brn 25.00 *22.50*
L140 A7 1pi on 1pi on 3pi dl red 40.00 *35.00*
 b. ¼pi on 1pi on 3pi dl red 110.00
L141 A7 10pi on 10pi on 5pi ol grn 20.00 *16.00*
 b. 1pi on 10 pi on 5 pi 95.00
 Nos. L135-L141 (6) 205.00 *181.00*

The printed surcharge (a) reads "The Hejaz Government. October 4, 1924." with new denomination in third line. This surcharge alone was used for the first issue (Nos. L135a-L141a). The new denomination was so small and indistinct that its equivalent in larger characters was soon added by handstamp (b) at bottom of each stamp for the second issue (Nos. L135-L141).

The handstamped surcharge (b) is found double, inverted, etc. It is also known in dark violet.

Without Handstamp "b"

L135a A7 ¼pi on ⅛pi red brn 90.00
L136b A7 ¼pi on ½pi red 90.00
L138e A7 1pi on 2pi orange 90.00
L139a A7 1pi on 3pi olive brn 90.00
L140a A7 1pi on 3pi dull red 90.00
L141a A7 10pi on 5pi olive grn 90.00
 Nos. L135a-L141a (6) 540.00

Stamps of 1922-24 Surcharged

Black Surcharge

L142 A7 ⅛pi on ½pi red 9.00 *7.25*
 a. Inverted surcharge 35.00
L143 A7 ¼pi on ½pi red 9.50 *7.25*
 a. Inverted surcharge 35.00
L144 A7 1pi on ½pi red 10.50 *7.25*
 a. Inverted surcharge 22.50
L145 A7 1pi on 1½pi vio 11.00 *7.25*
 a. Inverted surcharge 32.50
L146 A7 1pi on 2pi org 9.00 *7.25*
 a. "10pi" 77.50
 b. Inverted surcharge 35.00
 c. As "a," inverted surcharge 130.00
L147 A7 1pi on 3pi olive brn 10.00 *7.25*
 a. "10pi" 67.50
 b. Inverted surcharge 45.00
 c. As "a," inverted surcharge 130.00
L148 A7 10pi on 5pi olive grn 17.50 *14.00*
 a. Inverted surcharge 60.00
 Nos. L142-L148 (7) 76.50 *57.50*

Blue Surcharge

L149 A7 ⅛pi on ½pi red 15.00 *11.00*
 a. Inverted surcharge 60.00
 b. Double surcharge 200.00
L150 A7 ¼pi on ½pi red 12.50 *11.00*
 a. Inverted surcharge 45.00
L151 A7 1pi on ½pi red 12.50 *11.00*
 a. Inverted surcharge 45.00
 b. Double surcharge 90.00
L152 A7 1pi on 1½pi vio 15.00 *11.00*
 a. Inverted surcharge 60.00
L153 A7 1pi on 2pi org 15.00 *11.00*
 a. "10pi" 62.50
 b. Inverted surcharge 60.00
L154 A7 1pi on 3pi olive brn 25.00 *22.50*
 a. "10pi" 77.50
 b. Inverted surcharge 62.50
L155 A7 10pi on 5pi olive grn 30.00 *25.00*
 a. Inverted surcharge 55.00
 Nos. L149-L155 (7) 125.00 *102.50*

Red Surcharge

L156 A7 1pi on 1½pi vio 25.00 *22.50*
 a. Inverted surcharge 72.50
L157 A7 1pi on 2pi org 27.50 *22.50*
 a. "10pi" 72.50
 b. Inverted surcharge 72.50
L158 A7 1pi on 3pi olive brn 30.00 *22.50*
 a. "10pi" 90.00
 b. Inverted surcharge 72.50
L159 A7 10pi on 5pi olive grn 30.00 *22.50*
 a. Inverted surcharge 72.50
 Nos. L156-L159 (4) 112.50 *90.00*
 Nos. L142-L159 (18) 314.00 *250.00*

The "10pi" surcharge is found inverted on Nos. L146a, L147a. The existence of genuine inverted "10pi" surcharges on Nos. L153a, L154a, L157a and L158a is in doubt.

The 10pi on 1½pi is bogus.

King Ali Issue

A9

A10

A11

A12

1925, May-June *Perf. 11½*

Black Overprint

L160 A9 ⅛pi chocolate 2.00 *1.50*
L161 A9 ¼pi ultra 2.00 *1.50*
L162 A9 ½pi car rose 2.00 *1.50*
L163 A10 1pi yellow green 2.50 *1.75*
L164 A10 1½pi orange 2.50 *1.75*
L165 A10 2pi blue 3.00 *2.25*
L166 A11 3pi dark green 3.00 *2.25*
L167 A11 5pi orange brn 3.00 *2.25*
L168 A12 10pi red & green 5.00 *4.50*
a. Center inverted 67.50
Nos. L160-L168 (9) 25.00 *19.25*

Red Overprint

L169 A9 ⅛pi chocolate 3.50 *2.75*
L170 A9 ¼pi ultra 2.00 *1.60*
L171 A10 1pi yellow green 2.50 *2.00*
L172 A10 1½pi orange 2.50 *2.00*
L173 A10 2pi deep blue 3.00 *2.50*
L174 A11 3pi dark green 3.25 *2.75*
a. Horiz. pair, imperf. vert.
L175 A11 5pi org brn 3.50 *2.75*
L176 A12 10pi red & green 6.00 *5.50*
Nos. L169-L176 (8) 26.25 *21.85*

Blue Overprint

L177 A9 ⅛pi chocolate 2.25 *1.75*
L179 A9 ½pi car rose 2.25 *1.75*
L180 A10 1pi yellow green 2.25 *1.75*
L181 A10 1½pi orange 2.25 *1.75*
L182 A11 3pi dark green 2.25 *1.75*
L183 A11 5pi orange brn 6.25 *5.50*
L184 A12 10pi red & green 8.00 *7.25*
L185 A12 10pi red & org 275.00
Nos. L177-L184 (7) 25.50 *21.50*

Without Overprint

L186 A12 10pi red & green 7.50 *6.75*
a. Dbl. impression of center *90.00*

The overprint in the tablets on Nos. L160-L185 reads: "5 Rabi al'awwal, 1343" (Oct. 5, 1924), the date of the accession of King Ali.

The tablet overprints vary slightly in size. Each is found reading upward or downward and at either side of the stamp. These control overprints were first applied in Jedda by the government press.

They were later made from new plates by the stamp printer in Cairo. In the Jedda overprint, the bar over the "0" figure extends to the left.

Some values exist with 13m or 15mm instead of 18mm between tablets. They sell for more. The lines of the Cairo overprinting are generally wider, but more lightly printed, usually appearing slightly grayish and the bar is at center right. The Cairo overprints are believed not to have been placed in use.

Imperforates exist.

Nos. L160-L168 are known with the overprints spaced as on type D3 and aligned horizontally.

Copies of these stamps (perforated or imperforate) without the overprint, except No. L186 were not regularly issued and not available for postage.

No. L185 exists only with Cairo overprint. Imperfs of No. L185 sell for much less than No. L185. Fake perfs have been added to the imperfs.

The ¼pi with blue overprint is bogus.

No. L186 in other colors are color trials.

For overprints see #58B-58D, Jordan 122-129.

NEJDI ADMINISTRATION OF HEJAZ

Handstamped in Blue, Red, Black or Violet

The overprint reads: "1343. Barid al Sultanat an Nejdia" (1925. Post of the Sultanate of Nejd).

The overprints on this and succeeding issues are handstamped and, as usual, are found double, inverted, etc. These variations are scarce.

1925, Mar.-Apr. Unwmk. *Perf. 12*

On Stamp of Turkey, 1915, With Crescent and Star in Red

1 A22 5pa ocher (Bl) 40.00 27.50
2 A22 5pa ocher (R) 25.00 20.00
3 A22 5pa ocher (Bk) 30.00 22.50
4 A22 5pa ocher (V) 25.00 18.00

On Stamp of Turkey, 1913

5 A28 10pa green (Bl) 22.50 16.00
6 A28 10pa green (R) 18.00 12.50

On Stamps of Hejaz, 1922-24

Perf. 11½

7 A7 ⅛pi red brn (R) 24.00 24.00
8 A7 ⅛pi red brn (Bk) 35.00 35.00
9 A7 ⅛pi red brn (V) 24.00 24.00
10 A7 ⅛pi car (R) 30.00 30.00
11 A7 ⅛pi car (Bk) 35.00 35.00
12 A7 ⅛pi car (V) *27.50 27.50*
13 A7 ½pi red (Bl) 22.50 22.50
14 A7 ½pi red (V) 18.00 18.00
15 A7 1½pi vio (R) 24.00 24.00
16 A7 2pi yel buff (R) 57.50 57.50
a. 2pi orange (R) 35.00
17 A7 2pi yel buff (V) 57.50 57.50
a. 2pi orange (V) 32.50 32.50
18 A7 3pi brn red (Bl) 30.00 30.00
19 A7 3pi brn red (R) 22.50 22.50
20 A7 3pi brn red (V) 25.00 25.00

Many Hejaz stamps of the 1922 type were especially printed for this and following issues. The re-impressions are usually more clearly printed, in lighter shades than the 1922 stamps, and some are in new colors.

Counterfeits exist.

Arabic Inscriptions
R1 R2

On Hejaz Bill Stamp

22 R1 1pi violet (R) 15.00 15.00

On Hejaz Notarial Stamps

23 R2 1pi violet (R) 20.00 20.00
24 R2 2pi blue (R) 30.00 30.00
25 R2 2pi blue (V) 27.50 27.50

For overprint see No. 49.

Locomotive — R3

On Hejaz Railway Tax Stamps

26 R3 1pi blue (R) 37.50 9.00
27 R3 2pi ocher (R) 45.00 14.00
28 R3 2pi ocher (V) 37.50 14.00
29 R3 3pi lilac (R) 40.00 20.00
Nos. 1-20,22-29 (28) 845.50 698.50

There are two types of the basic stamps. The difference is in the locomotive.

For overprints and surcharges see Nos. 34, 50-54, 55, 59-68, J12-J15.

Pilgrimage Issue

Various Stamps Handstamp Surcharged in Blue and Red in Types "a" and "b" and with Tablets with New Values

a

b

Surcharge "a" reads: "Tezkar al Hajj al Awwal Fi 'ahd al Sultanat al Nejdia, 1343" (Commemorating the first pilgrimage under the Nejdi Sultanate, 1925).

"b" reads: "Al Arba" (Wednesday.)

1925, July 1 *Perf. 12*

On Stamps of Turkey, 1913

30 A28 1pi on 10pa grn (Bl & R) 75.00 55.00
31 A30 5pi on 1pi bl (Bl & R) 75.00 55.00

On Stamps of Hejaz, 1917-18

Serrate Roulette 13

32 A5 2pi on 1pa lil brn (R & Bl) 95.00 67.50
33 A4 4pi on ⅛pi org (R & Bl) 350.00 350.00

On Hejaz Railway Tax Stamp

Perf. 11½

34 R3 3pi lilac (Bl & R) 125.00 40.00
Nos. 30-34 (5) 720.00 567.50

No. 30 with handstamp "a" in black was a favor item. Nos. 30 and 33 with both handstamps in red is a forgery.

Handstamped in Blue, Red, Black or Violet

This overprint has practically the same meaning as that described over No. 1. The Mohammedan year (1343) is omitted.

This handstamp is said to be in private hands at this time. Extreme caution is advised before buying rare items.

1925, July-Aug. *Perf. 12*

On Stamp of Turkey, 1915, with Crescent and Star in Red

35 A22 5pa ocher (Bl) 24.00 24.00

On Stamps of Turkey, 1913

36 A28 10pa green (Bl) 20.00 20.00
a. Black overprint 85.00

On Stamps of Hejaz, 1922 (Nos. L28-L29)

Serrate Roulette 13

37 A3 1pi blue (R) 60.00 *67.50*
38 A6 2pi magenta (Bl) 60.00 *67.50*

On Stamps of Hejaz, 1922-24

Perf. 11½

38A A7 ⅛pi red brn (Bk) *4,250.*
38B A7 ⅛pi red brn (Bl) *3,500.*
39 A7 ½pi red (Bl) 10.00 10.00
a. Imperf., pair 22.50 22.50
39B A7 ½pi red (Bk) 18.00 18.00
c. Imperf., pair 37.50 37.50
40 A7 1pi gray vio (R) 29.00 29.00
a. 1pi black violet (R) *40.00*
41 A7 1½pi dk red (Bk) 30.00 30.00
a. 1½pi brick red (Bk) 45.00
42 A7 2pi yel buff (Bl) 47.50 47.50
a. 2pi orange (Bl) 55.00 55.00
43 A7 2pi deep vio (Bl) 52.50 52.50
44 A7 3pi brown red (Bl) 30.00 30.00
45 A7 5pi scarlet (Bl) 37.50 37.50
Nos. 35-38,39-45 (12) 418.50 *433.50*

Overprint on Nos. 38A, 39B, 39C is blue-black.

See note above No. 35.

With Additional Surcharge of New Value Typo. in Black:

c d

e

Color in parenthesis is that of overprint on basic stamp.

46 A7(c) 1pi on ½pi (Bl) 10.00 1.75
a. Imperf, pair 27.50
b. Ovpt. & surch. inverted 70.00
47 A7(d) 1½pi on ½pi (Bl) 15.00 7.25
a. Imperf., pair 27.50
b. Black overprint 18.00
48 A7(e) 2pi on 3pi (Bl) 16.00 16.00
Nos. 46-48 (3) 41.00 25.00

Several variations in type settings of "c," "d" and "e" exist, including inverted letters and values.

On Hejaz Notarial Stamp

49 R2 2pi blue (Bk) 20.00 20.00

On Hejaz Railway Tax Stamps

50 R3 1pi blue (R) 25.00 25.00
51 R3 1pi blue (Bk) 30.00 9.00
52 R3 2pi ocher (Bl) 27.50 9.00
53 R3 3pi lilac (Bl) 22.50 22.50
54 R3 5pi green (Bl) 20.00 20.00
Nos. 49-54 (6) 145.00 105.50

Hejaz Railway Tax Stamp Handstamped in Black

This overprint reads: "Al Saudia. — Al Sultanat al Nejdia." (The Saudi Sultanate of Nejd.)

1925-26

55 R3 1pi blue — *175.00*

On Nos. L34, L36-L37, L41

55A A7 ½ pi red — *325.00*
56 A7 1½pi violet — *350.00*
a. Violet overprint — *325.00*
57 A7 2pi orange — *350.00*
57A A7 10pi on 5pi ol grn — *325.00*

On Nos. L95 and L97

Color in parentheses is that of rectangular overprint on basic stamp

58 A7 3pi olive brn (Bk) — *350.00*
58A A7 5pi olive grn (Bk) — *325.00*

On Nos. L162-L163, L173

Perf. 11½

58B A9 ½pi car rose (Bk) — *325.00*
58C A10 1pi yel grn (Bk) — *190.00*
58D A10 2pi blue (R) — *325.00*

Nos. 55-58D were provisionally issued at Medina after its capitulation.

This overprint exists on Nos. L160-L161, L164-L172, L174-L175, L180-L183. These 17 are known as bogus items, but may exist genuine.

Lithographed overprints are forgeries.

Medina Issue

Hejaz Railway Tax Stamps Handstamped

and Handstamp Surcharged in Various Colors

The large overprint reads: "The Nejdi Posts — 1344 — Commemorating Medina, the Illustrious." The tablet shows the new value.

1925

59	R3	1pi on 10pi vio (Bk & V)	65.00	65.00
60	R3	2pi on 50pi lt bl (R & Bl)	65.00	65.00
61	R3	3pi on 100pi red brn (Bl & Bk)	65.00	65.00
62	R3	4pi on 500pi dull red (Bl & Bk)	65.00	65.00
63	R3	5pi on 1000pi dp red (Bl & Bk)	65.00	65.00
		Nos. 59-63 (5)	325.00	325.00

JEDDA ISSUE

Hejaz Railway Tax Stamps Handstamped and Tablet with New Value in Various Colors

This handstamp reads: "Commemorating Jedda — 1344 — The Nejdi Posts."

1925

64	R3	1pi on 10pi vio (Bk & Bl)	55.00	55.00
65	R3	2pi on 50pi lt bl (R & Bk)	55.00	55.00
66	R3	3pi on 100pi red brn (R & Bl)	55.00	55.00
67	R3	4pi on 500pi dl red (Bk & Bl)	55.00	55.00
68	R3	5pi on 1000pi dp red (Bk & Bl)	55.00	55.00
		Nos. 64-68 (5)	275.00	275.00

Nos. 59-63 and 64-68 were prepared in anticipation of the surrender of Medina and Jedda.

Kingdom of Hejaz-Nejd

Arabic Inscriptions and Value — A1

A2

Inscriptions in upper tablets: "Barid al Hejaz wa Nejd" (Posts of the Hejaz and Nejd)

1926, Feb. Typo. Unwmk. *Perf. 11*

69	A1	¼pi violet	11.00	8.25
70	A1	½pi gray	11.00	8.25
71	A1	1pi deep blue	14.00	10.00
72	A2	2pi blue green	12.00	8.25
73	A2	3pi carmine	14.00	9.00
74	A2	5pi maroon	7.50	5.75
		Nos. 69-74 (6)	69.50	49.50

Nos. 69-71, 74 exist imperf. Value, each $30.
Used values are for favor cancels.

1926, Mar. *Perf. 11*

75	A1	¼pi orange	5.75	3.25
76	A1	½pi blue green	2.25	1.40
77	A1	1pi carmine	1.75	1.10
78	A2	2pi violet	2.25	1.40
79	A2	3pi dark blue	2.25	1.40
80	A2	5pi lt brown	5.75	3.25
a.		5pi olive brown		
		Nos. 75-80 (6)	20.00	11.80

Nos. 75-80 also exist with perf. 14, 14x11, 11x14 and imperf. All of these sell for 10 times the values quoted.

Counterfeits of types A1 and A2 are perf. 11½. They exist with and without overprints.

Types A1 and A2 in colors other than listed are proofs.

Pan-Islamic Congress Issue

Stamps of 1926 Handstamped

1926 *Perf. 11*

92	A1	¼pi orange	4.75	2.75
93	A1	½pi blue green	4.75	2.75
94	A1	1pi carmine	4.75	2.75
95	A2	2pi violet	4.75	2.75
96	A2	3pi dark blue	4.75	2.75
97	A2	5pi light brown	4.75	2.75
		Nos. 92-97 (6)	28.50	16.50

The overprint reads: "al Mootamar al Islami 20 Zilkada, Sanat 1344." (The Islamic Congress, June 1, 1926.)

See counterfeit note after No. 80.

Tughra of King Abdul Aziz — A3

1926-27 Typo. *Perf. 11½*

98	A3	⅛pi ocher	3.25	.45
99	A3	¼pi gray green	3.50	1.10
100	A3	½pi dull red	3.50	1.10
101	A3	1pi deep violet	3.50	1.10
102	A3	1½pi gray blue	11.00	1.75
103	A3	3pi olive green	9.00	3.50
104	A3	5pi brown orange	18.00	4.00
105	A3	10pi dark brown	50.00	5.50
		Nos. 98-105 (8)	101.75	18.50

Inscription at top reads: "Al Hukumat al Arabia" (The Arabian Government). Inscription below tughra reads: "Barid al Hejaz wa Nejd" (Post of the Hejaz and Nejd).

Stamps of 1926-27 Handstamped in Black or Red

1927

107	A3	⅛pi ocher	11.00	4.50
108	A3	¼pi gray grn	11.00	4.50
109	A3	½pi dull red	11.00	4.50
110	A3	1pi deep violet	11.00	4.50
111	A3	1½pi gray bl (R)	11.00	4.50
112	A3	3pi olive green	11.00	4.50
113	A3	5pi brown orange	11.00	4.50
114	A3	10pi dark brown	11.00	4.50
		Nos. 107-114 (8)	88.00	36.00

The overprint reads: "In commemoration of the Kingdom of Nejd and Dependencies, 25th Rajab 1345."

Inverted varieties have not been authenticated.

Turkey No. 258 Surcharged in Violet

1925 *Perf. 12*

115	A28	1g on 10pa green	175.00	

Similar surcharges of 6g and 20g were made in red, but were not known to have been issued.

A4

A5

1929-30 Typo. *Perf. 11½*

117	A4	1¾g gray blue	18.00	2.25
119	A4	20g violet	22.50	5.00
120	A4	30g green	35.00	11.00

1930 *Perf. 11, 11½*

125	A5	½g rose	14.00	2.75
126	A5	1½g violet	14.00	1.75
127	A5	1¾g ultra	14.00	2.25
128	A5	3½g emerald	14.00	3.50

Perf. 11

129	A5	5g black brown	22.50	5.50
		Nos. 125-129 (5)	78.50	15.75

Anniversary of King Ibn Saud's accession to the throne of the Hejaz, January 8, 1926.

A6

A7

1931-32 *Perf. 11½*

130	A6	⅛g ocher ('32)	12.50	2.25
131	A6	¼g blue green	12.50	1.75
133	A6	1¾g ultra	16.00	2.25
		Nos. 130-133 (3)	41.00	6.25

1932 *Perf. 11½*

135	A7	¼g blue green	5.50	1.75
a.		Perf 11		
136	A7	½g scarlet	16.00	2.75
a.		Perf 11		
137	A7	2¼g ultra	37.50	4.50
a.		Perf 11		
		Nos. 135-137 (3)	59.00	9.00

Kingdom of Saudi Arabia

A8

1934, Jan. *Perf. 11½, Imperf.*

138	A8	¼g yellow green	8.00	7.25
139	A8	½g red	8.00	7.25
140	A8	1½g light blue	15.00	14.00
141	A8	3g blue green	15.00	14.00
142	A8	3½g ultra	27.50	5.50
143	A8	5g yellow	35.00	27.50
144	A8	10g red orange	65.00	
145	A8	20g bright violet	80.00	
146	A8	¼s claret	160.00	
147	A8	30g dull violet	100.00	
148	A8	½s chocolate	350.00	
149	A8	1s violet brown	775.00	
		Nos. 138-149 (12)	1,638.	

Proclamation of Emir Saud as Heir Apparent of Arabia. Perf. and imperf. stamps were issued in equal quantities.

Favor cancels exist on Nos. 144-149.

Tughra of King Abdul Aziz — A9

1934-57 *Perf. 11, 11½*

159	A9	⅛g yellow	4.00	.35
160	A9	¼g yellow grn	4.00	.35
161	A9	½g rose red ('43)	3.00	.20
a.		½g dark carmine	12.00	1.40
162	A9	⅞g lt blue ('56)	5.00	.45
163	A9	1g blue green	4.00	.35
164	A9	2g olive grn ('57)	7.00	1.75
a.		2g olive bister ('57)	25.00	7.25
165	A9	2⅞g violet ('57)	5.00	.45
166	A9	3g ultra ('38)	5.00	.20
a.		3g light blue	20.00	1.75
167	A9	3½g lt ultra	27.50	1.75
168	A9	5g orange	5.00	.45
169	A9	10g violet	15.00	1.40
170	A9	20g purple brn	25.00	.90
a.		20g purple black	25.00	2.25
171	A9	100g red vio ('42)	70.00	4.00
172	A9	200g vio brn ('42)	90.00	5.50
		Nos. 159-172 (14)	269.50	18.10

The ½g has two types differing in position of the tughra.

No. 162 measures 31x22mm. No. 164 30½x21½mm. No. 165, 30½x22mm. No. 166 30x21mm. No. 171, 31x22mm. No. 172, 30½x21½mm. Rest of set, 29x20½mm. Grayish paper was used in 1946-49 printings.

No. 168 exists with pin-perf 6.

For overprint see No. J24.

HEJAZ POSTAGE DUE STAMPS

From Old Door at El Ashraf Barsbai in Shari el Ashrafiya, Cairo — D1

Serrate Roulette 13

1917, June 27 Typo. Unwmk.

LJ1	D1	20pa red	3.25	2.00
LJ2	D1	1pi blue	3.50	2.00
LJ3	D1	2pi magenta	3.75	2.00
		Nos. LJ1-LJ3 (3)	10.50	6.00

For overprints see Nos. LJ4-LJ10, LJ17-LJ25, J9,

a

b

Nos. LJ1-LJ3 Overprinted Type "a" in Black or Red

1921, Dec.

LJ4	D1	20pa red	20.00	2.75
a.		Double overprint, one at left	140.00	
b.		Overprint at left	30.00	20.00
LJ5	D1	1pi blue (R)	7.00	3.50
LJ6	D1	1pi bl, ovpt. at left	30.00	18.00
a.		Overprint at right	27.50	32.50
LJ7	D1	2pi magenta	12.50	7.25
a.		Double overprint, one at left	62.50	
b.		Overprint at left	27.50	
		Nos. LJ4-LJ7 (4)	69.50	31.50

Nos. LJ1-LJ3 Overprinted Type "b" in Black

1922, Jan.

LJ8	D1	20pa red	25.00	27.50
a.		Overprint at left	35.00	
LJ9	D1	1pi blue	5.00	3.25
a.		Overprint at left	45.00	
LJ10	D1	2pi magenta	5.00	3.25
a.		Overprint at left	32.50	
		Nos. LJ8-LJ10 (3)	35.00	34.00

Regular issue of 1922 Overprinted

Black Overprint

1923 *Perf. 11½*

LJ11	A7	½pi red	4.25	1.40
a.		Inverted overprint	50.00	
LJ12	A7	1pi dark blue	7.50	1.40
a.		Inverted overprint	80.00	
b.		Double overprint	125.00	
LJ13	A7	2pi orange	5.00	1.75
a.		Inverted overprint	47.50	
		Nos. LJ11-LJ13 (3)	16.75	4.55

1924

Blue Overprint

LJ14	A7	½pi red	17.50	2.75
a.		Inverted overprint	80.00	
LJ15	A7	1pi dark blue	37.50	2.75
a.		Inverted overprint	100.00	
LJ16	A7	2pi orange	27.50	4.50
a.		Inverted overprint	80.00	
		Nos. LJ14-LJ16 (3)	82.50	10.00

This overprint reads "Mustahaq" (Due).

Jedda Issues

Nos. LJ1-LJ3 Overprinted in Red or Blue (Overprint reads up in illustration)

Jedda issues were also used in Medina and Yambo. **Used values for #L51-L186 and LJ17-LJ39 are for genuine cancels. Privately applied cancels exist for "Mekke" (Mecca, bilingual or all Arabic), Khartoum, Cairo, as well as for Jeddah. Many private cancels have wrong dates, some as early as 1916. These are worth half the used values.**

1925, Jan. ***Serrate Roulette 13***

LJ17	D1	20pa red (R)	375.00	*350.00*
LJ19	D1	1pi blue (R)	20.00	*18.00*
LJ20	D1	1pi blue (Bl)	27.50	*25.00*
LJ21	D1	2pi mag (Bl)	15.00	*14.00*

Overprint Reading Down

LJ17a	D1	20pa	*550.00*	*550.00*
LJ18	D1	20pa red (Bl)	*450.00*	
LJ19a	D1	1pi	18.00	*18.00*
LJ20a	D1	1pi	67.50	*80.00*
LJ21a	D1	2pi	60.00	*60.00*

Nos. LJ1-LJ3 Overprinted in Blue or Red

1925

LJ22 D1	20pa red (Bl)	450.00	*425.00*
a.	Inverted overprint	325.00	*325.00*
LJ24 D1	1pi blue (R)	25.00	*27.50*
a.	Inverted overprint	32.50	*32.50*
LJ25 D1	2pi magenta (Bl)	20.00	*18.00*
a.	Inverted overprint	35.00	*45.00*
b.	Double overprint	350.00	

No. LJ2 with this overprint in blue is bogus.

Regular Issues of 1922-24 Overprinted

a

and Handstamped

b

1925 ***Perf. 11½***

LJ26	A7	⅛pi red brown	20.00	*18.00*
LJ27	A7	½pi red	27.50	*25.00*
LJ28	A7	1pi dark blue	20.00	*18.00*
LJ29	A7	1½pi violet	22.50	*18.00*
LJ30	A7	2pi orange	25.00	*20.00*
LJ31	A7	3pi olive brown	25.00	*20.00*
LJ32	A7	3pi dull red	50.00	*45.00*
LJ33	A7	5pi olive green	25.00	*20.00*
LJ34	A7	10pi vio & dk brn	30.00	*25.00*
		Nos. LJ26-LJ34 (9)	245.00	*209.00*

The printed overprint *(a)*, consisting of the three top lines of Arabic, was used alone for the first issue (Nos. LJ26a-LJ34a). The "postage due" box was so small and indistinct that its equivalent in larger characters was added by boxed handstamp *(b)* at bottom of each stamp for the second issue (Nos. LJ26-LJ34).

The handstamped overprint *(b)* is found double, inverted, etc. It is also known in dark violet.

Counterfeits exist of both overprint and handstamp.

Without Boxed Handstamp "b"

LJ26a	A7	⅛pi red brown	42.50
LJ27a	A7	½pi red	42.50
LJ28a	A7	1pi dark blue	42.50
LJ29a	A7	1½pi violet	42.50
LJ30a	A7	2pi orange	42.50
LJ31a	A7	3pi olive brown	42.50
LJ32a	A7	3pi dull red	42.50
LJ33a	A7	5pi olive green	55.00
LJ34a	A7	10pi vio & dk brn	55.00
		Nos. LJ26a-LJ34a (9)	407.50

Regular Issue of 1922 Overprinted

and Handstamped

LJ35 A7	½pi red	*150.00*	*140.00*
LJ36 A7	1½pi violet	*150.00*	*140.00*
a.	Overprint in red, boxed handstamp violet		*1,400.*
LJ37 A7	2pi orange	*190.00*	*175.00*
LJ38 A7	3pi olive brown	*150.00*	*140.00*
LJ39 A7	5pi olive green	*150.00*	*140.00*
	Nos. LJ35-LJ39 (5)	*790.00*	*735.00*

Counterfeits exist of Nos. LJ4-LJ39.

Arabic Numeral of Value

D2 D3

1925, May-June ***Perf. 11½***

LJ40 D2	½pi light blue	3.00
LJ41 D2	1pi orange	3.00
LJ42 D2	2pi lt brown	3.00
LJ43 D2	3pi pink	3.00
	Nos. LJ40-LJ43 (4)	12.00

Nos. LJ40-LJ43 exist imperforate. Impressions in colors other than issued are trial color proofs.

Black Overprint

1925

LJ44 D3	½pi light blue	3.00
LJ45 D3	1pi orange	3.00
LJ46 D3	2pi light brown	3.00
LJ47 D3	3pi pink	3.75
	Nos. LJ44-LJ47 (4)	12.75

Nos. LJ44-LJ47 exist with either Jedda or Cairo overprints and the tablets normally read upward. Values are for Cairo overprints; Jedda overprints sell for more.

Red Overprint

LJ48 D3	½pi light blue	3.75
LJ49 D3	1pi orange	3.75
LJ50 D3	2pi light brown	3.75
LJ51 D3	3pi pink	3.75

Blue Overprint

LJ52 D3	½pi light blue	3.75
LJ53 D3	1pi orange	3.75
LJ54 D3	2pi light brown	3.75
LJ55 D3	3pi pink	3.75
	Nos. LJ40-LJ55 (16)	54.75

Red and blue overprints are from Cairo. Nos. LJ44-LJ55 exist imperf.

NEJDI ADMINISTRATION OF HEJAZ POSTAGE DUE STAMPS

Handstamped in Blue, Red or Black

On Hejaz Postage Due Stamps Typographed or Handstamped in Black

1925, Apr.-June Unwmk. ***Perf. 11½***

J1	A7	½pi red (Bl)	27.50	27.50
a.		1pi dark blue (R)	35.00	35.00
J2	A7	1pi lt blue (R)	55.00	55.00
J3	A7	2pi yel buff (Bl)	55.00	55.00
a.		2pi orange (Bl)	47.50	47.50
		Nos. J1-J3 (3)	137.50	137.50

Same, with Postage Due Overprint in Blue

J4	A7	½pi red (Bl)	*140.00*
J5	A7	1pi dk blue (R)	—
J6	A7	2pi orange (Bl)	*175.00*

On Hejaz Stamps of 1922-24

Handstamped in Blue

J7	A7	½pi red (Bl & Bl)	16.00	16.00
J8	A7	3pi brn red (Bl & Bl)	19.00	19.00

Handstamped in Blue, Black or Violet

See note before No. 35.

On Hejaz No. LJ9

Serrate Roulette 13½

J9	D1	1pi blue (V)	60.00	27.50

Same Overprint on Hejaz Stamps of 1924 with additional Handstamp in Black, Blue or Red

Perf. 11½

J10	A7	3pi brn red (Bl & Bk)	11.00	11.00
J11	A7	3pi brn red (Bk & Bl)	11.00	11.00

Same Handstamps on Hejaz Railway Tax Stamps

J12	R3	1pi blue (Bk & R)	12.00	12.00
J13	R3	2pi ocher (Bl & Bk)	12.00	12.00
J14	R3	5pi green (Bk & R)	20.00	20.00
J15	R3	5pi green (V & BK)	20.00	9.00
		Nos. J10-J15 (6)	86.00	75.00

The second handstamp, which is struck on the lower part of the Postage Due Stamps, is the word Mustahaq (Due) in various forms.

No. J13 exists with second handstamp in blue.

Hejaz-Nejd

D1

1926 **Typo.** ***Perf. 11***

J16	D1	½pi carmine	4.00	.65
J17	D1	2pi orange	4.00	.65
J18	D1	6pi light brown	4.00	.65
		Nos. J16-J18 (3)	12.00	1.95

Nos. J16-J18 exist with perf. 14, 14x11 and 11x14, and imperf. These sell for six times the values quoted.

Nos. J16-J18 in colors other than listed (both perf. and imperf.) are proofs.

Counterfeit note after No. 80 also applies to Nos. J16-J21.

Pan-Islamic Congress Issue

Postage Due Stamps of 1926 Handstamped like Regular Issue

J19	D1	½pi carmine	5.50	4.50
J20	D1	2pi orange	5.50	4.50
J21	D1	6pi light brown	5.50	4.50
		Nos. J19-J21 (3)	16.50	13.50

D2

1927 ***Perf. 11½***

J22 D2	1pi slate	18.00	.45
a.	Inscription reads "2 piastres" in upper right circle	175.00	100.00
J23 D2	2pi dark violet	5.75	.45

Saudi Arabia

Saudi Arabia No. 161 Handstamped in Black

1935

J24	A9	½g dark carmine	275.00

Two types of overprint.

D3

1937-39 **Unwmk.**

J25	D3	½g org brn ('39)	12.00	12.00
J26	D3	1g light blue	12.00	12.00
J27	D3	2g rose vio ('39)	17.00	8.00
		Nos. J25-J27 (3)	41.00	32.00

OFFICIAL STAMPS

Official stamps were normally used only on external correspondence.

O1

O2

1939	**Unwmk.**	**Typo.**		***Perf. 11½***
O1	O1	3g deep ultra	3.50	1.60
		Perf. 11, 11½		
O2	O1	5g red violet	4.50	2.10
		Perf. 11		
O3	O1	20g brown	9.50	4.25
O4	O1	50g blue green	18.00	8.75
O5	O1	100g olive grn	75.00	40.00
O6	O1	200g purple	60.00	27.50
		Nos. O1-O6 (6)	170.50	84.20

NEWSPAPER STAMPS

Nos. 8, 9 and 14 with Additional Overprint in Black

1925	**Unwmk.**			***Perf. 11½***
P1	A7	⅛pi red brown (Bk)	*1,800.*	*1,800.*
P2	A7	⅛pi red brown (V)	*1,400.*	*900.*
P3	A7	⅛pi red (V)	*2,750.*	*1,800.*

Overprint reads: "Matbu'a" (Newspaper), but these stamps were normally used for regular postage. Counterfeits exist.

The status of this set in question. The government may have declared it to be unauthorized.

POSTAL TAX STAMPS

PT1

1934, May 15	**Unwmk.**			***Perf. 11½***
RA1	PT1	⅛g scarlet	*175.00*	4.50

No. RA1 collected a "war tax" to aid wounded of the 1934 Saudi-Yemen war.

Nos. RA2-RA8 raised funds for the Medical Aid Society.

General Hospital, Mecca PT2

1936, Oct.

Size: 37x20mm

RA2	PT2	⅛g scarlet	*625.00*	9.00

Type of 1936, Redrawn

1937-42

Size: 30½x18mm

RA3	PT2	⅛g scarlet	60.00	.90
a.		⅛g rose ('39)	*110.00*	*1.75*
b.		⅛g rose car, perf. 11 ('42)	*175.00*	*6.75*

SCHLESWIG

'shles-ˌwig

LOCATION — In the northern part of the former Schleswig-Holstein Province, in northern Germany.

Schleswig was divided into North and South Schleswig after the Versailles Treaty, and plebiscites were held in 1920. North Schleswig (Zone 1) voted to join Denmark, South Schleswig to stay German.

100 Pfennig = 1 Mark
100 Ore = 1 Krone

Watermark

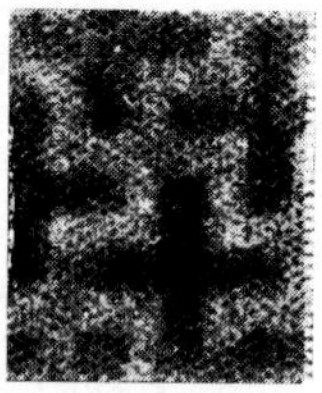
Wmk. 114 — Multiple Crosses

Plebiscite Issue

Arms — A11

View of Schleswig A12

Perf. 14x15

1920, Jan. 25		**Typo.**		**Wmk. 114**
1	A11	2½pf gray	.20	.20
		Never hinged	.40	
		On cover		6.00
2	A11	5pf green	.20	.20
		Never hinged	.40	
		On cover		3.75
3	A11	7½pf yellow brown	.20	.20
		Never hinged	.40	
		On cover		6.00
4	A11	10pf deep rose	.20	.20
		Never hinged	.40	
		On cover		3.75
5	A11	15pf red violet	.20	.20
		Never hinged	.40	
		On cover		3.75
6	A11	20pf deep blue	.20	.25
		Never hinged	.45	
		On cover		3.75
7	A11	25pf orange	.35	.25
		Never hinged	.75	
		On cover		7.50
8	A11	35pf brown	.45	.40
		Never hinged	1.10	
		On cover		15.00
9	A11	40pf violet	.35	.20
		Never hinged	.75	
		On cover		9.25
10	A11	75pf greenish blue	.40	.35
		Never hinged	1.10	
		On cover		19.00
11	A12	1m dark brown	.40	.35
		Never hinged	1.10	
		On cover		19.00
12	A12	2m deep blue	.65	.50
		Never hinged	1.50	
		On cover		52.50
13	A12	5m green	1.40	.85
		Never hinged	2.75	
		On cover		125.00
14	A12	10m red	2.50	1.75
		Never hinged	5.25	
		On cover		—
		Nos. 1-14 (14)	7.70	5.90
		Set, never hinged	17.00	

The colored portions of type A11 are white, and the white portions are colored, on Nos. 7-10.

Types of 1920 Overprinted in Blue

1920, May 20				
15	A11	1o dark gray	.20	*1.75*
		Never hinged	.40	
		On cover		19.00
16	A11	5o green	.20	*.65*
		Never hinged	.40	
		On cover		19.00
17	A11	7o yellow brn	.20	*1.10*
		Never hinged	.40	
		On cover		19.00
18	A11	10o rose red	.20	*1.10*
		Never hinged	.45	
		On cover		19.00
19	A11	15o lilac rose	.20	*1.75*
		Never hinged	.45	
		On cover		19.00
20	A11	20o dark blue	.20	*2.00*
		Never hinged	.45	
		On cover		26.00
21	A11	25o orange	.20	*5.50*
		Never hinged	.75	
		On cover		60.00
22	A11	35o brown	.85	*9.50*
		Never hinged	3.75	
		On cover		75.00
23	A11	40o violet	.25	*3.50*
		Never hinged	1.50	
		On cover		75.00
24	A11	75o greenish blue	.45	*5.50*
		Never hinged	1.90	
		On cover		110.00
25	A12	1k dark brown	.65	*9.50*
		Never hinged	2.75	
		On cover		140.00
26	A12	2k deep blue	7.00	*35.00*
		Never hinged	26.00	
		On cover		—
27	A12	5k green	3.50	*35.00*
		Never hinged	17.00	
		On cover		—
28	A12	10k red	8.00	*65.00*
		Never hinged	25.00	
		On cover		—
		Nos. 15-28 (14)	22.10	*176.85*
		Set, never hinged	80.00	

OFFICIAL STAMPS

Nos. 1-14 Overprinted **C·I·S**

1920		**Wmk. 114**		***Perf. 14x15***
O1	A11	2½pf gray	65.00	*92.50*
		Never hinged	110.00	
		On cover		*450.00*
O2	A11	5pf green	65.00	*110.00*
		Never hinged	110.00	
		On cover		*425.00*
O3	A11	7½pf yellow brn	65.00	*92.50*
		Never hinged	110.00	
		On cover		*525.00*
O4	A11	10pf deep rose	65.00	*120.00*
		Never hinged	110.00	
		On cover		*500.00*
O5	A11	15pf red violet	42.50	*60.00*
		Never hinged	75.00	
		On cover		*240.00*
O6	A11	20pf dp blue	65.00	*67.50*
		Never hinged	110.00	
		On cover		*240.00*
a.		Double overprint	1,200.	
O7	A11	25pf orange	125.00	*175.00*
		Never hinged	260.00	
		On cover		*575.00*
a.		Inverted overprint	*850.00*	
O8	A11	35pf brown	125.00	*175.00*
		Never hinged	260.00	
		On cover		*650.00*
O9	A11	40pf violet	110.00	100.00
		Never hinged	190.00	
		On cover		*500.00*
O10	A11	75pf grnsh blue	125.00	*250.00*
		Never hinged	225.00	
		On cover		*750.00*
O11	A12	1m dark brown	125.00	*250.00*
		Never hinged	225.00	
		On cover		*750.00*
O12	A12	2m deep blue	185.00	*275.00*
		Never hinged	350.00	
		On cover		*1,000.*
O13	A12	5m green	275.00	*425.00*
		Never hinged	500.00	
		On cover		—
O14	A12	10m red	500.00	*625.00*
		Never hinged	925.00	
		On cover		—
		Nos. O1-O14 (14)	1,937.	*2,817.*
		Set, never hinged	3,600.	

The letters "C.I.S." are the initials of "Commission Interalliée Slesvig," under whose auspices the plebiscites took place.

Counterfeit overprints exist.

SENEGAL

ˌse-ni-'gäl

LOCATION — West coast of Africa, bordering on the Atlantic Ocean
GOVT. — Republic
AREA — 76,000 sq. mi.
POP. — 6,300,000 (est. 1984)
CAPITAL — Dakar

The former French colony of Senegal became part of French West Africa in 1943. The Republic of Senegal was established Nov. 25, 1958. From Apr. 4, 1959, to June 20, 1960, the Republic of Senegal and the Sudanese Republic together formed the Mali Federation. After its breakup, Senegal resumed issuing its own stamps in 1960.

100 Centimes = 1 Franc

French Colonies Nos. 48, 49, 51, 52, 55, Type A9, Surcharged:

a

b

c

d

5
e

1887	**Unwmk.**			***Perf. 14x13½***
	Black Surcharge			
1	(a)	5c on 20c red, *grn*	175.00	175.00
		On cover		*550.00*
a.		Double surcharge		
2	(b)	5c on 20c red, *grn*	300.00	300.00
		On cover		—
3	(c)	5c on 20c red, *grn*	975.00	975.00
		On cover		—
4	(d)	5c on 20c red, *grn*	210.00	210.00
		On cover		—
5	(e)	5c on 20c red, *grn*	400.00	400.00
		On cover		—
6	(a)	5c on 30c brn, *bis*	250.00	250.00
		On cover		*750.00*
7	(b)	5c on 30c brn, *bis*	1,100.	1,100.
		On cover		—
8	(d)	5c on 30c brn, *bis*	375.00	375.00
		On cover		—
		Nos. 1-8 (8)	3,785.	3,785.

See Madagascar #6-7 for stamps with surcharge like "d" on 10c and 25c stamps.

f

g

h

i

10 10 10 10
j k l m

9	(f)	10c on 4c cl, *lav*	110.00	110.00
		On cover		*500.00*
10	(g)	10c on 4c cl, *lav*	165.00	165.00
		On cover		*500.00*
11	(h)	10c on 4c cl, *lav*	82.50	82.50
		On cover		*500.00*
12	(i)	10c on 4c cl, *lav*	75.00	75.00
		On cover		—
a.		"1" without top stroke		
13	(f)	10c on 20c red, *grn*	600.00	600.00
		On cover		—
14	(g)	10c on 20c red, *grn*	625.00	625.00
		On cover		—
15	(h)	10c on 20c red, *grn*	525.00	525.00
		On cover		—
16	(i)	10c on 20c red, *grn*	*3,350.*	*3,350.*
		On cover		—
17	(j)	10c on 20c red, *grn*	625.00	625.00
		On cover		—
18	(k)	10c on 20c red, *grn*	2,250.	2,250.
		On cover		—
19	(l)	10c on 20c red, *grn*	750.00	750.00
		On cover		—
20	(m)	10c on 20c red, *grn*	750.00	750.00
		On cover		—

15 15 15 15
n o p q

15 15 15 15
r s t u

1515
v w

21 (n) 15c on 20c red, *grn* 90.00 90.00
On cover *500.00*
22 (o) 15c on 20c red, *grn* 75.00 75.00
On cover *500.00*
23 (p) 15c on 20c red, *grn* 62.50 62.50
On cover *500.00*
24 (q) 15c on 20c red, *grn* 110.00 110.00
On cover *500.00*
25 (r) 15c on 20c red, *grn* 67.50 67.50
On cover *500.00*
26 (s) 15c on 20c red, *grn* 67.50 67.50
On cover *500.00*
27 (t) 15c on 20c red, *grn* 187.50 187.50
On cover *600.00*
28 (u) 15c on 20c red, *grn* 60.00 60.00
On cover *500.00*
29 (v) 15c on 20c red, *grn* 88.50 88.50
On cover *500.00*
30 (w) 15c on 20c red, *grn* 325.00 325.00
On cover —
Nos. 21-30 (10) 1,133. 1,133.

Counterfeits exist of Nos. 1-34.

Surcharged:

1892

Black Surcharge

31 A9 75c on 15c blue 375.00 150.00
On cover *650.00*
32 A9 1fr on 5c grn, *grnsh* 375.00 150.00
On cover *650.00*

"SENEGAL" in Red

33 A9 75c on 15c blue *12,000. 4,500.*
On cover *8,250.*
34 A9 1fr on 5c grn, *grnsh* *5,250. 1,200.*
On cover *2,750.*

Navigation and Commerce — A24

1892-1900 Typo. *Perf. 14x13½*

Name of Colony in Blue or Carmine

35 A24 1c blk, *lil bl* 1.00 .90
On cover *32.50*
36 A24 2c brn, *buff* 2.10 1.75
On cover *32.50*
37 A24 4c claret, *lav* 2.10 1.50
On cover *32.50*
38 A24 5c grn, *grnsh* 2.75 1.75
On cover *16.00*
39 A24 5c yel grn ('00) 1.75 1.00
On cover *16.00*
40 A24 10c blk, *lav* 6.75 5.25
On cover *16.00*
41 A24 10c red ('00) 4.25 1.40
On cover *16.00*
42 A24 15c bl, quadrille paper 12.00 1.75
On cover *16.00*
43 A24 15c gray ('00) 5.00 1.75
On cover *16.00*
44 A24 20c red, *grn* 9.25 5.25
On cover —
45 A24 25c blk, *rose* 15.00 5.75
On cover *22.50*
46 A24 25c blue ('00) 34.00 30.00
On cover *82.50*
47 A24 30c brn, *bis* 15.50 7.25
On cover —
48 A24 40c red, *straw* 21.00 18.00
On cover *55.00*
49 A24 50c car, *rose* 35.00 25.00
On cover *55.00*
50 A24 50c brn, *az* ('00) 40.00 37.50
On cover *100.00*
51 A24 75c vio, *org* 16.50 16.50
On cover *90.00*
52 A24 1fr brnz grn, *straw* 18.50 17.00
On cover —
Nos. 35-52 (18) 242.45 179.30

Perf. 13½x14 stamps are counterfeits.
For surcharges see Nos. 53-56, 73-78.

Stamps of 1892 Surcharged:

1903

53 A24 5c on 40c red, *straw* 13.50 13.50
On cover *55.00*
54 A24 10c on 50c car, *rose* 19.00 19.00
On cover *55.00*
55 A24 10c on 75c vio, *org* 19.00 19.00
On cover *55.00*
56 A24 10c on 1fr brnz grn, *straw* 70.00 70.00
On cover *110.00*
Nos. 53-56 (4) 121.50 121.50

General Louis Faidherbe A25

Oil Palms — A26

Dr. Noel Eugène Ballay A27

1906 Typo.

"SÉNÉGAL" in Red or Blue

57 A25 1c slate 1.00 .95
a. "SENEGAL" omitted 100.00 100.00
58 A25 2c choc (R) 1.40 1.00
58A A25 2c choc (Bl) 2.50 1.75
59 A25 4c choc, *gray bl* 2.00 1.50
60 A25 5c green 2.40 .75
61 A25 10c car (Bl) 10.00 .75
a. "SENEGAL" omitted 375.00 375.00
62 A25 15c violet 6.25 3.50
63 A26 20c blk, *az* 7.50 4.00
64 A26 25c bl, *pnksh* 3.00 2.25
65 A26 30c choc, *pnksh* 7.50 4.75
66 A26 35c blk, *yellow* 26.50 2.25
67 A26 40c car, *az* (Bl) 9.25 5.75
67A A26 45c choc, *grnsh* 20.00 13.50
68 A26 50c dp violet 10.00 6.50
69 A26 75c bl, *org* 7.50 6.75
70 A27 1fr blk, *azure* 25.00 24.00
71 A27 2fr blue, *pink* 30.00 29.00
72 A27 5fr car, *straw* (Bl) 57.50 55.00
Nos. 57-72 (18) 229.30 163.95

Stamps of 1892-1900 Surcharged in Carmine or Black

1912

Spacing between figures of surcharge 1.5mm (5c), 2mm (10c)

73 A24 5c on 15c gray (C) .85 .85
74 A24 5c on 20c red, *grn* 1.25 1.25
75 A24 5c on 30c brn, *bis* (C) 1.00 1.00
76 A24 10c on 40c red, *straw* 1.40 1.40
77 A24 10c on 50c car, *rose* 3.25 3.25
78 A24 10c on 75c vio, *org* 5.25 5.25
Nos. 73-78 (6) 13.00 13.00

Spacing between figures of surcharge 2.25mm (5c), 2.75mm (10c)

73a A24 5c on 15c gray (C) 19.00 19.00
74a A24 5c on 20c red, *grn* 225.00 225.00
75a A24 5c on 30c brn, *bis* (C) 70.00 70.00
76a A24 10c on 40c red, *straw* 35.00 35.00
77a A24 10c on 50c car, *rose* 65.00 65.00
78a A24 10c on 75c vio, *org* 200.00 200.00
Nos. 73a-78a (6) 614.00 614.00

Senegalese Preparing Food A28

1914-33 Typo.

79 A28 1c ol brn & vio .20 .20
80 A28 2c black & blue .25 .20
81 A28 4c gray & brn .25 .20
82 A28 5c yel grn & bl grn .40 .20
83 A28 5c blk & rose ('22) .20 .20
84 A28 10c org red & rose 1.00 .20
85 A28 10c yel grn & bl grn ('22) .25 .20
86 A28 10c red brn & bl ('25) .25 .20
87 A28 15c red org & brn vio ('17) .25 .20
88 A28 20c choc & blk .25 .20
89 A28 20c grn & bl grn ('26) .35 .25
90 A28 20c db & lt bl ('27) .40 .40
91 A28 25c ultra & bl .90 .40
92 A28 25c red & blk ('22) .45 .20
93 A28 30c black & rose .55 .20
94 A28 30c red org & rose ('22) .50 .20
95 A28 30c gray & bl ('26) .45 .20
96 A28 30c dl grn & dp grn ('28) .55 .40
97 A28 35c orange & vio .55 .40
98 A28 40c violet & grn .65 .40
99 A28 45c bl & ol brn 1.40 1.10
100 A28 45c rose & bl ('22) .70 .30
101 A28 45c rose & ver ('25) .70 .45
102 A28 45c ol brn & org ('28) 3.00 2.50
103 A28 50c vio brn & bl 1.40 .95
104 A28 50c ultra & bl ('22) 1.75 1.60
105 A28 50c red org & grn ('26) .40 .20
106 A28 60c vio, *pnksh* ('26) .40 .20
107 A28 65c rose red & dp grn ('28) 1.40 1.25
108 A28 75c gray & rose .85 .60
109 A28 75c dk bl & lt bl ('25) .75 .60
110 A28 75c rose & gray bl ('26) 1.50 .50
111 A28 90c brn red & rose ('30) 4.50 4.00
112 A28 1fr violet & blk .90 .60
113 A28 1fr blue ('26) .75 .60
114 A28 1fr blk & gray bl ('26) 1.50 .55
115 A28 1.10fr bl grn & blk ('28) 3.25 3.25
116 A28 1.25fr dp grn & dp org ('33) 1.00 .95
117 A28 1.50fr dk bl & bl ('30) 2.25 2.25
118 A28 1.75fr dk brn & Prus bl ('33) 5.75 1.00
119 A28 2fr carmine & bl 2.75 2.10
120 A28 2fr lt bl & brn ('22) 2.10 .75
121 A28 3fr red vio ('30) 3.50 1.75
122 A28 5fr green & vio 4.25 1.50
Nos. 79-122 (44) 55.40 34.60

Nos. 79, 82, 84 and 97 are on both ordinary and chalky paper.
For surcharges see Nos. 123-137, B1-B2.

No. 108 and Type of 1914 Surcharged:

1922-25

123 A28 60c on 75c vio, *pnksh* .75 .75
124 A28 65c on 15c red org & dl vio ('25) 1.00 1.00
125 A28 85c on 15c red org & dl vio ('25) 1.00 1.00
126 A28 85c on 75c ('25) 1.10 1.10

No. 87 Surcharged in Various Colors

1922

127 A28 1c on 15c (Bk) .55 .55
128 A28 2c on 15c (Bl) .55 .55
129 A28 4c on 15c (G) .55 .55
130 A28 5c on 15c (R) .55 .55
Nos. 123-130 (8) 6.05 6.05

Stamps and Type of 1914 Surcharged with New Value and Bars in Black or Red

1924-27

131 A28 25c on 5fr grn & vio .70 .70
132 A28 90c on 75c brn red & cer ('27) 1.10 .85
a. Double surcharge 100.00 90.00
133 A28 1.25fr on 1fr bl & lt bl (R) ('26) .90 .70
134 A28 1.50fr on 1fr dk bl & ultra ('27) 1.00 .85
135 A28 3fr on 5fr mag & ol brn ('27) 3.00 1.50
136 A28 10fr on 5fr dk bl & red org ('27) 6.75 2.50
137 A28 20fr on 5fr vio & ol bis ('27) 6.75 6.25
Nos. 131-137 (7) 20.20 13.35

Common Design Types pictured following the introduction

Colonial Exposition Issue

Common Design Types

Name of Country Typographed in Black

1931 Engr. *Perf. 12½*

138 CD70 40c deep green 3.00 3.00
139 CD71 50c violet 3.00 3.00
140 CD72 90c red orange 3.00 3.00
a. "SENEGAL" double 110.00
141 CD73 1.50fr dull blue 3.00 3.00
Nos. 138-141 (4) 12.00 12.00

Faidherbe Bridge, St. Louis A29

Diourbel Mosque A30

1935-40 *Perf. 12½x12*

142 A29 1c violet blue .20 .20
143 A29 2c brown .20 .20
144 A29 3c violet ('40) .40 .20
145 A29 4c gray blue .20 .20
146 A29 5c orange red .20 .20
147 A29 10c violet .20 .20
148 A29 15c black .20 .20
149 A29 20c dk carmine .20 .20
150 A29 25c black brn .40 .20
151 A29 30c green .40 .25
152 A29 40c rose lake .40 .25
153 A29 45c dk blue grn .40 .25
154 A30 50c red orange .30 .20
155 A30 60c violet ('40) .30 .25
156 A30 65c dk violet .45 .25
157 A30 70c red brn ('40) .70 .50
158 A30 75c brown .80 .45
159 A30 90c rose car 2.75 1.40
160 A30 1fr violet 10.50 2.00
161 A30 1.25fr redsh brn 1.60 .75
162 A30 1.25fr rose car ('39) .80 .55
163 A30 1.40fr dk bl grn ('40) .80 .55
164 A30 1.50fr dk blue .30 .30
165 A30 1.60fr pck bl ('40) .80 .55
166 A30 1.75fr dk blue grn .30 .30
167 A30 2fr blue .80 .30
168 A30 3fr green .70 .40
169 A30 5fr black brn .80 .55
170 A30 10fr rose lake 1.75 .95
171 A30 20fr grnsh slate 1.75 .95
Nos. 142-171 (30) 29.60 13.75

Nos. 143, 148 and 156 surcharged with new values are listed under French West Africa.
For surcharges see Nos. B9, B11-B12.

Paris International Exposition Issue

Common Design Types

1937 *Perf. 13*

172 CD74 20c deep violet 1.00 1.00
173 CD75 30c dark green 1.00 1.00
174 CD76 40c car rose 1.00 1.00
175 CD77 50c dark brown 1.00 1.00
176 CD78 90c red 1.00 1.00
177 CD79 1.50fr ultra 1.75 1.75
Nos. 172-177 (6) 6.75 6.75

Colonial Arts Exhibition Issue

Souvenir Sheet

Common Design Type

1937 Unwmk. *Imperf.*

178 CD76 3fr rose violet 5.50 6.50

Senegalese Woman — A31

1938-40 ***Perf. 12x12½, 12½x12***

179	A31	35c green	.55	.55
180	A31	55c chocolate	.55	.55
181	A31	80c violet	1.00	.55
182	A31	90c lt rose vio ('39)	.55	.55
183	A31	1fr car lake	1.90	1.00
184	A31	1fr cop brn ('40)	.60	.55
185	A31	1.75fr ultra	1.00	.60
186	A31	2.25fr ultra ('39)	.75	.75
187	A31	2.50fr black ('40)	1.25	1.25
		Nos. 179-187 (9)	8.15	6.35

For surcharge see No. B10.

Caillié Issue
Common Design Type

1939 **Engr.** ***Perf. 12½x12***

188	CD81	90c org brn & org	.60	.60
189	CD81	2fr brt vio	.80	.80
190	CD81	2.25fr ultra & dk bl	.95	.95
		Nos. 188-190 (3)	2.35	2.35

For No. 188 surcharged 20fr and 50fr, see French West Africa.

New York World's Fair Issue
Common Design Type

1939 ***Perf. 12½x12***

191	CD82	1.25fr car lake	.60	.60
192	CD82	2.25fr ultra	.60	.60

SEMI-POSTAL STAMPS

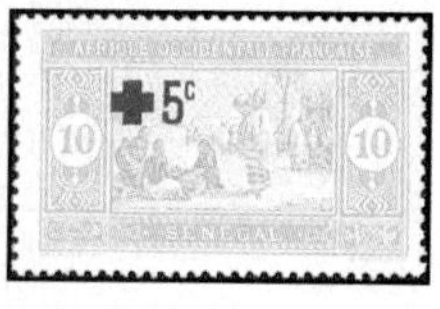

No. 84 Surcharged in Red

1915 **Unwmk.** ***Perf. 14x13½***

B1 A28 10c + 5c org red & rose 1.50 1.40

No. B1 is on both ordinary and chalky paper.

Same Surcharge on No. 87

1918

B2 A28 15c + 5c red org & brn vio 1.50 1.40

Curie Issue
Common Design Type

1938 **Engr.** ***Perf. 13***

B3 CD80 1.75fr + 50c brt ultra 9.50 *10.00*

French Revolution Issue
Common Design Type

Photo., Name & Value Typo. in Black

1939

B4	CD83	45c + 25c green	8.00	8.00
B5	CD83	70c + 30c brown	8.00	8.00
B6	CD83	90c + 35c red org	8.00	8.00
B7	CD83	1.25fr + 1fr rose pink	8.00	8.00
B8	CD83	2.25fr + 2fr blue	8.00	8.00
		Nos. B4-B8 (5)	40.00	40.00

AIR POST STAMPS

Landscape AP1

Caravan AP2

Perf. 12½x12, 12x12½

1935 **Engr.** **Unwmk.**

C1	AP1	25c dk brown	.25	.20
C2	AP1	50c red orange	.55	.35
C3	AP1	1fr rose lilac	.25	.20
C4	AP1	1.25fr yellow grn	.25	.20
C5	AP1	2fr blue	.25	.20
C6	AP1	3fr olive grn	.40	.20
C7	AP2	3.50fr violet	.40	.20
C8	AP2	4.75fr orange	.85	.35
C9	AP2	6.50fr dk blue	1.00	.85
C10	AP2	8fr black	1.50	1.40
C11	AP2	15fr rose lake	1.25	.90
		Nos. C1-C11 (11)	6.95	5.05

No. C8 surcharged "ENTR' AIDE FRANCAIS + 95f 25" in green, red violet or blue, was never issued in this colony.

Common Design Type

1940 **Engr.** ***Perf. 12½x12***

C12	CD85	1.90fr ultra	.40	.40
C13	CD85	2.90fr dk red	.40	.40
C14	CD85	4.50fr dk gray grn	.45	.50
C15	CD85	4.90fr yellow bis	.75	.85
C16	CD85	6.90fr dp orange	1.00	1.25
		Nos. C12-C16 (5)	3.00	3.40

AIR POST SEMI-POSTAL STAMPS

French Revolution Issue
Common Design Type

1939 **Unwmk.** **Photo.** ***Perf. 13***

Name and Value Typo. in Orange

CB1 CD83 4.75 + 4fr brn blk 12.00 12.00

Surtax used for the defense of the colonies.

POSTAGE DUE STAMPS

Postage Due Stamps of French Colonies Surcharged

1903 **Unwmk.** ***Imperf.***

J1	D1	10c on 50c lilac	62.50	65.00
J2	D1	10c on 60c brown, *buff*	62.50	65.00
J3	D1	10c on 1fr rose, *buff*	350.00	375.00
		Nos. J1-J3 (3)	475.00	505.00

D2

D3

1906 **Typo.** ***Perf. 14x13½***

J4	D2	5c green, *grnsh*	4.50	3.25
J5	D2	10c red brown	6.25	4.00
J6	D2	15c dark blue	6.75	7.50
J7	D2	20c black, *yellow*	7.25	4.50
J8	D2	30c red, *straw*	9.00	9.00
J9	D2	50c violet	10.00	10.00
J10	D2	60c black, *buff*	13.50	14.50
J11	D2	1fr black, *pinkish*	20.00	20.00
		Nos. J4-J11 (8)	77.25	72.75

1914

J12	D3	5c green	.35	.35
J13	D3	10c rose	.35	.35
J14	D3	15c gray	.55	.55
J15	D3	20c brown	.65	.55
J16	D3	30c blue	1.10	.85
J17	D3	50c black	1.25	1.25
J18	D3	60c orange	1.50	1.10
J19	D3	1fr violet	1.60	1.40
		Nos. J12-J19 (8)	7.35	6.40

Type of 1914 Issue Surcharged

1927

J20	D3	2fr on 1fr lilac rose	5.00	5.00
J21	D3	3fr on 1fr orange brown	5.00	5.00

D4

1935 **Engr.** ***Perf. 12½x12***

J22	D4	5c yellow green	.20	.20
J23	D4	10c red orange	.20	.20
J24	D4	15c violet	.20	.20
J25	D4	20c olive green	.20	.20
J26	D4	30c reddish brown	.20	.20
J27	D4	50c rose lilac	.75	.75
J28	D4	60c orange	1.00	1.00
J29	D4	1fr black	.75	.75
J30	D4	2fr dark blue	.75	.75
J31	D4	3fr dark carmine	1.00	1.00
		Nos. J22-J31 (10)	5.25	5.25

SENEGAMBIA & NIGER

ˌse-nə-ˈgam-bē-ə and ˈnī-jər

A French Administrative unit for the Senegal and Niger possessions in Africa during the period when the French possessions in Africa were being definitively divided into colonies and protectorates. The name was dropped in 1904 when this territory was consolidated with part of French Sudan, under the name Upper Senegal and Niger.

100 Centimes = 1 Franc

Covers
Values are for commercial covers bearing correct frankings. Philatelic covers sell for less.

Navigation and Commerce — A1

1903 **Unwmk.** **Typo.** ***Perf. 14x13½***

Name of Colony in Blue or Carmine

1	A1	1c black, *lil bl*	1.50	1.50
		On cover		—
2	A1	2c brown, *buff*	1.50	1.50
		On cover		—
3	A1	4c claret, *lav*	4.50	*4.50*
		On cover		—
4	A1	5c yel grn	5.25	*5.25*
		On cover		60.00
5	A1	10c red	6.00	6.00
		On cover		60.00
6	A1	15c gray	11.50	11.50
		On cover		70.00
7	A1	20c red, *green*	9.75	9.75
		On cover		—
8	A1	25c blue	15.00	15.00
		On cover		100.00
9	A1	30c brn, *bister*	13.00	*13.00*
		On cover		—
10	A1	40c red, *straw*	18.75	*18.75*
		On cover		150.00
11	A1	50c brn, *azure*	37.50	37.50
		On cover		—
12	A1	75c deep vio, *org*	42.00	*42.00*
		On cover		250.00
13	A1	1fr brnz grn, *straw*	52.50	52.50
		On cover		—
		Nos. 1-13 (13)	218.75	218.75

Perf. 13½x14 stamps are counterfeits.

SERBIA

ˈsər-bē-ə

LOCATION — In southeastern Europe, bounded by Romania and Bulgaria on the east, the former Austro-Hungarian Empire on the north, Greece on the south, and Albania and Montenegro on the west
GOVT. — Kingdom
AREA — 18,650 sq. mi.
POP. — 2,911,701 (1910)
CAPITAL — Belgrade

Following World War I, Serbia united with Montenegro, Bosnia and Herzegovina, Croatia, Dalmatia and Slovenia to form Yugoslavia.

100 Paras = 1 Dinar

Coat of Arms — A1

Prince Michael (Obrenovich III) — A2

1866 **Unwmk.** **Typo.** ***Imperf.***

Paper colored Through

1	A1	1p dk green, *dk vio rose*	45.00	

Surface Colored Paper, Thin or Thick

2	A1	1p dk green, *lil rose*	50.00	
a.		1p olive green, *rose*	50.00	
b.		1p yel grn, *pale rose* (thick paper)	300.00	
3	A1	2p red brown, *lilac*	60.00	
a.		2p red brn, *lil gray* (thick paper)	250.00	
b.		2p dl grn, *lil gray* (thick paper)	800.00	
		Nos. 1-3 (3)	155.00	

Vienna Printing
Perf. 12

4	A2	10p orange	750.00	500.00
5	A2	20p rose	425.00	17.50
6	A2	40p blue	475.00	125.00
a.		Half used as 20p on cover		
		Nos. 4-6 (3)	1,650.	642.50

Belgrade Printing
Perf. 9½

7	A2	1p green	15.00	
8	A2	2p bister brn	22.50	
9	A2	20p rose	15.00	15.00
a.		Pair, imperf. between		
10	A2	40p ultra	160.00	175.00
a.		Half used as 20p on cover		
		Nos. 7-10 (4)	212.50	

Pelure Paper

11	A2	10p orange	65.00	70.00
12	A2	20p rose	60.00	8.75
a.		Pair, imperf. between		
13	A2	40p ultra	35.00	25.00
a.		Pair, imperf. between		
b.		Half used as 20p on cover		
		Nos. 11-13 (3)	160.00	103.75

Nos. 1-3, 7-8, 14-16, 25-26 were used only as newspaper tax stamps.

1868-69 **Ordinary Paper** ***Imperf.***

14	A2	1p green	35.00	
a.		1p olive green ('69)	*2,000.*	
15	A2	2p brown	50.00	
a.		2p bister brown ('69)	160.00	

Counterfeits of type A2 are common.

Prince Milan (Obrenovich IV)
A3 A4

Perf. 9½, 12 and Compound

1869-78

16	A3	1p yellow	3.75	*95.00*
17	A3	10p red brown	7.50	3.75
a.		10p yellow brown	*350.00*	35.00
18	A3	10p orange ('78)	1.25	3.25
19	A3	15p orange	85.00	15.00
20	A3	20p gray blue	1.50	2.50
a.		20p ultramarine	3.25	2.00
b.		Half used as 10p on cover		
21	A3	25p rose	1.50	5.75
22	A3	35p lt green	3.00	3.50

23 A3 40p violet 1.50 2.75
a. Half used as 20p on cover
24 A3 50p blue green 5.00 3.75
Nos. 16-24 (9) 110.00 *135.25*

The first setting, which included all values except No. 18, had the stamps 2-2½mm apart.

A new setting, introduced in 1878, had the stamps 3-4mm apart, providing wider margins. Only Nos. 17, 18, 20 and 21 exist in this new setting, which differs also in shades from the earlier setting.

The narrow-spaced Nos. 17, 20 and 21 are rarer, especially unused, as are the early shades of Nos. 23 and 24.

All values except Nos. 19 and 24 are known in various partly perforated varieties.

Counterfeits exist.

See No. 25.

1872-79 ***Imperf.***

25 A3 1p yellow 4.50 8.75
a. Tête bêche pair
26 A4 2p blk, thin paper ('79) .50 .50
a. Thick paper ('73) 1.50 *10.00*

Used value of No. 26 is for canceled-to-order.

King Milan I — A5

King Alexander (Obrenovich V) — A6

1880 ***Perf. 13x13½***

27 A5 5p green .50 .20
a. 5p olive green 475.00 2.00
28 A5 10p rose 1.50 .20
29 A5 20p orange .50 .20
a. 20p yellow 3.00 1.25
30 A5 25p ultra 1.00 .75
a. 25p blue 1.25 .75
31 A5 50p brown 1.00 *3.75*
a. 50p brown violet 140.00 3.00
32 A5 1d violet 6.75 6.00
Nos. 27-32 (6) 11.25 11.10

1890

33 A6 5p green .20 .20
34 A6 10p rose red .50 .20
35 A6 15p red violet .50 .20
36 A6 20p orange .35 .20
37 A6 25p blue .60 .25
38 A6 50p brown 2.00 2.00
39 A6 1d dull lilac 7.50 6.25
Nos. 33-39 (7) 11.65 9.30

King Alexander — A7

1894-96 ***Perf. 13x13½***

Granite Paper

40 A7 5p green 3.25 .20
a. Perf. 11½ 3.50 .40
41 A7 10p car rose 3.50 .20
b. Perf. 11½ 45.00 .75
42 A7 15p violet 5.00 .20
43 A7 20p orange 52.50 .50
a. Half used as 10p on cover *375.00*
44 A7 25p blue 10.50 .20
45 A7 50p brown 11.00 .45
46 A7 1d dk green 1.50 2.50
47 A7 1d red brn, *bl* ('96) 11.00 3.75
Nos. 40-47 (8) 98.25 8.00

1898-1900 ***Perf. 13x13½, 11½***

Ordinary Paper

48 A7 1p dull red .25 .25
49 A7 5p green 1.50 .20
50 A7 10p rose 42.50 .20
51 A7 15p violet 7.00 .20
52 A7 20p orange 6.25 .25
53 A7 25p deep blue 7.00 .30
54 A7 50p brown 12.50 3.00
Nos. 48-54 (7) 77.00 4.40

Nos. 49-54 exist imperf.

Nos. 49-51, 53 and 56-57 exist with perf. 13x13½x11½x13½.

Type of 1900 Stamp Surcharged

1900

56 A7 10p on 20p rose 2.50 .20

Same, Surcharged

1901

57 A7 10p on 20p rose 1.75 .20
58 A7 15p on 1d red brn, *bl* 3.75 1.00
a. Inverted surcharge *100.00* *110.00*

King Alexander (Obrenovich V)
A8 A9

1901-03 **Typo.** ***Perf. 11½***

59 A8 5p green .20 .20
60 A8 10p rose .20 .20
61 A8 15p red violet .20 .20
62 A8 20p orange .20 .20
63 A8 25p ultra .20 .20
64 A8 50p bister .20 .20
65 A9 1d brown .70 .60
66 A9 3d brt rose 6.75 5.75
67 A9 5d deep violet 5.25 5.75
Nos. 59-67 (9) 13.90 13.30

Counterfeits of Nos. 66-67 exist. Nos. 59-67 imperf. value of set of pairs, $100.

Arms of Serbia on Head of King Alexander — A10

Two Types of the Overprint

Type I — Overprint 12mm wide. Bottom of mantle defined by a single line. Wide crown above shield.

Type II — Overprint 10mm wide. Double line at bottom of mantle. Smaller crown above shield.

Arms Overprinted in Blue, Black, Red and Red Brown

1903-04 **Type I** ***Perf. 13½***

68 A10 1p red lil & blk (Bl) .50 .50
a. Inverted overprint 10.00
69 A10 5p yel grn & blk (Bl) .35 .20
70 A10 10p car & blk (Bk) .20 .20
a. Double overprint 8.75
71 A10 15p ol gray & blk (Bk) .20 .20
a. Double overprint 8.75
72 A10 20p org & blk (Bk) .25 .20
73 A10 25p bl & blk (Bk) .25 .20
a. Double overprint 10.00
74 A10 50p gray & blk (R) 2.50 .65

There were two printings of the type I overprint on Nos. 68-74, one typographed and one lithographed.

Type II

75 A10 1d bl grn & blk (Bk) 7.50 2.50

#68-75 with overprint omitted, value, set $75.

Perf. 11½

Type I

75A A10 5p (Bl) .25 .35
75B A10 50p (R) .75 2.00
75C A10 1d (Bk) 1.50 4.00

Type II

76 A10 3d vio & blk (R Br) 1.50 1.75
a. Perf. 13½ *90.00* *90.00*
77 A10 5d lt brn & blk (Bl) 1.50 2.00

Type I With Additional Surcharge

78 A10 1p on 5d (R) .75 2.75
a. Perf. 13½ *275.00* *275.00*
Nos. 68-78 (14) 18.00 17.50

Karageorge and Peter I — A11

Insurgents, 1804 A12

1904 **Typo.**

79 A11 5p yellow green .20 .20
80 A11 10p rose red .20 .20
81 A11 15p red violet .35 .30
82 A11 25p blue .50 .35
83 A11 50p gray brown .60 .60
84 A12 1d bister 1.00 1.25
85 A12 3d blue green 2.00 3.50
86 A12 5d violet 2.50 4.00
Nos. 79-86 (8) 7.35 10.40

Centenary of the Karageorgevich dynasty and the coronation of King Peter. Counterfeits of Nos. 79-86 exist.

King Peter I Karageorgevich
A13 A14

Perf. 11½, 12x11½

1905 **Wove Paper**

87 A13 1p gray & blk .20 .20
88 A13 5p yel grn & blk .50 .20
89 A13 10p red & blk 1.50 .20
90 A13 15p red lil & blk 1.75 .20
91 A13 20p yellow & blk 3.00 .20
92 A13 25p ultra & blk 4.25 .20
93 A13 30p sl grn & blk 2.50 .20
94 A13 50p dk brown & blk 3.00 .20
95 A13 1d bister & blk .60 .25
96 A13 3d blue grn & blk .60 .60
97 A13 5d violet & blk 2.50 1.90
Nos. 87-97 (11) 20.40 4.35

Counterfeits of Nos. 87-97 abound.

The stamps of this issue may be found on both thick and thin paper.

1908 **Laid Paper**

98 A13 1p gray & blk .25 .20
99 A13 5p yel grn & blk 2.25 .20
100 A13 10p red & blk 6.75 .20
101 A13 15p red lilac & blk 6.75 .20
102 A13 20p yellow & blk 7.25 .20
103 A13 25p ultra & blk 6.75 .20
104 A13 30p gray grn & blk 10.00 .20
105 A13 50p dk brn & blk 13.00 .60
Nos. 98-105 (8) 53.00 2.00

Nos. 90, 98-100, 102-104 are known imperforate but are not believed to have been issued in this condition.

Values of Nos. 98-105 are for horizontally laid paper. Four values also exist on vertically laid paper (1p, 5p, 10p, 30p).

1911-14

Thick Wove Paper

108 A14 1p slate green .20 .20
109 A14 2p dark violet .20 .20
110 A14 5p green .20 .20
111 A14 5p pale yel grn ('14) .20 .20
112 A14 10p carmine .20 .20
113 A14 10p red ('14) .20 .20
114 A14 15p red violet .20 .20
115 A14 15p slate blk ('14) .20 .20
a. 15p red (error)
116 A14 20p yellow .20 .20
117 A14 20p brown ('14) .40 .20
118 A14 25p deep blue .30 .20
119 A14 25p indigo ('14) .20 .20
120 A14 30p blue green .20 .20
121 A14 30p olive grn ('14) .20 .20
122 A14 50p dk brown .20 .20
123 A14 50p brn red ('14) .20 .20
124 A14 1d orange 15.00 *25.00*
125 A14 1d slate ('14) 2.00 *2.75*
126 A14 3d lake 27.50 *77.50*
127 A14 3d olive yel ('14) 77.50 *475.00*
128 A14 5d violet 27.50 *42.50*
129 A14 5d dk violet ('14) 2.00 *14.00*
Nos. 108-129 (22) 155.00 *639.95*

Counterfeits exist.

King Peter and Military Staff — A15

1915 ***Perf. 11½***

132 A15 5p yellow green .20 —
133 A15 10p scarlet .20 —
134 A15 15p slate 3.75
135 A15 20p brown .60
136 A15 25p blue 7.50
137 A15 30p olive green 5.00
138 A15 50p orange brown 20.00
Nos. 132-138 (7) 37.25

Nos. 134-138 were prepared but not issued for postal use. Instead they were permitted to be used as wartime emergency currency. Some are known imperf. The 15p also exists in blue from an erroneous cliche in the 25p plate; value $250.

POSTES SERBES

Stamps of France, 1900-1907, with this handstamped control were used in 1916-1918 by the Serbian Postal Bureau, in the Island of Corfu. On the 1c to 35c, the handstamp covers 2 or 3 stamps. It was applied after the stamps were on the cover.

King Peter and Prince Alexander — A16

1918-20 **Typo.** ***Perf. 11, 11½***

155 A16 1p black .20 .20
156 A16 2p olive brown .20 .20
157 A16 5p apple green .20 .20
158 A16 10p red .20 .20
159 A16 15p black brown .20 .20
160 A16 20p red brown .20 .20
161 A16 20p violet ('20) 1.10 .60
162 A16 25p deep blue .20 .20
163 A16 30p olive green .20 .20
164 A16 50p violet .20 .20
165 A16 1d violet brown .25 .20
166 A16 3d slate green .75 .60
167 A16 5d red brown 1.25 .80
Nos. 155-167 (13) 5.15 4.00

#157-160, 164 exist imperf. Value each $6.

1920 **Pelure Paper** ***Perf. 11½***

169 A16 1p black .20 .20
170 A16 2p olive brown .20 .20

POSTAGE DUE STAMPS

Coat of Arms
D1 D2

1895 Unwmk. Typo. *Perf. 13x13½*

Granite Paper

J1 D1 5p red lilac	2.50	.80
J2 D1 10p blue	2.50	.20
J3 D1 20p orange brown	30.00	5.00
J4 D1 30p green	.20	.35
J5 D1 50p rose	.30	.40
a. Cliché of 5p in plate of 50p	75.00	*95.00*
Nos. J1-J5 (5)	35.50	6.75

No. J1 exists imperf. Value $35.

1898-1904

Ordinary Paper

J6 D1 5p magenta ('04)	.70	.70
J7 D1 20p brown	3.00	.70
a. Tête bêche pair	150.00	*150.00*
J8 D1 20p dp brn ('04)	3.00	.70
Nos. J6-J8 (3)	6.70	2.10

1906 Granite Paper *Perf. 11½*

J9 D1 5p magenta	5.25	1.00

1909

Laid Paper

J10 D1 5p magenta	.60	.60
J11 D1 10p pale blue	3.00	1.60
J12 D1 20p pale brown	.40	.40
Nos. J10-J12 (3)	4.00	2.60

1914

White Wove Paper

J13 D1 5p rose	.25	.50
J14 D1 10p deep blue	3.75	6.25

1918-20 *Perf. 11*

J15 D2 5p red	.40	.85
J16 D2 5p red brown ('20)	.40	.85
J17 D2 10p yellow green	.40	.85
J18 D2 20p olive brown	.40	.85
J19 D2 30p slate green	.40	.85
J20 D2 50p chocolate	.80	1.25
Nos. J15-J20 (6)	2.80	5.50

NEWSPAPER STAMPS

N1

Overprinted with Crown-topped Shield in Black

1911 Unwmk. Typo. *Perf. 11½*

P1 N1 1p gray	.45	.45
P2 N1 5p green	.45	.45
P3 N1 10p orange	.45	.45
a. Cliché of 1p in plate of 10p	*200.00*	
P4 N1 15p violet	.45	.45
P5 N1 20p yellow	.45	.45
a. Cliché of 50p in plate of 20p	75.00	*125.00*
P6 N1 25p blue	.50	.50
P7 N1 30p slate	5.25	5.25
P8 N1 50p brown	4.50	4.50
P9 N1 1d bister	4.50	4.50
P10 N1 3d rose red	4.50	4.50
P11 N1 5d gray vio	4.50	4.50
Nos. P1-P11 (11)	26.00	26.00

ISSUED UNDER AUSTRIAN OCCUPATION

100 Heller = 1 Krone

Stamps of Bosnia, 1912-14, Overprinted

1916 Unwmk. *Perf. 12½*

1N1 A23 1h olive green	1.60	2.25
1N2 A23 2h brt blue	1.60	2.25
1N3 A23 3h claret	1.60	1.75
1N4 A23 5h green	.40	.45
1N5 A23 6h dk gray	.80	1.50
1N6 A23 10h rose carmine	.40	.40
1N7 A23 12h dp olive grn	.80	1.50
1N8 A23 20h orange brown	.50	.90
1N9 A23 25h ultra	.50	.80
1N10 A23 30h orange red	.50	.80
1N11 A24 35h myrtle grn	.50	.80
1N12 A24 40h dk violet	.50	.80
1N13 A24 45h olive brown	.50	.80
1N14 A24 50h slate blue	.50	.80
1N15 A24 60h brown violet	.50	.80
1N16 A24 72h dark blue	.50	.80
1N17 A25 1k brn vio, *straw*	.70	1.00
1N18 A25 2k dk gray, *bl*	.70	1.00
1N19 A26 3k carmine, *grn*	.70	1.00
1N20 A26 5k dk vio, *gray*	.70	1.00
1N21 A25 10k dk ultra, *gray*	10.00	19.00
Nos. 1N1-1N21 (21)	24.50	40.40

Stamps of Bosnia, 1912-14, Overprinted "SERBIEN" Horizontally at Bottom

1916

1N22 A23 1h olive green	6.75	8.00
1N23 A23 2h bright blue	6.75	8.00
1N24 A23 3h claret	6.75	8.00
1N25 A23 5h green	.50	.65
1N26 A23 6h dark gray	6.75	8.00
1N27 A23 10h rose carmine	.50	.65
1N28 A23 12h dp olive grn	6.75	8.00
1N29 A23 20h orange brn	6.75	8.00
1N30 A23 25h ultra	6.75	8.00
1N31 A23 30h orange red	6.75	8.00
1N32 A24 35h myrtle green	6.75	8.00
1N33 A24 40h dark violet	6.75	8.00
1N34 A24 45h olive brown	6.75	8.00
1N35 A24 50h slate blue	6.75	8.00
1N36 A24 60h brown violet	6.75	8.00
1N37 A24 72h dark blue	6.75	8.00
1N38 A25 1k brn vio, *straw*	14.00	19.00
1N39 A25 2k dk gray, *bl*	16.00	19.00
1N40 A26 3k carmine, *grn*	18.00	19.00
1N41 A26 5k dk vio, *gray*	27.50	30.00
1N42 A25 10k dk ultra, *gray*	42.50	45.00
Nos. 1N22-1N42 (21)	213.50	245.30

Nos. 1N22-1N42 were prepared in 1914, at the time of the 1st Austrian occupation of Serbia. They were not issued at that time because of the retreat. The stamps were put on sale in 1916, at the same time as Nos. 1N1-1N21.

SEYCHELLES

sā-'shelz

LOCATION — A group of islands in the Indian Ocean, off the coast of Africa north of Madagascar.
GOVT. — British Colony
AREA — 156 sq. mi.
POP. — 64,718 (est. 1984)
CAPITAL — Victoria

The islands were attached to the British colony of Mauritius from 1810 to 1903, when they became a separate colony.

100 Cents = 1 Rupee

Catalogue values for unused stamps in this country are for Never Hinged items, beginning with Scott 149 in the regular postage section and Scott J1 in the postage due section.

STAMPS OF MAURITIUS USED IN SEYCHELLES

Various Issues Canceled B64

1861 Post Paid

A1 2p blue (#4b)	*11,000.*

1861 Britannia *Imperf.*

A2 6p blue (#18)	975.00
A3 6p gray violet (#20)	*2,500.*
A4 1sh vermilion (#19)	*1,500.*

1861-63 *Perf. 14*

A5 1p brown lilac (#24)	225.00
A6 2p blue (#25)	275.00
A7 4p rose (#26)	225.00
A8 6p green (#27)	1,000.
A9 6p lilac (#28)	650.00
A10 9p dull lilac (#29)	125.00
A11 1sh buff (#30)	350.00
A12 1sh green (#31)	750.00

1862 *Perf. 14 to 16*

A13 6p slate (#22)	*925.00*

1863-72 Wmk. 1

A14 1p lilac brown (#32)	125.00
a. 1p bister brown (#32a)	110.00
b. 1p brown (#32b)	110.00
A15 2p blue (#33)	140.00
A16 3p vermilion (#34)	97.50
a. 3p deep red (#34a)	160.00
A17 4p rose (#35)	55.00
A18 6p lilac (#36)	275.00
A19 6p blue grn (#37)	85.00
a. 6p yellow green (#37a)	125.00
A20 9p green (#38)	1,600.
A21 10p claret (#42)	375.00
A22 1sh org yel (#39)	125.00
a. 1sh yellow (#39a)	120.00
A23 1sh blue (#40)	325.00
A24 5sh red violet (#41)	925.00
a. 5sh bright violet (#41a)	*925.00*

1876-77 Surcharges

A25 ½p on 9p (#43)	*325.00*
A26 ½p on 10p claret (#46)	*300.00*
A27 ½p on 10p claret (#47)	*650.00*
A28 1p on 4p rose (#48)	—
A29 1sh on 5sh red vio (#49)	—
a. 1sh on 5sh violet (#49a)	—

1878 Decimal Surcharges

A30 2c claret (#50)	97.50
A31 4c on 1p bister brn (#51)	425.00
A32 8c on 2p blue (#52)	47.50
A33 13c on 3p org red (#53)	140.00
A34 17c on 4p rose (#54)	47.50
A35 25c on 6p sl blue (#55)	110.00
A36 38c on 9p violet (#56)	*550.00*
A37 50c on 1sh green (#57)	125.00
A38 2r50c on 5sh violet (#58)	525.00

1879-80 Wmk. 1 New Designs

A39 2c red brown (#59)	150.00
A40 4c orange (#60)	150.00
A41 8c blue (#61)	47.50
A42 13c slate (#62)	1,300.
A43 17c rose (#63)	100.00
A44 25c bister (#64)	210.00
A45 38c violet (#65)	1,800.
A46 50c green (#66)	925.00
A47 2r50c brn vio (#67)	*925.00*

1882-93 Wmk. 2

A48 2c red brown (#69)	110.00
A49 2c green (#70)	200.00
A50 4c orange (#71)	75.00
A51 4c rose (#72)	110.00
A52 25c bister (#74)	125.00
A53 50c deep orange (#75)	1,000.

1883 Surcharges

A54 16c on 17c rose, "16 CENTS" (#76)	150.00
A55 16c on 17c rose, "SIXTEEN CENTS" (#79)	50.00

1885

A56 16c orange brown (#82)	62.50

1885-87 Wmk. 1

A57 2c on 38c violet (#64)	—
A58 2c on 13c slate (R) (#84)	—

Issued under British Administration

Queen Victoria — A1

Two dies of 2c, 4c, 8c, 10c, 13c, 16c:

Die I — Shading lines at right of diamond in tiara band.
Die II — No shading lines in this rectangle.

1890-1900 Typo. Wmk. 2 *Perf. 14*

1 A1 2c grn & rose (II)	3.00	1.00
a. Die I	3.50	*10.50*
2 A1 2c org brn & grn ('00)	2.25	1.40
3 A1 3c dk vio & org ('93)	1.75	.60
4 A1 4c car rose & grn (II)	3.00	1.10
a. Die I	29.00	*12.50*
5 A1 6c car rose ('00)	4.00	*.60*
6 A1 8c brn vio & ultra (II)	9.00	2.00
a. 8c brn vio & bl (I)	9.75	*4.00*
7 A1 10c ultra & brn (II)	11.00	3.75
a. 10c bl & brn (I)	7.50	*20.00*
8 A1 12c ol gray & grn ('93)	3.00	.70
9 A1 13c slate & blk (II)	3.75	2.00
a. Die I	7.00	*12.50*
10A1 15c ol grn & vio ('93)	5.25	2.25
11A1 15c ultra ('00)	5.25	3.75
12A1 16c org brn & bl (I)	6.25	4.75
a. 16c org brn & ultra (II)	47.50	12.50
13A1 18c ultra ('97)	6.00	1.10
14A1 36c brn & rose ('97)	30.00	5.25
15A1 45c brn & rose ('93)	26.00	*40.00*
16A1 48c ocher & green	22.50	13.50
17A1 75c yel & pur ('00)	62.50	*80.00*
18A1 96c violet & car	57.50	55.00
19 A1 1r vio & red ('97)	15.00	5.00
20 A1 1.50r blk & rose ('00)	80.00	*97.50*
21 A1 2.25r vio & grn ('00)	110.00	*97.50*
Nos. 1-21 (21)	467.00	418.75

Numerals of 75c, 1r, 1.50r and 2.25r of type A1 are in color on plain tablet.

For surcharges see Nos. 22-37.

Surcharged in Black

1893

22 A1 3c on 4c car rose & green (II)	1.25	1.75
a. Inverted surcharge	350.00	*425.00*
b. Double surcharge	550.00	
d. Pair, one without surcharge	*9,750.*	
23 A1 12c on 16c org brn & ultra (II)	12.50	3.00
a. 12c on 16c org brn & bl (I)	2.75	*4.25*
b. Inverted surcharge (I)	525.00	
d. Double surcharge (I)	—	*10,500.*
e. Double surcharge (II)	5,250	5,250
24 A1 15c on 16c org brn & ultra (II)	15.00	3.50
a. 15c on 16c org brn & bl (I)	10.50	15.00
b. Inverted surcharge (I)	375.00	350.00
c. Inverted surcharge (II)	975.00	1,050.
d. Double surcharge (I)	1,250.	1,250.
e. Double surcharge (II)	750.00	800.00
f. Triple surcharge (II)	*4,750.*	
25 A1 45c on 48c ocher & grn	29.00	6.25
26 A1 90c on 96c vio & car	62.50	37.50
Nos. 22-26 (5)	120.25	52.00

No. 15 Surcharged in Black

1896

27 A1 18c on 45c brn & rose	8.00	3.25
a. Double surcharge	1,600.	1,600.
b. Triple surcharge	*2,300.*	
28 A1 36c on 45c brn & rose	9.25	*57.50*
a. Double surcharge	1,850.	

Surcharged in Black:

1901

29 A1 3c on 10c bl & brn (II)	1.60	.70
a. Double surcharge	800.00	
30 A1 3c on 16c org brn & ultra (II)	3.50	*4.75*
a. "3 cents" omitted (II)	625.00	625.00
b. Inverted surcharge (II)	750.00	750.00
c. Double surcharge (II)	575.00	
31 A1 3c on 36c brn & rose	.80	.90
a. Without bars		
b. Double surcharge	850.00	*975.00*
c. "3 cents" omitted	750.00	800.00
32 A1 6c on 8c brn vio & ultra (II)	1.25	*3.50*
a. Inverted surcharge	750.00	*875.00*
Nos. 29-32 (4)	7.15	*9.85*

Stamps of 1890-1900 Surcharged

1902, June

33 A1 2c on 4c car rose & grn (II)	1.90	3.25
34 A1 30c on 75c yel & pur	1.75	*4.50*
a. Narrow "0" in "30"	11.50	*52.50*
35 A1 30c on 1r vio & red	5.50	*30.00*
a. Narrow "0" in "30"	25.00	*100.00*
b. Double surcharge	*1,600.*	

36 A1 45c on 1r vio & red 7.75 *32.50*
37 A1 45c on 2.25r vio & grn 47.50 *97.50*
a. Narrow "5" in "45" 225.00 425.00
Nos. 33-37 (5) 64.40 *167.75*

King Edward VII — A6

Numerals of 75c, 1.50r and 2.25r of type A6 are in color on plain tablet.

1903, May 26 Typo. Wmk. 2

38 A6 2c red brn & grn 2.00 2.25
39 A6 3c green 1.10 *1.50*
40 A6 6c carmine rose 3.25 1.50
41 A6 12c ol gray & grn 3.25 *3.00*
42 A6 15c ultra 4.50 3.00
43 A6 18c pale yel grn & rose 4.75 *7.50*
44 A6 30c purple & grn 8.00 *12.50*
45 A6 45c brown & rose 8.00 *12.50*
46 A6 75c yel & pur 11.50 *32.50*
47 A6 1.50r black & rose 47.50 80.00
48 A6 2.25r red vio & grn 35.00 *97.50*
Nos. 38-48 (11) 128.85 *253.75*

Nos. 42-43, 45 Surcharged

1903

49 A6 3c on 15c 1.10 *3.50*
50 A6 3c on 18c 3.25 *42.50*
51 A6 3c on 45c 3.50 *3.50*
Nos. 49-51 (3) 7.85 *49.50*

Type of 1903

1906 Wmk. 3

52 A6 2c red brn & grn 1.60 *4.75*
53 A6 3c green 1.60 1.60
54 A6 6c car rose 2.25 .90
55 A6 12c ol gray & grn 3.50 3.50
56 A6 15c ultra 3.50 *2.25*
57 A6 18c pale yel grn & rose 3.50 *7.25*
58 A6 30c purple & grn 6.75 *9.00*
59 A6 45c brown & rose 3.50 *7.25*
60 A6 75c yellow & pur 9.50 *62.50*
61 A6 1.50r black & rose 57.50 *67.50*
62 A6 2.25r red vio & grn 35.00 *67.50*
Nos. 52-62 (11) 128.20 *234.00*

King George V
A7 A8

Numerals of 75c, 1.50r and 2.25r of type A7 are in color on plain tablet.

1912 *Perf. 14*

63 A7 2c org brn & grn .75 *5.75*
64 A7 3c green 2.75 .70
65 A7 6c car rose 4.75 .65
66 A7 12c ol gray & grn 1.40 *4.50*
67 A7 15c ultra 4.00 .70
68 A7 18c pl yel grn & rose 3.50 *6.00*
69 A7 30c pur & grn 5.75 1.40
70 A7 45c brn & rose 3.00 *40.00*
71 A7 75c yell & pur 3.25 *6.00*
72 A7 1.50r blk & rose 8.50 1.10
73 A7 2.25r vio & grn 62.50 2.75
Nos. 63-73 (11) 100.15 69.55

Die I

For description of dies I and II see Dies of British Colonial Stamps in the Table of Contents.

The 5c of type A8 has a colorless numeral on solid-color tablet. Numerals of 9c, 20c, 25c, 50c, 75c, and 1r to 5r of type A8 are in color on plain tablet.

1917-20

74 A8 2c org brn & grn .55 *3.00*
75 A8 3c green 2.25 *1.40*
76 A8 5c brown ('20) 2.50 *7.25*
77 A8 6c carmine rose 2.25 1.60
78 A8 12c gray 1.10 *1.10*
79 A8 15c ultra 1.90 1.60
80 A8 18c violet, *yel* 4.00 *25.00*
a. Die II ('20) 1.90 *14.00*
81 A8 25c blk & red, *yel* ('20) 1.90 *35.00*
a. Die II ('20) 1.50 *9.00*
82 A8 30c dull vio & ol grn 1.60 *9.50*
83 A8 45c dull vio & org 3.50 *40.00*
84 A8 50c dull vio & blk ('20) 6.00 *27.50*
85 A8 75c blk, *bl grn*, ol back 1.75 *17.00*
a. 75c blk, *emer* (Die II) ('20) 5.00 *17.50*
86 A8 1r dl vio & red ('20) 12.250 *50.00*
87 A8 1.50r vio & bl, *bl* 12.50 *57.00*
a. Die II ('20) 10.00 *30.00*
88 A8 2.25r gray grn & dp vio 55.00 *150.00*
89 A8 5r gray grn & ultra ('20) 95.00 *250.00*
Nos. 74-89 (16) 206.30 *676.95*

Die II

1921-32 Wmk. 4

Ordinary Paper

91 A8 2c org brn & grn .30 .20
92 A8 3c green 1.90 .20
93 A8 3c black ('22) 1.10 .35
94 A8 4c green ('22) 1.10 *2.75*
95 A8 4c ol grn & rose red ('28) 7.25 *19.00*
96 A8 5c dk brown 1.25 *6.00*
97 A8 6c car rose 3.00 *10.00*
98 A8 6c violet ('22) .70 .20
99 A8 9c rose red ('27) 3.50 *4.75*
100 A8 12c gray 3.00 .20
a. Die I ('32) 7.50 .65
101 A8 12c carmine ('22) 1.40 .35
102 A8 15c ultra 2.25 *60.00*
103 A8 15c yellow ('22) 1.10 *3.00*
104 A8 18c violet, *yel* 2.75 *13.50*
105 A8 20c ultra ('22) 1.60 .25

Chalky Paper

106 A8 25c blk & red, *yel* ('22) 3.00 *16.00*
107 A8 30c dull vio & ol grn 1.60 *17.00*
108 A8 45c dull vio & org 1.40 *5.75*
109 A8 50c dull vio & blk 2.75 *2.50*
110 A8 75c blk, *emerald* 9.00 *24.00*
111 A8 1r dull vio & red 16.00 *20.00*
a. Die I ('32) 12.00 *30.00*
112 A8 1.50r vio & bl, *bl* 16.00 *25.00*
113 A8 2.25r green & vio 15.00 *16.00*
114 A8 5r green & ultra 92.50 *175.00*
Nos. 91-114 (24) 189.45 *422.00*

Common Design Types pictured following the introduction.

Silver Jubilee Issue
Common Design Type

1935, May 6 Engr. *Perf. 11x12*

118 CD301 6c black & ultra .65 *1.75*
119 CD301 12c indigo & green 1.75 1.25
120 CD301 20c ultra & brown 1.50 1.75
121 CD301 1r brn vio & indigo 4.50 *10.00*
Nos. 118-121 (4) 8.40 *14.75*
Set, never hinged 20.00

Coronation Issue
Common Design Type

1937, May 12 *Perf. 11x11½*

122 CD302 6c olive green .20 .20
123 CD302 12c deep orange .30 *.50*
124 CD302 20c deep ultra .40 *.95*
Nos. 122-124 (3) .90 *1.65*
Set, never hinged 2.00

Coco-de-mer Palm — A9

Seychelles Giant Tortoise — A10

Fishing Canoe — A11

Perf. 13½x14½, 14½x13½

1938-41 Photo. Wmk. 4

125 A9 2c violet brown .35 .20
126 A10 3c green 4.25 1.40
127 A10 3c orange .40 .25
128 A11 6c orange 4.25 2.75
129 A11 6c green 1.00 .25
130 A9 9c rose red 5.00 *2.25*
131 A9 9c peacock blue 2.50 .50
132 A10 12c violet 20.00 1.50
133 A10 15c copper red 3.00 .20
134 A9 18c rose lake 2.50 .75
135 A11 20c bright blue 21.00 5.50
136 A11 20c ocher 1.60 .35
137 A9 25c ocher 25.00 15.00
138 A10 30c rose lake 25.00 10.00
139 A9 30c bright blue 1.60 .40
140 A11 45c brown 3.50 .60
141 A9 50c dull violet 1.50 .30
142 A10 75c gray blue 42.50 42.50
143 A10 75c dull violet 2.25 .45
144 A11 1r yellow green 50.00 55.00
145 A11 1r gray 2.75 .60
146 A9 1.50r ultra 5.00 2.75
147 A10 2.25r olive bister 8.00 6.50
148 A11 5r copper red 5.50 *7.00*
Nos. 125-148 (24) 238.45 157.00
Set, never hinged 600.00

Issued: #126, 128, 132, 135, 137, 1/1; #125, 130, 138, 140-142, 144, 146-148, 2/10; others, 8/8/41.

See Nos. 158-169, 174-188.

Catalogue values for unused stamps in this section, from this point to the end of the section, are for Never Hinged items.

Peace Issue
Common Design Type
Perf. 13½x14

1946, Sept. 23 Engr. Wmk. 4

149 CD303 9c light blue .20 .20
150 CD303 30c dark blue .35 .20

Silver Wedding Issue
Common Design Types

1948, Nov. 11 Photo. *Perf. 14x14½*

151 CD304 9c bright ultra .20 .20

Engraved; Name Typographed
Perf. 11½x11

152 CD305 5r rose carmine 13.00 *27.50*

UPU Issue
Common Design Types
Perf. 13½, 11x11½

1949, Oct. 10 Engr.

153 CD306 18c red violet .20 .25
154 CD307 50c dp rose violet 2.00 .90
155 CD308 1r gray .35 .35
156 CD309 2.25r olive .45 *.90*
Nos. 153-156 (4) 3.00 2.40

Types of 1938-41 Redrawn and

Sailfish — A12

Map — A13

Perf. 14½x13½, 13½x14½

1952, Mar. 3 Photo. Wmk. 4

157 A12 2c violet .70 .55
158 A10 3c orange .70 .25
159 A9 9c peacock blue .70 *1.25*
160 A11 15c yellow green .60 *.70*
161 A13 18c rose lake 1.50 .25
162 A11 20c ocher 1.25 .75
163 A10 25c bright red .80 .90
164 A12 40c ultra 1.00 1.00
165 A11 45c violet brown 1.00 .35
166 A9 50c brt violet 1.40 1.00
167 A13 1r gray 3.50 2.50
168 A9 1.50r brt blue 7.50 *14.00*
169 A10 2.25r olive bister 13.00 *14.00*
170 A13 5r copper red 14.00 *15.00*
171 A12 10r green 22.50 *30.00*
Nos. 157-171 (15) 70.15 *82.50*

The redrawn design shows a new portrait of King George VI surmounted by crown, as on type A12.

Nos. 157-170 exist with watermark 4a.

POSTAGE DUE STAMPS

Catalogue values for unused stamps in this section are for Never Hinged items.

D1

Engr.; Denomination Typo. in Carmine

1951, Mar. 1 Wmk. 4 *Perf. 11½*

J1 D1 2c carmine 1.90 *4.25*
J2 D1 3c blue green 1.90 *4.25*
J3 D1 6c ocher 1.25 *2.00*
J4 D1 9c brown orange 1.60 *6.50*
J5 D1 15c purple 1.90 *8.00*
J6 D1 18c deep blue 2.40 *9.00*
J7 D1 20c black brown 2.50 *10.50*
J8 D1 30c red brown 3.00 *13.50*
Nos. J1-J8 (8) 16.45 *58.00*

SIBERIA

sī-ˈbir-ē-ə

LOCATION — A vast territory of Russia lying between the Ural Mountains and the Pacific Ocean.

The anti-Bolshevist provisional government set up at Omsk by Adm. Aleksandr V. Kolchak issued Nos. 1-10 in 1919. The monarchist, anti-Soviet government in Priamur province issued Nos. 51-118 in 1921-22.

(Stamps of the Czechoslovak Legion are listed under Czechoslovakia.)

100 Kopecks = 1 Ruble

Russian Stamps of 1909-18 Surcharged

a

b

On Stamps of 1909-12

1919 Unwmk. *Perf. 14x14½*
Wove Paper
Lozenges of Varnish on Face

1 A14(a) 35k on 2k dull grn .55 *3.00*
a. Inverted surcharge 35.00
b. "5" omitted 80.00
c. Double surcharge —
2 A14(a) 50k on 3k car .55 *2.75*
a. Inverted surcharge 40.00
3 A14(a) 70k on 1k dl org yel .80 *5.50*
a. Inverted surcharge 35.00
4 A15(b) 1r on 4k car .90 *2.75*
a. Dbl. surch., one inverted 110.00 *110.00*
b. Inverted surcharge 55.00
c. Double surcharge 80.00
5 A14(b) 3r on 7k blue 1.50 *5.50*
a. Double surcharge 35.00 *30.00*
b. Inverted surcharge 30.00 *25.00*
c. Pair, one without surcharge —
d. "3" omitted —
6 A11(b) 5r on 14k dk bl & car 3.00 *14.00*
a. Double surcharge 30.00 *30.00*
b. Inverted surcharge 30.00 *30.00*

On Stamps of 1917
Imperf

7 A14(a) 35k on 2k gray grn .90 *5.50*
a. Inverted surcharge 80.00
8 A14(a) 50k on 3k red .90 *5.50*
a. Inverted surcharge 100.00
b. Double surcharge —
9 A14(a) 70k on 1k orange .75 *5.50*
a. Inverted surcharge 40.00
b. Dbl. surch., one inverted —
10 A15(b) 1r on 4k car 4.50 *7.75*
Nos. 1-10 (10) 14.35 *57.75*

Nos. 1-10, were first issued in Omsk during the regime of Admiral Kolchak. Later they were used along the line of the Trans-Siberian railway to Vladivostok.

Some experts question the postal use of most off-cover canceled copies of Nos. 1-10.

Similar surcharges, handstamped as above are bogus.

Priamur Government Issues
Nikolaevsk Issue

A5

A6

A7

Russian Stamps Handstamp Surcharged or Overprinted
On Stamps of 1909-17

1921 Unwmk. *Perf. 14x14½, 13½*

51	A5	10k on 4k carmine	*120.00*	
52	A5	10k on 10k dark blue	*1,200.*	
53	A6	15k on 14k dark blue & carmine	*150.00*	
54	A6	15k on 15k red brown & deep blue	*75.00*	
55	A6	15k on 35k red brown & green	*80.00*	
56	A6	15k on 50k brown violet & green	*100.00*	
57	A6	15k on 70k brown & red orange	*250.00*	
58	A7	15k on 1r brn & org	*200.00*	
59	A5	on 20k dull blue & dark carmine	*200.00*	
60	A5	on 20k on 14k dk blue & car (#118)	*175.00*	
a.		15k on 20k on 14k dark blue & carmine (error)	—	
61	A7	20k on 3½r maroon & light green	*250.00*	
62	A7	20k on 5r indigo, grn & lt blue	*950.00*	
63	A7	20k on 7r dark green & pink	*700.00*	

Nos. 59-60 are overprinted with initials but original denominations remain.

A 10k on 5k claret (Russia No. 77) and a 15k on 20k blue & carmine (Russia No. 82a) were not officially issued. Some authorities consider them bogus.

No evidence found of genuine usage of #51-72.

Reprints exist.

On Semi-Postal Stamp of 1914

64	SP6	20k on 3k mar & gray grn, *pink*	*775.00*	

On Stamps of 1917
Imperf

65	A5	10k on 1k orange	*60.00*	
66	A5	10k on 2k gray green	*70.00*	
67	A5	10k on 3k red	*70.00*	
68	A5	10k on 5k claret	*700.00*	
69	A6	15k on 1r pale brn, brn & red org	*100.00*	
70	A7	20k on 1r pale brn, brn & red org	*175.00*	
71	A7	20k on 3½r maroon & light green	*275.00*	
72	A7	20k on 7r dark green & pink	*700.00*	

The letters of the overprint are the initials of the Russian words for "Nikolaevsk on Amur Priamur Provisional Government."

As the surcharges on Nos. 51-72 are handstamped, a number exist inverted or double.

A 20k blue & carmine (Russia No. 126) with Priamur overprint and a 15k on 20k (Russia No. 126) were not officially issued. Some authorities consider them bogus.

No evidence found of genuine usage of #51-72.

Stamps of Far Eastern Republic Overprinted

1922

78	A2	2k gray green	25.00	25.00
a.		Inverted overprint	125.00	
79	A2a	4k rose	25.00	25.00
a.		Inverted overprint	*110.00*	
80	A2	5k claret	25.00	25.00
81	A2a	10k blue	25.00	25.00
		Nos. 78-81 (4)	100.00	100.00

Anniv. of the overthrow of the Bolshevik power in the Priamur district.

The letters of the overprint are the initials of "Vremeno Priamurski Pravitel'stvo" i.e. Provisional Priamur Government, 26th May.

Russian Stamps of 1909-21 Overprinted in Dark Blue or Vermilion

On Stamps of 1909-18

1922 ***Perf. 14x14½***

85	A14	1k dull org yel	45.00	50.00
86	A14	2k dull green	80.00	65.00
87	A14	3k carmine	25.00	30.00
88	A15	4k carmine	12.50	15.00
89	A14	5k dk claret	25.00	27.50
90	A14	7k blue (V)	25.00	27.50
91	A15	10k dark blue (V)	35.00	40.00
92	A11	14k dk bl & car	45.00	55.00
93	A11	15k red brn & dp bl	12.50	15.00
94	A8	20k dl bl & dk car	12.50	15.00
95	A11	20k on 14k dark blue & carmine	100.00	100.00
96	A11	25k dull green & dark violet (V)	25.00	30.00
97	A11	35k red brn & grn	7.50	10.00
a.		Inverted overprint	80.00	
98	A8	50k brn vio & grn	12.50	15.00
99	A11	70k brn & red org	25.00	30.00
		Nos. 85-99 (15)	487.50	525.00

On Stamps of 1917
Imperf

100	A14	1k orange	4.25	5.00
a.		Inverted overprint	65.00	85.00
101	A14	2k gray green	9.00	9.00
102	A14	3k red	12.00	12.00
103	A15	4k carmine	65.00	65.00
104	A14	5k claret	19.00	15.00
105	A11	15k red brn & dp bl	110.00	100.00
106	A8	20k blue & car	47.50	40.00
107	A9	1r pale brn, brn & red org	14.00	15.00
		Nos. 100-107 (8)	280.75	261.00

On Stamps of Siberia, 1919
Perf. 14½x15

108	A14	35k on 2k green	60.00	60.00

Imperf

109	A14	70k on 1k orange	85.00	85.00

On Stamps of Far Eastern Republic, 1921

110	A2	2k gray green	6.00	5.50
111	A2a	4k rose	6.00	5.50
112	A2	5k claret	6.00	5.50
a.		Inverted overprint	100.00	
113	A2a	10k blue (R)	4.00	3.50
		Nos. 109-113 (5)	107.00	105.00

Same, Surcharged with New Values

114	A2	1k on 2k gray grn	4.00	3.50
115	A2a	3k on 4k rose	4.00	3.50

The overprint is in a rectangular frame on stamps of 1k to 10k and 1r; on the other values the frame is omitted. It is larger on the 1 ruble than on the smaller stamps.

The overprint reads "Priamurski Zemski Krai," Priamur Rural Province.

Far Eastern Republic Nos. 30-32 Overprinted in Blue

Perf. 14½x15

116	A14	35k on 2k green	5.00	6.50

Imperf

117	A14	35k on 2k green	90.00	110.00
118	A14	70k on 1k orange	8.25	11.50
		Nos. 116-118 (3)	103.25	128.00

Counterfeits of Nos. 51-118 abound.

SIERRA LEONE

sē-ˌer-ə lē-ˈōn

LOCATION — West coast of Africa, between Guinea and Liberia
GOVT. — British Colony
AREA — 27,925 sq. mi.
POP. — 3,354,000 (est. 1982)
CAPITAL — Freetown

Sierra Leone was a British colony and protectorate.

12 Pence = 1 Shilling
20 Shillings = 1 Pound

Catalogue values for unused stamps in this country are for Never Hinged items, beginning with Scott 186 in the regular postage section.

Queen Victoria
A1 A2

1859-74 Unwmk. Typo. *Perf. 14*

1	A1	6p bright violet ('74)	55.00	30.00
a.		6p dull violet ('59)	220.00	55.00
b.		6p gray lilac ('65)	300.00	45.00

1872 ***Perf. 12½***

5	A1	6p violet	425.00	70.00

1872 Wmk. 1 Sideways *Perf. 12½*

6	A2	1p rose	85.00	40.00
8	A2	3p yellow buff	160.00	42.50
9	A2	4p blue	200.00	45.00
10	A2	1sh yellow green	525.00	62.50

1873 Wmk. 1 Upright

6a	A2	1p	140.00	35.00
7	A2	2p magenta	150.00	55.00
8a	A2	3p	550.00	95.00
9a	A2	4p	375.00	57.50
10a	A2	1sh	525.00	110.00

1876-96 Wmk. 1 Upright *Perf. 14*

11	A2	½p bister	3.50	9.50
12	A2	1p rose	55.00	16.00
13	A2	1½p violet ('77)	55.00	10.00
14	A2	2p magenta	72.50	4.50
15	A2	3p yellow buff	55.00	5.00
16	A2	4p blue	190.00	7.25
17	A1	6p brt violet ('85)	67.50	27.50
a.		Half used as 3p on cover		2,750.
18	A1	6p violet brn ('90)	21.00	16.00
19	A1	6p brown vio ('96)	3.00	7.75
20	A2	1sh green	67.50	7.25
		Nos. 11-20 (10)	590.00	110.75

For surcharge see No. 32.

1883-93 Wmk. Crown and C A (2)

21	A2	½p bister	27.50	57.50
22	A2	½p dull green ('84)	3.50	2.00
23	A2	1p carmine ('84)	5.50	1.10
a.		1p rose carmine	32.50	9.50
b.		1p rose	225.00	40.00
24	A2	1½p violet ('93)	3.25	7.25
25	A2	2p magenta	57.50	9.50
26	A2	2p slate ('84)	42.50	3.00
27	A2	2½p ultra ('91)	13.50	1.75
28	A2	3p org yel ('92)	4.00	11.00
29	A2	4p blue	1,000.	32.50
30	A2	4p bister ('84)	2.75	2.25
31	A2	1sh org brn ('88)	25.00	13.50
		Nos. 21-28,30-31 (10)	185.00	108.85

For surcharge see No. 33.

Nos. 13 and 24 Surcharged in Black

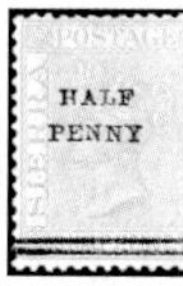

1893 Wmk. 1

32	A2	½p on 1½p violet	525.00	*800.00*
a.		"PFNNY"	3,300.	*4,500.*

Wmk. 2

33	A2	½p on 1½p violet	5.00	3.50
a.		"PFNNY"	82.50	*82.50*
b.		Inverted surcharge	125.00	125.00
c.		Same as "a," inverted	2,750.	*5,500.*
d.		Double surcharge	*1,200.*	

A4

1896-97

34	A4	½p lilac & grn ('97)	2.75	3.50
35	A4	1p lilac & car	4.75	2.00
36	A4	1½p lilac & blk ('97)	4.50	24.00
37	A4	2p lilac & org	2.75	5.50
38	A4	2½p lilac & ultra	2.75	1.40
39	A4	3p lilac & sl ('97)	9.50	7.75
40	A4	4p lilac & car ('97)	10.50	14.50
41	A4	5p lilac & blk	14.50	16.00
42	A4	6p lilac ('97)	9.00	27.50
43	A4	1sh green & blk	6.75	22.50
44	A4	2sh green & ultra	27.50	67.50
45	A4	5sh green & car	77.50	200.00
46	A4	£1 violet, *red*	190.00	500.00
		Nos. 34-46 (13)	362.75	892.15

Numerals of Nos. 39-46 of type A4 are in color on plain tablet.

A5

A6

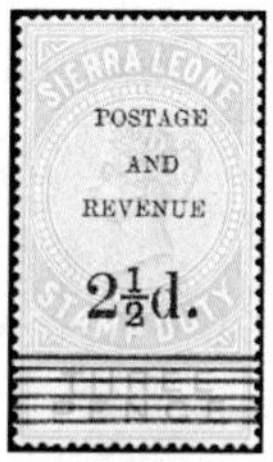
a

b

c

d

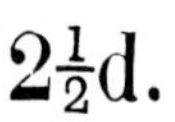
e

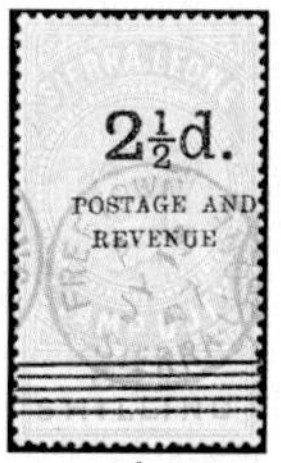
f

1897 Wmk. C A over Crown (46)

47	A5	1p lilac & grn	5.25	4.25
a.		Double overprint	*1,800.*	*1,800.*
48	A6(a)	2½p on 3p lil & grn	13.50	*17.50*
a.		Double surcharge	*35,000.*	
49	A6(b)	2½p on 3p	67.50	*80.00*
50	A6(c)	2½p on 3p	200.00	*215.00*
51	A6(d)	2½p on 3p	400.00	*525.00*
52	A6(a)	2½p on 6p lil & grn	10.50	*17.50*
53	A6(b)	2½p on 6p	50.00	*67.50*
54	A6(c)	2½p on 6p	150.00	175.00

No.	Type	Description	Unused	Used
55	A6(d)	2½p on 6p	325.00	*400.00*
56	A6(a)	2½p on 1sh lilac	110.00	80.00
57	A6(b)	2½p on 1sh lilac	1,100.	1,100.
58	A6(c)	2½p on 1sh lilac	525.00	500.00
59	A6(e)	2½p on 1sh lilac	1,750.	2,000.
59A	A6(f)	2½p on 1sh lilac	1,750.	1,500.
60	A6(a)	2½p on 2sh lilac	2,100.	2,500.
61	A6(b)	2½p on 2sh lilac	*20,000.*	
62	A6(c)	2½p on 2sh lilac	*11,500.*	*13,500.*
63	A6(e)	2½p on 2sh lilac	*47,500.*	*50,000.*
63A	A6(f)	2½p on 2sh lilac	*47,500.*	*50,000.*

The words "POSTAGE AND REVENUE" on Nos. 56-63A are set in two lines and overprinted below instead of above "2½d."

The "d" in type "f" is 3½mm wide; that in type "a" is 3mm.

Very fine examples of Nos. 47-63A will have perforations touching the frameline on one or more sides.

Nos. 56-59A are often found discolored. Such copies sell for about half the values quoted.

King Edward VII — A7

Numerals of 3p to £1 of type A7 are in color on plain tablet.

1903 Wmk. Crown and C A (2)

No.	Type	Description	Unused	Used
64	A7	½p violet & grn	3.25	*5.00*
65	A7	1p violet & car	2.25	1.10
66	A7	1½p violet & blk	1.50	*11.00*
67	A7	2p violet & brn org	4.50	*17.50*
68	A7	2½p violet & ultra	5.00	*9.00*
69	A7	3p violet & gray	11.00	*15.00*
70	A7	4p violet & car	8.00	*16.00*
71	A7	5p violet & blk	9.00	*35.00*
72	A7	6p violet & dull vio	12.50	*17.50*
73	A7	1sh green & blk	18.00	*67.50*
74	A7	2sh green & ultra	50.00	*67.50*
75	A7	5sh green & car	80.00	*110.00*
76	A7	£1 violet, *red*	225.00	275.00
		Nos. 64-76 (13)	430.00	647.10

1904-05 Wmk. 3

Chalky Paper

No.	Type	Description	Unused	Used
77	A7	½p violet & grn	5.75	5.25
78	A7	1p violet & car	4.50	1.75
a.		On ordinary paper	1.75	1.00
79	A7	1½p violet & blk	3.50	*15.00*
80	A7	2p violet & brn org	4.75	4.50
81	A7	2½p violet & ultra	5.25	2.25
82	A7	3p violet & gray	40.00	4.00
83	A7	4p violet & car	8.00	8.00
84	A7	5p violet & blk	14.00	*30.00*
85	A7	6p violet & dl vio	4.50	*3.50*
86	A7	1sh green & blk	8.50	*10.00*
87	A7	2sh green & ultra	25.00	30.00
88	A7	5sh green & car	35.00	57.50
89	A7	£1 violet, *red*	240.00	260.00
		Nos. 77-89 (13)	398.75	431.75

The 1p also exists on ordinary paper.

1907-10

Ordinary Paper

No.	Type	Description	Unused	Used
90	A7	½p green	1.00	.60
91	A7	1p carmine	6.25	.80
92	A7	1½p orange ('10)	1.40	2.25
93	A7	2p gray	1.40	1.75
94	A7	2½p ultra	4.00	3.25

Chalky Paper

No.	Type	Description	Unused	Used
95	A7	3p violet, *yel*	8.50	*3.25*
a.		On ordinary paper	12.00	*15.00*
96	A7	4p blk & red, *yel*	2.60	1.75
97	A7	5p vio & ol grn	9.00	5.75
98	A7	6p vio & red vio	10.00	9.00
99	A7	1sh black, *green*	6.25	5.75
100	A7	2sh vio & bl, *bl*	17.50	22.50
101	A7	5sh grn & red, *yel*	47.50	62.50
102	A7	£1 vio & blk, *red*	300.00	210.00
		Nos. 90-102 (13)	415.40	329.15

The 3p also exists on ordinary paper.

King George V and Seal of the Colony

A8 A9

Die I

For description of dies I and II see "Dies of British Colonial Stamps" in Table of Contents.

Numerals of 3p, 4p, 5p, 6p and 10p of type A8 are in color on plain tablet. Numerals of 7p and 9p are on solid-color tablet.

1912-24 Ordinary Paper Wmk. 3

No.	Type	Description	Unused	Used
103	A8	½p green	2.50	*2.50*
104	A8	1p scarlet	4.00	.80
a.		1p carmine	2.00	.45
105	A8	1½p orange	2.25	*2.75*
106	A8	2p gray	1.50	.25
107	A8	2½p ultra	1.25	1.00
a.		2½p deep blue	10.50	3.00

Chalky Paper

No.	Type	Description	Unused	Used
108	A9	3p violet, *yel*	3.50	*3.75*
109	A8	4p blk & red, *yel*	3.25	*9.50*
a.		Die II ('24)	5.00	*6.00*
110	A8	5p violet & ol grn	1.50	*7.00*
111	A8	6p vio & red vio	3.75	*6.75*
112	A8	7p violet & org	3.50	*9.50*
113	A8	9p violet & blk	5.75	*14.00*
114	A8	10p violet & red	3.50	*20.00*
115	A9	1sh black, *green*	5.00	*5.25*
a.		1sh black, *emerald*		*190.00*
116	A9	2sh vio & ultra, *bl*	15.00	6.25
117	A9	5sh grn & red, *yel*	15.00	*30.00*
118	A9	10sh grn & red, *grn*	80.00	*140.00*
119	A9	£1 vio & blk, *red*	175.00	*260.00*
120	A9	£2 violet & ultra	575.00	*775.00*
121	A9	£5 gray grn & org	*1,400.*	*2,000.*
		Nos. 103-119 (17)	326.25	519.30

The status of #115a has been questioned.

Die II

1921-27 Wmk. 4

Ordinary Paper

No.	Type	Description	Unused	Used
122	A8	½p green	1.40	1.10
123	A8	1p violet ('26)	3.50	.20
a.		Die I ('24)	1.75	*2.50*
124	A8	1½p scarlet	2.00	1.50
125	A8	2p gray ('22)	1.10	.20
126	A8	2½p ultra	1.40	*9.00*
127	A8	3p ultra ('22)	1.40	1.40
128	A8	4p blk & red, *yel*	2.00	*3.75*
129	A8	5p vio & ol grn	1.40	1.40

Chalky Paper

No.	Type	Description	Unused	Used
130	A8	6p dp vio & red vio	1.40	*2.75*
131	A8	7p vio & org ('27)	3.25	*22.50*
132	A8	9p dl vio & blk ('22)	3.25	*16.00*
133	A8	10p violet & red	4.00	*30.00*
134	A9	1sh blk, *emerald*	9.00	8.00
135	A9	2sh vio & ultra, *bl*	11.00	11.50
136	A9	5sh grn & red, *yel*	11.00	*57.50*
137	A9	10sh grn & red, *grn*	105.00	*200.00*
138	A9	£2 violet & ultra	550.00	*750.00*
139	A9	£5 gray grn & org	*1,300.*	*2,000.*
		Nos. 122-137 (16)	162.10	366.80

Rice Field — A10

Palms and Kola Tree — A11

1932, Mar. 1 Engr. *Perf. 12½*

No.	Type	Description	Unused	Used
140	A10	½p green	.20	.20
141	A10	1p dk violet	.30	.20
142	A10	1½p rose car	.35	*1.40*
143	A10	2p yellow brn	.35	.20
144	A10	3p ultra	.75	*2.00*
145	A10	4p orange	.75	*8.00*
146	A10	5p olive green	1.00	*3.50*
147	A10	6p light blue	.75	*3.50*
148	A10	1sh red brown	2.75	*6.50*

Perf. 12

No.	Type	Description	Unused	Used
149	A11	2sh dk brown	6.00	*8.25*
150	A11	5sh indigo	14.00	*22.50*
151	A11	10sh deep green	70.00	*140.00*
152	A11	£1 deep violet	120.00	*225.00*
		Nos. 140-152 (13)	217.20	421.25

Wilberforce Issue

Arms of Sierra Leone — A12

Slave Throwing Off Shackles — A13

Map of Sierra Leone — A14

Old Slave Market, Freetown A15

Fruit Seller — A16

Government Sanatorium — A17

Bullom Canoe — A18

Punting near Banana Islands — A19

Government Buildings, Freetown A20

Old Slavers' Resort, Bunce Island — A21

African Elephant — A22

George V A23

Freetown Harbor — A24

1933, Oct. 2

No.	Type	Description	Unused	Used
153	A12	½p deep green	.80	*1.40*
154	A13	1p brown & blk	.70	.20
155	A14	1½p orange brn	5.25	5.25
156	A15	2p violet	3.50	.20
157	A16	3p ultra	3.50	2.10
158	A17	4p dk brown	7.50	*11.50*
159	A18	5p red brn & sl grn	8.00	*15.00*
160	A19	6p dp org & blk	9.00	9.00
161	A20	1sh dk violet	5.50	*21.00*
162	A21	2sh bl & dk brn	25.00	*45.00*
163	A22	5sh red vio & blk	175.00	*190.00*
164	A23	10sh green & blk	200.00	*275.00*
165	A24	£1 yel & dk vio	400.00	*475.00*
		Nos. 153-165 (13)	843.75	*1,050.*

Abolition of slavery in the British colonies and cent. of the death of William Wilberforce, English philanthropist and agitator against the slave trade.

Common Design Types

For description of dies I and II see "Dies of British Colonial Stamps" in Table of Contents.

Silver Jubilee Issue

Common Design Type

1935, May 6 *Perf. 11x12*

No.	Type	Description	Unused	Used
166	CD301	1p black & ultra	.85	*2.50*
167	CD301	3p ultra & brown	.90	*9.50*
168	CD301	5p indigo & green	1.25	*12.50*
169	CD301	1sh brown vio & ind	5.00	5.50
		Nos. 166-169 (4)	8.00	30.00
		Set, never hinged	12.50	

Coronation Issue

Common Design Type

1937, May 12 *Perf. 11x11½*

No.	Type	Description	Unused	Used
170	CD302	1p deep orange	.40	.40
171	CD302	2p dark violet	.60	.45
172	CD302	3p deep ultra	.80	2.25
		Nos. 170-172 (3)	1.80	3.10
		Set, never hinged	3.00	

Freetown Harbor A25

Rice Harvesting A26

1938-44 *Perf. 12½*

No.	Type	Description	Unused	Used
173	A25	½p green & blk	.20	.40
174	A25	1p dp cl & blk	.25	.60
175	A26	1½p rose red	15.00	1.00
175A	A26	1½p red vio ('41)	.20	*.60*
176	A26	2p red violet	30.00	2.50
176A	A26	2p dark red ('41)	.20	*1.75*
177	A25	3p ultra & blk	.25	*.50*
178	A25	4p red brn & blk	.50	*4.75*
179	A26	5p olive green	3.50	3.75
180	A26	6p gray	.50	.50
181	A25	1sh ol grn & blk	1.25	.75
181A	A26	1sh3p org yel ('44)	.25	.50
182	A25	2sh sepia & blk	3.25	3.00
183	A26	5sh red brown	7.00	8.00
184	A26	10sh emerald	12.50	9.50
185	A25	£1 dk blue	12.50	*22.50*
		Nos. 173-185 (16)	87.35	60.60
		Set, never hinged	120.00	

Catalogue values for unused stamps in this section, from this point to the end of the section, are for Never Hinged items.

Peace Issue

Common Design Type

Perf. 13½x14

1946, Oct. 1 Engr. Wmk. 4

186	CD303	1½p lilac	.20	.20
187	CD303	3p bright ultra	.20	.20

Silver Wedding Issue

Common Design Types

1948, Dec. 1 Photo. *Perf. 14x14½*

188	CD304	1½p brt red violet	.20	.20

Engraved; Name Typographed

Perf. 11½x11

189	CD305	£1 dark blue	19.00	*17.50*

UPU Issue

Common Design Types

Engr.; Name Typo. on 3p, 6p

1949, Oct. 10 *Perf. 13½, 11x11½*

190	CD306	1½p rose violet	.20	.25
191	CD307	3p indigo	.35	1.25
192	CD308	6p gray	.60	1.50
193	CD309	1sh olive	1.00	.75
		Nos. 190-193 (4)	2.15	3.75

SINGAPORE

'siŋ-ə-ˌpor

LOCATION — An island just off the southern tip of the Malay Peninsula, south of Johore

GOVT. — British Colony

AREA — 239 sq. mi.

POP. — 2,529,100 (est. 1984)

CAPITAL — Singapore

Singapore, Malacca and Penang were the British settlements which, together with the Federated Malay States, composed the former colony of Straits Settlements. On April 1, 1946, Singapore became a separate colony when the Straits Settlements colony was dissolved. Malacca and Penang joined the Malayan Union, which was renamed the Federation of Malaya in 1948.

See Straits Settlements for stamps of India canceled Singapore.

100 Cents = 1 Dollar

Catalogue values for all unused stamps in this country are for Never Hinged items.

King George VI — A1

1948 Wmk. 4 Typo. *Perf. 14*

1	A1	1c	black	.20	*1.00*
2	A1	2c	orange	.25	*.50*
3	A1	3c	green	.35	*.80*
4	A1	4c	chocolate	.35	*1.25*
6	A1	6c	gray	.35	*.85*
7	A1	8c	rose red	.45	*.85*
9	A1	10c	plum	.40	.20
11	A1	15c	ultra	11.00	.20
12	A1	20c	dk green & blk	7.00	.40
14	A1	25c	org & rose lilac	1.50	.20
16	A1	40c	dk vio & rose red	13.00	*9.00*
17	A1	50c	ultra & black	8.50	.25
18	A1	$1	vio brn & ultra	12.50	4.00
19	A1	$2	rose red & emer	72.50	5.00
20	A1	$5	chocolate & emer	150.00	6.00
			Nos. 1-20 (15)	278.35	30.50
			Set, hinged	150.00	

1949-52 *Perf. 18*

1a	A1	1c	black ('52)	.70	3.00
2a	A1	2c	orange	.90	1.25
4a	A1	4c	chocolate	1.00	.20
5	A1	5c	rose violet ('52)	4.00	1.50
6a	A1	6c	gray ('52)	1.60	1.25
8	A1	8c	green ('52)	9.00	3.00
9a	A1	10c	plum ('50)	.55	.20
10	A1	12c	rose red ('52)	11.00	8.50
11a	A1	15c	ultra ('50)	18.00	.30
12a	A1	20c	dark green & black	4.00	3.00
13	A1	20c	ultra ('52)	6.50	.75
14a	A1	25c	org & rose lil ('50)	1.10	.20
15	A1	35c	dk vio & rose red ('52)	6.00	3.00
16a	A1	40c	dk vio & rose red ('51)	40.00	15.00
17a	A1	50c	ultra & black ('50)	9.50	.20
18a	A1	$1	violet brown & ultra	19.00	.75
b.			Wmk. 4a (error)	*6,000.*	
19a	A1	$2	rose red & emer ('51)	120.00	3.00
b.			Wmk. 4a (error)	*6,000.*	
20a	A1	$5	choc & emerald ('51)	235.00	3.75
			Nos. 1a-20a (18)	487.85	48.85
			Set, hinged	275.00	

Common Design Types pictured following the introduction.

Silver Wedding Issue

Common Design Types

Inscribed: "Singapore"

1948, Oct. 25 Photo. *Perf. 14x14½*

21	CD304	10c purple	1.00	.20

Engraved; Name Typographed

Perf. 11½x11

22	CD305	$5 light brown	130.00	45.00

UPU Issue

Common Design Types

Inscribed: "Malaya-Singapore"

Engr.; Name Typo. on 15c, 25c

Perf. 13½, 11x11½

1949, Oct. 10 Wmk. 4

23	CD306	10c rose violet	.75	.25
24	CD307	15c indigo	7.25	.75
25	CD308	25c orange	7.25	1.25
26	CD309	50c slate	7.25	4.25
		Nos. 23-26 (4)	22.50	6.50

SLOVAKIA

slō-'vä-kē-ə

LOCATION — Central Europe

GOVT. — Independent republic

AREA — 18,932 sq. mi.

POP. — 5,296,768 (est. 1992)

CAPITAL — Bratislava

Formerly a province of Czechoslovakia, Slovakia declared its independence in Mar., 1939. A treaty was immediately concluded with Germany guaranteeing Slovakian independence but providing for German "protection" for 25 years.

100 Halierov = 1 Koruna

Catalogue values for unused stamps in this country are for never hinged items, beginning with Scott 26 in the regular postage section, Scott B1 in the semi-postal section, Scott C1 in the airmail section, Scott EX1 in the personal delivery section, Scott J1 in the postage due section, and Scott P10 in the newspaper section.

Watermark

Wmk. 263 — Double-Barred Cross Multiple

Stamps of Czechoslovakia, 1928-39, Overprinted in Red or Blue

1939 *Perf. 10, 12½, 12x12½*

2	A29	5h	dk ultra	1.00	.90
3	A29	10h	brown	.20	.20
4	A29	20h	red (Bl)	.20	.20
5	A29	25h	green	5.00	4.00
6	A29	30h	red violet (Bl)	.20	.20
7	A61a	40h	dark blue	.20	.20
8	A73	50h	deep green	.20	.20
9	A63	50h	deep green	.20	.20
10	A63	60h	dull violet	.20	.20
11	A63	60h	dull blue	8.00	*8.75*
12	A60	1k	rose lake (Bl) (On No. 212)	.20	.20

Overprinted Diagonally

13	A64	1.20k	rose lilac (Bl)	1.00	1.00
14	A65	1.50k	carmine (Bl)	1.00	1.00
15	A79	1.60k	olive grn (Bl)	1.75	*2.50*
16	A66	2k	dk blue green	1.75	*2.50*
17	A67	2.50k	dark blue	1.00	1.00
18	A68	3k	brown	1.00	1.00
19	A69	3.50k	dk violet	22.50	22.50
20	A69	3.50k	dk violet (Bl)	30.00	30.00
21	A70	4k	dk violet	10.00	10.00
22	A71	5k	green	15.00	*15.00*
23	A72	10k	blue	125.00	125.00
			Nos. 2-23 (22)	225.60	*226.75*

Excellent counterfeit overprints exist.

Andrej Hlinka

A1 A2

Overprinted in Red or Blue

Perf. 12½

1939, Apr. Unwmk. Photo.

24	A1	50h dark green (R)	.40	.40
a.		Perf. 10½	4.00	2.00
b.		Perf. 10½x12½	20.00	10.00
25	A1	1k dk car rose (Bl)	60.00	50.00
a.		Perf. 10½	650.00	—
		Never hinged	800.00	
b.		Perf. 10½x12½	25.00	15.00

Catalogue values for unused stamps in this section, from this point to the end of the section, are for Never Hinged items.

1939 Unwmk. *Perf. 12½*

26	A2	5h	brt ultra	.50	*.45*
27	A2	10h	olive green	.80	*.65*
a.			Perf. 10½x12½	80.00	50.00
b.			Perf. 10½	250.00	80.00
28	A2	20h	orange red	.80	*.65*
a.			Imperf.	.85	*.80*
29	A2	30h	dp violet	.80	*.65*
a.			Imperf.	1.00	*1.25*
b.			Perf. 10½x12½	20.00	10.00
c.			Perf. 10½	25.00	12.00
30	A2	50h	dk green	.80	*.65*
31	A2	1k	dk carmine rose	1.00	*.65*
32	A2	2.50k	brt blue	1.00	.30
a.			Perf. 10½x12½	100.00	70.00
33	A2	3k	black brown	3.00	.50
a.			Perf. 10½x12½	10.00	5.00
b.			Perf. 10½	3.00	1.50
			Nos. 26-33 (8)	8.70	*4.50*

On Nos. 32 and 33 a pearl frame surrounds the medallion. See Nos. 55-57, and 69 in the Scott Standard Catalogue, Vol. 5.

General Stefánik and Memorial Tomb — A3

Rev. Josef Murgas and Radio Towers — A4

1939, May *Perf. 12½*

Size: 25x20mm

34	A3	40h dark blue	.90
35	A3	60h slate green	.90
36	A3	1k gray violet	.90

Size: 30x23¾mm

37	A3	2k bl vio & sepia	1.25
		Nos. 34-37 (4)	3.95

20th anniv. of the death of Gen. Milan Stefánik, but not issued.

1939 Unwmk.

38	A4	60h purple	.25	.30
39	A4	1.20k slate black	.50	.20

10th anniv. of the death of Rev. Josef Murgas. See No. 65 in the Scott Standard Catalogue, Vol. 5.

Girl Embroidering A5

Woodcutter A6

Girl at Spring — A7

1939-44 Wmk. 263 *Perf. 12½*

40	A5	2k	dk blue green	6.25	.50
41	A6	4k	copper brown	1.40	1.00
42	A7	5k	orange red	1.00	.50
a.			Perf. 10 ('44)	1.25	1.00
			Nos. 40-42 (3)	8.65	2.00

Dr. Josef Tiso — A8

Presidential Residence — A9

1939-44 Wmk. 263 *Perf. 12½*

43	A8	50h slate green	.45	.30
43A	A8	70h dk red brn ('42)	.30	.20
b.		Perf. 10½ ('44)	.50	.35

See No. 88.

1940, Mar. 14

44	A9	10k deep blue	1.00	.75

Tatra Mountains A10

Krivan Peak A11

Edelweiss in the Tatra Mountains A12

Chamois A13

Church at Javorina — A14

1940-43 Wmk. 263 *Perf. 12½*

Size: 17x21mm

45	A10	5h dk olive grn	.25	.20
46	A11	10h deep brown	.20	.20
47	A12	20h blue black	.20	.20
48	A13	25h olive brown	.45	.25

49	A14	30h chestnut brown	.30	.25
a.		Perf. 10½ ('43)	2.50	1.00
		Nos. 45-49 (5)	1.40	1.10

See Nos. 84-87, 103-107 in the Scott Standard Catalogue, Vol. 5.

Hlinka Type of 1939

1940-42 Wmk. 263 *Perf. 12½*

55	A2	1k dk car rose	.80	.60
56	A2	2.50k brt blue ('42)	1.00	.75
a.		Perf. 10½	.60	.60
57	A2	3k black brn ('41)	1.00	1.00
a.		Perf. 10½	1.00	.90

On Nos. 56 and 57 a pearl frame surrounds the medallion.

SEMI-POSTAL STAMPS

Catalogue values for unused stamps in this section are for Never Hinged items.

Josef Tiso — SP1

Wmk. 263

1939, Nov. 6 Photo. *Perf. 12½*

B1	SP1	2.50k + 2.50k royal blue	3.25	*3.50*

The surtax was used for Child Welfare.

AIR POST STAMPS

Catalogue values for unused stamps in this section are for Never Hinged items.

Planes over Tatra Mountains
AP1 AP2

Perf. 12½

1939, Nov. 20 Photo. Unwmk.

C1	AP1	30h violet	.35	.35
C2	AP1	50h dark green	.35	.35
C3	AP1	1k vermilion	.35	.35
C4	AP2	2k grnsh black	.55	.55
C5	AP2	3k dark brown	.80	.80
C6	AP2	4k slate blue	1.60	1.60
		Nos. C1-C6 (6)	4.00	*4.00*

See No. C10 in the Scott Standard Catalogue, Vol. 5.

Plane in Flight — AP3

1940, Nov. 30 Wmk. 263 *Perf. 12½*

C7	AP3	5k dk violet brn	1.40	1.40
C8	AP3	10k gray black	1.60	1.60
C9	AP3	20k myrtle green	2.00	2.00
		Nos. C7-C9 (3)	5.00	*5.00*

PERSONAL DELIVERY STAMPS

Catalogue values for unused stamps in this section are for Never Hinged items.

PD1

1940 Wmk. 263 Photo. *Imperf.*

EX1	PD1	50h indigo & blue	.90	*1.60*
EX2	PD1	50h carmine & rose	.90	*1.60*

POSTAGE DUE STAMPS

Catalogue values for unused stamps in this section are for Never Hinged items.

D1

Letter, Post Horn — D2

1939 Unwmk. Photo. *Perf. 12½*

J1	D1	5h bright blue	1.00	.55
J2	D1	10h bright blue	.50	.55
J3	D1	20h bright blue	.50	.55
J4	D1	30h bright blue	3.00	1.00
J5	D1	40h bright blue	.70	.75
J6	D1	50h bright blue	2.50	.80
J7	D1	60h bright blue	2.00	.80
J8	D1	1k dark carmine	14.00	8.25
J9	D1	2k dark carmine	14.00	2.50
J10	D1	5k dark carmine	8.00	2.50
J11	D1	10k dark carmine	55.00	7.50
J12	D1	20k dark carmine	18.00	9.25
		Nos. J1-J12 (12)	119.20	35.00

1940-41 Wmk. 263

J13	D1	5h bright blue ('41)	.75	.55
J14	D1	10h bright blue ('41)	.30	.30
J15	D1	20h bright blue ('41)	.50	.30
J16	D1	30h bright blue ('41)	4.00	2.00
J17	D1	40h bright blue ('41)	.60	.55
J18	D1	50h bright blue ('41)	.75	.95
J19	D1	60h bright blue	.90	.95
J20	D1	1k dark carmine ('41)	.90	1.10
J21	D1	2k dark carmine ('41)	20.00	9.00
J22	D1	5k dark carmine ('41)	4.00	2.75
J23	D1	10k dark carmine ('41)	3.00	3.25
		Nos. J13-J23 (11)	35.70	21.70

NEWSPAPER STAMPS

Newspaper Stamps of Czechoslovakia, 1937, Overprinted in Red or Blue

1939, Apr. Unwmk. *Imperf.*

P1	N2	2h bister brn (Bl)	.30	*.40*
P2	N2	5h dull blue (R)	.30	*.40*
P3	N2	7h red org (Bl)	.30	*.40*
P4	N2	9h emerald (R)	.30	*.40*
P5	N2	10h henna brn (Bl)	.30	*.40*
P6	N2	12h ultra (R)	.30	*.40*
P7	N2	20h dk green (R)	.60	*.85*
P8	N2	50h dk brown (Bl)	2.00	*2.50*
P9	N2	1k grnsh gray (R)	10.00	*12.00*
		Nos. P1-P9 (9)	14.40	*17.75*

Excellent counterfeits exist of Nos. P1-P9.

Catalogue values for unused stamps in this section, from this point to the end of the section, are for Never Hinged items.

Arms of Slovakia
N1

Type Block "N" (for "Noviny" - Newspaper)
N2

1939 Typo.

P10	N1	2h ocher	.20	*.20*
P11	N1	5h ultra	.25	*.40*
P12	N1	7h red orange	.20	*.30*
P13	N1	9h emerald	.20	*.30*
P14	N1	10h henna brown	.95	1.10
P15	N1	12h dk ultra	.20	*.35*
P16	N1	20h dark green	.95	1.10
P17	N1	50h red brown	1.10	1.25
P18	N1	1k grnsh gray	1.10	1.10
		Nos. P10-P18 (9)	5.15	6.10

1940-41 Wmk. 263

P20	N1	5h ultra	.20	.20
P23	N1	10h henna brown	.20	.20
P24	N1	15h brt purple ('41)	.20	.20
P25	N1	20h dark green	.35	.35
P26	N1	25h lt blue ('41)	.35	.35
P27	N1	40h red org ('41)	.35	.35
P28	N1	50h chocolate	.60	.55
P29	N1	1k grnsh gray ('41)	.60	.55
P30	N1	2k emerald ('41)	1.25	1.40
		Nos. P20-P30 (9)	4.10	4.15

SOLOMON ISLANDS

'sä-lə-mən 'ī-lənds

British Solomon Islands

LOCATION — West Pacific Ocean, east of Papua
GOVT. — British Protectorate
AREA — 11,500 sq. mi.
POP. — 258,193 (1984)
CAPITAL — Honiara

The Solomons include 10 large islands and four groups of small islands extending over an area of 375,000 square miles.

12 Pence = 1 Shilling
20 Shillings = 1 Pound

Catalogue values for unused stamps in this country are for Never Hinged items, beginning with Scott 80 in the regular postage section.

War Canoe — A1

Unwmk.

1907, Feb. 14 Litho. *Perf. 11*

1	A1	½p ultra	10.50	*16.00*
2	A1	1p red	26.00	*30.00*
3	A1	2p dull blue	32.50	*35.00*
a.		Horiz. pair, imperf. btwn.	*12,500.*	
4	A1	2½p orange	37.50	*47.50*
a.		Vert. pair, imperf. btwn.	*4,500.*	
b.		Horiz. pair, imperf. btwn.	*6,250.*	*4,750.*
5	A1	5p yellow green	65.00	*77.50*
6	A1	6p chocolate	60.00	*72.50*
a.		Vertical pair, imperf. btwn.	*4,250.*	
7	A1	1sh violet	85.00	*90.00*
		Nos. 1-7 (7)	316.50	368.50

Imperf. between varieties should be accompanied by certificates of authenticity issued by competent authorities. Excellent counterfeits are plentiful.

War Canoe
A2

George V
A3

Wmk. Multiple Crown and CA (3)

1908-11 Engr. *Perf. 14*

8	A2	½p green	1.75	1.10
9	A2	1p carmine	1.50	1.10
10	A2	2p gray	1.50	1.10
11	A2	2½p ultra	4.25	2.25
12	A2	4p red, *yel* ('11)	3.75	12.50
13	A2	5p olive green	10.50	8.00
14	A2	6p claret	11.50	7.50
15	A2	1sh black, *green*	9.75	*8.00*
16	A2	2sh vio, *bl* ('10)	47.50	*65.00*
17	A2	2sh6p red, *bl* ('10)	57.50	*85.00*
18	A2	5sh bl, *yel* ('10)	90.00	*120.00*
		Nos. 8-18 (11)	239.50	*311.55*
		Set, ovptd. "SPECIMEN"	290.00	

Inscribed "POSTAGE - POSTAGE"

1913-24 Typo.

19	A3	½p green	.95	*4.00*
20	A3	1p carmine	1.75	*16.00*
21	A3	3p violet, *yel*	1.00	*4.75*
a.		3p violet, *orange buff*	9.25	*27.50*
22	A3	11p dull violet & red	5.75	*13.50*

Wmk. 4

23	A3	1½p scarlet ('24)	2.50	.80
		Nos. 19-23 (5)	11.95	*39.05*
		Nos. 19-22, ovptd. "SPECIMEN"	80.00	

Inscribed "POSTAGE - REVENUE"

1914-23 Wmk. 3

28	A3	½p green	.95	*13.50*
a.		½p yellow green ('17)	5.25	*21.00*
29	A3	1p carmine	1.75	1.50
a.		1p scarlet ('17)	5.50	*7.50*
30	A3	2p gray	3.50	*10.50*
31	A3	2½p ultra	2.25	*5.75*

Chalky Paper

32	A3	3p violet, *yel* ('23)	22.50	*97.50*
33	A3	4p blk & red, *yel*	2.25	3.00
34	A3	5p dull vio & ol grn	22.50	*35.00*
a.		5p brown purple & olive green	22.50	*35.00*
35	A3	6p dull vio & red vio	7.00	*16.00*
36	A3	1sh blk, *green*	5.50	*8.00*
a.		1sh blk, *bl grn, ol back*	8.50	*27.50*
37	A3	2sh dull vio & ultra, *bl*	8.00	*11.50*
38	A3	2sh6p blk & red, *bl*	11.00	*22.50*
39	A3	5sh grn & red, *yel*	37.50	*55.00*
a.		5sh green & red, *orange buff*	52.50	*80.00*
40	A3	10sh grn & red, *grn*	95.00	*92.50*
41	A3	£1 vio & blk, *red*	275.00	140.00
		Nos. 28-41 (14)	494.70	*512.25*
		Set, ovptd. "SPECIMEN"	450.00	

Inscribed "POSTAGE - REVENUE"

1922-31 Wmk. 4

43	A3	½p green	.40	*4.00*
44	A3	1p carmine ('23)	12.50	12.50
45	A3	1p violet ('27)	1.10	*8.50*
46	A3	2p gray ('23)	4.50	*17.00*
47	A3	3p ultra ('23)	.85	*5.25*

Chalky Paper

48	A3	4p blk & red, *yel* ('27)	4.00	*26.00*
49	A3	4½p red brn ('31)	3.50	*22.50*
50	A3	5p dull vio & ol grn	3.50	*30.00*
51	A3	6p dull vio & red vio	4.25	*30.00*
52	A3	1sh black, *emer*	3.25	*14.00*
53	A3	2sh dull vio & ultra, *bl* ('27)	9.25	*42.50*
54	A3	2sh6p blk & red, *bl*	8.50	*45.00*
55	A3	5sh grn & red, *yel*	30.00	*62.50*
56	A3	10sh grn & red, *emer* ('25)	110.00	*110.00*
		Nos. 43-56 (14)	195.60	*429.75*

No. 49 is on ordinary paper.

Common Design Types
pictured following the introduction.

Silver Jubilee Issue
Common Design Type

1935, May 6 Engr. *Perf. 13½x14*

60	CD301	1½p car & dk bl	1.25	1.00
61	CD301	3p blue & brown	3.50	*6.50*
62	CD301	6p ol grn & lt bl	10.50	*13.00*
63	CD301	1sh brt vio & ind	8.50	*12.00*
		Nos. 60-63 (4)	23.75	32.50
		Set, never hinged	42.50	
		Set, perforated "SPECIMEN"	110.00	

Coronation Issue
Common Design Type

1937, May 13 *Perf. 11x11½*

64	CD302	1p dark purple	.25	*.60*
65	CD302	1½p dark carmine	.25	*.50*
66	CD302	3p deep ultra	.40	*.40*
		Nos. 64-66 (3)	.90	1.50
		Set, never hinged	1.25	
		Set, perforated "SPECIMEN"	80.00	

Spears and Shield — A4

Policeman and Chief — A5

Artificial Island, Malaita — A6

Canoe House, New Georgia A7

Roviana War Canoe — A8

View of Munda Point — A9

Meeting House, Reef Islands A10

Coconut Plantation A11

Breadfruit A12

Tinakula Volcano, Santa Cruz Islands A13

Scrub Fowl — A14

Malaita Canoe — A15

Perf. 12½, 13½ (A7, A13, A14)

1939-51 Wmk. 4

67	A4	½p deep grn & ultra	.20	*1.10*
		Never hinged	.25	
68	A5	1p dk pur & choc	.20	*1.75*
		Never hinged	.30	
69	A6	1½p car & sl grn	.30	*1.50*
		Never hinged	.55	
70	A7	2p blk & org brn	.35	*1.60*
		Never hinged	.70	
a.		2p black & red brown ('43)	.35	*1.75*
		Never hinged	.65	
b.		Perf. 12 ('51)	.20	*1.60*
		Never hinged	.35	
71	A8	2½p ol grn & rose vio	1.00	*2.50*
		Never hinged	1.50	
a.		Vert. pair, imperf. horiz.	*11,500.*	
72	A9	3p ultra & blk, perf. 13½	.55	*1.75*
		Never hinged	.90	
a.		Perf. 12 ('51)	.85	*2.75*
		Never hinged	1.75	
73	A10	4½p dk brn & yel grn	3.25	*14.00*
		Never hinged	5.00	
74	A11	6p rose lil & dk pur	.30	*1.10*
		Never hinged	.60	
75	A12	1sh blk & grn	.70	*1.10*
		Never hinged	1.25	
76	A13	2sh dp org & blk	4.25	*4.50*
		Never hinged	6.50	
a.		2sh dp org & vio blk ('43)	4.25	*5.00*
		Never hinged	5.50	
77	A14	2sh6p dull vio & blk	17.00	6.00
		Never hinged	25.00	
78	A15	5sh red & brt bl grn	20.00	13.00
		Never hinged	30.00	
79	A10	10sh red lil & ol ('42)	6.00	*9.50*
		Never hinged	6.50	
		Nos. 67-79 (13)	54.10	59.40
		Set, never hinged	100.00	

Catalogue values for unused stamps in this section, from this point to the end of the section, are for Never Hinged items.

Peace Issue
Common Design Type
Perf. 13½x14

1946, Oct. 15 Wmk. 4 Engr.

80	CD303	1½p carmine	.20	.70
81	CD303	3p deep blue	.20	.30
		Set, perforated "SPECIMEN"	70.00	

Silver Wedding Issue
Common Design Types

1949, Mar. 14 Photo. *Perf. 14x14½*

82	CD304	2p black	.40	.40

Perf. 11½x11
Engr.; Name Typo.

83	CD305	10sh red violet	17.50	13.50

UPU Issue
Common Design Types
Engr.; Name Typo. on 3p and 5p
Perf. 13½, 11x11½

1949, Oct. 10 Wmk. 4

84	CD306	2p red brown	1.00	.85
85	CD307	3p indigo	2.40	.85
86	CD308	5p green	1.00	*1.25*
87	CD309	1sh slate	1.00	.85
		Nos. 84-87 (4)	5.40	3.80

POSTAGE DUE STAMPS

D1

Perf. 12

1940, Sept. 1 Typo. Wmk. 4

J1	D1	1p emerald	4.00	*7.25*
J2	D1	2p dark red	4.25	*7.25*
J3	D1	3p chocolate	4.25	*12.00*
J4	D1	4p dark blue	6.50	*12.00*
J5	D1	5p deep green	7.25	*22.50*
J6	D1	6p brt red vio	7.25	*17.50*
J7	D1	1sh dull violet	9.00	*27.50*
J8	D1	1sh6p turq green	16.00	*50.00*
		Nos. J1-J8 (8)	58.50	*156.00*
		Set, never hinged	100.00	
		Set, perforated "SPECIMEN"	175.00	

SOMALIA

sō-'mä-lē-ə

(Italian Somaliland)

(Benadir)

LOCATION — Eastern Africa, bordering on the Indian Ocean and the Gulf of Aden
GOVT. — Italian Colony
AREA — 246,201 sq. mi.
POP. — 3,862,000 (est. 1982)
CAPITAL — Mogadiscio

The former Italian colony which included the territory west of the Juba River became known as Oltre Giuba (Trans-Juba), was absorbed into Italian East Africa in 1936.

4 Besas = 1 Anna
16 Annas = 1 Rupee
100 Besas = 1 Rupee (1922)
100 Centesimi = 1 Lira (1905, 1925)

Used values in italics are for postally used Italian Somalia stamps. CTO's sell for about the same as unused, hinged stamps.

Watermark

Wmk. 140 — Crown

Italian Somaliland

Elephant — A1

Lion — A2

Wmk. 140

1903, Oct. 12 Typo. *Perf. 14*

1	A1	1b brown	52.50	12.00
		Never hinged	130.00	
		On cover		225.00
2	A1	2b blue green	1.50	*7.50*
		Never hinged	3.75	
		On cover		165.00
3	A2	1a claret	1.50	*9.00*
		Never hinged	3.75	
		On cover		225.00
4	A2	2a orange brown	1.75	*16.00*
		Never hinged	4.50	
		On cover		325.00
5	A2	2½a blue	1.50	*16.00*
		Never hinged	3.75	
		On cover		600.00
6	A2	5a orange	1.75	*37.50*
		Never hinged	4.50	
		On cover		1,350.
7	A2	10a lilac	1.75	*37.50*
		Never hinged	4.50	
		On cover		—
		Nos. 1-7 (7)	62.25	*135.50*
		Set on overfranked cover		*600.00*

Covers: Cover values are for properly franked and traveled covers. Overpaid and other philatelic souvenirs sell for much less.

For surcharges see Nos. 8-27, 40-50, 70-77.

Surcharged

1905, Dec. 29

8	A2	15c on 5a orange	*3,000.*	825.00
		Never hinged	3,750.	
		On cover		2,750.
9	A2	40c on 10a lilac	600.00	250.00
		Never hinged	1,200.	
		On cover		2,000.

Covers: Cover values are for properly franked and traveled covers, generally abroad. Internal covers, normally overpaid and not traveled, and other philatelic souvenirs sell for much less.

Surcharged

1906-07

10	A1	2c on 1b brown	6.00	*15.00*
		Never hinged	15.00	
		On cover		165.00
11	A1	5c on 2b blue grn	6.00	10.50
		Never hinged	15.00	
		On cover		80.00
a.		Double surcharge	300.00	
b.		Double surcharge, one invtd.		*3,000.*
c.		Pair, one without surcharge	*3,000.*	

Surcharges on No. 11c are virtually on top of top of each other. Certificates are necessary.

Surcharged

12	A2	10c on 1a claret	6.00	10.50
		Never hinged	15.00	
		On cover		80.00
13	A2	15c on 2a brn org ('06)	6.00	10.50
		Never hinged	15.00	
		On cover		95.00
14	A2	25c on 2½a blue	15.00	10.50
		Never hinged	37.50	
		On cover		110.00
15	A2	50c on 5a yellow	22.50	26.00
		Never hinged	55.00	
		On cover		225.00

Surcharged

16 A2 1 l on 10a lilac 22.50 *32.50*
Never hinged 55.00
On cover 525.00
Nos. 10-16 (7) 84.00 *115.50*

Covers: Cover values are for properly franked and traveled covers. Overpaid and other philatelic souvenirs sell for much less.

Nos. 15 and 16 with bars over former Surcharge and

1916, Apr.
18 A2 5c on 50c on 5a yel 32.50 37.50
Never hinged 82.50
On cover 225.00
a. Double surcharge, one invtd. 2,750.
b. Lower left bar of surcharge omitted 90.00
19 A2 20c on 1 l on 10a dl lil 9.00 *30.00*
Never hinged 22.50
On cover 140.00
a. Bar of surcharge at top of stamp 120.00 120.00
b. Bar of surcharge omitted 475.00

No. 4 Surcharged

20 A2 20c on 2a org brn 18.00 11.00
Never hinged 45.00
Nos. 18-20 (3) 59.50 *78.50*

Nos. 11-16 Surcharged:

a

b

1922, Feb. 1
22 A1(a) 3b on 5c on 2b 10.50 *19.00*
Never hinged 26.00
On cover 100.00
23 A2(b) 6c on 10c on 1a 18.00 15.00
Never hinged 45.00
On cover 120.00
24 A2(b) 9b on 15c on 2a 18.00 19.00
Never hinged 45.00
On cover 120.00
25 A2(b) 15b on 25c on 2½a 18.00 15.00
Never hinged 45.00
On cover 165.00
26 A2(b) 30b on 50c on 5a 20.00 *37.50*
Never hinged 50.00
On cover 225.00
27 A2(b) 60b on 1 l on 10a 20.00 *67.50*
Never hinged 50.00
On cover 475.00
Nos. 22-27 (6) 104.50 *173.00*

Victory Issue

Italy Nos. 136-139 Surcharged

1922, Apr. ***Perf. 14***
28 A64 3b on 5c olive grn 1.75 *6.75*
Never hinged 4.50
On cover 90.00
29 A64 6b on 10c red 1.75 *6.75*
Never hinged 4.50
On cover 150.00
30 A64 9b on 15c slate grn 1.75 *10.50*
Never hinged 4.50
On cover 165.00
31 A64 15b on 25c ultra 1.75 *10.50*
Never hinged 4.50
On cover 200.00
Nos. 28-31 (4) 7.00 *34.50*

Perf. 14x13½

28a A64 3b on 5c olive grn 4.50 *14.50*
Never hinged 9.00
29a A64 6b on 10c red 4.50 *14.50*
Never hinged 9.00
30a A64 9b on 15c slate grn 4.50 *22.50*
Never hinged 9.00
31a A64 15b on 25c ultra 4.50 *22.50*
Never hinged 9.00
Nos. 28a-31a (4) 18.00 *74.00*

Perf. 13½

29b A64 6b on 10c red 110.00
Never hinged 225.00
31b A64 15b on 25c ultra 110.00
Never hinged 225.00

Nos. 10-16 Surcharged with Bars and

c

d

1923, July 1
40 A1 1b brown 9.00 *27.50*
Never hinged 22.50
On cover 165.00
41 A1(c) 2b on 2c on 1b 9.00 *27.50*
Never hinged 22.50
On cover 110.00
42 A1(c) 3b on 2c on 1b 9.00 *16.00*
Never hinged 22.50
On cover 110.00
43 A2(d) 5b on 50c on 5a 9.00 *15.00*
Never hinged 22.50
On cover 82.50
44 A1(c) 6b on 5c on 2b 13.50 15.00
Never hinged 32.50
On cover 90.00
45 A2(d) 18b on 10c on 1a 13.50 15.00
Never hinged 32.50
On cover 120.00
46 A2(d) 20b on 15c on 2a 16.00 15.00
Never hinged 40.00
On cover 165.00
47 A2(d) 25b on 15c on 2a 16.00 15.00
Never hinged 40.00
On cover 165.00
48 A2(d) 30b on 25c on 2½a 18.00 15.00
Never hinged 45.00
On cover 165.00
49 A2(d) 60b on 1 l on 10a 18.00 *40.00*
Never hinged 45.00
On cover 300.00
50 A2(d) 1r on 1 l on 10a 45.00 *52.50*
Never hinged 110.00
On cover 475.00
Nos. 40-50 (11) 176.00 *253.50*

No. 40 is No. 10 with bars over the 1907 surcharge.

Propagation of the Faith Issue

Italy Nos. 143-146 Surcharged

1923, Oct. 24 **Wmk. 140**
51 A68 6b on 20c ol grn & brn org 7.50 *37.50*
Never hinged 18.50
On cover —
52 A68 13b on 30c cl & brn org 7.50 *37.50*
Never hinged 18.50
On cover —
53 A68 20b on 50c vio & brn org 4.50 *45.00*
Never hinged 11.00
On cover —
54 A68 30b on 1 l bl & brn org 4.50 *55.00*
Never hinged 11.00
On cover —
Nos. 51-54 (4) 24.00 *175.00*

Fascisti Issue

Italy Nos. 159-164 Surcharged in Red or Black

1923, Oct. 29 **Unwmk.** ***Perf. 14***
55 A69 3b on 10c dk grn (R) 9.00 *13.00*
Never hinged 22.50
On cover 190.00
56 A69 13b on 30c dk vio (R) 9.00 *13.00*
Never hinged 22.50
On cover 190.00
57 A69 20b on 50c brn car 9.00 *15.00*
Never hinged 22.50
On cover 190.00

Wmk. 140

58 A70 30b on 1 l blue 9.00 *37.50*
Never hinged 22.50
On cover 325.00
59 A70 1r on 2 l brown 9.00 *45.00*
Never hinged 22.50
On cover 475.00
60 A71 3r on 5 l blk & bl (R) 9.00 *60.00*
Never hinged 22.50
On cover —
Nos. 55-60 (6) 54.00 *183.50*
Set on overfranked philatelic cover *475.00*

Manzoni Issue

Italy Nos. 165-170 Surcharged in Red

1924, Apr. 1
61 A72 6b on 10c brn red & blk 12.00 *37.50*
Never hinged 30.00
62 A72 9b on 15c bl grn & blk 12.00 *37.50*
Never hinged 30.00
63 A72 13b on 30c blk & sl 12.00 *37.50*
Never hinged 30.00
64 A72 20b on 50c org brn & blk 12.00 *37.50*
Never hinged 30.00

Surcharged

65 A72 30b on 1 l bl & blk 75.00 *250.00*
Never hinged 190.00
66 A72 3r on 5 l vio & blk 475.00 *2,000.*
Never hinged 1,200.
Nos. 61-66 (6) 598.00 *2,400.*

Covers bearing stamps of this issue are very scarce.

Victor Emmanuel Issue

Italy Nos. 175-177 Overprinted

1925-26 **Unwmk.** ***Perf. 13½, 11***
67 A78 60c brown car 1.50 *7.50*
Never hinged 3.75
On cover 120.00
a. Perf. 11 90.00 *150.00*
Never hinged 225.00
On cover 375.00
68 A78 1 l dk bl, perf. 11 2.25 *11.00*
Never hinged 5.50
On cover 190.00
a. Perf. 13½ 7.50 *37.50*
Never hinged 19.00
On cover 375.00
69 A78 1.25 l dk blue ('26) 1.50 *18.00*
Never hinged 3.75
On cover 260.00
a. Perf. 11 600.00 *825.00*
Never hinged 1,200.
On cover 2,000.
Nos. 67-69 (3) 5.25 *36.50*

Stamps of 1907-16 with Bars over Original Values

1926, Mar. 1 **Wmk. 140** ***Perf. 14***
70 A1 2c on 1b brown 20.00 *45.00*
Never hinged 50.00
On cover 190.00
71 A1 5c on 2b blue grn 15.00 *22.50*
Never hinged 37.50
On cover 110.00
72 A2 10c on 1a rose red 9.00 7.50
Never hinged 22.50
On cover 90.00
73 A2 15c on 2a org brn 9.00 10.50
Never hinged 22.50
On cover 110.00
74 A2 20c on 2a org brn 10.50 10.50
Never hinged 26.00
On cover 90.00
75 A2 25c on 2½a blue 10.50 *15.00*
Never hinged 26.00
On cover 140.00
76 A2 50c on 5a yellow 15.00 *26.00*
Never hinged 37.50
On cover 225.00
77 A2 1 l on 10a dull lil 20.00 *37.50*
Never hinged 50.00
On cover 400.00
Nos. 70-77 (8) 109.00 *174.50*

Saint Francis of Assisi Issue

Italy Nos. 178-180 Overprinted

1926, Apr. 12 ***Perf. 14***
78 A79 20c gray green 2.25 *10.50*
Never hinged 5.50
On cover 97.50
79 A80 40c dark violet 2.25 *10.50*
Never hinged 5.50
On cover 110.00
80 A81 60c red brown 2.25 *18.00*
Never hinged 5.50
On cover 110.00

Italy Nos. 182 and Type of 1926 Overprinted in Red

Unwmk. ***Perf. 11***
81 A82 1.25 l dark blue 2.25 *26.00*
Never hinged 5.50
On cover 200.00

Perf. 14

82 A83 5 l + 2.50 l ol grn 6.00 *52.50*
Never hinged 15.00
On cover —
Nos. 78-82 (5) 15.00 *117.50*
Set on overfranked philatelic cover *340.00*

Italian Stamps of 1901-26 Overprinted

1926-30 **Wmk. 140**
83 A43 2c orange brown 3.75 6.00
Never hinged 9.25
On cover 47.50
84 A48 5c green 3.75 6.00
Never hinged 9.25
On cover 40.00
85 A48 10c claret 3.00 .35
Never hinged 7.50
On cover 40.00
86 A49 20c violet brown 3.00 2.25
Never hinged 7.50
On cover 75.00
87 A46 25c grn & pale grn 3.00 1.50
Never hinged 7.50
On cover 52.50
88 A49 30c gray ('30) 13.50 *30.00*
Never hinged 32.50
On cover 190.00
89 A49 60c brown orange 4.50 9.00
Never hinged 11.00
On cover 225.00
a. Double overprint 2,750.

90 A46 75c dk red & rose 97.50 30.00
Never hinged 240.00
On cover 200.00
91 A46 1 l brown & grn 4.50 .75
Never hinged 11.00
On cover 82.50
92 A46 1.25 l blue & ultra 10.50 2.25
Never hinged 26.00
On cover 165.00
93 A46 2 l dk grn & org 22.50 13.50
Never hinged 55.00
On cover 375.00
94 A46 2.50 l dk grn & org 22.50 18.00
Never hinged 55.00
On cover 475.00
95 A46 5 l blue & rose 60.00 37.50
Never hinged 150.00
On cover 1,900.
96 A51 10 l gray grn & red 60.00 60.00
Never hinged 150.00
On cover —
Nos. 83-96 (14) 312.00 217.10

Volta Issue

Type of Italy, 1927, Overprinted

1927, Oct. 10
97 A84 20c purple 4.50 *30.00*
Never hinged 11.00
On cover 165.00
98 A84 50c deep orange 7.50 *18.00*
Never hinged 19.00
On cover 165.00
a. Double overprint 160.00
Never hinged 340.00
99 A84 1.25 l brt blue 10.50 *47.50*
Never hinged 26.00
On cover 300.00
Nos. 97-99 (3) 22.50 *95.50*
Set on overfranked philatelic cover *300.00*

Italian Stamps of 1927-28 Overprinted in Black or Red

1928-30
100 A86 7½c lt brown 18.00 *52.50*
Never hinged 45.00
On cover 225.00
a. Double overprint 400.00
Never hinged 850.00
101 A85 50c brn & sl (R) 18.00 6.00
Never hinged 45.00
On cover 45.00
102 A86 50c brt violet ('30) 37.50 *52.50*
Never hinged 92.50
On cover 120.00

Perf. 11
Unwmk.
103 A85 1.75 l deep brown 70.00 18.00
Never hinged 175.00
On cover 67.50
Nos. 100-103 (4) 143.50 *129.00*

Monte Cassino Issue

Types of Monte Cassino Issue of Italy Overprinted in Red or Blue

1929, Oct. 14 Wmk. 140 *Perf. 14*
104 A96 20c dk green (R) 4.50 *16.00*
Never hinged 11.00
On cover 190.00
105 A96 25c red org (Bl) 4.50 *16.00*
Never hinged 11.00
On cover 140.00
106 A98 50c + 10c crim (Bl) 4.50 *18.00*
Never hinged 11.00
On cover 100.00
107 A98 75c + 15c ol brn (R) 4.50 *18.00*
Never hinged 11.00
On cover 190.00
108 A96 1.25 l + 25c dk vio (R) 10.50 *32.50*
Never hinged 26.00
On cover 240.00
109 A98 5 l + 1 l saph (R) 10.50 *37.50*
Never hinged 26.00
On cover —

Overprinted in Red

Unwmk.
110 A100 10 l + 2 l gray brn 10.50 *52.50*
Never hinged 26.00
On cover —
Nos. 104-110 (7) 49.50 *190.50*

Royal Wedding Issue

Type of Italian Royal Wedding Stamps of 1930 Overprinted

1930, Mar. 17 Wmk. 140
111 A101 20c yellow green 1.50 *4.50*
Never hinged 3.75
On cover 95.00
112 A101 50c + 10c dp org 1.10 *7.50*
Never hinged 2.75
On cover 120.00
113 A101 1.25 l + 25c rose red 1.10 *15.00*
Never hinged 2.75
On cover 200.00
Nos. 111-113 (3) 3.70 *27.00*
Set on overfranked philatelic cover *150.00*

Ferrucci Issue

Types of Italian Stamps of 1930 Overprinted in Red or Blue

1930, July 26
114 A102 20c violet (R) 3.00 *3.75*
Never hinged 7.50
On cover 90.00
115 A103 25c dark green (R) 3.00 *3.75*
Never hinged 7.50
On cover 100.00
116 A103 50c black (R) 3.00 *7.50*
Never hinged 7.50
On cover 90.00
117 A103 1.25 l deep blue (R) 3.00 *15.00*
Never hinged 7.50
On cover 225.00
118 A104 5 l + 2 l dp car (bl) 7.50 *26.00*
Never hinged 19.00
On cover —
Nos. 114-118 (5) 19.50 *56.00*
Set on overfranked philatelic cover *200.00*

Virgil Issue

Types of Italian Stamps of 1930 Overprinted in Red or Blue

1930, Dec. 4 Photo. Wmk. 140
119 A106 15c violet blue 1.10 *7.50*
Never hinged 2.75
On cover 100.00
120 A106 20c orange brown 1.10 *3.00*
Never hinged 2.75
On cover 67.50
121 A106 25c dark green 1.10 *3.00*
Never hinged 2.75
On cover 60.00
122 A106 30c lt brown 1.10 *3.00*
Never hinged 2.75
On cover 67.50
123 A106 50c dull violet 1.10 *3.00*
Never hinged 2.75
On cover 52.50
124 A106 75c rose red 1.10 *6.00*
Never hinged 2.75
On cover 140.00
125 A106 1.25 l gray blue 1.10 *7.50*
Never hinged 2.75
On cover 200.00

Engr.
Unwmk.
126 A106 5 l + 1.50 l dk vio 3.25 *37.50*
Never hinged 8.25
On cover —
127 A106 10 l + 2.50 l ol brn 3.25 *55.00*
Never hinged 8.25
On cover —
Nos. 119-127 (9) 14.20 *125.50*
Set on overfranked philatelic cover *375.00*

Saint Anthony of Padua Issue

Types of Italian Stamps of 1931 Overprinted in Blue or Red

1931, May 7 Photo. Wmk. 140
129 A116 20c brown (Bl) 1.50 *16.00*
Never hinged 3.75
On cover 82.50
130 A116 25c green (R) 1.50 *6.00*
Never hinged 3.75
On cover 82.50
131 A118 30c gray brn (Bl) 1.50 *6.00*
Never hinged 3.75
On cover 120.00
132 A118 50c dull vio (Bl) 1.50 *6.00*
Never hinged 3.75
On cover 82.50
133 A120 1.25 l slate bl (R) 1.50 *30.00*
Never hinged 3.75
On cover 250.00

Overprinted in Red or Black

Engr. Unwmk.
134 A121 75c black (R) 1.50 *16.00*
Never hinged 3.75
On cover 225.00
135 A122 5 l + 2.50 l dk brn (Bk) 6.00 *62.50*
Never hinged 6.00
On cover —
Nos. 129-135 (7) 15.00 *142.50*
Set on overfranked philatelic cover *450.00*

Italy Nos. 218, 221 Overprinted in Red

1931 Wmk. 140
136 A94 25c dk green (R) 11.00 *18.00*
Never hinged 27.50
On cover 190.00
137 A95 50c purple (R) 11.00 4.00
Never hinged 27.50
On cover 97.50

Lighthouse at Cape Guardafui — A3

Tower at Mnara Ciromo — A4

Governor's Palace at Mogadishu — A5

Termite Nest — A6

Ostrich — A7

Hippopotamus — A8

Greater Kudu — A9

Lion — A10

1932 Wmk. 140 Photo. *Perf. 12*
138 A3 5c deep brown 6.00 *7.50*
Never hinged 15.00
On cover 47.50
139 A3 7½c violet 9.00 *18.00*
Never hinged 22.50
On cover 140.00
140 A3 10c gray black 11.00 .35
Never hinged 27.50
On cover 4.50
141 A3 15c olive green 4.50 1.10
Never hinged 11.00
On cover 19.00
142 A4 20c carmine 225.00 .35
Never hinged 550.00
On cover 2.25
143 A4 25c deep green 4.50 .35
Never hinged 11.00
On cover 2.25
144 A4 30c dark brown 37.50 1.10
Never hinged 92.50
On cover 6.00
145 A5 35c dark blue 6.00 *11.00*
Never hinged 15.00
On cover 47.50
146 A5 50c violet 300.00 .35
Never hinged 750.00
On cover 2.25
147 A5 75c carmine 6.00 .75
Never hinged 15.00
On cover 11.00
148 A6 1.25 l dark blue 18.00 .75
Never hinged 45.00
On cover 11.00
149 A6 1.75 l red orange 11.00 .75
Never hinged 27.50
On cover 11.00
150 A6 2 l carmine 6.00 .35
Never hinged 15.00
On cover 13.50
151 A7 2.55 l indigo 30.00 *60.00*
Never hinged 75.00
On cover 475.00
152 A7 5 l carmine 18.00 7.50
Never hinged 45.00
On cover 250.00
153 A8 10 l violet 26.00 18.00
Never hinged 65.00
On cover 1,000.
154 A9 20 l dark green 67.50 *82.50*
Never hinged 165.00
On cover —
155 A10 25 l dark blue 67.50 *125.00*
Never hinged 165.00
On cover —
Nos. 138-155 (18) 853.50 335.70
Set, never hinged 2,075.
Set on overfranked philatelic cover *1,200.*

1934-37 *Perf. 14*
138a A3 5c deep brown 2.25 .75
Never hinged 5.50
On cover 7.50
139a A3 7½c violet 2.25 *22.50*
Never hinged 5.50
On cover 82.50
140a A3 10c gray black 2.25 .35
Never hinged 5.50
On cover 2.25
141a A3 15c olive green 2.25 *2.10*
Never hinged 5.50
On cover 18.50
142a A4 20c carmine 2.25 .20
Never hinged 5.50
On cover 5.00
143a A4 25c deep green 2.25 .35
Never hinged 5.50
On cover 3.75
144a A4 30c dark brown 3.75 .35
Never hinged 9.00
On cover 6.00
145a A5 35c dark blue 7.50 *30.00*
Never hinged 18.50
On cover 52.50
146a A5 50c violet 22.50 .35
Never hinged 55.00
On cover 2.25
147a A5 75c carmine 37.50 .35
Never hinged 92.50
On cover 12.00

148a A6 1.25 l dark blue 60.00 1.10
Never hinged 150.00
On cover 12.00
149a A6 1.75 l red orange 150.00 18.00
Never hinged 375.00
On cover 30.00
150a A6 2 l carmine 45.00 .75
Never hinged 110.00
On cover 18.50
151a A7 2.55 l indigo 175.00 450.00
Never hinged 450.00
On cover 1,900.
152a A7 5 l carmine 15.00 3.00
Never hinged 37.50
On cover 100.00
153a A8 10 l violet 150.00 30.00
Never hinged 375.00
On cover 525.00
154a A9 20 l dark green 12,000. 1,350.
Never hinged 15,000.
On cover —
155a A10 25 l dark blue 675.00 400.00
Never hinged 1,650.
On cover —
Nos. 138a-153a,155a (17) 1,354. 960.15
Set, never hinged 3,350.
Set on overfranked philatelic cover 400.00

Eleven denominations in the foregoing series exist perf. 12x14 or 14x12.

Types of 1932 Issue Overprinted in Black or Red

1934, May **Perf. 14**
156 A3 10c brown (Bk) 9.00 18.00
Never hinged 22.50
On cover 250.00
157 A4 25c green 9.00 18.00
Never hinged 22.50
On cover 250.00
158 A5 50c dull vio (Bk) 7.50 18.00
Never hinged 19.00
On cover 190.00
159 A6 1.25 l blue 7.50 18.00
Never hinged 19.00
On cover 300.00
160 A7 5 l brown black 4.25 18.00
Never hinged 22.50
On cover —
161 A8 10 l car rose (Bk) 9.00
Never hinged 22.50
On cover —
162 A9 20 l dull blue 9.00
Never hinged 22.50
On cover —
163 A10 25 l dark green 9.00
Never hinged 22.50
On cover —
Nos. 156-163 (8) 64.25 90.00
Set, never hinged 160.00
Set on overfranked philatelic cover(s) 400.00

Duke of the Abruzzi (Luigi Amadeo, 1873-1933).

Mother and Child A11

1934, Oct.
164 A11 5c ol grn & brn 3.75 18.00
Never hinged 9.25
On cover 225.00
165 A11 10c yel brn & blk 3.75 18.00
Never hinged 9.25
On cover 190.00
166 A11 20c scarlet & blk 3.75 15.00
Never hinged 9.25
On cover 190.00
167 A11 50c dk violet & brn 3.75 15.00
Never hinged 9.25
On cover 165.00
168 A11 60c org brn & blk 3.75 22.50
Never hinged 9.25
On cover 225.00
169 A11 1.25 l dk blue & grn 3.75 37.50
Never hinged 9.25
On cover 250.00
Nos. 164-169,C1-C6 (12) 45.00 250.50
Set, never hinged 55.00
Nos. 164-169 on overfranked philatelic cover(s) 300.00

Second Colonial Arts Exhibition, Naples.

SEMI-POSTAL STAMPS

Italy Nos. B1-B4 Overprinted

1916 **Wmk. 140** **Perf. 14**
B1 SP1 10c + 5c rose 11.00 30.00
Never hinged 27.50
On cover 110.00
B2 SP2 15c + 5c slate 32.50 40.00
Never hinged 100.00
On cover 150.00
B3 SP2 20c + 5c orange 11.00 37.50
Never hinged 27.50
On cover 225.00
B4 SP2 20c on 15c + 5c slate 32.50 62.50
Never hinged 100.00
On cover 190.00
Nos. B1-B4 (4) 87.00 170.00
Set on overfranked philatelic cover(s) 250.00

Holy Year Issue

Italy Nos. B20-B25 Surcharged in Black or Red

1925, June 1 **Perf. 12**
B5 SP4 6b + 3b on 20c + 10c 3.00 18.00
Never hinged 7.50
On cover 150.00
B6 SP4 13b + 6b on 30c + 15c 3.00 21.00
Never hinged 7.50
On cover 150.00
B7 SP4 15b + 8b on 50c + 25c 3.00 18.00
Never hinged 7.50
On cover 150.00
B8 SP4 18b + 9b on 60c + 30c 3.00 24.00
Never hinged 7.50
On cover 200.00
B9 SP8 30b + 15b on 1 l +50c (R) 3.00 30.00
Never hinged 7.50
On cover —
B10 SP8 1r + 50b on 5 l +2.50 l (R) 3.00 45.00
Never hinged 7.50
On cover —
Nos. B5-B10 (6) 18.00 156.00
Set on overfranked philatelic cover(s) 375.00

Colonial Institute Issue

"Peace" Substituting Spade for Sword — SP10

1926, June 1 **Typo.** **Perf. 14**
B11 SP10 5c + 5c brown .90 7.50
Never hinged 2.25
On cover 130.00
B12 SP10 10c + 5c olive grn .90 7.50
Never hinged 2.25
On cover 100.00
B13 SP10 20c + 5c blue grn .90 7.50
Never hinged 2.25
On cover 82.50
B14 SP10 40c + 5c brown red .90 7.50
Never hinged 2.25
On cover 82.50
B15 SP10 60c + 5c orange .90 7.50
Never hinged 2.25
On cover 130.00
B16 SP10 1 l + 5c blue .90 7.50
Never hinged 2.25
On cover 225.00
Nos. B11-B16 (6) 5.40 45.00
Set on overfranked philatelic cover(s) 225.00

The surtax was for the Italian Colonial Institute.

Types of Italian Semi-Postal Stamps of 1926 Overprinted

1927, Apr. 21 **Unwmk.** **Perf. 11½**
B17 SP10 40c + 20c dk brn & blk 2.25 30.00
Never hinged 5.50
On cover 120.00
B18 SP10 60c + 30c brn red & ol brn 2.25 30.00
Never hinged 5.50
On cover 140.00
B19 SP10 1.25 l + 60c dp bl & blk 2.25 47.50
Never hinged 5.50
On cover 250.00
B20 SP10 5 l + 2.50 l dk grn & blk 3.75 67.50
Never hinged 9.25
On cover —
Nos. B17-B20 (4) 10.50 175.00
Set on overfranked philatelic cover(s) 400.00

The surtax was for the charitable work of the Voluntary Militia for Italian National Defense.

Allegory of Fascism and Victory — SP11

1928, Oct. 15 **Wmk. 140** **Perf. 14**
B21 SP11 20c + 5c blue grn 2.25 11.00
Never hinged 5.50
On cover 120.00
B22 SP11 30c + 5c red 2.25 11.00
Never hinged 5.50
On cover 120.00
B23 SP11 50c + 10c purple 2.25 11.00
Never hinged 5.50
On cover 110.00
B24 SP11 1.25 l + 20c dk blue 3.00 21.00
Never hinged 7.50
On cover 300.00
Nos. B21-B24 (4) 9.75 54.00
Set on overfranked philatelic cover(s) 260.00

46th anniv. of the Societa Africana d'Italia. The surtax aided that society.

Types of Italian Semi-Postal Stamps of 1928 Overprinted

1929, Mar. 4 **Unwmk.** **Perf. 11**
B25 SP10 30c + 10c red & blk 3.75 18.00
Never hinged 9.25
On cover 130.00
B26 SP10 50c + 20c vio & blk 3.75 22.00
Never hinged 9.25
On cover 130.00
B27 SP10 1.25 l + 50c brn & bl 4.50 37.50
Never hinged 11.00
On cover 275.00
B28 SP10 5 l + 2 l ol grn & blk 4.50 67.50
Never hinged 11.00
On cover —
Nos. B25-B28 (4) 16.50 145.00
Set on overfranked philatelic cover(s) 400.00

The surtax was for the charitable work of the Voluntary Militia for Italian National Defense.

Types of Italian Semi-Postal Stamps of 1926 Overprinted in Black or Red

1930, Oct. 20 **Perf. 14**
B29 SP10 30c + 10c dk grn & bl grn (Bk) 19.00 30.00
Never hinged 47.50
On cover 190.00
B30 SP10 50c + 10c dk grn & vio (R) 19.00 40.00
Never hinged 47.50
On cover 200.00
B31 SP10 1.25 l + 30c ol brn & red brn (R) 19.00 52.50
Never hinged 47.50
On cover 300.00
B32 SP10 5 l + 1.50 l ind & grn (R) 60.00 150.00
Never hinged 150.00
On cover —
Nos. B29-B32 (4) 117.00 272.50
Set on overfranked philatelic cover(s) 525.00

The surtax was for the charitable work of the Voluntary Militia for Italian National Defense.

Irrigation Canal SP14

1930, Nov. 27 **Photo.** **Wmk. 140**
B33 SP14 50c + 20c olive brn 3.75 18.00
Never hinged 9.25
On cover 190.00
B34 S414 1.25 l + 20c dp blue 3.75 18.00
Never hinged 9.25
On cover 190.00
B35 SP14 1.75 l + 20c green 3.75 20.00
Never hinged 9.25
On cover 240.00
B36 SP14 2.55 l + 50c purple 6.00 32.50
Never hinged 15.00
On cover 375.00
B37 SP14 5 l + 1 l dp car 6.00 47.50
Never hinged 15.00
On cover —
Nos. B33-B37 (5) 23.25 136.00
Set on overfranked philatelic cover(s) 300.00

25th anniv. of the Italian Colonial Agricultural Institute. The surtax was for the aid of that institution.

SP15

King Victor Emmanuel III — SP16

1935, Jan. 1
B38 SP15 5c + 5c blk brn 3.00 18.00
Never hinged 7.50
On cover 200.00
B39 SP15 7½c + 7½c vio 3.00 18.00
Never hinged 7.50
On cover 240.00
B40 SP15 15c + 10c ol blk 3.00 18.00
Never hinged 7.50
On cover 165.00
B41 SP15 20c + 10c rose red 3.00 18.00
Never hinged 7.50
On cover 165.00
B42 SP15 25c + 10c dp grn 3.00 18.00
Never hinged 7.50
On cover 190.00
B43 SP15 30c + 10c brn 3.00 18.00
Never hinged 7.50
On cover 200.00
B44 SP15 50c + 10c pur 3.00 18.00
Never hinged 7.50
On cover 200.00
B45 SP15 75c + 15c rose car 3.00 18.00
Never hinged 7.50
On cover 240.00
B46 SP15 1.25 l + 15c dp bl 3.00 18.00
Never hinged 7.50
On cover 300.00
B47 SP15 1.75 l + 25c red org 3.00 18.00
Never hinged 7.50
On cover 450.00

B48 SP15 2.75 l + 25c gray 18.00 *75.00*
Never hinged 45.00
On cover —
B49 SP15 5 l + 1 l dp cl 18.00 *75.00*
Never hinged 45.00
On cover —
B50 SP15 10 l + 1.80 l red brn 18.00 *75.00*
Never hinged 45.00
On cover —
B51 SP16 25 l + 2.75 l brn & red 150.00 *300.00*
Never hinged 375.00
On cover —
Nos. B38-B51 (14) 234.00 *705.00*
Set, never hinged 575.00
Set on overfranked philatelic cover(s) *1,900.*

Visit of King Victor Emmanuel III.

AIR POST STAMPS

View of Coast AP1

Cheetahs AP2

Wmk. 140
1934, Oct. Photo. *Perf. 14*

C1 AP1 25c sl bl & red org 3.75 *18.00*
Never hinged 9.25
On cover 165.00
C2 AP1 50c dk grn & blk 3.75 *15.00*
Never hinged 9.25
On cover 140.00
C3 AP1 75c brn & red org 3.75 *15.00*
Never hinged 9.25
On cover 190.00
a. Imperf. 1,800.
Never hinged 2,250.
C4 AP2 80c org brn & blk 3.75 *18.00*
Never hinged 9.25
On cover 225.00
C5 AP2 1 l scar & blk 3.75 *21.00*
Never hinged 9.25
On cover 240.00
C6 AP2 2 l dk bl & brn 3.75 *37.50*
Never hinged 9.25
On cover 325.00
Nos. C1-C6 (6) 22.50 *124.50*
Set, never hinged 55.00
Set, on flown cover 375.00

2nd Colonial Arts Exhibition, Naples.
For overprint see No. CO1.

Banana Tree and Airplane AP3

Designs: 25c, 1.50 l, Banana tree and plane. 50c, 2 l, Plane over cotton field. 60c, 5 l, Plane over orchard. 75c, 10 l, Plane over field workers. 1 l, 3 l, Small girl watching plane.

1936 Photo.

C7 AP3 25c slate green 1.50 *6.00*
Never hinged 3.75
On cover 75.00
C8 AP3 50c brown .75 .20
Never hinged 1.90
On cover 2.25
C9 AP3 60c red orange 2.25 *9.00*
Never hinged 5.50
On cover 140.00
C10 AP3 75c orange brn 1.50 2.25
Never hinged 3.75
On cover 18.50
C11 AP3 1 l deep blue .75 .20
Never hinged 1.90
On cover 2.25
C12 AP3 1.50 l purple 1.50 .75
Never hinged 3.75
On cover 18.50
C13 AP3 2 l slate blue 4.50 1.10
Never hinged 11.00
On cover 110.00
C14 AP3 3 l copper red 15.00 9.00
Never hinged 37.50
On cover 190.00
C15 AP3 5 l yellow green 16.00 13.50
Never hinged 40.00
On cover 300.00
C16 AP3 10 l dp rose red 18.00 22.50
Never hinged 45.00
On cover 600.00
Nos. C7-C16 (10) 61.75 *64.50*
Set, never hinged 150.00
Set, on flown cover 375.00

AIR POST SEMI-POSTAL STAMPS

King Victor Emmanuel III — SPAP1

Wmk. 140
1934, Nov. 5 Photo. *Perf. 14*

CB1 SPAP1 25c + 10c gray grn 6.00 *13.50*
Never hinged 15.00
On cover 190.00
CB2 SPAP1 50c + 10c brn 6.00 *13.50*
Never hinged 15.00
On cover 190.00
CB3 SPAP1 75c + 15c rose red 6.00 *13.50*
Never hinged 15.00
On cover 200.00
CB4 SPAP1 80c + 15c blk brn 6.00 *13.50*
Never hinged 15.00
On cover 240.00
CB5 SPAP1 1 l + 20c red brn 6.00 *13.50*
Never hinged 15.00
On cover 260.00
CB6 SPAP1 2 l + 20c brt bl 6.00 *13.50*
Never hinged 15.00
On cover —
CB7 SPAP1 3 l + 25c pur 21.00 *67.50*
Never hinged 52.50
On cover —
CB8 SPAP1 5 l + 25c org 21.00 *67.50*
Never hinged 52.50
On cover —
CB9 SPAP1 10 l + 30c rose vio 21.00 *67.50*
Never hinged 52.50
On cover —
CB10 SPAP1 25 l + 2 l dp grn 21.00 *67.50*
Never hinged 52.50
On cover —
Nos. CB1-CB10 (10) 120.00 *351.00*
Set, never hinged 300.00
Set, on flown cover 1,100.

65th birthday of King Victor Emmanuel III; non-stop flight from Rome to Mogadishu.
For overprint see No. CBO1.

AIR POST OFFICIAL STAMP

No. C1 Overprinted

Wmk. 140
1934, Nov. 11 Photo. *Perf. 14*

CO1 AP1 25c sl bl & red org *2,500.* *3,350.*
Never hinged 3,750.
On flown cover *5,000.*
Pair on flown cover *10,000.*

Forgeries of this overprint exist.

AIR POST SEMI-POSTAL OFFICIAL STAMP

Type of Air Post Semi-Postal Stamps, 1934 Overprinted Crown and "SERVIZIO DI STATO" in Black

1934, Nov. 5 Wmk. 140 *Perf. 14*

CBO1 SPAP1 25 l + 2 l cop red 2,500. *3,750.*
Never hinged 3,000.
On flown cover *5,250.*

SPECIAL DELIVERY STAMPS

Italy No. E3 Surcharged

1923, July 16 Wmk. 140 *Perf. 14*

E1 SD1 30b on 60c dl red 24.00 *20.00*
Never hinged 60.00
On cover 165.00

Italy, Type of 1908 Special Delivery Stamp Surcharged

E2 SD2 60b on 1.20 l bl & red 35.00 *42.50*
Never hinged 90.00
On cover 400.00

"Italia" SD3

1924, June Engr. Unwmk.

E3 SD3 30b dk red & brn 9.00 *15.00*
Never hinged 22.50
On cover 165.00
E4 SD3 60b dk blue & red 15.00 *22.50*
Never hinged 37.50
On cover 375.00

Nos. E3-E4 Surcharged in Black or Red with Bars and

1926, Oct.

E5 SD3 70c on 30b (Bk) 10.00 *16.00*
Never hinged 25.00
On cover 225.00
E6 SD3 2.50 l on 60b (R) 13.50 *20.00*
Never hinged 32.50
On cover 375.00
a. Imperf., pair 375.00

Same Surcharge on No. E3

1927 *Perf. 11*

E7 SD3 1.25 l on 30b 13.50 12.00
Never hinged 32.50
On cover 140.00
a. Perf. 14 175.00 *450.00*
Never hinged 375.00
On cover 22.50
b. Imperf., pair 750.00
Never hinged 1,150.

AUTHORIZED DELIVERY STAMP

Italy No. EY2 Overprinted in Black

1939 Wmk. 140 *Perf. 14*

EY1 AD2 10c brown 40.00 —
Never hinged 150.00
On cover *375.00*

No. EY1 has yellowish gum. A 1941 printing in grayish brown, with white gum, was not issued. Value: unused, 60 cents; never hinged, $1.50.

POSTAGE DUE STAMPS

Values for Nos. J1-J41 are for examples with perforations touching or cutting into the design on at least one side. Examples with perforations clear of the design on all four sides are scarce and command considerable premiums.

Postage Due Stamps of Italy Overprinted

1906-08 Wmk. 140 *Perf. 14*

J1 D3 5c buff & magenta 15.00 *37.50*
Never hinged 37.50
On cover 525.00
J2 D3 10c buff & magenta 52.50 45.00
Never hinged 77.50
On cover 450.00
J3 D3 20c org & magenta 37.50 *55.00*
Never hinged 55.00
On cover 375.00
J4 D3 30c buff & magenta 30.00 *60.00*
Never hinged 45.00
On cover 475.00
J5 D3 40c buff & magenta 225.00 60.00
Never hinged 325.00
On cover 525.00
J6 D3 50c buff & magenta 60.00 *75.00*
Never hinged 90.00
On cover 525.00
J7 D3 60c buff & mag ('08) 52.50 *75.00*
Never hinged 77.50
On cover —
J8 D3 1 l blue & magenta 1,125. 325.00
Never hinged 1,700.
On cover —
J9 D3 2 l blue & magenta 1,050. 325.00
Never hinged 1,600.0
On cover —
J10 D3 5 l blue & magenta 1,050. 325.00
Never hinged 1,600.
On cover —
J11 D3 10 l blue & magenta 185.00 *300.00*
Never hinged 275.00
On cover —
Nos. J1-J11 (11) 3,882. *1,682.*

Postage Due Stamps of Italy Overprinted at Top of Stamps

1909-19

J12 D3 5c buff & magenta 7.50 *18.00*
Never hinged 11.25
On cover 450.00
c. Overprint at center of stamp 22.50
Never hinged 32.50
J13 D3 10c buff & magenta 7.50 *18.00*
Never hinged 11.25
On cover 300.00
J14 D3 20c buff & magenta 6.00 *37.50*
Never hinged 25.00
On cover 325.00
J15 D3 30c buff & magenta 37.50 37.50
Never hinged 55.00
On cover 450.00
J16 D3 40c buff & magenta 37.50 *40.00*
Never hinged 55.00
On cover 475.00
J17 D3 50c buff & magenta 37.50 *60.00*
Never hinged 55.00
On cover 325.00
J18 D3 60c buff & mag ('19) 45.00 *52.50*
Never hinged 67.50
On cover —
J19 D3 1 l blue & magenta 115.00 60.00
Never hinged 175.00
On cover 525.00
J20 D3 2 l blue & magenta 160.00 160.00
Never hinged 250.00
On cover —
J21 D3 5 l blue & magenta 175.00 175.00
Never hinged 275.00
On cover —

J22 D3 10 l blue & magenta 45.00 *60.00*
Never hinged 67.50
On cover —
Nos. J12-J22 (11) 673.50 *718.50*

Same with Overprint at Bottom of Stamps

1920

J12a D3 5c buff & magenta 90.00 125.00
Never hinged 140.00
On cover 225.00
b. Double overprint 175.00
Never hinged 675.00
J13a D3 10c buff & magenta 90.00 125.00
Never hinged 140.00
On cover 190.00
J14a D3 20c buff & magenta 125.00 90.00
Never hinged 200.00
On cover 160.00
J15a D3 30c buff & magenta 150.00 90.00
Never hinged 225.00
On cover 190.00
J16a D3 40c buff & magenta 150.00 125.00
Never hinged 225.00
On cover 210.00
J17a D3 50c buff & magenta 125.00 115.00
Never hinged 200.00
On cover 160.00
J18a D3 60c buff & magenta 150.00 115.00
Never hinged 225.00
On cover —
J19a D3 1 l blue & magenta 150.00 175.00
Never hinged 225.00
On cover 325.00
'b. Overprint at center of stamp 300.00
Never hinged 450.00
J20a D3 2 l blue & magenta 150.00 175.00
Never hinged 225.00
On cover —
J21a D3 5 l blue & magenta 150.00 210.00
Never hinged 225.00
On cover —
Nos. J12a-J21a (10) 1,330. 1,345.

D4

1923, July 1

J23 D4 1b buff & black 1.50 *6.00*
Never hinged 2.25
On cover 325.00
J24 D4 2b buff & black 1.50 *6.00*
Never hinged 2.25
On cover 260.00
a. Inverted numeral and ovpt. 450.00
Never hinged 675.00
J25 D4 3b buff & black 1.50 *6.00*
Never hinged 2.25
On cover 260.00
J26 D4 5b buff & black 3.00 *6.00*
Never hinged 4.50
On cover 260.00
J27 D4 10b buff & black 3.00 *6.00*
Never hinged 4.50
On cover 375.00
J28 D4 20b buff & black 3.00 *6.00*
Never hinged 4.50
On cover 375.00
J29 D4 40b buff & black 3.00 *6.00*
Never hinged 4.50
On cover 525.00
J30 D4 1r blue & black 3.75 *30.00*
Never hinged 5.50
On cover —
Nos. J23-J30 (8) 20.25 *72.00*

Type of Postage Due Stamps of Italy Overprinted

1926, Mar. 1

J31 D3 5c buff & black 19.00 *26.00*
Never hinged 29.00
On cover 375.00
J32 D3 10c buff & black 19.00 18.00
Never hinged 29.00
On cover 240.00
J33 D3 20c buff & black 19.00 *27.50*
Never hinged 29.00
On cover 225.00
J34 D3 30c buff & black 19.00 18.00
Never hinged 29.00
On cover 260.00
J35 D3 40c buff & black 19.00 18.00
Never hinged 29.00
On cover 300.00
J36 D3 50c buff & black 30.00 18.00
Never hinged 45.00
On cover 225.00
J37 D3 60c buff & black 30.00 18.00
Never hinged 45.00
On cover 450.00
J38 D3 1 l blue & black 45.00 27.50
Never hinged 67.50
On cover 475.00
J39 D3 2 l blue & black 67.50 27.50
Never hinged 100.00
On cover —
J40 D3 5 l blue & black 75.00 40.00
Never hinged 110.00
On cover —
J41 D3 10 l blue & black 90.00 52.50
Never hinged 140.00
On cover —
Nos. J31-J41 (11) 432.50 291.00

Numerals and Ovpt. Invtd.

J32a D3 10c 175.00
Never hinged 275.00
J33a D3 20c 525.00
Never hinged 775.00
J34a D3 30c 175.00
Never hinged 275.00
J35a D3 40c 175.00
Never hinged 275.00
J36a D3 50c 175.00
Never hinged 275.00
J37a D3 60c 175.00
Never hinged 275.00

Postage Due Stamps of Italy, 1934, Overprinted in Black

1934, May 12

J42 D6 5c brown .75 *3.75*
Never hinged 1.90
On cover 375.00
J43 D6 10c blue .75 *3.75*
Never hinged 1.90
On cover 240.00
J44 D6 20c rose red 3.00 7.50
Never hinged 7.50
On cover 200.00
J45 D6 25c green 3.00 7.50
Never hinged 7.50
On cover 165.00
J46 D6 30c red orange 7.50 *11.00*
Never hinged 19.00
On cover 240.00
J47 D6 40c black brown 7.50 *15.00*
Never hinged 19.00
On cover 375.00
J48 D6 50c violet 13.50 4.50
Never hinged 32.50
On cover 150.00
J49 D6 60c black 16.00 *30.00*
Never hinged 40.00
On cover 400.00
J50 D7 1 l red orange 21.00 13.50
Never hinged 52.50
On cover 225.00
J51 D7 2 l green 37.50 30.00
Never hinged 92.50
On cover 375.00
J52 D7 5 l violet 40.00 *60.00*
Never hinged 100.00
On cover —
J53 D7 10 l blue 40.00 *67.50*
Never hinged 100.00
On cover —
J54 D7 20 l carmine 45.00 *82.50*
Never hinged 110.00
On cover —
Nos. J42-J54 (13) 235.50 *336.50*

PARCEL POST STAMPS

These stamps were used by affixing them to the way bill so that one half remained on it following the parcel, the other half staying on the receipt given the sender. Most used halves are right halves. Complete stamps were and are obtainable canceled, probably to order. Both unused and used values are for complete stamps.

Parcel Post Stamps of Italy, 1914-17, Overprinted

1917-19 **Wmk. 140** ***Perf. 13½***

Q1 PP2 5c brown 4.50 *37.50*
Never hinged 6.75
a. Double overprint 375.00
Never hinged 550.00
Q2 PP2 10c blue 6.00 *26.00*
Never hinged 9.00
Q3 PP2 20c black ('19) 260.00 110.00
Never hinged 400.00
Q4 PP2 25c red 11.00 *45.00*
Never hinged 16.50
a. Double overprint —
Never hinged —
Q5 PP2 50c orange 110.00 60.00
Never hinged 275.00
Q6 PP2 1 l lilac 37.50 *60.00*
Never hinged 92.50
Q7 PP2 2 l green 52.50 *60.00*
Never hinged 130.00
Q8 PP2 3 l bister 60.00 *90.00*
Never hinged 150.00
Q9 PP2 4 l slate 67.50 *90.00*
Never hinged 165.00
Nos. Q1-Q9 (9) 609.00 *578.50*

Halves Used

Q1, Q4 .20
Q2 .20
Q3, Q5 2.75
Q6-Q7 .30
Q8 .50
Q9 1.25

Nos. Q5-Q9 were overprinted in 1922 with a slightly different type in which the final "A" of SOMALIA is directly over the final "A" of ITALIANA. They were not regularly issued. Value for set, $400.

Parcel Post Stamps of Italy, 1914-17, Overprinted

1923

Q10 PP2 25c red 22.50 *25.00*
Never hinged 77.50
Q11 PP2 50c orange 19.00 *25.00*
Never hinged 110.00
Q12 PP2 1 l violet 27.50 25.00
Never hinged 140.00
Q13 PP2 2 l green 27.50 25.00
Never hinged 130.00
Q14 PP2 3 l bister 47.50 25.00
Never hinged 225.00
Q15 PP2 4 l slate 47.50 25.00
Never hinged 225.00
Nos. Q10-Q15 (6) 191.50 *150.00*

Halves Used

Q10 1.10
Q11, Q12 .30
Q13 .40
Q14 .85
Q15 1.60

Parcel Post Stamps of Italy, 1914-17, Surcharged

1923

Q16 PP2 3b on 5c brown 11.00 22.50
Never hinged 17.00
Q17 PP2 5b on 5c brown 11.00 22.50
Never hinged 17.00
Q18 PP2 10b on 10c blue 11.00 18.00
Never hinged 17.00
Q19 PP2 25b on 25c red 22.50 32.50
Never hinged 32.50
Q20 PP2 50b on 50c org 30.00 *40.00*
Never hinged 45.00
Q21 PP2 1r on 1 l lilac 37.50 47.50
Never hinged 55.00
Q22 PP2 2r on 2 l green 60.00 67.50
Never hinged 90.00
Q23 PP2 3r on 3 l bister 60.00 67.50
Never hinged 90.00
Q24 PP2 4r on 4 l slate 75.00 67.50
Never hinged 110.00
Nos. Q16-Q24 (9) 318.00 385.50

Halves Used

Q16-Q17 .20
Q18-Q19 .20
Q20-Q21 .30
Q22 .60
Q23 1.10
Q24 1.60

No. Q16 has the numeral "3" at the left also.

Parcel Post Stamps of Italy, 1914-22 Overprinted

1926-31

Red Overprint

Q25 PP2 5c brown 22.50 *45.00*
Never hinged 32.50
Q26 PP2 10c blue 22.50 *45.00*
Never hinged 32.50
Q27 PP2 20c black 52.50 45.00
Never hinged 77.50
Q28 PP2 25c red 52.50 45.00
Never hinged 77.50
Q29 PP2 50c orange 52.50 45.00
Never hinged 77.50
Q30 PP2 1 l violet 67.50 45.00
Never hinged 100.00
Q31 PP2 2 l green 115.00 45.00
Never hinged 180.00
Q32 PP2 3 l yellow 18.00 *45.00*
Never hinged 27.50
Q33 PP2 4 l slate 18.00 *45.00*
Never hinged 27.50
Q34 PP2 10 l vio brn ('30) 37.50 *60.00*
Never hinged 55.00
Q35 PP2 12 l red brn '31) 37.50 *60.00*
Never hinged 55.00
Q36 PP2 15 l olive ('31) 37.50 *95.00*
Never hinged 55.00
Q37 PP2 20 l dull vio ('31) 37.50 *95.00*
Never hinged 55.00
Nos. Q25-Q37 (13) 571.00 *715.00*

Halves Used

Q25-Q26 .30
Q27-Q28, Q33 .70
Q29, Q34 .90
Q30-Q31 .50
Q32 .40
Q35-Q36 1.10
Q37 1.25

Nos. Q25-Q31 come with two types of overprint: I — The first "I" and last "A" of ITALIANA extend slightly at both sides of SOMALIA. II — Only the I" extends. These seven stamps with type I overprint were not regularly issued, and Nos. Q27-Q31 (type I) sell for less than with type II overprint.

Black Overprint

Q38 PP2 10 l violet brown 75.00 55.00
Never hinged 110.00
Q39 PP2 12 l red brown 52.50 55.00
Never hinged 77.50
Q40 PP2 15 l olive 52.50 55.00
Never hinged 77.50
Q41 PP2 20 l dull violet 52.50 55.00
Never hinged 77.50
Nos. Q38-Q41 (4) 232.50 220.00

Halves Used

Q38 .45
Q39-Q41 .30

Same Overprint on Parcel Post Stamps of Italy, 1927-38

1928-39

Black Overprint

Q42 PP3 25c red ('31) 40.00 *30.00*
Never hinged 60.00
Q43 PP3 30c ultra 2.25 *3.75*
Never hinged 3.25
Q43A PP3 50c orange *11,250.*
Never hinged *14,000.*
Q44 PP3 60c red 2.25 *6.00*
Never hinged 3.25
Q45 PP3 1 l lilac brn ('31) 600.00 *1,300.*
Never hinged 900.00
a. 1 l lilac 2,250.
Never hinged 2,750.
Q46 PP3 2 l green ('31) 600.00 *2,000.*
Never hinged 900.00
Q47 PP3 3 l bister 4.50 *15.00*
Never hinged 6.75
Q48 PP3 4 l gray black 4.50 *15.00*
Never hinged 6.75
Q49 PP3 10 l rose lil ('34) 400.00 *425.00*
Never hinged 600.00
Q50 PP3 20 l lil brn ('34) 400.00 *450.00*
Never hinged 600.00
Nos. Q42-Q43,Q44-Q50 (9) 2,053. *4,244.*

Halves Used

Q42, Q50 1.00
Q43, Q44 .20
Q43A 40.00
Q45-Q48 .30
Q49 2.00

The 25c, 1 l and 2 l come with both types of overprint (see note below No. Q37). Both types were regularly issued. Values are for type I on 25c, type II on 1 l and 2 l.

Red Overprint

Q51 PP3 5c brown ('39) 14.50
Never hinged 22.50
Q52 PP3 3 l bister ('30) 30.00 *55.00*
Never hinged 45.00
Half stamp .30
Q53 PP3 4 l gray black ('30) 30.00 *55.00*
Never hinged 45.00
Half stamp .30
Nos. Q51-Q53 (3) 74.50

Same Overprint in Black on Italy Nos. Q24-Q25

1940 ***Perf. 13***

Q54 PP3 5c brown 2.25 *7.50*
Never hinged 3.25
Half stamp .20
Q55 PP3 10c deep blue 3.00 *7.50*
Never hinged 4.50
Half stamp .20

SOMALI COAST

sō-'mä-lē 'kōst

(Djibouti)

LOCATION — Eastern Africa, bordering on the Gulf of Aden
GOVT. — French Overseas Territory
AREA — 8,500 sq. mi.
POP. — 86,000 (est. 1963)
CAPITAL — Djibouti (Jibuti)

The port of Obock, which issued postage stamps in 1892-1894, was included in the territory and began to use stamps of Somali Coast in 1902.

100 Centimes = 1 Franc

Navigation and Commerce
A1 A2

A3

Camel and Rider
A4

Obock Nos. 32-33, 35, 45 with Overprint or Surcharge Handstamped in Black, Blue or Red

1894 Unwmk. *Perf. 14x13½*

1	A1	5c grn & red, *grnsh* (with bar)	135.00	120.00
		On cover		1,500.
a.		Without bar	1,000.	700.00
2	A2	25c on 2c brn & bl, *buff* (Bl & Bk)	335.00	200.00
		On cover		1,000.
a.		"25" omitted	850.00	700.00
b.		"DJIBOUTI" omitted	850.00	700.00
c.		"DJIBOUTI" inverted	975.00	900.00
3	A3	50c on 1c blk & red, *bl* (R & Bl)	350.00	225.00
		On cover		1,250.
a.		"5" instead of "50"	1,350.	1,000.
b.		"0" instead of "50"	1,350.	975.00
c.		"DJIBOUTI" omitted	1,350.	975.00

Imperf

4	A4	1fr on 5fr car	600.00	475.00
a.		"DJIBOUTI" omitted	3,500.	
5	A4	5fr carmine	1,650.	1,200.

The overprint on No. 1 includes a bar to obliterate "OBOCK."

"DJIBOUTI" is in blue on No. 2, in red on No. 3.

Counterfeits exist of Nos. 4-5.

View of Djibouti, Somali Warriors — A5

French Gunboat
A7

Crossing Desert (Size: 66mm wide, including simulated perfs.) — A8

Designs: 15c, 25c, 30c, 40c, 50c, 75c, Different views of Djibouti. 1fr, 2fr, Djibouti quay.

Imperf. (Simulated Perforations in Frame Color)

1894-1902 Typo.

Quadrille Lines Printed on Paper

6	A5	1c blk & claret	3.25	2.50
		On cover		125.00
7	A5	2c claret & blk	3.25	2.50
		On cover		125.00
8	A5	4c vio brn & bl	12.50	7.50
		On cover		125.00
9	A5	5c bl grn & red	12.50	6.00
		On cover		85.00
10	A5	5c grn & yel grn ('02)	9.00	7.50
		On cover		85.00
11	A5	10c brown & grn	16.50	7.50
		On cover		85.00
a.		Half used as 5c on cover		125.00
12	A5	15c violet & grn	16.50	7.50
		On cover		85.00
13	A5	25c rose & blue	25.00	9.00
		On cover		85.00
14	A5	30c gray brn & rose	16.50	9.00
		On cover		150.00
a.		Half used as 15c on cover		400.00
15	A5	40c org & bl ('00)	49.00	32.50
		On cover		150.00
a.		Half used as 20c on cover		650.00
16	A5	50c blue & rose	25.00	15.00
		On cover		150.00
a.		Half used as 25c on cover		1,450.
17	A5	75c violet & org	42.50	31.50
		On cover		250.00
18	A5	1fr ol grn & blk	20.00	15.00
		On cover		250.00
19	A5	2fr gray brn & rose	87.50	67.50
		On cover		—
a.		Half used as 1fr on cover		1,750.
20	A7	5fr rose & blue	180.00	125.00
21	A8	25fr rose & blue	850.00	*875.00*
22	A8	50fr blue & rose	575.00	575.00

High values are found with the overprint "S" (Specimen) erased and, usually, a cancellation added.

The 1c, 2c and 4c come on thick paper. Value, 1c, 2c, each $9 unused or used; 4c, $17.50 unused, $12.50 used.

Values for bisects are for complete covers, newspapers or other printed matter.

For surcharges see Nos. 24-27B.

A9

1899

Black Surcharge

23	A9	40c on 4c brn & bl	*2,950.*	27.50
		On cover		100.00
a.		Double surcharge	*5,500.*	1,275.
b.		Pair, one without surcharge		2,250.

Nos. 17-20 Surcharged

1902 Blue Surcharge

24	A5	0.05c on 75c	62.50	36.00
		On cover		200.00
a.		Inverted surcharge	525.00	475.00
b.		Double surcharge	525.00	475.00
c.		Pair, one without surcharge	2,000.	
25	A5	0.10c on 1fr	70.00	47.50
		On cover		250.00
a.		Inverted surcharge	500.00	375.00
b.		Double surcharge	400.00	375.00
26	A5	0.40c on 2fr	575.00	375.00
		On cover		*950.00*
a.		Double surcharge	1,900.	1,725.

Black Surcharge

27	A7	0.75c on 5fr	500.00	375.00
		On cover		*950.00*
a.		Inverted surcharge	2,500.	2,000.
c.		Double surcharge	2,500.	2,000.

Obock No. 57 Surcharged in Blue

27B	A7	0.05c on 75c gray lil & org	1,350.	975.00
		On cover		*2,250.*

A10

Nos. 15-16 Surcharged in Black

28	A10	5c on 40c	7.50	4.50
		On cover		125.00
a.		Double surcharge	120.00	100.00
29	A10	10c on 50c	25.00	25.00
		On cover		125.00
a.		Inverted surcharge	450.00	450.00
b.		Double surcharge	450.00	

Surcharged on Stamps of Obock

Group of Warriors
A11

Black Surcharge

30	A11	5c on 30c bis & yel grn	13.50	9.75
		On cover		125.00
a.		Inverted surcharge	225.00	225.00
b.		Double surcharge	200.00	175.00
c.		Triple surcharge		

A12

Red Surcharge

31	A12	10c on 25c blk & bl	13.50	11.50
		On cover		125.00
a.		Inverted surcharge	225.00	225.00
b.		Double surcharge	250.00	250.00
c.		Triple surcharge	1,500.	1,500.

A13

Black Surcharge

32	A13	10c on 10fr org & red vio	32.50	26.50
		On cover		150.00
a.		Double surcharge	210.00	200.00
b.		Triple surch., one invtd.	1,800.	1,700.

A14

Black Surcharge

33	A14	10c on 2fr dl vio & org	60.00	47.50
		On cover		150.00
a.		"DJIBOUTI" inverted	250.00	200.00
b.		Large "0" in "10"	110.00	82.50
c.		Double surcharge	400.00	375.00
j.		As "b," double surcharge	1,100.	850.00

Same Surcharge on Obock No. 53 in Red

33D	A7	10c on 25c blk & bl	*30,000.*	*20,000.*

A14a

Black Surcharge on Obock Nos. 63-64

33E	A14a	5c on 25fr brn & bl	57.50	47.50
		On cover		200.00
33F	A14a	10c on 50fr red vio & grn	75.00	52.50
		On cover		200.00
g.		"01" instead of "10"	190.00	165.00
h.		"CENTIMES" inverted	2,500.	2,500.
i.		Double surcharge	2,250.	2,250.
k.		Double surcharge, one inverted	2,000.	1,900.

Tadjoura Mosque
A15

Somalis on Camel
A16

Warriors — A17

1902 Engr. *Perf. 11½*

34	A15	1c brn vio & org	.75	.75
		On cover		85.00
35	A15	2c yel brn & yel grn	.90	.75
		On cover		85.00
36	A15	4c bl & carmine	2.00	1.50
		On cover		85.00
37	A15	5c bl grn & yel grn	2.00	1.00
		On cover		60.00
38	A15	10c car & red org	5.25	3.25
		On cover		60.00
39	A15	15c brn org & bl	5.25	3.25
		On cover		60.00
40	A16	20c vio & green	11.50	6.00
		On cover		85.00
41	A16	25c blue	17.00	10.50
		On cover		60.00
a.		25c indigo & blue ('03)	20.00	11.00
42	A16	30c red & black	5.00	4.00
		On cover		85.00
43	A16	40c orange & blue	11.50	7.25
		On cover		85.00
44	A16	50c grn & red org	35.00	35.00
		On cover		125.00

No.	Type	Description	Unused	Used
45	A16	75c orange & vio	6.50	4.00
		On cover		100.00
46	A17	1fr red org & vio	20.00	12.50
		On cover		150.00
47	A17	2fr yel grn & car	30.00	22.50
		On cover		—
a.		Without names of designer and engraver at bottom	100.00	100.00
48	A17	5fr orange & blue	18.00	16.00
		On cover		—
		Nos. 34-48 (15)	170.65	128.25

1903

No.	Type	Description	Unused	Used
49	A15	1c brn vio & blk	.75	.65
		On cover		85.00
50	A15	2c yel brn & blk	1.10	.80
		On cover		85.00
51	A15	4c lake & blk	1.50	1.25
		On cover		85.00
a.		4c red & black	1.50	1.25
52	A15	5c bl grn & blk	3.25	2.25
		On cover		60.00
53	A15	10c carmine & blk	6.50	2.50
		On cover		60.00
54	A15	15c org brn & blk	14.50	7.25
		On cover		60.00
55	A16	20c dl vio & blk	20.00	14.50
		On cover		85.00
56	A16	25c ultra & blk	10.00	7.25
		On cover		60.00
58	A16	40c orange & blk	7.25	7.25
		On cover		85.00
59	A16	50c green & blk	18.00	11.00
		On cover		85.00
60	A16	75c buff & blk	9.25	8.50
		On cover		125.00
a.		75c brown orange & black	60.00	60.00
61	A17	1fr orange & blk	15.00	14.50
		On cover		150.00
62	A17	2fr yel grn & blk	8.00	6.25
		On cover		—
a.		Without names of designer and engraver at bottom	35.00	35.00
63	A17	5fr red org & blk	17.00	14.50
		On cover		—
a.		5fr ocher & black	20.00	20.00
		Nos. 49-63 (14)	132.10	98.45

Imperforates, transposed colors and inverted centers exist in the 1902 and 1903 issues. Most of these were issued from Paris and some are said to have been fraudulently printed.

Tadjoura Mosque A18

Somalis on Camel — A19

Warriors — A20

1909 Typo. *Perf. 14x13½*

No.	Type	Description	Unused	Used
64	A18	1c maroon & brn	.65	.60
65	A18	2c vio & ol gray	.65	.60
66	A18	4c ol gray & bl	.85	.80
67	A18	5c grn & gray grn	1.10	.75
68	A18	10c car & ver	3.25	1.25
69	A18	20c blk & red brn	5.25	4.25
70	A19	25c bl & pale bl	4.00	2.50
71	A19	30c brn & scar	6.00	4.25
72	A19	35c vio & grn	7.25	4.50
73	A19	40c rose & vio	6.50	4.25
74	A19	45c brn & bl grn	6.50	4.25
75	A19	50c maroon & brn	6.50	5.25
76	A19	75c scarlet & grn	14.50	10.00
77	A20	1fr vio & brn	18.00	16.00
78	A20	2fr brn & rose	29.00	22.50
79	A20	5fr vio brn & bl grn	47.50	32.50
		Nos. 64-79 (16)	157.50	114.25

Drummer A21

Somali Girl A22

Djibouti-Addis Ababa Railroad Bridge — A23

1915-33 *Perf. 13½x14*

Chalky Paper

No.	Type	Description	Unused	Used
80	A21	1c brt vio & red brn	.20	.20
81	A21	2c ocher & ind	.20	.20
82	A21	4c dk brn & red	.20	.20
83	A21	5c yel grn & grn	.80	.75
84	A21	5c org & dl red ('22)	.45	.45
85	A22	10c car & dk red	1.25	.75
86	A22	10c ap grn & grn ('22)	.75	.75
87	A22	10c ver & grn ('25)	.20	.20
88	A22	15c brn vio & car	.65	.35
89	A22	20c org & blk brn	.20	.20
90	A22	20c dp grn & bl grn ('25)	.20	.20
91	A22	20c dk grn & red ('27)	.35	.35
92	A22	25c ultra & dl bl	.75	.45
93	A22	25c blk & bl grn ('22)	.80	.80
94	A22	30c blk & bl grn	1.60	1.25
95	A22	30c rose & red brn ('22)	1.00	1.00
96	A22	30c vio & ol grn ('25)	.20	.20
97	A22	30c grn & dl grn ('27)	.35	.35
98	A22	35c lt grn & dl rose	.45	.35
99	A22	40c bl & brn vio	.60	.45
100	A22	45c red brn & dk bl	.65	.55
101	A22	50c car rose & blk	8.00	5.25
102	A22	50c ultra & ind ('24)	.90	.90
103	A22	50c dk brn & red vio ('25)	.55	.55
104	A22	60c ol grn & red vio ('25)	.35	.20
105	A22	65c car rose & ol grn ('25)	.55	.35
106	A22	75c dl vio & choc	.55	.45
107	A22	75c ind & ultra ('25)	.45	.35
108	A22	75c brt vio & ol brn ('27)	1.25	.85
109	A22	85c vio brn & bl grn ('25)	.85	.75
110	A22	90c brn red & brt red ('30)	6.25	4.50
111	A23	1fr bis brn & red	1.25	.75
112	A23	1.10fr lt brn & ultra ('28)	3.25	3.25
113	A23	1.25fr dk bl & blk brn ('33)	7.25	6.00
114	A23	1.50fr lt bl & dk bl ('30)	1.00	.75
115	A23	1.75fr gray grn & lt red ('33)	6.25	4.00
116	A23	2fr bl vio & blk	2.25	1.75
117	A23	3fr red vio ('30)	8.25	5.75
118	A23	5fr rose red & blk	4.25	2.10
		Nos. 80-118 (39)	65.30	48.50

No. 99 is on ordinary paper.

For surcharges and overprints see Nos. 119-134, and 183-193 in the Scott Standard Catalogue, Vol. 6.

Nos. 83, 92 Surcharged in Green or Blue

1922

No.	Type	Description	Unused	Used
119	A21	10c on 5c (G)	.45	.45
a.		Double surcharge	65.00	65.00
120	A22	50c on 25c (Bl)	.45	.45

Type of 1915 Surcharged in Various Colors

1922

No.	Type	Description	Unused	Used
121	A22	0,01c on 15c vio & rose (Bk)	.20	.20
122	A22	0,02c on 15c vio & rose (Bl)	.35	.35
123	A22	0,04c on 15c vio & rose (G)	.45	.45
124	A22	0,05c on 15c vio & rose (R)	.45	.45
		Nos. 121-124 (4)	1.45	1.45

Nos. 88, 99 and Type of 1915 Surcharged

1923-27

No.	Type	Description	Unused	Used
125	A22	60c on 75c ol grn & vio	.35	.35
126	A22	65c on 15c ('25)	1.40	1.40
127	A22	85c on 40c ('25)	1.10	1.10
128	A22	90c on 75c brn red & red ('27)	3.50	3.50
		Nos. 125-128 (4)	6.35	6.35

No. 118 and Type of 1915-17 Surcharged with New Value and Bars in Black or Red

1924-27

No.	Type	Description	Unused	Used
129	A23	25c on 5fr	.80	.80
130	A23	1.25fr on 1fr dk bl & ultra (R) ('26)	.75	.75
131	A23	1.50fr on 1fr lt bl & dk bl ('27)	.80	.80
132	A23	3fr on 5fr ver & red vio ('27)	3.50	3.50
133	A23	10fr on 5fr brn red & ol brn ('27)	6.00	6.00
134	A23	20fr on 5fr gray grn & lil rose ('27)	10.00	10.00
		Nos. 129-134 (6)	21.85	21.85

Common Design Types pictured following the introduction.

Colonial Exposition Issue

Common Design Types

Engr., Name of Country Typo. in Black

1931 *Perf. 12½*

No.	Type	Description	Unused	Used
135	CD70	40c deep green	4.00	4.00
136	CD71	50c violet	4.00	4.00
137	CD72	90c red orange	4.25	4.25
138	CD73	1.50fr dull blue	4.25	4.25
		Nos. 135-138 (4)	16.50	16.50

Paris International Exposition Issue

Common Design Types

1937 Engr. *Perf. 13*

No.	Type	Description	Unused	Used
139	CD74	20c deep violet	1.25	1.25
140	CD75	30c dark green	1.25	1.25
141	CD76	40c carmine rose	1.25	1.25
142	CD77	50c dk brn & bl	1.25	1.25
143	CD78	90c red	1.40	1.40
144	CD79	1.50fr ultra	1.40	1.40
		Nos. 139-144 (6)	7.80	7.80

Colonial Arts Exhibition Issue

Souvenir Sheet

Common Design Type

1937 *Imperf.*

No.	Type	Description	Unused	Used
145	CD75	3fr dull violet	8.50	*10.00*

Mosque of Djibouti — A24

Somali Warriors — A25

Governor Léonce Lagarde — A26

View of Djibouti — A27

1938-40 *Perf. 12x12½, 12½*

No.	Type	Description	Unused	Used
146	A24	2c dull red vio	.20	.20
147	A24	3c slate grn	.20	.20
148	A24	4c dull red brn	.20	.20
149	A24	5c carmine	.20	.20
150	A24	10c blue gray	.20	.20
151	A24	15c slate black	.20	.20
152	A24	20c dark orange	.20	.20
153	A25	25c dark brown	.55	.45
154	A25	30c dark blue	.20	.20
155	A25	35c olive grn	.65	.55
156	A24	40c org brn ('40)	.20	.20
157	A24	45c dull grn ('40)	.20	.20
158	A25	50c red	.45	.35
159	A25	55c dull red vio	.65	.55
160	A25	60c black ('40)	.45	.45
161	A25	65c orange brown	.75	.65
162	A25	70c lt violet ('40)	1.00	1.00
163	A26	80c gray blk	1.60	1.25
164	A25	90c rose vio ('39)	1.10	1.10
165	A26	1fr carmine	2.50	1.50

166 A26 1fr black ('40) .35 .35
167 A26 1.25fr magenta ('39) .80 .80
168 A26 1.40fr pck bl ('40) .85 .85
169 A26 1.50fr dull green .65 .65
170 A26 1.60fr brn car ('40) .85 .85
171 A26 1.75fr ultra .85 .80
172 A26 2fr dk orange .75 .60
173 A26 2.25fr ultra ('39) 1.10 1.10
174 A26 2.50fr org brn ('40) 1.60 1.60
175 A26 3fr dull violet .75 .60
176 A27 5fr brn & pale cl 1.60 1.60
177 A27 10fr ind & pale bl 1.90 1.90
178 A27 20fr car lake & gray 1.90 1.90
Nos. 146-178 (33) 25.65 23.45

For overprints and surcharge see Nos. 194-223 in the Scott Standard Catalogue, Vol. 6.

New York World's Fair Issue
Common Design Type

1939 Engr. *Perf. 12½x12*
179 CD82 1.25fr car lake .85 .85
180 CD82 2.25fr ultra .85 .85

SEMI-POSTAL STAMPS

Somali Girl — SP1

1915 Unwmk. *Perf. 13½x14*
Chalky Paper
B1 SP1 10c + 5c car & dk red 6.50 5.50

Curie Issue
Common Design Type

1938 Engr. *Perf. 13*
B2 CD80 1.75fr + 50c brt ultra 6.00 6.00

French Revolution Issue
Common Design Type

Photo., Name and Value Typo. in Black

1939
B3 CD83 45c + 25c green 7.00 7.00
B4 CD83 70c + 30c brown 7.00 7.00
B5 CD83 90c + 35c red org 7.00 7.00
B6 CD83 1.25fr + 1fr rose pink 7.00 7.00
B7 CD83 2.25fr + 2fr blue 7.00 7.00
Nos. B3-B7 (5) 35.00 35.00

POSTAGE DUE STAMPS

D1

1915 Unwmk. Typo. *Perf. 14x13½*
Chalky Paper
J1 D1 5c deep ultra .20 .20
J2 D1 10c brown red .35 .35
J3 D1 15c black .55 .55
J4 D1 20c purple 1.10 1.10
J5 D1 30c orange 1.10 1.10
J6 D1 50c maroon 2.25 2.25
J7 D1 60c green 3.25 3.25
J8 D1 1fr dark blue 3.50 3.50
Nos. J1-J8 (8) 12.30 12.30

See Nos. J11-J20.

Type of 1915 Issue Surcharged

1927
J9 D1 2fr on 1fr light red 6.00 6.00
J10 D1 3fr on 1fr lilac rose 6.00 6.00

Type of 1915

1938 Engr. *Perf. 12½x13*
J11 D1 5c light ultra .20 .20
J12 D1 10c dark carmine .20 .20
J13 D1 15c brown black .20 .20
J14 D1 20c violet .20 .20
J15 D1 30c orange yellow .85 .85
J16 D1 50c brown .55 .55
J17 D1 60c emerald .85 .85
J18 D1 1fr indigo 1.75 1.75
J19 D1 2fr red .80 .80
J20 D1 3fr dark brown 1.10 1.10
Nos. J11-J20 (10) 6.70 6.70
Set, never hinged 12.00

Inscribed "Inst de Grav" below design.

SOMALILAND PROTECTORATE

sō-ˈmä-lē-ˌland

prə-ˈtek-t(ə-)rət

LOCATION — Eastern Africa, bordering on the Gulf of Aden
GOVT. — British Protectorate
AREA — 68,000 sq. mi.
POP. — 640,000 (estimated)
CAPITAL — Hargeisa

Formerly administered by the Indian Government, the territory was taken over by the British Foreign Office in 1898 and transferred to the Colonial Office in 1905.

16 Annas = 1 Rupee
100 Cents = 1 Shilling (1951)

Catalogue values for unused stamps in this country are for Never Hinged items, beginning with Scott 108.

Stamps of India, 1882-1900, Overprinted at Top of Stamp

1903 Wmk. 39 *Perf. 14*
1 A17 ½a light green 3.00 *4.50*
2 A19 1a carmine rose 3.00 *4.00*
3 A21 2a violet 2.50 1.60
a. Double overprint 725.00
4 A28 2½a ultra 2.25 *1.90*
5 A22 3a brown orange 3.50 3.50
6 A23 4a olive green 4.00 3.00
7 A25 8a red violet 4.25 *5.50*
8 A26 12a brown, *red* 3.50 *8.00*
a. Inverted overprint *1,200.*
9 A29 1r car rose & grn 7.50 *11.00*
10 A30 2r yel brn & car rose 30.00 *52.50*
11 A30 3r green & brown 25.00 *62.50*
12 A30 5r violet & blue 42.50 *72.50*
Wmk. Elephant's Head (38)
13 A14 6a bister 5.50 *5.25*
Nos. 1-13 (13) 136.50 *235.75*

Nos. 1-5 exist without the 2nd "I" of "BRITISH."

Same, but Overprinted at Bottom of Stamp

1903 Wmk. 39
14 A28 2½a ultra 3.50 *7.25*
15 A26 12a violet, *red* 8.00 *14.00*
16 A29 1r car rose & grn 4.00 *17.50*
17 A30 2r yel brn & car rose 90.00 *140.00*
18 A30 3r green & brn 90.00 *150.00*
a. Inverted overprint 675.00
19 A30 5r violet & blue 85.00 *110.00*
Wmk. 38
20 A14 6a bister 6.75 *6.25*
Nos. 14-20 (7) 287.25 *445.00*

Stamps of India, 1902-03, Ovptd.

1903 Wmk. 39
21 A33 ½a light green 2.50 .60
22 A34 1a car rose 1.40 .35
23 A35 2a violet 1.90 *2.75*
24 A37 3a brown orange 2.75 *2.75*
25 A38 4a olive green 1.60 *4.50*
26 A40 8a red violet 1.90 *2.50*
Nos. 21-26 (6) 12.05 *13.45*

The above overprints vary in length, also in the relative positions of the letters. Nos. 21-23 exist without the second "I" of "British."

A1

King Edward VII — A2

1904 Wmk. 2 Typo.
27 A1 ½a dl grn & grn 2.10 *4.50*
28 A1 1a carmine & blk 13.00 3.50
29 A1 2a red vio & dull vio 2.25 *2.40*
30 A1 2½a ultramarine 4.50 *4.00*
31 A1 3a gray grn & vio brn 2.40 *2.75*
32 A1 4a black & gray grn 2.50 *5.00*
33 A1 6a vio & gray grn 5.75 *18.00*
34 A1 8a pale blue & blk 4.50 *5.75*
35 A1 12a ocher & blk 7.50 *11.50*
Wmk. Crown and C C (1)
36 A2 1r gray grn 14.00 *47.50*
37 A2 2r red vio & dull vio 47.50 *85.00*
38 A2 3r blk & gray grn 47.50 *95.00*
39 A2 5r carmine & blk 47.50 *95.00*
Nos. 27-39 (13) 201.00 *379.90*
Set, ovptd. "SPECIMEN" 210.00

1905 Wmk. 3
Ordinary Paper
40 A1 ½a dl grn & grn 2.00 *8.00*
41 A1 1a carmine & blk 13.00 1.75
42 A1 2a red vio & dull vio 8.25 *10.00*
43 A1 2½a ultramarine 4.50 *11.00*
44 A1 3a gray grn & vio brn 2.50 *16.00*
45 A1 4a black & gray grn 5.00 *16.00*
46 A1 6a violet & gray grn 6.00 *27.50*
47 A1 8a pale blue & blk 6.75 *10.00*
48 A1 12a ocher & black 7.25 *11.00*
Nos. 40-48 (9) 55.25 *111.25*
Chalky Paper
41a A1 1a carmine & black ('06) 13.50 1.75
42a A1 2a red violet & dull violet ('09) 15.00 *16.00*
44a A1 3a gray green & violet brown ('11) 11.50 *32.50*
45a A1 4a black & gray green ('11) 16.00 *42.50*
46a A1 6a violet & gray green ('11) 30.00 *62.50*
47a A1 8a blue & black ('11) 30.00 *80.00*
48a A1 12a orange brown & black ('11) 19.00 *75.00*

1909
49 A1 ½a bluish green 26.00 *30.00*
50 A1 1a carmine 3.00 2.25
Ovptd. "SPECIMEN" 32.50

For overprints see Nos. O11-O16.

A3

King George V — A4

The ½, 1 and 2½a of type A3 are on ordinary paper, the other values of types A3 and A4 are on chalky paper.

1912-19
51 A3 ½a green .70 9.25
52 A3 1a carmine 2.75 .60
a. 1p scarlet ('17) 3.50 1.40
53 A3 2a red vio & dull vio 3.75 *16.00*
a. 2a violet purple & dull purple ('19) 25.00 *40.00*
54 A3 2½a ultramarine 1.10 *9.75*
55 A3 3a gray grn & vio brn 2.50 *7.50*
56 A3 4a blk & grn ('13) 2.75 *11.50*
57 A3 6a violet & green 2.75 *5.75*
58 A3 8a lt blue & blk 4.00 *17.50*
59 A3 12a ocher & blk 3.75 *24.00*
60 A4 1r dull grn & grn 12.00 *18.00*
61 A4 2r red vio & dull vio ('19) 20.00 *75.00*
62 A4 3r blk & gray grn ('19) 67.50 *125.00*
63 A4 5r car & blk ('19) 65.00 *175.00*
Nos. 51-63 (13) 188.55 *494.85*
Set, ovptd. "SPECIMEN" 225.00

1921 Wmk. 4
64 A3 ½a blue green 3.00 *11.50*
65 A3 1a scarlet 3.75 .80
66 A3 2a vio & dull vio 4.50 1.10
67 A3 2½a ultramarine 1.10 *5.25*
68 A3 3a gray grn & vio brown 2.75 *8.50*
69 A3 4a black & grn 2.75 *8.50*
70 A3 6a violet & grn 1.60 *15.00*
71 A3 8a lt blue & blk 2.25 *6.25*
72 A3 12a ocher & blk 9.00 *17.50*
73 A4 1r dull grn & grn 8.50 *55.00*
74 A4 2r vio & dull vio 25.00 *55.00*
75 A4 3r blk & gray grn 37.50 *110.00*
76 A4 5r scarlet & blk 72.50 *190.00*
Nos. 64-76 (13) 174.20 *484.40*
Set, ovptd. "SPECIMEN" 225.00

Common Design Types
pictured following the introduction.

Silver Jubilee Issue
Common Design Type

1935, May 6 Engr. *Perf. 11x12*
77 CD301 1a car & dk blue 2.50 *3.75*
78 CD301 2a black & ultra 3.00 *3.75*
79 CD301 3a ultra & brown 2.50 *13.50*
80 CD301 1r brown vio & ind 7.50 *13.50*
Nos. 77-80 (4) 15.50 *34.50*
Set, never hinged 25.00

Coronation Issue
Common Design Type

1937, May 13 *Perf. 13½x14*
81 CD302 1a carmine .20 *.25*
82 CD302 2a black .35 *1.75*
83 CD302 3a bright ultra .40 *.90*
Nos. 81-83 (3) .95 *2.90*
Set, never hinged 2.25

Blackhead Sheep — A5

Greater Kudu — A6

Map of Somaliland Protectorate A7

1938, May 10 Wmk. 4 *Perf. 12½*
84 A5 ½a green .30 *5.50*
85 A5 1a carmine .30 *1.60*
86 A5 2a deep claret 1.50 *1.90*
87 A5 3a ultra 5.75 *11.00*
88 A6 4a dark brown 3.50 *8.75*
89 A6 6a purple 5.00 *13.00*
90 A6 8a gray black 1.25 *13.50*
91 A6 12a orange 5.00 *16.00*
92 A7 1r green 6.00 *55.00*
93 A7 2r rose violet 11.00 *55.00*
94 A7 3r ultramarine 13.00 *32.50*
95 A7 5r black 14.00 *32.50*
a. Horiz. pair, imperf. btwn. *11,000.*
Nos. 84-95 (12) 66.60 *246.25*
Set, never hinged 125.00

A8

A9

A10

1942, Apr. 22

96 A8 ½a green .20 *.50*
97 A8 1a carmine .20 .20
98 A8 2a deep claret .40 .25
99 A8 3a ultramarine 1.25 .25
100 A9 4a dark brown 1.75 .25
101 A9 6a purple 1.75 .25
102 A9 8a gray 2.00 *.25*
103 A9 12a orange 2.00 *.50*
104 A10 1r green 1.25 *.90*
105 A10 2r rose violet 1.25 *5.25*
106 A10 3r ultra 2.25 *9.00*
107 A10 5r black 5.25 *8.25*
Nos. 96-107 (12) 19.55 *25.85*
Set, never hinged 37.50

For surcharges see Nos. 116-126.

Catalogue values for unused stamps in this section, from this point to the end of the section, are for Never Hinged items.

Peace Issue
Common Design Type
Perf. 13½x14

1946, Oct. 15 Engr. Wmk. 4
108 CD303 1a carmine .20 .20
a. Perf. 13½ 15.00 *62.50*
109 CD303 3a deep blue .20 .20

Silver Wedding Issue
Common Design Types

1949, Jan. 28 Photo. *Perf. 14x14½*
110 CD304 1a scarlet .25 .20

Engraved; Name Typographed
Perf. 11½x11
111 CD305 5r gray black 6.50 *9.25*

UPU Issue
Common Design Types
Surcharged in Black or Carmine with New Values in Annas
Engr.; Name Typo. on 3a, 6a

1949, Oct. 10 *Perf. 13½, 11x11½*
112 CD306 1a on 10c rose car .25 .20
113 CD307 3a on 30c ind (C) 1.40 .85
114 CD308 6a on 50c rose vio .50 *1.10*
115 CD309 12a on 1sh red org .50 .60
Nos. 112-115 (4) 2.65 2.75

Nos. 96 and 98 to 107 Surcharged with New Value in Black or Carmine

1951, Apr. 2 Wmk. 4 *Perf. 12½*
116 A8 5c on ½a green .40 *1.25*
117 A8 10c on 2a deep claret .40 *.50*
118 A8 15c on 3a ultramarine 1.40 1.40
119 A9 20c on 4a dark brown 2.10 .25
120 A9 30c on 6a purple 2.25 .60
121 A9 50c on 8a gray 2.50 .25
122 A9 70c on 12a red 4.75 *4.50*
123 A10 1sh on 1r green 2.25 .65
124 A10 2sh on 2r rose violet 6.00 *15.00*
125 A10 2sh on 3r ultra 7.50 6.50
126 A10 5sh on 5r black (C) 11.00 8.50
Nos. 116-126 (11) 40.55 39.40

OFFICIAL STAMPS

Official Stamps of India, 1883-1900, Overprinted

1903, June 1 Wmk. 39 *Perf. 14*
O1 A17 ½a light green 7.50 *55.00*
O2 A19 1a carmine rose 17.50 *9.25*
O3 A21 2a violet 9.25 *55.00*
O4 A25 8a red violet 11.50 *425.00*
O5 A29 1r car rose & grn 11.50 *625.00*
Nos. O1-O5 (5) 57.25 *1,169.*

India Nos. 61-63, 68, 49 Overprinted

1903
O6 A33 ½a green .50
O7 A34 1a carmine rose .50
O8 A35 2a violet .80
O9 A40 8a red violet 5.00
O10 A29 1r car rose & grn 20.00
Nos. O6-O10 (5) 26.80

Nos. O6-O10 were not regularly issued.

Regular Issue of 1904 Overprinted

1904 Wmk. Crown and C A (2)
O11 A1 ½a gray green 4.75 *55.00*
O12 A1 1a carmine & blk 3.75 *8.00*
O13 A1 2a red vio & dull vio 200.00 *70.00*
O14 A1 8a pale blue & blk 70.00 *150.00*
Nos. O11-O14 (4) 278.50 *283.00*

Wmk. Crown and C C (1)
O15 A2 1r gray green 190.00 *675.00*

Same Overprint on No. 42

1905 Wmk. 3
O16 A1 2a red vio & dull vio 90.00 *900.00*

The period after "M" may be found missing on Nos. O11-O14 and O16.

SOUTH AFRICA

sauth 'a-fri-kə

LOCATION — Southern Africa
GOVT. — Republic
AREA — 433,678 sq. mi.
POP. — 26,749,000 (est. 1984)
CAPITAL — Pretoria (administrative); Cape Town (legislative)

The union was formed on May 31, 1910, comprising the former British colonies of Cape of Good Hope, Natal, Transvaal and the Orange Free State, which became provinces.

For previous listings, see individual headings.

12 Pence = 1 Shilling
20 Shillings = 1 Pound

Catalogue values for unused stamps in this country are for Never Hinged items, beginning with Scott 74 in the regular postage section, Scott B1 in the semi-postal section, Scott J22 in the postage due section, and Scott O21 in the officials section.

Watermarks

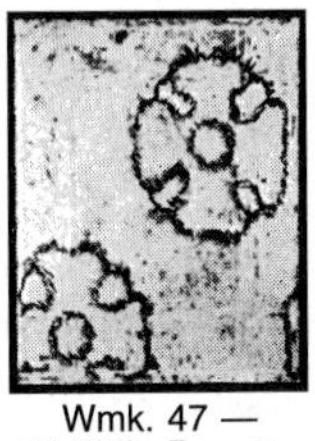
Wmk. 47 — Multiple Rosette

Wmk. 177 — Springbok's Head

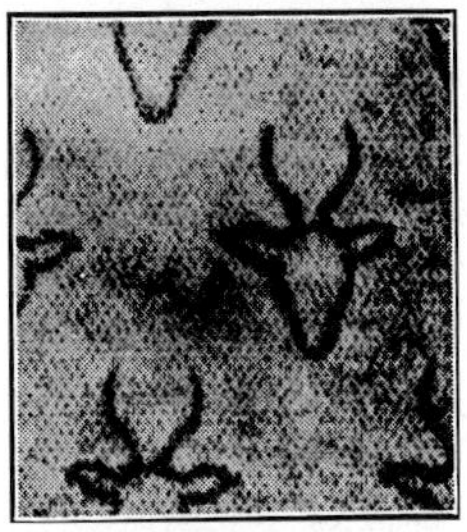
Wmk. 201 — Multiple Springbok's Head

STAMPS OF GREAT BRITAIN USED IN SOUTH AFRICA

Stamps of Great Britain used in South Africa during the Boer War, 1899-1902, with circular or octagonal postmarks "British Army South Africa" or "Natal Field Force" in several types.

1881
A1 1p lilac (16 dots) (#89) 5.75

1883-84
A2 2sh6p lilac (#96) 225.00
A3 5sh rose (#108) 250.00
A4 10sh ultramarine (#109) 525.00

1887-92
A5 ½p vermilion (#111) 7.00
A6 1½p violet & green (#112) 24.00
A7 2p green & carmine rose (#113) 16.00
A8 2½p violet, *blue* (#114) 7.50
A9 3p violet, *yellow* (#115) 14.00
A10 4p brown & green (#116) 19.00
A11 4½p carmine rose & green (#117) 55.00
A12 5p lilac blue, type II (#118) 16.00
A13 6p violet, *rose* (#119) 12.50
A14 9p blue & lilac (#120) 57.50
A15 10p carmine rose & lilac (#121) 55.00
A16 1sh green (#122) 80.00
A17 £1 green (#142) 850.00

1900
A18 ½p blue green (#125) 7.50
A19 1sh carmine rose & green (#126) 150.00

1902
A20 ½p blue green (#127a) 8.00
A21 1p scarlet(#128) 5.75
A22 1½p violet & green (#129) —
A23 2p yellow green & carmine (#130) —
A24 2½p ultramarine (#131) 11.50
A25 3p dull purple *orange yellow* (#132) —
A26 4p gray brown & green (#133) —
A27 5p dull purple & ultramarine (#134) —
A28 6p pale dull violet (#135) 20.00
A29 9p ultramarine & dull violet (#136) —
A30 10p carmine & dull purple (#137) —
A31 1sh carmine & dull green (#138) —

ARMY OFFICIAL STAMPS

1896-1901
AO1 ½p vermilion (#O54) 110.00
AO2 ½p blue green (#O57) 110.00
AO3 1p lilac (#O55) 100.00
AO4 6p purple, *rose red* (#O58) —

Union of South Africa

George V
A1 A2

1910 Engr. Wmk. 47 *Perf. 14*
1 A1 2½p blue 3.00 1.75
a. 2½ deep blue 3.00 2.75
Handstamped "SPECIMEN" *375.00*

Union Parliament opening, Nov. 4, 1910.

Type A2 stamps have very small margins at top and bottom. Values are for copies with perfs close to, or touching the frame.

1913-24 Typo. Wmk. 177
2 A2 ½p green 1.50 .20
a. Double impression *15,000.*
b. ½p blue green 1.80 .20
c. ½p yellow green 2.00 .50
d. ½p dark mossy green *125.00* *100.00*
3 A2 1p rose red 1.50 .20
a. 1p scarlet 1.50 .30
b. 1p carmine red 1.75 .20
c. 1p deep carmine lake 10.00 1.00
4 A2 1½p org brn ('20) .75 .20
a. Tête bêche pair 4.50 *15.00*
b. 1½p dark chestnut 2.00 .50
5 A2 2p dull violet 2.25 .20
a. 2p deep purple 2.25 .20
b. 2p reddish purple 2.40 .25
c. 2p deep plum *140.00* *120.00*
6 A2 2½p ultra 5.50 1.60
a. 2½p deep blue 5.00 3.00
7 A2 3p brn org & blk 13.00 .55
a. 3p dull orange red & black 10.00 .70
8 A2 3p ultra ('22) 4.75 1.60
9 A2 4p ol grn & org 11.00 .55
a. 4p sage green & orange 7.00 .45
10 A2 6p violet & black 9.50 .70
a. 6p bright violet & black 8.00 .60
b. 6p reddishviolet & black 9.00 1.00
11 A2 1sh orange 20.00 .70
a. 1sh orange yellow 22.50 1.00
12 A2 1sh3p violet ('20) 17.50 11.00
a. 1sh3p deep violet 17.00 9.00
13 A2 2sh6p green & cl 70.00 5.50

14 A2 5sh blue & claret 140.00 9.00
a. 5sh light blue * reddish purple 110.00 10.00
15 A2 10sh ol grn & blue 225.00 14.50
16 A2 £1 red & dp grn ('16) 850.00 450.00
a. £1 lt red & gray green ('24) 1,100. *1,600.*
Nos. 2-16 (15) 1,372. 496.50

The ½p, 1p and 1½p have the words "Revenue" and "Inkomst" on the stamps. On other stamps of this type these words are replaced by short vertical lines.

All values exist in many shades. No. 4a exists with and without gutter between.

Unwatermarked copies of the 1p are the result of misplaced watermarks.

All values except the 2sh6p and £1 exist with watermark inverted.

Nos. 3, 7 and 8 exist bisected. These are philatelic creations and have little value.

For overprint see No. O1.

Coil Stamps

Perf. 14 Horizontally

17 A2 ½p green 9.25 1.90
a. ½p blue green 5.00 1.00
b. ½p yellow green 5.00 1.25
18 A2 1p rose red ('14) 11.50 6.25
a. 1p scarlet 8.00 6.00
b. 1p carmine red 10.00 8.00
19 A2 1½p org brown ('20) 17.00 27.50
20 A2 2p dull violet ('21) 18.00 9.00
a. 2p deep purple 11.00 5.00
b. 2p reddish purple 11.00 5.25
Nos. 17-20 (4) 55.75 44.65

"Hope" — A3

Design: No. 22, inscribed SUIDAFRIKA.

1926 Engr. Wmk. 201 *Imperf.*

21 A3 4p blue gray 2.00 1.40
22 A3 4p blue gray 2.00 1.40

Nos. 21 and 22 were privately rouletted and perforated, but such varieties were not officially made.

No. 21 (English inscription) was printed in a separate sheet from No. 22 (Afrikaans inscription).

English-Afrikaans Se-Tenant

Stamps with English inscriptions and with Afrikaans inscriptions were printed alternately in the same sheets, starting with No. 23. Major-number listings and values are for horizontal pairs (vertical pairs sell for about one-third less) of such stamps consisting of one English and one Afrikaans-inscribed stamp, unless otherwise described.

Values are for pairs with no fold marks between stamps and no perf separations.

Beware of pairs that have been rejoined.

Springbok
A5

Jan van Riebeek's Ship, Drommedaris — A6

Orange Tree — A7

1926 Typo. *Perf. 14½x14*

23 A5 ½p dk grn & blk, pair 3.00 *3.50*
a. Single, English .25 .20
b. Single, Afrikaans .25 .20
c. Tete beche pair 1,500.
d. Center omitted 1,400.
e. Booklet pane of 6 190.00
f. As "e," perf. 14 300.00
24 A6 1p car & blk, pair 3.00 *3.00*
a. Single, English .25 .20
b. Single, Afrikaans .25 .20
c. Imperf., pair 1,350.
d. Tete beche pair 1,750.
e. Center omitted 275.00
f. Booklet pane of 6 160.00
g. As "f," perf. 14 250.00
25 A7 6p org & grn, pair 42.50 *47.50*
a. Single, English 3.00 2.25
b. Single, Afrikaans 3.00 2.25
Nos. 23-25 (3) 48.50 54.00

Nos. 23c and 24d are from uncut sheets printed for the perf. 14 booklet panes of 1928, Nos. 23f and 24g.

See Nos. 33-35, 42, 45-50, 59-61, 98-99. For overprints see Nos. O2-O4, O6-O9, O12-O15, O18, O21-O25, O30-O32, O42-O45, O48.

Government Buildings, Pretoria — A8

"Groote Schuur," Rhodes's Home — A9

Native Kraal — A10

Gnu — A11

Trekking — A12

Ox Wagon — A13

Cape Town and Table Mountain — A14

Perf. 14, 14x13½

1927-28 Engr. Wmk. 201

26 A8 2p vio brn & gray, pair 13.50 *26.00*
a. Single, English 2.10 1.40
b. Single, Afrikaans 2.10 1.40
27 A9 3p red & blk, pair 24.00 *37.50*
a. Single, English 2.10 1.40
b. Single, Afrikaans 2.10 1.40
c. Perf. 14x13½, pair 67.50 *82.50*
d. As "c," single, English 3.25 2.75
e. As "c," single, Afrikaans 3.25 2.75
28 A10 4p brown, pair ('28) 32.50 *67.50*
a. Single, English 3.25 1.90
b. Single, Afrikaans 3.25 1.90
29 A11 1sh dp bl & bis brn, pair 47.50 *87.50*
a. Single, English 6.75 2.75
b. Single, Afrikaans 6.75 2.75
30 A12 2sh6p brn & bl grn, pair 140.00 *400.00*
a. Single, English 20.00 24.00
b. Single, Afrikaans 20.00 24.00
c. Perf. 14x13½, pair 475.00 675.00
d. As "c," single, English 32.50 37.50
e. As "c," single, Afrikaans 32.50 37.50
31 A13 5sh dp grn & blk, pair 275.00 *650.00*
a. Single, English 30.00 40.00
b. Single, Afrikaans 30.00 40.00
c. Perf. 14x13½, pair 525.00 750.00
d. As "c," single, English 47.50 52.50
e. As "c," single, Afrikaans 47.50 52.50
32 A14 10sh ol brn & bl, pair 200.00 200.00
a. Single, English 20.00 16.00
b. Single, Afrikaans 20.00 16.00
c. Perf. 14x13½, pair 275.00 375.00
d. As "c," single, English 24.00 20.00
e. As "c," single, Afrikaans 24.00 20.00
Nos. 26-32 (7) 732.50 1,468.

See Nos. 36-41, 43-44, 53-54, 58, 62-66. For overprints see Nos. O5, O10-O111, O16-O17, O19-O20, O28, O33-O35, O39, O41, O49-O53.

Types of 1926-28 Redrawn
"SUIDAFRIKA" (No Hyphen) on Afrikaans Stamps

The photogravure, unhyphenated stamps of 1930-45 are distinguished from the 1926-28 typographed or engraved stamps (also unhyphenated) by the following characteristics:

½p, 1p, 6p. Leg of "R" in AFRICA or AFRIKA ends in a straight line in the photogravure set; in a curved line in the typographed. No. 35 differs from No. 34, having 2mm space between POSSEEL—INKOMSTE instead of 1mm.

2p. A memorial statue has been added just above and leftward of the "2" in value tablet on Nos. 36-37 (photogravure).

3p. Top frame on No. 38 consists of 3 heavy lines. On No. 27 it has 3 heavy and 2 very thin lines.

4p. On Nos. 40-41 the background in upper corners is solid. On No. 28 it consists of horizontal and vertical lines. No. 41 has pretzel-shaped scroll endings at bottom. On No. 40 these scroll endings enclose a solid mass of color.

1sh. No. 43 has no fine shading lines projecting from the curved top of the left inner frame, as No. 29 has. On No. 43 the shading of the last "A" of the country name partly covers the flower below it.

2sh6p. On No. 44 the shading below the country name is solid or shows signs of wear. On No. 30 it is composed of fine lines.

The engraved pictorials are much more finely executed and show details more clearly than the photogravure.

Perf. 15x14 (½p, 1p, 6p), 14

1930-45 Photo. Wmk. 201

33 A5 ½p bl grn & blk, pair 3.50 3.50
a. Single, English .20 .20
b. Single, Afrikaans .20 .20
c. Tete-beche pair 1,250.
d. As "c," gutter between 1,750.
e. Booklet pane of 6 40.00 40.00
f. Vert. pair, monolingual 5.00 5.00
34 A6 1p car & blk, pair 4.00 3.50
a. Single, English .20 .20
b. Single, Afrikaans .20 .20
c. Center omitted 2,500.
d. Frame omitted 2,500.
e. Tete-beche pair 1,800.
f. As "e," gutter between 1,500.
g. Booklet pane of 6 16.00 16.00
35 A6 1p rose & blk, pair ('32) 35.00 4.50
a. Single, English 1.00 .20
b. Single, Afrikaans 1.00 .20
c. Center omitted 750.00
36 A8 2p vio & gray, pair ('31) 24.00 16.00
a. Single, English 1.10 .40
b. Single, Afrikaans 1.10 .40
c. Frame omitted 1,000.
d. Tete-beche pair 6,500.
e. Booklet pane of 4 200.00 200.00
37 A8 2p vio & ind, pair ('38) 250.00 100.00
a. Single, English 12.50 7.25
b. Single, Afrikaans 12.50 7.25
38 A9 3p red & blk, pair ('31) 72.50 *95.00*
a. Single, English 6.75 6.75
b. Single, Afrikaans 6.75 6.75
39 A9 3p ultra & bl, pair ('33) 22.50 10.00
a. Single, English 1.10 .80
b. Single, Afrikaans 1.10 .80
c. Center omitted 1,000.
40 A10 4p redsh brn, pair ('32) 250.00 210.00
a. Single, English 25.00 11.00
b. Single, Afrikaans 25.00 11.00
41 A10 4p brn, pair ('36) 6.50 5.00
a. Single, English 1.10 .45
b. Single, Afrikaans 1.10 .45
42 A7 6p org & grn, pair ('31) 20.00 6.50
a. Single, English 1.10 .45
b. Single, Afrikaans 1.10 .45
43 A11 1sh dl bl & yel brn, pair 140.00 57.50
a. Single, English 7.25 1.10
b. Single, Afrikaans 7.25 1.10
c. 1sh dp bl & brn, pair ('32) 72.50 32.50
d. As "c," single, English 5.25 .40
e. As "c," single, Afrikaans 5.25 .40
44 A12 2sh 6p brn & bl, pair ('45) 29.00 19.00
a. Single, English 1.75 .70
b. Single, Afrikaans 1.75 .70
c. 2sh6p brn & sl grn ('36), pair 85.00 50.00
d. As "c," single, English 10.00 4.00
e. As "c," single, Afrikaans 10.00 4.00
f. 2sh6p choc & dp grn ('37), pair 75.00 40.00
g. As "f," single, English 9.00 4.00
h. As "f," single, Afrikaans 9.00 4.00
i. 2sh6p red brn & grn, pair ('32) 210.00 200.00
j. As "i," single, English 17.00 6.50
k. As "i," single, Afrikaans 17.00 6.50
Nos. 33-44 (12) 857.00 530.50

No. 34 unwatermarked, or watermarked multiple clover leaf, is a proof.

Types of 1926-28 with "SUID-AFRIKA" Hyphenated on Afrikaans Stamps, and

Gold Mine — A15

Government Buildings, Pretoria — A16

Groote Schuur — A17

Groot Constantia — A18

½p. No. 45 shading in leaves and ornaments strengthened; 40 lines in center background. Size: 18½x22½mm.

No. 46 has 28 heavy horizontal shading lines in center background and similar thicker lines in frame. Top and bottom green bars are scored by a white horizontal line. Size: 18½x22½mm.

No. 47 is smaller, 18x22mm.

1p. No. 48, size 18½x22½mm.

No. 49, size 18x22mm.

No. 50. Size: 17½x21½mm.

2p. On Nos. 53-54, S's in SOUTH and POSTAGE are narrower than on Nos. 36-37.

6p. Die I, "SUID-AFRIKA" 16½mm. Shading in leaves framing oval very faint and broken. Size: 18½x22½mm.

Die II, "SUID-AFRIKA" 17mm. Leaves strongly shaded. Heavy lines of shading in background of tree. Size: 18½x22½mm.

Die III, "question mark" scrolls below top panel are cleanly defined without intrusion of background shading. Size: 18x22mm.

Nos. 45-67 were printed in many shades. Some denominations in some printings were partly or wholly screened. Except for No. 47, the screened stamps were issued after 1947.

5sh. No. 65. Type I, letters "U" and "A" in SOUTH AFRICA have projections. Size: 27x21½mm.

No. 66. Type II, letters "U" and "A" redrawn to eliminate projections. Size: 26½x21½mm.

Perf. 15x14 (½p, 1p, 6p), 14

1933-54 Photo. Wmk. 201

45 A5 ½p grn & gray, pair ('36) 4.00 .80
a. Single, English .25 .20
b. Single, Afrikaans .25 .20
c. Bklt. pane of 6, marginal ads 25.00 25.00
d. Perf. 13½x14 (coil), pair 30.00 *47.50*
e. As "d," single, English 1.75 1.25
f. As "d," single, Afrikaans 1.75 1.25
46 A5 ½p grn & gray, redrawn, pair ('37) 4.00 .40
a. Single, English .20 .20
b. Single, Afrikaans .20 .20

c.	Booklet pane of 6	37.50	30.00
d.	Booklet pane of 2	8.00	1.00
e.	As "c," 4 blank margins	35.00	35.00
f.	Perf. 14½x14 (coil), pair	12.50	7.25
g.	As "f," single, English	2.25	.80
h.	As "f," single, Afrikaans	2.25	.80
47	A5 ½p grn & gray, pair ('47)	1.25	.40
a.	Single, English	.20	.20
b.	Single, Afrikaans	.20	.20
c.	Bklt. pane of 6, marginal ads	4.00	3.50
d.	As "c," no horiz. margins	5.00	3.00
48	A6 1p car & gray, pair ('34)	1.10	.65
a.	Single, English	.20	.20
b.	Single, Afrikaans	.20	.20
c.	Booklet pane of 6	37.50	37.50
d.	Booklet pane of 2	3.00	1.25
e.	Perf. 13½x14 (coil), pair	30.00	52.50
f.	As "e," single, English	1.40	1.00
g.	As "e," single, Afrikaans	1.40	1.00
h.	Center omitted, pair	325.00	
j.	Bklt. pane of 6, marginal ads	27.50	27.50
k.	As "j," 4 blank margins	30.00	30.00
m.	Perf. 14½x14 (coil), pair	11.00	11.00
n.	As "m," single, English	1.40	1.40
p.	As "m," single, Afrikaans	1.40	1.40
49	A6 1p rose car & gray blk, pair ('40)	1.50	.30
a.	Single, English	.20	.20
b.	Single, Afrikaans	.20	.20
c.	Unwmkd., pair	325.00	325.00
d.	Booklet pane of 6	3.75	2.75
e.	Perf. 14½x14 (coil), pair	4.00	6.00
f.	As "e," single, English	1.40	.90
g.	As "e," single, Afrikaans	1.40	.90
h.	As "d," marginal ads	5.00	4.25
50	A6 1p car & blk, pair ('51)	.75	.20
a.	Single, English	.20	.20
b.	Single, Afrikaans	.20	.20
51	A15 1½p dk grn & gold, 27x21½mm, pair ('36)	2.00	1.40
a.	Single, English	.25	.20
b.	Single, Afrikaans	.25	.20
c.	Booklet pane of 4	9.00	8.00
d.	Center omitted, pair	1,000.	
52	A15 1½p sl grn & och, 22x18mm, pair ('41)	1.25	.25
a.	Single, English	.20	.20
b.	Single, Afrikaans	.20	.20
c.	Center omitted, pair	900.00	
d.	Booklet pane of 6	5.75	4.50
53	A8 2p bl vio & dl bl, pair ('38)	40.00	32.50
a.	Single, English	3.00	1.25
b.	Single, Afrikaans	3.00	1.25
54	A8 2p dl vio & gray, pair ('41)	24.00	*45.00*
a.	Single, English	.90	.50
b.	Single, Afrikaans	.90	.50
55	A16 2p pur & sl bl, 27x21½mm, pair ('45)	1.50	*4.00*
a.	Single, English	.20	.20
b.	Single, Afrikaans	.20	.20
56	A16 2p same, 21½ x 17¼mm, pair ('50)	1.00	*4.50*
a.	Single, English	.20	.20
b.	Single, Afrikaans	.20	.20
c.	Booklet pane of 6 ('51)	3.75	2.75
57	A17 3p ultra, pair ('40)	5.00	1.75
a.	Single, English	.20	.20
b.	Single, Afrikaans	.20	.20
c.	3p bl, pair ('49)	2.00	*4.00*
d.	As "c," single, English	.20	.20
e.	As "c," single, Afrikaans	.20	.20
58	A10 4p choc brn, pair ('52)	1.25	*5.50*
a.	Single, English	.20	.20
b.	Single, Afrikaans	.20	.20
59	A7 6p org & bl grn, I, pair ('37)	50.00	22.50
a.	Single, English	3.75	1.10
b.	Single, Afrikaans	3.75	1.10
60	A7 6p org & grn, II, pair ('38)	22.50	3.00
a.	Single, English	1.50	.25
b.	Single, Afrikaans	1.50	.25
61	A7 6p red org & bl grn, III ('50), pair	1.75	1.00
a.	Single, English	.20	.20
b.	Single, Afrikaans	.20	.20
c.	6p org & grn, III, pair ('46)	13.50	1.90
d.	As "c," single, English	1.00	.20
e.	As "c," single, Afrikaans	1.00	.20
62	A11 1sh chlky bl & lt brn ('50), pair	9.00	6.00
a.	As "f," single, English	.55	.20
b.	As "f," single, Afrikaans	.55	.20
c.	1sh lt bl & ol brn, pair ('39)	35.00	7.50
d.	As "c," single, English	1.00	.20
e.	As "c," single, Afrikaans	1.00	.20
f.	1sh vio bl & brnsh blk, pair	16.00	10.00
g.	Single, English	.50	.30
h.	Single, Afrikaans	.50	.30
63	A12 2sh6p brn & brt grn, pair ('49)	7.50	*24.00*
a.	Single, English	1.25	.75
b.	Single, Afrikaans	1.25	.75
64	A13 5sh grn & blk, I, pair	55.00	55.00
a.	Single, English	2.50	2.00
b.	Single, Afrikaans	2.50	2.00
65	A13 5sh bl grn & blk, I, pair ('49)	42.50	*62.50*
a.	Single, English	4.00	3.50
b.	Single, Afrikaans	4.00	3.50
66	A13 5sh grn & blk, II, pair ('54)	55.00	*75.00*
a.	Single, English	4.00	3.50
b.	Single, Afrikaans	4.00	3.50
67	A18 10sh ol blk & bl, pair ('39)	50.00	17.50
a.	Single, English	3.00	1.00
b.	Single, Afrikaans	3.00	1.00
	Nos. 45-67 (23)	381.85	364.15

See Nos. 98-99. For overprints see Nos. O26-O27, O29, O36-O38, O40, O46-O47, O54.

George V and Springboks — A19

1935, May 1 Wmk. 201 *Perf. 15x14*

68	A19 ½p Prus grn & blk, pair	3.00	*8.50*
a.	Single, English top	.25	.25
b.	Single, Afrikaans top	.25	.25
69	A19 1p car rose & blk, pair	3.00	*8.00*
a.	Single, English top	.25	.25
b.	Single, Afrikaans top	.25	.25
70	A19 3p bl & dk bl, pair	14.00	*45.00*
a.	Single, English top	1.40	2.75
b.	Single, Afrikaans top	1.40	2.75
71	A19 6p org & grn, pair	30.00	*72.50*
a.	Single, English top	2.10	*3.00*
b.	Single, Afrikaans top	2.10	*3.00*
	Nos. 68-71 (4)	50.00	*134.00*
	Set, never hinged	100.00	

25th anniv. of the reign of George V.

English and Afrikaans inscriptions are transposed on alternate stamps. On the ½p, 3p and 6p with "SOUTH AFRICA" at top, "SILWER JUBILEUM" is at left of medallion, but on 1p with English at top, it is at the right.

Johannesburg International Philatelic Exhibition Issue

Souvenir Sheets

A20

A21

Black Overprint, "JIPEX 1936"

1936, Nov. 2 *Perf. 15x14*

72	A20 Sheet of 6 (½p)	5.00	9.50
73	A21 Sheet of 6 (1p)	4.00	6.50
	Set, never hinged	19.00	

Sheets made by overprinting booklet panes Nos. 45c and 48j. Sheets exist with and without horizontal perforations through right margin. Sheet size: 81x72½mm.

Catalogue values for unused stamps in this section, from this point to the end of the section, are for Never Hinged items.

George VI — A22

"KRONING SUID-AFRIKA" on alternate stamps.

1937, May 12 *Perf. 14*

74	A22 ½p grn & ol blk, pair	.55	.40
a.	Single, English	.20	.20
b.	Single, Afrikaans	.20	.20
75	A22 1p car & ol blk, pair	.85	.40
a.	Single, English	.20	.20
b.	Single, Afrikaans	.20	.20
76	A22 1½p Prus grn & org, pair	.85	.70
a.	Single, English	.20	.20
b.	Single, Afrikaans	.20	.20
77	A22 3p bl & ultra, pair	1.75	*2.00*
a.	Single, English	.20	.20
b.	Single, Afrikaans	.20	.20
78	A22 1sh Prus bl & org brn, pair	5.00	3.50
a.	Single, English	.50	.25
b.	Single, Afrikaans	.50	.25
	Nos. 74-78 (5)	9.00	7.00

Coronation of George VI and Queen Elizabeth.

Wagon Wheel A23

Voortrekker Family A24

Alternate stamps inscribed "SOUTH AFRICA," "SUID-AFRIKA."

1938, Dec. 14 *Perf. 15x14*

79	A23 1p rose & slate, pair	7.00	5.50
a.	Single, English	.30	.30
b.	Single, Afrikaans	.30	.30
80	A24 1½p red brn & Prus bl, pair	8.00	6.50
a.	Single, English	.30	.35
b.	Single, Afrikaans	.30	.35

Issued to commemorate the Voortrekkers.

Infantry A25

Nurse and Ambulance A26

Airman and Spitfires (Flight Lt. Robert Kershaw) A27

Sailor A28

Women's Services A29

Artillery — A30

Welder — A31

Tank Corps A32

Signal Corps — A33

Bilingual inscriptions on 2p and 1sh.

Perf. 14 (2p, 4p, 6p), 15x14

1941-43 Photo. Wmk. 201

81	A25 ½p dp bl grn, pair	.90	.40
a.	Single, English	.20	.20
b.	Single, Afrikaans	.20	.20
82	A26 1p brt rose, pair	1.75	.70
a.	Single, English	.20	.20
b.	Single, Afrikaans	.20	.20
83	A27 1½p Prus grn, pair ('42)	1.10	.40
a.	Single, English	.20	.20
b.	Single, Afrikaans	.20	.20
84	A28 2p dk violet	.50	.20
85	A29 3p dp blue, pair	14.00	11.50
a.	Single, English	.50	.50
b.	Single, Afrikaans	.50	.50
86	A30 4p org brn, pair	12.25	8.75
a.	Single, English	.75	.20
b.	Single, Afrikaans	.75	.20
c.	4p red brown, pair	32.50	32.50
d.	As "c," single, English	1.50	1.00
e.	As "c," single, Afrikaans	1.50	1.00
87	A31 6p brt red org, pair	11.75	6.75
a.	Single, English	.50	.20
b.	Single, Afrikaans	.50	.20
88	A32 1sh dark brown	2.25	.50
89	A33 1sh3p dk ol brn, pair ('43)	10.00	6.00
a.	Single, English	.50	.30
b.	Single, Afrikaans	.50	.30
c.	1sh3p dark brown, pair	6.00	6.50
d.	As "c," single, English	.50	.30
e.	As "c," single, Afrikaans	.50	.30
	Nos. 81-89 (9)	54.50	35.20

A34

A35

A36

Infantry-Nurse-Airman-Sailor — A37

Women's Services — A38

Artillery — A39

Welder — A40

Tank Corps — A41

Bilingual inscriptions on 4p and 1sh.

Pairs: Perf. 14, Roul. 6½ btwn. Strips of 3: Perf. 15x14, Roul. 6½ btwn.

1942-43 Photo. Wmk. 201

90	A34 ½p Horiz. strip of 3	.70	.55
a.	Single, English	.20	.20
b.	Single, Afrikaans	.20	.20
c.	As #90, imperf. between	350.00	

91 A35 1p Horiz. strip of 3 ('43) .90 .60
a. Single, English .20 .20
b. Single, Afrikaans .20 .20
c. As #91, imperf. between 350.00
92 A36 1½p Horiz. pair .70 .60
a. Single, English .20 .20
b. Single, Afrikaans .20 .20
c. As #92, roul. 13 4.50 4.50
d. As #92, imperf. btwn. 350.00 375.00
93 A37 2p Horiz. pair ('43) .70 .50
a. Single, English .20 .20
b. Single, Afrikaans .20 .20
c. As #93, imperf. btwn. 350.00
94 A38 3p Vert strip of 3 5.50 *8.50*
a. Single, English .20 .20
b. Single, Afrikaans .20 .20
95 A39 4p Vert. strip of 3 16.00 9.00
a. Single .20 .20
96 A40 6p Horiz. pair 3.00 2.75
a. Single, English .20 .20
b. Single, Afrikaans .20 .20
97 A41 1sh Vert. pair 12.50 3.50
a. Single .20 .20
Nos. 90-97 (8) 40.00 26.00

Because of the rouletting these are collected as pairs or strips of three, even on the bilingual stamps.

Types of 1926, Redrawn
"SUID-AFRIKA" Hyphenated
Coil Stamps

1943 Photo. *Perf. 15x14*
98 A5 ½p myrtle grn, vert. pair 1.25 *3.00*
a. Single, English .20 .20
b. Single, Afrikaans .20 .20
99 A6 1p rose pink, vert. pair 2.00 *3.00*
a. Single, English .20 .20
b. Single, Afrikaans .20 .20

"Victory" — A42

"Peace" — A43

Design: 3p, Profiles of couple ("Hope").

1945, Dec. 3 Photo. *Perf. 14*
100 A42 1p rose pink & choc, pair .25 .25
a. Single, English .20 .20
b. Single, Afrikaans .20 .20
101 A43 2p vio & sl bl, pair .25 .25
a. Single, English .20 .20
b. Single, Afrikaans .20 .20
102 A43 3p ultra & dp ultra, pair .35 .35
a. Single, English .20 .20
b. Single, Afrikaans .20 .20
Nos. 100-102 (3) .85 .85

World War II victory of the Allies.

George VI — A44

King George VI and Queen Elizabeth A45

Princesses Margaret Rose and Elizabeth A46

Perf. 15x14
1947, Feb. 17 Wmk. 201
103 A44 1p cer & gray, pair .25 .25
a. Single, English .20 .20
b. Single, Afrikaans .20 .20
104 A45 2p purple, pair .25 .25
a. Single, English .20 .20
b. Single, Afrikaans .20 .20
105 A46 3p dk blue, pair .35 .35
a. Single, English .20 .20
b. Single, Afrikaans .20 .20
Nos. 103-105 (3) .85 .85

Visit of the British Royal Family, Mar.-Apr., 1947.

George VI, Elizabeth — A47

Gold Mine — A48

1948, Apr. 26 Photo. *Perf. 14*
106 A47 3p dp chlky bl & sil, pair .50 .50
a. Single, English .20 .20
b. Single, Afrikaans .20 .20

25th anniv. of the marriage of George VI and Queen Elizabeth.

Vertical Pairs Perf. 14 all around, Rouletted 6½ between
1948, Apr.
107 A48 1½p sl & och, vert. pair 1.25 *2.00*
a. Single, English .20 .20
b. Single, Afrikaans .20 .20

"Wanderer" in Port Natal A49

1949, May 2 Photo. *Perf. 15x14*
108 A49 1½p red brown, pair .45 .45
a. Single, English .20 .20
b. Single, Afrikaans .20 .20

Mercury and Globe — A50

1949, Oct. 1 *Perf. 14x15*
109 A50 ½p dk green, pair .50 .50
a. Single, English .20 .20
b. Single, Afrikaans .20 .20
110 A50 1½p dk red, pair .75 .75
a. Single, English .20 .20
b. Single, Afrikaans .20 .20
111 A50 3p ultra, pair 1.25 1.25
a. Single, English .20 .20
b. Single, Afrikaans .20 .20
Nos. 109-111 (3) 2.50 2.50

75th anniv. of the UPU.

Except for Nos. 216, 310-313, 518a, 669a this is the end of bi-lingual multiples in the postage section.

Voortrekkers en Route to Natal — A51

Voortrekker Monument, Pretoria A52

Voortrekkers Looking Toward Natal, and Open Bible — A53

1949, Dec. 1 *Perf. 15x14*
112 A51 1p magenta .20 .20
113 A52 1½p dull green .20 .20
114 A53 3p dark blue .20 .20
Nos. 112-114 (3) .60 .60

Inauguration of the Voortrekker Monument at Pretoria.

Riebeeck's Seal and Dutch East India Company Monogram A54

Maria de la Quellerie — A55

2p, van Riebeeck's Ships. 4½p, Jan van Riebeeck. 1sh, Landing of van Riebeeck.

Perf. 15x14, 14x15
1952, Mar. 14 Wmk. 201
115 A54 ½p dk brn & red vio .20 .20
116 A55 1p dark green .20 .20
117 A54 2p dark purple .20 .20
118 A55 4½p dark blue .20 .20
119 A54 1sh brown .55 .50
Nos. 115-119 (5) 1.35 1.30

300th anniv. of the landing of Jan van Riebeeck at the Cape of Good Hope.

Nos. 116-117 Overprinted "SATISE" (1p) and "SADIPU" (2p)

1952, Mar. 26
120 A55 1p dark green .30 .55
121 A54 2p dark purple .35 .70

South African Tercentenary Intl. Stamp Exhib., Cape Town, Mar. 26-Apr. 5, 1952.

SEMI-POSTAL STAMPS

Catalogue values for unused stamps in this section are for Never Hinged items.

English-Afrikaans Se-Tenant Stamps with English inscriptions and with Afrikaans inscriptions of Nos. B1-B11 were printed alternately in the same sheets. Major-number listings and values are for pairs consisting of one English and one Afrikaans-inscribed stamp.

Church of the Vow — SP1

Cradock's Pass — SP2

Voortrekker — SP3

Voortrekker Woman — SP4

1933-36 Photo. Wmk. 201 *Perf. 14*
B1 SP1 ½p + ½p grn & blk, pair ('36) 8.00 3.25
a. Single, English .45 .45
b. Single, Afrikaans .45 .45
B2 SP2 1p + ½p rose & blk, pair 5.25 2.40
a. Single, English .35 .25
b. Single, Afrikaans .35 .25
B3 SP3 2p + 1p dull vio & gray, pair 8.75 3.25
a. Single, English .45 .45
b. Single, Afrikaans .45 .45
B4 SP4 3p + 1½p dp blue & gray, pair 13.00 7.25
a. Single, English 1.10 .90
b. Single, Afrikaans 1.10 .90
Nos. B1-B4 (4) 35.00 16.15

Issued to commemorate the Voortrekkers. Surtax went to the National Memorial Fund for a national Voortrekker monument.

Voortrekker Plowing — SP5

Crossing the Drakensberg — SP6

Signing Dingaan-Retief Treaty — SP7

Proposed Monument — SP8

1938, Dec. 14 *Perf. 14*
B5 SP5 ½p + ½p dl grn & ind, pair 5.50 5.25
a. Single, English .55 .45
b. Single, Afrikaans .55 .45
B6 SP6 1p + 1p rose & sl, pair 7.25 6.00
a. Single, English .65 .55
b. Single, Afrikaans .65 .55

Perf. 15x14
B7 SP7 1½p + ½p Prus grn & choc, pair 17.50 10.50
a. Single, English 1.10 1.10
b. Single, Afrikaans 1.10 1.10

B8 SP8 3p + 3p chlky bl, pair 20.00 12.50
a. Single, English 1.40 1.60
b. Single, Afrikaans 1.40 1.60
Nos. B5-B8 (4) 50.25 34.25

Voortrekker centenary. Surtax went to the Natl. Memorial Fund for a Voortrekker monument.

"The Old Vicarage," Huguenot Museum — SP9

Rising Sun and Cross — SP10

Huguenot Dwelling, Drakenstein Mountain Valley — SP11

1939, July 17 Photo. *Perf. 14*

B9 SP9 ½p + ½p Prus grn & gray brn, pair 6.50 4.75
a. Single, English .50 .50
b. Single, Afrikaans .50 .50
B10 SP10 1p + 1p rose car & Prus grn, pair 10.00 6.25
a. Single, English .60 .60
b. Single, Afrikaans .60 .60

Perf. 15x14

B11 SP11 1½p + 1½p, pair 16.00 9.00
a. Single, English .95 .95
b. Single, Afrikaans .95 .95
Nos. B9-B11 (3) 32.50 20.00

250th anniv. of the landing of the Huguenots in South Africa. Surtax went to a fund to build a Huguenot memorial at Paarl.

AIR POST STAMPS

Mail Plane — AP1

Biplane in Flight — AP2

Unwmk.
1925, Feb. 26 Litho. *Perf. 12*

C1 AP1 1p red 1.50 5.25
C2 AP1 3p ultramarine 8.00 *8.75*
C3 AP1 6p violet 12.75 *17.50*
C4 AP1 9p gray green 21.00 *32.50*
Nos. C1-C4 (4) 43.25 *64.00*

Forgeries exist.

1929, Aug. 16 Typo. *Perf. 14x13½*

C5 AP2 4p blue green 3.00 2.00
C6 AP2 1sh orange 17.00 13.00

POSTAGE DUE STAMPS

On cover values are for properly franked commercial covers. Philatelic usages also exist and sell for less.

D1

D2

Wmk. Springbok's Head (177)
1914-15 Typo. *Perf. 14*

J1 D1 ½p green & blk .90 3.50
On cover 70.00
J2 D1 1p red & blk .90 .20
On cover 20.00
J3 D1 2p vio & blk ('14) 4.50 .65
On cover 20.00
J4 D1 3p ultra & blk .70 .65
On cover 35.00
J5 D1 5p brown & blk 1.75 *15.00*
On cover *600.00*
J6 D1 6p gray & blk 8.75 *15.00*
On cover *650.00*
J7 D1 1sh black & red 62.50 *125.00*
On cover *2,000.*
Nos. J1-J7 (7) 80.00 *160.00*

1922 Unwmk. Litho. *Rouletted 7-8*

J8 D1 ½p blue grn & blk 1.00 *7.75*
On cover *60.00*
J9 D1 1p dull red & blk 1.10 .75
On cover 30.00
J10 D1 1½p yellow brn & blk 1.25 1.50
On cover 40.00
Nos. J8-J10 (3) 3.35 *10.00*

1922-26 *Perf. 14*

J11 D1 ½p blue grn & blk .20 .20
On cover 20.00
J12 D1 1p rose & blk ('23) .35 .20
On cover 15.00
J13 D1 1½p yel brn & blk ('24) 1.00 .80
On cover 40.00
J14 D1 2p vio & blk ('23) .85 .40
On cover 20.00
a. Imperf. pair 250.00
J15 D1 3p blue & blk ('26) 5.00 5.00
On cover 35.00
J16 D1 6p gray & blue ('23) 10.00 5.00
On cover 80.00
Nos. J11-J16 (6) 17.40 11.60

1927-28 Typo.

J17 D2 ½p blue green & blk .40 .50
On cover 20.00
J18 D2 1p rose & black .40 .40
On cover 15.00
J19 D2 2p violet & black .70 .60
On cover 20.00
J20 D2 3p ultra & black 6.50 6.50
On cover 35.00
J21 D2 6p gray & black 12.00 10.00
On cover 90.00
Nos. J17-J21 (5) 20.00 18.00

Type of 1927-28 Redrawn
Perf. 15x14
1932-40 Photo. Wmk. 201

J22 D2 ½p blue grn & blk ('34) 1.00 1.25
On cover 20.00
J23 D2 1p rose car & blk ('34) .95 .95
On cover 15.00
J24 D2 2p blk violet & blk 4.00 .30
On cover 15.00
a. 2p dark purple & black ('40) 11.00 .20
J25 D2 3p dp blue & blk 18.00 12.00
On cover 100.00
J26 D2 3p ultra & dk bl ('35) 3.50 .40
On cover 20.00
J27 D2 3p blue & dk bl ('40) 21.00 2.00
On cover 50.00
J28 D2 6p brn org & grn ('33) 18.00 6.00
On cover 70.00
J29 D2 6p red org & grn ('38) 8.50 2.00
On cover 50.00
Nos. J22-J29 (8) 74.95 24.90

The ½p No. J22 photogravure has larger but thinner numeral and the "d" is taller and thinner than on No. J17.

The 1p No. J23 photogravure has numeral with parallel sides. The "d" is taller and thicker than on No. J18.

On Nos. J25 and J27 the numeral is followed by a large "d" with thick lines and a large round period below it.

Nos. J22, J24 and J25 have frame in photogravure, value typographed.

Catalogue values for unused stamps in this section, from this point to the end of the section, are for Never Hinged items.

See "English-Afrikaans Se-tenant" note preceding No. 23.

D3

Horiz. strips of Three, Perf. 15x14 All Around, Rouletted 6½ Between
1943-44 Photo. Wmk. 201

J30 D3 ½p Prus green ('44) 8.50 *22.50*
On cover *400.00*
a. Single .20 .20
J31 D3 1p brt carmine 9.50 5.25
On cover 400.00
a. Single .20 .20
J32 D3 2p dark purple 9.00 9.00
On cover 650.00
a. Single .20 .20
J33 D3 3p dark blue 55.00 62.50
On cover 800.00
a. Single .20 .20
Nos. J30-J33 (4) 82.00 99.25

Catalogued as strips of 3 because of the perforations.

Type of 1932-38, Redrawn
Thick Numerals, Capital "D"
1948-49 *Perf. 15x14*

J34 D2 ½p blue green & blk 9.00 6.00
On cover 40.00
J35 D2 1p deep rose & blk 10.50 2.50
On cover 30.00
J36 D2 2p dk pur & blk ('49) 14.00 2.50
On cover 30.00
J37 D2 3p ultra & dk blue 12.00 9.00
On cover 60.00
J38 D2 6p dp org & grn ('49) 37.50 7.00
On cover 80.00
Nos. J34-J38 (5) 83.00 27.00

Redrawn Type of 1948-49
Hyphen between Suid-Afrika
1950-58 *Perf. 15x14*

J40 D2 1p car rose & blk 1.10 .40
On cover 20.00
J41 D2 2p dk pur & blk ('51) .75 .25
On cover 15.00
J42 D2 3p ultra & dk blue 5.75 2.25
On cover 25.00
J43 D2 4p emer & dk grn ('58) 13.00 10.00
On cover 60.00
J44 D2 6p dp org & grn ('52) 10.50 10.50
On cover 60.00
J45 D2 1sh brn red & dk brn ('58) 16.00 13.00
On cover 100.00
Nos. J40-J45 (6) 47.10 36.40

OFFICIAL STAMPS

Type A2 stamps have very small margins at top and bottom. IdsrtValues are for copies with perfs close to, or touching the frame.

Regular Issues Overprinted in Black

Periods in Overprint
On No. 5
1926 Wmk. 177 *Perf. 14*

O1 A2 2p dull violet 18.00 2.00

See "English-Afrikaans Se-tenant" note preceding No. 23.

On Nos. 23-25
Perf. 14½x14
Wmk. 201

O2 A5 ½p dk grn & blk, pair 6.00 *12.00*
a. Single, English .75 1.25
b. Single, Afrikaans .75 1.25
O3 A6 1p car & blk, pair 4.00 *7.00*
a. Single, English .25 .50
b. Single, Afrikaans .25 .50
O4 A7 6p org & grn, pair 550.00 75.00
a. Single, English 25.00 9.00
b. Single, Afrikaans 25.00 9.00

Nos. 26 and 25 Overprinted (Reading Up)

b

No Periods in Overprint
1928-29 *Perf. 14, 14½x14*
Space between words 19mm

O5 A8 2p vio brn & gray, pair ('29) 3.50 *10.00*
a. Single, English .50 *1.50*
b. Single, Afrikaans .50 *1.50*
c. Space 17½mm, pair 4.00 *12.50*
d. As "c," single, English .50 *2.00*
e. As "c," single, Afrikaans .50 *2.00*

Space between words 11½mm

O6 A7 6p org & grn, pair 18.00 *25.00*
a. Single, English 2.00 *2.75*
b. Single, Afrikaans 2.00 *2.75*

#23-25 Ovptd. type "b" Reading Down
Space between words 13½-14mm
1929 *Perf. 14½x14*

O7 A5 ½p grn & blk, pair 2.00 *2.75*
a. Single, English .25 .30
b. Single, Afrikaans .25 .30
c. Period after "OFFISIEEL" on English stamp 3.25 3.25
d. Pair, "c" + normal ½p 30.00 30.00
e. Period after "OFFICIAL." on Afrikaans stamp 3.25 3.25
f. Pair, "e" + normal ½p 35.00 35.00
O8 A6 1p car & blk, pair 2.50 *3.50*
a. Single, English .30 .40
b. Single, Afrikaans .30 .40
O9 A7 6p org & grn, pair 7.75 *26.00*
a. Single, English 1.25 *3.00*
b. Single, Afrikaans 1.25 *3.00*
c. Period after "OFFISIEEL." on English stamp 8.00 *10.00*
d. Pair, "c" + normal 6p 60.00 *100.00*
e. Period after "OFFISIEEL." on Afrikaans stamp 9.00 *12.00*
f. Pair, "e" + normal 6p 70.00 *110.00*
Nos. O7-O9 (3) 12.25 *32.25*

#29-30 Ovptd. type "b" Reading Down
Space between words 17½-19mm
1931 Engr. *Perf. 14, 14x13½*

O10 A11 1sh dp bl & bis brn, pair 30.00 *85.00*
a. Single, English 3.00 *9.00*
b. Single, Afrikaans 3.00 *9.00*
c. Period after "OFFICIAL." on Afrikaans stamp 50.00 50.00
d. Pair, "c" + normal 1sh 100.00 *225.00*
O11 A12 2sh6p brn & bl grn, pair 60.00 *150.00*
a. Single, English 7.50 *17.50*
b. Single, Afrikaans 7.50 *17.50*
c. Period after "OFFICIAL." on Afrikaans stamp 72.50 72.50
d. Pair, "c" + normal 2sh6p 275.00 *475.00*

Regular Issues of 1930-45 Overprinted type "b" Reading Down ("SUIDAFRIKA" on Afrikaans stamps)
Perf. 15x14 (½p, 1p, 6p), 14
1930-47 Photo. Wmk. 201
Space between words 9½-12mm
(Various spacings occur in same setting)

O12 A5 ½p bl grn & blk (#33), pair ('31) 2.00 *3.50*
a. Single, English .20 *.40*
b. Single, Afrikaans .20 *.40*
c. Period after "OFFISIEEL." on English stamp 3.50 *4.00*
d. Pair, "c" + normal ½p 25.00 *42.50*
e. Period after "OFFISIEEL." on Afrikaans stamp 3.25 *3.50*
f. Pair, "e" + normal ½p 25.00 *40.00*

Space between words 12½-13½mm

O13 A5 ½p bl grn & blk, pair (#33) 3.00 4.00
a. Single, English .25 .50
b. Single, Afrikaans .25 .50
O14 A6 1p car & blk, pair (#34) 3.50 3.50
a. Single, English .40 .50
b. Single, Afrikaans .40 .50
c. Period after "OFFISIEEL." on English stamp 3.75 *4.00*
d. Pair, "c" + normal 1p 25.00 *32.50*
e. Period after "OFFISIEEL." on Afrikaans stamp 3.00 *3.50*
f. Pair, "e" + normal 1p 25.00 *32.50*
O15 A6 1p rose & blk, pair (#35) ('33) 7.50 9.00
a. Single, English .75 1.00
b. Single, Afrikaans .75 1.00
c. Double ovpt., pair 275.00 *300.00*
d. As "c," English 45.00

e. As "c," Afrikaans 45.00

Space between words 20½-22mm

O16 A8 2p vio & gray, pair (#36) ('31) 4.50 10.00
a. Single, English .60 1.25
b. Single, Afrikaans .60 1.25
O17 A8 2p vio & ind, pair (#37) 75.00 85.00
a. Single, English 6.00 9.00
b. Single, Afrikaans 6.00 9.00

Space between words 12½-13½mm

O18 A7 6p org & grn, pair (#42) 7.00 8.50
a. Single, English .75 .90
b. Single, Afrikaans .75 .90
c. Period after "OFFISIEEL." on English stamp 6.50 6.50
d. Pair, "c" + normal 6p 50.00 60.00
e. Period after "OFFISIEEL." on Afrikaans stamp 5.50 5.50
f. Pair, "e" + normal 6p 40.00 50.00

Space between words 21mm

O19 A11 1sh dp bl & brn, pair (#43c) ('32) 42.50 75.00
a. Single, English 4.00 7.50
b. Single, Afrikaans 4.00 7.50
c. 1sh dk bl & yel brn (#43), 19mm, pair 42.50 75.00
d. As "c," single, English 3.00 7.50
e. As "c," single, Afrikaans 3.00 7.50
f. As "c," spaced 21mm, pair 42.50 65.00
g. As "f," single, English 6.00 7.50
h. As "f," single, Afrikaans 6.00 7.50

Space between words 17½-18½mm

O20 A12 2sh6p brn & sl grn (#44c) ('37), pair 65.00 100.00
a. Single, English 10.00 12.50
b. Single, Afrikaans 10.00 12.50
c. Spaced 21mm, pair 45.00 70.00
d. As "c," single, English 4.50 8.00
e. As "c," single, Afrikaans 4.50 8.00
f. 2sh6p red brn & grn, pair (#44i) ('33) 50.00 90.00
g. As "f," single, English 5.00 8.50
h. As "f," single, Afrikaans 5.00 8.50
j. 2sh6p brn & bl, 19-20mm (#44) ('47), pair 30.00 60.00
k. As "j," single, English 3.00 5.00
m. As "j," single, Afrikaans 3.00 5.00
Nos. O12-O20 (9) 210.00 298.50

Catalogue values for unused stamps in this section, from this point to the end of the section, are for Never Hinged items.

Regular Issue of 1933-54 Overprinted type "b" Reading Down ("SUID-AFRIKA" Hyphenated)

1935-50 Photo. *Perf. 15x14, 14*

Space between words given with each listing

O21 A5 ½p grn & gray (#45), 12½-13mm, pair ('36) 3.25 15.00
a. Single, English .25 1.60
b. Single, Afrikaans .25 1.60
O22 A5 ½p grn & gray, (#46), 11½-13mm, pair ('38) 12.00 12.50
a. Single, English .50 1.25
b. Single, Afrikaans .50 1.25
O23 A5 ½p grn & gray (#47), 11½mm, pair ('48) 1.25 5.00
a. Single, English .20 .70
b. Single, Afrikaans .20 .70
O24 A6 1p car & gray (#48), 11-13mm, pair 1.00 1.00
a. Single, English .20 .20
b. Single, Afrikaans .20 .20
O25 A6 1p rose car & gray blk (#49), 11½-12mm, pair ('41) 1.00 .50
a. Single, English .20 .20
b. Single, Afrikaans .20 .20
O26 A15 1½p dk grn & gold (#51), 19-21mm, pair ('37) 30.00 22.50
a. Single, English 2.25 1.75
b. Single, Afrikaans 2.25 1.75
O27 A15 1½p sl grn & ocher (#52), 16mm, pair ('44) 3.00 8.00
a. Single, English .30 .45
b. Single, Afrikaans .30 .45
c. Ovpt. spaced 14-14½mm, pair 3.00 5.00
d. As "c," single, English .25 .80
e. As "c," single, Afrikaans .25 .80
O28 A8 2p bl vio & dl bl (#53), 20-21mm, pair ('39) 80.00 30.00
a. Single, English 7.50 2.50
b. Single, Afrikaans 7.50 2.50
O29 A16 2p pur & sl (#55), 19-21mm, pair ('48) 4.50 16.00
a. Single, English .25 1.50
b. Single, Afrikaans .25 1.50

O30 A7 6p org & bl grn, I (#59), 12-13mm, pair ('38) 80.00 40.00
a. Single, English 6.50 3.75
b. Single, Afrikaans 6.50 3.75
O31 A7 6p org & grn, II (#60), 12-13mm, pair ('39) 12.00 10.00
a. Single, English 1.25 1.25
b. Single, Afrikaans 1.25 1.25
O32 A7 6p org & grn III (#61), 11½-12mm, pair ('47) 5.50 8.00
a. Single, English .50 .90
b. Single, Afrikaans .50 .90
O33 A11 1sh lt bl & ol brn (#62c), 19-21mm, pair ('40) 65.00 27.50
a. Single, English 4.50 2.00
b. Single, Afrikaans 4.50 2.00
c. "OFFICIAL" on both sides 500.00
d. "OFFISIEEL" on both sides 500.00
e. 1sh chlky bl & lt brn (#62) ('50), pair 10.00 25.00
f. As "e," single, English .90 2.50
g. As "e," single, Afrikaans .90 2.50
h. 1sh vio bl & brnsh blk (#62f), 18-19mm, pair 65.00 27.50
j. As "h," single, English 4.50 2.00
k. As "h," single, Afrikaans 4.50 2.00
O34 A13 5sh grn & blk (#64) 19-20mm, pair 55.00 110.00
a. Single, English 3.50 12.50
b. Single, Afrikaans 3.50 12.50
O35 A13 5sh bl grn & blk (#65), 20mm, pair 40.00 110.00
a. Single, English 3.50 12.50
b. Single, Afrikaans 3.50 12.50
O36 A18 10sh ol blk & bl (#67), 19½-20mm, pair ('48) 85.00 175.00
a. Single, English 7.50 22.50
b. Single, Afrikaans 7.50 22.50
Nos. O21-O36 (16) 478.50 591.00

Nos. 52 and 56 Overprinted type "b" Reading Up

Space between words 16mm

1949-50 Size: 22x18mm *Perf. 14*

O37 A15 1½p sl grn & ocher, pair 35.00 40.00
a. Single, English 2.25 3.50
b. Single, Afrikaans 2.25 3.50

Size: 21½x17½mm

O38 A16 2p pur & sl bl, pair ('50) 1,500. 1,750.
a. Single, English 125. 175.
b. Single, Afrikaans 125. 175.

Nos. 64, 67 Overprinted

c

Space between words 18-19mm

1940 *Perf. 14*

O39 A13 5sh grn & blk, pair 85.00 100.00
a. Single, English 3.00 10.00
b. Single, Afrikaans 3.00 10.00
O40 A18 10sh ol brn & bl, pair 375.00 350.00
a. Single, English 25.00 35.00
b. Single, Afrikaans 25.00 35.00

No. 54 Overprinted type "c" Reading Up

Space between words 19mm

1945 *Perf. 14*

O41 A8 2p dl vio & gray, pair 8.00 22.50
a. Single, English .50 2.25
b. Single, Afrikaans .50 2.25

No. 47 Overprinted

1947 *Perf. 15x14*

O42 A5 ½p grn & gray, pair 22.50 20.00
a. Single, English 1.00 2.00
b. Single, Afrikaans 1.00 2.00

Stamps of 1937-54 Overprinted

1950-54 *Perf. 15x14, 14*

Space between words 10mm

O43 A5 ½p grn & gray, pair (#47) .90 1.50
a. Single, English .20 .20
b. Single, Afrikaans .20 .20
O44 A6 1p rose car & gray blk, pair (#49) 1.00 2.00
a. Single, English .20 .20
b. Single, Afrikaans .20 .20
O45 A6 1p car & blk, pair (#50) 1.00 1.50
a. Single, English .20 .20
b. Single, Afrikaans .20 .20

Space between words 14½mm

O46 A15 1½p sl grn & ocher, pair (#52) 1.50 3.00
a. Single, English .20 .35
b. Single, Afrikaans .20 .35
O47 A16 2p pur & sl bl, pair (#56) 1.00 2.00
a. Single, English .20 .20
b. Single, Afrikaans .20 .20
c. Ovpt. reading up, pair

Space between words 10mm

O48 A7 6p red org & bl grn, III, pair (#61c) 2.00 3.00
a. Single, English .35 .35
b. Single, Afrikaans .35 .35

Space between words 19mm

O49 A11 1sh chlky bl & lt brn, pair (#62) 6.75 15.00
a. Single, English .50 1.75
b. Single, Afrikaans .50 1.75
c. 1sh vio bl & brnsh blk (#62f), pair 140.00 150.00
d. As "c," single, English 12.50 17.50
e. As "c," single, Afrikaans 12.50 17.50
O50 A12 2sh6p brn & brt grn, pair (#63) 10.00 32.50
a. Single, English 1.00 3.25
b. Single, Afrikaans 1.00 3.25
O51 A13 5sh grn & blk, pair (#64) 175.00 90.00
a. Single, English 2.00 9.00
b. Single, Afrikaans 2.00 9.00
O52 A13 5sh bl grn & blk, I, pair (#65) 65.00 75.00
a. Single, English 3.00 6.50
b. Single, Afrikaans 3.00 6.50
O53 A13 5sh grn & blk, II, pair (#66) 80.00 80.00
a. Single, English 4.00 9.00
b. Single, Afrikaans 4.00 9.00
O54 A18 10sh ol blk & bl, pair (#67) 80.00 200.00
a. Single, English 5.00 21.00
b. Single, Afrikaans 5.00 21.00
Nos. O43-O54 (12) 424.15 505.50

SOUTH AUSTRALIA

ˈsauth o-ˈstrāl-yə

LOCATION — Central part of southern Australia
GOVT. — British Colony
AREA — 380,070 sq. mi.
POP. — 358,346 (1901)
CAPITAL — Adelaide

South Australia was one of the six British colonies that united in 1901 to form the Commonwealth of Australia.

12 Pence = 1 Shilling
20 Shillings = 1 Pound

Values for unused stamps are for examples with original gum as defined in the catalogue introduction.

Very fine examples of Nos. 10-60 and O1-O60 will have perforations slightly cutting into the framelines or design on one or more sides due to the narrow spacing of the stamps on the plates.

Stamps with perfs clear on all sides are scarce to rare and will command higher to substantially higher prices.

Watermarks

Wmk. 6 — Star with Long Narrow Points

Wmk. 7 — Star with Short Broad Points

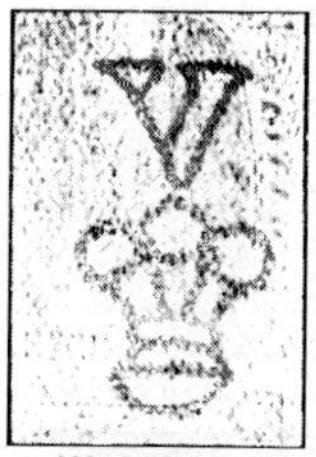

Wmk. 70 — Crown and V

Wmk. 72 — Crown and SA

Wmk. 73 — Crown and SA, Letters Close

Wmk. 74 — Crown and Single-lined A

Queen Victoria — A1

1855-56 Engr. Wmk. 6 *Imperf.*

London Print

1 A1 1p dark green 4,500. 575.
2 A1 2p dull carmine 700. 100.00
3 A1 6p deep blue 2,700. 200.
4 A1 1sh violet ('56) *7,750.*

No. 4 was never put in use. Nos. 1 and 3 without watermark are proofs.

Six copies each of Nos. 1-4 were hand-stamped "CANCELLED" in oval in 1855-56 by the printers, Perkins Bacon, for presentation to members of Sir Rowland Hill's family. Values, *from* $5,750.

1856-59 Local Print

5 A1 1p deep yel grn ('58) *7,250.* 650.00
a. 1p yellow green ('58) *6,000.* 775.00
6 A1 2p blood red 1,600. 90.00
a. Printed on both sides *1,000.*
b. 2p orange red ('56) 1,700. 100.00
7 A1 2p pale red ('57) 775.00 55.00
a. Printed on both sides *775.00*
8 A1 6p slate blue ('57) 1,900. 200.00
9 A1 1sh orange ('57) 5,250. 475.00
a. Printed on both sides — —
b. 1sh red orange — 600.00

1858-59 *Rouletted*

10 A1 1p yellow grn ('59) 775.00 72.50
a. Horiz. pair, imperf. between — —
b. 1p pale yellow green ('59) 775.00 77.50
11 A1 2p pale red ('59) 160.00 25.00
a. Printed on both sides *775.00*

12 A1 6p slate blue 575.00 45.00
13 A1 1sh orange ('59) 1,200. 50.00
c. Printed on both sides 1,400.

See #14-16, 19-20, 25-26, 28-29, 32, 35-36, 41-43, 47, 51-52, 69-70, 73, 113, 118. For overprints see #O1-O2, O5, O7, O9, O11-O13, O17, O20, O27, O30, O32, O39-O40, O42, O52, O76, O85.

A2

A3

Surcharge on #22-24, 34, 49-50

1860-69 *Rouletted*

14 A1 1p dull blue green 65.00 37.50
a. 1p deep green 350.00 95.00
b. 1p bright green 72.50 40.00
15 A1 1p sage green 90.00 50.00
a. 1p deep yellow green ('69) 140.00
b. 1p pale sage green ('65) 72.50
16 A1 2p vermilion ('62) 80.00 4.75
a. Horiz. pair, imperf. btwn. 1,750. 550.00
b. Rouletted and perf. all around 1,725. 500.00
c. 2p pale red 97.50 4.75
d. As "c," printed on both sides — 475.00
e. 2p bright vermilion ('64) 75.00 3.75
18 A2 4p dull violet ('67) 90.00 26.00
19 A1 6p grnsh bl ('63) 100.00 4.75
20 A1 6p dull blue 140.00 7.50
a. 6p sky blue 140.00 7.75
b. 6p Prussian blue 700.00 57.50
c. Horiz. pair, imperf btwn. 800.00
d. 6p ultramarine 95.00 4.75
e. Horiz. pair, imperf. btwn. (#20f) — 425.00
f. 6p indigo blue — 65.00
g. Rouletted and perf. all around (#20f) 375.00
h. 6p violet blue 200.00 8.00
i. 6p violet ultramarine ('68) 190.00 7.00
21 A3 9p gray lilac ('69) 85.00 10.50
a. Double impression — —
b. Horiz. pair, imperf between 1,375.
c. Rouletted and perf. all around 1,850. 250.00
22 A3 10p on 9p red org (Bl) ('66) 275.00 42.50
23 A3 10p on 9p yel (Bl) ('67) 425.00 32.50
24 A3 10p on 9p yel (Blk) ('69) 2,200. 55.00
a. Inverted surcharge — 3,750.
c. Printed on both sides — 1,050.
d. Rouletted x perf. 10 —
24E A1 1sh yellow ('61) 600.00 35.00
f. Vert. pair, imperf. btwn. — 1,600.
25 A1 1sh lake brn ('65) 140.00 14.50
a. Horiz. pair, imperf. btwn. — 575.00
26 A1 1sh brown ('63) 180.00 23.00
a. 1sh chestnut ('64) 190.00 13.50
b. 1sh gray brown ('63) 200.00 22.00
27 A2 2sh carmine ('67) 160.00 35.00
a. Vert. pair, imperf. btwn. 1,200.

There are six varieties of the surcharge "TEN PENCE" in this and subsequent issues.

Nos. 16b, 20g, 21c, 28a, 32c, 33a are rouletted remainders that were later perforated.

See #31, 33, 46, 48, 53, 63, 68, 72, 74, 112, 113B, 119-120. For surcharges & overprints see #34, 44-45, 49-50, 59, 67, 71, O4, O6, O8, O10, O16-O19, O18, O21, O26, O28-O29, O31, O33, O36-O38, O41, O41B, O43, O53. Compare with design A6a.

1867-72 *Perf. 11½ to 12½xRoulette*

28 A1 1p blue green 300.00 50.00
a. Rouletted and perf. all around 625.00
29 A1 1p grayish green ('70) 210.00 29.00
a. 1p bright green ('68) 175.00 25.00
b. 1p pale bright green ('67) 210.00 26.00
31 A2 4p dull violet ('68) 1,925. 175.00
a. 4p purple ('69) — 120.00
32 A1 6p Prus blue 500.00 23.00
a. 6p sky blue 575.00 23.00
b. Printed on both sides
c. Rouletted and perf. all around — 300.00
d. 6p indigo blue ('69) 650.00 30.00
e. As "d," rouletted and perf. all around — 375.00
33 A3 9p gray lilac ('72) — 250.00
34 A3 10p on 9p yel (Bl) ('68) 850.00 42.50
a. Printed on both sides — 750.00
35 A1 1sh chestnut ('68) 325.00 27.50
36 A1 1sh lake brown ('69) 325.00 22.50
a. Rouletted and perf. all around — —

#44-45

1867-74 *Perf. 11½-12½*

41 A1 1p yellow green 90.00 26.50
42 A1 1p blue green 95.00 26.50
a. Printed on both sides
b. Horiz. pair, imperf between 1,750.
c. 1p pale bright green ('68) 200.00 35.00
d. 1p gray green ('68) 160.00 57.50
43 A1 2p vermilion 1,150.
44 A2 3p on 4p sky blue (Blk) ('70) 360.00 16.00
a. 3p on 4p ultra, black surcharge 95.00 11.00
b. Surcharge omitted 24,000. 13,500.
c. Double surcharge 4,000.
d. Surcharged on both sides 3,250.
e. Rouletted — 850.00
f. 3p on 4p Prussian blue ('71) 1,000.
46 A2 4p dull violet 77.50 9.50
a. 4p dull purple ('68) 80.00 17.50
47 A1 6p Prussian blue 130.00 8.50
a. 6p sky blue 400.00 13.50
b. Imperf. vert., pair —
c. Horiz. pair, imperf x perf 11½ 1,250.
d. 6p indigo ('69) 160.00 20.00
48 A3 9p red lilac ('72) 85.00 9.50
a. 9p violet 130.00 9.50
b. 9p red violet 130.00 10.00
c. Printed on both sides —
49 A3 10p on 9p yel (Bl) ('68) 1,400. 42.50
50 A3 10p on 9p yel (Blk) ('69) 225.00 35.00
51 A1 1sh deep brown 120.00 13.50
52 A1 1sh red brown 135.00 13.50
a. 1sh chestnut 155.00 20.00
b. 1sh lake brown ('68) 190.00 12.50
53 A2 2sh carmine 110.00 16.00
a. Printed on both sides 450.00
b. Horiz. pair, imperf. vert. —
c. 2sh pale rose pink ('69) 1,150. 190.00
d. 2sh deep rose pink ('69) — 125.00
e. 2sh carmine red ('69) 115.00 21.00

Perf. 10

42e A1 1p bright green ('71) 175.00 19.00
42f A1 1p pale br green ('70) 175.00 19.00
42g A1 1p gray green ('70) 175.00 19.00
44g A2 3p on 4p pale ultra (Blk) ('71) 375.00 24.00
44h A2 3p on 4p ultra (Blk) ('71) 160.00 26.00
44i A2 3p on 4p Pruss bl (Blk) ('71) 1,150.
45 A2 3p on 4p sl bl (Red) ('70) 600.00 95.00
46b A2 4p dull lilac ('70) 140.00 12.50
46c A2 4p dull pur ('71) 125.00 12.50
47e A1 6p br blue ('70) 210.00 19.50
47f A1 6p indigo ('71) 290.00 18.50
52c A1 1sh chestnut ('71) 190.00 30.00

Perf. 10x11½-12½, 11½-12½x10, or compound

42h A1 1p pale br grn 200.00 16.00
i Printed on both sides —
42j A1 1p deep green 100.00 11.50
42k A1 1p gray green 180.00 17.50
44j A2 3p on 4p ultramarine (Blk) 290.00 62.50
46d A2 4p dull lilac — 22.50
46e A2 4p slate lilac 150.00 20.50
47g A1 6p Prussian blue 175.00 9.50
47h A1 6p br Pruss blue 190.00 12.00
50a A3 10p on 9p yel (Blk) 300.00 48.00
52d A1 1sh chestnut 260.00 57.50
53f A2 2sh carmine 175.00 42.50
53g A2 2sh rose pink — 225.00

See Nos. 67, O14, O28, O36.

A6

A6a

1868 Typo. Wmk. 72 *Rouletted*

54 A6a 2p orange red 85.00 3.50
a. Imperf.
b. Printed on both sides 500.00
c. Horiz. pair, imperf. btwn. 850.00
d. 2p deep brick red 90.00 5.25

1869 *Perf. 11½ to 12½xRoulette*

55 A6a 2p orange red 170.00

1870 *Perf. 10xRoulette*

56 A6a 2p orange red 325.00 32.50

Perf. 10, 11½, 12½ and Compound

1868-75

57 A6 1p bl grn ('75) 55.00 6.50
58 A6a 2p orange red 15.50 1.25
a. Printed on both sides 375.00
b. Horiz. pair, imperf. vert.

Engr.

59 A3 10p on 9p yel (Bl) 1,500.

1869 Typo. Wmk. 6 *Rouletted*

60 A6a 2p orange red 95.00 22.00
a. Imperf.
b. Printed on both sides

Perf. 11½ to 12½xRoulette

61 A6a 2p orange red 125.00

Perf. 11½ to 12½

61B A6a 2p orange red 1,000.

See #62, 64-66, 97-98, 105-106, 115-116, 133-134, 145-146. For surcharges & overprints see #75, O3, O22-O25, O34-O35, O44-O47, O49, O55-O56, O62-O63, O68-O69, O74, O78-O79.

1871 Wmk. 70 *Perf. 10*

62 A6a 2p orange red 95.00 27.50

Engr.

63 A2 4p dull violet 2,600. 325.00
a. Printed on both sides —

Copies of the 4p from edge of sheet sometimes lack watermark.

Perf. 10, 11½, 12½ and Compound

1876-80 Typo. Wmk. 73

64 A6 1p green 18.00 .50
65 A6a 2p orange 19.00 .45
66 A6a 2p blood red ('80) 275.00 6.75
Nos. 64-66 (3) 312.00 7.70

See #97-98, 105-106, 115-116, 133-134, 145-146.

No. 71

No. 75

1876-84 Engr. Wmk. 7

67 A2 3p on 4p ultra (Blk) 100.00 24.00
a. 3p on 4p deep blue 15.00
b. Double surcharge 1,600.
68 A2 4p reddish violet 72.50 6.50
a. 4p dull violet 72.50 8.00
b. 4p slate violet ('79) 125.00 19.00
69 A1 6p deep blue 85.00 4.50
a. Horiz. pair, imperf. between —
b. Imperf.
c. 6p bright blue, perf 10 150.00 17.00
d. 6p Prussian blue, perf 10 125.00 17.00
70 A1 6p pale ultra ('84) 62.50 2.50
71 A3 8p on 9p bister brn 110.00 8.00
a. 8p on 9p yellow brown 100.00 8.00
b. 8p on 9p gray brown ('80) 92.50 8.00
d. Double surcharge 625.00
e. Vert. pair, imperf between 750.00
72 A3 9p rose lilac 12.00 5.00
a. Printed on both sides 450.00
73 A1 1sh red brown 50.00 3.25
a. 1sh brown 55.00 3.75
b. 1sh chocolate 30.00 3.50
c. As "b," horiz. pair, imperf. btwn. 275.00
d. 1sh sepia 29.00 3.50
e. As "d," vert. pair, imperf. btwn. 290.00
f. 1sh reddish lake brown, perf 10 350.00
74 A2 2sh carmine 46.00 6.00
a. Horiz. pair, imperf. vert. 1,400.
b. Imperf., pair

For overprint see No. O41.

1882 Wmk. 73 *Perf. 10*

Black Surcharge

75 A6 ½p on 1p green 15.00 11.00

A9

A10

A11

A12

Perf. 10, 11½, 12½ and Compound

1883-90 Typo.

76 A9 ½p chocolate brown 7.00 1.60
a. ½p red brown ('89) 6.00 1.50
b. ½p bister brown 5.50 1.50
78 A10 3p deep green ('93) 11.00 3.25
a. 3p olive green ('90) 16.00 3.25
b. 3p sage green ('86) 18.00 2.75
79 A11 4p violet ('90) 25.00 4.00
a. 4p aniline violet ('93) 21.00 3.50
80 A12 6p pale blue ('87) 22.50 3.00
a. 6p blue ('87) 19.00 1.00
Nos. 76-80 (4) 65.50 11.85

See #96, 100-101, 104, 108-109, 111. For surcharges & overprints see #94-95, 99, O48, O50-O51, O54, O57-O61, O64, O66-O67, O71, O73, O75, O81-O82.

A13

1886-96 *Perf. 11½ to 12½*

81 A13 2sh6p violet 50.00 10.00
82 A13 5sh rose 62.50 21.00
83 A13 10sh green 160.00 60.00
84 A13 15sh buff 450.00 225.00
85 A13 £1 blue 325.00 160.00
86 A13 £2 red brown 1,450. 450.00
87 A13 50sh rose red 2,100. 550.00
88 A13 £3 olive green 2,250. 550.00
89 A13 £4 lemon 4,250. 1,050.
90 A13 £5 gray 4,250.
90A A13 £5 brown ('96) 3,250. 1,100.
91 A13 £10 bronze 3,900. 1,200.
92 A13 £15 silver 11,000. 2,000.
93 A13 £20 lilac 13,000. 2,100.

Perf. 10

81b A13 2sh6p violet 62.50 13.00
82a A13 5sh rose 85.00 21.00
83a A13 10sh green 190.00 65.00
84a A13 15sh buff 510.00 360.00
85a A13 £1 blue 400.00 175.00
86a A13 £2 red brown 1,600. 500.00
87a A13 50sh rose red 2,250. 650.00
88a A13 £3 olive green 2,400. 650.00
89a A13 £4 lemon 4,900.
90b A13 £5 gray 4,250.
91a A13 £10 bronze 4,900. 1,350.
92a A13 £15 silver 12,000.
93a A13 £20 lilac 14,500.

For overprints see Nos. O83-O84.

#94, 99

#95

Perf. 10, 11½x12½ and Compound

1891

Brown Surcharge

94 A11 2½p on 4p green 10.00 2.75
a. "½" nearer the "2" 35.00 24.00
b. Pair, imperf. between 1,500.
c. Fraction bar omitted 125.00 90.00

Carmine Surcharge

95 A12 5p on 6p red brn 21.00 6.50
a. No period after "D" 210.00

See #99. For overprints see #O48, O57, O59.

Many stamps of the issues of 1855-91 have been reprinted; they are all on paper watermarked Crown and SA, letters wide apart, and are overprinted "REPRINT."

1893 Typo. *Perf. 15*

96 A9 ½p brown 6.00 1.40
a. Horiz. pair, imperf. btwn 200.00
b. Pair, perf. 12 btwn; perf. 15 around 240.00 60.00
97 A6 1p green 14.50 1.40
98 A6a 2p orange 14.50 1.00
a. Vert. pair, imperf. between 450.00
99 A11 2½p on 4p green 29.00 3.75
a. "½" nearer the "2" 72.50 29.00
b. Fraction bar omitted
100 A11 4p gray violet 23.50 4.00
101 A12 6p blue 47.50 4.50
Nos. 96-101 (6) 135.00 16.05

Kangaroo, Palm — A16

Coat of Arms — A17

1894, Mar. 1

102 A16 2½p blue violet 29.00 3.25
103 A17 5p dull violet 32.50 4.25

See Nos. 107, 110, 117, 135-136, 147, 151. For overprints see Nos. O65, O70, O72, O80.

1895-97 *Perf. 13*

104 A9 ½p pale brown 3.75 .45
105 A6 1p green 9.75 .45
a. Vert. pair, imperf. between
106 A6a 2p orange 7.50 .25
107 A16 2½p blue violet 24.00 1.10
108 A10 3p olive green ('97) 7.50 2.25
109 A11 4p bright violet 8.00 .70
110 A17 5p dull violet 8.50 1.40
111 A12 6p blue 9.00 2.00
a. 6p pale blue ('96) 9.00 2.00
Nos. 104-111 (8) 78.00 8.60

Some authorities regard the so-called redrawn 1p stamps with thicker lettering (said to have been issued in 1897) as impressions from a new or cleaned plate.

Perf. 11½, 12½, Clean-Cut, Compound

1896 Engr. Wmk. 7

112 A3 9p lilac rose 13.00 6.00
113 A1 1sh dark brown 32.50 5.25
a. Horiz. pair, imperf. vert. 300.00
c. Vert. pair, imperf. btwn. 325.00
113B A2 2sh carmine 40.00 8.50
Nos. 112-113B (3) 85.50 19.75

Adelaide Post Office — A18

1899 Typo. Wmk. 73 *Perf. 13*

114 A18 ½p yellow green 2.75 .75
115 A6 1p carmine 5.50 .35
a. 1p scarlet 5.50 .50
116 A6a 2p purple 5.50 .30
117 A16 2½p dark blue 8.00 2.40
Nos. 114-117 (4) 21.75 3.80

See #132, 144. For overprint see #O77.

Perf. 11½, 12½

1901 Engr. Wmk. 72

118 A1 1sh dark brown 29.00 16.00
a. 1sh red brown 32.50 17.00
b. Horiz. pair, imperf. vert.
119 A2 2sh carmine 32.50 15.00

1902

120 A3 9p magenta 21.00 21.00

A19

A20

Perf. 11½, 12½ and Compound

1902-03 Typo. Wmk. 73

121 A19 3p olive grn 8.50 2.00
122 A19 4p red org 14.00 2.00
123 A19 6p blue grn 10.00 2.00
124 A19 8p ultra (value 19mm long) 11.00 5.75
124A A19 8p ultra (value 16½mm long) ('03) 13.00 11.00
b. "EIGNT" 1,700. 2,900.
125 A19 9p claret 11.00 6.00
a. Vert. pair, imperf. between 1,100.
b. Horiz. pair, imperf. between
c. 9p claret, perf 12 80.00 14.00
126 A19 10p org buff 16.00 10.00
127 A19 1sh brn ('03) 21.00 6.00
a. Horiz. pair, imperf. btwn.
b. Vert. pair, imperf. btwn. 1,200.
128 A19 2sh6p purple 32.50 17.00
129 A19 5sh rose 85.00 55.00
130 A19 10sh grn ('03) 160.00 85.00
131 A19 £1 blue 375.00 200.00
Nos. 121-131 (12) 757.00 401.75

1904 *Perf. 12x11½*

132 A18 ½p yellow green 4.25 1.75
133 A6 1p rose 8.00 .60
134 A6a 2p purple 8.50 1.00
135 A16 2½p dark blue 10.00 3.25
136 A17 5p dull violet 18.00 2.75
Nos. 132-136 (5) 48.75 9.35

1904-08 *Perf. 12 and 12x11½*

137 A20 6p blue green 18.00 4.00
138 A20 8p ultra ('06) 12.50 10.50
139 A20 9p claret 18.00 6.25
139A A20 10p org buff ('07) 21.00 17.00
b. Vert. pair, imperf. between 1,900.
c. Horiz. pair, imperf. between 1,300. 1,300.
140 A20 1sh brown 25.00 4.00
a. Vert. pair, imperf between 975.00
b. Horiz. pair, imperf between 1,200.
141 A20 2sh6p purple ('05) 72.50 21.00
142 A20 5sh scarlet 65.00 40.00
142B A20 10sh green ('08) 160.00 190.00
143 A20 £1 deep blue 200.00 160.00
Nos. 137-143 (9) 592.00 452.75

See Nos. 148-150, 152-157.

1906-12 Wmk. 74

144 A18 ½p green 7.25 .75
145 A6 1p carmine 6.50 .40
146 A6a 2p purple 6.00 .40
a. Horiz. pair, imperf. between
147 A16 2½p dk blue ('11) 12.00 6.75
148 A20 3p ol grn (value 19mm long) 16.00 4.50
a. Horiz. pair, imperf. between 3,900.
149 A20 3p ol grn (value 17mm long) ('09) 9.50 3.75
150 A20 4p red orange 13.50 3.00
151 A17 5p dull vio ('08) 21.50 5.00
152 A20 6p blue grn ('07) 9.75 3.00
a. Vert. pair, imperf. between 1,100. 1,100.
153 A20 8p ultra ('09) 14.00 16.00
154 A20 9p claret 14.00 6.00
a. Vert. pair, imperf. between 1,050.
b. Horiz. pair, imperf. between 1,750.
155 A20 1sh brown 14.50 6.25
a. Pair, imperf. between 1,500.
156 A20 2sh6p purple ('09) 72.50 18.00
a. 2sh6p pale violet, perf 12 ('10) 92.50 19.00
b. 2sh6p pale violet, perf 12½ ('12) 75.00 47.50
157 A20 5sh lt red ('12) 97.50
Nos. 144-157 (14) 314.50 73.80

OFFICIAL STAMPS

For Departments

Regular Issues Overprinted in Red, Black or Blue:

A. (Architect), A. G. (Attorney General), A. O. (Audit Office), B. D. (Barracks Department), B. G. (Botanical Gardens), B. M. (Bench of Magistrates), C. (Customs), C. D. (Convict Department), C. L. (Crown Lands), C. O. (Commissariat Officer), C. S. (Chief Secretary), C. Sgn. (Colonial Surgeon), C. P. (Commissioner of Police), C. T. (Commissioner of Titles), D. B. (Destitute Board), D. R. (Deed Registry), E. (Engineer), E. B. (Education Board),

G. P. (Government Printer), G. S. (Government Storekeeper), G. T. (Goolwa Tramway), G. F. (Gold Fields), H. (Hospital), H. A. (House of Assembly), I. A. (Immigration Agent), I. E. (Intestate Estates), I. S. (Inspector of Sheep), L. A. (Lunatic Asylum), L. C. (Legislative Council), L. L. (Legislative Library), L. T. (Land Titles), M. (Military), M. B. (Marine Board), M. R. (Manager of Railways), M. R. G. (Main Roads Gambierton), N. T. (Northern Territory),

O. A. (Official Assignee), P. (Police), P. A. (Protector of Aborigines), P. O. (Post Office), P. S. (Private Secretary), P. W. (Public Works), R. B. (Road Board), R. G. (Registrar General of Births, &c.), S. (Sheriff), S. C. (Supreme Court), S.G. (Surveyor General), S. M. (Stipendiary Magistrate), S. T. (Superintendent of Telegraph), T. (Treasurer), T. R. (Titles Registry), V. (Volunteers), V. A. (Valuator), V. N. (Vaccination), W. (Waterworks).

1868-74 Wmk. 6 *Rouletted*

O1 A1 1p green *180.00*
O2 A1 2p pale red *140.00*
O3 A6a 2p vermilion *60.00*
O4 A2 4p dull violet *140.00*
O5 A1 6p slate blue *140.00*
O6 A3 9p gray lilac *250.00*
O7 A1 1sh brown *140.00*
O8 A2 2sh carmine *140.00*

Perf. 11½ to 12½ x Roulette

O9 A1 1p green *140.00*
O10 A2 4p dull violet *425.00*
O11 A1 6p blue *110.00*
O12 A1 1sh brown *100.00*

Perf. 10, 11½, 12½ and Compound

O13 A1 1p green *80.00*
O14 A2 3p on 4p slate blue (Red) *375.00*
O15 A2 3p on 4p slate blue (Blk) *140.00*
O16 A2 4p dull violet *100.00*
O17 A1 6p deep blue *140.00*
O18 A3 9p violet *250.00*
O19 A3 10p on 9p yellow (Blk) *250.00*
O20 A1 1sh brown *120.00 140.00*
O21 A2 2sh carmine *100.00*

Rouletted

Wmk. 72

O22 A6a 2p orange *60.00*

Perf. 11 ½ x Roulette

O23 A6a 2p orange *80.00*
a. Perf 10 x Roulette *140.00*

Perf. 10, 11½, 12½ and Compound

O24 A6a 2p orange *20.00*

Wmk. 70

Perf. 10

O25 A6a 2p orange *55.00*
O26 A2 4p dull violet *140.00*

For General Use

Overprinted in Black

Perf. 10, 11½, 12½ and Compound

1874 Wmk. 6

O27 A1 1p green — *600.00*
a. Printed on both sides 900.00
b. 1p green, perf 11½-12½x10 — *700.00*
O28 A2 3p on 4p ultra 3,250. 1,500.
a. No period after "S" 2,000.
O29 A2 4p dull violet 65.00 12.50
a. Inverted overprint
b. No period after "S" 55.00
c. Perf. 10 1,600. 400.00
O30 A1 6p deep blue 125.00 17.00
a. No period after "S" 62.50
b. 6p Prussian blue, perf 11½-12½x10 110.00 10.00
O31 A3 9p violet 1,600. 850.00
a. No period after "S" 2,250. 1,300.
O32 A1 1sh red brown 90.00 8.00
a. Double overprint 145.00
b. No period after "S" 225.00 62.50
O33 A2 2sh carmine 185.00 27.50
a. Double overprint
b. No period after "S" 100.00
c. 2sh carmine, perf 11½-12½x10 145.00

1874-75 Wmk. 72

O34 A6 1p blue green 115.00 29.00
a. Inverted overprint
O35 A6a 2p orange 27.50 4.00

1876-86 Wmk. 7

O37 A2 4p dull violet 90.00 8.75
O38 A2 4p reddish vio 50.00 3.75
a. Double overprint
b. Inverted overprint
c. Dbl. ovpt., one inverted
O39 A1 6p dark blue 90.00 7.00
a. Double overprint 95.00
b. Inverted overprint
O40 A1 6p ultramarine 85.00 6.00
a. Double overprint
b. Inverted overprint
O41B A3 9p violet *4,250.*
O42 A1 1sh red brown 46.00 9.25
a. Inverted overprint 450.00 160.00
b. Double overprint
O43 A2 2sh carmine 145.00 11.00
a. Double overprint 145.00
b. Inverted overprint 160.00
c. No period after "S" 150.00

1880-91 Wmk. 73

O44 A6 1p blue green 18.00 1.40
a. Inverted overprint 62.50
b. Double overprint 90.00 55.00
c. Dbl. ovpt., one inverted
O45 A6 1p yellow green 22.50 1.40
O46 A6a 2p orange 11.00 1.40
a. Inverted overprint 29.00
b. Double overprint 110.00 42.50
c. Overprinted sideways
d. Dbl. ovpt., one inverted
e. Dbl. ovpt., both inverted 160.00
O47 A6a 2p blood red 77.50 14.50
O48 A11 2½p on 4p green 90.00 12.50
a. "½" nearer the "2" 70.00
b. Double overprint
c. Pair, one without ovpt.
Nos. O44-O48 (5) 219.00 31.20

1882-90 *Perf. 10*

O49 A6 ½p on 1p green 85.00 20.00
a. Inverted overprint
O50 A11 4p violet 90.00 6.50
O51 A12 6p blue 32.50 1.75
a. Double overprint
b. No period after "S"
Nos. O49-O51 (3) 207.50 28.25

Overprinted in Black

Perf. 10, 11½, 12½ and Compound

1891 Wmk. 7

O52 A1 1sh red brown 42.50 7.25
a. No period after "S" 85.00
b. 1sh lake brown, perf 11½-12½ 72.50 17.50
O53 A2 2sh carmine 97.50 14.00
a. Double overprint
b. No period after "S"

1891-95 Wmk. 73

O54 A9 ½p brown 29.00 6.75
a. No period after "S" 75.00 45.00
O55 A6 1p blue green 30.00 2.75
a. Double overprint 95.00 50.00
b. No period after "S" 65.00 15.00
O56 A6a 2p orange 30.00 2.25
a. No period after "S" 17.50
O57 A11 2½p on 4p green 50.00 17.50
a. "½" nearer the "2" 125.00 50.00
b. Inverted overprint 235.00
O58 A11 4p violet 65.00 4.50
a. Double overprint
O59 A12 5p on 6p red brn 57.50 24.00
O60 A12 6p blue 27.50 3.25
a. Double overprint
b. No period after "S"
Nos. O54-O60 (7) 289.00 61.00

1893 *Perf. 15*

O61	A9	½p brown	40.00	12.00
O62	A6	1p green	16.00	1.75
O63	A6a	2p orange	29.00	.75
a.		Inverted overprint		27.50
b.		Double overprint		37.50
O64	A11	4p gray violet	85.00	6.00
a.		Double overprint	240.00	50.00
O65	A17	5p dull violet	90.00	14.50
O66	A12	6p blue	35.00	5.00
		Nos. O61-O66 (6)	295.00	40.00

1896 *Perf. 13*

O67	A9	½p brown	22.50	8.00
a.		Triple overprint	240.00	
O68	A6	1p green	29.00	.85
a.		No period after "S"	85.00	13.00
O69	A6a	2p orange	29.00	.75
a.		No period after "S"	80.00	13.00
O70	A16	2½p blue violet	65.00	9.25
a.		No period after "S"		45.00
O71	A11	4p brt violet	85.00	4.00
a.		Double overprint	200.00	50.00
b.		No period after "S"	200.00	37.50
O72	A17	5p dull violet	92.50	18.00
a.		No period after "S"		
O73	A12	6p blue	42.50	2.75
a.		No period after "S"	125.00	72.00
		Nos. O67-O73 (7)	365.50	43.60

On No. O67a, one overprint is upright, two sideways.

Same Overprint in Dark Blue

1891-95 *Perf. 10*

O74	A6	1p green	260.00	7.75
O75	A12	6p blue		

Black Overprint

Perf. 11½, 12½, Clean-Cut

1897 **Wmk. 7**

O76	A1	1sh brown	42.50	7.25
a.		Double overprint		
b.		No period after "S"		

Overprinted in Black

1900 **Wmk. 73** *Perf. 13*

O77	A18	½p yellow green	20.00	8.00
O78	A6	1p carmine rose	18.00	2.10
a.		Inverted overprint	72.50	50.00
b.		Double overprint		300.00
c.		No period after "S"	55.00	20.00
O79	A6a	2p purple	22.50	1.10
a.		Inverted ovpt.	62.50	50.00
b.		No period after "S"	50.00	
O80	A16	2½p dark blue	72.50	25.00
a.		Inverted overprint		100.00
O81	A11	4p violet	65.00	7.25
a.		Inverted overprint	160.00	
O82	A12	6p blue	29.00	7.25
		Nos. O77-O82 (6)	227.00	50.70

1901 *Perf. 10*

O83	A13	2sh6p violet	*4,500.*	*3,750.*
O84	A13	5sh rose	*4,500.*	*3,750.*

On Nos. O77-O82 the letters "O.S." are 11½mm apart; on Nos. O83-O84, 14½mm apart.

Overprinted in Black

1903 **Wmk. 72** *Perf. 11½, 12½*

O85	A1	1sh red brown	72.50	17.50

SOUTHERN NIGERIA

'sə-t͟hərn nī-'jir-ē-ə

LOCATION — In western Africa bordering on the Gulf of Guinea
GOVT. — British Crown Colony and Protectorate
AREA — 90,896 sq. mi.
POP. — 8,590,545
CAPITAL — Lagos

The Protectorate of Southern Nigeria, formed in 1900, absorbed in that year the Niger Coast Protectorate. In 1906 it united with Lagos and became the Colony and Protectorate of Southern Nigeria. An amalgamation was effected in 1914 between Northern and Southern Nigeria to form the Colony and Protectorate of Nigeria. See Nigeria, Northern Nigeria, Niger Coast Protectorate and Lagos.

12 Pence = 1 Shilling
20 Shillings = 1 Pound

Victoria
A1

Edward VII
A2

Wmk. Crown and C A (2)

1901, Mar. **Typo.** *Perf. 14*

1	A1	½p yel grn & blk	2.00	2.50
a.		½p yel grn & sepia ('02)	2.50	3.00
2	A1	1p car rose & blk	1.60	1.75
a.		1p carmine rose & sepia ('02)	2.50	2.00
3	A1	2p org brn & blk	3.75	*4.25*
4	A1	4p ol grn & blk	3.25	*18.00*
5	A1	6p red vio & blk	3.25	*7.50*
6	A1	1sh blk & gray grn	9.25	*30.00*
7	A1	2sh6p brn & blk	52.50	*92.50*
8	A1	5sh yellow & blk	55.00	*110.00*
9	A1	10sh vio & blk, *yel*	100.00	*200.00*
		Nos. 1-9 (9)	230.60	*466.50*

1903-04

10	A2	½p yel grn & blk	1.10	.35
11	A2	1p car rose & blk	1.50	.80
12	A2	2p org brn & blk	7.50	1.75
13	A2	2½p ultra & blk ('04)	2.25	.85
14	A2	4p ol grn & blk	3.25	*6.25*
15	A2	6p red vio & blk	4.50	*9.25*
16	A2	1sh blk & gray grn	35.00	22.50
17	A2	2sh6p brown & blk	30.00	*70.00*
18	A2	5sh yellow & blk	70.00	*160.00*
19	A2	10sh vio & blk, *yel*	35.00	*100.00*
20	A2	£1 pur & gray grn	375.00	*750.00*
		Nos. 10-20 (11)	565.10	1,121.

1904-07 **Wmk. 3**

Chalky Paper

21	A2	½p yel grn & blk	.60	.20
22	A2	1p carmine & blk	14.00	.25
23	A2	2p org brn & blk	3.00	.50
24	A2	2½p ultra & blk	1.10	1.10
24A	A2	3p vio & org brn ('07)	11.00	1.50
25	A2	4p ol grn & blk ('05)	16.00	*29.00*
26	A2	6p red vio & blk	13.50	4.00
27	A2	1sh blk & gray grn	3.75	*4.00*
28	A2	2sh6p brn & blk ('05)	27.50	*20.00*
29	A2	5sh yellow & blk	47.50	*85.00*
30	A2	10sh vio & blk, *yel* ('08)	110.00	*200.00*
31	A2	£1 pur & gray grn ('05)	225.00	*250.00*
		Nos. 21-31 (12)	472.95	*595.55*

#23 and 24 are on ordinary paper, #24A and 25 on chalky, and the other values on both papers.

1907-10

Ordinary Paper

32	A2	½p green ('08)	2.00	.25
33	A2	1p carmine	4.00	.70
34	A2	2p gray	3.00	.80
35	A2	2½p ultra	2.25	*4.25*

Chalky Paper

36	A2	3p violet, *yel*	2.25	.35
37	A2	4p scar & blk, *yel*	2.50	.90
38	A2	6p red vio & dl vio	29.00	3.75
39	A2	1sh black, *green*	8.00	.50
40	A2	2sh6p car & blk, *bl*	5.75	1.10
41	A2	5sh scar & grn, *yel*	45.00	*55.00*
42	A2	10sh red & grn, *grn*	75.00	*110.00*
43	A2	£1 blk & vio, *red*	210.00	250.00
		Nos. 32-43 (12)	388.75	*427.60*

1910 **Ordinary Paper** **Redrawn**

44	A2	1p carmine	.85	.20

In the redrawn stamp the "1" of "1d" is not as thick as in No. 33 but the "d" is taller and broader.

King George V — A3

1912

45	A3	½p green	2.50	.20
46	A3	1p carmine	2.25	.20
47	A3	2p gray	.85	.95
48	A3	2½p ultra	3.25	3.25
49	A3	3p violet, *yel*	1.10	.35
50	A3	4p scar & blk, *yel*	1.50	*2.40*
51	A3	6p red vio & dl vio	1.50	1.50
52	A3	1sh black, *green*	3.25	.85
53	A3	2sh6p red & blk, *bl*	9.25	*35.00*
54	A3	5sh red & grn, *yel*	22.50	*87.50*
55	A3	10sh red & grn, *grn*	52.50	100.00
56	A3	£1 blk & vio, *red*	190.00	*250.00*
		Nos. 45-56 (12)	290.45	482.20

Stamps of Southern Nigeria were replaced in 1914 by those of Nigeria.

SOUTHERN RHODESIA

'sə-t͟hərn rō-'dē-zh͏ē-͏ə

LOCATION — Southeastern Africa between Northern Rhodesia and Mozambique
GOVT. — British Colony
AREA — 150,333 sq. mi.
POP. — 4,010,000 (est. 1963)
CAPITAL — Salisbury

Prior to 1923 this territory was administered by the British South Africa Company. The colony was created in that year by the British Government at the request of the inhabitants.

12 Pence = 1 Shilling
20 Shillings = 1 Pound

Catalogue values for unused stamps in this country are for Never Hinged items, beginning with Scott 56 in the regular postage section and Scott J1 in the postage due section.

King George V — A1

1924-30 **Unwmk.** **Engr.** *Perf. 14*

1	A1	½p dark green	2.50	.20
a.		Vert. pair, imperf. btwn.	950.00	1,050.
b.		Horiz. pair, imperf. btwn.	950.00	1,050.
c.		Horiz. pair, imperf. vert.	1,100.	
2	A1	1p scarlet	2.00	.20
a.		Horiz. pair, imperf. btwn.	850.00	950.00
b.		Perf. 12½ (coil) ('30)	3.25	*92.50*
c.		Vert. pair, imperf. btwn.	1,500.	
d.		Vert. pair, imperf. horiz.	950.00	
3	A1	1½p bister brown	2.50	.90
a.		Horiz. pair, imperf. btwn.	*10,000.*	
b.		Vert. pair, imperf. btwn.	*6,250.*	
4	A1	2p vio blk & blk	3.50	.80
a.		Horiz. pair, imperf. btwn.	*12,500.*	
5	A1	3p deep blue	2.75	3.50
6	A1	4p org red & blk	3.00	*3.25*
7	A1	6p lilac & blk	2.25	*4.75*
a.		Horiz. pair, imperf. btwn.	*40,000.*	
8	A1	8p gray grn & vio	12.50	*50.00*
9	A1	10p rose red & bl	13.50	*57.50*
10	A1	1sh turq bl & blk	5.75	*7.50*
11	A1	1sh6p yellow & blk	22.50	*37.50*
12	A1	2sh brown & blk	20.00	20.00
13	A1	2sh6p blk brn & bl	35.00	70.00
14	A1	5sh bl grn & bl	70.00	*175.00*
		Nos. 1-14 (14)	197.75	431.10

Values for imperf between pairs are for stamps from the same pane. Stamps separated by wide margins are cross-gutter pairs and sell for much lower prices.

George V
A2

Victoria Falls
A3

1931-37 *Perf. 11½, 14 (1p)*

16	A2	½p dp green ('33)	.75	.20
a.		Bklt. pane of 6 ('32)	*150.00*	
b.		Perf. 12	.95	1.10
c.		Perf. 14 ('35)	1.90	.35
17	A2	1p scarlet ('35)	.60	.20
a.		Bklt. pane of 6 ('32)	*150.00*	
b.		Perf. 11½ ('33)	2.00	.20
c.		Perf. 12	1.10	.80
18	A2	1½p dp brown ('32)	3.00	.90
a.		Bklt. pane of 6 ('32)	*600.00*	
b.		Perf. 12 ('33)	62.50	*47.50*

Typo. *Perf. 14½x14*

19	A3	2p blk brn & blk	4.75	1.75
20	A3	3p dark blue	11.50	12.50

Perf. 12, 11½ (2sh6p)

Engr.

21	A2	4p org red & blk	1.50	1.75
a.		Perf. 14 ('37)	37.50	55.00
b.		Perf. 11½ ('35)	20.00	5.75
22	A2	6p rose lilac & blk	2.50	3.50
a.		Perf. 14 ('36)	8.00	1.00
b.		Perf. 11½ ('33)	17.50	1.75
23	A2	8p green & violet	2.00	*3.75*
a.		Perf. 11½ ('34)	20.00	*37.50*
24	A2	9p gray grn & ver ('34)	7.00	10.50
25	A2	10p car & ultra	8.00	2.75
a.		Perf. 11½ ('33)	7.00	*15.00*
26	A2	1sh turq bl & blk	2.25	3.00
a.		Perf. 11½ ('36)	125.00	70.00
b.		Perf. 14 ('37)	225.00	160.00
27	A2	1sh6p ocher & blk	11.50	*17.50*
a.		Perf. 11½ ('36)	57.50	*125.00*
28	A2	2sh dk brn & blk	24.00	7.50
a.		Perf. 11½ ('33)	42.50	35.00
29	A2	2sh6p ol brn & ultra ('33)	32.50	35.00
a.		Perf. 12	37.50	40.00
30	A2	5sh bl grn & ultra	55.00	55.00
		Nos. 16-30 (15)	166.85	155.80

Victoria Falls — A4

1932, May *Perf. 12½*

31	A4	2p dark brn & grn	4.75	1.10
32	A4	3p dark blue	4.75	2.10
a.		Vert. pair, imperf. horiz.	*9,000.*	*11,000.*
b.		Vert. pair, imperf. btwn.	*21,500.*	
		Set, never hinged	18.00	

See Nos. 37-37A.

Silver Jubilee Issue

Victoria Falls and George V
A5

1935, May 6 *Perf. 11x12*

33	A5	1p car rose & olive	2.75	1.50
34	A5	2p blk brn & lt grn	4.25	4.00
35	A5	3p blue & violet	5.50	*9.50*
36	A5	6p dp violet & blk	7.50	*12.50*
		Nos. 33-36 (4)	20.00	*27.50*
		Set, never hinged	37.50	

25th anniv. of the reign of George V.

"Postage and Revenue"
A6

1935-41 *Perf. 14*

37	A6 2p dk brn & grn ('41)	1.10	.25
b.	Perf. 12½	1.75	10.00
	Never hinged	3.00	
37A	A6 3p deep blue ('38)	1.75	.25
	Set, never hinged	6.50	

Queen Elizabeth, George VI — A7

1937, May 12 *Perf. 12½*

38	A7 1p carmine & gray grn	.60	.70
39	A7 2p brown & green	.65	*1.75*
40	A7 3p lt blue & violet	3.00	*8.00*
41	A7 6p red violet & blk	1.75	*3.75*
	Nos. 38-41 (4)	6.00	14.20
	Set, never hinged	9.00	

Coronation of George VI & Elizabeth.

King George VI — A8

1937, Nov. 25 *Perf. 14*

42	A8	½p yellow green	.35	.20
43	A8	1p red	.35	.20
44	A8	1½p red brown	.65	.35
45	A8	4p orange red	.85	.20
46	A8	6p dark gray	.85	.60
47	A8	8p blue green	1.25	2.25
48	A8	9p blue	1.25	.80
49	A8	10p violet	1.60	*3.00*
50	A8	1sh green & blk	1.25	.20
51	A8	1sh6p ocher & blk	7.25	2.50
52	A8	2sh brown & blk	10.50	.70
53	A8	2sh6p violet & blue	7.25	5.50
54	A8	5sh green & blue	16.00	2.75
		Nos. 42-54 (13)	49.40	19.25
		Set, never hinged	75.00	

Catalogue values for unused stamps in this section, from this point to the end of the section, are for Never Hinged items.

Seal of British South Africa Co. — A9

Fort Salisbury, 1890 — A10

Cecil John Rhodes — A11

Pioneer Fort and Mail Coach A12

Rhodes Makes Peace, 1896 — A13

Victoria Falls Bridge — A14

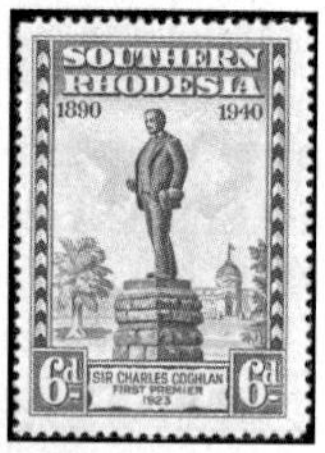

Sir Charles Coghlan — A15

Queen Victoria, George VI, Lobengula's Kraal and Government House A16

Unwmk.

1940, June 3 Engr. *Perf. 14*

56	A9	½p dp grn & dull vio	.20	.40
57	A10	1p red & vio blue	.20	.20
58	A11	1½p cop brn & blk	.20	.50
59	A12	2p pur & brt grn	.50	.40
60	A13	3p dk blue & blk	.80	1.00
61	A14	4p brn & bl grn	1.00	*1.50*
62	A15	6p sepia & dull grn	1.00	1.40
63	A16	1sh dk bl & brt grn	1.10	1.40
		Nos. 56-63 (8)	5.00	6.80

50th anniv. of the founding of Southern Rhodesia by Cecil John Rhodes.

Pioneer — A17

1943, Nov. 1 Photo. Wmk. 201

64	A17 2p Prus grn & choc	.20	.35

50th anniv. of Matabeleland under British control.

Princess Elizabeth and Princess Margaret Rose A18

King George VI and Queen Elizabeth A19

Unwmk.

1947, Apr. 1 Engr. *Perf. 14*

65	A18 ½p dk green & blk	.30	.60
66	A19 1p carmine & blk	.30	.60

Visit of the British Royal Family, Apr., 1947.

Victory Issue

Queen Elizabeth A20

George VI A21

Princess Elizabeth A22

Princess Margaret Rose A23

1947, May 8

67	A20 1p deep carmine	.20	.20
68	A21 2p slate black	.20	.20
69	A22 3p deep blue	.60	*.50*
70	A23 6p red orange	.40	*.75*
	Nos. 67-70 (4)	1.40	1.65

Victory of the Allied Nations in WW II.

Common Design Types pictured following the introduction.

UPU Issue

Common Design Types

Engr.; Name Typo.

1949, Oct. 10 Wmk. 4 ***Perf. 11x11½***

71	CD307 2p slate black	.70	.50
72	CD308 3p slate blue	1.25	*1.75*

75th anniv. of the UPU.

Queen Victoria and King George VI A24

Unwmk.

1950, Sept. 12 Engr. ***Perf. 14***

73	A24 2p choc & blue grn	.55	*1.10*

60th anniversary of Rhodesia.

Hospital, Doctor and Natives A25

Designs: 1p, African Scene. 2p, Native Houses, Modern City and Cecil Rhodes. 4½p, Dam and Natives. 1sh, Transportation.

1953, Apr. 15

74	A25	½p dk brown & blue	.20	*.40*
75	A25	1p blue grn & fawn	.20	.20
76	A25	2p vio & dk bl grn	.35	.20
77	A25	4½p dk bl & bl grn	1.50	*2.25*
78	A25	1sh chestnut & blk	2.00	.70
		Nos. 74-78 (5)	4.25	3.75

#77 is inscribed Matabeleland Diamond Jubilee.

POSTAGE DUE STAMPS

Catalogue values for unused stamps in this section are for Never Hinged items.

Great Britain Postage Due Stamps of 1938-51 Overprinted in Black

1951 Wmk. 251 ***Perf. 14x14½***

J1	D1 ½p emerald	3.00	*10.00*
	On cover		*500.00*
J2	D1 1p violet blue	2.75	*2.75*
	On cover		*175.00*
J3	D1 2p black brown	3.00	*1.65*
	On cover		*125.00*
J4	D1 3p violet	3.25	*1.25*
	On cover		*200.00*
J5	D1 4p brt blue	2.00	*2.25*
	On cover		*250.00*
a.	4p slate green	150.00	*300.00*
	On cover		*1,200.*
J6	D1 1sh blue	3.25	*2.00*
	On cover		*300.00*
	Nos. J1-J6 (6)	17.25	*19.90*

Covers are for properly franked commercial items. Philatelic usages sell for less.

SOUTH RUSSIA

sauth 'rəsh-ə

LOCATION — An area in southern Russia bordering on the Caspian and Black Seas.

A provisional government set up and maintained by General Denikin in opposition to the Bolshevik forces in Russia following the downfall of the Empire. The stamps were used in the field postal service established for carrying on communication between the various armies united in the revolt. These armies included the Don Cossacks, the Kuban Cossacks, and also the neighboring southern Russian people in favor of the counter-revolution against the Bolsheviks.

100 Kopecks = 1 Ruble

Values for used stamps are for canceled to order copies. Postally used specimens sell for considerably more.

Watermark

Wmk. 171 — Diamonds

Don Government (Novocherkassk) Rostov Issue

Russian Stamps of 1909-17 Surcharged

1918 Unwmk. ***Perf. 14x14½***

1	A14 25k on 1k dl org yel	2.00	*1.90*
a.	Inverted surcharge	30.00	*40.00*
2	A14 25k on 2k dl grn	.50	*.60*
a.	Inverted surcharge	30.00	*30.00*
3	A14 25k on 3k car	.75	*.75*
a.	Double surcharge	35.00	*60.00*
4	A15 25k on 4k car	2.50	*3.50*
a.	Inverted surcharge	25.00	*35.00*
5	A14 50k on 7k blue	5.00	*6.50*
	Impert		
6	A14 25k on 1k orange	.60	*1.25*
a.	Inverted surcharge	30.00	*40.00*
7	A14 25k on 2k gray grn	7.50	*12.50*
8	A14 25k on 3k red	4.50	*3.00*
	Nos. 1-8 (8)	23.35	30.00

Counterfeits exist of Nos. 1-8.

Ermak, Cossack Leader — A1

Inscription on Back

1919 *Perf. 11½*
10 A1 20k green 40.00 *85.00*

This stamp was available for both postage and currency.

Novocherkassk Issue

25 1P. 1P.

Russian stamps with these surcharges are bogus.

Kuban Government
Ekaterinodar Issues

Russian Stamps of 1909-17 Surcharged:

d

e

f

g

h

i

1918-20 Unwmk. *Perf. 14x14½*
20 A14(d) 25k on 1k dl org yel .40 *.65*
 a. Inverted surcharge 30.00 *27.50*
 b. Dbl. surch., one inverted 30.00 *25.00*
21 A14(d) 50k on 2k dl grn 6.00 *6.00*
 a. Inverted surcharge 30.00 *27.50*
 b. Double surcharge 25.00 *20.00*
 c. Dbl. surcharge inverted 25.00 *20.00*
22 A14(e) 70k on 5k dk cl 2.40 *6.00*
23 A14(f) 1r on 3k car 2.40 *4.75*
 a. Inverted surcharge 25.00 *20.00*
 b. Double surcharge 25.00 *15.00*
 c. Pair, one without surch. 25.00 *15.00*
24 A14(g) 1r on 3k car .60 *1.00*
 a. Inverted surcharge 25.00 *20.00*
 b. Double surcharge 25.00 *20.00*
 c. Pair, one without surcharge 20.00 *20.00*
25 A15(h) 3r on 4k rose 12.00 *18.00*
 b. Inverted surcharge 40.00 *50.00*
 c. Double surcharge 40.00 *60.00*
 d. Dbl. surcharge inverted 40.00 *60.00*
26 A15(i) 10r on 4k rose 4.00 *5.00*
 a. 10r on 4k carmine 8.00 *13.00*
 b. Inverted surcharge 40.00 *55.00*
27 A11(i) 10r on 15k red brn & dp bl 1.25 *1.60*
 a. Surchd. on face & back 25.00 15.00
 b. Dbl. surch., one inverted 40.00 *60.00*
28 A14(i) 25r on 3k car 2.25 2.00
 a. Inverted surcharge 15.00 *20.00*
29 A14(i) 25r on 7k bl 30.00 *27.50*
 a. Inverted surcharge 55.00 *60.00*
30 A11(i) 25r on 14k bl & car 60.00 *65.00*
 a. Inverted surcharge 80.00 *80.00*
31 A11(i) 25r on 25k dl grn & dk vio 30.00 *60.00*
 a. Inverted surcharge 65.00 *70.00*
 Nos. 20-31 (12) 151.30 197.50

Imperf

35 A14(d) 25d on 1k org 1.25 *2.00*
36 A14(d) 50k on 2k gray grn .30 *.35*
 a. Inverted surcharge 30.00 25.00
 b. Double surcharge 30.00 25.00
 c. Pair, one without surch. 30.00 *30.00*
37 A14(e) 70k on 5k claret 2.40 *3.25*
38 A14(f) 1r on 3k red 1.25 *2.00*
 a. Inverted surcharge 30.00 20.00
 b. Double surcharge 20.00 *15.00*
 c. Pair, one without surch. 20.00 *15.00*
39 A14(g) 1r on 3k red .50 *.65*
 a. Double surcharge 15.00 *20.00*
 b. Pair, one without surch. 15.00 *20.00*
 c. As "a," inverted 30.00 *45.00*
40 A11(i) 10r on 15k red brn & dp bl 4.75 *6.00*
41 A14(i) 25r on 3k red 6.00 *9.50*
 a. Inverted surcharge 42.50
 Nos. 35-41 (7) 16.45 23.75

Russian Stamps of 1909-17 Surcharged

1919 *Perf. 14, 14½x15*
45 A14 70k on 1k dl org yel 1.25 1.00

Imperf

46 A14 70k on 1k orange 1.25 *2.40*
 a. Inverted surcharge 20.00 *20.00*
 b. Double surch., one inverted 30.00 25.00

The 1k postal savings stamp with this surcharge inverted is a proof.
Counterfeits exist of Nos. 20-46.

Postal Savings Stamps Surcharged for Postal Use

A2

1919 Wmk. 171 *Perf. 14½x15*
47 A2 10r on 1k red, *buff* 18.00 *24.00*
 a. Inverted surcharge 75.00
48 A2 10r on 5k grn, *buff* 40.00 *45.00*
 a. Double surcharge 250.00
49 A2 10r on 10k brn, *buff* 120.00 *150.00*
 Nos. 47-49 (3) 178.00 219.00

Counterfeits exist of Nos. 47-49.

Crimea

Russian Stamp of 1917 Surcharged

35 коп.

1919 Unwmk. ***Imperf.***
51 A14 35k on 1k orange .30 *1.00*
 a. Comma, instead of period in surcharge 1.00

A3

Paper with Buff Network
Inscription on Back

1919 ***Imperf.***
52 A3 50k brown 40.00 *75.00*

Available for both postage and currency.

Russia Nos. 77, 82, 123, 73, 119 Surcharged

Nos. 53-57

Nos. 58-59

1920 *Perf. 14x14½*
53 A14 5r on 5k dk claret 1.25 *2.40*
 a. Inverted surcharge 40.00
 b. Double surcharge 45.00
54 A8 5r on 20k dl bl & dk car 1.25 *2.40*
 a. Inverted surcharge 30.00
 b. Double surcharge 40.00
 c. "5" omitted 30.00

Imperf

55 A14 5r on 5k claret 1.25 *2.40*
 a. Double surcharge 25.00

Same Surcharge on Stamp of Denikin Issue, No. 64

57 A5 5r on 35k lt bl 12.00 *14.00*
 a. Double surcharge 80.00
 Nos. 53-57 (4) 15.75 21.20

1920 *Perf. 14x14½*
58 A14 100r on 1k dl org yel 3.75
 a. "10" in place of "100" 55.00
 b. Inverted surcharge 35.00
 c. Double surcharge 55.00

Imperf

59 A14 100r on 1k orange 2.75

Nos. 53-57 were issued at Sevastopol during the occupation by General Wrangel's army. Nos. 58-59 were prepared but not used.

Denikin Issue

A5

St. George — A6

1919 Unwmk. ***Imperf.***
61 A5 5k orange .20 *.25*
62 A5 10k green .20 *.25*
63 A5 15k red .20 *.35*
64 A5 35k light blue .20 *.25*
65 A5 70k dark blue .20 *.35*
 a. Tête bêche pair 65.00
66 A6 1r brown & red .50 *.50*
67 A6 2r gray vio & yellow .70 *.75*
68 A6 3r dl rose & green .50 *.75*
69 A6 5r slate & violet .80 *1.10*
70 A6 7r gray grn & rose 1.50 *2.75*
71 A6 10r red & gray 1.25 *2.00*
 Nos. 61-71 (11) 6.25 9.30

Perf. 11½

68a A6 3r dull rose & green 1.25 *1.25*
69a A6 5r slate & violet 2.00 *2.00*
71a A6 10r red & gray 1.40 *1.60*
 Nos. 68a-71a (3) 4.65 4.85

Nos. 61-71 were issued at Ekaterinodar and used in all parts of South Russia that were occupied by the People's Volunteer Army under Gen. Anton Ivanovich Denikin. The inscription on the stamps reads "United Russia."

Stamps of type A6 with rosettes instead of numerals in the small circles at the sides may be essays. Perforated copies of Nos. 61-67 and 70 are of private origin.

For surcharges see Russia, Offices in Turkish Empire Nos. 303-319.

SOUTH WEST AFRICA

sauth 'west 'a-fri-kə

LOCATION — Southwestern Africa between Angola and Cape of Good Hope, bordering on the Atlantic Ocean
GOVT. — Administered by the Republic of South Africa under a mandate of the League of Nations
AREA — 318,261 sq. mi.
POP. — 1,039,800 (1982)
CAPITAL — Windhoek

Formerly a German possession, South West Africa was occupied by South African forces in 1915 and by the Treaty of Versailles was mandated to the Union of South Africa.

12 Pence = 1 Shilling
20 Shillings = 1 Pound

Catalogue values for unused stamps in this country are for Never Hinged items, beginning with Scott 125 in the regular postage section, Scott B1 in the semi-postal section, Scott J86 in the postage due section, and Scott O13 in the officials section.

Watermarks

Watermarks 177 and 201 can be found at the beginning of South Africa.

Stamps of South Africa, Nos. 2-3, 5 and 9-16, Overprinted in English or Afrikaans alternately throughout the sheets.

Major-number listings and values of Nos. 1-40 and 85-93 are for pairs with both overprints.

Setting I

a

b

"South West" 14½mm wide
"Zuid-West" 13mm wide
Overprint Spaced 14mm

1923, Jan. 2 Wmk. 177 *Perf. 14*
1 A2 ½p green, pair 3.00 *10.50*
 a. Single, Dutch 1.10 *1.10*
2 A2 1p red, pair 3.75 *10.50*
 a. Single, Dutch 1.10 *1.10*
 b. Inverted overprint, pair 550.00
 c. As "b," single, English 125.00
 d. As "b," single, Dutch 125.00
 e. "Af.rica" 175.00 210.00
 f. Double overprint, pair 1,000.
 g. As "f," single, English 500.00
 h. As "f," single, Dutch 500.00
3 A2 2p dull vio, pair 4.75 *14.00*
 a. Single, Dutch 1.75 *1.75*
 b. Inverted overprint, pair 625.00 700.00
 c. As "b," single, English 110.00
 d. As "b," single, Dutch 110.00
4 A2 3p ultra, pair 8.50 *19.00*
 a. Single, Dutch 3.25 *3.25*
5 A2 4p ol grn & org, pair 15.00 *52.50*
 a. Single, Dutch 4.50 *4.50*
6 A2 6p vio & blk, pair 9.25 *50.00*
 a. Single, Dutch 4.75 *4.75*
7 A2 1sh orange, pair 27.50 *55.00*
 a. Single, Dutch 5.75 *5.75*
8 A2 1sh3p violet, pair 35.00 *62.50*
 a. Single, Dutch 6.50 *6.50*
 b. Inverted overprint, pair 375.00
 c. As "b," single, English 45.00
 d. As "b," single, Dutch 45.00
9 A2 2sh6p grn & cl, pair 70.00 *150.00*
 a. Single, Dutch 22.50 *22.50*
10 A2 5sh blue & cl, pair 175.00 *375.00*
 a. Single, Dutch 57.50 *57.50*
11 A2 10sh ol grn & bl, pair 1,500. *2,900.*
 a. Single, Dutch 475.00 *500.00*
12 A2 £1 red & dp grn, pair 800.00 *2,000.*
 a. Single, Dutch 300.00 *300.00*
 Nos. 1-12 (12) 2,651. *5,699.*

Most values exist with "t" of "West" partly or totally missing. Vertical displacement in overprinting accounts for the copies with only one line of overprint.

For English from setting I "a," see note after No. 27.

Setting II

c

Zuid-West

d

Afrika.

Words Same Width as Setting I
Overprint Spaced 9½-10mm

1923, Apr.
13 A2 5sh blue & cl, pair 160.00 *300.00*
 a. Single, English 52.50 *52.50*
 b. Single, Dutch 52.50 *52.50*
 c. As #13, without period after "Afrika" 1,200. 1,300.
14 A2 10sh ol grn & bl, pair 575.00 *1,000.*
 a. Single, English 160.00 *160.00*
 b. Single, Dutch 160.00 *160.00*
 c. As #14, without period after "Afrika" 2,600. *3,250.*

15 A2 £1 red & green, pair 1,150. *1,700.*
- *a.* Single, English 225.00 *225.00*
- *b.* Single, Dutch 225.00 *225.00*
- *c.* As #15, without period after "Afrika" 6,000. 5,750.

Setting III

e

f

English as in Setting I
"Zuidwest" 11mm wide, No Hyphen
Overprint Spaced 14mm

1923-24

16 A2 ½p grn, pair ('24) 7.00 *40.00*
- *a.* Single, English .30 *4.25*
- *b.* Single, Dutch .30 *4.25*

17 A2 1p red, pair 6.25 *10.50*
- *a.* Single, English .30 *1.60*
- *b.* Single, Dutch .30 *1.60*

18 A2 2p dull vio, pair 6.25 *10.50*
- *a.* Single, English .30 *1.50*
- *b.* Single, Dutch .30 *1.50*
- *c.* Dbl. ovpt., pair 1,200.
- *d.* As "c," single, English 90.00
- *e.* As "c," single, Dutch 90.00

19 A2 3p ultra, pair 5.75 *11.50*
- *a.* Single, English .50 *1.50*
- *b.* Single, Dutch .50 *1.50*

20 A2 4p ol grn & org, pair 7.00 *24.00*
- *a.* Single, English .50 *3.25*
- *b.* Single, Dutch .50 *3.25*

21 A2 6p vio & blk, pair 16.00 *52.50*
- *a.* Single, English 1.00 *5.75*
- *b.* Single, Dutch 1.00 *5.75*

22 A2 1sh orange, pair 16.00 *52.50*
- *a.* Single, English 1.00 *5.75*
- *b.* Single, Dutch 1.00 *5.75*

23 A2 1sh3p violet, pair 32.50 *52.50*
- *a.* Single, English 1.75 *6.25*
- *b.* Single, Dutch 1.75 *6.25*

24 A2 2sh6p grn & cl, pair 52.50 *92.50*
- *a.* Single, English 4.00 *11.50*
- *b.* Single, Dutch 4.00 *11.50*

25 A2 5sh blue & cl, pair 70.00 *150.00*
- *a.* Single, English 7.50 *21.00*
- *b.* Single, Dutch 7.50 *21.00*

26 A2 10sh ol grn & bl, pair 190.00 *300.00*
- *a.* Single, English 30.00 *47.50*
- *b.* Single, Dutch 30.00 *47.50*

27 A2 £1 red & green, pair 350.00 *450.00*
- *a.* Single, English 40.00 *70.00*
- *b.* Single, Dutch 40.00 *70.00*

Nos. 16-27 (12) 759.25 *1,246.*

The English overprint of Setting III is the same as that of Setting I.

Setting IV

South West **Zuidwest**

Africa. **Afrika.**

g h

"South West" 16mm wide
"Zuidwest" 12mm wide
Overprint Spaced 14mm

1924, July

28 A2 2sh6p grn & cl, pair 92.50 *175.00*
- *a.* Single, English 13.00 *32.50*
- *b.* Single, Dutch 13.00 *32.50*

Setting VI

k

l

"South West" 16, 16½mm wide
"Zuidwest" 12½mm wide
Overprint Spaced 9½mm

1924, Dec.

29 A2 ½p green, pair 8.00 *45.00*
- *a.* Single, English .35 *5.75*
- *b.* Single, Dutch .35 *5.75*

30 A2 1p red, pair 3.75 *11.50*
- *a.* Single, English .25 *1.60*
- *b.* Single, Dutch .25 *1.60*

31 A2 2p dull vio, pair 5.75 *25.00*
- *a.* Single, English .30 *2.00*
- *b.* Single, Dutch .30 *2.00*

32 A2 3p ultra, pair 5.25 *32.50*
- *a.* Single, English .45 *3.25*
- *b.* Single, Dutch .45 *3.25*

33 A2 4p ol grn & org, pair 7.50 *52.50*
- *a.* Single, English .50 *4.50*
- *b.* Single, Dutch .50 *4.50*

34 A2 6p vio & blk, pair 10.50 *55.00*
- *a.* Single, English .75 *5.75*
- *b.* Single, Dutch .75 *5.75*

35 A2 1sh orange, pair 12.50 *55.00*
- *a.* Single, English .75 *5.75*
- *b.* Single, Dutch .75 *5.75*

36 A2 1sh3p violet, pair 17.50 *55.00*
- *a.* Single, English .75 *5.75*
- *b.* Single, Dutch .75 *5.75*

37 A2 2sh6p grn & cl, pair 32.50 *80.00*
- *a.* Single, English 3.00 *11.50*
- *b.* Single, Dutch 3.00 *11.50*

38 A2 5sh blue & cl, pair 47.50 *110.00*
- *a.* Single, English 6.00 *16.00*
- *b.* Single, Dutch 6.00 *16.00*

39 A2 10sh ol grn & bl, pair 75.00 *150.00*
- *a.* Single, English 10.00 *22.50*
- *b.* Single, Dutch 10.00 *22.50*

40 A2 £1 red & grn, pair 250.00 *475.00*
- *a.* Single, English 40.00 *75.00*
- *b.* Single, Dutch 40.00 *75.00*

Nos. 29-40 (12) 475.75 *1,146.*

Setting VII
South Africa Nos. 21-22 Overprinted:

m

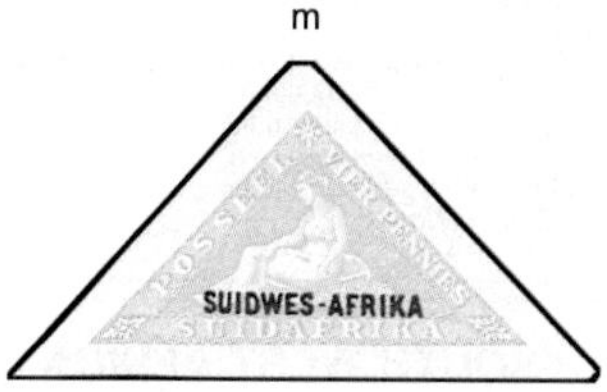

n

o

1926-27 **Wmk. 201** ***Imperf.***

81 A3 (m) 4p blue gray .85 *3.50*
82 A3 (n) 4p blue gray .85 *3.50*
83 A3 (o) 4p blue gray ('27) 7.00 *22.50*
Nos. 81-83 (3) 8.70 *29.50*

Nos. 81-83 were not officially perforated, but firms and individuals applied various forms of perforation and rouletting for their own convenience. Perf. 11 examples of Nos. 81-82 were made by John Meinert, Ltd., Windhoek, same values.

Setting VIII
South Africa Nos. 23-25 Overprinted Alternately with type "p" on English-inscribed Stamps and type "q" on Afrikaans-inscribed Stamps

p

p

"South West" 16½mm wide
"Suidwes" 11mm wide
Overprint Spaced 11½mm

1926 **Typo.** ***Perf. 14½x14***

85 A5 ½p dk grn & blk, pair 1.90 *7.50*
- *a.* Single, English .35 *1.00*
- *b.* Single, Afrikaans .35 *1.00*
- *c.* Ovpt. "q" on English stamp .35 *1.00*
- *d.* Ovpt. "p" on Afrikaans stamp .35 *1.00*
- *e.* Pair, "c" + "d" 1.75 *6.00*
- *f.* As "e," without period after "Africa" 175.00

86 A6 1p car & blk, pair 2.25 *3.00*
- *a.* Single, English .35 *.60*
- *b.* Single, Afrikaans .35 *.60*
- *c.* Ovpt. "q" on English stamp .35 *.60*
- *d.* Ovpt. "p" on Afrikaans stamp .35 *.60*
- *e.* Pair, "c" + "d" 1.75 *5.00*
- *f.* As "e," without period after "Africa" 325.00

87 A7 6p org & grn, pair 27.50 *35.00*
- *a.* Single, English 2.50 *5.00*
- *b.* Single, Afrikaans 2.50 *5.00*
- *c.* Ovpt. "q" on English stamp 2.00 *3.50*
- *d.* Ovpt. "p" on Afrikaans stamp 2.00 *3.50*
- *e.* Pair, "c" + "d" 12.50 *27.50*
- *f.* As "e," without period after "Africa" 200.00

Nos. 85-87 (3) 31.65 *45.50*

For overprints see Nos. O1-O3.

Setting IX
South Africa Nos. 26-27, 29-32 Overprinted in Blue with types "p" and "q" Spaced 16mm

1927 **Engr.** ***Perf. 14***

88 A8 2p vio brn & gray, pair 5.50 *17.50*
- *a.* Single, English .25 *2.00*
- *b.* Single, Afrikaans .25 *2.00*

89 A9 3p red & blk, pair 5.50 *32.50*
- *a.* Single, English .50 *3.00*
- *b.* Single, Afrikaans .50 *3.00*

90 A11 1sh dp bl & bis brn, pair 17.50 *37.50*
- *a.* Single, English 1.25 *4.50*
- *b.* Single, Afrikaans 1.25 *4.50*

91 A12 2sh6p brn & bl grn, pair 40.00 *97.50*
- *a.* Single, English 5.50 *15.00*
- *b.* Single, Afrikaans 5.50 *15.00*

92 A13 5sh dp grn & blk, pair 85.00 *200.00*
- *a.* Single, English 10.00 *22.50*
- *b.* Single, Afrikaans 10.00 *22.50*

93 A14 10sh ol brn & bl, pair 75.00 *160.00*
- *a.* Single, English 9.00 *22.50*
- *b.* Single, Afrikaans 9.00 *22.50*

Nos. 88-93 (6) 228.50 *545.00*

South Africa Nos. 12 and 16a Overprinted at Foot

r

1927 **Typo.** **Wmk. 177**

94 A2 1sh3p violet 1.40 *7.50*
- *a.* Without period after "A" 110.00

95 A2 £1 lt red & gray grn 110.00 190.00
- *a.* Without period after "A" 1,750. *2,600.*

South Africa Nos. 23-25 Overprinted type "r" at Foot

1927 **Wmk. 201** ***Perf. 14½x14***

96 A5 ½p green & blk, pair 2.25 *7.50*
- *a.* Single, English .20 *.90*
- *b.* Single, Afrikaans .20 *.90*
- *c.* As #96, without period after "A" on one stamp 47.50 85.00

97 A6 1p car & blk, pair 1.50 *3.75*
- *a.* Single, English .20 *.65*
- *b.* Single, Afrikaans .20 *.65*
- *c.* As #97, without period after "A" on one stamp 47.50 85.00
- *d.* Ovpt. at top, pair ('30) 2.00 *16.00*
- *e.* As "d," single, English .35 *1.90*
- *f.* As "d," single, Afrikaans .35 *1.90*

98 A7 6p org & grn, pair 13.00 *26.00*
- *a.* Single, English 1.25 *3.25*
- *b.* Single, Afrikaans 1.25 *3.25*
- *c.* As #98, without period after "A" on one stamp 125.00

Nos. 96-98 (3) 16.75 *37.25*

For overprints see Nos. O5-O7.

South Africa Nos. 26-32 Overprinted type "r" at Top

1927-28 **Engr.** ***Perf. 14***

99 A8 2p vio brn & gray, pair 10.50 *27.50*
- *a.* Single, English 1.00 *1.75*
- *b.* Single, Afrikaans 1.00 *1.75*
- *c.* As #99, without period after "A" on one stamp 85.00 125.00
- *d.* Double ovpt., one inverted 800.00 1,050.

100 A9 3p red & blk, pair 7.00 *26.00*
- *a.* Single, English .50 *3.75*
- *b.* Single, Afrikaans .50 *3.75*
- *c.* As #100, without period after "A" on one stamp 92.50 150.00

101 A10 4p brn, pair ('28) 17.50 *45.00*
- *a.* Single, English 1.25 *8.00*
- *b.* Single, Afrikaans 1.25 *8.00*
- *c.* As #101, without period after "A" on one stamp 97.50 *150.00*

102 A11 1sh dp bl & bis brn, pair 22.50 *55.00*
- *a.* Single, English 1.50 *5.75*
- *b.* Single, Afrikaans 1.50 *5.75*
- *c.* As #102, without period after "A" on one stamp 1,500.

103 A12 2sh6p brn & bl grn, pair 47.50 *97.50*
- *a.* Single, English 6.00 *14.00*
- *b.* Single, Afrikaans 6.00 *14.00*
- *c.* As #103, without period after "A" on one stamp 190.00 *325.00*

104 A13 5sh dp grn & blk, pair 70.00 *140.00*
- *a.* Single, English 8.00 *21.00*
- *b.* Single, Afrikaans 8.00 *21.00*
- *c.* As #104, without period after "A" on one stamp 275.00 425.00

105 A14 10sh ol brn & bl, pair 110.00 225.00
- *a.* Single, English 20.00 *32.50*
- *b.* Single, Afrikaans 20.00 *32.50*
- *c.* As #105, without period after "A" on one stamp 375.00 625.00

Nos. 99-105 (7) 285.00 *616.00*

For overprint see No. O8.

South Africa Nos. 33-34 Overprinted type "r" at Foot

1930 **Photo.** ***Perf. 15x14***

106 A5 ½p bl grn & blk, pair 9.25 *32.50*
- *a.* Single, English .50 *3.25*
- *b.* Single, Afrikaans .50 *3.25*

107 A6 1p car rose & blk, pair 7.50 *30.00*
- *a.* Single, English .50 *3.25*
- *b.* Single, Afrikaans .50 *3.25*

Kori Bustard — A15

Cape Cross — A16

Mail Transport — A17

Bogenfels — A18

Windhoek — A19

Waterberg — A20

Lüderitz Bay — A21

Bush Scene — A22

Elands — A23

Zebras and Brindled Gnus — A24

Herero Houses — A25

Welwitschia Plant — A26

Okuwahakan Falls — A27

Perf. 14x13½

1931-37 Wmk. 201 Engr.

108 A15 ½p grn & blk, pair 2.75 3.00
a. Single, English .20 .20
b. Single, Afrikaans .20 .20
109 A16 1p red & ind, pair 2.75 3.00
a. Single, English .20 .20
b. Single, Afrikaans .20 .20
110 A17 1½p vio brn, pair ('37) 25.00 3.50
a. Single, English .20 .30
b. Single, Afrikaans .20 .30
111 A18 2p dk brn & dk bl, pair .80 *4.25*
a. Single, English .20 .20
b. Single, Afrikaans .20 .20
112 A19 3p dp bl & gray blk, pair .80 *4.75*
a. Single, English .20 .20
b. Single, Afrikaans .20 .20
113 A20 4p brn vio & grn, pair 2.10 *8.00*
a. Single, English .20 .25
b. Single, Afrikaans .20 .25
114 A21 6p ol brn & bl, pair 1.75 *10.50*
a. Single, English .20 .25
b. Single, Afrikaans .20 .25
115 A22 1sh bl & vio brn, pair 1.75 *11.00*
a. Single, English .20 .30
b. Single, Afrikaans .20 .30
116 A23 1sh3p ocher & pur, pair 8.75 12.50
a. Single, English .45 .60
b. Single, Afrikaans .45 .60
117 A24 2sh6p dk gray & rose, pair 22.50 27.50
a. Single, English 1.25 2.00
b. Single, Afrikaans 1.25 2.00
118 A25 5sh vio brn & ol grn, pair 19.00 *45.00*
a. Single, English 1.25 *3.25*
b. Single, Afrikaans 1.25 *3.25*
119 A26 10sh grn & brn, pair 52.50 *57.50*
a. Single, English 4.50 *7.00*
b. Single, Afrikaans 4.50 *7.00*
120 A27 20sh bl grn & mar, pair 85.00 95.00
a. Single, English 12.50 12.50
b. Single, Afrikaans 12.50 12.50
Nos. 108-120 (13) 225.45 *285.50*

For overprints see Nos. O13-O27.

George V — A28

1935, May 6 ***Perf. 14x13½***

121 A28 1p carmine & blk 1.25 .30
122 A28 2p dk brown & blk 1.25 .30
123 A28 3p blue & blk 10.00 *21.00*
124 A28 6p violet & blk 4.50 *11.50*
Nos. 121-124 (4) 17.00 *33.10*
Set, never hinged 30.00

25th anniv. of the reign of George V.

Catalogue values for unused stamps in this section, from this point to the end of the section, are for Never Hinged items.

Coronation Issue

Inscribed alternately in English and Afrikaans

George VI — A29

1937, May 12 Engr. ***Perf. 13½x14***

125 A29 ½p emer & blk, pair .45 .25
a. Single, English .20 .20
b. Single, Afrikaans .20 .20
126 A29 1p car & blk, pair .45 .25
a. Single, English .20 .20
b. Single, Afrikaans .20 .20
127 A29 1½p org & blk, pair .45 .25
a. Single, English .20 .20
b. Single, Afrikaans .20 .20
128 A29 2p dk brn & blk, pair .45 .30
a. Single, English .20 .20
b. Single, Afrikaans .20 .20
129 A29 3p brt bl & blk, pair .55 .30
a. Single, English .20 .20
b. Single, Afrikaans .20 .20
130 A29 4p dk vio & blk, pair .55 .35
a. Single, English .20 .20
b. Single, Afrikaans .20 .20
131 A29 6p yel & blk, pair .55 *2.75*
a. Single, English .20 .30
b. Single, Afrikaans .20 .30
132 A29 1sh gray & blk, pair 2.00 *3.25*
a. Single, English .20 .75
b. Single, Afrikaans .20 .75
Nos. 125-132 (8) 5.45 7.70

George VI & Queen Elizabeth coronation.

Voortrekker Issue

South Africa Nos. 79-80 Overprinted type "r"

1938, Dec. 14 Photo. ***Perf. 15x14***

133 A23 1p rose & sl, pair 13.00 11.50
a. Single, English 1.00 *1.25*
b. Single, Afrikaans 1.00 *1.25*
134 A24 1½p red brn & Prus bl, pair 16.00 13.50
a. Single, English 1.50 1.50
b. Single, Afrikaans 1.50 1.50

Issued to commemorate the Voortrekkers.

South Africa Nos. 81-89 Overprinted

s 

Perf. 14 (2p, 4p, 6p); 15x14

1941-43 Wmk. 201

135 A25 ½p dp blue grn, pair 1.75 2.10
a. Single, English .20 .20
b. Single, Afrikaans .20 .20
136 A26 1p brt rose, pair 2.00 2.25
a. Single, English .20 .20
b. Single, Afrikaans .20 .20
137 A27 1½p Prus grn, pair ('42) 3.00 3.25
a. Single, English .20 .20
b. Single, Afrikaans .20 .20
138 A28 2p dk violet .60 .50
139 A29 3p dp blue, pair 15.00 10.00
a. Single, English .75 *1.00*
b. Single, Afrikaans .75 *1.00*
140 A30 4p brown, pair 6.00 8.25
a. Single, English .30 *.75*
b. Single, Afrikaans .30 *.75*
141 A31 6p brt red org, pair 3.50 4.00
a. Single, English .30 *1.00*
b. Single, Afrikaans .30 *1.00*
142 A32 1sh dk brown 1.25 1.00
143 A33 1sh3p dk ol brn, pair ('43) 15.00 16.00
a. Single, English 1.00 1.25
b. Single, Afrikaans 1.00 1.25
Nos. 135-143 (9) 48.10 47.35

South Africa Nos. 90-97 Overprinted

t

u

Pairs or Strips of 3 Perf. 14 or 15x14 all around, Rouletted 6½ or 13 btwn.

1942-45 Wmk. 201

144 A34(t) ½p dp grn, horiz. strip of 3 .75 .60
a. Single, English .20 .20
b. Single, Afrikaans .20 .20
c. ½p dp bl grn, horiz. strip of 3 1.50 2.25
d. As "c," single, English .20 .20
e. As "c," single, Afrikaans .20 .20
145 A35(t) 1p brt car, horiz. strip of 3 .75 .60
a. Single, English .20 .20
b. Single, Afrikaans .20 .20
c. 1p rose car, horiz. strip of 3 1.25 *2.00*
d. As "c," single, English .20 .20
e. As "c," single, Afrikaans .20 .20
146 A36(u) 1½p cop brn, horiz. pair .75 .60
a. Single, English .20 .20
b. Single, Afrikaans .20 .20
147 A37(t) 2p dk vio, horiz. pair .75 .75
a. Single, English .20 .20
b. Single, Afrikaans .20 .20
148 A38(t) 3p dp bl, vert. strip of 3 4.00 *4.25*
a. Single, English .20 *.40*
b. Single, Afrikaans .20 *.40*
149 A39(t) 4p sl grn, vert. strip of 3 5.00 *6.50*
a. Single .20 *.30*
b. As "c," single 50.00
c. Invtd. ovpt., strip of 3 500.00 300.00
150 A40(t) 6p brt red org, horiz. pair 2.75 1.60
a. Single, English .20 *.30*
b. Single, Afrikaans .20 *.30*
c. Inverted overprint, pair 425.00
d. As "c," single, English 50.00 50.00
e. As "c," single, Afrikaans 50.00 50.00
151 A41(u) 1sh dk brn, vert. pair 12.00 11.00
a. Single .75 1.50
b. As "c," single 70.00
c. Inverted overprint, pair 450.00 325.00
152 A41(t) 1sh dk brn, vert. pair 2.25 1.60
a. Single .20 *.30*
b. As "c," single 45.00 40.00
c. Invtd. ovpt., vert. pair 375.00 275.00
Nos. 144-152 (9) 29.00 27.50

Issue years: #144-145, 147-151, 1943; #152, 1944; #144c, 145c, 149c, 1945.

Peace Issue

South Africa Nos. 100-102 Overprinted Type "w"

1945, Dec. 3 Wmk. 201 ***Perf. 14***

153 A42 1p rose pink & choc, pair .40 .40
a. Single, English .20 .20
b. Single, Afrikaans .20 .20
c. Inverted overprint, pair 300.00 300.00
d. As "c," single, English 37.50
e. As "c," single, Afrikaans 37.50
154 A43 2p vio & sl bl, pair .40 .40
a. Single, English .20 .20
b. Single, Afrikaans .20 .20
155 A43 3p ultra & dp ultra, pair 1.25 1.25
a. Single, English .20 .20
b. Single, Afrikaans .20 .20
Nos. 153-155 (3) 2.05 2.05

WW II victory of the Allies.

Royal Visit Issue

South Africa Nos. 103-105 Overprinted

1947, Feb. 17 ***Perf. 15x14***

156 A44 1p cerise & gray, pair .30 .20
a. Single, English .20 .20
b. Single, Afrikaans .20 .20
157 A45 2p purple, pair .30 .25
a. Single, English .20 .20
b. Single, Afrikaans .20 .20
158 A46 3p dk blue, pair .35 .30
a. Single, English .20 .20
b. Single, Afrikaans .20 .20
Nos. 156-158 (3) .95 .75

Visit of the British Royal Family, Mar.-Apr., 1947.

South Africa No. 106 Overprinted

1948, Apr. 26 ***Perf. 14***

159 A47 3p dp chalky bl & sil, pair 1.25 .30
a. Single, English .20 .20
b. Single, Afrikaans .20 .20

25th anniv. of the marriage of George VI and Queen Elizabeth.

UPU Issue

South Africa Nos. 109-111 Overprinted type "w" 13mm wide

1949, Oct. 1 ***Perf. 14x15***

160 A50 ½p dk green, pair 1.10 *1.50*
a. Single, English .20 *.25*
b. Single, Afrikaans .20 *.25*
161 A50 1½p dk red, pair 1.10 *1.50*
a. Single, English .20 .20
b. Single, Afrikaans .20 .20
162 A50 3p ultra, pair 1.75 *2.00*
a. Single, English .20 *.25*
b. Single, Afrikaans .20 *.25*
Nos. 160-162 (3) 3.95 5.00

75th anniv. of the UPU.

Except for Nos. 312-313, 423-428, this ends the bi-lingual multiples in the postage section.

Voortrekker Monument Issue

South Africa Nos. 112-114 Overprinted

1949, Dec. 1 ***Perf. 15x14***

163 A51 1p magenta .20 .20
164 A52 1½p dull green .20 .20
165 A53 3p dark blue .30 .30
Nos. 163-165 (3) .70 .70

Inauguration of the Voortrekker Monument at Pretoria.

South Africa Nos. 115-119 Overprinted

w 

x 

1952, Mar. 14 ***Perf. 15x14, 14x15***

166 A54(w) ½p dk brown & red vio .40 .40
167 A55(x) 1p dark green .40 .40
168 A54(w) 2p dark purple .85 .40
169 A55(x) 4½p dark blue 1.00 1.00
170 A54(w) 1sh brown 2.00 2.00
Nos. 166-170 (5) 4.65 4.20

300th anniv. of the landing of Jan van Riebeeck at the Cape of Good Hope.

SEMI-POSTAL STAMPS

Catalogue values for unused stamps in this section are for Never Hinged items.

Voortrekker Monument Issue

South Africa Nos. B1-B4 Overprinted

1935-36 Wmk. 201 *Perf. 14*

B1 SP1 ½p + ½p grn & blk, pair 3.00 *6.25*
- a. Single, English .25 *.85*
- b. Single, Afrikaans .25 *.85*

B2 SP2 1p + ½p rose & blk, pair 4.00 3.75
- a. Single, English .30 .45
- b. Single, Afrikaans .30 .45

B3 SP3 2p + 1p dl vio & gray, pair 13.00 7.00
- a. Single, English .75 .90
- b. Single, Afrikaans .75 .90

B4 SP4 3p + 1½p dp bl & gray, pair 25.00 37.50
- a. Single, English 1.50 *4.50*
- b. Single, Afrikaans 1.50 *4.50*

Nos. B1-B4 (4) 45.00 54.50

Voortrekker Centenary Issue

South Africa Nos. B5-B8 Overprinted

1938, Dec. 14 *Perf. 14*

B5 SP5 ½p + ½p dl grn & indigo, pair 9.00 8.75
- a. Single, English .75 1.25
- b. Single, Afrikaans .75 1.25

Perf. 15x14

B6 SP6 1p + 1p rose & sl, pair 20.00 13.00
- a. Single, English .50 *1.00*
- b. Single, Afrikaans .50 *1.00*

B7 SP7 1½p + 1½p Prus grn & choc, pair 26.00 18.00
- a. Single, English 1.25 2.50
- b. Single, Afrikaans 1.25 2.50

B8 SP8 3p + 3p chlky bl, pair 50.00 37.50
- a. Single, English 2.75 5.00
- b. Single, Afrikaans 2.75 5.00

Nos. B5-B8 (4) 105.00 77.25

Same Overprint on South Africa Nos. B9-B11

1939, July 17 *Perf. 14*

B9 SP9 ½p + ½p Prus grn & gray brn, pair 8.50 6.75
- a. Single, English .85 .85
- b. Single, Afrikaans .85 .85

B10 SP10 1p + 1p rose car & Prus grn, pair 16.00 12.50
- a. Single, English 1.00 1.00
- b. Single, Afrikaans 1.00 1.00

Perf. 15x14

B11 SP11 1½p + 1½p rose vio, dk vio & Prus grn, pair 28.00 20.00
- a. Single, English 1.25 1.25
- b. Single, Afrikaans 1.25 1.25

Nos. B9-B11 (3) 52.50 39.25

250th anniv. of the landing of the Huguenots in South Africa. Surtax went to a fund to build a Huguenot memorial at Paarl.

AIR POST STAMPS

South Africa Nos. C5-C6 Overprinted

1930 Unwmk. *Perf. 14x13½*

C1 AP2 4p blue green 8.00 *32.50*
- a. Without period after "A" 80.00 150.00

C2 AP2 1sh orange 12.50 *57.50*
- a. Without period after "A" 475.00 *625.00*

Overprinted

C3 AP2 4p blue green 1.50 *7.00*
- a. Double overprint 200.00
- b. Inverted overprint 200.00
- c. Small "I" in "AIR" 6.00

C4 AP2 1sh orange 4.25 *17.50*
- a. Double overprint 575.00

Monoplane over Windhoek — AP3

Biplane over Windhoek — AP4

Wmk. 201

1931, Mar. 5 Engr. *Perf. 14*

C5 AP3 3p blue & dk brn, pair 30.00 *35.00*
- a. Single, English 2.00 *3.00*
- b. Single, Afrikaans 2.00 *3.00*

C6 AP4 10p brn vio & blk, pair 45.00 *75.00*
- a. Single, English 3.00 *6.00*
- b. Single, Afrikaans 3.00 *6.00*

POSTAGE DUE STAMPS

STAMPS OF TRANSVAAL USED IN SOUTH WEST AFRICA

Prior to the issue of Nos. J1-J9, postage due stamps of South Africa and Transvaal were used in South West Africa.

1915-23

AJ7 6p Transvaal #J6, on cover 500.00

AJ8 1sh Transvaal #J7, on cover 700.00

Values are for covers commercially used in South West Africa during 1915-1923.

REGULAR ISSUES

Postage Due Stamps of South Africa and Transvaal Overprinted like Regular Issues.

Setting I

On South Africa Nos. J11, J14

***Perf.* 14 Unwmk.**

1923

J1 D1 ½p blue grn & blk, pair 5.00 *15.00*
- a. Single, English .35 *4.00*
- b. Single, Dutch .35 *4.00*
- c. As #J1, without period after "Afrika" 100.00
- d. Inverted ovpt., pair 325.00

J2 D1 2p violet & blk, pair 3.00 *20.00*
- a. Single, English .20 *4.00*
- b. Single, Dutch .20 *4.00*
- c. As #J2, without period after "Afrika" 70.00 70.00

On South Africa Nos. J9-J10

Rouletted 7-8

J3 D1 1p dull red & blk, pair 7.00 *12.00*
- a. Single, English .20 *3.00*
- b. Single, Dutch .20 *3.00*
- c. As #J3, without period after "Afrika" 70.00 70.00
- d. Pair, imperf. between 825.00

J4 D1 1½p yel brn & blk, pair 1.00 *8.00*
- a. Single, English .20 *1.75*
- b. Single, Dutch .20 *1.75*
- c. As #J4, without period after "Afrika" 42.50 42.50

On South Africa Nos. J3-J4, J6

Perf. 14

Wmk. 177

J5 D1 2p violet & blk, pair 17.00 *27.50*
- a. Single, English 1.75 *7.50*
- b. Single, Dutch 1.75 *7.50*
- c. As #J5, without period after "Afrika" 150.00

J6 D1 3p ultra & blk, pair 9.00 *27.50*
- a. Single, English .85 *7.50*
- b. Single, Dutch .85 *7.50*

J7 D1 6p gray & blk, pair 24.00 *40.00*
- a. Single, English 2.50 *12.50*
- b. Single, Dutch 2.50 *12.50*

Nos. J5-J7 (3) 50.00 *95.00*

On Transvaal Nos. J5-J6

Wmk. Multiple Crown and C A (3)

J8 D1 5p violet & blk, pair 4.00 *27.50*
- a. Single, English .50 *7.50*
- b. Single, Dutch .50 *7.50*
- c. As #J8, without period after "Afrika" 85.00 85.00

J9 D1 6p red brn & blk, pair 17.00 *27.50*
- a. Single, Dutch 1.75 *7.50*
- b. As #J9, without period after "Afrika" 140.00

For No. J9 single in English see No. J17a and note after No. 27.

The "t" of "West" may be found partly or entirely missing on Nos. J1, J3-J6, J8-J9.

Setting II

On South Africa No. J9

Rouletted

Unwmk.

J10 D1 1p dull red & blk, pair *8,000.*
- a. Single, English 800.00 —
- b. Single, Dutch 800.00 —

On South Africa Nos. J3-J4

Perf. 14

Wmk. 177

J11 D1 2p violet & blk, pair 14.00 *25.00*
- a. Single, English 1.25 *7.00*
- b. Single, Dutch 1.25 *7.00*
- c. As #J11, without period after "Afrika" 110.00 125.00

J12 D1 3p ultra & blk, pair 7.00 20.00
- a. Single, English .75 5.00
- b. Single, Dutch .75 5.00
- c. As #J12, without period after "Afrika" 70.00 80.00

On Transvaal No. J5

Wmk. Multiple Crown and C A (3)

J13 D1 5p violet & blk, pair 75.00 140.00
- a. Single, English 15.00
- b. Single, Dutch 15.00

Setting III

On South Africa Nos. J11, J12, J9

Unwmk.

J14 D1 ½p blue grn & blk, pair 7.00 *17.50*
- a. Single, Dutch .75 *4.50*

J15 D1 1p rose & black, pair 8.00 *20.00*
- a. Single, English .75 *4.50*
- b. Single, Dutch .75 *4.50*

Rouletted 7

J16 D1 1p dull red & blk, pair 2.00 *20.00*
- a. Single, Dutch .20 *4.00*

For Nos. J14 and J16 singles in English see Nos. J1a and J3a and note after No. 27.

On Transvaal No. J6

Perf. 14

Wmk. 3

J17 D1 6p red brown & blk, pair 17.00 *60.00*
- a. Single, English 1.75 *17.50*
- b. Single, Dutch 1.75 *17.50*

See note below No. 27.

Setting IV

On South Africa Nos. J11-J12, J16

1924 Unwmk.

J18 D1 ½p blue grn & blk, pair 3.50 *20.00*
- a. Single, English .45 *5.00*
- b. Single, Dutch .45 *5.00*

J19 D1 1p rose & blk, pair 5.00 *20.00*
- a. Single, English .60 *5.00*
- b. Single, Dutch .60 *5.00*

J20 D1 6p gray & blk, pair 2.25 *27.50*
- a. Single, English .30 *8.00*
- b. Single, Dutch .30 *8.00*

On Transvaal No. J5

Wmk. Multiple Crown and C A (3)

J21 D1 5p violet & blk, pair 400.00 *1,000.*
- a. Single, English 100.00
- b. Single, Dutch 100.00

Setting V

i

j

"South West" 16mm wide

"Zuidwest" 12mm wide

Overprint Spaced 12mm

On South Africa Nos. J4, J11, J13

1924 Unwmk.

J22 D1 ½p green & blk, pair 2.00 *22.50*
- a. Single, English .25 *6.50*
- b. Single, Dutch .25 *6.50*

J23 D1 1½p yel brown & blk 4.00 *22.50*
- a. Single, English .50 *6.50*
- b. Single, Dutch .50 *6.50*

Wmk. Springbok's Head (177)

J24 D1 3p ultra & black, pair 12.50 *37.50*
- a. Single, English 1.40 *10.00*
- b. Single, Dutch 1.40 *10.00*

On Transvaal No. J5

Wmk. Multiple Crown and C A (3)

J25 D1 5p violet & blk, pair 3.00 *25.00*
- a. Single, English .40 *7.50*
- b. Single, Dutch .40 *7.50*

Setting VI

On South Africa Nos. J4, J11-J16

1924, Dec. Unwmk.

J26 D1 ½p blue grn & blk, pair 5.00 *25.00*
- a. Single, English .60 *6.00*
- b. Single, Dutch .60 *6.00*

J27 D1 1p rose & black, pair 1.50 *7.50*
- a. Single, English .20 *1.75*
- b. Single, Dutch .20 *1.75*
- c. As #J27, without period after "Africa" 87.50

J28 D1 1½p yel brown & blk, pair 2.50 *22.50*
- a. Single, English .30 *5.50*
- b. Single, Dutch .30 *5.50*
- c. As #J28, without period after "Africa" 75.00

J29 D1 2p violet & blk, pair 2.50 *12.50*
- a. Single, English .30 *3.00*
- b. Single, Dutch .30 *3.00*
- c. As #J29, without period after "Africa" 55.00

J30 D1 3p blue & black, pair 3.00 *15.00*
- a. Single, English .75 *3.50*
- b. Single, Dutch .75 *3.50*
- c. As #J30, without period after "Africa" 70.00

J31 D1 6p gray & black, pair 8.00 *45.00*
- a. Single, English 1.00 *12.50*
- b. Single, Dutch 1.00 *12.50*
- c. As #J31, without period after "Africa" 100.00

Nos. J26-J31 (6) 22.50 *127.50*

Wmk. Springbok's Head (177)

J32 D1 3p ultra & black, pair 6.00 *35.00*
- a. Single, English .75 *9.00*
- b. Single, Dutch .75 *9.00*

On Transvaal No. J5

Wmk. 3

J33 D1 5p violet & blk, pair 2.00 *12.50*
- a. Single, English .25 *3.00*
- b. Single, Dutch .25 *3.00*
- c. As #J33, without period after "Africa" 55.00 *75.00*

Setting VIII

On South Africa Nos. J18, J13-J16

1927 Unwmk.

J34 D2 1p rose & black, pair .90 *9.00*
- a. Single, English .20 *2.00*
- b. Single, Afrikaans .20 *2.00*
- c. As #J34, without period after "Africa" 10.50 *17.50*

J35 D1 1½p yel brown & blk, pair .90 *10.00*
- a. Single, English .20 *2.50*
- b. Single, Afrikaans .20 *2.50*
- c. As #J35, without period after "Africa" 50.00 *60.00*

J36 D1 2p violet & blk, pair 2.50 *12.50*
- a. Single, English .30 *3.25*
- b. Single, Afrikaans .30 *3.25*
- c. As #J36, without period after "Africa" 50.00 *60.00*

J37 D1 3p blue & black, pair 10.00 *40.00*
- a. Single, English 1.25 *10.00*
- b. Single, Afrikaans 1.25 *10.00*
- c. As #J37, without period after "Africa" 70.00 70.00

J38 D1 6p gray & black, pair 7.50 *27.50*
- a. Single, English 1.00 *8.00*
- b. Single, Afrikaans 1.00 *8.00*

c. As #J38, without period after "Africa" 100.00 115.00
Nos. J34-J38 (5) 21.80 *99.00*

On Transvaal No. J5

Wmk. Multiple Crown and C A (3)

J39 D1 5p violet & blk, pair 16.00 *75.00*
a. Single, English 1.75 *20.00*
b. Single, Afrikaans 1.75 *20.00*

South Africa Nos. J15-J16 Overprinted

1928 **Unwmk.**

J79 D1 3p blue & black 1.65 *12.00*
a. Without period after "A" 30.00 35.00
J80 D1 6p gray & black 7.50 *22.50*
a. Without period after "A" 125.00

Same Overprint on South Africa Nos. J17-J21

J81 D2 ½p blue grn & blk .40 *6.00*
J82 D2 1p rose & black .50 *3.00*
a. Without period after "A" 40.00 *45.00*
J83 D2 2p violet & black .65 *3.75*
a. Without period after "A" 60.00
J84 D2 3p ultra & black 1.50 *17.50*
J85 D2 6p gray & black 1.75 *15.00*
a. Without period after "A" 40.00 *55.00*
Nos. J81-J85 (5) 4.80 *45.25*

Catalogue values for unused stamps in this section, from this point to the end of the section, are for Never Hinged items.

D3

D4

Wmk. 201

1931, Feb. 23 **Litho.** ***Perf. 12***

Size: 19x22mm

J86 D3 ½p yel green & blk .85 *8.50*
On cover *120.00*
J87 D3 1p rose & black .85 *1.65*
On cover *90.00*
J88 D3 2p violet & black .85 *3.25*
On cover *90.00*
J89 D3 3p blue & black 3.25 *18.00*
On cover *130.00*
J90 D3 6p gray & black 13.00 *27.50*
On cover *275.00*
Nos. J86-J90 (5) 18.80 *58.90*

Cover values are for properly franked commercial items. Philatelic usages alo exist and sell for less.

OFFICIAL STAMPS

Nos. 85-87 (Setting VIII) Overprinted at top with type "c" on English-inscribed Stamps and type "d" on Afrikaans-inscribed Stamps

c d

Without Periods after Words

1927 **Wmk. 201** ***Perf. 14½x14***

O1 A5 ½p dk green & blk, pair 75.00 *175.00*
a. Single, English 9.00 *25.00*
b. Single, Afrikaans 9.00 *25.00*
O2 A6 1p car & blk, pair 75.00 *175.00*
a. Single, English 9.00 *25.00*
b. Single, Afrikaans 9.00 *25.00*
O3 A7 6p org & grn, pair 90.00 *175.00*
a. Single, English 9.50 *25.00*
b. Single, Afrikaans 9.50 *25.00*

South Africa No. 5 Overprinted As Nos. 85-87 plus "c" and "d"

Perf. 14

Wmk. 177

O4 A2 2p dull violet 190.00 *275.00*
a. Single, English 22.50 *40.00*
b. Single, Afrikaans 22.50 *40.00*

Nos. 96-98 Overprinted like Nos. J79-J85 at foot, Overprinted Types "c" and "d" at Top

1929 **Wmk. 201** ***Perf. 14½x14***

O5 A5 ½p green & blk, pair .85 *10.00*
a. Single, English .20 *2.50*
b. Single, Afrikaans .20 *2.50*
O6 A6 1p car & blk, pair 1.00 *11.00*
a. Single, English .20 *2.50*
b. Single, Afrikaans .20 *2.50*
O7 A7 6p org & grn, pair 3.75 *15.00*
a. Single, English .75 *3.50*
b. Single, Afrikaans .75 *3.50*
Nos. O5-O7 (3) 5.60 *36.00*

No. 99 Overprinted like Nos. J79-J85 at foot, Overprinted at top

OFFICIAL. **OFFISIEEL.**

With Periods after Words

Perf. 14

O8 A8 2p vio brn & gray, pair 2.50 *17.00*
a. Single, English .30 *3.75*
b. Single, Afrikaans .30 *3.75*
c. Without period after "OFFICIAL" 5.00 *30.00*
d. Pair, "c" + normal 2p 15.00 *80.00*
e. Without period after "OFFISIEEL" 5.00 *30.00*
f. Pair, "e" + normal 2p 15.00 *80.00*
g. Pair, "c" + "e" 15.00 *80.00*

In each sheet of 120 stamps there were 12 No. O8c and 10 No. O8e.

South Africa Nos. 23-25 Overprinted

Without Periods after Words

1929 **Wmk. 201** ***Perf. 14½x14***

O9 A5 ½p green & blk, pair .60 *11.00*
a. Single, English .20 *2.50*
b. Single, Afrikaans .20 *2.50*
O10 A6 1p car & blk, pair .70 *11.00*
a. Single, English .20 *2.50*
b. Single, Afrikaans .20 *2.50*
O11 A7 6p org & grn, pair 2.50 *25.00*
a. Single, English .30 *6.00*
b. Single, Afrikaans .30 *6.00*
Nos. O9-O11 (3) 3.80 *47.00*

South Africa No. 26 Overprinted

With Periods after Words

Perf. 14

O12 A8 2p vio brn & gray, pair 1.00 *15.00*
a. Single, English .20 *3.50*
b. Single, Afrikaans .20 *3.50*
c. Without period after "OFFICIAL" 3.50 *35.00*
d. Pair, "c" + normal 2p 12.50 *70.00*
e. Without period after "OFFISIEEL" 3.50 *35.00*
f. Pair, "e" + normal 2p 12.50 *70.00*
g. Pair, "c" + "e" 17.50 *80.00*

Catalogue values for unused stamps in this section, from this point to the end of the section, are for Never Hinged items.

Nos. 108-109, 111 and 114 Overprinted in Red

OFFICIAL **OFFISIEEL**

1931

O13 A15 ½p green & blk, pair 8.50 *15.00*
a. Single, English 1.00 *3.50*
b. Single, Afrikaans 1.00 *3.50*
O14 A16 1p red & indigo, pair .65 *15.00*
a. Single, English .20 *3.50*
b. Single, Afrikaans .20 *3.50*
O15 A18 2p dk brn & dk bl, pair 1.00 *9.00*
a. Single, English .20 *2.00*
b. Single, Afrikaans .20 *2.00*
O16 A21 6p ol brn & bl, pair 2.00 *13.00*
a. Single, English .25 *3.00*
b. Single, Afrikaans .25 *3.00*
Nos. O13-O16 (4) 12.15 *52.00*

No. 110 Overprinted in Red

1938, July 1 **Wmk. 201**

O17 A17 1½p violet brn, pair 25.00 *35.00*
a. Single, English 2.75 *6.00*
b. Single, Afrikaans 2.75 *6.00*

Nos. 108-111, 114 Ovptd. in Red

1945-50 **Wmk. 201** ***Perf. 14x13½***

O18 A15 ½p green & blk, pair 8.00 *21.00*
a. Single, English 1.00 *4.25*
b. Single, Afrikaans 1.00 *4.25*
O19 A16 1p red & ind, pair ('50) 2.00 *12.50*
a. Single, English .25 *3.00*
b. Single, Afrikaans .25 *3.00*
O20 A17 1½p vio brown, pair 30.00 27.50
a. Single, English 5.00 5.00
b. Single, Afrikaans 5.00 5.00
O21 A18 2p dk brn & dk bl, pair ('47) 425.00 *600.00*
a. Single, English 75.00 *100.00*
b. Single, Afrikaans 75.00 *100.00*
O22 A21 6p ol brn & bl, pair 7.00 *27.50*
a. Single, English .80 *5.00*
b. Single, Afrikaans .80 *5.00*
Nos. O18-O20,O22 (4) 47.00 *88.50*

Nos. 108-111, 114 Ovptd. in Red

1951-52

O23 A15 ½p grn & blk, pair ('52) 11.00 *15.00*
a. Single, English 1.25 *4.00*
b. Single, Afrikaans 1.25 *4.00*
O24 A16 1p red & ind, pair 2.25 *9.00*
a. Single, English .30 *1.75*
b. Single, Afrikaans .30 *1.75*
c. Ovpt. transposed, pair 50.00 *82.50*
d. As "c," single, English ovpt. 10.00
e. As "c," single, Afrikaans ovpt. 10.00
O25 A17 1½p violet brn, pair 22.50 22.50
a. Single, English 3.00 5.00
b. Single, Afrikaans 3.00 5.00
c. Ovpt. transposed, pair 60.00 75.00
d. As "c," single, English ovpt. 7.50
e. As "c," single, Afrikaans ovpt. 7.50
O26 A18 2p dk brn & dk bl, pair 1.50 *13.00*
a. Single, English .20 *3.50*
b. Single, Afrikaans .20 *3.50*
c. Ovpt. transposed, pair 32.50 *90.00*
d. As "c," single, English ovpt. 4.50
e. As "c," single, Afrikaans ovpt. 4.50
O27 A21 6p ol brn & blue, pair 2.75 *30.00*
a. Single, English .35 *7.00*
b. Single, Afrikaans .35 *7.00*
c. Ovpt. transposed, pair 20.00 *110.00*
d. As "c," single, English ovpt. 4.00
e. As "c," single, Afrikaans ovpt. 4.00
Nos. O23-O27 (5) 40.00 *89.50*

"Overprint transposed" means English inscription on Afrikaans stamp, or vice versa.
Use of official stamps ceased in Jan. 1955.

SPAIN

'spān

LOCATION — Southwestern Europe, Iberian Peninsula
GOVT. — Monarchy
AREA — 194,884 sq. mi.
POP. — 38,219,534 (est. 1983)
CAPITAL — Madrid

Spain was a monarchy until about 1931, when a republic was established. After the Civil War (1936-39), the Spanish State of Gen. Francisco Franco was recognized.

32 Maravedis = 8 Cuartos = 1 Real
1000 Milesimas = 100 Centimos = 1 Escudo (1866)
100 Milesimas = 1 Real
4 Reales = 1 Peseta
100 Centimos = 1 Peseta (1872)

Watermarks

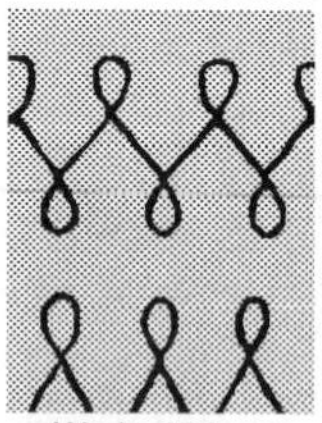

Wmk. 104 — Loops

Wmk. 105 — Crossed Lines

Wmk. 116 — Crosses and Circles

Wmk. 178 — Castle

Stamps punched with a small round hole have done telegraph service. In this condition most of these sell for 20 cents to $20 apiece.

Stamps of 1854 to 1882 canceled with three parallel horizontal bars or two thin lines are remainders. Most of these are valued through No. 101.

CANCELLATIONS

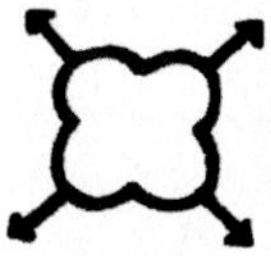

"Spider"

Town (c-d-s)

Grid

Cartwheel

Several types of cancellations were used on early Spanish issues. Most common are the so-called "Spider" cancels, applied in red, blue or black. Circular date stamp (c-d-s) cancellations and grid cancellations were also generally used. In addition, a variety of pre-philatelic cancels may be found. These sell for more than the other types.

Kingdom

Queen Isabella II
A1 A2

6 CUARTOS:
Type I — "T" and "O" of CUARTOS separated.
Type II — "T" and "O" joined.

Unwmk.

1850, Jan. 1 Litho. *Imperf.*

1	A1	6c blk, thin paper (II)	675.00	15.00
		On cover		90.00
a.		Thick paper (II)	675.00	25.00
		On cover		125.00
b.		Thick paper (I)	800.00	20.00
		On cover		90.00
c.		Thin paper (I)	800.00	25.00
		On cover		125.00
d.		6c intense black (II)	800.00	17.50
e.		6c intense black (I)	800.00	22.50
2	A2	12c lilac	2,300.	260.
		On cover		1,250.
a.		Thin paper	*3,200.*	275.00
		On cover		1,400.
b.		12c violet	*3,250.*	275.00
		On cover		1,700.
3	A2	5r red	2,300.	250.
		On cover		2,500.
		On cover, single franking		*6,000.*
a.		5r pale red	2,300.	275.00
b.		5r deep dark red	2,600.	300.00
4	A2	6r blue	3,000.	725.
		On cover		4,000.
		On cover, single franking		*8,750.*
a.		6r deep dark blue	3,000.	775.00
5	A2	10r green	4,100.	2,100.
		On cover		*5,250.*
		On cover, single franking		
a.		10r dark green	4,100.	2,250.
b.		10r pale green	4,100.	2,100.

Full margins = ¾mm.

Stamps of types A2, A3, A4, A6, A7a and A8 are inscribed "FRANCO" on the cuarto values and "CERTIFICADO," "CERTIFO" or "CERT DO" on the reales values.

Values for Singles and Covers Spider Cancellations

Scott No.	Black	Blue	Red
1	15.00	65.00	70.00
Cover	90.00	150.00	150.00
1b	20.00	85.00	95.00
Cover	90.00	150.00	140.00
2	260.00	750.00	675.00
Cover	1,250.	-	-
2b	275.00	750.00	675.00
Cover	1,700.	-	-
3	250.00	600.00	1,200.
Cover	2,500.	-	-
4	725.00	1,450.	1,250.
Cover	4,000.	-	-
5	2,100.	4,400.	5,250.
Cover	5,250.	-	-

Circular Date Stamp Cancellations

Scott No.	Black	Blue	Red
1	23.00	-	-
Cover	90.00	-	-
1b	35.00	950.00	775.00
Cover	90.00	2,900.	
2	2,500.	-	-
Cover	-	-	-
2b	2,600.	-	-
Cover	-	-	-
3	300.00	-	-
Cover	-	-	-
4	900.00	-	-
Cover	-	-	-
5	6,250.	-	-
Cover	-	-	-

Values for pairs

1	A1	6c blk, thin paper (II)	1,500.	57.50
a.		Thick paper (II)	*2,000.*	125.00
b.		Thick paper (I)	1,800.	72.00
c.		Thin paper (I)	*2,400.*	125.00
d.		6c intense black (II)	*1,850.*	
e.		6c intense black (I)	*2,100.*	
2	A2	12c lilac	4,750.	650.00
a.		Thin paper		675.00
b.		12c violet	*6,500.*	750.00
3	A2	5r red	4,000.	525.00
a.		5r pale red	4,750.	625.00
b.		5r deep dark red	5,750.	725.00
4	A2	6r blue	6,000.	1,450.
a.		6r deep dark blue	7,500.	1,900.
5	A2	10r green	—	4,750.
a.		10r dark green	—	5,500.
b.		10r pale green		4,500.

Values for strips of 3

1	A1	6c blk, thin paper (II)	2,300.	110.00
a.		Thick paper (II)	*3,000.*	*200.00*
b.		Thick paper (I)	2,750.	150.00
c.		Thin paper (I)	*3,500.*	*190.00*
d.		6c intense black (II)	*2,900.*	150.00
e.		6c intense black (I)	*3,200.*	190.00
2	A2	12c lilac		1,100.
a.		Thin paper		—
b.		12c violet		1,300.
3	A2	5r red		1,000.
a.		5r pale red		1,200.
b.		5r deep dark red		1,250.
4	A2	6r blue		2,300.
a.		6r deep dark blue		*3,000.*
5	A2	10r green	—	*6,000.*
a.		10r dark green	—	*8,750.*
b.		10r pale green		*7,000.*

Values for blocks of 4

1	A1	6c blk, thin paper (II)	*4,500.*	*550.00*
a.		Thick paper (II)	*5,000.*	*800.00*
b.		Thick paper (I)	*5,500.*	*600.00*
c.		Thin paper (I)	*6,500.*	*8,250.*
d.		6c intense black (II)	*5,500.*	650.00
e.		6c intense black (I)	*6,000.*	725.00
2	A2	12c lilac		*1,900.*
a.		Thin paper		*2,400.*
b.		12c violet		2,500.
3	A2	5r red		*1,800.*
a.		5r pale red		*2,250.*
b.		5r deep dark red		*2,500.*
4	A2	6r blue	*13,500.*	*5,200.*
a.		6r deep dark blue	*15,000.*	*7,500.*

5	A2	10r green		*11,500.*
a.		10r dark green		*15,000.*
b.		10r pale green		*12,500.*

A3

A4

1851, Jan. 1 Typo.

Thin Paper

6	A3	6c black	250.00	2.50
		On cover		27.50
a.		Thick paper	475.00	10.00
		On cover		40.00
b.		6c gray black	250.00	2.50
c.		6c intense black	350.00	3.50
7	A3	12c lilac	4,250.	140.00
		On cover		800.00
		On cover, single franking		1,000.
a.		12c violet	4,400.	140.00
b.		12c gray	4,400.	180.00
c.		12c dark lilac	4,000.	140.00
8	A3	2r red	*17,500.*	*9,500.*
		On cover		*30,000.*
a.		2r deep orange red	*18,000.*	*10,000.*
		On cover		*29,000.*
9	A3	5r rose	2,100.	225.00
		On cover		1,850.
		On cover, single franking		*6,000.*
a.		5r red brown (error)	*13,000.*	—
b.		5r rose carmine	2,300.	240.00
10	A3	6r blue	3,600.	900.00
		On cover		*3,300.*
		On cover, single franking		*10,000.*
a.		Cliche of 2r in plate of 6r	*125,000.*	*100,000.*
b.		Pair, #10, 10a		*110,000.*
c.		6r deep blue	3,750.	900.00
d.		6r pale blue	3,600.	800.00
11	A3	10r green	2,600.	375.00
		On cover		2,200.
		On cover, single franking		*9,000.*
a.		10r deep green	2,750.	425.00
b.		10r pale green	2,600.	375.00

Full margins = ¾mm.

Values for Singles and Covers Spider Cancellations

Scott No.	Black	Blue	Red
6	2.50	27.50	17.50
Cover	27.50	100.00	100.00
7	140.00	290.00	290.00
Cover	800.00	1,750.	-
8	9,500.	17,500.	19,000.
Cover	30,000.	-	-
9	225.00	750.00	550.00
Cover	1,850.	-	-
10	900.00	2,400.	2,200.
Cover	3,300.	-	-
11	375.00	1,300.	850.00
Cover	2,200.	-	-

Circular Date Stamp Cancellations

Scott No.	Red
6	140.00
7	325.00
8	18,000.
9	775.00

Grid Cancellations

Scott No.	Black	Blue	Red
6	200.00	160.00	325.00
7	-	1,000.	-

Values for pairs

6	A3	6c black	550.00	13.00
a.		Thick paper	1,100.	62.50
b.		6c gray black	550.00	16.00
c.		6c intense black	775.00	22.00
7	A3	12c lilac		325.00
a.		12c violet		350.00
b.		12c gray		475.00
c.		12c dark lilac		350.00
8	A3	2r red		22,000.
a.		2r deep orange red		23,500.
9	A3	5r rose	4,500.	500.00
b.		5r rose carmine	5,000.	575.00
10	A3	6r blue		2,000.
c.		6r deep blue		2,250.
d.		6r pale blue		2,000.
11	A3	10r green		900.00
a.		10r deep green	6,000.	900.00
b.		10r pale green		900.00

Values for strips of 3

6	A3	6c black	850.00	32.50
a.		Thick paper	1,900.	100.00
b.		6c gray black	850.00	42.50
c.		6c intense black	1,300.	75.00
7	A3	12c lilac		500.00
a.		12c violet		550.00
b.		12c gray		750.00
c.		12c dark lilac		550.00
8	A3	2r red		—
a.		2r deep orange red		—
9	A3	5r rose		750.00
b.		5r rose carmine		925.00
10	A3	6r blue		3,200.
c.		6r deep blue		3,500.
d.		6r pale blue		3,200.
11	A3	10r green		1,350.
a.		10r deep green		1,600.
b.		10r pale green		1,350.

Values for blocks of 4

6	A3	6c black	1,100.	200.00
a.		Thick paper		—
b.		6c gray black	1,100.	240.00
c.		6c intense black	1,750.	350.00
7	A3	12c lilac	20,000.	650.00
a.		12c violet	25,000.	675.00
b.		12c gray	21,000.	1,100.
c.		12c dark lilac	20,000.	725.00
8	A3	2r red		—
a.		2r deep orange red		—
9	A3	5r rose	10,000.	1,100.
b.		5r rose carmine	12,500.	1,475.
10	A3	6r blue		4,500.
c.		6r deep blue		5,750.
d.		6r pale blue		4,500.
11	A3	10r green	12,500.	3,000.
a.		10r deep green	15,000.	3,300.
b.		10r pale green	13,500.	3,000.

1852, Jan. 1

Thick Paper

12	A4	6c rose	350.00	2.25
		On cover, single franking		17.00
		On cover, in combination with other values		200.00
a.		Thin paper	400.00	3.50
		On cover		22.50
b.		6c deep rose	375.00	4.00
		On cover		27.50
c.		6c carmine lake	500.00	5.75
		On cover		32.50
13	A4	12c lilac	1,800.	120.00
		On cover, single franking		725.00
		On cover, in combination with other values		750.00
a.		12c gray lilac	2,000.	140.00
		On cover		950.00
b.		12c dark lilac	1,900.	125.00
		On cover		675.00
14	A4	2r pale red	15,000.	4,500.
		On cover		18,000.
		On cover, single franking		—
a.		2r orange red	15,000.	4,750.
		On cover		18,500.
15	A4	5r yellowish green	1,900.	85.00
		On cover		3,250.
		On cover, single franking		3,250.
a.		5r green	2,100.	100.00
		On cover		2,900.
b.		5r deep green	2,100.	110.00
		On cover		2,950.
16	A4	6r grnsh blue	3,100.	375.00
		On cover		5,000.
a.		6r blue	3,100.	425.00
		On cover		4,900.
b.		6r dark bluish grn	3,250.	425.00
		On cover		5,000.

Full margins = ¾mm.

Values for pairs

12	A4	6c rose	775.00	11.00
b.		6c deep rose	925.00	32.50
c.		6c carmine lake	1,300.	45.00
13	A4	12c lilac	3,750.	275.00
a.		12c gray lilac	5,000.	350.00
b.		12c dark lilac	5,000.	325.00
14	A4	2r pale red	30,000.	11,000.
a.		2r orange red	32,500.	14,750.
15	A4	5r yellowish green	4,250.	225.00
a.		5r green	4,400.	240.00
b.		5r deep green	4,400.	250.00
16	A4	6r greenish blue		925.00
a.		6r blue		1,000.
b.		6r dark bluish green		1,100.

Values for strips of 3

12	A4	6c rose	1,200.	25.00
b.		6c deep rose	1,500.	75.00
c.		6c carmine lake	2,100.	110.00
13	A4	12c lilac		450.00
a.		12c gray lilac		575.00
b.		12c dark lilac		550.00
14	A4	2r pale red		17,500.
a.		2r orange red		23,500.
15	A4	5r yellowish green		350.00
a.		5r green		375.00
b.		5r deep green		475.00
16	A4	6r greenish blue		1,450.
a.		6r blue		1,600.
b.		6r dark bluish green		1,750.

Values for blocks of 4

12	A4	6c rose	2,000.	160.00
b.		6c deep rose	2,300.	525.00
c.		6c carmine lake	3,250.	725.00
13	A4	12c lilac		600.00
a.		12c gray lilac		875.00
b.		12c dark lilac		850.00
14	A4	2r pale red		27,500.
a.		2r orange red		32,500.
15	A4	5r yellowish green		475.00
a.		5r green		475.00
b.		5r deep green		600.00
16	A4	6r greenish blue		1,725.
a.		6r blue		1,750.
b.		6r dark bluish green		2,200.

Arms of Madrid — A5

Isabella II — A6

1853, Jan. 1

Thin Paper

17	A5	1c bronze	2,400.	450.00
		On cover		1,250.
a.		1c golden bronze	3,250.	500.00
18	A5	3c bronze	12,500.	6,250.
		On cover		9,500.
a.		3c golden bronze	12,500.	6,500.
19	A6	6c carmine rose	400.00	1.75
		On cover		11.50
a.		Thick paper	525.00	11.00
b.		Thick bluish paper	775.00	16.00
c.		6c rose red, thin paper	400.00	4.00
20	A6	12c red violet	1,950.	100.00
		On cover		700.00
a.		12c dark violet	2,000.	190.00
b.		Thick paper	1,900.	200.00
21	A6	2r vermilion	10,500.	2,750.
		On cover		17,500.
		On cover, single franking		40,000.
a.		2r bright vermilion	10,500.	2,750.
22	A6	5r lt green	2,200.	85.00
		On cover		2,900.
		On cover, single franking		6,400.
a.		5r deep green	2,200.	100.00
23	A6	6r deep blue	3,000.	325.00
		On cover		4,750.
		On cover, single franking		7,500.
a.		6r blackish blue	3,000.	425.00

Full margins = ¾mm.

Nos. 17-18 were issued for use on Madrid city mail only. *They were reprinted on this white paper in duller colors.*

Values for Singles and Covers Grid Cancellations

Scott No.	Black	Red	Blue
17	450.00	1,400.	875.00
Cover	1,250.		-
18	6,300.		
Cover	9,400.		
19	1.75	67.50	30.00
Cover	11.50	57.50	110.00
20	100.00	400.00	275.00
Cover	675.00		-
21	2,750.		5,400.
Cover	17,000.		
22	100.00	400.00	375.00
Cover	2,900.		-
23	350.00	1,000.	800.00
Cover	4,750.		

Circular Date Stamp Cancellations

Scott No.	Red	Black
17	1,150.	1,150.
19	350.00	350.00
20	700.00	
23		875.00

Values for Pairs

17	A5	1c bronze	12,000.	
17a	A5	1c golden bronze	16,000.	
19	A6	6c carmine rose	1,100.	6.50
19c	A6	6c rose lake	1,150.	17.00
20	A6	12c red violet	—	275.00
20a	A6	12c dark violet	—	350.00
21	A6	2r vermilion		8,250.
21a	A6	2r bright vermilion		8,750.
22	A6	5r light green	5,250.	225.00
22a	A6	5r deep green	5,500.	300.00
23	A6	6r deep blue	7,500.	825.00
23a	A6	6r blackish blue	8,250.	1,100.

Values for Strips of 3

17	A5	1c bronze	19,000.	
17a	A5	1c golden bronze	25,000.	
19	A6	6c carmine rose	1,750.	24.00
19c	A6	6c rose lake	1,900.	70.00
20	A6	12c red violet	—	450.00
20a	A6	12c dark violet	—	600.00
21	A6	2r vermilion		14,000.
21a	A6	2r bright vermilion		14,500.
22	A6	5r light green		450.00
22a	A6	5r deep green		600.00
23	A6	6r deep blue		1,600.
23a	A6	6r blackish blue		2,100.

Values for Blocks of 4

17	A5	1c bronze	25,000.	
17a	A5	1c golden bronze	35,000.	
19	A6	6c carmine rose	2,500.	160.00
19c	A6	6c rose lake	2,750.	500.00
20	A6	12c red violet	—	675.00
20a	A6	12c dark violet	—	850.00
21	A6	2r vermilion		20,000.
21a	A6	2r bright vermilion		21,000.
22	A6	5r light green	12,000.	675.00
22a	A6	5r deep green	16,000.	925.00
23	A6	6r deep blue		2,300.
23a	A6	6r blackish blue		3,000.

A7

A7a

Coat of Arms of Spain — A8

1854

Thin White Paper

24	A7	2c green	2,650.	400.00
		On cover, single franking		900.00
		On cover, in combination with other values		2,500.
a.		2c dark green	3,300.	525.00
		On cover, single franking		1,000.
25	A7a	4c carmine	375.00	1.75
		On cover, single franking		10.00
		On cover, in combination with other values		50.00
b.		4c dark carmine lake	450.00	2.75
		On cover		10.00
		Bar cancellation		3.25
26	A8	6c carmine	275.00	1.40
		On cover		15.00
		Pair, on cover		25.00
		On cover, in combination with other values		225.00
c.		6c dark carmine	325.00	2.00
		On cover		16.00
d.		6c pale red	325.00	3.75
		Bar cancellation		1.40
		On cover		18.00
27	A7a	1r indigo	3,300.	250.00
		On cover		1,850.
		On cover, single franking		2,500.
a.		1r blue black	3,600.	300.00
		Bar cancellation		12.00
		On cover		1,900.
28	A8	2r scarlet	1,400.	90.00
		On cover		1,100.
		On cover, single franking		—
a.		2r vermilion	1,600.	110.00
		On cover		1,000.
b.		2r pale red	2,000.	110.00
		On cover		1,000.
		Bar cancellation, #28, 28a or 28b		5.50
29	A8	5r green	1,325.	90.00
		Bar cancellation		8.50
		On cover		1,100.
		On cover, single franking		3,250.
a.		5r dark green	1,650.	100.00
		Bar cancellation		8.50
		On cover		1,150.
30	A8	6r blue	2,200.	260.00
		Bar cancellation		12.50
		On cover		3,400.
		On cover, single franking		6,750.
a.		6r dark blue	2,600.	325.00
		Bar cancellation		12.50
		On cover		3,500.

Full margins = ¾mm.

Thick White Paper

24c	A7	2c green	1,750.	425.00
25a	A7a	4c carmine	400.00	10.00
		Bar cancellation		3.75
28c	A8	2r scarlet	—	125.00

See boxed note on bar cancellation before #1.

Thick Bluish Paper

31	A7	2c green	11,000.	1,700.
		On cover, single franking		4,750.
a.		2c dark green	11,750.	1,700.
		On cover, single franking		4,750.
32	A7a	4c carmine	350.00	4.75
		On cover, single franking		30.00
		On cover, in combination with other values		65.00
b.		4c dark carmine lake	350.00	4.50
		On cover, single franking		32.50
32A	A8	6c carmine	525.00	11.00
		Bar cancellation		1.40
33	A7a	1r pale blue		6,500.
		Bar cancellation		100.00
		On cover, single franking		22,000.
34	A8	2r dull red	4,500.	450.00
		On cover		2,250.

Full margins = ¾mm.

The 2c with watermark 104 is a proof.

Thin Bluish Paper

31b	A7	2c green	5,000.	1,300.
32c	A7a	4c carmine	250.00	8.50
32Ad	A8	6c carmine	—	55.00
33a	A7a	1r pale blue	—	6,000.
34a	A8	2r dull red	4,500.	450.00

Values for Singles and Covers Grid Cancellations

Scott No.	Black	Red	Blue
24	425.00		650.00
Cover	875.00		-
25	1.75	42.50	23.00
Cover	9.50	300.00	70.00
26	1.25	32.50	9.00
Cover	15.00	200.00	35.00
27	275.00		575.00
Cover	1,750.		-
28	90.00	400.00	200.00
Cover	1,050.		
29	90.00	400.00	250.00
Cover	1,050.		-
30	260.00	700.00	475.00
Cover	3,250.		
31	1,200.		
Cover	3,600.		
32	3.50	42.50	23.00
Cover	25.00	300.00	70.00
33	6,500.		7,000.
Cover	21,000.		
34	400.00		
Cover	2,100.		

Circular Date Stamp Cancellations

Scott No.	Black	Red	Blue
24	1,500.		9,500.
25	30.00		65.00
Cover	160.00		-
26	50.00	65.00	
Cover	525.00	875.00	
27	750.00		
28	375.00		
29	375.00		
32	75.00		80.00
Cover	260.00		-

Values for Pairs

24	A7	2c green	6,500.	1,100.
24a	A7	2c dark green	7,500.	1,300.
25	A7a	4c carmine	900.00	5.25
25b	A7a	4c dk carmine lake	1,150.	8.00
26	A8	6c carmine	700.00	4.25
		On cover		35.00
26c	A8	6c dark carmine	900.00	6.25
26d	A8	6c pale red	900.00	8.00
27	A7a	1r indigo		750.00

27a	A7a	1r blue black		900.00
28	A8	2r scarlet	3,250.	240.00
		On cover		1,100.
28a	A8	2r vermilion	3,750.	300.00
28b	A8	2r pale red	5,000.	300.00
29	A8	5r green		240.00
29a	A8	5r dark green		275.00
30	A8	6r blue		700.00
30a	A8	6r dark blue		950.00
31	A7	2c green		*4,900.*
32	A7a	4c carmine	775.00	12.00
32a	A7a	4c dk carmine lake	1,000.	16.00

Values for Strips of 3

24	A7	2c green		2,300.
24a	A7	2c dark green		3,000.
25	A7a	4c carmine		20.00
25b	A7a	4c dk carmine lake		30.00
26	A8	6c carmine	1,200.	18.00
26c	A8	6c dark carmine	1,450.	26.00
26d	A8	6c pale red	1,450.	35.00
27	A7a	1r indigo		1,200.
27a	A7a	1r blue black		1,400.
32	A7a	4c carmine		22.50
32a	A7a	4c dk carmine lake		30.00
33	A7a	1r pale blue		*24,000.*

Values for Blocks of 4

24	A7	2c green	9,500.	5,200.
24a	A7	2c dark green	11,750.	6,400.
25	A7a	4c carmine		40.00
25b	A7a	4c dk carmine lake		600.00
26	A8	6c carmine	1,750.	32.50
26c	A8	6c dark carmine	2,100.	50.00
26d	A8	6c pale red	2,100.	62.50
27	A7a	1r indigo		1,900.
27a	A7a	1r blue black		2,300.
28	A8	2r scarlet		550.00
28a	A8	2r vermilion		700.00
28b	A8	2r pale red		700.00
29	A8	5r green		550.00
29a	A8	5r dark green		625.00
30	A8	6r blue		1,750.
30a	A8	6r dark blue		2,200.
32	A7a	4c carmine		57.50
32a	A7a	4c dk carmine lake		80.00
33	A7a	1r pale blue		*43,000.*

Isabella II — A9

1855, Apr. 1 **Wmk. 104**

Blue Paper

36 A9 2c green *2,250.* 100.00
On cover, single franking 325.00
a. 2c yellow green *2,350.* 125.00
On cover, single franking 350.00
Bar cancellation, #36 or 36a 6.00
37 A9 4c brown red 225.00 .65
On cover, single franking 8.00
a. 4c carmine 240.00 1.40
On cover, single franking 10.00
b. 4c lake 240.00 .90
On cover, single franking 10.00
Bar cancellation, #37, 37a or 37b 1.50
c. 4c brown red, white to grayish paper 250.00 3.25
d. 4c lake red, white to grayish paper 250.00 5.00
Bar cancellation 1.50
38 A9 1r green blue 975.00 14.00
On cover, single franking 90.00
a. 1r blue 1,000. 14.50
On cover, single franking 110.00
Bar cancellation, #38 or 38a 3.00
b. Cliché of 2r in plate of 1r *13,000.* *2,000.*
Bar cancellation, #38b 500.00
39 A9 2r reddish violet 725.00 12.50
On cover, single franking 90.00
a. 2r deep violet 750.00 13.00
On cover, single franking 92.50
b. 2r grayish violet 725.00 13.00

On cover, single franking 95.00
Bar cancellation, #39, 39a or 39b 2.25

Full margins = ¾mm.

Values for Singles and Covers Grid Cancellations

Scott No.	Black	Red	Blue
36	110.00	325.00	110.00
Cover	325.00		-
37	65	21.00	2.25
Cover	3.50	110.00	27.50
38	12.00	67.50	22.00
Cover	90.00	-	190.00
39	12.00	10.00	24.00
Cover	90.00		210.00

Circular Date Stamp and Cartwheel Cancellations

Scott No.	Black c.d.s.	Blue c.d.s.	Cartwheel
36	600.00		290.00
Cover	875.00		525.00
37	21.00	42.50	27.50
Cover	70.00	110.00	70.00
38	62.50	110.00	62.50
Cover	150.00		110.00
39	42.50	110.00	62.50
Cover	125.00		110.00

Values for Pairs

36	A9	2c green	*5,600.*	400.00
36a	A9	2c yellow green	*6,800.*	525.00
37	A9	4c brown red	550.00	2.25
37a	A9	4c carmine	700.00	4.50
37b	A9	4c lake red	550.00	3.50
38	A9	1r green blue	2,400.	35.00
38a	A9	1r blue	2,500.	45.00
39	A9	2r reddish violet	2,000.	30.00
39a	A9	2r deep violet	2,600.	37.50
39b	A9	2r grayish violet	2,600.	37.50

Values for Strips of 3

36	A9	2c green	*8,100.*	1,400.
36a	A9	2c yellow green	*9,750.*	1,800.
37	A9	4c brown red	850.00	3.50
37a	A9	4c carmine	1,000.	700.00
37b	A9	4c lake red	850.00	6.00
38	A9	1r green blue	3,500.	62.50
38a	A9	1r blue	3,600.	72.50
39	A9	2r reddish violet	2,600.	45.00
39a	A9	2r deep violet	3,600.	57.50
39b	A9	2r grayish violet	3,600.	57.50

Values for Blocks of 4

36	A9	2c green		3,000.
36a	A9	2c yellow green		3,700.
37	A9	4c brown red	1,300.	14.00
37a	A9	4c carmine	1,600.	700.00
37b	A9	4c lake red	1,300.	11.50
38	A9	1r green blue	5,600.	80.00
38a	A9	1r blue	6,000.	95.00
39	A9	2r reddish violet	5,300.	70.00
39a	A9	2r deep violet	5,300.	85.00
39b	A9	2r grayish violet	5,300.	85.00

1856, Jan. 1 **Wmk. 105**

Rough Yellowish Paper

40 A9 2c green *2,750.* 200.00
On cover, single franking 725.00
a. 2c pale green *2,750.* 200.00
On cover, single franking 725.00
Bar cancellation, #40 or 40a 8.50
41 A9 4c rose 7.25 1.75
On cover, single franking 11.00
a. 4c deep rose 11.00 2.00
On cover, single franking 12.00
Bar cancellation, #41 or 41a 1.50
42 A9 1r grnsh blue *2,900.* 160.00
On cover 650.00
a. 1r dull blue *3,400.* 180.00
On cover 775.00
Bar cancellation, #42 or 42a 5.00
43 A9 2r brown violet 425.00 20.00
On cover, single franking 110.00
a. 2r dark reddish violet 425.00 30.00
On cover, single franking 150.00
b. 2r gray violet 425.00 30.00
On cover, single franking 150.00
Bar cancellation, #43, 43a or 43b 5.00

Full margins = ¾mm.

1856, Apr. 11 **Unwmk.**

White Smooth Paper

44 A9 2c blue green 450.00 35.00
On cover, single franking 95.00
On cover with other values, from 100.00
a. 2c yellow green 475.00 37.50
On cover, single franking 100.00
Bar cancellation, #44 or 44a 5.00
45 A9 4c rose 3.75 .30
On cover, single franking 4.00
On cover with other values, from 32.50
a. 4c carmine ('59) 25.00 17.50
On cover, single franking 67.50
On cover with other values, from 75.00
46 A9 1r blue 17.50 19.00
On cover, single franking 87.50
On cover with other values, from 95.00
a. 1r pale greenish blue 19.00 20.00
On cover, single franking 100.00
Bar cancellation, #46 or 46a 2.25

47 A9 2r brown lilac 57.50 21.00
On cover, single franking 85.00
On cover with other values, from 95.00
a. 2r dull lilac 65.00 22.50
On cover, single franking 110.00
Bar cancellation, #47 or 47a 4.75

Full margins = ¾mm.

Three types of No. 45.

1859

48 A9 12c dark orange 137.50 27.50
Bar cancellation 30.00
a. Tete-beche pair (#48) 2,750.
b. 12c light orange 1,000.00

Full margins = ¾mm.

Nos. 48-48b were never put in use. All canceled examples have the bar cancellation.

Stamps of the 1st printing (#48b), may be distinguished by shade and by a break at lower left, which is not on the 2nd printing (#48).

Reprints exist.

A10

A11

1860-61

Tinted Paper

49 A10 2c green, *grn* 275.00 17.50
Bar cancellation 2.00
On cover, single franking 70.00
On cover with other values, from 75.00
50 A10 4c orange, *grn* 30.00 .65
On cover, single franking 4.75
On cover with other values, from 17.50
51 A10 12c car, *buff* 290.00 11.00
Bar cancellation 2.25
On cover, single franking 40.00
On cover with other values, from 90.00
52 A10 19c brn, *buff* ('61) 2,400. 1,100.
On cover, single franking 7,250.
53 A10 1r blue, *grn* 260.00 11.00
Bar cancellation 2.00
On cover, single franking 120.00
On cover with other values, from 125.00
a. 1r dark blue, *green* 260.00 11.00
b. 1r pale blue, *green* 300.00 12.00
54 A10 2r lilac, *lil* 325.00 9.00
Bar cancellation 2.00
On cover, single franking 60.00
On cover with other values, from 95.00
a. 2r dark violet, *mauve* 325.00 9.50
b. 2r lilac, *blue,* thick paper 350.00 32.50

Full margins = ¾mm.

1862, July 16

55 A11 2c dp bl, *yel* 27.50 9.00
On cover, single franking 67.50
On cover with other values, from 95.00
56 A11 4c dk brn, *redsh buff* 1.90 .50
On cover, single franking 4.00
On cover with other values, from 18.50
a. 4c brown, *white* 17.50 5.00
Bar cancellation 1.50
On cover, single franking 30.00
57 A11 12c blue, *pnksh* 37.50 7.50
Bar cancellation 2.25
On cover, single franking 30.00
On cover with other values, from 90.00
58 A11 19c car, *lil* 160.00 200.00
On cover, single franking 3,000.
a. 19c carmine, *white* 225.00 210.00
On cover, single franking 3,250.
Bar cancellation, #58 or 58a 90.00
59 A11 1r brown, *yel* 50.00 17.50
Bar cancellation 2.50
On cover, single franking 115.00
On cover with other values, from 110.00
a. 1r brown, *yellow gold* 125.00 55.00
60 A11 2r green, *pnksh* 29.00 11.00
Bar cancellation 2.25
On cover, single franking 60.00
On cover with other values, from 75.00
a. 2r yellow green, *rose* 32.50 12.00
b. 2r dark yellow green, *rose* 40.00 17.50

Full margins = ¾mm.

A12

A13

1864, Jan. 1

61 A12 2c dk bl, *lil* 37.50 16.00
On cover, single franking 67.50
On cover with other values, from 120.00
62 A12 4c rose, *redsh buff* 2.00 .60
On cover, single franking 5.00
On cover with other values, from 17.50
a. 4c carmine, *reddish buff* 12.50 4.00
Bar cancellation, #62 or 62a 2.50
63 A12 12c green, *pnksh* 37.50 9.50
On cover, single franking 45.00
On cover with other values, from 90.00
64 A12 19c violet, *pnksh* 160.00 160.00
On cover, single franking 3,750.
65 A12 1r brown, *grn* 145.00 57.50
Bar cancellation 3.00
On cover, single franking 325.00
On cover with other values, from 250.00
66 A12 2r blue, *pnksh* 37.50 9.50
On cover, single franking 60.00
On cover with other values, from 95.00
a. 2r deep blue 42.50 11.75
Bar cancellation, #66 or 66a 2.50

Full margins = 1mm.

1865, Jan. 1 **Litho.** ***Imperf.***

67 A13 2c rose 250.00 25.00
On cover, single franking 125.00
On cover with other values, from 110.00
68 A13 4c blue *2,400.*
69 A13 12c blue & rose 325.00 17.50
Bar cancellation 4.50
On cover, single franking 65.00
On cover with other values, from 90.00
a. Frame inverted *13,500.* 900.00
Bar cancellation —
b. Pair, #69, 69a 1,550.
70 A13 19c brown & rose 1,200. 600.00
Bar cancellation 60.00
On cover, single franking *5,250.*
71 A13 1r yellow grn 350.00 45.00
Bar cancellation 17.50
On cover, single franking 225.00
On cover with other values, from 225.00
72 A13 2r red lilac 350.00 25.00
Bar cancellation 16.00
On cover, single franking 140.00
On cover with other values, from 140.00
73 A13 2r rose 375.00 55.00
Bar cancellation 8.50
On cover, single franking 250.00
On cover with other values, from 250.00
a. 2r salmon 350.00 57.50
Bar cancellation 12.50
On cover, single franking 275.00
On cover with other values, from 250.00
b. 2r orange 400.00 62.50
c. 2r yellow brown 400.00 70.00

Full margins = 1mm.

No. 68 is without gum and was never put in use.

A majority of the perforated stamps from 1865 to about 1950 are rather poorly centered. The very fine examples that are valued will be fairly well centered. Poorly centered stamps sell for less. Stamps of some issues are almost always badly centered, and our values will be for examples with fine centering. Such issues will be noted.

1865, Jan. 1 ***Perf. 14***

74 A13 2c rose red 450.00 90.00
Bar cancellation 8.50
On cover, single franking 250.00
On cover with other values, from 275.00
75 A13 4c blue 32.50 .65
On cover, single franking 3.00
On cover with other values, from 19.00
76 A13 12c blue & rose 450.00 47.50
Bar cancellation 7.00
On cover, single franking 80.00
On cover with other values, from 110.00
a. Frame inverted *16,500.* *1,650.*
As "a," bar cancel 50.00
77 A13 19c brown & rose *3,250.* *1,750.*
On cover, single franking *11,000.*
78 A13 1r yellow grn 1,300. 400.00
Bar cancellation 17.50
On cover, single franking 850.00
On cover with other values, from 725.00
79 A13 2r violet 1,000. 175.00
Bar cancellation 16.00
On cover, single franking 725.00
On cover with other values, from 875.00
80 A13 2r rose 1,100. 250.00
On cover, single franking 1,100.
On cover with other values, from 1,100.
a. 2r salmon 1,100. 250.00
On cover, single franking 1,000.
On cover with other values, from 1,100.
b. 2r dull orange 1,100. 250.00
On cover, single franking 1,000.

On cover with other values, from 1,100.
Bar cancellation, #80, 80a or 80b 22.50

Values for Nos. 74-80 are for stamps with perforations touching the frame on at least one side.

A14

A14a

1866, Jan. 1

81 A14 2c rose 170.00 22.50
On cover, single franking 65.00
On cover with other values, from 75.00
a. 2c dark carmine 240.00 22.50
On cover, single franking 72.50
On cover with other values, from 80.00
Bar cancellation, #81 or 81a 3.50
82 A14 4c blue 32.50 .65
On cover, single franking 2.50
On cover with other values, from 17.50
83 A14 12c orange 185.00 9.50
On cover, single franking 37.50
On cover with other values, from 37.50
a. 12c orange yellow 275.00 19.00
On cover, single franking 62.50
On cover with other values, from 80.00
84 A14 19c brown 850.00 325.00
Bar cancellation 32.50
On cover, single franking 1,300.
On cover with other values, from *1,300.*

1866

85 A14 10c green 225.00 19.00
Bar cancellation 3.00
On cover, single franking 100.00
On cover with other values, from 95.00
86 A14 20c lilac 150.00 15.00
Bar cancellation 3.00
On cover, single franking 95.00
On cover with other values, from 90.00
87 A14a 20c dull lilac 850.00 57.50
On cover, single franking 175.00
On cover with other values, from 190.00
a. 20c dark lilac 950.00 90.00
Bar cancellation, #87 or 87a 2.25

A15

A15a

A15b

A15c

1867-68

88 A15 2c yellow brown 375.00 37.50
On cover, single franking 80.00
On cover with other values, from 90.00
89 A15a 4c blue 27.50 1.00
On cover, single franking 3.00
On cover with other values, from 19.00
90 A15b 12c orange yellow 190.00 7.75
On cover, single franking 32.50
On cover with other values, from 35.00
a. 12c dark orange 250.00 12.00
On cover, single franking 42.50
On cover with other values, from 55.00
b. 12c red orange ('68) 850.00 37.50
On cover, single franking 110.00
On cover with other values, from 165.00
91 A15c 19c rose 1,100. 425.00
Bar cancellation 29.00
On cover, single franking 1,000.

See Nos. 100-102. For overprints see Nos. 114a-115a, 124-128, 124a-128a, 124c-124c, 124e-126e.

A15d

A15e

92 A15d 10c blue green 250.00 20.00
Bar cancellation 2.00
On cover, single franking 72.50
On cover with other values, from 65.00
a. 10c dark green 250.00 24.00
93 A15e 20c lilac 130.00 8.75
On cover, single franking 37.50
On cover with other values, from 40.00
a. 20c dark lilac 150.00 10.00
b. 20c gray lilac 150.00 10.00
Bar cancellation, #93, 93a or 93b 2.00

For overprints see Nos. 116-117, 116a-117a, 116c-117c, 117d, 117e, 117f.

A16

A17

A18

A19

94 A16 5m green 42.50 17.00
On cover or newsprint, single franking 57.50
On cover with other values, from 85.00
a. 5m bluish green 47.50 19.00
Bar cancellation, #94 or 94a 2.00
95 A17 10m brown 42.50 17.00
On cover or newsprint, single franking 60.00
On cover with other values, from 85.00
a. Tête bêche pair *16,500.*
b. 10m yellow brown 40.00 17.50
c. 10m dark brown 47.50 19.00
96 A18 25m blue & rose 225.00 20.00
Bar cancellation 5.00
On cover, single franking 70.00
On cover with other values, from 72.50
a. Frame inverted *16,000.*
97 A18 50m bister brown 20.00 .75
On cover, single franking 4.50
On cover with other values, from 18.00
a. 50m dark brown 22.50 .85
Bar cancellation, #97 or 97a 2.00

See No. 98. For overprints see Nos. 118-122, 118a-122a, 120c-122c, 122d, 120e, 122e, 119f, 122f.

1868-69

98 A18 25m blue 250.00 15.00
Bar cancellation 3.00
On cover, single franking 70.00
On cover with other values, from 70.00
99 A19 50m violet 25.00 .60
On cover, single franking 3.00
On cover with other values, from 18.00
a. 50m blackish violet 26.00 .80
Bar cancellation, #99 or 99a 2.00
100 A15b 100m brown 525.00 65.00
Bar cancellation 2.00
On cover, single franking 175.00
On cover with other values, from 160.00
101 A15c 200m green 190.00 14.00
Bar cancellation 2.00
On cover, single franking 42.50
On cover with other values, from 42.50
102 A15c 19c brown 2,250. 500.00
On cover, single franking 3,000.
On cover with other values, from 4,000.

For overprints see #123, 123a, 123c, 123e.

Provisional Government

Excellent counterfeits exist of the provisional and provincial overprints.

Regular Issues Handstamped in Black

1868-69

116	A15d	10c green	22.50	14.50
117	A15e	20c lilac	19.00	11.00
118	A16	5m green	14.50	5.00
119	A17	10m brown	11.00	5.00
120	A18	25m blue & rose	32.50	13.00
121	A18	25m blue	32.50	11.00
122	A18	50m bister brn	6.50	4.50
123	A19	50m violet	6.50	4.50
124	A15b	100m brown	65.00	26.00
125	A15c	200m green	22.50	8.25
126	A15b	12c orange	45.00	15.00
127	A15c	19c rose	300.00	125.00
128	A15c	19c brown	650.00	150.00
		Nos. 116-128 (13)	1,227.	392.75

Nos. 116-128 exist with handstamp in blue, a few in red. These sell for more.

For Andalusian Provinces

Regular Issues Handstamped Vertically in Blue

114a	A15	2c brown	65.00	32.50
115a	A15a	4c blue	30.00	22.50
116a	A15d	10c green	32.50	13.00
117a	A15e	20c lilac	25.00	14.00
118a	A16	5m green	17.00	7.25
119a	A17	10m brown	11.50	5.00
120a	A18	25m blue & rose	37.50	13.00
b.		Frame inverted	*22,000.*	
121a	A18	25m blue	37.50	14.00
122a	A18	50m bister brown	8.25	5.00
123a	A19	50m violet	8.25	5.00
124a	A15b	100m brown	82.50	30.00
125a	A15c	200m green	27.50	11.00
126a	A15b	12c org yel	30.00	12.00
127a	A15c	19c rose	375.00	190.00
128a	A15c	19c brown	700.00	250.00
		Nos. 114a-128a (15)	1,487.	624.25

For Valladolid Province

Regular Issues Handstamped in Black

(Two types of overprint)

116c	A15d	10c green	35.00	15.00
117c	A15e	20c lilac	32.50	16.00
120c	A18	25m blue & rose	50.00	13.00
121c	A18	25m blue	50.00	19.00
122c	A18	50m bister brown	13.00	8.25
123c	A19	50m violet	13.00	6.50
124c	A15b	100m brown	100.00	32.50
125c	A15c	200m green	32.50	13.00
126c	A15b	12c orange	35.00	11.50
127c	A15c	19c rose	*325.00*	*160.00*
128c	A15c	19c brown	*850.00*	*210.00*
		Nos. 116c-126c (9)	361.00	134.75

For Asturias Province Llanes (Oviedo)

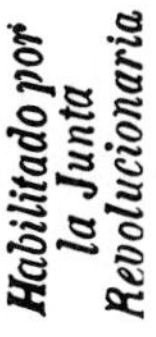

Regular Issues Handstamped in Black

117d	A15e	20c lilac	160.00	110.00
122d	A18	50m bister brown	175.00	110.00

For Teruel Province

Regular Issues Handstamped in Black

117e	A15e	20c lilac	65.00	50.00
120e	A18	25m blue & rose	82.50	50.00
122e	A18	50m bister brown	60.00	30.00
123e	A19	50m violet	60.00	30.00
124e	A15b	100m brown	140.00	65.00
125e	A15c	200m green	100.00	40.00
126e	A15b	12c orange	82.50	55.00
		Nos. 117e-126e (7)	590.00	320.00

For Salamanca Province

Regular Issues Handstamped in Blue

117f	A15e	20c lilac	65.00	50.00
119f	A17	10m brown	60.00	37.50
122f	A18	50m bister brown	65.00	45.00
		Nos. 117f-122f (3)	190.00	132.50

Duke de la Torre Regency

"España" — A20

1870, Jan. 1 **Typo.**

159 A20 1m brn lil, *buff* 6.50 6.50
Bar cancellation 2.00
On cover, single franking 110.00
On cover with other values, from 125.00
b. 1m brown lilac, *pinkish buff* 7.00 7.75
On cover, single franking 125.00
161 A20 2m blk, *pinkish* 7.75 8.00
On cover, single franking 110.00
On cover with other values, from 125.00
a. 2m black, *buff* 8.75 9.00
On cover, single franking 120.00
163 A20 4m bister brn 15.00 13.50
On cover, single franking 140.00
On cover with other values, from 150.00
164 A20 10m rose 17.00 6.00
On cover, single franking 85.00
On cover with other values, from 95.00
a. 10m carmine 21.00 7.50
On cover, single franking 100.00
165 A20 25m lilac 52.50 6.50
Bar cancellation 2.00
On cover, single franking 35.00
a. 25m gray lilac 55.00 6.50
On cover, single franking 30.00
On cover with other values, from 27.50
b. 25m aniline violet 85.00 8.25
On cover, single franking 35.00
166 A20 50m ultra 10.00 .35
On cover, single franking 3.50
On cover with other values, from 7.50
a. 50m dull blue 125.00 5.00
On cover, single franking 75.00
167 A20 100m red brown 29.00 5.25
Bar cancellation 1.40
On cover, single franking 27.50
On cover with other values, from 19.00
a. 100m claret 30.00 6.25
On cover, single franking 32.50
b. 100m orange brown 30.00 5.50
On cover, single franking 27.50
168 A20 200m pale brown 27.50 5.25
Bar cancellation 2.00
On cover, single franking 22.50
On cover with other values, from 19.00
169 A20 400m green 250.00 22.50
Bar cancellation 3.00
On cover, single franking 110.00
On cover with other values, from 85.00
170 A20 1e600m dull lilac 1,350. 850.00
Bar cancellation 27.50
On cover, single franking *7,000.*
171 A20 2e blue 1,100. 525.00
Bar cancellation 27.50
On cover —
172 A20 12c red brown 225.00 6.50
On cover, single franking 30.00
On cover with other values, from 40.00
a. 12c deep brown 235.00 7.00
On cover, single franking 35.00
173 A20 19c yellow green 300.00 160.00
On cover, single franking 1,750.
a. 19c bright green 310.00 210.00
On cover, single franking 2,100.

The 12c carmine rose and 12c blue on pink paper were not put in use. Value $1,000. and $1,250., respectively.

Kingdom

A21

A22

King Amadeo
A23 A24

1872, Oct. 1 ***Imperf.***

174 A21 ¼c ultra 2.25 2.25
On cover, pair of ¼c only 60.00
a. Complete 1c (block of 4 ¼c) 100.00 82.50
Bar cancellation 5.00
On cover 110.00
b. As "a," one cliche inverted 1,800. *1,750.*

See No. 221A.

1872-73 ***Perf. 14***

176 A22 2c gray lilac 17.50 7.75
On cover or newsprint 75.00
On cover with other values, from 70.00
a. 2c violet 27.50 17.00
On cover or newsprint, single franking 110.00
b. Imperf. 70.00
177 A22 5c green 125.00 60.00
On cover, single franking 175.00
On cover with other values, from 175.00
a. Imperf. 160.00
178 A23 5c rose ('73) 20.00 5.50
On cover, single franking 42.50
On cover with other values, from 40.00
179 A23 6c blue 120.00 37.50
On cover, single franking 110.00
On cover with other values, from 140.00
180 A23 10c brown lilac 350.00 225.00
On cover, single franking 450.00
On cover with other values, from 425.00
181 A23 10c ultra ('73) 7.50 .50
On cover, single franking 2.50
On cover with other values, from 6.50
182 A23 12c gray lilac 17.50 2.10
Bar cancellation 2.00
On cover, single franking 7.50
On cover with other values, from 18.00
183 A23 20c gray vio ('73) 140.00 82.50
Bar cancellation 5.00
On cover, single franking 175.00
On cover with other values, from 160.00
184 A23 25c brown 70.00 11.50
Bar cancellation 2.00
On cover, single franking 32.50
On cover with other values, from 32.50
185 A23 40c pale red brn 62.50 10.00
Bar cancellation 2.00
On cover, single franking 27.50
186 A23 50c deep green 100.00 10.50
Bar cancellation 2.00
On cover, single franking 65.00
On cover with other values, from 47.50
187 A24 1p lilac 100.00 52.50
Bar cancellation 3.25
On cover, single franking 200.00
On cover with other values, from 140.00
188 A24 4p red brown 625.00 600.00
Bar cancellation 7.50
On cover —
189 A24 10p deep green 2,200. 2,300.
Bar cancellation 250.00
On cover *15,000.*

First Republic

Mural Crown
A25

"España"
A26

1873, July 1 ***Imperf.***

190 A25 ¼c green 1.00 1.00
a. Complete 1c (block of 4 ¼c) 37.50 19.00
As "a," bar cancellation 2.50
As "a," on cover 85.00
b. As "a," deep green 45.00 35.00
c. As "a," bluish green 52.50 25.00
d. As "a," ultra (error) 190.00 160.00

1873, July 1 ***Perf. 14***

191 A26 2c orange 13.00 6.00
On cover, single franking 75.00
On cover with other values, from 50.00
192 A26 5c claret 29.00 6.00
Bar cancellation 2.00
On cover, single franking 50.00
On cover with other values, from 27.50
193 A26 10c green 6.50 .35
On cover, single franking 3.25
On cover with other values, from 13.00
a. Tête bêche pair *32,500.*
194 A26 20c black 80.00 22.50
Bar cancellation 3.75
On cover, single franking 140.00
On cover with other values, from 140.00
195 A26 25c deep brown 30.00 6.00
Bar cancellation 2.00
On cover, single franking 40.00
On cover with other values, from 30.00
196 A26 40c brown vio 32.50 6.00
Bar cancellation 2.00
On cover, single franking 32.50
On cover with other values, from 30.00
197 A26 50c ultra 16.50 6.75
Bar cancellation 2.00
On cover, single franking 32.50
On cover with other values, from 30.00
198 A26 1p lilac 52.50 30.00
Bar cancellation 2.00
On cover, single franking 190.00
On cover with other values, from 110.00
a. 1p deep lilac 47.50 32.50
b. 1p gray 55.00 45.00
199 A26 4p red brown 575.00 475.00
Bar cancellation 12.50
On cover —
200 A26 10p violet brn 1,750. 1,750.
Bar cancellation 17.50
On cover —

Only one example of No. 193a is known, and it is in a block of six stamps.

"Justice"
A27

Coat of Arms
A28

1874, July 1

201 A27 2c yellow 17.50 8.00
Bar cancellation 2.00
On cover, single franking 70.00
On cover with other values, from 40.00
202 A27 5c violet 32.50 6.50
Bar cancellation 2.00
On cover, single franking 35.00
On cover with other values, from 32.50
a. 5c red violet 30.00 9.50
On cover, single franking 45.00
203 A27 10c ultra 9.75 .35
On cover, single franking 3.25
On cover with other values, from 13.00
a. Imperf. 12.00
204 A27 20c dark green 140.00 42.50
Bar cancellation 3.75
On cover, single franking 225.00
On cover with other values, from 150.00
205 A27 25c red brown 30.00 6.50
Bar cancellation 2.00
On cover, single franking 32.50
On cover with other values, from 27.50
a. 25c lilac (error) 300.00
As "a," bar cancellation 27.50
b. Imperf. 55.00
206 A27 40c violet 300.00 7.50
Bar cancellation 2.00
On cover, single franking 30.00
On cover with other values, from 27.50
a. 40c brown (error) 225.00
b. Imperf. 175.00
207 A27 50c yellow 95.00 7.75
Bar cancellation 2.00
On cover, single franking 32.50
On cover with other values, from 30.00
a. Imperf. 110.00
b. 50c orange 100.00 9.00
208 A27 1p yellow green 75.00 32.50
Bar cancellation 2.00
On cover, single franking 190.00
On cover with other values, from 100.00
a. 1p emerald 85.00 45.00
On cover, single franking 250.00
b. Imperf. 160.00
209 A27 4p rose 625.00 390.00
Bar cancellation 8.50
On cover, single franking —
On cover with other values, from *1,900.*
a. 4p carmine 725.00 575.00
On cover, single franking —
210 A27 10p black 2,750. 1,800.
Bar cancellation 12.50
On cover, single franking —
On cover with other values, from *4,000.*

1874, Oct. 1

211 A28 10c red brown 22.50 .65
Bar cancellation 1.50
On cover 3.75
a. 10c brown 37.50 3.25
On cover 13.00
b. Imperf. 75.00

Kingdom

Nos. 212-221 are almost always badly centered and are often irregularly perforated. Values are for stamps with complete perforations and fine centering. Sound stamps with average centering are worth about 50% of these values. Stamps with very fine centering sell for more.

King Alfonso XII — A29

1875, Aug. 1

Blue Framed Numbers on Back, 1-100 on Each Sheet

212 A29 2c orange brown 22.50 11.00
On cover, single franking 60.00
On cover with other values, from 55.00
a. 2c chocolate brown 30.00 15.00
On cover, single franking 85.00
b. Imperf. 45.00 45.00
213 A29 5c lilac 77.50 13.00
On cover, single franking 45.00
On cover with other values, from 37.50
a. Imperf. 87.50 87.50
214 A29 10c blue 9.25 .40
Bar cancellation 2.00
On cover, single franking 3.75
On cover with other values, from 13.00
a. Imperf. 22.50 22.50
215 A29 20c brown orange 275.00 125.00
On cover, single franking 300.00
On cover with other values, from 275.00
216 A29 25c rose 65.00 8.00
Bar cancellation 2.00
On cover, single franking 30.00
On cover with other values, from 25.00
217 A29 40c deep brown 125.00 37.50
Bar cancellation 4.50
On cover, single franking 65.00
On cover with other values, from 50.00
a. Imperf. 140.00 140.00
218 A29 50c gray lilac 175.00 42.50
Bar cancellation 5.25
On cover, single franking 65.00
On cover with other values, from 65.00
219 A29 1p black 190.00 80.00
Bar cancellation 3.00
On cover, single franking 140.00
On cover with other values, from 130.00
220 A29 4p dark green 475.00 525.00
On cover, single franking —
On cover, with other values, from *1,000.*
221 A29 10p ultra 1,500. 1,750.
On cover, single franking —
On cover, with other values, from *3,500.*

1876, June 1 ***Imperf.***

221A A21 ¼c green .25 .20
On cover 9.00
b. Complete 1c (block 4 ¼c) 1.10 .30
As "b," on cover 30.00
c. As "b," two ¼c sideways, one invtd. 110.00 110.00
d. As "b," both upper ¼c invtd. 140.00 140.00
e. As "b," upper left ¼c invtd. 1,000. 500.00
f. As "b," both lower ¼c invtd. 140.00 140.00

No. 221Ac has one stamp upright, one inverted, one facing right and one facing left.

Nos. 222-230 are almost always badly centered. Values are for stamps with fine centering, fresh color and, in the case of mint stamps, full original gum. Sound stamps with average centering are worth about 50% of these values. Stamps with very fine centering sell for more.

King Alfonso XII
A30 A31

ONE PESETA:
Type I — Thin figures of value and "PESETA" in thick letters.
Type II — Thick figures of value and "PESETA" in thin letters.

Wmk. 178

1876, June 1 **Engr.** ***Perf. 14***

222 A30 5c yellow brown 14.00 3.75
On cover, single franking 35.00
On cover with other values, from 25.00
223 A30 10c blue 3.75 .45
Bar cancellation 50.00
On cover, single franking 2.75
On cover with other values, from 13.00
224 A30 20c bronze green 17.50 13.00
On cover, single franking 50.00
On cover with other values, from 40.00
a. 20c dark green 19.00 15.00
On cover, single franking 65.00
225 A30 25c brown 7.75 5.50
On cover, single franking 15.00
On cover with other values, from 19.00
226 A30 40c black brown 75.00 100.00
On cover, single franking —
On cover with other values, from 290.00
227 A30 50c green 15.00 6.75
On cover, single franking 19.00
On cover with other values, from 27.50
228 A30 1p dp blue, I 20.00 9.00
On cover, single franking 42.50
On cover with other values, from 37.50
a. 1p ultra, II 27.50 13.00
On cover, single franking 45.00
229 A30 4p brown violet 47.50 55.00
On cover, single franking —
On cover with other values, from *1,500.*
230 A30 10p vermilion 125.00 125.00
On cover, single franking —
On cover with other values, from *2,600.*

Imperf

222a	A30	5c	11.00
223a	A30	10c	5.50
225a	A30	25c	12.00
227a	A30	50c	17.00
228b	A30	1p	25.00
229a	A30	4p	87.50
230a	A30	10p	190.00

Two plates each were used for the 5c, 10c, 25c, 50c, 1p and 10p. The 1p plates are most easily distinguished.

The 20c value also exists imperf. Value $500.

Unwmk.

1878, July 1 **Typo.** ***Perf. 14***

232 A31 2c mauve 32.50 11.00
On cover, single franking 35.00
a. Imperf. 60.00
b. 2c lilac 35.00 13.00
233 A31 5c orange 40.00 14.00
On cover 30.00
On cover, single franking 45.00
a. 5c yellow gold 50.00 10.00
234 A31 10c brown 7.75 .50
Bar cancellation 3.00
On cover 3.00
235 A31 20c black 160.00 125.00
On cover 290.00
a. Imperf. 275.00
236 A31 25c olive bister 22.50 2.75
Bar cancellation 6.25
On cover 8.50
237 A31 40c red brown 150.00 140.00
On cover 375.00
238 A31 50c blue green 87.50 11.00
Bar cancellation 2.00
On cover 32.50
239 A31 1p gray 72.50 21.00
Bar cancellation 2.00
On cover 80.00
On cover, single franking 100.00
240 A31 4p violet 190.00 125.00
On cover 1,200.
241 A31 10p blue 375.00 350.00
On cover 1,900.
a. Imperf. 450.00

A32

A33

1879, May 1

242 A32 2c black 8.25 4.50
Bar cancellation 3.00
On cover 22.50
243 A32 5c gray green 14.00 1.10
Bar cancellation 3.00
On cover 14.00
On cover, single franking 17.50
244 A32 10c rose 13.50 .45
Bar cancellation 2.00
On cover 2.50
245 A32 20c red brown 110.00 15.00
Bar cancellation 2.00
On cover 45.00
246 A32 25c bluish gray 14.00 .45
Bar cancellation 2.00
On cover 13.50
247 A32 40c brown 26.00 5.50
Bar cancellation 2.00
On cover 22.50
248 A32 50c dull buff 170.00 5.00
Bar cancellation 2.00
On cover 22.50
On cover, single franking 27.50
a. 50c yellow 170.00 7.00

On cover 32.50
On cover, single franking 37.50
249 A32 1p brt rose 125.00 2.25
Bar cancellation 2.00
On cover 32.50
On cover, single franking 90.00
250 A32 4p lilac gray 575.00 32.50
Bar cancellation 3.00
On cover *1,200.*
251 A32 10p olive bister 1,650. *175.00*
Bar cancellation 6.25
On cover *5,000.*

1882, Jan. 1

252 A33 15c salmon 7.75 .20
Bar cancellation 2.00
On cover 1.75
a. 15c reddish orange 27.50 .45
On cover 5.50
b. 15c yellow 40.00 .85
On cover 11.00
253 A33 30c red lilac 310.00 5.25
Bar cancellation 2.00
On cover 60.00
On cover, single franking 65.00
254 A33 75c gray lilac 210.00 4.75
Bar cancellation 2.00
On cover 55.00
a. Imperf. 300.00
b. 75c gray 250.00 5.75
On cover 140.00

Nos. 255-270 are usually poorly centered and often exhibit defective perforations. Values are for fine to very fine examples, well centered but not very fine, fresh and without perforation faults. Average copies sell for about half these values.

King Alfonso XIII
A34 A35

1889-99

255 A34 2c blue green 6.00 .45
On cover 7.00
On cover, single franking 13.00
256 A34 2c black ('99) 35.00 7.25
On cover 30.00
On cover, single franking 65.00
257 A34 5c blue 11.00 .20
On cover 3.25
On cover, single franking 6.50
258 A34 5c blue grn ('99) 125.00 1.40
On cover 7.75
On cover, single franking 19.00
259 A34 10c yellow brown 13.00 .20
On cover 2.75
a. 10c red brown 17.50 .45
On cover 5.50
260 A34 10c red ('99) 225.00 4.50
On cover 22.50
261 A34 15c violet brown 4.75 .20
On cover 1.00
262 A34 20c yellow green 45.00 4.75
On cover 25.00
On cover, single franking 27.50
263 A34 25c blue 17.50 .20
On cover 3.25
264 A34 30c olive gray 72.50 5.25
On cover 35.00
On cover, single franking 45.00
265 A34 40c brown 72.50 3.00
On cover 22.50
On cover, single franking 32.50
266 A34 50c rose 70.00 2.10
On cover 15.00
267 A34 75c orange 210.00 4.25
On cover 30.00
On cover, single franking 32.50
268 A34 1p dark violet 55.00 .45
On cover 45.00
On cover, single franking 65.00
a. 1p carmine rose (error) 350.00
269 A34 4p carmine rose 650.00 47.50
On cover 725.00
270 A34 10p orange red 1,050. 110.00
On cover 1,750.

The 15c yellow, type A34 is an official stamp listed as No. O9.
No. 270 exists perf 10. Value, unused $1,000.
Several values exist imperf.

Nos. 272-286 are almost always badly centered. Values are for stamps with fine centering, fresh color and, if unused, full original gum. Sound stamps with average centering sell for about half these values. Very fine copies sell more more.

Control Number on Back

1900-05 Engr. Unwmk.

272 A35 2c bister brown 3.25 .20
Never hinged 5.50
On cover 3.25
273 A35 5c dark green 5.75 .20
Never hinged 8.75
On cover 3.25
274 A35 10c rose red 8.75 .20
Never hinged 5.50
On cover 3.25
275 A35 15c blue black 14.00 .20
Never hinged 20.00
On cover 3.25
276 A35 15c dull lilac ('02) 10.50 .20
Never hinged 16.00
On cover 3.25
277 A35 15c purple ('05) 5.75 .20
Never hinged 8.75
On cover 1.75
278 A35 20c grnsh black 32.50 2.75
Never hinged 47.50
On cover, single franking 30.00
279 A35 25c blue 5.25 .40
Never hinged 10.00
On cover 3.25
b. 25c green (error) *4,000.*
280 A35 30c deep green 37.50 .35
Never hinged 45.00
On cover 3.50
a. 30c pale bluish green 35.00 .40
Never hinged 55.00
On cover 3.75
c. 30c yellow green 32.50 .30
Never hinged 45.00
On cover 3.50
281 A35 40c olive bister 125.00 5.00
Never hinged 150.00
On cover 22.50
On cover, single franking 70.00
282 A35 40c rose ('05) 300.00 4.50
Never hinged 375.00
On cover 22.50
On cover, single franking 450.00
283 A35 50c slate blue 32.50 .55
Never hinged 45.00
On cover 4.50
b. 50c blue green (error) *2,250.* *1,100.*
c. 50c pale greenish blue 35.00 .60
Never hinged 50.00
On cover 5.00
284 A35 1p lake 30.00 .80
Never hinged 45.00
On cover 4.50
285 A35 4p dk violet 250.00 22.50
Never hinged 325.00
On cover 300.00
286 A35 10p brown orange 225.00 72.50
Never hinged 325.00
On cover 450.00
Nos. 272-286 (15) 1,085. 110.55
Set, never hinged 1,650.

Imperf

272a	A35	2c	57.50
273a	A35	5c	25.00
274a	A35	10c	25.00
275a	A35	15c	110.00
276a	A35	15c	22.50
277a	A35	15c	17.00
278a	A35	20c	90.00
279a	A35	25c	17.00
280b	A35	30c	110.00
282a	A35	40c	300.00
283a	A35	50c	125.00
284a	A35	1p	57.50
285a	A35	4p	200.00
286a	A35	10p	190.00

The 15c in red brown (value $850), 30c blue ($1,100), 1p olive ($1,000), 1p blue green ($750) and 1p dark violet ($900) were prepared but not issued.

Nos. 287-296 are almost always badly centered. Values are for stamps with fine centering, fresh color and, if unused, full original gum. Sound stamps with average centering sell for about half these values. Very fine copies sell more more.

Don Quixote Starts Forth A36

10c, Don Quixote attacks windmill. 15c, Meets country girls. 25c, Sancho Panza tossed in blanket. 30c, Don Quixote knighted. 40c, Tilting at sheep. 50c, On Wooden horse. 1p, Adventure with lions. 4p, In bullock cart, 10p, The Enchanted Lady.

Control Number on Back

1905, May 1 Typo.

287 A36 5c dark green 1.25 1.10
Never hinged 2.50
On cover 25.00
a. Imperf. 55.00
288 A36 10c orange red 2.50 1.75
Never hinged 4.50
On cover 35.00
a. 10c pale red 6.75 3.75
Never hinged 13.50
On cover 70.00
289 A36 15c violet 2.50 1.75
Never hinged 4.00
On cover 37.50
a. Imperf. 82.50
b. 15c pale violet 6.75 3.75
Never hinged 13.00
On cover 75.00
290 A36 25c dark blue 6.50 3.25
Never hinged 12.00
On cover 26.00
291 A36 30c dk blue green 47.50 9.25
Never hinged 75.00
On cover 100.00
a. 30c pale blue green 62.50 40.00
Never hinged 150.00
On cover 200.00
292 A36 40c bright rose 75.00 30.00
Never hinged 150.00
On cover 200.00
293 A36 50c slate 19.00 6.25
Never hinged 32.50
On cover 90.00
294 A36 1p rose red 250.00 80.00
Never hinged 500.00
On cover 500.00
295 A36 4p dk violet 120.00 80.00
Never hinged 150.00
On cover 250.00
296 A36 10p brown orange 175.00 125.00
Never hinged 260.00
On cover 300.00
Nos. 287-296 (10) 699.25 338.35
Set, never hinged 1,350.

300th anniversary of the publication of Cervantes' "Don Quixote."
Counterfeits exist of Nos. 287-296.
For surcharges see Nos. 586-588, C91.

Six stamps picturing King Alfonso XIII and Queen Victoria Eugenia were put on sale Oct. 1, 1907, at the Madrid Industrial Exhibition. They were not valid for postage. Value, unused $40, mint never hinged $60.
The original labels were engraved and perf 11½. Examples printed by other methods or with other perfs are reprints. Value $2.

Alfonso XIII — A46

A47

Blue Control Number on Back

Perf. 13x12½, 13, 13½x13, 14

1909-22 Engr.

297 A46 2c dark brown .55 .55
Never hinged 1.00
a. No control number .55 .20
Never hinged 1.00
298 A46 5c green 1.25 .20
Never hinged 2.50
299 A46 10c carmine 2.10 .20
Never hinged 3.25
300 A46 15c violet 9.50 .20
Never hinged 16.00
301 A46 20c olive green 50.00 .90
Never hinged 80.00
302 A46 25c deep blue 4.75 .20
Never hinged 8.50
303 A46 30c blue green 8.50 .20
Never hinged 15.00
304 A46 40c rose 15.50 .65
Never hinged 26.00
305 A46 50c blue ('22) 11.50 .40
Never hinged 21.00
a. 50c slate blue 12.50 .40
Never hinged 18.50
306 A46 1p lake 30.00 .40
Never hinged 52.50
307 A46 4p deep violet 80.00 12.00
Never hinged 165.00
309 A46 10p orange 100.00 26.00
Never hinged 210.00
Nos. 297-309 (12) 313.65 41.90
Set, never hinged 725.00

Nos. 297-309 exist imperforate. Value $500.
The 5c exists in carmine; the 10c in yellow orange (value $400); the 15c in blue (value $400); the 4p in lake (value $1,000). The 5c and 15c are unissued trial colors, privately perforated and back-numbered. The 4p lake is known only with perfin "B.H.A." (Banco Hispano-Americano). 100 copies of the 4p exist, most poorly centered.
See Nos. 310, 315-317. For overprints see Nos. C1-C5, C58-C61.
Counterfeits exist.

Control Number on Back in Red or Orange

1917

310 A46 15c yellow ocher 3.50 .35
Never hinged 6.00
a. Control number in blue 14.50 1.10
Never hinged 22.50

Control Number on Back in Blue

1918

313 A46 40c light red 82.50 5.75
Never hinged 150.00

1920 Typo. *Imperf.*

314 A47 1c blue green .20 .20
Never hinged .30

Perf. 13x12½,
Litho.

315 A46 2c bister 5.00 .20
Never hinged 15.00
316 A46 20c violet 42.50 .20
Never hinged 110.00
Nos. 314-316 (3) 47.70 .60

Nos. 314-315 have no control number on back.
For overprints and surcharge see Nos. 358, 449, 457, 468, 10L1, 11LB1.

1921 Engr.

317 A46 20c violet 30.00 .20
Never hinged 52.50

Madrid Post Office — A48

1920, Oct. 1 Typo. *Perf. 13½*
Center and Portrait in Black

318 A48 1c blue green .20 .25
Never hinged .45
319 A48 2c olive bister .20 .25
Never hinged .45

Control Number on Back

320 A48 5c green .85 .90
Never hinged 2.25
321 A48 10c red .85 .90
Never hinged 2.25
322 A48 15c yellow 1.40 1.10
Never hinged 3.00
323 A48 20c violet 1.60 1.50
Never hinged 5.00
324 A48 25c gray blue 2.25 2.50
Never hinged 5.25
325 A48 30c dark green 6.25 4.75
Never hinged 16.00
326 A48 40c rose 25.00 6.50
Never hinged 65.00
327 A48 50c brt blue 27.50 17.50
Never hinged 75.00
328 A48 1p brown red 27.50 14.50
Never hinged 75.00
329 A48 4p brown violet 85.00 60.00
Never hinged 225.00
330 A48 10p orange 175.00 125.00
Never hinged 475.00
Nos. 318-330 (13) 353.60 235.65
Set, never hinged 1,050.

Perf. 14

318a A48 1c blue green .20 .20
Never hinged .45
320a A48 5c green .85 .90
Never hinged 2.40
322a A48 15c yellow 1.75 1.40
Never hinged 4.00
323a A48 20c violet 2.50 1.50
Never hinged 7.75
324a A48 25c gray blue 2.60 2.50
Never hinged 7.75
325a A48 30c dark green 5.75 4.25
Never hinged 15.00
326a A48 40c rose 30.00 7.25
Never hinged 100.00
330a A48 10p orange 350.00 250.00
Never hinged 1,000.

Universal Postal Union Congress, Madrid, Oct. 10-Nov. 30.
Nos. 318-330 exist imperforate. Value, $2,500.

King Alfonso XIII
A49 A49a

FIFTEEN CENTIMOS:
Die I — Narrow "5."
Die II — Wide "5."

TWENTY FIVE CENTIMOS:
Die I — "25" is 2¾mm high. Vertical stroke of "5" is 1mm long.
Die II — "25" is 3mm high. Vertical stroke of "5" is 1½mm long.

Perf. 11 to 14, Compound

1922-26 Engr. Unwmk.

331 A49 2c olive green .75 .20
Never hinged 1.75
a. 2c deep orange (error) 87.50 *210.00*
Never hinged *110.00*
b. 2c bronze green 1.10 .20
Never hinged 2.50

Control Number on Back

332 A49 5c red violet 3.50 .20
Never hinged 6.50

333 A49 5c claret 1.50 .20
Never hinged 3.25
334 A49 10c carmine 1.50 1.00
Never hinged 3.25
335 A49 10c yellow green 1.40 .20
Never hinged 5.00
a. 10c blue green ('23) 2.25 .20
Never hinged 5.50
336 A49 15c slate bl (I) 6.50 .20
Never hinged 13.00
a. 15c black green (II) 27.50 2.25
Never hinged 47.50
b. 15c dk slate grn (I) 55.00 19.00
Never hinged 110.00
337 A49 20c violet 3.25 .20
Never hinged 7.50
a. 20c lilac 5.00 .20
Never hinged 11.00
338 A49 25c carmine (I) 3.25 .20
Never hinged 7.75
a. 25c rose red (II) 5.50 1.00
Never hinged 11.00
b. 25c lilac rose (error) 100.00 160.00
Never hinged *175.00*
339 A49 30c black brn ('26) 12.00 .20
Never hinged 24.00
340 A49 40c deep blue 3.75 .20
Never hinged 8.25
341 A49 50c orange 16.00 .20
Never hinged 32.50
a. 50c orange red 77.50 1.90
Never hinged 110.00
342 A49a 1p blue black 15.00 .20
Never hinged 37.50
343 A49a 4p lake 70.00 3.50
Never hinged 140.00
344 A49a 10p brown 30.00 12.00
Never hinged 65.00
Nos. 331-344 (14) 168.40 18.70
Set, never hinged 390.00

Nos. 331, 334, 336-344 exist imperf.
The 5c exists in vermilion (value $110); the 25c in dark blue (value $200). The 50c exists in red brown, the 4p in brown and 10p in lake; value, each $90. These five were not regularly issued.
For overprints see Nos. 359-370, 467.

"Santa Maria" and View of Seville A50

Herald of Barcelona — A51

Exposition Buildings — A52

King Alfonso XIII and View of Barcelona A53

1929, Feb. 15 ***Perf. 11***
345 A50 1c grnsh blue 2.25 2.25
Never hinged 3.75
346 A51 2c pale yel grn .25 .25
Never hinged .50
347 A52 5c rose lake .45 .45
Never hinged .75

Control Number on Back

348 A53 10c green .45 .45
Never hinged .85
349 A50 15c Prus blue .75 .75
Never hinged 1.50
350 A51 20c purple .50 .50
Never hinged .85
351 A50 25c brt rose .50 .50
Never hinged .85
352 A52 30c black brn 3.75 4.25
Never hinged 9.00
353 A53 40c dark blue 7.00 7.25
Never hinged 15.00
354 A51 50c deep orange 3.75 4.25
Never hinged 8.75
355 A52 1p blue black 10.50 11.00
Never hinged 25.00
356 A53 4p deep rose 22.50 22.50
Never hinged 47.50
357 A53 10p brown 60.00 62.50
Never hinged 110.00
Nos. 345-357,E2 (14) 130.15 136.90
Set, never hinged 250.00

Perf. 14

345a A50 1c greenish blue .70 .70
Never hinged 1.10
348a A53 10c green 20.00 37.50
Never hinged 32.50
349a A50 15c Prus blue 22.50 22.50
Never hinged 32.50
350a A51 20c purple 26.00 37.50
Never hinged 45.00
351a A50 25c bright rose 32.50 37.50
Never hinged 45.00
352a A52 30c black brown 32.50 37.50
Never hinged 45.00
353a A53 40c dark blue 70.00 90.00
Never hinged 100.00
354a A51 50c deep orange 32.50 37.50
Never hinged 45.00
355a A52 1p blue black 32.50 37.50
Never hinged 45.00
356a A53 4p deep rose 25.00 25.00
Never hinged 55.00
357a A53 10p brown 110.00 140.00
Never hinged 225.00
Nos. 345a-357a,E2a (12) 433.20 535.70
Set, never hinged 700.00

Seville and Barcelona Exhibitions.
Nos. 345-357 exist imperf. Values about 8 times those of perf. stamps. See note after No. 432.

Nos. 314, 331, 333, 335-344 Overprinted in Red or Blue

1929, June 10 ***Imperf.***
358 A47 1c blue green .50 .80
Never hinged 1.00

Perf. 13½x12½

359 A49 2c olive green .50 .90
Never hinged 1.00
360 A49 5c claret (Bl) .50 .90
Never hinged 1.00
361 A49 10c yellow green .50 .90
Never hinged 1.00
362 A49 15c slate blue .50 .90
Never hinged 1.00
363 A49 20c violet .50 .90
Never hinged 1.00
364 A49 25c carmine (Bl) .50 .90
Never hinged 1.00
365 A49 30c black brown 2.10 3.50
Never hinged 4.00
366 A49 40c deep blue 2.10 3.50
Never hinged 4.00
367 A49 50c orange (Bl) 2.10 3.50
Never hinged 4.00
368 A49a 1p blue black 10.00 17.50
Never hinged 19.00
369 A49a 4p lake (Bl) 10.00 19.00
Never hinged 19.00
370 A49a 10p brown (Bl) 35.00 65.00
Never hinged 70.00
Nos. 358-370,E4 (14) 76.80 143.20

55th assembly of League of Nations at Madrid June 10-16. The stamps were available for postal use only on those days.
Nos. 359-370 values are for off-center copies.

Exposition Building — A54

1930 **Litho.** ***Perf. 11***
371 A54 5c dk blue & salmon 5.50 5.00
Never hinged 8.50
372 A54 5c dk violet & blue 5.50 5.00
Never hinged 8.50

Barcelona Philatelic Congress and Exhibition. "C. F. y E. F." are the initials of "Congreso Filatelico y Exposicion Filatelica." For each admission ticket, costing 2.75 pesetas, the holder was allowed to buy one of each of these stamps.

A55

Locomotives A56

1930, May 10 ***Perf. 14***
373 A55 1c light blue .50 .60
Never hinged .70
374 A55 2c apple green .50 .60
Never hinged .70

Control Number on Back

375 A55 5c lake .50 .60
Never hinged .70
376 A55 10c yellow green .50 .60
Never hinged .70
377 A55 15c bluish gray .50 .60
Never hinged .70
378 A55 20c purple .50 .60
Never hinged .70
379 A55 25c brt rose .50 .60
Never hinged .70
380 A55 30c olive gray 1.60 1.40
Never hinged 2.50
381 A55 40c dark blue 1.60 1.50
Never hinged 2.00
382 A55 50c dk orange 3.50 4.50
Never hinged 5.50
383 A56 1p dark gray 4.25 5.00
Never hinged 7.00
384 A56 4p deep rose 77.50 60.00
Never hinged 190.00
385 A56 10p bister brn 300.00 300.00
Never hinged 650.00
Nos. 373-385,C12-C17,E6 (20) 526.20 510.85

11th Intl. Railway Congress, Madrid, 1930.
These stamps were on sale May 10-21, 1930, exclusively at the Palace of the Senate in Madrid and at the Barcelona and Seville expositions.

Francisco de Goya at Age 80 ("1746 1828") ("1828 1928")
A57 A59

"La Maja Desnuda" — A58

1930, June 15 **Litho.** ***Perf. 12½***
Inscribed "Correos Espana"

386 A57 1c yellow .20 .20
Never hinged .20
387 A57 2c bister brn .20 .20
Never hinged .20
388 A57 5c lilac rose .20 .20
Never hinged .20
389 A57 10c green .20 .20
Never hinged .20

Engr.

390 A57 15c lt blue .20 .20
Never hinged .20
391 A57 20c brown violet .20 .20
Never hinged .20
392 A57 25c red .20 .20
Never hinged .20
393 A57 30c brown 4.25 4.25
Never hinged 5.75
394 A57 40c dark blue 4.25 4.25
Never hinged 5.75
395 A57 50c vermilion 4.25 4.25
Never hinged 5.75
396 A57 1p black 5.25 5.25
Never hinged 5.75
397 A58 1p dark violet .75 .65
Never hinged .90
398 A58 4p slate gray .55 .50
Never hinged .65
399 A58 10p red brown 10.50 8.00
Never hinged 12.50

Inscribed "1828 Goya 1928"
Litho.

400 A59 2c olive green .20 .20
Never hinged .20
401 A59 5c gray violet .20 .20
Never hinged .20

Engr.

402 A59 25c rose carmine .25 .25
Never hinged .30
Nos. 386-402,C18-C30,CE1,E7 (32) 46.60 44.05

To commemorate the death of Francisco de Goya y Lucientes, painter and engraver.
Nos. 386-399 were issued in connection with the Spanish-American Exposition at Seville.
Nos. 386-402 exist imperf. Value, set $300.
See note after No. 432.

King Alfonso XIII — A61

Two types of the 40c:

Type I

Type II

1930 ***Perf. 11½, 12x11½***
406 A61 2c red brown .20 .20
Never hinged .20

Control Number on Back

407 A61 5c black brown .65 .20
Never hinged 1.25
408 A61 10c green 3.00 .20
Never hinged 7.50
409 A61 15c slate green 10.00 .20
Never hinged 35.00
410 A61 20c dark violet 5.50 .65
Never hinged 15.00
411 A61 25c carmine .65 .20
Never hinged 1.25
412 A61 30c brown lake 14.00 1.60
Never hinged 35.00
413 A61 40c dk blue (I) 19.00 1.00
Never hinged 40.00
a. Type II 25.00 1.00
Never hinged 55.00
414 A61 50c orange 17.50 1.75
Never hinged 50.00
Nos. 406-414 (9) 70.50 6.00

Nos. 406-414 exist imperf. Value for set, $350.
For overprints see #450-455, 458-466, 469-487.

Bow of "Santa Maria" — A63

Stern of "Santa Maria" — A64

"Santa Maria," "Niña," "Pinta" — A65

Columbus Leaving Palos — A66

Columbus Arriving in America — A67

1930, Sept. 29 Litho. *Perf. 12½*

418	A63	1c olive gray	.20	.20
		Never hinged	.55	
419	A64	2c olive green	.20	.20
		Never hinged	.55	
420	A63	2c olive green	.20	.20
		Never hinged	.55	
421	A64	5c red brown	.20	.20
		Never hinged	.55	
422	A63	5c red brown	.20	.20
		Never hinged	.55	
423	A64	10c blue green	.85	.70
		Never hinged	1.40	
424	A63	15c ultra	.85	.90
		Never hinged	1.40	
425	A64	20c violet	1.25	1.10
		Never hinged	1.75	

Engr.

426	A65	25c dark red	1.25	1.10
		Never hinged	1.75	
427	A66	30c bis brn, bl & blk brn	6.00	5.25
		Never hinged	12.50	
428	A65	40c ultra	5.50	5.75
		Never hinged	12.50	
429	A66	50c dk vio, bl & vio brn	7.75	5.75
		Never hinged	12.50	
430	A65	1p black	7.75	5.75
		Never hinged	12.50	
431	A67	4p blk & dk blue	8.75	6.50
		Never hinged	12.50	
432	A67	10p red brn & dk brn	35.00	32.50
		Never hinged	62.50	
		Nos. 418-432,E8 (16)	77.70	68.05

Christopher Columbus tribute.

Nos. 418 to 432 were privately produced. Their promoters presented a certain quantity of these labels to the Spanish Postal Authorities, who placed them on sale and allowed them to be used for three days, retaining the money obtained from the sale.

This note will also apply to Nos. 345-357, 386-402, 433-448, 557-571, B1-B105, C18-C57, C73-C87, CB1-CB5, CE1, E2, E7-E9, E15 and EB1.

Many so-called "errors" of color and perforation are known.

Nos. 418-432 exist imperf. Value, set $450. stamps.

See Nos. 2671, B194.

Arms of Spain, Bolivia, Paraguay A68

Pavilion and Map of Central America — A69

Exhibition Pavilion of Ecuador — A70

Colombia Pavilion — A71

Dominican Republic Pavilion A72

Uruguay Pavilion A73

Argentina Pavilion A74

Chile Pavilion A75

Brazil Pavilion A76

Mexico Pavilion A77

Cuba Pavilion A78

Peru Pavilion A79

U.S. Pavilion A80

Exhibition Pavilion of Portugal — A81

King Alfonso XIII and Queen Victoria — A82

Unwmk.

1930, Oct. 10 Photo. *Perf. 14*

433	A68	1c blue green	.20	.20
		Never hinged	.30	
434	A69	2c bister brown	.20	.20
		Never hinged	.30	
435	A70	5c olive brown	.20	.20
		Never hinged	.30	
436	A71	10c dark green	.30	.30
		Never hinged	.85	
437	A72	15c indigo	.30	.30
		Never hinged	.85	
438	A73	20c violet	.30	.30
		Never hinged	.85	
439	A74	25c car rose	.30	.30
		Never hinged	.85	
440	A75	25c car rose	.30	.30
		Never hinged	.85	
441	A76	30c rose lilac	1.50	1.50
		Never hinged	3.50	
442	A77	40c slate blue	.90	.90
		Never hinged	1.50	
443	A78	40c slate blue	.90	.90
		Never hinged	1.50	
444	A79	50c brown org	1.50	1.50
		Never hinged	3.50	
445	A80	1p ultra	2.25	2.25
		Never hinged	4.50	
446	A81	4p brown violet	30.00	27.50
		Never hinged	87.50	
447	A82	10p brown	2.10	2.10
		Never hinged	4.50	

Perf. 11, 14

Engr.

448	A82	10p dk reddish brn	42.50	42.50
		Never hinged	95.00	
		Nos. 433-448,C50-C57,E9 (25)	104.30	96.00
		Set, never hinged	265.00	

Spanish-American Union Exhibition, Seville.

The note after No. 432 will also apply to Nos. 433-448. All values exist imperforate. Value, set: hinged $250; never hinged $350.

Reprints of Nos. 433-448 have blurred colors, yellowish paper and an inferior, almost invisible gum. They sell for about $1 per set.

Revolutionary Issues
Madrid Issue

Regular Issues of 1920-30 Overprinted in Black, Green or Red

On No. 314

1931 *Imperf.*

449	A47	1c blue green	.20	.20
		Never hinged	.30	

On Nos. 406-411

Perf. 11½

450	A61	2c red brown (G)	.30	.25
		Never hinged	.60	
451	A61	5c black brn (R)	.40	.40
		Never hinged	.70	
452	A61	10c green	.70	.70
		Never hinged	1.25	
453	A61	15c slate grn (R)	1.40	1.50
		Never hinged	2.50	
454	A61	20c dk violet (R)	1.40	1.50
		Never hinged	2.50	
455	A61	25c carmine (G)	1.90	2.25
		Never hinged	3.50	
		Nos. 449-455,E10 (8)	10.80	11.30
		Set, never hinged	22.50	

The status of Nos. 449-455, E10 has been questioned.

First Barcelona Issue

Regular Issues of 1920-30 Overprinted in Black or Red

On No. 314

1931 *Imperf.*

457	A47	1c blue green	.20	.20
		Never hinged	.30	

On Nos. 406-414

Perf. 11½

458	A61	2c red brown	.20	.20
		Never hinged	.30	
459	A61	5c black brown	.20	.20
		Never hinged	.30	
460	A61	10c green	.55	.55
		Never hinged	1.00	
461	A61	15c slate grn (R)	.60	.60
		Never hinged	1.25	
462	A61	20c dk violet (R)	.60	.60
		Never hinged	1.25	
463	A61	25c carmine	.60	.60
		Never hinged	1.25	
464	A61	30c brown lake	4.50	4.50
		Never hinged	10.00	
465	A61	40c dk blue (R)	1.25	1.25
		Never hinged	2.50	
466	A61	50c orange	1.25	1.25
		Never hinged	2.50	

On Stamp of 1922-26

467	A49a	1p blue blk (R)	7.50	6.25
		Never hinged	16.00	
		Nos. 457-467,E11 (12)	22.45	21.20

Nos. 457-467 are known both with and without accent over "U."

The status of Nos. 457-467, E11 has been questioned.

Second Barcelona Issue

Regular Issues of 1920-30 Overprinted in Black or Red

On No. 314

Imperf

468	A47	1c blue green	.20	.20
		Never hinged	.30	

On Nos. 406-414

Perf. 11½

469	A61	2c red brown	.20	.20
		Never hinged	.30	
470	A61	5c black brown (R)	.20	.20
		Never hinged	.30	
471	A61	10c green	.20	.20
		Never hinged	.40	
472	A61	15c slate grn (R)	1.40	1.25
		Never hinged	2.50	
473	A61	20c dark violet (R)	.40	.45
		Never hinged	.70	
474	A61	25c carmine	.40	.45
		Never hinged	.70	
475	A61	30c brown lake	5.75	5.75
		Never hinged	11.00	

476 A61 40c dark blue (R) 1.25 1.25
Never hinged 2.25
477 A61 50c orange 4.50 3.50
Never hinged 10.00
Nos. 468-477 (10) 14.50 13.45

The status of Nos. 469-477, C58-C61 has been questioned.

General Issue of the Republic

Nos. 406-414, 342 Overprinted in Blue or Red

1931, May 27

478 A61 2c red brown .20 .20
Never hinged .20
479 A61 5c black brn (R) .20 .20
Never hinged .50
480 A61 10c green (R) .25 .20
Never hinged .70
481 A61 15c slate grn (R) 2.75 .20
Never hinged 4.50
482 A61 20c dk violet (R) 1.25 .75
Never hinged 2.50
483 A61 25c carmine .40 .20
Never hinged .70
484 A61 30c brown lake 3.50 .75
Never hinged 7.00
485 A61 40c dk blue (R) 3.50 .45
Never hinged 7.00
486 A61 50c orange 6.00 .45
Never hinged 15.00
487 A49a 1p blue blk (R) 45.00 .75
Never hinged 95.00
Nos. 478-487,E12 (11) 68.55 5.15

The setting contained 18 repetitions of "Republica Espanola" for each vertical row of 10 stamps. According to its sheet position, a stamp received different parts of the overprinted words.

Overprint position varieties include: reading down on 25c, 30c, 40c and 50c; double on 1p; double, both reading down, on 25c, 40c and 50c.

"Republica Espanola"
Stamps of various Spanish colonies overprinted "Republica Espanola" are listed with the colonies.

Fountain of Lions, The Alhambra, Granada
A84

Interior of Mosque, Córdoba — A85

Alcántara Bridge and Alcazar, Toledo
A86

Francisco García y Santos
A87

Puerta del Sol, Madrid, on April 14, 1931 as Republic Was Proclaimed
A88

Perf. 12½

1931, Oct. 10 Unwmk. Engr.

491 A84 5c violet brown .20 .25
Never hinged .20
492 A85 10c blue green .30 .30
Never hinged .90
493 A86 15c dark violet .30 .30
Never hinged .90
494 A85 25c deep red .30 .30
Never hinged .90
495 A87 30c olive green .30 .30
Never hinged .90
496 A84 40c indigo .90 .90
Never hinged 2.25
497 A85 50c orange red .90 .90
Never hinged 2.25
498 A86 1p black 1.75 1.75
Never hinged 4.50
499 A88 4p red violet 8.50 8.50
Never hinged 22.50
500 A88 10p red brown 27.50 *30.00*
Never hinged 70.00
Nos. 491-500,C62-C67,CO1-CO6,O20-O29 (32) 93.20 97.15

3rd Pan-American Postal Union Cong., Madrid.

Nos. 491-500 exist imperforate. Value, set: hinged $150; never hinged $250.

Symbolical of Montserrat Cut With a Saw — A89

Abbott Oliva and Monastery Workman — A90

"Black Virgin"
A91 A92

Montserrat Monastery — A93

1931, Dec. 9 ***Perf. 11, 14***

501 A89 1c myrtle green 1.10 1.40
Never hinged 2.25
a. Perf. 14 19.00 19.00
Never hinged 37.50
502 A89 2c red brown .65 1.00
Never hinged 1.25
a. Perf. 14 14.00 15.00
Never hinged 27.50

Control Number on Back

503 A89 5c black brown .75 1.25
Never hinged 1.60
a. Perf. 14 14.00 15.00
Never hinged 27.50
504 A89 10c yellow green .85 1.25
Never hinged 1.60
a. Perf. 14 14.00 17.00
Never hinged 27.50
505 A90 15c myrtle green 1.10 1.60
Never hinged 2.00
a. Perf. 14 19.00 22.50
Never hinged 37.50
506 A91 20c dark violet 2.25 2.25
Never hinged 4.25
a. Perf. 11 100.00 140.00
Never hinged *190.00*
507 A92 25c lake 3.25 3.25
Never hinged 6.00
a. Perf. 14 5.75 6.50
Never hinged 11.50
508 A91 30c deep red 35.00 32.50
Never hinged 62.50
a. Perf. 14 37.50 37.50
Never hinged 77.50
509 A93 40c dull blue 20.00 17.50
Never hinged 35.00
a. Perf. 11 140.00 160.00
Never hinged *275.00*
510 A90 50c dark orange 45.00 42.50
Never hinged 82.50
a. Perf. 14 62.50 72.50
Never hinged *125.00*
511 A92 1p gray black 45.00 42.50
Never hinged 82.50
a. Perf. 11 80.00 100.00
Never hinged *160.00*
512 A93 4p lilac rose 450.00 450.00
Never hinged 825.00
a. Perf. 14 475.00 825.00
Never hinged *875.00*
513 A92 10p deep brown 350.00 300.00
Never hinged 650.00
a. Perf. 14 725.00 875.00
Never hinged *1,400.*
Nos. 501-511,C68-C72,E13 (17) 244.20 236.25
Set, never hinged 375.00
Nos. 501-513,C68-C72,E13 (19) 1,044. 986.25
Set, never hinged 2,100.

Commemorative of the building of the old Monastery at Montserrat, started in 1031, and of the image of the Black Virgin (said to have been carved by St. Luke) which was crowned by Pope Leo XIII in 1881.

Nos. 501-513 exist imperforate. Value, set $4,000.

For surcharges see Nos. 589, C92-C96.

Francisco Pi y Margall — A95

Joaquín Costa — A96

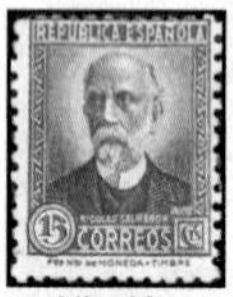

Nicolás Salmerón
A97

Pablo Iglesias
A99

Emilio Castelar — A100

1931-32 ***Perf. 11½***

Control Number on Back

516 A95 5c brnsh black 3.00 .30
Never hinged 5.50
517 A96 10c yellow green 7.25 .30
Never hinged 15.00
518 A97 15c slate green 4.75 .20
Never hinged 17.50
520 A99 25c lake 22.50 .70
Never hinged 50.00
b. Imperf. 175.00
Never hinged 225.00
521 A99 30c carmine rose 7.25 .20
Never hinged 15.00
c. Imperf. 82.50
Never hinged 125.00
522 A100 40c dark blue 42.50 4.50
Never hinged 110.00
523 A97 50c orange 52.50 7.75
Never hinged 140.00
Nos. 516-523 (7) 139.75 13.95
Set, never hinged 400.00

Without Control Number

516a A95 5c brownish blk ('32) 4.50 .20
Never hinged 7.75
517a A96 10c yellow green ('32) 4.00 .20
Never hinged 7.75
518a A97 15c slate green ('32) .60 .20
Never hinged 1.10
520a A99 25c lake 32.50 .20
Never hinged 72.50
521a A99 30c carmine rose 1.90 .20
Never hinged 3.25
522a A100 40c dark blue ('32) .20 .20
Never hinged .25
523a A97 50c orange ('32) 26.00 .50
Never hinged 57.50
Nos. 516a-523a (7) 69.70

Without Control Number, Imperf.

516b A95 5c 6.50
Never hinged 13.00
517b A96 10c 11.00
Never hinged 22.50
518b A97 15c 6.25
Never hinged 12.50
520c A99 25c *110.00*
Never hinged 210.00
521b A99 30c 5.50
Never hinged 11.00
522b A100 40c 14.00
Never hinged 25.00
523b A97 50c 125.00
Never hinged 250.00
Nos. 516b-523b (7) 278.25

See Nos. 532, 538, 550, 579, 579a.

For overprints and surcharges see Nos. 7LC12-7LC13, 7LC15-7LC16, 7LC18, 7LE4, 8LB6, 8LB9-8LB10, 9LC17-9LC18, 10L7, 10L10-10L12, 10L16-10L18, 10L22-10L23, 11L7, 11L10-11L12, 11LB8, 12L4, 12L8, 12L11-12L12, 13L8, 14L6, 14L10-14L12, 14L18, 14L22-14L24.

Blasco Ibáñez
A103

Manuel Ruiz-Zorrilla
A104

Without Control Number

1931-34 ***Perf. 11½***

526 A103 2c red brown ('32) .20 .20
Never hinged .40
528 A103 5c chocolate ('34) .20 .20
Never hinged .40
532 A95 20c dark violet .25 .20
Never hinged .50
534 A104 25c lake ('34) .45 .20
Never hinged .80
538 A100 60c apple green ('32) .20 .20
Never hinged .40
Nos. 526-538 (5) 1.30 1.00
Set, never hinged 2.50

Imperf

526a A103 2c 14.00
Never hinged 27.50
528a A103 5c 2.75
Never hinged 5.50
532a A95 20c 6.25
Never hinged 13.00
534a A104 25c 5.25
Never hinged 10.50
538a A100 60c 6.25
Never hinged 13.00
Nos. 526a-538a (5) 34.50

For overprints and surcharges see Nos. 8LB3, 8LB7, 9LC3, 9LC8-9LC9, 9LC14, 10L6, 10L13, 11L4, 11L8, 11LB5, 11LB9, 12L5, 12L9, 13L5, 13L7, 14L3, 14L7, 14L15, 14L19.

Cliff Houses, Cuenca — A105

Alcázar of Segovia — A106

Gate of the Sun at Toledo — A107

1932-38 ***Perf. 10***

539 A105 1p gray black ('38) .20 .20
Never hinged .40
540 A106 4p magenta ('38) .30 .40
Never hinged .60
541 A107 10p deep brown ('38) .65 .70
Never hinged 1.75
Nos. 539-541 (3) 1.15 1.30

Imperf

539a A105 1p 5.25 2.75
Never hinged 11.50
540a A106 4p 9.00 6.50
Never hinged 20.00

541a	A107	10p	6.50	6.00
		Never hinged	14.00	
		Nos. 539a-541a (3)	20.75	15.25

Perf. 11½

539b	A105	1p	.20	.20
		Never hinged	.20	
540b	A106	4p	.70	.85
		Never hinged	1.40	
541b	A107	10p	1.90	3.00
		Never hinged	3.50	
		Nos. 539b-541b (3)	2.80	4.05

For overprints and surcharge see Nos. 9LC19, 10L19, 13L9, 14L25, 14L27-14L28.

Numeral
A108

Santiago Ramón y Cajal
A109

1933 Unwmk. Typo. *Imperf.*

542 A108 1c blue green	.20	.20
Never hinged	.20	

Perf. 11½

543 A108 2c buff	.20	.20
Never hinged	.40	
a. Perf. 13½x13	.65	.20
Never hinged	1.40	

See Nos. 592-597. For surcharges and overprints see Nos. 590-590A, 634A-634D, 8LB1-8LB2, 9LC1-9LC2, 9LC4-9LC7, 9LC11-9LC12, 9LC20, 9LC26, 10L2-10L4, 11L1-11L2, 11LB2-11LB3, 12L1-12L2, 13L1-13L3, 14L1, 14L13.

1934 Engr. *Perf. 11½x11*

545 A109 30c black brown	6.00	1.10
Never hinged	15.00	
a. Perf. 14	22.50	30.00
Never hinged	42.50	
b. Imperf.	32.50	
Never hinged	55.00	

Type of 1931 and

Mariana Pineda
A110

Concepción Arenal
A111

Gumersindo de Azcarate
A112

Gaspar Melchor de Jovellanos
A113

1935

546 A110 10c green	.20	.20
Never hinged	.20	
b. 10c blue green ('36)	.20	.20
Never hinged	.20	
547 A111 15c green	.20	.20
Never hinged	.30	
b. 15c yellow green ('36)	.20	.20
Never hinged	.30	
548 A112 30c carmine rose	7.25	.20
Never hinged	17.00	
549 A113 30c rose red	.20	.20
Never hinged	.20	
550 A97 50c dark blue	1.00	.30
Never hinged	2.25	
Nos. 546-550 (5)	8.85	1.10

Imperf

546a	A110 10c	1.60	
	Never hinged	3.00	
547a	A111 15c	5.25	
	Never hinged	9.50	
548a	A112 30c	26.00	
	Never hinged	47.50	
549a	A113 30c	1.90	
	Never hinged	3.50	
550a	A97 50c	*225.00*	
	Never hinged	450.00	
	Nos. 546a-550a (5)	259.75	

Shades exist.

For overprints and surcharges see Nos. 7LE3, 8LB4-8LB5, 8LB8, 10L8-10L9, 10L14, 10L20-10L21, 11L5-11L6, 11L9, 11LB6-11LB7, 11LB10, 12L6-12L7, 12L10, 13L6, 14L4-14L5, 14L8, 14L16-14L17, 14L20.

Lope's Bookplate
A116

Lope de Vega
A117

Alcántara and Alcázar, Toledo
A118

1935, Oct. 12 *Perf. 11½x11, 11x11½*

552 A116 15c myrtle green	5.75	.30
Never hinged	10.00	
553 A117 30c rose red	2.50	.30
Never hinged	4.00	
554 A117 50c dark blue	11.00	3.00
Never hinged	27.50	
555 A118 1p blue black	21.00	2.00
Never hinged	37.50	
Nos. 552-555 (4)	40.25	5.60
Set, never hinged	95.00	

Imperf

552a	A116 15c	400.00	
	Never hinged	625.00	
553a	A117 30c	11.00	
	Never hinged	20.00	
554a	A117 50c	65.00	
	Never hinged	100.00	
555a	A118 1p	60.00	
	Never hinged	90.00	
	Nos. 552a-555a (4)	536.00	

Perf. 14

553b	A117 30c	6.50	14.50
	Never hinged	14.00	
554b	A117 50c	29.00	45.00
	Never hinged	62.50	
555b	A118 1p	32.50	50.00
	Never hinged	75.00	
	Nos. 553b-555b (3)	68.00	109.50
	Set, never hinged	150.00	

Lope Felix de Vega Carpio (1562-1635), Spanish dramatist and poet.

For surcharge see No. 11LB11.

Map of Amazon by Bartolomeo Oliva, 16th Century
A119

1935, Oct. 12 *Perf. 11½*

556 A119 30c rose red	1.90	.95
Never hinged	3.75	
a. Perf. 14	22.50	
Never hinged	45.00	
b. Imperf.	32.50	
Never hinged	60.00	

Proposed Iglesias Amazon Expedition.

Miguel Moya — A120

Torcuato Luca de Tena — A121

José Francos Rodríguez
A122

Alejandro Lerroux
A123

Nazareth School and Rotary Press — A124

1936, Feb. 14 Photo. *Perf. 12½*

Size: 22x26mm

557 A120 1c crimson	.20	.20
Never hinged	.20	
558 A121 2c orange brown	.20	.20
Never hinged	.20	
559 A122 5c black brown	.20	.20
Never hinged	.20	
560 A123 10c emerald	.20	.20
Never hinged	.20	

Size: 24x28½mm

561 A120 15c blue green	.20	.20
Never hinged	.20	
562 A121 20c violet	.20	.20
Never hinged	.20	
563 A122 25c red violet	.20	.20
Never hinged	.20	
564 A123 30c crimson	.20	.20
Never hinged	.20	

Size: 25½x30½mm

565 A120 40c orange	.50	.35
Never hinged	.75	
566 A121 50c ultra	.20	.20
Never hinged	.40	
567 A122 60c olive green	.50	.35
Never hinged	.75	
568 A123 1p gray black	.50	.35
Never hinged	.80	
569 A124 2p lt blue	6.50	3.00
Never hinged	9.50	
570 A124 4p lilac rose	6.50	6.00
Never hinged	9.50	
571 A124 10p red brown	17.00	14.00
Never hinged	24.00	
Nos. 557-571,E15 (16)	33.55	26.15
Nos. 557-571,C73-C87,E15 (31)	61.25	45.00

Madrid Press Association, 40th anniversary.

Nos. 557-571 exist imperf. Values about 7 times those of perf. stamps.

See note after No. 432. See Nos. C73-C87.

Arms of Madrid — A125

1936, Apr. 2 Engr. *Imperf.*

572 A125 10c brown black	42.50	42.50
Never hinged	55.00	
573 A125 15c dark green	42.50	42.50
Never hinged	55.00	
Set, never hinged	120.00	

1st National Philatelic Exhibition which opened in Madrid, Apr. 2, 1936.

For overprints see Nos. C88-C89.

"Republica Espanola"
A126

Gregorio Fernández
A127

1936 Litho. *Perf. 11½, 13½x13*

574 A126 2c orange brown	.20	.20
Never hinged	.30	

For surcharges & overprints see #591, 9LC24, 10L5, 11L3, 11LB4, 12L3, 13L4, 14L2, 14L14.

1936, Mar. 10 Engr. *Perf. 11½*

576 A127 30c carmine	1.10	.85
Never hinged	2.00	
a. Perf. 14	9.00	8.25
Never hinged	17.50	
b. Imperf.	15.00	
Never hinged	22.50	

Tercentenary of the death of Gregorio Fernandez, sculptor.

For overprints see Nos. 7LC20-7LC21.

Type of 1931 and

Pablo Iglesias
A128 A129

Velázquez
A130

Fermín Salvoechea
A131

1936-38 *Perf. 11, 11½, 11½x11*

577 A128 30c rose red	.20	.20
Never hinged	.20	
578 A129 30c car rose	1.10	.50
Never hinged	3.00	
579 A100 40c car rose ('37)	1.10	.50
Never hinged	3.00	
580 A129 45c carmine ('37)	.20	.20
Never hinged	.20	
581 A130 50c dark blue	.20	.20
Never hinged	.20	
582 A131 60c indigo ('37)	.75	.90
Never hinged	2.00	
583 A131 60c dp orange ('38)	6.00	5.00
Never hinged	15.00	
Nos. 577-583 (7)	9.55	7.50
Set, never hinged	26.00	

Perf. 14

577a	A128 30c rose red	6.50	
	Never hinged	13.00	
578a	A129 30c carmine rose	6.75	
	Never hinged	13.50	
579a	A100 40c carmine rose	6.50	
	Never hinged	13.50	
580a	A129 45c carmine	6.00	
	Never hinged	12.00	
582a	A131 60c indigo	6.00	
	Never hinged	12.00	
583a	A131 60c deep orange	9.50	
	Never hinged	19.00	
	Nos. 577a-583a (6)	41.25	

Nos. 577-583 exist imperf. Value, set $70, never hinged $150.

For overprints see Nos. C90, 7LC17, 7LC22-7LC23, 10L15, 14L21.

Statue of Liberty, Spanish and US Flags — A132

1938, June 1 Photo. *Perf. 11½*

585 A132 1p multicolored	15.00	16.00
Never hinged	26.00	
a. Imperf., pair	75.00	50.00
Never hinged	100.00	
b. Horiz. pair, imperf. vert.	57.50	75.00
Never hinged	85.00	
c. Souvenir sheet of 1	25.00	30.00
Never hinged	40.00	
d. As "c," imperf.	275.00	225.00
Never hinged	475.00	

150th anniv. of the US Constitution.

For surcharge see No. C97.

No. 289 Surcharged in Black

1938 *Perf. 14*

586 A36 45c on 15c violet	14.00	14.00
Never hinged	17.50	

7th anniversary of the Republic.

Values are for examples with perforations nearly touching the design on one or two sides.

No. 289 Surcharged in Black:

a 

b 

1938, May 1

587 A36 45c on 15c violet 3.00 3.00
Never hinged 4.00
588 A36 1p on 15c violet 5.25 5.25
Never hinged 7.00
Set, never hinged 12.00

Issued to commemorate Labor Day.

Values are for examples with perforations nearly touching the design on one or two sides.

No. 507 Surcharged in Black

1938, Nov. 10 ***Perf. 11½***

589 A92 2.50p on 25c lake .20 .20
Never hinged .20
b. Perf. 14 3.50 6.00
Never hinged 6.00

Types of 1933-36 Surcharged in Blue or Red

1938 ***Perf. 10, 11, 13½x13, 13x14***

590 A108 45c on 1c grn (R) .40 .25
Never hinged .90
b. Imperf. 6.00 5.00
Never hinged 10.00
590A A108 45c on 2c buff (Bl) 17.00 14.00
Never hinged 27.50
591 A126 45c on 2c org brn (Bl) .20 .20
Never hinged .60
Nos. 590-591 (3) 17.60 14.45
Set, never hinged 29.00

Many overprint varieties exist.

Numeral Type of 1933

1938-39 Litho. ***Perf. 11½, 13***

White or Gray Paper

592 A108 5c gray brown .20 .20
Never hinged .20
593 A108 10c yellow green .20 .20
Never hinged .20
594 A108 15c slate green .20 .20
Never hinged .25
595 A108 20c vio, gray paper .20 .20
Never hinged .25
596 A108 25c red violet .20 .20
Never hinged .25
597 A108 30c scarlet .20 .20
Never hinged .25
Nos. 592-597 (6) 1.20 1.20
Set, never hinged 1.40

"Republic" — A133

1938 ***Perf. 11½***

598 A133 40c rose red .20 .20
Never hinged .20
599 A133 45c car rose .20 .20
Never hinged .20
a. Printed on both sides 11.00 11.00
Never hinged 27.50
600 A133 50c ultra .20 .20
Never hinged .20
601 A133 60c dp ultra .50 .30
Never hinged .60
Nos. 598-601 (4) 1.10 .90
Set, never hinged 1.10

Nos. 598-601 exist imperf. Value for set $22.50

Machine Gunners A134

Infantry — A135

Perf. 11½x11, 11x11½, Imperf.

1938, Sept. 1 **Photo.**

602 A134 25c dark green 9.25 9.25
Never hinged 20.00
603 A135 45c red brown 9.25 9.25
Never hinged 20.00

43rd Division of the Republican Army. Sold only at the Philatelic Agency and for foreign exchange.

Blast Furnace A136

Steel Mill and Sculpture, "Defenders of Numantia" A137

1938, Aug. 9 ***Perf. 16***

604 A136 45c black .20 .20
Never hinged .20
605 A137 1.25p dark blue .20 .20
Never hinged .20

Issued in honor of the workers of Sagunto.

Submarine — A137a

Designs: 1p, 15p, U-Boat D1. 2p, 6p, U-Boat A1. 4p, 10p, U-Boat B2.

1938, Aug. 11 ***Perf. 16***

605A A137a 1p blue 5.50 5.50
605B A137a 2p red brown 10.00 10.00
605C A137a 4p red orange 12.00 12.00
605D A137a 6p deep blue 27.50 27.50
605E A137a 10p magenta 45.00 45.00
605F A137a 15p dp gray green 500.00 500.00
Nos. 605A-605F (6) 600.00 600.00
Set, never hinged 725.00

Souvenir Sheet

Perf. 10½

605G A137a Sheet of 3 550.00 550.00
Never hinged 700.00
a. 4p carmine & gray black 125.00 125.00
b. 6p dull blue & gray black 125.00 125.00
c. 15p green & gray black 125.00 125.00

Nos. 605A-605G were issued for use on a proposed submarine mail service between Barcelona and Mahon, Minorca. One voyage was made on this mail route, carrying 300 agency-prepared covers. The stamps were also valid for ordinary mail.

Nos. 605A-605G were sold only at the Philatelic Agency in Barcelona, for double their face value.

Nos. 605A-605G exist imperf. Value: set of 6 stamps, $775 unused, $1,000 never hinged; souvenir sheet, $2,250 unused, $2,900.

Riflemen A138

Machine Gunners A139

Bomb Throwing — A140

1938, Nov. 25 Engr. ***Perf. 10***

606 A138 5c sepia 3.50 3.50
Never hinged 5.50
607 A138 10c dp violet 3.50 3.50
Never hinged 5.50
608 A138 25c blue green 3.50 3.50
Never hinged 5.50
609 A139 45c rose red 3.50 3.50
Never hinged 5.50
610 A139 60c dark blue 6.25 6.25
Never hinged 8.25
611 A139 1.20p black 125.00 125.00
Never hinged 170.00
612 A140 2p orange 37.50 37.50
Never hinged 57.50
613 A140 5p dark brown 220.00 220.00
Never hinged 290.00
614 A140 10p dk blue grn 40.00 40.00
Never hinged 55.00
Nos. 606-614 (9) 442.75 442.75
Set, never hinged 725.00

Honoring the Militia. Sold only at the Philatelic Agency and for foreign exchange. Exist imperf. Value unused $1,200, never hinged $1,800.

Spanish State

Arms of Spain — A141

1936 Litho. ***Imperf.***

Thin Transparent Paper

615 A141 30c blue 190.00
Never hinged 275.00
616 A141 30c pale green 190.00
Never hinged 275.00

Perf. 11

Thick Wove Paper

617 A141 30c dark blue 550.00 110.00
Never hinged 650.00
Set, never hinged 1,200.

Issued in Granada during siege. After the city was liberated, these stamps were used throughout the province of Granada.

A143

Cathedral of Burgos — A145

University of Salamanca A146

Cathedral del Pilar, Zaragoza — A147

"La Giralda," Seville — A148

Xavier Castle, Navarre — A149

Court of Lions, Alhambra at Granada A150

Mosque, Córdoba A151

Alcántara Bridge and Alcázar, Toledo — A152

Soldier Carrying Flag — A153

Troops Landing at Algeciras A154

Two types of 30c:

Type I — Imprint 12mm long; "3" does not touch frame.

Type II — Imprint 8mm long; "3" touches frame.

1936 Unwmk. Litho. ***Imperf.***

623 A143 1c green 6.00 4.50
Never hinged 7.25

Perf. 11½

624 A143 2c orange brown .60 .45
Never hinged .90
625 A145 5c gray brown .60 .55
Never hinged .90
626 A146 10c green .60 .45
Never hinged .90
627 A147 15c dull green .60 .45
Never hinged .90
628 A148 25c rose lake .85 .45
Never hinged 1.60
629 A149 30c carmine (I) .60 .45
Never hinged .90
a. Type II .70 .55
Never hinged 1.40
630 A150 50c deep blue 14.00 8.75
Never hinged 23.00
631 A151 60c yellow green .95 .70
Never hinged 1.40
632 A152 1p black 5.25 3.75
Never hinged 9.00
633 A153 4p rose vio, red & yel 52.50 29.00
Never hinged 95.00
634 A154 10p light brown 52.50 29.00
Never hinged 95.00
Nos. 623-634 (12) 135.05 78.50
Set, never hinged 240.00

Nos. 624-634 exist imperf. Value, set $275.

Nos. 625-631, 633-634 were privately overprinted "VIA AEREA" and plane, supposedly for use in Ifni.

For surcharges see Nos. 9LC21, 9LC23.

Nos. 542-543 Surcharged "Habilitado 0'05 ptas." in Two Lines

1936 *Imperf., Perf. 11½*

634A A108 5c on 1c bl grn 2.25 3.00
Never hinged 3.25
634B A108 5c on 2c buff 2.25 3.00
Never hinged 3.25
634C A108 10c on 1c bl grn 2.25 3.00
Never hinged 3.25
634D A108 15c on 2c buff 2.25 3.00
Never hinged 3.25
Nos. 634A-634D (4) 9.00 12.00

Issued in the Balearic Islands to meet a shortage of these values. Nos. 634A and 634C are imperf., Nos. 634B and 634D are perf. 11½.

St. James of Compostela — A155

St. James Cathedral A156

Pórtico de la Gloria A157

Two types of 30c:
I — No dots in "1937."
II — Dot before and after "1937."

1937 *Perf. 11½, 11x11½*

635 A155 15c violet brown .95 1.25
Never hinged 2.25
636 A156 30c rose red (I) 5.00 .55
Never hinged 12.00
a. Type II 17.50 14.00
Never hinged 35.00
637 A157 1p blue & orange 14.50 3.25
Never hinged 35.00
a. Center inverted 275.00 250.00
Never hinged 425.00
Nos. 635-637 (3) 20.45 5.05
Set, never hinged 50.00

Holy Year of Compostela. Nos. 635-637 exist imperf. Value for set $150.

"Estado Espanol"
A159 A160

"El Cid" — A161

Isabella I — A162

Two types of 5c, 30c and 10p:
5 Centimos: Type I Imprint 9½mm long. Type II Imprint 14mm long.
30 Centimos: Type I Imprint, "Hija De B. Fournier Burgos." Type II Imprint, "Fournier Burgos".
10 Pesetas: Type I "10" 2½mm high. Type II "10" 3mm high.

With Imprint

1936-40 *Imperf.*

638 A159 1c green .20 .20
Never hinged .30

Perf. 11

640 A160 2c brown .20 .20
Never hinged .30

Perf. 11, 11½, 11½x11, 11½x10½

641 A161 5c brown (I) .45 .20
Never hinged 1.00
642 A161 5c brown (II) .20 .20
Never hinged .30
643 A161 10c green .20 .20
Never hinged .30

Perf. 11, 11x11½

644 A162 15c gray black .20 .20
Never hinged .30
645 A162 20c dark violet .40 .20
Never hinged .70
646 A162 25c brown lake .20 .20
Never hinged .40
647 A162 30c rose (I) .50 .20
Never hinged .95
648 A162 30c rose (II) 17.50 2.10
Never hinged 40.00
649 A162 40c orange 1.60 .20
Never hinged 4.00
650 A162 50c dark blue 1.60 .20
Never hinged 4.00
651 A162 60c yellow .30 .20
Never hinged .70
652 A162 1p blue 16.50 .50
Never hinged 32.50
653 A162 4p magenta 21.00 5.25
Never hinged 40.00
654 A161 10p dk bl (I) ('37) 75.00 40.00
Never hinged 130.00
655 A161 10p dp bl (II) ('40) 32.50 15.00
Never hinged 65.00
Nos. 638-655 (17) 168.55 65.25
Set, never hinged 375.00

No. 638 was privately perforated. See Nos. 662-667. For overprint and surcharges see Nos. E18, 9LC10, 9LC13, 9LC15-9LC16, 9LC22, 9LC25, 9LC27-9LC30, 9LC34-9LC53.

Ferdinand the Catholic A163

Emblem of the Falange A164

1938 *Perf. 10½, 11½x11*

Imprint: "Lit Fournier Vitoria"

656 A163 15c deep green 1.25 .20
Never hinged 4.50
657 A163 30c deep red 3.75 .20
Never hinged 11.00

Imprint: "Fournier Vitoria"

Perf. 10

658 A163 15c deep green 1.25 .20
Never hinged 4.50
659 A163 20c purple 8.25 1.25
Never hinged 17.00
660 A163 25c brown car .60 .20
Never hinged 1.00
661 A163 30c deep red 3.75 .20
Never hinged 16.00
Nos. 656-661 (6) 18.85 2.25

Nos. 656-661 exist imperf.; value for set, $150. Part-perf. varieties exist.

For overprints see Nos. C98-C99.

Without Imprint

1938-48 *Perf. 11, 13½*

Two types of the 15 Centimos:

Type I — Medieval style numerals with diagonal line through "5."

Type II — Modern numerals. Narrower "5" without diagonal line.

662 A159 1c green, imperf. .20 .20
Never hinged .20
663 A160 2c brn (18½x22mm; '40) .20 .20
Never hinged .20
a. 2c bis brn (17½x21mm; '48) .20 .20
Never hinged .20
664 A161 5c gray brn ('39) .20 .20
Never hinged .20
665 A161 10c dk carmine .20 .20
Never hinged .25
a. 10c rose .35 .20
Never hinged .75
666 A161 15c dk green (I) .90 .20
Never hinged 1.40
666A A161 15c dk green (II) .60 .20
Never hinged 1.40
b. Perf 13½x13¼ ('50) .65 .20
667 A162 70c dk blue ('39) .75 .20
Never hinged .85
Nos. 662-667 (7) 3.05 1.40

1938, July 17 *Perf. 10*

668 A164 15c bl grn & lt grn 4.25 3.75
Never hinged 7.25
669 A164 25c rose red & rose 4.25 3.75
Never hinged 7.25
670 A164 30c bl & lt bl 2.25 2.50
Never hinged 3.50
671 A164 1p brown & yellow 90.00 80.00
Never hinged 140.00
Nos. 668-671 (4) 100.75 90.00

Second anniversary of the Civil War.
Imperforate 4-value set also exists, value $725, $950 never hinged.

Isabella I A165

Gen. Francisco Franco A166

1938-39 **Litho.** *Perf. 10*

672 A165 20c brt violet ('39) .50 .20
Never hinged 3.75
673 A165 25c brown carmine 5.25 .60
Never hinged 15.00
674 A165 30c rose red .20 .20
Never hinged .40
675 A165 40c dull violet .25 .20
Never hinged .50
676 A165 50c indigo ('39) 22.50 2.50
Never hinged 52.50
677 A165 1p deep blue 7.50 .90
Never hinged 19.00
Nos. 672-677 (6) 36.20 4.60

Nos. 672-677 exist imperf. Value set, $225 hinged, $300 never hinged.

Imprint: "Sanchez Toda"

1939-40 *Perf. 10*

678 A166 20c brt violet .30 .20
Never hinged .40
679 A166 25c rose lake .30 .20
Never hinged .40
680 A166 30c rose carmine .25 .20
Never hinged .35
681 A166 40c slate green .20 .20
Never hinged .25
682 A166 45c vermilion ('40) 1.75 1.60
Never hinged 2.50
683 A166 50c indigo .25 .20
Never hinged .40
684 A166 60c orange 2.75 2.50
Never hinged 3.75
685 A166 70c blue .35 .20
Never hinged .45
686 A166 1p black 11.00 .20
Never hinged 16.00
687 A166 2p dark brown 16.50 1.10
Never hinged 21.00
688 A166 4p dark violet 87.50 16.00
Never hinged 140.00
689 A166 10p light brown 45.00 40.00
Never hinged 60.00
Nos. 678-689 (12) 166.15 62.60
Set, never hinged 290.00

#686-689 have value & "Pta." on 1 line while #702-705 have value & "Pta." on 2 lines.
Nos. 678-689 exist imperf. Value set, $525 hinged, $650 never hinged.

Without Imprint

Perf. 9½x10½

1939-47 **Litho.** **Unwmk.**

690 A166 5c dull brn vio .40 .20
Never hinged .50
691 A166 10c brown orange 1.75 .60
Never hinged 2.10
692 A166 15c lt green .45 .20
Never hinged .55
693 A166 20c brt violet ('40) .40 .20
Never hinged .50
694 A166 25c dp claret ('40) .40 .20
Never hinged .50
695 A166 30c blue ('40) .40 .20
Never hinged .50
697 A166 40c Prus grn ('40) .40 .20
Never hinged .50
a. 40c greenish black .55 .20
Never hinged .65
698 A166 45c ultra ('41) .45 .20
Never hinged .55
699 A166 50c indigo ('40) .40 .20
Never hinged .50
a. Perf. 11½ ('47) 30.00 3.00
Never hinged 50.00
700 A166 60c dull org ('40) .55 .20
Never hinged .65
701 A166 70c blue ('40) .65 .20
Never hinged .85
702 A166 1p gray blk ('40) 6.25 .20
Never hinged 6.50
703 A166 2p dull brn ('41) 7.75 .20
Never hinged 8.25
704 A166 4p dull rose ('40) 29.00 .20
Never hinged 32.50
705 A166 10p lt brown ('40) 140.00 2.50
Never hinged 190.00
Nos. 690-705 (15) 189.25 5.70
Set, never hinged 300.00

The 40c exists in three types, with variations in the value tablet: I. "CTS" does not touch bottom line. II. Light background in tablet. "CTS" touches bottom line. III. As type I, but with well defined lines of white and color around rectangle.

The 60c exists in two types: I. Top and left side of value tablet touch rest of design. II. Tablet separated from rest of design by white lines.

Five values exist with perf. 10: 5c, 10c, 45c, 4p and 10p.

The imperforate 10c dull claret, type A166, without imprint, is a postal tax stamp, RA14.

SEMI-POSTAL STAMPS

Red Cross Issue

Princesses María Cristina and Beatrice SP1

Queen as a Nurse — SP2

Queen Victoria Eugénia — SP3

Prince of Asturias — SP4

King Alfonso XIII — SP5

Perf. 12½

1926, Sept. 15 **Unwmk.** **Engr.**

B1 SP1 1c black 2.00 1.90
B2 SP2 2c ultra 2.00 1.90
B3 SP3 5c violet brn 4.50 3.25
B4 SP4 10c green 3.75 3.25
B5 SP1 15c indigo 1.50 1.25
B6 SP4 20c dull violet 1.50 1.25
a. 20c violet brown (error) 500.00 375.00
B7 SP5 25c rose red .25 .25
B8 SP1 30c blue green 35.00 32.50
B9 SP3 40c dark blue 20.00 17.50
B10 SP2 50c red orange 20.00 17.00
B11 SP4 1p slate 1.50 .90
B12 SP3 4p magenta 1.10 .65
B13 SP5 10p brown 1.10 .90
Nos. B1-B13,EB1 (14) 102.95 91.25
Set, never hinged 185.00

The 20c was printed in violet brown for use in the colonies (Cape Juby, Spanish Guinea, Spanish Morocco and Spanish Sahara). No. B6a, the missing overprint error, is listed here because it is not known to which colony it belongs.

For overprints see Nos. B19-B46.

Airplane and Map of Madrid-Manila Flight — SP6

1926, Sept. 15

B14 SP6 15c dp ultra & org .30 .30
B15 SP6 20c car & yel grn .30 .30
B16 SP6 30c dk brn & ultra .30 .30

B17 SP6 40c dk grn & brn org .30 .30
B18 SP6 4p magenta & yel 82.50 82.50
Nos. B14-B18,CB1-CB5 (10) 91.20 91.20
Set, never hinged 160.00

Madrid to Manila flight of Captains Eduardo G. Gallarza and Joaquim Loriga y Taboada.

Nos. B1-B18, CB1-CB5 and EB1 were used for regular postage on Sept. 15, 16, 17, 1926. Subsequently the unsold stamps were given to the Spanish Red Cross Society, by which they were sold uncanceled but they then had no franking power.

For overprints see Nos. B47-B53.

Coronation Silver Jubilee Issue

Red Cross Stamps of 1926 Overprinted "ALFONSO XIII," Dates and Ornaments in Various Colors

1927, May 27

B19 SP1 1c black (R) 4.50 4.00
B20 SP2 2c ultra (Bl) 7.75 7.75
B21 SP3 5c vio brn (R) 1.90 1.90
a. Double overprint 37.50
B22 SP4 10c green (Bl) 55.00 55.00
B23 SP1 15c indigo (R) 1.60 1.60
B24 SP4 20c dull vio (Bl) 3.00 3.00
B25 SP5 25c rose red (Bl) .45 .45
B26 SP1 30c blue grn (Bl) .85 .85
B27 SP3 40c dk blue (R) .85 .85
B28 SP2 50c red org (Bl) .85 .85
B29 SP4 1p slate (R) 1.60 1.60
B30 SP3 4p magenta (Bl) 8.25 8.25
B31 SP5 10p brown (G) 32.50 32.50
Nos. B19-B31 (13) 119.10 118.60
Set, never hinged 240.00

Same with Additional Surcharges of New Values

B32 SP2 3c on 2c (G) 9.50 9.50
B33 SP2 4c on 2c (Bk) 9.50 9.50
B34 SP5 10c on 25c (Bk) .55 .55
B35 SP5 25c on 25c (Bl) .55 .55
B36 SP2 55c on 2c (R) 1.00 1.00
B37 SP4 55c on 10c (Bk) 55.00 55.00
B38 SP4 55c on 20c (Bk) 55.00 55.00
B39 SP1 75c on 15c (R) .70 .70
B40 SP1 75c on 30c (R) 140.00 140.00
B41 SP3 80c on 5c (R) 52.50 50.00
B42 SP3 2p on 40c (R) 1.00 1.00
B43 SP4 2p on 1p (R) 1.00 1.00
B44 SP2 5p on 50c (G) 1.90 1.90
B45 SP3 5p on 4p (Bk) 3.25 3.25
B46 SP5 10p on 10p (G) 27.50 27.50
Nos. B32-B46 (15) 358.95 356.45
Set, never hinged 625.00

Nos. B14-B18 Overprinted

B47 SP6 15c (Br) .40 .40
a. Double overprint 30.00
B48 SP6 20c (Bl) .40 .40
a. Brown overprint (error) 65.00
b. Inverted overprint 30.00
B50 SP6 30c (R) .40 .40
a. Blue overprint (error) 65.00
b. Double overprint 30.00
B52 SP6 40c (Br) .40 .40
a. Inverted overprint 30.00
b. Double ovpt. (Bl + Br) 95.00
B53 SP6 4p (Bl) 95.00 95.00
a. Inverted overprint 160.00

Semi-Postal Special Delivery Stamp Overprinted "ALFONSO XIII," Dates and Ornaments in Violet

B54 SPSD1 20c 5.50 5.50
Nos. B47-B54 (6) 102.10 102.10

Nos. CB1-CB5 Overprinted in Various Colors

B55 SPAP1 5c (R) 1.90 1.60
a. Inverted overprint 30.00
B56 SPAP1 10c (R) 2.25 2.25
a. Inverted overprint 30.00
B57 SPAP1 25c (Bl) .40 .40
B58 SPAP1 50c (Bl) .40 .40
a. Double ovpt., one invtd. 72.50
B59 SPAP1 1p (R) 2.50 2.50
a. Inverted overprint 95.00

Same with Additional Surcharges of New Values

B60 SPAP1 75c on 5c (R) 4.50 3.25
a. Inverted surcharge 30.00
B61 SPAP1 75c on 10c (R) 17.00 13.00
a. Inverted surcharge 30.00
B62 SPAP1 75c on 25c (Bl) 32.50 27.50
a. Double surcharge 55.00
B63 SPAP1 75c on 50c (Bl) 15.00 13.00
Nos. B55-B63 (9) 76.45 63.90
Set, never hinged 225.00

Nos. B54-B63 were available for ordinary postage.

Stamps of Spanish Offices in Morocco and Spanish Colonies, 1926 (Spain Types SP3, SP5) Surcharged in Various Colors with New Values and

On Spanish Morocco

B64 SP3 55c on 4p bis (Bl) 21.00 17.50
B65 SP5 80c on 10p vio (Br) 21.00 17.50

On Spanish Tangier

B66 SP5 1p on 10p vio (Br) 110.00 90.00
B67 SP3 4p bis (G) 37.50 32.50

On Cape Juby

B68 SP3 5p on 4p bis (R) 70.00 57.50
B69 SP5 10p on 10p vio (R) 37.50 32.50

On Spanish Guinea

B70 SP5 1p on 10p vio (Bl) 21.00 17.50
B71 SP3 2p on 4p bis (G) 21.00 17.50

On Spanish Sahara

B72 SP5 80c on 10p vio (R) 32.50 27.50
B73 SP3 2p on 4p bis (R) 21.00 17.50
Nos. B64-B73 (10) 392.50 327.50
Set, never hinged 800.00

Nos. B64-B73 were available for postage in Spain only.

Nos. B19-B73 were for the 25th year of the reign of King Alfonso XIII.

Counterfeits of Nos. B64-B73 abound.

Catacombs Restoration Issues

Pope Pius XI and King Alfonso XIII SP7

1928, Dec. 23 Engr. *Perf. 12½*

Santiago Issue

B74 SP7 2c violet & blk .25 .25
B75 SP7 2c lake & blk .30 .30
B76 SP7 3c bl blk & vio .25 .25
B77 SP7 3c dl bl & vio .30 .30
B78 SP7 5c ol grn & vio .65 .65
B79 SP7 10c yel grn & blk 1.10 1.10
B80 SP7 15c bl grn & vio 3.75 3.75
B81 SP7 25c dp rose & vio 3.75 3.75
B82 SP7 40c ultra & blk .25 .25
B83 SP7 55c ol brn & vio .25 .25
B84 SP7 80c red & blk .25 .25
B85 SP7 1p gray blk & vio .25 .25
B86 SP7 2p red brn & blk 5.25 5.25
B87 SP7 3p pale rose & vio 5.25 5.25
B88 SP7 4p vio brn & blk 5.25 5.25
B89 SP7 5p grnsh blk & vio 5.25 5.25

Toledo Issue

B90 SP7 2c bl blk & car .25 .25
B91 SP7 2c ultra & car .30 .30
B92 SP7 3c bis brn & ultra .25 .25
B93 SP7 3c ol grn & ultra .30 .30
B94 SP7 5c red vio & car .65 .65
B95 SP7 10c yel grn & ultra 1.10 1.10
B96 SP7 15c slate bl & car 3.75 3.75
B97 SP7 25c red brn & ultra 3.75 3.75
B98 SP7 40c ultra & car .25 .25
B99 SP7 55c dk brn & ultra .25 .25
B100 SP7 80c black & car .25 .25
B101 SP7 1p yellow & car .25 .25
B102 SP7 2p dk gray & ultra 5.25 5.25
B103 SP7 3p violet & car 5.25 5.25
B104 SP7 4p vio brn & car 5.25 5.25
B105 SP7 5p bister & ultra 5.25 5.25
Nos. B74-B105 (32) 64.70 64.70
Set, never hinged 105.00

Nos. B74-B105 replaced regular stamps from Dec. 23, 1928 to Jan. 6, 1929. The proceeds from their sale were given to a fund to restore the catacombs of Saint Damasus and Saint Praetextatus at Rome.

Nos. B74-B105 exist imperf. Value set, $325 hinged, $375 never hinged.

Issues of the Republic

SP13

1938, Apr. 15 *Perf. 11½*

B106 SP13 45c + 2p bl & grnsh bl .75 .65
a. Imperf., pair 15.00 12.50
b. Souv. sheet of 1 22.50 22.50
c. Souv. sheet of 1, imperf. 625.00 575.00
Never hinged 775.00

Surtax for the defenders of Madrid.

For overprint and surcharge see Nos. B108, CB6.

Nurse and Orderly Carrying Wounded Soldier — SP14

1938, June 1 Engr. *Perf. 10*

B107 SP14 45c + 5p cop red .55 .55
a. Imperf., pair 220.00

For surcharge see No. CB7.

No. B106 Overprinted in Black

1938, Nov. 7 *Perf. 11½*

B108 SP13 45c + 2p 3.25 3.25
Never hinged 5.00

Defense of Madrid, 2nd anniversary.

A similar but larger overprint was applied to cover blocks of four. Value, $15 hinged, $30 never hinged.

Values for souvenir sheets of 1937-38 are for copies with some faults. Undamaged sheets are very hard to find.

Spanish State

Souvenir Sheets

Alcazar, Toledo SP15

Design: No. B108C, A patio of Alcazar after Civil War fighting.

1937 Unwmk. Photo. *Perf. 11½*

Control Numbers on Back

B108A SP15 2p org brn 19.00 19.00
b. Imperf. 450.00 400.00
B108C SP15 2p dark green 19.00 19.00
d. Imperf. 450.00 400.00
Never hinged 95.00

Set, never hinged 95.00
Set, B108Ab, B108Cd, never hinged 1,100.

Nos. B108A-B108C sold for 4p each.

SP16

Designs: 20c, Covadongas Cathedral. 30c, Palma Cathedral, Majorca. 50c, Alcazar of Segovia. 1p, Leon Cathedral.

1938 Unwmk. Photo. *Perf. 12½*

Control Numbers on Back

B108E SP16 Sheet of 4 42.50 42.50
f. 20c dull violet 5.00 5.00
g. 30c rose red 5.00 5.00
h. 50c bright blue 5.00 5.00
i. 1p greenish gray 5.00 5.00
j. Imperf. sheet 72.50 65.00
Never hinged 115.00

Each sheet sold for 4p.

SP17

Designs, alternating in sheet: Flag bearer. Battleship "Admiral Cervera." Soldiers in trenches. Moorish guard.

1938, July 1 Unwmk. *Perf. 13*

Control Numbers on Back

B108K SP17 Sheet of 20 35.00 35.00
Never hinged 45.00
l. Imperf. sheet 160.00 160.00
Never hinged 210.00

Sheet measures 175x132mm. Consists of five vertical rows of four 2c violet, 3c deep blue, 5c olive gray, 10c deep green and 30c red orange, with each denomination appearing in two different designs. Marginal inscription: "Homenaje al Ejercito y a la Marina" (Honoring the Army and Navy). Sold for 4p, or double face value.

Souvenir Sheets

Don Juan of Austria — SP18

Battle of Lepanto SP19

Perf. 12½

1938, Dec. 15 Unwmk. Engr.

Control Numbers on Back

B108M SP18 30c dk car 22.50 22.50
B108N SP19 50c blue black 22.50 22.50
Nos. B108M-B108N (2) 45.00 45.00
Set, never hinged 77.50

Imperf

B108O SP18 30c black vio 550.00 550.00
B108P SP19 50c dk sl grn 550.00 550.00
Nos. B108O-B108P (2) 1,100. 1,100.
Set, never hinged 1,300.

Victory over the Turks in the Battle of Lepanto, 1571.

Nos. B108M-B108P contain one stamp. The dates "1571-1938" appear in the lower sheet margin. Size: 89x74mm. Sold for 10p a pair.

LOCAL CHARITY STAMPS

Hundreds of different charity stamps were issued by local organizations and cities during the Civil War, 1936-39. Some had limited franking value, but most were simply charity labels. They are of three kinds: 1. Local semipostals. 2. Obligatory surtax stamps. 3. Propaganda or charity labels.

Ruins of Belchite SP20

Miracle of Calanda — SP21

Designs: 10c+5c, 70c+20c, Ruins of Belchite. 15c+10c, 80c+20c, The Rosary. 20c+10c, 1.50p+50c, El Pilar Cathedral. 25c+10c, 1p+30c, Mother Raffols praying. 40c+10c, 2.50p+50c, The Little Chamber. 45c+15c, 1.40p+40c, Oath of the Besieged. 10p+4p, The Apparition.

Perf. 10½, 11½x10½, 11½

1940, Jan. 29 Litho. Unwmk.

Design SP20

B109	10c + 5c dp bl & vio brn	.20	.20
B110	15c + 10c rose vio & dk grn	.25	.25
B111	20c + 10c vio & dp bl	.25	.25
B112	25c + 10c dp rose & vio brn	.25	.25
B113	40c + 10c sl grn & rose vio	.20	.20
B114	45c + 15c vio & dp rose	.30	.30
B115	70c + 20c multi	.30	.30
B116	80c + 20c dp rose & vio	.40	.40
B117	1p + 30c dk sl grn & pur	.40	.40
B118	1.40p + 40c pur & gray blk	32.50	32.50
B119	1.50p + 50c lt bl & brn vio	.50	.50
B120	2.50p + 50c choc & bl	.50	.50

Design SP21

B121	4p + 1p rose lil & sl grn	11.00	11.00
B122	10p + 4p ultra & chnt	160.00	160.00
	Nos. B109-B122,CB8-CB17,EB2 (25)	444.60	444.50
	Set, never hinged	850.00	

19th centenary of the Virgin of the Pillar.

The surtax was used to help restore the Cathedral at Zaragoza, damaged during the Civil War.

No. B121 exists in violet & slate green, No. B122 in ultramarine & brown violet. Value, $42.50 each.

Nos. B109-B122 exist imperf. Value, $750.

See No. 743, CB8-CB17.

General Franco — SP23

Knight and Lorraine Cross — SP24

1940, Dec. 23 Unwmk. *Perf. 10*

B123	SP23 20c + 5c dk grn & red	.65	.65
B124	SP23 40c + 10c dk bl & red	.90	.40
	Set, never hinged	3.25	

The surtax was for the tuberculosis fund. See Nos. RA15, RAC1.

AIR POST STAMPS

Regular Issue of 1909-10 Overprinted in Red or Black

Perf. 13x12½, 14

1920, Apr. 4 Unwmk.

C1	A46 5c green (R)	1.25	.80
a.	Imperf., pair	105.00	105.00
b.	Double overprint	35.00	35.00
c.	Inverted overprint	90.00	90.00
d.	Double ovpt., one invtd.	35.00	35.00
e.	Triple overprint	35.00	35.00
C2	A46 10c car (Bk)	1.50	1.00
a.	Imperf., pair	105.00	105.00
b.	Double overprint	35.00	35.00
d.	Double ovpt., one invtd.	35.00	35.00
C3	A46 25c dp blue (R)	2.75	1.40
a.	Inverted overprint	90.00	90.00
b.	Double overprint	35.00	35.00
C4	A46 50c sl blue (R)	11.00	5.00
a.	Imperf., pair	105.00	105.00
C5	A46 1p lake (Bk)	35.00	19.00
a.	Imperf., pair	385.00	385.00
	Nos. C1-C5 (5)	51.50	27.20
	Set, never hinged	110.00	

Dangerous counterfeits are plentiful.

A 30c green was authorized, but not issued. Value: hinged $550; never hinged $750.

For overprints see Nos. C58-C61.

"Spirit of St. Louis" over Coast of Europe - AP1

Plane and Congress Seal — AP2

Seville-Barcelona Exposition Issue

Control Numbers on Back

1929, Feb. 15 Engr. *Perf. 11*

C6	AP1 5c brown	5.00	5.00
C7	AP1 10c rose	5.00	5.00
C8	AP1 25c dark blue	5.50	5.50
C9	AP1 50c purple	5.75	5.75
C10	AP1 1p green	30.00	25.00
C11	AP1 4p black	21.00	20.00
	Nos. C6-C11 (6)	72.25	66.25
	Set, never hinged	175.00	

Nos. C6 to C11 exist imperforate. Value set, $575.

The so-called errors of color of Nos. C10, C18-C21, C23-C24, C28-C31, C37, C40, C42, C44, C46, C48, C50, C52, C55, C62-C67 are believed to have been irregularly produced.

Railway Congress Issue

Control Numbers on Back

1930, May 10 Litho. *Perf. 14*

C12	AP2 5c bister brn	5.25	5.25
	Never hinged	8.25	
C13	AP2 10c rose	5.25	5.25
	Never hinged	8.25	
C14	AP2 25c dark blue	5.25	5.25
	Never hinged	8.25	
C15	AP2 50c purple	13.50	13.50
	Never hinged	26.00	
a.	Vert. pair, imperf. between	300.00	
	Never hinged	*600.00*	
C16	AP2 1p yellow green	27.50	27.50
	Never hinged	52.50	
C17	AP2 4p black	27.50	27.50
	Never hinged	52.50	
	Nos. C12-C17 (6)	84.25	84.25
	Set, never hinged	175.00	

The note after No. 385 will apply here also. Dangerous counterfeits exist.

Goya Issue

Fantasy of Flight AP3

Asmodeus and Cleofas — AP4

Fantasy of Flight AP5

Fantasy of Flight — AP6

1930, June 15 Engr. *Perf. 12½*

C18	AP3 5c brn red & yel	.20	.20
	Never hinged	.20	
C19	AP3 15c blk & red org	.20	.20
	Never hinged	.20	
C20	AP3 25c brn car & dp red	.20	.20
	Never hinged	.20	
C21	AP4 5c ol grn & grnsh bl	.20	.20
	Never hinged	.20	
C22	AP4 10c sl grn & yel grn	.20	.20
	Never hinged	.20	
C23	AP4 20c ultra & rose red	.20	.20
	Never hinged	.20	
C24	AP4 40c vio bl & lt bl	.30	.30
	Never hinged	.35	
C25	AP5 30c brown & vio	.30	.30
	Never hinged	.35	
C26	AP5 50c ver & grn	.30	.30
	Never hinged	.35	
C27	AP5 4p brn car & blk	2.10	2.10
	Never hinged	2.65	
C28	AP6 1p vio brn & vio	.30	.30
	Never hinged	.35	
C29	AP6 4p bl blk & sl grn	2.10	2.10
	Never hinged	2.50	
C30	AP6 10p blk brn & bis brn	7.75	7.75
	Never hinged	10.00	
	Nos. C18-C30,CE1 (14)	14.55	14.55
	Set, never hinged	23.50	

Nos. C18-C30 exist imperf. Value for set, $150.

Christopher Columbus Issue

La Rábida Monastery — AP7

Martín Alonso Pinzón — AP8

Vicente Yanez Pinzón — AP9

Columbus in His Cabin — AP10

1930, Sept. 29 Litho.

C31	AP7 5c lt red brn	.25	.20
	Never hinged	.30	
C32	AP7 5c olive bister	.25	.20
	Never hinged	.30	
C33	AP7 10c blue green	.25	.20
	Never hinged	.45	
C34	AP7 15c dark violet	.25	.20
	Never hinged	.45	
C35	AP7 20c ultra	.25	.20
	Never hinged	.45	

Engr.

C36	AP8 25c carmine rose	.25	.20
	Never hinged	.45	
C37	AP9 30c dp red brn	1.75	1.75
	Never hinged	2.50	
C38	AP8 40c indigo	1.75	1.75
	Never hinged	2.50	
C39	AP9 50c orange	1.75	1.75
	Never hinged	2.50	
C40	AP8 1p dull violet	1.75	1.75
	Never hinged	2.50	
C41	AP10 4p olive green	1.75	1.75
	Never hinged	2.50	
C42	AP10 10p light brown	10.00	11.00
	Never hinged	15.00	
	Nos. C31-C42 (12)	20.25	20.95
	Set, never hinged	30.00	

Nos. C31-C42 exist imperf. Value for set, $190.

Spanish-American Issue

AP11

Columbus AP12

Columbus and Pinzón Brothers AP13

1930, Sept. 29 Litho.

C43	AP11 5c lt red	.20	.20
	Never hinged	.25	
C44	AP11 10c dull green	.20	.20
	Never hinged	.25	

Engr.

C45	AP12 25c scarlet	.20	.20
	Never hinged	.25	
C46	AP12 50c slate gray	2.25	1.90
	Never hinged	3.75	
C47	AP12 1p fawn	2.25	1.90
	Never hinged	3.75	
C48	AP13 4p slate blue	2.25	1.90
	Never hinged	3.75	
C49	AP13 10p brown violet	10.00	9.25
	Never hinged	16.00	
	Nos. C43-C49 (7)	17.35	15.55
	Set, never hinged	27.50	

Nos. C43-C49 exist imperf. Value for set, $160.

Spanish-American Exhibition Issue

Santos-Dumont and First Flight of His Airplane — AP14

Teodoro Fels and His Airplane AP15

Dagoberto Godoy and Pass over Andes — AP16

Sacadura Cabral and Gago Coutinho and Their Airplane AP17

Sidar of Mexico and Map of South America — AP18

Ignacio Jiménez and Francisco Iglesias — AP19

Charles A. Lindbergh, Statue of Liberty, Spirit of St. Louis and Cat AP20

Santa Maria, Plane and Torre del Oro, Seville AP21

1930, Oct. 10 Photo. *Perf. 14*

C50 AP14 5c gray black .80 .50
Never hinged 3.50
C51 AP15 10c dk olive grn .80 .50
Never hinged 3.50
C52 AP16 25c ultra .80 .50
Never hinged 3.50
C53 AP17 50c blue gray 1.75 1.25
Never hinged 5.50
C54 AP18 50c black 1.75 1.25
Never hinged 5.50
C55 AP19 1p car lake 3.75 2.75
Never hinged 8.50
a. 1p brown violet 65.00 65.00
Never hinged 140.00
C56 AP20 1p deep green 3.75 2.75
Never hinged 7.00
C57 AP21 4p slate blue 6.75 5.00
Never hinged 20.00
Nos. C50-C57 (8) 20.15 14.50

Exist imperf. Value, set $110.
Note after No. 432 also applies to Nos. C31-C57.
Reprints of Nos. C50-C57 have blurred impressions, yellowish paper. Value: one-tenth of originals.

Nos. C1-C4 Overprinted in Red or Black

1931 *Perf. 13x12½*

C58 A46 5c green (R) 11.00 10.00
Never hinged 22.50
C59 A46 10c carmine (Bk) 11.00 10.00
Never hinged 22.50
C60 A46 25c deep blue (R) 15.00 14.50
Never hinged 32.50
C61 A46 50c slate blue (R) 30.00 22.50
Never hinged 62.50
Nos. C58-C61 (4) 67.00 57.00

Counterfeits of overprint exist.
The status of Nos. C58-C61 has been questioned.

Plane and Royal Palace, Madrid AP22

Madrid Post Office and Cibeles Fountain AP23

Plane over Calle de Alcalá, Madrid AP24

1931, Oct. 10 Engr. *Perf. 12*

C62 AP22 5c brown violet .20 .30
Never hinged .25
C63 AP22 10c deep green .20 .30
Never hinged .25
C64 AP22 25c dull red .20 .30
Never hinged .25
C65 AP23 50c deep blue .40 .45
Never hinged .75
C66 AP23 1p deep violet .60 .55
Never hinged 1.25
C67 AP24 4p black 7.75 10.00
Never hinged 15.00
Nos. C62-C67 (6) 9.35 11.90

3rd Pan-American Postal Union Congress, Madrid.
Exist imperf. Value, set $45.
For overprints see Nos. CO1-CO6.

Montserrat Issue

Plane over Montserrat Pass — AP25

1931, Dec. 9 *Perf. 11½*

Control Number on Back

C68 AP25 5c black brown .50 .50
Never hinged .75
C69 AP25 10c yellow green 2.25 2.25
Never hinged 3.25
C70 AP25 25c deep rose 9.00 9.00
Never hinged 12.00
C71 AP25 50c orange 32.50 32.50
Never hinged 42.50
C72 AP25 1p gray black 22.50 22.50
Never hinged 27.50
Nos. C68-C72 (5) 66.75 66.75
Set, never hinged 85.00

Perf. 14

C68a AP25 5c 6.75 *13.00*
Never hinged 9.00
C69a AP25 10c 37.50 40.00
Never hinged 45.00
C70a AP25 25c 67.50 67.50
Never hinged 75.00
C71a AP25 50c 67.50 67.50
Never hinged 75.00
C72f AP25 1p 67.50 67.50
Never hinged 75.00
Nos. C68a-C72f (5) 246.75 255.50

900th anniv. of Montserrat Monastery.
Nos. C68-C72 exist imperf. Value set, $525.

Autogiro over Seville — AP26

1935-39 *Perf. 11½*

C72A AP26 2p gray blue 20.00 4.50
Never hinged 37.50
g. Imperf., pair 300.00

Re-engraved

C72B AP26 2p dk blue ('38) .65 .25
Never hinged 2.50
c. Imperf., pair 20.00
d. Perf. 10 ('39) 1.50 1.10
Never hinged 3.00

The sky has heavy horizontal lines of shading. Entire design is more heavily shaded than No. C72A.
No. C72B exists privately perforated 14. Value, $9 unused, $9 used.
For overprints see Nos. 7LC14, 7LC19, 14L26.

Eagle and Newspapers — AP27

Press Building, Madrid — AP28

Don Quixote and Sancho Panza Flying on the Wooden Horse — AP29

Design: 15c, 30c, 50c, 1p, Autogiro over House of Nazareth.

1936, Mar. 11 Photo. *Perf. 12½*

C73 AP27 1c rose car .20 .20
Never hinged .20
C74 AP28 2c dark brown .20 .20
Never hinged .20
C75 AP27 5c black brown .20 .20
Never hinged .20
C76 AP28 10c dk yellow grn .20 .20
Never hinged .20
C77 AP28 15c Prus blue .20 .20
Never hinged .20
C78 AP27 20c violet .20 .20
Never hinged .20
C79 AP28 25c magenta .20 .20
Never hinged .20
C80 AP28 30c red orange .20 .20
Never hinged .20
C81 AP27 40c orange .50 .20
Never hinged .75
C82 AP28 50c light blue .30 .20
Never hinged .50
C83 AP28 60c olive green .65 .40
Never hinged 1.10
C84 AP28 1p brnsh black .65 .45
Never hinged 1.10
C85 AP29 2p brt ultra 5.00 2.25
Never hinged 7.75
C86 AP29 4p lilac rose 5.00 2.75
Never hinged 7.75
C87 AP29 10p violet brown 14.00 11.00
Never hinged 21.00
Nos. C73-C87 (15) 27.70 18.85

Madrid Press Association, 40th anniv.
Exist imperf. Value, set $250 hinged, and $325 never hinged.
See note after No. 432.

Types of Regular Postage of 1936 Overprinted in Blue or Red

1936 *Imperf.*

C88 A125 10c dk red (Bl) 150.00 150.00
Never hinged 225.00
C89 A125 15c dk blue (R) 150.00 150.00
Never hinged 225.00

1st National Philatelic Exhibition which opened in Madrid, Apr. 2, 1936.

No. 577 Overprinted in Black

1936, Aug. 1 *Perf. 11½*

C90 A128 30c rose red 3.00 3.75
Never hinged 6.00
b. Imperf., pair 140.00

Issued in commemoration of the flight of aviators Antonio Arnaiz and Juan Calvo from Manila to Spain.
Counterfeit overprints exist.
Exists privately perforated 14. Value, $50 unused, $50 used.

No. 288 Surcharged in Black

1938, Apr. 13 *Perf. 14*

C91 A36 2.50p on 10c 80.00 72.50
Never hinged 150.00

7th anniversary of the Republic.
Values are for examples with perforations nearly touching the design on one or two sides.

No. 507 Surcharged in Various Colors

1938, Aug. *Perf. 11½*

C92 A92 50c on 25c (Bk) 25.00 25.00
Never hinged 45.00
C93 A92 1p on 25c (G) 1.90 1.90
Never hinged 2.75
C94 A92 1.25p on 25c (R) 1.90 1.90
Never hinged 2.75
C95 A92 1.50p on 25c (Bl) 1.90 1.90
Never hinged 2.75

C96 A92 2p on 25c (Bk & R) 35.00 30.00
Never hinged 47.50
Nos. C92-C96 (5) 65.70 60.70

No. 585 Surcharged

1938, June 1 ***Perf. 11***

C97	A132 5p on 1p multi	250.	250.
	Never hinged	375.	
a.	Imperf., pair	550.	550.
b.	Inverted surcharge	350.	350.
c.	Souvenir sheet	3,000.	3,000.
	Never hinged	6,000.	
d.	As "c," imperf.	6,500.	6,500.
e.	As "c," inverted surcharge	6,000.	6,000.

Counterfeit surcharges exist.

Type of 1938-39 Overprinted in Red or Carmine

1938, May ***Perf. 10, 10½***

C98	A163 50c indigo (R)	.70	.55
	Never hinged	1.00	
C99	A163 1p dk blue (C)	3.00	.70
	Never hinged	3.00	

Exist imperf. Value, each $100.
Copies without overprint are proofs.

Juan de la Cierva and his Autogiro over Madrid AP30

1939, Jan. Unwmk. Litho. ***Perf. 11***

C100	AP30 20c red orange	.60	.40
	Never hinged	.70	
C101	AP30 25c dk carmine	.45	.20
	Never hinged	.55	
C102	AP30 35c brt violet	.65	.40
	Never hinged	.75	
C103	AP30 50c dk brown	.65	.25
	Never hinged	.75	
C105	AP30 1p blue	.65	.25
	Never hinged	.75	
C107	AP30 2p green	3.25	1.75
	Never hinged	5.00	
C108	AP30 4p dull blue	5.00	2.75
	Never hinged	9.00	
	Nos. C100-C108 (7)	11.25	6.00
	Set, never hinged	19.00	

Exist imperf. Value, set $325.

1941-47 ***Perf. 10***

C109	AP30 20c dk red orange	.20	.20
	Never hinged	.30	
C110	AP30 25c redsh brown	.20	.20
	Never hinged	.30	
C111	AP30 35c lilac rose	1.60	.50
	Never hinged	2.25	
C112	AP30 50c brown	.45	.20
	Never hinged	.55	
C113	AP30 1p chalky blue	1.40	.20
	Never hinged	2.00	
C114	AP30 2p lt gray grn	1.60	.20
	Never hinged	2.25	
C115	AP30 4p gray blue	5.00	.30
	Never hinged	8.75	
C116	AP30 10p brt purple ('47)	3.75	.65
	Never hinged	7.50	
	Nos. C109-C116 (8)	14.20	2.45
	Set, never hinged	26.00	

Issued in honor of Juan de la Cierva (1895-1936), inventor of the autogiro.

Nos. C109-C115 exist imperf. Value, set $300.

The overprint "EXPOSICION NACIONAL DE FILATELIA 1948 SAN SEBASTIAN" multiple, in parallel horizontal lines, on Nos. C109 to C113 and other airmail stamps, was privately applied.

AIR POST SEMI-POSTAL STAMPS

Red Cross Issue

Ramon Franco's Plane Plus Ultra SPAP1

Perf. 12½, 13

1926, Sept. 15 Engr. Unwmk.

CB1	SPAP1 5c black & vio	1.40	1.40
CB2	SPAP1 10c ultra & blk	3.00	3.00
CB3	SPAP1 25c carmine & blk	.30	.30
CB4	SPAP1 50c red org & blk	.30	.30
CB5	SPAP1 1p black & green	2.50	2.50
	Nos. CB1-CB5 (5)	7.50	7.50
	Set, never hinged	10.00	

For overprints and surcharges see Nos. B55-B63.

No. B106 Surcharged in Black

1938, Apr. 15 ***Perf. 11½***

CB6	SP13 45c + 2p + 5p	250.	225.
	Never hinged	450.	
a.	Imperf., pair	1,150.	900.
b.	Souvenir sheet of 1	*4,500.*	*4,500.*
c.	Souvenir sheet, imperf.	*6,000.*	*6,000.*
d.	Souv. sheet, surch. invtd.	*6,500.*	*5,750.*

The surtax was used to benefit the defenders of Madrid.

This issue has been extensively counterfeited.

No. B107 Surcharged

1938, June 1 ***Perf. 10***

CB7	SP14 45c + 5p + 3p	10.00	9.75
	Never hinged	17.50	

Monument SPAP2

Dome Fresco by Goya, Cathedral of Zaragoza SPAP3

#CB9, CB14, Caravel Santa Maria. #CB10, CB12, The Ascension. #CB13, The Coronation. #CB17, Bombardment of Cathedral of Zaragoza.

Perf. 10½, 11½x10½, 11½

1940, Jan. 29 Litho. Unwmk.

Bicolored

CB8	SPAP2 25c + 5c	.25	.25
CB9	SPAP2 50c + 5c	.25	.25
CB10	SPAP2 65c + 15c	.25	.25
CB11	SPAP2 70c + 15c	.25	.25
CB12	SPAP2 90c + 20c	.25	.25
CB13	SPAP2 1.20p + 30c	.25	.25
CB14	SPAP2 1.40p + 40c	.50	.50
CB15	SPAP2 2p + 50c	.40	.40
CB16	SPAP3 4p + 1p sl grn & rose lil	9.75	9.75
CB17	SPAP3 10p + 4p chnt & ultra	225.00	225.00
	Nos. CB8-CB17 (10)	237.15	237.15
	Set, never hinged	350.00	

19th centenary of the Pillar Virgin. The surtax was used to help restore the Cathedral at Zaragoza, damaged during the Civil War.

No. CB16 exists in slate green & violet, No. CB17 in red violet & ultramarine. Value, $32.50 each.

Nos. CB8-CB17 exist imperf. Value, set $350.

AIR POST SPECIAL DELIVERY STAMP

Goya Commemorative Issue

Type of Air Post Stamp of 1930 Overprinted

1930 Unwmk. ***Perf. 12½***

CE1	AP4 20c bl blk & lt brn (Bk)	.20	.20
	Never hinged	.25	
a.	Blue overprint	15.00	7.75
	Never hinged	21.00	
b.	Overprint omitted	15.00	22.50
	Never hinged	25.00	

See note after No. 432.

AIR POST OFFICIAL STAMPS

Pan-American Postal Union Congress Issue

Types of Air Post Stamps of 1931 Overprinted in Red or Blue

1931 Unwmk. ***Perf. 12***

CO1	AP22 5c red brown (R)	.20	.20
CO2	AP22 10c blue grn (Bl)	.20	.20
CO3	AP22 25c rose (Bl)	.20	.20
CO4	AP23 50c lt blue (R)	.20	.20
CO5	AP23 1p violet (R)	.20	.20
CO6	AP24 4p gray blk (R)	3.25	3.25
	Nos. CO1-CO6 (6)	4.25	4.25
	Set, never hinged	9.00	

Shades exist.
Exist imperf. Value, set $22.50

SPECIAL DELIVERY STAMPS

Pegasus and Coat of Arms — SD1

1905-25 Unwmk. Typo. ***Perf. 14***

Control Number on Back

E1	SD1 20c deep red	40.00	.30
	Never hinged	75.00	
a.	20c rose red, litho. ('25)	35.00	.30
b.	Imperf., pair	275.00	
c.	As "a," imperf., pair	275.00	

Gazelle SD2

Pegasus — SD3

1929 Engr. ***Perf. 11***

Control Number on Back

E2	SD2 20c dull red	17.50	20.00
	Never hinged	35.00	
a.	Perf. 14	29.00	32.50
	Never hinged	55.00	

Seville and Barcelona Exhibitions. See note after No. 432.

1929-32 ***Perf. 13½x12½, 11½***

Control Number on Back

E3	SD3 20c red	19.00	3.75
	Never hinged	37.50	
a.	Imperf., pair	375.00	
b.	Without control number, perf. 11½ ('32)	55.00	1.40
	Never hinged	87.50	
c.	As "b," imperf., pair	*875.00*	

No. E3 Overprinted like Nos. 358-370

E4	SD3 20c red (Bl)	12.00	25.00
	Never hinged	25.00	

League of Nations 55th assembly.
For overprints see Nos. E5, E10-E12.

No. E3 Overprinted in Blue

1930 ***Perf. 13½x12½, 11½***

E5	SD3 20c red	12.00	.65
	Never hinged	32.50	

Railway Congress Issue

Electric Locomotive — SD4

1930, May 10 Litho. ***Perf. 14***

Control Number on Back

E6	SD4 20c brown orange	50.00	50.00
	Never hinged	95.00	

See note after No. 385.

Goya Issue

Type of Regular Issue of 1930 Overprinted

1930 ***Perf. 12½***

E7	A57 20c lilac rose	.20	.30
	Never hinged	.40	

Christopher Columbus Issue

Type of Regular Issue of 1930 Overprinted

1930 Sept. 29

E8 A64 20c brown violet 1.75 1.75
Never hinged 2.75

See note after No. 432.

Spanish-American Exhibition Issue

View of Seville Exhibition — SD5

1930, Oct. 10 Photo. *Perf. 14*

E9 SD5 20c orange .40 .25
Never hinged .65

See note after No. 432.

Madrid Issue

No. E5 Overprinted in Green

1931 *Perf. 11½*

E10 SD3 20c red 4.50 4.50
Never hinged 7.25

The status of No. E10 has been questioned.

Barcelona Issue

No. E3 Overprinted

E11 SD3 20c red 5.00 5.00
Never hinged 11.00

No. E11 also exists with accent over "U."
The status of No. E11 has been questioned.

No. E3 Overprinted in Blue

E12 SD3 20c red 5.50 1.00
Never hinged 19.00

Montserrat Issue

Pegasus — SD6

1931 Engr. *Perf. 11*
Control Number on Back

E13 SD6 20c vermilion 22.50 22.50
Never hinged 35.00
a. Perf. 14 55.00 60.00

SD7

1934 *Perf. 10*

E14 SD7 20c vermilion .20 .20
Never hinged .20
a. Imperf., pair 32.50

For overprints see #10LE1, 11LE1-11LE4, 14LE1.

Newsboy — SD8

Pegasus SD9

1936 Photo. *Perf. 12½*

E15 SD8 20c rose carmine .25 .30
Never hinged .50

40th anniversary of the Madrid Press Association.
See note after No. 432.

Spanish State

1937-38 Unwmk. Litho. *Perf. 11*
With imprint "Hija. deB Fournier-Burgos"

E16 SD9 20c violet brn 7.75 4.50
Never hinged 11.00
a. Imperf., pair 77.50

Without Imprint

E17 SD9 20c dk vio brn ('38) 1.50 .30
Never hinged 2.75
a. Imperf., pair 50.00

No. 645 Overprinted in Black

1937

E18 A162 20c dark violet 11.00 11.00
Never hinged 14.50

Pegasus SD10

1939-42 *Perf. 10½*
Imprint: "SANCHEZ TODA"

E19 SD10 25c carmine 4.50 .70
Never hinged 6.25
a. Imperf., pair 50.00

Without Imprint
Perf. 10

E20 SD10 25c carmine ('42) .20 .20
Never hinged .30
a. Imperf., pair 8.50

SEMI-POSTAL SPECIAL DELIVERY STAMPS

Red Cross Issue

Royal Family Group SPSD1

1926 Unwmk. Engr. *Perf. 12½, 13*

EB1 SPSD1 20c red vio & vio brn 8.75 8.75
Never hinged 17.00

See notes after Nos. 432 and B18.
For overprint see No. B54.

Motorcyclist and Zaragoza Cathedral SPSD2

1940 Litho. *Perf. 11½*

EB2 SPSD2 25c + 5c rose red & buff .40 .30

19th cent. of the Pillar Virgin. The surtax was used to help restore the Cathedral at Zaragoza, damaged during the Civil War.

DELIVERY TAX STAMPS

D1

1931 Unwmk. Litho. *Perf. 11½*

ER1 D1 5c black 7.25 .20
Never hinged 12.00

For overprints see Nos. ER2-ER3, 7LE5-7LE6.

No. ER1 Overprinted in Red

1931

ER2 D1 5c black 1.25 1.40
Never hinged 2.25

No. ER2 also exists with accent over "U."

No. ER1 Overprinted in Red

ER3 D1 5c black 3.00 3.00
Never hinged 5.50

These stamps were originally issued for Postage Due purpose but were later used as regular postage stamps.

WAR TAX STAMPS

These stamps did not pay postage but represented a fiscal tax on mail matter in addition to the postal fees. Their use was obligatory.

Coat of Arms
WT1 WT2

Unwmk.

1874, Jan. 1 Typo. *Perf. 14*

MR1 WT1 5c black 9.50 .95
On cover 6.50
a. Imperf. pair 14.00
MR2 WT1 10c pale blue 10.50 1.60
On cover 9.00
a. Imperf., pair 62.50

1875, Jan. 1

MR3 WT2 5c green 5.25 .60
On cover 4.00
a. Imperf., pair 27.50
MR4 WT2 10c lilac 11.00 2.75
On cover 10.00
a. Imperf., pair 55.00

King Alfonso XII
WT3 WT4

1876, June 1

MR5 WT3 5c pale green 6.25 1.00
On cover 5.50
MR6 WT3 10c blue 6.25 1.00
On cover 5.50
a. Cliche of 5c in plate of 10c 125.00
MR7 WT3 25c black 50.00 17.00
MR8 WT3 1p lilac 475.00 110.00
MR9 WT3 5p rose 775.00 300.00

Nos. MR5-MR9 exist imperforate. Value, $1,100.

1877, Sept. 1

MR10 WT4 15c claret 27.50 1.00
On cover 5.00
a. Imperf., pair 100.00
MR11 WT4 50c yellow 775.00 110.00

WT5 WT6

1879

MR12 WT5 5c blue 42.00
MR13 WT5 10c rose 25.00
MR14 WT5 15c violet 15.50
MR15 WT5 25c brown 25.00
MR16 WT5 50c olive green 15.50
MR17 WT5 1p bister 25.00
MR18 WT5 5p gray 90.00
Nos. MR12-MR18 (7) 238.00

Nos. MR12-MR18 were never placed in use.
Mr17 and MR18 exist imperforate. Value, $225.

Inscribed "1897 A 1898"

1897 *Perf. 14*

MR19 WT6 5c green 3.00 1.90
On cover 3.25
MR20 WT6 10c green 3.00 1.90
On cover 3.25
MR21 WT6 15c green 450.00 190.00
MR22 WT6 20c green 7.50 3.00
On cover 7.00

Nos. MR19-MR22 exist imperf. Value for set $825.

Inscribed "1898-99"

1898

MR23 WT6 5c black 2.25 1.75
On cover 3.75
MR24 WT6 10c black 2.25 1.75
On cover 3.75
MR25 WT6 15c black 50.00 9.50
MR26 WT6 20c black 3.50 3.00
Nos. MR23-MR26 (4) 58.00 16.00

Nos. MR23-MR26 exist imperf. Value about $275 a pair.

King Alfonso XIII — WT7

1898

MR27	WT7	5c black	7.50	.60
		On cover		3.00
a.		Imperf., pair	85.00	

OFFICIAL STAMPS

Coat of Arms
O1 O2

Unwmk.

1854, July 1 Typo. *Imperf.*

O1	O1	½o blk, *yellow*	2.10	2.75
		On cover		20.00
O2	O1	1o blk, *rose*	2.75	3.25
		On cover		22.50
a.		1o black, *blue*	29.00	
O3	O1	4o blk, *green*	7.50	9.25
		On cover		35.00
O4	O1	1 l blk, *blue*	52.50	60.00
		On cover		300.00
		Nos. O1-O4 (4)	64.85	75.25
		Set, never hinged	100.00	

1855-63

O5	O2	½o blk, *yellow*	1.50	1.75
		On cover		10.50
a.		½o black, *straw* ('63)	1.75	1.90
		On cover		12.00
O6	O2	1o blk, *rose*	1.50	1.75
		On cover		10.50
a.		1o black, *salmon rose*	3.25	1.90
		On cover		12.00
O7	O2	4o blk, *green*	3.25	1.90
		On cover		17.50
a.		4o black, *yellow green*	8.75	1.90
		On cover		17.50
O8	O2	1 l blk, *gray blue*	14.50	17.50
		On cover		70.00
		Nos. O5-O8 (4)	20.75	22.90
		Set, never hinged	25.00	

Full margins of Nos. O1-O8 = ¾mm.

The "value indication" on Nos. O1-O8 actually is the weight of the mail in onzas (ounces, "o") and libras (pounds, "l") for which they were valid.

Type of Regular Issue of 1889

1895 *Perf. 14*

O9	A34	15c yellow	10.00	6.00
		Never hinged	15.00	
		On cover		17.50
a.		Imperf., pair	250.00	

Coat of Arms — O5

1896-98

O10	O5	rose	5.25	1.75
		On cover		20.00
a.		Imperf., pair	87.50	
O11	O5	dk blue ('98)	17.50	6.00
		On cover		32.50

Cervantes Issue

Chamber of Deputies O6

Statue of Cervantes — O7

Cervantes — O9

National Library O8

1916, Apr. 22 Engr. *Perf. 12*

For the Senate

O12	O6	green & blk	1.10	.90
O13	O7	brown & blk	1.10	.90
O14	O8	carmine & blk	1.10	.90
O15	O9	brown & blk	1.10	.90

For the Chamber of Deputies

O16	O6	violet & blk	1.10	.90
O17	O7	carmine & blk	1.10	.90
O18	O8	green & blk	1.10	.90
O19	O9	violet & blk	1.10	.90
		Nos. O12-O19 (8)	8.80	7.20

Exist imperf. Value set of pairs, $110.

Exist with centers inverted. Value for set, $87.50

Pan-American Postal Union Congress Issue

Types of Regular Issue of 1931 Overprinted in Red or Blue

1931 *Perf. 12½*

O20	A84	5c dk brown (R)	.40	.20
O21	A85	10c brt green (Bl)	.40	.20
O22	A86	15c dull violet (R)	.40	.20
O23	A85	25c deep rose (Bl)	.40	.20
O24	A87	30c olive green (Bl)	.40	.20
O25	A84	40c ultra (R)	.55	.50
O26	A85	50c deep orange (Bl)	.55	.50
O27	A86	1p blue black (R)	.55	.50
O28	A88	4p magenta (Bl)	12.50	12.50
O29	A88	10p lt brown (R)	22.50	22.50
		Nos. O20-O29 (10)	38.65	37.50
		Set, never hinged	55.00	

Nos. O22-O29 exist imperf. Values about 3 times those quoted.

POSTAL TAX STAMPS

PT5

PT6

Perf. 10½x11½

1937, Dec. 23 Litho.

RA11	PT5	10c blk, pale bl & red	7.25	4.50
		Never hinged	19.00	
a.		Imperf. pair	72.50	
		Never hinged	110.00	

The tax was for the tuberculosis fund.

1938, Dec. 23 *Perf. 11½*

RA12	PT6	10c multicolored	4.50	1.75
		Never hinged	10.00	
a.		Imperf. pair	45.00	
		Never hinged	55.00	

The tax was for the tuberculosis fund.

"Spain" Holding Wreath of Peace over Marching Soldiers PT7

1939, July 18 *Perf. 11*

RA13	PT7	10c blue	.20	.20
		Never hinged	.25	
a.		Imperf. pair	65.00	
		Never hinged	82.50	

Type of Regular Issue, 1939 Without Imprint

Unwmk.

1939, Dec. 23 Litho. *Imperf.*

RA14	A166	10c dull claret	.20	.20
		Never hinged	.25	

Tuberculosis Fund Issue

Types of Corresponding Semi-Postal Stamps

1940, Dec. 23 *Perf. 10*

RA15	SP23	10c violet & red	.20	.20
		Never hinged	.25	

POSTAL TAX AIR POST STAMPS

Tuberculosis Fund Issues

Franco Type of Semi-Postal Stamps

Unwmk.

1940, Dec. 23 Litho. *Perf. 10*

RAC1	SP23	10c bright pink & red	.90	.90
		Never hinged	2.50	

FRANCHISE STAMPS

F1

F2

1869 Unwmk. Litho. *Imperf.*

S1	F1	blue	47.50	35.00
a.		Tête bêche pair	125.00	110.00

The franchise of No. S1 was granted to Diego Castell to use in distributing his publications on Spanish postal history.

1881

S2	F2	black, *buff*	32.50	14.00

The franchise of No. S2 was granted to Antonio Fernandez Duro for his book, "Resena histórico-descriptiva de los sellos correos de Espana."

Reprints of No. S2 have been made on carmine, blue, gray, fawn and yellow paper.

CARLIST STAMPS

From the beginning of the Civil War (April 21, 1872) until separate stamps were issued on July 1, 1873, stamps of France were used on all mail from the provinces under Carlist rule.

King Carlos VII — A1

Tilde on N — A1a

Unwmk.

1873, July 1 Litho. *Imperf.*

X1	A1	1r blue	550.00	
X2	A1a	1r blue	450.00	300.00

These stamps were reprinted three times in 1881 and once in 1887. The originals have 23 white lines and dots in the lower right spandrel. They are thin and of even width and spacing. The first reprint has 17 to 20 lines in the spandrel, most of them thick and of irregular width and length. The second and third reprints have 21 very thin lines, the second from the bottom being almost invisible. In the fourth reprint the lower right spandrel is an almost solid spot of color.

Originals of type A1 have the curved line above "ESPANA" broken at the left of the "E." All reprints of this type have the curved line continuous.

The reprints exist in various shades of blue, rose, red, violet and black.

King Carlos VII
A2 A3

A4

A5

1874

X3	A2	1r violet	240.00	240.00
X4	A3	16m rose	4.75	*72.50*
X5	A4	½r rose	100.00	100.00

Nos. X3 and X6-X7 were for use in the Basque Provinces and Navarra; No. X4 in Catalonia, and No. X5 in Valencia.

Two types of No. X5, alternating in each sheet.

No. X4 with favor cancellation (lozenge of dots) sells for same price as unused.

1875

White Paper

X6	A5	50c green	8.00	*82.50*
a.		50c blue green	25.00	*100.00*
b.		Bluish paper	50.00	
X7	A5	1r brown	8.00	*82.50*
a.		Bluish paper	50.00	
		Set, #X6-X7, never hinged	24.00	

Fake cancellations exist on Nos. X1-X7.

REVOLUTIONARY OVERPRINTS

Issued by the Nationalist (Revolutionary) Forces

Many districts or cities made use of the stamps of the Republic overprinted in various forms. Most such overprinting was authorized by military or postal officials but some were without official sanction. These overprints were applied in patriotic celebration and partly as a protection from the use of unoverprinted stamps seized or stolen by soldiers.

BURGOS AIR POST STAMPS

RAP1

Revenue Stamps Overprinted in Red, Blue or Black

1936, Dec. 1 Unwmk. *Perf. 11½*

Control Number on Face of Stamp

7LC1 RAP1 25c gray grn & blk (R) 42.50 42.50
a. Blue overprint 42.50 42.50
7LC2 RAP1 1.50p bl & blk (R) 5.50 5.50
7LC3 RAP1 3p rose & blk (Bl) 5.50 5.50
Nos. 7LC1-7LC3 (3) 53.50 53.50
Set, never hinged 95.00

RAP2

RAP4

Perf. 13½

Blue Control Number on Back

7LC4 RAP2 15c green (R) 3.75 3.75
7LC5 RAP2 25c blue (R) 27.50 27.50
Set, never hinged 45.00

Perf. 11½

Without Control Number

Overprint in Black

7LC6 RAP4 1.50p dk blue 6.50 6.50
7LC7 RAP4 3p carmine 6.50 6.50
Set, never hinged 21.00

RAP5

RAP6

Overprint in Black

Perf. 13½, 11½

7LC8 RAP5 1.20p green 25.00 25.00
Never hinged 37.50

Perf. 14

Control Number on Back

7LC9 RAP6 1.20p green 25.00 25.00
7LC10 RAP6 2.40p green 25.00 25.00
Set #7LC9-7LC10, never hinged 70.00

No. 7LC9 is inscribed "CLASE 8a."

RAP7

1937 Unwmk. *Perf. 11½*

Control Number on Back

7LC11 RAP7 25c ultra (R) 225.00 225.00

Stamps of Spain, 1931-36, Overprinted in Red or Black (10p)

Perf. 11, 11½, 11x11½

1937 Unwmk.

Overprint 13mm high

7LC12 A100 40c blue 1.10 1.10
a. Ovpt. 15mm high 1.10 1.10
7LC13 A97 50c dark blue 1.40 1.40
a. Ovpt. 15mm high 1.40 1.40
7LC14 A130 50c dark blue 1.75 1.75
a. Ovpt. 15mm high 1.75 1.75
7LC15 A100 60c apple green 2.50 2.50
a. Ovpt. 15mm high 2.50 2.50
7LC16 AP26 2p gray blue 32.50 32.50
a. Ovpt. 15mm high 32.50 32.50
7LC17 A49a 10p brown 82.50 82.50
a. Ovpt. 15mm high 82.50 82.50
Nos. 7LC12-7LC17 (6) 121.75 121.75

Issue dates: Nos. 7LC12-7LC17, 4/1. Nos. 7LC12a-7LC17a, 5/1.

Spain Nos. 576, 578 and 541b overprinted in Blue or Black

Nos. 7LC18, 7LC19

Nos. 7LC20, 7LC21

Perfs as on Basic Stamps

1937, May

7LC18 A127 30c carmine (Bk) 1.40 1.40
7LC19 A127 30c carmine (Bl) .70 .70
7LC20 A129 30c car rose (Bk) 1.40 1.40
7LC21 A129 30c car rose (Bl) .70 .70
7LC22 A107 10p dp brn (Bk) 11.00 11.00
Nos. 7LC18-7LC22 (5) 15.20 15.20

Spain Nos. 539b and 540b, the 1p and 4p values, were prepared with this overprint in January, 1938, but were not issued. Value, each $4.50.

BURGOS ISSUE SPECIAL DELIVERY STAMPS

Pair of Spain No. 546 Overprinted in Black

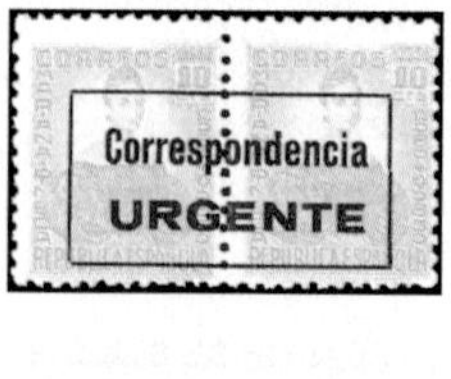

1936 Unwmk. *Perf. 11½x11*

7LE3 A110 20c (10c+10c) emer 4.50 4.50
Never hinged 9.00
a. Overprint inverted 14.00

Type of Regular Stamp of 1931 Overprinted in Red

7LE4 A95 20c dark violet 10.00 10.00

Type of Delivery Tax Stamp of 1931 Overprinted in Red on four 5c stamps

Perf. 11½

7LE5 D1 20c black 8.75 8.00
Never hinged 13.50

Same Overprinted in Red on four 5c stamps

7LE6 D1 20c black 30.00 25.00
Never hinged 50.00

SD1

1936 Unwmk. *Perf. 11½*

7LE7 SD1 20c green & blk 7.25 5.50
7LE8 SD1 20c green & red 7.25 5.50
Set, never hinged 25.00

Nos. 7LE7-7LE8 exist with control number on back. Value $42.50 each.

CADIZ ISSUE SEMI-POSTAL STAMPS

Stamps of Spain, 1931-36, Surcharged in Black or Red

1936 Unwmk. *Imperf.*

8LB1 A108 1c + 5c blue grn .20 .20

Perf. 11½x11, 11½

8LB2 A108 2c + 5c orange brn .20 .20
8LB3 A103 5c + 5c choc (R) .45 .45
8LB4 A110 10c + 5c green .45 .45
8LB5 A111 15c + 5c Prus grn (R) 2.75 2.75
8LB6 A95 20c + 5c dk vio (R) 3.25 3.25
8LB7 A104 25c + 5c lake 2.50 2.50
8LB8 A113 30c + 5c rose red 1.40 1.40
8LB9 A100 40c + 5c dk blue (R) 3.25 3.25
8LB10 A97 50c + 5c dk blue (R) 6.50 6.50
Nos. 8LB1-8LB10 (10) 20.95 20.95

CANARY ISLANDS AIR POST STAMPS

Issued for Use via the Lufthansa Service

Stamps of Spain, 1932-34, Surcharged in Blue

VIVA ESPAÑA
18 JULIO 1936
HABILITADO
AVIÓN
Pts. 0'50

1936, Oct. 27 Unwmk. *Imperf.*

9LC1 A108 50c on 1c bl grn 27.50 17.50

Perf. 11½x11

9LC2 A108 80c on 2c buff 14.50 6.50
9LC3 A103 1.25p on 5c choc 30.00 17.50
Nos. 9LC1-9LC3 (3) 72.00 41.50
Set, never hinged 82.50

The date July 18, 1936, in the overprints of Nos. 9LC1-9LC22 marks the beginning of the Franco insurrection.

Spain Nos. 542, 543, 528 and 641 Surcharged in Black, Red or Green

The surcharge on Nos. 9LC4 and 9LC6 exists in two types: Type I, 2½-3mm space between numerals and "Cts.". Type II, 1½-2mm space between numerals and "Cts."

1936-37 *Imperf.*

9LC4 A108 50c on 1c bl grn (I) 4.50 2.75
a. Overprint type II 11.00 7.75
9LC5 A108 50c on 1c bl grn (R) ('37) 4.50 2.75

Perf. 11, 11½x11

9LC6 A108 80c on 2c buff (I) 2.25 1.60
a. Overprint type II 5.50 3.25
9LC7 A108 80c on 2c buff (G) ('37) 3.25 1.60
9LC8 A103 1.25 Pts on 5c choc (R) 6.25 4.50
9LC9 A103 Pts 1.25 on 5c choc (R) ('37) 17.00 11.00
9LC10 A161 1.25p on 5c brn (G) ('37) 3.25 1.40
Nos. 9LC4-9LC10 (7) 41.00 25.60
Set, never hinged 65.00

Issued: Nos. 9LC4, 9LC6, 11/28/36; No. 9LC8, 1/7/37; Nos. 9LC4a, 9LC6a, 9LC9, 2/12/37; Nos. 9LC5, 9LC7, 9LC10, 3/2/37.

Spain Nos. 542, 543 and 641 Surcharged in Blue

1937, Mar. 31 *Imperf.*

The surcharge on Nos. 9LC11-9LC13 exists in two types: Type I, 18mm tall. Type II, 20mm tall.

9LC11 A108 50c on 1c bl grn (I) 11.00 5.50
a. Overprint type II 4.50 2.25

Perf. 11

9LC12 A108 80c on 2c buff (I) 11.00 4.50
a. Overprint type II 2.75 1.10
9LC13 A161 1.25p on 5c brown (I) 3.25 1.10
Nos. 9LC11-9LC13 (3) 25.25 11.10
Set, never hinged 40.00

Type II overprints issued 4/17/37.

Stamps of Spain, 1931-1936, Surcharged in Blue or Red (#9LC17, 9LC19)

The surcharge on Nos. 9LC15 and 9LC18 exists in two types: Type I, 2mm space between "+" and denomination. Type II, "+" abuts surcharged denomination. Other values are Type I.

1937

9LC14 A104 25c + 50c lake 50.00 10.00
9LC15 A162 30c + 80c rose 17.50 7.75
a. Overprint type II 17.50 7.75
9LC16 A162 30c + 1.25p rose 22.50 8.25
9LC17 A97 50c + 1.25p dp bl 29.00 11.00
9LC18 A100 60c + 80c ap grn 22.50 8.75
a. Overprint type II 25.00 10.00
9LC19 A105 1p + 1.25p bl blk 72.50 22.50
Nos. 9LC14-9LC19 (6) 214.00 68.25
Set, never hinged 300.00

The surcharge represents the airmail rate and the basic stamp the postage rate.

Issued: 9LC15a, 9LC18a, 4/15. 9LC14-9LC19, 5/5.

Spain Nos. 542, 624 and 641 Surcharged in Black

1937, May 25 Unwmk. *Imperf.*

9LC20	A108	50c on 1c bl grn	7.75	4.50

Perf. 11½, 11½x11

9LC21	A143	80c on 2c org brn	6.50	2.25
9LC22	A161	1.25p on 5c gray brn	6.50	2.25
		Nos. 9LC20-9LC22 (3)	20.75	9.00
		Set, never hinged	30.00	

Stamps and Type of Spain, 1933-36, Surcharged in Black

1937, July *Perf. 13½x13, 11, 11½*

9LC23	A143	50c on 2c org brn	3.25	2.25
9LC24	A126	80c on 2c org brn	325.00	180.00
9LC25	A161	80c on 5c gray brn	3.25	2.25
9LC26	A108	1.25p on 1c bl grn	3.75	2.25
9LC27	A161	2.50p on 10c grn	14.50	8.75

Spain Nos. 647, 650 and 652 Surcharged in Black or Red

Perf. 11

9LC28	A162	30c + 80c rose	2.75	1.40
9LC29	A162	50c + 1.25p dk bl (R)	9.50	5.00
9LC30	A162	1p + 1.25p bl (R)	14.50	8.75
		Nos. 9LC23-9LC30 (8)	376.50	210.65
		Set, never hinged	375.00	

See note after No. 9LC19.

AP1

Perf. 14x13½

1937, July 16 Wmk. 116

Surcharge in Various Colors

9LC31	AP1	50c on 5c ultra (Br)	2.75	2.50
9LC32	AP1	80c on 5c ultra (G)	1.90	1.75
9LC33	AP1	1.25p on 5c ultra (V)	2.25	2.25
		Nos. 9LC31-9LC33 (3)	6.90	6.50
		Set, never hinged	10.00	

Spain Nos. 641, 643 and 640 Surcharged in Green or Orange

1937, Oct. 29 Unwmk. *Perf. 11*

9LC34	A161	50c on 5c (G)	8.50	3.75
9LC35	A161	80c on 10c (O)	5.25	2.75
9LC36	A160	1.25p on 2c (G)	9.50	7.25
		Nos. 9LC34-9LC36 (3)	23.25	13.75
		Set, never hinged	35.00	

Spain Nos. 638, 640 and 643 Surcharged in Red, Blue or Violet

1937, Dec. 23 *Imperf.*

9LC37	A159	50c on 1c (R)	9.50	4.50

Perf. 11, 11x11½

9LC38	A160	80c on 2c (Bl)	3.75	2.75
9LC39	A161	1.25p on 10c (V)	8.50	3.50
		Nos. 9LC37-9LC39 (3)	21.75	10.75
		Set, never hinged	32.50	

Spain Nos. 647, 650 to 652 Surcharged in Black, Green or Brown

1937, Dec. 29

9LC40	A162	30c + 30c rose	4.50	3.75
9LC41	A162	50c + 2.50p dk bl (G)	29.00	21.00
9LC42	A162	60c + 2.30p yel (G)	29.00	21.00
9LC43	A162	1p + 5p bl (Br)	35.00	21.00
		Nos. 9LC40-9LC43 (4)	97.50	66.75
		Set, never hinged	110.00	

See note after No. 9LC19.

Stamps of Spain, 1936, Surcharged in Black, Green, Blue or Red

1938, Feb. 2 *Perf. 11, 11½, 11x11½*

9LC44	A160	50c on 2c brn	5.00	3.75
9LC45	A161	80c on 5c brn (G)	3.75	3.25
9LC46	A162	80c on 30c rose (Bl)	4.50	2.50
9LC47	A161	1.25p on 10c grn (Bl)	4.50	3.25
9LC48	A162	1.25p on 50c dk bl (R)	4.50	2.75
		Nos. 9LC44-9LC48 (5)	22.25	15.50
		Set, never hinged	27.50	

Spain Nos. 645, 646 and 649 Surcharged in Brown, Green or Violet

1938, Feb. 14

9LC51	A162	2.50p on 20c (Br)	50.00	25.00
9LC52	A162	5p on 25c (G)	50.00	25.00
9LC53	A162	10p on 40c (V)	50.00	25.00
		Nos. 9LC51-9LC53 (3)	150.00	75.00
		Set, never hinged	175.00	

MALAGA ISSUE

Stamps of 1920-36 Overprinted in Black or Red

1937 Unwmk. *Imperf.*

10L1	A47	1c blue green	.20	.20
10L2	A108	1c blue green	.20	.20
10L3	A108	1c lt green (R)	.20	.20

Perf. 13½, 13½x13, 11, 11½x11

10L4	A108	2c orange brn	14.50	14.50
10L5	A126	2c orange brn	.20	.20
10L6	A103	5c chocolate (R)	.20	.20
10L7	A96	10c yellow green	12.00	12.00
10L8	A110	10c emerald	.30	.30
10L9	A111	15c Prus grn (R)	.55	.55
10L10	A97	15c blue grn (R)	.55	.55
10L11	A95	20c dk violet (R)	.50	.50
10L12	A99	25c lake	1.50	1.50
10L13	A104	25c lake	.50	.50
10L14	A113	30c carmine	.50	.50
10L15	A129	30c carmine rose	2.50	2.50
10L16	A100	40c blue (R)	.45	.45
10L17	A97	50c dk blue (R)	2.50	2.50
10L18	A100	60c apple green	1.40	1.40
10L19	A105	1p black (R)	2.75	2.75
		Nos. 10L1-10L19 (19)	41.50	41.50

Stamps of 1932-35 Overprinted in Red or Black in panes of 25, reading down. "8.2.37" and "!Arriba Espana!" form the lower half of all overprints. The upper half varies.

Overprint a (1st and 2nd rows): "MALAGA AGRADECIDA A TRANQUILLO-BIANCHI"
Overprint b (3rd row): "MALAGA A SU SALVADOR QUEIPO DE LLANO"
Overprint c (4th and 5th rows): "MALAGA A SU CAUDILLO FRANCO"
Values are for vertical strips of 3 containing examples of each overprint type.

1937 *Perf. 11½*

10L20	A111	15c Prus grn (R)	5.50	5.50
a.		15c single stamp, ovpt. a	.85	.85
b.		15c single stamp, ovpt. b	1.60	1.60
c.		15c single stamp, ovpt. c	.85	.85
10L21	A113	30c rose red (Bk)	5.50	5.50
a.		30c single stamp, ovpt. a	.85	.85
b.		30c single stamp, ovpt. b	1.60	1.60
c.		30c single stamp, ovpt. c	.85	.85
10L22	A97	50c dk blue (R)	8.75	8.75
a.		50c single stamp, ovpt. a	1.60	1.60
b.		50c single stamp, ovpt. b	3.25	3.25
c.		50c single stamp, ovpt. c	1.60	1.60
10L23	A100	60c apple grn (Bk)	11.00	11.00
a.		60c single stamp, ovpt. a	1.60	1.60
b.		60c single stamp, ovpt. b	3.25	3.25
c.		60c single stamp, ovpt. c	1.60	1.60
		Nos. 10L20-10L23 (4)	30.75	30.75

SPECIAL DELIVERY STAMP

Overprinted like Nos. 10L1-10L19 on Type of Special Delivery Stamp of 1934

1937 *Perf. 10*

10LE1	SD7	20c rose red (Bk)	.45	.45

ORENSE ISSUE

Stamps of 1931-36 Overprinted in Red, Blue or Black

1936 *Imperf.*

11L1	A108	1c blue grn (Bl)	.45	.45
a.		Red overprint	1.10	1.10

Perf. 11½, 13½x13

11L2	A108	2c org brn (Bk)	3.50	3.25
11L3	A126	2c org brn (Bk)	.65	.65
11L4	A103	5c brown (R)	1.50	1.50
11L5	A110	10c lt green (Bl)	2.25	2.25
a.		Red overprint	11.00	11.00
11L6	A111	15c Prus grn (R)	3.25	3.25
11L7	A95	20c violet (Bl)	3.25	3.25
11L8	A104	25c lake (Bk)	3.75	3.75
11L9	A113	30c rose red (Bl)	2.75	2.75
a.		Black overprint	5.50	5.50
11L10	A100	40c blue (R)	3.75	3.75
a.		Imperf., pair	50.00	
11L11	A97	50c dark blue (R)	6.50	6.50
11L12	A100	60c apple grn (Bk)	4.75	4.75
a.		Red overprint	17.00	17.00
b.		As "a," Imperf, pair	50.00	
		Nos. 11L1-11L12 (12)	36.35	36.10

SEMI-POSTAL STAMPS

Stamps of Spain, 1931-36, Surcharged in Blue on front and on back of stamp

1936-37 Unwmk. *Imperf.*

11LB1	A47	1c + 5c bl grn	2.25	2.25
11LB2	A108	1c + 5c green	.40	.40

Perf. 13½x13, 11½, 11½x11

11LB3	A108	2c + 5c org brn	.45	.45
11LB4	A126	2c + 5c red brn	.45	.45
11LB5	A103	5c + 5c choc	.65	.65
11LB6	A110	10c + 5c emer	.65	.65
11LB7	A111	15c + 5c Prus grn	.95	.95
11LB8	A95	20c + 5c violet	.65	.65
11LB9	A104	25c + 5c lake	.95	.95
11LB10	A113	30c + 5c rose red	2.75	2.75
11LB11	A117	30c + 5c rose red	42.50	42.50
11LB12	A100	60c + 5c apple grn	190.00	190.00
		Nos. 11LB1-11LB12 (12)	242.65	242.65

SPECIAL DELIVERY STAMPS

Type of Special Delivery Stamp of 1934 Overprinted "!VIVA ESPANA!" in Blue or Black

1936 *Perf. 10*

11LE1	SD7	20c rose red (Bl)	1.90	1.90
11LE2	SD7	20c rose red (Bk)	4.25	4.25

Same with Surcharge "+ 5 cts."

11LE3	SD7	20c + 5c rose red	1.00	1.00

Same Surcharge, Overprint Repeated at Right

11LE4	SD7	20c + 5c rose red	1.10	1.10
		Nos. 11LE1-11LE4 (4)	8.25	8.25

SAN SEBASTIAN ISSUE

For Use in Province of Guipuzcoa

Stamps of 1931-36 Overprinted in Red or Blue

1937 Unwmk. *Imperf.*

12L1	A108	1c bl grn (R)	.65	.65

Perf. 11, 13½

12L2	A108	2c buff (Bl)	1.00	1.50
12L3	A126	2c org brn (Bl)	2.10	2.10
12L4	A95	5c chocolate (R)	5.00	5.00
12L5	A103	5c chocolate (R)	1.75	1.75
12L6	A110	10c emerald (R)	1.75	1.75
12L7	A111	15c Prus grn (R)	2.10	2.10
12L8	A95	20c dk violet (R)	2.75	2.75
12L9	A104	25c car lake (Bl)	2.75	2.75
12L10	A113	30c rose red (Bl)	2.75	2.75
12L11	A100	40c blue (R)	5.50	5.50
12L12	A97	50c dark blue (R)	5.50	5.50
		Nos. 12L1-12L12 (12)	33.60	34.10

SANTA CRUZ DE TENERIFE ISSUE

Stamps of Spain, 1931-36 Overprinted in Black or Red

1936 Unwmk. *Imperf.*

13L1	A108	1c bl grn (R)	.75	.75
13L2	A108	1c bl grn (Bk)	2.75	2.75

Perf. 11, 13½

13L3	A108	2c buff (Bk)	5.50	5.50
13L4	A126	2c org brn (Bk)	.95	.95
13L5	A103	5c choc (R)	3.00	3.00
13L6	A110	10c green (R)	3.00	3.00
13L7	A104	25c lake (Bk)	11.00	11.00
13L8	A100	40c dk blue (R)	3.25	3.25
13L9	A107	10p dp brn (Bk)	225.00	225.00
		Nos. 13L1-13L9 (9)	255.20	255.20

Many forgeries of #13L9 exist.

SEVILLE ISSUE

Stamps of Spain, 1931-36, Overprinted in Black or Red

1936 *Imperf.*

14L1	A108	1c blue grn (Bk)	.25	.25

Perf. 13½x13, 11, 11½x11

14L2	A126	2c org brn (Bk)	.30	.30
14L3	A103	5c chocolate (R)	.40	.40
14L4	A110	10c emerald (Bk)	.50	.50
14L5	A111	15c Prus grn (R)	1.25	1.25
14L6	A95	20c violet (R)	1.25	1.25
14L7	A104	25c lake (Bk)	1.25	1.25
14L8	A113	30c carmine (Bk)	1.25	1.25
14L9	A128	30c rose red (Bk)	7.50	7.50
14L10	A100	40c blue (R)	5.00	5.00

14L11	A97	50c dk blue (R)	5.00	5.00
14L12	A100	60c apple grn (Bk)	6.00	6.00
		Nos. 14L1-14L12 (12)	29.95	29.95

Stamps of Spain, 1931-36, Handstamped in Black

Imperf

14L13	A108	1c blue grn	.25	.25

Perf. 13½x13, 11, 11x11½, 11½x11

14L14	A126	2c orange brn	.40	.40
14L15	A103	5c chocolate	.40	.40
14L16	A110	10c emerald	.40	.40
14L17	A111	15c Prus green	.50	.50
14L18	A95	20c violet	.50	.50
14L19	A104	25c lake	.50	.50
14L20	A113	30c carmine	.50	.50
14L21	A128	30c rose red	2.75	2.75
14L22	A100	40c blue	.95	.95
14L23	A97	50c dk blue	2.75	2.75
14L24	A100	60c apple grn	.90	.90
14L25	A105	1p black	2.75	2.75
14L26	AP26	2p gray blue	12.00	12.00
14L27	A106	4p magenta	6.50	6.50
14L28	A107	10p deep brown	9.50	9.50
		Nos. 14L13-14L28,14LE1 (17)	42.00	42.00

The date "Julio-1936" in the overprints of Nos. 14L1-14L28 and 14LE1 marks the beginning of the Franco insurrection.

SPECIAL DELIVERY STAMP

Overprinted like Nos. 14L13-14L25 on Type of Special Delivery Stamp of 1934

1936 *Perf. 10*

14LE1	SD7	20c rose red	1.75	1.75

SPANISH GUINEA

'spa-nish 'gi-nē

LOCATION — In western Africa, bordering on the Gulf of Guinea
GOVT. — Spanish Colony
AREA — 10,852 sq. mi.
POP. — 212,000 (est. 1957)
CAPITAL — Santa Isabel

Spanish Guinea Nos. 1-84 were issued for and used only in the continental area later called Rio Muni. From 1909 to 1960, Spanish Guinea also included Fernando Po, Elobey, Annobon and Corisco.

100 Centimos = 1 Peseta

King Alfonso XIII
A1 A2

1902 **Unwmk.** **Typo.** *Perf. 14*

Blue Control Numbers on Back

1	A1	5c dark green	11.00	6.25
2	A1	10c indigo	11.00	6.25
3	A1	25c claret	82.50	47.50
4	A1	50c deep brown	82.50	47.50
5	A1	75c violet	82.50	47.50
6	A1	1p carmine rose	120.00	47.50
7	A1	2p olive green	155.00	100.00
8	A1	5p dull red	250.00	175.00
		Nos. 1-8 (8)	794.50	477.50
		Set, never hinged	1,400.	

Exists imperf, value set $1,750.

Revenue Stamps Surcharged

1903 *Imperf.*

Blue or Black Control Numbers on Back

8A	10c on 25c blk (R)	550.00	210.00
8B	10c on 50c org (Bl)	125.00	35.00
8D	10c on 1p 25c car (Bk)	750.00	350.00
8F	10c on 2p cl (Bk)	800.00	550.00
g.	Blue surcharge	1,300.	750.00
8H	10c on 2p 50c red brn (Bl)	1,250.	675.00
8J	10c on 5p ol blk (R)	1,500.	475.00

Nos. 8A-8J are surcharged on stamps inscribed "Posesiones Espanolas de Africa Occidental" and "1903," with arms at left.

This surcharge was also applied to revenue stamps of 10, 15, 25, 50, 75 and 100 pesetas and in other colors.

See Nos. 98-101C.

1903 **Typo.** *Perf. 14*

Blue Control Numbers on Back

9	A2	¼c black	1.25	.75
10	A2	½c blue green	1.25	.75
11	A2	1c claret	1.25	.65
12	A2	2c dark olive	1.25	.65
13	A2	3c dark brown	1.25	.65
14	A2	4c vermilion	1.25	.65
15	A2	5c black brown	1.25	.65
16	A2	10c red brown	2.00	.75
17	A2	15c dark blue	7.00	5.75
18	A2	25c orange buff	7.00	5.75
19	A2	50c carmine lake	13.00	12.50
20	A2	75c violet	17.50	12.50
21	A2	1p blue green	30.00	20.00
22	A2	2p dark green	30.00	20.00
23	A2	3p scarlet	80.00	26.00
24	A2	4p dull blue	92.50	45.00
25	A2	5p dark violet	175.00	65.00
26	A2	10p carmine rose	240.00	90.00
		Nos. 9-26 (18)	702.75	308.00
		Set, never hinged	1,300.	

1905

Same, Dated "1905"

Blue Control Numbers on Back

27	A2	1c black	.20	.20
28	A2	2c blue grn	.20	.20
29	A2	3c claret	.20	.20
30	A2	4c bronze grn	.20	.20
31	A2	5c dark brown	.20	.20
32	A2	10c red	1.10	.65
33	A2	15c black brown	3.25	2.25
34	A2	25c chocolate	3.25	2.25
35	A2	50c dark blue	7.25	5.25
36	A2	75c orange buff	7.75	5.25
37	A2	1p carmine rose	7.75	5.25
38	A2	2p violet	19.00	11.00
39	A2	3p blue green	50.00	22.50
40	A2	4p dark green	50.00	32.50
40A	A2	5p vermilion	80.00	35.00
41	A2	10p dull blue	140.00	110.00
		Nos. 27-41 (16)	370.35	232.90
		Set, never hinged	675.00	

Stamps of Elobey, 1905, Overprinted in Violet or Blue

1906

42	A1	1c rose	3.25	1.90
43	A1	2c deep violet	3.25	1.90
44	A1	3c black	3.25	1.90
45	A1	4c orange red	3.25	1.90
46	A1	5c deep green	3.25	1.90
47	A1	10c blue green	7.25	4.25
48	A1	15c violet	12.50	7.50
49	A1	25c rose lake	12.50	7.50
50	A1	50c orange buff	17.50	10.50
51	A1	75c dark blue	21.00	12.00
52	A1	1p red brown	37.50	21.00
53	A1	2p black brown	55.00	32.50
54	A1	3p vermilion	77.50	45.00
55	A1	4p dark brown	350.00	210.00
56	A1	5p bronze green	350.00	210.00
57	A1	10p claret	*1,400.*	*850.00*
		Nos. 42-54 (13)	257.00	149.75

King Alfonso XIII
A3 A4

1907 **Typo.**

Blue Control Numbers on Back

58	A3	1c dark green	.60	.20
59	A3	2c dull blue	.60	.20
60	A3	3c violet	.60	.20
61	A3	4c yellow grn	.60	.20
62	A3	5c carmine lake	.60	.20
63	A3	10c orange	3.25	1.00
64	A3	15c brown	2.50	.65
65	A3	25c dark blue	2.50	.65
66	A3	50c black brown	2.50	.65
67	A3	75c blue green	2.50	.65
68	A3	1p red	4.75	1.10
69	A3	2p dark brown	8.00	5.00
70	A3	3p olive gray	8.00	5.00
71	A3	4p maroon	10.50	5.00
72	A3	5p green	11.00	7.50
73	A3	10p red violet	16.50	9.75
		Nos. 58-73 (16)	75.00	37.95
		Set, never hinged	135.00	

Issue of 1907 Surcharged in Black or Red

1908-09

74	A3	05c on 1c dk grn (R)	2.75	1.50
75	A3	05c on 2c blue (R)	2.75	1.50
76	A3	05c on 3c violet	2.75	1.50
77	A3	05c on 4c yel grn	2.75	1.50
78	A3	05c on 10c orange	2.75	1.50
a.		Red surcharge	5.00	2.75
84	A3	15c on 10c orange	13.50	9.00
		Nos. 74-84 (6)	27.25	16.50

Many stamps of this issue are found with the surcharge inverted, sideways, double and in both black and red. Other stamps of the 1907 issue are known with this surcharge but are not believed to have been put in use. Value, each $17.

1909 **Typo.** *Perf. 14½*

Blue Control Numbers on Back

85	A4	1c orange brown	.20	.20
86	A4	2c rose	.20	.20
87	A4	5c dark green	1.00	.20
88	A4	10c vermilion	.30	.20
89	A4	15c dark brown	.30	.20
90	A4	20c violet	.55	.25
91	A4	25c dull blue	.55	.25
92	A4	30c chocolate	.65	.20
93	A4	40c lake	.40	.20
94	A4	50c dark violet	.40	.20
95	A4	1p blue green	11.00	5.50
96	A4	4p orange	2.75	3.25
97	A4	10p red	2.75	3.25
		Nos. 85-97 (13)	21.05	14.10
		Set, never hinged	37.50	

For overprints see Nos. 102-114.

Revenue Stamps Surcharged like Nos. 8A-8J in Black

1909 *Imperf.*

With or Without Control Numbers on Back

98	10c on 50c bl grn	80.00	52.50
a.	Red or violet surcharge	100.00	72.50
99	10c on 1p 25c violet	100.00	72.50
100	10c on 2p dk brn	550.00	325.00
100A	10c on 5p dk vio	550.00	325.00
101	10c on 25p red brn	*725.00*	*525.00*
101A	10c on 50p brn lil	*2,500.*	*1,450.*
101B	10c on 75p carmine	*2,500.*	*1,450.*
101C	10c on 100p orange	*2,500.*	*1,450.*

Nos. 98-101C are surcharged on undated stamps, arms centered. Stamps inscribed: "Territorios Espanoles del Africa Occidental." Basic revenue stamps similar to Rio de Oro type A3.

Stamps of 1909 Overprinted with Handstamp in Black, Blue, Green or Red

1911

102	A4	1c orange brn (Bl)	.25	.20
103	A4	2c rose (G)	.25	.20
104	A4	5c dk green (R)	1.25	.20
105	A4	10c vermilion	.70	.30
106	A4	15c dk brown (R)	1.25	.50
107	A4	20c violet	1.50	.70
108	A4	25c dull blue (R)	1.75	1.60
109	A4	30c choc (Bl)	2.50	2.25
110	A4	40c lake (Bl)	2.75	2.25
111	A4	50c dark violet	4.50	3.25
112	A4	1p blue grn (R)	37.50	27.50
113	A4	4p orange (R)	19.00	15.00
114	A4	10p red (G)	25.00	27.50
		Nos. 102-114 (13)	98.20	81.45
		Set, never hinged	180.00	

The date "1911" is missing from the overprint on the first stamp in each row, or ten times in each sheet of 100 stamps. This variety occurs on all stamps of the series. Value, set $450.

King Alfonso XIII
A5 A6

1912 **Typo.** *Perf. 13½*

Blue Control Numbers on Back

115	A5	1c black	.20	.20
116	A5	2c dark brown	.20	.20
117	A5	5c deep green	.20	.20
118	A5	10c red	.20	.20
119	A5	15c claret	.20	.20
120	A5	20c red	.30	.20
121	A5	25c dull blue	.20	.20
122	A5	30c lake	2.50	1.40
123	A5	40c car rose	1.60	.75
124	A5	50c brown org	1.40	.25
125	A5	1p dark violet	1.60	.95
126	A5	4p lilac	3.75	1.90
127	A5	10p blue green	7.75	7.00
		Nos. 115-127 (13)	20.10	13.65
		Set, never hinged	32.50	

For overprints and surcharges see Nos. 141-157.

1914 *Perf. 13*

Blue Control Numbers on Back

128	A6	1c dull violet	.20	.20
129	A6	2c car rose	.20	.20
130	A6	5c deep green	.20	.20
131	A6	10c vermilion	.20	.20
132	A6	15c dark violet	.20	.20
133	A6	20c dark brown	.70	.40
134	A6	25c dark blue	.30	.20
135	A6	30c brown orange	1.10	.40
136	A6	40c blue green	1.10	.40
137	A6	50c dp claret	.55	.25
138	A6	1p vermilion	1.25	1.50
139	A6	4p maroon	5.00	3.25
140	A6	10p olive black	5.50	6.00
		Nos. 128-140 (13)	16.50	13.40
		Set, never hinged	25.00	

Stamps with these or similar overprints are unauthorized and fraudulent.

Stamps of 1912 Overprinted

1917 *Perf. 13½*

141	A5	1c black	90.00	60.00
142	A5	2c dark brown	90.00	60.00
143	A5	5c deep green	.25	.20
144	A5	10c red	.25	.20
145	A5	15c claret	.25	.20
146	A5	20c red	.25	.20
147	A5	25c dull blue	.20	.20
148	A5	30c lake	.25	.20
149	A5	40c carmine rose	.50	.25
150	A5	50c brown orange	.25	.20
151	A5	1p dark violet	.50	.25

152	A5	4p lilac	6.25	3.00
153	A5	10p blue green	6.25	3.00
		Nos. 141-153 (13)	195.20	127.90
		Set, never hinged	260.00	

Nos. 143-153 exist with overprint double, inverted, in dark blue, reading "9117" and in pairs one without overprint.

Stamps of 1917 Surcharged

1918

154	A5	5c on 40c car rose	27.50	11.00
155	A5	10c on 4p lilac	27.50	11.00
156	A5	15c on 20c red	50.00	19.00
157	A5	25c on 10p bl grn	50.00	19.00
a.		"52" for "25"	375.00	325.00
		Nos. 154-157 (4)	155.00	60.00
		Set, never hinged	260.00	

The varieties "Gents" and "Censt" occur on Nos. 154-157. Values 50 percent more.

King Alfonso XIII
A7 A8

1919 **Typo.** ***Perf. 13***

Blue Control Numbers on Back

158	A7	1c lilac	.85	.25
159	A7	2c rose	.85	.25
160	A7	5c vermilion	.85	.25
161	A7	10c violet	1.40	.25
162	A7	15c brown	1.40	.40
163	A7	20c blue	1.40	.65
164	A7	25c green	1.40	.65
a.		25c blue (error)	52.50	
165	A7	30c orange	1.75	.65
166	A7	40c orange	3.75	.65
167	A7	50c red	3.75	.65
168	A7	1p light green	3.75	2.25
169	A7	4p claret	8.25	8.50
170	A7	10p brown	17.00	16.00
		Nos. 158-170 (13)	46.40	31.40
		Set, never hinged	60.00	

1920

Blue Control Numbers on Back

171	A8	1c brown	.20	.20
172	A8	2c dull rose	.20	.20
173	A8	5c gray green	.20	.20
174	A8	10c dull rose	.20	.20
175	A8	15c orange	.20	.20
176	A8	20c yellow	.20	.20
177	A8	25c dull blue	.75	.20
178	A8	30c greenish blue	27.50	17.50
179	A8	40c lt brown	1.25	.20
180	A8	50c lilac	1.40	.20
181	A8	1p light red	1.40	.20
182	A8	4p bright rose	4.50	4.50
183	A8	10p gray lilac	6.50	8.75
		Nos. 171-183 (13)	44.50	32.75
		Set, never hinged	72.50	

A9

Nipa House — A10

1922

Blue Control Numbers on Back

184	A9	1c dark brown	.50	.20
185	A9	2c claret	.50	.20
186	A9	5c blue green	.50	.20
187	A9	10c pale red	3.50	.95
188	A9	15c orange	.50	.20
189	A9	20c lilac	2.25	.85
190	A9	25c dark blue	3.75	1.00
191	A9	30c violet	3.50	1.10
192	A9	40c turq blue	2.50	.55
193	A9	50c deep rose	2.50	.55
194	A9	1p myrtle green	2.50	.55
195	A9	4p red brown	10.50	10.50
196	A9	10p yellow	21.00	20.00
		Nos. 184-196 (13)	54.00	36.85
		Set, never hinged	85.00	

1924

Blue Control Numbers on Back

197	A10	5c choc & bl	.20	.20
198	A10	10c gray grn & bl	.20	.20
199	A10	15c rose & blk	.20	.20
200	A10	20c violet & blk	.20	.20
201	A10	25c org red & blk	.40	.25
202	A10	30c orange & blk	.40	.20
203	A10	40c dl bl & blk	.40	.20
204	A10	50c claret & blk	.40	.20
205	A10	60c red brn & blk	.40	.20
206	A10	1p dk vio & blk	1.60	.20
a.		Center inverted	275.00	125.00
207	A10	4p brt bl & blk	3.75	2.25
208	A10	10p bl grn & blk	8.75	4.50
		Nos. 197-208 (12)	16.90	8.80
		Set, never hinged	25.00	

Seville-Barcelona Issue of Spain, 1929, Overprinted in Red or Blue

1929 ***Perf. 11***

209	A52	5c rose lake	.25	.30
210	A53	10c green (R)	.25	.30
211	A50	15c Prus bl (R)	.25	.30
212	A51	20c purple (R)	.25	.30
213	A50	25c brt rose	.25	.30
214	A52	30c black brn	.25	.30
215	A53	40c dk blue (R)	.50	.45
216	A51	50c dp orange	.50	.45
217	A52	1p blue blk (R)	8.50	4.50
218	A53	4p deep rose	17.50	8.75
219	A53	10p brown	32.50	17.00
		Nos. 209-219 (11)	61.00	32.95
		Set, never hinged	120.00	

Porter
A11

Drummers
A12

King Alfonso XIII and Queen Victoria — A13

1931 **Engr.** ***Perf. 14***

220	A11	1c blue green	.20	.20
221	A11	2c red brown	.20	.20

Blue Control Numbers on Back

222	A11	5c brown black	.20	.20
223	A11	10c light green	.20	.20
224	A11	15c dark green	.20	.20
225	A11	20c deep violet	.20	.20
226	A12	25c carmine	.20	.20
227	A12	30c lake	.30	.20
228	A12	40c dark blue	.70	.55
229	A12	50c red orange	1.50	1.10
230	A13	80c blue violet	2.50	1.60
231	A13	1p black	4.50	4.50
232	A13	4p violet rose	30.00	17.00
233	A13	5p dark brown	13.00	12.00
		Nos. 220-233 (14)	53.90	38.35
		Set, never hinged	110.00	

Exist imperf. Value for set, $300.

See Nos. 262-271. For overprints and surcharges see Nos. 234-277, 282-283, 298.

Stamps of 1931 Overprinted

1931

234	A11	1c blue green	.20	.20
235	A11	2c red brown	.20	.20
236	A11	5c brown black	.20	.20
237	A11	10c light green	.20	.20
238	A11	15c dark green	.20	.20
239	A11	20c deep violet	.20	.20
240	A12	25c carmine	.20	.20
241	A12	30c lake	.40	.20
242	A12	40c dark blue	1.40	.45
243	A12	50c red orange	9.75	5.50
244	A13	80c blue violet	3.00	1.60
245	A13	1p black	10.00	3.50
246	A13	4p violet rose	17.50	10.50
247	A13	5p dark brown	17.50	10.50
		Nos. 234-247 (14)	60.95	33.65
		Set, never hinged	100.00	

Stamps of 1931 Overprinted in Red or Blue

1933

248	A11	1c blue grn (R)	.20	.20
249	A11	2c red brown (Bl)	.20	.20
250	A11	5c brown blk (R)	.20	.20
251	A11	10c lt green (Bl)	.20	.20
252	A11	15c dk green (R)	.20	.20
253	A11	20c dp violet (R)	.40	.20
254	A12	25c carmine (Bl)	.40	.20
255	A12	30c lake (Bl)	.45	.20
256	A12	40c dk blue (R)	2.75	.70
257	A12	50c red orange (Bl)	17.00	3.50
258	A13	80c blue vio (R)	5.50	3.00
259	A13	1p black (R)	19.00	3.25
260	A13	4p violet rose (Bl)	35.00	15.00
261	A13	5p dk brown (Bl)	35.00	15.00
		Nos. 248-261 (14)	116.50	42.05
		Set, never hinged	175.00	

Types of 1931
Without Control Number

1934-35 **Engr.** ***Perf. 10***

262	A11	1c blue green ('35)	8.25	.20
263	A11	2c red brown ('35)	8.25	.20
264	A11	5c black brn	1.50	.20
265	A11	10c light green	1.50	.20
266	A11	15c dark green	2.75	.20
267	A12	30c rose red	3.25	.20
268	A12	50c indigo ('35)	7.25	.70
		Nos. 262-268 (7)	32.75	1.90
		Set, never hinged	47.50	

Types of 1931

1941 **Litho.** **Unwmk.**

269	A11	5c olive gray	2.10	.20
270	A11	20c violet	2.10	.20
271	A12	40c gray green	.85	.20
		Nos. 269-271 (3)	5.05	.60
		Set, never hinged	6.25	

Stamps of 1931-33 Surcharged in Black

a

1

peseta.

b

1936-37 ***Perf. 10, 14***

272	A12	30c on 40c (#228)	3.75	2.25
273	A12	30c on 40c (#242)	15.00	3.50
274	A12	30c on 40c (#256)	57.50	17.50
		Nos. 272-274 (3)	76.25	23.25
		Set, never hinged	110.00	

The surcharge on Nos. 272-274 exists in two types, differing in the "3" which is scarcer in italic.

No. 268 Surcharged Type "b" in Red

275	A12	1p on 50c indigo	22.50
276	A12	4p on 50c indigo	72.50
277	A12	5p on 50c indigo	42.50
		Nos. 275-277 (3)	137.50

Nos. 275-277 were not issued.

Stamps of Spain, 1936, Overprinted in Black or Carmine

1938 ***Perf. 11***

278	A161	10c gray green	1.50	.45
279	A162	15c gray black (C)	1.50	.45
280	A162	20c dark violet	3.50	1.40
281	A162	25c brown lake	3.50	1.40
		Nos. 278-281 (4)	10.00	3.70
		Set, never hinged	13.00	

Nos. 278-281 exist imperf. Value $175.

Stamps of 1931-33, Surcharged in Black

1939

282	A13	40c on 80c (#244)	11.00	7.25
283	A13	40c on 80c (#258)	11.00	4.50
		Set, never hinged	30.00	

A14

A15

Revenue Stamps Surcharged in Black

1940-41 ***Perf. 11½***

284	A14	5c on 35c pale grn	5.75	1.90
285	A14	25c on 60c org brn	5.75	2.25
286	A14	50c on 75c blk brn	8.00	2.50
		Nos. 284-286 (3)	19.50	6.65

Red Surcharge

287	A15	10c on 75c blk brn	8.00	2.50
288	A15	15c on 1.50p lt vio	5.75	2.25
289	A15	25c on 60c org brn	10.00	3.25
		Nos. 287-289 (3)	23.75	8.00

A16

A17

Black or Carmine Surcharge
Perf. 11

290	A16	1p on 17p deep red	45.00	13.50
291	A17	1p on 40p yel grn (C)	11.00	3.50

See No. C1.

A18

A19

Black Surcharge
Perf. 11, 13x12½

292	A18	5c carmine	5.50	1.40
293	A19	1p yellow	87.50	32.50

A20

General Francisco Franco — A21

Black Surcharge

294	A20	1p on 15c gray grn	9.50	3.25

1940 ***Perf. 11½, 13½***

295	A21	5c olive brown	2.50	.40
296	A21	40c blue	3.75	.40
297	A21	50c green	4.50	.40
a.		50c greenish gray	19.00	7.25
		Nos. 295-297 (3)	10.75	1.20
		Set, never hinged	24.50	

Nos. 295-297 exist imperf. Values $45.

SEMI-POSTAL STAMPS

Red Cross Issue

Types of Semi-Postal Stamps of Spain, 1926, Overprinted in Black or Blue

1926 **Unwmk.** ***Perf. 12½, 13***

B1	SP3	5c black brown	9.50	6.25
B2	SP4	10c dark green	9.50	6.25
B3	SP1	15c dark vio (Bl)	2.10	1.40
B4	SP4	20c violet brown	2.10	1.40
B5	SP5	25c deep carmine	2.10	1.40
B6	SP1	30c olive green	2.10	1.40
B7	SP3	40c ultra	.45	.20
B8	SP2	50c red brown	.45	.20
B9	SP5	60c myrtle green	.45	.20
B10	SP4	1p vermilion	.45	.20
B11	SP3	4p bister	1.75	1.25
B12	SP5	10p light violet	6.25	4.25
		Nos. B1-B12 (12)	37.20	24.40
		Set, never hinged	52.50	

See Spain No. B6a for No. B4 without overprint. For surcharges see Spain Nos. B70-B71.

SPANISH MOROCCO

'spa-nish mə-'rä-ˌkō

LOCATION — Northwest coast of Africa
GOVT. — Spanish Protectorate
AREA — 17,398 sq. mi. (approx.)
POP. — 1,010,117 (1950)
CAPITAL — Tetuán

100 Centimos = 1 Peseta

Spanish Offices in Morocco

Spain No. 221A Overprinted in Carmine

1903-09 **Unwmk.** ***Imperf.***

1	A21	¼c blue green	.50	.20
a.		Complete 1c (block 4 ¼c)	2.00	1.25

See Nos. 26, 39, 52, Tetuan 1, 7.

Stamps of Spain Overprinted in Carmine or Blue

a

On Stamps of 1900
Perf. 14

2	A35	2c bister brown	1.40	1.10
3	A35	5c green	1.60	.60
4	A35	10c rose red (Bl)	1.75	.25
5	A35	15c brt violet	2.50	.60
6	A35	20c grnsh black	10.00	2.75
7	A35	25c blue	.80	.65
8	A35	30c blue green	6.00	2.75
9	A35	40c rose (Bl)	10.00	4.75
10	A35	50c slate grn	6.00	4.50
11	A35	1p lake (Bl)	12.00	6.25
12	A35	4p dull violet	32.50	11.00
13	A35	10p brown org (Bl)	32.50	27.50
		Nos. 1-13 (13)	117.55	62.90
		Set, never hinged	175.00	

Many varieties of overprint exist. Nos. 7-13 exist imperf. Value, $500.

See Tetuan Nos. 2-6, 8-15.

On Stamps of 1909-10

1909-10 ***Perf. 13x12½, 14***

14	A46	2c dark brown	.55	.20
15	A46	5c green	2.75	.20
16	A46	10c carmine (Bl)	3.25	.20
17	A46	15c violet	7.50	.45
18	A46	20c olive green	19.00	.95
19	A46	25c deep blue	65.00	
20	A46	30c blue green	6.00	.45
21	A46	40c rose (Bl)	6.00	.45
22	A46	50c slate blue	10.50	10.00
23	A46	1p lake (Bl)	25.00	21.00
24	A46	4p deep violet	65.00	
25	A46	10p orange (Bl)	65.00	
		Nos. 14-18,20-23 (9)	80.55	33.90
		Set, never hinged	110.00	
		Nos. 14-25 (12)	275.55	

The stamps overprinted "Correo Espanol Marruecos" were used in all Morocco until the year 1914. After the issue of special stamps for the Protectorate the "Correo Espanol" stamps were continued in use solely in the city of Tangier.

Many varieties of overprint exist.

Nos. 19, 24 and 25 were not regularly issued.

See Nos. 27-38, 40-51, 53-67, 75-76, 78.

Spanish Morocco

Spain No. 221A Overprinted in Carmine

1914 ***Imperf.***

26	A21	¼c green	.20	.20
a.		Complete 1c (block 4 ¼c)	1.25	.90

Stamps of Spain 1909-10 Overprinted in Carmine or Blue

Perf. 13x12½, 14

27	A46	2c dark brown (C)	.20	.20
28	A46	5c green (C)	.20	.20
29	A46	10c carmine (Bl)	.20	.20
30	A46	15c violet (C)	1.10	.75
31	A46	20c olive grn (C)	2.10	1.50
32	A46	25c deep blue (C)	2.10	1.10
33	A46	30c blue grn (C)	4.25	2.10
34	A46	40c rose (Bl)	9.75	3.00
35	A46	50c slate blue (C)	5.00	2.10
36	A46	1p lake (Bl)	5.00	3.00
37	A46	4p dp violet (C)	25.00	21.00
38	A46	10p orange (Bl)	37.50	27.50
		Nos. 26-38,E1 (14)	96.35	64.60
		Set, never hinged	165.00	

Many varieties of overprint exist, including inverted.

#27-38 exist imperf. Value for set, $525.

Stamps of Spain 1876 and 1909-10 Overprinted in Red or Blue

1915 ***Imperf.***

39	A21	¼c blue grn (R)	.20	.20
a.		Complete 1c (block 4 ¼c)	1.25	.95

Perf. 13x12½, 14

40	A46	2c dk brown (R)	.20	.25
41	A46	5c green (R)	.25	.25
42	A46	10c carmine (Bl)	.25	.25
43	A46	15c violet (R)	.25	.25
44	A46	20c olive grn (R)	.95	.25
45	A46	25c deep blue (R)	.95	.40
46	A46	30c blue grn (R)	1.10	.45
47	A46	40c rose (Bl)	3.00	.45
48	A46	50c slate blue (R)	5.00	.40
49	A46	1p lake (Bl)	5.00	.45
50	A46	4p deep violet (R)	32.50	21.00
51	A46	10p orange (Bl)	47.50	22.50
		Nos. 39-51,E2 (14)	99.65	48.50
		Set, never hinged	155.00	

One stamp in the setting on Nos. 39-51 has the first "R" of "PROTECTORADO" inverted. Many other varieties of overprint exist, including double and inverted.

Nos. 40-51 exist imperf. Value, set $650.

Stamps of Spain 1877 and 1909-10 Overprinted in Red or Blue

b

1916-18 ***Imperf.***

52	A21	¼c blue grn (R)	1.10	.20
a.		Complete 1c (block 4 ¼c)	1.75	1.25

Perf. 13x12½, 14

53	A46	2c dk brown (R)	1.10	.20
54	A46	5c green (R)	5.00	.20
55	A46	10c carmine (Bl)	5.50	.20
56	A46	15c violet (R)	125.00	
57	A46	20c olive grn (R)	125.00	
58	A46	25c dp blue (R)	19.00	3.00
59	A46	30c blue grn (R)	25.00	20.00
60	A46	40c rose (Bl)	26.00	.45
61	A46	50c slate blue (R)	12.00	.20
62	A46	1p lake (Bl)	30.00	2.10
63	A46	4p dp violet (R)	50.00	29.00
64	A46	10p orange (Bl)	100.00	65.00
		Nos. 52-55,58-64 (11)	274.70	120.55
		Set, never hinged	400.00	
		Nos. 52-64 (13)	524.70	
		Set, never hinged	1,000.	

Nos. 56-57 were not regularly issued.

Varieties of overprint, including double and inverted, exist for several denominations.

The 5c exists in olive brown. Value $525.

Same Overprint on Spain No. 310

1920

65	A46	15c ocher (Bl)	5.50	.30

Exists imperf.; also with overprint inverted.

Nos. 44, 46 Perforated through the middle and each half Surcharged "10 céntimos" in Red

1920

66	A46	10c on half of 20c	5.00	1.90
67	A46	15c on half of 30c	11.00	7.25

No. E2 Divided and Surcharged in Black

68	SD1	10c on half of 20c	12.00	7.75
a.		"10/cts." surcharge added	145.00	45.00
		Nos. 66-68 (3)	28.00	16.90

Values of Nos. 66-68 are for pairs, both halves of the stamp. Varieties were probably made deliberately.

"Justice" — A1

Revenue Stamps Perforated through the Middle and each half Surcharged with New Value in Red or Green

1920 ***Perf. 11½***

69	A1	5c on 5p lt bl	9.50	1.90
70	A1	5c on 10p green	.40	.20
71	A1	10c on 25p dk grn	.40	.20
a.		Inverted surcharge	11.00	10.00
72	A1	10c on 50p indigo	.45	.30
73	A1	15c on 100p red (G)	.45	.30
74	A1	15c on 500p cl (G)	12.50	6.50
		Nos. 69-74 (6)	23.70	9.40
		Set, never hinged	37.50	

Values of Nos. 69-74 are for pairs, both halves of the stamp.

Stamps of Spain 1917-20 Overprinted Type "a" in Blue or Red

1921-24 ***Perf. 13***

75	A46	15c ocher (Bl)	1.25	.20
76	A46	20c violet (R)	1.90	.20

Stamps of Spain 1920-21 Overprinted Type "b" in Red

Imperf

77	A47	1c blue green	1.40	.20

Engr.

Perf. 13

78	A46	20c violet	10.00	.20

See No. 92.

Stamps of Spain, 1922 Overprinted Type "a" in Red or Blue

1923-28 ***Perf. 13½x12½***

79	A49	2c olive green (R)	3.50	.20
80	A49	5c red violet (Bl)	3.50	.20
81	A49	10c yellow green (R)	4.25	.20
82	A49	20c violet (R)	6.00	.90
		Nos. 79-82 (4)	17.25	1.50

Same Overprinted Type "b"

1923-25

83	A49	2c olive green (R)	.65	.20
84	A49	5c red violet (Bl)	.65	.20
85	A49	10c yellow grn (R)	2.75	.20
86	A49	15c blue (R)	2.75	.20
87	A49	20c violet (R)	6.00	.20
88	A49	25c carmine (Bl)	12.00	1.40
89	A49	40c deep blue (R)	12.50	4.50
90	A49	50c orange (Bl)	32.50	7.75
91	A49a	1p blue black (R)	50.00	4.50
		Nos. 83-91,E3 (10)	130.30	27.40
		Set, never hinged	210.00	

Spain No. 314 Overprinted Type "a" in Red

1927 ***Imperf.***

92	A47	1c blue green	.20	.20

Mosque of Alcazarquivir
A2

Moorish Gateway at Larache
A3

Well at Alhucemas
A4

View of Xauen — A5

View of Tetuan — A6

1928-32 **Engr.** ***Perf. 14, 14½***

93	A2	1c red ("Cs")	.20	.20
94	A2	1c car rose ("Ct") ('32)	.30	.30
95	A2	2c dark violet	.20	.20
96	A2	5c deep blue	.20	.20
97	A2	10c dark green	.20	.20
98	A2	15c orange brown	.50	.20
99	A3	20c olive green	.50	.20
100	A3	25c copper red	.50	.20
102	A3	30c black brown	1.75	.20
103	A3	40c dull blue	2.25	.20
104	A3	50c brown violet	4.75	.20
105	A4	1p yellow green	7.00	.25
106	A5	2.50p red violet	22.00	7.50
107	A6	4p ultra	16.50	4.50
		Nos. 93-107,E4 (15)	61.10	15.95
		Set, never hinged	85.00	

For surcharges see Nos. 164-167.

Seville-Barcelona Issue of Spain, 1929, Overprinted in Red or Blue

1929 *Perf. 11, 14*

108	A50	1c	greenish blue	.25	.25
109	A51	2c	pale yel grn	.25	.25
110	A52	5c	rose lake (Bl)	.25	.25
111	A53	10c	green	.25	.25
112	A50	15c	Prussian blue	.25	.25
113	A51	20c	purple	.25	.25
114	A50	25c	bright rose (Bl)	.25	.25
115	A52	30c	black brown (bl)	.70	.55
116	A53	40c	dark blue	.70	.55
117	A51	50c	deep orange (Bl)	.70	.55
118	A52	1p	blue black	5.75	4.25
119	A53	4p	deep rose (Bl)	12.50	9.75
120	A53	10p	brown (Bl)	27.50	21.00
			Nos. 108-120 (13)	49.60	38.40
			Set, never hinged	87.50	

See Nos. L1-L11.

Stamps of Spain, 1922-31, Overprinted Type "a" in Black, Blue or Red

1929-34 *Perf. 11½, 13x12½*

121	A49	5c	claret (Bk)	3.25	.20
122	A61	10c	green (R)	2.75	.40
123	A61	15c	slate grn (R)	97.50	1.00
124	A61	20c	violet (R)	2.75	.45
125	A61	30c	brown lake (Bl)	3.00	1.00
126	A61	40c	dark blue (R)	11.00	5.00
127	A49	50c	orange (Bl)	27.50	4.75
128	A49a	10p	brown (Bl)	2.75	4.25
			Nos. 121-128 (8)	150.50	17.05
			Set, never hinged	210.00	

Stamps of Spain, 1922-26, overprinted diagonally as above, and with no control number, or with "A000,000" on back, were not issued but were presented to the delegates at the 1929 UPU Congress in London. Value of complete set of 16, #3,250.

Stamps of Spain 1931-32, Overprinted in Black

1933-34 *Imperf.*

130	A108	1c	blue green	.20	.20

Perf. 11½

131	A108	2c	buff	.20	.20
132	A95	5c	brnsh black	.20	.20
133	A96	10c	yellow green	.20	.20
134	A97	15c	slate green	.20	.20
135	A95	20c	dark violet	.20	.20
136	A104	25c	lake	.20	.20
137	A99	30c	carmine rose	50.00	5.00
138	A100	40c	dark blue	.50	.20
139	A97	50c	orange	.95	.20
140	A100	60c	apple green	.95	.20
141	A105	1p	blue black	.95	.40
142	A106	4p	magenta	2.10	2.10
143	A107	10p	deep brown	3.00	4.75
			Nos. 130-143,E7 (15)	61.10	14.45
			Set, never hinged	100.00	

Street Scene in Tangier — A7

View of Xauen A8

Gate in Town Wall, Arzila — A9

Street Scene in Tangier A10

Mosque of Alcazarquivir A11

Caliph and His Guard A12

View of Tangier A13

Green Control Numbers Printed on Gum

1933-35 **Photo.** *Perf. 14, 13½*

144	A7	1c	brt rose	.20	.20
145	A8	2c	green ('35)	.20	.20
146	A9	5c	magenta ('35)	.20	.20
147	A10	10c	dark green	.30	.20
148	A11	15c	yellow ('35)	1.90	.20
149	A7	20c	slate green	.80	.20
150	A12	25c	crimson ('35)	20.00	.20
151	A10	30c	red brown	6.00	.20
152	A13	40c	deep blue	9.25	.20
153	A13	50c	red orange	30.00	3.75
154	A8	1p	slate blk ('35)	13.00	.20
155	A9	2.50p	brown ('35)	22.50	3.75
156	A11	4p	yel grn ('35)	22.50	3.75
157	A12	5p	black ('35)	30.00	3.75
			Nos. 144-157,E5 (15)	157.85	17.20
			Set, never hinged	230.00	

For surcharge see No. CB1.

Mosque — A14

Landscape A15

Green Control Numbers Printed on Gum

1935

158	A14	25c	violet	.85	.20
159	A15	30c	crimson	12.00	.20
160	A14	40c	orange	6.00	.20
161	A15	50c	bright blue	6.00	.20
162	A14	60c	dk blue green	6.00	.20
163	A15	2p	brown lake	30.00	4.25
			Nos. 158-163 (6)	60.85	5.25
			Set, never hinged	87.50	

See No. 174.

Regular Issue and Special Delivery Stamp of 1928, Surcharged in Blue, Green or Red with New Values and Ornaments

1936

164	A6	1c on 4p	ultra (Bl)	.25	.20
165	A5	2c on 2.50p	red vio (G)	.25	.20
166	A3	5c on 25c	cop red (R)	.20	.20
167	A4	10c on 1p	yel grn (G)	8.50	3.50
168	SD2	15c on 20c	blk (Bl)	6.50	1.75
			Nos. 164-168 (5)	15.70	5.85
			Set, never hinged	20.00	

Caliph and Viziers — A16

View of Bokoia A17

View of Alcazarquivir — A18

Sidi Saida Mosque A19

Caliph and Procession A20

Without Control Numbers

1937 **Photo.** *Perf. 13½*

169	A16	1c	green	.20	.20
170	A17	2c	red violet	.20	.20
171	A18	5c	orange	.20	.20
172	A16	15c	violet	.20	.20
173	A19	30c	red	.60	.20
a.			Souvenir sheet of 4, #170-173	18.00	10.00
174	A14	1p	ultra	6.00	.20
a.			Souv. sheet of 4, #169-171, 174	18.00	10.00
175	A20	10p	brown	50.00	15.00
			Nos. 169-175 (7)	57.40	16.20
			Set, never hinged	75.00	

Nos. 173a, 174a for 1st year of the Spanish Civil War.

Nos. 173a, 174a were privately overprinted "TANGER" in black on each stamp in the sheet for "use" in the International City of Tangier, and "GUINEA" for "use" in Spanish Guinea.

Harkeno Rifleman — A21

Troops Marching A22

Designs: 2c, Legionnaires. 5c, Cavalryman leading his mount. 10c, Moroccan phalanx. 15c, Legion flag-bearer. 20c, Colonial soldier. 25c, Ifni sharpshooters. 30c, Mounted trumpeters. 40c, Cape Juby Dromedary Corps. 50c, Regular infantry. 60c, Caliphate guards. 1p, Orderly on guard. 2p, Sentry. 2.50p, Regular cavalry. 4p, Orderly.

1937 *Perf. 13½*

176	A21	1c	dull blue	.20	.20
177	A21	2c	orange brn	.20	.20
178	A21	5c	cerise	.20	.20
179	A21	10c	emerald	.20	.20
180	A21	15c	brt blue	.20	.20
181	A21	20c	red brown	.20	.20
182	A21	25c	magenta	.20	.20
183	A21	30c	red orange	.20	.20
184	A21	40c	orange	.20	.20
185	A21	50c	ultra	.20	.20
186	A21	60c	yellow grn	.20	.20
187	A21	1p	blue violet	.20	.20
188	A21	2p	Prus blue	8.50	3.50
189	A21	2.50p	gray black	8.50	3.50
190	A21	4p	dark brown	8.50	3.50
191	A22	10p	black	8.50	3.50
			Nos. 176-191,E6 (17)	36.60	16.60
			Set, never hinged	52.50	

First Year of Spanish Civil War.

Exists imperf. Value, set $250.

For overprints see Nos. 214-229.

Spanish Quarter — A25

Designs: 10c, Moroccan quarter. 15c, Street scene, Larache. 20c, Tetuan.

1939 **Unwmk.** **Photo.** *Perf. 13½*

194	A25	5c	orange	.20	.20
195	A25	10c	brt blue grn	.20	.20
196	A25	15c	golden brown	.40	.20
197	A25	20c	brt ultra	.40	.20
			Nos. 194-197 (4)	1.20	.80

Postman — A26

Mail Box — A27

Landscape A28

Street Scene, Alcazarquivir A29

View of Xauen — A30

Sentry Guarding Palace at Sat — A31

The Chieftain — A32

Market Place, Larache — A33

Tetuán — A34

Ancient Gateway at Xauen — A35

Scene in Alcazarquivir A36

Post Office A37

Spanish War Veterans — A38

Victory Flag Bearers — A39

Cavalry — A40

Day of Court — A41

1940 Unwmk. Photo. *Perf. 11½x11*

198	A26	1c dark brown	.20	.20
199	A27	2c olive grn	.20	.20
200	A28	5c dk blue	.20	.20
201	A29	10c dk red lilac	.20	.20
202	A30	15c dk green	.25	.20
203	A31	20c purple	.20	.20
204	A32	25c black brown	.20	.20
205	A33	30c brt green	.20	.20
206	A34	40c slate green	1.75	.20
207	A35	45c orange ver	.70	.20
208	A36	50c brown orange	.70	.20
209	A37	70c sapphire	.70	.20
210	A38	1p indigo & brn	2.00	.20
211	A39	2.50p choc & dk grn	12.00	3.00
212	A40	5p dk cerise & sep	2.25	.20
213	A41	10p dk ol grn & brn org	20.00	5.00
		Nos. 198-213,E8 (17)	42.35	11.00
		Set, never hinged	70.00	

"ZONA" printed in black on back.
Exists imperf. Value, set $250.

Stamps of 1937 Overprinted in Various Colors

1940 Unwmk. *Perf. 13½*

214	A21	1c dull blue (Bk)	.70	.55
215	A21	2c org brn (Bk)	.70	.55
216	A21	5c cerise (Bk)	.70	.55
217	A21	10c emerald (Bk)	.70	.55
218	A21	15c brt blue (Bk)	.70	.55
219	A21	20c red brn (Bk)	.70	.55
220	A21	25c mag (Bk)	.70	.55
221	A21	30c red org (V)	.70	.55
222	A21	40c orange (V)	1.25	1.00
223	A21	50c ultra (Bk)	1.25	1.00
224	A21	60c yel grn (Bk)	1.25	1.00
225	A21	1p blue vio (V)	1.25	1.00
226	A21	2p Prus bl (Bl)	38.00	38.00
227	A21	2.50p gray blk (V)	38.00	38.00
228	A21	4p dk brn (Bl)	38.00	38.00
229	A22	10p black (R)	38.00	38.00
		Nos. 214-229,E10 (17)	172.10	167.65
		Set, never hinged	290.00	

4th anniversary of Spanish Civil War.

SEMI-POSTAL STAMPS

Types of Semi-Postal Stamps of Spain, 1926, Overprinted in Black or Blue

1926 Unwmk. *Perf. 12½, 13*

B1	SP1	1c orange	7.00	4.50
B2	SP2	2c rose	10.00	8.25
B3	SP3	5c black brn	3.50	3.00
B4	SP4	10c dark grn	3.50	3.00
B5	SP1	15c dk violet (Bl)	.65	.55
B6	SP4	20c violet brn	.65	.55
B7	SP5	25c deep carmine	.65	.55
B8	SP1	30c olive grn	.65	.55
B9	SP3	40c ultra	.20	.20
B10	SP2	50c red brown	.20	.20
B11	SP4	1p vermilion	.20	.20
B12	SP3	4p bister	.65	.55
B13	SP5	10p light violet	2.75	2.25
		Nos. B1-B13,EB1 (14)	33.10	26.45
		Set, never hinged	57.50	

See Spain No. B6a for No. B6 without overprint. For surcharges see Spain Nos. B64-B65.

AIR POST STAMPS

Mosque de Baja and Plane — AP1

View of Tetuán and Plane AP2

10c, Stork of Alcazar. 25c, Shore scene, plane. 40c, Desert tribesmen watching plane. 75c, View of shoreline at Larache. 1p, Arab mailman, plane above. 1.50p, Arab farmers, stork. 2p, Plane at twilight. 3p, Shadow of plane over city.

1938 Unwmk. Photo. *Perf. 13½*

C1	AP1	5c red brown	.20	.20
C2	AP1	10c emerald	.20	.20
C3	AP1	25c crimson	.20	.20
C4	AP1	40c dull blue	1.75	.50
C5	AP2	50c cerise	.20	.20
C6	AP2	75c ultra	.20	.20
C7	AP1	1p dark brown	.20	.20
C8	AP1	1.50p purple	.60	.30
C9	AP1	2p brown lake	.35	.20
C10	AP1	3p gray black	1.60	.20
		Nos. C1-C10 (10)	5.50	2.40

Nos. C1-C10 exist imperf. Value of set, $140.
For surcharge see No. C32.

AIR POST SEMI-POSTAL STAMPS

No. 150 Surcharged in Black

1936 Unwmk. *Perf. 14*

CB1	A12	25c + 2p on 25c	11.00	4.50
		Never hinged	25.00	
a.		Bars at right omitted	45.00	32.50
b.		Blue surcharge	35.00	11.50

25c was for postage, 2p for air post.

Nos. C1-C10 surcharged "Lucha Antituberculosa," a Lorraine cross and surtax are stated to be bogus.

SPECIAL DELIVERY STAMPS

Special Delivery Stamp of Spain Overprinted in Blue

1914 Unwmk. *Perf. 14*

E1	SD1	20c red	3.75	1.75

Special Delivery Stamp of Spain Overprinted in Blue

1915

E2	SD1	20c red	2.50	1.40

For bisected surcharge see No. 68.

Special Delivery Stamp of Spain Overprinted in Blue

1923

E3	SD1	20c red	10.50	8.25

Mounted Courier SD2

1928 Engr. *Perf. 14, 14½*

E4	SD2	20c black	4.25	1.40

For surcharge see No. 168.

Moorish Postman — SD3

Mounted Courier — SD4

1935 Photo. *Perf. 14*

Green Control Number on Back

E5	SD3	20c vermilion	1.00	.20

See No. E9.

1937 *Perf. 13½*

E6	SD4	20c bright carmine	.20	.20

1st Year of the Spanish Civil War.
For surcharge see No. E10.

Spain No. E14 Overprinted in Black

1938 *Perf. 10*

E7	SD7	20c vermilion	1.25	.20

Arab Postman SD5

Airmail 1935 SD6

1940 Photo. *Perf. 11½x11*

E8	SD5	25c scarlet	.60	.20

"ZONA" printed on back in black.

Type of 1935

1940 Litho. *Perf. 10*

E9	SD3	20c black brown	1.40	

No. E9 was prepared but not issued.

No. E6 Surcharged with New Value, Bars and

1940 *Perf. 13½*

E10	SD4	25c on 20c brt car	9.50	7.25

4th anniversary of Spanish Civil War.

SEMI-POSTAL SPECIAL DELIVERY STAMP

Type of Semi-Postal Special Delivery Stamp of Spain, 1926, Overprinted like #B1-B13

1926 Unwmk. *Perf. 12½, 13*

EB1	SPSD1	20c ultra & black	2.50	2.10

POSTAL TAX STAMPS

General Francisco Franco — PT1

1937-39	Unwmk.	Photo.	*Perf. 12½*	
RA1	PT1	10c sepia	.45	.20
a.		Sheet of 4, imperf.	4.00	1.60
RA2	PT1	10c copper brn ('38)	.45	.20
a.		Sheet of 4, imperf.	4.00	1.60
RA3	PT1	10c blue ('39)	.45	.20
a.		Sheet of 4, imperf.	4.00	1.60
		Nos. RA1-RA3 (3)	1.35	.60
		Set, never hinged	1.75	
		Set, RA1a-RA3a	12.00	

The tax was used for the disabled soldiers in North Africa.

TANGIER

For the International City of Tangier

Seville-Barcelona Issue of Spain, 1929, Overprinted in Blue or Red

TANGER

1929			*Perf. 11*	
L1	A52	5c rose lake	.25	.25
L2	A53	10c green (R)	.25	.25
L3	A50	15c Prus blue (R)	.25	.25
L4	A51	20c purple (R)	.25	.25
L5	A50	25c brt rose	.25	.25
L6	A52	30c black brn	.25	.25
L7	A53	40c dk blue (R)	.65	.65
L8	A51	50c deep org	.65	.65
L9	A52	1p blue blk (R)	7.00	7.00
L10	A53	4p deep rose	19.00	19.00
L11	A53	10p brown	27.50	27.50
		Nos. L1-L11 (11)	56.30	56.30
		Set, never hinged	95.00	

Overprints of 1937-39

The following overprints on stamps of Spain exist in black or in red:

"TANGER" vertically on Nos. 517-518, 522-523, 528, 532, 534, 539-543, 549.

"Correo Espanol Tanger" horizontally or vertically in three lines on Nos. 540, 592-597 (gray paper), 598-601.

"Tanger" horizontally on Nos. 539-541, 592-601.

"Correo Tanger" horizontally in two lines on five consular stamps.

TANGIER SEMI-POSTAL STAMPS

Types of Semi-Postal Stamps of Spain, 1926, Overprinted

1926			*Perf. 12½, 13*	
LB1	SP1	1c orange	6.00	6.50
LB2	SP2	2c rose	6.00	6.50
LB3	SP3	5c black brn	3.00	3.25
LB4	SP4	10c dk green	3.00	3.25
LB5	SP1	15c dk violet	1.00	1.25
LB6	SP4	20c violet brn	1.00	1.25
LB7	SP5	25c dp carmine	1.00	1.25
LB8	SP1	30c olive grn	1.00	1.25
LB9	SP3	40c ultra	.25	.25
LB10	SP2	50c red brn	.25	.25
LB11	SP4	1p vermilion	.60	.60
LB12	SP3	4p bister	.60	.60
LB13	SP5	10p lt violet	2.75	3.00
		Nos. LB1-LB13,LEB1 (14)	29.45	32.20
		Never hinged	50.00	

For overprints & surcharges see Spain Nos. B66-B67.

TANGIER SEMI-POSTAL SPECIAL DELIVERY STAMP

Types of Semi-Postal Special Delivery Stamp of Spain, 1926, Overprinted like #LB1-LB13

1926	Unwmk.	*Perf. 12½, 13*		
LEB1	SPSD1	20c ultra & black	3.00	3.00
		Never hinged	5.00	

TETUAN

Stamps of Spanish Offices in Morocco, 1903-09, Handstamped in Black, Blue or Violet

1908		Unwmk.	*Imperf.*	
1	A21	¼c blue green	13.00	10.00
		Perf. 14		
2	A35	2c bister brown	150.00	60.00
3	A35	5c green	140.00	35.00
4	A35	10c rose red	140.00	35.00
5	A35	20c grnsh black	300.00	125.00
6	A35	25c blue	100.00	35.00
		Nos. 1-6 (6)	843.00	300.00

Same Handstamp On Stamps of Spain, 1876 and 1900-05, in Black, Blue or Violet

1908			*Imperf.*	
7	A21	¼c deep green	7.50	3.25
		Perf. 14		
8	A35	2c bister brn	40.00	13.00
9	A35	5c dark green	55.00	22.50
10	A35	10c rose red	52.50	22.50
11	A35	15c purple	52.50	25.00
12	A35	20c grnsh black	150.00	110.00
13	A35	25c blue	80.00	35.00
14	A35	30c blue green	175.00	60.00
15	A35	40c olive bister	225.00	110.00
		Nos. 7-15 (9)	837.50	401.25

Counterfeits of this overprint are plentiful.

SPANISH SAHARA

'spa-nish sə-'har-ə

(Spanish Western Sahara)

LOCATION — Northwest Africa, bordering on the Atlantic
GOVT. — Spanish possession.
AREA — 102,703 sq. mi.
POP. — 32,000 (1940)
CAPITAL — Aaiún.

Spanish Sahara was a subdivision of Spanish West Africa. It included the colony of Rio de Oro and the territory of Saguiet el Hamra. Spanish Sahara was formerly known as Spanish Western Sahara, which superseded the older title of Rio de Oro.

100 Centimos = 1 Peseta

Tuareg and Camel — A1

1924	Unwmk.	Typo.	*Perf. 13*	
		Control Number on Back		
1	A1	5c blue green	2.25	.70
2	A1	10c gray green	2.25	.70
3	A1	15c turq blue	2.25	.70
4	A1	20c dark violet	2.25	1.00
5	A1	25c red	2.25	1.00
6	A1	30c red brown	2.25	1.00
7	A1	40c dark blue	2.25	1.00
8	A1	50c orange	2.25	1.00
9	A1	60c violet	2.25	1.00
10	A1	1p rose	12.00	5.50
11	A1	4p chocolate	55.00	27.50
12	A1	10p claret	140.00	85.00
		Nos. 1-12 (12)	227.25	126.10
		Set, never hinged	300.00	

#1-12 were for use in La Aguera & Rio de Oro.

An unissued set of 10, similar to Nos. 3-12, exists perf. 10 or imperf, and no control number except on 50c. The set also exists perf 14. Value, $200.

Nos. 1-12 also exist perf 14. Value, unused $300.

For overprints see Nos. 24-35.

Seville-Barcelona Issue of Spain, 1929 Overprinted in Blue or Red

1929			*Perf. 11*	
13	A52	5c rose lake	.25	.25
14	A53	10c green (R)	.25	.25
15	A50	15c Prus blue (R)	.25	.25
16	A51	20c purple (R)	.25	.25
17	A50	25c bright rose	.25	.25
18	A52	30c black brown	.25	.25
19	A53	40c dark blue (R)	.60	.40
20	A51	50c deep orange	.60	.40
21	A52	1p blue black (R)	2.50	1.60
22	A53	4p deep rose	20.00	15.00
23	A53	10p brown	37.50	30.00
		Nos. 13-23 (11)	62.70	48.90
		Set, never hinged	90.00	

Stamps of 1924 Overprinted in Red or Blue

1931			*Perf. 13*	
24	A1	5c blue grn (R)	.70	.55
25	A1	10c gray grn (R)	.70	.55
26	A1	15c turq blue (R)	.70	.55
27	A1	20c dark violet (R)	.70	.55
28	A1	25c red	.75	.55
29	A1	30c red brown	.75	.55
30	A1	40c dark blue (R)	3.50	.75
31	A1	50c orange	3.50	1.90
32	A1	60c violet	3.50	1.90
33	A1	1p rose	3.50	1.90
34	A1	4p chocolate	37.50	19.00
35	A1	10p claret	72.50	42.50
		Nos. 24-35 (12)	128.30	71.25
		Set, never hinged	175.00	

The stamps of the 1931 issue exist with the overprint reading upward, downward, or horizontally. Some values also exist with double overprint, double overprint, one inverted and diagonal overprint.

SEMI-POSTAL STAMPS

Red Cross Issue

Types of Semi-Postal Stamps of Spain, 1926, Overprinted

1926	Unwmk.		*Perf. 12½, 13*	
B1	SP3	5c black brown	8.00	8.00
B2	SP4	10c dark green	8.00	8.00
B3	SP1	15c dark violet	2.50	2.50
B4	SP4	20c violet brown	2.50	2.50
B5	SP5	25c deep carmine	2.50	2.50
B6	SP1	30c olive green	2.50	2.50
B7	SP3	40c ultra	.20	.20
B8	SP2	50c red brown	.20	.20
B9	SP5	60c myrtle green	.20	.20
B10	SP4	1p vermilion	.20	.20
B11	SP3	4p bister	2.50	1.90
B12	SP5	10p light violet	6.50	5.50
		Nos. B1-B12 (12)	35.80	34.20
		Set, never hinged	52.50	

See Spain No. B6a for No. B4 without overprint. For surcharges see Spain #B72-B73.

STELLALAND

'ste-lə-,land

LOCATION — South Africa
GOVT. — Republic
AREA — 5,000 sq. mi. (approx.)
CAPITAL — Vryburg

This short-lived republic was set up by the Boers in an effort to annex territory ruled by the Bechuana chiefs. Great Britain refused to recognize it and in 1885 sent an expeditionary force which ended the political career of the country.

Stellaland was annexed by Great Britain in 1885 and became a part of British Bechuanaland.

12 Pence = 1 Shilling

Coat of Arms

A1 A2

1884, Feb.	Unwmk.	Typo.	*Perf. 12*	
1	A1	1p red	225.00	*375.00*
a.		Horiz. pair, imperf. vert.	4,250.	
b.		Vert. pair, imperf. horiz.	4,600.	
2	A1	3p orange	25.00	*375.00*
a.		Horiz. pair, imperf. vert.	800.00	
b.		Vert. pair, imperf. horiz.	1,450.	
3	A1	4p gray	24.00	*400.00*
a.		Horiz. pair, imperf. vert.	750.00	
b.		Vert. pair, imperf. horiz.	*1,900.*	
4	A1	6p lilac	25.00	*400.00*
a.		Horiz. pair, imperf. vert.	1,400.	
b.		Vert. pair, imperf. horiz.	1,600.	
5	A1	1sh green	62.50	*750.00*
		Nos. 1-5 (5)	361.50	2,300.

Imperf. varieties are believed to be proofs.

No. 3 Handstamped "Twee" in Blackish Violet

1885				
6	A2	2p on 4p gray	*4,000.*	

The status of No. 6 has long been questioned.

STRAITS SETTLEMENTS

'strāts 'se-tᵊl-mənt

LOCATION — Malay Peninsula in southeastern Asia
GOVT. — British Colony
AREA — 1,356 sq. mi.
POP. — 1,435,895 (estimated)
CAPITAL — Singapore

The colony comprised the settlements of Malacca, Singapore and Penang, which were incorporated under one government in 1826 and the administration transferred from India to the Secretary of State for the Colonies in 1867.

Stamps of India were used in Malacca, Penang and Singapore, 1854-67.

The colony was dissolved in 1946 when Singapore became a separate crown colony. Malacca and Penang were incorporated into the Malayan Union, which became the Federation of Malaya in 1948.

See Malaya for stamps of the Federated Malay States, Johore, Kedah, Kelantan, Negri Sembilan, Pahang, Penang, Perak, Selangor, Sungei Ujong and Trengganu.

100 Cents = 1 Dollar

STAMPS OF INDIA USED IN STRAITS SETTLEMENTS

SINGAPORE

Stamps of India canceled with the Octagonal postmark "B/172"

1854 Wmk. 37 *Imperf.*

A1	½a blue (#2)	190.00
A2	1a red (#4)	125.00
A4	1a red (#7)	1,500.
A5	2a green (#5)	92.50
a.	Half used as 1a on cover	*150,000.*
A6	4a red & blue (#6)	925.00

1855-64 Unwmk. Typo. *Perf. 14*
Blue Glazed Paper

A9	4a black (#9)	45.00
a.	Half used as 2a on cover (#9b, '59)	*9,000.*
A10	8a rose (#10)	45.00
a.	Half used as 4a on cover (#10b, '59)	*62,500.*

1855-64 White Paper

A11	½a blue (#11)	47.50
A12	1a brown (#12)	27.50
a.	Half used as ½a on cover (#12c, '59)	*69,000.*
A13	2a dull rose (#13)	47.50
A14	2a buff (#15)	40.00
a.	2a orange (#15a)	42.50
A16	4a black (#16)	27.50
a.	Diagonal half used as 2a on cover (#16b, '59)	*24,000.*
A17	4a green ('64) (#17)	140.00
A18	8a rose (#18)	35.00
a.	Half used as 4a on cover (#18a, '59)	*62,500.*

1860-64 Unwmk. *Perf. 14*

A19	8p lilac (#19)	75.00
a.	Diagonal half used as 4p on cover (#19a)	*62,500.*
A20	8p lilac, *bluish* (#)	575.00

1865-67 Wmk. 38 (Elephant)

A22	½a blue (#20)	57.50
A23	8p lilac (#21)	150.00
A24	1a brown (#22)	45.00
A25	2a orange (#23)	47.50
a.	2a yellow (#23a)	47.50
A26	4a green (#24)	125.00
A27	8a rose (#25)	310.00

1866-67

A28	4a green, type I (#26)	160.00
A29	6a8p slate (#27)	350.00

1866 Official Stamps

A30	½a blue (#O5)	450.00
A31	2a yellow (#O8)	625.00

Stamps of India canceled with the Singapore Duplex Town Datestamp and Numeral "172" in adjacent diamond-shaped canceler

1855-64 White Paper

A32	1a brown (#12)	310.00
A33	2a orange (#15a)	400.00
A34	4a black (#16)	400.00
A35	8a rose (#18)	400.00

1860-64 Unwmk. *Perf. 14*

A36	8p lilac (#19)	425.00

1865-67

A37	2a orange (#23)	375.00
a.	2a yellow (#23a)	375.00
A38	4a green (#24)	450.00

PENANG

Stamps of India canceled with the Octagonal postmark "B/147"

1854 Wmk. 37 *Imperf.*

A50	½a blue (#2)	475.00
A51	1a red (#4)	195.00
A52	2a green (#5)	310.00
A53	4a red & blue (#6)	*1,800.*

1855-64 Unwmk. *Perf. 14*
Blue Glazed Paper

A56	4a black (#9)	100.00
A57	8a rose (#10)	92.50
a.	Half used as 4a on cover (#10b)	*69,000.*

1855-64 White Paper

A58	½a blue (#11)	97.50
A59	1a brown (#12)	57.50
A60	2a dull rose (#13)	85.00
A61	2a buff (#15)	80.00
a.	2a orange (#15a)	80.00
A63	4a black (#16)	57.50
A64	8a rose (#18)	75.00

1860-64 Unwmk. *Perf. 14*

A65	8p lilac (#19)	175.00

Stamps of India canceled with the Penang Duplex Town Datestamp and Numeral "147" in adjacent diamond-shaped canceler

1854 Wmk. 37 *Imperf.*

A66	1a red (#4)	3,100.

1855-64 White Paper

A67	½a blue (#2)	210.00
A68	1a brown (#12)	62.50
A69	2a orange (#15a)	75.00
A70	4a black (#16)	62.50
A71	4a green (#17)	180.00
A72	8a rose (#18)	70.00

1860-64 Unwmk. *Perf. 14*

A73	8p lilac (#19)	100.00

1865-67 Wmk. 38

A75	8p lilac (#21)	—
A76	1a brown (#22)	62.50
A77	2a yellow (#23a)	75.00
A78	4a green (#24)	195.00
A79	8a rose (#25)	—

1866-67

A80	4a green (#26)	210.00

MALACCA

Stamps of India canceled with the Octagonal postmark "B/109"

1854 Wmk. 37 *Imperf.*

A90	½a blue (#2)	*1,500.*
A91	1a red (#4)	*1,150.*
A93	2a green (#5)	*1,750.*
A94	4a red & blue, cut to shape (#6)	*1,800.*

1855-64 Unwmk. *Perf. 14*
Blue Glazed Paper

A97	8a rose (#10)	510.00

1855-64 White Paper

A98	½a blue (#11)	350.00
A99	1a brown (#12)	225.00
A100	2a dull rose (#13)	375.00
A101	2a buff (#15)	260.00
a.	2a orange (#15a)	290.00
A103	4a green (#17)	490.00
A104	8a rose (#18)	350.00

1860-64 Unwmk. *Perf. 14*

A105	8p lilac (#19)	425.00
A106	8p lilac, *bluish* (#19C)	850.00

1865-67 Wmk. 38

A107	4a green (#24)	490.00

Issued under British Administration

Stamps of India Surcharged in Red, Blue, Black Violet or Green:

Nos. 1-7

Nos. 8-9

1867, Sept. 1 Wmk. 38 *Perf. 14*

1	A7 1½c on ½a bl (R)		97.50	*190.00*
	Postal cancel, no company chop			*225.00*
2	A7 2c on 1a brn (R)		130.00	75.00
	Postal cancel, no company chop			92.50
3	A7 3c on 1a brn (Bl)		140.00	80.00
	Postal cancel, no company chop			95.00
4	A7 4c on 1a brn (Bk)		275.00	*250.00*
	Postal cancel, no company chop			300.00
5	A7 6c on 2a yel (V)		625.00	225.00
	Postal cancel, no company chop			275.00
6	A7 8c on 2a yel (G)		200.00	40.00
	Postal cancel, no company chop			50.00
7	A9 12c on 4a grn (R)		1,050.	275.00
	Postal cancel, no company chop			350.00
a.	Double surcharge		2,250.	
8	A7 24c on 8a rose (Bl)		450.00	72.50
	Postal cancel, no company chop			92.50
9	A7 32c on 2a yel (Bk)		375.00	80.00
	Postal cancel, no company chop			100.00

Manuscript Surcharge, Pen Bar Across "THREE HALF" of No. 1

9A	A7 2(c) on 1½c on ½a	*10,500.*	*5,000.*

Values for Nos. 1-9A are for stamps with perforations touching the frame line on one or two sides. Used values for Nos. 1-9 are for stamps with company chops in addition to postal cancellations.

Covers: Covers of this issue are very rare and seldom offered. Values start at about $1,500.

A2

A3

A4

A5

1867-72 Typo. Wmk. 1 *Perf. 14*

10	A2 2c bister brown	30.00	4.50
a.	2c yellow brown	30.00	4.50
b.	2c deep brown	87.50	12.00
11	A2 4c rose	50.00	7.75
a.	4c deep rose	65.00	10.25
12	A2 6c violet	87.50	16.50
a.	6c bright lilac	92.50	16.50
13	A3 8c yellow	150.00	10.00
a.	8c orange	150.00	11.00
14	A3 12c blue	125.00	10.00
a.	12c ultra	125.00	10.00
15	A3 24c green	125.00	5.75
a.	24c yellow green	250.00	22.50
16	A4 30c claret ('72)	225.00	12.50
17	A5 32c pale red	500.00	75.00
18	A5 96c olive gray	300.00	45.00
	Nos. 10-18 (9)	1,592.	187.00

Corner ornaments of types A2, A3 and A5 differ for each value.

See Nos. 19, 40-44, 48-50, 52-57. For surcharges see Nos. 20-35, 58-59, 61-66, 73-82, 91. For overprints see Malaya, Johore No. 1, Perak Nos. 1, O1-O2, Selangor Nos. 1-2, Sungei Ujong Nos. 2-3.

Stamps of Straits Settlements, 1867-82, overprinted "B" are listed under Bangkok.

1871 *Perf. 12½*

19	A5 96c olive gray	2,300.	275.00

Stamps of 1867-72 Surcharged:

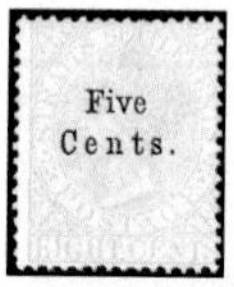

1879, May *Perf. 14*

20	A3 5c on 8c yellow	100.00	160.00
a.	No period after "CENTS"	825.00	875.00
21	A5 7c on 32c pale red	125.00	150.00
a.	No period after "CENTS"	1,100.	1,200.

No. 16 Surcharged:

10
g

10 10 10 10
j k m h

1880

22	A4(e) 10c on 30c	175.00	55.00
23	A4(f) 10c on 30c	550.00	125.00
24	A4(g) 10c on 30c	190.00	55.00
25	A4(h) 10c on 30c		—
25A	A4(j) 10c on 30c	3,800.	925.00
25B	A4(k) 10c on 30c	3,800.	925.00
25C	A4(m) 10c on 30c	3,800.	925.00

Surcharges e & f and g, h, j & m are virtually identical. These must have an expert certificate identifying them. Values can be suspect because of misidentifications.

Unused examples are valued without gum.

With Additional Surcharge *cents*

26	A4(e) 10c on 30c	325.00	82.50
27	A4(f) 10c on 30c	4,750.	700.00
27A	A4(g) 10c on 30c	3,000.	500.00
28	A4(h) 10c on 30c	*8,750.*	1,425.
28A	A4(j) 10c on 30c	*8,750.*	1,425.
28B	A4(k) 10c on 30c	*8,750.*	1,425.
28C	A4(m) 10c on 30c	*8,750.*	1,425.

Unused examples are valued without gum.

No. 13 Surcharged:

5
cents.
o

1880

29	A3(n) 5c on 8c yellow	125.00	150.00
30	A3(o) 5c on 8c yellow	450.00	525.00
31	A3(p) 5c on 8c yellow	130.00	160.00

No. 11 Surcharged

5
cents.

1882, Jan.

32	A2 5c on 4c rose	275.00	300.00

Nos. 12, 14a, 16 Surcharged

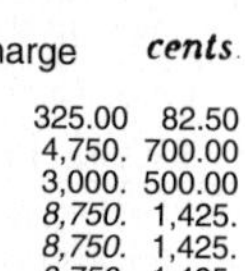

1880-81

33	A2 10c on 6c violet ('81)	65.00	7.50
a.	Double surcharge	—	2,100.
34	A3 10c on 12c blue ('81)	52.50	12.00
a.	10c on 12c ultra ('81)	70.00	19.00
35	A4 10c on 30c claret	400.00	97.50
	Nos. 33-35 (3)	517.50	117.00

A6

A7

1882, Jan. Typo. *Perf. 14*

38	A6	5c violet brown	87.50	100.00
39	A7	10c slate	400.00	75.00

See Nos. 45-47, 51. For surcharges see Nos. 60, 67-72, 89-92.

1882-99 Wmk. Crown and C A (2)

40	A2	2c bister brown	250.00	45.00
41	A2	2c car rose ('83)	7.00	1.00
a.		2c rose	40.00	4.00
42	A2	4c rose	125.00	6.00
43	A2	4c car rose ('99)	5.25	1.40
44	A2	4c bister brn ('83)	27.50	1.50
45	A6	5c ultra ('83)	13.00	1.10
46	A6	5c brown ('94)	5.50	1.10
47	A6	5c magenta ('99)	2.75	*2.40*
48	A2	6c violet	2.25	*4.00*
a.		6c lilac ('84)	27.50	10.50
49	A3	8c orange	3.50	1.10
50	A3	8c ultra ('94)	5.25	.60
a.		8c bright blue	7.75	.95
51	A7	10c slate	5.50	1.50
52	A3	12c vio brn ('83)	70.00	12.00
53	A3	12c claret ('94)	12.00	*9.75*
54	A3	24c blue grn ('83)	4.75	*4.50*
a.		24c yellow green ('84)	77.50	7.00
55	A4	30c claret ('91)	10.00	11.00
56	A5	32c red org ('87)	8.00	3.00
57	A5	96c olive gray ('88)	82.50	52.50
		Nos. 40-57 (18)	639.75	159.45

For overprints see Malaya, Perak Nos. O3-O9, Selangor Nos. 3-4, Sungei Ujong Nos. 6-7, 11.

Preceding Issues Surcharged

Surcharged Vertically

1883-84 Wmk. 2, 1

58	A3	2c on 8c orange	125.00	77.50
a.		Double surcharge	*2,750.*	*1,100.*
59	A5	2c on 32c pale red	650.00	190.00
a.		Double surcharge		
60	A6	2c on 5c ultra ('84)	130.00	140.00
a.		Pair, one without surcharge		
b.		Double surcharge		
		Nos. 58-60 (3)	905.00	407.50

Five types of surcharge on No. 58, two types on No. 59 and three types on No. 60.

Surcharged in Black

1883 Wmk. 2

61	A2	2c on 4c rose	85.00	*97.50*
b.		"s" of "Cents." inverted	1,325.	1,425.

Wmk. 1

62	A3	2c on 12c blue	275.00	140.00
a.		"s" of "Cents." inverted	4,000.	2,000.

Surcharged in Black or Blue

1884

63	A3	8c on 12c blue	475.00	130.00

Wmk. 2

64	A3	8c on 12c vio brn	325.00	130.00

With Additional Surcharge Handstamped in Red **8**

65	A3	8c on 8c on 12c vio brn (R + Bk)	275.00	300.00
66	A3	8c on 8c on 12c vio brn (R + Bl)	7,250.	

Surcharged in Black or Red **4 Cents**

1884

67	A6	4c on 5c ultra (Bk)	3,250.	*4,250.*
68	A6	4c on 5c ultra (R)	125.00	110.00

No. 68 Surcharged in Red **4**

69	A6	4c on 4c on 5c ultra	*24,000.*	

No. 69 may be a trial printing. "Usage" seems to been restricted to less than 10 letters known sent from the Postmaster General to his wife.

Surcharged in Black

1885-87

70	A6	3c on 5c ultra	125.00	*250.00*
a.		Double surcharge	2,500.	

Surcharged in Black **3 cents**

71	A6	3c on 5c vio brn ('86)	210.00	*225.00*

Surcharged

72	A6	2c on 5c ultra ('87)	25.00	*70.00*
a.		Double surcharge	1,200.	1,100.
b.		"C" omitted		*3,000.*

In the surcharged issues of 1883 to 1887, Nos. 59, 62, 63 and 71 are on stamps watermarked Crown and C C, the others are watermarked Crown and C A.

Surcharged

1885-94 Wmk. Crown and C A (2)

73	A5	3c on 32c magenta	1.50	1.10
a.		3c on 32c pale magenta	3.50	4.25
		Ovptd. "SPECIMEN"	225.00	
74	A5	3c on 32c rose ('94)	2.75	.85
a.		Without surcharge	*4,000.*	
		Ovptd. "SPECIMEN"	65.00	

No. 74a value is for copy with perfs touching frame line.

Surcharged

1891

75	A3	10c on 24c green	3.50	1.40
a.		Narrow "0" in "10"	32.50	32.50

Surcharged

76	A5	30c on 32c red orange	8.25	4.25

Surcharged

1892

77	A2	1c on 2c rose	2.25	*4.25*
78	A2	1c on 4c bister brn	5.75	*6.25*
a.		Double surcharge	1,300.	
79	A2	1c on 6c violet	1.60	*5.50*
a.		Dbl. surch., one invtd.	1,425.	1,325.
80	A3	1c on 8c orange	1.25	1.50
81	A3	1c on 12c vio brown	5.75	*10.50*
		Nos. 77-81 (5)	16.60	28.00

Surcharged

82	A3	1c on 8c gray green	1.10	*1.75*

Queen Victoria — A13

1892-99 Typo.

83	A13	1c gray green	3.75	.80
84	A13	3c car rose ('95)	12.50	.55
85	A13	3c brown ('99)	6.50	.70
a.		3c yellow brown	5.00	.75
86	A13	25c dk vio & grn	26.00	7.50
a.		25c purple brown & green	26.00	7.00
87	A13	50c ol grn & car	22.50	3.00
88	A13	$5 org & car ('98)	500.00	275.00
		Nos. 83-88 (6)	571.25	287.55
		Set ovptd. "SPECIMEN"	240.00	

Denomination of $5, is in color on plain tablet.

Stamps of 1883-94 Surcharged

1899

89	A6	4c on 5c ultra	4.00	*15.00*
a.		Double surcharge	—	1,400.
90	A6	4c on 5c brown	3.25	*5.25*
91	A3	4c on 8c brt blue	1.50	*1.25*
a.		4c on 8c ultra	1.00	*3.25*
b.		Double surcharge	*1,100.*	*1,000.*
		Nos. 89-91 (3)	8.75	*21.50*

Type of 1882 Issue Surcharged

92	A6	4c on 5c rose	.85	.40
a.		Without surcharge	*30,000.*	
		Ovptd. "SPECIMEN"	50.00	

King Edward VII — A14

Numerals of 5c, 8c, 10c, 30c, $1 and $5, type A14, are in color on plain tablet.

1902 Wmk. 2 Typo.

93	A14	1c green	3.25	*3.50*
a.		1c pale green	4.00	2.75
94	A14	3c vio & org	4.00	.25
95	A14	4c violet, *red*	5.50	.35
96	A14	5c violet	6.25	.95
97	A14	8c violet, *blue*	4.50	.30
98	A14	10c vio & blk, *yel*	29.00	1.75
99	A14	25c violet & grn	14.00	7.00
100	A14	30c gray & car rose	21.00	9.25
101	A14	50c grn & car rose	22.50	22.50
a.		50c dull green & carmine	21.00	20.00
102	A14	$1 green & blk	25.00	*75.00*
103	A14	$2 violet & blk	80.00	80.00
104	A14	$5 grn & brn org	225.00	190.00
104A	A14	$100 dl vio & grn, *yel*	*11,000.*	
		Nos. 93-104 (12)	440.00	390.85
		Nos. 93-104 ovptd. "SPECIMEN"	275.00	

High values of the 1902 and 1904 issues with revenue cancellations are of minimal value. No. 104A is inscribed "Postage & Revenue" but the limit of weight probably precluded its use postally.

See Nos. 113, 115-128B, 133.

A15

A16

A17

A18

1903-04

105	A15	1c gray green	2.00	9.25
106	A16	3c dull violet	12.50	5.25
107	A17	4c violet, *red*	5.50	.35
108	A18	8c violet, *blue*	55.00	1.50
		Nos. 105-108 (4)	75.00	16.35

See Nos. 109-112, 114, 129-132, 134.

1904-11 Wmk. 3

Chalky Paper

109	A15	1c gray green	3.25	.20
110	A16	3c dull violet	2.75	.35
111	A17	4c violet, *red*	11.50	.85
112	A17	4c dull vio ('08)	6.25	.20
113	A14	5c violet ('06)	12.50	2.75
114	A18	8c violet, *bl*	32.50	1.75
115	A14	10c vio & blk, *yel*	9.25	.90
116	A14	10c vio, *yel* ('08)	8.50	1.10
117	A14	25c vio & grn	37.50	24.00
118	A14	25c violet ('09)	16.00	8.00
119	A14	30c gray & car rose	55.00	3.00
120	A14	30c vio & org ('09)	45.00	4.50
121	A14	50c grn & car rose	62.50	17.50
122	A14	50c blk, *grn* ('10)	5.75	5.50
123	A14	$1 green & blk	62.50	21.00
124	A14	$1 blk & red, *bl* ('11)	17.00	5.75
125	A14	$2 violet & blk	110.00	97.50
		Revenue cancel		12.00
126	A14	$2 grn & red, *yel* ('09)	27.50	27.50
127	A14	$5 grn & brn org	225.00	160.00
128	A14	$5 grn & red, *grn* ('10)	140.00	85.00
		Revenue cancel		5.00
128A	A14	$25 green & blk	1,725.	1,600.
		Revenue cancel		55.00
128B	A14	$100dl vio & grn, *yel*	*12,650.*	
		Revenue cancel		200.00
		Nos. 109-128 (20)	890.25	467.35

Nos. 125, 128A and 128B are on chalky paper, the other values are on both ordinary and chalky. The note about No. 104A will apply to No. 128B.

1906-11

Ordinary Paper

129	A15	1c blue grn ('10)	26.00	1.25
130	A16	3c carmine ('08)	3.75	.20
131	A17	4c carmine ('07)	6.25	3.00
132	A17	4c lake ('11)	2.25	.95
133	A14	5c orange ('09)	3.25	2.25
134	A18	8c ultra ('06)	4.00	.60
		Nos. 129-134 (6)	45.50	8.25

Stamps of Labuan 1902-03, Overprinted or Surcharged in Red or Black

a

b

c

Perf. 12½ to 16 and Compound

1907 **Unwmk.**

134A	A38(a)	1c	violet & blk	70.00	*200.00*
135	A38(a)	2c	grn & blk	350.00	*350.00*
136	A38(a)	3c	brn & blk	22.50	*97.50*
137	A38(c)	4c	on 12c yel & blk	2.75	*7.00*
a.			No period after "CENTS"	350.00	—
138	A38(c)	4c	on 16c org brn & grn (Bk)	5.25	*9.25*
a.			With additional name in red	750.00	800.00
139	A38(c)	4c	on 18c bis & blk	3.25	*7.50*
a.			No period after "CENTS"	325.00	—
b.			"FOUR CENTS." & bar double	8,650.	
140	A38(a)	8c	orange & blk	3.50	*9.25*
141	A38(b)	10c	sl bl & brn	8.50	*8.00*
a.			No period after "Settlements"	375.00	
142	A38(a)	25c	grnsh bl & grn	17.00	*45.00*
143	A38(a)	50c	gray lil & vio	18.00	*80.00*
144	A38(a)	$1	org & red brn	52.50	*125.00*
			Nos. 134A-144 (11)	553.25	*938.50*

A19

A20

1908-11 **Typo.** **Wmk. 3** ***Perf. 14***

Chalky Paper

145	A19	$25	bl & vio, *bl* ('11)	1,600.	1,250.
146	A19	$500	violet & org	*92,000.*	
			Revenue cancel		275.

No. 146 is inscribed "Postage-Revenue" but was probably used only for revenue.

Excellent forgeries of No. 146 exist.

1910

Chalky Paper

147	A20	21c	maroon & vio	7.50	*40.00*
148	A20	45c	black, *green*	3.00	4.50

King George V
A21 A22

A23

A24

A25

A26

Die I (Type A24).

For description of dies I and II see front section of the Catalogue.

The 25c, 50c and $2 denominations of type A24 show the numeral on horizontally-lined tablet.

1912-18 **Chalky Paper** **Wmk. 3**

149	A21	1c	green	7.00	1.50
150	A21	1c	black ('18)	1.75	1.10
151	A25	2c	dp green ('18)	1.10	.60
152	A22	3c	scarlet	2.50	.40
a.			3c carmine	3.25	1.00
153	A23	4c	gray violet	1.75	.40
154	A23	4c	scarlet ('18)	2.75	.20
a.			Booklet pane of 1		
b.			Booklet pane of 12		
c.			4c carmine ('18)	2.75	.20
155	A24	5c	orange	2.00	.60
156	A25	6c	claret ('18)	2.00	.60
157	A25	8c	ultra	2.25	.90
158	A24	10c	violet, *yel*	1.75	.60
159	A24	10c	ultra ('18)	7.00	.60
160	A26	21c	maroon & vio	5.75	*11.00*
161	A24	25c	vio & red vio	14.00	9.75
162	A24	30c	vio & org ('14)	9.25	2.25
163	A26	45c	blk, *bl grn,* ol back ('14)	3.75	*22.50*
a.			45c black, *emerald* ('17)	3.75	*15.00*
164	A24	50c	black, *grn* ('14)	6.50	3.25
a.			50c black, *bl grn,* olive back	21.00	8.50
b.			50c black, *emerald*	14.00	11.00
c.			Die II	3.50	4.50
165	A24	$1	blk & red, *bl* ('14)	10.50	9.75
166	A24	$2	grn & red, *yel* ('15)	11.50	50.00
167	A24	$5	grn & red, *grn* ('15)	92.50	70.00
a.			$5 grn & red, *bl grn,* ol back	175.00	97.50
b.			$5 grn & red, *emer* ('15)	92.50	110.00
c.			Die II	110.00	75.00
			Nos. 149-167 (19)	185.60	186.00

The 1c, 3c, 5c and 8c are on ordinary paper.

Surface-colored Paper

168	A24	10c	violet, *yel*	1.75	1.10
169	A26	45c	black, *grn* ('14)	7.50	*21.00*
170	A24	$2	grn & red, *yel* ('14)	9.75	*50.00*
171	A24	$5	grn & red, *grn*	92.50	50.00
			Nos. 168-171 (4)	111.50	*122.10*

See Nos. 179-201. For surcharges see Nos. B1-B2.

A27

1915

172	A27	$25	bl & vio, *bl*	1,400.	500.00
			Revenue cancel		5.75
173	A27	$100	red & blk, *bl*	*5,750.*	
			Revenue cancel		90.00
174	A27	$500	org & dl vio	*46,000.*	
			Revenue cancel		200.00

Although Nos. 173 and 174 were available for postage, it is probable that they were used only for fiscal purposes.

See Nos. 202-204.

Die II (Type A24)

1921-32 **Wmk. 4**

Ordinary Paper

179	A21	1c	black	.60	.20
180	A25	2c	green	.60	.20
181	A25	2c	brown	8.00	3.00
182	A22	3c	green	1.75	.90
183	A23	4c	scarlet	2.25	*4.75*
184	A23	4c	dp violet ('25)	.70	.20
185	A23	4c	orange ('29)	1.10	.20
186	A24	5c	orange ('23)	2.75	1.50
a.			Die I	1.75	.20
187	A24	5c	dk brown ('32)	3.25	.20
a.			Die I ('32)	5.75	.20
188	A25	6c	claret	2.25	.25
189	A25	6c	scarlet ('27)	3.00	.20
a.			6c rose red ('25)	22.50	11.00
190	A24	10c	ultra (I)	2.00	3.00

Chalky Paper

191	A24	10c	vio, *yel* ('27)	2.25	.35
a.			Die I ('25)	3.00	*7.50*
192	A25	12c	ultra	1.10	.20
193	A26	21c	maroon & vio	7.00	*55.00*
194	A24	25c	vio & red vio	5.75	2.00
a.			Die I	32.50	80.00
195	A24	30c	violet & org	2.25	1.50
a.			Die I	26.00	*40.00*
196	A26	35c	orange & vio	14.00	7.00
197	A26	35c	vio & car ('31)	11.50	8.00
198	A24	50c	blk, *emerald*	2.00	.45
199	A24	$1	blk & red, *bl*	7.00	.75
200	A24	$2	grn & red, *yel*	11.50	9.25
201	A24	$5	grn & red, *grn*	100.00	37.50
202	A27	$25	bl & vio, *bl*	800.00	140.00
203	A27	$100	red & blk, *bl*	4,600.	1,900.
204	A27	$500	org & dl vio	*37,000.*	
			Nos. 179-201 (23)	192.60	136.60

No. 192 is on ordinary paper.

Nos. 203 and 204 were probably used only for fiscal purposes.

Stamps of 1912-21 Overprinted in Black: "MALAYA-BORNEO EXHIBITION," in Three Lines

1922 **Wmk. 3**

151d	A25	2c	deep green	32.50	*85.00*
154d	A23	4c	scarlet	8.50	*26.00*
155d	A24	5c	orange	5.75	*22.50*
157d	A25	8c	ultra	2.00	*8.50*
161d	A24	25c	vio & red vio	3.75	*35.00*
163d	A26	45c	blk, *bl grn,* ol back	3.50	*30.00*
165d	A24	$1	blk & red, *bl*	225.00	*800.00*
166d	A24	$2	grn & red, *yel*	30.00	*125.00*
167d	A24	$5	grn & red, *grn*	275.00	*450.00*

Wmk. 4

179d	A21	1c	black	3.50	*14.00*
180d	A25	2c	green	2.75	*16.00*
183d	A23	4c	scarlet	4.00	*30.00*
186d	A24	5c	orange (II)	3.25	*45.00*
190d	A24	10c	ultra	2.75	*29.00*
199d	A24	$1	blk & red, *bl*	22.50	*140.00*
			Nos. 151d-199d (15)	624.75	*1,856.*

Industrial fair at Singapore, Mar. 31-Apr. 15, 1922.

Common Design Types

pictured following the introduction.

Silver Jubilee Issue

Common Design Type

1935, May 6 **Engr.** ***Perf. 11x12***

213	CD301	5c	black & ultra	3.50	.35
214	CD301	8c	indigo & green	3.75	*3.50*
215	CD301	12c	ultra & brown	3.75	4.25
216	CD301	25c	brown vio & ind	4.00	*5.75*
			Nos. 213-216 (4)	15.00	*13.85*
			Set, never hinged	24.00	

George V
A28

George VI
A29

1936-37 **Typo.** ***Perf. 14***

Chalky Paper

217	A28	1c	black ('37)	.90	.20
218	A28	2c	green	1.00	.80
220	A28	4c	orange brn	2.00	.80
221	A28	5c	brown	.80	.35
222	A28	6c	rose red	1.10	1.25
223	A28	8c	gray	1.50	.80
224	A28	10c	dull vio	1.75	.70
225	A28	12c	ultra	2.00	3.00
226	A28	25c	rose red & vio	1.60	.60
227	A28	30c	org & dk vio	1.10	3.50
229	A28	40c	dk vio & car	1.10	2.75
230	A28	50c	blk, *emerald*	4.00	1.40
232	A28	$1	red & blk, *blue*	17.00	1.90
233	A28	$2	rose red & gray grn	37.50	11.50
234	A28	$5	grn & red, *grn* ('37)	80.00	11.50
			Nos. 217-234 (15)	153.35	41.05
			Set, never hinged	290.00	

Coronation Issue

Common Design Type

1937, May 12 **Engr.** ***Perf. 13½x14***

235	CD302	4c	deep orange	.20	.20
236	CD302	8c	gray black	.30	.20
237	CD302	12c	bright ultra	.50	.65
			Nos. 235-237 (3)	1.00	1.05
			Set, never hinged	2.00	

Two Dies

Die I. Printed in two operations. Lines of background touch outside of central oval. Foliage of palms touches outer frame line. Palm frond in front of King's eye has two points.

Die II. Printed from a single plate. Lines of background separated from central oval by a white line. Foliage of palms does not touch outer frame line. Palm frond in front of King's eye has one point.

1937-41 **Typo.** ***Perf. 14***

238	A29	1c	black (I)	2.75	.20
239	A29	2c	green (I)	9.00	.20
c.			Die II ('38)	35.00	.45
239A	A29	2c	brown org ('41) (II)	1.25	*5.00*
239B	A29	3c	green ('41) (II)	2.25	3.00
240	A29	4c	brown org (I)	8.00	.25
a.			Die II ('38)	50.00	.25
241	A29	5c	brown (I)	10.00	.35
a.			Die II ('39)	27.50	.20
242	A29	6c	rose red ('38) (I)	5.50	.50
243	A29	8c	gray ('38) (I)	19.00	.25
244	A29	10c	dull vio (I)	4.00	.20
245	A29	12c	ultra ('38) (I)	8.00	.35
245A	A29	15c	ultra ('41) (II)	3.25	*6.25*
246	A29	25c	rose red & vio (I)	40.00	1.10
247	A29	30c	org & vio (I)	25.00	2.00
248	A29	40c	dk vio & rose red (I)	10.00	2.25
249	A29	50c	blk, *emer* ('38) (I)	10.00	.45
250	A29	$1	red & blk, *bl* ('38) (I)	15.00	.40
251	A29	$2	rose red & gray grn ('38) (I)	30.00	4.25
252	A29	$5	grn & red, *grn* ('38) (I)	25.00	4.50
			Nos. 238-252 (18)	228.00	31.50
			Set, never hinged	375.00	

For overprints see #256-271, N1-N29 and Malaya, Malacca #N1-N14, Penang #N1-N26.

Stamps and Type of 1937-41 Overprinted in Red or Black

1945-48

256	A29	1c	black (R)	.20	.20
257	A29	2c	brown org (II)	.25	.20
a.			Die I ('46)	7.50	*3.75*
258	A29	3c	green	.25	.25
259	A29	5c	brown	.75	.60
260	A29	6c	gray	.25	.20
261	A29	8c	rose red	.25	.20
262	A29	10c	dull vio (I)	.30	.20
a.			10c claret (II) ('48)	*10.00*	1.25
263	A29	12c	ultra	1.75	*3.25*
264	A29	15c	ultra (Bk)	2.25	*4.75*
265	A29	15c	ultra (R)	.25	.20
266	A29	25c	rose red & vio	1.40	.25
a.			Double overprint	400.00	
267	A29	50c	blk, *emer* (R)	.60	.20
268	A29	$1	rose red & blk	2.00	.25
269	A29	$2	rose red & gray grn	2.50	.65
270	A29	$5	grn & red, *grn*	72.50	72.50
271	A29	$5	brn org & vio	3.75	2.75
			Nos. 256-271 (16)	89.25	86.65

The letters "B M A" are initials of "British Military Administration".

An 8c gray with BMA overprint was prepared but not issued. Value $5.

The 6c gray, 8c rose red and $5 brown orange & violet exist without BMA overprint, but were issued only with it.

No. 262a does not exist without overprint. No. 262 exists in at least three shades.

SEMI-POSTAL STAMPS

Nos. 152-153 Surcharged

1917 Wmk. 3 *Perf. 14*

B1	A22	3c + 2c scarlet	3.00	*29.00*
a.		No period after "C"	375.00	*575.00*
B2	A23	4c + 2c gray violet	4.00	*29.00*
a.		No period after "C"	400.00	*575.00*

POSTAGE DUE STAMPS

D1

1924-26 Typo. Wmk. 4 *Perf. 14*

J1	D1	1c violet	5.75	*7.50*
		On cover		90.00
J2	D1	2c black	3.75	1.50
		On cover		30.00
J3	D1	4c green ('26)	2.25	*5.50*
		On cover		60.00
J4	D1	8c red	5.25	.60
		On cover		40.00
J5	D1	10c orange	7.00	.95
		On cover		40.00
J6	D1	12c ultramarine	8.00	.75
		On cover		50.00
		Nos. J1-J6 (6)	32.00	*16.80*
		Set never hinged	55.00	

Cover values are for properly franked commercial covers. Philatelic usages also exist and sell for less.

OCCUPATION STAMPS

Issued Under Japanese Occupation

Straits Settlements Nos. 238, 239A, 239B, 243 and 245A Handstamped in Red

1942, Mar. 16 Wmk. 4 *Perf. 14*

N1	A29	1c black	16.00	20.00
N2	A29	2c brown orange	16.00	16.00
N3	A29	3c green	70.00	*85.00*
N4	A29	8c gray	27.50	22.50
N5	A29	15c ultra	20.00	20.00
		Nos. N1-N5 (5)	149.50	163.50
		Set, never hinged	200.00	

Other denominations with this handstamp are believed to be proofs.

The handstamp reads: "Seal of Post Office of Malayan Military Department."

Stamps of Straits Settlements, 1937-41, Handstamped in Red, Black, Violet or Brown

1942, Apr. 3

N6	A29	1c black	4.00	4.00
N6A	A29	2c green (V)	2,875.	500.00
N7	A29	2c brown org	3.50	3.50
N8	A29	3c green	3.25	3.50
N9	A29	5c brown	25.00	30.00
N10	A29	8c gray	5.00	3.50
N11	A29	10c dull violet	55.00	45.00
N12	A29	12c ultra	92.50	90.00
N13	A29	15c ultra	4.50	4.00
N14	A29	30c orange & vio	2,200.	350.00
N15	A29	40c dk vio & rose red	100.00	125.00
N16	A29	50c blk, *emerald*	60.00	60.00
N17	A29	$1 red & blk, *bl*	87.50	80.00
N18	A29	$2 rose red & gray grn	150.00	150.00
N19	A29	$5 grn & red, *grn*	200.00	165.00

Nos. N6-N7, N9, N11-N12, N15-N19 with red handstamp were used in Sumatra. The 2c green with red handstamp was not regularly issued.

Straits Settlements Nos. 239A, 239B, 243 and 245A Overprinted in Black

1942

N20	A29	2c brown orange	2.00	6.00
a.		Inverted overprint	14.50	21.00
b.		Dbl. ovpt., one invtd.	55.00	70.00
N21	A29	3c green	62.50	*75.00*
N22	A29	8c gray	5.75	2.75
a.		Inverted overprint	17.00	32.50
N23	A29	15c ultra	15.00	9.25
		Nos. N20-N23 (4)	85.25	93.00
		Set never hinged	100.00	

Straits Settlements Nos. 239A and 243 Overprinted in Black

1942, Nov. 3

N24	A29	2c brown orange	14.00	*25.00*
a.		Inverted overprint	375.00	375.00
N25	A29	8c gray	15.00	*20.00*
a.		Inverted overprint	375.00	375.00

Agricultural-Horticultural Exhibition held at Kuala Lumpur, Selangor, Nov. 1-2, 1942. Sold only at a temporary post office at the exhibition.

Straits Settlements Nos. 243, 245 and 248 Overprinted in Black or Red

1943

N26	A29	8c gray (Bk)	1.60	.60
a.		Inverted overprint	52.50	62.50
N27	A29	8c gray (R)	2.50	3.00
N28	A29	12c ultramarine	1.40	10.50
N29	A29	40c dk vio & rose red	2.00	4.50
		Nos. N26-N29 (4)	7.50	18.60
		Set never hinged	10.00	

The Japanese characters read: "Japanese Postal Service."

SUDAN

sü-'dan

LOCATION — Northeastern Africa, south of Egypt
GOVT. — Administered jointly by Egypt and Great Britain
AREA — 967,500 sq. mi.
POP. — 20,564,364 (1983)
CAPITAL — Khartoum

10 Milliemes = 1 Piaster
100 Piasters = 1 Egyptian Pound

Watermarks

Wmk. 71 — Rosette

Wmk. 179 — Multiple Crescent and Star

Wmk. 214 — Multiple S G

Egyptian Stamps of 1884-93 Overprinted in Black

1897, Mar. 1 Wmk. 119 *Perf. 14*

1	A18	1m brown	2.50	*2.00*
a.		Inverted overprint	300.00	
2	A19	2m green	2.50	*2.25*
3	A21	3m orange	1.75	*1.75*
4	A22	5m carmine rose	2.25	1.50
a.		Inverted overprint	300.00	
5	A14	1p ultra	9.00	2.00
6	A15	2p orange brown	55.00	15.00
7	A16	5p gray	45.00	17.50
a.		Double overprint	*4,500.*	
8	A22	10p violet	32.50	*40.00*
		Nos. 1-8 (8)	150.50	82.00

Counterfeits of Nos. 1-8 are plentiful.

Camel Post — A1

1898, Mar. 1 Typo. Wmk. 71

9	A1	1m rose & brn	1.00	1.25
10	A1	2m brown & grn	2.50	1.75
11	A1	3m green & vio	2.75	2.00
12	A1	5m black & rose	2.25	.75
13	A1	1p yel brn & ultra	6.00	3.50
14	A1	2p ultra & blk	25.00	6.75
15	A1	5p grn & org brn	30.00	16.00
16	A1	10p dp vio & blk	27.50	2.50
		Nos. 9-16 (8)	97.00	34.50

See Nos. 17-27, 43-50. For overprints see Nos. C3, MO1-MO15, O1-O9, O17-O24. For surcharges see Nos. 28, 62, C16.

1902-21 Wmk. 179

17	A1	1m car rose & brn ('05)	1.50	.50
18	A1	2m brown & grn	2.00	.20
19	A1	3m grn & vio ('03)	2.75	.30
20	A1	4m ol brn & bl ('07)	2.00	*2.50*
21	A1	4m brn & red ('07)	2.00	.80
22	A1	5m blk & rose red ('03)	2.50	.20
23	A1	1p brn & ultra ('03)	3.00	.30
24	A1	2p ultra & blk ('08)	27.50	2.00
25	A1	2p org & vio brn, chalky paper ('21)	5.00	*10.00*
26	A1	5p grn & org brn ('08)	25.00	.30
a.		On chalky paper	37.50	4.50
27	A1	10p dp vio & blk ('11)	25.00	4.00
a.		On chalky paper	32.50	10.0
		Nos. 17-27 (11)	98.25	21.10

No. 15 Surcharged in Black

1903, Sept. Wmk. 71

28	A1	5m on 5p	8.00	*10.00*
a.		Inverted surcharge	325.00	*260.00*

A2

1921-22 Typo. Wmk. 179

29	A2	1m orange & blk ('22)	1.25	*4.50*
30	A2	2m dk brn & org ('22)	11.00	*12.00*
a.		2m dark brown & yellow ('23)	12.00	12.00
31	A2	3m green & vio ('22)	3.00	*10.00*
32	A2	4m brown & grn ('22)	7.00	5.50
33	A2	5m blk & ol brn ('22)	3.00	.20
34	A2	10m black & car ('22)	5.00	.20
35	A2	15m org brn & ultra	4.00	1.25
		Nos. 29-35 (7)	34.25	33.65

See Nos. 36-42. For overprints see Nos. C1-C2, O10-O16.

For surcharges see Nos. 60-61.

1927-40 Wmk. 214

Chalky Paper

36	A2	1m org yel & blk	1.00	.20
37	A2	2m dk brn & org	.90	.20
38	A2	3m green & violet	1.00	.20
39	A2	4m brown & green	.90	.20
40	A2	5m blk & ol brn	.75	.20
a.		Booklet pane of 4		
41	A2	10m black & car	2.00	.20
42	A2	15m org brn & ultra	2.00	.20
43	A1	2p orange & vio brn	2.00	.20
44	A1	3p dk bl & red brn ('40)	3.00	.20
45	A1	4p black & ultra ('36)	3.50	.20
46	A1	5p dk grn & org brn	1.75	.20
47	A1	6p blk & pale bl ('36)	6.00	1.00
48	A1	8p blk & pck grn ('36)	7.00	2.50
49	A1	10p dp vio & blk	4.00	.20
50	A1	20p bl & lt bl ('35)	4.00	.20
		Nos. 36-50 (15)	39.80	6.10

Thick, Smooth, Unsurfaced Paper ('41)

36a	A2	1m org yel & blk	1.00	.20
37a	A2	2m dk brn & org	1.60	.20
38a	A2	3m green & violet	3.00	.35
39a	A2	4m brown & green	3.75	.35
40b	A2	5m blk & ol brn	2.75	.20
41a	A2	10m black & car	3.25	.20
42a	A2	15m org brn & ultra	1.60	.20
43a	A1	2p orange & vio brn	4.25	.20
44a	A1	3p dk bl & red brn	18.00	.20
46a	A1	5p dk grn & org brn	5.50	2.25
47a	A1	6p blk & pale blue	37.50	2.25
48a	A1	8p blk & pck grn	50.00	4.50
49a	A1	10p bright mauve & blk	9.50	.75
50a	A1	20p bl & lt blue	5.50	.20
		Nos. 36a-50a (14)	147.20	12.05

Charles George Gordon — A3

Gordon Memorial College A4

Memorial Service at Khartoum — A5

1935, Jan. 1 Engr. *Perf. 13½x14*

51	A3	5m deep green	.50	.20
52	A3	10m brown	.90	.20
53	A3	13m ultra	2.00	*11.00*
54	A3	15m carmine	1.50	.20
55	A4	2p deep blue	1.50	.20
56	A4	5p orange	1.75	.35
57	A4	10p dull violet	8.00	*8.00*
58	A5	20p black	30.00	*50.00*
59	A5	50p red brown	90.00	*110.00*
		Nos. 51-59 (9)	136.15	180.15

50th anniv. of the death of Gen. Charles George ("Chinese") Gordon (1833-85).

No. 41 Surcharged in Black

Wmk. Multiple S G (214)

1940, Feb. 25 Typo. *Perf. 14*

60	A2	5m on 10m black & car	.75	.50

Nos. 40 and 48 Surcharged in Black

a

b

1940-41

61	A2(a)	4½p on 5m ('41)	55.00	4.50
62	A1(b)	4½p on 8p	45.00	7.50

AIR POST STAMPS

Nos. 40-41, 43 Overprinted in Black

Nos. C1-C2

No. C3

1931 Wmk. 214 *Perf. 11½x12½, 14*

C1	A2	5m blk & olive brown	.75	*1.00*
C2	A2	10m blk & carmine	1.25	*4.00*
C3	A1	2p org & vio brown	2.00	*3.50*
		Nos. C1-C3 (3)	4.00	*8.50*

Statue of Gen. C. G. Gordon AP3

1931-35 Engr. *Perf. 14*

C4	AP3	3m dk brn & grn ('33)	3.00	*6.00*
C5	AP3	5m grn & blk	1.10	.20
C6	AP3	10m car rose & blk	1.10	.25
C7	AP3	15m dk brn & brn	.45	.20
C8	AP3	2p org & blk	.40	.20
C9	AP3	2½p bl & red vio ('33)	3.25	.20
C10	AP3	3p gray & blk	.65	.20
C11	AP3	3½p dl vio & blk	1.50	.90
C12	AP3	4½p gray & brn	11.00	*16.00*
C13	AP3	5p ultra & blk	1.10	.35
C14	AP3	7½p pck grn & dk grn ('35)	10.00	6.00
C15	AP3	10p peacock bl & sep ('35)	10.00	.75
		Nos. C4-C15 (12)	43.55	31.25

See Nos. C23-C30. For surcharges see Nos. C17-C22, C31-C34.

No. 43 Surcharged in Black

1932, July 18 Typo.

C16	A1	2½p on 2p	2.00	*4.00*

Nos. C6, C4-C5, C12 Surcharged

1935 Engr. *Perf. 14*

C17	AP3	15m on 10m	.45	.20
a.		Double surcharge	700.00	*775.00*
b.		Arabic characters omitted	650.00	
C18	AP3	2½p on 3m	.95	*6.00*
a.		"½" 2¼mm high instead of 3mm	2.50	*20.00*
b.		Second Arabic character of surcharge omitted	55.00	*125.00*
C19	AP3	2½p on 5m	.50	*1.75*
a.		"½" 2¼mm high instead of 3mm	1.50	*9.00*
b.		Second Arabic character of surcharge omitted	30.00	*60.00*
c.		Inverted surcharge	900.00	*900.00*
d.		As "a," inverted	4,000.	
e.		As "b," inverted	*1,500.*	*1,600.*
f.		Pair, C19c and C19d	*5,750.*	
C20	AP3	3p on 4½p	2.00	*10.00*
C21	AP3	7½p on 4½p	6.50	*45.00*
a.		"7¼" instead of "7½"		
C22	AP3	10p on 4½p	6.50	*45.00*
		Nos. C17-C22 (6)	16.90	*107.95*

Type of 1931-35

1936-37 *Perf. 11½x12½*

C23	AP3	15m dk brn & brn ('37)	4.00	.20
C24	AP3	2p org & blk ('37)	5.00	*15.00*
C25	AP3	2½p bl & red vio	3.00	.20
C26	AP3	3p gray & blk ('37)	1.00	.40
C27	AP3	3½p dl vio & blk ('37)	2.50	*12.00*
C28	AP3	5p ultra & blk ('37)	4.00	.40
C29	AP3	7½p pck grn & dk grn ('37)	4.50	*10.00*
C30	AP3	10p pck bl & sep ('37)	4.50	*20.00*
		Nos. C23-C30 (8)	28.50	*58.20*

Nos. C25, C11, C14 and C15 Surcharged as in 1935

1938 Wmk. 214 *Perf. 11½x12½, 14*

C31	AP3	5m on 2½p	1.00	.25
C32	AP3	3p on 3½p	15.00	*30.00*
a.		On No. C27	400.00	*500.00*
C33	AP3	3p on 7½p	6.00	6.00
a.		On No. C29	400.00	*500.00*
C34	AP3	5p on 10p	1.00	5.00
a.		On No. C30	400.00	*500.00*
		Nos. C31-C34 (4)	23.00	41.25

POSTAGE DUE STAMPS

Postage Due Stamps of Egypt, 1889, Overprinted in Black

1897 Wmk. 119 *Perf. 14*

J1	D3	2m green	1.50	*5.00*
J2	D3	4m maroon	1.50	*5.00*
J3	D3	1p ultra	10.00	*4.00*
J4	D3	2p orange	10.00	*8.50*
		Nos. J1-J4 (4)	23.00	22.50

Steamboat on Nile River — D1

1901 Typo. Wmk. 179

J5	D1	2m orange brn & blk	.70	.50
J6	D1	4m blue green & brn	2.00	1.00
J7	D1	10m blue vio & blue grn	4.00	3.50
J8	D1	20m car rose & ultra	3.75	3.75
		Nos. J5-J8 (4)	10.45	8.75

1927-30 Wmk. Multiple S G (214)

J9	D1	2m org brn & blk ('30)	2.50	2.50
J10	D1	4m blue grn & brn	1.00	.75
J11	D1	10m violet & blue grn	1.50	*1.60*
		Nos. J9-J11 (3)	5.00	4.85

ARMY OFFICIAL STAMPS

Regular Issues of 1898 and 1902-08 Overprinted in Black:

Nos. MO1, MO3 and MO2, MO4

1905 Wmk. 71 *Perf. 14*

MO1	A1	1m rose & brown	150.00	125.00
a.		"OFFICIAL"	3,250.	1,750.
b.		Pair, #MO1 and #MO2	2,750.	
MO2	A1	1m rose & brown	1,800.	*1,800.*

Wmk. 179

MO3	A1	1m car rose & brn	3.00	2.00
a.		"OFFICIAL"	45.00	30.00
b.		Inverted overprint	70.00	60.00
c.		Horizontal overprint	375.00	
MO4	A1	1m car rose & brn	40.00	24.00
a.		Inverted overprint	350.00	375.00

Regular Issues of 1902-11 Overprinted in Black

1906-11

MO5	A1	1m car rose & brn	1.25	.30
a.		"Army" and "Service" 14mm apart	275.00	200.00
b.		Inverted overprint	425.00	*450.00*
c.		Pair, one without ovpt.		*3,750.*
d.		Double overprint		800.00
e.		"Service" omitted		*3,750.*
MO6	A1	2m brn & grn	10.00	.95
a.		Pair, one without ovpt.	2,500.	
b.		"Army" omitted	3,000.	
MO7	A1	3m green & violet	16.00	.40
a.		Inverted overprint	2,000.	
MO8	A1	5m blk & rose red	1.40	.20
a.		Inverted overprint		225.00
b.		Double overprint	225.00	225.00
c.		Double ovpt., one invtd.	875.00	400.00
MO9	A1	1p yel brn & ultra	12.00	.40
a.		"Army" omitted	2,000.	2,000.
MO10	A1	2p ultra & blk ('09)	45.00	12.50
a.		Double overprint		—
MO11	A1	5p grn & org brn ('08)	100.00	60.00
MO12	A1	10p dp vio & blk ('11)	600.00	*600.00*
		Nos. MO5-MO12 (8)	785.65	674.75

Same Overprint On Regular Issue of 1898

Wmk. 71

MO13	A1	2p ultra & black	60.00	10.00
a.		Inverted overprint		
MO14	A1	5p grn & org brn	95.00	*175.00*
MO15	A1	10p dp vio & blk	140.00	375.00

There are two types of this overprint which may be distinguished by the size and shape of the "y."

PERFORATED ARMY OFFICIAL STAMPS

Stamps of Sudan punched with "AS" (Army Service) replaced the overprinted Army Official stamps Jan. 1, 1912.

These perforated Official stamps were used on internal military mail until the return of the Egyptian Army to Egypt in 1924. They continued to be used on mail to foreign destinations until supplies of individual denominations were exhausted or until 1936, when remaining stocks were destroyed. They were replaced by stamps overprinted or punched "SG."

Catalogue numbers are "MOA" plus Scott No. of basic, unoverprinted stamps.

1912-22

On Second Large Camel Post Issue

23 holes: 12 in "A," 11 in "S"

MOA17	A1	1m car rose & brn	65.00	7.25
MOA18	A1	2m brn & grn	7.50	.75
MOA19	A1	3m grn & vio	50.00	3.50
MOA22	A1	5m blk & rose red	11.00	.55
MOA23	A1	1p brn & ultra	22.50	.80
MOA24	A1	2p ultra & blk	45.00	4.50
MOA25	A1	2p org & vio brn ('22)	65.00	60.00
MOA26	A1	5p grn & org brn	45.00	30.00
a.		Chalky paper (#26a)	45.00	30.00
MOA27	A1	10p dp vio & blk	450.00	275.00
		Nos. MOA17-MOA27 (9)	761.00	382.35

1922-24

On Small Camel Post Issue

17 holes: 8 in "A," 9 in "S"

MOA30	A2	2m dk brn & org	70.00	45.00
MOA33	A2	5m blk & ol brn	13.00	4.50
MOA34	A2	10m black & car	20.00	5.50
		Nos. MOA30-MOA34 (3)	103.00	55.00

OFFICIAL STAMPS

PERFORATED OFFICIAL STAMPS

Stamps of Sudan punched with "SG" (Sudan Government) were issued for franking official mail in 1900-1901 and again in 1913-30. They were used on internal correspondence until 1932 and for foreign correspondence until 1936.

The perforated initials can appear upright, inverted, reversed, and inverted and reversed on the 1900-01 stamps, but upright only on later issues.

Values are for very fine examples, well-centered and free of encroaching perfin holes.

Catalogue numbers are "OA" plus Scott No. of basic, unoverprinted stamps.

1900, Feb. 8
On 1897 Ovpt. on Egypt
26 holes: 14 in "S," 12 in "G"

OA4	A22	5m carmine rose	55.00	17.50

1901, Jan.
On First Large Camel Post
26 holes: 14 in "S," 12 in "G"

OA9	A1	1m rose & brown	45.00	32.50

Regular Issue of 1898 Overprinted in Black

1902-06 Wmk. 71 *Perf. 14*

O1	A1	1m rose & brown	2.00	*7.50*
a.		Inverted overprint	325.00	*400.00*
b.		Round periods	7.50	*30.00*
c.		Double overprint	650.00	
d.		Oval "O" in overprint	90.00	
e.		As "d," inverted overprint	5,500.	
O2	A1	10p dp vio & blk ('06)	13.00	*20.00*

Same Ovpt. on Stamps of 1902-11

1903-12 Wmk. 179

O3	A1	1m car rose & brn ('04)	.45	.20
a.		Double overprint		
O4	A1	3m grn & vio ('04)	2.25	.20
a.		Double overprint		
O5	A1	5m blk & rose red	2.25	.20
O6	A1	1p yel brn & ultra	2.25	.20
O7	A1	2p ultra & blk	20.00	.20
O8	A1	5p grn & org brn	1.75	.25
O9	A1	10p dp vio & blk	3.75	47.50
		Nos. O3-O9 (7)	32.70	48.75

1913-22
On Second Large Camel Post
25 holes: 12 in "S," 13 in "G"

OA17	A1	1m car rose & brn	9.00	.30
OA18	A1	2m brown & grn ('15)	8.50	8.00
OA19	A1	3m grn & vio	15.00	.75
OA22	A1	5m blk & rose red	5.00	.20
OA23	A1	1p brn & ultra	7.50	.40
OA24	A1	2p ultra & blk	16.00	.70
OA25	A1	2p org & vio brn ('22)	55.00	8.00
OA26	A1	5p grn & org brn	32.50	1.50
a.		On chalky paper	32.50	4.50
OA27	A1	10p dp vio & blk ('14)	42.50	35.00
a.		On chalky paper	42.50	35.00
		Nos. OA17--OA27 (9)	191.00	54.85

1922
On First Small Camel Post Issue
19 holes: 9 in "S," 10 in "G"

OA31	A2	3m green & vio	17.50	15.00
OA32	A2	4m brown & grn	22.50	10.00
OA33	A2	5m blk & ol brn	3.00	1.60
OA34	A2	10m black & car	3.00	1.60
		Nos. OA31--OA34 (4)	46.00	28.20

1927-30
19 holes: 9 in "S," 10 in "G"

OA38	A2	3m org yel & blk ('28)	15.00	3.75
OA39	A2	4m brown & grn ('30)	75.00	50.00
OA40	A2	5m blk & ol brn	6.00	.20
OA41	A2	10m black & car	19.00	.40
		25 holes: 12 in "S," 13 in "G"		
OA43	A1	2p orange & vio brn	21.00	1.10
OA46	A1	5p dk grn & org brn	20.00	3.75
OA49	A1	10p dp vio & blk	42.50	11.00
		Nos. OA38--OA49 (7)	198.50	70.20

Regular Issue of 1927-40 Overprinted in Black

Perf. 14, 13½x 14
1936-46 Wmk. 214

O10	A2	1m dk org & int blk ('46)	.75	*3.50*
O11	A2	2m dk brn & dk org ('45)	.25	.20
O12	A2	3m green & vio ('37)	1.25	.20
O13	A2	4m brown & green	1.60	.20
O14	A2	5m blk & ol brn ('40)	.35	.20
O15	A2	10m blk & car ('46)	.35	.20
O16	A2	15m org brn & ultra ('37)	3.00	.20

O17	A1	2p org & vio brn ('37)	5.00	.20
O18	A1	3p dk bl & red brn ('46)	2.75	.50
O19	A1	4p blk & ultra ('46)	12.50	1.00
O20	A1	5p dk grn & org brn	6.75	.20
O21	A1	6p blk & pale bl ('46)	4.00	2.00
O22	A1	8p blk & pck grn ('46)	2.75	9.00
O23	A1	10p dp vio & blk ('37)	15.00	2.50
O24	A1	20p bl & lt bl ('46)	13.00	9.00
		Nos. O10-O24 (15)	69.30	29.10

SURINAM

'sur-ə-ˌnam

(Dutch Guiana)

LOCATION — On the northeast coast of South America, bordering on the Atlantic Ocean
GOVT. — Dutch Colony
AREA — 70,087 sq. mi.
POP. — 370,000 (est. 1984)
CAPITAL — Paramaribo

100 Cents = 1 Gulden (Florin)

Watermark

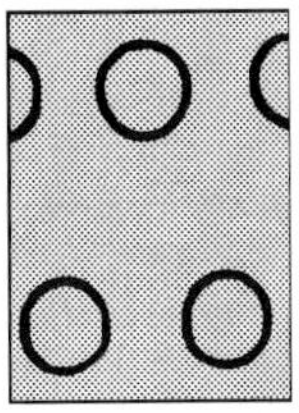

Wmk. 202 — Circles

Early issues of Surinam were sent to the colony without gum. Many of these were subsequently gummed locally.

King William III — A1

Numeral of Value — A2

Perf. 11½, 11½x12, 12½x12, 13½, 14
1873-89 Typo. Unwmk.
Without Gum

1	A1	1c lil gray ('85)	2.10	2.40
2	A1	2c yellow ('85)	1.40	1.40
3	A1	2½c rose	1.40	1.40
4	A1	3c green	17.50	15.00
5	A1	5c dull violet	15.00	4.75
6	A1	10c bister	3.25	2.25
7	A1	12½c sl bl ('85)	17.00	6.75
8	A1	15c gray ('89)	20.00	6.75
9	A1	20c green ('89)	30.00	27.50
10	A1	25c grnsh blue	70.00	8.00
11	A1	25c ultra	240.00	20.00
12	A1	30c red brn ('88)	30.00	32.50
13	A1	40c dk brn ('89)	27.50	26.00
14	A1	50c brown org	26.00	17.00
15	A1	1g red brn & gray ('89)	42.50	42.50
16	A1	2.50g grn & org ('79)	65.00	57.50
		Nos. 1-16 (16)	608.65	271.70

Perf. 14, Small Holes

3b	A1	2½c rose	10.00	11.50
4b	A1	3c green	18.00	24.00
5b	A1	5c dull violet	18.00	15.00
6b	A1	10c bister	17.00	20.00
11b	A1	25c ultra	225.00	60.00
14b	A1	50c brown org	47.50	40.00
		Nos. 3b-14b (6)	335.50	170.50

The paper of Nos. 3-6, 11 and 14 sometimes has an accidental bluish tinge of varying strength. During its manufacture a chemical whitener (bluing agent) was added in varying quantities. No particular printing was made on bluish paper.

"Small hole" varieties have the spaces between the holes wider than the diameter of the holes.

Nos. 1-16 and 3b-14b exist with gum.
For surcharges see Nos. 23, 31-35, 39-42.

1890 *Perf. 11½x11, 12½*
Without Gum

17	A2	1c gray	1.60	1.10
18	A2	2c yellow brn	2.50	2.00
19	A2	2½c carmine	2.00	1.60
20	A2	3c green	4.75	3.25
21	A2	5c ultra	21.00	1.10
		Nos. 17-21 (5)	31.85	9.05

Nos. 17-21 exist with gum.
For surcharges see Nos. 63-64.

A3

1892, Aug. 11 *Perf. 10½*
Without Gum

22	A3	2½c black & org	1.50	1.00
a.		First and fifth vertical words have fancy "F"	22.50	14.00
b.		Imperf.	2.00	
c.		As "a," imperf.	27.50	

No. 14 Surcharged in Black

2½
C E N T.

1892, Aug. 1 *Perf. 14*
Without Gum

23	A1	2½c on 50c	210.00	10.00
a.		Perf. 12½x12	300.00	9.00
b.		Perf. 11½x12	350.00	12.50
c.		Double surcharge	300.00	225.00
d.		Perf. 14, small holes	225.00	12.50

Nos. 23-23c were issued without gum.

Queen Wilhelmina — A5

1892-93 Typo. *Perf. 12½*
Without Gum

25	A5	10c bister	35.00	2.75
26	A5	12½c rose lilac	40.00	4.75
27	A5	15c gray	3.25	2.25
28	A5	20c green	3.75	2.75
29	A5	25c blue	8.25	4.75
30	A5	30c red brown	4.75	4.00
		Nos. 25-30 (6)	95.00	21.25

Nos. 25-30 exist with gum.
For surcharges see Nos. 65-66.

Nos. 7-12 Surcharged

1898 *Perf. 11½x12, 12½x12, 13½*
Without Gum

31	A1	10c on 12½c sl bl	22.50	3.25
32	A1	10c on 15c gray	52.50	45.00
33	A1	10c on 20c green	4.25	4.25
34	A1	10c on 25c grnsh bl	9.00	5.25
c.		Perf. 11½x12	10.00	10.00
34A	A1	10c on 25c ultra	475.00	425.00
b.		Perf. 11½x12	550.00	475.00
35	A1	10c on 30c red brn	4.25	4.25
a.		Double surcharge	275.00	

Dangerous counterfeits exist.

Netherlands Nos. 80, 83-84 Surcharged

50 C^T

SURINAME

No. 36

Nos. 37-38

1900, Jan. 8 *Perf. 12½*
Without Gum

36	A11	50c on 50c	22.50	8.50

Engr.
Perf. 11½x11

37	A12	100c on 1g dk grn	22.50	13.50
38	A12	2.50g on 2½g brn lil	20.00	12.50
		Nos. 36-38 (3)	65.00	34.50

For surcharge see No. 67.

Nos. 13-16 Surcharged

Perf. 11½, 11½x12, 12½x12, 14
1900 Typo.
Without Gum

39	A1	25c on 40c	5.00	3.50
40	A1	25c on 50c	5.00	3.50
a.		Perf. 14, small holes	110.00	125.00
b.		Perf. 11½x12	3.75	3.75

41	A1	50c on 1g	40.00	35.00
42	A1	50c on 2.50g	140.00	160.00
		Nos. 39-42 (4)	190.00	202.00

Counterfeits of No. 42 exist.

A9

A10

Queen Wilhelmina — A11

1902-08 Typo. *Perf. 12½*

Without Gum

44	A9	½c violet	1.00	.90
45	A9	1c olive grn	2.10	1.25
46	A9	2c yellow brn	11.50	4.50
47	A9	2½c blue grn	5.00	.45
48	A9	3c orange	8.25	5.25
49	A9	5c red	8.25	.45
50	A9	7½c gray ('08)	18.00	8.25
51	A10	10c slate	12.00	.95
52	A10	12½c deep blue	4.50	.45
53	A10	15c dp brown	30.00	10.50
54	A10	20c olive grn	27.50	5.25
55	A10	22½c brn & ol grn	24.00	13.00
56	A10	25c violet	20.00	1.25
57	A10	30c orange brn	47.50	15.00
58	A10	50c lake brown	37.50	9.25

Engr.

Perf. 11

59	A11	1g violet	60.00	20.00
60	A11	2½g slate blue	60.00	65.00
		Nos. 44-60 (17)	377.10	161.70

Nos. 44-60 exist with gum.

A12

1909 Typeset *Serrate Roulette 13½*

Without Gum

61	A12	5c red	13.50	11.50
a.		Tête bêche pair	190.00	175.00

Perf. 11½x10½

62	A12	5c red	14.50	12.00
a.		Tête bêche pair	140.00	140.00

Nos. 17-18, 29-30, 38 Surcharged in Red

Nos. 63-64

Nos. 65-66

No. 67

1911, July 15 Typo. *Perf. 12½*

Without Gum

63	A2	½c on 1c	1.75	1.10
64	A2	½c on 2c	12.25	9.00
65	A5	15c on 25c	75.00	57.50
66	A5	20c on 30c	14.00	9.50

Engr.

Perf. 11½x11

67	A12	30c on 2.50g on 2½g	125.00	110.00
		Nos. 63-67 (5)	228.00	187.10

A13

1912, July Typeset *Perf. 11½*

Without Gum

70	A13	½c lilac	.95	.95
a.		Horiz. pair, imperf. btwn.	200.00	
71	A13	2½c dk green	.95	.95
72	A13	5c pale red	8.75	8.75
a.		Vert. pair, imperf. btwn.	240.00	
73	A13	12½c deep blue	11.00	11.00
		Nos. 70-73 (4)	21.65	21.65

Numeral of Value — A14

Queen Wilhelmina
A15 A16

1913-31 Typo. *Perf. 12½*

74	A14	½c violet	.40	.25
75	A14	1c olive green	.40	.20
76	A14	1½c blue, perf 11½ ('21)	.40	.20
a.		Perf. 12½ ('32)	1.10	.85
77	A14	2c yellow brn	1.60	1.10
78	A14	2½c green	.95	.20
79	A14	3c yellow	.80	.65
80	A14	3c green ('26)	3.25	2.50
81	A14	4c chlky bl ('26)	8.25	5.00
82	A14	5c rose	1.60	.20
83	A14	5c green ('22)	2.00	1.00
84	A14	5c lilac ('26)	1.60	.20
85	A14	6c bister ('26)	2.75	2.50
86	A14	6c red org ('31)	2.25	.50
87	A14	7½c drab	1.00	.40
a.		Perf. 11x11½	1.40	.65
88	A14	7½c orange ('27)	1.40	.40
89	A14	7½c yellow ('31)	9.25	9.25
90	A14	10c violet ('22)	5.00	5.00
91	A14	10c rose ('26)	4.00	.55
92	A15	10c car rose	1.40	.65
93	A15	12½c blue	1.90	.65
94	A15	12½c red ('22)	2.00	2.25
95	A15	15c olive grn	.55	.70
96	A15	15c lt blue ('26)	7.75	4.75
97	A15	20c green	3.50	3.25
98	A15	20c blue ('22)	2.40	2.00
99	A15	20c ol grn ('26)	3.50	2.75
100	A15	22½c orange	2.50	2.50
101	A15	25c red violet	4.00	.40
102	A15	30c slate	5.00	1.10
103	A15	32½c vio & org ('22)	15.00	17.50
104	A15	35c sl & red ('26)	5.00	5.00

Perf. 11, 11½, 11½x11, 12½

Engr.

105	A16	50c green	4.00	.85
a.		Perf. 12½ ('32)	14.00	1.60
106	A16	1g brown	5.50	.50
a.		Perf. 12½ ('32)	15.00	1.00
107	A16	1½g dp vio ('26)	35.00	35.00
108	A16	2½g carmine ('23)	30.00	26.00
a.		Perf. 11½x11	35.00	32.50
		Nos. 74-108 (35)	175.90	135.95

Nos. 74, 75, 77-79, 82, 87, 105, 106 and 108 were issued both with and without gum.

Early printings of Nos. 74-104 had water soluble ink.

For surcharges see Nos. 116-120, 139.

Queen Wilhelmina — A17

1923, Oct. 5 *Perf. 11, 11x11½, 11½*

109	A17	5c green	1.10	.70
110	A17	10c car rose	1.75	1.50
111	A17	20c indigo	3.50	3.00
112	A17	50c brown org	19.00	19.00
113	A17	1g brown vio	26.00	17.00
114	A17	2½g gray blk	75.00	*200.00*
115	A17	5g brown	100.00	*240.00*
		Nos. 109-115 (7)	226.35	*481.20*

25th anniv. of the assumption of the government of the Netherlands by Queen Wilhelmina, at age 18.

Values for Nos. 114-115 used are for copies clearly dated before July 15, 1924.

Nos. 83, 93-94, 98 Surcharged in Black or Red:

j

k

m

1925, Dec. 19 Typo. *Perf. 12½*

116	A14	3c on 5c green	1.10	1.10
117	A15	10c on 12½c red	2.25	2.25
118	A15	15c on 12½c blue (R)	1.60	1.60
119	A15	15c on 20c blue	1.60	1.60
		Nos. 116-119 (4)	6.55	6.55

No. 100 Surcharged in Blue

1926, Jan. 1

120	A15	12½c on 22½c org	27.50	27.50

Postage Due Stamps Nos. J14 and J29 Surcharged in Blue or Black:

o

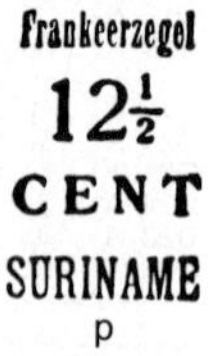

p

121	D2(o)	12½c on 40c (Bl)	3.25	3.25
122	D2(p)	12½c on 40c (Bk)	30.00	30.00
		Nos. 120-122 (3)	60.75	60.75

No. 121 issued without gum.

Queen Wilhelmina — A21

1927-30 Engr. *Perf. 11½*

123	A21	10c carmine	1.00	.40
124	A21	12½c red orange	1.75	1.90
125	A21	15c dark blue	2.00	.60
126	A21	20c indigo	2.00	.80
127	A21	21c dk brown ('30)	19.00	19.00
128	A21	22½c brown ('28)	8.00	9.75
129	A21	25c dk violet	3.00	.70
130	A21	30c dk green	3.00	1.10
131	A21	35c black brown	3.00	3.00
		Nos. 123-131 (9)	42.75	37.25

Types of Netherlands Marine Insurance Stamps Inscribed "SURINAME" and Surcharged

1927, Oct. 26

132	MI1	3c on 15c dk grn	.65	.65
133	MI1	10c on 60c car rose	.65	.65
134	MI1	12½c on 75c gray brn	.65	.65
135	MI2	15c on 1.50 dk blue	2.75	2.75
136	MI2	25c on 2.25g org brn	7.25	7.25
137	MI3	30c on 4½g black	9.00	7.25
138	MI3	50c on 7½g red	7.25	7.25
		Nos. 132-138 (7)	28.20	26.45

Nos. 135-137 have "FRANKEERZEGEL" in small capitals in one line. Nos. 135 and 136 have a heavy bar across the top of the stamp.

No. 88 Surcharged

1930, Mar. 1 Typo. *Perf. 12½*

139	A14	6c on 7½c orange	1.90	1.00

Prince William I (Portrait by Van Key) — A22

1933, Apr. 24 Photo.

141	A22	6c deep orange	6.75	1.90

400th birth anniv. of Prince William I, Count of Nassau and Prince of Orange, frequently referred to as William the Silent.

Van Walbeeck's Ship A23

Queen Wilhelmina A24

1936-41 Litho. *Perf. 13½x12½*

142	A23	½c yellow brn	.30	.30
143	A23	1c lt yellow grn	.40	.20
144	A23	1½c brt blue	.55	.40
145	A23	2c black brown	.60	.25
146	A23	2½c green	.25	.20
a.		Perf. 13 ('41)	9.00	3.25
147	A23	3c dark ultra	.60	.40
148	A23	4c orange	.60	.75
149	A23	5c gray	.60	.20
150	A23	6c red	2.50	2.00
151	A23	7½c red violet	.25	.20
a.		7½c plum, perf. 13 ('41)	3.00	.25

Engr.

Perf. 14, 12½

Size: 20x30mm

152	A24	10c vermilion	.85	.20
a.		Perf. 12½ ('39)	60.00	11.50
153	A24	12½c dull green	3.50	1.25
154	A24	15c dark blue	1.25	.60
155	A24	20c yellow org	2.10	.60
156	A24	21c dk gray	3.25	3.00
a.		Perf. 12½ ('39)	3.75	3.75
157	A24	25c brown lake	2.40	1.00
158	A24	30c brown vio	3.75	1.00
159	A24	35c olive brown	4.00	4.00

Perf. 12½x14
Size: 22x33mm

160	A24	50c dull yel grn	4.00	2.00
161	A24	1g dull blue	8.25	3.00
162	A24	1.50g black brown	22.50	18.00
163	A24	2.50g rose lake	13.50	9.50
		Nos. 142-163 (22)	76.00	49.05

For surcharges see Nos. 181-183, B37-B40.

Queen Wilhelmina — A25

Perf. 12½x12
1938, Aug. 30 Photo. Wmk. 202

164	A25	2c dull purple	.50	.30
165	A25	7½c red orange	1.50	1.25
166	A25	15c royal blue	3.00	3.00
		Nos. 164-166 (3)	5.00	4.55

Reign of Queen Wilhelmina, 40th anniv.

SEMI-POSTAL STAMPS

SP1

SP2

Green Cross — SP3

Perf. 12½
1927, Aug. 1 Unwmk. Photo.

B1	SP1	2c (+ 2c) bl blk & grn	1.10	1.00
B2	SP2	5c (+ 3c) vio & grn	1.10	1.00
B3	SP3	10c (+ 3c) ver & grn	2.00	1.75
		Nos. B1-B3 (3)	4.20	3.75
		Set, never hinged	10.50	

Surtax was given to the Green Cross Society, which promotes public health services.

Nurse and Patient SP4

Good Samaritan SP5

1928, Dec. 1 *Perf. 11½*

B4	SP4	1½c (+ 1½c) ultra	4.50	4.50
B5	SP4	2c (+ 2c) bl grn	4.50	4.50
B6	SP4	5c (+ 3c) vio	4.50	4.50
B7	SP4	7½c (+ 2½c) ver	4.50	4.50
		Nos. B4-B7 (4)	18.00	18.00
		Set, never hinged	67.50	

The surtax on these stamps was for a fund to combat indigenous diseases.

1929, Dec. 1 *Perf. 12½*

B8	SP5	1½c (+ 1½c) grn	6.75	6.75
B9	SP5	2c (+ 2c) scar	6.75	6.75
B10	SP5	5c (+ 3c) ultra	6.75	6.75
B11	SP5	6c (+ 4c) blk	6.75	6.75
		Nos. B8-B11 (4)	27.00	27.00
		Set, never hinged	72.50	

Surtax for the Green Cross Society.

Surinam Mother and Child — SP6

1931, Dec. 14

B12	SP6	1½c (+ 1½c) blk	4.75	4.75
B13	SP6	2c (+ 2c) car rose	4.75	4.75
B14	SP6	5c (+ 3c) ultra	4.75	4.75
B15	SP6	6c (+ 4c) dp grn	4.75	4.75
		Nos. B12-B15 (4)	19.00	19.00
		Set, never hinged	45.00	

The surtax was for Child Welfare Societies.

Designs Symbolical of the Creed of the Moravians
SP7 SP8

1935, Aug. 1 *Perf. 13x14*

B16	SP7	1c (+ ½c) dk brn	6.00	6.00
B17	SP7	2c (+ 1c) dp ultra	6.00	6.00
B18	SP8	3c (+ 1½c) grn	7.50	7.50
B19	SP8	4c (+ 2c) red org	7.50	7.50
B20	SP8	5c (+ 2½c) blk brn	9.00	9.00
B21	SP7	10c (+ 5c) car	9.00	9.00
		Nos. B16-B21 (6)	45.00	45.00
		Set, never hinged	90.00	

200th anniv. of the founding of the Moravian Mission in Surinam.

Surinam Child — SP9

1936, Dec. 14 *Perf. 12½*

B22	SP9	2c (+ 1c) dk grn	2.75	2.75
B23	SP9	3c (+ 1½c) dk bl	2.75	2.75
B24	SP9	5c (+ 2½c) brn blk	4.00	4.00
B25	SP9	10c (+ 5c) lake	4.00	4.00
		Nos. B22-B25 (4)	13.50	13.50
		Set, never hinged	26.50	

Surtax for baby food and the Green Cross Society.

"Emancipation" SP10

Surinam Girl SP11

1938, June 1 Litho. *Perf. 12½x12*

B26	SP10	2½c (+ 2c) dk bl grn	2.40	1.90

Photo.

B27	SP11	3c (+ 2c) vio blk	2.40	1.90
B28	SP11	5c (+ 3c) dk brn	2.60	2.25
B29	SP11	7½c (+ 5c) indigo	2.60	2.25
		Nos. B26-B29 (4)	10.00	8.30
		Set, never hinged	20.00	

75th anniv. of the abolition of slavery in Surinam. Surtax to Slavery Remembrance Committee.

Creole Woman — SP12

Javanese Woman — SP13

Hindustani Woman — SP14

American Indian Woman — SP15

1940, Jan. 8 Engr. *Perf. 13x14*

B30	SP12	2½c (+ 2c) dk grn	3.00	3.00
B31	SP13	3c (+ 2c) red org	3.00	3.00
B32	SP14	5c (+ 3c) dp bl	3.00	3.00
B33	SP15	7½c (+ 5c) henna brn	3.00	3.00
		Nos. B30-B33 (4)	12.00	12.00
		Set, never hinged	25.00	

Surtax to leper care and baby food.

AIR POST STAMPS

Allegory of Flight — AP1

Perf. 12½
1930, Sept. 3 Unwmk. Engr.

C1	AP1	10c dull red	3.75	.50
C2	AP1	15c ultra	3.75	.75
C3	AP1	20c dull green	.20	.20
C4	AP1	40c orange	.20	.35
C5	AP1	60c brown violet	.55	.40
C6	AP1	1g gray black	1.60	1.75
C7	AP1	1½g deep brown	1.75	1.90
		Nos. C1-C7 (7)	11.80	5.85

Nos. C1-C7 Overprinted in Black or Red

1931, Aug. 8

C8	AP1	10c red (Bk)	19.00	15.00
	a.	Double overprint	425.00	
C9	AP1	15c ultra (Bk)	19.00	15.00
C10	AP1	20c dull grn (R)	19.00	15.00
C11	AP1	40c orange (Bk)	29.00	22.50
	a.	Double overprint	425.00	
C12	AP1	60c brn vio (R)	62.50	52.50
C13	AP1	1g gray blk (R)	72.50	65.00
C14	AP1	1½g deep brn (Bk)	72.50	67.50
		Nos. C8-C14 (7)	293.50	252.50

The variety with period omitted after "Do" occurs twice on each sheet.

Warning: The red overprint may dissolve in water.

POSTAGE DUE STAMPS

D1

D2

Type I — 34 loops. "T" of "BETALEN" over center of loop; top branch of "E" of "TE" shorter than lower branch.

Type II — 33 loops. "T" of "BETALEN" over space between two loops.

Type III — 32 loops. "T" of "BETALEN" slightly to the left of center of loop; top branch of first "E" of "BETALEN" shorter than lower branch.

Type IV — 37 loops and letters of "PORT" larger than in the other 3 types.

Value in Black
Perf. 12½x12
1886-88 Typo. Unwmk.
Type III

J1	D1	2½c lilac	3.00	3.00
J2	D1	5c lilac	9.00	9.00
J3	D1	10c lilac	100.00	65.00
J4	D1	20c lilac	9.00	9.00
J5	D1	25c lilac	12.50	12.50
J6	D1	30c lilac ('88)	2.50	2.50
J7	D1	40c lilac	6.00	6.00
J8	D1	50c lilac ('88)	3.00	3.00
		Nos. J1-J8 (8)	145.00	110.00

Type I

J1a	D1	2½c	6.00	6.00
J2a	D1	5c	11.00	11.00
J3a	D1	10c	125.00	90.00
J4a	D1	20c	22.50	22.50
J5a	D1	25c	19.00	19.00
J6a	D1	30c	22.50	22.50
J7a	D1	40c	12.50	12.50
J8a	D1	50c	4.00	4.00
		Nos. J1a-J8a (8)	222.50	187.50

Type II

J1b	D1	2½c	5.00	5.00
J2b	D1	5c	10.00	10.00
J3b	D1	10c	1,250.	1,250.
J4b	D1	20c	9.00	9.00
J5b	D1	25c	300.00	300.00
J6b	D1	30c	75.00	75.00
J7b	D1	40c	350.00	350.00
J8b	D1	50c	5.00	5.00

Type IV

J3c	D1	10c	350.00	250.00
J5c	D1	25c	160.00	150.00
J7c	D1	40c	150.00	150.00
		Nos. J3c-J7c (3)	660.00	550.00

Nos. J1-J16 were issued without gum. For surcharges, see Nos. J15-J16.

1892-96 Value in Black *Perf. 12½*
Type III

J9	D2	2½c lilac	.40	.40
J10	D2	5c lilac	1.25	1.00
J11	D2	10c lilac	24.00	22.50
J12	D2	20c lilac	2.50	2.25
J13	D2	25c lilac	10.00	10.00

Type I

J9a	D2	2½c	.40	.40
J10a	D2	5c	2.00	2.00
J11a	D2	10c	24.00	20.00
J12a	D2	20c	5.00	5.00
J13a	D2	25c	13.00	12.50
J14	D2	40c ('96)	3.25	4.50

Type II

J9b	D2	2½c	.80	.80
J10b	D2	5c	3.00	3.00
J11b	D2	10c	40.00	42.50
J12b	D2	20c	90.00	90.00
J13b	D2	25c	100.00	100.00

For surcharges, see Nos. 121-122.

Stamps of 1888 Surcharged in Red

10
cent

1911, July 15

J15	D1	10c on 30c lil (III)	80.00	80.00
	a.	10c on 30c lilac (I)	200.00	225.00
	b.	10c on 30c lilac (II)	*1,800.*	*1,800.*
J16	D1	10c on 50c lil (III)	110.00	110.00
	a.	10c on 50c lilac (I)	115.00	115.00
	b.	10c on 50c lilac (II)	115.00	115.00

D3

Type I
Value in Color of Stamp
1913-31 *Perf. 12½, 13½x12½*

J17	D2	½c lilac ('30)	.25	.25
J18	D2	1c lilac ('31)	.25	.35
J19	D2	2c lilac ('31)	.25	.25
J20	D2	2½c lilac	.25	.25
J21	D2	5c lilac	.25	.25
J22	D2	10c lilac	.25	.25
J23	D2	12c lilac ('31)	.25	.25
J24	D2	12½c lilac ('22)	.25	.25
J25	D2	15c lilac ('26)	.55	.45
J26	D2	20c lilac	.85	.45
J27	D2	25c lilac	.45	.25

J28 D2 30c lilac ('26)	.45	.60
J29 D2 40c lilac	14.50	14.00
J30 D2 50c lilac ('26)	1.25	1.25
J31 D2 75c lilac ('26)	1.50	1.50
J32 D3 1g lilac ('26)	1.75	1.50
Nos. J17-J32 (16)	23.30	22.10

SWAZILAND

'swə-zē-,land

LOCATION — Southeast Africa bordered by the Transvaal and Zululand in South Africa and by Mozambique
GOVT. — Constitutional monarchy
AREA — 6,705 sq. mi.
POP. — 626,000 (est. 1984)
CAPITAL — Mbabane

An independent state in the 19th century, Swaziland was administered by Transvaal from 1894 to 1906, when the administration was transferred to the British High Commissioner for South Africa. In 1934 Swaziland and Bechuanaland Protectorate came under the administration of the British High Commissioner for Basutoland. The issuing of individual postage stamps had been resumed in 1933.

12 Pence = 1 Shilling
20 Shillings = 1 Pound

Catalogue values for unused stamps in this country are for Never Hinged items, beginning with Scott 38 in the regular postage section.

Coat of Arms — A1

George V — A2

Black Overprint

1889 Unwmk. *Perf. 12½, 12½x12*

1 A1 ½p gray	10.50	*21.00*
a. Inverted overprint	925.00	725.00
b. "Swazielan"	1,350.	850.00
c. As "b," inverted overprint		5,000.
2 A1 1p rose	20.00	19.00
a. Inverted overprint	800.00	*750.00*
3 A1 2p olive bister	20.00	18.00
a. Inverted overprint	900.00	525.00
b. "Swazielan"	550.00	475.00
c. Perf. 12½x12	100.00	25.00
d. As "c," "Swazielan"	1,250.	725.00
e. As "d," inverted overprint		1,250.
f. As "b," inverted overprint	5,100.	4,600.
g. Double overprint	2,600.	
4 A1 6p gray blue	25.00	*50.00*
5 A1 1sh green	12.50	*16.00*
a. Inverted overprint	850.00	525.00
6 A1 2sh6p yellow	275.00	*300.00*
7 A1 5sh slate	175.00	*225.00*
a. Inverted overprint	*1,900.*	*2,500.*
b. "Swazielan"	*5,250.*	
c. As "b," inverted overprint	*5,750.*	
8 A1 10sh lt brown	*5,750.*	*3,750.*

1892 Red Overprint

9 A1 ½p gray	8.50	19.00
a. Inverted overprint	575.00	
b. Double overprint	525.00	*525.00*
c. Pair, one without overprint		1,900.

Beware of counterfeits.
Reprints have a period after "Swazieland."

Stamps of Swaziland were replaced by those of Transvaal in 1895. Swaziland issues were resumed in 1933.

Perf. 14

1933, Jan. 2 Engr. Wmk. 4

10 A2 ½p green	.35	*.35*
11 A2 1p carmine	.35	.25
12 A2 2p lt brown	.35	.50
13 A2 3p ultra	.50	3.00
14 A2 4p orange	3.25	*3.50*
15 A2 6p rose violet	1.50	*1.10*
16 A2 1sh olive green	1.75	*3.25*
17 A2 2sh6p violet	17.50	*25.00*
18 A2 5sh gray	35.00	*57.50*
19 A2 10sh black brown	92.50	*125.00*
Nos. 10-19 (10)	153.05	*219.45*

Common Design Types pictured following the introduction.

Silver Jubilee Issue
Common Design Type

1935, May 4 *Perf. 11x12*

20 CD301 1p carmine & blue	.60	1.75
21 CD301 2p black & ultra	.60	1.50
22 CD301 3p ultra & brown	.65	*5.75*
23 CD301 6p brown, vio & ind	.75	*1.75*
Nos. 20-23 (4)	2.60	10.75
Set, never hinged	5.00	

Coronation Issue
Common Design Type

1937, May 12 *Perf. 11x11½*

24 CD302 1p dark carmine	.35	*.55*
25 CD302 2p brown	.35	*.20*
26 CD302 3p deep ultra	.35	.55
Nos. 24-26 (3)	1.05	1.30
Set, never hinged	1.60	

George VI — A3

1938, Apr. 1 *Perf. 13, 13x13½*

27 A3 ½p green	.25	*1.50*
28 A3 1p rose carmine	.80	*1.50*
29 A3 1½p light blue	.30	*.85*
a. Perf. 14 ('42)	1.40	1.25
Never hinged	3.25	
30 A3 2p brown	.30	*.45*
31 A3 3p ultra	2.75	2.00
32 A3 4p red orange	.40	*1.60*
33 A3 6p rose violet	3.50	1.75
34 A3 1sh olive green	.95	.75
35 A3 2sh6p dark violet	10.50	2.75
36 A3 5sh gray	20.00	15.00
37 A3 10sh black brown	4.75	*6.50*
Nos. 27-37 (11)	44.50	34.65
Set, never hinged	57.50	

Catalogue values for unused stamps in this section, from this point to the end of the section, are for Never Hinged items.

Peace Issue

South Africa, Nos. 100-102 Overprinted

Basic stamps inscribed alternately in English and Afrikaans.

1945, Dec. 3 Wmk. 201 *Perf. 14*

38 A42 1p rose pink & choc, pair	.55	*.85*
a. Single, English	.20	.20
b. Single, Afrikaans	.20	.20
39 A43 2p vio & sl blue, pair	.55	*.85*
a. Single, English	.20	.20
b. Single, Afrikaans	.20	.20
40 A43 3p ultra & dp ultra, pair	.55	*2.75*
a. Single, English	.20	.25
b. Single, Afrikaans	.20	.25
Nos. 38-40 (3)	1.65	*4.45*

World War II victory of the Allies.

Royal Visit Issue
Type of Basutoland, 1947

Perf. 12½

1947, Feb. 17 Wmk. 4 Engr.

44 A3 1p red	.20	.20
45 A4 2p green	.20	.20
46 A5 3p ultramarine	.20	.20
47 A6 1sh dark violet	.20	.20
Nos. 44-47 (4)	.80	.80

Visit of the British Royal Family, 3/25/47.

Silver Wedding Issue
Common Design Types

1948, Dec. 1 Photo. *Perf. 14x14½*

48 CD304 1½p bright ultra	.20	.20

Perf. 11½x11

Engraved; Name Typographed

49 CD305 10sh violet brown	50.00	*30.00*

UPU Issue
Common Design Types
Engr.; Name Typo. on 3p, 6p
Perf. 13½, 11x11½

1949, Oct. 10 Wmk. 4

50 CD306 1½p blue	.35	.20
51 CD307 3p indigo	.65	.65
52 CD308 6p red lilac	.85	.65
53 CD309 1sh olive	.95	.65
Nos. 50-53 (4)	2.80	2.15

POSTAGE DUE STAMPS

Catalogue values for unused stamps in this section are for Never Hinged items.

D1

1933 Typo. Wmk. 4 *Perf. 14*

J1 D1 1p carmine rose	.30	*4.00*
On cover		*175.00*
a. Wmk. 4a (error)	275.00	
J2 D1 2p violet	2.25	*15.00*
On cover		*225.00*

On cover values are for properly franked commercial covers. Philatelic usages sell for less.

SWEDEN

'swē-dᵊn

LOCATION — Northern Europe, occupying the eastern half of the Scandinavian Peninsula
GOVT. — Constitutional Monarchy
AREA — 173,341 sq. mi.
POP. — 8,330,577 (est. 1983)
CAPITAL — Stockholm

48 skilling banco = 1 rixdaler banco (until 1858)
100 öre = 1 rixdaler (1858 to 1874)
100 öre = 1 krona (since 1874)

Watermarks

Wmk. 180 — Crown

Wmk. 181 — Wavy Lines

Values for unused stamps are for examples with original gum as defined in the catalogue introduction except Nos. 1-5, excluding reprints, and LX1 which are valued without gum.

Coat of Arms
A1 A2

1855 Unwmk. Typo. *Perf. 14*

1 A1 3s blue green, thin paper	*7,500.*	*3,000.*
On cover		*33,000.*
a. 3s orange (error)		*3,000,000.*
b. 3s pale bluish green, thin paper	7,500.	*2,750.*
On cover		*33,000.*
2 A1 4s lt blue, thin paper	1,250.	70.00
On cover		80.00
a. 4s blue, thin paper	1,250.	70.00
On cover		80.00
b. 4s bright blue, dense background, thin paper	1,900.	160.00
On cover		350.00
c. 4s dull blue, dense background, thick paper	—	180.00
On cover		400.00
d. 4s bright blue, dense background, thick paper ('56)	2,000.	225.00
On cover		400.00
e. 4s grayish ultramarine, thick paper ('57)	*5,400.*	275.00
On cover		450.00
f. 4s dark grayish ultramarine, thick paper ('57)		450.00
On cover		2,250.
g. 4s turquoise, blurred print, thick paper ('57)	—	975.00
On cover		*5,000.*
h. 4s greenish blue, thick paper ('57)	1,200.	87.50
On cover		100.00
i. 4s blue, clear print, thick paper ('58)	*1,250.*	77.50
On cover		92.50
3 A1 6s gray, thin paper	*8,000.*	975.00
On cover		*8,750.*
a. 6s gray black, thin paper		*2,500.*
On cover		10,000.
b. 6s pale gray, thin paper	*8,000.*	975.00
On cover		8,750.
c. 6s gray brown ('56)	—	2,250.
On cover		*9,000.*
d. 6s brownish gray, thick paper ('58)	—	975.00
On cover		—
e. 6s gray brown, thick paper ('58)		1,250.
On cover		*9,000.*
f. Imperf.		—
4 A1 8s red orange, thin paper	4,250.	550.00
On cover		1,000.
a. 8s brownish orange, thin paper ('56)	4,250.	550.00
On cover		1,000.
b. 8s lemon yellow, *greenish*, thin paper ('56)	—	1,200.
On cover		2,500.
c. 8s bright yellow, thin paper ('56)	—	850.00
On cover		1,600.
d. 8s dull olive yellow, thin paper ('56)	—	750.00
On cover		—
e. 8s yellow orange, thick paper ('57)	4,250.	450.00
On cover		1,150.
f. 8s orange yellow, blurred print, thick paper ('57)		650.00
On cover		1,500.
g. 8s orange yellow, clear print, thick paper ('58)		500.00
On cover		—
h. Imperf.		—
5 A1 24s dull red, thin paper	*6,500.*	1,500.
On cover		8,500.
a. 24s orange red, thin paper ('56)	6,500.	1,500.
On cover		*8,500.*
b. 24s brick red, thck paper ('57)		1,500.
On cover		*8,500.*
c. 24s light orange red, thick paper ('57)		1,500.
On cover		*8,500.*
d. 24s brownish red, blurred print, thick paper ('58)		2,200.
On cover		*9,000.*

Nos. 1-5 were reprinted two or three times perf. 14, once perf. 13. Value of the lowest cost perf. 14 reprints, $375 each. Perf. 13, $325 each.

The reprints were made after Nos. 1-5 were withdrawn, but before being demonitized. Used copies are known.

1858-62 *Perf. 14*

6 A2 5o green	160.00	18.00
On cover		190.00
a. 5o deep green	575.00	140.00
On cover		550.00
7 A2 9o violet	350.00	225.00
On cover		775.00
a. 9o red lilac	450.00	275.00
On cover		1,000.
b. 9o bluish lilac	350.00	260.00
On cover		750.00
c. 9o blue violet ('64-'72)	350.00	225.00
On cover		750.00
8 A2 12o blue	175.00	1.90
On cover		5.00
a. 12o greenish dark blue	700.00	35.00
On cover		100.00
9 A2 12o ultra ('61)	310.00	12.50
On cover		18.00
10 A2 24o orange	400.00	27.50
On cover		60.00
a. 24o yellow	400.00	35.00
On cover		72.50
b. 24o dark orange ('58-'60)	450.00	45.00
On cover		150.00
11 A2 30o brown	400.00	27.50
On cover		190.00
a. 30o dark red brown	450.00	45.00

On cover 275.00
b. 30o rose red brown('60-'62) 60.00
On cover 325.00
12 A2 50o rose 500.00 90.00
On cover 500.00
a. 50o carmine 550.00 95.00
On cover 575.00
b. 50o gright darkcarmine ('61-'64) 650.00 97.50
On cover 600.00
Nos. 6-12 (7) 2,295. 402.40

Nos. 6 and 8 exist with double impressions. No. 8 is known printed on both sides. No. 11 exists imperf.

Nos. 6-8, 10-12 were reprinted in 1885, perf. 13. Value $100 each. Also reprinted in 1963, perf. 13½, with lines in stamp color crossing denominations, and affixed to book page. Value $12.50 each.

Lion and Arms
A3 A4

1862-69

3 Ore:
Type I — The horizontal inner frameline in the upper right corner extends beyond the curved spiral.
Type II — The horizontal inner frameline in the upper right corner does not extend beyond the curved spiral.

13 A3 3o bister brown, type II ('63) 200.00 13.50
On cover 30.00
a. Printed on both sides, type II 2,300.
b. 3o brown, type I 500.00 400.00
On cover 600.00
c. 3o orange brown, type I ('62) 450.00 360.00
On cover 600.00
d. 3o olive gray brown, type II ('63) 300.00 150.00
On cover 360.00
14 A4 17o red violet ('66) 600.00 160.00
On cover 600.00
a. 17o bluish red lilac ('66) 450.00 95.00
On cover 500.00
15 A4 17o gray ('69) 650.00 *650.00*
On cover *16,000.*
16 A4 20o vermilion ('66) 225.00 16.00
On cover 175.00
a. 20o brownish orange red ('66) 200.00 25.00
On cover 400.00
Nos. 13-16 (4) 1,675. 839.50

Nos. 13-15 were reprinted in 1885, perf. 13. Values $65, $100 and $65, respectively.

Numeral of Value — A5

Coat of Arms — A6

1872-77 ***Perf. 14***

17 A5 3o bister brown 60.00 8.00
On cover 25.00
18 A5 4o gray ('76) 425.00 135.00
On cover 600.00
19 A5 5o blue green 310.00 4.50
On cover 175.00
a. 5o emerald 500.00 55.00
On cover 400.00
20 A5 6o violet 325.00 40.00
On cover 42.50
a. 6o dark violet 325.00 40.00
On cover 42.50
21 A5 6o gray ('74) 900.00 87.50
On cover 115.00
22 A5 12o blue 175.00 1.00
On cover 5.00
23 A5 20o vermilion 800.00 7.00
On cover 60.00
a. 20o dull org yel ('75) 3,500. 35.00
On cover 600.00
b. Double impression, dull yel & ver ('76) 3,250 45.00
On cover 300.00
24 A5 24o orange 700.00 35.00
On cover 60.00
a. 24o yellow 700.00 35.00
On cover 60.00
25 A5 30o pale brown 600.00 9.25
On cover 95.00
a. 30o black brown 600.00 11.50
On cover 100.00
26 A5 50o rose 650.00 40.00
On cover 325.00
a. 50o carmine 750.00 40.00
On cover 325.00
27 A6 1rd bister & blue 800.00 75.00
On cover 2,250.
a. 1rd bister & ultra 800.00 75.00
On cover 2,250.
Nos. 17-27 (11) 5,745. 442.25

1877-79 ***Perf. 13***

28 A5 3o yellow brown 75.00 5.00
On cover 16.00
29 A5 4o gray ('79) 190.00 3.50
On cover 19.00
30 A5 5o dark green 125.00 1.00
On cover 22.50
31 A5 6o lilac 140.00 4.00
On cover 26.00
a. 6o red lilac 150.00 4.50
On cover 30.00
32 A5 12o blue 26.00 .80
On cover 4.00
33 A5 20o vermilion 225.00 1.00
On cover 30.00
a. "TRETIO" instead of "TJUGO" ('79) 8,250. 5,250.
On cover *18,000.*
34 A5 24o orange ('78) 55.00 25.00
On cover 67.50
a. 24o lemon yellow ('83) 400.00 45.00
On cover 250.000
35 A5 30o pale brown 350.00 1.90
On cover 26.00
a. 30o black brown 400.00 2.50
On cover 30.00
36 A5 50o carmine ('78) 260.00 7.00
On cover 70.00
37 A6 1rd bister & blue 1,850. 400.00
On cover 9,250.
38 A6 1k bister & bl ('78) 500.00 16.00
On cover 260.00
Nos. 28-36,38 (10) 1,946. 65.20

Imperf., Pairs

28a	A5	3o	750.00	
29a	A5	4o	750.00	
30a	A5	5o	750.00	
31b	A5	6o	750.00	
32a	A5	12o	750.00	
33b	A5	20o	750.00	
34b	A5	24o	750.00	
35b	A5	30o	750.00	*2,900.*
36a	A5	50o	750.00	
38a	A6	1k	750.00	

See Nos. 40-44, 46-49. For surcharges see Nos. B1-B10, B22-B31.

No. 37 has been reprinted in yellow brown and dark blue; perforated 13. Value, $325.

King Oscar II — A7

1885 **Typo.**

39 A7 10o dull rose 190.00 .65
On cover 7.50
a. Imperf., pair *2,000.*

Numeral Type with Post Horn on Back

1886-91

40 A5 2o orange ('91) 2.10 *7.50*
On cover 40.00
a. Period before "FRIMARKE" 11.00 *22.50*
b. Imperf., pair 725.00
41 A5 3o yellow brn ('87) 11.00 *21.00*
On cover 80.00
42 A5 4o gray 25.00 1.40
On cover 10.00
43 A5 5o green 55.00 .65
On cover 7.50
44 A5 6o red lilac ('88) 27.50 55.00
On cover 100.00
a. 6o violet 30.00 55.00
On cover 100.00
45 A7 10o pink 77.50 .25
On cover 3.00
a. 10o rose 77.50 .25
On cover 3.00
b. Imperf. 1,750.
46 A5 20o vermilion 100.00 .65
On cover 7.50
47 A5 30o pale brown 175.00 1.50
On cover 7.50
48 A5 50o rose 150.00 4.25
On cover 60.00
49 A6 1k bister & dk bl 82.50 2.50
On cover 40.00
a. Imperf., pair 600.00
Nos. 40-49 (10) 705.60 94.70

Nos. 32, 34 with Blue Surcharge

1889, Oct. 1

50 A5 10o on 12o blue 3.25 *4.50*
On cover 30.00
51 A5 10o on 24o orange 11.00 *42.50*
On cover 80.00

A9

King Oscar II
A10 A11

Wmk. 180

1891-1904 **Typo.** ***Perf. 13***

52 A9 1o brown & ultra ('92) 1.40 .65
On cover 2.50
53 A9 2o blue & yellow org 3.25 .30
On cover 1.50
54 A9 3o brown & orange ('92) .55 1.50
On cover 3.00
55 A9 4o carmine & ultra ('92) 4.75 .30
On cover 1.00

Engr.

56 A10 5o yellow green 2.75 .20
On cover .50
a. 5o blue green 11.50 .20
On cover .50
d. 5o brown (error) *6,000.*
e. Booklet pane of 6 140.00
57 A10 8o red violet ('03) 3.25 1.25
On cover 12.50
58 A10 10o carmine 4.50 .20
On cover .50
c. Booklet pane of 6 240.00
59 A10 15o red brown ('96) 22.50 .30
On cover 2.50
60 A10 20o blue 22.50 .30
On cover 3.00
b. 20o ultramarine 60.00 .60
On cover 6.00
61 A10 25o red orange ('96) 27.50 .40
On cover 4.00
62 A10 30o brown 50.00 .30
On cover 3.00
63 A10 50o slate 80.00 .85
On cover 5.50
64 A10 50o olive gray ('04) 80.00 .85
On cover 5.50
65 A11 1k car & sl ('00) 140.00 2.25
On cover 25.00
Nos. 52-65 (14) 442.95 9.65

Imperf., Pairs

52a	A9	1o	82.50
53a	A9	2o	*275.00*
54a	A9	3o	*275.00*
55a	A9	4o	250.00
56b	A10	5o No. 56	82.50
c.		No. 56a	300.00
57a	A10	8o	325.00
58a	A10	10o	52.50
59a	A10	15o	375.00
60a	A10	20o	140.00
61a	A10	25o	475.00
62a	A10	30o	450.00
63a	A10	50o	525.00
64a	A10	50o	375.00
65a	A11	1k	525.00

No. 56d may be a proof.

A booklet pane of 6 invalid stamps similar to No. 56 but with engraved lines through the denominations was released in 2004 to commemorate the 100th anniversary of the first Swedish booklet. This booklet pane is unwatermarked.

See Nos. 75-76.

Stockholm Post Office — A12

1903, Oct. 26

66 A12 5k blue 225.00 25.00
a. Imperf., pair 1,900.

Opening of the new General Post Office at Stockholm.

For surcharge see No. B11.

Arms — A13

Gustaf V — A14

Perf. 13, 13x13½

1910-14 **Typo.** **Wmk. 180**

67 A13 1o black ('11) .65 *1.50*
68 A13 2o orange 1.75 *3.50*
69 A13 4o violet 2.50 1.10

Engr.

70 A14 5o green ('11) 14.00 *29.00*
71 A14 10o carmine 9.50 .50
72 A14 1k black, *yel* ('11) 87.50 .50
73 A14 5k claret, *yel* ('14) 1.75 *3.00*
Nos. 67-73 (7) 117.65 *39.10*

See #77-98. For surcharges see #99-104, Q1-Q2.

1911 **Unwmk.**

75 A10 20o blue 20.00 14.00
76 A10 25o red orange 25.00 3.50

1910-19

77 A14 5o green ('11) 1.90 .20
a. Booklet pane of 10 225.00
b. Booklet pane of 4 125.00
78 A14 7o gray grn ('18) .20 .20
a. Booklet pane of 10 8.75
79 A14 8o magenta ('12) .20 .20
80 A14 10o carmine ('10) 1.90 .20
a. Booklet pane of 10 225.00
b. Booklet pane of 4 125.00
81 A14 12o rose lake ('18) .25 .20
a. Booklet pane of 10 8.75
82 A14 15o red brown ('11) 6.50 .20
a. Booklet pane of 10 325.00
83 A14 20o deep blue ('11) 9.50 .20
a. Booklet pane of 10 350.00
84 A14 25o orange red ('11) .25 .20
85 A14 27o pale blue ('18) .40 .90
86 A14 30o claret brn ('11) 20.00 .20
87 A14 35o dk violet ('11) 17.00 .20
88 A14 40o olive green ('17) 32.50 .20
89 A14 50o gray ('12) 57.50 .20
90 A14 55o pale blue ('18) *1,550.* *4,750.*
91 A14 65o pale ol grn ('18) .65 1.90
92 A14 80o black ('18) *1,550.* *4,750.*
93 A14 90o gray green ('18) .60 .65
94 A14 1k black, *yel* ('19) 92.50 .30
Nos. 77-89,91,93-94 (16) 241.85 6.15

Excellent forgeries of Nos. 90 and 92 exist.

1911-19 **Typo.** **Wmk. 181** ***Perf. 13***

95 A13 1o black .20 .20
96 A13 2o orange .20 .20
97 A13 3o pale brown ('19) .20 .20
98 A13 4o pale violet .20 .20
Nos. 95-98 (4) .80 .80

Remainders of Nos. 95-98 received various private overprints, mostly as publicity for stamp exhibitions. They were not postally valid.

Unwatermarked Stamps with Watermarks

Stamps of these and later issues through the UPU Congress issue of 1924, are frequently found with watermark showing parts of the words "Kungl Postverket" in double-lined capitals. This watermark is normally located in the margins of the sheets of unwatermarked paper or paper watermarked wavy lines or crown.

Nos. 80, 84, 91, 90, 92 Surcharge:

a

b

1918 **Unwmk.**

99 A14(a) 7o on 10o .20 .20
100 A14(b) 12o on 25o 1.90 .40
a. Inverted surcharge 300.00 500.00
101 A14(a) 12o on 65o .85 *1.40*
102 A14(a) 27o on 55o .75 *1.60*
103 A14(a) 27o on 65o 1.40 *3.50*
104 A14(a) 27o on 80o .85 *1.60*
Nos. 99-104 (6) 5.95 8.70

Arms
A15

Heraldic Lion Supporting Arms of Sweden
A16

Two types each of 5o green, 5o copper red and 10o violet, type A16.

Perf. 10 Vertically

1920-25 Engr. Unwmk.

115	A15	3o copper red	.20	.30
116	A16	5o green ('25)		3.75
117	A16	5o copper red ('21)	6.25	.25
118	A16	10o green ('21)	21.00	.30
a.		Tête bêche pair	*1,550.*	*2,500.*
119	A16	10o violet ('25)	5.25	.20
120	A16	25o orange ('21)	13.00	.40
121	A16	30o brown	.45	.45

Wmk. 181

122	A16	5o green	2.50	.90
123	A16	5o copper red ('21)	8.25	1.00
124	A16	10o green ('21)	2.50	1.10
125	A16	30o brown	8.25	16.00
		Nos. 115-125 (11)	71.40	21.15

Coil Stamps

Unless part of a booklet pane any stamp perforated only horizontally or vertically is a coil stamp.

1920-26 Unwmk. *Perf. 10*

126	A16	5o green	4.00	1.00
a.		Booklet pane of 10	80.00	
127	A16	10o green ('21)	11.50	3.50
a.		Booklet pane of 10	225.00	
128	A16	10o violet ('25)	6.50	.85
a.		Booklet pane of 10	180.00	
129	A16	30o brown	32.50	3.25

Wmk. 181

130	A16	5o green	11.50	26.00
131	A16	10o green ('21)	45.00	*90.00*
a.		Booklet pane of 10	425.00	

Perf. 13 Vertically

Unwmk.

132	A16	5o green ('25)	16.00	8.50
133	A16	5o copper red ('21)	425.00	140.00
134	A16	10o violet ('26)	25.00	32.50

Wmk. 181

135	A16	5o green ('25)	1.60	*6.50*
136	A16	5o copper red ('22)	1.90	5.50
137	A16	10o green ('24)	9.00	*35.00*
138	A16	10o violet ('25)	8.00	*22.50*
		Nos. 126-138 (13)	597.50	375.10

The paper used for the earlier printings of types A16, A17, A18, A18a and A20 is usually tinted by the color of the stamp. Printings of 1934 and later are on white paper in slightly different shades.

King Gustaf V — A17

1920-21 Unwmk. *Perf. 10 Vertically*

139	A17	10o rose	32.50	.35
140	A17	15o claret	.30	.45
141	A17	20o blue	35.00	.50

Perf. 10

142	A17	10o rose	12.50	5.50
143	A17	20o blue ('21)	29.00	9.00
a.		Booklet pane of 10	550.00	
		Nos. 139-143 (5)	109.30	15.80

Wmk. 181

144	A17	20o blue		*4,000.*

Crown and Post Horn — A18a
A18

See note after No. 138 regarding paper. There are 2 types of the 35, 40, 45 and 60o.

1920-34 Unwmk. *Perf. 10 Vert.*

145	A18	35o yellow ('22)	42.50	.75
146	A18	40o olive green	32.50	.75
147	A18	45o brown ('22)	1.25	.55
148	A18	60o claret	19.00	.30
149	A18	70o red brn ('22)	.60	2.50
150	A18	80o deep green	.40	.25
151	A18	85o myrtle grn ('29)	3.75	.45
152	A18	90o lt blue ('25)	55.00	.30
153	A18a	1kr dp org ('21)	7.75	.25
154	A18	110o ultra	.50	.40
155	A18	115o red brn ('29)	9.00	.45
156	A18	120o gray blk ('25)	62.50	.60
157	A18	120o lil rose ('33)	14.00	.60
158	A18	140o gray black	.90	.30
159	A18	145o brt grn ('30)	8.50	.55

Wmk. 181

160	A18	35o yellow ('23)	60.00	7.50
161	A18	60o red violet	95.00	*110.00*
162	A18	80o blue green	8.25	15.00
163	A18	110o ultra	3.50	3.75
		Nos. 145-163 (19)	424.90	145.25

The value for #147 is for the 2nd type, issued in 1925.

Gustavus Adolphus
A19

King Gustaf V
A20

Perf. 10 Vertically

1920, July 28 Unwmk.

164	A19	20o deep blue	2.25	.40

Wmk. 181

165	A19	20o blue	150.00	32.50

Unwmk.

Perf. 10

166	A19	20o blue	6.25	2.25
a.		Booklet pane of 10	130.00	
		Nos. 164-166 (3)	158.50	35.15

Tercentenary of Swedish post which first ran between Stockholm and Hamburg.

1921-36 Unwmk. *Perf. 10 Vert.*

See note after No. 138 regarding paper. There are two types each of the 15o rose and 40o olive green.

167	A20	15o violet ('22)	17.00	.30
168	A20	15o rose ('28)	5.50	.45
169	A20	15o brown ('36)	4.75	.45
170	A20	20o violet	.20	.20
171	A20	20o rose ('22)	22.50	.50
172	A20	20o orange ('25)	.20	.35
174	A20	25o rose red ('22)	.55	1.50
175	A20	25o dk bl ('25)	17.00	.20
176	A20	25o ultra ('34)	17.00	.65
177	A20	25o yel org ('36)	32.50	.45
178	A20	30o blue ('23)	19.00	.45
179	A20	30o brown ('25)	22.50	.35
180	A20	30o lt ultra ('36)	6.00	.70
181	A20	35o red vio ('30)	24.00	.45
182	A20	40o blue	.45	.70
183	A20	40o ol grn ('29)	45.00	1.25
184	A20	45o brown ('29)	5.00	.90
185	A20	50o gray	1.75	1.00
186	A20	85o myrtle grn ('25)	17.00	1.75
187	A20	115o brn red ('25)	11.00	1.75
188	A20	145o apple grn ('25)	8.25	1.75
		Nos. 167-188 (21)	277.15	16.10

Wmk. 181

189	A20	15o violet ('22)	2,650.	850.00
189A	A20	20o violet		*4,500.*

1922-36 Unwmk. *Perf. 10*

190	A20	15o violet	17.50	.70
a.		Booklet pane of 10	400.00	
191	A20	15o rose red ('25)	22.50	.85
a.		Booklet pane of 10	600.00	
192	A20	15o brown ('36)	5.75	1.25
a.		Booklet pane of 10	175.00	
193	A20	20o violet ('22)	.50	*1.50*
a.		Booklet pane of 10	10.00	
		Nos. 190-193 (4)	46.25	4.30

Gustavus Vasa — A21

1921, June *Perf. 10 Vertically*

194	A21	20o violet	12.50	*25.00*
195	A21	110o ultra	55.00	7.50
196	A21	140o gray black	30.00	7.50
		Nos. 194-196 (3)	97.50	40.00

400th anniversary of Gustavus Vasa's war of independence from the Danes.

Universal Postal Union Congress

Composite View of Stockholm's Skyline
A22

King Gustaf V — A23

1924, July 4 Unwmk. *Perf. 10*

197	A22	5o red brown	1.60	*3.25*
198	A22	10o green	1.60	*3.25*
199	A22	15o dk violet	1.60	*2.50*
200	A22	20o rose red	12.50	*17.00*
201	A22	25o dp orange	15.00	*21.00*
202	A22	30o deep blue	14.50	*21.00*
a.		30o greenish blue	87.50	125.00
203	A22	35o black	19.00	*26.00*
204	A22	40o olive green	29.00	*32.50*
205	A22	45o deep brown	32.50	32.50
206	A22	50o gray	32.50	32.50
207	A22	60o violet brn	47.50	*55.00*
208	A22	80o myrtle grn	35.00	35.00
209	A23	1k green	57.50	*87.50*
210	A23	2k rose red	140.00	*250.00*
211	A23	5k deep blue	300.00	*450.00*

Wmk. 181

212	A22	10o green	26.00	*55.00*
		Nos. 197-212 (16)	765.80	*1,124.*
		Set, never hinged	1,200.	

Postrider Watching Airplane
A24

Carrier Pigeon and Globe — A25

1924, Aug. 16 Engr. Unwmk.

213	A24	5o red brown	2.75	4.50
214	A24	10o green	2.75	5.75
215	A24	15o dk violet	3.00	3.00
216	A24	20o rose red	21.00	32.50
217	A24	25o deep orange	26.00	32.50
218	A24	30o deep blue	26.00	32.50
a.		30o greenish blue	90.00	52.50
219	A24	35o black	32.50	47.50
220	A24	40o olive green	32.50	32.50
221	A24	45o deep brown	37.50	35.00
222	A24	50o gray	50.00	62.50
223	A24	60o violet brown	50.00	77.50
224	A24	80o myrtle green	37.50	35.00
225	A25	1k green	75.00	87.50
226	A25	2k rose red	140.00	75.00
227	A25	5k deep blue	275.00	210.00

Wmk. 181

228	A24	10o green	22.50	*60.00*
		Nos. 213-228 (16)	834.00	833.25
		Set, never hinged	1,450.	

Universal Postal Union issue.

Royal Palace at Stockholm
A26

Death of Gustavus Adolphus — A27

1931, Nov. 26 Unwmk. *Perf. 10*

229	A26	5k dark green	110.00	12.50
		Never hinged	300.00	
a.		Booklet pane of 10	2,500.	

1932, Nov. 1

230	A27	10o dark violet	2.50	5.50
a.		Booklet pane of 10	40.00	
231	A27	15o dark red	4.50	1.90
a.		Booklet pane of 10	110.00	

Perf. 10 Vertically

232	A27	10o dark violet	1.90	.20
233	A27	15o dark red	2.50	.20
234	A27	25o dark blue	6.00	.95
235	A27	90o dark green	22.50	2.25
		Nos. 230-235 (6)	39.90	11.00
		Set, never hinged	80.00	

300th anniv. of the death of King Gustavus Adolphus II who was killed on the battlefield of Lützen, Nov. 6, 1632.

Catching Sunlight in Bowl — A28

1933, Dec. 6 *Perf. 10*

236	A28	5o green	2.50	1.75
a.		Booklet pane of 10	60.00	

There are two types of No. 236.

Perf. 10 Vertically

237	A28	5o green	2.50	.30

Perf. 13 Vertically

238	A28	5o green	3.50	7.25
		Nos. 236-238 (3)	8.50	9.30
		Set, never hinged	17.50	

50th anniv. of the Swedish Postal Savings Bank.

The Old Law Courts — A29

The "Four Estates" and Arms of Engelbrekt
A34

Designs: 10o, Stock exchange. 15o, Parish church (Storkyrkan). 25o, House of the Nobility. 35o, House of Parliament.

1935, Jan. 10 *Perf. 10*

239	A29	5o green	2.25	1.40
a.		Booklet pane of 10	55.00	
240	A29	10o dull violet	4.25	*5.75*
a.		Booklet pane of 10	60.00	
241	A29	15o carmine	4.75	1.10
a.		Booklet pane of 10	125.00	

Perf. 10 Vertically

242	A29	5o green	1.25	.20
243	A29	10o dull violet	5.75	.20
244	A29	15o carmine	2.25	.20
245	A29	25o ultra	6.00	.60
246	A29	35o deep claret	12.00	2.25
247	A34	60o deep claret	17.50	2.50
		Nos. 239-247 (9)	56.00	14.20
		Set, never hinged	110.00	

500th anniv. of the Swedish Parliament.

Chancellor Axel Oxenstierna
A35

Post Runner — A36

Mounted Courier — A37

Old Sailing Packet — A38

Mail Paddle Steamship A39

Mail Coach — A40

1855 Stamp Model — A41

Mail Train — A42

Postmaster General A. W. Roos — A43

Mail Truck and Trailer — A44

Modern Swedish Liner — A45

Junkers Plane with Pontoons — A46

1936, Feb. 20 Engr. *Perf. 10*

248	A35	5o green	1.75	.85
a.		Booklet pane of 18	72.50	
249	A36	10o dk violet	2.10	2.75
a.		Booklet pane of 18	95.00	
250	A37	15o dk carmine	3.00	.55
a.		Booklet pane of 18	250.00	

Perf. 10 Vertically

251	A35	5o green	1.75	.20
252	A36	10o dk violet	1.75	.20
253	A37	15o dk carmine	3.25	.20
254	A38	20o lt blue	8.25	5.00
255	A39	25o lt ultra	5.25	.50
256	A40	30o yellow brn	17.50	3.25
257	A41	35o plum	5.50	1.25
258	A42	40o olive grn	5.75	2.75
259	A43	45o myrtle grn	7.75	1.50
260	A44	50o gray	22.50	2.75
261	A45	60o maroon	29.00	.70
262	A46	1k deep blue	8.25	8.50
		Nos. 248-262 (15)	123.35	30.95
		Set, never hinged	300.00	

300th anniv. of the Swedish Postal Service.
See Nos. 946-950, B55-B56.

Airplane over Bromma Airport A47

Emanuel Swedenborg — A48

1936, May 23 *Perf. 10 Vert.*

263	A47	50o ultra	5.50	8.50
		Never hinged	10.50	

Opening of Bromma Airport near Stockholm.

Swedish Booklets

Before 1940, booklets were hand-made and usually held two panes of 10 stamps (2x5). About every third booklet contained one row of stamps with straight edges at right or left side. Se-tenant pairs may be obtained with one stamp perforated on 4 sides and one perforated on 3 sides.

Starting in 1940, booklet stamps have one or more straight edges.

1938, Jan. 29 *Perf. 12½*

264	A48	10o violet	1.50	.35
a.		Perf. on 3 sides	10.00	3.00
		Never hinged	17.00	
b.		Booklet pane of 10	30.00	

Perf. 12½ Vertically

266	A48	10o violet	1.10	.20
267	A48	100o green	3.75	1.40
		Nos. 264-267 (3)	6.35	1.95
		Set, never hinged	12.00	

250th anniv. of the birth of Swedenborg, scientist, philosopher and religious writer.

Johann Printz and Indian Chief — A49

"Kalmar Nyckel" Sailing from Gothenburg A50

Symbolizing the Settlement of New Sweden — A51

Holy Trinity Church, Wilmington, Del. — A52

Queen Christina — A53

1938, Apr. 8 *Perf. 12½ Vert.*

268	A49	5o green	.65	.20
269	A50	15o brown	.90	.20
270	A51	20o red	1.60	.70
271	A52	30o ultra	5.25	.85
272	A53	60o brown lake	8.25	.35

Perf. 12½

273	A49	5o green	1.60	1.00
a.		Perf. on 3 sides	10.00	7.50
		Never hinged	17.00	
b.		Booklet pane of 18	67.50	
274	A50	15o brown	2.75	.70
a.		Perf. on 3 sides	17.00	4.75
		Never hinged	26.00	
b.		Booklet pane of 18	115.00	
		Nos. 268-274 (7)	21.00	4.00
		Set, never hinged	32.50	

Tercentenary of the Swedish settlement at Wilmington, Del. See No. B54.

King Gustaf V — A54

1938, June 16 *Perf. 12½ Vert.*

275	A54	5o green	.65	.20
276	A54	15(o) brown	.75	.20
277	A54	30(o) ultra	17.50	.75

Perf. 12½

278	A54	5o green	1.40	.25
a.		Perf. on 3 sides	13.00	5.50
		Never hinged	22.50	
b.		Booklet pane of 10	45.00	
279	A54	15(o) brown	1.90	.30
a.		Perf. on 3 sides	20.00	1.40
		Never hinged	65.00	
b.		Booklet pane of 10	37.50	
		Nos. 275-279 (5)	22.20	1.70
		Set, never hinged	29.00	

80th birthday of King Gustaf V.

King Gustaf V — A55

Three Crowns — A56

1939 *Perf. 12½ Vertically*

280	A55	10o violet	.65	.20
281	A55	20o carmine	2.25	.60
282	A56	60o lake	.65	.20
283	A56	85o dk green	.30	.20
284	A56	90o peacock blue	.30	.20
285	A56	1k orange	.30	.20
286	A56	1.15k henna brn	.30	.20
287	A56	1.20k brt rose vio	1.60	.20
288	A56	1.45k lt yel grn	2.25	.80

Perf. 12½

289	A55	10o violet	1.60	3.00
a.		Perf. on 3 sides	47.50	65.00
		Never hinged	77.50	
b.		Bklt. pane of 10, perf. on 4 sides	30.00	
		Nos. 280-289 (10)	10.20	5.80
		Set, never hinged	17.50	

See Nos. 394-398, 416-417, 425-426, 431, 439-441, 473, 588-591, 656-664.

Per Henrik Ling — A57

1939, Feb. 25 *Perf. 12½ Vert.*

290	A57	5o green	.20	.20
291	A57	25(o) brown	1.10	.40

Perf. 12½

292	A57	5o green	.90	.40
a.		Perf. on 3 sides	14.00	3.75
		Never hinged	29.00	
b.		Booklet pane of 10	37.50	
		Nos. 290-292 (3)	2.20	1.00
		Set, never hinged	3.50	

Centenary of the death of P. H. Ling, father of Swedish gymnastics.

J. J. Berzelius A58

Carl von Linné A59

Perf. 12½ Vertically

1939, June 2 Engr.

293	A58	10o violet	3.75	.30
294	A59	15o fawn	.20	.20
295	A58	30o ultra	11.50	.45
296	A59	50o gray	13.00	1.00

Perf. 12½

297	A58	10o violet	2.10	.65
a.		Perf. on 3 sides	72.50	19.00
		Never hinged	125.00	
b.		Booklet pane of 10	65.00	
298	A59	15o fawn	3.00	.30
a.		Perf. on 3 sides	11.50	.45
		Never hinged	19.00	
b.		Booklet pane of 10	100.00	
c.		As "a," bklt. pane of 20	450.00	
		Nos. 293-298 (6)	33.55	2.90
		Set, never hinged	60.00	

200th anniv. of the founding of the Royal Academy of Science at Stockholm.

King Gustaf V — A60

Type A55 Re-engraved

1939-46 *Perf. 12½*

299	A60	5o dp green ('46)	.30	.20
b.		Perf. on 3 sides ('41)	.40	.20
		Never hinged	.50	
c.		As "b," bklt. pane of 20	12.00	
300	A60	10(o) violet ('46)	.20	.20
a.		Bklt. pane of 10, perf. on 4 sides	55.00	
		Never hinged	2.25	
c.		Perf. on 3 sides	2.25	.20
i.		As "c," booklet pane of 20	50.00	
300D	A60	15(o) chestnut ('46)	.20	.20
f.		Perf. on 3 sides ('45)	.40	.20
		Never hinged	.65	
j.		As "f," booklet pane of 20	7.75	
300G	A60	20(o) red ('42)	.30	.20
h.		Booklet pane of 20	6.50	
		Nos. 299-300G (4)	1.00	.80
		Set, never hinged	1.40	

No. 300 differs slightly from the original due to deeper engraving. No. 300G was issued only in booklets; all copies have one straight edge.

Nos. 299, 300, 300D exist in booklet panes of 20 made from sheets of stamps. These can be collected as booklets.

1940-42 *Perf. 12½ Vertically*

301	A60	5o dp green ('41)	.25	.20
302	A60	10(o) violet	.20	.20
302A	A60	15(o) chestnut ('42)	.20	.20
303	A60	20(o) red	.20	.20
304	A60	25(o) orange	1.00	.20
305	A60	30(o) ultra	.40	.20
306	A60	35(o) red vio ('41)	.60	.20
307	A60	40(o) olive grn	.60	.20
308	A60	45(o) dk brown	.60	.20
309	A60	50(o) gray blk ('41)	3.25	.20
		Nos. 301-309 (10)	7.30	2.00
		Set, never hinged	11.50	

Numerals measure 4½mm high. Less shading around head gives a lighter effect. Horizontal lines only as background for "SVERIGE."

See Nos. 391-393, 399.

Carl Michael Bellman A61

Tobias Sergel A62

1940, Feb. 4 Engr. *Perf. 12½ Vert.*

310 A61 5o green .25 .25
311 A61 35(o) rose red 1.00 .40

Perf. 12½

312 A61 5o green 1.25 .60
a. Perf. on 3 sides 10.00 .75
Never hinged 21.00
b. Booklet pane of 10 50.00
c. As "a," bklt. pane of 20 425.00
Nos. 310-312 (3) 2.50 1.25
Set, never hinged 3.00

Bellman (1740-95), lyric poet.

1940, Sept. 5 *Perf. 12½ on 3 Sides*

313 A62 15o lt brown 7.50 .25
a. Booklet pane of 20 275.00

Perf. 12½ Vertically

314 A62 15o lt brown 3.25 .20
315 A62 50o gray black 17.00 1.20
Nos. 313-315 (3) 27.75 1.65
Set, never hinged 47.50

Bicentenary of birth of Johan Tobias von Sergel (1740-1814), sculptor.

SEMI-POSTAL STAMPS

Type of 1872-91 Issues Surcharged in Dark Blue

Perf. 13x13½

1916, Dec. 21 Wmk. 181

B1 A5 5o + 5o on 2o org 5.50 *7.75*
B2 A5 5o + 5o on 3o yel brn 5.50 *7.75*
B3 A5 5o + 5o on 4o gray 5.50 *7.75*
B4 A5 5o + 5o on 5o grn 5.50 *7.75*
B5 A5 5o + 5o on 6o lilac 5.50 *7.75*
B6 A5 10o + 10o on 12o pale bl 5.50 *7.75*
B7 A5 10o + 10o on 20o red org 5.50 *7.75*
B8 A5 10o + 10o on 24o yel 5.50 *7.75*
B9 A5 10o + 10o on 30o brn 5.50 *7.75*
B10 A5 10o + 10o on 50o rose red 5.50 *7.75*
Nos. B1-B10 (10) 55.00 77.50

The surtax on Nos. B1-B31 was for the militia. See note after No. B21.
For surcharges see Nos. B22-B31.

No. 66 Surcharged in Dark Blue

1916, Dec. 21 Wmk. 180 *Perf. 13*

B11 A12 10o + 4.90k on 5k 150.00 *325.00*

Nos. J12-J22 Surcharged in Dark Blue

1916, Dec. 21 Unwmk. *Perf. 13*

B12 D1 5o + 5o on 1o 18.50 10.50
B13 D1 5o + 5o on 3o 5.00 5.50
B14 D1 5o + 5o on 5o 8.25 5.50
B15 D1 5o + 10o on 6o 5.00 6.00
B16 D1 5o + 15o on 12o 42.50 27.50
B17 D1 10o + 20o on 20o 15.00 21.00
B18 D1 10o + 40o on 24o 60.00 *82.50*
B19 D1 10o + 20o on 30o 5.50 6.00
B20 D1 10o + 40o on 50o 22.50 *37.50*
B21 D1 10o + 90o on 1kr 140.00 *375.00*
Nos. B12-B21 (10) 322.25 *577.00*

The surtax on Nos. B12-B21 is indicated not in figures, but in words at bottom of surcharge: Fem, 5; Tio, 10; Femton, 15; Tjugo, 20; Fyrtio, 40; Nittio, 90.

Nos. B1-B10 Surcharged

1918, Dec. 18 Wmk. 181

B22 A5 7o + 3o on #B1 8.75 8.25
B23 A5 7o + 3o on #B2 2.75 1.25
B24 A5 7o + 3o on #B3 2.75 1.25
B25 A5 7o + 3o on #B4 2.75 1.25
B26 A5 7o + 3o on #B5 2.75 1.25
B27 A5 12o + 8o on #B6 2.75 1.25
B28 A5 12o + 8o on #B7 2.75 1.25
B29 A5 12o + 8o on #B8 2.75 1.25
B30 A5 12o + 8o on #B9 2.75 1.25
B31 A5 12o + 8o on #B10 2.75 1.25
Nos. B22-B31 (10) 33.50 19.50

The 12o+8o surcharge exists on Nos. B1-B5 and the 7o+3o surcharge exists on Nos. B6-B10. Value, each $72.50.
Nos. B24, B26, B28 and B30 exist with surcharge inverted. Value unused, each $140.

King Gustaf V — SP1

Unwmk.

1928, June 16 Engr. *Perf. 10*

B32 SP1 5o (+ 5o) yel grn 2.75 *6.00*
B33 SP1 10o (+ 5o) dk vio 2.75 *6.00*
B34 SP1 15o (+ 5o) car 2.75 *4.50*
Complete booklet, pane of 8 ea. #B32, B33, B34 275.00
B35 SP1 20o (+ 5o) org 4.75 2.75
B36 SP1 25o (+ 5o) dk bl 4.75 3.25
Nos. B32-B36 (5) 17.75 *22.50*
Set, never hinged 27.50

70th birthday of King Gustaf V. The surtax was used for anti-cancer work.

AIR POST STAMPS

Official Stamps Surcharged in Dark Blue

1920, Sept. 17 Wmk. 181 *Perf. 13*

C1 O3 10o on 3o brn 2.75 *7.75*
a. Inverted surcharge 275.00 *700.00*
C2 O3 20o on 2o org 4.50 *11.00*
a. Inverted surcharge 275.00 *700.00*
C3 O3 50o on 4o vio 20.00 25.00
a. Inverted surcharge 275.00 *700.00*
Nos. C1-C3 (3) 27.25 *43.75*
Set, never hinged 55.00

Wmk. 180

C4 O3 20o on 2o org 2,250.
C5 O3 50o on 4o vio 160.00 *350.00*

Airplane over Stockholm oldst — AP2

Perf. 10 Vertically

1930, May 9 Engr. Unwmk.

C6 AP2 10o deep blue .20 .60
C7 AP2 50o dark violet .65 1.75
Set, never hinged 1.50

POSTAGE DUE STAMPS

D1

1874 Unwmk. Typo. *Perf. 14*

J1 D1 1o black 50.00 40.00
J2 D1 3o rose 50.00 40.00
J3 D1 5o brown 50.00 35.00
J4 D1 6o yellow 100.00 77.50
J5 D1 12o pale red 7.75 5.25
J6 D1 20o blue 62.50 40.00
J7 D1 24o violet 450.00 260.00
J8 D1 24o gray 55.00 52.50
J9 D1 30o dk grn 52.50 40.00
J10 D1 50o brown 175.00 57.50
J11 D1 1k blue & bister 225.00 72.50
Nos. J1-J11 (11) 1,277. 720.25

1877-86 *Perf. 13*

J12 D1 1o black ('80) 2.75 4.00
J13 D1 3o rose 6.25 7.25
J14 D1 5o brown 4.50 4.50
J15 D1 6o yellow 4.50 4.50
a. Printed on both sides 1,000.
J16 D1 12o pale red ('82) 14.50 17.00
J17 D1 20o pale blue ('78) 5.25 4.50
J18 D1 24o red lilac ('86) 26.00 29.00
a. 24o violet ('84) 26.00 29.00
J19 D1 24o gray lil ('82) 125.00 150.00
J20 D1 30o yellow green 6.50 4.50
J21 D1 50o yellow brown 10.50 5.75
J22 D1 1k blue & bister 30.00 17.50
Nos. J12-J22 (11) 235.75 248.50

Nos. J12-J17, J19-J22 exist imperf. Value, pairs, each $400.
For surcharges see Nos. B12-B21.

STAMPS FOR CITY POSTAGE

S1

Perf. 14x13½

1856-62 Typo. Unwmk.

LX1 S1 (1sk) (3o) blk, medium thick paper 950.00 450.00
On cover 600.00
On cover, before July 1, 1858 750.00
a. (1sk) gray black, thin paper ('56) *5,000.* 900.00
On cover 2,750.
LX2 S1 (3o) bis brn ('62) 600.00 475.00
On cover 675.00
a. (3o) olive brown ('62) 675.00 475.00
On cover 675.00

From 1856 to 1858 Nos. LX1, LX1a were sold at 1sk, from 1858 to 1862 No. LX1 was sold for 3o.

No. LX1 was reprinted three times with perf. 14, once with perf. 13. No. LX2 was reprinted once with each perforation. Value of lowest-cost Perf. 14 reprints, $250 each. Perf. 13, $175 each.

OFFICIAL STAMPS

O1

O3

1874-77 Unwmk. Typo. *Perf. 14*

O1 O1 3o bister 72.50 40.00
On cover 32.50
O2 O1 4o gray ('77) 250.00 70.00
On cover 52.50
O3 O1 5o yel green 140.00 52.50
On cover 125.00
O4 O1 6o lilac 250.00 65.00
On cover 65.00
O5 O1 6o gray 525.00 175.00
On cover 160.00
O6 O1 12o blue 160.00 2.50
On cover 7.75
O7 O1 20o pale red 950.00 90.00
On cover 275.00
O8 O1 24o yellow 950.00 20.00
On cover 55.00
a. 24o orange 950.00 22.50
On cover 60.00
O9 O1 30o pale brn 425.00 35.00
On cover 200.00
O10 O1 50o rose 575.00 125.00
On cover 325.00
O11 O1 1k bl & bis 1,650. 65.00
On cover 650.00
Nos. O1-O11 (11) 5,947. 740.00

Imperf., Pairs

O1a O1 3o 575.
O2a O1 4o 575.
O3a O1 5o 900.
O4a O1 6o 900.
O6a O1 12o 575.
O7a O1 20o 2,350.
O8b O1 24o 1,800.
O9a O1 30o 1,050.
O10a O1 50o 1,300.
O11a O1 1k 3,250.

1881-95 *Perf. 13*

O12 O1 2o org ('91) 1.40 2.00
On cover 22.50
O13 O1 3o bis brn 1.40 2.25
On cover 16.00
O14 O1 4o gray blk ('93) 2.50 .70
On cover 8.00
a. 4o gray ('82) 16.00 2.25
On cover 8.00
O15 O1 5o grn ('84) 5.25 .60
On cover 8.00
O16 O1 6o red lil ('82) 40.00 60.00
On cover 62.50
a. 6o lilac ('81) 45.00 65.00
On cover *75.00*
O17 O1 10o car ('95) 3.00 .20
On cover 4.00
b. 10o rose ('85) 45.00 1.25
On cover 11.00
O18 O1 12o blue 57.50 21.00
On cover 22.50
O19 O1 20o ver ('82) 200.00 2.50
On cover 55.00
O20 O1 20o dk bl ('91) 5.75 .60
On cover 10.00
O21 O1 24o yellow 72.50 22.50
On cover 65.00
a. 24o orange 65.00 22.50
On cover *125.00*
O22 O1 30o brown 26.00 .70
On cover 12.50
O23 O1 50o pale rose 140.00 22.50
On cover 100.00
O24 O1 50o pale gray ('93) 18.00 1.90
On cover 17.50
O25 O1 1k dk bl & yel brn 9.00 6.50
On cover 25.00
Nos. O12-O25 (14) 582.30 143.95

Imperf., Pairs

O12a O1 2o 250.00
O17a O1 10o No. O17 300.00
c. No. O17b 300.00
O20a O1 20o 45.00
O24a O1 50o 250.00

Surcharged in Dark Blue

1889

O26 O1 10o on 12o blue 11.50 *15.00*
On cover 500.00
a. Inverted surcharge 1,000. *2,250.*
On cover —
b. Perf. 14 — *3,500.*
O27 O1 10o on 24o yel 15.00 *22.00*
On cover 1,200.
a. Inverted surcharge *3,000.* *2,500.*
b. Perf. 14 *3,000.* *3,000.*

1910-12 Wmk. 180 Typo.

O28 O3 1o black .20 .45
Never hinged .30
On cover 15.00
O29 O3 2o orange 1.40 *3.00*
Never hinged 2.00
On cover 24.00
O30 O3 4o pale violet 2.10 *4.00*
Never hinged 3.25
On cover 15.00
O31 O3 5o green .65 *1.10*
Never hinged 1.10
On cover 10.00
O32 O3 8o claret .65 *1.10*
Never hinged 1.00
On cover 30.00
O33 O3 10o red 12.00 .70
Never hinged 24.00
On cover 15.00
O34 O3 15o red brown 1.10 .85
Never hinged 1.60
On cover 25.00
O35 O3 20o deep blue 8.25 1.60
Never hinged 15.00
On cover 30.00

O36	O3 25o red orange	8.25	2.10
	Never hinged	15.00	
	On cover		35.00
O37	O3 30o chocolate	8.00	3.25
	Never hinged	16.00	
	On cover		50.00
O38	O3 50o gray	8.25	3.25
	Never hinged	15.00	
	On cover		25.00
O39	O3 1k black, *yellow*	7.75	7.75
	Never hinged	15.00	
	On cover		30.00
O40	O3 5k claret, *yellow*	11.00	4.00
	Never hinged	21.00	
	On cover		40.00
	Nos. O28-O40 (13)	69.60	33.15

1910-19 Wmk. Wavy Lines (181)

O41	O3 1o black	3.00	*3.25*
	Never hinged	3.50	
	On cover		15.00
O42	O3 2o orange	.30	*.40*
	Never hinged	.40	
	On cover		5.00
O43	O3 3o pale brown	.40	*1.00*
	Never hinged	.50	
	On cover		7.50
O44	O3 4o pale violet	.30	*.40*
	Never hinged	.40	
	On cover		4.00
O45	O3 5o green	.30	*.40*
	Never hinged	.40	
	On cover		2.50
O46	O3 7o gray green	.45	*1.25*
	Never hinged	.55	
	On cover		13.00
O47	O3 8o rose	20.00	*27.50*
	Never hinged	24.00	
	On cover		8.00
O48	O3 10o red	.30	.20
	Never hinged	.40	
	On cover		4.00
O49	O3 12o rose red	.30	.30
	Never hinged	.40	
	On cover		5.00
O50	O3 15o org brown	.30	.30
	Never hinged	.60	
	On cover		7.50
O51	O3 20o deep blue	.45	.30
	Never hinged	.50	
	On cover		7.50
O52	O3 25o orange	1.00	.50
	Never hinged	1.60	
	On cover		10.00
O53	O3 30o chocolate	.55	.55
	Never hinged	1.00	
	On cover		10.00
O54	O3 35o dark violet	.85	*1.00*
	Never hinged	1.50	
	On cover		10.00
O55	O3 50o gray	3.25	2.10
	Never hinged	6.50	
	On cover		13.00
	Nos. O41-O55 (15)	31.75	39.45

For surcharges see Nos. C1-C5.

Use of official stamps ceased on July 1, 1920.

PARCEL POST STAMPS

Regular Issue of 1914 Surcharged

1917 Wmk. 180 *Perf. 13*

Q1	A14 1.98k on 5k claret, *yel*	1.40	*5.25*
Q2	A14 2.12k on 5k claret, *yel*	1.40	*5.25*

SWITZERLAND

'swit-sər-lənd

(Helvetia)

LOCATION — Central Europe, between France, Germany and Italy
GOVT. — Republic
AREA — 15,943 sq. mi.
POP. — 6,423,100 (est. 1983)
CAPITAL — Bern

100 Rappen or Centimes = 1 Franc

Watermarks

Wmk. 182 — Cross in Oval

Wmk. 183 — Swiss Cross

Watermark 182 is not a true watermark, having been impressed after the paper was manufactured. There are two types: 1- width just under 9mm. 2- width just under 8½mm. There are many other differences of 1/10mm to 1/3mm.

CANTONAL ADMINISTRATION

Unused values of Nos. 1L1-3L1 are for stamps without gum.
Counterfeit and repaired copies of Nos. 1L1-3L1 abound.

Zurich

A1 A2 Numerals of Value —

1843 Unwmk. Litho. *Imperf.*
Red Vertical Lines

1L1	A1 4r black	*20,000.*	*17,500.*
	On cover		*34,500.*
1L2	A2 6r black	*6,500.*	*1,750.*
	On cover		*4,300.*

1846 Red Horizontal Lines

1L3	A1 4r black	*17,500.*	*22,500.*
	On cover		*46,000.*
1L4	A2 6r black	1,900.	1,600.
	On cover		*3,900.*

Full margins = ½mm. There are dividing lines between stamps.

Five varieties of each value.

Reprints of the Zurich stamps show signs of wear and lack the red lines. Values 4r, $6,500; 6r, $2,150.

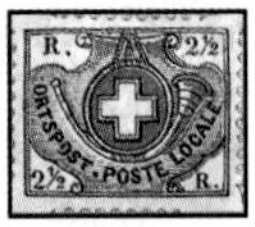

Coat of Arms — A3

1850 Unwmk. *Imperf.*

1L5	A3 2½r black & red	*6,500.*	*4,000.*
	On cover, single franking		*40,000.*
	Pair	29,000.	*11,000.*
	On cover, pair		*25,000.*

Full margins = 1¼mm.

No. 1L5 has separation designs in the margins between stamps as shown. Values are for stamps showing part of the separation design on all four sides.

Geneva

Coat of Arms — A4

1843 Unwmk. Litho. *Imperf.*

2L1	A4 10c blk, *yel grn*	*60,000.*	*40,000.*
	On cover		*60,000.*
a.	Either half	*22,500.*	*9,000.*
	On cover		*18,000.*
b.	Stamp composed of right half at left & left half at right	*85,000.*	*62,500.*
	On cover		*110,000.*

Full margins = ¾mm. There are dividing lines between stamps.

A5

A6

1845-48

2L2	A5 5c blk, *yel grn*	2,750.	1,750.
	On cover		3,400.
2L3	A6 5c blk, *yel grn* ('46)	2,100.	1,750.
	On cover		3,500.
2L4	A6 5c blk, *dk grn* ('48)	4,000.	3,000.
	On cover		6,000.

Full margins: No. 2L2 = 1¾mm; Nos. 2L3-2L4 = ½mm.

A7

Coat of Arms — A8

1849-50

2L5	A7 4c black & red	*35,000.*	*21,000.*
	On cover		*43,000.*
2L6	A7 5c blk & red ('50)	2,500.	1,750.
	On cover		3,400.

Full margins = 1mm. There are dividing lines between stamps.

1851

2L7	A8 5c black & red	*9,750.*	*4,000.*
	On cover		8,000.

Full margins = 1mm. There are dividing lines between stamps.

ENVELOPE STAMP USED AS ADHESIVE

E1

1847 Unwmk. *Imperf.*

2LU1	E1 5c yel grn, see footnote		*21,000.*

Value is for cut-out stamp used on folded letters. This use was authorized and is known from Feb. 19, 1847. Value of unused envelope cut-out, $450. Value of used cut-out off cover, $3,300.

Basel

Dove of Basel — A9

Typo. & Embossed
1845 Unwmk. *Imperf.*

3L1	A1 2½r blk, crim & bl	*14,000.*	*12,500.*
	On cover		*25,000.*
a.	2½r blk, crim & brt blue	*16,000.*	*15,000.*
	On cover		*27,000.*

Full margins = 1¼mm.

Proofs are black, vermilion and green. Value, $5,700.

FEDERAL ADMINISTRATION

Due to its tendency to damage the paper and/or the color of the stamps, the gum on Nos. 1-40 very often is removed. Unused values for Nos. 1-40 are for stamps without gum. Stamps with original gum sell for about the same prices.

A10

A11

1850 Unwmk. Litho. *Imperf.*
Full Black Frame Around Cross

1	A10 2½r black & red	3,000.	1,600.
	On cover, single franking		6,100.
	On cover, pair		6,800.
2	A11 2½r black & red	2,500.	1,500.
	On cover, single franking		4,500.
	On cover, pair		4,700.

Without Frame Around Cross

3	A10 2½r black & red	5,750.	2,750.
	On cover, single franking		7,900.
	On cover, pair		9,700.
4	A11 2½r blk & red	*42,500.*	*25,000.*
	On cover		*79,000.*
	On cover, pair		*160,000.*

Full margins = ¾mm. There are dividing lines between stamps.

Forty types of each.

A12

A13

1850
Full Black Frame Around Cross

5	A12 5r dk bl, blk & red	5,000.	1,250.
	On cover		3,000.

a. 5r dk grayish bl, blk & red 5,000. 1,250.
On cover 3,000.
6 A13 10r yel, blk & red *110,000.*
On cover *190,000.*

Full margins = ¾mm. There are dividing lines between stamps.

No. 6 used, with only parts of frame around cross showing, value $175 to $900.
Beware of copies of Nos. 7-8 with faked frame added.

Without Frame Around Cross

7 A12 5r lt bl, blk & red 1,750. 500.
On cover 1,100.
a. 5r dp bl, blk & red *3,500.* 1,000.
On cover 2,300.
b. 5r pur bl, blk & red — *5,500.*
On cover *10,500.*
c. 5r grnsh bl, blk & red 2,000. 575.
On cover 1,250.
d. 5r grayish vio, blk & red 2,150. 625.
On cover 1,400.
8 A13 10r yel, blk & red 925. 125.
On cover 275.
a. 10r buff, blk & red 1,275. 225.
On cover 340.
b. 10r org yel, blk & red 1,250. 250.
On cover 500.
c. Half used as 5r on cover, 5r rate *13,500.*
As "c," 15r rate *12,500.*
As "c," 25r rate *15,500.*
As "c," 30r rate *16,000.*

Full margins = ¾mm. There are dividing lines between stamps.

1851
Full Blue Frame Around Cross

9 A12 5r light blue & red *140,000.*
On cover *300,000.*

Full margins = ¾mm. There are dividing lines between stamps.

No. 9 used, with only parts of frame around cross showing, value $180 to $3,750.
Beware of copies of No. 10 with faked frame added.

Without Frame Around Cross

10 A12 5r lt blue & red 575. 125.00
On cover 275.00
a. Thin paper 1,000. 290.00
On cover 500.00

Full margins = ¾mm. There are dividing lines between stamps.

Forty types of each.

A14

A15

A16

1852
Vermilion Frame Around Cross

11 A14 15r vermilion *15,000.* 700.
On cover 1,700.
12 A15 15r vermilion 2,500. 125.
On cover 275.
13 A16 15c vermilion *14,000.* 1,000.
On cover 2,550.

Full margins = ¾mm. There are dividing lines between stamps.

Ten types of each.
On October 1st, 1854, all stamps of the preceding issues were declared obsolete.

Helvetia — A17

1854 Embossed. Unwmk.
Thin Paper, Fine Impressions
Emerald Silk Threads

14 A17 5r orange brn *8,000.* *1,600.*
On cover 3,200.
15 A17 5r red brown 550.00 140.00
On cover 260.00
16 A17 10r blue 775.00 80.00
On cover 140.00
17 A17 15r carmine rose 1,250. 175.00
On cover 325.00
a. 15r pale rose 1,250. 175.00
On cover 325.00
18 A17 40r pale yel grn *10,000.* 1,250.
On cover 3,200.
19 A17 40r yellow grn 1,250. 275.00
On cover 575.00

Full margins = ¼mm.

1854-55
Emerald Silk Threads
Medium Thick Paper
Fine Impressions

20 A17 5r pale yel brn 650.00 150.00
On cover 275.00
21 A17 10r blue 1,600. 110.00
On cover 200.00
22 A17 15r rose 925.00 100.00
On cover 175.00
23 A17 20r pale orange 1,400. 175.00
On cover 300.00

Full margins = ¼mm.

1855-57
Colored ( ) Silk Threads
Medium Thick Paper
Fine to Rough Impressions

24 A17 5r yel brn (yel) 575.00 100.00
On cover 190.00
25 A17 5r dk brown (blk) 325.00 35.00
On cover 70.00
26 A17 10r mlky bl (red) 925.00 175.00
On cover 325.00
27 A17 10r blue (car) 300.00 45.00
On cover 80.00
a. Thin paper 5,000. 425.00
On cover 800.00
28 A17 15r rose (bl) 550.00 65.00
On cover 125.00
29 A17 40r yel grn (mar) 1,000. 100.00
On cover 190.00
30 A17 1fr lav (blk) 1,400. 925.00
On cover 1,850.
31 A17 1fr lav (yel) 1,400. 925.00
On cover *1,850.*
a. Thin paper *20,000.* 7,250.
On cover *18,500.*

Full margins = ¼mm.

1857
Thin (Emergency) Paper
Rough Impressions
Green Silk Threads

32 A17 5r pale gray brn 4,500. 1,000.
On cover 2,000.
32A A17 10r blue 6,500. 925.
On cover 1,750.
33 A17 15r pale dl rose 3,250. 325.
On cover 600.
34 A17 20r pale dl org 3,500. 250.
On cover 500.

Full margins = ¼mm.

1858-62
Thick Ordinary Paper
Rough Impressions
Green Silk Threads

35 A17 2r gray 250.00 *550.00*
On newspaper or wrapper, single franking 1,000.
a. One and one-half used as 3r on newspaper or wrapper *14,000.*
c. Half used as 1r on cover
36 A17 5r brown 225.00 20.00
On cover 42.50
a. 5r black brown 275.00 40.00
On cover 75.00
b. Half used as 2r on cover *1,400.*
37 A17 10r dark blue 240.00 20.00
On cover 42.50
a. Half used as 5r on cover *7,250.*
38 A17 15r dark rose 375.00 65.00
On cover 130.00
39 A17 20r dark orange 475.00 70.00
On cover 140.00
a. Half used as 10r on cover *17,500.*
40 A17 40r dk yellow grn 450.00 85.00
On cover 160.00
a. Half used as 20r on cover *27,500.*
Nos. 35-40 (6) 2,015. 810.00

Full margins = ¼mm.

Helvetia — A18

Double transfer errors, Nos. 43c, 44a, 55b, 60a, 61a, 61b, 67b, have the design impressed twice. These do not refer to the "embossed" watermark.

1862-64 Wmk. 182 *Perf. 11½*
White Wove Paper

41 A18 2c gray 140.00 4.25
Never hinged 225.00
On cover 13.00
42 A18 3c black 14.50 *125.00*
Never hinged 21.00
On cover 325.00
On cover, single franking 575.00
On newspaper 210.00
43 A18 5c dark brown 3.50 .85
Never hinged 6.50
On cover 3.00
a. 5c bister brown 110.00 6.75
Never hinged 200.00
On cover 13.00
b. 5c gray brown 110.00 32.50
On cover 45.00
c. Dbl. transfer, one invtd. 4,000. 425.00
On cover 850.00
d. Dbl. transfer of lower left "5" 1,450.
On cover 3,200.
44 A18 10c blue 725.00 .85
Never hinged 1,250.
On cover 2.10
a. Dbl. transfer, one invtd. *8,000.*
45 A18 20c orange 2.50 2.75
Never hinged 4.25
On cover 13.00
a. 20c yellow orange 350.00 2.90
Never hinged 675.00
On cover 13.00
46 A18 30c vermilion 1,700. 40.00
Never hinged 3,600.
On cover 100.00
47 A18 40c green 1,600. 65.00
Never hinged 3,600.
On cover 125.00
48 A18 60c bronze 1,450. 180.00
Never hinged 3,600.
On cover 350.00
50 A18 1fr gold 20.00 *120.00*
Never hinged 42.50
On cover 350.00
a. 1fr yellowish bronze ('64) 1,450. 425.00
Never hinged 2,500.
On cover 850.00
b. 1fr reddish bronze 1,050. 375.00
Never hinged 2,900.
On cover 850.00

1867-78

52 A18 2c bister brown 2.50 1.80
Never hinged 4.25
On cover 3.50
a. 2c red brown 675.00 275.00
Never hinged 1,750
On cover 350.00
53 A18 10c carmine 3.50 1.00
Never hinged 7.25
On cover 2.10
54 A18 15c lemon 4.25 *42.50*
Never hinged 7.25
On cover 110.00
55 A18 25c blue green 1.80 *4.25*
Never hinged 2.90
On cover 18.00
a. 25c yellow green 60.00 40.00
On cover 125.00
b. Dbl. transfer, one invtd. 575.00
56 A18 30c ultra 575.00 10.00
Never hinged 1,450.
On cover 21.00
a. 30c blue *2,000.* 250.00
Never hinged *5,400.*
On cover 500.00
58 A18 40c gray 1.80 *160.00*
Never hinged 2.90
On cover 425.00
59 A18 50c violet 57.50 65.00
Never hinged 100.00
On cover 210.00
Nos. 52-59 (7) 646.35 *284.55*

1881
Granite Paper

60 A18 2c bister .55 *25.00*
Never hinged .75
On cover 42.50
a. Dbl. transfer, one invtd. 350.00
Never hinged 550.00
61 A18 5c brown .55 *13.00*
Never hinged .75
On cover 21.00
a. Dbl. transfer, one invtd. 30.00 *425.00*
Never hinged 42.50
On cover 850.00
b. Double transfer of lower left "5" *1,150.*
On cover 2,500.
62 A18 10c rose 5.00 *10.50*
Never hinged 11.50
On cover 20.00
63 A18 15c lemon 10.50 *475.00*
Never hinged 18.50
On cover 650.00
64 A18 20c orange .55 *160.00*
Never hinged .75
On cover 310.00
65 A18 25c green .55 *105.00*
Never hinged .75
On cover 190.00
66 A18 40c gray 1.80 *3,400.*
Never hinged 2.90
On cover 14,500.
67 A18 50c deep violet 18.00 *575.00*
Never hinged 25.00
On cover 1,150.
b. Dbl. transfer, one invtd. 250.00 *4,500.*
Never hinged 350.00
On cover 10,500.
68 A18 1fr gold 21.50 *1,300.*
Never hinged 32.50
On cover *5,400.*

The granite paper contains fragments of blue and red silk threads.
Forged or backdated cancellations are found frequently on Nos. 42, 50, 54, 58 and 60-68.
All stamps of the preceding issues were declared obsolete on October 1st, 1883. Some of the remainders of Nos. 41-68 were overprinted "AUSSER KURS" (Obsolete) diagonally in black.

Numeral — A19

1882-99 Typo. *Perf. 11½*
Granite Paper

69 A19 2c bister 1.80 .60
Never hinged 3.50
On cover 3.50
70 A19 3c gray brown 3.00 *8.50*
Never hinged 6.00
On cover 18.00
a. 3c gray 47.50 45.00
On cover *100.00*
71 A19 5c maroon 18.00 .60
Never hinged 35.00
On cover 3.00
a. Tête bêche pair —
72 A19 5c deep grn ('99) 8.00 .60
Never hinged 16.00
On cover 1.75
73 A19 10c red 7.25 .60
Never hinged 14.50
On cover 3.00
a. 10c carmine 55.00 .90
Never hinged 110.00
On cover 3.50
b. 10c light rose 250.00 5.00

		Never hinged	500.00	
		On cover		12.50
74	A19	12c ultra	8.00	.60
		Never hinged	16.00	
		On cover		5.75
a.		12c chalky blue	22.50	19.00
		On cover		40.00
b.		12c greenish blue	*450.00*	22.50
75	A19	15c yellow	140.00	29.00
		Never hinged	290.00	
		On cover		50.00
a.		15c orange	*14,500.*	*4,000.*
		On cover		*9,000.*
b.		Tête bêche pair	—	—
76	A19	15c violet ('89)	45.00	2.25
		Never hinged	90.00	
		On cover		27.50
		Nos. 69-76 (8)	231.05	*42.75*

1882

White Paper

77	A19	2c bister	375.00	300.00
		Never hinged	750.00	
		On cover		475.00
78	A19	5c maroon	825.00	100.00
		Never hinged	1,650.	
		On cover		180.00
79	A19	10c rose	2,100.	70.00
		Never hinged	4,000.	
		On cover		120.00
80	A19	12c chalky blue	150.00	26.00
		Never hinged	325.00	
		On cover		45.00
81	A19	15c yellow	225.00	250.00
		Never hinged	475.00	
		On cover		375.00

See Nos. 113-118.

Helvetia (Large numerals) A20

Helvetia (Small numerals) A21

1882-1904 Engr. *Perf. 11½ - 11¾*

82	A20	20c orange	150.00	5.50
		Never hinged	300.00	
		On cover		22.50
83	A20	25c green	82.50	3.00
		Never hinged	160.00	
		On cover		16.50
95b	A20	30c brown	—	*16,750.*
		On cover		—
84	A20	40c gray	120.00	40.00
		Never hinged	250.00	
		On cover		110.00
85	A21	40c gray ('04)	37.50	21.00
		Never hinged	75.00	
		On cover		125.00
86	A20	50c blue	125.00	21.00
		Never hinged	250.00	
		On cover		75.00
87	A20	1fr claret	210.00	6.00
		Never hinged	425.00	
		On cover		250.00
		On cover, single franking		*325.00*
88	A20	3fr yellow brn ('91)	180.00	19.00
		Never hinged	375.00	
		On cover		900.00
		On cover, single franking		*1,750.*

1888 *Perf. 9½*

89	A20	20c orange	800.00	100.00
		Never hinged	1,500.	
		On cover		165.00
90	A20	25c yellow grn	150.00	15.00
		Never hinged	275.00	
		On cover		50.00
91	A20	40c gray	800.00	650.00
		Never hinged	1,450.	
		On cover		1,450.
92	A20	50c blue	1,100.	325.00
		Never hinged	2,100.	
		On cover		800.00
93	A20	1fr claret	850.00	87.50
		Never hinged	1,650.	
		On cover		550.00
		On cover, single franking		650.00

Values for Nos. 89-93 are for well-centered stamps with slightly uneven perforations. Stamps missing perforations sell for much less.

1891-99 *Perf. 11½x11*

82a	A20	20c orange	47.50	1.75
		Never hinged	100.00	
		On cover		18.00
83a	A20	25c green	10.00	1.75
		Never hinged	20.00	
		On cover		17.50
94	A20	25c blue ('99)	11.00	1.75
		Never hinged	22.50	
		On cover		16.50
95	A20	30c red brn ('92)	30.00	1.90
		Never hinged	60.00	
		On cover		27.50
84a	A20	40c gray	67.50	4.75
		Never hinged	140.00	
		On cover		75.00
86a	A20	50c blue	40.00	11.00
		Never hinged	80.00	
		On cover		60.00
96	A20	50c green ('99)	42.50	21.00
		Never hinged	90.00	
		On cover		90.00
87a	A20	1fr claret	37.50	4.00
		Never hinged	75.00	
		On cover		*150.00*
		On cover, single franking		*175.00*
97	A20	1fr carmine	80.00	8.00
		Never hinged	160.00	
		On cover		*175.00*
		On cover, single franking		*225.00*
88a	A20	3fr yellow brown	135.00	25.00
		Never hinged	275.00	
		On cover		*750.00*
		On cover, single franking		*900.00*

1901-03 *Perf. 11½x12*

82b	A20	20c orange	25.00	1.60
		Never hinged	50.00	
		On cover		15.00
94a	A20	25c blue	12.00	1.10
		Never hinged	25.00	
		On cover		12.50
95a	A20	30c red brown	35.00	1.90
		Never hinged	75.00	
		On cover		24.00
84b	A20	40c gray	75.00	30.00
		Never hinged	150.00	
		On cover		120.00
96a	A20	50c green	60.00	7.00
		Never hinged	125.00	
		On cover		55.00
87b	A20	1fr claret	*2,000.*	250.00
		Never hinged	3,250.	
		On cover		*750.00*
		On cover, single franking		*900.00*
97a	A20	1fr carmine ('03)	375.00	32.50
		Never hinged	725.00	
		On cover		425.00
88b	A20	3fr yellow brown	180.00	19.00
		Never hinged	375.00	
		On cover		*750.00*
		On cover, single franking		*850.00*

Numerous retouches and plate flaws exist on all values of this issue.

Nos. 82-88 have wmk. type 1 and are ½mm taller (paper size) than Nos. 82b-88b, which have wmk. type 2.

See Nos. 105-112, 119-125.

UPU Allegory — A22

1900 *Perf. 11½*

98	A22	5c gray green	30.00	1.60
		Never hinged	60.00	
		On cover		4.00
99	A22	10c carmine rose	10.00	1.60
		Never hinged	20.00	
		On cover		4.00
100	A22	25c blue	25.00	30.00
		Never hinged	50.00	
		On cover		72.50
		Nos. 98-100 (3)	65.00	33.20

Re-engraved

101	A22	5c gray green	3.00	1.50
		Never hinged	6.00	
		On cover		4.00
102	A22	10c carmine rose	45.00	35.00
		Never hinged	90.00	
		On cover		90.00
a.		10c red purple	775.00	*6,000.*
103	A22	25c blue	700.00	*10,000.*
		Never hinged	1,200.	
		On cover		*13,000.*

Universal Postal Union, 25th anniv.

The impression of the re-engraved stamps is much clearer, especially the horizontally lined background. The figures of value are lined instead of being solid.

Helvetia Types of 1882-1904

1905 Wmk. 183 *Perf. 11½x11*

White Paper

105	A20	20c orange	3.75	2.25
		Never hinged	7.25	
		On cover		16.50
106	A20	25c blue	5.00	*9.00*
		Never hinged	10.00	
		On cover		45.00
107	A20	30c brown	5.00	2.00
		Never hinged	10.00	
		On cover		20.00
108a	A21	40c gray	90.00	*140.00*
		Never hinged	175.00	
		On cover		325.00
109	A20	50c green	30.00	7.25
		Never hinged	65.00	
		On cover		75.00
110	A20	1fr carmine	77.50	3.00
		Never hinged	160.00	
		On cover		55.00
		On cover, single franking		175.00
111	A20	3fr yellow brn	200.00	110.00
		Never hinged	400.00	
		On cover		175.00
		On cover, single franking		*1,000.*

Some clichés in the plates of the 20c, 25c, 30c, 50c and 3fr have been retouched.

1906 Re-engraved *Perf. 11½x11*

112	A20	25c pale blue	6.00	2.25
		Never hinged	12.50	
		On cover		22.50

In the re-engraved stamp the stars are larger and the background below "FRANCO" is of horiz. or horiz. and vert. crossed lines, instead of horiz. and curved lines.

1906 *Perf. 11½*

112a	A20	25c pale blue	85.00	7.50
		Never hinged	175.00	
		On cover		20.00
108	A21	40c gray	27.50	11.00
		Never hinged	55.00	
		On cover		110.00

1907 *Perf. 11½x12*

105a	A20	20c orange	6.00	6.00
		Never hinged	12.00	
		On cover		20.00
109a	A20	50c green	37.50	12.00
		Never hinged	72.50	
		On cover		77.50
110a	A20	1fr carmine	100.00	9.00
		Never hinged	200.00	
		On cover		110.00
		On cover, single franking		*240.00*
111a	A20	3fr yellow brown	240.00	190.00
		Never hinged	500.00	
		On cover		400.00
		On cover, single franking		*1,350.*

Numeral Type of 1882-99

1905 Typo. *Perf. 11½*

Granite Paper

113	A19	2c dull bister	4.25	1.90
		Never hinged	9.00	
		On cover		8.50
114	A19	3c gray brown	4.50	*60.00*
		Never hinged	9.00	
		On cover		90.00
115	A19	5c green	4.25	.50
		Never hinged	9.00	
		On cover		3.00
116	A19	10c scarlet	4.25	.50
		Never hinged	9.00	
		On cover		3.00
117	A19	12c ultra	5.50	2.00
		Never hinged	11.00	
		On cover		10.00
118	A19	15c brown vio	60.00	13.50
		Never hinged	120.00	
		On cover		72.50
a.		15c red lilac	240.00	140.00
		Never hinged	300.00	
		On cover		210.00
		Nos. 113-118 (6)	82.75	*78.40*

Helvetia Types of 1882-1904

1907 Engr. *Perf. 11½x12*

Granite Paper

119	A20	20c orange	2.25	3.75
120	A20	25c blue	7.75	*10.00*
121	A20	30c red brown	6.50	*17.50*
122	A21	40c gray	21.00	*45.00*
a.		Helvetia without diadem	300.00	*1,050.*
123	A20	50c gray green	5.50	*17.50*
124	A20	1fr carmine	19.00	9.25
125a	A20	3fr yellow brown		*10,500.*

There are retouches and plate flaws on all values.

Perf. 11½x11

120a	A20	25c deep blue	10.00	6.50
121a	A20	30c red brown	140.00	*325.00*
122b	A21	40c gray		*13,000.*
124a	A20	1fr carmine		*10,000.*
125	A20	3fr yel brn	100.00	65.00

William Tell's Son — A23

Helvetia
A24 A25

1907-25 Typo. *Perf. 11½*

Granite Paper

126	A23	2c pale bister	.30	.55
127	A23	3c lilac brn	.25	*10.00*
128	A23	5c yellow grn	2.25	.50
129	A24	10c rose red	1.50	.50
130	A24	12c ocher	.30	*3.50*
131	A24	15c red vio	3.00	*13.00*
132	A25	20c red & yel ('08)	2.25	1.00
133	A25	25c dp blue ('08)	1.90	.65
a.		Tête bêche pair	17.00	*55.00*
134	A25	30c yel brn & pale grn ('08)	1.60	.50
135	A25	35c yel grn & yel ('08)	1.90	1.40
136	A25	40c red vio & yel ('08)	12.50	1.00
a.		Designer's name in full on the rock ('08)	6.00	*82.50*
137	A25	40c deep blue ('22)	1.75	.50
a.		40c light blue ('21)	5.50	1.90
138	A25	40c red vio & grn ('25)	25.00	.50
139	A25	50c dp grn & pale grn ('08)	11.00	.50
140	A25	60c brn org & buff ('18)	9.25	.65
141	A25	70c dk brn & buff ('08)	55.00	17.00
142	A25	70c vio & buff ('24)	14.50	2.25
143	A25	80c slate & buff ('15)	9.75	1.10
144	A25	1fr dp cl & pale grn ('08)	7.00	.55
145	A25	3fr bis & yel ('08)	275.00	2.10
		Nos. 126-145 (20)	436.00	*57.75*

No. 136 has two leaves and "CL" below sword hilt. No. 136a has three leaves and designer's full name below hilt.

For surcharges and overprints see Nos. 189, 199, O10-O13, O15, 1O6-1O8, 1O14-1O16, 2O18-2O26, 3O14-3O22.

1933

With Grilled Gum

135a	A25	35c yel grn & yel	1.40	*12.50*
138a	A25	40c red vio & grn	32.50	1.50
139a	A25	50c dp grn & pale grn	9.00	1.50
140a	A25	60c brn org & buff	12.00	1.50
142a	A25	70c vio & buff	17.50	3.75
143a	A25	80c slate & buff	13.00	4.25
144a	A25	1fr dp cl & pale grn	19.00	6.50
		Nos. 135a-144a (7)	104.40	31.50

"Grilled" Gum

In 1930-44 many Swiss stamps were treated with a light grilling process, applied with the gumming to counteract the tendency to curl. It resembles a faint grill of vertical and horizontal ribs covering the entire back of the stamp, and can be seen after the gum has been removed. Listings of the grilled gum varieties begin with No. 135a.

William Tell's Son — A26

Bow-string in front of stock

1909 *Perf. 11½, 12*

Granite Paper

146 A26 2c bister .25 1.40
a. Tête bêche pair 3.25 *17.50*
147 A26 3c dark violet .25 *14.00*
148 A26 5c green 3.75 .20
a. Tête bêche pair 14.00 *50.00*
Nos. 146-148 (3) 4.25 *15.60*

See Nos. 149-163. For surcharges and overprints see Nos. 186, 193-195, 207-208, 1O1-1O3, 1O9-1O11, 2O1-2O7, 3O1-3O5.

First Redrawing

Bow-string behind stock. Thin loop above crossbow. Letters of "HELVETIA" without serifs.

1910-17

Granite Paper

149 A26 2c bister ('10) 8.75 8.00
150 A26 3c dk violet ('10) .20 .20
a. Tête bêche pair 2.75 2.75
b. Booklet pane of 6 12.50
151 A26 3c brown org ('17) .20 .20
a. Tête bêche pair 8.25 11.00
152 A26 5c green ('10) 21.00 6.50
a. Tête bêche pair 92.50 175.00
Nos. 149-152 (4) 30.15 14.90

Second Redrawing

Bow-string behind stock. Thick loop above crossbow. Letters of "HELVETIA" have serifs.

7½ CENTIMES:

Type I — Top of "7" is ½mm thick. The "1" of "½" has only traces of serifs. The two base plates of the statue are of even thickness.

Type II — Top of "7" is 1mm thick. The "1" of "½" has distinct serifs. The upper base plate is thinner than the lower.

1911-30

Granite Paper

153 A26 2c bister ('11) .20 .20
a. Tête bêche pair 3.25 1.60
154 A26 2½c claret ('18) .20 *1.10*
155 A26 2½c ol, *buff* ('28) .55 *2.10*
156 A26 3c ultra, *buff* ('30) 2.75 *6.00*
157 A26 5c green ('11) 1.75 .20
a. Tête bêche pair 5.50 *10.00*
158 A26 5c org, *buff* ('21) .20 .20
a. Bklt. pane of 6 (5 #158, 168) 14.00 *47.50*
159 A26 5c gray vio, *buff* ('24) .20 .20
a. Bklt. pane of 6 (5 #159, 168) 6.50 *19.00*
160 A26 5c red vio, *buff* ('27) .20 .20
a. Bklt. pane 6 (5 #160, 168) 30.00 *65.00*
161 A26 5c dk grn, *buff* ('30) .30 .25
a. Bklt. pane 6 (5 #161, 169) 27.50 *70.00*
162 A26 7½c gray (I) ('18) 1.10 .20
a. Tête bêche pair 13.00 *45.00*
c. 7½c slate (II) 4.50 2.75
163 A26 7½c dp grn, *buff* (I) ('28) .30 *3.25*
Nos. 153-163 (11) 7.75 *13.90*

1933 **With Grilled Gum**

156a A26 3c ultra, *buff* 4.75 *17.50*
161b A26 5c dark green, *buff* .55 *5.00*

Helvetia A27

William Tell A28

1909

Granite Paper

164 A27 10c carmine .60 .40
a. Tête bêche pair 2.25 *6.00*
165 A27 12c bister brn .85 .40
166 A27 15c red violet 26.00 1.10
Nos. 164-166 (3) 27.45 1.90

For surcharge see No. 187.

1914-30 **Granite Paper** *Perf. 11½*

TEN CENTIMES:

Type I — Bust 16½mm high. "HELVETIA" 15½mm wide. Cross bar of "H" at middle of the letter.

Type II — Bust 15mm high. "HELVETIA" 15mm wide. Cross bar of "H" above middle of the letter.

167 A28 10c red, *buff* (type II) .75 .20
a. 10c red, *buff* (type I) 2.50 *26.00*
b. Tête bêche pair (II) 3.25 4.25
d. Bklt. pane 6 (5 #167, 172) 50.00 *160.00*
168 A28 10c grn, *buff* (type II) ('21) .20 .20
a. Tête bêche pair 1.10 1.40
168C A28 10c bl grn, *buff* (type II) ('28) .20 .20
d. Tête bêche pair 2.50 2.50
169 A28 10c vio, *buff* (type II) ('30) 2.25 .20
a. Tête bêche pair 9.25 1.40
170 A28 12c brn, *buff* .20 *3.25*
171 A28 13c ol grn, *buff* ('15) 1.40 .50
172 A28 15c vio, *buff* 3.50 .20
b. 15c dk vio, *buff* 32.50 4.25
c. Tête bêche pair 87.50 125.00
173 A28 15c brn red, *buff* ('28) 2.50 2.75
174 A28 20c red vio, *buff* ('21) 3.25 .20
a. Tête bêche pair 6.50 7.50
175 A28 20c ver, *buff* ('24) 1.00 .50
a. Tête bêche pair 5.75 9.25
176 A28 20c car, *buff* ('25) .25 .20
a. Tête bêche pair 2.50 .55
177 A28 25c ver, *buff* ('21) 2.25 1.60
178 A28 25c car, *buff* ('22) 1.10 .85
179 A28 25c brn, *buff* ('25) 3.25 1.25
180 A28 30c dp bl, *buff* ('24) 9.25 .50
Nos. 167-180 (15) 31.35 12.60

1932-33 **With Grilled Gum**

169c A28 10c violet, *buff* 4.50 1.50
173a A28 15c brn red, *buff* ('33) 50.00 *52.50*
176c A28 20c carmine, *buff* 7.25 1.50
179a A28 25c brown, *buff* ('33) 125.00 35.00
180a A28 30c deep blue, *buff* 72.50 2.50
Nos. 169c-180a (5) 259.25 93.00

For surcharges and overprints see Nos. 188, 196-198, 1O4-1O5, 1O12-1O13, 2O8-2O17, 3O6-3O13.

The Mythen A29

The Rütli — A30

The Jungfrau A31

1914-30 **Engr.** **Granite Paper**

181 A29 3fr dk green 650.00 6.50
182 A29 3fr red ('18) 87.50 1.40
183 A30 5fr dp ultra 35.00 3.00
184 A31 10fr dull violet 100.00 3.25
185 A31 10fr gray grn ('30) 225.00 37.50
Nos. 181-185 (5) 1,097. 51.65

See No. 206. For overprints see Nos. 2O27-2O30, 3O23-3O26.

Stamps of 1909-14 Surcharged

a

b

c

1915

186 A26(a) 1c on 2c bister .25 1.25
187 A27(b) 13c on 12c bis brn .25 *9.25*
188 A28(c) 13c on 12c brn, *buff* .30 .90
Nos. 186-188 (3) .80 *11.40*

No. 141 Surcharged

189 A25 80c on 70c 25.00 17.50

Significant of Peace A32

"Peace" A33

"Dawn of Peace" A34

Perf. 11½

1919, Aug. 1 **Typo.** **Unwmk.**

190 A32 7½c olive drab & blk .80 *2.25*
191 A33 10c red & yel 1.10 *8.75*
192 A34 15c violet & yel 1.90 2.75
Nos. 190-192 (3) 3.80 13.75

Commemorating Peace after World War I.

Nos. 151, 149, 162, 171-172, 133 Surcharged in Black, Red or Dark Blue

a

b

c

1921 **Wmk. 183**

193 A26(a) 2½c on 3c (Bl) .20 1.10
a. Tête bêche pair 1.10 *3.25*
b. Inverted surcharge 800.00 *1,550.*
c. Double surcharge 550.00 *775.00*
194 A26(a) 5c on 2c (R) .20 *4.50*
a. Double surcharge 450.00 450.00
195 A26(a) 5c on 7½c (R) .20 .55
a. Tête bêche pair 6.50 *55.00*
b. Double surcharge 550.00 550.00
c. 5c on 7½c slate (II) 2,200. 4,500.
196 A28(b) 10c on 13c (R) .20 *2.25*
a. Double surcharge 550.00 550.00
197 A28(c) 20c on 15c (Bk) .55 2.75
a. Tête bêche pair 2.50 *55.00*
b. Double surcharge 875.00 *875.00*
198 A28(c) 20c on 15c (Bl) 2.25 5.50
b. Double surcharge 875.00 875.00
199 A25(c) 20c on 25c dp bl (R) .20 .55
a. Tête bêche pair 1.50 4.50
Nos. 193-199 (7) 3.80 *17.20*

A36

1924 **Typo.** *Perf. 11½*

Granite Paper, Surface Colored

200 A36 90c grn & red, *grn* 15.00 2.75
201 A36 1.20fr brn rose & red, *rose* 5.25 5.25
202 A36 1.50fr bl & red, *bl* 37.50 6.50
203 A36 2fr gray blk & red, *gray* 47.50 6.75
Nos. 200-203 (4) 105.25 21.25
Set, never hinged 325.00

1933 **With Grilled Gum**

200a A36 90c 17.50 3.25
201a A36 1.20fr 47.50 5.50
202a A36 1.50fr 32.50 6.50
203a A36 2fr 27.50 8.25
Nos. 200a-203a (4) 125.00 23.50
Set, never hinged 300.00

For overprints see Nos. O16-O18, 2O31-2O34, 3O27-3O30.

Building in Bern, Location of 1st UPU Congress, 1874
A37 A38

1924, Oct. 9 **Engr.** **Wmk. 183**

Granite Paper

204 A37 20c vermilion .55 1.60
205 A38 30c dull blue 1.10 6.25
Set, never hinged 3.25

50th anniv. of the UPU.

The Rütli — A39

Type of 1914 Issue

1928 **Re-engraved** *Perf. 11½*

206 A39 5fr blue 110.00 9.75
Never hinged 300.00
a. Imperf., pair, never hinged *10,000.*

In the re-engraved stamp the picture is clearer and lighter than on No. 183. "HELVETIA" is in smaller letters. The names at foot of the stamp are "Grasset-J. Sprenger" instead of "E. GRASSET-A. BURKHARD."

For overprints see Nos. 2O35, 3O31.

Nos. 155 and 163 Surcharged

1930, June *Perf. 11½*

207 A26 3c on 2½c ol grn, *buff* .20 *2.75*
208 A26 5c on 7½c dp grn, *buff* .20 *8.00*
Set, never hinged 1.10

The Mythen A40

1931 **Engr.** **Granite Paper**

209 A40 3fr orange brown 65.00 5.25
Never hinged 150.00

For overprints see Nos. 2O56, 3O47.

Dove on Broken Sword — A41

"Peace" A42

1932, Feb. 2 Typo. *Perf. 11½*

Granite Paper

210	A41	5c peacock blue	.20	.20
211	A41	10c orange	.20	.20
212	A41	20c cerise	.25	.20
213	A41	30c ultra	2.25	1.60
214	A41	60c olive brown	17.50	8.75

Unwmk.

Photo.

215	A42	1fr olive gray & bl	17.50	8.75
		Nos. 210-215 (6)	37.90	19.70
		Set, never hinged	95.00	

Intl. Disarmament Conf., Geneva, Feb. 1932.

For overprints see #2O36-2O41, 3O32-3O37.

Louis Favre — A43

Alfred Escher — A44

Design: 30c, Emil Welti.

Wmk. 183

1932, May 31 Engr. *Perf. 11½*

Granite Paper

216	A43	10c red brown	.20	.20
217	A44	20c vermilion	.25	.20
218	A44	30c deep ultra	.55	*2.10*
		Nos. 216-218 (3)	1.00	*2.50*
		Set, never hinged	3.00	

Completion of the St. Gotthard tunnel, 50th anniv.

Nos. 216-218 exist imperforate.

Staubbach Falls A46

Mt. Pilatus A47

Chillon Castle A48

Rhone Glacier A49

St. Gotthard Railroad A50

Via Mala Gorge A51

Rhine Falls — A52

1934, July 2 Typo. *Perf. 11½*

Granite Paper

219	A46	3c olive	.20	*3.00*
220	A47	5c emerald	.20	.20
221	A48	10c brt violet	.40	.20
222	A49	15c orange	.50	3.25
223	A50	20c red	.60	.60
224	A51	25c brown	7.75	8.25
225	A52	30c ultra	25.00	2.10
		Nos. 219-225 (7)	34.65	17.60
		Set, never hinged	100.00	

Tête bêche Pairs

220a	A47	5c	1.60	1.60
221a	A48	10c	1.50	.85
222a	A49	15c	1.75	3.00
223a	A50	20c	3.50	2.25

Souvenir Sheet

1934, Sept. 29

226	Sheet of 4	500.00	*550.00*
	Never hinged	825.00	

No. 226 was issued in connection with the Swiss National Philatelic Exhibition at Zurich, Sept. 29 to Oct. 7, 1934. It contains one each of Nos. 220-223. Size: 62x72mm.

For overprints see Nos. 2O42-2O46, 3O48.

Staubbach Falls A53

Mt. Pilatus A54

Chillon Castle A55

Rhone Glacier A56

St. Gotthard Railroad A57

Via Mala Gorge A58

Rhine Falls — A59

Balsthal Pass — A60

Alpine Lake of Säntis — A61

Two types of 10c red violet:

I — Shading inside "0" of 10 has only vertical lines.

II — Shading in "0" includes two diagonal lines.

1936-42 Unwmk. Engr. *Perf. 11½*

227	A53	3c olive	.20	.20
228	A54	5c blue green	.20	.20
229	A55	10c red vio (II)	.85	.20
b.		Type I	.85	.20
230	A55	10c dk red brn ('39)	.20	.20
230B	A55	10c org brn ('42)	.20	.20
231	A56	15c orange	.40	1.10
232	A57	20c carmine	4.75	.20
233	A58	25c lt brown	.50	1.10
234	A59	30c ultra	.90	.20
235	A60	35c yellow grn	1.10	1.25
236	A61	40c gray	6.00	.20
		Nos. 227-236 (11)	15.30	5.05
		Set, never hinged	37.50	

Two types of the 20c. See Nos. 316-321.

For overprints see Nos. O1-O4, O6-O9, O19-O19-O22, O24-O27, 2O47-2O55, 2O68-2O68A, 2O70-2O73, 2O75-2O78, 3O38-3O46, 3O60-3O60A, 3O62-3O65, 3O67-3O70, 4O1-4O4, 4O6-4O9, 4O23-4O24, 4O27-4O28, 5O1-5O2, 5O5.

Tête bêche Pairs

228a	A54	5c blue green	.45	.30
229a	A55	10c red violet (II)	4.50	5.50
230a	A55	10c dark red brown	1.75	1.10
230d	A55	10c orange brown	.50	.60
232a	A57	20c carmine	25.00	35.00

1936-40 With Grilled Gum

227a	A53	3c olive	.65	*6.25*
228d	A54	5c blue green	.30	.25
229d	A55	10c red violet (II)	.30	.25
e.		Type I	1.00	.25
230e	A55	10c dark red brown ('40)	1.90	*25.00*
231a	A56	15c orange	.30	1.10
232c	A57	20c carmine	6.75	.25
233a	A58	25c light brown	1.00	*5.00*
234a	A59	30c ultra	.95	.25
235a	A60	35c yellow green	1.40	3.25
236a	A61	40c gray	9.25	.50
		Nos. 227a-236a (10)	22.80	*42.10*
		Set, never hinged	47.50	

Mobile Post Office A62

1937, Sept. 5 Photo.

Granite Paper

237	A62	10c black & yellow	.25	.50
		Never hinged	.55	

No. 237 was sold exclusively by the traveling post office. It exists on two kinds of granite paper, black and red fibers or blue and red fibers. See No. 307 for type A62 redrawn.

View of Labor Building from Lake Geneva A63

Palace of League of Nations A64

Main Building, Palace of League of Nations A65

Labor Building and Albert Thomas Monument A66

1938, May 2 *Perf. 11½*

Granite Paper

238	A63	20c red & buff	.20	.20
239	A64	30c blue & lt blue	.45	.20
240	A65	60c brown & buff	1.75	*2.25*
241	A66	1fr black & buff	7.50	*17.00*
		Nos. 238-241 (4)	9.90	*19.65*
		Set, never hinged	25.00	

Opening of Assembly Hall of the Palace of the League of Nations.

For overprints see #2O57-2O64, 3O49-3O56.

Souvenir Sheet

A67

Engraved and Typographed

1938, Sept. 17 Unwmk. *Perf. 11½*

Granite Paper

242	A67	Sheet of 3	37.50	32.50
		Never hinged	70.00	
a.		AP4 10c on 65c gray bl & dp bl	19.00	*25.00*
b.		A68 20c red	1.10	*2.50*

Natl. Phil. Exhib. at Aarau, Sept. 17-25, and 25th anniv. of Swiss air mail. No. 242 contains 2 No. 243, but on granite paper, and a 10c on 65c similar to No. C22 but redrawn, with wing tips 1½mm from side frame lines; overall size 37x20½mm; no watermark.

On No. C22, wing tips touch frame lines; size is 36x21½mm; Wmk. 183.

Lake Lugano — A68

First Federal Pact, 1291 A69

Diet of Stans, 1481
A70

Citizens Voting
A71

1938, Sept. 17 Engr. *Perf. 11½*

243 A68 20c red		.25	.25
a.	"c,"tête bêche pair	.50	*.85*
c.	Grilled gum	.40	*.40*
d.	As "c," tête bêche pair	1.40	*15.00*

Granite Paper

244 A69 3fr brn car, *grnsh*	11.00	8.75
245 A70 5fr slate bl, *grnsh*	7.50	6.00
246 A71 10fr grn, *grnsh*	47.50	35.00
Nos. 243-246 (4)	66.25	50.00
Set, never hinged	190.00	

No. 243 is printed on ordinary paper. Nos. 244-246 are on granite surface-colored paper. The greenish surface coating has faded on most copies.

For type A68 in orange brown, see No. 318.

See Nos. 242b, 284-286. For overprints see Nos. O5, O23, 2O65-2O67, 2O69, 2O74, 2O88-2O90, 3O57-3O59, 3O61, 3O66, 3O80-3O82, 4O5, 4O19-4O21, O4O25, 5O3, 5O23-5O25, 7O18-7O20.

Deputation of Trades and Professions — A72

Swiss Family
A73

Alpine Scenery
A74

Engr., Photo. (30c)

1939, Feb. 1 *Perf. 11½*

Inscribed in French

247 A72 10c dl pur & red	.20	.20
248 A73 20c lake & red	.50	.20
249 A74 30c dp blue & red	2.50	*3.00*

Inscribed in German

250 A72 10c dl pur & red	.20	.20
251 A73 20c lake & red	.40	.20
252 A74 30c dp blue & red	2.10	*8.25*

Inscribed in Italian

253 A72 10c dl pur & red	.20	.20
254 A73 20c lake & red	1.90	.20
255 A74 30c dp blue & red	2.25	*9.25*
Nos. 247-255 (9)	10.25	21.70
Set, never hinged	27.50	

National Exposition of 1939, Zurich.

Tree and Crossbow — A75

1939, May 6 Photo. *Perf. 11½*

Granite Paper

Inscribed in French

256 A75 5c deep green	.55	*1.60*
257 A75 10c gray brown	.55	*1.90*
258 A75 20c brt carmine	1.10	*1.60*
259 A75 30c violet blue	3.00	*8.00*

Inscribed in German

260 A75 5c deep green	.55	*2.50*
261 A75 10c gray brown	.55	*2.50*
262 A75 20c brt carmine	1.10	*3.50*
263 A75 30c violet blue	8.75	*9.50*

Inscribed in Italian

264 A75 5c deep green	.85	*4.50*
265 A75 10c gray brown	.55	*3.50*
266 A75 20c brt carmine	1.10	*4.25*
267 A75 30c violet blue	3.25	*11.00*
Nos. 256-267 (12)	21.90	*54.35*
Set, never hinged	32.50	

National Exposition of 1939.

The 5c, 10c and 20c stamps in the three languages exist se-tenant in coils.

1939 With Grilled Gum

256a A75 5c deep green	.75	*2.25*
257a A75 10c gray brown	.75	*2.25*
258a A75 20c bright carmine	1.90	*3.00*
260a A75 5c deep green	.75	*1.60*
262a A75 20c bright carmine	1.90	1.60
264a A75 5c deep green	1.10	*3.75*
265a A75 10c gray brown	1.00	*3.00*
266a A75 20c bright carmine	1.90	*3.25*
Nos. 256a-266a (8)	10.05	*20.70*

View of Geneva
A76

Perf. 11½

1939, Aug. 22 Photo. Unwmk.

Granite Paper

268 A76 20c red, car & buff	.20	.20
269 A76 30c blue, car & gray	.30	*2.75*
Set, never hinged	1.40	

75th anniv. of the founding of the Intl. Red Cross Society.

SEMI-POSTAL STAMPS

Nos. B1-B76, B81-B84 were sold at premiums of 2c for 3c stamps, 5c for 5c-20c stamps and 10c for 30c-40c stamps.

Helvetia and Matterhorn — SP2

Perf. 11½, 12

1913, Dec. 1 Typo. Wmk. 183

Granite Paper

B1 SP2 5c green	2.75	*8.25*
Never hinged	7.75	

Boy (Appenzell)
SP3

Girl (Lucerne)
SP4

1915, Dec. 1 *Perf. 11½*

B2 SP3 5c green, *buff*		3.25	*8.25*
a.	Tête bêche pair	82.50	*875.00*
l	Never hinged	160.00	
B3 SP4 10c red, *buff*		100.00	87.50
Set, never hinged		225.00	

Girl (Fribourg)
SP5

Dairy Boy (Bern)
SP6

Girl (Vaud) — SP7

1916, Dec. 1

B4 SP5 3c vio, *buff*	5.00	*37.50*
B5 SP6 5c grn, *buff*	11.00	9.25
B6 SP7 10c brn red, *buff*	47.50	*77.50*
Nos. B4-B6 (3)	63.50	*124.25*
Set, never hinged	175.00	

Girl (Valais)
SP8

Girl (Unterwalden)
SP9

Girl (Ticino) — SP10

1917, Dec. 1

B7 SP8 3c vio, *buff*	3.25	*50.00*
B8 SP9 5c green, *buff*	7.75	5.50
B9 SP10 10c red, *buff*	19.00	22.50
Nos. B7-B9 (3)	30.00	*78.00*
Set, never hinged	87.50	

Uri
SP11

Geneva
SP12

1918, Dec. 1

Straw-Surfaced Paper

B10 SP11 10c red, org & blk	7.75	*25.00*
B11 SP12 15c vio, red, org & blk	9.25	*11.00*
Set, never hinged	52.50	

Nidwalden
SP13

Vaud
SP14

Obwalden — SP15

1919, Dec. 1

Cream-Surfaced Paper

B12 SP13 7½c gray, red & blk	2.50	*14.00*
B13 SP14 10c lake, grn & blk	2.50	*14.00*
B14 SP15 15c pur, red & blk	5.00	*7.25*
Nos. B12-B14 (3)	10.00	*35.25*
Set, never hinged	22.50	

Schwyz
SP16

Zürich
SP17

Ticino — SP18

1920, Dec. 1

Cream-Surfaced Paper

B15 SP16 7½c gray & red	3.75	*11.50*
B16 SP17 10c red & lt bl	5.00	*12.50*
B17 SP18 15c violet, red & bl	2.75	*6.00*
Nos. B15-B17 (3)	11.50	*30.00*
Set, never hinged	25.00	

Valais
SP19

Bern
SP20

Switzerland — SP21

1921, Dec. 1

Cream-Surfaced Paper

B18 SP19 10c grn, red & blk	.65	*3.00*
B19 SP20 20c vio, red, org & blk	1.90	*3.50*
B20 SP21 40c blue & red	7.25	*47.50*
Nos. B18-B20 (3)	9.80	*54.00*
Set, never hinged	25.00	

Zug
SP22

Fribourg
SP23

Lucerne
SP24

Switzerland
SP25

1922, Dec. 1

Cream-Surfaced Paper

B21 SP22 5c org, pale bl & blk	.50	*5.50*
B22 SP23 10c ol grn & blk	.60	*2.50*
B23 SP24 20c vio, pale bl & blk	1.00	*2.50*
B24 SP25 40c bl & red	8.75	*47.50*
Nos. B21-B24 (4)	10.85	*58.00*
Set, never hinged	26.00	

Basel
SP26

Glarus (St. Fridolin)
SP27

Neuchâtel
SP28

Switzerland
SP29

1923, Dec. 1

Cream-Surfaced Paper

B25 SP26 5c org & blk	.40	*3.50*
B26 SP27 10c multi	.40	*1.90*
B27 SP28 20c multi	.45	*1.90*
B28 SP29 40c dk bl & red	7.75	*37.50*
Nos. B25-B28 (4)	9.00	*44.80*
Set, never hinged	21.00	

Appenzell SP30

Solothurn SP31

Schaffhausen SP32

Switzerland SP33

1924, Dec. 1

Cream-Surfaced Paper

B29 SP30 5c dk vio & blk	.25	*1.60*
B30 SP31 10c grn, red & blk	.40	*1.00*
B31 SP32 20c car, yel & blk	.65	*1.00*
B32 SP33 30c bl, red & blk	1.40	*11.00*
Nos. B29-B32 (4)	2.70	*14.60*
Set, never hinged	6.50	

St. Gallen (Canton) SP34

Appenzell-Ausser-Rhoden SP35

Grisons SP36

Switzerland SP37

1925, Dec. 1

Cream-Surfaced Paper

B33 SP34 5c vio, grn & blk	.25	*1.10*
B34 SP35 10c grn & blk	.25	*.85*
B35 SP36 20c multi	.25	*.85*
B36 SP37 30c dk bl, red & blk	1.10	*8.25*
Nos. B33-B36 (4)	1.85	*11.05*
Set, never hinged	4.50	

Thurgau SP38

Basel SP39

Aargau SP40

Switzerland SP41

1926, Dec. 1

Cream-Surfaced Paper

B37 SP38 5c vio, bis & grn	.25	*1.40*
B38 SP39 10c gray grn, red & blk	.25	*1.40*
B39 SP40 20c red, blk & bl	.25	*1.40*
B40 SP41 30c dk bl & red	1.10	*12.50*
Nos. B37-B40 (4)	1.85	*16.70*
Set, never hinged	4.50	

Orphan SP42

Orphan at Pestalozzi School SP43

SP44

J. H. Pestalozzi SP45

1927, Dec. 1 Typo. Wmk. 183

Granite Paper

B41 SP42 5c red vio & yel, *grysh*	.20	*1.60*
B42 SP43 10c grn & fawn, *grnsh*	.20	*.60*

Engr.

B43 SP44 20c red	.20	*.60*

Unwmk.

Photo.

B44 SP45 30c gray bl & blk	1.10	*6.50*
Nos. B41-B44 (4)	1.70	*9.30*
Set, never hinged	3.25	

Nos. B43-B44 for the centenary of the death of Johann Heinrich Pestalozzi, the Swiss educational reformer.

Lausanne SP46

Winterthur SP47

St. Gallen (City) — SP48

J. H. Dunant SP49

1928, Dec. 1 Typo. Wmk. 183

Cream-Surfaced Paper.

B45 SP46 5c dk vio, red & blk	.20	*1.60*
B46 SP47 10c bl grn, org red & blk	.20	*.90*
B47 SP48 20c brn red, blk & yel	.20	*.90*

Unwmk.

Photo.

Thick White Paper

B48 SP49 30c dl bl & red	1.10	*7.00*
Nos. B45-B48 (4)	1.70	*10.40*
Set, never hinged	3.50	

No. B48 for the centenary of the birth of Jean Henri Dunant, Swiss author, philanthropist and founder of the Red Cross Society.

Lake Lugano and Mt. Salvatore SP50

Lake Engstlen and Mt. Titlis SP51

Mt. Lyskamm SP52

Nicholas von der Flüe SP53

1929, Dec. 1 ***Perf. 11x11½***

B49 SP50 5c dk vio & red org	.20	*1.40*
B50 SP51 10c ol brn & gray bl	.20	*1.10*
B51 SP52 20c brn garnet & bl	.25	*1.10*
B52 SP53 30c dk blue	1.25	*12.50*
Nos. B49-B52 (4)	1.90	*16.10*
Set, never hinged	4.50	

No. B52 for Nicholas von der Flüe, the Swiss patriot. By his advice the Swiss Confederation was continued and Swiss independence was saved.

Fribourg SP54

Altdorf SP55

Schaffhausen SP56

Jeremias Gotthelf SP57

Wmk. 183

1930, Dec. 1 Typo. ***Perf. 11½***

Cream-Surfaced Paper

B53 SP54 5c dp grn, dl bl & blk	.20	*1.40*
B54 SP55 10c multicolored	.20	*.90*
B55 SP56 20c multicolored	.30	*.90*

Engr.

White Paper

B56 SP57 30c slate blue	1.25	*6.00*
Nos. B53-B56 (4)	1.95	*9.20*
Set, never hinged	4.00	

No. B56 for Jeremias Gotthelf, pen name of Albrecht Bitzius, pastor and author.

Lakes Silvaplana and Sils SP58

Wetterhorn SP59

Lake Geneva SP60

Alexandre Vinet SP61

1931, Dec. 1 Photo. Unwmk.

Granite Paper

B57 SP58 5c dp grn	.45	*1.60*
B58 SP59 10c dk vio	.40	*.85*
B59 SP60 20c brn red	.55	*1.10*

Wmk. 183

Engr.

B60 SP61 30c ultra	4.50	*19.00*
Nos. B57-B60 (4)	5.90	*22.55*
Set, never hinged	14.00	

No. B60 for Alexandre Rudolph Vinet, critic and theologian.

Flag Swinger SP62

Putting the Stone SP63

Wrestling SP64

Eugen Huber SP65

1932, Dec. 1 Typo. Unwmk.

Granite Paper

B61 SP62 5c dk grn & red	.30	*1.90*
B62 SP63 10c orange	.45	*2.25*
B63 SP64 20c scarlet	.55	*1.90*

Wmk. 183

Engr.

B64 SP65 30c ultra	2.25	*8.75*
Nos. B61-B64 (4)	3.55	*14.80*
Set, never hinged	9.50	

No. B64 for Eugen Huber, jurist and author of the Swiss Civil Law Book.

Girl of Vaud — SP66

Girl of Bern — SP67

Girl of Ticino SP68

Jean Baptiste Girard (Le Père Grégoire) SP69

1933, Dec. 1 Photo. Unwmk.

Granite Paper

B65 SP66 5c grn & buff	.30	*1.50*
B66 SP67 10c vio & buff	.30	*1.10*
B67 SP68 20c red & buff	.45	*2.10*

Wmk. 183

Engr.

B68 SP69 30c ultra	2.50	*8.50*
Nos. B65-B68 (4)	3.55	*13.20*
Set, never hinged	8.25	

Girl of Appenzell
SP70

Girl of Valais
SP71

Girl of Grisons
SP72

Albrecht von Haller
SP73

1934, Dec. 1 Photo. Unwmk.

B69 SP70	5c grn & buff	.30	*1.60*
B70 SP71	10c vio & buff	.45	*1.10*
B71 SP72	20c red & buff	.45	*1.60*

Wmk. 183

Engr.

B72 SP73	30c ultra	2.50	*8.75*
	Nos. B69-B72 (4)	3.70	*13.05*
	Set, never hinged	8.25	

Girl of Basel
SP74

Girl of Lucerne
SP75

Girl of Geneva
SP76

Stefano Franscini
SP77

1935, Dec. 1 Photo. Unwmk.

Granite Paper

B73 SP74	5c grn & buff	.25	*1.75*
B74 SP75	10c vio & buff	.45	*1.10*
B75 SP76	20c red & buff	.45	*2.75*

Wmk. 183

Engr.

B76 SP77	30c ultra	2.50	*8.75*
	Nos. B73-B76 (4)	3.65	*14.35*
	Set, never hinged	8.25	

No. B76 honors Stefano Franscini (1796-1857), political economist and educator.

Alpine Herdsman — SP78

Perf. 11½

1936, Oct. 1 Photo. Unwmk.

Granite Paper

B77 SP78	10c + 5c vio	.55	*1.00*
B78 SP78	20c + 10c dk red	.85	*4.25*
B79 SP78	30c + 10c ultra	3.75	*20.00*
	Nos. B77-B79 (3)	5.15	*25.25*
	Set, never hinged	11.00	

Souvenir Sheet

B80 SP78	Sheet of 3	35.00	*125.00*
	Never hinged	70.00	
a.	Block of 4 sheets	190.00	*875.00*
	Never hinged	300.00	

Swiss National Defense Fund Drive.

No. B80 contains stamps similar to Nos. B77-B79, but on grilled granite paper with blue and red fibers instead of black and red. Sold for 2fr. Size: 120x130mm.

Johann Georg Nägeli
SP79

Girl of Neuchâtel
SP80

Girl of Schwyz
SP81

Girl of Zurich
SP82

Wmk. 183

1936, Dec. 1 Engr. *Perf. 11½*

Granite Paper

B81 SP79	5c grn	.55	*.70*

Unwmk.

Photo.

B82 SP80	10c vio & buff	.55	*.70*
B83 SP81	20c red & buff	.25	*1.90*
B84 SP82	30c ultra & buff	3.50	*30.00*
	Nos. B82-B84 (3)	4.30	*32.60*
	Set, never hinged	11.00	

Gen. Henri Dufour — SP83

Nicholas von der Flüe — SP84

Boy
SP85

Girl
SP86

Perf. 11½

1937, Dec. 1 Unwmk. Engr.

B85 SP83	5c + 5c bl grn	.20	*.55*
B86 SP84	10c + 5c red vio	.20	*.55*

Photo.

Granite Paper

B87 SP85	20c + 5c red & silver	.30	*.55*
B88 SP86	30c + 10c ultra & sil	1.25	*5.50*
	Nos. B85-B88 (4)	1.95	*7.15*
	Set, never hinged	3.50	

25th anniv. of the Pro Juventute (child welfare) stamps.

Souvenir Sheet

1937, Dec. 20 *Imperf.*

B89	Sheet of 2	6.50	*57.50*
a.	SP85 20c + 5c red & silver	1.60	*17.00*
b.	SP86 30c + 10c ultra & silver	1.60	*17.00*
	Never hinged	7.50	

Simulated perforation in silver. Sheet sold for 1fr.

Tell Chapel, Lake Lucerne
SP87

1938, June 15 *Perf. 11½*

Granite Paper

B90 SP87	10c + 10c brt vio & yel	.45	*1.10*
	Never hinged	1.10	
a.	Grilled gum	22.50	*77.50*
	Never hinged	32.50	

National Fête Day.

Salomon Gessner
SP88

Girl of St. Gallen
SP89

Girl of Uri — SP90

Girl of Aargau — SP91

1938, Dec. 1 Engr. *Perf. 11½*

B91 SP88	5c + 5c dp bl grn	.20	*.50*

Photo.

Granite Paper

B92 SP89	10c + 5c pur & buff	.25	*.55*
B93 SP90	20c + 5c red & buff	.25	*.55*
B94 SP91	30c + 10c ultra	1.60	*6.50*
	Nos. B91-B94 (4)	2.30	*8.10*
	Set, never hinged	4.50	

Castle at Laupen
SP92

1939, June 15

B95 SP92	10c + 10c brn, gray & red	.30	*1.10*
	Never hinged	1.10	

600th anniversary of the Battle of Laupen. The surtax was used to aid needy mothers.

Hans Herzog
SP93

Girl of Fribourg
SP94

Girl of Nidwalden
SP95

Girl of Basel
SP96

Perf. 11½

1939, Dec. 1 Unwmk. Engr.

B96 SP93	5c + 5c dk grn	.20	*.45*

Photo.

Granite Paper

B97 SP94	10c + 5c rose vio & buff	.20	*.45*
B98 SP95	20c + 5c org red	.30	*1.40*
B99 SP96	30c + 10c ultra & buff	1.60	*11.50*
	Nos. B96-B99 (4)	2.30	*13.80*
	Set, never hinged	5.00	

Sempach, 1386 — SP97

Giornico, 1478 — SP98

Calven, 1499
SP99

WWI Ranger
SP100

1940, Mar. 20 Photo.

Granite Paper

B100 SP97	5c + 5c emer, blk & red	.30	*1.25*
B101 SP98	10c + 5c brn org, blk & car	.30	*.55*
B102 SP99	20c + 5c brn red, blk & car	2.25	.95
B103 SP100	30c + 10c brt bl, brn blk & red	1.60	*8.25*

National Fête Day. The surtax was for the National Fund and the Red Cross.

Redrawn

B104 SP99	20c + 5c brn red, blk & car	9.75	6.50
	Nos. B100-B104 (5)	14.20	*17.50*
	Set, never hinged	26.00	

The base of statue has been heavily shaded "Calven 1499" moved nearer to bottom line of base. Top line of base removed.

Souvenir Sheet

Unwmk.

1940, July 16 Photo. *Imperf.*

Granite Paper

B105	Sheet of 4	250.00	*575.00*
	Never hinged	425.00	
a.	SP97 5c+5c yel grn, blk & red	11.00	*26.00*
b.	SP98 10c+5c org yel, blk & red	47.50	*210.00*
c.	SP99 20c+5c brn red, blk & red (redrawn)	47.50	*210.00*
d.	SP100 30c+10c chlky bl, blk & red	11.00	*26.00*

National Fete Day. Sheets measure 125x65mm and sold for 5fr.

Gottfried Keller
SP102

Girl of Thurgau
SP103

Girl of Solothurn
SP104

Girl of Zug
SP105

1940, Dec. 1 Engr. *Perf. 11½*

B106 SP102	5c + 5c dk bl grn	.20	*.40*

Photo.

B107 SP103	10c + 5c brn & buff	.20	*.30*
B108 SP104	20c + 5c org red & buff	.20	*.40*

B109 SP105 30c + 10c dp ultra & buff 1.40 *9.50*
Nos. B106-B109 (4) 2.00 *10.60*
Set, never hinged 4.00

AIR POST STAMPS

Nos. 134 and 139 Overprinted in Carmine

1919-20 **Wmk. 183** ***Perf. 11½***

Granite Paper

C1 A25 30c yel brn & pale grn ('20) 110.00 *1,250.*
C2 A25 50c dp & pale grn 32.50 110.00
Set, never hinged 350.00

Counterfeits of overprint and fraudulent cancellations exist.

Airplane AP1

Pilot at Controls of Airplane AP2

Biplane against Sky — AP3

Allegorical Figure of Flight AP4

Perf. 11½, 12 and Compound

1923-25 **Typo.**

C3 AP1 15c brn red & ap grn 2.25 8.25
C4 AP1 20c grn & lt grn ('25) .90 *6.00*
C5 AP1 25c dk bl & bl 7.75 *22.50*
C6 AP2 35c brn & buff 11.00 *42.50*
C7 AP2 40c vio & gray vio 14.50 *45.00*
C8 AP3 45c red & ind 1.60 *7.25*
C9 AP3 50c blk & red 12.50 17.00

Perf. 11½

C10 AP4 65c gray bl & dp bl ('24) 3.25 *16.00*
C11 AP4 75c org & brn red ('24) 15.00 *55.00*
C12 AP4 1fr vio & dp vio ('24) 42.50 32.50
Nos. C3-C12 (10) 111.25 *252.00*
Set, never hinged 275.00

For surcharges see Nos. C19, C22, C26.

1933-37 **With Grilled Gum**

C4a AP1 20c grn & lt grn ('37) .30 .40
C5a AP1 25c dk bl & bl ('34) 5.00 *50.00*
C8a AP3 45c red & indigo ('37) 2.50 *52.50*
C9a AP3 50c gray grn & scar ('35) 1.10 1.60
C10a AP4 65c gray bl & dp bl ('37) 2.75 *8.50*
C11a AP4 75c org & brn red ('36) 27.50 *175.00*
C12a AP4 1fr vio & deep vio 2.10 3.25
Nos. C4a-C12a (7) 41.25 *291.25*
Set, never hinged 65.00

See Grilled Gum note after No. 145.

Allegory of Air Mail — AP5

Bird Carrying Letter AP6

1929-30 **Granite Paper**

C13 AP5 35c red brn, bis & claret 15.00 42.50
C14 AP5 40c dl grn, yel grn & bl 57.50 82.50
C15 AP6 2fr blk brn & red brn, *gray* ('30) 85.00 85.00
Nos. C13-C15 (3) 157.50 210.00
Set, never hinged 425.00

1933-35 **With Grilled Gum**

C13a AP5 35c red brn, bis & cl 5.00 *50.00*
C14a AP5 40c dk grn, yel grn & bl 37.50 77.50
C15a AP6 2fr blk brn & red brn ('35) 7.25 12.00
Nos. C13a-C15a (3) 49.75 *139.50*
Set, never hinged 140.00

Front View of Airplane AP7

1932, Feb. 2 **Granite Paper**

C16 AP7 15c dp grn & lt grn .55 *1.60*
C17 AP7 20c dk red & buff 1.10 *2.50*
C18 AP7 90c dp bl & gray 7.25 *30.00*
Nos. C16-C18 (3) 8.90 *34.10*
Set, never hinged 22.50

Intl. Disarmament Conf., Geneva, Feb. 1932.
For surcharges see Nos. C20-C21, C23-C25.

Nos. C3, C10, C16-C18 Surcharged with New Values and Bars in Black or Red

1935-38

C19 AP1 10c on 15c 4.75 *37.50*
C20 AP7 10c on 15c .40 .55
a. Inverted surcharge *6,500.* *12,000.*
C21 AP7 10c on 20c ('36) .45 *2.25*
C22 AP4 10c on 65c ('38) .20 .40
C23 AP7 30c on 90c ('36) 3.00 *14.00*
C24 AP7 40c on 20c ('37) 3.75 *15.00*
C25 AP7 40c on 90c ('36) (R) 3.25 *14.50*
a. Vermilion surcharge 92.50 *800.00*
Never hinged, #C25a 150.00
Nos. C19-C25 (7) 15.80 *84.20*
Set, never hinged 40.00

Stamp similar to No. C22, but from souvenir sheet, is listed as No. 242a.

Type of Air Post Stamp of 1923 Surcharged in Black

1938, May 22 **Wmk. 183** ***Perf. 11½***

C26 AP3 75c on 50c gray & scar 6.50

"Pro Aero" Meeting, May 21-22.
No. C26 was not sold to the public in the ordinary way, but affixed to air mail letters by postal officials. It was not regularly obtainable unused.

POSTAGE DUE STAMPS

D1

D2

Wmk. 182

1878-80 **Typo.** ***Perf. 11½***

J1 D1 1c ultra 1.90 1.60
On cover 27.50
J2 D2 2c ultra 1.90 1.60
On cover 25.00
J3 D2 3c ultra 17.00 16.00
On cover 75.00
J4 D2 5c ultra 17.00 6.75
On cover 35.00
J5 D2 10c ultra 180.00 6.00
On cover 45.00
J6 D2 20c ultra 210.00 6.00
On cover 45.00
J7 D2 50c ultra 400.00 20.00
On cover 90.00
J8 D2 100c ultra 525.00 17.00
On cover 340.00
J9 D2 500c ultra 475.00 27.50
On cover 2,250.

A 5c in design D1 exists.

1882-83

Granite Paper

J10 D2 10c ultra 175.00 40.00
On cover 130.00
J11 D2 20c ultra 400.00 52.50
On cover 165.00
J12 D2 50c ultra 2,400. 525.00
On cover 1,100.
J13 D2 100c ultra 800.00 400.00
On cover 850.00
J14 D2 500c ultra *13,750.* 210.00
On cover 2,600.

1883-84

Numerals in Red

J15 D2 5c blue green 42.50 30.00
On cover 90.00
J16 D2 10c blue green 65.00 25.00
On cover 80.00
J17 D2 20c blue green 120.00 22.50
On cover 90.00
J18 D2 50c blue green 140.00 72.50
On cover 400.00
J19 D2 100c blue green 350.00 350.00
On cover 1,100.
J20 D2 500c blue green 775.00 190.00
On cover 1,750.

1884-97

Numerals in Red

J21 D2 1c olive green .65 .65
On cover 20.00
J22 D2 3c olive green 5.75 6.50
On cover 32.50
J23 D2 5c olive green 1.60 .65
On cover 6.50
a. 5c yellow green 25.00 12.50
On cover 55.00
J24 D2 10c olive green 3.75 .85
On cover 6.50
a. 10c yellow green 110.00 16.00
On cover 120.00
J25 D2 20c olive green 8.25 1.30
On cover 6.50
a. 20c yellow green 110.00 16.00
On cover 120.00
J26 D2 50c olive green 12.00 2.50
On cover 30.00
a. 50c yellow green 100.00 32.50
On cover 175.00
J27 D2 100c olive green 14.00 2.75
On cover 175.00
a. 100c yellow green 100.00 80.00
On cover 275.00
J28 D2 500c olive green 150.00 160.00
On cover —
a. 500c yellow green 125.00 60.00
On cover 2,250.

1908-09 **Wmk. 183**

Numerals in Red

J29 D2 1c olive green .30 1.10
Never hinged .35
On cover 11.00
J30 D2 5c olive green .60 .90
Never hinged 1.00
On cover 5.50
J31 D2 10c olive green 1.50 2.25
Never hinged 2.75
On cover 8.50
J32 D2 20c olive green 3.00 5.00
Never hinged 11.00
On cover 22.50
J33 D2 50c olive green 15.00 1.10
Never hinged 45.00
On cover 55.00
J34 D2 100c olive green 30.00 2.25
Never hinged 55.00
On cover 85.00
Nos. J29-J34 (6) 50.40 12.60

D3

1910 ***Perf. 11½, 12***

Numerals in Red

J35 D3 1c blue green .20 .20
J36 D3 3c blue green .20 .20
J37 D3 5c blue green .20 .20
J38 D3 10c blue green 11.00 .20
J39 D3 15c blue green .65 1.10
J40 D3 20c blue green 17.50 .20
J41 D3 25c blue green 1.25 .65
J42 D3 30c blue green 1.25 .55
J43 D3 50c blue green 1.50 1.10
Nos. J35-J43 (9) 33.75 4.40

See Nos. S1-S12.

No. J36 Surcharged

1916

J44 D3 5c on 3c bl grn & red .40 .25

Nos. J35-J36, J43 Surcharged

1924

J45 D3 10c on 1c .25 *8.25*
J46 D3 10c on 3c .25 *1.50*
J47 D3 20c on 50c .95 1.50
Nos. J45-J47 (3) 1.45 11.25

D4

D5

Wmk. 183

1924-26 **Typo.** ***Perf. 11½***

Granite Paper

J48 D4 5c ol grn & red .65 .25
J49 D4 10c ol grn & red 2.75 .20
J50 D4 15c ol grn & red ('26) 2.50 .55
J51 D4 20c ol grn & red 6.00 .20
J52 D4 25c ol grn & red 2.75 .55
J53 D4 30c ol grn & red 2.75 .85
J54 D4 40c ol grn & red ('26) 3.75 .70
J55 D4 50c ol grn & red 3.75 .70
Nos. J48-J55 (8) 24.90 4.00

1924 **With Grilled Gum**

J48a D4 5c olive green & red .65 .60
J49a D4 10c olive green & red 2.50 1.10
J51a D4 20c olive green & red 4.75 1.50
J52a D4 25c olive green & red 7.25 *65.00*
Nos. J48a-J52a (4) 15.15 *68.20*

See Grilled Gum note after No. 145.

Nos. J50, J53 and J55 Surcharged with New Value in Black

1937

J56 D4 5c on 15c .90 *4.25*
J57 D4 10c on 30c .90 *1.50*
J58 D4 20c on 50c 1.50 *5.00*
J59 D4 40c on 50c 2.50 *12.00*
Nos. J56-J59 (4) 5.80 *22.75*
Set, never hinged 10.50

1938 **Engr.** **Unwmk.**

J60 D5 5c scarlet .40 .20
J61 D5 10c scarlet .55 .20
J62 D5 15c scarlet 1.25 *2.25*
J63 D5 20c scarlet .95 .20
J64 D5 25c scarlet 1.40 *1.90*
J65 D5 30c scarlet 1.40 1.25
J66 D5 40c scarlet 1.60 .45
J67 D5 50c scarlet 1.90 2.25
Nos. J60-J67 (8) 9.45 *8.70*
Set, never hinged 19.00

1938

With Grilled Gum

J60a D5 5c scarlet .65 *1.60*
J61a D5 10c scarlet .65 *1.25*
J62a D5 15c scarlet 1.40 *2.50*
J63a D5 20c scarlet 1.25 .55
J64a D5 25c scarlet 1.40 *9.50*
J65a D5 30c scarlet 1.40 *2.25*
J66a D5 40c scarlet 2.10 2.10
J67a D5 50c scarlet 2.50 *3.50*
Nos. J60a-J67a (8) 11.35 *23.25*
Set, never hinged 29.00

See Grilled Gum note after No. 145.

OFFICIAL STAMPS

For General Use

With Perforated Cross
In 1935 the government authorized the use of regular postage issues perforated with a nine-hole cross for all government departments. Twenty-seven different stamps were so perforated. These were succeeded in 1938 by the cross overprints.

Values for canceled Official Stamps are for those canceled to order. Postally used stamps sell for considerably less. This note does not apply to Nos. 1O1-1O16, 2O27-2O30, 3O23-3O26.

Counterfeit overprints exist of most official stamps.

Official stamps without unused values were not made available to the public unused.

Regular Issues of 1908-36 Overprinted in Black

1938 Unwmk. *Perf. 11½*

O1 A53 3c olive .20 .20
O2 A54 5c blue green .20 .20
O3 A55 10c red violet .95 .45
O4 A56 15c orange .25 *1.60*
O5 A68 20c red .45 .25
O6 A58 25c brown .45 *1.40*
O7 A59 30c ultra .60 *1.00*
O8 A60 35c yellow green .60 *1.25*
O9 A61 40c gray .60 *1.00*

Wmk. 183

With Grilled Gum

O10 A25 50c dp grn & pale grn .60 *1.50*
O11 A25 60c brn org & buff 1.25 *2.50*
O12 A25 70c vio & buff 1.25 *4.25*
O13 A25 80c sl & buff 1.25 *3.25*
O14 A36 90c grn & red, *grn* 3.00 *3.25*
O15 A25 1fr dp cl & pale grn 1.50 *3.25*
O16 A36 1.20fr brn rose & red, *rose* 1.50 *4.50*
O17 A36 1.50fr bl & red, *bl* 2.50 *6.00*
O18 A36 2fr gray blk & red, *gray* 3.00 *7.00*
Nos. O1-O18 (18) 20.15 *42.85*
Set, never hinged 65.00

Nos. O14, O16, O17 and O18 are on surface-colored paper.

1938 Unwmk. With Grilled Gum

O1a A53 3c olive 4.50 .45
O2a A54 5c blue green 1.25 .45
O3a A55 10c red violet 1.50 .55
O4a A56 15c orange 2.75 1.25
O5a A68 20c red 1.50 .70
O6a A58 25c brown 75.00 7.75
O7a A59 30c ultra 2.50 1.10
O8a A60 35c yellow green 1.90 1.90
O9a A61 40c gray 2.50 1.00
Nos. O1a-O9a (9) 93.40 15.15
Set, never hinged 190.00

See Grilled Gum note after No. 145.

FOR THE WAR BOARD OF TRADE

Regular Issues of 1908-18 Overprinted

1918 Wmk. 183 *Perf. 11½, 12*

1O1 A26 3c brown org 110.00 *225.00*
1O2 A26 5c green 10.00 *32.50*
1O3 A26 7½c gray (I) 300.00 *450.00*
a. 7½c slate (II) 550.00 *950.00*
1O4 A28 10c red, *buff* 15.00 *40.00*
1O5 A28 15c vio, *buff* 12.50 *45.00*
1O6 A25 20c red & yel 125.00 *500.00*
1O7 A25 25c dp bl 125.00 *500.00*
1O8 A25 30c yel brn & pale grn 125.00 *450.00*
Nos. 1O1-1O8 (8) 822.50 *2,242.*

Most unused copies of Nos. 1O1-1O8 are reprints made using the original overprint forms.
Counterfeits exist.

Overprinted

1918

1O9 A26 3c brown orange 4.25 *35.00*
1O10 A26 5c green 12.00 *52.50*
1O11 A26 7½c gray 4.50 *22.50*
1O12 A28 10c red, *buff* 45.00 *87.50*
1O13 A28 15c vio, *buff* 82.50
1O14 A25 20c red & yel 8.75 *52.50*
1O15 A25 25c dp blue 8.75 *52.50*
1O16 A25 30c yel brn & pale grn 14.50 *87.50*
Nos. 1O9-1O16 (8) 180.25 390.00

No. 1O13 was never placed in use.
Fraudulent cancellations are found on Nos. 1O1-1O16.

FOR THE LEAGUE OF NATIONS

Regular Issues Overprinted

On 1908-30 Issues

1922-31 Wmk. 183 *Perf. 11½, 12*

2O1 A26 2½c ol, *buff* ('28) .45
2O2 A26 3c ultra, *buff* ('30) 8.25
2O3 A26 5c orange, *buff* 5.50
2O4 A26 5c gray vio, *buff* ('26) 2.75
2O5 A26 5c red vio, *buff* ('27) 2.25
2O6 A26 5c dk grn, *buff* ('31) 25.00
2O7 A26 7½c dp grn, *buff* ('28) .55
2O8 A28 10c green, *buff* .55
2O9 A28 10c bl grn, *buff* ('28) 1.10
2O10 A28 10c vio, *buff* ('31) 2.75
2O11 A28 15c brn red, *buff* ('28) 1.10
2O12 A28 20c red vio, *buff* 8.25
2O13 A28 20c car, *buff* ('26) 2.25
2O14 A28 25c ver, *buff* 8.25
2O15 A28 25c car, *buff* 1.10
2O16 A28 25c brn, *buff* ('27) 17.00
2O17 A28 30c dp bl, *buff* ('25) 8.25
2O18 A25 30c yel brn & pale grn 14.00
2O19 A25 35c yel grn & yel 10.00
2O20 A25 40c deep blue 1.40
2O21 A25 40c red vio & grn ('28) 14.00
2O22 A25 50c dp grn & pale grn 11.00
2O23 A25 60c brn org & buff 30.00 1.60
2O24 A25 70c vio & buff ('25) 26.00
2O25 A25 80c slate & buff 2.75
2O26 A25 1fr dp cl & pale grn 6.75
2O27 A29 3fr red 32.50
2O28 A30 5fr ultra 60.00
2O29 A31 10fr dull violet 140.00
2O30 A31 10fr gray grn ('30) 140.00
Nos. 2O1-2O30 (30) 555.35

1930-44 With Grilled Gum

2O2a A26 3c ultra, *buff* ('33) 10.00
2O6a A26 5c dk grn, *buff* ('33) 19.00
2O17a A28 30c dp bl,*buff* 425.00
2O22a A25 50c dp grn & pale grn ('35) .90 2.25
2O23a A25 60c brn org & buff ('44) 25.00 *225.00*
2O24a A25 70c violet & buff ('32) 1.60 2.25
2O25a A25 80c slate & buff ('42) 2.75 2.50
2O26a A25 1fr dp cl & pale grn ('42) 5.25

1935-36

With Grilled Gum

2O31 A36 90c grn & red, *grn* ('36) 5.00
2O32 A36 1.20fr brn rose & red, *rose* ('36) 2.75 *4.50*
b. Inverted overprint *4,250.*
2O33 A36 1.50fr bl & red, *bl* 2.75 *4.50*
2O34 A36 2fr gray blk & red, *gray* ('36) 2.75 *5.25*

1922-25 Ordinary Gum

2O31a A36 90c 14.00
2O32a A36 1.20fr ('25) 14.00
2O33a A36 1.50fr ('25) 13.00
2O34a A36 2fr ('25) 12.00

1928

2O35 A39 5fr blue 87.50

On 1932 Issue

1932

2O36 A41 5c peacock bl 19.00
2O37 A41 10c orange 1.60
2O38 A41 20c cerise 1.60
2O39 A41 30c ultra 55.00
2O40 A41 60c olive brn 15.00

Unwmk.

2O41 A42 1fr ol gray & bl 15.00
Nos. 2O36-2O41 (6) 107.20

On 1934 Issue

1934-35 Wmk. 183

2O42 A46 3c olive .25
2O43 A47 5c emerald .65
2O44 A49 15c orange ('35) 1.50
2O45 A51 25c brown 19.00
2O46 A52 30c ultra 1.60
Nos. 2O42-2O46 (5) 23.00

On 1936 Issue

1937 Unwmk.

2O47 A53 3c olive .20 .25
2O48 A54 5c blue green .25 .25
2O49 A55 10c red violet 1.10
2O50 A56 15c orange .45 .55
2O51 A57 20c carmine 1.90
2O52 A58 25c brown .65 1.10
2O53 A59 30c ultra .65 1.00
2O54 A60 35c yellow green .65 1.00
2O55 A61 40c gray .95 1.25
Nos. 2O47-2O55 (9) 8.40

1937 With Grilled Gum

2O47a A53 3c olive .30
2O48a A54 5c blue green .45
2O49a A55 10c red violet 6.25
2O50a A56 15c orange .70
2O51a A57 20c carmine 2.25
2O52a A58 25c brown 1.40
2O53a A59 30c ultra 1.10
2O54a A60 35c yellow green 4.25
2O55a A61 40c gray 4.25
Nos. 2O47a-2O55a (9) 20.95

On 1931 Issue

1937 Wmk. 183

2O56 A40 3fr orange brown 190.00

On 1938 Issue

1938 Unwmk. *Perf. 11½*

Granite Paper

2O57 A63 20c red & buff 1.90
2O58 A64 30c blue & lt blue 3.00
2O59 A65 60c brown & buff 5.75
2O60 A66 1fr black & buff 9.25
Nos. 2O57-2O60 (4) 19.90

Regular Issue of 1938 Overprinted in Black or Red

Granite Paper

2O61 A63 20c red & buff 2.25
2O62 A64 30c blue & lt blue 4.00
2O63 A65 60c brown & buff 7.25
2O64 A66 1fr black & buff (R) 12.50
Nos. 2O61-2O64 (4) 26.00

Regular Issue of 1938 Overprinted in Black

1939

2O65 A69 3fr brn car, *buff* 3.25 *11.00*
2O66 A70 5fr slate bl, *buff* 5.50 *15.00*
2O67 A71 10fr green, *buff* 11.00 *32.50*
Nos. 2O65-2O67 (3) 19.75 *58.50*

FOR THE INTERNATIONAL LABOR BUREAU

Regular Issues Overprinted

On 1908-30 Issues

1923-30 Wmk. 183 *Perf. 11½, 12*

3O1 A26 2½c ol grn, *buff* ('28) .30
3O2 A26 3c ultra, *buff* ('30) 1.10
3O3 A26 5c org, *buff* .55
3O4 A26 5c red vio, *buff* ('28) .20
3O5 A26 7½c dp grn, *buff* ('28) .45
3O6 A28 10c grn, *buff* .55
3O7 A28 10c bl grn, *buff* ('28) 1.10
3O8 A28 15c brn red, *buff* ('28) 1.10
3O9 A28 20c red vio, *buff* 17.00
3O10 A28 20c car, *buff* ('27) 5.00
3O11 A28 25c car, *buff* 1.25
3O12 A28 25c brn, *buff* ('28) 3.00
3O13 A28 30c dp bl, *buff* ('25) 2.50
3O14 A25 30c yel brn & pale grn 65.00
3O15 A25 35c yel grn & yel 11.00
3O16 A25 40c deep blue 1.25
3O17 A25 40c red vio & grn ('28) 17.00
3O18 A25 50c dp grn & pale grn 5.00
3O19 A25 60c brn org & buff 1.60 *1.90*
3O20 A25 70c vio & buff ('24) 26.00
3O21 A25 80c slate & buff 14.00 2.25
3O22 A25 1fr dp cl & pale grn 2.75
3O23 A29 3fr red 25.00
3O24 A30 5fr ultra 37.50
3O25 A31 10fr dull violet 150.00
3O26 A31 10fr gray grn ('30) 150.00
Nos. 3O1-3O26 (26) 528.75

1937-44 With Grilled Gum

3O18a A25 50c dp grn & pale grn ('42) 1.75 2.25
3O20a A25 70c vio & buff 1.75 2.25
3O21a A25 80c slate & buff ('44) 25.00 *175.00*
3O22a A25 1fr dp cl & pale grn ('42) 3.25

1925-42

With Grilled Gum

3O27 A36 90c grn & red, *grn* ('37) 9.75
a. Ordinary gum 5.00
3O28 A36 1.20fr brn rose & red, *rose* ('42) 14.00 4.00
a. Ordinary gum 4.50
3O29 A36 1.50fr bl & red, *bl* ('37) 2.75 *3.00*
a. Ordinary gum 14.00
3O30 A36 2fr gray blk & red, *gray* ('36) 3.25 *6.25*
a. Ordinary gum 32.50
Nos. 3O27-3O30 (4) 23.00

1928

3O31 A39 5fr blue 82.50

On 1932 Issue

1932

3O32 A41 5c peacock blue 1.10
3O33 A41 10c orange .90
3O34 A41 20c cerise 1.25
3O35 A41 30c ultra 7.75
3O36 A41 60c olive brown 7.75

Unwmk.

3O37 A42 1fr ol gray & bl 10.00
Nos. 3O32-3O37 (6) 28.75

On 1936 Issue

1937

3O38 A53 3c olive .20 .55
3O39 A54 5c blue green .20 .55
3O40 A55 10c red violet 2.75
3O41 A56 15c orange .45 1.10
3O42 A57 20c carmine 2.25
3O43 A58 25c brown .60 *1.40*
3O44 A59 30c ultra .60 *1.10*
3O45 A60 35c yellow green .60 *1.60*
3O46 A61 40c gray .95 *1.90*
Nos. 3O38-3O46 (9) 3.60 *13.20*

1937 With Grilled Gum

3O38a A53 3c olive 1.10
3O39a A54 5c blue green 1.10
3O40a A55 10c red violet 1.60
3O41a A56 15c orange 1.90
3O42a A57 20c carmine 1.60
3O43a A58 25c brown 2.25
3O44a A59 30c ultra 2.25
3O45a A60 35c yellow green 2.75
3O46a A61 40c gray 2.25
Nos. 3O38a-3O46a (9) 16.80

On 1931 Issue

1937 Wmk. 183

3O47 A40 3fr orange brown 175.00

On 1934 Issue

3O48 A46 3c olive 5.50

On 1938 Issue

1938 Unwmk. *Perf. 11½*
Granite Paper

3O49 A63 20c red & buff 1.60
3O50 A64 30c blue & lt blue 3.25
3O51 A65 60c brown & buff 6.00
3O52 A66 1fr black & buff 8.75
Nos. 3O49-3O52 (4) 19.60

Regular Issue of 1938 Overprinted in Black or Red

3O53 A63 20c red & buff (Bk) 3.25
3O54 A64 30c bl & lt bl (Bk) 3.25
3O55 A65 60c brn & buff (Bk) 6.50
3O56 A66 1fr blk & buff (R) 7.00
Nos. 3O53-3O56 (4) 20.00

Regular Issue of 1938 Overprinted in Black

S.d.N. Bureau international du Travail

1939

3O57 A69 3fr brn car, *buff* 4.50 *8.25*
3O58 A70 5fr slate bl, *buff* 5.50 *17.00*
3O59 A71 10fr green, *buff* 10.00 *30.00*
Nos. 3O57-3O59 (3) 20.00 *55.25*

FRANCHISE STAMPS

These stamps were distributed to many institutions and charitable societies for franking their correspondence.

F1

Control Figures Overprinted in Black

214

Perf. 11½, 12

1911-21 Typo. Wmk. 183
Blue Granite Paper

S1 F1 2c ol grn & red .20 .25
S2 F1 3c ol grn & red 2.50 .55
S3 F1 5c ol grn & red 1.10 .20
S4 F1 10c ol grn & red 1.40 .20
S5 F1 15c ol grn & red 21.00 4.00
S6 F1 20c ol grn & red 5.00 .60
Nos. S1-S6 (6) 31.20 5.80

Without Control Figures

S1a F1 2c olive green & red .55 *19.00*
S2a F1 3c olive green & red .55 *25.00*
S3a F1 5c olive green & red 4.75 *32.50*
S4a F1 10c olive green & red 8.25 *50.00*
S5a F1 15c olive green & red 5.25 *125.00*
S6a F1 20c olive green & red 9.50 *50.00*
Nos. S1a-S6a (6) 28.85 *301.50*

Control Figures Overprinted in Black

1926

S7 F1 5c ol grn & red 12.50 4.50
S8 F1 10c ol grn & red 7.75 3.25
S9 F1 20c ol grn & red 10.00 3.75
Nos. S7-S9 (3) 30.25 11.50

Control Figures Overprinted in Black

1927

White Granite Paper

S10 F1 5c green & red 5.00 .40
S11 F1 10c green & red 2.50 .20
b. Grilled gum 325.00 *725.00*
S12 F1 20c green & red 3.50 .30
Nos. S10-S12 (3) 11.00 .90

Without Control Figures

S10a F1 5c green & red 32.50 *140.00*
S11a F1 10c green & red 32.50 *140.00*
c. Grilled gum 150.00 *650.00*
S12a F1 20c green & red 32.50 *140.00*

Nurse — F2

Nun — F3

J. H. Dunant — F4

Control Figures Overprinted in Black

1935 *Perf. 11½*

S13 F2 5c turq green 2.25 *5.50*
b. Grilled gum 3.25 .40
S14 F3 10c lt violet 2.25 *5.50*
b. Grilled gum 3.25 .20
S15 F4 20c scarlet 2.25 *6.50*
b. Grilled gum 3.75 .45
Nos. S13-S15 (3) 6.75 *17.50*
Nos. S13b-S15b (3) 10.25 1.05

Without Control Figures

S13a F2 5c turquoise green 1.40 *3.75*
c. Grilled gum 15.00 1.40
S14a F3 10c light violet 1.40 *3.75*
c. Grilled gum 15.00 1.40
S15a F4 20c scarlet 1.40 *5.00*
c. Grilled gum 15.00 1.50
Nos. S13a-S15a (3) 4.20 *12.50*
Nos. S13c-S15c (3) 45.00 4.30

SYRIA

'sir-ē-ə

LOCATION — Asia Minor, bordering on Turkey, Iraq, Lebanon, Israel and the Mediterranean Sea
GOVT. — Republic
AREA — 71,498 sq. mi.
POP. — 9,840,000 (est. 1983)
CAPITAL — Damascus

Syria was originally part of the Turkish province of Sourya conquered by British and Arab forces in late 1918 and later partitioned. The British assumed control of the Palestine and Transjordan regions; the French were permitted to occupy the sanjaks of Lebanon. Alaouites and Alexandretta; and the remaining territory, including the vilayets of Damascus and Aleppo, was established as an independent Arab kingdom, under which the first Syrian stamps were issued.

French forces from Beirut deposed King Faisal in July 1920, and two years of military occupation followed until Syria was mandated to France in July 1922. Syrian autonomy was substituted for the mandate in 1934, but full independence was not again achieved until 1946.

10 Milliemes = 1 Piaster
40 Paras = 1 Piaster (Arabian Govt.)
100 Centimes = 1 Piaster (1920)

Issued under French Occupation

Stamps of France, 1900-07, Surcharged

Perf. 14x13½

1919, Nov. 21 Unwmk.

1 A16 1m on 1c gray 200.00 200.00
2 A16 2m on 2c vio brn 550.00 *550.00*
3 A16 3m on 3c red org 240.00 240.00
4 A20 4m on 15c gray grn 47.50 47.50
5 A22 5m on 5c dp grn 25.00 22.50
6 A22 1p on 10c red 37.50 32.50
7 A22 2p on 25c blue 17.50 15.00
8 A18 5p on 40c red & pale bl 25.00 22.50
9 A18 9p on 50c bis brn & lav 55.00 50.00
10 A18 10p on 1fr cl & ol grn 87.50 80.00
Nos. 1-10 (10) 1,285. 1,260.

The letters "T.E.O." are the initials of "Territoires Ennemis Occupés." There are two types of the numerals in the surcharges on Nos. 2, 3, 8 and 9.

Stamps of French Offices in Turkey, 1902-03, Surcharged

1919

11 A2 1m on 1c gray 1.10 .80
a. Inverted surcharge 17.00 17.00
12 A2 2m on 2c violet brn 1.10 .80
a. Inverted surcharge 17.00 17.00
13 A2 3m on 3c red orange 2.50 1.40
14 A3 4m on 15c pale red 1.10 .80
a. Inverted surcharge 17.00 17.00
15 A2 5m on 5c green 1.10 .80

Overprinted

16 A5 1p on 25c blue 1.00 .75
a. Inverted overprint 17.00 17.00
17 A6 2p on 50c bis brn & lav 1.90 1.25
18 A6 4p on 1fr claret & ol grn 3.25 2.50
19 A6 8p on 2fr gray vio & yel 10.00 8.00
a. "T.E.O." double 75.00 75.00
20 A6 20p on 5fr dk bl & buff 300.00 210.00
Nos. 11-20 (10) 323.05 227.10

On Nos. 17-20 "T.E.O." reads vertically up.

Nos. 1-20 were issued in Beirut and mainly used in Lebanon. Nos. 16-20 were also used in Cilicia.

Stamps of France, 1900-07, Surcharged

1920

21 A16 1m on 1c gray 5.00 4.50
a. Inverted surcharge 45.00 45.00
b. Double surcharge
22 A16 2m on 2c vio brn 6.00 4.75
a. Double surcharge 25.00
23 A22 3m on 5c green 12.00 12.00
a. Double surcharge 40.00 40.00
24 A18 20p on 5fr dk bl & buff 450.00 450.00
Nos. 21-23 (3) 23.00 21.25

The letters "O.M.F." are the initials of "Occupation Militaire Francaise."

Stamps of France, 1900-07, Surcharged in Black or Red

1920

25 A16 1m on 1c gray 1.10 .95
26 A16 2m on 2c violet brn 1.25 1.00
27 A22 3m on 5c green 2.00 2.00
28 A22 5m on 10c red 2.25 2.25
a. Inverted surcharge
29 A18 20p on 5fr dk bl & buff 70.00 70.00
30 A18 20p on 5fr dk bl & buff (R) 275.00 250.00
Nos. 25-30 (6) 351.60 326.20

Stamps of France, 1900-21, Surcharged in Black or Red:

1920-22

31 A16 25c on 1c gray 1.75 1.00
32 A16 50c on 2c vio brn 1.75 1.00
33 A16 75c on 3c red org 1.75 1.00
34 A22 1p on 5c green (R) 2.00 2.00
35 A22 1p on 5c green 1.00 1.00
36 A22 1p on 20c red brn ('21) .50 .25
37 A22 1.25p on 25c bl ('22) 1.25 .95
38 A22 1.50p on 30c org ('22) 1.40 .80
39 A22 2p on 10c red 1.00 1.00
40 A22 2p on 25c bl (R) 1.00 1.00
41 A18 2p on 40c red & pale bl ('21) 1.40 .75
42 A20 2.50p on 50c dl bl ('22) 1.10 1.10
a. Final "S" of "Piastres" omitted 10.00 10.00
43 A22 3p on 25c bl (R) 1.10 1.10
44 A18 3p on 60c vio & ultra ('21) 1.50 1.10
45 A20 5p on 15c gray grn 2.25 2.25
46 A18 5p on 1fr cl & ol grn ('21) 2.50 1.50
47 A18 10p on 40c red & pale bl 3.25 3.25
48 A18 10p on 2fr org & pale bl ('21) 5.00 3.00
49 A18 25p on 50c bis brn & lav 4.50 4.00
50 A18 25p on 5fr dk bl & buff ('21) 100.00 95.00
51 A18 50p on 1fr cl & ol grn 22.50 20.00
a. "PIASRTES" *1,650.* *1,650.*
52 A18 100p on 5fr dk bl & buff (R) 45.00 45.00

53 A18 100p on 5fr dk bl & buff (Bk) 240.00 225.00
a. "PIASRTES" *1,650. 1,650.*
Nos. 31-53 (23) 443.50 413.05

In first printing, space between "Syrie" and numeral is 2mm, second printing, 1mm.
Surcharge is found inverted on Nos. 32, 35-38, 42, 44-45. Value, each $2-$3.
Surcharge is found double on Nos. 31, 37, 40, 42. Value, each $2.
For overprints see Nos. C1-C9.

Surcharged in Black or Red

1920-23

54 A16 10c on 2c violet ('23) 1.10 .90
55 A22 10c on 5c org (R) ('23) .80 .65
56 A16 25c on 1c dk gray .90 .90
a. 50c on 1c dk gray (error) 4.50 4.50
57 A22 25c on 5c green ('21) .90 .60
58 A22 25c on 5c orange ('22) .80 .80
a. "CENTIEMES" omitted 26.00 26.00
59 A16 50c on 2c vio brn .90 .90
60 A22 50c on 10c red ('21) 1.00 .55
61 A22 50c on 10c green ('22) 1.25 1.25
62 A16 75c on 3c red orange 2.50 2.00
63 A20 75c on 15c sl grn ('21) 1.10 .90
Nos. 54-63 (10) 11.25 9.45

Surcharge is found inverted on Nos. 54-55, 58-59, 62-63; double on Nos. 60, 62. Value $1.50-$2.

Preceding Issues Overprinted

1920

Black Overprint

64 A16 25c on 1c sl gray 11.00 10.00
65 A16 50c on 2c vio brn 12.00 11.00
66 A22 1p on 5c green 10.00 9.00
67 A22 2p on 25c blue 16.00 14.50
68 A20 5p on 15c gray grn 50.00 47.50
69 A18 10p on 40c red & pale bl 77.50 75.00
70 A18 25p on 50c bis brn & lav 200.00 190.00
71 A18 50p on 1fr cl & ol grn 650.00 625.00
72 A18 100p on 5fr dk bl & buff 2,000. 1,900.
Nos. 64-72 (9) 3,026. 2,882.

Red Overprint

73 A16 25c on 1c sl gray 11.00 10.00
74 A16 50c on 2c vio brn 9.50 8.50
75 A22 1p on 5c green 9.50 8.50
76 A22 2p on 25c blue 7.50 6.50
77 A20 5p on 15c gray grn 50.00 47.50
78 A18 10p on 40c red & pale bl 77.50 75.00
79 A18 25p on 50c bis brn & lav 200.00 180.00
80 A18 50p on 1fr cl & ol grn 450.00 425.00
81 A18 100p on 5fr dk bl & buff 1,650. 1,650.
Nos. 73-81 (9) 2,465. 2,411.

Nos. 64-81 were used only in the vilayet of Aleppo where Egyptian gold currency was still in use.

A1

Black or Red Surcharge

1921 *Perf. 11½*

82 A1 25c on ¹⁄₁₀p lt brn 1.00 .85
a. "25 Centiemes" omitted
83 A1 50c on ²⁄₁₀p grn 1.00 .85
84 A1 1p on ³⁄₁₀p yel 1.40 .85
a. "²⁄₁₀" for "³⁄₁₀" 12.50 12.50

85 A1 1p on 5m rose 1.75 1.10
86 A1 2p on 5m rose 2.25 1.25
a. Tête bêche pair 110.00 110.00
87 A1 3p on 1p gray bl 2.75 1.25
88 A1 5p on 2p bl grn 4.75 3.50
89 A1 10p on 5p vio brn 10.00 5.75
90 A1 25p on 10p gray (R) 12.00 8.00
Nos. 82-90 (9) 36.90 23.40

Nos. 82-90 are surcharged on stamps of the Arabian Government Nos. 85, 87-93 and have the designs and sizes of those stamps.
Surcharge is found inverted on Nos. 84-88, 90; double on No. 86.

Kilis Issue

A2

Sewing Machine Perf. 9

1921 **Handstamped**

Pelure Paper

91 A2 (1p) violet *50.00 45.00*

Issued at Kilis to meet a shortage of the regular issue, caused by the sudden influx of a large number of Armenian refugees from Turkey. The Kilis area was restored to Turkey in Oct. 1923.

Stamps of France, Surcharged

1921-22 ***Perf. 14x13½***

92 A18 2p on 40c red & pale bl 1.00 .90
93 A18 2.50p on 50c bis brn & lav ('22) 1.10 1.00
a. 2p on 50c bister brown & lavender (error) 60.00 47.50
94 A18 3p on 60c vio & ultra 1.00 .90
95 A18 5p on 1fr cl & ol grn 6.50 6.00
96 A18 10p on 2fr org & pale bl 13.00 11.00
97 A18 25p on 5fr dk bl & buff 12.00 10.00
Nos. 92-97 (6) 34.60 29.80

On No. 93 the surcharge reads: "2 PIASTRES 50."
Surcharge is found inverted on Nos. 92-95; double on No. 94. Value $2-$3.
For overprints see Nos. C10-C17.

French Mandate

French Stamps of 1900-23 Surcharged

1923

104 A16 10c on 2c vio brn .40 .25
105 A22 25c on 5c orange .75 .75
106 A22 50c on 10c green .90 .85
a. 25c on 10c green (error) 170.00
107 A20 75c on 15c sl grn 1.60 1.50
108 A22 1p on 20c red brn .75 .70
109 A22 1.25p on 25c blue 1.40 1.25
110 A22 1.50p on 30c orange 1.10 .90
111 A22 1.50p on 30c red 1.10 .90
112 A20 2.50p on 50c dl bl .70 .60

On Pasteur Stamps of 1923

113 A23 50c on 10c green 2.00 1.75
114 A23 1.50p on 30c red 1.75 1.50
115 A23 2.50p on 50c blue 2.00 1.75

Surcharge is found inverted on #104-108, 110, 115; double on #104, 106. Value $1.50-$2.

Surcharged

116 A18 2p on 40c red & pale bl .75 .70
a. Inverted surcharge 14.00
b. Double surcharge 17.00
c. "Liabn" *450.00 450.00*
117 A18 3p on 60c vio & ultra 1.50 1.25
a. "Liabn" *450.00 450.00*
118 A18 5p on 1fr cl & ol grn 2.00 1.50
a. "Liabn" *450.00 450.00*
119 A18 10p on 2fr org & pale bl 7.50 7.00
a. "Liabn" *450.00 450.00*
120 A18 25p on 5fr dk bl & buff 22.50 20.00
a. Inverted surcharge
Nos. 104-120 (17) 48.70 43.15

Stamps of France, 1900-21, Surcharged

1924 ***Perf. 14x13½***

121 A16 10c on 2c vio brn .40 .25
a. Double surcharge —
122 A22 25c on 5c orange .70 .60
a. "25" omitted 16.50
123 A22 50c on 10c green .70 .60
124 A20 75c on 15c sl grn .70 .60
125 A22 1p on 20c red brn .60 .50
a. "1 PIASTRES" 15.00
126 A22 1.25p on 25c blue 1.10 .90
127 A22 1.50p on 30c orange 1.10 .90
128 A22 1.50p on 30c red 1.00 .85
129 A20 2.50p on 50c dl bl 1.00 .85

Same on Pasteur Stamps of France, 1923

1924

130 A23 50c on 10c grn .90 .70
131 A23 1.50p on 30c red 1.40 1.10
132 A23 2.50p on 50c blue .75 .70
Nos. 121-132 (12) 10.35 8.55

Olympic Games Issue

Stamps of France, 1924, Surcharged "SYRIE" and New Values

1924

133 A24 50c on 10c gray grn & yel grn 30.00 27.50
134 A25 1.25p on 25c rose & dk rose 30.00 27.50
135 A26 1.50p on 30c brn red & blk 30.00 27.50
136 A27 2.50p on 50c ultra & dk bl 30.00 27.50
Nos. 133-136 (4) 120.00 110.00

See Nos. 166-169.

Stamps of France 1900-20 Surcharged

137 A18 2p on 40c red & pale bl .90 .50
138 A18 3p on 60c vio & ultra .70 .65
139 A18 5p on 1fr claret & ol grn 3.50 3.25
140 A18 10p on 2fr org & pale bl 3.50 3.00
141 A18 25p on 5fr dk bl & buff 5.25 4.50
Nos. 137-141 (5) 13.85 11.90

For overprints see Nos. C18-C21.

Stamps of France 1900-21, Surcharged

or

1924-25

143 A16 10c on 2c vio brn .40 .25
a. Double surcharge 20.00
b. Inverted surcharge 22.50
144 A22 25c on 5c orange .40 .25
a. Double surcharge 20.00
145 A22 50c on 10c green .75 .50
b. Inverted surcharge 22.50
146 A20 75c on 15c gray grn .90 .70
a. Double surcharge 20.00
b. Inverted surcharge 22.50
147 A22 1p on 20c red brn .60 .40
a. Inverted surcharge 22.50
148 A22 1.25p on 25c blue .95 .75
a. Inverted surcharge 22.50
149 A22 1.50p on 30c red .90 .70
a. Double surcharge 20.00
150 A22 1.50p on 30c orange 26.00 25.00
151 A22 2p on 35c violet ('25) 1.00 .80
152 A18 2p on 40c red & pale bl .75 .50
a. Arabic "Piastre" in singular 1.75 1.75
153 A18 2p on 45c grn & bl ('25) 5.00 4.00
154 A18 3p on 60c vio & ultra 1.10 .75
155 A20 3p on 60c lt vio ('25) 1.25 .75
156 A20 4p on 85c ver .45 .25
157 A18 5p on 1fr cl & ol grn 1.25 .75
158 A18 10p on 2fr org & pale bl 2.00 1.50
159 A18 25p on 5fr dk bl & buff 2.75 1.50
Nos. 143-159 (17) 46.45 39.35

On No. 152a, the surcharge is as illustrated. The correct fourth line ("2 Piastres" -plural), as it appears on Nos. 151, 152 and 153, has four characters, the third resembling "9."
For overprints see Nos. C22-C25.

Same Surcharge on Pasteur Stamps of France

1924-25

160 A23 50c on 10c green 1.25 1.00
161 A23 75c on 15c grn ('25) 1.25 1.00
162 A23 1.50p on 30c red 1.25 1.00
163 A23 2p on 45c red ('25) 1.25 1.00
164 A23 2.50p on 50c blue 1.75 1.25
165 A23 4p on 75c blue 1.75 1.25
Nos. 160-165 (6) 8.50 6.50

Olympic Games Issue

Stamps of France, 1924, Surcharged "Syrie" and New Values in French and Arabic

1924

Same Colors as #133-136

166 A24 50c on 10c 29.00 29.00
167 A25 1.25p on 25c 29.00 29.00
168 A26 1.50p on 30c 29.00 29.00
169 A27 2.50p on 50c 29.00 29.00
Nos. 166-169 (4) 116.00 116.00

Ronsard Issue

Same Surcharge on France No. 219

1925

170 A28 4p on 75c bl, *bluish* 1.00 .75

Mosque at Hama
A3

Mosque at Damascus
A5

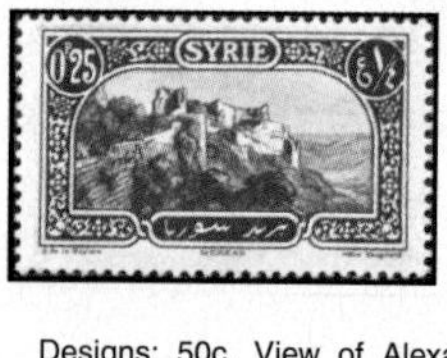

View of Merkab
A4

Designs: 50c, View of Alexandretta. 75c, View of Hama. 1p, Omayyad Mosque, Damascus. 1.25p, Latakia Harbor. 1.50p, View of Damascus. 2p, View of Palmyra. 2.50p, View of Kalat Yamoun. 3p, Bridge of Daphne. 5p, View of Aleppo. 10p, View of Aleppo. 25p, Columns at Palmyra.

Perf. 12½, 13½

1925 Litho. Unwmk.

173	A3	10c	dark violet	.35	.20

Photo.

174	A4	25c	olive black	.75	.55
175	A4	50c	yellow green	.30	.25
176	A4	75c	brown orange	.40	.20
177	A5	1p	magenta	.40	.20
178	A4	1.25p	deep green	1.25	1.10
179	A4	1.50p	rose red	.50	.20
180	A4	2p	dark brown	1.00	.20
181	A4	2.50p	peacock blue	.90	.50
182	A4	3p	orange brn	.90	.20
183	A4	5p	violet	.80	.20
184	A4	10p	violet brown	1.75	.30
185	A4	25p	ultra	2.25	1.25
			Nos. 173-185 (13)	11.55	5.35

For surcharges see Nos. 186-206, B1-B12, C26-C45, CB1-CB4.

Surcharged in Black or Red

1926-30

186	A4	1p	on 3pi org brn ('30)	.90	.50
187	A4	2p	on 1p25 dp grn (R) ('28)	.60	.40
a.			Double surcharge	16.00	16.00
188	A4	3.50p	on 75c org brn	.50	.35
a.			Double surcharge	16.00	16.00
189	A4	4p	on 25c ol blk	.85	.35
190	A4	4p	on 25c ol blk ('27)	.75	.45
191	A4	4p	on 25c ol blk (R) ('28)	.70	.35
192	A4	4.50p	on 75c brn org	.75	.35
193	A4	6p	on 2p50 pck bl	.55	.35
194	A4	7.50p	on 2p50 pck bl	.60	.35
195	A4	7.50p	on 2p50 pck bl (R) ('28)	1.75	.90
a.			Double surcharge	29.00	
196	A4	12p	on 1p25 dp grn	.75	.40
a.			Surcharge on face and back	50.00	42.50
197	A4	15p	on 25p ultra	1.40	.90
198	A4	20p	on 1p25 dp grn	1.10	.70
			Nos. 186-198 (13)	11.20	6.35

Size of numerals and arrangement of this surcharge varies on the different denominations.

No. 189 has slanting foot on "4."

No. 190, foot straight.

No. 173 Surcharged in Red

1928

199	A3	05c	on 10c dk vio	.50	.20

Stamps of 1925 Issue Overprinted in Red or Blue

1929 *Perf. 13½*

200	A4	50c	yellow grn (R)	2.60	2.00
201	A5	1p	magenta (Bl)	2.60	2.00
202	A4	1.50p	rose red (Bl)	2.60	2.00
203	A4	3p	orange brn (Bl)	2.60	2.00
204	A4	5p	violet (R)	2.60	2.00
205	A4	10p	violet brn (Bl)	2.60	2.00
206	A4	25p	ultra (R)	2.60	2.00
			Nos. 200-206 (7)	18.20	14.00

Industrial Exhibition, Damascus, Sept. 1929.

View of Hama — A6

View of Alexandretta — A9

Citadel at Aleppo A10

Great Mosque of Damascus A11

Ruins of Bosra A13

Mosque at Homs A15

View of Sednaya A16

Citadel at Aleppo A17

Ancient Bridge at Antioch A18

Mosque at Damascus A22

Designs: 20c, Great Mosque, Aleppo. 25c, Minaret, Hama. 2p, View of Antioch. 4p, Square at Damascus. 15p, Mosque at Hama. 25p, Monastery of St. Simeon the Stylite (ruins). 50p, Sun Temple (ruins), Palmyra.

Perf. 12x12½

1930-36 Litho. Unwmk.

208	A6	10c	red violet	.35	.20
209	A6	10c	vio brn ('33)	.35	.35
209A	A6	10c	vio brn, redrawn ('35)	.35	.20
210	A6	20c	dark blue	.35	.20
211	A6	20c	brn org ('33)	.35	.20
212	A6	25c	gray green	.35	.20
213	A6	25c	dk bl gray ('33)	.55	.45

Photo.

Perf. 13

214	A9	50c	violet	.35	.20
215	A15	75c	org red ('32)	.35	.20
216	A10	1p	green	.40	.20
217	A10	1p	bis brn ('36)	.90	.40
218	A11	1.50p	bister brown	4.25	3.00
219	A11	1.50p	dp grn ('33)	.60	.50
220	A9	2p	dark violet	.40	.25
221	A13	3p	yellow green	1.10	.70
222	A10	4p	yellow orange	.40	.25
223	A15	4.50p	rose carmine	1.00	.55
224	A16	6p	grnsh black	1.40	.50
225	A17	7.50p	dull blue	1.40	.70
226	A18	10p	dark brown	1.10	.50
227	A10	15p	deep green	1.90	1.00
228	A18	25p	violet brown	1.75	1.10
229	A15	50p	olive brown	6.00	4.50
230	A22	100p	red orange	11.50	9.75
			Nos. 208-230 (24)	37.45	26.10

On No. 209A Arabic inscriptions, upper right, are entirely redrawn with lighter lines. Hyphen added in "Helio-Vaugirard" imprint. Lines in buildings and background more distinct.

On No. 215 the letters of "VAUGIRARD" in the imprint are reversed as in a mirror.

For overprints and surcharges see Nos. 253-268, 346, M1-M2.

Autonomous Republic

Parliament Building A23

abu-al-Ala al-Maarri — A24

President Ali Bek el Abed — A25

Saladin — A26

1934, Aug. 2 Engr. *Perf. 12½*

232	A23	10c	olive green	.90	*1.00*
233	A23	20c	black	.90	*1.00*
234	A23	25c	red orange	.95	*1.00*
235	A23	50c	ultra	1.00	*1.00*
236	A23	75c	plum	1.00	*1.00*
237	A24	1p	vermilion	3.00	3.00
238	A24	1.50p	green	3.50	3.50
239	A24	2p	red brown	3.50	3.50
240	A24	3p	Prus blue	3.50	3.50
241	A24	4p	brt violet	3.75	3.50
242	A24	4.50p	carmine	4.00	3.75
243	A24	5p	dark blue	4.00	3.75
244	A24	6p	dark brown	4.00	3.75
245	A24	7.50p	dark ultra	4.25	3.75
246	A25	10p	dark brown	6.25	6.00
247	A25	15p	dull blue	8.75	8.50
248	A25	25p	rose red	13.50	13.00
249	A26	50p	dark brown	20.00	20.00
250	A26	100p	lake	32.50	32.50
			Nos. 232-250 (19)	119.25	117.00

Proclamation of the Republic. See Nos. C57-C66. For surcharge see No. M3.

Stamps of 1930-36 Overprinted in Red or Black

1936, Apr. 15

253	A9	50c	violet (R)	1.75	1.50
254	A10	1p	bister brn (Bk)	1.75	1.50
255	A9	2p	dk violet (R)	1.75	1.50
256	A13	3p	yellow grn (Bk)	2.00	1.50
257	A10	4p	yellow org (Bk)	2.00	1.50
258	A15	4.50p	rose car (Bk)	2.00	1.50
259	A16	6p	grnsh blk (R)	2.40	2.00
260	A17	7.50p	dull blue (R)	3.00	2.75
261	A18	10p	dk brown (Bk)	3.75	3.75
			Nos. 253-261 (9)	20.40	17.50

Industrial Exhibition, Damascus, May 1936. See Nos. C67-C71.

Stamps of 1930 Surcharged in Black

1937-38 *Perf. 13½x13*

262	A10	2.50p	on 4p yel org ('38)	.55	.40
263	A22	10p	on 100p red orange	1.00	.90

Stamps of 1930-33 Surcharged in Red or Black

1938 *Perf. 13½*

264	A15	25c	on 75c org red (Bk)	.30	.20
265	A11	50c	on 1.50p dp grn (R)	.40	.30
266	A17	2p	on 7.50p dl bl (R)	.70	.60
267	A17	5p	on 7.50p dl bl (R)	1.10	.90
268	A15	10p	on 50p ol brn (Bk)	1.10	.95
			Nos. 264-268 (5)	3.60	2.95

President Hashem Bek el Atassi — A27

1938-43 Photo. Unwmk.

268A	A27	10p	dp blue ('43)	.85	.85
269	A27	12.50p	on 10p dp bl (R)	.90	.90
270	A27	20p	dark brown	.85	.85
			Nos. 268A-270 (3)	2.60	2.60

The 10pi and 20pi exist imperf.

Columns at Palmyra A28

1940 Litho. *Perf. 11½*

271	A28	5p	pale rose	1.00	.65

Exists imperf.

Museum at Damascus — A29

Hotel at Bloudan A30

Kasr-el-Heir A31

1940 Typo. *Perf. 13x14*

272 A29 10c bright rose .25 .20
273 A29 20c light blue .25 .20
274 A29 25c fawn .30 .20
275 A29 50c ultra .30 .20

Engr.

Perf. 13

276 A30 1p peacock blue .35 .20
277 A30 1.50p chocolate .70 .70
278 A30 2.50p dark green .35 .30
279 A31 5p violet .40 .40
280 A31 7.50p vermilion .90 .40
281 A31 50p sepia 1.50 1.25
Nos. 272-281 (10) 5.30 4.05

For overprints see Nos. 298-299.

SEMI-POSTAL STAMPS

Nos. 174-185 Surcharged in Red or Black

1926 Unwmk. *Perf. 12½, 13½*

B1 A4 25c + 25c ol blk (R) 2.25 2.00
B2 A4 50c + 25c yel grn 2.25 2.00
B3 A4 75c + 25c brown org 2.25 2.00
B4 A5 1p + 50c magenta 2.25 2.00
B5 A4 1.25p + 50c dp grn (R) 2.25 2.00
B6 A4 1.50p + 50c rose red 2.25 2.00
B7 A4 2p + 75c dk brn (R) 2.25 2.00
B8 A4 2.50p + 75c pck bl (R) 2.25 2.00
B9 A4 3p + 1p org brn (R) 2.25 2.00
B10 A4 5p + 1p violet 2.25 2.00
B11 A4 10p + 2p vio brn 2.25 2.00
B12 A4 25p + 5p ultra (R) 2.25 2.00
Nos. B1-B12 (12) 27.00 24.00
Set, never hinged 36.00

On No. B4 the surcharge is set in six lines to fit the shape of the stamp.

The surcharge was a contribution to the relief of refugees from the Djebel Druze War. See Nos. CB1-CB4.

AIR POST STAMPS

POSTE
PAR
AVION

a

b

Nos. 35, 45, 47 Handstamped Type "a" in Violet

1920, Dec. Unwmk. *Perf. 13½*

C1 A22 1p on 5c 160.00 40.00
C2 A20 5p on 15c 290.00 47.50
C3 A18 10p on 40c 425.00 77.50
Nos. C1-C3 (3) 875.00 165.00

Nos. 36, 46, 48 Overprinted Type "a" in Violet

1921, June 12

C4 A22 1p on 20c 87.50 40.00
C5 A18 5p on 1fr 425.00 150.00
C6 A18 10p on 2fr 425.00 150.00
Nos. C4-C6 (3) 937.50 340.00

Excellent counterfeits exist of Nos. C1-C6.

Nos. 36, 46, 48 Overprinted Type "b"

1921, Oct. 5

C7 A22 1p on 20c 60.00 18.50
C8 A18 5p on 1fr 150.00 37.50
a. Inverted overprint 325.00 240.00
C9 A18 10p on 2fr 200.00 47.50
a. Double overprint 475.00 400.00
Nos. C7-C9 (3) 410.00 103.50

Nos. 92, 94-96 Overprinted

c

1922, May 28

C10 A18 2p on 40c 25.00 25.00
a. Inverted overprint
C11 A18 3p on 60c 25.00 25.00
C12 A18 5p on 1fr 25.00 25.00
C13 A18 10p on 2fr 25.00 25.00
Nos. C10-C13 (4) 100.00 100.00

Nos. 116-119 Overprinted Type "c"

1923, Nov. 22

C14 A18 2p on 40c 29.00 29.00
b. Inverted surcharge
C15 A18 3p on 60c 29.00 29.00
C16 A18 5p on 1fr 29.00 29.00
C17 A18 10p on 2fr 29.00 29.00
b. Double overprint
Nos. C14-C17 (4) 116.00 116.00

Overprinted "Liabn"

C14a A18 2p on 40c 400.00 400.00
C15a A18 3p on 60c 400.00 400.00
C16a A18 5p on 1fr 400.00 400.00
C17a A18 10p on 2fr 400.00 400.00

Nos. 137-140 Overprinted Type "c"

1924, Jan. 13

C18 A18 2p on 40c 3.50 3.50
a. Double overprint *27.50*
C19 A18 3p on 60c 3.50 3.50
a. Inverted overprint 47.50
C20 A18 5p on 1fr 3.50 3.50
a. Double overprint *50.00 30.00*
C21 A18 10p on 2fr 3.50 3.50
Nos. C18-C21 (4) 14.00 14.00

Nos. 152, 154, 157-158 Overprinted

1924, July 17

C22 A18 2p on 40c 5.00 5.00
a. Inverted overprint 32.50
C23 A18 3p on 60c 5.00 5.00
a. Inverted overprint 32.50
b. Double overprint 20.00
C24 A18 5p on 1fr 5.00 5.00
C25 A18 10p on 2fr 5.00 5.00
a. Inverted overprint 32.50
Nos. C22-C25 (4) 20.00 20.00

Regular Issue of 1925 Overprinted in Green

1925, Mar. 1

C26 A4 2p dark brown 1.90 1.90
C27 A4 3p orange brown 1.90 1.90
C28 A4 5p violet 1.90 1.90
C29 A4 10p violet brown 1.90 1.90
Nos. C26-C29 (4) 7.60 7.60

Regular Issue of 1925 Overprinted in Red

f

1926

C30 A4 2p dark brown 1.50 1.50
a. Inverted overprint 32.50
C31 A4 3p orange brown 1.60 1.60
a. Inverted overprint 32.50
C32 A4 5p violet 1.75 1.75
a. Inverted overprint 32.50
b. Double overprint
C33 A4 10p violet brown 1.75 1.75
a. Inverted overprint 32.50
b. Double overprint
Nos. C30-C33 (4) 6.60 6.60

Nos. C30-C33 received their first airmail use June 16, 1929, at the opening of the Beirut-Marseille line.

For surcharges see Nos. CB1-CB4.

Regular Issue of 1925 Overprinted Type "f" in Red or Black

1929

C34 A4 50c yellow green (R) 1.00 1.00
a. Inverted overprint 40.00
b. Overprinted on face and back 22.50
c. Double overprint 40.00
d. Double overprint, one inverted 60.00
e. Pair, one without overprint
C35 A5 1p magenta (Bk) 1.10 1.10
a. Reversed overprint
b. Red overprint
C36 A4 25p ultra (R) 4.00 4.00
a. Inverted overprint 82.50
b. Pair, one without overprint
Nos. C34-C36 (3) 6.10 6.10

On No. C35, the overprint is vertical, with plane nose down.

No. 197 Overprinted Type "f" in Red

1929, July 9

C37 A4 15p on 25p ultra 2.40 2.40
a. Inverted overprint

Air Post Stamps of 1926-29 Overprinted in Various Colors

1929, Sept. 5

C38 A4 50c yellow grn (R) 2.25 2.25
C39 A5 1p magenta (Bl) 2.25 2.25
C40 A4 2p dk brown (V) 2.25 2.25
C41 A4 3p orange brn (Bl) 2.25 2.25
a. Inverted overprint 70.00
C42 A4 5p violet (R) 2.25 2.25
C43 A4 10p violet brn (Bl) 2.25 2.25
C44 A4 25p ultra (R) 2.25 2.25
Nos. C38-C44 (7) 15.75 15.75

Damascus Industrial Exhibition.

AP1

Red Surcharge

1930, Jan. 30

C45 AP1 2p on 1.25p dp grn 2.25 2.25
a. Inverted surcharge
b. Double surcharge 60.00

Plane over Homs
AP2

Designs: 1pi, City Wall, Damascus. 2pi, Euphrates River. 3pi, Temple Ruins, Palmyra. 5pi, Deir-el-Zor. 10pi, Damascus. 15pi, Aleppo, Citadel. 25pi, Hama. 50pi, Zebdani. 100pi, Telebisse.

1931-33 Photo. Unwmk.

C46 AP2 50c ocher .60 .35
C47 AP2 50c black brn ('33) 1.00 .85
C48 AP2 1p chestnut brown .85 .50
C49 AP2 2p Prus blue 1.75 1.50
C50 AP2 3p blue grn 1.10 .80
C51 AP2 5p red violet 1.10 .80
C52 AP2 10p slate grn 1.10 .80
C53 AP2 15p orange red 1.50 1.00
C54 AP2 25p orange brn 1.75 1.50
C55 AP2 50p black 2.25 2.00
C56 AP2 100p magenta 2.50 2.00
Nos. C46-C56 (11) 15.50 12.10

Nos. C46 to C56 exist imperforate. Value, $425.

For overprints see Nos. C67-C71, C110-C112, C114-C115, MC1-MC4.

Village of Bloudan
AP12

1934, Aug. 2 Engr. *Perf. 12½*

C57 AP12 50c yel brown 1.25 1.25
C58 AP12 1p green 1.50 1.50
C59 AP12 2p peacock bl 1.75 1.75
C60 AP12 3p red 2.00 2.00
C61 AP12 5p plum 2.25 2.25
C62 AP12 10p brt violet 15.00 15.00
C63 AP12 15p orange brn 18.50 18.50
C64 AP12 25p dk ultra 23.00 23.00
C65 AP12 50p black 42.50 42.50
C66 AP12 100p red brown 77.50 77.50
Nos. C57-C66 (10) 185.25 185.25

Proclamation of the Republic. Exist imperf.

Air Post Stamps of 1931-33 Overprinted in Red or Black

1936, Apr. 15 *Perf. 13½x13, 13½*

C67 AP2 50c black brown 3.75 3.75
C68 AP2 1p chnt brown (Bk) 3.75 3.75
C69 AP2 2p Prus blue 3.75 3.75
C70 AP2 3p blue green 3.75 3.75
C71 AP2 5p red violet (Bk) 3.75 3.75
Nos. C67-C71 (5) 18.75 18.75

Industrial Exhibition, Damascus, May 1936.

Syrian Pavilion at Paris Exposition
AP13

1937, July 1 Photo. *Perf. 13½*

C72 AP13 ½p yellow green 1.75 1.75
C73 AP13 1p green 1.75 1.75
C74 AP13 2p lt brown 1.75 1.75
C75 AP13 3p rose red 1.75 1.75
C76 AP13 5p brown orange 1.75 1.75
C77 AP13 10p grnsh black 3.25 3.25
C78 AP13 15p blue 4.00 4.00
C79 AP13 25p dark violet 4.50 4.50
Nos. C72-C79 (8) 20.50 20.50

Paris International Exposition. Exist imperf.

Ancient Citadel at Aleppo
AP14

Omayyad Mosque and Minaret of Jesus at Damascus
AP15

1937 Engr. *Perf. 13*

C80 AP14 ½ dark violet .50 .50
C81 AP15 1p black .50 .50
C82 AP14 2p deep green .50 .50
C83 AP15 3p deep ultra .50 .50
C84 AP14 5p rose lake 1.50 1.50
C85 AP15 10p red brown .85 .85
C86 AP14 15p lake brown 3.25 3.25
C87 AP15 25p dark blue 4.00 4.00
Nos. C80-C87 (8) 11.60 11.60

No. C80 to C87 exist imperforate.

For overprint see No. C109.

Maurice Noguès and Route of France-Syria Flight — AP16

1938, July Photo. *Perf. 11*

C88 AP16 10p dark green 2.25 2.25
a. Souv. sheet of 4, perf. 13½ 17.50 17.50
b. Perf. 13½ 4.00 4.00

10th anniversary of first Marseille-Beirut flight, by Maurice Noguès.

No. C88a exists imperf.; value $800.

Bridge at Deir-el-Zor
AP17

1940 **Engr.** ***Perf. 13***

C89	AP17	25c brown black	.20	.20
C90	AP17	50c peacock blue	.20	.20
C91	AP17	1p deep ultra	.25	.20
C92	AP17	2p dk orange brn	.40	.30
C93	AP17	5p green	.65	.50
C94	AP17	10p rose carmine	1.00	.90
C95	AP17	50p dark violet	2.25	1.75
		Nos. C89-C95 (7)	4.95	4.05

Exist imperf.

AIR POST SEMI-POSTAL STAMPS

Nos. C30-C33 Surcharged Like Nos. B1-B12 in Black and Red

1926, Apr. 1 **Unwmk.** ***Perf. 13½***

CB1	A4	2p + 1p dk brown	3.00	2.75
CB2	A4	3p + 2p org brn	2.75	2.75
CB3	A4	5p + 3p violet	2.75	2.75
CB4	A4	10p + 5p vio brn	2.75	2.75
		Nos. CB1-CB4 (4)	11.25	11.00

The new value is in red and rest of the surcharge in black on Nos. CB1-CB3. The entire surcharge is black on No. CB4.

See note following Nos. B1-B12.

POSTAGE DUE STAMPS

Under French Occupation

Stamps of French Offices in the Turkish Empire, 1902-03, Surcharged

O. M. F
Syrie
Ch. taxe
1 PIASTRE

1920 **Unwmk.** ***Perf. 14x13½***

J1	A3	1p on 10c rose red	160.00	160.00
J2	A3	2p on 20c brn vio	160.00	160.00
J3	A3	3p on 30c lil	160.00	160.00
J4	A4	4p on 40c red & pale bl	160.00	160.00
		Nos. J1-J4 (4)	640.00	640.00

Postage Due Stamps of France, 1893-1920, Surcharged in Black or Red

1920

J5	D2	1p on 10c brown	3.25	3.25
J6	D2	2p on 20c ol grn (R)	3.25	3.25
a.		"PIASTRE"	900.00	900.00
J7	D2	3p on 30c red	3.25	3.25
a.		"PIASTRE"		
J8	D2	4p on 50c brn vio	4.75	4.75
a.		3p in setting of 4p	525.00	525.00
		Nos. J5-J8 (4)	14.50	14.50

1921-22

J9	D2	50c on 10c brown	1.40	1.40
a.		"75" instead of "50"	90.00	
b.		"CENTI MES" instead of "CENTIEMES"	7.50	
J10	D2	1p on 20c ol grn	1.40	1.40
J11	D2	2p on 30c red	3.25	3.25
J12	D2	3p on 50c brn vio	3.50	3.50
J13	D2	5p on 1fr red brn, *straw*	5.00	5.00
		Nos. J9-J13 (5)	14.55	14.55

D3

D4

1921 ***Perf. 11½***

Red Surcharge

J14	D3	50c on 1p black	3.75	3.75
J15	D3	1p on 1p black	3.75	3.75

1922

J16	D4	2p on 5m rose	10.00	6.50
a.		"AX" of "TAXE" inverted	175.00	175.00
J17	D4	3p on 1p gray bl	15.00	12.00

French Mandate

Postage Due Stamps of France, 1893-1920, Surcharged

1923

J18	D2	50c on 10c brown	1.50	1.50
J19	D2	1p on 20c ol grn	2.25	2.25
J20	D2	2p on 30c red	1.90	1.90
J21	D2	3p on 50c vio brn	1.90	1.90
J22	D2	5p on 1fr red brn, *straw*	3.75	3.75
		Nos. J18-J22 (5)	11.30	11.30

Postage Due Stamps of France, 1893-1920, Surcharged

1924

J23	D2	50c on 10c brown	1.00	1.00
J24	D2	1p on 20c ol grn	1.00	1.00
J25	D2	2p on 30c red	1.10	1.10
J26	D2	3p on 50c vio brn	1.50	1.50
J27	D2	5p on 1fr red brn, *straw*	1.50	1.50
		Nos. J23-J27 (5)	6.10	6.10

Postage Due Stamps of France, 1893-1920, Surcharged

1924

J28	D2	50c on 10c brown	.75	.75
J29	D2	1p on 20c ol grn	.75	.75
J30	D2	2p on 30c red	1.00	1.00
J31	D2	3p on 50c vio brn	1.40	1.40
J32	D2	5p on 1fr red brn, *straw*	1.75	1.75
		Nos. J28-J32 (5)	5.65	5.65

Water Wheel at Hama
D5

Bridge at Antioch — D6

Designs: 2p, The Tartous. 3p, View of Banias. 5p, Chevaliers' Castle.

1925 **Photo.** ***Perf. 13½***

J33	D5	50c brown, *yel*	.25	.25
J34	D6	1p violet, *rose*	.25	.25
J35	D5	2p black, *blue*	.55	.55
J36	D5	3p black, *red org*	1.25	1.25
J37	D5	5p black, *bl grn*	1.50	1.50
		Nos. J33-J37 (5)	3.80	3.80

D7

Lion — D8

1931

J38	D7	8p black, *gray blue*	3.50	3.50
J39	D8	15p black, *dull rose*	6.00	6.00

ISSUES OF THE ARABIAN GOVERNMENT

The following issues replaced the British Military Occupation (E.E.F.) stamps (Palestine Nos. 2-14) which were used in central and eastern Syria from Nov. 1918 until Jan. 1920.

Turkish Stamps of 1913-18 Handstamped in Various Colors

Also Handstamp Surcharged with New Values as:

1 millieme

1 Egyptian piaster

The Seal reads: "Hakuma al Arabie" (The Arabian Government)

Perf. 11½, 12, 12½, 13½

1919-20 **Unwmk.**

1	A24	1m on 2pa red lil (254)	.85	.85
2	A25	1m on 4pa dk brn (255)	.85	.85
3	A26	2m on 5pa vio brn (256)	1.40	1.40
4	A15	2m on 5pa on 10pa gray grn (291)	.95	.95
5	A18	2m on 5pa ocher (304)	22.50	22.50
6	A41	2m on 5pa grn (345)	*275.00*	*250.00*
7	A18	2m on 5pa ocher (378)	*47.50*	*47.50*
8	A28	4m on 10pa grn (258)	6.50	6.50
9	A28	4m on 10pa grn (271)	.85	.85
10	A22	4m on 10pa bl grn (329)	1.75	1.75
11	A41	4m on 10pa car (346)	37.50	37.50
12	A23	4m on 10pa grn (415)	7.25	7.25
13	A44	4m on 10pa grn (424)	1.25	1.25
14	A11	4m on 10pa on 20pa vio brn (B38)	1.25	1.25
15	A41	4m on 10pa car (B42)	.85	.85
16	SP1	4m on 10pa red vio (B46)	1.40	1.40
17	SP1	4m on 10pa on 20pa car rose (B47)	1.40	1.40
19	A21	5pa ocher (317)		
21	A21	20pa car rose (153)	*92.50*	*110.00*
22	A29	20pa red (259)	1.40	1.40
23	A29	20pa red (272)	*275.00*	*275.00*
24	A17	20pa car (299)	2.75	2.75
25	A21	20pa car rose (318)	2.75	2.75
26	A22	20pa car rose (330)	11.00	11.00
27	A21	20pa car rose (342)	5.00	5.00
28	A41	20pa ultra (347)	2.75	2.75
29	A16	20pa mag (363)	11.00	11.00
30	A17	20pa car (371)		
31	A18	20pa car (379)	7.75	7.75
32	A45	20pa dp rose (425)	3.75	3.75
33	A21	20pa car rose (B8)	2.75	2.75
34	A22	20pa car rose (B33)	2.75	2.75
35	A22	20pa car rose (B36)	13.00	13.00
36	A41	20pa ultra (B43)	.55	.55
37	A16	20pa mag (P140)	2.75	2.75
38	A17	20pa car (P144)	*250.00*	*250.00*
39	A30	1pi bl (260)	2.75	2.75
40	A31	1pi on 1½pi car & blk (261)	*375.00*	*375.00*
41	A30	1pi bl (273)	92.50	92.50
42	A30	1pi on 1pi bl (273)	125.00	125.00
43	A17	1pi blue (300)	4.75	4.75
44	A18	1pi blue (307)	57.50	57.50
45	A22	1pi ultra (331)	5.75	5.75
46	A21	1pi ultra (343)	10.00	10.00
47	A41	1pi vio & blk (348)	1.75	1.75
48	A18	1pi brt bl (389)	5.75	5.75
49	A46	1pi dl vio (426)	1.75	1.75
50	A47	1pi on 50pa ultra (428)	1.10	1.10
51	A21	1pi ultra (B9)	6.00	6.00
52	A22	1pi ultra (B15)	10.00	10.00
53	A18	1pi brt bl (B21)	6.00	6.00
54	A18	1pi blue (B23)	15.00	15.00
55	A22	1pi ultra (B34)	12.50	12.50
56	A41	1pi vio & blk (B44)	2.75	2.75
57	A33	2pi grn & blk (263)	72.50	72.50
58	A13	2pi brn org (289)	2.00	2.00
59	A18	2pi slate (308)	27.50	27.50
60	A18	2pi slate (314)	27.50	27.50
61	A21	2pi bl blk (320)	5.25	5.25
62	A17	2pi org (373)	4.25	4.25
63	A18	5pi brn (310)	12.00	12.00
64	A22	5pi dl vio (333)	23.50	23.50
65	A41	5pi yel brn & blk (349)	4.75	4.75
66	A41	5pi yel brn & blk (418)	4.75	4.75
67	A53	5pi on 2pa Prus bl (547)	7.75	7.75
68	A21	5pi dk vio (B10)	275.00	275.00
69	A17	5pi lil rose (B20)	47.50	47.50
70	A41	5pi yel brn & blk (B45)	4.75	4.75
72	A50	10pi dk grn (431)	130.00	130.00
73	A50	10pi dk vio (432)	110.00	110.00
74	A50	10pi dk brn (433)	*375.00*	
75	A18	10pi org brn (B2)	350.00	350.00
76	A37	25pi ol grn (267)	*350.00*	*350.00*
77	A40	25pi on 200pi grn & blk (287)	*500.00*	*500.00*
78	A17	25pi brn (303)	375.00	375.00
79	A51	25pi car, *straw* (434)	92.50	92.50
81	A52	50pi ind (438)	200.00	200.00

The variety "surcharge omitted" exists on Nos. 1-5, 12-13, 16, 32, 49-50, 67.

A few copies of No. 377 (50pi) and No. 269 (100pi) were overprinted but not regularly issued.

Overprinted

The Inscription reads "Hakum Soria Arabie" (Syrian-Arabian Government)

On Stamp of 1913

83	A26	2m on 5pa vio brn (256)	5.00	5.00

On Stamp of 1916-18

84	A45	20pa dp rose (425)	.55	.55

A1

Litho. ***Perf. 11½***

85	A1	5m rose	.55	.55
a.		Tête bêche pair	22.50	10.00
b.		Imperf.		

Independence Issue

Arabic Overprint in Green: "Souvenir of Syrian Independence March 8, 1920"

86	A1	5m rose	250.00	150.00
a.		Tête bêche pair		
b.		Inverted overprint	375.00	375.00

A2

Litho.
Size: 22x18mm

87 A2 1/10pi lt brn .25 .20

Size: 28x22mm

88 A2 2/10pi yel grn .30 .20
a. 2/10pi yellow (error) 10.00 10.00
89 A2 3/10pi yellow .40 .30
90 A2 1pi gray blue .35 .25
91 A2 2pi blue grn 2.00 1.00

Size: 31x25mm

92 A2 5pi vio brn 2.75 1.50
93 A2 10pi gray 2.75 2.00
Nos. 86-93 (8) 258.80 155.45

Nos. 86-93 exist imperf.
For overprint see No. J5.

PF1

PF2

Revenue Stamps Surcharged as on Postage Stamps, for Postal Use

1920 Unwmk. *Perf. 11½*

94 PF1 5m on 5pa red .50 .35
95 PF2 1m on 5pa red .50 .20
96 PF2 2m on 5pa red .40 .25
97 PF2 1pi on 5pa red 1.00 .65

Surcharged in Syrian Piasters

98 PF2 2pi on 5pa red .35 .20
99 PF2 3pi on 5pa red .35 .20
Nos. 94-99 (6) 3.10 1.85

ISSUES OF THE ARABIAN GOVERNMENT POSTAGE DUE STAMPS

Postage Due Stamps of Turkey, 1914, Handstamped and Surcharged with New Value

1920 Unwmk. *Perf. 12*

J1 D1 2m on 5pa claret 6.75 6.75
J2 D2 20pa red 6.75 6.75
J3 D3 1pi dark blue 6.75 6.75
J4 D4 2pi slate 6.75 6.75
Nos. J1-J4 (4) 27.00 27.00

Type of Regular Issue
Perf. 11½
Litho.

J5 A2 1pi black 1.25 1.25

TAHITI

tə-'hēt-ē

LOCATION — An island in the South Pacific Ocean, one of the Society group
GOVT. — A part of the French Oceania Colony
AREA — 600 sq. mi.
POP. — 19,029
CAPITAL — Papeete

The stamps of Tahiti were replaced by those of French Oceania.

100 Centimes = 1 Franc

Covers
Values are for commercial covers bearing correct frankings. Philatelic covers sell for less.

Counterfeits exist of surcharges and overprints on Nos. 1-31.

Stamps of French Colonies Surcharged in Black:

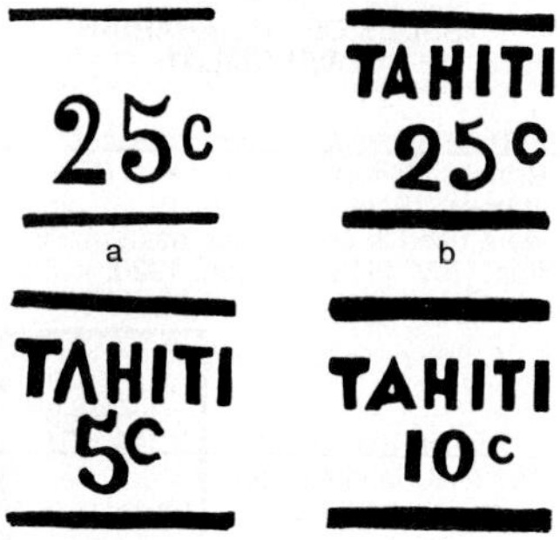
a b c d

1882 Unwmk. *Imperf.*

1 A8(a) 25c on 35c dk vio, *org* 325. 275.
On cover, single franking 6,500.
1A A8(b) 25c on 35c dk vio, *org* 3,500. 3,500.
On cover —
1B A8(a) 25c on 40c ver, *straw* 5,000. 5,750.
On cover —

Surcharge Inverted

1c A8(a) 25c on 35c dk vio, *org* 375. 300.
1Ad A8(b) 25c on 35c dk vio, *org* 4,000. 4,000.
1Be A8(a) 25c on 40c ver, *straw* 3,250. 3,500.

Surcharge Reading Up

1f A8(a) 25c on 35c dk vio, *org* 350. 300.
1Ag A8(b) 25c on 35c dk vio, *org* 4,100. 4,100.

Surcharge Reading Down

1h A8(a) 25c on 35c dk vio, *org* 350. 300.
1Ai A8(b) 25c on 35c dk vio, *org* 4,000. 4,000.

Double Surcharge, One Inverted

1Bj A8(a) 25c on 40c ver, *straw* 6,500. 6,900.

1884 *Perf. 14x13½*

2 A9(c) 5c on 20c red, *grn* 200. 175.
On cover, single franking 9,500.
3 A9(d) 10c on 20c red, *grn* 275. 225.
On cover, single franking 3,750.
On wrapper 6,000.

Imperf

4 A8(b) 25c on 1fr brnz grn, *straw* 625. 550.
On cover, single franking 9,500.

Covers: Only one cover each is recorded for Nos. 2 and 4, 8 covers recorded for No. 3.

Surcharge Inverted

2a 5c on 20c red, *grn* 200.00 175.00
3a 10c on 20c red, *grn* 275.00 225.00
4a 25c on 1fr brnz grn, *straw* 625.00 500.00

Surcharge Reading Up

2b 5c on 20c red, *grn* 200.00 175.00
3b 10c on 20c red, *grn* 275.00 225.00
4b 25c on 1fr brnz grn, *straw* 625.00 500.00

Surcharge Reading Up

2c 5c on 20c red, *grn* 200.00 175.00
3c 10c on 20c red, *grn* 275.00 225.00
4c 25c on 1fr brnz grn, *straw* 625.00 500.00

Handstamped in Black

1893 *Perf. 14x13½*

5 A9 1c blk, *lil bl* 800.00 725.00
6 A9 2c brown, *buff* 2,500. 1,900.
7 A9 4c claret, *lav* 1,175. 875.00
8 A9 5c green, *grnsh* 40.00 35.00
On cover, single franking 725.00
9 A9 10c black, *lav* 40.00 35.00
On cover, single franking 900.00
10 A9 15c blue 40.00 35.00
On cover, single franking 750.00
11 A9 20c red, *green* 57.50 50.00
On cover, single franking 900.00
12 A9 25c yel, *straw* 6,500. 5,500.
13 A9 25c blk, *rose* 40.00 35.00
On cover, single franking 450.00
14 A9 35c violet, *org* 1,900. 1,700.
15 A9 75c carmine, *rose* 70.00 57.50
On cover, single franking 675.00
16 A9 1fr brnz grn, *straw* 80.00 65.00
On cover, single franking 750.00

Surcharge Inverted

6a A9 2c brown, *buff* 3,500. 3,300.
8a A9 5c green, *grnsh* 110.00 110.00
9a A9 10c black, *lav* 190.00 175.00
10a A9 15c blue 190.00 175.00
11a A9 20c red, *green* 210.00 190.00
12a A9 25c yel, *straw* 8,500. 8,500.
13a A9 25c blk, *rose* 190.00 175.00
15a A9 75c carmine, *rose* 210.00 190.00
16a A9 1fr brnz grn, *straw* 240.00 240.00

Nearly all values of this set are known with overprint sloping up, sloping down and horizontal. Some occur double. Values the same as for the normal stamps.

Overprinted in Black

1893

17 A9 1c blk, *lil bl* 725.00 650.00
18 A9 2c brn, *buff* 2,900. 2,300.
19 A9 4c claret, *lav* 1,450. 1,250.
20 A9 5c grn, *grnsh* 875.00 725.00
21 A9 10c black, *lav* 275.00 275.00
22 A9 15c blue 40.00 35.00
On cover, single franking 750.00
23 A9 20c red, *grn* 40.00 35.00
On cover, single franking 775.00
24 A9 25c yel, *straw* 40,000. 30,000.
25 A9 25c black, *rose* 40.00 35.00
On cover, single franking 450.00
26 A9 35c violet, *org* 1,900. 1,700.
27 A9 75c carmine, *rose* 40.00 35.00
On cover, single franking 675.00
b. Double overprint 275.00
28 A9 1fr brnz grn, *straw* 45.00 40.00
On cover, single franking 750.00

Inverted Overprint

17a A9 1c blk, *lil bl* 1,000. 950.
18a A9 2c brn, *buff* 3,300. 3,100.
19a A9 4c claret, *lav* 1,600. 1,550.
20a A9 5c grn, *grnsh* 1,150. 1,150.
21a A9 10c black, *lav* 725. 650.
22a A9 15c blue 175. 160.
23a A9 20c red, *grn* 175. 160.
25a A9 25c black, *rose* 175. 160.
26a A9 35c violet, *org* 2,350. 2,250.
27a A9 75c carmine, *rose* 175. 160.
28a A9 1fr brnz grn, *straw* 190. 170.

Stamps of French Polynesia Surcharged in Black or Carmine:

g

h

1903

29 A1 (g) 10c on 15c bl (Bk) 7.25 7.25
On cover, single franking 140.00
a. Double surcharge 42.50 42.50
b. Inverted surcharge 42.50 42.50
30 A1 (h) 10c on 25c blk, *rose* (C) 7.25 7.25
On cover, single franking 140.00
a. Double surcharge 47.50 47.50
b. Inverted surcharge 72.50 72.50
31 A1 (h) 10c on 40c red, *straw* (Bk) 8.75 8.75
On cover, single franking 140.00
a. Double surcharge 55.00 55.00
b. Inverted surcharge 52.50 52.50
Nos. 29-31 (3) 23.25 23.25

In the surcharges on Nos. 29-31 there are two varieties of the "1" in "10," i. e. with long and short serif.

SEMI-POSTAL STAMPS

Stamps of French Polynesia Overprinted in Red

1915 Unwmk. *Perf. 14x13½*

B1 A1 15c blue 225.00 225.00
On cover, single franking 550.00
a. Inverted overprint 800.00 800.00
B2 A1 15c gray 25.00 25.00
On cover, single franking 200.00
a. Inverted overprint 325.00 325.00

Values are for commercial covers bearing correct frankings. Philatelic covers also exist and generally sell for less than the values quoted.
Counterfeits exist.

POSTAGE DUE STAMPS

Counterfeits exist of overprints on Nos. J1-J26.

Postage Due Stamps of French Colonies Handstamped in Black like Nos. 5-16

1893 Unwmk. *Imperf.*

J1 D1 1c black 310. 310.
J2 D1 2c black 330. 330.
J3 D1 3c black 350. 350.
J4 D1 4c black 350. 350.
J5 D1 5c black 350. 350.
J6 D1 10c black 350. 350.
J7 D1 15c black 350. 350.
J8 D1 20c black 290. 290.
On cover 8,000.
J9 D1 30c black 350. 350.
J10 D1 40c black 350. 350.
J11 D1 60c black 400. 400.
J12 D1 1fr brown 800. 800.
J13 D1 2fr brown 800. 800.
Nos. J1-J13 (13) 5,380. 5,380.

Surcharge Inverted

J1a D1 1c black 600. 600.
J2a D1 2c black 600. 600.
J3a D1 3c black 600. 600.
J4a D1 4c black 600. 600.
J5a D1 5c black 600. 600.
J6a D1 10c black 600. 600.
J7a D1 15c black 600. 600.
J8a D1 20c black 600. 600.
J9a D1 30c black 600. 600.
J10a D1 40c black 600. 600.
J11a D1 60c black 600. 600.
J12a D1 1fr brown 1,300. 1,300.
J13a D1 2fr brown 1,300. 1,300.

Surcharge Double

J6b D1 10c black 850. 850.
J7b D1 15c black 850. 850.

Covers: Only two covers are recorded for No. J8.

Overprinted in Black like Nos. 17-28

1893

J14 D1 1c black 1,900. 1,900.
J15 D1 2c black 450. 450.
J16 D1 3c black 450. 450.
J17 D1 4c black 450. 450.
J18 D1 5c black 450. 450.
J19 D1 10c black 450. 450.
J20 D1 15c black 450. 450.
J21 D1 20c black 450. 450.
On cover, single franking 6,750.
J22 D1 30c black 450. 450.
J23 D1 40c black 450. 450.
J24 D1 60c black 450. 450.
J25 D1 1fr brown 450. 450.
J26 D1 2fr brown 450. 450.
Nos. J14-J26 (13) 7,300. 7,300.

Surcharge Inverted

J14a D1 1c black 2,800. 2,800.
J15a D1 2c black 850. 850.
J19a D1 10c black 925. 925.
J20a D1 15c black 925. 925.
J21a D1 20c black 925. 925.
J23a D1 40c black 925. 925.
J24a D1 60c black 925. 925.
J25a D1 1fr brown 925. 925.
J26a D1 2fr brown 925. 925.

Surcharge Double

J15b D1 2c black 925. 925.
J16b D1 3c black 925. 925.
J17b D1 4c black 925. 925.
J18b D1 5c black 925. 925.
J19b D1 10c black 925. 925.
J20b D1 15c black 925. 925.
J22b D1 30c black 925. 925.
J25b D1 1fr brown 925. 925.
J26b D1 2fr brown 925. 925.

TANGANYIKA

ˌtan-gə-ˈnyē-kə

LOCATION — Southeastern Africa bordering on the Indian Ocean
AREA — 362,688 sq. mi.
POP. — 9,404,000 (est. 1961)
CAPITAL — Dar es Salaam

Before World War I, this area formed part of German East Africa It was mandated to Britain after World War I and (in 1946) became a trust territory under the United Nations. In 1935, stamps of the mandate were replaced by those used jointly by Kenya, Uganda and Tanganyika (see Kenya, Uganda and Tanzania).

100 Cents = 1 Rupee
100 Cents = 1 Shilling (1922)
20 Shillings = 1 Pound

Stamps of East Africa & Uganda Protectorates Overprinted

1921 Wmk. 4 *Perf. 14*

1	A1	12c gray	7.50	110.00
2	A1	15c ultra	3.75	6.25
3	A1	50c dull violet & blk	11.50	97.50

Overprinted

4	A2	2r black & red, *blue*	37.50	140.00
5	A2	3r gray green & violet	80.00	210.00
7	A2	5r dull violet & ultra	110.00	290.00
		Nos. 1-7 (6)	250.25	853.75

Overprinted in Red or Black

1922

8	A1	1c black (R)	.90	21.00
9	A1	10c orange (Bk)	.90	16.00

A3

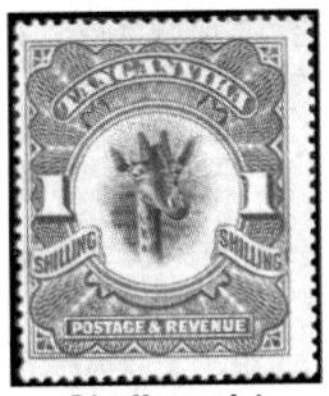

Giraffe — A4

Perf. 14½x14

1922-25 Engr. Wmk. 4

10	A3	5c dk violet & blk	2.75	.20
11	A3	5c grn & blk ('25)	3.75	1.75
12	A3	10c green & blk	2.75	.95
13	A3	10c yel & blk ('25)	5.25	1.75
14	A3	15c carmine & blk	2.25	.20
15	A3	20c orange & blk	2.00	.20
16	A3	25c black	6.25	7.50
17	A3	25c blue & blk ('25)	4.50	20.00
18	A3	30c blue & blk	5.75	5.75
19	A3	30c dull vio & blk ('25)	4.75	16.00
20	A3	40c brown & black	3.25	5.25
21	A3	50c gray black	2.75	1.75
22	A3	75c bister & black	3.75	21.00

Perf. 14

23	A4	1sh green & black	3.50	12.50
a.		Wmk. sideways	4.75	16.00
24	A4	2sh brn vio & blk	5.25	29.00
a.		Wmk. sideways	6.25	17.50
25	A4	3sh blk, wmk. sideways	21.00	32.50
26	A4	5sh red & black	18.00	85.00
a.		Wmk. sideways	37.50	97.50
27	A4	10sh dp blue & blk	62.50	125.00
a.		Wmk. sideways	140.00	250.00
28	A4	£1 orange & black	200.00	375.00
a.		Wmk. sideways	225.00	400.00
		Nos. 10-28 (19)	360.00	741.30

On No. 28 the words of value are in a curve between the circle and "POSTAGE & REVENUE."

King George V
A5 A6

1927-31 Typo.

29	A5	5c green & black	2.00	.20
30	A5	10c yellow & black	2.25	.20
31	A5	15c red & black	2.00	.20
32	A5	20c orange & black	3.00	.20
33	A5	25c ultra & black	4.25	2.25
34	A5	30c dull violet & blk	3.25	3.00
35	A5	30c ultra & blk ('31)	29.00	.35
36	A5	40c brown & black	2.25	5.25
37	A5	50c gray & black	2.90	1.10
38	A5	75c olive grn & blk	2.25	17.50
39	A6	1sh green & black	4.75	3.25
40	A6	2sh violet brn & blk	22.50	5.25
41	A6	3sh black	26.00	70.00
42	A6	5sh scarlet & blk	22.50	21.00
43	A6	10sh ultra & black	62.50	110.00
44	A6	£1 brown org & blk	175.00	350.00
		Nos. 29-44 (16)	366.40	589.75

TANNU TUVA

ˈtä-nə ˈtü-və

(Tuva People's Republic)

LOCATION — Between Siberia and northwestern Mongolia at the sources of the Yenisei, in the basin formed by the Tannu-Ola and Sayan Mountains.
GOVT. — A republic closely identified with Soviet Russia in Asia
AREA — 64,000 sq. mi. (approx.)
POP. — 95,000 (1941 est.)
CAPITAL — Kyzyl

This region, traditionally called Uriankhai, was ruled by the Mongols until the mid-18th century, when it became part of the Chinese Empire. Russia and China struggled for control of the country 1914-21, until it became independent as the Tannu Tuva People's Republic in 1921. In 1944 it was incorporated into the U.S.S.R. as an autonomous region of the Russian Soviet Federated Socialist Republic.

Russian, later Soviet, stamps were used in Tuva prior to 1926 and after 1944.

100 Mongo=1 Tugrik
100 Kopecks = 1 Ruble
100 Kopecks = 1 Tugrik (1934)
100 Kopecks = 1 Aksha (1936)

Watermarks

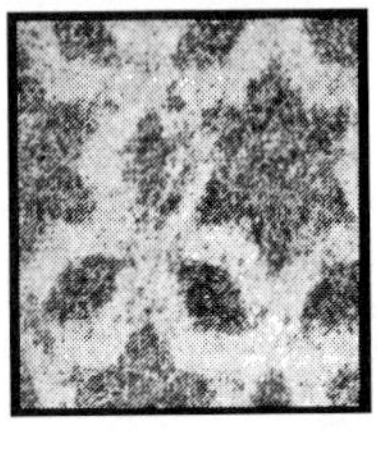

Wmk. 204 — Stars and Diamonds

Wmk. 170 — Greek Border and Rosettes

Values for covers are for properly franked covers with correct rates, usually addressed to Moscow. Because most have philatelic addresses, some leeway in proper rates is to be expected, and covers that vary slightly from proper rates are generally accepted as commercial covers.

For valuation of covers with multiple franking, see "Catalogue Values for Stamps on Covers" in the Introduction to this catalogue.

Most used examples of Nos. 1-38, 45-52a, 54-92 and C1-C18 on the market are cancelled to order, and the used values below are for such stamps.

Tuvan stamps, except for Nos. 117-123 and most of the overprints, were printed by the State Security Printers in Moscow.

Wheel of Truth — A1

1926 Litho. Wmk. 204 *Perf. 13½*
Size: 20x26mm

1	A1	1k red	1.25	1.00
		Never hinged	2.50	
		Postal cancel		1.60
		On cover		250.00
2	A1	2k light blue	1.50	1.00
		Never hinged	3.00	
		Postal cancel		1.50
		On cover		250.00
3	A1	5k orange	1.50	1.00
		Never hinged	3.00	
		Postal cancel		1.50
		On cover		250.00
4	A1	8k yel green	1.75	1.00
		Never hinged	3.50	
		Postal cancel		1.50
		On cover		250.00
5	A1	10k violet	2.00	1.00
		Never hinged	4.00	
		Postal cancel		1.50
		On cover		250.00
6	A1	30k dark brown	1.75	1.00
		Never hinged	3.50	
		Postal cancel		1.50
		On cover		250.00
7	A1	50k gray black	2.00	1.25
		Never hinged	4.00	
		Postal cancel		2.00
		On cover		250.00

Size: 22½x30mm
Perf. 10½

8	A1	1r blue green	5.50	2.50
		Never hinged	11.00	
		Postal cancel		7.50
		On cover		400.00
9	A1	3r red brown	8.00	4.00
		Never hinged	16.00	
		Postal cancel		8.00
		On cover		—
10	A1	5r dark ultra	13.50	6.00
		Never hinged	27.00	
		Postal cancel		13.50
		On cover		—
a.		Imperf, pair	180.00	
		Nos. 1-10 (10)	38.75	19.75
		Set, never hinged	77.50	

Nos. 1-10 have crackled white gum. Reprints can be distinguished by their smooth gum.

Nos. 1-10 in different colors are proofs.

Nos. 7-10 Surcharged in Red or Black

Surcharged in Kyzyl.

1927 *Perf. 13½*

11	A1	8k on 50k	25.00	12.50
		Never hinged	50.00	
		Postal cancel		27.50
		On cover		275.00
a.		Inverted surcharge	65.00	
b.		Double surcharge	100.00	

Perf. 10½

12	A1	14k on 1r	25.00	12.50
		Never hinged	50.00	
		Postal cancel		30.00
		On cover		350.00
a.		Inverted surcharge	75.00	
b.		Double surcharge	85.00	
13	A1	18k on 3r (Bk)	25.00	12.50
		Never hinged	50.00	
		Postal cancel		30.00
		On cover		350.00
a.		Inverted surcharge	90.00	
b.		Double surcharge	75.00	
14	A1	28k on 5r (Bk)	25.00	12.50
		Never hinged	50.00	
		Postal cancel		30.00
		On cover		350.00
a.		Inverted surcharge	90.00	
b.		Double surcharge	75.00	
		Nos. 11-14 (4)	100.00	50.00
		Set, never hinged	200.00	

Nos. 11-14 were surcharged with a shiny ink. Reprints are overprinted with a dull ink and are often smudged.

Tuvan Woman — A3

Map of Tannu Tuva A8

Sheep Herding — A11

Fording a Stream — A13

Tuvan Riding Reindeer — A16

Designs: 2k, Stag. 3k, Mountain goat. 4k, Tuvan and tent. 5k, Tuvan man. 10k, Archery competition. 14k, Camel caravan. 28k, Landscape. 50k, Weaving. 70k, Tuvan on horseback.

Printed in Moscow.

1927 Litho. *Perf. 12½*

15	A3	1k black, lt brown & red	1.00	.60
		Never hinged	2.00	
		Postal cancel		2.00
		On cover		125.00

16 A3 2k purple, dp brown & green 1.20 .55
Never hinged 2.40
Postal cancel 2.00
On cover 125.00
17 A3 3k black, bl grn & yellow 2.00 .60
Never hinged 4.00
Postal cancel 3.00
On cover 125.00
18 A3 4k vio bl & choc .90 .60
Never hinged 1.80
Postal cancel 1.50
On cover 125.00
19 A3 5k org, blk & dk bl .90 .65
Never hinged 1.80
Postal cancel 1.80
On cover 125.00

Perf. 12½x12

20 A8 8k ol brn, pale bl & red brn 1.00 .65
Never hinged 2.00
Postal cancel 1.00
On cover 150.00
21 A8 10k black, green & brn red 5.50 1.00
Never hinged 11.00
Postal cancel 1.50
On cover 200.00
22 A8 14k vio bl & red org 10.00 3.50
Never hinged 20.00
Postal cancel 5.00
On cover, *from* 150.00

Perf. 10½

23 A11 18k dk bl & red brn 10.00 5.00
Never hinged 20.00
Postal cancel 10.00
On cover, *from* 225.00
a. Perf 10 *70.00* *70.00*
Never hinged *140.00*
b. Perf compound 10, 10½ 15.00 8.00
Never hinged 30.00
Postal cancel 15.00
24 A11 28k emer & blk brn 7.25 2.75
Never hinged 14.50
Postal cancel 4.50
On cover, *from* 200.00
25 A13 40k rose & bl grn 5.00 2.50
Never hinged 10.00
Postal cancel 5.00
On cover, *from* 275.00
a. Perf 10 8.50 4.00
Never hinged 17.00
Postal cancel —
b. Perf 10x10½ 9.00 5.00
Never hinged 18.00
Postal cancel —
26 A13 50k black, green & red brown 3.50 2.00
Never hinged 7.00
Postal cancel 7.00
On cover, *from* 275.00
a. Perf 10 5.00 2.75
Never hinged 10.00
Postal cancel 5.00
b. Perf 10x10½ 7.00 3.75
Never hinged 14.00
Postal cancel 7.00
27 A13 70k dl red & bis 7.00 4.00
Never hinged 14.00
Postal cancel 10.00
On cover, *from* 350.00
28 A16 1r yel brn & vio 16.00 6.75
Never hinged 32.00
Postal cancel 20.00
On cover, *from* 350.00
Nos. 15-28 (14) 71.25 31.15
Set, never hinged 142.50

Nos. 15-28 were issued with a crackled white gum. Reprints of the 1k-5k values exist and can be distinguished by their smooth gum.

Nos. 15-28 in different colors are proofs.

Nos. 25-27, 20-22 Surcharged "Tuva", "Posta" and New Values in Various Colors

Surcharged in Moscow.

1932

29 A13 1k on 40k (Bk) 9.00 *10.00*
Never hinged 18.00
Postal cancel 30.00
On cover *175.00*
a. Perf 10 10.00 10.00
Never hinged 20.00
Postal cancel —
b. Perf 10x10½ 10.00 10.00
Never hinged 20.00
Postal cancel —
30 A13 2k on 50k (Br) 10.00 10.00
Never hinged 20.00
Postal cancel 30.00
On cover *175.00*
a. Perf 10 10.00 *20.00*
Never hinged 20.00
Postal cancel 30.00
b. Perf 10x10½ 45.00 25.00
Never hinged 90.00
Postal cancel 35.00
31 A13 3k on 70k (Bl) 10.00 10.00
Never hinged 20.00
Postal cancel 25.00
On cover *175.00*
a. Inverted surcharge *300.00*
Never hinged *600.00*
32 A8 5k on 8k (Bk) 10.00 10.00
Never hinged 20.00
Postal cancel 25.00
On cover *175.00*
33 A8 10k (Bk) 10.00 10.00
Never hinged 20.00
Postal cancel 25.00
On cover *175.00*
34 A8 15k on 14k (Bk) 15.00 15.00
Never hinged 30.00
Postal cancel 25.00
On cover *175.00*
Nos. 29-34 (6) 64.00 65.00
Set, never hinged 128.00
#29-34 on philatelic cover *300.00*

Issued in connection with the Romanization of the alphabet.

No. 31 with black surcharge was prepared but not issued.

#20//24 Surcharged in Black

Surcharged by numbering machine in Kyzyl.

No. 37

No. 38

1932-33 **Wmk. 204**

35 A8 10k on 8k 180.00 100.00
Never hinged 350.00
Postal cancel 300.00
36 A8 15k on 14k 300.00 200.00
Never hinged 600.00
Postal cancel 600.00
37 A11 35k on 18k (#23) 140.00 100.00
Never hinged 275.00
Postal cancel 140.00
On cover —
a. Perf 10 (#23a) 150.00 150.00
Never hinged 300.00
Postal cancel —
b. Pair, one without surcharge —
c. Inverted surcharge *500.00*
38 A11 35k on 28k 140.00 100.00
Never hinged 275.00
Postal cancel 140.00
On cover —
a. Pair, one without surcharge —
Nos. 35-38 (4) 760.00 500.00
Set, never hinged 1,550.

— A19

Three types: type 1, figures of value 6.7mm high; type 2, figures of value 6.7mm high, letter "p" lengthened at bottom; type 3, figures of value 5.1mm high.

Surcharged in Kyzyl.

1933 ***Perf. 12x12½***

39 A19 15k on 6k org yel, type 1 300.00 150.00
On cover —
a. "Posta" omitted — —
40 A19 15k on 6k org yel, type 2 300.00 150.00
On cover —
a. "Posta" omitted — —
b. Inverted surcharge — —
41 A19 15k on 6k org yel, type 3 500.00 300.00
On cover —
42 A19 35k on 15k red brn, type 1 — *4,000.*
On cover —
43 A19 35k on 15k red brn, type 2 — *4,000.*
On cover —
44 A19 35k on 15k red brn, type 3 *1,500.* 800.00
On cover —

Mounted Hunter — A20

Tuvan Inside of Yurt — A21

Tuvan Milking Yak — A22

Designs: 2k, Hunter stalking game. 4k, Tractor. 10k, Camel caravan. 15k, Herdsman lassoing reindeer. 20k, Hunter shooting fox with arrow.

Two dies on 10k: Die I, Crown at center top is light and matches the shade of the sky below; Die II, Crown at center top is bold, consistent with rest of design and darker than the sky.

Printed by State Security Printers, Moscow.

Wmk. 170

1934, Apr. **Photo.** ***Perf. 12***

45 A20 1k red orange 1.25 1.00
Never hinged 4.00
Postal cancel 2.00
On cover 100.00
46 A20 2k olive green 1.25 1.00
Never hinged 10.00
Postal cancel 6.00
On cover 100.00
47 A21 3k rose red 1.25 1.00
Never hinged 5.00
Postal cancel 1.50
On cover 100.00
48 A21 4k slate purple 3.00 1.75
Never hinged 6.00
Postal cancel 3.00
On cover 100.00
49 A22 5k ultramarine 3.00 1.75
Never hinged 8.00
Postal cancel 2.50
On cover 100.00
50 A22 10k brown, die II 3.00 1.75
Never hinged 10.00
Postal cancel 8.00
On cover 125.00
a. Perf 13¾ 25.00 —
b. Perf 11 — —
c. 10k brown, die I 8.00 2.00
Never hinged 16.00
Postal cancel 8.00
On cover 150.00
51 A22 15k dark lilac 3.00 1.75
Never hinged 14.00
Postal cancel 3.50
On cover 100.00
52 A22 20k gray black 4.00 2.75
Never hinged 20.00
Postal cancel 4.00
On cover 100.00
Nos. 45-52 (8) 19.75 12.75
Set, never hinged 50.00

Imperf

45a A20 1k red orange 2.25 1.50
Never hinged 4.50
Postal cancel 4.00
On cover 100.00
46a A20 2k olive green 10.00 6.50
Never hinged 20.00
Postal cancel 13.50
On cover —
47a A21 3k rose red 2.25 1.25
Never hinged 4.50
Postal cancel 4.00
On cover 100.00
48a A21 4k slate purple 4.00 1.75
Never hinged 8.00
Postal cancel 4.50
On cover 100.00
49a A22 5k ultramarine 4.00 2.00
Never hinged 8.00
Postal cancel 5.25
On cover 125.00
50d A22 10k brown, die II 5.00 3.50
Never hinged 10.00
Postal cancel 8.00
On cover 150.00
e. 10k brown, die I 8.50
Never hinged 18.00
Postal cancel 10.00
On cover 200.00
51a A22 15k dark lilac 5.00 3.50
Never hinged 10.00
Postal cancel 7.00
On cover 150.00
52a A22 20k gray black 17.50 6.00
Never hinged 35.00
Postal cancel 20.00
On cover —
Nos. 45a-52a (8) 50.00 26.00
Set, never hinged 135.00

Nos. 45-52a are inscribed "REGISTERED," but were used as regular postage stamps.

Nos. 46, 48 and 50 exist perf 11, and No. 50 also exists perf 11x10. No. 48 exists perf 11½, reportedly as a color trial proof.

#51 Surcharged in Black

Surcharged by numbering machine in Kyzyl.

1935

53 A22 20k on 15k *175.00* *325.00*
a. Inverted surcharge *400.00*

Map of Tuva — A23

Rocky Outcropping — A24

Designs: 3k, 5k, 10k, Different scenes of Yenisei River. 25k, Bei-kem rapids. 50k, Mounted hunters.

Printed by State Security Printers, Moscow.

Wmk. 170

1935, Mar. **Photo.** ***Perf. 14***

54 A23 1k yellow orange 1.20 .90
Never hinged 2.50
Postal cancel 1.50
On cover 100.00
55 A23 3k deep green 1.20 .90
Never hinged 2.50
Postal cancel 3.00
On cover 100.00
56 A23 5k carmine red 1.50 1.00
Never hinged 3.00
Postal cancel 1.50
On cover 100.00
57 A23 10k violet 1.60 1.00
Never hinged 3.50
Postal cancel 2.00
On cover 100.00
a. Perf 14x10x14 *35.00*
b. Pair, imperf between —
58 A24 15k olive green 1.75 1.25
Never hinged 3.50
Postal cancel 2.00
On cover 100.00
59 A24 25k violet blue 2.00 1.25
Never hinged 4.00
Postal cancel 2.00
On cover 100.00
60 A24 50k dark brown 3.00 1.50
Never hinged 6.00
Postal cancel 4.00
On cover 150.00
Nos. 54-60 (7) 12.25 7.80
Set, never hinged 25.00

Nos. 54-60 in different colors, perf and imperf, are proofs.

Badger
A25

Squirrel — A26

Fox — A27

Elk — A28

Yak — A29

Designs: 5k, Ermine. 25k, Otter. 50k, Lynx. 3t, Bactrian camels. 5t, Bear.

Printed by State Security Printers, Moscow.

1935, Mar.

61 A25 1k orange 1.60 1.00
Never hinged 3.25
Postal cancel 2.00
On cover 100.00
62 A26 3k emerald green 1.60 1.00
Never hinged 3.25
Postal cancel 2.00
On cover 100.00
a. Imperf, pair 300.00
63 A25 5k rose red 1.60 1.10
Never hinged 4.00
Postal cancel 2.00
On cover 100.00
64 A27 10k crimson red 1.60 1.10
Never hinged 5.00
Postal cancel 2.50
On cover 100.00
65 A27 25k orange red 2.50 1.20
Never hinged 5.00
Postal cancel 3.00
On cover 100.00
66 A27 50k deep blue 2.50 1.20
Never hinged 6.00
Postal cancel 3.50
On cover 125.00
67 A28 1t violet 2.50 1.20
Never hinged 8.00
a. Pair, imperf between —
68 A29 2t royal blue 3.50 1.20
Never hinged 7.00
69 A29 3t red brown 4.00 1.35
Never hinged 8.00
70 A28 5t indigo 5.00 1.75
Never hinged 10.00
a. Imperf, pair 300.00
b. Pair, imperf between —
Nos. 61-70 (10) 26.40 12.10
Set, never hinged 50.00

Nos. 61-70 in different colors are proofs.

Tuvan Arms — A30

Wrestlers — A31

Herdsman on Bull — A32

Athletic Competitions — A33

Soldiers A34

Designs: 2k, Pres. Ch(aumlaut char='u')rmit-Dazhy. 3k, Tuvan with Bactrian camel. 5k, 8k, Archer. 10k, 15k, Spearfishing. 12k, 20k, Bear-hunting. 30k, Camel and train. 40k, 50k, Horse race. 80k, Partisans. 3t, Partisans confiscating cattle. 5t, 1921 battle scene.

Printed by State Security Printers, Moscow.

1936, July ***Perf. 14***

71 A30 1k bronze green 1.50 .70
Never hinged 3.00
Postal cancel 2.00
On cover 90.00
72 A30 2k dark brown 2.00 1.50
Never hinged 4.00
Postal cancel 3.00
On cover 100.00
74 A31 4k orange red — 35.00
On cover
75 A31 5k brown purple 4.00 .70
Never hinged 8.00
Postal cancel 2.50
On cover 90.00
76 A31 6k myrtle green 3.75 .70
Never hinged 7.50
Postal cancel 3.00
On cover 90.00
77 A31 8k plum 3.75 .70
Never hinged 7.50
Postal cancel 3.00
On cover 90.00
78 A31 10k rose red 4.25 1.00
Never hinged 8.50
Postal cancel 2.50
On cover 90.00
79 A31 12k black brown 5.00 1.25
Never hinged 10.00
Postal cancel 4.00
On cover 90.00
80 A31 15k bronze green 7.00 1.50
Never hinged 14.00
Postal cancel 7.00
On cover 100.00
81 A31 20k deep blue 6.00 1.20
Never hinged 12.00
Postal cancel 3.00
On cover 90.00
82 A32 25k orange red 6.00 1.20
Never hinged 12.00
Postal cancel 6.00
On cover 100.00
83 A32 30k plum 18.00 1.25
Never hinged 36.00
Postal cancel 6.00
On cover 100.00
84 A32 35k rose red 6.00 1.50
Never hinged 12.00
Postal cancel 4.00
On cover 100.00
85 A32 40k deep brown 6.00 1.50
Never hinged 12.00
Postal cancel 6.00
On cover 100.00
86 A32 50k indigo blue 35.00 35.00
Never hinged 70.00
Postal cancel —
On cover —
87 A33 70k plum 7.25 2.00
Never hinged 14.50
Postal cancel 5.00
On cover 125.00
88 A33 80k green 7.00 2.00
Never hinged 14.00
Postal cancel 5.00
On cover 250.00
89 A34 1a orange red 7.00 2.00
Never hinged 14.00
Postal cancel 4.00
On cover 125.00
a. 1a rose red (error) — —
90 A34 2a rose red 7.00 3.00
Never hinged 14.00
Postal cancel 10.00
On cover 250.00
92 A33 5a black brown 7.25 2.50
Never hinged 14.50
Postal cancel 20.00
On cover 300.00

Perf. 11

72a A30 2k dark brown — 50.00
73 A30 3k indigo blue 2.00 .75
Never hinged 4.00
Postal cancel 2.50
74a A31 4k orange red 2.50 .75
Never hinged 5.00
Postal cancel 3.00
75a A31 5k brown purple 35.00 —
Never hinged 70.00
Postal cancel —
76a A31 6k myrtle green 4.00 .75
Never hinged 8.00
Postal cancel 3.00
78a A31 10k rose red 4.50 .75
Never hinged 9.00
Postal cancel 2.00
On cover 90.00
80a A31 15k bronze green 6.00 1.25
Never hinged 12.00
Postal cancel 6.00
81a A31 20k deep blue — —
82a A32 25k orange red 6.00 .90
Never hinged 12.00
Postal cancel 3.00
84a A32 35k rose red 6.00 1.25
Never hinged 12.00
Postal cancel 4.00
On cover —
85a A32 40k deep brown 6.00 1.50
Never hinged 12.00
Postal cancel 6.00
On cover 100.00
86a A32 50k indigo blue 6.00 1.50
Never hinged 12.00
Postal cancel 5.00
On cover
87a A33 70k plum 8.00 2.50
Never hinged 17.00
Postal cancel 8.00
88a A33 80k green 8.00 2.50
Never hinged 16.00
Postal cancel 8.00
89b A34 1a orange red 8.00 3.00
Never hinged 16.00
Postal cancel 8.00
90a A34 2a rose red 10.00 3.00
Never hinged 20.00
Postal cancel 10.00
91 A33 3a indigo blue 15.00 2.00
Never hinged 30.00
Postal cancel 15.00
Set of 22, cheapest vars. 129.50 30.15
Set of 22, never hinged 260.00

15th anniversary of independence.

Imperfs are remainders, later sold by the Soviet Postal Museum.

Values for Nos. 93-98 and 104-116 are for genuine examples. Expertization is essential for these issues.

Issues of 1934-36 Handstamped with Large Numerals and Old Values Obliterated with Bars or Blocks

1938, Aug.

93 A34 5k on 2a (#90a) *300.00*
94 AP5 5k on 2a (#C17) *225.00*
95 AP1 10k on 1t (#C8) *200.00*
96 A24 20k on 50k (#60) *200.00*
On cover —
97 AP5 30k on 2a (#C17) *200.00*
98 AP5 30k on 3a (#C18) *175.00*

Types of 1935-36 with Modified Designs and New Colors

1938, Dec. Unwmk. ***Perf. 12½***

99 A25 5k deep green 60.00 —
Never hinged *90.00*
100 A31 10k indigo (dates removed) 60.00 —
Never hinged *90.00*
101 AP3 15k red brown ("AIR MAIL," dates removed) 60.00 —
Never hinged *90.00*
102 A31 20k orange red (dates removed) 85.00 —
Never hinged *140.00*
103 A33 30k maroon (dates removed) 60.00 —
Never hinged *90.00*
Nos. 99-103 (5) 325.00
Set, never hinged 500.00

Some experts believe that these stamps were issued in March 1941.

A few commercial covers exist, dated between 1941 and 1943.

Stamps of 1934-35 Handstamp Surcharged with New Values in Black or Violet at Kyzyl

1939

104 AP1 10k on 1t (#C8) 225.00
a. 10k on 1t, #C8a —
105 AP1 10k on 1t (#B8) (V) 225.00
106 A24 20k on 50k (#60) (V) 200.00
On cover —

Old values obliterated on Nos. 104-106.

Stamps of 1934-36 Handstamp Surcharged with New Values at Kyzyl

1940, Oct.-1941

107 AP1 10k on 1t (#C8) — 90.00
a. Double surcharge — —
108 A24 20k on 50k (#60) 100.00
109 A27 20k on 50k (#66) 300.00
110 A32 20k on 50k (#86a) 300.00
111 AP4 20k on 50k (#C14) 65.00
112 A33 20k on 70k (#87a) —
113 AP4 20k on 75k (#C15) 75.00
114 A33 20k on 80k (#88) — *500.00*

The old values are not obliterated on Nos. 107 or 108.

Nos. 91, 92 Handstamp Surcharged with New Values at Kyzyl

1942

115 A33 25k on 3a (#91) 1,200. —
116 A33 25k on 5a (#92) —

Government House — A35

Exhibition Hall — A36

Tuvan Woman — A37

1942 Typo. Unwmk. ***Imperf.***

117 A35 25k steel blue 750.00 100.00
118 A36 25k steel blue 750.00 100.00
119 A37 25k steel blue 750.00 150.00
Nos. 117-119 (3) 2,250. 350.00

21st anniversary of independence.

Nos. 117-119 were hand-printed together in small sheetlets of five (117+119+118+117+119), so various se-tenant combinations are possible. Value, pane $2,000.

Two additional values, a 25k depicting a Tuvan man and a 50k depicting a soldier on a horse, were prepared, but not issued. A collective proof sheetlet of five, containing Nos. 117-119 and these two values, in the same color as the issued stamps, is also known.

Coat of Arms — A38

Government Building — A39

1943 ***Perf. 11 (1 or 2 Sides)***

Buff Paper

120	A38 25k slate blue	—	—
	Vertical strip of 5	900.00	
121	A38 25k black	100.00	—
	Vertical strip of 5	600.00	
122	A38 25k blue green	90.00	—
123	A39 50k blue green	90.00	—
	Vertical pair, 122 + 123	175.00	
	Nos. 120-123 (3)	280.00	

White Paper

120a	A38 25k slate blue	90.00	—
b.	Strip of 3, imperf between	*250.00*	
	Sheet of 5	500.00	
121a	A38 25k black	125.00	—
	Vertical strip of five	600.00	
122a	A38 25k blue green	95.00	—
123a	A39 50k blue green	95.00	—
	With gum	*175.00*	
	Nos. 120a-123a (4)	405.00	

22nd anniversary of independence.

Nos. 120 and 121 were each printed in vertical strips of five, perforated 11 between stamps and imperf on outside edges, so that these stamps may be perforated on top edge only, bottom edge only, or on both top and bottom edges. To make maximum use of limited wartime paper supplies, they were sometimes printed in strips of four. These smaller strips are rare.

Nos. 122 and 123 were printed together in blocks of four, containing a vertical pair of the 25k and a vertical pair of the 50k, perforated internally both vertically and horizontally and imperf on the outer edges. Setenant pairs, Value $225 (#122+123), $275 (#122a+123a).

Nos. 121 and 123a were issued with gum, No. 123a both with and without gum, and the balance of the set without gum.

Used examples and covers exist but are extremely rare.

AIR POST STAMPS

Airplane and Yaks — AP1

Airplane and Capercaillie — AP2

Designs, airplane over: 5k, 15k, Camels. 25k, Argali (wild sheep). 75k, Ox and cart. 2t, Roe deer.

Tuvan Leading Laden Yak — AP3

Horseman and Zeppelin AP4

Seaplane Above Dragon — AP5

Designs: 10k, Tuvan plowing. 50k, Villagers with biplane overhead.

Printed by State Security Printers, Moscow.

Printed by State Security Printers, Moscow.

Wmk. 170

1934, Apr. 4 **Photo.** ***Perf. 14***

C1	AP1 1k orange red	1.40	1.00
	Never hinged	5.00	
	Postal cancel		2.50
	On cover		*100.00*
C2	AP1 5k emer green	1.40	1.00
	Never hinged	5.00	
	Postal cancel		2.50
	On cover		*100.00*
C3	AP2 10k purple brown	4.50	3.00
	Never hinged	9.00	
	Postal cancel		3.00
	On cover		*100.00*
C4	AP1 15k rose red	2.75	1.00
	Never hinged	6.00	
	Postal cancel		3.00
	On cover		*100.00*
C5	AP2 25k slate purple	2.75	1.00
	Never hinged	6.00	
	Postal cancel		3.50
	On cover		*100.00*
C6	AP1 50k dp bl green	2.75	1.00
	Never hinged	6.00	
	Postal cancel		4.00
	On cover		*100.00*
C7	AP2 75k lake	2.75	1.00
	Never hinged	6.00	
	Postal cancel		4.00
	On cover		*100.00*
C8	AP1 1t royal blue	3.50	2.00
	Never hinged	5.00	
	Postal cancel		5.00
	On cover		*100.00*
a.	Perf 12½	77.50	—
	Never hinged	155.00	
C9	AP2 2t ultra, 61x31mm	20.00	*25.00*
	Never hinged	40.00	
	Postal cancel		40.00
	On cover		—
a.	54.5x29mm	40.00	—
	Never hinged	80.00	
	Nos. C1-C9 (9)	41.80	36.00
	Set, never hinged	55.00	

Nos. C1-C9 imperf or perf 11½ and stamps printed in different colors are proofs.

1936 **Unwmk.**

C10	AP3 5k indigo & beige	2.00	1.50
	Never hinged	4.00	
	Postal cancel		2.00
	On cover		*100.00*
C11	AP3 10k purple & cinnamon	3.00	1.50
	Never hinged	6.00	
	Postal cancel		2.00
	On cover		*100.00*
C12	AP3 15k black brown & pale gray	3.00	1.50
	Never hinged	6.00	
	Postal cancel		2.00
	On cover		*100.00*
C13	AP4 25k plum & cream	5.00	2.00
	Never hinged	10.00	
	Postal cancel		5.00
	On cover		*100.00*
a.	Perf 11	4.50	2.00
	Never hinged	9.00	
	Postal cancel		4.50
b.	Perf compound 14x11		—
c.	Horiz. pair, perf 11, imperf between	—	—
C14	AP4 50k rose red & cream	5.00	2.00
	Never hinged	10.00	
	Postal cancel		7.50
	On cover		*125.00*
C15	AP4 75k emer grn & pale yellow	5.00	2.00
	Never hinged	10.00	
	Postal cancel		10.00
	On cover		*200.00*
C16	AP5 1a blue green & pale bl grn	8.00	4.00
	Never hinged	16.00	
	Postal cancel		—
	On cover		—
C17	AP5 2a rose red & cream	7.50	3.00
	Never hinged	15.00	
	Postal cancel		30.00
	On cover		*350.00*
C18	AP5 3a dark brown & beige	8.00	3.00
	Never hinged	16.00	
	Postal cancel		35.00
	On cover		*400.00*
	Nos. C10-C18 (9)	46.50	20.50
	Set, never hinged	93.00	

15th anniversary of independence.

Nos. C10-C18 exist imperf.

TASMANIA

taz-ˈmā-nē-ə

LOCATION — An island off the southeastern coast of Australia
GOVT. — British Colony
AREA — 26,215 sq. mi.
POP. — 172,475 (1901)
CAPITAL — Hobart

Tasmania was one of the six British colonies that united in 1901 to form the Commonwealth of Australia. The island was originally named Van Diemen's Land by its discoverer, Abel Tasman, the present name having been adopted in 1853. Stamps of Australia are now used.

12 Pence = 1 Shilling
20 Shillings = 1 Pound

Watermarks

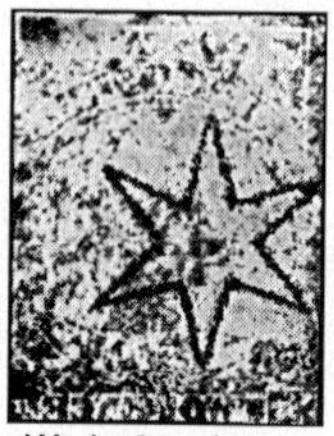

Wmk. 6 — Large Star

Wmk. 49 — Double-lined Numeral

Wmk. 75 — Double-lined Numeral

Wmk. 50 — Single-lined "2"

Wmk. 51 — Single-lined "4"

Wmk. 52 — Single-lined "10"

Wmk. 70 — V and Crown

Wmk. 13 — Crown & Double-lined A

Wmk. 76 — TAS

Wmk. 77 — TAS

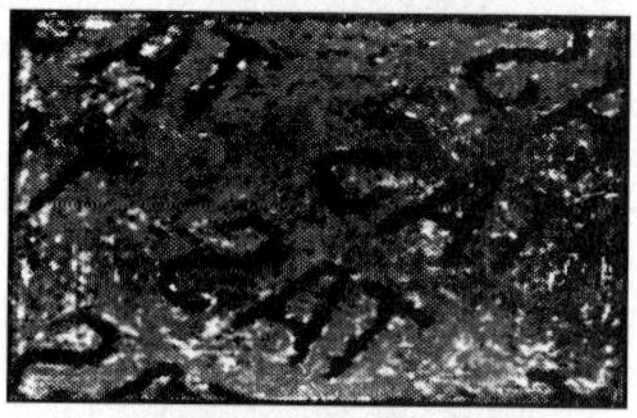

Wmk. 78 — Multiple TAS

Values for unused stamps are for examples with original gum as defined in the catalogue introduction except for Nos. 1-2b and 10 which are valued without gum as few examples exist with any remaining original gum. Very fine examples of Nos. 17-75a will have perforations touching the design on one or more sides due to the narrow spacing of the stamps on the plates. Stamps with perfs clear of the design on all four sides are scarce and command higher prices.

Queen Victoria
A1 A2

Unwmk.

1853, Nov. 1 **Engr.** ***Imperf.***

1	A1 1p blue, fine impression, soft paper	5,750.	1,300.
a.	1p blue, blurred impression, hard paper	5,750.	1,200.
2	A2 4p red orange	3,250.	500.00
a.	4p yellow orange	3,250.	500.00
	Cut to shape		40.00
b.	4p orange, blurred impression ('55)	2,300.	450.00
	Cut to shape		17.50

Twenty-four varieties of each.

No. 1 is the first printing, which was printed on a solt yellowish paper. Background lines are clear and distinct. The second printing, No. 1a, was made on thin hard white paper and demonstrates a wearing of the plate, with blurred background lines.

Two plates were made for No. 2. Plate I (Nos. 2, 2a) is finely engraved, with all lines clear ans sharp. Plate II (No. 2b) is more coarsely done, with blurred impressions and thicker background lines.

The 4p on vertically laid paper is believed to be a proof. Value, unused, $7,500.

The reprints are made from defaced plates and show marks across the face of each stamp. They are on thin and thick, unwatermarked paper and thin cardboard; only the first are perforated. Nearly all the reprints of Tasmania may be found with and without the overprint "REPRINT."

Nos. 1-47A with pen or revenue cancellations sell for a small fraction of the price of postally used specimens. Copies are found with pen cancellation removed.

Queen Victoria — A3

1855 Wmk. 6 Wove Paper
4 A3 1p dark carmine 6,000. 1,050.
5 A3 2p green 2,900. 600.00
 a. 2p deep green 2,900. 675.00
6 A3 4p deep blue 2,100. 130.00
 a. 4p blue 2,100. 150.00

1856-57 Unwmk.
7 A3 1p pale red 7,250. 775.00
8 A3 2p emerald ('57) 8,500. 1,200.
9 A3 4p blue ('57) 850.00 130.00
 a. 4p deep blue ('57) 1,100. 130.00
 b. 4p pale blue ('57) — 160.00

1856 Pelure Paper
10 A3 1p brown red 6,000. 900.00

1857 Wmk. 49, 75
11 A3 1p carmine 160.00 50.00
 a. 1p orange red 225.00 40.00
 b. 1p brown red 575.00 42.50
 c. Double impression 185.00
 d. 1p brick red 250.00 50.00
 e. Wmk. 50 (error) ('69) —
12 A3 2p sage green 250.00 100.00
 a. 2p yellow green 475.00 110.00
 b. 2p green — 62.50
 c. 2p dull emerald green 130.00
 d. As "b," double impression 225.00
13 A3 4p pale blue 200.00 29.00
 a. 4p blue 200.00 32.00
 b. Printed on both sides —
 c. 4p deep blue — 125.00
 d. As "a," double impression 225.00
 e. As "c," double impression 225.00
 g. 4p cobalt blue — 100.00
 Nos. 11-13 (3) 610.00

See #17-19, 23-25, 29-31, 35-37, 39-41, 45-47A.

A4

A4a

1858-67
14 A4 6p gray lilac 550.00 72.50
 a. 6p red violet 925.00 200.00
 b. Double impression 400.00
 c. 6p dull lilac 925.00 110.00
15 A4 6p blue gray 575.00 90.00
16 A4a 1sh vermilion 725.00 100.00
 Nos. 14-16 (3) 1,850. 262.50

No. 15 watermarked large star was not regularly issued.
Issued: #14c, 16, 1/58; #14, 4/63; #15, 2/65; #14a, 4/67.

1864 *Rouletted*
17 A3 1p carmine 525.00 210.00
 a. 1p brick red — 300.00
18 A3 2p yellow grn — 800.00
19 A3 4p blue — 260.00
21 A4 6p gray lilac — 325.00
22 A4a 1sh vermilion — 950.00

1864-69 *Perf. 10*
23 A3 1p brick red 100.00 45.00
 a. 1p carmine 85.00 35.00
 b. 1p orange red 100.00 40.00
 c. As "b," double impression —
24 A3 2p yellow green 525.00 150.00
 a. 2p sage green 550.00 240.00
25 A3 4p blue 185.00 18.00
 a. Double impression 175.00
26 A4 6p lilac 290.00 26.00
 a. 6p red lilac 525.00 110.00
27 A4 6p slate blue 475.00 90.00
28 A4a 1sh vermilion 210.00 35.00
 a. Horiz. pair, imperf. vert.
 Nos. 23-28 (6) 1,785. 364.00

1864-69 *Perf. 12, 12½*
29 A3 1p carmine 92.50 20.00
 a. 1p orange red 100.00 35.00
 b. 1p brick red 110.00 42.50
 c. Double impression —
 d. Wmkd. "2" 1,800.
 As "d," pen cancel 140.00
30 A3 2p yellow green 260.00 77.50
 a. 2p dark green 425.00 160.00
 b. 2p sage green 425.00 160.00
31 A3 4p blue 150.00 26.00

Perf. 11½, 12½
32 A4 6p red lilac 37.50 17.00
 a. 6p purple 125.00 40.00
 b. 6p violet 90.00 35.00
 d. Horiz. pair, imperf. vert. —
 e. Double impression —
33 A4 6p slate blue, perf. 12½ 425.00 110.00
34 A4a 1sh vermilion 210.00 50.00
 a. Double impression 225.00
 b. Horiz. pair, imperf. vert. —
 Nos. 29-34 (6) 1,175. 300.50

The reprints are on unwatermarked paper, perforated 11½, and on thin cardboard, imperforate and perforated.

Pin-perf. 5½ to 9½, 13½ to 14½
1867
35 A3 1p carmine 650.00 175.00
36 A3 2p yellow green 575.00
37 A3 4p blue 325.00
38 A4 6p gray 300.00
38A A4 6p red lilac 800.00
38B A4a 1sh vermilion —

Oblique Roulette
39 A3 1p carmine 600.00
40 A3 2p yellow green 800.00
41 A3 4p blue 650.00
42 A4 6p gray 1,050.
43 A4 6p red lilac —
44 A4a 1sh vermilion 1,300.

1868 *Serrate Perf. 19*
45 A3 1p carmine 500.00 185.00
46 A3 2p yellow green 525.00
47 A3 4p blue 1,200. 170.00
47A A3 6p purple 725.00

Queen Victoria — A5

1870-71 Typo. Wmk. 50 *Perf. 11½*
48 A5 2p blue green 92.50 6.00
 a. Double impression —
 b. Perf. 12 110.00 9.25
 c. 2p green 170.00 9.25
 d. As "c," perf. 12 100.00 9.25
 e. As "d," imperf, pair —

See Nos. 49-75, 98, 108-109.

Wmk. 51
49 A5 1p rose ('71) 77.50 21.00
 a. Imperf., pair 850.00 850.00
50 A5 4p blue 975.00 550.00

Wmk. 52
51 A5 1p rose 52.50 12.50
 a. Imperf. pair 850.00 850.00
 c. Perf. 11½ 1,400.
52 A5 10p black 30.00 30.00
 a. Imperf. pair 400.00
 b. Perf. 11½ 35.00 35.00

The reprints are on unwatermarked paper. The 4p has also been reprinted on thin cardboard, imperf and perf.

1871-76 Wmk. 76 *Perf. 11½*
53 A5 1p rose 9.75 1.35
 a. Imperf.
 c. Perf. 12 115.00 11.50
53B A5 1p vermilion ('73) 325.00 95.00
54 A5 2p deep green ('72) 37.50 1.35
 a. 2p yellow green 210.00 4.00
 b. 2p blue green 40.00 1.75
 c. Imperf. pair 1,100.
 d. 2p green, perf. 12 725.00 180.00
 e. Double impression
55 A5 3p brown 62.50 5.25
 a. 3p purple brown 62.50 5.00
 b. As "a," imperf. pair 850.00
56 A5 3p red brown ('71) 62.50 5.25
 a. 3p indian red 62.50 5.50
 b. Imperf. pair 400.00
 c. Vert. pair, imperf. horiz.
 d. Perf. 12 120.00 21.00
57 A5 4p dull yellow ('76) 85.00 12.00
 a. Perf. 12 325.00 22.50
58 A5 9p blue 22.00 9.75
 a. Imperf. pair 325.00
 b. Perf. 12 37.50 37.50
59 A5 5sh bright violet 325.00 175.00
 a. Imperf.
 b. Horiz. pair, imperf. vert.
 c. Perf. 12 475.00 350.00
 Pen cancel 7.50
 Nos. 53-59 (8) 929.25 304.95

The reprints are on unwatermarked paper, the 5sh has also been reprinted on thin cardboard; all are perforated.

1878 Wmk. 77 *Perf. 14*
60 A5 1p rose 5.25 2.00
61 A5 2p deep green 6.25 2.00
62 A5 8p violet brown 21.00 10.00
 Nos. 60-62 (3) 32.50 14.00

The 8p has been reprinted on thin unwatermarked paper, perforated 11½.

1880-83 *Perf. 12, 11½*
63 A5 3p indian red, perf. 12 14.00 5.75
 a. Imperf. pair 260.00
 b. Horiz. pair, imperf. between 1,050.
 c. Perf. 11½ 17.50 5.00
64 A5 4p lem, perf. 11½ ('83) 60.00 30.00
 a. 4p olive yellow, perf. 11½ 150.00 30.00
 b. Printed on both sides 925.00
 c. Imperf.
 d. 4p deep yellow, perf. 12 100.00 17.50

Type of 1871 Surcharged in Black

1889 *Perf. 14*
65 A5 ½p on 1p carmine 20.00 *20.00*
 a. "al" sideways in surcharge 1,450. *1,200.*

No. 65 has been reprinted on thin cardboard, perforated 12, with the surcharge "Halfpenny" 19mm long.

1889-96 *Perf. 11½*
66 A5 ½p red orange 4.00 3.75
 a. ½p yellow orange 4.00 3.75
 b. Perf. 12 3.75 *5.00*
67 A5 1p dull red 8.00 3.25
 a. 1p vermilion 7.25 3.25
68 A5 1p car, perf. 12 18.00 4.25
 a. 1p pink, perf. 12 25.00 6.25
 b. 1p salmon rose, perf. 12 22.50 5.50
 c. Imperf. pair 240.00 *260.00*

Perf. 12
69 A5 4p bister ('96) 20.00 14.00
70 A5 9p chalky bl ('96) 11.00 5.00
 Nos. 66-70 (5) 61.00 30.25

1891 Wmk. 76 *Perf. 11½*
71 A5 ½p orange 40.00 24.00
 a. ½p brown orange 32.50 17.00
 b. Imperf. pair 175.00
 c. Perf. 12 32.50 25.00
72 A5 1p salmon rose 22.50 11.00
 a. 1p carmine, perf. 12 27.50 20.00
73 A5 4p ol bis, perf. 12 22.50 15.00
 Nos. 71-73 (3) 85.00 50.00

See Nos. 98, 108-109.

Surcharged in Black

1891 Wmk. 77 *Perf. 11½*
Surcharge 14mm High
74 A5 2½p on 9p lt blue 12.00 6.50
 a. Dbl. surcharge, one invtd. 550.00 *625.00*
 b. Imperf. pair —

Perf. 12
Surcharge 15mm High
75 A5 2½p on 9p lt blue 6.00 5.00
 a. Surcharged in blue 7.00 4.75

No. 74 has been reprinted on thin unwatermarked paper, imperforate. There is also a reprint on thin cardboard, in deep ultramarine, with surcharge 16½mm high, and perforated 12.

A8

A9

1892-99 Typo. *Perf. 14*
76 A8 ½p orange & vio 3.00 3.00
77 A9 2½p magenta 5.00 5.00
78 A8 5p pale bl & brn 8.25 5.00
79 A8 6p blue vio & blk 11.00 5.00
80 A8 10p red brn & grn ('99) 20.00 15.00
81 A8 1sh rose & green 11.00 5.00
82 A8 2sh6p brown & blue 35.00 25.00
83 A8 5sh brn vio & red 65.00 30.00
84 A8 10sh brt vio & brn 125.00 85.00
85 A8 £1 green & yel 600.00 350.00
 Nos. 76-85 (10) 883.25 528.00

No. 80 shows the numeral on white tablet.
See Nos. 99, 110-111.

Lake Marion — A10

Mt. Wellington — A11

View of Hobart — A12

Tasman's Arch — A13

Spring River, Port Davey — A14

Russell Falls — A15

Mt. Gould and Lake St. Clair — A16

Dilston Falls — A17

1899-1900 Engr. Wmk. 78 *Perf. 14*
86 A10 ½p dark green 11.50 8.50
87 A11 1p carmine 7.50 2.25
88 A12 2p violet 18.50 2.50
89 A13 2½p dark blue 24.00 12.00
90 A14 3p dark brown 13.50 6.25
91 A15 4p ocher 22.50 8.50

92 A16 5p ultramarine 35.00 20.00
93 A17 6p lake 32.50 26.00
Nos. 86-93 (8) 165.00 86.00

See Nos. 94-97, 102-107, 114-117.

Perf. 11, 12½, 11x12½

1902-03 Litho., Typo. Wmk. 70

94 A10 ½p green 5.75 2.00
95 A11 1p carmine 11.00 1.75
96 A11 1p dull red 16.00 2.25
97 A12 2p violet 10.00 1.00
98 A5 9p blue 11.00 5.00
a. 9p ultramarine 525.00
b. 9p indigo 210.00
c. Perf. 11 11.00 11.00
d. Perf 12½, wmkd. sideways 35.00 15.00
99 A8 1sh rose & green 21.00 7.50
a. Perf. 11 52.50 52.50
Nos. 94-99 (6) 74.75 19.50

Nos. 94, 97 are litho., Nos. 96, 98-99 typo. No. 95 was printed both ways.

No. 78 Surcharged in Black

1904 Wmk. 77 *Perf. 14*

100 A8 1½p on 5p blue & brn 2.00 2.00

Perf. 11, 12, 12½ and Compound

1905-08 Typo. Wmk. 13

102 A10 ½p dull green 3.00 .65
a. Booklet pane of 12
103 A11 1p carmine 2.50 .40
a. Booklet pane of 18
104 A12 2p violet 13.00 .40
105 A14 3p dark brown 11.00 6.25
106 A15 4p ocher 18.00 5.00
107 A17 6p lake 45.00 9.00
108 A5 8p violet brown 25.00 11.50
109 A5 9p blue 9.50 5.75
110 A8 1sh rose & green 17.50 6.50
111 A8 10sh brt vio & brn 200.00 *225.00*
a. Perf. 11 325.00
Nos. 102-111 (10) 344.50 270.45

Nos. 104-107 also printed litho.

1911 Redrawn

114 A12 2p bright violet 10.50 5.25
115 A15 4p dull yellow 50.00 50.00
116 A17 6p lake 25.00 *32.50*
Nos. 114-116 (3) 85.50 87.75

The redrawn 2p measures 33½x25mm instead of 32½x24½mm. There are many slight changes in the clouds and other parts of the design.

The 4p is much lighter, especially the waterfall and trees above it. This appears to be a new or cleaned plate rather than a redrawn one.

In the redrawn 6p there are more colored lines in the waterfall and the river and more white dots in the trees.

No. 114 Surcharged in Red

1912

117 A12 1p on 2p bright violet 2.00 2.00

FISCAL STAMPS

Authorised for postal use by Act of November 1, 1882. Authorization withdrawn Nov. 30, 1900.

Used values are for examples with postal cancellations used from Nov. 1, 1882 through Nov. 30, 1900.

Beware of copies with a pen cancellation removed, often regummed or with a fake postmark added.

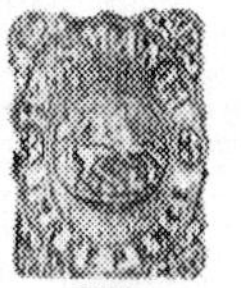

PF1

PF2

St. George and the Dragon
PF3 PF4

1863-80 Engr. Wmk. 139 *Imperf.*

AR1 PF1 3p green *700.00 425.00*
AR2 PF2 2sh 6p car *525.00 325.00*
AR3 PF3 5sh green *600.00 425.00*
AR4 PF3 5sh brown *500.00 425.00*
AR5 PF4 10sh salmon ('80) *550.00 475.00*
a. 10sh orange *825.00 475.00*

For overprint see No. AR32.

Perf. 10

AR6 PF1 3p green *325.00 200.00*
AR7 PF2 2sh 6p car *300.00*
AR8 PF3 5sh brown *475.00 325.00*
AR9 PF4 10sh orange *375.00*

Perf. 12

AR10 PF1 3p green *350.00 275.00*
AR11 PF2 2sh 6p car *350.00 300.00*
AR12 PF3 5sh green *350.00 240.00*
AR13 PF3 5sh brown *675.00*
AR14 PF4 10sh orange *425.00 275.00*

Perf. 12½

AR15 PF1 3p green *525.00*
AR16 PF2 2sh 6p car *275.00*
AR17 PF3 5sh brown *450.00*
AR18 PF4 10sh orange *400.00*

Perf. 11½

AR19 PF1 3p green
AR20 PF2 2sh 6p car *525.00 300.00*
AR21 PF3 5sh green *200.00 150.00*
AR22 PF4 10sh salmon *250.00 200.00*
a. 10sh orange *250.00 125.00*

Wmk. 77

Perf. 12

AR23 PF2 2sh 6p car 50.00 37.50

For overprint see No. AR33.

Duck-billed Platypus — PF5

1880 Engr. Wmk. 77 *Perf. 14*

AR24 PF5 1p slate 20.00 9.50
AR25 PF5 3p brown 25.00 5.50
AR26 PF5 6p lilac 100.00 15.00
AR27 PF5 1sh rose 150.00 25.00

For overprints see Nos. AR28-AR31.

Nos. AR24-AR27, AR2, AR23, 85 Overprinted "REVENUE"

1900, Nov. 15

AR28 PF5 1p slate 30.00 30.00
AR29 PF5 3p brown 40.00 *30.00*
AR30 PF5 6p lilac *200.00* 100.00
AR31 PF5 1sh rose *350.00* 175.00
AR32 PF2 2sh 6p car (#AR2) *475.00* 375.00
AR33 PF2 2sh 6p car (#AR23) *300.00*
AR34 PF4 10sh orange 675.00 675.00
AR35 A8 £1 grn & yel (#85) 275.00 *240.00*

Nos. AR28-AR35 were not supposed to be postally used. Because of imprecise terminology, postal use was tolerated until all postal use of revenues ceased on Nov. 30, 1900.

Other denominations and watermarks were overprinted after postal use was no longer allowed.

TETE

'tāt-ə

LOCATION — In southeastern Africa between Nyasaland and Southern Rhodesia.
GOVT. — A district of the Portuguese East Africa Colony.
AREA — 46,600 sq. mi. (approx.)
POP. — 367,000 (approx.)
CAPITAL — Tete

This district was formerly a part of Zambezia. Stamps of Mozambique replaced those of Tete. See Mozambique.

100 Centavos = 1 Escudo

Vasco da Gama Issue of Various Portuguese Colonies Surcharged as

1913 Unwmk. *Perf. 12½, 16*

On Stamps of Macao

1 CD20 ¼c on ½a bl grn 5.00 *5.00*
2 CD21 ½c on 1a red 1.75 *2.10*
3 CD22 1c on 2a red vio 1.75 *2.10*
4 CD23 2½c on 4a yel grn 1.75 *2.10*
5 CD24 5c on 8a dk blue 1.75 *2.10*
6 CD25 7½c on 12a vio brn 2.40 *3.00*
7 CD26 10c on 16a bis brn 1.75 *2.10*
8 CD27 15c on 24a bister 1.75 *2.10*
Nos. 1-8 (8) 17.90 *20.60*

On Stamps of Portuguese Africa

9 CD20 ¼c on 2½r bl grn 1.75 *2.10*
10 CD21 ½c on 5r red 1.75 *2.10*
11 CD22 1c on 10r red vio 1.75 *2.10*
12 CD23 2½c on 25r yel grn 1.75 *2.10*
13 CD24 5c on 50r dk blue 1.75 *2.10*
14 CD25 7½c on 75r vio brn 2.40 *3.00*
15 CD26 10c on 100r bis brn 1.75 *2.10*
16 CD27 15c on 150r bister 1.75 *2.10*
Nos. 9-16 (8) 14.65 *17.70*

On Stamps of Timor

17 CD20 ¼c on ½a bl grn 1.75 *2.10*
18 CD21 ½c on 1a red 1.75 *2.10*
19 CD22 1c on 2a red vio 1.75 *2.10*
a. Inverted overprint 30.00 30.00
20 CD23 2½c on 4a yel grn 1.75 *2.10*
21 CD24 5c on 8a dk blue 1.75 *2.10*
22 CD25 7½c on 12a vio brn 2.40 *3.00*
23 CD26 10c on 16a bis brn 1.75 *2.10*
24 CD27 15c on 24a bister 1.75 *2.10*
Nos. 17-24 (8) 14.65 *17.70*
Nos. 1-24 (24) 47.20 *56.00*

Common Design Types pictured following the introduction.

Ceres — A1

1914 Typo. *Perf. 15x14*

Name and Value in Black

25 A1 ¼c olive brn 1.40 *2.25*
26 A1 ½c black 1.40 *2.25*
27 A1 1c blue grn 1.40 *2.25*
28 A1 1½c lilac brn 1.40 *2.25*
29 A1 2c carmine 1.40 *2.25*
30 A1 2½c light vio 1.40 *2.25*
31 A1 5c deep blue 1.40 *2.25*
32 A1 7½c yel brn 2.25 *3.25*
33 A1 8c slate 2.25 *3.25*
34 A1 10c org brn 2.75 *4.00*
35 A1 15c plum 3.25 *4.50*
36 A1 20c yel green 3.25 *4.50*
37 A1 30c brn, *green* 3.25 *4.50*
38 A1 40c brn, *pink* 4.00 *7.00*
39 A1 50c org, *salmon* 7.00 *9.00*
40 A1 1e grn, *blue* 10.00 *10.00*
Nos. 25-40 (16) 47.80 *65.75*

THAILAND

'tī-,land

(Siam)

LOCATION — Western part of the Malay peninsula in southeastern Asia
GOVT. — Republic
AREA — 198,250 sq. mi.
POP. — 50,000,000 (est. 1984)
CAPITAL — Bangkok

32 Solot = 16 Atts = 8 Sio = 4 Sik = 2 Fuang = 1 Salung
4 Salungs = 1 Tical
100 Satangs (1909) = 1 Tical = 1 Baht (1912)

Watermarks

Wmk. 176 — Chakra

Wmk. 233 — Harrison & Sons, London in Script Letters

King Chulalongkorn
A1 A2

A4

Perf. 14½, 15

1883, Aug. 4 Unwmk. Engr.

1 A1 1sol blue 9.00 9.00
b. Imperf., pair *4,500.*
2 A1 1att carmine 9.00 9.00
3 A1 1sio vermilion 20.00 18.00
4 A2 1sik yellow 12.00 15.00
5 A4 1sa orange 45.00 45.00
a. 1sa ocher 50.00 50.00
Nos. 1-5 (5) 95.00 96.00

There are three types of No. 1, differing mainly in the background of the small oval at the top.

A 1 fuang red, of similar design to the foregoing, was prepared but not placed in use. Value, $900.

For surcharges see Nos. 6-8, 19.

No. 1 Handstamp Surcharged in Red:

1 TICAL
a

1 Tical
b

1 Tical
c

1 Tical
d

1 Tical
e

1885, July 1

6 A1 (a) 1t on 1sol blue *425.* *425.*
7 A1 (b) 1t on 1sol blue *350.* *350.*
c. "1" inverted *1,100.* *1,100.*
8 A1 (c) 1t on 1sol blue *450.* *450.*

Surcharges of Nos. 6-8 have been counterfeited.

Types "d" and "e" are typeset *official reprints.*

As is usual with handstamps, double impressions, etc., exist.

King Chulalongkorn — A7

1887-91 Typo. Wmk. 176 *Perf. 14*

11	A7	1a green ('91)	3.00	1.00
12	A7	2a green & car	4.50	1.00
13	A7	3a grn & blue	11.00	4.00
14	A7	4a grn & org brn	9.00	3.00
15	A7	8a green & yel	9.00	7.00
16	A7	12a lilac & car	15.00	1.50
17	A7	24a lilac & blue	21.00	1.75
18	A7	64a lil & org brn	80.00	25.00
		Nos. 11-18 (8)	152.50	44.25

The design of No. 11 has been redrawn and differs from the illustration in many minor details.

Issue dates: #12-18, Apr. 1; #11, Feb.

For surcharges see Nos. 20-69, 109, 111, 126.

No. 3 Handstamp Surcharged

1889, Aug. Unwmk. *Perf. 15*

19	A1	1a on 1sio	18.00	18.00

Three different handstamps were used. Doubles, etc. exist.

Nos. 12 and 13 Handstamp Surcharged ๑ อัฐ 1

1889-90 Wmk. 176 *Perf. 14*

20	A7	1a on 2a	4.00	3.00
a.		"1" omitted	*250.00*	*250.00*
c.		1st Siamese character invtd.		
d.		First Siamese character omitted	*300.00*	*300.00*
21	A7	1a on 3a ('90)	9.00	9.00
a.		Inverted "1"	*150.00*	*150.00*

For surcharge see No. 29.

๑ อัฐ 1

22	A7	1a on 2a grn & car	*450.00*	*450.00*

๑ อัฐ 1

24	A7	1a on 2a grn & car	*175.00*	*175.00*

๑ อัฐ 1

25	A7	1a on 2a grn & car	*1,000.*	*1,000.*

๑ อัฐ 1

26	A7	1a on 3a grn & bl		

Some authorities consider No. 26 a forgery.

Doubles, etc., exist in this issue.

Issue dates: Nov. 1889. Sept. 1890.

No. 13 Handstamp Surcharged ๒ อัฐ 2

1891

27	A7	2a on 3a grn & bl	55.00	55.00

๒ อัฐ 2

28	A7	2a on 3a grn & bl	50.00	50.00
a.		Double surcharge	*250.00*	*250.00*
b.		"2" omitted	*250.00*	

No. 21 with Additional 2 Att Surcharge

๒ อัฐ 2

29	A7	2a on 1a on 3a grn & bl	*1,500.*	*1,500.*

On No. 29 the 2a surcharge consists of Siamese numeral like No. 27 and English numeral like No. 28.

Most examples of No. 29 show attempts to remove the "1" of the first surcharge.

๒ อัฐ 2

Typeset Surcharge

30	A7	2a on 3a grn & bl	40.00	40.00

There are 7 types of this surcharge in the setting.

Issued: #27-28, Jan.; #29, Feb.; #30, Mar.

No. 17 Handstamp Surcharged:

ราคา๔อัฐ f   ราคา๔อัฐ g

1892, Oct.

33	A7 (f)	4a on 24a lil & bl	50.00	50.00
34	A7 (g)	4a on 24a lil & bl	35.00	35.00

Surcharges exist double on Nos. 33-34 and inverted on No. 33.

Nos. 33-34 Handstamp Surcharged in English

4 atts

1892, Nov.

35	A7	4a on 24a lil & bl	8.00	8.00
c.		Inverted "s"	*45.00*	*45.00*

36	A7	4a on 24a lil & bl	13.00	9.00
a.		Inverted "s"	*40.00*	*40.00*

37	A7	4a on 24a lil & bl	12.00	12.00

4 atts.

38	A7	4a on 24a lil & bl	13.00	15.00

Numerous inverts., doubles, etc., exist.

Nos. 18 and 17 Typeset Surcharged in English (Shown) and Siamese

1 Atts

1894

39	A7	1a on 64a lil & org brn	3.50	3.50
a.		Inverted "s"	*42.50*	*42.50*
b.		Inverted surcharge	*900.00*	*900.00*
d.		Italic "s"	*55.00*	*55.00*
e.		Italic "1"	*55.00*	*55.00*

1 Att.

40	A7	1a on 64a lil & org brn	2.00	2.00
a.		Inverted capital "S" added to the surcharge	*175.00*	*200.00*

2 Atts. *h*   2 Atts. *i*

2 Atts. *j*   2 Atts. *k*

2. Atts. *l*   2 Atts. *m*

41	A7 (h)	2a on 64a	24.00	24.00
a.		Inverted "s"	*42.50*	*42.50*
b.		Double surcharge	*100.00*	*100.00*
42	A7 (i)	2a on 64a	*3,000.*	*3,000.*
43	A7 (j)	2a on 64a	60.00	60.00
44	A7 (k)	2a on 64a	35.00	35.00
45	A7 (l)	2a on 64a	55.00	55.00
46	A7 (m)	2a on 64a	2.00	2.00
a.		"Att.s"	*42.50*	*42.50*

Nos. 41-46 were in one plate of 120 subjects. The quanrtities were: h, 38; i, 1; j, 8; k, 18; l, 11 and m, 44.

1 Att.

1894, Oct. 12

47	A7	1a on 64a	2.50	2.50
a.		Surcharged on face and back	*150.00*	
b.		Surcharge on back inverted	*200.00*	
c.		Double surcharge	*475.00*	
d.		Inverted surcharge	*500.00*	
e.		Siamese surcharge omitted	*400.00*	

2 Atts.

48	A7	2a on 64a	3.00	3.00
a.		"Att"	*35.00*	*35.00*
b.		Inverted surcharge	*300.00*	*300.00*
c.		Surch. on face and back	*400.00*	*400.00*
d.		Surcharge on back inverted	*400.00*	*400.00*
e.		Double surcharge	*300.00*	*300.00*
f.		Double surch., one inverted	*1,100.*	*1,100.*
g.		Inverted "s"	*42.50*	*42.50*

10 Atts.

1895, July 23

49	A7	10a on 24a lil & bl	7.00	2.00
a.		Inverted "s"	*42.50*	*42.50*
b.		Surch. on face and back	*175.00*	*175.00*
c.		Surcharge on back inverted	*175.00*	*175.00*

No. 16 Surcharged in English (Shown) and Siamese

4 Atts.

1896

50	A7	4a on 12a lil & car	15.00	7.00
a.		Inverted "s"	50.00	50.00
b.		Surcharged on face and back	175.00	175.00
c.		Double surcharge on back	175.00	175.00

Two types of surcharge.

Nos. 16-18 Surcharged in English (Shown) and Siamese Antique Surcharges:

1 Atts. *a*   1 Att. *b*   2 Atts. *c*

3 Atts. *d*   4 Atts. *e*   10 Atts. *f*

Atts.

Antique Letters

Atts.

Roman Letters

1898-99

51	A7 (a)	1a on 12a	350.00	350.00
52	A7 (b)	1a on 12a	17.50	7.00
53	A7 (c)	2a on 64a ('99)	30.00	9.00
54	A7 (d)	3a on 12a	12.00	4.00
a.		Double surcharge	*350.00*	*350.00*
55	A7 (e)	4a on 12a	12.00	5.00
a.		Double surcharge	*350.00*	*350.00*
56	A7 (e)	4a on 24a ('99)	35.00	12.00
57	A7 (f)	10a on 24a ('99)	775.00	775.00

Roman Surcharges:

1 Atts. *g*   1 Att. *h*   2 Atts. *i*

3 Atts. *j*   4 Atts. *k*   10 Atts. *l*

58	A7 (g)	1a on 12a	425.00	425.00
59	A7 (h)	1a on 12a	42.50	20.00
60	A7 (i)	2a on 64a ('99)	35.00	10.00
61	A7 (j)	3a on 12a	85.00	19.00
62	A7 (k)	4a on 12a	40.00	14.00
a.		Double surcharge	*175.00*	*175.00*
b.		No period after "Atts."	*35.00*	*35.00*
63	A7 (k)	4a on 24a ('99)	60.00	25.00
64	A7 (l)	10a on 24a ('99)	725.00	725.00
		Nos. 58-64 (7)	1,412.	1,238.

In making the settings to surcharge Nos. 51 to 64 two fonts were mixed. Antique and Roman letters are frequently found on the same stamp.

Issue dates: Nos. 54-55, 61-62, Feb. 22. Nos. 51-52, 58-59, June 4. Nos. 56-57, 63-64, Oct. 3.

Nos. 16 and 18 Surcharged in English (Shown) and Siamese Surcharged:

1 Att. *m*   1 Att. *n*

1 Att. *o*

2 Atts. *p*   2 Atts. *r*

1894-99

65	A7 (m)	1a on 12a	20.00	4.00
66	A7 (n)	1a on 12a	18.00	8.00
a.		Inverted "l"	*150.00*	*150.00*
b.		Inverted 1st "t"	*150.00*	*150.00*
67	A7 (o)	1a on 64a	5.00	5.00
68	A7 (p)	2a on 64a	9.00	9.00
a.		"1 Atts."	*500.00*	*500.00*
69	A7 (r)	2a on 64a	24.00	5.00
		Nos. 65-69 (5)	76.00	31.00

Issued: #67, 10/12/94; others, 2/14/99.

A13

A14

1899, Oct. Typo. Unwmk.

70	A13	1a dull green	130.	80.
71	A13	2a dl grn & rose	225.	120.
72	A13	3a carmine & blue	325.	175.
73	A13	4a black & grn	2,000.	625.
74	A13	10a carmine & grn	2,300.	900.
		Nos. 70-74 (5)	4,980.	1,900.

The King rejected Nos. 70-74 in 1897, but some were released by mistake to three post offices in Oct. 1899. Used values are for copies canceled to order at Korat in Dec. 1899. Postally used examples sell for more.

1899-1904

75	A14	1a gray green	2.00	1.00
76	A14	2a yellow green	2.25	1.25
77	A14	2a scarlet & bl	3.75	1.75

78 A14 3a red & blue 7.00 2.00
79 A14 3a green 20.00 12.00
80 A14 4a dark rose 4.00 1.50
81 A14 4a vio brn & rose 8.00 2.00
82 A14 6a dk rose 35.00 14.00
83 A14 8a dk grn & org 9.00 1.50
84 A14 10a ultra 9.00 3.00
85 A14 12a brn vio & rose 40.00 2.00
86 A14 14a ultra 22.50 18.00
87 A14 24a brn vio & bl 325.00 26.00
88 A14 28a vio brn & bl 25.00 25.00
89 A14 64a brn vio & org brn 70.00 11.00
Nos. 75-89 (15) 582.50 122.00

Two types of 1a differ in size and shape of Thai "1" are in drawing of spandrel ornaments.
Issue dates: 6a, 14a, 28a, Nos. 77, 79, 81, Jan. 1, 1904; others, Sept. 1899.
For surcharges see Nos. 90-91, 112, 125, 127.

Nos. 78 and 85 With Typewritten Surcharge of 6 or 7 Siamese Characters (1 line) in Violet

1902
78a A14 2a on 3a *4,000. 4,500.*
85a A14 10a on 12a *4,000. 4,500.*

Nos. 78a and 85a were authorized provisionals, surcharged and issued by the Battambang postmaster.

Nos. 86 and 88 Surcharged in Black

1905, Feb.
90 A14 1a on 14a 10.00 8.00
a. No period after "Att" 35.00 35.00
91 A14 2a on 28a 12.00 12.00
a. Double surcharge *125.00 125.00*

A15

King Chulalongkorn — A16

1905-08 **Engr.**
92 A15 1a orange & green 2.00 1.00
93 A15 2a violet & slate 3.00 1.00
94 A15 2a green ('08) 11.00 4.00
95 A15 3a green 3.00 2.00
96 A15 3a vio & sl ('08) 10.00 5.00
97 A15 4a gray & red 4.00 1.00
98 A15 4a car & rose ('08) 6.00 1.50
99 A15 5a carmine & rose 8.00 3.00
100 A15 8a blk & ol bis 8.00 1.50
101 A15 9a blue ('08) 22.50 9.00
102 A15 12a blue 18.00 4.00
103 A15 18a red brn ('08) 55.00 16.00
104 A15 24a red brown 32.50 7.00
105 A15 1t dp bl & brn org 45.00 10.00
Nos. 92-105 (14) 228.00 66.00

Issue dates: Dec. 1905, Apr. 1, 1908.
For surcharges and overprints see Nos. 110, 113-117, 128-138, 161-162, B15, B21.

1907, Apr. 24
Black Surcharge
106 A16 10t gray green *325.00 100.00*
107 A16 20t gray green *3,300. 290.00*
108 A16 40t gray green *2,400. 450.00*
Nos. 106-108 (3) 6,025. 840.00

Counterfeits of Nos. 106-108 exist. In the genuine, the surcharged figures correspond to the Siamese value inscriptions on the basic revenue stamps.

No. 17 Surcharged

1907, Dec. 16
109 A7 1a on 24a lil & bl 2.00 1.00
a. Double surcharge 400.00

No. 99 Surcharged

1908, Sept.
110 A15 4a on 5a car & rose 11.00 4.00

The No. 110 surcharge is found in two spacings of the numerals: normally 15mm apart, and a narrow, scarcer spacing of 13½mm.

Nos. 17 and 84 Surcharged in Black:

111 A7 2a on 24a lil & bl 2.00 1.00
a. Inverted surcharge *325.00 325.00*
112 A14 9a on 10a ultra 12.00 5.00
a. Inverted surcharge *325.00 325.00*

Jubilee Issue

Nos. 92, 95, 110, 100 and 103 Overprinted in Black or Red

1908, Nov. 11
113 A15 1a 2.00 1.00
a. Siamese date "137" instead of "127" *900.00 900.00*
b. Pair, one without ovpt.
114 A15 3a 3.00 2.00
115 A15 4a on 5a 4.50 3.00
a. Horiz. pair, imperf. btwn. *500.00*
116 A15 8a (R) 21.00 21.00
117 A15 18a 30.00 18.00
Nos. 113-117 (5) 60.50 45.00

40th year of the reign of King Chulalongkorn.
Nos. 113 to 117 exist with a small "i" in "Jubilee."

Statue of King Chulalongkorn A19

1908, Nov. 11 **Engr.** ***Perf. 13½***
118 A19 1t green & vio 29.00 3.00
119 A19 2t red vio & org 57.50 11.00
120 A19 3t pale ol & bl 85.00 14.00
121 A19 5t dl vio & dk grn 120.00 25.00
122 A19 10t bister & car *1,250.* 87.50
123 A19 20t gray & red brn 300.00 85.00
124 A19 40t sl bl & blk brn 475.00 290.00
Nos. 118-124 (7) 2,316. 515.50

The inscription at the foot of the stamps reads: "Coronation Commemoration-Forty-first year of the reign-1908."

Stamps of 1887-1904 Surcharged

1909 ***Perf. 14***
125 A14 6s on 6a dk rose 2.00 2.00
126 A7 14s on 12a lil & car 100.00 100.00
127 A14 14s on 14a ultra 18.00 18.00
Nos. 125-127 (3) 120.00 120.00

Nos. 92-102 Surcharged with Bar and

1909, Aug. 15
128 A15 2s on 1a #92 2.00 1.00
129 A15 2s on 2a #93 57.50 57.50
130 A15 2s on 2a #94 2.00 1.00
a. "2" omitted *85.00*
131 A15 3s on 3a #95 3.00 1.00
132 A15 3s on 3a #96 3.00 1.00
133 A15 6s on 4a #97 60.00 60.00
134 A15 6s on 4a #98 4.00 1.00
135 A15 6s on 5a #99 3.00 3.00
136 A15 12s on 8a #100 7.00 1.00
137 A15 14s on 9a #101 11.00 2.00
138 A15 14s on 12a #102 21.00 21.00
Nos. 128-138 (11) 173.50 149.50

King Chulalongkorn — A20

1910 **Engr.** ***Perf. 14x14½***
139 A20 2s org & green 1.50 .50
140 A20 3s green 2.00 .50
141 A20 6s carmine 3.00 .50
142 A20 12s blk & ol brn 6.00 1.00
143 A20 14s blue 19.00 2.00
144 A20 28s red brown 45.00 9.00
Nos. 139-144 (6) 76.50 13.50

Issue dates: 12s, June 5. Others, May 5.
For surcharges see Nos. 163, 223-224.

A21

King Vajiravudh — A22

Printed at the Imperial Printing Works, Vienna

1912 ***Perf. 14½***
145 A21 2s brown orange 1.25 .20
a. Vert. pair, imperf. btwn. *500.00 500.00*
b. Horiz. pair, imperf. btwn. *500.00 500.00*
146 A21 3s yellow green 1.25 .20
a. Horiz. pair, imperf. btwn. *500.00 500.00*
147 A21 6s carmine rose 2.25 .55
148 A21 12s gray blk & brn 3.25 .60
149 A21 14s ultramarine 5.25 .80
150 A21 28s chocolate 20.00 8.00
151 A22 1b blue & blk 20.00 2.00
a. Pair, imperf. btwn. *1,250. 1,250.*
152 A22 2b car rose & ol brn 24.00 3.00
153 A22 3b yel grn & bl blk 32.50 6.00
154 A22 5b vio & blk 50.00 7.00
155 A22 10b ol grn & vio brn 250.00 85.00
156 A22 20b sl bl & red brn 410.00 85.00
Nos. 145-156 (12) 819.75 198.35

See Nos. 164-175.
For surcharges and overprints see Nos. 157-160, 176-186, 206, B1-B14, B16-B20, B22, B31-B33.

Nos. 147-150 Surcharged in Red or Blue

1914-15
157 A21 2s on 14s (R) ('15) 1.75 .35
a. Vert. pair, imperf. btwn. *900.00 900.00*
b. Double surcharge 62.50 40.00
158 A21 5s on 6s (Bl) 3.25 .35
a. Horiz. pair, imperf. btwn. *900.00 900.00*
b. Double surcharge 67.50 67.50
159 A21 10s on 12s (R) 4.00 .45
a. Double surcharge 67.50 67.50
160 A21 15s on 28s (Bl) 5.00 .60
Nos. 157-160 (4) 14.00 1.75

The several settings of the surcharges on Nos. 157 to 160 show variations in the figures and letters.

Nos. 92-93 Surcharged

1915, Apr. 3
161 A15 2s on 1a org & grn 5.00 3.00
a. Pair, one without surcharge *350.00 350.00*
162 A15 2s on 2a vio & slate 5.00 3.00

No. 143 Surcharged in Red

1916, Oct.
163 A20 2s on 14s blue 2.50 1.10

Printed by Waterlow & Sons, London
Types of 1912 Re-engraved

1917, Jan. 1 ***Perf. 14***
164 A21 2s orange brown .65 .25
165 A21 3s emerald .95 .35
166 A21 5s rose red 2.50 .25
167 A21 10s black & olive 2.00 .25
168 A21 15s blue 4.00 .50
170 A22 1b bl & gray blk 17.50 2.00
171 A22 2b car rose & brn 70.00 26.00
172 A22 3b yellow grn & blk 500.00 250.00
173 A22 5b dp violet & blk 125.00 85.00
174 A22 10b ol gray & vio brn 400.00 10.00
a. Perf. 12½ 500.00 37.50
175 A22 20b sea green & brn 500.00 50.00
a. Perf. 12½ 600.00 85.00
Nos. 164-175 (11) 1,622. 424.60

The re-engraved design of the satang stamps varies in numerous minute details from the 1912 issue. Four lines of the background appear between the vertical strokes of the "M" of "SIAM" in the 1912 issue and only three lines in the 1917 stamps.
The 1912 stamps with value in bahts are 37½mm high; those of 1917 are 39mm. In the latter the king's features, especially the eyes and mouth, are more distinct and the uniform and decorations are more sharply defined.
The 1912 stamps have seven pearls between the earpieces of the crown. On the 1917 stamps there are nine pearls in the same place. Nos. 174 and 175 exist imperforate.

Nos. 164-173 Overprinted in Red

1918, Dec. 2
176 A21 2s orange brown .55 .45
a. Double overprint 110.00 110.00

177 A21 3s emerald .85 .75
178 A21 5s rose red 1.40 1.25
a. Double overprint 150.00 150.00
179 A21 10s black & olive 1.40 1.25
180 A21 15s blue 2.75 2.50
181 A22 1b bl & gray blk 22.50 17.00
182 A22 2b car rose & brn 45.00 35.00
183 A22 3b yellow grn & blk 110.00 65.00
184 A22 5b dp vio & blk 375.00 275.00
Nos. 176-184 (9) 559.45 398.20

Counterfeits of this overprint exist.

Nos. 147-148 Surcharged in Green or Red

1919-20
185 A21 5s on 6s (G) 1.75 .30
186 A21 10s on 12s (R) ('20) 6.00 1.00

Issue dates: 5s, Nov. 11. 10s, Jan. 1.

King Vajiravudh
A23

Throne Room
A24

1920-26 Engr. *Perf. 14-15, 12½*
187 A23 2s brn, *yel* ('21) 2.00 .40
188 A23 3s grn, *grn* ('21) 3.25 .55
189 A23 3s chocolate ('24) 3.25 .40
190 A23 5s rose, *pale rose* 3.75 .40
191 A23 5s green ('22) 30.00 5.00
192 A23 5s dk vio, *lil* ('26) 7.50 .40
193 A23 10s black & org ('21) 5.75 .40
194 A23 15s bl, *bluish* ('21) 8.50 .40
195 A23 15s carmine ('22) 40.00 5.00
196 A23 25s chocolate ('21) 24.00 2.00
197 A23 25s dk blue ('22) 27.50 1.00
198 A23 50s ocher & blk ('21) 25.00 2.00
Nos. 187-198 (12) 180.50 17.95

For overprints see Nos. 205, B23-B30.

1926, Mar. 5 *Perf. 12½*
199 A24 1t gray vio & grn 12.00 2.00
200 A24 2t car & org red 27.50 6.00
201 A24 3t ol grn & bl 45.00 25.00
202 A24 5t dl vio & ol grn 65.00 19.00
203 A24 10t red & ol bis 300.00 22.50
204 A24 20t gray bl & brn 325.00 67.50
Nos. 199-204 (6) 774.50 142.00

This issue was intended to commemorate the fifteenth year of the reign of King Vajiravudh. Because of the King's death the stamps were issued as ordinary postage stamps.

Nos. 195 and 150 with Surcharge similar to 1914-15 Issue in Black or Red

1928, Jan.
205 A23 5s on 15s car 4.00 2.00
206 A21 10s on 28s choc (R) 9.00 1.00

King Prajadhipok
A25 A26

1928 Engr. *Perf. 12½*
207 A25 2s deep red brown .60 .20
208 A25 3s deep green .75 .20
209 A25 5s dark violet .60 .20
210 A25 10s deep rose .75 .20
211 A25 15s dark blue .90 .40
212 A25 25s black & org 3.50 .60
213 A25 50s brn org & blk 1.75 1.25
214 A25 80s blue & black 3.00 .80
216 A26 1b dk blue & blk 6.00 1.25
217 A26 2b car rose & blk brn 12.00 3.00
218 A26 3b yellow grn & blk 9.00 3.00
219 A26 5b dp vio & gray blk 20.00 5.00
220 A26 10b ol grn & red vio 37.50 10.00
221 A26 20b Prus grn & brn 80.00 17.50
222 A26 40b dk grn & ol brn 160.00 47.50
Nos. 207-222 (15) 336.35 91.10
Set, never hinged 450.00

On the single colored stamps, type A25, the lines in the background are uniform; those of the bicolored values are shaded and do not extend to the frame.

Issue dates: 5s, 10s, 2b-40b, Apr. 15; 2s, 3s, 15s, 25s, 50s, May 1; 1b, June 1; 80s, Nov. 15.

For overprints & surcharge see #300-301, B34.

Nos. 142, 144 Surcharged in Red or Blue

1930 *Perf. 14*
223 A20 10s on 12s blk & ol brn 6.00 1.00
224 A20 25s on 28s red brn (Bl) 30.00 2.00
Set, never hinged 37.50

King Prajadhipok and Chao P'ya Chakri
A27 A28

Statue of Chao P'ya Chakri — A29

1932, Apr. 1 Engr. *Perf. 12½*
225 A27 2s dark brown 1.00 .25
226 A27 3s deep green 2.00 .40
227 A27 5s dull violet 1.25 .25
228 A28 10s red brn & blk 2.00 .25
229 A28 15s dull blue & blk 7.75 .95
230 A28 25s violet & black 11.00 1.40
231 A28 50s claret & black 50.00 5.00
232 A29 1b blue black 75.00 12.50
Nos. 225-232 (8) 150.00 21.00
Set, never hinged 225.00

150th anniv. of the Chakri dynasty, the founding of Bangkok in 1782, and the opening of the memorial bridge across the Chao Phraya River.

Assembly Hall, Bangkok
A30

1939, June 24 Litho. *Perf. 11, 12*
233 A30 2s dull red brown 3.25 1.00
234 A30 3s green 6.75 2.25
235 A30 5s dark violet 3.25 .20
236 A30 10s carmine 13.50 .20
237 A30 15s dark blue 32.50 2.00
Nos. 233-237 (5) 59.25 5.65
Set, never hinged 70.00

7th anniv. of the Siamese Constitution.

Chakri Palace, Bangkok — A31

1940 Typo. *Perf. 12½*
238 A31 2s dull brown 3.25 1.00
239 A31 3s dp yellow grn 6.25 2.25
a. Cliché of 5s in plate of 3s 900.00 *725.00*
240 A31 5s dark violet 4.75 .20
241 A31 10s carmine 17.50 .20
242 A31 15s dark blue 37.50 1.00
Nos. 238-242 (5) 69.25 4.65
Set, never hinged 90.00

Issued: 2s, 3s, 5/13; 5s, 5/24; 15s, 5/28; 10s, 5/30.

SEMI-POSTAL STAMPS

Nos. 164-175 Overprinted in Red

1918, Jan. 11 Unwmk. *Perf. 14*
B1 A21 2s orange brown 2.00 1.00
B2 A21 3s emerald 2.00 1.00
B3 A21 5s rose red 4.50 2.00
B4 A21 10s black & olive 7.00 3.00
B5 A21 15s blue 7.00 3.00
B6 A22 1b blue & gray blk 35.00 15.00
B7 A22 2b car rose & brn 60.00 25.00
B8 A22 3b yel grn & blk 90.00 40.00
B9 A22 5b dp vio & blk 225.00 65.00
a. Double overprint 775.00 400.00
B10 A22 10b ol grn & vio brn 575.00 175.00
B11 A22 20b sea grn & brn 2,100. 600.00
Nos. B1-B11 (11) 3,107. 930.00

Excellent counterfeit overprints are known.

These stamps were sold at an advance over face value, the excess being given to the Siamese Red Cross Society.

Stamps of 1905-19 Handstamp Overprinted

1920, Feb.

On Nos. 164, 146, 168
B12 A21 2s (+ 3s) org brn 37.50 37.50
B13 A21 3s (+ 2s) green 40.00 40.00
B14 A21 15s (+ 5s) blue 90.00 90.00

On No. 105
B15 A15 1t (+ 25s) 325.00 290.00

On Nos. 185-186
B16 A21 5s on 6s (+ 5s) 55.00 55.00
a. Overprint inverted
B17 A21 10s on 12s (+ 5s) 60.00 60.00
Nos. B12-B17 (6) 607.50 572.50
Set, never hinged 850.00

Stamps of 1905-20 Handstamp Overprinted

On Nos. 164, 146, 168
B18 A21 2s (+ 3s) org brn 35.00 35.00
B19 A21 3s (+ 2s) green 35.00 35.00
a. Pair, one without ovpt.
B20 A21 15s (+ 5s) blue 52.50 52.50

On No. 105
B21 A15 1t (+ 25s) 260.00 260.00

On No. 186
B22 A21 10s on 12s (+ 5s) 55.00 55.00

On No. 190
B23 A23 5s (+ 5s) 85.00 85.00
Nos. B18-B23 (6) 522.50 522.50
Set, never hinged 800.00

Nos. 187-188, 190, 193-194, 196, 198 Overprinted in Blue or Red

1920, Dec. 21
B24 A23 2s brown, *yel* 13.00 13.00
B25 A23 3s grn, *grn* (R) 13.00 13.00
B26 A23 5s rose, *pale rose* 13.00 13.00
B27 A23 10s blk & org (R) 13.00 13.00
B28 A23 15s bl, *bluish* (R) 25.00 25.00
B29 A23 25s chocolate 85.00 85.00
B30 A23 50s ocher & blk (R) 190.00 190.00
Nos. B24-B30 (7) 352.00 352.00
Set, never hinged 550.00

Nos. B12 to B30 were sold at an advance over face value, the excess being for the benefit of the Wild Tiger Corps. Counterfeits exist.

Nos. 170-172 Surcharged in Red

1939, Apr. 6 Unwmk. *Perf. 14*
B31 A22 5s + 5s on 1b 20.00 20.00
B32 A22 10s + 5s on 2b 26.00 26.00
B33 A22 15s + 5s on 3b 26.00 26.00
Nos. B31-B33 (3) 72.00 72.00
Set, never hinged 110.00

Founding of the Intl. Red Cross Soc., 75th anniv.

Bottom line of overprint is different on Nos. B32-B33.

AIR POST STAMPS

Garuda — AP1

1925 Unwmk. Engr. *Perf. 14, 14½*
C1 AP1 2s brown, *yel* 2.00 .50
C2 AP1 3s dark brown 2.00 .50
C3 AP1 5s green 6.00 .50
C4 AP1 10s black & org 17.50 1.00
C5 AP1 15s carmine 5.00 1.50
C6 AP1 25s dark blue 5.00 1.50
C7 AP1 50s brown org & blk 35.00 9.00
C8 AP1 1b blue & brown 32.50 11.00
Nos. C1-C8 (8) 105.00 25.50
Set, never hinged 165.00

Issue dates: 2s, 50s, Apr. 21; others, Jan. 3.

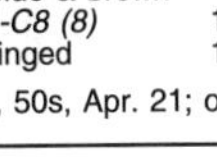

Nos. C1-C8 received this overprint ("Government Museum 2468") in 1925, but were never issued. The death of King Vajiravudh caused cancellation of the fair at which this set was to have been released.

They were used during 1928 only in the interdepartmental service for accounting purposes of the money-order sections of various Bangkok post offices, and were never sold to the public. Value for canceled set, $25.

1930-37 *Perf. 12½*
C9 AP1 2s brown, *yel* 5.00 1.00
C10 AP1 5s green 1.25 .20
C11 AP1 10s black & org 2.50 .20
C12 AP1 15s carmine 25.00 6.00
C13 AP1 25s dark blue ('37) 1.50 1.00
a. Vert. pair, imperf. btwn. 450.00

C14 AP1 50s brn org & blk ('37)		3.00	1.50
Nos. C9-C14 (6)		38.25	9.90
Set, never hinged		62.50	

THRACE

'thrās

LOCATION — In southeastern Europe between the Black and Aegean Seas
GOVT. — Former Turkish Province
AREA — 89,361 sq. mi. (approx.)

Thrace underwent many political changes during the Balkan Wars and World War I. It was finally divided among Turkey, Greece and Bulgaria.

100 Lepta = 1 Drachma
40 Paras = 1 Piaster
100 Stotinki = 1 Leva (1919)

Giumulzina District Issue

Turkish Stamps of 1909 Surcharged in Blue or Red

1913 Unwmk. *Perf. 12, 13½*

1	A21 10 l on 20pa rose (Bl)	20.00	*30.00*
2	A21 25 l on 10pa bl grn	47.50	*47.50*
3	A21 25 l on 20pa rose (Bl)	60.00	60.00
4	A21 25 l on 1pi ultra	80.00	*92.50*
	Nos. 1-4 (4)	207.50	230.00

Counterfeits exist of Nos. 1-4.

Turkish Inscriptions
A1 A2

1913 Litho. *Imperf.*
Laid Paper
Control Mark in Rose
Without Gum

5	A1 1pi blue	17.00	17.00
6	A1 2pi violet	20.00	20.00

Wove Paper

7	A2 10pa vermilion	35.00	32.50
8	A2 20pa blue	35.00	32.50
9	A2 1pi violet	37.50	32.50
	Nos. 5-9 (5)	144.50	134.50

Turkish Stamps of 1908-13 Surcharged in Red or Black

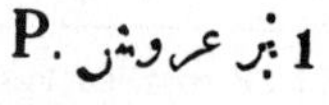

1913 *Perf. 12*

10	A22 1pi on 2pa ol grn (R)	12.00	12.00
10A	A22 1pi on 2pa ol grn	12.00	12.00
11	A22 1pi on 5pa ocher	16.00	14.50
11A	A22 1pi on 5pa ocher (R)	17.50	17.00
12	A22 1pi on 20pa rose	26.00	25.00
13	A21 1pi on 5pi dk vio (R)	60.00	60.00
13A	A21 1pi on 5pi dk vio	55.00	55.00
14	A21 1pi on 10pi dl red	90.00	90.00
15	A19 1pi on 25pi dk grn	425.00	425.00
	Nos. 10-15 (9)	713.50	710.50

On Nos. 13-15 the surcharge is vertical, reading up. No. 15 exists with double surcharge, one black, one red.

Nos. 10-15 exist with forged surcharges.

Bulgarian Stamps of 1911 Handstamp Surcharged in Red or Blue

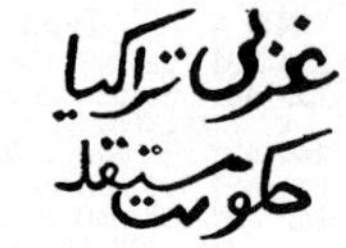

1913

16	A20	10pa on 1s myr grn (R)	20.00	20.00
17	A21	20pa on 2s car & blk	20.00	20.00
18	A23	1pi on 5s grn & blk (R)	20.00	20.00
19	A22	2pi on 3s lake & blk	26.00	26.00
20	A24	2½pi on 10s dp red & blk	40.00	40.00
21	A25	5pi on 15s brn bis	62.50	62.50
		Nos. 16-21 (6)	188.50	188.50

Same Surcharges on Greek Stamps
On Issue of 1911

1913 *Serrate Roulette 13½*

22	A24	10pa on 1 l grn (R)	21.00	21.00
23	A24	10pa on 1 l grn	22.50	22.50
25	A25	10pa on 25 l ultra (R)	30.00	30.00
26	A25	20pa on 2 l car rose	20.00	20.00
27	A24	1pi on 3 l ver	20.00	20.00
28	A26	2pi on 5 l grn (R)	47.50	47.50
29	A24	2½pi on 10 l car rose	47.50	47.50
30	A25	5pi on 40 l dp bl (R)	82.50	82.50
		Nos. 22-30 (8)	291.00	291.00

On Occupation Stamps of 1912

31	O1	10pa on 1 l brn	14.00	14.00
32	O1	20pa on 1 l brn	14.00	14.00
33	O1	1pi on 1 l brn	14.00	14.00
		Nos. 31-33 (3)	42.00	42.00

These surcharges were made with handstamps, two of which were required for each surcharge. One or both parts may be found inverted, double or omitted.

Nos. 16-33 exist with forged surcharges.

OCCUPATION STAMPS

Issued under Allied Occupation

Bulgarian Stamps of 1915-19 Handstamped in Violet Blue

Perf. 11½, 11½x12, 14

1919 Unwmk.

N1	A43	1s black	2.00	2.00
N2	A43	2s olive green	2.00	2.00
N3	A44	5s green	.75	.75
N4	A44	10s rose	.75	.75
N5	A44	15s violet	.85	.85
N6	A26	25s indigo & black	.85	.85
		Nos. N1-N6 (6)	7.20	7.20

The overprint on Nos. N1-N6 is frequently inverted and known in other positions.

Bulgarian Stamps of 1911-19 Overprinted in Red or Black

1919

N7	A43	1s black (R)	.20	.20
N8	A43	2s olive green	.20	.20
N9	A44	5s green	.20	.20
N10	A44	10s rose	.20	.20
N11	A44	15s violet	.20	.20
N12	A26	25s indigo & black	.25	.25
N13	A29	1 l chocolate	4.00	4.00
N14	A37a	2 l brown orange	6.00	6.00
N15	A38	3 l claret	10.00	10.00
		Nos. N7-N15 (9)	21.25	21.25

Overprint is vertical, reading up, on Nos. N9-N13.

The following varieties are found in the setting of "INTERALLIEE": Inverted "V" for "A," second "L" inverted, "F" instead of final "E."

Bulgarian Stamps of 1919 Overprinted

1920

N16	A44	5s green	.25	.25
N17	A44	10s rose	.25	.25
N18	A44	15s violet	.25	.25
N19	A44	50s yellow brown	.70	.70
		Nos. N16-N19 (4)	1.45	1.45

The varieties: "Irteraliiee" and final "e" inverted are found on all values.

Bulgarian Stamps of 1919 Overprinted

1920 *Perf. 12x11½*

N20	A44	5s green	.25	.25
a.		Inverted overprint	*19.00*	
N21	A44	10s rose	.25	.25
a.		Inverted overprint	*19.00*	
N22	A44	15s violet	.25	.25
N23	A44	25s deep blue	.25	.25
N24	A44	50s ocher	.25	.25

Imperf

N25	A44	30s chocolate	.75	.75
		Nos. N20-N25 (6)	2.00	2.00

No. N25 is not known without overprint.

ISSUED UNDER GREEK OCCUPATION

For Use in Western Thrace

Greek Stamps of 1911-19 Overprinted

Serrate Roulette 13½

1920 Litho. Unwmk.

N26	A24	1 l green	.20	*.35*
a.		Inverted overprint	15.00	
N27	A25	2 l rose	.20	*.35*
N28	A24	3 l vermilion	.20	*.35*
N29	A26	5 l green	.20	*.35*
N30	A24	10 l rose	.30	*.50*
N31	A25	15 l dull blue	.35	*.65*
a.		Inverted overprint	16.00	
b.		Dbl. ovpt., one inverted	24.00	
N32	A25	25 l blue	.40	*.75*
N33	A26	30 l rose	29.00	*50.00*
N34	A25	40 l indigo	1.90	*4.00*
N35	A26	50 l violet brn	1.90	*5.00*
N36	A27	1d ultra	6.50	*14.00*
N37	A27	2d vermilion	17.50	*32.50*

Engr.

N38	A25	2 l car rose	.60	.60
N39	A24	3 l vermilion	.60	.60
N40	A27	1d ultra	25.00	*52.50*
N41	A27	2d vermilion	25.00	*55.00*
N42	A27	3d car rose	37.50	*70.00*
N43	A27	5d ultra	14.50	*22.50*
N44	A27	10d deep blue	14.00	*20.00*
		Nos. N26-N44 (19)	175.85	*330.00*

Nos. N42-N44 are overprinted on the reissues of Greece Nos. 210-212. See footnote below Greece No. 213. Counterfeits exist of Nos. N26-N84.

Overprinted **ΔΙΟΙΚΗΣΙΣ ΔΥΤΙΚΗΣ ΘΡΑΚΗΣ**

N45	A28	25d deep blue	40.00	*65.00*

This overprint reads: "Administration Western Thrace."

With Additional Overprint

Litho.

N46	A24	1 l green	.55	*1.10*
N47	A25	2 l rose	.20	*.40*
a.		Inverted overprint	77.50	
N48	A24	10 l rose	.55	*.65*
N49	A25	20 l slate	.55	*.65*
N50	A26	30 l rose	.65	*1.00*

Engr.

N51	A27	2d vermilion	19.00	*32.50*
N52	A27	3d car rose	8.50	*22.50*
N53	A27	5d ultra	25.00	*42.50*
N54	A27	10d deep blue	19.00	*32.50*
a.		Double overprint	45.00	
		Nos. N46-N54 (9)	74.00	*133.80*

For Use in Eastern and Western Thrace

Greek Stamps of 1911-19 Overprinted

1920 Litho.

N55	A24	1 l green	.20	*.30*
a.		Pair, one without ovpt.	22.50	
N56	A25	2 l rose	.20	*.30*
N57	A24	3 l vermilion	.20	*.30*
a.		Double overprint	11.50	
N58	A26	5 l green	.25	*.45*
a.		Pair, one without ovpt.	24.00	
N59	A24	10 l rose	.40	*.70*
a.		Double overprint	27.50	
N60	A25	20 l slate	.65	*1.25*
a.		Inverted overprint	15.00	
N61	A25	25 l blue	1.25	*2.00*
N62	A25	40 l indigo	2.40	*6.50*
N63	A26	50 l violet brn	3.00	*8.50*
N64	A27	1d ultra	12.00	*20.00*
N65	A27	2d vermilion	22.50	*35.00*

Engr.

N66	A24	3 l vermilion	2.75	*4.75*
N67	A25	20 l gray lilac	9.50	*22.50*
N68	A28	25d deep blue	47.50	*90.00*
		Nos. N55-N68 (14)	102.80	*192.55*

This overprint reads "Administration Thrace."

With Additional Overprint as Nos. N46-N54

Litho.

N69	A25	2 l car rose	.25	*.50*
N70	A26	5 l green	1.50	*3.00*
N71	A25	20 l slate	.25	*.50*
N72	A26	30 l rose	.25	*.50*

Engr.

N73	A27	3d car rose	7.50	*14.00*
N74	A27	5d ultra	18.00	*30.00*
N75	A27	10d deep blue	32.50	*60.00*
		Nos. N69-N75 (7)	60.25	*108.50*

Turkish Stamps of 1916-20 Surcharged in Blue, Black or Red

1920 *Perf. 11½, 12½*

N76	A43	1 l on 5pa org (Bl)	.40	*.50*
N77	A32	5 l on 3pi blue	.40	*.50*
N78	A30	20 l on 1pi bl grn	.50	*.70*
N79	A53	25 l on 5pi on 2pa Prus bl (R)	.60	*.75*
N80	A49	50 l on 5pi bl & blk (R)	4.75	*4.75*
N81	A45	1d on 20pa dp rose (Bl)	1.60	1.40
N82	A22	2d on 10pa on 2pa ol grn (R)	2.50	*2.50*
N83	A57	3d on 1pi dp bl (R)	9.50	*9.50*
N84	A23	5d on 20pa rose	9.00	*9.00*
		Nos. N76-N84 (9)	29.25	29.60

Nos. N77, N78 and N84 are on the 1920 issue with designs modified. Nos. N81, N82 and N83 are on stamps with the 1919 overprints.

Varieties found on some values of this issue include: inverted surcharge, double surcharge with one inverted, and surcharge on both face and back.

POSTAGE DUE STAMPS

Issued under Allied Occupation

Bulgarian Postage Due Stamps of 1919 Overprinted like Nos. N7-N15 Reading Vertically Up

1919		Unwmk.	*Perf. 12x11½*	
NJ1	D6	5s emerald	.30	.30
NJ2	D6	10s purple	.70	.70
NJ3	D6	50s blue	.70	.60
		Nos. NJ1-NJ3 (3)	1.70	1.60

Type of Bulgarian Postage Due Stamps of 1919-22 Overprinted

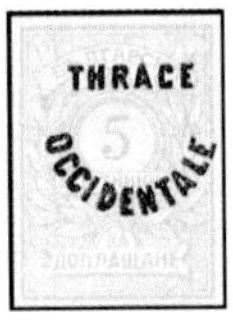

1920			*Imperf.*	
NJ4	D6	5s emerald	.20	.20
NJ5	D6	10s deep violet	1.40	1.40
NJ6	D6	20s salmon	.25	.25
NJ7	D6	50s blue	1.25	1.10
		Perf. 12x11½		
8	D6	10s deep violet	1.00	.80
		Nos. NJ4-NJ8 (5)	4.10	3.75

TIBET

tə-ˈbet

LOCATION — A high tableland in Central Asia
GOVT. — A semi-independent state, nominally under control of China.
AREA — 463,200 sq. mi.
POP. — 1,500,000 (approx.)
CAPITAL — Lhasa

Tibet's postage stamps were valid only within its borders.

6 2/3 Trangka = 1 Sang

Excellent counterfeits of Nos. 1-18 exist. Numerous shades of all values.

All stamps issued without gum

Small bits of foreign matter (inclusions) are to be expected in Native Paper. These do not reduce the value of the stamp unless they have caused serious damage to the design or paper.

A1

Lion — A2

1912-50		Unwmk. Typo. Native Paper	*Imperf.*	
1	A1	⅙t green	35.00	*40.00*
2	A1	⅓t blue	40.00	*45.00*
a.		⅓t ultramarine	45.00	*55.00*
3	A1	½t violet	40.00	*45.00*
4	A1	⅔t carmine	45.00	*50.00*
a.		"POTSAGE"	140.00	*150.00*
5	A1	1t vermilion	50.00	*60.00*
6	A1	1s sage green ('50)	90.00	*100.00*
		Nos. 1-6 (6)	300.00	*340.00*

The "POTSAGE" error is found on all shades of the ⅔t (positions 6 and 7).

Pin-perf. copies of Nos. 1 and 3 exist.

Issued in sheets of 12.

Beware of private reproductions of #1-5 that were printed in the US around 1986. Sheets of 12 bear "J. Crow Co." imprint. The set of 5 sheets was sold for $5.

Printed Using Shiny Enamel Paint

1920				
1a	A1	⅙t green	50.00	30.00
2b	A1	⅓t blue	450.00	450.00
3d	A1	½t purple	90.00	*100.00*
4h	A1	⅔t carmine	90.00	*100.00*
i.		"POTSAGE"	*200.00*	*225.00*
5c	A1	1t carmine	300.00	300.00

In some 1920-30 printings, European enamel paint was used instead of ink. It has a glossy surface.

1914				
7	A2	4t milky blue	675.	*725.*
a.		4t dark blue	1,000.	1,000.
8	A2	8t carmine rose	160.	160.
a.		8t carmine	1,000.	*1,100.*

Issued in sheets of 6.

Printed Using Shiny Enamel Paint

1920				
7b	A2	4t blue	1,200.	*1,250.*
8b	A2	8t carmine	1,200.	*1,250.*

See note following No. 5c.

A3

Thin White Native Paper

1933			*Pin-perf.*	
9	A3	½t orange	82.50	*95.00*
10	A3	⅔t dark blue	82.50	*110.00*
11	A3	1t rose carmine	82.50	*110.00*
12	A3	2t scarlet	82.50	*110.00*
13	A3	4t emerald	82.50	*110.00*
		Nos. 9-13 (5)	412.50	*535.00*

Issued in sheets of 12.

Exist imperf.

Heavy Toned Native Paper

1934			*Imperf.*	
14	A3	½t yellow	13.00	*16.00*
15	A3	⅔t blue	10.00	*11.00*
16	A3	1t orange ver	8.75	*10.00*
a.		1t carmine	11.00	11.00
17	A3	2t red	10.00	10.00
a.		2t orange vermilion	7.75	7.75
18	A3	4t green	7.75	7.75
a.		25x25mm instead of 24x24mm	50.00	*60.00*
		Nos. 14-18 (5)	49.50	*54.75*

Nos. 14-18 are also known with a private pin-perf.

The ½t and 1t exist printed on both sides.

Issued in sheets of 12.

TIMOR

ˈtē-ˌmor

LOCATION — The eastern part of Timor island, Malay archipelago
GOVT. — Portuguese Overseas Territory
AREA — 7,330 sq. mi.
POP. — 660,000 (est. 1974)
CAPITAL — Dili

1000 Reis = 1 Milreis
78 Avos = 1 Rupee (1895)
100 Avos = 1 Pataca

Watermark

Wmk. 232 — Maltese Cross

Stamps of Macao Overprinted in Black or Carmine **TIMOR**

1885		Unwmk.	*Perf. 12½, 13½*	
1	A1	5r black (C)	5.50	1.60
a.		Double overprint	37.50	37.50
b.		Triple overprint	115.00	
2	A1	10r green	8.00	3.50
a.		Overprint on Mozambique stamp	*22.50*	*14.00*
b.		Overprinted on Portuguese India stamp	*210.00*	*150.00*
3	A1	20r rose, perf. 13½	9.00	4.50
a.		Double overprint	22.50	
b.		Perf. 12½	9.50	5.00
4	A1	25r violet	2.25	1.10
a.		Perf. 13½	22.00	11.00
5	A1	40r yellow	5.50	3.00
a.		Double overprint	17.50	
b.		Inverted overprint	*21.00*	*21.00*
c.		Perf. 13½	14.00	11.00
6	A1	50r blue	4.50	1.50
a.		Perf. 13½	12.00	9.50
7	A1	80r slate	11.00	3.00
8	A1	100r lilac	5.50	1.50
a.		Double overprint	22.50	
b.		Perf. 13½	9.00	3.50
9	A1	200r org, perf. 13½	9.00	3.50
a.		Perf. 12½	11.00	3.50
10	A1	300r brown	8.00	3.00
		Nos. 1-10 (10)	68.25	26.20

The 20r brown, 25r rose and 50r green were prepared for use but not issued.

The reprints are printed on a smooth white chalky paper, ungummed, with rough perforation 13½, and on thin white paper with shiny white gum and clean-cut perforation 13½.

King Luiz — A2

King Carlos — A3

1887		Embossed	*Perf. 12½*	
11	A2	5r black	2.00	1.75
12	A2	10r green	3.50	3.00
13	A2	20r bright rose	3.50	3.00
14	A2	25r violet	6.75	3.50
15	A2	40r chocolate	11.50	4.50
16	A2	50r blue	14.00	5.50
17	A2	80r gray	14.00	7.50
18	A2	100r yellow brown	20.00	9.00
19	A2	200r gray lilac	25.00	16.00
20	A2	300r orange	25.00	16.00
		Nos. 11-20 (10)	125.25	69.75

Reprints of Nos. 11, 16, 18 and 19 have clean-cut perforation 13½.

For surcharges see Nos. 34-43, 83-91.

Macao No. 44 Surcharged in Black

1892		Without Gum	*Perf. 12½, 13*	
21	A7	30r on 300r orange	8.25	5.50

For surcharge see No. 44.

1894		Typo.	*Perf. 11½*	
22	A3	5r yellow	1.10	.65
23	A3	10r red violet	1.50	.65
24	A3	15r chocolate	2.75	.95
25	A3	20r lavender	3.50	1.10
26	A3	25r green	4.25	.80
27	A3	50r light blue	5.50	3.50
a.		Perf. 13½	*150.00*	*125.00*
28	A3	75r rose	6.75	2.75
29	A3	80r light green	7.25	4.25
30	A3	100r brown, *buff*	5.50	2.75
31	A3	150r car, *rose*	12.00	6.75
32	A3	200r dk bl, *lt bl*	12.50	8.00
33	A3	300r dk bl, *salmon*	14.00	9.50
		Nos. 22-33 (12)	76.60	41.65

For surcharges and overprints see Nos. 92-102, 120-122, 124-128, 131-133, 183-193, 199.

Stamps of 1887 Surcharged in Red, Green or Black

1895		Without Gum	*Perf. 12½*	
34	A2	1a on 5r black (R)	1.00	.85
35	A2	2a on 10r green	1.25	.85
a.		Double surcharge	17.50	
36	A2	3a on 20r brt rose (G)	2.75	1.75
37	A2	4a on 25r violet	2.75	1.10
38	A2	6a on 40r choc	4.50	2.50
39	A2	8a on 50r blue (R)	4.00	2.25
40	A2	13a on 80r gray	14.00	9.00
41	A2	16a on 100r yellow brn	15.00	6.75
42	A2	31a on 200r gray lilac	27.50	17.50
43	A2	47a on 300r org (G)	27.50	20.00
		Nos. 34-43 (10)	100.25	62.55

No. 21 Surcharged

5 avos
PROVISORIO
仙伍

1895		Without Gum	*Perf. 12½, 13*	
44	A7	5a on 30r on 300r org	8.50	5.00

Common Design Types pictured following the introduction.

Vasco da Gama Issue

Common Design Types

1898		Engr.	*Perf. 14 to 15*	
45	CD20	½a blue green	1.50	.85
46	CD21	1a red	1.50	.85
47	CD22	2a red violet	1.50	.85
48	CD23	4a yellow green	1.50	.85
49	CD24	8a dark blue	3.00	1.25
50	CD25	12a violet brown	3.50	1.40
51	CD26	16a bister brown	4.00	1.90
52	CD27	24a bister	5.00	2.50
		Nos. 45-52 (8)	21.50	10.45

400th anniversary of Vasco da Gama's discovery of the route to India.

For overprints and surcharge see Nos. 148-155.

King Carlos
A5 A6

1898-1903 Typo. *Perf. 11½*
Name & Value in Black Except #79

53 A5 ½a gray .35 .25
a. Perf. 12½ 2.50 1.75
54 A5 1a orange .35 .30
a. Perf. 12½ 2.50 1.75
55 A5 2a light green .35 .30
56 A5 2½a brown 1.25 1.10
57 A5 3a gray violet 1.25 1.10
58 A5 3a gray green ('03) 1.50 1.00
59 A5 4a sea green 1.60 1.00
60 A5 5a rose ('03) 1.50 1.00
61 A5 6a pale yel brn ('03) 1.50 1.00
62 A5 8a blue 2.00 1.10
63 A5 9a red brown ('03) 1.50 1.25
64 A5 10a slate blue ('00) 2.00 1.10
65 A5 10a gray brown ('03) 1.50 1.00
66 A5 12a rose 4.25 3.00
67 A5 12a dull blue ('03) 15.00 8.50
68 A5 13a violet 4.50 3.75
69 A5 13a red lilac ('03) 3.50 1.75
70 A5 15a gray lilac ('03) 5.50 3.75
71 A5 16a dark bl, *bl* 4.50 3.75
72 A5 20a brn, *yelsh* ('00) 5.25 3.75
73 A5 22a brn org, *pink* ('03) 5.25 3.50
74 A5 24a brown, *buff* 5.50 3.75
75 A5 31a red lil, *pinkish* 5.50 3.75
76 A5 31a brn, *straw* ('03) 5.75 3.00
77 A5 47a dk blue, *rose* 9.00 4.25
78 A5 47a red vio, *pink* ('03) 6.50 3.50
79 A5 78a blk & red, *bl* ('00) 11.00 6.00
80 A5 78a dl bl, *straw* ('03) 14.00 8.00
Nos. 53-80 (28) 121.65 76.00

Most of Nos. 53-80 were issued without gum.
For surcharges & overprints see #81-82, 104-119, 129-130, 134-147, 195-196.

1899

Black Surcharge

81 A6 10a on 16a dk bl, *bl* 3.00 2.50
82 A6 20a on 31a red lil, *pnksh* 3.00 2.50

Surcharged in Black

1902

On Issue of 1887

83 A2 5a on 25r violet 2.50 1.75
84 A2 5a on 200r gray lil 4.00 2.50
85 A2 6a on 10r blue grn 75.00 40.00
86 A2 6a on 300r orange 3.75 3.50
87 A2 9a on 40r choc 4.50 3.50
88 A2 9a on 100r yel brn 4.50 3.50
89 A2 15a on 20r rose 4.50 3.50
90 A2 15a on 50r blue 75.00 40.00
91 A2 22a on 80r gray 7.50 5.00
Nos. 83-91 (9) 181.25 103.25

Reprints of Nos. 83-88, 90-91, 104A have clean-cut perf. 13½.

On Issue of 1894

92 A3 5a on 5r yellow 1.90 1.10
a. Inverted surcharge 40.00 30.00
93 A3 5a on 25r green 2.25 1.10
94 A3 5a on 50r lt blue 2.25 1.40
95 A3 6a on 20r lavender 2.25 1.40
96 A3 9a on 15r choc 2.25 1.40
97 A3 9a on 75r rose 2.25 1.40
98 A3 15a on 10r red vio 4.00 2.25
99 A3 15a on 100r brn, *buff* 4.00 2.25
100 A3 15a on 300r bl, *sal* 4.00 2.25
101 A3 22a on 80r lt green 6.00 4.00
102 A3 22a on 200r bl, *blue* 8.00 4.00

On Newspaper Stamp of 1893

103 N2 6a on 2½r brn 1.00 .85
a. Inverted surcharge 27.50 27.50
Nos. 92-103 (12) 40.15 23.40

Nos. 93-97, 99-102 issued without gum.

Stamps of 1898 Overprinted in Black

104 A5 3a gray violet 3.00 1.40
104A A5 12a rose 6.00 3.75

Reprint noted after No. 91.

No. 67 Surcharged in Black

1905

105 A5 10a on 12a dull blue 3.50 2.50

Stamps of 1898-1903 Overprinted in Carmine or Green

1911

106 A5 ½a gray .30 .30
a. Inverted overprint *20.00 20.00*
107 A5 1a orange .30 .30
a. Perf. 12½ *16.00 16.00*
108 A5 2a light green .40 .35
109 A5 3a gray green .50 .35
110 A5 5a rose (G) .50 .35
111 A5 6a yel brown .50 .35
112 A5 9a red brown .75 .45
113 A5 10a gray brown .75 .45
114 A5 13a red lilac .80 .50
115 A5 15a gray lilac 1.60 1.25
116 A5 22a brn org, *pink* 1.60 1.25
117 A5 31a brown, *straw* 1.60 1.25
118 A5 47a red vio, *pink* 3.00 2.50
119 A5 78a dl bl, *straw* 4.75 3.50
Nos. 106-119 (14) 17.35 13.15

Preceding Issues Overprinted in Red

1913

Without Gum

On Provisional Issue of 1902

120 A3 5a on 5r yellow 4.00 4.00
121 A3 5a on 25r green 4.00 4.00
122 A3 5a on 50r lt bl 6.00 7.00
123 N2 6a on 2½r brn 6.00 7.00
124 A3 6a on 20r lavender 4.00 4.00
125 A3 9a on 15r choc 4.00 4.00
126 A3 15a on 100r brn, *buff* 6.00 5.50
127 A3 22a on 80r lt grn 9.00 8.00
128 A3 22a on 200r bl, *bl* 8.00 7.50

On Issue of 1903

129 A5 3a gray green 5.00 *7.50*

On Issue of 1905

130 A5 10a on 12a dull bl 4.50 *4.00*
Nos. 120-130 (11) 60.50 *62.50*

Overprinted in Green or Red

1913

On Provisional Issue of 1902

131 A3 9a on 75r rose (G) 4.50 4.50
132 A3 15a on 10r red vio (G) 3.75 3.75
a. Inverted overprint *35.00 35.00*
133 A3 15a on 300r bl, *sal* (R) 6.50 6.50
a. "REUBPLICA" 19.00 19.00
b. "REPBLICAU" 19.00 19.00

On Issue of 1903

134 A5 5a rose (G) 3.00 3.00
Nos. 131-134 (4) 17.75 17.75

Stamps of 1898-1903 Overprinted in Red

1913

135 A5 6a yellow brown 4.00 1.75
136 A5 9a red brown 4.00 1.75
137 A5 10a gray brown 4.00 1.75
138 A5 13a violet 6.00 2.50
a. Inverted overprint 40.00 40.00
139 A5 13a red lilac 5.00 2.50
140 A5 15a gray lilac 6.00 3.25
141 A5 22a brn org, *pnksh* 7.00 3.50
142 A5 31a red lil, *pnksh* 7.00 3.50
143 A5 31a brown, *straw* 9.00 5.50
144 A5 47a blue, *pink* 10.00 5.50
145 A5 47a red vio, *pink* 12.00 8.00
146 A5 78a dl bl, *straw* 12.00 6.50

No. 79 Overprinted in Red

147 A5 78a blk & red, *bl* 12.00 8.00
Nos. 135-147 (13) 98.00 54.00

Vasco da Gama Issue of 1898 Overprinted or Surcharged in Black:

1913

148 CD20 ½a blue green .65 .60
149 CD21 1a red .65 .60
150 CD22 2a red violet .65 .60
151 CD23 4a yellow green .65 .60
152 CD24 8a dark blue 1.40 1.10
153 CD25 10a on 12a vio brn 2.50 2.00
154 CD26 16a bister brown 2.00 1.75
155 CD27 24a bister 2.75 2.25
Nos. 148-155 (8) 11.25 9.50

Ceres — A7

1914-23 Typo. *Perf. 15x14, 12x11½*
Name and Value in Black

156 A7 ½a olive brown .20 .20
157 A7 1a black .20 .20
158 A7 1½a yel grn ('23) .60 *1.10*
159 A7 2a blue green .25 .25
160 A7 3a lilac brown 1.00 .75
161 A7 4a carmine 1.00 .75
162 A7 6a light violet 1.00 .75
163 A7 7a lt green ('23) 1.75 *1.75*
164 A7 7½a ultra ('23) 3.25 *3.50*
165 A7 9a blue ('23) 4.00 *6.75*
166 A7 10a deep blue 1.25 .75
167 A7 11a gray ('23) 4.00 *6.75*
168 A7 12a yellow brown 1.50 1.25
169 A7 15a lilac ('23) 8.00 *7.25*
170 A7 16a slate 2.00 3.75
171 A7 18a dp blue ('23) 10.00 6.25
172 A7 19a gray grn ('23) 10.00 5.50
173 A7 20a org brown 15.00 6.00
174 A7 36a turq blue ('23) 9.00 4.25
175 A7 40a plum 9.00 4.50
176 A7 54a choc ('23) 10.00 6.25
177 A7 58a brown, *grn* 10.00 5.00
178 A7 72a brt rose ('23) 16.00 16.00
179 A7 76a brown, *rose* 11.50 6.50
180 A7 1p org, *salmon* 20.00 11.00
181 A7 3p green, *blue* 35.00 25.00
182 A7 5p car rose ('23) 70.00 52.50
Nos. 156-182 (27) 255.50 184.50

For surcharges see Nos. 200-201, MR1.

Preceding Issues Overprinted in Carmine

1915 *Perf. 11½*

On Provisional Issue of 1902

183 A3 5a on 5r yellow 1.00 .55
184 A3 5a on 25r green 1.00 .55
185 A3 5a on 50r lt blue 1.00 .55
186 A3 6a on 20r lavender 1.00 .55
187 A3 9a on 15r chocolate 1.00 .55
188 A3 9a on 75r rose 1.50 .55
189 A3 15a on 10r red vio 1.50 1.50
190 A3 15a on 100r brn, *buff* 2.00 1.50
191 A3 15a on 300r bl, *sal* 2.00 3.00
192 A3 22a on 80r lt grn 3.25 2.75
193 A3 22a on 200r bl, *bl* 5.00 5.00

On No. 103

194 N2 6a on 2½r, perf. 13½ 1.00 .55
a. Perf. 12½ 2.00 1.25
b. Perf. 11½ 4.00 1.75

On No. 104

195 A5 3a gray violet 1.00 .60

On No. 105

196 A5 10a on 12a dull bl 1.10 .60
Nos. 183-196 (14) 23.35 18.80

Type of 1915 with Additional Surcharge in Black

Perf. 11½

199 A3 ½a on 5a on 50r lt bl 12.50 7.00
a. Perf. 13½ 35.00 12.50

Nos. 178 and 169 Surcharged

1932 *Perf. 12x11½*

200 A7 6a on 72a brt rose 1.50 1.25
201 A7 12a on 15a lilac 1.50 1.25

"Portugal" and Vasco da Gama's Flagship "San Gabriel" — A8

Perf. 11½x12
1935 Typo. Wmk. 232

202 A8 ½a bister .20 .20
203 A8 1a olive brown .20 .20
204 A8 2a blue green .20 .20
205 A8 3a red violet .60 .60
206 A8 4a black .60 .30
207 A8 5a gray .70 .65
208 A8 6a brown .85 .60
209 A8 7a bright rose 1.00 1.00
210 A8 8a bright blue 1.10 1.10
211 A8 10a red orange 1.60 1.20
212 A8 12a dark blue 2.75 2.10
213 A8 14a olive green 3.25 2.10
214 A8 15a maroon 3.00 2.75
215 A8 20a orange 3.50 2.75
216 A8 30a apple green 4.00 2.75
217 A8 40a violet 7.50 4.50
218 A8 50a olive bister 8.75 4.50
219 A8 1p light blue 21.00 12.00
220 A8 2p brn orange 42.50 22.50
221 A8 3p emerald 52.50 32.50
222 A8 5p dark violet 82.50 45.00
Nos. 202-222 (21) 238.30 139.50

Common Design Types

1938 Unwmk. Engr. *Perf. 13½x13*

Name and Value in Black

223 CD34 1a gray green .20 .20
224 CD34 2a orange brown .20 .30
225 CD34 3a dk violet brn .20 .30
226 CD34 4a brt green .20 .65
227 CD35 5a dk carmine .20 1.75
228 CD35 6a slate .45 .20
229 CD35 8a rose violet .65 1.10
230 CD37 10a brt red violet .65 1.75
231 CD37 12a red 1.10 2.50
232 CD37 15a orange 1.75 2.50
233 CD36 20a blue 1.75 .80
234 CD36 40a gray black 3.75 1.25
235 CD36 50a brown 3.75 1.25
236 CD38 1p brown carmine 7.00 4.50
237 CD38 2p olive green 14.00 3.50
238 CD38 3p blue violet 17.50 8.00
239 CD38 5p red brown 35.00 11.50
Nos. 223-239 (17) 88.35 42.05

For overprints see Nos. 245A-245K.

AIR POST STAMPS

Common Design Type

1938 Unwmk. Engr. *Perf. 13½x13*

Name and Value in Black

C1 CD39 1a scarlet .85 .45
C2 CD39 2a purple .90 .55
C3 CD39 3a orange .90 .60
C4 CD39 5a ultra 1.00 .65
C5 CD39 10a lilac brown 1.60 1.10
C6 CD39 20a dark green 3.00 1.40
C7 CD39 50a red brown 6.00 4.00
C8 CD39 70a rose carmine 7.00 5.25
C9 CD39 1p magenta 13.00 6.00
Nos. C1-C9 (9) 34.25 20.00

No. C7 exists with overprint "Exposicao Internacional de Nova York, 1939-1940" and Trylon and Perisphere. Counterfeits exist.

For overprints see Nos. C15-C23.

POSTAGE DUE STAMPS

D1

1904 Unwmk. Typo. *Perf. 12*

Without Gum

Name and Value in Black

J1 D1 1a yellow green .50 .50
J2 D1 2a slate .50 .50
J3 D1 5a yellow brown 2.25 1.50
J4 D1 6a red orange 2.25 2.25
J5 D1 10a gray brown 2.50 2.00
J6 D1 15a red brown 3.75 2.75
J7 D1 24a dull blue 6.25 5.50
J8 D1 40a carmine 7.50 5.50
J9 D1 50a orange 10.50 7.50
J10 D1 1p dull violet 17.00 13.00
Nos. J1-J10 (10) 53.00 41.00

Overprinted in Carmine or Green

1911 Without Gum

J11 D1 1a yellow green .25 .25
J12 D1 2a slate .30 .25
a. Inverted overprint
J13 D1 5a yellow brown .60 .40
J14 D1 6a deep orange .80 .50
J15 D1 10a gray brown 1.50 .70
J16 D1 15a brown 1.75 1.10
J17 D1 24a dull blue 2.50 2.00
J18 D1 40a carmine (G) 3.25 2.50
J19 D1 50a orange 3.75 2.50
J20 D1 1p dull violet 7.50 7.00
Nos. J11-J20 (10) 22.20 17.20

Nos. J1-J10 Overprinted in Red or Green

1913 Without Gum

J21 D1 1a yellow green 8.00 *9.00*
J22 D1 2a slate 8.00 *9.00*
J23 D1 5a yellow brown 4.50 *4.50*
J24 D1 6a deep orange 4.50 *4.50*
a. Inverted surcharge 30.00
J25 D1 10a gray brown 4.50 *6.00*
J26 D1 15a red brown 4.50 *6.00*
J27 D1 24a dull blue 6.00 *6.00*
J28 D1 40a carmine (G) 6.00 *6.00*
J29 D1 50a orange 10.00 *12.00*
J30 D1 1p gray violet 10.00 *12.00*
Nos. J21-J30 (10) 66.00 75.00

WAR TAX STAMP

Regular Issue of 1914 Surcharged in Red

1919 Unwmk. *Perf. 15x14*

Without Gum

MR1 A7 2a on ½a ol brn 22.50 20.00

See note after Macao No. MR2.

NEWSPAPER STAMPS

King Luiz — N1

Stamps of Macao Surcharged in Black

1892 Unwmk. *Perf. 12½*

Without Gum

P1 N1 2½r on 20r brt rose 2.00 .75
a. "TIMOR" inverted
P2 N1 2½r on 40r chocolate 2.00 .75
a. "TIMOR" inverted
b. Perf. 13½ 4.50 3.00
c. As "a," perf. 13½
P3 N1 2½r on 80r gray 2.00 .75
a. "TIMOR" inverted
b. Perf. 13½ 12.50 8.00
Nos. P1-P3 (3) 6.00 2.25

N2

N3

1893-95 Typo. *Perf. 11½, 13½*

P4 N2 2½r brown .40 .35
a. Perf. 12½ 2.00 1.50
P5 N3 ½a on 2½r brn ('95) .45 .30

For surcharges see Nos. 103, 123, 194.

POSTAL TAX STAMPS

Pombal Issue

Common Design Types

1925 Unwmk. *Perf. 12½*

RA1 CD28 2a lake & black .30 .30
RA2 CD29 2a lake & black .30 .30
RA3 CD30 2a lake & black .30 .30
Nos. RA1-RA3 (3) .90 .90

Type of War Tax Stamp of Portuguese India Overprinted in Red

1934-35 *Perf. 12*

RA4 WT1 2a green & blk 6.50 *8.00*
RA5 WT1 5a green & blk 8.00 8.00

Surcharged in Black

RA6 WT1 7a on ½a rose & blk ('35) 9.00 7.50
Nos. RA4-RA6 (3) 23.50 *23.50*

The tax was for local education.

Type of War Tax Stamp of Portuguese India Overprinted in Black

1936 *Perf. 12x11½*

RA7 WT1 10a rose & black 7.00 *9.00*

1937 *Perf. 11½*

RA8 WT1 10a green & blk 5.50 *8.25*

POSTAL TAX DUE STAMPS

Pombal Issue

Common Design Types

1925 Unwmk. *Perf. 12½*

RAJ1 CD28 4a lake & black .40 *1.00*
RAJ2 CD29 4a lake & black .40 *1.00*
RAJ3 CD30 4a lake & black .40 *1.00*
Nos. RAJ1-RAJ3 (3) 1.20 *3.00*

TOBAGO

tə-ˈbā-ˌgō

LOCATION — An island in the West Indies lying off the Venezuelan coast north of Trinidad
GOVT. — British Colony
AREA — 116 sq. mi.
POP. — 25,358
CAPITAL — Scarborough (Port Louis)

In 1889 Tobago, then an independent colony, was united with Trinidad under the name of Colony of Trinidad and Tobago. It became a ward of that colony January 1, 1899.

12 Pence = 1 Shilling
20 Shillings = 1 Pound

PRE-STAMP POSTAL MARKINGS

Crowned Circle handstamp types I and V are pictured in the Crowned Circle Handstamps and Great Britain Used Abroad section.

Scarborough

1851-75

A1 I "Tobago" crowned circle handstamp in red, on cover 1,000.
A2 V "Tobago" crowned circle handstamp in red, on cover ('75) 4,250.

STAMPS OF GREAT BRITAIN USED IN TOBAGO

Numeral cancellation type A is pictured in the Crowned Circle Handstamps and Great Britain Used Abroad section.

1858-60

A14 (Scarborough)

A3 A 1p rose red (#20) 925.
A4 A 4p rose (#26) 400.
A5 A 6p lilac (#27) 290.
A6 A 1sh green (#28) 1,750.

Issued under British Administration

Queen Victoria
A1 A2

Wmk. Crown and C C (1)

1879 Typo. *Perf. 14*

1 A1 1p rose 97.50 77.50
2 A1 3p blue 97.50 62.50
3 A1 6p orange 47.50 *67.50*
4 A1 1sh green 425.00 75.00
a. Half used as 6p on cover
5 A1 5sh slate 775.00 700.00
6 A1 £1 violet *4,500.*

Stamps of the above set with revenue cancellations sell for a small fraction of the price of postally used copies.

Stamps of Type A1, watermarked Crown and C A, are revenue stamps.

1880

Manuscript Surcharge

7 A1 1p on half of 6p org *5,250.* *875.*

1880

8 A2 ½p brown violet 47.50 *72.50*
9 A2 1p red brown 125.00 62.50
a. Half used as ½p on cover *2,250.*
10 A2 4p yellow green 290.00 30.00
a. Half used as 2p on cover *2,250.*
11 A2 6p bister brown 400.00 125.00
12 A2 1sh bister 77.50 *87.50*
a. Imperf.
Nos. 8-12 (5) 940.00 377.50

No. 11 Surcharged in Black

1883

13 A2 2½p on 6p bister brn 62.50 62.50
a. Double surcharge 3,250. 1,500.

1882-96 Wmk. Crown and C A (2)

14 A2 ½p brown vio ('82) 2.25 *14.50*
15 A2 ½p dull green ('86) 2.75 1.40
16 A2 1p red brown ('82) 4.75 2.50
a. Diagonal half used as ½p on cover —
17 A2 1p rose ('89) 3.50 1.40
18 A2 2½p ultra ('83) 8.50 1.10
a. 2½p dull blue ('83) 40.00 2.25
b. 2½p bright blue 8.50 1.10
19 A2 4p yel grn ('82) 210.00 100.00
20 A2 4p gray ('85) 3.25 2.25
a. Imperf., pair 2,000.
21 A2 6p bis brn ('84) 625.00 550.00
a. Imperf.
22 A2 6p brn org ('86) 2.75 *5.75*
23 A2 1sh olive bis ('94) 3.25 *19.00*
24 A2 1sh brn org ('96) 11.00 *77.50*

Stamps of 1882-96 Surcharged in Black:

Nos. 25-29

No. 30

1886-92

25 A2 ½p on 2½p ultra 6.50 *16.00*
a. Inverted surcharge
b. Pair, one without surcharge 11,000.
c. Space between "½" and "PENNY" 3mm 30.00 *67.50*
d. Double surcharge 2,400. 1,900.

26 A2 ½p on 4p gray 22.50 *62.50*
a. Space between "½" and "PENNY" 3mm
b. Double surcharge 2,250.
27 A2 ½p on 6p bis brn 3.50 *22.50*
a. Inverted surcharge 1,600.
b. Space between "½" and "PENNY" 3mm 30.00 *125.00*
c. Double surcharge 1,900.
28 A2 ½p on 6p brn org 110.00 150.00
a. Space between "½" and "PENNY" 3mm 350.00 *375.00*
b. Double surcharge 1,400.
29 A2 1p on 2½ ultra 70.00 19.00
a. Space between "1" and "PENNY" 4mm 175.00 *85.00*
b. Half used as ½p on cover *1,650.*
30 A2 2½p on 4p gray 10.00 *9.00*
a. Double surcharge 2,250. 2,250.
Nos. 25-30 (6) 222.50 *279.00*

Revenue Stamp Type A1 Surcharged in Black

1896

31 A1 ½p on 4p lilac & rose 72.50 40.00
a. Space between "½" and "d" 1½ to 2½mm 140.00 80.00

Tobago stamps were replaced by those of Trinidad or Trinidad and Tobago.

TOGO

ˈtō-ˌgō

LOCATION — Western Africa, bordering on the Gulf of Guinea
GOVT. — Republic
AREA — 20,400 sq. mi.
POP. — 2,890,000 (est. 1984)
CAPITAL — Lome

The German Protectorate of Togo was occupied by Great Britain and France in World War I, and later mandated to them. The British area became part of Ghana.

100 Pfennig = 1 Mark
12 Pence = 1 Shilling
100 Centimes = 1 Franc

Watermark

Wmk. 125 — Lozenges

German Protectorate

AREA — 34,934 sq. mi.
POP. — 1,000,368 (1913)

Stamps of Germany Overprinted in Black

1897 Unwmk. *Perf. 13½x14½*

1	A9	3pf dark brown	4.75	*6.25*
		Never hinged	13.50	
		On cover		30.00
a.		3pf yellow brown	8.25	*22.50*
		Never hinged	26.00	
		On cover		110.00
b.		3pf reddish brown	32.50	*95.00*
		Never hinged	120.00	
		On cover		260.00
c.		3pf pale gray brown	1,300.	*800.00*
		Never hinged	3,400.	
		On cover		1,600.
2	A9	5pf green	4.50	*2.50*
		Never hinged	8.25	
		On cover		15.00
3	A10	10pf carmine	5.25	*2.75*
		Never hinged	12.50	
		On cover		15.00
4	A10	20pf ultra	5.25	*12.00*
		Never hinged	15.00	
		On cover		37.50
5	A10	25pf orange	30.00	*52.50*
		Never hinged	97.50	
		On cover		165.00
6	A10	50pf red brown	30.00	*52.50*
		Never hinged	90.00	
		On cover		165.00
		Nos. 1-6 (6)	79.75	*128.50*

Covers: Value for No. 6 on cover is for overfranked complete covers, usually philatelic.

A3

Kaiser's Yacht, the "Hohenzollern" — A4

1900 Typo. *Perf. 14*

7	A3	3pf brown	.90	*1.10*
		Never hinged	1.90	
		On cover		52.50
8	A3	5pf green	10.50	*1.75*
		Never hinged	22.50	
		On cover		19.00
9	A3	10pf carmine	19.00	1.50
		Never hinged	45.00	
		On cover		19.00
10	A3	20pf ultra	.90	*1.25*
		Never hinged	3.75	
		On cover		22.50
11	A3	25pf org & blk, *yel*	.90	*9.00*
		Never hinged	3.75	
		On cover		45.00
12	A3	30pf org & blk, *sal*	1.10	*9.00*
		Never hinged	4.50	
		On cover		45.00
13	A3	40pf lake & blk	.90	*9.00*
		Never hinged	3.75	
		On cover		45.00
14	A3	50pf pur & blk, *sal*	1.10	*6.75*
		Never hinged	4.50	
		On cover		37.50
15	A3	80pf lake & blk, *rose*	2.25	*15.00*
		Never hinged	5.25	
		On cover		45.00

Engr.
Perf. 14½x14

16	A4	1m carmine	3.00	*47.50*
		Never hinged	9.00	
		On cover		90.00
17	A4	2m blue	4.75	*82.50*
		Never hinged	15.00	
		On cover		110.00
18	A4	3m black vio	6.25	*125.00*
		Never hinged	19.00	
		On cover		180.00
19	A4	5m slate & car	95.00	*450.00*
		Never hinged	310.00	
		On cover		675.00
		Nos. 7-19 (13)	146.55	*759.35*

Counterfeit cancellations are found on Nos. 10-19 and 22.

Covers: Values for Nos. 14-19 on cover are for overfranked complete covers, usually philatelic.

1909-19 Wmk. 125 Typo. *Perf. 14*

20	A3	3pf brown ('19)	.75	
		Never hinged	1.90	
21	A3	5pf green	1.10	*2.00*
		Never hinged	2.40	
		On cover		15.00
22	A3	10pf carmine ('14)	1.50	*95.00*
		Never hinged	3.25	
		On cover		600.00

Engr.
Perf. 14½x14

23	A4	5m slate & carmine, (25x17 holes) ('19)	21.00	
		Never hinged	82.50	
a.		5m slate & carmine (26x17 holes) ('15)	24.00	
		Never hinged	100.00	
		Nos. 20-23 (4)	24.35	

Nos. 20 and 23 were never placed in use.

British Protectorate

Nos. 7, 10-19, 21-22 Overprinted or Surcharged

First (Wide) Setting
3mm between Lines
2mm between "Anglo" & "French"

Wmk. 125 (5pf, 10pf); Unwmkd.

1914, Oct. 1 *Perf. 14, 14½*

33	A3	½p on 3pf brown	225.00	175.00
a.		Thin "y" in "penny"	*500.00*	*450.00*
34	A3	1p on 5pf green	*225.00*	*175.00*
a.		Thin "y" in "penny"	*500.00*	*500.00*
35	A3	3pf brown	*130.00*	*100.00*
36	A3	5pf green	*125.00*	*100.00*
37	A3	10pf carmine	*150.00*	*110.00*
a.		Inverted overprint	*8,500.*	*4,000.*
b.		Unwmk.		*6,250.*
38	A3	20pf ultra	*30.00*	*37.50*
39	A3	25pf org & blk, *yel*	*30.00*	*30.00*
40	A3	30pf org & blk, *sal*	*32.50*	*47.50*
41	A3	40pf lake & blk	*275.00*	*275.00*
42	A3	50pf pur & blk, *sal*	*10,000.*	*8,500.*
43	A3	80pf lake & blk, *rose*	*275.00*	*300.00*
44	A4	1m carmine	*5,750.*	*2,800.*
45	A4	2m blue	*9,000.*	*10,000.*
a.		Inverted overprint	—	—
b.		"Occupation" double	—	—

On Nos. 33-34, the surcharge line ("Half penny" or "One penny") was printed separately and its position varies in relation to the 3-line overprint. On Nos. 46-47, the surcharge and overprint lines were printed simultaneously.

Second (Narrow) Setting
2mm between Lines
2mm between "Anglo" & "French"

1914, Oct.

46	A3	½p on 3pf brown	*40.00*	*30.00*
a.		Thin "y" in "penny"	*70.00*	*70.00*
b.		"TOG"	*475.00*	*350.00*
47	A3	1p on 5pf green	*5.00*	*5.00*
a.		Thin "y" in "penny"	*15.00*	*17.50*
b.		"TOG"	*150.00*	125.00
48	A3	3pf brown	*5,250.*	*1,000*
a.		"Occupation" omitted		
49	A3	5pf green	*1,400.*	*800.00*
50	A3	10pf carmine		*3,100.*
51	A3	20pf ultra	*20.00*	*14.00*
a.		"TOG"	*4,750.*	*4,750.*
b.		Vert. pair, #51 & #38	*7,250.*	
52	A3	25pf org & blk, *yel*	*27.50*	*35.00*
a.		"TOG"	*13,750.*	
53	A3	30pf org & blk, *sal*	*22.50*	*32.50*
54	A3	40pf lake & blk	*5,250.*	*1,750.*
55	A3	50pf pur & blk, *sal*		*6,750.*
56	A3	80pf lake & blk, *rose*	*2,100.*	*2,100.*
57	A4	1m carmine	*8,500.*	*4,500.*
58	A4	2m blue		*10,000.*
59	A4	3m black violet		*45,000.*
60	A4	5m slate & car		*45,000.*

Third Setting
1¼mm btwn. "Anglo" & "French"
2mm between Lines
"Anglo-French" 15mm Wide

1915, Jan. 7

61	A3	3pf brown	*8,500.*	*3,250.*
62	A3	5pf green	*225.00*	*150.00*
63	A3	10pf carmine	*225.00*	*150.00*
64	A3	20pf ultra	*1,600.*	*600.*
64A	A3	40pf lake & blk		*8,500.*
65	A3	50pf pur & blk, *sal*	*14,000.*	*1,000.*

Stamps of Gold Coast Overprinted Locally

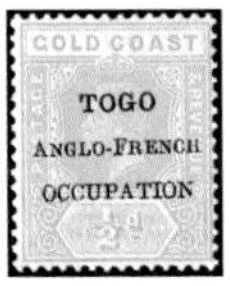

1915, May Wmk. 3 *Perf. 14*

66	A7	½p green	.35	*1.90*
a.		Double overprint	*525.00*	*550.00*
67	A8	1p scarlet	.35	*.55*
a.		Double ovpt.	*375.00*	*500.00*
b.		Inverted ovpt.	*200.00*	*275.00*
c.		As "b," "Togo" omitted		
68	A7	2p gray	.35	1.40
69	A7	2½p ultra	2.25	*4.00*

Chalky Paper

70	A7	3p violet, *yel*	2.25	*3.00*
71	A7	6p dl vio & red vio	1.60	*2.00*
72	A7	1sh black, *grn*	2.50	*6.00*
a.		Double overprint	*1,300.*	
73	A7	2sh vio & bl, *bl*	11.00	*16.00*
74	A7	2sh6p blk & red, *bl*	5.25	*25.00*
75	A7	10sh grn & red, *grn*	42.50	*70.00*
76	A7	20sh vio & blk, *red*	150.00	*175.00*

Surfaced-Colored Paper

77	A7	3p violet, *yel*	4.50	*20.00*
78	A7	5sh grn & red, *yel*	9.25	*17.50*
		Nos. 66-78 (13)	232.15	*342.35*

Nos. 66-78 exist with small "F" in "French" and thin "G" in "Togo." Several values are known without the hyphen between "Anglo-French" and all but No. 77 without the first "O" in "Occupation."

Stamps of Gold Coast Overprinted in London

1916, Apr.

Ordinary Paper

80	A7	½p green	.35	*2.90*
81	A8	1p scarlet	.35	*1.00*
a.		Inverted overprint		
82	A7	2p gray	.60	*.90*
83	A7	2½p ultra	.65	*1.75*

Chalky Paper

84	A7	3p violet, *yel*	3.00	1.80
85	A7	6p dl vio & red vio	2.25	1.10
86	A7	1sh black, *grn*	4.00	*7.50*
a.		1sh black, *emerald*	*350.00*	*750.00*
b.		1sh black, *bl grn,* ol back	*7.50*	*17.50*
87	A7	2sh vio & ultra, *bl*	5.25	9.75
88	A7	2sh6p blk & red, *bl*	5.25	*8.00*
89	A7	5sh grn & red, *yel*	21.00	*30.00*
90	A7	10sh grn & red, *bl grn,* ol back	20.00	*80.00*
a.		10sh green & red, *grn*	*27.50*	*75.00*
91	A7	20sh vio & blk, *red*	150.00	*180.00*
		Nos. 80-91 (12)	212.70	*324.70*

The overprint on Nos. 80-91 is in heavier letters than on Nos. 66-78 and the 2nd and 3rd lines are each ½mm longer. The letter "O" on Nos. 80-91 is narrower and more oval.

Issued under French Occupation

Stamps of German Togo Surcharged:

c

d

e

f

g

h

i

Wmk. Lozenges (5pf and 10pf) (125), Unwmk. (other values)

1914 *Perf. 14, 14½*

151	A3(c+d)	5c on 3pf brn	57.50	57.50
152	A3(c+e)	5c on 3pf brn	57.50	57.50
153	A3(c+f)	5c on 3pf brn	60.00	60.00
154	A3(c+g)	10c on 5pf grn	19.00	19.00
a.		Double surcharge	1,050.	1,050.
155	A3(c+h)	10c on 5pf grn	19.00	19.00
156	A3(c+i)	10c on 5pf grn	26.00	26.00
158	A3(c)	20pf ultra	45.00	45.00
a.		3 ½mm between "TOGO" and "Occupation"	700.00	*700.00*
159	A3(c)	25pf org & blk, *yel*	52.50	52.50
160	A3(c)	30pf org & blk, *sal*	95.00	95.00
161	A3(c)	40pf lake & black	575.00	525.00
162	A3(c)	80pf lake & blk, *rose*	575.00	525.00
		Nos. 151-162 (11)	1,581.	1,481.

Surcharged or Overprinted in Sans-Serif Type:

TOGO
Occupation
franco anglaise
05

1915

164	A3	5c on 3pf brown	*14,000.*	*4,400.*
165	A3	5pf green	900.	425.
166	A3	10pf carmine	1,050.	425.
a.		Inverted overprint	*27,000.*	*15,000.*
167	A3	20pf ultra	*1,300.*	900.
168	A3	25pf org & blk, *yel*	*14,000.*	*7,000.*
169	A3	30pf org & blk, *sal*	*14,000.*	*7,000.*
170	A3	40pf lake & blk	*14,000.*	*7,000.*
171	A3	50pf pur & blk, *sal*	*20,000.*	*12,000.*
172	A4	1m carmine		*75,000.*
173	A4	2m blue		*21,000.*
174	A4	3m black vio		*29,000.*
175	A4	5m slate & car	*27,000.*	*29,000.*

Stamps of Dahomey, 1913-17, Overprinted

1916-17 **Unwmk.** *Perf. 13½x14*

176	A5	1c violet & blk	.25	.25
177	A5	2c choc & rose	.25	.25
178	A5	4c black & brn	.35	.35
a.		Double overprint	425.00	425.00
179	A5	5c yel grn & bl grn	.60	.60
180	A5	10c org red & rose	.55	.55
181	A5	15c brn org & dk vio	1.50	1.50
182	A5	20c gray & choc	.60	.60
183	A5	25c ultra & dp bl	.90	.90
184	A5	30c choc & vio	.90	.90
185	A5	35c brown & blk	1.50	1.50
186	A5	40c blk & red org	1.25	1.25
187	A5	45c gray & ultra	1.40	1.40
188	A5	50c choc & brn	1.40	1.40
189	A5	75c blue & vio	6.00	6.00
190	A5	1fr bl grn & blk	7.50	7.50
191	A5	2fr buff & choc	11.00	11.00
192	A5	5fr vio & do bl	13.00	13.00
		Nos. 176-192 (17)	48.95	48.95

All values of the 1916-17 issue exist on chalky paper and all but the 15c, 25c and 35c on ordinary paper.

French Mandate

AREA — 21,893 sq. mi.
POP. — 780,497 (1938)

Type of Dahomey, 1913-39, Overprinted

1921

193	A5	1c gray & yel grn	.20	.20
a.		Overprint omitted	100.00	
194	A5	2c blue & org	.20	.20
195	A5	4c ol grn & org	.25	.25
196	A5	5c dull red & blk	.25	.25
a.		Overprint omitted	325.00	
197	A5	10c bl grn & yel grn	.55	.55
198	A5	15c brown & car	.60	.60
199	A5	20c bl grn & org	1.00	1.00
200	A5	25c slate & org	1.00	1.00
201	A5	30c dp rose & ver	1.10	1.10
202	A5	35c red brn & yel grn	1.00	1.00
203	A5	40c bl grn & ol	1.40	1.40
204	A5	45c red brn & ol	1.25	1.25
205	A5	50c deep blue	1.25	1.25
206	A5	75c dl red & ultra	1.40	1.40
207	A5	1fr gray & ultra	1.60	1.60
208	A5	2fr ol grn & rose	5.00	5.00
209	A5	5fr orange & blk	9.00	9.00
		Nos. 193-209 (17)	27.05	27.05

Stamps and Type of 1921 Surcharged

1922-25

210	A5	25c on 15c ol brn & rose red	.30	.30
211	A5	25c on 2fr ol grn & rose	.45	.45
212	A5	25c on 5fr org & blk	.45	.45
213	A5	60c on 75c vio, *pnksh*	.75	.75
a.		"60" omitted	175.00	175.00
214	A5	65c on 45c red brn & ol	1.25	1.25
a.		"TOGO" omitted	150.00	
215	A5	85c on 75c dull red & ultra	2.00	2.00
		Nos. 210-215 (6)	5.20	5.20

Issue years: #213, 1922; #211-212, 1924; others, 1925.

Coconut Grove A6

Cacao Trees — A7

Oil Palms A8

1924-38 **Typo.**

216	A6	1c yellow & blk	.20	.20
217	A6	2c dp rose & blk	.20	.20
218	A6	4c dk blue & blk	.20	.20
219	A6	5c dp org & blk	.20	.20
220	A6	10c red vio & blk	.20	.20
221	A6	15c green & blk	.20	.20
222	A7	20c gray & blk	.25	.25
223	A7	25c grn & blk, *yel*	.55	.55
224	A7	30c gray grn & blk	.25	.25
225	A7	30c dl grn & lt grn ('27)	.40	.40
226	A7	35c lt brown & blk	.60	.60
227	A7	35c dp bl grn & grn ('38)	.55	.45
228	A7	40c red org & blk	.25	.25
229	A7	45c carmine & blk	.25	.25
230	A7	50c ocher & blk, *bluish*	.40	.40
231	A7	55c vio bl & car rose ('38)	.75	.60
232	A7	60c vio brn & blk, *pnksh*	.25	.25
233	A7	60c dp red ('26)	.40	.40
234	A7	65c gray lil & brn	.55	.55
235	A7	75c blue & black	.55	.55
236	A7	80c ind & dl vio ('38)	1.60	1.50
237	A7	85c brn org & brn	1.00	1.00
238	A7	90c brn red & cer ('27)	.75	.75
239	A8	1fr red brn & blk, *bluish*	.70	.70
240	A8	1fr blue ('26)	.60	.60
241	A8	1fr gray lil & grn ('28)	2.25	1.90
242	A8	1fr dk red & red org ('38)	.75	.55
243	A8	1.10fr vio & dk brn ('28)	3.50	3.50
244	A8	1.25fr mag & rose ('33)	1.25	1.25
245	A8	1.50fr bl & lt bl ('27)	.60	.60
246	A8	1.75fr bis & pink ('33)	7.50	4.25
247	A8	1.75fr vio bl & ultra ('38)	1.25	1.00
248	A8	2fr bl blk & blk, *bluish*	1.00	1.00
249	A8	3fr bl grn & red org ('27)	1.25	1.25
250	A8	5fr red org & blk, *bluish*	1.75	1.75
251	A8	10fr ol brn & rose ('26)	2.25	2.25
252	A8	20fr brn red & blk, *yel* ('26)	2.50	2.50
		Nos. 216-252 (37)	37.70	33.30

For surcharges see Nos. 253, 301-302, B8-B9.

No. 240 Surcharged with New Value and Bars in Red

1926

253	A8	1.25fr on 1fr lt bl	.60	.60

Common Design Types pictured following the introduction.

Colonial Exposition Issue

Common Design Types

Engr., "TOGO" Typo. in Black

1931, Apr. 13 *Perf. 12½*

254	CD70	40c deep green	5.00	5.00
255	CD71	50c violet	5.00	5.00
256	CD72	90c red orange	5.00	5.00
257	CD73	1.50fr dull blue	5.00	5.00
		Nos. 254-257 (4)	20.00	20.00

Paris International Exposition Issue

Common Design Types

1937 *Perf. 13*

258	CD74	20c deep violet	1.50	1.50
259	CD75	30c dark green	1.50	1.50
260	CD76	40c carmine rose	1.50	1.50
261	CD77	50c dark brown	1.50	1.50
262	CD78	90c red	1.50	1.50
263	CD79	1.50fr ultra	1.50	1.50
		Nos. 258-263 (6)	9.00	9.00

Colonial Arts Exhibition Issue

Souvenir Sheet

Common Design Type

1937 *Imperf.*

264	CD77	3fr Prus bl & blk	6.00	*7.50*

Caillié Issue

Common Design Type

1939, Apr. 5 *Perf. 12½x12*

265	CD81	90c org brn & org	.75	.75
266	CD81	2fr brt violet	.75	.75
267	CD81	2.25fr ultra & dk bl	.75	.75
		Nos. 265-267 (3)	2.25	2.25

New York World's Fair Issue

Common Design Type

1939, May 10

268	CD82	1.25fr carmine lake	.90	.90
269	CD82	2.25fr ultra	.90	.90

SEMI-POSTAL STAMPS

Curie Issue

Common Design Type

1938 **Unwmk.** **Engr.** *Perf. 13*

B1	CD80	1.75fr + 50c brt ultra	16.00	16.00

French Revolution Issue

Common Design Type

Photo., Name and Value Typo. in Black

1939

B2	CD83	45c + 25c green	8.00	8.00
B3	CD83	70c + 30c brown	8.00	8.00
B4	CD83	90c + 35c red org	8.00	8.00
B5	CD83	1.25fr + 1fr rose pink	8.00	8.00
B6	CD83	2.25fr + 2fr blue	8.00	8.00
		Nos. B2-B6 (5)	40.00	40.00

French Revolution, 150th anniv. Surtax for defense of the colonies.

AIR POST STAMPS

Common Design Type

1940 **Unwmk.** **Engr.** *Perf. 12½x12*

C1	CD85	1.90fr ultra	.25	.25
C2	CD85	2.90fr dark red	.45	.25
C3	CD85	4.50fr dk gray grn	.60	.40
C4	CD85	4.90fr yellow bister	.60	.60
C5	CD85	6.90fr deep orange	1.00	1.00
		Nos. C1-C5 (5)	2.90	2.50

POSTAGE DUE STAMPS

Postage Due Stamps of Dahomey, 1914 Overprinted

1921 **Unwmk.** *Perf. 14x13½*

J1	D2	5c green	.60	.60
J2	D2	10c rose	.60	.60
J3	D2	15c gray	1.25	1.25
J4	D2	20c brown	2.25	2.25
J5	D2	30c blue	2.50	2.50
J6	D2	50c black	2.00	2.00
J7	D2	60c orange	2.00	2.00
J8	D2	1fr violet	3.75	3.75
		Nos. J1-J8 (8)	14.95	14.95

Cotton Field — D3

1925 **Typo.** **Unwmk.**

J9	D3	2c blue & blk	.20	.20
J10	D3	4c dl red & blk	.20	.20
J11	D3	5c ol grn & blk	.20	.20
J12	D3	10c cerise & blk	.25	.25
J13	D3	15c orange & blk	.60	.60
J14	D3	20c red vio & blk	.40	.40
J15	D3	25c gray & blk	.75	.75
J16	D3	30c ocher & blk	.40	.40
J17	D3	50c brown & blk	.85	.85
J18	D3	60c green & blk	.85	.85
J19	D3	1fr dk vio & blk	.85	.85
		Nos. J9-J19 (11)	5.55	5.55

Type of 1925 Issue Surcharged

1927

J20	D3	2fr on 1fr rose red & vio	5.00	5.00
J21	D3	3fr on 1fr org brn, blk & ultra	5.00	5.00

TONGA

ˈtäŋ-gə

LOCATION — A group of islands in the south Pacific Ocean, south of Samoa
GOVT. — Kingdom in British Commonwealth
AREA — 289 sq. mi.
POP. — 98,750 (est. 1983)
CAPITAL — Nuku'alofa

This group, also known as the Friendly Islands, became a British Protectorate in 1900 under the Anglo-German Agreement of 1899.

12 Pence = 1 Shilling
20 Shillings = 1 Pound

Catalogue values for unused stamps in this country are for Never Hinged items, beginning with Scott 87 in the regular postage section.

Watermarks

Wmk. 62 — NZ and Small Star Wide Apart

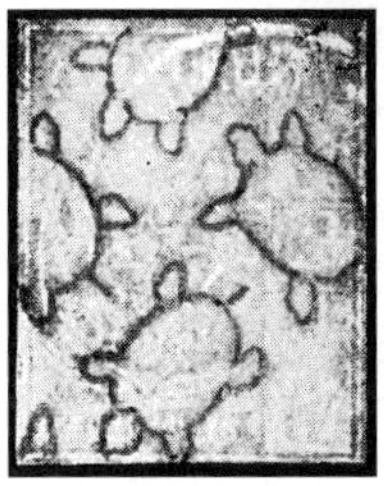

Wmk. 79 — Turtles

King George I — A1

Perf. 12x11½

1886-92 Typo. Wmk. 62

1	A1	1p car rose ('87)	11.50	4.00
a.		Perf. 12½	450.00	7.00
b.		Perf. 12½x10		
2	A1	2p violet ('87)	32.50	3.50
a.		Perf. 12½	57.50	14.00
3	A1	6p ultra ('88)	57.50	2.75
a.		Perf. 12½	67.50	4.00
4	A1	6p org yel ('92)	18.00	*30.00*
5	A1	1sh blue grn ('88)	62.50	7.25
a.		Perf. 12½	110.00	4.50
b.		Half used as 6p on cover		
		Nos. 1-5 (5)	182.00	*47.50*

For surcharges and overprints see #6-9, 24.

Nos. 1 and 2 Surcharged or Overprinted in Black:

a

b

1891, Nov. 10 ***Perf. 12x11½***

6	A1(a)	4p on 1p car rose	3.50	*12.50*
a.		No period after "PENCE"	57.50	*125.00*
7	A1(a)	8p on 2p violet	40.00	*100.00*

1891, Nov. 23 ***Perf. 12½***

Two types of overprint:
I — Solid stars, rays pointed and short.
II — Open-center stars, rays blunt and long.

8	A1(b)	1p car rose (I)	50.00	*57.50*
a.		Overprinted with 3 stars (I)	375.00	
b.		Overprinted with 4 stars (I)	475.00	
c.		Overprinted with 5 stars (I)	750.00	
d.		Type II	50.00	*57.50*
e.		Perf. 12x11½ (I or II)	350.00	
9	A1(b)	2p violet (I)	80.00	*42.50*
a.		Type II	80.00	*42.50*
b.		Perf. 12x11½ (I or II)	425.00	

Coat of Arms A4

George I A5

1892, Nov. 10 Typo. ***Perf. 12x11½***

10	A4	1p rose	14.00	*19.00*
a.		Diagonal half used as ½p on cover		975.00
11	A5	2p olive gray	18.00	*18.00*
12	A4	4p red brown	55.00	*80.00*
13	A5	8p violet	62.50	*200.00*
14	A5	1sh brown	90.00	*125.00*
		Nos. 10-14 (5)	239.50	442.00

For surcharges and overprints see Nos. 15-23, 25-28, 36-37, O1-O10.

Types A4 and A5 Surcharged in Carmine or Black:

c

d

f

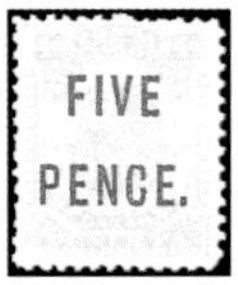

1893

15	A4	½p on 1p ultra (C)	26.00	*30.00*
a.		Surcharge omitted		
16	A4	½p on 1p ultra	50.00	*55.00*
17	A5	2½p on 2p blue grn (C)	16.00	*13.50*
18	A5	2½p on 2p blue grn	19.00	19.00
a.		Double surcharge		2,000.
19	A4	5p on 4p org yel (C)	4.50	*7.50*
20	A5	7½p on 8p rose (C)	27.50	*85.00*
		Nos. 15-20 (6)	143.00	210.00

Stamps of 1886-92 Surcharged in Blue or Black:

g

h

1894

21	A4	½p on 4p red brn (Bl)	2.25	*8.00*
a.		"SURCHARCE"	10.00	*22.50*
b.		Pair, one without surcharge		
c.		"HALF PENNY" omitted		
22	A5	½p on 1sh brn (Bk)	2.75	*12.50*
a.		Double surcharge	310.00	
b.		"SURCHARCE"	11.50	45.00
c.		As "b," double surcharge	1,000.	
23	A5	2½p on 8p vio (Bk)	5.75	*9.25*
a.		No period after "SURCHARGE"	35.00	*62.50*
24	A1	2½p on 1sh blue grn (Bk)	62.50	*27.50*
a.		No period after "SURCHARGE"	200.00	
b.		Perf. 12x11½	17.50	47.50
		Nos. 21-24 (4)	73.25	*57.25*

Type A5 with Same Surcharges in Carmine

1895 **Unwmk.**

25	A5(g)	1p on 2p lt blue	50.00	25.00
26	A5(h)	1½p on 2p lt bl, perf. 12x11	55.00	32.50
a.		Perf. 12	70.00	32.50
27	A5(h)	2½p on 2p lt blue	45.00	50.00
b.		Without period	250.00	250.00
28	A5(h)	7½p on 2p lt bl, perf. 12x11	70.00	50.00
a.		Perf. 12	450.00	
		Nos. 25-28 (4)	220.00	157.50

King George II — A13

1895, Aug. 16 ***Perf. 12***

29	A13	1p gray green	22.50	*30.00*
a.		Diagonal half used as ½p on cover		*850.00*
b.		Horiz. pair, imperf. btwn.	—	*6,900.*
30	A13	2½p dull rose	22.50	15.00
31	A13	5p brt blue, perf. 12x11	26.00	*57.50*
a.		Perf. 12	25.00	*57.50*
b.		Perf. 11	400.00	
32	A13	7½p yellow	35.00	*55.00*
		Nos. 29-32 (4)	106.00	*157.50*

Type A13 Redrawn and Surcharged "g" or "h" in Black

33	A13(g)	½p on 2½p red	35.00	*37.50*
a.		"SURCHARCE"	80.00	
b.		Period after "Postage"	85.00	
34	A13(g)	1p on 2½p red	70.00	45.00
a.		Period after "Postage"	125.00	
35	A13(h)	7½p on 2½p red	62.50	*70.00*
a.		Period after "Postage"	110.00	
		Nos. 33-35 (3)	167.50	*152.50*

Nos. 26 and 28 with Additional Surcharge in Violet and Black

1896, May ***Perf. 12x11***

36	A5	½p on 1½p on 2p	500.00	
a.		Tongan surch. reading up	475.00	475.00
b.		Perf. 12	475.00	*475.00*
c.		As "a," perf. 12	500.00	*500.00*
d.		"Haalf"	2,100.	
37	A5	½p on 7½p on 2p	97.50	*125.00*
a.		"Half penny" inverted	2,100.	
b.		"Half penny" double		
c.		Tongan surch. reading up	97.50	*125.00*
d.		Tongan surcharge as "c" and double		
e.		"Hafl Penny"	1,750.	*1,800.*
f.		"Hafl" only	3,750.	
g.		"Hwlf"		
h.		Periods instead of hyphens after words	1,000.	
j.		Perf. 12	925.00	

Coat of Arms — A17

Ovava Tree — A18

George II — A19

Prehistoric Trilithon, Tongatabu — A20

Breadfruit A21

Coral Formations A22

View of Haabai A23

Red-breasted Musk Parrot — A24

View of Vavau — A25

Two types of 2p:
I — Top of sword hilt shows above "2."
II — No hilt shows.

Wmk. 79 Sideways

1897-1934 Engr. ***Perf. 14***

38	A17	½p dark blue	4.75	3.00
39	A17	½p green ('34)	1.10	*1.40*
40	A18	1p dp red & blk	.90	.90
41	A19	2p bis & sep (I)	18.00	6.25
a.		bister & gray, type II	35.00	3.75
42	A19	2½p lt blue & blk	7.00	1.60
a.		"½" without fraction bar	110.00	75.00
43	A20	3p ol grn & blk	4.00	*9.75*
44	A21	4p dull vio & grn	4.25	*4.50*
45	A19	5p orange & blk	35.00	16.00
46	A22	6p red	15.00	*7.00*
47	A19	7½p green & blk	18.00	*26.00*
a.		Center inverted	5,500.	
48	A19	10p carmine & blk	50.00	55.00
49	A19	1sh red brn & blk	16.00	8.50
50	A23	2sh dk ultra & blk	70.00	*75.00*
51	A24	2sh6p dk violet	57.50	35.00
52	A25	5sh dull red & blk	55.00	55.00
		Nos. 38-52 (15)	356.50	304.90

See Nos. 73-74, 77-78, 80-81. For surcharges see Nos. 63-69.

Stamp of 1897 Overprinted in Black

1899, June 1

53	A18	1p red & black	35.00	*72.50*
a.		"1889" instead of "1899"	225.00	*400.00*
b.		Comma omitted after June		
c.		Double overprint		

Marriage of George II to Lavinia, June 1, 1899. The letters "T L" are the initials of Taufa'ahau, the King's family name, and Lavinia.

Queen Salote — A26

Dies of 2p:
Die I - Ball of "2" smaller.
Die II - Ball of "2" larger. "U" has spur at left.

1920-35 Engr. Wmk. 79

54	A26	1½p gray blk ('35)	.55	*3.50*
55	A26	2p violet & sepia	9.75	*15.00*
56	A26	2p dl vio & blk (I) ('24)	9.75	2.75
a.		Die II	5.00	*7.50*
57	A26	2½p blue & black	5.50	*45.00*
58	A26	2½p ultra ('34)	2.25	1.10
59	A26	5p red org & blk	3.75	*5.50*
60	A26	7½p green & blk	2.00	2.00
61	A26	10p carmine & blk	2.90	*5.50*
62	A26	1sh red brown & blk	1.40	2.90
		Nos. 54-62 (9)	37.85	83.25

See Nos. 75-76, 79.

Stamps of 1897 Surcharged in Dark Blue or Red

1923

63	A19	2p on 5p org & blk	1.10	1.00
64	A19	2p on 7½p grn & blk	20.00	32.50
65	A19	2p on 10p car & blk	12.50	*57.50*
66	A19	2p on 1sh red brn & blk	55.00	25.00
67	A23	2p on 2sh ultra & blk (R)	22.50	*22.50*
68	A24	2p on 2sh6p dk vio (R)	35.00	7.50
69	A25	2p on 5sh dull red & blk (R)	16.00	16.00
		Nos. 63-69 (7)	162.10	162.00

Queen Salote — A27

Inscribed "1918-1938"

1938, Oct. 12 ***Perf. 14***

70	A27	1p carmine & blk	.50	*4.00*
71	A27	2p violet & blk	4.50	3.00
72	A27	2½p ultra & blk	4.50	3.75
		Nos. 70-72 (3)	9.50	10.75
		Set, never hinged	18.00	

Accession of Queen Salote Tupou, 20th anniv.

See Nos. 82-86.

Types of 1897-1920

1942 Engr. Wmk. 4

Die III of 2p:
Foot of "2" longer than in Die II, extending beyond curve of loop.

73	A17	½p green	.30	*2.75*
74	A18	1p scarlet & blk	1.25	*2.75*
75	A26	2p dull vio & blk (II)	2.25	*3.00*
a.		Die III	4.25	*8.25*
76	A26	2½p ultra	.90	*2.00*
77	A20	3p green & black	.30	*3.75*
78	A22	6p orange red	1.50	*2.25*
79	A26	1sh red brown & gray blk	1.40	*3.50*
80	A24	2sh6p dk violet	22.50	*24.00*
81	A25	5sh dull red & brn blk	14.00	*50.00*
		Nos. 73-81 (9)	44.40	94.00
		Set, never hinged	62.50	

Type of 1938, Inscribed "1918-1943"

1944, Jan. 25

82	A27	1p rose car & blk	.20	*1.10*
83	A27	2p purple & blk	.20	*1.10*
84	A27	3p dk yel grn & blk	.20	*1.10*
85	A27	6p red orange & blk	.25	*2.00*
86	A27	1sh dk red brn & blk	.25	*2.00*
		Nos. 82-86 (5)	1.10	7.30
		Set, never hinged	2.00	

25th anniv. of the accession of Queen Salote.

Catalogue values for unused stamps in this section, from this point to the end of the section, are for Never Hinged items.

UPU Issue

Common Design Types

Engr.; Name Typo. on 3p, 6p

Perf. 13½, 11x11½

1949, Oct. 10 Wmk. 4

87	CD306	2½p ultra	.40	*.90*
88	CD307	3p deep olive	1.75	*3.25*
89	CD308	6p deep carmine	.55	.55
90	CD309	1sh red brown	.55	.55
		Nos. 87-90 (4)	3.25	5.25

Common Design Types pictured following the introduction.

A28

A29

Queen Salote — A30

1950, Nov. 1 Photo. *Perf. 12½*

91	A28	1p cerise	1.00	*2.25*
92	A29	5p green	1.00	*2.50*
93	A30	1sh violet	1.00	*3.00*
		Nos. 91-93 (3)	3.00	7.75

50th anniv. of the birth of Queen Salote.

Map and Island Scene — A31

Badges and Royal Palace A32

2½p, Queen Salote & coastal scene. 3p, Queen Salote & ship "Bellona." 5p, Flag of Tonga, island view. 1sh, Arms of Tonga & Great Britain.

Perf. 13x13½ (1p), 13½x13, 12½ (3p)

1951, July 2 Engr. Wmk. 4

94	A31	½p deep green	.30	3.00
95	A32	1p carmine & black	.30	*3.00*
96	A32	2½p choc & dp grn	.60	*3.00*
97	A31	3p ultra & org yel	2.25	*3.00*
98	A32	5p dp green & car	1.75	1.10
99	A32	1sh purple & orange	2.50	1.10
		Nos. 94-99 (6)	7.70	14.20

50th anniv. of the treaty of friendship between Tonga and Great Britain.

OFFICIAL STAMPS

Types of Postage Issue of 1892 Overprinted in Carmine

Perf. 12x11½

1893, Feb. 13 Wmk. 62

O1	A4	1p ultra	11.50	*55.00*
a.		Half used as ½p on cover		
O2	A5	2p ultra	30.00	*62.50*
O3	A4	4p ultra	55.00	*110.00*
O4	A5	8p ultra	100.00	*200.00*
O5	A5	1sh ultra	110.00	*210.00*
		Nos. O1-O5 (5)	306.50	*637.50*

Values are for copies of good color. Faded and discolored copies sell for much less.

The overprinted initials stand for "Gaue Faka Buleaga" (On Government Service).

Nos. O1-O5 with Additional Surcharge Handstamped in Black

1893

O6	A4	½p on 1p ultra	20.00	*57.50*
O7	A5	2½p on 2p ultra	27.50	*50.00*
O8	A4	5p on 4p ultra	27.50	*50.00*
O9	A5	7½p on 8p ultra	27.50	*92.50*
O10	A5	10p on 1sh ultra	32.50	*95.00*
		Nos. O6-O10 (5)	135.00	*345.00*

TRANSCAUCASIAN FEDERATED REPUBLICS

ˌtranˌt͟s-ko-ˈkā-zhən

ˈfe-də-rāted ri-ˈpə-blik

(Armenia, Georgia, Azerbaijan)

LOCATION — In southeastern Europe, south of the Caucasus Mountains between the Black and Caspian Seas
GOVT. — Republic
AREA — 71,255 sq. mi.
POP. — 5,851,000 (approx.)
CAPITAL — Tiflis

The Transcaucasian Federation was made up of the former autonomies of Armenia, Georgia and Azerbaijan. Its stamps were replaced by those of Russia.

100 Kopecks = 1 Ruble

Russian Stamps of 1909-17 Overprinted in Black or Red

1923 Unwmk. *Perf. 14½x15*

1	A15	10k dark blue	3.00	*5.00*
2	A14	10k on 7k lt bl	3.00	*5.00*
3	A11	25k grn & gray vio	3.00	*5.00*
4	A11	35k red brn & grn (R)	3.00	*5.00*
a.		Double overprint	40.00	40.00
5	A8	50k brn red & grn	3.00	*5.00*
6	A9	1r pale brn, brn & org	8.25	*10.00*
7	A12	3½r mar & lt grn	35.00	

Imperf

8	A9	1r pale brn, brn & red org	3.50	*6.00*
		Nos. 1-8 (8)	61.75	
		Nos. 1-6,8 (7)		41.00

No. 7 was prepared but not issued.

Overprinted on Stamps of Armenia Previously Handstamped:

a

c

Perf. 14½x15

9	A11(c)	25k grn & gray vio	*240.00*	*225.00*
10	A8(c)	50k vio & grn	*175.00*	*150.00*

Perf. 13½

11	A9(a)	1r pale brn, brn & org	*75.00*	*50.00*
12	A9(c)	1r pale, brn, brn & org	*75.00*	*50.00*

Imperf

13	A9(c)	1r pale brn, brn & red org	*35.00*	*35.00*
		Nos. 9-13 (5)	600.00	510.00

Counterfeit overprints exist.

Oil Fields — A1

Soviet Symbols — A2

1923 *Perf. 11½*

14	A1	40,000r red violet	1.50	*4.00*
15	A1	75,000r dark grn	1.50	*4.00*
16	A1	100,000r blk vio	1.50	*4.00*
17	A1	150,000r red	1.50	*4.00*
18	A2	200,000r dull grn	1.50	*4.00*
19	A2	300,000r blue	1.50	*4.00*
20	A2	350,000r dark brn	1.50	*4.00*
21	A2	500,000r rose	1.50	*4.00*
		Nos. 14-21 (8)	12.00	*32.00*

Nos. 14-15 Surcharged in Brown

1923

22 A1 700,000r on 40,000r 3.00 *5.00*
a. Imperf., pair 13.00
23 A1 700,000r on 75,000r 3.00 *5.00*
a. Imperf., pair 13.00

Types of Preceding Issue with Values in Gold Kopecks

1923, Oct. 24

25 A2 1k orange 1.75 *5.00*
26 A2 2k blue green 1.75 *5.00*
27 A2 3k rose 2.50 *5.00*
28 A2 4k gray brown 1.50 *5.00*
29 A1 5k dark violet 1.50 *5.00*
30 A1 9k deep blue 1.50 *5.00*
31 A1 18k slate 1.50 *5.00*
Nos. 25-31 (7) 12.00 *35.00*

Nos. 14-21, 25-31 exist imperf. but are not known to have been issued in that condition. Value, $12 each.

TRANSVAAL

tran͵t͵s-ˈväl

(South African Republic)

LOCATION — Southern Africa
AREA — 110,450 sq. mi.
POP. — 1,261,736 (1904)
CAPITAL — Pretoria

Transvaal was known as the South African Republic until 1877 when it was occupied by the British. The republic was restored in 1884 and continued until 1900 when it was annexed to Great Britain and named "The Transvaal."

12 Pence = 1 Shilling
20 Shillings = 1 Pound

Most unused stamps between Nos. 1-96, 119-122 and 136-137 were issued with gum, but do not expect gum on scarcer stamps as few examples retain their original gum. In many cases removal of the remaining gum may enhance the preservation of the stamps. Otherwise, values for unused stamps are for examples with original gum as defined in the catalogue introduction.

Very fine imperforate stamps will have adequate to large margins. However, rouletted stamps are valued as partly rouletted, with straight edges, and rouletted just into the design, as the rouletting methods were quite inaccurate.

First Republic

Coat of Arms
A1 A2

Mecklenburg Printings
By Adolph Otto, Gustrow
Fine Impressions
Thin Paper

A1 has spread wings on eagle.

1869 Unwmk. *Imperf.*

1 A1 1p brown lake 475.00
a. 1p red 625.00 625.00
2 A1 6p ultra 200.00 200.00
3 A1 1sh dark green 750.00 750.00
a. Tete beche pair

Rouletted 15½, 16

4 A1 1p red 110.00
a. 1p brown lake 150.00
5 A1 6p ultra 100.00 100.00
6 A1 1sh blue green 125.00 125.00
a. 1sh yellow green 175.00 160.00
b. 1sh deep green 210.00 225.00

Nos. 1-6 were printed from 2 sets of plates, differing in the spacing between the stamps.

The only known example of No. 3a is in a museum.

See Nos. 9-24, 26-33, 35-36, 38-39, 41-42, 43-49, 119, 122. For overprints see Nos. 53-61, 63-66, 68-72, 75-78, 81-83, 86-87, 90-91, 94.

1871-74

7 A2 3p lilac 90.00 *100.00*
a. 3p violet 100.00 110.00
8 A2 6p brt ultra ('74) 67.50 27.50
a. Half used as 3p on cover *1,600.*

Many forgeries exist in colors duller or lighter than the genuine stamps.

In forgeries of type A1, all values, the "D" of "EENDRAGT" is not noticeably larger than the other letters and does not touch the top of the ribbon. In type A1 genuine stamps, the "D" is large and touches the ribbon top. The eagle's eye is a dot and its face white on the genuine stamps; the eye is a loop or blob attached to the beak, and the beak is strongly hooked, on the forgeries. Many forgeries of the 1sh have the top line of the ribbon broken above "EENDRAGT."

Forgeries of type A2 usually can be detected only by color.

A sharply struck cancellation of a numeral in three rings is found on many of these forgeries. The similar genuine cancellation is always roughly or heavily struck.

See Nos. 25, 34, 437, 40, 42B, 120-121. For overprints see Nos. 50-52, 62, 67, 73-74, 79-80, 84-85, 88-89, 92-93, 95-96.

Local Printings

(A) By M. J. Viljoen, Pretoria
Poor Impressions,
Overinked and Spotted
Thin Soft Paper

1870 *Imperf.*

9 A1 1p pink 100.00
a. 1p rose red 77.50
b. 1p carmine 80.00 72.50
10 A1 6p dull ultra 350.00 80.00
a. Tete beche pair

The only known examples of No. 10a are in museums.

Rouletted 15½, 16

11 A1 1p carmine 775.00 300.00
a. Rouletted 6½ 1,100.
12 A1 6p dull ultra 225.00 110.00

Hard Paper, Thick to Medium

Imperf

13 A1 1p carmine 80.00 90.00
14 A1 6p ultra
15 A1 1sh gray green 125.00 110.00
a. 1sh dark green *650.00 300.00*
b. Tete beche pair *23,000.*
c. Half used as 6p on cover *2,000.*

The existence of No. 14 is questionable.

Rouletted 15½, 16

16 A1 1p light carmine 80.00 97.50
a. 1p carmine 57.50 62.50
17 A1 6p ultra 100.00 95.00
a. Tete beche pair *20,000. 15,000.*
18 A1 1sh dark green 140.00 85.00
a. 1sh gray green 575.00 175.00

Copies of Nos. 16 to 18 are sometimes so heavily inked as to be little more than blots of color.

(B) By J. P. Borrius, Potchefstroom
Clearer Impressions Though Often Overinked
Thick Porous Paper

1870 *Imperf.*

19 A1 1p black 150.00 125.00
20 A1 6p indigo 250.00

Rouletted 15½, 16

21 A1 1p black 20.00 30.00
22 A1 6p gray blue 160.00 70.00
a. 6p indigo 100.00 90.00
b. 6p bright ultra

Thin Transparent Paper

23 A1 1p black 225.00 *750.00*
24 A1 1p brt carmine 175.00 62.50
a. 1p deep carmine 75.00 45.00
25 A2 3p gray lilac 110.00 57.50
26 A1 6p ultra 75.00 35.00
27 A1 1sh yellow green 92.50 47.50
a. 1sh deep green 92.50 47.50
b. Half used as 6p on cover —

Thick Soft Paper

28 A1 1p dull rose 450.00 85.00
a. 1p brown rose 575.00 140.00
b. Printed on both sides
29 A1 6p dull blue 100.00 50.00
a. 6p bright blue 225.00 75.00
b. 6p ultramarine 210.00 75.00
c. Rouletted 6½
30 A1 1sh yellow green 950.00 750.00

The paper of Nos. 28 to 30 varies considerably in thickness.

(C) By P. Davis & Son, Natal
Thin to Medium Paper

1874 *Perf. 12½*

31 A1 1p red 110.00 45.00
a. 1p brownish red 110.00 45.00
32 A1 6p deep blue 160.00 70.00
a. 6p blue 150.00 62.50
b. Horiz. pair, imperf. between

(D) By the Stamp Commission, Pretoria
Pelure Paper

1875-76 *Imperf.*

33 A1 1p pale red 57.50 57.50
a. 1p orange red 50.00 27.50
b. 1p brown red 62.50 35.00
c. Pin perf. — 400.00
34 A2 3p gray lilac 57.50 47.50
a. 3p dull violet 60.00 45.00
b. Pin perf. 70.00 47.50
35 A1 6p blue 57.50 47.50
a. 6p pale blue 57.50 57.50
b. 6p dark blue 62.50 50.00
c. Tete beche pair
d. Pin perf. 400.00

The only known examples of No. 35c are in museums.

Rouletted 15½, 16

36 A1 1p orange red 400.00 140.00
a. Rouletted 6½ 1,100. 225.00
37 A2 3p dull violet 450.00 150.00
a. Rouletted 6½ *1,000.* 275.00
38 A1 6p blue 175.00 110.00
a. Rouletted 6½ 1,100. 125.00

The paper of this group varies slightly in thickness and is sometimes divided into pelure and semipelure. We believe there was only one lot of the paper and that the separation is not warranted.

Thick Hard Paper

Imperf

39 A1 1p orange red ('76) 27.50 20.00
40 A2 3p lilac 425.00 125.00
41 A1 6p deep blue 70.00 22.50
a. 6p blue 110.00 27.50
b. Tete beche pair *19,000.*

Rouletted 15½, 16

42 A1 1p orange red ('76) 450.00 175.00
a. Rouletted 6½ ('75) 700.00 175.00
42B A2 3p lilac 400.00
43 A1 6p deep blue *675.00* 300.00
a. 6p blue *850.00* 125.00
b. Rouletted 6½ ('75) *750.00* 275.00

Soft Porous Paper

Imperf

44 A1 1p orange red 150.00 62.50
45 A1 6p deep blue 225.00 60.00
a. 6p dull blue 400.00 100.00
46 A1 1sh yellow green 400.00 125.00
a. Half used as 6p on cover 1,800.

Rouletted 15½, 16

47 A1 1p orange red 425.00
a. Rouletted 6½ 500.00
48 A1 6p deep blue 175.00
a. Rouletted 6½ 1,250.
49 A1 1sh yellow grn 800.00 400.00
a. Rouletted 6½ 1,400.
b. Rouletted 15½-16x16½ 500.00 325.00

First British Occupation

Stamps and Types of 1875 Overprinted

Red Overprint
Pelure Paper

1877 Unwmk. *Imperf.*

50 A2 3p lilac 1,500. 210.00
a. Overprinted on back 3,750. *3,750.*
b. Double ovpt., red and black *7,000.*

Rouletted 15½, 16

51 A2 3p lilac 1,800.
a. Rouletted 6½ 1,500.

Thin Hard Paper

Imperf

52 A2 3p lilac 1,500. 350.00

Soft Porous Paper

53 A1 6p blue 1,800. 200.00
a. 6p deep blue 275.00
b. Inverted overprint *6,250.*
c. Double overprint 5,100. 1,100.
54 A1 1sh yellow grn 700.00 210.00
a. Inverted overprint *5,100.*
b. Half used as 6p on cover *2,000.*

Rouletted 15½, 16

55 A1 6p blue 1,900.
a. Rouletted 6½ 1,400.
56 A1 1sh yellow grn 1,800. 850.00
a. Rouletted 6½ 3,500. 1,200.

Black Overprint

Pelure Paper

Imperf

57 A1 1p red 300.00 110.00

Rouletted 15½, 16

58 A1 1p red 1,200.

Thick Hard Paper

Imperf

59 A1 1p red 27.50 25.00
a. Inverted overprint 625.00 575.00

Rouletted 15½, 16

60 A1 1p red 175.00 57.50
a. Rouletted 6½ 750.00 225.00
b. Inverted overprint
c. Double overprint — 1,250.

Soft Porous Paper

Imperf

61 A1 1p red 29.00 25.00
a. Double overprint 1,300.
62 A2 3p lilac 92.50 47.50
a. 3p deep lilac 200.00 97.50
b. Inverted overprint —
63 A1 6p dull blue 100.00 35.00
a. 6p bright blue 175.00 35.00
b. 6p dark blue 175.00 35.00
d. Inverted overprint — 850.00
e. Double overprint *4,000.*
64 A1 6p blue, *rose* 92.50 55.00
a. Tete beche pair
b. Inverted overprint 110.00 55.00
c. Overprint omitted 4,000. 2,900.
d. Half used as 3p on cover
65 A1 1sh yellow grn 110.00 57.50
a. Tete beche pair *22,500. 22,500.*
b. Inverted overprint 1,250. 500.00
c. Half used as 6p on cover 1,250.

The only known examples of No. 64a are in museums.

Rouletted 15½, 16

66 A1 1p red 85.00 85.00
a. Rouletted 6½ 750.00 175.00
67 A2 3p lilac 200.00 75.00
a. Rouletted 6½ 850.00
68 A1 6p dull blue 225.00 62.50
a. Inverted overprint — 850.00
b. Rouletted 6½ — 1,350.
c. As "a," rouletted 6½ 4,500.
69 A1 6p blue, *rose* 200.00 80.00
a. Inverted overprint 625.00 80.00
b. Rouletted 6½
c. Tete beche pair
d. Overprint omitted
e. As "a," rouletted 6½ 750.00
f. As "d," rouletted 6½
70 A1 1sh yellow grn 225.00 100.00
a. Inverted overprint 1,250. 575.00
b. Rouletted 6½ 525.00 150.00
c. As "a," rouletted 6½ 1,750. 700.00

In this issue the space between "V. R." and "TRANSVAAL" is normally 8½mm but in position 11 it is 12mm. In this and the following issues there are numerous minor varieties of the overprint, missing periods, etc.

The only known examples of No. 69c are in museums.

Types A1 and A2 Overprinted

1877-79 *Imperf.*

71 A1 1p red, *blue* 62.50 35.00
a. "Transvral" *6,250. 2,900.*
b. Inverted overprint *900.00* 450.00
c. Double overprint *4,500.*
d. Overprint omitted
72 A1 1p red, *org* ('78) 22.50 22.50
a. Printed on both sides
b. Pin perf.
73 A2 3p lilac, *buff* 57.50 30.00
a. Inverted overprint 850.00
b. Pin perf.
74 A2 3p lilac, *grn* ('79) 175.00 50.00
a. Inverted overprint 2,250.
b. Double overprint
c. Pin perf.
75 A1 6p blue, *grn* 97.50 42.50
a. Tete beche pair *20,000.*
b. Inverted overprint 1,250.
c. Half used as 3p on cover
d. Pin perf.
76 A1 6p blue, *bl* ('78) 62.50 30.00
a. Tete beche pair
b. Overprint omitted 2,500.
c. Inverted overprint 1,100.
d. Half used as 3p on cover 900.00
e. Double overprint 3,750.
f. Pin perf.
Nos. 71-76 (6) 477.50 210.00

The only known examples of No. 76a are in museums.

Rouletted 15½, 16

77 A1 1p red, *blue* 100.00 42.50
a. "Transvral" 3,500.
b. Inverted overprint
c. Double overprint
78 A1 1p red, *org* ('78) 35.00 30.00
a. Horiz. pair, imperf. vert. 700.00
b. Rouletted 6½ 275.00 125.00
79 A2 3p lilac, *buff* 110.00 30.00
a. Inverted overprint 3,500.
b. Vert. pair, imperf. horiz.
c. Rouletted 6½ 125.00
80 A2 3p lilac, *grn* ('79) 700.00 175.00
a. Inverted overprint
b. Rouletted 6½ 750.00 300.00
81 A1 6p blue, *green* 97.50 32.50
a. Inverted overprint 75.00
b. Overprint omitted 4,500.
c. Tete beche pair
d. Half used at 3p on cover 800.00
e. Rouletted 6½ — 1,100.

82 A1 6p blue, *bl* ('78) 250.00 62.50
a. Inverted overprint — 1,000.
b. Overprint omitted — 4,000.
c. Tete beche pair
d. Horiz. pair, imperf. vert.
e. Half used as 3p on cover 850.00
f. Double overprint
g. Rouletted 6½ 350.00
h. As "a," rouletted 6½
Nos. 77-82 (6) 1,292. 372.50

The only known examples of No. 81c are in museums. The existence of No. 82c is questioned.

Types A1 and A2 Overprinted

Imperf

83 A1 1p red, *org* ('78) 62.50 50.00
84 A2 3p lilac, *buff* ('78) 75.00 40.00
a. Pin perf. 850.00 850.00
85 A2 3p lilac, *grn* ('79) 125.00 40.00
a. Inverted overprint 2,250.
b. Overprint omitted 4,000.
c. Printed on both sides 1,100.
86 A1 6p blue, *bl* ('78) 125.00 35.00
a. Tete beche pair *17,500.*
b. Inverted overprint 700.00
Nos. 83-86 (4) 387.50 165.00

Rouletted 15½, 16

87 A1 1p red, *org* ('78) 160.00 140.00
a. Rouletted 6½ 350.00
88 A2 3p lilac, *buff* ('78) 175.00 125.00
a. Vert. pair, imperf. horiz.
b. Rouletted 6½ 400.00
89 A2 3p lilac, *grn* ('79) 700.00 175.00
a. Inverted overprint
b. Overprint omitted
c. Rouletted 6½ ('97) 350.00
90 A1 6p blue, *bl* ('78) 425.00 125.00
a. Tete beche pair
b. Inverted overprint — 1,250.
d. Rouletted 6½ 400.00
e. As "b," rouletted 6½

Types A1 and A2 Overprinted

1879 *Imperf.*
91 A1 1p red, *orange* 45.00 35.00
a. 1p red, *yellow* 50.00 42.50
b. Small capital "T" 350.00 225.00
92 A2 3p lilac, *green* 45.00 29.00
a. Small capital "T" 250.00 125.00
93 A2 3p lilac, *blue* 50.00 35.00
a. Small capital "T" 275.00 100.00
Nos. 91-93 (3) 140.00 99.00

Rouletted 15½, 16

94 A1 1p red, *yellow* 400.00 225.00
a. 1p red, *orange* 850.00 425.00
b. Small capital "T" 1,100. 750.00
c. Rouletted 6½ 750.00 750.00
d. Pin perf. 850.00
95 A2 3p lilac, *green* 850.00 275.00
a. Small capital "T"
b. Rouletted 6½
96 A2 3p lilac, *blue* 200.00
a. Small capital "T" 800.00
b. Rouletted 6½ 950.00
c. Pin perf.

Queen Victoria — A3

1878-80 **Engr.** *Perf. 14, 14½*
97 A3 ½p vermilion ('80) 25.00 *90.00*
98 A3 1p red brown 14.00 4.50
99 A3 3p claret 17.50 5.00
100 A3 4p olive green 24.00 6.25
101 A3 6p slate 12.50 4.50
a. Half used as 3p on cover
102 A3 1sh green 140.00 42.50
103 A3 2sh blue 175.00 85.00
Nos. 97-103 (7) 408.00 237.75

For surcharges see Nos. 104-118, 138-139.

No. 101 Surcharged in Red or Black:

(a) Surcharged

1879
104 A3 1p on 6p slate (R) 82.50 65.00
105 A3 1p on 6p slate (Bk) 35.00 24.00

(b) Surcharged **1 Penny**

106 A3 1p on 6p slate (R) 350.00 275.00
107 A3 1p on 6p slate (Bk) 160.00 85.00

(c) Surcharged **1 Penny**

108 A3 1p on 6p slate (R) 200.00 115.00
109 A3 1p on 6p slate (Bk) 65.00 32.50

(d) Surcharged

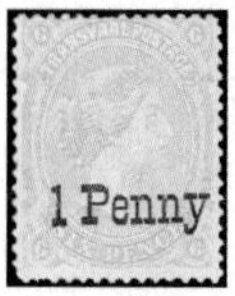

110 A3 1p on 6p slate (R) 210.00 125.00
111 A3 1p on 6p slate (Bk) 55.00 50.00
a. Pair, one without surcharge

(e) Surcharged ***1 Penny***

112 A3 1p on 6p slate (R) 350.00 225.00
113 A3 1p on 6p slate (Bk) 150.00 75.00

(f) Surcharged **1 Penny**

114 A3 1p on 6p slate (R) 325.00 150.00
115 A3 1p on 6p slate (Bk) 90.00 55.00

(g) Surcharged **1 Penny**

116 A3 1p on 6p slate (R) *1,500.*
117 A3 1p on 6p slate (Bk) 500.00 150.00

Surcharge distinctions: a, "PENNY" in gothic capitals. b, "1" has heavy serif at base; "P," thin serif at base. c, No serif at base of "1." d, Heavy serifs at base of "1" and "p." e, Italics. f, "1" has long, sloping serif at top, thin serif at base. g, Tail of "y" missing.

Second Republic

No. 100 Surcharged

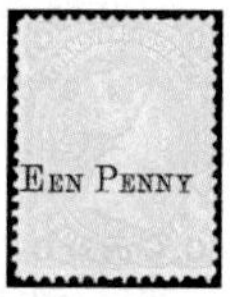

1882 **Unwmk.** *Perf. 14, 14½*
118 A3 1p on 4p olive grn 15.00 5.00
a. Inverted surcharge 350.00 250.00

1883 *Perf. 12*
119 A1 1p black 5.75 2.00
a. Imperf.
b. Vert. pair, imperf. horiz. 625.00 400.00
c. Horiz. pair, imperf. vert. 275.00
120 A2 3p red 11.00 2.50
a. Horiz. pair, imperf. vert.
b. Half used as 1p on cover 700.00
121 A2 3p black, *rose* 26.00 5.75
a. Half used as 1p on cover 750.00
122 A1 1sh green 62.50 4.50
a. Tete beche pair 950.00 175.00
b. Half used as 6p on cover 500.00
Nos. 119-122 (4) 105.25 14.75

The so-called reprints of this issue are forgeries. They were made from the counterfeit plates described in the note following No. 8, plus a new false plate for the 3p. The false 3p plate has many small flaws and defects.

Forgeries of No. 120 are in dull orange red, clearly printed on whitish paper, and those of No. 121 in brownish or grayish black on bright rose. Genuine copies of No. 120 lack the orange tint and the paper is yellowish; genuine copies of No. 121 are in black without gray or brown shade, on dull lilac rose paper.

A 6p in slate on white, apparently of this issue, is a late print from the counterfeit plate.

A4

Perf. 13½, 11½x12, 12½, 12½x12

1885-93 **Typo.**
123 A4 ½p gray .80 .20
124 A4 1p rose .80 .20
125 A4 2p brown 2.00 *2.75*
126 A4 2p olive bis ('87) 1.40 .20
127 A4 2½p purple ('93) 2.50 .55
128 A4 3p violet 2.75 1.40
129 A4 4p bronze green 4.25 .90
130 A4 6p blue 4.25 2.25
a. Imperf.
131 A4 1sh green 2.75 .70
132 A4 2sh6p yellow 9.00 2.50
133 A4 5sh steel blue 9.00 4.50
134 A4 10sh pale brown 35.00 9.00
135 A4 £5 dark green ('92) 3,750. 210.00
Nos. 123-134 (12) 74.50 25.15

Reprints of Nos. 123-137, 140-163, 166-174 closely resemble the originals. Paper is whiter; perf. 12½, large holes.

Excellent counterfeits of No. 135 exist.

For overprint and surcharges see Nos. 140-147, 163, 213.

Nos. 120, 122 Surcharged

1885 *Perf. 12*
136 A2 ½p on 3p red 5.75 *11.00*
a. Surcharge reading down 5.75 *11.00*
137 A1 ½p on 1sh green 25.00 57.50
a. Surcharge reading down 25.00 57.50
b. Tete beche pair 850.00 400.00

Almost all copies of No. 137b have telegraph cancellations. Postally used examples are rare.

Nos. 101, 128 Surcharged in Red or Black

Perf. 14

138 A3 ½p on 6p slate 62.50 *97.50*
139 A3 2p on 6p slate 6.25 *12.50*
a. Horiz. pair, imperf. vert.

Perf. 11½x12, 12½x12

140 A4 ½p on 3p vio (Bk) 4.50 4.50
a. "PRNNY" 45.00 *70.00*
b. 2nd "N" of "PENNY" invtd. 97.50 *110.00*

No. 128 Surcharged

No. 141

No. 142

1887
141 A4 2p on 3p violet 1.75 3.75
a. Double surcharge 200.00 200.00
142 A4 2p on 3p violet 8.50 8.50
a. Double surcharge 300.00

Nos. 126, 130, 131 Surcharged

Nos. 143-144

Nos. 145-146

No. 147

Red Surcharge

1893
143 A4 ½p on 2p olive bis .90 2.00
a. Inverted surcharge 2.75 2.75
b. Bars 14mm apart 1.75 2.75
c. As "b," inverted 5.75 11.00

Black Surcharge

144 A4 ½p on 2p olive bis .95 2.00
a. Inverted surcharge 5.00 5.75
b. Bars 14mm apart 1.25 2.25
c. As "b," inverted 22.50 17.50
145 A4 1p on 6p blue .80 .85
a. Inverted surcharge 1.75 2.25
b. Double surcharge 62.50 50.00
c. Pair, one without surcharge 250.00
d. Bars 14mm apart 1.10 1.10
e. As "d," inverted 5.75 4.50
f. As "d," double 90.00
146 A4 2½p on 1sh green 1.40 *4.25*
a. Inverted surcharge 7.50 *8.50*
b. Fraction line misplaced "2/1 2" 35.00 70.00
c. As "b," inverted 400.00 350.00
d. Bars 14mm apart 1.75 4.25
e. As "d," inverted 8.50 *18.00*
147 A4 2½p on 1sh green 5.50 4.75
a. Inverted surcharge 8.50 8.50
b. Bars 14mm apart 9.00 9.50
c. As "b," inverted 22.50 22.50
d. Double surcharge 85.00 *95.00*
Nos. 143-147 (5) 9.55 13.85

A13

Wagon with Two Shafts

1894 **Typo.** *Perf. 12½*
148 A13 ½p gray .50 .40
149 A13 1p rose 1.00 .20
150 A13 2p olive bister 1.00 .20
151 A13 6p blue 1.75 .40
152 A13 1sh yellow grn 10.00 *12.00*
Nos. 148-152 (5) 14.25 13.20

Counterfeits of #148-152 are plentiful.

See note following No. 135 for reprints.

1895-96 **Wagon with Pole**
153 A13 ½p gray .75 .20
154 A13 1p rose .75 .20
155 A13 2p olive bister .80 .20
156 A13 3p violet 1.50 .20
157 A13 4p slate 2.00 .45
158 A13 6p blue 2.00 .30
159 A13 1sh green 3.00 .90
160 A13 5sh slate blue ('96) 13.00 *20.00*
161 A13 10sh red brown ('96) 13.00 3.50
Nos. 153-161 (9) 36.80 25.95

Most of the unused specimens of Nos. 153-161 now on the market are reprints.

See Nos. 166-174. For surcharge and overprints see Nos. 162, 214-220, 232-235.

See note following No. 135 for reprints.

Nos. 159, 127 Surcharged in Red or Green

1895
162 A13 ½p on 1sh green (R) .30 .20
a. Inverted surcharge 5.25 5.25
b. "Pennij" instead of "Penny" 60.00 60.00
c. Double surcharge 60.00 60.00
163 A4 1p on 2½p pur (G) .60 .20
a. Inverted surcharge 20.00 20.00
b. Surcharge sideways
c. Surcharge on back
d. Space between "1" and "d" 1.25 1.25

A16

1895 *Perf. 11½*
164 A16 6p rose (G) .80 .80
a. Vertical pair, imperf. between

Counterfeits of No. 164 are on the 6p dark red revenue stamp of 1898, and have a shiny green ink for the overprint. The false overprint is also found on other revenue denominations, though only the 6p rose was converted to postal use.

Coat of Arms, Wheat Field and Railroad Train — A17

1895, Sept. 6 **Litho.**

165 A17 1p red		1.00	1.00
a.	Imperf.		
b.	Vertical pair, imperf. between	80.00	85.00

Penny Postage in Transvaal. Horiz. pair, imperf. between also exists.
For overprint see No. 245.

With Pole

1896 **Typo.** ***Perf. 12½***

166	A13	½p green	.25	.20
167	A13	1p rose & grn	.25	.20
168	A13	2p brown & grn	.25	.20
169	A13	2½p ultra & grn	.40	.20
170	A13	3p red vio & grn	1.00	.75
171	A13	4p olive & grn	1.00	.75
172	A13	6p violet & grn	.50	.40
173	A13	1sh bister & grn	.75	.20
174	A13	2sh6p lilac & grn	1.10	1.00
		Nos. 166-174 (9)	5.50	3.90

See note following No. 135 for reprints.
For overprints and surcharges see Nos. 202-212, 214-235, 237-244, 246-251, Cape of Good Hope Nos. N5-N8.

Pietersburg Issue

Date large; "P" in Postzegel large — A18

Date small; "P" in Postzegel large — A19

Date small; "P" in Postzegel small — A20

1901 **Typeset** ***Imperf.***

Initials in Red

175	A18	½p black, *green*	37.50
a.		Initials omitted	125.00
b.		Initials in black	45.00
176	A19	½p black, *green*	50.00
a.		Initials omitted	125.00
b.		Initials in black	45.00
177	A20	½p black, *green*	50.00
a.		Initials omitted	125.00
b.		Initials in black	45.00

Initials in Black

178	A18	1p black, *rose*	10.00
179	A19	1p black, *rose*	13.00
180	A20	1p black, *rose*	16.00
181	A18	2p black, *orange*	15.00
182	A19	2p black, *orange*	20.00
183	A20	2p black, *orange*	22.50
184	A18	4p black, *dull blue*	25.00
185	A19	4p black, *dull blue*	30.00
186	A20	4p black, *dull blue*	40.00
187	A18	6p black, *green*	32.50
188	A19	6p black, *green*	47.50
189	A20	6p black, *green*	65.00
190	A18	1sh black, *yellow*	75.00
191	A19	1sh black, *yellow*	55.00
192	A20	1sh black, *yellow*	140.00

Perf. 11½

Initials in Red

193	A18	½p black, *green*	13.00
194	A19	½p black, *green*	15.00
195	A20	½p black, *green*	20.00

Initials in Black

196	A18	1p black, *rose*	10.00
a.		Horiz. pair, imperf. vert.	125.00
197	A19	1p black, *rose*	13.00
a.		Horiz. pair, imperf. vert.	150.00
198	A20	1p black, *rose*	13.00
a.		Horiz. pair, imperf. vert.	150.00
199	A18	2p black, *orange*	15.00
200	A19	2p black, *orange*	17.00
201	A20	2p black, *orange*	17.00

Nos. 193 to 201 inclusive are always imperforate on one side.
The setting consisted of 12 stamps of type A18, 6 of type A19, and 6 of type A20. Numerous type-setting varieties exist. The perforated stamps are from the first printing and were put into use first. Used copies are not valued as all seen show evidence of having been canceled to order.

Second British Occupation
Issued under Military Authority

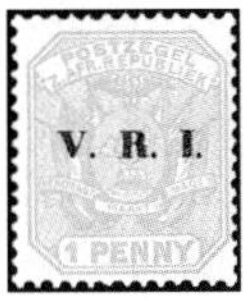

Nos. 166-174, 160-161, 135 Overprinted

1900 **Unwmk.** ***Perf. 12½***

202	A13	½p green	.20	.20
a.		"V.I.R."	650.00	
203	A13	1p rose & grn	.20	.20
204	A13	2p brown & grn	1.40	.40
a.		"V.I.R."	650.00	
205	A13	2½p ultra & grn	.50	.40
206	A13	3p red vio & grn	.50	.20
207	A13	4p olive & grn	1.10	.20
a.		"V.I.R."	650.00	
208	A13	6p violet & grn	1.10	.40
209	A13	1sh bister & grn	1.10	.80
210	A13	2sh6p hel & grn	1.75	2.25
211	A13	5sh slate blue	3.50	4.00
212	A13	10sh red brown	5.25	4.50
213	A4	£5 dark green		
		Nos. 202-212 (11)	16.60	13.55

Nos. 202 to 213 have been extensively counterfeited. The overprint on the forgeries is clear and clean, with small periods and letters showing completely. In the genuine, letters are worn and lack many or all serifs; the periods are large and oval.
The genuine overprint exists inverted; double; with period missing after "V," after "R," after "I," etc.

Issued in Lydenburg

Overprinted in Black

1900

214	A13	½p green	110.00	110.00
215	A13	1p rose & grn	100.00	80.00
216	A13	2p brown & grn	800.00	700.00
217	A13	2½p ultra & grn		800.00
218	A13	4p olive & grn	2,250.	650.00
219	A13	6p violet & grn	2,250.	575.00
220	A13	1sh bister & grn	2,500.	

Beware of counterfeits.

No. 167 Surcharged

221	A13	3p on 1p rose & green	80.00	70.00

Issued in Rustenburg

Nos. 166-170, 172-174 Handstamped in Violet

1900 ***Perf. 12½***

223	A13	½p green	100.00	100.00
224	A13	1p rose & grn	95.00	60.00
225	A13	2p brown & grn	200.00	190.00
226	A13	2½p ultra & grn	120.00	80.00
227	A13	3p red vio & grn	190.00	110.00
229	A13	6p violet & grn	650.00	500.00
230	A13	1sh bister & grn	1,300.	650.00
231	A13	2sh6p hel & grn		*4,250.*

Issued in Schweizer Reneke

Nos. 166-168 and 172 Handstamped "BESIEGED" in Black

1900 **Typo.** ***Perf. 12½***

232	A13	½p green	250.00
233	A13	1p rose & green	275.00
234	A13	2p brown & green	450.00
235	A13	6p violet & green	900.00
		Nos. 232-235 (4)	1,875.

Same Overprint on Cape of Good Hope No. 59 and Type of 1893

Perf. 14

236	A15	½p green	650.00
236A	A15	1p carmine	650.00

In 1902 five revenue stamps overprinted "V.R.I." are said to have been used postally in Volksrust. There seems to be some doubt that this issue was properly authorized for postal use.

Issued in Wolmaransstad

Nos. 166-173 Handstamped in Blue or Red

1900

237	A13	½p green	175.00	
238	A13	1p rose & grn	160.00	*175.00*
239	A13	2p brown & grn	1,400.	*1,400.*
240	A13	2½p ultra & grn (R)	2,000.	*2,000.*
241	A13	3p red vio & grn	2,500.	
242	A13	4p olive & grn	3,000.	*3,750.*
243	A13	6p violet & grn	2,750.	*4,250.*
244	A13	1sh bister & grn		

No. 165 Overprinted in Blue

245	A17	1p red	160.00	*150.00*

Regular Issues

No. 166-168, 170-171, 174 Surcharged or Overprinted

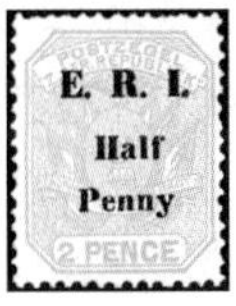

1901-02

246	A13	½p on 2p brn & grn	.80	.65
247	A13	½p green	.40	*.80*
248	A13	1p rose & grn	.40	.20
a.		Overprint "E" omitted	65.00	
249	A13	3p red vio & grn	2.00	1.50
250	A13	4p olive & grn	2.25	1.50
251	A13	2sh6p hel & grn	7.75	*10.00*
		Nos. 246-251 (6)	13.60	14.65

Excellent counterfeits of Nos. 246 to 251 are plentiful. See note after No. 213 for the recognition marks of the counterfeits.

Edward VII — A27

Nos. 260, 262 to 267 and 275 to 280 have "POSTAGE" at each side; the other stamps of type A27 have "REVENUE" at the right.

Wmk. Crown and C A (2)

1902-03 **Typo.** ***Perf. 14***

252	A27	½p gray grn & blk	1.40	.20
253	A27	1p rose & blk	1.25	.20
254	A27	2p violet & blk	3.25	.30
255	A27	2½p ultra & blk	5.75	.80
256	A27	3p ol grn & blk	6.00	.30
257	A27	4p choc & blk	4.75	.35
258	A27	6p brn org & blk	3.50	.50
259	A27	1sh ol grn & blk	12.00	6.00
260	A27	1sh red brn & blk	11.00	1.25
261	A27	2sh brown & blk	37.50	37.50
262	A27	2sh yel & blk	15.00	*9.00*
263	A27	2sh6p black & vio	13.00	10.00
264	A27	5sh vio & blk, *yel*	20.00	20.00
265	A27	10sh vio & blk, *red*	47.50	22.50
266	A27	£1 violet & grn	175.00	100.00
267	A27	£5 violet & org	1,300.	575.00
		Nos. 252-266 (15)	356.90	208.90

Issue dates: 3p, 4p, Nos. 260, 262, £1, £5, 1903. Others, Apr. 1, 1902.

1904-09 **Wmk. 3**

268	A27	½p gray grn & blk	4.00	1.75
269	A27	1p rose & blk	2.75	.20
270	A27	2p violet & blk	5.50	.50
271	A27	2½p ultra & blk	7.50	2.25
272	A27	3p ol grn & blk	2.50	.20
273	A27	4p choc & blk	3.00	.50
274	A27	6p brn org & blk	2.25	.30
275	A27	1sh red brn & blk	4.50	.30
276	A27	2sh yellow & blk	15.00	4.00
277	A27	2sh6p blk & red vio	35.00	3.00
278	A27	5sh vio & blk, *yel*	16.00	1.25
279	A27	10sh vio & blk, *red*	37.50	2.00
280	A27	£1 violet & grn	160.00	17.50
		Nos. 268-280 (13)	295.50	33.75

The 2p and 3p are on chalky paper, the 2½p, 4p, 6p and £1 on both chalky and ordinary, and the other values on ordinary paper only.
Issue years: ½p, 1p, 5sh, 1904. 2½p, 6p, 1sh, 1905. 2p, 3p, 4p, 2sh, 1906. 10sh, 1907. £1, 1908. 2sh6p, 1909.

1905-10

281	A27	½p green	1.50	.20
a.		Booklet pane of 6		
282	A27	1p carmine	1.00	.20
a.		Wmk. 16 (anchor) ('07)		275.00
b.		Booklet pane of 6		
283	A27	2p dull vio ('10)	3.00	.40
284	A27	2½p ultra ('10)	11.00	4.00
		Nos. 281-284 (4)	16.50	4.80

Wmk. 16 is illustrated in the Cape of Good Hope.
Some of the above stamps are found with the overprint "C. S. A. R." for use by the Central South African Railway, the control mark being applied after the stamps had left the post office.

POSTAGE DUE STAMPS

D1

Wmk. Multiple Crown and C A (3)

1907 **Typo.** ***Perf. 14***

J1	D1	½p green & blk	3.50	1.10
		On cover		25.00
J2	D1	1p carmine & blk	4.25	.65
		On cover		25.00
J3	D1	2p brown & org	4.25	1.00
		On cover		90.00
J4	D1	3p blue & blk	7.50	2.75
		On cover		125.00
J5	D1	5p violet & blk	2.25	10.00
		On cover		200.00
J6	D1	6p red brown & blk	4.50	11.00
		On cover		200.00
J7	D1	1sh black & car	10.00	7.00
		On cover		300.00
		Nos. J1-J7 (7)	36.25	33.50

Most canceled copies of #J1-J7 were used outside the Transvaal under the Union of South Africa administration in 1910-16. Values on cover are for commercial usages in the Transvaal, prior to the South African union.
The stamps of Transvaal were replaced by those of South Africa.

TRINIDAD

ˈtri-nə-ˌdad

LOCATION — West Indies, off the Venezuelan coast
GOVT. — British Colony which became part of the Colony of Trinidad and Tobago in 1889
AREA — 1,864 sq. mi.
POP. — 387,000
CAPITAL — Port of Spain

12 Pence = 1 Shilling
20 Shillings = 1 Pound

PRE-STAMP POSTAL MARKINGS

Crowned Circle handstamp type VII is pictured in the Crowned Circle Handstamps and Great Britain Used Abroad section.

Port of Spain

1850

A1 VII "Trinidad" crowned circle handstamp in red, on cover 3,100.

Though postage stamps were available in 1851, this handstamp was used on outgoing foreign mail covers which lacked postage stamps until 1858. However, most foreign mail covers did bear an adhesive, and covers with this handstamp and an additional adhesive stamp sell for less.

In 1847 David Bryce, owner of the "Lady McLeod," issued a blue, lithographed, imperf. stamp to prepay his 5-cent rate for carrying letters on his sail-equipped steamer between Port of Spain and San Fernando, another Trinidad port. The stamp pictures the "Lady McLeod" above the monogram "LMcL," expressing no denomination. Value: unused, $50,000; used (pen canceled), $12,500; on cover (pen caneled), $24,000; used stamps canceled by having a corner skinned off, $5,500; cover bearing skimmed stamp, $10,000.

Values for unused stamps are for examples with original gum as defined in the catalogue introduction. However, Nos. 9-12 are seldom found with gum, and these are valued without gum.

Values for Nos. 18-26 are for stamps with pin perforations on two or three sides. Stamps with pin perforations on all four sides are not often seen and command large premiums.

Very fine examples of Nos. 27-47 will have perforations touching the design on one or more sides due to the narrow spacing of the stamps on the plates and imperfect perforating methods. These stamps with perfs clear of the design on all four sides are scarce and command substantially higher prices.

"Britannia"
A1 A2

1851-56 Unwmk. Engr. *Imperf.*

Blued Paper

1 A1 (1p) brick red ('56) 200.00 85.00
a. (1p) brown red ('53) 360.00 77.50
2 A1 (1p) purple brown 18.00 *90.00*
3 A1 (1p) blue 18.00 *72.50*
a. (1p) deep blue, deeply blued paper 175.00 95.00
4 A1 (1p) gray brn ('53) 57.50 *90.00*
a. (1p) gray ('52) 90.00 77.50
Nos. 1-4 (4) 293.50 *337.50*

1854-57

White Paper

6 A1 (1p) brown red ('57) 3,250. 77.50
7 A1 (1p) gray 50.00 *95.00*
8 A1 (1p) black violet 30.00 *100.00*

See Nos. 14, 18, 22, 27, 33, 39, 43, 45, 48, 58. For surcharges see Nos. 62-64.

1852 Litho.

Fine Impressions

Yellowish Paper

9 A2 (1p) blue *11,500.* 1,950.
a. (1p) deep blue *11,500.* 1,950.
b. White paper 1,950.

1853

Bluish Paper

10 A2 (1p) blue *10,000.* 2,400.

Same, Lines of Background More or Less Worn

1855-60

Thin Paper

11 A2 (1p) slate blue *5,500.* 800.00
12 A2 (1p) blue *5,000.* 500.00
a. (1p) greenish blue 800.00
13 A2 (1p) rose 17.50 *750.00*
a. (1p) dull red 17.50 *725.00*

A3

1859 Engr. *Imperf.*

White Paper

14 A1 (1p) dull rose — —
15 A3 4p gray lilac 125.00 *400.00*
a. 4p dull lilac —
16 A3 6p green *15,000.* 525.00
17 A3 1sh slate blue 125.00 *425.00*

Pin-perf. 12½

18 A1 (1p) dull rose red *2,000.* 70.00
a. (1p) lake *2,250.* 70.00
19 A3 4p brown lilac — 1,250.
a. 4p dull purple 7,500. 1,250.
20 A3 6p deep green *3,500.* 250.00
a. 6p yellow green 3,500. 250.00
21 A3 1sh black violet *9,000.* 1,750.

Pin-perf. 14

22 A1 (1p) rose red 275.00 35.00
a. (1p) carmine 2,500. 37.50
23 A3 4p brown lilac 250.00 *150.00*
a. 4p violet 600.00 160.00
b. 4p dull violet 1,650. 125.00
24 A3 6p deep green 800.00 100.00
25 A3 6p yellow green 200.00 160.00
a. Vert. pair, imperf. between *8,000.*
26 A3 1sh black violet *9,000.* *1,150.*

1860 *Clean-cut Perf. 14 to 15½*

27 A1 (1p) dull rose 175.00 67.50
a. (1p) lake 100.00 40.00
b. Horiz. pair, imperf. vert. *3,000.*
29 A3 4p violet brown 200.00 95.00
a. 4p dull violet 375.00
30 A3 6p deep green 300.00 175.00
31 A3 6p yellow green 475.00 100.00
32 A3 1sh black violet

1861 *Rough Perf. 14 to 16½*

33 A1 (1p) dull rose 160.00 32.50
34 A3 4p gray lilac 750.00 100.00
35 A3 4p brown lilac 325.00 85.00
a. 4p dull violet 750.00 115.00
36 A3 6p green 475.00 85.00
a. 6p blue green 325.00 95.00
37 A3 1sh indigo 1,000. 350.00
a. 1sh purplish blue 1,675. 550.00

1863 *Perf. 11½ to 12*

Thick Paper

39 A1 (1p) carmine 160.00 24.00
a. Perf. 11½-12x11 2,000. *600.00*
40 A3 4p dull violet 225.00 72.50
41 A3 6p dp blue green *1,350.* 100.00
a. Perf. 11½-12x11 *8,000.*
42 A3 1sh indigo 2,750. 110.00

Perf. 12½

43 A1 (1p) lake 57.50 24.00

Perf. 13

45 A1 (1p) lake 27.50 15.00
46 A3 6p emerald 300.00 42.50
47 A3 1sh brt violet 4,000. 225.00

1864-72 Wmk. 1 *Perf. 12½*

48 A1 (1p) red 65.00 3.00
a. (1p) lake 65.00 7.25
b. (1p) rose 65.00 3.00
c. (1p) carmine 65.00 3.25
d. Imperf., pair *800.00* *800.00*
49 A3 4p brt violet 140.00 14.50
a. 4p pale violet 250.00 20.00
b. Imperf. *600.00*
50 A3 4p lilac 200.00 20.00
a. 4p gray lilac
51 A3 4p gray ('72) 160.00 6.75
52 A3 6p blue green 160.00 9.00
a. 6p emerald 110.00 17.50
53 A3 6p yellow grn 100.00 5.50
a. 6p dp grn 500.00 9.00
b. Imperf., pair *800.00*
54 A3 1sh purple 200.00 10.00
a. 1sh lilac 150.00 10.00
b. 1sh violet 150.00 10.00
c. 1sh red lilac 160.00 10.00
d. Imperf. *750.00*
55 A3 1sh orange yel ('72) 175.00 1.75
Nos. 48-55 (8) 1,200. 70.50

See Nos. 59-61A, 65. For surcharge see No. 67.

Queen Victoria — A4

1869-94 Typo. *Perf. 12½*

56 A4 5sh dull lake 200.00 90.00
a. Imperf., pair *1,250.*

Perf. 14

57 A4 5sh claret ('94) 67.50 *100.00*

For overprint see No. O7.

1876 Engr. *Perf. 14*

58 A1 (1p) carmine 32.50 1.75
a. (1p) red 57.50 1.75
b. (1p) lake 32.50 1.75
c. Half used as ½p on cover 750.00
59 A3 4p gray 140.00 .85
60 A3 6p yellow green 115.00 2.25
a. 6p deep green 150.00 2.10
61 A3 1sh orange yellow 150.00 4.00
Nos. 58-61 (4) 437.50 8.85

Perf. 14x12½

61A A3 6p yellow green *6,750.*

Value for No. 61A is for stamp with perfs barely touching the design.

Type A1 Surcharged in Black

1879 Wmk. 1 *Perf. 14*

62 A1 ½p lilac 14.50 10.00

Same Surcharge

1882 Wmk. Crown and C A (2)

63 A1 ½p lilac *250.00* 90.00
64 A1 1p carmine 42.50 1.75
a. Half used as ½p on cover 675.00

Type of 1859

1882 Wmk. 2

65 A3 4p gray 215.00 10.00

No. 60 Surcharged by pen and ink in Black or Red

1882 Wmk. 1

67 A3 1p on 6p green (R) 11.00 6.75
a. Half used as ½p on cover 400.00
b. Black surcharge *1,900.*

Counterfeits of No. 67b are plentiful. Various handwriting exists on both 60 and 60a.

A7 A8

A9

1883-84 Typo. Wmk. 2

68 A7 ½p green 6.00 1.50
69 A7 1p rose 12.00 .60
a. Half used as ½p on cover 950.00
70 A7 2½p ultra 15.00 .70
a. 2½p blue 15.00 .75
71 A7 4p slate 3.00 .70
72 A7 6p olive brn ('84) 4.75 *5.50*
73 A7 1sh orange brn ('84) 5.75 3.50
Nos. 68-73 (6) 46.50 12.50

For overprints see Nos. O1-O6.

1896-1904 *Perf. 14*

ONE PENNY:
Type I — Round "O" in "ONE."
Type II — Oval "O" in "ONE."

74 A8 ½p lilac & green 4.00 .35
75 A8 ½p gray grn ('02) .75 *2.40*
76 A8 1p lil & car, type I 4.25 .20
77 A8 1p lil & car, type II ('00) 400.00 4.75
78 A8 1p blk, *red,* type II ('01) 1.50 .20
a. Value omitted *36,000.*
79 A8 2½p lilac & ultra 7.25 .25
80 A8 2½p vio & bl, *bl* ('02) 20.00 .75
81 A8 4p lilac & orange 7.75 *21.00*
82 A8 4p grn & ultra, *buff* ('02) 2.00 *20.00*
83 A8 5p lilac & violet 9.50 *16.00*
84 A8 6p lilac & black 9.00 6.50
85 A8 1sh grn & org brn 8.25 7.75
86 A8 1sh blk & bl, *yel* ('04) 22.50 6.50

Wmk. C A over Crown (46)

87 A9 5sh green & org 55.00 90.00
88 A9 5sh lil & red vio ('02) 60.00 77.50
89 A9 10sh grn & ultra 210.00 400.00
Revenue cancel 25.00
90 A9 £1 grn & car 175.00 240.00
Nos. 74-90 (17) 996.75 894.15

No. 82 also exists on chalky paper. Nos. 88 and 90 exist on both ordinary and chalky paper.

Circular "Registrar General" cancels are revenue usage and of minimal value.

See Nos. 92-104.

Landing of Columbus — A10

1898 Engr. Wmk. 1

91 A10 2p gray vio & yel brn 2.50 1.25

400th anniv. of the discovery of the island of Trinidad by Columbus, July 31, 1498.

1904-09 Wmk. 3

Chalky Paper

92 A8 ½p gray green 4.25 1.25
93 A8 1p blk, *red,* type II 6.00 .20
94 A8 2½p vio & bl, *bl* 27.50 1.10
95 A8 4p blk & car, *yel* ('06) 2.00 10.00
96 A8 6p lilac & blk ('05) 19.00 18.00
97 A8 6p vio & dp vio ('06) 8.50 *12.00*
98 A8 1sh blk & bl, *yel* 24.00 9.50
99 A8 1sh vio & bl, *yel* 13.00 19.00
100 A8 1sh blk, *grn* ('06) 2.00 1.50
101 A9 5sh lil & red vio ('07) 55.00 110.00
102 A9 £1 grn & car ('07) 175.00 300.00
Nos. 92-102 (11) 336.25 482.55

The ½p and 1p also exist on ordinary paper.
For overprints see Nos. O8-O9.

1906-07

103	A8	1p carmine ('07)	1.75	.20
104	A8	2½p ultramarine	4.50	.20

A11

A12

1909

Ordinary Paper

105	A11	½p gray green	5.00	.20
106	A12	1p carmine	5.00	.20
107	A11	2½p ultramarine	16.00	3.75
		Nos. 105-107 (3)	26.00	4.15

For overprint see No. O10.

POSTAGE DUE STAMPS

D1

Wmk. Crown and C A (2)

1885, Jan. 1 Typo. *Perf. 14*

J1	D1	½p black	22.50	55.00
J2	D1	1p black	7.75	.25
J3	D1	2p black	35.00	.25
J4	D1	3p black	60.00	.50
J5	D1	4p black	42.50	4.75
J6	D1	5p black	27.50	.70
J7	D1	6p black	45.00	6.50
J8	D1	8p black	65.00	4.00
J9	D1	1sh black	77.50	9.00
		Nos. J1-J9 (9)	382.75	80.95

1906-07 Wmk. 3

J10	D1	1p black	5.50	.25
J11	D1	2p black	32.50	.25
J12	D1	3p black	15.00	3.25
J13	D1	4p black	15.00	16.00
J14	D1	5p black	15.00	16.00
J15	D1	6p black	7.25	12.00
J16	D1	8p black	14.50	16.00
J17	D1	1sh black	15.00	42.50
		Nos. J10-J17 (8)	119.75	106.25

See Trinidad and Tobago Nos. J1-J16.

OFFICIAL STAMPS

Postage Stamps of 1869-84 Overprinted in Black

1893-94 Wmk. 2 *Perf. 14*

O1	A7	½p green	42.50	65.00
O2	A7	1p rose	45.00	72.50
O3	A7	2½p ultra	55.00	110.00
O4	A7	4p slate	57.50	115.00
O5	A7	6p olive brown	57.50	115.00
O6	A7	1sh orange brown	77.50	150.00

Wmk. Crown and C C (1)

Perf. 12½

O7	A4	5sh dull lake	190.00	575.00
		Nos. O1-O7 (7)	525.00	1,202.

Nos. 92 and 103 Overprinted

1909-10 Wmk. 3 *Perf. 14*

O8	A8	½p gray green	1.25	9.00
O9	A8	1p carmine	1.25	9.00
a.		Double overprint		375.00
b.		Inverted overprint	900.00	275.00
c.		Vertical overprint	125.00	150.00

Same Overprint on No. 105

1910

O10	A11	½p gray green	6.50	9.00

Stamps of Trinidad have been superseded by those inscribed "Trinidad and Tobago."

TRINIDAD AND TOBAGO

'tri-nə-ˌdad and tə-'bā-ˌgō

LOCATION — West Indies off the coast of Venezuela
GOVT. — British Colony
AREA — 1,980 sq. mi.
POP. — 1,160,000 (est. 1984)
CAPITAL — Port-of-Spain

The two British colonies of Trinidad and Tobago were united from 1889 until 1899, when Tobago became a ward of the united colony. From 1899 until 1913 postage stamps of Trinidad were used.

12 Pence = 1 Shilling
20 Shillings = 1 Pound
100 Cents = 1 Dollar (1935)

Catalogue values for unused stamps in this country are for Never Hinged items, beginning with Scott 62 in the regular postage section and Scott J9 in the postage due section.

"Britannia"
A1 A2

1913 Typo. Wmk. 3 *Perf. 14*

Ordinary Paper

1	A1	½p green	3.50	.20
2	A1	1p scarlet	1.75	.20
a.		1p carmine	2.75	.20
4	A1	2½p ultra	8.00	.50

Chalky Paper

5	A1	4p scar & blk, *yel*	.80	7.00
6	A1	6p red vio & dull vio	11.00	5.00
7	A1	1sh black, *emerald*	1.75	3.50
a.		1sh black, *green*	2.00	5.00
b.		1sh black, *bl grn, ol back*	9.50	10.00
		Nos. 1-2,4-7 (6)	26.80	16.40

1914

Surface-colored Paper

8	A1	4p scar & blk, *yel*	2.00	11.00
9	A1	1sh black, *green*	1.60	3.50

Chalky Paper

10	A2	5sh dull vio & red vio	70.00	110.00
11	A2	£1 green & car	160.00	210.00
		Nos. 8-11 (4)	233.60	334.50

1921-22 Wmk. 4

Ordinary Paper

12	A1	½p green	3.00	2.50
13	A1	1p scarlet	.70	.35
14	A1	1p brown ('22)	.70	1.75
15	A1	2p gray ('22)	1.10	1.40
16	A1	2½p ultra	.90	17.50
17	A1	3p ultra ('22)	4.00	3.50

Chalky Paper

18	A1	6p red vio & dull vio	2.25	17.50
19	A2	5sh dull vio & red vio	57.50	175.00
20	A2	£1 green & car	110.00	290.00
		Nos. 12-20 (9)	180.15	509.50

For overprints see #B2-B3, MR1-MR13, O1-O5.

"Britannia" and King George V — A3

1922-28

Ordinary Paper

21	A3	½p green	.55	.20
22	A3	1p brown	.55	.20
23	A3	1½p rose red	2.50	.20
24	A3	2p gray	.55	1.40
25	A3	3p ultra	.55	1.40

Chalky Paper

26	A3	4p red & blk, *yel* ('28)	3.75	3.75
27	A3	6p red vio & dl vio	2.50	29.00
28	A3	6p red & grn, *emer* ('24)	1.40	.70
29	A3	1sh blk, *emer* ('25)	6.25	2.00
30	A3	5sh vio & dull vio	25.00	42.50
31	A3	£1 rose & green	125.00	225.00

Wmk. Multiple Crown and C A (3)

Chalky Paper

32	A3	4p red & blk, *yel*	3.75	11.00
33	A3	1sh blk, *emerald*	4.00	11.00
		Nos. 21-33 (13)	176.35	328.35

First Boca — A4

Designs: 2c, Agricultural College. 3c, Mt. Irvine Bay, Tobago. 6c, Discovery of Lake Asphalt. 8c, Queen's Park, Savannah. 12c, Town Hall, San Fernando. 24c, Government House. 48c, Memorial Park. 72c, Blue Basin.

1935-37 Engr. Wmk. 4 *Perf. 12*

34	A4	1c emer & bl, perf. 12½ ('36)	.35	.20
a.		Perf. 12	.45	1.00
35	A4	2c lt brn & ultra, perf. 12	.85	1.10
a.		Perf. 12½ ('36)	1.10	.20
36	A4	3c red & black, perf. 12½ ('36)	3.00	.35
a.		Perf. 12	1.50	.35
37	A4	6c bl & brn, perf. 12	4.75	2.75
a.		Perf. 12½ ('37)	9.00	5.00
38	A4	8c red org & yel grn	4.25	4.00
39	A4	12c dk violet & blk	3.75	2.00
a.		Perf. 12½ ('37)	9.00	7.00
40	A4	24c ol grn & blk	3.75	1.75
a.		Perf. 12½ ('37)	15.00	11.00
41	A4	48c slate green	10.00	17.00
42	A4	72c mag & sl grn	32.50	35.00
		Nos. 34-42 (9)	63.20	64.15

Common Design Types pictured following the introduction.

Silver Jubilee Issue

Common Design Type

1935, May 6 *Perf. 11x12*

43	CD301	2c black & ultra	.35	.85
44	CD301	3c car & blue	.35	1.60
45	CD301	6c ultra & brn	1.75	2.75
46	CD301	24c brn vio & ind	7.00	17.50
		Nos. 43-46 (4)	9.45	22.70
		Set, never hinged	20.00	

Coronation Issue

Common Design Type

1937, May 12 *Perf. 13½x14*

47	CD302	1c deep green	.20	.20
48	CD302	2c yellow brown	.20	.20
49	CD302	8c deep orange	.50	.50
		Nos. 47-49 (3)	.90	.90
		Set, never hinged	1.50	

First Boca — A13

George VI — A14

Various Frames and: 2c, Agricultural College. 3c, Mt. Irvine Bay, Tobago. 4c, Memorial Park. 5c, General Post Office and Treasury. 6c, Discovery of Lake Asphalt. 8c, Queen's Park, Savannah. 12c, Town Hall, San Fernando. 24c, Government House. 60c, Blue Basin.

Perf. 11½x11

1938-41 Wmk. 4 Engr.

50	A13	1c emer & blue	.25	.20
51	A13	2c lt brn & ultra	.25	.20
52	A13	3c dk car & blk	7.75	1.10
52A	A13	3c vio brn & bl grn ('41)	.20	.20
53	A13	4c brown	20.00	1.10
53A	A13	4c red ('41)	.25	.25
54	A13	5c mag ('41)	.20	.20
55	A13	6c brt bl & sep	1.00	.65
56	A13	8c red org & yel grn	.95	.85
57	A13	12c dk vio & blk	1.75	.20
58	A13	24c dk ol grn & blk	.50	.20
59	A13	60c mag & sl grn	6.00	1.50

Perf. 12

60	A14	$1.20 dk grn ('40)	7.00	1.00
61	A14	$4.80 rose pink ('40)	14.00	25.00
		Nos. 50-61 (14)	60.10	32.65
		Set, never hinged	95.00	

Watermark sideways on Nos. 50-59.

Catalogue values for unused stamps in this section, from this point to the end of the section, are for Never Hinged items.

Peace Issue

Common Design Type

Perf. 13½x14

1946, Oct. 1 Engr. Wmk. 4

62	CD303	3c brown	.20	.20
63	CD303	6c deep blue	.25	.25

Silver Wedding Issue

Common Design Types

1948, Nov. 22 Photo. *Perf. 14x14½*

64	CD304	3c red brown	.20	.20

Engr. *Perf. 11½x11*

65	CD305	$4.80 rose car	22.50	32.50

UPU Issue

Common Design Types

Engr.; Name Typo. on 6c, 12c

Perf. 13½, 11x11½

1949, Oct. 10 Wmk. 4

66	CD306	5c red violet	.40	.40
67	CD307	6c indigo	2.00	2.00
68	CD308	12c rose violet	.50	.50
69	CD309	24c olive	.50	.50
		Nos. 66-69 (4)	3.40	3.40

University Issue

Common Design Types

Inscribed: "Trinidad"

1951, Feb. 16 Engr. *Perf. 14x14½*

70	CD310	3c chocolate & grn	.25	.20
71	CD311	12c purple & blk	.60	.50

SEMI-POSTAL STAMPS

Emblem of Red Cross
SP1

Perf. 11, 12

1914, Sept. 18 Typo. Unwmk.

B1	SP1	(½p) red (on cover)	210.00

This stamp was allowed to pay ½p postage on one day, Sept. 18, 1914, on circulars distributed by the Red Cross. Value on cover is for proper Red Cross usage. Value unused, $12.50.

No. 2 Overprinted in Red (Cross) and Black (Date):

a

b

1915, Oct. 21 Wmk. 3 *Perf. 14*
B2 A1 (a) 1p scarlet 1.50 1.50

1916, Oct. 19
B3 A1 (b) 1p scarlet .50 *2.00*
a. Date omitted

POSTAGE DUE STAMPS

D1

1923-45 Typo. Wmk. 4 *Perf. 14*

J1	D1 1p black	.75	*1.50*
J2	D1 2p black	1.50	1.50
J3	D1 3p black ('25)	1.50	*2.25*
J4	D1 4p black ('29)	2.75	*20.00*
J5	D1 5p black ('45)	55.00	*92.50*
J6	D1 6p black ('45)	55.00	35.00
J7	D1 8p black ('45)	42.50	*160.00*
J8	D1 1sh black ('45)	72.50	*110.00*
	Nos. J1-J8 (8)	231.50	422.75

Catalogue values for unused stamps in this section, from this point to the end of the section, are for Never Hinged items.

Denominations in Cents

1947, Sept. 1

J9	D1 2c black	1.40	.75
J10	D1 4c black	.80	1.00
J11	D1 6c black	1.00	2.00
J12	D1 8c black	1.00	*6.00*
J13	D1 10c black	1.00	*.90*
J14	D1 12c black	1.00	*5.00*
J15	D1 16c black	1.90	*11.50*
J16	D1 24c black	6.75	*2.50*
	Nos. J9-J16 (8)	14.85	*29.65*

Nos. J9-J16 also exist on chalky paper.

Wmk. 4a (error)

J9a	D1	2c	50.00
J11a	D1	6c	100.00
J14a	D1	12c	125.00

WAR TAX STAMPS

Nos. 1-2 Overprinted

1917 Wmk. 3 *Perf. 14*
MR1 A1 1p scarlet 2.00 *2.75*
a. Invtd. overprint 175.00 *225.00*

Overprinted

MR2 A1 ½p green .20 .20
a. Overprinted on face and back 400.00
b. Pair, one without overprint 250.00
MR3 A1 1p scarlet .60 *1.75*
a. Pair, one without overprint 400.00 750.00
b. Double overprint 110.00

Overprinted

MR4 A1 ½p green .20 *5.00*
MR5 A1 1p scarlet .20 *.75*

Overprinted

MR6 A1 ½p green .20 *2.50*
MR7 A1 1p scarlet 2.75 1.00

Overprinted

MR8 A1 ½p green .20 *2.50*
MR9 A1 1p scarlet 27.50 22.50

Overprinted

MR10 A1 1p scarlet .60 *1.00*
a. Inverted overprint 92.50 *92.50*

Overprinted

MR11 A1 1p scarlet 1.25 .20
a. Double overprint 175.00 *175.00*
b. Inverted overprint 100.00 100.00

Overprinted

1918
MR12 A1 ½p green .20 *1.60*
MR13 A1 1p scarlet .75 *1.25*
a. Double overprint 110.00

The War Tax Stamps show considerable variations in the colors, thickness of the paper, distinctness of the watermark, and the gum. Counterfeits exist of the errors of Nos. MR1-MR13.

OFFICIAL STAMPS

Regular Issue of 1913 Overprinted

1913 Wmk. 3 *Perf. 14*
O1 A1 ½p green .80 5.50

Same Overprinted

1914
O2 A1 ½p green 1.50 10.00

Same Overprinted

1916
O3 A1 ½p green 1.00 2.50
a. Double overprint 22.50

Same Overprint without Period

1917
O4 A1 ½p green .50 5.50

Same Overprinted

1917, Aug. 22
O5 A1 ½p green 1.00 14.00

The official stamps are found in several shades of green and on paper of varying thickness.

TRIPOLITANIA

tri-ˌpä-lə-ˈtā-nyə

LOCATION — In northern Africa, bordering on Mediterranean Sea
GOVT. — Italian Colony
AREA — 350,000 sq. mi. (approx.)
POP. — 570,716 (1921)
CAPITAL — Tripoli

Formerly a Turkish province, Tripolitania became part of Italian Libya. See Libya.

100 Centesimi = 1 Lira

Watermark

Wmk. 140 — Crowns

Propaganda of the Faith Issue

Italian Stamps Overprinted

1923, Oct. 24 Wmk. 140 *Perf. 14*

1	A68 20c ol grn & brn org	7.50	*37.50*
	Never hinged	19.00	
	On cover		—
2	A68 30c claret & brn org	7.50	*37.50*
	Never hinged	19.00	
	On cover		—
3	A68 50c vio & brn org	4.50	*45.00*
	Never hinged	11.00	
	On cover		—
4	A68 1 l blue & brn org	4.50	*55.00*
	Never hinged	11.00	
	On cover		—
	Nos. 1-4 (4)	24.00	*175.00*
	Set, never hinged	57.50	

Fascisti Issue

Italian Stamps Overprinted in Red or Black

1923, Oct. 29 Unwmk.

5	A69 10c dk green (R)	9.00	*13.50*
	Never hinged	22.50	
	On cover		190.00
6	A69 30c dk violet (R)	9.00	*13.50*
	Never hinged	22.50	
	On cover		190.00
7	A69 50c brown car	9.00	*15.00*
	Never hinged	22.50	
	On cover		190.00
	Wmk. 140		
8	A70 1 l blue	9.00	*37.50*
	Never hinged	22.50	
	On cover		340.00
9	A70 2 l brown	9.00	*45.00*
	Never hinged	22.50	
	On cover		*500.00*
10	A71 5 l blk & bl (R)	9.00	*60.00*
	Never hinged	22.50	
	On cover		—
	Nos. 5-10 (6)	54.00	*184.50*
	Set, never hinged	125.00	

Manzoni Issue

Stamps of Italy, 1923, Overprinted in Red

1924, Apr. 1 Wmk. 140 *Perf. 14*

11	A72 10c brown red & blk	12.00	*37.50*
	Never hinged	30.00	
	On cover		—
12	A72 15c blue grn & blk	12.00	*37.50*
	Never hinged	30.00	
	On cover		—
13	A72 30c black & slate	12.00	*37.50*
	Never hinged	30.00	
	On cover		—
14	A72 50c org brn & blk	12.00	*37.50*
	Never hinged	30.00	
	On cover		—
15	A72 1 l blue & blk	75.00	*275.00*
	Never hinged	75.00	
16	A72 5 l violet & blk	500.00	*2,000.*
	Never hinged	1,250.	
	Nos. 11-16 (6)	623.00	*2,425.*
	Set, never hinged	1,530.	

On Nos. 15 and 16 the overprint is placed vertically at the left side.

Victor Emmanuel Issue

Italy Nos. 175-177 Overprinted

1925-26 Unwmk. *Perf. 11*

17	A78 60c brown car	.75	*6.75*
	Never hinged	1.90	
	On cover		140.00
18	A78 1 l dark blue	1.50	*6.75*
	Never hinged	3.75	
	On cover		1.90
a.	Perf. 13½	4.50	*22.50*
	Never hinged	11.00	
	On cover		225.00
	Perf. 13½		
19	A78 1.25 l dk blue ('26)	2.25	*21.00*
	Never hinged	5.50	
	On cover		375.00
a.	Perf. 11	1,050.	*1,350.*
	Never hinged	2,100.	
	On cover		2,250.
	Nos. 17-19 (3)	4.50	*34.50*
	Set, #17-19, 18a, 19a, never hinged	2,115.	

Saint Francis of Assisi Issue

Italy Nos. 178-180 Overprinted

1926, Apr. 12 Wmk. 140 *Perf. 14*

20 A79 20c gray green 2.25 *10.50*
Never hinged 5.50
On cover 97.50
21 A80 40c dark violet 2.25 *10.50*
Never hinged 5.50
On cover 110.00
22 A81 60c red brown 2.25 *18.00*
Never hinged 5.50
On cover 110.00

Italy No. 182 and Type of A83 Overprinted in Red

Unwmk.

23 A82 1.25 l dark blue 2.25 *26.00*
Never hinged 5.50
On cover 200.00
24 A83 5 l + 2.50 l ol grn 6.00 *52.50*
Never hinged 15.00
On cover —
Nos. 20-24 (5) 15.00 *117.50*
Set, never hinged 35.00

Volta Issue

Type of Italy Overprinted

1927, Oct. 10 Wmk. 140 *Perf. 14*

25 A84 20c purple 4.50 *30.00*
Never hinged 11.00
On cover 165.00
26 A84 50c deep orange 7.50 *18.00*
Never hinged 19.00
On cover 165.00
a. Double overprint 165.00
Never hinged 250.00
27 A84 1.25 l brt blue 10.50 *50.00*
Never hinged 26.00
On cover 300.00
Nos. 25-27 (3) 22.50 *98.00*
Set, never hinged 42.50

Monte Cassino Issue

Types of Italy Overprinted in Red or Blue

1929, Oct. 14

28 A96 20c dk green (R) 4.50 *16.00*
Never hinged 11.00
On cover 190.00
29 A96 25c red org (Bl) 4.50 *16.00*
Never hinged 11.00
On cover 140.00
30 A98 50c + 10c crim (Bl) 4.50 *18.00*
Never hinged 11.00
On cover 100.00
31 A98 75c + 15c ol brn (R) 4.50 *18.00*
Never hinged 11.00
On cover 190.00
32 A96 1.25 l + 25c dk vio (R) 10.50 *32.50*
Never hinged 26.00
On cover 250.00
33 A98 5 l + 1 l saph (R) 10.50 *37.50*
Never hinged 26.00
On cover —

Overprinted in Red

Unwmk.

34 A100 10 l + 2 l gray brn 10.50 *52.50*
Never hinged 26.00
On cover —
Nos. 28-34 (7) 49.50 *190.50*
Set, never hinged 115.00

Royal Wedding Issue

Type of Italy Overprinted

1930, Mar. 17 Wmk. 140

35 A101 20c yellow green 1.50 *4.50*
Never hinged 3.75
On cover 97.50
36 A101 50c + 10c dp org 1.10 *7.50*
Never hinged 2.75
On cover 120.00
37 A101 1.25 l + 25c rose red 1.10 *15.00*
Never hinged 2.75
On cover 200.00
Nos. 35-37 (3) 3.70 *27.00*
Set, never hinged 9.25

Ferrucci Issue

Types of Italy Overprinted in Red or Blue

1930, July 26

38 A102 20c violet (R) 3.00 *3.75*
Never hinged 7.50
On cover 90.00
39 A103 25c dk green (R) 3.00 *3.75*
Never hinged 7.50
On cover 105.00
40 A103 50c black (R) 3.00 *7.50*
Never hinged 7.50
On cover 90.00
41 A103 1.25 l deep blue (R) 3.00 *15.00*
Never hinged 7.50
On cover 225.00
42 A104 5 l + 2 l dp car (Bl) 7.50 *26.00*
Never hinged 19.00
On cover —
Nos. 38-42,C1-C3 (8) 42.00 124.50
Set, never hinged 100.00

Virgil Issue

Types of Italy Overprinted in Red or Blue

1930, Dec. 4 Photo.

43 A106 15c violet black 1.10 *7.50*
Never hinged 2.75
On cover 105.00
44 A106 20c orange brown 1.10 *3.00*
Never hinged 2.75
On cover 67.50
45 A106 25c dark green 1.10 *3.00*
Never hinged 2.75
On cover 60.00
46 A106 30c lt brown 1.10 *3.00*
Never hinged 2.75
On cover 67.50
47 A106 50c dull violet 1.10 *3.00*
Never hinged 2.75
On cover 52.50
48 A106 75c rose red 1.10 *6.00*
Never hinged 2.75
On cover 140.00
49 A106 1.25 l gray blue 1.10 *7.50*
Never hinged 2.75
On cover 200.00

Unwmk.
Engr.

50 A106 5 l + 1.50 l dk vio 3.25 *37.50*
Never hinged 8.50
On cover —
51 A106 10 l + 2.50 l ol brn 3.25 *55.00*
Never hinged 8.50
On cover —
Nos. 43-51,C4-C7 (13) 30.70 233.50
Set, never hinged 77.50

Saint Anthony of Padua Issue

Types of Italy Overprinted in Blue or Red

1931, May 7 Photo. Wmk. 140

52 A116 20c brown (Bl) 1.50 *16.00*
Never hinged 3.75
On cover 92.50
53 A116 25c green (R) 1.50 *6.00*
Never hinged 3.75
On cover 82.50
54 A118 30c gray brn (Bl) 1.50 *6.00*
Never hinged 3.75
On cover 120.00
55 A118 50c dull vio (Bl) 1.50 *6.00*
Never hinged 3.75
On cover 82.50
56 A120 1.25 l slate bl (R) 1.50 *30.00*
Never hinged 3.75
On cover 260.00

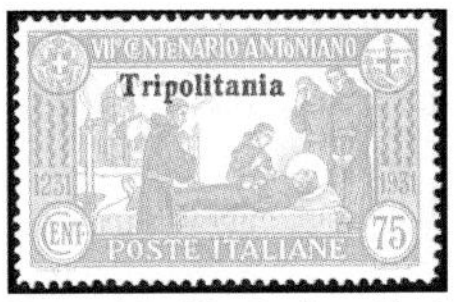

Overprinted in Red or Black

Unwmk. Engr.

57 A121 75c black (R) 1.50 *16.00*
Never hinged 3.75
On cover 225.00
58 A122 5 l + 2.50 l dk brn (Bk) 6.00 *65.00*
Never hinged 15.00
On cover —
Nos. 52-58 (7) 15.00 *145.00*
Set, never hinged 37.50

Native Village Scene A14

1934, Oct. 16 Wmk. 140

73 A14 5c ol grn & brn 3.75 *18.00*
Never hinged 9.25
On cover 225.00
74 A14 10c brown & black 3.75 *18.00*
Never hinged 9.25
On cover 190.00
75 A14 20c scar & indigo 3.75 *15.00*
Never hinged 9.25
On cover 190.00
76 A14 50c purple & brown 3.75 *15.00*
Never hinged 9.25
On cover 165.00
77 A14 60c org brn & ind 3.75 *22.50*
Never hinged 9.25
On cover 225.00
78 A14 1.25 l dk bl & grn 3.75 *37.50*
Never hinged 9.25
On cover 260.00
Nos. 73-78,C43-C48 (12) 45.00 252.00
Set, never hinged 110.00

2nd Colonial Arts Exhibition, Naples.

SEMI-POSTAL STAMPS

Many issues of Italy and Italian Colonies include one or more semipostal denominations. To avoid splitting sets, these issues are generally listed as regular postage, airmail, etc., unless all values carry a surtax.

Holy Year Issue

Italian Stamps of 1924 Overprinted in Black or Red

1925 Wmk. 140 *Perf. 12*

B1 SP4 20c + 10c dk grn & brn 3.00 *18.00*
Never hinged 7.50
On cover 150.00
B2 SP4 30c + 15c dk brn & brn 3.00 *21.00*
Never hinged 7.50
On cover 150.00
B3 SP4 50c + 25c vio & brn 3.00 *18.00*
Never hinged 7.50
On cover 150.00
B4 SP4 60c + 30c dp rose & brn 3.00 *24.00*
Never hinged 7.50
On cover 210.00
B5 SP8 1 l + 50c dp bl & vio (R) 3.00 *30.00*
Never hinged 7.50
On cover —
B6 SP8 5 l + 2.50 l org brn & vio (R) 3.00 *45.00*
Never hinged 7.50
On cover —
Nos. B1-B6 (6) 18.00 *156.00*
Set, never hinged 42.50

Colonial Institute Issue

Peace Substituting Spade for Sword — SP1

1926, June 1 Typo. *Perf. 14*

B7 SP1 5c + 5c brown .90 *7.50*
Never hinged 2.25
On cover 130.00
B8 SP1 10c + 5c ol brn .90 *7.50*
Never hinged 2.25
On cover 100.00
B9 SP1 20c + 5c bl grn .90 *7.50*
Never hinged 2.25
On cover 82.50
B10 SP1 40c + 5c brn red .90 *7.50*
Never hinged 2.25
On cover 82.50
B11 SP1 60c + 5c orange .90 *7.50*
Never hinged 2.25
On cover 140.00
B12 SP1 1 l + 5c blue .90 *16.00*
Never hinged 2.25
On cover 225.00
Nos. B7-B12 (6) 5.40 *53.50*
Set, never hinged 13.50

The surtax was for the Italian Colonial Institute.

Fiera Campionaria Tripoli
See Libya for stamps with this inscription.

Types of Italian Semi-Postal Stamps of 1926 Overprinted like Nos. 17-19

1927, Apr. 21 Unwmk. *Perf. 11*

B19 SP10 40c + 20c dk brn & blk 2.25 *30.00*
Never hinged 5.50
On cover 120.00
B20 SP10 60c + 30c brn red & ol brn 2.25 *30.00*
Never hinged 5.50
On cover 140.00
B21 SP10 1.25 l + 60c dp bl & blk 2.25 *47.50*
Never hinged 5.50
On cover 260.00
B22 SP10 5 l + 2.50 l dk grn & blk 3.75 *67.50*
Never hinged 5.50
On cover —
Nos. B19-B22 (4) 10.50 *175.00*
Set, never hinged 25.00

Th e surtax was for the charitable work of the Voluntary Militia for Italian National Defense.

Allegory of Fascism and Victory — SP2

1928, Oct. 15 Wmk. 140

B29 SP2 20c + 5c bl grn 2.25 *11.00*
Never hinged 5.50
On cover 120.00
B30 SP2 30c + 5c red 2.25 *11.00*
Never hinged 5.50
On cover 120.00
B31 SP2 50c + 10c pur 2.25 *18.00*
Never hinged 5.50
On cover 110.00
B32 SP2 1.25 l + 20c dk bl 3.00 *22.50*
Never hinged 7.50
On cover 300.00
Nos. B29-B32 (4) 9.75 *62.50*
Set, never hinged 24.00

46th anniv. of the Societa Africana d'Italia. The surtax aided that society.

Types of Italian Semi-Postal Stamps of 1928 Overprinted

1929, Mar. 4 Unwmk. *Perf. 11*

B33 SP10 30c + 10c red & blk 3.75 *18.00*
Never hinged 9.25
On cover 130.00
B34 SP10 50c + 20c vio & blk 3.75 *22.50*
Never hinged 9.25
On cover 130.00
B35 SP10 1.25 l + 50c brn & bl 4.50 *37.50*
Never hinged 11.00
On cover 275.00
B36 SP10 5 l + 2 l ol grn & blk 4.50 *67.50*
Never hinged 11.00
On cover —
Nos. B33-B36 (4) 16.50 *145.50*
Set, never hinged 40.00

The surtax on these stamps was for the charitable work of the Voluntary Militia for Italian National Defense.

Types of Italian Semi-Postal Stamps of 1926, Overprinted in Black or Red Like Nos. B33-B36

1930, Oct. 20

B50 SP10 30c + 10c dp grn & bl grn (Bk) 19.00 *30.00*
Never hinged 47.50
On cover 190.00
B51 SP10 50c + 10c dk grn & vio (R) 19.00 *40.00*
Never hinged 47.50
On cover 200.00
B52 SP10 1.25 l + 30c blk brn & red brn (R) 19.00 *52.50*
Never hinged 47.50
On cover 325.00
B53 SP10 5 l + 1.50 l ind & grn (R) 60.00 *150.00*
Never hinged 150.00
On cover —
Nos. B50-B53 (4) 117.00 *272.50*
Set, never hinged 290.00

Ancient Arch — SP3

1930, Nov. 27 Photo. Wmk. 140

B54 SP3 50c + 20c ol brn 3.75 *18.00*
Never hinged 9.25
On cover 140.00
B55 SP3 1.25 l + 20c dp bl 3.75 *18.00*
Never hinged 9.25
On cover 190.00
B56 SP3 1.75 l + 20c green 3.75 *21.00*
Never hinged 9.25
On cover 250.00
B57 SP3 2.55 l + 50c purple 6.00 *32.50*
Never hinged 15.00
On cover 375.00
B58 SP3 5 l + 1 l deep car 6.00 *47.50*
Never hinged 15.00
On cover —
Nos. B54-B58 (5) 23.25 *137.00*
Set, never hinged 57.50

25th anniv. of the Italian Colonial Agricultural Institute. The surtax was for the benefit of that institution.

AIR POST STAMPS

Ferrucci Issue

Type of Italian Air Post Stamps Overprinted in Blue or Red like #38-42

1930, July 26 Wmk. 140 *Perf. 14*

C1 AP7 50c brown vio (Bl) 3.75 *7.50*
Never hinged 9.25
On cover 150.00
C2 AP7 1 l dk blue (R) 3.75 *13.50*
Never hinged 9.25
On cover 260.00
C3 AP7 5 l + 2 l dp car (Bl) 15.00 *47.50*
Never hinged 37.50
On cover —
Nos. C1-C3 (3) 22.50 *68.50*
Set, never hinged 55.00
Set, on flown cover 260.00

Virgil Issue

Types of Italian Air Post Stamps Overprinted in Red or Blue like #43-51

1930, Dec. 4 Photo.

C4 AP8 50c deep green 2.25 *9.00*
Never hinged 5.50
On cover 120.00
C5 AP8 1 l rose red 2.25 *9.00*
Never hinged 5.50
On cover 165.00

Unwmk.
Engr.

C6 AP8 7.70 l + 1.30 l dk brn 6.00 *45.00*
Never hinged 15.00
On cover 400.00
C7 AP8 9 l + 2 l gray 6.00 *45.00*
Never hinged 15.00
On cover 625.00
Nos. C4-C7 (4) 16.50 *108.00*
Set, never hinged 40.00
Set, on flown cover 340.00

Airplane over Columns of the Basilica, Leptis — AP1

Arab Horseman Pointing at Airplane AP2

1931-32 Photo. Wmk. 140

C8 AP1 50c rose car .75 .20
Never hinged 1.90
On cover 2.50
C9 AP1 60c red org 2.25 *7.50*
Never hinged 5.50
On cover 100.00
C10 AP1 75c dp bl ('32) 2.25 *6.00*
Never hinged 5.50
On cover 90.00
C11 AP1 80c dull violet 6.00 *11.00*
Never hinged 15.00
On cover 165.00
C12 AP2 1 l deep blue 1.50 .20
Never hinged 3.75
On cover 5.50
C13 AP2 1.20 l dk brown 18.00 *15.00*
Never hinged 45.00
On cover 225.00
C14 AP2 1.50 l org red 7.50 *15.00*
Never hinged 19.00
On cover 250.00
C15 AP2 5 l green 22.50 *22.50*
Never hinged 55.00
On cover 500.00
Nos. C8-C15 (8) 60.75 *77.40*
Set, never hinged 150.00

For surcharges and overprint see Nos. C29-C32.

Agricultural Institute, 25th Anniv. AP3

1931, Dec. 7

C16 AP3 50c dp blue 3.00 *18.00*
Never hinged 7.50
On cover 190.00
C17 AP3 80c violet 3.00 *18.00*
Never hinged 7.50
On cover 225.00
C18 AP3 1 l gray black 3.00 *26.00*
Never hinged 7.50
On cover 275.00
C19 AP3 2 l deep green 6.00 *37.50*
Never hinged 15.00
On cover 500.00
C20 AP3 5 l + 2 l rose red 9.00 *67.50*
Never hinged 22.50
On cover —
Nos. C16-C20 (5) 24.00 *167.00*
Set, never hinged 60.00
Set, on flown cover 300.00

Graf Zeppelin Issue

Mercury, by Giovanni da Bologna, and Zeppelin AP4

Designs: 3 l, 12 l, Mercury. 10 l, 20 l, Guido Reni's "Aurora." 5 l, 15 l, Arch of Marcus Aurelius.

1933, May 5

C21 AP4 3 l dark brown 7.50 *95.00*
Never hinged 19.00
On cover 340.00
C22 AP4 5 l purple 7.50 *95.00*
Never hinged 19.00
On cover 400.00
C23 AP4 10 l deep green 7.50 *175.00*
Never hinged 19.00
On cover 625.00
C24 AP4 12 l deep blue 7.50 *200.00*
Never hinged 19.00
On cover 900.00
C25 AP4 15 l carmine 7.50 *200.00*
Never hinged 19.00
On cover 900.00
C26 AP4 20 l gray black 7.50 *260.00*
Never hinged 19.00
On cover 900.00
Nos. C21-C26 (6) 45.00 *1,025.*
Set, never hinged 110.00
Set, on flown cover *3,600.*

For overprints and surcharges see Nos. C38-C42.

North Atlantic Flight Issue

Airplane, Lion of St. Mark AP7

1933, June 1

C27 AP7 19.75 l blk & ol brn 15.00 *500.00*
Never hinged 37.50
On cover 2,250.
C28 AP7 44.75 l dk bl & lt grn 15.00 *500.00*
Never hinged 37.50
On cover 2,250.
Set, never hinged 75.00
Set, on flown cover *4,250.*

Type of 1931 Overprinted or Surcharged

1934, Jan. 20

C29 AP2 2 l on 5 l org brn 3.00 *60.00*
Never hinged 7.50
On cover 250.00
C30 AP2 3 l on 5 l grn 3.00 *60.00*
Never hinged 7.50
On cover 250.00
C31 AP2 5 l ocher 3.00 *67.50*
Never hinged 7.50
On cover 275.00
C32 AP2 10 l on 5 l rose 4.50 *67.50*
Never hinged 11.00
On cover 400.00
Nos. C29-C32 (4) 13.50 *255.00*
Set, never hinged 25.00
Set, on flown cover 1,200.

For use on mail to be carried on a special flight from Rome to Buenos Aires.

Types of Libya Airmail Issue Overprinted in Black or Red

1934, May 1 Wmk. 140

C38 AP4 50c rose red 9.00 *92.50*
Never hinged 22.50
On cover 260.00
C39 AP4 75c lemon 9.00 *92.50*
Never hinged 22.50
On cover 275.00
C40 AP4 5 l + 1 l brn 9.00 *92.50*
Never hinged 22.50
On cover 425.00
C41 AP4 10 l + 2 l dk bl 175.00 *525.00*
Never hinged 450.00
On cover —
C42 AP5 25 l + 3 l pur 175.00 *525.00*
Never hinged 450.00
On cover —
Nos. C38-C42,CE1-CE2 (7) 395.00 1,512.
Set, never hinged 1,030.
Set, on flown cover *3,250.*

"Circuit of the Oases."

Plane Shadow on Desert AP11

Designs: 25c, 50c, 75c, Plane shadow on desert. 80c, 1 l, 2 l, Camel corps.

1934, Oct. 16 Photo.

C43 AP11 25c sl bl & org red 3.75 *18.00*
Never hinged 9.25
On cover 165.00
C44 AP11 50c dk grn & ind 3.75 *15.00*
Never hinged 9.25
On cover 140.00
C45 AP11 75c dk brn & org red 3.75 *15.00*
Never hinged 9.25
On cover 190.00
C46 AP11 80c org brn & ol grn 3.75 *18.00*
Never hinged 9.25
On cover 225.00
C47 AP11 1 l scar & ol grn 3.75 *22.50*
Never hinged 9.25
On cover 250.00
C48 AP11 2 l dk bl & brn 3.75 *37.50*
Never hinged 9.25
On cover 325.00
Nos. C43-C48 (6) 22.50 *126.00*
Set, never hinged 55.00
Set, on flown cover 375.00

Second Colonial Arts Exhibition, Naples.

AIR POST SEMI-POSTAL STAMPS

King Victor Emmanuel III SPAP1

1934, Nov. 5 Wmk. 140 *Perf. 14*

CB1 SPAP1 25c + 10c gray grn 6.00 *13.50*
Never hinged 15.00
On cover 190.00
CB2 SPAP1 50c + 10c brn 6.00 *13.50*
Never hinged 15.00
On cover 190.00
CB3 SPAP1 75c + 15c rose red 6.00 *13.50*
Never hinged 15.00
On cover 200.00
CB4 SPAP1 80c + 15c blk brn 6.00 *13.50*
Never hinged 15.00
On cover 250.00
CB5 SPAP1 1 l + 20c red brn 6.00 *13.50*
Never hinged 15.00
On cover 260.00
CB6 SPAP1 2 l + 20c brt bl 6.00 *13.50*
Never hinged 15.00
On cover —
CB7 SPAP1 3 l + 25c pur 21.00 *67.50*
Never hinged 52.50
On cover —
CB8 SPAP1 5 l + 25c org 21.00 *67.50*
Never hinged 52.50
On cover —
CB9 SPAP1 10 l + 30c rose vio 21.00 *67.50*
Never hinged 52.50
On cover —
Never hinged 52.50
On cover —

CB10	SPAP1 25 l + 2 l dp grn	21.00	*67.50*
	Nos. CB1-CB10 (10)	120.00	*351.00*
	Set, never hinged	210.00	
	Set, on flown cover		1,150.

65th birthday of King Victor Emmanuel III; non-stop flight from Rome to Mogadiscio.

For overprint see No. CBO1.

AIR POST SEMI-POSTAL OFFICIAL STAMP

Type of Air Post Semi-Postal Stamps Overprinted Crown and "SERVIZIO DI STATO" in Black

1934 Wmk. 140 *Perf. 14*

CBO1	SPAP1 25 l + 2 l cop red	2,450.	*3,750.*
	Never hinged	3,000.	
	On cover		5,250.

AIR POST SPECIAL DELIVERY STAMPS

Type of Libya Overprinted in Black Like Nos. C38-c42

1934, May 1 Wmk. 140 *Perf. 14*

CE1	APSD1 2.25 l red orange	9.00	*92.50*
	Never hinged	22.50	
	On cover		550.00
CE2	APSD1 4.50 l + 1 l dp rose	9.00	*92.50*
	Never hinged	22.50	
	On cover		—
	Set, never hinged	45.00	

AUTHORIZED DELIVERY STAMP

Authorized Delivery Stamp of Italy 1930, Overprinted like Nos. 38-42

1931, Mar. Wmk. 140 *Perf. 14*

EY1	AD2 10c dark brown	9.00	18.00
	Never hinged	22.50	
	On cover		*1,200.*

TRISTAN DA CUNHA

ˌtris-tən-də-ˈkü-nə

LOCATION — Group of islands in the south Atlantic Ocean midway between the Cape of Good Hope and South America
GOVT. — A dependency of St. Helena
AREA — 40 sq. mi.
POP. — 325 (1982)

12 Pence = 1 Shilling

Catalogue values for all unused stamps in this country are for Never Hinged items.

Stamps of St. Helena, 1938-49, Overprinted in Black

1952, Jan. 1 Wmk. 4 *Perf. 12½*

1	A24 ½p purple	.20	*2.10*
2	A24 1p blue grn & blk	.80	*1.90*
3	A24 1½pcar rose & blk	.80	*1.90*
4	A24 2p carmine & blk	.80	*1.90*
5	A24 3p gray	1.10	*1.90*
6	A24 4p ultra	4.25	3.00
7	A24 6p gray blue	5.00	3.00
8	A24 8p olive	4.50	*6.50*
9	A24 1sh sepia	5.00	*2.50*
10	A24 2sh6p deep claret	22.50	*16.00*
11	A24 5sh brown	24.00	*25.00*
12	A24 10sh violet	45.00	*35.00*
	Nos. 1-12 (12)	113.95	*100.70*
	Set, hinged	70.00	

TUNISIA

tü-ˈnē-zhˌēˌə

LOCATION — Northern Africa, bordering on the Mediterranean Sea
GOVT. — French protectorate
AREA — 63,362 sq. mi.
POP. — 6,966,173 (1984)
CAPITAL — Tunis

100 Centimes = 1 Franc

Covers

Values are for commercial covers bearing correct frankings. Philatelic covers sell for less.

Coat of Arms — A1

Perf. 14x13½

1888-97 Typo. Unwmk.

1	A1 1c black, *blue*	3.00	2.25
	On cover, single franking		—
a.	Horiz. ruled line background	9.00	9.00
2	A1 2c pur brn, *buff*	3.00	2.25
	On cover, single franking		—
a.	Horiz. ruled line background	9.00	9.00
3	A1 5c green, *grnsh*	22.50	9.25
	On cover, single franking		32.50
a.	Horiz. ruled line background	24.00	17.50
4	A1 15c blue, *grysh*	45.00	17.50
	On cover, single franking		19.00
5	A1 25c black, *rose*	92.50	52.50
	On cover, single franking		50.00
a.	Horiz. ruled line background	350.00	350.00
6	A1 40c red, *straw*	92.50	60.00
	On cover, single franking		70.00
7	A1 75c car, *rose*	85.00	65.00
	On cover, single franking		80.00
a.	Horiz. ruled line background	140.00	140.00
8	A1 5fr gray vio, *grysh*	425.00	300.00
	On cover, single franking		—
a.	Horiz. ruled line background	525.00	500.00
	Nos. 1-8 (8)	768.50	508.75

All values exist imperforate.

Issued: Nos. 1-8, 7/1/88; Nos. 1a//8a, 1897.

Reprints were made in 1893 and some values have been reprinted twice since then. The shades usually differ from those of the originals. Stamps from the 1897 printing are on thicker paper, with white gum instead of grayish, and have a background of horizontal ruled lines.

A2

A3

1888-1902

9	A2 1c blk, *lil bl*	1.50	.85
	On cover, single franking		—
10	A2 2c pur brn, *buff*	1.50	.85
	On cover, single franking		—
11	A2 5c grn, *grnsh*	6.50	.85
	On cover, single franking		13.50
12	A2 5c yellow grn ('99)	5.75	.85
	On cover, single franking		13.50
13	A2 10c blk, *lav* ('93)	9.25	1.00
	On cover, single franking		7.00
14	A2 10c red ('01)	5.75	.85
	On cover, single franking		4.00
15	A2 15c blue, *grysh*	45.00	.85
	On cover, single franking		4.00
16	A2 15c gray ('01)	9.25	1.25
	On cover, single franking		4.00
17	A2 20c red, *grn* ('99)	17.00	1.50
	On cover		*15.00*
18	A2 25c blk, *rose*	22.50	1.90
	On cover, single franking		7.50
19	A2 25c blue ('01)	17.00	1.90
	On cover, single franking		8.00
20	A2 35c brown ('02)	45.00	1.90
	On cover, single franking		14.00
21	A2 40c red, *straw*	19.00	1.50
	On cover, single franking		10.00
22	A2 75c car, *rose*	160.00	75.00
	On cover		*250.00*
23	A2 75c dp vio, *org* ('93)	25.00	7.25
	On cover, single franking		20.00
24	A3 1fr olive, *olive*	30.00	8.50
	On cover, single franking		—
25	A3 2fr dull violet ('02)	160.00	140.00
	On cover, single franking		—
26	A3 5fr red lil, *lav*	190.00	75.00
	Bar cancellation		.50
	On cover, single franking		—

Quadrille Paper

27	A2 15c bl, *grysh* ('93)	45.00	.75
	On cover, single franking		7.50
	Nos. 9-27 (19)	815.00	322.55

For surcharges see Nos. 28, 58-61.

No. 27 Surcharged in Red

1902

28	A2 25c on 15c blue	3.00	3.00

Mosque at Kairouan A4

Plowing A5

Ruins of Hadrian's Aqueduct A6

Carthaginian Galley — A7

1906-26 Typo.

29	A4 1c blk, *yel*	.20	.20
30	A4 2c red brn, *straw*	.20	.20
31	A4 3c lt red ('19)	.20	.20
32	A4 5c grn, *grnsh*	.30	.20
33	A4 5c orange ('21)	.20	.20
34	A5 10c red	.30	.20
35	A5 10c green ('21)	.35	.25
36	A5 15c vio, *pnksh*	1.10	.25
a.	Imperf., pair		
37	A5 15c brn, *org* ('23)	.25	.25
38	A5 20c brn, *pnksh*	.25	.25
39	A5 25c deep blue	1.60	.60
a.	Imperf., pair		
40	A5 25c violet ('21)	.35	.25
41	A6 30c red brn & vio ('19)	.70	.60
42	A5 30c pale red ('21)	.90	.60
43	A6 35c ol grn & brn	8.75	1.75
44	A6 40c blk brn & red brn	4.25	.60
45	A5 40c blk, *pnksh* ('23)	1.10	.60
46	A5 40c gray grn ('26)	.20	.20
47	A5 50c blue ('21)	.60	.60
48	A6 60c ol grn & vio ('21)	.60	.60
49	A6 60c ver & rose ('25)	.60	.35
50	A6 75c red brn & red	.75	.60
51	A6 75c ver & dl red ('26)	.35	.35
52	A7 1fr red & dk brn	.90	.60
53	A7 1fr ind & ultra ('25)	.35	.35
54	A7 2fr brn & ol grn	5.25	1.50
55	A7 2fr grn & red, *pink* ('25)	.75	.35
56	A7 5fr violet & blue	9.50	4.50
57	A7 5fr gray vio & grn ('25)	.75	.60
	Nos. 29-57 (29)	41.60	17.80

For surcharges and overprints see Nos. 62-64, 70-73115-116, B1-B23, B25-B27, B29-B30, B32-B36, C1-C6.

Stamps and Type of 1888-1902 Surcharged

1908, Sept.

58	A2 10c on 15c gray, *lt gray* (R)	1.40	1.40
59	A3 35c on 1fr ol, *ol* (R)	3.25	3.25
60	A3 40c on 2fr dl vio (Bl)	6.00	6.00
61	A3 75c on 5fr red lil, *lav* (Bl)	4.50	4.50
	Nos. 58-61 (4)	15.15	15.15

No. 36 Surcharged

1911

62	A5 10c on 15c vio, *pinkish*	1.50	.60

No. 34 Surcharged

1917, Mar. 16

63	A5 15c on 10c red	.75	.20
a.	"15c" omitted	37.50	
b.	Double surcharge	75.00	

No. 36 Surcharged

1921

64	A5 20c on 15c vio, *pinkish*	.90	.25

Arab and Ruins of Dougga — A9

1922-26 Typo. *Perf. 13½x14*

65	A9 10c green	.20	.20
66	A9 10c rose ('26)	.25	.25
67	A9 30c rose	1.10	1.10
68	A9 30c lilac ('26)	.40	.40
69	A9 50c blue	.65	.65
	Nos. 65-69 (5)	2.60	2.60

For surcharges see Nos. 117, B24, B28, B31.

Stamps and Type of 1906 Surcharged in Red or Black

a

b

1923-25

70	A4(a) 10c on 5c grn, *grnsh* (R)	.35	.35
a.	Double surcharge	57.50	
71	A5(b) 20c on 15c violet (Bk)	.85	.25
72	A5(b) 30c on 20c yel brn (Bk) ('25)	.35	.35
73	A5(b) 50c on 25c blue (R)	.85	.25
	Nos. 70-73 (4)	2.40	1.20

Arab Woman Carrying Water — A10

Grand Mosque at Tunis — A11

Mosque, Tunis — A12

Roman Amphitheater, El Djem (Thysdrus) — A13

1926-46 Typo. *Perf. 14x13½*

74 A10 1c lt red .20 .20
75 A10 2c olive grn .20 .20
76 A10 3c slate blue .20 .20
77 A10 5c yellow grn .20 .20
78 A10 10c rose .20 .20
78A A12 10c brown ('46) .20 .20
79 A11 15c gray lilac .20 .20
80 A11 20c deep red .25 .20
81 A11 25c gray green .35 .25
82 A11 25c lt violet ('28) .60 .25
83 A11 30c lt violet .35 .35
84 A11 30c blue grn ('28) .35 .25
84A A12 30c dk ol grn ('46) .20 .20
85 A11 40c deep brown .25 .20
85A A12 40c lil rose ('46) .25 .25
86 A11 45c emerald ('40) .85 .85
87 A12 50c black .25 .20
88 A12 50c ultra ('34) .70 .25
88B A12 50c emerald ('40) .20 .20
88C A12 50c lt blue ('46) .25 .25
89 A12 60c red org ('40) .20 .20
89A A12 60c ultra ('45) .20 .20
90 A12 65c ultra ('38) .55 .25
91 A12 70c dark red ('40) .20 .20
92 A12 75c vermilion .35 .35
93 A12 75c lilac rose ('28) 1.00 .25
94 A12 80c blue green 1.00 .35
94A A12 80c blk brn ('40) .25 .25
94B A12 80c emerald ('45) .35 .25
95 A12 90c org red ('28) .25 .20
96 A12 90c ultra ('39) 8.50 8.50
97 A12 1fr brown violet .70 .35
97A A12 1fr rose ('40) .20 .20
98 A13 1.05fr dl bl & mag .60 .45
98A A12 1.20fr blk brn ('45) .35 .25
99 A13 1.25fr gray bl & dk bl .60 .35
100 A13 1.25fr car rose ('40) 1.00 1.00
100A A13 1.30fr bl & vio bl ('42) .25 .25
101 A13 1.40fr brt red vio ('40) 1.10 1.10
102 A13 1.50fr bl & dp bl ('28) 1.00 .35
102A A13 1.50fr rose red & red org ('42) .45 .45
102B A12 1.50fr rose lil ('46) .20 .20
103 A13 2fr rose & ol brn 1.40 .25
104 A13 2fr red orange ('39) .30 .30
104A A12 2fr Prus grn ('45) .25 .20
105 A13 2.25fr ultra ('39) .90 .90
105A A13 2.40fr red ('46) .55 .35
106 A13 2.50fr green ('40) .85 .85
107 A13 3fr dl bl & org 1.60 .60
108 A13 3fr violet ('39) .25 .25
108A A13 3fr black brn ('46) .20 .20
108B A13 4fr ultra ('45) .90 .55
109 A13 5fr red & grn, *grnsh* 2.75 .80
110 A13 5fr dp red brn ('40) 1.10 1.10
110A A13 5fr dk green ('46) .85 .20
110B A13 6fr dp ultra ('45) .60 .35
111 A13 10fr brn red & blk, *bluish* 9.50 2.75
112 A13 10fr rose pink ('40) .60 .60
112A A13 10fr ver ('46) .55 .35
112B A13 10fr ultra ('46) .55 .25
112C A13 15fr rose lil ('45) .35 .20
113 A13 20fr lil & red, *pnksh* ('28) 1.75 .85
113A A13 20fr dk green ('45) .70 .35
113B A13 25fr violet ('45) .70 .55
113C A13 50fr carmine ('45) 1.25 .70
113D A13 100fr car rose ('45) 1.50 .90
Nos. 74-113D (66) 55.50 35.45

See Nos. 152A-162, 185-189, 199-206.
For surcharges and overprints see Nos. 114, 118-121, 143-152, B74-B77, B87-B88, B91-B95, B98, C7-C12.

No. 99 Surcharged with New Value and Bars in Red

1927, Mar. 24
114 A13 1.50fr on 1.25fr .55 .25

Stamps of 1921-26 Surcharged

1928, May 1
115 A4 3c on 5c orange .25 .20
116 A5 10c on 15c brn, *org* .60 .25
117 A9 25c on 30c lilac .55 .35
118 A12 40c on 80c bl grn .55 .35
119 A12 50c on 75c ver .75 .55
Nos. 115-119 (5) 2.70 1.70

No. 83 Surcharged

1929
120 A11 10c on 30c lt violet 3.50 2.00

No. 120 exists precanceled only. The value in first column is for a stamp which has not been through the post and has original gum. The value in the second column is for a postally used, gumless stamp. See No. 199a.

No. 85 Surcharged with New Value and Bars

1930
121 A11 50c on 40c dp brn 5.00 .85

A14

A15

A16

A17

Perf. 11, 12½, 12½x13

1931-34 Engr.
122 A14 1c deep blue .20 .20
123 A14 2c yellow brn .20 .20
124 A14 3c black .35 .35
125 A14 5c yellow grn .20 .20
126 A14 10c red .20 .20
127 A15 15c dull violet .60 .55
128 A15 20c dull brown .20 .20
129 A15 25c rose red .25 .20
130 A15 30c deep green .55 .45
131 A15 40c red orange .25 .25
132 A16 50c ultra .25 .25
133 A16 75c yellow 2.10 1.90
134 A16 90c red .60 .60
135 A16 1fr olive black .45 .35
136 A16 1fr dk brown ('34) .45 .35
137 A17 1.50fr brt ultra .75 .55
138 A17 2fr deep brown .70 .70
139 A17 3fr blue green 8.50 8.50
140 A17 5fr car rose 22.50 18.00
a. Perf. 12½ 35.00 30.00
141 A17 10fr black 40.00 30.00
142 A17 20fr dark brown 52.50 42.50
Nos. 122-142 (21) 131.80 106.50

For surcharges see Nos. B54-B73.

Nos. 88, 102 Surcharged in Red or Black:

1937 *Perf. 14x13½*
143 A12 65c on 50c (R) .55 .20
b. Double surcharge 75.00 65.00
144 A13 1.75fr on 1.50fr (R) 5.00 1.25
a. Double surcharge 70.00 70.00

1938
145 A12 65c on 50c (Bk) .75 .25
146 A13 1.75fr on 1.50fr (R) 7.75 6.50

Stamps of 1938-39 Surcharged in Red or Carmine:

1940
147 A12 25c on 65c ultra (C) .20 .20
148 A12 1fr on 90c ultra (R) .35 .35

SEMI-POSTAL STAMPS

No. 36 Overprinted in Red

1915, Feb. Unwmk. *Perf. 14x13½*
B1 A5 15c vio, *pnksh* 1.00 1.00

No. 32 Overprinted in Red

1916, Feb. 15
B2 A4 5c grn, *grnsh* 1.25 1.25

Types of Regular Issue of 1906 in New Colors and Surcharged

1916, Aug.
B3 A5 10c on 15c brn vio, *bl* 1.00 1.00
B4 A5 10c on 20c brn, *org* 1.00 1.00
B5 A5 10c on 25c bl, *grn* 3.25 3.25
B6 A6 10c on 35c ol grn & vio 6.50 6.50
B7 A6 10c on 40c bis & blk 3.00 3.00
B8 A6 10c on 75c vio brn & grn 8.50 8.50
B9 A7 10c on 1fr red & grn 3.50 3.50
B10 A7 10c on 2fr bis & bl 75.00 75.00
B11 A7 10c on 5fr vio & red 100.00 100.00
Nos. B3-B11 (9) 201.75 201.75

Nos. B3 to B11 were sold at their face value but had a postal value of 10c only. The excess was applied to the relief of prisoners of war in Germany.

Types of Regular Issue of 1906 in New Colors and Surcharged in Carmine

1918
B12 A5 15c on 20c blk, *grn* 1.90 1.90
B13 A5 15c on 25c dk bl, *buff* 1.90 1.90
B14 A6 15c on 35c gray grn & red 1.90 1.90
B15 A6 15c on 40c brn & lt bl 4.25 4.25
B16 A6 15c on 75c red brn & blk 7.50 7.50
B17 A7 15c on 1fr red & vio 22.50 22.50
B18 A7 15c on 2fr bis brn & red 70.00 70.00
B19 A7 15c on 5fr vio & blk 125.00 125.00
Nos. B12-B19 (8) 234.95 234.95

The different parts of the surcharge are more widely spaced on the stamps of types A6 and A7. These stamps were sold at their face value but had a postal value of 15c only. The excess was intended for the relief of prisoners of war in Germany.

Types of 1906-22 Surcharged

1923
B20 A4 0c on 1c blue .75 .75
B21 A4 0c on 2c ol brn .75 .75
B22 A4 1c on 3c green .75 .75
B23 A4 2c on 5c red vio .75 .75
B24 A9 3c on 10c vio, *bluish* .75 .75
B25 A5 5c on 15c ol grn .75 .75
B26 A5 5c on 20c bl, *pink* 1.50 1.50
B27 A5 5c on 25c vio, *bluish* 1.50 1.50
B28 A9 5c on 30c orange 1.60 1.60
B29 A6 5c on 35c bl & vio 2.25 2.25
B30 A6 5c on 40c bl & brn 2.25 2.25
B31 A9 10c on 50c blk, *bluish* 3.00 3.00
B32 A6 10c on 60c ol brn & bl 3.00 3.00
B33 A6 10c on 75c vio & lt grn 5.00 5.00
B34 A7 25c on 1fr mar & vio 5.00 5.00
B35 A7 25c on 2fr bl & rose 16.00 16.00
B36 A7 25c on 5fr grn & ol brn 57.50 57.50
Nos. B20-B36 (17) 103.10 103.10

These stamps were sold at their original values but had postal franking values only to the amounts surcharged on them. The difference was intended to be used for the benefit of wounded soldiers.

This issue was entirely speculative. Before the announced date of sale most of the stamps were taken by postal employees and practically none of them were offered to the public.

Mail Delivery — SP1

Type of Parcel Post Stamps, 1906, with Surcharge in Black

1925, June 7 *Perf. 13½x14*
B37 SP1 1c on 5c brn & red, *pink* .55 .55
a. Surcharge omitted 110.00 *110.00*
B38 SP1 2c on 10c brn & bl, *yel* .55 .55
B39 SP1 3c on 20c red vio & rose, *lav* 1.00 1.00
B40 SP1 5c on 25c sl grn & rose, *bluish* 1.00 1.00
B41 SP1 5c on 40c rose & grn, *yel* 1.00 1.00
B42 SP1 10c on 50c vio & bl, *lav* 2.00 2.00
B43 SP1 10c on 75c grn & ol, *grnsh* 1.50 1.50
B44 SP1 25c on 1fr bl & grn, *bluish* 1.50 1.50
B45 SP1 25c on 2fr rose & vio, *pnksh* 7.50 7.50
B46 SP1 25c on 5fr red & brn, *lem* 35.00 35.00
Nos. B37-B46 (10) 51.60 51.60

These stamps were sold at their original values but paid postage only to the amount of the surcharged values. The difference was given to Child Welfare societies.

Tunis-Chad Motor Caravan SP2

1928, Feb. Engr. *Perf. 13½*

B47 SP2 40c + 40c org brn 1.00 1.00
B48 SP2 50c + 50c dp vio 1.40 1.40
B49 SP2 75c + 75c dk bl 1.40 1.40
B50 SP2 1fr + 1fr carmine 1.40 1.40
B51 SP2 1.50fr + 1.50fr brt bl 1.40 1.40
B52 SP2 2fr + 2fr dk grn 1.50 1.50
B53 SP2 5fr + 5fr red brn 1.90 1.90
Nos. B47-B53 (7) 10.00 10.00

The surtax on these stamps was for the benefit of Child Welfare societies.

Nos. 122-135, 137-142 Surcharged in Black

a

b

1938 *Perf. 11, 12½, 12½x13*

B54 A14(a) 1c + 1c 1.50 1.50
B55 A14(a) 2c + 2c 1.50 1.50
B56 A14(a) 3c + 3c 1.50 1.50
B57 A14(a) 5c + 5c 1.50 1.50
B58 A14(a) 10c + 10c 1.50 1.50
B59 A15(a) 15c + 15c 1.50 1.50
B60 A15(a) 20c + 20c 1.50 1.50
B61 A15(a) 25c + 25c 1.50 1.50
B62 A15(a) 30c + 30c 1.50 1.50
B63 A15(a) 40c + 40c 1.50 1.50
B64 A16(a) 50c + 50c 1.50 1.50
B65 A16(a) 75c + 75c 1.50 1.50
B66 A16(a) 90c + 90c 1.50 1.50
B67 A16(a) 1fr + 1fr 1.50 1.50
B68 A17(b) 1.50fr + 1fr 1.50 1.50
B69 A17(b) 2fr + 1.50fr 3.00 3.00
B70 A17(b) 3fr + 2fr 3.75 3.75
B71 A17(b) 5fr + 3fr 18.00 18.00
a. Perf. 12½ 92.50 92.50
B72 A17(b) 10fr + 5fr 35.00 35.00
B73 A17(b) 20fr + 10fr 60.00 60.00
Nos. B54-B73 (20) 142.25 142.25

50th anniversary of the post office.

AIR POST STAMPS

No. 43 Surcharged in Red

1919, Apr. Unwmk. *Perf. 14x13½*

C1 A6 30c on 35c ol grn & brn 1.25 1.25
a. Inverted surcharge 130.00 130.00
b. Double surcharge 130.00 130.00
c. Double inverted surcharge 150.00 150.00
d. Double surcharge, one inverted 130.00 130.00

Type A6, Overprinted in Rose

1920, Apr.

C2 A6 30c ol grn, bl & rose .40 .40

Nos. 53 and 55 Overprinted in Red

1927, Mar. 24

C3 A7 1fr indigo & ultra .90 .65
C4 A7 2fr grn & red, *pink* 3.00 1.90

Nos. 51 and 57 Surcharged in Black or Red

C5 A6 1.75fr on 75c (Bk) 1.00 .55
C6 A7 1.75fr on 5fr (R) 3.00 2.00

Type A13 Ovptd. like #C3-C4 in Blue

1928, Feb.

C7 A13 1.30fr org & lt vio 3.50 1.40
C8 A13 1.80fr gray grn & red 4.25 .85
C9 A13 2.55fr lil & ol brn 1.90 .95
Nos. C7-C9 (3) 9.65 3.20

Type A13 Surcharged like #C5-C6 in Blue

1930, Aug.

C10 A13 1.50fr on 1.30fr org & lt vio 2.40 .75
C11 A13 1.50fr on 1.80fr gray grn & red 4.25 .60
C12 A13 1.50fr on 2.55fr lil & ol brn 7.75 1.75
Nos. C10-C12 (3) 14.40 3.10

POSTAGE DUE STAMPS

During 1888-1901, postage due stamps were created by perforating regular postage stamps with the letter "T." Generally, panes were folded before perforation, so that the "T" is either upright or inverted on equal numbers of stamps. The high values (75c, 1fr and 5fr) were perforated as needed, not always in full panes, and so examples of these values with inverted "T" command a modest premium.

All values exist perforated with a smaller "T," apparently used in Gafsa. These are rare.

Nos. 1-8 perforated "T"

1888-97

JA1 A1 1c black, *blue* 5.25 3.75
a. "T" inverted 5.25 3.75
b. Horiz. ruled line background ('97) 11.50 11.50
c. As "b," "T" inverted 11.50 11.50
JA2 A1 2c pur brn, *buff* 5.25 3.75
a. "T" inverted 5.25 3.75
b. Horiz. ruled line background ('97) 14.00 14.00
c. As "b," "T" inverted 14.00 14.00
JA3 A1 5c green, *grnsh* 17.00 13.00
a. "T" inverted 17.00 13.00
b. Horiz. ruled line background ('97) 21.00 21.00
c. As "b," "T" inverted 21.00 21.00
JA4 A1 15c blue, *grysh* 42.50 23.00
a. "T" inverted 42.50 23.00
JA5 A1 25c black, *rose* 60.00 37.50
a. "T" inverted 60.00 37.50
b. Horiz. ruled line background ('97) 240.00 200.00
c. As "b," "T" inverted 240.00 200.00
JA6 A1 40c red, *straw* 45.00 37.50
a. "T" inverted 45.00 37.50
JA7 A1 75c car, *rose* 60.00 42.50
a. "T" inverted 19.00 15.00
b. Horiz. ruled line background ('97) 140.00 100.00
c. As "b," "T" inverted 160.00 110.00
JA8 A1 5fr gray vio, *grysh* 350.00 225.00
a. "T" inverted 400.00 250.00
b. Horiz. ruled line background ('97) 400.00 325.00
c. As "b," "T" inverted 450.00 375.00
Nos. JA1-JA8 (8) 585.00 386.00

See footnote following No. 8

Nos. 9//27 perforated "T"

1888-1901

JA9 A2 1c blk, *lil bl* 1.30 1.30
a. "T" inverted 1.30 1.30
b. Tête-bêche pair, JA9 & JA9a 4.50 4.50
JA10 A2 2c pur brn, *buff* 1.90 1.30
a. "T" inverted 1.90 1.30
b. Tête-bêche pair, JA10 & JA10a 7.50 6.00
JA11 A2 5c grn, *grnsh* 8.50 1.50
a. "T" inverted 8.50 1.50
b. Tête-bêche pair, JA11 & JA11a 27.50 7.50
JA12 A2 5c yellow grn ('99) 6.50 .75
a. "T" inverted 6.50 .75
b. Tête-bêche pair, JA12 & JA12a 27.50 3.75
JA13 A2 10c blk, *lav* ('93) 8.50 4.25
a. "T" inverted 8.50 4.25
b. Tête-bêche pair, JA13 & JA13a 27.50 13.50
JA14 A2 10c red ('01) 1.40 .70
a. "T" inverted 1.40 .70
b. Tête-bêche pair, JA14 & JA14a 6.00 3.00
JA15 A2 15c blue, *grysh* 12.50 4.25
a. "T" inverted 12.50 4.25
b. Tête-bêche pair, JA15 & JA15a 35.00 13.50
JA16 A2 15c gray ('01) 1.40 .70
a. "T" inverted 1.40 .70
b. Tête-bêche pair, JA16 & JA16a 6.00 3.00
JA17 A2 20c red, *grn* ('99) 15.00 5.00
a. "T" inverted 15.00 5.00
b. Tête-bêche pair, JA17 & JA17a 45.00 15.00
JA18 A2 25c blk, *rose* 15.00 5.00
a. "T" inverted 15.00 5.00
b. Tête-bêche pair, JA18 & JA18a 45.00 15.00
JA19 A2 25c blue ('01) 2.25 .90
a. "T" inverted 2.25 .90
b. Tête-bêche pair, JA19 & JA19a 11.50 4.50
JA20 A2 40c red, *straw* 17.00 4.25
a. "T" inverted 17.00 4.25
b. Tête-bêche pair, JA20 & JA20a 52.50 15.00
JA21 A2 75c car, *rose* 175.00 125.00
a. "T" inverted 190.00 140.00
JA22 A2 75c dp vio, *org* ('93) 30.00 8.50
a. "T" inverted 32.50 9.25
JA23 A3 1fr olive, *olive* 30.00 9.25
a. "T" inverted 32.50 10.00
JA24 A3 5fr red lil, *lav* 150.00 85.00
a. "T" inverted 165.00 92.50

Quadrille Paper

JA25 A2 15c bl, *grysh* ('93) 17.00 4.25
a. "T" inverted 17.00 4.25
b. Tête-bêche pair, JA25 & JA25a 52.50 13.50
Nos. JA9-JA25 (17) 493.25 261.90

D1

D2

Perf. 14x13½

1901-03 Unwmk. Typo.

J1 D1 1c black .40 .40
J2 D1 2c orange .85 .55
J3 D1 5c blue .60 .40
J4 D1 10c brown .60 .55
J5 D1 20c blue green 3.50 .75
J6 D1 30c carmine 3.00 .75
J7 D1 50c brown violet 1.75 .85
J8 D1 1fr olive green 1.25 .85
J9 D1 2fr carmine, *grn* 3.50 1.50
J10 D1 5fr blk, *yellow* 45.00 35.00
Nos. J1-J10 (10) 60.45 41.60

No. J10 Surcharged in Blue

1914, Nov.

J11 D1 2fr on 5fr blk, *yellow* 1.00 1.00

In Jan. 1917 regular 5c postage stamps were overprinted "T" in an inverted triangle and used as postage due stamps.

1922-49

J12 D2 1c black .25 .25
J13 D2 2c black, *yellow* .25 .25
J14 D2 5c violet brown .55 .25
J15 D2 10c blue .40 .25
J16 D2 10c yel green ('45) .20 .20
J17 D2 20c orange, *yel* .40 .40
J18 D2 30c brown ('23) .40 .25
J19 D2 50c rose red .75 .40
J20 D2 50c blue vio ('45) .20 .20
J21 D2 60c violet ('28) .75 .40
J22 D2 80c bister ('28) .60 .30
J23 D2 90c orange red ('28) .85 .55
J24 D2 1fr green .55 .25
J25 D2 2fr olive grn, *straw* 1.00 .40
J26 D2 2fr car rose ('45) .25 .25
J27 D2 3fr vio, *pink* ('29) .40 .25
J28 D2 4fr grnsh bl ('45) .40 .40
J29 D2 5fr violet .60 .40
J30 D2 10fr cerise ('49) .40 .40
J31 D2 20fr olive gray ('49) 1.10 .90
Nos. J12-J31 (20) 10.30 6.95

PARCEL POST STAMPS

Mail Delivery — PP1

Gathering Dates — PP2

1906 Unwmk. Typo. *Perf. 13½x14*

Q1 PP1 5c grn & vio brn .60 .40
Q2 PP1 10c org & red .75 .40
Q3 PP1 20c dk brn & org 1.10 .40
Q4 PP1 25c blue & brn 1.90 .40
Q5 PP1 40c gray & rose 2.40 .40
Q6 PP1 50c vio brn & vio 1.90 .40
Q7 PP1 75c bis brn & bl 3.00 .40
Q8 PP1 1fr red brn & red 2.90 .25
Q9 PP1 2fr carmine & bl 6.75 .60
Q10 PP1 5fr vio & vio brn 20.00 1.25
Nos. Q1-Q10 (10) 41.30 4.90

1926

Q11 PP2 5c pale brn & dk bl .40 .40
Q12 PP2 10c rose & vio .40 .40
Q13 PP2 20c yel grn & blk .40 .40
Q14 PP2 25c org brn & blk .40 .40
Q15 PP2 40c dp rose & dp grn 1.50 .65
Q16 PP2 50c lt vio & blk 1.50 .65
Q17 PP2 60c ol & brn red 1.50 .65
Q18 PP2 75c gray vio & bl grn 1.50 .65
Q19 PP2 80c ver & ol brn 1.50 .65
Q20 PP2 1fr Prus bl & dp rose 1.50 .65
Q21 PP2 2fr vio & mag 3.75 .65
Q22 PP2 4fr red & blk 4.50 .65
Q23 PP2 5fr red brn & dp vio 6.00 .65
Q24 PP2 10fr dl red & grn, *grnsh* 12.50 .65
Q25 PP2 20fr yel grn & dp vio, *lav* 24.00 1.25
Nos. Q11-Q25 (15) 61.35 9.35

Parcel post stamps were discontinued July 1, 1940.

TURKEY

'tər-kē

LOCATION — Southeastern Europe and Asia Minor, between the Mediterranean and Black Seas
GOVT. — Republic
AREA — 300,947 sq. mi.
POP. — 48,000,000 (est. 1984)
CAPITAL — Ankara

The Ottoman Empire ceased to exist in 1922, and the Republic of Turkey was inaugurated in 1923.

40 Paras = 1 Piaster
40 Paras = 1 Ghurush (1926)
40 Paras = 1 Kurush (1926)
100 Kurush = 1 Lira

Catalogue values for unused stamps in this country are for Never Hinged items, beginning with Scott 817 in the regular postage section, Scott C1 in the airpost section, and Scott J97 in the postage due section.

Turkish Numerals

"Tughra," Monogram of Sultan Abdul-Aziz
A1 A2

A3 A4

1863 Unwmk. Litho. *Imperf.*
Red Band: 20pa, 1pi, 2pi
Blue Band: 5pi
Thin Paper

1	A1 20pa blk, *yellow*	75.00	20.00
a.	Tête bêche pair	250.00	200.00
b.	Without band	100.00	
c.	Green band		
2	A2 1pi blk, *dl vio*	125.00	20.00
a.	1pi black, *gray*	125.00	21.00
b.	Tête bêche pair	400.00	300.00
c.	Without band	140.00	
d.	Design reversed		*175.00*
e.	1pi blk, *yel* (error)	250.00	150.00
4	A3 2pi blk, *grnsh bl*	110.00	20.00
a.	2pi black, *ind*	110.00	21.00
b.	Tête bêche pair	400.00	300.00
c.	Without band	140.00	
5	A4 5pi blk, *rose*	225.00	45.00
a.	Tête bêche pair	500.00	400.00
b.	Without band	250.00	
c.	Green band	*275.00*	
d.	Red band	*275.00*	

Thick, Surface Colored Paper

6	A1 20pa blk, *yellow*	250.00	37.50
a.	Tête bêche pair	450.00	450.00
b.	Design reversed	325.00	325.00
c.	Without band	225.00	225.00
d.	Paper colored through	225.00	225.00
7	A2 1pi blk, *gray*	275.00	35.00
a.	Tête bêche pair	900.00	900.00
b.	Design reversed		
c.	Without band		
d.	Paper colored through	300.00	225.00
	Nos. 1-7 (6)	1,060.	177.50

Full margins: Nos. 1, 2, 4, 5 = 1mm at sides and top, 3mm at bottom (includes part of band); Nos. 6-7 = ¾mm at sides and top, 3¼ at bottom (includes part of band). Height of colored bands is 6mm. Full margins for items without band = 3mm at bottom.

Full margins of first printings: No. 4 = 1mm; No. 5 = ½mm.

The 2pi and 5pi had two printings. In the common printing, the stamps are more widely spaced and alternate horizontal rows of 12 are inverted. In the first and rare printing, the stamps are more closely spaced and no rows are tête bêche.

See Nos. J1-J4.

Crescent and Star, Symbols of Turkish Caliphate — A5

Surcharged

The bottom characters of this and the following surcharges denote the denomination. The characters at top and sides translate, "Ottoman Empire Posts."

1865 Typo. *Perf. 12½*

8	A5 10pa deep green	8.50	*35.00*
c.	"1" instead of "10" in each corner	*300.00*	*300.00*
9	A5 20pa yellow	4.00	3.00
a.	Star without rays	4.00	*3.00*
10	A5 1pi lilac	12.50	4.00
a.	Star without rays	17.50	3.00
c.	1pi gray	11.00	3.00
11	A5 2pi blue	5.50	4.00
12	A5 5pi carmine	4.00	4.50
d.	Inverted surcharge		
13	A5 25pi red orange	325.00	250.00

Imperf., Pairs

8b	A5 10pa	125.00	125.00
9b	A5 20pa	125.00	125.00
10b	A5 1pi	*100.00*	*90.00*
11a	A5 2pi	*100.00*	*90.00*
12b	A5 5pi	*110.00*	*110.00*
13a	A5 25pi	750.00	*750.00*

See Nos. J6-J35. For overprints and surcharges see Nos. 14-52, 64-65, 446-461, 467-468, J71-J77, Eastern Rumelia 1.

Surcharged

1867

14	A5 10pa gray green	7.50	
a.	Imperf., pair	55.00	
15	A5 20pa yellow	12.50	
a.	Imperf., pair	75.00	
16	A5 1pi lilac	20.00	
a.	Imperf., pair	110.00	
b.	Imperf., with surcharge of 5pi	25.00	
17	A5 2pi blue	4.50	*40.00*
a.	Imperf.		
18	A5 5pi rose	3.50	*40.00*
a.	Imperf.		
19	A5 25pi orange	*3,500.*	
	Nos. 14-18 (5)	48.00	

Nos. 14, 15, 16 and 19 were never placed in use.

Surcharged

1869 *Perf. 13½*

20	A5 10pa dull violet	100.00	7.00
a.	Printed on both sides		
b.	Imperf., pair	*90.00*	*80.00*
c.	Inverted surcharge		*90.00*
d.	Double surcharge		
e.	10pa yellow (error)		*300.00*
f.	10pa gray brown	60.00	1.25
21	A5 20pa pale green	400.00	3.00
a.	Printed on both sides	*450.00*	*275.00*
22	A5 1pi yellow	10.00	2.50
	No gum	2.00	
c.	Inverted surcharge	*100.00*	
d.	Double surcharge		
e.	Surcharged on both sides		
f.	Printed on both sides		
23	A5 2pi orange red	200.00	6.50
b.	Imperf., pair	125.00	125.00
c.	Printed on both sides		125.00
d.	Inverted surcharge	70.00	70.00
e.	Surcharged on both sides		140.00
24	A5 5pi blue	2.50	*10.00*
25	A5 5pi gray	25.00	37.50
26	A5 25pi dull rose	37.50	125.00
	Nos. 20-26 (7)	775.00	*191.50*

Pin-perf., Perf. 5 to 11 and Compound

1870-71

27	A5 10pa lilac	*550.00*	*25.00*
28	A5 10pa brown	*500.00*	*8.00*
a.	10pa brown, *lilac*	*3,500.*	*57.50*
b.	10pa purple, *lilac*	*3,500.*	*70.00*
c.	10pa gray, *lilac*	*5,000.*	*92.50*
29	A5 20pa gray green	75.00	*2.50*
a.	Printed on both sides		
30	A5 1pi yellow	*550.00*	*2.50*
a.	Inverted surcharge	*500.00*	*80.00*
b.	Without surcharge		
31	A5 2pi red	5.00	5.00
a.	Imperf.	20.00	20.00
b.	Printed on both sides		*40.00*
c.	Surcharged on both sides		
32	A5 5pi blue	2.50	*12.50*
a.	5pi greenish blue	2.75	*8.00*
33	A5 5pi slate	40.00	50.00
a.	Printed on both sides		
b.	Surcharged on both sides		*40.00*
34	A5 25pi dull rose	40.00	*75.00*
	Nos. 27-34 (8)	1,762.	*180.50*

1873 *Perf. 12, 12½*

35	A5 10pa dark lilac	90.00	25.00
a.	Inverted surcharge		90.00
36	A5 10pa olive brown	110.00	17.50
a.	10pa bister	110.00	11.00
37	A5 2pi vermilion	2.50	3.50
a.	Surcharged on both sides	22.50	22.50
	Nos. 35-37 (3)	202.50	*46.00*

Surcharged

1874-75 *Perf. 13½*

38	A5 10pa red violet	35.00	7.50
a.	Imperf., pair	70.00	50.00
39	A5 20pa yellow green	15.00	4.00
b.	Inverted surcharge	30.00	13.00
c.	Double surcharge		
40	A5 1pi yellow	45.00	15.00
a.	Imperf., pair	100.00	80.00

Perf. 12, 12½

41	A5 10pa red violet	25.00	10.00
a.	Inverted surcharge	45.00	60.00
	Nos. 38-41 (4)	120.00	36.50

Surcharged

1876, Apr. *Perf. 13½*

42	A5 10pa red lilac	1.50	.50
a.	Inverted surcharge	70.00	
b.	Imperf., pair	15.00	15.00
43	A5 20pa pale green	1.50	.50
b.	Inverted surcharge	70.00	
c.	Imperf., pair	15.00	15.00
44	A5 1pi yellow	1.50	.50
a.	Imperf., pair	27.50	27.50
46	A5 5pi gray blue	*1,000.*	
47	A5 25pi dull rose	*1,000.*	
	Nos. 42-44 (3)	4.50	

Nos. 46 and 47 were never placed in use.
See Nos. 64-65.

Surcharged

1876, Jan.

48	A5 ¼pi on 10pa violet	2.50	2.50
49	A5 ½pi on 20pa yel grn	6.25	2.50
50	A5 1¼pi on 50pa rose	1.50	2.50
a.	Imperf., pair	60.00	
51	A5 2pi on 2pi redsh brn	40.00	7.50
52	A5 5pi on 5pi gray blue	*30.00*	*50.00*
	Nos. 48-52 (5)	80.25	*65.00*

The surcharge on Nos. 48-52 restates in French the value originally expressed in Turkish characters.

A7

1876, Sept. Typo. *Perf. 13½*

53	A7 10pa black & rose lil	2.00	6.00
54	A7 20pa red vio & grn	62.50	5.00
55	A7 50pa blue & yellow	.75	*10.00*
56	A7 2pi black & redsh brn	1.25	*5.00*
57	A7 5pi red & blue	3.00	*10.00*
b.	Cliché of 25pi in plate of 5pi	400.00	375.00
58	A7 25pi claret & rose	15.00	75.00
a.	Imperf.	160.00	
	Nos. 53-58 (6)	84.50	111.00

Nos. 56-58 exist perf. 11½, but were not regularly issued.

See Nos. 59-63, 66-91, J36-J38. For overprints see Nos. 462-466, 469-476, J78-J79, P10-P14, Eastern Rumelia 2-40.

1880-84 *Perf. 13½*

59	A7 5pa black & ol ('81)	2.50	6.50
a.	Imperf.	30.00	
60	A7 10pa black & grn ('84)	2.00	3.50
61	A7 20pa black & rose	55.00	1.00
62	A7 1pi blk & bl *(piastres)*	75.00	2.00
a.	1pi black & gray blue	75.00	
b.	Imperf.	40.00	
63	A7 1pi blk & bl *(piastre)* ('81)	110.00	3.00
	Nos. 59-63 (5)	244.50	16.00

A cliché of No. 63 was inserted in a plate of the Eastern Rumelia 1pi (No. 13). This was found in the remainder stock.

Nos. 60-61 and 63 exist perf. 11½, but were not regularly issued.

1881-82
Surcharged like Apr., 1876 Issue

64	A5 20pa gray	3.00	.50
a.	Inverted surcharge	13.50	
b.	Imperf., pair	25.00	
65	A5 2pi pale salmon	2.00	.50
a.	Inverted surcharge	22.50	

1884-86 *Perf. 11½, 13½*

66	A7 5pa lil & pale lil ('86)	200.00	*150.00*
67	A7 10pa grn & pale grn	1.25	1.25
68	A7 20pa rose & pale rose	1.25	1.25
69	A7 1pi blue & lt blue	1.25	1.25

Perf. 11½

70	A7 2pi ocher & pale ocher	2.00	1.25
71	A7 5pi red brn & pale brn	20.00	9.00
c.	5pi ocher & pale ocher (error)	12.00	12.00

Perf. 11½, 13½

73	A7 25pi blk & pale gray ('86)	300.00	*425.00*
	Nos. 66-73 (7)	525.75	*589.00*

Imperf

66a	A7 5pa	60.00	
67a	A7 10pa	20.00	
68b	A7 20pa	20.00	
69b	A7 1pi	20.00	
73a	A7 25pi	150.00	

1886 *Perf. 13½*

74	A7 5pa black & pale gray	1.25	2.50
75	A7 2pi orange & lt bl	1.25	2.00
76	A7 5pi grn & pale grn	3.00	25.00
77	A7 25pi bis & pale bis	30.00	*150.00*
	Nos. 74-77 (4)	35.50	*179.50*

Imperf

74a	A7 5pa	20.00	
75b	A7 2pi	20.00	
76b	A7 5pi	20.00	
77a	A7 25pi	35.00	

Stamps of 1884-86, bisected and surcharged as above, 10pa, 20pa, 1pi and 2pi or surcharged "2" in red are stated to have been made privately and without authority. With the aid of employees of the post office, copies were passed through the mails.

1888 *Perf. 13½*

83 A7 5pa green & yellow 2.50 5.00
84 A7 2pi red lilac & bl 1.50 1.50
85 A7 5pi dk brown & gray 5.00 *20.00*
86 A7 25pi red & yellow 30.00 *150.00*
Nos. 83-86 (4) 39.00 *176.50*

Imperf

83a A7 5pa 20.00
84a A7 2pi 20.00
85a A7 5pi 20.00
86a A7 25pi 25.00

Nos. 74-86 exist perf. 11½, but were not regularly issued.

1890 *Perf. 11½, 13½*

87 A7 10pa green & gray 5.00 1.00
88 A7 20pa rose & gray 1.25 1.00
89 A7 1pi blue & gray 75.00 1.00
90 A7 2pi yellow & gray 70.00 7.50
91 A7 5pi buff & gray 5.00 *22.50*
Nos. 87-91 (5) 156.25 *33.00*

Imperf

87a A7 10pa 20.00
88a A7 20pa 20.00
89a A7 1pi 20.00
90b A7 2pi 25.00
91a A7 5pi 25.00

Arms and Tughra of "El Gazi" (The Conqueror) Sultan Abdul Hamid
A10 A11

A12

A13

A14

No. 100

1892-98 **Typo.** *Perf. 13½*

95 A10 10pa gray green 1.50 .50
96 A11 20pa violet brn ('98) 1.25 .50
a. 20pa dark pink 7.50 .30
b. 20pa pink 10.00 .30
97 A12 1pi pale blue 110.00 .50
98 A13 2pi brown org 2.00 .50
a. Tête bêche pair *30.00 30.00*
99 A14 5pi dull violet 3.00 *15.00*
a. Turkish numeral in upper right corner reads "50" instead of "5" 30.00 15.00
Nos. 95-99 (5) 117.75 *17.00*

See Nos. J39-J42. For surcharges and overprints see Nos. 100, 288-291, 350, 355-359, 477-478, B38, B41, J80-J82, P25-P34, P36, P121-P122, P134-P137, P153-P154.

Red Surcharge

1897

100 A10 5pa on 10pa gray grn 3.00 1.25
a. "Cniq" instead of "Cinq" 10.00 10.00

Turkish stamps of types A11, A17-A18, A21-A24, A26, A28-A39, A41 with or without Turkish overprints and English surcharges with "Baghdad" or "Iraq" are listed under Mesopotamia in Vol. 4.

Turkish stamps of types A19 and A21 with Double-headed Eagle and "Shqipenia" handstamp are listed under Albania in Vol. 1.

A16

A17

1901 **Typo.** *Perf. 13½*

For Foreign Postage

102 A16 5pa bister 1.25 .60
103 A16 10pa yellow green 1.25 .60
104 A16 20pa magenta 1.25 .60
a. Perf. 12 1.25 .60
105 A16 1pi violet blue 1.50 1.00
106 A16 2pi gray blue 2.50 1.00
107 A16 5pi ocher 7.50 3.00
108 A16 25pi dark green 100.00 30.00
109 A16 50pi yellow 250.00 100.00
Nos. 102-109 (8) 365.25 136.80

For Domestic Postage

Perf. 12, 13½

110 A17 5pa purple 1.25 .50
111 A17 10pa green 1.25 .50
112 A17 20pa carmine 1.25 .50
113 A17 1pi blue 1.25 .50
a. Imperf. 20.00
114 A17 2pi orange 2.00 .50
115 A17 5pi lilac rose 5.75 1.00

Perf. 13½

116 A17 25pi brown 10.00 2.00
a. Perf. 12 12.50 5.25
117 A17 50pi yellow brown 32.50 3.50
a. Perf. 12 45.00 15.00
Nos. 110-117 (8) 55.25 9.00

Nos. 110-113 exist perf. 12x13½.

For overprints and surcharges see Nos. 165-180, 292-303, 340-341, 361-377, 479-493, B19-B20, B37, J43-J46, P37-P48, P69-P80, P123-P126, P138-P146, P155-P164.

A18

A19

1905 *Perf. 12, 13½ and Compound*

118 A18 5pa ocher 1.00 .50
119 A18 10pa dull green 1.00 .50
a. Imperf. 4.00 3.50
120 A18 20pa carmine 1.00 .50
a. Imperf. 4.00 3.50
121 A18 1pi blue 1.00 .50
122 A18 2pi slate 1.50 .50
123 A18 2½pi red violet 1.50 .50
a. Imperf. 11.00 9.00
124 A18 5pi brown 2.00 .50
125 A18 10pi orange brn 3.75 .50
126 A18 25pi olive green 12.50 15.00
127 A18 50pi deep violet 50.00 30.00

See Nos. J47-J48. For overprints and surcharges see Nos. 128-131, 181-182, 304-314, 351-354, 378-389, 494-508, B1-B3, B21-B23, B39-B40, P49-P54, P127-P129, P147-P150, P165-P171.

Overprinted in Carmine or Blue

1906

128 A18 10pa dull green (C) 3.00 1.00
129 A18 20pa carmine (Bl) 3.00 1.00
130 A18 1pi blue (C) 3.00 1.00
131 A18 2pi slate (C) 17.50 5.00
Nos. 118-131 (14) 101.75 57.00

Stamps bearing this overprint were sold to merchants at a discount from face value to encourage the use of Turkish stamps on foreign correspondence, instead of those of the various European powers which maintained post offices in Turkey. The overprint is the Arab "B," for "Béhié," meaning "discount."

1908

132 A19 5pa ocher 1.25 .50
133 A19 10pa blue green 1.75 .30
134 A19 20pa carmine 40.00 .50
135 A19 1pi bright blue 15.00 .50
a. 1pi ultramarine 50.00 10.00
136 A19 2pi blue black 10.00 .50
137 A19 2½pi violet brown 3.00 .50
138 A19 5pi dark violet 80.00 .50
139 A19 10pi red 70.00 2.50
140 A19 25pi dark green 10.00 5.00
141 A19 50pi red brown 50.00 35.00

See Nos. J49-J50. For overprints and surcharges see Nos. 142-145, 314B-316B, 390-396, 509-516A, B4-B6, B17, B24-B27, P55-P60, P130-P131, P151, P172, Thrace 15.

Overprinted in Carmine or Blue

142 A19 10pa blue green (C) 7.50 2.50
143 A19 20pa carmine (Bl) 7.50 2.50
144 A19 1pi brt blue (C) 15.00 2.50
145 A19 2pi blue black (C) 25.00 12.50
Nos. 132-145 (14) 336.00 65.80

A20

Perf. 12, 13½ & Compound

1908, Dec. 17

146 A20 5pa ocher .75 .50
147 A20 10pa blue green 1.50 .50
148 A20 20pa carmine 2.00 1.00
149 A20 1pi ultra 3.00 1.00
150 A20 2pi gray black 12.50 15.00
Nos. 146-150 (5) 19.75 18.00

Imperf

146a A20 5pa 3.00 3.00
147a A20 10pa 4.00 4.00
148a A20 20pa 5.50 5.50
149a A20 1pi 3.00 3.00

Granting of a Constitution, the date of which is inscribed on the banderol: "324 Temuz 10" (July 24, 1908).

For overprints see Nos. 397, 517.

Tughra and "Reshad" of Sultan Mohammed V — A21

1909, Dec.

151 A21 5pa ocher 1.00 .50
152 A21 10pa blue green 1.00 .50
a. Imperf. 3.00 3.00
153 A21 20pa carmine rose 1.00 .50
154 A21 1pi ultra 3.00 .50
a. 1pi bright blue 12.50 .50
155 A21 2pi blue black 3.00 .50
156 A21 2½pi dark brown 90.00 20.00
157 A21 5pi dark violet 3.00 1.00
158 A21 10pi dull red 37.50 1.00
159 A21 25pi dark green 350.00 100.00
160 A21 50pi red brown 125.00 80.00

The 2pa olive green, type A21, is a newspaper stamp, No. P68.

Two types exist for the 10pa, 20pa and 1pi. In the second type, the damaged crescent is restored.

See Nos. J51-J52. For overprints and surcharges see Nos. 161-164, 317-327, 342-343, 398-406, 518-528, 567, B7-B14, B18, B28-B32, P61-P68, P81, P132-P133, P152, P173, Turkey in Asia 67, 72, Thrace 1-4, 13, 13A, 14.

Overprinted in Carmine or Blue

161 A21 10pa blue grn (C) 1.75 .75
a. Imperf.
162 A21 20pa car rose (Bl) 1.75 .75
a. Imperf.
163 A21 1pi ultra (C) 3.50 2.00
a. Imperf. 4.00
b. 1pi bright blue 6.50 3.00
164 A21 2pi blue black (C) 75.00 30.00
a. Imperf.
Nos. 151-164 (14) 696.50 238.00

Stamps of 1901-05 Overprinted in Carmine or Blue

The overprint was applied to 18 denominations in four settings with change of city name, producing individual sets for each city: "MONASTIR," "PRISTINA," "SALONIKA" and "USKUB."

1911, June 26 *Perf. 12, 13½*

"Monastir"

165 A16 5pa bister 2.50 3.75
166 A16 10pa yel grn 1.00 1.00
167 A16 20pa magenta 6.00 7.50
168 A16 1pi violet blue 6.00 7.50
169 A16 2pi gray blue 6.00 7.50
170 A16 5pi ocher 40.00 60.00
171 A16 25pi dark green 60.00 75.00
172 A16 50pi yellow 100.00 125.00
173 A17 5pa purple 2.50 3.75
174 A17 10pa green 2.50 3.75
175 A17 20pa carmine 6.00 7.50
176 A17 1pi blue 6.00 7.50
177 A17 2pi orange 6.00 7.50
178 A17 5pi lilac rose 40.00 60.00
179 A17 25pi chocolate 85.00 125.00
180 A17 50pi yel brn 100.00 125.00
181 A18 2½pi red violet 65.00 100.00
182 A18 10pi org brn 60.00 60.00
Nos. 165-182 (18) 594.50 787.25

"Pristina"

165a A16 5pa bister 1.00 1.00
166a A16 10pa yel grn 1.00 1.00
167a A16 20pa magenta 6.00 6.00
168a A16 1pi violet blue 6.00 6.00
169a A16 2pi gray blue 6.00 6.00
170a A16 5pi ocher 35.00 35.00
171a A16 25pi dark green 60.00 60.00
172a A16 50pi yellow 100.00 100.00
173a A17 5pa purple 1.00 1.00
174a A17 10pa green 1.00 1.00
175a A17 20pa carmine 6.00 6.00
176a A17 1pi blue 6.00 6.00
177a A17 2pi orange 6.00 6.00
178a A17 5pi lilac rose 40.00 40.00
179a A17 25pi chocolate 80.00 80.00
180a A17 50pi yel brn 100.00 100.00
181a A18 2½pi red violet 60.00 60.00
182a A18 10pi org brn 60.00 60.00
Nos. 165a-182a (18) 575.00 575.00

"Salonika"

165b A16 5pa bister 1.00 1.00
166b A16 10pa yel grn 1.00 1.00
167b A16 20pa magenta 6.00 6.00
168b A16 1pi violet blue 6.00 6.00
169b A16 2pi gray blue 6.00 6.00
170b A16 5pi ocher 35.00 35.00
171b A16 25pi dark green 60.00 60.00
172b A16 50pi yellow 100.00 100.00
173b A17 5pa purple 1.00 1.00
174b A17 10pa green 1.00 1.00
175b A17 20pa carmine 6.00 6.00
176b A17 1pi blue 6.00 6.00
177b A17 2pi orange 6.00 6.00
178b A17 5pi lilac rose 40.00 40.00
179b A17 25pi chocolate 80.00 80.00
180b A17 50pi yel brn 100.00 100.00
181b A18 2½pi red violet 60.00 60.00
182b A18 10pi org brn 60.00 60.00
Nos. 165b-182b (18) 575.00 575.00

"Uskub"

165c A16 5pa bister 1.00 1.00
166c A16 10pa yel grn 1.00 1.00
167c A16 20pa magenta 6.00 6.00
168c A16 1pi violet blue 6.00 6.00
169c A16 2pi gray blue 6.00 6.00
170c A16 5pi ocher 35.00 35.00
171c A16 25pi dark green 60.00 60.00
172c A16 50pi yellow 100.00 100.00
173c A17 5pa purple 1.00 1.00
174c A17 10pa green 1.00 1.00
175c A17 20pa carmine 6.00 6.00
176c A17 1pi blue 6.00 6.00
177c A17 2pi orange 6.00 6.00
178c A17 5pi lilac rose 40.00 40.00
179c A17 25pi chocolate 80.00 80.00
180c A17 50pi yel brn 100.00 100.00
181c A18 2½pi red violet 60.00 60.00
182c A18 10pi org brn 60.00 60.00
Nos. 165c-182c (18) 575.00 575.00

Sultan's visit to Macedonia. The Arabic overprint reads: "Souvenir of the Sultan's Journey, 1329." See Nos. P69-P81.

General Post Office, Constantinople
A22

1913, Mar. 14 ***Perf. 12***

237	A22	2pa	olive green	1.00	.50
238	A22	5pa	ocher	1.00	.50
239	A22	10pa	blue green	1.00	.50
240	A22	20pa	carmine rose	1.00	.50
241	A22	1pi	ultra	1.00	.50
242	A22	2pi	indigo	2.00	.50
243	A22	5pi	dull violet	3.50	.50
244	A22	10pi	dull red	6.00	1.00
245	A22	25pi	gray green	22.50	22.50
246	A22	50pi	orange brown	85.00	125.00

See Nos. J53-J58. For overprints and surcharges see Nos. 247-250, 328-339, 344, 407-414, 529-538, 568, B15-B16, B33-B36, Turkey in Asia 68, Thrace 10, 10A, 11, 11A, 12, N82.

Overprinted in Carmine or Blue

247	A22	10pa	blue green (C)	1.00	.50
248	A22	20pa	car rose (Bl)	1.00	.50
249	A22	1pi	ultra (C)	1.00	.50
250	A22	2pi	indigo (C)	17.50	7.50
			Nos. 237-250 (14)	144.50	161.00

Mosque of Selim, Adrianople — A23

1913, Oct. 23 **Engr.**

251	A23	10pa	green	1.50	1.00
252	A23	20pa	red	2.50	2.00
253	A23	40pa	blue	6.00	3.00
			Nos. 251-253 (3)	10.00	6.00

Recapture of Adrianople (Edirne) by the Turks.

See Nos. 592, J59-J62. For overprints and surcharge see Nos. 415-417, 539-540, J59-J62, J67-J70, J83-J86, Thrace N84.

Obelisk of Theodosius in the Hippodrome A24

Column of Constantine A25

Leander's Tower — A26

One of the Seven Towers — A27

Fener Bahçe (Garden Lighthouse) A28

The Castle of Europe on the Bosporus A29

Mosque of Sultan Ahmed — A30

Monument to the Martyrs of Liberty A31

Fountains of Suleiman A32

Cruiser "Hamidie" A33

View of Kandili on the Bosporus A34

War Ministry (Later Istanbul University) A35

Sweet Waters of Europe Park A36

Mosque of Suleiman A37

The Bosporus A38

Sultan Ahmed's Fountain A39

Sultan Mohammed V — A40

Designs A24-A39: Views of Constantinople.

1914, Jan. 14 **Litho.**

254	A24	2pa	red lilac	.50	.40
255	A25	4pa	dark brown	.50	.40
256	A26	5pa	violet brown	.50	.40
257	A27	6pa	dark blue	.50	.40
			Engr.		
258	A28	10pa	green	2.00	.40
259	A29	20pa	red	1.75	.40
260	A30	1pi	blue	.50	.40
b.			Booklet pane of 2+2 labels		
261	A31	1½pi	car & blk	1.00	.40
262	A32	1¾pi	sl & red brn	1.00	.40
263	A33	2pi	green & blk	2.00	.40
264	A34	2½pi	org & ol grn	1.50	.40
265	A35	5pi	dull violet	3.00	.40
266	A36	10pi	red brown	7.00	.40
267	A37	25pi	olive green	125.00	5.50
268	A38	50pi	carmine	6.00	2.25
269	A39	100pi	deep blue	75.00	27.50
			Cut cancellation		12.00
270	A40	200pi	green & blk	550.00	*400.00*
			Cut cancellation		25.00
			Nos. 254-270 (17)	777.75	440.45

See Nos. 590-591, 593-598.

For overprints and surcharges see Nos. 271-287, 419, 541, 552-553, 574A, 601, 603-604, P174, Turkey in Asia 1-3, 5-9, 73-74, Thrace N77, N78.

Stamps of Preceding Issue Overprinted in Red or Blue

271	A28	10pa	green (R)	2.00	.50
272	A29	20pa	red (Bl)	10.00	.50
273	A30	1pi	blue (R)	2.00	.50
275	A32	1¾pi	sl & red brn (Bl)	2.00	1.25
276	A33	2pi	green & blk (R)	50.00	3.25
			Nos. 271-276 (5)	66.00	6.00

No. 261 Surcharged

1914, July 23

277	A31	1pi on 1½pi car & blk	3.25	2.50
a.		"1330" omitted	2.50	1.50
b.		Double surcharge		
c.		Triple surcharge	5.00	5.00

7th anniv. of the Constitution. The surcharge reads "10 July, 1330, National fête" and has also the numeral "1" at each side, over the original value of the stamp.

Stamps of 1914 Overprinted in Black or Red

278	A26	5pa	violet brn (Bk)	1.75	.50
279	A28	10pa	green (R)	3.25	.50
280	A29	20pa	red (Bk)	4.00	.50
281	A30	1pi	blue (R)	10.00	1.50
282	A33	2pi	grn & blk (R)	15.00	1.50
283	A35	5pi	dull violet (R)	50.00	4.25
284	A36	10pi	red brown (R)	190.00	65.00
			Nos. 278-284 (7)	274.00	73.75

This overprint reads "Abolition of the Capitulations, 1330".

No. 269 Surcharged

1915

286	A39	10pi on 100pi	62.50	22.50
a.		Inverted surcharge	—	—

No. 270 Surcharged

287	A40	25pi on 200pi	25.00	8.00

Preceding Issues Overprinted in Carmine or Black

1915

On Stamps of 1892

288	A10	10pa	gray green	1.00	.50
a.			Inverted overprint	7.50	7.50
289	A13	2pi	brown orange	1.50	.50
a.			Inverted overprint	7.50	7.50
290	A14	5pi	dull violet	4.00	.50
a.			On No. 99a	17.00	17.00

On Stamp of 1897

291	A15	5pa	on 10pa gray grn	1.00	.50
a.			Inverted overprint	5.00	5.00
b.			On No. 100a	10.00	10.00

On Stamps of 1901

292	A16	5pa	bister	1.00	.50
293	A16	1pi	violet blue	3.00	.50
294	A16	2pi	gray blue	2.50	.50
295	A16	5pi	ocher	20.00	.50
296	A16	25pi	dark green	50.00	20.00
297	A17	5pa	purple	1.00	.50
298	A17	10pa	green	1.50	.50
299	A17	20pa	carmine	1.50	.50
a.			Inverted overprint	7.50	7.50
300	A17	1pi	blue	1.50	.50
a.			Inverted overprint	5.00	5.00
301	A17	2pi	orange	2.00	.50
a.			Inverted overprint	7.50	7.50
b.			Double ovpt. (R and Bk)	5.00	5.00
302	A17	5pi	lilac rose	2.50	.50
303	A17	25pi	brown	12.50	2.00

On Stamps of 1905

304	A18	5pa	ocher	1.00	.50
305	A18	10pa	dull green	1.00	.50
a.			Inverted overprint	5.00	5.00
306	A18	20pa	carmine	1.00	.50
a.			Inverted overprint	5.00	5.00
307	A18	1pi	brt blue	1.50	.50
a.			Inverted overprint	5.00	5.00
308	A18	2pi	slate	2.50	.50
a.			Inverted overprint	10.00	10.00
309	A18	2½pi	red violet	1.50	.50
310	A18	5pi	brown	2.00	.50
a.			Inverted overprint	10.00	10.00
311	A18	10pi	orange brown	12.50	.50
312	A18	25pi	olive green	50.00	8.00

On Stamps of 1906

313	A18	10pa	dull green	2.00	.50
314	A18	2pi	slate	5.00	.50
a.			Inverted overprint	5.00	5.00

On Stamps of 1908

314B	A19	2pi	blue black	225.00	50.00
315	A19	2½pi	violet brown	3.00	.50
315A	A19	5pi	dark violet	100.00	35.00
315B	A19	10pi	red	15.00	7.50
316	A19	25pi	dark green	30.00	5.00
a.			Inverted overprint	17.00	17.00

With Additional Overprint

316B	A19	2pi	blue black	15.00	5.00

On Stamps of 1909

317	A21	5pa	ocher	1.00	.50
a.			Inverted overprint	10.00	10.00
b.			Double overprint	10.00	5.00
318	A21	20pa	car rose	1.00	.50
a.			Inverted overprint	5.00	5.00
319	A21	1pi	ultra	2.00	.50
a.			Inverted overprint	5.00	5.00
320	A21	2pi	blue black	2.00	.50
a.			Inverted overprint	5.00	5.00
321	A21	2½pi	dark brown	67.50	25.00

322 A21 5pi dark violet .30 .20
a. Inverted overprint 6.50 6.50
323 A21 10pi dull red 10.00 .50
324 A21 25pi dark green 1,750. 1,200.

With Additional Overprint

325 A21 20pa carmine rose 2.00 .50
a. Inverted overprint 5.00 5.00
326 A21 1pi ultra 2.00 .50
327 A21 2pi blue black 3.50 .50

On Stamps of 1913

328 A22 5pa ocher 1.00 .50
a. Inverted overprint 7.50 7.50
329 A22 10pa blue green 1.00 .50
a. Inverted overprint 10.00 10.00
330 A22 20pa carmine rose 1.00 .50
a. Inverted overprint 7.50 7.50
331 A22 1pi ultra 1.00 .50
a. Inverted overprint 5.00 5.00
332 A22 2pi indigo 1.50 .50
a. Inverted overprint 5.00 5.00
333 A22 5pi dull violet 3.00 .50
334 A22 10pi dull red 10.00 .50
a. Inverted overprint 10.00 10.00
335 A22 25pi gray green 30.00 20.00

With Additional Overprint

336 A22 10pa blue green 1.00 .50
337 A22 20pa carmine rose 1.00 .50
338 A22 1pi ultra 2.00 .50
339 A22 2pi indigo 7.50 3.00
a. Inverted overprint 10.00 10.00

See Nos. P121-P133.

Stamps of 1901-13 Overprinted

1916

340 A17 5pa purple 1.00 .50
a. 5pa purple, #P43 80.00 80.00
341 A17 10pa green 1.00 .50
a. Double overprint 6.50 6.50
b. 10pa yellow green, #103 80.00 80.00
342 A21 20pa car rose, #153 2.00 .50
a. 20pa carmine rose, #162 110.00 110.00
343 A21 1pi ultra 5.50 1.00
344 A22 5pi dull violet 10.00 3.00
Nos. 340-344 (5) 19.50 5.50

Occupation of the Sinai Peninsula.

Old General Post Office of Constantinople A41

1916, May 29 Litho. *Perf. 12½, 13½*

345 A41 5pa green .75 .50
346 A41 10pa carmine .75 .50
347 A41 20pa ultra .75 .50
348 A41 1pi violet & blk 1.50 .50
349 A41 5pi yel brn & blk 20.00 2.50
Nos. 345-349 (5) 23.75 4.50

Introduction of postage in Turkey, 50th anniv.
For overprints see Nos. 418, B42-B45.

Stamps of 1892-1905 Overprinted

1916

350 A10 10pa gray grn (R) 2.00 2.00
351 A18 20pa carmine (Bl) 3.75 2.50
352 A18 1pi blue (R) 10.00 5.00
353 A18 2pi slate (Bk) 12.50 1.00
354 A18 2½pi red violet (Bk) 20.00 1.50
Nos. 350-354 (5) 48.25 12.00

National Fête Day. Overprint reads "10 Temuz 1332" (July 23, 1916).

Preceding Issues Overprinted or Surcharged in Red or Black:

a

b

1916

On Stamps of 1892-98

355 A10(a) 10pa gray green 1.00 .50
355A A11(a) 20pa violet brown .75 .50
b. Inverted overprint 10.00 10.00
356 A12(a) 1pi gray blue 50.00 50.00
357 A13(a) 2pi brown org 5.00 1.50
358 A14(a) 5pi dull violet 50.00 50.00

On Stamp of 1897

359 A15(b) 5pa on 10pa gray grn .75 .50

On Stamps of 1901

361 A16(a) 5pa bister .75 .50
a. Double overprint 7.50 7.50
362 A16(a) 10pa yel grn 1.00 .50
363 A16(a) 20pa magenta .75 .50
364 A16(a) 1pi violet blue 1.00 .50
a. Inverted overprint 7.50 7.50
365 A16(a) 2pi gray blue 5.00 .50
366 A16(b) 5pi on 25pi dk grn 55.00 55.00
367 A16(b) 10pi on 25pi dk grn 55.00 55.00
368 A16(a) 25pi dark green 55.00 55.00
369 A17(a) 5pa purple 75.00 50.00
370 A17(a) 10pa green 1.50 1.50
371 A17(a) 20pa carmine .75 .50
a. Inverted overprint 7.50 7.50
372 A17(a) 1pi blue .75 .50
a. Inverted overprint 7.50 7.50
373 A17(a) 2pi orange 1.50 .50
374 A17(b) 10pi on 25pi brown 5.00 1.50
375 A17(b) 10pi on 50pi yel brn 7.50 1.50
376 A17(a) 25pi brown 7.50 1.50
377 A17(a) 50pi yel brn 10.00 2.50

On Stamps of 1905

378 A18(a) 5pa ocher .75 .50
379 A18(a) 20pa carmine .75 .50
a. Inverted overprint 10.00 5.00
380 A18(a) 1pi brt blue 2.00 .50
a. Inverted overprint 10.00 5.00
381 A18(a) 2pi slate 1.00 .50
382 A18(a) 2½pi red violet 7.50 1.50
383 A18(b) 10pi on 25pi ol grn 7.50 2.50
384 A18(b) 10pi on 50pi dp vio 7.50 2.00
385 A18(a) 25pi olive green 7.50 3.00
386 A18(a) 50pi deep violet 6.00 3.00

On Stamps of 1906

387 A18(a) 10pa dull green 1.00 .60
388 A18(a) 20pa carmine 1.00 .60
389 A18(a) 1pi brt blue 1.00 .60

On Stamps of 1908

390 A19(a) 2½pi violet brown 67.50 67.50
391 A19(b) 10pi on 25pi dk grn 20.00 12.50
392 A19(b) 10pi on 50pi red brn 67.50 67.50
393 A19(b) 25pi on 50pi red brn 67.50 67.50
394 A19(a) 25pi dark green 7.50 2.50
395 A19(a) 50pi red brown 50.00 50.00

With Additional Overprint

396 A19(a) 2pi blue black 67.50 67.50

On Stamps of 1908-09

397 A20(a) 5pa ocher 67.50 67.50
398 A21(a) 5pa ocher .75 2.50
399 A21(a) 10pa blue green 50.00 50.00
400 A21(a) 20pa carmine rose 50.00 50.00
401 A21(a) 1pi ultra 1.00 .50
402 A21(a) 2pi blue black 3.00 1.50
403 A21(a) 2½pi dark brown 50.00 50.00
404 A21(a) 5pi dark violet 50.00 50.00

With Additional Overprint

405 A21(a) 1pi ultra 67.50 67.50
406 A21(a) 2pi blue black 50.00 50.00

On Stamps of 1913

407 A22(a) 5pa ocher .75 .50
408 A22(a) 20pa carmine rose 1.50 .50
409 A22(a) 1pi ultra 1.50 .50
410 A22(a) 2pi indigo 3.00 1.00
411 A22(b) 10pi on 50pi org brn 12.50 10.00
412 A22(a) 25pi gray green 7.50 5.00
413 A22(a) 50pi orange brown 15.00 12.50

With Additional Overprint 

414 A22(a) 1pi ultra 1.00 1.00

On Commemorative Stamps of 1913

415 A23(a) 10pa green 1.25 .50
416 A23(a) 20pa red 2.00 .50
417 A23(a) 40pa blue 6.00 2.50

On Commemorative Stamp of 1916

418 A41(a) 5pi yel brn & blk 1.00 .50

No. 277 Surcharged in Blue

419 A31 60pa on 1pi on 1½pi 2.50 3.50
a. "1330" omitted 40.00 40.00

See Nos. P134-P152, J67-J70.

Turkish Artillery A42

Mosque at Orta Köy, Constantinople — A43

Lighthouse on Bosporus — A44

Monument to Martyrs of Liberty — A45

Map of the Dardanelles; Sultan Mohammed V — A46

Map of the Dardanelles A47

Istanbul Across the Golden Horn A48

Pyramids of Egypt A49

Dolma Bahçe Palace and Mohammed V — A50

Sentry and Shell — A51

Sultan Mohammed V — A52

1916-18 Typo. *Perf. 11½, 12½*

420 A42 2pa violet 1.25 .50
421 A43 5pa orange .75 .50
424 A44 10pa green .75 1.00

Engr.

425 A45 20pa deep rose .75 .50
426 A46 1pi dull violet 2.50 .50

Typo.

428 A47 50pa ultra 1.25 .50
429 A48 2pi org brn & ind 3.00 .50
430 A49 5pi pale blue & blk 17.50 1.00

Engr.

431 A50 10pi dark green 8.75 5.00
432 A50 10pi dark violet 32.50 2.50
433 A50 10pi dark brown 14.00 2.50
434 A51 25pi carmine, *straw* 2.25 1.50
437 A52 50pi carmine 5.00 5.00
438 A52 50pi indigo 2.00 2.50
439 A52 50pi green, *straw* 2.50 10.00
Nos. 420-439 (15) 94.75 34.00

For overprints and surcharges see Nos. 541B-541E, 554-560, 565-566, 569-574, 575, 577-578, 579A-580, Turkey in Asia 4, 10, 64-66, Thrace N76, N80, N81. Compare designs A42-A43 with A53-A54.

Forgeries of Nos. 446-545 abound.

Preceding Issues Overprinted or Surcharged in Red, Black or Blue:

d

e

f

g

1917

On Stamps of 1865

446 A5(d) 20pa yellow (R) 45.00 67.50
a. Star without rays (R) 50.00 57.50

447 A5(d) 1pi pearl gray (R) 45.00 67.50
a. Star without rays (R) 50.00 57.50
448 A5(d) 2pi blue (R) 45.00 67.50
449 A5(d) 5pi carmine (Bk) 45.00 67.50

On Stamp of 1867

450 A5(d) 5pi rose (Bk) 45.00 67.50

On Stamps of 1870-71

451 A5(d) 2pi red (Bl) 45.00 67.50
452 A5(d) 5pi blue (Bk) 45.00 67.50
453 A5(d) 25pi dull rose (Bl) 45.00 67.50

On Stamp of 1874-75

454 A5(d) 10pa red violet (Bl) 45.00 67.50

On Stamps of April, 1876

455 A5(d) 10pa red lilac (Bl) 45.00 67.50
a. 10pa red violet (Bl) 50.00 67.50
457 A5(d) 20pa pale green (R) 45.00 67.50
458 A5(d) 1pi yellow (Bl) 45.00 67.50

On Stamps of January, 1876

459 A5(d) ¼pi on 10pa rose lil (Bl) 45.00 67.50
460 A5(d) ½pi on 20pa yel grn (R) 45.00 67.50
461 A5(d) 1¼pi on 50pa rose (Bl) 45.00 67.50

On Stamps of September, 1876

462 A7(d) 50pa blue & yel (R) 45.00 67.50
463 A7(d) 2pi blk & redsh brn (R) 45.00 67.50
464 A7(d) 25pi claret & rose (Bk) 45.00 67.50

On Stamps of 1880-84

465 A7(d) 5pa black & ol (R) 45.00 67.50
466 A7(d) 10pa black & grn (R) 45.00 67.50

On Stamps of 1881-82

467 A5(d) 20pa gray (Bl) 45.00 67.50
468 A5(d) 2pi pale sal (Bl) 45.00 67.50

On Stamps of 1884-86

469 A7(d) 10pa grn & pale grn (Bk) 45.00 67.50
470 A7(d) 2pi ocher & pale ocher (Bk) 45.00 67.50
471 A7(d) 5pi red brn & pale brn (Bk) 45.00 67.50

On Stamps of 1886

472 A7(d) 5pa blk & pale gray (R) 2.00 1.75
a. Inverted overprint 30.00 30.00
473 A7(d) 2pi org & bl (Bk) 3.00 2.50
a. Inverted overprint 35.00 35.00
474 A7(d) 5pi grn & pale grn (R) 45.00 67.50
475 A7(d) 25pi bis & pale bis (Bk) 45.00 67.50

On Stamp of 1888

476 A7(d) 5pi dk brn & gray (Bk) 45.00 67.50

On Stamps of 1892-98

477 A11(d) 20pa vio brn (R) 4.00 3.00
478 A13(d) 2pi brn org (R) 4.00 3.50
a. Tête bêche pair 13.50 13.50

On Stamps of 1901

479 A16(d) 5pa bister (R) 3.00 3.00
a. Inverted overprint 20.00 20.00
480 A16(d) 20pa mag (Bk) 2.00 1.50
a. Inverted overprint 25.00 25.00
481 A16(d) 1pi vio bl (R) 3.00 3.00
a. Inverted overprint 20.00 20.00
482 A16(d) 2pi gray bl (R) 5.00 5.00
483 A16(d) 5pi ocher (R) 32.50 50.00
484 A16(e) 10pi on 50pi yel (R) 32.50 50.00
485 A16(d) 25pi dk grn (R) 100.00 50.00
486 A17(d) 5pa purple (Bk) 32.50 50.00
487 A17(d) 10pa green (R) 5.00 5.00
488 A17(d) 20pa car (Bk) 2.00 1.50
a. Inverted overprint 20.00 20.00
489 A17(d) 1pi blue (R) 1.00 .90
490 A17(d) 2pi org (Bk) 3.00 3.00
a. Inverted overprint 20.00 20.00
491 A17(d) 5pi lil rose (R) 32.50 50.00
492 A17(e) 10pi on 50pi yel brn (R) 32.50 50.00
493 A17(d) 25pi brown (R) 5.00 5.00

On Stamps of 1905

494 A18(d) 5pa ocher (R) 2.00 1.00
a. Inverted overprint 20.00 20.00
495 A18(d) 10pa dl grn (R) 32.50 50.00
496 A18(d) 20pa car (Bk) 1.00 1.00
a. Double ovpt., one invtd. 35.00 35.00
b. Inverted overprint 35.00 35.00
497 A18(d) 1pi blue (R) 1.50 1.00
a. Inverted overprint 35.00 35.00
498 A18(d) 2pi slate (R) 5.00 5.00
499 A18(d) 2½pi red vio (Bk) 5.00 5.00
a. Inverted overprint 20.00 20.00
500 A18(d) 5pi brown (R) 35.00 45.00
501 A18(d) 10pi orange brn (R) 35.00 50.00
502 A18(e) 10pi on 50pi dp vio (R) 35.00 50.00
503 A18(d) 25pi ol grn (R) 35.00 50.00

On Nos. 128-131

504 A18(d) 10pa dl grn (R) 1.50 1.00
a. Inverted overprint 20.00 20.00
505 A18(d) 20pa car (Bk) 1.00 .75
a. Double ovpt., one invtd. 20.00 20.00
b. Inverted overprint 20.00 20.00
506 A18(d) 1pi brt bl (Bk) 1.00 .75
a. Inverted overprint 20.00 20.00
507 A18(d) 1pi brt bl (R) 1.50 1.25
a. Inverted overprint 20.00 20.00
508 A18(d) 2pi slate (Bk) 35.00 50.00
Nos. 494-508 (15) 227.00 311.75

On Stamps of 1908

509 A19(d) 5pa ocher (R) 1.50 1.25
510 A19(d) 10pa bl grn (R) 20.00 20.00
510A A19(d) 1pi brt blue (R) *125.00* 140.00
511 A19(d) 2pi bl blk (R) 35.00 50.00
512 A19(d) 2½pi violet brn (Bk) 35.00 35.00
512A A19(d) 10pi red (R) *150.00* 225.00
513 A19(e) 10pi on 50pi red brn (R) 35.00 50.00
514 A19(d) 25pi dark green (R) 35.00 50.00

With Additional Overprint

514A A19(d) 10pa bl grn (Bk) 150.00 225.00
515 A19(d) 1pi brt bl (Bk) 35.00 50.00
516 A19(d) 2pi bl blk (R) 5.00 5.00
516A A19(d) 2pi bl blk (Bk) 35.00 67.50

On Stamps of 1908-09

517 A20(d) 5pa ocher (R) 3.00 3.00
518 A21(d) 5pa ocher (R) 2.00 1.50
a. Double overprint 20.00 20.00
b. Dbl. ovpt., one inverted 20.00 20.00
519 A21(d) 10pa bl grn (R) 2.00 1.50
520 A21(d) 20pa carmine rose (Bk) 2.00 1.50
a. Double overprint 35.00 35.00
521 A21(d) 1pi ultra (R) 1.00 .75
a. 1p bright blue (R) 30.00 30.00
522 A21(d) 2pi bl blk (R) 5.00 5.00
523 A21(d) 2½pi dk brn (Bk) 35.00 50.00
524 A21(d) 5pi dk vio (R) 35.00 50.00
525 A21(d) 10pi dull red (R) 35.00 50.00

With Additional Overprint 

525A A21(d) 10pa bl grn (Bk) 175.00 225.00
526 A21(d) 1pi ultra (Bk) 125.00 190.00
527 A21(d) 1pi ultra (R) 2.50 2.50
a. 1pi bright blue (R) 125.00 140.00
528 A21(d) 2pi bl blk (Bk) 35.00 50.00

On Stamps of 1913

529 A22(d) 5pa ocher (R) 1.25 1.25
530 A22(d) 10pa bl grn (R) 35.00 50.00
531 A22(d) 20pa car rose (Bk) 1.50 2.50
532 A22(d) 1pi ultra (R) 1.50 3.50
533 A22(d) 2pi indigo (R) 3.50 3.50
534 A22(d) 5pi dl vio (R) 35.00 50.00
535 A22(d) 10pi dl red (Bk) 45.00 50.00

With Additional Overprint

536 A22(d) 10pa bl grn (Bk) 1.50 1.50
a. Inverted overprint 20.00 20.00
537 A22(d) 1pi ultra (Bk) 3.00 3.00
a. Inverted overprint 20.00 20.00
538 A22(d) 2pi indigo (Bk) 35.00 100.00

On Commemorative Stamps of 1913

539 A23(d) 10pa green (R) 5.00 5.00
a. Inverted overprint 20.00 20.00
540 A23(d) 40pa blue (R) 7.00 7.00
a. Inverted overprint 20.00 20.00

On No. 277, with Addition of New Value

541 A31 60pa on 1pi on 1½pi (Bk) 1.50 1.50
a. "1330" omitted 45.00 45.00

On Stamps of 1916-18

541B A51(f) 25pi car, *straw* 5.00 5.00
541C A52(g) 50pi carmine 17.50 17.50
541D A52(g) 50pi indigo 35.00 50.00
541E A52(g) 50pi green, *straw* 15.00 27.50

Ovptd. on Eastern Rumelia No. 12

542 A4(d) 20pa blk & rose (Bl) 35.00 35.00

Ovptd. in Black on Eastern Rumelia #15-17

543 A4(d) 5pa lilac & pale lilac 45.00 45.00
544 A4(d) 10pa green & pale green 45.00 45.00
545 A4(d) 20pa carmine & pale rose 45.00 45.00

Some experts question the status of Nos. 510A, 512A and 525A.

See Nos. J71-J86, P153-P172.

Soldiers in Trench — A52a 545Asrch

1917

545A A52a 5pa on 1pi red .75 .50

It is stated that No. 545A was never issued without surcharge.

See Nos. 548f, 545A, 602.

Turkish Artillery A53

1917 **Typo.** ***Perf. 11½, 12½***

546 A53 2pa Prussian blue 100.00

In type A42 the Turkish inscription at the top is in one group, in type A53 it is in two groups. It is stated that No. 546 was never placed in use. Copies were distributed through the Universal Postal Union at Bern.

For surcharges see Nos. 547-548, Turkey in Asia 69-70.

Surcharged

547 A53 5pi on 2pa Prus bl 12.50 .90
a. Inverted surcharge 9.00 9.00
b. Turkish "5" omitted at lower left

Surcharged

1918

548 A53 5pi on 2pa Prus blue 12.50 .90
g. Inverted surcharge 10.00 10.00

Top line of surcharge on Nos. 547-548 reads "Ottoman Posts."

For surcharge see Thrace No. N79.

No. 545A Surcharged

1918

548A A52a 2pa on 5pa on 1pi red 1.50 1.50
b. Double surcharge 10.00 10.00
c. Inverted surcharge 10.00 10.00
d. Double surcharge inverted 10.00 10.00
e. Dbl. surch., one inverted 10.00 10.00
f. In pair with No. 545A 17.50 17.50

Enver Pasha and Kaiser Wilhelm II on Battlefield A54

St. Sophia and Obelisk of the Hippodrome A55

1918 **Typo.** ***Perf. 12, 12½***

549 A54 5pa brown red 75.00
550 A55 10pa gray green 75.00

The stamps, of which very few saw postal use, were converted into paper money by pasting on thick yellow paper and reperforating.

Values are for copies with original gum. Copies removed from the yellow paper are worth $8 each.

Armistice Issue

Overprinted in Black or Red

1919, Nov. 30

On Stamps of 1913

552 A34 2½pi org & ol grn 125.00 300.00
553 A38 50pi carmine 125.00 300.00

On Stamps of 1916-18

554 A46 1pi dull violet (R) 7.50 10.00
555 A47 50pa ultra (R) .75 1.50
556 A48 2pi org brn & ind .75 1.50
557 A49 5pi pale bl & blk (R) .75 1.50
558 A50 10pi dark green (R) 6.25 10.00
559 A51 25pi carmine, *straw* 6.25 10.00
560 A52 50pi grn, *straw* (R) 6.25 10.00

Fountain in Desert near Sinai — A56

Sentry at Beersheba — A57

Turkish Troops at Sinai A58

Typo.

562	A56	20pa claret	.75	1.50
563	A57	1pi blue (R)	125.00	150.00
564	A58	25pi slate blue (R)	125.00	150.00
		Nos. 552-564 (12)	529.25	946.00

The overprint reads: "Souvenir of the Armistice, 30th October 1334." Nos. 562 to 564 are not known to have been regularly issued without overprint.

See No. J87. For overprints and surcharges see Nos. 576, 579, 582, 583-584, 586, Turkey in Asia 71, Thrace N83.

Stamps of 1911-19 Overprinted in Turkish "Accession to the Throne of His Majesty, 3rd July 1334-1918," the Tughra of Sultan Mohammed VI and sometimes Ornaments and New Values

Dome of the Rock, Jerusalem A59

1919

565	A42	2pa violet	.75	2.50
566	A43	5pa orange	.50	.50
567	A21	5pa on 2pa ol grn	.50	.50
a.		Inverted surcharge	10.00	10.00
568	A22	10pa on 2pa ol grn	.50	.50
569	A44	10pa green	1.25	1.50
a.		Inverted overprint	25.00	25.00
570	A45	20pa deep rose	.75	.50
a.		Inverted overprint	12.00	12.00
571	A46	1pi dull violet	1.25	1.00
572	A47	60pa on 50pa ultra	1.25	1.00
573	A48	60pa on 2pi org brn & ind	.50	.50
574	A48	2pi orange brn & ind	.50	1.00
574A	A34	2½pi orange & ol grn	25.00	37.50
575	A49	5pi pale blue & blk	.50	1.00
576	A56	10pi on 20pa cl	.50	1.00
577	A50	10pi dark brown	2.50	2.50
578	A51	25pi carmine, *straw*	2.00	2.00
579	A57	35pi on 1pi blue	1.50	2.50
579A	A52	50pi carmine	25.00	37.50
580	A52	50pi green, *straw*	6.00	5.00
581	A59	100pi on 10pa green	6.00	5.00
582	A58	250pi on 25pi sl bl	6.00	5.00
		Nos. 565-582 (20)	82.75	108.50

See note after #586. See #J88-J91.
For overprint and surcharge see Nos. 585, Thrace N82.

Surcharged with Ornaments, New Values and

Perf. 11½, 12½

583	A56	20pa claret	1.75	10.00
584	A57	1pi deep blue	2.50	17.50
585	A59	60pa on 10pa green	1.50	7.50
586	A58	25pi slate blue	7.50	50.00
a.		Inverted overprint		100.00
		Nos. 583-586 (4)	13.25	85.00

#576, 579, 581, 582, 583-586 were prepared in anticipation of the invasion and conquest of Egypt by the Turks. They were not issued at that time but subsequently received various overprints in commemoration of Sultan Mehmet Sadi's accession to the throne (#565-582) and of the 1st anniv. of this event (#583-586).
For surcharge see Thrace No. N83.

Designs of 1913 Modified

1920 **Litho.** ***Perf. 11, 12***

590	A26	5pa brown orange	1.00	.50

Engr.

591	A28	10pa green	1.00	.50
592	A23	20pa rose	1.00	.50
593	A30	1pi blue green	3.75	.50
594	A32	3pi blue	1.00	.50
595	A34	5pi gray	50.00	.50
596	A36	10pi gray violet	12.50	.50
597	A37	25pi dull violet	5.00	2.50
598	A38	50pi brown	5.00	10.00
		Nos. 590-598 (9)	80.25	16.00

On most stamps of this issue the designs have been modified by removing the small Turkish word at right of the tughra of the Sultan. In the 3pi and 5pi the values have been altered, while for the 25pi the color has been changed.
For surcharges see Thrace Nos. N77, N78, N84.

Black Surcharge

1921-22

600	SP1	30pa on 10pa red vio	1.25	.50
a.		Double surcharge	37.50	37.50
b.		Imperf.		
601	A28	60pa on 10pa green	1.25	.50
a.		Double surcharge	22.50	22.50
602	A52a	4½pi on 1pi red	2.50	.50
a.		Inverted surcharge	20.00	20.00
603	A32	7½pi on 3pi blue	12.50	1.00
604	A32	7½pi on 3pi bl (R) ('22)	20.00	2.50
a.		Double surcharge	30.00	30.00
		Nos. 600-604 (5)	37.50	5.00

ΕΛΛΗΝΙΚΗ
ΚΑΤΟΧΗ
ΛΕΠΤΑ·5ο

Turkish Stamps of 1916-21 with Greek surcharge as above in blue or black are of private origin.

Issues of the Republic

Crescent and Star — A64

TWO PIASTERS:
Type I — "2" measures 3¼x1¾mm
Type II — "2" measures 2¾x1½mm

FIVE PIASTERS:
Type I — "5" measures 3½x2¼mm
Type II — "5" measures 3x1¾mm

Perf. 11, 12, 13½, 13½x12

1923-25 **Litho.**

605	A64	10pa gray black	.25	.25
606	A64	20pa citron	.25	.25
607	A64	1pi deep violet	.25	.25
a.		Slanting numeral in lower left corner	.50	.25
608	A64	1½pi emerald	.25	1.50
609	A64	2pi bluish grn (I)	2.00	.50
a.		2pi deep green (II)	.75	.25
610	A64	3pi yel brn	1.00	.50
611	A64	3¾pi lilac brown	2.50	2.50
612	A64	4½pi carmine	.75	1.00
613	A64	5pi purple (I)	3.50	1.50
a.		5pi violet (II)	12.50	1.00
614	A64	7½pi blue	2.50	.50
615	A64	10pi slate	7.50	1.00
a.		10pi blue	7.50	1.00
616	A64	11¼pi dull rose	2.50	2.00
617	A64	15pi brown	10.00	1.00
618	A64	18¾pi myrtle green	4.50	3.00
619	A64	22½pi orange	6.00	2.00
620	A64	25pi black brown	30.00	2.50
621	A64	50pi gray	75.00	4.00
622	A64	100pi dark violet	150.00	8.50
624	A64	500pi deep green	500.00	160.00
		Cut cancellation		1.60
		Nos. 605-624 (19)	798.75	192.75
		Set, never hinged	3,000.	

#605-610, 612-617 exist imperf. & part perf.

Bridge of Sakarya and Mustafa Kemal — A65

1924, Jan. 1 ***Perf. 12***

625	A65	1½pi emerald	.50	.30
626	A65	3pi purple	.60	.50
627	A65	4½pi pale rose	2.00	1.60
628	A65	5pi yellow brown	2.00	1.60
629	A65	7½pi deep blue	2.00	1.60
630	A65	50pi orange	22.50	10.00
631	A65	100pi brown violet	52.50	20.00
632	A65	200pi olive brown	72.50	35.00
		Nos. 625-632 (8)	154.60	70.60
		Set, never hinged	750.00	

Signing of Treaty of Peace at Lausanne.

The Legendary Blacksmith and his Gray Wolf — A66

Sakarya Gorge — A67

Fortress of Ankara — A68

Mustafa Kemal Pasha — A69

1926 **Engr.**

634	A66	10pa slate	.50	.20
635	A66	20pa orange	.50	.20
636	A66	1g brt rose	.50	.20
637	A67	2g green	1.50	.25
638	A67	2½g gray black	2.00	.25
639	A67	3g copper red	2.50	.25
640	A68	5g lilac gray	3.00	.50
641	A68	6g red	1.00	.25
642	A68	10g deep blue	7.50	.50
643	A68	15g deep orange	10.00	.50
644	A69	25g dk green & blk	15.00	1.25
645	A69	50g carmine & blk	20.00	1.50
646	A69	100g olive grn & blk	35.00	2.00
647	A69	200g brown & blk	90.00	5.50
		Nos. 634-647 (14)	189.00	13.35
		Set, never hinged	800.00	

Stamps of 1926 Overprinted in Black, Silver or Gold

1927, Sept. 9

648	A66	1g brt rose	.50	.50
649	A67	2g green	.50	1.00
650	A67	2½g gray black	1.50	2.00
651	A67	3g copper red	2.00	2.50
652	A68	5g lilac gray	2.50	4.00
653	A68	6g red	1.50	1.50
654	A68	10g deep blue	3.50	3.50
655	A68	15g deep orange	5.00	5.00
656	A69	25g dk green & blk (S)	15.00	20.00
657	A69	50g car & blk (S)	27.50	37.50
658	A69	100g ol grn & blk (G)	60.00	75.00
		Nos. 648-658 (11)	119.50	152.50
		Set, never hinged	425.00	

Agricultural and industrial exhibition at Izmir, Sept. 9-20, 1927.
The overprint reads: "1927" and the initials of "Izmir Dokuz Eylul Sergisi" (Izmir Exhibition, September 9).

Second Izmir Exhibition Issue

Nos. 634-647 Overprinted in Red or Black

On A66-A68

On A69

1928, Sept. 9

659	A66	10pa slate (R)	.50	.40
660	A66	20pa orange	.50	.40
661	A66	1g brt rose	1.00	.50
662	A67	2g green (R)	1.50	1.50
663	A67	2½g gray blk (R)	1.50	1.50
664	A67	3g copper red	1.50	1.50
665	A68	5g lilac gray (R)	2.00	3.00
666	A68	6g red	.50	.50
667	A68	10g deep blue	3.50	3.00
668	A68	15g deep orange	5.00	2.00
669	A69	25g dk grn & blk (R)	15.00	6.25
670	A69	50g car & blk	17.50	20.00
671	A69	100g ol grn & blk (R)	40.00	50.00
672	A69	200g brn & blk (R)	62.50	62.50
		Nos. 659-672 (14)	152.50	153.05
		Set, never hinged	650.00	

The overprint reads "Izmir, September 9, 1928."

Nos. 636, 652, 654 Surcharged in Black (#673) or Red (#674-675)

1929

673	A66	20pa on 1g brt rose	.50	.25
a.		Inverted surcharge	3.50	3.50
674	A68	2½k on 5g lilac gray	1.00	.50
a.		Inverted surcharge	7.50	7.50
675	A68	6k on 10g deep blue	6.00	.75
		Nos. 673-675 (3)	7.50	1.50
		Set, never hinged	40.00	

Railroad Bridge over Kizil Irmak — A70

A71

A72

A73

Latin Inscriptions
Without umlaut over first "U" of "CUMHURIYETI"

1929 **Engr.**

676 A70 2k gray black 5.00 1.00
677 A70 2½k green 3.00 1.00
678 A70 3k violet brown 4.00 1.50
679 A71 6k dark violet 25.00 1.00
680 A72 12½k deep blue 35.00 3.75
681 A73 50k carmine & blk 60.00 8.75
Nos. 676-681 (6) 132.00 17.00
Set, never hinged 400.00

See Nos. 682-691, 694-695, 697, 699. For surcharges & overprints see #705-714, 716-717, 719, 721, 727, 765-766, 770-771, 777, C2, C7.

Sakarya Gorge — A74

Mustafa Kemal Pasha — A75

With umlaut over first "U" of "CUMHURIYETI"

1930

682 A71 10pa green .25 .25
683 A70 20pa gray violet .25 .25
684 A70 1k olive green .50 .50
685 A71 1½k olive black .50 .40
686 A70 2k dull violet 3.00 .50
687 A70 2½k deep green 2.00 .50
688 A70 3k brown orange 20.00 1.50
689 A71 4k deep rose 7.50 .50
690 A72 5k rose lake 11.50 .50
691 A71 6k indigo 7.50 .50
692 A74 7½k red brown .25 .25
694 A72 12½k deep ultra .75 .25
695 A72 15k deep orange .75 .50
696 A74 17½k dark gray .75 .50
697 A72 20k black brown 50.00 2.00
698 A74 25k olive brown 1.00 1.00
699 A72 30k yellow brown 1.75 1.00
700 A74 40k red violet 1.50 1.00
701 A75 50k red & black 3.50 1.25
702 A75 100k olive grn & blk 3.50 1.25
703 A75 200k dk green & blk 3.75 1.50
704 A75 500k chocolate & blk 17.50 22.50
Nos. 682-704 (22) 138.00 38.40
Set, never hinged 400.00

For surcharges and overprints see Nos. 715, 718, 720, 722-726, 767-769, 772-773, 775-776, 778-780, 823-828, 848-850, C1, C3-C6, C8-C11.

Nos. 682-704 Surcharged in Red or Black:

Sivas
D. Y.
30 ag. 930
1 K.
a

D. Y. Sivas
30 ag. 930
10 P.
b

Sivas

D. Y.

30 ag. 930
40 K.
c

1930, Aug. 30

705 A71(a) 10pa on 10pa (R) .50 1.25
706 A70(b) 10pa on 20pa .50 1.50
707 A70(b) 20pa on 1ku 1.00 1.50
708 A71(a) 1k on 1½k (R) .50 1.25
709 A70(b) 1½k on 2k 1.00 1.50
710 A70(b) 2k on 2½k (R) 2.50 2.00
711 A70(b) 2½k on 3k 2.00 1.50
712 A71(a) 3k on 4k 2.00 1.00
713 A72(a) 4k on 5k 2.50 1.00
714 A71(a) 5k on 6k (R) 3.50 4.00
715 A74(a) 6k on 7½k .75 .50
716 A72(a) 7½k on 12½k (R) 1.25 1.00
717 A72(a) 12½k on 15k 1.25 1.00
718 A74(b) 15k on 17½k (R) 5.00 4.00
719 A72(b) 17½k on 20k (R) 5.00 2.00
720 A74(b) 20k on 25k (R) 7.50 2.00
721 A72(b) 25k on 30k 5.00 2.50
722 A74(b) 30k on 40k 7.50 2.50
723 A75(c) 40k on 50k 15.00 7.50
724 A75(c) 50k on 100k (R) 70.00 16.00
725 A75(c) 100k on 200k (R) 85.00 27.50
726 A75(c) 250k on 500k (R) 75.00 35.00
Nos. 705-726 (22) 294.25 118.00
Set, never hinged 800.00

Inauguration of the railroad between Ankara and Sivas.

There are numerous varieties in these settings as: "309," "390," "930" inverted, no period after "D," no period after "Y" and raised period before "Y."

No. 685 Surcharged in Red

1931, Apr. 1

727 A71 1k on 1½k olive blk .60 .20

Olive Tree with Roots Extending to All Balkan Capitals — A76

1931, Oct. 20 **Engr.** ***Perf. 12***

728 A76 2½k dark green .40 .20
729 A76 4k carmine .50 .20
730 A76 6k steel blue .50 .20
731 A76 7½k dull red .50 .20
732 A76 12k deep orange 1.00 .25
733 A76 12½k dark blue 1.00 .25
734 A76 30k dark violet 1.75 1.50
735 A76 50k dark brown 3.00 .75
736 A76 100k brown violet 6.25 1.50
Nos. 728-736 (9) 14.90 5.05
Set, never hinged 20.00

Second Balkan Conference.

A77

A78

Mustafa Kemal Pasha (Kemal Atatürk) — A79

1931-42 **Typo.** ***Perf. 11½, 12***

737 A77 10pa blue green .20 .20
738 A77 20pa deep orange .20 .20
739 A77 30pa brt violet ('38) .25 .20
740 A78 1k dk slate green .20 .20
740A A77 1½k magenta ('42) .55 .20
741 A78 2k dark violet .50 .20
741A A78 2k yel grn ('40) .25 .25
742 A77 2½k green .50 .20
743 A78 3k brn org ('38) 1.50 .20
744 A78 4k slate 2.50 .20
745 A78 5k rose red .25 .25
745A A78 5k brown blk ('40) 2.00 .50
746 A78 6k deep blue 3.00 .20
746A A78 6k rose ('40) .80 .30
747 A77 7½k deep rose ('32) .25 .20
747A A78 8k brt blue ('38) 3.50 .20
b. 8k dark blue ('36) 3.50 .20
748 A77 10k black brn ('32) .60 .20
748A A77 10k deep blue ('40) 7.00 .60
749 A77 12k bister ('32) .40 .20
750 A79 12½k indigo ('32) .40 .20
751 A77 15k org yel ('32) .40 .20
752 A77 20k olive grn ('32) .40 .20
753 A77 25k Prus blue ('32) 2.00 .25
754 A77 30k magenta ('32) 7.50 .50
755 A79 100k maroon ('32) 200.00 5.50
756 A79 200k purple ('32) 3.75 2.00
757 A79 250k chocolate ('32) 100.00 11.50
Nos. 737-757 (27) 338.90 25.05
Set, never hinged 750.00

See Nos. 1015-1033, 1117B-1126. For overprints see Nos. 811-816.

Symbolizing 10th Anniversary of Republic — A80

President Atatürk — A81

1933, Oct. 29 ***Perf. 10***

758 A80 1½k blue green 1.25 1.00
759 A80 2k olive brown 1.25 1.00
760 A81 3k red brown 1.25 1.00
761 A81 6k deep blue 1.25 1.00
762 A80 12½k dark blue 3.25 2.50
763 A80 25k dark brown 8.00 5.00
764 A81 50k orange brown 20.00 15.00
Nos. 758-764 (7) 36.25 26.50
Set, never hinged 55.00

10th year of the Turkish Republic. The stamps were in use for three days only.

Nos. 682, 685, 692, 694, 696-698, 702 Overprinted or Surcharged in Red:

1934, Aug. 26 ***Perf. 12***

765 A71 10pa green .50 1.00
766 A71 1k on 1½k 1.00 .75
767 A74 2k on 25k 1.50 1.25
768 A74 5k on 7½k 5.00 5.00
769 A74 6k on 17½k 2.50 2.00
770 A72 12½k deep ultra 7.50 5.00
771 A72 15k on 20k 50.00 45.00
772 A74 20k on 25k 35.00 37.50
773 A75 50k on 100k 40.00 37.50
Nos. 765-773 (9) 143.00 135.00
Set, never hinged 600.00

Izmir Fair, 1934.

Nos. 696, 698, 701-704 Surcharged in Black

1936, Oct. 26

775 A74 4k on 17½k 1.00 .50
776 A74 5k on 25k 1.00 .50
777 A73 6k on 50k 1.00 .50
778 A75 10k on 100k 1.75 1.00
779 A75 20k on 200k 5.50 2.00
780 A75 50k on 500k 10.00 3.25
Nos. 775-780 (6) 20.25 7.75
Set, never hinged 67.50

"1926" in Overprint

775a A74 4k on 17½k 6.50 3.75
776a A74 5k on 25k 7.00 3.75
777a A73 6k on 50k 7.00 3.75
778a A75 10k on 100k 9.00 4.50
779a A75 20k on 200k 20.00 10.00
780a A75 50k on 500k 55.00 27.50
Nos. 775a-780a (6) 104.50 53.25
Set, never hinged 250.00

Re-militarization of the Dardanelles.

Hittite Bronze Stag — A82

Thorak's Bust of Kemal Atatürk — A83

1937, Sept. 20 **Litho.** ***Perf. 12***

781 A82 3k light violet 1.75 1.25
782 A83 6k blue 3.00 2.00
783 A82 7½k bright pink 4.75 3.75
784 A83 12½k indigo 10.00 7.50
Nos. 781-784 (4) 19.50 14.50
Set, never hinged 32.50

2nd Turkish Historical Congress, Istanbul, Sept. 20-30.

Arms of Turkey, Greece, Romania and Yugoslavia — A84

1937, Oct. 29 ***Perf. 11½***

785 A84 8k carmine 6.75 3.50
786 A84 12½k dark blue 15.00 4.75

The Balkan Entente.

Street in Izmir A85

Fig Tree — A87

30pa, View of Fair Buildings. 3k, Tower, Government Square. 5k, Olive branch. 6k, Woman with grapes. 7½k, Woman picking grapes. 8k, Izmir Harbor through arch. 12k, Statue of Pres. Ataturk. 12½k, Pres. Ataturk.

1938, Aug. 20 **Photo.** ***Perf. 11½***
Inscribed: "Izmir Enternasyonal Fuari 1938"

789 A85 10pa dark brown .50 .60
790 A85 30pa purple .75 .50
791 A87 2½k brt green 1.25 1.00
792 A87 3k brown orange 1.25 .50
793 A87 5k olive green 2.25 .75
794 A85 6k brown 5.00 .40
795 A87 7½k scarlet 5.00 2.50
796 A87 8k brown lake 3.50 1.50
797 A87 12k rose violet 6.25 3.50
798 A87 12½k deep blue 10.00 8.50
Nos. 789-798 (10) 35.75 19.75
Set, never hinged 70.00

Izmir International Fair.

President Atatürk Teaching Reformed Turkish Alphabet A95

1938, Nov. 2

799	A95	2½k brt green	1.00	.55
800	A95	3k orange	1.00	.55
801	A95	6k rose violet	1.10	.65
802	A95	7½k deep rose	1.10	1.00
803	A95	8k red brown	1.40	1.10
804	A95	12½k brt ultra	2.00	1.25
		Nos. 799-804 (6)	7.60	5.10
		Set, never hinged	18.00	

Reform of the Turkish alphabet, 10th anniv.

Army and Air Force A96

Atatürk Driving Tractor — A98

3k, View of Kayseri. 7½k, Railway bridge. 8k, Scout buglers. 12½k, President Ataturk.

1938, Oct. 29

Inscribed: "Cumhuriyetin 15 inc yil donumu hatirasi"

805	A96	2½k dark green	.45	.35
806	A96	3k red brown	.45	.35
807	A98	6k bister	.75	.35
808	A96	7½k red	1.25	.90
809	A96	8k rose violet	4.00	2.50
810	A98	12½k deep blue	2.25	1.75
		Nos. 805-810 (6)	9.15	6.20
		Set, never hinged	20.00	

15th anniversary of the Republic.

Stamps of 1931-38 Overprinted in Black

1938, Nov. 21 *Perf. 11½x12*

811	A78	3k brown orange	.50	.35
812	A78	5k rose red	.50	.35
813	A78	6k deep blue	.75	.50
814	A77	7½k deep rose	.80	.55
815	A78	8k dark blue	2.00	.75
a.		8k bright blue	225.00	*150.00*
816	A79	12½k indigo	3.75	1.75
		Nos. 811-816 (6)	8.30	4.25
		Set, never hinged	15.00	

President Kemal Atatürk (1881-1938). The date is that of his funeral.

Catalogue values for unused stamps in this section, from this point to the end of the section, are for Never Hinged items.

Turkish and American Flags — A102

Presidents Inönü and F. D. Roosevelt and Map of North America A103

Designs: 3k, 8k, Inonu and Roosevelt. 7½k, 12½k, Kemal Ataturk and Washington.

1939, July 15 **Photo.** *Perf. 14*

817	A102	2½k ol grn, red & bl	.25	.20
818	A103	3k dk brn & bl grn	.50	.20
819	A102	6k purple, red & bl	.50	.20
820	A103	7½k org ver & bl grn	1.00	.40
821	A103	8k dp cl & bl grn	.75	.40
822	A103	12½k brt bl & bl grn	2.00	.85
		Nos. 817-822 (6)	5.00	2.25

US constitution, 150th anniversary.

Nos. 698, 702-704 Surcharged in Black

1939, July 23 **Unwmk.** *Perf. 13*

823	A74	3k on 25k	.40	.25
824	A75	6k on 200k	.65	.50
825	A74	7½k on 25k	.75	.50
826	A75	12k on 100k	1.00	.50
827	A75	12½k on 200k	2.00	.50
828	A75	17½k on 500k	3.00	1.00
		Nos. 823-828 (6)	7.80	3.25

Annexation of Hatay.

Railroad Bridge A105

Locomotive A106

Track Through Mountain Pass A107

Design: 12½k, Railroad tunnel, Atma Pass.

1939, Oct. 20 **Typo.** *Perf. 11½*

829	A105	3k lt orange red	3.25	3.25
830	A106	6k chestnut	3.75	3.75
831	A107	7½k rose pink	5.25	5.25
832	A107	12½k dark blue	8.75	8.75
		Nos. 829-832 (4)	21.00	21.00

Completion of the Sivas to Erzerum link of the Ankara-Erzerum Railroad.

Atatürk Residence in Ankara — A109

Kemal Atatürk — A110

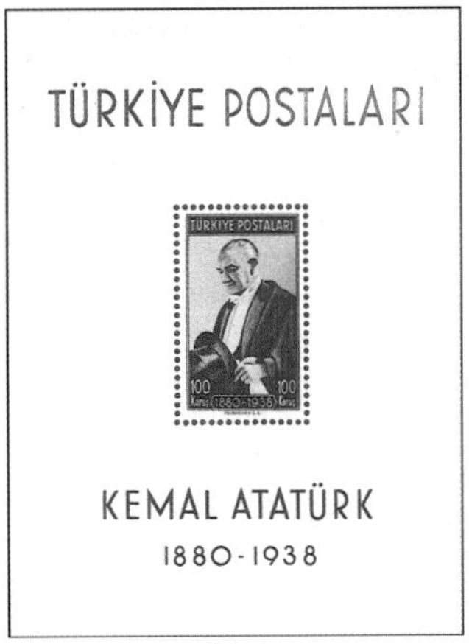

A111

Designs: 5k, 6k, 7½k, 8k, 12½k, 17½k, Various portraits of Ataturk, "1880-1938."

1939-40 **Photo.**

833	A109	2½k brt green	1.00	.50
834	A110	3k dk blue gray	1.00	.50
835	A110	5k chocolate	1.25	.75
836	A110	6k chestnut	1.25	.75
837	A110	7½k rose red	3.75	1.00
838	A110	8k gray green	1.75	1.00
839	A110	12½k brt blue	2.00	1.50
840	A110	17½k brt rose	6.50	2.00
		Nos. 833-840 (8)	18.50	8.00

Souvenir Sheet

841	A111	100k blue black	70.00	100.00

Death of Kemal Ataturk, first anniversary. Size of No. 841: 90x120mm.

Issued: 2½k, 6k, 12½k, 11/11/39; others, 1/3/40.

Namik Kemal A118

Arms of Turkey, Greece, Romania and Yugoslavia A119

1940, Jan. 3

842	A118	6k chestnut	1.25	.60
843	A118	8k dk olive grn	3.00	1.50
844	A118	12k brt rose red	3.50	2.00
845	A118	12½k brt blue	7.50	3.00
		Nos. 842-845 (4)	15.25	7.10

Birth cent. of Namik Kemal, poet and patriot.

Perf. 11½

1940, Jan. 1 **Typo.** **Unwmk.**

846	A119	8k light blue	3.00	1.00
847	A119	10k deep blue	5.50	1.00

The Balkan Entente.

Nos. 703-704 Surcharged in Red or Black

1940, Aug. 20 *Perf. 12*

848	A75	6k on 200k dk grn & blk (R)	.50	1.00
849	A75	10k on 200k dk grn & blk	.75	1.50
850	A75	12k on 500k choc & blk	1.25	2.50
		Nos. 848-850 (3)	2.50	5.00

13th International Izmir Fair.

Map of Turkey and Census Figures A120

1940, Oct. 1 **Typo.** *Perf. 11½*

851	A120	10pa dark blue green	.25	.25
852	A120	3k orange	1.25	1.25
853	A120	6k carmine rose	1.50	1.50
854	A120	10k dark blue	2.50	2.50
		Nos. 851-854 (4)	5.50	5.50

Census of Oct. 20, 1940.

Runner — A121

Pole Vaulter — A122

Hurdler A123

Discus Thrower — A124

1940, Oct. 5

855	A121	3k olive green	2.50	2.50
856	A122	6k rose	7.50	3.50
857	A123	8k chestnut brown	3.50	4.00
858	A124	10k dark blue	5.50	10.00
		Nos. 855-858 (4)	19.00	20.00

11th Balkan Olympics.

Mail Carriers on Horseback A125

Postman of 1840 and 1940 — A126

Old Sailing Vessel and Modern Mailboat — A127

Design: 12k, Post Office, Istanbul.

1940, Dec. 31 **Typo.** *Perf. 10*

859	A125	3k gray green	.50	.50
860	A126	6k rose	.75	.75
861	A127	10k dark blue	1.00	1.00
862	A127	12k olive brown	1.50	1.50
		Nos. 859-862 (4)	3.75	3.75

Centenary of the Turkish post.

SEMI-POSTAL STAMPS

Regular Issues Overprinted in Carmine or Black

Overprint reads: "For War Orphans"

Perf. 12, 13½ and Compound

1915 **Unwmk.**

On Stamps of 1905

B1 A18 10pa dull grn (#119) .75 .50
B2 A18 10pi orange brown 12.50 .80

On Stamp of 1906

B3 A18 10pa dull grn (#128) 40.00 25.00

On Stamps of 1908

B4 A19 10pa blue green 1.50 .75
B5 A19 5pi dark violet 75.00 12.50
Nos. B1-B5 (5) 129.75 39.55

With Additional Overprint

B6 A19 10pa blue green 240.00 175.00

On Stamps of 1909

B7 A21 10pa blue green 1.00 .75
a. Inverted overprint 22.50 22.50
b. Double overprint, one invtd. 30.00 30.00
B8 A21 20pa carmine rose 1.00 .75
a. Inverted overprint 27.50 27.50
B9 A21 1pi ultra 1.00 .75
B10 A21 5pi dark violet 8.75 1.50
Nos. B7-B10 (4) 11.75 3.75

With Additional Overprint

B11 A21 10pa blue green 1.00 .75
b. Double overprint, one inverted 5.00 5.00
B12 A21 20pa carmine rose 1.50 .75
B13 A21 1pi ultra 2.00 .75

On Stamps of 1913

B14 A22 10pa blue green 1.00 .75
a. Inverted overprint 22.50 22.50
B15 A22 1pi ultra 1.00 .75
a. Double overprint 5.00 5.00
Nos. B11-B15 (5) 6.50 3.75

With Additional Overprint

B16 A22 10pa blue green 1.25 .75
a. Inverted overprint 27.50 27.50

On Newspaper Stamp of 1908

B17 A19 10pa blue green 360.00 175.00

On Newspaper Stamp of 1909

B18 A21 10pa blue green 1.25 1.00

Regular Issues Overprinted in Carmine or Black

1916

On Stamps of 1901

B19 A17 1pi blue 1.00 .50
B20 A17 5pi lilac rose 10.00 1.50

On Stamps of 1905

B21 A18 1pi brt blue 7.50 2.00
B22 A18 5pi brown 7.50 5.00

On Stamp of 1906

B23 A18 1pi brt blue 1.00 .75

On Stamps of 1908

B24 A19 20pa carmine (Bk) *300.00*
B25 A19 10pi red 500.00 200.00

With Additional Overprint

B26 A19 20pa carmine 1.00 .75
B27 A19 1pi brt blue (C) 20.00 5.00

On Stamps of 1909

B28 A21 20pa carmine rose 1.00 .75
B29 A21 1pi ultra .50 .75
B30 A21 10pi dull red 175.00 100.00

With Additional Overprint

B31 A21 20pa carmine rose .75 .50
B32 A21 1pi ultra 1.00 .75

On Stamps of 1913

B33 A22 20pa carmine rose 1.00 .75
B34 A22 1pi ultra 1.00 .35
a. Inverted overprint 5.00 5.00
B35 A22 10pi dull red 22.50 15.00

With Additional Overprint

B36 A22 20pa carmine rose 1.00 .75

On Newspaper Stamps of 1901

B37 A16 5pi ocher 11.50 6.00
a. 5pa bister, No. P37 150.00 150.00

Regular Issues Surcharged in Black

On Stamp of 1899

B38 A11 10pa on 20pa vio brn 1.00 .75

On Stamp of 1905

B39 A18 10pa on 20pa carmine 1.00 .75

On Stamp of 1906

B40 A18 10pa on 20pa carmine .90 .75

On Newspaper Stamp of 1893-99

B41 A11 10pa on 20pa violet brn 2.00 1.50
Nos. B38-B41 (4) 4.90 3.75

Nos. 346-349 Overprinted

B42 A41 10pa carmine 1.00 .75
a. Inverted overprint 6.75 6.75
B43 A41 20pa ultra 1.00 .75
a. Inverted overprint 6.75 6.75
B44 A41 1pi violet & blk 1.00 .90
a. Inverted overprint 6.75 6.75
B45 A41 5pi yel brn & blk 1.00 .75
a. Inverted overprint 11.00 11.00
Nos. B42-B45 (4) 4.00 3.15

Nos. B42-B45 formed part of the Postage Commemoration issue of 1916.

A Soldier's Farewell — SP1

1917, Feb. 20 **Engr.** ***Perf. 12½***

B46 SP1 10pa red violet 1.25 .50

For surcharges see Nos. 600, B47.

Stamp of Same Design Surcharged

B47 SP1 10pa on 20pa car rose 2.00 .50

Badge of the Society — SP9

School Teacher — SP10

Marie Sklodowska Curie — SP16

Kemal Atatürk — SP23

Designs: 2k+2k, Woman farmer. 2½k+2½k, Typist. 4k+4k, Aviatrix and policewoman. 5k+5k, Women voters. 7½k+7½k, Yildiz Palace, Istanbul. 10k+10k, Carrie Chapman Catt. 12½k+12½k, Jane Addams. 15k+15k, Grazia Deledda. 20k+20k, Selma Lagerlof. 25k+25k, Bertha von Suttner. 30k+30k, Sigrid Undset.

1935, Apr. 17 **Photo.** ***Perf. 11½***

Inscribed: "XII Congres Suffragiste International"

B54 SP9 20pa + 20pa brn .50 .50
B55 SP10 1k + 1k rose car .75 .50
B56 SP10 2k + 2k sl bl 1.00 .75
B57 SP10 2½k + 2½k yel grn 1.00 .75
B58 SP10 4k + 4k blue 1.50 1.00
B59 SP10 5k + 5k dl vio 2.50 2.00
B60 SP10 7½k + 7½k org red 2.50 2.00
B61 SP16 10k + 10k org 2.50 2.50
B62 SP16 12½k + 12½k dk bl 2.50 2.50
B63 SP16 15k + 15k violet 5.00 5.00
B64 SP16 20k + 20k red org 7.50 6.25
B65 SP16 25k + 25k grn 15.00 14.00
B66 SP16 30k + 30k ultra 90.00 100.00
B67 SP16 50k + 50k dk sl grn 175.00 150.00
B68 SP23 100k + 100k brn car 125.00 140.00
Nos. B54-B68 (15) 432.25 427.75
Set, never hinged 675.00

12th Congress of the Women's Intl. Alliance.

AIR POST STAMPS

Catalogue values for unused stamps in this section are for Never Hinged items.

Nos. 692, 695, 698, 700 Overprinted or Surcharged in Brown or Blue

1934, July 15 **Unwmk.** ***Perf. 12***

C1 A74 7½k (Br) .75 .20
C2 A72 12½k on 15k (Br) .75 .25
C3 A74 20k on 25k (Br) .75 .25
C4 A74 25k (Bl) 1.00 .40
C5 A74 40k (Br) 2.25 1.25
Nos. C1-C5 (5) 5.50 2.35

Regular Stamps of 1930 Surcharged in Brown

1937

C6 A74 4½k on 7½k red brn 5.00 1.00
C7 A72 9k on 15k dp org 40.00 20.00
C8 A74 35k on 40k red vio 10.00 4.25
Nos. C6-C8 (3) 55.00 25.25

POSTAGE DUE STAMPS

Same Types as Regular Issues of Corresponding Dates

1863 **Unwmk.** ***Imperf.***

Blue Band

J1 A1 20pa blk, *red brn* 100.00 32.50
a. Tête bêche pair 225.00 225.00
b. Without band 50.00
c. Red band 90.00 45.00
J2 A2 1pi blk, *red brn* 150.00 22.50
a. Tête bêche pair 225.00 225.00
b. Without band 50.00
J3 A3 2pi blk, *red brn* 500.00 70.00
a. Tête bêche pair 650.00 450.00
J4 A4 5pi blk, *red brn* 300.00 80.00
a. Tête bêche pair 425.00 425.00
b. Without band 100.00
c. Red band 150.00
Nos. J1-J4 (4) 1,050. 205.00

Full margins = 1mm at sides and top, 3mm at bottom (includes part of band). Height of colored bands is 6mm. Full margins for items without band = 3mm at bottom.

1865 ***Perf. 12½***

J6 A5 20pa brown 2.50 5.00
J7 A5 1pi brown 2.50 5.00
b. Half used as 20pa on cover
c. Printed on both sides 25.00
J8 A5 2pi brown 12.50 25.00
a. Half used as 1pi on cover
J9 A5 5pi brown 5.00 30.00
a. Half used as 2½pi on cover
J10 A5 25pi brown 45.00 100.00
Nos. J6-J10 (5) 67.50 165.00

Exist imperf. Values, $60 to $100 each.

The 10pa brown is an essay. Value about $2,750.

1867

J11 A5 20pa bister brn 7.50 100.00
J12 A5 1pi bister brn 7.50
a. With surcharge of 5pi 13.50
b. Imperf., pair 65.00

J13 A5 2pi fawn 75.00
J14 A5 5pi fawn 17.50
J15 A5 25pi bister brn *21,250.*
Nos. J11-J14 (4) 107.50

Nos. J12-J15 were not placed in use.

1869 ***Perf. 13½***

With Yellow-Brown Border

J16 A5 20pa bister brn 10.00 10.00
a. Without surcharge
J17 A5 1pi bister brn 550.00 5.00
a. Without surcharge
J18 A5 2pi bister brn 800.00 5.00
J19 A5 5pi bister brn 1.50 12.50
b. Without border
c. Printed on both sides 15.00
J20 A5 25pi bister brn — —
Nos. J16-J20 (4) 1,361. 32.50

With Brown Border

Color of border ranges from brown to reddish brown and black brown.

J21 A5 20pa bister brn 125.00 20.00
a. Inverted surcharge
b. Without surcharge
J22 A5 1pi bister brn 550.00 12.50
a. Without surcharge
J23 A5 2pi bister brn 450.00 12.50
b. Inverted surcharge
J24 A5 5pi bister brn 2.50 15.00
b. Without surcharge
J25 A5 25pi bister brn 37.50 100.00
Nos. J21-J25 (5) 1,165. 160.00

Pin-perf., Perf. 5 to 11½ and Compound

1871

With Brick Red Border

J26 A5 20pa bister brn 875.00 50.00
J27 A5 1pi bister brn *5,000.*
J28 A5 2pi bister brn 110.00 140.00
J29 A5 5pi bister brn 7.50 25.00

With Black Brown Border

J31 A5 20pa bister brn 150.00 2.50
a. Half used as 10pa on cover
b. Imperf., pair 16.50
c. Printed on both sides 40.00 40.00
J32 A5 1pi bister brn 225.00 2.50
a. Half used as 20pa on cover
c. Inverted surcharge 50.00 35.00
d. Printed on both sides
J33 A5 2pi bister brn 6.00 9.00
a. Half used as 1pi on cover
c. Imperf., pair 16.50
J34 A5 5pi bister brn 2.50 20.00
a. Half used as 2½pi on cover
c. Printed on both sides
J35 A5 25pi bister brn 40.00 125.00
a. Inverted surcharge
Nos. J31-J35 (5) 423.50 *159.00*

1888 ***Perf. 11½ and 13½***

J36 A7 20pa black 3.00 12.50
J37 A7 1pi black 3.00 12.50
J38 A7 2pi black 3.00 15.00
b. Diagonal half used as 1pi
Nos. J36-J38 (3) 9.00 40.00

Imperf

J36a A7 20pa 11.00
J37a A7 1pi 11.00
J38a A7 2pi 11.00

1892 ***Perf. 13½***

J39 A11 20pa black 7.00 12.50
J40 A12 1pi black 22.50 12.50
a. Printed on both sides
J41 A13 2pi black 17.50 12.50
Nos. J39-J41 (3) 47.00 *37.50*

1901

J42 A11 20pa black, *deep rose* 2.50 20.00

1901

J43 A17 10pa black, *deep rose* 4.00 6.00
J44 A17 20pa black, *deep rose* 3.75 8.75
J45 A17 1pi black, *deep rose* 3.00 10.00
J46 A17 2pi black, *deep rose* 1.75 15.00
Nos. J43-J46 (4) 12.50 39.75

1905 ***Perf. 12***

J47 A18 1pi black, *deep rose* 3.00 10.00
J48 A18 2pi black, *deep rose* 4.50 20.00

1908, ***Perf. 12, 13½ and Compound***

J49 A19 1pi black, *deep rose* 80.00 7.50
J50 A19 2pi black, *deep rose* 12.50 45.00

1909

J51 A21 1pi black, *deep rose* 15.00 *50.00*
J52 A21 2pi black, *deep rose* *150.00* *175.00*
a. Imperf. 65.00

1913 ***Perf. 12***

J53 A22 2pa black, *deep rose* 1.00 .50
J54 A22 5pa black, *deep rose* 1.00 .50
J55 A22 10pa black, *deep rose* 1.00 .50
J56 A22 20pa black, *deep rose* 1.00 .50
J57 A22 1pi black, *deep rose* 4.50 10.00
J58 A22 2pi black, *deep rose* 8.00 17.50
Nos. J53-J58 (6) 16.50 29.50

Adrianople Issue

Nos. 251-253 Surcharged in Black, Blue or Red

1913

J59 A23 2pa on 10pa green (Bk) 3.25 .35
J60 A23 5pa on 20pa red (Bl) 3.25 .35
J61 A23 10pa on 40pa blue (R) 10.00 .80
J62 A23 20pa on 40pa blue (Bk) 32.50 11.00
Nos. J59-J62 (4) 49.00 12.50

For surcharges see Nos. J67-J70, J83-J86.

D1

D2

D3

D4

1914 **Engr.**

J63 D1 5pa claret 1.25 10.00
J64 D2 20pa red 1.25 10.00
J65 D3 1pi dark blue 1.25 10.00
J66 D4 2pi slate 1.25 10.00
Nos. J63-J66 (4) 5.00 40.00

For surcharges and overprints see Nos. J87-J91.

Nos. J59 to J62 Surcharged in Red or Black

1916

J67 A23 10pa on 2pa on 10pa (R) 55.00 55.00
J68 A23 20pa on 5pa on 20pa 55.00 55.00
J69 A23 40pa on 10pa on 40pa 55.00 55.00
J70 A23 40pa on 20pa on 40pa (R) 55.00 55.00
Nos. J67-J70 (4) 220.00 220.00

Preceding Issues Overprinted in Red, Black or Blue

1917

On Stamps of 1865

J71 A5 20pa red brn (Bl) 45.00 67.50
J72 A5 1pi red brn (Bl) 45.00 67.50
J73 A5 2pi bis brn (Bl) 45.00 67.50
J74 A5 5pi bis brn (Bl) 45.00 67.50
J75 A5 25pi dk brn (Bl) 45.00 67.50
Nos. J71-J75 (5) 225.00 337.50

On Stamp of 1869

Red Brown Border

J76 A5 5pi bis brn (R) 45.00 67.50

On Stamp of 1871

Black Brown Border

J77 A5 5pi bis brn 75.00 50.00

On Stamps of 1888

J78 A7 1pi black (R) 45.00 67.50
J79 A7 2pi black (R) 45.00 67.50

On Stamps of 1892

J80 A11 20pa black (R) 2.50 2.50
J81 A12 1pi black (R) 2.50 2.50
J82 A13 2pi black (R) 2.50 2.50
Nos. J80-J82 (3) 7.50 7.50

Adrianople Issue

On Nos. J59 to J62 with Addition of New Value

J83 A23 10pa on 2pa on 10pa (R) 1.00 1.00
J84 A23 20pa on 5pa on 20pa (Bk) 1.00 1.00
J85 A23 40pa on 10pa on 40pa (Bk) 1.50 1.50
a. "40pa" double
J86 A23 40pa on 20pa on 40pa (R) 3.50 3.50
Nos. J83-J86 (4) 7.00 7.00

Nos. J71-J86 were used as regular postage stamps.

Armistice Issue

No. J65 Overprinted

1919, Nov. 30

J87 D3 1pi dark blue 125.00 150.00

Accession to the Throne Issue

Postage Due Stamps of 1914 Overprinted in Turkish "Accession to the Throne of His Majesty. 3rd July, 1334-1918"

1919

J88 D1 10pa on 5pa claret 25.00 37.50
J89 D2 20pa red 25.00 37.50
J90 D3 1pi dark blue 25.00 37.50
J91 D4 2pi slate 25.00 37.50
Nos. J88-J91 (4) 100.00 150.00

Railroad Bridge over Kizil Irmak — D5

Kemal Atatürk — D6

1926 **Engr.**

J92 D5 20pa ocher 1.00 2.50
J93 D5 1g red 1.50 5.00
J94 D5 2g blue green 2.50 5.00
J95 D5 3g lilac brown 2.50 12.50
J96 D5 5g lilac 5.00 20.00
Nos. J92-J96 (5) 12.50 45.00
Set, never hinged 30.00

Catalogue values for unused stamps in this section, from this point to the end of the section, are for Never Hinged items.

1936 **Litho.** ***Perf. 11½***

J97 D6 20pa brown .20 .20
J98 D6 2k light blue .20 .20
J99 D6 3k bright violet .20 .20
J100 D6 5k Prussian blue .20 .20
J101 D6 12k bright rose .35 .20
Nos. J97-J101 (5) 1.15 1.00

For surcharges see Nos. 1461-1465.

Local Issues

Type I

Type II

Type III

Type IV

Type V

Type VI

During 1873//1882 Turkish stamps with the above overprints were used for local postage in Constantinople (types 1-5) and Mount Athos (type 6).

MILITARY STAMPS

For the Army in Thessaly

Tughra and Bridge at Larissa — M1

1898, Apr. 21 **Unwmk.** ***Perf. 13***

M1 M1 10pa yellow green 10.00 7.50
M2 M1 20pa rose 10.00 7.50
M3 M1 1pi dark blue 10.00 7.50
M4 M1 2pi orange 10.00 7.50
M5 M1 5pi violet 10.00 7.50
Nos. M1-M5 (5) 50.00 37.50

Issued for Turkish occupation forces to use in Thessaly during the Greco-Turkish War of 1897-98.

Forgeries of Nos. M1-M5 are perf. 11½.

NEWSPAPER STAMPS

N1

Black Overprint

1879 **Unwmk.** ***Perf. 11½ and 13½***

P1 N1 10pa blk & rose lilac 225.00 225.00

Other stamps found with this "IMPRIMES" overprint were prepared on private order and have no official status as newspaper stamps.

Counterfeits exist of No. P1.

The 10pa surcharge, on half of 20pa rose and pale rose was made privately. See note after No. 77.

Regular Issue of 1890 Handstamped in Black

There are two types of this handstamp, varying slightly in size.

1891 *Perf. 13½, 11½*

P10 A7 10pa grn & gray 40.00 12.50
a. Imperf. 22.50 12.50
P11 A7 20pa rose & gray 75.00 15.00
P12 A7 1pi blue & gray 200.00 150.00
P13 A7 2pi yel & gray *500.00 400.00*
P14 A7 5pi buff & gray *1,000. 750.00*
Nos. P10-P14 (5) *1,815. 1,327.*

Blue Handstamp

P10b A7 10pa green & gray 200.00 *125.00*
P11a A7 20pa rose & gray 300.00 *250.00*
P12a A7 1pi blue & gray *400.00* 375.00
Nos. P10b-P12a (3) *900.00 750.00*

This overprint in red and on 2pi and 5pi in blue is considered bogus.

Same Handstamp on Regular Issue of 1892

1892 *Perf. 13½*

P25 A10 10pa gray green *400.00 100.00*
P26 A11 20pa rose *1,250. 375.00*
P27 A12 1pi pale blue *110.00 150.00*
P28 A13 2pi brown org *200.00 175.00*
P29 A14 5pi pale violet *1,800. 1,250.*
a. On No. 99a *500.00*
Nos. P25-P29 (5) 3,760. 2,050.

The handstamps on Nos. P10-P29 are found double, inverted and sideways. Counterfeit overprints comprise most of the copies offered for sale in the marketplace.

Regular Issues of 1892-98 Overprinted in Black

1893-98

P30 A10 10pa gray grn 3.75 2.50
P31 A11 20pa vio brn ('98) 3.00 1.50
a. 20pa dark pink .60 .60
b. 20pa pink 225.00 15.00
P32 A12 1pi pale blue 3.00 1.50
P33 A13 2pi brown org 27.50 12.50
a. Tete beche pair 22.50
P34 A14 5pi pale violet 85.00 75.00
a. On No. 99a 140.00 65.00
Nos. P30-P34 (5) 122.25 93.00

For surcharge and overprints see Nos. B41, P134-P136, P153-P154.

No. 95 Surcharged

1897

P36 A10 5pa on 10pa gray grn 4.00 2.00
a. "Cniq" instead of "Cinq" 15.00 15.00

For overprint see No. P137.

Nos. 102-107 Overprinted in Black

1901 *Perf. 12, 13½ and Compound*

P37 A16 5pa bister 1.00 1.00
a. Inverted overprint
P38 A16 10pa yellow grn 6.25 6.25
P39 A16 20pa magenta 32.50 7.50
P40 A16 1pi violet blue 60.00 22.50
P41 A16 2pi gray blue 42.50 37.50
P42 A16 5pi ocher 300.00 90.00
Nos. P37-P42 (6) 442.25 164.75

For overprints see Nos. B37, P69-P74, P123, P138-P141, P155-P158.

Same Overprint on Nos. 110-115

1901

P43 A17 5pa purple 8.75 2.00
P44 A17 10pa green 32.50 2.50
P45 A17 20pa carmine 8.75 1.50
a. Overprinted on back
P46 A17 1pi blue 25.00 2.00
P47 A17 2pi orange 87.50 4.00
a. Inverted overprint
P48 A17 5pi lilac rose 160.00 27.50
Nos. P43-P48 (6) 322.50 39.50

For overprints see Nos. P75-P80, P124-P126, P142-P146, P159-P164.

Same Overprint on Regular Issue of 1905

1905

P49 A18 5pa ocher 2.50 1.00
P50 A18 10pa dull green 30.00 1.50
P51 A18 20pa carmine 2.50 1.25
P52 A18 1pi pale blue 2.50 1.25
P53 A18 2pi slate 70.00 10.00
P54 A18 5pi brown 175.00 20.00
Nos. P49-P54 (6) 282.50 35.00

For overprints see Nos. P127-P129, P147-P150, P165-P171.

Regular Issue of 1908 Overprinted in Carmine or Blue

1908

P55 A19 5pa ocher (Bl) 10.00 .50
P56 A19 10pa blue grn (C) 17.50 .50
P57 A19 20pa carmine (Bl) 22.50 1.00
P58 A19 1pi brt blue (C) 100.00 2.50
P59 A19 2pi blue blk (C) 150.00 7.50
P60 A19 5pi dk violet (C) 200.00 17.50
Nos. P55-P60 (6) 500.00 29.50

For overprints see Nos. B17, P130-P131, P151, P172.

Same Overprint on Regular Issue of 1909

1909

P61 A21 5pa ocher (Bl) 3.00 1.00
a. Imperf.
P62 A21 10pa blue grn (C) 8.75 1.50
P63 A21 20pa car rose (Bl) 60.00 1.75
a. Imperf.
P64 A21 1pi brt blue (C) 100.00 5.00
P65 A21 2pi blue blk (C) 250.00 30.00
P66 A21 5pi dk violet (C) 500.00 65.00
Nos. P61-P66 (6) 921.75 104.25

For surcharge and overprints see Nos. B18, P67-P68, P81, P132-P133, P152.

No. 151 Surcharged in Blue

1910 *Perf. 12, 13½ and Compound*

P67 A21 2pa on 5pa ocher .75 .75

1911 *Perf. 12*

P68 A21 2pa olive green 1.00 .50

Newspaper Stamps of 1901-11 Overprinted in Carmine or Blue

The overprint was applied to 13 denominations in four settings with change of city name, producing individual sets for each city: "MONASTIR," "PRISTINA," "SALONIKA" and "USKUB."

1911, June 26 *Perf. 12, 13½*

"Monastir"

P69 A16 5pa bister 15.00 22.50
P70 A16 10pa yellow grn 15.00 22.50
P71 A16 20pa magenta 15.00 22.50
P72 A16 1pi violet blue 15.00 22.50
P73 A16 2pi gray blue 20.00 30.00
P74 A16 5pi ocher 40.00 60.00
P75 A17 5pa purple 7.50 12.50
P76 A17 10pa green 7.50 12.50
P77 A17 20pa carmine 7.50 12.50
P78 A17 1pi blue 7.50 12.50
P79 A17 2pi orange 10.00 15.00
P80 A17 5pi lilac rose 20.00 30.00
P81 A21 2pa olive green 2.50 3.75
Nos. P69-P81 (13) 182.50 278.75

"Pristina"

P69a A16 5pa bister 5.00 5.00
P70a A16 10pa yellow grn 5.00 5.00
P71a A16 20pa magenta 5.00 5.00
P72a A16 1pi violet blue 5.25 5.25
P73a A16 2pi gray blue 6.50 6.50
P74a A16 5pi ocher 13.00 13.00
P75a A17 5pa purple 5.00 5.00
P76a A17 10pa green 5.00 5.00
P77a A17 20pa carmine 5.00 5.00
P78a A17 1pi blue 6.50 6.50
P79a A17 2pi orange 6.50 6.50
P80a A17 5pi lilac rose 13.00 13.00
P81a A21 2pa olive green .35 .35
Nos. P69a-P81a (13) 81.10 81.10

"Salonika"

P69b A16 5pa bister 5.00 5.00
P70b A16 10pa yellow grn 5.00 5.00
P71b A16 20pa magenta 5.00 5.00
P72b A16 1pi violet blue 5.25 5.25
P73b A16 2pi gray blue 6.50 6.50
P74b A16 5pi ocher 13.00 13.00
P75b A17 5pa purple 5.00 5.00
P76b A17 10pa green 5.00 5.00
P77b A17 20pa carmine 5.00 5.00
P78b A17 1pi blue 6.50 6.50
P79b A17 2pi orange 6.50 6.50
P80b A17 5pi lilac rose 13.00 13.00
P81b A21 2pa olive green .35 .35
Nos. P69b-P81b (13) 81.10 81.10

"Uskub"

P69c A16 5pa bister 5.00 5.00
P70c A16 10pa yellow grn 5.00 5.00
P71c A16 20pa magenta 5.00 5.00
P72c A16 1pi violet blue 5.25 5.25
P73c A16 2pi gray blue 6.50 6.50
P74c A16 5pi ocher 13.00 13.00
P75c A17 5pa purple 5.00 5.00
P76c A17 10pa green 5.00 5.00
P77c A17 20pa carmine 5.00 5.00
P78c A17 1pi blue 6.50 6.50
P79c A17 2pi orange 6.50 6.50
P80c A17 5pi lilac rose 13.00 13.00
P81c A21 2pa olive green .35 .35
Nos. P69c-P81c (13) 81.10 81.10

The note after No. 182 will also apply to Nos. P69-P81.

Preceding Newspaper Issues with additional Overprint in Carmine or Black

1915

On Stamps of 1893-98

P121 A10 10pa gray green 6.00 .50
a. Inverted overprint 10.00 10.00
P122 A13 2pi yellow brn 1.50 1.00
a. Inverted overprint 10.00 10.00

On Stamps of 1901

P123 A16 10pa yellow grn 1.00 .50
P124 A17 5pa purple 1.00 1.00
P125 A17 20pa carmine 2.00 1.00
P126 A17 5pi lilac rose 20.00 5.00

On Stamps of 1905

P127 A18 5pa ocher 1.00 .50
a. Inverted overprint 7.50 7.50
P128 A18 2pi slate 17.50 5.00
P129 A18 5pi brown 10.00 .60

On Stamps of 1908

P130 A19 2pi blue blk *1,375. 550.00*
P131 A19 5pi dk violet 10.00 1.25

On Stamps of 1909

P132 A21 5pa ocher 1.00 .50
P133 A21 5pi dk violet 100.00 35.00
Nos. P121-P129,P131-P133 (12) 171.00 51.85

Preceding Newspaper Issues with additional Overprint in Red or Black

1916

On Stamps of 1893-98

P134 A10 10pa gray green 1.00 .50
P135 A11 20pa violet brn .50 .50
P136 A14 5pi dull violet 50.00 50.00

On Stamp of 1897

P137 A10 5pa on 10pa gray grn .60 .50

On Stamps of 1901

P138 A16 5pa bister .50 .30
P139 A16 10pa yellow grn .90 .90
P140 A16 20pa magenta 1.00 .90
a. Inverted overprint 10.00 10.00
P141 A16 1pi violet blue 1.00 1.00
P142 A17 5pa purple 50.00 50.00
P143 A17 10pa green 50.00 50.00
P144 A17 20pa carmine 1.50 .90
P145 A17 1pi blue 1.50 .90
P146 A17 2pi orange 1.50 .90

On Stamps of 1905

P147 A18 5pa ocher 1.00 .75
P148 A18 10pa dull green 50.00 50.00
P149 A18 20pa carmine 50.00 50.00
P150 A18 1pi pale blue 1.75 1.00

On Stamp of 1908

P151 A19 5pa ocher 62.50 62.50

On Stamp of 1909

P152 A21 5pa ocher 62.50 62.50
Nos. P134-P152 (19) 387.75 384.05

Preceding Newspaper Issues with additional Overprint in Red or Black

1917

On Stamps of 1893-98

P153 A12 1pi gray (R) 2.50 2.00
P154 A11 20pa vio brn (R) 3.75 3.75

On Stamps of 1901

P155 A16 5pa bister (Bk) 1.50 1.25
a. Inverted overprint 20.00 20.00
P156 A16 10pa yellow grn (R) 1.50 1.25
P157 A16 20pa magenta (Bk) 1.50 1.25
P158 A16 2pi gray blue (R) 40.00 30.00
P159 A17 5pa purple (Bk) 2.25 2.25
a. Inverted overprint 20.00 20.00
b. Double overprint 20.00 20.00
c. Double ovpt., one inverted 25.00 25.00
P160 A17 10pa green (R) 22.50 35.00
P161 A17 20pa carmine (Bk) 1.50 1.25
P162 A17 1pi blue (R) 3.00 3.00
P163 A17 2pi orange (Bk) 2.50 2.50
P164 A17 5pi lilac rose (R) 32.50 50.00

On Stamps of 1905

P165 A18 5pa ocher (R) 2.50 2.00
a. Inverted overprint 10.00 10.00
P166 A18 5pa ocher (Bk) 3.00 2.50
a. Inverted overprint 10.00 10.00
P167 A18 10pa dull green (R) 2.50 2.00
P168 A18 20pa carmine (Bk) 2.50 2.00
a. Double overprint 15.00 15.00
P169 A18 1pi blue (R) 2.50 2.00
a. Inverted overprint 25.00 25.00
P170 A18 2pi slate (R) 32.50 50.00
P171 A18 5pi brown (R) 32.50 50.00

On Stamp of 1908

P172 A19 5pa ocher (R) 32.50 50.00
Nos. P153-P172 (20) *225.50 294.00*

Nos. P153-P172 were used as regular postage stamps.

#P173

#P174

1919

Blue Surcharge and Red Overprint

P173 A21 5pa on 2pa ol grn .75 .75
a. Red overprint double 12.50 5.00
b. Blue surcharge double 12.50 5.00

1920 **Red Surcharge**

P174 A25 5pa on 4pa brn 1.25 .50

POSTAL TAX STAMPS

Map of Turkey and Red Crescent
PT1

1928 Unwmk. Typo. *Perf. 14*

Crescent in Red

RA1	PT1	½pi lt brown	.30	.20
RA2	PT1	1pi red violet	.30	.20
RA3	PT1	2½pi orange	.30	.20

Engr.

Various Frames

RA4	PT1	5pi dk brown	.60	.45
RA5	PT1	10pi yellow green	.75	.55
RA6	PT1	20pi slate	1.25	.60
RA7	PT1	50pi dark violet	3.75	1.40
		Nos. RA1-RA7 (7)	7.25	3.60
		Set, never hinged	13.00	

The use of these stamps on letters, parcels, etc. in addition to the regular postage, was obligatory on certain days in each year.

For surcharges see Nos. RA16, RA21-RA22.

Cherubs Upholding Star — PT2

1932

RA8	PT2	1k ol bis & red	.50	.20
RA9	PT2	2½k dk brn & red	.65	.20
RA10	PT2	5k green & red	.85	.20
RA11	PT2	25k black & red	2.75	.90
		Nos. RA8-RA11 (4)	4.75	1.50
		Set, never hinged	7.50	

For surcharges and overprints see Nos. RA12-RA15, RA28-RA29, RA36-RA38.

No. RA8 Surcharged

RA12	PT2	20pa on 1k	.25	.20
RA13	PT2	3k on 1k	1.00	.40
a.		3 "kruus"	2.50	2.50

By a law of Parliament the use of these stamps on letters and telegraph forms, in addition to the regular fees, was obligatory from Apr. 20-30 of each year. The inscription in the tablet at the bottom of the design states that the money derived from the sale of the stamps is devoted to child welfare work.

No. RA8 Surcharged

1933

RA14	PT2	20pa on 1k ol bis & red	.25	.20
RA15	PT2	3k on 1k ol bis & red	1.00	.60

No. RA5 Surcharged

RA16	PT1	5k on 10pi yel grn & red	.95	.45
		Nos. RA14-RA16 (3)	2.20	1.25

PT3

PT4

1933 *Perf. 11, 11½*

RA17	PT3	20pa gray vio & red	.65	.20
RA18	PT4	1k violet & red	.80	.20
RA19	PT4	5k dk brown & red	2.50	.50
RA20	PT3	15k green & red	3.50	.50
		Nos. RA17-RA20 (4)	7.45	1.40
		Set, never hinged	11.00	

Nos. RA17 and RA20 were issued in Ankara; Nos. RA18 and RA19 in Izmir.

For overprint see No. RA27.

Nos. RA3, RA1 Surcharged in Black

1933-34

RA21	PT1	1k on 2½pi orange	.25	.20
RA22	PT1	5k on ½pi lt brown	.70	.25

Map of Turkey
PT5

1934-35 Crescent in Red *Perf. 12*

RA23	PT5	½k blue ('35)	.20	.20
RA24	PT5	1k red brown	.20	.20
RA25	PT5	2½k brown ('35)	.50	.20
RA26	PT5	5k blue green ('35)	1.25	.20
		Nos. RA23-RA26 (4)	2.15	.80
		Set, never hinged	5.00	

Frame differs on No. RA26.

See Nos. RA30-RA35B. For surcharge see No. RA63.

Nos. RA17, RA8-RA9 Overprinted "P.Y.S." in Roman Capitals

1936 *Perf. 11, 14*

RA27	PT3	20pa gray vio & red	.40	.20
RA28	PT2	1k ol bis & red	.40	.20
RA29	PT2	3k on 2½k dk brn & red	.75	.30
		Nos. RA27-RA29 (3)	1.55	
		Set, never hinged	12.00	

Type of 1934-35, Inscribed "Türkiye Kizilay Cemiyeti"

1938-46 *Perf. 8½-11½*

Type I — Imprint, "Devlet Basimevi". Crescent red.

Type II — Imprint, "Alaeddin Kiral Basimevi". Crescent carmine.

Type III — Imprint, "Damga Matbaasi". Crescent red.

Crescent in Red or Carmine

RA30	PT5	½k blue (I)	.20	.20
a.		Type II	3.50	1.00
b.		Type III	.30	.20
RA31	PT5	1k red vio (I)	.20	.20
a.		Type II	6.50	2.00
b.		Type III	.30	.20
RA32	PT5	2½k orange (I)	.20	.20
a.		Type III	1.25	.25
RA33	PT5	5k blue grn (I)	.35	.20
RA33A	PT5	5k choc (III) ('42)	1.00	.20
RA34	PT5	10k pale grn (I)	.95	.30
a.		Type III	1.25	.30
RA35	PT5	20k black (I)	1.40	.45
RA35A	PT5	50k pur (III) ('46)	5.00	.55
RA35B	PT5	1 l blue (III) ('44)	22.50	2.50
		Nos. RA30-RA35B (9)	31.80	4.80
		Set, never hinged	75.00	

No. RA9 Surcharged in Black

1938 *Perf. 14*

RA36	PT2	20pa on 2½k	.40	.20
RA37	PT2	1k on 2½k	.60	.20

No. RA9 Surcharged in Black

1938 Unwmk. *Perf. 14*

RA37A	PT2	20pa on 2½k	.90	.50
RA37B	PT2	1k on 2½k	1.10	.65

No. RA9 Surcharged "1 Kurus" in Black

1939 *Perf. 14*

RA38	PT2	1k on 2½k dk brn & red	.50	.50

Child — PT6

Nurse with Child — PT7

1940 Typo. *Perf. 12*

Star in Carmine

RA39	PT6	20pa bluish grn	.30	.20
RA40	PT6	1k violet	.30	.20
RA41	PT7	1k lt blue	.30	.20
RA42	PT7	2½k pale red lil	.30	.20
RA43	PT6	3k black	.35	.20
RA44	PT7	5k pale violet	.30	.20
RA45	PT7	10k blue green	1.00	.40
RA46	PT6	15k dark blue	.75	.30
RA47	PT7	25k olive bister	2.50	1.25
RA48	PT7	50k olive gray	6.00	2.50
		Nos. RA39-RA48 (10)	12.10	5.65
		Set, never hinged	30.00	

POSTAL TAX AIR POST STAMPS

Air Fund Issues

These stamps were obligatory on all air mail for 21 days a year. Tax for the Turkish Aviation Society: 20pa for a postcard, 1k for a regular letter, 2 1/2k for a registered letter, 3k for a telegram, 5k-50k for a package, higher values for air freight. Postal tax air post stamps were withdrawn Aug. 21, 1934 and remainders destroyed later that year.

Biplane
PTAP1

Perf. 11, Pin Perf.

1926 Unwmk. Litho.

Type PTAP1

Size: 35x25mm

RAC1	20pa brn & pale grn	2.25	.30
RAC2	1g blue grn & buff	1.25	.30

Size: 40x29mm

RAC3	5g vio & pale grn	5.00	1.00
RAC4	5g car lake & pale grn	25.00	15.00
	Nos. RAC1-RAC4 (4)	33.50	16.60
	Set, never hinged	275.00	

PTAP2

PTAP3

1927-29

Type PTAP2

RAC5	20pa dl red & pale grn	.50	.20
RAC6	1k green & yel	.45	.20

Type PTAP3

Perf. 11½

RAC7	2k dp cl & yel grn	.60	.35
RAC8	2½k red & yel grn	4.50	1.60
RAC9	5k dk bl gray & org	.45	.45
RAC10	10k dk grn & rose	3.75	1.25
RAC11	15k green & yel	3.75	1.00
RAC12	20k ol brn & yel	5.00	2.00
RAC13	50k dk bl & cob bl	8.00	4.50
RAC14	100k car & lt bl	110.00	80.00
	Nos. RAC5-RAC14 (10)	137.00	91.55
	Set, never hinged	825.00	

#RAC1, RAC5, RAC7 and RAC11 Surcharged in Black (RAC15-RAC16, RAC18-RAC19) or Red (Others)

1930-31

RAC15	1k ("Bir kurus") on RAC1	200.00	75.00
RAC16	1k ("Bir Kurus") on RAC5	.75	.50
RAC17	100pa ("Yuz Para") on RAC7	1.00	.75
RAC18	5k ("Bes Kurus") on RAC5	5.00	1.50
RAC19	5k ("5 Kurus") on RAC5	1.00	.75
RAC20	10k ("On kurus") on RAC7	1.50	1.25
RAC21	50k ("Elli kurus") on RAC7	8.00	4.00
RAC22	1 l ("Bir lira") on RAC7	*25.00*	*9.00*
RAC23	5 l ("Bes lira") on RAC11	*2,000.*	*400.00*
	Nos. RAC15-RAC23 (9)	*2,242.*	*492.75*
	Set, never hinged	5,000.	

PTAP4

PTAP5

1931-32 Litho. *Perf. 11½*

RAC24	PTAP4	20pa black	5.00	1.75

Typo.

RAC25	PTAP5	1k brown car ('32)	1.00	.50
RAC26	PTAP5	5k red ('32)	2.00	.75
RAC27	PTAP5	10k green ('32)	3.00	1.50
		Nos. RAC24-RAC27 (4)	11.00	4.50

PTAP6

1933

Type PTAP6

RAC28 10pa ("On Para") grn 3.50 2.00
RAC29 1k ("Bir Kurus") red 8.00 2.75
RAC30 5k ("Bes Kurus") lil 12.00 3.00
Nos. RAC28-RAC30 (3) 23.50 7.75

TURKEY IN ASIA

'tər-kē in 'ā-zhə

(Anatolia)

40 Paras = 1 Piaster

This designation, which includes all of Turkey in Asia Minor, came into existence during the uprising of 1919, led by Mustafa Kemal Pasha. Actually there was no separation of territory, the Sultan's sovereignty being almost immediately reduced to a small area surrounding Constantinople. The formation of the Turkish Republic and the expulsion of the Sultan followed in 1923. Subsequent issues of postage stamps are listed under Turkey (Republic).

Issues of the Nationalist Government

Turkish Stamps of 1913-18 Surcharged in Black or Red

(The Surcharge reads "Angora 3 Piastres")

1920 Unwmk. *Perf. 12*

On Stamps of 1913

1 A24 3pi on 2pa red lilac 2.50 3.50
2 A25 3pi on 4pa dk brn 37.50 *37.50*
3 A27 3pi on 6pa dk bl 250.00 *150.00*

On Stamp of 1916-18

4 A42 3pi on 2pa vio (Bk) 15.00 10.00
Nos. 1-4 (4) 305.00 201.00

Turkish Stamps of 1913-18 Handstamped in Black or Red

(The Surch. reads "Post, Piastre 3")

1921 *Perf. 12*

On Stamps of 1913

5 A24 3pi on 2pa red lilac 25.00 25.00
a. On No. 1 45.00 67.50
b. As #5, surcharge in red 900.00
c. As #5a, surcharge in red 900.00
6 A25 3pi on 4pa dk brown 30.00 30.00
a. On No. 2 150.00 160.00
7 A25 3pi on 4pa dk brn (R) 150.00 175.00
a. On No. 2 150.00 160.00
8 A27 3pi on 6pa dk blue 125.00 150.00
a. On No. 3 275.00 300.00
9 A27 3pi on 6pa dk bl (R) 62.50 75.00
a. On No. 3 100.00 125.00

On Stamps of 1916-18

10 A42 3pi on 2pa vio (R) 62.50 75.00
a. On No. 4 90.00 110.00
Nos. 5-10 (6) 455.00 530.00

Turkish Revenue Stamps Handstamped in Turkish "Osmanli Postalari, 1336" (Ottoman Post, 1920).

Dash at upper left is set high. Bottom (date) line is 8½mm long.

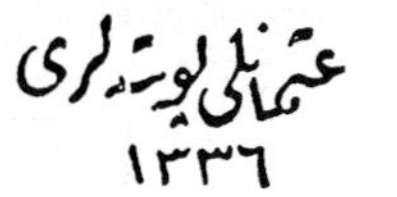

Dash at upper left is set lower. Bottom (date) line is 10mm long.

Dash at upper left is set lower. Bottom (date) line is 9mm long.

Religious Tribunals Revenue — R1

12 R1 1pi grn (a, b, c) 750.00 300.00
13 R1 5pi ultra (a, b) *16,000.* *15,500.*
14 R1 50pi gray grn (a, b, c) 25.00 35.00
Cut cancellation 1.50
15 R1 100pi buff (a) 140.00 90.00
a. 100pi yellow (a) 90.00 67.50
Cut cancellation 7.50
16 R1 500pi org (a) 225.00 150.00
Cut cancellation 19.00
17 R1 1000pibrn (a) 3,000. 1,750.
Cut cancellation 175.00

See Nos. 29-32.

Court Costs Revenue — R2

Black Overprint

18 R2 10pa grn (b, c) 110.00 100.00
19 R2 1pi ultra (a, c) — *15,000.*
20 R2 5pi rose (c) *15,000.* —
21 R2 50pi ocher (a, b, c) 50.00 50.00
a. 50pi yellow (a, b, c) 12.00 16.00
Cut cancellation, #21, 21a 2.00
22 R2 100pi brown (a) 150.00 100.00
Cut cancellation 20.00
23 R2 500pi slate (a) 325.00 325.00
Cut cancellation 20.00

See Nos. 24, 33-39.

Notary Public Revenue R3

Design R2 Overprinted "Katibi Adliye Masus dur" in Red

24 R3 50pi ocher (a) 1,250. 150.00
Cut cancellation 20.00

Laborer's Passport Tax Stamp — R4

Notary Public Revenue — R5

Black Overprint

25 R4 2pi emerald (a, c) — *20,000.*
26 R5 100pi yellow brn (a) 1,250. 150.00
Cut cancellation 20.00

See Nos. 46-48.

Theater Tax Stamp — R6

Land Registry Revenue — R7

27 R6 20pa black *5,000.* *5,000.*
a. 20pa black *grayish* — —
28 R7 2pi blue black *6,250.* *6,250.*

See Nos. 40, 45.

Hejaz Railway Tax Stamp — R8

Perf. 11½

28A R8 2pi dk red & bl (b) 1,750. *1,750.*

Turkish Revenue Stamps Overprinted in Turkish "Osmanli Postalari, 1337" (Ottoman Post, 1921)

On #29-63

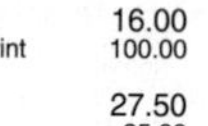

Perf. 12

29 R1 10pa slate 16.00 *13.50*
a. Handstamped overprint 100.00 *50.00*
b. Double overprint
30 R1 1pi green 27.50 18.00
a. Inverted overprint 35.00 22.50
b. Handstamped overprint *3,250.* *3,250.*
31 R1 5pi ultra 27.50 13.50
a. "1337" inverted 100.00 90.00
b. Half used as 2½pi on cover
c. Handstamped overprint 875.00 875.00
Nos. 29-31 (3) 71.00 45.00

Handstamped Overprint

32 R1 50pi green *6,250.* *6,250.*

Design R2 Overprinted

33 R2 10pa green 22.50 22.50
a. Handstamped overprint 3,500. *3,500.*
34 R2 1pi ultra 45.00 22.50
a. Handstamped overprint 875.00 875.00
35 R2 5pi red 22.50 22.50
a. Inverted overprint
b. "1337" inverted *100.00* 100.00
c. Half used as 2½pi on cover
d. Handstamped overprint 6,750 *6,750.*
e. 5pi rose 67.50 22.50
f. As "e," handstamped overprint *5,000.* *5,000.*
36 R2 50pi ocher, handtamped ovpt. 500.00 100.00
Cut cancellation 10.00
Nos. 33-36 (4) 590.00 167.50

Design R3 Overprinted

Additional Turkish Overprint in Red or Black

37 R3 10pa green (R) *90.00* 57.50
38 R3 1pi ultra (R) 67.50 45.00
39 R3 5pi rose (Bk) 67.50 45.00
a. "1337" inverted *200.00* *200.00*
b. Handstamped overprint *6,250.* *6,250.*
c. 5pi carmine 90.00 57.50
d. As "c," handstamped overprint *7,750.*
Nos. 37-39 (3) 225.00 147.50

Design R7 Overprinted

40 R7 2pi blue black 110.00 100.00
a. Handstamped overprint *5,000.* *5,000.*

R12

1921 *Perf. 12*

Overprinted in Black

41 R12 5pi green 150.00 125.00
Cut cancellation 15.00
a. Handstamped overprint *5,000.* *5,000.*

Museum Tax Stamp R13

Overprinted in Black

42 R13 1pi ultra 400.00 400.00
a. Handstamped overprint *5,000.* *5,000.*
43 R13 5pi deep green 450.00 450.00
a. Handstamped overprint *5,000.* *5,000.*

Handstamped Overprint

44 R13 5pi dark vio *6,250.* *6,250.*

The overprint variety "337" for "1337" exists on Nos. 42-43.

Design R6 Overprinted

Perf. 12, 12½

45 R6 20pa black 12.50 4.25
a. Date 4½mm high 15.00
b. "337" for "1337" 25.00
c. Silk paper 500.00 500.00
d. White paper 12.50 6.75

Design R5 Overprinted

46 R5 10pa green 25.00 25.00
a. Overprint 21mm long
b. "131" for "1337"
47 R5 1pi ultra 37.50 25.00
a. "13" for "1337" *50.00* *50.00*
b. "131" for "1337" *50.00* *50.00*
c. Inverted overprint *90.00* *90.00*
d. Handstamped overprint *4,000.* *4,000.*

48	R5 5pi red	62.50	25.00
a.	Inverted overprint	*90.00*	*90.00*
b.	"131" for "1337"	*85.00*	*85.00*
c.	Handstamped overprint	*4,000.*	*4,000.*
d.	5pi pink	425.00	275.00
e.	As "d," handstamped overprint	*5,000.*	*5,000.*
	Nos. 46-48 (3)	125.00	75.00

R16

Perf. 11½, 11½x11

Overprinted in Black

49	R16 10pa pink	4.00	1.50
a.	Imperf.		
b.	Date "1237"	5.00	2.00
d.	Inverted overprint		
e.	Handstamped overprint	*1,750.*	*1,750.*
50	R16 1pi yellow	10.00	5.00
a.	Overprint 18mm long	10.00	5.00
b.	Date "1332"	12.00	
c.	Date "1317"		
d.	Inverted overprint		
e.	Handstamped overprint	*1,750.*	*1,750.*
51	R16 2pi yellow grn	12.50	5.00
a.	Date "1237"	15.00	
b.	Date "1317"		
c.	Imperf.		
d.	Inverted overprint	40.00	9.00
e.	Handstamped overprint	—	—
52	R16 5pi red	20.00	1.00
a.	Horiz. pair, imperf. vert.		
b.	Inverted overprint	25.00	7.50
c.	Double overprint	30.00	12.50
d.	Date "1332"	45.00	
e.	Half used as 2½pi on cover		
f.	Overprint 18mm long	20.00	7.50
g.	Handstamped overprint	*1,750.*	*1,750.*
	Nos. 49-52 (4)	46.50	12.50

Design R8 Overprinted TURKISH INSCRIPTIONS:

20 Paras

1 Piaster

2 Piasters

5 Piasters

1921 ***Perf. 11½***

Dark Red & Blue

53	R8 20pa on 1pi	75.00	75.00
54	R8 1pi on 1pi	4.00	3.00
55	R8 2pi on 1pi	4.00	3.00
a.	Inverted surcharge		
56	R8 5pi on 1pi	6.00	5.00
	Nos. 53-56 (4)	89.00	86.00

See No. 57.

No. 54 Overprinted

57	R8 1pi on 1pi dk red & bl	45.00	45.00

Hejaz Railway Tax Stamp — R19

Overprinted in Black

58	R19 1pi grn & brn red	4.00	3.00
a.	Double overprint		
b.	Handstamped overprint		

The errors "1307," "1331" and "2337" occur once in each sheet of Nos. 53-58.

Naval League Labels — R20

1921 ***Perf. 12x11½***

Overprinted in Black

59	R20 1pa orange	10.00	15.00
a.	Date "1327"	15.00	3.50
60	R20 2pa indigo	10.00	15.00
61	R20 5pa green	12.50	17.50
62	R20 10pa brown	25.00	30.00
63	R20 40pa red brown	175.00	190.00
	Nos. 59-63 (5)	232.50	267.50

The error "2337" occurs on all values of this issue.

The Naval League stamps have pictures of three Turkish warships. They were sold for the benefit of sailors of the fleet but did not pay postage until they were overprinted in 1921.

Turkish Stamps of 1915-20 Overprinted

a

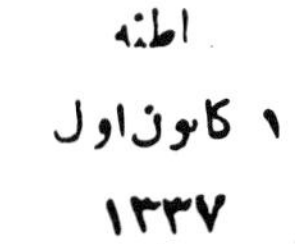
b

The overprints on Nos. 64-77 read "Adana December 1st, 1921." This issue commemorated the withdrawal of the French from Cilicia.

On No. 71 the lines of the overprint are further apart than on Nos. 68-70 and 73-74.

1921 ***Perf. 12***

64	A44 (a) 10pa grn (424)	6.00	6.00
65	A45 (a) 20pa deep rose (425)	6.00	6.00
a.	Inverted overprint	17.00	
66	A51 (a) 25pi car, *straw* (434)	15.00	20.00
a.	Double overprint		
b.	Inverted overprint	37.50	37.50
	Nos. 64-66 (3)	27.00	32.00

On Newspaper Stamp of 1915

67	A21 (a) 5pa och (P132)	90.00	150.00

On Stamp of 1915

68	A22 (b) 5pa och (328)	350.00	400.00

On Stamps of 1917-18

69	A53 (b) 5pi on 2pa (547)	12.50	15.00
70	A53 (b) 5pi on 2pa (548)	12.50	15.00

On Stamp of 1919

71	A57 (b) 35pi on 1pi bl (Bk; 579)	40.00	45.00
a.	Inverted surcharge		

On Newspaper Stamp of 1915

72	A21 (b) 5pa och (P132)	*200.00*	*200.00*

On No. 72 the overprint is vertical, half reading up and half reading down.

On Stamps of 1920

73	A32 (b) 3pi blue (594)	10.00	10.00
74	A36 (b) 10pi gray vio (596)	12.50	15.00

On Postage Due Stamps of 1914

75	D1 (a) 5pa claret (J63)	350.00	350.00
76	D2 (a) 20pa red (J64)	350.00	400.00
a.	Inverted overprint		
77	D3 (b) 1pi dk bl (J65)	350.00	400.00
a.	Inverted overprint	*750.00*	*750.00*
	Nos. 75-77 (3)	1,050.	1,150.

Withdrawal of the French from Cilicia. Forged overprints exist.

Pact of Revenge, Burning Village at Top — A21

Izmir Harbor — A22

Mosque of Selim, Adrianople A23

Mosque of Selim, Konya — A24

Soldier — A25

Legendary Gray Wolf — A26

Snake Castle and Seyhan River, Adana — A27

Parliament Building at Sivas — A28

A29

Mosque at Urfa — A30

Map of Anatolia — A31

Declaration of Faith from the Koran — A32

1922 **Litho.** ***Perf. 11½***

78	A21 10pa violet brn	1.00	.25
	Never hinged	2.25	
79	A22 20pa blue grn	1.00	.25
	Never hinged	2.25	
80	A23 1pi dp blue	1.00	.25
	Never hinged	2.25	
81	A24 2pi red brown	3.00	.50
	Never hinged	13.50	
82	A25 5pi dk blue	3.00	.50
	Never hinged	13.50	
83	A26 10pi dk brown	12.50	.75
	Never hinged	45.00	
a.	Vert. pair, imperf between	*100.00*	
b.	Vert. strip of 3, imperf between	*300.00*	
84	A27 25pi rose	15.00	1.00
	Never hinged	67.50	
85	A28 50pi indigo	1.00	15.00
	Never hinged	4.50	
86	A29 50pi dk gray	1.00	1.25
	Never hinged	4.50	
87	A30 100pi violet	75.00	5.00
	Never hinged	350.00	
	Cut cancellation		1.25
88	A31 200pi slate	200.00	62.50
	Never hinged	950.00	
	Cut cancellation		1.50
89	A32 500pi green	125.00	27.50
	Never hinged	500.00	
	Cut cancellation		3.00
	Nos. 78-89 (12)	438.50	114.75
	Set, ovptd. "SPECIMEN"	650.00	

Imperf

79a	A22 20pa	25.00	*30.00*
80a	A23 1pi	15.00	*20.00*
82a	A25 5pi	15.00	*20.00*
84a	A27 25pi	35.00	*30.00*
85a	A28 50pi	27.50	*30.00*

Stamps of Type A23 Overprinted

1922

90	A23 1pi deep blue	7.00	15.00
	Never hinged	13.50	
91	A23 5pi deep blue	7.00	20.00
	Never hinged	13.50	
92	A23 10pi brown	7.00	20.00
	Never hinged	13.50	
93	A23 25pi rose	10.00	25.00
	Never hinged	13.50	
94	A23 50pi slate	12.50	25.00
	Never hinged	22.50	
95	A23 100pi violet	17.50	37.50
	Never hinged	32.50	
96	A23 200pi black vio	17.50	50.00
	Never hinged	32.50	
97	A23 500pi blue green	25.00	75.00
	Never hinged	47.50	
	Nos. 90-97 (8)	103.50	

Withdrawal of the French from Cilicia and the return of the Kemalist Natl. army. The overprint reads: "Adana, Jan. 5, 1922."

No. 90-97 without overprint were presented to some high government officials.

First Parliament House, Ankara — A33

1922 **Litho.**

98	A33 5pa violet	.50	2.50
	Never hinged	1.75	
99	A33 10pa green	1.00	2.50
	Never hinged	3.50	
100	A33 20pa pale red	1.50	2.00
	Never hinged	5.50	

101	A33	1pi brown org		10.00	1.50
		Never hinged		36.00	
102	A33	2pi red brown		20.00	4.25
		Never hinged		72.50	
103	A33	3pi rose		2.50	.50
		Never hinged		9.00	
a.		Arabic "13" in right corner		10.00	7.50
b.		Thin grayish paper		55.00	7.50
		Never hinged		200.00	
		Nos. 98-103 (6)		35.50	13.25

Nos. 98-103, 103b exist imperf. In 1923 several stamps of Turkey and Turkey in Asia were overprinted in Turkish for advertising purposes. The overprint reads: "Izmir Economic Congress, 17 Feb., 1339."

POSTAGE DUE STAMPS

D1

1922 Litho. *Perf. 11½*

J1	D1	20pa dull green	.50	5.00
		Never hinged	2.25	
a.		Imperf.		—
J2	D1	1pi gray green	.50	5.00
		Never hinged	2.25	
J3	D1	2pi red brown	1.50	17.50
		Never hinged	6.75	
J4	D1	3pi rose	3.50	25.00
		Never hinged	16.00	
J5	D1	5pi dark blue	4.50	55.00
		Never hinged	22.50	
		Nos. J1-J5 (5)	10.50	
		Set, ovptd. "SPECIMEN"	175.00	

TURKS AND CAICOS ISLANDS

'tərks ən‚d‚ ' kā-kəs 'ī-ləndz

LOCATION — A group of islands in the West Indies, at the southern extremity of the Bahamas
GOVT. — British colony; a dependency of Jamaica until 1959
AREA — 192 sq. mi.
POP. — 7,436 (1980)
CAPITAL — Grand Turk

12 Pence = 1 Shilling
20 Shillings = 1 Pound

Catalogue values for unused stamps in this country are for Never Hinged items, beginning with Scott 90.

Dependency's Badge
A6 A7

1900-04 Engr. Wmk. 2 *Perf. 14*

1	A6	½p green	3.00	*4.50*
2	A6	1p rose	4.00	.85
3	A6	2p black brown	1.10	*1.40*
4	A6	2½p gray blue ('04)	2.00	1.10
a.		2½p blue ('00)	8.50	*17.50*
5	A6	4p orange	4.25	*8.00*
6	A6	6p violet	2.75	*7.50*
7	A6	1sh purple brn	3.75	*20.00*

Wmk. 1

8	A7	2sh violet	45.00	*67.50*
9	A7	3sh brown lake	62.50	*85.00*
		Nos. 1-9 (9)	128.35	*195.85*

1905-08 Wmk. 3

10	A6	½p green	5.75	.20
11	A6	1p carmine	18.00	.55
12	A6	3p violet, *yel* ('08)	2.50	*7.00*
		Nos. 10-12 (3)	26.25	*7.75*

King Edward VII — A8

1909, Sept. 2 *Perf. 14*

13	A8	½p yellow green	.85	.45
14	A8	1p carmine	1.40	.45
15	A8	2p gray	3.50	1.60
16	A8	2½p ultra	4.25	4.25
17	A8	3p violet, *yel*	2.75	2.75
18	A8	4p red, *yel*	3.75	*8.00*
19	A8	6p violet	8.00	7.00
20	A8	1sh black, *green*	8.00	*9.50*
21	A8	2sh red, *grn*	40.00	*55.00*
22	A8	3sh black, *red*	40.00	*45.00*
		Nos. 13-22 (10)	112.50	*134.00*

Turk's-Head Cactus
A9

George V
A10

1910-11 Wmk. 3

23	A9	¼p claret	2.00	1.10
24	A9	¼p red ('11)	.70	.50

See Nos. 36, 44.

1913-16

25	A10	½p yellow green	.55	*2.00*
26	A10	1p carmine	1.10	*2.50*
27	A10	2p gray	2.50	*4.00*
28	A10	2½p ultra	2.50	*3.50*
29	A10	3p violet, *yel*	2.50	*12.50*
30	A10	4p scarlet, *yel*	1.10	*11.00*
31	A10	5p olive grn ('16)	7.50	*25.00*
32	A10	6p dull violet	2.75	*4.00*
33	A10	1sh orange	1.75	*5.75*
34	A10	2sh red, *bl grn*	8.50	*30.00*
a.		2sh red, *grnsh white* ('19)	30.00	*80.00*
b.		2sh red, *emerald* ('21)	55.00	*80.00*
35	A10	3sh black, *red*	17.50	30.00
		Nos. 25-35 (11)	48.25	130.25

Issued: 5p, 5/18/16; others, 4/1/13.
For overprints see Nos. MR1-MR13.

1921, Apr. 23 Wmk. 4

36	A9	¼p red	2.75	*17.50*
37	A10	½p green	3.00	*6.25*
38	A10	1p scarlet	1.10	*6.25*
39	A10	2p gray	1.10	*21.00*
40	A10	2½p ultra	2.00	*8.50*
41	A10	5p olive green	9.00	*57.50*
42	A10	6p dull violet	7.50	*57.50*
43	A10	1sh brown orange	7.50	*32.50*
		Nos. 36-43 (8)	33.95	*207.00*

A11

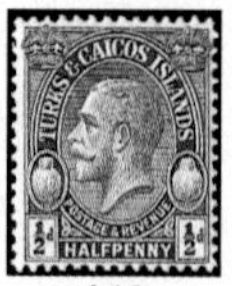
A12

Inscribed "Postage"

1922-26

44	A9	¼p gray black ('26)	.90	*1.10*
45	A11	½p green	2.50	*3.75*
46	A11	1p brown	.55	*3.75*
47	A11	1½p rose red ('25)	7.50	*18.00*
48	A11	2p gray	.55	*5.75*
49	A11	2½p violet, *yel*	.55	*2.00*
50	A11	3p ultra	.55	*5.75*
51	A11	4p red, *yel*	1.40	*18.00*
52	A11	5p yellow grn	1.00	*25.00*
53	A11	6p dull violet	.80	*7.00*
54	A11	1sh orange	.90	*21.00*
55	A11	2sh red, *green*	2.25	*10.50*

Wmk. 3

56	A11	2sh red, *green* ('25)	29.00	*80.00*
57	A11	3sh black, *red* ('25)	5.75	*32.50*
		Nos. 44-57 (14)	54.20	*234.10*

Issued: #47, 56-57, 11/24; #44, 10/11; others, 11/20.

Inscribed "Postage and Revenue"

1928, Mar. 1 Wmk. 4

60	A12	½p green	.85	.55
61	A12	1p brown	.85	.80
62	A12	1½p red	.85	*3.75*
63	A12	2p dk gray	.85	.55
64	A12	2½p vio, *yel*	.85	*5.75*
65	A12	3p ultra	.85	*8.00*
66	A12	6p brown vio	.85	*8.50*
67	A12	1sh brown org	4.25	*8.50*
68	A12	2sh red, *grn*	7.00	*40.00*
69	A12	5sh green, *yel*	12.50	*40.00*
70	A12	10sh violet, *bl*	57.50	*110.00*
		Nos. 60-70 (11)	87.20	*226.40*

Common Design Types pictured following the introduction.

Silver Jubilee Issue
Common Design Type

1935, May 6 *Perf. 11x12*

71	CD301	½p green & blk	.35	.50
72	CD301	3p ultra & brn	1.75	3.25
73	CD301	6p ol grn & lt bl	1.75	3.75
74	CD301	1sh brn vio & ind	3.50	2.50
		Nos. 71-74 (4)	7.35	10.00
		Set, never hinged	12.00	

Coronation Issue
Common Design Type

1937, May 12 *Perf. 13½x14*

75	CD302	½p deep green	.20	.20
76	CD302	2p gray	.30	.25
77	CD302	3p brt ultra	.40	.25
		Nos. 75-77 (3)	.90	.70
		Set, never hinged	1.25	

Raking Salt — A13

Salt Industry — A14

1938-45 Wmk. 4 *Perf. 12½*

78	A13	¼p black	.20	.20
79	A13	½p green	1.90	.20
80	A13	1p brown	.35	.20
81	A13	1½p carmine	.35	.20
82	A13	2p gray	.55	.25
83	A13	2½p orange	2.00	.90
84	A13	3p ultra	.25	.25
85	A13	6p rose violet	4.75	1.40
85A	A13	6p blk brn ('45)	.20	.20
86	A13	1sh bister	1.90	*8.00*
86A	A13	1sh dk ol grn ('45)	.20	.20
87	A14	2sh rose car	20.00	13.50
88	A14	5sh green	24.00	15.00
89	A14	10sh dp violet	6.00	*6.75*
		Nos. 78-89 (14)	62.65	47.25
		Set, never hinged	90.00	

Catalogue values for unused stamps in this section, from this point to the end of the section, are for Never Hinged items.

Peace Issue
Common Design Type

1946, Nov. 4 Engr. *Perf. 13½x14*

90	CD303	2p gray black	.20	.20
91	CD303	3p deep blue	.25	.20

Silver Wedding Issue
Common Design Types

1948, Sept. 13 Photo. *Perf. 14x14½*

92	CD304	1p red brown	.20	.25

Perf. 11½x11

Engr.; Name Typo.

93	CD305	10sh purple	8.50	*13.00*

Dependency's Badge — A17

Flag and Merchant Ship — A18

Map of the Islands A19

Victoria and George VI A20

1948, Dec. 14 Engr. *Perf. 12½*

94	A17	½p green	.20	.20
95	A17	2p carmine	.25	.20
96	A18	3p deep blue	.40	.40
97	A19	6p violet	.50	.45
98	A20	2sh ultra & blk	.75	*.75*
99	A20	5sh blue grn & blk	2.25	2.00
100	A20	10sh chocolate & blk	3.50	*5.00*
		Nos. 94-100 (7)	7.85	*9.00*

Cent. of political separation from the Bahamas.

UPU Issue
Common Design Types
Engr.; Name Typo. on 3p, 6p
Perf. 13½, 11x11½

1949, Oct. 10 Wmk. 4

101	CD306	2½p red orange	.20	.20
102	CD307	3p indigo	1.40	1.40
103	CD308	6p chocolate	.55	.55
104	CD309	1sh olive	.55	.55
		Nos. 101-104 (4)	2.70	2.70

Loading Bulk Salt — A21

Dependency's Badge — A22

Designs: 1p, Salt Cay. 1½p, Caicos mail. 2p, Grand Turk. 2½p, Sponge diving. 3p, South Creek. 4p, Map. 6p, Grand Turk Light. 1sh, Government House. 1sh6p, Cockburn Harbor. 2sh, Government offices. 5sh, Salt Loading.

1950, Aug. 2 Engr. *Perf. 12½*

105	A21	½p deep green	.70	.50
106	A21	1p chocolate	.60	*1.00*
107	A21	1½p carmine	1.00	.75
108	A21	2p red orange	.50	*.50*
109	A21	2½p olive green	.90	.65
110	A21	3p ultra	.25	*.40*
111	A21	4p rose car & blk	3.00	.95
112	A21	6p ultra & blk	2.25	.65
113	A21	1sh bl gray & blk	1.00	.50
114	A21	1sh6p red & blk	9.00	4.50
115	A21	2sh ultra & emer	3.25	*4.75*
116	A21	5sh black & ultra	20.00	9.50
117	A22	10sh purple & blk	20.00	*22.50*
		Nos. 105-117 (13)	62.45	*47.15*

WAR TAX STAMPS

Regular Issue of 1913-16 Overprinted

1917 Wmk. 3 *Perf. 14*

Black Overprint at Bottom of Stamp

MR1 A10 1p carmine .20 *1.75*
a. Double overprint 200.00 *275.00*
b. "TAX" omitted
c. Pair, one without ovpt.
MR2 A10 3p violet, *yel* 1.40 *5.75*
a. Double overprint 110.00

Black Overprint at Top or Middle of Stamp

1917

MR3 A10 1p carmine .20 *1.40*
a. Inverted overprint 55.00
b. Double overprint 50.00 *62.50*
c. Pair, one without overprint 625.00
MR4 A10 3p violet, *yel* .70 *2.00*
a. Double overprint 50.00
b. Dbl. ovpt., one inverted 375.00

Same Overprint in Violet or Red

1918-19

MR5 A10 1p car (V) ('19) .20 *1.10*
a. Double overprint 24.00
b. "WAR" omitted 175.00
MR6 A10 3p violet, *yel* (R) 11.00 *30.00*
a. Double overprint 375.00

Regular Issue of 1913-16 Overprinted in Black

1918

MR7 A10 1p carmine .20 *1.40*
MR8 A10 3p violet, *yel* 2.75 *4.25*

Same Overprint in Red

1919

MR9 A10 3p violet, *yel* .20 *2.75*

Regular Issue of 1913-16 Overprinted in Black

MR10 A10 1p carmine .20 *1.10*
a. Double overprint 160.00 *190.00*
MR11 A10 3p violet, *yel* .35 *3.00*

Regular Issue of 1913-16 Overprinted

MR12 A10 1p carmine .20 2.75
a. Double overprint *100.00*
MR13 A10 3p violet, *yel* .55 3.00

TURKS ISLANDS

'tərks 'ī-ləndz

LOCATION — West Indies, at the southern extremity of the Bahamas
AREA — 616 sq. mi.
POP. — 2,000 (approx.)
CAPITAL — Grand Turk

In 1848 the Turks Islands together with the Caicos group, lying to the northwest, were made a British colony. In 1873 the Colony became a dependency under the government of Jamaica although separate stamp issues were continued. Postage stamps inscribed Turks and Caicos Islands have been used since 1900.

12 Pence = 1 Shilling

PRE-STAMP POSTAL MARKINGS

Crowned Circle handstamp type V is pictured in the Crowned Circle Handstamps and Great Britain Used Abroad section.

Grand Turk

1857

A1 V "Turks Islands" crowned circle handstamp, on cover 6,250.

Values for unused stamps are for examples with original gum as defined in the catalogue introduction. Very fine examples of Nos. 1-42 will have generally rough perforations that cut into the design on one or more sides due to the narrow spacing of the stamps on the plates and imperfect perforating methods. Stamps with perfs clear of the design on all four sides are extremely scarce and will command substantially higher prices.

Because of the printing and imperfect perforating methods, stamps are often found scissor separated. Prices will not be adversely affected on those stamps where the scissor cut does not remove the perforations.

Watermark

Wmk. 5 — Small Star

Queen Victoria — A1

Perf. 11½ to 13

1867 Unwmk. Engr.

1 A1 1p rose 62.50 62.50
2 A1 6p gray black 110.00 *140.00*
3 A1 1sh slate blue 105.00 67.50
Nos. 1-3 (3) 277.50 270.00

Perf. 11 to 13x14 to 15

1873-79 Wmk. 5

4 A1 1p lake 57.50 57.50
5 A1 1p dull red ('79) 62.50 67.50
a. Horiz. pair, imperf. btwn. *19,000.*
b. Perf. 11-12 *1,100.*
6 A1 1sh violet *5,750. 2,250.*

Stamps offered as No. 6 are often copies from which the surcharge has been removed.

Stamps of 1867-79 Surcharged in Black:

a

b

c

d

e

12 settings of the ½p, 9 of 2½p, and 6 of 4p.

1881 Unwmk. *Perf. 11 to 13*

7 (a) ½p on 6p gray blk 85.00 *140.00*
7A (b) ½p on 6p gray blk 80.00 *120.00*
8 (b) ½p on 1sh slate bl 110.00 *180.00*
a. Double surcharge *5,750.*
8B (c) ½p on 1sh slate bl *11,000.*
c. Without fraction bar

Perf. 11 to 13x14 to 15

Wmk. 5

9 (a) ½p on 1p dull red 150.00 200.00
a. Double surcharge
10 (b) ½p on 1p dull red 55.00 *90.00*
11 (c) ½p on 1p dull red 210.00 *275.00*
a. Double surcharge *4,250.*
12 (d) ½p on 1p dull red 260.00
a. Without fraction bar 1,150.
b. Double surcharge
13 (e) ½p on 1p dull red 600.00
14 (a) ½p on 1sh violet 175.00 225.00
a. Double surcharge 4,000.
15 (b) ½p on 1sh violet 140.00 *225.00*
a. Without fraction bar 625.00
16 (c) ½p on 1sh violet 105.00 *190.00*

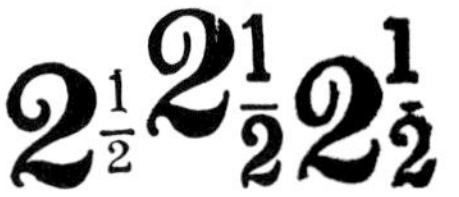

f g h

Perf. 11 to 13

Unwmk.

17 (f) 2½p on 6p gray blk *9,500.*
18 (g) 2½p on 6p gray blk 375.00 *450.00*
a. Horiz. pair, imperf. between *19,000.*
b. Double surcharge *9,500.*
19 (h) 2½p on 6p gray blk 175.00 *325.00*
a. Double surcharge *9,500.*

i

j

Perf. 11 to 13x14 to 15

Wmk. 5

20 (i) 2½p on 1sh violet *2,600.*
21 (h) 2½p on 1sh violet 625.00 *950.00*
22 (j) 2½p on 1sh violet *9,500.*

k

l

m

n

Perf. 11 to 13

Unwmk.

24 (k) 2½p on 6p gray blk *8,500.*
25 (k) 2½p on 1sh slate bl *15,000.*
26 (l) 2½p on 1sh slate bl 850.00
27 (m) 2½p on 1sh slate bl *2,200.*
a. Without fraction bar *8,000.*
28 (n) 2½p on 1sh slate bl *6,500.*

o

Perf. 11 to 13x14 to 15

Wmk. 5

29 (l) 2½p on 1p dull red 600.00
30 (o) 2½p on 1p dull red 1,350.
31 (l) 2½p on 1sh violet 850.00
a. Double surcharge of "½" *4,000.*
32 (o) 2½p on 1sh violet 1,350.
b. Double surcharge of "½" *5,750.*

p

q

r

Perf. 11 to 13

Unwmk.

33 (p) 4p on 6p gray black 85.00 120.00
34 (q) 4p on 6p gray black 375.00 *475.00*
35 (r) 4p on 6p gray black 475.00 *350.00*

Copies of No. 33 with top of "4" painted in are sometimes offered as No. 35.

Perf. 11 to 13x14 to 15

Wmk. 5

36 (r) 4p on 1p dull red 950.00 625.00
a. Inverted surcharge 3,250.
37 (p) 4p on 1p dull red 850.00 550.00
a. Inverted surcharge
38 (p) 4p on 1sh violet 450.00 *625.00*
39 (q) 4p on 1sh violet *2,750.*

Wmk. Crown and C C (1)

1881 Engr. *Perf. 14*

40 A1 1p brown red 67.50 95.00
a. Diagonal half used as ½p on cover
41 A1 6p olive brown 110.00 170.00
42 A1 1sh slate green 170.00 140.00
Nos. 40-42 (3) 347.50 405.00

A2

A3

1881 Typo.

43 A2 4p ultramarine 140.00 67.50

1882-95 Engr. Wmk. 2

44 A1 1p orange brn ('83) 77.50 35.00
a. Half used as ½p on cover 4,750.
45 A1 1p car lake ('89) 1.75 *2.25*
46 A1 6p yellow brn ('89) 2.25 3.00
47 A1 1sh black brn ('87) 3.50 3.00
a. 1sh deep brown 3.50 3.00

Typo.

Die A

48 A2 ½p dull green ('85) 2.50 4.00
a. ½p blue green ('82) 10.50 25.00
49 A2 2½p red brown ('82) 21.00 15.00
50 A2 4p gray ('84) 20.00 2.75
a. Half used as 2p on cover 4,750.

Die B

51 A2 ½p gray green ('94) 2.75 2.00
52 A2 2½p ultra ('93) 2.75 2.75
53 A2 4p dk vio & bl ('95) 11.00 15.00

For explanation of dies A and B see back of this volume.

1887 Engr. *Perf. 12*

54 A1 1p carmine lake 14.00 3.25

No. 49 Surcharged in Black

1889

55 A2 1p on 2½p red brn 10.00 *11.00*
a. Double surcharge
b. Double surcharge, one inverted
c. "One" omitted 1,800.
d. Half used as ½p on cover 5,500.

No. 55c caused by the misplacement of the surcharge. Stamps also exist from the same sheet reading "Penny One."

No. 50 Surcharged in Black

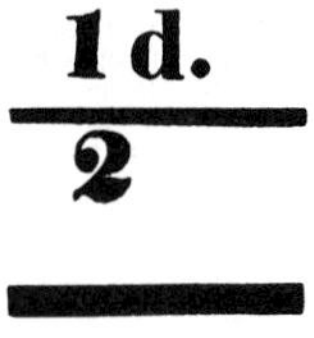

Two types of surcharge:
Type I — Upper bar continuous across sheet.

Type II — Upper bar breaks between stamps.

1893

56 A2 ½p on 4p gray (I) 160.00 150.00
a. Type II 2,600. 1,150.

This surcharge exists in five settings.

1894 **Typo.**

57 A3 5p olive grn & carmine 6.00 *16.50*
a. Diag. half used as 2½p on cover *4,250.*

UBANGI-SHARI

ü-'baŋ-gē 'shär-ē

(Ubangi-Shari-Chad)

LOCATION — In Western Africa, north of the equator
GOVT. — French Colony
AREA — 238,767 sq. mi.
POP. — 833,916
CAPITAL — Bangui

In 1910 French Congo was divided into the three colonies of Gabon, Middle Congo and Ubangi-Shari and officially named "French Equatorial Africa." Under that name in 1934 the group, with the territory of Chad included, became a single administrative unit. See Gabon.

100 Centimes = 1 Franc

Stamps of Middle Congo Overprinted in Black

1915-22 **Unwmk.** ***Perf. 14x13½***
Chalky Paper

1 A1 1c ol gray & brn .25 .25
a. Double overprint 160.00
b. Imperf. 47.50
2 A1 2c violet & brn .25 .25
3 A1 4c blue & brn .45 .45
4 A1 5c dk grn & bl .45 .45
5 A1 5c yel & bl ('22) .75 .75
6 A1 10c carmine & bl .85 .85
7 A1 10c dp grn & bl grn ('22) .80 .80
8 A1 15c brn vio & rose 1.25 1.25
9 A1 20c brown & blue 3.00 3.00

No. 8 is on ordinary paper.

Overprinted

10 A2 25c blue & grn 1.40 1.40
11 A2 25c bl grn & gray ('22) 1.00 1.00
12 A2 30c scarlet & grn 1.10 1.10
13 A2 30c dp rose & rose ('22) 1.00 1.00
14 A2 35c vio brn & bl 4.00 4.00
15 A2 40c dl grn & brn 5.25 5.25
16 A2 45c vio & red 5.25 5.25
17 A2 50c bl grn & red 5.00 5.00
18 A2 50c blue & grn ('22) .90 .90
19 A2 75c brown & bl 11.00 11.00
20 A3 1fr dp grn & vio 11.00 11.00
21 A3 2fr vio & gray grn 12.50 12.50
22 A3 5fr blue & rose 32.50 32.50
Nos. 1-22 (22) 99.95 99.95

For surcharges see Nos. B1-B2.

Types of Middle Congo, 1907-22, Overprinted in Black or Red

1922

23 A1 1c violet & grn .45 .45
a. Overprint omitted 150.00
b. Imperf. 30.00
24 A1 2c grn & salmon .60 .60
25 A1 4c ol brn & brn .85 .85
a. Overprint omitted 175.00
26 A1 5c indigo & rose .85 .65
27 A1 10c dp grn & gray grn 1.40 1.40
28 A1 15c lt red & dl bl 1.50 1.50
29 A1 20c choc & salmon 4.50 4.50

Overprinted

30 A2 25c vio & salmon 6.50 6.50
31 A2 30c rose & pale rose 2.40 2.40
32 A2 35c vio & grn 4.00 4.00
33 A2 40c ind & vio (R) 4.00 4.00
34 A2 45c choc & vio 4.00 4.00
35 A2 50c dk bl & pale bl 2.40 2.40
36 A2 60c on 75c vio, *pnksh* 3.00 3.00
37 A2 75c choc & sal 4.75 4.75
38 A3 1fr grn & dl bl (R) 7.50 7.50
a. Overprint omitted
39 A3 2fr grn & salmon 9.75 9.75
40 A3 5fr grn & ol brn 16.50 16.50
Nos. 23-40 (18) 74.95 74.75

Stamps of 1922 Issue with Additional Overprint in Black, Blue or Red

1924-33

41 A1 1c vio & grn (Bl) .25 .25
a. "OUBANGUI CHARI" omitted 100.00
42 A1 2c grn & sal (Bl) .25 .25
a. "OUBANGUI CHARI" omitted 125.00
b. Double overprint 115.00
43 A1 4c ol brn & brn (Bl) .35 .35
a. Double overprint (Bl + Bk) 150.00
b. "OUBANGUI CHARI" omitted 180.00
44 A1 5c ind & rose .35 .35
a. "OUBANGUI CHARI" omitted 100.00
45 A1 10c dp grn & gray grn .45 .45
46 A1 10c red org & bl ('25) .65 .65
47 A1 15c sal & dl bl .75 .75
48 A1 15c sal & dl bl (Bl) ('26) .55 .55
49 A1 20c choc & salmon (Bl) .85 .85

On Nos. 41-49 the color in ( ) refers to the overprint "Afrique Equatoriale Francaise."

50 A2 25c vio & salmon (Bl) .60 .60
a. Imperf.
51 A2 30c rose & pale rose (Bl) .30 .30
52 A2 30c choc & red ('25) .60 .60
a. "OUBANGUI CHARI" omitted 115.00
53 A2 30c dk grn & grn ('27) 1.00 1.00
54 A2 35c vio & grn (Bl) .60 .60
a. "OUBANGUI CHARI" omitted
55 A2 40c ind & vio (Bl) .60 .60
56 A2 45c choc & vio (Bl) .75 .75
57 A2 50c dk bl & pale bl (R) .40 .40
58 A2 50c gray & bl vio ('25) (R) 1.10 1.10
59 A2 60c on 75c dk vio, *pnksh* (R) .40 .40
60 A2 65c org brn & bl ('28) 1.25 1.25
61 A2 75c choc & sal (Bl) 1.40 1.40
62 A2 75c dp bl & lt bl ('25) (R) .90 .90
a. "OUBANGUI CHARI" omitted 115.00
63 A2 75c rose & dk brn ('28) 2.00 2.00
64 A2 90c brn red & pink ('30) 4.00 4.00
65 A3 1fr grn & ind (Bk + Bl) .60 .60
66 A3 1fr grn & ind (R + Bl) 1.10 1.10
67 A3 1.10fr bister & bl ('28) 2.00 2.00
68 A3 1.25fr mag & lt grn ('33) 7.50 7.50
69 A3 1.50fr ultra & bl ('30) 5.50 5.50
70 A3 1.75fr dk brn & dp buff ('33) 9.25 9.25
71 A3 2fr grn & red 1.10 1.10
a. "OUBANGUI CHARI" omitted 950.00 750.00
72 A3 3fr red vio ('30) 4.75 4.75
73 A3 5fr grn & ol brn (Bl) 3.50 3.50
Nos. 41-73 (33) 55.65 55.65

On Nos. 65, 66 the first overprint color refers to OUBANGUI CHARI.
For surcharges see Nos. 74-81.

Types of 1924 Issue Surcharged with New Values in Black or Red

1925-26

74 A3 65c on 1fr vio & ol 1.75 1.75
a. "65" omitted 100.00
75 A3 85c on 1fr vio & ol 1.75 1.75
a. "AFRIQUE EQUATORIALE FRANCAISE" omitted 100.00
b. Double surcharge 115.00
76 A3 1.25fr on 1fr dk bl & ultra (R) ('26) 1.00 1.00
a. "1f25" omitted 125.00 125.00

Bars cover old denomination on No. 76.

Types of 1924 Issue Surcharged with New Values and Bars

1927

77 A2 90c on 75c brn red & rose red 1.75 1.75
78 A3 1.50fr on 1fr ultra & bl 1.75 1.75
79 A3 3fr on 5fr org brn & dl red 2.60 2.60
80 A3 10fr on 5fr ver & vio 15.00 14.00
81 A3 20fr on 5fr vio & gray 22.50 21.00
Nos. 77-81 (5) 43.60 41.10

Common Design Types pictured following the introduction.

Colonial Exposition Issue
Common Design Types

1931 **Engr.** ***Perf. 12½***
Name of Country Typo. in Black

82 CD70 40c deep green 4.25 4.25
83 CD71 50c violet 4.25 4.25
84 CD72 90c red orange 4.25 4.25
a. Imperf. 80.00
85 CD73 1.50fr dull blue 4.25 4.25
Nos. 82-85 (4) 17.00 17.00

SEMI-POSTAL STAMPS

Regular Issue of 1915 Surcharged

1916 **Unwmk.** ***Perf. 14x13½***
Chalky Paper

B1 A1 10c + 5c car & blue 2.40 2.40
a. Inverted surch. 100.00 100.00
b. Double surcharge 100.00 100.00
c. Double surch., one invtd. 130.00 130.00
d. Vertical surcharge 100.00 100.00
e. No period under "C" 12.00 12.00

Regular Issue of 1915 Surcharged in Carmine

B2 A1 10c + 5c car & blue 1.40 1.40

POSTAGE DUE STAMPS

Postage Due Stamps of France Overprinted

1928 **Unwmk.** ***Perf. 14x13½***

J1 D2 5c light blue 1.25 1.25
J2 D2 10c gray brown 1.40 1.40
J3 D2 20c olive green 1.60 1.60
J4 D2 25c bright rose 1.60 1.60
J5 D2 30c light red 1.60 1.60
J6 D2 45c blue green 1.60 1.60
J7 D2 50c brown violet 2.10 *2.10*
J8 D2 60c yellow brown 2.40 *2.40*
J9 D2 1fr red brown 3.00 *3.00*
J10 D2 2fr orange red 4.25 *4.25*
J11 D2 3fr bright violet 4.25 *4.25*
Nos. J1-J11 (11) 25.05 25.05

Landscape D3

Emile Gentil — D4

1930 **Typo.**

J12 D3 5c dp bl & olive .70 .70
J13 D3 10c dk red & brn .90 .90
J14 D3 20c green & brn 1.00 1.00
J15 D3 25c lt bl & brn 1.10 1.10
J16 D3 30c bis brn & Prus bl 2.25 2.25
J17 D3 45c Prus bl & ol 2.50 2.50
J18 D3 50c red vio & brn 4.50 4.50
J19 D3 60c gray lil & bl blk 4.75 4.75
J20 D4 1fr bis brn & bl blk 4.25 4.25
J21 D4 2fr violet & brown 5.25 5.25
J22 D4 3fr dp red & brn 6.00 6.00
Nos. J12-J22 (11) 33.20 33.20

Stamps of Ubangi-Shari were replaced in 1936 by those of French Equatorial Africa.

UGANDA

ü-'gan-də

LOCATION — East Africa, at the Equator and separated from the Indian Ocean by Kenya and Tanzania
AREA — 91,343 sq. mi.
POP. — 13,990,000 (est. 1983)
CAPITAL — Kampala

Stamps of 1898-1902 were replaced by those issued for Kenya, Tanganyika and Uganda.

Cowries (50 = 4 Pence)
16 Annas = 1 Rupee (1896)

Unused values for Nos. 2-68 are for copies without gum. Very fine examples will be evenly cut and will show at least two full typewritten framelines.

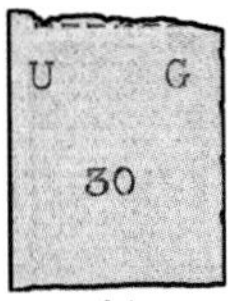
A1

A2

Nos. 1-53 were produced with a typewriter by Rev. Ernest Millar of the Church Missionary Society. They were 20-26mm wide, with nine stamps in a horizontal row. Later two more were added to each row, and the stamps became narrower, 16-18mm.

Rev. Millar got a new typewriter in 1895, and the stamps he typed on it have a different appearance. A violet ribbon in the machine, inserted late in 1895, resulted in Nos. 35-53.

Nos. 1-53 are on thin, tough, white paper, laid horizontally with traces of a few vertical lines.

Forgeries of Nos. 1-53 are known.

Without Gum
Wide Letters
Typewritten on Thin Laid Paper
Stamps 20 to 26mm wide

1895		**Unwmk.**	***Imperf.***	
1	A1	10(c) black	*5,750.*	3,750.
2	A1	20(c) black	*5,250.*	*1,600.*
3	A1	30(c) black	*1,800.*	*1,800.*
4	A1	40(c) black	*3,250.*	1,550.
5	A1	50(c) black	*1,550.*	*1,300.*
6	A1	60(c) black	*2,100.*	2,100.

Surcharged with New Value in Black, Pen-written

9	A1	10 on 30(c) black	—
10	A1	10 on 50(c) black	—
11	A1	15 on 10(c) black	—
12	A1	15 on 20(c) black	—
13	A1	15 on 40(c) black	—
14	A1	15 on 50(c) black	—
15	A1	25 on 50(c) black	—
16	A1	50 on 60(c) black	—

Stamps 16 to 18mm wide

17	A1	5(c) black	*1,750.*	*1,100.*
18	A1	10(c) black	*1,750.*	*1,150.*
19	A1	15(c) black	*1,150.*	*1,150.*
20	A1	20(c) black	*1,500.*	*750.*
21	A1	25(c) black	*1,100.*	*1,100.*
22	A1	30(c) black	*8,750.*	*8,750.*
23	A1	40(c) black	*8,000.*	*8,000.*
24	A1	50(c) black	*3,750.*	*5,750.*
25	A1	60(c) black	*7,500.*	

Narrow Letters
Stamps 16 to 18mm wide

26	A2	5(c) black	*1,000.*	
27	A2	10(c) black	*1,000.*	
28	A2	15(c) black	*1,000.*	
29	A2	20(c) black	*800.*	
30	A2	25(c) black	*1,000.*	
31	A2	30(c) black	*1,100.*	
32	A2	40(c) black	*1,100.*	
33	A2	50(c) black	*950.*	
34	A2	60(c) black	*1,900.*	
35	A2	5(c) violet	*575.*	*575.*
36	A2	10(c) violet	*550.*	*550.*
37	A2	15(c) violet	*700.*	*500.*
38	A2	20(c) violet	*425.*	*325.*
39	A2	25(c) violet	*800.*	*800.*
40	A2	30(c) violet	*1,100.*	*800.*
41	A2	40(c) violet	*925.*	*925.*
42	A2	50(c) violet	*1,000.*	1,150.
43	A2	100(c) violet	*3,250.*	3,750.

As a favor to a philatelist, 35c and 45c denominations were made in black and violet. They were not intended for postal use and no rate called for those denominations.

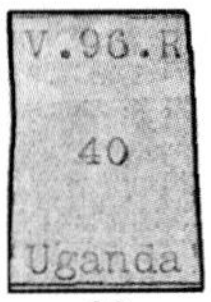
A3

A4

1896				
44	A3	5(c) violet	*550.*	*375.*
45	A3	10(c) violet	*500.*	*325.*
46	A3	15(c) violet	*550.*	*375.*
47	A3	20(c) violet	*325.*	*200.*
48	A3	25(c) violet	*325.*	
49	A3	30(c) violet	*525.*	*1,150.*
50	A3	40(c) violet	*625.*	*1,150.*
51	A3	50(c) violet	*700.*	*900.*
52	A3	60(c) violet	*1,600.*	
53	A3	100(c) violet	*1,500.*	2,250.

Overprinted "L" in Black

1896		**Typeset**	**White Paper**	
54	A4	1a black (thin "1")	200.	175.
a.		Small "O" in "POSTAGE"	1,350.	1,000.
55	A4	2a black	110.	*140.*
a.		Small "O" in "POSTAGE"	475.	*525.*
56	A4	3a black	275.	*350.*
a.		Small "O" in "POSTAGE"	1,500.	*1,800.*
57	A4	4a black	110.	*175.*
a.		Small "O" in "POSTAGE"	525.	
		Yellowish Paper		
58	A4	8a black	210.	*250.*
a.		Small "O" in "POSTAGE"	1,250.	*1,500.*
59	A4	1r black	425.	*475.*
a.		Small "O" in "POSTAGE"	1,750.	
60	A4	5r black	37,500.	37,500.

Without Overprint

		White Paper		
61	A4	1a black (thin "1")	125.00	110.00
a.		Small "O" in "POSTAGE"	700.00	625.00
62	A4	1a black (thick "1")	21.00	*27.50*
a.		Small "O" in "POSTAGE"	90.00	*110.00*
63	A4	2a black	29.00	*32.50*
a.		Small "O" in "POSTAGE"	110.00	*140.00*
64	A4	3a black	30.00	*35.00*
a.		Small "O" in "POSTAGE"	125.00	*160.00*
65	A4	4a black	30.00	*35.00*
a.		Small "O" in "POSTAGE"	110.00	*140.00*
		Yellowish Paper		
66	A4	8a black	32.50	*35.00*
a.		Small "O" in "POSTAGE"	140.00	*160.00*
67	A4	1r black	87.50	*110.00*
a.		Small "O" in "POSTAGE"	350.00	*450.00*
68	A4	5r black	250.00	*400.00*
a.		Small "O" in "POSTAGE"	850.00	*1,050.*

A5

Queen Victoria — A6

1898-1902		**Engr. Wmk. 2**	***Perf. 14***	
69	A5	1a red	2.25	*2.50*
70	A5	1a car rose ('02)	2.25	1.10
71	A5	2a brown	4.00	*8.00*
72	A5	3a gray	13.00	*30.00*
a.		3a bluish gray ('02)	13.00	*15.00*
73	A5	4a dark green	7.00	*7.50*
74	A5	8a olive gray	9.00	*27.50*
a.		8a gray green ('02)	13.00	*32.50*
		Wmk. 1		
75	A6	1r ultra	45.00	*47.50*
a.		1r bright blue (02)	*47.50*	*52.50*
76	A6	5r brown	80.00	*110.00*
		Nos. 69-76 (8)	162.50	*234.10*

A7

1902		**Wmk. 2**	**Black Overprint**	
77	A7	½a yellow green	2.25	1.60
a.		Inverted overprint	*2,000.*	
b.		Double overprint	*2,250.*	
c.		Pair, one without overprint	*4,750.*	
		Red Overprint		
78	A7	2½a dark blue	3.25	*3.50*
a.		Double overprint	750.00	

UKRAINE

yü-'krān

LOCATION — In southeastern Europe, bordering on the Black Sea
GOVT. — Republic
AREA — 170,998 sq. mi.
POP. — 48,760,474 (2001)
CAPITAL — Kiev

Following the collapse of the Russian Empire, a national assembly met at Kiev and declared the Ukrainian National Republic on Jan. 22, 1918. During three years of civil war, the Ukrainian army, as well as Bolshevik, White Russian, Allied and Polish armies, fought back and forth across the country. By November, 1920, Ukraine was finally occupied by Soviet forces and on July 6, 1923, it was incorporated into the Soviet Union. Soviet stamps were used until March 1, 1992, when newly independent Ukraine again began issuing its own stamps.

200 Shahiv = 100 Kopiyok (Kopecks)
= 1 Karbovanets (Ruble)
100 Shahiv = 1 Hryvnia

Watermark

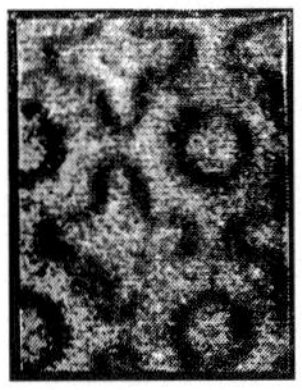
Wmk. 116- Crosses and Circles

Republic's Trident Emblem — A1

Ukrainian Peasant — A2

Allegorical Ukraine — A3

Trident — A4

Inscription of Value — A5

1918, July		**Typo.**	***Imperf.***	
		Thin Paper		
1	A1	10sh buff	.20	*.25*
2	A2	20sh brown	.20	*.25*
3	A3	30sh ultra	.20	*.25*
a.		30sh blue	.65	*1.25*
4	A4	40sh green	.20	*.25*
5	A5	50sh red	.20	*.25*
		Nos. 1-5 (5)	1.00	*1.25*

The stamps of this issue exist perforated or pin-perforated unofficially.

Forgeries of this set exist on a very thin, glossy paper.

These designs were earlier (April, 1918) utilized for money tokens, printed on thin cardboard, perforated 11½, and bearing an inscription on the reverse "Circulates on par with coins" in Ukrainian. These tokens exist favor canceled but were not postage stamps. Value uncanceled, $6 each.

TRIDENT OVERPRINTS

Stamps of Russia Overprinted in Violet, Black, Blue, Red, Brown or Green

This trident-shaped emblem was taken from the arms of the Grand Prince Volodymyr and adopted as the device of the Ukrainian Republic.

In the early months of independence, Russian stamps were commonly used, but the influx of large quantities of stamps from Russia made it necessary to take measures to protect postal revenue. In August, 1918, local post offices were ordered to send their existing stocks of Russian stamps to regional centers, where they were overprinted with the trident arms. Unoverprinted Russian stamps were declared invalid after October 1, although they were often accepted for use.

Nos. 6-47 represent the basic Russian stamps that received these overprints. Values are for the most common overprint variety.

Following this basic Trident listing are detailed listings for the major regional and city types (Nos. 6a-44s).

The basic Russian stamps to which Trident overprints were applied:

A8

A9

A11

A12

A13

A14

A15

On Stamps of 1902-03

1918		**Wmk. 168**	***Perf. 13½***	
6	A12	3½r black & gray	27.00	*30.00*
7	A12	7r black & yellow	17.00	*20.00*

On Stamps of 1909-18
Lozenges of Varnish on Face
Perf. 14, 14½x15
Unwmk.

8	A14	1k orange	.20	*.25*
9	A14	2k green	.20	*.25*
10	A14	3k red	.20	*.25*
11	A15	4k carmine	.20	*.25*
12	A14	5k claret	.20	*.25*
13	A14	7k light blue	.20	*.25*
14	A15	10k dark blue	.20	*.25*
15	A11	14k blue & rose	.20	*.40*
16	A11	15k red brn & bl	.20	*.25*
17	A8	20k blue & car	.20	*.25*

18	A11	25k	grn & gray vio	.20	.25
19	A11	35k	red brn & grn	.20	.25
20	A8	50k	violet & grn	.20	.25
21	A11	70k	brown & org	.20	.25

Perf. 13½

22	A9	1r	lt brn, brn & org	.35	.60
23	A12	3½r	mar & lt grn	.75	1.75
24	A13	5r	dk bl, grn & pale bl	5.00	7.00
25	A12	7r	dk grn & pink	6.00	8.00
26	A13	10r	scar, yel & gray	7.00	10.00
			Nos. 6-26 (21)	65.90	81.00

On Stamps of 1917

Perf. 14, 14½x15

27	A14	10k	on 7k light blue	.25	.30
28	A11	20k	on 14k bl & rose	.20	.25

On Stamps of 1917-18

Imperf

29	A14	1k	orange	.20	.25
30	A14	2k	gray green	.20	.25
31	A14	3k	red	.20	.25
32	A15	4k	carmine	.20	.25
33	A14	5k	claret	.75	1.00
34	A11	15k	red brn & bl	.20	.25
35	A8	20k	bl & car	.50	1.50
36	A11	25k	grn & gray vio	50.00	—
37	A11	35k	red brn & grn	.20	.25
38	A8	50k	violet & grn	.25	.75
39	A11	70k	brown & org	.20	.25
40	A9	1r	pale brn, brn & red org	.30	.35
41	A12	3½r	mar & lt grn	.45	1.00
42	A13	5r	dk bl, grn & pale bl	.50	1.25
43	A12	7r	dk grn & pink	1.50	1.75
44	A13	10r	scar, yel & gray	40.00	50.00
			Nos. 29-44 (16)	95.65	59.35

On Postal Savings Bank Stamps

Wmk. 171 **Litho.**

Perf. 14, 14½x14¾

45	1k	red, *buff*	.75	15.00
46	5k	green, *buff*	7.00	70.00
47	10k	brown, *buff*	1.75	200.00
		Nos. 45-47 (3)	9.50	285.00

Nos. 45-47 were used and accepted as postage stamps during stamp shortages.

REGIONAL ISSUES

Katerynoslav I — Handstamped in black with a rubber device

8a	A14	1k	orange	.35	2.50
9a	A14	2k	green	.20	.25
10a	A14	3k	red	.25	.35
11a	A15	4k	carmine	.20	1.40
12a	A14	5k	claret	.20	.35
13a	A14	7k	light blue	.20	.35
14a	A15	10k	dark blue	.20	.25
15a	A11	14k	blue & rose	.20	.75
16a	A11	15k	red brn & bl	.20	.25
17a	A8	20k	blue & car	.25	.35
18a	A11	25k	grn & gray vio	.25	.75
19a	A11	35k	red brn & grn	5.00	8.50
20a	A8	50k	violet & grn	.20	.25
21a	A11	70k	brown & org	.20	.35
27a	A14	10k	on 7k light blue	.20	.75
28a	A11	20k	on 14k bl & rose	.25	1.50
29a	A14	1k	orange	.20	.25
30a	A14	2k	gray green	3.50	10.00
31a	A14	3k	red	.20	.25
32a	A15	4k	carmine	60.00	65.00
33a	A14	5k	claret	4.00	5.00
34a	A11	15k	red brn & bl	.45	1.50
35a	A8	20k	bl & car	.50	1.50
37a	A11	35k	red brn & grn	2.00	4.00
38a	A8	50k	violet & grn	60.00	65.00
39a	A11	70k	brown & org	60.00	65.00

Katerynoslav II — Handstamped in black with a rubber device

6a	A12	3½r	black & gray	—	200.00
7a	A12	7r	black & yellow	70.00	75.00
22a	A9	1r	lt brn, brn & org	100.00	135.00
23a	A12	3½r	mar & lt grn	8.50	13.50
25a	A12	7r	dk grn & pink	13.50	27.00
40a	A9	1r	pale brn, brn & red org	1.35	1.75
41a	A12	3½r	mar & lt grn	1.50	3.50
42a	A12	7r	dk grn & pink	27.00	35.00
43a	A12	7r	dk grn & pink	85.00	—

Kharkiv I — Handstamped in black with a metal device

8b	A14	1k	orange	.50	3.50
9b	A14	2k	green	1.35	2.00
10b	A14	3k	red	.20	.75
11b	A15	4k	carmine	.75	3.50
12b	A14	5k	claret	3.50	5.00
13b	A14	7k	light blue	17.00	60.00
14b	A15	10k	dark blue	1.75	2.75
15b	A11	14k	blue & rose	17.00	45.00
16b	A11	15k	red brn & bl	.20	.25
17b	A8	20k	blue & car	.85	1.50
18b	A11	25k	grn & gray vio	30.00	40.00
19b	A11	35k	red brn & grn	.20	.25
20b	A8	50k	violet & grn	.20	.25
21b	A11	70k	brown & org	.35	1.00
27b	A14	10k	on 7k light blue	1.50	2.00
28b	A11	20k	on 14k bl & rose	1.00	2.75
29b	A14	1k	orange	.20	.75
30b	A14	2k	gray green	1.00	2.75
31b	A14	3k	red	.20	1.00
33b	A14	5k	claret	.85	2.75
34b	A11	15k	red brn & bl	3.50	5.00
37b	A11	35k	red brn & grn	17.00	50.00
45b	A6	1k	red, *buff*	.75	
46b	A6	5k	green, *buff*	7.00	
47b	A6	10k	brown, *buff*	1.75	

Kharkiv II — Handstamped in black with a metal device

6c	A12	3½r	black & gray	—	
7c	A12	7r	black & yellow	70.00	85.00
9c	A14	2k	green	—	
10c	A14	3k	red	—	
16c	A11	15k	red brn & bl	—	
22c	A9	1r	lt brn, brn & org	1.75	10.00
23c	A12	3½r	mar & lt grn	17.00	27.00
24c	A13	5r	dk bl, grn & pale bl		170.00
25c	A12	7r	dk grn & pink	10.00	17.00
26c	A13	10r	scar, yel & gray	170.00	135.00
40c	A9	1r	pale brn, brn & red org	.20	.75
41c	A12	3½r	mar & lt grn	.45	1.35
42c	A13	5r	dk bl, grn & pale bl	.75	1.50
43c	A12	7r	dk grn & pink	10.00	17.00
44c	A13	10r	scar, yel & gray	85.00	100.00

Kharkiv III — Handstamped in black with a metal device

6d	A12	3½r	black & gray	200.00	170.00
7d	A12	7r	black & yellow	—	170.00
9d	A14	2k	green	—	
10d	A14	3k	red	—	
16d	A11	15k	red brn & bl	—	
22d	A9	1r	lt brn, brn & org	4.00	27.00
23d	A12	3½r	mar & lt grn	20.00	27.00
24d	A13	5r	dk bl, grn & pale bl	—	—
25d	A12	7r	dk grn & pink	12.00	17.00
26d	A13	10r	scar, yel & gray	70.00	85.00
30d	A14	2k	gray green	70.00	
40d	A9	1r	pale brn, brn & red org	.25	1.00
41d	A12	3½r	mar & lt grn	.50	1.35
42d	A13	5r	dk bl, grn & pale bl	.50	1.50
43d	A12	7r	dk grn & pink	14.00	27.00
44d	A13	10r	scar, yel & gray	40.00	50.00

Kiev I — Handstamped in violet with a rubber device

6e	A12	3½r	black & gray	200.00	170.00
7e	A12	7r	black & yellow	170.00	100.00
8e	A14	1k	orange	.20	.25
9e	A14	2k	green	.75	.50
10e	A14	3k	red	2.50	1.35
11e	A15	4k	carmine	1.25	1.35
12e	A14	5k	claret	.25	.30
13e	A14	7k	light blue	10.00	13.50
14e	A15	10k	dark blue	.45	.55
15e	A11	14k	blue & rose	8.50	10.00
16e	A11	15k	red brn & bl	.35	.55
17e	A8	20k	blue & car	1.35	.75
18e	A11	25k	grn & gray vio	17.00	13.50
19e	A11	35k	red brn & grn	13.50	10.00
20e	A8	50k	violet & grn	.25	.30
21e	A11	70k	brown & org	.25	.30
22e	A9	1r	lt brn, brn & org	3.50	4.00
23e	A12	3½r	mar & lt grn	.75	2.00
24e	A13	5r	dk bl, grn & pale bl	27.00	35.00
25e	A12	7r	dk grn & pink	27.00	35.00
26e	A13	10r	scar, yel & gray	7.00	10.00
27e	A14	10k	on 7k light blue	2.00	2.75
28e	A11	20k	on 14k bl & rose	.45	.55
29e	A14	1k	orange	1.00	1.50
30e	A14	2k	gray green	.20	.25
31e	A14	3k	red	.20	.25
32e	A15	4k	carmine	.20	.25
33e	A14	5k	claret	10.00	13.50
34e	A11	15k	red brn & bl	2.75	3.50
35e	A8	20k	bl & car	10.00	13.50
36e	A11	25k	bl & car	—	—
37e	A11	35k	red brn & grn	.35	.40
38e	A8	50k	violet & grn	10.00	9.00
39e	A11	70k	brown & org	17.00	20.00
40e	A9	1r	pale brn, brn & red org	.50	.60
41e	A12	3½r	mar & lt grn	13.50	17.00
42e	A13	5r	dk bl, grn & pale bl	1.00	1.25
43e	A12	7r	dk grn & pink	1.50	1.75
44e	A13	10r	scar, yel & gray	175.00	—
45e	A6	1k	red, *buff*	—	
46e	A6	5k	green, *buff*	—	—
47e	A6	10k	brown, *buff*	17.00	

Kiev II — Handstamped in violet with a rubber device

6f	A12	3½r	black & gray	27.00	30.00
7f	A12	7r	black & yellow	17.00	20.00
8f	A14	1k	orange	.20	.25
9f	A14	2k	green	.20	.25
10f	A14	3k	red	.20	.25
11f	A15	4k	carmine	.20	.25
12f	A14	5k	claret	.20	.25
13f	A14	7k	light blue	7.00	12.00
14f	A15	10k	dark blue	.20	.25
15f	A11	14k	blue & rose	.30	.40
16f	A11	15k	red brn & bl	.20	.25
17f	A8	20k	blue & car	.20	.25
18f	A11	25k	grn & gray vio	.50	.40
19f	A11	35k	red brn & grn	.20	.25
20f	A8	50k	violet & grn	.20	.25
21f	A11	70k	brown & org	.20	.25
22f	A9	1r	lt brn, brn & org	.35	1.00
23f	A12	3½r	mar & lt grn	2.00	12.00
24f	A13	5r	dk bl, grn & pale bl	17.00	75.00
25f	A12	7r	dk grn & pink	7.00	12.00
26f	A13	10r	scar, yel & gray	10.00	13.50
27f	A14	10k	on 7k light blue	.25	.30
28f	A11	20k	on 14k bl & rose	.20	.25
29f	A14	1k	orange	.20	.25
30f	A14	2k	gray green	.20	.25
31f	A14	3k	red	.20	.25
32f	A15	4k	carmine	.50	.75
33f	A14	5k	claret	.75	1.00
34f	A11	15k	red brn & bl	.20	.25
36f	A11	25k	bl & car	50.00	—
37f	A11	35k	red brn & grn	.20	.25
38f	A8	50k	violet & grn	—	40.00
39f	A11	70k	brown & org	.20	.25
40f	A9	1r	pale brn, brn & red org	.30	.35
41f	A12	3½r	mar & lt grn	1.00	1.35
42f	A13	5r	dk bl, grn & pale bl	1.25	1.50
43f	A12	7r	dk grn & pink	2.00	3.00
44f	A13	10r	scar, yel & gray	—	—
45f	A6	1k	red, *buff*	13.50	
46f	A6	5k	green, *buff*	10.00	
47f	A6	10k	brown, *buff*	27.00	

Kiev III — Lithographed in black

6g	A12	3½r	black & gray	50.00	100.00
8g	A14	1k	orange	.20	.25
9g	A14	2k	green	.50	.75
10g	A14	3k	red	.50	.75
11g	A15	4k	carmine	.20	.25
12g	A14	5k	claret	.25	.75
13g	A14	7k	light blue	1.35	1.75
14g	A15	10k	dark blue	2.00	2.75
15g	A11	14k	blue & rose	2.00	2.75
16g	A11	15k	red brn	.20	.25
17g	A8	20k	blue & car	2.75	3.50
18g	A11	25k	grn & gray vio	2.75	3.50
19g	A11	35k	red brn & grn	.20	.25
20g	A8	50k	violet & grn	.20	.25
21g	A11	70k	brown & org	.20	.25
23g	A12	3½r	mar & lt grn	70.00	100.00
24g	A13	5r	dk bl, grn & pale bl	200.00	220.00
25g	A12	7r	dk grn & pink	50.00	75.00
26g	A13	10r	scar, yel & gray	200.00	220.00
27g	A14	10k	on 7k light blue	4.00	7.00
28g	A11	20k	on 14k bl & rose	.45	.75
29g	A14	1k	orange	.20	.25
30g	A14	2k	gray green	.20	.25
31g	A14	3k	red	.20	.25
32g	A15	4k	carmine	1.35	2.75
33g	A14	5k	claret	12.00	10.00
34g	A11	15k	red brn & bl	10.00	12.00
37g	A11	35k	red brn & grn	13.50	15.00
39g	A11	70k	brown & org	10.00	12.00
40g	A9	1r	pale brn, brn & red org	.40	2.75
41g	A12	3½r	mar & lt grn	60.00	75.00
42g	A13	5r	dk bl, grn & pale bl	50.00	75.00
43g	A12	7r	dk grn & pink	100.00	125.00

Overinked or worn plates produced impressions where the thin outer line of the trident cannot be distinguished.

Odessa I — Typographed in black

9h	A14	2k	green	.20	.25
11h	A15	4k	carmine	27.00	—
12h	A14	5k	claret	70.00	—
13h	A14	7k	light blue	.30	.75
14h	A15	10k	dark blue	.50	1.00
15h	A11	14k	blue & rose	27.00	35.00
16h	A11	15k	red brn	.40	.70
17h	A8	20k	blue & car	40.00	100.00
19h	A11	35k	red brn & grn	.40	.70
20h	A8	50k	violet & grn	.30	.50
21h	A11	70k	brown & org	13.50	
27h	A14	10k	on 7k light blue	1.75	7.00
29h	A14	1k	orange	.20	.25
31h	A14	3k	red	.20	.25
34g	A11	15k	red brn & bl	1.35	2.75
37h	A11	35k	red brn & grn	10.00	27.00
38h	A8	50k	violet & grn	65.00	125.00
39h	A11	70k	brown & org	85.00	100.00

Odessa II — Typographed in black

8i	A14	1k	orange	.20	1.00
9i	A14	2k	green	.20	.25
10i	A14	3k	red	.75	2.00
11i	A15	4k	carmine	.20	.25
12i	A14	5k	claret	.20	.25
13i	A14	7k	light blue	.20	.25
14i	A15	10k	dark blue	.30	.35
15i	A11	14k	blue & rose	.30	.75
16i	A11	15k	red brn	.20	.25
17i	A8	20k	blue & car	.20	.25
18i	A11	25k	grn & gray vio	.30	.75
19i	A11	35k	red brn & grn	.20	.30
20i	A8	50k	violet & grn	.20	.25
21i	A11	70k	brown & org	.35	.75
27i	A14	10k	on 7k light blue	.30	.75
28i	A11	20k	on 14k bl & rose	.20	.35
29i	A14	1k	orange	.20	.25
30i	A14	2k	gray green	.75	2.00
31i	A14	3k	red	.20	.25
33i	A14	5k	claret	8.50	—
34i	A11	15k	red brn & bl	.25	.35
37i	A11	35k	red brn & grn	.20	.75
38i	A8	50k	violet & grn	.25	.75
39i	A11	70k	brown & org	.50	2.75

Odessa III — Lithographed in black

8j	A14	1k	orange	.45	2.75
9j	A14	2k	green	10.00	70.00
12j	A14	5k	claret	.25	.45
14j	A15	10k	dark blue	.20	.25
15j	A11	14k	blue & rose	.25	.45
16j	A11	15k	red brn	.50	2.50
17j	A8	20k	blue & car	.25	.40
18j	A11	25k	grn & gray vio	1.75	2.00
19j	A11	35k	red brn & grn	.20	2.00
20j	A8	50k	violet & grn	.20	.30
21j	A11	70k	brown & org	.25	.50
27j	A14	10k	on 7k light blue	.50	3.00
29j	A14	1k	orange	.30	.50
34j	A11	15k	red brn & bl	1.00	2.00
37j	A11	35k	red brn & grn	.35	1.00
38j	A8	50k	violet & grn	.50	2.75
39j	A11	70k	brown & org	.45	1.75

Odessa IV — Handstamped in black with a metal device

6k	A12	3½r	black & gray	50.00	60.00
7k	A12	7r	black & yellow	100.00	120.00
8k	A14	1k	orange	.45	1.75
9k	A14	2k	green	.60	1.30
10k	A14	3k	red	1.00	1.35
11k	A15	4k	carmine	2.00	5.50
12k	A14	5k	claret	1.75	5.50
13k	A14	7k	light blue	40.00	80.00
14k	A15	10k	dark blue	.75	1.00
15k	A11	14k	blue & rose	1.75	2.50
16k	A11	15k	red brn	1.25	1.50
17k	A8	20k	blue & car	.60	2.25
18k	A11	25k	grn & gray vio	2.75	2.25
19k	A11	35k	red brn & grn	1.75	10.00
20k	A8	50k	violet & grn	1.00	2.75
21k	A11	70k	brown & org	2.25	4.00
22k	A9	1r	lt brn, brn & org	.75	1.00
23k	A12	3½r	mar & lt grn	30.00	80.00
24k	A13	5r	dk bl, grn & pale bl	5.00	7.00
25k	A12	7r	dk grn & pink	6.00	8.00
26k	A13	10r	scar, yel & gray	100.00	150.00
27k	A14	10k	on 7k light blue	.75	2.00
28k	A11	20k	on 14k bl & rose	1.35	5.00
29k	A14	1k	orange	.25	1.00
30k	A14	2k	gray green	.50	2.75
31k	A14	3k	red	.70	1.75
32k	A15	4k	carmine	70.00	120.00
33k	A14	5k	claret	2.75	10.00
34k	A11	15k	red brn & bl	.75	2.75
35k	A8	20k	bl & car	70.00	100.00
37k	A11	35k	red brn & grn	2.00	8.50
38k	A8	50k	violet & grn	4.00	13.50
39k	A11	70k	brown & org	22.00	40.00
40k	A9	1r	pale brn, brn & red org	.40	.50
41k	A12	3½r	mar & lt grn	12.00	6.00
42k	A13	5r	dk bl, grn & pale bl	13.00	20.00
43k	A12	7r	dk grn & pink	—	
44k	A13	10r	scar, yel & gray	100.00	150.00

Odessa V — Handstamped in black with a metal device

6m	A12	3½r	black & gray	60.00	65.00

7m	A12	7r	black & yellow	150.00	*160.00*
8m	A14	1k	orange	40.00	
9m	A14	2k	green	8.00	*37.00*
10m	A14	3k	red	1.50	*12.00*
11m	A15	4k	carmine	30.00	
12m	A14	5k	claret	2.00	*70.00*
13m	A14	7k	light blue	—	—
14m	A15	10k	dark blue	30.00	*80.00*
15m	A11	14k	blue & rose	14.00	*35.00*
16m	A11	15k	red brn	10.00	*22.00*
17m	A8	20k	blue & car	5.00	*8.00*
18m	A11	25k	grn & gray vio	—	—
19m	A11	35k	red brn & grn	80.00	*90.00*
20m	A8	50k	violet & grn	14.00	*90.00*
21m	A11	70k	brown & org	25.00	*90.00*
22m	A9	1r	lt brn, brn & org	.50	*.60*
23m	A12	3½r	mar & lt grn	1.25	*1.75*
24m	A13	5r	dk bl, grn & pale bl	9.00	*12.00*
25m	A12	7r	dk grn & pink	8.00	*12.00*
26m	A13	10r	scar, yel & gray	14.00	*30.00*
27m	A14	10k	on 7k light blue	7.00	*12.00*
28m	A11	20k	on 14k bl & rose	7.00	*18.00*
29m	A14	1k	orange	4.50	*5.00*
30m	A14	2k	gray green	4.50	*5.00*
31m	A14	3k	red	4.50	*5.00*
33m	A14	5k	claret	4.50	*5.00*
34m	A11	15k	red brn & bl	12.00	*15.00*
37m	A11	35k	red brn & grn	100.00	—
38m	A8	50k	violet & grn	90.00	
39m	A11	70k	brown & org	20.00	*40.00*
40m	A9	1r	pale brn, brn & red org	.35	*.40*
41m	A12	3½r	mar & lt grn	.75	*1.00*
42m	A13	5r	dk bl, grn & pale bl	70.00	*80.00*
43m	A12	7r	dk grn & pink	—	
44m	A13	10r	scar, yel & gray	80.00	*100.00*

Odessa VI — Handstamped in black with a metal device

6n	A12	3½r	black & gray	150.00	125.00
7n	A12	7r	black & yellow	—	—
8n	A14	1k	orange	100.00	
9n	A14	2k	green	3.00	*10.00*
10n	A14	3k	red	120.00	*150.00*
11n	A15	4k	carmine	—	
12n	A14	5k	claret	120.00	
13n	A14	7k	light blue	150.00	
14n	A15	10k	dark blue	2.00	*5.00*
15n	A11	14k	blue & rose	8.00	
16n	A11	15k	red brn	25.00	*140.00*
17n	A8	20k	blue & car	30.00	*35.00*
19n	A11	35k	red brn & grn		90.00
20n	A8	50k	violet & grn	125.00	*140.00*
21n	A11	70k	brown & org	150.00	—
22n	A9	1r	lt brn, brn & org	.75	*1.00*
23n	A12	3½r	mar & lt grn	2.00	*3.00*
24n	A13	5r	dk bl, grn & pale bl	80.00	*150.00*
25n	A12	7r	dk grn & pink	45.00	*150.00*
26n	A13	10r	scar, yel & gray	90.00	*150.00*
27n	A14	10k	on 7k light blue	6.00	*60.00*
28n	A11	20k	on 14k bl & rose	20.00	*25.00*
29n	A14	1k	orange	6.00	*7.00*
30n	A14	2k	gray green	6.00	*7.00*
31n	A14	3k	red	6.00	*7.00*
32n	A15	4k	carmine	80.00	*140.00*
33n	A14	5k	claret	6.00	*7.00*
34n	A11	15k	red brn & bl	8.00	*12.00*
35n	A8	20k	bl & car	100.00	*120.00*
38n	A8	50k	violet & grn	120.00	*130.00*
39n	A11	70k	brown & org	27.00	*35.00*
40n	A9	1r	pale brn, brn & red org	.50	*.75*
41n	A12	3½r	mar & lt grn	.75	*1.50*
42n	A13	5r	dk bl, grn & pale bl	—	—
43n	A12	7r	dk grn & pink	—	
44n	A13	10r	scar, yel & gray	150.00	—

Podillia Ia — Handstamped in black with a metal device

Over 60 additional Podillia trident types and subtypes have been identified by specialists. The majority of these types were made with single-subject overprinting devices composed of non-durable wood or rubber, which quickly deteriorated with use, resulting in subtypes, necessitating the creation of new handstamp types. Because of the rapid wear of the handstamp devices, often only partial trident impressions appear on stamps. The Podillia Ia metal handstamp overprinted far more stamps than any of the wooden or rubber types.

6o	A12	3½r	black & gray		—
7o	A12	7r	black & yellow	150.00	*175.00*
8o	A14	1k	orange	.35	*2.50*
9o	A14	2k	green	.20	*.25*
10o	A14	3k	red	.45	*.80*
11o	A15	4k	carmine	50.00	*150.00*
12o	A14	5k	claret	60.00	2.50
13o	A14	7k	light blue	.20	*.45*
14o	A15	10k	dark blue	.40	*1.00*
15o	A11	14k	blue & rose	—	—
16o	A11	15k	red brn	.20	*.25*
17o	A8	20k	blue & car	.35	*.50*
18o	A11	25k	grn & gray vio	.30	*1.35*
19o	A11	35k	red brn & grn	.20	*.25*
20o	A8	50k	violet & grn	.20	*.25*
21o	A11	70k	brown & org	.20	*.25*
22o	A9	1r	lt brn, brn & org	.45	*.75*
23o	A12	3½r	mar & lt grn	3.00	*7.00*
24o	A13	5r	dk bl, grn & pale bl	25.00	—
25o	A12	7r	dk grn & pink	17.00	—
26o	A13	10r	scar, yel & gray	—	
27o	A14	10k	on 7k light blue	.25	2.75
28o	A11	20k	on 14k bl & rose	1.00	*10.00*
29o	A14	1k	orange	.50	*2.75*
30o	A14	2k	gray green	20.00	—
31o	A14	3k	red	.30	*1.75*
33o	A14	5k	claret	1.00	
34o	A11	15k	red brn & bl	85.00	
37o	A11	35k	red brn & grn	—	—
38o	A8	50k	violet & grn	75.00	30.00
40o	A9	1r	pale brn, brn & red org	.35	*.50*
41o	A12	3½r	mar & lt grn	6.00	4.00
42o	A13	5r	dk bl, grn & pale bl	15.00	*20.00*
43o	A12	7r	dk grn & pink	17.00	10.00

Poltava I — Handstamped in violet with a rubber device (kopeck values) or with a metal device (ruble values)

8p	A14	1k	orange	150.00	—
9p	A14	2k	green	.30	*.40*
10p	A14	3k	red	6.00	*7.00*
11p	A15	4k	carmine	12.00	*15.00*
12p	A14	5k	claret	7.00	*8.50*
13p	A14	7k	light blue	130.00	*150.00*
14p	A15	10k	dark blue	7.50	*8.50*
15p	A11	14k	blue & rose		150.00
16p	A11	15k	red brn	4.00	*8.00*
17p	A8	20k	blue & car	1.00	*2.00*
18p	A11	25k	grn & gray vio	2.00	*10.00*
19p	A11	35k	red brn & grn	60.00	50.00
20p	A8	50k	violet & grn	1.00	*.75*
21p	A11	70k	brown & org	.50	*.75*
22p	A9	1r	lt brn, brn & org		70.00
24p	A13	5r	dk bl, grn & pale bl		—
25p	A12	7r	dk grn & pink	13.50	*17.00*
27p	A14	10k	on 7k light blue	50.00	40.00
28p	A11	20k	on 14k bl & rose	12.00	*15.00*
29p	A14	1k	orange	2.50	*4.00*
30p	A14	2k	gray green	6.00	*110.00*
31p	A14	3k	red	.75	*1.00*
33p	A14	5k	claret	85.00	*150.00*
34p	A11	15k	red brn & bl	6.00	*9.00*
35p	A8	20k	bl & car		—
37p	A11	35k	red brn & grn	4.00	*9.00*
38p	A8	50k	violet & grn		—
40p	A9	1r	pale brn, brn & red org	80.00	50.00
41p	A12	3½r	mar & lt grn		—
43p	A12	7r	dk grn & pink		—
44p	A13	10r	scar, yel & gray		—
45p	A6	1k	red, *buff*	10.00	*15.00*
46p	A6	5k	green, *buff*	150.00	70.00

Poltava I — Handstamped in black with a rubber device (kopeck values) or with a metal device (ruble values)

6q	A12	3½r	black & gray		200.00
7q	A12	7r	black & yellow	—	200.00
8q	A14	1k	orange	—	150.00
9q	A14	2k	green	9.00	*18.00*
10q	A14	3k	red	14.00	*28.00*
11q	A15	4k	carmine	70.00	*150.00*
12q	A14	5k	claret	75.00	40.00
13q	A14	7k	light blue	—	—
14q	A15	10k	dark blue	60.00	35.00
15q	A11	14k	blue & rose	—	—
16q	A11	15k	red brn	3.00	*5.00*
17q	A8	20k	blue & car	70.00	35.00
18q	A11	25k	grn & gray vio	—	*120.00*
19q	A11	35k	red brn & grn	100.00	70.00
20q	A8	50k	violet & grn	100.00	50.00
21q	A11	70k	brown & org	100.00	35.00
22q	A9	1r	lt brn, brn & org	5.00	4.00
23q	A12	3½r	mar & lt grn	5.00	*7.00*
24q	A13	5r	dk bl, grn & pale bl	—	*135.00*
25q	A12	7r	dk grn & pink	15.00	*20.00*
26q	A13	10r	scar, yel & gray	—	—
27q	A14	10k	on 7k light blue	100.00	*110.00*
28q	A11	20k	on 14k bl & rose	100.00	*120.00*
29q	A14	1k	orange	13.00	*75.00*
30q	A14	2k	gray green	—	—
31q	A14	3k	red	35.00	*40.00*
32q	A15	4k	carmine		—
33q	A14	5k	claret	120.00	*140.00*
34q	A11	15k	red brn & bl	25.00	*80.00*
35q	A8	20k	bl & car		—
37q	A11	35k	red brn & grn	120.00	80.00
38q	A8	50k	violet & grn	—	—
39q	A11	70k	brown & org	—	—
40q	A9	1r	pale brn, brn & red org	1.00	*1.50*
41q	A12	3½r	mar & lt grn	—	
42q	A13	5r	dk bl, grn & pale bl	—	—
43q	A12	7r	dk grn & pink	—	
44q	A13	10r	scar, yel & gray	—	*150.00*
45q	A6	1k	red, *buff*	—	—
47q	A6	10k	brown, *buff*		*200.00*

Poltava I — Handstamped in green with a rubber device

9r	A14	2k	green		150.00
14r	A15	10k	dark blue	170.00	—
20r	A8	50k	violet & grn	125.00	—
21r	A11	70k	brown & org	125.00	—
27r	A14	10k	on 7k light blue	—	170.00
28r	A11	20k	on 14k bl & rose		—
29r	A14	1k	orange		175.00
45r	A6	1k	red, *buff*	—	—
46r	A6	5k	green, *buff*		—

Poltava II — Handstamped in black with a rubber device

7s	A12	7r	black & yellow	200.00	—
9s	A14	2k	green	175.00	—
10s	A14	3k	red	—	—
12s	A14	5k	claret	—	—
13s	A14	7k	light blue	—	
14s	A15	10k	dark blue	—	—
16s	A11	15k	red brn	75.00	*160.00*
17s	A8	20k	blue & car	—	—
19s	A11	35k	red brn & grn	175.00	—
20s	A8	50k	violet & grn	75.00	*50.00*
21s	A11	70k	brown & org	—	—
22s	A9	1r	lt brn, brn & org	30.00	25.00
23s	A12	3½r	mar & lt grn	75.00	60.00
24s	A13	5r	dk bl, grn & pale bl	125.00	*150.00*
25s	A12	7r	dk grn & pink	125.00	100.00
27s	A14	10k	on 7k light blue	—	175.00
28s	A11	20k	on 14k bl & rose	175.00	
29s	A14	1k	orange	—	
31s	A14	3k	red	125.00	*150.00*
34s	A11	15k	red brn & bl	—	100.00
37s	A11	35k	red brn & grn	—	100.00
40s	A9	1r	pale brn, brn & red org	9.00	*10.00*
44s	A13	10r	scar, yel & gray	175.00	*200.00*

The trident overprint was applied by favor to Russia Nos. 88-104, 110-111, the Romanov issue.

For surcharges see Russian Offices in the Turkish Empire Nos. 320-339.

A6

1919, Jan. **Litho.**

48	A6	20hr red & green	3.00	*20.00*

Because of its high face value, No. 48 was used primarily on money transfer forms or parcel receipts.

Nos. 1 and 5 Surcharged

1919 **Unwmk.** ***Imperf.***

49	A1	35k on 10sh buff	7.50	*15.00*
50	A5	70k on 50sh red	20.00	*35.00*
a.		Surcharge inverted	50.00	

Some authorities state that Nos. 49-50 were issued by the Soviets in the Ukraine in April 1919.

Excellent forged surcharges exist.

Nos. 1-5 surcharged in grivni (hryven) with the Polish eagle were sold as Polish occupation issues. They are of private origin.

Nos. 1-3 and 5 overprinted diagonally as above ("South Russia") are believed to be of private origin.

A lithographed set of 14 stamps (1hr-200hr) of these types, perf. 11½, was prepared in 1920, but never placed in use. Value, set $3.

All values exist imperf., some with inverted centers. Trial printings exist on various papers, including inverted, multiple, omitted and misaligned center vignettes. These are from the printer's waste.

This set handstamped "VILNA UKRAINA / 1921" and 6 values additionally overprinted "DOPLATA" are of private origin.

In 1923 the Ukrainian government-in-exile in Warsaw prepared an 11-value set, consisting of the 10h, 20h and 40h denominations surcharged and overprinted with the Cyrillic "UPP," supposedly intended as a Field Post issue for a planned invasion of the Ukraine. The invasion never occurred, and the stamps were never issued.

SEMI-POSTAL STAMPS

Ukrainian Soviet Socialist Republic

"Famine" — SP1

Taras H. Shevchenko SP2

"Death" Stalking Peasant — SP3

"Ukraine" Distributing Food — SP4

Perf. 14½x13½, 13½x14½

1923, June **Litho.** **Unwmk.**

B1	SP1	10k + 10k gray bl & blk	.75	*5.00*
B2	SP2	20k + 20k vio brn & org brn	.75	*5.00*
B3	SP3	90k + 30k db & blk, *straw*	.75	*5.00*
B4	SP4	150k + 50k red brn & blk	.75	*5.00*
		Nos. B1-B4 (4)	3.00	*20.00*

Imperf., Pairs

B1a	SP1	10k + 10k	80.00	*100.00*
B2a	SP2	20k + 20k	80.00	*100.00*
B3a	SP3	90k + 30k	80.00	*100.00*
B4a	SP4	150k + 50k	80.00	*100.00*

The values of these stamps are in karbovanets, which by 1923 converted to rubles at 100 to 1.

Wmk. 116
Same Colors

B5	SP1	10k + 10k	*40.00*	*60.00*
B6	SP2	20k + 20k	*40.00*	*60.00*
a.		Imperf., pair	2,000.	
B7	SP3	90k + 30k	*30.00*	*60.00*
B8	SP4	150k + 50k	*30.00*	*60.00*
		Nos. B5-B8 (4)	*140.00*	*240.00*

MILITARY STAMPS

COURIER FIELD POST ISSUE

Nos. 1-5, 48 Surcharged

1920, Aug. 26

M1	A1	10hr on 10sh buff	15.00	—
a.		Inverted surcharge	60.00	
M2	A2	10hr on 20sh brown	30.00	—
M3	A3	10hr on 30sh ultramarine	35.00	—
M4	A4	10hr on 40sh green	40.00	—
a.		Inverted surcharge	160.00	
M5	A5	10hr on 50sh red	35.00	—
M6	A1	20hr on 10sh buff	40.00	—
M7	A2	20hr on 20sh brown	10.00	—
a.		Inverted surcharge	40.00	
M8	A3	20hr on 30sh ultramarine	30.00	—
a.		Inverted surcharge	120.00	
M9	A4	20hr on 40sh green	30.00	—
M10	A5	20hr on 50sh red	30.00	—
a.		Inverted surcharge	120.00	
M11	A1	40hr on 10sh buff	150.00	—
M12	A2	40hr on 20sh brown	75.00	—
M13	A3	40hr on 30sh ultramarine	300.00	—
M14	A4	40hr on 40sh green	150.00	—
M15	A5	40hr on 50sh red	300.00	—
M16	A6	40hr on 20hr red & green	—	—

Nos. M1-M16 were prepared to facilitate communications between the Ukrainian government-in-exile at Tarnow, Poland, and its military units in the field.

Only two copies of No. M16 are known, one unused and one used on cover.

Forged surcharges and cancellations exist.

UPPER SENEGAL AND NIGER

'ə-pər ˌse-nə-gäl and 'nī-jər

LOCATION — In Northwest Africa, north of French Guinea and Ivory Coast
GOVT. — French Colony
AREA — 617,600 sq. mi.
POP. — 2,474,142
CAPITAL — Bamako

In 1921 the name of this colony was changed to French Sudan and postage stamps so inscribed were placed in use.

100 Centimes = 1 Franc

Gen. Louis Faidherbe A1

Oil Palms — A2

Dr. N. Eugène Ballay — A3

Perf. 14x13½

1906-07 Unwmk. Typo.

Name of Colony in Red or Blue

1	A1	1c slate	1.25	1.25
2	A1	2c brown	1.40	1.25
3	A1	4c brn, *gray bl*	2.00	1.25
4	A1	5c green	5.00	2.25
5	A1	10c car (B)	5.00	2.40
6	A1	15c vio ('07)	4.00	4.00
7	A2	20c bluish gray	5.00	3.75
8	A2	25c bl, *pnksh*	15.00	3.75
9	A2	30c vio brn, *pnksh*	6.25	4.50
10	A2	35c blk, *yellow*	5.00	3.75
11	A2	40c car, *az* (B)	8.50	6.00
12	A2	45c brn, *grnsh*	9.50	8.00
13	A2	50c dp vio	9.50	8.00
14	A2	75c bl, *org*	9.50	9.50
15	A3	1fr blk, *azure*	22.50	20.00
16	A3	2fr bl, *pink*	42.50	42.50
17	A3	5fr car, *straw* (B)	87.50	87.50
		Nos. 1-17 (17)	239.40	209.65

Camel with Rider — A4

1914-17 ***Perf. 13½x14***

18	A4	1c brn vio & vio	.25	.25
19	A4	2c gray & brn vio	.25	.25
20	A4	4c black & blue	.25	.25
21	A4	5c yel grn & bl grn	.75	.35
22	A4	10c red org & rose	2.00	1.60
23	A4	15c choc & org ('17)	1.75	.60
24	A4	20c brn vio & blk	1.90	1.10
25	A4	25c ultra & bl	1.25	1.10
26	A4	30c ol brn & brn	1.50	1.10
27	A4	35c car rose & vio	2.40	1.60
28	A4	40c gray & car rose	2.00	.80
29	A4	45c bl & ol brn	1.75	1.60
30	A4	50c black & green	2.00	1.60
31	A4	75c org & ol brn	2.00	1.60
32	A4	1fr brown & brn vio	2.00	1.60
33	A4	2fr green & blue	2.50	2.25
34	A4	5fr violet & black	11.00	9.50
		Nos. 18-34 (17)	35.55	27.15

See Upper Volta for types of this issue that escaped overprinting.

For surcharge see No. B1.

SEMI-POSTAL STAMP

Regular Issue of 1914 Surcharged in Red

1915 Unwmk. ***Perf. 13½x14***

B1	A4	10c + 5c red orange & rose	1.50	1.50

POSTAGE DUE STAMPS

Natives — D1

D2

1906 Unwmk. Typo. ***Perf. 14x13½***

J1	D1	5c green, *greenish*	3.00	2.25
J2	D1	10c red brown	6.50	6.00
J3	D1	15c dark blue	8.75	8.00
J4	D1	20c black, *yellow*	12.00	4.25
J5	D1	50c violet	21.50	20.00
J6	D1	60c black, *buff*	15.00	15.00
J7	D1	1fr black, *pinkish*	30.00	26.00
		Nos. J1-J7 (7)	96.75	81.50

1914

J8	D2	5c green	.95	.95
J9	D2	10c rose	.95	.95
J10	D2	15c gray	.95	.95
J11	D2	20c brown	1.10	1.10
J12	D2	30c blue	1.85	1.85
J13	D2	50c black	1.50	1.50
J14	D2	60c orange	5.50	5.50
J15	D2	1fr violet	5.50	5.50
		Nos. J8-J15 (8)	18.30	18.30

Stamps of Upper Senegal and Niger were superceded in 1921 by those of French Sudan.

UPPER SILESIA

'ə-pər sī'lē-zhˌē-ˌə

LOCATION — Formerly in eastern Germany and prior to World War I a part of Germany.

A plebiscite held under the terms of the Treaty of Versailles failed to determine the status of the country, the voting resulting about equally in favor of Germany and Poland. Accordingly, the League of Nations divided the territory between Germany and Poland.

100 Pfennig = 1 Mark
100 Fennigi = 1 Marka

Plebiscite Issues

A1

Perf. 14x13½

1920, Feb. 20 Typo. Unwmk.

1	A1	2½pf slate	.40	*.55*
		Never hinged	1.00	
		On cover		11.00
2	A1	3pf brown	.40	*.85*
		Never hinged	1.00	
		On cover		11.00
3	A1	5pf green	.30	*.35*
		Never hinged	.60	
		On cover		3.75
4	A1	10pf dull red	.40	*.90*
		Never hinged	1.00	
		On cover		3.75
5	A1	15pf violet	.20	*.40*
		Never hinged	.60	
		On cover		3.75
6	A1	20pf blue	.20	*.40*
		Never hinged	.60	
		On cover		3.75
a.		Imperf., pair	275.00	—
b.		Half used as 10pf on cover		85.00
c.		20pf prussian blue	1.10	*5.00*
		Never hinged	5.00	
		On cover		26.00
d.		As "c," half used as 10pf on cover		875.00
7	A1	50pf violet brn	3.50	*6.50*
		Never hinged	14.50	
		On cover		30.00
a.		50pf red brown	18.00	*45.00*
		Never hinged	45.00	
		On cover		150.00
8	A1	1m claret	5.00	*9.25*
		Never hinged	14.00	
		On cover		45.00
9	A1	5m orange	4.25	*9.25*
		Never hinged	13.00	
		On cover		140.00
		Nos. 1-9 (9)	14.65	*28.45*
		Set, never hinged	45.00	

Black Surcharge

5 Pf. I — 5 Pf. II — 5 Pf. III — 5 Pf. IV

10	A1	5pf on 15pf vio (I)	13.00	*42.50*
		Never hinged	35.00	
		On cover		525.00
a.		Type II	13.00	*42.50*
		Never hinged	40.00	
		On cover		*600.00*
b.		Type III	13.00	*42.50*
		Never hinged	40.00	
		On cover		*600.00*
c.		Type IV	13.00	*42.50*
		Never hinged	40.00	
		On cover		*600.00*
11	A1	5pf on 20pf blue (I)	.65	*2.00*
		Never hinged	1.60	
		On cover		*10.00*
a.		Type II	.80	*2.25*
		Never hinged	2.00	
		On cover		*13.50*
b.		Type III	1.00	*2.50*
		Never hinged	2.40	
		On cover		*17.00*
c.		Type IV	1.25	*3.25*
		Never hinged	2.60	
		On cover		*27.00*

Red Surcharge

10 Pf. I — 10 Pf. II — 10 Pf. III — 10 Pf. IV

12	A1	10pf on 20pf bl (I)	.65	*1.60*
		Never hinged	1.60	
		On cover		*13.50*
a.		Type II	.65	*1.60*
		Never hinged	1.60	
		On cover		*17.00*
b.		Type III	.65	*1.60*
		Never hinged	1.60	
		On cover		*10.00*
c.		Type IV	.65	*1.60*
		Never hinged	1.60	
		On cover		*11.50*
d.		Imperf.	50.00	
		Never hinged	80.00	
		On cover		*800.00*

Black Surcharge

50 Pf. I — 50 Pf. II — 50 Pf. III — 50 Pf. IV — 50 Pf. V

13	A1	50pf on 5m org (I), shiny ovpt.	14.00	*42.50*
		Never hinged	80.00	
		On cover		*200.00*
a.		Type II	15.00	*45.00*
		Never hinged	72.50	
		On cover		*210.00*
b.		Type III	16.00	*80.00*
		Never hinged	140.00	
		On cover		*300.00*
c.		Type IV	16.00	*80.00*
		Never hinged	140.00	
		On cover		*300.00*
d.		Type V	25.00	*100.00*
		Never hinged	190.00	
		On cover		*375.00*
e.		Type I, matte ovpt.	32.50	*80.00*
		Never hinged	110.00	
		On cover		525.00

Nos. 10-13 are found with many varieties including surcharges inverted, double and double inverted.

Dove with Olive Branch Flying over Silesian Terrain — A2

A3

1920, Mar. 26 Typo. ***Perf. 13½x14***

15	A2	2½pf gray	.25	*.40*
		Never hinged	1.40	
		On cover		7.50
16	A2	3pf red brown	.25	*.40*
		Never hinged	1.40	
		On cover		7.50
17	A2	5pf green	.25	*.40*
		Never hinged	1.40	
		On cover		3.75
18	A2	10pf dull red	.25	*.40*
		Never hinged	1.40	
		On cover		4.50

19 A2 15pf violet	.25	*.40*
Never hinged	1.40	
On cover		4.50
20 A2 20pf blue	.65	*1.60*
Never hinged	2.25	
On cover		4.50
21 A2 25pf dark brown	.25	*.40*
Never hinged	1.40	
On cover		7.50
22 A2 30pf orange	.25	*.40*
Never hinged	1.40	
On cover		6.00
23 A2 40pf olive green	.25	*1.00*
Never hinged	1.40	
On cover		6.00

Perf. 14x13½

24 A3 50pf gray	.25	*.40*
Never hinged	1.50	
On cover		19.00
25 A3 60pf blue	.25	*1.60*
Never hinged	1.40	
On cover		19.00
26 A3 75pf deep green	.85	*2.00*
Never hinged	3.50	
On cover		23.00
a. 75pf blackish green	*750.00*	*1,150.*
Never hinged	*1,500.*	
b. 75pf bluish green	*1,150.*	*1,150.*
Never hinged	*1,700.*	
c. 75pf deep gray green	*2,700.*	*2,300.*
Never hinged	*3,000.*	
27 A3 80pf red brown	.65	*1.00*
Never hinged	3.00	
On cover		15.00
28 A3 1m claret	.50	.40
Never hinged	3.00	
On cover		15.00
29 A3 2m dark brown	.50	.40
Never hinged	2.75	
On cover		11.50
30 A3 3m violet	.70	.40
Never hinged	2.75	
On cover		23.00
31 A3 5m orange	2.75	*4.00*
Never hinged	10.50	
On cover		37.50
Nos. 15-31 (17)	9.10	15.60
Set, never hinged	40.00	

Nos. 18-28 Overprinted in Black or Red

1921, Mar. 20

32 A2 10pf dull red	3.25	*10.00*
Never hinged	13.00	
On cover		92.50
33 A2 15pf violet	3.25	*10.00*
Never hinged	13.00	
On cover		92.50
34 A2 20pf blue	4.50	*14.00*
Never hinged	23.00	
On cover		92.50
35 A2 25pf dk brn (R)	12.00	*32.50*
Never hinged	42.50	
On cover		110.00
36 A2 30pf orange	9.00	*20.00*
Never hinged	42.50	
On cover		110.00
37 A2 40pf olive grn (R)	11.00	*20.00*
Never hinged	42.50	
On cover		110.00

Overprinted

38 A3 50pf gray (R)	11.00	*27.50*
Never hinged	55.00	
On cover		—
39 A3 60pf blue	12.00	*22.50*
Never hinged	60.00	
On cover		—
40 A3 75pf deep green	12.00	*27.50*
Never hinged	92.50	
On cover		—
a. 75pf blue green	*1,500.*	*1,700.*
41 A3 80pf red brown	19.00	*35.00*
Never hinged	110.00	
On cover		—
42 A3 1m claret	22.50	*65.00*
Never hinged	125.00	
On cover		—
Nos. 32-42 (11)	119.50	*284.00*
Set, never hinged	625.00	

Inverted or double overprints exist on Nos. 32-33, 35-40. Counterfeit overprints exist.

Type of 1920 and Surcharged

1922, Mar.

45 A3 4m on 60pf ol grn	.80	*1.60*
Never hinged	2.75	
On cover		23.00
46 A3 10m on 75pf red	.80	*2.50*
Never hinged	3.00	
On cover		110.00
47 A3 20m on 80pf orange	6.25	*13.00*
Never hinged	18.50	
On cover		350.00
Nos. 45-47 (3)	7.85	*17.10*
Set, never hinged	25.00	

Stamps of the above design were a private issue not recognized by the Inter-Allied Commission of Government. Value, set of 7, $45 unused, $140 never hinged, $180 used.

OFFICIAL STAMPS

German Stamps of 1905-20 Handstamped in Blue

1920, Feb. Wmk. 125 *Perf. 14, 14½*

On Stamps of 1906-19

O1	A22	2pf gray	1.10	*1.25*
O3	A22	2½pf gray	.55	*.65*
O4	A16	3pf brown	.55	*.65*
O5	A16	5pf green	.55	*.65*
O6	A22	7½pf orange	.55	*.65*
O7	A16	10pf car rose	.55	*.65*
O8	A22	15pf dk violet	.55	*.65*
O9	A16	20pf blue violet	.55	*.65*
O10	A16	25pf org & blk, *yel*	5.25	*6.50*
O11	A16	30pf org & blk, *buff*	.55	*.65*
O12	A22	35pf red brown	.55	*.65*
O13	A16	40pf lake & blk	.55	*.65*
O14	A16	50pf vio & blk, *buff*	.55	*.65*
O15	A16	60pf magenta	.55	*.65*
O16	A16	75pf green & blk	.55	*.65*
O17	A16	80pf lake & blk, *rose*	6.50	*8.00*
O18	A17	1m car rose	1.10	*1.25*
O19	A21	2m gray blue	5.25	*6.50*

On National Assembly Stamps of 1919-20

O25	A23	10pf car rose	.90	*1.10*
O26	A24	15pf choc & bl	1.60	*2.00*
O27	A25	25pf green & red	3.25	*4.00*
O28	A25	30pf red vio & red	2.50	*3.00*

On Semi-Postal Stamps of 1919

O30	A16	10pf + 5pf carmine	6.50	*8.00*
O31	A22	15pf + 5pf dk vio	6.50	*8.00*
		Nos. O1-O31 (24)	47.60	*58.05*

Red Handstamp

O5a	A16	5pf	10.00	*14.00*
O8a	A22	15pf	6.50	*10.00*
O9a	A16	20pf	6.50	*10.00*
O13a	A16	40pf	20.00	*30.00*
O16a	A16	75pf	20.00	*30.00*
O26a	A24	15pf	1.10	*1.25*
		Nos. O5a-O26a (6)	64.10	*95.25*

Values of Nos. O1-O31 are for reprints made with a second type of handstamp differing in minor details from the original (example: period after "S" is round instead of the earlier triangular form). Originals are scarce. Counterfeits exist.

Germany No. 65C with this handstamp is considered bogus by experts.

Local Official Stamps of Germany, 1920, Overprinted

1920, Apr. *Perf. 14*

O32	LO2	5pf green	.30	*.45*
O33	LO3	10pf carmine	.30	*.45*
O34	LO4	15pf violet brn	.30	*.45*
O35	LO5	20pf deep ultra	.30	*.45*
O36	LO6	30pf orange, *buff*	.30	*.45*
O37	LO7	50pf violet, *buff*	.30	*1.40*
O38	LO8	1m red, *buff*	6.00	*10.00*
		Nos. O32-O38 (7)	8.00	*13.65*

Same Overprint on Official Stamps of Germany, 1920-21

1920-21

O39	O1	5pf green	1.00	*2.40*
O40	O2	10pf carmine	.20	.20
O41	O3	15pf violet brn	.20	.20
O42	O4	20pf deep ultra	.20	.20
O43	O5	30pf orange, *buff*	.20	.20
O44	O6	40pf carmine rose	.20	.20
O45	O7	50pf violet, *buff*	.20	.20
O46	O8	60pf red brown	.20	.20
O47	O9	1m red, *buff*	.20	.20
O48	O10	1.25m dk blue, *yel*	.20	.20
O49	O11	2m dark blue	7.00	*8.00*
O50	O12	5m brown, *yel*	.20	.20

1922, Feb. Wmk. 126

O51	O11	2m dark blue	.20	.20
		Nos. O39-O51 (13)	10.20	*12.60*

This overprint is found both horizontal, reading upright or inverted, and vertical, reading up or down. These variations generally command no premium over the values above.

The overprint also exists on most values double and double, one inverted, in the above formats, as well as at a 45 degree angle, upreading and downreading, either upright or inverted. These varieties generally sell for 25-100 percent over the value of normal examples.

UPPER VOLTA

LOCATION — Northwestern Africa, north of Gold Coast
GOVT. — French Colony
AREA — 105,869 sq. mi.
POP. — 6,695,500 (est. 1984)
CAPITAL — Ouagadougou

In 1919 the French territory of Upper Volta was detached from the southern section of Upper Senegal and Niger and made a separate colony. In 1933 the colony was divided among its neighbors: French Sudan, Ivory Coast, and Niger Territory.

100 Centimes = 1 Franc

Stamps and Types of Upper Senegal and Niger, 1914-17, Overprinted in Black or Red

1920-28 Unwmk. *Perf. 13½x14*

1	A4	1c brn vio & vio	.20	.20
2	A4	2c gray & brn vio (R)	.20	.20
3	A4	4c blk & bl	.20	.20
4	A4	5c yel grn & bl grn	.75	.40
5	A4	5c ol brn & dk brn ('22)	.20	.20
6	A4	10c red org & rose	1.25	.60
		On cover		35.00
7	A4	10c yel grn & bl grn ('22)	.20	.20
		On cover		35.00
8	A4	10c claret & bl ('25)	.35	.35
		On cover		35.00
	a.	Overprint omitted	130.00	
9	A4	15c choc & org	.55	.55
10	A4	20c brn vio & blk (R)	.75	.70
11	A4	25c ultra & bl	1.70	.70
		On cover		35.00
12	A4	25c blk & bl grn ('22)	.60	.55
		On cover		35.00
	a.	Overprint omitted	120.00	
13	A4	30c ol brn & brn (R)	2.50	2.25
14	A4	30c red org & rose ('22)	1.00	1.00
15	A4	30c vio & brn red ('25)	.70	.70
16	A4	30c dl grn & bl grn ('27)	1.00	1.00
17	A4	35c car rose & vio	.75	.50
18	A4	40c gray & car rose	.75	.55
19	A4	45c bl & brn (R)	.75	.70
20	A4	50c blk & grn	2.50	2.50
21	A4	50c ultra & bl ('22)	.90	.80
22	A4	50c red org & bl ('25)	.90	.80
23	A4	60c org red ('26)	.40	.35
24	A4	65c bis & pale bl ('28)	.90	.75
25	A4	75c org & brn	1.10	.75
26	A4	1fr brn & brn vio	1.10	1.10
27	A4	2fr grn & bl	1.50	1.00
28	A4	5fr vio & blk (R)	3.00	3.00
		Nos. 1-28 (28)	26.70	22.60

No. 9 Surcharged in Various Colors

1922

29 A4 0,01c on 15c (Bk)		.70	.70
a.	Double surcharge	110.00	110.00
30 A4 0,02c on 15c (Bl)		.70	.70
31 A4 0,05c on 15c (R)		.70	.70
	Nos. 29-31 (3)	2.10	2.10

Type of 1920 Surcharged

1922

32 A4 60c on 75c vio, *pnksh*	.55	.55

Stamps and Types of 1920 Surcharged with New Value and Bars

1924-27

33	A4	25c on 2fr grn & bl	.60	.60
34	A4	25c on 5fr vio & blk	.60	.60
35	A4	65c on 45c bl & brn ('25)	1.00	1.00
36	A4	85c on 75c org & brn ('25)	1.25	1.25
37	A4	90c on 75c brn red & sal pink ('27)	1.25	1.25
38	A4	1.25fr on 1fr dp bl & lt bl (R) ('26)	.85	.85
39	A4	1.50fr on 1fr dp bl & ultra ('27)	2.25	2.25
40	A4	3fr on 5fr dl red & brn org ('27)	3.50	3.50
41	A4	10fr on 5fr ol grn & lil rose ('27)	11.50	11.50
42	A4	20fr on 5fr org brn & vio ('27)	15.00	15.00
		Nos. 33-42 (10)	37.80	37.80

Hausa Chief — A5

Hausa Woman — A6

Hausa Warrior A7

1928 Typo. *Perf. 13½x14*

43	A5	1c indigo & grn	.20	.20
44	A5	2c brn & lil	.20	.20
45	A5	4c blk & yel	.25	.25
46	A5	5c indigo & gray bl	.25	.25
47	A5	10c indigo & pink	.75	.75
48	A5	15c brn & bl	1.25	1.25
49	A5	20c brn & grn	1.25	1.25
50	A6	25c brn & yel	1.75	1.75
51	A6	30c dp grn & grn	1.60	1.60
52	A6	40c blk & pink	1.60	1.60
53	A6	45c brn & blue	2.25	2.25
54	A6	50c blk & grn	1.90	1.90
55	A6	65c indigo & bl	2.25	2.25
56	A6	75c blk & lil	2.00	2.00
57	A6	90c brn red & lil	2.25	2.25

Perf. 14x13½

58	A7	1fr brn & grn	1.75	1.75
59	A7	1.10fr indigo & lil	2.00	2.00
60	A7	1.50fr ultra & grysh	3.00	3.00
61	A7	2fr blk & bl	3.50	3.50
62	A7	3fr brn & yel	3.50	3.50
63	A7	5fr brn & lil	3.00	3.00

64	A7	10fr blk & grn	15.00	15.00
65	A7	20fr blk & pink	20.00	20.00
		Nos. 43-65 (23)	71.50	71.50

Common Design Types pictured following the introduction.

Colonial Exposition Issue

Common Design Types

1931 Engr. *Perf. 12½*

Country Name Typo. in Black

66	CD70	40c dp grn	2.25	2.25
67	CD71	50c violet	2.75	2.75
68	CD72	90c red org	2.75	2.75
69	CD73	1.50fr dull blue	4.00	4.00
		Nos. 66-69 (4)	11.75	11.75

POSTAGE DUE STAMPS

Postage Due Stamps of Upper Senegal and Niger, 1914, Overprinted in Black or Red

1920 Unwmk. *Perf. 14x13½*

J1	D2	5c green	.35	.35
J2	D2	10c rose	.35	.35
J3	D2	15c gray	.50	.50
J4	D2	20c brown (R)	.55	.55
J5	D2	30c blue	.55	.55
J6	D2	50c black (R)	.95	.95
J7	D2	60c orange	.95	.95
J8	D2	1fr violet	1.25	1.25
		Nos. J1-J8 (8)	5.45	5.45

Type of 1914 Issue Surcharged

1927

J9	D2	2fr on 1fr lilac rose	2.25	2.25
J10	D2	3fr on 1fr orange brn	2.75	2.75

D3

1928 Typo.

J11	D3	5c green	.50	.50
J12	D3	10c rose	.50	.50
J13	D3	15c dark gray	.70	.70
J14	D3	20c dark brown	.70	.70
J15	D3	30c dark blue	1.10	1.10
J16	D3	50c black	2.25	2.25
J17	D3	60c orange	2.75	2.75
J18	D3	1fr dull violet	4.25	4.25
J19	D3	2fr lilac rose	7.25	7.25
J20	D3	3fr orange brn	9.00	9.00
		Nos. J11-J20 (10)	29.00	29.00

URUGUAY

ˈyur-ə-ˌgwā

LOCATION — South America, between Brazil and Argentina and bordering on the Atlantic Ocean
GOVT. — Republic
AREA — 72,172 sq. mi.
POP. — 2,991,341 (est. 1983)
CAPITAL — Montevideo

120 Centavos = 1 Real
8 Reales = 1 Peso
100 Centesimos = 1 Peso (1859)
1000 Milesimos = 1 Peso (1898)

Watermarks

Wmk. 187 — R O in Diamond

Wmk. 188 — REPUBLICA O. DEL URUGUAY

Wmk. 189 — Caduceus

Wmk. 227 — Greek Border and REPUBLICA O. DEL URUGUAY in Alternate Curved Lines

PRE-STAMP POSTAL MARKINGS

Crowned Circle handstamp type VI is pictured in the Crowned Circle Handstamps and Great Britain Used Abroad section.

1851

A1	VI	Crowned Circle handstamp inscribed "PAID AT MONTEVIDEO" in black, on cover		1,000.
A2	VI	Crowned Circle handstamp inscribed "PAID AT MONTEVIDEO" in red, on cover		—

Carrier Issues

Issued by Atanasio Lapido, Administrator-General of Posts

"El Sol de Mayo"
A1 A1a

Unwmk.

1856, Oct. 1 Litho. *Imperf.*

1	A1	60c blue	350.	
		On cover		*5,000.*
a.		60c deep blue	500.	
		On cover		*6,500.*
b.		60c indigo	800.	
		On cover		—
c.		60c pale blue	500.	
		On cover		—
2	A1	80c green	325.	
		On cover		*8,000.*
a.		80c deep green	350.	
		On cover		—
b.		80c emerald green	400.	
		On cover		—
3	A1	1r vermilion	300.	
		On cover		*11,000.*
a.		1r carmine vermilion	350.	
		On cover		—

1857, Oct. 1

3B	A1a	60c blue	*2,500.*	
		On cover		—
c.		60c pale blue	*2,750.*	
		On cover		—
d.		60c indigo	*3,000.*	
		On cover		—

Nos. 1-3d were spaced very closely on the stone. Very fine examples will have clear margins on three sides and touching or slightly cut into the frames on the fourth (consult the grading illustrations in the catalogue introduction). All genuinely used examples are pen canceled. Certification by a recognized authority is recommended.

Stamps with tiny faults, such as small thin spots, sell for about 75% of the values of sound copies.

See Nos. 410-413.

A2

1858, Mar.

4	A2	120c blue	250.00	*300.00*
		On cover		*7,500.*
a.		120c deep blue	275.00	*300.00*
		On cover		—
b.		120c greensih blue	300.00	—
		On cover		—
c.		Tête bêche pair	—	
5	A2	180c green	100.00	*200.00*
		On cover		—
a.		180c deep green	200.00	*350.00*
		On cover		—
b.		80c pale green	120.00	—
		On cover		—
b.		As "b," thick paper	450.00	—
		On cover		—
c.		Tête bêche pair	—	
6	A2	240c dull ver	150.00	*1,500.*
		On cover		—
a.		240c deep vermilion	175.00	
		On cover		—
b.		240c brick red	300.00	
		On cover		—
c.		180c dl ver in stone of 240c	—	
d.		Thick paper (dull ver)	—	—
e.		240c setenant with a vacant space	*5,000.*	
		Nos. 4-6 (3)	500.00	*2,000.*

Nos. 4-6e have been extensively forged. Certification by a recognized authority is recommended.

Government Issues

A3

A4

1859, June 26

Thin Numerals

7	A3	60c lilac	25.00	20.00
		On cover		250.00
a.		60c gray lilac	25.00	20.00
		On cover		250.00
8	A3	80c orange	190.00	35.00
		On cover		800.00
a.		80c yellow	275.00	50.00
		On cover		1,500.
9	A3	100c brown lake	55.00	45.00
		On cover		1,500.
a.		100c brown rose	55.00	45.00
		On cover		1,500.
10	A3	120c blue	35.00	15.00
		On cover		250.00
a.		120c slate blue	50.00	17.50
		On cover		600.00
b.		120c greenish blue	75.00	25.00
		On cover		350.00
11	A3	180c green	15.00	17.50
		On cover		1,200.
12	A3	240c vermilion	50.00	50.00
		On cover		1,500.
		Nos. 7-12 (6)	370.00	*182.50*

Very fine examples of Nos. 7-12 have 1.5mm margins on all sides.

1860

Thick Numerals

13	A4	60c dull lilac	15.00	8.00
		On cover		200.00
a.		60c gray lilac	17.50	10.00
		On cover		250.00
b.		60c brown lilac	17.50	12.00
		On cover		250.00
c.		60c red lilac	17.50	12.00
		On cover		250.00
d.		As "a," fine impression (1st printing)	70.00	40.00
		On cover		350.00
e.		60c chocolate brown	75.00	37.50
		On cover		350.00
14	A4	80c yellow	20.00	16.00
		On cover		400.00
a.		80c orange	45.00	18.00
		On cover		500.00
15	A4	100c rose	45.00	35.00
		On cover		*1,200.*
a.		100c carmine	45.00	35.00
		On cover		*1,200.*
16	A4	120c blue	21.00	16.00
		On cover		200.00
17	A4	180c yellow grn	175.00	225.00
		On cover		*2,000.*
a.		180c deep green	225.00	250.00
		On cover		*2,000.*
		Nos. 13-17 (5)	276.00	*300.00*

No. 13 was first printed (1860) in sheets of 192 (16x12) containing 24 types. The impressions are very clear; paper is whitish and of better quality than that of the later printings. In the 1861-62 printings, the layout contains 12 types and the subjects are spaced farther apart.

Very fine examples of Nos. 13-17 have 1.5mm margins on all sides.

Coat of Arms — A5

1864, Apr. 13

18	A5	6c rose	12.00	7.00
		On cover		150.00
a.		6c carmine	32.50	25.00
		On cover		150.00
b.		6c red	32.50	25.00
		On cover		—
c.		6c brick red	32.50	25.00
		On cover		1,200.
d.		On laid paper	30.00	20.00
		On cover		—
20	A5	6c salmon	300.00	*385.00*
		On cover		—
21	A5	8c green	17.00	17.00
		On cover		750.00
a.		Tête bêche pair	775.00	
b.		8c yellow green	15.00	15.00
		On cover		900.00
c.		8c dark green	15.00	15.00
		On cover		900.00
22	A5	10c yellow	25.00	20.00
		On cover		1,200.
a.		10c ocher	25.00	20.00
		On cover		—
23	A5	12c blue	15.00	8.00
		On cover		200.00
a.		12c dark blue	25.00	15.00
		On cover		250.00
b.		12c slate blue	30.00	50.00
		On cover		600.00
c.		12c pale blue	25.00	15.00
		On cover		250.00
d.		On laid paper	30.00	20.00
		On cover		—

No. 20, which is on thicker paper, was never placed in use.

Stamps of 1864 Surcharged in Black

1866, Jan. 1

24	A5	5c on 12c blue	20.00	*42.50*
a.		5c on 12c slate blue	25.00	*45.00*
b.		Inverted surcharge	150.00	
c.		Double surcharge	150.00	
d.		Pair, one without surcharge		
e.		Triple surcharge	55.00	
25	A5	10c on 8c brt grn	20.00	*42.50*
a.		10c on 8c dl grn	20.00	*42.50*
b.		Tête bêche pair	300.00	
c.		Double surcharge	150.00	
26	A5	15c on 10c ocher	20.00	*67.50*
a.		15c on 10c yellow	20.00	*67.50*
b.		Inverted surcharge	150.00	
c.		Double surcharge	150.00	
27	A5	20c on 6c rose	27.00	*67.50*
a.		20c on 6c rose red	30.00	*50.00*
b.		Inverted surcharge	150.00	
c.		Double surcharge	150.00	
d.		Pair, one without surcharge		
28	A5	20c on 6c brick red	*350.00*	
a.		Double surcharge	400.00	
		Nos. 24-27 (4)	87.00	*220.00*

Many counterfeits exist.
No. 28 was not issued.

Coat of Arms and Numeral of Value — A7

A8

A8a

A8b

A8c

ONE CENTESIMO:

Type I — The wavy lines behind "CENTESIMO" are clear and distinct. Stamps 4mm apart.

Type II — The wavy lines are rough and blurred. Stamps 3mm apart.

1866, Jan. 10 ***Imperf.***

29	A7	1c black (type II)	4.00	*15.00*
a.		1c black (type I)	4.00	*15.00*
30	A8	5c blue	4.00	2.00
a.		5c dull blue	4.00	2.00
b.		5c ultramarine	25.00	10.00
c.		Numeral with white flag	25.00	12.00
d.		"ENTECIMOS"	25.00	12.00
e.		"CENTECIMO"	25.00	12.00
f.		"CENTECIMOS" with small "S"	25.00	12.00
g.		Pelure paper	100.00	100.00
h.		Thick paper		
31	A8a	10c yellow green	15.00	5.00
a.		10c blue green	17.00	6.00
b.		"I" of "CENTECIMOS" omitted	27.50	14.00
c.		"CENIECIMOS"	27.50	14.00
d.		"CENTRCIMOS"	27.50	14.00
32	A8b	15c orange yel	25.00	9.00
a.		15c yellow	25.00	9.00
33	A8c	20c rose	30.00	10.00
a.		20c lilac rose	30.00	10.00
b.		Thick paper	35.00	15.00
		Nos. 29-33 (5)	78.00	41.00

See Nos. 34-38. For overprint see No. O11.

Engraved plates were prepared for Nos. 30 to 33 but were not put in use. The stamps were printed from lithographic transfers from the plate. In 1915 a few reprints of the 15c were made from the engraved plate by a California philatelic society, each sheet being numbered and signed by officers of the society; then the plate was defaced.

1866-67 ***Perf. 8½ to 13½***

34	A7	1c black	5.00	20.00
35	A8	5c blue	5.00	1.00
a.		5c dark blue	5.00	1.00
b.		Numeral with white flag	15.00	8.00
c.		"ENTECIMOS"	15.00	8.00
d.		"CENTECIMO"	15.00	8.00
e.		"CENTECIMOS" with small "S"	15.00	8.00
f.		Pelure paper	90.00	20.00
36	A8a	10c green	12.00	4.00
a.		10c yellow green	14.00	4.00
b.		"CENIECIMOS"	20.00	10.00
c.		"I" of "CENTECIMOS" omitted	20.00	10.00
d.		"CENTRCIMOS"	20.00	10.00
e.		Pelure paper	90.00	20.00
37	A8b	15c orange yel	21.00	6.00
a.		15c yellow	21.00	6.00
b.		Thin paper	25.00	10.00
38	A8c	20c rose	25.00	10.00
a.		20c brown rose	25.00	10.00
b.		Thin paper	30.00	15.00
c.		Thick paper	30.00	15.00
		Nos. 34-38 (5)	68.00	41.00

A9

A10

A11

A12

1877-79 **Engr.** ***Rouletted 8***

39	A9	1c red brown	.55	.40
40	A10	5c green	.65	.40
a.		Thick paper	4.00	2.00
41	A11	10c vermilion	1.00	.65
42	A11	20c bister	1.10	.65
43	A11	50c black	7.00	3.00
43A	A12	1p blue ('79)	35.00	20.00
		Nos. 39-43A (6)	45.30	25.10

The first printing of the 1p had the coat of arms smaller with quarterings reversed. These "error" stamps were not issued, and all were ordered burned. A copy is known to have been in a celebrated Uruguayan collection and a few others exist.

See No. 44. For overprints and surcharges see Nos. 52-53, O1-O8, O10, O19.

1880, Nov. 10 **Engr.** ***Rouletted 6***

44	A9	1c brown	.40	.40
a.		Imperf., pair	10.00	
b.		Rouletted 12½	2.50	

Joaquin Suárez — A13

1881, Aug. 25 ***Perf. 12½***

45	A13	7c blue	1.75	1.75
a.		Imperf., pair	9.00	9.00

For overprint see No. O9.

Devices from Coat of Arms
A14 A14a

1882, May 15

46	A14	1c green	1.25	1.25
a.		1c yellow green	4.00	2.00
b.		Imperf., pair	13.00	
47	A14a	2c rose	1.00	.75
a.		Imperf., pair	15.00	

These stamps bear numbers from 1 to 100 according to their position on the sheet.

Counterfeits of Nos. 46 and 47 are plentiful.

See Nos. 1132-1133. For overprints see Nos. 54, O12-O13, O20.

Coat of Arms
A15 A16

Gen. Máximo Santos — A17

General José Artigas — A18

Perf. 12, 12x12½, 12x13, 13x12

1883, Mar. 1

48	A15	1c green	1.25	1.00
49	A16	2c red	1.50	1.25
50	A17	5c blue	2.50	1.75
51	A18	10c brown	3.00	2.10
		Nos. 48-51 (4)	8.25	6.10

Imperf., Pairs

48a	A15	1c	7.00
49a	A16	2c	7.00
50a	A17	5c	6.50
51a	A18	10c	11.00

For overprints see Nos. O14-O18.

No. 40 Overprinted in Black

1883, Sept. 24 ***Rouletted 8***

52	A10	5c green	1.00	.75
a.		Double overprint	15.00	15.00
b.		Overprint reading down	6.00	6.00
c.		"Provisorio" omitted	7.00	7.00
d.		"1883" omitted	4.50	4.50

No. 52 with overprint in red is a color essay.

No. 41 Surcharged in Black

1884, Jan. 15

53	A11	1c on 10c ver	.50	.50
a.		Small figure "1"	4.25	4.25
b.		Inverted surcharge	4.25	4.25
c.		Double surcharge	8.00	5.00

No. 47 Overprinted in Black

Perf. 12½

54	A14a	2c rose	.75	.75
a.		Double overprint	14.00	
b.		Imperf., pair	40.00	

A22

A23

Thick Paper

1884, Jan. 25 **Litho.** **Unwmk.**

55	A22	5c ultra	2.00	1.00
a.		Imperf., pair	7.50	4.00

Thin Paper

Perf. 12½, 13 and Compound

56	A23	5c blue	1.50	.70
a.		Imperf., pair	14.00	

For overprints see Nos. O21-O22.

A24

A24a

A24b

Artigas — A25

Santos — A26

A27

A28

1884-88 **Engr.** ***Rouletted 8***

57	A24	1c gray	.80	.50
58	A24	1c olive	.75	.40
59	A24	1c green	.65	.40
60	A24a	2c vermilion	.40	.25
60A	A24a	2c rose ('88)	.40	.25
61	A24b	5c deep blue	.80	.30
61A	A24b	5c blue, *blue*	2.00	.85
62	A24b	5c violet ('86)	.50	.20
63	A24b	5c lt bl ('88)	.50	.20
64	A25	7c dk brown	2.00	.85
65	A25	7c org ('88)	2.00	.75
66	A26	10c olive brn	.80	.35
67	A27	20c red violet	2.00	1.00
68	A27	20c bis brn ('88)	2.00	1.00
69	A28	25c gray violet	4.00	1.50
70	A28	25c ver ('88)	3.00	1.00
		Nos. 57-70 (16)	22.60	9.80

Water dissolves the blue in the paper of No. 61A.

For overprints see Nos. 73, 98-99, O23-O34, O36-O39, O61.

A29

A30

1887, Oct. 17 **Litho.** ***Rouletted 9***

71	A29	10c lilac	2.50	1.25
a.		10c gray lilac	3.00	1.25

For overprint see No. O40.

1888, Jan. 1 **Engr.** ***Rouletted 8***

72	A30	10c violet	.60	.25

For overprint see No. O35.

No. 62 Overprinted in Black

1889, Oct. 14

73	A24b	5c violet	.40	.40
a.		Inverted overprint	8.00	6.00
b.		Inverted "A" for "V" in "Provisorio"	4.00	4.00

No. 73 with overprint in red is a color essay.

Coat of Arms — A32

Numeral of Value — A33

A34

A35

A36

A37

Justice A38

Mercury A39

A40

Perf. 12½ to 15½ and Compound

1889-1901 **Engr.**

74	A32	1c green	.50	.20
a.		Imperf., pair	13.00	
75	A32	1c dull bl ('94)	.50	.20
76	A33	2c rose	.50	.20
77	A33	2c red brn ('94)	.55	.25
78	A33	2c org ('99)	.55	.25
79	A34	5c dp blue	.50	.20

80	A34	5c rose ('94)	.55	.20
81	A35	7c bister brn	1.00	.30
82	A35	7c green ('94)	4.75	2.75
83	A35	7c car ('00)	4.00	1.75
84	A36	10c blue grn	3.50	.85
a.		Printed on both sides	20.00	
85	A36	10c org ('94)	3.25	.60
86	A37	20c orange	2.50	.60
87	A37	20c brown ('94)	4.75	1.75
88	A37	20c lt blue ('00)	2.75	.40
a.		20c greenish blue	3.00	.40
89	A38	25c red brown	3.25	.85
90	A38	25c ver ('94)	6.75	3.50
91	A38	25c bis brn ('01)	3.75	.50
92	A39	50c lt blue	7.50	5.00
93	A39	50c lilac ('94)	11.00	5.50
94	A39	50c car ('01)	6.75	1.00
95	A40	1p lilac	18.00	5.00
96	A40	1p lt blue ('94)	25.00	7.00
97	A40	1p dp grn ('01)	20.00	2.25
a.		Imperf., pair	30.00	
		Nos. 74-97 (24)	132.15	41.10

For surcharges and overprints see Nos. 100-101, 142, 180, 185, C1-C3, O41-O60, O89-O91, O108-O109.

Nos. 59 and 62 Overprinted in Red

a

b

1891-92 ***Rouletted 8***

98	A24 (a)	1c green ('92)	.40	.40
a.		Inverted overprint	6.00	6.00
b.		Double overprint	7.75	7.75
c.		Double ovpt., one invtd.	3.00	2.50
d.		"PREVISORIO"	4.00	4.00
99	A24b (b)	5c violet	.20	.20
a.		"1391"	4.00	2.75
b.		Double overprint	4.00	2.75
c.		Inverted overprint	4.00	2.75
d.		Double ovpt., one invtd.	5.00	3.00

Nos. 86 and 81 Surcharged in Black or Red

c

d

Perf. 12½ to 15½ and Compound

1892

100	A37 (c)	1c on 20c org (Bk)	.40	.40
a.		Inverted surcharge	3.00	3.00
101	A35 (d)	5c on 7c bis brn (R)	.40	.40
a.		Inverted surcharge	1.00	1.00
b.		Double surcharge, one invtd.	3.00	3.00
c.		Double surcharge	3.00	3.00
d.		Vertical surcharge	10.00	
e.		"PREVISORIO"	3.00	3.00
f.		"Cinco" omitted	4.50	

No. 101 with surcharge in green is a color essay.

Several surcharge errors of date and misspelling of "Centésimos" exist. Value $15.

A45

A46

Arms
A47

Peace
A48

1892 **Engr.**

102	A45	1c green	.50	.20
103	A46	2c rose	.50	.20
104	A47	5c blue	.50	.20
105	A48	10c orange	2.00	.85
		Nos. 102-105 (4)	3.50	1.45

Issued: 1c, 2c, 3/9; 5c, 4/19; 10c, 12/15.

Liberty
A49

Arms
A50

1894, June 2

106	A49	2p carmine	27.50	17.00
107	A50	3p dull violet	27.50	17.00

Gaucho
A51

Solis Theater
A52

Locomotive
A53

Bull's Head
A54

Ceres — A55

Sailing Ship — A56

Liberty
A57

Mercury
A58

Coat of Arms — A59

Montevideo Fortress — A60

Cathedral in Montevideo
A61

Perf. 12 to 15½ and Compound

1895-99

108	A51	1c bister	.50	.20
109	A51	1c slate bl ('97)	.50	.20
a.		Printed on both sides	14.00	
110	A52	2c blue	.50	.20
111	A52	2c claret ('97)	.50	.20
112	A53	5c red	.50	.20
113	A53	5c green ('97)	.65	.20
a.		Imperf., pair	3.50	
114	A53	5c grnsh bl ('99)	1.00	.40
115	A54	7c deep green	7.75	2.50
116	A54	7c orange ('97)	3.50	1.25
117	A55	10c brown	2.00	.50
118	A56	20c green & blk	7.00	.85
119	A56	20c cl & blk ('97)	4.75	.60
120	A57	25c red brn & blk	5.50	1.50
a.		Center inverted	2,000.	
121	A57	25c pink & bl ('97)	3.50	.60
122	A58	50c blue & blk	7.00	3.50
123	A58	50c grn & brn ('97)	5.00	1.25
124	A59	1p org brn & blk	14.00	5.50
125	A59	1p yel brn & bl ('97)	9.50	3.50
126	A60	2p violet & grn	32.50	20.00
127	A60	2p bis & car ('97)	9.50	2.00
128	A61	3p carmine & blue	32.50	20.00
129	A61	3p lil & car ('97)	12.50	2.50
		Nos. 108-129 (22)	160.65	67.65

All values of this issue exist imperforate but they were not issued in that form.

For overprints and surcharges see Nos. 138-140, 143, 145, 147, O62-O78.

President Joaquin Suárez
A62 A63

Statue of President Suárez — A64

Perf. 12½ to 15 and Compound

1896, July 18

130	A62	1c brown vio & blk	.25	.20
131	A63	5c pale bl & blk	.25	.20
132	A64	10c lake & blk	1.00	.30
		Nos. 130-132 (3)	1.50	.70

Dedication of Pres. Suárez statue.

For overprints and surcharge see Nos. 133-135, 144, 146, 152, O79-O81.

Same Overprinted in Red:

e

f

1897, Mar. 1

133	A62 (e)	1c brn vio & blk	.40	.40
a.		Inverted overprint	6.00	6.00
134	A63 (e)	5c pale blue & blk	.50	.40
a.		Inverted overprint	9.50	6.00
135	A64 (f)	10c lake & blk	1.00	.60
a.		Inverted overprint	12.00	9.50
b.		Double overprint	7.50	
		Nos. 133-135 (3)	1.90	1.40

"Electricity" — A68

1897-99 **Engr.**

136	A68	10c red	1.75	.40
137	A68	10c red lilac ('99)	.75	.50

For overprints see Nos. 141, O82-O83.

Regular Issues Overprinted in Red or Blue

1897, Sept. 26

138	A51	1c slate bl (R)	.80	.60
a.		Inverted overprint	4.75	4.75
139	A52	2c claret (Bl)	1.25	1.25
a.		Inverted overprint	4.75	4.75
140	A53	5c green (Bl)	1.75	1.60
a.		Inverted overprint	7.75	7.75
b.		Double overprint		
141	A68	10c red (Bl)	2.75	2.75
a.		Inverted overprint	17.00	17.00
		Nos. 138-141 (4)	6.55	6.20

Commemorating the Restoration of Peace at the end of the Civil War.

Issue for use only on the days of the National Fête, Sept. 26-28, 1897.

Regular Issues Surcharged in Black, Blue or Red

1898, July 25

142	A32	½c on 1c bl (Bk)	.40	.40
a.		Inverted surcharge	3.00	3.00
143	A51	½c on 1c bis (Bl)	.40	.40
a.		Inverted surcharge	3.00	
b.		Double surcharge	2.50	
144	A62	½c on 1c brn vio & blk (R)	.40	.40
145	A52	½c on 2c blue (Bk)	.40	.40
146	A63	½c on 5c pale bl & blk (R)	.40	.40
a.		Double surcharge	6.25	
147	A54	½c on 7c dp grn (R)	.40	.40
		Nos. 142-147 (6)	2.40	2.40

The 2c red brown of 1894 (#77) was also surcharged like #142-147 but was not issued. Value $12.

Liberty — A69

Statue of Artigas — A70

1898-99 **Litho.** ***Perf. 11, 11½***

148	A69	5m rose	.25	.25
149	A69	5m purple ('99)	.25	.25

1899-1900 **Engr.** ***Perf. 12½, 14, 15***

150	A70	5m lt blue	.25	.25
151	A70	5m orange ('00)	.25	.25

No. 135 With Additional Surcharge in Black

1900, Dec. 1

152	A64	5c on 10c lake & blk	.50	.25
a.		Black bar covering "1897" omitted	15.00	

Cattle — A72

Girl's Head — A73

Shepherdess — A74

Perf. 13½ to 16 and Compound

1900-10 **Engr.**

153	A72	1c yellow green	.40	.20
154	A73	5c dull blue	.80	.20
155	A73	5c slate grn ('10)	.80	.20
156	A74	10c gray violet	1.00	.20
		Nos. 153-156 (4)	3.00	.80

For surcharges and overprints see Nos. 179, 184, O84, O86, O88, O106-O107.

Eros and Cornucopia A75

Basket of Fruit A76

1901, Feb. 11

157	A75 2c vermilion	.50	.20
158	A76 7c brown orange	1.75	.25

For surcharges and overprints see Nos. 197-198, O85, O87, O105.

General Artigas — A78

Cattle — A79

Eros — A80

Cow — A81

Shepherdess A82

Numeral A83

Justice — A84

1904-05 Litho. *Perf. 11½*

160	A78 5m orange	.40	.20
a.	5m yellow	.40	.20
161	A79 1c green	.50	.20
a.	Imperf., pair	3.50	
162	A80 2c dp orange	.20	.20
a.	2c orange red	.20	.20
b.	Imperf., pair	3.00	
163	A81 5c blue	.80	.20
a.	Imperf., pair	3.50	
164	A82 10c dk violet ('05)	.50	.20
165	A83 20c gray grn ('05)	2.50	.50
166	A84 25c olive bis ('05)	3.25	.80
	Nos. 160-166 (7)	8.15	2.30

For overprints see Nos. 167-169, O92-O98, O101-O103.

Overprinted Diagonally in Carmine or Black

1904, Oct. 15

167	A79 1c green (C)	.40	.40
168	A80 2c deep orange (Bk)	.65	.40
169	A81 5c dark blue (C)	1.25	.60
	Nos. 167-169 (3)	2.30	1.40

End of the Civil War of 1904. In the first overprinting, "Paz 1904" appears at a 50-degree angle; in the second, at a 63-degree angle.

A85

A86

1906, Feb. 23 Litho. Unwmk.

170	A85 5c dark blue	1.10	.20
a.	Imperf., pair	6.00	

1906-07

171	A86 5c deep blue	.30	.30
172	A86 7c orange brn ('07)	.70	.50
173	A86 50c rose	5.00	1.25
	Nos. 171-173 (3)	6.00	2.05

Cruiser "Montevideo" — A87

1908, Aug. 23 Typo. *Rouletted 13*

174	A87 1c car & dk grn	2.00	1.50
175	A87 2c green & dk grn	2.00	1.50
176	A87 5c org & dk grn	2.00	1.50
	Nos. 174-176 (3)	6.00	4.50

Center Inverted

174a	A87 1c	300.00	300.00
175a	A87 2c	300.00	300.00
176a	A87 5c	300.00	300.00
	Nos. 174a-176a (3)	900.00	900.00

Imperf., Pairs

174b	A87 1c	30.00	
175b	A87 2c	30.00	
176b	A87 5c	30.00	

Independence of Uruguay, declared Aug. 25, 1825. Counterfeits exist.
For surcharges and overprints see Nos. 186, O99-O100, O104, O110.

View of the Port of Montevideo — A88

Wmk. 187

1909, Aug. 24 Engr. *Perf. 11½*

177	A88 2c lt brown & blk	1.25	1.00
178	A88 5c rose red & blk	1.25	1.00

Issued to commemorate the opening of the Port of Montevideo, Aug. 25, 1909.

Nos. 156, 91 Surcharged

Perf. 14 to 16

1909, Sept. 13 Unwmk.

179	A74 8c on 10c dull vio	.75	.20
a.	"Contesimos"	4.00	2.00
180	A38 23c on 25c bis brn	1.75	.60

Centaur — A89

Wmk. 187

1910, May 22 Engr. *Perf. 11½*

182	A89 2c carmine red	.60	.40
183	A89 5c deep blue	.60	.40

Cent. of Liberation Day, May 25, 1810.
The 2c in deep blue and 5c in carmine red were prepared for collectors.

Stamps of 1900-06 Surcharged

a

b

c

Perf. 14 to 16, 11½

1910, Oct. 6 Unwmk.

Black Surcharge

184	A72 (a) 5m on 1c yel grn	.20	.20
a.	Inverted surcharge	4.50	3.75

Dark Blue Surcharge

185	A39 (b) 5c on 50c dull red	.40	.20
a.	Inverted surcharge	4.50	4.50

Blue Surcharge

186	A86 (c) 5c on 50c rose	.80	.45
a.	Double surcharge	20.00	
b.	Inverted surcharge	10.00	8.75
	Nos. 184-186 (3)	1.40	.85

Artigas A90

"Commercial Progress" A91

1910, Nov. 21 Engr. *Perf. 14, 15*

187	A90 5m dk violet	.20	.20
188	A90 1c dp green	.20	.20
189	A90 2c orange red	.20	.20
190	A90 5c dk blue	.20	.20
191	A90 8c gray blk	.40	.20
192	A90 20c brown	.60	.20
193	A91 23c dp ultra	2.75	.40
194	A91 50c orange	4.00	1.25
195	A91 1p scarlet	7.50	1.25
	Nos. 187-195 (9)	16.05	4.10

See Nos. 199-210. For overprints see Nos. 211-213, O118-O124.

Symbolical of the Posts — A92

1911, Jan. 6 Wmk. 187 *Perf. 11½*

196	A92 5c rose car & blk	.80	.60

1st South American Postal Cong., at Montevideo, Jan. 1911.

No. 158 Surcharged in Red or Dark Blue

Perf. 14 to 16

1911, May 17 Unwmk.

197	A76 2c on 7c brn org (R)	.40	.40
198	A76 5c on 7c brn org (Bl)	.40	.20
a.	Inverted surcharge	8.50	8.50

Centenary of the battle of Las Piedras, won by the forces under Gen. Jose Gervasio Artigas, May 8, 1811.

Types of 1910

FOUR AND FIVE CENTESIMOS:
Type I — Large numerals about 3mm high.
Type II — Small numerals about 2¼mm high.

1912-15 Typo. *Perf. 11½*

199	A90 5m violet	.20	.20
a.	5m purple	.20	.20
200	A90 5m magenta	.20	.20
a.	5m dull rose	.20	.20
201	A90 1c green ('13)	.20	.20
202	A90 2c brown org	.20	.20
203	A90 2c rose red ('13)	.20	.20
a.	2c deep red ('14)	.20	.20
204	A90 4c org (I) ('14)	.20	.20
a.	4c orange (II) ('15)	.20	.20
b.	4c yellow (II) ('13)	.20	.20
205	A90 5c dull bl (I)	.40	.20
a.	5c blue (II)	.40	.20
206	A90 8c ultra ('13)	.50	.20
207	A90 20c brown ('13)	1.40	.20
a.	20c chocolate	1.40	.20
208	A91 23c dk blue ('15)	3.50	.60
209	A91 50c orange ('14)	3.50	1.50
210	A91 1p vermilion ('15)	10.50	1.25
	Nos. 199-210 (12)	21.00	5.15

Stamps of 1912-15 Overprinted

1913, Apr. 4

211	A90 2c brown orange	.85	.50
a.	Inverted overprint	5.00	4.50
212	A90 4c yellow	.85	.50
213	A90 5c blue	.85	.50
	Nos. 211-213 (3)	2.55	1.50

Cent. of the Buenos Aires Cong. of 1813.

Liberty Extending Peace to the Country — A93

1918, Jan. 3 Litho.

214	A93 2c green & red	.85	.50
215	A93 5c buff & blue	.85	.50

Promulgation of the Constitution.

Statue of Liberty, New York Harbor A94

Harbor of Montevideo A95

Perf. 14, 15, 13½

1919, July 15 Engr.

217	A94 2c carmine & brn	.55	.20
218	A94 4c orange & brn	.55	.20
219	A94 5c blue & brn	.80	.40
220	A94 8c org brn & ind	.80	.40
221	A94 20c ol bis & blk	2.00	.80
222	A94 23c green & blk	4.00	1.25
	Nos. 217-222 (6)	8.70	3.25

Peace at end of World War I.
Perf 13½ used only on 2c, 20c, 23c.

1919-20 Litho. *Perf. 11½*

225	A95 5m violet & blk	.20	.20
226	A95 1c green & blk	.20	.20
227	A95 2c red & blk	.20	.20
228	A95 4c orange & blk	.35	.20
229	A95 5c ultra & slate	.40	.20
230	A95 8c gray bl & lt brn	.50	.20
231	A95 20c brown & blk	1.60	.35
232	A95 23c green & brn	2.75	.65

233	A95	50c brown & blue	5.00	2.00
234	A95	1p dull red & bl	10.00	3.00
		Nos. 225-234 (10)	21.20	7.20

For overprints see Nos. O125-O131.

José Enrique Rodó — A96

Mercury — A97

1920, Feb. 28 Engr. *Perf. 14, 15*

235	A96	2c car & blk	.55	.40
236	A96	4c org & bl	.65	.50
237	A96	5c bl & brn	.75	.55
		Nos. 235-237 (3)	1.95	1.45

Issued to honor José Enrique Rodó, author.
For surcharges see Nos. P2-P4.

1921-22 Litho. *Perf. 11½*

238	A97	5m lilac	.20	.20
239	A97	5m gray blk ('22)	.20	.20
240	A97	1c lt grn	.20	.20
241	A97	1c vio ('22)	.20	.20
242	A97	2c fawn	.40	.20
243	A97	2c red ('22)	.40	.20
244	A97	3c bl grn ('22)	.60	.20
245	A97	4c orange	.40	.20
246	A97	5c ultra	.50	.20
247	A97	5c choc ('22)	.60	.20
248	A97	12c ultra ('22)	2.40	.60
249	A97	36c ol grn ('22)	7.75	2.75
		Nos. 238-249 (12)	13.85	5.35

See Nos. 254-260. For overprint and surcharge see Nos. E1, P1.

Dámaso A. Larrañaga (1771-1848), Bishop, Writer, Scientist and Physician — A98

1921, Dec. 10 Unwmk.

250	A98	5c slate	1.25	1.00

Mercury Type of 1921-22

1922-23 Wmk. 188

254	A97	5m gray blk	.20	.20
255	A97	1c violet ('23)	.20	.20
a.		1c red violet	.20	.20
256	A97	2c pale red	.25	.20
257	A97	2c deep rose ('23)	.30	.20
259	A97	5c yel brn ('23)	.65	.20
260	A97	8c salmon pink ('23)	1.00	.90
		Nos. 254-260 (6)	2.60	1.90

Equestrian Statue of Artigas — A99

Unwmk.

1923, Feb. 26 Engr. *Perf. 14*

264	A99	2c car & sepia	.40	.25
265	A99	5c vio & sepia	.40	.25
266	A99	12c blue & sepia	.40	.25
		Nos. 264-266 (3)	1.20	.75

Southern Lapwing A100

Battle Monument A101

Perf. 12½, 11½x12½

1923, June 25 Litho. Wmk. 189

Size: 18x22½mm

267	A100	5m gray	.20	.20
268	A100	1c org yel	.20	.20
269	A100	2c lt vio	.20	.20
270	A100	3c gray grn	.40	.20
271	A100	5c lt bl	.40	.20
272	A100	8c rose red	.80	.50
273	A100	12c dp bl	.80	.50
274	A100	20c brn org	2.00	.50
275	A100	36c emerald	4.00	1.75
276	A100	50c orange	6.75	2.75
277	A100	1p brt rose	32.50	20.00
278	A100	2p lt grn	47.50	20.00
		Nos. 267-278 (12)	95.75	47.00

See #285-298, 309-314, 317-323, 334-339. For surcharges and overprints see Nos. 345-348, O132-O148, P5-P7.

1923, Oct. 12 Wmk. 188 *Perf. 11½*

279	A101	2c dp grn	.55	.40
280	A101	5c scarlet	.55	.40
281	A101	12c dk bl	.55	.40
		Nos. 279-281 (3)	1.65	1.20

Unveiling of the Sarandi Battle Monument by José Luis Zorrilla, Oct. 12, 1923.

"Victory of Samothrace" — A102

Unwmk.

1924, July 29 Typo. *Perf. 11*

282	A102	2c rose	20.00	10.00
283	A102	5c mauve	20.00	10.00
284	A102	12c brt bl	20.00	10.00
		Nos. 282-284 (3)	60.00	30.00

Olympic Games. Sheets of 20 (5x4).
Five hundred sets of these stamps were printed on yellow paper for presentation purposes. They were not on sale at post offices. Value for set, $650.

Lapwing Type of 1923
First Redrawing
Imprint: "A. BARREIRO Y RAMOS"

1924, July 26 Litho. *Perf. 12½, 11½*

Size: 17¼x21½mm

285	A100	5m gray blk	.20	.20
286	A100	1c fawn	.20	.20
287	A100	2c rose lil	.30	.20
288	A100	3c gray grn	.20	.20
289	A100	5c chalky blue	.20	.20
290	A100	8c pink	.50	.20
291	A100	10c turq blue	.40	.20
292	A100	12c slate blue	.50	.25
293	A100	15c lt vio	.50	.20
294	A100	20c brown	.75	.30
295	A100	36c salmon	3.00	.70
296	A100	50c greenish gray	5.00	2.00
297	A100	1p buff	12.00	4.00
298	A100	2p dl vio	20.00	10.00
		Nos. 285-298 (14)	43.75	18.85

Landing of the 33 "Immortals" Led by Juan Antonio Lavalleja — A103

Perf. 11, 11½

1925, Apr. 19 Wmk. 188

300	A103	2c salmon pink & blk	1.40	.80
301	A103	5c lilac & blk	1.40	.80
302	A103	12c blue & blk	1.40	.80
		Nos. 300-302 (3)	4.20	2.40

Cent. of the landing of the 33 Founders of the Uruguayan Republic.

Legislative Palace — A104

Perf. 11½

1925, Aug. 24 Unwmk. Engr.

303	A104	5c vio & blk	1.25	.80
304	A104	12c bl & blk	1.25	.80

Dedication of the Legislative Palace.

General Fructuoso Rivera — A105

Wmk. 188

1925, Sept. 24 Litho. *Perf. 11*

305	A105	5c light red	.50	.40

Centenary of Battle of Rincón. See No. C9.

Battle of Sarandí A106

1925, Oct. 12 *Perf. 11½*

306	A106	2c bl grn	1.25	1.00
307	A106	5c dl vio	1.25	1.00
308	A106	12c dp bl	1.25	1.00
		Nos. 306-308 (3)	3.75	3.00

Centenary of the Battle of Sarandi.

Lapwing Type of 1923
Second Redrawing
Imprint: "Imprenta Nacional"

1925-26 *Perf. 11, 11½, 10½*

Size: 17½x21¾mm

309	A100	5m gray blk	1.00	.25
310	A100	1c dl vio	1.25	.25
311	A100	2c brt rose	1.60	.25
312	A100	3c gray grn	1.25	.40
313	A100	5c dl bl ('26)	2.00	.25
314	A100	12c slate blue	4.00	.40
		Nos. 309-314 (6)	11.10	1.80

The design differs in many small details from that of the 1923-24 issues. These stamps may be readily identified by the imprint and perforation.

Lapwing Type of 1923
Third Redrawing
Imprint: "Imp. Nacional" at center

1926-27 *Perf. 11, 11½, 10½*

Size: 17½x21¾mm

317	A100	5m gray	.40	.20
318	A100	1c lt vio ('27)	2.40	.55
319	A100	2c red	1.75	.40
320	A100	3c gray grn	2.40	.65
321	A100	5c lt bl	.75	.20
322	A100	8c pink ('27)	3.50	.80
323	A100	36c rose buff	8.00	4.00
		Nos. 317-323 (7)	19.20	6.80

These stamps may be distinguished from preceding stamps of the same design by the imprint.

Philatelic Exhibition Issue

Post Office at Montevideo A107

Unwmk.

1927, May 25 Engr. *Imperf.*

330	A107	2c green	4.75	3.50
a.		Sheet of 4	20.00	20.00
331	A107	5c dull red	4.75	3.50
a.		Sheet of 4	20.00	20.00
332	A107	8c dark blue	4.75	3.50
a.		Sheet of 4	20.00	20.00
		Nos. 330-332 (3)	14.25	10.50

Printed in sheets of 4 and sold at the Montevideo Exhibition. Lithographed counterfeits exist.

Lapwing Type of 1923
Fourth Redrawing
Imprint: "Imp. Nacional" at right

Perf. 11, 11½

1927, May 6 Litho. Wmk. 188

Size: 17¾x21¾mm

334	A100	1c gray vio	.40	.25
335	A100	2c vermilion	.40	.25
336	A100	3c gray grn	.80	.35
337	A100	5c blue	.40	.25
338	A100	8c rose	3.00	.80
339	A100	20c gray brn	4.00	1.60
		Nos. 334-339 (6)	9.00	3.50

The design has been slightly retouched in various places. The imprint is in italic capitals and is placed below the right numeral of value.

No. 292 Surcharged in Red

Inauguración
Ferrocarril
SAN CARLOS
a ROCHA
14/1/928
5 cts. 5

1928, Jan. 13 Unwmk. *Perf. 11½*

345	A100	2c on 12c slate blue	2.00	2.00
346	A100	5c on 12c slate blue	2.00	2.00
347	A100	10c on 12c slate blue	2.00	2.00
348	A100	15c on 12c slate blue	2.00	2.00
		Nos. 345-348 (4)	8.00	8.00

Issued to celebrate the inauguration of the railroad between San Carlos and Rocha.

General Rivera — A108

1928, Apr. 19 Engr. *Perf. 12*

349	A108	5c car rose	.50	.35

Centenary of the Battle of Las Misiones.

Artigas (7 dots in panels below portrait.) — A109

Imprint:
"Waterlow & Sons. Ltd., Londres"

Perf. 11, 12½, 13x13½, 12½x13, 13x12½

1928-43

Size: 16x19½mm

350	A109	5m black	.20	.20
350A	A109	5m org ('43)	.20	.20
351	A109	1c dk vio	.20	.20
352	A109	1c brn vio ('34)	.20	.20
352A	A109	1c vio bl ('43)	.20	.20
353	A109	2c dp grn	.20	.20
353A	A109	2c brn red ('43)	.20	.20
354	A109	3c bister	.20	.20
355	A109	3c dp grn ('32)	.20	.20
355A	A109	3c brt grn ('43)	.20	.20
356	A109	5c red	.20	.20
357	A109	5c ol grn ('33)	.20	.20
357A	A109	5c dl pur ('43)	.20	.20
358	A109	7c car ('32)	.20	.20
359	A109	8c dk bl	.20	.20
360	A109	8c brn ('33)	.20	.20
361	A109	10c orange	.25	.20
362	A109	10c red org ('32)	.60	.40
363	A109	12c dp bl ('32)	.40	.20
364	A109	15c dl bl	.40	.20
365	A109	17c dk vio ('32)	.80	.20
366	A109	20c ol brn	.65	.20
367	A109	20c red brn ('33)	1.25	.50
368	A109	24c car rose	.90	.35
369	A109	24c yel ('33)	.80	.40
370	A109	36c ol grn ('33)	1.40	.50
371	A109	50c gray	2.40	1.25
372	A109	50c blk ('33)	3.50	1.60
373	A109	50c blk brn ('33)	3.00	1.25
374	A109	1p yel grn	7.00	4.00
		Nos. 350-374 (30)	26.55	14.45

1929-33 *Perf. 12½*

Size: 22 to 22½x28½ to 29½mm

375	A109	1p ol brn ('33)	6.00	4.00
376	A109	2p dk grn	17.00	9.00
377	A109	2p dl red ('32)	20.00	16.00
378	A109	3p dk bl	25.00	17.00
379	A109	3p blk ('32)	23.00	20.00
380	A109	4p violet	28.00	17.00
381	A109	4p dk ol grn ('32)	23.00	20.00
382	A109	5p car brn	32.50	23.00
383	A109	5p red org ('32)	30.00	20.00

384	A109 10p lake ('33)		92.50	70.00
385	A109 10p dp ultra ('33)		92.50	70.00
	Nos. 375-385 (11)		389.50	286.00

See Nos. 420-423, 462. See type A135.

Equestrian Statue of Artigas — A110

1928, May 1

386	A110 2p Prus bl & choc	16.00	7.75
387	A110 3p dp rose & blk	23.00	12.00

Symbolical of Soccer Victory — A111

Gen. Eugenio Garzón — A112

1928, July 29

388	A111 2c brn vio	16.00	9.25
389	A111 5c dp red	16.00	9.25
390	A111 8c ultra	16.00	9.25
	Nos. 388-390 (3)	48.00	27.75

Uruguayan soccer victories in the Olympic Games of 1924 and 1928. Printed in sheets of 20, in panes of 10 (5x2).

1928, Aug. 25 ***Imperf.***

391	A112 2c red	1.40	1.40
a.	Sheet of 4	6.50	6.50
392	A112 5c yel grn	1.40	1.40
a.	Sheet of 4	6.50	6.50
393	A112 8c dp bl	1.40	1.40
a.	Sheet of 4	6.50	6.50
	Nos. 391-393 (3)	4.20	4.20

Dedication of monument to Garzon. Issued in sheets of 4. Lithographed counterfeits exist.

Black River Bridge A113

Gauchos Breaking a Horse — A114

Peace A115

Montevideo A116

Liberty and Flag of Uruguay A117

Liberty with Torch and Caduceus A118

Statue of Artigas A124

Artigas Dictating Instructions for 1813 Congress A119

Seascape A120

Montevideo Harbor, 1830 — A121

Liberty and Coat of Arms A122

Montevideo Harbor, 1930 — A123

1930, June 16 ***Perf. 12½, 12***

394	A113 5m gray blk	.20	.20
395	A114 1c dk brn	.20	.20
396	A115 2c brn rose	.20	.20
397	A116 3c yel grn	.20	.20
398	A117 5c dk bl	.20	.20
399	A118 8c dl red	.35	.20
400	A119 10c dk vio	.50	.35
401	A120 15c bl grn	.65	.50
402	A121 20c indigo	.80	.65
403	A122 24c red brn	1.10	.80
404	A123 50c org red	3.00	2.00
405	A124 1p black	6.00	3.00
406	A124 2p bl vio	14.00	8.50
407	A124 3p dk red	20.00	14.00
408	A124 4p red org	23.00	19.00
409	A124 5p lilac	35.00	22.50
	Nos. 394-409 (16)	105.40	72.50

Cent. of natl. independence and the promulgation of the constitution.

Type of 1856 Issue
Values in Centesimos

Wmk. 227

1931, Apr. 11 Litho. ***Imperf.***

410	A1 2c gray blue	3.00	2.00
a.	Sheet of 4	15.00	15.00
411	A1 8c dull red	3.00	2.00
a.	Sheet of 4	15.00	15.00
412	A1 15c blue black	3.00	2.00
a.	Sheet of 4	15.00	15.00

Wmk. 188

413	A1 5c light green	3.00	2.00
a.	Sheet of 4	15.00	15.00
	Nos. 410-413 (4)	12.00	8.00

Sold only at the Philatelic Exhibition, Montevideo, Apr. 11-15, 1931. Issued in sheets of 4.

Juan Zorrilla de San Martin, Uruguayan Poet — A125

1932, June 6 Unwmk. ***Perf. 12½***

414	A125 1½c brown violet	.20	.20
415	A125 3c green	.20	.20
416	A125 7c dk blue	.25	.20
417	A125 12c lt blue	.40	.25
418	A125 1p deep brown	20.00	13.00
	Nos. 414-418 (5)	21.05	13.85

Semi-Postal Stamp No. B2 Surcharged

1932, Nov. 1 ***Perf. 12***

419	SP1 1½c on 2c + 2c dp grn	.35	.35

Artigas Type of 1928
Imprint: "Imprenta Nacional" at center

1932-35 Litho. ***Perf. 11, 12½***
Size: 15¾x19¼mm

420	A109 5m lt brown ('35)	.20	.20
421	A109 1c pale violet ('35)	.20	.20
422	A109 15m black	.25	.20
423	A109 5c bluish grn ('35)	.50	.20
	Nos. 420-423 (4)	1.15	.80

Gen. J. A. Lavalleja A126

Flag of the Race and Globe A127

1933, July 12 Engr. ***Perf. 12½***

429	A126 15m brown lake	.20	.20

Perf. 11, 11½, 11x11½

1933, Aug. 3 Litho.

430	A127 3c blue green	.50	.25
431	A127 5c rose	.50	.25
432	A127 7c lt blue	.50	.25
433	A127 8c dull red	1.00	.55
434	A127 12c deep blue	.65	.25
435	A127 17c violet	1.75	.80
436	A127 20c red brown	3.50	1.60
437	A127 24c yellow	3.50	1.75
438	A127 36c orange	5.00	2.40
439	A127 50c olive gray	5.50	3.00
440	A127 1p bister	13.00	6.25
	Nos. 430-440 (11)	35.40	17.35

Raising of the "Flag of the Race" and of the 441st anniv. of the sailing of Columbus from Palos, Spain, on his first voyage to America.

Sower A128

Juan Zorrilla de San Martin A129

1933, Aug. 28 Unwmk. ***Perf. 11½***

441	A128 3c blue green	.25	.20
442	A128 5c dull violet	.40	.25
443	A128 7c lt blue	.40	.25
444	A128 8c deep red	.80	.50
445	A128 12c ultra	2.00	1.00
	Nos. 441-445 (5)	3.85	2.20

3rd Constituent National Assembly.

1933, Nov. 9 Engr. ***Perf. 12½***

446	A129 7c slate	.20	.20

Albatross Flying over Map of the Americas — A130

1933, Dec. 3 Typo. ***Perf. 11½***

447	A130 3c green, blk & brn	2.75	2.00
448	A130 7c turq bl, brn & blk	1.60	.80
449	A130 12c dk bl, gray & ver	2.40	1.60
450	A130 17c ver, gray & vio	5.00	2.75
451	A130 20c yellow, bl & grn	6.00	3.50
452	A130 36c red, blk & yel	7.75	5.50
	Nos. 447-452 (6)	25.50	16.15

7th Pan-American Conf., Montevideo. Issued in sheets of 6. Value $200. For overprints see Nos. C61-C62.

General Rivera — A131

1934, Feb. Engr. ***Perf. 12½***

453	A131 3c green	.20	.20

Stars Representing the Three Constitutions — A132

1934, Mar. 23 Typo.

454	A132 3c yellow grn & grn	.60	.40
455	A132 7c org red & red	.60	.40
456	A132 12c ultra & blue	2.00	.80

Perf. 11½

457	A132 17c brown & rose	2.50	1.25
458	A132 20c yellow & gray	3.50	1.60
459	A132 36c dk vio & bl grn	3.50	1.60
460	A132 50c black & blue	7.00	3.25
461	A132 1p dk car & vio	16.00	6.75
	Nos. 454-461 (8)	35.70	16.05

First Year of Third Republic.

Artigas Type of 1928
Imprint: "Barreiro & Ramos S. A."

1934, Nov. 28 Litho.

462	A109 50c brown black	6.00	2.50

"Uruguay" and "Brazil" Holding Scales of Justice A133

Florencio Sánchez A134

1935, May 30 Unwmk. ***Perf. 11***

463	A133 5m brown	.80	.40
464	A133 15m black	.40	.20
465	A133 3c green	.40	.20
466	A133 7c orange	.40	.20
467	A133 12c ultra	.80	.60
468	A133 50c yellow green	4.00	2.50
	Nos. 463-468 (6)	6.80	4.10

Visit of President Vargas of Brazil.

1935, Nov. 7

469	A134 3c green	.20	.20
470	A134 7c brown	.20	.20
471	A134 12c blue	.55	.35
	Nos. 469-471 (3)	.95	.75

Florencio Sanchez (1875-1910), author.

Artigas (6 dots in panels below portrait) — A135

Imprint: "Imprenta Nacional" at center

1936-44 *Perf. 11, 12½*

474	A135	5m	org brn ('37)	.20	.20
475	A135	5m	lt brown ('39)	.20	.20
476	A135	1c	lt violet ('37)	.20	.20
477	A135	2c	dk brown ('37)	.20	.20
478	A135	2c	green ('39)	.20	.20
479	A135	5c	brt blue ('37)	.20	.20
480	A135	5c	bluish grn ('39)	.40	.20
481	A135	12c	dull blue ('38)	.40	.20
482	A135	20c	fawn	1.40	.35
482A	A135	20c	rose ('44)	1.00	.40
483	A135	50c	brown black	3.00	.80

Size: 21½x28½mm

483A	A135	1p	brown	8.50	3.00
483B	A135	2p	blue	14.00	12.00
483C	A135	3p	gray black	20.00	16.00
			Nos. 474-483C (14)	49.90	34.15

See Nos. 488, and 576 in the Scott Standard Catalogue, Vol. 6. See type A109.

Power Dam on Black River — A136

1937-38

484	A136	1c	dull violet	.20	.20
485	A136	10c	blue	.50	.20
486	A136	15c	rose	1.25	.65
487	A136	1p	choc ('38)	6.25	2.50
			Nos. 484-487 (4)	8.20	3.55

Imprint: "Imprenta Nacional" at right

1938

488	A135	1c	bright violet	.40	.20

International Law Congress, 1889 — A137

1939, July 16 **Litho.** *Perf. 12½*

489	A137	1c	brown orange	.20	.20
490	A137	2c	dull green	.25	.20
491	A137	5c	rose ver	.25	.20
492	A137	12c	dull blue	.65	.40
493	A137	50c	lt violet	2.50	1.50
			Nos. 489-493 (5)	3.85	2.50

50th anniversary of the Montevideo Congress of International Law.

Artigas
A138 A138a

1939-43 **Litho.** **Unwmk.**

Size: 15¾x19mm

494	A138	5m	dl brn org ('40)	.20	.20
495	A138	1c	lt blue	.20	.20
496	A138	2c	lt violet	.20	.20
497	A138	5c	violet brn	.20	.20
498	A138	8c	rose red	.25	.20
499	A138	10c	green	.50	.20
500	A138	15c	dull blue	1.25	.60

Size: 24x29½mm

501	A138	1p	dull brn ('41)	2.50	1.00
502	A138	2p	dl rose vio ('40)	7.00	3.00
503	A138	4p	orange ('43)	9.25	4.00
504	A138	5p	ver ('41)	14.00	6.00
			Nos. 494-504 (11)	35.55	15.80

See No. 578 in the Scott Standard Catalogue, Vol. 6.

Redrawn: Horizontal lines in portrait background

1940-44

Size: 17x21mm

505	A138a	5m	brn org ('41)	.20	.20
506	A138a	1c	lt blue	.20	.20
507	A138a	2c	lt violet ('41)	.20	.20
508	A138a	5c	violet brn	.20	.20
509	A138a	8c	sal pink ('44)	.20	.20
510	A138a	10c	green ('41)	.40	.20
511	A138a	50c	olive bis ('42)	6.25	1.75
511A	A138a	50c	yel grn ('44)	4.75	1.75
			Nos. 505-511A (8)	12.40	4.70

See Nos. 568-575, 577, 601, 632, 660-661 in the Scott Standard Catalogue, Vol. 6. For surcharges see Nos. 523, 726 in the Scott Standard Catalogue, Vol. 6.

SEMI-POSTAL STAMPS

Indigent Old Man — SP1

Unwmk.

1930, Nov. 13 **Engr.** *Perf. 12*

B1	SP1	1c + 1c	dark violet	.20	.20
B2	SP1	2c + 2c	deep green	.20	.20
B3	SP1	5c + 5c	red	.30	.30
B4	SP1	8c + 8c	gray violet	.30	.30
			Nos. B1-B4 (4)	1.00	1.00

The surtax on these stamps was for a fund to assist the aged.

For surcharge see No. 419.

AIR POST STAMPS

No. 91 Overprinted in Dark Blue, Red or Green

1921-22 **Unwmk.** *Perf. 14*

C1	A38 25c bister brn (Bl)		15.00	12.00
	a.	Black overprint	*625.00*	*625.00*
C2	A38 25c bister brn (R)		6.50	5.00
	a.	Inverted overprint	*77.50*	*77.50*
C3	A38 25c bister brn (G) ('22)		6.50	5.00
		Nos. C1-C3 (3)	28.00	22.00

This overprint also exists in light yellow green.

No. C1a was not issued. Some authorities consider it an overprint color trial.

AP2

Wmk. 188

1924, Jan. 2 **Litho.** *Perf. 11½*

C4	AP2	6c	dark blue	2.50	2.00
C5	AP2	10c	scarlet	3.50	3.00
C6	AP2	20c	deep green	5.00	5.00
			Nos. C4-C6 (3)	11.00	10.00

Heron — AP3

1925, Aug. 24 *Perf. 12½*

Inscribed "MONTEVIDEO"

C7	AP3	14c blue & blk	30.00	14.00

Inscribed "FLORIDA"

C8	AP3	14c blue & blk	30.00	14.00

These stamps were used only on Aug. 25, 1925, the cent. of the Assembly of Florida, on letters intended to be carried by airplane between Montevideo and Florida, a town 60 miles north. The stamps were not delivered to the public but were affixed to the letters and canceled by post office clerks. Later uncanceled copies came on the market.

One authority believes Nos. C7-C8 served as registration stamps on these two attempted special flights.

Gaucho Cavalryman at Rincón — AP4

1925, Sept. 24 *Perf. 11*

C9	AP4	45c blue green	15.00

Centenary of Battle of Rincon. Used only on Sept. 24. No. C9 was affixed and canceled by post office clerks.

Albatross — AP5

1926, Mar. 3 **Wmk. 188** ***Imperf.***

C10	AP5	6c	dark blue	1.50	1.50
C11	AP5	10c	vermilion	2.00	2.00
C12	AP5	20c	blue green	2.50	2.50
C13	AP5	25c	violet	4.00	4.00
			Nos. C10-C13 (4)	10.00	10.00

Excellent counterfeits exist.

1928, June 25 *Perf. 11*

C14	AP5	10c	green	2.50	2.00
C15	AP5	20c	orange	4.00	3.00
C16	AP5	30c	indigo	4.00	3.00
C17	AP5	38c	green	7.00	6.00
C18	AP5	40c	yellow	8.00	6.00
C19	AP5	50c	violet	9.00	7.00
C20	AP5	76c	orange	17.00	15.00
C21	AP5	1p	red	20.00	18.00
C22	AP5	1.14p	indigo	45.00	40.00
C23	AP5	1.52p	yellow	70.00	65.00
C24	AP5	1.90p	violet	90.00	75.00
C25	AP5	3.80p	red	200.00	150.00
			Nos. C14-C25 (12)	476.50	390.00

Counterfeits of No. C25 exist.

1929, Aug. 23 **Unwmk.**

C26	AP5	4c	olive brown	2.50	2.00

The design was redrawn for Nos. C14-C26. The numerals are narrower, "CENTS" is 1mm high instead of 2½mm and imprint letters touch the bottom frame line.

Pegasus AP6

1929-43 **Engr.** *Perf. 12½*

Size: 34x23mm

C27	AP6	1c	red lilac ('30)	.40	.40
C28	AP6	1c	dk blue ('32)	.40	.40
C29	AP6	2c	yellow ('30)	.40	.40
C30	AP6	2c	olive grn ('32)	.40	.40
C31	AP6	4c	Prus blue ('30)	.70	.70
C32	AP6	4c	car rose ('32)	.70	.70
C33	AP6	6c	dull vio ('30)	.70	.70
C34	AP6	6c	red brown ('32)	.70	.70
C35	AP6	8c	red orange	3.00	2.50
C36	AP6	8c	gray ('30)	4.00	3.00
C36A	AP6	8c	brt green ('43)	2.50	2.00
C37	AP6	16c	indigo	.50	.50
C38	AP6	16c	rose ('30)	3.25	3.00
C39	AP6	24c	claret	4.25	3.50
C40	AP6	24c	brt violet ('30)	3.00	2.50
C41	AP6	30c	bister	3.00	2.75
C42	AP6	30c	dk green ('30)	2.00	1.50
C43	AP6	40c	dk brown	5.50	5.00
C44	AP6	40c	yel org ('30)	6.00	5.00
C45	AP6	60c	blue green	5.00	3.25
C46	AP6	60c	emerald ('30)	8.50	7.00
C47	AP6	60c	dp orange ('31)	3.00	2.00
C48	AP6	80c	dk ultra	8.00	7.00
C49	AP6	80c	green ('30)	15.00	12.00
C50	AP6	90c	light blue	8.00	6.00
C51	AP6	90c	dk olive grn ('30)	15.00	12.00
C52	AP6	1p	car rose ('30)	10.00	7.50
C53	AP6	1.20p	olive grn	22.00	20.00
C54	AP6	1.20p	dp car ('30)	30.00	26.00
C55	AP6	1.50p	red brown	25.00	20.00
C56	AP6	1.50p	blk brn ('30)	20.00	15.00
C57	AP6	3p	deep red	40.00	35.00
C58	AP6	3p	ultra ('30)	30.00	25.00
C59	AP6	4.50p	black	75.00	55.00
C60	AP6	4.50p	violet ('30)	45.00	35.00
C60A	AP6	10p	dp ultra ('43)	17.00	12.00
			Nos. C27-C60A (36)	417.90	335.40

See Nos. C63-C82. For surcharges see Nos. C106-C112, C114 in the Scott Standard Catalogue, Vol. 6.

Nos. 450, 452 Overprinted in Red

1934, Jan. 1 *Perf. 11½*

C61	A130 17c ver, gray & vio		20.00	15.00
	a.	Sheet of 6	140.00	
	b.	Gray omitted	150.00	
	c.	Double overprint	150.00	
C62	A130 36c red, blk & yel		20.00	15.00
	a.	Sheet of 6	140.00	

7th Pan-American Conference, Montevideo.

Pegasus Type of 1929

1935 **Engr.** *Perf. 12½*

Size: 31½x21mm

C63	AP6	15c	dull yellow	2.50	2.00
C64	AP6	22c	brick red	1.50	1.40
C65	AP6	30c	brown violet	2.50	2.00
C66	AP6	37c	gray lilac	1.40	1.00
C67	AP6	40c	rose lake	2.00	1.40
C68	AP6	47c	rose	4.00	3.50
C69	AP6	50c	Prus blue	1.40	.80
C70	AP6	52c	dp ultra	4.00	3.50
C71	AP6	57c	grnsh blue	2.00	1.75
C72	AP6	62c	olive green	1.75	.80
C73	AP6	87c	gray green	5.00	4.00
C74	AP6	1p	olive	3.50	2.25
C75	AP6	1.12p	brown red	3.50	2.25
C76	AP6	1.20p	bister brn	15.00	12.00
C77	AP6	1.27p	red brown	15.00	13.00
C78	AP6	1.62p	rose	10.00	9.00
C79	AP6	2p	brown rose	17.00	14.00
C80	AP6	2.12p	dk slate grn	17.00	14.00
C81	AP6	3p	dull blue	15.00	13.00
C82	AP6	5p	orange	60.00	60.00
			Nos. C63-C82 (20)	184.05	161.65

Counterfeits exist.

Power Dam on Black River — AP7

Imprint: "Imp. Nacional" at center

1937-41 **Litho.**

C83	AP7	20c	lt green ('38)	5.50	4.00
C84	AP7	35c	red brown	8.00	6.50
C85	AP7	62c	blue grn ('38)	.80	.30
C86	AP7	68c	yel org ('38)	2.00	1.50
C86A	AP7	68c	pale vio brn ('41)	1.75	.70
C87	AP7	75c	violet	7.50	5.00
C88	AP7	1p	dp pink ('38)	2.50	1.75

C89	AP7	1.38p rose ('38)	25.00	20.00
C90	AP7	3p dk blue ('40)	17.00	12.00
		Nos. C83-C90 (9)	70.05	51.75

Imprint at left

C91	AP7	8c pale green ('39)	.60	.50
C92	AP7	20c lt green ('38)	2.00	1.50

For surcharge and overprint see Nos. 545, C120 in the Scott Standard Catalogue, Vol. 6.

Plane over Sculptured Oxcart — AP8

1939-44 ***Perf. 12½***

C93	AP8	20c slate	.50	.40
C94	AP8	20c lt violet ('43)	.80	.80
C95	AP8	20c blue ('44)	.60	.40
C96	AP8	35c red	1.00	.80
C97	AP8	50c brown org	1.00	.30
C98	AP8	75c deep pink	1.10	.20
C99	AP8	1p dp blue ('40)	3.25	.60
C100	AP8	1.38p brt vio	5.50	2.25
C101	AP8	1.38p yel org ('44)	5.00	4.00
C102	AP8	2p blue	8.00	1.40
a.		Perf. 11	7.00	1.10
C103	AP8	5p rose lilac	10.00	2.25
C104	AP8	5p blue grn ('44)	15.00	7.00
C105	AP8	10p rose ('40)	100.00	65.00
		Nos. C93-C105 (13)	151.75	85.40

Counterfeits exist.

For surcharges see Nos. C116-C119 in the Scott Standard Catalogue, Vol. 6.

SPECIAL DELIVERY STAMPS

No. 242 Overprinted **MENSAJERIAS**

1921, Aug. **Unwmk.** ***Perf. 11½***

E1	A97	2c fawn	.55	.20
a.		Double overprint	3.25	

Caduceus — SD1

Imprint: "IMP. NACIONAL."

1922, Dec. 2 **Litho.** **Wmk. 188**

Size: 21x27mm

E2	SD1	2c light red	.40	.20

1924, Oct. 1

E3	SD1	2c pale ultra	.40	.20

1928 **Unwmk.** ***Perf. 11***

E4	SD1	2c light blue	.40	.20

Imprint: "IMPRA. NACIONAL."

1928-36 **Wmk. 188**

Size: 16½x19½mm.

E5	SD1	2c black, *green*	.20	.20

Unwmk.

E6	SD1	2c blue green ('29)	.20	.20

Perf. 11½, 12½

E7	SD1	2c blue ('36)	.20	.20
		Nos. E5-E7 (3)	.60	.60

LATE FEE STAMPS

Galleon and Modern Steamship — LF1

Wmk. Crossed Keys in Sheet

1936, May 18 **Litho.** ***Perf. 11***

I1	LF1	3c green	.20	.20
I2	LF1	5c violet	.20	.20
I3	LF1	6c blue green	.20	.20
I4	LF1	7c brown	.25	.25
I5	LF1	8c carmine	.50	.50
I6	LF1	12c deep blue	.65	.65
		Nos. I1-I6 (6)	2.00	2.00

POSTAGE DUE STAMPS

D1

1902 **Unwmk.** **Engr.** ***Perf. 14 to 15***

Size: 21¼x18½mm

J1	D1	1c blue green	.40	.20
J2	D1	2c carmine	.40	.20
J3	D1	4c gray violet	.65	.20
J4	D1	10c dark blue	.95	.25
J5	D1	20c ocher	1.50	.80
		Nos. J1-J5 (5)	3.90	1.65

Surcharged in Red

1904

J6	D1	1c on 10c dk bl	.80	.80
a.		Inverted surcharge	7.75	7.75

1913-15 **Litho.** ***Perf. 11½***

Size: 22½x20mm

J7	D1	1c lt grn	.50	.20
J8	D1	2c rose red	.50	.25
J9	D1	4c dl vio	.65	.25
J10	D1	6c dp brn	.80	.40

Size: 21¼x19mm

J11	D1	10c dl bl	.80	.40
		Nos. J7-J11 (5)	3.25	1.50

Imprint: "Imprenta Nacional"

1922

Size: 20x17mm

J12	D1	1c bl grn	.20	.20
J13	D1	2c red	.25	.20
J14	D1	3c red brn	.40	.25
J15	D1	4c brn vio	.25	.20
J16	D1	5c blue	.40	.25
J17	D1	10c gray grn	.40	.20
		Nos. J12-J17 (6)	1.90	1.30

1926-27 **Wmk. 188** ***Perf. 11***

Size: 20x17mm

J18	D1	1c bl grn ('27)	.40	.20
J19	D1	3c red brn ('27)	.40	.20
J20	D1	5c slate blue	.40	.20
J21	D1	6c light brown	.40	.40
		Nos. J18-J21 (4)	1.60	1.00

1929 **Unwmk.** ***Perf. 10½, 11***

J22	D1	1c blue green	.20	.20
J23	D1	10c gray green	.40	.20

Figure of Value Redrawn (Flat on sides)

1932 **Wmk. 188**

J24	D1	6c yel brn	.40	.25

Imprint: "Casa A. Barreiro Ramos S. A."

1935 **Unwmk.** **Litho.** ***Perf. 12½***

Size: 20x17mm

J25	D1	4c violet	.40	.25
J26	D1	5c rose	.40	.25

Type of 1935

Imprint: "Imprenta Nacional" at right

1938

J27	D1	1c blue green	.20	.20
J28	D1	2c red brown	.20	.20
J29	D1	3c deep pink	.20	.20
J30	D1	4c light violet	.20	.20
J31	D1	5c blue	.20	.20
J32	D1	8c rose	.20	.20
		Nos. J27-J32 (6)	1.20	1.20

OFFICIAL STAMPS

Regular Issues Handstamped in Black, Red or Blue

Many double and inverted impressions exist of the handstamped overprints on Nos. O1-O83. Prices are the same as for normal stamps or slightly more.

On Stamps of 1877-79

1880-82 **Unwmk.** ***Rouletted 8***

O1	A9	1c red brown	4.00	3.50
O2	A10	5c green	3.00	2.50
O3	A11	20c bister	2.50	2.00
O4	A11	50c black	18.00	15.00
O5	A12	1p blue	20.00	16.00
		Nos. O1-O5 (5)	47.50	39.00

On No. 44

Rouletted 6

O6	A9	1c brown ('81)	4.75	4.25

On Nos. 43-43A

Rouletted 8

O7	A11	50c black (R)	17.00	16.00
O8	A12	1p blue (R)	22.50	20.00

On Nos. 45, 41, 37a

Perf. 12½

O9	A13	7c blue (R) ('81)	3.25	2.50

Rouletted 8

O10	A11	10c ver (Bl)	1.75	1.50

Perf. 13½

O11	A8b	15c yellow (Bl)	5.00	4.00

On Nos. 46-47

1883 ***Perf. 12½***

O12	A14	1c green	6.00	6.00
O13	A14a	2c rose	7.00	7.00

On Nos. 50-51

Perf. 12½, 12x12½, 13

O14	A17	5c blue (R)	3.00	3.00
a.		Imperf., pair	4.50	
O15	A18	10c brown (Bl)	5.00	5.00
a.		Imperf., pair	6.00	

No. 48 Handstamped

1884 ***Perf. 12½***

O16	A15	1c green	29.00	25.00

Overprinted Type "a" in Black

On Nos. 48-49

1884 ***Perf. 12, 12x12½, 13***

O17	A15	1c green	29.00	25.00
O18	A16	2c red	10.00	8.00

On Nos. 53-56

Rouletted 8

O19	A11	1c on 10c ver	1.50	1.25
a.		Small "1" (No. 53a)	5.00	

Perf. 12½

O20	A14a	2c rose	5.00	5.00
O21	A22	5c ultra	5.00	5.00
O22	A23	5c blue	3.75	1.75
		Nos. O17-O22 (6)	54.25	46.00

On Stamps of 1884-88

1884-89 ***Rouletted 8***

O23	A24	1c gray	9.25	4.25
O24	A24	1c green ('88)	1.90	.95
O25	A24	1c olive grn	2.50	1.50
O26	A24a	2c vermilion	.80	.50
O27	A24a	2c rose ('88)	1.75	.95
O28	A24b	5c slate blue	1.75	.95
O29	A24b	5c slate bl, *bl*	5.00	2.50
O30	A24b	5c violet ('88)	5.00	2.50
O31	A24b	5c lt blue ('89)	5.00	2.50
O32	A25	7c dk brown	5.00	2.50
O33	A25	7c orange ('89)	2.50	1.50
O34	A26	10c olive brn	1.50	.70
O35	A30	10c violet ('89)	12.50	7.50
O36	A27	20c red violet	2.50	1.50
O37	A27	20c bister brn ('89)	12.50	5.50
O38	A28	25c gray violet	3.50	2.50
O39	A28	25c vermilion ('89)	12.50	8.00
		Nos. O23-O39 (17)	85.45	46.30

The OFICIAL handstamp, type "a," was also applied to No. 73, the 5c violet with "Provisorio" overprint, but it was not regularly issued.

On No. 71

1887 ***Rouletted 9***

O40	A29	10c lilac	5.00	

No. O40 was not regularly issued.

On Stamps of 1889-1899

Perf. 12½ to 15 and Compound

1890-1900

O41	A32	1c green	.80	.20
O43	A32	1c blue ('95)	2.00	2.00
O44	A33	2c rose	.80	.20
O45	A33	2c red brn ('95)	2.50	2.50
O46	A33	2c orange ('00)	.80	.80
O47	A34	5c deep blue	1.50	1.50
O48	A34	5c rose ('95)	2.00	2.00
O49	A35	7c bister brown	1.25	.80
O50	A35	7c green ('95)	25.00	
O51	A36	10c blue green	1.25	.80
O52	A36	10c orange ('95)	25.00	
O53	A37	20c orange	1.25	.80
O54	A37	20c brown ('95)	25.00	
O55	A38	25c red brown	1.25	.80
O56	A38	25c ver ('95)	55.00	
O57	A39	50c lt blue	4.50	4.50
O58	A39	50c lilac ('95)	5.50	5.50
O59	A40	1p lilac	7.00	5.00
O60	A40	1p lt blue ('95)	40.00	22.50

Nos. O50, O52, O54, O56 and O60 were not regularly issued.

On No. 99

1891 ***Rouletted 8***

O61	A24b	5c violet	1.50	1.25
a.		"1391"	9.00	

On Stamps of 1895-99

Perf. 12½ to 15 and Compound

1895-1900

O62	A51	1c bister	.60	.60
O63	A51	1c slate blue ('97)	1.25	.55
O64	A52	2c blue	.25	.25
O65	A52	2c claret ('97)	1.25	.55
O66	A53	5c red	.80	.55
O67	A53	5c green ('97)	1.25	.55
O68	A53	5c grnsh blue ('00)	.95	.75
O69	A54	7c deep green	.50	.50
O70	A55	10c brown	.50	.50
O71	A56	20c green & blk	.80	.80
O72	A56	20c claret & blk ('97)	4.50	2.25
O73	A57	25c red brn & blk	.80	.80
O74	A57	25c pink & bl ('97)	4.50	2.25
O75	A58	50c blue & blk	.95	.95
O76	A58	50c grn & brn ('97)	5.75	2.75
O77	A59	1p org brn & blk	4.75	4.75
O78	A59	1p yel brn & bl ('97)	9.25	5.75
a.		Inverted overprint		
		Nos. O62-O78 (17)	38.65	25.10

On Nos. 133-135

1897, Sept.

O79	A62	1c brown vio & blk	1.25	1.00
O80	A63	5c pale bl & blk	1.75	1.00
O81	A64	10c lake & blk	1.75	1.10
		Nos. O79-O81 (3)	4.75	3.10

On Nos. 136-137

Perf. 12½ to 15 and Compound

1897-1900

O82	A68	10c red	2.50	1.50
O83	A68	10c red lilac ('00)	1.25	1.25

Regular Issue of 1900-01 Overprinted

1901 ***Perf. 14 to 16***

O84	A72	1c yellow green	.50	.20
O85	A75	2c vermilion	.60	.20
O86	A73	5c dull blue	.60	.20
O87	A76	7c brown orange	.85	.50
O88	A74	10c gray violet	.90	.55
O89	A37	20c lt blue	7.75	4.00
O90	A38	25c bister brown	1.50	.80
O91	A40	1p deep green	10.00	5.75
a.		Inverted overprint	12.50	8.00
		Nos. O84-O91 (8)	22.70	12.20

Most of the used official stamps of 1901-1928 have been punched with holes of various shapes, in addition to the postal cancellations.

Regular Issue of 1904-05 Overprinted

1905 ***Perf. 11½***

O92	A79	1c green	.50	.20
O93	A80	2c orange red	.50	.20
O94	A81	5c deep blue	.50	.20
O95	A82	10c dark violet	1.00	.40
O96	A83	20c gray green	3.00	1.00
a.		Inverted overprint		
O97	A84	25c olive bister	2.00	.80
		Nos. O92-O97 (6)	7.50	2.80

Regular Issues of 1904-07 Overprinted

1907, Mar.

O98	A79	1c green	.25	.20
O99	A86	5c deep blue	.25	.20
O100	A86	7c orange brown	.25	.20
O101	A82	10c dark violet	.25	.20
O102	A83	20c gray green	.40	.35
a.		Inverted overprint	4.00	
O103	A84	25c olive bister	.50	.40
O104	A86	50c rose	.95	.70
		Nos. O98-O104 (7)	2.85	2.25

Regular Issues of 1900-10 Overprinted

1910, July 15 ***Perf. 14½ to 16***

O105	A75	2c vermilion	8.50	4.00
O106	A73	5c slate green	5.00	3.00
O107	A74	10c gray violet	2.50	1.25
O108	A37	20c grnsh blue	2.50	1.25
O109	A38	25c bister brown	4.25	2.40

Perf. 11½

O110	A86	50c rose	5.75	2.50
a.		Inverted overprint	20.00	15.00
		Nos. O105-O110 (6)	28.50	14.40

Peace—O1

1911, Feb. 18 **Litho.**

O111	O1	2c red brown	.40	.25
O112	O1	5c dark blue	.40	.40
O113	O1	8c slate	.40	*.60*
O114	O1	20c gray brown	.55	*.95*
O115	O1	23c claret	.80	*.95*
O116	O1	50c orange	1.50	1.25
O117	O1	1p red	4.00	1.50
		Nos. O111-O117 (7)	8.05	5.90

Regular Issue of 1912-15 Overprinted

1915, Sept. 16

O118	A90	2c carmine	.55	.40
O119	A90	5c dark blue	.55	.40
O120	A90	8c ultra	.55	.40
O121	A90	20c dark brown	1.25	.50
O122	A91	23c dark blue	4.00	3.50
O123	A91	50c orange	6.00	3.50
O124	A91	1p vermilion	8.00	4.00
		Nos. O118-O124 (7)	20.90	12.70

Regular Issue of 1919 Overprinted

1919, Dec. 25

O125	A95	2c red & black	.80	.40
a.		Inverted overprint	3.50	
O126	A95	5c ultra & blk	.95	.40
O127	A95	8c gray bl & lt brn	.95	.40
a.		Inverted overprint	3.50	
O128	A95	20c brown & blk	2.00	.80
O129	A95	23c green & brn	2.00	.80
O130	A95	50c brown & bl	4.00	2.00
O131	A95	1p dull red & bl	10.00	4.00
a.		Double overprint	15.00	
		Nos. O125-O131 (7)	20.70	8.80

Regular Issue of 1923 Overprinted

1924 **Wmk. 189** ***Perf. 12½***

O132	A100	2c violet	.20	.20
O133	A100	5c light blue	.20	.20
O134	A100	12c deep blue	.30	.20
O135	A100	20c buff	.40	.20
O136	A100	36c blue green	1.75	1.25
O137	A100	50c orange	3.50	2.50
O138	A100	1p pink	6.25	5.00
O139	A100	2p lt green	12.00	10.00
		Nos. O132-O139 (8)	24.60	19.55

Same Overprint on Regular Issue of 1924

1926-27 **Unwmk.** ***Imperf.***

O140	A100	2c rose lilac	.40	.20
O141	A100	5c pale blue	.60	.20
O142	A100	8c pink ('27)	.80	.20
O143	A100	12c slate blue	.95	.20
O144	A100	20c brown	2.00	.40
O145	A100	36c dull rose	3.00	.95
		Nos. O140-O145 (6)	7.75	2.15

Regular Issue of 1924 Overprinted

1928 ***Perf. 12½***

O146	A100	2c rose lilac	1.50	.95
O147	A100	8c pink	1.50	.50
O148	A100	10c turq blue	2.00	.50
		Nos. O146-O148 (3)	5.00	1.95

Since 1928, instead of official stamps, Uruguay has used envelopes with "S. O." printed on them, and stamps of many issues which are punched with various designs such as star or crescent.

NEWSPAPER STAMPS

No. 245 Surcharged

1922, June 1 **Unwmk.** ***Perf. 11½***

P1	A97	3c on 4c orange	.40	.40
a.		Inverted surcharge	9.25	9.25
b.		Double surcharge	2.50	2.50

Nos. 235-237 Surcharged

1924, June 1 ***Perf. 14½***

P2	A96	3c on 2c car & blk	.40	.40
P3	A96	6c on 4c red org & bl	.40	.40
P4	A96	9c on 5c bl & brn	.40	.40
		Nos. P2-P4 (3)	1.20	1.20

Nos. 288, 291, 293 Overprinted or Surcharged in Red:

1926 ***Imperf.***

P5	A100	3c gray green	.80	.25
a.		Double overprint	1.00	1.00
P6	A100	9c on 10c turq bl	.95	.40
a.		Double surcharge	1.00	1.00
P7	A100	15c light violet	1.25	.50
		Nos. P5-P7 (3)	3.00	1.15

PARCEL POST STAMPS

Mercury — PP1

Imprint: "IMPRENTA NACIONAL"

Perf. 11½

1922, Jan. 15 **Litho.** **Unwmk.**

Size: 20x29½mm

Inscribed "Exterior"

Q1	PP1	5c grn, *straw*	.20	.20
Q2	PP1	10c grn, *bl gray*	.40	.20
Q3	PP1	20c grn, *rose*	2.00	.55
Q4	PP1	30c grn, *grn*	2.00	.20
Q5	PP1	50c grn, *blue*	3.50	.40
Q6	PP1	1p grn, *org*	5.00	1.50
		Nos. Q1-Q6 (6)	13.10	3.05

Inscribed "Interior"

Q7	PP1	5c grn, *straw*	.25	.20
Q8	PP1	10c grn, *bl gray*	.25	.20
Q9	PP1	20c grn, *rose*	1.00	.25
Q10	PP1	30c grn, *grn*	1.40	.25
Q11	PP1	50c grn, *blue*	2.25	.35
Q12	PP1	1p grn, *org*	5.75	1.25
		Nos. Q7-Q12 (6)	10.90	2.50

Imprint: "IMP. NACIONAL"
Inscribed "Exterior"

1926, Jan. 20 ***Perf. 11½***

Q13	PP1	20c grn, *rose*	1.75	.50

Inscribed "Interior"

Perf. 11

Q14	PP1	5c grn, *yellow*	.40	.20
Q15	PP1	10c grn, *bl gray*	.50	.20
Q16	PP1	20c grn, *rose*	1.00	.20
Q17	PP1	30c grn, *bl grn*	1.75	.40
		Nos. Q13-Q17 (5)	5.40	1.50

Inscribed "Exterior"

1926 ***Perf. 11½***

Q18	PP1	5c blk, *straw*	.40	.20
Q19	PP1	10c blk, *bl gray*	.50	.20
Q20	PP1	20c blk, *rose*	1.10	.20

Inscribed "Interior"

Q21	PP1	5c blk, *straw*	.40	.20
Q22	PP1	10c blk, *bl gray*	.50	.20
Q23	PP1	20c blk, *rose*	1.00	.20
Q24	PP1	30c blk, *bl grn*	1.75	.40
		Nos. Q18-Q24 (7)	5.65	1.60

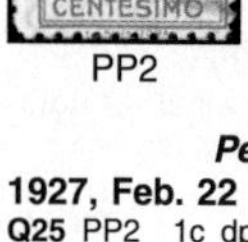

PP2

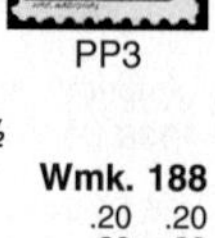

PP3

Perf. 11, 11½

1927, Feb. 22 **Wmk. 188**

Q25	PP2	1c dp bl	.20	.20
Q26	PP2	2c lt grn	.20	.20
Q27	PP2	4c violet	.20	.20
Q28	PP2	5c red	.25	.20
Q29	PP2	10c dk brn	.40	.20
Q30	PP2	20c orange	.60	.40
		Nos. Q25-Q30 (6)	1.85	1.40

See Nos. Q35-Q38, Q51-Q54.

1928, Nov. 20 ***Perf. 11***

Size: 15x20mm

Q31	PP3	5c blk, *straw*	.20	.20
Q32	PP3	10c blk, *gray blue*	.20	.20
Q33	PP3	20c blk, *rose*	.50	.20
Q34	PP3	30c blk, *green*	.80	.20
		Nos. Q31-Q34 (4)	1.70	.80

Type of 1927 Issue

1929-30 **Unwmk.** ***Perf. 11, 12½***

Q35	PP2	1c violet	.20	.20
Q36	PP2	1c ultra ('30)	.20	.20
Q37	PP2	2c bl grn ('30)	.20	.20
Q38	PP2	5c red ('30)	.20	.20
		Nos. Q35-Q38 (4)	.80	.80

Nos. Q35-Q38, and possibly later issues, occasionally show parts of a papermaker's watermark.

PP4

1929, July 27 **Wmk. 188** ***Perf. 11***

Q39	PP4	10c orange	.50	.50
Q40	PP4	15c slate blue	.50	.50
Q41	PP4	20c ol brn	.50	.50
Q42	PP4	25c rose red	1.00	.50
Q43	PP4	50c dark gray	2.00	1.00
Q44	PP4	75c violet	8.00	6.00
Q45	PP4	1p gray green	7.50	3.00
		Nos. Q39-Q45 (7)	20.00	12.00

For overprints see Nos. Q57-Q63 in the Scott Standard Catalogue, Vol. 6.

Ship and Train — PP5

Numeral of Value — PP6

1938-39 **Unwmk.** ***Perf. 12½***

Q46	PP5	10c scarlet	.40	.20
Q47	PP5	20c dk bl	.60	.20
Q48	PP5	30c lt vio ('39)	.95	.20
Q49	PP5	50c green	1.75	.20
Q50	PP5	1p brn org	2.50	1.10
		Nos. Q46-Q50 (5)	6.20	1.90

See #Q70-Q73, Q80, Q88-Q90, Q92-Q93, Q95 in the Scott Standard Catalogue, Vol. 6.

VATICAN CITY

'va-ti-kən 'si-tē

LOCATION — Western Italy, directly outside the western boundary of Rome
GOVT. — Independent state subject to certain political restrictions under a treaty with Italy
AREA — 108.7 acres
POP. — 1,000 (est.)

100 Centesimi = 1 Lira

Catalogue values for unused stamps in this country are for Never Hinged items, beginning with Scott 68 in the regular postage section, Scott C1 in the airpost section, and Scott E3 in the special delivery section.

Watermark

Wmk. 235 — Crossed Keys

Papal Arms — A1

Pope Pius XI — A2

Unwmk.

1929, Aug. 1 Engr. *Perf. 14*

Surface-Colored Paper

1	A1	5c dk brn & pink	.20	.25
2	A1	10c dk grn & lt grn	.25	.30
3	A1	20c violet & lilac	.55	.40
4	A1	25c dk bl & lt bl	.70	.45
5	A1	30c indigo & yellow	.80	.60
6	A1	50c ind & sal buff	1.25	.65
7	A1	75c brn car & gray	1.60	1.00

Photo.

White Paper

8	A2	80c carmine rose	1.25	.40
9	A2	1.25 l dark blue	2.00	.75
10	A2	2 l olive brown	3.75	1.40
11	A2	2.50 l red orange	3.25	2.50
12	A2	5 l dk green	3.75	*8.50*
13	A2	10 l olive blk	8.00	*11.50*
		Nos. 1-13,E1-E2 (15)	53.35	*52.20*
		Set, never hinged	150.00	

The stamps of Type A1 have, in this and subsequent issues, the words "POSTE VATICANE" in rows of colorless letters in the background.

For surcharges and overprints see Nos. 14, 35-40, 61-67, J1-J6, Q1-Q13.

No. 5 Surcharged in Red

1931, Oct. 1

14	A1	25c on 30c ind & yel	2.10	1.40
		Never hinged	6.75	

Arms of Pope Pius XI — A5

Vatican Palace and Obelisk — A6

Vatican Gardens — A7

Pope Pius XI A8

St. Peter's Basilica A9

1933, May 31 Engr. Wmk. 235

19	A5	5c copper red	.20	.20
a.		Imperf., pair	250.00	*275.00*
20	A6	10c dk brn & blk	.20	.20
21	A6	12½c dp grn & blk	.20	.20
22	A6	20c orange & blk	.20	.20
a.		Vertical pair imperf. between and at bottom	250.00	250.00
23	A6	25c dk olive & blk	.20	.20
a.		Imperf., pair	150.00	175.00
24	A7	30c blk & dk brn	.20	.20
25	A7	50c vio & dk brn	.20	.20
26	A7	75c brn red & dk brn	.20	.20
27	A7	80c rose & dk brn	.20	.20
28	A8	1 l violet & blk	3.25	2.75
29	A8	1.25 l dk bl & blk	11.00	5.00
30	A8	2 l dk brn & blk	27.50	20.00
31	A8	2.75 l dk vio & blk	32.50	*40.00*
32	A9	5 l blk brn & dk grn	.20	.25
33	A9	10 l dk bl & dk grn	.20	.30
34	A9	20 l blk & dp grn	.25	.35
		Nos. 19-34,E3-E4 (18)	77.40	71.35
		Set, never hinged	210.00	

Nos. 8-13 Surcharged in Black

1934, June 16 Unwmk.

35	A2	40c on 80c	3.25	1.90
36	A2	1.30 l on 1.25 l	57.50	37.50
a.		Small figures "30" in "1.30"	*10,000.*	*7,250.*
		Never hinged	*12,500.*	
37	A2	2.05 l on 2 l	125.00	14.00
a.		No comma btwn. 2 & 0	275.00	20.00
		Never hinged	850.00	
38	A2	2.55 l on 2.50 l	82.50	150.00
a.		No comma btwn. 2 & 5	150.00	275.00
		Never hinged	475.00	
39	A2	3.05 l on 5 l	275.00	275.00
40	A2	3.70 l on 10 l	250.00	*400.00*
a.		No comma btwn. 3 & 7	—	—
		Nos. 35-40 (6)	793.25	878.40
		Set, never hinged	2,300.	

A second printing of Nos. 36-40 was made in 1937. The 2.55 l and 3.05 l of the first printing and 1.30 l of the second printing sell for more.

The status of No. 40a has been questioned. The editors would like to examine an authenticated copy of this variety.

Forged surcharges of Nos. 35-40 are plentiful.

Tribonian Presenting Pandects to Justinian I A10

Pope Gregory IX Promulgating Decretals A11

1935, Feb. 1 Photo.

41	A10	5c red orange	1.25	.75
42	A10	10c purple	1.25	.75
43	A10	25c green	12.50	12.50
44	A11	75c rose red	45.00	27.50
45	A11	80c dark brown	35.00	21.00
46	A11	1.25 l dark blue	45.00	20.00
		Nos. 41-46 (6)	140.00	82.50
		Set, never hinged	500.00	

Intl. Juridical Congress, Rome, 1934.

Doves and Bell — A12

Allegory of Church and Bible — A13

St. John Bosco — A14

St. Francis de Sales — A15

1936, June 22

47	A12	5c blue green	.75	1.00
48	A13	10c black	.75	1.00
49	A14	25c yellow green	40.00	8.50
50	A12	50c rose violet	.75	1.00
51	A13	75c rose red	40.00	40.00
52	A14	80c orange brn	1.50	2.00
53	A15	1.25 l dark blue	2.00	2.00
54	A15	5 l dark brown	2.00	*6.25*
		Nos. 47-54 (8)	87.75	61.75
		Set, never hinged	300.00	

Catholic Press Conference, 1936.

Crypt of St. Cecilia in Catacombs of St. Calixtus A16

Basilica of Sts. Nereus and Achilleus in Catacombs of St. Domitilla A17

1938, Oct. 12 *Perf. 14*

55	A16	5c bister brown	.20	.20
56	A16	10c deep orange	.20	.20
57	A16	25c deep green	.25	.25
58	A17	75c deep rose	5.50	5.50
59	A17	80c violet	17.00	17.00
60	A17	1.25 l blue	22.50	22.50
		Nos. 55-60 (6)	45.65	45.65
		Set, never hinged	125.00	

Intl. Christian Archaeological Congress, Rome, 1938.

Interregnum Issue

Nos. 1-7 Overprinted in Black

1939, Feb. 20 *Perf. 14*

61	A1	5c dk brn & pink	27.50	6.00
62	A1	10c dk grn & lt grn	.30	.20
63	A1	20c violet & lilac	.30	.20
64	A1	25c dk bl & lt bl	3.00	*3.50*
65	A1	30c indigo & yellow	.60	.20
a.		Pair, one without ovpt.	*1,300.*	
66	A1	50c indigo & sal buff	.60	.20
67	A1	75c brn car & gray	.60	.20
		Nos. 61-67 (7)	32.90	10.50
		Set, never hinged	92.50	

Catalogue values for unused stamps in this section, from this point to the end of the section, are for Never Hinged items.

Coronation of Pope Pius XII — A18

1939, June 2 Photo.

68	A18	25c green	2.25	.30
69	A18	75c rose red	.50	.45
70	A18	80c violet	6.25	3.00
71	A18	1.25 l deep blue	.50	.45
		Nos. 68-71 (4)	9.50	4.20

Coronation of Pope Pius XII, Mar. 12, 1939.

Arms of Pope Pius XII — A19

Pope Pius XII
A20 A21

Wmk. 235

1940, Mar. 12 Engr. *Perf. 14*

72	A19	5c dark carmine	.20	.20
73	A20	1 l purple & blk	.20	.20
74	A21	1.25 l slate bl & blk	.20	.20
a.		Imperf., pair	*450.00*	*500.00*
75	A20	2 l dk brn & blk	1.40	.85
76	A21	2.75 l dk rose vio & blk	2.00	1.75
		Nos. 72-76 (5)	4.00	3.20

See #91-98. For surcharges see #102-109.

SEMI-POSTAL STAMPS

Holy Year Issue

Cross and Orb
SP1 SP2

1933 Unwmk. Engr. *Perf. 13x13½*

B1	SP1	25c + 10c green	3.50	*3.50*
B2	SP1	75c + 15c scarlet	6.25	*11.50*
B3	SP2	80c + 20c red brown	22.50	16.00
B4	SP2	1.25 l + 25c ultra	7.00	*12.00*
		Nos. B1-B4 (4)	39.25	*43.00*
		Set, never hinged	100.00	

AIR POST STAMPS

Catalogue values for unused stamps in this section are for Never Hinged items.

Statue of St. Peter AP1

Dove of Peace over Vatican AP2

Elijah's Ascent into Heaven AP3

Our Lady of Loreto and Angels Moving the Holy House AP4

Wmk. 235

1938, June 22 Engr. *Perf. 14*

C1 AP1 25c brown .20 .20
C2 AP2 50c green .20 .20
C3 AP3 75c lake .20 .20
C4 AP4 80c dark blue .20 .20
C5 AP1 1 l violet .45 .45
C6 AP2 2 l ultra 1.00 .60
C7 AP3 5 l slate blk 2.25 1.50
C8 AP4 10 l dk brown vio 2.25 1.90
Nos. C1-C8 (8) 6.75 5.25

SPECIAL DELIVERY STAMPS

Pius XI SD1

Unwmk.

1929, Aug. 1 Photo. *Perf. 14*

E1 SD1 2 l carmine rose 14.00 11.50
E2 SD1 2.50 l dark blue 12.00 12.00

For overprints see Nos. Q14-Q15.

Catalogue values for unused stamps in this section, from this point to the end of the section, are for Never Hinged items.

Aerial View of Vatican City SD2

1933 Wmk. 235 Engr.

E3 SD2 2 l rose red & brn .35 .35
E4 SD2 2.50 l dp blue & brn .35 *.55*

POSTAGE DUE STAMPS

Regular Issue of 1929 Overprinted in Black and Brown

1931 Unwmk. *Perf. 14*

J1 A1 5c dk brown & pink .20 .20
a. Double frame
J2 A1 10c dk grn & lt grn .20 .20
a. Frame omitted *675.00*
J3 A1 20c violet & lilac 5.75 2.00

Surcharged

J4 A1 40c on 30c indigo & yel 1.50 *4.00*

Surcharged

J5 A2 60c on 2 l olive brn 27.50 18.00
J6 A2 1.10 l on 2.50 l red org 3.75 *16.00*
Nos. J1-J6 (6) 38.90 *40.40*
Set, never hinged 100.00

In addition to the surcharges, #J4-J6 are overprinted with ornamental frame as on #J1-J3.

PARCEL POST STAMPS

Regular Issue of 1929 Overprinted

1931 Unwmk. *Perf. 14*

Q1 A1 5c dk brown & pink .40 .30
Q2 A1 10c dk grn & lt grn .40 .30
Q3 A1 20c violet & lilac 4.75 5.50
Q4 A1 25c dk bl & lt bl 6.25 4.25
Q5 A1 30c indigo & yel 9.25 4.25
Q6 A1 50c indigo & sal buff 9.25 4.25
Q7 A1 75c brn car & gray 2.75 2.75

Overprinted

Q8 A2 80c carmine rose 1.60 1.90
Q9 A2 1.25 l dark blue 2.75 2.00
Q10 A2 2 l olive brown .55 .85
a. Inverted overprint 325.00 475.00
Q11 A2 2.50 l red orange .55 .85
a. Double overprint 225.00
b. Inverted overprint 500.00
Q12 A2 5 l dark green .55 .85
Q13 A2 10 l olive black .55 .85
a. Double overprint 325.00

Special Delivery Stamps of 1929 Overprinted Vertically

Q14 SD1 2 l carmine rose .55 .85
Q15 SD1 2.50 l dark blue .55 .85
Nos. Q1-Q15 (15) 40.70 30.60
Set, never hinged 95.00

VENEZUELA

ˌve-nə-ˈzwā-lə

LOCATION — Northern coast of South America, bordering on the Caribbean Sea
GOVT. — Republic
AREA — 352,143 sq. mi.
POP. — 15,260,000 (est. 1984)
CAPITAL — Caracas

100 Centavos = 8 Reales = 1 Peso
100 Centesimos = 1 Venezolano (1879)
100 Centimos = 1 Bolivar (1880)

Catalogue values for unused stamps in this country are for Never Hinged items, beginning with Scott 743 in the regular postage section.

PRE-STAMP POSTAL MARKINGS

Crowned Circle handstamp type II is pictured in the Crowned Circle Handstamps and Great Britain Used Abroad section.

La Guayra

1841

A1 II "PAID AT LA GUAYRA" crowned circle handstamp in black, on cover 2,000.

Coat of Arms — A1

Fine Impression
No Dividing Line Between Stamps

Unwmk.

1859, Jan. 1 Litho. *Imperf.*

1 A1 ½r yellow 23.00 9.25
On cover *3,000.*
a. ½r orange 27.00 11.00
On cover *750.00*
b. Greenish paper *225.00*
2 A1 1r blue 325.00 20.00
On cover 500.00
a. Half used as ½r on cover *7,500.*
3 A1 2r red 42.50 15.00
On cover *1,500.*
a. 2r dull rose red 55.00 17.00
On cover *1,500.*
b. Half used as 1r on cover *1,250.*
c. Greenish paper 225.00 140.00
Nos. 1-3 (3) 390.50 44.25

Coarse Impression

1859-62

Thick Paper

4 A1 ½r orange ('61) 12.00 4.00
On cover 75.00
a. ½r yellow ('59) 500.00 30.00
On cover 125.00
b ½r olive yellow 750.00 35.00
On cover 200.00
c. Bluish paper 575.00
d. ½r dull rose (error)
5 A1 1r blue ('62) 20.00 12.50
On cover *2,500.*
a. 1r pale blue 35.00 15.00
On cover *2,500.*
b. 1r dark blue 35.00 15.00
On cover *2,500.*
c. Half used as ½r on cover *7,500.*
d. Bluish paper 200.00
6 A1 2r red ('62) 30.00 20.00
On cover *1,500.*
a. 2r dull rose 42.50 20.00
On cover *1,500.*
b. Tête bêche pair *10,000.*
c. Half used as 1r on cover *400.00*
d. Bluish paper *225.00*
Nos. 4-6 (3) 62.00 36.50

In the fine impression, the background lines of the shield are more sharply drawn. In the coarse impression, the shading lines at each end of the scroll inscribed "LIBERTAD" are usually very heavy. Stamps of the coarse impression are closer together, and there is usually a dividing line between them.

Nos. 1-3 exist on thick paper and on bluish paper. Nos. 1-6 exist on pelure paper.

The greenish paper varieties (Nos. 1b and 3c) and the bluish paper varieties were not regularly issued.

Arms — A2

Eagle — A3

1862 Litho.

7 A2 ¼c green 20.00 *110.00*
On newsprint —
8 A2 ½c dull lilac 30.00 *190.00*
On newsprint —
a. ½c violet 40.00 210.00
On newsprint —
9 A2 1c gray brown 42.50 *225.00*
On newsprint —
Nos. 7-9 (3) 92.50 *525.00*

Counterfeits are plentiful. Forged cancellations abound on Nos. 7-17.

1863-64

10 A3 ½c pale red ('64) 55.00 *125.00*
On cover —
a. ½c red 60.00 *125.00*
On cover —
11 A3 1c slate ('64) 62.50 *160.00*
On cover —
12 A3 ½r orange 7.75 3.50
On cover 150.00
13 A3 1r blue 17.00 8.50
On cover *500.00*
a. 1r pale blue 30.00 13.00
On cover *600.00*
b. Half used as ½r on cover *750.00*
14 A3 2r green 23.00 20.00
On cover *2,000.*
a. 2r deep yellow green 30.00 20.00
On cover *2,000.*
b. Quarter used as ½r on cover *7,500.*
c. Half used as 1r on cover *2,000.*

Counterfeits exist.

Redrawn

1865

15 A3 ½r orange 4.00 *2.50*
On cover *3,000.*

The redrawn stamp has a broad "N" in "FEDERACION." "MEDIO REAL" and "FEDERACION" are in thin letters. There are 52 instead of 49 pearls in the circle.

No. 15 in yellow is a postal forgery.

A4

Simón Bolívar — A5

1865-70

16 A4 ½c yel grn ('67) 200.00 *300.00*
On cover —
17 A4 1c bl grn ('67) 200.00 *250.00*
On cover —
18 A4 ½r brn vio (thin paper) 9.25 2.00
On cover 50.00
19 A4 ½r lil rose ('70) 9.25 2.50
On cover 50.00
a. ½r brownish rose 9.25 3.00
On cover 50.00
b. Tête bêche pair 110.00 *150.00*
On cover *5,000.*
20 A4 1r vermilion 42.50 15.00
On cover *1,000.*
a. Half used as ½r on cover *500.00*
21 A4 2r yellow 160.00 77.50
On cover *3,000.*
a. Half used as 1r on cover *3,000.*
Nos. 16-21 (6) 621.00 *647.00*

This issue is known unofficially rouletted.
Postal forgeries exist of the ½r.
One quarter of #21 used as ½r is a postal forgery.
For overprints see Nos. 37-48.

Overprinted in Very Small Upright Letters "Bolivar Sucre Miranda dash> Decreto de 27 de Abril de 1870", or "Decreto de 27 de Junio 1870" in Slanting Letters

(The "Junio" overprint is continuously repeated, in four lines arranged in two pairs, with the second line of each pair inverted.)

Un	1	Siete	7
Dos	2	Nueve	9
Tres	3	Quince	15
Cuatro	4	Veinte	20
Cinco	5	Cincuenta	50

1871-76 Litho.

22 A5 1c yellow 1.50 .40
On cover *1,000.*
a. 1c orange 2.10 .45
b. 1c brown orange ('76) 2.10 .30
c. 1c pale buff ('76) 2.10 .45
d. Laid paper 1.00 .75
23 A5 2c yellow 2.00 .45
On cover *1,000.*
a. 2c orange 4.00 .45
b. 2c brown orange 3.50 .75
c. 2c pale buff ('76) 3.50 .45
d. Laid paper 3.50 .55
e. Frame inverted *4,000.* *3,000.*
24 A5 3c yellow 3.00 .75
On cover *1,000.*
a. 3c orange 3.00 1.40
b. 3c pale buff ('76) 5.50 1.75
25 A5 4c yellow 4.00 .75
On cover *1,000.*
a. 4c orange 4.50 1.25

b. 4c brown orange ('76)	4.50	1.25
c. 4c buff ('76)	4.50	1.25
26 A5 5c yellow	4.00	.75
On cover		500.00
a. 5c orange	4.00	.90
On cover		500.00
b. 5c pale buff ('76)	4.00	.90
On cover		500.00
c. Laid paper	7.50	.90
27 A5 1r rose	4.00	2.00
On cover		1,000.
a. 1r pale red	4.00	2.00
On cover		1,000.
b. Laid paper	6.00	2.50
c. Half used as ½r on cover		1,500.
28 A5 2r rose	4.50	2.00
a. 2r pale red	4.50	2.00
b. Laid paper	12.00	2.50
29 A5 3r rose	6.00	2.00
a. 3r pale red	6.00	2.00
30 A5 5r rose	5.75	1.00
a. 5r pale red	5.75	1.00
31 A5 7r rose	22.50	4.00
a. 7r pale red	22.50	4.00
32 A5 9r green	22.50	4.25
a. 9r olive green	22.50	6.00
33 A5 15r green	55.00	8.50
a. 15r gray green ('76)	55.00	8.50
b. Frame inverted	8,000.	6,500.
34 A5 20r green	77.50	20.00
a. Laid paper	110.00	35.00
35 A5 30r green	375.00	110.00
a. 30r gray green ('76)	600.00	160.00
b. Double overprint		
36 A5 50r green	1,200.	300.00
a. 50r gray green ('76)		
Nos. 22-34 (13)	212.25	46.85
Nos. 22-35 (14)	587.25	156.85

These stamps were made available for postage and revenue by official decree, and were the only stamps sold for postage in Venezuela from Mar., 1871 to Aug., 1873.

Due to lack of canceling handstamps, the majority of stamps were canceled with pen marks. Fiscal cancellations were also made with the pen. The values quoted are for pen-canceled copies.

Different settings were used for the different overprints. Stamps with the upright letters were issued in 1871. Those with the slanting letters in one double line were issued in 1872-73. Those with the slanting overprint in two double lines were issued starting in 1874 from several different settings, those of 1877-78 showing much coarser impressions of the design than the earlier issues. The 7r and 9r are not known with this overprint. Stamps on laid paper (1875) are from a separate setting.

Stamps and Types of 1866-67 Overprinted in Two Lines of Very Small Letters Repeated Continuously

Overprinted "Estampillas de Correo — Contrasena"

1873, July 1

37 A4 ½r pale rose	70.00	13.00
On cover		2,500.
a. ½r rose	70.00	13.00
On cover		2,500.
b. Inverted overprint	175.00	75.00
c. Tête bêche pair	3,000.	2,000.
38 A4 1r vermilion	85.00	25.00
On cover		3,500.
a. Inverted overprint	—	—
b. Half used as ½r on cover		5,500.
39 A4 2r yellow	300.00	125.00
On cover		—
a. Inverted overprint	—	—
b. Half used as 1r on cover		12,000.
Nos. 37-39 (3)	455.00	163.00

Covers: Only one cover is recorded of No. 39b. Two examples are known on fragments.

Overprinted

"Contrasena — Estampillas de Correo"

1873, Nov.

40 A4 1c gray lilac	30.00	32.50
On cover		—
a. Inverted overprint	6.50	17.00
On cover		3,000.
41 A4 2c green	125.00	90.00
On cover		3,000.
a. Inverted overprint	40.00	50.00
On cover		3,000.
b. As "a," half used as 1c on cover		7,500.
42 A4 ½r rose	72.50	13.00
On cover		100.00
a. Inverted overprint	30.00	4.00
On cover		50.00
b. ½r pink	60.00	11.00
On cover		100.00
43 A4 1r vermilion	85.00	23.00
On cover		500.00
a. Inverted overprint	35.00	9.00
On cover		300.00
b. Half used as ½r on cover		300.00
44 A4 2r yellow	325.00	160.00
On cover		—
a. Inverted overprint	110.00	50.00
On cover		10,000.
b. Half used as 1r on cover		10,000.
Nos. 40-44 (5)	637.50	318.50

Overprinted

"Contrasena — Estampilla de Correos"

1875

45 A4 ½r rose	85.00	10.00
On cover		200.00
a. Inverted overprint	125.00	25.00
On cover		500.00
b. Double overprint	160.00	90.00
46 A4 1r vermilion	160.00	15.00
On cover		700.00
a. Inverted overprint	200.00	80.00
On cover		2,500.
b. Tête bêche pair	3,500.	3,000.
c. Half used as ½r on cover		3,500.

Overprinted

"Estampillas de correo — Contrasena"

1876-77

47 A4 ½r rose	77.50	9.25
On cover		200.00
a. ½r pink	65.00	7.50
On cover		200.00
b. Inverted overprint	65.00	7.50
On cover		200.00
c. Both lines of overprint read "Contrasena"	75.00	17.50
On cover		3,500.
d. Both lines of overprint read "Estampillas de correo"	75.00	17.50
On cover		3,500.
e. Double overprint	125.00	35.00
48 A4 1r vermilion ('77)	92.50	23.00
On cover		700.00
a. Inverted overprint	85.00	24.00
On cover		700.00
b. Tête bêche pair	2,250.	2,500.
c. Half used as ½r on cover		—

On Nos. 47 and 48 "correo" has a small "c" instead of a capital. Nos. 45 and 46 have the overprint in slightly larger letters than the other stamps of the 1873-76 issues.

Simón Bolívar

A6 A7

Overprinted

"Decreto de 27 Junio 1870"

Twice, One Line Inverted

1879 *Imperf.*

49 A6 1c yellow	4.00	1.00
Multiple, on cover		—
a. 1c orange	5.00	1.50
Multiple, on cover		1,500.
b. 1c olive yellow	5.50	1.75
Multiple, on cover		—
50 A6 5c yellow	3.50	.50
On cover		75.00
a. 5c orange	2.50	.75
On cover		75.00
b. Double overprint	20.00	10.00
51 A6 10c blue	5.00	.50
On cover		1,500.
52 A6 30c blue	7.75	1.00
On cover		3,000.
53 A6 50c blue	7.75	1.00
54 A6 90c blue	40.00	12.00
55 A7 1v rose red	77.50	18.00
56 A7 3v rose red	130.00	55.00
57 A7 5v rose red	225.00	77.50
Nos. 49-57 (9)	500.50	166.50

In 1879 and the early part of 1880 there were no regular postage stamps in Venezuela and the stamps inscribed "Escuelas" were permitted to serve for postal as well as revenue purposes. Postally canceled copies are extremely scarce. Values quoted are for stamps with cancellations of banks or business houses or with pen cancellations. Copies with pen marks removed are sometimes offered as unused stamps, or may have fraudulent postal cancellations added.

Nos. 49-57 exist without overprint. These are proofs.

Covers: Nos. 53-57 are not known on cover.

A8 A9

1880 *Perf. 11*

58 A8 5c yellow	1.50	.50
On cover		500.00
a. 5c orange	1.50	.50
On cover		500.00
b. Printed on both sides	150.00	85.00
59 A8 10c yellow	2.50	.60
On cover		1,000.
a. 10c orange	2.50	.60
On cover, pair		1,000.
60 A8 25c yellow	2.50	.60
On cover		60.00
a. 25c orange	2.75	.70
On cover		60.00
b. Printed on both sides	110.00	52.50
c. Impression of 5c on back	175.00	90.00
61 A8 50c yellow	4.75	.80
On cover		2,000.
a. 50c orange	5.25	.85
On cover		2,000.
b. Half used as 25c on cover		—
c. Printed on both sides	150.00	90.00
d. Impression of 25c on back	150.00	90.00
62 A9 1b pale blue	12.00	1.40
On cover		3,000.
63 A9 2b pale blue	17.00	1.75
On cover		5,000.
64 A9 5b pale blue	40.00	5.75
a. Half used as 2½b on cover		—
65 A9 10b rose red	200.00	70.00
66 A9 20b rose red	1,200.	200.00
67 A9 25b rose red	5,000.	500.00
Nos. 58-65 (8)	280.25	81.40

See note on used values below No. 57.

Covers: Nos. 64-67 are not known on cover.

Bolívar — A10

1880 **Litho.** ***Perf. 11***

Thick or Thin Paper

68 A10 5c blue	15.00	7.25
On cover		200.00
a. Printed on both sides	225.00	140.00
69 A10 10c rose	20.00	12.00
On cover		200.00
a. 10c carmine	20.00	12.00
On cover		250.00
b. Double impression	90.00	75.00
c. Horiz. pair, imperf. btwn.	75.00	75.00
70 A10 10c scarlet	20.00	12.00
On cover		250.00
a. Horiz. pair, imperf. btwn.	75.00	75.00
71 A10 25c yellow	15.00	7.25
On cover		250.00
b. Thick paper	20.00	10.00
On cover		250.00
72 A10 50c brown	92.50	40.00
On cover		1,000.
a. 50c deep brown	92.50	.40
On cover		1,000.
b. Printed on both sides	225.00	140.00
c. Half used as 25c on cover		5,000.
73 A10 1b green	140.00	50.00
On cover		2,000.
a. Horiz. pair, imperf. btwn.	300.00	300.00
Nos. 68-73 (6)	302.50	128.50

Nos. 68 to 73 were used for the payment of postage on letters to be sent abroad and the Escuelas stamps were then restricted to internal use.

Counterfeits of this issue exist in a great variety of shades as well as in wrong colors. They are on thick and thin paper, white or toned, and imperf. or perforated 11, 12 and compound. They are also found téte bêche. Counterfeits of Nos. 68 to 72 inclusive often have a diagonal line across the "S" of "CENTS" and a short line from the bottom of that letter to the frame below it. Originals of No. 73 show parts of a frame around "BOLIVAR."

Simón Bolívar

A11 A12

A13 A14

A15

1882, Aug. 1 **Engr.** ***Perf. 12***

74 A11 5c blue	.70	.35
On cover		100.00
75 A12 10c red brown	.70	.35
On cover		100.00
76 A13 25c yellow brown	1.00	.40
On cover		20.00
a. Printed on both sides	50.00	27.50
77 A14 50c green	2.40	.70
On cover		200.00
a. Half used as 25c on cover		500.00
78 A15 1b violet	3.25	1.75
On cover		1,000.
Nos. 74-78 (5)	8.05	3.55

Nos. 75-78 exist imperf. Value, set $32.50.

See Nos. 88, 92-95. For surcharges and overprints see Nos. 100-103, 108-112.

A16 A17

A18 A19

A20 A21

A22 A23

1882-88

79 A16 5c blue green	.20	.20
On cover		100.00
80 A17 10c brown	.20	.20
On cover		100.00
81 A18 25c orange	.20	.20
On cover		50.00
82 A19 50c blue	.20	.20
On cover		200.00
83 A20 1b vermilion	.25	.20
84 A21 3b dull vio ('88)	.25	.20
85 A22 10b dark brn ('88)	1.25	.80
86 A23 20b plum ('88)	1.50	.95
Nos. 79-86 (8)	4.05	2.95

By official decree, dated Apr. 14, 1882, stamps of types A11 to A15 were to be used for foreign postage and those of types A16 to A23 for inland correspondence and fiscal use.

Issue date: Nos. 79-83, Aug. 1.

See Nos. 87, 89-91, 96-99. For surcharges and overprints see Nos. 104-107, 114-122.

1887-88 **Litho.** ***Perf. 11***

87 A16 5c gray green	.25	.20
On cover		100.00
88 A13 25c yellow brown	42.50	15.00
On cover		100.00
89 A18 25c orange	.40	.35
On cover		100.00
90 A20 1b orange red ('88)	3.50	.75
On cover		100.00
Nos. 87-90 (4)	46.65	16.30

Perf. 14

91 A16 5c gray green	70.00	22.50

Stamps of type A16, perf. 11 and 14, are from a new die with "ESCUELAS" in smaller letters. Stamps of the 1887-88 issue, perf. 12, and a 50c dark blue, perf. 11 or 12, are believed by experts to be from printer's waste.

Counterfeits of No. 91 have been made by perforating printers waste of No. 96.

Rouletted 8

92 A11 5c blue	40.00	17.00
On cover		200.00
93 A13 25c yel brown	15.00	10.00
On cover		200.00
94 A14 50c green	15.00	10.00
On cover		500.00
95 A15 1b purple	30.00	20.00
On cover		500.00
Nos. 92-95 (4)	100.00	57.00

1887-88

96	A16	5c green	.20	.20
		On cover		200.00
97	A18	25c orange	.20	.20
		On cover		100.00
98	A19	50c dark blue	.70	.70
		On cover		200.00
99	A21	3b purple ('88)	3.00	3.00
		On overfranked cover		*1,000.*
		Nos. 96-99 (4)	4.10	4.10

The so-called imperforate varieties of Nos. 92 to 99, and the pin perforated 50c dark blue, type A19, are believed to be from printer's waste.

Stamps of 1882-88 Handstamp Surcharged in Violet

1892 *Perf. 12*

100	A11	25c on 5c blue	*40.00*	*40.00*
101	A12	25c on 10c red brn	*16.00*	*16.00*
102	A13	1b on 25c yel brn	*16.00*	*16.00*
103	A14	1b on 50c green	*20.00*	*20.00*
		Nos. 100-103 (4)	*92.00*	*92.00*

See note after No. 107.

1892

104	A16	25c on 5c bl grn	*10.00*	*6.00*
105	A17	25c on 10c brown	*10.00*	*6.00*
106	A18	1b on 25c orange	*15.00*	*12.00*
107	A19	1b on 50c blue	*23.00*	*12.00*
		Nos. 104-107 (4)	*58.00*	*36.00*

Counterfeits of this surcharge abound.

Stamps of 1882-88 Overprinted in Red or Black:

1893

108	A11	5c blue (R)	.55	.25
		On cover		*500.00*
a.		Inverted overprint	3.25	3.25
b.		Double overprint	16.00	16.00
109	A12	10c red brn (Bk)	.90	.90
		On cover		*500.00*
a.		Inverted overprint	4.00	4.00
b.		Double overprint	16.00	16.00
110	A13	25c yel brn (R)	.80	.50
		On cover		*100.00*
a.		Inverted overprint	5.25	5.25
b.		Double overprint	16.00	16.00
c.		25c yel brn (Bk)	*500.00*	*500.00*
111	A14	50c green (R)	1.25	.80
		On cover		*500.00*
a.		Inverted overprint	5.25	5.25
b.		Double overprint	27.50	27.50
112	A15	1b pur (R)	3.00	1.20
		On cover		*2,000.*
a.		Inverted overprint	10.00	10.00
		Nos. 108-112 (5)	6.50	3.65

1893

114	A16	5c bl grn (R)	.20	.20
		On cover		*500.00*
a.		Inverted overprint	3.25	3.25
b.		Double overprint	5.25	5.25
115	A17	10c brn (R)	.20	.20
		On cover		*500.00*
a.		Inverted overprint	3.25	3.25
116	A18	25c org (R)	.20	.20
		On cover		*500.00*
a.		Inverted overprint	3.25	3.25
117	A18	25c org (Bk)	5.75	2.75
		On cover		*500.00*
a.		Inverted overprint	8.25	5.00
118	A19	50c blue (R)	.20	.20
		On cover		*500.00*
a.		Inverted overprint	3.25	3.25
119	A20	1b ver (Bk)	.60	.40
a.		Inverted overprint	4.00	4.00
120	A21	3b dl vio (R)	.90	.40
a.		Double overprint	8.25	8.25
121	A22	10b dk brn (R)	3.50	2.25
a.		Double overprint	10.00	10.00
b.		Inverted overprint	20.00	20.00
122	A23	20b plum (Bk)	3.00	3.00
a.		Double overprint	10.00	20.00
b.		Inverted overprint		
		Nos. 114-122 (9)	14.55	9.60

Counterfeits exist.

Simón Bolívar
A24 A25

1893 **Engr.**

123	A24	5c red brn	.90	.25
		On cover		100.00
124	A24	10c blue	3.25	1.25
		On cover		100.00
125	A24	25c magenta	15.00	.50
		On cover		20.00
126	A24	50c brn vio	4.25	.55
		On cover		50.00
127	A24	1b green	5.75	1.25
		On cover		*750.00*
		Nos. 123-127 (5)	29.15	3.80

Many shades exist in this issue, but their values do not vary.

1893

128	A25	5c gray	.20	.20
		On cover		100.00
129	A25	10c green	.20	.20
		On cover		100.00
130	A25	25c blue	.20	.20
		On cover		100.00
131	A25	50c orange	.20	.20
		On cover		100.00
132	A25	1b red vio	.20	.20
133	A25	3b red	.55	.20
134	A25	10b dl vio	.90	.80
135	A25	20b red brn	4.25	2.75
		Nos. 128-135 (8)	6.70	4.75

By decree of Nov. 28, 1892, the stamps inscribed "Correos" were to be used for external postage and those inscribed "Instruccion" were for internal postage and revenue purposes.

For surcharge see No. 230.

After July 1, 1895, stamps inscribed "Escuelas" or "Instruccion" were no longer available for postage. Stamps of design A25 in shades different than those listed were printed after 1895.

Landing of Columbus
A26

1893 *Perf. 12*

136	A26	25c magenta	11.00	.60
		On cover		100.00

4th cent. of the discovery of the mainland of South America, also participation of Venezuela in the Intl. Exhib. at Chicago in 1893.

Map of Venezuela
A27

1896 **Litho.**

137	A27	5c yel grn	3.00	2.75
		On cover		250.00
a.		5c apple green	3.00	2.75
		On cover		250.00
138	A27	10c blue	4.00	3.00
		On cover		250.00
139	A27	25c yellow	4.00	5.50
		On cover		50.00
a.		25c orange	4.00	5.50
		On cover		50.00
b.		Tête bêche pair	125.00	125.00
		On cover		*2,000.*
140	A27	50c rose red	52.50	27.00
		On cover		500.00
a.		50c red	52.50	52.50
		On cover		500.00
b.		Tête bêche pair	375.00	375.00
141	A27	1b violet	40.00	27.00
		On cover		*1,000.*
		Nos. 137-141 (5)	103.50	65.25

Gen. Francisco Antonio Gabriel de Miranda (1752-1816).

These stamps were in use from July 4 to Nov. 4, 1896. Later usage is known.

There are many forgeries of this issue. They include faked errors, imperforate stamps and many tête bêche. The paper of the originals is thin, white and semi-transparent. The gum is shiny and crackled. The paper of the reprints is often thick and opaque. The gum is usually dull, smooth, thin and only slightly adhesive.

Bolívar — A28

1899-1901 **Engr.**

142	A28	5c dk grn	1.00	.25
		On cover		50.00
143	A28	10c red	1.25	.40
		On cover		50.00
144	A28	25c blue	1.50	.55
		On cover		75.00
145	A28	50c gray blk	2.00	1.00
		On cover		200.00
146	A28	50c org ('01)	1.75	.50
		On cover		25.00
147	A28	1b yel grn	32.50	15.00
		On cover		*1,000.*
149	A28	2b orange	375.00	225.00
		On cover		—
		Nos. 142-147,149 (7)	415.00	242.70

Stamps of 1899 Overprinted in Black

1900

150	A28	5c dk grn	1.25	.40
		On cover		50.00
a.		Inverted overprint	4.75	4.75
151	A28	10c red	1.25	.40
		On cover		50.00
a.		Inverted overprint	6.50	6.50
b.		Double overprint	10.50	10.50
152	A28	25c blue	7.75	1.25
		On cover		50.00
a.		Inverted overprint	13.00	13.00
153	A28	50c gray blk	4.00	.55
		On cover		*500.00*
a.		Inverted overprint	12.00	12.00
154	A28	1b yel grn	1.75	.80
		On cover		*1,000.*
a.		Double overprint	13.00	13.00
b.		Inverted overprint	12.00	12.00
155	A28	2b orange	2.75	2.25
		On cover		—
a.		Inverted overprint	35.00	35.00
b.		Double overprint	32.50	32.50
		Nos. 150-155 (6)	18.75	5.65

Initials are those of R. T. Mendoza.

Counterfeit overprints exist, especially of inverted and doubled varieties.

Bolivar Type of 1899-1903 Overprinted

1900

156	A28	5c dk grn	200.00	200.00
		On cover		—
157	A28	10c red	200.00	200.00
		On cover		—
158	A28	25c blue	350.00	175.00
		On cover		—
159	A28	50c yel orange	23.00	1.60
		On cover		30.00
160	A28	1b slate	1.25	1.00
		On cover		200.00
a.		Without overprint	*4,000.*	—
		Nos. 156-160 (5)	774.25	577.60

Overprinted

1900, Aug. 14

161	A28	5c green	7.75	.55
		On cover		50.00
162	A28	10c red	7.00	1.00
		On cover		50.00
163	A28	25c blue	7.75	1.00
		On cover		50.00
		Nos. 161-163 (3)	22.50	2.55

Inverted Overprint

161a	A28	5c	9.25	6.50
162a	A28	10c	9.25	6.50
163a	A28	25c	12.00	7.25
		Nos. 161a-163a (3)	30.50	20.25

Overprint exists on each value without "Castro" or without "1900."

Type of 1893 Surcharged

1904, Jan. *Perf. 12*

230	A25	5c on 50c green	.80	.60
		On cover		20.00
a.		"Vele"	23.00	23.00
b.		Surcharge reading up	1.00	.50
c.		Double surcharge	18.00	18.00

Gen. José de Sucre — A35

Pres. Cipriano Castro — A37

1904-09 **Engr.**

231	A35	5c bl grn	.50	.20
		On cover		20.00
232	A35	10c carmine	.55	.20
		On cover		20.00
233	A35	15c violet	.90	.40
		On cover		50.00
234	A35	25c dp ultra	6.50	.40
		On cover		10.00
235	A35	50c plum	1.00	.50
		On cover		20.00
236	A35	1b plum	1.10	.50
		On cover		75.00
		Nos. 231-236 (6)	10.55	2.20

Issue date: 15c, Dec. 1909. Others, July 1, 1904.

1905, July 5 **Litho.** *Perf. 11½*

245	A37	5c vermilion	3.25	3.25
		On cover		100.00
a.		5c carmine	5.00	5.00
246	A37	10c dark blue	5.50	4.25
		On cover		100.00
247	A37	25c yellow	2.00	1.50
		On cover		100.00
		Nos. 245-247 (3)	10.75	9.00

National Congress. Issued for interior postage only. Valid only for 90 days.

Various part-perforate varieties of Nos. 245-247 exist. Value, $15-$30.

Liberty — A38

1910, Apr. 19 **Engr.** *Perf. 12*

249	A38	25c dark blue	13.00	.60
		On cover		50.00

Centenary of national independence.

Francisco de Miranda
A39

Rafael Urdaneta
A40

Bolívar — A41

1911 Litho. Perf. 11½x12

250 A39 5c dp grn .50 .20
On cover 30.00
251 A39 10c carmine .50 .20
On cover 30.00
252 A40 15c gray 5.75 .40
On cover 20.00
253 A40 25c dp bl 3.25 .60
On cover 20.00
a. Imperf., pair 40.00 50.00
254 A41 50c purple 3.50 .40
On cover 30.00
255 A41 1b yellow 3.50 1.50
On cover 75.00
Nos. 250-255 (6) 17.00 3.30

The 50c with center in blue was never issued although copies were postmarked by favor.

The centers of Nos. 250-255 were separately printed and often vary in shade from the rest of the design. In a second printing of the 5c and 10c, the entire design was printed at one time.

Redrawn

1913

255A A40 15c gray 3.50 2.25
255B A40 25c deep blue 2.00 .65
255C A41 50c purple 2.00 .65
Nos. 255A-255C (3) 7.50 3.55

The redrawn stamps have two berries instead of one at top of the left spray; a berry has been added over the "C" and "S" of "Centimos"; and the lowest leaf at the right is cut by the corner square.

Simón Bolívar
A42 A43

1914, July Engr. Perf. 13½, 14, 15

256 A42 5c yel grn 37.50 .55
257 A42 10c scarlet 35.00 .50
258 A42 25c dark blue 5.75 .25
Nos. 256-258 (3) 78.25 1.30

Printed by the American Bank Note Co.

Different frames.

1915-23 Perf. 12

259 A43 5c green 4.25 .25
260 A43 10c vermilion 10.00 .60
261 A43 10c claret ('22) 10.00 .90
262 A43 15c dull ol grn 9.25 .60
263 A43 25c ultra 6.50 .25
a. 25c blue 13.00 .60
264 A43 40c dull green 23.00 11.50
265 A43 50c dp violet 6.50 .80
266 A43 50c ultra ('23) 17.00 4.75
267 A43 75c lt blue 57.50 23.00
a. 75c greenish blue 57.50 23.00
268 A43 1b dark gray 35.00 5.25
Nos. 259-268 (10) 179.00 47.90

See Nos. 269-285. For surcharges see Nos. 307, 309-310.

Type of 1915-23 Issue
Printed by Waterlow & Sons, Ltd.
Re-engraved

1924-39 Perf. 12½

269 A43 5c orange brn .55 .20
a. 5c yellow brown .55 .20
b. Horiz. pair, imperf. between 25.00 40.00
270 A43 5c green ('39) 12.00 1.00
271 A43 7½c yel grn ('39) 1.25 .40
272 A43 10c dk green .25 .20
273 A43 10c dk car ('39) 4.00 .25
274 A43 15c olive grn 2.25 .50
275 A43 15c brown ('27) .30 .20
276 A43 25c ultra 2.25 .25
277 A43 25c red ('28) .25 .20
a. Horiz. pair, imperf. btwn. 50.00 85.00
278 A43 40c dp blue ('25) .55 .25
279 A43 40c slate bl ('39) 7.75 1.25
280 A43 50c dk blue .55 .25
281 A43 50c dk pur ('39) 7.75 .85
282 A43 1b black .55 .25
283 A43 3b yel org ('25) 1.75 .95
284 A43 3b red org ('39) 12.00 4.25
285 A43 5b dull vio ('25) 16.00 8.50
Nos. 269-285 (17) 70.00 19.75

Perf. 14

269c A43 5c 7.00 2.00
272a A43 10c 7.00 2.00
274a A43 15c 8.25 2.75
276a A43 25c 12.00 4.75
280a A43 50c 35.00 14.00
282a A43 1b 42.50 27.00
Nos. 269c-282a (6) 111.75 52.50

The re-engraved stamps may readily be distinguished from the 1915 issue by the perforation and sometimes by the colors. The designs differ in many minor details which are too minute for illustration or description.

Bolívar and Sucre
A44

Perf. 11½x12, 12

1924, Dec. 1 Litho.

286 A44 25c grayish blue 2.75 .55

Redrawn

286A A44 25c ultra 3.50 .85

Centenary of the Battle of Ayacucho.

The redrawn stamp has a whiter effect with less shading in the faces. Bolivar's ear is clearly visible and the outline of his aquiline nose is broken.

A45

A46

Revenue Stamps Surcharged in Black or Red

1926 Perf. 12, 12½

287 A45 5c on 1b ol grn .65 .40
a. Double surcharge 8.00 8.00
b. Pair, one without surcharge 12.00 12.00
c. Inverted surcharge 8.00 8.00
288 A46 25c on 5c dk brn (R) .65 .40
a. Inverted surcharge 8.00 8.00
b. Double surcharge 8.00 8.00

View of Ciudad Bolívar and General J.V. Gómez — A47

1928, July 21 Litho. Perf. 12

289 A47 10c deep green 1.00 .65
a. Imperf., pair 40.00

25th anniversary of the Battle of Ciudad Bolívar and the foundation of peace in Venezuela.

Simón Bolívar
A48 A49

1930, Dec. 9

290 A48 5c yellow 1.00 .35
291 A48 10c dark blue 1.00 .25
292 A48 25c rose red 1.00 .25
Nos. 290-292 (3) 3.00 .85

Imperf., Pairs

290a A48 5c 5.25 5.25
291a A48 10c 6.50 6.50
292a A48 25c 10.50 10.50

Death centenary of Simón Bolívar (1783-1830), South American liberator.

Nos. 290-292 exist part-perforate, including pairs imperf. between, imperf. horiz., imperf. vert. Value range, $6-12.

Various Frames
Bluish Winchester Security Paper

1932-38 Engr. Perf. 12½

293 A49 5c violet .50 .20
294 A49 7½c dk green ('37) 1.00 .40
295 A49 10c green .60 .20
296 A49 15c yellow 1.50 .25
297 A49 22½c dp car ('38) 3.50 .50
298 A49 25c red 1.25 .20
299 A49 37½c ultra ('36) 4.50 2.00
300 A49 40c indigo 4.50 .25
301 A49 50c olive grn 4.50 .40
302 A49 1b lt blue 6.00 .70
303 A49 3b brown 40.00 13.00
304 A49 5b yellow brn 50.00 17.00
Nos. 293-304 (12) 117.85 35.10

For surcharges see Nos. 308, 318-319, C223.

Arms of Bolívar — A50

1933, July 24 Litho. Perf. 11

306 A50 25c brown red 3.00 2.40
a. Imperf., pair 32.50 32.50

150th anniv. of the birth of Simón Bolívar. Valid only to Aug. 21.

Stamps of 1924-32 Surcharged in Black: (Blocks of Surcharge in Color of stamps)

1933

307 A43 7½c on 10c grn .50 .25
a. Double surcharge 2.50 2.50
b. Inverted surcharge 4.25 4.25
308 A49 22½c on 25c (#298) 2.00 .85
309 A43 22½c on 25c (#277) 1.50 1.50
a. Double surcharge 10.00 10.00
310 A43 37½c on 40c dp bl 2.00 .95
a. Double surcharge 11.50 11.50
b. Inverted surcharge 10.00 10.00
Nos. 307-310 (4) 6.00 3.55

Nurse and Child — A51

River Scene — A52

Gathering Cacao Pods — A53

Cattle Raising A54

Plowing A55

Perf. 11, 11½ or Compound

1937, July 1 Litho.

311 A51 5c deep violet .55 .35
312 A52 10c dk slate grn .55 .20
313 A53 15c yellow brn 1.00 .55
314 A51 25c cerise 1.00 .35
315 A54 50c yellow grn 6.50 4.25
316 A55 3b red orange 12.00 7.75
317 A51 5b lt brown 23.00 15.00
Nos. 311-317 (7) 44.60 28.45

Nos. 311-317 exist imperforate. Value for set $75. Nos. 311-315 exist in pairs, imperf. between; value range, $20-$30.

For overprints and surcharges see Nos. 321-324, 345, 376-377, 380-384.

No. 300 Surcharged in Black

1937
VALE 25 POR

1937, July Perf. 12½

318 A49 25c on 40c indigo 7.75 .95
a. Double surcharge 16.00 16.00
b. Inverted surcharge 13.00 13.00
c. Triple surcharge 32.50 32.50

Surcharged

1937
VALE 25 POR

319 A49 25c on 40c indigo 400.00 325.00
a. Double surcharge

A56

1937, Oct. 28 Litho. Perf. 10½

320 A56 25c blue 1.25 .45

Acquisition of the Port of La Guaira by the Government from the British Corporation, June 3, 1937. Exists imperf. See Nos. C64-C65.

A redrawn printing of No. 320, with top inscription beginning "Nacionalización . . ." was prepared but not issued. Value, $40.

For surcharge see No. 385.

Stamps of 1937 Overprinted in Black

RESELLADO
1937-1938

1937, Dec. 17 Perf. 11, 11½

321 A51 5c deep violet 5.75 3.25
322 A52 10c dk slate grn 1.75 .75
a. Inverted overprint 13.00 13.00
323 A51 25c cerise 1.50 .55
a. Inverted overprint 16.00 16.00
324 A55 3b red orange 375.00 225.00
Nos. 321-324 (4) 384.00 229.55

Part-perforate pairs exist of Nos. 321-322 and 324. Value range, $12.50 to $125.

See Nos. C66-C78.

Gathering Coffee Beans — A57

Simón Bolívar — A58

Post Office, Caracas — A59

1938	Engr.		Perf. 12	
325	A57	5c green	.40	.20
326	A57	5c deep green	.40	.20
327	A58	10c car rose	.70	.20
328	A58	10c dp rose	.70	.20
329	A59	15c dk violet	1.40	.25
330	A59	15c olive grn	.85	.25
331	A58	25c lt blue	.40	.20
332	A58	25c dk blue	.40	.20
333	A58	37½c dk blue	8.50	4.00
334	A58	37½c lt blue	2.75	.85
335	A59	40c sepia	20.00	7.75
336	A59	40c black	17.00	7.75
337	A57	50c olive grn	27.50	7.75
338	A57	50c dull violet	9.25	.85
339	A58	1b dp brown	12.00	5.50
340	A58	1b black brown	17.00	1.50
341	A57	3b orange	92.50	50.00
342	A59	5b black	15.00	7.75
		Nos. 325-342 (18)	226.75	95.40

See Nos. 400 and 412.

Teresa Carreño — A60

Bolívar Statue — A61

1938, June 12			Perf. 11½x12	
343	A60	25c blue	5.75	.60

Teresa Carreno, Venezuelan pianist, whose remains were repatriated Feb. 14, 1938.

For surcharge see No. 386.

1938, July 24			Perf. 12	
344	A61	25c dark blue	6.50	.60

"The Day of the Worker."

For surcharge see No. 387.

Type of 1937 Surcharged in Black

VALE
Bs. 0,40
1938

1938	Litho.		Perf. 11, 11½	
345	A51	40c on 5b lt brn	8.50	4.50
a.		Inverted surcharge	21.00	21.00

Gen. José I. Paz Castillo, Postmaster of Venezuela, 1859 — A62

1939, Apr. 19	Engr.		Perf. 12½	
348	A62	10c carmine	2.50	.70

80th anniv. of the first Venezuelan stamp.

View of Ojeda A63

1939, June 24			Photo.	
349	A63	25c dull blue	9.25	.75

Founding of city of Ojeda.

Cristóbal Mendoza A64

Diego Urbaneja A65

1939, Oct. 14	Engr.		Perf. 13	
350	A64	5c green	.40	.20
351	A64	10c dk car rose	.40	.20
352	A64	15c dull lilac	1.00	.25
353	A64	25c brt ultra	.80	.20
354	A64	37½c dark blue	15.00	6.25
355	A64	50c lt olive grn	16.00	4.00
356	A64	1b dark brown	6.50	3.50
		Nos. 350-356 (7)	40.10	14.60

Mendoza (1772-1839), postmaster general.

1940-43			Perf. 12	
357	A65	5c Prus green	.45	.20
357A	A65	7½c dk bl grn ('43)	.65	.25
358	A65	15c olive	.80	.25
359	A65	37½c deep blue	1.25	.60
360	A65	40c violet blue	.95	.30
361	A65	50c violet	5.50	1.40
362	A65	1b dk violet brn	2.75	.75
363	A65	3b scarlet	8.00	3.25
		Nos. 357-363 (8)	20.35	7.00

See Nos. 399, 408, 410 and 411. For surcharges see Nos. 396, C226.

Battle of Carabobo, 1821 — A67

1940, June 13				
365	A67	25c blue	6.00	.70

Birth of General JoséAntonio Páez, 150th anniv.

"Crossing the Andes" by Tito Salas — A68

1940, June 13				
366	A68	25c dark blue	6.00	.70

Death cent. of General Francisco Santander.

Monument and Urn containing Ashes of Simón Bolívar — A69

Bed where Simón Bolívar was Born — A70

Designs: 15c, "Christening of Bolivar" by Tito Salas. 20c, Bolivar's birthplace, Caracas. 25c, "Bolivar on Horseback" by Salas. 30c, Patio of Bolivar House, Caracas. 37½c, Patio of Bolivar's Birthplace. 50c, "Rebellion of 1812" by Salas.

1940-41				
367	A69	5c turq green	.25	.20
368	A70	10c rose pink	.25	.20
369	A69	15c olive	.60	.20
370	A70	20c blue ('41)	1.00	.20
371	A69	25c lt blue	.60	.20
372	A70	30c plum ('41)	1.50	.25
373	A70	37½c dk blue	3.00	1.00
374	A70	50c purple	2.00	.50
		Nos. 367-374 (8)	9.20	2.75

110th anniv. of the death of Simón Bolívar.

See #397, 398, 403, 405-407, 409. For surcharges see #375, 401-402, C224, C237-C238.

AIR POST STAMPS

Air post stamps of 1930-42 perforated "GN" (Gobierno Nacional) were for official use.

Airplane and Map of Venezuela
AP1 AP2

1930	Unwmk.	Litho.	Perf. 12	
C1	AP1	5c bister brn	.20	.20
C2	AP1	10c yellow	.20	.20
a.		10c salmon	32.50	32.50
C3	AP1	15c gray	.20	.20
C4	AP1	25c lilac	.20	.20
C5	AP1	40c olive grn	.20	.20
a.		40c slate blue	40.00	
b.		40c slate green	40.00	
C6	AP1	75c dp red	.25	.20
C7	AP1	1b indigo	.40	.20
C8	AP1	1.20b blue grn	.60	.30
C9	AP1	1.70b dk blue	.75	.40
C10	AP1	1.90b blue grn	.75	.45
C11	AP1	2.10b dk blue	1.50	.60
C12	AP1	2.30b vermilion	1.50	.45
C13	AP1	2.50b dk blue	1.50	.45
C14	AP1	3.70b blue grn	1.50	1.00
C15	AP1	10b dull vio	4.50	2.25
C16	AP1	20b gray grn	7.00	4.25
		Nos. C1-C16 (16)	21.25	11.55

Nos. C1-C16 exist imperforate or partly perforated. See Nos. C119-C126.

Issued: 10b, 6/8; 20b, 6/16; others, 4/5.

Bluish Winchester Security Paper

1932, July 12	Engr.		Perf. 12½	
C17	AP2	5c brown	.40	.20
C18	AP2	10c org yel	.40	.20
C19	AP2	15c gray lilac	.40	.20
C20	AP2	25c violet	.40	.20
C21	AP2	40c ol grn	.80	.20
C22	AP2	70c rose	.55	.20
C23	AP2	75c red org	1.00	.20
C24	AP2	1b dk bl	1.10	.20
C25	AP2	1.20b green	2.25	.85
C26	AP2	1.70b red brn	4.50	.55
C27	AP2	1.80b ultra	2.25	.35
C28	AP2	1.90b green	5.50	3.50
C29	AP2	1.95b blue	6.50	2.75
C30	AP2	2b blk brn	4.00	2.25
C31	AP2	2.10b blue	9.25	5.50
C32	AP2	2.30b red	4.00	2.25
C33	AP2	2.50b dk bl	5.50	1.40
C34	AP2	3b dk vio	5.50	.85
C35	AP2	3.70b emerald	7.75	5.50
C36	AP2	4b red org	5.50	1.40
C37	AP2	5b black	6.50	2.25
C38	AP2	8b dk car	13.00	4.50
C39	AP2	10b dk vio	25.00	7.75
C40	AP2	20b grnsh slate	55.00	20.00
		Nos. C17-C40 (24)	167.05	63.25

Pairs imperf. between exist of the 1b (value $150); the 25c and 4b (value $300 each).

Air Post Stamps of 1932 Surcharged in Black

1937, June 4				
C41	AP2	5c on 1.70b red brn	11.00	7.00
C42	AP2	10c on 3.70b emer	11.00	7.00
C43	AP2	15c on 4b red org	5.00	3.50
C44	AP2	25c on 5b blk	5.00	3.50
C45	AP2	1b on 8b dk car	4.00	3.50
C46	AP2	2b on 2.10b bl	30.00	23.00
		Nos. C41-C46 (6)	66.00	47.50

Various varieties of surcharge exist, including double and triple impressions. No. C43 exists in pair imperf. between; value $30 unused, $50 used.

Allegory of Flight AP3

Allegory of Flight AP4

National Pantheon at Caracas AP5

Airplane — AP6

AP7

Perf. 11, 11½ and Compound

1937, July 1				Litho.
C47	AP3	5c brn org	.30	.40
C48	AP4	10c org red	.25	.20
C49	AP5	15c gray blk	.60	.40
C50	AP6	25c dk vio	.60	.40
C51	AP4	40c yel grn	1.10	.55
C52	AP3	70c red	1.10	.40
C53	AP5	75c bister	2.50	1.30
C54	AP3	1b dk gray	1.50	.55
C55	AP4	1.20b pck grn	6.50	4.25
C56	AP3	1.80b dk ultra	3.25	2.00
C57	AP5	1.95b lt ultra	10.00	7.75
C58	AP6	2b chocolate	4.25	2.75
C59	AP6	2.50b gray bl	11.50	11.50
C60	AP4	3b lt vio	6.50	4.50
C61	AP6	3.70b rose red	11.50	15.00
C62	AP5	10b red vio	25.00	15.00
C63	AP3	20b gray	30.00	23.00
		Nos. C47-C63 (17)	116.45	89.95

All values exist imperf, and all except the 3.70b part-perf.

Counterfeits exist.

For overprints & surcharges see #C66-C78, C114-C118, C164-C167, C169-C172, C174-C180.

1937, Oct. 28			Perf. 11	
C64	AP7	70c emerald	1.40	.55
C65	AP7	1.80b ultra	2.25	1.00

Acquisition of the Port of La Guaira by the Government from the British Corporation, June 3, 1937. Exist imperf.

A redrawn printing of #C64-C65, with lower inscription beginning "Nacionalización . ." was prepared but not issued. Price, $40 each.

For overprints see Nos. C168, C173.

Air Post Stamps of 1937 Overprinted in Black

1937, Dec. 17			Perf. 11, 11½	
C66	AP4	10c org red	1.00	.70
a.		Inverted overprint	15.00	12.00
C67	AP6	25c dk vio	2.00	1.00
C68	AP4	40c yel grn	2.00	1.40
C69	AP3	70c red	1.50	1.00
a.		Inverted overprint	15.00	14.00
b.		Double overprint	20.00	16.00
C70	AP3	1b dk gray	2.00	1.40
a.		Inverted overprint	16.00	13.00
b.		Double overprint	13.00	
C71	AP4	1.20b pck grn	30.00	20.00
a.		Inverted overprint	77.50	
C72	AP3	1.80b dk ultra	5.75	2.40
C73	AP5	1.95b lt ultra	7.75	4.25
a.		Inverted overprint	60.00	40.00
C74	AP6	2b chocolate	50.00	23.00
a.		Inverted overprint	100.00	90.00
b.		Double overprint	82.50	82.50

C75	AP6	2.50b gray bl	50.00	19.00
a.		Double overprint	70.00	
b.		Inverted overprint	100.00	82.50
C76	AP4	3b lt vio	30.00	12.00
C77	AP5	10b red vio	72.50	40.00
C78	AP3	20b gray	77.50	47.50
a.		Double overprint	150.00	150.00
		Nos. C66-C78 (13)	332.00	173.65

Counterfeit overprints exist on #C77-C78.

View of La Guaira AP8

National Pantheon AP9

Oil Wells AP10

1938-39 Engr. *Perf. 12*

C79	AP8	5c green	1.00	.50
C80	AP8	5c dk grn	.20	.20
C81	AP9	10c car rose	1.40	.80
C82	AP9	10c scarlet	.20	.20
C83	AP8	12½c dull vio	.60	.55
C84	AP10	15c slate vio	3.00	1.25
C85	AP10	15c dk bl	.85	.20
C86	AP8	25c dk bl	3.00	1.25
C87	AP8	25c bis brn	.25	.20
C88	AP10	30c vio ('39)	2.00	.20
C89	AP9	40c dk vio	3.50	1.25
C90	AP9	40c redsh brn	2.50	.20
C91	AP8	45c Prus grn ('39)	1.00	.20
C92	AP9	50c blue ('39)	1.25	.20
C93	AP10	70c car rose	.85	.25
C94	AP8	75c bis brn	6.00	2.00
C95	AP8	75c ol bis	1.40	.20
C96	AP10	90c red org ('39)	1.00	.20
C97	AP9	1b ol & bis	7.00	2.75
C98	AP9	1b dk vio	1.25	.20
C99	AP10	1.20b orange	20.00	5.75
C100	AP10	1.20b green	2.00	.55
C101	AP8	1.80b ultra	2.00	.55
C102	AP9	1.90b black	5.50	2.75
C103	AP10	1.95b lt bl	4.25	2.50
C104	AP8	2b ol gray	45.00	15.00
C105	AP8	2b car rose	1.75	.70
C106	AP9	2.50b red brn	45.00	20.00
C107	AP9	2.50b orange	10.00	2.75
C108	AP10	3b bl grn	20.00	4.75
C109	AP10	3b ol gray	5.50	2.00
C110	AP8	3.70b gray blk	7.75	5.50
C111	AP10	5b red brn ('39)	7.75	2.00
C112	AP9	10b vio brn	20.00	2.40
C113	AP10	20b red org	57.50	25.00
		Nos. C79-C113 (35)	292.25	105.00

See Nos. C227a, C235-C236, C254-C255. For surcharge see No. C227.

Nos. C51, C56, C58-C59, C61 Surcharged

1938, Apr. 15 *Perf. 11, 11½*

C114	AP3	5c on 1.80b	.85	.60
a.		Inverted surcharge	12.50	7.50
C115	AP6	10c on 2.50b	3.00	1.40
a.		Inverted surcharge	10.00	7.50
C116	AP6	15c on 2b	1.40	1.10
C117	AP4	25c on 40c	1.75	1.40
C118	AP6	40c on 3.70b	3.50	3.25
		Nos. C114-C118 (5)	10.50	7.75

Plane & Map Type of 1930
White Paper; No Imprint

1938-39 Engr. *Perf. 12½*

C119	AP1	5c dk grn ('39)	.25	.20
C120	AP1	10c org yel ('39)	.55	.20
C121	AP1	12½c rose vio ('39)	1.10	.85
C122	AP1	15c dp bl	.95	.20
C123	AP1	25c brown	1.10	.20
C124	AP1	40c olive ('39)	2.75	.40
C125	AP1	70c rose car ('39)	20.00	7.75
C126	AP1	1b dk bl ('39)	7.75	3.00
		Nos. C119-C126 (8)	34.45	12.80

Monument to Sucre — AP11

Monuments at Carabobo
AP12 AP13

1938, Dec. 23 *Perf. 13½*

C127	AP11	20c brn blk	.80	.30
C128	AP12	30c purple	1.20	.30
C129	AP13	45c dk bl	1.75	.25
C130	AP11	50c lt ultra	1.50	.25
C131	AP13	70c dk car	26.00	7.50
C132	AP12	90c red org	2.50	.75
C133	AP13	1.35b gray blk	3.00	1.00
C134	AP11	1.40b slate gray	12.00	2.75
C135	AP12	2.25b green	6.00	2.00
		Nos. C127-C135 (9)	54.75	15.10

For surcharge see No. C198.

Simón Bolívar and Carabobo Monument AP14

1940, Mar. 30 *Perf. 12*

C136	AP14	15c blue	.75	.20
C137	AP14	20c olive bis	.75	.20
C138	AP14	25c red brn	2.75	.40
C139	AP14	40c blk brn	2.25	.20
C140	AP14	1b red lilac	5.00	.55
C141	AP14	2b rose car	11.00	1.40
		Nos. C136-C141 (6)	22.50	2.95

"The Founding of Grand Colombia" AP15

1940, June 13

C142	AP15	15c copper brown	1.25	.45

Founding of the Pan American Union, 50th anniv.

Statue of Simón Bolívar, Caracas — AP16

1940-44

C143	AP16	5c dk grn ('42)	.20	.20
C144	AP16	10c scar ('42)	.20	.20
C145	AP16	12½c dull purple	.60	.25
C146	AP16	15c blue ('43)	.40	.20
C147	AP16	20c bis brn ('44)	.40	.20
C148	AP16	25c bis brn ('42)	.40	.20
C149	AP16	30c dp vio ('43)	.40	.20
C150	AP16	40c blk brn ('43)	.50	.20
C151	AP16	45c turq grn ('43)	.50	.20
C152	AP16	50c blue ('44)	.50	.20
C153	AP16	70c rose pink	1.50	.25
C154	AP16	75c ol bis ('43)	6.00	1.25
C155	AP16	90c red org ('43)	1.00	.25
C156	AP16	1b dp red lil ('42)	.50	.20
C157	AP16	1.20b dp yel grn ('43)	1.90	.60
C158	AP16	1.35b gray blk ('42)	8.00	3.75
C159	AP16	2b rose pink ('43)	1.50	.20
C160	AP16	3b ol blk ('43)	2.50	.60
C161	AP16	4b black	2.00	.60
C162	AP16	5b red brn ('44)	16.00	6.25
		Nos. C143-162 (20)	45.00	16.00

See #C232-C234, C239-C253. For surcharges see #C225, C873.

REGISTRATION STAMPS

Bolívar — R1

1899, May Unwmk. Engr. *Perf. 12*

F1	R1	25c yellow brown	3.00	2.50

No. F1 Overprinted like Nos. 150-155

1900

F2	R1	25c yellow brown	1.50	1.50
a.		Inverted overprint	22.50	22.50
b.		Double overprint	30.00	30.00

Counterfeit overprints exist, especially of the varieties.

OFFICIAL STAMPS

Coat of Arms
O1 O3

Lithographed, Center Engraved

1898, May 1 Unwmk. *Perf. 12*

O1	O1	5c bl grn & blk	.80	.55
O2	O1	10c rose & blk	.95	.85
O3	O1	25c bl & blk	1.50	1.40
O4	O1	50c yel & blk	2.50	2.25
O5	O1	1b vio & blk	2.75	2.50
		Nos. O1-O5 (5)	8.50	7.55

Nos. O4 and O5 Handstamp Surcharged in Magenta or Violet

1899, Nov.

O6	O1	5c on 50c yel & blk	4.75	4.50
O7	O1	5c on 1b vio & blk	20.00	18.00
O8	O1	25c on 50c yel & blk	20.00	18.00
O9	O1	25c on 1b vio & blk	12.00	11.00
		Nos. O6-O9 (4)	56.75	51.50

Inverted Surcharge

O6a	O1	5c on 50c	15.00	15.00
O7a	O1	5c on 1b	40.00	40.00
O8a	O1	25c on 50c	32.50	32.50
O9a	O1	25c on 1b	32.50	32.50
		Nos. O6a-O9a (4)	120.00	120.00

Nos. O6-O9 exist with double surcharge. Value each $18.50-$37.50.

Many of the magenta overprints have become violet. There are intermediate shades.

Counterfeit overprints exist.

1900 Litho., Center Engr.

O14	O3	5c bl grn & blk	.40	.40
O15	O3	10c rose & blk	.55	.55
O16	O3	25c bl & blk	.55	.55
O17	O3	50c yel & blk	.55	.55
O18	O3	1b dl vio & blk	.65	.65
		Nos. O14-O18 (5)	2.70	2.70

O4 No Stars Above Shield — O5

Imprint: "American Bank Note Co., N.Y."

1904, July Engr.

O19	O4	5c emerald & blk	.25	.25
O20	O4	10c rose & blk	.65	.65
O21	O4	25c blue & blk	.65	.65
O22	O4	50c red brn & blk	4.25	4.25
a.		50c claret & black	4.25	4.25
O23	O4	1b red brn & blk	2.00	2.00
a.		1b claret & black	2.00	2.00
		Nos. O19-O23 (5)	7.80	7.80

1912 Lithographed in Caracas

O24	O5	5c grn & blk	.55	.30
O25	O5	10c car & blk	.55	.30
O26	O5	25c dk bl & blk	.55	.30
O27	O5	50c pur & blk	.55	.40
a.		Center double	19.00	
O28	O5	1b yel & blk	1.30	.80
		Nos. O24-O28 (5)	3.50	2.10

Perforated Initials

After 1925, Venezuela's official stamps consisted of regular postage stamps, some commemoratives and air post stamps of 1930-42 punched with "GN" (Gobierno Nacional) in large perforated initials.

LOCAL STAMPS FOR THE PORT OF CARUPANO

In 1902 Great Britain, Germany and Italy, seeking compensation for revolutionary damages, established a blockade of La Guaira and seized the custom house. Carúpano, a port near Trinidad, was isolated and issued the following provisionals. A treaty effected May 7, 1903, referred the dispute to the Hague Tribunal.

A1

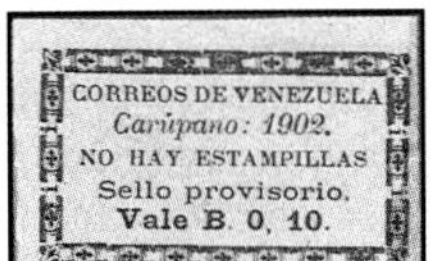

A2

1902 Typeset *Imperf.*

1	A1	5c purple, *orange*	27.00
2	A2	10c black, *orange*	40.00
a.		Tête bêche pair	82.50
3	A1	25c purple, *green*	32.50
4	A1	50c green, *yellow*	80.00
5	A1	lb blue, *rose*	100.00
		Nos. 1-5 (5)	279.50

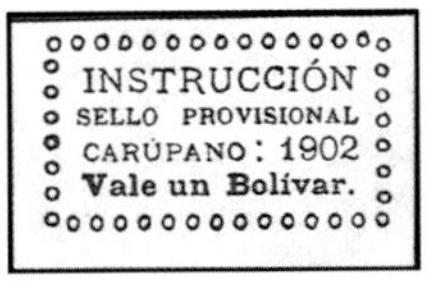

A3

1902

6	A3	1b black, *yellow*	200.00
a.		Tête bêche pair	

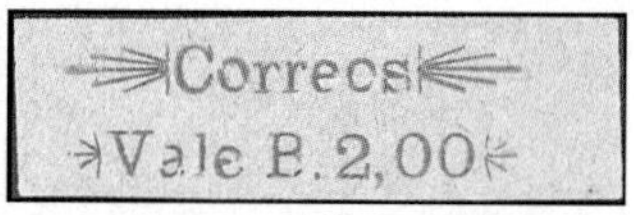

A4

1903		Handstamped	
7	A4 5c carmine, *yellow*	40.00	40.00
8	A4 10c green, *yellow*	92.50	92.50
9	A4 25c green, *orange*	45.00	45.00
10	A4 50c blue, *rose*	45.00	45.00
11	A4 1b violet, *gray*	45.00	45.00
12	A4 2b carmine, *green*	45.00	45.00
13	A4 5b violet, *blue*	45.00	45.00
	Nos. 7-13 (7)	357.50	357.50

Dangerous counterfeits exist of Nos. 1-13.

LOCAL STAMPS FOR THE STATE OF GUAYANA

Revolutionary Steamship "Banrigh" — A1

Control Mark

1903	Typo.		Perf. 12
1	A1 5c black, *gray*	19.00	19.00
2	A1 10c black, *orange*	47.50	47.50
3	A1 25c black, *pink*	19.00	19.00
4	A1 50c black, *blue*	30.00	30.00
5	A1 1b black, *straw*	25.00	25.00
	Nos. 1-5 (5)	140.50	140.50

Nos. 1-5 can be found with or without the illustrated control mark which covers four stamps.

Counterfeits include the 10c and 50c in red and are from different settings from the originals. They are on papers differing in colors from the originals. All 5c on granite paper are bogus.

Coat of Arms A2

1903		
11	A2 5c black, *pink*	40.00
12	A2 10c black, *orange*	50.00
13	A2 25c black, *gray blue*	40.00
a.	25c black, *blue*	40.00
14	A2 50c black, *straw*	40.00
15	A2 1b black, *gray*	30.00
	Nos. 11-15 (5)	200.00

Postally used examples are very scarce, as are specimens having 9 ornaments in horizontal borders. Nos. 11-15 pen canceled sell for same values as unused.

See note on controls after No. 5.

Counterfeits exist of Nos. 11-15. Stamps with 10 ornaments in horizontal borders are counterfeits.

Nos. 1-5, 11-15 were issued by a group of revolutionists and had a limited local use. The dates on the stamps commemorate the declaration of Venezuelan independence and a compact with Spain against Joseph Bonaparte.

VICTORIA

vik-'tōr-ē-ə

LOCATION — In the extreme southeastern part of Australia
GOVT. — British Colony
AREA — 87,884 sq. mi.
POP. — 1,201,341 (1901)
CAPITAL — Melbourne

Victoria was one of the six former British colonies which united on Jan. 1, 1901, to form the Commonwealth of Australia.

12 Pence = 1 Shilling
20 Shillings = 1 Pound

Unused values for Nos. 1-16 are for stamps without gum as these stamps are seldom found with original gum. Otherwise, unused values are for stamps with original gum as defined in the catalogue introduction.

Very fine examples of all rouletted, perforated and serrate perforated stamps from Nos. 9-109 and F2 will have roulettes, perforations or serrate perforations touching the design. Examples clear on four sides range from scarce to rare and will command higher prices.

Watermarks

Wmk. 6 — Large Star

Wmk. 80

Wmk. 50

Wmk. 80a

Wmk. 81

Wmk. 139

Wmk. 49

Wmk. 75

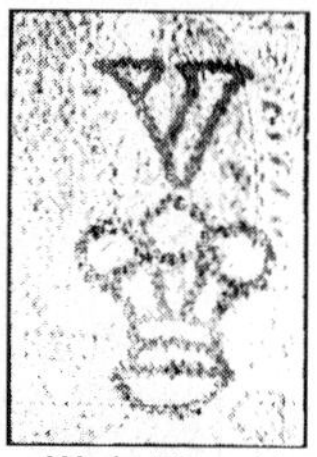

Wmk. 70 — V and Crown

Wmk. 13 — Crown & Double-lined A

Queen Victoria A1

Victoria on Throne A2

A1 TYPES

1p:

Type I — "VICTORIA" very close to top of design, with very thin line of color between "VICTORIA" and frameline.

Type II — Thicker line of color between "VICTORIA" and frameline at top.

2p:

Type I — Border, two sets of nine wavy lines crisscrossing. Background, 22 groups of wavy triple lines below "VICTORIA."

Type II — Border, same. Background, 15 groups of wavy triple lines below "VICTORIA."

Type III — Border, two sets of five wavy lines crisscrossing. Background, same as type II.

3p:

Type I — Orb poorly defined, with white area at right and thicker at left. Central band of orb does not protrude at left.

Type II — Orb clearly defined, with white outlines at left and right. Central band of orb protrudes at left.

1850	Litho. Unwmk.		Imperf.
1	A1 1p dull red, II	1,600.	190.00
a.	1p dull org ver, II	2,900.	650.00
b.	1p brownish red, II ('51)	1,000.	160.00
c.	1p dull brown, I	*10,000.*	2,100.
d.	1p orange vermilion, I	*30,000.*	3,900.
e.	1p orange brown, I		1,900.
2	A1 1p rose, II	900.00	150.00
a.	1p pink, II	700.00	140.00
b.	1p reddish brown, II ('51)	950.00	140.00
3	A1 3p blue, I	*3,750.*	325.00
a.	3p light blue, II ('52)	650.00	82.50
b.	3p bright blue, I	3,750.	525.00
4	A1 3p indigo, II	900.00	82.50
a.	3p pale grnsh blue, II ('52)	1,100.	165.00
	Nos. 1-4 (4)	7,150.	747.50

Nos. 1-4 exist with and without frame line.

5	A1 2p lilac, I	*5,000.*	400.00
a.	2p brn lilac, I	*3,750.*	400.00
b.	2p orange brown, I		*1,900.*
6	A1 2p brn lilac, II	1,500.	1,900.
a.	2p gray lilac, II	1,500.	150.00
7	A1 2p brn lilac, III	*800.00*	140.00
a.	2p gray lilac, III	*900.00*	375.00
b.	Value omitted, III		*13,000.*
8	A1 2p yel brn, III	725.00	140.00

A used pair of No. 5b, the 2 pence, type I, orange brown shade, issued in January 1850, realized the equivalent of U.S. $10,400 at an Australian auction in 2004.

A used example of No. 7b, with "butterfly" cancellation, realized the equivalent of U.S. $12,910 at an Australian auction in 2004.

Rouletted 7

9	A1 1p vermilion		*2,500.*
10	A1 3p blue		210.00
a.	3p deep blue	*1,750.*	225.00

Perf. 12

12	A1 3p blue	*1,600.*	140.00
a.	3p deep blue	*1,600.*	140.00

1852	Engr.		Imperf.
14	A2 2p reddish brown	300.00	40.00
a.	2p chestnut		150.00
b.	2p purple brown	375.00	35.00

#14 was reprinted on paper with watermark 70, imperf. & perf. 12½, overprinted "REPRINT."

1854			Litho.
15	A2 2p gray brown	320.00	32.50
a.	2p purple black		32.50
16	A2 2p brown lilac	200.00	30.00
a.	2p red lilac	300.00	32.50
b.	As "a," "TVO" for "TWO"	*7,500.*	1,250.

Fifty varieties.

A3

A4

1854-58			Typo.
17	A3 6p yellow orange	225.00	27.50
a.	6p dull orange	225.00	25.00
b.	6p reddish brown	425.00	52.50

See Nos. 19-20, 22-24A, 26-28

Lithographed

18	A4 1sh blue	850.00	28.00
a.	1sh greenish blue	950.00	28.00
b.	1sh indigo blue	—	150.00

See Nos. 21, 25.

Typographed

19	A3 2sh green	1,800.	190.00

1857-58			*Rouletted 7, 9½*
20	A3 6p orange	—	60.00
a.	6p yellow orange	—	65.00
b.	6p reddish brown	—	75.00

Lithographed

21	A4 1sh blue	—	110.00
a.	1sh greenish blue	—	110.00

Typographed

22	A3 2sh green ('58)	*5,250.*	500.00

Small Serrate Perf. 19

23	A3 6p orange	—	100.00

Large Serpentine Perf. 10½

24	A3 6p orange	—	95.00

Serrate x Serpentine Perf.

24A	A3 6p orange	—	150.00

1859	Litho.		*Perf. 12*
25	A4 1sh blue	175.00	18.00
a.	1sh greenish blue	200.00	15.00
b.	1sh indigo blue	—	37.50

Typographed

26	A3 2sh green	350.00	45.00

1861	Wmk. "SIX PENCE" (80)		
27	A3 6p black	250.00	52.50

Wmk. Single-lined "2" (50)

1864			*Perf. 12, 13*
28	A3 2sh blue, *green*	225.00	8.50

A5

Wmk. Large Star (6)

1856, Oct.	Engr.		*Imperf.*
29	A5 1p green	190.00	29.00

1858			*Rouletted 5½-6½*
30	A5 6p blue	225.00	17.50
a.	6p light blue	300.00	30.00

Nos. 29 and 30 have been reprinted on paper watermarked V and Crown. They are imperforate and overprinted "REPRINT."

A6

A7

1857-61	Typo.		*Imperf.*
	Wove Paper		
31	A6 1p yellow green	130.00	19.00
a.	Printed on both sides		*1,500.*
b.	1p deep green	150.00	35.00
32	A6 4p vermilion	325.00	13.50
a.	Printed on both sides		*1,500.*
b.	4p brownish vermilion	290.00	10.50

33 A6 4p rose 240.00 11.00
a. 4p dull red 200.00 8.50

Rouletted 7 to 9½

34 A6 1p yellow green 375.00 110.00
35 A6 4p rose — 40.00
a. 4p vermilion 110.00
b. 4p dull red 42.50
35A A6 4p vermilion 400.00

Perf. 12

36 A6 1p yellow green — 325.00

Unwmk. ***Imperf.***

37 A6 1p blue green 300.00 14.50
a. 1p emerald green 16.00
38 A6 2p lilac 275.00 14.50
a. 2p gray lilac 275.00 14.50
39 A6 4p rose *400.00* 35.00
a. 4p rose pink 400.00 30.00
b. 4p reddish pink 35.00

Copies of No. 39 printed in dull carmine on thin paper are regarded as printer's waste and of little value. They are also found printed on both sides.

Rouletted 7 to 9½

40 A6 1p emerald green 375.00 25.00
a. 1p pale emerald 340.00 24.00
41 A6 2p lilac 850.00 500.00
42 A6 4p rose pink 275.00 8.25
a. Vert.. pair, imperf. btwn. *575.00*
b. 4p reddish pink 12.50
c. 4p bright rose 275.00 8.25

Perf. 12

43 A6 1p blue green 145.00 12.50
a. 1p yellow green 210.00 16.00
b. Horiz. pair, imperf. btwn. —
c. As "a," on thin, glazed "Bordeaux" paper 175.00
44 A6 2p lilac 300.00
a. 2p gray lilac 275.00
45 A6 4p rose 190.00 5.75
b. Vert. pair, imperf. btwn. —

Rouletted 5½-6½

45C A6 4p dull rose 950.00

Serrate Rouletted 19

45A A6 2p lilac 750.00 450.00

Laid Paper

Imperf

46 A6 4p rose 550.00 22.50

Rouletted 5 to 7

47 A6 2p violet 180.00 7.50
a. 2p brown lilac 150.00 11.00
b. 2p dark lilac 210.00 20.00
48 A6 4p rose 180.00 5.00
a. 4p pale dull red, vertically laid paper 180.00 5.00
b. 4p pale dull red, horizontally laid paper *1,000.*
c. 4p dull rose red 150.00 4.50

Serrate Rouletted 19

48D A6 4p rose red *550.00*

Perf. 12

49 A6 1p green 210.00 17.00
a. Laid lines close together 29.00
50 A6 4p rose 135.00 11.00
a. Laid lines close together 11.50

Wove Paper

1860 Wmk. Value in Words (80)

51 A6 1p pale yellowish green 90.00 7.50
a. Wmk. "FOUR PENCE" (error) *7,200.*
b. 1p yellow green 85.00 5.00
52 A6 2p gray lilac 140.00 7.00
a. 2p brown lilac ('61) — 35.00
b. 2p bluish slate ('61) 140.00 6.75
c. 2p slate gray ('62) 6.75
d. 2p bluish gray ('63) 160.00 18.00

Wmk. "THREE PENCE" (80)

53 A6 2p gray lilac 225.00 15.00

Single-lined "2" (50)

54 A6 2p lilac 175.00 13.50
a. 2p gray lilac 165.00 16.00
b. 2p brown lilac 160.00 15.00
c. As "a," wmkd. single-lined "6" *5,750.*
d. 2p gray violet ('63) 190.00 17.50
e. 2p slate ('63) 195.00 24.00

1860 Unwmk. Laid Paper

56 A7 3p deep blue 400.00 50.00

Wmk. Value in Words (80)

Perf. 11½ to 12

1860-64 Wove Paper

57 A7 3p blue ('63) 160.00 9.00
a. "TRREE" instead of "THREE" in watermark 525.00
b. 3p pale blue ('61) 160.00 10.00
c. 3p bright blue ('61) 160.00 10.00
d. 3p deep blue ('64) 175.00 9.00
58 A7 3p claret 160.00 32.50
a. Perf. 13 175.00 35.00
59 A7 4p rose 140.00 5.00
a. 4p rose pink 9.50
b. 4p rose red 125.00 4.50
c. 4p rose carmine 10.50

60 A7 6p orange *4,500.* 325.00
61 A7 6p black 190.00 7.25
a. 6p gray black 200.00 7.00

Wmk. "FIVE SHILLINGS" (80)

62 A7 4p rose *2,000.* 24.00

Wmk. Single-lined "4" (80a)

1863 ***Imperf.***

63 A7 4p rose — *125.00*

Rouletted

64 A7 4p rose *2,500.* 300.00

Perf. 11½ to 12

65 A7 4p rose 120.00 7.50

1863 Unwmk. ***Perf. 12***

66 A7 4p rose 400.00 20.00
a. 4p rose pink, thin glazed "Bordeaux" paper 15.00
b. 4p rose, thick coarse paper 400.00 15.00

A8

A9

1861-63 Wmk. 80 ***Perf. 11½ to 12***

67 A8 1p green 110.00 11.00
a. 1p olive green 11.50
68 A9 6p black 100.00 10.00
a. 6p gray black 100.00 11.00
b. 6p jet black 110.00 12.50

Wmk. Double-lined "1" (139)

69 A8 1p green 180.00 12.00
a. 1p dull green — 12.00
b. Horiz. pair, imperf between —

Wmk. Single-lined Figures (50)

70 A8 1p green 80.00 7.50
a. 1p apple green 80.00 7.00
b. 1p olive green 80.00 13.50
71 A9 6p gray black 140.00 6.50
a. 6p jet black — 8.50
b. 6p jet black, perf 13 140.00 8.50
c. 6p gray black, perf 13 140.00 7.00

The 1p and 6p of 1861-63 are known on paper without watermark but were probably impressions on the margins of watermarked sheets.

A10

A11

A12

A13

Wmk. Single-lined Figures (50, 80a, 81)

1863-67 ***Perf. 11½ to 13***

74 A10 1p green 85.00 5.50
a. Double impression 1,050.
75 A10 2p gray lilac 95.00 11.00
a. 2p violet 77.50 8.00
76 A10 4p rose 100.00 3.50
a. Double impression 1,050.
77 A11 6p blue 80.00 3.00
78 A10 8p orange 450.00 72.50
79 A12 10p brn, *rose* 140.00 6.75
80 A13 1sh blue, *blue* 140.00 4.25
Nos. 74-80 (7) 1,090. 106.50

See Nos. 81-82, 84-96, 99-101, 108-112, 115-119, 124-126, 144, 188. Compare type A11 with type A54.

A14

Wmk. Double-lined "1" (139)

81 A10 1p green 90.00 4.50
82 A10 2p gray lilac 225.00 7.50
83 A14 3p lilac 210.00 65.00
84 A11 6p blue 77.50 5.50
Nos. 81-84 (4) 602.50 82.50

See Nos. 97, 113, 114, 155, 186. Compare type A14 with type A51.

Wmk. Double-lined "2" (49)

85 A11 6p blue *3,250.*

Wmk. Single-lined "4" (80a)

86 A10 1p green 140.00 20.00
87 A10 2p gray lilac 175.00 7.00
88 A11 6p blue *2,100.*

Wmk. Double-lined "4" (75)

89 A10 1p green 1,800. 140.00
90 A10 2p gray lilac 180.00 5.75
91 A10 4p rose 200.00 6.75
92 A11 6p blue 210.00 22.50

Wmk. Single-lined "6" (50)

93 A10 1p green 225.00 29.00
94 A10 2p gray lilac 225.00 8.00

Wmk. Single-lined "8" (50)

95 A10 1p green 200.00 20.00
96 A10 2p gray lilac 225.00 7.25
97 A14 3p lilac 175.00 35.00
99 A12 10p slate 650.00 140.00

Wmk. "SIX PENCE" (80)

100 A10 1p green 725.00 37.50
100A A10 2p slate gray *14,500.*
101 A11 6p blue 525.00 29.00

All values of the 1864-67 series except the 3p and 8p are known on unwatermarked paper. They are probably varieties from watermarked sheets which had been so placed on the printing press that some of the stamps escaped the watermark.

One copy of the 2p gray lilac, type A10, is reported to exist with only "PENCE" of watermark 80 showing. Some believe this is part of the "SIX PENCE" watermark.

1870 Wmk. "THREE PENCE" (80)

108 A11 6p blue 290.00 11.50

Wmk. "FOUR PENCE" (80)

109 A11 6p blue 525.00 37.50

A15

1867-78 Wmk. (70) ***Perf. 11½ to 13***

110 A10 1p green 75.00 4.00
111 A10 2p lilac 72.50 3.50
a. 2p gray lilac 90.00 6.75
112 A10 2p lilac, *lilac* 92.50 10.00
113 A14 3p red lilac 275.00 47.50
a. 3p lilac 325.00 50.00
114 A14 3p orange 32.50 2.75
a. 3p yellow 55.00 5.00
115 A10 4p rose 95.00 7.25
116 A11 6p blue 40.00 3.00
117 A11 6p ultra 47.50 3.50
a. 6p lilac blue 92.50 11.50
118 A10 8p brn, *rose* 100.00 7.50
119 A13 1sh bl, *blue* 225.00 11.50
120 A15 5sh bl, *yel* 2,400. 400.00
121 A15 5sh bl & rose 260.00 21.00
a. Without blue line under crown 250.00 20.00
122 A15 5sh ultra & rose 240.00 20.00

See #126, 144, 188. For surcharge see #124.

For additional stamps of type A15, see No. 191. Compare type A15 with type A58.

A16

A19

1870 ***Perf. 13***

123 A16 2p lilac 77.50 1.40
a. Perf. 12 85.00 3.00

No. 110 Surcharged in Red

1873, July 19 ***Perf. 13, 12***

124 A10 ½p on 1p green 65.00 17.50

No. 79 Surcharged in Blue

1871 Wmk. Single-lined "10" (81)

125 A12 9p on 10p brn, *rose* 425.00 18.00
a. Double surcharge *1,500.*

1873-78 Typo.

126 A10 8p brown, *rose* ('78) 125.00 6.75
127 A19 9p brown, *rose* 125.00 18.00

For additional stamps of type A19, see Nos. 128-129, 174-175. Compare type A19 with type A55.

1875 Wmk. V and Crown (70)

128 A19 9p brown, *rose* 150.00 18.00

No. 128 Surcharged in Blue

8d 8d
EIGHTPENCE

1876

129 A19 8p on 9p brn, *rose* 225.00 21.00

A21

A22

A23

A24

A25

1873-81 ***Perf. 13, 12***

130 A21 ½p rose ('74) 16.00 1.50
131 A21 ½p rose, *rose* ('78) 45.00 29.00
132 A22 1p grn ('75) 35.00 2.25
133 A22 1p grn, *gray* ('78) 160.00 72.50
134 A22 1p grn, *yel* ('78) 110.00 20.00
135 A23 2p violet 50.00 1.00
136 A23 2p vio, *grnsh* ('78) 225.00 27.50
137 A23 2p vio, *buff* ('78) 200.00 27.50
137A A23 2p vio, *lil* ('78) — *900.00*
138 A24 1sh bl, *bl* ('76) 82.50 4.75
139 A25 2sh bl, *grn* ('81) 175.00 24.00

See Nos. 140, 156A-159, 184, 189-190. Compare design A21 with design A46, A24 with A56, A25 with A57.

1878

Double-lined Outer Oval

140 A23 2p violet 50.00 2.75
b. Vert. pair, lower stamp imperf horiz. *2,250.*

A26

A27

A28

1881-83 ***Perf. 12½***

141	A26 1p green ('83)		30.00	2.50
142	A27 2p brown		32.50	1.00
143	A27 2p lilac		25.00	1.50
144	A10 4p car rose		200.00	5.50
145	A28 4p car rose		75.00	6.50
	Nos. 141-145 (5)		362.50	17.00

See Nos. 156, 185, 187. Compare design A26 with design A47, A27 with A49, A28 with A52.

A29

A30

A31

A32

A33

A34

1884-86

146	A29 ½p rose	12.50	1.50
147	A30 1p green	19.00	1.75
148	A31 2p violet	18.00	.75
a.	2p lilac rose	20.00	.85
149	A30 3p bister	14.00	1.75
a.	3p ocher	13.00	1.75
150	A32 4p magenta	72.50	4.25
a.	4p violet (error)	*4,500.*	*975.00*
151	A30 6p bright blue ('85)	75.00	3.50
a.	6p ultramarine ('85)	55.00	3.00
b.	6p gray blue ('85)	45.00	3.00
152	A33 8p rose, *rose*	35.00	9.50
153	A34 1sh blue, *yel*	125.00	17.50
154	A33 2sh olive, *grn*	75.00	4.50
	Nos. 146-154 (9)	446.00	45.00

See Nos. 177-178, 192A. Compare designs A31-A32 with designs A37-A38.

Nos. 114, 145, 138-139 Overprinted "STAMP / DUTY" Vertically in Blue or Black

1885

155	A14 3p orange (Bl)	80.00	32.50
156	A28 4p car rose (Bl)	72.50	50.00
156A	A24 1sh bl, *bl* (Bl)		2,250.
157	A24 1sh bl, *bl* (Bk)	120.00	27.50
158	A25 2sh bl, *grn* (Bk)	120.00	25.00
	Nos. 155-156,157-158 (4)	392.50	135.00

Reprints of 4p and 1sh have brighter colors than originals. They lack the overprint "REPRINT."

A35

A36

A37

A38

A39

A40

1886-87 ***Perf. 12½***

159	A35 ½p lilac	27.50	6.75
160	A35 ½p rose	12.00	1.00
160A	A35 ½p scarlet	5.50	1.00
161	A36 1p green	11.50	1.00
162	A37 2p violet	14.00	.25
a.	2p red lilac	8.00	.50
b.	Imperf.		*900.00*
163	A38 4p red	15.00	1.75
164	A39 6p blue	22.50	.85
165	A39 6p ultra	18.50	.75
166	A40 1sh lilac brown	22.50	2.75
	Nos. 159-166 (9)	149.00	16.10

See No. 180.

A41

A42

1889

167	A41 1sh6p blue	185.00	100.00
168	A41 1sh6p orange	25.00	10.00

Southern Cross
A43

Queen Victoria
A44

1890-95 ***Perf. 12½***

169	A42 1p org brn	7.00	.55
a.	1p chocolate brown	9.00	.75
170	A42 1p yel brn	9.00	.40
171	A42 1p brn org, *pink* ('91)	7.50	3.25
172	A43 2½p brn red, *yel*	13.00	1.25
173	A44 5p choc ('91)	11.00	2.75
174	A19 9p green ('92)	32.50	11.50
175	A19 9p rose red	22.50	4.25
a.	9p rose ('95)	27.50	8.00
176	A40 1sh deep claret	27.50	1.75
a.	1sh red brown	22.50	1.00
b.	1sh maroon	60.00	3.75
177	A33 2sh yel grn	27.50	12.00
178	A33 2sh emerald	24.00	13.00
	Nos. 169-178 (10)	181.50	50.70

In 1891 many stamps of the early issues were reprinted. They are on paper watermarked V and Crown, perforated 12, 12½, and overprinted "REPRINT."

See Nos. 181, 183, 192. Compare type A43 with type A50, A44 with A53.

A45

1897

179	A45 1½p yellow green	4.25	*4.75*

See No. 182. Compare type A45 with type A48.

1899

180	A35 ½p emerald	16.00	4.00
181	A42 1p brt rose	8.00	.40
182	A45 1½p red, *yel*	4.00	2.25
183	A43 2½p dark blue	10.00	2.00
	Nos. 180-183 (4)	38.00	8.65

1901

184	A21 ½p blue green	2.75	2.00
a.	"VICTCRIA"	75.00	32.50
185	A27 2p violet	10.00	2.00
186	A14 3p brown org	17.50	3.50
187	A28 4p bister	30.00	18.00
188	A11 6p emerald	12.00	9.00
189	A24 1sh orange yel	60.00	45.00
190	A25 2sh blue, *rose*	50.00	32.50
191	A15 5sh rose red & bl	62.50	50.00
	Nos. 184-191 (8)	244.75	162.00

1901

192	A42 1p olive green	8.00	5.25
192A	A30 3p sage green	29.00	13.00

Nos. 192-192A were available for postal use until June 30, 1901, and thereafter restricted to revenue use.

A46

A47

A48

A49

A50

A51

A52

A53

A54

A55

A56

A57

A58

1901 ***Perf. 11, 12½ and Compound***

193	A46 ½p blue green	4.00	1.00
194	A47 1p rose red	3.00	.45
a.	1p rose	3.25	.55
195	A48 1½p red, *yellow*	2.75	.90
a.	Perf. 11	75.00	75.00
196	A49 2p violet	9.50	.75
197	A50 2½p blue	10.00	.75
198	A51 3p brown org	10.00	1.60
199	A52 4p bister	7.50	.90
200	A53 5p chocolate	12.00	.80
201	A54 6p emerald	15.00	1.75
202	A55 9p rose	19.50	2.00
203	A56 1sh org yel	20.00	3.50
204	A57 2sh blue, *rose*	29.00	3.50
205	A58 5sh rose red & bl	75.00	25.00
a.	5sh carmine & blue	75.00	19.00
	Nos. 193-205 (13)	217.25	42.90

See Nos. 209-229, 232.

King Edward VII
A59 A60

1901-05

206	A59 £1 deep rose	325.00	160.00
a.	Perf. 11 ('05)	450.00	200.00
208	A60 £2 dk blue ('02)	750.00	400.00
a.	Perf. 11 ('05)	2,000.	1,300.

See Nos. 230-231.

1903 **Redrawn**

209	A56 1sh yellow	24.00	4.00
a.	1sh orange	22.50	3.25

No. 209 has the network lighter than No. 203. In the latter the "P" and "E" of "POSTAGE" are in a position more nearly horizontal than on No. 209.

Perf. 11, 12x12½, 12½, 12½x11

1905-10 **Wmk. 13**

218	A46 ½p blue green	3.25	.55
219	A47 1p rose red	1.75	.25
a.	1p carmine rose	11.00	2.00
220	A49 2p violet	6.50	.55
a.	2p purple	7.00	.65
221	A50 2½p blue	4.00	.75
222	A51 3p brown org	11.00	2.00
a.	3p dull yellow	12.00	2.00
223	A52 4p bister	9.00	1.25
224	A53 5p chocolate	9.00	3.25
225	A54 6p emerald	17.50	1.50
226	A55 9p orange brown	18.00	3.50
a.	9p brown rose	19.00	4.50
227	A55 9p car rose	12.50	2.00
228	A56 1sh yellow ('08)	17.00	3.00
229	A58 5sh orange red & ultra	95.00	13.00
a.	5sh rose red & ultra	110.00	15.00
230	A59 £1 pale red ('07)	325.00	175.00
a.	£1 rose ('10)	325.00	175.00
231	A60 £2 dull blue	800.00	500.00
	Nos. 218-229 (12)	204.50	31.60

No. 220 Surcharged in Red

1912, July 1

232	A49 1p on 2p violet	1.25	.90

POSTAL-FISCAL STAMPS

On Jan. 1, 1884, all postage and fiscal stamps were made available for either purpose. Fiscal stamps became invalid after June 30, 1901.

Used values are for examples with postal cancellations used from Jan. 1, 1884 through June 30, 1901.

Beware of copies with a pen cancellation removed, often regummed or with a fake postmark added.

Stamps inscribed "Stamp Duty" that were issued primarily in postal rates in the normal postage stamp size are listed in the postage section (Nos. 146-178, 180-183, 192-192A). The stamps meeting primarily fiscal rates and in the larger fiscal stamp size, are listed here in the Postal-Fiscal section.

Stamps Inscribed "Stamp Statute"

Victoria — PF1

PF1a

Coat of Arms — PF2

PF3

Frames differ on design PF1.

Wmk. V and Crown (70)

1870-83 Typo. *Perf. 13*

AR1 PF1a 1p green 57.50 37.50
Revenue cancel 5.00
a. Perf. 12½ 100.00 80.00

AR2 PF1 3p lilac 750.00 425.00
Revenue cancel 100.00

AR3 PF1a 4p red 650.00 325.00
Revenue cancel 90.00

AR4 PF1a 6p blue 90.00 30.00
Revenue cancel 10.00
a. Perf. 12 110.00 17.50
Revenue cancel 7.50

AR5 PF1a 1sh blue, *blue* 95.00 30.00
Revenue cancel 10.00
a. Perf. 12 100.00 35.00
Revenue cancel 12.00
b. Perf. 12½ 95.00 30.00
Revenue cancel 10.00
c. Wmk. 50, perf. 13 110.00 20.00
Revenue cancel 8.00
d. Wmk. 50, perf. 12 110.00 25.00
Revenue cancel 9.00

AR6 PF1a 2sh blue, *grn* 150.00 92.50
Revenue cancel 20.00
a. Perf. 12 150.00 *110.00*
Revenue cancel 25.00
b. Wmk. 50, perf. 13 210.00 30.00
Revenue cancel 12.50
c. Wmk. 50, perf. 12 225.00 37.50
Revenue cancel 15.00

AR7 PF2 2sh 6p orange, *yel* 425.00 175.00
Revenue cancel 50.00
a. Perf. 12 425.00 175.00
Revenue cancel 50.00
b. Perf. 12½ — 190.00
Revenue cancel 60.00

AR8 PF1a 5sh blue, *yel* 400.00 100.00
Revenue cancel 50.00
a. Perf. 12 400.00
b. Perf. 12½ 400.00 100.00
Revenue cancel 50.00

AR9 PF1a 10sh brn, *rose* 1,200. 300.00
Revenue cancel 75.00
a. Perf. 12
b. Wmk. 50, perf. 13 1,200. 175.00
Revenue cancel 60.00
c. Wmk. 50, perf. 12

AR10 PF1a £1 lilac, *yel* 850.00 240.00
Revenue cancel 80.00
a. Perf. 12 850.00 240.00
Revenue cancel 80.00
b. Perf. 12½ 850.00 240.00
Revenue cancel 80.00

AR11 PF3 £5 black, *grn* 4,750. 1,100.
Revenue cancel 125.00
a. Perf. 12
b. Perf. 12½ 4,750. 1,100.
Revenue cancel 130.00

Nos. AR1-AR12 distributed for postal use from Jan. 1, 1884 through Apr. 23, 1884.

No. AR1 Surcharged "½d/HALF"

1879-96

AR12 PF1 ½p on 1p grn 80.00 70.00
Revenue cancel 30.00

Stamps Inscribed "Stamp Duty"

PF4

PF5

PF6

PF7

PF8

PF9

PF10

PF11

PF12

PF13

PF14

PF15

PF16

PF17

PF18

PF23

PF19

PF24

PF20

PF25

PF21

PF26

PF22

PF27

PF28

Wmk. V and Crown (70)

1879-96 Litho. *Perf. 13*

AR13 PF4 1p green 95.00 30.00
Revenue cancel 10.00
a. Perf. 12 95.00 30.00
Revenue cancel 10.00
b. Perf. 12½

AR14 PF8 1sh 6p pink 240.00 32.50
Revenue cancel 15.00
a. Perf. 12 — 42.50
Revenue cancel 18.00
b. Perf. 12½

AR15 PF11 3sh violet, *blue* 550.00 55.00
Revenue cancel 15.00
a. Perf. 12 650.00 65.00
Revenue cancel 15.00
b. Perf. 12½

AR16 PF12 4sh orange 125.00 25.00
Revenue cancel 9.00
a. Perf. 12 125.00 25.00
Revenue cancel 9.00
b. Perf. 12½

AR17 PF14 6sh green 400.00 45.00
Revenue cancel 10.00
a. Perf. 12½

AR18 PF15 10sh brown, *pink* 600.00 125.00
Revenue cancel 50.00
a. Perf. 12
b. Perf. 12½

AR19 PF16 15sh lilac 1,600. 260.00
Revenue cancel 100.00

AR20 PF17 £1 orange 600.00 110.00
Revenue cancel 20.00
a. Perf. 12½ 600.00 110.00

AR21 PF18 £1 5sh pink 1,500. 300.00
Revenue cancel 110.00

AR22 PF19 £1 10sh olive 1,600. 190.00
Revenue cancel 60.00

AR23 PF20 35sh lilac *7,000.*
Revenue cancel 275.00

AR24 PF21 £2 blue — 160.00
Revenue cancel 30.00

AR25 PF22 45sh violet 3,250. 250.00
Revenue cancel 75.00

AR26 PF23 £5 rose 4,000. 600.00
Revenue cancel 100.00

AR27 PF24 £6 blue, *pink* — 900.00
Revenue cancel 150.00

AR28 PF25 £7 violet, *blue* — 900.00
Revenue cancel 150.00

AR29 PF26 £8 scarlet, *yel* — 1,100.
Revenue cancel 160.00

AR30 PF27 £9 green, *grn* — 1,100.
Revenue cancel 160.00

Typo.

AR31 PF4 1p green 70.00 30.00
Revenue cancel 6.00
a. Perf. 12 70.00 30.00
Revenue cancel 6.00
b. Perf. 12½

AR32 PF5 1p brown 24.00 5.00
Revenue cancel 1.00
a. Perf. 12 24.00 6.00
Revenue cancel 1.00
b. Perf. 12½

AR33 PF6 6p blue 100.00 15.00
Revenue cancel 4.00
a. Perf. 12 110.00 25.00
Revenue cancel 4.00
b. Perf. 12½

AR34 PF7 1sh blue, *blue* 110.00 7.25
Revenue cancel 4.00
a. Perf. 12 110.00 9.00
Revenue cancel 4.00
b. Perf. 12½ 110.00 8.50
Revenue cancel 4.00

AR35 PF7 1sh blue, *yel*, perf 12½ 125.00 32.50
Revenue cancel 12.00

AR36 PF8 1sh 6p pink 190.00 35.00
Revenue cancel 12.00

AR37 PF9 2sh blue, *grn* 210.00 30.00
Revenue cancel 9.00
a. Perf. 12 — 35.00
Revenue cancel 9.00
b. Perf. 12½ — 37.50
Revenue cancel 9.00

AR38 PF10 2sh 6p orange, perf 12½ 125.00 27.50
a. 2sh6p yellow ('85) 80.00 11.00
6. 2sh6p lemon yellow ('92) 80.00 11.50
Revenue cancel 4.00

AR39 PF11 3sh violet, *bl*, perf 12½ 450.00 42.50
Revenue cancel 10.00

AR40 PF11 3sh bister 90.00 21.00
Revenue cancel 15.00

AR41 PF12 4sh org, perf 12½ 110.00 19.00
Revenue cancel 5.00

AR42 PF13 5sh claret, *yel* 72.50 8.00
Revenue cancel 4.00
a. Perf. 12 90.00 16.00
Revenue cancel 4.00
b. Perf. 12½ 65.00 16.00
Revenue cancel 4.00

AR43 PF13 5sh car rose 95.00 25.00
Revenue cancel 5.00

AR44 PF14 6sh green	150.00	55.00
Revenue cancel		11.50
AR45 PF15 10sh brn, *pink*	—	120.00
Revenue cancel		40.00
a. Perf. 12		
b. Perf. 12½		
AR46 PF15 10sh green	190.00	40.00
Revenue cancel		14.00
AR47 PF16 15sh brown	850.00	130.00
Revenue cancel		35.00
AR48 PF17 £1 org, *yel,* perf 12½	525.00	72.50
Revenue cancel		20.00
a. Perf. 12	800.00	95.00
Revenue cancel		25.00
AR49 PF18 £1 5sh pink	1,600.	125.00
Revenue cancel		60.00
AR50 PF19 £1 10sh olive	1,100.	120.00
Revenue cancel		40.00
AR51 PF21 £2 blue	1,100.	110.00
Revenue cancel		22.50
a. Perf. 12	—	160.00
Revenue cancel		22.50
AR52 PF22 45sh gray lilac	3,500.	150.00
Revenue cancel		50.00
AR53 PF23 £5 rose, perf. 12	—	550.00
Revenue cancel		85.00
a. perf. 12½	—	725.00
Revenue cancel		120.00
AR54 PF28 £10 lilac	3,500.	160.00
Revenue cancel		50.00
a. Perf. 12	3,500.	210.00
Revenue cancel		50.00

Nos. AR49-AR52, AR54, used, are valued cto.

PF29

PF30

PF31

Wmk. V and Crown (70)

1879-1900 Engr. *Perf. 12½*

AR55 PF29 £25 green	—	725.00
Revenue cancel		95.00
a. Perf. 13		
b. Perf. 12		
AR56 PF30 £50 violet	—	725.00
Revenue cancel		110.00
a. Perf. 13		
AR57 PF31 £100 red	—	725.00
Revenue cancel		200.00
a. Perf. 13		
b. Perf. 12		
Revenue cancel		200.00

Typo.

AR58 PF29 £25 green	—	210.00
a. Lithographed		
Revenue cancel		75.00
AR59 PF30 £50 violet	—	325.00
a. Lithographed		
Revenue cancel		100.00
AR60 PF31 £100 red	—	425.00
a. Lithographed		
Revenue cancel		150.00

Nos. AR55-AR60, used, are valued cto.

PF32

1887-90 Typo.

AR61 PF32 £5 cl & ultra	*2,600.*	125.00
Revenue cancel		75.00
AR62 PF32 £6 blue & yel	*3,000.*	160.00
Revenue cancel		85.00
AR63 PF32 £7 blk & red	*3,250.*	175.00
Revenue cancel		100.00
AR64 PF32 £8 org & lil	*3,500.*	210.00
Revenue cancel		110.00
AR65 PF32 £9 red & green	*4,000.*	225.00
Revenue cancel		125.00

Nos. AR61-AR65, used, are valued cto.

SEMI-POSTAL STAMPS

SP1

Queen Victoria and Figure of Charity SP2

Wmk. V and Crown (70)

1897, Oct. Typo. *Perf. 12½*

B1 SP1 1p deep blue	22.50	22.50
B2 SP2 2½p red brown	110.00	110.00

These stamps were sold at 1sh and 2sh6p respectively. The premium was given to a charitable institution.

Victoria Cross — SP3

Scout Reporting SP4

1900

B3 SP3 1p brown olive	95.00	60.00
B4 SP4 2p emerald	200.00	190.00

These stamps were sold at 1sh and 2sh respectively. The premium was given to a patriotic fund in connection with the South African War.

REGISTRATION STAMPS

R1

Unwmk.

1854, Dec. 1 Typo. *Imperf.*

F1 R1 1sh rose & blue	1,700.	190.00

1857 *Rouletted 7*

F2 R1 1sh rose & blue	6,500.	325.00

LATE FEE STAMP

LF1

Unwmk.

1855, Jan. 1 Typo. *Imperf.*

I1 LF1 6p lilac & green	1,300.	225.00

POSTAGE DUE STAMPS

D1

Wmk. V and Crown (70)

1890 Typo. *Perf. 12½*

J1 D1 ½p claret & blue	5.75	4.50
J2 D1 1p claret & blue	7.75	1.90
J3 D1 2p claret & blue	13.00	2.25
J4 D1 4p claret & blue	18.00	3.00
J5 D1 5p claret & blue	17.00	2.50
J6 D1 6p claret & blue	18.00	4.25
J7 D1 10p claret & blue	100.00	62.50
J8 D1 1sh claret & blue	62.50	9.00
J9 D1 2sh claret & blue	140.00	65.00
J10 D1 5sh claret & blue	210.00	110.00
Nos. J1-J10 (10)	592.00	264.90

1891-94

J11 D1 ½p lake & blue	3.50	*5.00*
J12 D1 1p brown red & blue ('93)	11.00	2.00
J13 D1 2p brown red & blue ('93)	17.00	1.40
J14 D1 4p lake & blue ('94)	21.00	8.00
Nos. J11-J14 (4)	52.50	16.40

1894-96

J15 D1 ½p bl grn & rose	6.25	2.10
J16 D1 1p bl grn & rose	5.75	2.00
J17 D1 2p bl grn & rose	12.00	2.25
J18 D1 4p bl grn & rose	12.50	2.25
J19 D1 5p bl grn & rose	15.00	15.00
J20 D1 6p bl grn & rose	13.00	8.00
J21 D1 10p bl grn & rose	29.00	13.50
J22 D1 1sh bl grn & rose	21.00	4.25
J23 D1 2sh yel green & rose	80.00	27.50
J24 D1 5sh yel green & rose	140.00	52.50
Nos. J15-J24 (10)	334.50	129.35

1894-96

J15a D1 ½p yel grn & pale scar	3.75	1.50
J16a D1 1p yel grn & pale scar	4.75	1.00
J17a D1 2p yel grn & pale scar	7.50	1.00
J18a D1 4p yel grn & pale scar	9.50	2.00
J19a D1 5p yel grn & pale scar	10.00	6.00
J20a D1 6p yel grn & pale scar	8.75	4.00
Nos. J15a-J20a (6)	44.25	15.50

1906 Wmk. 13

J25 D1 ½p yel grn & rose	7.25	*8.50*
a. ½p pale green & pink	17.00	15.00
J26 D1 1p yel grn & rose	8.50	3.25
a. 1p pale green & pink	65.00	8.00
J27 D1 2p yel grn & rose	13.50	3.75
J28 D1 4p yel grn & rose	24.00	15.00
Nos. J25-J28 (4)	53.25	30.50

A 5p with wmk. 13 exists but was not issued.

VIRGIN ISLANDS

'vər-jən 'ī-lənds

LOCATION — West Indies, southeast of Puerto Rico
GOVT. — British colony
AREA — 59 sq. mi.
POP. — 12,034 (1980)
CAPITAL — Road Town

The British Virgin Islands constituted one of the presidencies of the Leeward Islands colony. For many years stamps of Leeward Islands were used concurrently.

The Virgin Islands group is divided between Great Britain and the United States. See Danish West Indies.

12 Pence = 1 Shilling
20 Shillings = 1 Pound
100 Cents = 1 Dollar (1951)

Catalogue values for unused stamps in this country are for Never Hinged items, beginning with Scott 88 in the regular postage section.

PRE-STAMP POSTAL MARKINGS

Crowned Circle handstamp types I and VI are pictured in the Crowned Circle Handstamps and Great Britain Used Abroad section.

1842-58

A1 I "Tortola" crowned circle handstamp in red, on cover		6,250.
A2 VI "Tortola" crowned circle handstamp in red, on cover		11,500.

No. A2, in black, was used for the payment of official postage during 1900-18. Value, on cover $1,000.

STAMPS OF GREAT BRITAIN USED IN VIRGIN ISLANDS

Numeral cancellation type A is pictured in the Crowned Circle Handstamps and Great Britain Used Abroad section.

1858-60

A13 (Tortola)

A3 A 1p rose red (#20)		4,250.
A4 A 4p rose (#26)		4,600.
A5 A 6p lilac (#27)		1,600.
A6 A 1sh green (#28)		—

Issued under British Administration

Values for unused stamps are for examples with original gum as defined in the catalogue introduction. However, Nos. 1-2c are valued without gum as the vast majority of examples are found thus.

Virgin and Lamps — A1

St. Ursula — A2

A3

A4

1866 Litho. Unwmk. *Perf. 12*

Toned or White Paper

1 A1 1p green	50.00	*65.00*
a. Toned paper	52.50	*65.00*
c. Perf. 15x12, toned paper	6,000.	*7,750.*

2 A3 6p rose 65.00 100.00
a. Large "V" in "VIRGIN" 300.00 400.00
b. White paper 100.00 120.00
c. As "a," white paper 410.00 525.00

Copies offered as No. 1c frequently have forged perfs.

1867-70 *Perf. 15*

3 A1 1p blue grn ('70) 65.00 75.00
4 A1 1p yel grn ('68) 80.00 75.00
a. Toned paper 92.50 85.00
5 A2 4p lake, *buff* 45.00 65.00
a. 4p lake, *rose* 55.00 75.00
6 A3 6p rose 650.00 650.00
a. Toned paper ('68) 325.00 375.00
7 A4 1sh rose & blk 300.00 400.00
a. Toned paper 300.00 400.00
b. Double lined frame 300.00 400.00
c. As "b," bluish paper 300.00 400.00

Colored Margins

8 A4 1sh rose & blk 70.00 82.50
a. White paper 70.00 82.50
b. Bluish paper 825.00 1,000.
c. Central figure omitted 92,500.
Nos. 3-8 (6) 1,210. 1,347.

Copies of No. 8c have perfs. trimmed on one or two sides.

1878 **Wmk. 1** *Perf. 14*

9 A1 1p green 90.00 110.00

See #16-17, 19-20. For surcharge see #18.

Queen Victoria — A5

1880 **Typo.**

10 A5 1p green 80.00 95.00
11 A5 2½p red brown 100.00 125.00

1883-84 **Wmk. 2**

12 A5 ½p yellow 92.50 92.50
13 A5 ½p green 6.00 11.00
a. Imperf., pair 1,750.
14 A5 1p rose 27.50 32.50
15 A5 2½p ultra ('84) 3.00 17.50
Nos. 12-15 (4) 129.00 153.50

No. 13a probably is a plate proof.

1887 **Litho.**

16 A2 4p brick red 40.00 70.00
a. 4p brown red 50.00 80.00
17 A3 6p violet 17.50 50.00

No. 8 Handstamp Surcharged in Violet

1888 **Unwmk.** *Perf. 15*

18 A4 4p on 1sh dp rose & blk, toned paper 140.00 175.00
a. Double surcharge 7,500.
b. Inverted surcharge 47,500.
c. White paper 200.00 250.00

1889 **Wmk. 2** *Perf. 14*

19 A1 1p carmine 2.75 8.25
20 A4 1sh brown 50.00 80.00
a. 1sh black brown 90.00 110.00

St. Ursula with Sheaf of Lilies A7

Edward VII A8

1899 **Engr.**

21 A7 ½p yellow grn 2.75 .60
a. "PFNNY" 92.50 140.00
b. "F" without cross bar 92.50 140.00
c. Horiz. pair, imperf. between 9,250.
22 A7 1p red 3.25 2.75
23 A7 2½p ultra 13.00 3.00
24 A7 4p chocolate 4.50 20.00
a. "PENCF" 825. 1,200.
25 A7 6p dark violet 5.00 3.50
26 A7 7p slate green 9.25 6.50
27 A7 1sh ocher 25.00 37.50
28 A7 5sh dark blue 80.00 95.00
Nos. 21-28 (8) 142.75 168.85

1904 **Typo.** **Wmk. 3**

29 A8 ½p violet & bl grn .85 .55
30 A8 1p violet & scar 2.75 .45
31 A8 2p violet & bis 6.50 4.00
32 A8 2½p violet & ultra 2.25 2.25
33 A8 3p violet & blk 4.00 2.75
34 A8 6p violet & brn 3.00 2.75
35 A8 1sh green & scar 4.50 5.50
36 A8 2sh6p green & blk 27.50 60.00
37 A8 5sh green & ultra 52.50 72.50
Nos. 29-37 (9) 103.85 150.75

Numerals of 2p, 3p, 1sh and 2sh6p of type A8 are in color on plain tablet.

George V A9

Colony Seal A10

Die I

For description of dies I and II see back of this volume.

1913

Ordinary Paper

38 A9 ½p green 1.75 4.50
39 A9 1p scarlet 2.50 16.00
a. 1p carmine 52.50 30.00
40 A9 2p gray 4.50 27.50
41 A9 2½p ultra 6.00 10.00

Chalky Paper

42 A9 3p vio, *yel* 3.00 7.25
43 A9 6p dl vio & red vio 5.50 12.50
44 A9 1sh blk, *green* 3.50 10.00
45 A9 2sh6p blk & red, *bl* 52.50 55.00
46 A9 5sh grn & red, *yel* 37.50 120.00
Nos. 38-46 (9) 116.75 262.75

Numerals of 2p, 3p, 1sh and 2sh6p of type A9 are in color on plain tablet.

1921 **Wmk. 4**

Die II

47 A9 ½p green 5.00 35.00
48 A9 1p carmine 4.00 27.50

For overprints see Nos. MR1-MR2.

1922 **Wmk. 3**

49 A10 3p violet, *yel* .90 19.00
50 A10 1sh black, *emerald* .85 16.00
51 A10 2sh6p blk & red, *bl* 6.00 12.50
52 A10 5sh grn & red, *yel* 35.00 110.00
Nos. 49-52 (4) 42.75 157.50

1922-28 **Wmk. 4**

53 A10 ½p green .90 3.00
54 A10 1p rose red .65 .65
55 A10 1p violet ('27) 1.10 4.00
56 A10 1½p rose red ('27) 1.60 2.75
57 A10 1½p fawn ('28) 1.90 1.60
58 A10 2p gray 1.10 6.50
59 A10 2½p ultra 2.25 20.00
60 A10 2½p orange ('23) 1.40 1.75
61 A10 3p dl vio, *yel* ('28) 2.50 12.50
62 A10 5p dl lil & ol grn 6.00 50.00
63 A10 6p dl vio & red vio 1.60 7.00
a. 6p brown lilac & red violet 1.60 7.00
64 A10 1sh blk, *emer* ('28) 2.75 16.00
65 A10 2sh6p blk & red, *bl* ('28) 21.00 52.50
66 A10 5sh grn & red, *yel* ('23) 21.00 80.00
Nos. 53-66 (14) 65.75 258.25

The ½, 1, 2 and 2½p are on ordinary paper, the others on chalky.

Numerals of 1½p of type A10 are in color on plain tablet.

Common Design Types pictured following the introduction.

Silver Jubilee Issue

Common Design Type

1935, May 6 **Engr.** *Perf. 11x12*

69 CD301 1p car & dk blue .50 1.75
70 CD301 1½p black & ultra .50 1.75
71 CD301 2½p ultra & brn 1.00 1.75
72 CD301 1sh brn vio & ind 6.50 7.25
Nos. 69-72 (4) 8.50 12.50
Set, never hinged 14.00

Coronation Issue

Common Design Type

1937, May 12 *Perf. 11x11½*

73 CD302 1p dark carmine .20 .50
74 CD302 1½p brown .20 1.50
75 CD302 2½p deep ultra .35 .50
Nos. 73-75 (3) .75 2.50
Set, never hinged 1.10

King George VI and Seal of the Colony — A11

1938-47 **Photo.** *Perf. 14*

76 A11 ½p green .20 .20
77 A11 1p scarlet .20 .20
78 A11 1½p red brown .35 .50
79 A11 2p gray .25 .40
80 A11 2½p ultra .35 .75
81 A11 3p orange .25 .50
82 A11 6p deep violet .90 .40
83 A11 1sh olive bister 1.00 .45
84 A11 2sh6p sepia 7.50 3.50
85 A11 5sh rose lake 10.00 4.50
86 A11 10sh brt blue ('47) 5.00 9.75
87 A11 £1 gray blk ('47) 8.00 16.00
Nos. 76-87 (12) 34.00 37.15
Set, never hinged 50.00

Catalogue values for unused stamps in this section, from this point to the end of the section, are for Never Hinged items.

Peace Issue

Common Design Type

Perf. 13½x14

1946, Nov. 1 **Engr.** **Wmk. 4**

88 CD303 1½p red brown .20 .20
89 CD303 3p orange .20 .20

Silver Wedding Issue

Common Design Types

1949, Jan. 3 **Photo.** *Perf. 14x14½*

90 CD304 2½p brt ultra .25 .25

Engr.; Name Typo.

Perf. 11½x11

91 CD305 £1 gray black 12.00 12.50

UPU Issue

Common Design Types

Engr.; Name Typo. on Nos. 93 & 94

1949, Oct. 10 *Perf. 13½, 11x11½*

92 CD306 2½p ultra .40 .40
93 CD307 3p deep orange 1.00 1.60
94 CD308 6p red lilac .65 .40
95 CD309 1sh olive .65 .40
Nos. 92-95 (4) 2.70 2.80

University Issue

Common Design Types

1951 **Engr.** *Perf. 14x14½*

96 CD310 3c red brn & gray blk .25 .25
97 CD311 12c purple & black .85 .85

Map of the Islands A12

1951, Apr. 2 **Wmk. 4** *Perf. 14½x14*

98 A12 6c red orange .25 .25
99 A12 12c purple .35 .35
100 A12 24c olive grn .50 .55
101 A12 $1.20 carmine 1.90 1.50
Nos. 98-101 (4) 3.00 2.65

Restoration of the Legislative Council, 1950.

Sombrero Lighthouse — A13

Map of Jost van Dyke — A14

Designs: 3c, Sheep. 4c, Map, Anegada. 5c, Cattle. 8c, Map, Virgin Gorda. 12c, Map, Tortola. 24c, Badge of the Presidency. 60c, Dead Man's Chest. $1.20, Sir Francis Drake Channel. $2.40, Road Town. $4.80, Map, Virgin Islands.

1952, Apr. 15 *Perf. 12½x13, 13x12½*

102 A13 1c gray black .25 .65
103 A14 2c deep green .55 .20
104 A14 3c choc & gray blk .30 .50
105 A14 4c red .45 .65
106 A14 5c gray blk & rose lake .90 .30
107 A14 8c ultra .55 .55
108 A14 12c purple 1.00 .65
109 A13 24c dk brown 1.10 .20
110 A14 60c blue & ol grn 1.75 7.00
111 A14 $1.20 ultra & blk 4.00 7.50
112 A14 $2.40 hn brn & dk grn 8.50 8.25
113 A14 $4.80 rose car & bl 14.00 9.00
Nos. 102-113 (12) 33.35 35.45

WAR TAX STAMPS

Regular Issue of 1913 Overprinted

1916-17 **Wmk. 3** *Perf. 14*

Die I

MR1 A9 1p scarlet .55 8.00
a. 1p carmine 2.50 20.00
MR2 A9 3p violet, *yellow* 3.50 16.00

WALLIS AND FUTUNA ISLANDS

'wä-ləs and fə-'tü-nə 'ī-ləndz

LOCATION — Group of islands in the South Pacific Ocean, northeast of Fiji
GOVT. — French Overseas Territory
AREA — 106 sq. mi.
POP. — 13,000 (est. 1984)
CAPITAL — Mata-Utu, Wallis Island

100 Centimes = 1 Franc

New Caledonia Stamps of 1905-28 Overprinted in Black or Red

1920-28 Unwmk. *Perf. 14x13½*

No.	Type	Description	Unused	Used
1	A16	1c black, *green*	.20	.20
a.		Double overprint	100.00	
2	A16	2c red brown	.20	.20
3	A16	4c blue, *org*	.30	.30
4	A16	5c green	.30	.30
5	A16	5c dull blue ('22)	.30	.30
6	A16	10c rose	.45	.45
7	A16	10c green ('22)	.60	.60
8	A16	10c red, *pink* ('25)	1.75	1.75
9	A16	15c violet	.85	.85
10	A17	20c gray brown	.75	.75
11	A17	25c blue, *grn*	1.10	1.10
12	A17	25c red, *yel* ('22)	.70	.70
13	A17	30c brown, *org*	1.25	1.25
14	A17	30c dp rose ('22)	1.10	1.10
15	A17	30c red orange ('25)	.60	.60
16	A17	30c lt green ('27)	1.90	1.90
17	A17	35c black, *yel* (R)	.75	.75
18	A17	40c rose, *grn*	.85	.85
19	A17	45c violet brn, *pnksh*	1.25	1.25
20	A17	50c red, *org*	1.25	1.25
21	A17	50c dark blue ('22)	1.50	1.50
22	A17	50c dark gray ('25)	1.75	1.75
23	A17	65c deep blue ('28)	5.25	5.25
24	A17	75c olive green	1.60	1.60

Overprinted

No.	Type	Description	Unused	Used
25	A18	1fr blue, *yel grn*	3.50	3.50
a.		Triple overprint	150.00	
26	A18	1.10fr orange brn ('28)	4.25	4.25
27	A18	2fr carmine, *bl*	5.75	5.75
28	A18	5fr black, *org* (R)	11.50	11.50
		Nos. 1-28 (28)	51.55	51.55

No. 9 Surcharged New Value and Bars in Various Colors

1922

No.	Type	Description	Unused	Used
29	A16	0.01c on 15c violet (Bk)	.60	.60
30	A16	0.02c on 15c violet (Bl)	.60	.60
31	A16	0.04c on 15c violet (G)	.60	.60
32	A16	0.05c on 15c violet (R)	.60	.60
		Nos. 29-32 (4)	2.40	2.40

Stamps and Types of 1920 Surcharged with New Values and Bars in Black or Red

1924-27

No.	Type	Description	Unused	Used
33	A18	25c on 2fr car, *bl*	.85	.85
34	A18	25c on 5fr black, *org*	.85	.85
35	A17	65c on 40c rose red, *grn* ('25)	1.40	1.40
36	A17	85c on 75c ol grn ('25)	1.10	1.10
37	A17	90c on 75c dp rose ('27)	1.75	1.75
38	A18	1.25fr on 1fr dp bl (R; '26)	.85	.85
39	A18	1.50fr on 1fr dp bl, *bl* ('27)	3.75	3.75
a.		Double surcharge	240.00	
b.		Surcharge omitted	200.00	
40	A18	3fr on 5fr red vio ('27)	6.00	6.00
a.		Surcharge omitted	175.00	
b.		Double surcharge	240.00	
41	A18	10fr on 5fr ol, *lav* ('27)	29.00	29.00
42	A18	20fr on 5fr vio rose, *yel* ('27)	35.00	35.00
		Nos. 33-42 (10)	80.55	80.55

New Caledonia Stamps and Types of 1928-40 Overprinted as in 1920

1930-40 *Perf. 13½, 14x13, 14x13½*

No.	Type	Description	Unused	Used
43	A19	1c brn vio & indigo	.20	.20
a.		Double overprint	140.00	
44	A19	2c dk brn & yel grn	.20	.20
45	A19	3c brn vio & ind ('40)	.20	.20
46	A19	4c org & Prus grn	.20	.20
47	A19	5c Prus bl & dp ol	.20	.20
48	A19	10c gray lil & dk brn	.20	.20
49	A19	15c yel brn & dp bl	.20	.20
50	A19	20c brn red & dk brn	.45	.45
51	A19	25c dk grn & dk brn	.85	.85
52	A20	30c gray grn & bl grn	.85	.85
53	A20	35c Prus grn & dk grn ('38)	.85	.85
a.		Without overprint	130.00	
54	A20	40c brt red & olive	.85	.85
55	A20	45c dp bl & red org	.85	.85
56	A20	45c bl grn & dl grn ('40)	.75	.75
57	A20	50c violet & brn	.85	.85
58	A20	55c bl vio & rose red ('38)	2.00	2.00
59	A20	60c vio bl & car ('40)	.25	.25
60	A20	65c org brn & bl	1.75	1.75
61	A20	70c dp rose & brn ('38)	1.10	1.10
62	A20	75c Prus bl & ol gray	2.75	2.75
63	A20	80c dk cl & grn ('38)	1.00	1.00
64	A20	85c green & brown	3.00	3.00
65	A20	90c dp red & brt red	2.00	2.00
66	A20	90c ol grn & rose red ('39)	.90	.90
67	A21	1fr dp ol & sal red	3.25	3.25
68	A21	1fr rose red & dk car ('38)	1.90	1.90
69	A21	1fr brn red & grn ('40)	.20	.20
70	A21	1.10fr dp grn & brn	26.00	26.00
71	A21	1.25fr brn red & grn ('33)	2.75	2.75
72	A21	1.25fr rose red & dk car ('39)	.75	.75
73	A21	1.40fr dk bl & red org ('40)	.90	.90
74	A21	1.50fr dp bl & bl	1.00	1.00
75	A21	1.60fr dp grn & brn ('40)	1.40	1.40
76	A21	1.75fr dk bl & red org ('33)	11.50	11.50
77	A21	1.75fr vio bl ('38)	1.90	1.90
78	A21	2fr red org & brn	1.40	1.40
79	A21	2.25fr vio bl ('39)	1.50	1.50
80	A21	2.50fr brn & lt brn ('40)	1.50	1.50
81	A21	3fr magenta & brn	1.40	1.40
82	A21	5fr dk bl & brn	1.90	1.90
83	A21	10fr vio & brn, *pnksh*	2.50	2.50
84	A21	20fr red & brn, *yel*	3.75	3.75
		Nos. 43-84 (42)	87.95	87.95

For overprints see Nos. 94-126 in the Scott Standard Catalogue, Vol. 6.

Common Design Types pictured following the introduction.

Colonial Exposition Issue
Common Design Types

1931, Apr. 13 Engr. *Perf. 12½*
Name of Country Typo. in Black

No.	Type	Description	Unused	Used
85	CD70	40c deep green	7.50	7.50
86	CD71	50c violet	7.50	7.50
87	CD72	90c red orange	7.50	7.50
88	CD73	1.50fr dull blue	7.50	7.50
		Nos. 85-88 (4)	30.00	30.00

Colonial Arts Exhibition Issue
Common Design Type
Souvenir Sheet

1937 *Imperf.*

No.	Type	Description	Unused	Used
89	CD78	3fr red violet	22.50	*27.50*
		Never hinged	27.50	

New York World's Fair Issue
Common Design Type

1939, May 10 Engr. *Perf. 12½x12*

No.	Type	Description	Unused	Used
90	CD82	1.25fr carmine lake	2.40	2.40
91	CD82	2.25fr ultramarine	2.40	2.40

SEMI-POSTAL STAMPS

French Revolution Issue
Common Design Type
Unwmk.

1939, July 5 Photo. *Perf. 13*
Name and Value Typo. in Black

No.	Type	Description	Unused	Used
B1	CD83	45c + 25c green	12.00	*16.00*
B2	CD83	70c + 30c brown	12.00	*16.00*
B3	CD83	90c + 35c red org	12.00	*16.00*
B4	CD83	1.25fr + 1fr rose pink	12.00	*16.00*
B5	CD83	2.25fr + 2fr blue	12.00	*16.00*
		Nos. B1-B5 (5)	60.00	80.00
		Set, never hinged	95.00	

POSTAGE DUE STAMPS

Postage Due Stamps of New Caledonia, 1906, Overprinted in Black or Red

1920 Unwmk. *Perf. 13½x14*

No.	Type	Description	Unused	Used
J1	D2	5c ultra, *azure*	.85	.85
J2	D2	10c brn, *buff*	.90	.90
J3	D2	15c grn, *grnsh*	.90	.90
J4	D2	20c blk, *yel* (R)	1.25	1.25
a.		Double overprint	150.00	
J5	D2	30c carmine rose	1.40	1.40
J6	D2	50c ultra, *straw*	2.00	2.00
J7	D2	60c olive, *azure*	2.50	2.50
a.		Double overprint	110.00	
J8	D2	1fr grn, *cream*	3.50	3.50
		Nos. J1-J8 (8)	13.30	13.30

2f

Type of 1920 Issue Surcharged

1927

No.	Type	Description	Unused	Used
J9	D2	2fr on 1fr brt vio	15.00	15.00
J10	D2	3fr on 1fr org brn	15.00	15.00

Postage Due Stamps of New Caledonia, 1928, Overprinted as in 1920

1930

No.	Type	Description	Unused	Used
J11	D3	2c sl bl & dp brn	.20	.20
J12	D3	4c brn red & bl grn	.20	.20
J13	D3	5c red org & bl blk	.20	.20
J14	D3	10c mag & Prus bl	.20	.20
J15	D3	15c dl grn & scar	.25	.25
J16	D3	20c maroon & ol grn	.60	.60
J17	D3	25c bis brn & sl bl	.60	.60
J18	D3	30c bl grn & ol grn	1.25	1.25
J19	D3	50c lt brn & dk red	.70	.70
J20	D3	60c mag & brt rose	1.25	1.25
J21	D3	1fr dl bl & Prus grn	1.25	1.25
J22	D3	2fr dk red & ol grn	1.25	1.25
J23	D3	3fr vio & brn	1.25	1.25
		Nos. J11-J23 (13)	9.20	9.20

WESTERN AUSTRALIA

'wes-tərn o-'strāl-yə

LOCATION — Western part of Australia, occupying about a third of that continent
GOVT. — British Colony
AREA — 975,920 sq. mi.
POP. — 184,124 (1901)
CAPITAL — Perth

Western Australia was one of the six British colonies that united on January 1, 1901, to form the Commonwealth of Australia.

12 Pence = 1 Shilling
20 Shillings = 1 Pound

Unused values for Nos. 1-10 are for stamps without gum as these stamps are seldom found with original gum. Otherwise, unused values are for stamps with original gum as defined in the catalogue introduction.

Very fine examples of all rouletted and perforated stamps from Nos. 6-34 have roulettes or perforations touching the design. Examples clear on all four sides range from scarce to rare and will command higher prices.

Watermarks

Wmk. 82 — Swan

Wmk. 83 — Crown and W A

Wmk. 70 — V and Crown

Wmk. 13 — Crown & Double-lined A

Wmk. 74 — Crown and Single-lined A

Swan

A1 A2

1854-57 Engr. Wmk. 82 *Imperf.*

No.	Type	Description	Unused	Used
1	A1	1p black	1,100.	240.

Litho.

No.	Type	Description	Unused	Used
2	A2	2p brown, *red* ('57)	3,000.	650.
a.		2p brown, *deep red* ('57)	3,250.	950.
b.		Printed on both sides	3,800.	1,000.

See Nos. 4, 6-7, 9, 14-39, 44-52, 54, 59-61. For surcharges see Nos. 41, 55-56.

A3 A4

No.	Type	Description	Unused	Used
3	A3	4p blue	350.	210.
a.		Frame inverted		*80,000.*
		As "a," cut to shape		*20,000.*
b.		4p slate blue	2,700.	1,100.
4	A2	6p bronze ('57)	*4,800.*	*775.*
5	A4	1sh pale brown	475.	350.
a.		1sh dark brown	650.	450.
b.		1sh dark red brown	1,800.	900.
c.		1sh pale red brown		3,000.

Engraved
Rouletted

No.	Type	Description	Unused	Used
6	A1	1p black	2,400.	600.00

Lithographed

No.	Type	Description	Unused	Used
7	A2	2p brown, *red* ('57)	*8,250.*	1,900.
a.		Printed on both sides		2,400.
8	A3	4p blue		600.00
9	A2	6p bronze ('57)	*8,250.*	1,100.
10	A4	1sh brown	3,900.	900.00

The 1p, 2p, 4p and 6p are known with pin-perforation but this is believed to be unofficial. No. 7a is only recorded used and with pin perforations.

1860 Engr. *Imperf.*

14 A1 2p vermilion 95.00 90.00
a. 2p pale orange 95.00 90.00
15 A1 4p blue 300.00 *2,000.*
16 A1 6p dull green 1,900. 600.00

Rouletted

17 A1 2p vermilion 650.00 240.00
a. 2p pale orange 575.00 225.00
18 A1 4p deep blue 4,000. —
19 A1 6p dull green 3,900. 725.00

1861 *Clean-Cut Perf. 14 to 16*

20 A1 1p rose 450.00 135.00
a. Imperf.
21 A1 2p blue 95.00 28.00
a. Imperf., pair
b. Horiz. pair, imperf. vert.
22 A1 4p vermilion 900.00 *2,000.*
a. Imperf.
23 A1 6p purple brn 350.00 60.00
a. Imperf.
24 A1 1sh green 550.00 90.00
a. Imperf.

Rough Perf. 14 to 16

24B A1 1p rose 275.00 60.00
24C A1 6p pur brn, *bluish* 3,000. 475.00
24D A1 1sh deep green 1,650. 350.00

Perf. 14

25 A1 1p rose 275.00 72.50
25A A1 2p blue 120.00 47.50
25B A1 4p vermilion 325.00 200.00

Unwmk. *Perf. 13*

26 A1 1p lake 75.00 5.50
28 A1 6p violet 165.00 47.50

1865-79 Wmk. 1 *Perf. 12½*

29 A1 1p bister 72.50 6.50
30 A1 1p yel ocher 90.00 9.50
31 A1 2p yellow 85.00 3.25
a. 2p lilac (error) ('79) *16,000.* *16,000.*
b. 2p chrome yellow 90.00 3.25
32 A1 4p carmine 90.00 6.00
a. Double impression *40,000.*
33 A1 6p violet 110.00 7.25
a. 6p lilac 190.00 7.25
b. 6p red lilac 190.00 7.25
c. Double impression *22,500.*
34 A1 1sh bright green 140.00 15.00
a. 1sh sage green 350.00 30.00
Nos. 29-34 (6) 587.50 47.50

An unused example of No. 31a realized the equivalent of U.S. $12,330 at an Australian auction in 2005.

A used example of No. 31a realized the equivalent of U.S. $16,180 at an Australian auction in 2005.

An unused example of No. 32a, with short perforations, realized the equivalent of U.S. $38,530 at an Australian auction in 2005.

A used example of No. 33c realized the equivalent of U.S. $27,740 at an Australian auction in 2005.

1872-78 *Perf. 14*

35 A1 1p bister 120.00 5.00
36 A1 1p yellow ocher 80.00 3.50
37 A1 2p yellow 75.00 1.75
38 A1 4p carmine 475.00 110.00
39 A1 6p lilac 140.00 4.50
Nos. 35-39 (5) 890.00 124.75

A5

A8

1872 Typo.

40 A5 3p red brown 47.50 4.75
a. 3p brown 47.50 5.50
Handstamped "SPECIMEN" 125.00

See #53, 92. For surcharges see #57, 69-72A.

No. 31 Surcharged in Green

1875 Engr. *Perf. 12½*

41 A1 1p on 2p yellow 500.00 65.00
a. Pair, one without surcharge
b. "O" of "ONE" omitted
c. Triple surcharge *4,800.*

Forged surcharges exist.

1882 Wmk. 2 *Perf. 12*

44 A1 1p ocher yellow 82.50 5.75
46 A1 2p yellow 110.00 5.50
47 A1 4p carmine 190.00 42.50
48 A1 6p pale violet 375.00 42.50
Nos. 44-48 (4) 757.50 96.25

1882 *Perf. 14*

49 A1 1p ocher yellow 30.00 2.00
50 A1 2p yellow 32.50 2.00
51 A1 4p carmine 120.00 11.50
52 A1 6p pale violet 110.00 4.50
a. 6p violet 110.00 3.50
Handstamped "SPECIMEN" 140.00

Typographed

53 A5 3p red brown 10.00 3.00
a. 3p brown 19.00 3.00
Nos. 49-53 (5) 302.50 23.00

1883 Engr. *Perf. 12x14*

54 A1 1p ocher yellow 1,700. 300.00

Nos. 44 and 49 Surcharged in Red

1884 *Perf. 12*

55 A1 ½p on 1p ocher yel 13.50 *22.50*

Perf. 14

56 A1 ½p on 1p ocher yel 20.00 *27.50*
a. Thin fraction bar 85.00 *100.00*

No. 40 Surcharged in Green

1885 Typo. Wmk. 1

57 A5 1p on 3p red brown 60.00 18.00
a. 1p on 3p brown 72.50 19.50
b. "1" with straight top 160.00 52.50
c. As "a," "1" with straight top 190.00 52.50

Wmk. Crown and C A (2)

1885 Typo. *Perf. 14*

58 A8 ½p green 4.75 .85

See No. 89.

1888 Engr.

59 A1 1p rose 24.00 4.00
60 A1 2p slate 57.50 1.50
61 A1 4p red brown 90.00 25.00
Nos. 59-61 (3) 171.50 30.50

A9

A10

A11

A12

1890-93 Typo.

62 A9 1p carmine rose 26.50 1.75
63 A10 2p slate 30.00 2.00
64 A11 2½p blue 16.00 2.75
65 A12 4p orange brown 12.00 2.00
66 A12 5p bister 12.00 4.25
67 A12 6p violet 18.00 5.50
68 A12 1sh olive green 22.50 6.50
Nos. 62-68 (7) 137.00 24.75

See Nos. 73-74, 76, 80, 90, 94.

Nos. 40 and 53a Surcharged in Green

1893 Wmk. Crown and C C (1)

69 A5 1p on 3p red brown 14.00 6.75
a. 1p on 3p brown 14.00 6.50
b. Double surcharge *1,400.*

Wmkd. Crown and C A (2)

70 A5 1p on 3p brown 60.00 9.00

Nos. 40a and 53a Surcharged in Green

1895 Wmk. Crown and C C (1)

71 A5 ½p on 3p brown 11.00 *30.00*
a. Double surcharge *1,150.*

Green and Red Surcharge

72 A5 ½p on 3p brown 125.00 *300.00*

Wmk. Crown and C A (2)

72A A5 ½p on 3p brown 85.00 *200.00*

After the supply of paper watermarked Crown and C C was exhausted, No. 72A was printed. Ostensibly this was to provide samples for Postal Union distribution, but a supply for philatelic demands was also made.

Types of 1890-93 and

A15

1899-1901 Typo. Wmk. 83

73 A9 1p carmine rose 6.75 1.50
74 A10 2p yellow 19.00 2.75
75 A15 2½p blue ('01) 9.25 4.00
Nos. 73-75 (3) 35.00 8.25

A16

A17

A18

A19

A20

A21

A22

Southern Cross — A23

Queen Victoria
A24 A25

Perf. 12½, 12x12½

1902-05 Wmk. 70

76 A9 1p car rose 14.50 .65
a. 1p salmon —
b. Perf. 11 275.00 23.50
c. Perf. 12½x11 775.00 450.00
77 A16 2p yellow 16.50 1.50
a. Perf. 11 275.00 40.00
b. Perf. 12½x11 *1,200.* *775.00*
79 A17 4p orange brn 19.00 2.75
a. Perf. 11 950.00 400.00
80 A12 5p ol bis, perf 12½ ('05) 120.00 85.00
a. Perf. 11 57.50 *65.00*
81 A18 8p pale yel grn 21.00 3.25
82 A19 9p orange 32.50 12.00
b. Perf. 11 120.00 *130.00*
83 A20 10p red 40.00 8.25
84 A21 2sh orange red, *yel* ('06) 55.00 12.00
a. Perf. 11 350.00 160.00
b. 2sh orange brown, *yel* ('11) 55.00 13.50
c. 2sh bright red 95.00 13.50
d. As "c," perf. 11 240.00 140.00
85 A22 2sh6p dk bl, *rose* 55.00 9.00
86 A23 5sh blue green 85.00 30.00
87 A24 10sh violet 210.00 90.00
a. 10sh bright purple 525.00 290.00
88 A25 £1 brown org 450.00 225.00
a. £1 orange 725.00 375.00
Nos. 76-88 (12) 1,118. 479.40

Perf. 12½, 12x12½

1905-12 Wmk. 13

89 A8 ½p dp green ('10) 5.25 *6.00*
a. Perf 11 *1,800.*
90 A9 1p rose 11.00 .85
e. Perf. 11 38.00 15.00
f. Perf. 12½x11 *725.00* 350.00
91 A16 2p yellow 8.50 2.10
a. Perf. 11 42.00 22.50
b. Perf. 12½x11 *650.00* 350.00
92 A5 3p brown 24.00 2.75
a. Perf. 11 20.00 6.00
b. Perf. 12½x11 — 900.00
93 A17 4p orange brn 22.50 6.50
a. 4p bister brown 24.00 8.00
b. Perf. 11 750.00 260.00
94 A12 5p olive bis 20.00 11.00
a. Perf. 11, pale olive bister 35.00 12.00
b. Perf. 11, olive green 22.00 16.00
95 A18 8p pale yel grn ('12) 21.00 *60.00*
96 A19 9p orange 30.00 6.00
b. Perf. 11 140.00 *160.00*
97 A20 10p red orange 27.50 21.50
98 A23 5s blue green 160.00 120.00
Nos. 89-98 (10) 329.75 236.70

For surcharge see No. 103.

A26

A27

1906-07 Wmk. 83 *Perf. 14*

99 A26 6p bright violet 27.50 2.25
100 A27 1sh olive green 32.50 4.50

1912 Wmk. 74 *Perf. 11½x12*

101 A26 6p bright violet 13.50 11.00
102 A27 1sh gray green 30.00 20.00
a. Perf. 12½ *1,750.*

No. 91 Surcharged

1912 Wmk. 13 *Perf. 12½*

103 A16 1p on 2p yellow 1.40 1.40
a. Perf compound 12½x11 *475.00* *325.00*

Stamps of Western Australia were replaced by those of Australia.

FISCAL STAMPS

Postal use of the 1p telegraph stamp was authorized beginning Oct. 25, 1886.

Used values are for examples with postal cancellations.

Beware of copies with a pen cancellation removed and a fake postmark added.

PF1

PF2

1886 **Wmk. 1** ***Perf. 14***

AR1 PF1 1p bister 40.00 6.00

Perf. 12½

AR2 PF1 1p bister 40.00 5.00

The 6p is known postally used but was not authorized.

Authorized for postal use by the Post and Telegraph Act of Sept. 5, 1893 were the current revenue stamps through the 1sh value.

Beware of copies with a pen cancellation removed and a fake postmark added.

Because the Act specified current stamps, postally used examples from the provisional issue of of 1881 are not included here.

1882 **Wmk. 2** ***Perf. 14***

AR3 PF2 1p purple 15.00 2.75
AR4 PF2 2p purple 160.00 70.00
AR5 PF2 3p purple 52.50 3.75
AR6 PF2 6p purple 65.00 5.00
AR7 PF2 1sh purple 110.00 10.00

Wmk. 83

AR8 PF2 1p purple 10.50 2.75
AR9 PF2 3p purple 47.50 3.75
AR10 PF2 6p purple 47.50 4.00
AR11 PF2 1sh purple 110.00 12.50

Nos. AR7, AR11 have a rectangular outer frame and a circular frame around the swan.

Higher values are known with postal cancels, some postally used, but these were not authorized.

WESTERN UKRAINE

ˈwes-tərn yü-ˈkrān

LOCATION — In Eastern Central Europe
GOVT. — A former short-lived independent State

A provisional government was established in 1918 in the eastern part of Austria-Hungary but the area later came under Polish administration.

100 Shahiv (Sotykiv) = 1 Hryvnia
100 Heller = 1 Krone

Forgeries of almost all Western Ukraine stamps are plentiful. Particularly dangerous forgeries have been noted for the Kolomyia Issue and for the First and Second Stanyslaviv Issues.

Lviv Issue

Austria Nos. 145-146, 148, 169 Overprinted

Nos. 1-4A are handstamped with an octagonal overprint that reads "ZAKHIDNO UKR. NARODNA REPUBLYKA" ("Western Ukrainian National Republic"), framing the image of a rearing crowned lion.

1918, Nov. 20

1 A37 3h bright violet 50.00 *350.00*
a. Inverted overprint 125.00
2 A37 5h light green 45.00 *275.00*
a. Inverted overprint 125.00
3 A37 10h magenta 35.00 *275.00*
a. Inverted overprint 125.00
4 A42 20h dark green 30.00 *300.00*
a. Inverted overprint 125.00
4A A42 20h light green 200.00 *750.00*
Nos. 1-4A (5) 360.00 *1,950.*

This issue was in circulation for only two days before Lviv was captured by the Poles on Nov. 22. No examples of Nos. 1-4A used in Lviv are known.

The Western Ukrainian National Republic (ZUNR) government evacuated to the city of Ternopil, which became the provisional capital. ZUNR postal operations were set up in other Western Ukrainian cities, and the Lviv Issue was used in Stanyslaviv (earliest known cancellation date, Dec. 8), Khodoriv and Kolomyia.

Nos. 1-4 exist in pairs with both normal and inverted overprints. Value $275.

Overprints in other colors (green, red and violet) are known, but these are probably essays. Violet-black overprints are likely transitional color impressions.

Kolomyia Issue

Austria Nos. 168, 145, 147, 149 Surcharged

Kolomyia is the main town of the Pokutia region of southwestern Ukraine. Cut off from ZUNR postal officials by wartime conditions and in urgent need of basic value stamps, the Kolomyia postmaster obtained permission from the District Military Command to surcharge remaining Austrian postage stamps to either 5 or 10 sotyks, the equivalent of 5 or 10 heller. These stamps were produced on Dec. 10, under very strict security, by preparing two distinct plates (one for each value) that overprinted 25 stamps at a time (5x5 quarter sections of the Austrian 100-stamp panes). The stamps were placed on sale two days later.

1918, Dec. 12 **Unwmk.** ***Perf. 12½***

5 A42 5sot on 15h dl red 75.00 *100.00*
a. Inverted overprint 500.00 *600.00*
b. Double overprint 500.00 *600.00*
6 A37 10sot on 3h vio 80.00 *100.00*
7 A37 10sot on 6h dp org *1,200.* *1,050.*
8 A37 10sot on 12h lt bl *1,400.* *1,250.*
Nos. 5-8 (4) 2,755. *2,500.*

10 sotyk on 15 heller values are essays; only six were produced.

All inverted surcharges on Nos. 6-8 are forgeries. Double surcharges are forgeries.

First Stanyslaviv Issue

Austrian Stamps of 1916-18 Surcharged in Shahiv (shown) and Hryvnia Currency

At the end of December, 1918, the national government again moved, this time to the city of Stanyslaviv (present-day Ivano-Frankivsk). A shortage of qualified postal personnel resulted in a considerable delay in the creation of new ZUNR postage stamps. In the interim, remaining unoverprinted Austrian stamps were used. Finally, on March 18, 1919, 20 different available Austrian definitive stamps were typograph surcharged at the Weidenfeld Printing Shop in Stanyslaviv.

1919, Mar. 18

9 A37 3sh on 3h bright violet 15.00 *20.00*
10 A37 5sh on 5h light green 15.00 *20.00*
11 A37 6sh on 6h deep orange 30.00 *50.00*
12 A37 10sh on 10h mag 25.00 *35.00*
13 A37 12sh on 12h lt blue 25.00 *35.00*
a. Double overprint 250.00 *350.00*
b. Double overprint, one on reverse 75.00 *175.00*
14 A42 15sh on 15h dull red 25.00 *35.00*
15 A42 20sh on 20h deep green 25.00 *35.00*
16 A42 30sh on 30h dull violet 150.00 *225.00*
17 A39 40sh on 40h olive green 25.00 *35.00*
18 A39 50sh on 50h dark green 25.00 *35.00*
19 A39 60sh on 60h deep blue 25.00 *35.00*
20 A39 80sh on 80h orange brown 25.00 *35.00*
a. Inverted overprint 250.00 *350.00*
21 A39 1hr on 1k car, *yel* 35.00 *40.00*
22 A40 2hr on 2k lt blue 35.00 *45.00*
23 A40 3hr on 3k claret (on #161) 2,500. *2,700.*
24 A40 3hr on 3k car rose (on #165) 75.00 75.00
25 A40 3hr on 3k car rose (on #173) 60.00 60.00
26 A40 4hr on 4k dk grn (on #162) 250.00 *300.00*
27 A40 4hr on 4k yel grn (on #166) 45.00 *50.00*
28 A40 10hr on 10k deep violet 550.00 *750.00*
a. Double overprint 2,500. *3,000.*
Nos. 9-28 (20) 3,960. *4,615.*

The 25sh on 25h, type A42, in both light and dull blue shades, never received this overprint. All such specimens are fantasies.

Second Stanyslaviv Issue

The overprinting of a second issue of postage stamps in Stanyslaviv was undertaken in early May. Stamps from several different Austrian stamp series were utilized to create four distinct sets. Most of the stamps available were Austrian postage due, charity or field post stamps.

Same Surcharge on Postage Due Stamps of Bosnia, 1904, but without Asterisks

1919, May 5

29 D1 1sh on 1h blk, red & yel 30.00 30.00
a. Inverted overprint 60.00 60.00
b. Double overprint 80.00 80.00
30 D1 2sh on 2h blk, red & yel 10.00 *12.00*
a. Inverted overprint 75.00 *125.00*
31 D1 3sh on 3h blk, red & yel 10.00 *12.00*
a. Inverted overprint 20.00 *30.00*
32 D1 4sh on 4h blk, red & yel 80.00 80.00
a. Inverted overprint 150.00 150.00
b. Double overprint 250.00 250.00
33 D1 5sh on 5h blk, red & yel *2,750.* *3,000.*
34 D1 6sh on 6h blk, red & yel 200.00 *225.00*
a. Inverted overprint 500.00 500.00
b. Double overprint 400.00 *425.00*
35 D1 7sh on 7h blk, red & yel 20.00 *25.00*
a. Inverted overprint 30.00 *35.00*
36 D1 8sh on 8h blk, red & yel 15.00 *20.00*
a. Inverted overprint 40.00 *50.00*
b. Vertical overprint 600.00 *800.00*
c. As "b," double overprint 800.00 *900.00*
37 D1 10sh on 10h blk, red & yel *900.00* *1,150.*
38 D1 15sh on 15h blk, red & yel *350.00* *350.00*
a. Inverted overprint 450.00 *500.00*
39 D1 20sh on 20h blk, red & yel *5,250.*
a. Double overprint 6,500. *14,000.*
40 D1 50sh on 50h blk, red & yel *175.00* *175.00*
a. Inverted overprint 300.00 250.00

Nos. 29-40 were created by overprinting Bosnian 1904 postage due stamps, which had been brought to Stanyslaviv by a Ukrainian military officer returning from the Serbian front. The same printing cliché was used as for the First Stanyslaviv Issue, but the asterisk obliterators were removed.

Most of the overprinting was made using 50-stamp panes (half of a sheet). After one half of the pane (25 positions) was overprinted, it would apparently be turned over and its second half overprinted with the same 25-position block, but as an inverted impression. After overprinting, the pane was torn into two equal 25-stamp halves.

Two types of surcharge on No. 61: Shahiv in singular (wara) and in plural (warib). Value the same.

Same Surcharge on Austrian Military Semipostal Stamps of 1918
Perf. 12½x13

41 MSP7 10sh on 10h gray green 100.00 *110.00*
a. Inverted overprint 100.00 *120.00*
b. Double overprint 150.00 *175.00*
42 MSP8 20sh on 20h magenta 90.00 *85.00*
a. Inverted overprint 85.00 *100.00*
b. Double overprint 120.00 *140.00*
43 MSP7 45sh on 45h blue 75.00 *85.00*
a. Inverted overprint 65.00 *85.00*

Nos. 41-43 were printed in the same manner as Nos. 29-40.

Same Surcharge on Austrian Military Stamps of 1917
Perf. 12½

44 M3 1sh on 1h grnsh blue *800.00* *800.00*
45 M3 2sh on 2h red orange 90.00 90.00
a. Inverted overprint 100.00 100.00
b. Double overprint 175.00 175.00
46 M3 3sh olive gray 150.00 *160.00*
a. Double overprint 300.00 *325.00*
47 M3 5sh on 5h olive grn 225.00 225.00
48 M3 6sh on 6h violet 130.00 *150.00*
49 M3 10sh on 10h org brn *750.00* *850.00*
50 M3 12sh on 12h blue 450.00 *500.00*
a. Inverted overprint 550.00 *600.00*
51 M3 15sh on 15h brt rose 425.00 *500.00*
a. Inverted overprint 525.00 *600.00*
52 M3 20sh on 20h red brown 15.00 *17.00*
a. Inverted overprint 75.00 *120.00*
b. Double overprint 40.00 *45.00*
53 M3 25sh on 25h ultra *2,750.* *3,250.*
54 M3 30sh on 30h slate *825.00* *1,000.*
55 M3 40sh on 40h olive bis *700.00* *700.00*
56 M3 50sh on 50h deep green 8.00 8.00
a. Inverted overprint 15.00 15.00
b. Double overprint 50.00 50.00
57 M3 60sh on 60h car rose 800.00 800.00
58 M3 80sh on 80h dull blue 40.00 40.00
a. Inverted overprint 70.00 *75.00*
59 M3 90sh on 90h dk vio *800.00* *850.00*
60 M4 2hr on 2k rose, *straw* 12.00 *16.00*
a. Inverted overprint 25.00 *32.50*
b. Imperforate 2,500.
61 M4 3hr on 3k blue, *grn* 20.00 *22.50*
a. Inverted overprint 24.00 *27.50*
b. Double overprint 55.00 *60.00*
62 M4 4hr on 4k rose, *grn* 20.00 *22.50*
a. Inverted overprint 24.00 *27.50*
b. Double overprint 55.00 *60.00*
63 M4 10hr on 10k dl violet, *gray* — —

Two examples of No. 63 were printed, and neither was ever postally used. The "used" specimen was cut from a document prepared by the Western Ukrainian economic bureau (Ekonomat) to display the stamps that made up the First, Second and Third Stanyslaviv issues. The specimen stamps on this document were tied with a double-ring bureau cancel that somewhat resembles a regular double-ring postal cancellation.

About half of this issue, where several sheets were available for printing, was overprinted in the manner of Nos. 29-43.

Same Surcharge on Austrian Stamps of 1916-18, but with two upper bars

64 A38 15sh on 36h vio (on #J61) 325.00 *400.00*
a. Double overprint 400.00 *450.00*
65 A38 50sh on 42h choc (on #J63) 4,500. *5,000.*
66 A37 3sh on 3h brt violet (on #145) 160.00 160.00
67 A37 5sh on 5h lt green (on #146) 160.00 160.00
a. Inverted overprint 240.00 240.00
68 A37 6sh on 6h deep org (on #147) 600.00 600.00
69 A37 10sh on 10h magenta (on #148) 175.00 175.00
a. Inverted overprint 210.00 210.00
70 A37 12sh on 12h lt blue (on #149) 350.00 350.00
71 A38 15sh on 15h rose red (on #150) (on #149) 160.00 160.00
a. Inverted overprint 190.00 190.00
72 A42 15sh on 15h dull red (on #168) 175.00 175.00
73 A42 30sh on 30h dull violet (on #171) 160.00 160.00
a. Double overprint 300.00 300.00
74 A39 40sh on 40h ol grn (on #154) 250.00 250.00
75 M3 50sh on 50h dp grn (on #M61) 400.00 400.00

The two bars in the surcharge were originally created to obliterate the "PORTO" on Nos. 64 and 65 but were subsequently retained for Nos. 66-75.

Third Stanyslaviv Issue

Austrian Stamps of 1916-18 Overprinted

1919, May

76 A37 3h brt violet .50 *1.00*
77 A37 5h light green .50 *1.00*
78 A37 6h deep orange .50 *1.00*
79 A37 10h magenta .50 *1.00*
80 A37 12h light blue .50 *1.00*
81 A42 15h dull red .50 *1.00*
82 A42 20h deep green .50 *1.00*
83 A42 25h blue .50 *1.00*
84 A42 30h dull vio .50 *1.00*
85 A39 40h olive green .75 *1.25*
86 A39 50h dark green .75 *1.25*
87 A39 60h deep blue .75 *1.25*
88 A39 80h orange brn 1.00 *1.25*
89 A39 90h red violet 1.00 *1.60*
90 A39 1k car, *yel* 1.25 *4.00*
91 A40 2k light blue 2.00 *6.00*
92 A40 3k carmine rose 2.50 *7.50*

93	A40	4k yellow grn	10.00	*15.00*
94	A40	10k deep violet	15.00	*40.00*
		Nos. 76-94 (19)	39.50	*88.10*

Issued: 3h-10h, 15h, 25h-40h, 60h-1k, 5/8; balance of set, 5/13.

A definitive set for Western Ukraine was ordered from the Austrian State Printing Office in March, 1919. Because of the time involved in designing and printing these stamps, Nos. 76-94 were overprinted in Vienna as a provisional issue and were delivered in two shipments. Because travel into and out of Stanyslaviv was becoming more difficult as the month wore on, it was not known whether or not the second shipment, which included the higher values, would arrive. Because of this, the Fourth Stanyslaviv Issue, Nos. 95-103, were overprinted locally.

Fourth Stanislaviv Issue

Black Surcharge on Austrian Military Stamps of 1917-18.

1919, May

95	A2	2hr on 2k rose, *straw*	12.00	*14.00*
96	A2	3hr on 2k rose, *straw*	12.00	*15.00*
97	A2	3hr on 3k grn, *blue*	80.00	*150.00*
98	A2	4hr on 2k rose, *straw*	12.00	*15.00*
99	A2	4hr on 4k rose, *grn*	1,100.	*1,600.*
100	A2	5hr on 2k rose, *straw*	12.00	*15.00*
a.		Inverted surcharge	250.00	
101	A2	10hr on 50h dp grn (Austria type M3)	15.00	*35.00*
a.		Double surcharge	150.00	

Same Surcharge on Austrian Postage Due Stamps of 1916, but without Rosettes and Numerals

102	D5	1hr ultra	120.00	*175.00*
103	D5	5hr ultra	1,200.	*1,800.*

REGISTRATION STAMPS

Kolomyia Issue

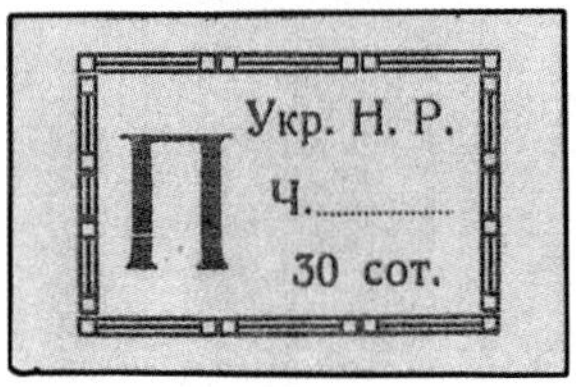

RS1

Without Gum

1918-19 Unwmk. Typeset *Imperf.*

F1	RS1	30sot black, *rose*	175.00	150.00
F2	RS1	50sot black, *rose* ('19)	100.00	*125.00*
a.		50sot black, *deep rose* ('19)	100.00	125.00

No. F1 was printed on Dec. 10 and issued Dec. 12, 1918, along with the regular Kolomyia Issue (Nos. 5-8). On Dec. 19, the ZUNR government approved an increase in the registered letter rate to 50 sotyks, effective January 1, 1919. Because of communication disruptions, the Kolomyia post office did not learn of this decree until about January 7, when it ordered new values in the higher denomination (No. F2). F1 continued to be used, usually in combination with 20h of Austrian stamps, until supplies were exhausted, at which point No. F2 was put into use. A second printing of the 50sot value, on darker rose paper, was made in late March.

Nos. F1-F2a were typographed in vertical panes of five stamps by the Wilhelm Brauner Print Ship in Kolomyia.

Forgeries exist.

OCCUPATION STAMPS

Romanian Occupation of Pokutia

Only the stamps listed below were officially created. Soon after the Romanian occupation ended on Aug. 20, 1919, the C.M.T. handstamps fell into the hands of speculators, and some 37 other Austrian stamps were overprinted. None of these privately-created stamps are known on authentic covers.

Austrian Stamps Surcharged in Dark Violet Blue

1919, June 14 Unwmk. *Perf. 12½*

On Stamps of 1916-18

N1	A37	40h on 5h lt grn	4.00	*5.00*
N2	A42	60h on 15h dl red	5.00	*6.00*
N3	A42	60h on 20h dp grn	2.00	*3.00*
a.		Inverted overprint	2,500.	
b.		Double overprint	20.00	
N4	A42	60h on 25h blue	11.00	*12.00*
a.		Inverted overprint	55.00	
b.		Double overprint	75.00	
N5	A42	60h on 30h dl vio	13.00	14.00
N6	A39	1k 20h on 50h dk grn	5.00	*6.00*
N7	A39	1k 20h on 60h dp bl	9.00	*11.00*
N8	A39	1k 20h on 1k car, *yel*	17.00	19.00

On Austrian Postage Due Stamps of 1910-1917

N9	D4	40h on 5h rose red	18.00	*20.00*
N10	D3	1k 20h on 25h carmine	150.00	*300.00*
N11	D4	1k 20h on 25h rose red	150.00	*300.00*
N12	D4	1k 20h on 30h rose red	1,200.	1,200.
N13	A38	1k 20h on 50h on 42h choc	1,300.	1,300.

First Vienna Issue, May 1919: Lithographed at the Austrian State Printing Office on unwatermarked white paper. Inscribed "Ukrainska Narodnia Respublika Z.O." ("Ukrainian National Republic W(estern) P(rovince)"). Design incorporates the heraldic arms of Ukraine (trident), Kiev (Archangel Michael) and Lviv (lion rampant). 10, 20 and 50 sotyk values imperf; 1 and 10 krone values perf 11½. Not issued. Value, set of 5, $5. Also exists on cream-colored paper.

Arms of Kiev

Arms of Ukraine

Arms of Lviv

Second Vienna Issue, May 1919: Lithographed at the Austrian State Printing Office on unwatermarked white paper. Inscribed "Ukrainska Narodnia Republyka Zakhidnia Oblast" ("Ukrainian National Republic Western Province"). Set of 12 values (four of each design), perf 11½ or imperf. Not issued. Value, set of 12: perf $300; imperf $475.

YEMEN

ˈye-mən

LOCATION — Arabian Peninsula, south of Saudi Arabia and bordering on the Red Sea
GOVT. — Kingdom
AREA — 73,300 sq. mi.
CAPITAL — San'a

40 Bogaches = 1 Imadi

Watermarks

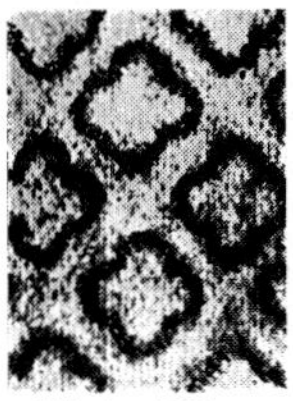

Wmk. 127 — Quatrefoils

Wmk. 258 — Arabic Characters and Y G Multiple

For Domestic Postage

A1

Crossed Daggers and Arabic Inscriptions — A2

1926 Unwmk. Typo. *Imperf.*

Laid Paper

Without Gum

1	A1	2½b black	40.00	40.00
2	A1	2½b black, *orange*	40.00	40.00
3	A2	5b black	40.00	40.00
		Nos. 1-3 (3)	120.00	120.00

No. 2 is known rouletted 7½ or 9.

Type A1 differs from A2 primarily in the inscription in the left dagger blade.

All come on wove paper.

For Foreign and Domestic Postage

Arabic Inscriptions

A3 A4

1930-31 Wmk. 127 *Perf. 14*

7	A3	½b orange ('31)	.30	.20
8	A3	1b green	.40	.30
9	A3	1b yellow grn ('31)	.35	.25
10	A3	2b olive grn	.40	.35
11	A3	2b olive brn ('31)	.35	.25
12	A3	3b dull vio ('31)	.40	.35
13	A3	4b red	.60	.50
14	A3	4b deep rose ('31)	.50	.40
15	A3	5b slate gray ('31)	.90	.50
16	A4	6b dull blue	1.25	1.00
17	A4	6b dp ultra ('31)	1.00	.75
18	A4	8b lilac rose ('31)	1.40	1.00
19	A4	10b lt brown	2.00	1.40
20	A4	10b brn org ('31)	1.75	1.00
21	A4	20b yel grn ('31)	4.50	2.50
22	A4	1i red brn & lt bl	8.00	6.00
23	A4	1i lil rose & yel grn ('31)	8.00	6.00
		Nos. 7-23 (17)	32.10	22.75

Some values exist imperforate.

For surcharges and overprints see Nos. 30, 59-62, 166-167, 169-171, 174-176 in the Scott Standard Catalogue, Vol. 6.

Flags of Saudi Arabia, Yemen and Iraq — A5

1939 Litho. Wmk. 258 *Perf. 12½*

24	A5	4b dl rose & ultra	.80	.50
25	A5	6b slate bl & ultra	.80	.50
26	A5	10b fawn & ultra	1.40	.75
27	A5	14b olive & ultra	2.25	1.25
28	A5	20b yel grn & ultra	3.25	1.75
29	A5	1i claret & ultra	6.50	3.50
		Nos. 24-29 (6)	15.00	8.25

2nd anniv. of the Arab Alliance. Nos. 24-29 exist imperforate.

For overprints see Nos. C29-C29D in the Scott Standard Catalogue, Vol. 6.

No. 7 Handstamped in Black

a-b-c

Three types of surcharge:
a. 11½x16mm
b. 13-13½x15½mm
c. 12x16mm

Values of surcharged stamps are for ordinary copies. Clear, legible surcharges command a premium.

1939 Wmk. 127 *Perf. 14*

30	A3	4b on ½b orange	*15.00*	*12.50*

See Nos. 44-48, 59-67, 82, 86-87 in the Scott Standard Catalogue, Vol. 6.

A6

A7

1940 Wmk. 258 Litho. *Perf. 12½*

31	A6	½b ocher & ultra	.20	.20
32	A6	1b lt grn & rose red	.20	.20
33	A6	2b bis brn & vio	.20	.20
34	A6	3b dl vio & ultra	.25	.20
35	A6	4b rose & yel grn	.35	.30
36	A6	5b dk gray grn & bis brn	.40	.35

37	A7	6b ultra & yel org	.45	.45
38	A7	8b claret & dull bl	.55	.50
39	A7	10b brn org & yel grn	.75	.75
40	A7	14b gray grn & vio	.95	.80
41	A7	18b emerald & blk	1.10	.90
42	A7	20b yel ol & cerise	1.50	1.50
43	A7	1i vio rose, yel grn & brn red	2.75	2.50
		Nos. 31-43 (13)	9.65	8.85
		Set, never hinged	20.00	

No. 36 was used as a 4b stamp in 1957.

For surcharges see Nos. 44-47 in the Scott Standard Catalogue, Vol. 6.

YUGOSLAVIA

ˌyü-gō-ˈslä-vē-ə

LOCATION — Southern Europe, bordering on the Adriatic Sea
GOVT. — Kingdom
AREA — 98,766 sq. mi.
POP. — 22,850,000 (est. 1983)
CAPITAL — Belgrade

On December 1, 1918, Bosnia and Herzegovina, Croatia, Dalmatia, Montenegro, Serbia and Slovenia united to form a kingdom which was later called Yugoslavia. Other listings may be found under all.

100 Heller = 1 Krone
(Bosnia & Herzegovina)
100 Filler = 1 Krone
(Croatia-Slavonia)
100 Paras = 1 Dinar (General Issues)

Catalogue values for unused stamps in this country are for Never Hinged items, beginning with Scott RA1 in the postal tax section, and Scott RAJ1 in the postal tax due section.

Counterfeits exist of most of the 1918-19 overprints for Bosnia and Herzegovina, Croatia-Slavonia and Slovenia.

BOSNIA AND HERZEGOVIA

Stamps of Bosnia and Herzegovina, 1910, Overprinted or Surcharged in Black or Red

a

b

c

1918 Unwmk. *Perf. 12½*

1L1	A4(a)	3h olive green	.40	.70
1L2	A4(b)	5h dk grn (R)	.20	.20
1L3	A4(a)	10h carmine	.20	.20
1L4	A4(a)	20h dk brn (R)	.20	.20
1L5	A4(a)	25h deep blue (R)	.20	.20
1L6	A4(b)	30h green	.20	.20
1L7	A4(b)	40h orange	.20	.20
1L8	A4(b)	45h brown red	.20	.20
1L9	A4(b)	50h dull violet	.20	.20
1L10	A4(a)	60h on 50h dl vio	.20	.20
1L11	A4(b)	80h on 6h org brown	.20	.30
1L12	A4(a)	90h on 35h myr green	.20	.20
1L13	A5(c)	2k gray green	.20	.35
1L14	A4(b)	3k on 3h ol grn	.80	1.25
1L15	A5(c)	4k on 1k mar	1.40	1.90
1L16	A4(b)	10k on 2h vio	2.25	2.50
		Nos. 1L1-1L16 (16)	7.25	9.00

Inverted and double overprints and assorted varieties exist on the stamps for Bosnia and Herzegovina.

Bosnian Girl — A1

1918 Typo. *Perf. 11½*

1L17	A1	2h ultramarine	.20	.20
1L18	A1	6h violet	.55	1.90
1L19	A1	10h rose	.20	.20
1L20	A1	20h green	.20	.20
		Nos. 1L17-1L20 (4)	1.15	2.50

Imperforate stamps of this type (A1) are newspaper stamps of Bosnia.

See Nos. 1L21-1L22, 1L43-1L45.

Bosnia and Herzegovina Nos. P1-P2 (Nos. 1L17-1L18, Imperf.) Surcharged

1918 *Imperf.*

1L21	A1	3h on 2h ultra	.20	.20
a.		Double surcharge	*14.00*	
1L22	A1	5h on 6h violet	.20	.20
a.		Double surcharge	*14.00*	

Stamps of Bosnia and Herzegovina, 1906-17, Overprinted or Surcharged in Black or Red:

d

e

f

1919 *Perf. 12½*

1L25	A23(d)	3h claret	.20	.50
1L26	A23(e)	5h green	.20	.20
1L27	A23(e)	10h on 6h dark gray	.20	.20
1L28	A24(d)	20h on 35h myr green	.20	.20
1L29	A23(e)	25h ultra	.20	.20
1L30	A23(d)	30h orange red	.45	.90
1L31	A24(d)	45h olive brn	.35	.45
1L32	A27(d)	45h on 80h org brown	.20	.20
a.		Perf. 11½	3.25	4.00
1L33	A24(e)	50h slate blue	20.00	24.00
1L34	A24(e)	50h on 72h dk blue (R)	.20	.20
1L35	A24(d)	60h brown violet	.20	.20
1L36	A27(e)	80h orange brown	.20	.25
a.		Perf. 11½	24.00	30.00
1L37	A27(d)	90h dark violet	.20	.20
a.		Perf. 11½	2.25	2.75
1L38	A17(f)	2k gray green	.20	.25
a.		Imperf.	27.50	
b.		Perf. 9½	4.50	5.00
1L39	A26(d)	3k car, *green*	.80	.90
1L40	A28(e)	4k car, *green*	1.75	2.50
1L41	A26(d)	5k dk vio, *gray*	1.75	2.75
1L42	A28(e)	10k dk vio, *gray*	2.00	2.75
		Nos. 1L25-1L42 (18)	29.30	36.85

Nos. 1L32, 1L36, 1L37, 1L40 and 1L42 have no bars in the overprint.

Nos. 1L25 to 1L42 exist with inverted overprint or surcharge.

Bosnia and Herzegovina Nos. P2-P4 (Nos. 1L18-1L20, Imperf.) Surcharged

1920 *Imperf.*

1L43	A1	2h on 6h violet	50.00	70.00
1L44	A1	2h on 10h rose	20.00	40.00
1L45	A1	2h on 20h green	1.10	2.75
		Nos. 1L43-1L45 (3)	71.10	112.75

SEMI-POSTAL STAMPS ISSUES FOR BOSNIA AND HERZEGOVINA

Leading Blind Soldier — SP1

Wounded Soldier — SP2

Semi-Postal Stamps of Bosnia and Herzegovina, 1918 Overprinted

1918 Unwmk. *Perf. 12½, 13*

1LB1	SP1	10h greenish bl	.65	1.00
a.		Overprinted as No. 1LB2	27.50	37.50
1LB2	SP2	15h red brown	1.75	1.75
a.		Overprinted as No. 1LB1	27.50	37.50

Bosnian Semi-Postal Stamps of 1916 Overprinted like No. 1LB2

1LB3	SP1	5h green	125.00	140.00
a.		Overprinted as No. 1LB1	240.00	300.00
1LB4	SP2	10h magenta	75.00	95.00
		Nos. 1LB1-1LB4 (4)	202.40	237.75

Inverted and double overprints exist on Nos. 1LB1-1LB4.

Mail Wagon SP3

Bridge at Mostar SP4

Scene near Sarajevo — SP5

Regular Issue of Bosnia, 1906 Surcharged in Black

1919

1LB5	SP3	10h + 10h on 40h org red	1.75	1.90
1LB6	SP4	20h + 10h on 20h dk brown	.60	.60
1LB7	SP5	45h + 15h on 1k mar	2.50	2.75
		Nos. 1LB5-1LB7 (3)	4.85	5.25

Nos. 1LB5-1LB7 exist with surcharge inverted. Value each $7.50.

SPECIAL DELIVERY STAMPS ISSUES FOR BOSNIA AND HERZEGOVINA

SD1

SD2

Lightning

Bosnian Special Delivery Stamps Overprinted in Black

1918 Unwmk. *Perf. 12½, 13*

1LE1	SD1	2h vermilion	4.75	5.00
a.		Inverted overprint	32.50	
b.		Overprinted as No. 1LE2	30.00	35.00
1LE2	SD2	5h deep green	1.40	1.50
a.		Inverted overprint	18.00	
b.		Overprinted as No. 1LE1	30.00	35.00

POSTAGE DUE STAMPS ISSUES FOR BOSNIA AND HERZEGOVINA

Postage Due Stamps of Bosnia and Herzegovina, 1916, Overprinted in Black or Red:

a

b

1918 Unwmk. *Perf. 12½, 13*

1LJ1	D2 (a)	2h red	.20	.20
1LJ2	D2 (b)	4h red	.25	.65
1LJ3	D2 (a)	5h red	.20	.20
1LJ4	D2 (b)	6h red	.30	.40
1LJ5	D2 (a)	10h red	.20	.20
1LJ6	D2 (b)	15h red	4.00	4.75
1LJ7	D2 (a)	20h red	.20	.20
1LJ8	D2 (b)	25h red	.25	.70
1LJ9	D2 (a)	30h red	.25	.70
1LJ10	D2 (b)	40h red	.20	.20
1LJ11	D2 (a)	50h red	.50	.80

c

d

1LJ12	D2 (c)	1k dark blue (R)	.25	.25
1LJ13	D2 (d)	3k dark blue (R)	.20	.20
		Nos. 1LJ1-1LJ13 (13)	7.00	9.45

Nos. 1LJ1-1LJ13 exist with overprint double or inverted. Value $3 to $7.

Nos. 1LJ1-1LJ11 exist with type "b" overprint instead of type "a," and vice versa. Value, each $10.

Stamps of Bosnia and Herzegovina, 1900-04, Surcharged

e

f

1919

1LJ14 A2 (e) 2h on 35h blue .25 1.10
1LJ15 A2 (e) 5h on 45h grnsh bl .40 .85
1LJ16 A2 (f) 10h on 10 red .20 .20
1LJ17 A2 (e) 15h on 40h org .20 .80
1LJ18 A2 (f) 20h on 5h green .20 .20
1LJ19 A2 (e) 25h on 20h pink .20 .50
1LJ20 A2 (f) 30h on 30h bis brn .20 .45
1LJ21 A2 (e) 1k on 50h red lil .20 .20
1LJ22 A2 (e) 3k on 25h blue .20 .30

Postage Due Stamps of Bosnia and Herzegovina, 1904 Surcharged:

g

h

1LJ23 D1 (g) 40h on 6h blk, red & yel .20 .20
1LJ24 D1 (h) 50h on 8h blk, red & yel .20 .20
1LJ25 D1 (h) 200h blk, red & grn 2.50 2.50
1LJ26 D1 (h) 4k on 7h blk, red & yel .20 .30
Nos. 1LJ14-1LJ26 (13) 5.15 7.80

Nos. 1LJ14-1LJ26 exist with overprint double or inverted. Value, $3 to $6.

CROATIA-SLAVONIA

Stamps of Hungary Overprinted in Blue

A1

1918 **Wmk. 137** ***Perf. 15***

On Stamps of 1913

2L1 A1 6f olive green 1.10 2.00
2L2 A1 50f lake, *blue* .85 1.75

A2

A3

On Stamps of 1916

2L3 A2 10f violet 20.00 27.50
2L4 A3 15f red 20.00 27.50

A4

On Hungary Nos. 106-107 White Numerals

2L4A A4 10f rose 240.00 300.00
2L5 A4 15f violet 22.50 27.50
a. Inverted overprint *125.00*

On Stamps of 1916-18 Colored Numerals

2L6 A4 2f brown orange .20 .20
2L7 A4 3f red lilac .20 .20
2L8 A4 5f green .20 .20
2L9 A4 6f greenish blue .20 .25
2L10 A4 10f rose red 1.60 2.75
2L11 A4 15f violet .20 .20
2L12 A4 20f gray brown .20 .30
2L13 A4 25f dull blue .20 .20
2L14 A4 35f brown .20 .20
2L15 A4 40f olive green .20 .45

The overprints and surcharges for Croatia-Slavonia exist inverted, double, double inverted, in wrong colors, on wrong stamps, on back, in pairs with one lacking overprint, etc.

A5

A6

2L16 A5 50f red vio & lilac .20 .20
2L17 A5 75f brt bl & pale bl .20 .25
2L18 A5 80f grn & pale grn .20 .20
2L19 A6 1k red brown & cl .20 .20
2L20 A6 2k olive brn & bis .20 .20
2L21 A6 3k dark vio & ind .40 1.00
2L22 A6 5k dk brn & lt brn 2.00 4.00
2L23 A6 10k vio brn & vio 7.50 14.00

Stamps of Hungary Overprinted in Blue, Black or Red

A7

A8

2L24 A7 10f scarlet (Bl) .20 .20
2L25 A7 20f dark brown (Bk) .20 .20
2L26 A7 25f deep blue (R) .80 2.50
2L27 A8 40f olive green (Bl) .20 .20
Nos. 2L6-2L27 (22) 15.70 28.10

Many other stamps of the 1913-18 issues of Hungary, the Semi-Postal Stamps of 1915-16 and Postage Due Stamps were surreptitiously overprinted but were never sold through the post office.

Freedom of Croatia-Slavonia
A9

1918 **Unwmk.** **Litho.** ***Perf. 11½***

2L28 A9 10f rose 1.00 1.00
2L29 A9 20f violet 1.25 1.25
2L30 A9 25f blue 2.50 2.50
2L31 A9 45f greenish blk 24.00 24.00
Nos. 2L28-2L31 (4) 28.75 28.75

Independence of Croatia, Slavonia and Dalmatia.

#2L28-2L31 exist imperforate, but were not officially issued in this condition.

Excellent counterfeits of #2L28-2L31 exist.

Allegory of Freedom
A10

Youth with Standard
A11

Falcon, Symbol of Liberty — A12

1919 ***Perf. 11½***

2L32 A10 2f brn orange .20 .20
2L33 A10 3f violet .20 .20
2L34 A10 5f green .20 .20
2L35 A11 10f red .20 .20
2L36 A11 20f black brown .20 .20
2L37 A11 25f deep blue .20 .20
2L38 A11 45f dark ol grn .20 .20
2L39 A12 1k carmine rose .20 .20
2L40 A12 3k dark violet .35 .35
2L41 A12 5k deep brown .85 .70
Nos. 2L32-2L41 (10) 2.80 2.65

Perf. 12½

2L32a A10 2f 1.25 1.25
2L33a A10 3f 1.25 1.25
2L34a A10 5f 40.00 52.50
2L35a A11 10f .35 .35
2L36a A11 20f .30 .25
Nos. 2L32a-2L36a (5) 43.15 55.60

#2L32-2L41 exist imperf. Value, set $25.

SEMI-POSTAL STAMPS ISSUES FOR CROATIA-SLAVONIA

SP1

SP2

SP3

1918 **Wmk. 137** ***Perf. 15***

2LB1 SP1 10f + 2f rose red .30 *2.75*
2LB2 SP2 15f + 2f dull violet .20 *.40*
2LB3 SP3 40f + 2f brn carmine .20 *.85*
Nos. 2LB1-2LB3 (3) .70 *4.00*

SPECIAL DELIVERY STAMP ISSUE FOR CROATIA-SLAVONIA

SD1

Hungary No. E1 Overprinted in Black

1918 **Wmk. 137** ***Perf. 15***

2LE1 SD1 2f gray green & red .20 .20

POSTAGE DUE STAMPS ISSUES FOR CROATIA-SLAVONIA

D1

Postage Due Stamps of Hungary Overprinted in Blue

1918 **Wmk. Crown (136)** ***Perf. 15***

2LJ1 D1 50f green & blk 175.00 175.00

Wmk. Double Cross (137)

2LJ2 D1 1f green & red 6.25 6.25
a. Inverted overprint 22.50 22.50
2LJ3 D1 2f green & red .75 .75
2LJ4 D1 10f green & red .55 .55
2LJ5 D1 12f green & red 25.00 25.00
2LJ6 D1 15f green & red .45 .45
2LJ7 D1 20f green & red .45 .45
2LJ8 D1 30f green & red 1.10 1.10
2LJ9 D1 50f green & blk 7.75 7.75
Nos. 2LJ2-2LJ9 (8) 42.30 42.30

NEWSPAPER STAMPS ISSUES FOR CROATIA-SLAVONIA

N1

N2

Hungary No. P8 Overprinted in Black

1918 **Wmk. 137** ***Imperf.***

2LP1 N1 (2f) orange .20 .30

1919 **Litho.** **Unwmk.**

2LP2 N2 2f yellow .20 .50

SLOVENIA

Chain Breaker
A1 A2

3, 5, 10, 15f: Chain on right wrist is short, extending only about half way to the frame.

10f: Numerals are 8½mm high.

20, 25, 30, 40f: Distant mountains show faintly between legs of male figure.

40f: Numerals 7mm high. The upright strokes of the "4" extend to the same height; the "0" is 3mm wide.

1919 **Unwmk.** ***Perf. 11½***

Lithographed at Ljubljana Fine Impression

3L1 A1 3f violet .20 .20
3L2 A1 5f green .20 .20
3L3 A1 10f carmine rose .20 .20
3L4 A1 15f blue .20 .20
3L5 A2 20f brown .20 .20
3L6 A2 25f blue .20 .20
3L7 A2 30f lilac rose .20 .20
3L8 A2 40f bister .20 .20
Nos. 3L1-3L8 (8) 1.60 1.60

Various stamps of this series exist imperforate and part perforate. Many shades exist.

See Nos. 3L9-3L17, 3L24-3L28. For surcharges see Nos. 3LJ15-3LJ32.

Allegories of Freedom
A3 A4

King Peter I — A5

3, 5, 15f: The chain on the right wrist touches the bottom tablet.

10f: Numerals are 7½mm high.

15f: Curled end of loin cloth appears above letter "H" in the bottom tablet.

20, 25, 30, 40f: The outlines of the mountains have been redrawn and they are more distinct than on the lithographed stamps.

40f: Numerals 8mm high. The left slanting stroke of the "4" extends much higher than the main vertical stroke. The "0" is 2½mm wide and encloses a much narrower space than on the lithographed stamp.

1919-20 ***Perf. 11½***

Typographed at Ljubljana and Vienna

Coarse Impression

3L9	A1	3f violet	.20	.20
3L10	A1	5f green	.20	.20
3L11	A1	10f red	.20	.20
3L12	A1	15f blue	.20	.20
3L13	A2	20f brown	.20	.20
3L14	A2	25f blue	.20	.20
3L15	A2	30f carmine rose	.20	.20
3L16	A2	30f dp red	2.75	.90
3L17	A2	40f orange	.25	.20
3L18	A3	50f green	.30	.20
a.		50f dark green	.30	.20
b.		50f olive green	3.50	1.10
3L19	A3	60f dark blue	.50	.20
a.		60f violet blue	.85	.20
3L20	A4	1k vermilion	.30	.20
a.		1k red orange	.45	.20
3L21	A4	2k blue	.30	.20
a.		2k dull ultramarine	.90	.20
3L22	A5	5k brown lake	.45	.20
a.		5k lake	12.00	1.60
b.		5k dull red	.60	.20
3L23	A5	10k deep ultra	2.75	.90
		Nos. 3L9-3L23 (15)	9.00	4.40

Nos. 3L9-3L23 exist imperf. Value, set $90.
Many of the series exist part perforate.
Many shades exist of lower values.
See Nos. 3L29-3L32, 3L40-3L41.

Serrate Roulette 13½

3L24	A1	5f light grn	.20	.20
3L25	A1	10f carmine	.20	.20
3L26	A1	15f slate blue	.20	.20
3L27	A2	20f dark brown	.30	.20
a.		Serrate x straight roul.	.55	.20
3L28	A2	30f car rose	.20	.20
a.		Serrate x straight roul.	.60	.20
3L29	A3	50f green	.30	.20
3L30	A3	60f dark blue	.45	.20
a.		60f violet blue	2.25	1.10
3L31	A4	1k vermilion	.65	.20
a.		1k rose red	.60	.20
3L32	A4	2k blue	13.00	1.50
		Nos. 3L24-3L32 (9)	15.50	3.10

Roulette x Perf. 11½

3L24a	A1	5f	125.00	140.00
3L25a	A1	10f	45.00	47.50
3L26a	A1	15f	140.00	150.00
3L28b	A2	30f	45.00	47.50
3L29a	A3	50f	5.25	4.00
3L30b	A3	60f	45.00	47.50
3L31b	A4	1k	45.00	47.50

Thick Wove Paper

1920 **Litho.** ***Perf. 11½***

3L40	A5	15k gray green	4.00	5.25
3L41	A5	20k dull violet	1.00	2.00

On Nos. 3L40-3L41 the horizontal lines have been removed from the value tablets. They are printed over a background of pale brown wavy lines.

Chain Breaker A7

Freedom A8

King Peter I — A9

Dinar Values:
Type I — Size: 21x30½mm.
Type II — Size: 22x32½mm.

Thin to Thick Wove Paper

1920 ***Serrate Roulette 13½***

3L42	A7	5p olive green	.20	.20
3L43	A7	10p green	.20	.20
3L44	A7	15p brown	.20	.20
3L45	A7	20p carmine	.75	1.00
3L46	A7	25p chocolate	.30	.30
3L47	A8	40p dark violet	.20	.20
3L48	A8	45p yellow	.20	.20
3L49	A8	50p dark blue	.20	.20
3L50	A8	60p red brown	.20	.20
3L51	A9	1d dark brown (I)	.20	.20

Perf. 11½

3L52	A9	2d gray vio (II)	.20	.20
3L53	A9	4d grnsh black (I)	.30	.30
3L54	A9	6d olive brn (II)	.20	.25
3L55	A9	10d brown red (II)	.30	.35
		Nos. 3L42-3L55 (14)	3.65	4.00

The 2d and 6d have a background of pale red wavy lines, the 10d of gray lines.
Counterfeits exist of No. 3L45.

POSTAGE DUE STAMPS ISSUES FOR SLOVENIA

D1

1919 **Litho.** **Unwmk.** ***Perf. 11½***

Ljubljana Print

Numerals 9½mm high

3LJ1	D1	5f carmine	.20	.20
3LJ2	D1	10f carmine	.20	.20
3LJ3	D1	20f carmine	.20	.20
3LJ4	D1	50f carmine	.20	.20

Nos. 3LJ1-3LJ4 were also printed in scarlet and dark red.

Numerals 8mm high

3LJ5	D1	1k dark blue	.45	.30
3LJ6	D1	5k dark blue	.65	.50
3LJ7	D1	10k dark blue	.90	.75
		Nos. 3LJ1-3LJ7 (7)	2.80	2.35

1920

Vienna Print

Numerals 11 to 12 mm high

3LJ8	D1	5f red	.20	.20
3LJ9	D1	10f red	.20	.20
3LJ10	D1	20f red	.20	.20
3LJ11	D1	50f red	1.25	.85

Numerals 7mm high

3LJ12	D1	1k Prussian blue	1.10	.70
a.		1k dark blue	5.00	4.50
3LJ13	D1	5k Prussian blue	1.60	1.25
a.		5k dark blue	8.00	6.75
3LJ14	D1	10k Prussian blue	3.75	3.25
a.		10k dark blue	14.00	15.00
		Nos. 3LJ8-3LJ14 (7)	8.30	6.65

Nos. 3LJ8-3LJ14 exist imperf. Value, set $40.

No. 3L4 Surcharged in Red

1920 ***Perf. 11½***

On Litho. Stamps

3LJ15	A1	5p on 15f blue	.20	.20
3LJ16	A1	10p on 15f blue	.60	.60
3LJ17	A1	20p on 15f blue	.20	.20
3LJ18	A1	50p on 15f blue	.20	.20
		Nos. 3LJ15-3LJ18 (4)	1.20	1.20

Nos. 3L7, 3L12, 3L26, 3L28, 3L28a Surcharged in Dark Blue

3LJ19	A2	1d on 30f lil rose	.20	.20
3LJ20	A2	3d on 30f lil rose	.20	.20
3LJ21	A2	8d on 30f lil rose	1.10	.60
		Nos. 3LJ19-3LJ21 (3)	1.50	1.00

On Typographed Stamps

Perf. 11½

3LJ22	A1	5p on 15f pale bl	12.00	2.50
3LJ23	A1	10p on 15f pale bl	27.50	22.50
3LJ24	A1	20p on 15f pale bl	11.00	4.00
3LJ25	A1	50p on 15f pale bl	6.00	7.00
		Nos. 3LJ22-3LJ25 (4)	56.50	36.00

Serrate Roulette 13½

3LJ26	A1	5p on 15f slate bl	2.75	.50
3LJ27	A1	10p on 15f slate bl	8.50	3.25
3LJ28	A1	20p on 15f slate bl	2.75	.50
3LJ29	A1	50p on 15f slate bl	2.75	.50
3LJ30	A2	1d on 30f dp rose	2.75	.65
a.		Serrate x straight roulette	7.00	4.50
3LJ31	A2	3d on 30f dp rose	5.75	1.75
a.		Serrate x straight roulette	8.00	5.50
3LJ32	A2	8d on 30f dp rose	95.00	6.50
a.		Serrate x straight roulette	90.00	7.50
		Nos. 3LJ26-3LJ32 (7)	120.25	13.65

The para surcharges were printed in sheets of 100, ten horizontal rows of ten. There were: 5p three rows, 10p one row, 20p three rows, 50p three rows. The dinar surcharges were in a setting of 50, arranged in vertical rows of five. There were: 1d five rows, 3d three rows, 8d two rows.

NEWSPAPER STAMPS ISSUES FOR SLOVENIA

Eros — N1

2 4 6 10

1919 **Unwmk.** **Litho.** ***Imperf.***

Ljubljana Print

3LP1	N1	2f gray	.20	.20
3LP2	N1	4f gray	.20	.20
3LP3	N1	6f gray	3.25	4.00
3LP4	N1	10f gray	.20	.20
3LP5	N1	30f gray	.20	.20
		Nos. 3LP1-3LP5 (5)	4.05	4.80

See Nos. 3LP6-3LP13. For surcharges see Nos. 3LP14-3LP23, 4LB1-4LB5.

2 4 6 10

1920

Vienna Print

3LP6	N1	2f gray	.20	.20
3LP7	N1	4f gray	6.50	10.00
3LP8	N1	6f gray	1.75	2.75
3LP9	N1	10f gray	14.00	21.00
3LP10	N1	2f blue	.20	.30
3LP11	N1	4f blue	.20	.20
3LP12	N1	6f blue	90.00	110.00
3LP13	N1	10f blue	.20	.20
		Nos. 3LP6-3LP13 (8)	113.05	144.65

Nos. 3LP1, 3LP10 Surcharged:

a

b

On Ljubljana Print

3LP14	N1 (a)	2p on 2f gray	.25	.40
3LP15	N1 (a)	4p on 2f gray	.25	.40
3LP16	N1 (a)	6p on 2f gray	.40	.65
3LP17	N1 (b)	10p on 2f gray	.65	.80
3LP18	N1 (b)	30p on 2f gray	.65	.85

On Vienna Print

3LP19	N1 (a)	2p on 2f blue	.20	.20
3LP20	N1 (a)	4p on 2f blue	.20	.20
3LP21	N1 (a)	6p on 2f blue	.20	.20
3LP22	N1 (b)	10p on 2f blue	.20	.20
3LP23	N1 (b)	30p on 2f blue	.20	.25
		Nos. 3LP14-3LP23 (10)	3.20	4.15

The five surcharges were arranged in a setting of 100, in horizontal rows of ten. There were: 2p three rows, 4p three rows, 6p two rows, 10p one row and 30p one row. The sheets were perforated 11½ horizontally between the groups of the different values.

SEMI-POSTAL STAMPS ISSUE FOR CARINTHIA PLEBISCITE

SP1

Nos. 3LP2, 3LP1 Surcharged With Various Designs in Dark Red

1920

4LB1	SP1	5p on 4f gray	.20	.20
4LB2	SP1	15p on 4f gray	.20	.20
4LB3	SP1	25p on 4f gray	.20	.20
4LB4	SP1	45p on 2f gray	.20	.20
4LB5	SP1	50p on 2f gray	.20	.20
4LB6	SP1	2d on 2f gray	1.25	1.60
		Nos. 4LB1-4LB6 (6)	2.25	2.60

Nos. 4LB1 to 4LB6 have a different surcharge on each stamp but each includes the letters "K.G.C.A." which signify Carinthian Governmental Commission, Zone A.
Sold at three times face value for the benefit of the Plebiscite Propaganda Fund.

GENERAL ISSUES

For Use throughout the Kingdom

King Alexander — A1

King Peter I — A2

Unwmk.

1921, Jan. 16 **Engr.** ***Perf. 12***

1	A1	2p olive brown	.20	.20
2	A1	5p deep green	.20	.20
3	A1	10p carmine	.20	.20
4	A1	15p violet	.20	.20
5	A1	20p black	.20	.20
6	A1	25p dark blue	.20	.20
7	A1	50p olive green	.20	.20
8	A1	60p vermilion	.20	.20
9	A1	75p purple	.20	.20
10	A2	1d orange	.20	.20
11	A2	2d olive bister	.25	.20
12	A2	4d dark green	.40	.20
13	A2	5d carmine rose	2.00	.20
14	A2	10d red brown	4.00	.55
		Nos. 1-14 (14)	8.65	3.15

Exist imperf. Value, set $22.50.
For surcharge see No. 27.

Nos. B1-B3 Surcharged in Black, Brown, Green or Blue:

a

b

1922-24

15	SP1(a)	1d on 10p	.20	.20
16	SP2(b)	1d on 15p ('24)	.20	.20
17	SP3(a)	1d on 25p (Br)	.20	.20
18	SP2(b)	3d on 15p (G)	.80	.20
a.		Blue surcharge	1.90	.20
19	SP2(b)	8d on 15p (G)	1.40	.20
a.		Double surcharge	32.50	30.00
b.		9d on 15p (error)	100.00	
20	SP2(b)	20d on 15p	6.50	1.00
21	SP2(b)	30d on 15p (Bl)	13.50	2.50
		Nos. 15-21 (7)	22.80	4.50

A3

1923, Jan. 23 **Engr.**

22	A3	1d red brown	.65	.20
23	A3	5d carmine	3.25	.20
24	A3	8d violet	6.25	.25
25	A3	20d green	16.00	.75
26	A3	30d red orange	42.50	2.00
		Nos. 22-26 (5)	68.65	3.40

For surcharge see No. 28.

Nos. 8 and 24 Surcharged in Black or Blue

1924, Feb. 18

27	A1	20p on 60p ver	.25	.20
28	A3	5d on 8d violet (Bl)	4.75	.60

The color of the surcharge on No. 28 varies, including blue, blue black, greenish black and black.

A4

A5

1924, July 1 ***Perf. 14***

29	A4	20p black	.90	.20
30	A4	50p dark brown	.90	.20
31	A4	1d carmine	.35	.20
32	A4	2d myrtle green	.75	.20
33	A4	3d ultramarine	.60	.20
34	A4	5d orange brown	2.50	.20
35	A5	10d dark violet	8.50	.20
36	A5	15d olive green	5.00	.20
37	A5	20d vermilion	4.50	.20
38	A5	30d dark green	4.50	1.10
		Nos. 29-38 (10)	28.50	2.90

No. 33 Surcharged

1925, June 5

39	A4	25p on 3d ultramarine	.20	.20
40	A4	50p on 3d ultramarine	.20	.20

King Alexander
A6 A7

1926-27 **Typo.** ***Perf. 13***

41	A6	25p deep green	.20	.20
42	A6	50p olive brown	.20	.20
43	A6	1d scarlet	.30	.20
44	A6	2d slate black	.30	.20
45	A6	3d slate blue	.40	.20
46	A6	4d red orange	2.00	.20
47	A6	5d violet	1.50	.20
48	A6	8d black brown	3.75	.20
49	A6	10d olive brown	3.50	.20
50	A6	15d brown ('27)	6.75	.20
51	A6	20d dark vio ('27)	8.25	.20
52	A6	30d orange ('27)	25.00	.45
		Nos. 41-52 (12)	52.15	2.65

For overprints and surcharges see Nos. 53-62, 87-101, B5-B16.

Semi-Postal Stamps of 1926 Overprinted over the Red Surcharge

1928, July

53	A6	1d scarlet	1.25	.20
a.		Surcharge "0.50" inverted		
54	A6	2d black	4.00	.20
55	A6	3d deep blue	3.00	.35
56	A6	4d red orange	9.25	.40
57	A6	5d bright vio	3.00	.20
58	A6	8d black brown	4.50	.65
59	A6	10d olive brown	6.00	.20
60	A6	15d brown	35.00	2.00
61	A6	20d violet	18.00	2.00
62	A6	30d orange	40.00	4.00
		Nos. 53-62 (10)	124.00	10.20

With Imprint at Foot

1931-34 ***Perf. 12½***

63	A7	25p black	.70	.20
64	A7	50p green	.60	.20
65	A7	75p slate green	.20	.20
66	A7	1d red	.65	.20
67	A7	1.50d pink	.30	.20
68	A7	1.75d dp rose ('34)	.55	.35
69	A7	3d slate blue	3.50	.20
70	A7	3.50d ultra ('34)	1.10	.25
71	A7	4d deep orange	2.00	.20
72	A7	5d purple	2.00	.20
73	A7	10d dark olive	5.50	.20
74	A7	15d deep brown	5.50	.20
75	A7	20d dark violet	9.25	.20
76	A7	30d rose	6.00	.45
		Nos. 63-76 (14)	37.85	3.25

Type of 1931 Issue Without Imprint at Foot

1932-33

77	A7	25p black	.20	.20
78	A7	50p green	.30	.20
79	A7	1d red	.65	.20
80	A7	3d slate bl ('33)	1.60	.20
81	A7	4d deep org ('33)	3.50	.20
82	A7	5d purple ('33)	5.25	.20
83	A7	10d dk olive ('33)	17.00	.20
84	A7	15d deep brn ('33)	21.00	.20
85	A7	20d dark vio ('33)	32.50	.20
86	A7	30d rose ('33)	37.50	.35
		Nos. 77-86 (10)	119.50	2.15

See Nos. 102-115.

ЈУГОСЛАВИЈА

Nos. 41 to 52 Overprinted

JUGOSLAVIJA

1933, Sept. 5 ***Perf. 13***

87	A6	25p deep green	.20	.20
88	A6	50p olive brown	.20	.20
89	A6	1d scarlet	.40	.20
90	A6	2d slate black	1.75	.70
91	A6	3d slate blue	1.60	.20
92	A6	4d red orange	1.10	.20
93	A6	5d violet	1.60	.20
94	A6	8d black brown	4.75	1.00
95	A6	10d olive brown	6.75	.20
96	A6	15d brown	8.25	1.75
97	A6	20d dark violet	15.00	.50
98	A6	30d orange	13.00	.65
		Nos. 87-98 (12)	54.60	6.00

Semi-Postal Stamps of 1926 Overprinted like Nos. 87 to 98 and Four Bars over the Red Surcharge of 1926

1933, Sept. 5

99	A6	25p green	.50	.20
100	A6	50p olive brown	.60	.20
101	A6	1d scarlet	1.25	.40
		Nos. 99-101 (3)	2.35	.80

Nos. 99-101 exist with double impression of bars. Value, each $5.50 unused, $4.50 used.

King Alexander Memorial Issue
Type of 1931-34 Issues
Borders in Black

1934, Oct. 17

102	A7	25p black	.20	.20
103	A7	50p green	.20	.20
104	A7	75p slate green	.20	.20
105	A7	1d red	.20	.20
106	A7	1.50d pink	.20	.20
107	A7	1.75d deep rose	.20	.20
108	A7	3d slate blue	.20	.20
109	A7	3.50d ultramarine	.25	.20
110	A7	4d deep orange	.40	.20
111	A7	5d purple	.45	.20
112	A7	10d dark olive	1.90	.20
113	A7	15d deep brown	3.25	.20
114	A7	20d dark violet	5.00	.20
115	A7	30d rose	3.25	.20
		Nos. 102-115 (14)	15.90	2.80

Cyrillic Characters

Latin and Cyrillic inscriptions are transposed within some sets. In some sets some stamps are inscribed in Latin, others in Cyrillic. This will be mentioned only if it is necessary to identify otherwise identical stamps.

King Peter II — A10

1935-36 ***Perf. 13x12½***

116	A10	25p brown black	.20	.20
117	A10	50p yel orange	.20	.20
118	A10	75p turq green	.20	.20
119	A10	1d brown red	.20	.20
120	A10	1.50d scarlet	.20	.20
121	A10	1.75d cerise	.20	.20
122	A10	2d magenta ('36)	.20	.20
123	A10	3d brn orange	.20	.20
124	A10	3.50d ultramarine	.20	.20
125	A10	4d yellow grn	.75	.20
126	A10	4d slate blue ('36)	.20	.20
127	A10	10d bright vio	.35	.20
128	A10	15d brown	.60	.20
129	A10	20d bright blue	2.25	.20
130	A10	30d rose pink	1.50	.20
		Nos. 116-130 (15)	7.45	3.00

For overprints see Nos. N12, 14, N29.

King Alexander — A11

Nikola Tesla — A12

1935, Oct. 9 ***Perf. 12½x11½, 11½***

131	A11	75p turq green	.20	.20
132	A11	1.50d scarlet	.20	.20
133	A11	1.75d dark brown	.70	1.00
134	A11	3.50d ultramarine	.70	1.00
135	A11	7.50d rose carmine	.70	1.00
		Nos. 131-135 (5)	2.50	3.40

Death of King Alexander, 1st anniv.

1936, May 28 **Litho.** ***Perf. 12½x11½***

136	A12	75p yel grn & dk brn	.20	.20
137	A12	1.75d dull blue & indigo	.25	.20

80th birthday of Nikola Tesla (1856-1943), electrical inventor.

Memorial Church, Oplenac — A13

Coats of Arms of Yugoslavia, Greece, Romania and Turkey — A14

1937, July 1

138	A13	3d Prussian grn	.60	.20
a.		Perf. 12½	7.25	5.00
139	A13	4d dark blue	.60	.20

"Little Entente," 16th anniversary.

Perf. 11, 11½, 12½

1937, Oct. 29 **Photo.**

140	A14	3d peacock grn	.35	.20
141	A14	4d ultramarine	.45	.30

Balkan Entente.

King Peter II — A16

1939-40 **Typo.** ***Perf. 12½***

142	A16	25p black ('40)	.20	.20
143	A16	50p orange ('40)	.20	.20
144	A16	1d yellow grn	.20	.20
145	A16	1.50d red	.20	.20
146	A16	2d dp mag ('40)	.20	.20
147	A16	3d dull red brn	.20	.20
148	A16	4d ultra	.20	.20
148A	A16	5d dk blue ('40)	.20	.20
148B	A16	5.50d dk vio brn ('40)	.20	.20
149	A16	6d slate blue	.40	.20
150	A16	8d sepia	.40	.20
151	A16	12d bright vio	.70	.20
152	A16	16d dull violet	1.00	.20
153	A16	20d blue ('40)	1.00	.20
154	A16	30d brt pink ('40)	2.25	.30
		Nos. 142-154 (15)	7.55	3.10

For overprints and surcharges see Nos. N1-N11, N13, N15-N28, N30-N35, Croatia 1-25.

Arms of Yugoslavia, Greece, Romania and Turkey
A17 A18

1940, June 1

155	A17	3d ultramarine	.65	.35
156	A18	3d ultramarine	.65	.35
a.		Pair, #155-156	2.50	2.50
157	A17	4d dark blue	.65	.35
158	A18	4d dark blue	.65	.35
a.		Pair, #157-158	2.50	2.50
		Nos. 155-158 (4)	2.60	1.40

Balkan Entente.

Bridge at Obod A19

1940, Sept. 29 **Litho.**

159	A19	5.50d slate grn & dull grn	1.50	1.75

Zagreb Phil. Exhib.; 500th anniv. of Johann Gutenberg's invention of printing. The first press in the Yugoslav area was located at Obod in 1493.

SEMI-POSTAL STAMPS

Giving Succor to Wounded SP1

Wounded Soldier SP2

Symbolical of National Unity — SP3

Unwmk.

1921, Jan. 30 **Engr.** ***Perf. 12***

B1 SP1 10p carmine .20 .20
B2 SP2 15p violet brown .20 .20
B3 SP3 25p light blue .20 .20
Nos. B1-B3 (3) .60 .60

Nos. B1-B3 were sold at double face value, the excess being for the benefit of invalid soldiers.

For surcharges see Nos. 15-21.

This overprint was applied to 500,000 copies of No. B1 in 1923 and they were given to the Society for Wounded Invalids (Uprava Ratnih Invalida) which sold them for 2d apiece. These overprinted stamps had no franking power, but some were used through ignorance.

Regular Issue of 1926-27 Surcharged in Dark Red

1926, Nov. 1 ***Perf. 13***

B5 A6 25p + 25p green .20 .20
B6 A6 50p + 50p olive brn .20 .20
B7 A6 1d + 50p scarlet .20 .20
B8 A6 2d + 50p black .60 .20
B9 A6 3d + 50p slate blue .50 .20
B10 A6 4d + 50p red org 1.40 .20
B11 A6 5d + 50p brt vio .75 .20
B12 A6 8d + 50p black brn 1.90 .60
B13 A6 10d + 1d olive brn 1.75 .60
B14 A6 15d + 1d brown 5.00 1.00
B15 A6 20d + 1d dark vio 4.50 .75
B16 A6 30d + 1d orange 15.00 1.90
a. Double surcharge
Nos. B5-B16 (12) 32.00 6.25

The surtax on these stamps was intended for a fund for relief of sufferers from floods.

For overprints see Nos. 99-101.

Cathedral at Duvno SP4

King Tomislav SP6

Kings Tomislav and Alexander SP5

Perf. 12½, 11½x12

1929, Nov. 1 **Typo.**

B17 SP4 50p (+ 50p) olive green .20 .20
B18 SP5 1d (+ 50p) red .20 .20
B19 SP6 3d (+ 1d) blue 1.25 1.10
Nos. B17-B19 (3) 1.65 1.50

Millenary of the Croatian kingdom. The surtax was used to create a War Memorial Cemetery in France and to erect a monument to Serbian soldiers who died there.

View of Dobropolje SP7

War Memorial — SP8

View of Kajmaktchalan SP9

1931, Apr. 1 ***Perf. 12½, 11½***

B20 SP7 50p + 50p blue grn .20 .20
B21 SP8 1d + 1d scarlet .20 .20
B22 SP9 3d + 3d deep blue .20 .20
Nos. B20-B22 (3) .60 .60

The surtax was added to a fund for a War Memorial to Serbian soldiers who died in France during World War I.

SP10

SP12

SP11

Black Overprint

1931, Nov. 1 ***Perf. 12½, 11½x12***

B23 SP10 50p (+ 50p) olive grn .20 *.20*
B24 SP11 1d (+ 50p) red .20 *.20*
B25 SP12 3d (+ 1d) blue .20 *.20*
Nos. B23-B25 (3) .60 *.60*

Surtax for War Memorial fund.

Rower on Danube at Smederevo SP13

Bled Lake SP14

Danube near Belgrade SP15

View of Split Harbor SP16

Zagreb Cathedral — SP17

Prince Peter — SP18

1932, Sept. 2 **Litho.** ***Perf. 11½***

B26 SP13 75p + 50p dl grn & lt blue .40 1.00
B27 SP14 1d + ½d scar & lt blue .40 1.10
B28 SP15 1½d + ½d rose & green .40 1.10
B29 SP16 3d + 1d bl & lt bl .80 2.00
B30 SP17 4d + 1d red org & lt blue 4.00 10.00
B31 SP18 5d + 1d dl vio & lilac 4.00 8.50
Nos. B26-B31 (6) 10.00 23.70

European Rowing Championship Races, Belgrade.

King Alexander SP19

Prince Peter SP20

1933, May 25 **Typo.** ***Perf. 12½***

B32 SP19 50p + 25p black 3.50 5.25
B33 SP19 75p + 25p yel grn 3.50 5.25
B34 SP19 1.50d + 50p rose 3.50 5.25
B35 SP19 3d + 1d bl vio 3.50 5.25
B36 SP19 4p + 1d dk grn 3.50 5.25
B37 SP19 5d + 1d orange 3.50 5.25
Nos. B32-B37 (6) 21.00 31.50

11th Intl. Congress of P.E.N. (Poets, Editors and Novelists) Clubs, Dubrovnik, May 25-27.

The labels at the foot of the stamps are printed in either Cyrillic or Latin letters and each bears the amount of a premium for the benefit of the local P.E.N. Club at Dubrovnik.

1933, June 28

B38 SP20 75p + 25p slate grn .20 .25
B39 SP20 1½d + ½d deep red .20 .25

60th anniv. meeting of the National Sokols (Sports Associations) at Ljubljana, July 1.

Eagle Soaring over City SP22

Athlete and Eagle SP23

1934, June 1 ***Perf. 12½***

B40 SP22 75p + 25p green 1.75 1.10
B41 SP22 1.50d + 50p car 3.50 1.60
B42 SP22 1.75d + 25p brown 5.50 2.25
Nos. B40-B42 (3) 10.75 4.95

20th anniversary of Sokols of Sarajevo.

1934, June 1

B43 SP23 75p + 25p Prus grn 1.60 .90
B44 SP23 1.50d + 50p car 3.50 1.75
B45 SP23 1.75d + 25p choc 5.50 2.50
Nos. B43-B45 (3) 10.60 5.15

60th anniversary of Sokols of Zagreb.

Mother and Children
SP24 SP25

Perf. 12½x11½

1935, Dec. 25 **Photo.**

B46 SP24 1.50d + 1d dk brn & brown .70 .55
a. Perf. 11½ 11.50 11.50
B47 SP25 3.50d + 1.50d bright ultra & bl 1.25 1.00

The surtax was for "Winter Help."

Queen Mother Marie SP26

Prince Regent Paul SP27

1936, May 3 **Litho.**

B48 SP26 75p + 25p grnsh bl .40 .40
B49 SP26 1.50d + 50p rose pink .45 .45
B50 SP26 1.75d + 75p brown .65 .65
B51 SP26 3.50d + 1d brt bl .50 .50
Nos. B48-B51 (4) 2.00 2.00

1936, Sept. 20 **Typo.**

B52 SP27 75p + 50p turq grn & red .20 *4.50*
B53 SP27 1.50d + 50p cer & red .20 *3.00*

Surtax for the Red Cross.

Princes Tomislav and Andrej
SP28 SP29

Perf. 11½x12½, 12½x11½

1937, May 1

B54 SP28 25p + 25p red brn .20 .25
B55 SP28 75p + 75p emerald .20 .30
B56 SP29 1.50d + 1d org red .25 .35
B57 SP29 2d + 1d magenta .25 .35
Nos. B54-B57 (4) .90 1.25

Souvenir Sheet

National Costumes — SP30

1937, Sept. 12 ***Perf. 14***

B57A SP30 Sheet of 4 1.75 2.75
b. 1d blue green .25 .35
c. 1.50d bright violet .25 .35
d. 2d rose red .25 .35
e. 4d dark blue .25 .35

1st Yugoslavian Phil. Exhib., Belgrade. Sold only at the exhibition post office at 15d each.

SP31

SP32

Perf. 11½x12½, 12½x11½

1938, May 1 **Photo.**

B58 SP31 50p + 50p dark brn .25 .30
B59 SP32 1d + 1d dk green .30 .35
B60 SP31 1.50d + 1.50d scar .35 .40
B61 SP32 2d + 2d magenta .40 .45
Nos. B58-B61 (4) 1.30 1.50

Surtax for the benefit of Child Welfare.
For overprints see Nos. B75-B78.

Bridge and Anti-aircraft Lights — SP33

1938, May 28 ***Perf. 11½x12½***

B62 SP33 1d + 50p dk grn .20 .25
B63 SP33 1.50d + 1d scarlet .35 .40
a. Perf. 11½ 17.50 17.50
B64 SP33 2d + 1d rose vio .45 .50
a. Perf. 11½ 16.00 16.00
B65 SP33 3d + 1.50d dp bl .50 .60
Nos. B62-B65 (4) 1.50 1.75

Intl. Aeronautical Exhib., Belgrade.

Cliff at Demir-Kapiya — SP34

Modern Hospital SP35

Runner Carrying Torch — SP36

Alexander I — SP37

Perf. 11½x12½, 12½x11½

1938, Aug. 1

B66 SP34 1d + 1d slate grn & dp grn .45 .55
B67 SP35 1.50d + 1.50d scar .60 .75
B68 SP36 2d + 2d claret & dp rose .75 .85
B69 SP37 3d + 3d dp bl .75 .85
Nos. B66-B69 (4) 2.55 3.00

The surtax was to raise funds to build a hospital for railway employees.

Runner SP38

Shot-Putter SP41

Hurdlers SP39

Pole Vaulter SP40

1938, Sept. 11

B70 SP38 50p + 50p org brn .70 .70
B71 SP39 1d + 1d sl grn & dp grn .90 .90
B72 SP40 1.50d + 1.50d rose & dk mag .90 .90
B73 SP41 2d + 2d dk blue 1.40 1.40
Nos. B70-B73 (4) 3.90 3.90

Ninth Balkan Games.

Stamps of 1938 Overprinted in Black

a

b

1938, Oct. 1

B75 SP31(a) 50p + 50p dk brn .35 .35
B76 SP32(b) 1d + 1d dk grn .35 .35
B77 SP31(a) 1.50d + 1.50d scar .35 .35
B78 SP32(b) 2d + 2d mag .50 .50
Nos. B75-B78 (4) 1.55 1.55

Surtax for the benefit of Child Welfare.

Postriders SP43

1d+1d, Rural mail delivery. 1.50d+1.50d, Mail train. 2d+2d, Mail bus. 4d+4d, Mail plane.

1939, Mar. 15 **Photo.** ***Perf. 11½***

B79 SP43 50p + 50p buff, bis & brown .40 .50
B80 SP43 1d + 1d sl grn & dp green .55 .75
B81 SP43 1.50d + 1.50d red, cop red & brn car .60 .90
B82 SP43 2d + 2d dp plum & rose lilac .70 1.25
B83 SP43 4d + 4d ind & sl bl 1.25 1.60
Nos. B79-B83 (5) 3.50 5.00

Centenary of the present postal system in Yugoslavia. The surtax was used for the Railway Benevolent Association.

The Cyrillic and Latin inscriptions are transposed on Nos. B82 and B83.

Child Eating SP48

Children at Seashore — SP49

Children in Crib — SP51

Boy Planing Board SP50

1939, May 1 ***Perf. 12½***

B84 SP48 1d + 1d blk & dp bl green 1.25 1.40
B85 SP49 1.50d + 1.50d org brn & sal .55 1.25
a. Perf. 11½ 40.00 22.50
B86 SP50 2d + 2d mar & vio rose 1.10 1.40
B87 SP51 4d + 4d ind & royal blue 1.40 1.90
Nos. B84-B87 (4) 4.30 5.95

The surtax was for the benefit of Child Welfare.

Czar Lazar of Serbia — SP52

Milosh Obilich — SP53

1939, June 28 ***Perf. 11½***

B88 SP52 1d + 1d sl grn & bl grn .55 .70
B89 SP53 1.50d + 1.50d mar & brt car .55 .70

Battle of Kosovo, 550th anniversary.

Training Ship "Jadran" SP54

Designs: 1d+50p, Steamship "King Alexander." 1.50d+1d, Freighter "Triglan." 2d+1.50d, Cruiser "Dubrovnik."

1939, Sept. 6 **Engr.**

B90 SP54 50p + 50p brn org .60 .70
B91 SP54 1d + 50p dull grn .80 .95
B92 SP54 1.50d + 1d dp rose .70 .80
B93 SP54 2d + 1.50d dark bl .80 1.10
Nos. B90-B93 (4) 2.90 3.55

Yugoslav Navy and Merchant Marine. The surtax aided a Marine Museum.

Motorcycle and Sidecar — SP58

Motorcycle SP60

Racing Car SP59

Racing Car SP61

1939, Sept. 3 **Photo.**

B94 SP58 50p + 50p multi .55 .60
B95 SP59 1d + 1d multi .60 .70
B96 SP60 1.50d + 1.50d multi .70 .85
B97 SP61 2d + 2d multi 1.25 1.50
Nos. B94-B97 (4) 3.10 3.65

Automobile and Motorcycle Races, Belgrade. The surtax was for the Race Organization and the State Treasury.

Unknown Soldier Memorial SP62

1939, Oct. 9 ***Perf. 12½***

B98 SP62 1d + 50p sl grn & green .60 .85
B99 SP62 1.50d + 1d red & rose red .70 .90
B100 SP62 2d + 1.50d dp cl & vio rose .85 1.00
B101 SP62 3d + 2d dp bl & bl .85 1.00
Nos. B98-B101 (4) 3.00 3.75

Assassination of King Alexander, 5th anniv. The surtax was used to aid World War I invalids.

Postman Delivering Mail — SP64

Postman Emptying Mail Box — SP65

Parcel Post Delivery Wagon SP66

Parcel Post SP67

Repairing Telephone Wires — SP68

1940, Jan. 1

B102	SP64	50p + 50p brn & deep org	.50	.55
B103	SP65	1d + 1d sl grn & blue grn	.55	.70
B104	SP66	1.50d + 1.50d red brn & scar	.70	.85
B105	SP67	2d + 2d dl vio & red lilac	.85	1.40
B106	SP68	4d + 4d sl bl & bl	1.40	1.75
		Nos. B102-B106 (5)	4.00	5.25

The surtax was used for the employees of the Postal System in Belgrade.

Croats' Arrival at Adriatic in 640 SP69

King Tomislav — SP70

Death of Matija Gubec — SP71

Anton and Stjepan Radic SP72

Map of Yugoslavia SP73

1940, Mar. 1 Typo. *Perf. 11½*

B107	SP69	50p + 50p brn org	.25	.30
B108	SP70	1d + 1d green	.25	.30
B109	SP71	1.50d + 1.50d brt red	.30	.30
B110	SP72	2d + 2d dk cerise	.35	.45
B111	SP73	4d + 2d dark blue	.40	.50
		Nos. B107-B111 (5)	1.55	1.85

The surtax was used for the benefit of postal employees in Zagreb.

Children Playing in Snow SP74

Children at Seashore — SP75

1940, May 1 Photo. *Perf. 11½, 12½*

B112	SP74	50p + 50p brn org & org yellow	.25	.30
B113	SP75	1d + 1d sl grn & dk green	.30	.40
B114	SP74	1.50d + 1.50d brn red & scarlet	.25	.30
B115	SP75	2d + 2d mar & vio rose	.35	.45
		Nos. B112-B115 (4)	1.15	1.45

The surtax was for Child Welfare.

Nos. C11-C14 Surcharged in Carmine

Perf. 11½x12½, 12½x11½

1940, Dec. 23

B116	AP6	50p + 50p on 5d	.30	.30
B117	AP7	1d + 1d on 10d	.30	.30
B118	AP8	1.50d + 1.50d on 20d	.35	.45
B119	AP9	2d + 2d on 30d	.35	.45
		Nos. B116-B119 (4)	1.30	1.50

The surtax was used to fight tuberculosis. For surcharges see Nos. NB1-NB4.

AIR POST STAMPS

Dubrovnik AP1

Lake Bled AP2

Falls of Jaice — AP3

Church at Oplenac — AP4

Bridge at Mostar — AP5

Perf. 12½

1934, June 15 Typo. Unwmk.

C1	AP1	50p violet brown	.20	.20
C2	AP2	1d green	.20	.20
C3	AP3	2d rose red	.45	.20
C4	AP4	3d ultramarine	.50	.25
C5	AP5	10d vermilion	1.50	1.40
		Nos. C1-C5 (5)	2.85	2.25

King Alexander Memorial Issue

1935, Jan. 1

Border in Black

C6	AP4	3d ultramarine	1.50	1.25

St. Naum Convent — AP6

Sarajevo AP8

Port of Rab — AP7

Ljubljana AP9

Perf. 12½, 11½x12½, 12½x11½

1937, Sept. 12 Photo.

C7	AP6	50p brown	.20	.20
C8	AP7	1d yellow grn	.20	.20
C9	AP8	2d blue gray	.20	.20
C10	AP9	2.50d rose red	.20	.20
C11	AP6	5d brn violet	.20	.20
C12	AP7	10d brown lake	.20	.20
C13	AP8	20d dark green	.35	.35
C14	AP9	30d ultramarine	.70	.70
		Nos. C7-C14 (8)	2.25	2.25

For surcharges see Nos. B116-B119, NB1-NB4, NC1-NC8.

Cathedral of Zagreb AP10

Bridge at Belgrade AP11

1940, Aug. 15 Litho. *Perf. 12½*

C15	AP10	40d Prus grn & pale green	.95	*1.40*
C16	AP11	50d slate bl & gray bl	1.10	*1.40*

For overprints see Nos. NC9-NC10.

POSTAGE DUE STAMPS

King Alexander — D1

1921 Typo. Unwmk. *Perf. 11½*

Red or Black Surcharge

J1	D1	10p on 5p green (R)	.20	.20
J2	D1	30p on 5p green (Bk)	.20	.20

D2

D3

1921-22 Typo. *Perf. 11½, Rough*

J3	D2	10p rose	.20	.20
J4	D2	30p yellow green	.20	.20
J5	D2	50p violet	.30	.20
J6	D2	1d brown	.35	.20
J7	D2	2d blue	.35	.20
J8	D3	5d orange	7.50	.40
J9	D3	10d violet brown	9.25	.45
a.		Cliche of 10p in sheet of 10d	75.00	*100.00*
J10	D3	25d pink	30.00	2.00
J11	D3	50d green	27.50	1.60
		Nos. J3-J11 (9)	75.65	5.45

1924 *Perf. 9, 10½, 11½, Clean-cut*

J12	D3	10p rose red	.20	.20
J13	D3	30p yellow green	.45	.35
J14	D3	50p violet	.20	.20
J15	D3	1d brown	.35	.20
J16	D3	2d deep blue	.55	.20
J17	D3	5d orange	9.25	.20
J18	D3	10d violet brown	21.00	.20
J19	D3	25d pink	42.50	1.00
J20	D3	50d green	57.50	.85
		Nos. J12-J20 (9)	132.00	3.40

Nos. J19-J20 do not exist perf 9. Nos. J18-J20 do not exist perf 11½.

Nos. J19-J20 Surcharged

1928

J21	D3	10d on 25d pink	3.25	.25
J22	D3	10d on 50d green	3.25	.25
a.		Inverted surcharge	30.00	18.00

A second type of "1" in surcharge has flag projecting horizontally. Value, each $15 unused, $3 used.

Coat of Arms — D4

Numeral of Value — D5

1931 Typo. *Perf. 12½*

With Imprint at Foot

J23	D4	50p violet	1.10	.20
J24	D4	1d deep magenta	2.00	.20
J25	D4	2d deep blue	5.00	.20
J26	D4	5d orange	2.00	.20
J27	D4	10d chocolate	6.75	.70
		Nos. J23-J27 (5)	16.85	1.50

For overprints see Nos. NJ1-NJ13, Croatia 26-29, J1-J5.

1932

Without Imprint at Foot

J28 D4 50p violet .20 .20
J29 D4 1d deep magenta .20 .20
J30 D4 2d deep blue .20 .20
J31 D4 5d orange .20 .20
J32 D4 10d chocolate .20 .20
Nos. J28-J32 (5) 1.00 1.00

1933 ***Perf. 9, 10½, 11½***

Overprint in Green, Blue or Maroon

J33 D5 50p vio (G) .20 .20
J34 D5 1d brown (Bl) .20 .20
a. Perf. 10½ 3.25 .85
J35 D5 2d blue (M) .35 .20
a. Perf. 10½ 1.60 .50
J36 D5 5d orange (Bl) 1.25 .20
J37 D5 10d violet brn (Bl) 6.00 1.00
Nos. J33-J37 (5) 8.00 1.80

POSTAL TAX STAMPS

Catalogue values for unused stamps in this section are for Never Hinged items.

The tax was for the Red Cross or The Olympic Fund unless otherwise noted.

Red Cross Emblem
PT1

Dr. Vladen Djordjevic
PT2

Unwmk.

1933, Sept. 17 Litho. *Perf. 13*
RA1 PT1 50p dark blue & red .30 .20

Obligatory on inland letters during Red Cross Week, Sept. 17-23.
See No. RAJ1.

1936, Sept. 20 Typo. *Perf. 12*
RA2 PT2 50p brn blk & red .35 .20

Obligatory on inland letters during Red Cross Week, Sept. 20-26.

Aiding the Wounded
PT3

1938, Sept. 18 Litho. *Perf. 12½*
RA3 PT3 50p dk bl, red, yel & grn .35 .20

1940, Sept. 15 Redrawn
RA4 PT3 50p slate blue & red 1.10 .20

The inscription at the upper right of this stamp and the numerals of value are in smaller characters.
Obligatory on all letters during the second week of September.

POSTAL TAX DUE STAMPS

Catalogue values for unused stamps in this section are for Never Hinged items.

Type of Postal Tax Stamp Inscribed "PORTO"

1933 Unwmk. Litho. *Perf. 13*
RAJ1 PT1 50p dull grn & red .80 .20

ZAMBEZIA

zam-ˈbē-zē-ə

LOCATION — A former district of the Mozambique Province in Portuguese East Africa

GOVT. — Part of the Portuguese East Africa Colony

The districts of Quelimane and Tete were created from Zambezia. Eventually stamps of Mozambique came into use. See Quelimane and Tete.

1000 Reis = 1 Milreis

King Carlos
A1 A2

Perf. 11½, 12½, 13½

1894 Typo. Unwmk.
1 A1 5r yellow .25 .25
2 A1 10r red violet .75 .45
3 A1 15r chocolate 1.00 .65
a. Perf. 12½ 27.50 19.00
4 A1 20r lavender 1.00 .65
5 A1 25r blue green 2.00 1.25
a. Perf. 11½
6 A1 50r lt blue 2.00 1.25
7 A1 75r carmine 4.50 3.25
a. Perf. 11½ 50.00 35.00
8 A1 80r yellow grn 5.00 2.50
9 A1 100r brown, *buff* 4.00 1.75
10 A1 150r car, *rose* 7.00 3.00
11 A1 200r dk blue, *bl* 8.00 3.00
a. Perf. 11½ 200.00 150.00
b. Perf. 13½ 32.50 24.00
12 A1 300r dk bl, *salmon* 10.00 4.50
a. Perf. 11½ 25.00 20.00
Nos. 1-12 (12) 45.50 22.50

For surcharges and overprints see Nos. 36-47, 73-74, 77-81, 84-88.

1898-1903 *Perf. 11½*

Name and Value in Black or Red (500r)

13 A2 2½r gray .45 .45
14 A2 5r orange .45 .45
15 A2 10r lt green .75 .50
16 A2 15r brown 1.25 1.00
17 A2 15r gray grn ('03) 1.60 1.40
18 A2 20r gray violet 1.25 1.00
19 A2 25r sea green 1.25 1.00
20 A2 25r carmine ('03) 1.00 .85
21 A2 50r blue 1.25 1.10
22 A2 50r brown ('03) 2.75 2.25
23 A2 65r dull bl ('03) 8.00 5.50
24 A2 75r rose 10.00 5.25
25 A2 75r lilac ('03) 3.25 2.75
26 A2 80r violet 5.00 3.00
27 A2 100r dk bl, *bl* 2.00 2.00
28 A2 115r org brn, *pink* ('03) 10.00 7.25
29 A2 130r brn, *straw* ('03) 10.00 7.25
30 A2 150r brn, *buff* 6.00 3.50
31 A2 200r red vio, *pnksh* 6.00 3.50
32 A2 300r dk bl, *rose* 8.00 3.50
33 A2 400r dull bl, *straw* ('03) 10.00 8.50
34 A2 500r blk, *bl* ('01) 12.00 6.75
35 A2 700r vio, *yelsh* ('01) 15.00 8.75
Nos. 13-35 (23) 117.25 77.50

For surcharges and overprints see Nos. 49-68, 72, 82-83, 93-107.

Stamps of 1894 Surcharged

1902 *Perf. 11½, 12½*
36 A1 65r on 10r red vio 9.00 7.00
37 A1 65r on 15r choc 9.00 7.00
38 A1 65r on 20r lav 9.00 7.00
39 A1 65r on 300r bl, *sal* 9.00 7.00
40 A1 115r on 5r yel 9.00 7.00
41 A1 115r on 25r bl grn 9.00 7.00
42 A1 115r on 80r yel grn 9.00 7.00
43 A1 130r on 75r car 7.00 7.00
44 A1 130r on 150r car, *rose* 5.25 5.25
45 A1 400r on 50r lt bl 2.00 3.25
46 A1 400r on 100r brn, *buff* 2.00 3.50
47 A1 400r on 200r bl, *bl* 2.00 3.50

Same Surcharge on No. P1
48 N1 130r on 2½r brn 9.00 7.00
Nos. 36-48 (13) 90.25 78.50

Stamps of 1898 Overprinted

1902 *Perf. 11½*
49 A2 15r brown 2.00 1.40
50 A2 25r sea green 2.00 1.40
51 A2 50r blue 2.00 1.40
52 A2 75r rose 6.00 3.75
Nos. 49-52 (4) 12.00 7.95

No. 23 Surcharged in Black

1905
53 A2 50r on 65r dull blue 5.75 4.00

Stamps of 1898-1903 Overprinted in Carmine or Green

1911
54 A2 2½r gray .35 .20
55 A2 5r orange .35 .20
56 A2 10r light green .40 .25
a. Inverted overprint 15.00 12.50
57 A2 15r gray green .40 .25
58 A2 20r gray violet .50 .30
59 A2 25r carmine (G) 1.50 .50
60 A2 50r brown .40 *.35*
61 A2 75r lilac 1.25 .90
62 A2 100r dk bl, *bl* 1.25 .90
63 A2 115r org brn, *pink* 1.25 .90
64 A2 130r brown, *straw* 1.25 .90
65 A2 200r red vio, *pnksh* 1.25 .90
66 A2 400r dull bl, *straw* 2.10 1.10
67 A2 500r blk & red, *bl* 2.10 1.10
68 A2 700r violet, *yelsh* 2.25 1.50
Nos. 54-68 (15) 16.60 *10.25*

Stamps of 1902-05 Overprinted in Carmine or Green

1914

Without Gum

72 A2 50r on 65r dl bl *1,200. 800.00*
73 A1 115r on 5r yellow 1.25 1.50
74 A1 115r on 25r bl grn 1.25 1.50
75 A1 115r on 80r yel grn 1.25 1.50
76 N1 130r on 2½r brn (G) 1.25 1.50
a. Carmine overprint 22.50 22.50
77 A1 130r on 75r car 1.75 1.50
a. Perf. 12½ 5.50 7.00
78 A1 130r on 150r car, *rose* 1.75 1.50
79 A1 400r on 50r lt bl 2.50 3.00
a. Perf. 12½ 11.00 11.00
80 A1 400r on 100r brn, *buff* 2.50 2.50
81 A1 400r on 200r bl, *bl* 2.50 2.50

On Nos. 51-52
82 A2 50r blue 1.50 1.50
83 A2 75r rose 1.50 1.50
Nos. 73-83 (11) 19.00 20.00

Preceding Issues Overprinted in Carmine

1915

On Provisional Issue of 1902
84 A1 115r on 5r yellow .85 .45
85 A1 115r on 25r bl grn .85 .45
86 A1 115r on 80r lt grn .85 .45
87 A1 130r on 75r carmine .85 .45
a. Perf. 12½ 4.50 2.25
88 A1 130r on 150r car, *rose* .85 .45
92 N1 130r on 2½r (down) .85 .45

On Nos. 51, 53
93 A2 50r blue .85 .50
a. "Republica" inverted 15.00 15.00
94 A2 50r on 65r dull bl 3.50 *4.50*
Nos. 84-94 (8) 9.45 *7.70*

Stamps of 1898-1903 Overprinted Locally in Carmine

1917

Without Gum
95 A2 2½r gray 1.50 *3.00*
96 A2 5r orange 7.00 6.50
97 A2 10r light green 7.00 6.00
98 A2 15r gray green 6.50 6.50
99 A2 20r gray violet 7.25 6.50
100 A2 25r sea green 13.50 15.00
101 A2 100r blue, *blue* 4.00 2.75
102 A2 115r org brn, *pink* 4.00 2.75
103 A2 130r brown, *straw* 4.00 2.75
104 A2 200r red vio, *pnksh* 4.00 2.75
105 A2 400r dull bl, *straw* 4.50 3.50
106 A2 500r blk & red, *bl* 5.50 3.75
107 A2 700r vio, *yelsh* 9.00 5.25
Nos. 95-107 (13) 77.75 67.00

NEWSPAPER STAMP

N1

1894 Unwmk. Typo. *Perf. 12½*
P1 N1 2½r brown .60 .35

For overprints and surcharges see Nos. 76, 92.

ZANZIBAR

'zan-zə-,bär

LOCATION — Group of islands about twenty miles off the coast of Tanganyika in East Africa
GOVT. — British protectorate
AREA — 1,044 sq. mi. (approx.)
POP. — 354,360 (est. 1967)
CAPITAL — Zanzibar

Before 1895, unoverprinted stamps of India were used in Zanzibar.

12 Pies = 1 Anna
16 Annas = 1 Rupee
100 Cents = 1 Rupee (1908)
100 Cents = 1 Shilling (1935)

Catalogue values for unused stamps in this country are for Never Hinged items, beginning with Scott 201 in the regular postage section and Scott J18 in the postage due section.

Watermarks

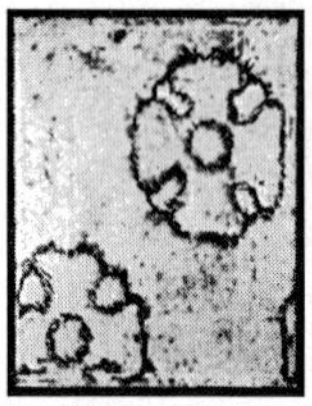

Wmk. 47 — Multiple Rosette

Wmk. 71 — Rosette

Stamps of British India Overprinted

On Stamps of 1882-95

1895 Wmk. Star (39) *Perf. 14*

Blue Overprint

1	A17 ½a green		*15,000.*	*4,500.*
2	A19 1a violet brown		2,600.	575.
a.	"Zanzidar"			*17,500.*

1895-96

Black Overprint

3	A17 ½a green	4.75	4.00
a.	"Zanzidar"	1,350.	725.00
b.	"Zanibar"	1,350.	*1,800.*
c.	"Zapzibar"		
4	A19 1a violet brn	4.50	4.00
a.	"Zanzidar"	—	*3,250.*
b.	"Zanibar"	1,750.	2,000.
5	A20 1a6p bister brn	5.25	3.75
a.	"Zanzidar"	3,750.	1,100.
b.	"Zanizbar"	1,750.	
c.	"Zanibar"	1,600.	1,750.
d.	"Zapzibar"		
6	A21 2a ultra	5.50	5.25
a.	"Zanzidar"	4,250.	2,100.
b.	"Zanibar"	4,250.	2,100.
c.	"Zapzibar"		
d.	Double overprint	280.00	
7	A28 2a6p green	8.50	5.50
a.	"Zanzidar"	3,750.	1,800.
b.	"Zanibar"	700.00	*1,250.*
c.	"Zapzibar"		
d.	"Zanzipar"	1,250.	
8	A22 3a orange	12.50	11.00
a.	"Zanzidar"	850.00	*1,600.*
b.	"Zanizbar"	4,000.	*4,500.*
9	A23 4a olive grn	12.50	15.00
a.	"Zanzidar"	7,000.	4,250.
10	A25 8a red vio	18.00	24.00
a.	"Zanzidar"	7,000.	7,000.
11	A26 12a vio, *red*	18.00	11.50
a.	"Zanzidar"	6,250.	4,250.
12	A27 1r gray	85.00	80.00
a.	"Zanzidar"	6,250.	4,750.
13	A29 1r car rose & grn	18.00	*27.50*
a.	Vertical overprint	475.00	
14	A30 2r brn & rose	62.50	*90.00*
a.	"Zanziba"	8,500.	4,750.
b.	Inverted "r"	4,250.	4,250.
c.	Pair, one without overprint		
15	A30 3r grn & brn	55.00	*67.50*
a.	"Zanziba"	8,500.	
b.	Inverted "r"	4,250.	4,500.
16	A30 5r vio & blue	62.50	*85.00*
a.	"Zanziba"	8,500.	
b.	Inverted "r"	3,750.	*4,500.*
c.	Dbl. ovpt., one invtd.	950.00	

On Stamp of 1873-76

Wmk. Elephant's Head (38)

17	A14 6a bister	21.00	12.50
a.	"Zanzidar"	7,000.	4,000.
b.	"Zanzibarr"	*4,250.*	*4,000.*
c.	"Zanibar"	725.00	*1,400.*
d.	"Zapzibar"		
e.	Double overprint	160.00	
	Nos. 3-17 (15)	393.50	446.50

Nos. 4-6 Surcharged:

a

b

c

d

e

f 2½

1896 Wmk. Star (39)

Black Surcharge

18	(a) 2½a on 1a	*175.00*	*110.00*
19	(b) 2½a on 1a	*450.00*	*350.00*
20	(c) 2½a on 1a	*180.00*	*125.00*

Red Surcharge

21	(a) 2½a on 1a	*260.00*	*675.00*
22	(b) 2½a on 1a	*500.00*	*1,000.*
23	(c) 2½a on 1a	*275.00*	*675.00*
24	(a) 2½a on 1a6p	*60.00*	*50.00*
a.	"Zanzidar"	*1,600.*	*1,400.*
b.	"Zanizbar"	*4,250.*	*2,250.*
24C	(b) 2½a on 1a6p	*210.00*	*500.00*
25	(c) 2½a on 1a6p	*130.00*	*275.00*
26	(d) 2½a on 1a6p	*150.00*	*125.00*
27	(e) 2½a on 1a6p	*425.00*	*400.00*
27A	(f) 2½a on 1a6p	*13,500.*	*9,000.*
28	(a) 2½a on 2a	*110.00*	*275.00*
28A	(b) 2½a on 2a	*225.00*	*525.00*
29	(c) 2½a on 2a	*125.00*	*350.00*
30	(d) 2½a on 2a	*65.00*	*35.00*
31	(e) 2½a on 2a	*200.00*	*125.00*
31A	(f) 2½a on 2a	*5,000.*	*2,250.*

Certain type varieties are found in the word "Zanzibar" on Nos. 1 to 31A viz: Inverted "q" for "b," broken "p" for "n," "i" without dot, small second "z" and tall second "z." These varieties are found on all values from ½a to 1r inclusive and the tall "z" is also found on the 2r, 3r and 5r.

Stamps of British East Africa, 1896, Overprinted in Black or Red

1896 Wmk. Crown and C A (2)

32	A8 ½a yellow grn	35.00	20.00
33	A8 1a carmine	30.00	18.00
34	A8 2½a dk blue (R)	85.00	50.00
35	A8 4½a orange	50.00	57.50
36	A8 5a dark ocher	57.50	37.50
37	A8 7½a lilac	42.50	57.50
	Nos. 32-37 (6)	300.00	240.50

Sultan Seyyid Hamed-bin-Thwain

A2 A3

1896, Sept. 20 Engr. Wmk. 71

38	A2 ½a yel grn & red	4.50	2.00
39	A2 1a indigo & red	3.00	1.75
40	A2 2a red brn & red	3.25	.85
41	A2 2½a ultra & red	12.50	1.60
42	A2 3a slate & red	10.50	5.75
43	A2 4a dk green & red	7.25	3.00
44	A2 4½a orange & red	5.25	5.50
45	A2 5a bister & red	5.00	2.75
a.	Half used as 2½a on cover		*3,750.*
46	A2 7½a lilac & red	4.00	3.00
47	A2 8a ol gray & red	11.00	8.00
48	A3 1r ultra & red	15.00	11.00
49	A3 2r green & red	26.00	11.00
50	A3 3r violet & red	26.00	11.00
51	A3 4r lake & red	21.00	18.00
52	A3 5r blk brn & red	27.50	18.00
	Nos. 38-52 (15)	181.75	103.20

No. 43 Surcharged in Red

1897

53	A2 (a) 2½a on 4a	67.50	*45.00*
54	A2 (b) 2½a on 4a	225.00	*200.00*
55	A2 (c) 2½a on 4a	85.00	*57.50*
	Nos. 53-55 (3)	377.50	*302.50*

1898 Engr. Wmk. 47

56	A2 ½a yel grn & red	1.75	.40
57	A2 1a indigo & red	2.50	.60
58	A2 2a red brn & red	4.50	2.00
58A	A2 2½a ultra & red	3.25	.35
59	A2 3a slate & red	6.25	.65
60	A2 4a dk grn & red	3.75	1.10
60A	A2 4½a orange & red	8.00	1.25
61	A2 5a bister & red	16.00	2.00
61A	A2 7½a lilac & red	9.50	3.00
61B	A2 8a ol gray & red	13.50	2.50
	Nos. 56-61B (10)	69.00	13.85

A4

Sultan Seyyid Hamoud-bin-Mahommed-bin-Said — A5

1899-1901

62	A4 ½a yel grn & red	2.25	.65
63	A4 1a indigo & red	5.00	.25
64	A4 1a car & red ('01)	2.25	.25
65	A4 2a red brn & red	2.50	.55
66	A4 2½a ultra & red	2.50	.65
67	A4 3a slate & red	3.25	2.50
68	A4 4a dk green & red	3.75	1.60
69	A4 4½a orange & red	14.00	4.00
70	A4 4½a ind & red ('01)	16.00	13.50
71	A4 5a bister & red	3.50	1.40
72	A4 7½a lilac & red	3.75	*4.25*
73	A4 8a ol gray & red	3.75	*5.00*

Wmk. 71

74	A5 1r ultra & red	21.00	17.50
75	A5 2r green & red	21.00	21.00
76	A5 3r violet & red	35.00	*40.00*
77	A5 4r lilac rose & red	55.00	*62.50*
78	A5 5r gray brown & red	62.50	*75.00*
	Nos. 62-78 (17)	257.00	*250.60*

For surcharges see Nos. 94-98.

A6

Monogram of Sultan Ali bin Hamoud — A7

1904, June 8 Typo. Wmk. 47

79	A6 ½a emerald	1.75	1.00
80	A6 1a rose red	1.75	.20
81	A6 2a bister brown	2.00	.50
82	A6 2½a ultra	3.00	.40
83	A6 3a gray	3.00	2.50
84	A6 4a blue green	2.75	1.75
85	A6 4½a black	3.75	2.75
86	A6 5a ocher	4.25	1.40
87	A6 7½a violet	5.25	*8.00*
88	A6 8a olive green	4.75	3.00
89	A7 1r ultra & red	24.00	14.00
90	A7 2r green & red	27.00	*42.50*
91	A7 3r violet & red	50.00	*85.00*
92	A7 4r magenta & red	55.00	*100.00*
93	A7 5r olive & red	55.00	*110.00*
	Nos. 79-93 (15)	243.25	*373.00*

Nos. 69-70, 72-73 Surcharged in Black or Lake:

g

h

i

1904

94	A4 (g) 1a on 4½a	4.75	*5.25*
95	A4 (g) 1a on 4½a (L)	5.25	*21.00*
96	A4 (h) 2a on 4a (L)	16.00	*21.00*
97	A4 (i) 2½a on 7½a	15.00	*22.50*
a.	"Hlaf"	12,500.	
98	A4 (i) 2½a on 8a	19.00	*35.00*
a.	"Hlaf"	11,500.	*9,000.*
	Nos. 94-98 (5)	60.00	*104.75*

Sultan Ali bin Hamoud
A8 A9

A10

Palace of the Sultan — A11

1908-09 Engr. Wmk. 47

99	A8	1c gray ('09)	2.50	.35
100	A8	3c yellow grn	6.75	.20
101	A8	6c carmine	10.50	.20
102	A8	10c org brn ('09)	2.75	2.25
103	A8	12c violet	16.00	3.50
104	A9	15c ultra	14.00	.45
105	A9	25c brown	4.25	1.10
106	A9	50c dp green	6.75	4.75
107	A9	75c slate ('09)	11.50	14.00
108	A10	1r yellow green	27.50	14.00
109	A10	2r violet	21.00	16.00
110	A10	3r yellow brown	27.50	52.50
111	A10	4r red	50.00	85.00
112	A10	5r blue	45.00	62.50
113	A11	10r brn & dk grn	160.00	280.00
114	A11	20r yel grn & blk	350.00	500.00
115	A11	30r dk brn & blk	375.00	675.00
116	A11	40r org brn & blk	525.00	
117	A11	50r lilac & blk	450.00	
118	A11	100r blue & blk	750.00	
119	A11	200r black & brn	1,150.	
		Nos. 99-112 (14)	246.00	256.80

It is probable that Nos. 118 and 119 were used only for fiscal purposes.

Sultan Khalifa bin Harub — A12

Dhow — A13

Dhow — A14

1913 *Perf. 14*

120	A12	1c gray	.45	.20
121	A12	3c yellow grn	.55	.20
122	A12	6c carmine	1.75	.20
123	A12	10c brown	1.25	2.10
124	A12	12c violet	1.10	.20
125	A12	15c ultra	1.40	.35
126	A12	25c black brn	1.10	1.10
127	A12	50c dk green	2.25	4.50
128	A12	75c dk gray	2.25	3.00
129	A13	1r yellow grn	8.00	10.00
130	A13	2r dk violet	12.50	27.50
131	A13	3r orange	15.00	45.00
132	A13	4r red	30.00	72.50
133	A13	5r blue	40.00	40.00
134	A14	10r brown & grn	125.00	210.00
135	A14	20r yel grn & blk	175.00	400.00
136	A14	30r dk brn & blk	190.00	475.00
137	A14	40r orange & blk	400.00	675.00
138	A14	50r dull vio & blk	375.00	675.00
139	A14	100r blue & blk	450.00	
140	A14	200r black & brn	725.00	
		Nos. 120-134 (15)	242.60	416.85

1914-22 Wmk. 3

141	A12	1c gray	.90	.30
142	A12	3c yellow grn	1.40	.20
143	A12	6c carmine	.95	.20
144	A12	8c vio, *yel* ('22)	.85	4.00
145	A12	10c dk grn, *yel* ('22)	.85	.40
146	A12	15c ultra	1.25	5.75
148	A12	50c dark green	5.00	4.75
149	A12	75c deep gray	3.50	26.00
150	A13	1r yellow grn	4.50	4.00
151	A13	2r dark violet	5.75	9.00
152	A13	3r brown org	18.00	37.50
153	A13	4r red	18.00	95.00
154	A13	5r blue	18.00	72.50
155	A14	10r brown & grn	125.00	450.00
		Nos. 141-155 (14)	203.95	709.60

1921-29 Wmk. 4

156	A12	1c gray	.20	8.00
157	A12	3c yellow grn	.55	3.75
158	A12	3c orange ('22)	.35	.20
159	A12	4c green ('22)	.55	.55
160	A12	6c carmine	.35	.55
161	A12	6c vio, *bl* ('22)	.45	.20
162	A12	10c lt brown	.80	9.50
163	A12	12c violet	.50	.35
164	A12	12c carmine ('22)	.50	.50
165	A12	15c ultra	.70	9.50
166	A12	20c dk blue ('22)	1.10	.40
167	A12	25c black brn	.85	11.50
168	A12	50c blue green	1.40	4.25
169	A12	75c dark gray	2.75	57.50
170	A13	1r yellow grn	4.75	4.00
171	A13	2r dk violet	3.75	9.50
172	A13	3r ocher	4.75	8.50
173	A13	4r red	14.00	40.00
174	A13	5r blue	22.50	72.50
175	A14	10r brown & grn	110.00	275.00
176	A14	20r green & blk	225.00	450.00
177	A14	30r dk brn & blk ('29)	210.00	575.00
		Nos. 156-175 (20)	170.80	516.25

Sultan Khalifa bin Harub ("CENTS" with Serifs) — A15

1926-27

184	A15	1c brown	.65	.20
185	A15	3c yellow org	.20	.20
186	A15	4c deep green	.25	.35
187	A15	6c dark violet	.35	.20
188	A15	8c slate	1.10	5.00
189	A15	10c olive green	1.10	.45
190	A15	12c deep red	1.60	.20
191	A15	20c ultra	.60	.35
192	A15	25c violet, *yel*	4.75	2.75
193	A15	50c claret	2.00	.40
194	A15	75c olive brown	28.00	25.00
		Nos. 184-194 (11)	40.60	35.10

Catalogue values for unused stamps in this section, from this point to the end of the section, are for Never Hinged items.

"CENTS" without Serifs — A16

Dhow — A17

Dhow — A18

1936 *Perf. 14*

201	A16	5c deep green	.20	.20
202	A16	10c black	.20	.20
203	A16	15c carmine	.30	.20
204	A16	20c brown org	.20	.20
205	A16	25c violet, *yel*	.20	.20
206	A16	30c ultra	.25	.20
207	A16	40c black brown	.25	.20
208	A16	50c claret	.40	.20
209	A17	1sh yellow grn	.65	.20
210	A17	2sh dark violet	1.25	2.00
211	A17	5sh red	17.50	6.75
212	A17	7.50sh blue	28.50	28.00
213	A18	10sh brn & grn	32.50	25.00
		Nos. 201-213 (13)	82.40	63.55

For overprints see Nos. 222-223.

A19

A20

1936, Dec. 9

214	A19	10c olive grn & blk	3.00	.30
215	A19	20c red violet & blk	5.00	1.10
216	A19	30c deep ultra & blk	13.00	.75
217	A19	50c red orange & blk	13.50	4.50
		Nos. 214-217 (4)	34.50	6.65

Reign of Sultan Khalifa bin Harub, 25th anniv.

Perf. 14

1944, Nov. 20 Engr. Wmk. 4

Dhow & Map Showing Zanzibar & Muscat.

218	A20	10c violet blue	.85	2.75
219	A20	20c brown orange	.90	3.50
220	A20	50c Prus green	.90	.35
221	A20	1sh dull purple	.90	.75
		Nos. 218-221 (4)	3.55	7.35

200th anniv. of the Al Busaid Dynasty.

Nos. 202 and 206 Overprinted in Red

1946, Nov. 11

222	A16	10c black	.20	.20
223	A16	30c ultra	.30	.30

Victory of the Allied Nations in WW II.

Common Design Types pictured following the introduction.

Silver Wedding Issue

Common Design Types

1949, Jan. 10 Photo. *Perf. 14x14½*

224	CD304	20c orange	.60	.60

Engraved; Name Typographed

Perf. 11½x11

225	CD305	10sh light brown	21.00	30.00

UPU Issue

Common Design Types

Engr.; Name Typo. on 30c, 50c

Perf. 13½, 11x11½

1949, Oct. 10 Wmk. 4

226	CD306	20c red orange	.35	2.50
227	CD307	30c indigo	2.00	1.00
228	CD308	50c red lilac	1.25	2.00
229	CD309	1sh blue green	1.25	3.50
		Nos. 226-229 (4)	4.85	9.00

Sultan Khalifa bin Harub — A21

Seyyid Khalifa Schools A22

Perf. 12x12½, 13x12½

1952, Aug. 26 Engr.

230	A21	5c black	.20	.20
231	A21	10c red orange	.20	.20
232	A21	15c green	.75	2.25
233	A21	20c carmine	.55	.20
234	A21	25c plum	1.10	.20
235	A21	30c blue green	1.10	.20
236	A21	35c ultra	.70	3.50
237	A21	40c chocolate	.70	1.25
238	A21	50c purple	2.50	.20
239	A22	1sh choc & bl grn	.65	.20
240	A22	2sh claret & ultra	2.50	2.75
241	A22	5sh carmine & blk	2.50	4.00
242	A22	7.50sh emer & gray	22.50	24.00
243	A22	10sh gray blk & rose red	12.00	13.00
		Nos. 230-243 (14)	47.95	52.15

POSTAGE DUE STAMPS

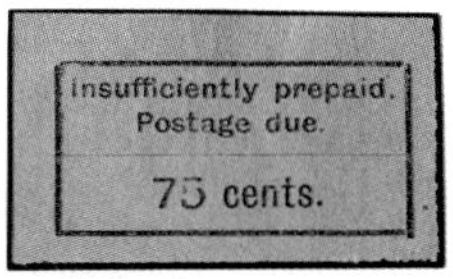

D1

Rouletted 10

1931 Typeset Unwmk.

Thin Paper

Without Gum

J1	D1	1c blk, *orange*	12.50	100.00
		On cover		1,250.
J2	D1	2c blk, *orange*	5.50	60.00
		On cover		600.00
J3	D1	3c blk, *orange*	5.75	47.50
		On cover		600.00
J3A	D1	6c blk, *orange*		8,000.
		On cover		10,000.
J4	D1	9c blk, *orange*	3.25	25.00
		On cover		500.00
J4A	D1	12c blk, *orange*	10,000.	9,500.
		On cover		12,500.
J4B	D1	12c blk, *green*	1,600.	675.00
		On cover		6,000.
J5	D1	15c blk, *orange*	3.25	27.50
		On cover		500.00
J6	D1	18c blk, *orange*	20.00	75.00
		On cover		750.00
a.		18c black, *salmon*	5.00	45.00
		On cover		600.00
J7	D1	20c blk, *orange*	4.50	65.00
		On cover		600.00
J8	D1	21c blk, *orange*	4.00	37.50
		On cover		500.00
J8A	D1	25c blk, *orange*	11,500.	11,500.
		On cover		—
J8B	D1	25c blk, *magenta*	3,250.	1,500.
		On cover		9,000.
J9	D1	31c blk, *orange*	11.00	85.00
		On cover		2,500.
J10	D1	50c blk, *orange*	24.00	160.00
		On cover		5,000.
J11	D1	75c blk, *orange*	72.50	375.00
		On cover		6,000.

The variety "cent.s" occurs once on each sheet of Nos. J3 to J11 inclusive.

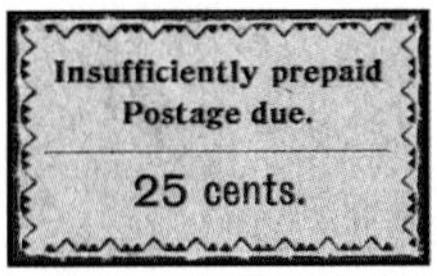

D2

D3

1931-33 *Rouletted 5*

Thick Paper

J12	D2	2c blk, *salmon*	17.50	32.50
		On cover		650.00
J13	D2	3c blk, *rose*	3.50	52.50
		On cover		1,000.
J14	D2	6c blk, *yellow*	3.50	37.50
		On cover		450.00
J15	D2	12c blk, *blue*	4.50	30.00
		On cover		450.00
J16	D2	25c blk, *pink*	11.00	85.00
		On cover		1,000.

J17 D2 25c blk, *dull violet*	16.00	*57.50*
On cover		850.00
Nos. J12-J17 (6)	56.00	295.00

Catalogue values for unused stamps in this section, from this point to the end of the section, are for Never Hinged items.

1936 Typo. Wmk. 4 *Perf. 14*

J18 D3 5c violet	4.75	*9.50*
On cover		275.00
J19 D3 10c carmine	4.00	*3.25*
On cover		275.00
J20 D3 20c green	2.50	*4.75*
On cover		325.00
J21 D3 30c brown	9.50	*21.00*
On cover		500.00
J22 D3 40c ultra	9.50	*27.50*
On cover		500.00
J23 D3 1sh gray	9.50	*32.50*
On cover		1,250.
Nos. J18-J23 (6)	39.75	*98.50*

Chalky paper was introduced in 1956 for the 5c, 30c, 40c, 1sh, and in 1962 for the 10c, 20c. Value for set of 6, unused $3.25, used $110.

See note after No. 300a.

ZULULAND

'zü-ˌlü-ˌland

LOCATION — Northeastern part of Natal, South Africa
GOVT. — British Colony
AREA — 10,427 sq. mi.
POP. — 230,000 (estimated 1900)
CAPITAL — Eshowe

12 Pence = 1 Shilling
20 Shillings = 1 Pound

Stamps of Great Britain Overprinted

1888-93 Wmk. 30 *Perf. 14*

1	A54	½p vermilion	4.25	3.00
2	A40	1p violet	29.00	4.50
3	A56	2p green & red	17.50	32.50
4	A57	2½p vio, *bl* ('91)	27.50	22.50
5	A58	3p violet, *yel*	29.00	25.00
6	A59	4p green & brn	50.00	65.00
7	A61	5p lil & bl ('93)	100.00	150.00
8	A62	6p vio, *rose*	15.00	20.00
9	A63	9p blue & lil ('92)	100.00	100.00
10	A65	1sh green ('92)	125.00	150.00

Wmk. 31

11	A51	5sh rose ('92)	600.00	*700.00*
		Nos. 1-10 (10)	497.25	572.50

Natal No. 66 Overprinted

1888-94 Wmk. 2

12 A14 ½p green, no period	26.00	*45.00*
a. Period after "Zululand"	62.50	*85.00*
b. As "a," double overprint	3,000.	1,750.
c. As "a," invtd. overprint	1,400.	
d. As "a," pair, one without ovpt.	*8,500.*	
e. As No. 12, double overprint	1,600.	*1,750.*

Natal No. 71 Ovptd. Like Nos. 1-11

13 A11 6p violet ('94)	55.00	55.00

A1

A2

1891

14 A1 1p lilac	3.50	3.50

By proclamation of the Governor of Zululand, dated June 27th, 1891, No. 14 was declared to be a postage stamp.

1894-96 Typo.

15	A2	½p lilac & grn	3.75	5.00
16	A2	1p lilac & rose	5.75	2.25
17	A2	2½p lilac & blue	16.00	9.75
18	A2	3p lilac & brn	9.25	4.00
19	A2	6p lilac & blk	22.50	22.50
20	A2	1sh green	45.00	45.00
21	A2	2sh6p grn & blk ('96)	85.00	*97.50*
22	A2	4sh grn & car rose	125.00	*175.00*
23	A2	£1 violet, *red*	550.00	625.00
24	A2	£5 vio & blk, *red*	5,250.	*1,750.*
		Nos. 15-23 (9)	862.25	986.00

Numerals of #19-24 are in color on plain tablet.

Purple or violet cancellations are not necessarily revenue cancels. 14 of the 17 post offices and agencies used violet as well as black postal cancellations.

Zululand was annexed to Natal in Dec. 1897 and separate stamps were discontinued June 30, 1898.

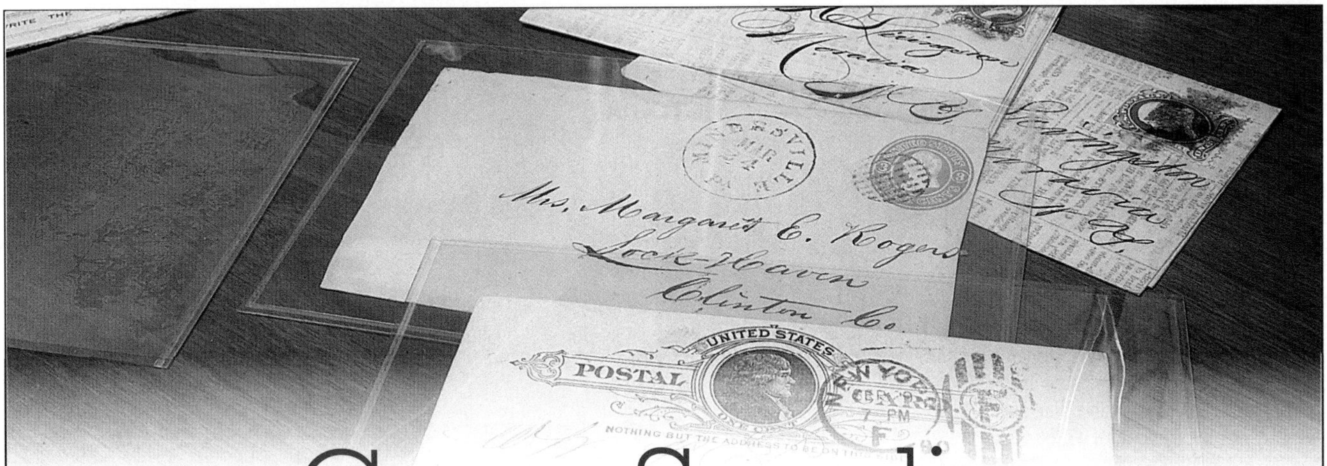

Cover Supplies

COVER SLEEVES
Protect your covers with clear polyethylene sleeves.
Sold in packages of 100.

U.S. POSTAL CARD

3¾" / 5⅞"

Item	*Retail*	*AA**
CV005	$3.95	$2.99

U.S. FIRST DAY COVER #6

4" / 6¾"

Item	*Retail*	*AA**
CV006	$3.95	$2.99

CONTINENTAL POSTCARD

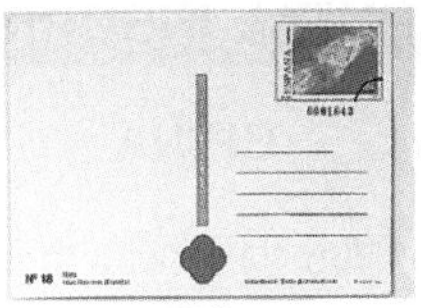

4¼" / 6¼"

Item	*Retail*	*AA**
CV007	$4.95	$3.74

EUROPEAN FIRST DAY COVER

5⅜" / 7"

Item	*Retail*	*AA**
CV009	$4.95	$3.74

#10 BUSINESS ENVELOPE

4¾" / 10"

Item	*Retail*	*AA**
CV010	$5.95	$4.49

COVER BINDERS AND PAGES
Padded, durable, 3-ring binders will hold up to 100 covers. Features the "D" ring mechanism on the right hand side of album so you don't have to worry about creasing or wrinkling covers when opening or closing binder. Cover pages sold separately. Available in two colors. Sold in packages of 25.

Item		*Retail*	*AA**
CBRD	Red	$11.99	$9.59
CBBL	Blue	$11.99	$9.59
CBGY	Gray	$11.99	$9.59
CBBK	Black	$11.99	$9.59
T2	Pages Black	$6.49	$5.49
T2C	Pages Clear	$6.49	$5.49

COVER BOX
Box measures
10½" x 7⅜" x 4¼"
and will hold hundreds of covers.

Item	*Retail*	*AA**
CVBOX	$7.74	$6.24

U.S. POSTAL HISTORY SAMPLER
An entertaining and informative introduction to the many different U.S. postal history topics cover collections can be built. Topics covered include train wreck covers, fancy cancels, APO markings, campaign covers, flag cancels and many more. Available in either hardbound or softcover format.

Item		*Retail*	*AA**
LIN36	Softcover	$14.95	**$13.45**
LIN36H	Hardbound	$30.00	**$27.00**

AMOS ADVANTAGE

1. AA* prices apply to paid subscribers of *Scott Stamp Monthly* and *Linn's*
2. Prices, terms and product availability subject to change.
3. **Shipping & Handling:**
   United States: 10% of order total. Minimum charge $5.99 Maximum charge $30.00.
   Canada: 15% of order total. Minimum charge $14.99 Maximum charge $45.00.
   Foreign orders are shipped via DHL and billed actual freight. Credit cards only.

To Order Call
1-800-572-6885
www.amosadvantage.com

Illustrated Identifier

This section pictures stamps or parts of stamp designs that will help identify postage stamps that do not have English words on them.

Many of the symbols that identify stamps of countries are shown here as well as typical examples of their stamps.

See the Index and Identifier on the previous pages for stamps with inscriptions such as "sen," "posta," "Baja Porto," "Helvetia," "K.S.A.", etc.

Linn's Stamp Identifier is now available. The 144 pages include more 2,000 inscriptions and over 500 large stamp illustrations. Available from Linn's Stamp News, P.O. Box 29, Sidney, OH 45365-0029.

1. HEADS, PICTURES AND NUMERALS

GREAT BRITAIN

Great Britain stamps never show the country name, but, except for postage dues, show a picture of the reigning monarch.

Victoria

Edward VII George V Edward VIII

George VI

Some George VI stamps are surcharged in annas, new paisa or rupees. These are listed under Oman.

VICTORIA

Queen Victoria

INDIA

Other stamps of India show this portrait of Queen Victoria and the words "Service" and "Annas."

AUSTRIA

YUGOSLAVIA

(Also BOSNIA & HERZEGOVINA if imperf.)

BOSNIA & HERZEGOVINA

Denominations also appear in top corners instead of bottom corners.

HUNGARY

Another stamp has posthorn facing left

BRAZIL

AUSTRALIA

Kangaroo and Emu

SWITZERLAND

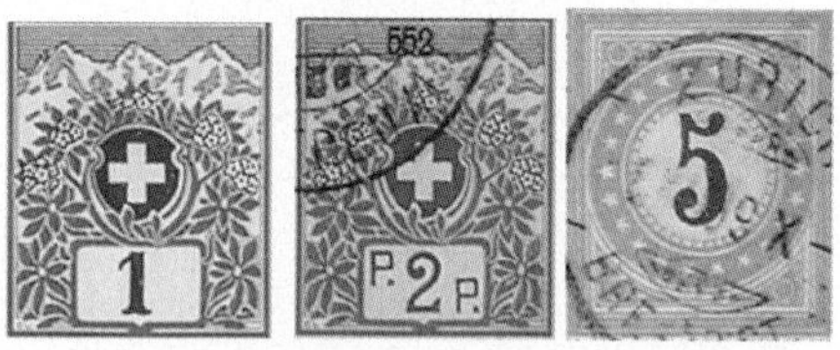

2. ORIENTAL INSCRIPTIONS

CHINA

中 中

Any stamp with this one character is from China (Imperial, Republic or People's Republic). This character appears in a four-character overprint on stamps of Manchukuo. These stamps are local provisionals, which are unlisted. Other overprinted Manchukuo stamps show this character, but have more than four characters in the overprints. These are listed in People's Republic of China.

Some Chinese stamps show the Sun.

Most stamps of Republic of China show this series of characters.

Chinese stamps without China character

REPUBLIC OF CHINA

MANCHUKUO

Temple

Emperor Pu-Yi

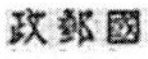

The first 3 characters are common to many Manchukuo stamps.

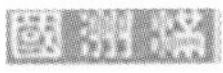

The last 3 characters are common to other Manchukuo stamps.

Orchid Crest

Manchukuo stamp without these elements

JAPAN

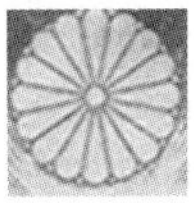

Chrysanthemum Crest

Country Name

Japanese stamps without these elements

The number of characters in the center and the design of dragons on the sides will vary.

KOREA

Yin Yang appears on some stamps.

THAILAND

Country Name

King Chulalongkorn

King Prajadhipok and Chao P'ya Chakri

3. CENTRAL AND EASTERN ASIAN INSCRIPTIONS

INDIA - FEUDATORY STATES

Alwar

Bhor

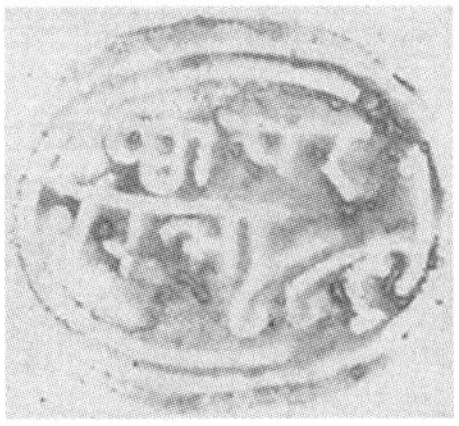

Bundi

Similar stamps come with different designs in corners and differently drawn daggers (at center of circle).

Dhar

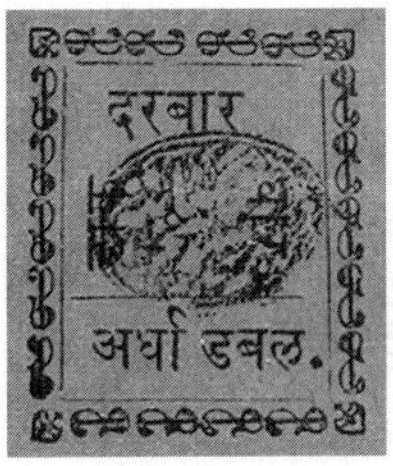

Faridkot

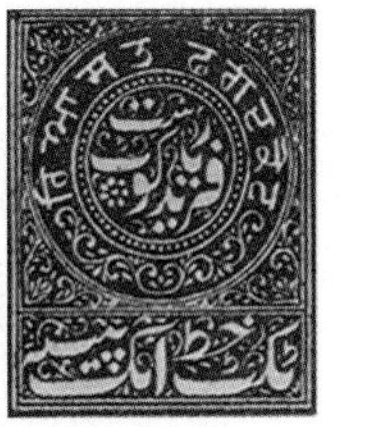

Hyderabad

Similar stamps exist with straight line frame around stamp, and also with different central design which is inscribed "Postage" or "Post & Receipt."

Indore

Jhalawar

A similar stamp has the central figure in an oval.

Nandgaon

Nowanuggur

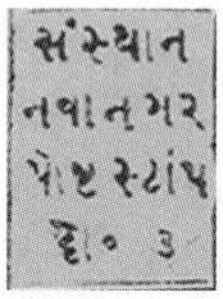

Poonch

Similar stamps exist in various sizes

Rajpeepla

Soruth

NEPAL

Similar stamps are smaller, have squares in upper corners and have five or nine characters in central bottom panel.

TANNU TUVA

GEORGIA

This inscription is found on other pictorial stamps.

ARMENIA

The four characters are found somewhere on pictorial stamps. On some stamps only the middle two are found.

4. AFRICAN INSCRIPTIONS

ETHIOPIA

5. ARABIC INSCRIPTIONS

AFGHANISTAN

Many early Afghanistan stamps show Tiger's head, many of these have ornaments protruding from outer ring, others show inscriptions in black.

Arabic Script

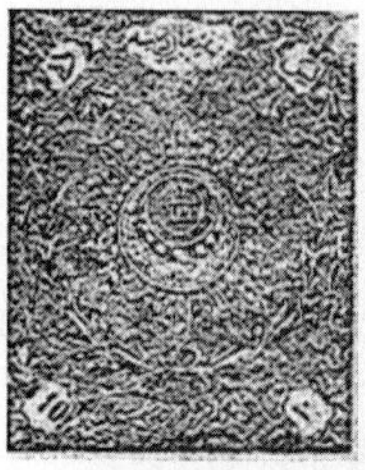

Mosque Gate & Crossed Cannons
The four characters are found somewhere on pictorial stamps. On some stamps only the middle two are found.

EGYPT

INDIA - FEUDATORY STATES

Jammu & Kashmir

Text and thickness of ovals vary. Some stamps have flower devices in corners.

India-Hyderabad

IRAN

Country Name

Royal Crown

SAUDI ARABIA

Tughra (Central design)

THRACE

YEMEN

TURKEY

Star & Crescent is a device found on many Turkish stamps, but is also found on stamps from other Arabic areas (see Pakistan-Bahawalpur)

Tughra (similar tughras can be found on stamps of Turkey in Asia, Afghanistan and Saudi Arabia)

Mohammed V

Mustafa Kemal

Plane, Star and Crescent

TURKEY IN ASIA

Other Turkey in Asia pictorials show star & crescent.
Other stamps show tughra shown under Turkey.

6. GREEK INSCRIPTIONS

GREECE

Country Name in various styles
(Some Crete stamps overprinted with the Greece country name are listed in Crete.)

Lepta

ΔΡΑΧΜΗ ΔΡΑΧΜΑΙ ΛΕΠΤΟΝ

Drachma Drachmas Lepton

Abbreviated Country Name ΕΛΛ

Other forms of Country Name

No country name

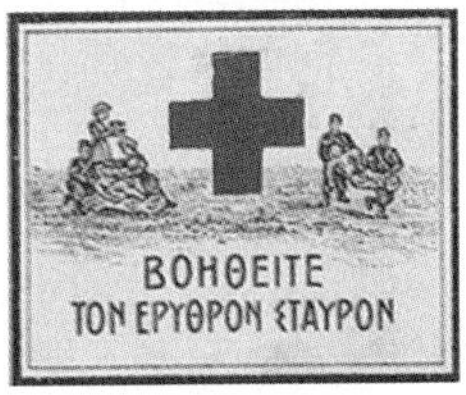

CRETE

Country Name

These words are on other stamps

Grosion

Crete stamps with a surcharge that have the year "1922" are listed under Greece.

EPIRUS

Country Name

IONIAN ISLANDS

7. CYRILLIC INSCRIPTIONS

RUSSIA

Postage Stamp

Imperial Eagle

Postage in various styles

Abbreviation for Kopeck

Abbreviation for Ruble

Russia

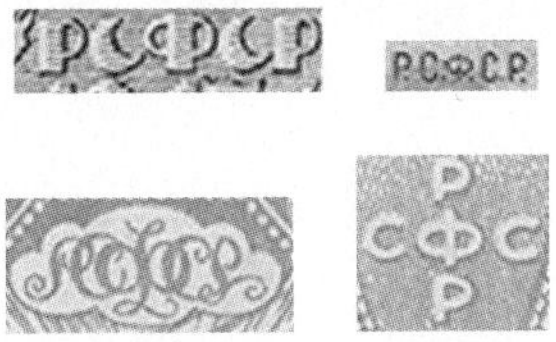

Abbreviation for Russian Soviet Federated Socialist Republic

RSFSR stamps were overprinted (see below)

Abbreviation for Union of Soviet Socialist Republics

This item is footnoted in Latvia

RUSSIA - Army of the North

"OKCA"

RUSSIA - Wenden

RUSSIAN OFFICES IN

THE TURKISH EMPIRE

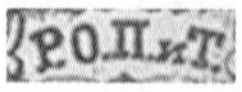

These letters appear on other stamps of the Russian offices.

The unoverprinted version of this stamp and a similar stamp were overprinted by various countries (see below).

ARMENIA

FAR EASTERN REPUBLIC

Country Name

SOUTH RUSSIA

Country Name

FINLAND

Circles and Dots on stamps similar to Imperial Russia issues

BATUM

Forms of Country Name

TRANSCAUCASIAN FEDERATED REPUBLICS

Abbreviation for Country Name

ROMANIA

UKRAINE

The trident appears on many stamps, usually as an overprint.

Abbreviation for Ukrainian Soviet Socialist Republic

WESTERN UKRAINE

Abbreviation for Country Name

AZERBAIJAN

Abbreviation for Azerbaijan Soviet Socialist Republic

MONTENEGRO

Country Name in various forms

Abbreviation for country name

No country name (A similar Montenegro stamp without country name has same vignette.)

SERBIA

Country Name in various forms

Abbreviation for country name

No country name

YUGOSLAVIA

Showing country name

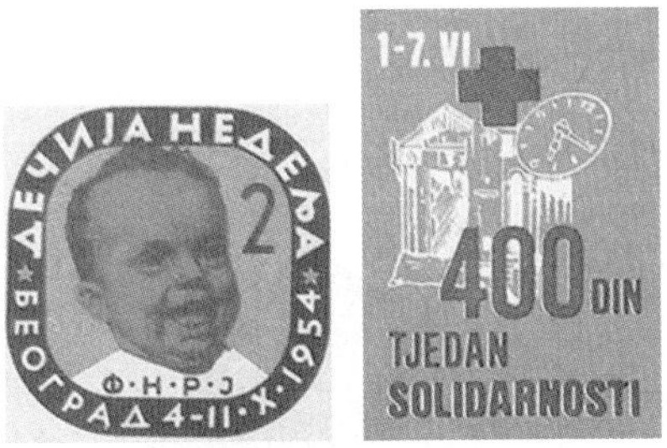

No Country Name

BULGARIA

Country Name

Postage

Stotinka

Stotinki (plural)

Abbreviation for Stotinki

Country Name in various forms and styles

No country name

Abbreviation for Lev, leva

MONGOLIA

No Country Name

MAGNIFIERS

5X FOLD-A-WAY POCKET MAGNIFIER

Item	*Retail*	*AA**
MG5X	$21.90	$19.75

10X STATIC MAGNIFIER

Item	*Retail*	*AA**
MG10	$17.95	$14.99

LIGHTED MAGNIFIER

This is a great, inexpensive tool for anyone who needs illuminated magnification. The spring-loaded lens is hidden within the body of the magnifier, until you push the button. The super-bright, white LED illuminates the magnified area. The light is activated by a locking on/off switch. The light is powered by two CR2032, replaceable, 3V lithium button cells (which are included with the magnifier). The magnifier comes with a belt clip and a slot for a lanyard. [working distance is about 2.5"]. Available in 4x or 10x magnification.

Item	*Description*	*Retail*	*AA**
MG4XL	Red 4x	$13.99	$10.99
MG10XL	Black 10x	$17.99	$13.99

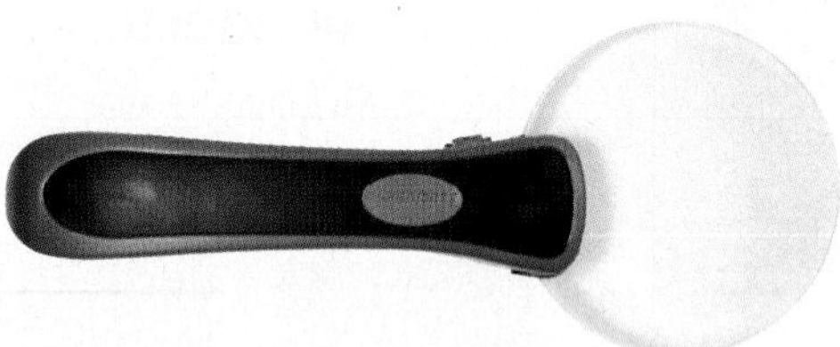

2.5X FRAMELESS LED ILLUMINATED MAGNIFIER

This 2.5x magnifier has a 3" high-quality acrylic lens attached to a modern, ergonomically designed handle. Illumination comes from two LEDs. The magnifier comes with a soft, protective pouch.

Item	*Retail*	*AA**
MG25XL	$18.90	$16.99

BAUSCH & LOMB MAGNIFIER

Handy 5x magnifier slides into carrying case.

Item	*Retail*	*AA**
MG1	$9.95	$6.97

10X LENSCOPE ILLUMINATED MAGNIFIER

The Lenscope 10x Magnifier is a precision inspection tool that provides a clear, distortion-free image. Magnification comes through a 10x Hastings Triplet lens housed in a plastic body. Illumination is provided by two angled lamps. A zippered storage case protects the Lenscope when it is not in use. Focal length is about 1". [2 AA batteries are not included.]

Item	*Retail*	*AA**
LNSCP10MG	$67.99	$57.99

Scales available for more precise measurements.

METRIC SCALE

Item	*Retail*	*AA**
METSCLE	$40.99	$36.99

PROTRACTOR SCALE

PROSCLE	$40.99	$36.99

GENERAL PURPOSE SCALE

GPSCLE	$40.99	$36.99

INCH SCALE

INCHSCLE	$40.99	$36.99

LENSCOPE & 4 SCALES

Item	*Retail*	*AA**
LNSCPSET	$199.99	$169.99

5X-20X FOLDING POCKET MAGNIFIER

Contains three separate glass lenses housed in a durable plastic swing-away case. Seven different powers of magnification from 5x to 20x can be created when the lenses are used in combination. Depending on magnification, the focal length is between .5" and 2".

Item	*Retail*	*AA**
MG520	$29.99	$25.99

2.5" CRYSTAL VIEW MAGNIFIER

Dome shaped 4x magnifier "draws light like a magnet," illuminating intricate details of stamps or coins. 2 1/2" diameter magnifier fits in handsome solid oak ring and slides easily across any flat surface.

Item	*Retail*	*AA**
MG25	$39.99	$31.99

3.5X HANDS FREE OPTIVISOR

The hands free Optivisor provides 3.5x magnification with a focal length of 4". The optical glass lenses are ground and polished to precise standards. The comfortable continuous headband is fully adjustable, as are the pivot knobs holding the visor. The visor can be pushed up and out of the way when not in use. The Optivisor can be worn and used by people who normally wear glasses.

Item	*Retail*	*AA**
MG35H	$44.99	$39.99
2.5X OPTI-LOUPE MAGNIFIER		
MG35HLP	$7.99	$6.99
VISOR LIGHT FOR OPTIVISOR		
MG35HVL	$22.99	$20.99
QUASAR LED LIGHTING SYSTEM FOR OPTIVISOR		
MG35LED	$24.95	$22.99

AMOS ADVANTAGE

1. *AA prices apply to paid subscribers of *Scott Stamp Monthly* and *Linn's*
2. Prices, terms and product availability subject to change.
3. **Shipping & Handling:**
   United States: 10% of order total. Minimum charge $5.99 Maximum charge $30.00.
   Canada: 15% of order total. Minimum charge $14.99 Maximum charge $45.00.
   Foreign orders are shipped via DHL and billed actual freight. Credit cards only.

To Order Call 1-800-572-6885

www.amosadvantage.com

INDEX AND IDENTIFIER

PRE-STAMP POSTAL MARKINGS

FORERUNNER USAGE IN COLONIES OF STAMPS OF PARENT STATES, ETC.

Numeral Cancellations

On Stamps of Great Britain

On Stamps of Ceylon

On Stamps of India

On Stamps of Mauritius

On Stamps of German Offices in China

On Stamps of Portugal

AUSTRIAN POST

in Albania

On Stamps of Lombardy-Venetia or Austrian Turkish Offices

in Bulgaria

On Stamps of Lombardy-Venetia

On Stamps of Austrian Levant

in Crete

On Stamps of Lombardy-Venetia or Austrian Turkish Offices

in Cyprus

On Stamps of Lombardy-Venetia or Austrian Turkish Offices

FRENCH IMPERIAL POST IN BULGARIA

On Stamps of France

GREAT BRITAIN CONSULAR POST IN THAILAND

GREEK CONSULAR POST IN EPIRUS

On Stamps of Greece

ITALIAN CONSULAR POST IN ARGENTINA

On Stamps of Italian Offices Abroad

INDEX TO ADVERTISERS 2008 CLASSIC SPECIALIZED

2008
CLASSIC SPECIALIZED DEALER DIRECTORY YELLOW PAGE LISTINGS

This section of your Scott Catalogue contains advertisements to help you conveniently find what you need, when you need it...!

Accessories

BROOKLYN GALLERY COIN & STAMP, INC.
8725 4th Ave.
Brooklyn, NY 11209
PH: 718-745-5701
FAX: 718-745-2775
info@brooklyngallery.com
www.brooklyngallery.com

Appraisals

COLONIAL STAMP COMPANY
5757 Wilshire Blvd. PH #8
Los Angeles, CA 90036
PH: 323-933-9435
FAX: 323-939-9930
Toll Free in North America
PH: 877-272-6693
FAX: 877-272-6694
info@colonialstampcompany.com
www.colonialstampcompany.com

Approvals-Personalized WW & US

THE KEEPING ROOM
PO Box 257
Trumbull, CT 06611
PH: 203-372-8436

Argentina

MARCELO LOEB
Maipu 466, Locales 19/21
1006 Buenos Aires
ARGENTINA
PH: +54 11 43939464
FAX: +54 11 43939464
marceloloeb@loebphilately.com
loebphilately@gmail.com

Asia

MICHAEL ROGERS, INC.
Mailing Address:
336 Grove Ave.
Suite B
Winter Park, FL 32789-3602
Walk-in Address:
Ranch Mall
325 S. Orlando Ave.
Suite 14
Winter Park, FL 32789-3608
PH: 407-644-2290
PH: 800-843-3751
FAX: 407-645-4434
Stamps@michaelrogersinc.com
www.michaelrogersinc.com

Auctions

COLONIAL STAMP COMPANY
5757 Wilshire Blvd. PH #8
Los Angeles, CA 90036
PH: 323-933-9435
FAX: 323-939-9930
Toll Free in North America
PH: 877-272-6693
FAX: 877-272-6694
info@colonialstampcompany.com
www.colonialstampcompany.com

Auctions

DANIEL F. KELLEHER CO., INC.
20 Walnut St.
Suite 213
Wellesley, MA 02481
PH: 781-235-0990
FAX: 781-235-0945

JACQUES C. SCHIFF, JR., INC.
195 Main St.
Ridgefield Park, NJ 07660
PH: 201-641-5566
PH from NYC: 212-662-2777
FAX: 201-641-5705

R. MARESCH & SON LTD.
5th Floor - 6075 Yonge St.
Toronto, ON M2M 3W2
CANADA
PH: 416-363-7777
FAX: 416-363-6511
www.maresch.com

SAM HOUSTON PHILATELICS
PO Box 820087
Houston, TX 77282
PH: 281-493-6386
PH: 800-231-5926
FAX: 281-496-1445
shduck@aol.com
www.shpauctions.com

THE STAMP CENTER DUTCH COUNTRY AUCTIONS
4115 Concord Pike
Wilmington, DE 19803
PH: 302-478-8740
FAX: 302-478-8779
auctions@thestampcenter.com
www.thestampcenter.com

Australia

ARON R. HALBERSTAM PHILATELISTS, LTD.
PO Box 150168
Van Brunt Station
Brooklyn, NY 11215-0168
PH: 718-788-3978
FAX: 718-965-3099
arh@arhstamps.com
www.arhstamps.com

COLONIAL STAMP COMPANY
5757 Wilshire Blvd. PH #8
Los Angeles, CA 90036
PH: 323-933-9435
FAX: 323-939-9930
Toll Free in North America
PH: 877-272-6693
FAX: 877-272-6694
info@colonialstampcompany.com
www.colonialstampcompany.com

NO LIMITS STAMPS
PO Box 8795
Madison, WI 53708
nlsc@nolimitsstamps.com
www.nolimitsstamps.com

Australian States

COLONIAL STAMP COMPANY
5757 Wilshire Blvd. PH #8
Los Angeles, CA 90036
PH: 323-933-9435
FAX: 323-939-9930
Toll Free in North America
PH: 877-272-6693
FAX: 877-272-6694
info@colonialstampcompany.com
www.colonialstampcompany.com

Auctions

Auctions-Mail Bid

DALE ENTERPRISES, INC.
PO Box 539-C
Emmaus, PA 18049
PH: 610-433-3303
FAX: 610-965-6089
daleent@ptd.net
www.dalestamps.com

Auctions - Public

ALAN BLAIR STAMPS/ AUCTIONS
5405 Lakeside Ave.
Suite 1
Richmond, VA 23228
PH/FAX: 800-689-5602
alanblair@prodigy.net

Austria

HENRY GITNER PHILATELISTS, INC.
PO Box 3077-S
Middletown, NY 10940
PH: 845-343-5151
PH: 800-947-8267
FAX: 845-343-0068
hgitner@hgitner.com
www.hgitner.com

Baltic States

NO LIMITS STAMPS
PO Box 8795
Madison, WI 53708
nlsc@nolimitsstamps.com
www.nolimitsstamps.com

Auctions - Public

Belgium

HENRY GITNER PHILATELISTS, INC.
PO Box 3077-S
Middletown, NY 10940
PH: 845-343-5151
PH: 800-947-8267
FAX: 845-343-0068
hgitner@hgitner.com
www.hgitner.com

THE STAMP & COIN SHOP
725 Pike St. #6
Seattle, WA 98101
PH: 206-624-1400
stampandcoin@mcleodusa.net
www.Stamp-Coin.com

Bermuda

ARON R. HALBERSTAM PHILATELISTS, LTD.
PO Box 150168
Van Brunt Station
Brooklyn, NY 11215-0168
PH: 718-788-3978
FAX: 718-965-3099
arh@arhstamps.com
www.arhstamps.com

Bermuda

COLONIAL STAMP COMPANY
5757 Wilshire Blvd. PH #8
Los Angeles, CA 90036
PH: 323-933-9435
FAX: 323-939-9930
Toll Free in North America
PH: 877-272-6693
FAX: 877-272-6694
info@colonialstampcompany.com
www.colonialstampcompany.com

British Asia

COLONIAL STAMP COMPANY
5757 Wilshire Blvd. PH #8
Los Angeles, CA 90036
PH: 323-933-9435
FAX: 323-939-9930
Toll Free in North America
PH: 877-272-6693
FAX: 877-272-6694
info@colonialstampcompany.com
www.colonialstampcompany.com

British Commonwealth

EMPIRE PHILATELICS

www.empire-philatelics.com

- BRITISH EMPIRE STAMPS & POSTAL HISTORY 1840-1960
- SPECIALIZED STOCK, INCLUDING RARITIES, AWAITING YOUR WANT LIST OR INQUIRY
- BUYING COLLECTIONS, ESTATES AND SINGLE ITEMS
- PRICE LISTS & SHOW SCHEDULE ON OUR WEB SITE

Barry Banks (Stamps)
P.O. Box 150013
Ogden, UT 84415 USA
Tel and FAX: (801) 479-3764

John Hart (Postal History)
P.O. Box 1162
Salt Lake City, UT 84110
Tel and FAX (801) 359-3459

e-mail: barry@empire-philatelics.com

British Commonwealth

BRITISH EMPIRE EXCLUSIVELY

Request a catalogue for our next Public Auction.
Please specify your interests.

Want lists invited from serious collectors of the BRITISH EMPIRE. References please.

Selling? Ask us about consigning *your* collection to a future sale.

Victoria Stamp Co.

PHOEBE A. MacGILLIVARY
P.O. BOX 745, RIDGEWOOD, NJ 07451
PHONE 201-652-7283 • FAX 201-612-0024
www.VictoriaStampCo.com
Email: VictoriaStampCo@aol.com

THE BRITISH COMMONWEALTH
O • F N • A • T • I • O • N • S

We are active buyers and sellers of stamps and postal history of all areas of pre-1960 British Commonwealth, including individual items, collections or estates. Want lists from all reigns are accepted with references.

"VISIT OUR BOOTH AT MOST MAJOR SHOWS"

L. W. Martin, Jr.

CROWN COLONY STAMPS

P.O. Box 1198
BELLAIRE, TEXAS 77402
PH. (713) 781-6563 • FAX (713) 789-9998
E-mail: lwm@crowncolony.com

British Colonies

THE STAMP & COIN SHOP
725 Pike St. #6
Seattle, WA 98101
PH: 206-624-1400
stampandcoin@mcleodusa.net
www.Stamp-Coin.com

British Commonwealth

ARON R. HALBERSTAM PHILATELISTS, LTD.
PO Box 150168
Van Brunt Station
Brooklyn, NY 11215-0168
PH: 718-788-3978
FAX: 718-965-3099
arh@arhstamps.com
www.arhstamps.com

British Commonwealth

Aron R. Halberstam Philatelists, Ltd.

Buying and Selling
Pre-1960 Stamps of the Entire

British Commonwealth

Visit our website to Browse, Search and Order securely online from our extensive inventory of superb quality stamps:

www.arhstamps.com

Not on the internet? No problem. Call or write for a free price list.

We are eager to buy pre-1960 British Commonwealth material.
Call or write to us first with a description of what you have to offer.

POB 150168, Van Brunt Station
Brooklyn, NY 11215-0168, USA
Email: arh@arhstamps.com
Tel: 1-718-788-3978
Fax: 1-718-965-3099
Toll Free: 1-800-343-1303

The British Empire
1840-1936

Aden to Zululand Mint & Used
Most complete stock in North America

For over 30 years we have helped our customers build some of the worlds finest known collections. Our expert ***Want Lists Services*** can do the same for you. With over 40 volumes filled with singles, sets and rare stamps, I am sure we have what you need. We welcome your Want Lists in Scott or Gibbons numbers. Monthly payment plans available for larger purchases.

Put our expertise to work for you today!
You'll be glad you did!!

Colonial Stamp Company
5757 Wilshire Blvd., Penthouse 8
Los Angeles, CA 90036 USA
Tel: +1 (323) 933-9435 Fax: +1 (323) 939-9930
Toll Free in North America
Tel: 1 (877) 272-6693 Fax: 1 (877) 272-6694
E-Mail: *info@colonialstampcompany.com*
URL: *www.colonialstampcompany.com*

British Empire Public Auctions Subscription: $35

CCNY, IFSDA, INTERNATIONAL SOCIETY OF APPRAISERS

Canada

COLONIAL STAMP COMPANY
5757 Wilshire Blvd. PH #8
Los Angeles, CA 90036
PH: 323-933-9435
FAX: 323-939-9930
Toll Free in North America
PH: 877-272-6693
FAX: 877-272-6694
info@colonialstampcompany.com
www.colonialstampcompany.com

NO LIMITS STAMPS
PO Box 8795
Madison, WI 53708
nlsc@nolimitsstamps.com
www.nolimitsstamps.com

Cape of Good Hope

COLONIAL STAMP COMPANY
5757 Wilshire Blvd. PH #8
Los Angeles, CA 90036
PH: 323-933-9435
FAX: 323-939-9930
Toll Free in North America
PH: 877-272-6693
FAX: 877-272-6694
info@colonialstampcompany.com
www.colonialstampcompany.com

China

MICHAEL ROGERS, INC.
Mailing Address:
336 Grove Ave.
Suite B
Winter Park, FL 32789-3602
Walk-in Address:
Ranch Mall
325 S. Orlando Ave.
Suite 14
Winter Park, FL 32789-3608
PH: 407-644-2290
PH: 800-843-3751
FAX: 407-645-4434
Stamps@michaelrogersinc.com
www.michaelrogersinc.com

THE STAMP & COIN SHOP
725 Pike St. #6
Seattle, WA 98101
PH: 206-624-1400
stampandcoin@mcleodusa.net
www.Stamp-Coin.com

Cuba

R.D.C. STAMPS
R. del Campo
Store Address:
3131 Coral Way
Miami, FL 33145
Mailing Address:
10535 SW 96th Ter.
Miami, FL 33176
PH: 305-815-0577
PH: 305-567-3131
FAX: 305-567-1416
rdcstamps@aol.com

Denmark

NO LIMITS STAMPS
PO Box 8795
Madison, WI 53708
nlsc@nolimitsstamps.com
www.nolimitsstamps.com

Ducks

MICHAEL JAFFE
PO Box 61484
Vancouver, WA 98666
PH: 360-695-6161
PH: 800-782-6770
FAX: 360-695-1616
mjaffe@brookmanstamps.com
www.brookmanstamps.com

SAM HOUSTON DUCK CO.
PO Box 820087
Houston, TX 77282
PH: 281-493-6386
PH: 800-231-5926
FAX: 281-496-1445
shduck@aol.com
www.shduck.com

Errors, Freaks & Oddities

SAM HOUSTON PHILATELICS
PO Box 820087
Houston, TX 77282
PH: 281-493-6386
PH: 800-231-5926
FAX: 281-496-1445
shduck@aol.com
www.shpauctions.com

Ethiopia

WINTER PARK STAMP SHOP
Ranch Mall (17-92)
325 S. Orlando Ave.
Suite 14
Winter Park, FL 32789-3608
PH: 407-628-1120
PH: 800-845-1819
FAX: 407-628-0091
stamps@winterparkstampshop.com
www.winterparkstampshop.com

Falkland Islands

ARON R. HALBERSTAM PHILATELISTS, LTD.
PO Box 150168
Van Brunt Station
Brooklyn, NY 11215-0168
PH: 718-788-3978
FAX: 718-965-3099
arh@arhstamps.com
www.arhstamps.com

COLONIAL STAMP COMPANY
5757 Wilshire Blvd. PH #8
Los Angeles, CA 90036
PH: 323-933-9435
FAX: 323-939-9930
Toll Free in North America
PH: 877-272-6693
FAX: 877-272-6694
info@colonialstampcompany.com
www.colonialstampcompany.com

France

HENRY GITNER PHILATELISTS, INC.
PO Box 3077-S
Middletown, NY 10940
PH: 845-343-5151
PH: 800-947-8267
FAX: 845-343-0068
hgitner@hgitner.com
www.hgitner.com

THE STAMP & COIN SHOP
725 Pike St. #6
Seattle, WA 98101
PH: 206-624-1400
stampandcoin@mcleodusa.net
www.Stamp-Coin.com

France & Colonies

WULFF'S STAMPS
PO Box 661746
Sacramento, CA 95866
PH/FAX: 800-884-0656
PH/FAX: 916-489-0656
service@wulffstamps.com
www.wulffstamps.com

German Colonies

COLONIAL STAMP COMPANY
View our on-line price list
at our website!
5757 Wilshire Blvd. PH #8
Los Angeles, CA 90036
PH: 323-933-9435
FAX: 323-939-9930
Toll Free in North America
PH: 877-272-6693
FAX: 877-272-6694
info@colonialstampcompany.com
www.colonialstampcompany.com

German States

COLONIAL STAMP COMPANY
5757 Wilshire Blvd. PH #8
Los Angeles, CA 90036
PH: 323-933-9435
FAX: 323-939-9930
Toll Free in North America
PH: 877-272-6693
FAX: 877-272-6694
info@colonialstampcompany.com
www.colonialstampcompany.com

Germany

HENRY GITNER PHILATELISTS, INC.
PO Box 3077-S
Middletown, NY 10940
PH: 845-343-5151
PH: 800-947-8267
FAX: 845-343-0068
hgitner@hgitner.com
www.hgitner.com

NO LIMITS STAMPS
PO Box 8795
Madison, WI 53708
nlsc@nolimitsstamps.com
www.nolimitsstamps.com

THE STAMP & COIN SHOP
725 Pike St. #6
Seattle, WA 98101
PH: 206-624-1400
stampandcoin@mcleodusa.net
www.Stamp-Coin.com

Great Britain

ARON R. HALBERSTAM PHILATELISTS, LTD.
PO Box 150168
Van Brunt Station
Brooklyn, NY 11215-0168
PH: 718-788-3978
FAX: 718-965-3099
arh@arhstamps.com
www.arhstamps.com

COLONIAL STAMP COMPANY
5757 Wilshire Blvd. PH #8
Los Angeles, CA 90036
PH: 323-933-9435
FAX: 323-939-9930
Toll Free in North America
PH: 877-272-6693
FAX: 877-272-6694
info@colonialstampcompany.com
www.colonialstampcompany.com

Hong Kong

COLONIAL STAMP COMPANY
5757 Wilshire Blvd. PH #8
Los Angeles, CA 90036
PH: 323-933-9435
FAX: 323-939-9930
Toll Free in North America
PH: 877-272-6693
FAX: 877-272-6694
info@colonialstampcompany.com
www.colonialstampcompany.com

Insurance

COLLECTIBLES INSURANCE AGENCY
11350 McCormick Rd.
Suite 700
Hunt Valley, MD 21031
PH: 888-837-9537
PH: 410-876-8833
FAX: 410-876-9233
info@insurecollectibles.com
www.collectinsure.com

Ireland

NO LIMITS STAMPS
PO Box 8795
Madison, WI 53708
nlsc@nolimitsstamps.com
www.nolimitsstamps.com

Insurance

Italy

HENRY GITNER PHILATELISTS, INC.
PO Box 3077-S
Middletown, NY 10940
PH: 845-343-5151
PH: 800-947-8267
FAX: 845-343-0068
hgitner@hgitner.com
www.hgitner.com

Japan

HENRY GITNER PHILATELISTS, INC.
PO Box 3077-S
Middletown, NY 10940
PH: 845-343-5151
PH: 800-947-8267
FAX: 845-343-0068
hgitner@hgitner.com
www.hgitner.com

MICHAEL ROGERS, INC.
Mailing Address:
336 Grove Ave.
Suite B
Winter Park, FL 32789-3602
Walk-in Address:
Ranch Mall
325 S. Orlando Ave.
Suite 14
Winter Park, FL 32789-3608
PH: 407-644-2290
PH: 800-843-3751
FAX: 407-645-4434
Stamps@michaelrogersinc.com
www.michaelrogersinc.com

THE STAMP & COIN SHOP
725 Pike St. #6
Seattle, WA 98101
PH: 206-624-1400
stampandcoin@mcleodusa.net
www.Stamp-Coin.com

Korea

MICHAEL ROGERS, INC.
Mailing Address:
336 Grove Ave.
Suite B
Winter Park, FL 32789-3602
Walk-in Address:
Ranch Mall
325 S. Orlando Ave.
Suite 14
Winter Park, FL 32789-3608
PH: 407-644-2290
PH: 800-843-3751
FAX: 407-645-4434
Stamps@michaelrogersinc.com
www.michaelrogersinc.com

Luxembourg

WWW.WORLDSTAMPS.COM
242 West Saddle River Road
Suite C
Upper Saddle River, NJ 07458
PH: 201-236-8122
FAX: 201-236-8133
by mail:
Frank Geiger Philatelists
info@WorldStamps.com
www.WorldStamps.com

Madagascar (British Issues)

COLONIAL STAMP COMPANY
5757 Wilshire Blvd. PH #8
Los Angeles, CA 90036
PH: 323-933-9435
FAX: 323-939-9930
Toll Free in North America
PH: 877-272-6693
FAX: 877-272-6694
info@colonialstampcompany.com
www.colonialstampcompany.com

Malaya

COLONIAL STAMP COMPANY
5757 Wilshire Blvd. PH #8
Los Angeles, CA 90036
PH: 323-933-9435
FAX: 323-939-9930
Toll Free in North America
PH: 877-272-6693
FAX: 877-272-6694
info@colonialstampcompany.com
www.colonialstampcompany.com

Manchukuo

MICHAEL ROGERS, INC.
Mailing Address:
336 Grove Ave.
Suite B
Winter Park, FL 32789-3602
Walk-in Address:
Ranch Mall
325 S. Orlando Ave.
Suite 14
Winter Park, FL 32789-3608
PH: 407-644-2290
PH: 800-843-3751
FAX: 407-645-4434
Stamps@michaelrogersinc.com
www.michaelrogersinc.com

Netherlands

HENRY GITNER PHILATELISTS, INC.
PO Box 3077-S
Middletown, NY 10940
PH: 845-343-5151
PH: 800-947-8267
FAX: 845-343-0068
hgitner@hgitner.com
www.hgitner.com

WWW.WORLDSTAMPS.COM
242 West Saddle River Road
Suite C
Upper Saddle River, NJ 07458
PH: 201-236-8122
FAX: 201-236-8133
by mail:
Frank Geiger Philatelists
info@WorldStamps.com
www.WorldStamps.com

New Issues

DAVIDSON'S STAMP SERVICE
PO Box 36355
Indianapolis, IN 46236-0355
PH: 317-826-2620
davidson@in.net
www.newstampissues.com

New Issues - Retail

BOMBAY PHILATELIC INC.
PO Box 480009
Delray Beach, FL 33448
PH: 561-499-7990
FAX: 561-499-7553
sales@bombaystamps.com
www.bombaystamps.com

New Zealand

COLONIAL STAMP COMPANY
5757 Wilshire Blvd. PH #8
Los Angeles, CA 90036
PH: 323-933-9435
FAX: 323-939-9930
Toll Free in North America
PH: 877-272-6693
FAX: 877-272-6694
info@colonialstampcompany.com
www.colonialstampcompany.com

Publications-Collector

THE AMERICAN PHILATELIST
Dept. TZ
100 Match Factory Pl.
Bellefonte, PA 16823-1367
PH: 814-933-3803
FAX: 814-933-6128
apsinfo@stamps.org
www.stamps.org

STAMP STORES

California

BROSIUS STAMP, COIN & SUPPLIES
2105 Main St.
Santa Monica, CA 90405
PH: 310-396-7480
FAX: 310-396-7455

COLONIAL STAMP CO./ BRITISH EMPIRE SPECIALIST
5757 Wilshire Blvd. PH #8
(by appt.)
Los Angeles, CA 90036
PH: 323-933-9435
FAX: 323-939-9930
Toll Free in North America
PH: 877-272-6693
FAX: 877-272-6694
info@colonialstampcompany.com
www.colonialstampcompany.com

FISCHER-WOLK PHILATELICS
22762 Aspan St.
Suite 211
Lake Forest, CA 92630
PH: 949-837-2932
fischerwolk@earthlink.net

NATICK STAMPS & HOBBIES
405 S. Myrtle Ave.
Monrovia, CA 91016
PH: 626-305-7333
natickco@earthlink.net

Colorado

ACKLEY'S ROCKS & STAMPS
3230 N. Stone Ave.
Colorado Springs, CO 80907
PH: 719-633-1153
ackl9@aol.com

SHOWCASE STAMPS
3865 Wadsworth
Wheat Ridge, CO 80033
PH: 303-425-9252
kbeiner@colbi.net
www.showcasestamps.com

Connecticut

SILVER CITY COIN & STAMP
41 Colony St.
Meriden, CT 06451
PH: 203-235-7634
FAX: 203-237-4915

Florida

R.D.C. STAMPS
R. del Campo
Store Address:
3131 Coral Way
Miami, FL 33145
Mailing Address:
10535 SW 96thTerrace
Miami, FL 33176
PH: 305-815-0577
PH: 305-567-3131
FAX: 305-567-1416
rdcstamps@aol.com

Florida

WINTER PARK STAMP SHOP
Ranch Mall (17-92)
325 S. Orlando Ave.
Suite 14
Winter Park, FL 32789-3608
PH: 407-628-1120
PH: 800-845-1819
FAX: 407-628-0091
stamps@winterparkstampshop.com
www.winterparkstampshop.com

Georgia

STAMPS UNLIMITED OF GEORGIA, INC.
100 Peachtree St.
Suite 1460
Atlanta, GA 30303
PH: 404-688-9161

Illinois

DR. ROBERT FRIEDMAN & SONS
2029 W. 75th St.
Woodridge, IL 60517
PH: 800-588-8100
FAX: 630-985-1588
drbobstamps@yahoo.com
www.drbobfriedmanstamps.com

Spain

STAMP STORES

Indiana

KNIGHT STAMP & COIN CO.
237 Main St.
Hobart, IN 46342
PH: 219-942-4341
PH: 800-634-2646
knight@knightcoin.com
www.knightcoin.com

Massachusetts

KAPPY'S COINS & STAMPS
534 Washington St.
Norwood, MA 02062
PH: 781-762-5552
FAX: 781-762-3292
kappyscoins@aol.com

Maryland

BULLDOG STAMP COMPANY
4641 Montgomery Ave.
Bethesda, MD 20814
PH: 301-654-1138

New Jersey

BERGEN STAMPS & COLLECTIBLES
717 American Legion Dr.
Teaneck, NJ 07666
PH: 201-836-8987

New Jersey

RON RITZER STAMPS INC.
Millburn Mall
2933 Vauxhall Rd.
Vauxhall, NJ 07088
PH: 908-687-0007
FAX: 908-687-0795
rritzer@comcast.net
www.ritzerstamps.com

TRENTON STAMP & COIN CO.
Thomas DeLuca
Store: Forest Glen Plaza
1804 Route 33
Hamilton Square, NJ 08690
Mail: PO Box 8574
Trenton, NJ 08650
PH: 800-446-8664
PH: 609-584-8100
FAX: 609-587-8664
TOMD4TSC@aol.com

New York

CHAMPION STAMP CO., INC.
432 W. 54th St.
New York, NY 10019
PH: 212-489-8130
FAX: 212-581-8130
championstamp@aol.com
www.championstamp.com

Florida

Stamp Shows

Ohio

HILLTOP STAMP SERVICE
Richard A. Peterson
PO Box 626
Wooster, OH 44691
PH: 330-262-8907
PH: 330-262-5378
hilltop@bright.net

THE LINK STAMP CO.
3461 E. Livingston Ave.
Columbus, OH 43227
PH/FAX: 614-237-4125
PH/FAX: 800-546-5726

Tennessee

HERRON HILL, INC.
5007 Black Rd.
Suite 140
Memphis, TN 38117
PH: 901-683-9644

Texas

SAM HOUSTON PHILATELICS
14780 Memorial Dr. #110
Houston, TX 77079
PH: 281-493-6386
PH: 800-231-5926
FAX: 281-496-1445
shduck@aol.com
www.shduck.com

Virginia

KENNEDY'S STAMPS & COINS, INC.
7059 Brookfield Plaza
Springfield, VA 22150
PH: 703-569-7300
FAX: 703-569-7644
j.w.kennedy@verizon.net

LATHEROW & CO., INC.
5054 Lee Hwy.
Arlington, VA 22207
PH: 703-538-2727
PH: 800-647-4624
FAX: 703-538-5210

Sweden

NO LIMITS STAMPS
PO Box 8795
Madison, WI 53708
nlsc@nolimitsstamps.com
www.nolimitsstamps.com

Switzerland

HENRY GITNER PHILATELISTS, INC.
PO Box 3077-S
Middletown, NY 10940
PH: 845-343-5151
PH: 800-947-8267
FAX: 845-343-0068
hgitner@hgitner.com
www.hgitner.com

Togo

COLONIAL STAMP COMPANY
5757 Wilshire Blvd. PH #8
Los Angeles, CA 90036
PH: 323-933-9435
FAX: 323-939-9930
Toll Free in North America
PH: 877-272-6693
FAX: 877-272-6694
info@colonialstampcompany.com
www.colonialstampcompany.com

Topicals

WINTER PARK STAMP SHOP
Ranch Mall (17-92)
325 S. Orlando Ave.
Suite 14
Winter Park, FL 32789-3608
PH: 407-628-1120
PH: 800-845-1819
FAX: 407-628-0091
stamps@winterparkstampshop.com
www.winterparkstampshop.com

Topicals-Columbus

MR. COLUMBUS
PO Box 1492
Fennville, MI 49408
PH: 269-543-4755
columbus@accn.org

Ukraine

MR. VAL ZABIJAKA
PO Box 3711
Silver Spring, MD 20918
PH/FAX: 301-593-5316
vtz@comcast.net

United States

BROOKMAN STAMP CO.
PO Box 90
Vancouver, WA 98666
PH: 360-695-1391
PH: 800-545-4871
FAX: 360-695-1616
larry@brookmanstamps.com
www.brookmanstamps.com

HENRY GITNER PHILATELISTS, INC.
PO Box 3077-S
Middletown, NY 10940
PH: 845-343-5151
PH: 800-947-8267
FAX: 845-343-0068
hgitner@hgitner.com
www.hgitner.com

THE STAMP & COIN SHOP
725 Pike St. #6
Seattle, WA 98101
PH: 206-624-1400
stampandcoin@mcleodusa.net
www.Stamp-Coin.com

U.S.-Collections Wanted

DR. ROBERT FRIEDMAN & SONS
2029 W. 75th St.
Woodridge, IL 60517
PH: 800-588-8100
FAX: 630-985-1588
drbobstamps@yahoo.com
www.drbobfriedmanstamps.com

Want Lists

BROOKMAN INTERNATIONAL
PO Box 450
Vancouver, WA 98666
PH: 360-695-1391
PH: 800-545-4871
FAX: 360-695-1616
larry@brookmanstamps.com
www.brookmanstamps.com

CHARLES P. SCHWARTZ
PO Box 165
Mora, MN 55051
PH: 320-679-4705
charlesp@ecenet.com

Want Lists-British Empire 1840-1935 German Cols./Offices

COLONIAL STAMP COMPANY
5757 Wilshire Blvd. PH #8
Los Angeles, CA 90036
PH: 323-933-9435
FAX: 323-939-9930
Toll Free in North America
PH: 877-272-6693
FAX: 877-272-6694
info@colonialstampcompany.com
www.colonialstampcompany.com

Wanted-Estates

BILL'S
59 Paulding Blvd.
Dallas, GA 30157
PH: 770-369-1001
cynthianix59@aol.com

COLONIAL STAMP COMPANY
5757 Wilshire Blvd. PH #8
Los Angeles, CA 90036
PH: 323-933-9435
FAX: 323-939-9930
Toll Free in North America
PH: 877-272-6693
FAX: 877-272-6694
info@colonialstampcompany.com
www.colonialstampcompany.com

Wanted-Worldwide Collections

DANIEL F. KELLEHER CO., INC.
20 Walnut St.
Suite 213
Wellesley, MA 02481
PH: 781-235-0990
FAX: 781-235-0945

DR. ROBERT FRIEDMAN & SONS
2029 W. 75th St.
Woodridge, IL 60517
PH: 800-588-8100
FAX: 630-985-1588
drbobstamps@yahoo.com
www.drbobfriedmanstamps.com

Wanted-Worldwide Collections

THE STAMP CENTER
DUTCH COUNTRY AUCTIONS
4115 Concord Pike
Wilmington, DE 19803
PH: 302-478-8740
FAX: 302-478-8779
auctions@thestampcenter.com
www.thestampcenter.com

Wanted-U.S. Collections

THE STAMP CENTER
DUTCH COUNTRY AUCTIONS
4115 Concord Pike
Wilmington, DE 19803
PH: 302-478-8740
FAX: 302-478-8779
auctions@thestampcenter.com
www.thestampcenter.com

Websites

ARON R. HALBERSTAM PHILATELISTS, LTD.
PO Box 150168
Van Brunt Station
Brooklyn, NY 11215-0168
PH: 718-788-3978
FAX: 718-965-3099
arh@arhstamps.com
www.arhstamps.com

Worldwide

B.J.'S STAMPS
Barbara J. Johnson
6342 W. Bell Rd.
Glendale, AZ 85308
PH: 623-878-2080
FAX: 623-412-3456
info@bjstamps.com
www.bjstamps.com

THE STAMP & COIN SHOP
725 Pike St. #6
Seattle, WA 98101
PH: 206-624-1400
stampandcoin@mcleodusa.net
www.Stamp-Coin.com

Worldwide Price List

NO LIMITS STAMPS
PO Box 8795
Madison, WI 53708
nlsc@nolimitsstamps.com
www.nolimitsstamps.com

United States

U.S.A.

BELOW MARKET PRICES!!

USED • UNUSED

MOST GRADES & PRICE RANGES!

Here is your opportunity to have the older and scarcer stamps of our country at low, reasonable prices. Issues prior to the year 1950 worth anywhere from 25¢ up to several hundred dollars each.

JUST SEND 41¢ POSTAGE for complete price list. Compare for PROOF OF LOWEST PRICES before ordering, and find out what you have missed until you discovered us!!!

LOWELL S. DONALD CO.
P.O. BOX 728
RUTLAND, VERMONT 05702

APS

Worldwide

All Countries A-Z

ALL TOPICS
VERY LARGE WORLDWIDE STOCK

For many years we have been a leader in this field. No sub-topic is strange to us! ... including varieties, cancels, covers, etc.

WANT LISTS WELCOME
... any Catalogue #, any main language.

ERCOLE GLORIA - srl Zuskis Family
Piazza Pio XI 1, 20123 Milan, ITALY
TEL. +39.02804106 • FAX +39.02864217
www.ercolegloria.it • E-MAIL: info@ercolegloria.it

PTS APS